TUFF STUFF 2003 Standard Catalog of

FOOTBALL CARDS

6TH EDITION

FROM THE PRICE GUIDE EDITORS OF TUFF STUFF® MAGAZINE

Published by

700 E. State Street • Iola, WI 54990-0001
Telephone: 715/445-2214
Web: www.krause.com

Please call or write for our free catalog of publications.
Our toll-free number to place an order or obtain a free catalog is 800-258-0929
or please use our regular business telephone 715-445-2214.

Library of Congress Catalog Number: 97-73033

ISBN: 0-87349-479-2

Printed in the United States of America

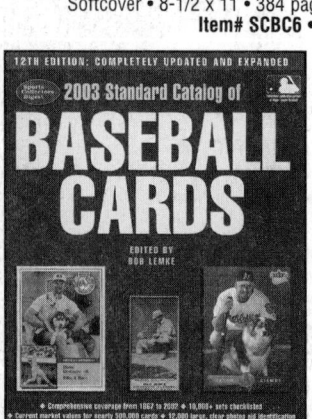
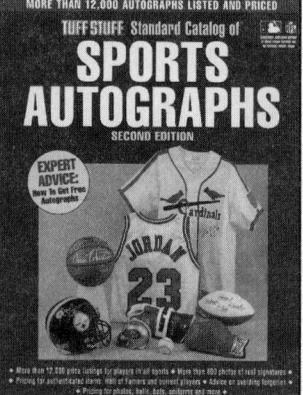
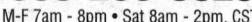

TABLE OF CONTENTS

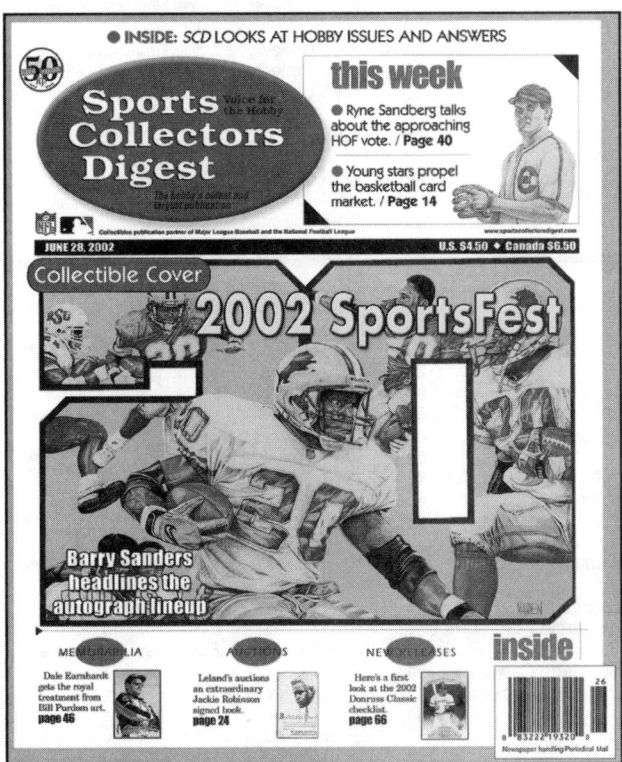

Q

R

S

TUFF STUFF® 2003 Standard Catalog of®
FOOTBALL CARDS

WELCOME!

Thank you for purchasing the sixth edition of Standard Catalog of Football Cards.

This book is the most comprehensive annual football card price guide in the industry, complete with listings for more than 425,000 cards and checklists for more than 3,000 sets. The entire Sports Collectors Digest price guide staff contributed to this book, including coordinator Jason Stonelake and staff members Steve Bloedow, Joe Clemens and Bert Lehman.

Krause Publications' Standard Catalog of Baseball Cards is widely accepted in the sports card hobby as the most comprehensive annual price guide, containing current values for over 450,000 cards and checklists of over 9,500 sets. Authored each year by Bob Lemke, the Standard Catalog of Baseball Cards is a standard tool of the trade for the serious baseball card dealer and collector.

Given the outstanding performance of the Standard Catalog of Baseball Cards and the rising popularity of football cards, it was only natural for the price guide staff to extend the successful formula for its baseball catalog to the Standard Catalog of Football Cards.

It is our hope that this book enhances both your collection and your enjoyment of the sports card hobby.

HOW TO USE THIS CATALOG

This catalog has been uniquely designed to serve the needs of beginning and advanced football card collectors. It provides a comprehensive guide to more than 80 years of sports card issues, arranged so that even the novice collector can use it with confidence and ease.

The following explanations summarize the general practices used in preparing this catalog's listings. However, because of specialized requirements which may vary from card set to card set, these explanations should not be considered ironclad, but used as guidelines.

ARRANGEMENT

Because the most important feature in identifying and pricing a sports card is its set of origin, this catalog has been alphabetically arranged according to the name by which the set is most popularly known.

Those sets that were issued for more than one year are then listed chronologically, from earliest to most recent.

Within each set, the cards are listed by their designated card number, or in the absence of card numbers, alphabetically according to the last name of the player pictured.

IDENTIFICATION

While the date and issue of most modern sports cards are well identified on front, back, or both, such has not always been the case. In general, the back of the card is more useful in identifying the set of origin than the front. The issuer or sponsor's name will usually appear on the back since, after all, sports cards were first produced as a promotional item to stimulate sales of other products. As often as not, that issuer's name is the name by which the set is known to collectors and under which it will be found listed in this catalog.

In some difficult cases identifying a sports card's general age, if not specific year of issue, can be fixed by studying the biological or statistical information on the back of the card. The last year mentioned in either the biography or stats is usually the year which preceded the year of issue.

PHOTOGRAPHS

A photograph of the front of at least one representative card from virtually every set listed in this catalog has been incorporated into the listings to aid in identification.

Photographs have been printed in reduced size. The actual size of cards in each set is given in the introductory text preceding its listing, unless the card is the standard size 1-1/2" by 3-1/2".

DATING

The dating of sports cards by year of issue on the front or back of the card itself is a relatively new phenomenon. In most cases, to accurately determine a date of issue for an unidentified card, it must be studied for clues. As mentioned, the biography, career summary or statistics on the back of the card are the best way to pinpoint a year of issue. In most cases, the year of issue will be the year after the last season mentioned on the card.

Luckily for today's collector, earlier generations have done much of the research in determining your year of issue for those cards which bear no clues. The painstaking task of matching players' listed and/or pictured teams against their career records often allowed an issue date to be determined.

In some cases, particular card sets were issued over a period of more than one calendar year, but since they are collected together as a single set, their specific year of issue is not important. Such sets will be listed with their complete known range of issue years.

NUMBERING

While many sports card issues as far back as the early 1900s have contained card numbers assigned by the issuer to facilitate the collecting of a complete set, the practice has by no means been universal. Even today, not every set bears card numbers.

Logically, those sports cards which were numbered by their manufacturer are presented in that numerical order within the listings of this catalog. The many unnumbered issues, however, have been assigned Sports Collectors Digest/Tuff Stuff Price Guide numbers to facilitate their universal identification within the hobby, especially when buying and selling by mail.

In all cases, numbers which have been assigned or which otherwise do not appear on the card through error or by design, are shown in this catalog within parentheses. In virtually all cases, unless a more natural system suggested itself by the unique matter of a particular set, the assignment of Sports Collectors Digest/Tuff Stuff Price Guide numbers by the cataloging staff has been done by alphabetical arrangement of the players' last names or the card's principal title.

Significant collectible variations for any particular card are noted within the listings by the application of a suffix letter within parentheses. In instances of variations, the suffix "a" is assigned to the variation which was created first.

NAMES

The identification of a player by full name on the front of his sports card has been a common practice only since the 1940s. Prior to that, the player's name and team were the usual information found on the card front.

As a general practice, the listings in the Sports Collectors Digest/Tuff Stuff Price Guide present the player's name as it is more commonly known. If the player's name only appears on the back, rather than on the front of the card, the listing corresponds to that designation.

In cases where only the player's last name is given on the card, the cataloging staff has included the first name by which he was most often known for ease of identification.

Cards which contain misspelled first or last names, or even wrong initials, will have included in their listings the in-

correct information, with a correction accompanying in parentheses. This extends, also, to cases where the name on the card does not correspond to the player actually pictured.

GRADING

The vast majority of cards in this book were issued between 1981 and 2001 and feature NFL players only. The term "card" is used rather loosely as in this context it is construed to include virtually any series of cardboard or paper product, of whatever size and/or shape, depicting football players. Further, "cards" printed on wood, metal, plastic and other materials are either by their association with other issues or by their compatibility in size with the current 2-1/2" x 3-1/2" card standard also listed here.

Because modern cards are generally not popularly collected in lower grades, cards in this section carry only a Mint (MT) value quote. In general, post-1980 cards which grade Near Mint (NM) will retail at about 75% of the Mint price, while Excellent (EX) condition cards bring 40%.

Here is a more detailed look at grading procedures:

Mint (MT): A perfect card. Well-centered, with parallel borders which appear equal to the naked eye. Four sharp, square corners. No creases, edge dents, surface scratches, paper flaws, loss of luster, yellowing or fading, regardless of age. No imperfectly printed card - out of register, badly cut or ink flawed - or card stained by contact with gum, wax or other substances can be considered truly Mint, even if new out of the pack.

Near Mint (NR MT): A nearly perfect card. At first glance, a Near Mint card appears perfect; upon a closer examination, however, a minor flaw will be discovered. On well-centered cards, three of the four corners must be perfectly sharp; only one corner shows a minor imperfection upon close inspection. A slightly off-center card with one or more borders being noticeably unequal - but still present - would also fit this grade.

Excellent (EX): Corners are still fairly sharp with only moderate wear. Card borders may be off center. No creases. May have very minor gum, wax or product stains, front or back. Surfaces may show slight loss of luster from rubbing across other cards.

Very Good (VG): Show obvious handling. Corners rounded and/or perhaps showing minor creases. Other minor creases may be visible. Surfaces may exhibit loss of luster, but all printing is intact. May show major gum, wax or other packaging stains. No major creases, tape marks or extraneous markings or writing. Exhibit honest wear.

Good (G - generally 50% of the VG price): A well-worn card, but exhibits no intentional damage or abuse. May have major or multiple creases. Corners rounded well beyond the border.

Fair (F - generally 50% of the Good price): Shows excessive wear, along with damage or abuse. Will show all the wear characteristics of a Good card, along with such damage as thumb tack holes in or near margins, evidence of having been taped or pasted, perhaps small tears around the edges, or creases so heavy as to break the cardboard. Backs may show minor added pen or pencil writing, or be missing small bits of paper. Still, basically a complete card.

Poor (P): A card that has been tortured to death. Corners or other areas may be torn off. Card may have been trimmed, show holes from a paper punch or have been used for BB gun practice. Front may have extraneous pen or pencil writing, or other defacement. Major portions of front or back design may be missing. In other words, not a pretty sight.

In addition to these terms, collectors may encounter intermediate grades, such as VG-EX or EX-MT. These cards usually have characteristics of both the lower and higher grades, and are generally priced midway between those two values.

VALUATIONS

Values quoted in this book represent the current retail market and are compiled from recommendations provided and verified through the authors' daily involvement in the publication of the hobby's leading advertising periodicals, as well as the input of specialized consultants.

It should be stressed, however, that this book is intended to serve only as an aid in evaluating cards; actual market conditions are constantly changing. This is especially true of the cards of current players, whose on-field performance during the course of a season can greatly affect the value of their cards - upwards or downward.

Publication of this book is not intended as a solicitation to buy or sell the listed cards by the editors, publishers or contributors.

Again, the values here are retail prices - what a collector can expect to pay when buying a card from a dealer. The wholesale price, that which a collector can expect to receive from a dealer when selling cards, will be significantly lower.

Most dealers operate on a 100 percent mark-up, generally paying about 50 percent of a card's retail value. On some high demand cards, dealers will pay up to 75 percent or even 100 percent or more of retail value, anticipating continued price increases. Conversely, for many low-demand cards, such as common players' cards of recent years, dealers may pay 25 percent or even less of retail.

SETS

Collectors may note that the complete set prices for newer issues quoted in these listings are usually significantly lower than the total of the value of the individual cards which comprise the set. This reflects two factors in the sports card market. First, a seller is often willing to take a lower composite price for a complete set as a "volume discount" and to avoid inventorying a large number of common player or other lower-demand cards.

Second, to a degree, the value of common cards can be said to be inflated as a result of having a built-in overhead charge to justify the dealer's time in sorting cards, carrying them in stock and filling orders. This accounts for the fact that even brand new sports cards, which cost the dealer around 1 cent each when bought in bulk, carry individual price tags of 3 cents or higher.

ERRORS/VARIATIONS

It is often hard for the beginning collector to understand that an error on a sports card, in and of itself, does not usually add premium value to that card. It is usually only when the correcting of an error in the subsequent printing creates a variation that premium value attaches to an error.

Minor errors, such as wrong stats or personal data, create a variation that attaches to an error. Misspellings, inconsistencies, etc. - usually affecting the back of the card - are very common, especially in recent years. Unless a corrected variation was also printed, these errors are not noted in the listings of this book because they are not generally perceived by collectors to have premium value.

On the other hand, major effort had been expended to include the most complete listings ever for collectible variation cards. Many scarce and valuable variations are included in these listings because they are widely collected and often have significant premium value.

COUNTERFEITS/REPRINTS

As the value of sports cards has risen in the past 10-20 years, certain cards and sets have become too expensive for the average collector to obtain. This, along with changes in the technology of color printing, has given rise to increasing numbers of counterfeit and reprint cards.

While both terms describe essentially the same thing - a modern day copy which attempts to duplicate as closely as possible an original sports card - there are differences which are important to the collector.

Generally, a counterfeit is made with the intention of deceiving somebody into believing it is genuine, and thus paying large amounts of money for it. The counterfeiter takes every pain to try to make his fakes look as authentic as possible.

A reprint, on the other hand, while it may have been made to look as close as possible to an original card, is made with the intention of allowing collectors to buy them as substitutes for cards they may never be otherwise able to afford. The big difference is that a reprint is generally marked as such, usually on the back of the card.

In other cases, like the Topps 1952 baseball reprint set, the replicas are printed in a size markedly different from the originals. Collectors should be aware, however, that unscrupulous persons will sometimes cut off or otherwise obliterate the distinguishing word - "Reprint," "Copy" - or modern copyright date on the back of a reprint card in an attempt to pass it as genuine.

A collector's best defense against reprints and counterfeits is to acquire a knowledge of the look and feel of genuine sports cards of various eras and issues.

UNLISTED CARDS

Readers who have cards or sets which are not covered in this edition are invited to correspond with the editor for purposes of adding to the compilation of work now in progress. Address: Tuff Stuff's Standard Catalog of Football Cards, 700 E. State St., Iola, WI 54990. Contributors will be acknowledged in future editions.

COLLECTOR ISSUES

Many cards do not fall under the scope of this catalog because they were issued solely for the collector market. Known as, "collector issues," these cards and sets are distinguished from "legitimate" issues by not having been created as a sales promotional item for another product - bubble gum, soda, snack cakes, dog food, cigarettes, gasoline, etc.

Because of their nature - the person issuing them is always free to print and distribute more if they should ever attain any real value - collector issues are generally regarded as having little or no premium value.

NEW ISSUES

Because new sports cards are being issued all the time, the cataloging of them is an ongoing challenge. Readers are invited to submit news of new issues, especially limited-edition or regionally issued cards, to the editors. Address: Tuff Stuff's Standard Catalog of Football Cards, 700 E. State St., Iola, WI 54990.

ACKNOWLEDGMENTS

The editors wish to thank the many collectors, dealers and hobbyists who helped us compile, list and price the data in this edition.

HISTORY OF FOOTBALL CARDS

THE EARLY YEARS

The history of football cards started more than 100 years ago with the 1890 Mayo Cut Plug set. That set consists of 36 cards of college football players from Yale, Harvard and Princeton. It looks like any other small tobacco issue of the era, except the players are wearing hooded sweatshirts or turtlenecks with big letters on them instead of uniforms. There are no big names in the set, but it is still very significant for its historical perspective.

The next major football set came nearly a half-century later. The 1935 National Chicle set also has 36 cards, but the cards are beautiful full-color renditions - much like the Diamond Stars baseball set - of better-known football players, with some very well-known names (Knute Rockne, Bronko Nagurski) and a few more Hall of Famers (Dutch Clark, Cliff Battles, Clarke Hinkle).

The 1948 Leaf set introduced football cards to the postwar generation. The set consists of 98 hand-colored cards that closely resemble the Leaf baseball sets of the era. It contains the cards of Hall of Famers: Sid Luckman, Bulldog Turner, Doak Walker, Bobby Layne, Steve Van Buren, Bob Waterfield, Sammy Baugh, Leo Nomellini, George Connor, Pete Pihos and George McAffee.

Leaf also issued a "slip-numbered" 49-card set in 1949 that contains the rookie card of Chuck Bednarik.

BOWMAN

Bowman was also on the scene in 1948 and issued a 108-card football set that has "short prints" scattered throughout the set. Key cards include Baugh, Waterfield, Alex Wojciechowicz, Pihos, Bill Dudley, Luckman and Van Buren.

Bowman failed to issue a football set in 1949, but returned in 1950 with a football card set that bears a very close resemblance to the 1949 Bowman baseball set, with 144 hand-colored player pictures on card fronts and player information on card backs. Its 144 cards contain an astonishing number of Hall of Famers, and are among the loveliest renditions of sports figures on pasteboard ever. Key cards in the set include Lou Groza, Y.A. Tittle, Bobby Layne, Joe Perry, Tom Fears, Glenn Davis and Elroy Hirsch.

The 144-card 1951 Bowman set does not closely resemble the 1951 Bowman baseball set. All other Bowman football sets from this point deviate even more markedly from their baseball counterparts. Norm Van Brocklin, Ernie Stautner and Emlen Tunnell are the key cards in the set.

Two sets of 1952 Bowman cards were issued. The 1952 Bowman "small" set has 144 cards; the 1952 Bowman "large" has the same number of cards - the same cards, in fact. The difference? Cards in the small set measure 2-1/16" by 3-1/8", while cards in the large set measure 2-1/2" by 3-3/4". The large set is scarcer, and therefore more expensive - in fact it is the single most expensive football set in this catalog. Key cards include Otto Graham, Frank Gifford, Gino Marchetti, Kyle Rote, Hugh McElhenny, Ollie Matson, Yale Lary, Tom Landry and Jim Lansford.

Set size was decreased to 96 cards in the 1953 Bowman set, while the card size remained large - Bowman-sized, in

other words. Trimmed cards are plentiful in this and subsequent Bowman sets.

The 128-card 1954 Bowman set was issued in four series of 32 cards each, with the third series being scarcest. Its key cards are the George Blanda rookie and a card of Whizzer White which actually shows Wilford White instead of the future Supreme Court justice. The set is the most common of all the Bowman sets.

Bowman's swan song as a company was the 160-card 1955 Bowman set. The company was purchased by Topps late in 1955 after it produced this set, which includes the rookie cards of Pat Summerall and John Henry Johnson. It was a scarce high-number series. Topps revived the Bowman name in 1991 and has had a set each year except for 1996 and 1997.

TOPPS

The trading card giant, Topps, entered the football card market in 1951 with its Topps Magic set, featuring 75 contemporary college football players.

The 1955 Topps All-American set also shows college football players, but in an all-time great format. Certain cards in the 100-card set were short-printed, a common practice in Topps football sets. Notable cards include Don Hutson, Knute Rockne, Jim Thorpe, Red Grange and Amos Alonzo Stagg.

There's a quirk in the 1956 Topps set: cards of St. Louis Cardinals and Washington Redskins are scarcer than other cards in the set. The set's key cards are Roosevelt Brown and Lenny Moore.

The 154-card 1957 Topps set has an unusual "splitscreen" format. High numbers are slightly scarcer.

Key cards are Bart Starr, John Unitas, Dick Lane, Ray Berry, Paul Hornung, Lenny Moore and Bob St. Clair.

Jim Brown's rookie card is far and away the key card in the 132-card 1958 Topps set, though there are others, most notably Sonny Jurgensen.

The 1959 Topps set has 176 cards, a high-number series and the rookie cards of Alex Karras and Sam Huff.

AFL and NFL players were included in the 198-card 1961 Topps set. AFL players are slightly scarcer in the set, which has the first cards of John Brodie, Don Maynard, Jim Otto and Lionel Taylor.

It was back to NFL-only status and a split-screen format for the 1962 Topps set, which contains a bundle of shortprinted cards along with the rookie cards of Ernie Davis, Don Meredith and Mike Ditka. The black-bordered set is exceptionally tough to find in top grade.

Topps' last NFL set for a while was the 1963 Topps set, which short-printed many Cleveland Browns and all New York Giants and Dallas Cowboys, including the Bob Lilly rookie. The rookie cards of Ray Nitschke, Willie Wood, Deacon Jones, and Jim Marshall are also in the 170-card set.

Short-prints were everywhere in the 1964 Topps set, which has 176 cards of AFL players. There are no special key cards in the set (Buck Buchanan and Bobby Bell are about it), but 86 short prints present quite a challenge in completing the 175-card set.

Probably the most unusual Topps set, and certainly one of the most significant and attractve, the 1965 Topps set has 175 tall (4-11/16") cards, along with the normal batch of short prints. The key card here, and perhaps the key card of the 1960s, is the Joe Namath rookie. The set also has rookie cards of Willie Brown and Fred Biletnikoff.

With a "television" design borrowed from the 1955 Bowman baseball set, the 132-card 1966 Topps set has no short-

prints, but one unusually scarce card - a checklist that everyone seemed to get in their packs but nobody saved.

The last of Topps' AFL-only sets, the 1967 Topps set, has no short prints and few significant rookie cards, save for the card of linebacker turned pro-wrestler Wahoo McDaniel. The set has 132 cards.

With Philadelphia Gum gone, Topps had the football card market all to itself, and responded with a 219-card set. First series cards have blue backs; key cards are the Jim Hart and Bob Griese cards.

One of the Topps' last classic football card sets, the 163-card 1969 Topps set was again split into two series, with an important distinction between the series: first-series cards have white borders; second-series cards have pictures that bleed out to the card edges. The set has Brian Piccolo's only card.

O.J. Simpson's rookie card is a highlight of the 263-card 1970 Topps set. There are no other significant cards (except for rookies of Alan Page, Jan Stenerud and Bubba Smith) in the set, which was issued in two series. The second series is slightly scarcer.

The 263-card 1971 Topps set was again split into two series, with the second series being slightly tougher to find. No cards are exceptionally scarce, though the set is notable for the rookie cards of Terry Bradshaw and Joe Greene.

Topps' most ambitious set to date, and one of its most interesting, the 351-card 1972 Topps set was split into three series: a common, low-number series, a slightly scarcer middle-number series, and a very scarcer high number series. The set also has rookie cards of Jim Plunkett, Lyle Alzado, Gene Upshaw, John Riggins, Ted Hendricks and Roger Staubach.

Topps sets through the rest of the 1970s fell into a relatively standard format. Set sizes were big, card sizes were uniform and designs followed a pattern. Key cards in the 528-card 1973 set include Franco Harris, Jack Ham and Art Shell. The 1974 set had the same number of cards and the rookie cards of Ahmad Rashad, Harold Carmichael, Ray Guy and John Matuszak. It was deja vu all over again with the 1975 set, which features the rookie cards of Mel Blount and Dan Fouts. The key card in the 1976 set, and maybe of the decade, is Walter Payton. The set also has rookie cards of Harvey Martin, Russ Francis, Randy White and Steve Grogan.

The 1977 set also has a key rookie card of Steve Largent, which accounts for about one-fourth of the total price. Similarly, the 1978 set contains the rookie card of Tony Dorsett.

The big rookie in the 528-card 1979 set is Earl Campbell. There were really no key rookie cards in the 1980 Topps set.

The string of flat sets with no key rookie cards changed in 1981 with the arrival of Joe Montana in a 528-card set that also features the rookie card of future Hall of Famer Art Monk and possible Hall of Famer Dan Hampton. Despite the big bucks you have to pump into the set for Montana, the set's a good buy for the secondary rookies and the added headroom left Montana.

Topps' last 528-card set was issued in 1982 and may be an even better buy than the 1981 set, considering it contains the rookie cards of Ronnie Lott, Lawrence Taylor, Cris Collinsworth and Anthony Munoz, in addition to Montana's second-year card.

The 1983 set represents a dip in both set size (328 cards) and interest. The top rookies are Mike Singletary and Marcus Allen. It's different with the 1984 set, which features the best assortment of rookies of any set of the 1980s, including John Elway, Eric Dickerson, Dan Marino and Roger Craig.

Topps also issued a 132-card set for the USFL in 1984, which includes rookie cards of Jim Kelly, Anthony Carter,

Reggie White and Herschel Walker, and is expensive because of its limited production.

Topps' 1985 NFL set is great-looking but a lot less significant, unless you attach a lot of importance to second-year cards. The biggest cards are second-year cards of Marino and Elway and the rookie cards of Richard Dent and Warren Moon. Its black-bordered, big-type design makes it hard to find in perfect shape. Topps issued another 132-card USFL set in 1985, that includes Doug Flutie's first card.

Jerry Rice's rookie card accounts for half of the value of the 1986 Topps set. Other top rookies include Boomer Esiason, Bernie Kosar and Steve Young.

The 396-card 1987 Topps set includes rookie cards of Jim Everett and Randall Cunningham.

There's no shortage of top running back rookies in the 1988 set. In addition to the first football card of Bo Jackson, the set features rookies of Christian Okoye, Neal Anderson, Chris Doleman, Vinny Testaverde and Cornelius Bennett.

An update set added some excitement to Topps' 1989 set, which is keyed by the rookie cards of John Taylor, Keith Jackson, Sterling Sharpe, Thurman Thomas, Anthony Miller and the update rookies of Troy Aikman, Barry Sanders, Michael Irvin and Eric Metcalf.

The 1990 Topps set was a big one: 528 cards, including several subsets highlighted by a series of 25 draft picks. A 132-card update set was also issued. An update set was not issued in 1991, but the regular set jumped to 660 cards, the largest ever at that point. The company topped that mark in 1992, issuing 759 cards over three series. In 1993, Topps reverted to a 660-card set.

The company's premium issue, under the name Stadium Club, debuted in 1991 with a 500-card glossy set. In 1992 the set jumped to 700 cards, issued over three series. The 1993 effort had two 250-card series.

Topps' Finest brand surfaced in 1992 with a 44-card set, while the first full set of Finest arrived two years later with 220 cards. While Topps, Stadium Club and Finest name brands have continued through 2000, Topps has also tried several brands like FantaSports in 1993, Archives in 1994 and Gilt Edge and Laser in 1996 that were not continued.

Topps also added Topps Chrome to its lineup of football cards in 1996, and that brand has become a mainstay in all sports. The product essentially reprints cards from Topps produce, but adds a chromium finish to the front and also adds Refractor parallels.

FLEER

Fleer issued football cards sets for four years (1960-63) and then again beginning in 1990. Fleer jumped from a 132-card set to a high of 220 and then down to two sets of 88 cards each, and featured the AFL exclusively three out of the four years.

The 1960 Fleer set contains 132 cards, including Ron Mix, Jack Kemp, George Blanda, Sid Gillman and Hank Stram.

Fleer showed both AFL and NFL players for the only time in this 1961 set. It's the most appealing of the four Fleer sets; it has the best photography and cards of players from both leagues. The 220-card set has several rookie cards - Don Meredith, Jim Otto, Johnny Robinson and Don Maynard and a scarce 87-card run of AFL players.

The 88-card 1962 Fleer set shows nothing but AFL players, most notably Gino Cappelletti. All cards in this set are relatively scarce, which accounts for its high price tag.

Fleer stayed at 88 cards for its 1963 football set, another rough set with two very scarce short prints - Charlie Long and Bob Dougherty This set also has a handful of significant

rookie cards - Nick Buoniconti, Cookie Gilchrist, Keith Lincoln, Len Dawson and Lance Alworth. This set, like its 1961 and 1962 predecessors, is difficult to find in Mint condition at any price.

The company returned its line of football cards again in 1990 and has continued them. Fleer introduced its premium set, Fleer Ultra, in 1991, and has continued that label also. The 1992 and 1993 cards are glossy.

In 1995, Fleer purchased SkyBox, which had produced football since 1992, when it broke in with Impact and Primetime. Once under the Fleer/SkyBox umbrella, SkyMotion was issued in 1996 and Impact Rookies in 1997.

In 1997, Fleer renamed its Flair brand, which hadn't appeared in 1996, to Flair Showcase and mixed up the format with 120 players featured on three different frontal designs. Fleer/SkyBox also produced two series of Goudey Football in 1997 under the SkyBox name as well as 1997 SkyBox EX2001. In addition, NFL Autographics debuted in 1997 with autograph cards being inserted into all SkyBox releases for the season.

PHILADELPHIA

Philadelphia Gum's four sets chronicle the history of the NFL in, if not the Golden Age of pro football, the age from which many present and future Hall of Famers will come. These are the key years of the storied men in the trenches: Lombardi, Karras, Starr, Unitas, Brown, Olsen, Gifford, Ditka and Jurgensen. The sets are attractive, all more than 20 years old, and considerably underpriced compared to more modem issues. Their prices generally match the Topps sets of the same years, and yet contain more popular NFL players.

Philly's first set, the clean-lined, attractive 1964 Philadelphia set, has 198 cards and no short prints. However, it does have the first cards of Herb Adderly, Willie Davis, Henry Jordan, Willie Wood, Merlin Olsen and Roman Gabriel.

The key card in the 198-card 1965 Philadelphia set - a virtual clone of the 1964 set - is Paul Warfield, though the set also has the first cards of Deacon Jones, Charlie Taylor, Paul Krause and Mel Renfro.

The 1966 Philadelphia set is another fine-looking set, noteworthy for two big rookies: Gale Sayers and Dick Butkus. However, the set also has Jim Brown's last card, as well as Bob Hayes' first card.

Philly's last set, the 1967 Philadelphia set, has an easy-to-spot yellow border, first cards for Tommy Nobis and Lee Roy Jordan, and no scarcities.

PRO SET

Pro Set entered the football card market along with Score in 1989, injecting a much-needed shot of excitement and marketing savvy. Pro Set kicked off the year with a set that checked in at 615 cards, making it the largest football set. The set consists of a 440-card first series; a 100-card second series, including 30 announcer cards; 23 Super Bowl insert cards; and a 20-card "Final Update" set, which includes cards of Sterling Sharpe, Dave Meggett and Raiders coach Art Shell. The set has a handful of scarce variations as well as the rookie cards of Barry Sanders, Troy Aikman and Deion Sanders.

Pro Set produced full sets up until 1993, when their chronic over-production finally caught up with them and killed collector interest. Their final offering was a seven-card (eight with header) National Promo set in 1994.

UPPER DECK

Upper Deck produced its first football card set in 1991, after debuting in baseball in 1989. The 1991 set included 700 cards, which were issued in two series, as well as factory sets. Series I had 500 cards, while Series II (called High Series) had 200.

In 1993, Upper Deck added SP to its football product line. SP featured super-premium cards and one insert, called All-Pros. The SP line erupted with popularity in 1993, with rookies like Drew Bledsoe, Natrone Means and Rick Mirer. In 1994, SP added Holoviews and Die-cut Holoviews to its mix. The popularity of the Holoview technology also eventually led to an SPx brand, which featured a 50-card, all Holoview die-cut set.

In 1994, Collector's Choice also entered Upper Deck's mix. Collector's Choice was a base brand, tailored toward kids with its 99-cent pack price.

SPx was introduced by Upper Deck in 1996 with a 50-card set issued in one-card packs. This brand continued each year. SP Authentic debuted in 1997 with a 198-card set that was oriented toward autographs and memorabilia.

PLAYOFF

Playoff entered the football card market in 1992 with its Tekchrome finish. Its inaugural set featured 150 cards on thicker-than-usual card stock. Playoff added Contenders to its lineup in 1993, with 150 cards in the regular-issue set.

In 1995, Playoff split its product into Absolute (hobby) and Prime (retail). Although the checklist was identical, the photos were slightly different for each product, and the inserts were different, with some being totally unique to the product and others split into both.

In 1997, Playoff produced Absolute, Contenders, Zone and 1st & 10.

In recent years Collector's Edge, Pacific, Motion Vision, Sage, Press Pass and many other companies have been added to the mix. In 1996 alone there were 11 companies that produced major football issues, including Topps, Fleer/SkyBox, Upper Deck, Pinnacle, Donruss/Leaf, MotionVision, Press Pass, Score Board, Playoff, Pacific, Collector's Edge.

Score Board went backrupt in 1997 to reduce the number of licensees to 10.

Product releases have grown at an even greater rate than the number of manufacturers. In 1989, for example, there were only three football card releases - Topps, Score and Pro Set. In 1990, this number doubled to six, and in 1991, it doubled again to 12. In 1992, there were 22 football card releases, in 1993 there were 24, in 1994 it was 31 and in 1995 it was 46.

In 1996 there were 64 football card releases, and those products contained 363 insert sets. In 1997 the number of products jumped to 66, and contained a mind-boggling 451 insert sets. For 2000 we are up to 75 sets.

A

1987 Ace Fact Pack Chicago Bears

Ace Fact Pack in West Germany printed card sets for 12 National Football League teams. The cards, which have rounded corners, were distributed throughout Great Britain and England. They were designed to look like a deck of playing cards and are unnumbered. There were 33 cards created for each of the 12 teams, which are listed below alphabetically. Twenty-two cards are players; 11 are informational. All but the cards for the Chicago Bears (2-1/2" x 3-1/2") measure 2-1/4" x 3-5/8".

		MT
Complete Set (33):		175.00
Common Player:		4.00
(1)	Todd Bell	5.00
(2)	Mark Bortz	4.00
(3)	Kevin Butler	5.00
(4)	Jim Covert	6.00
(5)	Richard Dent	10.00
(6)	Dave Duerson	4.00
(7)	Gary Fencik	5.00
(8)	Willie Gault	8.00
(9)	Dan Hampton	10.00
(10)	Jay Hilgenberg	4.00
(11)	Wilber Marshall	6.00
(12)	Jim McMahon	10.00
(13)	Steve McMichael	6.00
(14)	Emery Moorehead	4.00
(15)	Keith Ortega	4.00
(16)	Walter Payton	70.00
(17)	William Perry	8.00
(18)	Mike Richardson	4.00
(19)	Mike Singletary	10.00
(20)	Matt Suhey	5.00
(21)	Keith Van Horne	4.00
(22)	Otis Wilson	5.00
(23)	Bears Helmet	4.00
(24)	Bears Information	4.00
(25)	Bears Uniform	4.00
(26)	Game Record Holders	4.00
(27)	Season Record Holders	4.00
(28)	Career Record Holders	4.00
(29)	Bears 1967-86	4.00
(30)	1986 Team Statistics	4.00
(31)	All-Time Greats	4.00
(32)	Roll of Honour	4.00
(33)	Soldier Field	4.00

1987 Ace Fact Pack Denver Broncos

Measuring 2-1/4" x 3-5/8", the 33-card set features 22 player cards and 11 organizational cards. The front showcases the team's logo and player's name at the top, with a photo and the player's bio filling the remainder of the card front. The opposite side of the card has a playing card design. The cards are unnumbered. The set was released in Great Britain.

		MT
Complete Set (33):		175.00
Common Player:		4.00
(1)	Keith Bishop	4.00
(2)	Bill Bryan	4.00
(3)	Mark Cooper	4.00
(4)	John Elway	90.00
(5)	Steve Foley	5.00
(6)	Mike Harden	4.00
(7)	Rick Hunley	4.00
(8)	Vance Johnson	5.00
(9)	Rulon Jones	5.00
(10)	Rich Karlis	4.00
(11)	Clarence Kay	5.00
(12)	Ken Lanier	5.00
(13)	Karl Mecklenburg	8.00
(14)	Chris Norman	4.00
(15)	Jim Ryan	4.00
(16)	Dennis Smith	5.00
(17)	Dave Studdard	4.00
(18)	Andre Townsend	4.00
(19)	Steve Watson	5.00
(20)	Gerald Wilhite	4.00
(21)	Sammy Winder	5.00
(22)	Louis Wright	5.00
(23)	Team Helmet	4.00
(24)	Team Information	4.00
(25)	Broncos Uniform	4.00
(26)	Game Record Holders	4.00
(27)	Season Record Holders	4.00
(28)	Career Record Holders	4.00
(29)	Record 1967-86	4.00
(30)	Roll of Honour	4.00
(31)	All-Time Greats	4.00
(32)	1986 Team Statistics	4.00
(33)	Denver Mile High Stadium	4.00

1987 Ace Fact Pack Dallas Cowboys

Measuring 2-1/4" x 3-5/8", the 33-card set follows the same design as the Bears and Broncos. The set was released in Great Britain. It has 22 player cards in the set and 11 organizational cards. The cards are unnumbered.

		MT
Complete Set (33):		200.00
Common Player:		4.00
(1)	Bill Bates	5.00
(2)	Doug Cosbie	5.00
(3)	Tony Dorsett	25.00
(4)	Michael Downs	4.00
(5)	John Dutton	5.00
(6)	Ron Fellows	4.00
(7)	Mike Hegman	4.00
(8)	Tony Hill	6.00
(9)	Jim Jeffcoat	5.00
(10)	Ed "Too Tall" Jones	12.00
(11)	Crawford Ker	4.00
(12)	Eugene Lockhart	5.00
(13)	Phil Pozderac	4.00
(14)	Tom Rafferty	5.00
(15)	Jeff Rohrer	4.00
(16)	Mike Sherrard	6.00
(17)	Glen Titensor	4.00
(18)	Mark Tuinei	5.00
(19)	Herschel Walker	15.00
(20)	Everson Walls	5.00
(21)	Danny White	8.00
(22)	Randy White	16.00
(23)	Cowboys Helmet	4.00
(24)	Cowboys Information	4.00
(25)	Cowboys Uniform	4.00
(26)	Game Record Holders	4.00
(27)	Season Record Holders	4.00
(28)	Career Record Holders	4.00
(29)	1967-86 Team Record	4.00
(30)	1986 Team Statistics	4.00
(31)	All-Time Greats	4.00
(32)	Roll of Honour	4.00
(33)	Texas Stadium	4.00

1987 Ace Fact Pack Miami Dolphins

Measuring 2-1/4" x 3-5/8", the 33-card set follows the same design as the others. It was released in Great Britain. There are 22 player cards and 11 highlight cards. The cards are unnumbered.

		MT
Complete Set (33):		300.00
Common Player:		4.00
(1)	Bob Baumhower	5.00
(2)	Woody Bennett	4.00
(3)	Doug Betters	5.00
(4)	Glenn Blackwood	5.00
(5)	Bud Brown	4.00
(6)	Bob Brudzinski	4.00
(7)	Mark Clayton	7.00
(8)	Mark Duper	7.00
(9)	Roy Foster	4.00
(10)	Jim Giesler	4.00
(11)	Hugh Green	6.00
(12)	Lorenzo Hampton	5.00
(13)	Bruce Hardy	4.00
(14)	William Judson	4.00
(15)	Greg Koch	4.00
(16)	Paul Lankford	4.00
(17)	George Little	4.00
(18)	Dan Marino	175.00
(19)	John Offerdahl	5.00
(20)	Dwight Stephenson	6.00
(21)	Don Strock	5.00
(22)	T.J. Turner	4.00
(23)	Dolphins Helmet	4.00
(24)	Team Information	4.00
(25)	Dolphins Uniform	4.00
(26)	Game Record Holders	4.00
(27)	Season Record Holders	4.00
(28)	Career Record Holders	4.00
(29)	Dolphins 1967-86	4.00
(30)	1986 Team Statistics	4.00
(31)	Dolphin Greats	4.00
(32)	Roll of Honour	4.00
(33)	Joe Robbie Stadium	4.00

1987 Ace Fact Pack San Francisco 49ers

Measuring 2-1/4" x 3-5/8", this 33-card set was released in Great Britain. The design follows the same format of the other teams in the set. There are 22 player cards and 11 highlights cards. The cards are unnumbered.

		MT
Complete Set (33):		400.00
Common Player:		4.00
(1)	John Ayers	4.00
(2)	Dwaine Board	4.00
(3)	Michael Carter	6.00
(4)	Dwight Clark	12.00
(5)	Roger Craig	12.00
(6)	Joe Cribbs	5.00
(7)	Randy Cross	5.00
(8)	Riki Ellison	4.00
(9)	Jim Fahnhorst	4.00
(10)	Keith Fahnhorst	4.00
(11)	Russ Francis	5.00
(12)	Don Griffin	5.00
(13)	Ronnie Lott	14.00
(14)	Milt McColl	4.00
(15)	Tim McKyer	5.00
(16)	Joe Montana	175.00
(17)	Bubba Paris	4.00
(18)	Fred Quinlan	4.00
(19)	Jerry Rice	150.00
(20)	Manu Tuiasosopo	4.00
(21)	Keena Turner	6.00
(22)	Carlton Williamson	4.00
(23)	49er Helmet	4.00
(24)	49er Information	4.00
(25)	49er Uniform	4.00
(26)	Game Record Holders	4.00
(27)	Season Record Holders	4.00
(28)	Career Record Holders	4.00
(29)	49ers History 1967-86	4.00
(30)	1986 Team Statistics	4.00
(31)	All-Time Greats	4.00
(32)	Roll of Honour	4.00
(33)	Candlestick Park	4.00

1987 Ace Fact Pack New York Giants

Measuring 2-1/4" x 3-5/8", the 33-card set follows the same design as the other teams in the series. Released in Great Britain, the set includes 22 player cards and 11 highlight cards. The cards are unnumbered.

		MT
Complete Set (33):		150.00
Common Player:		4.00
(1)	Billy Ard	4.00
(2)	Carl Banks	8.00
(3)	Mark Bavaro	5.00
(4)	Brad Benson	4.00
(5)	Harry Carson	8.00
(6)	Maurice Carthon (misspelled Morris)	5.00
(7)	Mark Collins	5.00
(8)	Chris Godfrey	4.00
(9)	Kenny Hill	4.00
(10)	Erik Howard	5.00
(11)	Bobby Johnson	4.00
(12)	Leonard Marshall	6.00
(13)	George Martin	5.00
(14)	Joe Morris	5.00
(15)	Karl Nelson	4.00
(16)	Bart Oates (misspelled Oakes)	5.00
(17)	Gary Reasons	5.00
(18)	Stacy Robinson	4.00
(19)	Phil Simms	20.00
(20)	Lawrence Taylor	30.00
(21)	Herb Welch	4.00
(22)	Perry Williams	4.00
(23)	Giants Helmet	4.00
(24)	Giants Information	4.00
(25)	Giant Uniforms	4.00
(26)	Game Record Holders	4.00
(27)	Season Record Holders	4.00
(28)	Career Record Holders	4.00
(29)	Giants 1967-86	4.00
(30)	1986 Team Statistics	4.00
(31)	All-Time Greats	4.00
(32)	Roll of Honour	4.00
(33)	Giants Stadium	4.00

1987 Ace Fact Pack New York Jets

Measuring 2-1/4" x 3-5/8", the 33-card set follows the same design as the other teams in the series. Released in Great Britain, there are 22 player cards and 11 highlight cards. The cards are unnumbered.

		MT
Complete Set (33):		120.00
Common Player:		4.00
(1)	Dan Alexander	4.00
(2)	Tom Baldwin	4.00
(3)	Barry Bennett	4.00
(4)	Russell Carter	5.00
(5)	Kyle Clifton	6.00
(6)	Bob Crable	4.00
(7)	Joe Fields	5.00
(8)	Rusty Guilbeau	4.00
(9)	Harry Hamilton	5.00
(10)	Johnny Hector	7.00
(11)	Jerry Holmes	4.00
(12)	Gordon King	4.00
(13)	Lester Lyles	4.00
(14)	Marty Lyons	5.00
(15)	Kevin McArthur	4.00
(16)	Freeman McNeil	8.00
(17)	Ken O'Brien	7.00
(18)	Tony Paige	6.00
(19)	Mickey Shuler	5.00
(20)	Jim Sweeney	4.00
(21)	Al Toon	8.50
(22)	Wesley Walker	9.50
(23)	Jets Helmet	4.00
(24)	Jets Team Information	4.00
(25)	Jets Uniform	4.00
(26)	Game Record Holders	4.00
(27)	Season Record Holders	4.00
(28)	Career Record Holders	4.00
(29)	1986 Team Statistics	4.00
(30)	Jets 1967-86	4.00
(31)	All-Time Greats	4.00
(32)	Roll of Honour	4.00
(33)	Giants Stadium	4.00

1987 Ace Fact Pack Detroit Lions

Measuring 2-1/4" x 3-5/8", the 33-card set follows the same design as the other teams in the series. Issued in Great Britain, the set includes 22 player cards and 11 highlight cards. The cards are unnumbered.

		MT
Complete Set (33):		120.00
Common Player:		4.00
(1)	Carl Bland	4.00
(2)	Lomas Brown	6.00
(3)	Jeff Chadwick	5.00
(4)	Mike Cofer	6.00
(5)	Keith Dorney	4.00
(6)	Keith Ferguson	4.00
(7)	William Gay	6.00
(8)	James Harrell	4.00
(9)	Eric Harrell	5.00
(10)	Garry James	5.00
(11)	Demetrious Johnson	4.00
(12)	James Jones	6.00
(13)	Chuck Long	5.00
(14)	Vernon Maxwell	5.00
(15)	Bruce McNorton	4.00
(16)	Devon Mitchell	4.00
(17)	Steve Lott	4.00
(18)	Eddie Murray	6.00
(19)	Harvey Smith	4.00
(20)	Rich Stenger	4.00
(21)	Eric Williams	4.00
(22)	Jimmy Williams	4.00
(23)	Detroit Lions Helmet	4.00
(24)	Team Information	4.00
(25)	Uniform Design	4.00
(26)	Game Record Holders	4.00
(27)	Season Record Holders	4.00
(28)	Career Record Holders	4.00
(29)	1986 Team Statistics	4.00
(30)	Team Record 1967-86	4.00
(31)	Championship Seasons	4.00
(32)	Pontiac Silverdome	4.00
(33)	All-Time Greats	4.00

A card number in parentheses ( ) indicates the set is unnumbered.

1987 Ace Fact Pack Green Bay Packers

Measuring 2-1/4" x 3-5/8", the 33-card set follows the same design as the other teams in the series. Issued in Great Britain, there are 22 player cards and 11 highlight cards. The cards are unnumbered.

		MT
Complete Set (33):		120.00
Common Player:		4.00
(1)	John Anderson	6.00
(2)	Robbie Bosco	5.00
(3)	Don Bracken	4.00
(4)	John Cannon	5.00
(5)	Alphonso Carreker	4.00
(6)	Kenneth Davis	8.00
(7)	Al Del Greco	4.00
(8)	Gary Ellerson	4.00
(9)	Gerry Ellis	5.00
(10)	Phillip Epps	6.00
(11)	Ron Hallstrom	4.00
(12)	Mark Lee	5.00
(13)	Bobby Leopold	4.00
(14)	Charles Martin	4.00
(15)	Brian Noble	5.00
(16)	Ken Ruettgers	5.00
(17)	Randy Scott	4.00
(18)	Walter Stanley	5.00
(19)	Ken Stills	4.00
(20)	Keith Uecker	4.00
(21)	Ed West	5.00
(22)	Randy Wright	5.00
(23)	Packer Helmet	4.00
(24)	Packer Information	4.00
(25)	Packer Uniform	4.00
(26)	Game Record Holders	4.00
(27)	Season Record Holders	4.00
(28)	Career Record Holders	4.00
(29)	1967-86 Team Record	4.00
(30)	1986 Team Statistics	4.00
(31)	All-Time Greats	4.00
(32)	Roll of Honour	4.00
(33)	Lambeau Field/Milwaukee County Stadium	4.00

1987 Ace Fact Pack Los Angeles Rams

Measuring 2-1/4" x 3-5/8", the 33-card set follows the same design as the other teams in the series. Issued in Great Britain, it contains 22 player cards and 11 highlight cards, which are unnumbered.

		MT
Complete Set (33):		120.00
Common Player:		4.00
(1)	Nolan Cromwell	6.00
(2)	Eric Dickerson	18.00
(3)	Reggie Doss	4.00
(4)	Carl Ekern	4.00
(5)	Henry Ellard	10.00
(6)	Jim Everett	10.00
(7)	Jerry Gray	5.00
(8)	Dennis Harrah	5.00
(9)	David Hull	4.00
(10)	Kevin House	5.00
(11)	LeRoy Irvin	5.00
(12)	Mark Jerue	4.50
(13)	Shawn Miller	4.00
(14)	Tom Newberry	5.00
(15)	Vince Newsome	4.50
(16)	Mel Owens	5.00
(17)	Irv Pankey	4.00
(18)	Doug Reed	5.00
(19)	Doug Smith	5.00
(20)	Jackie Slater	6.00
(21)	Charles White	6.00
(22)	Mike Wilcher	4.00
(23)	Rams Helmet	4.00
(24)	Rams Information	4.50
(25)	Rams Uniform	4.00
(26)	Game Record Holders	4.00
(27)	Season Record Holders	4.00
(28)	Career Record Holders	5.00
(29)	Team Record 1967-86	4.00
(30)	1986 Team Statistics	4.00
(31)	All-Time Greats	4.00
(32)	Rams Roll of Honour	4.50
(33)	Anaheim Stadium	4.00

1987 Ace Fact Pack Washington Redskins

Measuring 2-1/4" x 3-5/8", the 33-card set follows the same design as the other teams in the series. Issued in Great Britain, the set is broken up into 22 player cards and 11 highlight cards, which are unnumbered.

		MT
Complete Set (33):		175.00
Common Player:		4.00
(1)	Jeff Bostic	5.00
(2)	Dave Butz	6.00
(3)	Gary Clark	20.00
(4)	Monte Coleman	5.00
(5)	Vernon Dean	4.00
(6)	Clint Didier	5.00
(7)	Darryl Grant	4.00
(8)	Darrell Green	7.50
(9)	Russ Grimm	6.00
(10)	Joe Jacoby	6.00
(11)	Curtis Jordan	4.00
(12)	Dexter Manley	5.00
(13)	Charles Mann	6.00
(14)	Mark May	5.00
(15)	Rich Milot	4.00
(16)	Art Monk	30.00
(17)	Neal Olkewicz	6.00
(18)	George Rogers	8.00
(19)	Jay Schroeder	8.00
(20)	R.C. Thielemann	6.00
(21)	Alvin Walton	4.00
(22)	Don Warren	4.00
(23)	Redskin Helmet	4.00
(24)	Redskin Information	4.00
(25)	Redskin Uniforms	4.00
(26)	Game Record Holders	4.00
(27)	Season Record Holders	4.00
(28)	Career Record Holders	4.00
(29)	Redskins 1867-86	4.00
(30)	1986 Team Statistics	4.00
(31)	All-Time Redskins	4.00
(32)	Roll of Honour	4.00
(33)	Robert F. Kennedy Stadium	4.00

1987 Ace Fact Pack Seattle Seahawks

Measuring 2-1/4" x 3-5/8", the 33-card set follows the same design as the other teams in the series. Issued in Great Britain, the set is broken up into 22 player and 11 highlight cards, which are unnumbered.

		MT
Complete Set (33):		150.00
Common Player:		4.00
(1)	Edwin Bailey	4.00
(2)	Dave Brown	6.00
(3)	Jeff Bryant	4.00
(4)	Blair Bush	5.00
(5)	Keith Butler	4.00
(6)	Kenny Easley	5.00
(7)	Greg Gaines	4.00
(8)	Jacob Green	6.00
(9)	Norm Johnson	5.00
(10)	Dave Krieg	8.00
(11)	Steve Largent	30.00
(12)	Reggie Kinlaw	4.00
(13)	Ron Mattes	4.00
(14)	Bryan Millard	4.00
(15)	Eugene Robinson	5.00
(16)	Bruce Scholtz	4.00
(17)	Terry Taylor	4.00
(18)	Mike Tice	5.00
(19)	Daryl Turner	5.00
(20)	Curt Warner	7.50
(21)	John L. Williams	12.00
(22)	Fredd Young	5.00
(23)	Seattle Helmet	4.00
(24)	Seahawk Information	4.00
(25)	Seahawk Uniform	4.00
(26)	Game Record Holder	4.00
(27)	Season Record Holders	4.00
(28)	Career Record Holders	4.00
(29)	1977-86 Team Record	4.00
(30)	1986 Team Statistics	4.00
(31)	All-Time Greats	4.00
(32)	Roll of Honour	4.00
(33)	Kingdome	4.00

1989 Action Packed Prototypes

These cards were produced as prototypes before Action Packed released its 1989 30-card test set. The gold-bordered front has a raised color action photo on it; the back has stats, a head shot, notes, a card number and a space for an autograph. These cards, numbered 72 and 101, can be distinguished from the test set by where the card number appears. On these cards, they are on the same side as the mug shot; on the test cards they are on the opposite side.

		MT
Complete Set (2):		75.00
Common Player:		45.00
72	Freeman McNeil	45.00
101	Phil Simms	45.00

1989 Action Packed Test

These 30 cards are standard size and were packaged in packs of six. Ten players from the Chicago Bears, New York Giants and Washington Redskins are represented in the set, which was copyrighted by Hi-Pro Marketing of Northbrook, Ill. Each front has a gold-border and a raised color action photo; the back has a head shot, statistics, informational notes, a card number and a space for an autograph.

		MT
Complete Set (30):		25.00
Common Player:		.50
Foil Pack (6):		2.50
Foil Wax Box (36):		40.00
1	Neal Anderson	4.00
2	Trace Armstrong	.60
3	Kevin Butler	.50
4	Richard Dent	.75
5	Dennis Gentry	.50
6	Dan Hampton	.75
7	Jay Hilgenberg	.60
8	Thomas Sanders	.60
9	Mike Singletary	.75
10	Mike Tomczak	.75
11	Raul Allegre	.50
12	Ottis Anderson	.75
13	Mark Bavaro	.60
14	Terry Kinard	.50
15	Lionel Manuel	.50
16	Leonard Marshall	.60
17	Dave Meggett	4.50
18	Joe Morris	.75
19	Phil Simms	1.00
20	Lawrence Taylor	1.75
21	Kelvin Bryant	.75
22	Darrell Green	1.00
23	Dexter Manley	.60
24	Charles Mann	.60
25	Wilber Marshall	.60
26	Art Monk	1.50
27	Jamie Morris	.60
28	Tracy Rocker	.60
29	Mark Rypien	12.00
30	Ricky Sanders	1.00

1990 Action Packed

Action Packed was released in two series over the summer, with the first available in June and the second available in August. The total of 280 cards was randomly split up between the two series. In the first series, 126 players were issued; 154 came out in Series II. A factory set was also issued. The cards are embossed, with a gold foil and rounded corners. Special cards included those honoring the retired Reggie Williams and Steve Largent; a card back for Christian Okoye with a phrase written in Nigerian; and a Braille card featuring the retired Jim Plunkett.

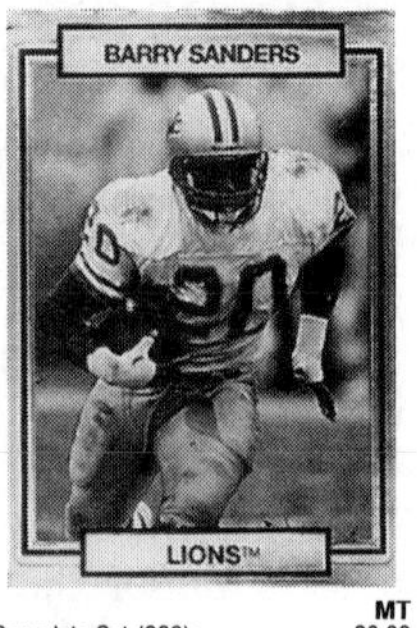

		MT
Complete Set (280):		20.00
Complete Factory (281):		20.00
Common Player:		.10
Minor Stars:		.20
Series 1 Foil Pack (6):		.75
Series 1 Foil Wax Box (36):		19.00
Series 2 Foil Pack (6):		.75
Series 2 Foil Wax Box (36):		19.00
1	Aundray Bruce	.10
2	Scott Case	.10
3	Tony Casillas	.10
4	Shawn Collins	.10
5	Marcus Cotton	.10
6	Bill Fralic	.10
7	Tim Green	.10
8	Chris Miller	.20
9	Deion Sanders	1.25
10	John Settle	.10
11	Cornelius Bennett	.20
12	Shane Conlan	.10
13	Kent Hill	.10
14	Jim Kelly	.50
15	Mark Kelso	.10
16	Scott Norwood	.10
17	Andre Reed	.20
18	Fred Smerlas	.10
19	Bruce Smith	.20
20	Thurman Thomas	.50
21	Neal Anderson	.20
22	Kevin Butler	.10
23	Richard Dent	.20
24	Dennis Gentry	.10
25	Dan Hampton	.10
26	Jay Hilgenberg	.10
27	Steve McMichael	.10
28	Brad Muster	.10
29	Mike Singletary	.20
30	Mike Tomczak	.10
31	James Brooks	.10
32	Rickey Dixon	.10
33	Boomer Esiason	.20
34	David Fulcher	.10
35	Rodney Holman	.10
36	Tim Krumrie	.10
37	Tim McGee	.10
38	Anthony Munoz	.20
39	Reggie Williams	.10
40	Ickey Woods	.10
41	Thane Gash	.10
42	Mike Johnson	.10
43	Bernie Kosar	.20
44	Reggie Langhorne	.10
45	Clay Matthews	.10
46	Eric Metcalf	.20
47	Frank Minnifield	.10
48	Ozzie Newsome	.20
49	Webster Slaughter	.10
50	Felix Wright	.10
51	Troy Aikman	2.00
52	James Dixon	.10
53	Michael Irvin	.50
54	Jim Jeffcoat	.10
55	Ed Jones	.10
56	Eugene Lockhart	.10
57	Danny Noonan	.10
58	Paul Palmer	.10
59	Everson Walls	.10
60	Steve Walsh	.20
61	Steve Atwater	.10
62	Tyrone Braxton	.10
63	John Elway	2.00
64	Bobby Humphrey	.10
65	Mark Jackson	.10
66	Vance Johnson	.10
67	Greg Kragen	.10
68	Karl Mecklenberg	.10
69	Dennis Smith	.10
70	David Treadwell	.10
71	Jim Arnold	.10
72	Jerry Ball	.10
73	Bennie Blades	.10
74	Mel Gray	.10
75	Richard Johnson	.10
76	Eddie Murray	.10
77	Rodney Peete	.10
78	Barry Sanders	5.00
79	Chris Spielman	.10
80	Walter Stanley	.10
81	Dave Brown	.10
82	Brent Fullwood	.10
83	Tim Harris	.10
84	Johnny Holland	.10
85	Don Majkowski	.10
86	Tony Mandarich	.10
87	Mark Murphy	.10
88	Brian Noble	.10
89	Ken Ruettgers	.10
90	Sterling Sharpe	.20
91	Ray Childress	.10
92	Ernest Givins	.10
93	Alonzo Highsmith	.10
94	Drew Hill	.10
95	Bruce Matthews	.10
96	Bubba McDowell	.10
97	Warren Moon	.50

98 Mike Munchak .10
99 Allen Pinkett .10
100 Mike Rozier .10
101 Albert Bentley .10
102 Duane Bickett .10
103 Bill Brooks .10
104 Chris Chandler .20
105 Ray Donaldson .10
106 Chris Hinton .10
107 Andre Rison .20
108 Keith Taylor .10
109 Clarence Verdin .10
110 Fredd Young .10
111 Deron Cherry .10
112 Steve DeBerg .10
113 Dino Hackett .10
114 Albert Lewis .10
115 Nick Lowery .10
116 Christian Okoye .10
117 Stephone Paige .10
118 Kevin Ross .10
119 Derrick Thomas .20
120 Mike Webster .10
121 Marcus Allen .20
122 Eddie Anderson .10
123 Steve Beuerlein .20
124 Tim Brown .50
125 Mervyn Fernandez .10
127 Bob Golic .10
128 Bo Jackson .50
129 Howie Long .20
130 Greg Townsend .10
131 Willie Anderson .10
132 Greg Bell .10
133 Robert Delpino .10
134 Henry Ellard .10
135 Jim Everett .20
136 Jerry Gray .10
137 Kevin Greene .20
138 Tom Newberry .10
139 Jackie Slater .10
140 Doug Smith .10
141 Mark Clayton .10
142 Jeff Cross .10
143 Mark Duper .10
144 Ferrell Edmunds .10
145 Jim Jensen .10
146 Dan Marino 3.50
147 John Offerdahl .10
148 Louis Oliver .10
149 Reggie Roby .10
150 Sammie Smith .10
151 Joey Browner .10
152 Anthony Carter .10
153 Chris Doleman .10
154 Steve Jordan .10
155 Carl Lee .10
156 Randall McDaniel .10
157 Keith Millard .10
158 Herschel Walker .20
159 Wade Wilson .10
160 Gary Zimmerman .10
161 Hart Lee Dykes .10
162 Irving Fryar .20
163 Steve Grogan .10
164 Maurice Hurst .10
165 Fred Marion .10
166 Stanley Morgan .10
167 Robert Perryman .10
168 John Stephens .10
169 Andre Tippett .10
170 Brent Williams .10
171 John Fourcade .10
172 Bobby Hebert .20
173 Dalton Hilliard .10
174 Rickey Jackson .10
175 Vaughan Johnson .10
176 Eric Martin .10
177 Robert Massey .10
178 Rueben Mayes .10
179 Sam Mills .10
180 Pat Swilling .10
181 Ottis Anderson .20
182 Carl Banks .10
183 Mark Bavaro .10
184 Mark Collins .10
185 Leonard Marshall .10
186 Dave Meggett .10
187 Gary Reasons .10
188 Phil Simms .20
189 Lawrence Taylor .50
190 Odessa Turner .10
191 Kyle Clifton .10
192 James Hasty .10
193 Johnny Hector .10
194 Jeff Lagemann .10
195 Pat Leahy .10
196 Erik McMillan .10
197 Ken O'Brien .10
198 Mickey Shuler .10
199 Al Toon .10
200 JoJo Townsell .10
201 Eric Allen .10
202 Jerome Brown .10
203 Keith Byars .10
204 Cris Carter 1.00
205 Wes Hopkins .10
206 Keith Jackson .20
207 Seth Joyner .10
208 Mike Quick .10
209 Andre Waters .10
210 Reggie White .50
211 Rich Carmarillo .10
212 Roy Green .10
213 Ken Harvey .10
214 Gary Hogeboom .10
215 Tim McDonald .10
216 Stump Mitchell .10
217 Luis Sharpe .10
218 Vai Sikahema .10
219 J.T. Smith .10
220 Ron Wolfley .10
221 Gary Anderson .10
222 Bubby Brister .10
223 Merril Hoge .10
224 Tunch Ilken .10
225 Louis Lipps .10
226 David Little .10
227 Greg Lloyd .10
228 Dwayne Woodruff .10
229 Rod Woodson .20
230 Tim Worley .10
231 Marion Butts .10
232 Gill Byrd .10
233 Burt Grossman .10
234 Jim McMahon .20
235 Anthony Miller .20
236 Leslie O'Neal .10
237 Gary Plummer .10
238 Billy Ray Smith .10
239 Tim Spencer .10
240 Lee Williams .10
241 Mike Cofer .10
242 Roger Craig .20
243 Charles Haley .10
244 Ronnie Lott .20
245 Guy McIntyre .10
246 Joe Montana 2.50
247 Tom Rathman .10
248 Jerry Rice 2.00
249 John Taylor .20
250 Michael Walter .10
251 Brian Blades .10
252 Jacob Green .10
253 Dave Krieg .10
254 Steve Largent .20
255 Joe Nash .10
256 Rufus Porter .10
257 Eugene Robinson .20
258 Paul Skansi .10
259 Curt Warner .10
260 John L. Williams .10
261 Mark Carrier .10
262 Reuben Davis .10
263 Harry Hamilton .10
264 Bruce Hill .10
265 Donald Igwebuike .10
266 Eugene Marve .10
267 Kevin Murphy .10
268 Mark Robinson .10
269 Lars Tate .10
270 Vinny Testaverde .50
271 Gary Clark .10
272 Monte Coleman .10
273 Darrell Green .20
274 Charles Mann .10
275 Wilbur Marshall .10
276 Art Monk .20
277 Gerald Riggs .10
278 Mark Rypien .20
279 Rickey Sanders .10
280 Alvin Walton .10
NNO Jim Plunkett BR (Braille) 4.00
NNO Checklist .10

1990 Action Packed Rookie Update

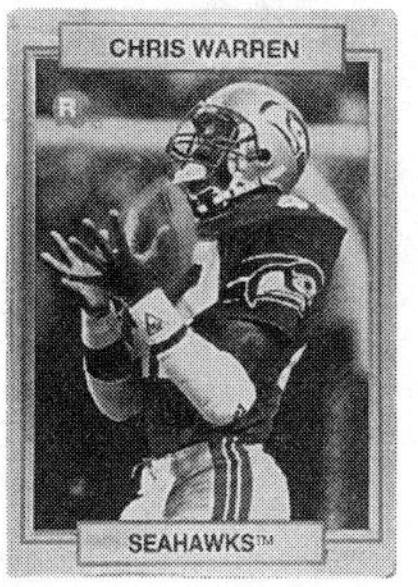

Issued in November 1990, the Update set includes each of the 1990 first-round draft choices, rookie prospects, and traded players. Randall Cunningham, who did not appear in the regular 1990 Action Packed set, signed a late contract with the NFL Players Association and does not appear in the Update set. Cards were issued in both wax packs and factory sets.

MT
Complete Set (84): 20.00
Complete Factory (84): 20.00
Common Player: .10
Minor Stars: .20
Foil Pack (6): 2.00
Foil Box (36): 55.00
1 Jeff George 2.00
2 Richmond Webb .20
3 James Williams .10
4 Tony Bennett .20
5 Darrell Thompson .10
6 Steve Broussard .10
7 Rodney Hampton .75
8 Rob Moore 3.00
9 Alton Montgomery .10
10 Leroy Butler .50
11 Anthony Johnson .50
12 Scott Mitchell 1.00
13 Mike Fox .10
14 Robert Blackmon .10
15 Blair Thomas .10
16 Tony Stargell .10
17 Peter Tom Willis .10
18 Harold Green .20
19 Bernard Clark .10
20 Aaron Wallace .10
21 Dennis Brown .10
22 Johnny Johnson .10
23 Chris Calloway .50
24 Walter Wilson .10
25 Dexter Carter .10
26 Percy Snow .10
27 Johnny Bailey .10
28 Mike Bellamy .10
29 Ben Smith .10
30 Mark Carrier .50
31 James Francis .10
32 Lamar Lathon .10
33 Bern Brostek .10
34 Emmitt Smith 15.00
35 Andre Collins .10
36 Alexander Wright .10
37 Fred Barnett .20
38 Junior Seau 3.00
39 Cortez Kennedy .50
40 Terry Wooden .10
41 Eric Davis .10
42 Fred Washington .10
43 Reggie Cobb .10
44 Andre Ware .20
45 Anthony Smith .10
46 Shannon Sharpe 8.00
47 Harlon Barnett .10
48 Greg McMurty .10
49 Stacey Simmons .10
50 Calvin Williams .20
51 Anthony Thompson .10
52 Ricky Proehl .50
53 Tony James .10
54 Ray Agnew .10
55 Tom Hodson .10
56 Ron Cox .10
57 Leroy Hoard 1.00
58 Eric Green .50
59 Barry Foster .10
60 Keith McCants .10
61 Oliver Barnett .10
62 Chris Warren 1.00
63 Pat Terrell .10
64 Renaldo Turnbull .10
65 Chris Chandler .20
66 Everson Walls .10
67 Alonzo Highsmith .10
68 Gary Anderson .20
69 Fred Smerlas .10
70 Jim McMahon .50
71 Curt Warner .20
72 Stanley Morgan .10
73 Dave Waymer .10
74 Billy Joe Tolliver .20
75 Tony Eason .10
76 Max Montoya .10
77 Greg Bell .10
78 Dennis McKinnon .10
79 Raymond Clayborn .10
80 Broderick Thomas .10
81 Timm Rosenbach .10
82 Tim McKyer .10
83 Andre Rison .50
84 Randall Cunningham .75

1990 Action Packed All-Madden

This 58-card set pictures players selected by CBS analyst and former coach John Madden. Cards were released in late February of 1991. Cards were issued in six-card wax packs and in complete sets. The set features Action Packed's first borderless set, previewing the 1991 set. Cards are standard-sized, embossed, and feature Madden's comments about each player on the back.

MT
Complete Set (58): 20.00
Common Player: .25
Wax Box: 20.00
1 Joe Montana 3.00
2 Jerry Rice 3.00
3 Charles Haley .40
4 Steve Wisniewski .25
5 Dave Meggett .40
6 Ottis Anderson .40
7 Nate Newton .25
8 Warren Moon 1.00
9 Emmitt Smith 6.00
10 Jackie Slater .25
11 Pepper Johnson .25
12 Lawrence Taylor .75
13 Sterling Sharpe 1.00
14 Sean Landeta .25
15 Richard Dent .40
16 Neal Anderson .50
17 Bruce Matthews .25
18 Matt Millen .25
19 Reggie White .50
20 Greg Townsend .25
21 Troy Aikman 3.00
22 Don Mosebar .25
23 Jeff Zimmerman .25
24 Rod Woodson .40
25 Keith Byars .40
26 Randall Cunningham .75
27 Reyna Thompson .40
28 Marcus Allen .60
29 Gary Clark .50
30 Anthony Carter .50
31 Bubba Paris .50
32 Ronnie Lott .50
33 Erik Howard .25
34 Ernest Givins .25
35 Mike Munchak .25
36 Jim Lachey .25
37 Merril Hoge .25
38 Darrell Green .25
39 Pierce Holt .25
40 Jerome Brown .25
41 William Perry .25
42 Michael Carter .25
43 Keith Jackson .40
44 Kevin Fagan .25
45 Mark Carrier .40
46 Fred Barnett .75
47 Barry Sanders 3.00
48 Pat Swilling, Rickey Jackson .50
49 Sam Mills, Vaughan Johnson .25
50 Jacob Green .25
51 Stan Brock .25
52 Dan Hampton .25
53 Brian Noble .25
54 John Elliott .25
55 Matt Bahr .25
56 Bill Parcells .25
57 Art Shell .25
58 All-Madden Team Trophy .25

1991 Action Packed

Action Packed issued a borderless card with a gold stripe protecting the back seam, both improving on the previous year's design. Cards are arranged in alphabetical order by city and player. Two unnumbered prototype cards were also created, for Randall Cunningham and Emmitt Smith. The cards are labeled on the back as being 1991 prototypes. Cunningham's is valued at $10; Smith's is $15. Eight Braille cards, numbers 281-288, were also produced. The cards, similar in design to the regular issue, feature statistical leaders but have different photos than the players' regular cards. The backs are written in Braille. The Braille cards were only available in factory sets.

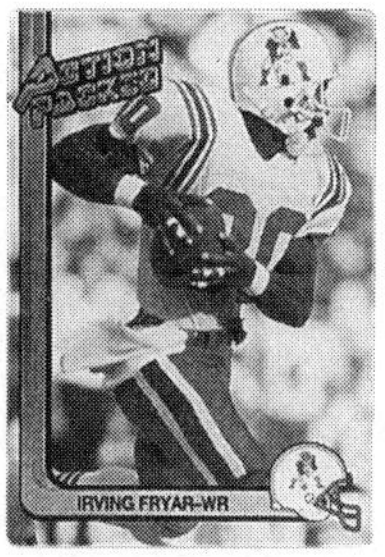

MT
Complete Set (280): 30.00
Complete Factory (291): 30.00
Common Player: .10
Minor Stars: .20
Pack (6): 1.00
Wax Box (24:) 20.00
1 Steve Broussard .10
2 Scott Case .10
3 Brian Jordan .20
4 Darion Conner .10
5 Tim Green .10
6 Chris Miller .20
7 Andre Rison .50
8 Mike Rozier .10
9 Deion Sanders 1.00
10 Jessie Tuggle .10
11 Leonard Smith .10
12 Shane Conlan .10
13 Kent Hull .10
14 Keith McKeller .10
15 James Lofton .20
16 Andre Reed .20
17 Bruce Smith .20
18 Darryl Talley .10
19 Steve Tasker .10
20 Thurman Thomas .50
21 Neal Anderson .10
22 Trace Armstrong .10
23 Mark Bortz .10
24 Mark Carrier (Chi.) .10
25 Wendell Davis .10
26 Richard Dent .10
27 Jim Harbaugh .20
28 Jay Hilgenberg .10
29 Brad Muster .10
30 Mike Singletary .20
31 Harold Green .10
32 James Brooks .10
33 Eddie Brown .10
34 Boomer Esiason .20
35 James Francis .10
36 David Fulcher .10
37 Rodney Holman .10
38 Tim McGee .10
39 Anthony Munoz .10
40 Ickey Woods .10
41 Rob Burnett .10
42 Thane Gash .10
43 Mike Johnson .10
44 Brian Brennan .10
45 Reggie Langhorne .10
46 Kevin Mack .10
47 Clay Matthews .10
48 Eric Metcalf .20
49 Anthony Pleasant .10
50 Ozzie Newsome .10
51 Troy Aikman 2.00
52 Issiac Holt .10
53 Michael Irvin .50
54 Jimmie Jones .10
55 Eugene Lockhart .10
56 Kelvin Martin .10
57 Ken Norton Jr. .10
58 Jay Novacek .10
59 Emmitt Smith 4.00
60 Daniel Stubbs .10
61 Steve Atwater .10
62 Michael Brooks .10
63 John Elway 2.00
64 Simon Fletcher .10
65 Bobby Humphrey .10
66 Mark Jackson .10
67 Vance Johnson .10
68 Karl Mecklenburg .10
69 Dennis Smith .10
70 Greg Kragen .10
71 Jerry Ball .10
72 Lomas Brown .10
73 Robert Clark .10
74 Michael Coper .10
75 Mel Gray .10
76 Richard Johnson .10
77 Rodney Peete .20
78 Barry Sanders 4.00
79 Chris Spielman .10
80 Andre Ware .10
81 Matt Brock .10
82 Leroy Butler .10
83 Tim Harris .10
84 Perry Kemp .10
85 Don Majkowski .10
86 Mark Murphy .10
87 Brian Noble .10
88 Sterling Sharpe .20
89 Darrell Thompson .10
90 Ed West .10
91 Ray Childress .10
92 Ernest Givins .10
93 Drew Hill .10
94 Haywood Jeffires .10
95 Richard Johnson .10
96 Sean Jones .10
97 Bruce Matthews .10
98 Warren Moon .20
99 Mike Munchak .10
100 Lorenzo White .10
101 Albert Bentley .10
102 Duane Bickett .10
103 Bill Brooks .10
104 Jeff George .50
105 Jon Hand .10
106 Jeff Herrod .10
107 Jessie Hester .10
108 Mike Prior .10
109 Rohn Stark .10
110 Clarence Verdin .10
111 Steve Deberg .10
112 Dan Saleaumua .10
113 Albert Lewis .10
114 Nick Lowery .10
115 Christian Okoye .10
116 Stephone Paige .10
117 Kevin Ross .10
118 Dino Hackett .10
119 Derrick Thomas .20
120 Barry Word .10
121 Marcus Allen .25
122 Mervyn Fernandez .10
123 Willie Gault .10
124 Bo Jackson .25
125 Terry McDaniel .10
126 Don Mosebar .10
127 Jay Schroeder .10
128 Greg Townsend .10
129 Aaron Wallace .10
130 Steve Wisniewski .10
131 Willie Anderson .10
132 Henry Ellard .10
133 Jim Everett .20
134 Cleveland Gary .10
135 Jerry Gray .10
136 Kevin Greene .10
137 Buford McGee .10
138 Vince Newsome .10
139 Jackie Slater .10
140 Frank Stams .10
141 Jeff Cross .10
142 Mark Duper .10
143 Ferrell Edmunds .10
144 Dan Marino 3.00
145 Louis Oliver .10
146 John Offerdahl .10
147 Tony Paige .10
148 Sammie Smith .10
149 Richmond Webb .10
150 Jarvis Williams .10
151 Joey Browner .10
152 Anthony Carter .10
153 Chris Doleman .10
154 Hassan Jones .10
155 Steve Jordan .10
156 Carl Lee .10
157 Randall McDaniel .10
158 Mike Merriweather .10
159 Herschel Walker .20
160 Wade Wilson .10
161 Ray Agnew .10
162 Bruce Armstrong .10
163 Marv Cook .10
164 Hart Lee Dykes .10
165 Irving Fryar .10
166 Tom Hodson .10
167 Ronnie Lippett .10
168 Fred Marion .10
169 John Stephens .10
170 Brent Williams .10
171 Morten Andersen .10
172 Gene Atkins .10
173 Craig Heyward .10
174 Rickey Jackson .10
175 Vaughan Johnson .10
176 Eric Martin .10
177 Rueben Mayes .10
178 Pat Swilling .10
179 Renaldo Turnbull .10
180 Steve Walsh .10
181 Ottis Anderson .10
182 Rodney Hampton .20
183 Jeff Hostetler .20
184 Pepper Johnson .10
185 Sean Landeta .10
186 Dave Meggett .10
187 Bart Oates .10
188 Phil Simms .10
189 Lawrence Taylor .20
190 Reyna Thompson .10
191 Brad Baxter .10
192 Dennis Byrd .10
193 Kylce Clifton .10
194 James Hasty .10
195 Pat Leahy .10
196 Erik McMillan .10
197 Rob Moore .50
198 Ken O'Brien .10
199 Mark Boyer .10
200 Al Toon .10
201 Fred Barnett .10
202 Jerome Brown .10
203 Keith Byars .10
204 Randall Cunningham .50
205 Wes Hopkins .10
206 Keith Jackson .10
207 Seth Joyner .10
208 Heath Sherman .10
209 Reggie White .50
210 Calvin Williams .10
211 Roy Green .10
212 Ken Harvey .10
213 Luis Sharpe .10
214 Ernie Jones .10
215 Tim McDonald .10
216 Freddie Joe Nunn .10
217 Ricky Proehl .10
218 Timm Rosenbach .10
219 Anthony Thompson .10
220 Lonnie Young .10
221 Gary Anderson .10
222 Bubby Brister .10
223 Eric Green .10
224 Merril Hoge .10
225 Carnell Lake .10
226 Louis Lipps .10
227 David Little .10
228 Greg Lloyd .10
229 Gerald Williams .10
230 Rod Woodson .10
231 Marion Butts .10
232 Gill Byrd .10
233 Burt Grossman .10
234 Courtney Hall .10
235 Ronnie Harmon .10
236 Anthony Miller .10
237 Leslie O'Neal .10
238 Junior Seau .50
239 Billy Joe Tolliver .10
240 Lee Williams .10
241 Dexter Carter .10
242 Kevin Fagan .10
243 Charles Haley .10
244 Brent Jones .10
245 Ronnie Lott .20
246 Guy McIntyre .10
247 Joe Montana 2.50
248 Jerry Rice 2.00
249 John Taylor .10
250 Roger Craig .20
251 Brian Blades .10
252 Derrick Penner .10
253 Nesby Glasgow .10
254 Jacob Green .10
255 Tommy Kane .10
256 Dave Krieg .10
257 Rufus Porter .10
258 Eugene Robinson .10
259 Cortez Kennedy .10
260 John L. Williams .10
261 Gary Anderson .10
262 Mark Carrier .10
263 Steve Christie .10
264 Reggie Cobb .10
265 Paul Gruber .10
266 Wayne Haddix .10
267 Bruce Hill .10
268 Keith McCants .10
269 Vinny Testaverde .50
270 Broderick Thomas .10
271 Earnest Byner .10
272 Gary Clark .10
273 Darrell Green .10
274 Jim Lachey .10
275 Chip Lohmiller .10
276 Charles Mann .10
277 Wilber Marshall .10
278 Art Monk .20
279 Mark Rypien .10
280 Alvin Walton .10
281 Randall Cunningham (Braille) .50
282 Warren Moon (Braille) .20
283 Barry Sanders (Braille) 5.00
284 Thurman Thomas (Braille) .50
285 Jerry Rice (Braille) 2.00
286 Haywood Jeffires (Braille) .20
287 Charles Haley (Braille) .20
288 Derrick Thomas (Braille) .20
289 NFC Logo Card .20
290 AFC Logo Card .20
291 Checklist .10

1991 Action Packed 24K Gold

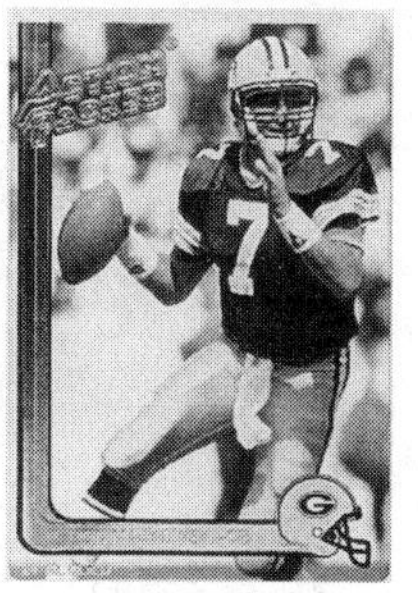

These cards were randomly issued in foil packs of 1991 Action Packed cards. Cards feature the regular-issue fronts, but the stripe has been done in 24k gold. Cards have also been stamped 24k on the front and are numbered 1G-42G on the back. It's estimated that less than 8,000 were made of each card. Generally, the cards are valued at about 15 times the amount of the corresponding regular Action Packed card.

MT
Complete Set (42): 500.00
Common Player: 5.00
Minor Stars: 10.00
1 Andre Rison 10.00
2 Deion Sanders 20.00
3 Andre Reed 5.00
4 Bruce Smith 5.00
5 Thurman Thomas 10.00
6 Neal Anderson 5.00
7 Mark Carrier 5.00
8 Mike Singletary 5.00
9 Boomer Esiason 5.00
10 James Francis 5.00
11 Anthony Munoz 5.00
12 Troy Aikman 40.00
13 Emmitt Smith 60.00
14 John Elway 40.00
15 Bobby Humphrey 5.00
16 Barry Sanders 80.00
17 Don Majikowski 5.00
18 Sterling Sharpe 10.00
19 Warren Moon 10.00
20 Jeff George 10.00
21 Christian Okoye 5.00
22 Derrick Thomas 10.00
23 Barry Word 5.00
24 Marcus Allen 10.00
25 Bo Jackson 10.00
26 Jim Everett 5.00
27 Cleveland Gary 5.00
28 Dan Marino 60.00
29 Herschel Walker 5.00
30 Ottis Anderson 5.00
31 Rodney Hampton 5.00
32 Dave Meggett 5.00
33 Marion Butts 5.00
34 Randall Cunningham 10.00
35 Reggie White 10.00
36 Jerry Rice 40.00
37 Eric Green 5.00
38 Charles Haley 5.00
39 Ronnie Lott 5.00
40 Joe Montana 60.00
41 Vinny Testaverde 10.00
42 Gary Clark 5.00

1991 Action Packed Rookie Update

This set features the first 26 top draft picks among its 74 rookie cards, plus 10 traded and update cards. Each card has an embossed helmet with a white "R" inside to indicate the player

is a rookie. The backs are written in red and have the player's collegiate statistics. An Emmitt Smith prototype card was included in each case of 1991 Action Packed Rookie/Update foil or factory set ordered. Special 24K gold cards were also made for the 26 first-round draft draft picks. They were inserted into update packs.

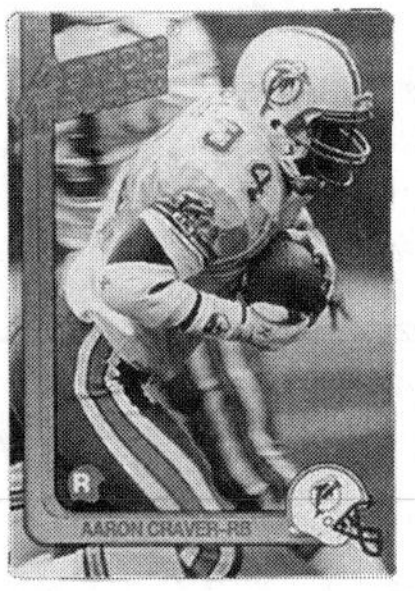

		MT
Complete Set (84):		15.00
Complete Factory (84):		15.00
Common Player:		.05
Minor Stars:		.10
Pack (6):		1.25
Wax Box (24):		25.00
1	*Herman Moore*	3.00
2	*Eric Turner*	.10
3	*Mike Croel*	.10
4	*Alfred Williams*	.05
5	*Stanley Richard*	.10
6	*Russell Maryland*	.25
7	*Pat Harlow*	.05
8	*Alvin Harper*	.25
9	*Mike Pritchard*	.25
10	*Leonard Russell*	.25
11	*Jarrod Bunch*	.10
12	*Dan McGwire*	.10
13	*Bobby Wilson*	.05
14	*Vinnie Clark*	.05
15	*Kelvin Pritchett*	.05
16	*Harvey Williams*	.25
17	*Stan Thomas*	.05
18	*Todd Marinovich*	.10
19	*Antone Davis*	.05
20	*Greg Lewis*	.05
21	*Brett Favre*	8.00
22	*Wesley Carroll*	.05
23	*Ed McCaffrey*	3.00
24	*Reggie Barrett*	.05
25	*Chris Zorich*	.05
26	*Kenny Walker*	.05
27	*Aaron Craver*	.05
28	*Browning Nagle*	.05
29	*Nick Bell*	.05
30	*Anthony Morgan*	.05
31	*Jesse Campbell*	.05
32	*Eric Bieniemy*	.10
33	*Ricky Ervins*	.10
34	*Kanavis McGhee*	.05
35	*Shawn Moore*	.05
36	*Todd Lyght*	.10
37	*Eric Swann*	.25
38	*Henry Jones*	.05
39	*Ted Washington*	.05
40	*Charles McRae*	.05
41	*Randal Hill*	.10
42	*Huey Richardson*	.05
43	*Roman Phifer*	.05
44	*Ricky Watters*	2.00
45	*Esera Tuaolo*	.05
46	*Michael Jackson*	.25
47	*Shawn Jefferson*	.25
48	*Tim Barnett*	.05
49	*Chuck Webb*	.05
50	*Moe Gardner*	.05
51	*Mo Lewis*	.05
52	*Mike Dumas*	.05
53	*Jon Vaughn*	.05
54	*Jerome Henderson*	.05
55	*Harry Colon*	.05
56	*David Daniels*	.05
57	*Phil Hansen*	.05
58	*Ernie Mills*	.05
59	*John Kasay*	.05
60	*Darren Lewis*	.05
61	*James Joseph*	.05
62	*Robert Wilson*	.05
63	*Lawrence Dawsey*	.05
64	*Mike Jones*	.05
65	*Dave McCloughan*	.05
66	*Erric Pegram*	.10
67	*Aeneas Williams*	.25
68	*Reggie Johnson*	.25
69	*Todd Scott*	.05
70	*James Jones*	.05
71	*Lamar Rogers*	.05
72	*Darryll Lewis*	.05
73	*Bryan Cox*	.25
74	*Leroy Thompson*	.05
75	*Mark Higgs*	.05
76	John Friesz	.25
77	Tim McKyer	.05
78	Roger Craig	.10
79	Ronnie Lott	.25
80	Steve Young	1.00
81	Percy Snow	.05
82	Cornelius Bennett	.10
83	Johnny Johnson	.10
84	Blair Thomas	.05

1991 Action Packed Rookie Update 24K Gold

These insert cards were randomly included in 1991 Action Packed Rookie Update foil packs and are devoted to first-round draft picks. Each card front has an embossed color photo, plus gold foil stamping. A "24K" is also stamped on the card to distinguish it as an insert card. The card back is in a horizontal format and includes the player's collegiate statistics, a color mug shot, a panel for an autograph, and a card number. The card is numbered according to the order the player was drafted and uses a "G" suffix.

		MT
Complete Set (26):		300.00
Common Player:		10.00
Minor Stars:		20.00
1	Russell Maryland	10.00
2	Eric Turner	10.00
3	Mike Croel	10.00
4	Todd Lyght	10.00
5	Eric Swann	20.00
6	Charles McRae	10.00
7	Antone Davis	10.00
8	Stanley Richard	10.00
9	Herman Moore	40.00
10	Pat Harlow	10.00
11	Alvin Harper	10.00
12	Mike Pritchard	10.00
13	Leonard Russell	10.00
14	Huey Richardson	10.00
15	Dan McGwire	10.00
16	Bobby Wilson	10.00
17	Alfred Williams	10.00
18	Vinnie Clark	10.00
19	Kelvin Pritchett	10.00
20	Harvey Williams	20.00
21	Stan Thomas	10.00
22	Randal Hill	10.00
23	Todd Marinovich	10.00
24	Ted Washington	10.00
25	Henry Jones	10.00
26	Jarrod Bunch	10.00

1991 Action Packed NFLPA Awards

1990 NFL award winners are recognized in this 16-card set produced by Action Packed. The cards, similar in design to the regular 1991 issue, were available as a boxed set; 5,000 individually-numbered sets were produced. Each box has the set number on it, plus "NFLPA/MDA Awards Dinner March 12, 1991" inscribed on it. Each card back has the award he won listed under his name.

		MT
Complete Set (16):		75.00
Common Player:		4.00
1	Jim Lachey	4.00
2	Anthony Munoz	5.00
3	Bruce Smith	6.00
4	Reggie White	6.00
5	Charles Haley	4.00
6	Derrick Thomas	6.00
7	Albert Lewis	4.00
8	Mark Carrier	5.00
9	Reyna Thompson	5.00
10	Steve Tasker	4.00
11	James Francis	6.00
12	Mark Carrier	7.50
13	Johnny Johnson	7.50
14	Eric Green	7.50
15	Warren Moon	9.00
16	Randall Cunningham	9.00

1991 Action Packed Whizzer White Greats

The 25 winners of the Justice Byron "Whizzer" White Humanitarian Award from 1967 to 1991 were pictured in this special Action Packed set issued in conjunction with the 1991 awards banquet in Chicago. The White award is given annually to a single NFL player who serves his team, community and country in the spirit of former NFL player and U.S. Supreme Court Justice Byron White. The card set features Action Packed's 1991 gold standard design with full color, embossed action photos. For the first time, however, the indicia is silver with the award year inscribed in a silver helmet. The card backs feature a color head shot, player biographical information, career and community contributions. A total of 3,500 sets were distributed at the dinner; another 5,000 were made available to collectors through Rotman Productions.

		MT
Complete Set (25):		75.00
Common Player:		2.00
1	Bart Starr (1967)	15.00
2	Willie Davis (1968)	4.00
3	Ed Meador (1969)	2.00
4	Gale Sayers (1970)	15.00
5	Kermit Alexander (1971)	2.00
6	Ray May (1972)	2.00
7	Andy Russell (1973)	3.00
8	Floyd Little (1974)	3.00
9	Rocky Bleier (1975)	3.00
10	Jim Hart (1976)	4.00
11	Lyle Alzado (1977)	4.00
12	Archie Manning (1978)	4.00
13	Roger Staubach (1979)	25.00
14	Gene Upshaw (1980)	4.00
15	Ken Houston (1981)	4.00
16	Franco Harris (1982)	10.00
17	Doug Dieken (1983)	2.00
18	Rolf Benirschke (1984)	2.00
19	Reggie Williams (1985)	2.00
20	Nat Moore (1986)	2.00
21	George Martin (1987)	2.00
22	Deron Cherry (1988)	2.00
23	Mike Singletary (1989)	5.00
24	Ozzie Newsome (1990)	4.00
25	Mike Kenn (1991)	2.00

A player's name in *italic type* indicates a rookie card.

1991 Action Packed All-Madden

This 52-card set is John Madden's second issue featuring the All-Madden team. The borderless fronts feature embossed color photos with gold and aqua border stripes. Cards, which are standard size, have the Madden logo and team helmet on the front. The back, which is numbered, has stats and a mug shot.

		MT
Complete Set (52):		25.00
Common Player:		.20
Wax Box:		15.00
1	Mark Rypien	.40
2	Erik Kramer	1.00
3	Jim McMahon	.40
4	Jesse Sapolu	.20
5	Jay Hilgenberg	.20
6	Howard Ballard	.20
7	Lomas Brown	.20
8	John Elliott	.20
9	Joe Jacoby	.20
10	Jim Lachey	.20
11	Anthony Munoz	.30
12	Nate Newton	.20
13	Will Wolford	.20
14	Jerry Ball	.20
15	Jerome Brown	.20
16	William Perry	.25
17	Charles Mann	.20
18	Clyde Simmons	.20
19	Reggie White	1.50
20	Eric Allen	.20
21	Darrell Green	.25
22	Bennie Blades	.20
23	Chuck Cecil	.20
24	Rickey Dixon	.30
25	David Fulcher	.20
26	Ronnie Lott	.75
27	Emmitt Smith	6.00
28	Neal Anderson	.30
29	Robert Delpino	.30
30	Barry Sanders	4.00
31	Thurman Thomas	1.00
32	Cornelius Bennett	.35
33	Rickey Jackson	.20
34	Seth Joyner	.20
35	Wilber Marshall	.20
36	Clay Matthews	.20
37	Chris Spielman	.20
38	Pat Swilling	.25
39	Fred Barnett	.50
40	Gary Clark	.40
41	Michael Irvin	1.50
42	Art Monk	.50
43	Jerry Rice	2.50
44	John Taylor	.50
45	Tom Waddle	.20
46	Kevin Butler	.20
47	Bill Bates	.20
48	Greg Manusky	.20
49	Elvis Patterson	.20
50	Steve Tasker	.20
51	John Daly	1.00
52	All-Madden Trophy	1.50

1992 Action Packed Prototypes

These standard-size cards were prototypes featuring the basic design for Action Packed's 1992 regular set. Each card has a card number (92) on the back, plus a suffix (A, N or P). The cards made their debut at the 1992 Super Bowl Show in Minneapolis and are labeled on the back as being prototypes.

		MT
Complete Set (3):		35.00
Common Player:		10.00
A	Thurman Thomas	10.00
N	Emmitt Smith	15.00
P	Barry Sanders	20.00

1992 Action Packed

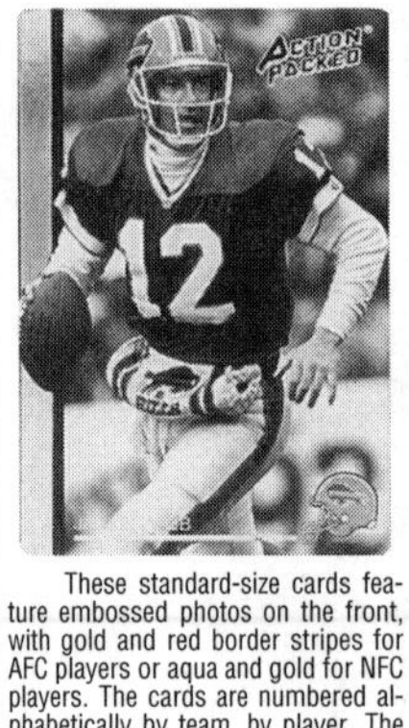

These standard-size cards feature embossed photos on the front, with gold and red border stripes for AFC players or aqua and gold for NFC players. The cards are numbered alphabetically by team, by player. The set has two subsets - eight Braille cards (#s 281-288) featuring league leaders and two logo cards (#s 289-290). There were 42 24K gold insert cards made, too.

		MT
Complete Set (280):		30.00
Complete Factory (292):		35.00
Common Player:		.15
Minor Stars:		.30
Pack (6):		1.00
Wax Box (24):		20.00
1	Steve Broussard	.15
2	Michael Haynes	.15
3	Tim McKyer	.15
4	Chris Miller	.30
5	Andre Rison	.50
6	Jessie Tuggle	.15
7	Mike Pritchard	.30
8	Moe Gardner	.15
9	Brian Jordan	.30
10	Mike Kenn, Chris Hinton	.15
11	Steve Tasker	.15
12	Cornelius Bennett	.30
13	Shane Conlan	.15
14	Darryl Talley	.15
15	Thurman Thomas	.50
16	James Lofton	.30
17	Don Beebe	.15
18	Jim Ritcher	.15
19	Keith McKeller	.15
20	Nate Odomes	.15
21	Mark Carrier	.15
22	Wendell Davis	.15
23	Richard Dent	.15
24	Jim Harbaugh	.30
25	Jay Hilgenberg	.15
26	Steve McMichael	.15
27	Tom Waddle	.15
28	Neal Anderson	.15
29	Brad Muster	.15
30	Shaun Gayle	.15
31	Jim Breech	.15
32	James Brooks	.15
33	James Francis	.15
34	David Fulcher	.15
35	Harold Green	.15
36	Rodney Holman	.15
37	Anthony Munoz	.30
38	Tim Krumrie	.15
39	Tim McGee	.15
40	Eddie Brown	.15
41	Kevin Mack	.15
42	James Jones	.15
43	Vince Newsome	.15
44	Ed King	.15
45	Eric Metcalf	.15
46	Leroy Hoard	.30
47	Stephen Braggs	.15
48	Clay Matthews	.15
49	David Brandon	.15
50	Rob Burnett	.15
51	Larry Brown	.15
52	Alvin Harper	.15
53	Michael Irvin	.50
54	Ken Norton Jr.	.15
55	Jay Novacek	.15
56	Emmitt Smith	4.00
57	Tony Tolbert	.15
58	Nate Newton	.15
59	Steve Beuerlein	.15
60	Tony Casillas	.15
61	Steve Atwater	.15
62	Mike Croel	.15
63	Gaston Green	.15
64	Mark Jackson	.15
65	Greg Kragen	.15
66	Karl Mecklenberg	.15
67	Dennis Smith	.15
68	Steve Sewell	.15
69	John Elway	2.00
70	Simon Fletcher	.15
71	Mel Gray	.15
72	Barry Sanders	4.00
73	Jerry Ball	.15
74	Bennie Blades	.15
75	Lomas Brown	.15
76	Erik Kramer	.30
77	Chris Spielman	.15
78	Ray Crockett	.15
79	Willie Green	.15
80	Rodney Peete	.15
81	Sterling Sharpe	.50
82	Tony Bennett	.15
83	Chuck Cecil	.15
84	Perry Kemp	.15
85	Brian Noble	.15
86	Darrell Thompson	.15
87	Mike Tomczak	.15
88	Vince Workman	.15
89	Esera Tuaolo	.15
90	Mark Murphy	.15
91	William Fuller	.15
92	Ernest Givins	.15
93	Drew Hill	.15
94	Al Smith	.15
95	Ray Childress	.15
96	Haywood Jeffires	.15
97	Cris Dishman	.15
98	Warren Moon	.50
99	Lamar Lathon	.15
100	Mike Munchak, Bruce Matthews	.15
101	Bill Brooks	.15
102	Duane Bickett	.15
103	Eugene Daniel	.15
104	Jeff Herrod	.15
105	Jessie Hester	.15
106	Donnell Thompson	.15
107	Anthony Johnson	.15
108	Jon Hand	.15
109	Rohn Stark	.15
110	Clarence Verdin	.15
111	Derrick Thomas	.50
112	Steve DeBerg	.15
113	Deron Cherry	.15
114	Chris Martin	.15
115	Christian Okoye	.15
116	Dan Saleaumua	.15
117	Neil Smith	.15
118	Barry Word	.15
119	Tim Barnett	.15
120	Albert Lewis	.15
121	Ronnie Lott	.30
122	Marcus Allen	.50
123	Todd Marinovich	.15
124	Nick Bell	.15
125	Tim Brown	.50
126	Ethan Horton	.15
127	Greg Townsend	.15
128	Jeff Gossett, Jeff Jaeger	.15
129	Scott Davis	.15
130	Steve Wisniewski, Don Mosebar	.15
131	Kevin Greene	.15
132	Roman Phifer	.15
133	Tony Zendejas	.15
134	Pat Terrell	.15
135	Willie Anderson	.15
136	Robert Delpino	.15
137	Jim Everett	.30
138	Larry Kelm	.15
139	Todd Lyght	.15
140	Henry Ellard	.15
141	Mark Clayton	.15
142	Jeff Cross	.15
143	Mark Duper	.15
144	John Offerdahl	.15
145	Louis Oliver	.15
146	Pete Stoyanovich	.15
147	Richmond Webb	.15
148	Mark Higgs	.15
149	Tony Paige	.15
150	Bryan Cox	.15
151	Anthony Carter	.15
152	Cris Carter	1.00
153	Rich Gannon	.15
154	Steve Jordan	.15
155	Mike Merriweather	.15
156	Henry Thomas	.15
157	Herschel Walker	.30
158	Randall McDaniel	.15
159	Terry Allen	.50
160	Joey Browner	.15
161	Leonard Russell	.30
162	Bruce Armstrong	.15
163	Vincent Brown	.15
164	Hugh Millen	.15
165	Andre Tippett	.15
166	Jon Vaughn	.15
167	Pat Harlow	.15
168	Marv Cook	.15
169	Irving Fryar	.30
170	Maurice Hurst	.15
171	Pat Swilling	.15
172	Vince Buck	.15
173	Rickey Jackson	.15
174	Sam Mills	.15
175	Bobby Hebert	.15
176	Vaughan Johnson	.15
177	Floyd Turner	.15
178	Fred McAfee	.15
179	Morten Andersen	.15
180	Eric Martin	.15
181	Rodney Hampton	.30
182	Pepper Johnson	.15
183	Leonard Russell	.15
184	Stephen Baker	.15
185	Mark Ingram	.15
186	Dave Meggett	.15
187	Bart Oates	.15
188	Mark Collins	.15
189	Myron Guyton	.15
190	Jeff Hostetler	.30
191	Jeff Lageman	.15
192	Brad Baxter	.15
193	Mo Lewis	.15
194	Chris Burkett	.15
195	James Hasty	.15
196	Rob Moore	.50
197	Kyle Clifton	.15
198	Terance Mathis	.15
199	Marvin Washington	.15
200	Lonnie Young	.15
201	Reggie White	.50
202	Eric Allen	.15
203	Fred Barnett	.30
204	Keith Byars	.15
205	Seth Joyner	.15
206	Clyde Simmons	.15
207	Jerome Brown	.15
208	Wes Hopkins	.15
209	Keith Jackson	.15
210	Calvin Williams	.15
211	Aeneas Williams	.15
212	Ken Harvey	.15
213	Ernie Jones	.15
214	Freddie Joe Nunn	.15
215	Rich Camarillo	.15
216	Johnny Johnson	.30
217	Tim McDonald	.15
218	Eric Swann	.15
219	Eric Hill	.15
220	Anthony Thompson	.15
221	Hardy Nickerson	.15
222	Barry Foster	.15
223	Louis Lipps	.15
224	Greg Lloyd	.15
225	Neil O'Donnell	.30
226	Jerrol Williams	.15
227	Eric Green	.15
228	Rod Woodson	.15
229	Carnell Lake	.15
230	Dwight Stone	.15
231	Marion Butts	.15
232	John Friesz	.30
233	Burt Grossman	.15
234	Ronnie Harmon	.15
235	Gill Byrd	.15
236	Rod Bernstine	.15
237	Courtney Hall	.15
238	Nate Lewis	.15
239	Joe Phillips	.15
240	Henry Rolling	.15
241	Keith Henderson	.15
242	Guy McIntyre	.15
243	Bill Romanowski	.15
244	Don Griffin	.15
245	Dexter Carter	.15
246	Charles Haley	.30
247	Brent Jones	.15
248	John Taylor	.15
249	Steve Young	1.50
250	Larry Roberts	.15
251	Brian Blades	.15
252	Jacob Green	.15
253	John Kasay	.15
254	Cortez Kennedy	.30
255	Rufus Porter	.15
256	John L. Williams	.15
257	Tommy Kane	.15
258	Eugene Robinson	.15
259	Terry Wooden	.15
260	Chris Warren	.50
261	Lawrence Dawsey	.15
262	Mark Carrier	.15
263	Keith McCants	.15
264	Jesse Solomon	.15
265	Vinny Testaverde	.50
266	Rickey Reynolds	.15
267	Broderick Thomas	.15
268	Gary Anderson	.15
269	Reggie Cobb	.15
270	Tony Covington	.15
271	Darrell Green	.30
272	Charles Mann	.15
273	Wilber Marshall	.15
274	Gary Clark	.15
275	Chip Lohmiller	.15
276	Earnest Byner	.15
277	Jim Lachey	.15
278	Art Monk	.30
279	Mark Rypien	.30
280	Mark Schlereth	.15
281	Mark Rypien (Braille)	.15
282	Warren Moon (Braille)	.30
283	Emmitt Smith (Braille)	2.00
284	Thurman Thomas (Braille)	.30
285	Michael Irvin (Braille)	.30
286	Haywood Jeffires (Braille)	.15
287	Pat Swilling (Braille)	.15
288	Ronnie Lott (Braille)	.15
289	NFC logo	.15
290	AFC Logo	.15

1992 Action Packed 24K Gold

These cards have a color embossed photo on the front, with gold foil stamping and a team helmet. The back has statistics, a mug shot, a biography and a caption which describes the photo on the front. A panel is also included for an autograph. Cards are numbered on the back, using a "G" suffix, and are checklisted alphabetically by team name. Cards were randomly inserted in foil packs. Detroit Lions star Barry Sanders autographed 1,000 of his card (#13G); they were randomly inserted in packs.

		MT
Complete Set (42):		650.00
Common Player:		7.00
Minor Stars:		14.00
1	Michael Haynes	7.00
2	Chris Miller	7.00
3	Andre Rison	14.00
4	Cornelius Bennett	7.00
5	James Lofton	7.00
6	Thurman Thomas	14.00
7	Neal Anderson	7.00
8	Michael Irvin	20.00
9	Emmitt Smith	75.00
10	Mike Croel	7.00
11	John Elway	50.00
12	Gaston Green	7.00
13	Barry Sanders	100.00
14	Sterling Sharpe	14.00
15	Ernest Givins	7.00
16	Drew Hill	7.00
17	Haywood Jeffires	7.00
18	Warren Moon	14.00
19	Christian Okoye	7.00
20	Derrick Thomas	14.00
21	Ronnie Lott	7.00
22	Todd Marinovich	7.00
23	Henry Ellard	7.00
24	Mark Clayton	7.00
25	Herschel Walker	7.00
26	Irving Fryar	7.00
27	Leonard Russell	7.00
28	Pat Swilling	7.00
29	Rodney Hampton	7.00
30	Rob Moore	14.00
31	Seth Joyner	7.00
32	Reggie White	20.00
33	Eric Green	7.00
34	Rod Woodson	7.00
35	Marion Butts	7.00
36	Charles Haley	7.00
37	John Taylor	7.00
38	Steve Young	40.00
39	Earnest Byner	7.00
40	Gary Clark	7.00
41	Art Monk	7.00
42	Mark Rypien	7.00

Rookie Cards are *italicized.* *Pricing for cards for 1980 and older is for Near Mint condition. 1981 cards and newer are priced as mint.*

1992 Action Packed Rookie Update

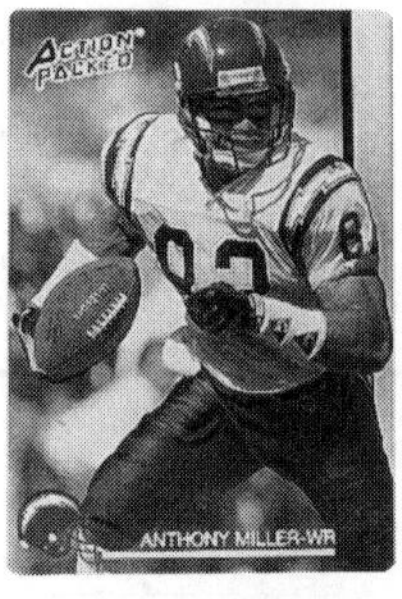

Twenty-five first-round draft picks are featured in their new teams' uniforms in this 84-card update set, which has 51 rookies in all and 33 NFL stars. The cards have a black-and-gold foil stripe along the side, and a red helmet with an "R" on the front. There were also 35 24K gold insert cards featuring ten NFL quarterbacks and 25 first-round draft picks. A special "Neon Deion Sanders" card, numbered 84N, was also made and features neon fluorescent orange.

		MT
Complete Set (84):		15.00
Common Player:		.15
Minor Stars:		.30
Pack (7):		1.00
Wax Box (24):		20.00
1	*Steve Emtman*	.30
2	*Quentin Coryatt*	.30
3	*Sean Gilbert*	.30
4	*John Fina*	.15
5	*Alonzo Spellman*	.30
6	*Amp Lee*	.30
7	*Robert Porcher*	.30
8	*Jason Hanson*	.15
9	*Ty Detmer*	.50
10	*Ray Roberts*	.15
11	*Bob Whitfield*	.15
12	*Greg Skrepenak*	.15
13	*Vaughn Dunbar*	.15
14	*Siran Stacy*	.15
15	*Mark D'Onofrio*	.15
16	*Tony Sacca*	.15
17	*Dana Hall*	.15
18	*Courtney Hawkins*	.30
19	*Shane Collins*	.15
20	*Tony Smith*	.15
21	*Rod Smith*	.15
22	*Troy Auzenne*	.15
23	*David Klingler*	.30
24	*Darryl Williams*	.15
25	*Carl Pickens*	2.00
26	*Ricardo McDonald*	.15
27	*Tommy Vardell*	.30
28	*Kevin Smith*	.30
29	*Rodney Culver*	.15
30	*Jimmy Smith*	4.00
31	*Robert Jones*	.15
32	*Tommy Maddox*	.30
33	*Shane Dronett*	.30
34	*Terrell Buckley*	.50
35	*Santana Dotson*	.50
36	*Edgar Bennett*	1.00
37	*Ashley Ambrose*	.15
38	*Dale Carter*	.50
39	*Chester McGlockton*	.15
40	*Steve Israel*	.15
41	*Marc Boutte*	.15
42	*Marco Coleman*	.30
43	*Troy Vincent*	.30
44	*Mark Wheeler*	.15
45	*Darren Perry*	.15
46	*Eugene Chung*	.15
47	*Derek Brown*	.15
48	*Phillippi Sparks*	.15
49	*Johnny Mitchell*	.15
50	*Kurt Barber*	.15
51	*Leon Searcy*	.15
52	*Chris Mims*	.30
53	Keith Jackson	.30
54	Charles Haley	.30
55	Dave Krieg	.15
56	Dan McGwire	.15
57	Phil Simms	.30
58	Bobby Humphrey	.15
59	Jerry Rice	2.50
60	Joe Montana	3.00
61	Junior Seau	.50
62	Leslie O'Neal	.15
63	Anthony Miller	.30
64	Timm Rosenbach	.15
65	Herschel Walker	.30
66	Randal Hill	.15
67	Randall Cunningham	.75
68	Al Toon	.15
69	Browning Nagle	.15
70	Lawrence Taylor	.50
71	Dan Marino	4.00
72	Eric Dickerson	.30
73	Harvey Williams	.30
74	Jeff George	.50
75	Russell Maryland	.30
76	Troy Aikman	2.00
77	Michael Dean Perry	.30
78	Bernie Kosar	.30
79	Boomer Esiason	.30
80	Mike Singletary	.30
81	Bruce Smith	.15
82	Andre Reed	.30
83	Jim Kelly	.50
84	Deion Sanders	1.00
84N	Deion Sanders Neon	10.00

1992 Action Packed Rookie Update 24K Gold

Quarterbacks and first-round draft picks are featured on these insert cards, randomly included in 1992 Action Packed Rookie Update foil packs. Cards have 24K gold foil-stamping on them.

		MT
Complete Set (35):		450.00
Common Player:		7.00
Minor Stars:		14.00
1	Steve Emtman	7.00
2	Quentin Coryatt	7.00
3	Sean Gilbert	14.00
4	Terrell Buckley	14.00
5	David Klingler	7.00
6	Troy Vincent	7.00
7	Tommy Vardell	14.00
8	Leon Searcy	7.00
9	Marco Coleman	7.00
10	Eugene Chung	7.00
11	Derek Brown	7.00
12	Johnny Mitchell	7.00
13	Chester McGlockton	7.00
14	Kevin Smith	7.00
15	Dana Hall	7.00
16	Tony Smith	7.00
17	Dale Carter	14.00
18	Vaughn Dunbar	7.00
19	Alonzo Spellman	14.00
20	Chris Mims	7.00
21	Robert Jones	7.00
22	Tommy Maddox	14.00
23	Robert Porcher	7.00
24	John Fina	7.00
25	Darryl Williams	7.00
26	Jim Kelly	20.00
27	Randall Cunningham	20.00
28	Dan Marino	75.00
29	Troy Aikman	40.00
30	Boomer Esiason	14.00
31	Bernie Kosar	14.00
32	Jeff George	20.00
33	Phil Simms	14.00
34	Ray Roberts	7.00
35	Bob Whitfield	7.00

1992 Action Packed NFLPA Mackey Awards

These standard-size 24K-gold cards were produced for those who attended the 1992 NFLPA Mackey Awards Banquet. Only 2,000 cards of each player were produced.

		MT
Complete Set (3):		125.00
(1)	John Mackey	35.00
(2)	Reggie White	65.00
(3)	Jack Kemp	85.00

1992 Action Packed 24K NFLPA MDA Awards

The 1991 NFL Players of the Year are honored in this 16-card set produced by Action Packed for distribution to those who attended the NFLPA/MDA Awards Dinner, March 5, 1992. The sets were packed in a black box and were stamped "Banquet Edition." The cards feature 24K gold stamping. Cards for players from the AFC are red and have the Action Packed logo in the upper left corner. Cards for the NFC players are blue and have the logo in the upper right corner. Only 1,000 sets were produced.

		MT
Complete Set (16):		375.00
Common Player:		15.00
1	Steve Wisniewski	15.00
2	Jim Lachey	15.00
3	Reggie White	25.00
4	William Fuller	15.00
5	Derrick Thomas	35.00
6	Pat Swilling	25.00
7	Darrell Green	25.00
8	Ronnie Lott	25.00
9	Steve Tasker	15.00
10	Mel Gray	15.00
11	Aeneas Williams	15.00
12	Mike Croel	35.00
13	Leonard Russell	50.00
14	Lawrence Dawsey	25.00
15	Barry Sanders	90.00
16	Thurman Thomas	75.00

1992 Action Packed All-Madden

This third John Madden set includes a card of the famed Madden Cruiser. Cards are standard size and were also made into 24K gold insert versions, too.

		MT
Complete Set (55):		20.00
Common Player:		.15
Wax Box:		18.00
1	Emmitt Smith	6.50
2	Reggie White	.75
3	Deion Sanders	1.25
4	Wilber Marshall	.15
5	Barry Sanders	3.00
6	Derrick Thomas	.50
7	Troy Aikman	3.50
8	Eric Allen	.15
9	Cris Carter	.15
10	Jerry Rice	2.50
11	Rickey Jackson	.15
12	Bubba McDowell	.15
13	Jack Del Rio	.15
14	Nate Newton	.15
15	John Elliott	.15
16	Fred Barnett	.40
17	Mike Singletary	.15
18	Lawrence Taylor	.40
19	Bruce Matthews	.15
20	Pat Swilling	.40
21	Charles Haley	.15
22	Andre Rison	1.25
23	Seth Joyner	.15
24	Steve Young	1.75
25	Gary Clark	.25
26	Jerry Ball	.15
27	Michael Irvin	1.50
28	Haywood Jeffires	.30
29	Kevin Ross	.15
30	Chris Doleman	.15
31	Vai Sikahema	.15
32	Ricky Watters	2.00
33	Henry Thomas	.15
34	Mike Kenn	.15
35	Erik Williams	.15
36	Neil Smith	.15
37	Mark Schlereth	.15
38	Steve Wallace	.15
39	Randall McDaniel	.15
40	Kurt Gouveia	.15
41	Al Noga	.15
42	Tom Rathman	.15
43	Harris Barton	.15
44	Mel Gray	.15
45	Keith Byars	.15
46	Todd Scott	.15
47	Brent Jones	.15
48	Audray McMillian	.15
49	Ray Childress	.15
50	Dennis Smith	.15
51	Mark McMillian	.15
52	Sean Gilbert	.15
53	Pierce Holt	.15
54	Daryl Johnston	.40
55	Madden Cruiser	.50

1993 Action Packed Troy Aikman Promos

The two-card, standard-size set highlights Dallas quarterback Troy Aikman, after he won the MVP award in Super Bowl XXVII. Aikman's name is printed along the left border. The card back has "1993 Prototype" printed over Aikman's statistics. The cards are numbered TA2 and TA3 as they were originally part of an 11-card promo sheet.

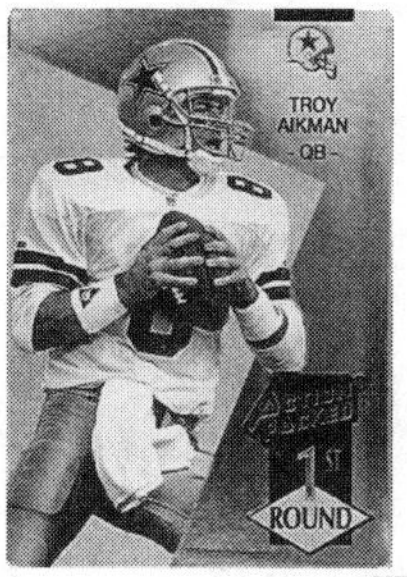

		MT
Complete Set (2):		40.00
Common Player:		20.00
2	Troy Aikman (Running with ball)	20.00
3	Troy Aikman (Pitching the ball)	20.00

1993 Action Packed Emmitt Smith Promos

The five-card, standard-size set features five Emmitt Smith cards to promote the All-Madden Team set. The word "Prototype" is printed on the card back and each card has the prefix "ES." ES1 and ES4 were available at the Super Bowl Card Show in 1993. ES5 was available to members of the Tuff Stuff Buyers Club.

		MT
Complete Set (5):		40.00
Common Player:		5.00
1	Emmitt Smith (Receiving handoff from quaterback; side view)	5.00
2	Emmitt Smith	10.00
3	Emmitt Smith	10.00
4	Emmitt Smith (Cutting to right to elude tackler; ball cradled in left arm)	5.00
5	Emmitt Smith (Running to right; ball in left arm)	10.00

1993 Action Packed Prototypes

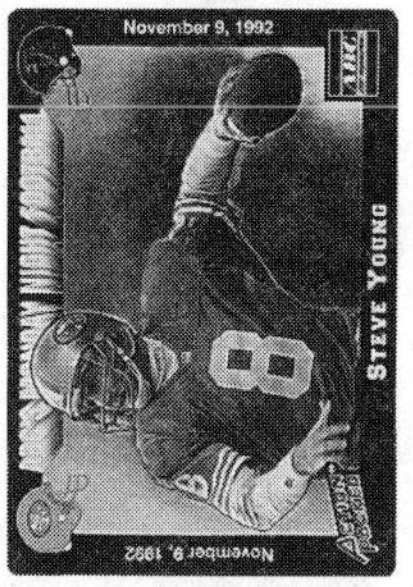

The six-card, standard-size set previewed the 1993 regular series. The player's last name is printed vertically on the card edge in gold foil. The card backs feature "1993 Prototype" and the prefix "FB." The bottom of the back includes a blank space for an autograph.

		MT
Complete Set (6):		40.00
Common Player:		5.00
1	Emmitt Smith	15.00
2	Thurman Thomas	5.00
3	Steve Young	8.00
4	Barry Sanders	10.00
5	Barry Foster	5.00
6	Warren Moon	6.00

1993 Action Packed

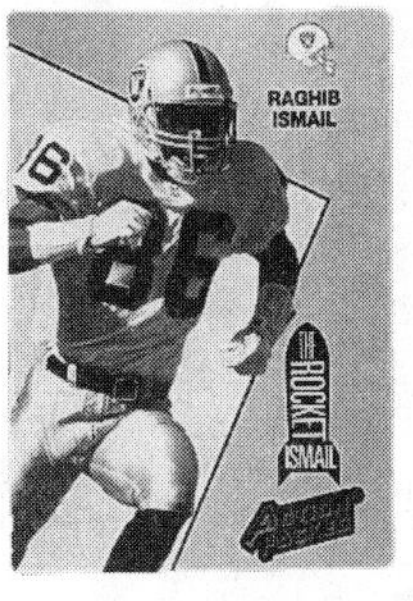

This 204-card set features 162 regular cards and 42 subset cards. The 42 subset cards are three types, each with its own numbering prefix - the "Quarterback Club" (18, with a QB prefix), "Moving Targets" (12, with an MT prefix) and 1,000-yard rushers (12, with an RB prefix). Each of these subset cards also has a 24K gold equivalent, with a G suffix. The Quarterback Club cards were also done in Braille (B suffix) and as Mint versions (500 each). The 1993 Rookie/Update set begins where the regular set ended, excluding subsets, by starting with #163. These cards have a gold, silver and bronze design theme designating the first three rounds of the NFL draft. First-rounders have gold foil accents, seconds have silver, and thirds have bronze. Prominent players who have been traded have also been included in the set; the year they were drafted is on the front of the card. There were six standard-size 1993 prototype cards also produced.

		MT
Complete Set (222):		75.00
Complete Series 1 (162):		45.00
Complete Series 2 (60):		30.00
Common Player:		.15
Minor Stars:		.25
Series 1 Pack (6):		2.25
Series 1 Wax Box (24):		45.00
Rook/Up. Pack (8):		2.00
Rook/Up. Wax Box (24):		42.00
1	Michael Haynes	.15
2	Chris Miller	.15
3	Andre Rison	.25
4	Jim Kelly	.50
5	Andre Reed	.25
6	Thurman Thomas	.50
7	Jim Harbaugh	.15
8	Harold Green	.15
9	David Klingler	.25
10	Bernie Kosar	.25
11	Troy Aikman	3.00
12	Michael Irvin	.50
13	Emmitt Smith	5.00
14	John Elway	1.50
15	Barry Sanders	4.00
16	Brett Favre	5.00
17	Sterling Sharpe	.75
18	Ernest Givins	.15
19	Haywood Jeffires	.15
20	Warren Moon	.50
21	Lorenzo White	.15
22	Jeff George	.50
23	Joe Montana	3.00
24	Jim Everett	.25
25	Cleveland Gary	.15
26	Dan Marino	4.00
27	Terry Allen	.15
28	Rodney Hampton	.50
29	Phil Simms	.15
30	Fred Barnett	.15
31	Randall Cunningham	.50
32	Gary Clark	.15
33	Barry Foster	.50
34	Neil O'Donnell	.50
35	Stan Humphries	.50
36	Anthony Miller	.15
37	Jerry Rice	3.00
38	Ricky Watters	.50
39	Steve Young	2.00
40	Chris Warren	1.00
41	Reggie Cobb	.15
42	Mark Rypien	.15
43	Deion Sanders	1.50
44	Henry Jones	.15
45	Bruce Smith	.15
46	Richard Dent	.15
47	Tommy Vardell	.15
48	Charles Haley	.15
49	Ken Norton	.15
50	Jay Novacek	.15
51	Simon Fletcher	.15
52	Pat Swilling	.15
53	Tony Bennett	.15
54	Reggie White	.40
55	Ray Childress	.15
56	Quentin Coryatt	.15
57	Steve Emtman	.15
58	Derrick Thomas	.25
59	James Lofton	.15
60	Marco Coleman	.15
61	Bryan Cox	.15
62	Troy Vincent	.15
63	Chris Doleman	.15
64	Audray McMillian	.15
65	Vaughn Dunbar	.15
66	Rickey Jackson	.15
67	Lawrence Taylor	.25
68	Ronnie Lott	.15
69	Rob Moore	.15
70	Browning Nagle	.15
71	Eric Allen	.15
72	Tim Harris	.15
73	Clyde Simmons	.15
74	Steve Beuerlein	.15
75	Randal Hill	.15
76	Darren Perry	.15
77	Rod Woodson	.25
78	Marion Butts	.15
79	Chris Mims	.15
80	Junior Seau	.50
81	Cortez Kennedy	.15
82	Santana Dotson	.15
83	Earnest Byner	.15
84	Charles Mann	.15
85	Pierce Holt	.15
86	Mike Pritchard	.15
87	Cornelius Bennett	.15
88	Neal Anderson	.15
89	Carl Pickens	1.50
90	Eric Metcalf	.15
91	Michael Dean Perry	.15
92	Alvin Harper	.25
93	Robert Jones	.15
94	Steve Atwater	.15
95	Rod Bernstine	.15
96	Herman Moore	1.50
97	Chris Spielman	.15
98	Terrell Buckley	.15
99	Dale Carter	.15
100	Terry McDaniel	.15
101	Tim Brown	.25
102	Gaston Green	.15
103	Howie Long	.15
104	Todd Marinovich	.15
105	Anthony Smith	.15
106	Willie Anderson	.15
107	Henry Ellard	.15
108	Mark Higgs	.15
109	Keith Jackson	.15
110	Irving Fryar	.15
111	Cris Carter	.25
112	Leonard Russell	.15
113	Wayne Martin	.15
114	Mark Jackson	.15
115	David Meggett	.15
116	Brad Baxter	.15
117	Boomer Esiason	.15
118	Johnny Johnson	.15
119	Seth Joyner	.15
120	Kevin Greene	.15
121	Ronnie Harmon, Greg Lloyd	.15
122	Brent Jones	.15
123	Amp Lee	.15
124	Tim McDonald	.15
125	Darrell Green	.15
126	Art Monk	.15
127	Tony Smith	.15
128	Bill Brooks	.15
129	Kenneth Davis	.15
130	Donnell Woolford	.15
131	Derrick Fenner	.15
132	Michael Jackson	.15
133	Mark Clayton	.15
134	Al Smith	.15
135	Curtis Duncan, Rodney Culver	.15
137	Harvey Williams	.15
138	Neil Smith	.15
139	Marcus Allen	.25
140	Eric Dickerson	.15
141	Sean Gilbert	.15
142	Shane Conlan	.15
143	Todd Scott	.15
144	Vincent Brown	.15
145	Andre Tippett	.15
146	Jon Vaughn	.15
147	Marv Cook	.15
148	Morten Anderson	.15
149	Sam Mills	.15
150	Mark Collins	.15
151	Heath Sherman	.15
152	Johnny Bailey	.15
153	Eric Green	.15
155	Gill Byrd	.15
156	Leslie O'Neal	.15
157	Rufus Porter	.15
158	Eugene Robinson	.15
159	Broderick Thomas	.15
160	Lawrence Dawsey	.15
161	Anthony Munoz	.15
162	Wilber Marshall	.15
163	*Drew Bledsoe*	8.00
164	*Rick Mirer*	.50
165	*Garrison Hearst*	3.00
166	*Marvin Jones*	.25
167	*John Copeland*	.25
168	*Eric Curry*	.25
169	*Curtis Conway*	2.50
170	*William Roaf*	.25
171	*Lincoln Kennedy*	.15
172	*Jerome Bettis*	3.00
173	*Dan Williams*	.15
174	*Patrick Bates*	.25
175	*Brad Hopkins*	.15
176	*Steve Everitt*	.25
177	*Wayne Simmons*	.15
178	*Tom Carter*	.25
179	*Ernest Dye*	.15
180	*Lester Holmes*	.15
181	*Irv Smith*	.25
182	*Robert Smith*	3.00
183	*Darrien Gordon*	.25
184	*Deon Figures*	.25
185	*Leonard Renfro*	.15
186	*O.J. McDuffie*	2.00
187	*Dana Stubblefield*	1.00
188	*Todd Kelly*	.15
189	*Thomas Smith*	.25
190	*George Teague*	.25
191	Wilber Marshall	.15
192	Reggie White	.25
193	*Carlton Gray*	.15
194	*Chris Slade*	.50
195	*Ben Coleman*	.15
196	*Ryan McNeil*	.15
197	*Demetrius DuBose*	.15
198	*Coleman Rudolph*	.15
199	*Tony McGee*	1.00
200	*Troy Drayton*	.25
201	*Natrone Means*	3.00
202	*Glyn Milburn*	1.00
203	*Chad Brown*	.50
204	*Reggie Brooks*	.25
205	*Kevin Williams*	2.50
206	*Michael Barrow*	.15
207	*Roosevelt Potts*	.25
208	*Victor Bailey*	.25
209	*Qadry Ismail*	1.00
210	*Vincent Brisby*	1.00
211	*Billy Joe Hobert*	1.00
212	*Lamar Thomas*	.25
213	*Jason Elam*	.15
214	*Andre Hastings*	1.00
215	*Terry Kirby*	1.00
216	Joe Montana	3.00
217	*Derrick Lassic*	.25
218	*Mark Brunell*	8.00
219	*Vaughn Hebron*	.25
220	*Troy Brown*	.15
221	*Derek Brown*	.25
222	Raghib Ismail	.25

1993 Action Packed 24K Gold

These cards are identical in format to the regular 1993 Action Packed cards, except they have "24K" written under the Action Packed logo on the card front. The cards use a "G" suffix for numbering; the card number appears on the back. Cards were random inserts in 1993 Action Packed foil packs and feature 24K versions of three insert sets - Quarterback Club (1G-18G), Moving Targets (19G-30G) and 1,000 Yard Rushers (31G-42G), plus 30 others.

		MT
Complete Set (72):		2000.
Complete Series 1 (42):		1200.
Complete Series 2 (30):		800.00
Common Player:		20.00
Minor Stars:		30.00
1	Troy Aikman	75.00
2	Randall Cunningham	20.00
3	John Elway	50.00
4	Jim Everett	20.00
5	Brett Favre	125.00
6	Jim Harbaugh	20.00
7	Jeff Hostetler	20.00
8	Jim Kelly	30.00
9	David Klingler	20.00
10	Bernie Kosar	20.00
11	Dan Marino	125.00
12	Chris Miller	20.00
13	Boomer Esiason	20.00
14	Warren Moon	30.00
15	Neil O'Donnell	30.00
16	Mark Rypien	20.00
17	Phil Simms	20.00
18	Steve Young	75.00
19	Fred Barnett	20.00
20	Gary Clark	20.00
21	Mark Clayton	20.00
22	Ernest Givins	20.00
23	Michael Haynes	20.00
24	Michael Irvin	30.00
25	Haywood Jeffires	20.00
26	Anthony Miller	20.00
27	Andre Reed	20.00
28	Jerry Rice	75.00
29	Andre Rison	20.00
30	Sterling Sharpe	30.00
31	Terry Allen	20.00
32	Reggie Cobb	20.00
33	Barry Foster	20.00
34	Cleveland Gary	20.00
35	Harold Green	20.00
36	Rodney Hampton	30.00
37	Barry Sanders	90.00
38	Emmitt Smith	125.00
39	Thurman Thomas	30.00
40	Chris Warren	30.00
41	Ricky Watters	30.00
42	Lorenzo White	20.00
43	Drew Bledsoe	75.00
44	Rick Mirer	35.00
45	Garrison Hearst	40.00
46	Marvin Jones	20.00
47	John Copeland	20.00
48	Eric Curry	20.00
49	Curtis Conway	35.00
50	William Roaf	20.00
51	Lincoln Kennedy	20.00
52	Jerome Bettis	35.00
53	Dan Williams	20.00
54	Patrick Bates	20.00
55	Brad Hopkins	20.00
56	Steve Everitt	20.00
57	Wayne Simmons	20.00
58	Tom Carter	20.00
59	Ernest Dye	20.00
60	Lester Holmes	20.00
61	Irv Smith	20.00
62	Robert Smith	35.00
63	Darrien Gordon	20.00
64	Deon Figures	20.00
65	Leonard Renfro	20.00
66	O.J. McDuffie	30.00
67	Dana Stubblefield	30.00
68	Todd Kelly	20.00
69	Thomas Smith	20.00
70	George Teague	20.00
71	Wilber Marshall	20.00
72	Reggie White	30.00

1993 Action Packed Moving Targets

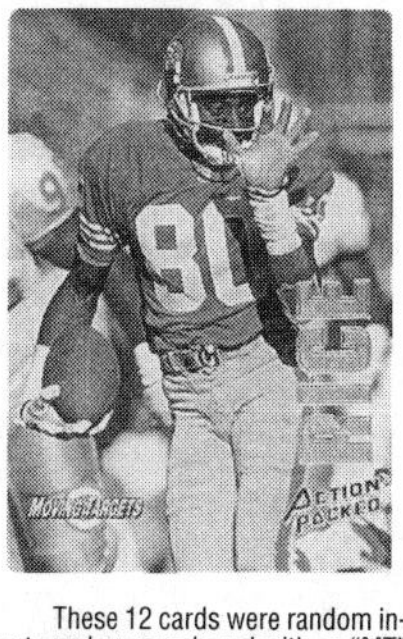

These 12 cards were random inserts and are numbered with an "MT" prefix. The "Moving Targets" logo appears on each card front, plus a full-bleed embossed photo, along with the player's name in gold foil. The back has a painted football scene, plus a color head shot of the player and career stats. An autograph slot is also included. There were also 24K versions created for these cards; they are random inserts and are numbered with a "G" prefix.

		MT
Complete Set (12):		12.00
Common Player:		.50
Minor Stars:		1.00
1	Fred Barnett	.50
2	Gary Clark	.50
3	Mark Clayton	.50
4	Ernest Givins	.50
5	Michael Haynes	.50
6	Michael Irvin	1.00
7	Haywood Jeffires	.50
8	Anthony Miller	.50
9	Andre Reed	.50
10	Jerry Rice	4.00
11	Andre Rison	1.00
12	Sterling Sharpe	1.00

1993 Action Packed Quarterback Club

These subset cards, numbered on the back using a "QB" prefix, were included in 1993 Action Packed boxes

at the same rate as the set's regular cards, but 24K versions were randomly inserted in fewer quantities. The gold versions have a "G" suffix after the card number. "Quarterback Club" cards follow the same format as the regular cards, but have the set logo on the front to distinguish them.

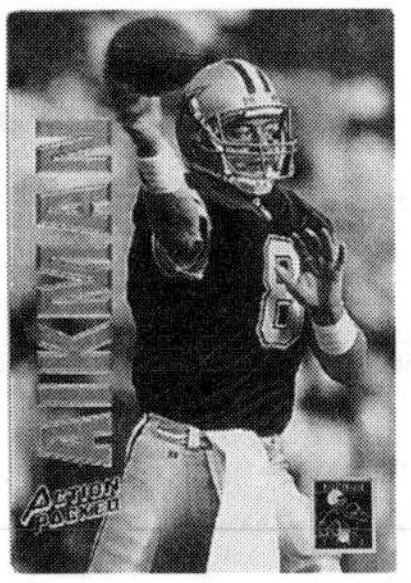

		MT
Complete Set (18):		20.00
Common Player:		.50
Minor Stars:		1.00
Braille Cards: 2x-3x		
1	Troy Aikman	4.00
2	Randall Cunningham	2.00
3	John Elway	3.00
4	Jim Everett	.50
5	Brett Favre	6.00
6	Jim Harbaugh	1.00
7	Jeff Hostetler	.50
8	Jim Kelly	1.00
9	David Klingler	.50
10	Bernie Kosar	.50
11	Dan Marino	6.00
12	Chris Miller	.50
13	Boomer Esiason	.50
14	Warren Moon	1.00
15	Neil O'Donnell	1.00
16	Mark Rypien	.50
17	Phil Simms	.50
18	Steve Young	4.00

1993 Action Packed Quarterback Club Braille

These 18 cards, which each have a "B" suffix after the card number, are identical to their regular version counterparts, except they are done in Braille. They are generally about two or three times more valuable than the regular cards. Cards were random inserts; some were donated to more than 400 schools for the blind.

		MT
Complete Set (18):		60.00
Common Player:		1.25
1	Troy Aikman	15.00
2	Randall Cunningham	4.00
3	John Elway	8.00
4	Jim Everett	1.25
5	Brett Favre	10.00
6	Jim Harbaugh	1.25
7	Jeff Hostetler	1.25
8	Jim Kelly	5.00
9	David Klingler	2.00
10	Bernie Kosar	2.00
11	Dan Marino	12.00
12	Chris Miller	1.25
13	Boomer Esiason	3.00
14	Warren Moon	3.50
15	Neil O'Donnell	3.00
16	Mark Rypien	1.25
17	Phil Simms	3.00
18	Steve Young	6.00

1993 Action Packed Rookies Previews

The three-card, standard-size set features Troy Aikman, Brett Favre and Neil O'Donnell. The round the quarterback was drafted in is done in gold (first round), silver (second) or bronze (third) on the card front. The card back has "1993 Prototype" printed with the prefix "RU." The set was available as a topper in select hobby boxes.

		MT
Complete Set (3):		6.00
Common Player:		1.00
1	Troy Aikman	2.00
2	Brett Favre	4.00
3	Neil O'Donnell	1.00

1993 Action Packed Rushers

Players who gained 1,000 or more yards rushing during the previous season are featured in this Action Packed insert set. Cards have a "1000 Yard Rushers" logo on the front, plus a full-bleed photo and the player's name in gold foil. Backs have a color head shot of the player and statistics for his team's single-season rushing leaders. Card backs have an autograph slot, and are numbered with an "RB" prefix. There were also 24K versions created of these cards; they are numbered with a "G" suffix and were random inserts.

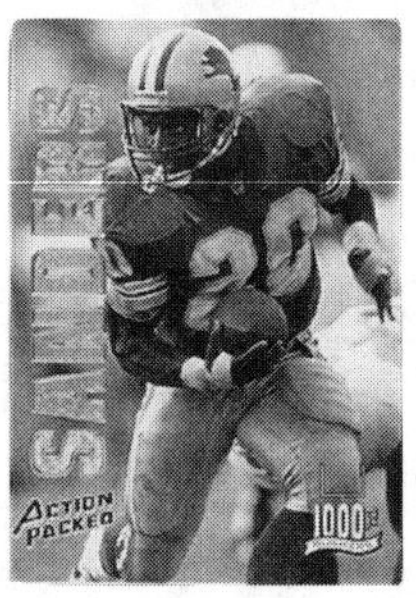

		MT
Complete Set (12):		15.00
Common Player:		.50
Minor Stars:		1.00
1	Terry Allen	.50
2	Reggie Cobb	.50
3	Barry Foster	.50
4	Cleveland Gary	.50
5	Harold Green	.50
6	Rodney Hampton	.50
7	Barry Sanders	4.00
8	Emmitt Smith	6.00
9	Thurman Thomas	1.00
10	Chris Warren	1.00
11	Ricky Watters	1.00
12	Lorenzo White	.50

1993 Action Packed NFLPA Awards

Outstanding players from the 1992 NFL season are honored in this 17-card Action Packed set. The cards, issued in a special box, have an embossed front; backs have a head shot, career summary and the position the player was selected as being the best at in 1992. A card number is also on the back. The cards were distributed at the 20th annual NFLPA banquet on March 4, 1993, in Washington, D.C. The District of Columbia's Special Olympics was the beneficiary.

		MT
Complete Set (17):		60.00
Common Player:		3.00
1	Randall McDaniel	3.00
2	Bruce Matthews	3.00
3	Richmond Webb	3.00
4	Cortez Kennedy	7.00
5	Clyde Simmons	3.00
6	Wilber Marshall	4.00
7	Junior Seau	8.00
8	Henry Jones	4.00
9	Audray McMillian	3.00
10	Mel Gray	4.00
11	Steve Tasker	3.00
12	Marco Coleman	6.00
13	Santana Dotson	6.00
14	Vaughn Dunbar	7.00
15	Carl Pickens	7.00
16	Barry Foster	8.00
17	Steve Young	10.00

1993 Action Packed All-Madden

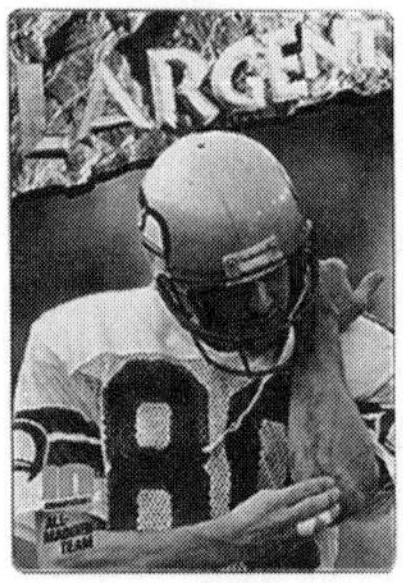

This 42-card set marks the 10th Anniversary All-Madden team and features the all-time favorites from the last 10 years as selected by the charismatic broadcaster and former coach, John Madden. Players' names are stamped in gold foil on a stone background. A 12-card insert was also done in a 24K gold equivalent. These cards have the suffix "G" used in their numbering. A five-card Emmitt Smith prototype set was also issued as a promotional for the All-Madden set. The All-Madden logo appears on each card front; the back is labeled as a prototype and is numbered ES1-ES5. Cards ES1 and ES4 were giveaways at the 1993 Super Bowl card show; ES5 was a giveaway to members of the Tuff Stuff Buyers Club.

		MT
Complete Set (42):		18.00
Common Player:		.15
1	Troy Aikman	3.00
2	Bill Bates	.15
3	Mark Bavaro	.15
4	Jim Burt	.15
5	Gary Clark	.15
6	Richard Dent	.15
7	Gary Fencik	.15
8	Darryl Green	.15
9	Roy Green	.15
10	Russ Grimm	.15
11	Charles Haley	.20
12	Dan Hampton	.20
13	Lester Hayes	.15
14	Michael Haynes	.50
15	Jay Hilgenberg	.15
16	Michael Irvin	.50
17	Joe Jacoby	.15
18	Steve Largent	.15
19	Howie Long	.15
20	Ronnie Lott	.25
21	Dan Marino	3.00
22	Jim McMahon	.15
23	Matt Millen	.15
24	Art Monk	.20
25	Joe Montana	2.50
26	Anthony Munoz	.15
27	Nate Newton	.15
28	Walter Payton	.50
29	William Perry	.15
30	Jack Reynolds	.15
31	Jerry Rice	1.50
32	Barry Sanders	3.00
33	Sterling Sharpe	1.00
34	Mike Singletary	.20
35	Jackie Slater	.15
36	Emmitt Smith	4.00
37	Pat Summerall	.25
38	Lawrence Taylor	.40
39	Jeff Van Note	.15
40	Reggie White	.40
41	Otis Wilson	.15
42	Jack Youngblood	.15

1993 Action Packed All-Madden 24K Gold

These 24K gold cards are identical in design to the regular 10th Anniversary All-Madden cards, except they have 24Kt. Gold stamped on the card front in gold foil. They were random inserts in 1993 Action Packed 10th Anniversary All-Madden Team packs and are numbered on the card back using a "G" suffix.

		MT
Complete Set (12):		500.00
Common Player:		20.00
1	Troy Aikman	125.00
2	Michael Irvin	70.00
3	Ronnie Lott	20.00
4	Dan Marino	75.00
5	Joe Montana	100.00
6	Walter Payton	30.00
7	Jerry Rice	100.00
8	Barry Sanders	90.00
9	Sterling Sharpe	30.00
10	Emmitt Smith	135.00
11	Lawrence Taylor	20.00
12	Reggie White	25.00

1993 Action Packed Monday Night Football Prototypes

The six-card, standard-size set promoted the Monday Night Football set with highlights from the 1992 season. The date of each game is printed on on each side border while the ABC logo is located in the bottom right corner. Helmets from each team from the Monday Night Game are found on the top corners. The card backs have "1993 Prototype" printed and feature the "MN" prefix.

		MT
Complete Set (6):		45.00
Common Player:		5.00
1	Barry Sanders	8.00
2	Steve Young	7.00
3	Emmitt Smith	15.00
4	Thurman Thomas	5.00
5	Barry Foster	5.00
6	Warren Moon	5.00

1993 Action Packed Monday Night Football

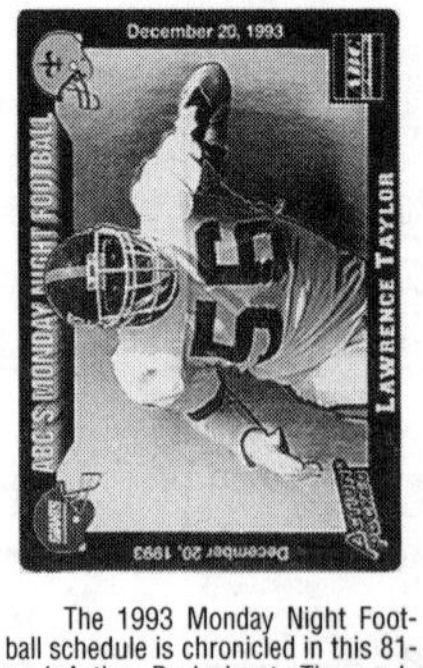

The 1993 Monday Night Football schedule is chronicled in this 81-card Action Packed set. The cards preview top players slated to appear in each game, plus ABC's game announcers. Each card gives the date of the game, along with helmets of the two opposing teams participating. A key player from one of the teams is featured on each card front. The back has a mug shot of the player and provides a summary of his performance against that particular opponent. A Monday Night Football trivia fact is also given. Each foil pack also had the chance of obtaining a randomly included gold mint card; there were 250 gold mint cards produced for each card in the set.

		MT
Complete Set (81):		22.00
Common Player:		.15
Wax Box:		25.00
1	Michael Irvin	1.25
2	Charles Haley	.15
3	Art Monk	.15
4	Earnest Byner	.15
5	Tom Rathman	.15
6	John Taylor	.30
7	Bernie Kosar	.15
8	Clay Matthews	.15
9	Simon Fletcher	.15
10	John Elway	.50
11	Joe Montana	2.00
12	Derrick Thomas	.40
13	Rod Woodson	.20
14	Gary Anderson	.15
15	Chris Miller	.15
16	Andre Rison	.50
17	Mark Rypien	.25
18	Charles Mann	.15
19	Mark Duper	.15
20	Pete Stoyanovich	.15
21	Warren Moon	.50
22	Lorenzo White	.15
23	Haywood Jeffires	.40
24	Andre Reed	.40
25	Darryl Talley	.15
26	Tim Brown	.15
27	Howie Long	.15
28	Steve Atwater	.15
29	Karl Mecklenberg	.15
30	Chris Doleman	.15
31	Terry Allen	.40
32	Richard Dent	.15
33	Neal Anderson	.15
34	Darrell Green	.15
35	Chip Lohmiller	.15
36	Jim Kelly	.75
37	Cornelius Bennett	.15
38	Brett Favre	3.00
39	Sterling Sharpe	1.00
40	Reggie White	.40
41	Neil Smith	.15
42	Nick Lowery	.15
43	Thurman Thomas	1.50
44	Bruce Smith	.20
45	Barry Foster	.90
46	Neil O'Donnell	.90
47	Rickey Jackson	.15
48	Morten Andersen	.15
49	Brent Jones	.15
50	Ricky Watters	1.50
51	Leslie O'Neil	.15
52	Marion Butts	.15
53	Anthony Miller	.15
54	Jeff George	.25
55	Steve Emtmann	.75
56	Herschel Walker	.15
57	Randall Cunningham	.50
58	Clyde Simmons	.15
59	Emmitt Smith	4.00
60	Ken Norton	.15
61	Troy Aikman	2.00
62	Eric Green	.15
63	Greg Lloyd	.15
64	Bryan Cox	.15
65	Mark Higgs	.15
66	Phil Simms	.15
67	Lawrence Taylor	.30
68	Rodney Hampton	.75
69	Wayne Martin	.15
70	Vaughn Dunbar	.15
71	Keith Jackson	.15
72	Dan Marino	1.00
73	Junior Seau	.50
74	Stan Humphries	.15
75	Fred Barnett	.40
76	Seth Joyner	.15
77	Steve Young	1.00
78	Jerry Rice	1.25
79	Dan Dierdorf	.40
80	Frank Gifford	.40
81	Al Michaels	.40
82	All Three Together	.40

1993 Action Packed Monday Night Football Mint

Each 1993 Action Packed Monday Night Football pack had the random chance of including a certificate good for one of 250 gold mint cards produced for each card in the set.

		MT
Complete Set (78):		3000.
Common Player:		40.00
1	Michael Irvin	60.00
2	Charles Haley	40.00
3	Art Monk	40.00
4	Earnest Byner	40.00
5	Tom Rathman	40.00
6	John Taylor	40.00
7	Bernie Kosar	40.00
8	Clay Matthews	40.00
9	Simon Fletcher	40.00
10	John Elway	40.00
11	Joe Montana	275.00
12	Derrick Thomas	40.00
13	Rod Woodson	40.00
14	Gary Anderson	40.00
15	Chris Miller	40.00
16	Andre Rison	75.00
17	Mark Rypien	40.00
18	Charles Mann	40.00
19	John Offerdahl	40.00
20	Pete Stoyanovich	40.00
21	Warren Moon	60.00
22	Lorenzo White	40.00
23	Haywood Jeffires	40.00
24	Andre Reed	40.00
25	Darryl Talley	40.00
26	Tim Brown	40.00
27	Howie Long	40.00
28	Steve Atwater	40.00
29	Karl Mecklenburg	40.00
30	Chris Doleman	40.00
31	Terry Allen	65.00
32	Richard Dent	40.00
33	Neal Anderson	40.00
34	Darrell Green	40.00
35	Chip Lohmiller	40.00
36	Jim Kelly	150.00
37	Cornelius Bennett	40.00
38	Brett Favre	175.00
39	Sterling Sharpe	100.00
40	Reggie White	40.00
41	Neil Smith	40.00
42	Nick Lowery	40.00
43	Thurman Thomas	150.00
44	Bruce Smith	40.00
45	Barry Foster	90.00
46	Neil O'Donnell	100.00
47	Rickey Jackson	40.00
48	Morten Anderson	40.00
49	Brent Jones	40.00
50	Ricky Watters	95.00
51	Leslie O'Neal	40.00
52	Marion Butts	40.00
53	Anthony Miller	40.00
54	Jeff George	40.00
55	Steve Emtman	95.00
56	Herschel Walker	40.00
57	Randall Cunningham	40.00
58	Clyde Simmons	40.00
59	Emmitt Smith	300.00
60	Ken Norton	40.00
61	Troy Aikman	40.00
62	Eric Green	40.00
63	Greg Lloyd	40.00
64	Bryan Cox	40.00
65	Mark Higgs	40.00
66	Phil Simms	40.00
67	Lawrence Taylor	40.00
68	Rodney Hampton	100.00
69	Wayne Martin	40.00
70	Vaughn Dunbar	40.00
71	Keith Jackson	40.00
72	Dan Marino	250.00
73	Junior Seau	50.00
74	Stan Humphries	40.00
75	Fred Barnett	40.00
76	Seth Joyner	40.00
77	Steve Young	185.00
78	Jerry Rice	200.00

1994 Action Packed Prototypes

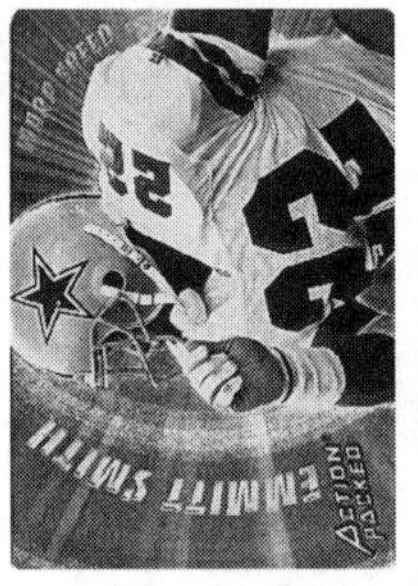

These 12 promotional cards preview Action Packed's 1994 design for its regular, subset and insert cards (the type of card is included in the checklist below). Each card is numbered on the back, using one of three different prefixes (FB, MNF or RU). The back is also labeled as a prototype. These cards were given to dealers and to those who attended the Super Bowl 28 card show. A set, which excluded Barry Foster's card, was also produced in its own display frame.

		MT
Complete Set (12):		70.00
Common Player:		3.00
FB941	(Troy Aikman) (1994 Action Packed)	15.00
FB942	Jeff Hostetler (Quarterback Challenge)	3.00
FB943	Emmitt Smith (Warp Speed)	12.00
FB944	(Jerry Rice) (Catching Fire)	7.00
FB945	(Barry Foster) (Fantasy Forecast Subset)	6.00
MNF941	(Steve Young) (Monday Night Football)	6.00
MNF942	(Steve Young) (Monday Night Moment)	6.00
MNF943	(Barry Foster) (Monday Night Moment)	6.00
RU941	(Drew Bledsoe) (Rookie Update)	10.00
RU942	(Derrick Lassic) (Rookie Update)	3.00
RU943	Rick Mirer (Golden Domers)	8.00
RU944	Jerome Bettis (Golden Domers)	8.00

1994 Action Packed

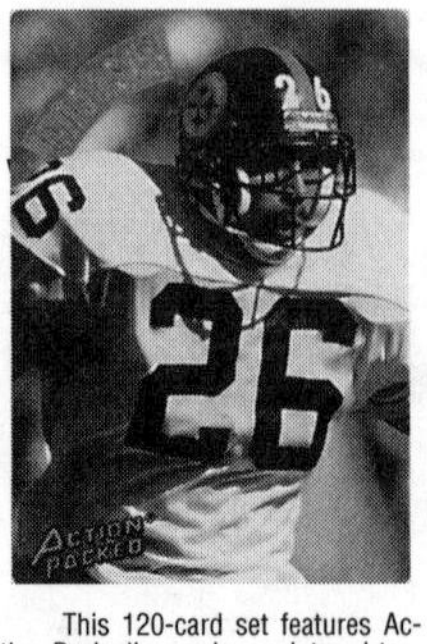

This 120-card set features Action Packed's regular sculptured texture, showing a full-bleed color photo on the card front, along with the player's name burnished in gold. Each card back has a metallic, foil background, a head shot of the player, 1993 statistics and an "Action Note." Insert sets include Quarterback Club, Catching Fire, Warp Speed, and Fantasy Forecast. There were 12 prototype cards made - each one says prototype on the back, and uses either an FB, MNF or RU prefix for the card number.

		MT
Complete Set (198):		60.00
Complete Series 1 (120):		35.00
Complete Series 2 (78):		25.00
Common Player:		.20
Minor Stars:		.40
Braille Cards:		2x
Gold Signature Cards:		3x
Inserted 1:1 Retail		
Series 1 Pack (8):		2.50
Series 1 Box (24):		45.00
Rook/Update Pack (8):		2.00
Rook/Update Wax Box (24):		40.00
1	Michael Haynes	.20
2	Andre Rison	.75
3	Mike Pritchard	.20
4	Erric Pegram	.20
5	Deion Sanders	1.00
6	Jim Kelly	.75
7	Andre Reed	.40
8	Thurman Thomas	.75
9	Bruce Smith	.20
10	Cornelius Bennett	.20
11	Nate Odomes	.20
12	Richard Dent	.20
13	Donnell Woolford	.20
14	Harold Green	.20
15	David Klingler	.20
16	Eric Metcalf	.20
17	Michael Dean Perry	.20
18	Michael Jackson	.40
19	Vinny Testaverde	.75
20	Troy Aikman	2.50
21	Michael Irvin	.75
22	Emmitt Smith	4.00
23	Jay Novacek	.20
24	Alvin Harper	.40
25	Charles Haley	.20
26	John Elway	3.00
27	Shannon Sharpe	.40
28	Rod Bernstine	.20
29	Simon Fletcher	.20
30	Barry Sanders	5.00
31	Herman Moore	1.00
32	Pat Swilling	.20
33	Chris Spielman	.20
34	Brett Favre	5.00
35	Sterling Sharpe	.40
36	Reggie White	.75
37	Jackie Harris	.20
38	Tony Bennett	.20
39	LeRoy Butler	.20
40	Warren Moon	.75
41	Ernest Givins	.20
42	Haywood Jeffires	.20
43	Webster Slaughter	.20
44	Ray Childress	.20
45	Gary Brown	.40
46	Jeff George	.75
47	Roosevelt Potts	.20
48	Quentin Coryatt	.20
49	Joe Montana	3.00
50	Derrick Thomas	.40
51	Neil Smith	.20
52	Marcus Allen	.75
53	Willie Davis	.20
54	Jerome Bettis	1.00
55	Sean Gilbert	.20
56	Chris Miller	.20
57	Jeff Hostetler	.40
58	Tim Brown	.75
59	Anthony Smith	.20
60	Greg Townsend	.20
61	Terry McDaniel	.20
62	Dan Marino	4.00
63	Irving Fryar	.20
64	Keith Jackson	.20
65	Terry Kirby	.20
66	Bryan Cox	.20
67	Chris Doleman	.20
68	Cris Carter	1.00
69	John Randle	.40
70	Drew Bledsoe	3.00
71	Ben Coates	.40
72	Vincent Brisby	.40
73	Rickey Jackson	.20
74	Eric Martin	.20
75	Renaldo Turnbull	.20
76	Rodney Hampton	.40
77	Mike Sherrard	.20
78	Phil Simms	.40
79	Keith Hamilton	.20
80	Rob Moore	.75
81	Brad Baxter	.20
82	Boomer Esiason	.40
83	Johnny Johnson	.20
84	Ronnie Lott	.40
85	Randall Cunningham	.75
86	Herschel Walker	.20
87	Eric Allen	.20
88	Clyde Simmons	.20
89	Seth Joyner	.20
90	Calvin Williams	.20
91	Garrison Hearst	1.00
92	Steve Beuerlein	.20
93	Ricky Proehl	.20
94	Ron Moore	.20
95	Barry Foster	.20
96	Neil O'Donnell	.40
97	Eric Green	.20
98	Rod Woodson	.40
99	Greg Lloyd	.20
100	Kevin Greene	.20
101	Stan Humphries	.40
102	Anthony Miller	.20
103	Junior Seau	.40
104	Leslie O'Neal	.20
105	Ronnie Harmon	.20
106	Jerry Rice	2.50
107	Ricky Watters	.75
108	Steve Young	2.00
109	Brent Jones	.20
110	John Taylor	.20
111	Rick Mirer	.40
112	Chris Warren	.40
113	Cortez Kennedy	.20
114	Brian Blades	.20

115	Eugene Robinson	.20
116	Reggie Cobb	.20
117	Hardy Nickerson	.20
118	Reggie Brooks	.20
119	Darrell Green	.20
120	Troy Aikman	2.50
121	*Dan Wilkinson*	.40
122	*Marshall Faulk*	7.00
123	*Heath Shuler*	.75
124	*Willie McGinest*	.40
125	*Trev Alberts*	.40
126	*Trent Dilfer*	4.00
127	*Bryant Young*	.75
128	*Sam Adams*	.40
129	*Antonio Langham*	.40
130	*Jamir Miller*	.20
131	*John Thierry*	.40
132	*Aaron Glenn*	.40
133	*Joe Johnson*	.20
134	*Bernard Williams*	.20
135	*Wayne Gandy*	.20
136	*Charles Johnson*	.75
137	*DeWayne Washington*	.40
138	*Todd Steussie*	.40
139	*Tim Bowens*	.40
140	*Johnnie Morton*	2.00
141	*Rob Fredrickson*	.40
142	*Shante Carver*	.40
143	*Thomas Lewis*	.40
144	*Greg Hill*	.75
145	*Henry Ford*	.20
146	*Jeff Burris*	.40
147	*William Floyd*	.75
148	*Derrick Alexander*	.75
149	*Darnay Scott*	2.50
150	*Isaac Bruce*	6.00
151	*Errict Rhett*	1.00
152	*Kevin Lee*	.40
153	*Chuck Levy*	.40
154	*David Palmer*	1.00
155	*Ryan Yarborough*	.40
156	*Charlie Garner*	3.00
157	*Mario Bates*	.75
158	*Bert Emanuel*	2.00
159	*Bucky Brooks*	.40
160	*Donnell Bennett*	1.00
161	*Tydus Winans*	.40
162	*Andre Coleman*	.40
163	*Calvin Jones*	.40
164	*LeShon Johnson*	.40
165	*Doug Brien*	.20
166	*Bam Morris*	.75
167	*Lake Dawson*	.75
168	*Perry Klein*	.40
169	*Doug Nussmeier*	.40
170	*Lamont Warren*	.20
171	*Gus Frerotte*	1.00
172	Troy Aikman	1.50
173	Randall Cunningham	.40
174	John Elway	1.50
175	Jim Everett	.20
176	Drew Bledsoe	1.50
177	Jim Kelly	.40
178	Dan Marino	2.00
179	Chris Miller	.20
180	Warren Moon	.20
181	Rick Mirer	.20
182	Jeff Hostetler	.20
183	Brett Favre	3.00
184	Steve Young	1.00
185	Anthony Miller	.20
186	Michael Haynes	.20
187	Mike Pritchard	.20
188	Jeff George	.40
189	Lewis Tillman	.20
190	Ken Norton	.20
191	Erik Kramer	.20
192	Richard Dent	.20
193	Rick Mirer	.20
194	Jerome Bettis	.40
195	Reggie Brooks	.20
196	Tom Carter	.20
197	Irv Smith	.20
198	Rocket Ismail	.20

1994 Action Packed 24K Gold

Action Packed made 24K gold versions for each of its insert sets - Quarterback Club (G1-G20); Catching Fire (G21-G30); and Warp Speed (G31-G42). These Quarterback Club cards feature gold foil fronts rather than in silver like the regular ones.

		MT
Complete Set (55):		1000.
Complete Series 1 (42):		700.00
Complete Series 2 (13):		300.00
Common Player:		5.00
Minor Stars:		10.00
Inserted 1:96		
1	Troy Aikman	30.00
2	Randall Cunningham	15.00
3	John Elway	40.00
4	Boomer Esiason	5.00
5	Jim Everett	5.00
6	Brett Favre	60.00
7	Jerry Rice	30.00
8	Jeff Hostetler	5.00
9	Jim Kelly	10.00
10	David Klingler	5.00
11	Bernie Kosar	5.00
12	Dan Marino	45.00
13	Chris Miller	5.00
14	Warren Moon	10.00
15	Neil O'Donnell	10.00
16	Michael Irvin	10.00
17	Phil Simms	5.00
18	Steve Young	20.00
19	Rick Mirer	10.00
20	Drew Bledsoe	30.00
21	Jerry Rice	30.00
22	Sterling Sharpe	10.00
23	Michael Irvin	10.00
25	Anthony Miller	5.00
26	Tim Brown	10.00
27	Andre Reed	5.00
28	Herman Moore	10.00
29	Irving Fryar	5.00
30	Shannon Sharpe	10.00
31	Emmitt Smith	45.00
32	Barry Sanders	60.00
33	Thurman Thomas	10.00
34	Jerome Bettis	10.00
35	Barry Foster	5.00
36	Ricky Watters	10.00
37	Rodney Hampton	5.00
38	Chris Warren	10.00
39	Erric Pegram	5.00
40	Reggie Brooks	5.00
41	Marcus Allen	10.00
42	Ron Moore	5.00
43	Troy Aikman	30.00
44	Randall Cunningham	10.00
45	John Elway	40.00
46	Jim Everett	5.00
47	Drew Bledsoe	30.00
48	Jim Kelly	10.00
49	Dan Marino	45.00
50	Chris Miller	5.00
51	Warren Moon	10.00
52	Rick Mirer	10.00
53	Jeff Hostetler	5.00
54	Brett Favre	60.00
55	Steve Young	20.00

1994 Action Packed Catching Fire

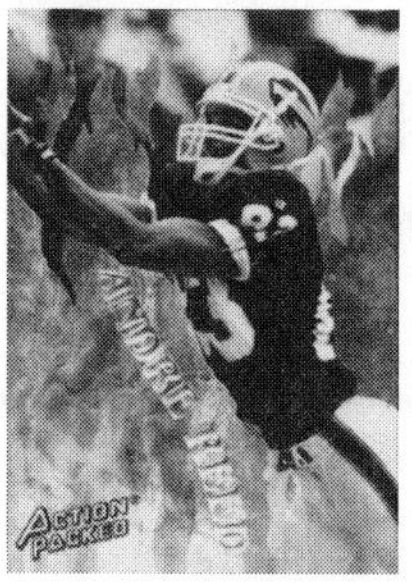

The NFL's top 10 wide receivers are featured in this insert set. The "Catching Fire" logo is on the card front, which shows the player surrounded by metallic foil flames. Card backs are numbered with an "R" prefix; except for 24K gold versions which were also created; they are numbered G21-G30.

		MT
Complete Set (10):		10.00
Common Player:		.50
Minor Stars:		1.00
1	Jerry Rice	5.00
2	Sterling Sharpe	1.00
3	Michael Irvin	1.00
4	Andre Rison	1.00
5	Anthony Miller	.50
6	Tim Brown	1.00
7	Andre Reed	.50
8	Herman Moore	2.00
9	Irving Fryar	.50
10	Shannon Sharpe	1.00

1994 Action Packed Fantasy Forecast

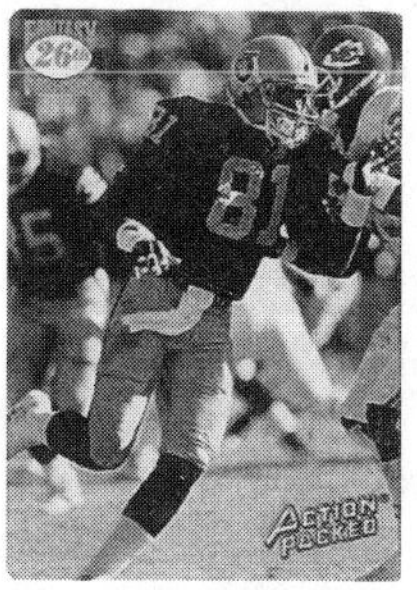

This Fantasy Forecast insert set provides a scouting report for 42 top NFL players. Each card front features the player with a football that is covered with heat-sensitive ink. Touching the football reveals how high you should draft the player if you were picking a fantasy football team. Cards are numbered FF1-FF42

		MT
Complete Set (42):		15.00
Common Player:		.25
Minor Stars:		.50
1	Rodney Hampton	.50
2	Steve Young	1.50
3	Michael Irvin	.50
4	Emmitt Smith	3.00
5	Troy Aikman	2.00
6	Jerry Rice	2.00
7	Brett Favre	4.00
8	Jerome Bettis	.50
9	Reggie Brooks	.25
10	John Elway	2.50
11	Jim Kelly	.50
12	Dan Marino	3.00
13	Randall Cunningham	.50
14	Sterling Sharpe	.50
15	Chris Warren	.50
16	Andre Rison	.50
17	Mike Pritchard	.25
18	Barry Sanders	4.00
19	Marcus Allen	.50
20	Thurman Thomas	.50
21	Erric Pegram	.25
22	Barry Foster	.25
23	Anthony Miller	.25
24	Shannon Sharpe	.50
25	Tim Brown	.50
26	Ricky Watters	.50
27	Ernest Givins	.25
28	Cris Carter	.50
29	Willie Davis	.50
30	Warren Moon	.50
31	Joe Montana	2.50
32	Herman Moore	.50
33	Terry Kirby	.25
34	Eric Green	.25
35	Michael Jackson	.25
36	Johnny Johnson	.25
37	Calvin Williams	.25
38	Michael Haynes	.25
39	Irving Fryar	.25
40	Gary Brown	.25
41	Jeff Hostetler	.25
42	Keith Jackson	.25

1994 Action Packed Quarterback Challenge

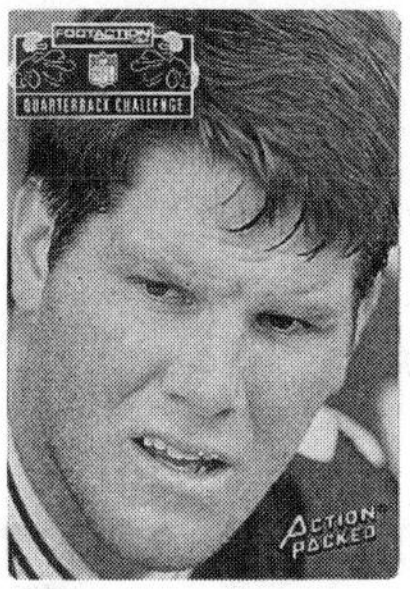

The 12-card, regular-size set was inserted in each retail pack that was available at Foot Action stores. The card fronts feature the quarterback's face - outlined in silver, while the backs include information from the Quarterback Challenge competition. All cards are numbered with the "FA" prefix.

		MT
Complete Set (12):		15.00
Common Player:		.25
Minor Stars:		.50
1	Steve Young	2.00
2	John Elway	3.00
3	Troy Aikman	2.50
4	Randall Cunningham	.75
5	Warren Moon	.50
6	Brett Favre	5.00
7	Rick Mirer	.25
8	Drew Bledsoe	3.00
9	Boomer Esiason	.25
10	Jeff Hostetler	.25
11	Jim Kelly	.50
12	Dan Marino	3.50

1994 Action Packed Quarterback Club

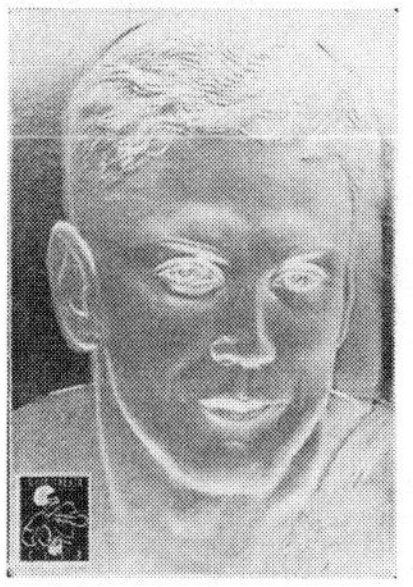

These Action Packed cards are printed with a silver foil front similar to, but far more sturdier and attractive, than Topps 1965 Embossed insert set. Cards were random inserts in 1994 packs and are numbered with a "QB" prefix. They feature the player's embossed portrait on the front. There were also 24K gold versions made for each Quarterback Club card. These cards feature gold foil on the front instead of silver.

		MT
Complete Set (20):		15.00
Common Player:		.25
Minor Stars:		.50
1	Troy Aikman	2.50
2	Randall Cunningham	.75
3	John Elway	3.00
4	Boomer Esiason	.50
5	Jim Everett	.25
6	Brett Favre	5.00
7	Jerry Rice	2.50
8	Jeff Hostetler	.25
9	Jim Kelly	.50
10	David Klingler	.25
11	Bernie Kosar	.25
12	Dan Marino	3.50
13	Chris Miller	.25
14	Warren Moon	.50
15	Neil O'Donnell	.50
16	Michael Irvin	.50
17	Phil Simms	.25
18	Steve Young	2.00
19	Rick Mirer	.50
20	Drew Bledsoe	3.00

1994 Action Packed Warp Speed

These 1994 Action Packed inserts feature 12 of the NFL's top running backs. Card fronts are printed using a colored foil design and have the "Warp Speed" and player's name in foil, too. Cards are numbered with a "WS" prefix. Gold versions were also made and are numbered G31-G42.

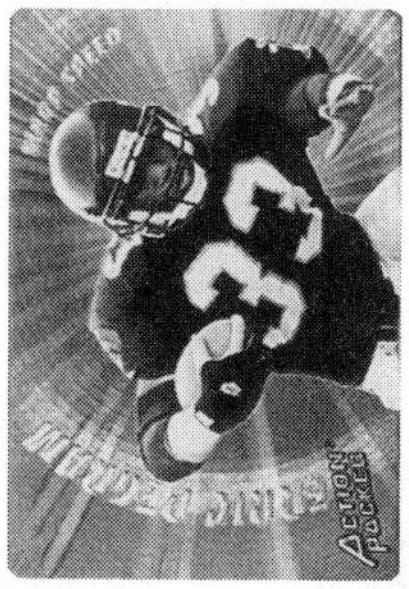

		MT
Complete Set (12):		15.00
Common Player:		.25
Minor Stars:		.50
1	Emmitt Smith	4.00
2	Barry Sanders	6.00
3	Thurman Thomas	.50
4	Jerome Bettis	1.00
5	Barry Foster	.25
6	Ricky Watters	.50
7	Rodney Hampton	.50
8	Chris Warren	.25
9	Erric Pegram	.25
10	Reggie Brooks	.25
11	Marcus Allen	.50
12	Ron Moore	.25

1994 Action Packed All-Madden

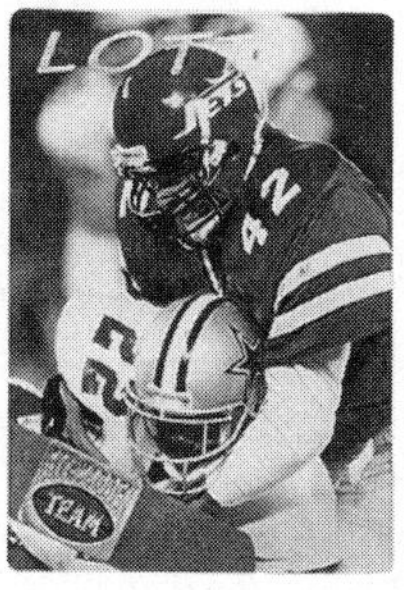

The 11th Annual All-Madden Team is a 41-card set from Action Packed that showcases Madden's hand-picked All-Pro Team. The fronts have a borderless design and incorporates a band-aid logo, exemplifying the toughness that was required to be selected by Madden. All 41 cards also have a 24kt gold equivalent, of which there is one per every box of the product. Cards were sold in packs of six. Each pack includes a "Smash Mouth" scratch-and-win game card which offers various prizes, including different television sets and 24kt gold cards.

		MT
Complete Set (41):		20.00
Common Player:		.15
Wax Box:		35.00
1	Emmitt Smith	4.00
2	Jerome Bettis	1.00
3	Steve Young	2.00
4	Jerry Rice	2.50
5	Richard Dent	.15
6	Junior Seau	.50
7	Harris Barton	.15
8	Steve Wallace	.15
9	Keith Byars	.15
10	Michael Irvin	1.00
11	Joe Montana	2.50
12	Jesse Sapolu	.15
13	Rickey Jackson	.15
14	Ronnie Lott	.50
15	Donnell Woolford	.15
16	Reggie White	1.50
17	John Taylor	.25
18	Bruce Matthews	.15
19	Ron Moore	.15
20	Bill Bates	.15
21	Steve Hendrickson	.15
22	Eric Allen	.25
23	Monte Coleman	.15
24	Mark Collins	.15
25	Barry Sanders	3.00
26	Erik Williams	.15
27	Phil Simms	.25
28	Chris Zorich	.15
29	Troy Aikman	3.00
30	Charles Haley	.15
31	Darrell Green	.15
32	Sean Gilbert	.15
33	Kevin Gogan	.15
34	Rodney Hampton	1.00
35	Chris Doleman	.15
36	Nate Newton	.15
37	Jackie Slater	.15
38	Ricky Watters	1.00
39	LeRoy Butler	.15
40	Gary Clark	.15
41	Sterling Sharpe	.50

A card number in parentheses ( ) indicates the set is unnumbered.

1994 Action Packed All-Madden 24k Gold

Each of the 41 cards in the 11th Annual All-Madden Team was created in a 24kt gold version for this parallel set. There was one 24kt gold card in each All-Madden product box.

		MT
Complete Set (41):		1000.
Common Player:		20.00
1	Emmitt Smith	150.00
2	Jerome Bettis	50.00
3	Steve Young	80.00
4	Jerry Rice	95.00
5	Richard Dent	20.00
6	Junior Seau	28.00
7	Harris Barton	20.00
8	Steve Wallace	20.00
9	Keith Byars	20.00
10	Michael Irvin	50.00
11	Joe Montana	95.00
12	Jesse Sapolu	20.00
13	Rickey Jackson	20.00
14	Ronnie Lott	28.00
15	Donnell Woolford	20.00
16	Reggie White	75.00
17	John Taylor	25.00
18	Bruce Matthews	20.00
19	Ron Moore	20.00
20	Bill Bates	20.00
21	Steve Hendrickson	20.00
22	Eric Allen	25.00
23	Monte Coleman	20.00
24	Mark Collins	20.00
25	Barry Sanders	95.00
26	Erik Williams	20.00
27	Phil Simms	25.00
28	Chris Zorich	20.00
29	Troy Aikman	95.00
30	Charles Haley	20.00
31	Darrell Green	20.00
32	Sean Gilbert	20.00
33	Kevin Gogan	20.00
34	Rodney Hampton	50.00
35	Chris Doleman	20.00
36	Nate Newton	20.00
37	Jackie Slater	20.00
38	Ricky Watters	50.00
39	LeRoy Butler	20.00
40	Gary Clark	20.00
41	Sterling Sharpe	28.00

1994 Action Packed Monday Night Football

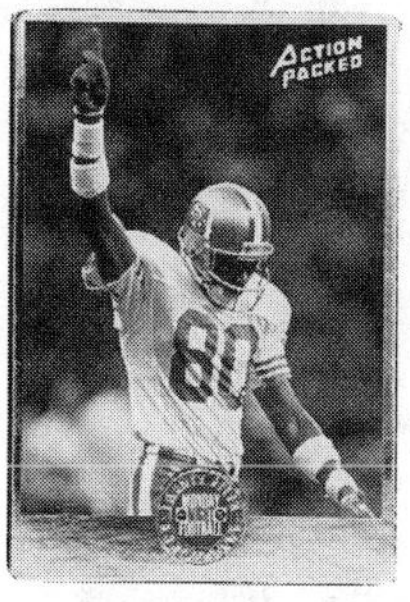

Action Packed released a 71-card, silver foil, football set celebrating 25 years of Monday Night Football. This set includes a randomly inserted .999 pure silver foil insert set and 25 certificates for a sterling silver card with Emmitt Smith, Troy Aikman and Michael Irvin. The card fronts feature a tight shot of each player. The back casts the player in moonlight and discusses specific challenges that player faced in the upcoming Monday night match-up. The set primarily consisted of players expected to shine in 1994 Monday Night match-ups. Also, as part of the 25th anniversary promotion, Action Packed included members of the announcing cast, such as Howard Cosell and Meredith.

		MT
Complete Set (71):		25.00
Common Player:		.20
Minor Stars:		.40
Wax Box:		35.00
1	Jeff Hostetler	.20
2	Terry McDaniel	.20
3	Steve Young	2.00
4	Jerry Rice	2.00
5	Donnell Woolford	.20
6	Eric Allen	.20
7	Herschel Walker	.20
8	Barry Sanders	3.00
9	Herman Moore	.75
10	Emmitt Smith	4.00
11	Michael Irvin	1.00
12	John Elway	1.00
13	Jim Kelly	.40
14	Andre Reed	.20
15	Gary Brown	.20
16	Ernest Givins	.20
17	Barry Foster	.20
18	Rod Woodson	.20
19	Warren Moon	.40
20	Cris Carter	.40
21	Rodney Hampton	.20
22	Derrick Thomas	.20
23	Marcus Allen	.40
24	Shannon Sharpe	.20
25	Cody Carlson	.20
26	Haywood Jeffires	.20
27	Randall Cunningham	.20
28	Calvin Williams	.20
29	Brett Favre	2.00
30	Sterling Sharpe	.40
31	Chris Zorich	.20
32	Dante Jones	.20
33	Mike Sherrard	.20
34	Keith Hamilton	.20
35	Charles Haley	.20
36	Thurman Thomas	.40
37	Bruce Smith	.20
38	Greg Lloyd	.20
39	Michael Brooks	.20
40	Jumbo Elliott	.20
41	Ray Childress	.20
42	Bruce Matthews	.20
43	Ricky Watters	.40
44	Brent Jones	.20
45	Morten Andersen	.20
46	Tim Brown	.40
47	Anthony Smith	.20
48	Natrone Means	1.50
49	Junior Seau	.40
50	Joe Montana	2.50
51	Neil Smith	.20
52	Dan Marino	4.00
53	Keith Jackson	.20
54	Troy Aikman	1.50
55	Jay Novacek	.20
56	Rickey Jackson	.20
57	John Taylor	.20
58	Tim McDonald	.20
59	John Randle	.20
60	Henry Thomas	.20
61	Prime Time Players	.20
62	The Don & Howard Show	.20
63	The Entertainers	.20
64	I Never Played the Game	.20
65	Monday Night Madness	.20
66	Whoa Nellie	.20
67	Dandy Don Meredith	.20
68	Speaking of Sports	.20
69	Donning a Dierdorf	.20
70	Half-Time Highlights	.20
71	Return to the Field	.20

1994 Action Packed Monday Night Football Silver

Action Packed randomly inserted a 12-card set into its foil packs, called .999 pure silver foil cards. These are comparable to the 24k gold cards randomly inserted into Action Packed's usual gold foil products.

		MT
Complete Set (12):		650.00
Common Player:		20.00
1	Steve Young	75.00
2	Jerry Rice	75.00
3	Barry Sanders	75.00
4	Emmitt Smith	100.00
5	John Elway	40.00
6	Jim Kelly	30.00
7	Warren Moon	20.00
8	Randall Cunningham	20.00
9	Brett Favre	75.00
10	Dan Marino	100.00
11	Troy Aikman	75.00
12	Speaking of Sports	20.00

1994 Action Packed Badge of Honor Pins

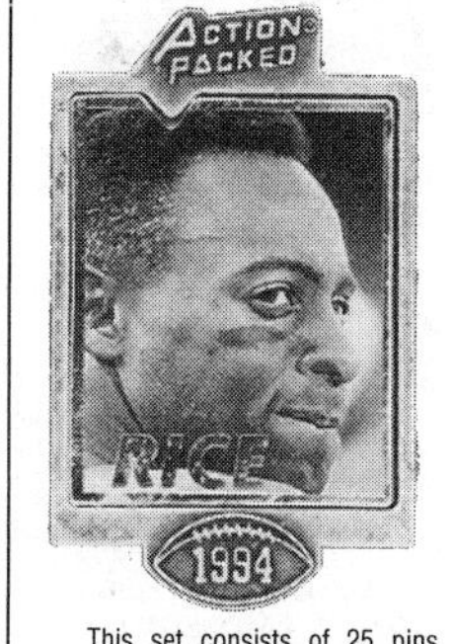

This set consists of 25 pins measuring 1-1/2" x 1". The front of each pin features a color player portrait with a gold border on a bronze background. The player's last name and Action Packed logo are also on the front. Each box of Action Packed contained three packs of four pins and one of five black pin albums to store five pins. Each pack of pins came in a cardboard holder with the set checklist on the back. A 24K Gold parallel of each pin was created and randomly seeded in packs.

		MT
Complete Set (25):		40.00
Common Pin:		.75
*24K Gold Pins:		10x-20x
1	Troy Aikman	3.00
2	Drew Bledsoe	3.00
3	Bubby Brister	.75
4	Randall Cunningham	1.00
5	John Elway	2.00
6	Boomer Esiason	1.00
7	Jim Everett	.75
8	Brett Favre	6.00
9	Jim Harbaugh	1.50
10	Jeff Hostetler	.75
11	Michael Irvin	1.50
12	Jim Kelly	1.50
13	David Klingler	.75
14	Bernie Kosar	.75
15	Dan Marino	5.00
16	Chris Miller	.75
17	Rick Mirer	.75
18	Warren Moon	1.00
19	Neil O'Donnell	1.00
20	Jerry Rice	3.00
21	Mark Rypien	.75

22 Barry Sanders 4.00
23 Phil Simms 1.00
24 Emmitt Smith 5.00
25 Steve Young 2.00

1994 Action Packed CoaStars

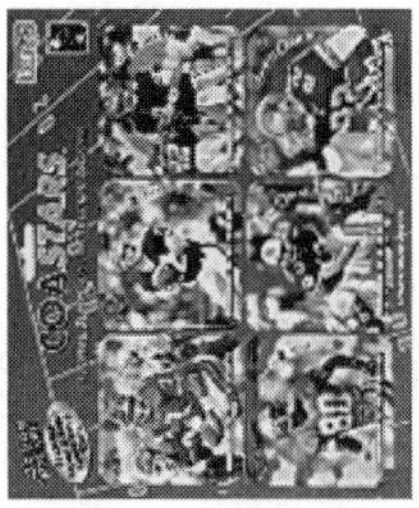

The set of 25 coaster cards were sold in six-card packs. Each coaster has rounded corners and measures 3-1/4" x 3-1/4". The front of the coaster features the player's name and position, while the back has an action shot with 1993 statistics.

MT
Complete Set (25): 25.00
Common Player: .25
1 Troy Aikman 2.50
2 Drew Bledsoe 2.50
3 Bubby Brister .25
4 Randall Cunningham .25
5 John Elway 1.25
6 Boomer Esiason .40
7 Jim Everett .40
8 Brett Favre 5.00
9 Jim Harbaugh .50
10 Jeff Hostetler .40
11 Michael Irvin .50
12 Jim Kelly .50
13 David Klingler .25
14 Bernie Kosar .40
15 Dan Marino 5.00
16 Rick Mirer 1.00
17 Chris Miller .40
18 Warren Moon .50
19 Neil O'Donnell .50
20 Jerry Rice 2.50
21 Mark Rypien .40
22 Barry Sanders 2.50
23 Phil Simms .40
24 Emmitt Smith 5.00
25 Steve Young 1.50

1994 Action Packed Mammoth

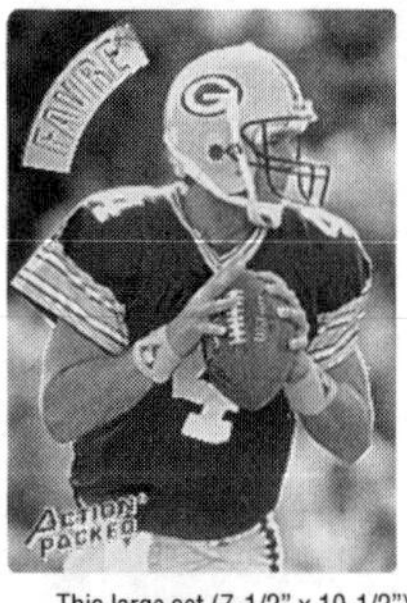

This large set (7-1/2" x 10-1/2") was offered to dealers by Action Packed. Each card has an "MM" prefix on the back and while it is a 25-card set, it's numbered from 1 to 26 as there is no card 25. Series 2 cards of Troy Aikman, Emmitt Smith and Michael Irvin are also included, while three prototypes, including two 24kt gold cards, were randomly inserted. Reportedly, only 25,000 of each base card was produced while less than 2,500 of the Aikman and Smith gold cards were issued.

MT
Complete Set (25): 120.00
Common Player: 4.00
1 Troy Aikman 10.00
2 Drew Bledsoe 10.00
3 Barry Sanders 10.00
4 Chris Miller 4.00
5 Randall Cunningham 4.00
6 John Elway 6.00
7 Boomer Esiason 4.00
8 Jim Everett 4.00
9 Brett Favre 16.00
10 Jim Harbaugh 4.00
11 Jeff Hostetler 4.00
12 Michael Irvin 4.00
13 Jim Kelly 4.00
14 David Klingler 4.00
15 Bernie Kosar 4.00
16 Dan Marino 16.00
17 Rick Mirer 4.00
18 Warren Moon 4.00
19 Neil O'Donnell 4.00
20 Jerry Rice 10.00
21 Mark Rypien 4.00
22 Phil Simms 4.00
23 Emmitt Smith 16.00
24 Steve Young 6.00
26 Bubby Brister 4.00
2MM1 Troy Aikman (Series 2 card numbered MM1-2) 10.00
2MM2 Michael Irvin (Series 2 card numbered MM2-2) 4.00
2MM6 Emmitt Smith (Series 2 card numbered MM6-2) 16.00
P1 Troy Aikman (Prototype Numbered MMP) 10.00
P2 Emmitt Smith (Prototype 24K Gold Numbered MMP1G report edly 2500 made) 60.00
P3 Troy Aikman (Prototype 24K Gold Numbered MMP2G report edly 1000 made) 35.00

1995 Action Packed Promos

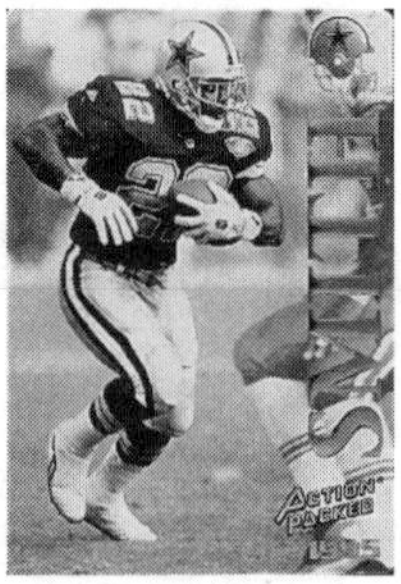

The four-card, standard-size set was issued as a preview for the 126-card base set. The set included two regular cards, one Armed Forces insert card and one advertisement card. The card fronts are the same as the base set, but the backs have a "Promo" stamp.

MT
Complete Set (4): 10.00
Common Player: .50
1 Jerry Rice 2.50
2 Emmitt Smith 5.00
AF4 Steve Young 1.75
NNO Action Packed Ad Card (Armed Forces card) .50

1995 Action Packed

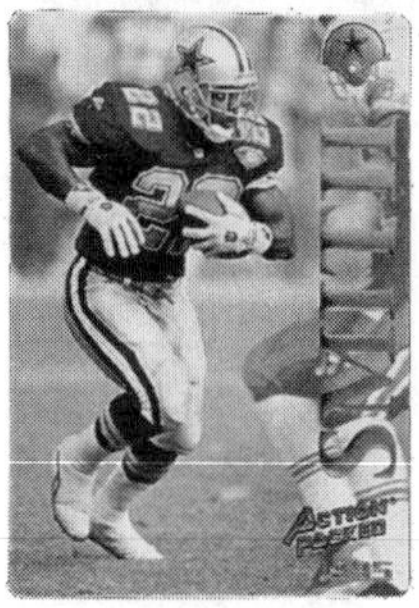

Action Packed Football returned in 1995 under new ownership, Pinnacle, which repeated the existing embossed technology and added its own improvements. The 126-card set captures game action and candid shots with embossed highlights. All 126 cards were also repeated in a metallized silver foil parallel (Quick Silver) set (one per every six packs). The regular cards feature an action shot on the front, with the player's team helmet in the upper right corner. The player's last name is written in gold foil down the side, with Action Packed and 1995 written below the name. The card back is horizontal, with a mug shot, statistics and a brief career summary included. A panel at the bottom includes his name, biographical information and a team logo. The card number is in the upper right corner. Insert sets include Armed Forces, which are also featured on a parallel Braille set, Rocket Men, G-Force and 24k Gold cards.

MT
Complete Set (126): 25.00
Common Player: .10
Minor Stars: .20
Complete Silver Set (126): 300.00
Silver Cards: 3x-6x
Pack (8): 3.50
Wax Box (24): 65.00
1 Jerry Rice 1.50
2 Emmitt Smith 3.00
3 Drew Bledsoe 2.00
4 Ben Coates .20
5 Jim Everett .10
6 Warren Moon .20
7 Herman Moore .75
8 Deion Sanders .75
9 Rick Mirer .20
10 Natrone Means .50
11 *Jeff Blake* 1.00
12 William Floyd .20
13 Steve Young 1.00
14 John Elway .75
15 Brett Favre 3.00
16 Marshall Faulk .75
17 Heath Shuler .20
18 Ricky Watters .50
19 Michael Haynes .10
20 Troy Aikman 1.25
21 Dan Marino 3.00
22 Bam Morris .10
23 Marcus Allen .20
24 Carl Pickens .20
25 Rodney Hampton .10
26 Dave Brown .10
27 Jerome Bettis .50
28 Jim Kelly .50
29 Andre Reed .20
30 Michael Irvin .50
31 Barry Sanders 3.00
32 Chris Warren .20
33 Jeff Hostetler .10
34 Alvin Harper .10
35 Rob Moore .20
36 *Steve McNair* 5.00
37 *Rashaan Salaam* .50
38 *Joey Galloway* 5.00
39 *J.J. Stokes* 2.00
40 *Michael Westbrook* 1.75
41 *Kerry Collins* 2.00
42 *Ki-Jana Carter* 1.00
43 Boomer Esiason .10
44 Chris Spielman .10
45 Vinny Testaverde .20
46 Kevin Williams .10
47 Ronnie Harmon .10
48 Fred Barnett .10
49 Harvey Williams .10
50 Reggie White .50
51 Brent Jones .10
52 Henry Ellard .10
53 Cris Carter .50
54 Leroy Hoard .10
55 Trent Dilfer .75
56 Desmond Howard .10
57 Garrison Hearst .50
58 Lewis Tillman .10
59 Mark Brunell 1.50
60 Bruce Smith .10
61 Lake Dawson .20
62 Bert Emanuel .20
63 Eric Green .10
64 Barry Foster .10
65 Jeff Graham .10
66 Curtis Conway .20
67 Herschel Walker .10
68 Edgar Bennett .10
69 Mario Bates .20
70 Irving Fryar .10
71 Gary Brown .10
72 Cortez Kennedy .10
73 John Taylor .10
74 Jeff George .50
75 Shannon Sharpe .50
76 Andre Rison .50
77 Mike Sherrard .10
78 Errict Rhett .20
79 Junior Seau .50
80 Willie Davis .10
81 Craig Erickson .10
82 Torrance Small .10
83 Randall Cunningham .50
84 Robert Brooks .10
85 Terance Mathis .10
86 Rod Woodson .20
87 Anthony Miller .10
88 Stan Humphries .20
89 Chris Miller .10
90 Steve Beuerlein .10
91 Steve Bono .20
92 Frank Reich .10
93 Corey Fleming .10
94 Isaac Bruce .50
95 Dave Meggett .10
96 Jackie Harris .10
97 J.J. Birden .10
98 Willie Anderson .10
99 Johnnie Morton .10
100 Michael Timpson .10
101 Derek Brown .10
102 Ricky Ervins .10
103 *Derrick Alexander* .50
104 *Dave Barr* .20
105 *Tony Boselli* .50
106 *Kyle Brady* .75
107 *Mark Bruener* .75
108 *Kevin Carter* .10
109 Neil O'Donnell .10
110 Derrick Alexander .20
111 Charlie Garner .20
112 Darnay Scott .20
113 Scott Mitchell .20
114 Charles Johnson .20
115 Greg Hill .20
116 *Ty Law* .20
117 *Frank Sanders* 1.75
118 *James Stewart Tenn* 2.00
119 *James Stewart Miami* .50
120 *Kordell Stewart* 6.00
121 *Rob Johnson* 3.00
122 *John Walsh* .25
123 *Stoney Case* .50
124 *Tyrone Wheatley* .50
125 *Sherman Williams* .50
126 *Ray Zellars* .50

1995 Action Packed Quick Silver

The 126-card, regular-size set was a parallel release to the 1995 base set, inserted every six packs. The cards have a silver-foil card front while the backs have "Quick Silver" printed.

MT
Complete Set (126): 450.00
Common Player: 1.50
Quick Silver Cards: 4x-8x

Values quoted in this guide reflect the retail price of a card — the price a collector can expect to pay when buying a card from a dealer. The wholesale price — that which a collector can expect to receive from a dealer when selling cards — will be significantly lower, depending on desirability and condition.

1995 Action Packed 24K Gold

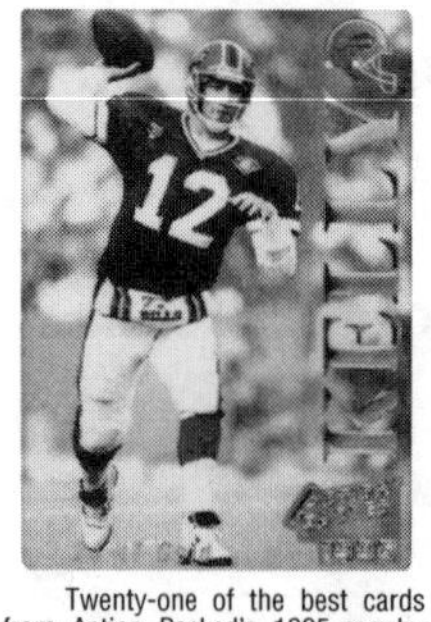

Twenty-one of the best cards from Action Packed's 1995 regular football set are showcased in this 24K Gold insert set. Inserts, which have special gold foil stamping, could be found one per every 72 packs. They are numbered using a "G" suffix.

MT
Complete Set (21): 450.00
Common Player: 7.50
Minor Stars: 15.00
Inserted 1:72
1 Jerry Rice 30.00
2 Emmitt Smith 45.00
3 Drew Bledsoe 30.00
4 Warren Moon 7.50
5 Deion Sanders 20.00
6 Natrone Means 7.50
7 Steve Young 25.00
8 John Elway 45.00
9 Brett Favre 60.00
10 Marshall Faulk 15.00
11 Heath Shuler 7.50
12 Troy Aikman 30.00
13 Dan Marino 45.00
14 Jerome Bettis 15.00
15 Jim Kelly 15.00
16 Michael Irvin 15.00
17 Barry Sanders 60.00
18 Steve McNair 30.00
19 Rashaan Salaam 15.00
20 Kerry Collins 15.00
21 Ki-Jana Carter 7.50

1995 Action Packed Armed Forces

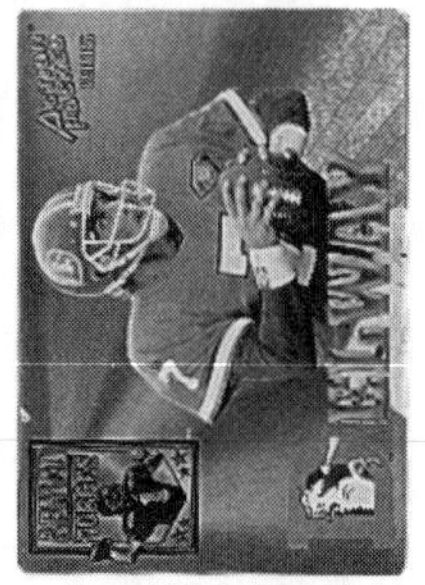

These 1995 Action Packed inserts feature 12 of the hottest arms in the NFL Quarterback Club. The cards were randomly included one per every 24 packs. The front is a horizontal design which features a full color raised photo in the center, flanked by the insert set logo and the set logo in the upper corners. The player's name appears in gold below his name, which is adjacent to a team logo in the lower left corner. The card back, numbered using an "AF" prefix, is vertical and includes a close-up shot of the player, plus a brief career summary. A panel along the right side of the card includes an action shot. A parallel Braille version set was also created for the Armed Forces set (1 in 96 packs).

MT
Complete Set (12): 100.00
Common Player: 5.00
Complete Braille Set (12): 150.00
Braille Cards: 1x-2x
1 Drew Bledsoe 10.00
2 Dan Marino 20.00
3 Troy Aikman 10.00
4 Steve Young 10.00
5 Brett Favre 20.00
6 Heath Shuler 5.00
7 Dave Brown 5.00
8 Jeff Blake 7.00
9 John Elway 8.00
10 Rick Mirer 5.00
11 Kerry Collins 10.00
12 Steve McNair 10.00

1995 Action Packed G-Force

Some of the NFL's best running backs are featured on these 1995 Action Packed inserts. The 12 cards, random inserts one per every 24 packs, have a horizontal front format. The card front has two photos on it; one is an action shot, the other is a close-up profile. The player's name, in gold foil, and the insert set logo are on the left side of the card. The back, numbered with a "GF" prefix, contains a color photo and recap of the player's accomplishments in 1994. A panel on the left side has the insert set logo at the top, with the player's name and his yards per carry average underneath.

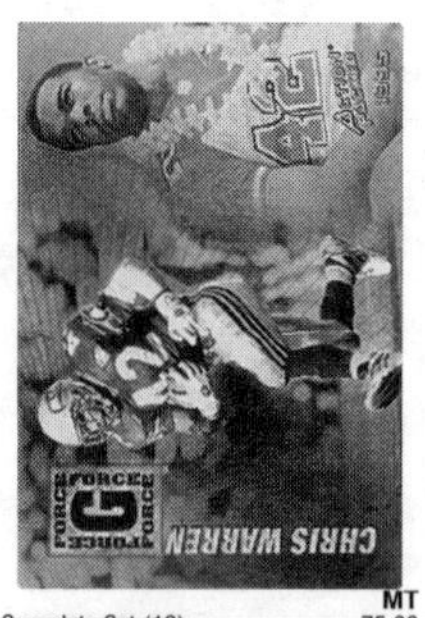

MT
Complete Set (12): 75.00
Common Player: 5.00
1 Emmitt Smith 20.00
2 Barry Sanders 10.00
3 Marshall Faulk 5.00
4 Natrone Means 5.00
5 Chris Warren 5.00
6 Jerome Bettis 5.00
7 Errict Rhett 5.00
8 Bam Morris 5.00
9 Ki-Jana Carter 5.00
10 Mario Bates 5.00
11 Ricky Watters 5.00
12 Tyrone Wheatley 5.00

1995 Action Packed Rocket Men

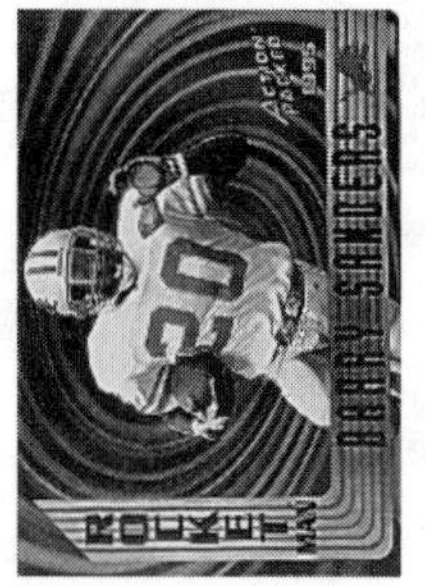

These horizontally-designed inserts feature 18 of the NFL's top stars. Cards were random inserts in 1995 Action Packed football, one every 12 jumbo packs. The card front has a color embossed photo with a swirled background. "Rocket Man" is written along the left side of the card, with the player's name and team logo along the bottom, below the photo. The vertical back, numbered using an "RM" prefix, has a panel on the right which includes the player's name, team logo, card number and "Rocket Man." An action photo and a closeup photo are also included on the back, which includes a quote from another player about the "Rocket Man."

MT
Complete Set (18): 175.00
Common Player: 5.00
1 Marshall Faulk 5.00
2 Emmitt Smith 20.00
3 Barry Sanders 12.00
4 Natrone Means 5.00
5 Errict Rhett 5.00
6 Ki-Jana Carter 5.00
7 Tyrone Wheatley 5.00
8 Drew Bledsoe 10.00
9 Dan Marino 20.00
10 Steve Young 10.00
11 Troy Aikman 10.00
12 Brett Favre 20.00
13 Kerry Collins 10.00
14 Steve McNair 10.00
15 Heath Shuler 10.00
16 Jerry Rice 10.00
17 Michael Irvin 5.00
18 Herman Moore 5.00

1995 Action Packed Monday Night Football Promos

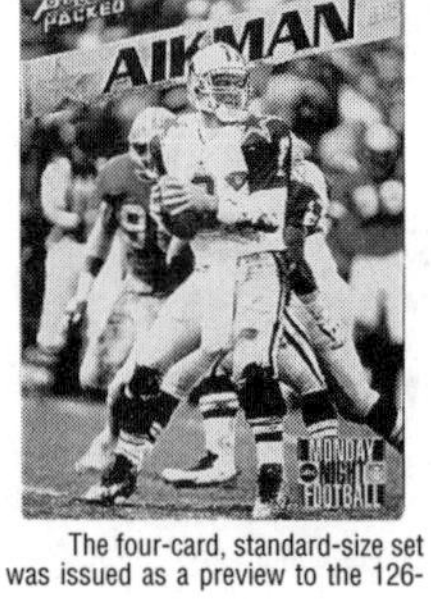

The four-card, standard-size set was issued as a preview to the 126-card Monday Night Football set. The set includes two base issues, one Night Flights insert card and one advertisement card. The card fronts are identical to the base set, but the backs have "Promo" printed.

MT
Complete Set (4): 10.00
Common Player: .50
1 Steve Young 2.00
3A Troy Aikman 4.00
3B Drew Bledsoe 4.00
NNO NMFB Ad Card (Night Flights card) .50

1995 Action Packed Monday Night Football

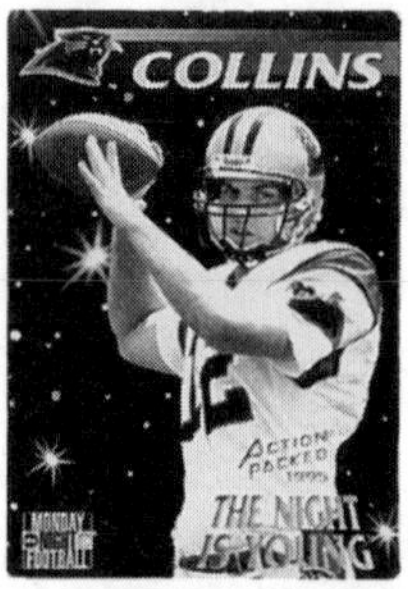

Action Packed's 1995 Monday Night Football set contains 26 cards, plus a parallel Highlights set which uses a prismatic foil background. These cards, found one per every six packs, have "Highlights" written in gold foil on the card back. The regular cards feature a full-bleed photo with a raised image of the player. A gold band runs across the top of the card; it includes the player's last name in black, alongside a gold team logo. The Monday Night Football icon appears in the lower right corner. The horizontal card back has a mug shot, statistics, biographical information and a brief player profile. A black band with the various sponsor logos runs across the bottom of the card. Insert sets include Night Flights, 24KT Team and Reverse Angle.

MT
Complete Set (126): 25.00
Common Player: .10
Minor Stars: .20
Complete Highlights (126): 200.00
Highlights Cards: 4x-8x
Wax Box: 50.00
1 Jerry Rice 1.00
2 Barry Sanders 2.00
3 Troy Aikman 1.00
4 Jerome Bettis .40
5 Tim Brown .20
6 Marcus Allen .20
7 *Jeff Blake* 2.00
8 Rodney Hampton .20
9 Reggie White .20
10 Warren Moon .20
11 William Floyd .40
12 Cris Carter .20
13 Stan Humphries .20
14 Herschel Walker .10
15 Dave Brown .10
16 Jim Everett .10
17 Mario Bates .40
18 Terance Mathis .10
19 Chris Spielman .10
20 Neil O'Donnell .20
21 Anthony Miller .10
22 Steve Bono .30
23 Henry Ellard .10
24 Dave Meggett .10
25 Flipper Anderson .10
26 Rocket Ismail .10
27 Leroy Hoard .10
28 Steve Young 1.00
29 Marshall Faulk 2.00
30 Dan Marino 2.50
31 Errict Rhett 1.50
32 Michael Irvin .20
33 Bam Morris .20
34 Heath Shuler 1.00
35 Jim Kelly .20
36 Deion Sanders .50
37 Jeff Hostetler .20
38 Jeff George .20
39 Alvin Harper .10
40 Barry Foster .10
41 Craig Erickson .10
42 Vinny Testaverde .10
43 Andre Reed .10
44 Eric Green .10
45 Bruce Smith .10
46 Frank Reich .10
47 Shannon Sharpe .10
48 Chris Miller .10
49 Darnay Scott .50
50 Eric Metcalf .10
51 Mike Sherrard .10
52 Lorenzo White .10
53 Scott Mitchell .20
54 Jay Novacek .10
55 Emmitt Smith 2.50
56 Drew Bledsoe 1.00
57 Natrone Means .75
58 John Elway .50
59 Herman Moore .30
60 Brett Favre 1.00
61 Ricky Watters .20
62 Andre Rison .10
63 Junior Seau .20
64 Randall Cunningham .10
65 Chris Warren .20
66 Garrison Hearst .10
67 Ben Coates .10
68 Rick Mirer .40
69 Johnny Mitchell .10

70	Trent Dilfer	.40
71	Carl Pickens	.25
72	Craig Heyward	.10
73	Greg Lloyd	.10
74	Boomer Esiason	.10
75	Greg Hill	.30
76	Lewis Tillman	.10
77	Willie Davis	.10
78	Brent Jones	.10
79	Michael Haynes	.10
80	Darryl Johnston	.10
81	Steve Beuerlein	.10
82	*Ki-Jana Carter* (The Night is Young)	.75
83	*Steve McNair* (The Night is Young)	4.00
84	*Michael Westbrook* (The Night is Young)	2.50
85	*Kerry Collins* (The Night is Young)	4.00
86	*Joey Galloway* (The Night is Young)	4.00
87	*Kyle Brady* (The Night is Young)	.40
88	*J.J. Stokes* (The Night is Young)	3.00
89	*Tyrone Wheatley* (The Night is Young)	.75
90	*Rashaan Salaam* (The Night is Young)	3.00
91	*Napoleon Kaufman* (The Night is Young)	1.50
92	*Frank Sanders* (The Night is Young)	1.25
93	*Stoney Case* (The Night is Young)	.50
94	*Todd Collins* (The Night is Young)	.20
95	*James Stewart* (The Night is Young)	1.50
96	*Kordell Stewart* (The Night is Young)	3.00
97	*Joe Aska* (The Night is Young)	.20
98	*Terrell Fletcher* (The Night is Young)	.20
99	*Rob Johnson* (The Night is Young)	1.50
100	Steve Young (Monday Night Classics)	.50
101	Jerry Rice (Monday Night Classics)	.50
102	Emmitt Smith (Monday Night Classics)	1.00
103	Barry Sanders (Monday Night Classics)	1.00
104	Marshall Faulk (Monday Night Classics)	.50
105	Drew Bledsoe (Monday Night Classics)	.50
106	Dan Marino (Monday Night Classics)	1.00
107	Troy Aikman (Monday Night Classics)	.40
108	John Elway (Monday Night Classics)	.30
109	Brett Favre (Monday Night Classics)	.50
110	Michael Irvin (Monday Night Classics)	.20
111	Heath Shuler (Monday Night Classics)	.40
112	Warren Moon (Monday Night Classics)	.20
113	Chris Warren (Monday Night Classics)	.20
114	Natrone Means (Monday Night Classics)	.30
115	Errict Rhett (Monday Night Classics)	.75
116	Bam Morris (Monday Night Classics)	.20
117	Randall Cunningham (Monday Night Classics)	.20
118	Jim Kelly (Monday Night Classics)	.20
119	Jeff Hostetler (Monday Night Classics)	.10
120	Barry Foster (Monday Night Classics)	.10
121	Jim Everett (Monday Night Classics)	.10
122	Neil O'Donnell (Monday Night Classics)	.10
123	Jerome Bettis (Monday Night Classics)	.20
124	Ricky Watters (Monday Night Classics)	.20
125	Joe Montana (Monday Night Classics)	.75
126	Howard Cosell (Monday Night Classics)	.20

1995 Action Packed Monday Night Football Highlights

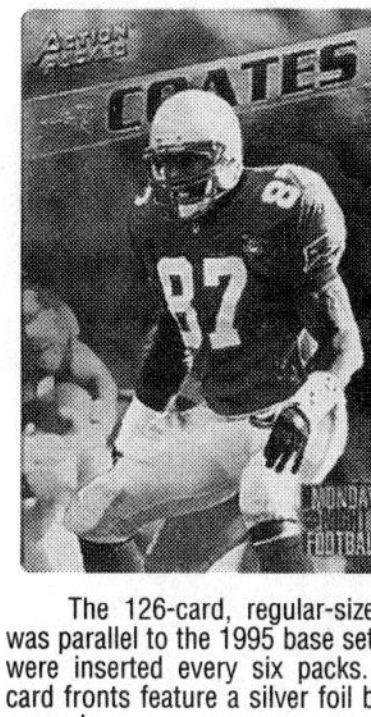

The 126-card, regular-size set was parallel to the 1995 base set and were inserted every six packs. The card fronts feature a silver foil background.

	MT
Complete Set (126):	275.00
Common Player:	1.00
Highlight Cards:	5x-10x

1995 Action Packed Monday Night Football 24KT Gold Team

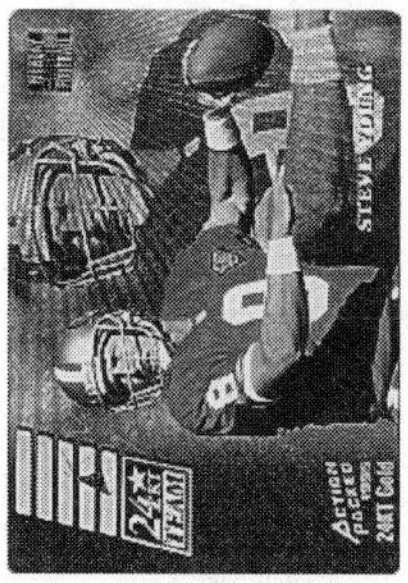

These inserts provide a golden rendition of 12 regular issue cards with micro-etched highlights on rainbow holographic foil with an exclusive gold logo that includes genuine gold leafing. The cards, randomly included in every 72 packs of 1995 Action Packed Monday Night Football, features members of the 24KT Team. Fewer than 2,000 sets were made. The card front is horizontal and includes a smaller photo in the foreground, with a larger image of the same photo in the background. The card back, numbered 1 of 12, etc., has a player photo and brief recap of a game in which the player had a key role. A vertical format is used for the back, which has the appropriate logos in a panel on the right.

		MT
Complete Set (12):		400.00
Common Player:		20.00
1	Emmitt Smith	50.00
2	Barry Sanders	70.00
3	Marshall Faulk	40.00
4	Dan Marino	60.00
5	Steve Young	40.00
6	Drew Bledsoe	40.00
7	Troy Aikman	35.00
8	John Elway	50.00
9	Brett Favre	70.00
10	Ki-Jana Carter	20.00
11	Steve McNair	30.00
12	Kerry Collins	35.00

1995 Action Packed Monday Night Football Night Flights

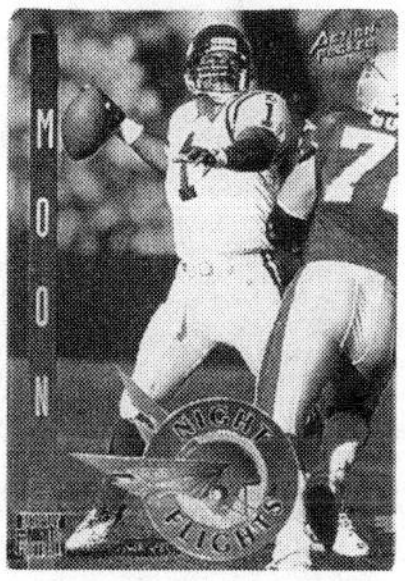

These 1995 Action Packed Monday Night Football inserts feature 12 members of the Quarterback Club on Dufex cards of textured gold foil. Each card front has a colored raised image, with the player's last name running in a gold strip along the left side of the card, which has the MNF logo at its bottom. The Night Flight logo is at the bottom of the card, too. The back is horizontal, with a mug shot, card number (1 of 12, etc.), and 1994 season recap.

		MT
Complete Set (12):		80.00
Common Player:		5.00
1	Steve Young	10.00
2	Dan Marino	17.00
3	Drew Bledsoe	10.00
4	Troy Aikman	10.00
5	John Elway	8.00
6	Brett Favre	10.00
7	Heath Shuler	8.00
8	Dave Brown	5.00
9	Steve McNair	10.00
10	Kerry Collins	12.00
11	Warren Moon	5.00
12	Jeff Hostetler	5.00

1995 Action Packed Monday Night Football Reverse Angle

These 18 insert cards could be found one per every 24 hobby packs of 1995 Action Packed Monday Night Football. They feature 18 NFL stars. Fewer than 1,500 sets of Reverse Angle inserts were made. The front has a raised color image, along with the set, insert set and MNF logos, against a metallic background. The player's name runs along the left side of the card. The back has a black panel along the left side, which also has his name and card number (1 of 18, etc.). A photo and brief player profile are also included on the back. Cards were random inserts, one per every 24 hobby packs.

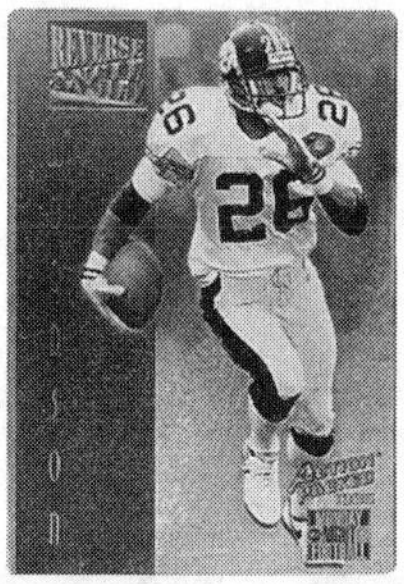

		MT
Complete Set (18):		50.00
Common Player:		3.00
1	Emmitt Smith	12.00
2	Barry Sanders	8.00
3	Steve Young	7.00
4	Marshall Faulk	10.00
5	Randall Cunningham	3.00
6	Deion Sanders	5.00
7	John Elway	5.00
8	Brett Favre	7.00
9	William Floyd	5.00
10	Ricky Watters	3.00
11	Ben Coates	3.00
12	Rod Woodson	3.00
13	Marcus Allen	3.00
14	Eric Metcalf	3.00
15	Keith Byars	3.00
16	Jerry Rice	7.00
17	Alvin Harper	3.00
18	Eric Green	3.00

1995 Action Packed Rookies/Stars

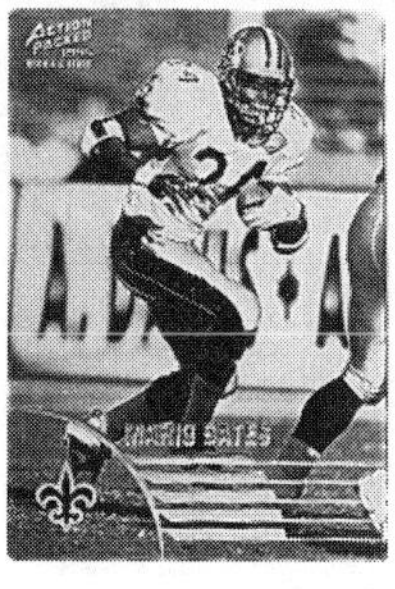

Action Packed's 1995 Rookies and Stars set features the NFL's top rookie draft choices, along with a parallel foiled Stargazers set (one card per six packs). The regular cards have a raised full-bleed color photo on the front, with the set name in the upper left corner and the player's team logo in the bottom left corner. The player's name is stamped in gold foil at the bottom. The horizontal back has a photo on two thirds of the card, with a player profile paragraph next to it. A black band at the bottom of the card contains the player's 1994 and career statistics. Insert sets include 24K Gold Team, Bustout, Closing Seconds and Instant Impressions.

		MT
Complete Set (105):		25.00
Common Player:		.10
Minor Stars:		.20
Stargazer Cards:		8x-16x
Stargazer Rookies:		4x-8x
Inserted 1:6		
Pack (8):		3.00
Wax Box (24):		60.00
1	Steve Young	1.00
2	Steve Bono	.30
3	Natrone Means	.50
4	Steve Beuerlein	.10
5	Neil O'Donnell	.10
6	Marshall Faulk	1.00
7	Ricky Watters	.20
8	Gary Brown	.10
9	Jeff Hostetler	.10
10	Robert Brooks	.25
11	Johnny Mitchell	.10
12	Barry Sanders	2.00
13	Dave Brown	.10
14	John Elway	2.00
15	Garrison Hearst	.10
16	Jim Everett	.10
17	Michael Irvin	.20
18	Dan Marino	2.50
19	Jeff George	.20
20	Ben Coates	.10
21	Charles Johnson	.30
22	Carl Pickens	.25
23	Deion Sanders	.75
24	Errict Rhett	.75
25	Steve Walsh	.10
26	Bruce Smith	.10
27	Andre Rison	.20
28	Warren Moon	.10
29	Terry Allen	.10
30	Desmond Howard	.10
31	Shannon Sharpe	.10
32	Dave Krieg	.10
33	Bam Morris	.20
34	Rodney Hampton	.10
35	Scott Mitchell	.20
36	Alvin Harper	.10
37	Robert Smith	.10
38	Troy Aikman	1.00
39	William Floyd	.40
40	Randall Cunningham	.10
41	Mario Bates	.30
42	Reggie White	.20
43	Chris Chandler	.10
44	Erik Kramer	.10
45	Emmitt Smith	2.50
46	Irving Fryar	.10
47	*Jeff Blake*	.50
48	Drew Bledsoe	1.50
49	Anthony Miller	.10
50	Marcus Allen	.20
51	Leroy Hoard	.10
52	Stan Humphries	.20
53	Eric Green	.10
54	Herschel Walker	.10
55	Junior Seau	.20
56	Terance Mathis	.10
57	Boomer Esiason	.10
58	Lorenzo White	.10
59	Tim Brown	.20
60	Brett Favre	3.00
61	Craig Erickson	.10
62	Rod Woodson	.10
63	Frank Reich	.10
64	Cris Carter	.20
65	Jerry Rice	1.00
66	Greg Hill	.30
67	Andre Reed	.10
68	Trent Dilfer	.40
69	Eric Metcalf	.10
70	Jim Kelly	.20
71	Herman Moore	.50
72	Vinny Testaverde	.10
73	Jeff Graham	.10
74	Edgar Bennett	.10
75	Jerome Bettis	.30
76	Heath Shuler	.75
77	Chris Warren	.20
78	Reggie Brooks	.10
79	Rick Mirer	.40
80	Chris Miller	.10
81	*Napoleon Kaufman*	3.00
82	*Christian Fauria*	.20
83	*Todd Collins*	.20
84	*J.J. Stokes*	1.00
85	*Mark Bruener*	.40
86	*Frank Sanders*	1.00
87	*Chad May*	.20
88	*Kordell Stewart*	4.00
89	*Ki-Jana Carter*	.50
90	*Curtis Martin*	3.00
91	*Sherman Williams*	.20
92	*Terrell Davis*	10.00
93	*Chris Sanders*	.50
94	*Kyle Brady*	.40
95	*Tyrone Wheatley*	.50
96	*Rodney Thomas*	.50
97	*James Stewart*	1.50
98	*Kerry Collins*	1.00
99	*Rashaan Salaam*	.75
100	*Stoney Case*	.20
101	*Steve McNair*	3.00
102	*Joey Galloway*	3.00
103	*Michael Westbrook*	1.00
104	*Eric Zeier*	.75
105	*Ray Zellars*	.50

1995 Action Packed Rookies & Stars Stargazers

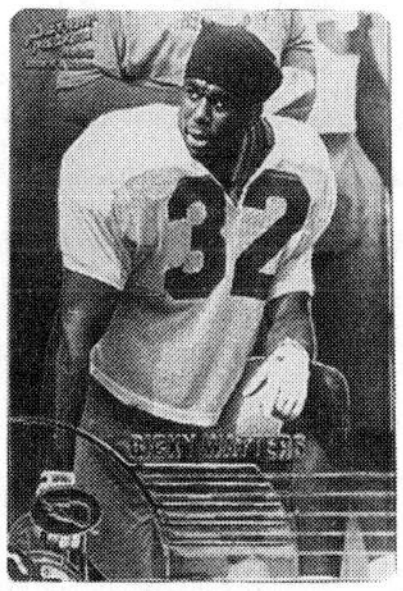

The 105-card, regular-size set was issued as a parallel release to the 1995 Rookies/Stars base set, inserted every six packs. The background of the card fronts contain silver foil while the backs each have a "Stargazers" stamp.

	MT
Complete Set (105):	475.00
Common Player:	.75
Stargazers:	6x-12x

1995 Action Packed Rookies/Stars 24K Gold

These 14 cards were the most exclusive of the 1995 Action Packed Rookies & Stars inserts, available at one per every 72 packs. Each card front has a raised color image on it, with part of it against a black background, and most of it against a gold foil panel along the right side of the card. "24 KT Gold Team" is inside the gold panel. The set logo is in the gold in the bottom right corner, opposite the player's name. The horizontal card back has mostly a black background which contains a mug shot and brief summary of the player's accomplishments. A jagged gold panel at the top of the card contains the words "24 KT Gold Team." A card number is in the lower right corner.

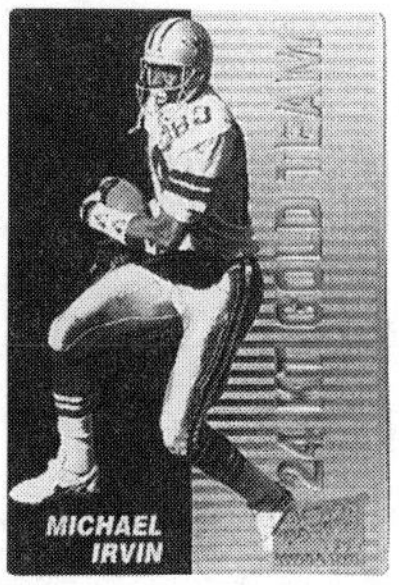

		MT
Complete Set (14):		575.00
Common Player:		10.00
Minor Stars:		20.00
Inserted 1:72		
1	Steve Young	30.00
2	Brett Favre	80.00
3	Rashaan Salaam	20.00
4	Tyrone Wheatley	10.00
5	Marshall Faulk	20.00
6	Rick Mirer	10.00
7	Troy Aikman	40.00
8	John Elway	60.00
9	Dan Marino	60.00
10	Barry Sanders	80.00
11	Jerry Rice	40.00
12	Emmitt Smith	60.00
13	Michael Irvin	20.00
14	Drew Bledsoe	40.00

1995 Action Packed Rookies/Stars Bustout

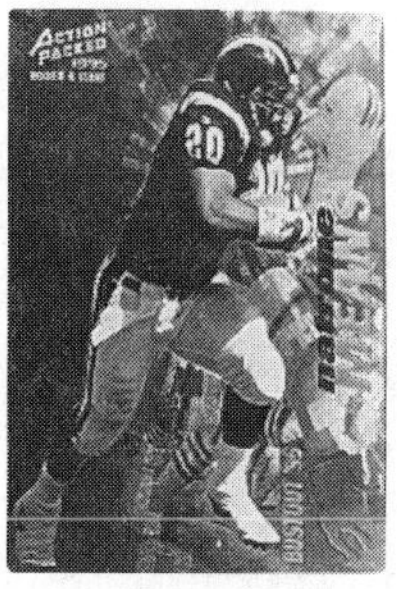

These insert cards were available in 12-card jumbo packs of 1995 Action Packed Rookies and Stars. The 12 cards, numbered on the back, feature top NFL running backs. The card front has a raised color photo against a metallic background. The player's name and the set logo are on the left side of the card. The player's name, card number and a team helmet are in a black strip along the left side of the card back; a photo is on the opposite side, along with an example of when the player "busted out" and had a big game.

		MT
Complete Set (12):		45.00
Common Player:		2.00
Minor Stars:		4.00
Inserted 1:12		
1	Marshall Faulk	5.00
2	Barry Sanders	20.00
3	Emmitt Smith	15.00
4	Natrone Means	4.00
5	Errict Rhett	2.00
6	Bam Morris	2.00
7	Terry Allen	4.00
8	Rodney Hampton	2.00
9	Ricky Watters	4.00
10	Chris Warren	2.00
11	Jerome Bettis	4.00
12	Gary Brown	2.00

1995 Action Packed Rookies/Stars Closing Seconds

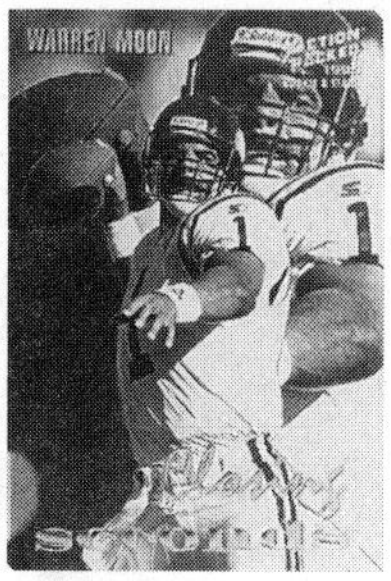

These 12 1995 Action Packed Rookies & Stars inserts feature players who pulled out victories for their teams in the final seconds. A raised color photo is on the front, with a ghosted, rainbow holographic-foiled larger image of the same photo as a background. "Closing Seconds" is written in gold foil. The player's name and set name are in the top corners. The card back has a black panel along the left side which contains a number and accounts of the game he helped win in the final seconds. A photo also appears on the back. Cards were exclusive to hobby packs, one per every 36 packs.

		MT
Complete Set (12):		125.00
Common Player:		3.00
Minor Stars:		6.00
Inserted 1:36 Hobby		
1	Dan Marino	18.00
2	Steve Young	10.00
3	Jerry Rice	12.00
4	Emmitt Smith	18.00
5	Barry Sanders	25.00
6	Brett Favre	25.00
7	Drew Bledsoe	12.00
8	Troy Aikman	12.00
9	John Elway	18.00
10	Dave Brown	3.00
11	Warren Moon	6.00
12	Jim Kelly	6.00

1995 Action Packed Rookies/Stars Instant Impressions

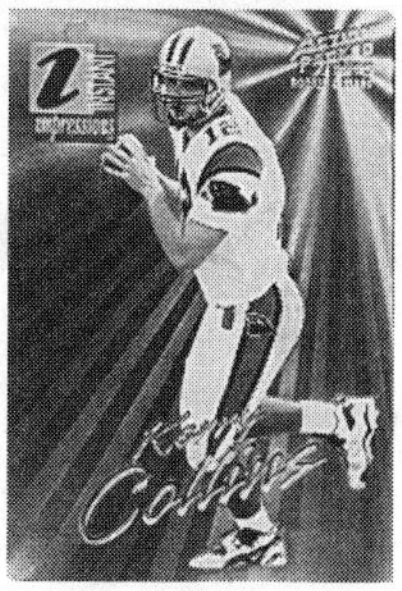

These 1995 Action Packed Rookies & Stars inserts have 12 rookies highlighted on Dufex cards. The front has a raised color image against a strobelight-like background. The set and insert set logos are in the upper corners; the player's name is at the bottom in gold foil. The back has a colored panel on the left side which contains the player's name, position and card number. A smaller horizontal picture is on the right side, with a brief player profile sandwiched between it and the colored panel. Cards were available one per every 24 packs.

		MT
Complete Set (12):		75.00
Common Player:		1.25
Minor Stars:		2.50
Inserted 1:24		
1	Ki-Jana Carter	2.50
2	Steve McNair	12.00
3	Kerry Collins	5.00
4	Michael Westbrook	4.00
5	Joey Galloway	10.00
6	J.J. Stokes	5.00
7	Rashaan Salaam	2.50
8	Tyrone Wheatley	1.25
9	Eric Zeier	4.00
10	Curtis Martin	12.00
11	Napoleon Kaufman	12.00
12	Kyle Brady	1.25

1996 Action Packed Promos

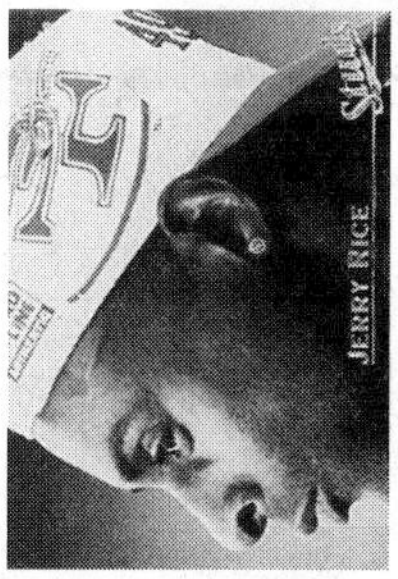

The four-card, regular-size set was released as a preview for the 1996 base set and includes three regular cards and one Studs card. The card fronts are identical to the regular issue cards, but "Promo" is printed on the back.

		MT
Complete Set (4):		12.00
Common Player:		1.00
1	Emmitt Smith	4.50
3	Jerry Rice (Studs Card)	6.00

16	Steve Young	2.00
105	Neil O'Donnell	1.00

1996 Action Packed

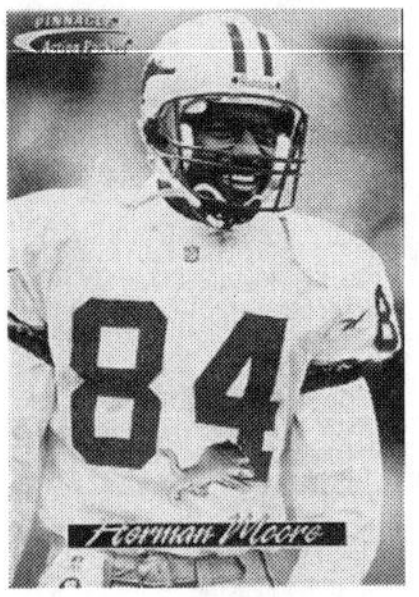

Action Packed's 1996 football set has 126 regular cards, plus a parallel Artist's Proofs set (one in 24 packs). Each card front has a set logo in the upper left corner, with the player's name, in a black bar, and his team logo stamped in gold foil at the bottom. The full-bleed color action photo on the front uses the company's raised photo format. The card back has a closeup photo of the player on the left, with his name and position below, followed by biographical information and statistics. A colored panel along the right side has a brief player profile. The card number is in the upper left corner. Insert sets include 24k Team, Studs, Sculptor's Proofs, Ball Hog and the Longest Yard.

		MT
Complete Set (126):		35.00
Common Player:		.20
Minor Stars:		.40
Comp. Artist's Proof (126):		1200.
Artist's Proof Cards:		15x-30x
Pack (5):		3.00
Wax Box (24):		65.00
1	Emmitt Smith	3.00
2	Dan Marino	3.00
3	Isaac Bruce	.40
4	Eric Zeier	.20
5	Ben Coates	.20
6	Jim Kelly	.20
7	Rodney Hampton	.20
8	Greg Lloyd	.20
9	Reggie White	.20
10	Derrick Thomas	.20
11	Jerry Rice	1.50
12	Drew Bledsoe	1.50
13	Cris Carter	.20
14	Troy Aikman	1.50
15	Steve McNair	1.50
16	Steve Young	1.50
17	Ricky Watters	.20
18	Brett Favre	3.00
19	Michael Westbrook	.40
20	Charles Haley	.20
21	Heath Shuler	.40
22	Tim Brown	.20
23	Kerry Collins	2.00
24	Hugh Douglas	.20
25	Marcus Allen	.40
26	Steve Bono	.20
27	Curtis Martin	3.00
28	Wayne Chrebet	.20
29	Dave Brown	.20
30	James Stewart	.20
31	Chris Sanders	.40
32	Deion Sanders	1.00
33	Rodney Thomas	.40
34	Rashaan Salaam	.40
35	Curtis Conway	.20
36	Harvey Williams	.20
37	William Floyd	.20
38	Carl Pickens	.40
39	Herman Moore	.40
40	Stan Humphries	.20
41	Orlanda Thomas	.20
42	Bert Emanuel	.20
43	Yancey Thigpen	1.00
44	Darick Holmes	.40
45	Mario Bates	.20
46	Greg Hill	.20
47	Errict Rhett	.40
48	Erik Kramer	.20
49	Garrison Hearst	.20
50	Jim Everett	.20
51	Barry Sanders	2.50
52	Eric Metcalf	.20
53	Marshall Faulk	1.50
54	Junior Seau	.20
55	Bruce Smith	.20
56	Kordell Stewart	2.00
57	Edgar Bennett	.20
58	Joey Galloway	1.50
59	Jeff Hostetler	.20
60	Frank Sanders	.40
61	John Elway	.75
62	Tyrone Wheatley	.20
63	Jeff George	.20
64	Ken Norton Jr.	.20
65	Bryan Cox	.20
66	Bryce Paup	.20
67	Larry Centers	.20
68	Bernie Parmalee	.20
69	Jeff Graham	.20
70	Rick Mirer	.20
71	Chris Warren	.40
72	Charlie Garner	.20
73	Robert Brooks	.20
74	Jim Harbaugh	.20
75	Tamarick Vanover	.40
76	Napoleon Kaufman	.40
77	Warren Moon	.20
78	Vincent Brisby	.20
79	Ki-Jana Carter	.40
80	Michael Irvin	.40
81	Trent Dilfer	.20
82	Bam Morris	.20
83	Mark Brunell	1.50
84	Jeff Blake	1.00
85	Kevin Williams	.20
86	Rod Woodson	.20
87	Andre Reed	.20
88	Erric Pegram	.20
89	Anthony Miller	.20
90	Gus Frerotte	.20
91	Quinn Early	.20
92	Daryl Johnston	.20
93	Tony Martin	.20
94	Terrell Davis	6.00
95	Brent Jones	.20
96	Mark Chmura	.40
97	Kyle Brady	.20
98	J.J. Stokes	.40
99	Rodney Peete	.20
100	Natrone Means	.40
101	Sherman Williams	.20
102	Brian Blades	.20
103	Brett Perriman	.20
104	Antonio Freeman	.20
105	Neil O'Donnell	.20
106	Craig Heyward	.20
107	Derek Loville	.20
108	Jay Novacek	.20
109	Scott Mitchell	.20
110	Bill Brooks	.20
111	Shannon Sharpe	.20
112	Jake Reed	.20
113	Derrick Moore	.20
114	Steve Atwater	.20
115	Darren Woodson	.20
116	Junior Seau	.20
117	Quentin Coryatt	.20
118	Bruce Smith	.20
119	Rod Woodson	.20
120	Charles Haley	.20
121	Derrick Thomas	.20
122	Ken Norton	.20
123	Steve Atwater	.20
124	Greg Lloyd	.20
125	Reggie White	.20
126	Bryan Cox	.20

1996 Action Packed Artist's Proof

The 126-card, regular-size set was issued as a parallel release to the 1996 base set. The cards were inserted every 24 hobby and retail packs and every 30 magazine packs. The cards have "Artist's Proof" printed on the fronts.

		MT
Complete Set (126):		1200.
Common Player:		5.00
Artist's Proof Cards:		15x-30x
1	Emmitt Smith	125.00
2	Dan Marino	125.00
3	Isaac Bruce	40.00
11	Jerry Rice	60.00
12	Drew Bledsoe	60.00
14	Troy Aikman	60.00
15	Steve McNair	40.00
16	Steve Young	50.00
18	Brett Favre	125.00
19	Michael Westbrook	25.00
23	Kerry Collins	60.00
27	Curtis Martin	80.00
32	Deion Sanders	40.00
34	Rashaan Salaam	25.00
43	Yancey Thigpen	25.00
47	Errict Rhett	40.00
51	Barry Sanders	70.00
53	Marshall Faulk	50.00
56	Kordell Stewart	50.00
58	Joey Galloway	40.00
61	John Elway	50.00
75	Tamarick Vanover	25.00
84	Jeff Blake	25.00
94	Terrell Davis	70.00
98	J.J. Stokes	25.00

1996 Action Packed 24kt Gold

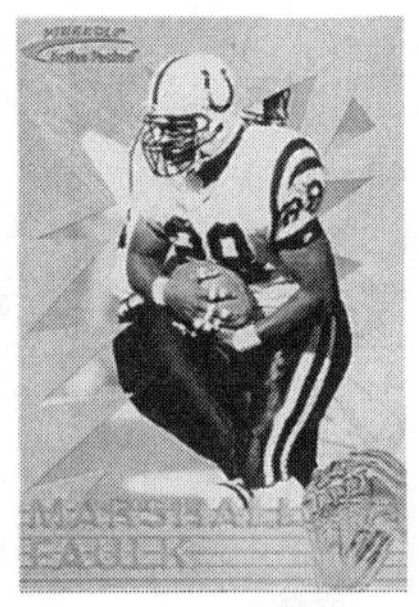

These insert cards feature the standard raised photo on the front, against a "Prime Frost" background with 24kt gold foil stamping used for the 24kt gold logo. The card back has the number at the top of a panel along the left side of the card. The player's name and position are also in the panel. The right side of the card has a mug shot at the top, along with an action photo. A recap of a memorable game from the previous season is underneath, along with the player's team name. Cards were seeded one per every 72 packs of 1996 Action Packed football.

		MT
Complete Set (14):		500.00
Common Player:		15.00
1	Brett Favre	80.00
2	Michael Irvin	15.00
3	Drew Bledsoe	45.00
4	Jerry Rice	45.00
5	Troy Aikman	45.00
6	Dan Marino	80.00
7	Errict Rhett	15.00
8	Curtis Martin	65.00
9	Steve Young	45.00
10	Barry Sanders	50.00
11	Marshall Faulk	30.00
12	Isaac Bruce	30.00
13	John Elway	30.00
14	Emmitt Smith	80.00

1996 Action Packed Ball Hog

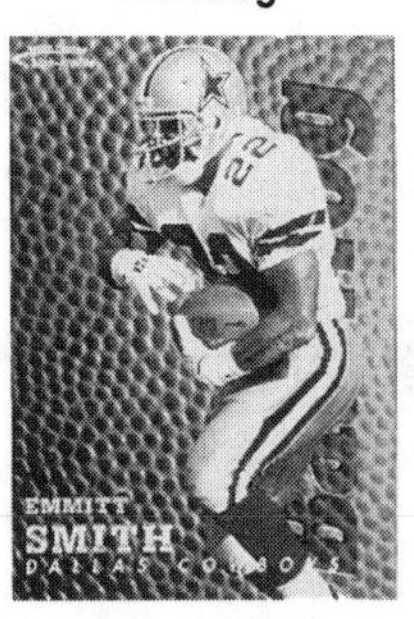

This 12-card 1996 Action Packed insert set highlights players who always seem to have the ball in their hands. The cards, seeded one per every 23 packs, use an embossed leather-looking print technology. The card front has a raised action photo against a football background. "Ball Hog" is written along the right side. The brand logo is stamped in gold in the upper left corner; the player's name and his team's name are stamped in gold in the bottom left corner. The back has the player's name written in a panel along the top, with a brief player profile and a player mug shot below.

		MT
Complete Set (12):		100.00
Common Player:		4.00
1	Carl Pickens	4.00
2	Terrell Davis	14.00
3	Jerry Rice	12.00
4	Barry Sanders	12.00
5	Marshall Faulk	6.00
6	Isaac Bruce	6.00
7	Michael Irvin	4.00
8	Cris Carter	4.00
9	Rashaan Salaam	6.00
10	Herman Moore	4.00
11	Chris Warren	4.00
12	Emmitt Smith	25.00

1996 Action Packed Jumbo Inserts

These cards were inserted one per retail box as a boxtopper insert. They are a parallel of each player's base set card except they are oversized and numbered differently.

		MT
Complete Set (4):		20.00
Common Player:		4.00
1	Emmitt Smith	6.00
2	Drew Bledsoe	4.00
3	Troy Aikman	4.00
4	Brett Favre	8.00

1996 Action Packed Longest Yard

The 12-card, regular-sized set was inserted every 24 magazine packs of 1996 Action Packed.

		MT
Complete Set (12):		180.00
Common Player:		5.00
1	Brett Favre	35.00
2	Tamarick Vanover	5.00
3	Joey Galloway	12.00
4	Kerry Collins	20.00
5	Jeff Blake	10.00
6	Jerry Rice	20.00
7	Barry Sanders	30.00
8	Rodney Thomas	5.00
9	Herman Moore	7.00
10	Emmitt Smith	35.00
11	Terrell Davis	20.00
12	Cris Carter	7.00

1996 Action Packed Sculptor's Proof

Sculptor's Proofs inserts are pewter metal-card renditions of 14 players' regular issue cards, except the card numbers on the back correspond to the checklist. These cards were available to consumers through a randomly-inserted redemption card found one per every 192 packs.

		MT
Complete Set (14):		1000.
Common Player:		30.00
1	Dan Marino	150.00
2	Deion Sanders	50.00
3	Joey Galloway	50.00
4	Brett Favre	150.00
5	Barry Sanders	80.00
6	Michael Irvin	30.00
7	Drew Bledsoe	75.00
8	Emmitt Smith	150.00
9	Curtis Martin	100.00
10	Steve Young	50.00
11	John Elway	50.00
12	Jerry Rice	75.00
13	Errict Rhett	40.00
14	Troy Aikman	75.00

1996 Action Packed Studs

These 1996 Action Packed insert cards feature six NFL stars and their diamond stud earrings. Studs cards contain a genuine diamond chip and are found one per every 161 packs. There were 1,500 sets produced. Each card front, in a horizontal format, has the set name in the upper right corner in gold foil; the player's name and "Studs" are in gold along the bottom. The card back is also horizontal. An action photo of the player is on the right, with his name, position, team logo and card number in a panel above. The left side of the card has a recap of a memorable game in the player's career, plus his team name in a black strip.

		MT
Complete Set (6):		325.00
Common Player:		20.00
1	Emmitt Smith	150.00
2	Deion Sanders	60.00
3	Jerry Rice	75.00
4	Michael Irvin	20.00
5	Kordell Stewart	75.00
6	Ricky Watters	20.00

1997 Action Packed Promos

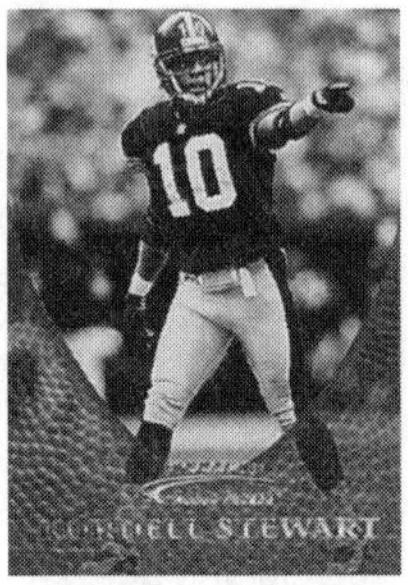

This three-card set was issued to promote sales of 1997 Action Packed. It included two base cards and one Studs insert. All three cards contained the words "Promo" in a black box across the back.

		MT
Complete Set (3):		5.00
Common Player:		.50
28	Kordell Stewart	1.50
45	Jim Harbaugh	.50
4 of 9	Jerry Rice (Studs)	4.00

1997 Action Packed

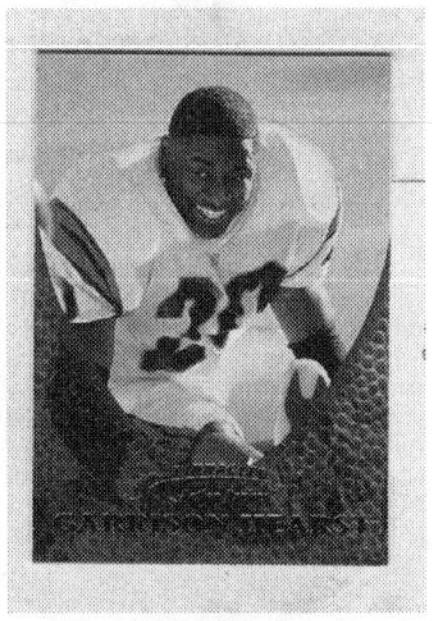

The 125-card set features a brown football pebble grain at the bottom of the card front. The player's photo is printed at the top, with the player embossed. The Pinnacle Action Packed logo is at the bottom center, with the player's name printed directly below. The card backs have a player photo with a ghosted photo in the background. The player's bio is listed along the upper right border. The player's name, position and stats are printed at the bottom left. The First Impressions silver-foil parallel of the base set was inserted 1:15 packs, while the Gold Impressions parallel set, which includes gold foil, was seeded 1:44 packs. A 15-card Down "N" Dirty subset was included as part of the base set.

		MT
Complete Set (125):		40.00
Common Player:		.10
Minor Stars:		.20
First Impressions:		5x-10x
Gold Impressions:		10x-20x
Pack (5):		3.00
Wax Box (24):		65.00
1	Jerry Rice	2.00
2	Troy Aikman	2.00
3	Ricky Watters	.20
4	Dan Marino	4.00
5	Emmitt Smith	4.00
6	Warren Moon	.20
7	Rashaan Salaam	.50
8	Drew Bledsoe	2.00
9	Eddie George	2.00
10	John Elway	1.25
11	Robert Brooks	.10
12	Scott Mitchell	.10
13	Isaac Bruce	.50
14	Marshall Faulk	.75
15	Steve Bono	.10
16	Barry Sanders	3.00
17	Brett Favre	4.00
18	Curtis Martin	3.00
19	Keyshawn Johnson	.75
20	Dave Brown	.10
21	Frank Sanders	.10
22	Gus Frerotte	.10
23	Eric Metcalf	.10
24	Thurman Thomas	.20
25	Steve Young	1.25
26	Alvin Harper	.10
27	Mark Brunell	2.00
28	Kordell Stewart	2.00
29	Terry Glenn	.30
30	Junior Seau	.20
31	Karim Abdul-Jabbar	.30
32	Jeff Hostetler	.10
33	Rodney Hampton	.10
34	Irving Fryar	.10
35	Cris Carter	.10
36	James Stewart	.10
37	Marcus Allen	.20
38	Napoleon Kaufman	.20
39	Shannon Sharpe	.20
40	LeShon Johnson	.10
41	Tony Banks	.50
42	Lawrence Phillips	.20
43	Kerry Collins	.30
44	Curtis Conway	.10
45	Jim Harbaugh	.10
46	Garrison Hearst	.10
47	Trent Dilfer	.20
48	Terance Mathis	.10
49	Jerome Bettis	.30
50	Chris Sanders	.10
51	Deion Sanders	1.00
52	Herman Moore	.30
53	Elvis Grbac	.10
54	O.J. McDuffie	.10
55	Ben Coates	.10
56	Jim Kelly	.20
57	J.J. Stokes	.10
58	Terrell Davis	3.00
59	Stan Humphries	.10
60	Carl Pickens	.20
61	Neil O'Donnell	.10
62	Edgar Bennett	.10
63	Yancey Thigpen	.10
64	Bert Emanuel	.10
65	Amani Toomer	.10
66	Jeff Blake	.20
67	Eddie Kennison	.75
68	Jason Dunn	.10
69	Rob Moore	.10
70	Andre Rison	.10
71	Vinny Testaverde	.10
72	Henry Ellard	.10
73	Dale Carter	.10
74	Tony Martin	.10
75	Jim Everett	.10
76	Joey Galloway	.50
77	Mike Alstott	.20
78	Kevin Hardy	.10
79	Jake Reed	.10
80	Tim Brown	.10
81	Sean Dawkins	.10
82	Bobby Engram	.10
83	Michael Irvin	.20
84	Rickey Dudley	.20
85	Chris Chandler	.10
86	Keith Jackson	.10
87	Muhsin Muhammad	.20
88	Tamarick Vanover	.20
89	Chris Warren	.10
90	Johnnie Morton	.10
91	Terry Allen	.20
92	Stanley Pritchett	.10
93	Charles Johnson	.10
94	Chris T. Jones	.10
95	Winslow Oliver	.10
96	Anthony Miller	.10
97	Tyrone Wheatley	.10
98	Robert Smith	.10
99	Eric Moulds	.10
100	Hardy Nickerson	.10
101	Derrick Alexander	.10
102	Michael Haynes	.10
103	Jamal Anderson	.20
104	Marvin Harrison	.75
105	Antonio Freeman	.20
106	Dorsey Levens	.20
107	Natrone Means	.20
108	Keenan McCardell	.10
109	Mark Chmura	.10
110	Darren Woodson	.10
111	Brett Favre	2.00
112	Emmitt Smith	2.00
113	Junior Seau	.10
114	Jerry Rice	1.00
115	Barry Sanders	1.50
116	Bruce Smith	.10
117	Troy Aikman	1.00
118	Bryan Cox	.10
119	Zach Thomas	.30
120	Reggie White	.10
121	Ben Coates	.10
122	Jerome Bettis	.10
123	Michael Irvin	.10
124	Quentin Coryatt	.10
125	Checklist	.10

1997 Action Packed First Impressions

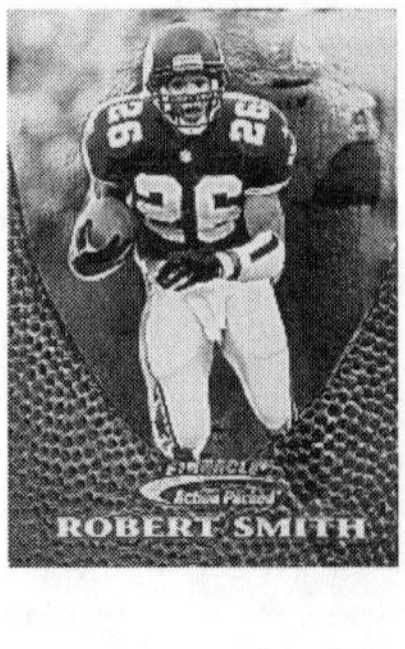

This 125-card parallel featured each card from the regular- issue set printed in a silver foil. First Impressions parallels were inserted one per 12 packs.

		MT
Complete Set (125):		400.00
First Impression Cards:		5x-10x

1997 Action Packed Gold Impressions

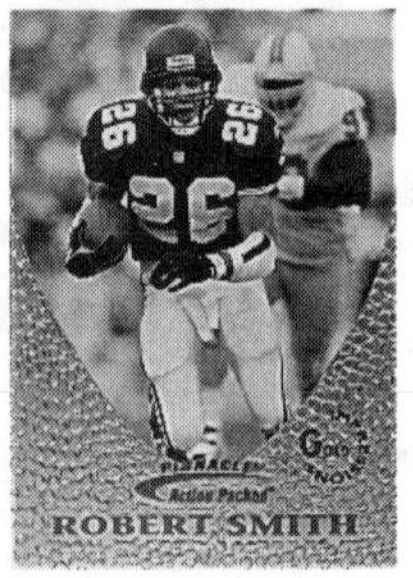

Gold Impressions was a 125-card parallel set to Action Packed that featured the bottom, football-textured part of each base card printed in gold foil. Each card featured a blue "Gold Impressions" logo and they were inserted one per 35 packs.

		MT
Complete Set (125):		800.00
Gold Cards:		10x-20x

1997 Action Packed Crash Course

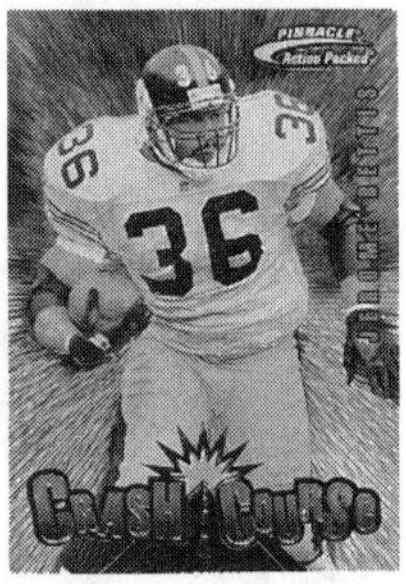

Inserted 1:23 packs, the 18-card set includes the Crash Course logo at the bottom center. The Action Packed logo is in the upper right. The player's name is printed vertically along the upper right side.

		MT
Complete Set (18):		200.00
Common Player:		5.00
Minor Stars:		10.00
1	Dan Marino	35.00
2	Troy Aikman	20.00
3	Barry Sanders	25.00
4	Emmitt Smith	35.00
5	Brett Favre	40.00
6	John Elway	15.00
7	Keyshawn Johnson	10.00
8	Jim Harbaugh	5.00
9	Kerry Collins	20.00
10	Karim Abdul-Jabbar	15.00
11	Eddie Kennison	10.00
12	Curtis Martin	20.00
13	Tony Banks	10.00
14	Dorsey Levens	5.00
15	Jerome Bettis	10.00
16	Drew Bledsoe	20.00
17	Marvin Harrison	10.00
18	Jerry Rice	20.00

1997 Action Packed Studs

Numbered as one of 1,500 sets, the nine-card chase set was inserted 1:167 packs. The cards include a real diamond chip in the ears of the player on the card front.

		MT
Complete Set (9):		800.00
Common Player:		35.00
1	Deion Sanders	60.00
2	Barry Sanders	120.00
3	Eddie George	130.00
4	Jerry Rice	110.00
5	Kordell Stewart	80.00
6	Emmitt Smith	225.00
7	Terrell Davis	100.00
8	Keyshawn Johnson	35.00
9	Robert Smith	35.00

1997 Action Packed 24K Team

The 15-card chase set was inserted 1:71 packs. The top of the card front has a gold banner, which includes "24KT Gold." The player's name is printed directly below the

banner. The player's photo is superimposed over a gold background and silver rays. The Action Packed logo is printed at the bottom center.

		MT
Complete Set (15):		550.00
Common Player:		15.00
1	Brett Favre	90.00
2	Steve Young	35.00
3	Terrell Davis	45.00
4	Barry Sanders	45.00
5	Isaac Bruce	25.00
6	Deion Sanders	30.00
7	Dan Marino	80.00
8	Jim Harbaugh	15.00
9	Jerry Rice	45.00
10	John Elway	35.00
11	Herman Moore	15.00
12	Troy Aikman	45.00
13	Emmitt Smith	80.00
14	Drew Bledsoe	45.00
15	Eddie George	50.00

1991 All-World Troy Aikman Promos

The six-card, regular size set used the same Troy Aikman photo, but with different crops and biography versions (English, French and Spanish). Each card is numbered with a "1" and A-F is used to distinguish the cards.

		MT
Complete Set (6):		15.00
Common Player:		2.50
1A	Troy Aikman (Green border, English bio)	2.50
1B	Troy Aikman (Green border, French bio)	2.50
1C	Troy Aikman (Green border, Spanish bio)	2.50
1D	Troy Aikman (Speckled border, English bio)	2.50
1E	Troy Aikman (Speckled border, French bio)	2.50
1F	Troy Aikman (Speckled border, Spanish bio)	2.50

1992 All-World

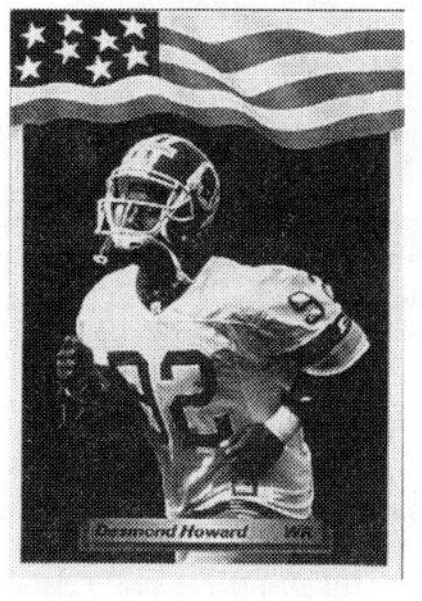

The 1992 All World set, which included 300 regular-size cards, was sold in 12-card packs and 26-card rack packs. The front of each card features an American flag on the top. Two insert sets, Greats/Rookies and Legends/Rookies were randomly inserted in packs, as were autographed cards from Joe Namath, Jim Brown and Desmond Howard. Subsets in the base set included Legends in the Making (LM), and Greats of the Game (GG).

		MT
Complete Set (300):		18.00
Common Player:		.05
1	Emmitt Smith (LM)	.75
2	Thurman Thomas (LM)	.10
3	Deion Sanders (LM)	.25
4	Randall Cunningham (LM)	.10
5	Michael Irvin (LM)	.10
6	Bruce Smith (LM)	.10
7	Jeff George (LM)	.10
8	Derrick Thomas (LM)	.10
9	Andre Rison (LM)	.20
10	Troy Aikman (LM)	.40
11	Quentin Coryatt	.25
12	Carl Pickens	1.50
13	Steve Emtman	.10
14	Derek Brown (TE)	.10
15	Desmond Howard	.75
16	Troy Vincent	.20
17	David Klingler	.20
18	Vaughn Dunbar	.10
19	Terrell Buckley	.10
20	Jimmy Smith	.50
21	Marquez Pope	.05
22	Kurt Barber	.05
23	Robert Harris	.05
24	Tony Sacca	.10
25	Alonzo Spellman	.20
26	Shane Collins	.05
27	Chris Mims	.20
28	Siran Stacy	.10
29	Edgar Bennett	.40
30	Sean Gilbert	.20
31	Eugene Chung	.05
32	Levon Kirkland	.10
33	Chuck Smith	.05
34	Chester McGlockton	.20
35	Ashley Ambrose	.10
36	Phillippi Sparks	.05
37	Darryl Williams	.10
38	Tracy Scroggins	.10
39	Mike Gaddis	.05
40	Tony Brooks	.05
41	Steve Israel	.05
42	Patrick Rowe	.05
43	Shane Dronett	.05
44	Mike Pawlawski	.05
45	Dale Carter	.20
46	Tyji Armstrong	.05
47	Kevin Smith	.20
48	Courtney Hawkins	.10
49	Marco Coleman	.10
50	Tommy Vardell	.10
51	Ray Ethridge	.05
52	Robert Porcher	.10
53	Todd Collins	.05
54	Robert Jones	.10
55	Tommy Maddox	.10
56	Dana Hall	.10
57	Leon Searcy	.10
58	Robert Brooks	2.00
59	Darren Woodson	.20
60	Jeremy Lincoln	.05
61	Sean Jones	.10
62	Howie Long	.10
63	Rich Gannon	.10
64	Keith Byars	.05
65	John Taylor	.10
66	Burt Grossman	.05
67	Chris Hinton	.05
68	Brad Muster	.05
69	Cris Dishman	.05
70	Russell Maryland	.10
71	Harvey Williams	.20
72	Broderick Thomas	.05
73	Louis Lipps	.05
74	Erik Kramer	.10
75	David Fulcher	.05
76	Andre Tippett	.05
77	Timm Rosenbach	.05
78	Mark Rypien	.10
79	James Lofton	.10
80	Dan Saleaumua	.05
81	John L. Williams	.05
82	Kevin Fagan	.05
83	Flipper Anderson	.05
84	Michael Dean Perry	.10
85	Mark Higgs	.05
86	Pat Swilling	.10
87	Pierce Holt	.05
88	John Elway	.75
89	Bill Brooks	.10
90	Rob Moore	.10
91	Junior Seau	.30
92	Wendell Davis	.05
93	Brian Noble	.05
94	Ernest Givins	.10
95	Phil Simms	.10
96	Eric Dickerson	.20
97	Bennie Blades	.05
98	Gary Anderson (RB)	.05
99	Erric Pegram	.20
100	Hart Lee Dykes	.05
101	Charles Haley	.10
102	Bruce Smith	.20
103	Nick Lowery	.05
104	Webster Slaughter	.05
105	Ray Childress	.10
106	Gene Atkins	.05
107	Bruce Armstrong	.05
108	Anthony Miller	.20
109	Eric Thomas	.05
110	Greg Townsend	.05
111	Anthony Carter	.10
112	James Hasty	.05
113	Chris Miller	.10
114	Sammie Smith	.05
115	Bubby Brister	.10
116	Mark Clayton	.10
117	Richard Johnson	.05
118	Bernie Kosar	.10
119	Lionel Washington	.05
120	Gary Clark	.20
121	Anthony Munoz	.10
122	Brent Jones	.10
123	Thurman Thomas	.20
124	Lee Williams	.05
125	Jessie Hester	.05
126	Andre Ware	.10
127	Patrick Hunter	.05
128	Erik Howard	.05
129	Keith Jackson	.10
130	Troy Aikman	.75
131	Mike Singletary	.10
132	Carnell Lake	.10
133	Jeff Hostetler	.10
134	Alonzo Highsmith	.05
135	Vaughn Johnson	.05
136	Louis Oliver	.05
137	Mel Gray	.05
138	Al Toon	.10
139	Bubba McDowell	.05
140	Ronnie Lott	.10
141	Deion Sanders	.50
142	Jim Harbaugh	.20
143	Gary Zimmerman	.05
144	Ernie Jones	.05
145	Cortez Kennedy	.20
146	Jeff Cross	.05
147	Floyd Turner (UER-Bio says he was drafted in 4th round)	.05
148	Mike Tomczak	.10
149	Lorenzo White	.10
150	Mark Carrier (DB)	.05
151	John Stephens	.05
152	Jerry Rice	.75
153	Jim Kelly	.20
154	Al Smith	.05
155	Duane Bickett	.05
156	Brett Perriman	.20
157	Boomer Esiason	.10
158	Neil Smith	.20
159	Eddie Anderson	.05
160	Browning Nagle	.05
161	John Friesz	.10
162	Robert Delpino	.05
163	Darren Lewis	.05
164	Roger Craig	.10
165	Keith McCants	.05
166	Stephone Paige	.05
167	Steve Broussard	.05
168	Gaston Green	.05
169	Ethan Horton	.05
170	Lewis Billups	.05
171	Mike Merriweather	.05
172	Randall Cunningham	.10
173	Leonard Marshall	.05
174	Jay Novacek	.20
175	Irving Fryar	.10
176	Randal Hill	.05
177	Keith Henderson	.05
178	Brad Baxter	.10
179	William Fuller	.10
180	Leslie O'Neal	.10
181	Steve Smith	.05
182	Joe Montana (UER-Born 1956, not 1965)	.75
183	Eric Green	.10
184	Rodney Peete	.10
185	Lawrence Dawsey	.10
186	Brian Mitchell	.10
187	Rickey Jackson	.05
188	Christian Okoye	.10
189	David Wyman	.05
190	Jessie Tuggle	.05
191	Ronnie Harmon	.05
192	Andre Reed	.20
193	Chris Doleman	.10
194	Leroy Hoard	.10
195	Mark Ingram	.05
196	Willie Gault	.10
197	Eugene Lockhart	.05
198	Jim Everett	.10
199	Doug Smith	.05
200	Clarence Verdin	.05
201	Steve Bono	1.00
202	Mark Vlasic	.05
203	Fred Barnett	.10
204	Henry Thomas	.05
205	Shaun Gayle	.05
206	Rod Bernstine	.05
207	Harold Green	.10
208	Dan McGwire	.05
209	Marv Cook	.05
210	Emmitt Smith	1.50
211	Merril Hoge	.05
212	Darion Conner	.05
213	Mike Sherrard	.10
214	Jeff George	.25
215	Craig Heyward	.10
216	Henry Ellard	.10
217	Lawrence Taylor	.20
218	Jerry Ball	.05
219	Tom Rathman	.05
220	Warren Moon	.20
221	Ricky Proehl	.05
222	Sterling Sharpe	.20
223	Earnest Byner	.05
224	Jay Schroeder	.05
225	Vance Johnson	.05
226	Cornelius Bennett	.10
227	Ken O'Brien	.05
228	Ferrell Edmunds	.05
229	Eric Allen	.05
230	Derrick Thomas	.20
231	Cris Carter	.20
232	Jon Vaughn	.10
233	Eric Metcalf	.20
234	William Perry	.10
235	Vinny Testaverde	.10
236	Chip Banks	.05
237	Brian Blades	.10
238	Calvin Williams	.10
239	Andre Rison	.20
240	Neil O'Donnell	.25
241	Michael Irvin	.25
242	Gary Plummer	.05
243	Nick Bell	.05
244	Ray Crockett	.05
245	Sam Mills	.05
246	Haywood Jeffires	.10
247	Steve Young	.50
248	Martin Bayless	.05
249	Dan Marino	1.50
250	Carl Banks	.05
251	Keith McKeller	.05
252	Aaron Wallace	.05
253	Lamar Lathon	.05
254	Derrick Fenner	.05
255	Vai Sikahema	.05
256	Keith Sims	.05
257	Rohn Stark	.05
258	Reggie Roby	.05
259	Tony Zendejas	.05
260	Harris Barton	.05
261	Checklist 1-100	.05
262	Checklist 101-200	.05
263	Checklist 201-300	.05
264	Rookies Checklist	.05
265	Greats Checklist	.05
266	Joe Namath (GG)	.10
267	Joe Namath (GG)	.10
268	Joe Namath (GG)	.10
269	Joe Namath (GG)	.10
270	Joe Namath (GG)	.10
271	Jim Brown (GG)	.10
272	Jim Brown (GG)	.10
273	Jim Brown (GG)	.10
274	Jim Brown (GG)	.10
275	Jim Brown (GG)	.10
276	Vince Lombardi (GG)	.05
277	Jim Thorpe (GG)	.05
278	Tom Fears (GG)	.05
279	John Henry Johnson (GG)	.05
280	Gale Sayers (GG)	.10
281	Willie Brown (GG)	.05
282	Doak Walker (GG)	.05
283	Dick Lane (GG)	.05
284	Otto Graham (GG)	.10
285	Hugh McElhenny (GG)	.05
286	Roger Staubach (GG)	.10
287	Steve Largent (GG)	.20
288	Otis Taylor (GG)	.05
289	Sam Huff (GG)	.05
290	Harold Carmichael (GG)	.05
291	Steve Van Buren (GG)	.05
292	Gino Marchetti (GG)	.05
293	Tony Dorsett (GG)	.05
294	Leo Nomellini (GG)	.05
295	Jack Lambert (GG)	.05
296	Joe Theismann (GG)	.05
297	Bobby Layne (GG)	.05
298	John Stallworth (GG)	.05
299	Paul Hornung (GG)	.05
300	Don Maynard (GG)	.05
A1	Desmond Howard (AU-Certified autograph)	75.00
A2	Jim Brown (AU-Certified autograph)	125.00
A3	Joe Namath (AU-Certified autograph)	175.00
P1	Desmond Howard (Promo)	3.00
TRI	Desmond Howard, Jim Brown, Joe Namath (Triplefolder)	5.00

1992 All-World Greats & Rookies

The 20-card, regular-size set was randomly inserted in the 1992 base set. The set features 15 current (as of 1992) players in color and five older players in black and white. The cards maintain the American flag card fronts, but with gold-foil embossed stars. The card backs lead with the "SG" prefix.

		MT
Complete Set (20):		12.00
Common Greats:		.50
Common Rookies:		.25
1	Troy Aikman	3.50
2	Thurman Thomas	1.00
3	Andre Rison	.50
4	Emmitt Smith	6.00
5	Derrick Thomas	.75
6	Joe Namath	.75
7	Jim Brown	.75
8	Roger Staubach	.50
9	Gale Sayers	.50
10	Jim Thorpe	.50
11	Quentin Coryatt	.50
12	Carl Pickens	3.50
13	Steve Emtman	.25
14	Derek Brown (TE)	.25
15	Desmond Howard	1.00
16	Troy Vincent	.25
17	David Klinger	.25
18	Vaughn Dunbar	.25
19	Terrell Buckley	.25
20	Jimmy Smith	.75

1992 All-World Legends & Rookies

The 20-card, standard-size set was randomly inserted in 1992 All-World packs. The first ten cards of the set feature Legends in the Making parallels (with gold stars) while cards 11-20 feature top rookies, also with gold stars on the card front's American flag. The card backs lead with the "L" prefix.

		MT
Complete Set (20):		25.00
Common Legends:		1.00
Common Rookies:		1.00
1	Emmitt Smith	10.00
2	Thurman Thomas	2.00
3	Deion Sanders	4.00
4	Randall Cunningham	1.00
5	Michael Irvin	1.50
6	Bruce Smith	1.00
7	Jeff George	1.50
8	Derrick Thomas	1.50
9	Andre Rison	1.00
10	Troy Aikman	6.00
11	Quentin Coryatt	1.00
12	Carl Pickens	6.00
13	Steve Emtman	1.00
14	Derek Brown (TE)	1.00
15	Desmond Howard	2.00
16	Troy Vincent	1.00
17	David Klinger	1.00
18	Vaughn Dunbar	1.00
19	Terrell Buckley	1.00
20	Jimmy Smith	2.00

1966 American Oil All-Pro

Released in 1966, the 15/16" x 1-1/8" 20-stamp set could be affixed to an 8-1/2" x 11" collection sheet. American Oil dealers distributed the stamps and collectors could win cash prizes and a 1967 Ford Mustang as a top prize. The stamps feature headshots of top players such as Bob Lilly, Deacon Jones, Alex Karras, Johnny Unitas and Gale Sayers.

		NM
Complete Set (15):		220.00
Common Player:		10.00
1	Herb Adderley (Winner 5.00)	
2	Gary Ballman	10.00
3	Dick Butkus (Winner 250.00)	
4	Gary Collins (Winner Car)	
5	Willie Davis	20.00
6	Tucker Frederickson	10.00
7	Sam Huff	28.00
8	Charlie Johnson	10.00
9	Deacon Jones	30.00
10	Alex Karras	30.00
11	Bob Lilly	35.00
12	Lenny Moore	35.00
13	Tommy Nobis	20.00
14	Dave Parks	10.00
15	Pete Retzlaff	10.00
16	Frank Ryan	10.00
17	Gale Sayers	45.00
18	Mick Tinglehoff	10.00
19	Johnny Unitas (Winner 25.00)	
20	Wayne Walker (Winner 1.00)	
NNO	Saver Sheet	25.00

1968 American Oil Mr. and Mrs.

The 32-card, 2-1/8" x 3-7/16" set featured 16 players and their wives. The cards were distributed by American Oil stations and collectors could win cash or a 1969 Ford. The player card fronts feature a horizontal action shot with the wife cards in domestic-type poses.

		NM
Complete Set (16):		100.00
Common Player:		5.00
Common Wife:		2.50
1	Kermit Alexander (Winner 100.00)	
2	Mrs. Kermit Alexander (Jogging with Family)	2.50
3	Jim Bakken	5.00
4	Mrs. Jim Bakken (Winner 1.00)	
5	Gary Collins (Winner 500.00)	
6	Mrs. Gary Collins (Enjoying the Outdoors)	2.50
7	Jim Grabowski (Winner 1969 Ford)	
8	Mrs. Jim Grabowski (At the Fireside)	2.50
9	Earl Gros (Winner 1.00)	
10	Mrs. Earl Gros (At the Park)	2.50
11	Deacon Jones	20.00
12	Mrs. Deacon Jones (Winner 500.00)	
13	Billy Lothridge (Winner 10.00)	
14	Mrs. Billy Lothridge and Baby Daughter	2.50
15	Tom Matte	10.00
16	Mrs. Tom Matte (Winner 50 cents)	
17	Bobby Mitchell (Winner 5.00)	
18	Mrs. Bobby Mitchell (At a Backyard Barbecue)	2.50
19	Joe Morrison	10.00
20	Mrs. Joe Morrison (Winner 1969 Ford)	
21	Dave Osborn	5.00
22	Mrs. Dave Osborn (Winner 5.00)	
23	Dan Reeves (Winner 50 cents)	
24	Mrs. Dan Reeves (Enjoying the Children)	2.50
25	Gale Sayers	30.00
26	Mrs. Gale Sayers (Winner 100.00)	
27	Norm Snead (Winner 1.00)	
28	Mrs. Norm Snead (On the Family Boat)	2.50
29	Steve Stonebreaker	5.00
30	Mrs. Steve Stonebreaker (Winner 10.00)	
31	Wayne Walker (Winner 50 cents)	
32	Mrs. Wayne Walker (At a Family Picnic)	2.50

1988 Athletes in Action

The 12-card, regular-sized set features six Dallas Cowboys and six Texas Rangers from 1988. The card fronts have a color action shot while the backs contain a player quote, a religious message and the player's favorite Bible verse. The top card in the set is Dallas head coach Tom Landry, featured one year before leaving the Cowboys after 29 years.

		MT
Complete Set (12):		10.00
Common Player:		.50
1	Pete O'Brien	.50
2	Scott Fletcher	.50
3	Oddibe McDowell	.75
4	Steve Buechele	.50
5	Jerry Browne	.50
6	Larry Parrish	.50
7	Tom Landry (CO)	3.00
8	Steve Pelluer	.50
9	Gordon Banks	.50
10	Bill Bates	.75
11	Doug Cosbie	.50
12	Herschel Walker	1.50

B

1990 Bandits Smokey

The Fresno Bandits, a semi-pro team, are featured in this 25-card set. The fronts feature a black-and-white player photo with the Smokey the Bear logo in the upper left and the team logo in the bottom right. The card backs have a black-and-white photo of the player with Smokey and a safety message.

		MT
Complete Set (25):		30.00
Common Player:		1.25
1	Allan Blades	1.25
2	Corey Clark	1.25
3	Darryl Duke	1.25
4	Heikoti Fakava	1.25
5	Charles Frazier	1.25
6	Chris Geile	1.25
7	Mike Henson	1.25
8	James Hickey	1.25
9	Anthony Howard	1.25
10	Derrick Jinks	1.25
11	Anthony Jones	1.25
12	Marvin Jones	1.25
13	Mike Jones	1.25
14	Steve Loop	1.25
15	Thomas Ireland	1.25
16	Jay Lynch	1.25
17	Sheldon Martin	1.25
18	Chuckie McCutchen	1.25
19	Lance Oberparleiter	1.25
20	Darrell Rosette	1.25
21	Fred Sims	1.25
22	Bryan Turner	1.25
23	Jim Woods CO	1.25
24	Rick Zumwalt	1.25
25	Coaching Staff	1.25

1959 Bazooka

These cards were found on the backs of Bazooka Bubble Gum boxes in 1959. The unnumbered cards are blank-backed and are checklisted alphabetically. Each card measures 2-13/16" x 4-15/16" and is part of the display box. Intact boxes are worth more than if the cards have been cut out.

		NM
Complete Set (18):		5000.
Common Player:		150.00
(1)	Alan Ameche	190.00
(2)	Jon Arnett	150.00
(3)	Jim Brown	675.00
(4)	Rick Casares	150.00
(5A)	Charley Connerly (error, Baltimore Colts)	450.00
(5B)	Charley Conerly (correct, New York Giants)	325.00
(6)	Howard Ferguson	150.00
(7)	Frank Gifford	450.00
(8)	Lou Groza	475.00
(9)	Bobby Layne	325.00
(10)	Eddie LeBaron	200.00
(11)	Woodley Lewis	150.00
(12)	Ollie Matson	250.00
(13)	Joe Perry	250.00
(14)	Pete Retzlaff	150.00
(15)	Kyle Rote	225.00
(16)	Y.A. Tittle	325.00
(17)	Tom Tracy	300.00
(18)	Johnny Unitas	500.00

1971 Bazooka

These cards were issued on the backs of Bazooka Bubble Gum as panels of three. The panels are 2-5/8" x 5-7/8"; each individual card is 1-15/16" x 2-5/8". The card front has a number, plus a color head shot of the player. The back is blank. Panels generally command a premium price which would be greater than the total of the three players combined. Individual card prices are listed.

		NM
Complete Set (36):		200.00
Common Player:		3.00
1	Joe Namath	35.00
2	Larry Brown	5.00
3	Bobby Bell	5.00
4	Dick Butkus	15.00
5	Charlie Sanders	3.00
6	Chuck Howley	4.00
7	Gale Gillingham	3.00
8	Leroy Kelly	6.00
9	Floyd Little	6.00
10	Dan Abramowicz	3.50
11	Sonny Jurgensen	15.00
12	Andy Russell	3.00
13	Tommy Nobis	3.00
14	O.J. Simpson	30.00
15	Tom Woodeshick	3.00
16	Roman Gabriel	4.50
17	Claude Humphrey	3.00
18	Merlin Olsen	8.00
19	Daryle Lamonica	4.00
20	Fred Cox	3.00
21	Bart Starr	16.00
22	John Brodie	8.00
23	Jim Nance	3.00
24	Gary Garrison	3.00
25	Fran Tarkenton	17.00
26	Johnny Robinson	3.00
27	Gale Sayers	18.00
28	John Unitas	20.00
29	Jerry LeVias	3.00
30	Virgil Carter	3.00
31	Bill Nelsen	3.00
32	Dave Osborn	3.00
33	Matt Snell	3.00
34	Larry Wilson	6.00
35	Bob Griese	15.00
36	Lance Alworth	8.00

1972 Bazooka Official Signals

The 12-card, 6-1/4" x 2-7/8" set was issued by Bazooka on the bottoms of bubble gum boxes in 1972. The first eight cards define football lingo for juveniles while cards 9-12 describe the responsibilities of the referees.

		NM
Complete Set (12):		85.00
Common Player:		8.00
1	Football Lingo (Automatic through Bread and Butter Play)	8.00
2	Football Lingo (Broken-Field Runner through Dive)	8.00
3	Football Lingo (Double-Coverage through Interference)	8.00
4	Football Lingo (Game Plan through Lateral Pass)	8.00
5	Football Lingo (Interception through Man-to-Man Coverage)	8.00
6	Football Lingo (Killing the Clock through Punt)	8.00
7	Football Lingo (Belly Series through Quick Whistle)	8.00
8	Football Lingo (Prevent Defense through Primary Receiver)	8.00
9	Officials' Duties (Reveree through Line Judge)	8.00
10	Officials' Duties	8.00
11	Officials' Signals	8.00
12	Officials' Signals	8.00

1976 Bears Coke Discs

The 24 circular-card set was issued in 1976 as part of a local Coca-Cola promotion in Chicago. Each one

of the 3-3/8" (diameter) discs feature Chicago Bears players, including a noteworthy disc of Walter Payton, whose rookie Topps card was also issued in 1976. The card front features a headshot with the Coca-Cola logo and a Bears helmet while the back has another Coca-Cola logo with the "Coke adds life to ... halftime fun."

		NM
Complete Set (24):		60.00
Common Player:		1.50
1	Lionel Antoine	1.50
2	Bob Avellini	3.00
3	Waymond Bryant	1.50
4	Doug Buffone	2.00
5	Wally Chambers	2.00
6A	Craig Clemons (Yellow border)	1.50
6B	Craig Clemons (Orange border)	1.50
7	Allan Ellis	1.50
8	Roland Harper	2.50
9	Mike Hartenstine	1.50
10	Noah Jackson	2.50
11	Virgil Livers	1.50
12	Jim Osborne	1.50
13	Bob Parsons	1.50
14	Walter Payton	45.00
15	Dan Peiffer	1.50
16A	Doug Plank (Yellow border)	3.00
16B	Doug Plank (Green border)	3.00
17	Bo Rather	1.50
18	Don Rives	1.50
19	Jeff Sevy	1.50
20	Ron Shanklin	1.50
21	Revie Sorey	1.50
22	Roger Stillwell	1.50

1981 Bears Police

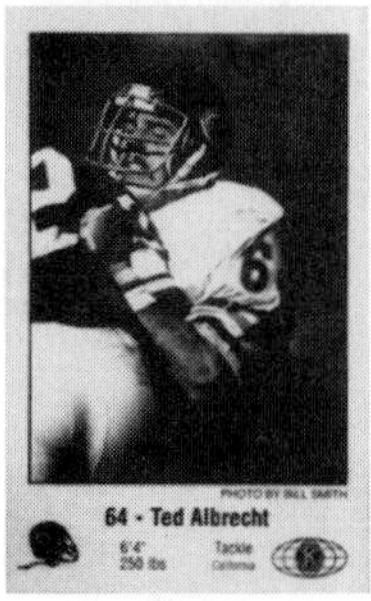

The 24-card, 2-5/8" x 4-1/8" set was released in 1981 and sponsored by the Kiwanis Club, the local law enforcement agency and the Chicago Bears. The card fronts feature an action shot while the backs have a Bears helmet and tips geared toward younger fans.

		MT
Complete Set (24):		25.00
Common Player:		.50
1	Ted Albrecht	.50
2	Neil Armstrong CO	.50
3	Brian Baschnagel	.50
4	Gary Campbell	.50
5	Robin Earl	.50
6	Allan Ellis	.50
7	Vince Evans	2.00
8	Gary Fencik	1.50
9	Dan Hampton	5.00
10	Roland Harper	.75
11	Mike Hartenstine	.50
12	Tom Hicks	.50
13	Noah Jackson	.75
14	Dennis Lick	.50
15	Jerry Muckensturm	.50
16	Dan Neal	.50
17	Jim Osborne	.50
18	Alan Page	3.50
19	Walter Payton	18.00
20	Doug Plank	.50
21	Terry Schmidt	.50
22	James Scott	.50
23	Revie Sorey	.50
24	Rickey Watts	.50

1994 Bears 75th Anniversary Sheets

The 10-card, 10-3/4" x 7-5/8" set was inserted into game programs for the 1994 75th anniversary season for the Chicago Bears. Each card in the set could be found on a perforated sheet for the eight regular-season Bears home games and two preseason home games. The card backs feature a WGN AM radio advertisement while the fronts have a light blue face with action shots of past Chicago Hall of Famers.

		MT
Complete Set (10):		50.00
Common Player:		2.50
1	George Halas OWN/CO (vs. Eagles; 8/5/94)	6.00
2	Doug Atkins, George Connor, George Blanda (vs. Giants; 8/27/94)	2.50
3	Walter Payton (vs. Bucs; 9/4/94)	8.00
4	Dan Fortmann, Mike Ditka, Paddy Driscoll (vs. Vikings; 9/18/94)	5.00
5	Dick Butkus (vs. Bills; 10/2/94)	7.00
6	Bill George, Red Grange, Ed Healey (vs. Saints; 10/9/94)	4.00
7	Gale Sayers (vs. Packers; 10/31/94)	7.00
8	Bill Hewitt, Stan Jones, Sid Luckman (vs. Lions; 11/20/94)	3.00
9	Link Lyman, George Musso, George McAfee (vs. Rams; 12/18/94)	2.50
10	Bronko Nagurski, Bulldog Turner, Joe Stydahar, George Trafton (vs. Patriots; 12/24/94)	4.00

1994 Bears Toyota

The two-card, standard-size set was sponsored by Toyota and commemorates October 31, 1994, the day Dick Butkus and Gale Sayers had their jerseys retired by the Bears. The card fronts have a Bears logo in the upper left corner and have a color action shot. The card backs feature a color headshot with a career summary and highlights.

		MT
Complete Set (2):		16.00
Common Player:		8.00
1	Dick Butkus	8.00
2	Gale Sayers	8.00

1995 Bears Program Sheets

The eight-sheet, 8" x 10" set was inserted in Bears game programs during the 1995 season to commemorate the 10th anniversary of Chicago's Super Bowl XX victory in January of 1986. The fronts contained color action shots of top players including Walter Payton, Jim McMahon and Mike Singletary.

		MT
Complete Set (8):		40.00
Common Player:		4.00
1	Mike Ditka (9/3/95 vs. Vikings)	6.00
2	Walter Payton (9/11/95 vs. Packers)	8.00
3	Jim McMahon (10/8/95 vs. Panthers)	5.00
4	Mike Singletary, Gary Fencik (10/22/95 vs. Oilers)	5.00
5	Richard Dent (11/5/95 vs. Steelers)	5.00
6	William Perry (11/19/95 vs. Lions)	5.00
7	Otis Wilson (12/17/95 vs. Buccaneers)	4.00
8	Wilber Marshall (12/24/95 vs. Eagles)	4.00

1995 Bears Super Bowl XX 10th Anniversary Kemper

The 20-card, regular-sized set released in 1995, commemorates the Chicago Bears Super Bowl XX win. Issued in conjunction with Kemper Mutual Funds, the fronts feature color action shots with the player's name, position and uniform number along the left border. The card backs have a player closeup with bio statistical information.

		MT
Complete Set (20):		25.00
Common Player:		1.00
1	Mark Bortz	1.00
2	Kevin Butler	1.00
3	Jim Covert	1.00
4	Richard Dent	1.50
5	Dave Duerson	1.00
6	Gary Fencik	1.00
7	Willie Gault	1.00
8	Dan Hampton	1.00
9	Jay Hilgenberg	1.00
10	Wilber Marshall	1.00
11	Dennis McKinnon	1.00
12	Jim McMahon	2.00
13	Steve McMichael	1.00
14	Walter Payton	4.00
15	William Perry	1.50
16	Mike Singletary	1.50
17	Matt Suhey	1.00
18	Tom Thayer	1.00
19	Keith Van Horne	1.00
20	Otis Wilson	1.00

1995 Bears Super Bowl XX Montgomery Ward Cards

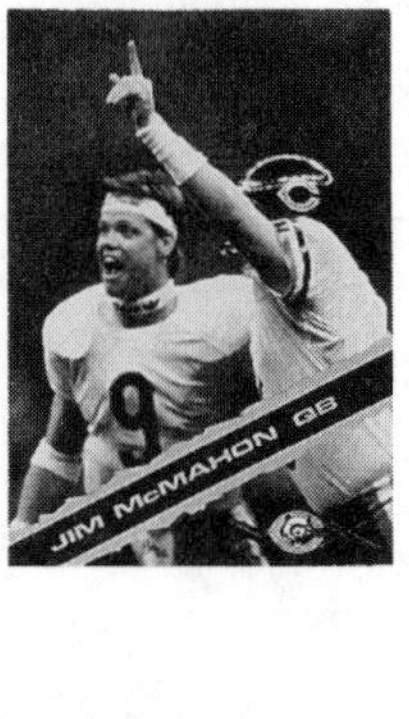

The eight-card, regular-sized set was released in conjunction with Montgomery Ward stores and commemorates Chicago's 10th anniversary of a win in Super Bowl XX. The card fronts have a color action shot with a diagonal blue and orange stripe which states the player's name and position. The card backs contain a checklist for the eight cards.

		MT
Complete Set (8):		12.00
Common Player:		1.00
1	Mike Ditka ('85 Super Bowl)	2.00
2	Kevin Butler	1.00
3	Dan Hampton	1.00
4	Richard Dent	1.50
5	Gary Fencik	1.00
6	Walter Payton	2.50
7	Jim McMahon	1.50
8	Mike Ditka	1.75

1995 Bears Super Bowl XX Montgomery Ward Coins

The eight-coin set was released in 1995 in conjunction with Montgomery Ward stores to commemorate Chicago's 10th anniversary of its Super Bowl XX victory. The coins parallel the eight-card set, also released in 1995. The coin fronts depict the player's name and uniform number while the backs have the Super Bowl XX logo.

		MT
Complete Set (8):		10.00
Common Player:		1.00
1	Kevin Butler	1.00
2	Richard Dent	1.25
3	Mike Ditka CO	1.75
4	Gary Fencik	1.00
5	Dan Hampton	1.00
6	Jim McMahon	1.50
7	Walter Payton	2.50
8	Super Bowl Trophy	1.00

1996 Bears Illinois State Lottery

These cards were Illinois State Lottery scratch-and-win tickets. The tickets feature a color photo of the player. They are usually found scratched.

		MT
Complete Set (5):		3.00
Common Player:		.25
1	Richard Dent	.50
2	Mike Ditka	1.00
3	Dan Hampton	.50
4	William Perry	.25
5	Gale Sayers	1.00

1968 Bengals Team Issue

The Cincinnati Bengals team-issued set consisted of 8-1/2" x 11" cards with a black and white player photo. The player's name and position are below the photo.

		NM
Complete Set (7):		35.00
Complete Player:		5.00
1	Frank Buncom	5.00
2	Sherrill Headrick	5.00
3	Warren McVea	5.00
4	Fletcher Smith	5.00
5	John Stofa	7.00
6	Dewey Warren	5.00
7	Ernie Wright	7.00

1969 Bengals Tresler Comet

The 20-card, standard-size cards were distributed by Tresler Comet gas stations. The card fronts feature a simulated autograph while the backs contain bio and career highlights. The card backs are not numbered and Bob Johnson's card is unusually higher in value than the other 19 because of its scarcity. Also, future Bengals' coach Sam Wyche is included along with football announcer Bob Trumpy.

		NM
Complete Set (20):		300.00
Common Player:		5.00
1	Al Beauchamp	5.00
2	Bill Bergey	10.00
3	Royce Berry	5.00
4	Paul Brown CO	35.00
5	Frank Buncom	5.00
6	Greg Cook	10.00
7	Howard Fest SP	25.00
8	Harry Gunner SP	20.00
9	Bobby Hunt	5.00
10	Bob Johnson SP	125.00
11	Charley King	5.00
12	Dale Livingston	5.00
13	Warren McVea SP	25.00
14	Bill Peterson	5.00
15	Jess Phillips	5.00
16	Andy Rice	5.00
17	Bill Staley	5.00
18	Bob Trumpy	20.00
19	Ernie Wright	5.00
20	Sam Wyche	25.00

1960 Bills Team Issue

Issued by the team, this set of 40 black and white 5" x 7" cards were delivered to the 1960 Buffalo Bills season ticketholders. The photos are not numbered and were frequently found autographed.

		NM
Complete Set (40):		180.00
Common Player:		5.00
1	Bill Atkins	5.00
2	Bob Barrett	5.00
3	Phil Blazer	5.00
4	Bob Brodhead	5.00
5	Dick Brubacher	5.00
6	Bernie Burzinski	5.00
7	Wray Carlton	8.00
8	Don Chelf	5.00
9	Monte Crockett	5.00
10	Bob Dove	5.00
11	Elbert Dubenion	10.00
12	Fred Ford	5.00
13	Dick Gallagher	5.00
14	Darrell Harper	5.00
15	Harvey Johnson	5.00
16	John Johnson	5.00
17	Billy Kinard	5.00
18	Joe Kulbacki	5.00
19	John Laraway	5.00
20	Richie Lucas	10.00
21	Archie Matsos	8.00
22	Richie McCabe	8.00
23	Dan McGrew	5.00
24	Chuck McMurtry	5.00
25	Ed Meyer	5.00
26	Ed Muelhaupt	5.00
27	Tom O'Connell	5.00
28	Harold Olson	5.00
29	Buster Ramsey CO	5.00
30	Floyd Reid	5.00
31	Tom Rychlec	5.00
32	Joe Schaeffer	5.00
33	John Scott	5.00
34	Bob Sedlock	5.00
35	Carl Smith	5.00
36	Jim Sorey	5.00
27	Lavern Torczon	5.00
38	Jim Wagstaff	5.00
39	Ralph Wilson OWN	8.00
40	Mack Yoho	5.00

1963 Bills Jones Dairy

The 40-card, circular cards were available as cardboard cut-outs on milk cartons. The 1" (diameter) discs are frequently found miscut and off-centered and are not numbered.

		NM
Complete Set (40):		1000.
Common Player:		20.00
1	Ray Abruzzese	20.00
2	Art Baker	20.00
3	Stew Barber	20.00
4	Glenn Bass	20.00
5	Dave Behrman	20.00
6	Al Bemiller	20.00
7	Wray Carlton	20.00
8	Carl Charon	20.00
9	Monte Crockett	20.00
10	Wayne Crow	20.00
11	Tom Day	20.00
12	Elbert Dubenion	25.00
13	Jim Dunaway	25.00
14	Booker Edgerson	20.00
15	Cookie Gilchrist	30.00
16	Dick Hudson	20.00
17	Frank Jackunas	20.00
18	Harry Jacobs	20.00
19	Jack Kemp	375.00
20	Roger Kochman	20.00
21	Daryle Lamonica	85.00
22	Charley Leo	20.00
23	Marv Matuszak	20.00
24	Bill Miller	20.00
25	Leroy Moore	20.00
26	Harold Olson	20.00
27	Herb Paterra	20.00
28	Ken Rice	20.00
29	Henry Rivera	20.00
30	Ed Rutkowski	20.00
31	George Saimes	25.00
32	Tom Sestak	25.00
33	Billy Shaw	25.00
34	Mike Stratton	20.00
35	Gene Sykes	20.00
36	John Tracey	20.00
37	Ernie Warlick	20.00
38	Willie West	20.00
39	Mack Yoho	20.00
40	Sid Youngelman	20.00

1965 Bills Super Duper Markets

The 10-card, 8-1/2" x 11" set was offered as a giveaway from Super Duper food stores in 1965. The fronts contain black and white action (posed) photos and the set is not numbered.

		NM
Complete Set (10):		180.00
Common Player:		5.00
1	Glenn Bass	5.00
2	Elbert Dubenion	10.00
3	Billy Joe	10.00
4	Jack Kemp	100.00
5	Daryle Lamonica	30.00
6	Tom Sestak	5.00
7	Billy Shaw	10.00
8	Mike Stratton	5.00
9	Ernie Warlick	5.00
10	Team Photo	25.00

1967 Bills Jones-Rich Milk

Through a special mail-in offer, Jones-Rich Milk offered the set of six Buffalo Bills 8-1/2" x 11" cards in 1967.

		NM
Complete Set (6):		100.00
Common Player:		15.00
1	George (Butch) Byrd	20.00
2	Wray Carlton	20.00
3	Hagood Clarke	15.00
4	Paul Costa	20.00
5	Jim Dunaway	20.00
6	Jack Spikes	20.00

1974 Bills Team Issue

The 12-card, 8-1/2" x 11" photo cards were issued through concession sales at Rich Stadium in Buffalo during the 1974 season.

		NM
Complete Set (12):		80.00
Common Player:		5.00
1	Jim Braxton	5.00
2	Bob Chandler	8.00
3	Jim Cheyunski	5.00
4	Earl Edwards	5.00
5	Joe Ferguson	12.00
6	Dave Foley	5.00
7	Robert James	5.00
8	Reggie McKenzie	5.00
9	Jerry Patton	5.00
10	Walt Patulski	5.00
11	John Skorupan	5.00
12	O.J. Simpson	30.00

1976 Bills McDonald's

The three-card set was issued by McDonald's in conjunction with WBEN-TV and was given away free with a purchase of a Quarter Pounder hamburger at particpating restaurants. The 8" x 10" color photos included statistical information on the backs.

		NM
Complete Set (3):		30.00
Common Player:		8.00
1	Bob Chandler	10.00
2	Joe Ferguson	15.00
3	Reggie McKenzie	8.00

1979 Bills Bell's Market

The 11-card, 7-5/8" x 10" photo cards were issued weekly by Bell's Markets during the 1979 season. The cards were printed on thin stock and were not numbered.

		NM
Complete Set (11):		50.00
Common Player:		4.00
(1)	Curtis Brown	4.00
(2)	Bob Chandler	5.00
(3)	Joe DeLamielleure	4.00
(4)	Joe Ferguson	10.00
(5)	Reuben Gant	4.00
(6)	Dee Hardison	4.00
(7)	Frank Lewis	4.00
(8)	Reggie McKenzie	5.00
(9)	Terry Miller	4.00
(10)	Shane Nelson	4.00
(11)	Lucius Sanford	4.00

1980 Bills Bell's Market

The 20-card, regular-sized set was issued by Bell's Markets in 1980 and arrived in 20-card packs or two-pack perforation sets. The card fronts contain color shots while the backs have career statistics.

		NM
Complete Set (20):		9.00
Common Player:		.40
1	Curtis Brown	.40
2	Shane Nelson	.40
3	Jerry Butler	.40
4	Joe Ferguson	.40
5	Joe Cribbs	.40
6	Reggie McKenzie	.40
7	Joe Devlin	.40
8	Ken Jones	.40
9	Steve Freeman	.40
10	Mike Kadish	.40
11	Jim Haslett	.40
12	Isiah Robertson	.40
13	Frank Lewis	.40
14	Jeff Nixon	.40
15	Nick Mike-Mayer	.40
16	Jim Ritcher	.40
17	Charles Romes	.40
18	Fred Smerlas	.40
19	Ben Williams	.40
20	Roland Hooks	.40

1986 Bills Sealtest

The six-card, 3-5/8" x 7-5/8" set was issued on sides of half-gallon Sealtest milk containers. The Freeman and Marve cards were found on vitamin D cartons while the Kelly and Romes cards appeared on lowfat (2%) cartons. The cards featured a black and white player headshot with bio information and stats.

		MT
Complete Set (6):		30.00
Common Player:		1.50
1	Greg Bell SP	5.00
2	Jerry Butler SP	5.00
3	Steve Freeman	1.50
4	Jim Kelly	20.00
5	Eugene Marve	1.50
6	Charles Romes	1.50

1987 Bills Police

The eight-card, 2-5/8" x 4-1/8" set was sponsored by the Bills, Erie and Niagara County Sheriff's Departments, Louis Rich Turkey products, Claussen Pickles and WBEN radio. The black and white photos on the card fronts were taken by Robert L. Smith, the Bills' official team photographer.

		MT
Complete Set (8):		12.00
Common Player:		1.00
1	Marv Levy CO	1.50
2	Bruce Smith	2.00
3	Joe Devlin	1.00
4	Jim Kelly	5.00
5	Eugene Marve	1.00
6	Andre Reed	2.00
7	Pete Metzelaars	1.00
8	John Kidd	1.00

1988 Bills Police

The eight-card, 2-5/8" x 4-1/8" set was sponsored by the Bills, Erie and Niagara County Sheriff's Departments, Louis Rich Turkey Products and WBEN radio. The fronts feature an action photo while the backs have bio and stat information.

		MT
Complete Set (8):		8.00
Common Player:		.75
1	Steve Tasker	1.50
2	Cornelius Bennett	2.00
3	Shane Conlan	1.25
4	Mark Kelso	.75
5	Will Wolford	.75
6	Chris Burkett	.75
7	Kent Hull	1.25
8	Art Still	.75

1989 Bills Police

The eight-card, regular-sized set was issued in conjunction with the Bills, Erie County Sheriff's Department and Louis Rich Turkey Products. The card fronts feature an action shot while the backs contain bio and stat information.

		MT
Complete Set (8):		10.00
Common Player:		.75
1	Leon Seals	.75
2	Thurman Thomas	6.00
3	Jim Ritcher	.75
4	Scott Norwood	.75
5	Darryl Talley	1.50
6	Nate Odomes	.75
7	Leonard Smith	.75
8	Ray Bentley	.75

1990 Bills Police

The eight-card, 4" x 6" set was sponsored by Blue Shield of New York. The card fronts feature a color action photo and the card backs contain highlights and career statistics.

		MT
Complete Set (8):		10.00
Common Player:		.50
1	Carlton Bailey	.50
2	Kirby Jackson	.50
3	Jim Kelly	5.00
4	James Lofton	1.50
5	Keith McKeller	.50
6	Mark Pike	.50
7	Andre Reed	2.50
8	Jeff Wright	.50

1991 Bills Police

The eight-card, regular-sized set was sponsored by Blue Shield of New York. The card fronts feature an action shot and bio information while the backs contain highlights and career statistics.

		MT
Complete Set (8):		5.00
Common Player:		.75
1	Howard Ballard	.75
2	Don Beebe	1.50
3	John Davis	.75
4	Kenneth Davis	1.00
5	Mark Kelso	.75
6	Frank Reich	1.50
7	Butch Rolle	.75
8	J.D. Williams	.75

1992 Bills Police

The seven-card, 4" x 6" set was sponsored by Blue Shield of New York. The card fronts feature an action photo and bio information while the backs have highlights and stats.

		MT
Complete Set (7):		5.00
Common Player:		.50
1	Carlton Bailey	.50
2	Steve Christie	.50
3	Shane Conlan	.75
4	Phil Hansen	.50
5	Henry Jones	.75
6	Chris Mohr	.50
7	Thurman Thomas	3.00

1994 Bills Police

The six-card, 3" x 5" set was sponsored by the Erie County Sheriff's Office and Coca-Cola. The card fronts feature color action shots with the Bills logo in the lower left corner. The backs feature a headshot with biographical and statistical information with "Tips from the Sheriff."

		MT
Complete Set (6):		5.00
Common Player:		.50
1	Bill Brooks	1.25
2	Kenneth Davis	1.00
3	John Fina	.50
4	Phil Hansen	.75
5	Pete Metzelaars	1.00
6	Marvcus Patton	.75

1995 Bills Police

The six-card, 4" x 6" set was sponsored by the Erie County Sheriff's Office and Coca-Cola. The card

fronts feature a color action shot with the Bills logo in the upper left corner. The card backs have a headshot with bio and stat information and a safety tip.

		MT
Complete Set (6):		5.00
Common Player:		.50
1	Jeff Burris	.75
2	Joe Ferguson (All-Time Great)	1.50
3	Kent Hull	.50
4	Adam Lingner	.50
5	Glenn Parker	.50
6	Andre Reed	2.50

1996 Bills Police

Coca-Cola and the Erie County Sheriff's Office sponsored this five-card set of the Buffalo Bills. The cards are 4" x 6" and feature a color player photo and the sponsors' logos on the front.

		MT
Complete Set (5):		4.00
Common Player:		.75
24	Kurt Schulz	.75
55	Mark Maddox	.75
79	Ruben Brown	1.25
94	Mark Pike	.75
95	Bryce Paup	1.50

1993-94 Bleachers Troy Aikman Promos

The four-card, standard-size promo set highlights the Dallas Cowboys quarterback in his UCLA uniform. Ten-thousand sets were produced and the card backs feature the same card-front image ghosted behind a text of career highlights. Card #4 was an exclusive promo for the 1994 Houston Tri-Star show and features "Houston 1994" in gold foil.

		MT
Complete Set (4):		10.00
Common Player:		2.50
1	Troy Aikman (Exclusive promo)	2.50
2	Troy Aikman (UCLA)	2.50
3	Troy Aikman (UCLA, Comicfest '93)	2.50
4	Troy Aikman (UCLA, Houston '94)	2.50

1993 Bleachers 23K Troy Aikman

This three-card set is sequentially-numbered to 10,000. The cards feature color photos of Aikman, a facsimile autograph printed in gold foil and golden borders. A promo card with Aikman pictured in his Cowboy uniform was also produced.

		MT
Complete Set (3):		20.00
Common Player:		5.00
1	Troy Aikman (Oklahoma)	5.00
2	Troy Aikman (UCLA)	5.00
3	Troy Aikman (Cowboys)	5.00
P1	Troy Aikman Promo (Cowboys)	5.00

1994 Bleachers 23K Troy Aikman

The three-card, standard-sized set features the Dallas Cowboys quarterback in collegiate color photos (#1 and #2) and a pro shot with Dallas (#3). The card fronts have a gold-foil border along with his name, team and position in gold on the bottom edge. The card backs are numbered in production "x of 10,000" and in the set "x of 3" and feature a facsimile Aikman autograph.

		MT
Complete Set (3):		15.00
Common Player:		5.00
1	Troy Aikman (Oklahoma)	5.00
2	Troy Aikman (UCLA)	5.00
3	Troy Aikman	5.00

1995 Bleachers 23K Emmitt Smith

The four-card, regular-sized set features the Dallas Cowboys running back in high school (#1), college (#2) and Dallas (#3). The card fronts feature a gold border while the card backs are numbered in production as "x of 10,000." A promo card, not numbered, featured Smith in his collegiate uniform.

		MT
Complete Set (3):		30.00
Common Player:		10.00
1	Emmitt Smith (Escambia High School)	10.00
2	Emmitt Smith (Florida Gators)	10.00
3	Emmitt Smith	10.00
NNO	Emmitt Smith (Promo, Escambia High School)	3.00

1983 Blitz Chicago

The eight-sheet, 10" x 8" set featured the United States Football League team. One set contains the coaching staff, including head coach George Allen, while the other seven feature the players. The sheets are unnumbered and the individual photos on the sheets are approximately 2-1/4" x 2-1/2".

		MT
Complete Set (8):		35.00
Common Player:		4.50
1	Coaching Staff (George Allen, Joe Haering, Paul Lanham, John Payne, John Teerlink, Dick Walker, Charlie Waller, Ray Wietecha)	4.50
2	Luther Bradley, Eddie Brown, Virgil Livers, Frank Minnifield, Lance Sheilds, Don Schwartz, Maurice Tyler, Ted Walton	4.50
3	Mack Boatner, Frank Collins, Frank Corral, Doug Cozen, Doug Dennison, John Roveto, Jim Stone, Tim Wrightman	4.50
4	Robert Barnes, Bruce Branch, Nick Eyre, Tim Norman, Wally Pesuit, Mark Stevenson, Rob Taylor, Steve Tobin	4.50
5	Junior Ah You, Mark Buben, Bob Cobb, Joe Ehrmann, Kit Lathrop, Karl Lorch, Troy Thomas	4.50
6	Jim Fahnhorst, Joe Federspiel, Doak Field, Bruce Gheesling, Andy Melontree, Ed Smith, Stan White, Kari Yli-Renko	4.50
7	Marcus Anderson, Larry Douglas, Mark May, Pat Schmidt, Lenny Willis, Warren Anderson, Chris Pagnucco, Bruce Allen GM	4.50

1948 Bowman

Considered to be the first true football set of the modern era, the 1948 Bowman set included only players from the National Football League (the first set to do so). Each of the 108 cards measures 2-1/16" x 2-1/2" and shows a player photo on the front with no name or team name. Backs have biographical information. This set was printed on three separate sheets, with the first sheet being plentiful, the second a little scarcer, and the third very difficult to find. So cards numbered 1, 4, 7, 10, etc., are easiest to find; cards numbered 2, 5, 8, 11, etc., are somewhat harder, and those divisible by three (3, 6, 9, 12, etc.) are extremely tough to find. Rookie cards in this set include Hall of Famers Steve Van Buren, Charley Trippi, Sammy Baugh, Bob Waterfield, Bulldog Turner, Alex Wojciechowicz, Pete Pihos, Bill Dudley, George McAfee and Sid Luckman. Other star rookie cards include Johnny Lujack and Charlie Conerly.

		NM
Complete Set (108):		6000.
Common Player:		20.00
SP Cards:		50.00
1	*Joe Tereshinski*	150.00
2	Larry Olsonoski	20.00
3	*John Lujack*	320.00
4	Ray Poole	20.00
5	Bill DeCorrevont	20.00
6	Paul Briggs	100.00
7	*Steve Van Buren*	150.00
8	*Kenny Washington*	50.00
9	Nolan Luhn	100.00
10	Chris Iversen	20.00
11	Jack Wiley	20.00
12	*Charlie Conerly*	320.00
13	*Hugh Taylor*	20.00
14	Frank Seno	20.00
15	Gil Bouley	100.00
16	*Tommy Thompson*	30.00
17	*Charlie Trippi*	100.00
18	Vince Banonis	100.00
19	Art Faircloth	20.00
20	Clyde Goodnight	20.00
21	Bill Chipley	100.00
22	*Sammy Baugh*	425.00
23	Don Kindt	20.00
24	John Koniszewski	100.00
25	Pat McHugh	20.00
26	*Bob Waterfield*	200.00
27	Tony Compagno	100.00
28	Paul Governali	20.00
29	*Pat Harder*	40.00
30	Vic Lindskog	100.00
31	Salvatore Rosato	20.00
32	John Mastrangelo	20.00
33	Fred Gehrke	100.00
34	Bosh Pritchard	20.00
35	Mike Micka	20.00
36	*Bulldog Turner*	250.00
37	Len Younce	20.00
38	Pat West	20.00
39	Russ Thomas	100.00
40	James Peebles	20.00
41	Bob Skoglund	20.00
42	Wat Stickle	100.00
43	*Whitey Wistert*	20.00
44	*Paul Christman*	45.00
45	Jay Rhodemyre	100.00
46	Skip Minisi	20.00
47	Bob Mann	20.00
48	Mal Kutner	100.00
49	Dick Poillon	20.00
50	Charles Cherundolo	20.00
51	Gerald Cowhig	100.00
52	*Neil Armstrong*	30.00
53	Frak Maznicki	20.00
54	John Sanchez	100.00
55	Frank Reagan	20.00
56	Jim Hardy	20.00
57	John Badaczewski	100.00
58	Robert Nussbaumer	20.00
59	Marvin Pregulman	20.00
60	*Elbert Nickel*	125.00
61	*Alex Wojciechowicz*	75.00
62	Walt Shclinkman	20.00
63	*Pete Pihos*	220.00
64	Joseph Sulaitis	20.00
65	*Mike Holovak*	50.00
66	Cecil Souders	100.00
67	Paul McKee	20.00
68	Bill Moore	20.00
69	Frank Minini	100.00
70	Jack Ferrante	20.00
71	*Leslie Horvath*	40.00
72	Ted Fritsch, Sr.	100.00
73	Tex Coulter	20.00
74	Boley Dancewicz	20.00
75	Dante Mangani	100.00
76	James Hefti	20.00
77	Paul Sarringhaus	20.00
78	Joe Scott	100.00
79	*Bucko Kilroy*	30.00
80	*Bill Dudley*	100.00
81	Marshall Goldberg	100.00
82	John Cannady	20.00
83	Perry Moss	20.00
84	Harold Crisler	100.00
85	Bill Gray	20.00
86	John Clement	20.00
87	Dan Sandifer	100.00
88	Ben Kish	20.00
89	Herbert Banta	20.00
90	Bill Garnaas	100.00
91	Jim White	20.00
92	Frank Barzilauskas	20.00
93	Vic Sears	100.00
94	John Adams	20.00
95	*George McAfee*	100.00
96	Ralph Heywood	100.00
97	Joe Muha	20.00
98	Fred Enke	20.00
99	*Harry Gilmer*	160.00
100	Bill Miklich	20.00
101	Joe Gottieb	20.00
102	Bud Angsman	100.00
103	Tom Farmer	20.00
104	*Bruce F. Smith*	50.00
105	Bob Cifers	100.00
106	Ernie Steele	20.00
107	*Sid Luckman*	220.00
108	*Buford Ray*	350.00

1950 Bowman

After a one-year absence, Bowman returned to football cards with the first of four straight 144-card sets. As with the '48 Bowman set, cards showed only the player on the front without any identification. Cards again measured 2-1/16" x 2-1/2". Rookie cards in this set include Y.A. Tittle, Lou Groza, Tony Canadeo, Joe Perry, Marion Motley, Otto Graham, Tom Fears, Elroy Hirsch, Dante Lavelli, Tobin Rote and Dub Jones.

		NM
Complete Set (144):		4250.
Common Player:		20.00
1	Doak Walker	175.00
2	John Greene	20.00
3	Bob Nowasky	20.00
4	Jonathan Jenkins	20.00
5	*Y.A. Tittle*	300.00
6	*Lou Groza*	180.00
7	*Alex Agase*	20.00
8	*Mac Speedie*	35.00
9	*Tony Canadeo*	55.00
10	Larry Craig	20.00
11	Ted Fritsch, Sr.	20.00
12	Joe Goldring	20.00
13	Martin Ruby	20.00
14	George Taliaferro	20.00
15	*Tank Younger*	50.00
16	*Glenn Davis*	130.00
17	Bob Waterfield	75.00
18	Val Jansante	20.00
19	Joe Geri	20.00
20	Jerry Nuzum	20.00
21	Elmer Angsman	20.00
22	Billy Dewell	20.00
23	Steve Van Buren	60.00
24	Cliff Patton	20.00
25	Bosh Pritchard	20.00
26	John Lujack	60.00
27	Sid Luckman	80.00
28	Bulldog Turner	45.00
29	Bill Dudley	45.00
30	Hugh Taylor	20.00
31	George Thomas	20.00
32	Ray Poole	20.00
33	Travis Tidwell	20.00
34	Gail Bruce	20.00
35	*Joe Perry*	160.00
36	*Frankie Albert*	35.00
37	Bobby Layne	190.00
38	Leon Hart	30.00
39	Bob Hoernschemeyer	20.00
40	*Dick Barwegan*	20.00
41	*Adrian Burk*	20.00
42	Barry French	20.00
43	*Marion Motley*	130.00
44	Jim Martin	20.00
45	*Otto Graham*	450.00
46	Al Baldwin	20.00
47	Larry Coutre	20.00
48	John Rauch	20.00
49	Sam Tamburo	20.00
50	Mike Swistowicz	20.00
51	*Tom Fears*	80.00
52	*Elroy Hirsch*	150.00
53	Dick Huffman	20.00
54	Bob Cage	20.00
55	Bob Tinsley	20.00
56	Bill Blackburn	20.00
57	John Cochran	20.00
58	Bill Fischer	20.00
59	Whitey Wistert	20.00
60	Clyde Scott	20.00
61	Walter Barnes	20.00
62	Bob Perina	20.00
63	Bill Wightkin	20.00
64	Bob Goode	20.00
65	Al Demao	20.00
66	Harry Gilmer	20.00
67	Bill Austin	20.00
68	Joe Scott	20.00
69	Tex Coulter	20.00
70	Paul Salata	20.00
71	Emil Sitko	20.00
72	Bill Johnson	20.00
73	*Don Doll*	20.00
74	Dan Sandifer	20.00
75	John Panelli	20.00
76	Bill Leonard	20.00
77	Bob Kelly	20.00
78	*Dante Lavelli*	80.00
79	Tony Adamle	20.00
80	Dick Wildung	20.00
81	*Tobin Rote*	35.00
82	Paul Burris	20.00
83	Lowell Tew	20.00
84	Barney Poole	20.00
85	Fred Naumetz	20.00
86	Dick Hoerner	20.00
87	Bob Reinhard	20.00
88	Howard Hartley	20.00
89	Darrell Hogan	20.00
90	Jerry Shipkey	20.00
91	Frank Tripucka	20.00
92	Garrard Ramsey	20.00
93	Pat Harder	20.00
94	Vic Sears	20.00
95	Tommy Thompson	20.00
96	Bucko Kilroy	20.00
97	George Connor	35.00
98	Fred Morrison	20.00
99	Jim Keane	20.00
100	Sammy Baugh	200.00
101	Harry Ulinski	20.00
102	Frank Spaniel	20.00
103	Charlie Conerly	60.00
104	Dick Hensley	20.00
105	Eddie Price	20.00
106	Ed Carr	20.00
107	Leo Nomellini	60.00
108	Verl Lillywhite	20.00
109	Wallace Triplett	20.00
110	Joe Watson	20.00
111	*Cloyce Box*	20.00
112	Billy Stone	20.00
113	Earl Murray	20.00
114	*Chet Mutryn*	20.00
115	Ken Carpenter	20.00
116	*Lou Rymkus*	20.00
117	*Dub Jones*	20.00
118	Clayton Tonnemaker	20.00
119	Walt Schlinkman	20.00
120	Billy Grimes	20.00
121	*George Ratterman*	20.00
122	Bob Mann	20.00
123	*Buddy Young*	50.00
124	Jack Zilly	20.00
125	Tom Kalmanir	20.00
126	Frank Sinkovitz	20.00
127	Elbert Nickel	20.00
128	*Jim Finks*	45.00
129	Charlie Trippi	45.00
130	Tom Wham	20.00
131	Ventan Yablonski	20.00
132	Chuck Bednarik	75.00
133	Joe Muha	20.00
134	Pete Pihos	45.00
135	Washington Serini	20.00
136	George Gulyanics	20.00
137	Ken Kavanaugh	20.00
138	Howie Livingston	20.00
139	Joe Tereshinski	20.00
140	Jim White	20.00
141	Gene Roberts	20.00
142	William Swiacki	20.00
143	Norm Standlee	20.00
144	*Knox Ramsey*	60.00

1951 Bowman

Bowman's third set was again 144 cards, but cards were increased in size to 2-1/16" x 3-1/8". Cards bear a close similarity to this year's Bowman baseball set on both fronts and backs. Rookies in this set include Norm Van Brocklin, Tom Landry, Arnie Weinmeister, Bill Walsh, Emlen Tunnell, and Ernie Stautner.

		NM
Complete Set (144):		3500.
Common Player:		18.00
1	*Weldon Humble*	60.00
2	Otto Graham	150.00
3	Mac Speedie	18.00
4	*Norm Van Brocklin*	250.00
5	Woodley Lewis	18.00
6	Tom Fears	35.00
7	George Musacco	18.00
8	George Taliaferro	18.00
9	Barney Poole	18.00
10	Steve Van Buren	60.00
11	Whitey Wistert	18.00
12	Chuck Bednarik	60.00
13	Bulldog Turner	40.00
14	Bob Williams	18.00
15	John Lujack	50.00
16	Roy "Rebel" Steiner	18.00
17	Earl "Jug" Girard	18.00
18	Bill Neal	18.00
19	Travis Tidwell	18.00
20	*Tom Landry*	500.00
21	*Arnie Weinmeister*	40.00
22	Joe Geri	18.00
23	*Bill Walsh*	18.00
24	Fran Rogel	18.00
25	Doak Walker	50.00
26	Leon Hart	18.00
27	Thurman McGraw	18.00
28	Buster Ramsey	18.00
29	Frank Tripucka	18.00
30	Don Paul	18.00
31	Alex Loyd	18.00
32	Y.A. Tittle	120.00
33	Verl Lillywhite	18.00
34	Sammy Baugh	150.00
35	Chuck Drazenovich	18.00
36	Bob Goode	18.00
37	Horace Gillom	18.00
38	Lou Rymkus	18.00
39	Ken Carpenter	18.00
40	Bob Waterfield	60.00
41	Vitamin Smith	18.00
42	Glenn Davis	50.00
43	Dan Edwards	18.00
44	John Rauch	18.00
45	Zollie Toth	18.00
46	Pete Pihos	30.00
47	Russ Craft	18.00
48	Walter Barnes	18.00
49	Fred Morrison	18.00
50	Ray Bray	18.00
51	*Ed Sprinkle*	18.00
52	Floyd Reid	18.00
53	Billy Grimes	18.00
54	Ted Fritsch, Sr.	18.00
55	Al DeRogatis	18.00
56	Charlie Conerly	50.00
57	Jon Baker	18.00
58	Tom McWilliams	18.00
59	Jerry Shipkey	18.00
60	Lynn Chandnois	18.00
61	Don Doll	18.00
62	Lou Creekmur	35.00
63	Bob Hoernschemeyer	18.00
64	Tom Wham	18.00
65	Bill Fischer	18.00
66	Robert Nussbaumer	18.00
67	Gordon Soltau	18.00
68	Visco Grgich	18.00
69	John Strzykalski	18.00
70	Pete Stout	18.00
71	Paul Lipscomb	18.00
72	Harry Gilmer	18.00
73	Dante Lavelli	40.00
74	Dub Jones	18.00
75	Lou Groza	70.00
76	Elroy Hirsch	60.00
77	Tom Kalmanir	18.00
78	Jack Zilly	18.00
79	Bruce Alford	18.00
80	Art Weiner	18.00
81	Brad Ecklund	18.00
82	Bosh Pritchard	18.00
83	John Green	18.00
84	H. Ebert Van Buren	18.00
85	Julie Rykovich	18.00
86	Fred Davis	18.00
87	John Hoffman	18.00
88	Tobin Rote	18.00
89	Paul Burris	18.00
90	Tony Canadeo	30.00
91	*Emlen Tunnell*	100.00
92	Otto Schnellbacher	18.00
93	Ray Poole	18.00
94	Darrell Hogan	18.00
95	Frank Sinkovitz	18.00
96	Ernie Stautner	70.00
97	Elmer Angsman	18.00
98	Jack Jennings	18.00
99	Jerry Groom	18.00
100	John Prchlik	18.00
101	J. Robert Smith	18.00
102	Bobby Layne	120.00
103	Frankie Albert	18.00
104	Gail Bruce	18.00
105	Joe Perry	60.00
106	Leon Heath	18.00
107	Ed Quirk	18.00
108	Hugh Taylor	18.00
109	Marion Motley	50.00
110	Tony Adamle	18.00
111	Alex Agase	18.00
112	Tank Younger	18.00
113	Bob Boyd	18.00
114	Jerry Williams	18.00
115	Joe Goldring	18.00
116	Sherman Howard	18.00
117	John Wozniak	18.00
118	Frank Reagan	18.00
119	Vic Sears	18.00
120	Clyde Scott	18.00
121	George Gulyanics	18.00
122	Bill Wightkin	18.00
123	Chuck Hunsinger	18.00
124	Jack Cloud	18.00
125	Abner Wimberly	18.00
126	Dick Wildung	18.00
127	Eddie Price	18.00
128	Joe Scott	18.00
129	Jerry Nuzum	18.00
130	Jim Finks	40.00
131	Bob Gage	18.00
132	William Swiacki	18.00
133	Joe Watson	18.00
134	Ollie Cline	18.00
135	Jack Lininger	18.00
136	Fran Polsfoot	18.00
137	Charlie Trippi	40.00
138	Ventan Yablonski	18.00
139	Emil Sitko	18.00
140	Leo Nomellini	50.00
141	Norm Standlee	18.00
142	Eddie Saenz	18.00
143	Al Demao	18.00
144	Bill Dudley	75.00

1952 Bowman Large

The player selection in the "Large" set exactly matches Bowman's 1952 "Small" issue. The card size, however, was increased from 2-1/16" x 3-1/8" to 2-1/2" x 3-3/4". A problem surfaced for Bowman while trying to produce the larger set: the company could not fit all the larger cards on one sheet the way it could with the smaller set. So certain cards were pulled. The short-printed cards are those with a factor of nine plus the card immediately following that number. In addition, the second series was issued in lesser quantities than the first. The 1952 Bowman Large set is easily the most valuable football card set ever produced. Card #144, Jim "Buck" Lansford, is practically impossible to find in mint condition, first because it was an odd number on the last sheet, second because it was the last card in the set.

		NM
Complete Set (144):		12000.
Common Player (1-72):		25.00
Common Player (73-144):		35.00
1	Norm Van Brocklin	425.00
2	Otto Graham	275.00
3	Doak Walker	75.00
4	*Steve Owen*	50.00
5	Frankie Albert	30.00
6	Laurie Niemi	25.00
7	Chuck Hunsinger	25.00
8	Ed Modzelewski	30.00
9	Joe Spencer (SP)	75.00
10	Chuck Bednarik (SP)	175.00
11	Barney Poole	25.00
12	Charlie Trippi	50.00
13	Tom Fears	50.00
14	*Paul Brown*	225.00
15	Leon Hart	30.00
16	*Frank Gifford*	475.00
17	Y.A. Tittle	175.00
18	Charlie Justice (SP)	150.00
19	George Connor (SP)	125.00
20	Lynn Chandnois	25.00
21	*Bill Howton*	35.00
22	Kenneth Snyder	25.00
23	*Gino Marchetti*	200.00
24	John Karras	25.00
25	Tank Younger	30.00
26	Tommy Thompson	25.00
27	*Bob Miller* (SP)	285.00
28	*Kyle Rote* (SP)	140.00
29	*Hugh McElhenny*	200.00
30	Sammy Baugh	350.00
31	Jim Dooley	25.00
32	Ray Matthews	25.00
33	Fred Cone	25.00
34	Al Pollard	25.00
35	Brad Ecklund	25.00
36	*John Lee Hancock*	350.00
37	Elroy Hirsch (SP)	150.00
38	Keever Jankovich	25.00
39	Emlen Tunnell	60.00
40	Steve Dowden	25.00
41	Claude Hipps	25.00
42	Norm Standlee	25.00
43	Dick Todd	25.00
44	Babe Parilli	30.00
45	Steve Van Buren (SP)	225.00
46	*Art Donovan* (SP)	350.00
47	Bill Fischer	25.00
48	*George Halas*	275.00
49	Jerrell Price	25.00
50	*John Sandusky*	35.00
51	Ray Beck	25.00
52	Jim Martin	25.00
53	Joe Back	25.00
54	Glen Christian (SP)	75.00
55	Andy Davis (SP)	75.00
56	Tobin Rote	30.00
57	*Wayne Millner*	70.00
58	Zollie Toth	25.00
59	Jack Jennings	25.00
60	Bill McColl	25.00
61	*Les Richter*	30.00
62	*Walt Michaels*	30.00
63	Charlie Conerly (SP)	475.00
64	Howard Hartley (SP)	75.00
65	Jerome Smith	25.00
66	James Clark	25.00
67	Dick Logan	25.00
68	Wayne Robinson	25.00
69	James Hammond	25.00
70	Gene Schroeder	25.00
71	Tex Coulter	25.00
72	*John Schweder* (SP)	500.00
73	Vitamin Smith (SP)	150.00
74	Joe Campanella	35.00
75	*Joe Kuharich*	35.00
76	Herman Clark	35.00
77	Dan Edwards	35.00
78	Bobby Layne	225.00
79	Bob Hoernschemeyer	35.00
80	John Carr Blount	35.00
81	John Kastan (SP)	150.00
82	*Harry Minarik* (SP)	130.00
83	Joe Perry	80.00
84	Ray Parker	35.00
85	*Andy Robustelli*	175.00
86	Dub Jones	40.00
87	Mal Cook	35.00
88	Billy Stone	35.00
89	George Taliaferro	35.00
90	Thomas Johnson (SP)	150.00
91	Leon Heath (SP)	100.00
92	Pete Pihos	75.00
93	Fred Benners	35.00
94	George Tarasovic	35.00
95	Lawrence Shaw	35.00
96	Bill Wightkin	35.00
97	John Wozniak	35.00
98	Bobby Dillon	35.00
99	*Joe Stydahar* (SP)	575.00
100	Dick Alban (SP)	150.00
101	Arnie Weinmeister	55.00
102	Robert Joe Cross	35.00
103	Don Paul	35.00
104	Buddy Young	50.00
105	Lou Groza	100.00
106	Ray Pelfrey	35.00
107	Maurice Nipp	35.00
108	*Hubert Johnston*	625.00
109	Volney Quinlan (SP)	100.00
110	Jack Simmons	35.00
111	George Ratterman	35.00
112	John Badaczewski	35.00
113	Bill Reichardt	35.00
114	Art Weiner	35.00
115	Keith Flowers	35.00
116	Russ Craft	35.00
117	Jim O'Donahue (SP)	150.00
118	Darrell Hogan (SP)	100.00
119	Frank Ziegler	35.00
120	Deacon Dan Towler	40.00
121	Fred Williams	35.00
122	Jimmy Phelan	35.00
123	Eddie Price	35.00
124	Chet Ostrowski	35.00
125	Leo Nomellini	70.00
126	*Steve Romanik* (SP)	300.00
127	*Ollie Matson* (SP)	300.00
128	Dante Lavelli	75.00
129	*Jack Christiansen*	150.00
130	Dom Moselle	35.00
131	John Rapacz	35.00
132	Chuck Ortman	35.00
133	Bob Williams	35.00
134	Chuck Ulrich	35.00
135	*Gene Ronzani* (SP)	625.00
136	Bert Rechichar (SP)	100.00
137	Bob Waterfield	120.00
138	*Bobby Walston*	40.00
139	Jerry Shipkey	35.00
140	*Yale Lary*	150.00
141	Gordon Soltau	40.00
142	Tom Landry	600.00
143	John Papit	35.00
144	*Jim Lansford* (SP)	2800.

1952 Bowman Small

This set was issued in two sizes, large and small, with the large size being much more scarce and expensive.

The Bowman Small set measures 2-1/16" x 3-1/8", and cards feature a flag motif, with flags pointing to the right (two years later, Bowman would use about the same theme, with flags pointing left). This 144-card set features an abdundance of rookie cards. They include Steve Owen, Paul Brown, Frank Gifford, Gino Marchetti, Kyle Rote, Hugh McElhenny, George Halas, Wayne Millner, Walt Michaels, Andy Robustelli, Joe Stydahar, Ollie Matson and Yale Lary.

	NM
Complete Set (144):	5000.
Common Player (1-72):	20.00
Common Player (73-144):	25.00

1	Norm Van Brocklin	200.00
2	Otto Graham	125.00
3	Doak Walker	35.00
4	*Steve Owen*	35.00
5	Frankie Albert	20.00
6	Laurie Niemi	20.00
7	Chuck Hunsinger	20.00
8	Ed Modzelewski	20.00
9	Joe Spencer	20.00
10	Chuck Bednarik	60.00
11	Barney Poole	20.00
12	Charlie Trippi	30.00
13	Tom Fears	30.00
14	*Paul Brown*	125.00
15	Leon Hart	17.50
16	*Frank Gifford*	325.00
17	Y.A. Tittle	80.00
18	Charlie Justice	30.00
19	George Connor	30.00
20	Lynn Chandnois	20.00
21	*Bill Howton*	30.00
22	Kenneth Snyder	20.00
23	*Gino Marchetti*	100.00
24	John Karras	20.00
25	Tank Younger	25.00
26	Tommy Thompson	25.00
27	Bob Miller	20.00
28	*Kyle Rote*	50.00
29	*Hugh McElhenny*	125.00
30	Sammy Baugh	200.00
31	Jim Dooley	25.00
32	Ray Matthews	20.00
33	Fred Cone	20.00
34	Al Pollard	20.00
35	Brad Ecklund	20.00
36	John Lee Hancock	20.00
37	Elroy Hirsch	50.00
38	Keever Jankovich	20.00
39	Emlen Tunnell	35.00
40	Steve Dowden	20.00
41	Claude Hipps	20.00
42	Norm Standlee	20.00
43	Dick Todd	20.00
44	Babe Parilli	25.00
45	Steve Van Buren	45.00
46	*Art Donovan*	150.00
47	Bill Fischer	20.00
48	*George Halas*	150.00
49	Jerrell Price	20.00
50	John Sandusky	20.00
51	Ray Beck	20.00
52	Jim Martin	20.00
53	Joe Back	20.00
54	Glen Christian	20.00
55	Andy Davis	20.00
56	Tobin Rote	25.00
57	*Wayne Millner*	35.00
58	Zollie Toth	20.00
59	Jack Jennings	20.00
60	Bill McColl	20.00
61	*Les Richter*	25.00
62	*Walt Michaels*	25.00
63	Charlie Conerly	50.00
64	Howard Hartley	20.00
65	Jerome Smith	20.00
66	James Clark	20.00
67	Dick Logan	20.00
68	Wayne Robinson	20.00
69	James Hammond	20.00
70	Gene Schroeder	20.00
71	Tex Coulter	20.00
72	John Schweder	20.00
73	Vitamin Smith	25.00
74	Joe Campanella	25.00
75	Joe Kuharich	25.00
76	Herman Clark	25.00
77	Dan Edwards	25.00
78	Bobby Layne	90.00
79	Bob Hoernschemeyer	25.00
80	John Carr Blount	25.00
81	John Kastan	25.00
82	Harry Minarik	25.00
83	Joe Perry	60.00
84	Ray Parker	25.00
85	*Andy Robustelli*	100.00
86	Dub Jones	25.00
87	Mal Cook	25.00
88	Billy Stone	25.00
89	George Taliaferro	25.00
90	Thomas Johnson	25.00
91	Leon Heath	25.00
92	Pete Pihos	40.00
93	Fred Benners	25.00
94	George Tarasovic	25.00
95	Lawrence Shaw	25.00
96	Bill Wightkin	25.00
97	John Wozniak	25.00
98	*Bobby Dillon*	25.00
99	*Joe Stydahar*	40.00
100	Dick Alban	25.00
101	Arnie Weinmeister	35.00
102	Robert Joe Cross	25.00
103	Don Paul	25.00
104	Buddy Young	30.00
105	Lou Groza	50.00
106	Ray Pelfrey	25.00
107	Maurice Nipp	25.00
108	Hubert Johnston	25.00
109	Volney Quinlan	25.00
110	Jack Simmons	25.00
111	George Ratterman	25.00
112	John Badaczewski	25.00
113	Bill Reichardt	25.00
114	Art Weiner	25.00
115	Keith Flowers	25.00
116	Russ Craft	25.00
117	Jim O'Donahue	25.00
118	Darrell Hogan	25.00
119	Frank Ziegler	25.00
120	Deacon Dan Towler	30.00
121	Fred Williams	25.00
122	Jimmy Phelan	25.00
123	Eddie Price	25.00
124	Chet Ostrowski	25.00
125	Leo Nomellini	50.00
126	Steve Romanik	25.00
127	*Ollie Matson*	120.00
128	Dante Lavelli	40.00
129	*Jack Christiansen*	75.00
130	Dom Moselle	25.00
131	John Rapacz	25.00
132	Chuck Ortman	25.00
133	Bob Williams	25.00
134	Chuck Ulrich	25.00
135	*Gene Ronzani*	28.00
136	Bert Rechichar	25.00
137	Bob Waterfield	60.00
138	*Bobby Walston*	30.00
139	Jerry Shipkey	25.00
140	*Yale Lary*	80.00
141	Gordon Soltau	25.00
142	Tom Landry	300.00
143	John Papit	25.00
144	*Jim Lansford*	125.00

1953 Bowman

The "name in a football" theme was one that would next be used by Topps in its 1960 set and again in the 1976 set. Bowman was the only company to issue football cards, but only a 96-card issue was produced (and 24 of those were short-printed).

	NM
Complete Set (96):	3200.
Common Player:	25.00
SP Cards:	40.00

1	*Eddie LeBaron*	100.00
2	John Dottley	25.00
3	Babe Parilli	25.00
4	Bucko Kilroy	25.00
5	Joe Tereshinski	25.00
6	Doak Walker	50.00
7	Fran Polsfoot	25.00
8	Sisto Averno	25.00
9	Marion Motley	50.00
10	Pat Brady	25.00
11	Norm Van Brocklin	80.00
12	Bill McColl	25.00
13	Jerry Groom	25.00
14	Al Pollard	25.00
15	Dante Lavelli	40.00
16	Eddie Price	25.00
17	Charlie Trippi	40.00
18	Elbert Nickel	25.00
19	George Taliaferro	25.00
20	Charlie Conerly	50.00
21	Bobby Layne	100.00
22	Elroy Hirsch	60.00
23	Jim Finks	35.00
24	Chuck Bednarik	60.00
25	Kyle Rote	30.00
26	Otto Graham	135.00
27	Harry Gilmer	25.00
28	Tobin Rote	25.00
29	Billy Stone	25.00
30	Buddy Young	25.00
31	Leon Hart	25.00
32	Hugh McElhenny	60.00
33	Dale Samuels	25.00
34	Lou Creekmur	25.00
35	Tom Catlin	25.00
36	Tom Fears	40.00
37	George Connor	35.00
38	Bill Walsh	25.00
39	Leo Sanford (SP)	40.00
40	Horace Gillom	25.00
41	John Schweder (SP)	40.00
42	Tom O'Connell	25.00
43	Frank Gifford (SP)	350.00
44	Frank Continetti (SP)	40.00
45	John Olszewski (SP)	40.00
46	Dub Jones	25.00
47	Don Paul (SP)	40.00
48	Gerald Weatherly	25.00
49	Fred Bruney (SP)	40.00
50	Jack Scarbath	25.00
51	John Karras	25.00
52	Al Conway	25.00
53	Emlen Tunnell (SP)	100.00
54	Gern Nagler (SP)	40.00
55	Kenneth Snyder (SP)	40.00
56	Y.A. Tittle	100.00
57	John Rapacz (SP)	40.00
58	Harley Sewell	40.00
59	Don Bingham	25.00
60	Darrell Hogan	25.00
61	Tony Curcillo	25.00
62	*Ray Renfro* (SP)	50.00
63	Leon Heath	25.00
64	Tex Coulter (SP)	40.00
65	Dewayne Douglas	25.00
66	J. Robert Smith (SP)	40.00
67	Bob McChesney (SP)	40.00
68	Dick Alban (SP)	40.00
69	Andy Kozar	25.00
70	Merwin Hodel (SP)	40.00
71	Thurman McGraw	25.00
72	Cliff Anderson	25.00
73	Pete Pihos	40.00
74	Julie Rykovich	25.00
75	John Kreamcheck (SP)	40.00
76	Lynn Chandnois (SP)	40.00
77	Cloyce Box (SP)	40.00
78	Ray Matthews	25.00
79	Bobby Walston	25.00
80	Jim Dooley	25.00
81	Pat Harder (SP)	40.00
82	Jerry Shipkey	25.00
83	Bobby Thomason	25.00
84	Hugh Taylor	25.00
85	George Ratterman	25.00
86	Don Stonesifer	25.00
87	John Williams (SP)	40.00
88	Leo Nomellini	45.00
89	Frank Ziegler	25.00
90	Don Paul	25.00
91	Tom Dublinski	25.00
92	Ken Carpenter	25.00
93	*Ted Marchibroda*	40.00
94	Chuck Drazenovich	25.00
95	Lou Groza (SP)	100.00
96	William Cross (SP)	75.00

1954 Bowman

This 128-card set has a flag motif that points left, almost a reversal of the 1952 theme. Issued in four series of 32 cards, numbers 65-96 are much tougher to find than the other three. Rookies in this set include Doug Atkins, George Blanda, Hawg Hanner and Whizzer White (actually not Whizzer White; see below). There's an error and a variation in this set. The error is on card #125 "Whizzer" White, his rookie card. It shows not the future Supreme Court Justice, but Wilford White. The variation involves #97, Tom Finnan. On the scarcer error version, his name was incorrectly spelled "Finnin." This was corrected.

	NM
Complete Set (128):	1600.
Common Player (1-64):	6.00
Common Player (65-96):	25.00
Common Player (97-128):	6.00

1	Ray Matthews	25.00
2	John Huzvar	6.00
3	Jack Scarbath	6.00
4	*Doug Atkins*	45.00
5	Bill Stits	6.00
6	Joe Perry	30.00
7	Kyle Rote	12.00
8	Norm Van Brocklin	45.00
9	Pete Pihos	20.00
10	Babe Parilli	10.00
11	*Zeke Bratkowski*	25.00
12	Ollie Matson	25.00
13	Pat Brady	6.00
14	Fred Enke	6.00
15	Harry Ulinski	6.00
16	Bobby Garrett	6.00
17	Bill Bowman	6.00
18	Leo Rucka	6.00
19	John Cannady	6.00
20	Tom Fears	20.00
21	Norm Willey	6.00
22	Floyd Reid	6.00
23	*George Blanda*	180.00
24	Don Doheney	6.00
25	John Schweder	6.00
26	Bert Rechichar	6.00
27	Harry Dowda	6.00
28	John Sandusky	6.00
29	*Les Bingaman*	10.00
30	Joe Arenas	6.00
31	Ray Wietecha	8.00
32	Elroy Hirsch	30.00
33	Harold Giancanelli	6.00
34	Bill Howton	10.00
35	Fred Morrison	6.00
36	Bobby Cavazos	6.00
37	Darrell Hogan	6.00
38	Buddy Young	7.00
39	Charlie Justice	14.00
40	Otto Graham	75.00
41	Doak Walker	25.00
42	Y.A. Tittle	50.00
43	Buford Long	6.00
44	Volney Quinlan	6.00
45	Bobby Thomason	7.00
46	Fred Cone	6.00
47	Gerald Weatherly	6.00
48	Don Stonesifer	6.00
49	Lynn Chandnois	6.00
50	George Taliaferro	6.00
51	Dick Alban	6.00
52	Lou Groza	25.00
53	Bobby Layne	50.00
54	Hugh McElhenny	30.00
55	Frank Gifford	100.00
56	Leon McLaughlin	6.00
57	Chuck Bednarik	30.00
58	Art Hunter	6.00
59	Bill McColl	6.00
60	Charlie Trippi	25.00
61	*Jim Finks*	10.00
62	Bill Lange	6.00
63	Laurie Niemi	6.00
64	Ray Renfro	6.00
65	Dick Chapman	25.00
66	Bob Hantla	25.00
67	Ralph Starkey	25.00
68	Don Paul	25.00
69	Kenneth Snyder	25.00
70	Tobin Rote	25.00
71	Arthur DeCarlo	25.00
72	Tom Keane	25.00
73	Hugh Taylor	25.00
74	*Warren Lahr*	25.00
75	Jim Neal	25.00
76	Leo Nomellini	50.00
77	Dick Yelvington	25.00
78	Les Richter	25.00
79	Bucko Kilroy	25.00
80	John Martinkovic	25.00
81	*Dale Dodrill*	25.00
82	Ken Jackson	25.00
83	Paul Lipscomb	25.00
84	John Bauer	25.00
85	Lou Creekmur	50.00
86	Eddie Price	25.00
87	Kenneth Farragut	25.00
88	*Dave Hanner*	25.00
89	Don Boll	25.00
90	Chet Hanulak	25.00
91	Thurman McGraw	25.00
92	*Don Heinrich*	25.00
93	Dan McKown	25.00
94	Bob Fleck	25.00
95	Jerry Hilgenberg	25.00
96	Bill Walsh	25.00
97	Tom Finnin	50.00
98	Paul Barry	6.00
99	Harry Jagade	6.00
100	Jack Christiansen	20.00
101	Gordon Soltau	6.00
102	Emlen Tunnell	20.00
103	Stan West	6.00
104	Jerry Williams	6.00
105	Veryl Switzer	6.00
106	Billy Stone	6.00
107	Jerry Watford	6.00
108	Elbert Nickel	6.00
109	Ed Sharkey	6.00
110	Steve Meilinger	6.00
111	Dante Lavelli	20.00
112	Leon Hart	14.00
113	Charlie Conerly	30.00
114	Richard Lemmon	6.00
115	Al Carmichael	6.00
116	George Conner	15.00
117	John Olszewski	6.00
118	Ernie Stautner	20.00
119	Ray Smith	6.00
120	Neil Worden	6.00
121	Jim Dooley	6.00
122	Arnold Galiffa	6.00
123	Kline Gilbert	6.00
124	Bob Hoernschemeyer	6.00
125	*Whizzer White*	15.00
126	Art Spinney	6.00
127	Joe Koch	6.00
128	*John Lattner*	75.00

1955 Bowman

An excellent run of football cards ended after this year when the Bowman Co. released its last set of 160 cards. (Its competitor, Topps Chewing Gum Co., bought it early in 1956). The first 64 cards are relatively easy to find, compared to numbers 65-160. Rookies in this set include Hall of Famers Mike McCormick, Len Ford, John Henry Johnson, Bob St. Clair, Jim Ringo, and Frank Gatski. Other rookies include Pat Summerall and Alan Ameche.

	NM
Complete Set (160):	1500.
Common Player (1-64):	4.50
Common Player (65-160):	6.00

1	Doak Walker	50.00
2	*Mike McCormack*	30.00
3	John Olszewski	4.50
4	Dorne Dibble	4.50
5	Lindon Crow	4.50
6	Hugh Taylor	4.50
7	Frank Gifford	75.00
8	*Alan Ameche*	30.00
9	Don Stonesifer	4.50
10	Pete Pihos	12.50
11	Bill Austin	4.50
12	Dick Alban	4.50
13	Bobby Walston	4.50
14	*Len Ford*	30.00
15	Jug Girard	4.50
16	Charlie Conerly	25.00
17	Volney Peters	4.50
18	Max Boydston	4.50
19	Leon Hart	6.00
20	Bert Rechichar	4.50
21	Lee Riley	4.50
22	Johnny Carson	4.50
23	Harry Thompson	4.50
24	Ray Wietecha	4.50
25	Ollie Matson	25.00
26	Eddie LeBaron	8.00
27	Jack Simmons	4.50
28	Jack Christiansen	12.50
29	Bucko Kilroy	4.50
30	Tom Keane	4.50
31	Dave Leggett	4.50
32	Norm Van Brocklin	35.00
33	Harlon Hill	6.00
34	Robert Haner	4.50
35	Veryl Switzer	4.50
36	Dick Stanfel	6.00
37	Lou Groza	24.00
38	Tank Younger	5.00
39	Dick Flanagan	4.50
40	Jim Dooley	4.50
41	Ray Collins	4.50
42	*John Henry Johnson*	40.00
43	Tom Fears	15.00
44	Joe Perry	25.00
45	Gene Brito	6.00
46	Bill Johnson	4.50
47	Deacon Dan Towler	6.00
48	Dick Moegle	4.50
49	Kline Gilbert	4.50
50	Les Gobel	4.50
51	Ray Krouse	4.50
52	*Pat Summerall*	55.00
53	*Ed Brown*	8.00
54	Lynn Chandnois	4.50
55	Joe Heap	4.50
56	John Hoffman	4.50
57	Howard Ferguson	4.50
58	Bobby Watkins	4.50
59	Charlie Ane	4.50
60	*Ken MacAfee*	6.00
61	*Ralph Guglielmi*	6.00
62	George Blanda	70.00
63	Kenneth Snyder	4.50
64	Chet Ostrowski	4.50
65	Buddy Young	5.00
66	Gordon Soltau	6.00
67	Eddie Bell	6.00
68	*Ben Agajanian*	8.00
69	Tom Dahms	6.00
70	*Jim Ringo*	35.00
71	Bobby Layne	60.00
72	Y.A. Tittle	60.00
73	Bob Gaona	6.00
74	Tobin Rote	10.00
75	Hugh McElhenny	20.00
76	John Kreamcheck	6.00
77	Al Dorow	6.00
78	Bill Wade	9.00
79	Dale Dodrill	6.00
80	Chuck Drazenovich	6.00
81	*Billy Wilson*	10.00
82	Les Richter	6.00
83	Pat Brady	6.00
84	Bob Hoernschemeyer	6.00
85	Joe Arenas	6.00
86	Len Szafaryn	6.00
87	*Rick Casares*	16.00
88	Leon McLaughlin	6.00
89	Charley Toogood	6.00
90	Tom Bettis	6.00
91	John Sandusky	6.00
92	Bill Wightkin	6.00
93	Darrell Brewster	6.00
94	Marion Campbell	8.00
95	Floyd Reid	6.00
96	Harry Jagade	6.00
97	George Taliaferro	6.00
98	Carleton Massey	6.00
99	Fran Rogel	6.00
100	Alex Sandusky	6.00
101	*Bob St. Clair*	35.00
102	Al Carmichael	6.00
103	Carl Taseff	8.00
104	Leo Nomellini	18.00
105	Tom Scott	6.00
106	Ted Marchibroda	16.00
107	Art Spinney	6.00
108	Wayne Robinson	6.00
109	Jim Ricca	6.00
110	Lou Ferry	6.00
111	Roger Zatkoff	6.00
112	Lou Creekmur	6.00
113	Kenny Konz	6.00
114	Doug Eggers	6.00
115	Bobby Thomason	6.00
116	Bill McPeak	6.00
117	William Brown	6.00
118	Royce Womble	6.00
119	*Frank Gatski*	28.00
120	Jim Finks	8.00
121	Andy Robustelli	20.00
122	Bobby Dillon	6.00
123	Leo Sanford	6.00
124	Elbert Nickel	6.00
125	Wayne Hansen	6.00
126	Buck Lansford	6.00
127	Gern Nagler	6.00
128	Jim Salsbury	6.00
129	Dale Atkeson	6.00
130	John Schweder	6.00
131	Dave Hanner	6.00
132	Eddie Price	6.00
133	Vic Janowicz	20.00
134	Ernie Stautner	20.00
135	James Parmer	6.00
136	Emlen Tunnell	20.00
137	Kyle Rote	14.00
138	Norm Willey	6.00
139	Charlie Trippi	18.00
140	Bill Howton	8.00
141	Bobby Clatterbuck	6.00
142	Bob Boyd	6.00
143	*Bob Toneff*	6.00
144	Jerry Helluin	6.00
145	Adrian Burk	6.00
146	Walt Michaels	8.00
147	Zillie Toth	6.00
148	*Frank Varrichione*	8.00
149	Dick Bielski	6.00
150	George Ratterman	6.00
151	Mike Jarmoluk	6.00
152	Tom Landry	175.00
153	Ray Renfro	6.00
154	Zeke Bratkowski	7.50
155	Jerry Norton	6.00
156	Maurice Bassett	6.00
157	Volney Quinlan	6.00
158	Chuck Bednarik	25.00
159	Don Colo	6.00
160	*L.G. Dupre*	30.00

1991 Bowman

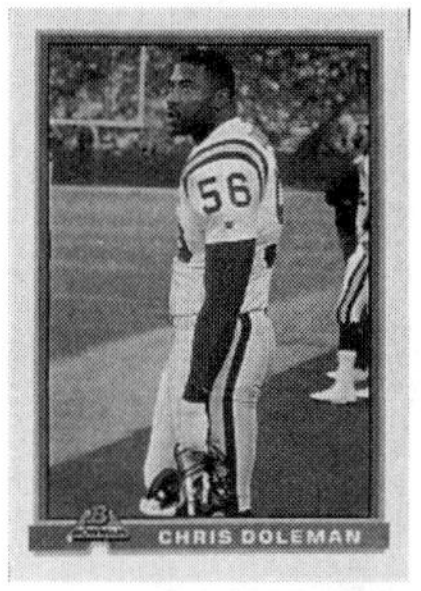

Topps produced this 561-card set in 1991 under the Bowman name. The standard-size cards have color photos on the front, with blue and orange borders. The player's name is in white in a purple stripe at the bottom. The grey backs, in green and black type, have a player profile, biography and statistics. The cards are numbered alphabetically by team, beginning with Atlanta and ending with Washington. Subsets include League Leaders (#s 273-283), Rookie Superstars (#s 1-11), and Road to the Super Bowl (#s 547-557). These 33 subset cards are gold-foil embossed, with one appearing in every pack.

	MT
Complete Set (561):	10.00
Common Player:	.03
Pack:	.30
Wax Box (36):	7.00

1	Jeff George (RS)	.10
2	Richmond Webb (RS)	.03
3	Emmitt Smith (RS)	1.00
4	Mark Carrier (RS)	.05
5	Steve Christie (RS)	.03
6	Keith Sims (RS)	.03
7	Rob Moore (RS)	.15
8	Johnny Johnson (RS)	.10
9	Eric Green (RS)	.03
10	Ben Smith (RS)	.03
11	Tory Epps (RS)	.03
12	Andre Rison	.25
13	Shawn Collins	.03
14	Chris Hinton	.03
15	Deion Sanders	.50
16	Darion Conner	.03
17	Michael Haynes	.30
18	Chris Miller	.03
19	Jessie Tuggle	.03
20	Scott Fulhage	.03
21	Bill Fralic	.03
22	Floyd Dixon	.03
23	Oliver Barnett	.03
24	Mike Rozier	.03
25	Tory Epps	.03
26	Tim Green	.03
27	Steve Broussard	.03
28	Bruce Pickens	.03
29	*Mike Pritchard*	.50
30	Andre Reed	.10
31	Darryl Talley	.03
32	Nate Odomes	.03
33	Jamie Mueller	.03
34	Leon Seals	.03
35	Keith McKeller	.03
36	Al Edwards	.03
37	Butch Rolle	.03
38	Jeff Wright	.10
39	Will Wolford	.03
40	James Williams	.03
41	Kent Hull	.03
42	James Lofton	.03
43	Frank Reich	.03
44	Bruce Smith	.03
45	Thurman Thomas	.50
46	Leonard Smith	.03
47	Shane Conlan	.03
48	Steve Tasker	.03
49	Ray Bentley	.03
50	Cornelius Bennett	.03
51	Stan Thomas	.03
52	Shaun Gayle	.03
53	Wendell Davis	.10
54	James Thornton	.03
55	Mark Carrier	.03
56	Richard Dent	.03
57	Ron Morris	.03
58	Mike Singletary	.03
59	Jay Hilgenberg	.03
60	Donnell Woolford	.03
61	Jim Covert	.03
62	Jim Harbaugh	.10
63	Neal Anderson	.10
64	Brad Muster	.03
65	Kevin Butler	.03
66	Trace Armstrong	.03
67	Ron Cox	.03
68	Peter Tom Willis	.03
69	Johnny Bailey	.03
70	Mark Bortz	.03
71	*Chris Zorich*	.25
72	Lamar Rogers	.03
73	David Grant	.03
74	Lewis Billups	.03
75	Harold Green	.15
76	Ickey Woods	.03
77	Eddie Brown	.03
78	David Fulcher	.03
79	Anthony Munoz	.03
80	Carl Zander	.03
81	Rodney Holman	.03
82	James Brooks	.03
83	Tim McGee	.03
84	Boomer Esiason	.15
85	Leon White	.03
86	James Francis	.10
87	Mitchell Price	.03
88	*Ed King*	.10
89	*Eric Turner*	.25
90	*Rob Burnett*	.10
91	Leroy Hoard	.10
92	Kevin Mack	.03
93	Thane Gash	.03
94	Gregg Rakoczy	.03
95	Clay Matthews	.03
96	Eric Metcalf	.03
97	Stephen Braggs	.03
98	Frank Minnifield	.03
99	Reggie Langhorne	.03
100	Mike Johnson	.03
101	Brian Brennan	.03
102	Anthony Pleasant	.03
103	Godfrey Myles	.03
104	*Russell Maryland*	.50
105	*James Washington*	.10
106	Nate Newton	.03
107	Jimmie Jones	.03
108	Jay Novacek	.15
109	Alexander Wright	.10
110	Jack Del Rio	.03
111	Jim Jeffcoat	.03
112	Mike Saxon	.03
113	Troy Aikman	1.00
114	Issiac Holt	.03
115	Ken Norton	.03
116	Kelvin Martin	.03
117	Emmitt Smith	2.00
118	Ken Willis	.03
119	Daniel Stubbs	.03
120	Michael Irvin	.15
121	Danny Noonan	.03
122	*Alvin Harper*	.50
123	*Reggie Johnson*	.10
124	Vance Johnson	.03
125	Steve Atwater	.03
126	Greg Kragen	.03
127	John Elway	.40
128	Simon Fletcher	.03
129	Wymon Henderson	.03
130	Ricky Nattiel	.03
131	Shannon Sharpe	.10
132	Ron Holmes	.03
133	Karl Mecklenburg	.03
134	Bobby Humphrey	.03
135	Clarence Kay	.03
136	Dennis Smith	.03
137	Jim Juriga	.03
138	Melvin Bratton	.03
139	Mark Jackson	.03
140	Michael Brooks	.03
141	Alton Montgomery	.03
142	*Mike Croel*	.15
143	Mel Gray	.03
144	Michael Cofer	.03
145	Jeff Campbell	.03
146	Dan Owens	.03
147	Robert Clark	.03
148	Jim Arnold	.03
149	William White	.03
150	Rodney Peete	.03
151	Jerry Ball	.03
152	Bennie Blades	.03
153	Barry Sanders	1.50
154	Andre Ware	.10
155	Lomas Brown	.03
156	Chris Spielman	.03
157	Kelvin Pritchett	.03
158	*Herman Moore*	3.50
159	Chris Jacke	.03
160	Tony Mandarich	.03
161	Perry Kemp	.03
162	Johnny Holland	.03
163	Mark Lee	.03
164	Anthony Dilweg	.03
165	Scott Stephen	.03
166	Ed West	.03
167	Mark Murphy	.03
168	Darrell Thompson	.15
169	James Campen	.03
170	Jeff Query	.03
171	Brian Noble	.03
172	Sterling Sharpe	.15
173	Robert Brown	.03
174	Tim Harris	.03
175	LeRoy Butler	.03
176	Don Majkowski	.03
177	Vinnie Clark	.03
178	Esera Tuaolo	.03
179	Lorenzo White	.10
180	Warren Moon	.25
181	Sean Jones	.03
182	Curtis Duncan	.03
183	Al Smith	.04
184	Richard Johnson	.03
185	Tony Jones	.03
186	Bubba McDowell	.03

187 Bruce Matthews .03
188 Ray Childress .03
189 Haywood Jeffires .25
190 Ernest Givins .03
191 Mike Munchak .03
192 Greg Montgomery .03
193 *Cody Carlson* .30
194 Johnny Meads .03
195 Drew Hill .03
196 Mike Dumas .03
197 *Darryll Lewis* .10
198 Rohn Stark .03
199 Clarence Verdin .03
200 Mike Prior .03
201 Eugene Daniel .03
202 Dean Biasucci .03
203 Jeff Herrod .03
204 Keith Taylor .03
205 Jon Hand .03
206 Pat Beach .03
207 Duane Bickett .03
208 Jessie Hester .03
209 Chip Banks .03
210 Ray Donaldson .03
211 Bill Brooks .03
212 Jeff George .30
213 Tony Siragusa .03
214 Albert Bentley .03
215 Joe Valerio .03
216 Chris Martin .03
217 Christian Okoye .03
218 Stephone Paige .03
219 Percy Snow .03
220 David Scott .03
221 Derrick Thomas .25
222 Todd McNair .03
223 Albert Lewis .03
224 Neil Smith .03
225 Barry Word .10
226 Robb Thomas .03
227 John Alt .03
228 Jonathan Hayes .03
229 Kevin Ross .03
230 Nick Lowery .03
231 Tim Grunhard .03
232 Dan Saleaumua .03
233 Steve DeBerg .03
234 *Harvey Williams* .50
235 *Nick Bell* .15
236 Mervyn Fernandez .03
237 Howie Long .03
238 Marcus Allen .03
239 Eddie Anderson .03
240 Ethan Horton .03
241 Lionel Washington .03
242 Steve Wisniewski .03
243 Bo Jackson .25
244 Greg Townsend .03
245 Jeff Jaeger .03
246 Aaron Wallace .03
247 Garry Lewis .03
248 Steve Smith .03
249 Willie Gault .03
250 Scott Davis .03
251 Jay Schroeder .03
252 Don Mosebar .03
253 *Todd Marinovich* .10
254 Irv Pankey .03
255 Flipper Anderson .03
256 Tom Newberry .03
257 Kevin Greene .03
258 Mike Wilcher .03
259 Bern Brostek .03
260 Buford McGee .03
261 Cleveland Gary .03
262 Jackie Slater .03
263 Henry Ellard .03
264 Alvin Wright .03
265 *Darryl Henley* .10
266 Damone Johnson .03
267 Frank Stams .03
268 Jerry Gray .03
269 Jim Everett .03
270 Pat Terrell .03
271 *Todd Lyght* .15
272 Aaron Cox .03
273 Barry Sanders (LL) .50
274 Jerry Rice (LL) .40
275 Derrick Thomas (LL) .10
276 Mark Carrier (LL) .05
277 Warren Moon (LL) .15
278 Randall Cunningham (LL) .10
279 Nick Lowery (LL) .03
280 Clarence Verdin (LL) .03
281 Thurman Thomas (LL) .25
282 Mike Horan (LL) .03
283 Flipper Anderson (LL) .03
284 John Offerdahl .03
285 Dan Marino 2.00
286 Mark Clayton .03
287 Tony Paige .03
288 Keith Sims .03
289 Jeff Cross .03
290 Pete Stoyanovich .03
291 Ferrell Edmunds .03
292 Reggie Roby .03
293 Louis Oliver .03
294 Jarvis Williams .03
295 Sammie Smith .03
296 Richmond Webb .03
297 J.B. Brown .03
298 Jim Jensen .03
299 Mark Duper .03
300 David Griggs .03
301 *Randal Hill* .35
302 *Aaron Craver* .10
303 Keith Millard .03
304 Steve Jordan .03
305 Anthony Carter .03
306 Mike Merriweather .03
307 *Audray McMillian* .35
308 Randall McDaniel .03
309 Gary Zimmerman .03
310 Carl Lee .03
311 Reggie Rutland .03
312 Hassan Jones .03
313 Kirk Lowdermilk .03
314 Herschel Walker .08
315 Chris Doleman .03
316 Joey Browner .03
317 Wade Wilson .03
318 Henry Thomas .03
319 Rich Gannon .08
320 Al Noga .03
321 *Pat Harlow* .08
322 Bruce Armstrong .03
323 Maurice Hurst .03
324 Brent Williams .03
325 Chris Singleton .03
326 Jason Staurovsky .03
327 Marvin Allen .03
328 Hart Lee Dykes .03
329 Johnny Rembert .03
330 Andre Tippett .03
331 Greg McMurtry .03
332 John Stephens .03
333 Ray Agnew .03
334 Tommy Hodson .03
335 Ronnie Lippett .03
336 Marv Cook .03
337 *Tommy Barnhardt* .08
338 Dalton Hilliard .03
339 Sam Mills .03
340 Morten Andersen .03
341 Stan Brock .03
342 Brett Maxie .03
343 Steve Walsh .03
344 Vaughan Johnson .03
345 Rickey Jackson .03
346 Renaldo Turnbull .03
347 Joel Hilgenberg .03
348 *Toi Cook* .10
349 Robert Massey .03
350 Pat Swilling .03
351 Eric Martin .03
352 Rueben Mayes .03
353 Vince Buck .03
354 Brett Perriman .03
355 *Wesley Carroll* .25
356 *Jarrod Bunch* .10
357 Pepper Johnson .03
358 Dave Meggett .03
359 Mark Collins .03
360 Sean Landeta .03
361 Maurice Carthon .03
362 Mike Fox .03
363 Jeff Hostetler .15
364 Phil Simms .08
365 Leonard Marshall .03
366 Gary Reasons .03
367 Rodney Hampton .50
368 *Greg Jackson* .08
369 Jumbo Elliott .03
370 *Bob Kratch* .08
371 Lawrence Taylor .10
372 Erik Howard .03
373 Carl Banks .03
374 Stephen Baker .03
375 Mark Ingram .03
376 *Browning Nagle* .25
377 Jeff Lageman .03
378 Ken O'Brien .03
379 Al Toon .03
380 Joe Prokop .03
381 Tony Stargell .03
382 Blair Thomas .10
383 Erik McMillan .03
384 Dennis Byrd .03
385 Freeman McNeil .03
386 Brad Baxter .08
387 Mark Boyer .03
388 Terance Mathis .10
389 Jim Sweeney .03
390 Kyle Clifton .03
391 Pat Leahy .03
392 Rob Moore .15
393 James Hasty .03
394 Blaise Bryant .03
395 Jesse Campbell (Error-Photo actually Dan McGwire, see 509 Corrected) .03
396 Keith Jackson .15
397 Jerome Brown .03
398 Keith Byars .03
399 Seth Joyner .03
400 Mike Bellamy .03
401 Fred Barnett .20
402 Reggie Singletary .03
403 Reggie White .15
404 Randall Cunningham .15
405 Byron Evans .03
406 Wes Hopkins .03
407 Ben Smith .03
408 Roger Ruzek .03
409 Eric Allen .03
410 Anthony Toney .03
411 Clyde Simmons .03
412 Andre Waters .03
413 Calvin Williams .15
414 *Eric Swann* .15
415 Eric Hill .03
416 Tim McDonald .03
417 Luis Sharpe .03
418 Ernie Jones .03
419 Ken Harvey .03
420 Ricky Proehl .15
421 Johnny Johnson .25
422 Anthony Bell .03
423 Timm Rosenbach .03
424 Rich Camarillo .03
425 Walter Reeves .03
426 Freddie Joe Nunn .03
427 Anthony Thompson .03
428 Bill Lewis .03
429 *Jim Wahler* .08
430 Cedric Mack .03
431 *Michael Jones* .08
432 Ernie Mills .08
433 Tim Worley .03
434 Greg Lloyd .03
435 Dermontti Dawson .03
436 Louis Lipps .03
437 Eric Green .08
438 Donald Evans .03
439 David Johnson .03
440 Tunch Ilkin .03
441 Bubby Brister .08
442 Chris Calloway .03
443 David Little .03
444 Thomas Everett .03
445 Carnell Lake .03
446 Rod Woodson .05
447 Gary Anderson .03
448 Merril Hoge .03
449 Gerald Williams .03
450 *Eric Moten* .08
451 Marion Butts .05
452 Leslie O'Neal .08
453 Ronnie Harmon .03
454 Gill Byrd .03
455 Junior Seau .25
456 *Nate Lewis* .25
457 Leo Goeas .03
458 Burt Grossman .03
459 Courtney Hall .08
460 Anthony Miller .06
461 Gary Plummer .03
462 Billy Joe Tolliver .03
463 Lee Williams .03
464 Arthur Cox .03
465 John Kidd .03
466 Frank Cornish .03
467 John Carney .03
468 *Eric Bieniemy* .10
469 Don Griffin .03
470 Jerry Rice 1.00
471 Keith DeLong .03
472 John Taylor .10
473 Brent Jones .03
474 Pierce Holt .03
475 Kevin Fagan .03
476 Bill Romanowski .03
477 Dexter Carter .03
478 Guy McIntyre .03
479 Joe Montana 1.00
480 Charles Haley .03
481 Mike Cofer .03
482 Jesse Sapolu .03
483 Eric Davis .03
484 Mike Sherrard .03
485 Steve Young .75
486 Darryl Pollard .03
487 Tom Rathman .03
488 Michael Carter .03
489 *Ricky Watters* 1.50
490 *John Johnson* .08
491 Eugene Robinson .03
492 Andy Heck .03
493 John L. Williams .03
494 Norm Johnson .03
495 David Wyman .03
496 Derrick Fenner .10
497 Rick Donnelly .03
498 Tony Woods .03
499 *Derek Loville* .75
500 Dave Krieg .03
501 Joe Nash .03
502 Brian Blades .03
503 Cortez Kennedy .25
504 Jeff Bryant .03
505 Tommy Kane .03
506 Travis McNeal .03
507 Terry Wooden .03
508 Chris Warren .50
509 *Dan McGwire* (Error-Photo actually Jesse Campbell; see 395 Corrected) .50
510 Mark Robinson .03
511 Ron Hall .03
512 Paul Gruber .03
513 Hary Hamilton .03
514 Keith McCants .03
515 Reggie Cobb .25
516 Steve Christie .03
517 Broderick Thomas .03
518 Mark Carrier .03
519 Vinny Testaverde .10
520 Ricky Reynolds .03
521 Jesse Anderson .03
522 Reuben Davis .03
523 Wayne Haddix .03
524 Gary Anderson .03
525 Bruce Hill .03
526 Kevin Murphy .03
527 *Lawrence Dawsey* .25
528 *Ricky Ervins* .35
529 Charles Mann .03
530 Jim Lachey .03
531 Mark Rypien .10
532 Darrell Green .03
533 Stan Humphries .40
534 Jeff Bostic .03
535 Earnest Byner .03
536 Art Monk .08
537 Don Warren .03
538 Darryl Grant .03
539 Wilber Marshall .03
540 *Kurt Gouveia* .10
541 Markus Koch .03
542 Andre Collins .03
543 Chip Lohmiller .03
544 Alvin Walton .03
545 Gary Clark .10
546 Ricky Sanders .03
547 Redskins vs. Eagles (Gary Clark) .03
548 Bengals vs. Oilers (Cody Carlson) .03
549 Dolphins vs. Chiefs (Mark Clayton) .03
550 Bears vs. Saints (Neal Anderson) .03
551 Bills vs. Dolphins (Thurman Thomas) .10
552 49ers vs. Redskins (Line Play) .03
553 Giants vs. Bears (Ottis Anderson) .03
554 Raiders vs. Bengals (Bo Jackson) .10
555 AFC Championship (Andre Reed) .03
556 NFC Championship (Jeff Hostetler) .03
557 Super Bowl XXV (Ottis Anderson) .03
558 Checklist 1-140 .03
559 Checklist 141-280 .03
560 Checklist 281-420 .03
561 Checklist 421-561 .03

1992 Bowman

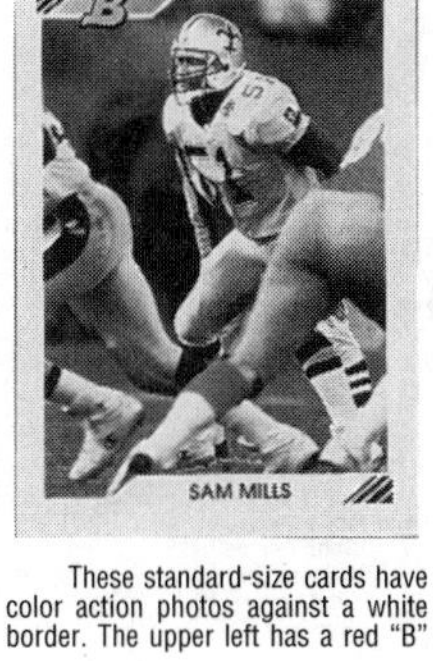

These standard-size cards have color action photos against a white border. The upper left has a red "B" on a green stripe, while the player's name is at the bottom in an orange-yellow stripe. There are 45 subset cards within the regular set - 28 Team Leader cards, 12 Playoff Star cards and five cards commemorating the longest plays of the 1991 season (punt, kick return, field goal, run and reception). These cards have gold-foil engraved borders and were randomly inserted one per 15-card pack.

MT
Complete Set (573): 160.00
Common Player: .25
Minor Stars: .50
Pack (12): 4.50
Wax Box (36): 150.00
1 Reggie White 1.00
2 Johnny Meads .25
3 Chip Lohmiller .25
4 James Lofton .50
5 Ray Horton .25
6 Rich Moran .25
7 Howard Cross .25
8 Mike Horan .25
9 Erik Kramer .50
10 Steve Wisniewski .25
11 Michael Haynes .25
12 Donald Evans .25
13 Michael Irvin (FOIL) 1.00
14 Gary Zimmerman .25
15 John Friesz .50
16 Mark Carrier .25
17 Mark Duper .25
18 James Thornton .25
19 Jon Hand .25
20 Sterling Sharpe 1.00
21 Jacob Green .25
22 Wesley Carroll .25
23 Clay Matthews .25
24 Kevin Greene .50
25 Brad Baxter .25
26 Don Griffin .25
27 (Robert Delpino) (FOIL SP) 1.50
28 Lee Johnson .25
29 Jim Wahler .25
30 Leonard Russell .50
31 Eric Moore .25
32 Dino Hackett .25
33 Simon Fletcher .25
34 Al Edwards .25
35 Brad Edwards .25
36 James Joseph .25
37 Rodney Peete .50
38 Ricky Reynolds .25
39 Eddie Anderson .25
40 Ken Clarke .25
41 (Tony Bennett) (FOIL) .50
42 Larry Brown .25
43 Ray Childress .25
44 Mike Kenn .25
45 Vestee Jackson .25
46 Neil O'Donnell 1.00
47 Bill Brooks .25
48 Kevin Butler .25
49 Joe Phillips .25
50 Cortez Kennedy .50
51 Rickey Jackson .25
52 Vinnie Clark .25
53 Michael Jackson .50
54 Ernie Jones .25
55 Tom Newberry .25
56 Pat Harlow .25
57 Craig Taylor .25
58 Joe Prokop .25
59 Warren Moon (FOIL SP) 2.00
60 Jeff Lageman .25
61 Neil Smith .50
62 Jim Jeffcoat .25
63 Bill Fralic .25
64 Mark Schlereth .25
65 Keith Byars .25
66 Jeff Hostetler .50
67 Joey Browner .25
68 Bobby Hebert (FOIL SP) 1.50
69 Keith Sims .25
70 Warren Moon 1.00
71 *Pio Sagapolutele* .25
72 Cornelius Bennett .50
73 Greg Davis .25
74 Ronnie Harmon .25
75 Ron Hall .25
76 Howie Long .50
77 Greg Lewis .25
78 Carnell Lake .25
79 Ray Crockett .25
80 Tom Waddle .25
81 Vincent Brown .25
82 (Bill Brooks) (FOIL) .50
83 John L. Williams .25
84 Floyd Turner .25
85 Scott Radecic .25
86 Anthony Munoz .50
87 Lonnie Young .25
88 Dexter Carter .25
89 Tony Zendejas .25
90 Tim Jorden .25
91 LeRoy Butler .50
92 *Richard Brown* .25
93 Eric Pegram .50
94 Sean Landeta .25
95 Clyde Simmons .25
96 Martin Mayhew .25
97 Jarvis Williams .25
98 (Barry Word) .25
99 John Taylor (FOIL) .50
100 Emmitt Smith 12.00
101 Leon Seals .25
102 Marion Butts .25
103 Mike Merriweather .25
104 Ernest Givins .25
105 Wymon Henderson .25
106 Robert Wilson .25
107 Bobby Hebert .25
108 Terry McDaniel .25
109 Jerry Ball .25
110 John Taylor .25
111 Rob Moore 1.00
112 Thurman Thomas (FOIL) 1.00
113 Checklist 1 .25
114 Brian Blades .25
115 Larry Kelm .25
116 James Francis .25
117 Rod Woodson .50
118 Trace Armstrong .25
119 Eugene Daniel .25
120 Andre Tippett .25
121 Chris Jacke .25
122 Jessie Tuggle .25
123 Chris Chandler 1.00
124 Tim Johnson .25
125 Mark Collins .25
126 (Aeneas Williams) (FOIL SP) 2.00
127 James Jones .25
128 George Jamison .25
129 Deron Cherry .25
130 Mark Clayton .25
131 Keith DeLong .25
132 Marcus Allen 1.00
133 Joe Walter .25
134 Reggie Rutland .25
135 Kent Hull .25
136 Jeff Feagles .25
137 Ronnie Lott (FOIL SP) 1.50
138 Henry Rolling .25
139 Gary Anderson .25
140 Morten Andersen .50
141 Cris Dishman .25
142 David Treadwell .25
143 Kevin Gogan .25
144 James Hasty .25
145 Robert Delpino .50
146 Patrick Hunter .25
147 Gary Anderson .25
148 Chip Banks .25
149 Dan Fike .25
150 Chris Miller .25
151 Hugh Millen .25
152 Courtney Hall .25
153 Gary Clark .25
154 Michael Brooks .25
155 Jay Hilgenberg .25
156 Tim McDonald .25
157 (Andre Tippett) (FOIL) .50
158 Doug Riesenberg .25
159 Bill Maas .25
160 Fred Barnett .50
161 Pierce Holt .25
162 Brian Noble .25
163 Harold Green .25
164 Joel Hilgenberg .25
165 Mervyn Fernandez .25
166 John Offerdahl .25
167 Shane Conlan .25
168 Mark Higgs (FOIL SP) 1.50
169 Bubba McDowell .25
170 Barry Sanders 12.00
171 Larry Roberts .25
172 Herschel Walker .50
173 Steve McMichael .25
174 Kelly Stouffer .25
175 Louis Lipps .25
176 Jim Everett .50
177 Tony Tolbert .25
178 Mike Baab .25
179 Eric Swann .25
180 Emmitt Smith (FOIL SP) 25.00
181 Tim Brown 1.00
182 Dennis Smith .25
183 Moe Gardner .25
184 Derrick Walker .25
185 Reyna Thompson .25
186 Esera Tuaolo .25
187 Jeff Wright .25
188 Mark Rypien .50
189 Quinn Early .25
190 Christian Okoye .25
191 Keith Jackson .50
192 Doug Smith .25
193 John Elway (FOIL) 12.00
194 Reggie Cobb .25
195 Reggie Roby .25
196 Clarence Verdin .25
197 Jim Breech .25
198 Jim Sweeney .25
199 Marv Cook .25
200 Ronnie Lott .50
201 Mel Gray .25
202 Maury Buford .25
203 Lorenzo Lynch .25
204 Jesse Sapolu .25
205 Steve Jordan .25
206 Don Majkowski .25
207 Flipper Anderson .25
208 Ed King .25
209 Tony Woods .25
210 Ron Heller .25
211 Greg Kragen .25
212 Scott Case .25
213 Tommy Barnhardt .25
214 Charles Mann .25
215 David Griggs .25
216 Kenneth Davis (FOIL SP) 1.50
217 Lamar Lathon .25
218 Nate Odomes .25
219 Vinny Testaverde 1.00
220 Rod Bernstine .25
221 Barry Sanders (FOIL) 20.00
222 Carlton Haselrig .25
223 Steve Beuerlein .25
224 John Alt .25
225 Pepper Johnson .25
226 Checklist 2 .25
227 Irv Eatman .25
228 Greg Townsend .25
229 Mark Jackson .25
230 Robert Blackmon .25
231 Terry Allen 2.50
232 Bennie Blades .25
233 (Sam Mills) (FOIL) .50
234 Richmond Webb .25
235 Richard Dent .50
236 Alonzo Mitz .25
237 Steve Young 6.00
238 Pat Swilling .25
239 James Campen .25
240 Earnest Byner .25
241 Pat Terrell .25
242 Carwell Gardner .25
243 Charles McRae .25
244 Vince Newsome .25
245 Eric Hill .25
246 Steve Young (FOIL) 8.00
247 Nate Lewis .25
248 William Fuller .25
249 Andre Waters .25
250 Dean Biasucci .25
251 Andre Rison 1.00
252 Brent Williams .25
253 Todd McNair .25
254 Jeff Davidson .25
255 Art Monk 1.00
256 Kirk Lowdermilk .25
257 Bob Golic .25
258 Michael Irvin 1.00
259 Eric Green .25
260 (David Fulcher) (FOIL) .50
261 Damone Johnson .25
262 Marc Spindler .25
263 Alfred Williams .25
264 Donnie Elder .25
265 Keith McKeller .25
266 *Steve Bono* 2.00
267 Jumbo Elliott .25
268 Randy Hilliard .25
269 Rufus Porter .25
270 Neal Anderson .25
271 Dalton Hilliard .25
272 Michael Zordich .25
273 (Cornelius Bennett) (FOIL) .75
274 Louie Aguiar .25
275 Aaron Craver .25
276 Tony Bennett .25
277 Terry Wooden .25
278 Mike Munchak .25
279 Chris Hinton .25
280 John Elway 6.00
281 Randall McDaniel .25
282 (Brad Baxter) (FOIL) .50
283 Wes Hopkins .25
284 Scott Davis .25
285 Mark Tuinei .25
286 Broderick Thompson .25
287 Henry Ellard .25
288 Adrian Cooper .25
289 Don Warren .25
290 Rodney Hampton 1.00
291 Kevin Ross .25
292 Mark Carrier .25
293 Ian Beckles .25
294 Gene Atkins .25
295 Mark Rypien (FOIL) .75
296 Eric Metcalf .50
297 Howard Ballard .25
298 Nate Newton .25
299 Dan Owens .25
300 Tim McGee .25
301 Greg McMurtry .25
302 Walter Reeves .25
303 Jeff Herrod .25
304 Darren Comeaux .25
305 Pete Stoyanovich .25
306 Johnny Holland .25
307 Jay Novacek .50
308 Steve Broussard .25
309 Darrell Green .50
310 Sam Mills .25
311 Tim Barnett .25
312 Steve Atwater .25
313 (Tom Waddle) (FOIL) .50
314 Felix Wright .25
315 Sean Jones .25
316 Jim Harbaugh 1.00
317 Eric Allen .25
318 Don Mosebar .25
319 Rob Taylor .25
320 Terance Mathis 1.00
321 Leroy Hoard 1.00
322 Kenneth Davis .25
323 Guy McIntyre .25
324 (Deron Cherry) (FOIL) .50
325 Tunch Ilkin .25
326 Willie Green .50
327 Darryl Henley .25
328 Shawn Jefferson .25
329 Greg Jackson .25
330 John Roper .25
331 Bill Lewis .25
332 Rodney Holman .25
333 Bruce Armstrong .25
334 Robb Thomas .25
335 Alvin Harper .50
336 Brian Jordan 1.00
337 (Morten Andersen) (FOIL) .75
338 Dermontti Dawson .25
339 Checklist 3 .25
340 Louis Oliver .25
341 Paul McJulien .25
342 Karl Mecklenburg .25
343 Lawrence Dawsey .25
344 Kyle Clifton .25
345 Jeff Bostic .25
346 Cris Carter 2.50
347 Al Smith .25
348 Mark Kelso .25
349 Art Monk (FOIL) 1.00
350 Michael Carter .25
351 Ethan Horton .25
352 Andy Heck .25
353 Gill Fenerty .25
354 David Brandon .25
355 Anthony Johnson .25
356 Mike Golic .25
357 Ferrell Edmunds .25
358 Dennis Gibson .25
359 Gill Byrd .25
360 Todd Lyght .25
361 Jayice Pearson .25
362 John Rade .25
363 Keith Van Horne .25
364 John Kasay .25
365 (Broderick Thomas) (FOIL SP) 1.50
366 Ken Harvey .25
367 Rich Gannon .25
368 Darrell Thompson .25
369 Jon Vaughn .25
370 Jesse Solomon .25
371 Erik McMillan .25
372 Bruce Matthews .25
373 Wilber Marshall .25
374 (Brian Blades) (FOIL SP) 1.50
375 Vance Johnson .25
376 Eddie Brown .25
377 Don Beebe .50
378 Brent Jones .50
379 Matt Bahr .25
380 Dwight Stone .25
381 Tony Casillas .25
382 Jay Schroeder .25
383 Byron Evans .25
384 Dan Saleaumua .25
385 Wendell Davis .25
386 Ron Holmes .25
387 George Thomas .25
388 Ray Berry .25
389 Eric Martin .25
390 Kevin Mack .25
391 Natu Tuatagaloa .25
392 Bill Romanowski .25
393 Nick Bell (FOIL SP) 1.50
394 Grant Feasel .25

395 Eugene Lockhart .25
396 Lorenzo White .25
397 Mike Farr .25
398 Eric Bieniemy .25
399 Kevin Murphy .25
400 Luis Sharpe .25
401 (Jessie Tuggle) (FOIL SP) 1.50
402 Cleveland Gary .25
403 Tony Mandarich .50
404 Bryan Cox .25
405 Marvin Washington .25
406 Fred Stokes .25
407 Duane Bickett .25
408 Leonard Marshall .25
409 Barry Foster .25
410 Thurman Thomas 1.00
411 Willie Gault .25
412 Vinson Smith .25
413 Mark Bortz .25
414 Johnny Johnson .25
415 Rodney Hampton (FOIL) 1.00
416 Steve Wallace .25
417 Fuad Reveiz .25
418 Derrick Thomas .50
419 *Jackie Harris* .50
420 Derek Russell .25
421 David Grant .25
422 Tommy Kane .25
423 Stan Brock .25
424 Haywood Jeffires .50
425 Broderick Thomas .25
426 John Kidd .25
427 (Shawn McCarthy) (FOIL) .50
428 Jim Arnold .25
429 Scott Fulhage .25
430 Jackie Slater .25
431 Scott Galbraith .25
432 Roger Ruzek .25
433 Irving Fryar .50
434A (Derrick Thomas) (FOIL ERR) 1.00
434B Derrick Thomas (FOIL COR) 1.00
435 David Johnson .25
436 Jim Jensen .25
437 James Washington .25
438 Phil Hansen .25
439 Rohn Stark .25
440 Jarrod Bunch .25
441 Todd Marinovich .25
442 Brett Perriman 1.00
443 Eugene Robinson .50
444 Robert Massey .25
445 Nick Lowery .25
446 Rickey Dixon .25
447 Jim Lachey .25
448 (Johnny Hector) (FOIL) .50
449 Gary Plummer .25
450 Robert Brown .25
451 Gaston Green .25
452 Checklist 4 .25
453 Darion Conner .25
454 Mike Cofer .25
455 Craig Heyward .25
456 Anthony Carter .25
457 Pat Coleman .25
458 Jeff Bryant .25
459 Mark Gunn .25
460 Stan Thomas .25
461 (Simon Fletcher) (FOIL SP) 1.50
462 Ray Agnew .25
463 Jessie Hester .25
464 Rob Burnett .25
465 Mike Croel .25
466 Mike Pitts .25
467 Darryl Talley .25
468 Rich Camarillo .25
469 Reggie White (FOIL) 1.50
470 Nick Bell .25
471 Tracy Hayworth .25
472 Eric Thomas .25
473 Paul Gruber .25
474 David Richards .25
475 T.J. Turner .25
476 Mark Ingram .25
477 Tim Grunhard .25
478 Marion Butts (FOIL) .50
479 Tom Rathman .25
480 Brian Mitchell .25
481 Bryce Paup .50
482 Mike Pritchard .25
483 Ken Norton Jr. .25
484 Roman Phifer .25
485 Greg Lloyd .50
486 Brett Maxie .25
487 Richard Dent (FOIL SP) 1.50
488 Curtis Duncan .25
489 Chris Burkett .25
490 Travis McNeal .25
491 Carl Lee .25
492 Clarence Kay .25
493 Tom Thayer .25
494 Erik Kramer (FOIL SP) 2.00
495 Perry Kemp .25
496 Jeff Jaeger .25
497 Eric Sanders .25
498 Burt Grossman .25
499 Ben Smith .25
500 Keith McCants .25
501 John Stephens .25
502 John Rienstra .25
503 Jim Ritcher .25
504 Harris Barton .25
505 Andre Rison (FOIL SP) 2.00
506 Chris Martin .25
507 Freddie Joe Nunn .25
508 Mark Higgs .25
509 Norm Johnson .25
510 Stephen Baker .25
511 Ricky Sanders .25
512 Ray Donaldson .25
513 David Fulcher .25
514 Gerald Williams .25
515 Toi Cook .25
516 Chris Warren 1.00
517 Jeff Gossett .25
518 Ken Lanier .25
519 Haywood Jeffires (FOIL SP) 1.50
520 Kevin Glover .25
521 Mo Lewis .25
522 Bern Brostek .25
523 *Bo Orlando* .25
524 Mike Saxon .25
525 Seth Joyner .25
526 John Carney .25
527 Jeff Cross .25
528 (Gary Anderson) (FOIL SP) 1.50
529 Chuck Cecil .25
530 Tim Green .25
531 Kevin Porter .25
532 Chris Spielman .25
533 Willie Drewrey .25
534 Chris Singleton .25
535 Matt Stover .25
536 Andre Collins .25
537 Erik Howard .25
538 Steve Tasker .25
539 Anthony Thompson .25
540 Charles Haley .50
541 (Mike Merriweather) (FOIL) .50
542 Henry Thomas .25
543 Scott Stephen .25
544 Bruce Kozerski .25
545 Tim McKyer .25
546 Chris Doleman .25
547 Riki Ellison .25
548 Mike Prior .25
549 Dwayne Harper .25
550 Bubby Brister .25
551 Dave Meggett .25
552 Greg Montgomery .25
553 (Kevin Mack) (FOIL) .50
554 Mark Stepnoski .25
555 Kenny Walker .25
556 Eric Moten .25
557 Michael Stewart .25
558 Calvin Williams .25
559 Johnny Hector .25
560 Tony Paige .25
561 Tim Newton .25
562 Brad Muster .25
563 Aeneas Williams .50
564 Herman Moore 8.00
565 Checklist 5 .25
566 Jerome Henderson .25
567 Danny Copeland .25
568 (Alexander Wright) (FOIL) .50
569 Tim Harris .25
570 Jonathan Hayes .25
571 Tony Jones .25
572 *Carlton Bailey* .25
573 Vaughan Johnson .25

1993 Bowman

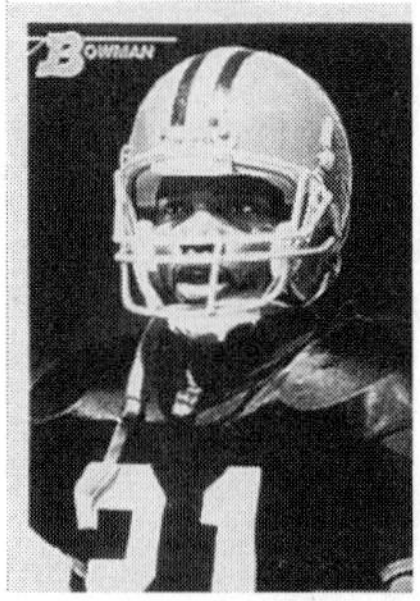

The 1993 Bowman set cut back to 423 cards with a numbered subset of 27 special foil-designed cards. These cards feature nine 1993 rookies, nine former #1 draft picks and nine superstars. Each pack of 1993 Bowman contains 14 cards, plus one special foil insert card. The regular cards are glossy and feature full-color photos on premium stock.

MT
Complete Set (423): 75.00
Common Player: .15
Minor Stars: .30
Pack (14): 3.00
Wax Box (24): 60.00
1 Troy Aikman 4.00
2 John Parella .15
3 *Dana Stubblefield* 1.00
4 Mark Higgs .15
5 *Tom Carter* .30
6 Nate Lewis .15
7 *Vaughn Hebron* .30
8 Ernest Givins .15
9 Vince Buck .15
10 Levon Kirkland .15
11 J.J. Birden .15
12 Steve Jordan .15
13 Simon Fletcher .15
14 Willie Green .15
15 Pepper Johnson .15
16 Roger Harper .15
17 Rob Moore .15
18 David Lang .15
19 David Klingler .15
20 *Garrison Hearst* 4.00
21 Anthony Johnson .15
22 *Eric Curry* .30
23 Nolan Harrison .15
24 Earl Dotson .15
25 Leonard Russell .15
26 Doug Riesenberg .15
27 Dwayne Harper .15
28 Richard Dent .30
29 *Victor Bailey* .30
30 Junior Seau .30
31 Steve Tasker .15
32 Kurt Gouveia .15
33 Renaldo Turnbull .15
34 Dale Carter .15
35 Russell Maryland .15
36 Dana Hall .15
37 Marco Coleman .15
38 Greg Montgomery .15
39 *Deon Figures* .30
40 *Troy Drayton* .50
41 Eric Metcalf .15
42 Michael Husted .15
43 Harry Newsome .15
44 Kelvin Pritchett .15
45 Andre Rison .30
46 *John Copeland* .30
47 Greg Biekert .15
48 Johnny Johnson .15
49 Chuck Cecil .15
50 *Rick Mirer* .50
51 Rod Bernstine .15
52 Steve McMichael .15
53 *Roosevelt Potts* .30
54 Mike Sherrard .15
55 Terrell Buckley .15
56 Eugene Chung .15
57 *Kimble Anders* 1.00
58 Daryl Johnston .15
59 Harris Barton .15
60 Thurman Thomas .30
61 Eric Martin .15
62 *Reggie Brooks* .30
63 Eric Bieniemy .15
64 John Offerdahl .15
65 Wilber Marshall .15
66 Mark Carrier .15
67 Merril Hoge .15
68 Cris Carter .30
69 Marty Thompson .15
70 Randall Cunningham .30
71 Winston Moss .15
72 Doug Pelfrey .15
73 Jackie Slater .15
74 Pierce Holt .15
75 Hardy Nickerson .15
76 Chris Burkett .15
77 Michael Brandon .15
78 Tom Waddle .15
79 Walter Reeves .15
80 Lawrence Taylor .30
81 *Wayne Simmons* .30
82 Brent Williams .15
83 Shannon Sharpe .30
84 Robert Blackmon .15
85 Keith Jackson .15
86 A.J. Johnson .15
87 *Ryan McNeil* .30
88 Michael Dean Perry .15
89 *Russell Copeland* .30
90 Sam Mills .15
91 Courtney Hall .15
92 *Gino Torretta* .30
93 *Artie Smith* .15
94 David Whitmore .15
95 Charles Haley .15
96 Rod Woodson .15
97 Lorenzo White .15
98 Tom Scott .15
99 Tyji Armstrong .15
100 Boomer Esiason .30
101 Raghib Ismail .15
102 Mark Carrier .15
103 Broderick Thompson .15
104 Bob Whitfield .15
105 Ben Coleman .15
106 Jon Vaughn .15
107 Marcus Buckley .15
108 Cleveland Gary .15
109 Ashley Ambrose .15
110 Reggie White .30
111 *Arthur Marshall* .30
112 Greg McMurtry .15
113 Mike Johnson .15
114 Tim McGee .15
115 John Carney .15
116 Neil Smith .15
117 Mark Stepnoski .15
118 Don Beebe .15
119 Scott Mitchell .30
120 Randall McDaniel .15
121 Chidi Ahanotu .15
122 Ray Childress .15
123 *Tony McGee* .30
124 Marc Boutte .15
125 Ronnie Lott .30
126 *Jason Elam* .30
127 *Martin Harrison* .30
128 Leonard Renfro .15
129 Jesse Armstead .15
130 Quentin Coryatt .15
131 Luis Sharpe .15
132 Bill Maas .15
133 Jesse Solomon .15
134 Kevin Greene .30
135 *Derek Brown* .30
136 Greg Townsend .15
137 Neal Anderson .15
138 John Williams .15
139 *Vincent Brisby* .50
140 Barry Sanders 6.00
141 Charles Mann .15
142 Ken Norton .15
143 Eric Moten .15
144 John Alt .15
145 *Dan Footman* .15
146 Bill Brooks .15
147 James Thornton .15
148 Martin Mayhew .15
149 Andy Harmon .15
150 Dan Marino 7.00
151 Michael Barrow .15
152 Flipper Anderson .15
153 Jackie Harris .15
154 Todd Kelly .15
155 *Dan Williams* .15
156 Harold Green .15
157 David Treadwell .15
158 Chris Doleman .15
159 Eric Hill .15
160 *Lincoln Kennedy* .30
161 Devon McDonald .15
162 *Natrone Means* 4.00
163 Rick Hamilton .15
164 Kelvin Martin .15
165 Jeff Hostetler .30
166 *Mark Brunell* 15.00
167 Tim Barnett .15
168 Ray Crockett .15
169 William Perry .15
170 Michael Irvin .30
171 Marvin Washington .15
172 Irving Fryar .15
173 Scott Sisson .15
174 Gary Anderson .15
175 Bruce Smith .15
176 Clyde Simmons .15
177 Russell White .15
178 *Irv Smith* .15
179 Mark Wheeler .15
180 Warren Moon .30
181 Del Speer .15
182 Henry Thomas .15
183 Keith Kartz .15
184 Ricky Ervins .15
185 Phil Simms .30
186 Tim Brown .30
187 Willis Peguese .15
188 Rich Moran .15
189 Robert Jones .15
190 Craig Heyward .15
191 Ricky Watters .30
192 Stan Humphries .30
193 Larry Webster .15
194 Brad Baxter .15
195 Randal Hill .15
196 Robert Porcher .15
197 Patrick Robinson .15
198 Ferrell Edmunds .15
199 Melvin Jenkins .15
200 Joe Montana 4.00
201 Marv Cook .15
202 Henry Ellard .15
203 Calvin Williams .15
204 Craig Erickson .15
205 Steve Atwater .15
206 Najee Mustafaa .15
207 Darryl Talley .15
208 Jarrod Bunch .15
209 Tim McDonald .15
210 *Patrick Bates* .30
211 Sean Jones .15
212 Leslie O'Neal .15
213 Mike Golic .15
214 Mark Clayton .15
215 Leonard Marshall .15
216 *Curtis Conway* 3.00
217 *Andre Hastings* .50
218 Barry Word .15
219 Will Wolford .15
220 Desmond Howard .30
221 Rickey Jackson .15
222 Alvin Harper .15
223 William White .15
224 Steve Broussard .15
225 Aeneas Williams .15
226 Michael Brooks .15
227 Reggie Cobb .15
228 Derrick Walker .15
229 Marcus Allen .30
230 Jerry Ball .15
231 J.B. Brown .15
232 Terry McDaniel .15
233 LeRoy Butler .15
234 Kyle Clifton .15
235 Henry Jones .15
236 Shane Conlan .15
237 *Michael Bates* .30
238 Vincent Brown .15
239 William Fuller .15
240 Ricardo McDonald .15
241 Gary Zimmerman .15
242 Fred Barnett .15
243 *Elvis Grbac* 6.00
244 Myron Baker .15
245 Steve Emtman .15
246 Mike Compton .15
247 Mark Jackson .15
248 Santo Stephens .15
249 Tommie Agee .15
250 Broderick Thomas .15
251 Fred Baxter .15
252 Andre Collins .15
253 Ernest Dye .15
254 Raylee Johnson .15
255 Rickey Dixon .15
256 Ron Heller .15
257 Joel Steed .15
258 Everett Lindsay .15
259 Tony Smith .15
260 Sterling Sharpe .30
261 Tommy Vardell .15
262 Morten Andersen .15
263 Eddie Robinson .15
264 *Jerome Bettis* 6.00
265 Alonzo Spellman .15
266 Harvey Williams .15
267 Jason Belser .15
268 Derek Russell .15
269 *Derrick Lassic* .30
270 Steve Young 3.00
271 *Adrien Murrell* 5.00
272 Lewis Tillman .15
273 *O.J. McDuffie* 3.00
274 Marty Carter .15
275 Ray Seals .15
276 Earnest Byner .15
277 Marion Butts .15
278 Chris Spielman .15
279 Carl Pickens 2.00
280 *Drew Bledsoe* 14.00
281 Mark Kelso .15
282 Eugene Robinson .15
283 Eric Allen .15
284 Ethan Horton .15
285 Greg Lloyd .15
286 Anthony Carter .15
287 Edgar Bennett .30
288 Bobby Hebert .15
289 Haywood Jeffires .15
290 *Glyn Milburn* 1.00
291 Bernie Kosar .15
292 Jumbo Elliott .15
293 Jessie Hester .15
294 Brent Jones .15
295 Carl Banks .15
296 Brian Washington .15
297 Steve Beuerlein .15
298 John Lynch .15
299 Troy Vincent .15
300 Emmitt Smith 7.00
301 Chris Zorich .15
302 Wade Wilson .15
303 *Darrien Gordon* .30
304 Fred Stokes .15
305 Nick Lowery .15
306 Rodney Peete .15
307 Chris Warren .30
308 Herschel Walker .15
309 Aundray Bruce .15
310 Barry Foster .15
311 *George Teague* .30
312 Darryl Williams .15
313 *Thomas Smith* .30
314 Dennis Brown .15
315 *Marvin Jones* .30
316 Andre Tippett .15
317 *Demetrius Dubose* .15
318 Kirk Lowdermilk .15
319 Shane Dronett .15
320 *Terry Kirby* 1.00
321 *Qadry Ismail* .50
322 Lorenzo Lynch .15
323 Willie Drewrey .15
324 Jessie Tuggle .15
325 Leroy Hoard .15
326 Mark Collins .15
327 Darrell Green .15
328 Anthony Miller .30
329 Brad Muster .15
330 Jim Kelly .50
331 Sean Gilbert .15
332 Tim McKyer .15
333 Scott Mersereau .15
334 Willie Davis .15
335 Brett Favre 8.00
336 Kevin Gogan .15
337 Jim Harbaugh .30
338 James Trapp .15
339 Pete Stoyanovich .15
340 Jerry Rice 4.00
341 Gary Anderson .15
342 *Carlton Gray* .15
343 Dermontti Dawson .15
344 Ray Buchanan .15
345 Derrick Fenner .15
346 Dennis Smith .15
347 Todd Rucci .15
348 Seth Joyner .15
349 Jim McMahon .30
350 Rodney Hampton .30
351 Al Smith .15
352 Steve Everitt .15
353 Vinnie Clark .15
354 Eric Swann .15
355 Brian Mitchell .15
356 Will Shields .15
357 Cornelius Bennett .15
358 *Darrin Smith* .30
359 Chris Mims .15
360 Blair Thomas .15
361 Dennis Gibson .15
362 Santana Dotson .15
363 Mark Ingram .15
364 Don Mosebar .15
365 Ty Detmer .30
366 Bob Christian .15
367 Adrian Hardy .15
368 Vaughan Johnson .15
369 Jim Everett .15
370 Ricky Sanders .15
371 Jonathan Hayes .15
372 Bruce Matthews .15
373 Darren Drozdov .15
374 Scott Brumfield .15
375 Cortez Kennedy .15
376 Tim Harris .15
377 Neil O'Donnell .30
378 *Robert Smith* 6.00
379 Mike Caldwell .15
380 Burt Grossman .15
381 Corey Miller .15
382 *Kevin Williams* .50
383 Ken Harvey .15
384 *Greg Robinson* .15
385 Harold Alexander .15
386 Andre Reed .30
387 Reggie Langhorne .15
388 Courtney Hawkins .15
389 James Hasty .15
390 Pat Swilling .15
391 *Chris Slade* .30
392 Keith Byars .15
393 Dalton Hilliard .15
394 David Williams .15
395 Terry Obee .15
396 Heath Sherman .15
397 John Taylor .15
398 Irv Eatman .15
399 Johnny Holland .15
400 John Elway 3.00
401 Clay Matthews .15
402 Dave Meggett .15
403 Eric Green .15
404 Bryan Cox .15
405 Jay Novacek .15
406 Kenneth Davis .15
407 *Lamar Thomas* .30
408 Lance Gunn .15
409 Audray McMillian .15
410 Derrick Thomas .30
411 Rufus Porter .15
412 Coleman Rudolph .15
413 Mark Rypien .15
414 Duane Bickett .15
415 Chris Singleton .15
416 Mitch Lyons .15
417 Bill Fralic .15
418 Gary Plummer .15
419 Ricky Proehl .15
420 Howie Long .15
421 *Willie Roaf* .30
422 Checklist 1 of 2 .15
423 Checklist 2 of 2 .15

1994 Bowman

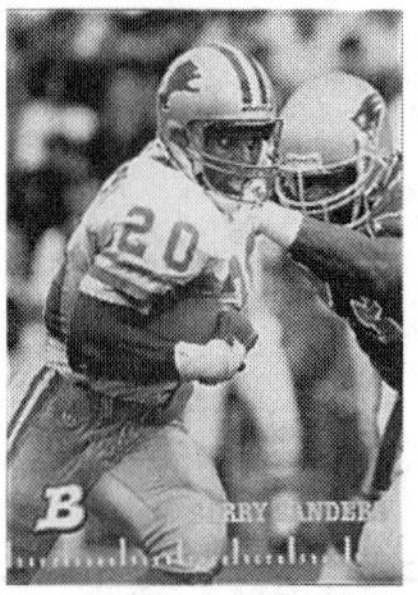

This 360-card set features 116 of this year's draft picks, plus a 30-card rookie subset (#s 215-244). Each card front has a glossy full-color action photo of the player, with a borderless design. Gold-foil stamped yard markers run across the bottom, while the Bowman logo appears in the lower left corner. The player's name is stamped in gold in the opposite corner. The card back has a smaller picture of the player on the left side; statistics are on the right side on top of a football background. The card number is in white in a red triangle in the upper right corner.

MT
Complete Set (390): 80.00
Common Player: .10
Minor Stars: .20
Pack (12): 4.00
Wax Box (24): 90.00
1 *Dan Wilkinson* .20
2 *Marshall Faulk* 20.00
3 *Heath Shuler* .75
4 *Willie McGinest* .20
5 *Trent Dilfer* 6.00
6 *Brent Jones* .20
7 *Sam Adams* .20
8 *Randy Baldwin* .20
9 *Jamir Miller* .20
10 *John Thierry* .20
11 *Aaron Glenn* .20
12 *Joe Johnson* .20
13 *Bernard Williams* .20
14 *Wayne Gandy* .20
15 *Aaron Taylor* .20
16 *Charles Johnson* 1.50
17 *Dewayne Washington* .20
18 Bernie Kosar .10
19 *Johnnie Morton* 1.50
20 *Rob Fredrickson* .20
21 *Shante Carver* .20
22 *Thomas Lewis* .20
23 *Greg Hill* .75
24 Cris Dishman .10
25 *Jeff Burris* .20
26 *Isaac Davis* .20
27 *Bert Emanuel* 2.00
28 *Allen Aldridge* .20
29 *Kevin Lee* .20
30 *Chris Brantley* .20
31 *Rich Braham* .20
32 Ricky Watters .20
33 Quentin Coryatt .10
34 Hardy Nickerson .10
35 Johnny Johnson .10
36 Ken Harvey .10
37 Chris Zorich .10
38 Chris Warren .20
39 *David Palmer* .20
40 Chris Miller .10
41 Ken Ruettgers .10
42 *Joe Panos* .20
43 *Mario Bates* .30
44 Harry Colon .10
45 Barry Foster .10
46 Steve Tasker .10
47 Richmond Webb .10
48 *James Folston* .20
49 Erik Williams .10
50 Rodney Hampton .20
51 Derek Russell .10
52 Greg Montgomery .10
53 Anthony Phillips .10
54 Andre Coleman .10
55 Gary Brown .10
56 Neil Smith .10
57 Myron Baker .10
58 *Sean Dawkins* .50
59 Marvin Washington .10
60 Steve Beuerlein .10
61 *Brenston Buckner* .20
62 William Gaines .10
63 *LeShon Johnson* .20
64 *Errict Rhett* 2.00
65 Jim Everett .10
66 Desmond Howard .10
67 Jack Del Rio .10
68 *Isaac Bruce* 20.00
69 *Van Moore* .20
70 Jim Kelly .20
71 Leon Lett .10
72 Greg Robinson .10
73 *Ryan Yarborough* .20
74 Terry Wooden .10
75 Eric Allen .10
76 Ernest Givins .10
77 *Marcus Spears* .20
78 *Thomas Randolph* .20
79 *Willie Clark* .20
80 John Elway 1.50
81 *Aubrey Beavers* .20
82 Jeff Cothran .10
83 Norm Johnson .10
84 *Donnell Bennett* .20
85 Phillippi Sparks .10
86 Scott Mitchell .10
87 *Bucky Brooks* .20
88 Courtney Hawkins .10
89 Kevin Greene .10
90 *Doug Nussmeier* .20
91 Floyd Turner .10
92 Anthony Newman .10
93 Vinny Testaverde .10
94 Ronnie Lott .10
95 Troy Aikman 3.00
96 John Taylor .10
97 Henry Ellard .10
98 Carl Lee .10
99 Terry McDaniel .10
100 Joe Montana 3.00
101 David Klingler .10
102 *Bruce Walker* .20
103 Rick Cunningham .10
104 Robert Delpino .10
105 Mark Ingram .10
106 Leslie O'Neal .10
107 Darrell Thompson .10
108 David Meggett .10
109 Chris Gardocki .10
110 Andre Rison .10
111 Kelvin Martin .10
112 Marcus Robertson .10
113 *Jason Gildon* .20
114 Mel Gray .10
115 Tommy Vardell .10
116 Dexter Carter .10
117 *Scottie Graham* .20
118 Horace Copeland .10
119 Cornelius Bennett .10
120 *Chris Maumalanga* .20
121 Mo Lewis .10
122 *Toby Wright* .20
123 *George Hegamin* .20
124 Chip Lohmiller .10
125 *Calvin Jones* .20
126 *Steve Shine* .20
127 *Chuck Levy* .20
128 Sam Mills .10
129 Terance Mathis .10
130 Randall Cunningham .10
131 John Fina .10
132 Reggie White .20
133 Tom Waddle .10
134 Chris Calloway .10
135 *Kevin Mawae* .20
136 *Lake Dawson* .50
137 *Alai Kalaniuhalu* .20
138 Tom Nalen .10
139 Cody Carlson .10

140 Dan Marino 5.00
141 Harris Barton .10
142 Don Mosebar .10
143 *Romeo Bandison* .20
144 Bruce Smith .10
145 Warren Moon .20
146 David Lutz .10
147 Dermontti Dawson .10
148 Ricky Proehl .10
149 *Lou Benfatti* .20
150 Craig Erickson .10
151 Sean Gilbert .10
152 *Zefros Moss* .20
153 *Darnay Scott* 3.00
154 Courtney Hall .10
155 Brian Mitchell .10
156 *Joe Burch* .20
157 *Terry Mickens* .20
158 Jay Novacek .10
159 Chris Gedney .10
160 Bruce Matthews .10
161 *Marlo Perry* .20
162 Vince Buck .10
163 Michael Bates .10
164 Willie Davis .10
165 Mike Pritchard .10
166 Doug Riesenberg .10
167 Herschel Walker .10
168 *Tim Ruddy* .20
169 *William Floyd* 1.50
170 John Randle .10
171 Winston Moss .10
172 Thurman Thomas .20
173 *Eric England* .20
174 Vincent Brisby .20
175 Greg Lloyd .10
176 Paul Gruber .10
177 *Brad Ottis* .20
178 George Teague .10
179 *Willie Jackson* .20
180 Barry Sanders 4.00
181 Brian Washington .10
182 Michael Jackson .10
183 *Jason Mathews* .20
184 Chester McGlockton .10
185 *Tydus Winans* .20
186 Michael Haynes .10
187 Erik Kramer .10
188 Chris Doleman .10
189 Haywood Jeffires .10
190 *Larry Whigham* .20
191 Shawn Jefferson .10
192 Pete Stoyanovich .10
193 Rod Bernstine .10
194 William Thomas .10
195 Marcus Allen .20
196 Dave Brown .10
197 *Harold Bishop* .20
198 Lorenzo Lynch .10
199 Dwight Stone .10
200 Jerry Rice 3.00
201 Raghib Ismail .10
202 LeRoy Butler .10
203 Glenn Parker .10
204 Bruce Armstrong .10
205 Shane Conlan .10
206 Russell Maryland .10
207 Herman Moore 1.00
208 Eric Martin .10
209 John Friesz .10
210 Boomer Esiason .10
211 Jim Harbaugh .10
212 Harold Green .10
213 *Perry Klein* .20
214 Eric Metcalf .10
215 Steve Everitt .10
216 Victor Bailey .10
217 Lincoln Kennedy .10
218 Glyn Milburn .10
219 John Copeland .10
220 Drew Bledsoe 3.00
221 Kevin Williams .20
222 Roosevelt Potts .10
223 Troy Drayton .10
224 Terry Kirby .10
225 Ron Moore .10
226 Tyrone Hughes .10
227 Wayne Simmons .10
228 Tony McGee .10
229 Derek Brown .10
230 Jason Elam .10
231 Qadry Ismail .10
232 O.J. McDuffie .20
233 Mike Caldwell .10
234 Reggie Brooks .10
235 Rick Mirer .20
236 Steve Tovar .10
237 Patrick Robinson .10
238 Tom Carter .10
239 Ben Coates .20
240 Jerome Bettis 1.25
241 Garrison Hearst 1.00
242 Natrone Means .75
243 Dana Stubblefield .20
244 William Roaf .10
245 Cortez Kennedy .10
246 *Todd Steussie* .20
247 Pat Coleman .10
248 David Wyman .10
249 Jeremy Lincoln .10
250 Carlester Crumpler .10
251 Dale Carter .10
252 Corey Raymond .10
253 Bryan Cox .10
254 *Charlie Garner* 6.00
255 Jeff Hostetler .20
256 Shane Bonham .10
257 Thomas Everett .10
258 John Jackson .10
259 *Terry Irving* .20
260 *Corey Sawyer* .20
261 Rob Waldrop .10
262 Curtis Conway .30
263 *Winfred Tubbs* .20
264 Sean Jones .10
265 James Washington .10
266 *Lonnie Johnson* .20
267 Rob Moore .10
268 Willie Anderson .10
269 Jon Hand .10
270 *Joe Patton* .20
271 Howard Ballard .10
272 *Fernando Smith* .20
273 Jessie Tuggle .10
274 John Alt .10
275 Corey Miller .10
276 *Gus Frerotte* 5.00
277 Jeff Cross .10
278 Kevin Smith .10
279 *Corey Louchiey* .20
280 Michael Barrow .10
281 *Jim Flanigan* .30
282 Calvin Williams .10
283 Jeff Jaeger .10
284 *John Reece* .20
285 Jason Hanson .10
286 *Kurt Haws* .20
287 Eric Davis .10
288 Maurice Hurst .10
289 Kirk Lowdermilk .10
290 Rod Woodson .10
291 Andre Reed .10
292 Vince Workman .10
293 Wayne Martin .10
294 *Keith Lyle* .20
295 Brett Favre 6.00
296 *Doug Brien* .20
297 Junior Seau .20
298 Randall McDaniel .10
299 Johnny Mitchell .10
300 Emmitt Smith 5.00
301 Michael Brooks .10
302 Steve Jackson .10
303 Jeff George .20
304 Irving Fryar .10
305 Derrick Thomas .10
306 Dante Jones .10
307 Darrell Green .10
308 Mark Bavaro .10
309 Eugene Robinson .10
310 Shannon Sharpe .20
311 Michael Timpson .10
312 Kevin Mitchell .10
313 Stevon Moore .10
314 Eric Swann .10
315 James Bostic .10
316 Robert Brooks 1.00
317 Pete Pierson .10
318 Jim Sweeny .10
319 Anthony Smith .10
320 Rohn Stark .10
321 Gary Anderson .10
322 Robert Porcher .10
323 Darryl Talley .10
324 Stan Humphries .20
325 Shelly Hammonds .10
326 Jim McMahon .10
327 Lamont Warren .10
328 *Chris Penn* .20
329 Tony Woods .10
330 *Raymont Harris* 2.00
331 *Mitch Davis* .20
332 Michael Irvin .20
333 Kent Graham .10
334 Brian Blades .10
335 Lomas Brown .10
336 Willie Drewrey .10
337 Russell Freeman .10
338 *Eric Zomalt* .20
339 Santana Dotson .10
340 Sterling Sharpe .20
341 *Ray Crittenden* .20
342 *Perry Carter* .20
343 *Austin Robbins* .20
344 *Mike Wells* .20
345 Toddrick McIntosh .10
346 Mark Carrier .10
347 Eugene Daniel .10
348 *Tre Johnson* .20
349 D.J. Johnson .10
350 Steve Young 1.50
351 Jim Pyne .10
352 Jocelyn Borgella .10
353 Pat Carter .10
354 *Sam Rogers* .20
355 *Jason Sehorn* .20
356 Darren Carrington .10
357 *Lamar Smith* 12.00
358 James Burton .10
359 Darrin Smith .10
360 Marco Coleman .10
361 Webster Slaughter .10
362 Lewis Tillman .10
363 David Alexander .10
364 *Bradford Banta* .20
365 Erric Pegram .10
366 Mike Fox .10
367 Jeff Lageman .10
368 Kurt Gouveia .10
369 Tim Brown .20
370 Seth Joyner .10
371 Irv Eatman .10
372 *Dorsey Levens* 12.00
373 Anthony Pleasant .10
374 Henry Jones .10
375 Cris Carter .20
376 Morten Andersen .10
377 Neil O'Donnell .10
378 *Tyronne Drakeford* .20
379 John Carney .10
380 Vincent Brown .10
381 J.J. Birden .10
382 Chris Spielman .10
383 Mark Bortz .10
384 Ray Childress .10
385 Carlton Bailey .10
386 Charles Haley .10
387 Shane Dronett .10
388 Jon Vaughn .10
389 Checklist 1 .10
390 Checklist 2 .10

1995 Bowman

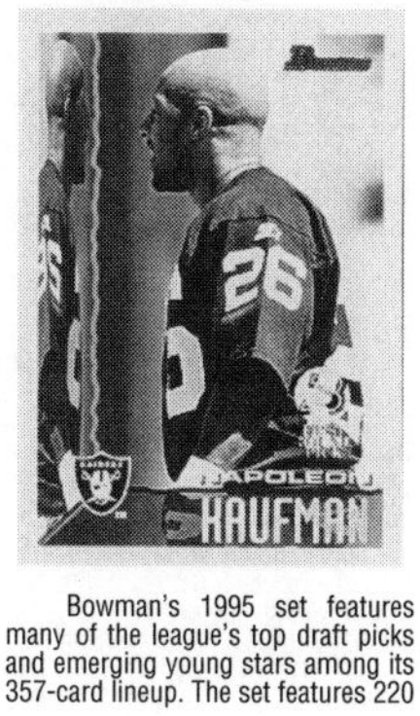

Bowman's 1995 set features many of the league's top draft picks and emerging young stars among its 357-card lineup. The set features 220 top players, 110 Draft Picks and 27 all-foil Expansion Team theme cards. Two insert sets were also made. Expansion Team cards are showcased utilizing an etched gold foil process with an embossed border (one per 12 packs), while 1st-Round Draft Picks highlights 22 players utilizing gold diffraction foil stamping (one per 12 packs). Each regular card in the set has a color action photo of the player on the right, with a smaller mirror image on a brown-shaded panel on the left. A team logo is in the lower left corner. The player's name is in the lower right corner, with his last name stamped in gold foil. The Bowman logo is in the upper right corner, stamped in red foil. The horizontal card back has biographical info, 1994 game-by-game stats and the player's name on one side; a color photo, team name, position and card number run along the right border.

MT
Complete Set (357): 125.00
Common Player: .10
Minor Stars: .20
Expansion Foils (221-247): .25
First Rounds: 1x-2x
Expansion Golds: 2x-4x
Pack (10): 4.00
Wax Box (24): 90.00
1 *Ki-Jana Carter* (1st Round Draft Picks) 1.00
2 *Tony Boselli* (1st Round Draft Picks) .50
3 *Steve McNair* (1st Round Draft Picks) 10.00
4 *Michael Westbrook* (1st Round Draft Picks) 3.00
5 *Kerry Collins* (1st Round Draft Picks) 5.00
6 *Kevin Carter* (1st Round Draft Picks) .50
7 *Mike Mamula* (1st Round Draft Picks) .10
8 *Joey Galloway* (1st Round Draft Picks) 5.00
9 *Kyle Brady* (1st Round Draft Picks) .50
10 *J.J. Stokes* (1st Round Draft Picks) 2.00
11 *Derrick Alexander* (1st Round Draft Picks) .10
12 *Warren Sapp* (1st Round Draft Picks) 2.00
13 *Mark Fields* (1st Round Draft Picks) .10
14 *Ruben Brown* (1st Round Draft Picks) .10
15 *Ellis Johnson* (1st Round Draft Picks) .10
16 *Hugh Douglas* (1st Round Draft Picks) .50
17 *Mike Pelton* (1st Round Draft Picks) .10
18 *Napoleon Kaufman* (1st Round Draft Picks) 6.00
19 *James Stewart* (1st Round Draft Picks) 5.00
20 *Luther Elliss* (1st Round Draft Picks) .10
21 *Rashaan Salaam* (1st Round Draft Picks) 1.00
22 *Tyrone Poole* (1st Round Draft Picks) .10
23 *Ty Law* (1st Round Draft Picks) .10
24 *Korey Stringer* .25
25 *Billy Milner* .10
26 *Devin Bush* .10
27 *Mark Bruener* .75
28 Derrick Brooks .10
29 Blake Brockermeyer .10
30 Alundis Brice .10
31 Trezelle Jenkins .10
32 *Craig Newsome* .40
33 Fred Barnett .10
34 Ray Childress .10
35 Chris Miller .10
36 Charles Haley .10
37 Ray Crittenden .10
38 Gus Frerotte .50
39 Jeff George .20
40 Dan Marino 3.00
41 Shawn Lee .10
42 Herman Moore .50
43 Chris Calloway .10
44 Jeff Graham .10
45 Ray Buchanan .10
46 Doug Pelfrey .10
47 Lake Dawson .25
48 Glenn Parker .10
49 Terry McDaniel .10
50 Rod Woodson .10
51 Santana Dotson .10
52 Anthony Miller .10
53 Bo Orlando .10
54 David Palmer .10
55 William Floyd .50
56 Edgar Bennett .10
57 *Jeff Blake* 1.00
58 Anthony Pleasant .10
59 Quinn Early .10
60 Bobby Houston .10
61 *Terrell Fletcher* .50
62 Gary Brown .10
63 Dwayne Sabb .10
64 Roman Phifer .10
65 *Sherman Williams* .50
66 Roosevelt Potts .10
67 Darnay Scott .40
68 Charlie Garner .10
69 Bert Emanuel .40
70 Herschel Walker .10
71 Lorenzo Styles .10
72 Andre Coleman .10
73 Tyronne Drakeford .10
74 Jay Novacek .10
75 Raymont Harris .10
76 *Tamarick Vanover* .50
77 Tom Carter .10
78 Eric Green .10
79 Patrick Hunter .10
80 Jeff Hostetler .20
81 Robert Blackmon .10
82 Anthony Cook .10
83 Craig Erickson .10
84 Glyn Milburn .10
85 Greg Lloyd .20
86 Brent Jones .10
87 Barrett Brooks .10
88 Alvin Harper .10
89 Sean Jones .10
90 Cris Carter .20
91 Russell Copeland .10
92 *Frank Sanders* 3.00
93 Mo Lewis .10
94 Michael Haynes .10
95 Andre Rison .10
96 Jesse James .10
97 Stan Humphries .20
98 James Hasty .10
99 Ricardo McDonald .10
100 Jerry Rice 1.50
101 Chris Hudson .10
102 David Meggett .10
103 Brian Mitchell .10
104 Mike Johnson .10
105 *Kordell Stewart* 10.00
106 Michael Brooks .10
107 Steve Walsh .10
108 Eric Metcalf .10
109 Ricky Watters .20
110 Brett Favre 3.00
111 Aubrey Beavers .10
112 Brian Williams .10
113 Eugene Robinson .10
114 Matt O'Dwyer .10
115 Michael Barrow .10
116 Raghib Ismail .10
117 Scott Gragg .10
118 Leon Lett .10
119 Reggie Roby .10
120 Marshall Faulk 1.00
121 Jack Jackson .10
122 Keith Byars .10
123 Eric Hill .10
124 Todd Sauerbrun .10
125 Dexter Carter .10
126 Vinny Testaverde .10
127 Shane Conlan .10
128 Terrance Shaw .10
129 William Roaf .10
130 Jim Kelly .20
131 Neil O'Donnell .20
132 Ray McElroy .10
133 Ed McDaniel .10
134 Brian Gelzheiser .10
135 Marcus Allen .20
136 Carl Pickens .20
137 Mike Verstegen .10
138 Chris Mims .10
139 Darryl Pounds .10
140 Emmitt Smith 3.00
141 Mike Frederick .10
142 Henry Ellard .10
143 Willie McGinest .10
144 Michael Roan .10
145 Chris Spielman .10
146 Darryl Talley .10
147 Randall Cunningham .10
148 Andrew Greene .10
149 George Teague .10
150 Tyrone Hughes .10
151 Ron Davis .10
152 Stevon Moore .10
153 Merton Hanks .10
154 Darren Perry .10
155 Dave Brown .10
156 Mike Morton .10
157 Seth Joyner .10
158 Bryan Cox .10
159 Corey Fuller .10
160 John Elway .50
161 Dewayne Washington .10
162 Chris Warren .25
163 Jeff Kopp .10
164 Sean Dawkins .10
165 Mark Carrier .10
166 Andre Hastings .10
167 Derek West .10
168 Glenn Montgomery .10
169 Trent Dilfer .40
170 *Rob Johnson* 8.00
171 Todd Scott .10
172 Charles Johnson .25
173 Kez McCorvey .10
174 Rob Fredrickson .10
175 Corey Sawyer .10
176 Brett Perriman .10
177 *Ken Dilger* .40
178 Dana Stubblefield .10
179 Eric Allen .10
180 Drew Bledsoe 1.50
181 Tyrone Davis .10
182 Reggie Brooks .10
183 Dale Carter .10
184 William Henderson .10
185 Reggie White .20
186 Lorenzo White .10
187 Leslie O'Neal .10
188 *Stoney Case* .50
189 Jeff Burris .10
190 Leroy Hoard .10
191 Thomas Randolph .10
192 *Rodney Thomas* .40
193 Quentin Coryatt .10
194 Terry Wooden .10
195 *David Sloan* .25
196 Bernie Parmalee .25
197 *Zack Crockett* .25
198 Troy Aikman 1.50
199 Bruce Smith .10
200 *Eric Zeier* .20
201 Anthony Smith .10
202 Jake Reed .10
203 Hardy Nickerson .10
204 Patrick Riley .10
205 Bruce Matthews .10
206 Larry Centers .10
207 Troy Drayton .10
208 John Burrough .10
209 Jason Elam .10
210 Donnell Woolford .10
211 Sam Shade .10
212 Kevin Greene .10
213 Ronald Moore .10
214 Shane Hannah .10
215 Jim Everett .10
216 Scott Mitchell .20
217 *Antonio Freeman* 15.00
218 Tony McGee .10
219 Clay Matthews .10
220 Neil Smith .10
221 Mark Williams (Expansion Team) .25
222 Derrick Graham (Expansion Team) .25
223 Mike Hollis (Expansion Team) .25
224 Darion Conner (Expansion Team) .25
225 Steve Beuerlein (Expansion Team) .25
226 Rod Smith (Expansion Team) .25
227 James Williams (Expansion Team) .25
228 Bob Christian (Expansion Team) .25
229 Jeff Lageman (Expansion Team) .25
230 Frank Reich (Expansion Team) .25
231 Harry Colon (Expansion Team) .25
232 Carlton Bailey (Expansion Team) .25
233 Mickey Washington (Expansion Team) .25
234 Shawn Bouwens (Expansion Team) .25
235 Don Beebe (Expansion Team) .25
236 Kelvin Pritchett (Expansion Team) .25
237 Tommy Barnhardt (Expansion Team) .25
238 Mike Dumas (Expansion Team) .25
239 Brett Maxie (Expansion Team) .25
240 Desmond Howard (Expansion Team) .25
241 Sam Mills (Expansion Team) .25
242 Keith Goganious (Expansion Team) .25
243 Bubba McDowell (Expansion Team) .25
244 Vinnie Clark (Expansion Team) .25
245 Lamar Lathon (Expansion Team) .25
246 Bryan Barker (Expansion Team) .25
247 Darren Carrington (Expansion Team) .25
248 Jay Barker .10
249 Eric Davis .10
250 Heath Shuler 1.00
251 Donta Jones .10
252 LeRoy Butler .10
253 Michael Zordich .10
254 Cortez Kennedy .10
255 Brian DeMarco .10
256 Randal Hill .10
257 Michael Irvin .50
258 Natrone Means 1.00
259 Linc Harden .10
260 Jerome Bettis .50
261 Tony Bennett .10
262 Dameian Jeffries .10
263 Cornelius Bennett .10
264 Chris Zorich .10
265 Bobby Taylor .10
266 Terrell Buckley .10
267 Troy Dumas .10
268 Rodney Hampton .10
269 Steve Everitt .10
270 Mel Gray .10
271 Antonio Armstrong .10
272 Jim Harbaugh .10
273 Gary Clark .10
274 Tau Pupua .10
275 Warren Moon .20
276 Corey Croom .10
277 Tony Berti .10
278 Shannon Sharpe .10
279 Boomer Esiason .10
280 Aeneas Williams .10
281 Lethon Flowers .10
282 Derek Brown .10
283 Charlie Williams .10
284 Dan Wilkinson .10
285 Mike Sherrard .10
286 Evan Pilgrim .10
287 Kimble Anders .10
288 Greg Jefferson .10
289 Ken Norton .10
290 Terance Mathis .10
291 Torey Hunter .10
292 Ken Harvey .10
293 Irving Fryar .10
294 Michael Reed .10
295 Andre Reed .10
296 Vencie Glenn .10
297 Corey Swinson .10
298 Harvey Williams .10
299 Willie Davis .10
300 Barry Sanders 3.00
301 *Curtis Martin* 10.00
302 Johnny Mitchell .10
303 Daryl Johnston .10
304 Lorenzo Lynch .10
305 *Christian Fauria* .50
306 Sean Gilbert .10
307 *Ray Zellars* .50
308 William Strong .10
309 Jack Del Rio .10
310 Junior Seau .20
311 Justin Armour .10
312 Eric Bjorson .10
313 Vincent Brown .10
314 Darius Holland .10
315 *Chad May* .50
316 Simon Fletcher .10
317 Roell Preston .10
318 John Thierry .10
319 Orlanda Thomas .10
320 Zach Wiegert .10
321 Derrick Alexander .10
322 Chris Cowart .10
323 *Chris Sanders* 1.50
324 Robert Brooks .25
325 *Todd Collins* .50
326 Ken Irvin .10
327 Erric Pegram .10
328 Damien Covington .10
329 Brendan Stai .10
330 *James Stewart* .50
331 Jessie Tuggle .10
332 Marco Coleman .10
333 Steve Young 1.50
334 Greg Hill .40
335 Darryl Williams .10
336 Calvin Williams .10
337 Cris Dishman .10
338 Anthony Morgan .10
339 Renaldo Turnbull .10
340 Rick Mirer .50
341 Tim Brown .20
342 Dennis Gibson .10
343 Brad Baxter .10
344 Henry Jones .10
345 Johnny Bailey .10
346 Qadry Ismail .10
347 Richmond Webb .10
348 Robert Jones .10
349 Garrison Hearst .20
350 Errict Rhett 1.00
351 Steve Atwater .10
352 Joe Cain .10
353 Ben Coates .10
354 Aaron Glenn .10
355 Antonio Langham .10
356 Eugene Daniel .10
357 Tim Bowens .10

1995 Bowman's Best

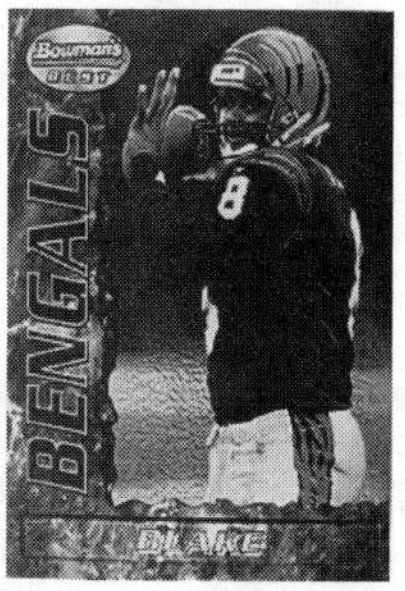

Ninety veterans, 90 rookies and 15 Mirror Image cards make up the debut set of Bowman's Best Football. Bowman's Best 1995 is divided into three subsets - Black Series (90 veterans), Blue Series (90 rookies) and Mirror Images, which show off one of this year's first-round draft choices on one side and last year's corresponding first-round pick on the other (1 per every four packs). The entire set was also done in a refractor version. Black and Blue Series Refractors could be found one per six packs, while Mirror Images Refractors were seeded one per 36 packs. The Black and Blue Series cards have the same format, except the L-shaped border containing the player's team name and his last name are in the corresponding color. An action photo completes the card front design. The back has an action photo, with biographical information, best skills, best stats and the player's name against the corresponding subset color. Mirror Images cards use a black background for the 1994 first-round picks and a blue background for the 1995 selections. A circle with the overall number the player was drafted at is also included.

MT
Complete Set (180): 220.00
Common Player: .50
Minor Stars: 1.00
Refractor Cards: 4x-8x
Refractor Rookies: 2x-4x
Inserted 1:6
Pack (7): 11.00
Wax Box (24): 250.00
V1 Rob Moore .50
V2 Craig Heyward .50
V3 Jim Kelly 1.00
V4 John Kasay .50
V5 Jeff Graham .50
V6 *Jeff Blake* 2.50
V7 Antonio Langham .50
V8 Troy Aikman 4.00
V9 Simon Fletcher .50
V10 Barry Sanders 8.00
V11 Edgar Bennett .50
V12 Ray Childress .50
V13 Ray Buchanan .50
V14 Desmond Howard .50
V15 Dale Carter .50
V16 Troy Vincent .50
V17 David Palmer .50
V18 Ben Coates .50
V19 Derek Brown .50
V20 Dave Brown .50
V21 Mo Lewis .50
V22 Harvey Williams .50
V23 Randall Cunningham .50
V24 Kevin Greene .50
V25 Junior Seau 1.00
V26 Merton Hanks .50
V27 Cortez Kennedy .50
V28 Troy Drayton .50
V29 Hardy Nickerson .50
V30 Brian Mitchell .50
V31 Raymont Harris .50
V32 Keith Goganious .50
V33 Andre Reed .50
V34 Terance Mathis .50
V35 Garrison Hearst 1.00
V36 Glyn Milburn .50
V37 Emmitt Smith 6.00
V38 Vinny Testaverde .50
V39 Darnay Scott 1.00
V40 Mickey Washington .50
V41 Craig Erickson .50
V42 Chris Chandler .50
V43 Brett Favre 8.00
V44 Scott Mitchell .50
V45 Chris Slade .50
V46 Warren Moon 1.00
V47 Dan Marino 6.00
V48 Greg Hill .50
V49 Raghib Ismail .50
V50 Bobby Houston .50
V51 Rodney Hampton .50
V52 Jim Everett .50
V53 Rick Mirer 1.00

V54	Steve Young	3.00
V55	Dennis Gibson	.50
V56	Rod Woodson	.50
V57	Calvin Williams	.50
V58	Tom Carter	.50
V59	Trent Dilfer	1.00
V60	Shane Conlan	.50
V61	Cornelius Bennett	.50
V62	Eric Metcalf	.50
V63	Frank Reich	.50
V64	Eric Hill	.50
V65	Erik Kramer	.50
V66	Michael Irvin	1.00
V67	Tony McGee	.50
V68	Andre Rison	.50
V69	Shannon Sharpe	.50
V70	Quentin Coryatt	.50
V71	Robert Brooks	1.50
V72	Steve Beuerlein	.50
V73	Herman Moore	2.00
V74	Jack Del Rio	.50
V75	David Meggett	.50
V76	Pete Stoyanovich	.50
V77	Neil Smith	.50
V78	Corey Miller	.50
V79	Tim Brown	1.00
V80	Tyrone Hughes	.50
V81	Boomer Esiason	.50
V82	Natrone Means	1.00
V83	Chris Warren	1.00
V84	Byron Morris	.50
V85	Jerry Rice	4.00
V86	Michael Zordich	.50
V87	Errict Rhett	2.00
V88	Henry Ellard	.50
V89	Chris Miller	.50
V90	John Elway	3.00
R1	*Ki-Jana Carter*	2.00
R2	*Tony Boselli*	1.00
R3	*Steve McNair*	18.00
R4	*Michael Westbrook*	4.00
R5	*Kerry Collins*	12.00
R6	*Kevin Carter*	1.00
R7	*Mike Mamula*	1.00
R8	*Joey Galloway*	8.00
R9	*Kyle Brady*	1.50
R10	*Ray McElroy*	.50
R11	*Derrick Alexander*	.50
R12	*Warren Sapp*	4.00
R13	*Mark Fields*	.50
R14	*Ruben Brown*	.50
R15	*Ellis Johnson*	.50
R16	*Hugh Douglas*	1.50
R17	*Alundis Brice*	.50
R18	*Napoleon Kaufman*	12.00
R19	*James Stewart*	15.00
R20	*Luther Elliss*	.50
R21	*Rashaan Salaam*	2.00
R22	*Tyrone Poole*	.50
R23	*Ty Law*	.50
R24	*Korey Stringer*	1.00
R25	*Billy Milner*	.50
R26	*Roell Preston*	.50
R27	*Mark Bruener*	1.00
R28	*Derrick Brooks*	.50
R29	*Blake Brockermeyer*	.50
R30	*Mike Frederick*	.50
R31	*Trezelle Jenkins*	.50
R32	*Craig Newsome*	1.00
R33	*Matt O'Dwyer*	.50
R34	*Terrance Shaw*	.50
R35	*Anthony Cook*	.50
R36	*Darick Holmes*	2.00
R37	*Cory Raymer*	.50
R38	*Zach Wiegert*	.50
R39	*Sam Shade*	.50
R40	*Brian DeMarco*	.50
R41	*Ron Davis*	.50
R42	*Orlanda Thomas*	.50
R43	*Derek West*	.50
R44	*Ray Zellars*	1.50
R45	*Todd Collins*	1.50
R46	*Linc Harden*	.50
R47	*Frank Sanders*	5.00
R48	*Ken Dilger*	1.50
R49	*Barrett Robbins*	.50
R50	*Bobby Taylor*	.50
R51	*Terrell Fletcher*	1.50
R52	*Jack Jackson*	.50
R53	*Jeff Kopp*	.50
R54	*Brendan Stai*	.50
R55	*Corey Fuller*	.50
R56	*Todd Sauerbrun*	.50
R57	*Dameian Jeffries*	.50
R58	*Troy Dumas*	.50
R59	*Charlie Williams*	.50
R60	*Kordell Stewart*	15.00
R61	*Jay Barker*	.50
R62	*Jesse James*	.50
R63	*Shane Hannah*	.50
R64	*Rob Johnson*	15.00
R65	*Darius Holland*	.50
R66	*William Henderson*	.50
R67	*Chris Sanders*	2.00
R68	*Darryl Pounds*	.50
R69	*Melvin Tuten*	.50
R70	*David Sloan*	.50
R71	*Chris Hudson*	.50
R72	*William Strong*	.50
R73	*Brian Williams*	.50
R74	*Curtis Martin*	20.00
R75	*Mike Verstegen*	.50
R76	*Justin Armour*	.50
R77	*Lorenzo Styles*	.50
R78	*Oliver Gibson*	.50
R79	*Zack Crockett*	1.00
R80	*Tau Pupua*	.50
R81	*Tamarick Vanover*	1.25
R82	*Steve McLaughlin*	.50
R83	*Sean Harris*	.50
R84	*Eric Zeier*	1.00
R85	*Rodney Young*	.50
R86	*Chad May*	1.00
R87	*Evan Pilgrim*	.50
R88	*James Stewart*	1.50
R89	*Torey Hunter*	.50
R90	*Antonio Freeman*	20.00

1995 Bowman's Best Refractors

Each of the 195 cards in Bowman's Best football was done in a Refractor version. Black and Blue Series Refractors were seeded one per six packs; Mirror Images Refractors were seeded one per 36 packs. Each Refractor, which has a shiny, rainbow effect, has the same format as its regular counterpart, except it is labeled on the back with the card number as being a Refractor.

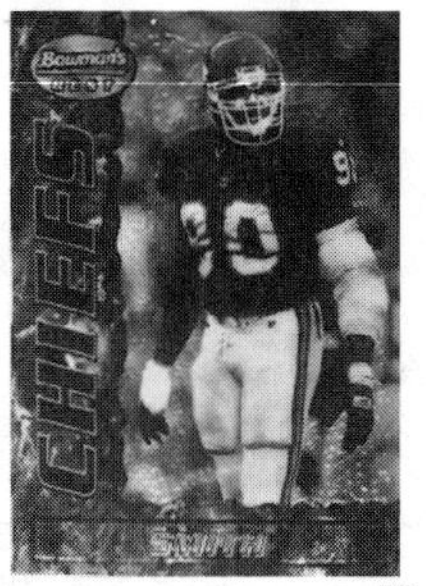

		MT
Complete Set (180):		1200.
Common Player:		4.00
Minor Stars:		8.00
Unlisted Cards:		4x-8x
V1	Rob Moore	4.00
V2	Craig Heyward	4.00
V3	Jim Kelly	8.00
V4	John Kasay	4.00
V5	Jeff Graham	4.00
V6	*Jeff Blake*	8.00
V7	Antonio Langham	4.00
V8	Troy Aikman	30.00
V9	Simon Fletcher	4.00
V10	Barry Sanders	60.00
V11	Edgar Bennett	4.00
V12	Ray Childress	4.00
V13	Ray Buchanan	4.00
V14	Desmond Howard	4.00
V15	Dale Carter	4.00
V16	Troy Vincent	4.00
V17	David Palmer	4.00
V18	Ben Coates	4.00
V19	Derek Brown	4.00
V20	Dave Brown	4.00
V21	Mo Lewis	4.00
V22	Harvey Williams	4.00
V23	Randall Cunningham	4.00
V24	Kevin Greene	4.00
V25	Junior Seau	8.00
V26	Merton Hanks	4.00
V27	Cortez Kennedy	4.00
V28	Troy Drayton	4.00
V29	Hardy Nickerson	4.00
V30	Brian Mitchell	4.00
V31	Raymont Harris	10.00
V32	Keith Goganious	4.00
V33	Andre Reed	4.00
V34	Terance Mathis	4.00
V35	Garrison Hearst	10.00
V36	Glyn Milburn	4.00
V37	Emmitt Smith	50.00
V38	Vinny Testaverde	4.00
V39	Darnay Scott	8.00
V40	Mickey Washington	4.00
V41	Craig Erickson	4.00
V42	Chris Chandler	4.00
V43	Brett Favre	60.00
V44	Scott Mitchell	8.00
V45	Chris Slade	4.00
V46	Warren Moon	8.00
V47	Dan Marino	50.00
V48	Greg Hill	8.00
V49	Raghib Ismail	4.00
V50	Bobby Houston	4.00
V51	Rodney Hampton	4.00
V52	Jim Everett	4.00
V53	Rick Mirer	8.00
V54	Steve Young	20.00
V55	Dennis Gibson	4.00
V56	Rod Woodson	4.00
V57	Calvin Williams	4.00
V58	Tom Carter	4.00
V59	Trent Dilfer	8.00
V60	Shane Conlan	4.00
V61	Cornelius Bennett	4.00
V62	Eric Metcalf	4.00
V63	Frank Reich	4.00
V64	Eric Hill	4.00
V65	Erik Kramer	4.00
V66	Michael Irvin	8.00
V67	Tony McGee	4.00
V68	Andre Rison	4.00
V69	Shannon Sharpe	4.00
V70	Quentin Coryatt	4.00
V71	Robert Brooks	8.00
V72	Steve Beuerlein	4.00
V73	Herman Moore	10.00
V74	Jack Del Rio	4.00
V75	David Meggett	4.00
V76	Pete Stoyanovich	4.00
V77	Neil Smith	4.00
V78	Corey Miller	4.00
V79	Tim Brown	8.00
V80	Tyrone Hughes	4.00
V81	Boomer Esiason	4.00
V82	Natrone Means	10.00
V83	Chris Warren	8.00
V84	Byron Morris	4.00
V85	Jerry Rice	30.00
V86	Michael Zordich	4.00
V87	Errict Rhett	8.00
V88	Henry Ellard	4.00
V89	Chris Miller	4.00
V90	John Elway	50.00
R1	*Ki-Jana Carter*	8.00
R2	*Tony Boselli*	8.00
R3	*Steve McNair*	60.00
R4	*Michael Westbrook*	35.00
R5	*Kerry Collins*	20.00
R6	*Kevin Carter*	8.00
R7	*Mike Mamula*	8.00
R8	*Joey Galloway*	60.00
R9	*Kyle Brady*	8.00
R10	*Ray McElroy*	4.00
R11	*Derrick Alexander*	8.00
R12	*Warren Sapp*	8.00
R13	*Mark Fields*	4.00
R14	*Ruben Brown*	4.00
R15	*Ellis Johnson*	4.00
R16	*Hugh Douglas*	4.00
R17	*Alundis Brice*	4.00
R18	*Napoleon Kaufman*	40.00
R19	*James Stewart*	40.00
R20	*Luther Elliss*	4.00
R21	*Rashaan Salaam*	10.00
R22	*Tyrone Poole*	4.00
R23	*Ty Law*	4.00
R24	*Korey Stringer*	8.00
R25	*Billy Milner*	4.00
R26	*Roell Preston*	4.00
R27	*Mark Bruener*	8.00
R28	*Derrick Brooks*	4.00
R29	*Blake Brockermeyer*	4.00
R30	*Mike Frederick*	4.00
R31	*Trezelle Jenkins*	4.00
R32	*Craig Newsome*	8.00
R33	*Matt O'Dwyer*	4.00
R34	*Terrance Shaw*	4.00
R35	*Anthony Cook*	4.00
R36	*Darick Holmes*	10.00
R37	*Cory Raymer*	4.00
R38	*Zach Wiegert*	4.00
R39	*Sam Shade*	4.00
R40	*Brian DeMarco*	4.00
R41	*Ron Davis*	4.00
R42	*Orlanda Thomas*	4.00
R43	*Derek West*	4.00
R44	*Ray Zellars*	8.00
R45	*Todd Collins*	8.00
R46	*Linc Harden*	4.00
R47	*Frank Sanders*	15.00
R48	*Ken Dilger*	8.00
R49	*Barrett Robbins*	4.00
R50	*Bobby Taylor*	4.00
R51	*Terrell Fletcher*	8.00
R52	*Jack Jackson*	4.00
R53	*Jeff Kopp*	4.00
R54	*Brendan Stai*	4.00
R55	*Corey Fuller*	4.00
R56	*Todd Sauerbrun*	4.00
R57	*Dameian Jeffries*	4.00
R58	*Troy Dumas*	4.00
R59	*Charlie Williams*	4.00
R60	*Kordell Stewart*	60.00
R61	*Jay Barker*	4.00
R62	*Jesse James*	4.00
R63	*Shane Hannah*	4.00
R64	*Rob Johnson*	25.00
R65	*Darius Holland*	4.00
R66	*William Henderson*	10.00
R67	*Chris Sanders*	8.00
R68	*Darryl Pounds*	4.00
R69	*Melvin Tuten*	4.00
R70	*David Sloan*	4.00
R71	*Chris Hudson*	4.00
R72	*William Strong*	4.00
R73	*Brian Williams*	4.00
R74	*Curtis Martin*	60.00
R75	*Mike Verstegen*	4.00
R76	*Justin Armour*	4.00
R77	*Lorenzo Styles*	4.00
R78	*Oliver Gibson*	4.00
R79	*Zack Crockett*	8.00
R80	*Tau Pupua*	4.00
R81	*Tamarick Vanover*	8.00
R82	*Steve McLaughlin*	4.00
R83	*Sean Harris*	4.00
R84	*Eric Zeier*	8.00
R85	*Rodney Young*	8.00
R86	*Chad May*	8.00
R87	*Evan Pilgrim*	4.00
R88	*James Stewart*	8.00
R89	*Torey Hunter*	4.00
R90	*Antonio Freeman*	60.00

1995 Bowman's Best Mirror Images

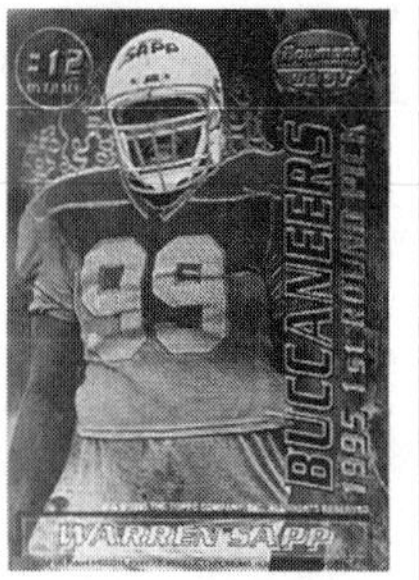

These cards feature one of 1995's first-round draft picks on one side, with the corresponding 1994 pick on the other. The 1994 picks use black for the background; the 1995 picks use blue. A circle with the overall number the player was selected at is also included on both sides. Regular Mirror Images cards were seeded one per four packs of 1995 Bowman's Best football. Mirror Images Refractors were seeded one per 36 packs.

		MT
Complete Set (15):		35.00
Common Player:		1.00
Minor Stars:		2.00
Inserted 1:4		
Refractor Cards:		3x-6x
Inserted 1:36		
1	Ki-Jana Carter, Dan Wilkinson	2.00
2	Marshall Faulk, Tony Boselli	2.00
3	Steve McNair, Heath Shuler	8.00
4	Michael Westbrook, Willie McGinist	3.00
5	Kerry Collins, Trev Alberts	3.00
6	Trent Dilfer, Kevin Carter	2.00
7	Mike Mamula, Bryant Young	1.00
8	Joey Galloway, Sam Adams	6.00
9	Kyle Brady, Antonio Langham	1.00
10	J.J. Stokes, Jamir Miller	3.00
11	Derrick Alexander, John Thierry	1.00
12	Warren Sapp, Aaron Glenn	1.00
13	Mark Fields, Joe Johnson	1.00
14	Ruben Brown, Bernard Williams	1.00
15	Ellis Johnson, Wayne Gandy	1.00

1996 Bowman's Best

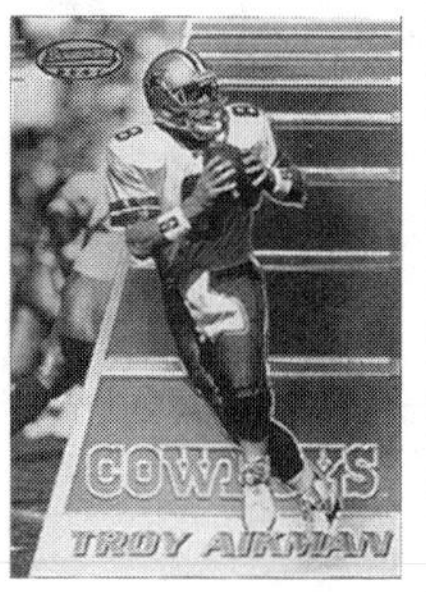

Bowman's Best contained 135 key veterans on gold designs and 45 1996 NFL draft picks on silver designed cards. All 180 cards are also found in a parallel Refractors and Atomic Refractors insert. The cards show the player in front of a fake field with yard markers running down the length of the card. The player's name and team logo are near the bottom. Bowman's Best had three inserts - Mirror Images, Best Bets and Best Cuts.

		MT
Complete Set (180):		110.00
Common Player:		.25
Minor Stars:		.50
Refractors:		5x-10x
Atomic Refractors:		15x-30x
Pack (6):		5.00
Wax Box (24):		115.00
1	Emmitt Smith	6.00
2	Kordell Stewart	4.00
3	Mark Chmura	.25
4	Sean Dawkins	.25
5	Steve Young	3.00
6	Tamarick Vanover	1.00
7	Scott Mitchell	.25
8	Aaron Hayden	.25
9	William Thomas	.25
10	Dan Marino	6.00
11	Curtis Conway	.25
12	Steve Atwater	.25
13	Derrick Brooks	.25
14	Rick Mirer	.25
15	Mark Brunell	3.00
16	Garrison Hearst	.25
17	Eric Turner	.25
18	Mark Carrier	.25
19	Darnay Scott	.25
20	Steve McNair	4.00
21	Jim Everett	.25
22	Wayne Chrebet	.25
23	Ben Coates	.25
24	Harvey Williams	.25
25	Michael Westbrook	.50
26	Kevin Carter	.25
27	Dave Brown	.25
28	Jake Reed	.25
29	Thurman Thomas	.50
30	Jeff George	.25
31	Carnell Lake	.25
32	J.J. Stokes	.50
33	Jay Novacek	.25
34	Brett Perriman	.25
35	Robert Brooks	.25
36	Neil Smith	.25
37	Chris Zorich	.25
38	Michael Barrow	.25
39	Quentin Coryatt	.25
40	Kerry Collins	.75
41	Aeneas Williams	.25
42	James Stewart	.25
43	Warren Moon	.25
44	Willie McGinest	.25
45	Rodney Hampton	.25
46	Jeff Hostetler	.25
47	Darrell Green	.25
48	Warren Sapp	.25
49	Troy Drayton	.25
50	Junior Seau	.25
51	Mike Mamula	.25
52	Antonio Langham	.25
53	Eric Metcalf	.25
54	Adrian Murrell	.25
55	Joey Galloway	1.00
56	Anthony Miller	.25
57	Carl Pickens	.25
58	Bruce Smith	.25
59	Merton Hanks	.25
60	Troy Aikman	3.00
61	Erik Kramer	.25
62	Tyrone Poole	.25
63	Michael Jackson	.25
64	Rob Moore	.25
65	Marcus Allen	.25
66	Orlando Thomas	.25
67	David Meggett	.25
68	Trent Dilfer	.25
69	Herman Moore	.75
70	Brett Favre	8.00
71	Blaine Bishop	.25
72	Eric Allen	.25
73	Bernie Parmalee	.25
74	Kyle Brady	.25
75	Terry McDaniel	.25
76	Rodney Peete	.25
77	Yancey Thigpen	.25
78	Stan Humphries	.25
79	Craig Heyward	.25
80	Rashaan Salaam	.75
81	Shannon Sharpe	.25
82	Jim Harbaugh	.25
83	Vinnie Clark	.25
84	Steve Bono	.25
85	Drew Bledsoe	3.00
86	Ken Norton	.25
87	Brian Mitchell	.25
88	Hardy Nickerson	.25
89	Todd Lyght	.25
90	Barry Sanders	5.00
91	Robert Blackmon	.25
92	Larry Centers	.25
93	Jim Kelly	.25
94	Lamar Lathon	.25
95	Cris Carter	.25
96	Hugh Douglas	.25
97	Michael Strahan	.25
98	Lee Woodall	.25
99	Michael Irvin	.25
100	Marshall Faulk	1.00
101	Terance Mathis	.25
102	Eric Zeier	.25
103	Marty Carter	.25
104	Steve Tovar	.25
105	Isaac Bruce	1.00
106	Tony Martin	.25
107	Dale Carter	.25
108	Terry Kirby	.25
109	Tyrone Hughes	.25
110	Bryce Paup	.25
111	Errict Rhett	.75
112	Ricky Watters	.50
113	Chris Chandler	.25
114	Edgar Bennett	.25
115	John Elway	3.00
116	Sam Mills	.25
117	Seth Joyner	.25
118	Jeff Lageman	.25
119	Chris Calloway	.25
120	Curtis Martin	4.00
121	Ken Harvey	.25
122	Eugene Daniel	.25
123	Tim Brown	.25
124	Mo Lewis	.25
125	Jeff Blake	.75
126	Jessie Tuggle	.25
127	Vinny Testaverde	.25
128	Chris Warren	.25
129	Terrell Davis	8.00
130	Greg Lloyd	.25
131	Deion Sanders	2.00
132	Derrick Thomas	.25
133	Darryll Lewis	.25
134	Reggie White	.50
135	Jerry Rice	3.00
136	*Tony Banks*	5.00
137	*Derrick Mayes*	3.00
138	*Leeland McElroy*	.75
139	*Bryan Still*	.25
140	*Tim Biakabutuka*	2.00
141	*Rickey Dudley*	2.00
142	*Troy James*	.25
143	*Lawyer Milloy*	.25
144	*Mike Ulufale*	.25
145	*Bobby Engram*	.75
146	*Willie Anderson*	1.00
147	*Terrell Owens*	15.00
148	*Jonathan Ogden*	1.00
149	*Darrius Johnson*	.25
150	*Kevin Hardy*	.50
151	*Simeon Rice*	.50
152	*Alex Molden*	.25
153	*Cedric Jones*	.25
154	*Duane Clemons*	.25
155	*Karim Abdul-Jabbar*	2.00
156	*Dedric Mathis*	.25
157	*John Michels*	.25
158	*Winslow Oliver*	.25
159	*Stepfret Williams*	.25
160	*Eddie Kennison*	1.00
161	*Marcus Coleman*	.25
162	*Tedy Bruschi*	.25
163	*Detron Smith*	.25
164	*Ray Lewis*	10.00
165	*Marvin Harrison*	15.00
166	*Je'Rod Cherry*	.25
167	*Jerris McPhail*	.25
168	*Eric Moulds*	10.00
169	*Walt Harris*	.50
170	*Eddie George*	20.00
171	*Jermaine Lewis*	3.00
172	*Jeff Lewis*	.75
173	*Ray Mickens*	.25
174	*Amani Toomer*	6.00
175	*Zach Thomas*	2.50
176	*Lawrence Phillips*	2.00
177	*John Mobley*	.25
178	*Anthony Dorsett Jr.*	.25
179	*DeRon Jenkins*	.25
180	*Keyshawn Johnson*	10.00

1996 Bowman's Best Refractors

All 180 cards in Bowman's Best Football had parallel Refractor versions, inserted every 12 packs. The fronts feature a refractive foil, while the backs contain the word "Refractor" within the white card number box.

	MT
Refractors:	5x-10x

1996 Bowman's Best Atomic Refractors

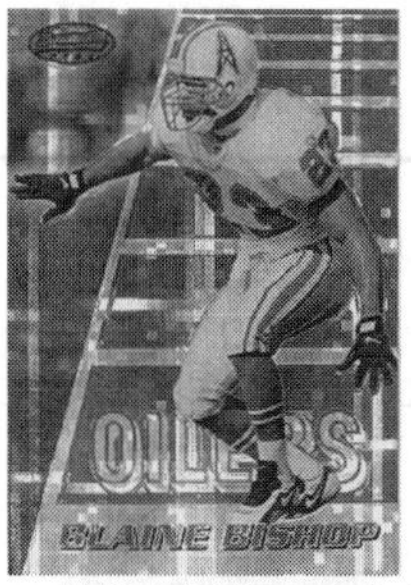

All 180 cards in Bowman's Best Football also had Atomic Refractor parallel versions, inserted every 48 packs. Atomic Refractors featured a prismatic refractive foil on the card fronts and the words "Atomic Refractor" on the back within the white card number box.

	MT
Atomic Refractors:	15x-30x

1996 Bowman's Best Mirror Images

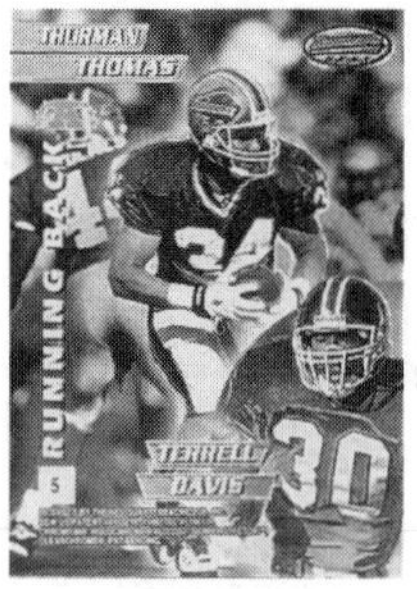

Bowman's Best Mirror Images was a nine-card insert that featured four players per card, with two on each side. Regular versions are seeded every 48 packs, Refractors are found every 96 packs and Atomic Refractors are seeded every 192 packs. Card No. 7 has Jerry Rice on the front with Isaac Bruce with him, but lists running back as their position. This card was an uncorrected error.

		MT
Complete Set (9):		175.00
Common Player:		12.00
Refractors:		2x
Atomic Refractors:		4x
1a	Steve Young, Kerry Collins	40.00
1b	Dan Marino, Mark Brunell	40.00
2a	Brett Favre, Elvis Grbac	40.00
2b	John Elway, Drew Bledsoe	40.00
3a	Troy Aikman, Gus Frerotte	20.00
3b	Jim Harbaugh, Jeff Blake	20.00
4a	Emmitt Smith, Errict Rhett	40.00
4b	Chris Warren, Curtis Martin	40.00
5a	Barry Sanders, Rashaan Salaam	25.00
5b	Thurman Thomas, Terrell Davis	25.00
6a	Rodney Hampton, Lawrence Phillips	12.00
6b	Marcus Allen, Marshall Faulk	12.00
7a	Jerry Rice, Isaac Bruce	20.00
7b	Tim Brown, Joey Galloway	20.00
8a	Cris Carter, Curtis Conway	12.00
8b	Carl Pickens, Keyshawn Johnson	12.00
9a	Robert Brooks, Michael Westbrook	12.00
9b	Anthony Miller, O.J. McDuffie	12.00

1996 Bowman's Best Best Cuts

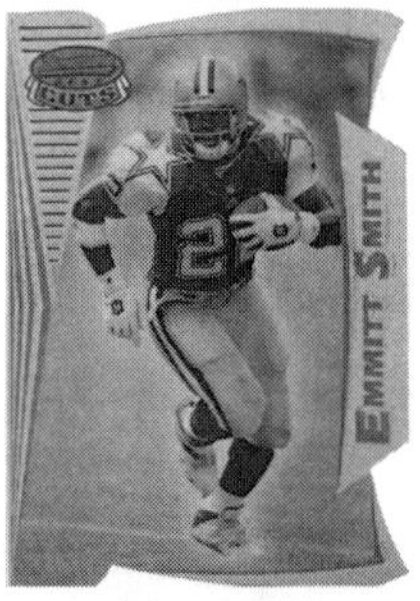

Bowman's Best Cuts displays 15 of the top players in the NFL on die-cut chromium cards. The player's name runs along the right side, with the majority of the die-cutting on that side. Regular versions are found every 24 packs, Refractors are seeded every 48 packs and Atomic Refractor versions are found every 96 packs.

		MT
Complete Set (15):		250.00
Common Player:		5.00
Refractors:		2x
Atomic Refractors:		4x
1	Dan Marino	40.00
2	Emmitt Smith	40.00
3	Rashaan Salaam	5.00
4	Herman Moore	5.00
5	Brett Favre	40.00
6	Marshall Faulk	10.00
7	John Elway	12.00
8	Curtis Martin	25.00
9	Deion Sanders	12.00
10	Jerry Rice	20.00
11	Terrell Davis	20.00
12	Kerry Collins	8.00
13	Steve Young	15.00
14	Troy Aikman	20.00
15	Barry Sanders	20.00

1996 Bowman's Best Best Bets

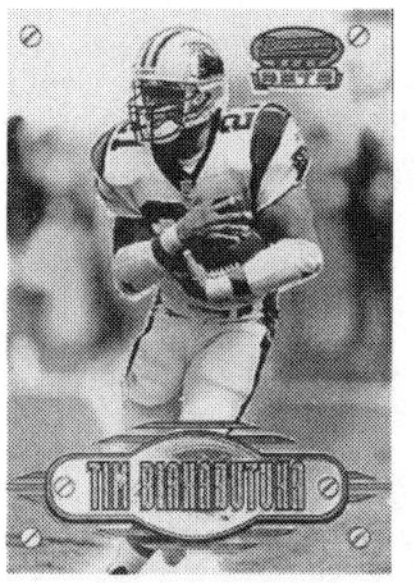

Bowman's Best Bets highlighted nine top rookies on a borderless design with "screws" in all four corners as if the card was in a screw-down holder. Regular versions are seeded every 12 packs, Refractors are found every 48 packs with Atomic Refractors every 96 packs.

		MT
Complete Set (9):		45.00
Common Player:		2.00
Refractors:		2x
Atomic Refractors:		4x
1	Keyshawn Johnson	10.00
2	Lawrence Phillips	4.00
3	Tim Biakabutuka	5.00
4	Eddie George	20.00
5	John Mobley	2.00
6	Eddie Kennison	6.00
7	Marvin Harrison	10.00
8	Amani Toomer	2.00
9	Bobby Engram	4.00

1997 Bowman's Best

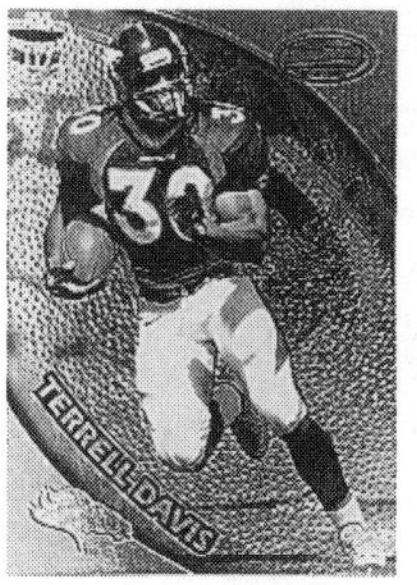

Bowman's Best Football is a 125-card set featuring 95 NFL veterans with a gold design and 30 rookies with a silver design. The base cards also come in Refractor (1:12) and Atomic Refractor (1:24) parallels. The insert sets include Bowman's Best Autographs, Laser Cuts and Mirror Image. Each of the insert cards has a Refractor and Atomic Refractor version. Bowman's Best Football was sold in six-card packs.

		MT
Complete Set (125):		100.00
Common Player:		.25
Minor Stars:		.50
Refractor Stars:		4x-8x
Refractor Rookies:		2x-4x
Atomic Ref. Stars:		8x-16x
Atomic Ref. Rookies:		4x-8x
Pack (6):		3.50
Wax Box (24):		80.00
1	Brett Favre	8.00
2	Larry Centers	.25
3	Trent Dilfer	.50
4	Rodney Hampton	.25
5	Wesley Walls	.25
6	Jerome Bettis	.50
7	Keyshawn Johnson	1.00
8	Keenan McCardell	.25
9	Terry Allen	.25
10	Troy Aikman	4.00
11	Tony Banks	1.50
12	Ty Detmer	.25
13	Chris Chandler	.25
14	Marshall Faulk	.50
15	Heath Shuler	.25
16	Stan Humphries	.25
17	Bryan Cox	.25
18	Chris Spielman	.25
19	Derrick Thomas	.25
20	Steve Young	2.50
21	Desmond Howard	.25
22	Jeff Blake	.50
23	Michael Jackson	.25
24	Cris Carter	.25
25	Joey Galloway	1.00
26	Simeon Rice	.25
27	Reggie White	.50
28	Dave Brown	.25
29	Mike Alstott	1.50
30	Emmitt Smith	7.00
31	Anthony Johnson	.25
32	Mark Brunell	4.00
33	Ricky Watters	.50
34	Terrell Davis	4.00
35	Ben Coates	.25
36	Gus Frerotte	.25
37	Andre Reed	.25
38	Isaac Bruce	.50
39	Junior Seau	.50
40	Eddie George	6.00
41	Adrian Murrell	.50
42	Jake Reed	.25
43	Karim Abdul-Jabbar	.75
44	Scott Mitchell	.25
45	Ki-Jana Carter	.25
46	Curtis Conway	.50
47	Jim Harbaugh	.25
48	Tim Brown	.50
49	Mario Bates	.25
50	Jerry Rice	4.00
51	Byron Morris	.25
52	Marcus Allen	.50
53	Errict Rhett	.25
54	Steve McNair	3.00
55	Kerry Collins	.75
56	Bert Emanuel	.25
57	Curtis Martin	4.00
58	Bryce Paup	.25
59	Brad Johnson	.50
60	John Elway	2.50
61	Natrone Means	.50
62	Deion Sanders	2.00
63	Tony Martin	.25
64	Michael Westbrook	.25
65	Chris Calloway	.25
66	Antonio Freeman	.25
67	Rick Mirer	.25
68	Kent Graham	.25
69	O.J. McDuffie	.25
70	Barry Sanders	4.00
71	Chris Warren	.25
72	Kordell Stewart	4.00
73	Thurman Thomas	.50
74	Marvin Harrison	1.00
75	Carl Pickens	.25
76	Brent Jones	.25
77	Irving Fryar	.25
78	Neil O'Donnell	.25
79	Elvis Grbac	.25
80	Drew Bledsoe	4.00
81	Shannon Sharpe	.25
82	Vinny Testaverde	.25
83	Chris Sanders	.25
84	Herman Moore	.50
85	Jeff George	.50
86	Bruce Smith	.25
87	Robert Smith	.25
88	Kevin Hardy	.25
89	Kevin Greene	.25
90	Dan Marino	7.00
91	Michael Irvin	.50
92	Garrison Hearst	.25
93	Lake Dawson	.25
94	Lawrence Phillips	.50
95	Terry Glenn	.75
96	*Jake Plummer*	7.00
97	*Byron Hanspard*	2.00
98	*Bryant Westbrook*	.50
99	*Troy Davis*	1.00
100	*Danny Wuerffel*	3.00
101	*Tony Gonzalez*	2.00
102	*Jim Druckenmiller*	4.00
103	*Kevin Lockett*	.25
104	*Renaldo Wynn*	.25
105	*James Farrior*	.25
106	*Rae Carruth*	3.00
107	*Tom Knight*	.25
108	*Corey Dillon*	7.00
109	*Kenny Holmes*	.25
110	*Orlando Pace*	.50
111	*Reidel Anthony*	4.00
112	*Chad Scott*	.25
113	*Antowain Smith*	5.00
114	*David LaFleur*	2.00
115	*Yatil Green*	1.50
116	*Darrell Russell*	.25
117	*Joey Kent*	1.00
118	*Darnell Autry*	1.00
119	*Peter Boulware*	.50
120	*Shawn Springs*	.25
121	*Ike Hilliard*	3.00
122	*Dwayne Rudd*	.25
123	*Reinard Wilson*	.25
124	*Michael Booker*	.25
125	*Warrick Dunn*	4.00

1997 Bowman's Best Autographs

This 10-card set features autographed versions of 10 base set cards. The cards were inserted 1:131. Refractor (1:1578) and Atomic Refractor (1:4733) parallels are also available.

		MT
Complete Set (10):		500.00
Common Player:		20.00
22	Jeff Blake	20.00
44	Scott Mitchell	20.00
47	Jim Harbaugh	20.00
99	Troy Davis	20.00
102	Jim Druckenmiller	80.00
113	Antowain Smith	80.00
114	David LaFleur	30.00
120	Shawn Springs	20.00
121	Ike Hilliard	50.00
125	Warrick Dunn	150.00

1997 Bowman's Best Cuts

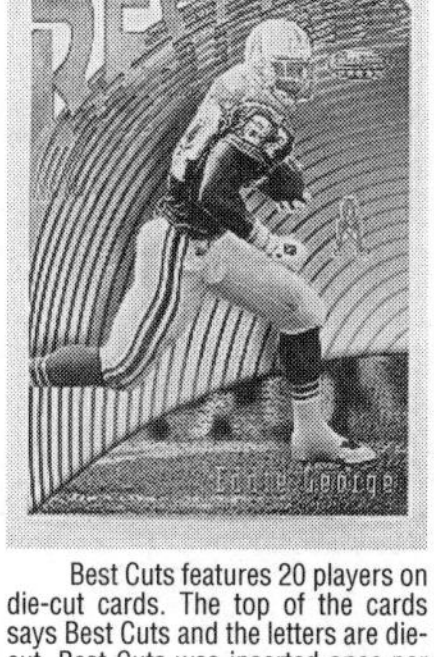

Best Cuts features 20 players on die-cut cards. The top of the cards says Best Cuts and the letters are die-cut. Best Cuts was inserted once per 24 packs. Refractor (1:48) and Atomic Refractor (1:96) parallels were also created. They are numbered with the "BC" prefix.

		MT
Complete Set (20):		200.00
Common Player:		3.00
Refractors:		2x
Atomic Refractors:		2x-4x
1	Orlando Pace	3.00
2	Eddie George	16.00
3	John Elway	8.00
4	Tony Gonzalez	3.00
5	Brett Favre	25.00
6	Shawn Springs	3.00
7	Warrick Dunn	20.00
8	Troy Aikman	12.00
9	Terry Glenn	6.00
10	Dan Marino	20.00
11	Jake Plummer	8.00
12	Ike Hilliard	8.00
13	Emmitt Smith	20.00
14	Steve Young	8.00
15	Barry Sanders	18.00
16	Jim Druckenmiller	10.00
17	Drew Bledsoe	12.00
18	Antowain Smith	8.00
19	Mark Brunell	12.00
20	Jerry Rice	12.00

1997 Bowman's Best Mirror Images

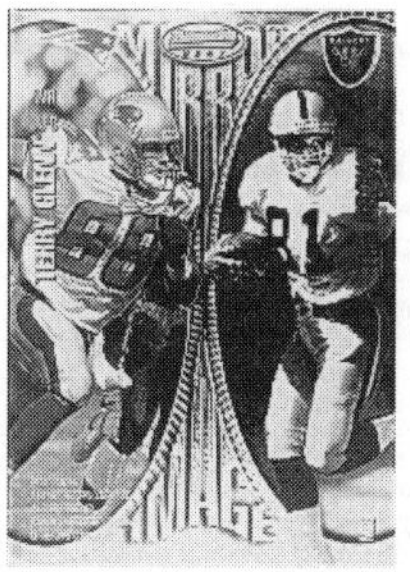

The 10, double-sided cards in Mirror Images showcase four top players from the same position. Two NFC players and two AFC players are featured on each card. The chromium cards (1:48) also had Refractor (1:96) and Atomic Refractor (1:192) parallels. They are numbered with the "MI" prefix.

		MT
Complete Set (10):		180.00
Common Player:		5.00
Refractors:		2x
Atomic Refractors:		2x-4x
1	Brett Favre, Gus Frerotte, John Elway, Mark Brunell	40.00
2	Steve Young, Tony Banks, Dan Marino, Drew Bledsoe	35.00
3	Troy Aikman, Kerry Collins, Vinny Testaverde, Kordell Stewart	20.00
4	Emmitt Smith, Dorsey Levens, Marcus Allen, Eddie George	35.00
5	Barry Sanders, Errict Rhett, Thurman Thomas, Curtis Martin	25.00
6	Ricky Watters, Jamal Anderson, Chris Warren, Terrell Davis	20.00
7	Jerry Rice, Isaac Bruce, Tony Martin, Marvin Harrison	20.00
8	Herman Moore, Curtis Conway, Tim Brown, Terry Glenn	15.00
9	Michael Irvin, Eddie Kennison, Carl Pickens, Keyshawn Johnson	5.00
10	Wesley Walls, Jason Dunn, Shannon Sharpe, Rickey Dudley	5.00

1998 Bowman

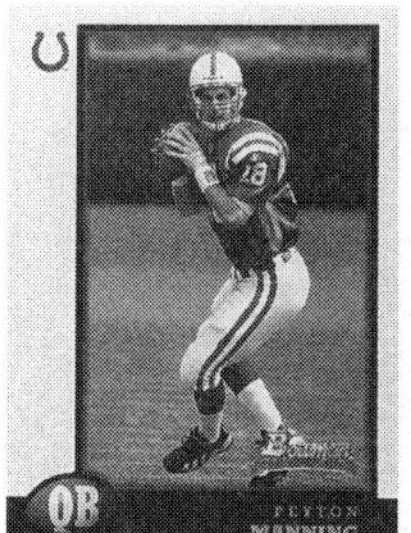

Bowman contained 220 cards, including 150 veterans and 70 rookies. Prospects were featured on a silver and blue design while veterans are shown on a silver and red design. Rookies contain a "Bowman Rookie Card" gold foil stamp. The set is paralleled in Inter-State and Golden Anniversary sets. Three insert sets are included in packs: Bowman Autographs, which come in blue, silver and gold foil versions, Scout's Choice and Bowman Chrome Preview.

		MT
Complete Set (220):		80.00
Common Player:		.25
Minor Stars:		.50
Common Rookie:		.50
Inter-State Cards:		3x
Inter-State Rookies:		2x
Inserted 1:1		
Golden Ann. Stars:		50x-100x
Golden Ann. Rookies:		10x-20x
Inserted 1:180		
Production 50 Sets		
Pack (10):		4.00
Wax Box (24):		80.00
1	*Peyton Manning*	20.00
2	*Keith Brooking*	.50
3	*Duane Starks*	.50
4	*Takeo Spikes*	.50
5	*Andre Wadsworth*	2.00
6	*Greg Ellis*	1.00
7	*Brian Griese*	10.00
8	*Germane Crowell*	3.00
9	*Jerome Pathon*	2.00
10	*Ryan Leaf*	5.00
11	*Fred Taylor*	8.00
12	*Robert Edwards*	4.00
13	*Grant Wistrom*	.50
14	*Robert Holcombe*	4.00
15	*Tim Dwight*	3.00
16	*Jacquez Green*	4.00
17	*Marcus Nash*	3.00
18	*Jason Peter*	.50
19	*Anthony Simmons*	.50
20	*Curtis Enis*	5.00
21	*John Avery*	3.00
22	*Patrick Johnson*	.50
23	*Joe Jurevicius*	2.00
24	*Brian Simmons*	2.00
25	*Kevin Dyson*	3.00
26	*Skip Hicks*	3.00
27	*Hines Ward*	3.00
28	*Tavian Banks*	3.00
29	*Ahman Green*	4.00
30	*Tony Simmons*	.50
31	Charles Johnson	.25
32	Freddie Jones	.25
33	Joey Galloway	.75
34	Tony Banks	.50
35	Jake Plummer	1.50
36	Reidel Anthony	.25
37	Steve McNair	.75
38	Michael Westbrook	.25
39	Chris Sanders	.25
40	Isaac Bruce	.50
41	Charlie Garner	.25
42	Wayne Chrebet	.25
43	Michael Strahan	.25
44	Brad Johnson	.50
45	Mike Alstott	.50
46	Tony Gonzalez	.50
47	Johnnie Morton	.25
48	Darnay Scott	.25
49	Rae Carruth	.25
50	Terrell Davis	2.50
51	Jermaine Lewis	.25
52	Frank Sanders	.25
53	Byron Hanspard	.25
54	Gus Frerotte	.25
55	Terry Glenn	.50
56	J.J. Stokes	.25
57	Will Blackwell	.25
58	Keyshawn Johnson	.50
59	Tiki Barber	.50
60	Dorsey Levens	.50
61	Zach Thomas	.25
62	Corey Dillon	1.25
63	Antowain Smith	1.00
64	Michael Sinclair	.25
65	Rod Smith	.25
66	Trent Dilfer	.50
67	Warren Sapp	.25
68	Charles Way	.25
69	Tamarick Vanover	.25
70	Drew Bledsoe	1.50
71	John Mobley	.25
72	Kerry Collins	.50
73	Peter Boulware	.25
74	Simeon Rice	.25
75	Eddie George	1.50
76	Fred Lane	.50
77	Jamal Anderson	.50
78	Antonio Freeman	.75
79	Jason Sehorn	.25
80	Curtis Martin	.75
81	Bobby Hoying	.25
82	Garrison Hearst	.25
83	Glenn Foley	.25
84	Danny Kanell	.25
85	Kordell Stewart	1.50
86	O.J. McDuffie	.25
87	Marvin Harrison	.75
88	Bobby Engram	.25
89	Chris Slade	.25
90	Warrick Dunn	1.50
91	Ricky Watters	.50
92	Rickey Dudley	.25
93	Terrell Owens	.50
94	Karim Abdul-Jabbar	.50
95	Napoleon Kaufman	.75
96	Darrell Green	.25
97	Levon Kirkland	.25
98	Jeff George	.50
99	Andre Hastings	.25
100	John Elway	2.00
101	John Randle	.25
102	Andre Rison	.25
103	Keenan McCardell	.25
104	Marshall Faulk	.75
105	Emmitt Smith	3.00
106	Robert Brooks	.25
107	Scott Mitchell	.25
108	Shannon Sharpe	.50
109	Deion Sanders	.75
110	Jerry Rice	2.00
111	Erik Kramer	.25
112	Michael Jackson	.25
113	Aeneas Williams	.25
114	Terry Allen	.25
115	Steve Young	1.25
116	Warren Moon	.50
117	Junior Seau	.50
118	Jerome Bettis	.50
119	Irving Fryar	.25
120	Barry Sanders	4.00
121	Tim Brown	.50
122	Chad Brown	.25
123	Ben Coates	.25
124	Robert Smith	.50
125	Brett Favre	4.00
126	Derrick Thomas	.25
127	Reggie White	.50
128	Troy Aikman	2.00
129	Jeff Blake	.50
130	Mark Brunell	1.50
131	Curtis Conway	.50
132	Wesley Walls	.25
133	Thurman Thomas	.50
134	Chris Chandler	.25
135	Dan Marino	3.00
136	Larry Centers	.25
137	Shawn Jefferson	.25
138	Andre Reed	.25
139	Jake Reed	.25
140	Cris Carter	.50
141	Elvis Grbac	.25
142	Mark Chmura	.50
143	Michael Irvin	.50
144	Carl Pickens	.50
145	Herman Moore	.50
146	Marvin Jones	.25
147	Terance Mathis	.25
148	Rob Moore	.25
149	Bruce Smith	.25
150	Checklist	.25
151	Leslie Shepherd	.25
152	Chris Spielman	.25
153	Tony McGee	.25
154	Kevin Smith	.25
155	Bill Romanowski	.25
156	Stephen Boyd	.25
157	James Stewart	.25
158	Jason Taylor	.25
159	Troy Drayton	.25
160	Mark Fields	.25
161	Jessie Armstead	.25
162	James Jett	.25
163	Bobby Taylor	.25
164	Kimble Anders	.25
165	Jimmy Smith	.25
166	Quentin Coryatt	.25
167	Bryant Westbrook	.25
168	Neil Smith	.25
169	Darren Woodson	.25
170	Ray Buchanan	.25
171	Earl Holmes	.25
172	Ray Lewis	.25
173	Steve Broussard	.25
174	Derrick Brooks	.25
175	Ken Harvey	.25
176	Darryll Lewis	.25
177	Derrick Rodgers	.25
178	James McKnight	.25
179	Cris Dishman	.25
180	Hardy Nickerson	.25
181	*Charles Woodson*	5.00
182	*Randy Moss*	20.00
183	*Stephen Alexander*	.50
184	*Samari Rolle*	.50
185	*Jamie Duncan*	.50
186	*Lance Schulters*	.50
187	*Tony Parrish*	.50
188	*Corey Chavous*	.50
189	*Jammi German*	.50
190	*Sam Cowart*	.50
191	*Donald Hayes*	.50
192	*R.W. McQuarters*	1.00
193	*Az-Zahir Hakim*	2.00
194	*Chris Fuamatu-Ma'afala*	2.00
195	*Allen Rossum*	.50
196	*Jon Ritchie*	.50
197	*Blake Spence*	.50
198	*Brian Alford*	.50
199	*Fred Weary*	.50
200	*Rod Rutledge*	.50
201	*Michael Myers*	.50
202	*Rashaan Shehee*	2.00
203	*Donovin Darius*	.50
204	*E.G. Green*	.50
205	*Vonnie Holliday*	2.00
206	*Charlie Batch*	8.00
207	*Michael Pittman*	.50
208	*Artrell Hawkins*	.50
209	*Jonathan Quinn*	.50
210	*Kailee Wong*	.50
211	*Deshea Townsend*	1.00
212	*Patrick Surtain*	.50
213	*Brian Kelly*	.50
214	*Tebucky Jones*	.50
215	*Pete Gonzalez*	1.00
216	*Shaun Williams*	.50
217	*Scott Frost*	.50
218	*Leonard Little*	.50
219	*Alonzo Mayes*	1.00
220	*Cordell Taylor*	.50

1998 Bowman Inter-State

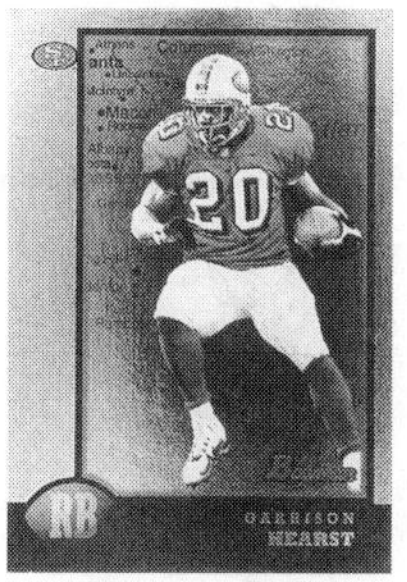

All 220 cards were reprinted in Inter-State parallel versions and seeded one per pack. These are printed on silver foil and included a background map of where the player was born on the front and a vanity plate on the back.

	MT
Inter-State Cards:	3x
Inter-State Rookies:	2x

A player's name in *italic type* indicates a rookie card.

1998 Bowman Blue Autographs

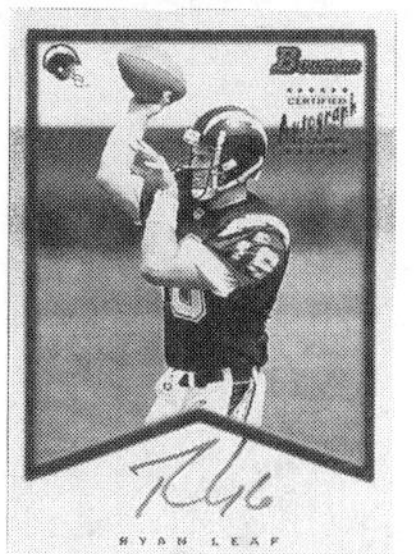

Eleven different players signed cards to be inserted into packs of Bowman. Card rarity was differentiated by blue (1:360 packs), silver (2,401) or gold foil Topps Certified Autograph Issue stamps (1:7,202).

		MT
Complete Set (11):		700.00
Common Player:		20.00
Inserted 1:360		
Silver Cards:		2x
Inserted 1:2,401		
Gold Cards:		4x
Inserted 1:7,202		
1	Peyton Manning	140.00
2	Andre Wadsworth	20.00
3	Brian Griese	50.00
4	Ryan Leaf	75.00
5	Fred Taylor	100.00
6	Robert Edwards	60.00
7	Randy Moss	250.00
8	Curtis Enis	60.00
9	Kevin Dyson	40.00
10	Charles Woodson	60.00
11	Tim Dwight	40.00

1998 Bowman Chrome Preview

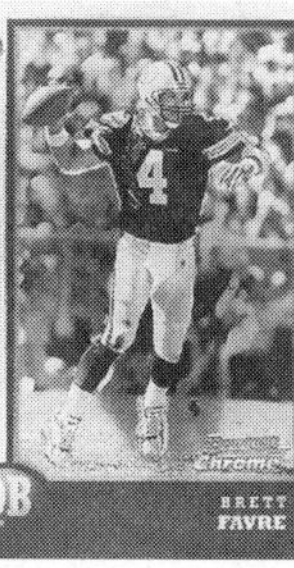

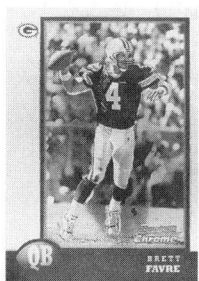

This 10-card insert set previewed the upcoming Bowman Chrome set. It included five veterans and five rookies, with regular versions seeded one per 12 packs and Refractors every 48 packs.

		MT
Complete Set (10):		50.00
Common Player:		4.00
Inserted 1:12		
Refractors:		2x
Inserted 1:48		
1	Peyton Manning	10.00
2	Curtis Enis	5.00
3	Charles Woodson	4.00
4	Robert Edwards	6.00
5	Ryan Leaf	7.00
6	Brett Favre	12.00
7	John Elway	6.00
8	Barry Sanders	12.00
9	Kordell Stewart	4.00
10	Terrell Davis	8.00

1998 Bowman Scout's Choice

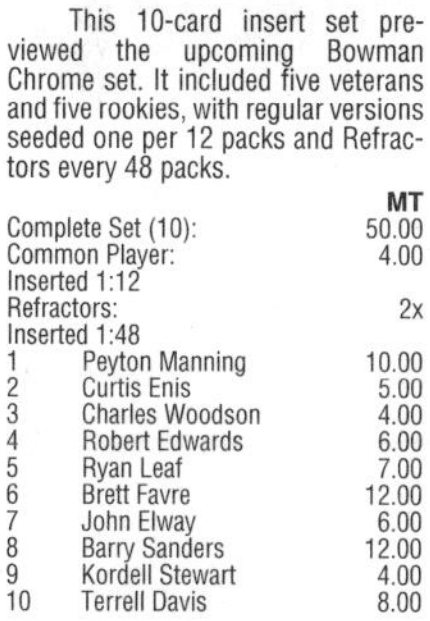

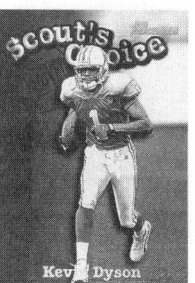

This 14-card insert set showcased the top rookies according to the Bowman Scouts. Cards featured a borderless, double-etched foil design and were inserted one per 12 packs.

	MT
Complete Set (14):	60.00
Common Player:	2.00
Inserted 1:12	

SC1 Peyton Manning 15.00
SC2 John Avery 3.00
SC3 Grant Wistrom 2.00
SC4 Kevin Dyson 3.00
SC5 Andre Wadsworth 3.00
SC6 Joe Jurevicius 2.00
SC7 Charles Woodson 6.00
SC8 Takeo Spikes 2.00
SC9 Fred Taylor 10.00
SC10 Ryan Leaf 8.00
SC11 Robert Edwards 6.00
SC12 Randy Moss 20.00
SC13 Patrick Johnson 2.00
SC14 Curtis Enis 6.00

1998 Bowman's Best

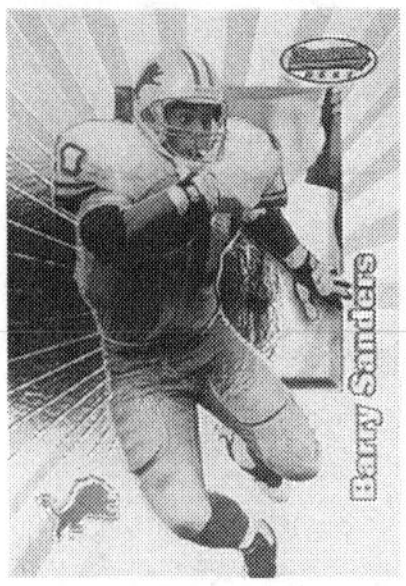

This super-premium set has a 125-card base set that is made up of 100 veterans and 25 rookies. Each veteran card has a gold design, while the rookies are in silver. Each card has a Refractor version that is sequentially numbered to 400 and inserted 1:25 packs. Each player also has a parallel Atomic Refractor version that is numbered to 100 and inserted 1:103 packs.

MT
Complete Set (125): 120.00
Common Player: .25
Minor Stars: .50
Common Rookie: 2.00
Inserted 1:2
Refractor Cards: 8x-16x
Refractor Rookies: 3x-6x
Inserted 1:25
Production 400 Sets
Atomic Ref. Cards: 25x-50x
Atomic Ref. Rookies: 10x-20x
Inserted 1:103
Production 100 Sets
Pack (6): 4.50
Wax Box (24): 95.00
1 Emmitt Smith 4.00
2 Reggie White .75
3 Jake Plummer 2.00
4 Ike Hilliard .25
5 Isaac Bruce .50
6 Trent Dilfer .50
7 Ricky Watters .50
8 Jeff George .50
9 Wayne Chrebet .50
10 Brett Favre 6.00
11 Terry Allen .50
12 Bert Emanuel .25
13 Andre Reed .25
14 Andre Rison .50
15 Jeff Blake .50
16 Steve McNair 1.50
17 Joey Galloway 1.00
18 Irving Fryar .25
19 Dorsey Levens .75
20 Jerry Rice 3.00
21 Kerry Collins .75
22 Michael Jackson .25
23 Kordell Stewart 2.00
24 Junior Seau .50
25 Jimmy Smith .75
26 Michael Westbrook .25
27 Eddie George 2.50
28 Cris Carter 1.00
29 Jason Sehorn .25
30 Warrick Dunn 2.00
31 Garrison Hearst .75
32 Erik Kramer .25
33 Chris Chandler .50
34 Michael Irvin .50
35 Marshall Faulk 1.00
36 Warren Moon .50
37 Rickey Dudley .25
38 Drew Bledsoe 2.50
39 Antowain Smith 1.00
40 Terrell Davis 5.00
41 Gus Frerotte .25
42 Robert Brooks .25
43 Tony Banks .50
44 Terrell Owens 1.50
45 Edgar Bennett .25
46 Rob Moore .50
47 J.J. Stokes .50
48 Yancey Thigpen .25
49 Elvis Grbac .25
50 John Elway 3.00
51 Charles Johnson .25
52 Karim Abdul-Jabbar .75
53 Carl Pickens .50
54 Peter Boulware .25
55 Chris Warren .25
56 Terance Mathis .25
57 Andre Hastings .25
58 Jake Reed .25
59 Mike Alstott 1.00
60 Mark Brunell 2.50
61 Herman Moore .75
62 Troy Aikman 3.00
63 Fred Lane .75
64 Rod Smith .75
65 Terry Glenn .75
66 Jerome Bettis .75
67 Derrick Thomas .50
68 Marvin Harrison .50
69 Adrian Murrell .50
70 Curtis Martin 1.25
71 Bobby Hoying .25
72 Darrell Green .25
73 Sean Dawkins .25
74 Robert Smith .50
75 Antonio Freeman 1.50
76 Scott Mitchell .25
77 Curtis Conway .50
78 Rae Carruth .25
79 Jamal Anderson 1.50
80 Dan Marino 4.00
81 Brad Johnson 1.00
82 Danny Kanell .25
83 Charlie Garner .25
84 Rob Johnson .50
85 Natrone Means .50
86 Tim Brown .75
87 Keyshawn Johnson 1.00
88 Ben Coates .50
89 Derrick Alexander .25
90 Steve Young 2.00
91 Shannon Sharpe .50
92 Corey Dillon 1.50
93 Bruce Smith .25
94 Errict Rhett .25
95 Jim Harbaugh .50
96 Napoleon Kaufman 1.25
97 Glenn Foley .50
98 Tony Gonzalez .25
99 Keenan McCardell .50
100 Barry Sanders 6.00
101 *Charles Woodson* 6.00
102 *Tim Dwight* 4.00
103 *Marcus Nash* 4.00
104 *Joe Jurevicius* 3.00
105 *Jacquez Green* 5.00
106 *Kevin Dyson* 4.00
107 *Keith Brooking* 2.00
108 *Andre Wadsworth* 2.50
109 *Randy Moss* 25.00
110 *Robert Edwards* 6.00
111 *Patrick Johnson* 2.50
112 *Peyton Manning* 25.00
113 *Duane Starks* 2.00
114 *Grant Wistrom* 2.00
115 *Anthony Simmons* 2.00
116 *Takeo Spikes* 2.00
117 *Tony Simmons* 3.00
118 *Jerome Pathon* 3.00
119 *Ryan Leaf* 7.00
120 *Skip Hicks* 3.00
121 *Curtis Enis* 5.00
122 *Germane Crowell* 4.00
123 *John Avery* 4.00
124 *Hines Ward* 3.00
125 *Fred Taylor* 8.00

1998 Bowman's Best Autographs

Ten players are in this set with each having two different cards. The only difference is the suffix "A" or "B" after the card number. Each of the 20 cards has a "Certified Autograph Issue" stamp on the fronts. Singles are found 1:158 packs, while Refractor versions are 1:840 and Atomic Refractors are 1:2,521.

MT
Complete Set (20): 450.00
Common Player: 15.00
Inserted 1:158
Refractor Cards: 2x
Inserted 1:840
Atomic Ref. Cards: 3x
Inserted 1:2,521
1A Jake Plummer 40.00
1B Jake Plummer 40.00
2A Jason Sehorn 15.00
2B Jason Sehorn 15.00
3A Corey Dillon 30.00
3B Corey Dillon 30.00
4A Tim Brown 25.00
4B Tim Brown 25.00
5A Keenan McCardell 15.00
5B Keenan McCardell 15.00
6A Kordell Stewart 35.00
6B Kordell Stewart 35.00
7A Peyton Manning 125.00
7B Peyton Manning 125.00
8A Danny Kanell 15.00
8B Danny Kanell 15.00
9A Fred Taylor 60.00
9B Fred Taylor 60.00
10A Curtis Enis 25.00
10B Curtis Enis 25.00

1998 Bowman's Best Mirror Image Fusion

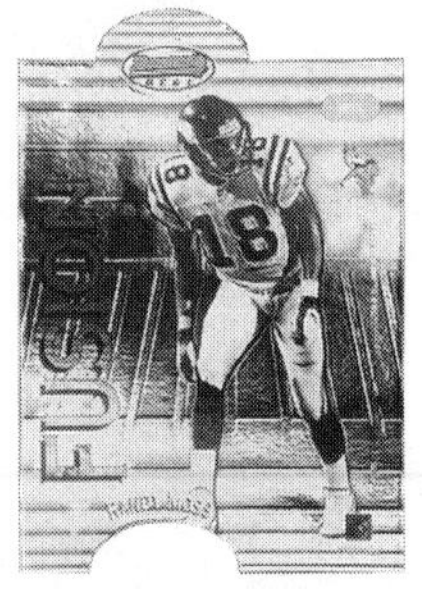

This insert is made up of 20 double-sided cards that feature two top players at the same position. Singles are found 1:48 packs, while the parallel Refractors are sequentially numbered to 100 and inserted 1:630. Atomic Refractors are numbered to 25 and found 1:2,521.

MT
Complete Set (20): 280.00
Common Player: 4.00
Minor Stars: 8.00
Inserted 1:48
Refractor Cards: 3x-5x
Inserted 1:630
Production 100 Sets
Atomic Ref. Cards: 6x-12x
Inserted 1:2,521
Production 25 Sets
MI1 Terrell Davis, John Avery 35.00
MI2 Emmitt Smith, Curtis Enis 35.00
MI3 Barry Sanders, Skip Hicks 50.00
MI4 Eddie George, Robert Edwards 12.00
MI5 Jerome Bettis, Fred Taylor 20.00
MI6 Mark Brunell, Ryan Leaf 20.00
MI7 John Elway, Brian Griese 25.00
MI8 Dan Marino, Peyton Manning 25.00
MI9 Brett Favre, Charlie Batch 50.00
MI10 Drew Bledsoe, Jonathan Quinn 20.00
MI11 Tim Brown, Kevin Dyson 10.00
MI12 Herman Moore, Germane Crowell 10.00
MI13 Joey Galloway, Jerome Pathon 8.00
MI14 Cris Carter, Jacquez Green 12.00
MI15 Jerry Rice, Randy Moss 60.00
MI16 Junior Seau, Takeo Spikes 4.00
MI17 John Randle, Jason Peter 4.00
MI18 Reggie White, Andre Wadsworth 8.00
MI19 Peter Boulware, Anthony Simmons 4.00
MI20 Derrick Thomas, Brian Simmons 4.00

1998 Bowman's Best Performers

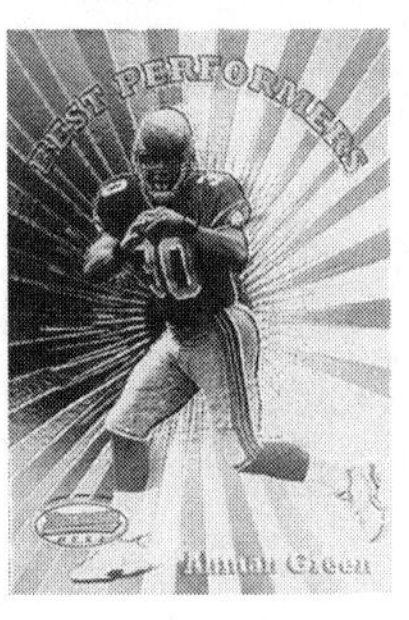

This insert showcases the top rookies who came up in '98. Singles were inserted 1:12 packs, while Refractors are numbered to 200 and can be found 1:630. Atomic Refractors are numbered to 50 and found 1:2,521.

MT
Complete Set (10): 60.00
Common Player: 2.00
Inserted 1:12
Refractor Cards: 3x-6x
Inserted 1:630
Production 200 Sets
Atomic Ref. Cards: 10x-20x
Inserted 1:2,521
Production 50 Sets
BP1 Peyton Manning 15.00
BP2 Charles Woodson 6.00
BP3 Skip Hicks 4.00
BP4 Andre Wadsworth 2.00
BP5 Randy Moss 25.00
BP6 Marcus Nash 5.00
BP7 Ahman Green 4.00
BP8 Anthony Simmons 2.00
BP9 Tavian Banks 4.00
BP10 Ryan Leaf 8.00

1998 Bowman's Best Super Bowl Show

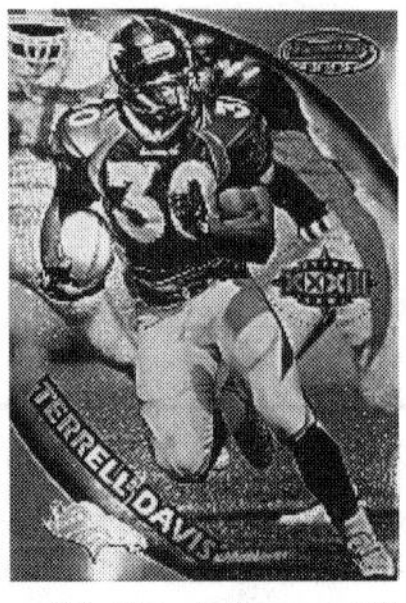

This 16-card set was available exclusively at the NFL Experience Card Show at Super Bowl XXXII. It features 4" x 5 1/2" Bowman's Best cards, with the Super Bowl logo on the front near the middle. Refractor versions of each of these cards was also available randomly. The cards were obtained by exchanging wrappers of Topps products at the Topps booth.

MT
Complete Set (16): 350.00
Common Player: 8.00
Refractors: 2x
1 Brett Favre 75.00
2 Barry Sanders 60.00
3 Emmitt Smith 60.00
4 John Elway 30.00
5 Tim Brown 8.00
6 Eddie George 30.00
7 Troy Aikman 30.00
8 Drew Bledsoe 30.00
9 Dan Marino 60.00
10 Jerry Rice 30.00
11 Junior Seau 8.00
12 Antowain Smith 20.00
13 Warrick Dunn 30.00
14 Jim Druckenmiller 20.00
15 Terrell Davis 30.00
16 Curtis Martin 25.00

1998 Bowman Chrome

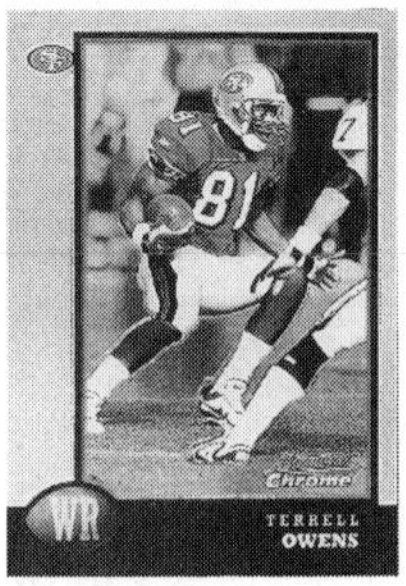

Bowman Chrome football is a 220-card base set that includes 150 veterans and 70 rookies. There are also Refractor parallel cards of every regular card in the set that are randomly inserted 1:12 packs. Rookies are designated with a silver and blue logo design, while the veteran cards are shown with a silver and red design.

MT
Complete Set (220): 300.00
Common Player: .30
Minor Stars: .60
Common Rookie: 3.50
Refractor Cards: 3x-6x
Refractor Rookies: 3x
Inserted 1:12
Inter-State Cards: 3x
Inter-State Rookies: 1.2x
Inserted 1:4
I.S. Refractor Cards: 5x-10x
I.S. Refractor Rookies: 3x
Inserted 1:24
Golden Ann. Stars: 30x-60x
Golden Ann. Rookies: 2x-4x
Inserted 1:138
Production 50 Sets
Pack (10): 7.00
Wax Box (24): 150.00
1 *Peyton Manning* 55.00
2 *Keith Brooking* 7.00
3 *Duane Starks* 5.00
4 *Takeo Spikes* 7.00
5 *Andre Wadsworth* 7.00
6 *Greg Ellis* 3.50
7 *Brian Griese* 25.00
8 *Germane Crowell* 15.00
9 *Jerome Pathon* 7.00
10 *Ryan Leaf* 10.00
11 *Fred Taylor* 15.00
12 *Robert Edwards* 10.00
13 *Grant Wistrom* 3.50
14 *Robert Holcombe* 10.00
15 *Tim Dwight* 10.00
16 *Jacquez Green* 10.00
17 *Marcus Nash* 10.00
18 *Jason Peter* 3.50
19 *Anthony Simmons* 3.50
20 *Curtis Enis* 15.00
21 *John Avery* 10.00
22 *Patrick Johnson* 7.00
23 *Joe Jurevicius* 7.00
24 *Brian Simmons* 4.00
25 *Kevin Dyson* 10.00
26 *Skip Hicks* 10.00
27 *Hines Ward* 10.00
28 *Tavian Banks* 7.00
29 *Ahman Green* 15.00
30 *Tony Simmons* 8.00
31 Charles Johnson .30
32 Freddie Jones .30
33 Joey Galloway 1.00
34 Tony Banks .60
35 Jake Plummer 2.50
36 Reidel Anthony .60
37 Steve McNair 1.00
38 Michael Westbrook .60
39 Chris Sanders .30
40 Isaac Bruce .60
41 Charlie Garner .30
42 Wayne Chrebet .60
43 Michael Strahan .30
44 Brad Johnson 1.00
45 Mike Alstott 1.00
46 Tony Gonzalez .60
47 Johnnie Morton .30
48 Darnay Scott .30
49 Rae Carruth .30
50 Terrell Davis 4.50
51 Jermaine Lewis .30
52 Frank Sanders .30
53 Byron Hanspard .30
54 Gus Frerotte .30
55 Terry Glenn .60
56 J.J. Stokes .60
57 Will Blackwell .30
58 Keyshawn Johnson 1.00
59 Tiki Barber .60
60 Dorsey Levens .60
61 Zach Thomas .30
62 Corey Dillon 1.50
63 Antowain Smith 1.00
64 Michael Sinclair .30
65 Rod Smith .60
66 Trent Dilfer .60
67 Warren Sapp .30
68 Charles Way .30
69 Tamarick Vanover .30
70 Drew Bledsoe 2.50
71 John Mobley .30
72 Kerry Collins .60
73 Peter Boulware .30
74 Simeon Rice .30
75 Eddie George 2.50
76 Fred Lane .60
77 Jamal Anderson 1.50
78 Antonio Freeman 1.00
79 Jason Sehorn .30
80 Curtis Martin 1.00
81 Bobby Hoying .30
82 Garrison Hearst 1.00
83 Glenn Foley .60
84 Danny Kanell .30
85 Kordell Stewart 2.50
86 O.J. McDuffie .30
87 Marvin Harrison .60
88 Bobby Engram .30
89 Chris Slade .30
90 Warrick Dunn 2.00
91 Ricky Watters .60
92 Rickey Dudley .30
93 Terrell Owens 1.00
94 Karim Abdul-Jabbar .60
95 Napoleon Kaufman 1.00
96 Darrell Green .30
97 Levon Kirkland .30
98 Jeff George .60
99 Andre Hastings .30
100 John Elway 3.00
101 John Randle .30
102 Andre Rison .30
103 Keenan McCardell .30
104 Marshall Faulk 1.00
105 Emmitt Smith 4.50
106 Robert Brooks .30
107 Scott Mitchell .30
108 Shannon Sharpe .60
109 Deion Sanders 1.00
110 Jerry Rice 3.00
111 Erik Kramer .30
112 Michael Jackson .30
113 Aeneas Williams .30
114 Terry Allen .60
115 Steve Young 1.75
116 Warren Moon .60
117 Junior Seau .60
118 Jerome Bettis .60
119 Irving Fryar .30
120 Barry Sanders 6.00
121 Tim Brown .60
122 Chad Brown .30
123 Ben Coates .30
124 Robert Smith .60
125 Brett Favre 6.00
126 Derrick Thomas .30
127 Reggie White 1.00
128 Troy Aikman 3.00
129 Jeff Blake .60
130 Mark Brunell 2.50
131 Curtis Conway .60
132 Wesley Walls .30
133 Thurman Thomas .60
134 Chris Chandler .30
135 Dan Marino 4.50
136 Larry Centers .30
137 Shawn Jefferson .30
138 Andre Reed .30
139 Jake Reed .30
140 Cris Carter 1.00
141 Elvis Grbac .30
142 Mark Chmura .60
143 Michael Irvin .60
144 Carl Pickens .60
145 Herman Moore .60
146 Marvin Jones .30
147 Terance Mathis .30
148 Rob Moore .60
149 Bruce Smith .30
150 Checklist .30
151 Leslie Shepherd .30
152 Chris Spielman .30
153 Tony McGee .30
154 Kevin Smith .30
155 Bill Romanowski .30
156 Stephen Boyd .30
157 James Stewart .30
158 Jason Taylor .30
159 Troy Drayton .30
160 Mark Fields .30
161 Jessie Armstead .30
162 James Jett .30
163 Bobby Taylor .30
164 Kimble Anders .30
165 Jimmy Smith .60
166 Quentin Coryatt .30
167 Bryant Westbrook .30
168 Neil Smith .30
169 Darren Woodson .30
170 Ray Buchanan .30
171 Earl Holmes .30
172 Ray Lewis .30
173 Steve Broussard .30
174 Derrick Brooks .30
175 Ken Harvey .30
176 Darryll Lewis .30
177 Derrick Rodgers .30
178 James McKnight .30
179 Cris Dishman .30
180 Hardy Nickerson .30
181 *Charles Woodson* 15.00
182 *Randy Moss* 55.00
183 *Stephen Alexander* 7.00
184 *Samari Rolle* 3.50
185 *Jamie Duncan* 3.50
186 *Lance Schulters* 3.50
187 *Tony Parrish* 3.50
188 *Corey Chavous* 3.50
189 *Jammi German* 7.00
190 *Sam Cowart* 3.50
191 *Donald Hayes* 6.00
192 *R.W. McQuarters* 6.00
193 *Az-Zahir Hakim* 10.00
194 *Chris Fuamatu-Ma'afala* 7.00
195 *Allen Rossum* 3.50
196 *Jon Ritchie* 7.00
197 *Blake Spence* 3.50
198 *Brian Alford* 3.50
199 *Fred Weary* 3.50
200 *Rod Rutledge* 3.50
201 *Michael Myers* 3.50
202 *Rashaan Shehee* 7.00
203 *Donovin Darius* 3.50
204 *E.G. Green* 7.00
205 *Vonnie Holliday* 7.00
206 *Charlie Batch* 15.00
207 *Michael Pittman* 7.00
208 *Artrell Hawkins* 3.50
209 *Jonathan Quinn* 10.00
210 *Kailee Wong* 3.50
211 *Deshea Townsend* 3.50
212 *Patrick Surtain* 3.50
213 *Brian Kelly* 3.50
214 *Tebucky Jones* 3.50
215 *Pete Gonzalez* 6.00
216 *Shaun Williams* 3.50
217 *Scott Frost* 6.00
218 *Leonard Little* 3.50
219 *Alonzo Mayes* 6.00
220 *Cordell Taylor* 3.50

1999 Bowman

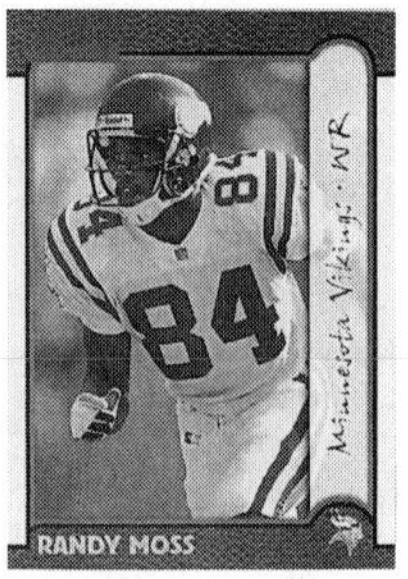

Bowman Football was a 220-card set that included 70 players who made their first appearance. Each of the rookie cards has the "Rookie Card Logo" on the front of the singles and are printed with a silver and blue logo design. The veterans are shown with a silver and red design. Parallel sets include the Inter-State and Gold singles. Other insert sets include: Autographs (Gold, Silver and Blue), Late Bloomers/Early Risers and Scout's Choice. Nine-card packs had an SRP of $3.00.

MT
Complete Set (220): 85.00
Common Player: .15
Minor Stars: .30
Common Rookie: .75
Pack (10): 3.00
Wax Box (24): 65.00
1 Dan Marino 2.00
2 Michael Westbrook .30
3 Yancey Thigpen .15
4 Tony Martin .15
5 Michael Strahan .15
6 Dedric Ward .15
7 Joey Galloway .50
8 Bobby Engram .15
9 Frank Sanders .15
10 Jake Plummer 1.50
11 Eddie Kennison .15
12 Curtis Martin .50
13 Ryan Leaf .50
14 Trent Dilfer .15
15 Tim Biakabutuka .15
16 Elvis Grbac .30
17 Charlie Batch 1.00
18 Takeo Spikes .15
19 Tony Banks .30
20 Doug Flutie 1.00
21 Ty Law .15
22 Isaac Bruce .30
23 James Jett .15
24 Kent Graham .15
25 Derrick Mayes .30
26 Amani Toomer .15
27 Ray Lewis .15
28 Shawn Springs .15
29 Warren Sapp .15
30 Jamal Anderson .50
31 Byron Morris .15
32 Johnnie Morton .15
33 Terance Mathis .15
34 Terrell Davis 2.00
35 John Randle .15
36 Vinny Testaverde .30
37 Junior Seau .30
38 Reidel Anthony .30
39 Brad Johnson .50
40 Emmitt Smith 2.00
41 Mo Lewis .15
42 Terry Glenn .50
43 Dorsey Levens .50
44 Thurman Thomas .30
45 Rob Moore .30
46 Corey Dillon .50
47 Jessie Armstead .15
48 Marshall Faulk .50
49 Charles Woodson .50
50 John Elway 2.00
51 Kevin Dyson .30
52 Tony Simmons .30
53 Keenan McCardell .30
54 O.J. Santiago .15
55 Jermaine Lewis .30
56 Herman Moore .50
57 Gary Brown .15
58 Jim Harbaugh .30
59 Mike Alstott .50
60 Brett Favre 3.00
61 Tim Brown .30
62 Steve McNair .75
63 Ben Coates .30
64 Jerome Pathon .15
65 Ray Buchanan .15
66 Troy Aikman 1.50
67 Andre Reed .30
68 Bubby Brister .30
69 Karim Abdul .30
70 Peyton Manning 2.00
71 Charles Johnson .15
72 Natrone Means .30
73 Michael Sinclair .15
74 Skip Hicks .30
75 Derrick Alexander .15
76 Wayne Chrebet .30
77 Rod Smith .30
78 Carl Pickens .30
79 Adrian Murrell .30

80 Fred Taylor 1.50
81 Eric Moulds .50
82 Erik Kramer .15
83 Marvin Harrison .50
84 Cris Carter .50
85 Ike Hilliard .15
86 Hines Ward .30
87 Terrell Owens .50
88 Ricky Proehl .15
89 Bert Emanuel .15
90 Randy Moss 3.00
91 Aaron Glenn .15
92 Robert Smith .30
93 Andre Hastings .15
94 Jake Reed .15
95 Curtis Enis .50
96 Andre Wadsworth .30
97 Ed McCaffrey .50
98 Zach Thomas .30
99 Kerry Collins .30
100 Drew Bledsoe 1.25
101 Germane Crowell .30
102 Bryan Still .15
103 Chad Brown .15
104 Jacquez Green .30
105 Garrison Hearst .30
106 Napoleon Kaufman .30
107 Ricky Watters .30
108 O.J. McDuffie .30
109 Keyshawn Johnson .50
110 Jerome Bettis .50
111 Duce Staley .30
112 Curtis Conway .30
113 Chris Chandler .30
114 Marcus Nash .30
115 Stephen Alexander .15
116 Darnay Scott .15
117 Bruce Smith .15
118 Priest Holmes .30
119 Mark Brunell 1.25
120 Jerry Rice 1.50
121 Randall Cunningham .50
122 Cameron Cleeland .30
123 Antonio Freeman .50
124 Kordell Stewart .75
125 Jon Kitna .75
126 Ahman Green .30
127 Warrick Dunn .75
128 Robert Brooks .15
129 Derrick Thomas .30
130 Steve Young 1.00
131 Peter Boulware .15
132 Michael Irvin .30
133 Shannon Sharpe .30
134 Jimmy Smith .30
135 John Avery .30
136 Fred Lane .15
137 Trent Green .30
138 Andre Rison .15
139 Antowain Smith .30
140 Eddie George .75
141 Jeff Blake .30
142 Raghib Ismail .15
143 Rickey Dudley .15
144 Courtney Hawkins .15
145 Mikhael Ricks .15
146 J.J. Stokes .30
147 Levon Kirkland .15
148 Deion Sanders .50
149 Barry Sanders 3.00
150 Tiki Barber .15
151 *David Boston* 4.00
152 *Chris McAlister* 1.50
153 *Peerless Price* 3.00
154 *D'Wayne Bates* 1.50
155 *Cade McNown* 4.00
156 *Akili Smith* 6.00
157 *Kevin Johnson* 4.00
158 *Tim Couch* 12.00
159 *Sedrick Irvin* 3.00
160 *Chris Claiborne* 1.50
161 *Edgerrin James* 12.00
162 *Michael Cloud* 1.50
163 *Cecil Collins* 6.00
164 *James Johnson* 3.00
165 *Rob Konrad* 1.50
166 *Daunte Culpepper* 6.00
167 *Kevin Faulk* 3.00
168 *Donovan McNabb* 6.00
169 *Troy Edwards* 4.00
170 *Amos Zereoue* 3.00
171 *Karsten Bailey* 1.50
172 *Brock Huard* 2.00
173 *Joe Germaine* 2.00
174 *Torry Holt* 4.00
175 *Shaun King* 5.00
176 *Jevon Kearse* 3.00
177 *Champ Bailey* 2.50
178 *Ebenezer Ekuban* 1.50
179 *Andy Katzenmoyer* 2.00
180 *Antoine Winfield* 1.50
181 *Jermaine Fazande* .75
182 *Ricky Williams* 12.00
183 *Joel Mackovicka* .75
184 *Reginald Kelly* .75
185 *Brandon Stokley* .75
186 *Shawn Bryson* .75
187 *Marty Booker* 1.50
188 *Jerry Azumah* .75
189 *Craig Yeast* .75
190 *Scott Covington* 1.50
191 *Rahim Abdullah* .75
192 *Darrin Chiaverini* .75
193 *Dat Nguyen* 1.50
194 *Wane McGarity* 1.50
195 *Al Wilson* 1.50
196 *Travis McGriff* 1.50
197 *Aaron Gibson* 1.50
198 *Antwan Edwards* .75
199 *Aaron Brooks* 10.00
200 *De'Mond Parker* .75
201 *Dee Miller* .75
202 *John Tait* .75
203 *Jim Kleinsasser* 1.50
204 *Michael Bishop* 3.00
205 *Joe Montgomery* 1.50
206 *Sean Bennett* 1.50
207 *Dameane Douglas* .75
208 *Na Brown* .75
209 *Jerame Tuman* .75
210 *Malcolm Johnson* .75
211 *Dre Bly* .75
212 *Terry Jackson* .75
213 *Tai Streets* .75
214 *Autry Denson* 1.50
215 *Darnell McDonald* 1.50
216 *Charlie Rogers* .75
217 *Reggie McGrew* .75
218 *Tony Bryant* .75
219 *Larry Parker* .75
220 *Martay Jenkins* .75

1999 Bowman Gold Parallel

This was a 220-card parallel to the base set with the team name stamped in gold foil. Each card was sequentially numbered to 99 and inserted 1:68 packs.

MT
Gold Cards: 20x-40x
Gold Rookies: 5x-10x
Production 99 Sets

1999 Bowman Interstate Parallel

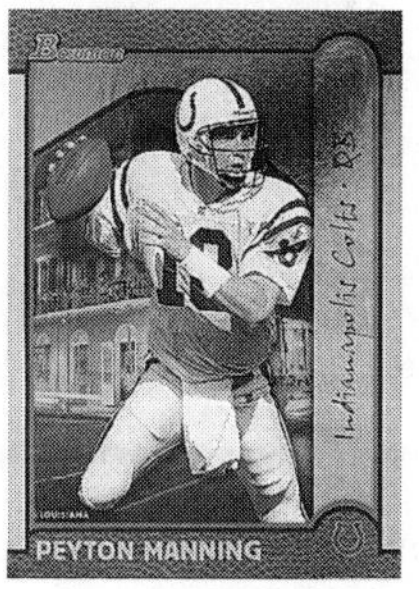

This was a 220-card parallel to the base set. The card fronts have a scenic landmark from the player's home state and the card backs feature a custom-tailored vanity plate from that state. Singles were inserted into every pack.

MT
Complete Set (220): 250.00
Interstate Cards: 3x
Interstate Rookies: 1.5x
Inserted 1:1

1999 Bowman Autographs

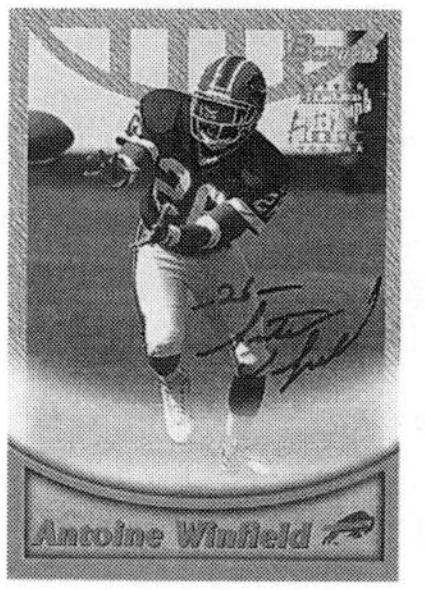

The 32-card autograph set was divdided into three sections with the first six cards in Gold and found 1:850 packs. The next 15 cards were printed in Silver and inserted 1:212 packs. The last 11 singles were in Blue and found 1:180 packs.

MT
Complete Set (32): 1850.
Common Gold (1-6): 100.00
Inserted 1:850
Common Silver (7-21): 20.00
Inserted 1:212
Common Blue (22-32): 12.00
Inserted 1:180
1 Randy Moss G 250.00
2 Akili Smith G 150.00
3 Edgerrin James G 275.00
4 Ricky Williams G 275.00
5 Torry Holt G 100.00
6 Daunte Culpepper G 150.00
7 Donovan McNabb S 85.00
8 Tim Couch S 175.00
9 Champ Bailey S 40.00
10 David Boston S 50.00
11 Chris Claiborne S 20.00
12 Chris McAlister S 20.00
13 Rob Konrad S 20.00
14 Michael Cloud S 20.00
15 Jermaine Fazande S 20.00
16 Brock Huard S 30.00
17 Joe Germaine S 30.00
18 Sedrick Irvin S 40.00
19 Cecil Collins S 80.00
20 Karsten Bailey S 20.00
21 Antoine Winfield S 20.00
22 Cade McNown B 60.00
23 Troy Edwards B 40.00
24 Jevon Kearse B 35.00
25 Andy Katzenmoyer B 20.00
26 Kevin Johnson B 40.00
27 James Johnson B 30.00
28 Kevin Faulk B 30.00
29 Shaun King B 25.00
30 Peerless Price B 30.00
31 D'Wayne Bates B 12.00
32 Amos Zereoue B 30.00

A card number in parentheses ( ) indicates the set is unnumbered.

1999 Bowman Late Bloomers/ Early Risers

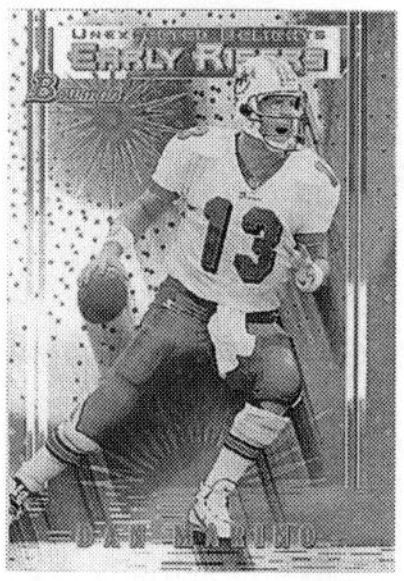

This 10-card set includes five Late Bloomers and five Early Risers. The Late Bloomer theme includes the best late-round selections and the Early Risers include impact players from past NFL Drafts. Singles were found 1:12 packs.

MT
Complete Set (10): 20.00
Common Player: 1.00
Inserted 1:12
1 Fred Taylor (Early Risers) 3.00
2 Peyton Manning (Early Risers) 4.00
3 Dan Marino (Early Risers) 4.00
4 Barry Sanders (Early Risers) 5.00
5 Randy Moss (Early Risers) 5.00
6 Mark Brunell (Late Bloomers) 2.00
7 Jamal Anderson (Late Bloomers) 1.00
8 Curtis Martin (Late Bloomers) 1.00
9 Wayne Chrebet (Late Bloomers) 1.00
10 Terrell Davis (Late Bloomers) 4.00

1999 Bowman Scout's Choice

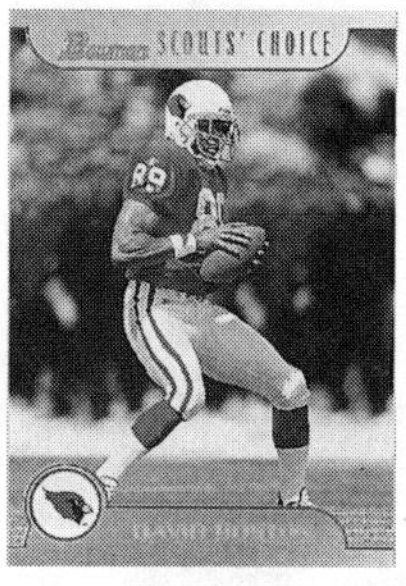

This 21-card set included the top rookies from the 1999 Draft. Each card was borderless and printed on double-etched foil board. Singles were inserted 1:12 packs.

MT
Complete Set (21): 50.00
Common Player: 1.00
Minor Stars: 2.00
Inserted 1:12
1 David Boston 4.00
2 Champ Bailey 2.50
3 Edgerrin James 10.00
4 Michael Cloud 1.00
5 Kevin Faulk 3.00
6 Troy Edwards 4.00
7 Joe Germaine 2.00
8 Peerless Price 3.00
9 Torry Holt 4.00
10 Rob Konrad 2.00
11 Akili Smith 6.00
12 Daunte Culpepper 6.00
13 D'Wayne Bates 2.00
14 Donovan McNabb 6.00
15 James Johnson 3.00
16 Cade McNown 6.00
17 Kevin Johnson 4.00
18 Ricky Williams 10.00
19 Karsten Bailey 1.00
20 Tim Couch 10.00
21 Shaun King 3.00

1999 Bowman's Best

Bowman's Best Football was a 133-card set that had each single printed on 26-pt. Serillusion stock. The set breakdown was 90 Star Veterans that were printed on gold stock and 10 Best Performance cards. The last 33 cards were rookies and they were printed on silver stock and included the "Bowman's Best Rookie Logo". Rookies were found one-per-pack. Parallel sets included Refractors and Atomic Refractors. Other inserts included: Autographs, Franchise Best, Franchise Favorites, Franchise Favorite Autographs, Future Foundations, Honor Roll, Legacy, Legacy Autographs, Locker Room Autographs and Locker Room Jerseys. Six-card packs had an SRP of $5.00.

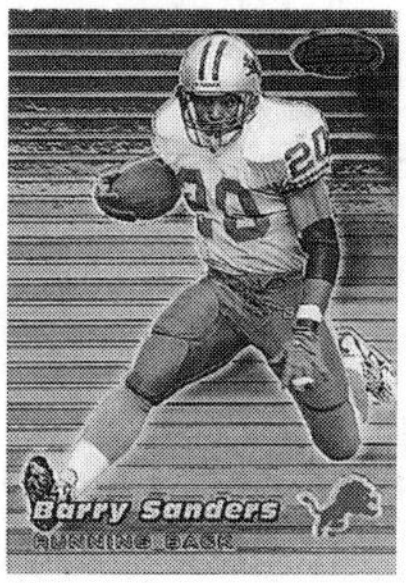

MT
Complete Set (133): 100.00
Common Player: .20
Minor Stars: .40
Common Rookie: 1.00
Pack (6): 4.00
Wax Box (24): 90.00
1 Randy Moss 3.00
2 Skip Hicks .40
3 Robert Smith .75
4 Drew Bledsoe 1.25
5 Tim Brown .40
6 Marshall Faulk .75
7 Terance Mathis .20
8 Sean Dawkins .20
9 Ed McCaffrey .50
10 Jamal Anderson .75
11 Antonio Freeman .75
12 Terry Kirby .20
13 Vinny Testaverde .40
14 Eddie George 1.00
15 Ricky Watters .50
16 Johnnie Morton .20
17 Natrone Means .50
18 Terry Glenn .75
19 Michael Westbrook .50
20 Doug Flutie 1.25
21 Jake Plummer 1.25
22 Darnay Scott .40
23 Andre Rison .40
24 Jon Kitna 1.00
25 Dan Marino 2.00
26 Ike Hilliard .20
27 Warrick Dunn .75
28 Jerome Bettis .75
29 Curtis Conway .40
30 Emmitt Smith 2.00
31 Jimmy Smith .75
32 Isaac Bruce .75
33 Jerry Rice 1.50
34 Curtis Martin .75
35 Steve McNair 1.00
36 Jeff Blake .40
37 Rob Moore .40
38 Dorsey Levens .75
39 Terrell Davis 2.00
40 John Elway 2.00
41 Trent Dilfer .50
42 Joey Galloway .75
43 Keyshawn Johnson .75
44 O.J. McDuffie .40
45 Fred Taylor 1.50
46 Andre Reed .40
47 Frank Sanders .40
48 Keenan McCardell .40
49 Elvis Grbac .40
50 Barry Sanders 3.00
51 Terrell Owens .75
52 Trent Green .50
53 Brad Johnson .75
54 Rich Gannon .40
55 Randall Cunningham .75
56 Tony Martin .20
57 Rod Smith .50
58 Eric Moulds .75
59 Yancey Thigpen .40
60 Brett Favre 3.00
61 Cris Carter .75
62 Marvin Harrison .75
63 Chris Chandler .40
64 Antowain Smith .50
65 Carl Pickens .40
66 Shannon Sharpe .50
67 Mike Alstott .75
68 J.J. Stokes .40
69 Ben Coates .40
70 Peyton Manning 2.00
71 Duce Staley .50
72 Michael Irvin .40
73 Tim Biakabutuka .40
74 Priest Holmes .75
75 Steve Young 1.25
76 Jerome Pathon .20
77 Wayne Chrebet .75
78 Bert Emanuel .20
79 Curtis Enis .75
80 Mark Brunell 1.25
81 Herman Moore .75
82 Corey Dillon .75
83 Jim Harbaugh .40
84 Gary Brown .40
85 Kordell Stewart .75
86 Garrison Hearst .50
87 Raghib Ismail .20
88 Charlie Batch 1.25
89 Napoleon Kaufman .75
90 Troy Aikman 1.50
91 Brett Favre 1.50
92 Randy Moss 1.50
93 Terrell Davis 1.00
94 Barry Sanders 1.50
95 Peyton Manning 1.00
96 Troy Edwards .75
97 Cade McNown 2.00
98 Edgerrin James 6.00
99 Torry Holt .75
100 Tim Couch 3.50
101 *Chris Claiborne* 2.00
102 *Brock Huard* 3.00
103 *Amos Zereoue* 2.00
104 *Sedrick Irvin* 2.00
105 *Kevin Faulk* 3.00
106 *Ebenezer Ekuban* 1.00
107 *Daunte Culpepper* 12.00
108 *Rob Konrad* 2.00
109 *James Johnson* 2.00
110 *Kurt Warner* 20.00
111 *Mike Cloud* 2.00
112 *Andy Katzenmoyer* 2.00
113 *Jevon Kearse* 4.00
114 *Akili Smith* 4.50
115 *Edgerrin James* 15.00
116 *Cecil Collins* 2.00
117 *Chris McAlister* 2.00
118 *Donovan McNabb* 8.00
119 *Kevin Johnson* 4.00
120 *Torry Holt* 5.00
121 *Antoine Winfield* 1.00
122 *Michael Bishop* 3.00
123 *Joe Germaine* 2.00
124 *David Boston* 4.00
125 *D'Wayne Bates* 2.00
126 *Champ Bailey* 2.50
127 *Cade McNown* 3.00
128 *Shaun King* 5.00
129 *Peerless Price* 3.00
130 *Troy Edwards* 3.00
131 *Karsten Bailey* 1.00
132 *Tim Couch* 10.00
133 *Ricky Williams* 10.00

1999 Bowman's Best Refractors Parallel

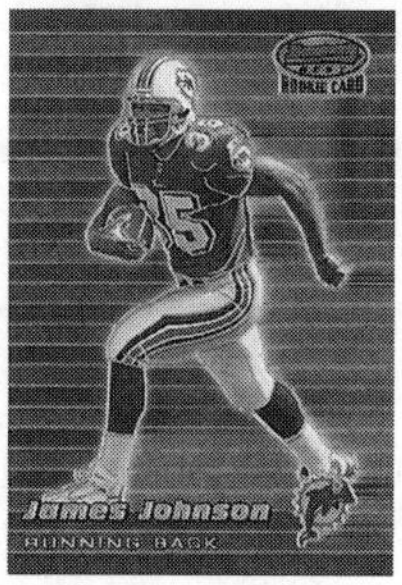

This was a parallel to the base set except that each single was printed on metalized refractor board. Singles were sequentially numbered to 400 and were inserted 1:17 packs.

MT
Complete Set (133): 550.00
Refractor Cards: 5x-10x
Refractor Rookies: 2x-4x
Inserted 1:17
Production 400 Sets

1999 Bowman's Best Atomic Refractors Parallel

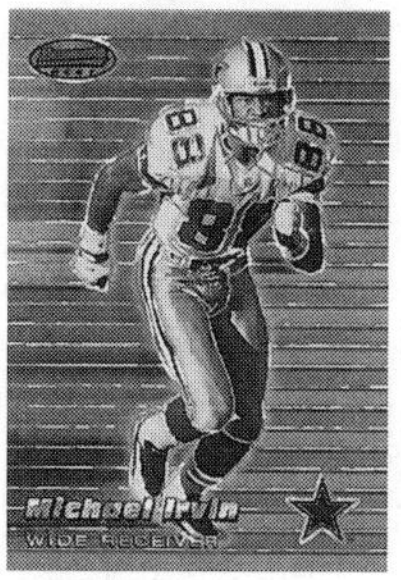

This was a parallel to the base set except that each single was printed on iridescent refractor foil board. Singles were sequentially numbered to 100 and inserted 1:69 packs.

MT
Atomic Cards: 15x-30x
Atomic Rookies: 8x-16x
Inserted 1:69
Production 100 Sets

1999 Bowman's Best Autographs

Each of the three autographs in this set include the stamp "Certified Autograph Issue" as well as the Topps-3M authentication sticker on the backs of the cards. The Fred Taylor and Jake Plummer singles were found 1:915 packs and the Randy Moss card was inserted 1:9,129 packs.

MT
Complete Set (3): 300.00
Common Player: 50.00
Inserted 1:915
Inserted 1:9,129 (Moss)
1 Fred Taylor 50.00
2 Jake Plummer 50.00
ROY1 Randy Moss 200.00

1999 Bowman's Best Franchise Best

This 9-card insert included the top players in the NFL and pictured them on die-cut cards. Singles were inserted 1:20 packs.

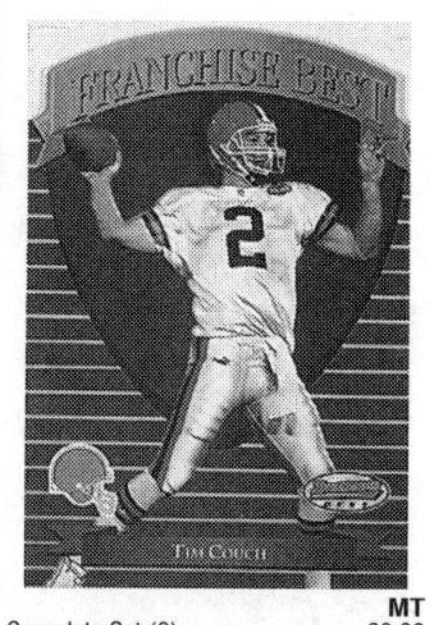

MT
Complete Set (9): 60.00
Common Player: 3.00
Inserted 1:20
1 Dan Marino 10.00
2 Fred Taylor 6.00
3 Emmitt Smith 10.00
4 Terrell Davis 10.00
5 Brett Favre 12.00
6 Tim Couch 12.00
7 Peyton Manning 10.00
8 Eddie George 3.00
9 Randy Moss 12.00

1999 Bowman's Best Franchise Favorites

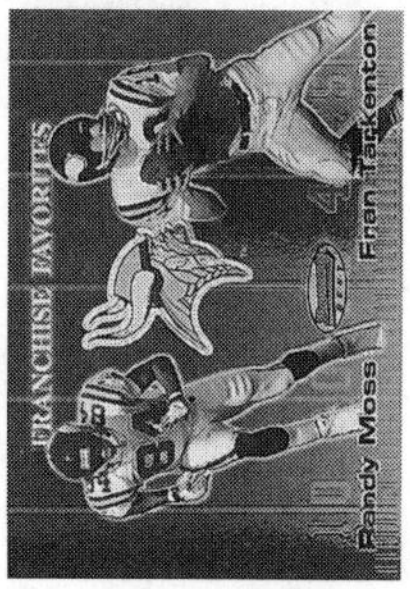

Singles from this insert set include both current and retired stars. Each is printed on prismatic holographic board with two players on each card. Singles were inserted 1:153 packs.

MT
Complete Set (2): 30.00
Common Player: 10.00
Inserted 1:153
1 Tony Dorsett, Roger Staubach 10.00
2 Randy Moss, Fran Tarkenton 20.00

1999 Bowman's Best Franchise Favorites Autographs

Each of the singles in this 6-card set are autographed and found at different ratios. The odds for the singles are as follows: #1 (1:4,599), #2, 5 (1:1,017) and #3, 4, 6 (1:9,129).

MT
Complete Set (6): 600.00
Common Player: 70.00
Inserted 1:703
1 Tony Dorsett 70.00
2 Roger Staubach 100.00
3 Tony Dorsett, Roger Staubach 150.00
4 Randy Moss 150.00
5 Fran Tarkenton 70.00
6 Randy Moss, Fran Tarkenton 200.00

1999 Bowman's Best Future Foundations

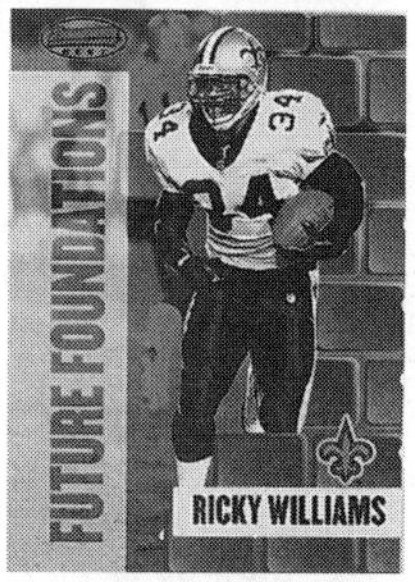

This 18-card insert set included the top rookies from the 1999 NFL Draft. Each card was printed on prismatic holographic stock with a die-cut pattern. Singles were inserted 1:20 packs.

MT
Complete Set (18): 50.00
Common Player: 1.00

Minor Stars:		2.00
Inserted 1:20		
1	Tim Couch	10.00
2	David Boston	3.00
3	Donovan McNabb	5.00
4	Troy Edwards	3.00
5	Ricky Williams	10.00
6	Daunte Culpepper	5.00
7	Torry Holt	3.00
8	Cade McNown	5.00
9	Akili Smith	5.00
10	Edgerrin James	15.00
11	Cecil Collins	3.00
12	Peerless Price	2.00
13	Kevin Johnson	3.00
14	Champ Bailey	2.00
15	Michael Cloud	1.00
16	D'Wayne Bates	1.00
17	Shaun King	5.00
18	James Johnson	2.00

1999 Bowman's Best Honor Roll

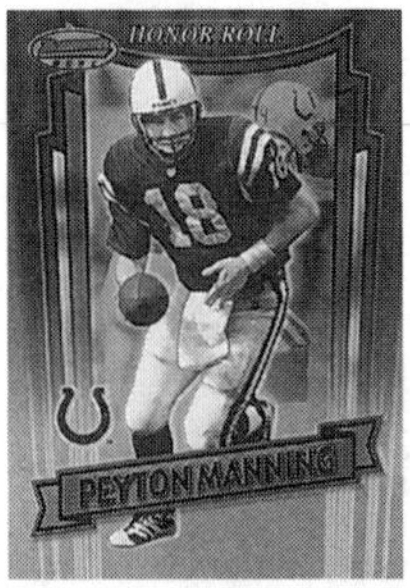

This 8-card insert set included only Heisman winners or first overall Draft Picks. Singles were found 1:40 packs.

		MT
Complete Set (8):		35.00
Common Player:		3.00
Inserted 1:40		
1	Peyton Manning	10.00
2	Drew Bledsoe	5.00
3	Doug Flutie	4.00
4	Tim Couch	12.00
5	Charles Woodson	3.00
6	Ricky Williams	12.00
7	Tim Brown	3.00
8	Eddie George	4.00

1999 Bowman's Best Legacy

This 3-card insert set included Texas legends and Heisman Trophy winners. Singles were inserted 1:102 packs.

		MT
Complete Set (3):		40.00
Common Player:		10.00
Inserted 1:102		
1	Ricky Williams	15.00
2	Earl Campbell	10.00
3	Ricky Williams, Earl Campbell	15.00

1999 Bowman's Best Legacy Autographs

This was a parallel to the Best Legacy insert. Each single is autographed and includes the "Certified Autograph Issue" stamp on the fronts and the Topps-3M sticker on the backs. Card #1 was found 1:4,599, card #2 was found 1:2,040 and card #3 was found 1:18,108.

		MT
Complete Set (3):		425.00
Common Player:		75.00
#1 Inserted 1:4,599		
#2 Inserted 1:2,040		
#3 Inserted 1:18,108		
1	Ricky Williams	150.00
2	Earl Campbell	75.00
3	Ricky Williams, Earl Campbell	250.00

1999 Bowman's Best Rookie Class Photo

This single card included the 1999 NFL Rookie Class with a group shot photo. It was inserted 1:100 packs.

		MT
Inserted 1:100		
Refractor:		8x
Inserted 1:7,429		
Production 125 Sets		
Atomic Refractor:		20x
Inserted 1:26,880		
Production 35 Sets		
C1	Rookie Class Photo	12.00

1999 Bowman's Best Rookie Locker Room Autographs

This 5-card insert set included autographs of the top rookies from 1999. Each card included the Topps "Certified Autograph Issue" stamp on the card fronts and the Topps-3M authentication sticker on the backs. Cards #1, 4 & 5 were inserted 1:305 packs and cards #2 & 3 were found 1:915 packs.

		MT
Complete Set (5):		300.00
Common Player:		25.00
#1,4,5 Inserted 1:305		
#2,3 Inserted 1:915		
1	Tim Couch	100.00
2	Donovan McNabb	60.00
3	Edgerrin James	200.00
4	David Boston	25.00
5	Torry Holt	25.00

1999 Bowman's Best Rookie Locker Room Jerseys

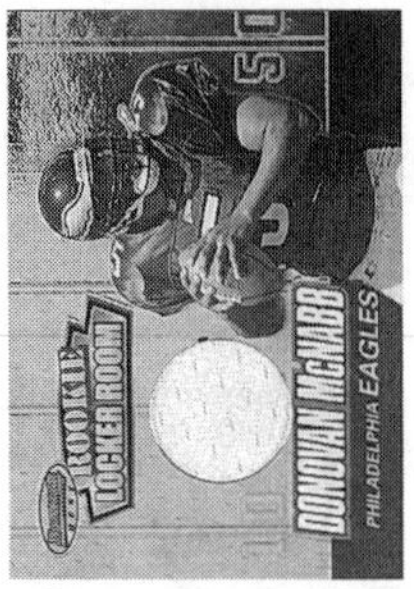

This 4-card set insert included rookies from 1999. Each card included the Topps-3M sticker on the card backs. Some of the singles could only be found through redemption cards. Singles were found 1:229 packs.

		MT
Complete Set (4):		225.00
Common Player:		50.00
Inserted 1:229		
1	Kevin Faulk	50.00
2	Donovan McNabb	75.00
3	Ricky Williams	100.00
4	Torry Holt	50.00

1999 Bowman Chrome

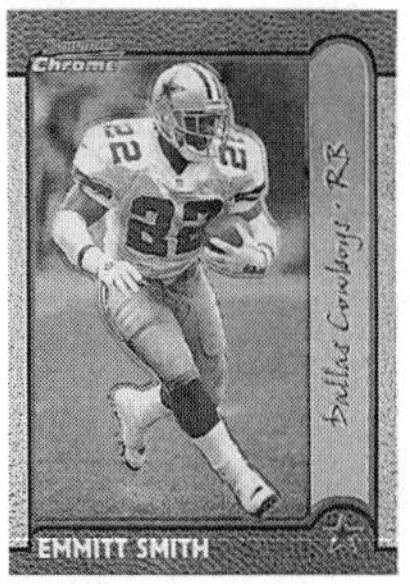

Bowman Chrome Football was a 220-card set that paralleled the regular Bowman issue. The set included 150 veterans and 70 rookies. Each rookie card had the "Bowman Chrome Rookie Card" logo. Parallel sets included: Refractors, Gold, Gold Refractors, Interstate and Interstate Refractors. Other insert sets included: Scout's Choice, Scout's Choice Refractors, Stock in the Game and Stock in the Game Refractors. Four-card packs had an SRP of $3.00.

		MT
Complete Set (220):		225.00
Common Player:		.25
Minor Stars:		.50
Common Rookie:		2.00
Pack (4):		4.00
Wax Box (24):		90.00
1	Dan Marino	3.00
2	Michael Westbrook	.50
3	Yancey Thigpen	.50
4	Tony Martin	.25
5	Michael Strahan	.25
6	Dedric Ward	.25
7	Joey Galloway	1.00
8	Bobby Engram	.25
9	Frank Sanders	.50
10	Jake Plummer	2.00
11	Eddie Kennison	.25
12	Curtis Martin	1.00
13	Chris Spielman	.25
14	Trent Dilfer	1.00
15	Tim Biakabutuka	.50
16	Elvis Grbac	.50
17	Charlie Batch	1.50
18	Takeo Spikes	.25
19	Tony Banks	1.00
20	Doug Flutie	1.50
21	Ty Law	.25
22	Isaac Bruce	1.00
23	James Jett	.25
24	Kent Graham	.25
25	Derrick Mayes	.50
26	Amani Toomer	.50
27	Ray Lewis	.25
28	Shawn Springs	.25
29	Warren Sapp	.50
30	Jamal Anderson	1.00
31	Byron Morris	.25
32	Johnnie Morton	.50
33	Terance Mathis	.25
34	Terrell Davis	3.00
35	John Randle	.50
36	Vinny Testaverde	1.00
37	Junior Seau	.75
38	Reidel Anthony	.50
39	Brad Johnson	1.00
40	Emmitt Smith	3.00
41	Mo Lewis	.25
42	Terry Glenn	1.00
43	Dorsey Levens	1.00
44	Thurman Thomas	.75
45	Rob Moore	.50
46	Corey Dillon	1.00
47	Jessie Armstead	.25
48	Marshall Faulk	1.00
49	Charles Woodson	1.00
50	John Elway	3.00
51	Kevin Dyson	.50
52	Tony Simmons	.50
53	Keenan McCardell	.50
54	O.J. Santiago	.25
55	Jermaine Lewis	.50
56	Herman Moore	1.00
57	Gary Brown	.25
58	Jim Harbaugh	.50
59	Mike Alstott	1.00
60	Brett Favre	4.00
61	Tim Brown	.75
62	Steve McNair	1.00
63	Ben Coates	.50
64	Jerome Pathon	.50
65	Ray Buchanan	.25
66	Troy Aikman	2.00
67	Andre Reed	.50
68	Bubby Brister	.50
69	Karim Abdul	.50
70	Peyton Manning	3.00
71	Charles Johnson	.25
72	Natrone Means	.75
73	Michael Sinclair	.25
74	Skip Hicks	.50
75	Derrick Alexander	.25
76	Wayne Chrebet	1.00
77	Rod Smith	1.00
78	Carl Pickens	1.00
79	Adrian Murrell	.50
80	Fred Taylor	2.00
81	Eric Moulds	1.00
82	Erik Kramer	.25
83	Marvin Harrison	1.00
84	Cris Carter	1.00
85	Ike Hillard	.50
86	Hines Ward	.75
87	Terrell Owens	1.00
88	Ricky Proehl	.25
89	Bert Emanuel	.25
90	Randy Moss	4.00
91	Aaron Glenn	.25
92	Robert Smith	1.00
93	Andre Hastings	.25
94	Jake Reed	.50
95	Curtis Enis	1.00
96	Andre Wadsworth	.50
97	Ed McCaffrey	1.00
98	Zach Thomas	.50
99	Kerry Collins	.50
100	Drew Bledsoe	1.50
101	Germane Crowell	.75
102	Bryan Still	.25
103	Chad Brown	.25
104	Jacquez Green	.50
105	Garrison Hearst	.50
106	Napoleon Kaufman	1.00
107	Ricky Watters	.50
108	O.J. McDuffie	.50
109	Keyshawn Johnson	1.00
110	Jerome Bettis	1.00
111	Duce Staley	1.00
112	Curtis Conway	.50
113	Chris Chandler	.50
114	Marcus Nash	.50
115	Stephen Alexander	.25
116	Darnay Scott	.50
117	Bruce Smith	.25
118	Priest Holmes	1.00
119	Mark Brunell	1.50
120	Jerry Rice	2.00
121	Randall Cunningham	1.00
122	Cameron Cleeland	.50
123	Antonio Freeman	1.00
124	Kordell Stewart	1.00
125	Jon Kitna	1.00
126	Ahman Green	.50
127	Warrick Dunn	1.00
128	Robert Brooks	.25
129	Derrick Thomas	.50
130	Steve Young	1.50
131	Peter Boulware	.25
132	Michael Irvin	.50
133	Shannon Sharpe	.50
134	Jimmy Smith	1.00
135	John Avery	.50
136	Fred Lane	.50
137	Trent Green	.50
138	Andre Rison	.50
139	Antowain Smith	1.00
140	Eddie George	1.25
141	Jeff Blake	.75
142	Raghib Ismail	.25
143	Rickey Dudley	.50
144	Courtney Hawkins	.25
145	Mikhael Ricks	.25
146	J.J. Stokes	.50
147	Levon Kirkland	.25
148	Deion Sanders	1.00
149	Barry Sanders	4.00
150	Tiki Barber	.50
151	*David Boston*	6.00
152	*Chris McAlister*	3.00
153	*Peerless Price*	5.00
154	*D'Wayne Bates*	3.00
155	*Cade McNown*	6.00
156	*Akili Smith*	8.00
157	*Kevin Johnson*	6.00
158	*Tim Couch*	15.00
159	*Sedrick Irvin*	3.00
160	*Chris Claiborne*	3.00
161	*Edgerrin James*	25.00
162	*Michael Cloud*	3.00
163	*Cecil Collins*	4.00
164	*James Johnson*	4.00
165	*Rob Konrad*	3.00
166	*Daunte Culpepper*	20.00
167	*Kevin Faulk*	6.00
168	*Donovan McNabb*	15.00
169	*Troy Edwards*	5.00
170	*Amos Zereoue*	4.00
171	*Karsten Bailey*	3.00
172	*Brock Huard*	6.00
173	*Joe Germaine*	4.00
174	*Torry Holt*	8.00
175	*Shaun King*	8.00
176	*Jevon Kearse*	8.00
177	*Champ Bailey*	5.00
178	*Ebenezer Ekuban*	3.00
179	*Andy Katzenmoyer*	4.00
180	*Antoine Winfield*	3.00
181	*Jermaine Fazande*	4.00
182	*Ricky Williams*	15.00
183	*Joel Mackovicka*	3.00
184	*Reginald Kelly*	2.00
185	*Brandon Stokley*	5.00
186	*L.C. Stevens*	2.00
187	*Marty Booker*	4.00
188	*Jerry Azumah*	2.00
189	*Ted White*	2.00
190	*Scott Covington*	3.00
191	*Tim Alexander*	2.00
192	*Darrin Chiaverini*	4.00
193	*Dat Nguyen*	3.00
194	*Wane McGarity*	3.00
195	*Al Wilson*	3.00
196	*Travis McGriff*	3.00
197	*Stacey Mack*	4.00
198	*Antwan Edwards*	3.00
199	*Aaron Brooks*	15.00
200	*De'Mond Parker*	4.00
201	*Jed Weaver*	2.00
202	*Madre Hill*	2.00
203	*Jim Kleinsasser*	4.00
204	*Michael Bishop*	5.00
205	*Michael Basnight*	2.00
206	*Sean Bennett*	3.00
207	*Dameane Douglas*	2.00
208	*Na Brown*	2.00
209	*Patrick Kerney*	2.00
210	*Malcolm Johnson*	2.00
211	*Dre Bly*	2.00
212	*Terry Jackson*	4.00
213	*Eugene Baker*	2.00
214	*Autry Denson*	4.00
215	*Darnell McDonald*	4.00
216	*Charlie Rogers*	3.00
217	*Joe Montgomery*	4.00
218	*Cecil Martin*	3.00
219	*Larry Parker*	2.00
220	*Mike Peterson*	2.00

1999 Bowman Chrome Gold Parallel

This was a parallel to the base set with each single printed in gold ink. Singles were found 1:24 packs.

	MT
Complete Set (220):	1000.
Gold Cards:	4x-8x
Gold Rookies:	2x
Inserted 1:24	

1999 Bowman Chrome Gold Refractors Parallel

This is a parallel to the Gold set except that each card is printed on refractor board. Singles were sequentially numbered to 25 and found 1:253 packs.

	MT
Complete Set (220):	3500.
Gold Ref. Cards:	35x-70x
Gold Ref. Rookies:	3x-6x
Inserted 1:253	
Production 25 Sets	

1999 Bowman Chrome Interstate Parallel

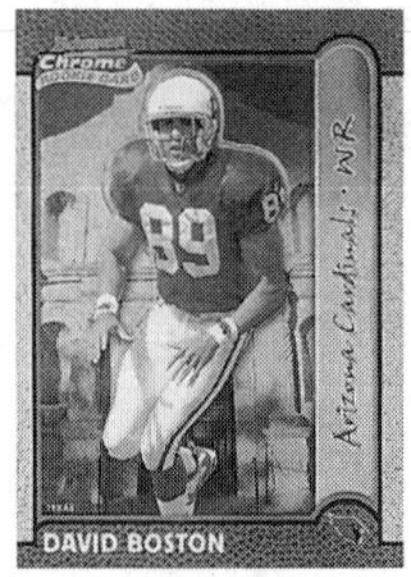

This set was a parallel to the base. The card fronts featured an image that related to that player's home state. The backs had a custom- tailored vanity plate from that state. Singles were found 1:4 packs.

	MT
Complete Set (220):	450.00
Interstate Cards:	2x-4x
Interstate Rookies:	1.5x
Inserted 1:4	

1999 Bowman Chrome Interstate Refractors Parallel

This was a parallel to the Interstate insert except that each single is printed on refractor board. Singles were sequentially numbered to 100 and found 1:63 packs.

	MT
Complete Set (220):	2200.
Interstate Ref. Cards:	15x-30x
Interstate Ref. Rookies:	3x
Inserted 1:63	
Production 100 Sets	

A card number in parentheses ( ) indicates the set is unnumbered.

1999 Bowman Chrome Refractors Parallel

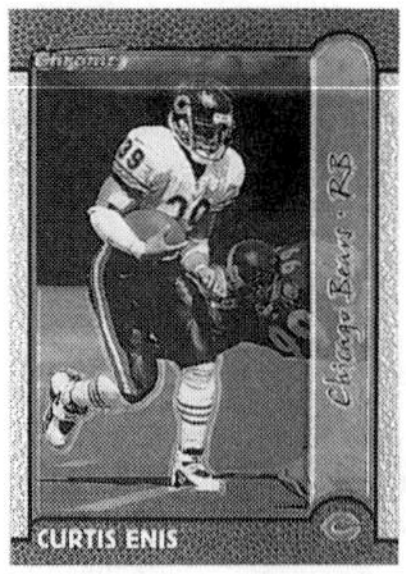

This was a parallel to the base set except that each single was printed on refractor board. Singles were found 1:12 packs.

	MT
Complete Set (220):	800.00
Refractor Cards:	4x-8x
Refractor Rookies:	2x
Inserted 1:12	

1999 Bowman Chrome Scout's Choice

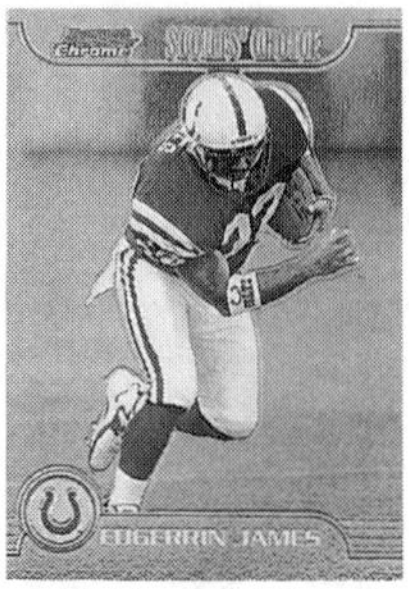

This 21-card set includes all of the top rookies from the 1999 NFL Draft. Each single was borderless and printed on double-etched foil board. Singles were found 1:12 packs.

		MT
Complete Set (21):		60.00
Common Player:		1.00
Minor Stars:		2.00
Inserted 1:12		
Refractors:		2x
Inserted 1:60		
1	David Boston	3.00
2	Champ Bailey	2.00
3	Edgerrin James	15.00
4	Michael Cloud	1.00
5	Kevin Faulk	2.00
6	Troy Edwards	3.00
7	Cecil Collins	3.00
8	Peerless Price	2.00
9	Torry Holt	3.00
10	Rob Konrad	1.00
11	Akili Smith	5.00
12	Daunte Culpepper	5.00
13	D'Wayne Bates	1.00
14	Donovan McNabb	5.00
15	James Johnson	2.00
16	Cade McNown	5.00
17	Kevin Johnson	3.00
18	Ricky Williams	10.00
19	Karsten Bailey	1.00
20	Tim Couch	10.00
21	Shaun King	5.00

1999 Bowman Chrome Scout's Choice Refractors Parallel

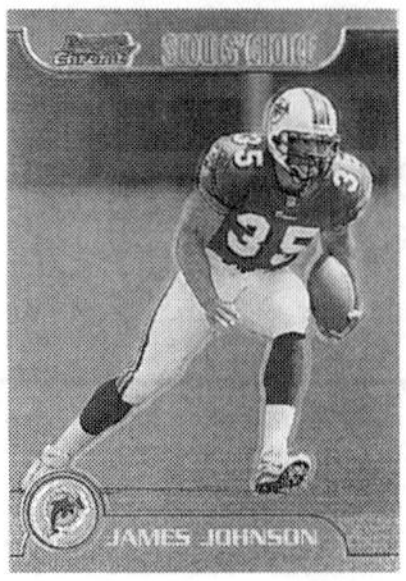

This was a parallel to the Scout's Choice insert. Singles were inserted 1:60 packs.

	MT
Refractor Cards:	2x
Inserted 1:60	

1999 Bowman Chrome Stock in the Game

This 18-card set was an exclusive to the Bowman Chrome line. The set was divided into three categories. I.P.O. included six rookies not found in the Scout's Choice insert. The Growth section included six young stars and the Blue Chips included six of the game's veterans. Singles were found 1:21 packs.

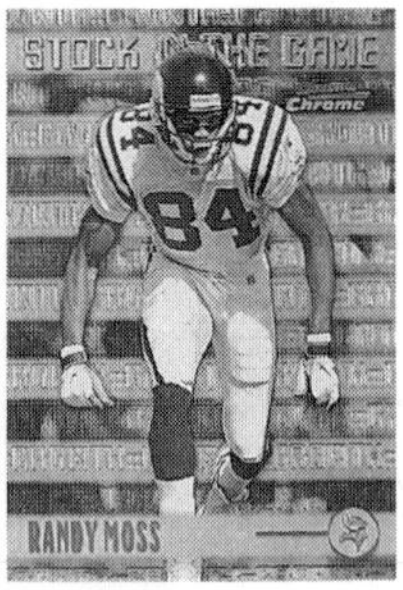

		MT
Complete Set (18):		40.00
Common Player:		2.00
Inserted 1:21		
Refractors:		3x
Inserted 1:105		
1	Joe Germaine	2.00
2	Madre Hill	2.00
3	Sedrick Irvin	2.00
4	Brock Huard	2.00
5	Amos Zereoue	2.00
6	Andy Katzenmoyer	2.00
7	Randy Moss	8.00
8	Jake Plummer	3.00
9	Keyshawn Johnson	2.00
10	Fred Taylor	4.00
11	Eddie George	2.00
12	Peyton Manning	6.00
13	Dan Marino	6.00
14	Terrell Davis	6.00
15	Brett Favre	8.00
16	Jamal Anderson	2.00
17	Steve Young	3.00
18	Jerry Rice	4.00

1999 Bowman Chrome Stock in the Game Refractors Paralle

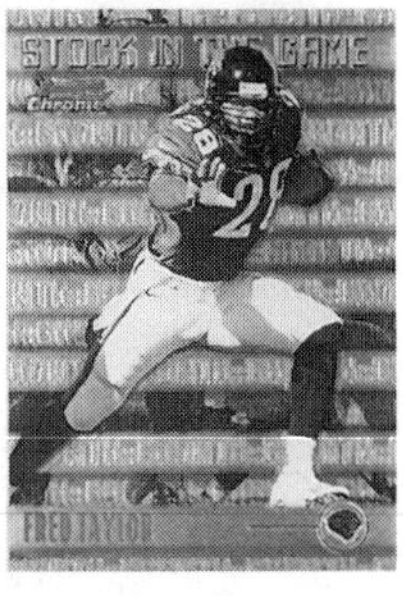

This was a parallel to the Stock in the Game insert. Each single was printed on refractor board and was found 1:105 packs.

	MT
Refractors:	3x
Inserted 1:105	

2000 Bowman

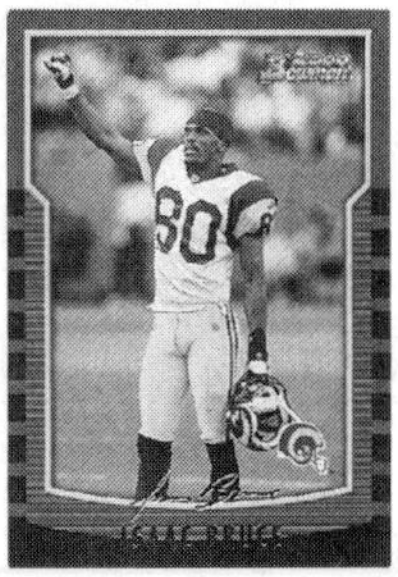

		MT
Complete Set (240):		60.00
Common Player:		.10
Minor Stars:		.20
Common Europe:		.40
Common Rookie:		.40
Pack (10):		3.00
Wax Box (24):		50.00
1	Eddie George	.60
2	Ike Hilliard	.20
3	Terrell Owens	.50
4	James Stewart	.30
5	Joey Galloway	.50
6	Jake Reed	.20
7	Derrick Alexander	.10
8	Jeff George	.30
9	Kerry Collins	.20
10	Tony Gonzalez	.20
11	Marcus Robinson	.50
12	Charles Woodson	.30
13	Germane Crowell	.30
14	Yancey Thigpen	.20

15	Tony Martin	.10
16	Frank Sanders	.20
17	Napoleon Kaufman	.30
18	Jay Fiedler	.50
19	Patrick Jeffers	.50
20	Steve McNair	.50
21	Herman Moore	.50
22	Tim Brown	.50
23	Olandis Gary	.60
24	Corey Dillon	.50
25	Warren Sapp	.20
26	Curtis Enis	.30
27	Vinny Testaverde	.30
28	Tim Biakabutuka	.20
29	Kevin Johnson	.30
30	Charlie Batch	.50
31	Jermaine Fazande	.20
32	Shaun King	.75
33	Errict Rhett	.20
34	O.J. McDuffie	.20
35	Bruce Smith	.10
36	Antonio Freeman	.50
37	Tim Couch	1.00
38	Duce Staley	.50
39	Jeff Blake	.20
40	Jim Harbaugh	.20
41	Jeff Graham	.10
42	Drew Bledsoe	.75
43	Mike Alstott	.50
44	Terance Mathis	.10
45	Antowain Smith	.20
46	Johnnie Morton	.20
47	Chris Chandler	.20
48	Keith Poole	.10
49	Ricky Watters	.30
50	Darnay Scott	.20
51	Damon Huard	.50
52	Peerless Price	.30
53	Brian Griese	.60
54	Frank Wycheck	.10
55	Kevin Dyson	.20
56	Junior Seau	.20
57	Curtis Conway	.20
58	Jamal Anderson	.50
59	Jim Miller	.10
60	Rob Johnson	.20
61	Mark Brunell	.75
62	Wayne Chrebet	.30
63	James Johnson	.20
64	Sean Dawkins	.10
65	Stephen Davis	.50
66	Daunte Culpepper	1.00
67	Doug Flutie	.50
68	Pete Mitchell	.10
69	Bill Schroeder	.20
70	Terrence Wilkins	.50
71	Cade McNown	.75
72	Muhsin Muhammad	.20
73	E.G. Green	.10
74	Edgerrin James	2.00
75	Troy Edwards	.30
76	Terry Glenn	.50
77	Tony Banks	.20
78	Derrick Mayes	.20
79	Curtis Martin	.50
80	Kordell Stewart	.60
81	Amani Toomer	.20
82	Dorsey Levens	.30
83	Brad Johnson	.50
84	Ed McCaffrey	.30
85	Charlie Garner	.30
86	Brett Favre	2.00
87	J.J. Stokes	.20
88	Steve Young	.75
89	Jonathon Linton	.20
90	Isaac Bruce	.50
91	Shawn Jefferson	.10
92	Rod Smith	.30
93	Champ Bailey	.30
94	Ricky Williams	1.25
95	Priest Holmes	.30
96	Corey Bradford	.20
97	Eric Moulds	.50
98	Warrick Dunn	.50
99	Jevon Kearse	.50
100	Albert Connell	.20
101	Az-Zahir Hakim	.20
102	Marvin Harrison	.50
103	Qadry Ismail	.10
104	Oronde Gadsden	.20
105	Rob Moore	.20
106	Marshall Faulk	.50
107	Steve Beuerlein	.20
108	Torry Holt	.50
109	Donovan McNabb	.75
110	Rich Gannon	.20
111	Jerome Bettis	.50
112	Peyton Manning	2.00
113	Cris Carter	.50
114	Jake Plummer	.50
115	Kent Graham	.10
116	Keenan McCardell	.20
117	Tim Dwight	.50
118	Fred Taylor	.75
119	Jerry Rice	1.25
120	Michael Westbrook	.20
121	Kurt Warner	2.50
122	Jimmy Smith	.50
123	Emmitt Smith	1.50
124	Terrell Davis	1.50
125	Randy Moss	2.00
126	Akili Smith	.50
127	Raghib Ismail	.10
128	Jon Kitna	.50
129	Elvis Grbac	.20
130	Wesley Walls	.10
131	Torrance Small	.10
132	Tyrone Wheatley	.20
133	Carl Pickens	.20
134	Zach Thomas	.20
135	Jacquez Green	.20
136	Robert Smith	.50
137	Keyshawn Johnson	.50
138	Matthew Hatchette	.20
139	Troy Aikman	1.25
140	Charles Johnson	.10
141	Terry Battle	.40
142	*Pepe Pearson*	.40
143	Cory Sauter	.40
144	Brian Shay	.40
145	*Marcus Crandell*	.40
146	Danny Wuerffel	.75
147	L.C. Stevens	.40
148	Ted White	.40
149	*Matt Lytle*	.40
150	*Vershan Jackson*	.40
151	Mario Bailey	.40
152	*Darryl Daniel*	.40
153	*Sean Morey*	.40
154	*Jim Kubiak*	.40
155	*Aaron Stecker*	1.50
156	Damon Dunn	.40
157	Kevin Daft	.40
158	Corey Thomas	.40
159	*Deon Mitchell*	.40
160	*Todd Floyd*	.40
161	*Norman Miller*	.40
162	Jeremaine Copeland	.40
163	Michael Blair	.40
164	Ron Powlus	.75
165	Pat Barnes	.75
166	*Dez White*	1.00
167	*Trung Canidate*	1.00
168	*Thomas Jones*	2.00
169	*Courtney Brown*	1.25
170	*Jamal Lewis*	5.00
171	*Chris Redman*	2.00
172	*Ron Dayne*	5.00
173	*Chad Pennington*	4.00
174	*Plaxico Burress*	2.50
175	*R. Jay Soward*	1.25
176	*Travis Taylor*	1.75
177	*Shaun Alexander*	3.50
178	*Brian Urlacher*	2.00
179	*Danny Farmer*	1.00
180	*Tee Martin*	1.25
181	*Sylvester Morris*	2.00
182	*Curtis Keaton*	.75
183	*Peter Warrick*	4.00
184	*Anthony Becht*	1.00
185	*Travis Prentice*	1.50
186	*J.R. Redmond*	1.50
187	*Bubba Franks*	1.50
188	*Ron Dugans*	1.00
189	*Reuben Droughns*	1.00
190	*Corey Simon*	1.00
191	*Joe Hamilton*	1.00
192	*Laveranues Coles*	1.25
193	*Todd Pinkston*	1.00
194	*Jerry Porter*	1.00
195	*Dennis Northcutt*	1.00
196	*Tim Rattay*	1.50
197	*Giovanni Carmazzi*	1.50
198	*Mareno Philyaw*	.40
199	*Avion Black*	.75
200	*Chafie Fields*	.40
201	*Rondell Mealey*	.75
202	*Troy Walters*	.75
203	*Frank Moreau*	1.00
204	*Vaughn Sanders*	.40
205	*Sherrod Gideon*	.40
206	*Doug Chapman*	.40
207	*Marcus Knight*	.75
208	*Jamel White*	.75
209	*Windrell Hayes*	.40
210	*Reggie Jones*	.75
211	*Jarious Jackson*	1.00
212	*Ronney Jenkins*	.40
213	*Quinton Spotwood*	.40
214	*Rob Morris*	.75
215	*Gari Scott*	.40
216	*Kevin Thompson*	.40
217	*Trevor Insley*	.40
218	*Frank Murphy*	.40
219	*Patrick Pass*	.75
220	*Mike Anderson*	8.00
221	*Derrius Thompson*	.40
222	*John Abraham*	.75
223	*Dante Hall*	.40
224	*Chad Morton*	1.25
225	*Ahmed Plummer*	.75
226	*Julian Peterson*	.40
227	*Mike Green*	.40
228	*Michael Wiley*	1.00
229	*Spergon Wynn*	1.00
230	*Trevor Gaylor*	1.00
231	*Doug Johnson*	1.25
232	*Marc Bulger*	.75
233	*Ron Dixon*	1.25
234	*Aaron Shea*	.75
235	*Thomas Hamner*	.40
236	*Tom Brady*	2.00
237	*Deltha O'Neal*	.75
238	*Todd Husak*	1.00
239	*Erron Kinney*	.40
240	*JaJuan Dawson*	1.25

2000 Bowman Gold Parallel

	MT
Gold Cards:	10x-20x
Gold Europe Cards:	6x-12x
Gold Rookies:	5x-10x
Inserted 1:60	
Production 99 Sets	

2000 Bowman ROY Promotion

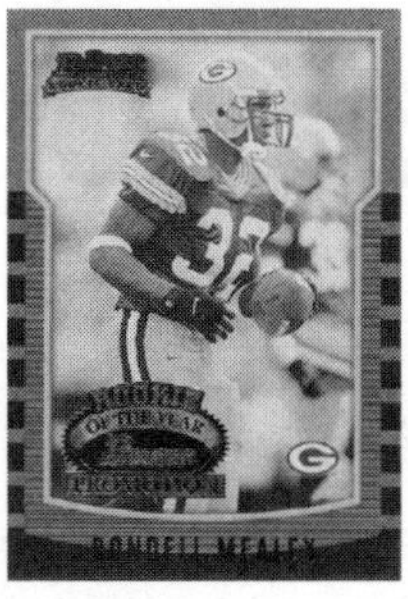

	MT
ROY Cards:	5x
Inserted 1:76	

2000 Bowman Autographs

		MT
Common Player:		6.00
Minor Stars:		12.00
Inserted 1:46		
SA	Shaun Alexander	45.00
AB	Anthony Becht	12.00
CB	Courtney Brown	18.00
MB	Marc Bulger	12.00
PB	Plaxico Burress	45.00
TC	Trung Canidate	15.00
GC	Giovanni Carmazzi	20.00
LC	Laveranues Coles	20.00
RD	Ron Dayne	85.00
RDR	Reuben Droughns	12.00
RDU	Ron Dugans	12.00
DF	Danny Farmer	12.00
DFR	Daniel "Bubba" Franks	20.00
TG	Trevor Gaylor	12.00
JH	Joe Hamilton	15.00
TJ	Thomas Jones	35.00
CK	Curtis Keaton	6.00
JL	Jamal Lewis	45.00
TM	Tee Martin	15.00
SM	Sylvester Morris	20.00
DN	Dennis Northcutt	15.00
CP	Chad Pennington	50.00
TPI	Todd Pinkston	18.00
JP	Jerry Porter	20.00
TP	Travis Prentice	15.00
TR	Tim Rattay	15.00
CR	Chris Redman	30.00
JR	J.R. Redmond	15.00
CS	Corey Simon	12.00
RS	R. Jay Soward	12.00
TT	Travis Taylor	20.00
BU	Brian Urlacher	25.00
PW	Peter Warrick	75.00
DW	Dez White	12.00

2000 Bowman Bowman's Best Previews

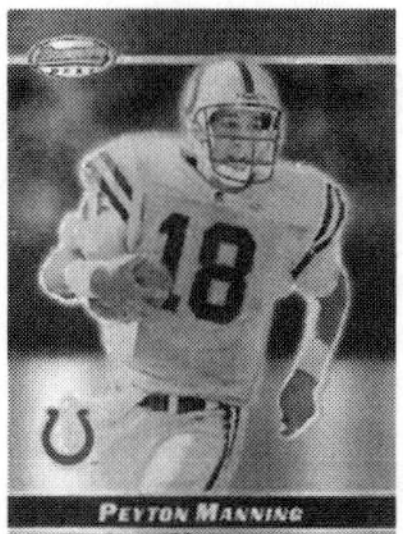

		MT
Complete Set (10):		25.00
Common Player:		1.50
Inserted 1:24		
BBP1	Peyton Manning	6.00
BBP2	Stephen Davis	1.50
BBP3	Marshall Faulk	1.50
BBP4	Marvin Harrison	1.50
BBP5	Brett Favre	6.00
BBP6	Terrell Davis	4.50
BBP7	Eddie George	2.00
BBP8	Kurt Warner	7.00
BBP9	Edgerrin James	6.00
BBP10	Randy Moss	6.00

2000 Bowman Breakthrough Discoveries

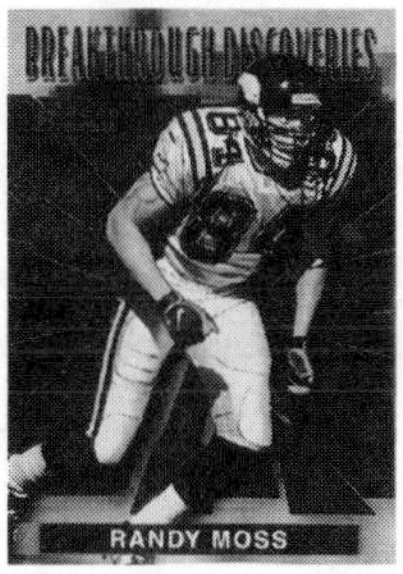

		MT
Complete Set (10):		10.00
Common Player:		.50
Minor Stars:		1.00
Inserted 1:12		
BD1	Jerry Rice	2.00
BD2	Kurt Warner	4.00
BD3	Wayne Chrebet	.50
BD4	Isaac Bruce	1.00
BD5	Steve McNair	1.00
BD6	Shannon Sharpe	.50
BD7	Andre Reed	.50
BD8	Jimmy Smith	1.00
BD9	Darrell Green	.50
BD10	Randy Moss	3.00

2000 Bowman Draft Day Jerseys

		MT
Complete Set (4):		85.00
Common Player:		15.00
Inserted 1:279		
CB	Courtney Brown	15.00
TJ	Thomas Jones	25.00
CS	Chris Samuels	15.00
PW	Peter Warrick	50.00

A player's name in *italic type* indicates a rookie card.

2000 Bowman Road to Success

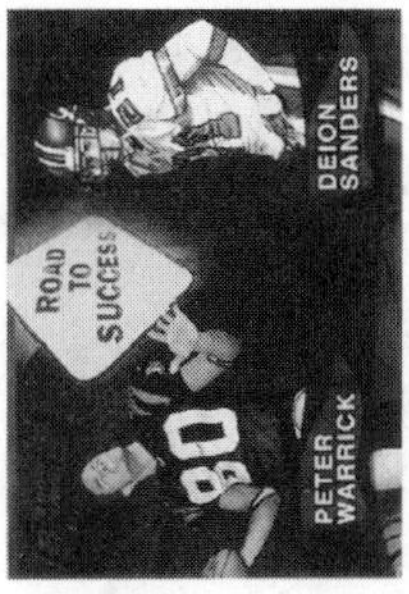

		MT
Complete Set (10):		20.00
Common Player:		1.50
Inserted 1:18		
R1	Chad Pennington, Randy Moss	5.00
R2	Jamal Lewis, Peyton Manning	5.00
R3	R. Jay Soward, Keyshawn Johnson	1.50
R4	Thomas Jones, Germane Crowell	3.00
R5	Giovanni Carmazzi, Wayne Chrebet	2.00
R6	Travis Taylor, Ike Hilliard	2.00
R7	Plaxico Burress, Muhsin Muhammad	3.00
R8	Todd Pinkston, Brett Favre	5.00
R9	Sylvester Morris, Jimmy Smith	2.50
R10	Peter Warrick, Deion Sanders	5.00

2000 Bowman Rookie Rising

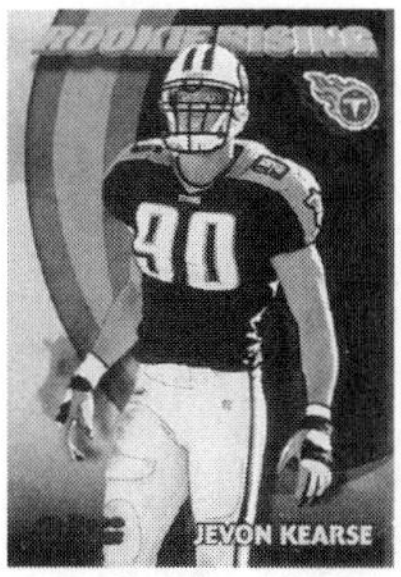

		MT
Complete Set (10):		8.00
Common Player:		.50
Minor Stars:		1.00
Inserted 1:12		
RR1	Jevon Kearse	1.00
RR2	Edgerrin James	4.00
RR3	Champ Bailey	1.00
RR4	Zach Thomas	.50
RR5	Marvin Harrison	1.00
RR6	Kevin Johnson	1.00
RR7	Curtis Martin	1.00
RR8	Jerome Bettis	1.00
RR9	Fred Taylor	1.75
RR10	Terry Glenn	1.00

2000 Bowman Scout's Choice

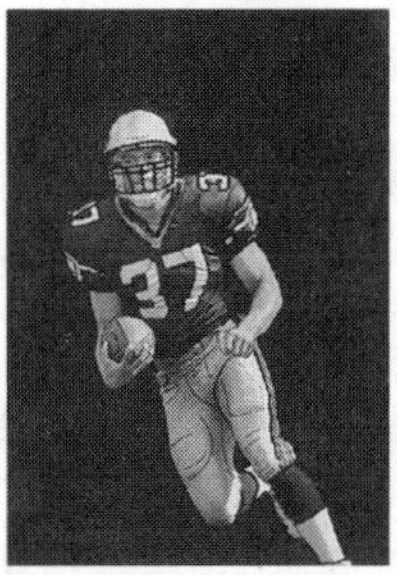

		MT
Complete Set (20):		35.00
Common Player:		1.50
Inserted 1:18		
SC1	Shaun Alexander	4.00
SC2	Bubba Franks	2.00
SC3	Travis Prentice	2.50
SC4	Peter Warrick	5.00
SC5	Plaxico Burress	3.00
SC6	Corey Simon	1.50
SC7	Courtney Brown	1.75
SC8	Tee Martin	2.00
SC9	Brian Urlacher	3.00
SC10	J.R. Redmond	2.00
SC11	Anthony Becht	1.50
SC12	Thomas Jones	2.50
SC13	Giovanni Carmazzi	2.00
SC14	Jamal Lewis	6.00
SC15	Ron Dayne	6.00
SC16	R. Jay Soward	1.50
SC17	Travis Taylor	2.50
SC18	Chad Pennington	4.50
SC19	Sylvester Morris	3.00
SC20	Chris Redman	2.50

2000 Bowman Chrome

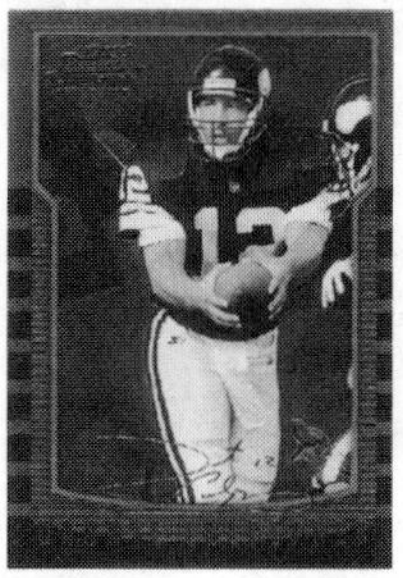

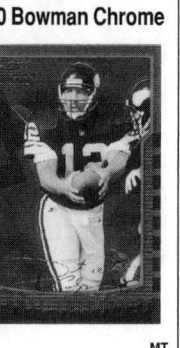

		MT
Complete Set (270):		1250.
Common Player:		.25
Minor Stars:		.50
Common Europe:		1.00
Common Rookie:		1.50
Common Rookie SP:		30.00
Inserted 1:134		
Pack (4):		3.00
Wax Box (24):		60.00
1	Eddie George	1.00
2	Ike Hilliard	.50
3	Terrell Owens	.75
4	James Stewart	.50
5	Joey Galloway	.75
6	Jake Reed	.25
7	Derrick Alexander	.25
8	Jeff George	.50
9	Kerry Collins	.50
10	Tony Gonzalez	.50
11	Marcus Robinson	.75
12	Charles Woodson	.50
13	Germane Crowell	.75
14	Yancey Thigpen	.50
15	Tony Martin	.25
16	Frank Sanders	.50
17	Napoleon Kaufman	.75
18	Jay Fiedler	.50
19	Patrick Jeffers	.75
20	Steve McNair	.75
21	Herman Moore	.50
22	Tim Brown	.75
23	Olandis Gary	.75
24	Corey Dillon	.75
25	Warren Sapp	.50
26	Curtis Enis	.50
27	Vinny Testaverde	.50
28	Tim Biakabutuka	.50
29	Kevin Johnson	.50
30	Charlie Batch	.75
31	Jermaine Fazande	.50
32	Shaun King	1.25
33	Errict Rhett	.50
34	O.J. McDuffie	.50
35	Bruce Smith	.50
36	Antonio Freeman	.75
37	Tim Couch	1.50
38	Duce Staley	.75
39	Jeff Blake	.50
40	Jim Harbaugh	.50
41	Jeff Graham	.25
42	Drew Bledsoe	1.25
43	Mike Alstott	.75
44	Terance Mathis	.25
45	Antowain Smith	.50
46	Johnnie Morton	.50
47	Chris Chandler	.50
48	Keith Poole	.25
49	Ricky Watters	.50
50	Darnay Scott	.50
51	Damon Huard	.50
52	Peerless Price	.50
53	Brian Griese	1.00
54	Frank Wycheck	.25
55	Kevin Dyson	.50
56	Junior Seau	.50
57	Curtis Conway	.50
58	Jamal Anderson	.75
59	Jim Miller	.25
60	Rob Johnson	.50
61	Mark Brunell	1.25
62	Wayne Chrebet	.75
63	James Johnson	.50
64	Sean Dawkins	.25
65	Stephen Davis	.75
66	Daunte Culpepper	1.50
67	Doug Flutie	1.00
68	Pete Mitchell	.25
69	Bill Schroeder	.25
70	Terrence Wilkins	.50
71	Cade McNown	.75
72	Muhsin Muhammad	.50
73	E.G. Green	.25
74	Edgerrin James	3.00
75	Troy Edwards	.50
76	Terry Glenn	.75
77	Tony Banks	.50
78	Derrick Mayes	.50
79	Curtis Martin	.75
80	Kordell Stewart	1.00
81	Amani Toomer	.50
82	Dorsey Levens	.75
83	Brad Johnson	.50
84	Ed McCaffrey	.50
85	Charlie Garner	.50
86	Brett Favre	3.00
87	J.J. Stokes	.50
88	Steve Young	1.25
89	Jonathon Linton	.50
90	Isaac Bruce	.75
91	Shawn Jefferson	.25
92	Rod Smith	.75
93	Champ Bailey	.50
94	Ricky Williams	2.00
95	Priest Holmes	.50
96	Corey Bradford	.25
97	Eric Moulds	.75
98	Warrick Dunn	.75
99	Jevon Kearse	.75
100	Albert Connell	.50
101	Az-Zahir Hakim	.50
102	Marvin Harrison	.75
103	Qadry Ismail	.25
104	Oronde Gadsden	.50
105	Rob Moore	.50
106	Marshall Faulk	.75
107	Steve Beuerlein	.50
108	Torry Holt	.75
109	Donovan McNabb	1.25
110	Rich Gannon	.50
111	Jerome Bettis	.75
112	Peyton Manning	2.50
113	Cris Carter	.75
114	Jake Plummer	.75
115	Kent Graham	.25
116	Keenan McCardell	.50
117	Tim Dwight	.50
118	Fred Taylor	1.25
119	Jerry Rice	1.75
120	Michael Westbrook	.50
121	Kurt Warner	3.00
122	Jimmy Smith	.50
123	Emmitt Smith	2.25
124	Terrell Davis	2.25
125	Randy Moss	2.50
126	Akili Smith	.75
127	Raghib Ismail	.25
128	Jon Kitna	.75
129	Elvis Grbac	.50
130	Wesley Walls	.50
131	Torrance Small	.25
132	Tyrone Wheatley	.50
133	Carl Pickens	.50
134	Zach Thomas	.50
135	Jacquez Green	.25
136	Robert Smith	.75
137	Keyshawn Johnson	.75
138	Matthew Hatchette	.50
139	Troy Aikman	1.75
140	Charles Johnson	.50
141	Terry Battle	1.00
142	*Pepe Pearson*	1.25
143	Cory Sauter	1.00
144	Brian Shay	1.00
145	*Marcus Crandell*	1.00
146	Danny Wuerffel	1.25
147	L.C. Stevens	1.00
148	Ted White	1.00
149	*Matt Lytle*	1.00
150	*Vershan Jackson*	1.00
151	Mario Bailey	1.00
152	*Darryl Daniel*	1.00
153	*Sean Morey*	1.00
154	*Jim Kubiak*	1.00
155	*Aaron Stecker*	1.50
156	Damon Dunn	1.00
157	Kevin Daft	1.00
158	Corey Thomas	1.00
159	*Deon Mitchell*	1.00
160	*Todd Floyd*	1.00
161	*Norman Miller*	1.00
162	*Jeremaine Copeland*	1.00
163	*Michael Blair*	1.00
164	*Ron Powlus*	3.00
165	Pat Barnes	1.50
166	*Dez White*	3.50
167	*Trung Canidate SP*	30.00
168	*Thomas Jones SP*	60.00
169	*Courtney Brown SP*	35.00
170	*Jamal Lewis SP*	200.00
171	*Chris Redman SP*	60.00
172	*Ron Dayne SP*	175.00
173	*Chad Pennington SP*	125.00
174	*Plaxico Burress SP*	75.00
175	*R. Jay Soward SP*	35.00
176	*Travis Taylor SP*	45.00
177	*Shaun Alexander SP*	100.00
178	*Brian Urlacher*	15.00
179	*Danny Farmer*	3.00
180	*Tee Martin SP*	35.00
181	*Sylvester Morris SP*	75.00
182	*Curtis Keaton*	2.50
183	*Peter Warrick SP*	150.00
184	*Anthony Becht*	3.00
185	*Travis Prentice SP*	50.00
186	*J.R. Redmond SP*	45.00
187	*Daniel "Bubba" Franks SP*	35.00
188	*Ron Dugans SP*	30.00
189	*Reuben Droughns*	3.00
190	*Corey Simon*	4.50
191	*Joe Hamilton*	4.50
192	*Laveranues Coles*	5.00
193	*Todd Pinkston SP*	35.00
194	*Jerry Porter SP*	35.00
195	*Dennis Northcutt*	4.00
196	*Tim Rattay*	6.00
197	*Giovanni Carmazzi*	6.00
198	*Mareno Philyaw*	1.50
199	*Avion Black*	2.00
200	*Chafie Fields*	2.00
201	*Rondell Mealey*	2.00
202	*Troy Walters*	2.50
203	*Frank Moreau*	4.00
204	*Vaughn Sanders*	1.50
205	*Sherrod Gideon*	1.50
206	*Doug Chapman*	2.00
207	*Marcus Knight*	1.50
208	*Jamel White*	3.00
209	*Windrell Hayes*	1.50
210	*Reggie Jones*	4.00
211	*Jarious Jackson*	4.00
212	*Ronney Jenkins*	3.00
213	*Quinton Spotwood*	1.50
214	*Rob Morris*	2.00
215	*Gari Scott*	1.50
216	*Kevin Thompson*	2.00
217	*Trevor Insley*	1.50
218	*Frank Murphy*	1.50
219	*Patrick Pass*	3.50
220	*Mike Anderson*	25.00
221	*Derrius Thompson*	2.50
222	*John Abraham*	2.50
223	*Dante Hall*	2.50
224	*Chad Morton*	4.00
225	*Ahmed Plummer*	3.00
226	*Julian Peterson*	3.00
227	*Mike Green*	1.50
228	*Michael Wiley*	4.00
229	*Spergon Wynn*	3.50
230	*Trevor Gaylor*	3.00
231	*Doug Johnson*	4.00
232	*Marc Bulger*	3.00
233	*Ron Dixon*	4.00
234	*Aaron Shea*	1.50
235	*Thomas Hamner*	2.00
236	*Tom Brady*	8.00
237	*Deltha O'Neal*	2.00
238	*Todd Husak*	3.50
239	*Erron Kinney*	2.50
240	*JaJuan Dawson*	5.00

241 Nick Williams .25
242 *Deon Grant* 1.50
243 *Brad Hoover* 20.00
244 Kamil Loud .25
245 *Rashard Anderson* 3.00
246 *Clint Stoerner* 10.00
247 *Antwain Harris* 1.50
248 *Jason Webster* 1.50
249 *Kevin McDougal* 1.50
250 *Tony Scott* 1.50
251 *Thabiti Davis* 1.50
252 *Ian Gold* 2.50
253 *Sammy Morris* 5.00
254 *Raynoch Thompson* 2.50
255 Jeremy McDaniel .25
256 *Terrelle Smith* 2.00
257 *Deon Dyer* 2.00
258 *Na'il Diggs* 3.00
259 *Brandon Short* 2.00
260 *Mike Brown* 2.00
261 *John Engelberger* 1.50
262 *Rogers Beckett* 2.00
263 *Jafuan Seider* 1.50
264 *Desmond Kitchings* 1.50
265 *Reggie Davis* 1.50
266 *Corey Moore* 1.50
267 *Cornelius Griffin* 1.50
268 *Stockar McDougle* 1.50
269 *James Williams* 1.50
270 *Darrell Jackson* 6.00

2000 Bowman Chrome Refractors Parallel

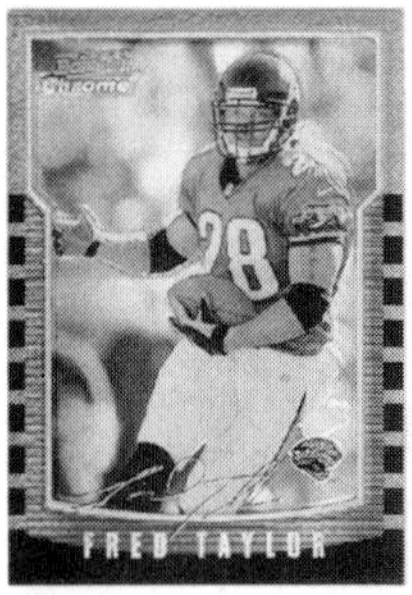

MT
Refractor Cards: 2x-4x
Inserted 1:12
Refractor Europe: 3x
Inserted 1:12
Refractor Rookie: 2x-4x
Inserted 1:281
Refractor Rookie SP: 1.5x
Inserted 1:659

2000 Bowman Chrome By Selection

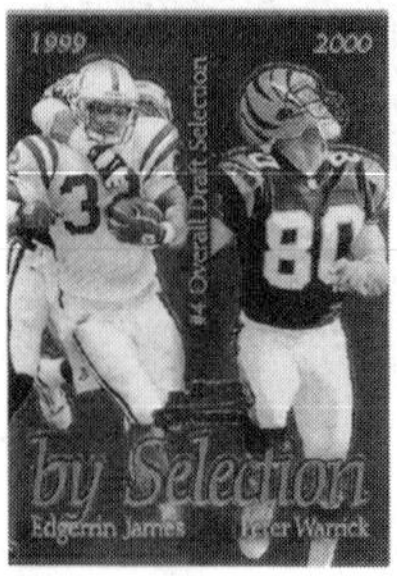

MT
Complete Set (10): 30.00
Common Player: 2.00
Inserted 1:24
Refractors: 4x
Inserted 1:240
B1 Troy Aikman, Drew Bledsoe 5.00
B2 Marshall Faulk, Donovan McNabb 3.00
B3 Ricky Williams, Jamal Lewis 10.00
B4 Randy Moss, Sylvester Morris 7.00
B5 Shaun Alexander, Marvin Harrison 4.00
B6 Tim Couch, Peyton Manning 6.00
B7 Edgerrin James, Peter Warrick 7.00
B8 Jimmy Smith, Todd Pinkston 2.00
B9 Steve McNair, Akili Smith 2.00
B10 Plaxico Burress, Joey Galloway 3.50

Values quoted in this guide reflect the retail price of a card — the price a collector can expect to pay when buying a card from a dealer. The wholesale price — that which a collector can expect to receive from a dealer when selling cards — will be significantly lower, depending on desirability and condition.

2000 Bowman Chrome Ground Breakers

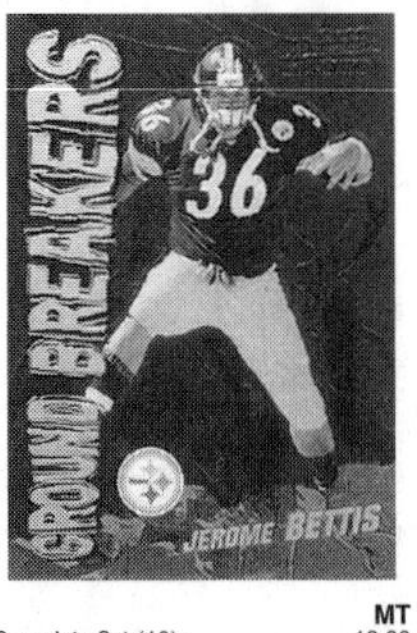

MT
Complete Set (10): 12.00
Common Player: .75
Minor Stars: 1.50
Inserted 1:12
Refractors: 4x
Inserted 1:120
GB1 Edgerrin James 5.00
GB2 Eddie George 1.75
GB3 Jerome Bettis 1.50
GB4 Fred Taylor 2.00
GB5 Curtis Martin 1.50
GB6 Errict Rhett .75
GB7 Marshall Faulk 1.50
GB8 Karim Abdul .75
GB9 Olandis Gary 1.50
GB10 Terrell Davis 3.00

2000 Bowman Chrome Rookie Autographs

MT
Common Player: 80.00
Production 25 Sets
Inserted 1:5,247
168 Thomas Jones 125.00
170 Jamal Lewis 500.00
172 Ron Dayne 400.00
173 Chad Pennington 300.00
175 R. Jay Soward 80.00
177 Shaun Alexander 225.00
181 Sylvester Morris 150.00
183 Peter Warrick 350.00
185 Travis Prentice 100.00

2000 Bowman Chrome Rookie of the Year

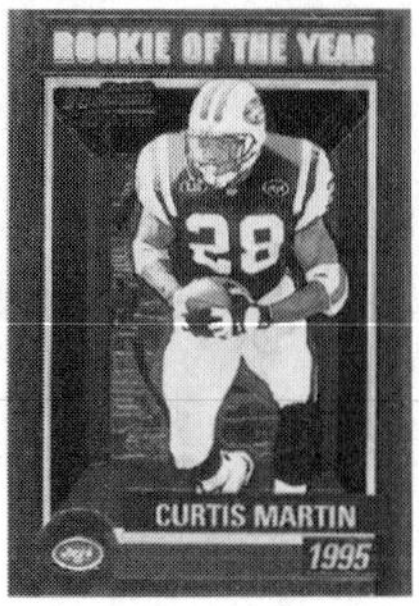

MT
Complete Set (10): 12.00
Common Player: .75
Minor Stars: 1.50
Inserted 1:Box
R1 Santana Dotson .75
R2 Jerome Bettis 1.50
R3 Marshall Faulk 1.50
R4 Curtis Martin 1.50
R5 Eddie George 2.00
R6 Warrick Dunn 1.50
R7 Charles Woodson .75
R8 Randy Moss 6.00
R9 Jevon Kearse 1.50
R10 Edgerrin James 6.00

2000 Bowman Chrome Scout's Choice Update

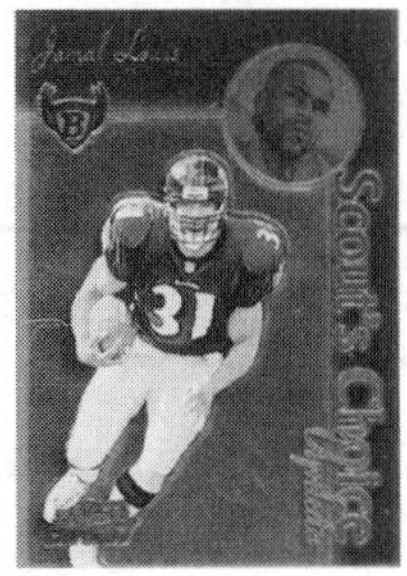

MT
Complete Set (10): 25.00
Common Player: 2.00
Inserted 1:24
Refractors: 4x
Inserted 1:240
SCU1 Shaun Alexander 5.00
SCU2 Brian Urlacher 5.00
SCU3 Courtney Brown 2.00
SCU4 Jamal Lewis 10.00
SCU5 Sylvester Morris 4.00
SCU6 Plaxico Burress 4.00
SCU7 Ron Dayne 8.00
SCU8 Thomas Jones 3.00
SCU9 Corey Simon 2.00
SCU10 Travis Taylor 2.50

2000 Bowman Chrome Shattering Performers

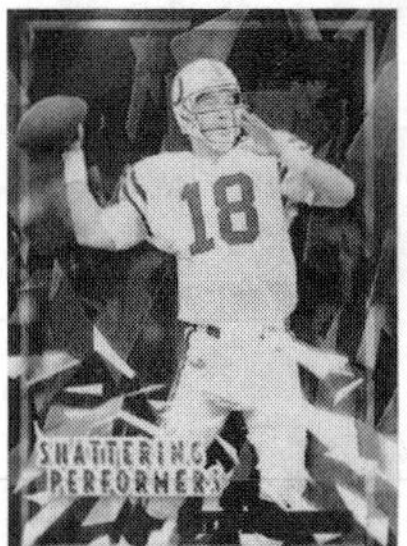

MT
Complete Set (20): 40.00
Common Player: 1.00
Minor Stars: 2.00
Inserted 1:16
Refractors: 4x
Inserted 1:160
SP1 Kurt Warner 8.00
SP2 Peyton Manning 7.00
SP3 Brian Griese 2.50
SP4 Daunte Culpepper 3.00
SP5 Elvis Grbac 1.00
SP6 Stephen Davis 2.00
SP7 Charlie Garner 1.00
SP8 Mike Anderson 10.00
SP9 Marshall Faulk 2.00
SP10 Robert Smith 2.00
SP11 Tiki Barber 1.00
SP12 Edgerrin James 7.00
SP13 Isaac Bruce 2.00
SP14 Rod Smith 2.00
SP15 Jimmy Smith 2.00
SP16 Torry Holt 2.00
SP17 Keenan McCardell 1.00
SP18 Marcus Robinson 2.00
SP19 Marvin Harrison 2.00
SP20 Randy Moss 7.00

2000 Bowman's Best

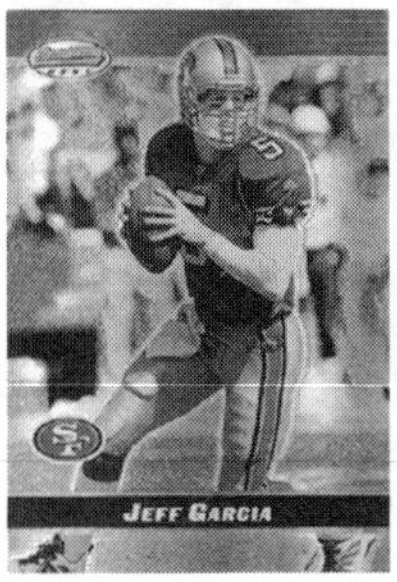

MT
Complete Set (150): 350.00
Common Player: .15
Minor Stars: .30
Common Rookie: 4.00
Production 1,499 Sets
Inserted 1:11
Pack (5): 5.00
Wax Box (24): 75.00
1 Troy Edwards .30
2 Kurt Warner 3.00
3 Steve McNair .50
4 Terry Glenn .50
5 Charlie Batch .50
6 Patrick Jeffers .50
7 Jake Plummer .50
8 Derrick Alexander .15
9 Joey Galloway .50
10 Tony Banks .30
11 Robert Smith .50
12 Jerry Rice 1.50
13 Jeff Garcia .50
14 Michael Westbrook .30
15 Curtis Conway .30
16 Brian Griese .75
17 Peyton Manning 2.50
18 Daunte Culpepper 1.50
19 Frank Sanders .30
20 Muhsin Muhammad .30
21 Corey Dillon .50
22 Brett Favre 2.50
23 Warrick Dunn .50
24 Tim Brown .50
25 Kerry Collins .30
26 Brad Johnson .50
27 Raghib Ismail .15
28 Jamal Anderson .50
29 Jimmy Smith .50
30 Torry Holt .50
31 Duce Staley .50
32 Drew Bledsoe 1.00
33 Jerome Bettis .50
34 Keyshawn Johnson .50
35 Fred Taylor 1.00
36 Akili Smith .50
37 Rob Johnson .30
38 Elvis Grbac .30
39 Antonio Freeman .50
40 Curtis Enis .50
41 Terance Mathis .15
42 Terrell Davis 1.75
43 Randy Moss 2.50
44 Jon Kitna .50
45 Curtis Martin .50
46 Terrell Owens .50
47 Robert Smith .50
48 Albert Connell .30
49 Edgerrin James 2.50
50 Tony Gonzalez .30
51 Eric Moulds .50
52 Natrone Means .15
53 Carl Pickens .30
54 Mark Brunell 1.00
55 Rob Moore .30
56 Marshall Faulk .50
57 Stephen Davis .50
58 Rich Gannon .30
59 Ricky Williams 1.50
60 Emmitt Smith 1.75
61 Germane Crowell .50
62 Doug Flutie .75
63 O.J. McDuffie .15
64 Chris Chandler .30
65 Qadry Ismail .15
66 Tim Couch 1.25
67 James Stewart .30
68 Marvin Harrison .50
69 Cris Carter .50
70 Cade McNown .75
71 Marcus Robinson .50
72 Steve Beuerlein .30
73 Jevon Kearse .50
74 Eddie George .75
75 Donovan McNabb 1.00
76 Jeff Blake .30
77 Wayne Chrebet .50
78 Kordell Stewart .60
79 Steve Young 1.00
80 Mike Alstott .50
81 Ricky Watters .30
82 Charlie Garner .30
83 Troy Aikman 1.50
84 Dorsey Levens .50
85 Ike Hilliard .30
86 Shaun King .50
87 Isaac Bruce .50
88 Tyrone Wheatley .30
89 Amani Toomer .30
90 Ed McCaffrey .50
91 Edgerrin James, Marshall Faulk 1.50
92 Drew Bledsoe, Brad Johnson .50
93 Jimmy Smith, Randy Moss 1.50
94 Eddie George, Stephen Davis .50
95 Mark Brunell, Troy Aikman 1.00
96 Marvin Harrison, Cris Carter .50
97 Curtis Martin, Emmitt Smith 1.25
98 Tim Brown, Isaac Bruce .50
99 Fred Taylor, Ricky Williams 1.00
100 Peyton Manning, Kurt Warner 1.50
101 *Shaun Alexander* 25.00
102 *Thomas Jones* 15.00
103 *Courtney Brown* 8.00
104 *Curtis Keaton* 5.00
105 *Jerry Porter* 7.00
106 *Corey Simon* 7.00
107 *Dez White* 5.00
108 *Jamal Lewis* 50.00
109 *Ron Dayne* 40.00
110 *R. Jay Soward* 8.00
111 *Tee Martin* 7.00
112 *Brian Urlacher* 25.00
113 *Reuben Droughns* 5.00
114 *Travis Taylor* 10.00
115 *Plaxico Burress* 18.00
116 *Chad Pennington* 30.00
117 *Sylvester Morris* 18.00
118 *Ron Dugans* 7.00
119 *Joe Hamilton* 8.00
120 *Chris Redman* 15.00
121 *Trung Canidate* 7.00
122 *J.R. Redmond* 10.00
123 *Danny Farmer* 7.00
124 *Todd Pinkston* 7.00
125 *Dennis Northcutt* 8.00
126 *Laveranues Coles* 8.00
127 *Bubba Franks* 8.00
128 *Travis Prentice* 12.50
129 *Peter Warrick* 35.00
130 *Anthony Becht* 7.00
131 *Ike Charlton* 4.00
132 *Shaun Ellis* 4.00
133 *Sean Morey* 4.00
134 *Sebastian Janikowski* 7.00
135 *Aaron Stecker* 5.00
136 *Ronney Jenkins* 4.00
137 *Jamel White* 4.00
138 *Nick Williams* 4.00
139 *Andy McCullough* 4.00
140 *Kevin Daft* 4.00
141 *Thomas Hamner* 4.00
142 *Tim Rattay* 8.00
143 *Spergon Wynn* 5.00
144 *Brandon Short* 4.00
145 *Chad Morton* 6.00
146 *Gari Scott* 4.00
147 *Frank Murphy* 4.00
148 *James Williams* 4.00
149 *Windrell Hayes* 4.00
150 *Doug Johnson* 5.00

2000 Bowman's Best Parallel Parallel

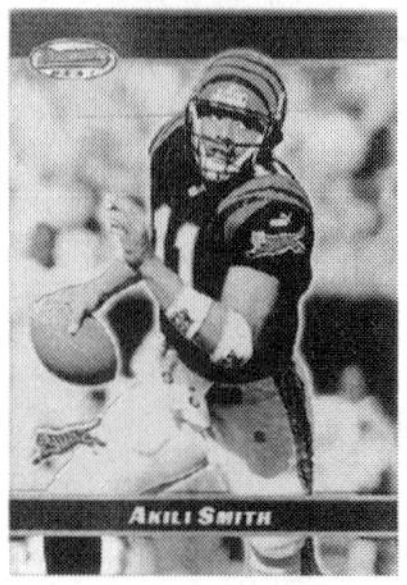

MT
Parallel Cards: 5x-10x
Parallel Rookies: 1.5x
Production 250 Sets
Inserted 1:22

2000 Bowman's Best Autographs

MT
Common Player: 100.00
Inserted 1:2,395
JM Joe Montana 200.00
RM Randy Moss 100.00

2000 Bowman's Best Best of the Game Autographs

MT
Common Player: 70.00
Inserted 1:837
BG1 Edgerrin James 70.00
BG2 Kurt Warner 100.00

2000 Bowman's Best Bets

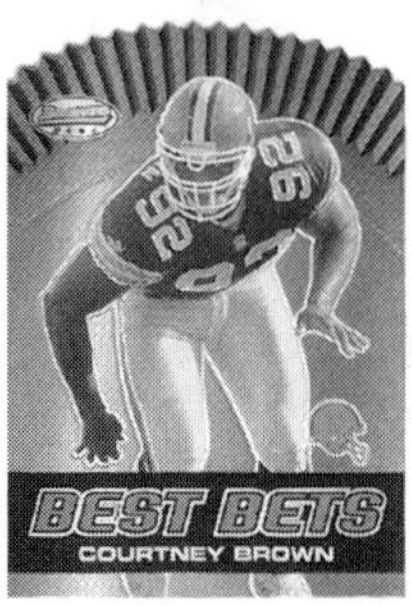

MT
Complete Set (13): 18.00
Common Player: .50
Minor Stars: 1.00
Inserted 1:19
B1 Jamal Lewis 5.00
B2 Plaxico Burress 2.00
B3 Chad Pennington 3.00
B4 Sylvester Morris 2.00
B5 Shaun Alexander 2.50
B6 Peter Warrick 3.50
B7 Travis Taylor 1.25
B8 Courtney Brown 1.00
B9 R. Jay Soward 1.00
B10 Ron Dayne 4.00
B11 Jerry Porter 1.00
B12 Curtis Keaton .50
B13 Thomas Jones 1.75

2000 Bowman's Best Franchise 2000

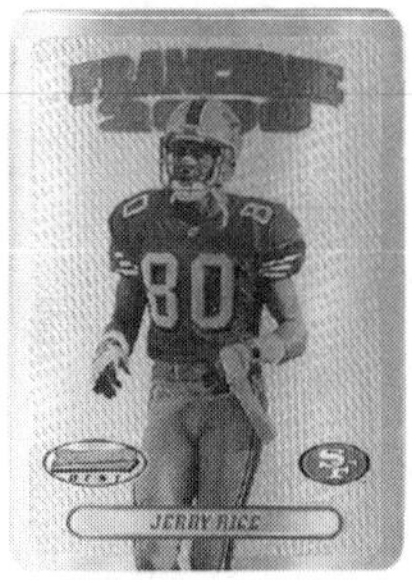

MT
Complete Set (20): 30.00
Common Player: .50
Minor Stars: 1.00
Inserted 1:12
F1 Curtis Martin 1.00
F2 Eddie George 1.50
F3 Emmitt Smith 3.00
F4 Stephen Davis 1.00
F5 Cade McNown 1.00
F6 Drew Bledsoe 2.00
F7 Zach Thomas .50
F8 Mark Brunell 2.00
F9 Tim Brown .50
F10 Akili Smith 1.00
F11 Peyton Manning 4.00
F12 Terrell Davis 3.00
F13 Brett Favre 5.00
F14 Randy Moss 4.00
F15 Kurt Warner 5.00
F16 Ricky Williams 2.50
F17 Jerry Rice 2.50
F18 Jake Plummer 1.00
F19 Tim Couch 2.00
F20 Warren Sapp .50

2000 Bowman's Best Pro Bowl Jerseys

MT
Complete Set (14): 300.00
Common Player: 20.00
Inserted 1:112
DB Derrick Brooks 20.00
IB Isaac Bruce 25.00
MB Mark Brunell 30.00
SD Stephen Davis 25.00
MF Marshall Faulk 30.00
MH Marvin Harrison 25.00
EJ Edgerrin James 60.00
BJ Brad Johnson 20.00
KJ Keyshawn Johnson 25.00
JK Jevon Kearse 25.00
RM Randy Moss 60.00
JS Jimmy Smith 25.00
KW Kurt Warner 70.00
CW Charles Woodson 20.00

2000 Bowman's Best Rookie Autographs

MT
Common Player: 12.00
Inserted 1:83
SA Shaun Alexander 25.00
CB Courtney Brown 30.00
PB Plaxico Burress 30.00
LC Laveranues Coles 18.00
RD Ron Dayne 50.00
RDR Reuben Droughns 12.00
RDU Ron Dugans 12.00
DF Danny Farmer 12.00
JH Joe Hamilton 12.00
TJ Thomas Jones 20.00
JL Jamal Lewis 75.00
TM Tee Martin 15.00
SM Sylvester Morris 30.00
CP Chad Pennington 40.00
TPR Travis Prentice 15.00
JR J.R. Redmond 18.00
RS R. Jay Soward 15.00
BU Brian Urlacher 50.00
PW Peter Warrick 45.00

2000 Bowman's Best Year by Year

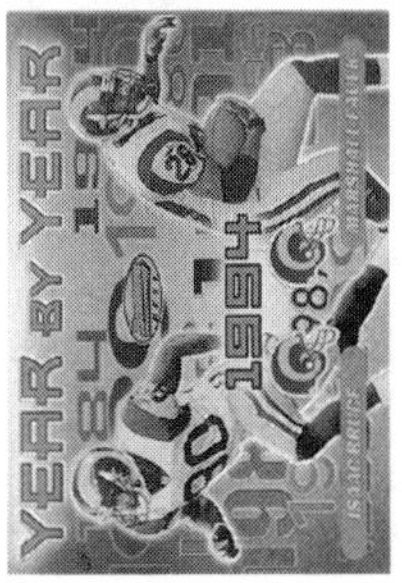

MT
Complete Set (12): 20.00
Common Player: 1.50
Inserted 1:20
Y1 Peyton Manning, Randy Moss 5.00
Y2 Keyshawn Johnson, Eddie George 2.00
Y3 Tim Brown, Thurman Thomas 1.50
Y4 Drew Bledsoe, Jerome Bettis 2.00
Y5 Edgerrin James, Ricky Williams 5.00
Y6 Troy Aikman, Deion Sanders 3.00
Y7 Isaac Bruce, Marshall Faulk 1.50
Y8 Junior Seau, Emmitt Smith 3.00
Y9 Curtis Martin, Terrell Davis 3.00
Y10 Brad Johnson, Jimmy Smith 1.50
Y11 Brett Favre, Ricky Watters 4.00
Y12 Peter Warrick, Plaxico Burress 3.50

2000 Bowman Reserve

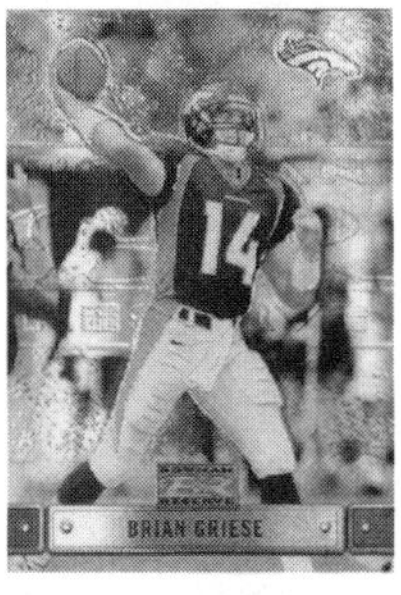

MT
Complete Set (125): 750.00
Common Player: .30
Minor Stars: .60
Common Rookies: 15.00
Production 999 Sets
Wax Box (10 + Mini Helmet): 150.00
1 *Chad Pennington* 70.00
2 *Shaun Alexander* 60.00
3 *Thomas Jones* 35.00
4 *Courtney Brown* 25.00
5 *Curtis Keaton* 15.00
6 *Jerry Porter* 20.00
7 *Jamal Lewis* 125.00
8 *Ron Dayne* 75.00
9 *R. Jay Soward* 20.00
10 *Tee Martin* 20.00
11 *Travis Taylor* 30.00
12 *Plaxico Burress* 35.00
13 *Giovanni Carmazzi* 25.00
14 *Sylvester Morris* 35.00
15 *Chris Redman* 35.00
16 *Trung Canidate* 20.00

17	*J.R. Redmond*	25.00
18	*Bubba Franks*	20.00
19	*Travis Prentice*	30.00
20	*Peter Warrick*	75.00
21	Frank Sanders	.60
22	Edgerrin James	5.00
23	Marcus Robinson	1.00
24	Mike Alstott	1.00
25	Jerry Rice	2.50
26	Marshall Faulk	1.00
27	Brad Johnson	1.00
28	Elvis Grbac	.60
29	Wayne Chrebet	1.00
30	Akili Smith	1.00
31	Rob Johnson	.60
32	Brett Favre	5.00
33	Ricky Williams	2.50
34	Donovan McNabb	2.00
35	Cris Carter	1.00
36	Ricky Watters	.60
37	Steve McNair	1.25
38	Stephen Davis	1.00
39	Fred Taylor	2.00
40	Raghib Ismail	.30
41	Terry Glenn	1.00
42	Ed McCaffrey	.75
43	Patrick Jeffers	1.00
44	Jake Plummer	1.00
45	Doug Flutie	1.50
46	Terrell Davis	3.50
47	Marvin Harrison	1.00
48	Amani Toomer	.60
49	Tyrone Wheatley	.60
50	Charlie Garner	1.00
51	Jevon Kearse	1.00
52	Michael Westbrook	1.00
53	Eddie George	1.50
54	Robert Smith	1.00
55	Keyshawn Johnson	1.00
56	Torry Holt	1.00
57	Jon Kitna	1.00
58	Curtis Conway	.60
59	Jeff Garcia	1.00
60	Randy Moss	5.00
61	Jimmy Smith	1.00
62	James Stewart	1.00
63	Troy Aikman	2.50
64	Cade McNown	1.75
65	Natrone Means	.60
66	Jamal Anderson	1.00
67	Warrick Dunn	1.00
68	Kordell Stewart	1.25
69	Duce Staley	1.00
70	Rich Gannon	.75
71	Curtis Martin	1.00
72	Kerry Collins	.60
73	Jeff Blake	.60
74	Drew Bledsoe	2.00
75	Kevin Dyson	.30
76	Tony Gonzalez	1.00
77	Mark Brunell	2.00
78	Peyton Manning	5.00
79	Dorsey Levens	1.00
80	Germane Crowell	1.00
81	Brian Griese	1.25
82	Steve Beuerlein	.60
83	Eric Moulds	1.00
84	Tony Banks	.60
85	Chris Chandler	.60
86	Isaac Bruce	1.00
87	Terrell Owens	1.00
88	Jerome Bettis	1.00
89	Daunte Culpepper	2.50
90	Emmitt Smith	3.50
91	Curtis Enis	.60
92	Shaun King	2.00
93	Tim Brown	1.00
94	Antonio Freeman	1.00
95	Charlie Batch	1.25
96	Tim Couch	2.50
97	Corey Dillon	1.00
98	Muhsin Muhammad	.60
99	Joey Galloway	1.00
100	Kurt Warner	6.00
101	David Boston	1.00
102	Rod Smith	.75
103	Derrick Mayes	.30
104	Tony Martin	.30
105	Darnay Scott	.60
106	Joe Horn	.60
107	Troy Edwards	.75
108	James Johnson	.60
109	Vinny Testaverde	.75
110	Qadry Ismail	.30
111	Andre Reed	.30
112	Zach Thomas	.75
113	Ike Hilliard	.30
114	Herman Moore	1.00
115	Kevin Johnson	1.00
116	Shawn Jefferson	.30
117	Terance Mathis	.30
118	Peerless Price	.75
119	Bert Emanuel	.30
120	Terrence Wilkins	1.00
121	*Mike Anderson*	100.00
122	*Dez White*	15.00
123	*Todd Pinkston*	20.00
124	*Reuben Droughns*	15.00
125	*Danny Farmer*	20.00

2000 Bowman Reserve Autographed Rookie Mini-Helmets

	MT
Common Helmet:	25.00
Inserted 1:Box	
Shaun Alexander	50.00
Mike Anderson	85.00
Courtney Brown SP	85.00
Plaxico Burress	45.00
Trung Canidate	25.00
Giovanni Carmazzi	35.00
Laveranues Coles	35.00
Ron Dayne	85.00
Danny Farmer	25.00
Darrell Jackson	40.00
Thomas Jones	35.00
Jamal Lewis	85.00
Sylvester Morris	40.00
Chad Pennington	75.00
Todd Pinkston	35.00
Travis Prentice	35.00
Chris Redman	45.00
J.R. Redmond	35.00
R. Jay Soward	30.00
Brian Urlacher	75.00
Peter Warrick SP	200.00
Dez White	25.00

2000 Bowman Reserve Autographs

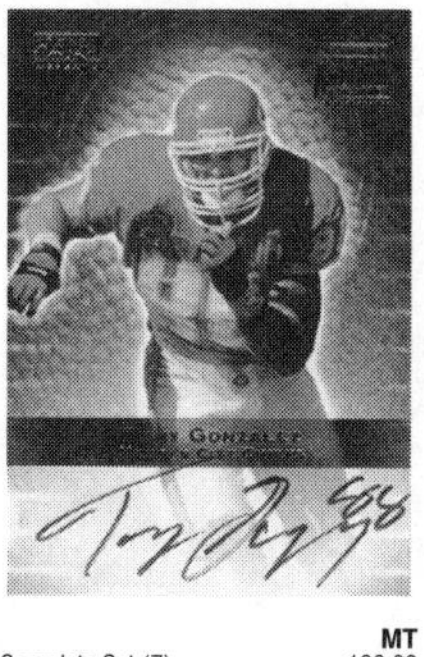

		MT
Complete Set (7):		130.00
Common Player:		8.00
Inserted 1:Box		
GC	Germane Crowell	8.00
DC	Daunte Culpepper	50.00
TG	Tony Gonzalez	8.00
TH	Torry Holt	25.00
EJ	Edgerrin James	60.00
KJ	Kevin Johnson	8.00
MR	Marcus Robinson	20.00

2000 Bowman Reserve Pro Bowl Jerseys

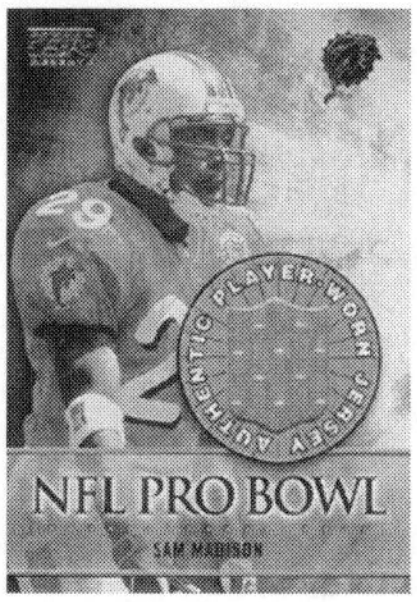

		MT
Complete Set (45):		600.00
Common Player:		8.00
Minor Stars:		15.00
Inserted 1:Box		
MA	Mike Alstott	25.00
JA	Jessie Armstead	8.00
SB	Steve Beuerlein	20.00
PB	Peter Boulware	8.00
CB	Chad Brown	8.00
IB	Isaac Bruce	20.00
MB	Mark Brunell	25.00
CC	Cris Carter	35.00
SD	Stephen Davis	25.00
MF	Marshall Faulk	30.00
RG	Rich Gannon	20.00
SG	Sam Gash	8.00
EG	Eddie George	35.00
TG	Tony Gonzalez	25.00
KH	Kevin Hardy	8.00
MH	Marvin Harrison	25.00
EJ	Edgerrin James	60.00
BJ	Brad Johnson	20.00
KJ	Keyshawn Johnson	25.00
JK	Jevon Kearse	30.00
CK	Cortez Kennedy	15.00
CL	Carnell Lake	15.00
TL	Todd Lyght	8.00
SM	Sam Madison	8.00
BM	Bruce Matthews	15.00
KM	Kevin Mawae	8.00
MM	Michael McCrary	8.00
RM	Randall McDaniel	8.00
GM	Glyn Milburn	8.00
LM	Lawyer Milloy	8.00
RM	Randy Moss	60.00
HN	Hardy Nickerson	8.00
RP	Robert Porcher	8.00
WR	William Roaf	15.00
DR	Darrell Russell	8.00
WS	Warren Sapp	15.00
EM	Emmitt Smith	50.00
JS	Jimmy Smith	20.00
MS	Michael Strahan	8.00
TT	Tom Tupa	8.00
WW	Wesley Walls	15.00
KW	Kurt Warner	75.00
CW	Charles Woodson	25.00
RW	Rod Woodson	15.00
FW	Frank Wycheck	15.00

2000 Bowman Reserve Rookie Autographs

		MT
Complete Set (15):		400.00
Common Player:		10.00
Inserted 1:41 Retail		
SA	Shaun Alexander	35.00
CB	Courtney Brown	12.00
PB	Plaxico Burress	25.00
TC	Trung Canidate	10.00
RDA	Ron Dayne	60.00
TJ	Thomas Jones	20.00
JL	Jamal Lewis	75.00
SM	Sylvester Morris	25.00
CP	Chad Pennington	50.00
TPR	Travis Prentice	18.00
CR	Chris Redman	20.00
JR	J.R. Redmond	15.00
RS	R. Jay Soward	12.00
PW	Peter Warrick	60.00
DW	Dez White	10.00

2000 Bowman Reserve Rookie Relic Jerseys

		MT
Complete Set (2):		60.00
Common Player:		20.00
Randomly Inserted		
RDU	Ron Dugans	20.00
PW	Peter Warrick	45.00

2001 Bowman

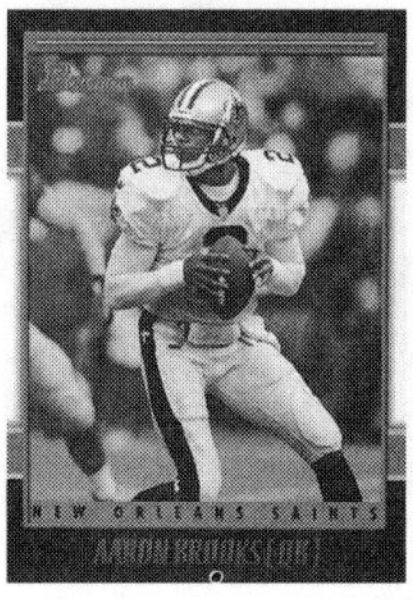

		MT
Complete Set (275):		85.00
Common Player:		.15
Minor Stars:		.30
Common Rookie:		.50
Pack (10):		3.00
Wax Box (24):		55.00
1	Emmitt Smith	1.25
2	James Stewart	.30
3	Jeff Graham	.15
4	Keyshawn Johnson	.50
5	Stephen Davis	.50
6	Chad Lewis	.30
7	Drew Bledsoe	.60
8	Fred Taylor	.50
9	Mike Anderson	1.25
10	Tony Gonzalez	.30
11	Aaron Brooks	.50
12	Vinny Testaverde	.30
13	Jerome Bettis	.50
14	Marshall Faulk	.60
15	Jeff Garcia	.50
16	Terry Glenn	.40
17	Jay Fiedler	.40
18	Ahman Green	.50
19	Cade McNown	.50
20	Rob Johnson	.30
21	Jamal Anderson	.50
22	Corey Dillon	.50
23	Jake Plummer	.50
24	Rod Smith	.50
25	Trent Green	.40
26	Ricky Williams	.50
27	Charlie Garner	.40
28	Shaun Alexander	.50
29	Jeff George	.30
30	Torry Holt	.50
31	James Thrash	.30
32	Rich Gannon	.50
33	Ron Dayne	.75
34	Dedric Ward	.30
35	Edgerrin James	1.25
36	Cris Carter	.50
37	Derrick Mason	.30
38	Brad Johnson	.40
39	Charlie Batch	.40
40	Joey Galloway	.50
41	James Allen	.30
42	Tim Biakabutuka	.30
43	Ray Lewis	.40
44	David Boston	.50
45	Kevin Johnson	.40
46	Jimmy Smith	.40
47	Joe Horn	.30
48	Terrell Owens	.50
49	Eddie George	.60
50	Brett Favre	2.00
51	Wayne Chrebet	.40
52	Hines Ward	.30
53	Warrick Dunn	.50
54	Matt Hasselbeck	.30
55	Tiki Barber	.50
56	Lamar Smith	.50
57	Tim Couch	.60
58	Eric Moulds	.50
59	Shawn Jefferson	.30
60	Donald Hayes	.30
61	Brian Urlacher	1.00
62	Steve McNair	.50
63	Kurt Warner	1.50
64	Tim Brown	.50
65	Troy Brown	.30
66	Albert Connell	.30
67	Peyton Manning	1.50
68	Peter Warrick	.60
69	Elvis Grbac	.40
70	Chris Chandler	.30
71	Akili Smith	.50
72	Keenan McCardell	.30
73	Kerry Collins	.40
74	Junior Seau	.30
75	Donovan McNabb	.75
76	Tony Banks	.30
77	Steve Beuerlein	.30
78	Daunte Culpepper	1.00
79	Darrell Jackson	.30
80	Isaac Bruce	.50
81	Tyrone Wheatley	.30
82	Derrick Alexander	.30
83	Germane Crowell	.40
84	Jon Kitna	.30
85	Jamal Lewis	1.50
86	Ed McCaffrey	.60
87	Mark Brunell	.60
88	Jeff Blake	.30
89	Duce Staley	.50
90	Doug Flutie	.60
91	Kordell Stewart	.50
92	Randy Moss	1.50
93	Marvin Harrison	.50
94	Muhsin Muhammad	.30
95	Brian Griese	.60
96	Antonio Freeman	.40
97	Amani Toomer	.30
98	Oronde Gadsden	.30
99	Curtis Martin	.50
100	Jerry Rice	1.25
101	Michael Pittman	.30
102	Shannon Sharpe	.30
103	Peerless Price	.30
104	Bill Schroeder	.30
105	Ike Hilliard	.30
106	Freddie Jones	.30
107	Tai Streets	.30
108	Ricky Watters	.40
109	Az-Zahir Hakim	.30
110	Jacquez Green	.30
111	Bobby Shaw	.30
112	Johnnie Morton	.30
113	Laveranues Coles	.30
114	Chad Pennington	1.00
115	Champ Bailey	.40
116	Charles Woodson	.40
117	Curtis Conway	.30
118	Marcus Robinson	.50
119	Michael Westbrook	.30
120	Mike Alstott	.50
121	Priest Holmes	.40
122	Qadry Ismail	.30
123	Raghib Ismail	.30
124	Shawn Bryson	.15
125	Jeff Lewis	.30
126	Jeremy McDaniel	.15
127	Terance Mathis	.30
128	Travis Prentice	.30
129	Warren Sapp	.30
130	Jevon Kearse	.40
131	*George Layne*	.75
132	*Correll Buckhalter*	1.50
133	*Tony Stewart*	1.00
134	*Chris Barnes*	1.00
135	*A.J. Feeley*	.75
136	*Margin Hooks*	.50
137	*Anthony Henry*	.50
138	*Dwight Smith*	.50
139	*Torrance Marshall*	1.00
140	*Gary Baxter*	.50
141	*Derek Combs*	1.00
142	*Marcus Bell*	.50
143	*DeLawrence Grant*	.50
144	*Jameel Cook*	.50
145	*Eric Downing*	.50
146	*Marlon McCree*	.50
147	*Tay Cody*	.50
148	*Mario Monds*	.50
149	*Kenny Smith*	.50
150	*Sedrick Hodge*	.50
151	*Marcus Stroud*	1.00
152	*Steve Smith*	.50
153	*Tyrone Robertson*	.50
154	*James Reed*	.50
155	*Kris Kocurek*	.50
156	*Dan O'Leary*	.50
157	*Harold Blackmon*	.50
158	*Fred Smoot*	1.00
159	*Billy Baber*	.50
160	*Jarrod Cooper*	.50
161	*Travis Henry*	2.00
162	*David Terrell*	3.00
163	*Josh Heupel*	1.75
164	*Drew Brees*	5.00
165	*T.J. Houshmandzadeh*	.75
166	*Rod Gardner*	2.00
167	*Richard Seymour*	.75
168	*Koren Robinson*	2.00
169	*Scotty Anderson*	.75
170	*Marques Tuiasosopo*	2.00
171	*John Capel*	1.00
172	*LaMont Jordan*	1.50
173	*James Jackson*	1.75
174	*Bobby Newcombe*	1.00
175	*Anthony Thomas*	5.00
176	*Dan Alexander*	1.00
177	*Quincy Carter*	2.50
178	*Morlon Greenwood*	.75
179	*Robert Ferguson*	1.00
180	*Sage Rosenfels*	1.00
181	*Michael Stone*	.50
182	*Chris Weinke*	3.50
183	*Travis Minor*	1.00
184	*Gerard Warren*	1.00
185	*Jamar Fletcher*	.75
186	*Andre Carter*	1.00
187	*Deuce McAllister*	2.50
188	*Dan Morgan*	1.00
189	*Todd Heap*	1.00
190	*Marvin "Snoop" Minnis*	1.50
191	*Will Allen*	.75
192	*Freddie Mitchell*	1.75
193	*Rudi Johnson*	1.25
194	*Kevan Barlow*	1.50
195	*Jamie Winborn*	.75
196	*Onomo Ojo*	.75
197	*Leonard Davis*	.75
198	*Santana Moss*	1.75
199	*Chris Chambers*	2.50
200	*Michael Vick*	5.00
201	*Michael Bennett*	2.50
202	*Mike McMahon*	2.00
203	*Jonathan Carter*	.50
204	*Jamal Reynolds*	1.00
205	*Justin Smith*	1.00
206	*Quincy Morgan*	1.75
207	*Chad Johnson*	1.25
208	*Jesse Palmer*	1.00
209	*Reggie Wayne*	1.50
210	*LaDainian Tomlinson*	4.00
211	*Andre King*	.75
212	*Richmond Flowers*	.50
213	*Derrick Blaylock*	.50
214	*Cedrick Wilson*	1.00
215	*Zeke Moreno*	.50
216	*Tommy Polley*	.75
217	*Damione Lewis*	1.00
218	*Aaron Schobel*	.50
219	*Alge Crumpler*	1.00
220	*Nate Clements*	.75
221	*Quentin McCord*	.75
222	*Ken-Yon Rambo*	1.00
223	*Milton Wynn*	.50
224	*Derrick Gibson*	.50
225	*Chris Taylor*	.75
226	*Corey Hall*	.50
227	*Vinny Sutherland*	1.00
228	*Kendrell Bell*	1.00
229	*Casey Hampton*	.75
230	*Demetric Evans*	.50
231	*Brian Allen*	.50
232	*Rodney Bailey*	.50
233	*Otis Leverette*	.50
234	*Ron Edwards*	.50
235	*Michael Jameson*	.50
236	*Markus Steele*	.50
237	*Jimmy Williams*	.50
238	*Roger Knight*	.50
239	*Randy Garner*	.50
240	*Raymond Perryman*	.50
241	*Karon Riley*	.50
242	*Adam Archuleta*	1.00
243	*Arnold Jackson*	.75
244	*Ryan Pickett*	.50
245	*Shad Meier*	.50
246	*Reggie Germany*	1.00
247	*Justin McCareins*	.50
248	*Idrees Bashir*	.50
249	*Josh Booty*	1.00
250	*Eddie Berlin*	1.00
251	*Heath Evans*	.75
252	*Alex Bannister*	1.00
253	*Corey Alston*	.50
254	*Reggie White*	1.00
255	*Orlando Huff*	.50
256	*Ken Lucas*	.50
257	*Matt Stewart*	.50
258	*Cedric Scott*	.75
259	*Ronney Daniels*	.75
260	*Kevin Kasper*	1.25
261	*Tony Driver*	.75
262	*Kyle Vanden Bosch*	1.00
263	*T.J. Turner*	.50
264	*Eric Westmoreland*	.50
265	*Ronald Flemons*	.50
266	*Eric Kelly*	.50
267	*Moran Norris*	.50
268	*Darnerian McCants*	.50
269	*James Boyd*	.50
270	*Keith Adams*	.50
271	*Brandon Manumaleuna*	.50
272	*Dee Brown*	.50
273	*Ross Kolodziej*	.50
274	*Eddie "Boo" Williams*	.50
275	*Patrick Chukwurah*	.50

2001 Bowman Gold

	MT
Gold Cards:	2x-4x
Gold Rookies:	2x
Inserted 1:1	

2001 Bowman Autographs

		MT
Common Player:		8.00
Inserted 1:61:		
BA-DA	Dan Alexander	10.00
BA-KB	Kevan Barlow	15.00
BA-MB	Michael Bennett	45.00
BA-JB	Josh Booty	10.00
BA-DB	Drew Brees	50.00
BA-QC	Quincy Carter	25.00
BA-CC	Chris Chambers	15.00
BA-RG	Rod Gardner	20.00
BA-TH	Travis Henry	20.00
BA-JH	Josh Heupel	12.00
BA-JJ	James Jackson	18.00
BA-CJ	Chad Johnson	15.00
BA-LJ	LaMont Jordan	15.00
BA-TM	Travis Minor	12.00
BA-FM	Freddie Mitchell	18.00
BA-DM	Dan Morgan	10.00
BA-QM	Quincy Morgan	20.00
BA-SM	Santana Moss	25.00
BA-BN	Bobby Newcombe	8.00
BA-JP	Jesse Palmer	15.00
BA-KYR	Ken-Yon Rambo	10.00
BA-DR	David Rivers	8.00
BA-KR	Koren Robinson	30.00
BA-DT	David Terrell	30.00
BA-AT	Anthony Thomas	45.00
BA-LT	LaDainian Tomlinson	60.00
BA-MV	Michael Vick	85.00
BA-KW	Kenyatta Walker	8.00
BA-RW	Reggie Wayne	25.00
BA-CW	Chris Weinke	30.00

2001 Bowman 1996 Rookies

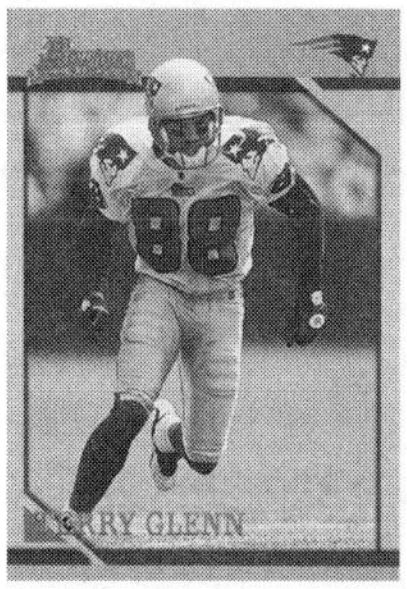

		MT
Complete Set (15):		30.00
Common Player:		1.00
Inserted 1:4		
BRC1	Eric Moulds	2.50
BRC2	Ray Lewis	3.00
BRC3	Tim Biakabutuka	1.50
BRC4	Eddie George	4.00
BRC5	Marvin Harrison	3.00
BRC6	Joe Horn	2.00
BRC7	Muhsin Muhammad	2.00
BRC8	Mike Alstott	2.50
BRC9	Amani Toomer	2.00
BRC10	Terrell Owens	3.50
BRC11	Keyshawn Johnson	2.50
BRC12	Terry Glenn	1.75
BRC13	Zach Thomas	1.75
BRC14	Stephen Davis	3.00
BRC15	La'Roi Glover	1.00

2001 Bowman Relics

		MT
Complete Set (2):		
Common Player:		
RRE-SB	Sammy Baugh	
RRE-GM	Gino Marchetti	

2001 Bowman Rookie Reprint

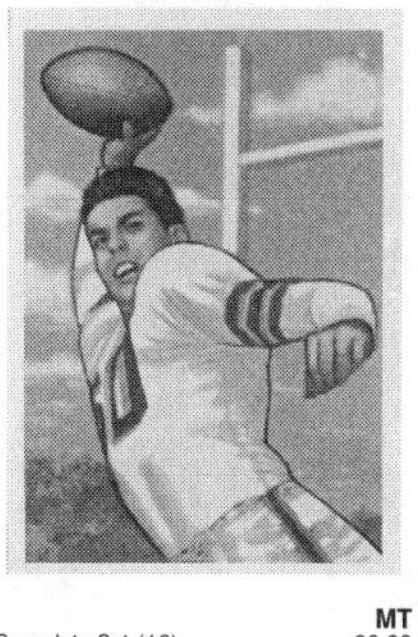

		MT
Complete Set (16):		30.00
Common Player:		1.50
Inserted 1:6		
R-AA	Alan Ameche	1.50
R-SB	Sammy Baugh	4.50
R-CC	Charlie Conerly	2.75
R-AD	Art Donovan	3.00
R-TF	Tom Fears	1.50
R-FG	Frank Gifford	5.00
R-OG	Otto Graham	3.50
R-LG	Lou Groza	3.00
R-EH	Elroy Hirsch	3.00
R-BH	Bill Howton	1.50
R-SL	Sid Luckman	2.75
R-GM	Gino Marchetti	2.00
R-YT	Y.A. Tittle	4.00
R-ET	Emlen Tunnell	1.50
R-BT	Bulldog Turner	2.50
R-NV	Norm Van Brocklin	3.50

2001 Bowman Senior Bowl/Hula Bowl Relics

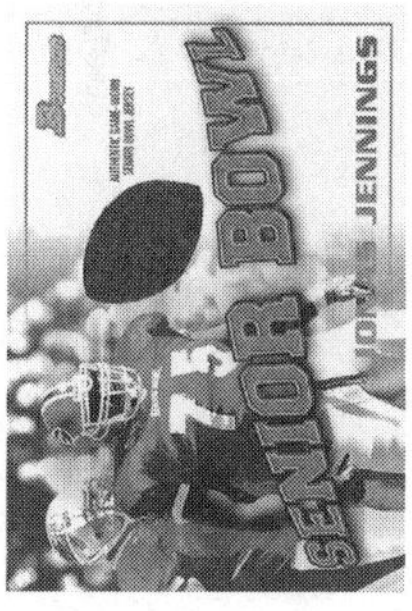

		MT
Common Player:		5.00
Inserted 1:25		
BJ-BA	Brian Allen	5.00
BJ-AA	Adam Archuleta	10.00
BJ-JB	Jeff Backus	7.00
BJ-DB	Drew Brees	30.00
BJ-DBU	Derrick Burgess	5.00
BJ-JC	Jarrod Cooper	5.00
BJ-AC	Alge Crumpler	10.00
BJ-TD	Tony Dixon	5.00
BJ-MF	Mario Fatafehi	8.00
BJ-RG	Reggie Germany	10.00
BJ-DG	Derrick Gibson	5.00
BJ-JHE	Jamie Henderson	5.00
BJ-JH	Jabari Holloway	7.00
BJ-SH	Steve Hutchinson	8.00
BJ-JJ	Jonas Jennings	5.00
BJ-LJ	LaMont Jordan	12.00
BJ-BJ	Bhawoh Jue	5.00
BJ-KK	Kevin Kasper	15.00
BJ-MM	CMike McMahon	12.00
BJ-TM	Travis Minor	10.00
BJ-ZM	Zeke Moreno	7.00
BJ-LM	Leonard Myers	5.00
BJ-BN	Bobby Newcombe	7.00
BJ-JP	Jesse Palmer	10.00
BJ-SR	Sage Rosenfels	12.00
BJ-SS	Steve Smith	7.00
BJ-FS	Fred Smoot	10.00
BJ-TS	Tony Stewart	8.00
BJ-MS	Michael Stone	5.00
BJ-CT	Chris Taylor	7.00
BJ-LT	LaDainian Tomlinson	45.00
BJ-RW	Reggie Wayne	15.00
BJ-EW	Eric Westmoreland	7.00

2001 Bowman Senior Bowl/Hula Bowl Relics Autographed

		MT
Common Player:		25.00
Inserted 1:1,780		
BJA-DB	Drew Brees	80.00
BJA-LJ	LaMont Jordan	25.00
BJA-BN	Bobby Newcombe	25.00
BJA-JP	Jesse Palmer	25.00
BJA-LT	LaDainian Tomlinson	125.00
BJA-RW	Reggie Wayne	30.00

Post-1980 cards in Near Mint condition will generally sell for about 75% of the quoted Mint value. Excellent-condition cards bring no more than 40%.

2001 Bowman's Best

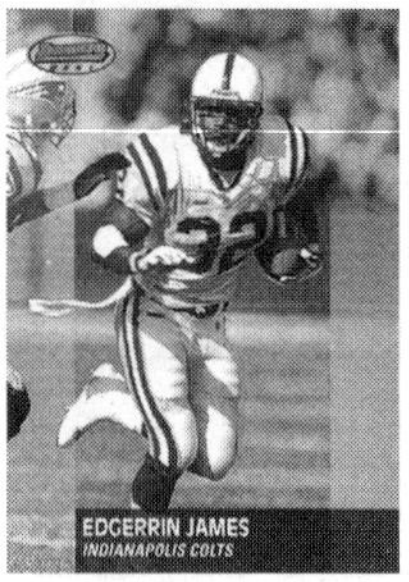
EDGERRIN JAMES
INDIANAPOLIS COLTS

MT
Complete Set (170): 375.00
Common Player: .15
Minor Stars: .30
Common Rookie JSY: 10.00
Production 999 Sets
Common Rookie (121-170): 3.00
Production 1,499 Sets
Pack (5): 5.00
Box (24): 85.00

1 Jerry Rice 1.50
2 Doug Flutie .75
3 Drew Bledsoe .75
4 Edgerrin James 1.50
5 Muhsin Muhammad .30
6 Charlie Batch .30
7 Marshall Faulk .75
8 Trent Green .30
9 Rich Gannon .50
10 Emmitt Smith 1.50
11 Steve McNair .50
12 Darrell Jackson .30
13 Amani Toomer .30
14 Jimmy Smith .30
15 Kevin Johnson .30
16 Ray Lewis .30
17 Peter Warrick .50
18 Cris Carter .50
19 Jerome Bettis .50
20 Keyshawn Johnson .50
21 Joey Galloway .50
22 Chris Chandler .15
23 Brett Favre 2.50
24 Aaron Brooks .75
25 Kurt Warner 2.00
26 Jeff Graham .15
27 Curtis Martin .50
28 Mike Anderson 1.00
29 Eric Moulds .30
30 David Boston .50
31 Elvis Grbac .30
32 James Stewart .15
33 Randy Moss 2.00
34 Donovan McNabb 1.25
35 Matt Hasselbeck .30
36 Stephen Davis .30
37 Brad Johnson .30
38 Jamal Anderson .30
39 Tim Biakabutuka .15
40 Antonio Freeman .30
41 Mark Brunell .75
42 Tiki Barber .30
43 Charlie Garner .30
44 Eddie George .75
45 Ricky Williams 1.00
46 Rob Johnson .30
47 Jake Plummer .30
48 Peyton Manning 2.00
49 Lamar Smith .30
50 Corey Dillon .50
51 Derrick Alexander .30
52 Troy Brown .30
53 Wayne Chrebet .50
54 Shaun Alexander 1.00
55 Jeff George .15
56 Tim Brown .50
57 Brian Griese .75
58 Cade McNown .15
59 Jamal Lewis 1.25
60 Germane Crowell .30
61 Junior Seau .30
62 Warrick Dunn .50
63 Isaac Bruce .50
64 Terry Glenn .30
65 Fred Taylor .75
66 Tim Couch .75
67 Akili Smith .15
68 Tony Gonzalez .30
69 Kerry Collins .30
70 James Thrash .30
71 Terrell Owens .50
72 Derrick Mason .30
73 Tyrone Wheatley .30
74 Oronde Gadsden .15
75 Ahman Green .50
76 Jon Kitna .15
77 Tony Banks .15
78 Marvin Harrison .50
79 Daunte Culpepper 1.25
80 Vinny Testaverde .30
81 Chad Lewis .15
82 Torry Holt .50
83 Jeff Garcia .75
84 Rod Smith .30
85 Marcus Robinson .30
86 Keenan McCardell .30
87 Joe Horn .30
88 Kordell Stewart .50
89 Jay Fiedler .30
90 Ed McCaffrey .30
91 Eddie George, Stephen Davis .50
92 Peyton Manning, Jeff Garcia 1.50
93 Rod Smith, Torry Holt .50
94 Edgerrin James, Marshall Faulk 1.00
95 Elvis Grbac, Daunte Culpepper .75
96 Marvin Harrison, Randy Moss 1.50
97 Mike Anderson, Emmitt Smith 1.00
98 Brian Griese, Kurt Warner 1.50
99 Muhsin Muhammad, Ed McCaffrey .30
100 Eric Moulds, Terrell Owens .50
101 *David Terrell JSY* 25.00
102 *Kevan Barlow JSY* 12.00
103 *Quincy Morgan JSY* 10.00
104 *Chris Weinke JSY* 15.00
105 *Josh Heupel JSY* 10.00
106 *Chris Chambers JSY* 20.00
107 *Reggie Wayne JSY* 15.00
108 *Gerard Warren JSY* 10.00
109 *Freddie Mitchell JSY* 15.00
110 *Anthony Thomas JSY* 40.00
111 *Robert Ferguson JSY* 10.00
112 *Deuce McAllister JSY* 15.00
113 *Travis Henry JSY* 12.00
114 *Rod Gardner JSY* 15.00
115 *Michael Bennett JSY* 20.00
116 *Santana Moss JSY* 15.00
117 *Chad Johnson JSY* 10.00
118 *Jesse Palmer JSY* 10.00
119 *James Jackson JSY* 10.00
120 *Dan Morgan JSY* 10.00
121 *Drew Brees* 25.00
122 *Travis Minor* 8.00
123 *Quincy Carter* 15.00
124 *LaDainian Tomlinson* 25.00
125 *Michael Vick* 30.00
126 *Ryan Pickett* 3.00
127 *Mike McMahon* 12.00
128 *Alex Bannister* 5.00
129 *A.J. Feeley* 5.00
130 *Shad Meier* 3.00
131 *Jamie Winborn* 3.00
132 *Fred Smoot* 5.00
133 *Milton Wynn* 3.00
134 *Onomo Ojo* 3.00
135 *Jonathan Carter* 3.00
136 *Todd Heap* 5.00
137 *Bobby Newcombe* 3.00
138 *Tony Stewart* 3.00
139 *Torrance Marshall* 3.00
140 *Jamal Reynolds* 3.00
141 *Jamar Fletcher* 3.00
142 *Richard Seymour* 5.00
143 *Tay Cody* 3.00
144 *Koren Robinson* 12.00
145 *Eddie Berlin* 3.00
146 *Damione Lewis* 3.00
147 *Marques Tuiasosopo* 12.00
148 *Marvin "Snoop" Minnis* 10.00
149 *Chris Barnes* 3.00
150 *Leonard Davis* 3.00
151 *Vinny Sutherland* 5.00
152 *Rudi Johnson* 5.00
153 *Derrick Gibson* 3.00
154 *Dan Alexander* 5.00
155 *Darnerian McCants* 3.00
156 *Adam Archuleta* 5.00
157 *Correll Buckhalter* 10.00
158 *LaMont Jordan* 8.00
159 *Quentin McCord* 3.00
160 *Justin Smith* 3.00
161 *Nate Clements* 3.00
162 *Alge Crumpler* 5.00
163 *Dan O'Leary* 3.00
164 *Sage Rosenfels* 8.00
165 *Andre Carter* 3.00
166 *Marcus Stroud* 3.00
167 *Will Allen* 3.00
168 *Tommy Polley* 5.00
169 *Justin McCareins* 3.00
170 *Josh Booty* 5.00

2001 Bowman's Best Autographs

MT
Common Player: 10.00
Inserted 1:23
BB-DA Dan Alexander 10.00
BB-KB Kevan Barlow 15.00
BB-MB Michael Bennett 25.00
BB-DBR Drew Brees 50.00
BB-QC Quincy Carter 20.00
BB-CC Chris Chambers 25.00
BB-SD Stephen Davis 15.00
BB-TD Tim Dwight 10.00
BB-RF Robert Ferguson 10.00
BB-RG Rod Gardner 20.00
BB-DH Donald Hayes 10.00
BB-TH Travis Henry 15.00
BB-JHE Josh Heupel 15.00
BB-JH Joe Horn 10.00
BB-JJ James Jackson 15.00
BB-CJ Chad Johnson 15.00
BB-LJ LaMont Jordan 15.00
BB-JL Jamal Lewis 20.00
BB-FM Freddie Mitchell 20.00
BB-DMO Dan Morgan 10.00
BB-QM Quincy Morgan 15.00
BB-SMO Sammy Morris 10.00
BB-RM Randy Moss 60.00
BB-SM Santana Moss 20.00
BB-EM Eric Moulds 15.00
BB-BN Bobby Newcombe 10.00
BB-TO Terrell Owens 20.00
BB-JP Jesse Palmer 15.00
BB-DR David Rivers 10.00
BB-KR Koren Robinson 25.00
BB-MR Marcus Robinson 15.00
BB-LS Lamar Smith 10.00
BB-TS Tai Streets 10.00
BB-DT David Terrell 25.00
BB-AT Anthony Thomas 50.00
BB-LT LaDainian Tomlinson 40.00
BB-BU Brian Urlacher 10.00
BB-MV Michael Vick 70.00
BB-RW Reggie Wayne 20.00
BB-CW Chris Weinke 25.00
BB-TW Terrence Wilkins 10.00

2001 Bowman's Best Bowman's Best Bets

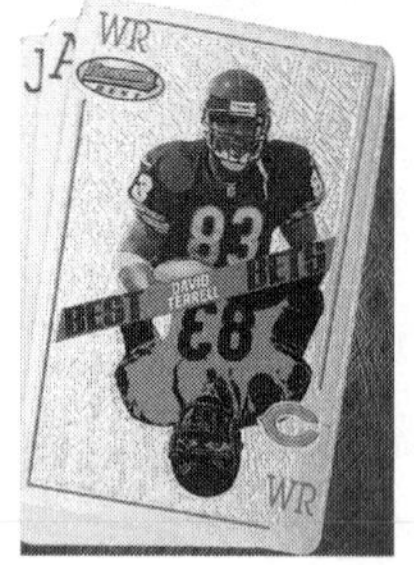

MT
Complete Set (13): 18.00
Common Player: 1.00
Inserted 1:12
BB1 Drew Brees 3.00
BB2 Michael Vick 4.00
BB3 David Terrell 2.50
BB4 Michael Bennett 2.00
BB5 LaDainian Tomlinson 3.00
BB6 Koren Robinson 1.50
BB7 Chris Weinke 1.50
BB8 Rod Gardner 1.50
BB9 Reggie Wayne 1.50
BB10 Deuce McAllister 1.50
BB11 Freddie Mitchell 1.50
BB12 Chad Johnson 1.00
BB13 Santana Moss 1.50

2001 Bowman's Best Franchise Favorites

MT
Common Player: 20.00
Inserted 1:414 H; 1:692 R
FF-CC Daunte Culpepper, Cris Carter 50.00
FF-GJ Eddie George, Edgerrin James 50.00
FF-SG Jimmy Smith, Tony Gonzalez 20.00
FF-WW Charles Woodson, Rod Woodson 20.00

2001 Bowman's Best Impact Players

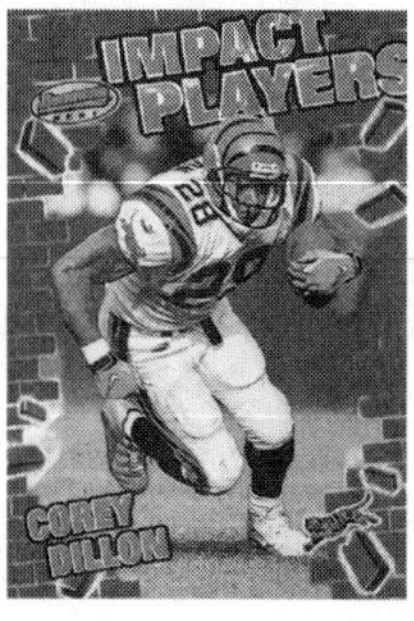
IMPACT PLAYERS
COREY DILLON

MT
Complete Set (20): 15.00
Common Player: .50
Inserted 1:4
IP1 Randy Moss 3.00
IP2 Peyton Manning 3.00
IP3 Eddie George 1.00
IP4 Elvis Grbac .50
IP5 Marshall Faulk 1.00
IP6 Marvin Harrison .75
IP7 Tony Gonzalez .50
IP8 Corey Dillon .50
IP9 Rod Smith .50
IP10 Daunte Culpepper 2.00
IP11 Edgerrin James 2.50
IP12 Terrell Owens .75
IP13 Eric Moulds .50
IP14 Kurt Warner 3.00
IP15 Donovan McNabb 2.00
IP16 Isaac Bruce .75
IP17 Jeff Garcia 1.00
IP18 Cris Carter .50
IP19 Stephen Davis .50
IP20 Torry Holt .75

Values quoted in this guide reflect the retail price of a card — the price a collector can expect to pay when buying a card from a dealer. The wholesale price — that which a collector can expect to receive from a dealer when selling cards — will be significantly lower, depending on desirability and condition.

2001 Bowman's Best Rookie Relics

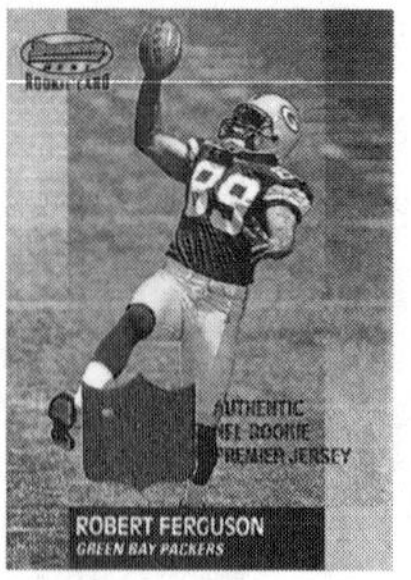
ROBERT FERGUSON
GREEN BAY PACKERS

MT
Complete Set (20):
Common Player: 10.00
101 David Terrell 25.00
102 Kevan Barlow 12.00
103 Quincy Morgan 10.00
104 Chris Weinke 15.00
105 Josh Heupel 10.00
106 Chris Chambers 20.00
107 Reggie Wayne 15.00
108 Gerard Warren 10.00
109 Freddie Mitchell 15.00
110 Anthony Thomas 40.00
111 Robert Ferguson 10.00
112 Deuce McAllister 15.00
113 Travis Henry 12.00
114 Rod Gardner 15.00
115 Michael Bennett 20.00
116 Santana Moss 15.00
117 Chad Johnson 10.00
118 Jesse Palmer 10.00
119 James Jackson 10.00
120 Dan Morgan 10.00

2001 Bowman's Best Vintage Best

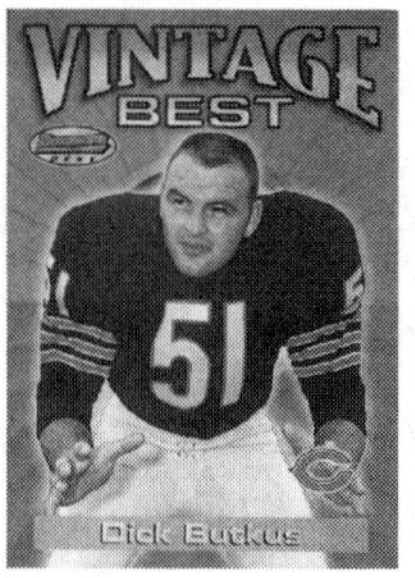
VINTAGE BEST
Dick Butkus

MT
Complete Set (10): 15.00
Common Player: 1.00
Inserted 1:4
VB JB Jim Brown 2.00
VB DB Dick Butkus 1.00
VB ED Eric Dickerson 2.00
VB FG Frank Gifford 2.00
VB PH Paul Hornung 2.00
VB DC Deacon Jones 2.00
VB JM Joe Montana 5.00
VB JN Joe Namath 3.00
VB GS Gale Sayers 2.00
VB LT Lawrence Taylor 2.00

2001 Bowman Chrome

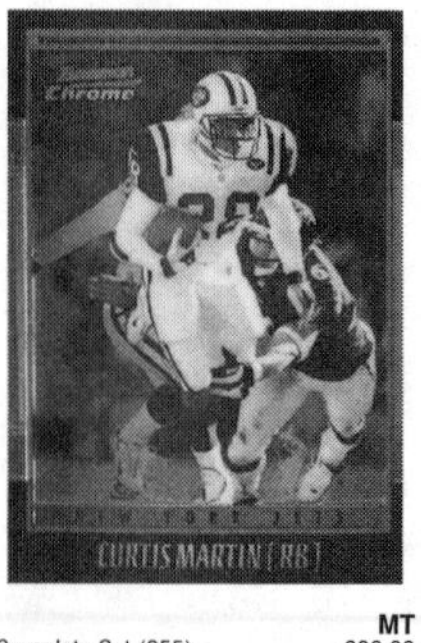
CURTIS MARTIN [RB]

MT
Complete Set (255): 600.00
Common Player: .20
Minor Stars: .40
Common Rookie (111-255): 2.00
Production 1,999 Sets
Inserted 1:3
Pack (4): 3.00
Box (24): 55.00
1 Emmitt Smith 2.00
2 James Stewart .40
3 Jeff Graham .20
4 Keyshawn Johnson .75
5 Stephen Davis .40
6 Chad Lewis .20
7 Drew Bledsoe 1.00
8 Fred Taylor .75
9 Mike Anderson 1.25
10 Tony Gonzalez .40
11 Aaron Brooks .75
12 Vinny Testaverde .40
13 Jerome Bettis .40
14 Marshall Faulk 1.00
15 Jeff Garcia .75
16 Terry Glenn .40
17 Jay Fiedler .20
18 Ahman Green .40
19 Cade McNown .20
20 Rob Johnson .20
21 Jamal Anderson .40
22 Corey Dillon .40
23 Jake Plummer .40
24 Rod Smith .40
25 Trent Green .20
26 Ricky Williams 1.25
27 Charlie Garner .20
28 Shaun Alexander 1.25
29 Jeff George .20
30 Torry Holt 75.00
31 James Thrash .20
32 Rich Gannon .20
33 Ron Dayne .40
34 Dedric Ward .20
35 Edgerrin James 2.00
36 Cris Carter .40
37 Derrick Mason .20
38 Brad Johnson .40
39 Charlie Batch .20
40 Joey Galloway .40
41 James Allen .20
42 Tim Biakabutuka .20
43 Ray Lewis .40
44 David Boston .75
45 Kevin Johnson .40
46 Jimmy Smith .40
47 Joe Horn .20
48 Terrell Owens .75
49 Eddie George 1.00
50 Brett Favre 3.00
51 Wayne Chrebet .40
52 Hines Ward .40
53 Warrick Dunn .40
54 Matt Hasselbeck .20
55 Tiki Barber .40
56 Lamar Smith .40
57 Tim Couch 1.00
58 Eric Moulds .40
59 Shawn Jefferson .20
60 Donald Hayes .20
61 Brian Urlacher 1.50
62 Steve McNair .40
63 Kurt Warner 2.50
64 Tim Brown .40
65 Troy Brown .20
66 Albert Connell .20
67 Peyton Manning 2.50
68 Peter Warrick .75
69 Elvis Grbac .40
70 Chris Chandler .20
71 Akili Smith .40
72 Keenan McCardell .20
73 Kerry Collins .40
74 Junior Seau .40
75 Donovan McNabb 1.50
76 Tony Banks .20
77 Steve Beuerlein .20
78 Daunte Culpepper 1.50
79 Darrell Jackson .20
80 Isaac Bruce .40
81 Tyrone Wheatley .20
82 Derrick Alexander .20
83 Germane Crowell .40
84 Jon Kitna .20
85 Jamal Lewis 1.50
86 Ed McCaffrey .40
87 Mark Brunell .75
88 Jeff Blake .40
89 Duce Staley .40
90 Doug Flutie 1.00
91 Kordell Stewart .75
92 Randy Moss 2.50
93 Marvin Harrison .75
94 Muhsin Muhammad .20
95 Brian Griese 1.00
96 Antonio Freeman .40
97 Amani Toomer .20
98 Oronde Gadsden .20
99 Curtis Martin .20
100 Jerry Rice 2.00
101 Michael Pittman .20
102 Shannon Sharpe .40
103 Peerless Price .20
104 Bill Schroeder .40
105 Ike Hilliard .40
106 Freddie Jones .20
107 Tai Streets .20
108 Ricky Watters .40
109 Az-Zahir Hakim .20
110 Jacquez Green .20
111 *George Layne* 2.00
112 *Correll Buckhalter* 10.00
113 *Tony Stewart* 2.00
114 *Chris Barnes* 2.00
115 *A.J. Feeley* 6.00
116 *Margin Hooks* 2.00
117 *Anthony Henry* 6.00
118 *Dwight Smith* 2.00
119 *Torrance Marshall* 2.00
120 *Gary Baxter* 2.00
121 *Derek Combs* 2.00
122 *Marcus Bell* 2.00
123 *DeLawrence Grant* 2.00
124 *Jameel Cook* 2.00
125 *Eric Downing* 2.00
126 *Marlon McCree* 2.00
127 *Tay Cody* 2.00
128 *Mario Monds* 2.00
129 *Kenny Smith* 2.00
130 *Sedrick Hodge* 2.00
131 *Marcus Stroud* 2.00
132 *Steve Smith* 4.00
133 *Tyrone Robertson* 2.00
134 *James Reed* 2.00
135 *Kris Kocurek* 2.00
136 *Dan O'Leary* 2.00
137 *Harold Blackmon* 2.00
138 *Fred Smoot* 2.00
139 *Billy Baber* 2.00
140 *Jarrod Cooper* 2.00
141 *Travis Henry* 10.00
142 *David Terrell* 20.00
143 *Josh Heupel* 8.00
144 *Drew Brees* 25.00
145 *T.J. Houshmandzadeh* 6.00
146 *Rod Gardner* 12.00
147 *Richard Seymour* 4.00
148 *Koren Robinson* 12.00
149 *Scotty Anderson* 2.00
150 *Marques Tuiasosopo* 12.00
151 *John Capel* 6.00
152 *LaMont Jordan* 6.00
153 *James Jackson* 8.00
154 *Bobby Newcombe* 4.00
155 *Anthony Thomas* 30.00
156 *Dan Alexander* 6.00
157 *Quincy Carter* 15.00
158 *Morlon Greenwood* 2.00
159 *Robert Ferguson* 6.00
160 *Sage Rosenfels* 8.00
161 *Michael Stone* 2.00
162 *Chris Weinke* 12.00
163 *Travis Minor* 8.00
164 *Gerard Warren* 4.00
165 *Jamar Fletcher* 4.00
166 *Andre Carter* 4.00
167 *Deuce McAllister* 12.00
168 *Dan Morgan* 4.00
169 *Todd Heap* 4.00
170 *Marvin "Snoop" Minnis* 10.00
171 *Will Allen* 4.00
172 *Freddie Mitchell* 12.00
173 *Rudi Johnson* 4.00
174 *Kevan Barlow* 10.00
175 *Jamie Winborn* 2.00
176 *Onome Ojo* 2.00
177 *Leonard Davis* 4.00
178 *Santana Moss* 12.00
179 *Chris Chambers* 15.00
180 *Michael Vick* 30.00
181 *Michael Bennett* 15.00
182 *Mike McMahon* 12.00
183 *Jonathan Carter* 8.00
184 *Jamal Reynolds* 2.00
185 *Justin Smith* 2.00
186 *Quincy Morgan* 8.00
187 *Chad Johnson* 6.00
188 *Jesse Palmer* 8.00
189 *Reggie Wayne* 12.00
190 *LaDainian Tomlinson* 25.00
191 *Andre King* 6.00
192 *Richmond Flowers* 2.00
193 *Derrick Blaylock* 2.00
194 *Cedrick Wilson* 2.00
195 *Zeke Moreno* 2.00
196 *Tommy Polley* 6.00
197 *Damione Lewis* 2.00
198 *Aaron Schobel* 2.00
199 *Alge Crumpler* 4.00
200 *Nate Clements* 4.00
201 *Quentin McCord* 2.00
202 *Ken-Yon Rambo* 4.00
203 *Milton Wynn* 2.00
204 *Derrick Gibson* 2.00
205 *Chris Taylor* 2.00
206 *Corey Hall* 2.00
207 *Vinny Sutherland* 6.00
208 *Kendrell Bell* 20.00
209 *Casey Hampton* 2.00
210 *Demetric Evans* 2.00
211 *Brian Allen* 2.00
212 *Rodney Bailey* 2.00
213 *Otis Leverette* 2.00
214 *Ron Edwards* 2.00
215 *Michael Jameson* 2.00
216 *Markus Steele* 2.00
217 *Jimmy Williams* 2.00
218 *Roger Knight* 2.00
219 *Randy Garner* 2.00
220 *Raymond Perryman* 2.00
221 *Karon Riley* 2.00
222 *Adam Archuleta* 4.00
223 *Arnold Jackson* 2.00
224 *Ryan Pickett* 2.00
225 *Shad Meier* 2.00
226 *Reggie Germany* 4.00
227 *Justin McCareins* 2.00
228 *Idrees Bashir* 2.00
229 *Josh Booty* 4.00
230 *Eddie Berlin* 2.00
231 *Heath Evans* 2.00
232 *Alex Bannister* 4.00
233 *Corey Alston* 2.00
234 *Reggie White* 2.00
235 *Orlando Huff* 2.00
236 *Ken Lucas* 2.00
237 *Matt Stewart* 2.00
238 *Cedric Scott* 2.00
239 *Ronney Daniels* 2.00
240 *Kevin Kasper* 6.00
241 *Tony Driver* 4.00
242 *Kyle Vanden Bosch* .20
243 *T.J. Turner* 2.00
244 *Eric Westmoreland* 2.00
245 *Ronald Flemons* 2.00
246 *Eric Kelly* 2.00
247 *Moran Norris* 2.00
248 *Darnerian McCants* 2.00
249 *James Boyd* 2.00
250 *Keith Adams* 2.00
251 *Brandon Manumaleuna* 2.00
252 *Dee Brown* 2.00
253 *Ross Kolodziej* 2.00
254 *Eddie "Boo" Williams* 2.00
255 *Patrick Chukwurah* 2.00

2001 Bowman Chrome Autographs

MT
Common Player: 12.00
Inserted 1:315
BC-DA Dan Alexander 20.00
BC-KB Kevan Barlow 25.00
BC-MB Michael Bennett 100.00
BC-DBO David Boston 25.00
BC-DB Drew Brees 125.00
BC-QC Quincy Carter 50.00
BC-CC Chris Chambers 60.00
BC-RG Rod Gardner 40.00
BC-RGE Reggie Germany 20.00
BC-TH Travis Henry 30.00
BC-JH Josh Heupel 25.00
BC-JHO Joe Horn 12.00
BC-JJ James Jackson 25.00
BC-CJ Chad Johnson 30.00
BC-LJ LaMont Jordan 30.00
BC-DM Deric Mason 10.00
BC-TM Travis Minor 25.00
BC-DM Dan Morgan 25.00
BC-QM Quincy Morgan 12.00
BC-SM Santana Moss 30.00
BC-BN Bobby Newcombe 20.00
BC-JP Jesse Palmer 20.00
BC-DT David Terrell 60.00
BC-AT Anthony Thomas 150.00
BC-LT LaDainian Tomlinson 125.00
BC-MV Michael Vick 250.00
BC-RW Reggie Wayne 30.00
BC-CW Chris Weinke 60.00

2001 Bowman Chrome 1996 Bowman Rookie

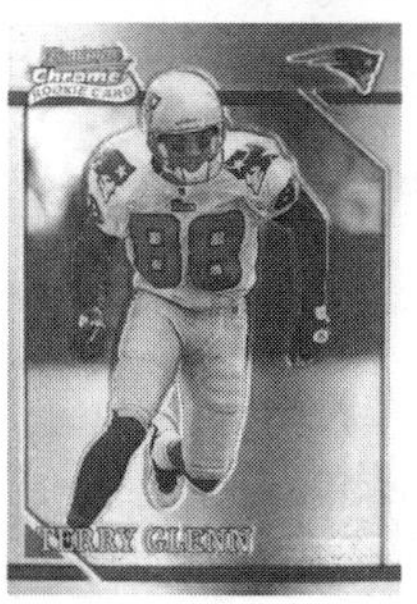

		MT
Complete Set (15):		45.00
Common Player:		2.00
Inserted 1:16		
BRC1	Eric Moulds	4.00
BRC2	Ray Lewis	4.00
BRC3	Tim Biakabutuka	2.00
BRC4	Eddie George	8.00
BRC5	Marvin Harrison	6.00
BRC6	Joe Horn	2.00
BRC7	Muhsin Muhammad	3.00
BRC8	Mike Alstott	4.00
BRC9	Amani Toomer	3.00
BRC10	Terrell Owens	6.00
BRC11	Keyshawn Johnson	6.00
BRC12	Terry Glenn	4.00
BRC13	Zach Thomas	2.00
BRC14	Stephen Davis	4.00
BRC15	La'Roi Glover	2.00

2001 Bowman Chrome Draft Day Relics

		MT
Common Player:		10.00
JSY Inserted 1:131		
HAT Inserted 1:2129		
DH-LD	Leonard Davis HAT	10.00
DJ-LD	Leonard Davis JSY	10.00
DH-JS	Justin Smith HAT	25.00
DJ-JS	Justin Smith JSY	10.00
DH-DT	David Terrell HAT	50.00
DJ-DT	David Terrell JSY	25.00
DH-LT	LaDainian Tomlinson HAT	60.00
DJ-LT	LaDainian Tomlinson JSY	30.00
DH-MV	Michael Vick HAT	125.00
DJ-MV	Michael Vick JSY	50.00
DH-KW	Kenyatta Walker HAT	25.00
DJ-KW	Kenyatta Walker JSY	10.00

2001 Bowman Chrome Rookie Reprint

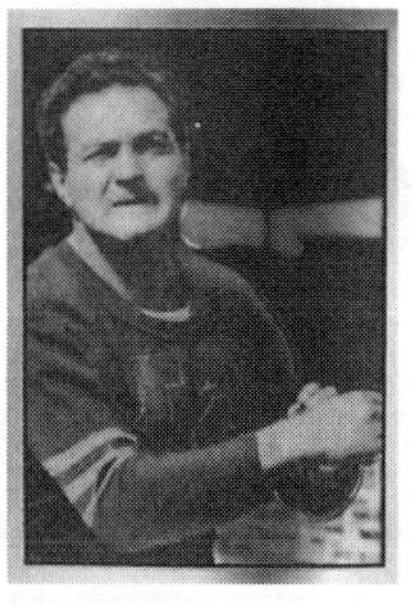

		MT
Common Player:		2.00
Inserted 1:24		
R-AA	Alan Ameche	4.00
R-SB	Sammy Baugh	6.00
R-CC	Charlie Conerly	2.00
R-AD	Art Donovan	4.00
R-TF	Tom Fears	2.00
R-FG	Frank Gifford	6.00
R-OG	Otto Graham	4.00
R-LG	Lou Groza	4.00
R-EH	Elroy Hirsch	6.00
R-BH	Bill Howton	2.00
R-SL	Sid Luckman	4.00
R-GM	Gino Marchetti	2.00
R-YT	Y.A. Tittle	6.00
R-ET	Emlen Tunnell	2.00
R-BT	Clyde "Bulldog" Turner	2.00
R-NV	Norm Van Brocklin	4.00

2001 Bowman Chrome Senior Bowl/Hula Bowl Relics

		MT
Common Player:		10.00
Inserted 1:78		
BCR-BA	Brian Allen	10.00
BCR-JB	Jeff Backus	10.00
BCR-DB	Drew Brees	30.00
BCR-DBU	Derrick Burgess	10.00
BCR-JC	Jarrod Cooper	10.00
BCR-TD	Tony Dixon	10.00
BCR-MF	Mario Fatafehi	10.00
BCR-RG	Reggie Germany	10.00
BCR-JH	Jamie Henderson	10.00
BCR-JH	Jabari Holloway	10.00
BCR-SH	Steve Hutchinson	10.00
BCR-JJ	Jonas Jennings	10.00
BCR-LJ	LaMont Jordan	15.00
BCR-BJ	Bhawoh Jue	10.00
BCR-KK	Kevin Kasper	15.00
BCR-ZM	Zeke Moreno	10.00
BCR-LM	Leonard Myers	10.00
BCR-JP	Jesse Palmer	15.00
BCR-SS	Steve Smith	12.00
BCR-TS	Tony Stewart	10.00
BCR-MS	Michael Stone	10.00
BCR-RW	Reggie Wayne	15.00
BCR-EW	Eric Westmoreland	10.00

1952 Bread For Health

These early 1950s bread end labels feature 32 NFL players. The cards, which measure 2-3/4" x 2-3/4", were found in loaves of Fisher's Bread (New Jersey, New York and Pennsylvania) and NBC Bread in Michigan. The cards are unnumbered and are blank-backed. A B.E.B. copyright is on the card front, along with an informational note.

		NM
Complete Set (32):		4300.
Common Player:		90.00
(1)	Frankie Albert	120.00
(2)	Elmer Angsman	90.00
(3)	Dick Barwegen	90.00
(4)	Sammy Baugh	350.00
(5)	Charley Conerly	200.00
(6)	Glenn Davis	150.00
(7)	Don Doll	90.00
(8)	Tom Fears	150.00
(9)	Harry Gilmer	100.00
(10)	Otto Graham	350.00
(11)	Pat Harder	110.00
(12)	Bobby Lane	300.00
(13)	Sid Luckman	200.00
(14)	Johnny Lujack	175.00
(15)	John Panelli	90.00
(16)	Barney Poole	90.00
(17)	George Ratterman	90.00
(18)	Tobin Rote	125.00
(19)	Jack Russell	90.00
(20)	Lou Rymkus	90.00
(21)	Joe Signiago	90.00
(22)	Mac Speedie	120.00
(23)	Bill Swiacki	90.00
(24)	Tommy Thompson	120.00
(25)	Y.A. Tittle	300.00
(26)	Clayton Tonnemaker	90.00
(27)	Charlie Trippi	110.00
(28)	Clyde Turner	150.00
(29)	Steve Van Buren	150.00
(30)	Bill Walsh	90.00
(31)	Bob Waterfield	200.00
(32)	Jim White	90.00

1992 Breyers Bookmarks

Breyers Bookmarks contained 66 bookmarks measuring 2" x 8". The set was used to promote reading in the city of 11 featured teams. Card fronts feature a cut-out of the player against a yellow background with books. Cards are numbered on the front and arranged in order by teams.

		MT
Complete Set (66):		150.00
Common Player:		1.50
1	Greg Townsend	1.50
2	Steve Wisniewski	1.50
3	Art Shell (CO)	2.50
4	Jeff Jaeger	1.50
5	Lisa O'Day (Cheerleader)	1.50
6	Los Angeles Raiders (Helmet and SB trophies)	1.50
7	Jerry Rice	12.00
8	Don Griffin	1.50
9	John Taylor	1.50
10	Joe Montana	18.00
11	Mike Walker	1.50
12	San Francisco 49ers (Helmet)	1.50
13	Junior Seau	3.00
14	John Friesz	1.50
15	Ronnie Harmon	1.50
16	Marion Butts	1.50
17	Gill Byrd	1.50
18	San Diego Chargers (Helmet)	1.50
19	Kelly Stouffer	1.50
20	John Kasay	1.50
21	Andy Heck	1.50
22	Jacob Green	1.50
23	Eugene Robinson	1.50
24	Seattle Seahawks (Helmet)	1.50
25	Pat Swilling	1.50
26	Vaughn Johnson	1.50
27	Bobby Hebert	1.50
28	Floyd Turner	1.50
29	Rickey Jackson	1.50
30	New Orleans Saints (Helmet)	1.50
31	Harvey Williams	1.50
32	Derrick Thomas	3.00
33	Bill Maas	1.50
34	Tim Grunhard	1.50
35	Jonathan Hayes	1.50
36	Kansas City Chiefs (Mascot)	1.50
37	Rich Gannon	1.50
38	Tim Irwin	1.50
39	Audray McMillian	1.50
40	Gary Zimmerman	1.50
41	Hassan Jones	1.50
42	Minnesota Vikings (Helmet)	1.50
43	Eric Green	1.50
44	Louis Lipps	1.50
45	Rod Woodson	1.50
46	Merril Hoge	1.50
47	Gary Anderson (RB)	1.50
48	Pittsburgh Steelers (60-Season Emblem)	1.50
49	Anthony Johnson	1.50
50	Bill Brooks	1.50
51	Jeff Herrod	1.50
52	Mike Prior	1.50
53	Jeff George	3.00
54	Indianapolis Colts (Ted Marchibroda) (CO)	1.50
55	Troy Aikman	12.00
56	Jay Novacek	1.50
57	Emmitt Smith	20.00
58	Michael Irvin	3.00
59	Dorie Braddy (Cheerleader)	1.50
60	Dallas Cowboys (Super Bowl trophy)	1.50
61	Clay Matthews	1.50
62	Tommy Vardell	1.50
63	Eric Turner	1.50
64	Mike Johnson	1.50
65	James Jones	1.50
66	Cleveland Browns (Helmet)	1.50

1990 British Petroleum

This 36-card set featured color fronts and black backs (with either contest rules or advertising). The cards were handed out two at a time in California, with the goal of the game to collect two adjacent numbers (1-2, 3-4). One of the two was difficult to find, with the contest expiring in October of 1991. There were also five instant win cards: Andre Tippett, Freeman McNeil, Clay Matthews, Tim Harris and Deion Sanders. Numbers 1, 3, 6, 8 and 10 had six different possible players.

		MT
Complete Set (36):		45.00
Common Player:		.50
1A	John Elway	3.00
1B	Boomer Esiason	.50
1C	Jim Everett	.50
1D	Bernie Kosar	.50
1E	Karl Mecklenburg	.50
1F	Bruce Smith	.50
2	Deion Sanders	
3A	Roger Craig	.50
3B	Randall Cunningham	.50
3C	Keith Jackson	.50
3D	Dan Marino	10.00
3E	Freddie Joe Nunn	.50
3F	Jerry Rice	5.00
3G	Vinny Testaverde	.50
3H	John L. Williams	.50
4	Tim Harris	
5	Clay Matthews	
6A	Neal Anderson	.50
6B	Duane Bickett	.50
6C	Ronnie Lott	.50
6D	Anthony Munoz	.50
6E	Christian Okoye	.50
6F	Barry Sanders	5.00
7	Freeman McNeil	
8A	Cornelius Bennett	.50
8B	Anthony Carter	.50
8C	Jim Kelly	1.00
8D	Louis Lipps	.50
8E	Phil Simms	.50
8F	Billy Ray Smith	.50
8G	Lawrence Taylor	1.00
9	Andre Tippett	
10A	Bo Jackson	1.50
10B	Howie Long	.50
10C	Don Majkowski	.50
10D	Art Monk	1.00
10E	Warren Moon	1.00
10F	Mike Singletary	1.00
10G	Al Toon	.50
10H	Herschel Walker	1.00
10I	Reggie White	1.50

1968-70 Broncos

This 53-card set contains black and white photos and black, unnumbered card backs. The cards measure 5" x 7" and include mostly posed shots.

		NM
Complete Set (53):		130.00
Common Player:		2.00
1	Bob Anderson	4.00
2	Tom Beer	4.00
3	Phil Brady	2.00
4	Sam Brunelli	3.00
5	George Burrell	2.00
6	Carter Campbell	2.00
7	Grady Cavness	3.00
8	Barney Chavous	6.00
9	Dave Costa	3.00
10	Ken Criter (Head shot)	2.00
11	Ken Criter (Head-and-shoulders)	2.00
12	Carl Cunningham	2.00
13	Mike Current (Left-side shot)	4.00
14	Mike Current (Right-side shot)	4.00
15	Joe Dawkins	4.00
16	Al Denson (Offensive end)	4.00
17	Al Denson (Wide receiver)	4.00
18	Wallace Dickey	2.00
19	John Embree	2.00
20	Fred Forsberg	2.00
21	Jack Gehrke	2.00
22	Cornell Gordon	3.00
23	John Grant	2.00
24	Charlie Greer (Head shot)	2.00
25	Charlie Greer (Head-and-shoulders)	2.00
26	Dwight Harrison	2.00
27	Walter Highsmith	2.00
28	Gus Hollomon	2.00
29	Larron Jackson (Left-side shot)	2.00
30	Larron Jackson (Right-side shot)	2.00
31	Calvin Jones	4.00
32	Larry Kaminski (Left-side shot)	2.00
33	Larry Kaminski (Right-side shot)	2.00
34	Bill Laskey	2.00
35	Pete Liske	4.00
36	Fran Lynch	2.00
37	Tom Lyons (Guard on front)	2.00
38	Tommy Lyons (Center on front)	2.00
39	Rex Mirich	2.00
40	Randy Montgomery (Left-side shot)	2.00
41	Randy Montgomery (Right-side shot)	2.00
42	Tom Oberg	2.00
43	Steve Ramsey	6.00
44	Frank Richter	2.00
45	Mike Schnitker	2.00
46	Roger Shoals	2.00
47	Jerry Simmons (Looking toward upper left corner of pict ure)	4.00
48	Jerry Simmons (Head turned slightly toward right)	4.00
49	Paul Smith (Head shot)	4.00
50	Paul Smith (Head-and-shoulders)	4.00
51	Olen Underwood	2.00
52	Dave Washington	2.00
53	Bob Young	2.00

1980 Broncos Stamps Police

This unnumbered set contains nine different stamps, with each stamp containing two players with a Broncos logo in between. The stamps were given away (one per week) at Albertson's food stores in the Denver area. The set measures 3" x 3" and is tri-sponsored by Albertson's, the Kiwanis Club and local police. There is a poster that the stamps fit on that sold at the time for 99 cents.

		NM
Complete Set (9):		12.00
Common Player:		1.00
1	Barney Chavous, Rubin Carter	1.00
2	Bernard Jackson, Haven Moses	1.00
3	Tom Jackson, Riley Odoms	3.00
4	Brison Manor, Steve Foley	1.00
5	Claudie Minor, Randy Gradishar	1.00
6	Craig Morton, Tom Glassic	2.00
7	Jim Turner, Bob Swenson	1.00
8	Rick Upchurch, Billy Thompson	1.00
9	Louis Wright, Joe Rizzo	1.00

1982 Broncos Police

Measuring 2-5/8" x 4-1/8", the 15-card set boasts the player's jersey number, name, position, team and Broncos' helmet under a photo. The unnumbered card backs feature Broncos Tips inside a box, which is topped by a Broncos' helmet. The set's sponsor is listed at the bottom center.

		MT
Complete Set (15):		150.00
Common Player:		2.00
7	Craig Morton	8.00
11	Luke Prestridge	2.00
20	Louis Wright	4.00
24	Rick Parros	2.00
36	Bill Thompson	4.00
41	Rob Lytle	2.00
46	Dave Preston (SP)	5.00
51	Bob Swenson	2.00
53	Randy Gradishar (SP)	45.00
57	Tom Jackson	12.00
60	Paul Howard	2.00
68	Rubin Carter	2.00
79	Barney Chavous (SP)	45.00
80	Rick Upchurch	8.00
88	Riley Odoms (SP)	12.00

1984 Broncos KOA

Handed out at Safeway or Dairy Queen stores, this 24-card set was part of the KOA Match 'N Win and KOA/Denver Broncos Silver Anniversary Sweepstakes. Measuring 2" x 4", with a bottom tab measuring 1-1/8", the card fronts showcase a black-and-white photo, with the player's name, number and position inside a banner under the photo. The American Football League and various sponsor logos appear under the photo. The card's tab featured three silver footballs that could be scratched off with a coin. The card backs feature the sweepstakes' rules. Besides the player's jersey number, the cards are unnumbered.

		MT
Complete Set (24):		90.00
Common Player:		1.00
7	Craig Morton	5.00
11	Bob Anderson (SP)	10.00
12	Charlie Johnson	4.00
15	Jim Turner	2.00
21	Gene Mingo	1.00
22	Fran Lynch	1.00
23	Goose Gonsoulin	2.00
24	Otis Armstrong	4.00
24	Willie Brown	6.00
25	Haven Moses	2.00
36	Billy Thompson	2.00
42	Bill Van Heusen	1.00
44	Floyd Little (SP)	16.00
53	Randy Gradishar (SP)	14.00
71	Claudie Minor (SP)	5.00
72	Sam Brunelli	1.00
74	Mike Current	1.00
75	Eldon Danenhauer	1.00
78	Marv Montgomery	1.00
81	Billy Masters	1.00
82	Bob Scarpitto	1.00
87	Lionel Taylor	2.00
87	Rich Jackson	1.00
88	Riley Odoms	2.00

1987 Broncos Orange Crush

This standard sized nine-card set honors former Denver Broncos players who are featured in the stadium's Ring of Fame. The card fronts feature a black-and-white photo bordered with blue and orange. The Orange Crush logo is on an angle at the top of the card front. The player's number, name, position and years played with the Broncos are printed underneath the photo. The Broncos' Ring of Fame logo is located at the bottom right. The backs feature "1st Annual Collector's Edition Ring of Famer" at the top, with his name, number, position, years played and highlights printed below. The info is packaged inside a box, with the Crush logo appearing at the bottom. The KOA Radio logo is printed at the very bottom of the card back. The cards were handed out for three weeks at 7-11 and Albertsons stores in the Denver area.

		MT
Complete Set (9):		4.50
Common Player:		.50
1	Billy Thompson	.50
2	Lionel Taylor	.50
3	Goose Gonsoulin	.50
4	Paul Smith	.50
5	Rich Jackson	.50
6	Charlie Johnson	.50
7	Floyd Little	.75
8	Frank Tripucka	.50
9	Gerald Phipps (Owner 1960-1981)	.50

1986 Brownell Heisman

Measuring 7-15/16" x 10", the black-and-white cards feature Art Brownell artwork of Heisman Trophy winners. The blank-backed cards are unnumbered. The cards are listed in chronological order. Even though Archie Griffin won the Heisman in both 1974 and 1975, he is featured on only one card. The fronts feature the year the player won the Heisman, plus a short write-up.

		MT
Complete Set (50):		250.00
Common Player:		5.00
1	Jay Berwanger	4.00
2	Larry Kelley	4.00
3	Clint Frank	4.00
4	Davey O'Brien	4.00
5	Niles Kinnick	10.00
6	Tom Harmon	5.00
7	Bruce Smith	4.00
8	Frank Sinkwich	4.00
9	Angelo Bertelli	4.00
10	Les Horvath	4.00
11	Doc Blanchard	8.00
12	Glenn Davis	8.00
13	Johnny Lujack	12.00
14	Doak Walker	10.00
15	Leon Hart	4.00
16	Vic Janowicz	10.00
17	Dick Kazmaier	4.00
18	Billy Vessels	4.00
19	John Lattner	8.00
20	Alan Ameche	6.00
21	Howard Cassady	5.00
22	Paul Hornung	18.00
23	John David Crow	4.00
24	Pete Dawkins	4.00
25	Billy Cannon	4.00
26	Joe Bellino	4.00
27	Ernie Davis	30.00
28	Terry Baker	4.00
29	Roger Staubach	35.00
30	John Huarte	4.00
31	Mike Garrett	4.00
32	Steve Spurrier	15.00
33	Gary Beban	4.00
34	O.J. Simpson	20.00
35	Steve Owens	5.00
36	Jim Plunkett	10.00
37	Pat Sullivan	4.00
38	Johnny Rodgers	4.00
39	John Cappelletti	4.00
40	Archie Griffin	6.00
41	Tony Dorsett	18.00
42	Earl Campbell	18.00
43	Billy Sims	8.00
44	Charles White	4.00
45	George Rogers	4.00
46	Marcus Allen	10.00
47	Herschel Walker	8.00
48	Mike Rozier	4.00
49	Doug Flutie	8.00
50	Bo Jackson	10.00

1946 Browns Sears

Measuring 2-1/2" x 4", the eight-card set was released by Sears and Roebuck. The set showcases players from the Cleveland Browns' initial season. Card fronts boast a black-and-white photo of the player and a slogan to follow the Browns and shop at Sears. The cards are unnumbered.

		NM
Complete Set (8):		280.00
Common Player:		35.00
(1)	Ernie Blandin	35.00
(2)	Jim Daniell	35.00
(3)	Fred Evans	35.00
(4)	Frank Gatski	50.00
(5)	Otto Graham	150.00
(6)	Dante Lavelli	75.00
(7)	Mel Maceau	35.00
(8)	George Young	35.00

1950 Browns Team Issue

Measuring 6-1/2" x 9", the five-card set showcases a black-and-white posed player photo, which is bordered in white. The player's name, printed in cursive, also is on the front of the blank-backed and unnumbered cards.

		NM
Complete Set (5):		75.00
Common Player:		10.00
1	Frank Gatski	15.00
2	Tommy James	10.00
3	Don Moselle	10.00
4	Marion Motley	30.00
5	Derrell F. Palmer	10.00

1951 Browns White Border

Measuring 6-1/2" x 9", the 25-card team-issued set was anchored by a posed black-and-white photo on the front, bordered in white. The player's name is printed in cursive on the front of the unnumbered and blank-backed cards. The set was housed in an off-white envelope with brown and orange trim. "Cleveland Browns Photographs" is also printed on the envelopes.

		NM
Complete Set (25):		250.00
Common Player:		5.00
1	Tony Adamle	8.00
2	Alex Agase	8.00
3	Rex Bumgardner	5.00
4	Emerson Cole	5.00
5	Len Ford	12.00
6	Frank Gatski	12.00
7	Horace Gillom	5.00
8	Ken Gorgal	5.00
9	Otto Graham	45.00
10	Forrest Gregg	5.00
11	Lou Groza	20.00
12	Hal Herring	5.00
13	Lin Houston	5.00
14	Weldon Humble	5.00
15	Tommy James	5.00
16	Dub Jones	8.00
17	Warren Lahr	5.00
18	Dante Lavelli	20.00
19	Cliff Lewis	5.00
20	Marion Motley	20.00
21	Lou Rymkus	8.00
22	Mac Speedie	10.00
23	Tommy Thompson	10.00
24	Bill Willis	15.00
25	George Young	15.00

1954-55 Browns White Border

Measuring 8-1/2" x 10", the 20-card set showcases posed player shots on the front, which are bordered in white. The unnumbered and blank-backed cards feature the player's name and position at the bottom inside a white border.

		NM
Complete Set (20):		125.00
Common Player:		5.00
1	Maurice Bassett	5.00
2	Harold Bradley	5.00
3	Darrell Brewster	5.00
4	Don Colo	5.00
5	Len Ford	10.00
6	Bob Gain	5.00
7	Frank Gatski	10.00
8	Abe Gibron	5.00
9	Tommy James	5.00
10	Dub Jones	7.00
11	Ken Konz	5.00
12	Warren Lahr	5.00
13	Dante Lavelli	15.00
14	Carlton Massey	5.00
15	Mike McCormack	10.00
16	Walt Michaels	5.00
17	Chuck Noll	25.00
18	Don Paul	5.00
19	Ray Renfro	10.00
20	George Ratterman	5.00

1955 Browns Carling Beer

Measuring 8-1/2" x 11-1/2", the 10-card set featured a large black-and-white photo on the front of the white-bordered cards. Carling's Black Label Beer and team name are printed below the photo in black. "DBL 54" is printed in the bottom right corner.

		NM
Complete Set (10):		200.00
Common Player:		10.00
1	Darrell Brewster	10.00
2	Tom Catlin	10.00
3	Len Ford	20.00
4	Otto Graham	45.00
5	Lou Groza	30.00
6	Kenny Konz	10.00
7	Dante Lavelli	25.00
8	Mike McCormack	20.00
9	Fred Morrison	10.00
10	Chuck Noll	45.00

1955 Browns Color Postcards

These six postcards, which measure 6" x 9", boast a full-bleed color photo on the front. The unnumbered backs have the player's name and team at the top left, with the "place stamp here" box in the upper left and "Giant Post Card" centered on

the right. The cards feature rounded corners.

		NM
Complete Set (6):		120.00
Common Player:		10.00
1	Mo Bassett	10.00
2	Don Colo	10.00
3	Frank Gatski	20.00
4	Lou Groza	45.00
5	Dante Lavelli	30.00
6	George Ratterman	15.00

1959 Browns Carling Beer

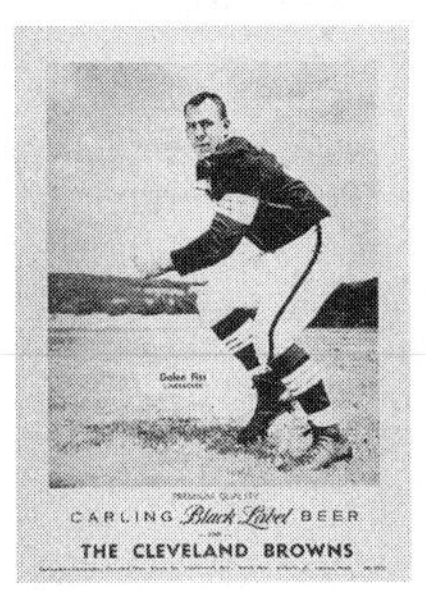

Measuring 8-1/2" x 11-1/2", the nine-card set featured a black-and-white posed photo, which was bordered in white. The player's name and position are printed in black inside a white rectangle inside the photo. Printed under the photo are "Carling Black Label Beer" and "The Cleveland Browns." The backs are usually blank, but can be stamped with "Henry M. Barr Studios, Berea, Ohio BE4-1330." The card fronts are numbered in the lower right corner, except for Jim Brown's photo card. The set was also reprinted in the late 1980s on thinner paper and most likely show the Henry M. Barr stamp on the back. Some sources say the Brown photo is only available in the reprint set.

		NM
Complete Set (9):		130.00
Common Player:		10.00
A	Leroy Bolden	10.00
B	Vince Costello	10.00
C	Galen Fiss	10.00
E	Lou Groza	30.00
F	Walt Michaels	15.00
G	Bobby Mitchell	30.00
J	Bob Gain	10.00
K	Billy Howton	15.00
NNO	Jim Brown (DP)	8.00

1961 Browns Carling Beer

Measuring 8-1/2" x 11-1/2", the 10 black-and-white cards feature posed photos on the front, with the player's name and position printed inside a white rectangle inside the photo. "Carling Back Label Beer" and "The Cleveland Browns" are printed underneath the photo on the card front. The card numbers appear in the lower right corner on the front, while the backs are blank.

		NM
Complete Set (10):		200.00
Common Player:		10.00
A	Milt Plum	20.00
B	Mike McCormack	20.00
C	Bob Gain	10.00
D	John Morrow	10.00
E	Jim Brown	80.00
F	Bobby Mitchell	35.00
G	Bobby Franklin	10.00
H	Jim Ray Smith	10.00
K	Jim Houston	18.00
L	Ray Renfro	15.00

1961 Browns National City Bank

Measuring 2-1/2" x 3-9/16", the 36-card set was released in sheets of six cards. Each sheet was numbered, while each individual card was numbered. The card fronts feature "Quarterback Club Brownie Card 1961 Cleveland Browns" at the top. The posed photos anchor the front, with "issued in 1961 by Cleveland's Oldest Bank National City Bank" printed underneath. The card backs are numbered at the top with a set number and a player (card) number. The player's name, position, bio and write-up are also on the back. The bottom of the card back includes the National City Bank logo.

		NM
Complete Set (36):		2000.
Common Player:		40.00
1	Mike McCormack	80.00
2	Jim Brown	575.00
3	Leon Clarke	40.00
4	Walt Michaels	40.00
5	Jim Ray Smith	40.00
6	Quarterback Club Membership Card	220.00
7	Len Dawson	225.00
8	John Morrow	40.00
9	Bernie Parrish	40.00
10	Floyd Peters	40.00
11	Paul Wiggin	40.00
12	John Wooten	40.00
13	Ray Renfro	40.00
14	Galen Fiss	40.00
15	Dave Lloyd	40.00
16	Dick Schafrath	40.00
17	Ross Fichtner	40.00
18	Gern Nagler	40.00
19	Rich Kreitling	40.00
20	Duane Putnam	40.00
21	Vince Costello	40.00
22	Jim Shofner	40.00
23	Sam Baker	40.00
24	Bob Gain	40.00
25	Lou Groza	100.00
26	Don Fleming	40.00
27	Tom Watkins	40.00
28	Jim Houston	40.00
29	Larry Stephens	40.00
30	Bobby Mitchell	100.00
31	Bobby Franklin	40.00
32	Charlie Ferguson	40.00
33	Johnny Brewer	40.00
34	Bob Crespino	40.00
35	Milt Plum	40.00
36	Preston Powell	40.00

1961 Browns White Border

Measuring 8-1/2" x 10-1/2", the 20-card set showcased black-and-white photos on the front, with the player's name and position listed inside a white box inside the photo. The fronts are bordered in white. The cards are unnumbered and blank-backed.

		NM
Complete Set (20):		160.00
Common Player:		5.00
1	Jim Brown	75.00
2	Galen Fiss	5.00
3	Don Fleming	5.00
4	Bobby Franklin	5.00
5	Bob Gain	5.00
6	Jim Houston	5.00
7	Rich Kreitling	5.00
8	Dave Lloyd	5.00
9	Mike McCormack	12.00
10	Bobby Mitchell	16.00
11	John Morrow	5.00
12	Bernie Parrish	5.00
13	Milt Plum	5.00
14	Ray Renfro	5.00
15	Dick Schafrath	5.00
16	Jim Shofner	5.00
17	Jim Ray Smith	5.00
18	Tom Watkins	5.00
19	Paul Wiggin	5.00
20	John Wooten	5.00

1963 Browns White Border

Measuring 7-1/2" x 9-1/2", the 26-card set showcases black-and-white photos on the front. The card backs are blank. Each card is unnumbered.

		NM
Complete Set (26):		120.00
Common Player:		5.00
1	Johnny Brewer	5.00
2	Monte Clark	5.00
3	Gary Collins	10.00
4	Vince Costello	5.00
5	Bob Crespino	5.00
6	Ross Fichtner	5.00
7	Galen Fiss	5.00
8	Bob Gain	5.00
9	Bill Glass	5.00
10	Ernie Green	10.00
11	Lou Groza	16.00
12	Gene Hickerson	7.00
13	Jim Houston	5.00
14	Tom Hutchinson	5.00
15	Rich Kreitling	5.00
16	Mike Lucci	5.00
17	John Morrow	5.00
18	Jim Ninowski	5.00
19	Frank Parker	5.00
20	Bernie Parrish	5.00
21	Ray Renfro	5.00
22	Dick Schafrath	5.00
23	Jim Shofner	5.00
24	Ken Webb	5.00
25	Paul Wiggin	5.00
26	John Wooten	5.00

1985 Browns Coke/Mr. Hero

Measuring 2-3/4" x 3-1/4", the 48-card set was released on six sheets of eight cards. The card fronts are anchored by a photo, with the player's name and position listed at the bottom center. The player's jersey number is printed in large numerals in the lower left. The unnumbered card backs spotlight the player's name, position, bio and career highlights. Coupons were included on each complete sheet.

		MT
Complete Set (48):		25.00
Common Player:		.50
7	Jeff Gossett (4)	.75
9	Matt Bahr (1)	.75
16	Paul McDonald (4)	.50
18	Gary Danielson (5)	.50
19	Bernie Kosar (6)	2.50
20	Don Rogers (4)	.50
22	Felix Wright (2)	.50
26	Greg Allen (3)	.50
27	Al Gross (2)	.50
29	Hanford Dixon (5)	.50
30	Boyce Green (1)	.50
31	Frank Minnifield (1)	.50
34	Kevin Mack (3)	1.00
37	Chris Rockins (1)	.50
38	Johnny Davis (5)	.50
44	Earnest Byner (2)	1.25
47	Larry Braziel (4)	.50
50	Tom Cousineau (6)	.50
51	Eddie Johnson (2)	.50
55	Curtis Weathers (1)	.50
56	Chip Banks (6)	.75
57	Clay Matthews (5)	1.75
58	Scott Nicolas (1)	.50
61	Mike Baab (4)	.50
62	George Lilja (5)	.50
63	Cody Risien (6)	.50
65	Mark Krerowicz (3)	.50
68	Robert Jackson (4)	.50
69	Dan Fike (2)	.50
72	Dave Puzzuoli (1)	.50
74	Paul Farren (2)	.50
77	Rickey Bolden (3)	.50
78	Carl Hairston (2)	.50
79	Bob Golic (6)	.50
80	Willis Adams (2)	.50
81	Harry Holt (3)	.50
82	Ozzie Newsome (3)	1.75
83	Fred Banks (3)	.50
84	Glen Young (1)	.50
85	Clarence Weathers (6)	.50
86	Brian Brennan (5)	.50
87	Travis Tucker (6)	.50
88	Reggie Langhorne (5)	.50
89	John Jefferson (4)	1.00
91	Sam Clancy (4)	.50
96	Reggie Camp (5)	.50
99	Keith Baldwin (6)	.50
NNO	Action Photo (Clay Matthews tackling Eric Dickerson, 3)	1.75

1987 Browns Louis Rich

Louis Rich produced this set to be a promotion in its products. After the cards were printed the promotion was pulled. After the set's cancellation, Oscar Mayer gave collectors who stopped into the Cleveland corporate office a set. The cards measure 5" x 7-1/8".

		MT
Complete Set (5):		45.00
Common Player:		5.00
1	Jim Brown, Bobby Mitchell	22.00
2	Otto Graham	15.00
3	Lou Groza	10.00
4	Dante Lavelli (Question Mark)	5.00
5	Marion Motley	5.00

1992 Browns Sunoco

NFL Properties produced this 24-card set as a promotion at Ohio-area Sunoco gas stations. Spotlighting Browns who have been inducted into the Hall of Fame, the player card fronts feature a full-bleed photo. The player's last name is printed in large orange letters at the bottom of the card, with a small Sunoco logo printed over the top of the name. The player card backs feature the player's career highlights and name printed over a ghosted image of the player. Logos for radio stations WMMS and WHK are printed at the bottom of the card backs. Player cards are numbered on the bottom right. The set was sold in three-card cello packs which included a cover card, player card and sweepstakes entry card. Randomly inserted in packs were autographed cards. The cover card fronts had "The Cleveland Browns' Collection" at the top, with a Browns' helmet at the center and the player's name underneath. The cover card backs showcase the sponsors' and Pro Football Hall of Fame logos. Cover card backs are not numbered. In addition, albums were issued to hold the set.

		MT
Complete Set (24):		16.00
Common Player (1-12):		.75
Common Cover (1C-12C):		.25
1	Otto Graham (Player card)	2.50
1C	Otto Graham (Cover card)	.25
2	Paul Brown (CO, Player card)	1.50
2C	Paul Brown (CO, Cover card)	.25
3	Marion Motley (Player card)	1.25
3C	Marion Motley (Cover card)	.25
4	Jim Brown (Player card)	4.00
4C	Jim Brown (Cover card)	.50
5	Lou Groza (Player card)	1.25
5C	Lou Groza (Cover card)	.25
6	Dante Lavelli (Player card)	1.00
6C	Dante Lavelli (Cover card)	.25
7	Len Ford (Player card)	1.00
7C	Len Ford (Cover card)	.25
8	Bill Willis (Player card)	1.00
8C	Bill Willis (Cover card)	.25
9	Bobby Mitchell (Player card)	1.50
9C	Bobby Mitchell (Cover card)	.25
10	Paul Warfield (Player card)	1.50
10C	Paul Warfield (Cover card)	.25
11	Mike McCormack (Player card)	1.00
11C	Mike McCormack (Cover card)	.25
12	Frank Gatski (Player card)	1.00
12C	Frank Gatski (Cover card)	.25

1980 Buccaneers Police

Measuring 2-5/8" x 4-1/8", the 56-card set boasts a photo on the front, with the player's name, position and bio underneath on the left. The Bucs' helmet is printed in the lower right. The unnumbered card backs have "Kids and Kops tips from the Buccaneers" at the top. A definition of a football term and a safety tip are included, while the Coca-Cola logo is printed above the various sponsor names at the bottom. Cards including the Paradyne Corp. name on the back are scarce variations, which are valued at two to three times more.

		NM
Complete Set (56):		150.00
Common Player:		3.00
1	Ricky Bell	8.00
2	Rick Berns	3.00
3	Tom Blanchard	3.00
4	Scot Brantley	3.00
5	Aaron Brown	3.00
6	Cedric Brown	3.00
7	Mark Cotney	3.00
8	Randy Crowder	3.00
9	Gary Davis	3.00
10	Johnny Davis	3.00
11	Tony Davis	3.00
12	Jerry Eckwood	5.00
13	Chuck Fusina	3.00
14	Jimmie Giles	5.00
15	Isaac Hagins	3.00
16	Charley Hannah	3.00
17	Andy Hawkins	3.00
18	Kevin House	3.00
19	Cecil Johnson	3.00
20	Gordon Jones	3.00
21	Curtis Jordan	3.00
22	Bill Kollar	3.00
23	Jim Leonard	3.00
24	David Lewis	3.00
25	Reggie Lewis	3.00
26	David Logan	3.00
27	Larry Mucker	3.00
28	Jim O'Bradovich	3.00
29	Mike Rae	3.00
30	Dave Reavis	3.00
31	Danny Reece	3.00
32	Greg Roberts	3.00
33	Gene Sanders	3.00
34	Dewey Selmon	3.00
35	Lee Roy Selmon	15.00
36	Ray Snell	3.00
37	Dave Stalls	3.00
38	Norris Thomas	3.00
39	Mike Washington	3.00
40	Doug Williams	10.00
41	Steve Wilson	3.00
42	Richard Wood	3.00
43	George Yarno	3.00
44	Garo Yepremian	6.00
45	Logo Card	3.00
46	Team Photo	5.00
47	Hugh Culverhouse (OWN)	3.00
48	John McKay (CO)	3.00
49	Mascot Capt. Crush	3.00
50	Cheerleaders: Swash-Buc-Lers	3.00
51	Swash-Buc-Lers (Buzz)	3.00
52	Swash-Buc-Lers (Check with me)	3.00
53	Swash-Buc-Lers (Gap Two)	3.00
54	Swash-Buc-Lers (Gas)	3.00
55	Swash-Buc-Lers (Pass Protection)	3.00
56	Swash-Buc-Lers (Post Pattern)	3.00

1982 Buccaneers Shell

Measuring 1-1/2" x 2-1/2", the 32-card set boasts a full-bleed color photo on the front, with a white stripe at the bottom which includes the Buccaneers' helmet on the left, the player's name in the center and Shell logo on the right. The card backs are blank and unnumbered.

		MT
Complete Set (32):		30.00
Common Player:		.50
1	Theo Bell	.75
2	Scot Brantley	.75
3	Cedric Brown	.50
4	Bill Capece	.50
5	Neal Colzie	.75
6	Mark Cotney	.50
7	Hugh Culverhouse	.75
8	Jeff Davis	.75
9	Jerry Eckwood	.75
10	Sean Farrell	.75
11	Jimmie Giles	1.00
12	Hugh Green	1.50
13	Charley Hannah	.50
14	Andy Hawkins	.50
15	John Holt	.50
16	Kevin House	1.00
17	Cecil Johnson	.50
18	Gordon Jones	.50
19	David Logan	.75
20	John McKay	1.50
21	James Owens	1.00
22	Greg Roberts	.50
23	Gene Sanders	.50
24	Lee Roy Selmon	4.00
25	Ray Snell	.50
26	Larry Swider	.50
27	Norris Thomas	.50
28	Mike Washington	.50
29	James Wilder	1.50
30	Doug Williams	2.00
31	Steve Wilson	.50
32	Richard Wood	1.00

1984 Buccaneers Police

Measuring 2-5/8" x 4-1/8", the 56-card set boasts a photo on the card front, with the player's name, position and bio on the bottom left. The Bucs' helmet is located in the lower right. The unnumbered card backs have "Kids and Kops tips from the Buccaneers" at the top, with a football term definition and safety tip below it. The various sponsors are listed at the bottom.

		MT
Complete Set (56):		65.00
Common Player:		1.00
1	Swash-Buc-Lers	2.00
2	Hugh Culverhouse (OWN)	1.75
3	John McKay (25 Years as Head Coach)	1.50
4	John McKay (CO)	1.50
5	Defensive Action	1.25
6	Fred Acorn	1.00
7	Obed Ariri	1.00
8	Adger Armstrong	1.00
9	Jerry Bell	1.00
10	Theo Bell	2.50
11	Byron Braggs	1.00
12	Scot Brantley	1.00
13	Cedric Brown	1.00
14	Keith Browner	1.50
15	John Cannon	1.00
16	Jay Carroll	1.00
17	Gerald Carter	1.00
18	Melvin Carter	1.00
19	Jeremiah Castille	1.50
20	Mark Cotney	1.00
21	Steve Courson	1.50
22	Jeff Davis	1.00
23	Steve DeBerg	5.00
24	Sean Farrell	1.75
25	Frank Garcia	1.00
26	Jimmie Giles	2.50
27	Hugh Green	3.00
28	Hugh Green (1A)	1.50
29	Randy Grimes	1.00
30	Ron Heller	1.50
31	John Holt	1.00
32	Kevin House	2.00
33	Noah Jackson	2.00
34	Cecil Johnson	1.00
35	Ken Kaplan	1.00
36	Blair Kiel	1.50
37	David Logan	1.50
38	Brison Manor	1.00
39	Michael Morton	1.00
40	James Owens	1.00
41	Beasley Reece	1.50
42	Gene Sanders	1.00
43	Lee Roy Selmon	5.00
44	Lee Roy Selmon (1A)	3.00
45	Danny Spradlin	1.00
46	Kelly Thomas	1.00
47	Norris Thomas	1.00
48	Jack Thompson	1.50
49	Perry Tuttle	1.00
50	Chris Washington	1.00
51	Mike Washington	1.00
52	James Wilder	2.50
53	James Wilder (1A)	1.25
54	Steve Wilson	1.00
44	Mark White	1.00
56	Richard Wood	1.50

1989 Buccaneers Police

Measuring 2-5/8" x 4-1/8", the 10-card set showcases a color action photo at the top, with the player's name, position and team, along with the Bucs' helmet printed inside a box under the photo. The card backs have the Polk County Sheriff's name at the top, with the card number underneath. Located in the center of the card back are the player's name, number, bio, highlights and stats. A safety tip and IMC Fertilizer are listed at the bottom of the card back.

		MT
Complete Set (10):		20.00
Common Player:		1.50
1	Vinny Testaverde	6.00
2	Mark Carrier (WR)	4.00
3	Randy Grimes	1.50
4	Paul Gruber	3.00
5	Ron Hall	2.00
6	William Howard	1.50
7	Curt Jarvis	1.50
8	Ervin Randle	1.50
9	Ricky Reynolds	1.50
10	Rob Taylor	1.50

1976 Buckmans Discs

Measuring 3-3/8 inches in diameter, the 20-disc set features a black-and-white headshot of the player on the front, with four stars printed at the top. The player's name is printed on the right side of the photo, with his team name on the left. His position is printed under the photo. A colored border surrounds the disc, except where the stars are at the top. Printed inside the border are the player's bio and "National Football League Players 1976." The unnumbered disc backs have "A collectors and traders item" at the top, with Buckmans and its address and phone number underneath.

		NM
Complete Set (20):		45.00
Common Player:		.50
1	Otis Armstrong	1.00
2	Steve Bartkowski	1.00
3	Terry Bradshaw	10.00
4	Doug Buffone	.50
5	Wally Chambers	.50
6	Chuck Foreman	1.00
7	Roman Gabriel	1.00
8	Mel Gray	1.00
9	Franco Harris	7.00
10	James Harris	1.00
11	Jim Hart	1.00
12	Gary Huff	.50
13	Billy Kilmer	1.00
14	Terry Metcalf	1.00
15	Jim Otis	.50
16	Jim Plunkett	1.50
17	Greg Pruitt	.50
18	Roger Staubach	10.00
19	Jan Stenerud	1.00
20	Roger Wehrli	.50

C

1960 Cardinals Mayrose Franks

Measuring 2-1/2" x 3-1/2", the 11-card set showcases a black-and-white photo printed over a red background. A box in the upper left includes the Cardinals' logo and card number. The player's name, position and bio are printed under the photo. The card backs describe the Mayrose Franks football contest. The cards are coated in plastic because they were inserted in hot dog and bacon packages. The cards feature rounded corners.

		NM
Complete Set (11):		100.00
Common Player:		8.00
1	Don Gillis	8.00
2	Frank Fuller	8.00
3	George Izo	10.00
4	Woodley Lewis	8.00
5	King Hill	12.00
6	John David Crow	16.00
7	Bill Stacy	8.00
8	Ted Bates	8.00
9	Mike McGee	8.00
10	Bobby Joe Conrad	12.00
11	Ken Panfil	8.00

1961 Cardinals Jay Publishing

Measuring 5" x 7", the 12-card set spotlights posed black-and-white photos on the front, while the backs were blank and unnumbered. The set was sold in 12-card packs for 25 cents in 1961.

		NM
Complete Set (12):		50.00
Common Player:		5.00
1	Joe Childress	5.00
2	Sam Etcheverry	5.00
3	Ed Henke	5.00
4	Jimmy Hill	5.00
5	Bill Koman	5.00
6	Roland McDole	5.00
7	Mike McGee	5.00
8	Dale Meinert	5.00
9	Jerry Norton	5.00
10	Sonny Randle	5.00
11	Joe Robb	5.00
12	Billy Stacy	5.00

1965 Cardinals Big Red Biographies

Half-gallon milk cartons from St. Louis' Adams Dairy featured these biographies on side panels. When cut from the carton, the panels measure 3-1/16" x 5-9/16". The panels spotlight "Big Red Biographies" in the upper left, with the Cardinals' logo in the upper right. The player's photo is printed on the left center, with his name, number, position and bio listed on the right. His highlights are printed under the photo. "Enjoy Cardinal Football get your tickets now!" and the team's address are printed at the bottom. The card backs are blank.

		NM
Complete Set (17):		1000.
Common Player:		50.00
1	Monk Bailey	50.00
2	Jim Bakken	100.00
3	Jim Burson	50.00
4	Willis Crenshaw	50.00
5	Bob DeMarco	50.00
6	Pat Fischer	100.00
7	Billy Gambrell	50.00
8	Ken Gray	75.00
9	Irv Goode	50.00
10	Mike Melinkovich	50.00
11	Bob Reynolds	50.00
12	Marion Rushing	50.00
13	Carl Silvestri	50.00
14	Dave Simmons	50.00
15	Jackie Smith	150.00
16	Bill (Thunder) Thornton	50.00
17	Herschel Turner	50.00

1965 Cardinals Team Issue

Measuring 7-3/8" x 9-3/8", the 10-card set is anchored by a black-and-white photo inside a white border on the front. The player's name, position and team are listed in the white border at the bottom. The unnumbered backs are also blank.

		NM
Complete Set (10):		40.00
Common Player:		4.00
1	Don Brumm	4.00
2	Bobby Joe Conrad	5.00
3	Bob DeMarco	4.00
4	Charley Johnson	7.00
5	Ernie McMillan	5.00
6	Dale Meinert	4.00
7	Luke Owens	4.00
8	Sonny Randle	4.00
9	Joe Robb	4.00
10	Jerry Stovall	4.00

1980 Cardinals Police

Measuring 2-5/8" x 4-1/8", the 15-card set showcases the player's name, jersey number, position, bio and team name under the photo. The Cardinals' helmet is printed in the lower left. The card backs feature Cardinal Tips inside a box, with the Cards' helmet at the top of it. The various sponsors are listed, along with their logos, at the bottom of the unnumbered card backs.

		NM
Complete Set (15):		16.00
Common Player:		.75
17	Jim Hart	2.00
22	Roger Wehrli	1.00
24	Wayne Morris	.75
32	Ottis Anderson	2.00
33	Theotis Brown	.75
37	Kevin Green	.75
55	Eric Williams	.75
56	Tim Kearney	.75
59	Calvin Favron	.75
68	Terry Stieve	.75
72	Dan Dierdorf	2.50
73	Mike Dawson	.75
82	Bob Pollard	.75
83	Pat Tilley	1.50
85	Mel Gray	2.00

1988 Cardinals Holsum

The standard sized 12-card set showcases the Holsum logo in the upper left, with "1988 Annual Collectors' Edition" in the upper right. The color headshot anchors the front, with the player's name and team listed in a box at the bottom. The backs have the player's facsimile autograph at the top, along with his jersey number, bio and card number. His stats are listed in the center. The NFLPA, MSA and Holsum logos are printed at the bottom of the card backs.

		MT
Complete Set (12):		50.00
Common Player:		4.00
1	Roy Green	7.00
2	Stump Mitchell	6.00
3	J.T. Smith	5.00
4	E.J. Junior	5.00
5	Cedric Mack	4.00
6	Curtis Greer	4.00
7	Lonnie Young	4.00
8	David Galloway	4.00
9	Luis Sharpe	4.00
10	Leonard Smith	4.00
11	Ron Wolfley	4.00
12	Earl Ferrell	4.00

1989 Cardinals Holsum

The standard-sized 16-card set showcases the Holsum logo in the upper left, with "1989 Annual Collectors' Edition" in the upper right. The player's name and team are printed inside a stripe underneath the photo. The card backs have the player's name, jersey number, card number, position and bio at the top. His stats are listed in the center, while the NFLPA logo is in the lower left.

		MT
Complete Set (16):		6.00
Common Player:		.25
1	Roy Green	1.00
2	J.T. Smith	.50
3	Neil Lomax	1.00
4	Stump Mitchell	.50
5	Vai Sikahema	.25
6	Lonnie Young	.25
7	Robert Awalt	.25
8	Cedric Mack	.25
9	Earl Ferrell	.25
10	Ron Wolfley	.25
11	Bob Clasby	.25
12	Luis Sharpe	.25
13	Steve Alvord	.25
14	David Galloway	.25
15	Freddie Joe Nunn	.25
16	Niko Noga	.25

1989 Cardinals Police

Measuring 2-5/8" x 4-3/16", the 15-card set has a photo bordered in white. The player's name and position are printed under the photo on the left, with his jersey number on the right. The bottom of the card front features the Phoenix Cardinals' logo. The unnumbered card backs feature the Cardinals' logo at the top, with his jersey number, name, position, bio and career highlights listed. The Cardinals rule is printed inside a box. The KTSP-TV and Louis Rich logos also appear at the bottom. The cards are listed here by uniform number. Two cards were distributed each week. Overall, 100,000 of each card was produced.

		MT
Complete Set (15):		25.00
Common Player:		1.00
5	Gary Hogeboom	1.25
24	Ron Wolfley	1.00
30	Stump Mitchell	1.25
31	Earl Ferrell	1.00
36	Vai Sikahema	1.00
43	Lonnie Young	1.00
46	Tim McDonald	1.50
65	David Galloway	1.00
67	Luis Sharpe	1.00
70	Derek Kennard (SP)	10.00
79	Bob Clasby	1.00
80	Robert Awalt	1.00
81	Roy Green	1.50
84	J.T. Smith	1.25
85	Jay Novacek	5.00

1990 Cardinals Police

Measuring 2-5/8" x 4-1/4", the 16-card set is bordered in maroon, with the Cardinals' logo in the upper left and NFL shield in upper right. Underneath the photo are the player's name, position and jersey number. The unnumbered card backs feature the Phoenix Cardinals' logo at the top, with the player's number, name, position, bio highlights underneath. The center of the card back has the Cardinal Rule in a box. KTSP, McGruff the Crime Dog and Louis Rich logos are printed at the bottom.

		MT
Complete Set (16):		10.00
Common Player:		.25
1	Anthony Bell	.25
2	Joe Bugel (CO)	.50
3	Rich Camarillo	.25
4	Roy Green	1.25
5	Ken Harvey	1.00
6	Eric Hill	1.25
7	Tim McDonald	.50
8	Tootie Robbins	.25
9	Timm Rosenbach	.75
10	Luis Sharpe	.50
11	Vai Sikahema	.50
12	J.T. Smith	.75
13	Lance Smith	.25
14	Jim Wahler	.25
15	Ron Wolfley	.25
16	Lonnie Young	.25

1992 Cardinals Police

The standard-sized 16-card set features a photo on the front that is bordered on the left by a stripe that changes from red to yellow. The NFL shield is in the upper left of the photo, with the player's jersey number and position on a scoreboard in the lower left. The Phoenix Cardinals logo and player name and number are printed in red and white, respectively, at the bottom right of the photo. The unnumbered card backs have the player's name, jersey number and position at the top, with his bio printed under a stripe. The Cards' logo is ghosted in the center. A red box at the bottom of the card includes a safety tip and sponsor logos.

		MT
Complete Set (16):		12.00
Common Player:		.50
1	Joe Bugel (CO)	.75
2	Rich Camarillo	.50
3	Ed Cunningham	.50
4	Greg Davis	.75
5	Ken Harvey	.75
6	Randal Hill	1.50
7	Ernie Jones	.50
8	Mike Jones	.50
9	Tim McDonald	1.00
10	Freddie Joe Nunn	.50
11	Ricky Proehl	1.00
12	Timm Rosenbach	.75
13	Tony Sacca	.75
14	Lance Smith	.50
15	Eric Swann	1.50
16	Aeneas Williams	1.00

1994 Cardinals Police

Collectors believe this set only contains four cards. The card fronts have a maroon and orange border, with a color photo, player name and number. The card backs are unnumbered and carry the player's name, number and bio.

		MT
Complete Set (4):		12.00
Common Player:		3.00
1	Greg Davis	3.00
2	Anthony Edwards	3.00
3	Terry Hoage	3.00
4	Aeneas Williams	4.00

1989 CBS Television Announcers

Measuring 2-3/4" x 3-7/8", this 10-card set showcases the 1989 CBS NFL announcers. The card fronts spotlight a color action shot from the announcer's pro career. The photo is bordered in orange and placed over a green and white football field. "Going the extra yard" is printed in red at the top. "NFL on CBS" is located in the bottom right. The horizontal card backs feature a black-and-white head shot of the announcer, with his bio and highlights bordered in red. Approximately 500 sets, which were divided into two five-card series, were given to CBS affiliates.

		MT
Complete Set (10):		250.00
Common Player:		10.00
1	Terry Bradshaw	50.00
2	Dick Butkus	45.00
3	Irv Cross	10.00
4	Dan Fouts	25.00
5	Pat Summerall	15.00
6	Gary Fencik	10.00
7	Dan Jiggetts	10.00
8	John Madden	45.00
9	Ken Stabler	35.00
10	Hank Stram	15.00

A card number in parentheses ( ) indicates the set is unnumbered.

1961 Chargers Golden Tulip

The 22-card, 2" x 3" set was found in bags of Golden Tulip potato chips. The cards featured top players from the San Diego Chargers in black and white with brief bio information also on the card fronts. The back explains how to upgrade to an 8" x 10" photo and win tickets to a Chargers home game. The set was also sponsored by XETV, an independent television station in San Diego.

		NM
Complete Set (22):		1500.
Common Player:		40.00
1	Ron Botchan	40.00
2	Howard Clark	40.00
3	Fred Cole	40.00
4	Sam DeLuca	40.00
5	Orlando Ferrante	40.00
6	Charlie Flowers	40.00
7	Dick Harris	40.00
8	Emil Karas	40.00
9	Jack Kemp	550.00
10	Dave Kocourek	40.00
11	Bob Laraba	40.00
12	Paul Lowe	60.00
13	Paul Maguire	70.00
14	Charlie McNeil	40.00
15	Ron Mix	100.00
16	Ron Nery	40.00
17	Don Norton	40.00
18	Volney Peters	40.00
19	Don Rogers	40.00
20	Maury Schleicher	40.00
21	Ernie Wright	40.00
22	Bob Zeman	40.00

1962 Chargers Union Oil

The 14-card, 6" x 8" set, sponsored by Union 76, features black and white player sketches by the artist, "Patrick." The card backs include a player bio and the Union 76 logo.

		NM
Complete Set (14):		450.00
Common Player:		8.00
1	Chuck Allen	10.00
2	Lance Alworth	100.00
3	John Hadl	30.00
4	Dick Harris	10.00
5	Bill Hudson	8.00
6	Jack Kemp	225.00
7	Dave Kocourek	10.00
8	Ernie Ladd	25.00
9	Keith Lincoln	18.00
10	Paul Lowe	18.00
11	Charlie McNeil	10.00
12	Ron Mix	25.00
13	Ron Nery	8.00
14	Team Photo	25.00

1966 Chargers White Border

The 50-card, 5-1/2" x 8-1/2" set was issued by the team and features black and white headshots of top players, such as Lance Alworth, with facsimile autographs. With the exception of card No. 16 (George Gross), the card backs are blank.

		NM
Complete Set (50):		225.00
Common Player:		3.00
1	Chuck Allen	5.00
2	James Allison	3.00
3	Lance Alworth	30.00
4	Tom Bass	3.00
5	Joe Beauchamp	3.00
6	Frank Buncom	5.00
7	Richard Degen	3.00
8	Steve DeLong	5.00
9	Les Duncan	3.00
10	John Farris	3.00
11	Gene Foster	3.00
12	Willie Frazier	5.00
13	Gary Garrison	5.00
14	Sid Gillman (CO)	10.00
15	Kenny Graham	3.00
16	George Gross	3.00
17	Sam Gruineisen	3.00
18	Walt Hackett (CO)	3.00
19	John Hadl	15.00
20	Dick Harris	5.00
21	Dan Henning	10.00
22	Bob Horton	3.00
23	Harry Johnston (CO)	3.00
24	Howard Kindig	3.00
25	Keith Lincoln	5.00
26	Paul Lowe	5.00
27	Jacque MacKinnon	3.00
28	Joseph Madro (CO)	3.00
29	Ed Mitchell	3.00
30	Bob Mitinger	3.00
31	Ron Mix	10.00
32	Fred Moore	3.00
33	Don Norton	3.00
34	Terry Owen	5.00
35	Bob Petrich	3.00
36	Dave Plump	3.00
37	Rick Redman	3.00
38	Houston Ridge	3.00
39	Pat Shea	3.00
40	Walt Sweeney	5.00
41	Sammy Taylor	3.00
42	Steve Tensi	3.00
43	Herb Travenio	3.00
44	John Travis	3.00
45	Dick Van Raaphorst	3.00
46	Charlie Waller (CO)	3.00
47	Bud Whitehead	3.00
48	Nat Whitmyer	3.00
49	Ernie Wright	3.00
50	Bob Zeman	3.00

A player's name in *italic type* indicates a rookie card.

1976 Chargers Dean's Photo

The 10-card, 5" x 8" set was sponsored by Dean's Photo Service and featured top Chargers players such as Dan Fouts and Joe Washington. The card fronts are black and white while the Chargers helmet in the lower left corner is in color. The backs are blank.

		NM
Complete Set (10):		28.00
Common Player:		2.00
1	Pat Curran	2.00
2	Chris Fletcher	2.00
3	Dan Fouts	12.00
4	Gary Garrison	2.00
5	Louie Kelcher	3.00
6	Joe Washington	3.00
7	Russ Washington	2.00
8	Doug Wilkerson	2.00
9	Don Woods	2.00
10	Schedule Card	2.00

1981 Chargers Police

The 24-card, 2-5/8" x 4-1/8" set was sponsored by San Diego law enforcement, Pepsi and Kiwanis. The card fronts feature an action shot with the player's name and position, along with the Chargers team logo. The backs contain a law enforcement tip. The Fouts and Winslow cards have two versions with different safety tips. The cards are numbered by the player's jersey number.

		MT
Complete Set (24):		50.00
Common Player:		1.00
6	Rolf Benirschke	2.00
14A	Dan Fouts (After a team...)	14.00
14B	Dan Fouts (Once you've...)	7.00
18	Charlie Joiner	4.00
25	John Cappelletti	2.00
28	Willie Buchanon	1.00
29	Mike Williams	1.00
43	Bob Gregor	1.00
44	Pete Shaw	1.00
46	Chuck Muncie	2.00
51	Woodrow Lowe	1.00
57	Linden King	1.00
59	Cliff Thrift	1.00
62	Don Macek	1.00
63	Doug Wilkerson	1.00
66	Billy Shields	1.00
67	Ed White	1.00
68	Leroy Jones	1.00
70	Russ Washington	1.00
74	Louie Kelcher	1.00
79	Gary Johnson	1.00
80A	Kellen Winslow (Go all out...)	14.00
80B	Kellen Winslow (The length of ...)	7.00
NNO	Don Coryell (CO)	2.00

1982 Chargers Police

The 16-card, 2-5/8" x 4-1/8" set is nearly identical in design with the 1981 Chargers Police set. The card fronts feature a Chargers player with his postion and San Diego helmet. The backs contain a law enforcement tip and are sponsored by San Diego law enforcement, Pepsi and Kiwanis.

		MT
Complete Set (16):		45.00
Common Player:		2.00
1	Rolf Benirschke	2.00
2	James Brooks	4.00
3	Wes Chandler	5.00
4	Dan Fouts	10.00
5	Tim Fox	2.00
6	Gary Johnson	2.00
7	Charlie Joiner	8.00
8	Louie Kelcher	2.00
9	Linden King	2.00
10	Bruce Laird	2.00
11	David Lewis	2.00
12	Don Macek	2.00
13	Billy Shields	2.00
14	Eric Sievers	2.00
15	Russ Washington	2.00
16	Kellen Winslow	10.00

1985 Chargers Kodak

The 15-card, 5-1/2" x 8-1/2" set, sponsored by Kodak, features color action shots and San Diego helmet in the lower left corner. The backs contain bio information.

		MT
Complete Set (15):		40.00
Common Player:		2.00
1	Carlos Bradley	2.00
2	Wes Chandler	6.00
3	Chuck Ehin	2.00
4	Mike Green	2.00
5	Pete Holohan	2.00
6	Lionel James	2.00
7	Charlie Joiner	12.00
8	Woodrow Lowe	2.00
9	Dennis McKnight	2.00
10	Miles McPherson	2.00
11	Derrie Nelson	2.00
12	Vince Osby	2.00
13	Billy Ray Smith	2.00
14	Danny Walters	2.00
15	Ed White	2.00

1986 Chargers Kodak

The 36-card, 5-1/2" x 8-1/2" set are similar to the 1985 Kodak Chargers cards, but have blank backs. The bio information is featured on the card fronts below the player's name and between the Chargers helmet and the Kodak logo.

		MT
Complete Set (36):		45.00
Common Player:		1.00
1	Curtis Adams	1.00
2	Gary Anderson (RB)	3.00
3	Jesse Bendross	1.00
4	Gill Byrd	1.00
5	Sam Claphan	1.00
6	Don Coryell (CO)	2.00
7	Jeffery Dale	1.00
8	Wayne Davis	1.00
9	Jerry Doerger	1.00
10	Chris Faulkner	1.00
11	Mark Fellows	1.00
12	Dan Fouts	8.00
13	Mike Guendling	1.00
14	John Hendy	1.00
15	Mark Hermann	1.00
16	Lionel James	1.00
17	Trumaine Johnson	1.00
18	David King	1.00
19	Linden King	1.00
20	Jim Lachey	2.00
21	Don Macek	1.00
22	Buford McGee	1.00
23	Dennis McKnight	1.00
24	Ralf Mojsiejenko	1.00
25	Ron O'Bard	1.00
26	Fred Robinson	1.00
27	Eric Sievers	1.00
28	Tony Simmons	1.00
29	Billy Ray Smith	1.00
30	Lucious Smith	1.00
31	Alex G. Spanos (PRES)	1.00
32	Tim Spencer	1.00
33	Rich Umphrey	1.00
34	Ed White	1.00
35	Lee Williams	1.00
36	Earl Wilson	1.00

1987 Chargers Junior Coke Tickets

The 12-card, 1-7/8" x 4-1/4" set was issued to members of the Coca-Cola Junior Chargers. The cards are in the form of a ticket, which was exchanged by members for actual game tickets. The card fronts included a color action photo, and had imitation ticket information, such as section, row and seat number. The card backs contain a Chargers logo and a description of how to exchange the coupon for a real ticket.

		MT
Complete Set (12):		12.00
Common Player:		1.00
1	Gary Anderson (RB)	1.50
2	Rolf Benirschke	1.00
3	Wes Chandler	1.75
4	Jeffery Dale	1.00
5	Dan Fouts	3.00
6	Pete Holohan	1.00
7	Lionel James	1.00
8	Don Macek	1.00
9	Dennis McKnight	1.00
10	Al Saunders (CO)	1.00
11	Billy Ray Smith	1.00
12	Kellen Winslow	3.00

1987 Chargers Police

The 21-card, 2-5/8" x 4-1/8" set, sponsored by the Chargers, Oscar Meyer and San Diego law enforcement, features top players from the 1987 Chargers squad. Even though the cards are numbered, there was no card No. 13 issued and card Nos. 3 and 17 were pulled during distribution. The card fronts feature an action shot and bio information while the backs have a brief player description with a safety tip.

		MT
Complete Set (22):		20.00
Common Player:		.75
1	Alex G. Spanos (OWN)	.75
2	Gary Anderson (RB)	1.00
3	Rolf Benirschke (SP)	5.00
4	Gill Byrd	.75
5	Wes Chandler	1.50
6	Sam Claphan	.75
7	Jeffery Dale	.75
8	Pete Holohan	.75
9	Lionel James	.75
10	Jim Lachey	.75
11	Woodrow Lowe	.75
12	Don Macek	.75
14	Dan Fouts	3.50
15	Eric Sievers	.75
16	Billy Ray Smith	.75
17	Danny Walters (SP)	4.00
18	Lee Williams	.75
19	Kellen Winslow	2.50
20	Al Saunders (CO)	.75
21	Dennis McKnight	.75
22	Chip Banks	.75

1987 Chargers Smokey

The 48-card, 5-1/2" x 8-1/2" sets were issued by the California Forestry Department and fronted color action shots. The card backs contain a safety tip cartoon with Smokey The Bear. Coach Don Coryell's card was pulled after the initial distribution after he was replaced. Also, the cards of Donald Brown, Mike Douglass and Fred Robinson were pulled after they were cut.

		MT
Complete Set (48):		100.00
Common Player:		1.00
Common SP:		8.00
1	Curtis Adams	1.00
2	Ty Allert	1.00
3	Gary Anderson (RB)	2.50
4	Rolf Benirschke	2.00
5	Thomas Benson	1.00
6	Donald Brown (SP)	8.00
7	Gill Byrd	1.50
8	Wes Chandler	4.00
9	Sam Claphan	1.00
10	Don Coryell (CO, SP)	10.00
11	Jeffery Dale	1.00
12	Wayne Davis	1.00
13	Mike Douglass (SP)	8.00
14	Chuck Ehin	1.00
15	James Fitzpatrick	1.00
16	Tom Flick	1.00
17	Dan Fouts	12.00
18	Dee Hardison	1.00
19	Andy Hawkins	1.00
20	John Hendy	1.00
21	Mark Hermann	1.00
22	Pete Holohan	1.00
23	Lionel James	1.50
24	Trumaine Johnson	1.00
25	Charlie Joiner	8.00
26	Gary Kowalski	1.00
27	Jim Lachey	1.50
28	Jim Leonard	1.00
29	Woodrow Lowe	1.00
30	Don Macek	1.00
31	Buford McGee	1.00
32	Dennis McKnight	1.00
33	Ralf Mojsiejenko	1.00
34	Derrie Nelson	1.00
35	Leslie O'Neal	5.00
36	Gary Plummer	1.50
37	Fred Robinson (SP)	8.00
38	Eric Sievers	1.00
39	Billy Ray Smith	1.50
40	Tim Spencer	1.50
41	Kenny Taylor	1.00
42	Terry Unrein	1.00
43	Jeff Walker	1.00
44	Danny Walters	1.00
45	Lee Williams	1.50
46	Earl Wilson	1.00
47	Kellen Winslow	8.00
48	Kevin Wyatt	1.00

1988 Chargers Police

The 12-card, 2-5/8" x 4" set features white and blue borders with color action shots. The card backs have career highlights and safety tips.

		MT
Complete Set (12):		12.00
Common Player:		.50
1	Gary Anderson (RB)	.75
2	Rod Bernstine	1.00
3	Gill Byrd	.75
4	Vencie Glenn	.75
5	Lionel James	.75
6	Babe Laufenberg	.75
7	Don Macek	.50
8	Mark Malone	1.00
9	Dennis McKnight	.50
10	Anthony Miller	5.00
11	Billy Ray Smith	.75
12	Lee Williams	.75

1988 Chargers Smokey

The 52-card, 5" x 8" set features color action shots on the card fronts and a forestry safety tip, along with a Smokey The Bear cartoon on the back. Two Alex Spanos cards exist, one stating incorrectly that he purchased the Chargers in 1987, and one stating the correct 1984. Also, 18 of the cards were short printed (Nos. 9, 23, 27, 36, 55, 56, 57, 74, 77, 78, 79, 81, 88, 89, 92, 96 and 98) as some of the players were cut, traded or put on injured reserve.

		MT
Complete Set (52):		45.00
Common Player:		.50
2	Ralf Mojsiejenko	.50
9	Mark Hermann (SP)	1.50
10	Vince Abbott	.50
13	Mark Vlasic	.50
14	Dan Fouts	4.00
20	Barry Redden	.50
22	Gill Byrd	.75
23	Danny Walters (SP)	1.50
25	Vencie Glenn	.50
26	Lionel James	.75
27	Daniel Hunter (SP)	1.50
34	Elvis Patterson	.50
36	Mike Davis (SP)	1.50
40	Gary Anderson (RB)	.75
42	Curtis Adams	.50
43	Tim Spencer	.50
44	Martin Bayless	.50
50	Gary Plummer	.50
52	Jeff Jackson	.50
54	Billy Ray Smith	.50
55	Steve Busick (SP)	1.50
56	Chip Banks (SP)	2.00
57	Thomas Benson (SP)	1.50
58	David Brandon	.50
60	Dennis McKnight	.50
61	Ken Dallafior	.50
62	Don Macek	.50
68	Gary Kowalski	.50
69	Les Miller	.50
70	James Fitzpatrick	.50
71	Mike Charles	.50
72	Karl Wilson	.50
74	Jim Lachey (SP)	2.00
75	Joe Phillips	.50
76	Broderick Thompson	.50
77	Sam Claphan (SP)	1.50
78	Chuck Ehin (SP)	1.50
79	Curtis Rouse (SP)	1.50
80	Kellen Winslow	4.00
81	Timmie Ware (SP)	1.50
82	Rod Bernstine	.75
85	Eric Sievers	.50
86	Jamie Holland	.50
88	Pete Holohan (SP)	1.50
89	Wes Chandler (SP)	4.00
92	Dee Hardison (SP)	1.50
94	Randy Kirk	.50
96	Keith Baldwin (SP)	1.50
98	Terry Unrein (SP)	1.50
99	Lee Williams	.50
NNO	Al Saunders (CO)	.50
NNO	Alex G. Spanos (ERR SP Chairman of the Board, Purchased team 1987)	4.00

NNO Alex G. Spanos (COR Chairman of the Board, Purchased tea m 1984) .50

1989 Chargers Junior Ralph's Tickets

The 12-card, 1-7/8" x 3-5/8" set was delivered in a perforated sheet which has all 12 cards. The set was sponsored by Ralph's and XTRA and the backs of the cards had coupons to local attractions. The fronts have a color action shot with the coupon description.

MT
Complete Set (12): 10.00
Common Player: .50
1 Gary Anderson (RB) .75
2 Gill Byrd .75
3 Quinn Early 1.50
4 Vencie Glenn .75
5 Jamie Holland .50
6 Don Macek .50
7 Dennis McKnight .50
8 Anthony Miller 5.00
9 Ralf Mojsiejenko .50
10 Leslie O'Neal 1.75
11 Billy Ray Smith .50
12 Lee Williams .50

1989 Chargers Police

The 12-card, 2-5/8" x 4-3/16" set has white borders with color action shots while the backs have bio information, career highlights and safety messages and are sponsored by Louis Rich. The cards were distributed in two, six-card sheets on Oct. 22 and Nov. 5 at Chargers home games.

MT
Complete Set (12): 10.00
Common Player: .50
1 Tim Spencer .50
2 Vencie Glenn .75
3 Gill Byrd .75
4 Jim McMahon 1.50
5 David Richards .50
6 Don Macek .50
7 Billy Ray Smith .75
8 Gary Plummer .75
9 Lee Williams .50
10 Leslie O'Neal 1.00
11 Anthony Miller 3.00
12 Broderick Thompson .50

1989 Chargers Smokey

The 48-card, 5" x 8" set has white borders with color action shots while the backs have bio information, career highlights and safety tips.

MT
Complete Set (48): 45.00
Common Player: 1.00
2 Ralf Mojsiejenko 1.00
6 Steve DeLine 1.00
10 Vince Abbott 1.00
13 Mark Vlasic 1.00
16 Mark Malone 1.00
20 Barry Redden 1.00
22 Gill Byrd 1.00
23 Roy Bennett 1.00
25 Vencie Glenn 1.00
26 Lionel James 1.00
30 Sam Seale 1.00
31 Leonard Coleman 1.00
34 Elvis Patterson 1.00
40 Gary Anderson (RB) 1.50
42 Curtis Adams 1.00
43 Tim Spencer 1.00
44 Martin Bayless 1.00
48 Pat Miller 1.00
50 Gary Plummer 1.00
51 Cedric Figaro 1.00
52 Jeff Jackson 1.00
53 Chuck Faucette 1.00
54 Billy Ray Smith 1.00
57 Keith Browner 1.00
58 David Brandon 1.00
59 Ken Woodard 1.00
60 Dennis McKnight 1.00
61 Ken Dallafior 1.00
65 David Richards 1.00
66 Dan Rosado 1.00
69 Les Miller 1.00
70 James Fitzpatrick 1.00
71 Mike Charles 1.00
72 Karl Wilson 1.00
73 Darrick Brilz 1.00
75 Joe Phillips 1.00
76 Broderick Thompson 1.00
82 Rod Bernstine 1.50
83 Anthony Miller 6.00
86 Jamie Holland 1.00
87 Quinn Early 1.50
88 Arthur Cox 1.00
89 Darren Flutie 2.50
91 Leslie O'Neal 2.50
93 Tyrone Keys 1.00
95 Joe Campbell 1.00
97 George Hinkle 1.00
99 Lee Williams 1.00

1990 Chargers Police

The 12-card, 2-5/8" x 4-1/8" set was sponsored by Louis Rich Meats. The card fronts have blue borders with color action shots while the backs have player descriptions and bio information, along with a safety tip.

MT
Complete Set (12): 10.00
Common Player: .75
1 Martin Bayless .75
2 Marion Butts 1.25
3 Gill Byrd .75
4 Burt Grossman .75
5 Ronnie Harmon 1.00
6 Anthony Miller 3.00
7 Leslie O'Neal 1.50
8 Joe Phillips .75
9 Gary Plummer .75
10 Billy Ray Smith .75
11 Billy Joe Tolliver 1.00
12 Lee Williams .75

1990 Chargers Smokey

The 36-card, 5" x 8" set was similar to the 1989 set with a fire safety cartoon and brief bio information on the back.

MT
Complete Set (36): 30.00
Common Player: .75
11 Billy Joe Tolliver 1.25
13 Mark Vlasic .75
15 David Archer 1.50
20 Darrin Nelson .75
22 Gill Byrd 1.00
24 Lester Lyles .75
25 Vencie Glenn 1.25
30 Sam Seale .75
31 Craig McEwen .75
35 Marion Butts 1.25
43 Tim Spencer .75
44 Martin Bayless .75
46 Joe Caravello .75
50 Gary Plummer .75
51 Cedric Figaro .75
53 Courtney Hall .75
54 Billy Ray Smith 1.00
58 David Brandon .75
59 Ken Woodard .75
60 Dennis McKnight .75
65 David Richards .75
69 Les Miller .75
75 Joe Phillips .75
76 Broderick Thompson .75
78 Joel Patten .75
79 Joey Howard .75
80 Wayne Walker .75
82 Rod Bernstine 1.00
83 Anthony Miller 5.00
85 Andy Parker .75
87 Quinn Early 1.75
88 Arthur Cox .75
91 Leslie O'Neal 1.75
92 Burt Grossman .75
97 George Hinkle .75
99 Lee Williams .75

1991 Chargers Vons

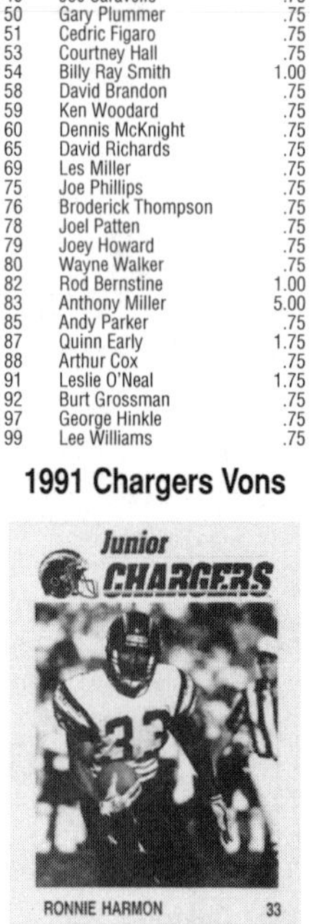

The twelve standard-sized cards were distributed by Vons in three-card sheets (6-5/8" x 3-1/2") with each sheet containing one card, one Junior Chargers Official Membership Card and a Sea World of California discount coupon. The card fronts have a color shot with a white border while the backs have bio and stat information.

MT
Complete Set (12): 10.00
Common Player: .75
1 Rod Berstine .75
2 Gill Byrd 1.00
3 Burt Grossman .75
4 Ronnie Harmon 1.00
5 Anthony Miller 2.00
6 Leslie O'Neal 1.50
7 Gary Plummer .75
8 Junior Seau 2.50
9 Billy Ray Smith .75
10 Broderick Thompson .75
11 Billy Joe Tolliver 1.00
12 Lee Williams .75

1992 Chargers Louis Rich

The 52-card, 5" x 8" set, distributed by Louis Rich, had glossy color fronts with the backs containing the Louis Rich logo.

MT
Complete Set (52): 30.00
Common Player: .50
1 Sam Anno .50
2 Johnnie Barnes .50
3 Rod Bernstine .75
4 Eric Bieniemy .75
5 Anthony Blaylock .50
6 Brian Brennan .50
7 Marion Butts 1.00
8 Gill Byrd .75
9 John Carney 1.00
10 Darren Carrington .50
11 Robert Claborne .50
12 Floyd Fields .50
13 Donald Frank .50
14 Bob Gagliano .50
15 Leo Goeas .50
16 Burt Grossman .50
17 Courtney Hall .50
18 Delton Hall .50
19 Ronnie Harmon 1.00
20 Steve Hendrickson .50
21 Stan Humphries 3.00
22 Shawn Jefferson 1.00
23 John Kidd .50
24 Shawn Lee .50
25 Nate Lewis .50
26 Eugene Marve .50
27 Deems May .50
28 Anthony Miller 2.00
29 Chris Mims 1.00
30 Eric Moten .50
31 Kevin Murphy .50
32 Pat O'Hara .50
33 Leslie O'Neal 1.50
34 Gary Plummer .50
35 Marquez Pope .50
36 Alfred Pupunu .50
37 Stanley Richard .75
38 David Richards .50
39 Henry Rolling .50
40 Bobby Ross (CO) 1.00
41 Junior Seau 2.50
42 Harry Swayne .75
43 Broderick Thompson .50
44 George Thornton .50
45 Peter Tuipulotu .50
46 Sean Vanhorse .50
47 Derrick Walker .50
48 Reggie E. White .50
49 Curtis Whitley .50
50 Blaise Winter .50
51 Duane Young .50
52 Mike Zandofsky .50

1993 Chargers Police

The 32-card, regular-sized set was sponsored by the highway patrol and contained the rookie card of running back Natrone Means. The fronts feature team color borders and the backs have bio information with a safe driving tip appearing in the lower right corner.

MT
Complete Set (32): 12.00
Common Player: .25
1 Darrien Gordon .50
2 Natrone Means 3.00
3 John Friesz .75
4 Stan Humphries 1.75
5 Anthony Miller 1.50
6 Marion Butts .75
7 Ronnie Harmon .75
8 Stanley Richard .50
9 Leslie O'Neal 1.00
10 Harry Swayne .25
11 Junior Seau 1.75
12 Courtney Hall .25
13 Gary Plummer .25
14 Eric Moten .25
15 Chris Mims .75
16 Burt Grossman .25
17 Blaise Winter .25
18 Donald Frank .25
19 Sean Vanhorse .25
20 John Carney .50
21 Floyd Fields .25
22 Gill Byrd .50
23 Shawn Jefferson .50
24 Shawn Lee .25
25 Alfred Pupunu .50
26 Marquez Pope .25
27 Darren Carrington .25
28 Duane Young .25
29 Derrick Walker .25
30 Deems May .25
31 Nate Lewis .25
32 Bobby Ross CO, Clarence Tuck (CHP Chief) .75

1994 Chargers Castrol Promos

The six-card, 5" x 8" set was sponsored by Pepboys and Castrol. The card fronts feature a color photo with the backs containing bio information and sponsor logos over the NFL emblem.

MT
Complete Set (6): 6.00
Common Player: .50
1 Courtney Hall .50
2 Ronnie Harmon .50
3 Stan Humphries 1.50
4 Natrone Means 2.50
5 Leslie O'Neal 1.00
6 Junior Seau 1.50

1994 Chargers Castrol

The 52-card, 5" x 8" set, as with the Promos set, was sponsored by Pepboys and Castrol with the card fronts containing a color shot. The card backs are similar to the Promos set, with bio information and sponsor logos over the NFL emblem.

MT
Complete Set (52): 30.00
Common Player: .50
1 Johnnie Barnes .50
2 Eric Bieniemy .75
3 David Binn .50
4 Stan Brock .50
5 Jeff Brohm .50
6 Lewis Bush .50
7 John Carney 1.00
8 Darren Carrington .50
9 Eric Castle .50
10 Willie Clark .50
11 Joe Cocozzo .50
12 Andre Coleman .75
13 Rodney Culver .75
14 Isaac Davis .50
15 Reuben Davis .50
16 Greg Engel .50
17 Dennis Gilbert .50
18 Gale Gilbert .50
19 Darrien Gordon 1.00
20 David Griggs .50
21 Courtney Hall .50
22 Ronnie Harmon 1.00
23 Dwayne Harper .50
24 Rodney Harrison .50
25 Steve Hendrickson .50
26 Stan Humphries 3.00
27 Shawn Jefferson 1.50
28 Raylee Johnson .50
29 Eric Jonassen .50
30 Aaron Laing .50
31 Shawn Lee .50
32 Deems May .50
33 Natrone Means 3.50
34 Joe Milinichik .50
35 Doug Miller .50
36 Chris Mims 1.00
37 Shannon Mitchell .50
38 Leslie O'Neal 1.50
39 Vaughn Parker .50
40 John Parrella .50
41 Alfred Pupunu .75
42 Stanley Richard .75
43 Junior Seau 3.50
44 Mark Seay 1.75
45 Harry Swayne .50
46 Cornell Thomas .50
47 Sean Vanhorse .50
48 Bryan Wagner .50
49 Reggie E. White .50
50 Curtis Whitley .50
51 Duane Young .50
52 Lonnie Young .50

1994 Chargers Pro Mags/Pro Tags

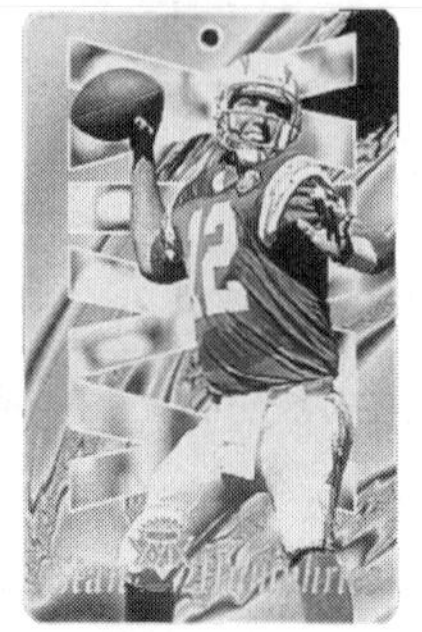

The 12-card, 2-1/8" x 3-3/8" set (with rounded corners) was issued in 750 boxes that contained six magnets and six "tag" cards. The magnet-card fronts feature the player's name and Super Bowl XXIX logo in gold foil, as do the tag cards which also have a closeup photo and a player profile on the backs.

MT
Complete Set (12): 20.00
Common Player: 1.50
1 Stan Humphries 3.00
2 Tony Martin 3.00
3 Natrone Means 4.00
4 Leslie O'Neal 2.00
5 Junior Seau 3.00
6 Mark Seay 1.50
7 Stan Humphries 3.00
8 Tony Martin 3.00
9 Natrone Means 4.00
10 Leslie O'Neal 2.00
11 Junior Seau 3.00
12 Mark Seay 1.50

1964-69 Chiefs Fairmont Dairy

The 19-card, 3-3/8" x 2-3/8" set was available on milk cartons by Fairmont Dairy between the years 1964-69. Most cards are printed in red ink, with some cards printed in black (3-7/16" x 1-9/16"). Although there are 19 cards listed below, there could have been more than that produced in the 1960s. The card fronts feature a player closeup with brief bio information, as well as a Chiefs schedule.

NM
Complete Set (19): 1800.
Common Player: 75.00
1 Fred Arbanas (Red printing) 75.00
2 Bobby Bell (Red printing) 175.00
3 Buck Buchanan (Black print) 160.00
4 Chris Burford (Red printing) 75.00
5 Len Dawson (Red printing) 260.00
6 Dave Grayson (Red printing) 75.00
7 Abner Haynes (Red printing) 100.00
8 Sherrill Headrick (Red printing) 100.00
9 Bobby Hunt (Red printing) 75.00
10 Frank Jackson (Red printing) 75.00
11 Curtis McClinton (Red printing) 75.00
12 Bobby Ply (Red printing) 75.00
13 Al Reynolds (Red printing) 75.00
14 Johnny Robinson (Red printing) 125.00
15 Noland Smith 75.00
16 Smokey Stover (Red printing) 75.00
17 Otis Taylor 150.00
18 Jim Tyrer (Red printing) 100.00
19 Jerrel Wilson (Red printing) 75.00

1969 Chiefs Kroger

The eight-card, 8" x 9-3/4" set was sponsored by Kroger and features card fronts with color paintings by artist John Wheeldon. The backs have biographical and statistical information and a brief note about the artist.

NM
Complete Set (8): 75.00
Common Player: 5.00
1 Buck Buchanan 10.00
2 Len Dawson 25.00
3 Mike Garrett 10.00
4 Willie Lanier 15.00
5 Jerry Mays 5.00
6 Johnny Robinson 10.00
7 Jan Stenerud 15.00
8 Jim Tyrer 5.00

1971 Chiefs Team Issue

The 10-card, 7" x 10" set features Chiefs players in black and white headshots with white borders. The backs contain bio information and career highlights and limited statistics.

NM
Complete Set (10): 45.00
Common Player: 5.00
1 Bobby Bell 10.00
2 Wendell Hayes 5.00
3 Ed Lothamer 5.00
4 Jim Lynch 5.00
5 Jack Rudnay 5.00
6 Sid Smith 5.00
7 Bob Stein 5.00
8 Jan Stenerud 12.00
9 Otis Taylor 10.00
10 Jim Tyrer 5.00

1973-74 Chiefs Team Issue

The 18-card, 5" x 7" set features black and white photos on the card fronts with white borders. The card backs are blank.

NM
Complete Set (18): 50.00
Common Player: 3.00
1 Robert Briggs 3.00
2 Larry Brunson 3.00
3 Gary Butler 3.00
4 Dean Carlson 3.00
5 Tom Condon 3.00
6 George Daney 3.00
7 Andy Hamilton 3.00
8 Dave Hill 3.00
9 Jim Kearney 3.00
10 Mike Livingston 3.00
11 Jim Marsalis 3.00
12 Barry Pearson 3.00
13 Francis Peay 3.00
14 Kerry Reardon 3.00
15 Mike Sensibaugh 3.00
16 Bill Thomas 3.00
17 Marvin Upshaw 3.00
18 Clyde Werner 3.00

1979 Chiefs Police

The 10-card, 2-5/8" x 4-1/8" set was issued by Hardee's Restaurants, the Chiefs and the Kansas City Police Department. The card fronts feature an action shot with the backs offering a safety tip.

NM
Complete Set (10): 10.00
Common Player: 1.00
1 Bob Grupp 1.00
4 Steve Fuller 1.00
22 Ted McKnight 1.00
24 Gary Green 1.00
26 Gary Barbaro 1.50
32 Tony Reed 1.00
58 Jack Rudnay 1.00
67 Art Still 1.50
73 Bob Simmons 1.00
NNO Marv Levy (CO) 3.00

1980 Chiefs Police

The 10-card, 2-5/8" x 4-1/8" set, sponsored by Frito-Lay, Kiwanis and area law enforcement, features action fronts with "Chiefs Tips" on the backs. The Stenerud card was limited in distribution.

NM
Complete Set (10): 12.00
Common Player: 1.00
1 Bob Grupp 1.00
3 Jan Stenerud (SP) 3.00
32 Tony Reed 1.00
53 Whitney Paul 1.00
59 Gary Spani 1.00
67 Art Still 1.75
86 J.T. Smith 1.00
99 Mike Bell 1.00
NNO Defensive Team 1.50
NNO Offensive Team 1.50

1981 Chiefs Police

The 10-card, 2-5/8" x 4-1/8" set, sponsored by Frito-Lay, Kiwanis and local law enforcement, features action shots on the card fronts and "Chiefs Tips" on the backs.

MT
Complete Set (10): 6.00
Common Player: .50
1 Warpaint and Carla (Mascots) .50
2 Art Still .75
3 Steve Fuller, Jack Rudnay .75
4 Gary Green .50
5 Tom Condon, Marv Levy (CO) 1.00
6 J.T. Smith .75
7 Gary Spani, Whitney Paul .50
8 Nick Lowery, Steve Fuller .75
9 Gary Barbaro .50
10 Henry Marshall .50

1982 Chiefs Police

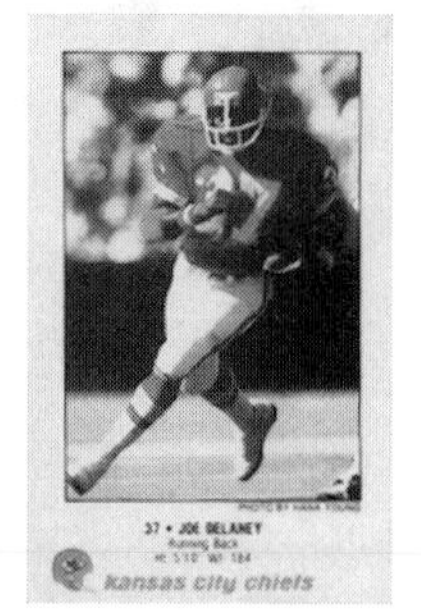

The 10-card, 2-5/8" x 4-1/8" set, sponsored by Frito-Lay, Kiwanis and local law enforcement, features action fronts while the backs contain cartoons in addition to "Chiefs Tips." Some of the card fronts feature two players (card Nos. 1 and 2).

MT
Complete Set (10): 6.00
Common Player: .50
1 Bill Kenney, Jack Rudnay .75
2 Steve Fuller, Nick Lowery .75
3 Matt Herkenhoff .50
4 Art Still .75
5 Gary Spani .50
6 James Hadnot .50
7 Mike Bell .50
8 Carol Canfield (Chiefette) .50
9 Gary Green .50
10 Joe Delaney .75

1983 Chiefs Police

The 10-card, 2-5/8" x 4-1/8" set, sponsored by Frito-Lay, KCTV-5, Kiwanis and local law enforcement, features action fronts with "Crime Tip" cartoons on the backs.

MT
Complete Set (10): 6.00
Common Player: .50
1 John Mackovic (CO) .75
2 Tom Condon .50
3 Gary Spani .50
4 Carlos Carson .75
5 Brad Budde .50
6 Lloyd Burruss .50
7 Gary Green .50
8 Mike Bell .50
9 Nick Lowery .75
10 Sandi Byrd (Chiefette) .50

1984 Chiefs Police

The 10-card, 2-5/8" x 4-1/8" set, sponsored by Frito-Lay and KCTV, features a "Chiefs Tip" and "Crime Tip" on the card backs.

MT
Complete Set (10): 6.00
Common Player: .50
1 John Mackovic (CO) .75
2 Deron Cherry .75
3 Bill Kenney .50
4 Henry Marshall .50
5 Nick Lowery .75
6 Theotis Brown .50
7 Stephone Paige 1.00
8 Gary Spani, Art Still .75
9 Albert Lewis .75
10 Carlos Carson .75

1984 Chiefs QuikTrip

The 16-card, 5" x 7" set was sponsored by QuickTrip and features black and white fronts with blank backs.

MT
Complete Set (16): 48.00
Common Player: 2.00
1 Mike Bell 2.00
2 Todd Blackledge 3.00
3 Brad Budde 2.00
4 Lloyd Burruss 2.00
5 Carlos Carson 3.00
6 Gary Green 2.00
7 Anthony Hancock 2.00
8 Eric Harris 2.00
9 Lamar Hunt (OWN) 5.00
10 Bill Kenney 3.00
11 Ken Kremer 2.00
12 Nick Lowery 4.50
13 John Mackovic (CO) 3.00
14 J.T. Smith 3.00
15 Gary Spani 2.00
16 Art Still 3.00

1985 Chiefs Police

The 10-card, 2-5/8" x 4-1/8" set, sponsored by Frito-Lay, KCTV and local law enforcement, features a "Chiefs Tip" and "Crime Tip" on the card backs.

MT
Complete Set (10): 6.00
Common Player: .50
1 John Mackovic (CO) .75
2 Herman Heard .50

3 Bill Kenney .75
4 Deron Cherry, Lloyd Burruss .75
5 Jim Arnold .50
6 Kevin Ross .50
7 David Lutz .50
8 Chiefettes Cheerleaders .75
9 Bill Maas .75
10 Art Still 1.00

1986 Chiefs Police

The 10-card, 2-5/8" x 4-1/8" set was sponsored by Frito-Lay, KCTV and local law enforcement and features "Chiefs Tip" and "Crime Tip" on the backs.

MT
Complete Set (10): 6.00
Common Player: .50
1 John Mackovic .50
2 Willie Lanier (Hall of Fame) 1.50
3 Stephone Paige 1.00
4 Brad Budde .50
5 Nick Lowery .75
6 Scott Radecic .50
7 Mike Pruitt .50
8 Albert Lewis .75
9 Todd Blackledge .75
10 Deron Cherry 1.25

1987 Chiefs Police

The 10-card, 2-5/8" x 4-1/8" set, sponsored by Frito-Lay, US Sprint, KCTV and local law enforcement, features a "Chiefs Tip" and "Crime Tip" on the backs.

MT
Complete Set (10): 5.00
Common Player: .50
1 Frank Gansz (CO) .50
2 Tim Cofield .50
3 Deron Cherry, Albert Lewis .75
4 Chiefs Cheerleaders .50
5 Jeff Smith .50
6 Rick Donnalley .50
7 Lloyd Burruss, Kevin Ross .50
8 Dino Hackett .50
9 Bill Maas .50
10 Carlos Carson .75

1988 Chiefs Police

The 10-card, 2-5/8" x 4-1/8" set was sponsored by Frito-Lay, KCTV, US Sprint and local law enforcement and has "Chiefs Tip" and "Crime Tip" on the backs.

MT
Complete Set (10): 6.00
Common Player: .50
1 Frank Gansz (CO) .50
2 Bill Kenney .75
3 Carlos Carson .75
4 Paul Palmer .50
5 Christian Okoye 1.00
6 Mark Adickes .50
7 Bill Maas .50
8 Albert Lewis .75
9 Deron Cherry .75
10 Stephone Paige .75

1989 Chiefs Police

The 10-card, 2-5/8" x 4-1/8" set, sponsored by Western Auto, KCTV and local law enforcement, features a "Chiefs Tip" and "Crime Tip" on the card backs.

MT
Complete Set (10): 5.00
Common Player: .50
1 Marty Schottenheimer (CO) 1.00
2 Irv Eatman .50
3 Kevin Ross .50
4 Bill Maas .50
5 Chiefs Cheerleaders .50
6 Carlos Carson .75
7 Steve DeBerg 1.00
8 Jonathan Hayes .50
9 Deron Cherry .75
10 Dino Hackett .50

1997 Chiefs Pocket Schedules

This 22-card set featured a Chiefs player on one side with the Kansas City Chiefs 1997 schedule on the other side. Pocket schedules were distributed in the Kansas City area early in the 1997 season.

MT
Complete Set (22): 7.00
Common Player: .25
Marcus Allen 2.00
Kimble Anders .25
Vaughn Booker .25
John Browning .25
Dale Carter .25
Anthony Davis .25
Troy Dumas .25
Donnie Edwards .25
Elvis Grbac 1.00
Tim Grunhard .25
James Hasty .25
Greg Hill .75
Chris Penn .25
Will Shields .25
Tracy Simien .25
Pete Styoyanovich .25
Dave Szott .25
Derrick Thomas 1.00
Reggie Tongue .50
Tamarick Vanover .50
K.C. Wolf .25
Jerome Woods .25

1972 Chiquita NFL Slides

The 13-slide, 3-9/16" x 1-3/4" set features two players on each slide. The slides have a slide image in each of the four corners with a player summary in the middle. The top two images are of the same player, while the bottom two are of the second player. A yellow viewer was also issued.

NM
Complete Set (13): 325.00
Common Player: 20.00
1 Joe Greene, Bob Lilly (2) 50.00
3 Bill Bergey, Gary Collins (4) 30.00
5 Walt Sweeney, Bubba Smith (6) 30.00
7 Larry Wilson, Fred Carr (8) 20.00
9 Mac Percival, John Brodie (10) 30.00
11 Lem Barney, Ron Yary (12) 30.00
13 Curt Knight, Alvin Haymond (14) 20.00
15 Floyd Little, Gerry Philbin (16) 30.00
17 Jim Mitchell, Paul Costa (18) 20.00
19 Jake Kupp, Ben Hawkins (20) 20.00
21 Johnny Robinson, George Webster (22) 20.00
23 Mercury Morris, Willie Brown (24) 40.00
25 Ron Johnson, Jon Morris (26) 20.00
NNO Yellow Viewer 30.00

1970 Clark Volpe

The 66-card, 7-1/2" x 9-15/16" set includes cards for eight of the teams in the league in 1970. The Chicago Bears (1-8), Cincinnati Bengals (9-14), Cleveland Browns (15-21), Detroit Lions (22-30), Green Bay Packers (31-39), Kansas City Chiefs (40-48), Minnesota Vikings (49-57) and St. Louis Cardinals (58-66). Cards with the mail tabs measure 7-1/2" x 14" and the backs have mail-in offers for other merchandise while the fronts feature player drawings by artist Nicholas Volpe.

NM
Complete Set (66): 325.00
Common Player: 3.00
1 Ron Bull 3.00
2 Dick Butkus 18.00
3 Lee Roy Caffey 3.00
4 Bobby Douglass 6.00
5 Dick Gordon 3.00
6 Bennie McRae 3.00
7 Ed O'Bradovich 3.00
8 George Seals 3.00
9 Bill Bergey 6.00
10 Jess Phillips 3.00
11 Mike Reid 6.00
12 Paul Robinson 6.00
13 Bob Trumpy 8.00
14 Sam Wyche 12.00
15 Erich Barnes 3.00
16 Gary Collins 6.00
17 Gene Hickerson 3.00
18 Jim Houston 3.00
19 Leroy Kelly 12.00
20 Ernie Kellerman 3.00
21 Bill Nelsen 6.00
22 Lem Barney 10.00
23 Mel Farr 6.00
24 Larry Hand 3.00
25 Alex Karras 12.00
26 Mike Lucci 6.00
27 Bill Munson 6.00
28 Charlie Sanders 6.00
29 Tommy Vaughn 3.00
30 Wayne Walker 6.00
31 Lionel Aldridge 3.00
32 Donny Anderson 6.00
33 Ken Bowman 3.00
34 Carroll Dale 6.00
35 Jim Grabowski 6.00
36 Ray Nitschke 15.00
37 Dave Robinson 6.00
38 Travis Williams 6.00
39 Willie Wood 10.00
40 Fred Arbanas 3.00
41 Bobby Bell 10.00
42 Aaron Brown 3.00
43 Buck Buchanan 10.00
44 Len Dawson 16.00
45 Jim Marsalis 3.00
46 Jerry Mays 3.00
47 Johnny Robinson 6.00
48 Jim Tyrer 6.00
49 Bill Brown 6.00
50 Fred Cox 3.00
51 Gary Cuozzo 6.00
52 Carl Eller 10.00
53 Jim Marshall 10.00
54 Dave Osborn 6.00
55 Alan Page 12.00
56 Mick Tingelhoff 6.00
57 Gene Washington 6.00
58 Pete Beathard 6.00
59 John Gilliam 6.00
60 Jim Hart 8.00
61 Johnny Roland 6.00
62 Jackie Smith 10.00
63 Larry Stallings 3.00
64 Roger Wehrli 6.00
65 Dave Williams 3.00
66 Larry Wilson 10.00

1991 Classic Promos

These promotional cards preview Classic's design for its debut set in 1991. The card back only has trademark information, plus the words "For Promotional Purposes Only! Not For Resale." The five cards were also featured together on a 7-1/2" x 7-1/8" promo sheet which was made available to collectors who attended the 12th National Sports Collectors Convention in Anaheim, Calif., in July 1991. Each sheet is serially-numbered (1 of 10,000, etc.) and is labeled on the back as being a promotional sheet.

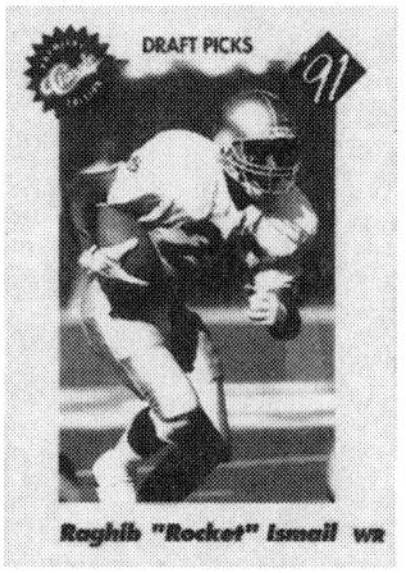

MT
Complete Set (7): 15.00
Common Player (1-5): 1.50
1 Antone Davis 1.50
2A Raghib Rocket Ismail 5.00
2B Raghib Rocket Ismail 5.00
3A Todd Lyght 2.00
3B Todd Lyght 2.00
4 Russell Maryland 2.00
5 Eric Turner 2.00

1991 Classic Fb

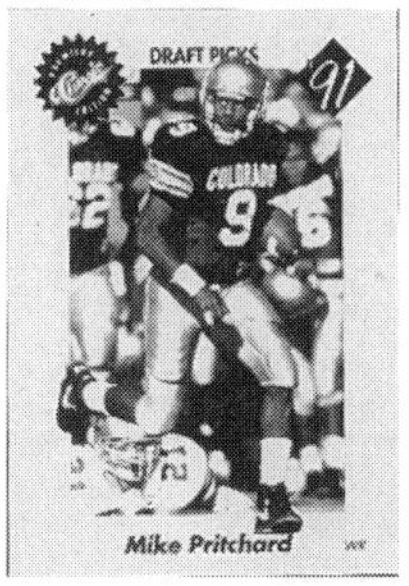

Classic's first venture into the football field resulted in this 50-card boxed set released in June. Classic reportedly paid several players for exclusive rights to appear in the set, including Raghib Ismail. No team names or college names are listed on the cards, which have a grey marble-like border on the front, plus the Classic logos. Each has biographical information, plus a player profile.

MT
Complete Set (50): 6.00
Common Player: .05
1 Rocket Ismail .50
2 Russell Maryland .30
3 Eric Turner .30
4 Bruce Pickens .10
5 Mike Croal .10
6 Todd Lyght .10
7 Eric Swann .30
8 Antone Davis .10
9 Stanley Richard .10
10 Pat Harlow .10
11 Alvin Harper .50
12 Mike Pritchard .30
13 Leonard Russell .10
14 Dan McGwire .10
15 Bobby Wilson .10
16 Alfred Williams .10
17 Vinnie Clark .10
18 Kelvin Pritchett .10
19 Harvey Williams .50
20 Stan Thomas .10
21 Randal Hill .25
22 Todd Marinovich .10
23 Henry Jones .05
24 Jarrod Bunch .05
25 Mike Dumas .10
26 Ed King .05
27 Reggie Jackson .05
28 Roman Phifer .10
29 Mike Jones .10
30 Brett Favre 2.00
31 Browning Nagle .10
32 Esera Tualolo .10
33 George Thornton .10
34 Dixon Edwards .10
35 Darryl Lewis .10
36 Eric Bieniemy .20
37 Shane Curry .10
38 Jerome Henderson .10
39 Wesley Carroll .10
40 Nick Bell .10
41 John Flannery .05
42 Ricky Watters 1.00
43 Jeff Graham .50
44 Eric Moten .05
45 Jesse Campbell .05
46 Chris Zorich .20
47 Doug Thomas .05
48 Phil Hansen .05
49 Kanavis McGhee .10
50 Reggie Barrett .10

1992 Classic Promos

The six-card, standard-size set was issued by Classic to preview the upcoming 1992 NFL Draft set. The card fronts contain black borders while the backs have collegiate summaries. The photos on the card fronts of the six promos differ from their card counterparts in the 100-card set.

MT
Complete Set (6): 8.00
Common Player: .50
1 Desmond Howard 2.00
2 David Klingler .50
3 Quentin Coryatt .50
4 Carl Pickens 4.00
5 Derek Brown .50
6 Casey Weldon .50

1992 Classic Fb

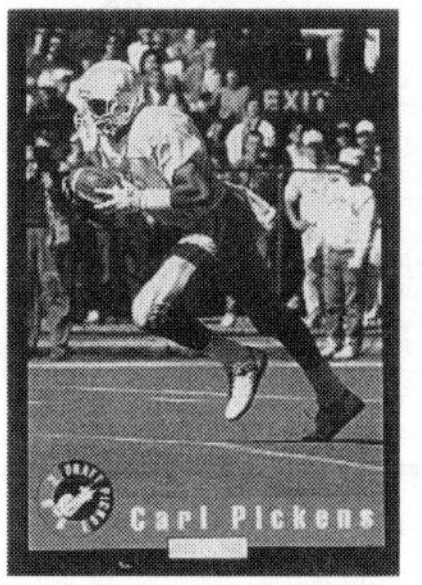

This set features 100 of the top collegiate players expected to be selected in the NFL draft. The card front has a color glossy photo surrounded by a black border. The player's name and position are at the bottom, along with a set logo. The card back has a summary of the player's collegiate successes and a color mug shot. Statistics, biographical information and a card number are also given. The background is a blurred image of a running back hitting the hole. These cards were sold in foil packs. Cards using the same design and card numbers, but different photos, were also sold in blister packs. There were six promo cards made, previewing the 1992 design but using different photos from the regular cards. Nuances in the card backs are what distinguishes these cards as promos - they are labeled as "For Promotional Purposes Only" and have an ad in place of a career summary.

MT
Complete Set (100): 8.00
Common Player: .05
1 Desmond Howard .30
2 David Klingler .20
3 Quentin Coryatt .30
4 Bill Johnson .05
5 Eugene Chung .05
6 Derek Brown .10
7 Carl Pickens 1.50
8 Chris Mims .10
9 Charles Davenport .05
10 Ray Roberts .05
11 Chuck Smith .05
12 Joe Bowden .05
13 Mirko Jurkovic .05
14 Tony Smith .05
15 Ken Swilling .05
16 Greg Skrepenak .05
17 Phillippi Sparks .05
18 Alonzo Spellman .20
19 Bernard Dafney .05
20 Edgar Bennett 1.00
21 Shane Dronett .05
22 Jeremy Lincoln .15
23 Dion Lambert .05
24 Siran Stacy .05
25 Tony Sacca .10
26 Sean Lumpkin .05
27 Tommy Vardell .10
28 Keith Hamilton .05
29 Ashley Ambrose .05
30 Sean Gilbert .75
31 Casey Weldon .20
32 Marc Boutte .05
33 Santana Dotson .05
34 Ronnie West .05
35 Michael Bankston .05
36 Mike Pawlawski .05
37 Dale Carter .10
38 Carlos Snow .05
39 Corey Barlow .05
40 Mark D'Onofrio .05
41 Matt Blundin .10
42 George Rooks .05
43 Patrick Rowe .10
44 Dwight Hollier .05
45 Joel Steed .05
46 Erick Anderson .10
47 Rodney Culver .10
48 Chris Hakel .05
49 Luke Fisher .05
50 Kevin Smith .05
51 Robert Brooks 1.00
52 Bucky Richardson .05
53 Steve Isreal .05
54 Marco Coleman .40
55 Johnny Mitchell .20
56 Scottie Graham .30
57 Keith Goganious .05
58 Tommy Maddox .20
59 Terrell Buckley .20
60 Dana Hall .05
61 Ty Detmer .25
62 Darryl Williams .10
63 Jason Hanson .30
64 Leon Searcy .10
65 Gene McGuire .05
66 Will Furrer .10
67 Darren Woodson .10
68 Tracy Scoggins .10
69 Corey Widmer .05
70 Robert Harris .05
71 Larry Tharpe .05
72 Lance Olberding .05
73 Stacey Dillard .05
74 Anthony Hamlet .05
75 Tommy Jeter .05
76 Mike Evans .05
77 Shane Collins .05
78 Mark Thomas .05
79 Chester McGlockton .10
80 Robert Porcher .10
81 Marquez Pope .10
82 Rico Smith .05
83 Tyrone Williams .05
84 Rod Smith .05
85 Tyrone Legette .05
86 Wayne Hawkins .05
87 Derrick Moore .25
88 Tim Lester .05
89 Calvin Holmes .05
90 Reggie Dwight .05
91 Eddie Robinson .05
92 Robert Jones .05
93 Ricardo McDonald .05
94 Howard Dinkins .05
95 Todd Collins .10
96 Eddie Blake .05
97 Classic Quarterbacks .10
98 Back to Back .10
99 Checklist .05
100 Checklist .05

1992 Classic Draft Blister

These 60 cards feature the top prospects entering the 1992 NFL draft. Each card front has a black border surrounding a glossy color action photo. The player's name and position are at the bottom of the card, along with the Classic logo. The back has a blurred action photo for a background, and gives collegiate statistics and a summary of the player's accomplishments at that level. Bio information, a mug shot, and a card number are also on the back. The cards have the same numbers as those in Classic's regular 100-card main set, but the photos on the front are different. The backgrounds on the backs of these cards also have a richer color tone, too; the regular cards' backgrounds are ghosted. These cards were sold in blister packs.

MT
Complete Set (60): 7.00
Common Player: .05
1 Desmond Howard .75
2 David Klingler .75
3 Quentin Coryatt .75
4 Bill Johnson .07
5 Eugene Chung .10
6 Derek Brown .50
7 Carl Pickens .75
8 Chris Mims .30
9 Charles Davenport .12
10 Ray Roberts .10
11 Chuck Smith .10
12 Joe Bowden .07
13 Mirko Jurkovic .05
14 Tony Smith .25
15 Ken Swilling .05
16 Greg Skrepenak .07
17 Phillippi Sparks .10
18 Alonzo Spellman .25
19 Bernard Dafney .07
20 Edgar Bennett .75
21 Shane Dronett .15
22 Jeremy Lincoln .12
23 Dion Lambert .07
24 Siran Stacy .07
25 Tony Sacca .12
26 Sean Lumpkin .07
27 Tommy Vardell .50
28 Keith Hamilton .12
29 Ashley Ambrose .12
30 John Rays .07
31 Casey Weldon .30
32 Marc Boutte .12
33 Santana Dotson .25
34 Ronnie West .05
35 Michael Bankston .10
36 Mike Pawlawski .05
37 Dale Carter .25
38 Carlos Snow .05
39 Corey Barlow .07
40 Mark D'Onofrio .05
41 Matt Blundin .20
42 George Rooks .05
43 Patrick Rowe .07
44 Dwight Hollier .12
45 Joel Steed .07
46 Erick Anderson .10
47 Rodney Culver .15
48 Chris Hakel .07
49 Luke Fisher .05
50 Kevin Smith .25
51 Robert Brooks .12
52 Bucky Richardson .05
53 Steve Israel .05
54 Tyrone Ashley .05
55 Johnny Mitchell .75
56 Scottie Graham .15
57 Keith Goganious .07
58 Tommy Maddox .50
59 Terrell Buckley .30
60 Dana Hall .12

A player's name in *italic type* indicates a rookie card.

1992 Classic LPs Fb

These gold-foiled stamps were randomly included inside 1992 Classic Draft Picks packs. Approximately 40,000 of each card was produced. Each is numbered on the back using LP 1/10, etc.. The players in the set were projected as top picks in the 1992 NFL draft.

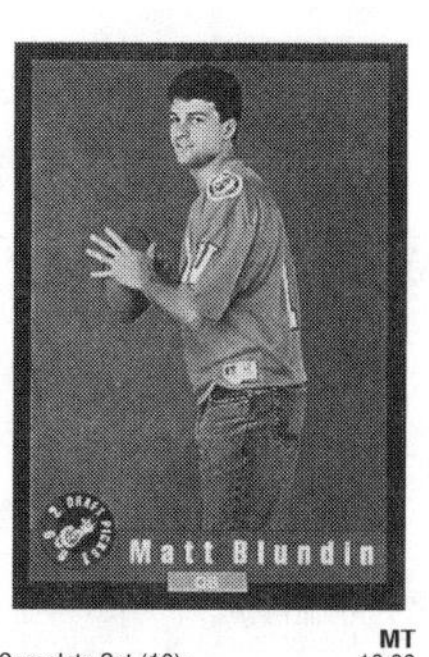

MT
Complete Set (10): 10.00
Common Player: .75
1 Desmond Howard 2.00
2 David Klingler 1.25
3 Siran Stacy .75
4 Casey Weldon 1.25
5 Sean Gilbert 3.00
6 Matt Blundin 1.25
7 Tommy Maddox 1.25
8 Derek Brown .75
9 Tony Smith .75
10 Tony Sacca .75

1992 Classic NFL Game

These standard-size cards were included as part of Classic's 1992 NFL football game. The card front has a color action photo framed by rose and dark blue borders. The player's name is also on the front, in a black panel at the bottom, along with a Classic logo, which is at the top. The card back has a player profile, action photo, a card number and five trivia questions. The game included a game board, die, player markers, a scoreboard, rules, and plays which could be used in the game. Two unnumbered cards - Cris Dishman and Andre Ware - had the game's rules on the back.

MT
Complete Set (62): 10.00
Common Player: .15
1 Steve Atwater .15
2 Louis Oliver .15
3 Ronnie Lott .25
4 Reggie White .50
5 Cortez Kennedy .30
6 Derrick Thomas .40
7 Pat Swilling .20
8 Cornelius Bennett .25
9 Mark Rypien .20
10 Todd Marinovich .15
11 Steve Young 1.00
12 Warren Moon .30
13 Mirko Jurkovic .15
14 Hugh Millen .15
15 John Friesz .25
16 John Elway .75
17 Chris Miller .25
18 Jim Everett .25
19 Emmitt Smith 2.00
20 Johnny Johnson .25
21 Thurman Thomas .60
22 Leonard Russell .25
23 Rodney Hampton .50
24 Marion Butts .30
25 Neal Anderson .25
26 Barry Sanders 1.00
27 Dexter Carter .15
28 Gaston Green .15
29 Barry Word .15
30 Eric Bieniemy .15
31 Nick Bell .20
32 Reggie Cobb .15
33 Jay Novacek .30
34 Keith Jackson .30
35 Eric Green .30
36 Lawrence Dawsey .20
37 Mike Pritchard .20
38 Michael Haynes .20
39 James Lofton .25
40 Art Monk .25
41 Herman Moore .40
42 Andre Rison .40
43 Wendell Davis .15
44 Sterling Sharpe .60
45 Fred Barnett .20
46 Rob Moore .30
47 Gary Clark .25
48 Wesley Carroll .15
49 Michael Irvin .75
50 John Taylor .25
51 Robert Brooks .15
52 Ray Bentley .15
53 Eric Swann .20
54 Amp Lee .20
55 Darryl Williams .15
56 Wilbur Marshall .15
57 Siran Stacy .15
58 Chip Lohmiller .15
59 Rodney Culver .15
60 Tommy Vardell .25
---- Cris Dishman (Rules on back) .15
---- Andre Ware (Rules on back) .20

1993 Classic Gold Promos

The two-card, standard-size set was made available to Classic Collectors Club members. The fronts feature color action shots while the backs contain another action photo, biography and player profile. The cards are stamped as "x of 5,000" and are numbered with the "PR" prefix.

		MT
Complete Set (2):		7.00
Common Player:		2.00
1	Terry Kirby	2.00
2	Jerome Bettis	5.00

1993 Classic Preview

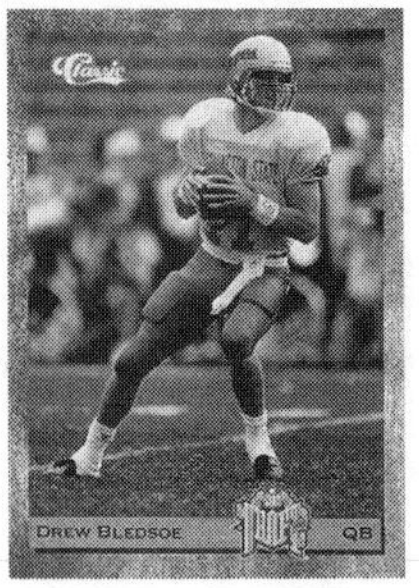

The one-card, standard size promo was issued as a preview to the base 1993 Classic set. The card, depicting Drew Bledsoe, has the same design as cards in the 1993 base set, although the Bledsoe photo is different from the base card photo.

		MT
Complete Set (1):		6.00
Common Player:		6.00
1	Drew Bledsoe	6.00

1993 Classic Fb

These Classic cards feature blue marble-like borders around color action photos. The players name and position are at the bottom of the card in a yellow stripe which contains the set logo. The Classic logo appears in the upper left corner. The back is numbered and is designed in a horizontal manner. Another action photo, collegiate summary, statistics, biographical information and the logo for the team which selected the player in the draft are also included. Inserts within the main set included 1993 Basketball Draft Pick Preview cards, 1,000 cards autographed by Dallas Cowboy quarterback Troy Aikman, 1993 Classic Pro Line Preview cards, and LP cards. Classic also made three types of promo cards - Classic Draft Preview; C3 Presidential Club; and Classic Draft Gold promos. There were 5,000 Gold promos made, each having the words "1 of 5,000" and set logo stamped in gold foil on the front. The back indicates the card is for "Promotional Purposes Only." These cards previewed Classic's gold version set, which parallels its main set. The gold cards were issued in a factory set box and included a certificate of authenticity. There were 5,000 sets made; star gold cards are three to six times more valuable than the regular cards. Drew Bledsoe and Rick Mirer also signed 5,000 of their cards.

		MT
Complete Set (100):		8.00
Common Player:		.05
Comp. Gold Set (102):		180.00
Gold Cards:		3x-6x
Drew Bledsoe Auto/5000		75.00
Rick Mirer Auto/5000		45.00
1	Drew Bledsoe	2.00
2	Rick Mirer	1.00
3	Garrison Hearst	.75
4	Marvin Jones	.10
5	John Copeland	.10
6	Eric Curry	.10
7	Curtis Conway	.75
8	Willie Roaf	.10
9	Lincoln Kennedy	.10
10	Jerome Bettis	.75
11	Mike Compton	.05
12	John Gerak	.05
13	Will Shields	.10
14	Ben Coleman	.05
15	Ernest Dye	.05
16	Lester Holmes	.05
17	Brad Hopkins	.05
18	Everett Lindsay	.05
19	Todd Rucci	.05
20	Lance Gunn	.05
21	Elvis Grbac	.40
22	Shane Matthews	.10
23	Rudy Harris	.05
24	Rich Anderson	.05
25	Derek Brown	.10
26	Roger Harper	.05
27	Terry Kirby	.30
28	Natrone Means	1.25
29	Glyn Milburn	.40
30	Adrian Murrell	1.00
31	Lorenzo Neal	.10
32	Roosevelt Potts	.20
33	Kevin Williams	.10
34	Russell Copeland	.10
35	Fred Baxter	.05
36	Troy Drayton	.25
37	Chris Gedney	.10
38	Irv Smith	.10
39	Olanda Truitt	.05
40	Victor Bailey	.20
41	Horace Copeland	.10
42	Ron Dickerson Jr.	.05
43	Willie Harris	.05
44	Tyrone Hughes	.10
45	Qadry Ismail	.25
46	Reggie Brooks	.15
47	Sean LaChapelle	.05
48	O.J. McDuffie	.75
49	Larry Ryans	.05
50	Kenny Shedd	.05
51	Brian Stablein	.05
52	Lamar Thomas	.10
53	Kevin Williams	.75
54	Othello Henderson	.05
55	Kevin Henry	.05
56	Todd Kelly	.05
57	Devon McDonald	.05
58	Michael Strahan	.05
59	Dan Williams	.05
60	Gilbert Brown	.05
61	Mark Caesar	.05
62	Ronnie Dixon	.05
63	John Parrella	.05
64	Leonard Renfro	.05
65	Coleman Rudolph	.05
66	Ronnie Bradford	.05
67	Tom Carter III	.10
68	Deon Figures	.10
69	Derrick Frazier	.05
70	Darrien Gordon	.10
71	Carlton Gray	.10
72	Adrian Hardy	.05
73	Mike Reid	.05
74	Thomas Smith	.05
75	Robert O'Neal	.05
76	Chad Brown	.40
77	Demetrius DuBose	.20
78	Reggie Givens	.05
79	Travis Hill	.05
80	Rich McKenzie	.05
81	Barry Minter	.05
82	Darrin Smith	.10
83	Steve Tovar	.10
84	Patrick Bates	.10
85	Dan Footman	.05
86	Ryan McNeil	.05
87	Danan Hughes	.05
88	Mark Brunell	1.00
89	Ron Moore	.15
90	Antonio London	.10
91	Steve Everitt	.10
92	Wayne Simmons	.20
93	Robert Smith	.50
94	Dana Stubblefield	.30
95	George Teague	.20
96	Carl Simpson	.10
97	Billy Joe Hobert	.20
98	Gino Torretta	.15
99	Checklist No. 1	.05
100	Checklist No. 2	.05
AU1	Troy Aikman Auto/1000	150.00

1993 Classic Draft Stars Fb

1993 Classic Football jumbo packs each contained one of these random inserts. The card front indicates the card is 1 of 20,000 made; the card back uses a DS prefix for the card number. The front has a color full-bleed photo, and foil stamping for the player's name, position and set logo. The card back has biographical information, a mug shot and a congratulatory note indicating the card is one of 20,000 made for each player. The logo of the team which selected the player is also on the card back. A Mirer/Bledsoe jumbo card, available one per every other box, was also produced.

		MT
Complete Set (20):		24.00
Common Player:		.50
DS1	Drew Bledsoe	7.00
DS2	Rick Mirer	4.00
DS3	Garrison Hearst	3.00
DS4	Marvin Jones	.50
DS5	John Copeland	.50
DS6	Eric Curry	.50
DS7	Curtis Conway	2.00
DS8	Jerome Bettis	3.00
DS9	Patrick Bates	.50
DS10	Tom Carter	.50
DS11	Irv Smith	.50
DS12	Robert Smith	2.00
DS13	O.J. McDuffie	2.00
DS14	Roosevelt Potts	.75
DS15	Natrone Means	4.00
DS16	Glyn Milburn	1.00
DS17	Reggie Brooks	.75
DS18	Kevin Williams	1.50
DS19	Qadry Ismail	1.00
DS20	Billy Joe Hobert	.50
----	Drew Bledsoe, Rick Mirer	12.00

1993 Classic LPs Fb

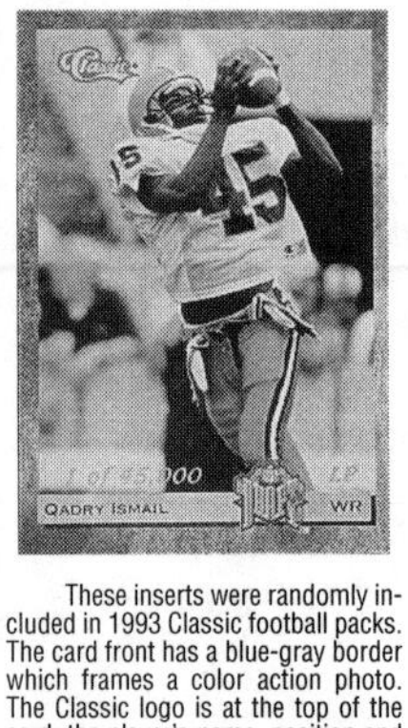

These inserts were randomly included in 1993 Classic football packs. The card front has a blue-gray border which frames a color action photo. The Classic logo is at the top of the card; the player's name, position and set logo are at the bottom in a gold foil stripe. "LP" and "1 of 45,000" are also stamped in gold foil at the bottom. The card back is horizontal and includes another action photo, career summary and card number. The logo of the team which selected the player in the draft is also on the back.

		MT
Complete Set (10):		35.00
Common Player:		1.50
1	Drew Bledsoe	12.00
2	Rick Mirer	6.00
3	Garrison Hearst	5.00
4	Marvin Jones	1.50
5	John Copeland	1.50
6	Eric Curry	1.50
7	Curtis Conway	4.00
8	Jerome Bettis	4.00
9	Reggie Brooks	2.00
10	Qadry Ismail	3.00

1993 Classic Superhero Comic Fb

These cards were random inserts in 1993 Classic Football packs. Each card front has a comic-book style drawing of the featured player, as illustrated by artist Neal Adams. The drawing is full-bleed and in color and includes the player's name and position at the bottom in a yellow bar. The card back is numbered with an "SH" prefix and features a ghosted image of the front photo as its background. A second color action photo and career summary are also included. There were 15,000 cards of each player made.

		MT
Complete Set (4):		50.00
Common Player:		7.00
1	Troy Aikman	20.00
2	Drew Bledsoe	20.00
3	Rick Mirer	12.00
4	Garrison Hearst	7.00

1993 Classic TONX

The 150-card, 1-5/8" in diameter set features color action shots on the circular fronts with the player's name, team helmet logo and NFL and Classic logos on the back.

		MT
Complete Set (150):		12.00
Common Player:		.05
1	Troy Aikman	1.00
2	Eric Allen	.05
3	Terry Allen	.25
4	Morten Anderson	.05
5	Neal Anderson	.05
6	Flipper Anderson	.05
7	Steve Atwater	.05
8	Carl Banks	.05
9	Patrick Bates	.05
10	Cornelius Bennett	.10
11	Rod Bernstine	.05
12	Jerome Bettis	.75
13	Steve Beuerlein	.05
14	Bennie Blades	.05
15	Brian Blades	.05
16	Drew Bledsoe	1.00
17	Tim Brown	.10
18	Terrell Buckley	.05
19	Marion Butts	.05
20	Mark Carrier (DB)	.05
21	Anthony Carter	.05
22	Cris Carter	.10
23	Dale Carter	.05
24	Ray Childress	.05
25	Gary Clark	.05
26	Reggie Cobb	.05
27	Marco Coleman	.05
28	Curtis Conway	.30
29	John Copeland	.05
30	Quentin Coryatt	.10
31	Randall Cunningham	.10
32	Eric Curry	.05
33	Lawrence Dawsey	.05
34	Chris Doleman	.05
35	Vaughn Dunbar	.05
36	Henry Ellard	.05
37	John Elway	.75
38	Steve Emtman	.05
39	Ricky Ervins	.05
40	Jim Everett	.05
41	Brett Favre	2.00
42	Barry Foster	.05
43	Gary Cleveland	.05
44	Jeff George	.10
45	Sean Gilbert	.05
46	Ernest Givins	.05
47	Harold Green	.05
48	Kevin Greene	.05
49	Paul Gruber	.05
50	Charles Haley	.05
51	Rodney Hampton	.10
52	Jim Harbaugh	.10
53	Ronnie Harmon	.05
54	Michael Haynes	.05
55	Garrison Hearst	.50
56	Randal Hill	.05
57	Merril Hoge	.05
58	Pierce Holt	.05
59	Jeff Hostetler	.05
60	Stan Humphries	.10
61	Michael Irvin	.15
62	Keith Jackson	.05
63	Rickey Jackson	.05
64	Haywood Jeffires	.05
65	Pepper Johnson	.05
66	Brent Jones	.05
67	Marvin Jones	.05
68	Seth Joyner	.05
69	Jim Kelly	.15
70	Cortez Kennedy	.05
71	David Klingler	.05
72	Bernie Kosar	.05
73	Reggie Langhorne	.05
74	Mo Lewis	.05
75	Howie Long	.10
76	Ronnie Lott	.10
77	Charles Mann	.05
78	Dan Marino	2.00
79	Todd Marinovich	.05
80	Eric Martin	.05
81	Clay Matthews	.05
82	Ed McCaffrey	.05
83	O.J. McDuffie	.30
84	Steve McMichael	.05
85	Audray McMillian	.05
86	Greg McMurtry	.05
87	Karl Mecklenburg	.05
88	Dave Meggett	.05
89	Eric Metcalf	.05
90	Anthony Miller	.10
91	Chris Miller	.05
92	Sam Mills	.05
93	Rick Mirer	.50
94	Johnny Mitchell	.05
95	Art Monk	.10
96	Joe Montana	1.00
97	Warren Moon	.15
98	Rob Moore	.05
99	Brad Muster	.05
100	Browning Nagle	.05
101	Ken Norton Jr.	.05
102	Jay Novacek	.05
103	Neil O'Donnell	.10
104	Leslie O'Neal	.05
105	Louis Oliver	.05
106	Rodney Peete	.05
107	Michael Dean Perry	.05
108	Carl Pickens	.30
109	Ricky Proehl	.05
110	Andre Reed	.10
111	Jerry Rice	1.00
112	Andre Rison	.10
113	Leonard Russell	.10
114	Mark Rypien	.05
115	Barry Sanders	1.00
116	Deion Sanders	.50
117	Junior Seau	.10
118	Shannon Sharpe	.10
119	Sterling Sharpe	.10
120	Clyde Simmons	.05
121	Wayne Simmons	.05
122	Phil Simms	.10
123	Bruce Smith	.10
124	Emmitt Smith	2.00
126	Alonzo Spellman	.10
127	Pat Swilling	.05
128	John Taylor	.05
129	Lawrence Taylor	.15
130	Broderick Thomas	.05
131	Derrick Thomas	.10
132	Thurman Thomas	.15
133	Andre Tippett	.05
134	Jessie Tuggle	.05
135	Tommy Vardell	.05
136	Jon Vaughn	.05
137	Clarence Verdin	.05
138	Herschel Walker	.10
139	Andre Ware	.05
140	Chris Warren	.10
141	Ricky Watters	.20
142	Lorenzen White	.05
143	Reggie White	.15
144	Alfred Williams	.05
145	Calvin Williams	.05
146	Harvey Williams	.05
147	John L. Williams	.05
148	Rod Woodson	.15
149	Barry Word	.05
150	Steve Young	.75

1994 Classic Previews

The five-card, standard-size set was issued by Classic to preview its 1994 NFL Draft Pick set. The card fronts feature the same design as the base set with the backs containing a congratulatory message for pulling the card, which was limited to "1 of 1,950" sets. They are numbered with the "PR" prefix.

		MT
Complete Set (5):		16.00
Common Player:		2.00
1	Heath Shuler	7.00
2	Trent Dilfer	4.00
3	Dan Wilkinson	2.00
4	David Palmer	2.00
5	Johnnie Morton	4.00

1994 Classic Promos

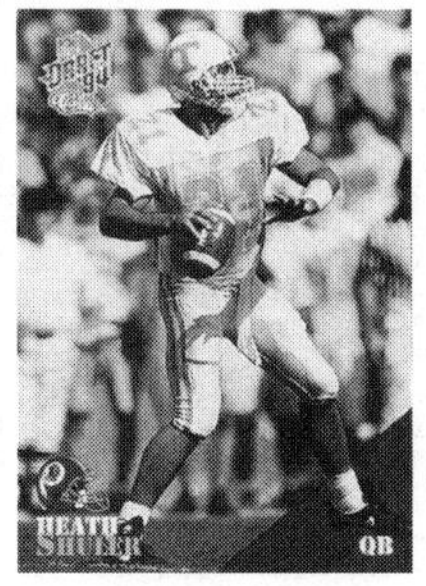

The three-card, standard-size set previewed the release of the 1994 base set. The card fronts feature the same design as the base set - as do the backs. The cards are numbered with the "PR" prefix.

		MT
Complete Set (3):		10.00
Common Player:		4.00
1	Marshall Faulk	5.00
2	Heath Shuler	4.00
3	Heath Shuler	4.00

1994 Classic Fb

This 105-card set features the first licensed cards of 93 NFL rookies. Each card front has a full-bleed color action photo, the player's name and position, the set logo, and a helmet of the team which drafted him. The card back has a ghosted image of the player, except for the player's head, which is full-color. Biographical information, stats, a card number and collegiate summary are also included. The set is limited to just under 10,000 cases. A parallel gold foil card was also made for each card in the set; one card was included in each pack. Other inserts included 1,994 autographed Jerry Rice cards; 9,994 numbered cards honoring Rice's records; sweepstakes Rookie of the Year cards, Classic LPs, Pro Line previews, Basketball previews and Classic Stars. There were also three Classic Draft promo cards produced, using the same design as the main cards also produced, and labeled with a "PR" prefix. The front format is similar to the regular and promo cards, but the back is different; it has a congratulatory message indicating the card is one of five of the 1,950 sets produced.

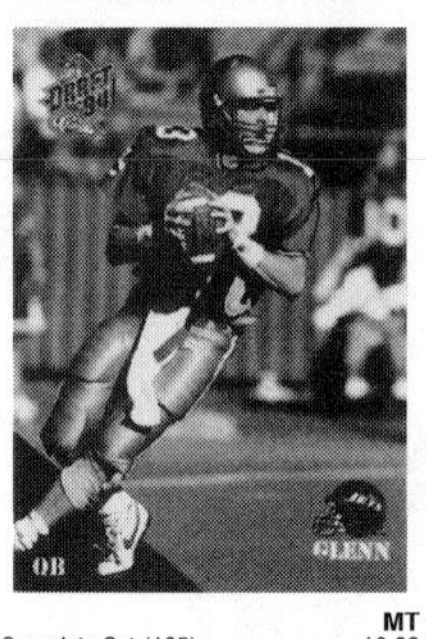

		MT
Complete Set (105):		10.00
Common Player:		.05
Comp. Gold Set (105):		30.00
Gold Cards:		1x-3x
Wax Box:		24.00
1	Heath Shuler	1.00
2	Trent Dilfer	.75
3	Marshall Faulk	2.00
4	Errict Rhett	1.25
5	Charlie Garner	.40
6	Sam Adams	.10
7	Shante Carver	.10
8	Dwayne Chandler	.05
9	Andre Coleman	.05
10	Carlester Crumpler	.05
11	Charles Johnson	.40
12	David Palmer	.10
13	Dan Wilkinson	.20
14	LeShon Johnson	.10
15	Mario Bates	.50
16	Glenn Foley	.05
17	William Gaines	.05
18	Wayne Gandy	.05
19	Jason Gildon	.05
20	Eric Gant	.05
21	Tre Johnson	.05
22	Calvin Jones	.05
23	Jake Kelchner	.05
24	Perry Klein	.05
25	Chuck Levy	.10
26	Corey Louchiey	.05
27	Chris Maumalanga	.05
28	Jamir Miller	.10
29	Jim Miller	.05
30	Johnnie Morton	.30
31	Doug Nussmeier	.05
32	Vaughn Parker	.05
33	Darnay Scott	.40
34	Fernando Smith	.05
35	Lamar Smith	.05
36	Marcus Spears	.05
37	Irving Spikes	.25
38	Todd Steussie	.10
39	Aaron Taylor	.10
40	John Thierry	.10
41	Dewayne Washington	.05
42	Jason Winrow	.05
43	Ronnie Woolfork	.05
44	Bryant Young	.30
45	Arthur Bussie	.05
46	Derrick Alexander	.25
47	Larry Allen	.05
48	Aubrey Beavers	.05
49	James Bostic	.10
50	Jeff Burris	.05
51	Lindsey Chapman	.05
52	Isaac Davis	.05
53	Lake Dawson	.30
54	Tyronne Drakeford	.05
55	William Floyd	.50
56	Henry Ford	.05
57	Rob Fredrickson	.20
58	Aaron Glenn	.05
59	Shelby Hill	.05
60	Willie Jackson	.20
61	Joe Johnson	.05
62	Aaron Laing	.05
63	Kevin Lee	.05
64	Eric Mahlum	.05
65	Steve Matthews	.05
66	Willie McGinest	.20
67	Kevin Mitchell	.05
68	Bam Morris	.75
69	Thomas Randolph	.05
70	Tony Richardson	.05
71	Corey Sawyer	.05
72	Jason Sehorn	.05
73	Rob Waldrop	.05
74	Jay Walker	.05
75	Bernard Williams	.05
76	Marvin Goodwin	.05
77	Romeo Bandison	.05
78	Bucky Brooks	.05
79	James Folston	.05
80	Donnell Bennett	.05
81	Charlie Ward	.20
82	Antonio Langham	.10
83	Greg Hill	.40
84	Darnay Scott	.10
85	Winfred Tubbs	.05
86	Trev Alberts	.10
87	Tim Bowens	.25
88	Thomas Lewis	.10
89	Allen Aldridge	.05
90	Bert Emanuel	.25
91	Ryan Yarborough	.10
92	Lonnie Johnson	.05
93	Isaac Bruce	1.00
94	Checklist #1	.05
95	Checklist #2	.05
96	Troy Aikman	.25
97	Steve Young	.25
98	Rick Mirer	.15
99	Drew Bledsoe	.40
100	Jerry Rice	.25
101	Heath Shuler	.75
102	Marshall Faulk	1.50
103	Trent Dilfer	.30
104	Dan Wilkerson	.10
105	David Palmer	.10
JR1	Jerry Rice Special	12.00
NNO	Jerry Rice Auto/1994	125.00

1994 Classic Football Gold

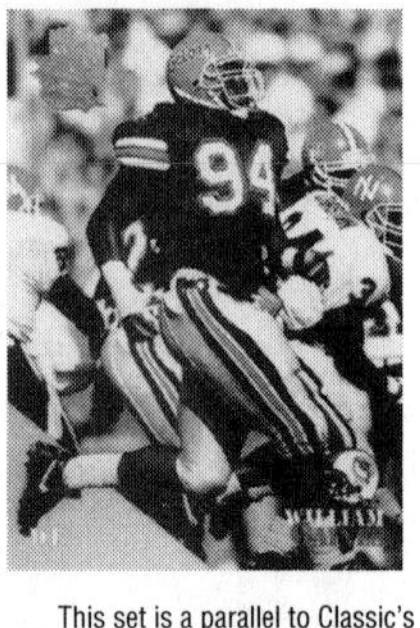

This set is a parallel to Classic's main 1994 Draft set; the cards are the same as the regular ones, except the set logo is stamped in gold foil on the card front. One gold card was in each pack.

		MT
Complete Set (105):		40.00
Common Player:		.15
Gold Cards:		2x

1994 Classic Draft Stars Fb

These cards feature a full-bleed color action photo on the front, along with the set logo. The player's name, position and helmet of the team which drafted him are at the bottom. The card back has another color photo, part of which is ghosted to allow for the player's name and biographical information.

		MT
Complete Set (20):		12.00
Common Player:		.25
1	Trev Alberts	.50
2	Jeff Burris	.25
3	Shante Carver	.25
4	Trent Dilfer	2.00
5	Marshall Faulk	5.00
6	William Floyd	1.50
7	Aaron Glenn	.25
8	Greg Hill	.50
9	Charles Johnson	.50
10	Calvin Jones	.25
11	Antonio Langham	.25
12	Thomas Lewis	.25
13	Willie McGinest	.50
14	Jamir Miller	.25
15	Johnnie Morton	.75
16	David Palmer	.50
17	Darnay Scott	1.00
18	Heath Shuler	2.00
19	Dan Wilkinson	.50
20	Bryant Young	.75
NNO	Rick Mirer Special	10.00

1994 Classic Picks Fb

These limited-edition cards were randomly included in Classic Draft football packs. Only 20,000 of each card was made, as noted in blue on the card back. The card front features a color action photo against a metallic background. The player's name appears in the upper left corner. The back has a player mug shot, collegiate highlights, and bio notes, all against a ghosted image of the photo on the front. A card number, using an "LP" prefix, is also included. An LP card was in every box.

		MT
Complete Set (5):		40.00
Common Player:		4.00
1	Heath Shuler	10.00
2	Trent Dilfer	7.00
3	Johnnie Morton	6.00
4	David Palmer	4.00
5	Marshall Faulk	20.00

1994 Classic ROY Sweepstakes Fb

These 20 sweepstakes cards, issued approximately 5 per case, feature players who were in the running for the NFL's 1994 Rookie of the Year Award. Collectors who obtained a card of the winner could redeem it for an autographed football of the player.

		MT
Complete Set (20):		100.00
Common Player:		2.50

1 Trent Dilfer 5.00
2 Mario Bates 4.00
3 Darnay Scott 4.00
4 Johnnie Morton 3.00
5 William Floyd 5.00
6 Errict Rhett 12.00
7 Greg Hill 5.00
8 Lake Dawson 4.00
9 Charlie Garner 5.00
10 Heath Shuler 10.00
11 Derrick Alexander 4.00
12 LeShon Johnson 2.50
13 Kevin Lee 2.50
14 David Palmer 2.50
15 Charles Johnson 5.00
16 Chuck Levy 2.50
17 Calvin Jones 2.50
18 Thomas Lewis 2.50
19 Marshall Faulk 25.00
20 "Field" card 2.50

1994 Classic Game Cards

The 10-card, regular-sized set was inserted in every jumbo pack of 1994 Classic. The card fronts have "Game Card" printed along the left border with a scratch-off section on the back. An unnumbered Drew Bledsoe card was randomly inserted as well, and winning cards could be redeemed for an uncut Gold NFL Draft sheet or a 1994 NFL Draft Day set. The cards are numbered with the "GC" prefix.

MT
Complete Set (10): 10.00
Common Player: .25
Scratched Cards: .5x
DB1 Drew Bledsoe Special 12.00
1 Trent Dilfer .75
2 Marshall Faulk 3.50
3 Heath Shuler 1.75
4 Dan Wilkinson .25
5 Antonio Langham .25
6 Willie McGinest .25
7 Greg Hill .50
8 Trev Alberts .25
9 Charles Johnson .50
10 Errict Rhett 2.50

1994 Images

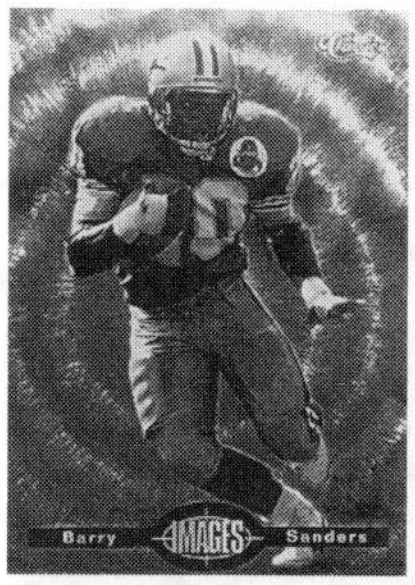

Only 1,994 cases of Classic Images Football were produced, with each card in the 125-card set printed on a specially designed 18-point, micro-lined foil board. The card front has an action shot on a foil background. The player's name is in a stripe at the bottom, with the Images logo in the middle. The card back has stats from the 1993 season and the player's career totals, plus a color photo and card number. Inserts were from two types - All-Pros and All-Pro Prospects cards, and NFL Experience Sneak Preview cards.

MT
Complete Set (125): 60.00
Common Player: .25
Pack (6): 8.00
Wax Box (24): 180.00
1 Emmitt Smith 4.00
2 Reggie White .40
3 Michael Haynes .25
4 Chris Warren .40
5 Jeff George .40
6 Sean Gilbert .25
7 Ricky Watters .40
8 Eric Metcalf .25
9 Randall Cunningham .40
10 Tim Brown .40
11 *Trent Dilfer* 1.00
12 *Marshall Faulk* 7.00
13 David Klingler .25
14 Barry Foster .40
15 John Elway 1.50
16 Joe Montana 4.00
17 Rodney Hampton .40
18 *Todd Steussie* .40
19 Bruce Smith .25
20 Wayne Gandy .25
21 Anthony Miller .25
22 Reggie Brooks .25
23 Johnny Johnson .25
24 *Byron Morris* 1.00
25 Drew Bledsoe 4.00
26 Jeff Hostetler .25
27 Alvin Harper .25
28 Cris Carter .25
29 *Bert Emanuel* 2.00
30 *Errict Rhett* 1.00
31 Scott Mitchell .25
32 Deion Sanders 1.50
33 Lewis Tillman .25
34 *Tim Bowens* .75
35 Charles Haley .25
36 Stan Humphries .25
37 Haywood Jeffires .25
38 Andre Reed .25
39 *Charles Johnson* 1.00
40 Ron Moore .25
41 Jim Everett .25
42 *Greg Hill* 1.00
43 Thurman Thomas .50
44 *Willie McGinest* 1.00
45 *Aaron Glenn* .40
46 Eric Pegram .25
47 Terry Kirby .25
48 Warren Moon .40
49 Clyde Simmons .25
50 Eric Turner .25
51 *Heath Shuler* .75
52 Rickey Jackson .25
53 *Johnnie Morton* 1.00
54 *Charlie Garner* 3.00
55 Mark Collins .25
56 Mike Pritchard .25
57 *Bryant Young* 1.00
58 *Joe Johnson* .40
59 Erik Kramer .25
60 Barry Sanders 3.00
61 Rod Woodson .40
62 Dave Brown .25
63 Gary Brown .25
64 Brett Favre 4.00
65 *Isaac Bruce* 5.00
66 Boomer Esiason .25
67 Jim Harbaugh .25
68 Jackie Harris .25
69 Art Monk .25
70 *Jamir Miller* .40
71 Neil O'Donnell 1.00
72 Neil Smith .25
73 Junior Seau .40
74 *Jerome Bettis* 1.50
75 *Bernard Williams* .25
76 *Jeff Burris* .75
77 Henry Ellard .25
78 Reggie Cobb .25
79 *Shante Carver* .40
80 Terry Allen .25
81 Cortez Kennedy .25
82 *Trev Alberts* .50
83 Michael Irvin 1.00
84 Herschel Walker .25
85 Dan Marino 4.00
86 Dave Meggett .25
87 Herman Moore 1.00
88 *Darnay Scott* 2.00
89 *Dewayne Washington* .50
90 *Rob Fredrickson* .50
91 Rick Mirer .50
92 *Thomas Lewis* .75
93 Chris Miller .25
94 Marion Butts .25
95 *Sam Adams* .75
96 Jerry Rice 2.50
97 Ben Coates .50
98 *David Palmer* 1.00
99 *Antonio Langham* 1.00
100 Curtis Conway 1.50
101 Derrick Thomas .40
102 Ken Norton .25
103 Ronnie Lott .25
104 Sterling Sharpe .40
105 Troy Aikman 3.00
106 Shannon Sharpe .40
107 Natrone Means 1.00
108 Derek Brown .40
109 Dan Wilkinson .75
110 Andre Rison .40
111 Quentin Coryatt .25
112 Cody Carlson .25
113 *William Floyd* .75
114 Marcus Allen .40
115 Steve Young 2.50
116 Jim Kelly .40
117 *LeShon Johnson* .50
118 Irving Fryar .25
119 Carl Pickens 1.00
120 Keith Jackson .25
121 *John Thierry* .40
122 Vinny Testaverde .25
123 *Derrick Alexander* 1.00
124 Seth Joyner .25
125 Checklist .25
TP1 Drew Bledsoe (NFL EX) 50.00
NNO Emmitt Smith (NFL EX) 15.00

1994 Images All-Pro

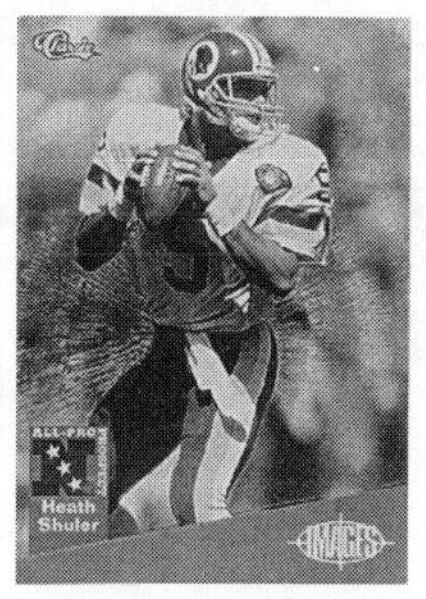

These cards were randomly included in packs of 1994 Classic Images football, either two cards per box or two All-Pro packs per case. Each card in this 25-card set is sequentially numbered up to 2,600. All-Pros have a colored foil stripe across the bottom which includes the Images logo. The player's name, his conference and All-Pro logo are in a box in the lower left corner. The card back has the sequential number, a color action photo, and card number, which uses an "A" prefix.

MT
Complete Set (25): 350.00
Common Player: 7.00
1 Heath Shuler 10.00
2 Steve Young 25.00
3 Trent Dilfer 10.00
4 Troy Aikman 25.00
5 Emmitt Smith 50.00
6 Barry Sanders 30.00
7 Jerome Bettis 12.00
8 Errict Rhett 15.00
9 Jerry Rice 25.00
10 Michael Irvin 7.00
11 Andre Rison 7.00
12 Sterling Sharpe 7.00
13 Reggie White 7.00
14 Rick Mirer 10.00
15 Drew Bledsoe 20.00
16 John Elway 15.00
17 Joe Montana 30.00
18 Dan Marino 50.00
19 Thurman Thomas 10.00
20 Marshall Faulk 20.00
21 Marcus Allen 7.00
22 Charles Johnson 7.00
23 Tim Brown 7.00
24 Anthony Miller 7.00
25 Derrick Thomas 7.00

1994 Images Update

The 10-card, standard-size set was randomly inserted in retail packs of 1995 Classic Images 4-Sport. The cards' numbering starts at No. 126 as an addition to the 1994 Images set.

MT
Complete Set (10): 100.00
Common Player: 4.00
126 Emmitt Smith 25.00
127 Troy Aikman 12.00
128 Steve Young 10.00
129 Deion Sanders 10.00
130 Ben Coates 4.00
131 Natrone Means 8.00
132 Drew Bledsoe 12.00
133 Cris Carter 5.00
134 Marshall Faulk 10.00
135 Errict Rhett 8.00

1994 Classic NFL Experience Promos

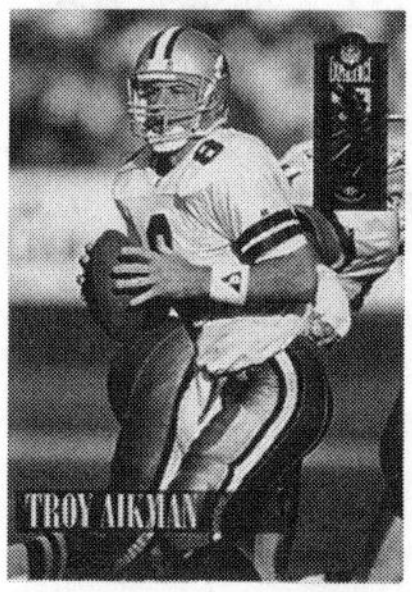

The six-card, standard-size set was issued to preview the 100-card 1994 Classic NFL Experience set. The fronts feature full-bleed action shots with "For Promotional Purposes Only" printed on the card backs.

MT
Complete Set (6): 18.00
Common Player: 1.25
1 Troy Aikman 5.00
2 Jerry Rice 5.00
3 Emmitt Smith 10.00
4 Derrick Thomas 1.25
5 Thurman Thomas 2.50
6 Rod Woodson 1.25

1994 Classic NFL Experience

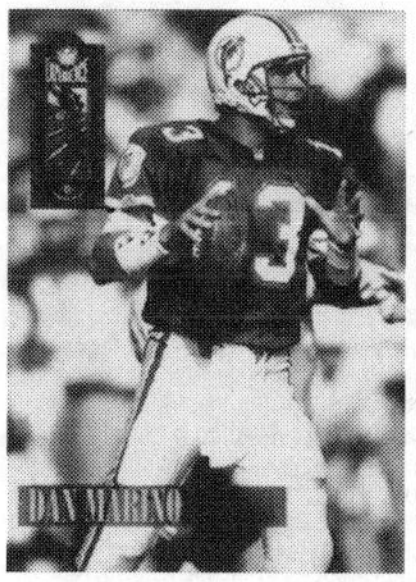

This limited-print 100-card set features the NFL's impact players and highlights 23 top rookies, along with 16 members of the NFL Quarterback Club. Each card front has a borderless color photo of the player, the set logo, and the player's name in a color bar at the bottom. The back has a color photo, a summary of the player's accomplishments during the 1993 season, and a card number. Both sides are UV coated. Classic produced only 1,500 numbered cases, available only through hobby dealers, in conjunction with Super Bowl XXVIII. A 10-card limited-print set of rookies was produced as inserts, as were 1,994 Troy Aikman Super Bowl MVP cards. Six promo cards were also produced to showcase the company's main set. The cards were given away during a Super Bowl card show.

MT
Complete Set (100): 12.00
Common Player: .06
Pack: .75
Wax Box (36): 24.00
1 Checklist 1 .06
2 Checklist 2 .06
3 Bobby Hebert .10
4 Erric Pegram .25
5 Andre Rison .30
6 Deion Sanders .15
7 Cornelius Bennett .08
8 Jim Kelly .25
9 Andre Reed .10
10 Bruce Smith .10
11 Thurman Thomas .40
12 Curtis Conway .30
13 Jim Harbaugh .06
14 John Copeland .10
15 David Klingler .20
16 Carl Pickens .10
17 Eric Metcalf .15
18 Vinny Testaverde .10
19 Eric Turner .08
20 Tommy Vardell .08
21 Troy Aikman 1.00
22 Michael Irvin .45
23 Emmitt Smith 2.00
24 Kevin Williams .10
25 John Elway .40
26 Glyn Milburn .15
27 Shannon Sharpe .10
28 Herman Moore .25
29 Rodney Peete .06
30 Barry Sanders 1.25
31 Pat Swilling .10
32 Brett Favre 1.00
33 Sterling Sharpe .10
34 Reggie White .15
35 Haywood Jeffires .10
36 Warren Moon .15
37 Webster Slaughter .06
38 Lorenzo White .06
39 Quentin Coryatt .06
40 Jeff George .10
41 Roosevelt Potts .06
42 Marcus Allen .10
43 Joe Montana 1.25
44 Neil Smith .08
45 Derrick Thomas .10
46 Tim Brown .25
47 Jeff Hostetler .08
48 Raghib Ismail .15
49 Anthony Smith .06
50 Jerome Bettis .50
51 Jim Everett .08
52 T.J. Rubley .06
53 Keith Jackson .10
54 Terry Kirby .45
55 Dan Marino 2.00
56 O.J. McDuffie .25
57 Scott Mitchell .35
58 Cris Carter .10
59 Chris Doleman .08
60 Robert Smith .10
61 Drew Bledsoe 1.50
62 Vincent Brisby .45
63 Derek Brown .20
64 Willie Roaf .08
65 Irv Smith .06
66 Renaldo Turnbull .06
67 Rodney Hampton .35
68 Phil Simms .10
69 Lawrence Taylor .10
70 Boomer Esiason .06
71 Marvin Jones .06
72 Ronnie Lott .10
73 Johnny Mitchell .06
74 Rob Moore .10
75 Victor Bailey .10
76 Randall Cunningham .10
77 Ken O'Brien .06
78 Steve Beuerlein .08
79 Garrison Hearst .50
80 Ron Moore .30
81 Rocky Proehl .08
82 Deon Figures .06
83 Barry Foster .20
84 Neil O'Donnell .12
85 Rod Woodson .10
86 Natrone Means .50
87 Anthony Miller .25
88 Junior Seau .06
89 Jerry Rice .75
90 Ricky Watters .20
91 Steve Young 1.00
92 Brian Blades .06
93 Cortez Kennedy .10
94 Rick Mirer .50
95 Reggie Cobb .06
96 Eric Curry .06
97 Craig Erickson .10
98 Reggie Brooks .40
99 Desmond Howard .10
100 Mark Rypien .06

1994 Classic NFL Experience LPs

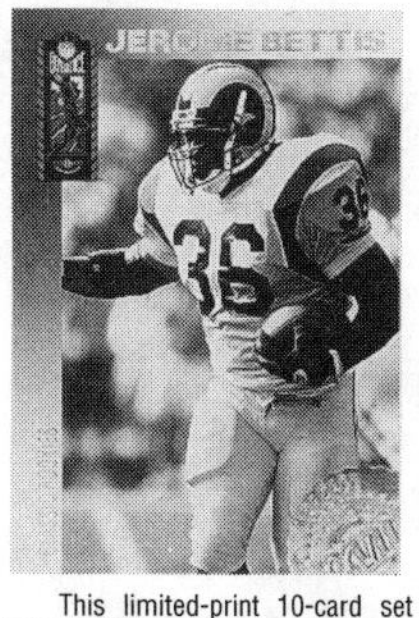

This limited-print 10-card set features 10 top NFL prospects. Only 2,400 of each card was produced, and each includes an embossed gold logo of Super Bowl XXVIII on the front. The card front also has a color action photo, the set logo, the player's name and "Classic Rookies" on it. The back, numbered using an "LP" prefix, has another color photo and brief player profile. Cards were random inserts in 1994 Classic NFL Experience packs.

MT
Complete Set (10): 90.00
Common Player: 3.00
Minor Stars: 6.00
1 Jerome Bettis 6.00
2 Drew Bledsoe 25.00
3 Reggie Brooks 3.00
4 Garrison Hearst 12.00
5 Derek Brown 3.00
6 Terry Kirby 6.00
7 Natrone Means 12.00
8 Glyn Milburn 3.00
9 Rick Mirer 12.00
10 Robert Smith 6.00

1995 Classic NFL Rookies Fb

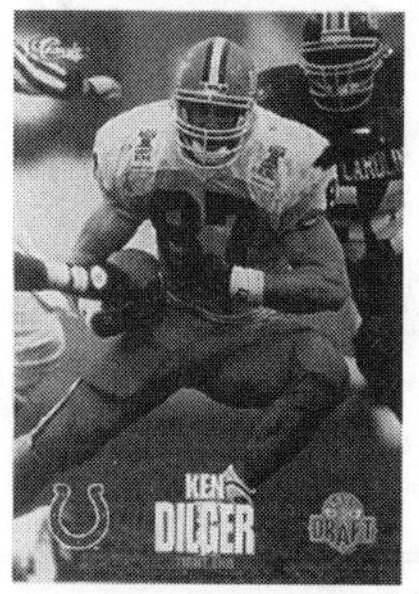

Each of these cards features the 1995 NFL Draft logo and the logo of the team the player was selected by during the draft, along with a full-bleed color action photo on the front. The player's name is in white at the bottom of the card; the Classic logo is in an upper corner. The back has the player's name, position, NFL team name, biographical information and collegiate statistics toward the top; a recap of the player's collegiate accomplishments and a color action photo are on the bottom half. The card number is in the upper left corner in an arrow. Two subsets were also created within the main set - NFL Draft Retro cards and Award Winners. Three parallel sets were also produced - a Silver Series (cards printed on silver foil board; one per pack); a Printer's Proof Series (one per 18 hobby); and a Printer's Proof Silver Series (one in 36 packs). An abbreviated Die-Cut Printer's Proof 1st Round Picks set of the first 32 cards was also made; only 97 sets were made. Only 595 of each regular card appears in a Printer's Proof format, while only 297 of each card was done in a Printer's Proof Silver Series format. Three insert sets were made - Rookie of the Year Redemption, Pro Line Game Breakers and oversized bonus rookie cards. Production of 1995 NFL Classic Rookies was limited to 2,950 hobby and 2,950 retail cases.

MT
Complete Set (110): 15.00
Common Player: .05
Comp. Silver Set (110): 50.00
Common Silver Player: .10
Silver Cards: 2x-4x
Comp. Prin. Proof (110): 325.00
Common Prin. Proof: 1.00
Prin. Proof Cards: 10x-20x
Comp. Prin. Proof Sil. (110): 550.00
Common Prin. Proof Sil.: 1.50
Prin. Proof Silvers: 15x-30x
1 Ki-Jana Carter 1.00
2 Tony Boseli .25
3 Steve McNair 1.00
4 Michael Westbrook .50
5 Kerry Collins 1.25
6 Kevin Carter .25
7 Mike Mamula .25
8 Joseph Galloway 1.25
9 Kyle Brady .20
10 J.J. Stokes 1.25
11 Derrick Alexander .25
12 Warren Sapp .30
13 Mark Fields .25
14 Ruben Brown .05
15 Ellis Johnson .25
16 Hugh Douglas .40
17 Tyrone Wheatley .75
18 Napoleon Kaufman .75
19 James Stewart .50
20 Luther Elliss .20
21 Rashaan Salaam 1.50
22 Tyrone Poole .10
23 Ty Law .10
24 Korey Stringer .10
25 Billy Milner .10
26 Devin Bush .10
27 Mark Bruener .30
28 Derrick Brooks .20
29 Blake Brockermeyer .10
30 Craig Powell .05
31 Trezelle Jenkins .10
32 Craig Newsome .20
33 Thomas Bailey .05
34 Chad May .10
35 J.J. Smith .05
36 Lorenzo Styles .05
37 Brian Williams .05
38 Damien Covington .05
39 Steve Stenstrom .05
40 Darius Holland .05
41 Pete Mitchell .05
42 Todd Collins .25
43 Kordell Stewart 1.00
44 Eric Zeier .75
45 Frank Sanders .50
46 Ben Talley .05
47 Billy Williams .05
48 Chris Jones .05
49 Tamarick Vanover .50
50 Jimmy Hitchcock .05
51 Chris Hudson .05
52 Terrell Fletcher .20
53 Brent Moss .05
54 Terrell Davis 1.00
55 Rodney Thomas .50
56 Larry Jones .10
57 Ray Zellars .20
58 David Sloan .05
59 Brandon Bennett .05
60 Brian DeMarco .05
61 Bryan Schwartz .05
62 Jack Jackson .05
63 Bobby Taylor .05
64 Kevin Hickman .05
65 Matt O'Dwyer .05
66 Patrick Riley .05
67 Ki-Jana Carter 1.00
68 Kerry Collins 1.25
69 Steve McNair 1.00
70 Tyrone Wheatley .75
71 Antonio Freeman .40
72 Clifton Abraham .05
73 Kez McCorvey .10
74 Lovell Pinkney .10
75 Lee DeRamus .05
76 John Walsh .10
77 Cory Raymer .10
78 Corey Fuller .10
79 Tyrone Davis .10
80 David Dunn .10
81 Dana Howard .05
82 Melvin Johnson .05
83 Robert Baldwin .05
84 Curtis Martin 1.50
85 Zack Crockett .10
86 Jay Barker .10
87 Christian Fauria .25
88 Zach Wiegert .05
89 Barrett Brooks .05
90 Ken Dilger .25
91 James Stewart .20
92 Ed Hervey .05
93 Torey Hunter .05
94 Sherman Williams .40
95 Shawn King .05
96 Dave Barr .05
97 Rob Johnson .10
98 Stoney Case .25
99 Checklist 1 (Ki-Jana Carter) .25
100 Checklist 2 (Steve McNair) .25
101 Rashaan Salaam .75
102 Kerry Collins .75
103 Rashaan Salaam .75
104 Kerry Collins .75
105 Jay Barker .10
106 Drew Bledsoe .50
107 Marshall Faulk .50
108 Steve Young .50
109 Troy Aikman .50
110 Emmitt Smith .75
101 Rashaan Salaam
102 Kerry Collins
103 Rashaan Salaam
104 Kerry Collins
105 Jay Barker
106 Drew Bledsoe
107 Marshall Faulk
108 Steve Young
109 Troy Aikman
110 Emmitt Smith

1995 Classic NFL Rookies Silver

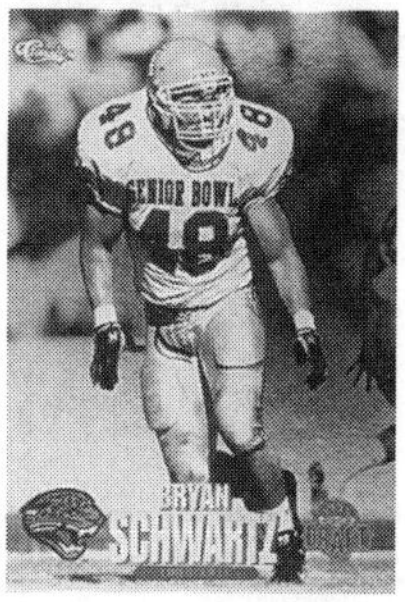

The 110-card, standard-size set is a parallel to the base set and features the same front and back designs as the base set, with the cards being printed on silver-foil stock. The cards were inserted one per pack.

MT
Complete Set (110): 40.00
Common Player: .10
Silver Cards: 3x

1995 Classic NFL Rookies Printer's Proofs

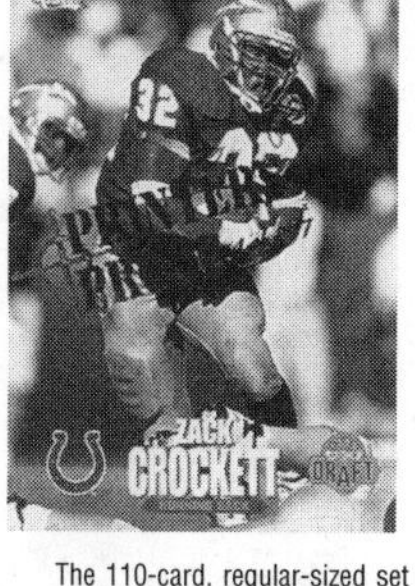

The 110-card, regular-sized set was a parallel set to the 1995 Classic

NFL Rookies set. Limited to 595 each, the cards feature "Printer's Proofs" printed across the front, which are the same fronts as found in the base set. The backs are also identical.

	MT
Complete Set (110):	280.00
Common Player:	1.00
Printer's Proofs:	10x-20x

1995 Classic NFL Rookies Printer's Proofs Silver

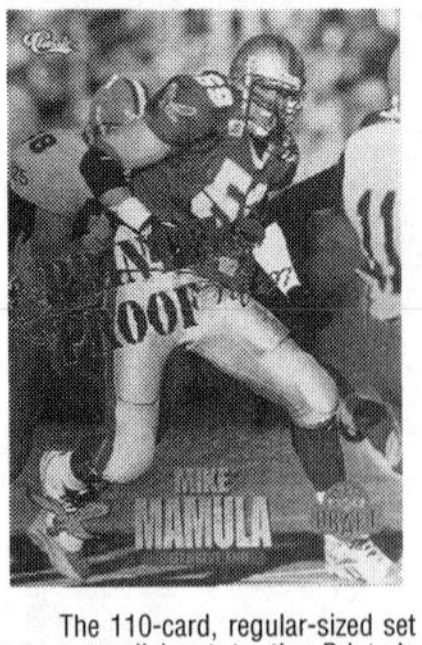

The 110-card, regular-sized set was a parallel set to the Printer's Proofs inserts, with the difference being "Printer's Proofs" is printed in silver foil across the card fronts. Each card was limited to 297 issues.

	MT
Complete Set (110):	425.00
Common Player:	1.50
Silver Cards:	15x-30x

1995 Classic NFL Rookies Die Cuts

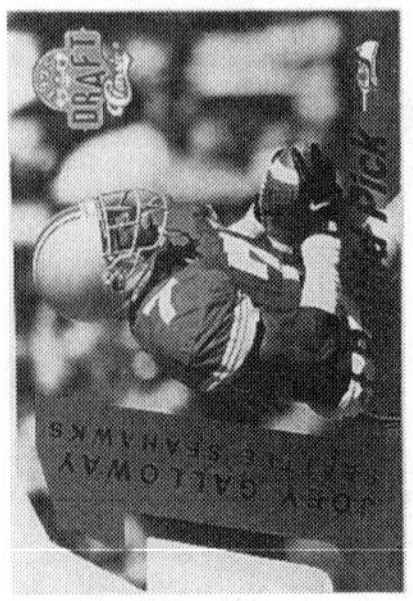

The 32-card, regular-size set featured the 32 players selected in the 1995 NFL Draft's first round. The cards are die cut in the form of a No. 1 and are sequentially numbered to 4,500. Cards in the set were inserted twice per box.

		MT
Complete Set (32):		85.00
Common Player:		.50
1	Ki-Jana Carter	6.00
2	Tony Boselli	1.50
3	Steve McNair	10.00
4	Michael Westbrook	4.00
5	Kerry Collins	12.00
6	Kevin Carter	1.00
7	Mike Mamula	1.00
8	Joey Galloway	10.00
9	Kyle Brady	1.00
10	J.J. Stokes	6.00
11	Derrick Alexander	1.00
12	Warren Sapp	1.50
13	Mark Fields	.50
14	Ruben Brown	.50
15	Ellis Johnson	.50
16	Hugh Douglas	2.00
17	Tyrone Wheatley	4.00
18	Napoleon Kaufman	4.00
19	James O. Stewart	2.00
20	Luther Ellis	1.00
21	Rashaan Salaam	8.00
22	Tyrone Poole	1.00
23	Ty Law	1.00
24	Korey Stringer	1.00
25	Billy Miner	.50
26	Devin Bush	.50
27	Mark Bruener	1.50
28	Derrick Brooks	1.00
29	Blake Brockermeyer	1.00
30	Craig Powell	.50
31	Trezelle Jenkins	.50
32	Craig Newsome	2.00

A card number in parentheses ( ) indicates the set is unnumbered.

1995 Classic NFL Rookies Die Cuts Printer's Proofs

The 32-card, regular-sized set, inserted every hobby case, paralleled the 1995 NFL Rookies Die Cut set with the exception being "Printer's Proofs" printed on the card fronts.

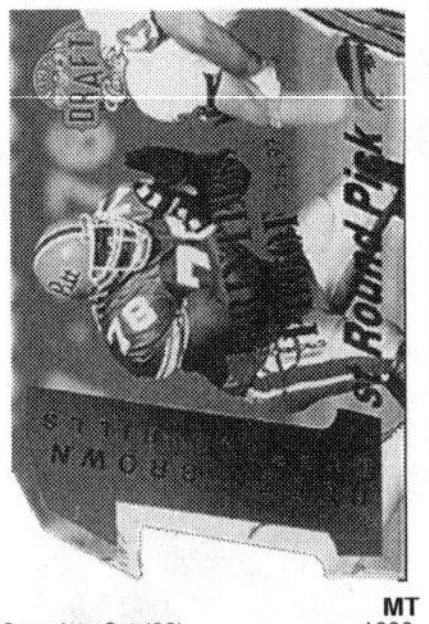

	MT
Complete Set (32):	1300.
Common Player:	10.00
Die-Cut Printer's Proofs:	8x-16x

1995 Classic NFL Rookies Die Cuts Silver Signatures

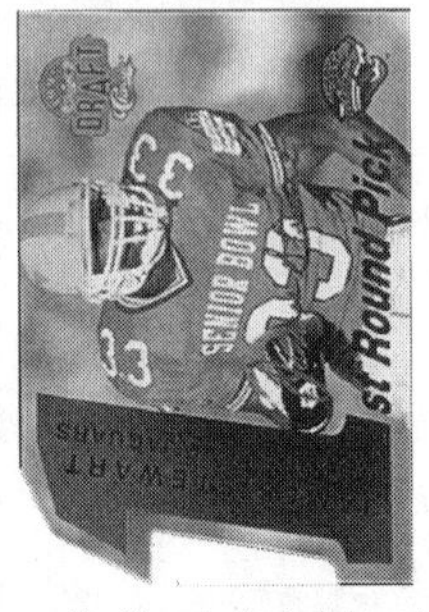

The 32-card, standard-size set paralleled the NFL Rookies set, except for the facsimile autographs stamped on each card front. Cards in the set were inserted every 48 packs and are sequentially numbered to 1,750.

	MT
Complete Set (32):	250.00
Common Player:	2.00
Die-Cut Silvers:	2x-3x

1995 Classic NFL Rookies Bonus Card Jumbos NFL Team's

As a special dealer bonus for Classic's 1995 NFL Rookies set, each hobby case of the product contains at least one of these three oversized rookie cards. Each card is sequentially numbered up to 2,500. The front has a photo of the player in his college uniform, with his NFL's team logo in the background. The brand logo is in the upper left corner; the player's name, position and team name are at the bottom. Cards are ticket size, measuring 4-3/4" x 2-1/2". They are printed on micro-lined foil board.

		MT
Complete Set (3):		30.00
Common Player:		10.00
1	Ki-Jana Carter	10.00
2	Steve McNair	12.00
3	Kerry Collins	10.00

1995 Classic NFL Rookies Draft Review

The first 14 cards of Draft Review were handed out to the media on NFL Draft Day, and were also later reissued in retail packs of Classic NFL Rookies, every one per three packs. Card No. 14, which was a checklist when first issued, was replaced by an Emmitt Smith card, while the eight additional cards updated team selections. The 14-card set that the media received came with a certificate of authenticity numbered up to 19,995 sets. Since it was not known which team would draft certain players, some are pictured in multiple pro uniforms, and updated in the final eight cards of this 22-card set.

		MT
Complete Set (23):		20.00
Common Player:		.25
1	Steve McNair (Oilers)	3.00
2	Steve McNair (Vikings)	1.50
3	Steve McNair (Jaguars)	1.50
4	Ki-Jana Carter (Panthers)	1.00
5	Ki-Jana Carter (Jaguars)	1.00
6	Kerry Collins (Bills)	1.75
7	Kerry Collins (Colts)	1.75
8	Kerry Collins (Cardinals)	1.75
9	John Walsh (Panthers)	.25
10	John Walsh (Vikings)	.25
11	John Walsh (Dolphins)	.25
12	J.J. Stokes (Seahawks)	1.00
13	J.J. Stokes (Rams)	1.00
14A	Checklist (John Walsh, Steve McNair, Kerry Collins)	1.75
14B	Emmitt Smith	2.50
15	Steve Young	1.00
16	Marshall Faulk	1.00
17	Troy Aikman	1.50
18	Ki-Jana Carter (Bengals)	1.50
19	Kerry Collins (Panthers)	3.50
20	J.J. Stokes (49ers)	1.50
21	Michael Westbrook (Redskins)	1.00
22	Kyle Brady (Jets)	.50

1995 Classic NFL Rookies Instant Energy

The 20-card, standard-sized set was inserted every rack pack of 1995 Classic NFL Rookies. The card fronts feature a color player image over a lightning background with the backs containing another player shot with a profile, also over a lightning background. They cards are numbered with the "IE" prefix.

		MT
Complete Set (20):		18.00
Common Player:		.50
1	Ki-Jana Carter	1.00
2	Steve McNair	3.00
3	Michael Westbrook	1.00
4	Joey Galloway	3.00
5	Tyrone Wheatley	1.00
6	Napoleon Kaufman	1.25
7	Warren Sapp	.75
8	Kevin Carter	.50
9	Todd Collins	.75
10	Rob Johnson	.50
11	Chad May	.50
12	Mike Mamula	.50
13	Sherman Williams	.50
14	Tony Boselli	.75
15	Kerry Collins	3.00
16	J.J. Stokes	1.50
17	Rashaan Salaam	2.00
18	Kordell Stewart	3.00
19	Derrick Brooks	.50
20	Frank Sanders	1.00

1995 Classic NFL Rookies ROY Redemption Fb

The top 19 offensive players and a field card are featured on these 1995 Classic NFL Rookies inserts. Each card in this set is limited to 2,500 produced and was inserted at a rate of one per every three boxes. Cards depicting the January 1996 NFL Offensive Rookie of the Year are redeemable for a $50 phone card of the player. The card front is horizontal, with "1 of 2,500" and "Rookie of the Year" on it. The back has the contest rules. The cards are numbered with "ROY" prefix.

		MT
Complete Set (20):		180.00
Common Player:		3.00
1	Ki-Jana Carter	10.00
2	Tony Boselli	4.00
3	Steve McNair	12.00
4	Michael Westbrook	8.00
5	Kerry Collins	18.00
6	Joseph Galloway	18.00
7	Kyle Brady	4.00
8	J.J. Stokes	12.00
9	Tyrone Wheatley	10.00
10	Napoleon Kaufman	10.00
11	Rashaan Salaam	16.00
12	Kordell Stewart	10.00
13	James Stewart	5.00
14	Frank Sanders	8.00
15	Ray Zellars	5.00
16	Zack Crockett	3.00
17	Tamarick Vanover	8.00
18	Chad May	3.00
19	Eric Zeier	10.00
20	Field Card	20.00

1995 Classic NFL Rookies Rookie Spotlight

The 30-card, standard-size set features a color action shot on the card fronts while the backs contain a color headshot with a player profile. The cards were inserted in every rack pack. The cards are numbered with the "RS" prefix.

		MT
Complete Set (30):		28.00
Common Player:		.50
Holographic Cards:		3x-6x
1	Ki-Jana Carter	1.50
2	Steve McNair	3.00
3	Michael Westbrook	1.00
4	Joey Galloway	3.00
5	Tyrone Wheatley	1.00
6	Napoleon Kaufman	1.00
7	Kordell Stewart	3.00
8	Frank Sanders	1.00
9	Zack Crockett	.50
10	Tamarick Vanover	1.00
11	Chad May	.50
12	Eric Zeier	.50
13	Mike Mamula	.50
14	Warren Sapp	.75
15	Kevin Carter	.50
16	Derrick Brooks	.50
17	Todd Collins	.50
18	Rob Johnson	.50
19	Chris T. Jones	1.00
20	Terrell Fletcher	.50
21	Sherman Williams	.50
22	Tony Boselli	.75
23	Kerry Collins	3.00
24	J.J. Stokes	1.50
25	Rashaan Salaam	2.00
26	James O. Stewart	1.00
27	Rodney Thomas	.50
28	Jack Jackson	.50
29	Lovell Pinkney	.50
30	Ruben Brown	.50

1995 Classic Draft Day Jaguars

The five-card, standard-size set was issued on Draft Day in 1995 to honor the Jacksonville Jaguars first NFL Draft. The card fronts feature color action photos of top 1995 NFL picks in their collegiate uniforms while the backs have the NFL Draft emblem, along with the Jaguars logo. The cards are numbered with the "JJ" prefix.

		MT
Complete Set (5):		20.00
Common Player:		2.00
1	Kerry Collins	6.00
2	Steve McNair	5.00
3	Tony Boselli	2.00
4	Kevin Carter	2.00
5	Ki-Jana Carter	5.00

1995 Classic Images Previews

These five micro-lined insert cards preview the design Classic used for its 1995 NFL Images set. Cards were seeded one per every 18 packs of 1995 Classic Pro Line II product.

		MT
Complete Set (5):		50.00
Common Player:		8.00
1	Emmitt Smith	20.00
2	Steve Young	8.00
3	Drew Bledsoe	10.00
4	Kerry Collins	10.00
5	Marshall Faulk	8.00

1995 Images Limited/Live

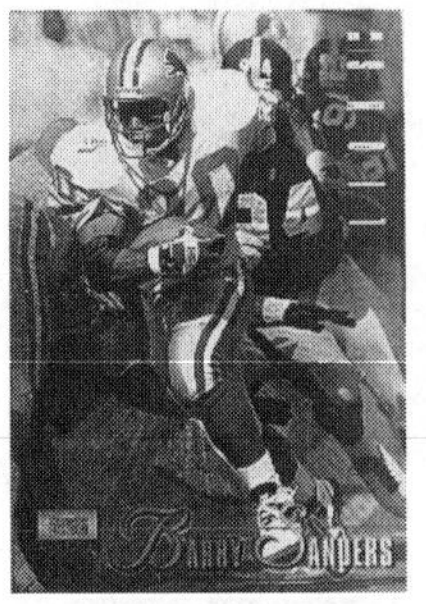

Classic's 1995 NFL Images Limited set has two versions - a hobby version called Limited and a retail version called Live. Both contain 125 cards in the regular issue, with an identical checklist, but slightly different designs. The set showcases top NFL veterans and 35 rookies in their pro uniforms. Limited card fronts have a slightly raised image against a metallic background. The player's team name and position are in the upper right corner, while the Images Limited logo is in the bottom left corner. The player's name runs along the bottom. The card back has the number in the upper left corner, with the player's name running along the left side of the card. A full-bleed color action photo is in the center, with 1994 and career statistics underneath. The Live versions have a slightly raised image with a metallic background. The player's name, team and position are at the bottom. The set icon is in the upper left corner. "Live" repeats itself along the left border. The card back has a photo in the center with a white frame. The player's name and position are underneath, followed by his 1994 and career statistics. The card number is in the upper left corner, while a team logo is in the upper right corner. Images Limited features a 20-card Icons insert set that is printed on fabric. Other insert sets include: DC Images, Silks, NFL Experience Sculpted Previews, Focused and Untouchables.

		MT
Complete Set (125):		30.00
Common Player:		.20
Minor Stars:		.40
Pack (6):		3.50
Wax Box (24):		65.00
1	Emmitt Smith	3.00
2	Steve Young	1.00
3	Drew Bledsoe	1.50
4	Dan Marino	3.00
5	John Elway	.75
6	Barry Sanders	2.00
7	Brett Favre	3.00
8	Troy Aikman	1.50
9	Jim Kelly	.40
10	Marshall Faulk	1.00
11	Jerry Rice	1.50
12	Warren Moon	.40
13	Jim Everett	.20
14	Rodney Hampton	.20
15	Jeff Hostetler	.20
16	Errict Rhett	.50
17	Jerome Bettis	.50
18	Byron Morris	.20
19	Randall Cunningham	.20
20	Rick Mirer	.50
21	Natrone Means	.75
22	Jeff George	.40
23	Garrison Hearst	.40
24	Michael Irvin	.75
25	Cris Carter	.40
26	Irving Fryar	.20
27	*Jeff Blake*	.75
28	Bruce Smith	.20
29	Shannon Sharpe	.20
30	Steve Beuerlein	.20
31	Stan Humphries	.40
32	Chris Warren	.40
33	Ben Coates	.20
34	Boomer Esiason	.20
35	Trent Dilfer	.75
36	Chris Miller	.20
37	Dave Brown	.20
38	Herman Moore	.75
39	Anthony Miller	.20
40	Andre Reed	.20
41	Reggie White	.40
42	Darnay Scott	.50
43	Erik Kramer	.20
44	Leroy Hoard	.20
45	Fred Barnett	.20
46	Junior Seau	.40
47	Vinny Testaverde	.20
48	Gus Frerotte	.50
49	William Floyd	.50
50	Mo Lewis	.20
51	Tim Brown	.40
52	Greg Lloyd	.20
53	Chester McGlockton	.20
54	Heath Shuler	.75
55	Rod Woodson	.20
56	Don Beebe	.20
57	Carl Pickens	.40
58	Charles Haley	.20
59	Steve Bono	.50
60	Harvey Williams	.20
61	Greg Hill	.50
62	Eric Metcalf	.20
63	Mario Bates	.50
64	Terry Allen	.20
65	Michael Timpson	.20
66	Mark Stepnoski	.20
67	Jeff Lageman	.20
68	Robert Smith	.20
69	Eric Allen	.20
70	Ricky Watters	.40
71	Derek Loville	.20
72	Bernie Parmalee	.40
73	Bryce Paup	.20
74	Frank Reich	.20
75	Henry Thomas	.20
76	Craig Erickson	.20
77	Eric Green	.20
78	Dave Meggett	.20
79	Deion Sanders	1.00
80	Herschel Walker	.20
81	Andre Rison	.40
82	*Ki-Jana Carter*	.75
83	*Tony Boselli*	.40
84	*Steve McNair*	4.00
85	*Michael Westbrook*	1.00
86	*Kerry Collins*	1.50
87	*Kevin Carter*	.40
88	*Warren Sapp*	.75
89	*Joey Galloway*	2.50
90	*J.J. Stokes*	1.00
91	*Derrick Brooks*	.40
92	*Kyle Brady*	.75
93	*Napoleon Kaufman*	2.00
94	*Tyrone Wheatley*	.75
95	*Mike Mamula*	.40
96	Desmond Howard	.20
97	*James Stewart*	2.00
98	Craig Newsome	.20
99	*Ty Law*	.20
100	Ellis Johnson	.20
101	*Hugh Douglas*	.50
102	*Mark Bruener*	.75
103	*Tyrone Poole*	.20
104	*Luther Elliss*	.20
105	*Mark Fields*	.20
106	*Frank Sanders*	.75
107	*Rashaan Salaam*	.75
108	*Craig Powell*	.20
109	*Sherman Williams*	.40
110	*Chad May*	.40
111	*Rob Johnson*	1.50
112	*Todd Collins*	.40
113	*Terrell Davis*	10.00
114	*Eric Zeier*	.40
115	*Curtis Martin*	4.00
116	*Kordell Stewart*	5.00
117	Troy Vincent	.20
118	*Ray Zellars*	.40
119	Dave Krieg	.20
120	Mike Sherrard	.20
121	Willie Davis	.20
122	Robert Brooks	.40
123	*Chris Sanders*	.75
124	(Drew Bledsoe CL)	.50
125	(Emmitt Smith CL)	1.00

1995 Images Limited/Live Die-Cuts

These 1995 NFL Images Limited die-cut cards were seeded one per every 99 packs. The card front has a color action photo on the left side, with the "Images" logo repeated throughout the background. An insert set logo is in the lower left corner. The right side of the card has a black panel with the player's name in it; the panel is die-cut like a puzzle piece. The card back repeats the die-cut design on the left side, with a color action photo on the right against a colored background which has the Images icon throughout it. A white box at the top has numbers which indicate the card is "x of 965" made. The cards are numbered with the "DC" prefix.

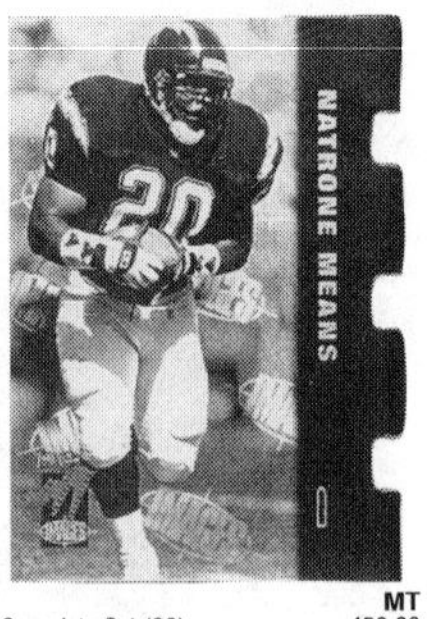

		MT
Complete Set (30):		450.00
Complete Series 1 (15):		225.00
Complete Series 2 (15):		225.00
Common Player:		7.00
1	Jim Kelly	10.00
2	Kerry Collins	35.00
3	Michael Irvin	10.00
4	Troy Aikman	25.00
5	John Elway	15.00
6	Barry Sanders	35.00
7	Marshall Faulk	10.00
8	James Stewart	7.00
9	Drew Bledsoe	25.00
10	Herman Moore	10.00
11	Bam Morris	7.00
12	Jerry Rice	25.00
13	Joey Galloway	25.00
14	Rick Mirer	7.00
15	Errict Rhett	10.00
16	Rob Moore	7.00
17	Jeff George	7.00
18	Rashaan Salaam	10.00
19	Andre Rison	7.00
20	Emmitt Smith	50.00
21	Brett Favre	50.00
22	Dan Marino	50.00
23	Warren Moon	10.00
24	Dave Brown	7.00
25	Napoleon Kaufman	10.00
26	Natrone Means	10.00
27	Steve Young	25.00
28	Reggie White	10.00
29	Jerome Bettis	10.00
30	Michael Westbrook	10.00

1995 Images Limited/Live Focused

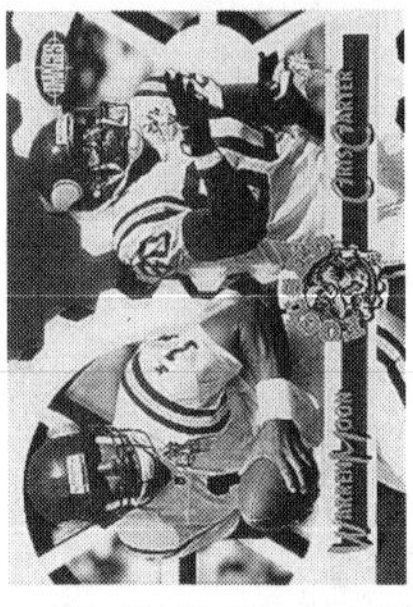

These plastic cards were seeded one per every 24 packs of 1995 NFL Images Limited football. The horizontal front shows two teammates against a background of two wheel cogs. The Images logo is in the upper right corner. A "Focused" icon is in the center of the card at the bottom, sandwiched between the players' names. The card back has ghosted, reversed images of the photos from the front, plus a card number, which is in the upper left corner. The number uses an "F" prefix.

		MT
Complete Set (30):		140.00
Common Player:		5.00
1	Erik Kramer, Rashaan Salaam	8.00
2	Frank Reich, Kerry Collins	10.00
3	Jim Kelly, Andre Reed	5.00
4	Jeff George, Craig Heyward	5.00
5	Garrison Hearst, Dave Krieg	5.00
6	Barry Sanders, Herman Moore	10.00
7	John Elway, Shannon Sharpe	7.00
8	Troy Aikman, Emmitt Smith	20.00
9	Andre Rison, Leroy Hoard	5.00
10	Jeff Blake, Carl Pickens	7.00
11	Steve Bono, Willie Davis	5.00
12	James Stewart, Steve Beuerlein	5.00
13	Marshall Faulk, Craig Erickson	14.00
14	Steve McNair, Chris Chandler	7.00
15	Brett Favre, Reggie White	20.00
16	Dave Brown, Rodney Hampton	5.00
17	Jim Everett, Mario Bates	5.00

18	Drew Bledsoe, Ben Coates	12.00
19	Warren Moon, Cris Carter	5.00
20	Dan Marino, Irving Fryar	20.00
21	Stan Humphries, Natrone Means	8.00
22	Bam Morris, Kevin Greene	5.00
23	Randall Cunningham, Ricky Watters	5.00
24	Jeff Hostetler, Tim Brown	5.00
25	Boomer Esiason, Kyle Brady	5.00
26	Terry Allen, Michael Westbrook	5.00
27	Errict Rhett, Trent Dilfer	8.00
28	Jerome Bettis, Kevin Carter	5.00
29	Steve Young, Jerry Rice	13.00
30	Rick Mirer, Joey Galloway	7.00

1995 Images Limited/Live Icons

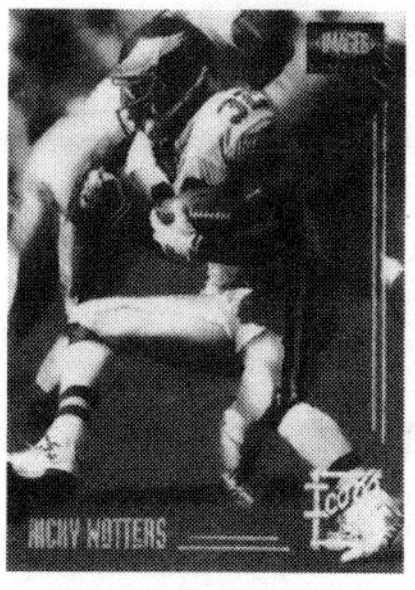

These 20 cards, numbered on the back using an "I" prefix, are printed on fabric cards which are extremely limited; they are seeded one per every 20 boxes of 1995 Classic NFL Images Limited. The set logo is in the upper right corner; the insert set icon is in the lower right corner, opposite the player's name. A full-bleed fabric action photo comprises the front. The back has the card number in the upper left corner, with a photo on the top half of the card. The player's name is below the photo, at the top of a box which includes a recap of the player's professional accomplishments.

		MT
Complete Set (20):		150.00
Common Player:		5.00
1	Jim Kelly	5.00
2	Rashaan Salaam	7.00
3	Andre Rison	5.00
4	Troy Aikman	12.00
5	Emmitt Smith	25.00
6	John Elway	7.00
7	Barry Sanders	12.00
8	Brett Favre	25.00
9	Marshall Faulk	10.00
10	Irving Fryar	5.00
11	Dan Marino	25.00
12	Drew Bledsoe	12.00
13	Rodney Hampton	5.00
14	Ricky Watters	5.00
15	Byron Morris	5.00
16	Natrone Means	7.00
17	Steve Young	12.00
18	Jerry Rice	12.00
19	Errict Rhett	7.00
20	Michael Westbrook	5.00

1995 Images Limited/Live Sculpted Previews

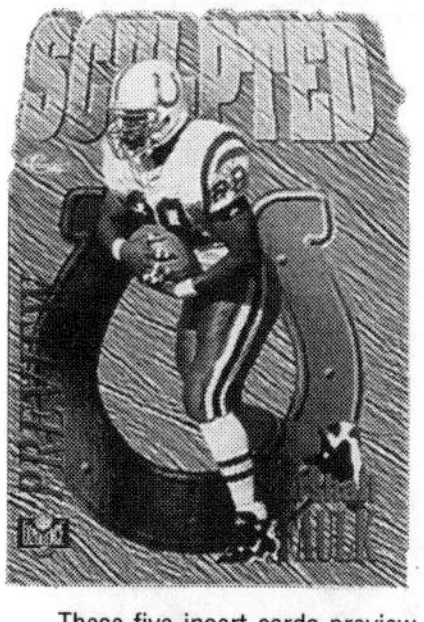

These five insert cards preview the 1996 Classic NFL Experience Sculpted insert cards. Cards, seeded one per every 24 packs, are numbered using an "NX" prefix. The cards, with a foil background, are die-cut around the top. The team logo is incorporated into the background, with an action photo in the forefront. "Sculpted" is written across the top of the card; the player's name is in the bottom right corner in red foil. The back has the player's name at the top, along with a card number. An action photo is on the right, a recap of the player's 1994 season is on the left.

		MT
Complete Set (5):		40.00
Common Player:		5.00
1	Emmitt Smith	15.00
2	Drew Bledsoe	10.00
3	Steve Young	7.00
4	Rashaan Salaam	5.00
5	Marshall Faulk	5.00

1995 Images Limited/Live Silks

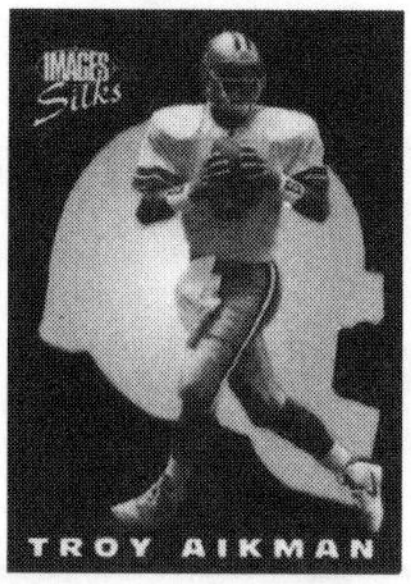

These 10 cards were extremely limited; they are seeded one per every 375 packs of 1995 Classic Images Limited/Live football. The card front has a fabric or "silk" action figure cutout of the player against an orange football helmet background. The rest of the card is black, and has a silk set logo in the upper left corner and the player's name in white silk along the bottom. The back, with a number using an "S" prefix in the upper left corner, has an action photo of the player on the right; his name and a summary of his career are on the left. S1-S5 were in Live Images packs; S6-S10 were in Limited packs.

		MT
Complete Set (10):		550.00
Complete Series 1 (5):		250.00
Complete Series 2 (5):		300.00
Common Player:		20.00
1	Troy Aikman	75.00
2	Marshall Faulk	50.00
3	Drew Bledsoe	75.00
4	Bam Morris	25.00
5	James Stewart	25.00
7	Steve Young	60.00
8	Rashaan Salaam	45.00
9	Natrone Means	35.00
10	Michael Westbrook	20.00

1995 Images Limited/Live Untouchables

These 25 cards feature some of the NFL's "untouchable" players. Cards were random inserts in 1995 Classic Images Limited/Live packs. The fronts have a large and small photo against a ghosted action background. The player's name and insert set icon are along the left side of the card. A brand logo is in the upper right corner. The back has a photo, stats, career recap, and card number, which uses a "U" prefix.

		MT
Complete Set (25):		180.00
Common Player:		3.00
1	Jim Kelly	3.00
2	Kerry Collins	8.00
3	Rashaan Salaam	6.00
4	Troy Aikman	12.00
5	Emmitt Smith	25.00
6	John Elway	6.00
7	Barry Sanders	20.00
8	Reggie White	3.00
9	Steve McNair	10.00
10	Marshall Faulk	8.00
11	Dan Marino	25.00
12	Drew Bledsoe	12.00
13	Ben Coates	3.00
14	Tyrone Wheatley	3.00
15	Chester McGlockton	3.00
16	Ricky Watters	3.00
17	Junior Seau	3.00
18	Natrone Means	3.00
19	Steve Young	12.00
20	Jerry Rice	12.00
21	Rick Mirer	3.00
22	Jerome Bettis	6.00
23	Warren Sapp	3.00
24	Michael Westbrook	3.00
25	Heath Shuler	3.00

1995 Classic NFL Experience

Classic limited production on these cards to 1,995 sequentially-numbered cases. Each card front shows an action shot of the player bordered by his team's colors. His team's name runs along the right side; the player's name is in a small pennant in the lower left corner. The set logo also appears on the card front. The back side has another color photo, a card number and highlights from the first 10 weeks of the 1994 season. Each pack included one gold card, which is part of a parallel set. Other inserts include Throwbacks, 1994 Classic Rookies, a Miami Dolphins commemorative card, an Emmitt Smith "Emmitt Zone" card, and an interactive game card awarding prizes based on the Super Bowl's final score.

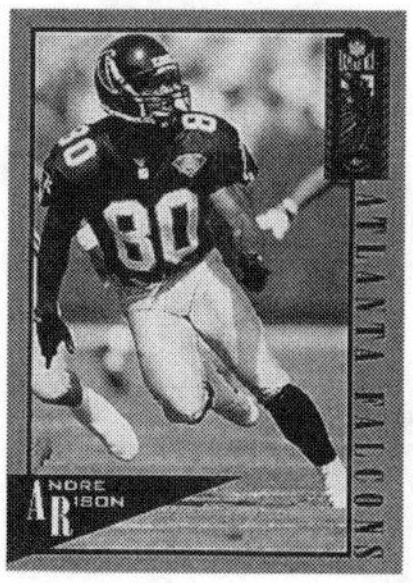

		MT
Complete Set (110):		10.00
Common Player:		.05
Minor Stars:		.10
Complete Gold Set (110):		35.00
Common Gold Player:		.20
Minor Gold Stars:		.40
Unlisted Gold Stars:		1x-3x
Pack (10):		1.75
Wax Box (24):		35.00
1	Seth Joyner	.05
2	Clyde Simmons	.05
3	Ron Moore	.05
4	Andre Rison	.10
5	Bert Emanuel	.05
6	Jeff George	.10
7	Terance Mathis	.10
8	Jim Kelly	.15
9	Thurman Thomas	.20
10	Andre Reed	.10
11	Bruce Smith	.05
12	Cornelius Bennett	.05
13	Steve Walsh	.05
14	Lewis Tillman	.05
15	Chris Zorich	.05
16	*Jeff Blake*	1.00
17	Darnay Scott	.25
18	Dan Wilkinson	.10
19	Eric Metcalf	.05
20	Antonio Langham	.05
21	Pepper Johnson	.05
22	Eric Turner	.05
23	Leroy Hoard	.05
24	Vinny Testaverde	.05
25	Troy Aikman	.75
26	Emmitt Smith	1.00
27	Michael Irvin	.20
28	Alvin Harper	.10
29	Charles Haley	.05
30	John Elway	.25
31	Leonard Russell	.05
32	Shannon Sharpe	.10
33	Herman Moore	.10
34	Barry Sanders	1.00
35	Brett Favre	1.00
36	Sterling Sharpe	.15
37	Reggie White	.10
38	Gary Brown	.05
39	Haywood Jeffires	.05
40	Quentin Coryatt	.05
41	Marshall Faulk	1.00
42	Tony Bennett	.05
43	Joe Montana	1.00
44	Marcus Allen	.10
45	Derrick Thomas	.10
46	Neil Smith	.05
47	Tim Brown	.10
48	Jeff Hostetler	.05
49	Terry McDaniel	.05
50	Jerome Bettis	.30
51	Sean Gilbert	.05
52	Dan Marino	1.50
53	Irving Fryar	.05
54	Keith Jackson	.05
55	Bernie Parmalee	.30
56	Tim Bowens	.05
57	Cris Carter	.10
58	Terry Allen	.05
59	Warren Moon	.15
60	John Randle	.05
61	Jake Reed	.05
62	Drew Bledsoe	1.00
63	Marion Butts	.05
64	Ben Coates	.05
65	Derek Brown	.05
66	Jim Everett	.05
67	Michael Haynes	.05
68	Darion Conner	.05
69	Rodney Hampton	.10
70	Dave Meggett	.05
71	Boomer Esiason	.05
72	Johnny Johnson	.05
73	Ronnie Lott	.05
74	Rob Moore	.05
75	Mo Lewis	.05
76	Randall Cunningham	.10
77	Herschel Walker	.10
78	Charlie Garner	.10
79	Calvin Williams	.05
80	Fred Barnett	.05
81	William Fuller	.05
82	Eric Allen	.05
83	Barry Foster	.10
84	Neil O'Donnell	.05
85	Rod Woodson	.05
86	Kevin Greene	.05
87	Byron Morris	.30
88	Darren Perry	.05
89	Greg Lloyd	.05
90	Steve Young	.40
91	Ricky Watters	.10
92	Jerry Rice	.60
93	Ken Norton	.05
94	Deion Sanders	.50
95	Stan Humphries	.10
96	Natrone Means	.50
97	Junior Seau	.10
98	Leslie O'Neal	.05
99	Chris Mims	.05
100	Rick Mirer	.40
101	Chris Warren	.05
102	Brian Blades	.05
103	Trent Dilfer	.40
104	Errict Rhett	.50
105	Heath Shuler	.50
106	Henry Ellard	.05
107	Ken Harvey	.05
108	Gus Frerotte	.25
109	Checklist 1	.05
110	Checklist 2	.05
MD1	Dan Marino, Don Shula	10.00
NNO	Zone 95 (Emmitt Smith)	80.00

1995 Classic NFL Experience Gold

The 110-card, regular-sized set is a parallel to the 1995 NFL Experience base set, inserted one per hobby pack. The player's name is printed in gold foil on the card fronts, distinguishing it from the base cards.

	MT
Complete Set (110):	45.00
Common Player:	.25
Gold Cards:	2x-3x

1995 Classic NFL Experience Rookies

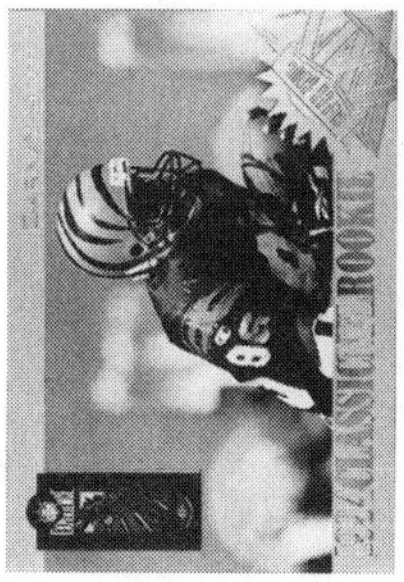

Ten rookies are showcased on these inserts, which were randomly included four per box of product. Each player is displayed on a horizontal design, with a grey border on the top and bottom and a foil embossed Super Bowl XXIX logo.

		MT
Complete Set (10):		20.00
Common Player:		1.00
1	Marshall Faulk	6.00
2	Bert Emanuel	1.00
3	Charlie Garner	4.00
4	Errict Rhett	4.00
5	Byron Morris	4.00
6	Heath Shuler	3.00
7	Trent Dilfer	3.00
8	Darnay Scott	2.00
9	Tim Bowens	1.00
10	Antonio Langham	1.00

1995 Classic NFL Experience Super Bowl Game

1995 Classic NFL Experience jumbo packs each had one of 20 of these inserts, based on an interactive game regarding the final score of Super Bowl XXIX. Each card has either an AFC or NFC logo, plus a number (0-9). If the last digit of the final score from the game corresponds with the conference and number of a card found by a collector, he could qualify for an assortment of prizes if he sent the card in by mail by March 6, 1995. The grand prize was to be a trip to Super Bowl XXX in Phoenix in 1996. Game cards submitted to Classic were not returned. The back had the rules and prizes for the game listed.

		MT
Complete Set (20):		20.00
Common Player:		.50
0	AFC (Marshall Faulk)	2.50
1	AFC (Natrone Means)	1.25
2	AFC (Thurman Thomas)	.50
3	AFC (Joe Montana)	2.00
4	AFC (John Elway)	1.00
5	AFC (Rick Mirer)	1.00
6	AFC (Drew Bledsoe)	2.00
7	AFC (Dan Marino)	3.00
8	AFC (Jim Kelly)	.50
9	AFC (Marcus Allen)	.50
0	NFC (Troy Aikman)	2.00
1	NFC (Steve Young)	2.00
2	NFC (Jerome Bettis)	1.00
3	NFC (Barry Sanders)	2.00
4	NFC (Randall Cunningham)	.50
5	NFC (Andre Rison)	.50
6	NFC (Jerry Rice)	2.00
7	NFC (Emmitt Smith)	3.00
8	NFC (Michael Irvin)	1.00
9	NFC (Sterling Sharpe)	1.00

Post-1980 cards in Near Mint condition will generally sell for about 75% of the quoted Mint value. Excellent-condition cards bring no more than 40%.

1995 Classic NFL Experience Throwbacks

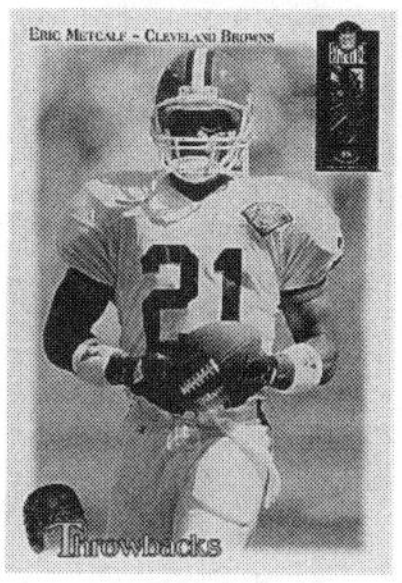

These 28 insert cards are printed on parchment to give each card a look and feel of an old-time card. This was done to commemorate the NFL's 75th anniversary. The set features one player from each team in his throwback uniform, bordered by a white frame. A brief history of the NFL franchise and the reason why the team chose that particular uniform are given on the back. The card number uses a "T" prefix. These inserts were included two per box.

		MT
Complete Set (28):		130.00
Common Player:		3.00
Minor Stars:		6.00
1	Seth Joyner	3.00
2	Andre Rison	6.00
3	Thurman Thomas	6.00
4	Lewis Tillman	3.00
5	Dan Wilkinson	6.00
6	Eric Metcalf	6.00
7	Emmitt Smith	20.00
8	John Elway	7.00
9	Barry Sanders	12.00
10	Reggie White	6.00
11	Haywood Jeffires	3.00
12	Marshall Faulk	12.00
13	Joe Montana	12.00
14	Jeff Hostetler	3.00
15	Jerome Bettis	6.00
16	Dan Marino	20.00
17	Warren Moon	6.00
18	Drew Bledsoe	12.00
19	Jim Everett	3.00
20	Dave Meggett	3.00
21	Ronnie Lott	3.00
22	Randall Cunningham	6.00
23	Rod Woodson	6.00
24	Natrone Means	10.00
25	Rick Mirer	6.00
26	Steve Young	12.00
27	Trent Dilfer	8.00
28	Henry Ellard	3.00

1996 Classic NFL Draft Day

The 15-card, regular-sized set was distributed by Classic in New York on the 1996 NFL Draft Day. The first nine cards feature the top three players in the draft with three different teams each. The final six cards feature former first-round draft picks.

		MT
Complete Set (15):		25.00
Common Player:		1.00
1A	Keyshawn Johnson (Jets)	2.50
1B	Keyshawn Johnson (Jaguars)	2.50
1C	Keyshawn Johnson (Redskins)	2.50
2A	Kevin Hardy (Jaguars)	1.25
2B	Kevin Hardy (Redskins)	1.25
2C	Kevin Hardy (Cardinals)	1.25
3A	Terry Glenn (Patriots)	2.00
3B	Terry Glenn (Giants)	2.00
3C	Terry Glenn (Jets)	2.00
4	Eddie George	5.00
5	Emmitt Smith	3.50
6	Troy Aikman	2.00
7	Drew Bledsoe	2.00
8	Kerry Collins	2.00
9	Title Card (Checklist back)	1.00

1996 Classic NFL Rookies

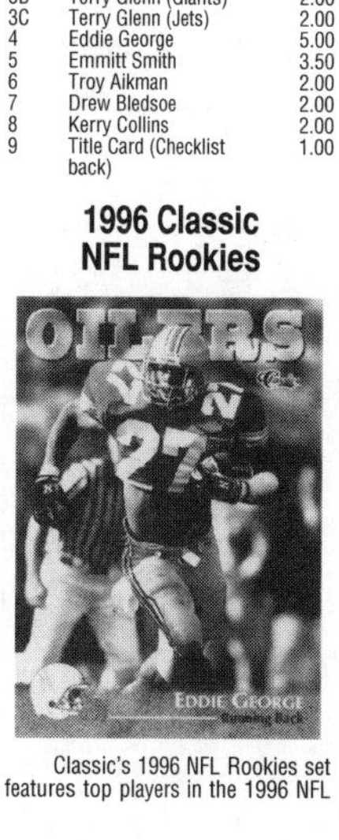

Classic's 1996 NFL Rookies set features top players in the 1996 NFL Draft, including two subsets called All-Americans and NFL Greats. Each card front has a full-bleed color action photo of the player in his college uniform, but his pro team's name is at the top, along with a team helmet at the bottom, next to his name. Backs have a color closeup photo of the player in a square which has his name, team name, position and draft selection number along the four sides. Below the photo is a ghosted body shot from the same closeup shot. A recap of his collegiate accomplishments are on one side; statistics and biographical information are on the other. A card number is in the upper left corner in a blue square. Hobby pack insert cards were Rookie of the Year Interactive, NFL Road Jerseys and Rookie Lasers. Retail pack inserts include Rookie #1 Die-Cuts and NFL Home Jerseys.

		MT
Complete Set (100):		10.00
Common Player:		.05
Minor Stars:		.10
1	Keyshawn Johnson	1.50
2	Jonathan Ogden	.20
3	Kevin Hardy	.20
4	Leeland McElroy	.30
5	Terry Glenn	1.00
6	Tim Biakabutuka	.50
7	Tony Brackens	.05
8	Duane Clemons	.10
9	Willie Anderson	.05
10	Karim Abdul-Jabbar	.75
11	Daryl Gardener	.05
12	Simeon Rice	.20
13	Eddie George	2.00
14	Andre Johnson	.05
15	Jon Runyan	.05
16	Jevon Langford	.05
17	Derrick Mayes	.40
18	Stephen Davis	.75
19	Ray Farmer	.05
20	Chris Doering	.10
21	Jimmy Herndon	.05
22	Jerome Woods	.05
23	Scott Greene	.05
24	Jamin Stephens	.05
25	Tommie Frazier	.20
26	Dusty Zeigler	.05
27	Alex Molden	.05
28	Dietrich Jells	.05
29	Brian Roche	.05
30	Danny Kanell	.50
31	Roman Oben	.05
32	Chris Darkins	.20
33	Christian Peter	.05
34	Jeff Hartings	.05
35	Bobby Hoying	.50
36	Steve Taneyhill	.05
37	Lance Johnstone	.05
38	Zach Thomas	.50
39	Donnie Edwards	.05
40	Eric Moulds	1.25
41	Amani Toomer	.40
42	Scott Slutzker	.05
43	Matt Stevens	.05
44	Randall Godfrey	.05
45	Orpheus Roye	.05
46	Jason Odom	.05
47	Jerod Cherry	.05
48	Jeff Lewis	.20
49	Mike Alstott	1.25
50	Tony Banks	.75
51	Stepfret Williams	.20
52	Michael Cheever	.05
53	Bryant Mix	.05
54	James Ritchey	.10
55	Marcus Coleman	.05
56	Sedric Clark	.05
57	Kyle Wachholz	.05
58	Johnny McWilliams	.10
59	Lawyer Milloy	.10
60	Alex Van Dyke	.30
61	Stanley Pritchett	.20
62	Ray Mickens	.10
63	Toraino Singleton	.05
64	Richard Huntley	.20
65	Eddie George	.75
66	Terry Glenn	.25
67	Keyshawn Johnson	.30
68	Jonathan Ogden	.05
69	Tommie Frazier	.10
70	Kevin Hardy	.05
71	Zach Thomas	.20
72	Tony Brackens	.05
73	Lawyer Milloy	.05
74	Leeland McElroy	.10
75	Emmitt Smith	.50
76	Steve McNair	.20
77	Kerry Collins	.10
78	Drew Bledsoe	.25
79	Marshall Faulk	.20
80	Pete Kendall	.05
81	Regan Upshaw	.05
82	Mercury Hayes	.05
83	Dou Innocent	.05
84	DeRon Jenkins	.05
85	Marco Battaglia	.10
86	John Mobley	.10
87	Cedric Jones	.05
88	Marvin Harrison	.50
89	Israel Ifeanyl	.05
90	Reggie Brown	.05
91	Jermain Mayberry	.05
92	Brian Dawkins	.05
93	Tedy Bruschi	.05
94	Terrell Owens	2.00
95	Jermaine Lewis	.50
96	Sean Boyd	.05
97	Phillip Daniels	.05
98	Lawrence Phillips	1.00
99	Keyshawn Johnson (Checklist 1)	.50
100	Terry Glenn (Checklist 2)	.25

1996 Classic NFL Rookies Rookie #1 Die-Cuts

Thirty top rookies are featured on these 1996 Classic NFL Rookies

inserts, seeded randomly in retail packs. The cards use a metallic stock and are die-cut around the number 1.

		MT
Complete Set (30):		300.00
Common Player:		5.00
1	Keyshawn Johnson	20.00
2	Kevin Hardy	5.00
3	Simeon Rice	5.00
4	Jonathan Ogden	5.00
5	Cedric Jones	5.00
6	Lawrence Phillips	10.00
7	Terry Glenn	25.00
8	Tim Biakabutuka	7.00
9	Emmitt Smith	25.00
10	Willie Anderson	5.00
11	Alex Molden	5.00
12	Regan Upshaw	5.00
13	Kerry Collins	10.00
14	Eddie George	60.00
15	John Mobley	5.00
16	Duane Clemons	5.00
17	Reggie Brown	5.00
18	Marshall Faulk	10.00
19	Marvin Harrison	10.00
20	Daryl Gardener	5.00
21	Pete Kendall	5.00
22	Joey Galloway	7.00
23	Jeff Hartings	5.00
24	Eric Moulds	5.00
25	Jermain Mayberry	5.00
26	Steve McNair	20.00
27	Kyle Brady	5.00
28	Jerome Woods	5.00
29	Jamin Stephens	5.00
30	Andre Johnson	5.00

1996 Classic NFL Rookies NFL Home Jerseys

These 30 cards were exclusive inserts to 1996 Classic NFL Rookies retail packs, one per every 15 packs. The card front is horizontal and shows the player in action while he was in college, alongside a home jersey of his new NFL team. Card backs are numbered using an "HJ" prefix.

		MT
Complete Set (30):		120.00
Common Player:		3.00
1	Keyshawn Johnson	30.00
2	Kevin Hardy	8.00
3	Jonathan Ogden	3.00
4	Terry Glenn	17.00
5	Tim Biakabutuka	10.00
6	Karim Abdul-Jabbar	10.00
7	Simeon Rice	8.00
8	Eric Moulds	8.00
9	Mike Alstott	7.00
10	Leeland McElroy	10.00
11	Daryl Gardener	3.00
12	Eddie George	17.00
13	Amani Toomer	8.00
14	Johnny McWilliams	3.00
15	Derrick Mayes	3.00
16	Duane Clemons	3.00
17	Chris Darkins	7.00
18	Ray Farmer	3.00
19	Danny Kanell	7.00
20	Bobby Hoying	10.00
21	Zach Thomas	3.00
22	Tony Banks	3.00
23	Alex Van Dyke	3.00
24	Stepfret Williams	3.00
25	Chris Doering	3.00
26	Lance Johnstone	3.00
27	Stephen Davis	3.00
28	Scott Greene	3.00
29	Tony Brackens	3.00
30	Jevon Langford	3.00

1996 Classic NFL Rookies NFL Road Jerseys

Each of these horizontally-designed cards shows the player on the front in his college uniform, but adjacent to a road jersey of the NFL team which drafted him in 1996. The cards were random inserts in 1996 Classic NFL Rookies packs, one per 15 packs. Card backs are numbered using an "RJ" prefix and have a color closeup photo, plus a recap of the player's collegiate accomplishments. Silver foil stamping is used on the front for the player's name and brand logo.

		MT
Complete Set (30):		120.00
Common Player:		3.00
1	Keyshawn Johnson	30.00
2	Kevin Hardy	8.00
3	Jonathan Ogden	3.00
4	Terry Glenn	17.00
5	Tim Biakabutuka	10.00
6	Karim Abdul-Jabbar	10.00
7	Simeon Rice	8.00
8	Eric Moulds	8.00
9	Mike Alstott	7.00
10	Leeland McElroy	10.00
11	Daryl Gardener	3.00
12	Eddie George	17.00
13	Amani Toomer	8.00
14	Marvin Harrison	3.00
15	Derrick Mayes	3.00
16	Dietrich Jells	3.00
17	Chris Darkins	7.00
18	Ray Farmer	3.00
19	Danny Kanell	7.00
20	Bobby Hoying	10.00
21	Zach Thomas	3.00
22	Kyle Wachholz	3.00
23	Alex Van Dyke	3.00
24	Stepfret Williams	3.00
25	Chris Doering	3.00
26	Lance Johnstone	3.00
27	Stephen Davis	3.00
28	Scott Greene	3.00
29	Tony Brackens	3.00
30	Jevon Langford	3.00

1996 Classic NFL Rookies Rookie Lasers

Rookie Lasers cards were seeded one per every 100 packs of 1996 Classic NFL Rookies hobby packs. The cards feature 10 of the best rookies and are numbered using an "RL" prefix.

		MT
Complete Set (10):		150.00
Common Player:		7.00
1	Keyshawn Johnson	45.00
2	Jonathan Ogden	7.00
3	Eddie George	35.00
4	Terry Glenn	35.00
5	Tommie Frazier	25.00
6	Karim Abdul-Jabbar	15.00
7	Duane Clemons	7.00
8	Leeland McElroy	25.00
9	Tim Biakabutuka	30.00
10	Kevin Hardy	10.00

1996 Classic NFL Rookies Rookie of the Year Contenders

The 10-card, regular-sized set was randomly inserted in retail packs of 1996 Classic NFL. Both the card fronts and backs feature action shots of the players with the player's name appearing in the lower right corner of the fronts. The cards are numbered with the "C" prefix.

		MT
Complete Set (10):		65.00
Common Player:		1.50
1	Keyshawn Johnson	15.00
2	Jonathan Ogden	1.50
3	Eddie George	20.00
4	Terry Glenn	16.00
5	Eric Moulds	4.00
6	Karim Abdul-Jabbar	14.00
7	Leeland McElroy	6.00
8	Tim Biakabutuka	10.00
9	Bobby Hoying	3.00
10	Stephen Davis	3.00

1996 Classic NFL Rookies Rookie of the Year Interactive

These interactive insert cards were randomly seeded in hobby packs of 1996 Classic NFL Rookies product. The cards feature 20 leading candidates to win the NFL Offensive Rookie of the Year award. If the player on the card wins, it is redeemable for an autographed collectible of the player. The card front has a full-bleed color or action photo, with the player's name towards the bottom of the card. "Rookie of the Year" and "Interactive" are spelled out along the right side of the card. Card backs, numbered using an "ROY" prefix, explain the rules of the redemption program.

		MT
Complete Set (20):		150.00
Common Player:		3.00
1	Keyshawn Johnson	30.00
2	Jonathan Ogden	3.00
3	Steve Taneyhill	3.00
4	Leeland McElroy	10.00
5	Terry Glenn	20.00
6	Tim Biakabutuka	15.00
7	Karim Abdul-Jabbar	10.00
8	Eddie George	20.00
9	Johnny McWilliams	3.00
10	Eric Moulds	8.00
11	Bobby Hoying	8.00
12	Chris Darkins	10.00
13	Derrick Mayes	10.00
14	Mike Alstott	3.00
15	Chris Doering	3.00
16	Danny Kanell	10.00
17	Stephen Davis	3.00
18	Amani Toomer	10.00
19	Dietrich Jells	3.00
20	Field Card	10.00

1996 Score Board Laser National Promos

Distributed at the Classic booth at the 1996 National Card Collector's Convention, this five-card set was available separately or in a lucite holder, which was numbered of 300.

		MT
Complete Set (5):		25.00
Complete Framed Set (5):		35.00
Common Player:		3.00
1	Kordell Stewart	5.00
2	Troy Aikman	5.00
3	Emmitt Smith	10.00
4	Lawrence Phillips	3.00
5	Keyshawn Johnson	4.00

1996 Score Board NFL Lasers

This 100-card set features some of the NFL's top stars, including seven who have autographed special inserts. The regular card front has a color action photo on it against a metallic background. The left frame of the card is green; the upper right and lower right corners are gold, with NFL Lasers and the player's team name in them. The player's name and position are above the bottom frame. The card back has a card number and the player's name at the top, with biographical information below. The right border has the player's name at the top, with his team name running horizontally toward the bottom. 1995 and career stats are along the bottom. A photo completes the back. The autographed cards, available at a rate of two per case, come in two versions - regular (400 each, one per 150 packs), and die-cuts (100 each, one per 930 packs). The other inserts are Laser Images and Sunday's Heroes.

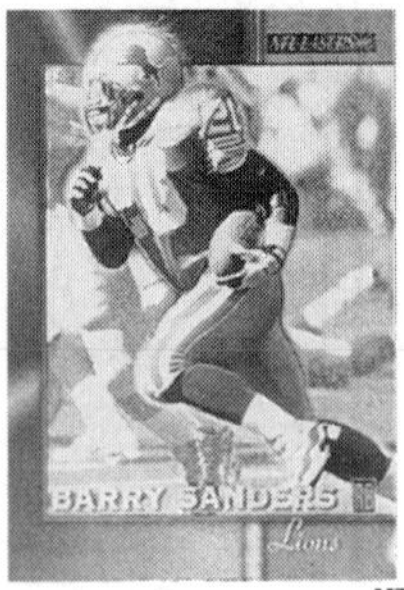

		MT
Complete Set (100):		30.00
Common Player:		.10
Minor Stars:		.20
Wax Box:		80.00
1	Brett Favre	2.50
2	Chris Warren	.10
3	J.J. Stokes	.25
4	Barry Sanders	1.25
5	Ben Coates	.10
6	Bryan Cox	.10
7	Carl Pickens	.10
8	Cris Carter	.10
9	Curtis Martin	2.00
10	Dan Marino	2.50
11	Dave Brown	.10
12	Drew Bledsoe	1.00
13	Edgar Bennett	.10
14	Herman Moore	.30
15	Jeff Blake	.30
16	Jerry Rice	1.25
17	Jim Kelly	.20
18	John Elway	.75
19	Junior Seau	.10
20	Kerry Collins	1.25
21	Kordell Stewart	1.00
22	Leonard Russell	.10
23	Mark Brunell	.50
24	Marshall Faulk	.30
25	Mike Tomczak	.10
26	Reggie White	.20
27	Ricky Watters	.20
28	Rod Woodson	.10
29	Rodney Peete	.10
30	Stan Humphries	.10
31	Steve McNair	.75
32	Terry Allen	.10
33	Thurman Thomas	.20
34	Troy Aikman	1.25
35	Vinny Testaverde	.10
36	Chris T. Jones	.10
37	Deion Sanders	.75
38	Eric Metcalf	.10
39	Erik Kramer	.10
40	Emmitt Smith	2.50
41	Gus Frerotte	.10
42	Jeff George	.10
43	Jerome Bettis	.20
44	Jim Harbaugh	.10
45	Isaac Bruce	.50
46	Jeff Hostetler	.10
47	Ki-Jana Carter	.20
48	Marcus Allen	.20
49	Neil O'Donnell	.10
50	Rashaan Salaam	.40
51	Robert Brooks	.10
52	Steve Bono	.10
53	Scott Mitchell	.10
54	Terrell Davis	1.50
55	Tim Brown	.10
56	Troy Vincent	.10
57	Warren Moon	.10
58	Tony Martin	.10
59	Rodney Hampton	.10
60	Steve Young	1.00
61	Rick Mirer	.10
62	Mark Chmura	.10
63	Larry Centers	.10
64	Ken Dilger	.10
65	Joey Galloway	1.00
66	Jim Everett	.10
67	Chris Chandler	.10
68	James Stewart	.10
69	Robert Smith	.10
70	Tamarick Vanover	.50
71	Wayne Chrebet	.10
72	*Keyshawn Johnson*	2.00
73	*Kevin Hardy*	.20
74	*Lawrence Phillips*	.50
75	*Jonathan Ogden*	.20
76	*Terry Glenn*	1.50
77	*Tim Biakabutuka*	1.00
78	*Eddie George*	3.00
79	*Eric Moulds*	1.50
80	*John Mobley*	.10
81	*Amani Toomer*	.20
82	*Marvin Harrison*	2.00
83	*Leeland McElroy*	.30
84	*Rickey Dudley*	.30
85	*Tony Banks*	.50
86	*Zach Thomas*	.75
87	*Alex Molden*	.10
88	*Daryl Gardener*	.10
89	*Jamal Anderson*	5.00
90	*Karim Abdul-Jabbar*	.50
91	*Simeon Rice*	.20
92	*Walt Harris*	.10
93	*Bobby Engram*	.30
94	Kevin Williams	.10
95	Sean Gilbert	.10
96	Kevin Greene	.10
97	Regan Upshaw	.10
98	Marcus Jones	.10
99	Ray Lewis	.30
100	Checklist	.10

1996 Score Board NFL Lasers Laser Images

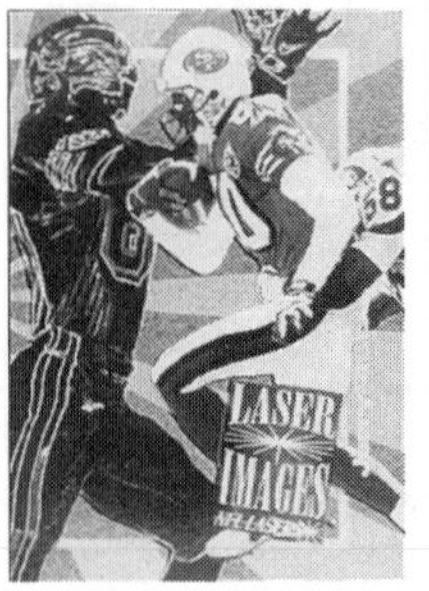

These cards are seeded one per every 30 packs of 1996 Score Board NFL Lasers. The card front has a color action photo of the player, with a ghosted black laser image of the player in the background, which is metallic. The card has gold foil stamped around three sides as a border; the player's name is also in gold foil on the right side. The Laser Images logo is also on the front. The card back has a color photo of the laser image from the front, with a column down the left side which has a recap of the player's accomplishments and a team logo at the bottom. The card number, using an "I" prefix, is in the upper left corner. The player's name is in a rectangle in the upper right corner. His last name is in scripted letter along the left side of the card.

		MT
Complete Set (30):		250.00
Common Player:		3.00
1	Steve Bono	3.00
2	Kerry Collins	20.00
3	Tim Biakabutuka	6.00
4	Rashaan Salaam	3.00
5	Jeff Blake	6.00
6	Emmitt Smith	30.00
7	Troy Aikman	20.00
8	Deion Sanders	12.00
9	John Elway	12.00
10	Herman Moore	3.00
11	Brett Favre	30.00
12	Eddie George	20.00
13	Marvin Harrison	12.00
14	Mark Brunell	12.00
15	Dan Marino	30.00
16	Karim Abdul-Jabbar	15.00
17	Cris Carter	3.00
18	Drew Bledsoe	15.00
19	Curtis Martin	20.00
20	Keyshawn Johnson	10.00
21	Chris T. Jones	3.00
22	Kordell Stewart	15.00
23	Junior Seau	3.00
24	Steve Young	15.00
25	Jerry Rice	20.00
26	Joey Galloway	12.00
27	Lawrence Phillips	12.00
28	Jonathan Ogden	3.00
29	Jim Harbaugh	3.00
30	Neil O'Donnell	3.00

1996 Score Board NFL Lasers Sunday's Heroes

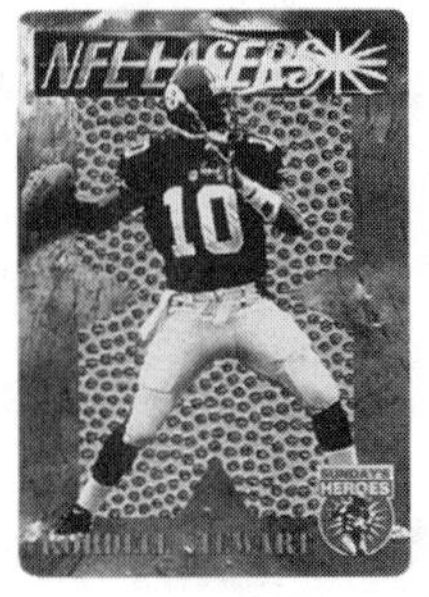

These cards, numbered using an "S" prefix, capture 25 stars on a thicker, embossed surface. Cards were seeded one per every 22 packs of 1996 Score Board NFL Lasers product.

		MT
Complete Set (25):		450.00
Common Player:		8.00
1	Tim Brown	8.00
2	Kerry Collins	30.00
3	Tim Biakabutuka	15.00
4	Rashaan Salaam	12.00
5	Jeff Blake	15.00
6	Ki-Jana Carter	12.00
7	Emmitt Smith	50.00
8	Troy Aikman	30.00
9	Deion Sanders	20.00
10	Terrell Davis	30.00
11	Barry Sanders	30.00
12	Brett Favre	50.00
13	Reggie White	12.00
14	Marshall Faulk	20.00
15	Mark Brunell	20.00
16	Kevin Hardy	8.00
17	Dan Marino	50.00
18	Drew Bledsoe	25.00
19	Curtis Martin	40.00
20	Keyshawn Johnson	20.00
21	Kordell Stewart	25.00
22	Steve Young	25.00
23	Jerry Rice	30.00
24	Chris Warren	8.00
25	Karim Abdul-Jabbar	30.00

1996 Score Board NFL Lasers Autographs

Seven players have autographed these 1996 Score Board inserts - Emmitt Smith, Troy Aikman, Keyshawn Johnson, Marshall Faulk, Drew Bledsoe, Steve Young and Kordell Stewart. The cards were available at a rate of two per case, in two different versions. Regular versions (400 each) were seeded one per 150 packs. Die-cut versions (100 each) were seeded one per 930 packs.

	MT
Complete Set (7):	850.00
Packs (8):	4.00
Wax Box (24):	80.00
Troy Aikman	150.00
Steve Young	120.00
Kordell Stewart	150.00
Keyshawn Johnson	100.00
Emmitt Smith	250.00
Marshall Faulk	100.00
Drew Bledsoe	150.00

1996 Score Board NFL Lasers Die-Cut Autographs

Also included in packs of NFL Lasers were die-cut versions of each of the seven players. Die-cut versions were limited to only 100 of each.

	MT
Complete Set (7):	1700.
Troy Aikman	300.00
Steve Young	240.00
Kordell Stewart	300.00
Keyshawn Johnson	200.00
Emmitt Smith	500.00
Marshall Faulk	200.00
Drew Bledsoe	300.00

1996 Classic NFL Experience

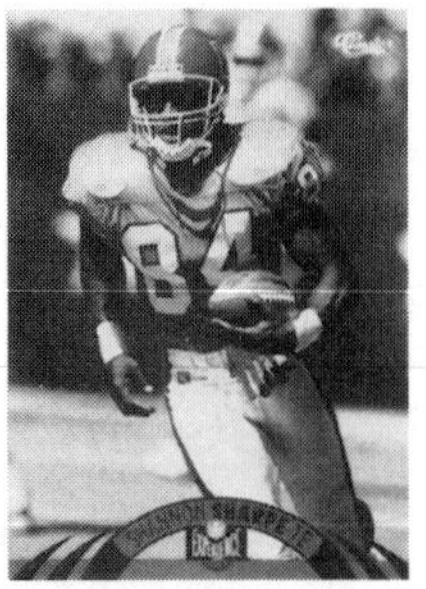

This 125-card 1996 Classic NFL Experience set is geared toward players who participated in the postseason. Each card front has a full-bleed color action photo on glossy stock. The Classic logo is in an upper corner; the player's name and position are in an arch at the bottom. Three-fourths of the card back has a format similar to the design used for the card front, except a number has been added in an upper corner. The bottom fourth of the card has a 1995 recap. Insert sets include: Sculpted, Super Bowl game cards, three oversized bonus cards, Emmitt Zone and The "X." 1996 Classic NFL Experience also continues the Hot Box program. There is an average of one Hot Box every five sealed cases, with each pack in a Hot Box containing 20-percent inserts. Each card in the regular set is also reprinted as part of a Printer's Proof parallel set. Only 499 of each card is printed, with an insert ratio of one per 10 packs.

		MT
Complete Set (125):		10.00
Common Player:		.05
Minor Stars:		.10
Comp. Prin. Proof Set (125):		200.00
Prin. Proof Cards:		10x-20x
Pack (10):		2.00
Wax Box (24):		38.00
1	Emmitt Smith	2.00
2	Jerry Rice	1.00
3	Carl Pickens	.15
4	Curtis Conway	.10
5	Isaac Bruce	.10
6	Marshall Faulk	.10
7	Errict Rhett	.10
8	Troy Aikman	.75
9	Jeff Hostetler	.05
10	Dan Marino	2.00
11	Barry Sanders	1.00
12	Drew Bledsoe	.50
13	Ricky Watters	.10
14	Natrone Means	.20
15	Chris Warren	.10
16	Jim Kelly	.10
17	Jeff George	.05
18	Garrison Hearst	.10
19	Brett Favre	2.00
20	John Elway	.50
21	Robert Smith	.05
22	Steve Bono	.10
23	Byron Morris	.20
24	Jim Everett	.05
25	Steve Young	.50
26	Rodney Hampton	.05
27	Terry Allen	.05
28	Chris Chandler	.05
29	Mark Carrier	.05
30	Desmond Howard	.05
31	Erik Kramer	.05
32	Irving Fryar	.05
33	Jeff Blake	.50
34	Vinny Testaverde	.05
35	Stan Humphries	.05
36	Tim Brown	.05
37	Trent Dilfer	.10
38	Jim Harbaugh	.05
39	Warren Moon	.10
40	Ben Coates	.05
41	Boomer Esiason	.05
42	Rodney Peete	.05
43	Gus Frerotte	.10
44	Jerome Bettis	.10
45	Dave Brown	.05
46	William Floyd	.10
47	Andre Rison	.05
48	Robert Brooks	.10
49	Marcus Allen	.10
50	Rick Mirer	.10
51	Alvin Harper	.05
52	Chris Miller	.05
53	Eric Metcalf	.05
54	Dave Krieg	.05
55	Darnay Scott	.10
56	Cris Carter	.05
57	Lake Dawson	.05
58	Haywood Jeffires	.05
59	Herman Moore	.20
60	Michael Irvin	.20
61	Anthony Miller	.05
62	Troy Vincent	.05
63	Jake Reed	.05
64	Michael Haynes	.05
65	Scott Mitchell	.05
66	Roman Phifer	.05
67	Harvey Williams	.05
68	Darren Perry	.05
69	Brian Mitchell	.05
70	Derek Loville	.05
71	Junior Seau	.10
72	Bruce Smith	.05
73	Willie Davis	.05
74	Charles Haley	.05
75	Mike Sherrard	.05
76	Pat Swilling	.05
77	Yancey Thigpen	.25
78	Bryce Paup	.05
79	Eric Green	.05
80	Deion Sanders	.40
81	Mario Bates	.05
82	John Randle	.05
83	Charlie Garner	.05
84	Chris Doleman	.05
85	Robert Porcher	.05
86	Rob Moore	.05
87	Anthony Pleasant	.05
88	Bryan Cox	.05
89	Greg Hill	.05
90	Reggie White	.10
91	Shannon Sharpe	.05
92	Leroy Hoard	.05
93	John Copeland	.05
94	Tony Martin	.05
95	Greg Lloyd	.05
96	Tony Bennett	.05
97	Alonzo Spellman	.05
98	Wayne Martin	.05
99	Craig Heyward	.05
100	Leslie O'Neal	.05
101	Andy Harmon	.05
102	Edgar Bennett	.05
103	Derrick Moore	.05
104	Terrell Davis	.75
105	Kerry Collins	.75
106	Rodney Thomas	.25
107	Mark Brunell	.50
108	Curtis Martin	2.00
109	Tyrone Wheatley	.20
110	Rashaan Salaam	.10
111	Kevin Carter	.10
112	Joey Galloway	.75
113	Mike Mamula	.10
114	Kyle Brady	.10
115	James Stewart	.10
116	Michael Westbrook	.10
117	J.J. Stokes	.10
118	Wayne Chrebet	.10
119	Warren Sapp	.10
120	Hugh Douglas	.05
121	Jim Flanigan	.10
122	Chester McGlockton	.05
123	Shawn Lee	.05
124	Checklist Card 1	.25
125	Checklist Card 2	.25

1996 Classic NFL Experience Printer's Proofs

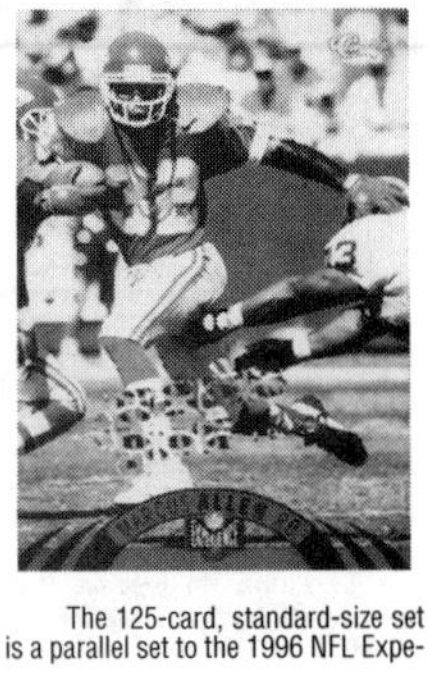

The 125-card, standard-size set is a parallel set to the 1996 NFL Expe-

rience base set, inserted every 20 packs. The card fronts are numbered as "x of 499."

	MT
Complete Set (125):	225.00
Common Player:	.75
Printer's Proofs Cards:	10x-20x

1996 Classic NFL Experience Super Bowl Gold/Red

The 125-card, regular-size set is a parallel to the 1996 NFL Experience set. The gold cards are numbered as "x of 799"' while the red cards are numbered as "x of 150."

	MT
Complete Gold Set (125):	125.00
Common Gold Player:	.50
Gold Cards:	5x-10x
Complete Red Set (125):	550.00
Common Red Player:	2.00
Red Cards: 25x-50x	

1996 Classic NFL Experience Class of 1995

This five-card set was included one per every 1996 Classic NFL Experience factory set. Cards are numbered using an "FI" prefix and have the set icon on the card front.

		MT
Complete Set (5):		10.00
Common Player:		1.00
1	Steve Young	2.00
2	Emmitt Smith	4.00
3	Deion Sanders	1.50
4	Rashaan Salaam	1.00
5	Kerry Collins	2.00

1996 Classic NFL Experience Emmitt Zone

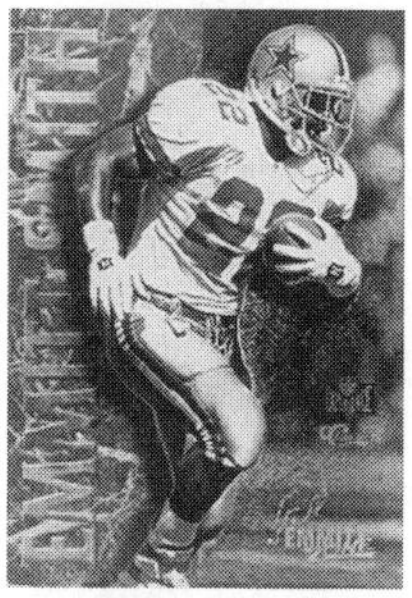

The five-card, standard-size set was randomly inserted in packs of 1996 NFL Experience. Smith's name is printed down the card front's left border while "Emmitt Zone" appears in the lower right corner. A $5 "Emmitt Zone" phone card was also inserted every 375 Super Bowl packs.

		MT
Complete Set (5):		250.00
Common Player:		50.00
1	Emmitt Smith (1990-91 ROY)	50.00
2	Emmitt Smith (1992 NFL Leading Rusher)	50.00
3	Emmitt Smith (1993 3rd NFL Rushing Title)	50.00
4	Emmitt Smith (1994 Leader in League Touchdowns)	50.00
5	Emmitt Smith (1995 Best Season Ever)	50.00

1996 Classic NFL Experience Oversized Bonus Cards

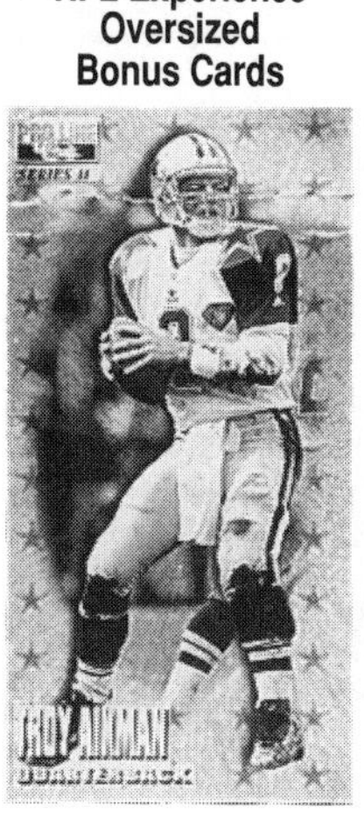

These cards, one of which is randomly placed in each case of 1996 Classic NFL Experience product, complete the company's bonus program for its 1995 NFL-licensed products. The cards feature Emmitt Smith, Michael Westbrook and Reggie White.

		MT
Complete Set (15):		15.00
Common Player:		2.00
13	Emmitt Smith	10.00
14	Michael Westbrook	2.00
15	Reggie White	5.00

1996 Classic NFL Experience Super Bowl Die Cut Promos

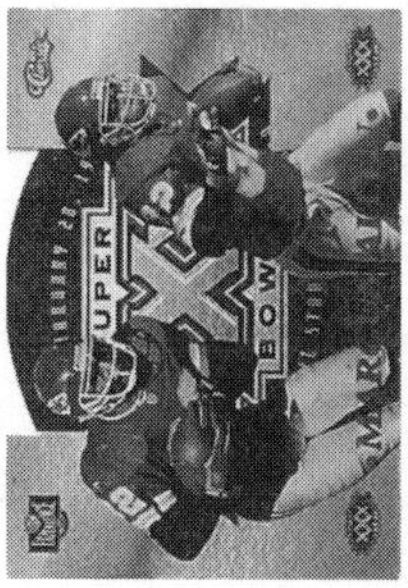

The 10-card, regular-sized set, given away at the Super Bowl Card Show in Tempe, Ariz., featured players from the NFL Experience Die Cut matched inserts. The card backs contain rules for prize giveaways and "Show Promo." The cards are numbered with the "C" suffix.

		MT
Complete Set (10):		45.00
Common Player:		2.00
1	Jim Kelly	3.00
2	Dan Marino	12.00
3	Greg Lloyd	2.00
4	Marcus Allen	3.00
5	Tim Brown	2.00
6	Emmitt Smith	12.00
7	Steve Young	4.00
8	Rashaan Salaam	3.00
9	Brett Favre	12.00
10	Isaac Bruce	4.00

1996 Classic NFL Experience Super Bowl Die Cut Contest

The 20-card, regular-size set features 10 players on two cards each and was inserted in every 12 packs of the Card Show version of 1996 NFL Experience. The cards are numbered 1A through 10A and 1B through 10B. When the cards are put together, they form the Super Bowl XXX logo. The card backs contain rules on how to redeem the cards for a prize.

		MT
Complete Set (20):		160.00
Common Player:		2.50
1A	Jim Kelly	5.00
1B	Jim Kelly	5.00
2A	Dan Marino	20.00
2B	Dan Marino	20.00
3A	Greg Lloyd	2.50
3B	Greg Lloyd	2.50
4A	Marcus Allen	4.00
4B	Marcus Allen	4.00
5A	Tim Brown	2.50
5B	Tim Brown	2.50
6A	Emmitt Smith	20.00
6B	Emmitt Smith	20.00
7A	Steve Young	8.00
7B	Steve Young	8.00
8A	Rashaan Salaam	6.00
8B	Rashaan Salaam	6.00
9A	Brett Favre	20.00
9B	Brett Favre	20.00
10A	Isaac Bruce	8.00
10B	Isaac Bruce	8.00

1996 Classic NFL Experience Super Bowl Game Cards

These interactive cards are based on the final score of Super Bowl XXX in 1996. The 20 cards were inserted one per pack of 1996 Classic NFL Experience product; each card has either an AFC or NFC logo, plus a number (0-9). If the last digit of the final score from the game corresponds with the conference and number of a card found by a collector, he could qualify for an assortment of prizes if he sent it in by March 8, 1996. The grand prize was to be a trip to Super Bowl XXXI in 1997 in New Orleans. Game cards submitted to Classic were not returned. Each card front has a silver metallic background, with a color action shot. The Super Bowl XXX logo is in the upper left corner. The player's name and conference logo/card number are at the bottom. The back has a set checklist, list of rules and prizes, and the card number again. The Super Bowl logo repeats itself in the background.

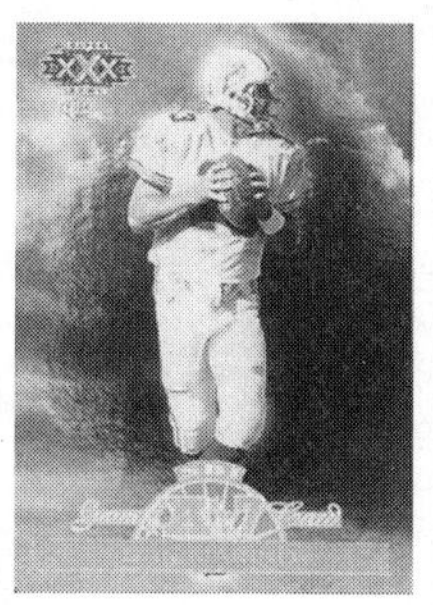

		MT
Complete Set (20):		2.50
Common Player:		.75
A0	Drew Bledsoe	2.50
A1	John Elway	1.25
A2	Harvey Williams	.75
A3	Marshall Faulk	2.50
A4	Jim Kelly	.75
A5	Carl Pickens	.75
A6	Stan Humphries	.75
A7	Dan Marino	6.00
A8	Steve Bono	.75
A9	Napoleon Kaufman	.75
N0	Isaac Bruce	2.50
N1	Steve Young	2.50
N2	Michael Westbrook	2.00
N3	Troy Aikman	3.00
N4	Barry Sanders	3.00
N5	Rashaan Salaam	2.00
N6	Emmitt Smith	6.00
N7	Jerry Rice	3.00
N8	Deion Sanders	2.50
N9	Kerry Collins	3.00

1996 Classic NFL Experience Sculpted

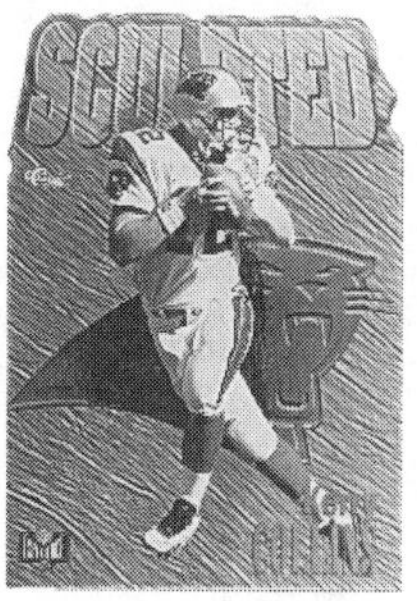

These die-cut foil-board insert cards were seeded one per every 15 packs of 1996 Classic NFL Experience. Cards were limited to 2,400 of each card. The card has a color action photo against a tan background which has the team logo incorporated into it. "Sculpted" is written at the top; the player's name is at the bottom. The card back has a color action photo on one side, with the player's name at the top in his team's primary color. A brief player profile, also using the team color, is given, as is a card number, which uses an "S" prefix.

		MT
Complete Set (20):		180.00
Common Player:		3.00
Minor Stars:		6.00
1	Kerry Collins	12.00
2	Jeff Blake	8.00
3	Vinny Testaverde	3.00
4	Emmitt Smith	20.00
5	Troy Aikman	10.00
6	Deion Sanders	8.00
7	John Elway	6.00
8	Barry Sanders	12.00
9	Brett Favre	20.00
10	Marshall Faulk	10.00
11	Steve Bono	6.00
12	Dan Marino	20.00
13	Robert Smith	3.00
14	Drew Bledsoe	10.00
15	Natrone Means	6.00
16	Steve Young	10.00
17	Jerry Rice	10.00
18	Isaac Bruce	10.00
19	Errict Rhett	6.00
20	Michael Westbrook	6.00

1996 Classic NFL Experience X

This 1996 Classic NFL Experience insert set exposes collectors to everything exceptional about the game. Each card is seeded one per every 45 packs; there were only 1,500 of each produced. The card front features a silver stamp, plus a color photo of the player and the set icon, an X. Backs are numbered using an "X" prefix.

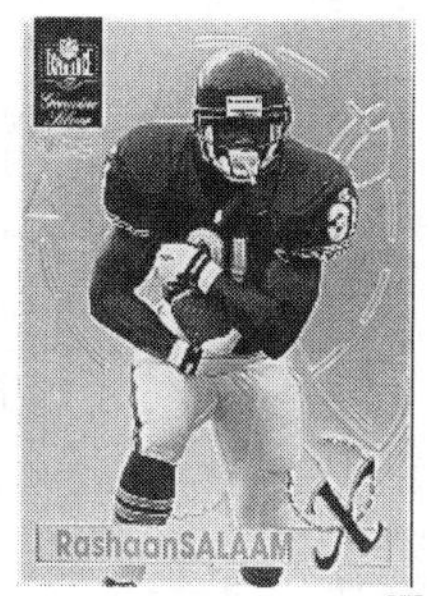

		MT
Complete Set (10):		300.00
Common Player:		20.00
1	Kerry Collins	25.00
2	Rashaan Salaam	20.00
3	Michael Westbrook	20.00
4	Terrell Davis	40.00
5	Joey Galloway	20.00
6	Deion Sanders	20.00
7	Steve Young	30.00
8	Dan Marino	60.00
9	Drew Bledsoe	30.00
10	Emmitt Smith	60.00

1996 Classic SP Autographs

The eight-card, regular-sized set was available as a mail-in from Score Board Inc. and Scott Paper Company. Each card was originally sold for $7.95 with two UPCs or $10.95 without UPC labels. The autographed cards came with Score Board's certificate of authenticity and the entire set was available for $64.95, or $54.95 with eight UPC labels. The cards are numbered with the "SP" prefix.

		MT
Complete Set (8):		80.00
Common Player:		12.00
1	Kyle Brady	12.00
2	Kerry Collins	16.00
3	Ron Jaworski	12.00
4	Napoleon Kaufman	12.00
5	Jim Kiick	12.00
6	Steve McNair	14.00
7	Jim Plunkett	12.00
8	Randy White	12.00

1997 Score Board NFL Experience

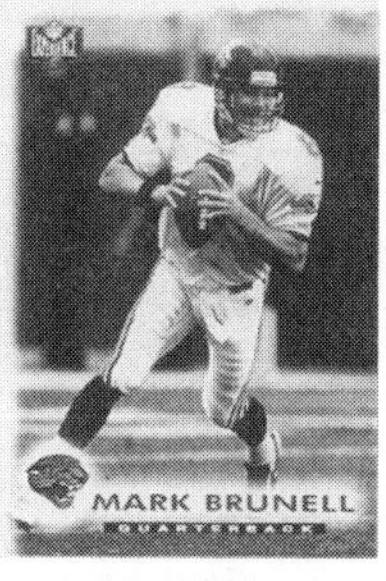

The 100-card, regular-sized set was sold in six-card packs. The card fronts feature a color action photo with the player's name and position printed on the bottom edge. The team's logo appears in the lower left corner. The card backs include another photo, a short highlight and a trivia question with answer. The base cards are printed on vintage-style cards. Inserts include Foundations, Teams Of The 90's and NFL Vintage cards.

		MT
Complete Set (100):		12.00
Common Player:		.05
Minor Stars:		.10
Pack (6):		1.50
Wax Box (36):		43.00
1	Emmitt Smith	1.50
2	Kordell Stewart	.75
3	Antonio Freeman	.05
4	William Thomas	.05
5	Simeon Rice	.25
6	Drew Bledsoe	.75
7	Elvis Grbac	.05
8	Ken Dilger	.05
9	John Elway	.50
10	Curtis Conway	.05
11	Adrian Murrell	.05
12	Karim Abdul-Jabbar	.25
13	Terry Allen	.05
14	Lawrence Phillips	.50
15	Barry Sanders	1.25
16	Shannon Sharpe	.05
17	Troy Aikman	.75
18	Kevin Greene	.05
19	Cris Carter	.05
20	Jim Kelly	.05
21	Eric Metcalf	.05
22	Joey Galloway	.50
23	Eddie George	1.00
24	Scott Mitchell	.05
25	Neil O'Donnell	.05
26	Ben Coates	.05
27	Andre Reed	.05
28	Michael Jackson	.05
29	Keith Jackson	.05
30	J.J. Stokes	.20
31	Rickey Dudley	.25
32	Ricky Watters	.10
33	Marcus Allen	.10
34	Brett Favre	1.25
35	Kevin Hardy	.05
36	Jim Everett	.05
37	Zach Thomas	.25
38	Lamar Lathon	.05
39	LeShon Johnson	.05
40	Bruce Smith	.05
41	Junior Seau	.05
42	Tony Banks	.50
43	Brian Mitchell	.05
44	Chris T. Jones	.05
45	Ty Detmer	.05
46	Robert Brooks	.05
47	Derrick Thomas	.05
48	Dan Wilkinson	.05
49	Michael Sinclair	.05
50	Dave Brown	.05
51	Carl Pickens	.05
52	Jim Harbaugh	.05
53	Wayne Chrebet	.05
54	Warren Moon	.05
55	Steve Young	.50
56	Sean Gilbert	.05
57	Jerome Bettis	.10
58	Dan Marino	1.50
59	Terrell Davis	.75
60	Mark Brunell	.20
61	Kent Graham	.05
62	Rashaan Salaam	.25
63	Tony Martin	.05
64	Robert Smith	.05
65	Thurman Thomas	.10
66	Marshall Faulk	.40
67	Dale Carter	.05
68	Stan Humphries	.05
69	Isaac Bruce	.40
70	Warren Sapp	.05
71	Kerry Collins	.25
72	Jamal Anderson	.40
73	Chris Chandler	.05
74	Herman Moore	.20
75	Rodney Hampton	.05
76	Tim Brown	.05
77	Keenan McCardell	.05
78	Anthony Miller	.05
79	Jake Reed	.05
80	Earnest Byner	.05
81	Chris Warren	.05
82	Deion Sanders	.50
83	Mike Tomczak	.05
84	Curtis Martin	1.00
85	John Friesz	.05
86	Gus Frerotte	.05
87	Vinny Testaverde	.05
88	Jason Dunn	.05
89	James Stewart	.05
90	Steve Bono	.05
91	Levon Kirkland	.05
92	Merton Hanks	.05
93	Marvin Harrison	.60
94	Reggie Brooks	.05
95	Reggie White	.10
96	Jeff Blake	.30
97	Terry Glenn	.25
98	Jerry Rice	.75
99	Keyshawn Johnson	.75
100	Checklist	.05

1997 Score Board NFL Experience Bayou Country

		MT
Complete Set (10):		150.00
Common Player:		5.00
1	Terry Allen	5.00
2	Emmitt Smith	30.00
3	Troy Aikman	15.00
4	Brett Favre	35.00
5	Jerry Rice	15.00
6	Curtis Martin	15.00
7	John Elway	12.00
8	Jerome Bettis	8.00
9	Kevin Greene	5.00
10	Karim Abdul-Jabbar	12.00

1997 Score Board NFL Experience Foundations

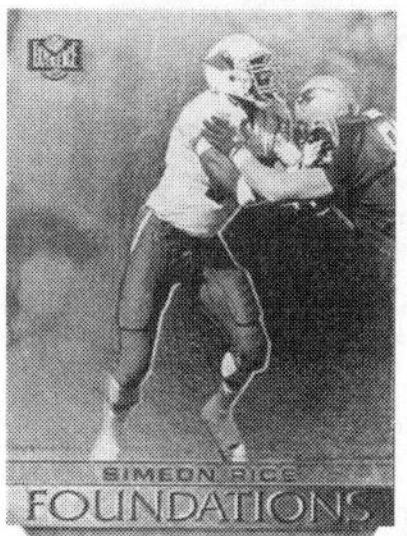

The 30-card, regular-sized set was inserted every 12 packs of Score Board's 1997 NFL Experience. The cards feature a key player from each of the league's 30 franchises. The card backs feature another player photo, imaged over a pedestal blueprint, and are numbered with an "F" prefix.

		MT
Complete Set (30):		150.00
Common Player:		2.00
1	Ray Lewis	2.00
2	Bruce Smith	2.00
3	Jeff Blake	6.00
4	Terrell Davis	10.00
5	Steve McNair	8.00
6	Marshall Faulk	8.00
7	Mark Brunell	5.00
8	Derrick Thomas	2.00
9	Karim Abdul-Jabbar	4.00
10	Curtis Martin	15.00
11	Keyshawn Johnson	8.00
12	Tim Brown	2.00
13	Kordell Stewart	10.00
14	Junior Seau	2.00
15	Joey Galloway	10.00
16	Simeon Rice	2.00
17	Jessie Tuggle	2.00
18	Kerry Collins	4.00
19	Rashaan Salaam	4.00
20	Emmitt Smith	20.00
21	Barry Sanders	10.00
22	Brett Favre	15.00
23	Cris Carter	2.00
24	Jim Everett	2.00
25	Amani Toomer	2.00
26	Ricky Watters	2.00
27	Tony Banks	5.00
28	Jerry Rice	10.00
29	Warren Sapp	2.00
30	Terry Allen	2.00

1997 Score Board NFL Experience Hard Target

Hard Target cards were distributed at the 1997 NFL Experience in New Orleans. The front of these 5" x 7" cards featured an NFL player and the backs described Score Board's Wrapper Redemption program. A different player was available each day of the show.

		MT
Complete Set (5):		20.00
Common Player:		3.00
1	Terrell Davis	4.00
2	Brett Favre	6.00
3	Eddie George	6.00
4	Keyshawn Johnson	3.00
5	Emmitt Smith	5.00

1997 Score Board NFL Experience Season's Heroes

Season's Heroes is a 20-card insert seeded 1:18. Each card features the Super Bowl XXXI logo and football-textured panel on the front. The cards are numbered with the "SH" prefix.

		MT
Complete Set (20):		150.00
Common Player:		3.00
1	Gus Frerotte	3.00
2	Terry Allen	3.00
3	Troy Aikman	12.00
4	Emmitt Smith	25.00
5	Ricky Watters	3.00
6	Brett Favre	30.00
7	Reggie White	5.00
8	Steve Young	10.00
9	Jerry Rice	12.00
10	Kevin Greene	3.00
11	Anthony Johnson	3.00
12	Thurman Thomas	5.00
13	Bruce Smith	3.00
14	Jerome Bettis	5.00
15	Rod Woodson	3.00
16	Eddie George	15.00
17	Terrell Davis	12.00
18	John Elway	10.00
19	Drew Bledsoe	12.00
20	Junior Seau	3.00

1997 Score Board NFL Experience Teams of the 90's

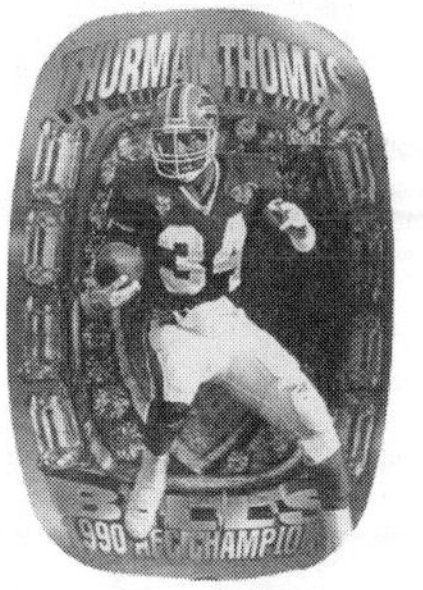

The 15-card, regular-sized set highlights players who have starred in Super Bowls of the 1990s. The cards were inserted in every 100 packs of Score Board's 1997 NFL Experience. The cards are die-cut into the shape of an oval ring. The card fronts feature the player over a common Super Bowl ring while the backs have another player shot with a short bio. The cards are numbered with the "T" prefix.

		MT
Complete Set (15):		300.00
Common Player:		15.00
1	Emmitt Smith	120.00
2	Bruce Smith	15.00
3	Steve Young	50.00
4	Thurman Thomas	15.00
5	Kordell Stewart	60.00
6	Ricky Watters	15.00
7	Ken Norton	15.00
8	Jeff Hostetler	15.00
9	Jim Kelly	15.00
10	Troy Aikman	60.00
11	Jerry Rice	60.00
12	Mark Rypien	15.00
13	Stan Humphries	15.00
14	Deion Sanders	40.00
15	Andre Reed	15.00

1995 Cleo Quarterback Club Valentines

The eight-card, regular-sized set was available through 38-card boxes of Cleo Valentines. The fronts feature a color action shot with a valentine heart with a catchy message. The set was found in perforated sheets with two rows of two cards each. The backs are blank.

MT
Complete Set (8): 5.00
Common Player: .25
1 Troy Aikman 1.00
2 John Elway .50
3 Brett Favre 1.50
4 Jim Kelly .25
5 Dan Marino 1.50
6 Warren Moon .25
7 Phil Simms .25
8 Steve Young .50

1996 Cleo Quarterback Club Valentines

These eight cards were sold in 40-card boxes. The cards are 2-1/2" x 5" (except the Marcus Allen card which measures 3-3/4" x 5"), feature a color photo with a white border and are unnumbered. Each box had two cards on the bottom which are identical to cards in the set.

MT
Complete Set (10): 2.50
Common Player: .15
1 Troy Aikman .40
2 Marcus Allen .15
3 Drew Bledsoe .40
4 John Elway .30
5 Jim Kelly .25
6A Junior Seau (Valentine) .15
6B Junior Seau (box bottom card) .25
7A Emmitt Smith (Valentine) .60
7B Emmitt Smith (box bottom card) .75
8 Steve Young .30

1981 Coke

Players from seven NFL teams are represented in this 84-card set produced by Topps for Coca-Cola. Each card is numbered from 1-11 within its own team, but has been checklisted below using #s 1-77, plus seven unnumbered header cards (one for each team). The Coca-Cola logo appears on both sides of the card, making it identifiable from the regular 1981 Topps card, which the set is patterned after.

MT
Complete Set (77): 50.00
Common Player: .20
(1) Raymond Butler .40
(2) Roger Carr .30
(3) Curtis Dickey .40
(4) Nesby Glasgow .20
(5) Bert Jones 1.00
(6) Bruce Laird .20
(7) Greg Landry .40
(8) Reese McCall .20
(9) Don McCauley .20
(10) Herb Orvis .20
(11) Ed Simonini .20
(12) Pat Donovan .20
(13) Tony Dorsett 2.50
(14) Billy Joe DuPree .40
(15) Tony Hill .40
(16) Ed "Too Tall" Jones .75
(17) Harvey Martin .35
(18) Robert Newhouse .30
(19) Drew Pearson .40
(20) Charlie Waters .30
(21) Danny White .70
(22) Randy White 1.75
(23) Mike Barber .30
(24) Elvin Bethea .30
(25) Gregg Bingham .20
(26) Robert Brazile .30
(27) Ken Burrough .30
(28) Rob Carpenter .30
(29) Leon Gray .30
(30) Vernon Perry .30
(31) Mike Renfro .30
(32) Carl Roaches .30
(33) Morris Towns .20
(34) Harry Carson .75
(35) Mike Dennis .20
(36) Mike Friede .20
(37) Earnest Gray .20
(38) Dave Jennings .30
(39) Gary Jeter .30
(40) George Martin .30
(41) Roy Simmons .20
(42) Phil Simms 2.50
(43) Billy Taylor .20
(44) Brad Van Pelt .30
(45) Ottis Anderson 1.50
(46) Rush Brown .20
(47) Theotis Brown .30
(48) Dan Dierdorf .75
(49) Mel Gray .30
(50) Ken Greene .20
(51) Jim Hart .50
(52) Doug Marsh .20
(53) Wayne Morris .20
(54) Pat Tilley .20
(55) Roger Wehrli .30
(56) Rolf Bernirschke .30
(57) Fred Dean .30
(58) Dan Fouts 1.25
(59) John Jefferson .40
(60) Gary Johnson .30
(61) Charlie Joiner .75
(62) Louie Kelcher .30
(63) Chuck Muncie .30
(64) Doug Wilkerson .20
(65) Clarence Williams .20
(66) Kellen Winslow 1.75
(67) Coy Bacon .20
(68) Wilbur Jackson .20
(69) Karl Lorch .20
(70) Rich Milot .20
(71) Art Monk 20.00
(72) Mark Moseley .30
(73) Mike Nelms .30
(74) Lemar Parrish .30
(75) Joe Theismann 1.25
(76) Ricky Thompson .20
(77) Joe Washington .30

1993 Coke Monsters of the Gridiron

The 30-card, standard-size set, sponsored by Coca-Cola, was available as a complete set at the Super Bowl Card Show in Atlanta. The card fronts feature players in uniforms, but with scary monster makeup. The card backs contain career highlights with the player's scary monster nickname. The set was available to the first 10,000 collectors who redeemed 10 1993 NFL-licensed trading card wrappers.

MT
Complete Set (30): 20.00
Common Player: .25
1 Title Card (Checklist) .50
2 Cornelius Bennett (Big Bear) .25
3 Terrell Buckley (Tiger) .25
4 Tony Casillas (Conde (Count)) .25
5 Reggie Cobb (Crossbones) .25
6 Marco Coleman (Cobra) .25
7 Shane Conlan (Conlan the Barbarian) .25
8 Randall Cunningham (Rocket Man) .50
9 Chris Doleman (Dr. Doomsday) .25
10 Steve Emtman (Beast-Man) .25
11 Harold Green (Slime) .25
12 Michael Haynes (Moonlight Flyer) .25
13 Garrison Hearst (Hearse) 2.00
14 Craig Heyward (Iron Head) .25
15 Rickey Jackson (The Jackal) .25
16 Joe Jacoby (Frankenstein) .25
17 Sean Jones (Ghost) .25
18 Cortez Kennedy (Tez Rex) .25
19 Howie Long (Howlin') .75
20 Ronnie Lott (The Rattler) .75
21 Karl Mecklenburg (Midnight Marauder) .25
22 Neil O'Donnell (Knight Raider) .50
23 Tom Rathman (Psycho) .25
24 Junior Seau (Stealth) 1.00
25 Emmitt Smith (Lone Star Sheriff) 10.00
26 Pat Swilling (Chillin') .25
27 Lawrence Taylor (Six Gun) .75
28 Derrick Thomas (Attack Cat) .75
29 Andre Tippett (Andre the Terrible) .25
30 Eric Turner (Bad Bone) .25

1994 Coke Monsters of the Gridiron

Coca-Cola and Classic teamed up for the promotion and distribution of Monsters of the Gridiron, which is a 30- card set featuring one player from each team transformed into a bizarre, supernatural creature. Two cards were inserted into specially marked multi-packs of Coca-Cola Classic, diet Coke, caffeine-free diet Coke and Sprite. The two additional cards feature a logo of the expansion Panthers and Jaguars. Classic used this promotion to launch its new line of pins, called PINHEADS. These pins were also offered in a parallel set to the cards.

MT
Complete Set (30): 12.00
Common Player: .25
(1) Eric "The Red" Swann .25
(2) Jessie " Tarantula" Tuggle .25
(3) Cornelius "Big Bear" Bennett .25
(4) Team mascot (Panther) .25
(5) Chris "Zorro" Zorich .25
(6) Dan Wilkinson .50
(7) Eric "Bad Bone" Turner .25
(8) Emmitt "Lone Star Sheriff" Smith 3.50
(9) Steve "The Bandit" Atwater .25
(10) Pat "Chillin" Swilling .25
(11) Sean "Ghost" Jones .25
(12) Ray "Scarecrow" Childress .25
(13) Marshall "The Missile" Faulk 3.00
(14) Team mascot (Jaguar) .25
(15) Derrick "Attack Cat" Thomas .50
(16) Chester "Renegade Raider" McGlockton .25
(17) Shane "The Barbarian" Conlan .25
(18) Marco "Cobra" Coleman .25
(19) John "Runaway Train" Randle .25
(20) Bruce "The Pile Driver" Armstrong .25
(21) Renaldo "Raging" Turnbull .25
(22) John "Jumbo" Elliot .25
(23) Ronnie "The Rattler" Lott .50
(24) Randall "Rocket Man" Cunningham .25
(25) Neil "Knight Rider" O'Donnell .25
(26) Junior "Stealth" Seau .50
(27) Ken "Commando" Norton Jr. .25
(28) Cortez "Tez Rex" Kennedy .25
(29) Hardy "Hyena" Nickerson .25
(30) Ken "Jackhammer" Harvey .25

1994 Collector's Choice

Upper Deck's Collector's Choice set was issued in one 384-card series, marking this brand's football debut. Each card has a color action photo on the front with a white frame. The set logo is in the upper left corner; a position icon is in the lower right corner. The player's name and team is in white letters along the bottom of the card. The card back has another photo, player profile, stats and a card number. All cards are UV coated and have the Upper Deck security hologram. Subsets within the main set include: 1994 Rookie Class, Images of '93, Traditions of Excellence, and Expansion cards. Two parallel sets to the main issue were also produced - silver-foil cards, one per pack, and gold-foil cards, one every 35 packs. Instant win "Crash the Game" cards were also made as random inserts. A Joe Montana prototype card was also produced to preview the regular set's design. The back, numbered 19, is somewhat different; the card back has a ghosted picture for its background and only has statistics.

MT
Complete Set (384): 25.00
Common Player: .05
Minor Stars: .10
Silver Cards: 3x
Silver Rookies: 2x
Inserted 1:1
Gold Cards: 15x-30x
Gold Rookies: 7x-14x
Inserted 1:36
Pack (12): 1.00
Wax Box (36): 30.00
1 *Antonio Langham* .50
2 *Aaron Glenn* .25
3 *Sam Adams* .25
4 *DeWayne Washington* .20
5 *Dan Wilkinson* .40
6 *Bryant Young* .50
7 *Aaron Taylor* .10
8 *Willie McGinest* .50
9 *Trev Alberts* .25
10 *Jamir Miller* .25
11 John Thierry .20
12 *Heath Shuler* .25
13 *Trent Dilfer* 2.00
14 *Marshall Faulk* 4.00
15 *Greg Hill* .50
16 *William Floyd* .30
17 *Chuck Levy* .25
18 *Charlie Gardner* .50
19 *Mario Bates* .20
20 *Donnell Bennett* .25
21 *LeShon Johnson* .40
22 *Calvin Jones* .25
23 *Darnay Scott* 1.00
24 *Charles Johnson* .50
25 *Johnnie Morton* .50
26 *Shante Carver* .15
27 *Derrick Alexander* .50
28 *David Palmer* .50
29 *Ryan Yarborough* .25
30 *Errict Rhett* .75
31 James Washington .05
32 Sterling Sharpe .10
33 Drew Bledsoe .50
34 Eric Allen .10
35 Jerome Bettis .30
36 Joe Montana .50
37 John Carney .05
38 Emmitt Smith 1.00
39 Chris Warren .05
40 Reggie Brooks .05
41 Gary Brown .05
42 Tim Brown .10
43 Erric Pegram .05
44 Ron Moore .10
45 Jerry Rice .50
46 Ricky Watters .10
47 Joe Montana .75
48 Reggie Brooks .05
49 Rick Mirer .50
50 Raghib Ismail .10
51 Curtis Conway .10
52 Junior Seau .10
53 Mark Carrier .05
54 Ronnie Lott .05
55 Marcus Allen .10
56 Michael Irvin .15
57 Bennie Blades .10
58 Randal Hill .05
59 Brian Blades .05
60 Russell Maryland .05
61 Jim Kelly .15
62 Arthur Marshall .05
63 Webster Slaughter .05
64 Dave Krieg .05
65 Steve Jordan .05
66 Neil O'Donnell .10
67 Andre Reed .10
68 Mike Croel .05
69 Al Smith .05
70 Joe Montana 1.00
71 Randall McDaniel .05
72 Greg Lloyd .05
73 Thomas Smith .05
74 Glyn Milburn .10
75 Lorenzo White .05
76 Neil Smith .05
77 John Randle .05
78 Rod Woodson .10
79 Russell Maryland .05
80 Rodney Peete .05
81 Jackie Harris .05
82 James Jett .05
83 Rodney Hampton .10
84 Bill Romanowski .05
85 Ken Norton Jr. .05
86 Barry Sanders 1.25
87 Johnny Holland .05
88 Terry McDaniel .05
89 Greg Jackson .05
90 Dana Stubblefield .10
91 Jay Novacek .05
92 Chris Spielman .05
93 Ken Ruettgers .05
94 Greg Robinson .05
95 Mark Jackson .05
96 John Taylor .10
97 Roger Harper .05
98 Jerry Ball .05
99 Keith Byars .05
100 Morten Andersen .05
101 Eric Allen .05
102 Marion Butts .05
103 Michael Haynes .05
104 Rob Burnett .05
105 Marco Coleman .05
106 Derek Brown .10
107 Andy Harmon .05
108 Darren Carrington .05
109 Bobby Hebert .05
110 Mark Carrier .05
111 Bryan Cox .05
112 Toi Cook .05
113 Tim Harris .05
114 John Friesz .05
115 Neal Anderson .05
116 Jerome Bettis .50
117 Bruce Armstrong .05
118 Brad Baxter .05
119 Johnny Bailey .05
120 Brian Blades .05
121 Mark Carrier .05
122 Shane Conlan .05
123 Drew Bledsoe 1.00
124 Chris Burkett .05
125 Steve Beuerlein .05
126 Ferrell Edmunds .05
127 Curtis Conway .10
128 Troy Drayton .05
129 Vincent Brown .05
130 Boomer Esiason .05
131 Larry Centers .05
132 Carlton Gray .05
133 Chris Miller .05
134 Eric Metcalf .05
135 Mark Higgs .05
136 Tyrone Hughes .05
137 Randall Cunningham .10
138 Ronnie Harmon .05
139 Andre Rison .10
140 Eric Turner .05
141 Terry Kirby .05
142 Eric Martin .05
143 Seth Joyner .05
144 Stan Humphries .10
145 Deion Sanders .50
146 Vinny Testaverde .05
147 Dan Marino 2.00
148 Renaldo Turnbull .05
149 Herschel Walker .05
150 Anthony Miller .10
151 Richard Dent .05
152 Jim Everett .05
153 Ben Coates .20
154 Jeff Lageman .05
155 Garrison Hearst .50
156 Kelvin Martin .05
157 Dante Jones .05
158 Sean Gilbert .05
159 Leonard Russell .05
160 Ronnie Lott .05
161 Randal Hill .05
162 Rick Mirer .50
163 Alonzo Spellman .05
164 Todd Lyght .05
165 Chris Slade .05
166 Johnny Mitchell .05
167 Ron Moore .20
168 Eugene Robinson .05
169 Chris Hinton .05
170 Dan Footman .05
171 Keith Jackson .05
172 Ricky Jackson .05
173 Heath Sherman .05
174 Chris Mims .05
175 Erric Pegram .05
176 Leroy Hoard .05
177 O.J. McDuffie .20
178 Wayne Martin .05
179 Clyde Simmons .05
180 Leslie O'Neal .05
181 Mike Pritchard .05
182 Michael Jackson .05
183 Scott Mitchell .10
184 Lorenzo Neal .05
185 William Thomas .05
186 Junior Seau .20
187 Chris Gedney .05
188 Tim Lester .05
189 Sam Gash .05
190 Johnny Johnson .05
191 Chuck Cecil .05
192 Cortez Kennedy .10
193 Jim Harbaugh .05
194 Roman Phifer .05
195 Pat Harlow .05
196 Rob Moore .05
197 Gary Clark .05
198 John Vaughn .05
199 Craig Heyward .05
200 Michael Stewart .05
201 Greg McCurty .05
202 Brian Washington .05
203 Ken Harvey .05
204 Chris Warren .05
205 Bruce Smith .05
206 Tom Rouen .05
207 Cris Dishman .05
208 Keith Cash .05
209 Carlos Jenkins .05
210 Levon Kirkland .05
211 Pete Metzelaars .05
212 Shannon Sharpe .10
213 Cody Carlson .05
214 Derrick Thomas .10
215 Emmitt Smith 2.00
216 Robert Porcher .05
217 Sterling Sharpe .20
218 Anthony Smith .05
219 Mike Sherrard .05
220 Tom Rathman .05
221 Nate Newton .05
222 Pat Swilling .05
223 George Teague .05
224 Greg Townsend .05
225 Eric Guliford .20
226 Leroy Thompson .05
227 Thurman Thomas .20
228 Dan Williams .05
229 Bubba McDowell .05
230 Tracy Simien .05
231 *Scottie Graham* .25
232 Eric Green .05
233 Phil Simms .05
234 Ricky Watters .10
235 Kevin Williams .40
236 Brett Perriman .05
237 Reggie White .10
238 Steve Wisniewski .05
239 Mark Collins .05
240 Steve Young .50
241 Steve Tovar .05
242 Jason Belser .05
243 Ray Seals .05
244 Earnest Byner .05
245 Ricky Proehl .05
246 Rich Miano .05
247 Alfred Williams .05
248 Ray Buchannan .05
249 Hardy Nickerson .05
250 Brad Edwards .05
251 Jerrol Williams .05
252 Marvin Washington .05
253 Tony McGhee .05
254 Jeff George .10
255 Ron Hall .05
256 Tim Johnson .05
257 Willie Roaf .05
258 Andre Tippett .05
259 Richardo McDonald .05
260 Jeff Herrod .05
261 Demetrius Dubose .05
262 Ricky Sanders .05
263 John L. Williams .05
264 John Lynch .05
265 Lance Gurn .05
266 Jessie Hester .05
267 Mark Wheeler .05
268 Chip Lohmiller .05
269 Eric Swann .05
270 Byron Evans .05
271 Gary Plummer .05
272 Roger Duffy .05
273 Irv Smith .05
274 Todd Collins .05
275 Robert Blackmon .05
276 Reggie Roby .05
277 Russell Copeland .05
278 Simon Fletcher .05
279 Ernest Givins .05
280 Tim Barnett .05
281 Chris Doleman .05
282 Jeff Graham .05
283 Kenneth Davis .05
284 Vance Johnson .05
285 Haywood Jeffires .05
286 Todd McNair .05
287 Daryl Johnston .05
288 Ryan McNeil .05
289 Terrell Buckley .05
290 Ethan Horton .05
291 Corey Miller .05
292 Marc Logan .05
293 *Lincoln Coleman* .10
294 Derrick Moore .05
295 Leroy Butler .05
296 Jeff Hostetler .05
297 Qadry Ismail .10
298 Andre Hastings .05
299 Henry Jones .05
300 John Elway .50
301 Warren Moon .15
302 Willie Davis .05
303 Vencie Glenn .05
304 Kevin Green .05
305 Marcus Buckley .05
306 Tim McDonald .05
307 Michael Irvin .30
308 Herman Moore .20
309 Brett Favre 2.00
310 Raghib Ismail .10
311 Jerrod Bunch .05
312 Don Beebe .05
313 Steve Atwater .05
314 Gary Brown .05
315 Marcus Allen .10
316 Terry Allen .05
317 Chad Brown .05
318 Cornelius Bennett .05
319 Rod Bernstine .05
320 Greg Montgomery .05
321 Kimble Anders .05
322 Charles Haley .05
323 Mel Gray .05
324 Edgar Bennett .05
325 Eddie Anderson .05
326 Derek Brown .05
327 Steve Bono .10
328 Alvin Harper .10
329 Willie Green .05
330 Robert Brooks .05
331 Patrick Bates .05
332 Anthony Carter .05
333 Barry Foster .10
334 Bill Brooks .05
335 Jason Elam .05
336 Ray Childress .05
337 J.J. Birden .05
338 Cris Carter .10
339 Deion Figures .10
340 Carlton Bailey .05
341 Brent Jones .05
342 Troy Aikman 1.00
343 Rodney Holman .05
344 Tony Bennett .05
345 Tim Brown .10
346 Michael Brooks .05
347 Martin Harrison .05
348 Jerry Rice 1.00
349 John Copeland .05
350 Kerry Cash .05
351 Reggie Cobb .05
352 Brian Mitchell .05
353 Derrick Fenner .05
354 Roosevelt Potts .05
355 Courtney Hawkins .05
356 Carl Banks .05
357 Harold Green .05
358 Steve Emtman .05
359 Santana Dotson .05
360 Reggie Brooks .10
361 Terry Obee .05
362 David Klingler .05
363 Quentin Coryatt .05
364 Craig Erickson .05
365 Desmond Howard .05
366 Carl Pickens .05
367 Lawrence Dawsey .05
368 Henry Ellard .05
369 Shaun Gayle .05
370 David Lang .05
371 Anthony Johnson .05
372 *Darnell Walker* .10
373 Pepper Johnson .05
374 Kurt Gouveia .05
375 Louis Oliver .05
376 Lincoln Kennedy .05
377 Anthony Pleasant .05
378 Irving Fryar .05
379 Carolina Panthers .25
380 Jacksonville Jaguars .25
381 Checklist .05
382 Checklist .05
383 Checklist .05
384 Checklist .05

1994 Collector's Choice Silver

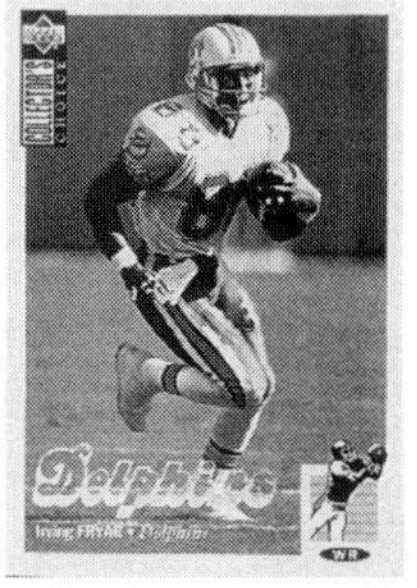

The 384-card, standard-sized set, parallel to the 1994 Collector's Choice base set, was available one per hobby pack, two per retail pack and three per jumbo pack. Unlike the base set, the Silver set has the team's name on the card front in silver foil.

MT
Complete Set (384): 75.00
Common Player: .20
Silver Cards: 2x-4x

1994 Collector's Choice Gold

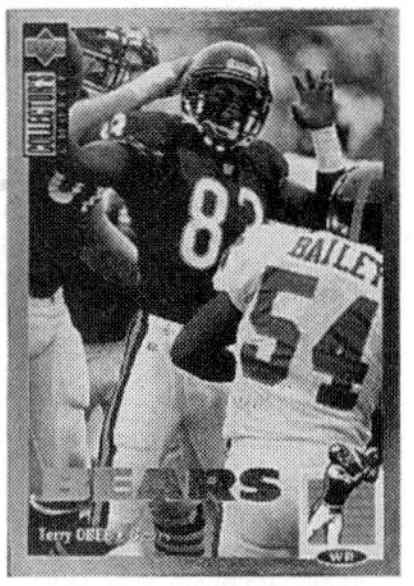

This 384-card set features each card in the base set, but includes a gold border around the card and the team name is printed in gold foil. Gold parallel cards were seeded every 35 packs of Collector's Choice.

MT
Complete Set (384): 1500.
Common Player: 2.00
Minor Stars: 4.00
Unlisted Stars: 20x-40x
1 *Antonio Langham* 10.00
2 *Aaron Glenn* 6.00
3 *Sam Adams* 6.00
4 *DeWayne Washington* 6.00
5 *Dan Wilkinson* 8.00
6 *Bryant Young* 10.00
7 *Aaron Taylor* 4.00
8 *Willie McGinest* 10.00
9 *Trev Alberts* 6.00
10 *Jamir Miller* 6.00
11 John Thierry 6.00
12 *Heath Shuler* 5.00
13 *Trent Dilfer* 30.00
14 *Marshall Faulk* 100.00
15 *Greg Hill* 15.00
16 *William Floyd* 35.00
17 *Chuck Levy* 6.00
18 *Charlie Gardner* 10.00
19 *Mario Bates* 25.00
20 *Donnell Bennett* 6.00
21 *LeShon Johnson* 8.00
22 *Calvin Jones* 6.00
23 *Darnay Scott* 30.00
24 *Charles Johnson* 20.00
25 *Johnnie Morton* 6.00

26	*Shante Carver*	4.00
27	*Derrick Alexander*	15.00
28	*David Palmer*	10.00
29	*Ryan Yarborough*	6.00
30	*Errict Rhett*	60.00
31	James Washington	2.00
32	Sterling Sharpe	4.00
33	Drew Bledsoe	20.00
34	Eric Allen	4.00
35	Jerome Bettis	15.00
36	Joe Montana	20.00
37	John Carney	2.00
38	Emmitt Smith	35.00
39	Chris Warren	2.00
40	Reggie Brooks	2.00
41	Gary Brown	2.00
42	Tim Brown	4.00
43	Erric Pegram	2.00
44	Ron Moore	4.00
45	Jerry Rice	25.00
46	Ricky Watters	4.00
47	Joe Montana	30.00
48	Reggie Brooks	2.00
49	Rick Mirer	15.00
50	Raghib Ismail	4.00
51	Curtis Conway	4.00
52	Junior Seau	4.00
53	Mark Carrier	2.00
54	Ronnie Lott	2.00
55	Marcus Allen	2.00
56	Michael Irvin	6.00
57	Bennie Blades	4.00
58	Randal Hill	2.00
59	Brian Blades	2.00
60	Russell Maryland	2.00
61	Jim Kelly	6.00
62	Arthur Marshall	2.00
63	Webster Slaughter	2.00
64	Dave Krieg	2.00
65	Steve Jordan	2.00
66	Neil O'Donnell	4.00
67	Andre Reed	4.00
68	Mike Croel	2.00
69	Al Smith	2.00
70	Joe Montana	40.00
71	Randall McDaniel	2.00
72	Greg Lloyd	2.00
73	Thomas Smith	2.00
74	Glyn Milburn	4.00
75	Lorenzo White	2.00
76	Neil Smith	2.00
77	John Randle	2.00
78	Rod Woodson	4.00
79	Russell Maryland	2.00
80	Rodney Peete	2.00
81	Jackie Harris	2.00
82	James Jett	2.00
83	Rodney Hampton	4.00
84	Bill Romanowski	2.00
85	Ken Norton Jr.	2.00
86	Barry Sanders	75.00
87	Johnny Holland	2.00
88	Terry McDaniel	2.00
89	Greg Jackson	2.00
90	Dana Stubblefield	4.00
91	Jay Novacek	2.00
92	Chris Spielman	2.00
93	Ken Ruettgers	2.00
94	Greg Robinson	2.00
95	Mark Jackson	2.00
96	John Taylor	4.00
97	Roger Harper	2.00
98	Jerry Ball	2.00
99	Keith Byars	2.00
100	Morten Andersen	2.00
101	Eric Allen	2.00
102	Marion Butts	2.00
103	Michael Haynes	2.00
104	Rob Burnett	2.00
105	Marco Coleman	2.00
106	Derek Brown	4.00
107	Andy Harmon	2.00
108	Darren Carrington	2.00
109	Bobby Hebert	2.00
110	Mark Carrier	2.00
111	Bryan Cox	2.00
112	Toi Cook	2.00
113	Tim Harris	2.00
114	John Friesz	2.00
115	Neal Anderson	2.00
116	Jerome Bettis	25.00
117	Bruce Armstrong	2.00
118	Brad Baxter	2.00
119	Johnny Bailey	2.00
120	Brian Blades	2.00
121	Mark Carrier	2.00
122	Shane Conlan	2.00
123	Drew Bledsoe	40.00
124	Chris Burkett	2.00
125	Steve Beuerlein	2.00
126	Ferrell Edmunds	2.00
127	Curtis Conway	4.00
128	Troy Drayton	2.00
129	Vincent Brown	2.00
130	Boomer Esiason	2.00
131	Larry Centers	2.00
132	Carlton Gray	2.00
133	Chris Miller	2.00
134	Eric Metcalf	2.00
135	Mark Higgs	2.00
136	Tyrone Hughes	2.00
137	Randall Cunningham	4.00
138	Ronnie Harmon	2.00
139	Andre Rison	4.00
140	Eric Turner	2.00
141	Terry Kirby	2.00
142	Eric Martin	2.00
143	Seth Joyner	2.00
144	Stan Humphries	4.00
145	Deion Sanders	20.00
146	Vinny Testaverde	2.00
147	Dan Marino	60.00
148	Renaldo Turnbull	2.00
149	Herschel Walker	2.00
150	Anthony Miller	4.00
151	Richard Dent	2.00
152	Jim Everett	2.00
153	Ben Coates	8.00
154	Jeff Lageman	2.00
155	Garrison Hearst	10.00
156	Kelvin Martin	2.00
157	Dante Jones	2.00
158	Sean Gilbert	2.00
159	Leonard Russell	2.00
160	Ronnie Lott	2.00
161	Randal Hill	2.00
162	Rick Mirer	6.00
163	Alonzo Spellman	2.00
164	Todd Lyght	2.00
165	Chris Slade	2.00
166	Johnny Mitchell	2.00
167	Ron Moore	6.00
168	Eugene Robinson	2.00
169	Chris Hinton	2.00
170	Dan Footman	2.00
171	Keith Jackson	2.00
172	Ricky Jackson	2.00
173	Heath Sherman	2.00
174	Chris Mims	2.00
175	Erric Pegram	2.00
176	Leroy Hoard	2.00
177	O.J. McDuffie	8.00
178	Wayne Martin	2.00
179	Clyde Simmons	2.00
180	Leslie O'Neal	2.00
181	Mike Pritchard	2.00
182	Michael Jackson	2.00
183	Scott Mitchell	4.00
184	Lorenzo Neal	2.00
185	William Thomas	2.00
186	Junior Seau	8.00
187	Chris Gedney	2.00
188	Tim Lester	2.00
189	Sam Gash	2.00
190	Johnny Johnson	2.00
191	Chuck Cecil	2.00
192	Cortez Kennedy	4.00
193	Jim Harbaugh	2.00
194	Roman Phifer	2.00
195	Pat Harlow	2.00
196	Rob Moore	2.00
197	Gary Clark	2.00
198	John Vaughn	2.00
199	Craig Heyward	2.00
200	Michael Stewart	2.00
201	Greg McCurty	2.00
202	Brian Washington	2.00
203	Ken Harvey	2.00
204	Chris Warren	2.00
205	Bruce Smith	2.00
206	Tom Rouen	2.00
207	Cris Dishman	2.00
208	Keith Cash	2.00
209	Carlos Jenkins	2.00
210	Levon Kirkland	2.00
211	Pete Metzelaars	2.00
212	Shannon Sharpe	4.00
213	Cody Carlson	2.00
214	Derrick Thomas	4.00
215	Emmitt Smith	60.00
216	Robert Porcher	2.00
217	Sterling Sharpe	8.00
218	Anthony Smith	2.00
219	Mike Sherrard	2.00
220	Tom Rathman	2.00
221	Nate Newton	2.00
222	Pat Swilling	2.00
223	George Teague	2.00
224	Greg Townsend	2.00
225	Eric Guliford	5.00
226	Leroy Thompson	2.00
227	Thurman Thomas	8.00
228	Dan Williams	2.00
229	Bubba McDowell	2.00
230	Tracy Simien	2.00
231	*Scottie Graham*	6.00
232	Eric Green	2.00
233	Phil Simms	2.00
234	Ricky Watters	4.00
235	Kevin Williams	4.00
236	Brett Perriman	2.00
237	Reggie White	4.00
238	Steve Wisniewski	2.00
239	Mark Collins	2.00
240	Steve Young	25.00
241	Steve Tovar	2.00
242	Jason Belser	2.00
243	Ray Seals	2.00
244	Earnest Byner	2.00
245	Ricky Proehl	2.00
246	Rich Miano	2.00
247	Alfred Williams	2.00
248	Ray Buchannan	2.00
249	Hardy Nickerson	2.00
250	Brad Edwards	2.00
251	Jerrol Williams	2.00
252	Marvin Washington	2.00
253	Tony McGhee	2.00
254	Jeff George	4.00
255	Ron Hall	2.00
256	Tim Johnson	2.00
257	Willie Roaf	2.00
258	Andre Tippett	2.00
259	Richardo McDonald	2.00
260	Jeff Herrod	2.00
261	Demetrius Dubose	2.00
262	Ricky Sanders	2.00
263	John L. Williams	2.00
264	John Lynch	2.00
265	Lance Gurn	2.00
266	Jessie Hester	2.00
267	Mark Wheeler	2.00
268	Chip Lohmiller	2.00
269	Eric Swann	2.00
270	Byron Evans	2.00
271	Gary Plummer	2.00
272	Roger Duffy	2.00
273	Irv Smith	2.00
274	Todd Collins	2.00
275	Robert Blackmon	2.00
276	Reggie Roby	2.00
277	Russell Copeland	2.00
278	Simon Fletcher	2.00
279	Ernest Givins	2.00
280	Tim Barnett	2.00
281	Chris Doleman	2.00
282	Jeff Graham	2.00
283	Kenneth Davis	2.00
284	Vance Johnson	2.00
285	Haywood Jeffires	2.00
286	Todd McNair	2.00
287	Daryl Johnston	2.00
288	Ryan McNeil	2.00
289	Terrell Buckley	2.00
290	Ethan Horton	2.00
291	Corey Miller	2.00
292	Marc Logan	2.00
293	*Lincoln Coleman*	4.00
294	Derrick Moore	2.00
295	Leroy Butler	2.00
296	Jeff Hostetler	2.00
297	Qadry Ismail	4.00
298	Andre Hastings	2.00
299	Henry Jones	2.00
300	John Elway	50.00
301	Warren Moon	6.00
302	Willie Davis	2.00
303	Vencie Glenn	2.00
304	Kevin Green	2.00
305	Marcus Buckley	2.00
306	Tim McDonald	2.00
307	Michael Irvin	10.00
308	Herman Moore	8.00
309	Brett Favre	80.00
310	Raghib Ismail	4.00
311	Jerrod Bunch	2.00
312	Don Beebe	2.00
313	Steve Atwater	2.00
314	Gary Brown	2.00
315	Marcus Allen	4.00
316	Terry Allen	2.00
317	Chad Brown	2.00
318	Cornelius Bennett	2.00
319	Rod Bernstine	2.00
320	Greg Montgomery	2.00
321	Kimble Anders	2.00
322	Charles Haley	2.00
323	Mel Gray	2.00
324	Edgar Bennett	2.00
325	Eddie Anderson	2.00
326	Derek Brown	2.00
327	Steve Bono	4.00
328	Alvin Harper	4.00
329	Willie Green	2.00
330	Robert Brooks	2.00
331	Patrick Bates	2.00
332	Anthony Carter	2.00
333	Barry Foster	4.00
334	Bill Brooks	2.00
335	Jason Elam	2.00
336	Ray Childress	2.00
337	J.J. Birden	2.00
338	Cris Carter	4.00
339	Deion Figures	2.00
340	Carlton Bailey	2.00
341	Brent Jones	2.00
342	Troy Aikman	40.00
343	Rodney Holman	2.00
344	Tony Bennett	2.00
345	Tim Brown	4.00
346	Michael Brooks	2.00
347	Martin Harrison	2.00
348	Jerry Rice	40.00
349	John Copeland	2.00
350	Kerry Cash	2.00
351	Reggie Cobb	2.00
352	Brian Mitchell	2.00
353	Derrick Fenner	2.00
354	Roosevelt Potts	2.00
355	Courtney Hawkins	2.00
356	Carl Banks	2.00
357	Harold Green	2.00
358	Steve Emtman	2.00
359	Santana Dotson	2.00
360	Reggie Brooks	4.00
361	Terry Obee	2.00
362	David Klingler	2.00
363	Quentin Coryatt	2.00
364	Craig Erickson	2.00
365	Desmond Howard	2.00
366	Carl Pickens	2.00
367	Lawrence Dawsey	2.00
368	Henry Ellard	2.00
369	Shaun Gayle	2.00
370	David Lang	2.00
371	Anthony Johnson	2.00
372	*Darnell Walker*	4.00
373	Pepper Johnson	2.00
374	Kurt Gouveia	2.00
375	Louis Oliver	2.00
376	Lincoln Kennedy	2.00
377	Anthony Pleasant	2.00
378	Irving Fryar	2.00
379	Carolina Panthers	6.00
380	Jacksonville Jaguars	6.00
381	Checklist	2.00
382	Checklist	2.00
383	Checklist	2.00
384	Checklist	2.00

1994 Collector's Choice Crash the Game

These instant-win sweepstakes cards were randomly inserted in 1994 Upper Deck Collector's Choice packs, one every 36th pack. More than 300,000 prizes were to be given away, including a grand prize of a $10,000 football card and memorabilia shopping spree at Upper Deck and Upper Deck Authenticated, plus an afternoon with Joe Montana.

		MT
Complete Set (30):		75.00
Common Player:		1.00
Minor Stars:		2.00
Bronze Cards:		.2x
Silver Cards:		.3x
Gold Cards:		.5x
1	Steve Young	2.50
2	Troy Aikman	3.00
3	Rick Mirer	1.00
4	Trent Dilfer	2.00
5	Dan Marino	6.00
6	John Elway	4.00
7	Heath Shuler	1.00
8	Joe Montana	4.00
9	Drew Bledsoe	3.00
10	Warren Moon	1.00
11	Marshall Faulk	4.00
12	Thurman Thomas	1.00
13	Barry Foster	1.00
14	Gary Brown	1.00
15	Emmitt Smith	6.00
16	Barry Sanders	6.00
17	Rodney Hampton	1.00
18	Jerome Bettis	2.00
19	Ricky Watters	1.00
20	Ron Moore	1.00
21	Jerry Rice	3.00
22	Andre Rison	1.00
23	Michael Irvin	1.00
24	Sterling Sharpe	2.00
25	Shannon Sharpe	1.00
26	Darnay Scott	1.00
27	Andre Reed	1.00
28	Tim Brown	1.00
29	Charles Johnson	1.00
30	Irving Fryar	1.00

1994 Collector's Choice Then and Now

The eight-card, regular-sized set was available to collectors by sending in a redemption card. The horizontal card fronts feature a current top player with a former great in a holographic image. The backs feature color shots of each player with highlights of each player.

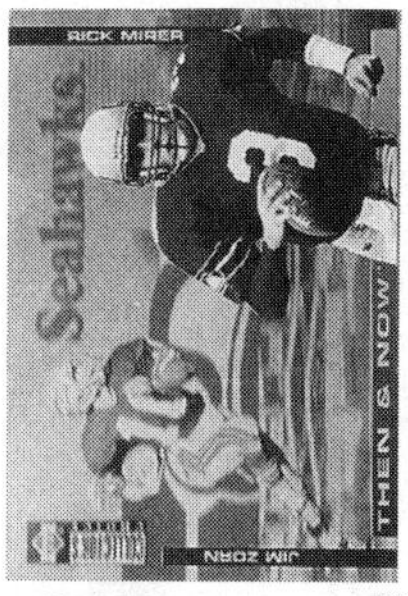

		MT
Complete Set (8):		10.00
Common Player:		.50
1	Eric Dickerson, Jerome Bettis	1.00
2	Fred Biletnikoff, Tim Brown	.50
3	Len Dawson, Joe Montana	2.00
4	Joe Montana, Steve Young	3.00
5	Bob Griese, Dan Marino	4.00
6	Jim Zorn, Rick Mirer	.50
NNO	Header Card (Joe Montana)	2.00
NNO	Then/Now Exch. Card	.50
NNO	Checklist (Eric Dickerson)	.50

1994-95 Collector's Choice Crash Super Bowl XXIX

The eight-card, standard-sized set, produced specifically for Super Bowl XXIX, were available at the NFL Experience card show in Miami, as well as other media outlets. The set features four players from the San Diego Chargers and four from the San Francisco 49ers. If a player featured in the set scored a touchdown in the Super Bowl, the card was redeemable for a special nine-card set.

		MT
Complete Set (9):		12.00
Common Player:		.50
1	Steve Young (WIN)	3.00
2	Jerry Rice (WIN)	4.00
3	Brent Jones	.50
4	Ricky Watters (WIN)	1.00
5	Stan Humphries (WIN)	1.00
6	Natrone Means (WIN)	1.50
7	Ronnie Harmon	.50
8	Tony Martin (WIN)	.50
NNO	Header Card	.50

1995 Collector's Choice

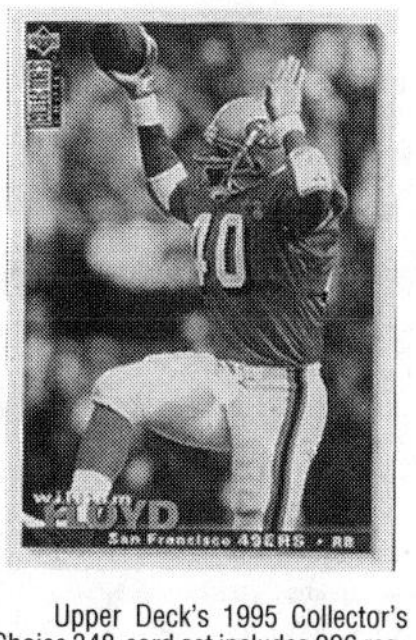

Upper Deck's 1995 Collector's Choice 348-card set includes 296 regular cards, plus 30 1995 Rookie Class and 20 Did You Know cards. Each regular card front has a color photo with a white frame. The brand logo is in the upper left corner; the player's name, team name and position are at the bottom. The card back has that information at the top, along with biographical information and a card number. The middle of the card has another action photo, with statistics and a brief summary of the player's accomplishments. Two parallel sets were also created - Players Club, which uses a silver stamp (one card every pack) and Platinum Players Club, which reproduces each card on silver-foil paper (one in 35 packs). Other inserts include eight of 20 Joe Montana Trilogy cards, and You Crash the Game cards. Once again, Collector's Choice features Crash Packs, which contain all types of insert cards. These packs are inserted one per 144 packs.

		MT
Complete Set (348):		25.00
Common Player:		.05
Minor Stars:		.10
Marino Chronicles (10):		15.00
Montana Chronicles (10):		15.00
1:1 Special Retail		
Player Club Cards: 2x		
Inserted 1:1		
PC Platinum Cards: 12x-24x		
PC Platinum Rookies: 6x-12x		
Inserted 1:35		
Pack (12):		.75
Wax Box (36):		20.00
1	*Ki-Jana Carter*	.30
2	*Tony Boselli*	.10
3	*Steve McNair*	2.50
4	*Michael Westbrook*	1.00
5	*Kerry Collins*	1.00
6	*Kevin Carter*	.10
7	*Mike Mamula*	.10
8	*Joey Galloway*	2.00
9	*Kyle Brady*	.40
10	*J.J. Stokes*	1.00
11	*Derrick Alexander*	.20
12	*Warren Sapp*	.50
13	*Mark Fields*	.10
14	*Tyrone Wheatley*	.30
15	*Napoleon Kaufman*	2.50
16	*James Stewart*	1.25
17	*Luther Elliss*	.10
18	*Rashaan Salaam*	.30
19	*Ty Law*	.10
20	*Mark Bruener*	.20
21	*Derrick Brooks*	.10
22	*Christian Fauria*	.10
23	*Ray Zellars*	.10
24	*Todd Collins*	.10
25	*Sherman Williams*	.10
26	*Frank Sanders*	1.00
27	*Rodney Thomas*	.10
28	*Rob Johnson*	1.75
29	*Steve Stenstrom*	.20
30	*James Stewart*	.10
31	Barry Sanders	1.00
32	Marshall Faulk	.20
33	Darnay Scott	.10
34	Joe Montana	.50
35	Michael Irvin	.10
36	Jerry Rice	.50
37	Errict Rhett	.20
38	Drew Bledsoe	.50
39	Dan Marino	.75
40	Terance Mathis	.10
41	Natrone Means	.20
42	Tim Brown	.10
43	Steve Young	.40
44	Mel Gray	.05
45	Jerome Bettis	.20
46	Aeneas Williams	.05
47	Charlie Gardner	.05
48	Deion Sanders	.20
49	Ken Harvey	.05
50	Emmitt Smith	.75
51	Andre Reed	.10
52	Sean Dawkins	.15
53	Irving Fryar	.05
54	Vincent Brisby	.05
55	Rob Moore	.05
56	Carl Pickens	.05
57	Vinny Testaverde	.05
58	Webster Slaughter	.05
59	Eric Green	.05
60	Anthony Miller	.05
61	Lake Dawson	.20
62	Tim Brown	.10
63	Stan Humphries	.10
64	Rick Mirer	.40
65	Gary Clark	.05
66	Troy Aikman	1.00
67	Mike Sherrard	.05
68	Fred Barnett	.05
69	Henry Ellard	.05
70	Terry Allen	.05
71	Jeff Graham	.05
72	Herman Moore	.10
73	Brett Favre	2.00
74	Trent Dilfer	.40
75	Derek Brown	.05
76	Andre Rison	.10
77	Willie Anderson	.05
78	Jerry Rice	1.00
79	Thurman Thomas	.20
80	Marshall Faulk	.50
81	O.J. McDuffie	.05
82	Ben Coates	.05
83	Johnny Mitchell	.05
84	Darnay Scott	.40
85	Derrick Alexander	.20
86	Michael Barrow	.05
87	Charles Johnson	.20
88	John Elway	1.00
89	Willie Davis	.05
90	James Jett	.05
91	Mark Seay	.05
92	Brian Blades	.05
93	Ricky Proehl	.05
94	Charles Haley	.05
95	Cris Calloway	.05
96	Calvin Williams	.05
97	Ethan Horton	.05
98	Cris Carter	.10
99	Curtis Conway	.05
100	Lomas Brown	.05
101	Edgar Bennett	.05
102	Craig Erickson	.05
103	Jim Everett	.05
104	Terance Mathis	.05
105	Wayne Gandy	.05
106	Brent Jones	.05
107	Bruce Smith	.05
108	Roosevelt Potts	.05
109	Dan Marino	1.50
110	Michael Timpson	.05
111	Boomer Esiason	.05
112	David Klingler	.05
113	Eric Metcalf	.05
114	Lorenzo White	.05
115	Neil O'Donnell	.10
116	Shannon Sharpe	.05
117	Joe Montana	1.00
118	Jeff Hostetler	.10
119	Ronnie Harmon	.05
120	Chris Warren	.10
121	Randal Hill	.05
122	Alvin Harper	.10
123	Dave Brown	.05
124	Randall Cunningham	.10
125	Heath Shuler	.50
126	Jake Reed	.05
127	Donnell Woolford	.05
128	Scott Mitchell	.05
129	Reggie White	.10
130	Lawrence Dawsey	.05
131	Michael Haynes	.05
132	Bert Emanuel	.20
133	Troy Drayton	.05
134	Merton Hanks	.05
135	Jim Kelly	.10
136	Tony Bennett	.05
137	Terry Kirby	.05
138	Drew Bledsoe	1.00
139	Johnny Johnson	.05
140	Dan Wilkinson	.05
141	Leroy Hoard	.05
142	Gary Brown	.05
143	Barry Foster	.05
144	Shane Dronett	.05
145	Marcus Allen	.10
146	Harvey Williams	.05
147	Tony Martin	.05
148	Rod Stephens	.05
149	Ronald Moore	.05
150	Michael Irvin	.20
151	Rodney Hampton	.05
152	Herschel Walker	.05
153	Reggie Brooks	.05
154	Qadry Ismail	.05
155	Chris Zorich	.05
156	Barry Sanders	2.00
157	Sean Jones	.05
158	Errict Rhett	.10
159	Tyrone Hughes	.05
160	Jeff George	.10
161	Chris Miller	.05
162	Steve Young	.75
163	Cornelius Bennett	.05
164	Trev Alberts	.05
165	Marco Coleman	.05
166	Marion Butts	.05
167	Aaron Glenn	.05
168	James Francis	.05
169	Eric Turner	.05
170	Darryll Lewis	.05
171	John L. Williams	.05
172	Simon Fletcher	.05
173	Neil Smith	.05
174	Chester McGlockton	.05
175	Natrone Means	.40
176	Michael Sinclair	.05
177	Larry Centers	.05
178	Daryl Johnston	.05
179	Dave Meggett	.05
180	Greg Jackson	.05
181	Ken Harvey	.05
182	Warren Moon	.10
183	Steve Walsh	.05
184	Chris Spielman	.05
185	Bryce Paup	.05
186	Courtney Hawkins	.05
187	Willie Roaf	.05
188	Chris Doleman	.05
189	Jerome Bettis	.40
190	Ricky Watters	.10
191	Henry Jones	.05
192	Quentin Coryatt	.05
193	Bryan Cox	.05
194	Kevin Turner	.05
195	Siupeli Malamala	.05
196	Louis Oliver	.05
197	Rob Burnett	.05
198	Cris Dishman	.05
199	Bam Morris	.40
200	Ray Crockett	.05
201	Jon Vaughn	.05
202	Nolan Harrison	.05
203	Leslie O'Neal	.05
204	Sam Adams	.05
205	Eric Swann	.05
206	Jay Novacek	.05
207	Keith Hamilton	.05
208	Charlie Garner	.05
209	Tom Carter	.05
210	Henry Thomas	.05
211	Lewis Tillman	.05
212	Pat Swilling	.05
213	Terrell Buckley	.05
214	Hardy Nickerson	.05
215	Mario Bates	.20
216	D.J. Johnson	.05
217	Robert Young	.05
218	Dana Stubblefield	.05
219	Jeff Burris	.05
220	Floyd Turner	.05
221	Troy Vincent	.05
222	Willie McGinest	.05
223	James Hasty	.05
224	*Jeff Blake*	1.00
225	Stevon Moore	.05
226	Ernest Givins	.05
227	Greg Lloyd	.05
228	Steve Atwater	.05
229	Dale Carter	.05
230	Terry McDaniels	.05
231	John Carney	.05
232	Cortez Kennedy	.05
233	Clyde Simmons	.05
234	Emmitt Smith	1.50
235	Thomas Lewis	.05
236	William Fuller	.05
237	Ricky Ervins	.05
238	John Randle	.05
239	John Thierry	.05
240	Mel Gray	.05
241	George Teague	.05
242	Charles Wilson	.05
243	Joe Johnson	.05
244	Chuck Smith	.05
245	Sean Gilbert	.05
246	Bryant Young	.05
247	Bucky Brooks	.05
248	Ray Buchanan	.05
249	Tim Bowens	.05
250	Vincent Brown	.05
251	Marcus Turner	.05
252	Derrick Fenner	.05
253	Antonio Langham	.05
254	Cody Carlson	.05
255	Kevin Greene	.05
256	Leonard Russell	.05
257	Donnell Bennett	.05
258	Raghib Ismail	.05
259	Alfred Pupunu	.20
260	Eugene Robinson	.05
261	Seth Joyner	.05
262	Darren Woodson	.05
263	Phillipi Sparks	.05
264	Andy Harmon	.05
		.05
266	Fuad Reveiz	.05
267	Mark Carrier	.05
268	Johnnie Morton	.05
269	LeShon Johnson	.05
270	Eric Curry	.05
271	Quinn Early	.05

272 Elbert Shelley .05
273 Roman Phifer .05
274 Ken Norton .05
275 Steve Tasker .05
276 Jim Harbaugh .05
277 Aubrey Beavers .05
278 Chris Slade .05
279 Mo Lewis .05
280 Alfred Williams .05
281 Michael Dean Perry .05
282 Marcus Robertson .05
283 Rod Woodson .10
284 Glyn Milburn .05
285 Greg Hill .25
286 Rob Fredrickson .05
287 Junior Seau .10
288 Rick Tuten .05
289 Aeneas Williams .05
290 Darrin Smith .05
291 John Booty .05
292 Eric Allen .05
293 Reggie Roby .05
294 David Palmer .05
295 Trace Armstrong .05
296 Dave Krieg .05
297 Robert Brooks .05
298 Brad Culpepper .05
299 Wayne Martin .05
300 Craig Heyward .05
301 Isaac Bruce .15
302 Deion Sanders .40
303 Matt Darby .05
304 Kirk Lowdermilk .05
305 Bernie Parmalee .20
306 Leroy Thompson .05
307 Ronnie Lott .05
308 Steve Tovar .05
309 Michael Jackson .05
310 Al Smith .05
311 Chad Brown .05
312 Elijah Alexander .05
313 Kimble Anders .05
314 Anthony Smith .05
315 Andre Coleman .05
316 Terry Wooden .05
317 Garrison Hearst .10
318 Russell Maryland .05
319 Michael Brooks .05
320 Bernard Williams .05
321 Andre Collins .05
322 DeWayne Washington .05
323 Raymont Harris .15
324 Brett Perriman .05
325 LeRoy Butler .05
326 Santana Dotson .05
327 Irv Smith .05
328 Ron George .05
329 Marquez Pope .05
330 William Floyd .25
331 Mickey Washington .05
332 Keith Goganious .05
333 Derek Brown .05
334 Steve Beuerlein .05
335 Reggie Cobb .05
336 Jeff Lageman .05
337 Kelvin Martin .05
338 Darren Carrington .05
339 Mark Carrier .05
340 Willie Green .05
341 Frank Reich .05
342 Don Beebe .05
343 Lamar Lathon .05
344 Tim McKyer .05
345 Pete Metzelaars .05
346 Vernon Turner .05
347 Checklist 1-174 .05
348 Checklist 175-348 .05

1995 Collector's Choice Player's Club

The 348-card, regular-size parallel set was inserted in each pack of 1995 Collector's Choice. The card fronts have a silver border with a silver "Player's Club" logo.

	MT
Complete Set (348):	45.00
Common Player:	.20
Player's Club Cards:	2x

1995 Collector's Choice Player's Club Platinum

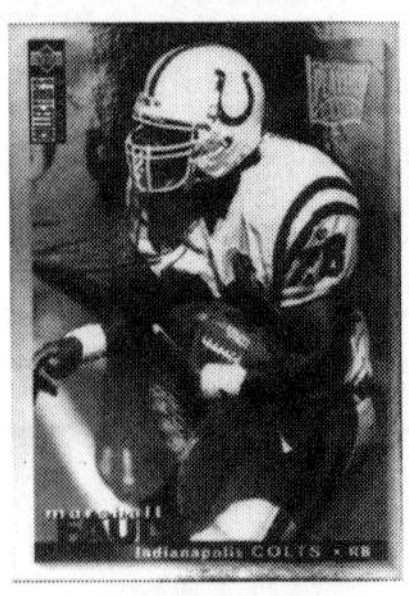

The 348-card, regular-sized parallel set was inserted every 35 packs of Collector's Choice. The card fronts feature a silver "Platinum Player's Club" logo, as well as a silver border.

	MT
Complete Set (348):	750.00
Common Player:	1.00
Player's Club Platinum:	10x-20x

A card number in parentheses ( ) indicates the set is unnumbered.

1995 Collector's Choice Crash The Game

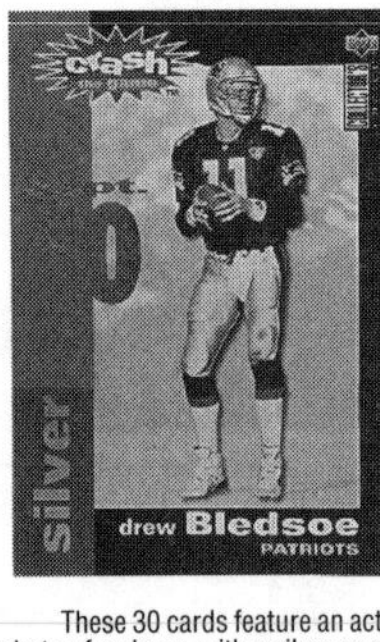

These 30 cards feature an action photo of a player, with a silver or gold foil date stamped into the design. If the player pictured scored a touchdown during his team's game on the date on the card front, a collector could redeem the card for a complete 30-card set. Odds of finding a silver version were one per every five packs; gold cards were inserted one per every 50 packs. The back of the card is numbered using a "C" prefix and includes the rules of the game.

	MT
Complete Silver Set (90):	60.00
Common Player:	.25
Minor Stars:	.50
Inserted 1:5	
Gold Cards:	3x
Inserted 1:50	
Silver Red. Cards:	.5x
Gold Red. Cards:	2x

1 Dan Marino 2.00
2 John Elway 2.00
3 Kerry Collins .50
4 Stan Humphries .25
5 Steve Young 1.00
6 Brett Favre 2.50
7 Troy Aikman 1.25
8 Warren Moon .50
9 Drew Bledsoe 1.25
10 Steve McNair 1.00
11 Chris Warren .25
12 Natrone Means .50
13 Thurman Thomas .50
14 Barry Sanders 2.50
15 Emmitt Smith 2.00
16 Jerome Bettis .50
17 Ki-Jana Carter .50
18 Napoleon Kaufman 1.00
19 Marshall Faulk .75
20 Errict Rhett .25
21 Cris Carter .75
22 Jerry Rice 1.25
23 Tim Brown .50
24 Andre Reed .25
25 Andre Rison .50
26 Ben Coates .25
27 Michael Irvin .50
28 Terance Mathis .25
29 Michael Westbrook .50
30 Herman Moore .50

1995 Collector's Choice Marino Chronicles

The 10-card, regular-sized set was inserted in specially marked retail packs and features Marino highlight cards. The card fronts feature an aqua border with "Marino" in gold foil. The cards are numbered with the "DM" prefix.

	MT
Complete Set (10):	10.00
Common Player:	1.25

1 Dan Marino (Rookie of the Year) 1.25
2 Dan Marino (5000 Yards Passing) 1.25
3 Dan Marino (48 TD Passes) 1.25
4 Dan Marino (Super Bowl XIX) 1.25
5 Dan Marino (30,000 Yards Passing) 1.25
6 Dan Marino (4000 Yard Season) 1.25
7 Dan Marino (40,000 Yards Passing) 1.25
8 Dan Marino (Marino's Back) 1.25
9 Dan Marino (300th TD Pass) 1.25
10 Dan Marino (More Records to Fall) 1.25

1995 Collector's Choice Montana Trilogy

Eight of 20 Joe Montana Trilogy cards were included in packs of 1995 Upper Deck Collector's Choice football cards. These cards are numbered 1-8, using an "MT" prefix. Cards recap Montana's career, and were included one per every 12 packs. A Montana Trilogy header card was also produced.

	MT
Complete Set (9):	30.00
Common Player:	4.00
Header Card:	5.00

1 1977 NCAA Champs 4.00
2 1978 Cotton Bowl 4.00
3 The 1978 NFL Draft 4.00
4 The Catch 4.00
5 Super Bowl XVI 4.00
6 Super Bowl XVI MVP 4.00
7 Super Bowl XIX 4.00
8 Super Bowl XIX MVP 4.00
CCH Trilogy Header 5.00

1995 Collector's Choice Update

The 1995 Upper Deck Collector's Choice set has 225 cards, including 103 regular player cards (featuring free agents, traded players and rookies in the uniforms of their new teams), 60 "Rookie Collection" cards (picturing first-year players in their NFL uniforms), 30 cards featuring players from the expansion team Carolina Panthers and Jacksonville Jaguars, two checklists and 30 "The Key" cards (describing what NFL teams do to stop "key" players on each team). The set is numbered U1-U225. Gold and silver parallel sets were made for two of the subsets; silver Rookie Collection cards are found one per three packs, while gold versions are one in every 35. Silver "The Key" cards are seeded one per every five packs, while gold ones are one per every 52. Also included as inserts are Stick-Ums, restickable stickers the size of a trading card which picture top stars, rookies and team helmets. Each one has either four mini-stickers on it, a large "superstar" sticker, or one with three players and a team helmet. One of these 90 cards was seeded in every pack of 1995 Upper Deck Collector's Choice Update product. Six different Stick-Ums sticker booklets were also available through a wrapper mail-in offer. A new version of the "You Crash the Game" interactive cards were redesigned for the playoffs. "You Crash the Playoffs" cards were randomly inserted every 18th pack; if the player on the card scored a touchdown during the playoffs the card could be redeemed for various prizes.

	MT
Complete Set (225):	20.00
Common Player:	.05
Minor Stars:	.10
Silver Cards:	3x
Inserted 1:3	
Gold Cards:	10x-20x
Gold Rookies:	5x-10x
Inserted 1:35	
Pack (10):	1.25
Wax Box (36):	35.00

1 Roell Preston .05
2 Lorenzo Styles .05
3 Todd Collins .10
4 *Darick Holmes* .75
5 Justin Armour .10
6 Tony Cline .05
7 Tyrone Poole .05
8 Kerry Collins .50
9 Sean Harris .05
10 Steve Stenstrom .05
11 Rashaan Salaam .30
12 Ki-Jana Carter .30
13 Craig Powell .05
14 *Eric Zeier* .50
15 Ernest Hunter .05
16 Sherman Williams .10
17 *Terrell Davis* 10.00
18 Luther Elliss .05
19 Craig Newsome .05
20 Steve McNair 1.00
21 *Chris Sanders* .30
22 Rodney Thomas .30
23 Ellis Johnson .05
24 *Ken Dilger* .40
25 *Zack Crockett* .20
26 Tony Boselli .10
27 Rob Johnson 1.00
28 James O. Stewart .20
29 Pete Mitchell .05
30 *Tamarick Vanover* .20
31 Napoleon Kaufman 1.00
32 Kevin Carter .05
33 Steve McLaughlin .05
34 Lovell Pinkney .05
35 James A. Stewart .05
36 *Chad May* .30
37 Derrick Alexander .05
38 *Curtis Martin* 2.50
39 Will Moore .05
40 Ty Law .05
41 Ray Zellars .05
42 Mark Fields .05
43 Tyrone Wheatley .30
44 Kyle Brady .05
45 Mike Mamula .05
46 Bobby Taylor .05
47 *Chris Jones* .30
48 Frank Sanders .50
49 *Stoney Case* .25
50 Mark Bruener .50
51 *Kordell Stewart* 3.50
52 Jimmy Oliver .05
53 Terrance Shaw .05
54 *Terrell Fletcher* .30
55 J.J. Stokes .50
56 Christian Fauria .05
57 Joey Galloway 1.00
58 Warren Sapp .05
59 Derrick Brooks .05
60 Michael Westbrook .50
61 Emmitt Smith .75
62 Barry Sanders 1.00
63 Marshall Faulk .30
64 Troy Aikman .50
65 Steve Young .40
66 Junior Seau .10
67 John Elway .50
68 Dan Marino .75
69 Drew Bledsoe .50
70 Errict Rhett .30
71 Natrone Means .10
72 Deion Sanders .30
73 Brett Favre 1.00
74 Cris Carter .25
75 Ben Coates .05
76 Jerome Bettis .20
77 Reggie White .20
78 Stan Humphries .05
79 Michael Westbrook .30
80 Steve McNair .75
81 Kevin Greene .05
82 Joey Galloway .50
83 Napoleon Kaufman .75
84 Jerry Rice .50
85 Andre Rison .05
86 Eric Metcalf .05
87 Kerry Collins .20
88 Chris Warren .10
89 Irving Fryar .05
90 Michael Irvin .10
91 Don Beebe .05
92 Pete Metzelaars .05
93 Mark Carrier .05
94 Frank Reich .05
95 Randy Baldwin .05
96 Bob Christian .05
97 John Kasay .05
98 Lamar Lathon .05
99 Sam Mills .05
100 Carlton Bailey .05
101 Darrion Conner .05
102 Blake Brockermeyer .05
103 Gerald Williams .05
104 Willie Green .05
105 Derrick Graham .05
106 Desmond Howard .05
107 Harry Colon .05
108 Steve Beuerlein .05
109 Reggie Cobb .05
110 Jeff Lageman .05
111 Mark Brunell 1.00
112 Darren Carrington .05
113 Brian DeMarco .05
114 Ernest Givins .05
115 LeShia Maston .05
116 Willie Jackson .05
117 Keith Goganious .05
118 Kelvin Pritchett .05
119 Ryan Christopherson .05
120 Brian Schwartz .05
121 Dave Kreig .05
122 Darryl Talley .05
123 Bryce Paup .05
124 Anthony Johnson .05
125 Eric Bieniemy .05
126 Andre Rison .05
127 Rodney Peete .05
128 Aaron Craver .05
129 Henry Thomas .05
130 *Antonio Freeman* 3.00
131 Chris Chandler .05
132 Craig Erickson .05
133 Roell Preston .05
134 Brian Washington .05
135 Eric Green .05
136 Broderick Thomas .05
137 Dave Meggett .05
138 Eric Allen .05
139 Herschel Walker .05
140 Dexter Carter .05
141 Kerry Cash .05
142 Kelvin Martin .05
143 Erric Pegram .05
144 Bo Orlando .05
145 Ricky Ervins .05
146 John Friesz .05
147 Alexander Wright .05
148 Alvin Harper .05
149 Gus Frerotte .25
150 Duval Love .05
151 Eric Metcalf .05
152 Ruben Brown .05
153 Marty Carter .05
154 James Joseph .05
155 Steve Emtman .05
156 Wade Wilson .05
157 Britt Hager .05
158 Mark Schlereth .05
159 Corey Scheliger .05
160 Mark Ingram .05
161 Mark Stepnoski .05
162 Willie Anderson .05
163 Donta Jones .05
164 James Hasty .05
165 Gary Clark .05
166 David Sloan .05
167 Jeff Dallenbach .05
168 Rufus Porter .05
169 Mike Croel .05
170 Charles Wilson .05
171 Pat Swilling .05
172 Kurt Gouveia .05
173 Norm Johnson .05
174 Shawn Gayle .05
175 Marquez Pope .05
176 Tyrone Stowe .05
177 Anthony Parker .05
178 Kenneth Gant .05
179 James Washington .05
180 Rob Moore .05
181 Alundis Brice .05
182 Lamont Warren .05
183 Michael Timpson .05
184 Lorenzo White .05
185 Charlie Williams .05
186 Ed McCaffrey .05
187 James Jones .05
188 Derrick Fenner .05
189 Mel Gray .05
190 James Williams .05
191 Jeff Criswell .05
192 Randal Hill .05
193 Terry Allen .05
194 Joel Smeenge .05
195 Ricky Watters .10
196 Don Sasa .05
197 Steve Bono .10
198 Steve Broussard .05
199 Carlos Jenkins .05
200 Reggie Roby .05
201 Stanley Richard .05
202 Vince Workman .05
203 Eric Guliford .05
204 Lionel Washington .05
205 Brian Williams .05
206 Ronnie Lott .05
207 Corey Harris .05
208 Harlon Barnett .05
209 Bubby Brister .05
210 Darren Bennett .05
211 Winston Moss .05
212 Leonard Russell .05
213 Ronald Davis .05
214 Curtis Whitley .05
215 Webster Slaughter .05
216 Korey Stringer .05
217 Don Davey .05
218 Mark Rypien .05
219 Chad Cota .05
220 Tim Ruddy .05
221 Corey Fuller .05
222 Mike Dumas .05
223 Eddie Murray .05
224 Checklist .05
225 Checklist .05

1995 Collector's Choice Update Silver

The 90-card, regular-sized set was inserted every three packs of Collector's Choice Update and paralleled the first 90 cards of the set with the card name in silver foil.

	MT
Complete Set (90):	45.00
Common Player:	.15
Silver Cards:	1.5x-3x

1995 Collector's Choice Update Gold

The 90-card, regular-size set was inserted every 35 packs of Collector's Choice Update and paralleled the first 90 cards of the Update set.

	MT
Complete Set (90):	475.00
Common Player:	1.50
Gold Cards:	15x-30x

1995 Collector's Choice Update Crash the Playoffs

Upper Deck's "You Crash the Game" interactive cards were redesigned for the 1995 Upper Deck Collector's Choice Update set to spotlight the playoffs. Called "You Crash the Playoffs," the cards allow fans holding the cards to redeem them for special card sets if any of the players pictured on the cards is involved in a scoring play during the playoffs (catching or throwing a touchdown pass, running for one). Each card pictures five players at one position (either quarterback, running back or wide receiver) for each division. The winning cards were redeemable for a 20-card set which highlights the playoffs and Super Bowl XXX. Two versions were made - silver (good for a silver set; one in five packs), or gold (good for a gold set; one in 50 packs). The cards are numbered with the "CP" prefix.

	MT
Complete Set (18):	20.00
Common Player:	.50
Minor Stars:	1.00
Inserted 1:5	
Gold Cards:	3x
Inserted 1:50	

1 AFC East QB 3.00
2 AFC Central QB 1.50
3 AFC West QB 2.00
4 NFC East QB 1.50
5 NFC Central QB 3.00
6 NFC West QB 1.50
7 AFC East RB 2.50
8 AFC Central RB .50
9 AFC West RB 3.00
10 NFC East RB 1.00
11 NFC Central RB .50
12 NFC West RB .50
13 AFC West WR .50
14 AFC Central WR .50
15 AFC West WR 1.00
16 NFC East WR 1.00
17 NFC Central WR 3.00
18 NFC West WR 1.50

1995 Collector's Choice Update Post Season Heroics

The 20-card, standard-size set was available by redeeming a winning Collector's Choice Update Crash The Playoffs silver or gold card. The cards are similar to the base set cards with "Post Season Heroics" printed along the card fronts in silver or gold foil.

	MT
Complete Set (20):	10.00
Common Player:	.25
Minor Stars:	.50
Gold Cards:	3x

1 Stan Humphries .25
2 Natrone Means .50
3 Tony Martin .25
4 Neil O'Donnell .25
5 Byron "Bam" Morris .25
6 Charles Johnson .25
7 Jim Harbaugh .25
8 Darick Holmes .50
9 Sean Dawkins .25
10 Steve Young 1.50
11 Craig Heyward .25
12 Jerry Rice 2.00
13 Brett Favre 4.00
14 Edgar Bennett .25
15 Robert Brooks .50
16 Troy Aikman 2.00
17 Emmitt Smith 3.00
18 Michael Irvin .50
19 Byron "Bam" Morris .25
20 Larry Brown .25

1995 Collector's Choice Update Stick-Ums

These 1995 Upper Deck Collector's Choice inserts were seeded one per every pack. The 90 restickable stickers are the size of a trading card and picture some of the NFL's biggest stars and top rookies, plus team helmets. Cards have either four mini-stickers on it, one large full-size superstar sticker, or three players and a team helmet sticker. Six different Stick-Ums booklets (one for each division) were also made to display the stickers. Each booklet, which contains team trivia and important dates in team history, were available as a mail-in offer for $2 and two Collector's Choice Update foil wrappers.

	MT
Complete Set (90):	10.00
Common Player:	.10
Minor Stars:	.20
Inserted 1:1	

1 Jeff George .20
2 Kerry Collins .20
3 Jerome Bettis .20
4 Mario Bates .10
5 Steve Young .50
6 Rashaan Salaam .20
7 Barry Sanders 1.00
8 Brett Favre 1.00
9 Warren Moon .20
10 Errict Rhett .20
11 Emmitt Smith .75
12 Rodney Hampton .10
13 Ricky Watters .20
14 Garrison Hearst .20
15 Michael Westbrook .20
16 Jim Kelly .20
17 Marshall Faulk .30
18 Dan Marino .75
19 Drew Bledsoe .50
20 Kyle Brady .10
21 Ki-Jana Carter .10
22 Andre Rison .20
23 Steve McNair .50
24 James O. Stewart .20
25 Bam Morris .10
26 John Elway .75
27 Marcus Allen .20
28 Tim Brown .20
29 Natrone Means .20
30 Chris Warren .20
31 Terance Mathis, Mark Carrier, Chris Miller, Jim Everett .10
32 Bert Emanuel, Pete Metzelaars, Isaac Bruce, Dana Stubblefield .20
33 Chris Doleman, Frank Reich, Derek Brown, Jerry Rice .30
34 Jessie Tuggle, Roman Phifer, Tyrone Hughes, Bryant Young .30
35 Sam Mills, Kevin Carter, Michael Haynes, Brent Jones .10
36 Falcons (Eric Metcalf, Tyrone Poole, Lovell Pinkney) .10
37 Panthers (Morten Andersen, John Kasay, Troy Drayton) .10
38 Vikings (Sean Gilbert, Mark Fields, J.J. Stokes) .10
39 Saints (Darion Conner, Willie Roaf, Ken Norton) .10
40 49ers (Craig Heyward, Renaldo Turnbull, William Floyd) .10
41 Raymont Harris, Herman Moore, Edgar Bennett, Cris Carter .10
42 Jeff Graham, Henry Thomas, Reggie White, Trent Dilfer .10
43 Curtis Conway, Scott Mitchell, Scottie Graham, Alvin Harper .10
44 Steve Walsh, Sean Jones, Qadry Ismail, Hardy Nickerson .10
45 John Randle, Mark Carrier, Chris Spielman, John Jurkovic .10
46 Bears (John Thierry, Luther Elliss, LeRoy Butler) .10
47 Lions (Johnnie Morton, Robert Brooks, Jake Reed) .10
48 Packers (LeShon Johnson, DeWayne Washington, Jackie Harris) .10
49 Vikings (Donnell Woolford, James A. Stewart, Eric Curry) .10
50 Buccaneers (Mark Carrier, Chris Spielman, Warren Sapp) .10
51 Troy Aikman, Mike Sherrard, Fred Barnett, Dave Kreig .30
52 Michael Irvin, Chris Calloway, Calvin Williams, Henry Ellard .10
53 Sherman Williams, Dave Brown, Rob Moore, Heath Shuler .10
54 Charles Haley, Randall Cunningham, Eric Swann, Ken Harvey .10
55 Thomas Lewis, Charlie Garner, Clyde Simmons, Tom Carter .10

56	Cowboys (Tyrone Wheatley, Bobby Taylor, Daryl Johnston)	.10
57	Giants (Mike Croel, Byron Evans, Aeneas Williams)	.10
58	Eagles (Mike Mamula, Larry Centers, Brian Mitchell)	.10
59	Cardinals (Jay Novacek, Frank Sanders, Terry Allen)	.10
60	Redskins (Deion Sanders, Herschel Walker, Sterling Palmer)	.20
61	Henry Jones, Craig Erickson, Terry Kirby, Ben Coates	.10
62	Andre Reed, Willie Anderson, Irving Fryar, Johnny Mitchell	.10
63	Russell Copeland, Sean Dawkins, Vincent Brisby, Boomer Esiason	.10
64	Bruce Smith, O.J. McDuffie, Willie McGinest, Ryan Yarborough	.10
65	Roosevelt Potts, Keith Byars, Curtis Martin, Brad Baxter	.75
66	Bills (Cornelius Bennett, Ray Buchanan, Marco Coleman)	.10
67	Colts (Quentin Coryatt, Bryan Cox, Chris Slade)	.10
68	Dolphins (Eric Green, Ty Law, Marvin Washington)	.10
69	Patriots (Todd Collins, Vincent Brown, Ronald Moore)	.10
70	Jets (Jeff Burris, Floyd Turner, Aaron Glenn)	.10
71	Carl Pickens, Vinny Testaverde, Haywood Jeffires, Desmond Howard	.10
72	Darnay Scott, Eric Turner, Gary Brown, Neil O'Donnell	.10
73	David Klingler, Leroy Hoard, Tony Boselli, Charles Johnson	.10
74	Steve Tovar, Al Smith, Derek Brown, John L. Williams	.10
75	Lorenzo White, Rodney Thomas, Steve Beuerlein, Kevin Greene	.10
76	Bengals (Jeff Blake, Derrick Alexander, Ray Childress)	.10
77	Browns (Eric Zeier, Mel Gray, Reggie Cobb)	.10
78	Oilers (Todd McNair, Jeff Lageman, Greg Lloyd)	.10
79	Jaguars (Dan Wilkinson, Rob Johnson, Rod Woodson)	.30
80	Steelers (Eric Bieniemy, Antonio Langham, Mark Bruener)	.10
81	Shannon Sharpe, Willie Davis, Jeff Hostetler, Stan Humphries	.10
82	Rod Bernstine, Ronnie Lott, Harvey Williams, Rick Mirer	.10
83	Anthony Miller, Neil Smith, Junior Seau, Brian Blades	.10
84	Mike Pritchard, Napoleon Kaufman, Leslie O'Neal, Sam Adams	.20
85	Greg Hill, Raghib Ismail, Alfred Pupunu, Cortez Kennedy	.10
86	Broncos (Steve Atwater, Tamarick Vanover, Chester McGlockton)	.10
87	Chiefs (Steve Bono, Rob Fredrickson, Tony Martin)	.10
88	Raiders (Terry McDaniel, Jimmy Oliver, Christian Fauria)	.10
89	Chargers (Glyn Milburn, John Carney, Joey Galloway)	.20
90	Seahawks (Simon Fletcher, Keith Cash, Eugene Robinson)	.10

1996 Collector's Choice

Upper Deck's 1996 Collector's Choice Series I contains 375 cards - broken down into 294 regular cards, 45 Rookie Class cards, two checklists and 34 Season to Remember cards. Each regular card front has a color action photo on it, with a brand logo in the upper right corner. The left side of the card has a team color-coded panel with the player's name and team helmet at the bottom; the top portion, which is black, has the player's position in it. The card back has biographical information at the top, along with a card number. A color action photo is underneath, followed by statistics and a football quiz. The right side of the card has a color-coded panel with the player's name at the bottom and the player's team name and position at the top. Insert sets created are MVPs (in gold and silver versions) and You Crash the Game redemption cards. Play Action Stick-Ums also return from the previous year's Update set. These re-stickable die-cut stickers allow collectors to create a football scene. The set consists of 30 NFL athletes and is seeded one per every three packs.

		MT
Complete Set (375):		25.00
Common Player:		.05
Minor Stars:		.10
Pack (14):		1.00
Wax Box (40):		40.00
1	*Keyshawn Johnson*	1.50
2	*Kevin Hardy*	.10
3	*Simeon Rice*	.10
4	*Jonathan Ogden*	.10
5	*Cedric Jones*	.05
6	*Lawrence Phillips*	1.00
7	*Tim Biakabutuka*	.50
8	*Terry Glenn*	1.00
9	*Rickey Dudley*	.50
10	*Regan Upshaw*	.05
11	*Walt Harris*	.05
12	*Eddie George*	3.00
13	*John Mobley*	.05
14	*Duane Clemons*	.05
15	*Marvin Harrison*	2.00
16	*Daryl Gardener*	.05
17	*Pete Kendall*	.05
18	*Marcus Jones*	.05
19	*Eric Moulds*	1.50
20	*Ray Lewis*	.50
21	*Alex Van Dyke*	.10
22	*Leeland McElroy*	.20
23	*Mike Alstott*	1.50
24	*Lawyer Milloy*	.05
25	*Marco Battaglia*	.05
26	*Je'Rod Cherry*	.05
27	*Israel Ifeanyl*	.05
28	*Bobby Engram*	.50
29	*Jason Dunn*	.25
30	*Derrick Mayes*	.75
31	*Stepfret Williams*	.25
32	*Bobby Hoying*	.75
33	*Karim Abdul-Jabbar*	1.00
34	*Danny Kanell*	.50
35	*Chris Darkins*	.10
36	*Charlie Jones*	.05
37	*Tedy Bruschi*	.05
38	*Stanley Pritchett*	.05
39	*Donnie Edwards*	.05
40	*Jeff Lewis*	.50
41	*Stephen Davis*	2.50
42	*Winslow Oliver*	.05
43	*Mercury Hayes*	.05
44	*Jon Runyan*	.05
45	*Steve Taneyhill*	.05
46	Eric Metcalf	.05
47	Bryce Paup	.05
48	Kerry Collins	.40
49	Rashaan Salaam	.25
50	Carl Pickens	.05
51	Emmitt Smith	1.00
52	Michael Irvin	.05
53	Troy Aikman	.50
54	Terrell Davis	.30
55	John Elway	.15
56	Herman Moore	.05
57	Brett Favre	.50
58	Rodney Thomas	.05
59	Jim Harbaugh	.05
60	Mark Brunell	.25
61	Marcus Allen	.05
62	Tamarick Vanover	.15
63	Steve Bono	.05
64	Dan Marino	1.00
65	Warren Moon	.05
66	Curtis Martin	.75
67	Tyrone Hughes	.05
68	Rodney Hampton	.05
69	Hugh Douglas	.05
70	Tim Brown	.05
71	Ricky Watters	.05
72	Kordell Stewart	.30
73	Andre Coleman	.05
74	Jerry Rice	.50
75	Joey Galloway	.30
76	Isaac Bruce	.40
77	Errict Rhett	.40
78	Michael Westbrook	.25
79	Brian Mitchell	.05
80	Aeneas Williams	.05
81	Andre Reed	.05
82	Brett Maxie	.05
83	Jim Flanigan	.05
84	Jeff Blake	.30
85	Mike Frederick	.05
86	Michael Irvin	.10
87	Aaron Craver	.05
88	Barry Sanders	1.00
89	Keith Jackson	.05
90	Chris Sanders	.25
91	Marshall Faulk	.75
92	Bryan Schwartz	.05
93	Tamarick Vanover	.20
94	Troy Vincent	.05
95	Robert Smith	.05
96	Drew Bledsoe	.75
97	Quinn Early	.05
98	Wayne Chrebet	.05
99	Tim Brown	.05
100	Charlie Garner	.05
101	Yancey Thigpen	.30
102	Isaac Bruce	.75
103	Natrone Means	.10
104	Jerry Rice	1.00
105	Chris Warren	.10
106	Errict Rhett	.50
107	Heath Shuler	.40
108	Eric Swann	.05
109	Jeff George	.10
110	Steve Tasker	.05
111	Sam Mills	.05
112	Jeff Graham	.05
113	Carl Pickens	.10
114	Vinny Testaverde	.05
115	Emmitt Smith	2.00
116	John Elway	.25
117	Henry Thomas	.05
118	LeRoy Butler	.05
119	Blaine Bishop	.05
120	Floyd Turner	.05
121	Jeff Lageman	.05
122	Kimble Anders	.05
123	Bryan Cox	.05
124	Qadry Ismail	.05
125	Ted Johnson	.05
126	Wesley Walls	.05
127	Rodney Hampton	.05
128	Adrian Murrell	.05
129	Daryl Hobbs	.05
130	Ricky Watters	.10
131	Carnell Lake	.05
132	Toby Wright	.05
133	Darren Bennett	.05
134	J.J. Stokes	.50
135	Eugene Robinson	.05
136	Eric Curry	.05
137	Tom Carter	.05
138	Dave Krieg	.05
139	Eric Metcalf	.05
140	Bill Brooks	.05
141	Pete Metzelaars	.05
142	Kevin Butler	.05
143	John Copeland	.05
144	Keenan McCardell	.05
145	Larry Brown	.05
146	Jason Elam	.05
147	Willie Clay	.05
148	Robert Brooks	.05
149	Chris Chandler	.05
150	Quentin Coryatt	.05
151	Pete Mitchell	.05
152	Martin Bayless	.05
153	Pete Stoyanovich	.05
154	Cris Carter	.10
155	Jimmy Hitchcock	.05
156	Mario Bates	.05
157	Mike Sherrard	.05
158	Boomer Esiason	.05
159	Chester McGlockton	.05
160	Bobby Taylor	.05
161	Kordell Stewart	.60
162	Kevin Carter	.05
163	Junior Seau	.10
164	Derek Loville	.05
165	Brian Blades	.05
166	Jackie Harris	.05
167	Michael Westbrook	.50
168	Rob Moore	.05
169	Jessie Tuggle	.05
170	Darick Holmes	.05
171	Tim McKyer	.05
172	Erik Kramer	.05
173	Harold Green	.05
174	Stevon Moore	.05
175	Deion Sanders	.40
176	Anthony Miller	.05
177	Herman Moore	.20
178	Brett Favre	2.00
179	Rodney Thomas	.30
180	Ken Dilger	.05
181	Mark Brunell	.50
182	Marcus Allen	.10
183	Dan Marino	2.00
184	John Randle	.05
185	Ben Coates	.05
186	Tyrone Hughes	.05
187	Dave Brown	.05
188	Johnny Mitchell	.05
189	Harvey Williams	.05
190	Andy Harmon	.05
191	Kevin Greene	.05
192	D'Marco Farr	.05
193	Andre Coleman	.05
194	Bryant Young	.05
195	Rick Mirer	.05
196	Horace Copeland	.05
197	Leslie Shepherd	.05
198	Jamir Miller	.05
199	Bert Emanuel	.05
200	Steve Christie	.05
201	Kerry Collins	.75
202	Rashaan Salaam	.50
203	Steve Tovar	.05
204	Michael Jackson	.05
205	Kevin Williams	.05
206	Glyn Milburn	.05
207	Johnnie Morton	.05
208	Antonio Freeman	.05
209	Cris Dishman	.05
210	Ellis Johnson	.05
211	Cedric Tillman	.05
212	Steve Bono	.10
213	Eric Green	.05
214	David Palmer	.05
215	Vincent Brisby	.05
216	Michael Haynes	.05
217	Chris Calloway	.05
218	Kyle Brady	.05
219	Terry McDaniel	.05
220	Calvin Williams	.05
221	Greg Lloyd	.05
222	Jerome Bettis	.05
223	Stan Humphries	.05
224	Lee Woodall	.05
225	Robert Blackmon	.05
226	Warren Sapp	.05
227	Brian Mitchell	.05
228	Garrison Hearst	.05
229	Terance Mathis	.05
230	Bryce Paup	.05
231	Derrick Moore	.05
232	Curtis Conway	.05
233	Darnay Scott	.05
234	Andre Rison	.05
235	Jay Novacek	.05
236	Terrell Davis	.60
237	David Sloan	.05
238	Reggie White	.05
239	Todd McNair	.05
240	Ray Buchanan	.05
241	Steve Beuerlein	.05
242	Dan Saleaumua	.05
243	Bernie Parmalee	.05
244	Warren Moon	.05
245	Ty Law	.05
246	Torrance Small	.05
247	Philippi Sparks	.05
248	Mo Lewis	.05
249	Jeff Hostetler	.05
250	Rodney Peete	.05
251	Bam Morris	.05
252	Chris Miller	.05
253	Tony Martin	.05
254	Eric Davis	.05
255	Joey Galloway	.60
256	Derrick Brooks	.05
257	Ken Harvey	.05
258	Frank Sanders	.10
259	Morten Andersen	.05
260	Marlon Kerner	.05
261	Mark Carrier	.05
262	Mark Carrier	.05
263	Tony McGee	.05
264	Eric Zeier	.05
265	Darren Woodson	.05
266	Shannon Sharpe	.05
267	Brett Perriman	.05
268	Edgar Bennett	.05
269	Darryll Lewis	.05
270	Jim Harbaugh	.05
271	Desmond Howard	.05
272	Derrick Thomas	.05
273	Irving Fryar	.05
274	Jake Reed	.05
275	Curtis Martin	1.50
276	Eric Allen	.05
277	Thomas Lewis	.05
278	Hugh Douglas	.05
279	Pat Swilling	.05
280	William Thomas	.05
281	Norm Johnson	.05
282	Roman Phifer	.05
283	Chris Mims	.05
284	Steve Young	1.00
285	Cortez Kennedy	.05
286	Trent Dilfer	.05
287	Terry Allen	.05
288	Clyde Simmons	.05
289	Craig Heyward	.05
290	Jim Kelly	.05
291	Tyrone Poole	.05
292	Chris Zorich	.05
293	Dan Wilkinson	.05
294	Antonio Langham	.05
295	Troy Aikman	1.00
296	Steve Atwater	.05
297	Scott Mitchell	.05
298	Mark Chmura	.20
299	Steve McNair	.50
300	Tony Bennett	.05
301	Willie Jackson	.05
302	Neil Smith	.05
303	Terry Kirby	.05
304	Orlanda Thomas	.05
305	Willie McGinest	.05
306	Wayne Martin	.05
307	Michael Brooks	.05
308	Marvin Washington	.05
309	Nolan Harrison	.05
310	William Fuller	.05
311	Willie Williams	.05
312	Troy Drayton	.05
313	Shawn Lee	.05
314	Ken Norton	.05
315	Terry Wooden	.05
316	Hardy Nickerson	.05
317	Gus Frerotte	.05
318	Oscar McBride	.05
319	Merton Hanks	.05
320	Justin Armour	.05
321	Willie Green	.05
322	Roger Jones	.05
323	Leroy Hoard	.05
324	Chris Boniol	.05
325	Jason Hanson	.05
326	Sean Jones	.05
327	Roosevelt Potts	.05
328	Greg Hill	.05
329	O.J. McDuffie	.05
330	Amp Lee	.05
331	Chris Slade	.05
332	Jim Everett	.05
333	Tyrone Wheatley	.10
334	Charles Wilson	.05
335	Napoleon Kaufman	.10
336	Fred Barnett	.05
337	Neil O'Donnell	.05
338	Sean Gilbert	.05
339	*Aaron Hayden*	.30
340	Brent Jones	.05
341	Christian Fauria	.05
342	Alvin Harper	.05
343	Henry Ellard	.05
344	Willie Davis	.05
345	Charles Haley	.05
346	Chris Jacke	.05
347	Allen Aldridge	.05
348	Jeff Herrod	.05
349	Raghib Ismail	.05
350	Leslie O'Neal	.05
351	Marquez Pope	.05
352	Brock Marion	.05
353	Ernie Mills	.05
354	Larry Centers	.05
355	Chris Doleman	.05
356	Bruce Smith	.05
357	John Kasay	.05
358	Donnell Woolford	.05
359	David Dunn	.05
360	Eric Turner	.05
361	Sherman Williams	.05
362	Chris Spielman	.05
363	Craig Newsome	.05
364	Sean Dawkins	.05
365	James O. Stewart	.05
366	Dale Carter	.05
367	Marco Coleman	.05
368	Dave Meggett	.05
369	Irv Smith	.05
370	Mike Mamula	.05
371	Erric Pegram	.05
372	Dana Stubblefield	.05
373	Terrance Shaw	.05
374	(Jerry Rice CL)	.25
375	(Dan Marino CL)	.25

1996 Collector's Choice A Cut Above

This 10-card set was seeded one per special retail pack and included 10 different players.

		MT
Complete Set (10):		10.00
Common Player:		.20
Minor Stars:		.40
Inserted 1:1 Special Retail		
1	Terrell Davis	3.00
2	Tim Biakabutuka	.20
3	Drew Bledsoe	1.00
4	Emmitt Smith	1.50
5	Marshall Faulk	.40
6	Brett Favre	2.00
7	Keyshawn Johnson	.75
8	Deion Sanders	.40
9	Curtis Martin	1.00
10	Jerry Rice	1.00

Post-1980 cards in Near Mint condition will generally sell for about 75% of the quoted Mint value. Excellent-condition cards bring no more than 40%.

1996 Collector's Choice Crash The Game

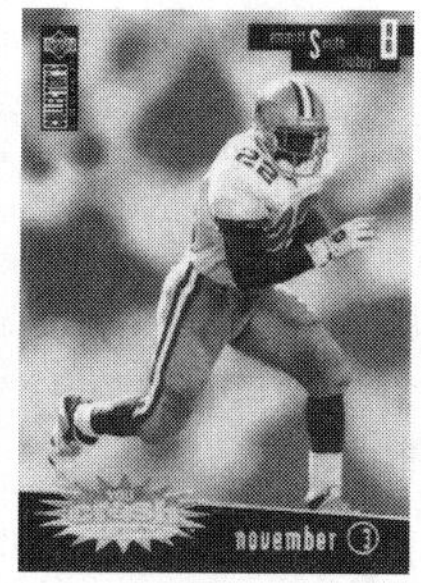

These inserts were available in 1996 Upper Deck Collector's Choice packs. If the player on the card throws for, runs for or catches a touchdown pass on the date specified, that card is redeemable for an exclusive Light F/X card of that player. Two versions were made - silver (one per five packs) and gold (one per 50). The basic card front design has a color action photo in the center, with the brand logo in the upper left corner. The player's name, team name and position are in the upper right corner. The bottom has a black panel which has the set icon in silver foil, along with the game date for the contest. The back, numbered using a "CG" prefix, has the rules of the redemption program.

		MT
Complete Set (90):		75.00
Common Player:		.50
Minor Stars:		1.00
Gold Cards:		2x-4x
Comp. Gold Redemption (22):		225.00
Gold Redemptions:		5x-10x
Comp. Silver Redemption (22):		75.00
Silver Redemptions:		1.5x-3x
1	Dan Marino	6.00
2	John Elway	3.00
3	Jeff Blake	1.00
4	Drew Bledsoe	3.00
5	Steve Young	4.00
6	Brett Favre	6.00
7	Jim Kelly	2.00
8	Scott Mitchell	.50
9	Jeff George	.50
10	Erik Kramer	.50
11	Jerry Rice	3.00
12	Michael Irvin	.50
13	Joey Galloway	3.00
14	Cris Carter	.50
15	Carl Pickens	.50
16	Herman Moore	.50
17	Isaac Bruce	2.00
18	Tim Brown	.50
19	Keyshawn Johnson	3.00
20	Terry Glenn	2.50
21	Emmitt Smith	6.00
22	Rodney Hampton	.50
23	Chris Warren	.50
24	Marshall Faulk	3.00
25	Curtis Martin	4.00
26	Barry Sanders	3.00
27	Rashaan Salaam	.50
28	Leeland McElroy	2.50
29	Tim Biakabutuka	2.50
30	Lawrence Phillips	2.50

1996 Collector's Choice Crash The Game Gold

You Crash the Game Golds ran parallel to the 90 cards in the silver version, but were inserted one per 50 packs. As the name indicates, gold versions are gold foil stamped instead of the silver foil used on regular versions. Similar to the rules for silver versions, if the player on the gold version throws for, runs for or catches a touchdown pass on the date specified, that card is redeemable for a gold Light F/X card of that player. Thirty different players are featured in this insert, with each having three specified dates.

	MT
Complete Set (90):	300.00
Gold Cards:	2x-4x
Gold Redemptions:	5x-10x

1996 Collector's Choice Cut Above Dan Marino

This 10-card insert features Miami Dolphins quarterback Dan Marino and highlights different moments in his Hall of Fame career. One Marino A Cut Above insert was found in each special retail pack of Collector's Choice Series I. The cards are numbered with the "CA" prefix.

		MT
Complete Set (10):		15.00
Common Player:		1.50
1	Dan Marino	1.50
2	Dan Marino	1.50
3	Dan Marino	1.50
4	Dan Marino	1.50
5	Dan Marino	1.50
6	Dan Marino	1.50
7	Dan Marino	1.50
8	Dan Marino	1.50
9	Dan Marino	1.50
10	Dan Marino	1.50

1996 Collector's Choice Jumbos

This nine-card set consists of enlarged versions (3-1/2" x 5") of the players' Season to Remember subset cards from the regular 1996 Collector's Choice set. The cards were inserted one per retail blister pack, which also included a team set and a foil pack of 1996 Collector's Choice.

		MT
Complete Set (9):		30.00
Common Player:		2.00
48	Kerry Collins	3.00
49	Rashaan Salaam	2.00
51	Emmitt Smith	5.00
57	Brett Favre	6.00
60	Mark Brunell	3.00
64	Dan Marino	5.00
70	Tim Brown	2.00
72	Kordell Stewart	3.00
74	Jerry Rice	3.00

1996 Collector's Choice MVPs

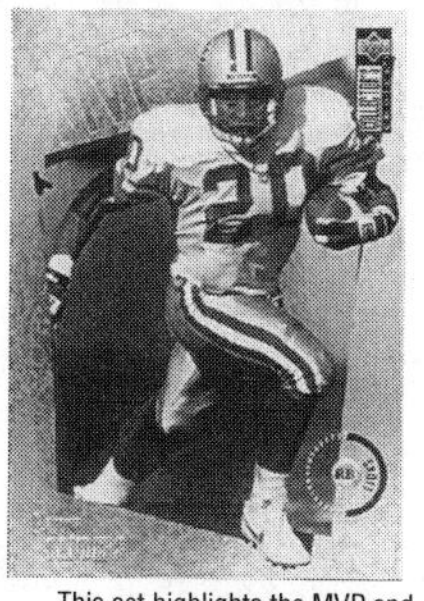

This set highlights the MVP and co-MVP of each NFL team in two different versions - gold or silver. The card has a marble-like background for the front, in either gold or silver. A player color photo is in the center. MVP is stamped into the upper left corner; the player's name is stamped in the lower left corner. A brand logo is in the upper right corner, while a circle towards the bottom has the player's position and team name inside it. Part of the circle's diameter is stamped in silver dots; the other is in the same color used to shadow the frame around the picture on the front. The back has biographical information, 1995 stats and a card number, which uses an "M" prefix. Gold versions were seeded one every 35 packs of 1996 Upper Deck Collector's Choice product; silver cards were in every pack.

		MT
Complete Set (45):		12.00
Common Player:		.20
Minor Stars:		.40
Gold Cards:		5x-10x
1	Larry Centers	.20
2	Jeff George	.20
3	Jim Kelly	.20
4	Bryce Paup	.20
5	Kerry Collins	.50
6	Erik Kramer	.20
7	Rashaan Salaam	.75
8	Jeff Blake	.75
9	Carl Pickens	.20
10	Vinny Testaverde	.20
11	Michael Irvin	.40
12	Emmitt Smith	2.00
13	John Elway	.50
14	Terrell Davis	1.00
15	Herman Moore	.40
16	Barry Sanders	1.50
17	Brett Favre	2.00
18	Edgar Bennett	.20
19	Rodney Thomas	.40
20	Jim Harbaugh	.20
21	Marshall Faulk	.75
22	Mark Brunell	1.00
23	Steve Bono	.20
24	Marcus Allen	.20
25	Dan Marino	2.00
26	Bryan Cox	.20
27	Cris Carter	.20
28	Drew Bledsoe	1.00
29	Curtis Martin	1.50
30	Jim Everett	.20
31	Rodney Hampton	.20
32	Adrian Murrell	.20
33	Tim Brown	.20
34	Rodney Peete	.20
35	Ricky Watters	.20
36	Yancey Thigpen	.75
37	Greg Lloyd	.20
38	Isaac Bruce	.75
39	Tony Martin	.20
40	Junior Seau	.20
41	Steve Young	1.00
42	Jerry Rice	1.00
43	Chris Warren	.40
44	Errict Rhett	.40
45	Brian Mitchell	.20

A player's name in *italic type* indicates a rookie card.

1996 Collector's Choice MVP Golds

This insert paralleled the MVP set, and is inserted every 35 packs of Series I. While regular versions are printed on silver foil, MVP Gold are printed on gold foil.

	MT
Complete Set (45):	120.00
Gold Cards:	5x-10x

1996 Collector's Choice Stick-Ums

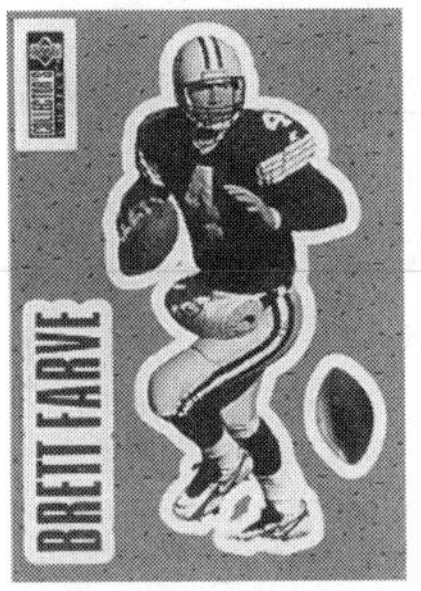

Stick-Ums featured 30 top NFL players on re-stickable, die-cut stickers. The stickers offer removable players, names, footballs, referees, yardage markers and play calls. One Stick-Ums insert is found in every three packs of Series I. The cards are numbered with the "S" prefix.

		MT
Complete Set (30):		10.00
Common Player:		.25
Minor Stars:		.50
1	Dan Marino	2.00
2	Mike Mamula	.25
3	Errict Rhett	.50
4	Drew Bledsoe	1.00
5	Anthony Smith	.25
6	Brett Favre	2.00
7	Morten Andersen	.25
8	Deion Sanders	.75
9	Jeff George	.25
10	Erik Kramer	.25
11	Jerry Rice	1.00
12	Michael Irvin	.50
13	Greg Lloyd	.25
14	Cris Carter	.25
15	Ken Norton	.25
16	Natrone Means	.50
17	Robert Brooks	.50
18	Action Words-Bomb	.25
19	Kordell Stewart	1.00
20	Referee	.25
21	Emmitt Smith	2.00
22	Reggie White	.50
23	Eric Metcalf	.25
24	Jesse Sapolu	.25
25	Curtis Martin	1.50
26	Neil Smith	.25
27	Junior Seau	.25
28	Action Words-TD	.25
29	Accessories-Yardmarkers	.25
30	Terry McDaniel	.25

1996 Collector's Choice Update

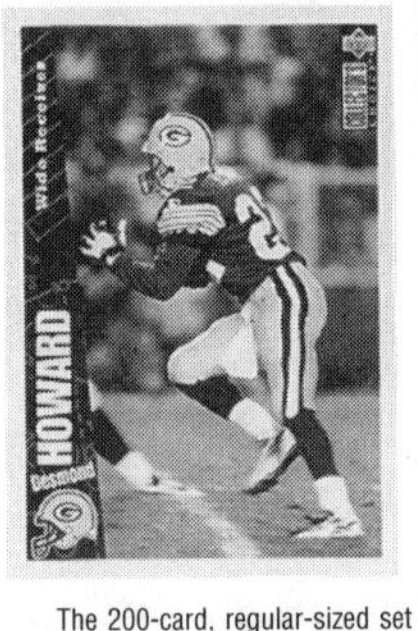

The 200-card, regular-sized set was issued as an update to the 375-card Collector's Choice set in 1996. The Update set included a 60-card rookies subset and 30 Franchise Play Makers subset. The base card fronts included the player's team colors along the left border with the player's position and team helmet. Inserts included were Play Action Stick-Ums, Play Action Stick-Ums Base Cards, Record-Breaking Trio, You Make the Play and Meet The Stars Trivia Game Cards.

		MT
Complete Set (200):		15.00
Common Player:		.05
Minor Stars:		.10
Pack (12):		1.00
Wax Box (36):		30.00
1	*Zack Thomas*	.75
2	Simeon Rice	.10
3	Jonathan Ogden	.05
4	Eric Moulds	.50
5	Tim Biakabutuka	.20
6	Walt Harris	.10
7	Willie Anderson	.05
8	Rickey Whittle	.05
9	John Mobley	.05
10	Reggie Brown	.05
11	John Michels	.05
12	Eddie George	1.00
13	Marvin Harrison	.50
14	Kevin Hardy	.10
15	Kavika Pittman	.05
16	Daryl Gardener	.05
17	Duane Clemons	.05
18	Terry Glenn	.75
19	Alex Molden	.05
20	Cedric Jones	.05
21	Keyshawn Johnson	.60
22	Rickey Dudley	.20
23	Jason Dunn	.05
24	Jermain Stephens	.05
25	Lawrence Phillips	.60
26	Bryan Still	.05
27	Isreal Ifeanyi	.05
28	Pete Kendall	.05
29	Regan Upshaw	.05
30	Andre Johnson	.05
31	Leeland McElroy	.20
32	Ray Lewis	.25
33	Sean Moran	.05
34	*Mushin Muhammad*	.50
35	Bobby Engram	.20
36	Marco Battaglia	.05
37	Stepfret Williams	.05
38	Jeff Lewis	.05
39	Derrick Mayes	.05
40	Reggie Tongue	.05
41	Tory James	.05
42	*Tony Banks*	.75
43	Tedy Bruschi	.05
44	Mike Alstott	.20
45	Anthony Dorsett Jr.	.05
46	*Tony Brackens*	.30
47	Bryant Mix	.05
48	Karim Abdul-Jabbar	.75
49	Moe Williams	.05
50	Lawyer Milloy	.05
51	Je'Rod Cherry	.05
52	*Amani Toomer*	.30
53	Alex Van Dyke	.20
54	Lance Johnstone	.05
55	Bobby Hoying	.05
56	John Wittman	.05
57	*Eddie Kennison*	.50
58	Brian Roche	.05
59	*Terrell Owens*	2.50
60	Stephen Davis	1.25
61	Jeff George	.05
62	Darick Holmes	.05
63	Kerry Collins	.40
64	Rashaan Salaam	.05
65	Jeff Blake	.20
66	Emmitt Smith	.75
67	Troy Aikman	.40
68	John Elway	.30
69	Terrell Davis	.50
70	Barry Sanders	1.00
71	Herman Moore	.05
72	Brett Favre	.75
73	Robert Brooks	.05
74	Steve McNair	.20
75	Marshall Faulk	.20
76	Marcus Allen	.05
77	Dan Marino	.75
78	Warren Moon	.05
79	Drew Bledsoe	.40
80	Curtis Martin	.50
81	Mario Bates	.05
82	Tim Brown	.05
83	Charlie Garner	.05
84	Kordell Stewart	.40
85	Isaac Bruce	.20
86	Tony Martin	.05
87	Jerry Rice	.40
88	J.J. Stokes	.05
89	Joey Galloway	.20
90	Errict Rhett	.15
91	Mike Pritchard	.05
92	Jerome Bettis	.10
93	Winslow Oliver	.05
94	David Klingler	.05
95	Lawrence Dawsey	.05
96	Charlie Jones	.05
97	Dave Krieg	.05
98	Chris Spielman	.05
99	Stanley Pritchett	.05
100	Sean Gilbert	.05
101	Tommy Vardell	.05
102	DeRon Jenkins	.05
103	Larry Bowie	.05
104	Kyle Wachholz	.05
105	Brady Smith	.05
106	Steve Walsh	.05
107	Wesley Walls	.05
108	Kevin Ross	.05
109	Willie Clay	.05
110	Olanda Truitt	.05
111	Calvin Williams	.05
112	Chris Doleman	.05
113	Irving Fryar	.05
114	Jimmy Spencer	.05
115	Reggie Barlow	.05
116	Reggie Brown	.05
117	Dixon Edwards	.05
118	Haywood Jeffires	.05
119	Santana Dotson	.05
120	Herschel Walker	.05
121	Darryl Williams	.05
122	Bryan Cox	.05
123	Lamar Thomas	.05
124	Hendrick Lusk	.05
125	Jahine Arnold	.05
126	Boomer Esiason	.05
127	Willie Davis	.05
128	Pete Stoyanovich	.05
129	Bill Romanowski	.05
130	Tim McKyer	.05
131	Patrick Sapp	.05
132	Natrone Means	.05
133	Quinn Early	.05
134	Leslie O'Neal	.05
135	Mark Seay	.05
136	Pete Metzelaars	.05
137	Jay Leuwenberg	.05
138	Buster Owens	.05
139	Todd McNair	.05
140	Eugene Robinson	.05
141	Sean Salisbury	.05
142	Eugene Robinson	.05
143	Jerris McPhail	.05
144	Ray Farmer	.05
145	Garrison Hearst	.05
146	Leonard Russell	.05
147	Ray Barker	.05
148	Larry Brown	.05
149	Webster Slaughter	.05
150	Roman Oben	.05
151	LeShon Johnson	.05
152	Patrick Bates	.05
153	Iheanyi Uwaezuoke	.05
154	Scott Slutzker	.05
155	John Jurkovic	.05
156	Brian Milne	.05
157	Mike Sherrard	.05
158	Neil O'Donnell	.05
159	Roger Harper	.05
160	Desmond Howard	.05
161	Alfred Williams	.05
162	Ronnie Harmon	.05
163	Sammie Burroughs	.05
164	Keenan McCardell	.05
165	Shane Dronett	.05
166	Jeff Graham	.05
167	Bill Brooks	.05
168	Shawn Jefferson	.05
169	Detron Smith	.05
170	Danny Kanell	.05
171	Jevon Langford	.05
172	Russell Maryland	.05
173	Scott Milanovich	.05
174	Eric Davis	.05
175	Ernie Conwell	.05
176	Kurt Gouveia	.05
177	Andre Rison	.05
178	Harold Green	.05
179	Frank Reich	.05
180	Glyn Milburn	.05
181	Nilo Silvan	.05
182	Cornelius Bennett	.05
183	Freddie Solomon	.05
184	Pat Terrell	.05
185	Miles Mecik	.05
186	Bo Orlando	.05
187	Kelvin Martin	.05
188	Todd Kinchen	.05
189	Reggie Brooks	.05
190	Steve Beuerlein	.05
191	Marco Coleman	.05
192	Johnnie Johnson	.05
193	Dedric Mathis	.05
194	Leon Searcy	.05
195	Kevin Greene	.05
196	Daniel Stubbs	.05
197	Ray Mickens	.05
198	Devin Wyman	.05
199	Lorenzo Lynch	.05
200	Checklist	.20

1996 Collector's Choice Update Record Breaking Trio

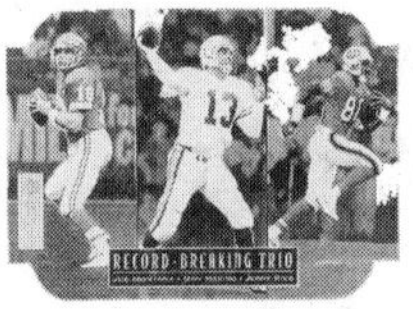

The four-card, regular-sized, die-cut set was inserted every 100 packs of Collector's Choice 1996 Update. The cards feature Joe Montana, Dan Marino, Jerry Rice and a fourth card including all three. The cards are numbered with the "RS" prefix.

		MT
Complete Set (4):		60.00
Common Player:		10.00
1	Joe Montana	10.00
2	Dan Marino	25.00
3	Jerry Rice	15.00
4	(Joe Montana, Dan Marino, Jerry Rice)	10.00

1996 Collector's Choice Update You Make The Play

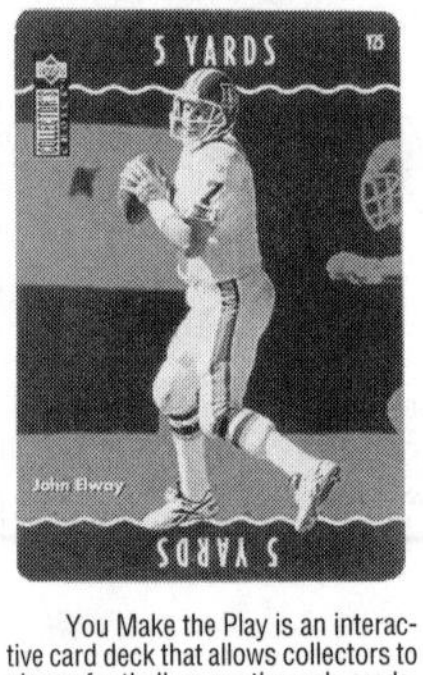

You Make the Play is an interactive card deck that allows collectors to play a football game through cards. The deck contains 90 cards and is found at a rate of one per pack.

		MT
Complete Set (90):		20.00
Common Player:		.10
Minor Stars:		.20
1	Norm Johnson	.10
2	Jerry Rice	1.00
3	Dan Marino	2.00
4	Marshall Faulk	.30
5	Neil Smith	.10
6	Herman Moore	.20
7	Brett Favre	2.00
8	Curtis Martin	1.50
9	Reggie White	.20
10	Cris Carter	.10
11	Rick Tuten	.10
12	Steve Young	.75
13	Barry Sanders	2.00
14	Deion Sanders	.50
15	Isaac Bruce	.30
16	Troy Aikman	1.00
17	Emmitt Smith	2.00
18	Junior Seau	.10
19	Joey Galloway	.30
20	Drew Bledsoe	1.00
21	Jason Elam	.10
22	Edgar Bennett	.10
23	Greg Lloyd	.10
24	Tamarick Vanover	.20
25	John Elway	.75
26	Larry Centers	.10
27	Derrick Thomas	.10
28	Michael Irvin	.20
29	Jeff George	.10
30	Thurman Thomas	.20
31	Darren Bennett	.10
32	Ken Norton	.10
33	Carl Pickens	.10
34	Jeff Blake	.20
35	Craig Heyward	.10
36	Aeneas Williams	.10
37	Terance Mathis	.10
38	Jim Kelly	.20
39	Marcus Allen	.20
40	Tim McDonald	.10
41	Jason Hanson	.10
42	Scott Mitchell	.10
43	Tim Brown	.10
44	Kordell Stewart	1.00
45	Eric Metcalf	.10
46	Norm Johnson	.10
47	Jerry Rice	1.00
48	Dan Marino	2.00
49	Marshall Faulk	.30
50	Neil Smith	.10
51	Herman Moore	.30
52	Brett Favre	2.00
53	Curtis Martin	1.50
54	Reggie White	.20
55	Cris Carter	.10
56	Rick Tuten	.10
57	Steve Young	.75
58	Barry Sanders	2.00
59	Deion Sanders	.50
60	Isaac Bruce	.30
61	Troy Aikman	1.00
62	Emmitt Smith	2.00
63	Junior Seau	.10
64	Joey Galloway	.30
65	Drew Bledsoe	1.00
66	Jason Elam	.10
67	Edgar Bennett	.10
68	Greg Lloyd	.10
69	Tamarick Vanover	.20
70	John Elway	.75
71	Larry Centers	.10
72	Derrick Thomas	.10
73	Michael Irvin	.20
74	Jeff George	.10
75	Thurman Thomas	.20
76	Darren Bennett	.10
77	Ken Norton	.10
78	Carl Pickens	.10
79	Jeff Blake	.20
80	Craig Heyward	.10
81	Aeneas Williams	.10
82	Terance Mathis	.10
83	Jim Kelly	.20
84	Marcus Allen	.20
85	Tim McDonald	.10
86	Jason Hanson	.10
87	Scott Mitchell	.10
88	Tim Brown	.10
89	Kordell Stewart	1.00
90	Eric Metcalf	.10

1996 Collector's Choice Update Stick-Ums

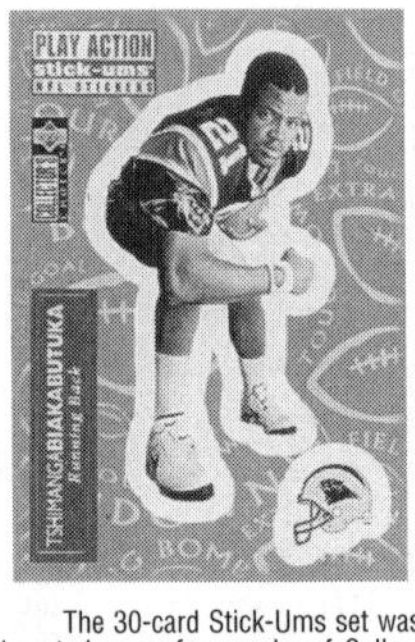

The 30-card Stick-Ums set was inserted every four packs of Collector's Choice 1996 Update. The regular-sized set came with peel-off stickers of the player, team helmet and name. Thirty base cards were also inserted every four packs. The base cards feature a white outline of the corresponding player and contain clues as to which player's sticker goes with which base card. The cards are numbered with the "S" prefix.

		MT
Complete Set (30):		15.00
Common Player:		.25
Minor Stars:		.50
Mystery Base Cards:		.5x
1	Jeff George	.25
2	Darren Bennett	.25
3	Marcus Allen	.50
4	Brett Favre	2.00
5	Carl Pickens	.25
6	Troy Aikman	1.00
7	John Elway	.75
8	Steve Young	.75
9	Norm Johnson	.25
10	Kordell Stewart	1.00
11	Drew Bledsoe	1.00
12	Jim Kelly	.50
13	Dan Marino	2.00
14	Joey Galloway	.50
15	Lawrence Phillips	.50
16	Reggie White	.50
17	Kevin Hardy	.25
18	Isaac Bruce	.50
19	Keyshawn Johnson	.50
20	Barry Sanders	1.50
21	Deion Sanders	.75
22	Emmitt Smith	2.00
23	Chris Warren	.25
24	Tim Biakabutuka	.50
25	Terry Glenn	1.00
26	Marshall Faulk	.50
27	Tamarick Vanover	.25
28	Curtis Martin	1.50
29	Terrell Davis	1.50
30	Jerry Rice	1.00

1996 Collector's Choice Update Stick-Ums Mystery Base

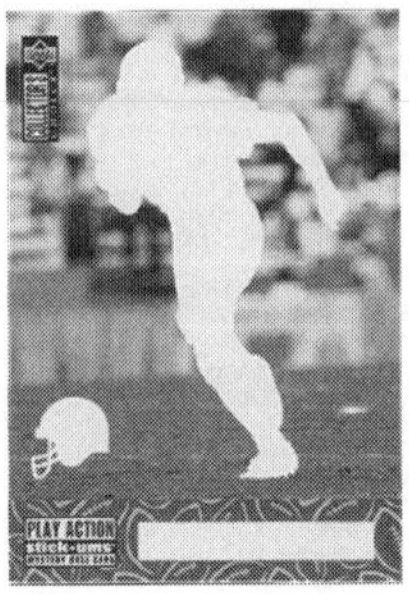

Each Stick-Ums card in Collector's Choice Update has a corresponding Mystery Base card. It is printed on cardboard stock like regular-issue cards and have a background of an action shot, with a white space where the player is supposed to be. The sticker is supposed to be used with the Mystery Base base to complete the football action scene. One Mystery Base card is included in every four packs of Collector's Choice Update.

	MT
Complete Set (30):	7.50
Mystery Base Cards:	.5x

1996 Collector's Choice Packers

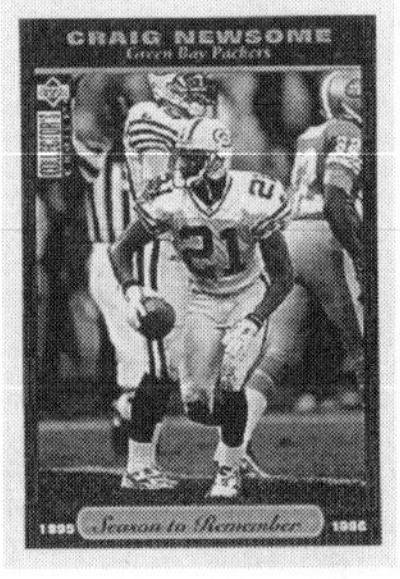

This 90-card set was exclusively available in ShopKo stores and contained all Green Bay Packers including current players and all-time greats. The set featured several different subsets, including A Season to Remember and Legends of the Green and Gold. The regular-issue set contained the first 69 cards, while the final 21 cards, called Leaders of the Pack, is considered an insert set. The cards are numbered with the "GB" prefix.

		MT
Complete Set (69):		14.00
Common Player:		.10
1	Brett Favre	1.50
2	Mark Chmura	.25
3	Edgar Bennett	.25
4	Robert Brooks	.50
5	Antonio Freeman	.25
6	Travis Jervey	.10
7	Craig Newsome	.10
8	Reggie White	.75
9	Sean Jones	.10
10	LeRoy Butler	.10
11	Chris Jacke	.10
12	Derrick Mayes	1.00
13	Chris Darkins	.10
14	Anthony Morgan	.10
15	Terry Mickens	.10
16	Dorsey Levens	.40
17	Jim McMahon	.10
18	Craig Hendricks	.10
19	George Koonce	.10
20	William Henderson	.10
21	Doug Evans	.10
22	Mike Prior	.10
23	Wayne Simmons	.10
24	Darius Holland	.10
25	Gilbert Brown	.10
26	Aaron Taylor	.10
27	Frank Winters	.10
28	Ken Ruettgers	.10
29	Earl Dotson	.10
30	Eugene Robinson	.10
31	Brett Favre (Season to Remember)	1.50
32	Brett Favre (Season to Remember)	1.50
33	Brett Favre (Season to Remember)	1.50
34	Edgar Bennett (Season to Remember)	.25
35	Edgar Bennett (Season to Remember)	.25
36	Robert Brooks (Season to Remember)	.50
37	Robert Brooks (Season to Remember)	.50
38	Mark Chmura (Season to Remember)	.25
39	Mark Chmura (Season to Remember)	.25
40	LeRoy Butler (Season to Remember)	.10
41	LeRoy Butler (Season to Remember)	.10
42	Craig Newsome (Season to Remember)	.10
43	Craig Newsome (Season to Remember)	.10
44	Reggie White (Season to Remember)	.75
45	Reggie White (Season to Remember)	.75
46	Sean Jones (Season to Remember)	.10
47	Sean Jones (Season to Remember)	.10
48	Antonio Freeman (Season to Remember)	.25
49	Chris Jacke (Season to Remember)	.10
50	Offensive Line (Season to Remember)	.10
51	Forrest Gregg (Legends of the Green & Gold)	.10
52	Paul Hornung (Legends of the Green & Gold)	.50
53	Jim Taylor (Legends of the Green & Gold)	.10
54	Vince Lombardi (Legends of the Green & Gold)	.50
55	Ray Nitschke (Legends of the Green & Gold)	.30
56	Willie Wood (Legends of the Green & Gold)	.10
57	Don Hutson (Legends of the Green & Gold)	.10
58	Don Majkowski (Legends of the Green & Gold)	.10
59	Bryce Paup (Legends of the Green & Gold)	.10
60	Sterling Sharpe (Legends of the Green & Gold)	.40
61	Ted Hendricks (Legends of the Green & Gold)	.10
62	Lynn Dickey (Legends of the Green & Gold)	.10
63	James Lofton (Legends of the Green & Gold)	.20
64	Brett Favre (Legends of the Green & Gold)	1.50
65	Edgar Bennett (Legends of the Green & Gold)	.25
66	Reggie White (Legends of the Green & Gold)	.75
67	John Jurkovic (Legends of the Green & Gold)	.20
68	Mike Holmgren (Legends of the Green & Gold)	.30
69	Ron Wolf (Legends of the Green & Gold)	.20

1996 Collector's Choice Leaders of the Pack

Leaders of the Pack consisted of the final 21 cards of the Collector's Choice Packers set that was exclusively available at ShopKo stores. Although it's numbered consecutively with the regular-issue set, it was considered an insert and seeded one per pack. The cards are identified by a thick gold-foil border across the top with the words "Leaders of the Pack." In addition, a color shot of the featured player is shown over a black-and-white dotted background, with a bold yellow strip at the bottom that contains the player's name.

		MT
Complete Set (21):		8.00
Common Player:		.15
70	Forrest Gregg	.15
71	Paul Hornung	1.50
72	Jim Taylor	.15
73	Ray Nitschke	.15
74	Willie Wood	.15
75	Don Hutson	.15
76	Sterling Sharpe	1.25
77	Don Majkowski	.15
78	Ted Hendricks	.15
79	Lynn Dickey	.15
80	James Lofton	.50
81	Brett Favre	4.50
82	Edgar Bennett	.75
83	Robert Brooks	1.50
84	Mark Chmura	.75
85	Reggie White	2.50
86	Sean Jones	.15
87	Chris Jacke	.15
88	LeRoy Butler	.15
89	Craig Newsome	.15
90	Checklist	.25

A player's name in *italic type* indicates a rookie card.

1997 Collector's Choice

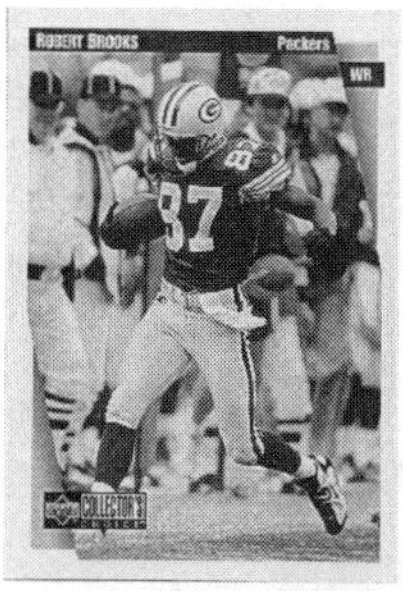

The 565-card set features white borders on the front. The player's name and team are printed inside a stripe at the top, while his position is located inside a rectangle at the upper right. The Collector's Choice logo is printed in the lower left on the front. The backs have a photo on the left, with the player's bio, "Did you know?" and stats along the right side. The cards feature a dual numbering system that helps collectors put players from their favorite team together. Series I also features a 45-card Rookie Class subset and a 40-card Names of the Game subset. Series II includes Checklist/Collector Info cards, 30 NFL Mini Standees and the StarQuest insert.

	MT
Complete Set (565):	40.00
Complete Series 1 (310):	25.00
Complete Series 2 (255):	15.00
Common Player:	.05
Minor Stars:	.10
Ser 1, 2 Pack (14):	1.30
Ser 1, 2 Wax Box (36):	40.00

1	*Orlando Pace*	.25
2	*Darrell Russell*	.05
3	*Shawn Springs*	.25
4	*Peter Boulware*	.05
5	*Bryant Westbrook*	.10
6	*Tom Knight*	.05
7	*Ike Hilliard*	1.00
8	*James Farrior*	.05
9	*Chris Naeole*	.05
10	*Michael Booker*	.05
11	*Warrick Dunn*	1.25
12	*Tony Gonzalez*	.75
13	*Reinard Wilson*	.05
14	*Yatil Green*	.75
15	*Reidel Anthony*	1.00
16	*Kenard Lang*	.05
17	*Kenny Holmes*	.05
18	*Tarik Glenn*	.05
19	*Dwayne Rudd*	.05
20	*Renaldo Wynn*	.05
21	*David LaFleur*	.20
22	*Antowain Smith*	1.50
23	*Jim Druckenmiller*	1.25
24	*Rae Carruth*	1.00
25	*Jared Tomich*	.05
26	*Chris Canty*	.05
27	*Jake Plummer*	2.50
28	*Troy Davis*	.50
29	*Sedrick Shaw*	.50
30	*Jamie Sharper*	.05
31	*Tiki Barber*	1.00
32	*Byron Hanspard*	.75
33	*Darnell Autry*	.50
34	*Corey Dillon*	2.50
35	*Joey Kent*	.30
36	*Nathan Davis*	.05
37	*Will Blackwell*	.30
38	*Kim Herring*	.05
39	*Pat Barnes*	.30
40	*Kevin Lockett*	.20
41	*Trevor Pryce*	.05
42	*Matt Russell*	.05
43	*Greg Jones*	.05
44	*Antonio Anderson*	.05
45	*George Jones*	.10
46	Steve Young	.20
47	Jerry Rice	.35
48	Curtis Conway	.05
49	Jeff Blake	.05
50	Carl Pickens	.05
51	Bruce Smith	.05
52	John Elway	.20
53	Terrell Davis	.50
54	Shannon Sharpe	.05
55	Junior Seau	.05
56	Darren Bennett	.05
57	Jim Harbaugh	.05
58	Marshall Faulk	.05
59	Emmitt Smith	.75
60	Troy Aikman	.35
61	Deion Sanders	.20
62	Dan Marino	.75
63	Ricky Watters	.05
64	Mark Brunell	.35
65	Keenan McCardell	.05
66	Keyshawn Johnson	.20
67	Barry Sanders	.50
68	Herman Moore	.05
69	Eddie George	.50
70	Steve McNair	.25
71	Brett Favre	1.00
72	Reggie White	.05
73	Edgar Bennett	.05
74	Kerry Collins	.35
75	Kevin Greene	.05
76	Drew Bledsoe	.35
77	Terry Glenn	.40
78	Curtis Martin	.50
79	Jeff Hostetler	.05
80	Napoleon Kaufman	.05
81	Isaac Bruce	.05
82	Terry Allen	.05
83	Joey Galloway	.20
84	Kordell Stewart	.20
85	Jerome Bettis	.05
86	Dana Stubblefield	.05
87	Merton Hanks	.05
88	Terrell Owens	.50
89	Brent Jones	.05
90	Ken Norton Jr.	.05
91	Jerry Rice	.75
92	Terry Kirby	.05
93	Bryant Young	.05
94	Raymont Harris	.05
95	Jeff Jaeger	.05
96	Curtis Conway	.10
97	Walt Harris	.05
98	Bobby Engram	.10
99	Donnell Woolford	.05
100	Rashaan Salaam	.10
101	Jeff Blake	.10
102	Tony McGee	.05
103	Ashley Ambrose	.05
104	Dan Wilkinson	.05
105	Jevon Langford	.05
106	Darnay Scott	.05
107	David Dunn	.05
108	Eric Moulds	.05
109	Darrick Holmes	.05
110	Thurman Thomas	.10
111	Quinn Early	.05
112	Jim Kelly	.10
113	Bryce Paup	.05
114	Bruce Smith	.05
115	Todd Collins	.05
116	Tory James	.05
117	Anthony Miller	.05
118	Terrell Davis	1.00
119	Tyrone Braxton	.05
120	John Mobley	.05
121	Bill Romanowski	.05
122	Vaughn Hebron	.05
123	Mike Alstott	.15
124	Errict Rhett	.10
125	Trent Dilfer	.10
126	Courtney Hawkins	.05
127	Hardy Nickerson	.05
128	Donnie Abraham	.05
129	Regan Upshaw	.05
130	Kent Graham	.05
131	Rob Moore	.05
132	Simeon Rice	.05
133	LeShon Johnson	.05
134	Frank Sanders	.05
135	Leeland McElroy	.05
136	Seth Joyner	.05
137	Andre Coleman	.05
138	Stan Humphries	.05
139	Charlie Jones	.05
140	Junior Seau	.10
141	Rodney Harrison	.05
142	Darren Gordon	.05
143	Terrell Fletcher	.05
144	Tamarick Vanover	.10
145	Greg Hill	.05
146	Marcus Allen	.10
147	Lake Dawson	.05
148	Dale Carter	.05
149	Kimble Anders	.05
150	Chris Penn	.05
151	Sean Dawkins	.05
152	Ken Dilger	.05
153	Marvin Harrison	.40
154	Jeff Herrod	.05
155	Jim Harbaugh	.05
156	Cary Blanchard	.05
157	Aaron Bailey	.05
158	Deion Sanders	.40
159	Jim Schwantz	.05
160	Michael Irvin	.10
161	Herschel Walker	.05
162	Emmitt Smith	1.50
163	Chris Boniol	.05
164	Eric Bjornson	.05
165	Karim Abdul-Jabbar	.60
166	O.J. McDuffie	.05
167	Troy Drayton	.05
168	Zach Thomas	.40
169	Irving Spikes	.05
170	Shane Burton	.05
171	Stanley Pritchett	.05
172	Ty Detmer	.05
173	Chris T. Jones	.05
174	Troy Vincent	.05
175	Brian Dawkins	.05
176	Irving Fryar	.05
177	Charlie Garner	.05
178	Bobby Taylor	.05
179	Jamal Anderson	.10
180	Terance Mathis	.05
181	Craig Heyward	.05
182	Cornelius Bennett	.05
183	Jessie Tuggle	.05
184	Devin Bush	.05
185	Dave Brown	.05
186	Danny Kanell	.05
187	Rodney Hampton	.05
188	Tyrone Wheatley	.05
189	Amani Toomer	.05
190	Phillipi Sparks	.05
191	Thomas Lewis	.05
192	Jimmy Smith	.05
193	Pete Mitchell	.05
194	Natrone Means	.10
195	Mark Brunell	.75
196	Kevin Hardy	.05
197	Tony Brackens	.05
198	Aaron Beasley	.05
199	Chris Hudson	.05
200	Wayne Chrebet	.05
201	Keyshawn Johnson	.40
202	Adrian Murrell	.05
203	Neil O'Donnell	.05
204	Hugh Douglas	.05
205	Mo Lewis	.05
206	Glenn Foley	.05
207	Aaron Glenn	.05
208	Johnnie Morton	.05
209	Reggie Brown	.05
210	Barry Sanders	1.25
211	Glyn Milburn	.05
212	Bennie Blades	.05
213	Steve McNair	.40
214	Frank Wycheck	.05
215	Chris Sanders	.05
216	Blaine Bishop	.05
217	Willie Davis	.05
218	Darryll Lewis	.05
219	Marcus Robertson	.05
220	Robert Brooks	.10
221	Antonio Freeman	.30
222	Keith Jackson (Retired)	.05
223	Mark Chmura	.05
224	Brett Favre	1.75
225	Sean Jones	.05
226	Reggie White	.10
227	LeRoy Butler	.05
228	Craig Newsome	.05
229	Wesley Walls	.05
230	Mark Carrier	.05
231	Muhsin Muhammad	.05
232	John Kasay	.05
233	Anthony Johnson	.05
234	Kerry Collins	.75
235	Kevin Greene	.05
236	Sam Mills	.05
237	Ben Coates	.05
238	Terry Glenn	.75
239	Willie McGinest	.05
240	Ted Johnson	.05
241	Lawyer Milloy	.05
242	Drew Bledsoe	.75
243	Willie Clay	.05
244	Chris Slade	.05
245	Tim Brown	.05
246	Daryl Hobbs	.05
247	Rickey Dudley	.05
248	Joe Aska	.05
249	Chester McGlockton	.05
250	Rob Fredrickson	.05
251	Terry McDaniel	.05
252	Tony Banks	.25
253	Lawrence Phillips	.10
254	Isaac Bruce	.15
255	Eddie Kennison	.25
256	Kevin Carter	.05
257	Roman Phifer	.05
258	Keith Lyle	.05
259	Vinny Testaverde	.05
260	Derrick Alexander	.05
261	Ray Lewis	.05
262	Jermaine Lewis	.05
263	Bam Morris	.05
264	Stevon Moore	.05
265	Antonio Langham	.05
266	Brian Mitchell	.05
267	Henry Ellard	.05
268	Leslie Shepherd	.05
269	Michael Westbrook	.05
270	Jamie Asher	.05
271	Ken Harvey	.05
272	Gus Frerotte	.05
273	Michael Haynes	.05
274	Ray Zellars	.05
275	Jim Everett	.05
276	Tyrone Hughes (Bears)	.05
277	Joe Johnson	.05
278	Eric Allen	.05
279	Brady Smith	.05
280	Mario Bates	.05
281	Torrance Small	.05
282	John Friesz	.05
283	Brian Blades	.05
284	Chris Warren	.05
285	Joey Galloway	.25
286	Michael Sinclair	.05
287	Lamar Smith	.05
288	Mike Pritchard	.05
289	Jerome Bettis	.10
290	Charles Johnson	.05
291	Mike Tomczak	.05
292	Levon Kirkland	.05
293	Carnell Lake	.05
294	Erric Pegram	.05
295	Kordell Stewart	.50
296	Greg Lloyd	.05
297	Dixon Edwards	.05
298	Cris Carter	.05
299	Brad Johnson	.05
300	Qadry Ismail	.05
301	John Randle	.05
302	Orlanda Thomas	.05
303	DeWayne Washington	.05
304	Jake Reed	.05
305	Derrick Alexander	.05
306	Eddie George	1.25
307	Dan Marino	1.50
308	Curtis Martin	1.00
309	Troy Aikman	.75
310	Marcus Allen	.10
311	Jim Druckenmiller	1.00
312	Greg Clark	.05
313	Darnell Autry	.30
314	Reinard Wilson	.05
315	Corey Dillon	1.50
316	Antowain Smith	.75
317	Trevor Pryce	.05
318	Warrick Dunn	1.75
319	Reidel Anthony	.75
320	Jake Plummer	1.75
321	Tom Knight	.05
322	Freddie Jones	.10
323	Tony Gonzalez	.30
324	Pat Barnes	.30
325	Kevin Lockett	.05
326	Tarik Glenn	.05
327	David LaFleur	.30
328	Antonio Anderson	.05
329	Yatil Green	.40
330	Jason Taylor	.05
331	Brian Manning	.05
332	Michael Booker	.05
333	Byron Hanspard	.40
334	Ike Hilliard	.40
335	Tiki Barber	.50
336	Renaldo Wynn	.05
337	Damon Jones	.05
338	James Farrior	.05
339	Dedric Ward	.05
340	Bryant Westbrook	.05
341	Matt Russell	.05
342	Joey Kent	.05
343	Kenny Holmes	.05
344	Darren Sharper	.05
345	Rae Carruth*	.40
346	Chris Canty	.05
347	Darrell Russell	.05
348	Orlando Pace	.05
349	Peter Boulware	.05
350	*Danny Wuerffel*	.75
351	Troy Davis	.40
352	Shawn Springs	.05
353	Walter Jones	.05
354	Will Blackwell	.05
355	Dwayne Rudd	.05
356	Cardinals	.05
357	Falcons	.05
358	Ravens	.05
359	Bills	.05
360	Panthers	.05
361	Bears	.05
362	Bengals	.05
363	Cowboys	.05
364	Broncos	.05
365	Lions	.05
366	Packers	.05
367	Oilers	.05
368	Colts	.05
369	Jaguars	.05
370	Chiefs	.05
371	Dolphins	.05
372	Vikings	.05
373	Patriots	.05
374	Saints	.05
375	Jets	.05
376	Giants	.05
377	Raiders	.05
378	Eagles	.05
379	Steelers	.05
380	Chargers	.05
381	49ers	.05
382	Seahawks	.05
383	Rams	.05
384	Buccaneers	.05
385	Redskins	.05
386	William Floyd	.05
387	Steve Young	.75
388	Lee Woodall	.05
389	J.J. Stokes	.05
390	Marc Edwards	.05
391	Rod Woodson	.05
392	Jim Schwantz	.05
393	Garrison Hearst	.05
394	Rick Mirer	.05
395	Alonzo Spellman	.05
396	Tom Carter	.05
397	Bryan Cox	.05
398	John Allred	.05
399	Ricky Proehl	.05
400	Tyrone Hughes	.05
401	Carl Pickens	.05
402	Tremain Mack	.05
403	Boomer Esiason	.05
404	Ki-Jana Carter	.05
405	Steve Tovar	.05
406	Billy Joe Hobert	.05
407	Andre Reed	.05
408	Marcelius Wiley	.05
409	Steve Tasker	.05
410	Chris Spielman	.05
411	Alfred Williams	.05
412	John Elway	.75
413	Shannon Sharpe	.05
414	Steve Atwater	.05
415	Neil Smith	.05
416	Darrien Gordon	.05
417	Jeff Lewis	.05
418	Flipper Anderson	.05
419	Willie Green	.05
420	Jackie Harris	.05
421	Steve Walsh	.05
422	Anthony Parker	.05
423	Ronde Barber	.05
424	Warren Sapp	.05
425	Aeneas Williams	.05
426	Larry Centers	.05
427	Eric Swann	.05
428	Kevin Williams	.05
429	Darren Bennett	.05
430	Tony Martin	.05
431	John Carney	.05
432	Jim Everett	.05
433	William Fuller	.05
434	Latario Rachel	.05
435	Erric Pegram	.05
436	Eric Metcalf	.05
437	Jerome Woods	.05
438	Derrick Thomas	.05
439	Elvis Grbac	.05
440	Terry Wooden	.05
441	Andre Rison	.05
442	Brett Perriman	.05
443	Roosevelt Potts	.05
444	Robert Blackman	.05
445	Carlton Gray	.05
446	Chris Gardocki	.05
447	Marshall Faulk	.10
448	Sammie Burroughs	.05
449	Quentin Coryatt	.05
450	Troy Aikman	1.00
451	Daryl Johnston	.05
452	Tony Tolbert	.05
453	Brock Marion	.05
454	Billy Davis	.05
455	Dexter Coakley	.05
456	Anthony Miller	.05
457	Dan Marino	2.00
458	Jerris McPhail	.05
459	Terrell Buckley	.05
460	Daryl Gardener	.05
461	George Teague	.05
462	Qadry Ismail	.05
463	Fred Barnett	.05
464	Darrin Smith	.05
465	Michael Timpson	.05
466	Jon Harris	.05
467	Jason Dunn	.05
468	Bobby Hoying	.05
469	Ricky Watters	.10
470	Derrick Witherspoon	.05
471	Chris Chandler	.05
472	Ray Buchanan	.05
473	Michael Haynes	.05
474	Nathan Davis	.05
475	Morten Andersen	.05
476	Bert Emanuel	.05
477	Chris Calloway	.05
478	Jason Sehorn	.05
479	John Jurkovic	.05
480	Keenan McCardell	.05
481	James O. Stewart	.05
482	Rob Johnson	.05
483	Mike Logan	.05
484	Deon Figures	.05
485	Kyle Brady	.05
486	Alex Van Dyke	.05
487	Jeff Graham	.05
488	Jason Hanson	.05
489	Herman Moore	.10
490	Scott Mitchell	.05
491	Tommy Vardell	.05
492	*Derrick Mason*	1.00
493	Rodney Thomas	.05
494	Ronnie Harmon	.05
495	Eddie George	1.50
496	Edgar Bennett	.05
497	William Henderson	.05
498	Dorsey Levens	.10
499	Gilbert Brown	.05
500	Steve Bono	.05
501	Derrick Mayes	.05
502	*Fred Lane*	.50
503	Ernie Mills	.05
504	Tshimanga Biakabutuka	.05
505	Michael Bates	.05
506	Winslow Oliver	.05
507	Ty Law	.05
508	Shawn Jefferson	.05
509	Vincent Brisby	.05
510	Henry Thomas	.05
511	Tedy Bruschi	.05
512	Curtis Martin	.75
513	Jeff George	.05
514	Desmond Howard	.05
515	Napoleon Kaufman	.10
516	Kenny Shedd	.05
517	Russell Maryland	.05
518	Lance Johnstone	.05
519	Chad Levitt	.05
520	Dexter McLeon	.05
521	Craig Heyward	.05
522	Ryan McNeil	.05
523	Mark Rypien	.05
524	Mike Jones	.05
525	Jamie Sharper	.05
526	Tony Siragusa	.05
527	Michael Jackson	.05
528	Floyd Turner	.05
529	Eric Green	.05
530	Michael McCrary	.05
531	Jay Graham	.05
532	Terry Allen	.05
533	Sean Gilbert	.05
534	Scott Turner	.05
535	Cris Dishman	.05
536	Jeff Hostetler	.05
537	Chris Mims	.05
538	Alvin Harper	.05
539	Daryl Hobbs	.05
540	Wayne Martin	.05
541	Heath Shuler	.05
542	Andre Hastings	.05
543	Jared Tomich	.05
544	Nicky Savoie	.05
545	Cortez Kennedy	.05
546	Warren Moon	.05
547	Chad Brown	.05
548	Willie Williams	.05
549	Bennie Blades	.05
550	Darren Perry	.05
551	Mark Bruener	.05
552	Yancey Thigpen	.05
553	Courtney Hawkins	.05
554	Chad Scott	.05
555	George Jones	.05
556	Robert Tate	.05
557	Torrian Gray	.05
558	Robert Griffith	.05
559	Leroy Hoard	.05
560	Robert Smith	.05
561	Randall Cunningham	.05
562	(Darrell Russell CL)	.05
563	(Troy Aikman CL)	.25
564	(Dan Marino CL)	.40
565	(Jim Druckenmiller CL)	.25

1997 Collector's Choice Crash the Game

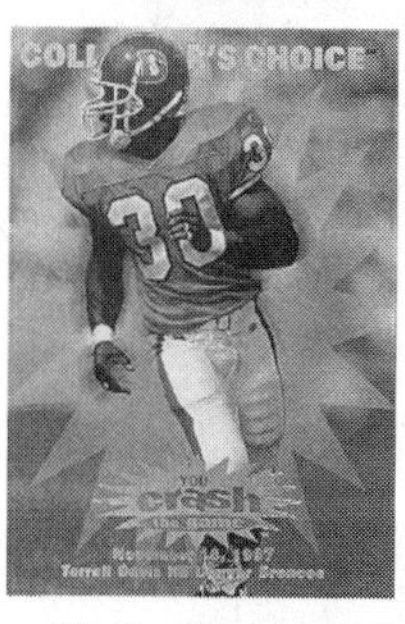

This 30-card chase set was inserted 1:5 packs. If the player featured on the front scored on the date shown on the front, the collector won a redemption card of the player. This insert appeared only in Series I.

		MT
Complete Set (30):		25.00
Common Player:		.50
Minor Stars:		1.00
Each player has three cards with 3 different dates.		
1	Troy Aikman	1.50
2	Dan Marino	3.00
3	Steve Young	1.25
4	Brett Favre	3.50
5	Drew Bledsoe	1.50
6	Jeff Blake	1.00
7	Mark Brunell	1.00
8	John Elway	1.25
9	Vinny Testaverde	.50
10	Steve McNair	1.25
11	Jerry Rice	1.50
12	Terry Glenn	1.00
13	Michael Jackson	.50
14	Tony Martin	.50
15	Isaac Bruce	1.00
16	Cris Carter	1.00
17	Shannon Sharpe	.50
18	Rae Carruth	1.00
19	Ike Hilliard	1.00
20	Yatil Green	.75
21	Terry Allen	.50
22	Emmitt Smith	3.00
23	Karim Abdul-Jabbar	1.00
24	Barry Sanders	1.50
25	Terrell Davis	1.50
26	Jerome Bettis	1.00
27	Ricky Watters	1.00
28	Curtis Martin	1.25
29	Byron Hanspard	1.00
30	Warrick Dunn	2.00

1997 Collector's Choice Mini-Standee

Inserted 1:5, the 30-card Mini Standee insert appeared in Series II. The cards can be folded into a football shaped stand-up card. The cards are numbered with the "ST" prefix.

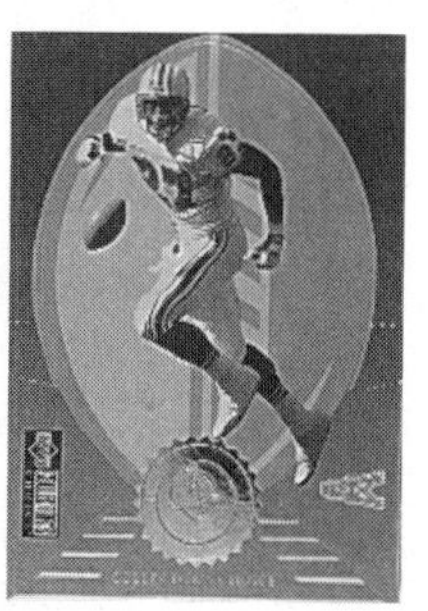

		MT
Complete Set (30):		25.00
Common Player:		.25
Minor Stars:		.50
1	Jerry Rice	1.50
2	Rashaan Salaam	.25
3	Jeff Blake	.50
4	Antowain Smith	1.25
5	John Elway	1.25
6	Errict Rhett	.25
7	Jake Plummer	1.25
8	Junior Seau	.25
9	Marcus Allen	.50
10	Marvin Harrison	.50
11	Emmitt Smith	3.00
12	Dan Marino	3.00
13	Ricky Watters	.50
14	Jamal Anderson	.25
15	Rodney Hampton	.25
16	Mark Brunell	1.50
17	Keyshawn Johnson	.50
18	Barry Sanders	2.00
19	Eddie George	2.00
20	Brett Favre	3.50
21	Kerry Collins	1.00
22	Drew Bledsoe	1.50
23	Napoleon Kaufman	.50
24	Tony Banks	.50
25	Vinny Testaverde	.25
26	Terry Allen	.25
27	Mario Bates	.25
28	Joey Galloway	.50
29	Jerome Bettis	.50
30	Robert Smith	.25

1997 Collector's Choice Star Quest

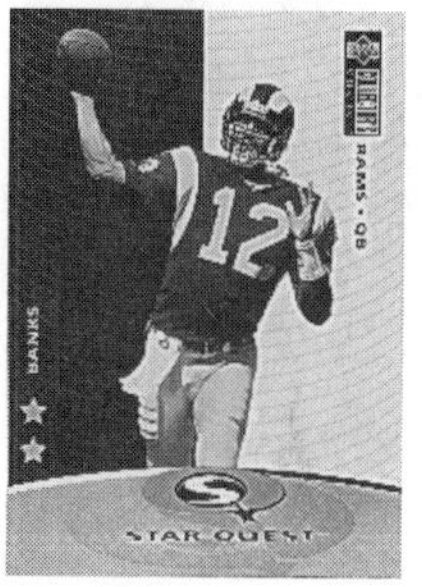

StarQuest is a four-tiered insert available in Series II. The tiers are indicated by the number of stars on the card - one per tier. Tier one includes 45 cards and were inserted 1:1. Tier two includes 20 cards inserted 1:21. The 15 tier three cards were inserted 1:71. Tier four had 10 cards and was inserted 1:145. The insert set totaled 90 cards, featuring the top players in the game. The cards are numbered with the "SQ" prefix.

		MT
Complete Set (90):		500.00
Common Player (1-45):		.25
Common Player (46-65):		2.00
Common Player (66-80):		5.00
Common Player (81-90):		10.00
1	Frank Sanders	.25
2	Jamal Anderson	.50
3	Bam Morris	.25
4	Thurman Thomas	.50
5	Muhsin Muhammad	.25
6	Bobby Engram	.25
7	Carl Pickens	.25
8	Deion Sanders	.75
9	Shannon Sharpe	.25
10	Herman Moore	.50
11	Robert Brooks	.25
12	Steve McNair	1.50
13	Marshall Faulk	.50
14	Keenan McCardell	.25
15	Tamarick Vanover	.25
16	Fred Barnett	.25
17	Orlanda Thomas	.25
18	Drew Bledsoe	1.50
19	Mario Bates	.25
20	Keyshawn Johnson	.50
21	Rodney Hampton	.25
22	Darrell Russell	.25
23	Irving Fryar	.25
24	Charles Johnson	.25
25	Stan Humphries	.25
26	Terrell Owens	.50
27	Chris Warren	.25
28	Isaac Bruce	.50
29	Warrick Dunn	2.50
30	Gus Frerotte	.25
31	Raghib Ismail	.25
32	Natrone Means	.50
33	Chris Sanders	.25
34	Vinny Testaverde	.25

35	Ken Norton	.25
36	Kevin Greene	.25
37	Marcus Allen	.50
38	Zach Thomas	.25
39	Derrick Thomas	.25
40	Tyrone Wheatley	.25
41	Dorsey Levens	.50
42	Darnay Scott	.25
43	Scott Mitchell	.25
44	Marvin Harrison	.50
45	Eddie Kennison	.50
46	Jake Reed	2.00
47	Andre Reed	2.00
48	Neil Smith	2.00
49	Anthony Johnson	2.00
50	Napoleon Kaufman	4.00
51	Terance Mathis	2.00
52	Tony Martin	2.00
53	Adrian Murrell	4.00
54	Bryant Westbrook	2.00
55	Errict Rhett	2.00
56	Kerry Collins	10.00
57	Curtis Conway	2.00
58	Eric Swann	2.00
59	Michael Jackson	2.00
60	Ty Detmer	2.00
61	Michael Irvin	4.00
62	Andre Coleman	2.00
63	Brian Mitchell	2.00
64	Tony Banks	4.00
65	Eddie George	20.00
66	Kordell Stewart	20.00
67	Greg Hill	5.00
68	Karim Abdul-Jabbar	12.00
69	Cris Carter	5.00
70	Terry Glenn	15.00
71	Emmitt Smith	60.00
72	Jim Harbaugh	5.00
73	Jeff Blake	8.00
74	Rashaan Salaam	5.00
75	Ricky Watters	5.00
76	Joey Galloway	8.00
77	Junior Seau	5.00
78	Dave Brown	5.00
79	Tim Brown	5.00
80	Troy Aikman	25.00
81	Dan Marino	70.00
82	Brett Favre	75.00
83	John Elway	30.00
84	Steve Young	25.00
85	Mark Brunell	35.00
86	Barry Sanders	40.00
87	Jerome Bettis	10.00
88	Terrell Davis	35.00
89	Curtis Martin	30.00
90	Jerry Rice	35.00

1997 Collector's Choice Stick-Ums

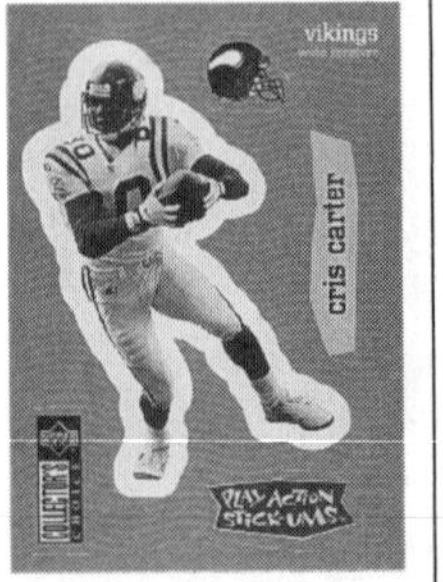

Inserted 1:3 packs in Series I, these 30 stickers featured a photo of the player on the front, the Stick-Ums logo, his name and team helmet which could be peeled off. The sticker number is printed on the upper left of the back. Directions on how to use the stickers are on the left of the back, while the checklist is on the right. Each of the stickers' numbers included an "S" prefix.

	MT
Complete Set (30):	15.00
Common Player:	.25
Minor Stars:	.50

1	Kerry Collins	.75
2	Troy Aikman	1.25
3	Steve Young	.75
4	Ricky Watters	.50
5	Cris Carter	.25
6	Terry Allen	.25
7	Bobby Engram	.50
8	Simeon Rice	.25
9	Mike Alstott	.25
10	Rodney Hampton	.25
11	Eddie Kennison	.50
12	Jamal Anderson	.50
13	Jim Everett	.25
14	Curtis Martin	1.25
15	Keenan McCardell	.25
16	Kordell Stewart	1.00
17	John Elway	.75
18	Terrell Davis	1.25
19	Thurman Thomas	.50
20	Marshall Faulk	.50
21	Marcus Allen	.50
22	Tony Martin	.25
23	Dan Marino	2.00
24	Karim Abdul-Jabbar	1.00
25	Carl Pickens	.25
26	Eddie George	1.50
27	Joey Galloway	.25
28	Napoleon Kaufman	.25
29	Vinny Testaverde	.25
30	Keyshawn Johnson	.50

1997 Collector's Choice Turf Champions

The 90-card chase set was broken up into four tiers. Tier one and two both contain 30 cards, while Tier three has 20. Tier four includes 10. The Tiers were inserted as follows: one (every pack), two (1:21), three (1:71) and four (1:145). The holofoil cards have a green-marble border at the top and bottom. The Collector's Choice logo is in the upper left, with the Turf Champions' logo in the lower left. The player's name, position and team are listed at the bottom center. The backs, which are numbered with a "TC" prefix, have the player's highlights printed over a green area on the left, with his achievement printed vertically in the center. The right has a photo and quote. Turf Champions appeared in Series I.

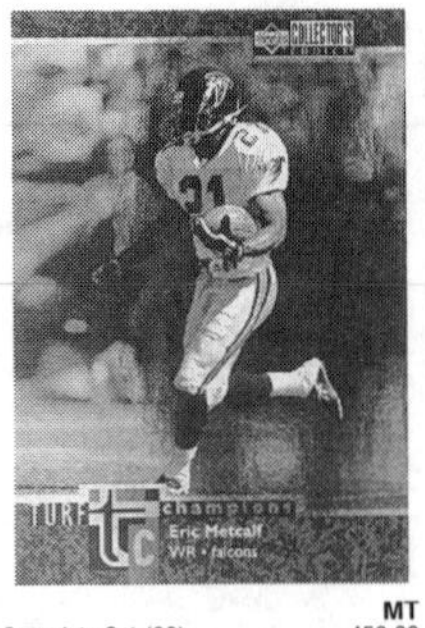

	MT
Complete Set (90):	450.00
Common Player (1-30):	.20
Inserted 1:1	
Common Player (31-60):	2.00
Inserted 1:21	
Common Player (61-80):	5.00
Inserted 1:71	
Common Player (81-90):	6.00
Inserted 1:145	

1	Kerry Collins	.50
2	Scott Mitchell	.20
3	Jim Schwantz	.20
4	Orlando Pace	.40
5	Troy Davis	.40
6	Vinny Testaverde	.50
7	Raghib Ismail	.20
8	Henry Ellard	.20
9	Kevin Turner	.20
10	Bobby Engram	.20
11	Keyshawn Johnson	.75
12	Trent Dilfer	.50
13	Elvis Grbac	.40
14	Trev Alberts	.20
15	Kevin Hardy	.20
16	Warren Sapp	.40
17	Chris Hudson	.20
18	Antonio Langham	.20
19	Jonathan Ogden	.20
20	Bruce Smith	.40
21	Marcus Allen	.50
22	Desmond Howard	.20
23	Eric Metcalf	.20
24	Terance Mathis	.20
25	LeShon Johnson	.20
26	Kevin Greene	.20
27	Alex Van Dyke	.20
28	Jeff Jaeger	.20
29	Jason Elam	.20
30	Thomas Lewis	.20
31	Rick Mirer	2.00
32	Warren Moon	5.00
33	Jim Kelly	5.00
34	Junior Seau	4.00
35	Jeff Hostetler	2.00
36	Neil O'Donnell	2.00
37	Jeff Blake	4.00
38	Kordell Stewart	10.00
39	Terry Glenn	6.00
40	Simeon Rice	2.00
41	Jimmy Smith	5.00
42	Natrone Means	4.00
43	Tony Martin	2.00
44	Charles Johnson	4.00
45	Napoleon Kaufman	6.00
46	Dale Carter	2.00
47	Brett Perriman	2.00
48	Cortez Kennedy	2.00
49	Bryce Paup	2.00
50	Greg Lloyd	2.00
51	Bryant Young	2.00
52	Steve McNair	8.00
53	Garrison Hearst	4.00
54	John Copeland	2.00
55	Eric Curry	2.00
56	Reggie White	5.00
57	Rod Woodson	4.00
58	Andre Rison	4.00
59	Herschel Walker	4.00
60	John Kasay	2.00
61	Emmitt Smith	35.00
62	Dan Marino	35.00
63	Michael Irvin	10.00
64	Drew Bledsoe	20.00
65	Mark Brunell	20.00
66	Jim Harbaugh	5.00
67	Herman Moore	8.00
68	Rashaan Salaam	5.00
69	Ty Detmer	8.00
70	Cris Carter	12.00
71	Chris Warren	7.00
72	Thurman Thomas	8.00
73	Ricky Watters	8.00
74	Tim Brown	10.00
75	Marshall Faulk	15.00
76	Jerome Bettis	10.00
77	Karim Abdul-Jabbar	8.00
78	Deion Sanders	12.00
79	Ben Coates	7.00
80	Andre Reed	7.00
81	Brett Favre	45.00
82	Terrell Davis	35.00
83	Troy Aikman	20.00
84	Carl Pickens	6.00
85	Barry Sanders	40.00
86	Jerry Rice	20.00
87	Curtis Martin	10.00
88	Steve Young	15.00
89	Eddie George	20.00
90	John Elway	35.00

1992 Collector's Edge Prototypes

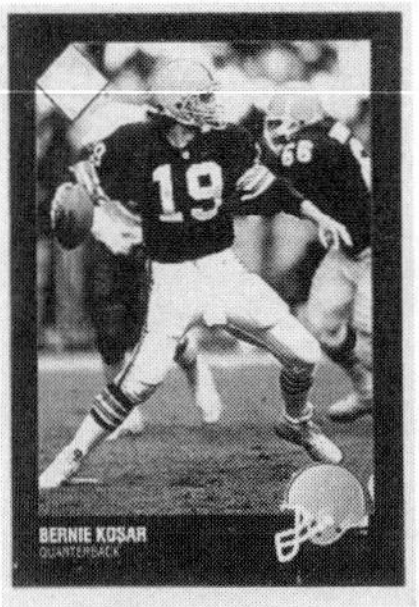

Two different versions of this six-card prototype set were issued. One version had a removable piece of paper glued to the card back, while the other version was not sticky. The paper-covered backs are tougher to find. Edge produced 8,000 of each card. The card fronts are bordered in black, with a color photo. The Edge '92 logo is in the upper left. The player's name and position are in the lower left. The player's team's helmet is located on the lower right of the card back. The backs have a player headshot at the top, with his name, position, team, bio and stats listed below. The cards are numbered in the upper right with a "prototype" suffix.

	MT
Complete Set (6):	25.00
Common Player:	2.00

1	Jim Kelly	3.00
2	Randall Cunningham	4.00
3	Warren Moon	2.00
4	John Elway	10.00
5	Dan Marino	10.00
6	Bernie Kosar	2.00

1992 Collector's Edge

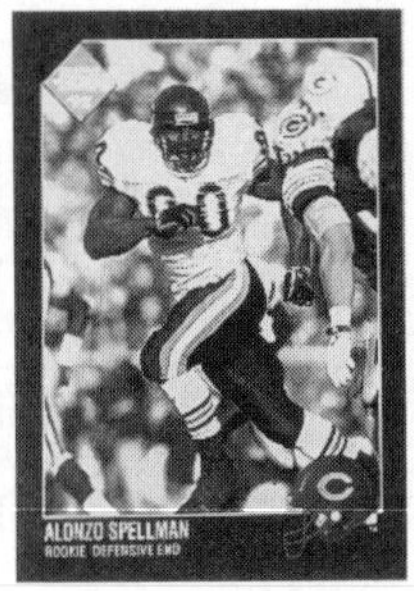

Each card in this 175-card set is individually numbered from 1-100,000. The standard-size cards are printed on a plastic stock and feature color action shots with black borders. A team helmet is on the lower right-hand corner. Backs, which have the card front image ghosted through, have a mug shot, statistics and a biography. John Elway and Ken O'Brien autographed 2,500 cards which were randomly inserted in factory sets and foil packs. Rookie/Update cards begin with #176 and are considered a second series. There were also 2,500 Ronnie Lott autographed cards in the series, plus 20,000 cards each for Terrell Buckley and Tommy Maddox.

	MT
Complete Set (250):	40.00
Complete Series 1 (175):	25.00
Complete Series 2 (75):	15.00
Common Player:	.10
Minor Stars:	.20
Elway Auto:	100.00
Lott Auto:	40.00
O'Brien Auto:	20.00
Series 1 Pack (6):	.75
Series 1 Wax Box (24):	15.00
Rookie/Update Pack (6):	.75
Rookie/Update Wax Box (24):	15.00

1	Chris Miller	.10
2	Steve Broussard	.20
3	Mike Pritchard	.20
4	Tim Green	.10
5	Andre Rison	.30
6	Deion Sanders	1.00
7	Jim Kelly	.50
8	James Lofton	.10
9	Andre Reed	.10
10	Bruce Smith	.10
11	Thurman Thomas	1.00
12	Cornelius Bennett	.10
13	Jim Harbaugh	.10
14	William Perry	.10
15	Mike Singletary	.10
16	Mark Carrier	.10
17	Kevin Butler	.10
18	Tom Waddle	.10
19	Boomer Esiason	.20
20	David Fulcher	.10
21	Anthony Munoz	.10
22	Tim McGee	.10
23	Harold Green	.10
24	Rickey Dixon	.10
25	Bernie Kosar	.10
26	Michael Dean Perry	.10
27	Mike Baab	.10
28	Brian Brennan	.10
29	Michael Jackson	.20
30	Eric Metcalf	.10
31	Troy Aikman	3.00
32	Emmitt Smith	6.00
33	Michael Irvin	1.00
34	Jay Novacek	.10
35	Issiac Holt	.10
36	Ken Norton	.10
37	John Elway	1.25
38	Gaston Green	.10
39	Charles Dimry	.10
40	Vance Johnson	.10
41	Dennis Smith	.10
42	David Treadwell	.10
43	Michael Young	.10
44	Bennie Blades	.10
45	Mel Gray	.10
46	Andre Ware	.10
47	Rodney Peete	.10
48	*Toby Caston*	.10
49	Herman Moore	2.00
50	Brian Noble	.10
51	Sterling Sharpe	.50
52	Mike Tomczak	.10
53	Vinnie Clark	.10
54	Tony Mandarich	.10
55	Ed West	.10
56	Warren Moon	.30
57	Ray Childress	.10
58	Haywood Jeffires	.10
59	Al Smith	.10
60	Cris Dishman	.10
61	Ernest Givins	.10
62	Richard Johnson	.10
63	Eric Dickerson	.10
64	Jessie Hester	.10
65	Robin Stark	.10
66	Clarence Verdin	.10
67	Dean Biasucci	.10
68	Duane Bickett	.10
69	Jeff George	.30
70	Christian Okoye	.10
71	Derrick Thomas	.30
72	Stephone Paige	.10
73	Dan Saleaumua	.10
74	Deron Cherry	.10
75	Kevin Ross	.10
76	Barry Word	.10
77	Ronnie Lott	.10
78	Greg Townsend	.10
79	Willie Gault	.10
80	Howie Long	.10
81	Winston Moss	.10
82	Steve Smith	.10
83	Jay Schroeder	.10
84	Jim Everett	.20
85	Willie Anderson	.10
86	Henry Ellard	.10
87	Tony Zendejas	.10
88	Robert Delpino	.10
89	Pat Terrel	.10
90	Dan Marino	5.00
91	Mark Clayton	.10
92	Jim Jensen	.10
93	Reggie Roby	.10
94	Sammie Smith	.10
95	Tony Martin	.10
96	Jeff Cross	.10
97	Anthony Carter	.10
98	Chris Doleman	.10
99	Wade Wilson	.10
100	Cris Carter	.20
101	Mike Meriweather	.10
102	Gary Zimmerman	.10
103	Chris Singleton	.10
104	Bruce Armstrong	.10
105	Marv Cook	.10
106	Andre Tippet	.10
107	Tom Hodson	.10
108	Greg McMurtry	.10
109	Jon Vaughn	.10
110	Vaughan Johnson	.10
111	Craig Heyward	.10
112	Floyd Turner	.10
113	Pat Swilling	.10
114	Ricky Jackson	.10
115	Steve Walsh	.10
116	Phil Simms	.10
117	Carl Banks	.10
118	Mark Ingram	.10
119	Bart Oates	.10
120	Lawrence Taylor	.20
121	Jeff Hostetler	.30
122	Rob Moore	.20
123	Ken O'Brien	.10
124	Bill Pickel	.10
125	Irv Eatman	.10
126	Browning Nagle	.10
127	Al Toon	.10
128	Randall Cunningham	.20
129	Eric Allen	.10
130	Mike Golic	.10
131	Fred Barnett	.10
132	Keith Byars	.10
133	Calvin Williams	.10
134	Randal Hill	.10
135	Ricky Proehl	.10
136	Lance Smith	.10
137	Ernie Jones	.10
138	Timm Rosenbach	.10
139	Anthony Thompson	.10
140	Bubby Brister	.10
141	Merril Hoge	.10
142	Louis Lipps	.10
143	Eric Green	.10
144	Gary Anderson	.10
145	Neil O'Donnell	.40
146	Rod Bernstine	.10
147	John Friesz	.10
148	Anthony Miller	.10
149	Junior Seau	.50
150	Leslie O'Neal	.10
151	Nate Lewis	.10
152	Steve Young	3.00
153	Kevin Fagan	.10
154	Charles Haley	.10
155	Tom Rathman	.10
156	Jerry Rice	3.00
157	John Taylor	.10
158	Brian Blades	.10
159	Patrick Hunter	.10
160	Cortez Kennedy	.20
161	Vann McElroy	.10
162	Dan McGwire	.10
163	John L. Williams	.10
164	Gary Anderson	.10
165	Broderick Thomas	.10
166	Vinny Testaverde	.10
167	Lawrence Dawsey	.10
168	Paul Gruber	.10
169	Keith McCants	.10
170	Mark Rypien	.10
171	Gary Clark	.10
172	Earnest Byner	.10
173	Brian Mitchell	.10
174	Monte Coleman	.10
175	Joe Jacoby	.10
176	*Tommy Vardell*	.20
177	*Troy Vincent*	.25
178	*Robert Jones*	.20
179	*Marc Boutte*	.10
180	*Marco Coleman*	.30
181	*Chris Mims*	.50
182	Tony Casillas	.10
183	*Shane Dronett*	.20
184	*Sean Gilbert*	.40
185	*Siran Stacy*	.10
186	*Tommy Maddox*	.20
187	Steve Israel	.10
188	Brad Muster	.10
189	*Shane Collins*	.20
190	*Terrell Buckley*	.25
191	*Eugene Chung*	.10
192	*Leon Searcy*	.20
193	*Chuck Smith*	.10
194	*Patrick Rowe*	.20
195	*Bill Johnson*	.10
196	*Gerald Dixon*	.20
197	*Robert Porcher*	.25
198	*Tracy Scroggins*	.40
199	*Jason Hanson*	.30
200	*Corey Harris*	.20
201	*Eddie Robinson*	.20
202	*Steve Emtman*	.30
203	*Ashley Ambrose*	.20
204	*Greg Skrepenak*	.20
205	*Todd Collins*	.20
206	*Derek Brown*	.25
207	*Kurt Barber*	.20
208	*Tony Sacca*	.20
209	*Mark Wheeler*	.20
210	*Kevin Smith*	.30
211	*John Fina*	.10
212	*Johnny Mitchell*	.50
213	*Dale Carter*	.30
214	*Bobby Spitulski*	.10
215	*Phillippi Sparks*	.10
216	*Levon Kirkland*	.10
217	Mike Sherrard	.10
218	*Marquez Pope*	.10
219	*Courtney Hawkins*	.30
220	*Tyji Armstrong*	.20
221	Keith Jackson	.20
222	*Clayton Holmes*	.10
223	*Quentin Coryatt*	.30
224	*Troy Auzenne*	.10
225	*David Klingler*	.25
226	*Darryl Williams*	.25
227	*Carl Pickens*	1.50
228	*Jimmy Smith*	3.50
229	*Chester McGlockton*	.50
230	*Robert Brooks*	2.00
231	*Alonzo Spellman*	.50
232	*Darren Woodson*	.30
233	Lewis Billups	.10
234	*Edgar Bennett*	.75
235	*Vaughn Dunbar*	.20
236	*Steve Bono*	1.00
237	Clarence Kay	.10
238	Chris Hinton	.10
239	Jimmie Jones	.10
240	Vai Sikahema	.10
241	Russell Maryland	.10
242	Neal Anderson	.10
243	Charles Mann	.10
244	Hugh Millen	.10
245	Roger Craig	.10
246	Rich Gannon	.10
247	Ricky Ervins	.10
248	Leonard Marshall	.10
249	Eric Dickerson	.20
250	Joe Montana	3.00

1992 Collector's Edge Special

Produced to promote Tuff Stuff's Buyer's Club, one of the four cards was inserted in all copies of the November 1992 magazine. Over 250,000 cards were issued of the first card. The other three cards were printed in quantities of approximately 40,000 each. One of each of the three cards were given as a bonus with each paid membership. The Elway card was also printed as "Proto 1," "John Elway Dealerships" and "Elway Foundation." Reportedly, less than 50,000 of these cards were issued. The card fronts have a dark blue border, with a color photo, the player's name and position in the lower left and his team's helmet in the lower right. The card backs are numbered with a "TS" prefix for the Buyer's Club. "Proto 1" is numbered as such, while the Elway Foundation and Elway Dealerships are not numbered. The card backs have a headshot, player's name, bio, position and stats. The card number is in the upper right.

	MT
Complete Set (4):	12.00
Common Player:	2.00

1	John Elway	2.00
2	Ronnie Lott	5.00
3	Jim Everett	3.00
4	Bernie Kosar	3.00
PROT1	John Elway	10.00
NNO	Elway Foundation	30.00
NNO	Elway Dealerships	25.00

1993 Collector's Edge Prototype

These cards, which promote the 1993 Collector's Edge set, are numbered from 1 to 40,000 on the backs. Each card front has a blue marble-like border and an action photo. The back uses a green marble-like border and also indicates that the card is a "Proto." In addition to these cards, there were 8-1/2" x 11" versions of these cards made, too. They, however, are not numbered and were included in dealer cases. They are generally two to four times more valuable than the smaller versions.

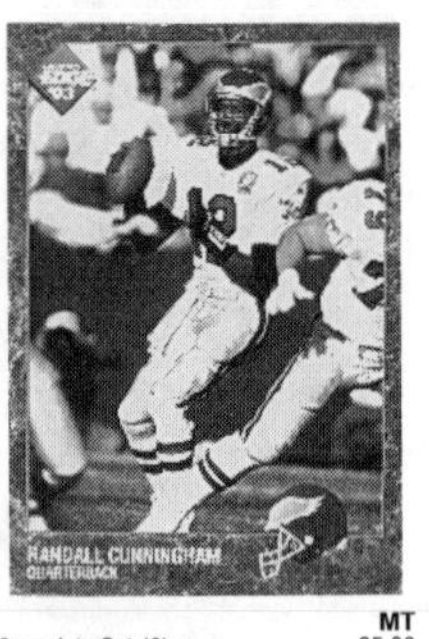

	MT
Complete Set (6):	25.00
Common Player:	4.00

1	John Elway	7.00
2	Derrick Thomas	4.00
3	Randall Cunningham	4.00
4	Thurman Thomas	6.00
5	Warren Moon	5.00
6	Barry Sanders	8.00

1993 Collector's Edge RU Prototypes

Blue-marble borders highlight the front of this five-card Rookie/Update set. The Edge logo is in the upper left, with his name and position in the lower left. The player's helmet is printed in the lower right. The card backs have the player's headshot on the upper left, with his team's logo, name, team, position, jersey number and card number, prefixed with "RU." The card's serial number is printed in the center above the player's bio and stats.

	MT
Complete Set (5):	6.00
Common Player:	1.00

1	Garrison Hearst	1.50
2	Reggie White	2.00
3	Boomer Esiason	1.00
4	Rod Bernstine	1.00
5	Dana Stubblefield	1.50

1993 Collector's Edge

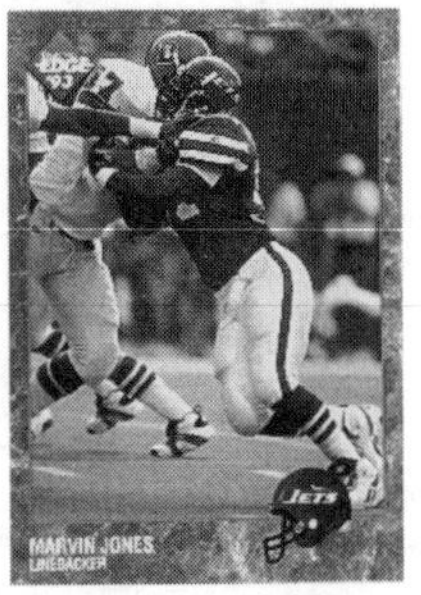

The second set from Collector's Edge uses the same features features as its first set in 1992 - the cards are plastic and are each individually numbered from 1-100,000. The fronts have an action photo with against a blue marble background. A team helmet is at the bottom of the card, while the Collector's Edge logo is at the top. The backs have statistics, a career summary and a mug shot. Rookie/Update cards are numbered from #251-325. Ten John Elway prism inserts were randomly included in packs; E1-E5 were in late packs, while S1-S5 were in early packs. Twenty-five Collector's Edge Rookies FX cards were randomly inserted in Rookie/Update packs and are numbered with an "FX" prefix. Five Collector's Edge checklists were also made and were randomly inserted in regular packs. Six promo cards were also made featuring Elway, Derrick Thomas, Randall Cunningham, Thurman Thomas, Warren Moon and Barry Sanders. There were 40,000 cards produced for each player.

	MT
Complete Set (325):	20.00
Complete Series 1 (250):	10.00
Complete Series 2 (75):	10.00
Common Player:	.05
Minor Stars:	.10
Comp. Checklists (5):	2.00
John Elway Auto.	75.00
Series 1 Pack (6):	.75
Series 1 Wax Box (24):	13.00
Rookie/Up. Pack (6):	.90
Rookie/Up. Wax Box (24):	16.00

1	Atlanta Team	.05
2	Michael Haynes	.05
3	Chris Miller	.05
4	Mike Pritchard	.05
5	Andre Rison	.10

6	Deion Sanders	.50
7	Chuck Smith	.05
8	Drew Hill	.05
9	Bobby Hebert	.05
10	Buffalo Team	.05
11	Matt Darby	.05
12	John Fina	.05
13	Jim Kelly	.15
14	*Marvcus Patton*	.10
15	Andre Reed	.10
16	Thurman Thomas	.15
17	James Lofton	.05
18	Bruce Smith	.05
19	Chicago Team	.05
20	Neal Anderson	.05
21	Troy Auzenne	.05
22	Jim Harbaugh	.05
23	Alonzo Spellman	.05
24	Tom Waddle	.05
25	Darren Lewis	.05
26	Wendell Davis	.05
27	Will Furrer	.05
28	Cincinnati Team	.05
29	David Klingler	.15
30	Ricardo McDonald	.05
31	Carl Pickens	.40
32	Harold Green	.05
33	Anthony Munoz	.05
34	Darryl Williams	.05
35	Cleveland Team	.05
36	Michael Jackson	.05
37	Pio Sagapolutele	.05
38	Tommy Vardell	.05
39	Bernie Kosar	.05
40	Michael Dean Perry	.05
41	Bill Johnson	.05
42	Vinny Testaverde	.05
43	Dallas team	.05
44	Troy Aikman	.75
45	Alvin Harper	.20
46	Michael Irvin	.10
47	Russell Maryland	.05
48	Emmitt Smith	2.00
49	Kenneth Gant	.05
50	Jay Novacek	.05
51	Robert Jones	.05
52	Clayton Holomes	.05
53	Denver Team	.05
54	Mike Croel	.05
55	Shane Dronett	.05
56	Kenny Walker	.05
57	Tommy Maddox	.05
58	Dennis Smith	.05
59	John Elway	.40
60	Karl Mecklenberg	.05
61	Steve Atwater	.05
62	Vance Johnson	.05
63	Detroit team	.05
64	Barry Sanders	1.25
65	Andre Ware	.05
66	Pat Swilling	.05
67	Jason Hanson	.05
68	Willie Green	.05
69	Herman Moore	.50
70	Rodney Peete	.05
71	Erik Kramer	.10
72	Robert Porcher	.05
73	Green Bay team	.05
74	Terrell Buckley	.10
75	Reggie White	.10
76	Brett Favre	2.00
77	Don Majkowski	.05
78	Edgar Bennett	.10
79	Ty Detmer	.05
80	Sanjay Beach	.05
81	Sterling Sharpe	.10
82	Houston team	.05
83	Gary Brown	.10
84	Ernest Givins	.05
85	Haywood Jeffires	.05
86	Corey Harris	.05
87	Warren Moon	.15
88	Eddie Robinson	.05
89	Lorenzo White	.05
90	Bo Orlando	.05
91	Indianapolis team	.05
92	Quentin Coryatt	.05
93	Steve Emtman	.05
94	Jeff George	.10
95	Jessie Hester	.05
96	Rohn Stark	.05
97	Ashley Ambrose	.05
98	John Baylor	.05
99	Kansas City team	.05
100	Tim Barnett	.05
101	Derrick Thomas	.10
102	Barry Word	.05
103	Dale Carter	.05
104	Jayice Pearson	.05
105	Tracy Simien	.05
106	Harvey Williams	.15
107	Dave Krieg	.05
108	Christian Okoye	.05
109	Joe Montana	1.00
110	Miami team	.05
111	J.B. Brown	.05
112	Marco Coleman	.05
113	Dan Marino	2.00
114	Mark Clayton	.05
115	Mark Higgs	.05
116	Bryan Cox	.05
117	Chuck Klingbeil	.05
118	Troy Vincent	.10
119	Keith Jackson	.10
120	Bruce Alexander	.05
121	Minnesota team	.05
122	Terry Allen	.10
123	Rich Gannon	.05
124	Todd Scott	.05
125	Cris Carter	.10
126	Sean Salisbury	.05
127	Jack Del Rio	.05
128	Chris Doleman	.05
129	Anthony Carter	.05
130	New England team	.05
131	Eugene Chung	.05
132	Todd Collins	.05
133	Tom Hodson	.05
134	Leonard Russell	.05
135	Jon Vaughn	.05
136	Andre Tippet	.05
137	New Orleans team	.05
138	Wesley Carroll	.05
139	Richard Cooper	.05
140	Vaughn Dunbar	.05
141	Fred McAfee	.05
142	Torrance Small	.05
143	Steve Walsh	.05
144	Vaughan Johnson	.05
145	New York Giants team	.05
146	Jarrod Bunch	.05
147	Phil Simms	.05
148	Carl Banks	.05
149	Lawrence Taylor	.10
150	Rodney Hampton	.10
151	Phillippi Sparks	.05
152	Derek Brown	.05
153	New York Jets team	.05
154	Boomer Esiason	.05
155	Johnny Mitchell	.05
156	Rob Moore	.05
157	Ronnie Lott	.05
158	Browning Nagle	.05
159	Johnny Johnson	.05
160	Dwayne White	.05
161	Blair Thomas	.05
162	Philadelphia team	.05
163	Randall Cunningham	.10
164	Fred Barnett	.05
165	Siran Stacy	.05
166	Keith Byars	.05
167	Calvin Williams	.05
168	Jeff Sydner	.05
169	Tommy Jeter	.05
170	Andre Waters	.05
171	Phoenix team	.05
172	Steve Beuerlein	.10
173	Randal Hill	.05
174	Timm Rosenbach	.05
175	Ed Cunningham	.05
176	Walter Reeves	.05
177	Michael Zordich	.05
178	Gary Clark	.05
179	Ken Harvey	.05
180	Pittsburgh team	.05
181	Barry Foster	.10
182	Neil O'Donnell	.15
183	Leon Searcy	.05
184	Bubby Brister	.05
185	Merril Hoge	.05
186	Joel Steed	.05
187	Los Angeles Raiders team	.05
188	Nick Bell	.05
189	Eric Dickerson	.05
190	Nolan Harrison	.05
191	Todd Marinovich	.05
192	Greg Skrepenak	.05
193	Howie Long	.05
194	Jay Schroeder	.05
195	Chester McGlockton	.05
196	Los Angeles Rams team	.05
197	Jim Everett	.05
198	Sean Gilbert	.05
199	Steve Israel	.05
200	Marc Boutte	.05
201	Joe Milinichik	.05
202	Henry Ellard	.05
203	Jackie Slater	.05
204	San Diego team	.05
205	Eric Bieniemy	.05
206	Marion Butts	.05
207	Nate Lewis	.05
208	Junior Seau	.15
209	Steve Hendrickson	.05
210	Chris Mims	.05
211	Harry Swayne	.05
212	Marquez Pope	.05
213	Donald Frank	.05
214	Anthony Miller	.05
215	Seattle team	.05
216	Cortez Kennedy	.10
217	Dan McGwire	.05
218	Kelly Stouffer	.05
219	Chris Warren	.20
220	Brian Blades	.05
221	Rod Stephens	.05
222	San Francisco team	.05
223	Jerry Rice	1.00
224	Ricky Watters	.20
225	Steve Young	1.00
226	Tom Rathman	.05
227	Dana Hall	.05
228	Amp Lee	.10
229	Brian Bollinger	.05
230	Keith DeLong	.05
231	John Taylor	.05
232	Tampa Bay Team	.05
233	Tyji Armstrong	.05
234	Lawrence Dawsey	.05
235	Mark Wheeler	.05
236	Vince Workman	.05
237	Reggie Cobb	.05
238	Tony Mayberry	.05
239	Marty Carter	.05
240	Courtney Hawkins	.05
241	Ray Seals	.05
242	Mark Carrier	.05
243	Washington Team	.05
244	Mark Rypien	.05
245	Ricky Ervins	.05
246	Gerald Riggs	.05
247	Art Monk	.10
248	Mark Schlereth	.05
249	Monte Coleman	.05
250	Wilber Marshall	.05
251	*Ben Coleman*	.05
252	*Curtis Conway*	1.25
253	*Ernest Dye*	.05
254	*Todd Kelly*	.05
255	*Patrick Bates*	.10
256	*George Teague*	.10
257	*Mark Brunell*	3.00
258	*Adrian Hardy*	.05
259	*Dana Stubblefield*	.50
260	*William Roaf*	.10
261	*Irv Smith*	.10
262	*Drew Bledsoe*	3.00
263	*Dan Williams*	.10
264	Jerry Ball	.05
265	Mark Clayton	.05
266	John Stephens	.05
267	Reggie White	.10
268	Jeff Hostetler	.10
269	Boomer Esiason	.05
270	Wade Wilson	.05
271	Steve Beuerlein	.05
272	Tim McDonald	.05
273	Craig Heyward	.05
274	Everson Walls	.05
275	Stan Humphries	.10
276	Carl Banks	.05
277	Brad Muster	.05
278	Tim Harris	.05
279	Gary Clark	.05
280	Joe Milinichik	.05
281	Leonard Marshall	.05
282	Joe Montana	1.00
283	Rod Bernstine	.05
284	Mark Carrier	.05
285	Michael Brooks	.05
286	*Marvin Jones*	.10
287	*John Copeland*	.20
288	*Eric Curry*	.10
289	*Steve Everitt*	.10
290	*Tom Carter*	.10
291	*Deon Figures*	.15
292	*Leonard Renfro*	.10
293	*Thomas Smith*	.10
294	*Carlton Gray*	.10
295	*Demetrius DeBose*	.10
296	*Coleman Rudolph*	.05
297	*John Parrella*	.05
298	*Glyn Milburn*	.30
299	*Reggie Brooks*	.20
300	*Garrison Hearst*	1.00
301	John Elway	.40
302	*Brad Hopkins*	.05
303	*Darrien Gordon*	.20
304	*Robert Smith*	.60
305	*Chris Slade*	.25
306	*Ryan McNeil*	.10
307	*Michael Barrow*	.10
308	*Roosevelt Potts*	.10
309	*Qadry Ismail*	.50
310	*Reggie Freeman*	.05
311	*Vincent Brisby*	.30
312	*Rick Mirer*	.30
313	*Billy Joe Hobert*	.25
314	*Natrone Means*	1.00
315	Gary Zimmerman	.05
316	Bobby Hebert	.05
317	Don Beebe	.05
318	Wilber Marshall	.05
319	Marcus Allen	.10
320	Ronnie Lott	.05
321	Ricky Sanders	.05
322	Charles Mann	.05
323	Simon Fletcher	.05
324	Johnny Johnson	.05
325	Gary Plummer	.05
326	Carolina Panthers	30.00

1993 Collector's Edge Elway Prisms

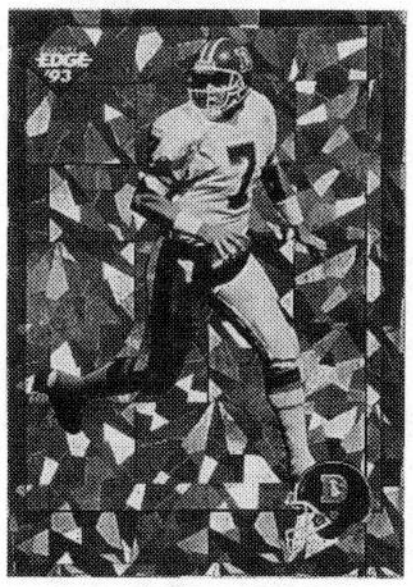

This five-card chase set was randomly seeded in 1993 Collector's Edge packs. The cards are bordered with blue prism foil. The photo of Elway is placed over a silver prism background. The Edge logo is in the upper left, while the Broncos' helmet is in the lower right. The card backs have an action shot at the top, with the card's serial number underneath it. Elway's highlights are printed inside a box in the center of the card. The cards are numbered with an "E" prefix. Two versions of each card were produced. Those cards with the "S" prefix were inserted in early packs, and tougher to locate. The "E" prefix cards were inserted in later runs. The backgrounds are different on the different versions of cards. Five "S" prefix cards were included with each box of All-Star Collection Manager software from Taurus Technologies. Approximately 500 sets were produced for this offer. Elway's best two-minute marches are featured in this Two-Minute Warning set.

		MT
Complete Set (5):		5.00
Common Player:		1.00
E1	John Elway (Both arms outstretched)	1.00
E2	John Elway (Passing, orange jersey)	1.00
E3	John Elway (Running, orange jersey)	1.00
E4	John Elway (Passing, white jersey)	1.00
E5	John Elway (Running, white jersey)	1.00
S1	John Elway (Both arms outstretched)	3.00
S2	John Elway (Passing, orange jersey)	3.00
S3	John Elway (Running, orange jersey)	3.00
S4	John Elway (Passing, white jersey)	3.00
S5	John Elway (Running, white jersey)	3.00
PRO1	John Elway (AU/3000)	80.00

1993 Collector's Edge Rookies FX

These inserts, randomly available in 1993 Collector's Edge Rookie Update foil packs, feature top rookies. Each card is clear plastic and features a color action photo within a maroon border. A team helmet, in the lower right corner, and player's name, in white letters in the upper right, are also given on the card front. A card number, using an "F/X" prefix, is also on the front. The card back is clear; the reverse image from the front photo can be seen. Cards with gold backgrounds also exist; they are generally about 10 to 20 times more valuable than the regular inserts.

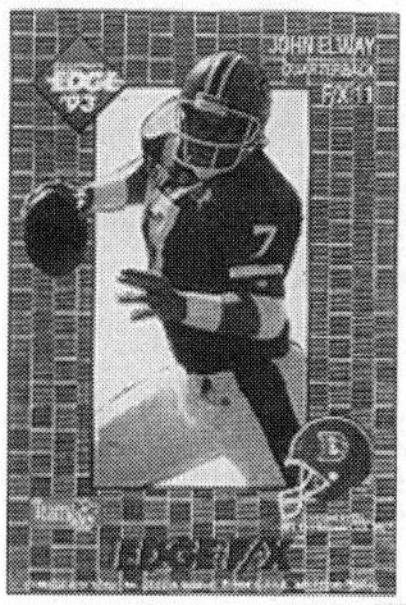

		MT
Complete Set (25):		15.00
Common Player:		.25
Minor Stars:		.50
Comp. Gold Set (25):		150.00
Gold Stars:		5x-10x
1	Garrison Hearst	2.00
2	Glyn Milburn	.50
3	Demetrius Debose	.25
4	Joe Montana	3.00
5	Thomas Smith	.25
6	Mark Clayton	.25
7	Curtis Conway	1.00
8	Drew Bledsoe	3.00
9	Todd Kelly	.25
10	Stan Humphries	.75
11	John Elway	1.50
12	Troy Aikman	3.00
13	Marion Butts	.25
14	Alvin Harper	.50
15	Drew Hill	.25
16	Michael Irvin	1.00
17	Warren Moon	.50
18	Andre Reed	.25
19	Andre Rison	.50
20	Emmitt Smith	4.00
21	Thurman Thomas	.75
22	Ricky Watters	.75
23	Calvin Williams	.25
24	Steve Young	1.50
25	Howie Long	.25

1994 Collector's Edge Boss Rookies Update Promos

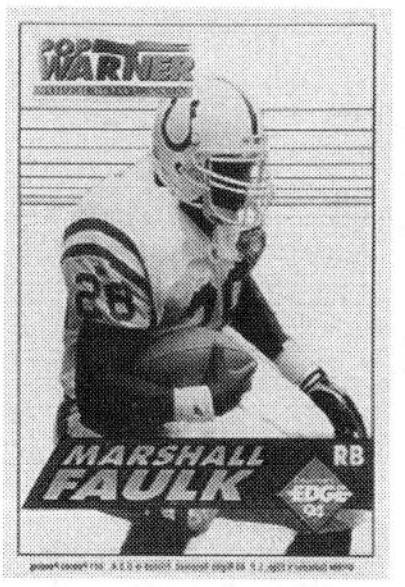

Printed on green plastic stock, the six-card set promoted the upcoming series. The cards have a photo of the player superimposed over the clear background. The player's name, position and Edge logo are included inside a stripe near the bottom of the card. The card number is located on the upper right of the card front. The cards are prefixed with either a "P" or "SHR." The card backs have the player's bio inside the stripe, along with the various logos.

		MT
Complete Set (6):		12.00
Common Player:		.50
1	Trent Dilfer	1.00
2	Marshall Faulk	4.00
3	Heath Shuler	3.00
4	Errict Rhett	3.00
5	Johnnie Morton	1.00
6	Charlie Garner	.50

1994 Collector's Edge

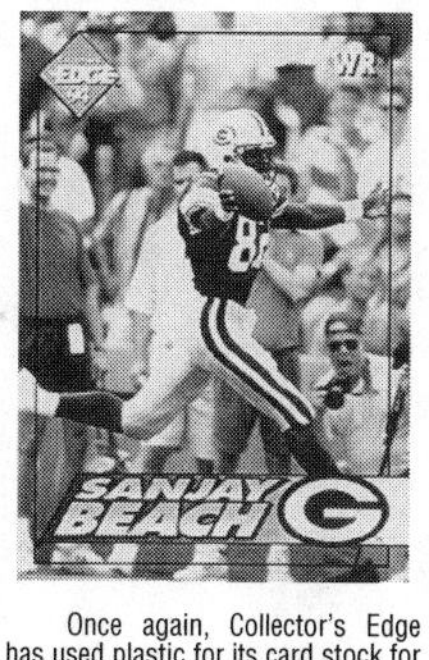

Once again, Collector's Edge has used plastic for its card stock for this 200-card set. Each card front has a full-color action shot, framed by a thin black border. The set logo appears in the upper right corner. The player's name and a team logo appear in a panel at the bottom of the card. Each card back has a player mug shot and statistics at the top of the page, with a stadium shot underneath. A serial number and card number are also on the back. A parallel 1st Day Production set was also created; these cards have a gold-foil stamp for the logo. Insert cards were Boss Squad, F/X player and F/X gold checklist cards, and Boss Rookies.

		MT
Complete Set (200):		17.00
Common Player:		.10
Gold Set (200):		35.00
Gold Cards:		2x
Retail Pack (6):		1.50
Retail Wax Box (24):		30.00
Silver/Pop Warner Pack (6):		1.75
Silver/Pop Warner Wax Box (36):		50.00
Gold Pack (7):		2.50
Gold Wax Box (36):		70.00
1	Mike Pritchard	.12
2	Erric Pegram	.10
3	Michael Haynes	.12
4	Bobby Hebert	.10
5	Deion Sanders	.75
6	Andre Rison	.20
7	Don Beebe	.10
8	Mark Kelso	.10
9	Darryl Talley	.10
10	Cornelius Bennett	.10
11	Jim Kelly	.40
12	Andre Reed	.15
13	Bruce Smith	.10
14	Thurman Thomas	.50
15	Craig Heyward	.10
16	Chris Zorich	.10
17	Alonzo Spellman	.10
18	Tom Waddle	.10
19	Neal Anderson	.10
20	Kevin Butler	.10
21	Curtis Conway	.30
22	Richard Dent	.10
23	Jim Harbaugh	.10
24	Derrick Fenner	.10
25	Harold Green	.10
26	David Klingler	.10
27	Daniel Stubbs	.10
28	Alfred Williams	.10
29	John Copeland	.10
30	Mark Carrier	.10
31	Michael Jackson	.10
32	Eric Metcalf	.10
33	Vinny Testaverde	.10
34	Tommy Vardell	.10
35	Alvin Harper	.12
36	Ken Norton	.10
37	Tony Casillas	.10
38	Leon Lett	.10
39	Jay Novacek	.10
40	Kevin Smith	.10
41	Troy Aikman	1.00
42	Michael Irvin	.50
43	Russell Maryland	.10
44	Emmitt Smith	2.00
45	Robert Delpino	.10
46	Simon Fletcher	.10
47	Greg Kragen	.10
48	Arthur Marshall	.10
49	Steve Atwater	.10
50	Rod Bernstine	.10
51	John Elway	1.00
52	Glyn Milburn	.20
53	Shannon Sharpe	.10
54	Bennie Blades	.10
55	Mel Gray	.10
56	Herman Moore	.15
57	Pat Swilling	.10
58	Chris Spielman	.10
59	Rodney Peete	.10
60	Andre Ware	.10
61	Brett Perriman	.10
62	Erik Kramer	.10
63	Barry Sanders	1.25
64	Mark Clayton	.10
65	Chris Jacke	.10
66	Terrell Buckley	.10
67	Ty Detmer	.10
68	Sanjay Beach	.10
69	Brian Noble	.10
70	Edgar Bennett	.10
71	Brett Favre	2.00
72	Sterling Sharpe	.55
73	Reggie White	.12
74	Ernest Givins	.10
75	Al Del Greco	.10
76	Chris Dishman	.10
77	Curtis Duncan	.10
78	Webster Slaughter	.10
79	Spencer Tillman	.10
80	Warren Moon	.10
81	Wilber Marshall	.10
82	Haywood Jeffires	.10
83	Lorenzo White	.10
84	Gary Brown	.10
85	Reggie Langhorne	.10
86	Dean Biasucci	.10
87	Steve Emtman	.10
88	Jessie Hester	.10
89	Quentin Coryatt	.10
90	Roosevelt Potts	.10
91	Jeff George	.10
92	Nick Lowery	.10
93	Willie Davis	.10
94	Joe Montana	1.00
95	Neil Smith	.10
96	Marcus Allen	.15
97	Derrick Thomas	.12
98	Greg Townsend	.10
99	Willie Gault	.10
100	Ethan Horton	.10
101	Jeff Hostetler	.10
102	Tim Brown	.12
103	Raghib Ismail	.25
104	Shane Conlan	.10
105	Henry Ellard	.10
106	T.J. Rubley	.15
107	Sean Gilbert	.10
108	Troy Drayton	.20
109	Jerome Bettis	.50
110	Terry Kirby	.15
111	Mark Ingram	.10
112	John Offerdahl	.10
113	Louis Oliver	.10
114	Irving Fryar	.10
115	Dan Marino	2.00
116	Keith Jackson	.10
117	O.J. McDuffie	.40
118	Jim McMahon	.10
119	Sean Salisbury	.10
120	Randell McDaniel	.10
121	Jack Del Rio	.10
122	Cris Carter	.10
123	Chris Doleman	.10
124	John Randle	.10
125	Vincent Brisby	.20
126	Greg McMurtry	.10
127	Drew Bledsoe	1.00
128	Leonard Russell	.10
129	Michael Brooks	.10
130	Mark Jackson	.10
131	Pepper Johnson	.10
132	Doug Riesenberg	.10
133	Phil Simms	.10
134	Rodney Hampton	.35
135	Leonard Marshall	.10
136	Rob Moore	.10
137	Chris Burkett	.10
138	Boomer Esiason	.10
139	Johnny Johnson	.10
140	Ronnie Lott	.10
141	Brad Muster	.10
142	Renaldo Turnbull	.10
143	William Roaf	.20
144	Ricky Jackson	.10
145	Morton Anderson	.10
146	Vaughn Dunbar	.10
147	Wade Wilson	.10
148	Eric Martin	.10
149	Seth Joyner	.10
150	Calvin Williams	.10
151	Vai Sikahema	.10
152	Herschel Walker	.10
153	Eric Allen	.10
154	Fred Barnett	.10
155	Randall Cunningham	.25
156	Steve Beurlein	.10
157	Gary Clark	.10
158	Anthony Edwards	.10
159	Randall Hill	.10
160	Freddie Joe Nunn	.10
161	Garrison Hearst	.50
162	Ricky Proehl	.10
163	Eric Green	.10
164	Levon Kirkland	.10
165	Joel Steed	.10
166	Deon Figures	.15
167	Leroy Thompson	.10
168	Barry Foster	.35
169	Neil O'Donnell	.10
170	Junior Seau	.10
171	Leslie O'Neil	.10
172	Stan Humphries	.10
173	Marion Butts	.10
174	Anthony Miller	.10
175	Natrone Means	.50
176	Odessa Turner	.10
177	Dana Stubblefield	.25
178	John Taylor	.10
179	Ricky Watters	.15
180	Steve Young	1.00
181	Jerry Rice	1.00
182	Tom Rathman	.10
183	Brian Blades	.10
184	Patrick Hunter	.10
185	Rick Mirer	.20
186	Chris Warren	.12
187	Cortez Kennedy	.12
188	Reggie Cobb	.10
189	Craig Erickson	.10
190	Hardy Nickerson	.10
191	Lawrence Dawsey	.10
192	Broderick Thomas	.10
193	Ricky Sanders	.10
194	Carl Banks	.10
195	Ricky Ervins	.10
196	Darrel Green	.10
197	Mark Rypien	.10
198	Desmond Howard	.15
199	Art Monk	.10
200	Reggie Brooks	.10

1994 Collector's Edge Silver

Randomly inserted into packs, this 200-card set was a parallel to the 1994 Edge base set. The card fronts have a silver-foil stamp on the front. The card backs resemble the base card backs.

	MT
Complete Set (200):	25.00
Common Player:	.10
Silver Cards:	1x

1994 Collector's Edge Gold

A parallel of the regular Collector's Edge set, the 200-card set features a gold-foil "First Day" logo on the front of the card. The backs resemble the base card backs.

	MT
Complete Set (200):	45.00
Common Player:	.15
Gold Cards:	2x

A player's name in *italic type* indicates a rookie card.

1994 Collector's Edge Pop Warner

This 200-card set was produced as a fund-raiser for Pop Warner football teams. The cards were available from participating dealers and Pop Warner players. Edge printed 1,000 cases of the product. An updated 25-card Boss Rookie chase set, printed on Edge-Glo card stock, was randomly seeded.

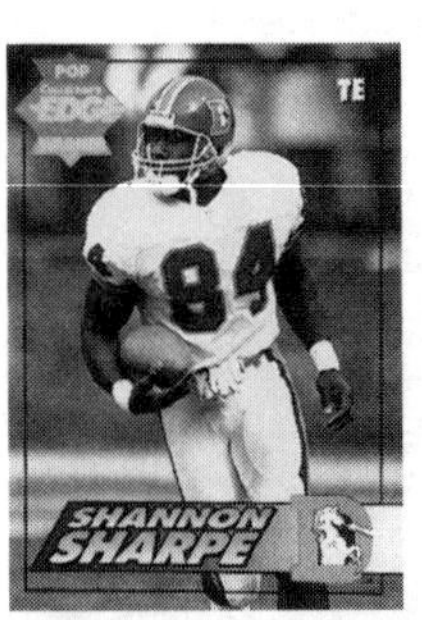

		MT
Complete Set (200):		25.00
Common Player:		.10
Pop Warner Cards:		1x

1994 Collector's Edge Pop Warner 22K Gold

The 200-card set was a parallel to the Edge Pop Warner base cards. The cards showcase the Pop Warner logo and a gold-foil helmet (with 22K printed under the helmet) on the card fronts.

		MT
Complete Set (200):		100.00
Common Player:		.40
Pop Warner 22K Cards:		2x-4x

1994 Collector's Edge Boss Rookies

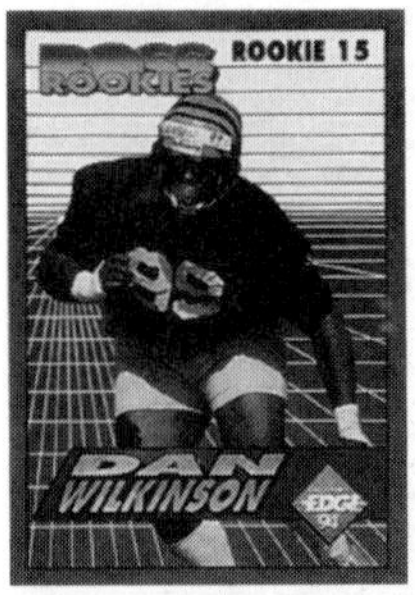

Top rookies are featured on these insert cards, which were randomly included in 1994 Collector's Edge packs. The cards are similar to the format used by the Boss Squad insert cards; "Boss Rookies" is written in the upper left corner and the card number, Rookie 1, etc., is in the upper right corner. The player's name, position and Collector's Edge logo are at the bottom of the card. The back of the card shows a reverse image of the photo on the front.

		MT
Complete Set (19):		15.00
Common Player:		.25
Minor Stars:		.50
Inserted 1:2		
1	Isaac Bruce	1.75
2	Jeff Burris	.25
3	Shante Carver	.25
4	Lake Dawson	.50
5	Bert Emanuel	.75
6	William Floyd	.75
7	Wayne Gandy	.25
8	Aaron Glenn	.25
9	Chris Maumalanga	.25
10	David Palmer	.50
11	Errict Rhett	.75
12	Heath Shuler	.75
13	DeWayne Washington	.25
14	Bryant Young	.50
15	Dan Wilkinson	.25
16	Rob Frederickson	.25
17	Calvin Jones	.25
18	James Folston	.25
19	Marshall Faulk	4.00

1994 Collector's Edge Boss Rookies Update

Randomly seeded in 1994 Pop Warner packs, this 25-card set was printed on Edge-Glo green plastic. The card fronts feature a purple Pop Warner logo in the upper left corner.

		MT
Complete Set (25):		30.00
Common Player:		.75
Minor Stars:		1.50
Diamond Cards:		2x
Green Cards:		1x
Inserted 1:3 Pop Warner		
1	Trent Dilfer	4.00
2	Jeff Burris	.75
3	Shante Carver	.75
4	Lake Dawson	1.50
5	Bert Emanuel	1.50
6	Marshall Faulk	7.00
7	William Floyd	1.50
8	Charlie Garner	1.50
9	Rob Fredrickson	.75
10	Wayne Gandy	.75
11	Aaron Glenn	.75
12	Greg Hill	1.50
13	Isaac Bruce	3.00
14	Charles Johnson	1.50
15	Johnnie Morton	1.50
16	Calvin Jones	.75
17	Tim Bowens	.75
18	David Palmer	1.50
19	Errict Rhett	1.50
20	Darnay Scott	2.50
21	Heath Shuler	1.50
22	John Thierry	.75
23	Bernard Williams	.75
24	Dan Wilkinson	.75
25	Bryant Young	1.50
NNO	Diamond Exch. Expired	1.50

1994 Collector's Edge Boss Squad Promos

Previewing the 1994 Edge Boss Squad insert, this six-card transparent plastic promo set showcases a cutout photo of a player over a background of lines which make a 3-D effect. The player's name, position and Edge logo are printed inside a stripe near the bottom of the front of the card. The card number is printed on the top right of the card front, prefixed by "Boss." The set was released on two uncut sheets.

		MT
Complete Set (6):		10.00
Common Player:		1.00
1	Marshall Faulk	4.00
2	Jerome Bettis	2.50
3	Erric Pegram	1.25
4	Sterling Sharpe	1.25
5	Shannon Sharpe	1.25
6	Leonard Russell	1.00

1994 Collector's Edge Boss Squad

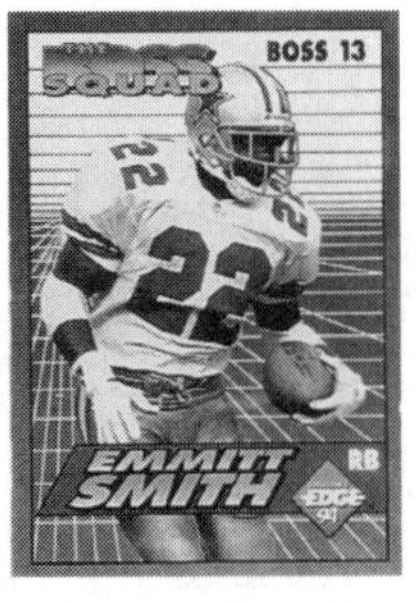

This transparent set features eight top quarterbacks, running backs and receivers for this insert set titled Boss Squad. If the player on the card finished the 1994 season in first or second place in statistics for that position, the card could be redeemed for prizes. Receptions were used for receivers, rushing yards were used for running backs, and quarterback ratings were used for quarterbacks. Cards are numbered with a "Boss" prefix. The card back shows a reversed image of the photo on the front.

		MT
Complete Set (24):		20.00
Common Player:		.50
Minor Stars:		1.00
Inserted 1:2		
Silver Cards:		1x
Inserted 1:2 Pop Warner		
Bronze EQII Cards:		1x
Gold Helmet Cards:		1x
1	John Elway	2.50
2	Joe Montana	2.50
3	Vinny Testaverde	1.00
4	Boomer Esiason	.50
5	Steve Young	1.50
6	Troy Aikman	2.00
7	Phil Simms	.50
8	Bobby Hebert	.50
9	Thurman Thomas	1.00
10	Leonard Russell	.50
11	Chris Warren	1.00
12	Gary Brown	.50
13	Emmitt Smith	3.00
14	Jerome Bettis	1.00
15	Erric Pegram	.50
16	Barry Sanders	4.00
17	Reggie Langhorne	.50
18	Anthony Miller	.50
19	Shannon Sharpe	1.00
20	Tim Brown	1.00
21	Sterling Sharpe	1.00
22	Jerry Rice	2.00
23	Michael Irvin	1.00
24	Andre Rison	1.00

1994 Collector's Edge EdgeQuest

Randomly seeded in packs and offered as a dealer promotion, the nine-card set showcased a letter on the front, with EdgeQuest II printed inside a bar near the bottom of the card. The "Q" card was released in smaller numbers in packs. The cards were redeemable for prizes. Card backs include the rules of the contest. The identical cards with a clear background were inserted into Pop Warner packs.

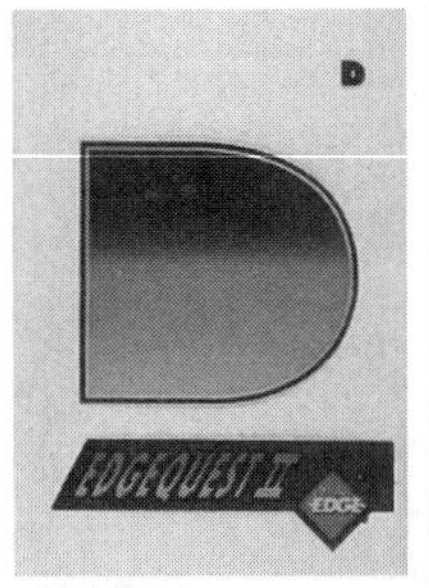

		MT
Complete Set (10):		4.00
Comm. Pack Insert (A/B/D/U):		.40
Comm. Box Insert (E/G/O/S):		.40
Clear Cards: 1x		
A	Letter A	.40
B	Letter B	.40
D	Letter D	.40
E	Letter E	.40
G	Letter G	.40
O	Letter O	.40
Q	Letter Q (SP, Expired)	1.00
S	Letter S	.40
U	Letter U	.40
WC	Clear Star Wild Card	1.00

1994 Collector's Edge FX

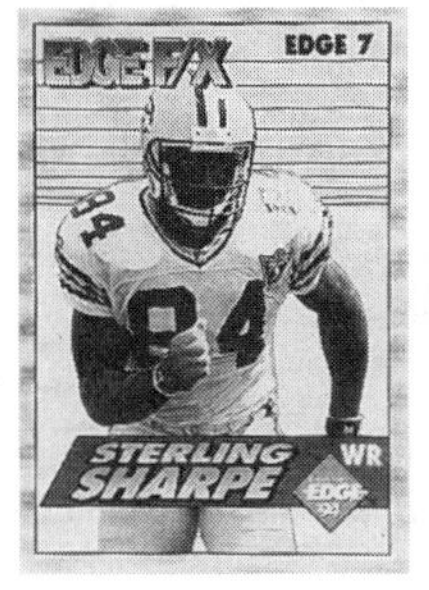

Two versions of these insert cards were made - a regular F/X card and a gold version. Seven top players are featured on these cards, which were random inserts.

		MT
Complete Set (7):		20.00
Common Player:		.75
Minor Stars:		1.50
Inserted 1:7 Gold		
Gold Shield Cards:		2x
Inserted 1:200 Gold		
White Back Cards:		1x
Inserted 1:7 Retail		
Silver Shield Cards:		5x
Inserted 1:200 Retail		
Silver Back Cards:		.5x
Inserted 1:7 Silver		
Gold Back Cards:		3x
Inserted 1:200 Silver		
Silver Letter Cards:		1x
Inserted 1:7 Pop Warner		
Gold Letter Cards:		2x
Inserted 1:200 Pop Warner		
Red Letter Cards:		1x
1	John Elway	5.00
2	Joe Montana	5.00
3	Troy Aikman	4.00
4	Emmitt Smith	6.00
5	Jerome Bettis	1.50
6	Anthony Miller	.75
7	Sterling Sharpe	1.50

1994 Collector's Edge Excalibur Elway Promos

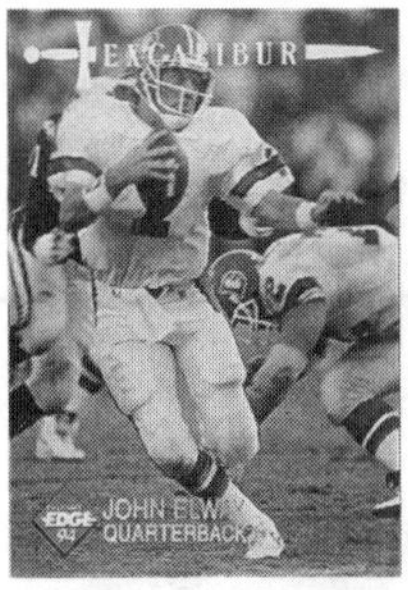

This three-card set previewed the 1994 Excalibur set. Each of the cards featured John Elway. The Excalibur logo is printed in silver foil at the top, with his name and position printed in silver foil at the bottom to the right of the Edge logo. The backs have his headshot inside a shield design on the left, which also includes his position and jersey number. The shield in the right corner has his name, the Broncos' logo and card number "of 3" prefixed by "SL." A quote about Elway from Dick Butkus is included above his stats. The card's serial number is printed under the stats.

		MT
Complete Set (3):		15.00
Common Player:		5.00
1	John Elway	5.00
2	John Elway (Looking to pass)	5.00
3	John Elway (Running with football)	5.00

1994 Excalibur

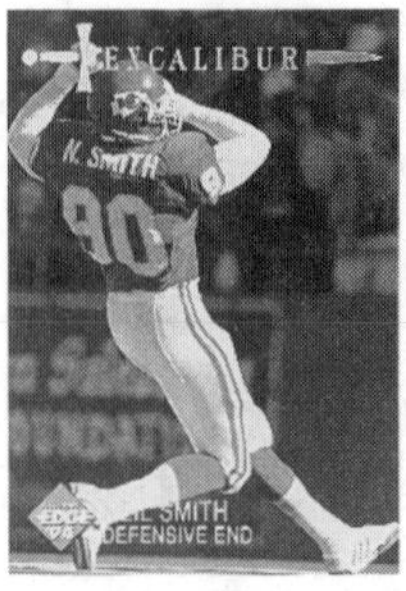

This 75-card NFL All-Star set involves a medieval theme and features the company's unique plastic cards. Each card front has a full-bleed action photo and silver foil on the front for the player's name and position. The card back has a statement about the player by Hall of Famer Dick Butkus. The set's theme is based on Excalibur, the sword pulled from the stone in the legend of King Arthur. A player mug shot also appears on the card back, along with a medieval shield containing his name. A knight is ghosted in the background. All of the teams in the NFL are represented in the set, except for the Minnesota Vikings. Insert cards randomly included in Excalibur packs are: EdgeQuest cards, Excalibur FX, and Excalibur Knights of the NFL.

		MT
Complete Set (75):		30.00
Common Player:		.25
Minor Stars:		.50
Pack (6):		8.00
Wax Box (24):		175.00
1	Bobby Hebert	.25
2	Deion Sanders	1.00
3	Andre Rison	.75
4	Cornelius Bennett	.25
5	Jim Kelly	.75
6	Andre Reed	.50
7	Bruce Smith	.25
8	Thurman Thomas	.75
9	Curtis Conway	.50
10	Richard Dent	.25
11	Jim Harbaugh	.50
12	Troy Aikman	2.50
13	Michael Irvin	.75
14	Russell Maryland	.25
15	Emmitt Smith	4.00
16	Steve Atwater	.25
17	Rod Bernstine	.25
18	John Elway	3.00
19	Glyn Milburn	.25
20	Shannon Sharpe	.75
21	Barry Sanders	5.00
22	Edgar Bennett	.25
23	Brett Favre	5.00
24	Sterling Sharpe	.75
25	Reggie White	.75
26	Warren Moon	.50
27	Wilber Marshall	.25
28	Haywood Jeffires	.25
29	Lorenzo White	.25
30	Quentin Coryatt	.25
31	Roosevelt Potts	.25
32	Jeff George	.75
33	Joe Montana	3.00
34	Neil Smith	.25
35	Marcus Allen	.75
36	Derrick Thomas	.50
37	Jeff Hostetler	.25
38	Tim Brown	.75
39	Raghib Ismail	.25
40	Howie Long	.25
41	Jerome Bettis	1.00
42	Dan Marino	4.00
43	Keith Jackson	.25
44	O.J. McDuffie	.50
45	Drew Bledsoe	3.00
46	Leonard Russell	.25
47	Wade Wilson	.25
48	Eric Martin	.25
49	Phil Simms	.50
50	Lawrence Taylor	.75
51	Rodney Hampton	.50
52	Boomer Esiason	.50
53	Johnny Johnson	.25
54	Ronnie Lott	.50
55	Fred Barnett	.25
56	Leroy Thompson	.25
57	Barry Foster	.25
58	Neil O'Donnell	.50
59	Stan Humphries	.50
60	Marion Butts	.25
61	Anthony Miller	.25
62	Natrone Means	1.00
63	Dana Stubblefield	.50
64	John Taylor	.25
65	Ricky Watters	.75
66	Steve Young	2.00
67	Jerry Rice	2.50
68	Tom Rathman	.25
69	Rick Mirer	.50
70	Chris Warren	.50
71	Cortez Kennedy	.25
72	Mark Rypien	.25
73	Desmond Howard	.25
74	Art Monk	.50
75	Reggie Brooks	.25

1994 Excalibur 22K

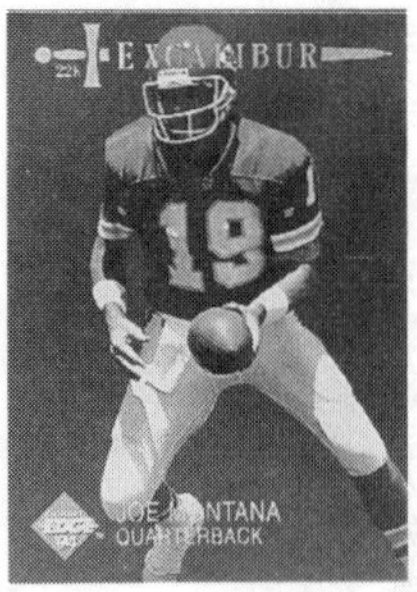

These 22K gold cards feature a color photo on the front against a background with a knight in shining armor. A gold sword appears at the top of the card; the player's name and position are at the bottom. The card back has a knight with a sword and shield as a background. The player's name and a team logo are in the foreground. Cards were random inserts in 1994 Collector's Edge foil packs. The set is titled Knights of the NFL.

		MT
Complete Set (25):		85.00
Common Player:		.75
Minor Stars:		1.50
Inserted 1:2		
1	Troy Aikman	4.00
2	Michael Irvin	1.50
3	Emmitt Smith	6.00
4	Edgar Bennett	.75
5	Brett Favre	8.00
6	Sterling Sharpe	1.50
7	Rodney Hampton	.75
8	Jerome Bettis	1.50
9	Jerry Rice	4.00
10	Steve Young	3.00
11	Ricky Watters	1.50
12	Thurman Thomas	1.50
13	John Elway	5.00
14	Shannon Sharpe	1.50
15	Joe Montana	5.00
16	Marcus Allen	1.50
17	Tim Brown	1.50
18	Raghib Ismail	.75
19	Barry Foster	.75
20	Natrone Means	1.50
21	Rick Mirer	1.50
22	Dan Marino	6.00
23	AFC Card	.75
24	NFC Card	.75
25	Excalibur card	.75

1994 Collector's Edge Excalibur EdgeQuest

Designed as a contest, this nine-card set was both inserted into packs and provided to dealers as a premium. The card fronts featured a letter and "EdgeQuest" at the bottom. The letter X was inserted in smaller quantities and was issued in both gold-foil and silver-foil versions. The letters C, E, L and U were printed as case promos for dealers. If a collector spelled out "Excalibur" with the cards, they could redeem the cards for a prize. A single card could be exchanged for a promo card. A gold version of "Excalibur" could be redeemed for an uncut sheet of 22K Gold insert cards. The card backs have the rules for the contest.

		MT
Complete Set (9):		5.00
Common Insert (A/B/I/R)		.50
Common Dealer (C/E/L/U)		.50
A	Letter A	.50
B	Letter B	.50
C	Letter C	.50
E	Letter E	.50
I	Letter I	.50
L	Letter L	.50
R	Letter R	.50
U	Letter U	.50
X	Letter X SP Expired	2.00

1994 Excalibur FX

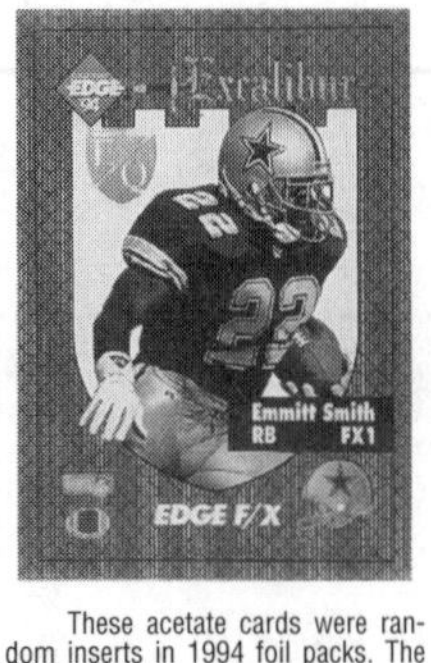

These acetate cards were random inserts in 1994 foil packs. The front has a photo of a player inside a shield. His name, team helmet, position and card number are in the bottom right corner. Cards are numbered on the front using an "FX" prefix. Special gold versions of each card were also made and are generally eight to 10 times more valuable than the regular inserts.

		MT
Complete Set (7):		30.00
Common Player:		1.00
Minor Stars:		2.00
Inserted 1:7		
FX Gold Shield Cards:		4x
Inserted 1:170		
EQ Gold Shield Cards:		1x
EQ Silver Shield Cards:		1x
1	Emmitt Smith	10.00
2	Rodney Hampton	1.00
3	Jerome Bettis	2.00
4	Steve Young	1.00
5	Rick Mirer	2.00
6	John Elway	8.00
7	Troy Aikman	7.00

1994 Collector's Edge Excalibur Redemption

These nine EdgeQuest insert redemption cards were randomly included in 1994 Collector's Edge Excalibur packs. Each of the nine cards is numbered using a letter from the word EXCALIBUR, not a number. The object of the game is to get each different letter insert, to spell out Excalibur. Those who obtained all nine cards could redeem them for an F/X subset or uncut press sheet. Individual cards could be redeemed for a Collector's Edge prototype card. The A, B, I, R and X cards were randomly inserted into every ninth foil pack. The C, E, L and U cards were given to dealers who purchased a case of the Excalibur cards.

		MT
Complete Set (9):		4.50
Common Player:		4.50
1	Dealer promo	4.50
2	Foil Pack Insert	4.50
3	Dealer promo	4.50
4	Foil Pack Insert	4.50
5	Dealer promo	4.50
6	Foil Pack Insert	4.50
7	Foil Pack Insert	4.50
8	Dealer promo	4.50
9	Foil Pack Insert	4.50

1995 Collector's Edge Junior Seau Promos

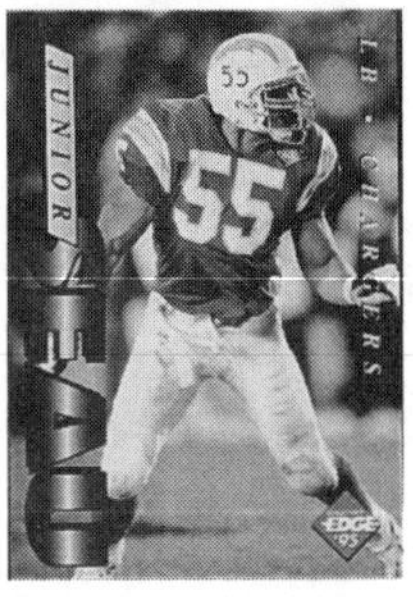

Each card in the five-card set showcased a full-bleed photo of Seau on the front, with his last name running along the left border of the card. "Seau" is printed in large letters, while "Junior" is in a stripe. The card backs feature a head shot, the player's name, team, position, bio and stats. The cards are numbered "/5," with a promo prefix. "Promo '95" is printed in a white stripe along the right side of the card back.

		MT
Complete Set (5):		5.00
Common Player:		1.00
1	Rookie Season 1990	1.00
2	Second Season 1991	1.00
3	Third Season 1992	1.00
4	Fourth Season 1993	1.00
5	Super Bowl Season 1994	1.00

1995 Collector's Edge

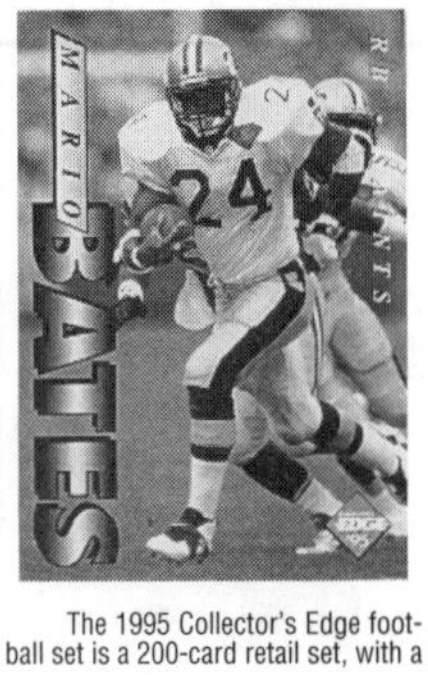

The 1995 Collector's Edge football set is a 200-card retail set, with a

Black Label hobby version also issued. The main cards in the set have a full-bleed color photo on the front, with the player's name along the left side and his position and team nickname along the right side. The horizontal back has a mug shot of the player in the upper right corner, and a ghosted image of him with his stats and biographical information superimposed over them. Two parallel sets were also made - a die-cut version (one per every 24 packs) and a gold foil-based set (one per every 20 packs). Insert sets include TimeWarp Matchups, Rookies, EdgeTech, and EdgeQuest 12th Man cards. Retail cards have the same card numbers as the hobby versions, but different photos and designs are used, plus a Black Label logo is foil-stamped into the hobby cards. This set has the same insert sets as the hobby brand does.

		MT
Complete Set (205):		15.00
Common Player:		.10
Minor Stars:		.20
Comp. Gold Set (205):		15.00
Gold Cards Equal Value		
Comp. Die Cut Set (205):		140.00
Die Cuts:		4x-8x
Comp. Black Label Set (205):		25.00
Black Label Cards:		1x-1.5x
Comp. BL Silv. Die Cut (205):		250.00
Silv. Die Cut Cards:		5x-10x
Comp. BL 22K Gold (205):		2200.
BL 22K Gold Cards:		40x-80x
Comp. EdgeQuest 12th Man (7):		15.00
Common EdgeQuest:		2.50
Hobby Pack (6):		1.25
Hobby Wax Box (36):		40.00
Retail Pack (6):		1.25
Retail Wax Box (24):		30.00
1	Anthony Edwards	.10
2	Garrison Hearst	.20
3	Seth Joyner	.10
4	Dave Krieg	.10
5	Chuck Levy	.10
6	Rob Moore	.10
7	J.J. Birden	.10
8	Jeff George	.20
9	Craig Heyward	.10
10	Norm Johnson	.10
11	Terance Mathis	.10
12	Eric Metcalf	.10
13	Chuck Smith	.10
14	Darryl Talley	.10
15	Cornelius Bennett	.10
16	Steve Christie	.10
17	Kenneth Davis	.10
18	Phil Hansen	.10
19	Jim Kelly	.20
20	Bryce Paup	.10
21	Andre Reed	.10
22	Bruce Smith	.10
23	Eric Ball	.10
24	Don Beebe	.10
25	Mark Carrier	.10
26	Tim McKyer	.10
27	Pete Metzelaars	.10
28	Sam Mills	.10
29	Jack Trudeau	.10
30	Mark Carrier	.10
31	Curtis Conway	.10
32	Eric Kramer	.10
33	Lewis Tillman	.10
34	Michael Timpson	.10
35	Steve Walsh	.10
36	Chris Zorich	.10
37	*Jeff Blake*	1.00
38	Harold Green	.10
39	David Klinger	.10
40	Carl Pickens	.20
41	Tom Waddle	.10
42	Dan Wilkinson	.10
43	Leroy Hoard	.10
44	Michael Jackson	.10
45	Antonio Langham	.10
46	Andre Rison	.20
47	Vinny Testaverde	.10
48	Eric Turner	.10
49	Tommy Vardell	.10
50	Troy Aikman	.75
51	Charles Haley	.10
52	Michael Irvin	.25
53	Daryl Johnston	.10
54	Leon Lett	.10
55	Jay Novacek	.10
56	Emmitt Smith	1.50
57	Kevin Williams	.10
58	Steve Atwater	.10
59	John Elway	.30
60	Simon Fletcher	.10
61	Glyn Milburn	.10
62	Anthony Miller	.10
63	Leonard Russell	.10
64	Shannon Sharpe	.10
65	Scott Mitchell	.10
66	Herman Moore	.20
67	Johnnie Morton	.10
68	Brett Perriman	.10
69	Barry Sanders	1.25
70	Edgar Bennett	.10
71	Brett Favre	1.50
72	Mark Ingram	.10
73	Chris Jacke	.10
74	Guy McIntyre	.10
75	Reggie White	.20
76	Gary Brown	.10
77	Ernest Givins	.10
78	Mel Gray	.10
79	Haywood Jeffires	.10
80	Webster Slaughter	.10
81	Craig Erickson	.10
82	Marshall Faulk	1.00
83	Jim Harbaugh	.10
84	Roosevelt Potts	.10
85	Floyd Turner	.10
86	Steve Beuerlein	.10
87	Reggie Cobb	.10
88	Jeff Lageman	.10
89	Mazio Royster	.10
90	Marcus Allen	.20
91	Steve Bono	.20
92	Willie Davis	.10
93	Lake Dawson	.25
94	Ronnie Lott	.10
95	Eric Martin	.10
96	Chris Penn	.10
97	Tim Brown	.20
98	Derrick Fenner	.10
99	Rob Fredrickson	.10
100	Nolan Harrison	.10
101	Jeff Hostetler	.10
102	Raghib Ismail	.10
103	James Jett	.10
104	Chester McGlockton	.10
105	Anthony Smith	.10
106	Harvey Williams	.10
107	Jerome Bettis	.25
108	Troy Drayton	.10
109	Chris Miller	.10
110	Robert Young	.10
111	Keith Byars	.10
112	Gary Clark	.10
113	Bryan Cox	.10
114	Jeff Cross	.10
115	Irving Fryar	.10
116	Randall Hill	.10
117	Terry Kirby	.10
118	Dan Marino	1.50
119	O.J. McDuffie	.10
120	Bernie Parmalee	.25
121	Terry Allen	.10
122	Cris Carter	.20
123	Qadry Ismail	.10
124	Warren Moon	.25
125	John Randle	.10
126	Jake Reed	.10
127	Fuad Reveiz	.10
128	Broderick Thomas	.10
129	Drew Bledsoe	1.00
130	Vincent Brisby	.10
131	Ben Coates	.10
132	David Meggett	.10
133	Chris Slade	.10
134	Leroy Thompson	.10
135	Eric Allen	.10
136	Mario Bates	.30
137	Quinn Early	.10
138	Jim Everett	.10
139	Michael Haynes	.10
140	Torrance Small	.10
141	Dave Brown	.10
142	Chris Calloway	.10
143	Keith Hamilton	.10
144	Rodney Hampton	.10
145	Mike Sherrard	.10
146	David Treadwell	.10
147	Herschel Walker	.10
148	Boomer Esiason	.10
149	Erik Howard	.10
150	Johnny Johnson	.10
151	Mo Lewis	.10
152	Johnny Mitchell	.10
153	Fred Barnett	.10
154	Randall Cunningham	.20
155	William Fuller	.10
156	Charlie Garner	.10
157	Greg Jackson	.10
158	Ricky Watters	.20
159	Calvin Williams	.10
160	Barry Foster	.10
161	Kevin Greene	.10
162	Greg Lloyd	.10
163	Bam Morris	.40
164	Neil O'Donnell	.10
165	Erric Pegram	.10
166	John L. Williams	.10
167	Rod Woodson	.10
168	John Carney	.10
169	Stan Humphries	.20
170	Natrone Means	.40
171	Chris Mims	.10
172	Leslie O'Neal	.10
173	Alfred Pupunu	.20
174	Junior Seau	.20
175	Mark Seay	.10
176	William Floyd	.40
177	Jerry Rice	.75
178	Deion Sanders	.40
179	Dana Stubblefield	.10
180	John Taylor	.10
181	Steve Young	.50
182	Bryant Young	.10
183	Brian Blades	.10
184	Cortez Kennedy	.10
185	Kelvin Martin	.10
186	Rick Mirer	.30
187	Ricky Proehl	.20
188	Michael Sinclair	.10
189	Chris Warren	.10
190	Trent Dilfer	.40
191	Alvin Harper	.10
192	Jackie Harris	.10
193	Hardy Nickerson	.10
194	Errict Rhett	.75
195	Reggie Roby	.10
196	Henry Ellard	.10
197	Ricky Ervins	.10
198	Darrell Green	.10
199	Brian Mitchell	.10
200	Heath Shuler	.50

1995 Collector's Edge Die Cuts

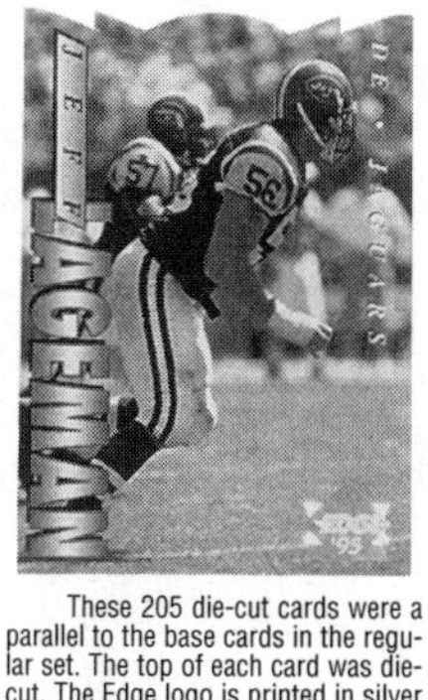

These 205 die-cut cards were a parallel to the base cards in the regular set. The top of each card was die-cut. The Edge logo is printed in silver foil on card fronts.

	MT
Complete Set (205):	150.00
Common Player:	.30
Die Cut Cards: 3x-6x	

1995 Collector's Edge Gold Logo

Randomly inserted into hobby and retail packs, the 205-card set was a parallel to the base cards. The card fronts each showcase a gold-foil Edge logo at the bottom right.

	MT
Complete Set (205):	18.00
Common Player:	.05
Gold Cards:	1x

1995 Collector's Edge 22K Gold

Randomly inserted into retail packs, the 205-card set was a parallel to the base set. Each card front has a gold-foil 22K logo on it.

	MT
Complete Set (205):	2200.
Common Player:	3.00
22K Gold Cards:	35x-70x

1995 Collector's Edge EdgeTech

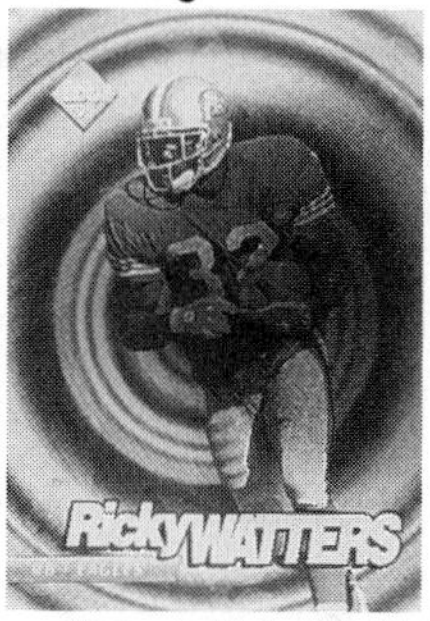

This insert set features 36 of the premier players in the game on cards with a prismatic background. Cards came in four versions - 22k Gold and Circular Prisms (in Edge packs) and Quantum and Die-Cuts (in Black Label packs).

		MT
Complete Set (36):		70.00
Common Player:		1.50
Black Label Same Price		
Comp. 22K Gold Set (36):		300.00
22K Gold Cards:		1x-3x
Comp. Quantum Set (36):		600.00
Quantum Cards:		2x-4x
Comp. Quantum Die Cut (36):		800.00
Quantum Die Cuts:		4x-8x
Comp. Circular Prisms (36):		50.00
Circular Prisms: Half Value		
1	Dan Marino	12.00
2	Steve Young	4.00
3	Rick Mirer	2.50
4	Emmitt Smith	12.00
5	John Elway	4.00
6	Neil O'Donnell	1.50
7	Marshall Faulk	3.00
8	Deion Sanders	3.00
9	Terance Mathis	1.50
10	Kevin Greene	1.50
11	Ricky Watters	2.00
12	Tim Brown	1.50
13	Antonio Langham	1.50
14	Lake Dawson	1.50
15	Jay Novacek	1.50
16	Herman Moore	2.50
17	Mark Seay	1.50
18	Bernie Parmalee	1.50
19	Drew Bledsoe	6.00
20	Troy Aikman	6.00
21	Brett Favre	12.00
22	Jerry Rice	6.00
23	Barry Sanders	6.00
24	Heath Shuler	2.50
25	Errict Rhett	2.50
26	Cris Carter	1.50
27	Jerome Bettis	2.50
28	Reggie White	2.00
29	Chris Warren	1.50
30	Ben Coates	1.50
31	Bryant Young	1.50
32	Mel Gray	1.50
33	Darryl Talley	1.50
34	Mike Sherrard	1.50
35	William Floyd	2.00
36	Alvin Harper	1.50

A card number in parentheses ( ) indicates the set is unnumbered.

1995 Collector's Edge Rookies

These 1995 Collector's Edge inserts come in three versions - two in the retail packs, including a gold version, and one in the hobby Black Label packs. The cards feature 25 of the top 1995 NFL draft picks. The front has a photo of the player in his college uniform, along with a set logo in the upper right corner. The horizontal card back has a closeup shot of the player, biographical information, and a synopsis of the player's selection in the draft.

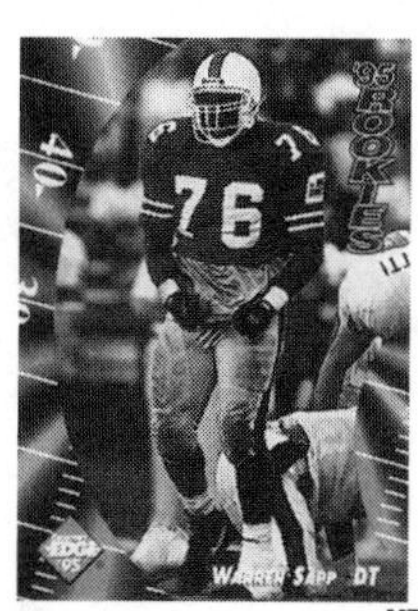

		MT
Complete Set (24):		35.00
Common Player:		.50
Minor Stars:		1.00
Comp. 22K Gold Set (24):		120.00
22K Gold Cards:		2x-4x
Black Label Same Price		
1	Derrick Alexander	.50
2	Tony Boselli	1.00
3	Ki-Jana Carter	3.00
4	Kevin Carter	.50
5	Kerry Collins	5.00
6	Steve McNair	4.00
7	Billy Milner	.50
8	Rashaan Salaam	4.00
9	Warren Sapp	1.00
10	James Stewart	.50
11	J.J. Stokes	3.00
12	Bobby Taylor	.50
13	Tyrone Wheatley	1.00
14	Derrick Brooks	.50
15	Reuben Brown	.50
16	Mark Bruener	1.00
17	Joey Galloway	4.00
18	Napolean Kaufman	1.00
19	Ty Law	.50
20	Craig Newsome	1.00
21	Kordell Stewart	5.00
22	Korey Stringer	.50
23	Zach Weigert	.50
24	Michael Westbrook	2.00

1995 Collector's Edge TimeWarp

These 1995 Collector's Edge inserts feature one star from today matched up against a former NFL star in game action, through the magic of computers. Three versions were made - two for Edge retail packs, including a gold version, and one for the hobby Black Label packs. Card fronts have a TimeWarp logo in the upper right corner, and show the two players competing against each other. The card back has mug shots of each player, with biographical information underneath. A quote from Hall of Fame linebacker Dick Butkus, the company's spokesman, is also given regarding the matchup.

		MT
Complete Set (20):		70.00
Common Player:		2.50
Minor Stars:		5.00
Comp. 22K Gold Set (20):		280.00
22K Gold Cards:		2x-4x
Black Label Same Price		
1	Emmitt Smith, Dick Butkus	14.00
2	Troy Aikman, Gino Marchetti	7.00
3	Natrone Means, Ray Nitschke	5.00
4	Chris Zorich, Steve Van Buren	2.50
5	Barry Sanders, Deacon Jones	14.00
6	Kevin Greene, Paul Hornung	2.50
7	Charles Haley, Len Dawson	2.50
8	Marshall Faulk, Willie Lanier	5.00
9	Ronnie Lott, Gale Sayers	5.00
10	Cris Carter, Jack Ham	2.50
11	Junior Seau, Gale Sayers	2.50
12	Reggie White, Otto Graham	2.50
13	Leslie O'Neil, Y.A. Tittle	2.50
14	Drew Bledsoe, Ted Hendricks	7.00
15	Heath Shuler, Bob Lilly	2.50
16	Ricky Watters, Daryle Lamonica	2.50
17	Marshall Faulk, Dick Butkus	5.00
18	Deion Sanders, Raymond Berry	7.00
19	Steve Young, Jack Youngblood	6.00
20	Bruce Smith, Sammy Baugh	2.50
NNO	Checklist	3.00
TW1	Gale Sayers, Junior Seau, Dick Butkus	3.00

1995 Collector's Edge TimeWarp Jumbos

Measuring 8 x 10 inches, the 42-card set has full-bleed photos on the front, with Time Warp in the upper right. The Time Warp logo also is in the lower right, with an Edge logo in the lower left. The cards resemble the regular sized Time Warp cards which were inserted into 1995 Collector's Edge. The backs have headshots of each featured player, along with the Time Warp logo, at the top. Each player's bio appears under the photo. A Dick Butkus quote appears in the lower center of the back. Overall, 5,000 of each card were issued and given to hobby dealers. Signed editions of each card were produced and autographed by a Hall of Famer. The cards were also offered through a 1996 Edge retail pack mail-in offer for $3.95 each with 12 wrappers.

		MT
Complete Set (42):		450.00
Common Player:		8.00
1	Dick Butkus, Emmitt Smith	20.00
2	Dick Butkus, Emmitt Smith	20.00
3	Gino Marchetti, Troy Aikman	14.00
4	Gino Marchetti, Troy Aikman	14.00
5	Ray Nitschke, Natrone Means	10.00
6	Ray Nitschke, Natrone Means	10.00
7	Steve Van Buren, Chris Zorich	8.00
8	Steve Van Buren, Chris Zorich	8.00
9	Deacon Jones, Barry Sanders	14.00
10	Deacon Jones, Barry Sanders	14.00
11	Paul Hornung, Kevin Greene	10.00
12	Paul Hornung, Kevin Greene	10.00
13	Len Dawson, Charles Haley	8.00
14	Len Dawson, Charles Haley	8.00
15	Willie Lanier, Marshall Faulk	12.00
16	Willie Lanier, Marshall Faulk	12.00
17	Gale Sayers, Ronnie Lott	10.00
18	Gale Sayers, Ronnie Lott	10.00
19	Jack Ham, Cris Carter	8.00
20	Jack Ham, Cris Carter	8.00
21	Gale Sayers, Junior Seau	10.00
22	Gale Sayers, Junior Seau	10.00
23	Otto Graham, Reggie White	10.00
24	Otto Graham, Reggie White	10.00
25	Y.A. Tittle, Leslie O'Neal	10.00
26	Y.A. Tittle, Leslie O'Neal	10.00
27	Daryle Lamonica, Ricky Watters	8.00
28	Daryle Lamonica, Ricky Watters	8.00
29	Dick Butkus, Marshall Faulk	12.00
30	Dick Butkus, Marshall Faulk	12.00
31	Raymond Berry, Deion Sanders	12.00
32	Raymond Berry, Deion Sanders	12.00
33	Jack Youngblood, Steve Young	12.00
34	Jack Youngblood, Steve Young	12.00
35	Sammy Baugh, Bruce Smith	10.00
36	Sammy Baugh, Bruce Smith	10.00
37	Ted Hendricks, Dan Marino	20.00
38	Bob Lilly, Dan Marino	20.00
39	Ted Hendricks, Drew Bledsoe	12.00
40	Bob Lilly, Heath Shuler	10.00
41	Dick Butkus, Jeff Blake	12.00
42	Dick Butkus, Michael Westbrook	12.00

1995 Collector's Edge TimeWarp Sunday Ticket

Offered for $19.95 per set through a mail order offer, the five-card set had a full-bleed photo on the front, with the Edge logo in the upper left and NFL Sunday Ticket logo in the lower right. The card backs resemble the Time Warp Jumbo backs, except the background has a prism effect. Overall, 2,500 sets were produced.

		MT
Complete Set (5):		15.00
Common Player:		2.00
1	Paul Hornung, Chris Zorich	2.00
2	Gale Sayers, Kevin Greene	2.00
3	Ted Hendricks, Ricky Watters	3.00
4	Sammy Baugh, Bruce Smith	3.00
5	Dick Butkus, Marshall Faulk	7.00

1995 Collector's Edge 12th Man Redempton

This redemption set was available through 1995 Black Label and retail version packs. If a collector compiled all the cards which spelled "12th Man," they could exchange them plus $19.95 for this complete 25-card set. The cards carry a 1996 copyright date, but are part of the 1995 set. The card fronts feature a cutout photo of the player over a multi-colored background, with "12th Man" printed at the top of the card. The card backs include a headshot, player name, bio and highlight. The card number is printed in the upper right.

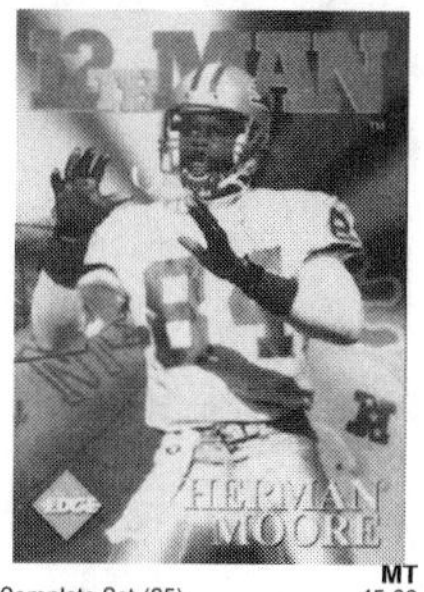

		MT
Complete Set (25):		45.00
Common Player:		.50
Comp. Letters Set (7):		2.50
1	Dan Marino	8.00
2	Jeff Blake	2.00
3	Steve Bono	1.00
4	Brett Favre	8.00
5	Steve Young	3.00
6	Scott Mitchell	1.00
7	Chris Warren	1.00
8	Marshall Faulk	2.00
9	Byron "Bam" Morris	.50
10	Emmitt Smith	8.00
11	Barry Sanders	4.00
12	Rashaan Salaam	2.00
13	Carl Pickens	1.00
14	Anthony Miller	.50
15	Tim Brown	1.00
16	Jerry Rice	4.00
17	Herman Moore	2.00
18	Isaac Bruce	2.00
19	Ben Coates	1.00
20	Shannon Sharpe	1.00
21	Alfred Pupunu	.50
22	Jackie Harris	.50
23	Jay Novacek	.50
24	Brent Jones	.50
25	Checklist	.50

1995 Collector's Edge Black Label

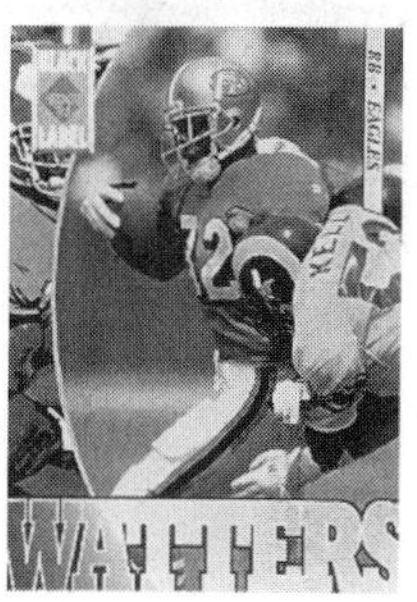

This was the hobby version of the Collector's Edge set. The 205-card set was sold in six-card packs. The card fronts spotlight a full-bleed photo, with the player's last name at the bottom. The Black Label logo is printed in the top left. Showcased on the horizontal card backs are the player's headshot and an action photo in the background. The player's bio and stats are on the back, too.

	MT
Complete Set (205):	25.00
Common Player:	.05
Black Label Cards:	1x
Pack (6):	1.00
Wax Box (36):	30.00

1995 Collector's Edge Black Label 22K Gold

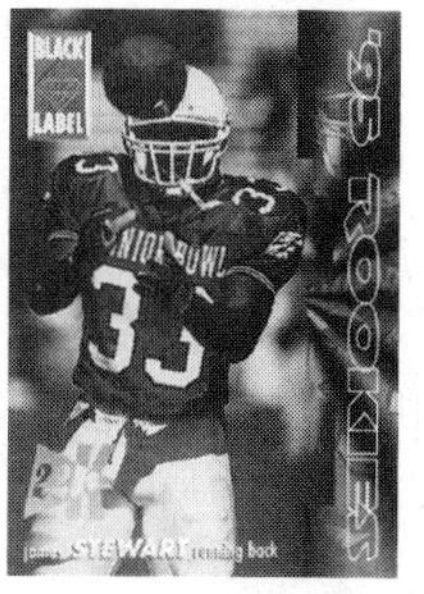

This parallel of the base set featured the Black Label logo in gold foil, along with a 22K logo, on the front of each card in the 205-card set.

	MT
Complete Set (205):	2200.
Common Player:	3.00
BL 22K Gold Cards:	35x-70x

1995 Collector's Edge Black Label Silver Die Cuts

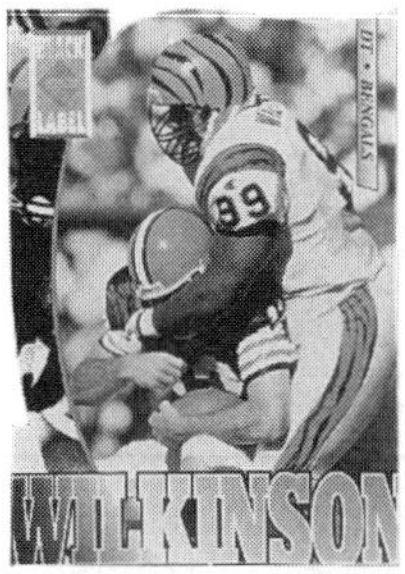

Randomly seeded one per 24 packs, the 205-card set was a parallel of the base set. Each front showcased a Black Label logo in silver foil. The top of each card was die-cut.

	MT
Complete Set (205):	325.00
Common Player:	.50
Silver Die Cuts:	7x-14x

1995 Excalibur

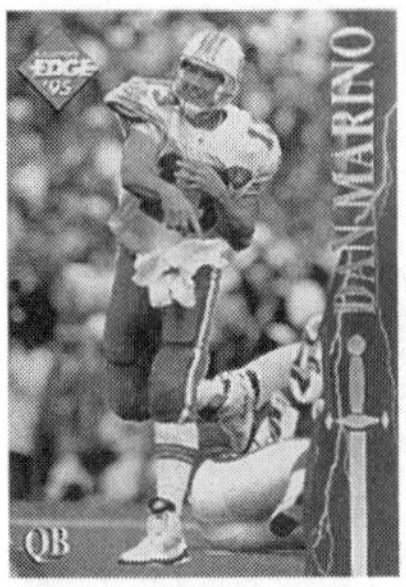

1995 Collector's Edge Excalibur was issued in two 75-card series - I, called the Sword, and II, called the Stone. The regular cards have a full-bleed color action photo on the front, with a Collector's Edge logo in the upper left corner. The player's name is in silver foil along the right side of the card, with a silver-foiled sword next to it. The card back indicates at the top which series the card is from and includes a mug shot of the player. Each player is addressed as "Sir" and has his statistics from 1991-1994 listed, along with a team logo. Each card was also reprinted in a die-cut version resembling a castle (one in every nine packs). Insert sets in both series include Rookie Roundtable and Knights of the NFL. Sword Challengers Draft Day Redemption cards were exclusive to Series I packs, while DragonSlayers could be found only in Series II packs. EdgeTech cards in Series I were continued in Series II, but were called TekTech and had a different design. "Stone" and "Sword" game cards were also randomly included in their respective series' packs.

		MT
Complete Set (150):		30.00
Comp. Series 1 (75):		15.00
Comp. Series 2 (75):		15.00
Common Player:		.20
Minor Stars:		.40
Die Cut Cards:		3x-6x
Inserted 1:9		
Series 1 Pack (7):		3.50
Series 1 Wax Box (36):		100.00
Series 2 Pack (7):		3.50
Series 2 Wax Box (36):		100.00
1	Gary Clark	.20
2	Randall Hill	.20
3	Anthony Edwards	.20
4	Terrance Mathis	.40
5	Erric Pegram	.20
6	Jeff George	.40
7	Pete Metzelaars	.20
8	Jim Kelly	.40
9	Andre Reed	.20
10	Lewis Tillman	.20
11	Curtis Conway	.50
12	Steve Walsh	.20
13	Derrick Fenner	.20
14	Harold Green	.20
15	Michael Jackson	.20
16	Eric Metcalf	.20
17	Antonio Langham	.20
18	Troy Aikman	3.00
19	Alvin Harper	.40
20	Jay Novacek	.20
21	John Elway	4.00
22	Glyn Milburn	.20
23	Steve Atwater	.20
24	Mel Gray	.20
25	Herman Moore	.75
26	Scott Mitchell	.40
27	Guy McIntyre	.20
28	Edgar Bennett	.20
29	Sterling Sharpe	.40
30	Gary Brown	.20
31	Haywood Jeffires	.20
32	Marshall Faulk	.75
33	Roosevelt Potts	.20
34	Marcus Allen	.40
35	Willie Davis	.20
36	Lake Dawson	.75
37	Jeff Hostetler	.20
38	Raghib Ismail	.20
39	Troy Drayton	.20
40	Jerome Bettis	.75
41	Dan Marino	5.00
42	Mark Ingram	.20
43	O.J. McDuffie	.20
44	Warren Moon	.40
45	Qadry Ismail	.20
46	Jake Reed	.20
47	Ben Coates	.20
48	Vincent Brisby	.20
49	Michael Timpson	.20
50	Brad Daluiso	.20
51	Rodney Hampton	.20
52	Chris Calloway	.20
53	Rob Moore	.20
54	Boomer Esiason	.20
55	Michael Haynes	.20
56	Vaughn Dunbar	.20
57	Calvin Williams	.20
58	Herschel Walker	.20
59	Charlie Garner	.20
60	Neil O'Donnell	.40
61	Deon Figures	.20
62	Bam Morris	1.50
63	Junior Seau	.40
64	Leslie O'Neil	.20
65	Natrone Means	1.75
66	Jerry Rice	3.00
67	Deion Sanders	1.50
68	William Floyd	1.00
69	Chris Warren	.40
70	Cortez Kennedy	.20
71	Hardy Nickerson	.20
72	Craig Erickson	.20
73	Heath Shuler	1.00
74	Reggie Brooks	.20
75	Henry Ellard	.20
76	Garrison Hearst	.20
77	Steve Beuerlein	.20
78	Seth Joyner	.20
79	Andre Rison	.20
80	Norm Johnson	.20
81	Craig Hayword	.20
82	Thurman Thomas	.40
83	Kenny Davis	.20
84	Bruce Smith	.20
85	Tom Waddle	.20
86	Erik Kramer	.20
87	Alonzo Spellman	.20
88	Dan Wilkinson	.20
89	*Jeff Blake*	2.00
90	Vinny Testaverde	.20
91	Tommy Vardell	.20
92	Mark Carrier	.20
93	Emmitt Smith	5.00
94	Michael Irvin	.75
95	Daryl Johnston	.20
96	Shannon Sharpe	.20
97	Anthony Miller	.20
98	Leonard Russell	.20
99	Barry Sanders	5.00
100	Brett Perriman	.40
101	Johnnie Morton	.20
102	Brett Favre	5.00
103	Bryce Paup	.40
104	Jackie Harris	.20
105	Ernest Givins	.20
106	Webster Slaughter	.20
107	Jim Harbaugh	.40
108	Joe Montana	4.00
109	J.J. Birden	.20
110	Tim Burnett	.20
111	James Jett	.20
112	Tim Brown	.40
113	Rob Fredrickson	.20
114	Chris Miller	.20
115	Bernie Parmalee	.50
116	Terry Kirby	.20
117	Keith Jackson	.20
118	Irving Fryer	.20
119	Terry Allen	.20
120	Cris Carter	.40
121	Fuad Reveiz	.20
122	Drew Bledsoe	3.00
123	Greg McMurtry	.20
124	Dave Brown	.20
125	David Meggett	.20
126	Johnnie Johnson	.20
127	Ronnie Lott	.20
128	Johnny Mitchell	.20
129	Eric Martin	.20
130	Jim Everett	.20
131	Randall Cunningham	.20
132	Fred Barnett	.20
133	Eric Allen	.20
134	Barry Foster	.20
135	Kevin Greene	.20
136	Eric Green	.20
137	Stan Humphries	.40
138	Mark Seay	.20
139	*Alfred Pupunu*	.50
140	Steve Young	2.00
141	John Taylor	.20
142	Ricky Watters	.50
143	Brian Blades	.20
144	Rick Mirer	.75
145	Cortez Kennedy	.20
146	Errict Rhett	2.00
147	Trent Dilfer	1.25
148	Brian Mitchell	.20
149	Ricky Ervins	.20
150	Desmond Howard	.20

A card number in parentheses ( ) indicates the set is unnumbered.

1995 Excalibur Die Cuts

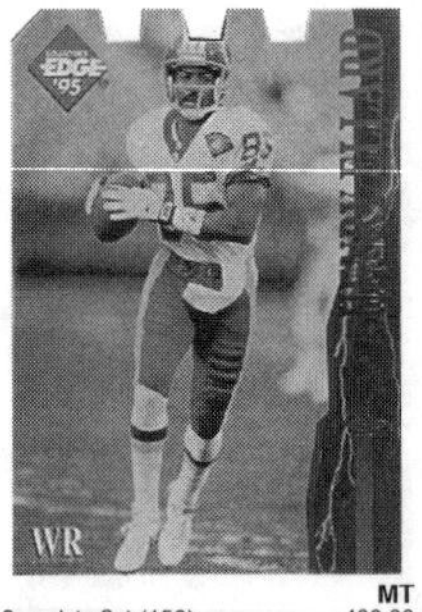

This 150-card set paralleled the base Excalibur set, and was inserted in packs at a rate of one per nine. Similar to the Excalibur set in 1995, this die-cut set was issued in two, 75-card series.

	MT
Complete Set (150):	400.00
Complete Sword Set (75):	200.00
Complete Stone Set (75):	200.00
Common Sword Card (1-75):	3.00
Common Stone Card (76-150):	3.00
Die Cuts	4x-8x

1995 Excalibur 22K Gold

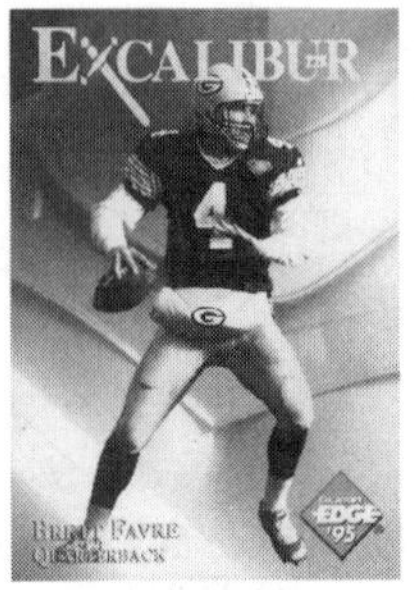

This 22K Knights of the NFL insert set was issued in two 25- card subsets; cards 1-25 were randomly included one per every 35 packs of Excalibur Series I product, while #s 26-50 were in Excalibur Series II packs at the same ratio. In addition to the regular versions, there were also limited editions of each card created in a prism format. The card front has "Excalibur 22K" stamped in gold foil at the top, with a colorful swirly-patterned background. The card back has a shield with the player's name and team logo in it, also against a background of a knight holding a football.

		MT
Complete Set (50):		1100.
Comp. Series 1 (25):		500.00
Comp. Series 2 (25):		600.00
Common Player:		10.00
Comp. Prism Set (50):		3600.
Comp. Prisms Ser. 1 (25):		1800.
Comp. Prisms Ser. 2 (25):		1800.
Prism Cards:		2x-3x
1	Steve Young	60.00
2	Barry Sanders	60.00
3	John Elway	30.00
4	Warren Moon	20.00
5	Chris Warren	10.00
6	Jim Kelly	20.00
7	Troy Aikman	60.00
8	Jerome Bettis	20.00
9	Marcus Allen	20.00
10	William Floyd	20.00
11	Terance Mathis	10.00
12	Antonio Langham	10.00
13	Sterling Sharpe	20.00
14	Leonard Russell	10.00
15	Drew Bledsoe	60.00
16	Rodney Hampton	10.00
17	Herschel Walker	10.00
18	Jim Everett	10.00
19	Eric Allen	10.00
20	Junior Seau	20.00
21	Natrone Means	30.00
22	Deion Sanders	30.00
23	Charlie Garner	10.00
24	Marshall Faulk	60.00
25	Ben Coates	10.00
26	Emmitt Smith	120.00
27	Jerry Rice	60.00
28	Stan Humphries	10.00
29	Joe Montana	75.00
30	Thurman Thomas	20.00
31	Eric Metcalf	10.00
32	Jay Novacek	10.00
33	Brett Favre	100.00
34	Dan Marino	120.00
35	Bam Morris	20.00
36	Heath Shuler	25.00
37	Trent Dilfer	20.00
38	Errict Rhett	25.00
39	Herman Moore	20.00
40	Terry Allen	10.00
41	Cris Carter	20.00
42	Ronnie Lott	10.00
43	Randall Cunningham	10.00
44	Barry Foster	10.00
45	John Taylor	10.00
46	Rick Mirer	20.00
47	Jerry Rice	60.00
48	Michael Irvin	30.00
49	Ricky Watters	20.00
50	Andre Rison	10.00

A player's name in *italic type* indicates a rookie card.

1995 Excalibur Challengers Draft Day Rookie Redemption

Each of these 1995 Collector's Edge Excalibur Series I Sword inserts could be exchanged for a card of its respective team's top draft choice. Cards were seeded one per every four Series I packs. The front shows the team's helmet three times; a larger one dominates the center of the card, while smaller ones appear in the upper right and lower left corners. The team name is printed into the background, too. The card back states the rules of the redemption program.

		MT
Complete Set (31):		45.00
Common Player:		1.00
Minor Stars:		2.00
Gold Cards: 2x		
1	(Derrick Alexander)	2.00
2	(Tony Boselli)	2.00
3	(Kyle Brady)	1.00
4	(Mark Bruener)	1.00
5	(Jamie Brown)	1.00
6	(Ruben Brown)	1.00
7	(Devin Bush)	1.00
8	(Kevin Carter)	1.00
9	(Ki-Jana Carter)	2.00
10	(Kerry Collins)	3.00
11	(Kordell Stewart)	10.00
12	(Mark Fields)	1.00
13	(Joey Galloway)	6.00
14	(Trezelle Jenkins)	1.00
15	(Ellis Johnson)	1.00
16	(Napoleon Kaufman)	6.00
17	(Ty Law)	2.00
18	(Mike Mamula)	1.00
19	(Steve McNair)	8.00
20	(Billy Milner)	1.00
21	(Craig Newsome)	2.00
22	(Craig Powell)	1.00
23	(Rashaan Salaam)	2.00
24	(Frank Sanders)	3.00
25	(Warren Sapp)	2.00
26	(Terrance Shaw)	1.00
27	(J.J. Stokes)	3.00
28	(Michael Westbrook)	2.00
29	(Tyrone Wheatley)	2.00
30	(Sherman Williams)	2.00

1995 Excalibur Dragon Slayers

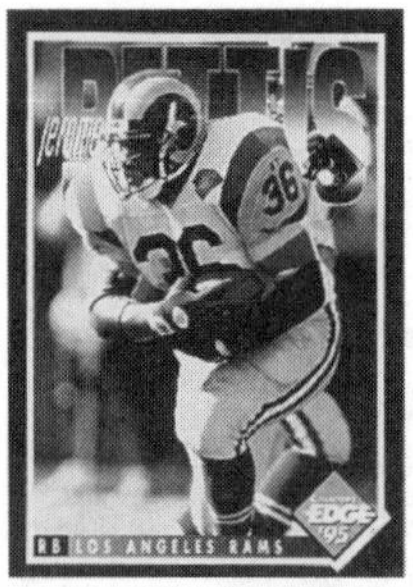

These 1995 Collector's Edge Excalibur Series II inserts were made by members of the art departments of hobby price guide editors, so each card has a different design. Fourteen players were spotlighted on the cards, which were random inserts one per every 12 packs.

		MT
Complete Set (14):		65.00
Common Player:		2.00
Minor Stars:		4.00
1	Troy Aikman	5.00
2	Jerome Bettis	4.00
3	Ricky Watters	4.00
4	Barry Sanders	6.00
5	Emmitt Smith	10.00
6	Marshall Faulk	5.00
7	Drew Bledsoe	5.00
8	Errict Rhett	5.00
9	Joe Montana	5.00
10	Junior Seau	4.00
11	Deion Sanders	5.00
12	Bam Morris	2.00
13	Jerry Rice	5.00
14	Natrone Means	4.00

1995 Excalibur EdgeQuest

Designed as an insert and a dealer promotion, the set was printed on clear acetate. The fronts have a large letter and EdgeQuest at the bottom. Collectors who spelled "Sword" or "Stone" with the cards could redeem them for prizes. The D, R and W cards were in Sword packs. The E, N and T cards were in Stone packs. The S and O cards were given to hobby dealers. "Sword" cards could be exchanged for a Rookie Roundtable set, while "Stone" cards could be exchanged for a Challengers Rookie set.

		MT
Complete Set (9):		5.00
Common Box Insert (O/S):		.40
Common Sword Insert (D/R/W):		.40
Common Stone Insert (E/N/T):		.40
1	Letter D	.40
2	Letter E	.40
3	Letter N	.40
4	Letter T	.40
5	Letter O	.40
6	Letter R	.40
7	Letter S	.40
8	Letter W	.40
9	Ampersand	1.50

1995 Excalibur EdgeTech

These 1995 Collector's Edge Excalibur Series I inserts were the rarest, seeded one per every 75 packs. The cards are continued as a TekTech series in Excalibur Series II packs, starting with #13, but the designs remain different.

		MT
Complete Set (12):		375.00
Common Player:		15.00
Minor Stars:		20.00
1	Emmitt Smith	100.00
2	Errict Rhett	40.00
3	Steve Young	50.00
4	Jerry Rice	50.00
5	Ben Coates	15.00
6	Marcus Allen	20.00
7	John Elway	40.00
8	Keith Jackson	15.00
9	Garrison Hearst	25.00
10	Natrone Means	25.00
11	Michael Haynes	15.00
12	Bam Morris	20.00

1995 Excalibur Rookie Roundtable

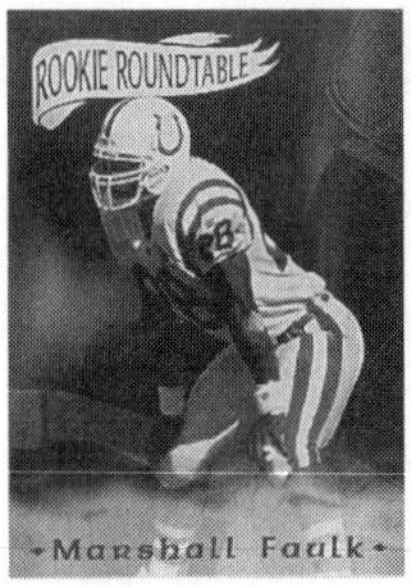

These 25 inserts, featuring the top sophomores heading into the 1995 season, were issued in both 1995 Collector's Edge Excalibur series packs. Cards 1-13 were seeded one per every nine packs in Series I; cards 14-25 were in every ninth Series II pack. The card front has the Rookie Roundtable banner stamped in silver foil in the upper left corner; the player's name is along the bottom. The card back has a mug shot of the player, with biographical information beside it, plus his 1994 statistics and a quote from Hall of Fame linebacker Dick Butkus, the company's spokesman. The player's team helmet is in the upper right corner.

		MT
Complete Set (25):		50.00
Comp. Series 1 (13):		15.00
Comp. Series 2 (12):		35.00
Common Player:		2.00
1	Sam Adams	2.00
2	Joe Johnson	2.00
3	Tim Bowens	2.00
4	Bryant Young	2.00
5	Aubrey Beavers	2.00
6	Willie McGinnest	2.00
7	Rob Fredrickson	2.00
8	Lee Woodall	2.00
9	Antonio Langham	2.00
10	DeWayne Washington	2.00
11	Darryl Morrison	2.00
12	Keith Lyle	2.00
13	Antonio Langham	2.00
14	Darnay Scott	6.00
15	Derrick Alexander	2.00
16	Todd Steussie	2.00
17	Larry Allen	2.00
18	Anthony Redmon	2.00
19	Joe Panos	2.00
20	Kevin Mawae	2.00
21	Andrew Jordan	2.00
22	Heath Shuler	6.00
23	Marshall Faulk	8.00
24	Errict Rhett	6.00
25	Marshall Faulk	8.00

1995 Excalibur TekTech

Like the Series I inserts, these cards were seeded one per 75 packs of 1995 Collector's Edge Excalibur Series II packs. The cards pick up where the first series left off, at #13, but have different designs from that series. The card front has a prism-like background, which contains ghosted images of the player in the background. The back has a mug shot of the player, with his name running down the left side of the card. Brief biographical information is underneath the photo.

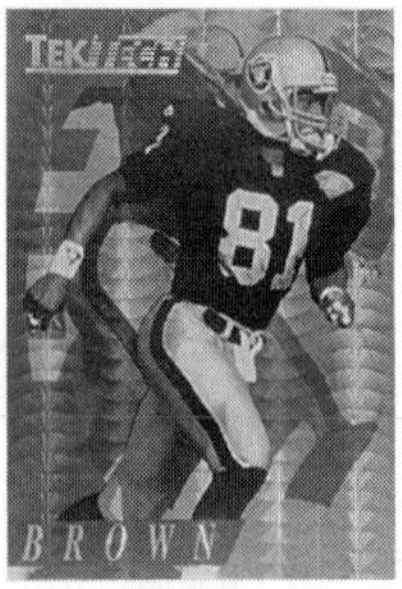

		MT
Complete Set (12):		100.00
Common Player:		2.50
Minor Stars:		5.00
1	Ricky Watters	5.00
2	Rick Mirer	2.50
3	Drew Bledsoe	15.00
4	Barry Sanders	20.00
5	Junior Seau	2.50
6	Dan Marino	30.00
7	Edgar Bennett	2.50
8	Haywood Jeffires	2.50
9	Deion Sanders	7.00
10	Tim Brown	2.50
11	Jerome Bettis	5.00
12	Marshall Faulk	5.00

1995 Collector's Edge Instant Replay

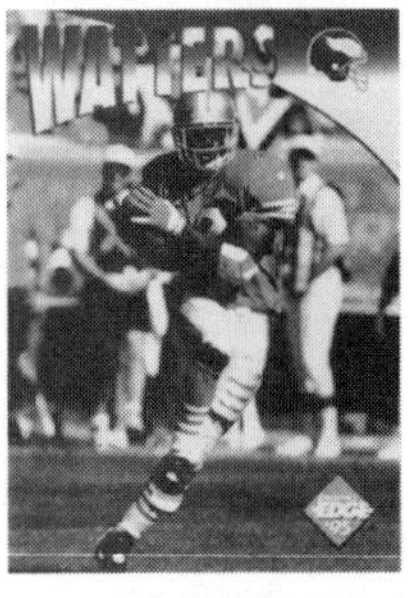

The 51-card set showcased the player's last name and team helmet at the top of the card fronts. The Edge logo is in the lower right. The card backs have the player's name, team, position and jersey number, along with a head shot, at the top. His bio is printed underneath. A quote is printed about the player's team logo background. Logos included on the back are Team NFL, Pop Warner and Edge. There is a Prism parallel of the set, which were seeded one per two packs. A Micro Mini set, an eight-card set of Black Label base cards, were found one per 14 packs. Each card showcased 50 mini-cards with 25 on each side.

		MT
Complete Set (51):		15.00
Common Player:		.05
Minor Stars:		.10
Prism Cards:		2x
Inserted 1:2		
Pack (8):		2.00
Wax Box (20):		35.00
1	Jeff George	.10
2	Eric Metcalf	.05
3	Jim Kelly	.20
4	Jeff Blake	.20
5	Andre Rison	.10
6	Troy Aikman	.75
7	Michael Irvin	.10
8	Emmitt Smith	1.00
9	John Elway	1.00
10	*Terrell Davis*	7.00
11	Herman Moore	.20
12	Barry Sanders	1.50
13	Brett Favre	1.50
14	Marshall Faulk	.30
15	Steve Beuerlein	.05
16	Steve Bono	.10
17	Tim Brown	.10
18	Jeff Hostetler	.05
19	Jerome Bettis	.20
20	Dan Marino	1.00
21	Cris Carter	.20
22	Drew Bledsoe	.75
23	Ben Coates	.10
24	Randall Cunningham	.20
25	Terry Kirby	.05
26	Ricky Watters	.10
27	Kyle Brady	.05
28	Byron "Bam" Morris	.05
29	Neil O'Donnell	.10
30	Natrone Means	.20
31	Junior Seau	.10
32	William Floyd	.10
33	Jerry Rice	.75

34 Deion Sanders .40
35 Steve Young .50
36 Rick Mirer .10
37 Chris Warren .10
38 Trent Dilfer .20
39 Errict Rhett .10
40 Heath Shuler .10
41 *Ki-Jana Carter* .10
42 *Kerry Collins* .75
43 *Steve McNair* 2.00
44 *Rashaan Salaam* .20
45 *James O. Stewart* .20
46 *J.J. Stokes* .50
47 *Tyrone Wheatley* .20
48 *Joey Galloway* 1.50
49 *Napoleon Kaufman* 2.00
50 *Michael Westbrook* .75
NNO Checklist .05

1995 Collector's Edge Instant Replay Edge Tech Die Cuts

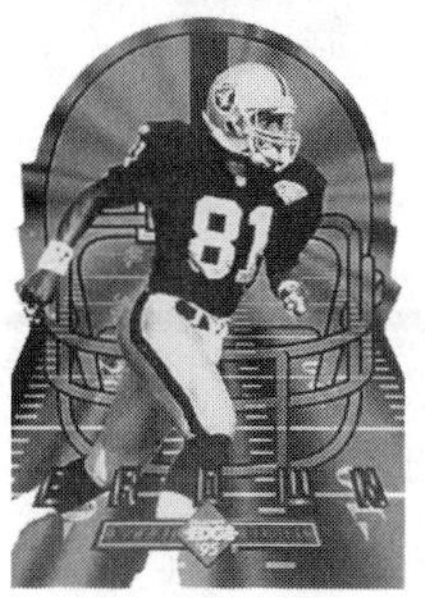

Randomly seeded one per four regular retail packs and one per special retail pack, the 13-card set showcased a die-cut in the shape of a helmet on the top of the card. The player's name is printed at the bottom of the card. A helmet also appears in the background. The card backs have "EdgeTech" at the top, with the player's headshot inside a circle. The player's name and bio are inside a stripe underneath his picture.

MT
Complete Set (13): 10.00
Common Player: .25
1 Troy Aikman 1.50
2 Drew Bledsoe 1.50
3 Tim Brown .50
4 Ben Coates .25
5 Marshall Faulk .75
6 William Floyd .25
7 Dan Marino 3.00
8 Errict Rhett 1.00
9 Deion Sanders 1.25
10 Emmitt Smith 3.00
11 Ricky Watters .50
12 Steve Young 1.25
NNO Checklist .25

1995 Collector's Edge Instant Replay Quantum Motion

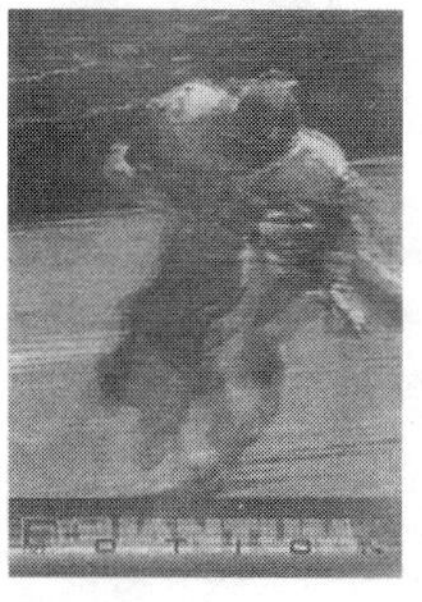

Cards Nos. 1-10 of the 22-card set were seeded one per 12 packs, while the remaining 11 cards were offered through a mail-in redemption. Card Nos. 1-10 include game action on the lenticular card fronts, with "Quantum Motion" printed at the bottom. The card backs have a headshot in the upper left, with the player's team's helmet on the right. The player's name and highlights are listed inside a box in the center of the card. The cards are numbered "of 21."

MT
Complete Set (22): 55.00
Complete Series 1 (11): 30.00
Complete Series 2 (11): 25.00
Common Player: 1.00
1 Troy Aikman 5.00
2 Drew Bledsoe 5.00
3 Marshall Faulk 3.00
4 Michael Irvin 2.00
5 Dan Marino 10.00
6 Jerry Rice 5.00
7 Rod Smith 1.00
8 Emmitt Smith 10.00
9 Michael Westbrook 2.50
10 Steve Young 3.50
11 Erik Kramer 1.00
12 Jeff Blake 3.00
13 Eric Metcalf 1.00
14 Steve Bono 1.00
15 Carl Pickens 2.00
16 Isaac Bruce 3.00
17 Errict Rhett 3.00
18 Kerry Collins 5.00
19 Rashaan Salaam 3.00
20 Gus Frerotte 1.00
21 Terry Kirby 1.00
NNO Checklist 1.00

1996 Collector's Edge Promos

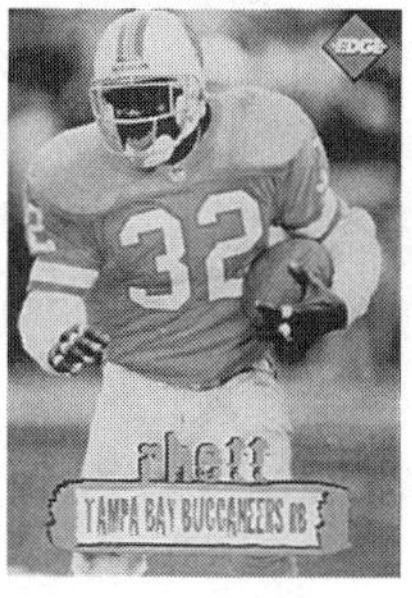

This six-card set gave a sampling of the Collector's Edge set for 1996. It included three regular-issue cards and a sampling of inserts that resemble that of the regular-issue series.

MT
Complete Set (4): 2.50
Common Player: .25
P1 Errict Rhett 1.00
P2 Junior Seau .75
P3 Terry Kirby .50
NNO Cover Card .25

1996 Collector's Edge

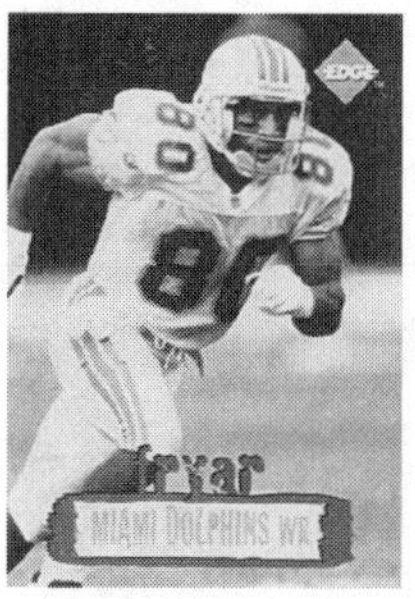

1996 Collector's Edge Series I football has 240 cards, consisting of veterans and rookies. Each regular card is also reprinted as part of a parallel Holofoil set, found one per every six packs. Three insert sets were also made - Quantum, Ripped and Too Cool Rookies.

MT
Complete Set (240): 20.00
Common Player: .05
Minor Stars: .10
Comp. Die Cut Set (240): 60.00
Die Cut Cards: 1.5x-3x
Comp. Holofoil Set (240): 600.00
Holofoil Cards: 15x-30x
Comp. Draft Redemp. (30): 100.00
Common Draft: 5.00
Pack (6): 1.25
Wax Box (24): 30.00
1 Larry Centers .05
2 Garrison Hearst .10
3 Dave Krieg .05
4 Rob Moore .05
5 Frank Sanders .05
6 Eric Swann .05
7 Morten Andersen .05
8 Chris Doleman .05
9 Bert Emanuel .05
10 Jeff George .10
11 Craig Heyward .05
12 Terance Mathis .05
13 Clay Matthews .05
14 Eric Metcalf .05
15 Bill Brooks .05
16 Todd Collins .05
17 Russell Copeland .05
18 Jim Kelly .10
19 Bryce Paup .05
20 Andre Reed .05
21 Bruce Smith .05
22 Mark Carrier .05
23 Kerry Collins .30
24 Willie Green .05
25 Eric Guliford .05
26 Brett Maxie .05
27 Tim McKyer .05
28 Derrick Moore .05
29 Curtis Conway .05
30 Jim Flanigan .05
31 Jeff Graham .05
32 Robert Green .05
33 Erik Kramer .05
34 Rashaan Salaam .50
35 Alonzo Spellman .05
36 Donnell Woolford .05
37 Chris Zorich .05
38 Eric Bieniemy .05
39 Jeff Blake .50
40 Ki-Jana Carter .25
41 John Copeland .05
42 Harold Green .05
43 Tony McGee .05
44 Carl Pickens .10
45 Darnay Scott .05
46 Bracey Walker .05
47 Dan Wilkinson .05
48 Rob Burnett .05
49 Leroy Hoard .05
50 Earnest Hunter .05
51 Michael Jackson .05
52 Stevon Moore .05
53 Anthony Pleasant .05
54 Andre Rison .05
55 Vinny Testaverde .05
56 Eric Zeier .05
57 Troy Aikman 1.00
58 Bill Bates .05
59 Shante Carver .05
60 Michael Irvin .10
61 Daryl Johnston .05
62 Jay Novacek .05
63 Deion Sanders .50
64 Emmitt Smith 2.00
65 Sherman Williams .05
66 Terrell Davis .50
67 John Elway .50
68 Ed McCaffrey .05
69 Glyn Milburn .05
70 Anthony Miller .05
71 Michael Dean Perry .05
72 Shannon Sharpe .05
73 Willie Clay .05
74 Scott Mitchell .05
75 Herman Moore .25
76 Johnnie Morton .05
77 Brett Perriman .05
78 Barry Sanders 1.25
79 Tracy Scroggins .05
80 Edgar Bennett .05
81 Robert Brooks .10
82 Brett Favre 2.00
83 Dorsey Levens .10
84 Craig Newsome .05
85 Wayne Simmons .05
86 Reggie White .10
87 Chris Chandler .05
88 Anthony Cook .05
89 Mel Gray .05
90 Haywood Jeffires .05
91 Darryll Lewis .05
92 Steve McNair .50
93 Todd McNair .05
94 Rodney Thomas .20
95 Trev Alberts .05
96 Tony Bennett .05
97 Quentin Coryatt .05
98 Sean Dawkins .05
99 Ken Dilger .05
100 Marshall Faulk .75
101 Jim Harbaugh .05
102 Ronald Humphrey .05
103 Floyd Turner .05
104 Steve Beuerlein .05
105 Tony Boselli .05
106 Mark Brunell .75
107 Willie Jackson .05
108 Jeff Lageman .05
109 James Stewart .05
110 Cedric Tillman .05
111 Marcus Allen .05
112 Kimble Anders .05
113 Steve Bono .05
114 Dale Carter .05
115 Willie Davis .05
116 Lake Dawson .05
117 Dan Saleaumua .05
118 Neil Smith .05
119 Derrick Thomas .05
120 Tamarick Vanover .30
121 Marco Coleman .05
122 Bryan Cox .05
123 Steve Emtman .05
124 Irving Fryar .05
125 Eric Green .05
126 Terry Kirby .05
127 Dan Marino 2.00
128 O.J. McDuffie .05
129 Bernie Parmalee .05
130 Troy Vincent .05
131 Cris Carter .05
132 Jack Del Rio .05
133 Qadry Ismail .05
134 Amp Lee .05
135 Warren Moon .05
136 John Randle .05
137 Jake Reed .05
138 Robert Smith .05
139 Drew Bledsoe .75
140 Vincent Brisby .05
141 Ben Coates .05
142 Curtis Martin 1.50
143 David Meggett .05
144 Will Moore .05
145 Chris Slade .05
146 Mario Bates .05
147 Quinn Early .05
148 Jim Everett .05
149 Michael Haynes .05
150 Tyrone Hughes .05
151 Wayne Martin .05
152 Renaldo Turnbull .05
153 Dave Brown .05
154 Chris Calloway .05
155 Rodney Hampton .05
156 Mike Sherrard .05
157 Michael Strahan .05
158 Herschel Walker .05
159 Tyrone Wheatley .05
160 Kyle Brady .05
161 Wayne Chrebet .05
162 Hugh Douglas .05
163 Adrian Murrell .05
164 Todd Scott .05
165 Charles Wilson .05
166 Tim Brown .05
167 Aundray Bruce .05
168 Andrew Glover .05
169 Jeff Hostetler .05
170 Napoleon Kaufman .05
171 Terry McDaniel .05
172 Chester McGlockton .05
173 Pat Swilling .05
174 Harvey Williams .05
175 Fred Barnett .05
176 Randall Cunningham .05
177 William Fuller .05
178 Charlie Garner .05
179 Andy Harmon .05
180 Rodney Peete .05
181 Ricky Watters .05
182 Calvin Williams .05
183 Chad Brown .05
184 Kevin Greene .05
185 Greg Lloyd .05
186 Bam Morris .05
187 Neil O'Donnell .05
188 Eric Pegram .05
189 Kordell Stewart .75
190 Yancey Thigpen .25
191 Rod Woodson .05
192 Darren Bennett .05
193 Ronnie Harmon .05
194 Stan Humphries .05
195 Tony Martin .05
196 Natrone Means .05
197 Leslie O'Neil .05
198 Junior Seau .10
199 Mark Seay .05
200 William Floyd .05
201 Merton Hanks .05
202 Brent Jones .05
203 Derek Loville .05
204 Ken Norton Jr. .05
205 Gary Plummer .05
206 Jerry Rice 1.00
207 J.J. Stokes .30
208 Dana Stubblefield .05
209 John Taylor .05
210 Bryant Young .05
211 Steve Young .75
212 Brian Blades .05
213 Joey Galloway .50
214 Carlton Gray .05
215 Cortez Kennedy .05
216 Rick Mirer .05
217 Chris Warren .10
218 Jerome Bettis .05
219 Isaac Bruce .40
220 Troy Drayton .05
221 D'Marco Farr .05
222 Sean Gilbert .05
223 Chris Miller .05
224 Roman Phifer .05
225 Trent Dilfer .05
226 Santana Dotson .05
227 Alvin Harper .05
228 Jackie Harris .05
229 John Lynch .05
230 Hardy Nickerson .05
231 Errict Rhett .50
232 Warren Sapp .05
233 Terry Allen .05
234 Henry Ellard .05
235 Gus Frerotte .05
236 Ken Harvey .05
237 Brian Mitchell .05
238 Heath Shuler .20
239 James Washington .05
240 Michael Westbrook .30

1996 Collector's Edge Die Cuts

Randomly seeded one per retail pack, the die-cut had a pink front, with a front that was similar to base set cards, except for the die-cut.

MT
Complete Set (240): 75.00
Common Player: .25
Die-Cut Cards: 2x-4x

1996 Collector's Edge Holofoil

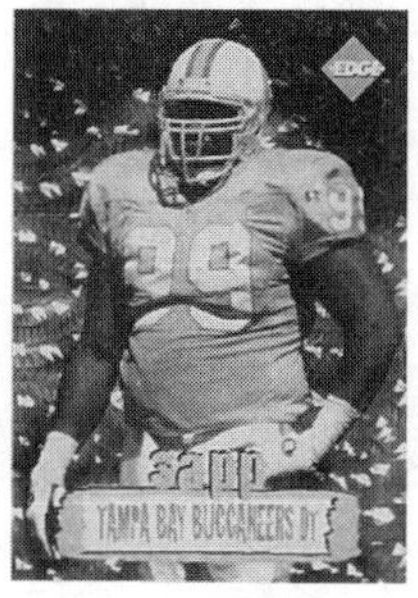

Seeded one per 48 retail, hobby or Cowboybilia packs, the 240-card set was a parallel to the Edge base cards.

MT
Complete Set (240): 500.00
Common Player: 2.00
Holofoil Cards: 15x-30x

1996 Collector's Edge All-Stars

This 13-card set (includes a checklist) was done on plastic stock and features two photos of the player on the front.

MT
Complete Set (13): 35.00
Common Player: 2.00
1 Junior Seau 3.00
2 Drew Bledsoe 6.00
3 Marshall Faulk 3.00
4 John Elway 5.00
5 Jerry Rice 6.00
6 Errict Rhett 2.00
7 Jerome Bettis 2.00
8 Deion Sanders 4.00
9 Byron "Bam" Morris 2.00
10 Cris Carter 3.00
11 Terrell Davis 6.00
12 Terance Mathis 2.00
--- Checklist Card 1.00

1996 Collector's Edge Big Easy

Big Easy cards were inserted in various 1996 Collector's Edge packs. Each card is numbered one of 2,000. A gold foil parallel was released through mail order. Each card in the parallel is numbered one of 3,100.

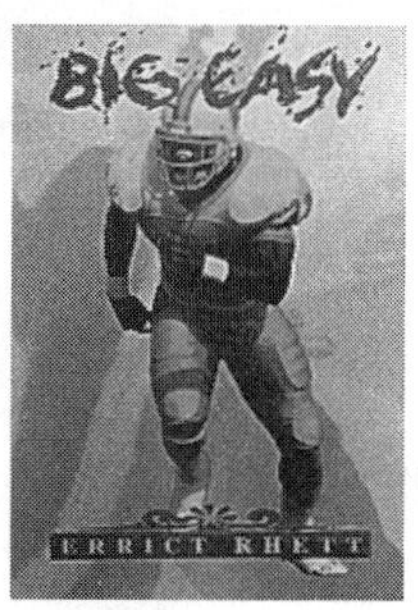

MT
Complete Set (19): 200.00
Common Player: 5.00
1 Kerry Collins 14.00
2 Rashaan Salaam 5.00
3 Troy Aikman 16.00
4 Deion Sanders 10.00
5 Emmitt Smith 30.00
6 Terrell Davis 16.00
7 Barry Sanders 16.00
8 Brett Favre 35.00
9 Marshall Faulk 8.00
10 Tamarick Vanover 8.00
11 Dan Marino 30.00
12 Drew Bledsoe 16.00
13 Curtis Martin 16.00
14 J.J. Stokes 8.00
15 Joey Galloway 8.00
16 Isaac Bruce 8.00
17 Errict Rhett 5.00
18 Carl Pickens 5.00
--- Checklist Card 1.50

1996 Collector's Edge Draft Day Redemption

This 30-card set features one 1996 draft pick from each NFL team. One card could be obtained via that team's redemption card. The redemption cards were inserted 1:8.

MT
Complete Set (30): 100.00
Common Player: 2.00
Trade Cards: .10
1 Simeon Rice 2.00
2 Richard Huntley 2.00
3 Jonathan Ogden 2.00
4 Eric Moulds 4.00
5 Tim Biakabutuka 4.00
6 Walt Harris 2.00
7 Marco Battaglia 2.00
8 Stepfret Williams 2.00
9 John Mobley 2.00
10 Reggie Brown LB 2.00
11 Derrick Mayes 2.00
12 Eddie George 8.00
13 Marvin Harrison 5.00
14 Kevin Hardy 3.00
15 Jerome Woods 2.00
16 Karim Abdul-Jabbar 6.00
17 Duane Clemons 2.00
18 Terry Glenn 7.00
19 Ricky Whittle 2.00
20 Amani Toomer 2.00
21 Keyshawn Johnson 5.00
22 Rickey Dudley 3.00
23 Bobby Hoying 4.00
24 Jahine Arnold 2.00
25 Tony Banks 5.00
26 Bryan Still 2.00
27 Terrell Owens 5.00
28 Reggie Brown RB 2.00
29 Mike Alstott 4.00
30 Stephen Davis 3.00

1996 Collector's Edge Proteges

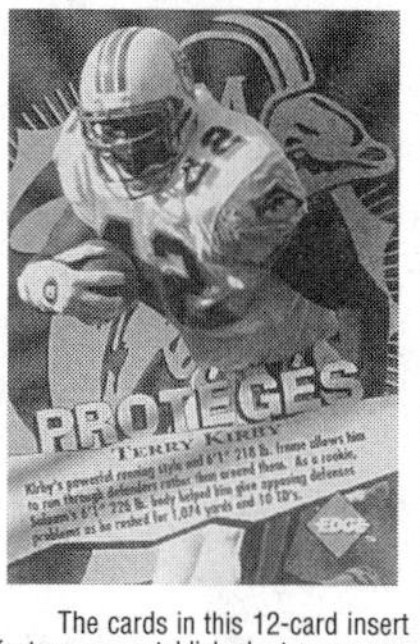

The cards in this 12-card insert feature an established star on one side and a young player with similar skills on the other. They were inserted 1:164 in 1996 Collector's Edge packs.

MT
Complete Set (13): 200.00
Common Player: 8.00
1 Eric Metcalf, Joey Galloway 12.00
2 Herman Moore, Michael Westbrook 12.00
3 Emmitt Smith, Errict Rhett 30.00
4 Kordell Stewart, John Elway 20.00
5 Terrell Davis, Marshall Faulk 20.00
6 Rashaan Salaam, Marcus Allen 12.00
7 Dan Marino, Drew Bledsoe 30.00
8 Brett Favre, Kerry Collins 30.00
9 Tim Brown, Isaac Bruce 12.00
10 Cris Carter, Chris Sanders 8.00
11 Curtis Martin, Chris Warren 18.00
12 Tamarick Vanover, Brian Mitchell 10.00
--- Checklist Card 2.00
P1 Rashaan Salaam Promo, Terry Kirby Promo 2.00

1996 Collector's Edge Ripped

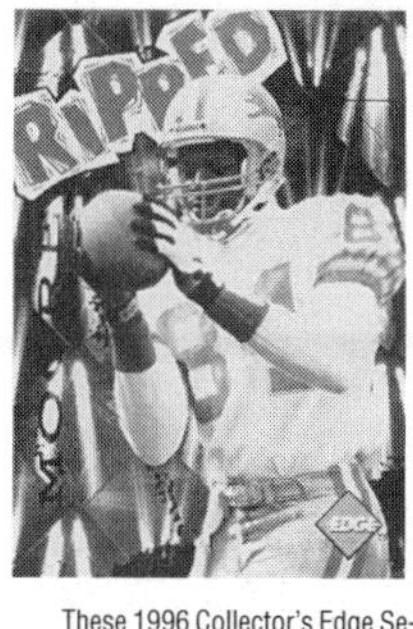

These 1996 Collector's Edge Series I inserts feature 36 of the NFL's top stars. Cards were seeded one per 18 packs of Series I product.

MT
Complete Set (36): 100.00
Complete Hobby (18): 50.00
Complete Retail (18): 50.00
Common Player: 2.00
1 Jeff Blake 3.00
2 Steve Bono 2.00
3 Terrell Davis 7.00
4 John Elway 4.00
5 Marshall Faulk 4.00
6 Brett Favre 12.00
7 Jeff Hostetler 2.00
8 Erik Kramer 2.00
9 Dan Marino 12.00
10 Natrone Means 2.00
11 Eric Metcalf 2.00
12 Anthony Miller 2.00
13 Herman Moore 3.00
14 Errict Rhett 2.00
15 Andre Rison 2.00
16 Barry Sanders 6.00
17 Yancey Thigpen 2.00
18 Michael Westbrook 2.00
19 Troy Aikman 6.00
20 Drew Bledsoe 6.00
21 Tim Brown 2.00
22 Mark Brunell 6.00
23 Cris Carter 2.00
24 Kerry Collins 3.00
25 Joey Galloway 3.00
26 Michael Irvin 2.00
27 Terry Kirby 2.00
28 Curtis Martin 8.00
29 Carl Pickens 2.00
30 Jerry Rice 6.00
31 Rashaan Salaam 3.00
32 Deion Sanders 4.00
33 Emmitt Smith 12.00
34 Kordell Stewart 6.00
35 Ricky Watters 2.00
36 Steve Young 4.00

1996 Collector's Edge Too Cool Rookies

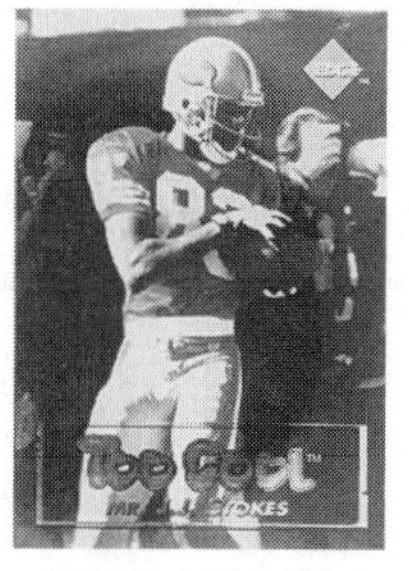

The NFL's top 25 rookies from 1995 are featured on these 1996 Collector's Edge Series I inserts. Cards were seeded one per every 25 packs of Series I product.

MT
Complete Set (25): 75.00
Common Player: 2.00
1 Tony Boselli 2.00
2 Kyle Brady 2.00
3 Ki-Jana Carter 4.00
4 Kerry Collins 4.00
5 Todd Collins 2.00
6 Terrell Davis 6.00
7 Hugh Douglas 2.00
8 Joey Galloway 6.00
9 Darius Holland 2.00
10 Napoleon Kaufman 2.00
11 Mike Mamula 2.00
12 Curtis Martin 10.00
13 Steve McNair 6.00
14 Billy Milner 2.00

15	Rashaan Salaam	5.00
16	Frank Sanders	2.00
17	Warren Sapp	2.00
18	James Stewart	2.00
19	Kordell Stewart	7.00
20	J.J. Stokes	5.00
21	Tamarick Vanover	3.00
22	Michael Westbrook	5.00
23	Tyrone Wheatley	2.00
24	Sherman Williams	2.00
25	Eric Zeier	2.00

1996 Collector's Edge Quantum

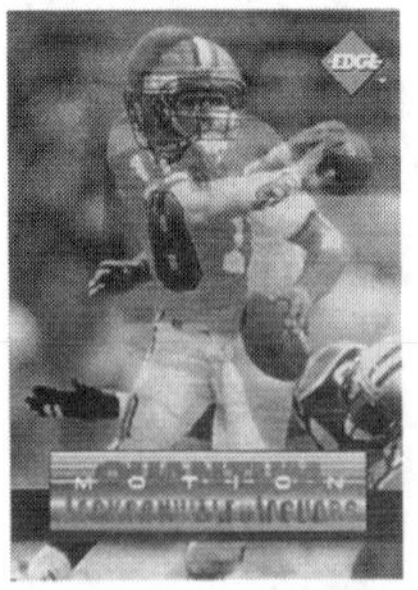

These 24 cards were seeded one per 36 packs of 1996 Collector's Edge Series I football. The cards change images; NFL stars are shown in their current pro team's uniform and also in their college uniforms.

		MT
Complete Set (24):		300.00
Common Player:		7.00
1	Troy Aikman	20.00
2	Jeff Blake	15.00
3	Drew Bledsoe	20.00
4	Steve Bono	7.00
5	Tim Brown	7.00
6	Isaac Bruce	14.00
7	Mark Brunell	18.00
8	Kerry Collins	10.00
9	Marshall Faulk	10.00
10	Brett Favre	40.00
11	Jeff George	7.00
12	Terry Kirby	7.00
13	Dan Marino	40.00
14	Natrone Means	10.00
15	Carl Pickens	7.00
16	Errict Rhett	10.00
17	Rashaan Salaam	10.00
18	Deion Sanders	15.00
19	Barry Sanders	20.00
20	Emmitt Smith	40.00
21	Kordell Stewart	20.00
22	Yancey Thigpen	10.00
23	Michael Westbrook	10.00
24	Steve Young	20.00

1996 Collector's Edge Advantage Promos

This three-card promo set featured one regular-issue card (EA1), one Role Models insert (RM1) and one Edge Video (PR1). The cards detailed what the Edge Advantage set for 1996 would look like.

		MT
Complete Set (3):		8.00
Common Player:		2.50
EA1	Jeff Blake	3.00
PR1	Rashaan Salaam	3.00
RM1	Michael Westbrook	2.50

1996 Collector's Edge Advantage

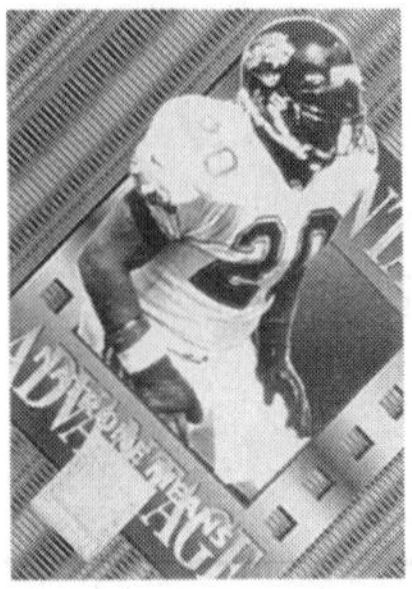

Collector's Edge's 1996 Advantage set includes 150 cards, including 25 cards of rookies in their NFL uniforms. Each card front and back is gold foil stamped and embossed, with the rookie cards featuring extra foil stamping. The base set is also paralleled by Perfect Play Holofoil inserts; these cards, seeded one per two packs, use prism art technology. Five other insert sets were also produced - Role Models, Edge Video, Crystal Cuts, Game Ball and Super Bowl Game Ball. Portions of the proceeds made from the sale of this product were donated to the Pop Warner Football program.

		MT
Complete Set (150):		25.00
Common Player:		.10
Minor Stars:		.20
Foil Cards:		3x-6x
Pack (6):		2.75
Wax Box (24):		58.00
1	Drew Bledsoe	1.00
2	Chris Warren	.10
3	*Eddie George*	3.50
4	Barry Sanders	1.75
5	Scott Mitchell	.10
6	Carl Pickens	.10
7	Tim Brown	.10
8	John Elway	.75
9	Michael Westbrook	.20
10	Cris Carter	.10
11	Troy Aikman	1.25
12	Ben Coates	.10
13	Brett Favre	2.50
14	Marshall Faulk	.40
15	Steve Young	1.00
16	Terrell Davis	2.00
17	*Keyshawn Johnson*	3.00
18	Mario Bates	.10
19	Steve McNair	.75
20	Kerry Collins	.30
21	Natrone Means	.10
22	Kordell Stewart	1.25
23	Jeff George	.10
24	Rick Mirer	.10
25	Herman Moore	.20
26	Rodney Peete	.10
27	Isaac Bruce	.50
28	Errict Rhett	.20
29	Jerry Rice	1.25
30	Rashaan Salaam	.50
31	Eric Metcalf	.10
32	Jim Kelly	.20
33	Jerome Bettis	.20
34	Deion Sanders	.75
35	J.J. Stokes	.20
36	Neil O'Donnell	.10
37	Marcus Allen	.20
38	Thurman Thomas	.20
39	Dan Marino	2.50
40	*Rickey Dudley*	.75
41	Napoleon Kaufman	.10
42	Kyle Brady	.10
43	Emmitt Smith	2.50
44	Tyrone Wheatley	.10
45	Jeff Blake	.20
46	Reggie White	.20
47	Joey Galloway	1.00
48	Antonio Langham	.10
49	Craig Heyward	.10
50	Curtis Martin	1.75
51	*Karim Abdul-Jabbar*	1.00
52	Antonio Freeman	.10
53	Ki-Jana Carter	.20
54	Willie Davis	.10
55	Jim Everett	.10
56	Gus Frerotte	.10
57	Daryl Gardener	.10
58	Charles Haley	.10
59	Michael Irvin	.20
60	Keith Jackson	.10
61	Cortez Kennedy	.10
62	Greg Lloyd	.10
63	Tony Martin	.10
64	Ken Norton Jr.	.10
65	Leslie O'Neal	.10
66	Bryce Paup	.10
67	Jake Reed	.10
68	Frank Sanders	.10
69	Vinny Testaverde	.10
70	Regan Upshaw	.10
71	Tamarick Vanover	.50
72	Walt Harris	.10
73	John Randle	.10
74	Ricky Watters	.20
75	Terry Allen	.10
76	Edgar Bennett	.10
77	Larry Centers	.10
78	Chris Penn	.10
79	*Bobby Engram*	.75
80	Irving Fryar	.10
81	Charlie Garner	.10
82	Rodney Hampton	.10
83	Michael Jackson	.10
84	O.J. McDuffie	.10
85	Shannon Sharpe	.10
86	Aaron Hayden	.10
87	*Mushin Muhammad*	1.00
88	Rodney Woodson	.10
89	Levon Kirkland	.10
90	Chad Brown	.10
91	Junior Seau	.10
92	Terry Kirby	.10
93	*Zach Thomas*	1.00
94	Harvey Williams	.10
95	Robert Brooks	.10
96	Darrell Green	.10
97	Chester McGlockton	.10
98	Neil Smith	.10
99	Eric Swann	.10
100	*Mike Alstott*	1.50
101	*Tim Biakabutuka*	1.00
102	Mark Brunell	1.00
103	Chris Doleman	.10
104	Sean Gilbert	.10
105	Jim Harbaugh	.10
106	Chris T. Jones	.10
107	Tyrone Hughes	.10
108	*Amani Toomer*	.40
109	Larry Brown	.10
110	Kevin Greene	.10
111	John Mobley	.10
112	*Danny Kanell*	.75
113	*Kevin Hardy*	.40
114	Brett Perriman	.10
115	*Simeon Rice*	.40
116	Chris Sanders	.10
117	Dave Brown	.10
118	Bryan Cox	.10
119	Yancey Thigpen	.10
120	Terance Mathis	.10
121	Warren Moon	.10
122	Derrick Thomas	.10
123	Trent Dilfer	.10
124	*Terry Glenn*	2.00
125	Jeff Hostetler	.10
126	*Leeland McElroy*	.50
127	Hardy Nickerson	.10
128	Steve Bono	.10
129	Stanley Pritchett	.10
130	Dana Stubblefield	.10
131	Andre Coleman	.10
132	Anthony Miller	.10
133	Stan Humphries	.10
134	Robert Smith	.10
135	Curtis Conway	.10
136	Derrick Holmes	.10
137	Pat Swilling	.10
138	Andre Rison	.10
139	Erik Kramer	.10
140	Jason Dunn	.10
141	Torrance Small	.10
142	Cedric Jones	.10
143	Derek Loville	.10
144	Brian Mitchell	.10
145	*Eric Moulds*	2.00
146	James Stewart	.10
147	Bruce Smith	.10
148	Keenan McCardell	.10
149	Warren Sapp	.10
150	*Marvin Harrison*	3.00

1996 Collector's Edge Advantage Perfect Play Holofoil

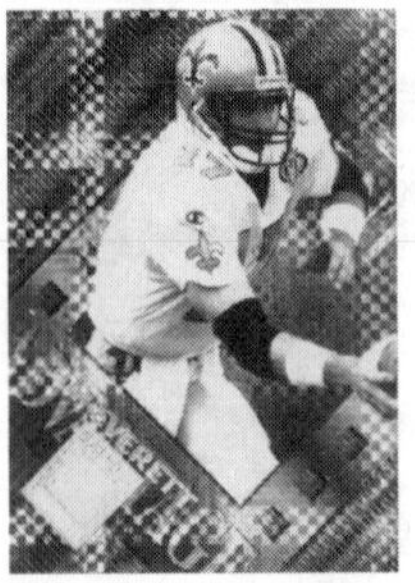

Perfect Play Holofoil cards put a prismatic finish on all 150 cards in the Advantage set. These parallel cards were inserted every two packs.

	MT
Complete Set (150):	150.00
Holofoil Cards:	3x-6x

1996 Collector's Edge Advantage Game Ball

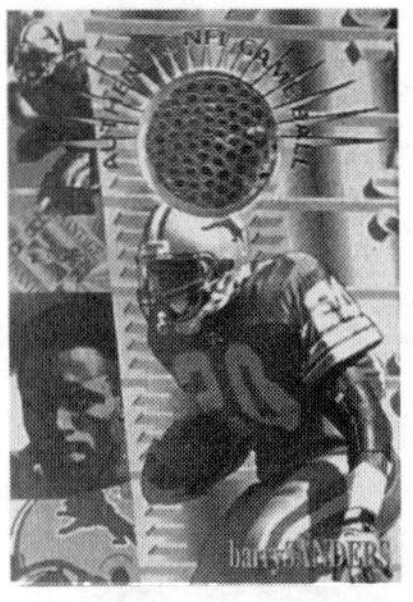

These 1996 Collector's Edge Advantage inserts feature a medallion cut from an authentic game-used NFL football, with highlights of the game in which the ball was used. The card front has a color photo on it, plus foil stamping. The background of the card has a football field, with smaller color photos along the left side. Each card back contains a statement of authentication for the ball and game in which it was used. The cards are limited to 400 individually dual-numbered cards, seeded one per 72 packs.

		MT
Complete Set (36):		1600.
Common Player:		25.00
1	Kordell Stewart	75.00
2	Emmitt Smith	150.00
3	Brett Favre	150.00
4	Steve Young	50.00
5	Barry Sanders	120.00
6	John Elway	40.00
7	Drew Bledsoe	60.00
8	Dan Marino	150.00
9	Keyshawn Johnson	40.00
10	Eddie George	85.00
11	Kevin Hardy	25.00
12	Terry Glenn	75.00
13	Michael Westbrook	25.00
14	Joey Galloway	50.00
15	John Mobley	25.00
16	Curtis Martin	80.00
17	Rashaan Salaam	25.00
18	J.J. Stokes	25.00
19	Kerry Collins	60.00
20	Deion Sanders	50.00
21	Shannon Sharpe	25.00
22	Terry Allen	25.00
23	Rickey Watters	25.00
24	Marshall Faulk	40.00
25	Tim Biakabutaka	30.00
26	Troy Aikman	60.00
27	Jerry Rice	60.00
28	Chris Warren	25.00
29	Jeff Blake	25.00
30	Carl Pickens	25.00
31	Isaac Bruce	35.00
32	Terrell Davis	80.00
33	Mark Brunell	75.00
34	Karim Abdul-Jabbar	50.00
35	Herman Moore	25.00
36	Cris Carter	25.00

A card number in parentheses ( ) indicates the set is unnumbered.

1996 Collector's Edge Advantage Super Bowl Game Ball

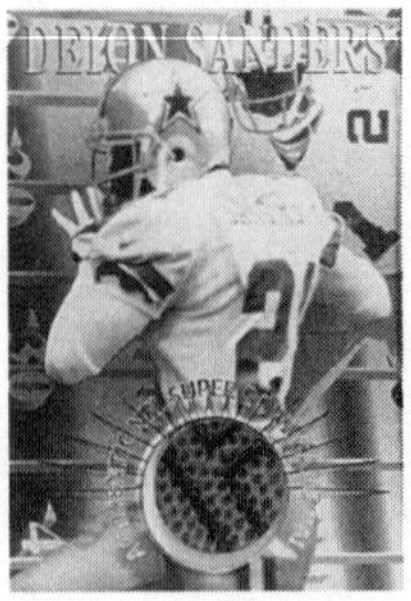

Collector's Edge obtained several footballs from the Super Bowl to create these 1996 inserts. Each card has a medallion cut from an authentic NFL Super Bowl game-used ball, with highlights of the game in which the ball was used. The 36 cards were limited to 200 individually-numbered cards each, with odds of one per 164 packs.

		MT
Complete Set (36):		2200.
Common Player:		30.00
1	Emmitt Smith	325.00
2	Troy Aikman	180.00
3	Michael Irvin	50.00
4	Deion Sanders	130.00
5	John Elway	160.00
6	Dan Marino	325.00
7	Marcus Allen	80.00
8	Kordell Stewart	180.00
9	Steve Young	130.00
10	Ricky Watters	50.00
11	Jerry Rice	180.00
12	Jim Kelly	80.00
13	Thurman Thomas	50.00
14	Bruce Smith	30.00
15	Stan Humphries	30.00
16	Junior Seau	50.00
17	Natrone Means	30.00
18	Neil O'Donnell	30.00
19	Rod Woodson	30.00
20	Andre Reed	30.00
21	Jeff Hostetler	30.00
22	Dave Meggett	30.00
23	Greg Lloyd	30.00
24	Kevin Green	30.00
25	Yancey Thigpen	30.00
26	Charles Haley	30.00
27	Bam Morris	30.00
28	Alvin Harper	30.00
29	Ken Norton Jr.	30.00
30	William Floyd	30.00
31	Leslie O'Neal	30.00
32	Jay Novacek	30.00
33	Irvin Fryar	30.00
34	Leon Lett	30.00
35	Tony Martin	30.00
36	Mark Collins	30.00

1996 Collector's Edge Advantage Role Models

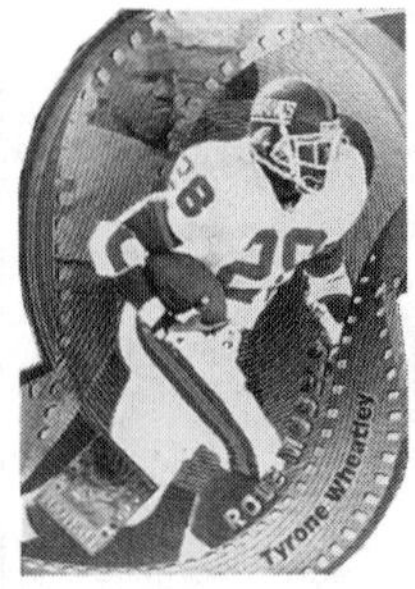

These 1996 Collector's Edge Advantage inserts were seeded one per 12 packs. Each card front has an action shot on it, on a die-cut, embossed metallized card. A smaller photo is in the background of the card front, which has the Collector's Edge logo stamped in gold foil.

		MT
Complete Set (12):		60.00
Common Player:		2.50
1	John Elway	7.00
2	Dan Marino	16.00
3	Jerry Rice	8.00
4	Emmitt Smith	16.00
5	Chris Warren	2.50
6	Tim Brown	2.50
7	Jeff George	2.50
8	Tyrone Wheatley	2.50
9	Steve Bono	2.50
10	Kerry Collins	5.00
11	Jerome Bettis	5.00
12	Steve Beuerlein	2.50

1996 Collector's Edge Advantage Edge Video

These 1996 Collector's Edge Advantage inserts depict real game action with an overlaid photograph. The card front has a stand-out player shot with a state-of-the-art "Edge Video" background showing actual in-motion footage. The cards, each limited to 1,200, were seeded one per 36 packs.

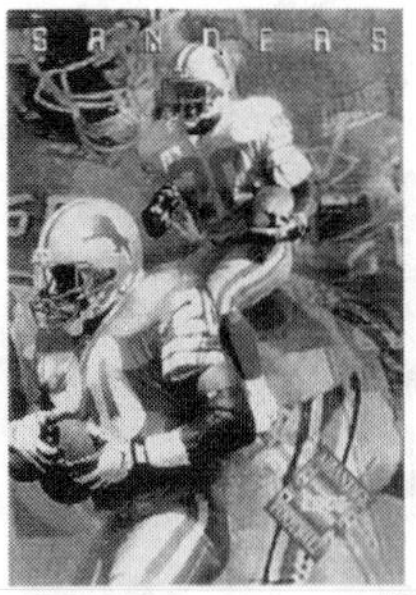

		MT
Complete Set (25):		200.00
Common Player:		4.00
1	Brett Favre	35.00
2	Keyshawn Johnson	10.00
3	Deion Sanders	10.00
4	Marcus Allen	4.00
5	Rashaan Salaam	8.00
6	Thurman Thomas	4.00
7	Emmitt Smith	35.00
8	Isaac Bruce	6.00
9	Michael Westbrook	4.00
10	Cris Carter	4.00
11	Marshall Faulk	6.00
12	Jerry Rice	17.00
13	Tim Brown	4.00
14	Steve Young	12.00
15	Eric Metcalf	4.00
16	Chris Warren	4.00
17	Drew Bledsoe	17.00
18	Barry Sanders	20.00
19	Herman Moore	6.00
20	Rodney Peete	4.00
21	Troy Aikman	17.00
22	Jerome Bettis	4.00
23	Errict Rhett	6.00
24	Dan Marino	35.00
25	Natrone Means	4.00

1996 Collector's Edge Advantage Crystal Cuts

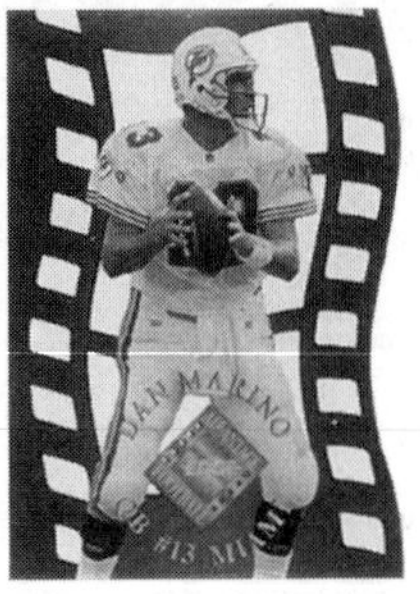

These 1996 Collector's Edge Advantage die-cut inserts are printed on clear plastic stock. The cards, dual numbered up to 5,000, were seeded one per eight packs. The card front has a color photo on it, with a background which makes the card look like a filmstrip. The player's name, position, number and team name are in gold foil and form a circle at the bottom of the card. The Collector's Edge logo is stamped in gold foil in the middle.

		MT
Complete Set (25):		125.00
Common Player:		2.50
1	Barry Sanders	8.00
2	Eddie George	12.00
3	Curtis Martin	12.00
4	J.J. Stokes	5.00
5	Kyle Brady	2.50
6	Chris Warren	2.50
7	Jerry Rice	7.00
8	Ben Coates	2.50
9	Terrell Davis	8.00
10	Marcus Allen	2.50
11	John Elway	6.00
12	Joey Galloway	5.00
13	Dan Marino	14.00
14	Napoleon Kaufman	2.50
15	Emmitt Smith	14.00
16	Eric Metcalf	2.50
17	Kerry Collins	7.00
18	Troy Aikman	7.00
19	Rickey Dudley	3.00
20	Steve McNair	6.00
21	Steve Young	6.00
22	Isaac Bruce	4.00
23	Kordell Stewart	7.00
24	LeShon Johnson	2.50
25	Scott Mitchell	2.50

1996 Collector's Edge Cowboybilia

Each of the 25 cards, except Troy Aikman, were signed by the featured player. They were seeded one per 2.5 packs in Cowboybilia. Other packs included a certificate for signed Cowboys items like jerseys, helmets, photos, footballs and pennants. In addition, 24K Prism parallel cards of Deion Sanders, Troy Aikman, Emmitt Smith and Michael Irvin were seeded four per case (one of each player per case). A Roger Staubach/Drew Pearson autographed Hail Mary card was found one per 192 packs. The cards are numbered with the "DC" prefix.

		MT
Complete Set (25):		450.00
Common Player:		8.00
1	Chris Boniol (4000)	8.00
2	John Jett (4000)	8.00
3	Sherman Williams (4000)	8.00
4	Chad Hennings (4000)	8.00
5	Larry Allen (4000)	10.00
6	Jason Garrett (4000)	8.00
7	Tony Tolbert (4000)	8.00
8	Kevin Williams (4000)	20.00
9	Mark Tuinei (4000)	8.00
10	Larry Brown (4000)	10.00
11	Kevin Smith (4000)	10.00
12	Darrin Smith (4000)	8.00
13	Robert Jones (4000)	8.00
14	Nate Newton (4000)	12.00
15	Darren Woodson (4000)	12.00
16	Leon Lett (4000)	12.00
17	Russell Maryland (4000)	10.00
18	Erik Williams (4000)	12.00
19	Bill Bates (4000)	12.00
20	Daryl Johnston (2300)	20.00
21	Jay Novacek (2300)	20.00
22	Charles Haley (2300)	20.00
23	Troy Aikman (600 all cards unsigned)	18.00
24	Michael Irvin (500)	60.00
25	Emmitt Smith (500)	175.00
NNO	Roger Staubach, Drew Pearson (Hail Mary Pass numbered of 1000)	200.00

1996 Collector's Edge Cowboybilia 24K Holofoil

Randomly seeded one per 48 1995 Edge Cowboybilia packs, the four cards parallel the players' 1995 Edge Holofoil card. The Cowboybilia 24K Holofoil cards have a 24K logo and are numbered with the "CB" prefix.

		MT
Complete Set (4):		200.00
Common Player:		20.00
57	Troy Aikman	50.00
60	Michael Irvin	20.00
63	Deion Sanders	30.00
64	Emmitt Smith	100.00

1996 Collector's Edge President's Reserve Promos

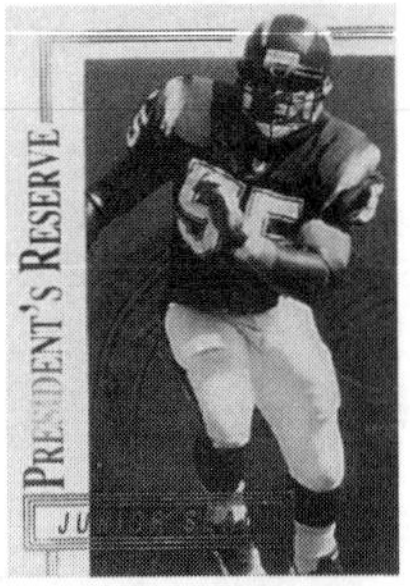

The 1996 Edge President's Reserve set was hyped by this six-card set, which included one card from each of the upcoming set's regular and chase sets. The cards each are numbered with the "PR" prefix.

		MT
Complete Set (6):		7.00
Common Player:		.50
1	Jeff Blake, Errict Rhett (Running Mates)	2.50
2	Dick Butkus, Steve Bono (TimeWarp)	2.50
3	Philadelphia Eagles (Candidates Rookie Redemption)	.50
4	Rashaan Salaam (New Regime)	1.00
5	Junior Seau (Base Brand)	.50
6	Michael Westbrook (Air Force One)	1.00

1996 Collector's Edge President's Reserve

1996 Collector's Edge President's Reserve Series I contains 200 cards. The cards replace the Excalibur series of the previous year. There were only 20,000 boxes made (1,000 cases). Boxes could be purchased by invitation only, with collectors being limited to one box and dealers to two. Consumers who were invited to purchase the product were to order through an authorized President's Reserve dealer, who displays a marker in

his store shop window. The cards are plastic, with gold foil used for the brand name, player's name and card trimmings and borders. An action photo is set against a color square. The card back uses that square as a box for biographical and statistical information about the player, plus a mug shot. Insert sets include: Air Force One; New Regime; Tan, Rested and Ready (Pro Bowl '96); Running Mates; Time Warp; and Candidates rookie redemption cards. These cards have a team logo on the front, with the team's colors as a background. The insert set and President's Reserve logos are also on the front. The back has the rules, which indicate the card can be returned for a set of "long shot" cards of players signed by the corresponding team pictured on the front. These cards, included in every fourth pack, were limited to 6,000 each.

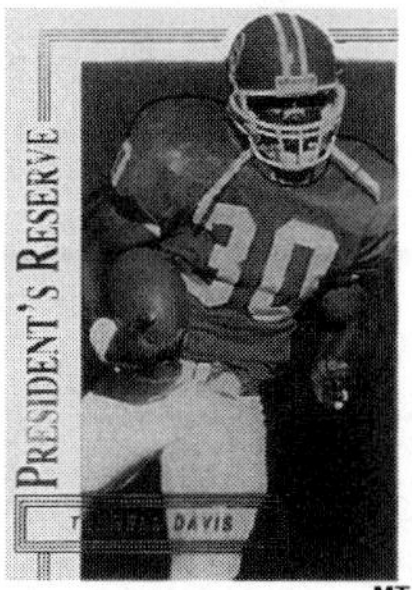

		MT
Complete Set (400):		110.00
Complete Series 1 (200):		60.00
Complete Series 2 (200):		50.00
Common Player:		.25
Minor Stars:		.50
Comp. Candidates (30):		80.00
Candidates Cards:		4.00
Series 1 or 2 Pack (6):		5.50
Series 1 or 2 Wax Box (32):		150.00
1	Larry Centers	.25
2	Frank Sanders	.50
3	Clyde Simmons	.25
4	Eric Swann	.25
5	Morten Andersen	.25
6	Lester Archambeau	.25
7	J.J. Birden	.25
8	Bert Emanuel	.50
9	Jumpy Geathers	.25
10	Jeff George	.50
11	Craig Heyward	.25
12	Bill Brooks	.25
13	Steve Christie	.25
14	Todd Collins	.50
15	Darick Holmes	.50
16	Andre Reed	.25
17	Bryce Paup	.25
18	Bruce Smith	.25
19	Blake Brockermeyer	.25
20	Mark Carrier	.25
21	Kerry Collins	.75
22	Darion Conner	.25
23	Eric Guliford	.25
24	Lamar Lathon	.25
25	Derrick Moore	.25
26	Frank Reich	.25
27	Kevin Butler	.25
28	Tony Carter	.25
29	Curtis Conway	.50
30	Robert Green	.25
31	Jay Leeuwenburg	.25
32	Alonzo Spellman	.25
33	Chris Zorich	.25
34	Eric Bieniemy	.25
35	Jeff Blake	2.00
36	Tony McGee	.25
37	Carl Pickens	.50
38	Rob Burnett	.25
39	Earnest Byner	.25
40	Michael Jackson	.25
41	Antonio Langham	.25
42	Anthony Pleasant	.25
43	Vinny Testaverde	.25
44	Troy Aikman	3.00
45	Larry Allen	.25
46	Bill Bates	.25
47	Chris Boniol	.25
48	Charles Haley	.25
49	Michael Irvin	.50
50	Robert Jones	.25
51	Leon Lett	.25
52	Russell Maryland	.25
53	Nate Newton	.25
54	Deion Sanders	2.00
55	Sherman Williams	.50
56	Darren Woodson	.25
57	Aaron Craver	.25
58	Terrell Davis	3.50
59	Jason Elam	.25
60	Simon Fletcher	.25
61	Anthony Miller	.25
62	Shannon Sharpe	.25
63	Tracy Scroggins	.25
64	Antonio London	.25
65	Scott Mitchell	.25
66	Johnnie Morton	.25
67	Barry Sanders	3.00
68	Edgar Bennett	.25
69	Mark Chmura	.25
70	Brett Favre	6.00
71	Mark Ingram	.25
72	Dorsey Levens	.50
73	Wayne Simmons	.25
74	Gary Brown	.25
75	Anthony Cook	.25
76	Al Del Greco	.25
77	Haywood Jeffires	.25
78	Steve McNair	3.00
79	Rodney Thomas	.50
80	Trev Alberts	.25
81	Quentin Coryatt	.25
82	Ken Dilger	.25
83	Jim Harbaugh	.25
84	Floyd Turner	.25
85	Lamont Warren	.25
86	Steve Beuerlein	.25
87	Mark Brunell	1.50
88	Eugene Chung	.25
89	Jeff Lageman	.25
90	Willie Jackson	.25
91	Kimble Anders	.25
92	Steve Bono	.50
93	Derrick Thomas	.25
94	Willie Davis	.25
95	Greg Hill	.25
96	Neil Smith	.25
97	Tamarick Vanover	.50
98	James Hasty	.25
99	Gary Clark	.25
100	Marco Coleman	.25
101	Steve Emtman	.25
102	Irving Fryar	.25
103	Randal Hill	.25
104	Terry Kirby	.25
105	Dan Marino	6.00
106	Cris Carter	.25
107	Jack Del Rio	.25
108	David Palmer	.25
109	Jake Reed	.25
110	Robert Smith	.25
111	Korey Stringer	.25
112	Orlanda Thomas	.25
113	Drew Bledsoe	3.00
114	Vincent Brisby	.25
115	Ted Johnson	.25
116	Curtis Martin	7.00
117	Chris Slade	.25
118	Jim Dombrowski	.25
119	Vaughn Dunbar	.25
120	Quinn Early	.25
121	Wesley Walls	.25
122	Wayne Martin	.25
123	Irv Smith	.25
124	Torrance Small	.25
125	Dave Brown	.25
126	Chris Calloway	.25
127	John Elliott	.25
128	Rodney Hampton	.25
129	Tyrone Wheatley	.50
130	Kyle Brady	.25
131	Hugh Douglas	.25
132	Todd Scott	.25
133	Adrian Murrell	.25
134	Wayne Chrebet	.25
135	Aundray Bruce	.25
136	Andrew Glover	.25
137	*Daryl Hobbs*	1.00
138	Napoleon Kaufman	.50
139	Chester McGlockton	.25
140	Rob Fredrickson	.25
141	Guy McIntyre	.25
142	Bobby Taylor	.25
143	Fred Barnett	.25
144	William Fuller	.25
145	Rodney Peete	.25
146	Daniel Stubbs	.25
147	Charlie Garner	.25
148	Myron Bell	.25
149	Rod Woodson	.25
150	Charles Johnson	.25
151	Ernie Mills	.25
152	Levon Kirkland	.25
153	Carnell Lake	.25
154	Kevin Greene	.25
155	Neil O'Donnell	.50
156	Erric Pegram	.25
157	Ray Seals	.25
158	Willie Williams	.25
159	Kordell Stewart	4.00
160	Yancey Thigpen	2.00
161	Darren Bennett	.25
162	Andre Coleman	.25
163	*Aaron Hayden*	1.00
164	Tony Martin	.25
165	Chris Mims	.25
166	Shawn Lee	.25
167	Junior Seau	.50
168	Merton Hanks	.25
169	Rickey Jackson	.25
170	Derek Loville	.25
171	Gary Plummer	.25
172	J.J. Stokes	.50
173	John Taylor	.25
174	Bryant Young	.25
175	Antonio Edwards	.25
176	Joey Galloway	.50
177	Carlton Gary	.25
178	Rick Mirer	.25
179	Winston Moss	.25
180	Jerome Bettis	.25
181	Troy Drayton	.25
182	Wayne Gandy	.25
183	Sean Gilbert	.25
184	Jessie Hester	.25
185	Sean Landeta	.25
186	Roman Phifer	.25
187	Alberto White	.25
188	Santana Dotson	.25
189	Jerry Ellison	.25
190	Jackie Harris	.25
191	Courtney Hawkins	.25
192	Horace Copeland	.25
193	Hardy Nickerson	.25
194	Warren Sapp	.25
195	Terry Allen	.25
196	Henry Ellard	.25
197	Gus Frerotte	.50
198	John Gesek	.25
199	Jim Lachey	.25
200	Brian Mitchell	.25
201	Garrison Hearst	.25
202	Dave Krieg	.25
203	Rob Moore	.25
204	Aeneas Williams	.25
205	Chris Doleman	.25
206	Terance Mathis	.25
207	Clay Matthews	.25
208	Eric Metcalf	.25
209	Jessie Tuggle	.25
210	Cornelius Bennett	.25
211	Ruben Brown	.25
212	Russell Copeland	.25
213	Phil Hansen	.25
214	Jim Kelly	.50
215	Don Beebe	.25
216	Willie Green	.25
217	Howard Griffith	.25
218	John Kasay	.25
219	Brett Maxie	.25
220	Tim McKyer	.25
221	Sam Mills	.25
222	Jim Flanigan	.25
223	Jeff Graham	.25
224	Erik Kramer	.25
225	Rashaan Salaam	.50
226	Steve Walsh	.25
227	Donnell Woolford	.25
228	Ki-Jana Carter	1.50
229	John Copeland	.25
230	Harold Green	.25
231	Doug Pelfrey	.25
232	Darney Scott	.25
233	Bracey Walker	.25
234	Dan Wilkinson	.25
235	Leroy Hoard	.25
236	Earnest Hunter	.25
237	Keenan McCardell	.25
238	Steven Moore	.25
239	Andre Rison	.25
240	Eric Zeier	.50
241	Larry Brown	.25
242	Shante Carver	.25
243	Chad Hennings	.25
244	John Jett	.25
245	Daryl Johnston	.25
246	Derek Kennard	.25
247	Brock Marion	.25
248	Jay Novacek	.25
249	Emmitt Smith	6.00
250	Tony Tolbert	.25
251	Mark Tuinei	.25
252	Erik Williams	.25
253	Kevin Williams	.25
254	John Elway	2.00
255	Ed McCaffrey	.25
256	Glyn Milburn	.25
257	Michael Dean Perry	.25
258	Mike Pritchard	.25
259	Willie Clay	.25
260	Jason Hanson	.25
261	Herman Moore	.75
262	Brett Perriman	.25
263	Lomas Brown	.25
264	Chris Spielman	.25
265	Henry Thomas	.25
266	Robert Brooks	.25
267	Sean Jones	.25
268	John Jurkovic	.25
269	Anthony Morgan	.25
270	Craig Newsome	.25
271	Reggie White	.25
272	Chris Chandler	.25
273	Mel Gray	.25
274	Darryll Lewis	.25
275	Bruce Matthews	.25
276	Todd McNair	.25
277	Chris Sanders	1.00
278	Mark Stepnoski	.25
279	Ashley Ambrose	.25
280	Tony Bennett	.25
281	Zack Crockett	.25
282	Sean Dawkins	.25
283	Marshall Faulk	3.00
284	Ronald Humphrey	.25
285	Tony Siragusa	.25
286	Roosevelt Potts	.25
287	Bryan Barker	.25
288	Tony Boselli	.25
289	Keith Goganious	.25
290	Desmond Howard	.25
291	Jeff Lageman	.25
292	Corey Mayfield	.25
293	James Stewart	.25
294	Cedric Tillman	.25
295	Marcus Allen	.50
296	Dale Carter	.25
297	Lake Dawson	.25
298	Darren Mickell	.25
299	Dan Saleaumua	.25
300	Webster Slaughter	.25
301	Keith Cash	.25
302	Bryan Cox	.25
303	Jeff Cross	.25
304	Eric Green	.25
305	O.J. McDuffie	.25
306	Bernie Parmalee	.25
307	Billy Milner	.25
308	Pete Stoyanovich	.25
309	Troy Vincent	.25
310	Qadry Ismail	.25
311	Amp Lee	.25
312	Warren Moon	.50
313	Scottie Graham	.25
314	John Randle	.25
315	Fuad Reveiz	.25
316	Broderick Thomas	.25
317	Ben Coates	.25
318	Willie McGinest	.25
319	David Meggett	.25
320	Will Moore	.25
321	Dave Wohlabaugh	.25
322	Mario Bates	.25
323	Jim Everett	.25
324	Tyrone Hughes	.25
325	William Roaf	.25
326	Renaldo Turnbull	.25
327	Michael Haynes	.25
328	Mike Sherrard	.25
329	Michael Strahan	.25
330	Herschel Walker	.25
331	Charles Wilson	.25
332	Otis Smith	.25
333	Mo Lewis	.25
334	Marvin Washington	.25
335	Tim Brown	.25
336	Greg Skrepenak	.25
337	Kevin Gogan	.25
338	Jeff Hostetler	.25
339	Terry McDaniel	.25
340	Anthony Smith	.25
341	Pat Swilling	.25
342	Harvey Williams	.25
343	Tom Hutton	.25
344	Mike Mamula	.25
345	Randall Cunningham	.25
346	Ricky Watters	.25
347	Andy Harmon	.25
348	William Thomas	.25
349	Calvin Williams	.25
350	Mark Breunner	.25
351	Dermonte Dawson	.25
352	Greg Lloyd	.25
353	Norm Johnson	.25
354	Bam Morris	.25
355	Thomas Newberry	.25
356	Darren Perry	.25
357	Rohn Stark	.25
358	Joel Steed	.25
359	Brenden Stal	.25
360	Justin Strzelczyk	.25
361	Leon Searcy	.25
362	Chad Brown	.25
363	John Carney	.25
364	Rodney Culver	.25
365	Ronnie Harmon	.25
366	Stan Humphries	.25
367	Leslie O'Neal	.25
368	Natrone Means	.75
369	Mark Seay	.25
370	William Floyd	.25
371	Brent Jones	.25
372	Tim McDonald	.25
373	Ken Norton Jr.	.25
374	Jerry Rice	3.00
375	Dana Stubblefield	.25
376	Steve Young	3.00
377	Brian Blades	.25
378	Cortez Kennedy	.25
379	Michael Sinclair	.25
380	Lamar Smith	.25
381	Chris Warren	.50
382	Johnny Bailey	.25
383	Isaac Bruce	.50
384	Kevin Carter	.25
385	Shane Conlan	.25
386	D'Marco Farr	.25
387	Todd Kinchen	.25
388	Chris Miller	.25
389	Lonnie Marts	.25
390	Trent Dilfer	.25
391	Alvin Harper	.25
392	John Lynch	.25
393	Errict Rhett	.50
394	Darnell Stephens	.25
395	Ken Harvey	.25
396	Eddie Murray	.25
397	Heath Shuler	1.50
398	Matt Turk	.25
399	Michael Westbrook	1.00
400	James Washington	.25

1996 Collector's Edge President's Reserve Air Force One

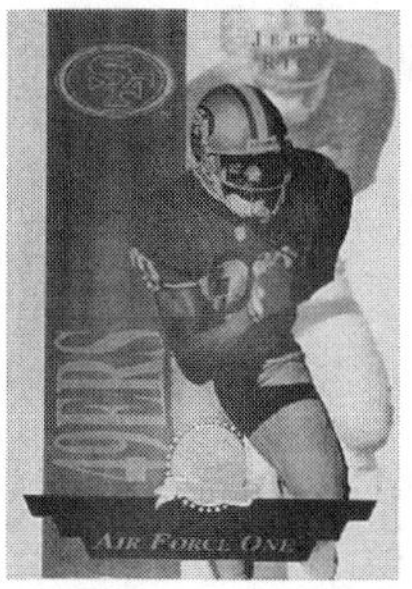

These 18 cards, randomly inserted into 1996 Collector's Edge President's Reserve packs, feature top wide receivers and quarterbacks in the NFL. Cards were seeded one per 16 packs. The card front has a color action photo, with the set icon at the bottom. The player's team logo is in the upper left corner, with the team name running down the side. The player's name is in the upper right corner. The back has a color action photo, plus a color panel on one side which includes the player's name, team logo, biographical information, a card number and recap of the player's achievements. There were only 2,500 of each card made.

		MT
Complete Set (36):		300.00
Complete Series 1 (18):		150.00
Complete Series 2 (18):		150.00
Common Player:		3.00
Jumbo Cards:		1.5x
1	Brett Favre	30.00
2	Neil O'Donnell	3.00
3	Steve Young	15.00
4	Dan Marino	30.00
5	Kerry Collins	6.00
6	Scott Mitchell	3.00
7	Deion Sanders	15.00
8	Cris Carter	3.00
9	Tim Brown	3.00
10	Joey Galloway	15.00
11	Robert Brooks	3.00
12	Tony Martin	3.00
13	Michael Westbrook	6.00
14	Eric Metcalf	3.00
15	Vincent Brisby	3.00
16	Anthony Miller	3.00
17	J.J. Stokes	6.00
18	Kordell Stewart	15.00
19	Troy Aikman	15.00
20	Drew Bledsoe	15.00
21	Jeff Blake	10.00
22	John Elway	12.00
23	Jim Harbaugh	3.00
24	Erik Kramer	3.00
25	Herman Moore	6.00
26	Carl Pickens	3.00
27	Michael Irvin	6.00
28	Jerry Rice	15.00
29	Isaac Bruce	3.00
30	Yancey Thigpen	6.00
31	Brett Perriman	3.00
32	Ben Coates	3.00
33	Jay Novacek	3.00
34	Tamarick Vanover	3.00
35	Terrell Davis	25.00
36	Jeff Graham	3.00

1996 Collector's Edge P.R. Candidates Top Picks

This 30-card set was available through the mail in exchange for team logo cards, which were inserted one per four President's Reserve Series II packs. Overall, 6,000 of each card was produced. According to the company, eight of these 30 cards were completed in time to be inserted directly into packs, including Simeon Rice, Tim Biakabutuka, Jonathan Ogden, John Mobley, Eddie George, Keyshawn Johnson, Daryl Gardener and Kevin Hardy. The card fronts feature the rookie on draft day holding his new team jersey, while the backs feature the rookie in college action and information about the draft pick.

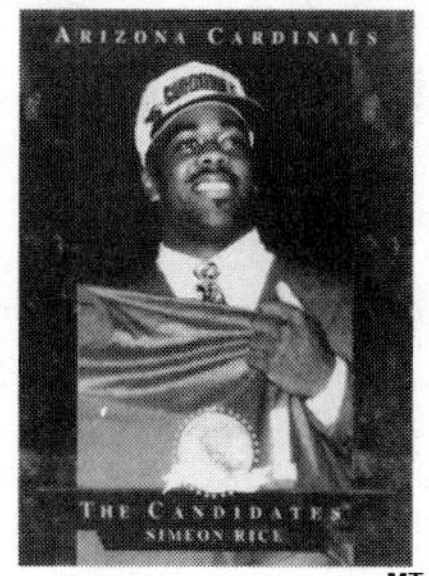

		MT
Complete Set (30):		100.00
Common Player:		2.00
Minor Stars:		4.00
1	Simeon Rice	4.00
2	Shannon Brown	2.00
3	Willie Anderson	2.00
4	Tim Biakabutuka	4.00
5	Eric Moulds	4.00
6	Kavika Pittman	2.00
7	Jonathan Ogden	2.00
8	Reggie Brown	2.00
9	John Mobley	2.00
10	John Michels	2.00
11	Walt Harris	2.00
12	Eddie George	10.00
13	Marvin Harrison	6.00
14	Kevin Hardy	2.00
15	Jerome Woods	2.00
16	Duane Clemons	2.00
17	Daryl Gardener	2.00
18	Terry Glenn	8.00
19	Alex Molden	2.00
20	Cedric Jones	2.00
21	Rickey Dudley	4.00
22	Keyshawn Johnson	5.00
23	Jermaine Mayberry	2.00
24	Jermain Stephens	2.00
25	Lawrence Phillips	4.00
26	Bryan Still	2.00
27	Isreal Ifeanyi	2.00
28	Pete Kendall	2.00
29	Regan Upshaw	2.00
30	Andre Johnson	2.00

1996 Collector's Edge P.R. Candidates Long Shots

This 30-card set was available through the mail in exchange for redemption cards which were inserted one per four packs in President's Reserve Series I. According to the company, 6,000 of each card was produced. The cards feature an action shot of the rookie in the NFL, while the backs feature the rookie in college action and information about the draft pick.

		MT
Complete Set (30):		75.00
Common Player:		2.00
Minor Stars:		4.00
1	Leeland McElroy	4.00
2	Richard Huntley	4.00
3	Ray Lewis	2.00
4	Sean Moran	2.00
5	Muhsin Muhammad	4.00
6	Bobby Engram	4.00
7	Marco Battaglia	2.00
8	Stepfret Williams	2.00
9	Jeff Lewis	4.00
10	Ryan Stewart	2.00
11	Derrick Mayes	4.00
12	Terry Killens	2.00
13	Scott Slutzker	2.00
14	Reggie Barlow	2.00
15	Joe Horn	2.00
16	Karim Abdul-Jabbar	5.00
17	Moe Williams	2.00
18	Kantroy Barber	2.00
19	Je'Rod Cherry	2.00
20	Amani Toomer	4.00
21	Alex Van Dyke	4.00
22	Tim Hall	2.00
23	Bobby Hoying	5.00
24	Jahine Arnold	2.00
25	Tony Banks	5.00
26	Freddie Bradley	2.00
27	Stephen Pitts	2.00
28	Reggie Brown	2.00
29	Mike Alstott	6.00
30	Stephen Davis	4.00

1996 Collector's Edge President's Reserve New Regime

These 1996 Collector's Edge President's Reserve cards were seeded one per every five packs. There were 12,000 cards produced for each of the 12 players in the set. The card front is die-cut around the words "New Regime," which appear along the left side of the card. The player's name, position, team name and set logo appear on the right, with a ghosted closeup shot of the player in the background. A set icon is stamped in gold foil in the lower right corner. An action photo is in the center of the card. The card back has a closeup shot of the player, with 1995 and career stats under it. To the right is biographical information, a brief player profile, plus the limited-edition number of 12,000.

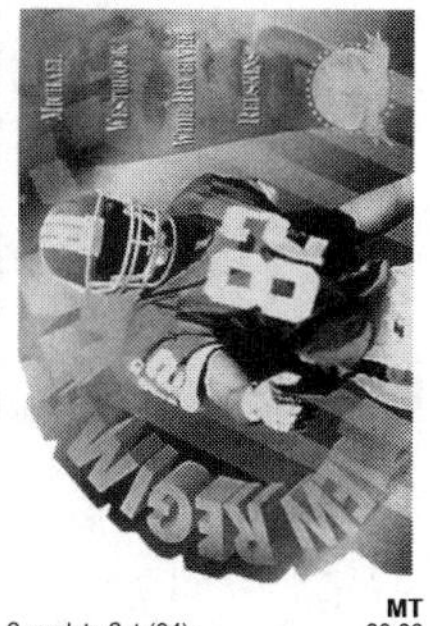

		MT
Complete Set (24):		60.00
Complete Series 1 (12):		30.00
Complete Series 2 (12):		30.00
Common Player:		1.00
Minor Stars:		2.00
1	Tamarick Vanover	2.00
2	Kerry Collins	4.00
3	J.J. Stokes	2.00
4	Napoleon Kaufman	2.00
5	Steve McNair	6.00
6	Todd Collins	1.00
7	Frank Sanders	2.00
8	Warren Sapp	1.00
9	Tony Boselli	1.00
10	Curtis Martin	6.00
11	Ki-Jana Carter	2.00
12	Zack Crockett	1.00
13	Joey Galloway	2.00
14	Terrell Davis	10.00
15	Chris Sanders	2.00
16	Rashaan Salaam	2.00
17	Michael Westbrook	2.00
18	Hugh Douglas	1.00
19	Eric Zeier	1.00
20	Kordell Stewart	8.00
21	Ted Johnson	1.00
22	Ken Dilger	1.00
23	Derrick Holmes	2.00
24	Wayne Chrebet	1.00

1996 Collector's Edge President's Reserve Honor Guard

This set was a bonus redemption from President's Reserve. Collectors could redeem wrappers for a Jumbo Running Mates card and receive one Honor Guard card as a bonus. Each Honor Guard card is numbered one of 1,000 with an "HG" prefix.

		MT
Complete Set (30):		75.00
Common Player:		2.00
1	(Troy Aikman)	5.00
2	Michael Irvin	3.00
3	Emmitt Smith	10.00
4	Brett Favre	12.00
5	Steve Young	4.00
6	Tim Brown	2.50
7	Errict Rhett	2.50
8	Curtis Martin	5.00
9	Carl Pickens	3.00
10	Herman Moore	3.00
11	Robert Brooks	2.00
12	Michael Westbrook	2.00
13	Leon Lett	2.00
14	Russell Maryland	2.00
15	Eric Swann	2.00
16	John Elway	4.00
17	Barry Sanders	5.00
18	Dan Marino	10.00
19	Drew Bledsoe	5.00
20	Jerry Rice	5.00
21	Deion Sanders	3.50
22	Rashaan Salaam	2.00
23	Marshall Faulk	2.50
24	Napoleon Kaufman	2.00
25	Ki-Jana Carter	2.00
26	Cris Carter	2.00
27	Joey Galloway	3.00
28	Eric Metcalf	2.00
29	Derrick Thomas	2.00
30	Bruce Smith	2.00

1996 Collector's Edge President's Reserve Running Mates

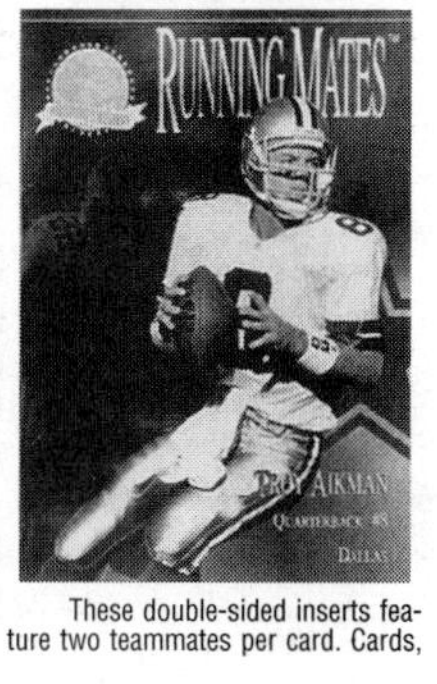

These double-sided inserts feature two teammates per card. Cards,

limited to 2,000 each, were randomly inserted into every 33rd pack of 1996 Collector's Edge President's Reserve. The cards match up a top NFL quarterback with a top running back from his team on the opposite side.

		MT
Complete Set (24):		400.00
Complete Series 1 (12):		200.00
Complete Series 2 (12):		200.00
Common Player:		8.00
Minor Stars:		16.00
1	Troy Aikman, Emmitt Smith	45.00
2	Jim Harbaugh, Marshall Faulk	16.00
3	John Elway, Terrell Davis	60.00
4	Stan Humphries, Natrone Means	16.00
5	Erik Kramer, Rashaan Salaam	8.00
6	Chris Miller, Jerome Bettis	16.00
7	Trent Dilfer, Errict Rhett	16.00
8	Jeff George, Craig Heyward	8.00
9	Gus Frerotte, Terry Allen	8.00
10	Drew Bledsoe, Curtis Martin	30.00
11	Jeff Blake, Ki-Jana Carter	16.00
12	Rick Mirer, Chris Warren	8.00
13	Brett Favre, Edgar Bennett	50.00
14	Neil O'Donnell, Bam Morris	8.00
15	Scott Mitchell, Barry Sanders	50.00
16	Steve Young, Derek Loville	25.00
17	Warren Moon, Robert Smith	8.00
18	Heath Shuler, Brian Mitchell	8.00
19	Rodney Peete, Ricky Watters	8.00
20	Kerry Collins, Derrick Moore	25.00
21	Dan Marino, Terry Kirby	50.00
22	Steve Bono, Marcus Allen	16.00
23	Jim Kelly, Darick Holmes	16.00
24	Kordell Stewart, Eric Pegram	40.00

1996 Collector's Edge President's Reserve Pro Bowl '96

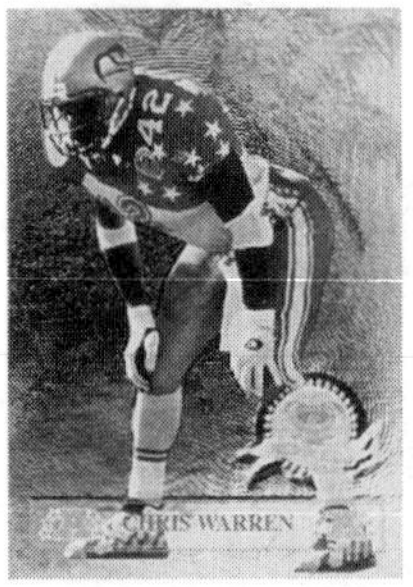

These cards feature participants in the 1996 Pro Bowl. Cards were seeded one per eight packs of 1996 Collector's Edge President's Reserve packs. The metallic card front has palm trees in the background, with the player in the center wearing his Pro Bowl uniform. The President's Reserve logo is stamped in gold at the bottom of the card. The player's name is written in a rectangle at the bottom which is flanked on each side by the appropriate football conference logo. The back has biographical information and a brief player profile on the left side, with 1995 and career stats below. A player close-up shot is on the right, along with the limited-edition number (1 of 7,500).

		MT
Complete Set (24):		100.00
Complete Series 1 (12):		50.00
Complete Series 2 (12):		50.00
Common Player:		2.00
1	Jeff Blake	5.00
2	Jim Harbaugh	2.00
3	Brett Favre	16.00
4	Steve Young	6.00
5	Emmitt Smith	16.00
6	Ricky Watters	2.00
7	Michael Irvin	2.00
8	Carl Pickens	2.00
9	Tim Brown	2.00
10	Anthony Miller	2.00
11	Darren Bennett	2.00
12	Yancey Thigpen	4.00
13	Bryce Paup	2.00
14	Warren Moon	2.00
15	Barry Sanders	8.00
16	Herman Moore	4.00
17	Cris Carter	2.00
18	Chris Warren	4.00
19	Marshall Faulk	6.00
20	Curtis Martin	12.00
21	Ben Coates	2.00
22	Brent Jones	2.00
23	Shannon Sharpe	2.00
24	Brian Mitchell	2.00
25	Ken Harvey	2.00

1996 Collector's Edge President's Reserve TimeWarp

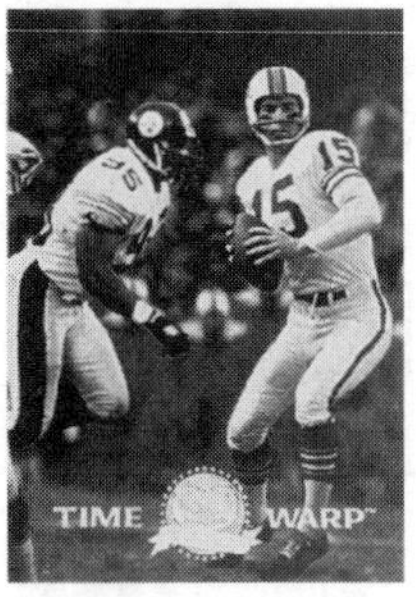

These cards feature a former NFL star matched up against a current NFL star, whose picture is superimposed into an action scene of the former star. The matchups are different from those produced last year. These cards were inserted one every 64th 1996 Collector's Edge President's Reserve pack and were limited in production to 2,000 each.

		MT
Complete Set (12):		300.00
Complete Series 1 (6):		150.00
Complete Series 2 (6):		150.00
Common Player:		8.00
1	Jack Kemp, Greg Lloyd	8.00
2	Sonny Jurgensen, Marshall Faulk	8.00
3	Fran Tarkenton, Bryce Paup	8.00
4	Roger Staubach, Emmitt Smith	50.00
5	Jack Lambert, Curtis Martin	25.00
6	Jack Youngblood, Brett Favre	60.00
7	Fran Tarkenton, Reggie White	8.00
8	Art Donovan, Steve Bono	8.00
9	Bobby Mitchell, Troy Aikman	25.00
10	Larry Csonka, Kordell Stewart	40.00
11	Dick Butkus, Deion Sanders	20.00
12	Deacon Jones, Dan Marino	50.00

1997 Collector's Edge Excalibur

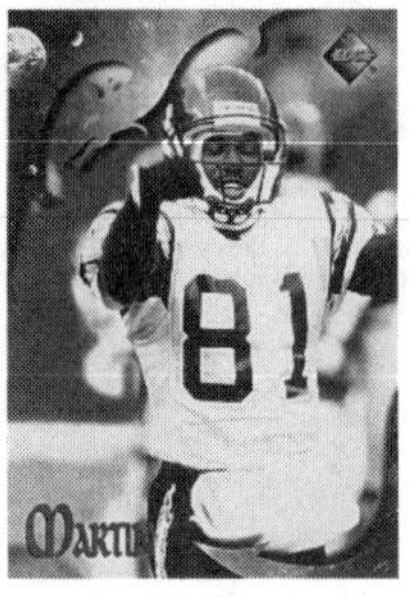

The 150-card base set appears in two versions. The base set includes a space-motif Excalibur dragon in the top corner, with the tail filling the bottom right of the card. The premium parallel set featured a gold-foil stamped dragon. The backs have the player's headshot on the left over an outer space background. An Excalibur medallion is pictured in the upper right, along with the card number, player's name and bio. His stats appear in six sword blades near the bottom of the card back.

		MT
Complete Set (150):		30.00
Common Player:		.10
Minor Stars:		.20
Pack (6):		4.50
Wax Box (24):		90.00
1	Larry Centers	.10
2	Leeland McElroy	.20
3	Simeon Rice	.10
4	Eric Swann	.10
5	Jamal Anderson	.30
6	Bert Emanuel	.10
7	Eric Metcalf	.10
8	Ray Lewis	.10
9	Derrick Alexander	.10
10	Michael Jackson	.10
11	Vinny Testaverde	.10
12	Todd Collins	.20
13	Jim Kelly	.20
14	Eric Moulds	.10
15	Andre Reed	.10
16	Bruce Smith	.10
17	Thurman Thomas	.20
18	Tim Biakabutuka	.20
19	Kerry Collins	.30
20	Kevin Greene	.10
21	Anthony Johnson	.10
22	Lamar Lathon	.10
23	Muhsin Muhammad	.10
24	Curtis Conway	.20
25	Bryan Cox	.10
26	Walt Harris	.10
27	Erik Kramer	.10
28	Rick Mirer	.10
29	Rashaan Salaam	.20
30	Jeff Blake	.30
31	Ki-Jana Carter	.20
32	Carl Pickens	.20
33	Troy Aikman	1.50
34	Michael Irvin	.20
35	Daryl Johnston	.10
36	Emmitt Smith	2.50
37	Broderick Thomas	.10
38	Terrell Davis	1.50
39	John Elway	1.00
40	Anthony Miller	.10
41	John Mobley	.10
42	Shannon Sharpe	.10
43	Neil Smith	.10
44	Scott Mitchell	.10
45	Herman Moore	.30
46	Brett Perriman	.10
47	Barry Sanders	4.00
48	Edgar Bennett	.10
49	Robert Brooks	.20
50	Brett Favre	3.00
51	Antonio Freeman	.30
52	Dorsey Levens	.20
53	Reggie White	.20
54	Eddie George	1.75
55	Darryll Lewis	.10
56	Steve McNair	1.25
57	Chris Sanders	.10
58	Marshall Faulk	.20
59	Jim Harbaugh	.10
60	Marvin Harrison	.75
61	Jimmy Smith	.10
62	Tony Brackens	.10
63	Mark Brunell	1.50
64	Kevin Hardy	.10
65	Keenan McCardell	.10
66	Natrone Means	.20
67	Marcus Allen	.20
68	Elvis Grbac	.10
69	Derrick Thomas	.10
70	Tamarick Vanover	.10
71	Karim Abdul-Jabbar	.30
72	Terrell Buckley	.10
73	Irving Fryar	.10
74	Dan Marino	2.50
75	O.J. McDuffie	.10
76	Zach Thomas	.50
77	Terry Kirby	.10
78	Cris Carter	.20
79	Brad Johnson	.10
80	John Randle	.10
81	Jake Reed	.10
82	Robert Smith	.10
83	Drew Bledsoe	1.50
84	Ben Coates	.10
85	Terry Glenn	.30
86	Ty Law	.10
87	Curtis Martin	1.50
88	Willie McGinest	.10
89	Mario Bates	.10
90	Jim Everett	.10
91	Wayne Martin	.10
92	Heath Shuler	.10
93	Torrance Small	.10
94	Ray Zellars	.10
95	Dave Brown	.10
96	Jason Sehorn	.10
97	Amani Toomer	.10
98	Tyrone Wheatley	.10
99	Hugh Douglas	.10
100	Aaron Glenn	.10
101	Jeff Graham	.10
102	Keyshawn Johnson	.75
103	Adrian Murrell	.10
104	Neil O'Donnell	.10
105	Tim Brown	.10
106	Jeff George	.10
107	Jeff Hostetler	.10
108	Napoleon Kaufman	.20
109	Chester McGlockton	.10
110	Fred Barnett	.10
111	Ty Detmer	.10
112	Chris T. Jones	.10
113	Ricky Watters	.20
114	Bobby Engram	.10
115	Jerome Bettis	.20
116	Charles Johnson	.10
117	Greg Lloyd	.10
118	Kordell Stewart	1.50
119	Yancey Thigpen	.10
120	Rod Woodson	.10
121	Stan Humphries	.10
122	Tony Martin	.10
123	Leonard Russell	.10
124	Junior Seau	.10
125	Chad Brown	.10
126	John Friesz	.10
127	Joey Galloway	.40
128	Cortez Kennedy	.10
129	Warren Moon	.10
130	Chris Warren	.10
131	Garrison Hearst	.10
132	Terrell Owens	1.00
133	Jerry Rice	1.50
134	Dana Stubblefield	.10
135	Bryant Young	.10
136	Steve Young	1.00
137	Tony Banks	.75
138	Isaac Bruce	.30
139	Eddie Kennison	.75
140	Keith Lyle	.10
141	Lawrence Phillips	.20
142	Mike Alstott	.20
143	Hardy Nickerson	.10
144	Errict Rhett	.20
145	Warren Sapp	.10
146	Gus Frerotte	.10
147	Sean Gilbert	.10
148	Ken Harvey	.10
149	Terry Allen	.10
150	Michael Westbrook	.20

1997 Collector's Edge Excalibur 22K Knights

The 25-card set includes a player photo superimposed over a foil background on the card front. The player's name is printed in gold foil at the top, while the "Excalibur 22k" logo is printed at the bottom center. The backs have the player's name printed vertically along the left border of the card. The player's head shot appears in the center, with his bio in the lower right. Edge produced 2,000 of each card. The cards were inserted 1:20 packs. A 22k Black Magnum Knights parallel version, which includes a prism logo printed above the Excalibur 22k logo on the card front, was inserted 1:75 packs in super premium boxes.

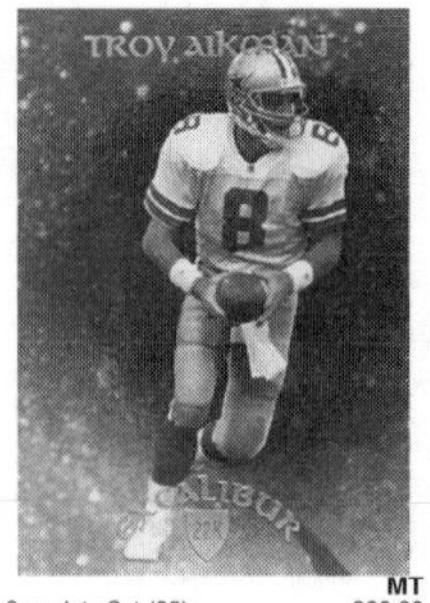

		MT
Complete Set (25):		200.00
Common Player:		2.50
Magnum Cards:		2x-3x
Supreme Edge Cards:		5x
Production 50 Sets		
1	Troy Aikman	15.00
2	John Elway	12.00
3	Brett Favre	30.00
4	Dan Marino	25.00
5	Barry Sanders	30.00
6	Emmitt Smith	25.00
7	Mark Brunell	15.00
8	Jerry Rice	15.00
9	Terrell Davis	15.00
10	Natrone Means	2.50
11	Joey Galloway	5.00
12	Keyshawn Johnson	2.50
13	Curtis Martin	10.00
14	Herman Moore	2.50
15	Eddie George	15.00
16	Terry Glenn	5.00
17	Steve McNair	8.00
18	Marshall Faulk	2.50
19	Ricky Watters	2.50
20	Karim Abdul-Jabbar	5.00
21	Gus Frerotte	2.50
22	Terry Allen	2.50
23	Andre Reed	2.50
24	Jerome Bettis	2.50
25	Tim Brown	2.50

1997 Collector's Edge Excalibur Crusaders

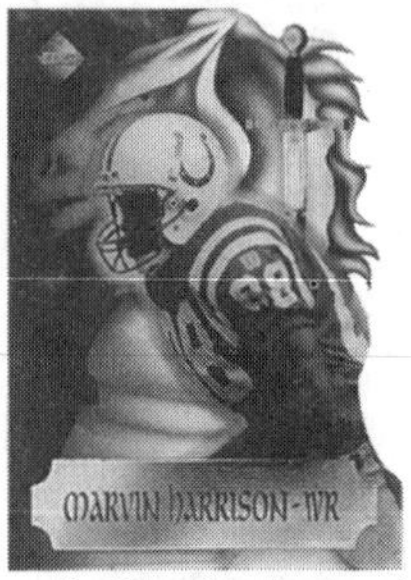

The 25 acetate die-cut cards have the player's photo superimposed over a chess piece background on the front. The Edge logo is printed in the upper left, with an Excalibur sword printed in the background on the right side. The player's name is printed inside a gold-foil "plaque" at the bottom of the front. The chess piece is printed in purple in the background. The backs are a reverse of the front, with the card number inside a diamond in the upper right. The card's individual number is printed at the bottom center. Edge produced 750 of each card.

		MT
Complete Set (25):		250.00
Common Player:		5.00
1	Brett Favre	50.00
2	Mark Brunell	25.00
3	Jim Kelly	10.00
4	Michael Westbrook	5.00
5	Emmitt Smith	40.00
6	Marshall Faulk	10.00
7	Kerry Collins	10.00
8	Jeff Hostetler	5.00
9	Rashaan Salaam	5.00
10	Garrison Hearst	5.00
11	Tamarick Vanover	5.00
12	Rodney Hampton	5.00
13	Leeland McElroy	5.00
14	Tony Banks	15.00
15	Deion Sanders	15.00
16	Errict Rhett	5.00
17	Thurman Thomas	10.00
18	Chris Warren	5.00
19	Andre Reed	5.00
20	Napoleon Kaufman	10.00
21	Terry Allen	5.00
22	Carl Pickens	5.00
23	Marvin Harrison	10.00
24	Lawrence Phillips	5.00
25	Troy Aikman	25.00

A player's name in *italic type* indicates a rookie card.

1997 Collector's Edge Excalibur Game Gear

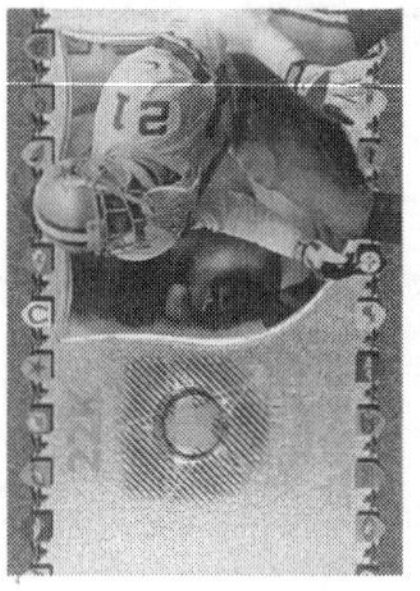

The 19 Game Gear chase cards are hard to miss, as they are as thick as six base cards. The fronts include a photo of the player along with a circular piece of the player's game-used helmet. Edge produced 500 of each card, which were inserted one per 60 packs. Autographed Game Gear cards were inserted one per 350 packs.

		MT
Complete Set (25):		900.00
Common Player:		12.00
1	Brett Favre	100.00
2	Mark Brunell	50.00
3	Barry Sanders	120.00
4	John Elway	40.00
5	Emmitt Smith	90.00
6	Drew Bledsoe	50.00
7	Troy Aikman	50.00
8	Dan Marino	90.00
9	Eddie George	60.00
10	Terry Glenn	25.00
11	Keyshawn Johnson	30.00
12	Terrell Davis	50.00
13	Curtis Martin	50.00
14	Steve McNair	40.00
15	Muhsin Muhammad	12.00
16	Antonio Freeman	20.00
17	Ricky Watters	12.00
18	Jerome Bettis	12.00
19	Herman Moore	12.00
20	Isaac Bruce	20.00
21	Deion Sanders	25.00
22	Cris Carter	12.00
23	Tim Biakabutuka	12.00
24	Karim Abdul-Jabbar	25.00
25	Mike Alstott	12.00

1997 Collector's Edge Excalibur Gridiron Sorcerers

Featuring the top 25 players from the 1997 draft, these chase cards include a photo superimposed over a purple background filled with lightning. "1997 NFL Draft" is printed at the top of the front, with the player's team helmet printed at the top center. His name appears across the bottom of the front. The backs have the team name at the top, with the logo in the background on the left. The card number is in the top right. The player's name and bio is printed in the lower left, with his photo appearing on the right center. The card's individual number is printed at the bottom right. Edge produced 1,000 of each card.

		MT
Complete Set (25):		125.00
Common Player:		2.00
1	Orlando Pace	2.00
2	Peter Boulware	2.00
3	Darrell Russell	2.00
4	Shawn Springs	2.00
5	Yatil Green	5.00
6	Jim Druckenmiller	7.00
7	Bryant Westbrook	2.00
8	Dwayne Rudd	2.00
9	David LaFleur	5.00
10	Rae Carruth	5.00
11	Corey Dillon	10.00
12	Antowain Smith	8.00
13	Tiki Barber	7.00
14	Marcus Harris	2.00
15	Warrick Dunn	15.00
16	Chris Canty	2.00
17	Tony Gonzalez	5.00
18	Danny Wuerffel	5.00
19	Ike Hilliard	5.00
20	James Farrior	2.00
21	Reidel Anthony	6.00
22	Jake Plummer	15.00
23	Troy Davis	5.00
24	Pat Barnes	5.00
25	Darnell Autry	5.00

A player's name in *italic type* indicates a rookie card.

1997 Collector's Edge Excalibur Gridiron Wizards

Similar to the Gridiron Sorcerers, this 25-card set included the top players from the 1997 draft. Like the Sorcerers cards, the Wizard cards were inserted one per 20 packs, the only difference being the Wizard cards were seeded in super premium boxes and the Sorcerers cards were inserted in premium packs.

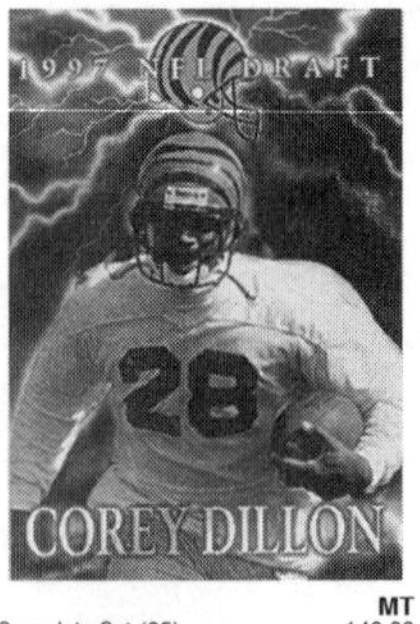

		MT
Complete Set (25):		140.00
Common Player:		2.50
1	Orlando Pace	5.00
2	Peter Boulware	2.50
3	Darrell Russell	2.50
4	Shawn Springs	5.00
5	Yatil Green	5.00
6	Jim Druckenmiller	10.00
7	Bryant Westbrook	2.50
8	Dwayne Rudd	2.50
9	David LaFleur	5.00
10	Rae Carruth	6.00
11	Corey Dillon	12.00
12	Antowain Smith	8.00
13	Tiki Barber	6.00
14	Marcus Harris	2.50
15	Warrick Dunn	12.00
16	Chris Canty	2.50
17	Tony Gonzalez	5.00
18	Danny Wuerffel	5.00
19	Ike Hilliard	6.00
20	James Farrior	2.50
21	Reidel Anthony	6.00
22	Jake Plummer	15.00
23	Troy Davis	5.00
24	Pat Barnes	5.00
25	Darnell Autry	5.00

1997 Collector's Edge Excalibur Marauders

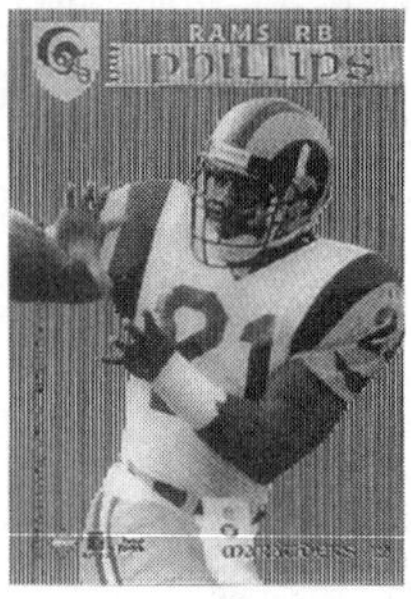

The 25-card set featured 50 players, as two appeared on each double-front card. The player's photo is superimposed over a blue lenticular background, which featured vertical black lines moving from side-to-side. The team's logo appears in the upper left inside a shield, while the team name and his position are printed in gold foil in the upper right. The player's last name is printed inside a gold-foil stripe in the upper right. The appropriate logos appear in the lower left, while "Marauders" and the card number are printed in the lower right in dark blue. The cards were inserted in one of 20 super premium packs.

		MT
Complete Set (25):		200.00
Common Player:		3.00
Supreme Edge Cards:		5x
Production 50 Sets		
1	Antonio Freeman, Tony Banks	8.00
2	Heath Shuler, Tim Biakabutuka	3.00
3	Brett Favre, Eddie Kennison	30.00
4	Marcus Allen, Todd Collins	3.00
5	Dan Marino, Shannon Sharpe	25.00
6	Desmond Howard, Napoleon Kaufman	6.00
7	Dorsey Levens, Muhsin Muhammad	3.00
8	Drew Bledsoe, Mike Alstott	15.00
9	Emmitt Smith, Michael Westbrook	25.00
10	Heath Shuler, Marvin Harrison	3.00
11	Jeff Blake, Marshall Faulk	3.00
12	Jeff George, Lawrence Phillips	3.00
13	Tony Martin, Edgar Bennett	3.00
14	Jerry Rice, Karim Abdul-Jabbar	15.00
15	Jim Harbaugh, Terrell Owens	6.00
16	John Elway, Isaac Bruce	15.00
17	Dave Brown, Eric Metcalf	3.00
18	Junior Seau, Eddie Kennison	6.00

19	Mark Brunell, Eddie George	15.00
20	Cris Carter, Deion Sanders	6.00
21	Steve Young, Eric Moulds	10.00
22	Ben Coates, Chris Warren	3.00
23	Robert Brooks, Carl Pickens	3.00
24	Tim Brown, Bobby Engram	3.00
25	Troy Aikman, Ben Coates	15.00

1997 Collector's Edge Excalibur Overlords

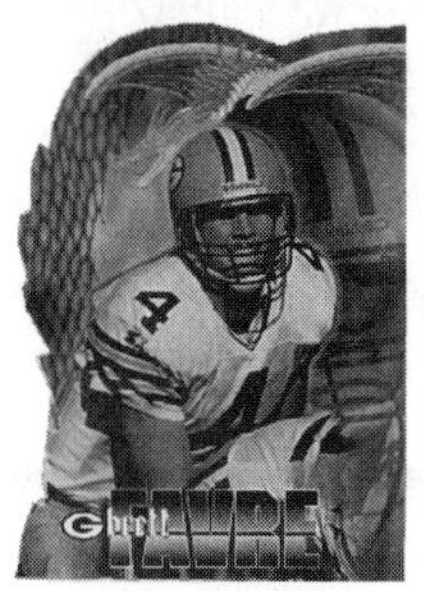

The 25-card set, which is printed on acetate, features a die-cut design in the shape of a dragon. The player's photo is superimposed over a orange and red dragon in the background on the front. The player's last name is printed in large capital letters at the bottom, with his first name printed in white in small letters. The team's logo is printed to the left of the player's name on the front. The backs have the player's headshot in the left center, with the team logo, his name and bio to the right of the photo. The top and bottom of the back have a brick design. The card's individual number appears at the bottom right. Edge produced 750 of each card.

		MT
Complete Set (25):		225.00
Common Player:		4.00
Minor Stars:		8.00
Inserted 1:30		
Production 750 Sets		
Castle Cards:		1x
Production 750 Sets		
1	Jeff Blake	4.00
2	Mark Brunell	25.00
3	Bobby Engram	4.00
4	Joey Galloway	8.00
5	Eddie Kennison	4.00
6	Terrell Davis	40.00
7	Joey Galloway	8.00
8	Hardy Nickerson	4.00
9	Errict Rhett	4.00
10	Emmitt Smith	35.00
11	Kordell Stewart	20.00
12	Steve Young	15.00
13	Marcus Allen	8.00
14	Edgar Bennett	4.00
15	Robert Brooks	4.00
16	Kerry Collins	8.00
17	Todd Collins	4.00
18	Brett Favre	50.00
19	Gus Frerotte	4.00
20	Elvis Grbac	4.00
21	Jeff Hostetler	4.00
22	Tony Martin	4.00
23	Terrell Owens	15.00
24	Dorsey Levens	8.00
25	Thurman Thomas	8.00

1997 Collector's Edge Extreme

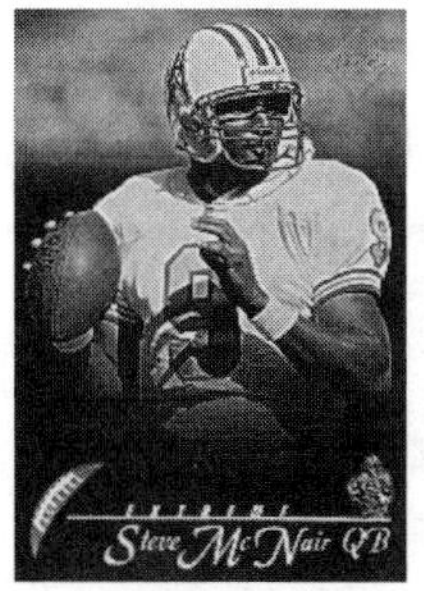

Extreme includes a 180-card base set. Three different parallel sets were made. Extreme Base Parallel 1 (1:2) parallels 108 base cards with a flat silver foil stamp. Extreme Base Parallel II (1:12) adds a gold foil stamp to 36 base cards redone on a silver card. Base Parallel III (1:36) parallels the other 36 base cards with a diamond etched foil stamp on a silver, die-cut card. The inserts include Force, Finesse, Fury, Forerunners and Gamegear Quads.

		MT
Complete Set (180):		30.00
Common Player:		.10
Minor Stars:		.20
Pack (6):		2.30
Wax Box (36):		70.00
1	Larry Centers	.10
2	Leeland McElroy	.10
3	*Jake Plummer*	2.50
4	Simeon Rice	.10
5	Eric Swann	.10
6	Jamal Anderson	.20
7	Bert Emanuel	.10
8	*Byron Hanspard*	.75
9	Derrick Alexander	.10
10	Peter Boulware	.10
11	Michael Jackson	.10
12	Ray Lewis	.10
13	Vinny Testaverde	.10
14	Todd Collins	.10
15	Eric Moulds	.10
16	Bryce Paup	.10
17	Andre Reed	.10
18	Bruce Smith	.10
19	*Antowain Smith*	1.25
20	Chris Spielman	.10
21	Thurman Thomas	.20
22	Tim Biakabutuka	.10
23	*Rae Carruth*	.75
24	Kerry Collins	.30
25	Anthony Johnson	.10
26	Lamar Lathon	.10
27	Muhsin Muhammad	.10
28	*Darnell Autry*	.50
29	Curtis Conway	.20
30	Bryan Cox	.10
31	Bobby Engram	.10
32	Walt Harris	.10
33	Erik Kramer	.10
34	Rashaan Salaam	.10
35	Jeff Blake	.20
36	Ki-Jana Carter	.10
37	*Corey Dillon*	2.50
38	Carl Pickens	.20
39	Troy Aikman	1.00
40	Dexter Coakley	.10
41	Michael Irvin	.20
42	Daryl Johnston	.10
43	*David LaFleur*	.50
44	Anthony Miller	.10
45	Deion Sanders	.50
46	Emmitt Smith	2.00
47	Broderick Thomas	.10
48	Terrell Davis	1.00
49	John Elway	.75
50	John Mobley	.10
51	Shannon Sharpe	.10
52	Neil Smith	.10
53	Checklist	.10
54	Scott Mitchell	.10
55	Herman Moore	.20
56	Barry Sanders	1.25
57	Edgar Bennett	.10
58	Robert Brooks	.20
59	Mark Chmura	.20
60	Brett Favre	2.25
61	Antonio Freeman	.20
62	Dorsey Levens	.20
63	Reggie White	.20
64	Eddie George	1.50
65	Darryll Lewis	.10
66	Steve McNair	.75
67	Chris Sanders	.10
68	Marshall Faulk	.20
69	Jim Harbaugh	.10
70	Marvin Harrison	.20
71	Tony Brackens	.10
72	Mark Brunell	1.00
73	Kevin Hardy	.10
74	Rob Johnson	.20
75	Keenan McCardell	.10
76	Natrone Means	.20
77	Jimmy Smith	.10
78	Marcus Allen	.20
79	*Pat Barnes*	.50
80	*Tony Gonzalez*	1.00
81	Elvis Grbac	.10
82	Brett Perriman	.10
83	Andre Rison	.10
84	Derrick Thomas	.10
85	Tamarick Vanover	.10
86	Karim Abdul-Jabbar	.50
87	Fred Barnett	.10
88	Terrell Buckley	.10
89	*Yatil Green*	.40
90	Dan Marino	2.00
91	O.J. McDuffie	.10
92	Jason Taylor	.10
93	Zach Thomas	.20
94	Cris Carter	.10
95	Brad Johnson	.20
96	John Randle	.10
97	Jake Reed	.10
98	Robert Smith	.10
99	Drew Bledsoe	1.00
100	Chris Canty	.10
101	Ben Coates	.10
102	Terry Glenn	.30
103	Ty Law	.10
104	Curtis Martin	1.00
105	Willie McGinest	.10
106	*Troy Davis*	.30
107	Wayne Martin	.10
108	Heath Shuler	.10
109	*Danny Wuerffel*	.75
110	Ray Zellars	.10
111	*Tiki Barber*	1.00
112	Dave Brown	.10
113	Checklist	.10
114	*Ike Hilliard*	.75
115	Jason Sehorn	.10
116	Amani Toomer	.10
117	Tyrone Wheatley	.10
118	Hugh Douglas	.10
119	Aaron Glenn	.10
120	Jeff Graham	.10
121	Keyshawn Johnson	.20
122	Adrian Murrell	.20
123	Neil O'Donnell	.10
124	Tim Brown	.10
125	Jeff George	.10
126	Desmond Howard	.10
127	Napoleon Kaufman	.20
128	Chester McGlockton	.10
129	Darrell Russell	.10
130	Ty Detmer	.10
131	Irving Fryar	.10
132	Chris T. Jones	.10
133	Ricky Watters	.20
134	Jerome Bettis	.20
135	Charles Johnson	.10
136	George Jones	.10
137	Greg Lloyd	.10
138	Kordell Stewart	.75
139	Yancey Thigpen	.10
140	Jim Everett	.10
141	Stan Humphries	.10
142	Tony Martin	.10
143	Eric Metcalf	.10
144	Junior Seau	.10
145	*Jim Druckenmiller*	1.50
146	Kevin Greene	.10
147	Garrison Hearst	.10
148	Terry Kirby	.10
149	Terrell Owens	.50
150	Jerry Rice	1.00
151	Dana Stubblefield	.10
152	Rod Woodson	.10
153	Bryant Young	.10
154	Steve Young	.50
155	Chad Brown	.10
156	John Friesz	.10
157	Joey Galloway	.20
158	Cortez Kennedy	.10
159	Warren Moon	.10
160	*Shawn Springs*	.20
161	Chris Warren	.10
162	Tony Banks	.50
163	Isaac Bruce	.20
164	Eddie Kennison	.20
165	Keith Lyle	.10
166	*Orlando Pace*	.20
167	Lawrence Phillips	.10
168	Checklist	.10
169	Mike Alstott	.50
170	*Reidel Anthony*	1.00
171	*Warrick Dunn*	1.25
172	Hardy Nickerson	.10
173	Errict Rhett	.10
174	Warren Sapp	.10
175	Terry Allen	.10
176	Gus Frerotte	.10
177	Sean Gilbert	.10
178	Ken Harvey	.10
179	Jeff Hostetler	.10
180	Michael Westbrook	.10

1997 Collector's Edge Extreme Foil

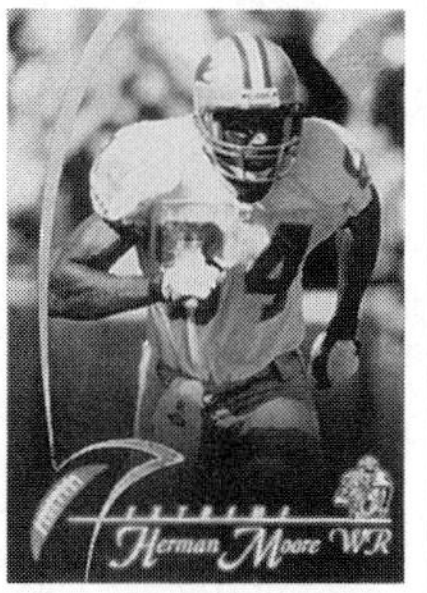

Collector's Edge ran three parallel sets to its Extreme set. The first parallel simply included a silver foil stripe up the left side and contained all 180 cards with an insert rate of one per two packs. The second parallel contained only 36 of the cards and featured a gold and silver strip on the left side, with the rest of the card done with a silver finish. These gold parallels are inserted every 12 packs. The third parallel level included a gold, silver and blue foil strip up the left side and was die-cut around the entire perimeter. The card fronts also featured a silver finish, with the cards inserted one per 36 packs. All three levels were numbered on the back with a "P" prefix.

	MT
Silver Cards:	2x
Gold Cards:	2x-4x
Die-Cut Stars:	8x-16x
Die-Cut Rookies:	4x-8x

1997 Collector's Edge Extreme Finesse

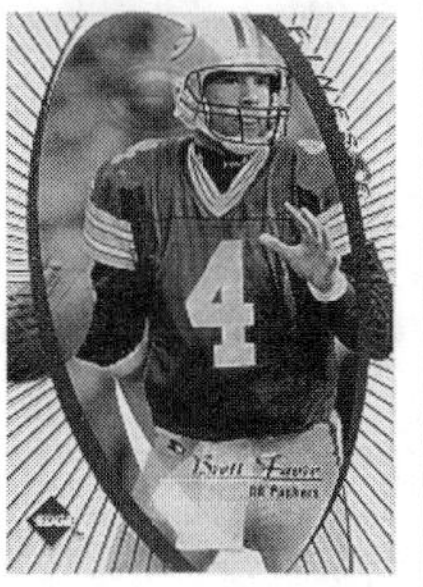

This 19-card insert is done on frosted, clear, foil-stamped cards. The cards were inserted 1:60 packs of Extreme.

		MT
Complete Set (25):		400.00
Common Player:		5.00
Minor Stars:		10.00
1	Troy Aikman	30.00
2	Marcus Allen	10.00
3	Ben Coates	5.00
4	Tony Banks	10.00
5	Jeff Blake	10.00
6	Tim Brown	5.00
7	Mark Brunell	30.00
8	Todd Collins	5.00
9	Terrell Davis	30.00
10	Jim Druckenmiller	20.00
11	John Elway	25.00
12	Marshall Faulk	10.00
13	Brett Favre	60.00
14	Antonio Freeman	10.00
15	Joey Galloway	10.00
16	Eddie George	40.00
17	Terry Glenn	15.00
18	Marvin Harrison	10.00
19	Garrison Hearst	5.00
20	Warrick Dunn	35.00
21	Muhsin Muhammad	5.00
22	Jerry Rice	30.00
23	Barry Sanders	40.00
24	Emmitt Smith	55.00
25	Shawn Springs	5.00

1997 Collector's Edge Extreme Force

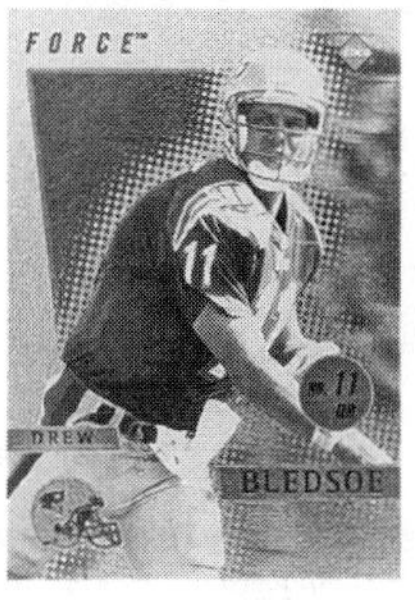

Force features 26 players on silver cards with flow etched designs. Force was inserted 1:8 packs of Extreme.

		MT
Complete Set (25):		75.00
Common Player:		.50
Minor Stars:		1.00
1	Marcus Allen	1.00
2	Chris Canty	.50
3	Jerome Bettis	1.00
4	Carl Pickens	.50
5	Drew Bledsoe	6.00
6	Robert Brooks	1.00
7	Shannon Sharpe	.50
8	Tim Brown	.50
9	Mark Brunell	6.00
10	Ben Coates	.50
11	Todd Collins	.50
12	Terrell Davis	6.00
13	John Elway	4.00
14	Brett Favre	12.00
15	Antonio Freeman	1.00
16	Joey Galloway	1.00
17	Warrick Dunn	6.00
18	Terry Glenn	3.00
19	Marvin Harrison	1.00
20	Dan Marino	10.00
21	Jerry Rice	6.00
22	Junior Seau	.50
23	Tony Banks	3.00
24	Emmitt Smith	10.00
25	Napoleon Kaufman	1.00

1997 Collector's Edge Extreme Forerunners

This 25-card redemption subset was made on clear two-way view cards with a large head shot on the back visible from the front. Gold foil was also added to the cards. The cards were available by redemption through instant win cards, of which 250 were made.

		MT
Complete Set (25):		300.00
Common Player:		5.00
Minor Stars:		10.00
1	Karim Abdul-Jabbar	10.00
2	Marcus Allen	5.00
3	Jerome Bettis	10.00
4	Drew Bledsoe	20.00
5	Robert Brooks	5.00
6	Mark Brunell	20.00
7	Todd Collins	5.00
8	Terrell Davis	20.00
9	John Elway	15.00
10	Brett Favre	45.00
11	Joey Galloway	10.00
12	Eddie George	30.00
13	Terry Glenn	12.00
14	Marvin Harrison	10.00
15	Keyshawn Johnson	10.00
16	Rob Johnson	5.00
17	Eddie Kennison	10.00
18	Dorsey Levens	10.00
19	Dan Marino	40.00
20	Steve McNair	15.00
21	Terrell Owens	10.00
22	Carl Pickens	5.00
23	Jerry Rice	20.00
24	Emmitt Smith	40.00
25	Kordell Stewart	20.00

Values quoted in this guide reflect the retail price of a card — the price a collector can expect to pay when buying a card from a dealer. The wholesale price — that which a collector can expect to receive from a dealer when selling cards — will be significantly lower, depending on desirability and condition.

1997 Collector's Edge Extreme Fury

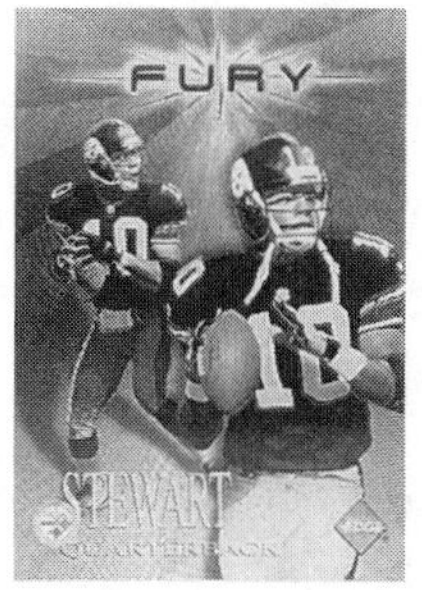

Fury is an 18-card insert with top players featured on a Deep Metal card with chromium finish. Fury was inserted 1:48 packs of Extreme.

		MT
Complete Set (18):		200.00
Common Player:		3.00
Minor Stars:		6.00
1	Jerome Bettis	6.00
2	Terry Glenn	12.00
3	Drew Bledsoe	20.00
4	Mark Brunell	20.00
5	Terrell Davis	20.00
6	Troy Davis	6.00
7	Marshall Faulk	6.00
8	Brett Favre	40.00
9	Antonio Freeman	6.00
10	Joey Galloway	6.00
11	Eddie George	30.00
12	Eddie Kennison	6.00
13	Errict Rhett	3.00
14	Rashaan Salaam	3.00
15	Emmitt Smith	35.00
16	Kordell Stewart	20.00
17	Danny Wuerffel	6.00
18	Steve Young	15.00

1997 Collector's Edge Masters

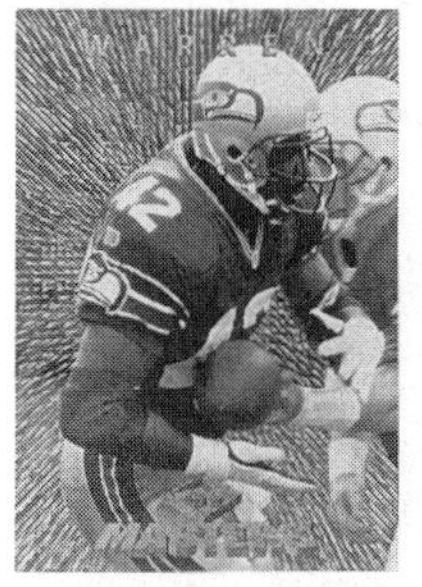

The 270 standard-sized cards include 240 player cards and 30 team flag cards. The fronts have a player photo superimposed over a background of etched foil that is in a "burst" design. The player's last name is printed in gold at the top center, while the Edge Masters' logo is located at the bottom center and printed in gold. The card backs have the player's headshot in the upper left, with the card number in the upper right. The player's name and bio runs vertically along the right side of the back. The stats are printed horizontally inside stripes along the left side of the back. All of the information is printed over a teal ghosted image of a Wilson football.

		MT
Complete Set (270):		25.00
Common Player:		.05
Minor Stars:		.10
Pack (6):		3.50
Wax Box (24):		70.00
1	Arizona Cardinals	.05
2	Larry Centers	.05
3	Rob Moore	.05
4	Frank Sanders	.05
5	Eric Swann	.05
6	Atlanta Falcons	.05
7	Morten Andersen	.05
8	Bert Emanuel	.05
9	Jeff George	.05
10	Craig Heyward	.05
11	Terance Mathis	.05
12	Clay Matthews	.05
13	Eric Metcalf	.05
14	Baltimore Ravens	.05
15	Rob Burnett	.05
16	Leroy Hoard	.05
17	Earnest Hunter	.05
18	Michael Jackson	.05
19	Stevon Moore	.05
20	Anthony Pleasant	.05
21	Vinny Testaverde	.05
22	Eric Zeier	.05
23	Buffalo Bills	.05
24	Todd Collins	.05
25	Russell Copeland	.05
26	Quinn Early	.05
27	Jim Kelly	.10
28	Bryce Paup	.05
29	Andre Reed	.05
30	Bruce Smith	.05
31	Carolina Panthers	.05
32	Steve Beuerlein	.05
33	Mark Carrier	.05
34	Kerry Collins	.30
35	Willie Green	.05
36	Kevin Greene	.05
37	Eric Guliford	.05
38	Brett Maxie	.05
39	Tim McKyer	.05
40	Derrick Moore	.05
41	Chicago Bears	.05
42	Curtis Conway	.05
43	Bryan Cox	.05
44	Jim Flanigan	.05
45	Robert Green	.05
46	Erik Kramer	.05
47	Dave Krieg	.05
48	Rashaan Salaam	.10
49	Alonzo Spellman	.05
50	Donnell Woolford	.05
51	Chris Zorich	.05
52	Cincinnati Bengals	.05
53	Eric Bieniemy	.05
54	Jeff Blake	.20
55	Ki-Jana Carter	.05
56	John Copeland	.05
57	Garrison Hearst	.05
58	Tony McGee	.05
59	Carl Pickens	.05
60	Darnay Scott	.05
61	Bracey Walker	.05
62	Dan Wilkinson	.05
63	Dallas Cowboys	.05
64	Troy Aikman	1.00
65	Bill Bates	.05
66	Shante Carver	.05
67	Michael Irvin	.10
68	Daryl Johnston	.05
		.05
70	Deion Sanders	.50
71	Emmitt Smith	2.00
72	Herschel Walker	.05
73	Sherman Williams	.05
74	Denver Broncos	.05
75	Terrell Davis	1.50
76	John Elway	.75
77	Ed McCaffrey	.05
78	Anthony Miller	.05
79	Michael Dean Perry	.05
80	Shannon Sharpe	.05
81	Mike Sherrard	.05
82	Detroit Lions	.05
83	Scott Mitchell	.05
84	Glyn Milburn	.05
85	Herman Moore	.20
86	Johnnie Morton	.05
87	Brett Perriman	.05
88	Barry Sanders	2.00
89	Tracy Scroggins	.05
90	Green Bay Packers	.05
91	Edgar Bennett	.05
92	Robert Brooks	.05
93	Santana Dotson	.05
94	Brett Favre	2.00
95	Dorsey Levens	.10
96	Craig Newsome	.05
97	Wayne Simmons	.05
98	Reggie White	.10
99	Houston Oilers	.05
100	Chris Chandler	.05
101	Anthony Cook	.05
102	Willie Davis	.05
103	Mel Gray	.05
104	Ronnie Harmon	.05
105	Darryll Lewis	.05
106	Steve McNair	1.00
107	Todd McNair	.05
108	Rodney Thomas	.05
109	Indianapolis Colts	.05
110	Trev Alberts	.05
111	Tony Bennett	.05
112	Quentin Coryatt	.05
113	Sean Dawkins	.05
114	Ken Dilger	.05
115	Marshall Faulk	.25
116	Jim Harbaugh	.05
117	Ronald Humphrey	.05
118	Floyd Turner	.05
119	Jacksonville Jaguars	.05
120	Tony Boselli	.05
121	Mark Brunell	1.00
122	Willie Jackson	.05
123	Jeff Lageman	.05
124	Natrone Means	.05
125	Andre Rison	.05
126	James Stewart	.05
127	Cedric Tillman	.05
128	Kansas City Chiefs	.05
129	Marcus Allen	.10
130	Kimble Anders	.05
131	Steve Bono	.05
132	Dale Carter	.05
133	Lake Dawson	.05
134	Dan Salesaumua	.05
135	Neil Smith	.05
136	Derrick Thomas	.05
137	Tamarick Vanover	.15
138	Miami Dolphins	.05
139	Fred Barnett	.05
140	Steve Emtman	.05
141	Eric Green	.05
142	Dan Marino	2.00
143	O.J. McDuffie	.05
144	Bernie Parmalee	.05
145	Minnesota Vikings	.05
146	Cris Carter	.05
147	Jack Del Rio	.05
148	Qadry Ismail	.05
149	Amp Lee	.05
150	Warren Moon	.05
151	John Randle	.05
152	Jake Reed	.05
153	Robert Smith	.05
154	New England Patriots	.05
155	Drew Bledsoe	1.00
156	Vincent Brisby	.05
157	Willie Clay	.05
158	Ben Coates	.05
159	Curtis Martin	1.50
160	Dave Meggett	.05
161	Will Moore	.05
162	Chris Slade	.05
163	New Orleans Saints	.05
164	Mario Bates	.05
165	Jim Everett	.05
166	Michael Haynes	.05
167	Tyrone Hughes	.05
168	Haywood Jeffires	.05
169	Wayne Martin	.05
170	Renaldo Turnbull	.05
171	New York Giants	.05
172	Dave Brown	.05
173	Chris Calloway	.05

174	Rodney Hampton	.05
175	Michael Strahan	.05
176	Tyrone Wheatley	.05
177	New York Jets	.05
178	Kyle Brady	.05
179	Wayne Chrebet	.05
180	Hugh Douglas	.05
181	Jeff Graham	.05
182	Adrian Murrell	.05
183	Neil O'Donnell	.05
184	Oakland Raiders	.05
185	Tim Brown	.05
186	Aundray Bruce	.05
187	Andrew Glover	.05
188	Jeff Hostetler	.05
189	Napoleon Kaufman	.05
190	Terry McDaniel	.05
191	Chester McGlockton	.05
192	Pat Swilling	.05
193	Harvey Williams	.05
194	Philadelphia Eagles	.05
195	Randall Cunningham	.05
196	Irving Fryar	.05
197	William Fuller	.05
198	Charlie Garner	.05
199	Andy Harmon	.05
200	Rodney Peete	.05
201	Mark Seay	.05
202	Troy Vincent	.05
203	Ricky Watters	.10
204	Calvin Williams	.05
205	Pittsburgh Steelers	.05
206	Jerome Bettis	.10
207	Chad Brown	.05
208	Greg Lloyd	.05
209	Bam Morris	.05
210	Erric Pegram	.05
211	Kordell Stewart	1.00
212	Yancey Thigpen	.05
213	Rod Woodson	.05
214	San Diego Chargers	.05
215	Darren Bennett	.05
216	Marco Coleman	.05
217	Stan Humphries	.05
218	Tony Martin	.05
219	Junior Seau	.05
220	San Francisco 49ers	.05
221	Chris Doleman	.05
222	William Floyd	.05
223	Merton Hanks	.05
224	Brent Jones	.05
225	Terry Kirby	.05
226	Derek Loville	.05
227	Ken Norton Jr.	.05
228	Gary Plummer	.05
229	Jerry Rice	1.00
230	J.J. Stokes	.10
231	Dana Stubblefield	.05
232	John Taylor	.05
233	Bryant Young	.05
234	Steve Young	.75
235	Seattle Seahawks	.05
236	Brian Blades	.05
237	Joey Galloway	.30
238	Carlton Gray	.05
239	Cortez Kennedy	.05
240	Rick Mirer	.05
241	Chris Warren	.05
242	St. Louis Rams	.05
243	Isaac Bruce	.20
244	Troy Drayton	.05
245	D'Marco Farr	.05
246	Harold Green	.05
247	Chris Miller	.05
248	Leslie O'Neal	.05
249	Roman Phifer	.05
250	Tampa Bay Buccaneers	.05
251	Trent Dilfer	.10
252	Alvin Harper	.05
253	Jackie Harris	.05
254	John Lynch	.05
255	Hardy Nickerson	.05
256	Errict Rhett	.20
257	Warren Sapp	.05
258	Todd Scott	.05
259	Charles Wilson	.05
260	Washington Redskins	.05
261	Terry Allen	.05
262	Bill Brooks	.05
263	Henry Ellard	.05
264	Gus Frerotte	.05
265	Sean Gilbert	.05
266	Ken Harvey	.05
267	Brian Mitchell	.05
268	Heath Shuler	.05
269	James Washington	.05
270	Michael Westbrook	.10

1997 Collector's Edge Masters '96 Rookies

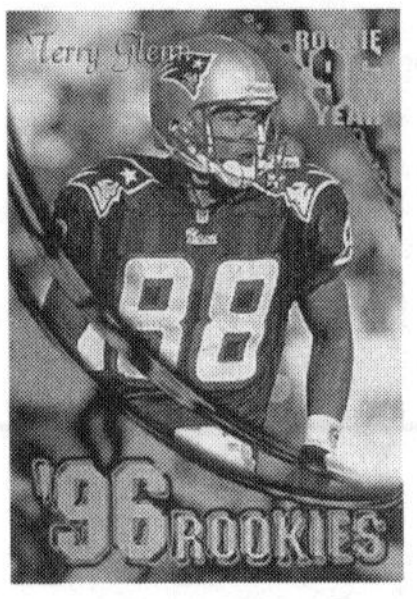

Inserted in retail packs, this chase set included a color photo of the player in the top center of the front. The photo is surrounded by holographic foil, with the Rookie Year '96 logo printed in the upper right. Printed at the bottom of the front is "'96 Rookies." The player's name is printed in yellow at the top center of the card. The backs have the player's name printed in yellow in the top center, followed by the team logo, his bio and stats. The card number is printed in the upper right. Each card is serial numbered, which is located along the left of the back. All the information on the back is printed over a ghosted image of a football player. Overall, 2,000 of each card was produced by Edge.

		MT
Complete Set (25):		45.00
Common Player:		1.00
1	Simeon Rice	1.00
2	Jonathan Ogden	1.00
3	Eric Moulds	2.00
4	Tim Biakabutuka	3.00
5	Walt Harris	1.00
6	John Mobley	1.00
7	Reggie Brown	1.00
8	Derrick Mayes	1.00
9	Eddie George	10.00
10	Marvin Harrison	4.00
11	Kevin Hardy	1.00
12	Jerome Woods	1.00
13	Karim Abdul-Jabbar	7.00
14	Duane Clemons	1.00
15	Terry Glenn	8.00
16	Rickey Whittle	1.00
17	Amani Toomer	1.00
18	Keyshawn Johnson	5.00
19	Rickey Dudley	1.00
20	Bobby Hoying	1.00
21	Eddie Kennison	4.00
22	Bryan Still	1.00
23	Terrell Owens	6.00
24	Reggie Brown	1.00
25	Mike Alstott	2.00

1997 Collector's Edge Masters Crucibles

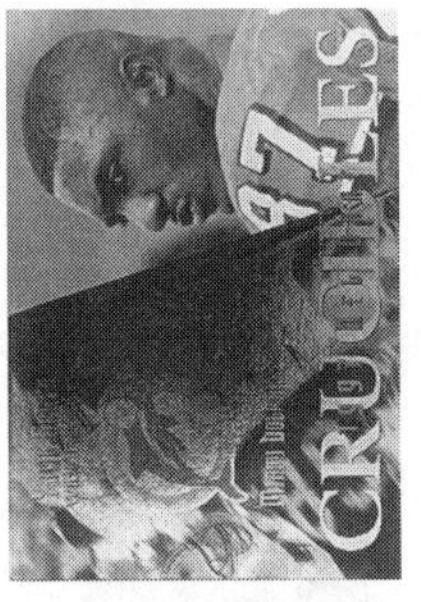

Inserted one per six hobby packs, the chase set includes a color photo of the player on the right. The left side of the front is printed in holographic foil, with a "rolled over" effect in the center. The player's name and position are in the upper left, while the team logo is in the center left and the team name printed directly underneath. "Crucibles" is printed in large capital letters along the bottom front, with "1997 NFL Draft" printed in red over "Crucibles." The backs have the player's write-up along the left and right, with his name, team helmet and bio printed in the center over a ghosted gray background. The card's serial number is printed in the lower right. Edge produced 3,000 of each card in the chase set.

		MT
Complete Set (25):		75.00
Common Player:		1.50
Minor Stars:		3.00
1	Jake Plummer	3.00
2	Byron Harnspard	4.00
3	Peter Boulware	1.50
4	Jay Graham	1.50
5	Antowain Smith	5.00
6	Rae Carruth	4.00
7	Darnell Autry	3.00
8	Corey Dillion	5.00
9	Bryant Westbrook	3.00
10	Joey Kent	3.00
11	Kevin Lockett	3.00
12	Pat Barnes	3.00
13	Tony Gonzalez	3.00
14	Yatil Green	3.00
15	Danny Wuerffel	6.00
16	Troy Davis	3.00
17	Tiki Barber	6.00
18	Ike Hilliard	6.00
19	Darrell Russell	1.50
20	Leon Johnson	1.50
21	Jim Druckenmiller	7.00
22	Shawn Springs	3.00
23	Orlando Pace	3.00
24	Warrick Dunn	10.00
25	Reidel Anthony	6.00

1997 Collector's Edge Masters Night Games

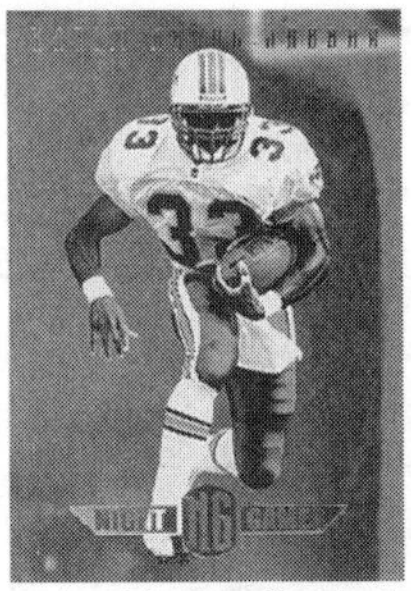

Inserted one per 20 packs, the 25-card chase set features a color photo of the player superimposed over a black and brown computer-generated background. The player's name is printed in gold foil at the top, while the Night Games' logo is printed at the bottom center. The backs have the player's name running vertically along the left. The player's bio runs vertically along the right border. The card number is in the upper right. A color photo of the player is located at the bottom center printed over a colored ghosted image of the player. The card's serial number is printed in the lower right. Edge produced 1,500 of each card in the chase set. A Prism parallel set was inserted 1:60 packs. Edge produced 250 of each Prism card.

		MT
Complete Set (25):		175.00
Common Player:		2.00
1	Terry Glenn	8.00
2	Eddie George	10.00
3	Ricky Watters	2.00
4	Barry Sanders	20.00
5	Curtis Martin	15.00
6	Brett Favre	20.00
7	Emmitt Smith	20.00
8	John Elway	8.00
9	Keyshawn Johnson	4.00
10	Kordell Stewart	8.00
11	Drew Bledsoe	10.00
12	Kerry Collins	5.00
13	Terrell Davis	15.00
14	Karim Abdul-Jabbar	7.00
15	Jerome Bettis	2.00
16	Antonio Freeman	2.00
17	Dorsey Levens	2.00
18	Herman Moore	2.00
19	Jerry Rice	10.00
20	Mark Brunell	10.00
21	Mike Alstott	2.00
22	Napoleon Kaufman	2.00
23	Terry Allen	2.00
24	Tony Banks	2.00
25	Vinny Testaverde	2.00

1997 Collector's Edge Masters Nitro-Hobby

This chase set was split between hobby and retail packs. The fronts resemble the base cards with a player photo superimposed over an etched-foil background. The player's name is printed in gold at the top, while a gold-foil burst is printed at bottom of the card and includes the Nitro logo and the player's outstanding stat. The backs are identical to the base cards.

		MT
Complete Set (18):		20.00
Common Player:		.75
2	Larry Centers	.75
24	Todd Collins	.75
34	Kerry Collins	1.25
59	Carl Pickens	.75
71	Emmitt Smith	5.00
76	John Elway	1.50
88	Barry Sanders	6.00
116	Jim Harbaugh	.75
121	Mark Brunell	2.50
137	Tamarick Vanover	.75
159	Curtis Martin	3.50
189	Napoleon Kaufman	.75
206	Jerome Bettis	1.00
211	Kordell Stewart	2.00
229	Jerry Rice	2.50
237	Joey Galloway	1.25
243	Isaac Bruce	1.25
264	Gus Frerotte	.75

1997 Collector's Edge Masters Nitro-Retail

This chase set was split between hobby and retail packs. The fronts are identical to the base cards, except for a gold-foil "burst" at the bottom of the card front. The Nitro logo and outstanding player stats are printed inside the burst. The backs are identical to the base cards.

		MT
Complete Set (18):		20.00
Common Player:		.75
18	Michael Jackson	.75
30	Bruce Smith	.75
36	Kevin Green	.75
64	Troy Aikman	2.50
75	Terrell Davis	3.50
85	Herman Moore	1.25
94	Brett Favre	5.00
98	Reggie White	1.00
106	Steve McNair	2.50
126	Derrick Thomas	.75
142	Dan Marino	5.00
155	Drew Bledsoe	2.50
167	Tyrone Huges	.75
203	Ricky Watters	.75
207	Chad Brown	.75
218	Tony Martin	.75
234	Steve Young	1.50
261	Terry Allen	.75

1997 Collector's Edge Masters Playoff Game Ball

Inserted one per 72 packs, the 19-card set features two player photos on the front. The horizontal cards have a gold-foil background at the top, with the NFC or AFC logo in the top center. The two teams which matched up in the playoff game are printed in black over the logo. A piece of a game-used ball from the contest is embedded into the card in the bottom center. The bottom half of the card front has a Wilson football background. The player's names are printed over their respective photos in the lower corners of the front. The backs have a photo of each of the players, their names, game summary, score and date. All of the information is printed over a football background. Edge produced 250 of each of the cards in the chase set.

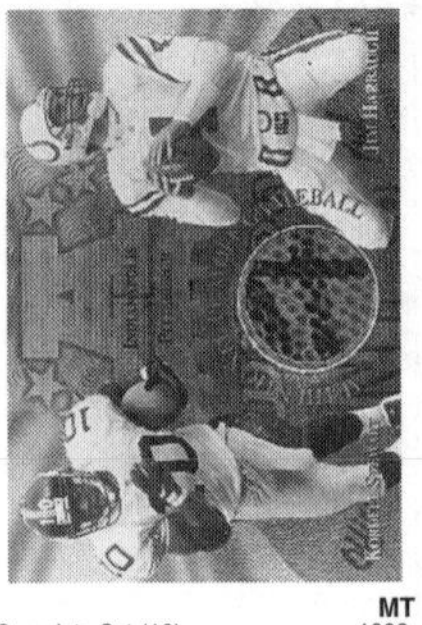

		MT
Complete Set (19):		1000.
Common Player:		15.00
1	Natrone Means, Thurman Thomas	15.00
2	Tony Boselli, Bruce Smith	15.00
3	Jerome Bettis, Marshall Faulk	15.00
4	Kordell Stewart, Jim Harbaugh	35.00
5	Natrone Means, Terrell Davis	50.00
6	Mark Brunell, John Elway	80.00
7	Curtis Martin, Jerome Bettis	50.00
8	Drew Bledsoe, Mark Brunell	100.00
9	Terry Glenn, Keenan McCardell	45.00
10	Troy Aikman, Brad Johnson	40.00
11	Steve Young, Ty Detmer	15.00
12	Jerry Rice, Irving Fryer	60.00
13	Dorsey Levens, Terry Kirby	15.00
14	Brett Favre, Steve Young	110.00
15	Andre Rison, Jerry Rice	60.00
16	Reggie White, Ken Norton Jr.	15.00
17	Kerry Collins, Troy Aikman	70.00
18	Kerry Collins, Brett Favre	120.00
19	Kevin Green, Reggie White	15.00

1997 Collector's Edge Masters Radical Rivals

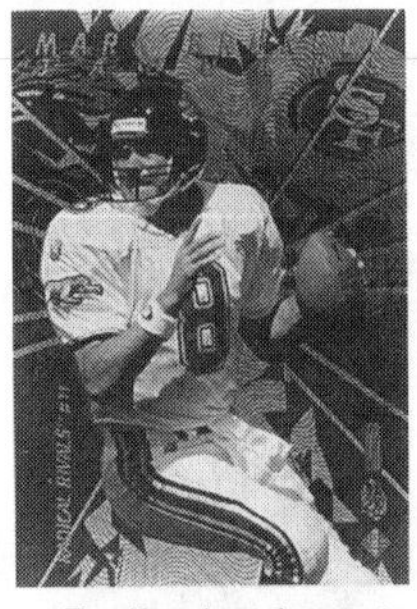

The 12-card set features two players on each card, one on each side. A player photo is superimposed over a background of the two players' teams' helmets. The player's name and team are printed at the top in gold, while "Radical Rivals" and the card number are printed vertically along the left. The card's serial number is printed along the left border on one side of the card. Edge produced 1,000 of each card. The cards were inserted one per 30 hobby packs.

		MT
Complete Set (12):		130.00
Common Player:		2.00
1	Emmitt Smith, Eddie George	25.00
2	Brett Favre, Kerry Collins	25.00
3	Jerry Rice, Antonio Freeman	12.00
4	Ricky Watters, Napoleon Kaufman	2.00
5	Herman Moore, Keyshawn Johnson	6.00
6	Dan Marino, John Elway	25.00
7	Jerome Bettis, Karim Abdul-Jabbar	10.00
8	Isaac Bruce, Carl Pickens	2.00
9	Barry Sanders, Terry Allen	25.00
10	Terry Glenn, Joey Galloway	10.00
11	Mark Brunell, Steve Young	12.00
12	Terrell Davis, Curtis Martin	18.00

1997 Collector's Edge Masters Ripped

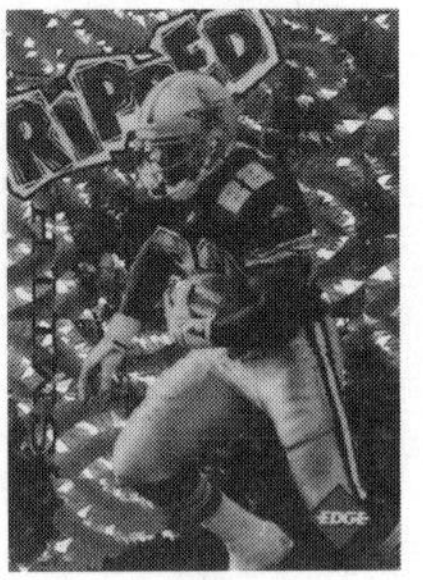

This retail-only chase set continues where the 1996 Ripped set left off, beginning with No. 19. The card fronts have the "Ripped" logo in the upper left, with the player's name printed vertically in black along the lower left border. A color photo of the player is superimposed over a background of red and blue prism-effect foil. The Edge logo is in the lower right of the front. The backs have the card number in gold in the upper right, with a quote about the player from Dick Butkus printed at the top. The player's head shot is printed in the right center, with the team's helmet and player's name, team, position and number printed to the left.

		MT
Complete Set (18):		150.00
Common Player:		3.00
19	Troy Aikman	15.00
20	Drew Bledsoe	15.00
21	Tim Brown	3.00
22	Mark Brunell	15.00
23	Cris Carter	6.00
24	Kerry Collins	5.00
25	Barry Sanders	20.00
26	Michael Irvin	3.00
27	Jeff Hostetler	3.00
28	Curtis Martin	20.00
29	Carl Pickens	3.00
30	Marshall Faulk	6.00
31	Rashaan Salaam	6.00
32	Deion Sanders	8.00
33	Emmitt Smith	30.00
34	Kordell Stewart	10.00
35	Ricky Watters	3.00
36	Steve Young	10.00

1997 Collector's Edge Masters Super Bowl XXXI Game Ball

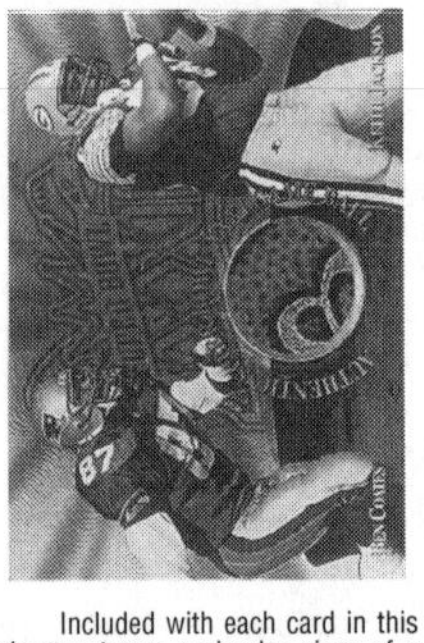

Included with each card in this chase set was a circular piece of a game-used football from Super Bowl XXXI. Featured on the fronts are photos of one New England player and one Green Bay player (one on each side of the front). The Super Bowl XXXI logo appears in the top center in gold foil. The football piece is embedded in the card in the lower center of the front. The players' names are printed in the bottom corners. The Superdome is printed in the background of the lower part of the front. The backs have the player photos over the Super Bowl logo on the left. On the right over gold foil are the players' names, game score, date, game summary and team logos. Edge produced 250 of each card. One card was inserted per 350 packs.

		MT
Complete Set (6):		475.00
Common Player:		30.00
1	Brett Favre, Drew Bledsoe	300.00
2	Dorsey Levens, Curtis Martin	125.00
3	Desmond Howard, Dave Meggett	30.00
4	Antonio Freeman, Terry Glenn	100.00
5	Keith Jackson, Ben Coates	30.00
6	Reggie White, Willie McGinest	30.00

1998 Collector's Edge Advantage

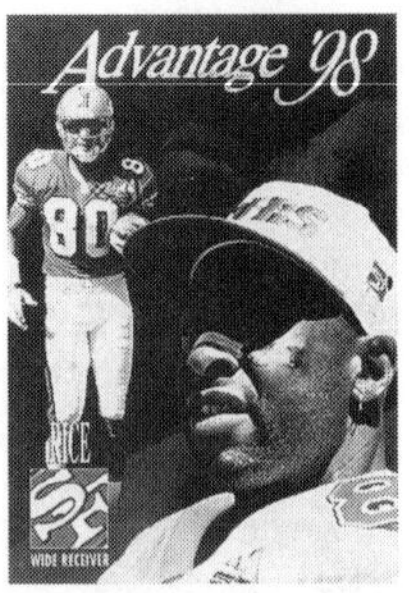

Edge Advantage was a 180-card set that included three different parallel sets and five insert sets. The base cards contain the words "Advantage '98" written in script across the top, with the player's name, team logo and position in the bottom left corner. An action shot of the player is on the left part of the card with a close-up head shot on the right side, with all of this over another closer shot of the player in the background. Advantage also has a silver parallel (one per two packs) that has the front in a silver foil, a gold parallel (one per six) that has the front printed on gold foil and a 50-point stock parallel (one per pack) with the words "Advantage '98" printed in gold foil. Advantage Football included five insert sets: Livin' Large, Memorable Moments, Personal Victory, Prime Connection and Showtime.

		MT
Complete Set (200):		90.00
Common Player:		.25
Minor Stars:		.50
Gold Cards:		5x
50-Point Cards:		3x
Silver Cards:		4x
Pack (6):		6.00
Wax Box (18):		90.00
1	Larry Centers	.25
2	Kent Graham	.25
3	LaShon Johnson	.25
4	Leeland McElroy	.25
5	Jake Plummer	2.50
6	Jamal Anderson	.50
7	Chris Chandler	.25
8	Bert Emanuel	.25
9	Byron Hanspard	.50
10	O.J. Santiago	.25
11	Derrick Alexander	.25
12	Peter Boulware	.25
13	Eric Green	.25
14	Michael Jackson	.25
15	Bam Morris	.25
16	Vinny Testaverde	.25
17	Todd Collins	.25
18	Quinn Early	.25
19	Jim Kelly	.50
20	Andre Reed	.25
21	Antowain Smith	1.75
22	Steve Tasker	.25
23	Thurman Thomas	.50
24	Steve Beuerlein	.25
25	Rae Carruth	.50
26	Kerry Collins	.50
27	Anthony Johnson	.25
28	Ernie Mills	.25
29	Wesley Walls	.25
30	Curtis Conway	.50
31	Bobby Engram	.25
32	Raymont Harris	.25
33	Erik Kramer	.25
34	Rick Mirer	.25
35	Darnay Scott	.25
36	Tony McGee	.25
37	Jeff Blake	.50
38	Corey Dillon	2.00
39	Carl Pickens	.25
40	Troy Aikman	2.50
41	Billy Davis	.25
42	David LaFleur	.50
43	Anthony Miller	.25
44	Emmitt Smith	4.00
45	Herschel Walker	.25
46	Sherman Williams	.25
47	Flipper Anderson	.25
48	Terrell Davis	2.50
49	Jason Elam	.25
50	John Elway	2.00
51	Darrien Gordon	.25
52	Ed McCaffrey	.25
53	Shannon Sharpe	.25
54	Neil Smith	.25
55	Rod Smith	.25
56	Maa Tanuvasa	.25
57	Glyn Milburn	.25
58	Scott Mitchell	.25
59	Herman Moore	.50
60	Johnnie Morton	.25
61	Barry Sanders	3.00
62	Tommy Vardell	.25
63	Bryant Westbrook	.25
64	Robert Brooks	.25
65	Mark Chmura	.50
66	Brett Favre	5.00
67	Antonio Freeman	.50
68	Dorsey Levens	.50
69	*Bill Schroeder*	4.00
70	Marshall Faulk	.50
71	Jim Harbaugh	.25
72	Marvin Harrison	.50
73	Derek Brown	.25
74	Mark Brunell	2.00
75	Rob Johnson	.50
76	Keenan McCardell	.25
77	Natrone Means	.50
78	Jimmy Smith	.25
79	James Stewart	.25

80	Marcus Allen	.50
81	Pat Barnes	.50
82	Tony Gonzalez	.50
83	Elvis Grbac	.25
84	Greg Hill	.25
85	Kevin Lockett	.25
86	Andre Rison	.25
87	Karim Abdul-Jabbar	.50
88	Fred Barnett	.25
89	Troy Drayton	.25
90	Dan Marino	4.00
91	Irving Spikes	.25
92	Cris Carter	.25
93	Matthew Hatchette	.25
94	Brad Johnson	.50
95	Jake Reed	.25
96	Robert Smith	.25
97	Drew Bledsoe	2.50
98	Keith Byars	.25
99	Ben Coates	.25
100	Terry Glenn	1.00
101	Shawn Jefferson	.25
102	Curtis Martin	2.00
103	Dave Meggett	.25
104	Troy Davis	.50
105	Danny Wuerffel	.50
106	Ray Zellers	.25
107	Tiki Barber	1.25
108	Rodney Hampton	.25
109	Ike Hilliard	.50
110	Danny Kanell	.25
111	Tyrone Wheatley	.25
112	Kyle Brady	.25
113	Wayne Chrebet	.25
114	Aaron Glenn	.25
115	Jeff Graham	.25
116	Keyshawn Johnson	.50
117	Adrian Murrell	.50
118	Neil O'Donnell	.25
119	Heath Shuler	.25
120	Tim Brown	.50
121	Rickey Dudley	.25
122	Jeff George	.50
123	Desmond Howard	.25
124	James Jett	.25
125	Napoleon Kaufman	.50
126	Chad Levitt	.25
127	Darrell Russell	.25
128	Ty Detmer	.25
129	Irving Fryar	.25
130	Charlie Garner	.25
131	Kevin Turner	.25
132	Ricky Watters	.50
133	Jerome Bettis	.50
134	Will Blackwell	.25
135	Mark Bruener	.25
136	Charles Johnson	.25
137	George Jones	.25
138	Kordell Stewart	2.50
139	Yancey Thigpen	.25
140	Gary Brown	.25
141	Jim Everett	.25
142	Terrell Fletcher	.25
143	Stan Humphries	.25
144	Freddie Jones	.25
145	Tony Martin	.25
146	Jim Druckenmiller	1.50
147	Garrison Hearst	.25
148	Brent Jones	.25
149	Terrell Owens	.50
150	Jerry Rice	2.50
151	J.J. Stokes	.25
152	Steve Young	1.50
153	Steve Broussard	.25
154	Joey Galloway	.50
155	Jon Kitna	.25
156	Warren Moon	.50
157	Shawn Springs	.25
158	Chris Warren	.25
159	Tony Banks	.50
160	Isaac Bruce	.50
161	Eddie Kennison	.50
162	Orlando Pace	.25
163	Lawrence Phillips	.25
164	Mike Alstott	.50
165	Reidel Anthony	1.25
166	Horace Copeland	.25
167	Trent Dilfer	.50
168	Warrick Dunn	3.00
169	Hardy Nickerson	.25
170	Karl Williams	.25
171	Eddie George	2.50
172	Ronnie Harmon	.25
173	Joey Kent	.25
174	Steve McNair	2.00
175	Chris Sanders	.25
176	Terry Allen	.25
177	Jamie Asher	.25
178	Stephen Davis	.25
179	Gus Frerotte	.25
180	Leslie Shepherd	.25
181	*Victor Reilly*	.50
182	*Curtis Enis*	2.00
183	*Brian Griese*	3.50
184	*Eric Brown*	.50
185	*Jacquez Green*	1.50
186	*Andre Wadsworth*	.75
187	*Ryan Leaf*	2.00
188	*Rashaan Shehee*	.75
189	*Peyton Manning*	8.00
190	*Flozell Adams*	.50
191	*Fred Taylor*	5.00
192	*Charlie Batch*	3.00
193	*Kevin Dyson*	1.50
194	*Charles Woodson*	2.00
195	*Ahman Green*	.75
196	*Randy Moss*	8.00
197	*Robert Edwards*	.75
198	*Reidel Anthony*	1.00
199	*Jerome Pathon*	.75
200	*Samari Rolle*	.50

Post-1980 cards in Near Mint condition will generally sell for about 75% of the quoted Mint value. Excellent-condition cards bring no more than 40%.

1998 Collector's Edge Advantage Gold

The 180-card Advantage base set has a lacquered gold parallel version. The cards were inserted one per six packs.

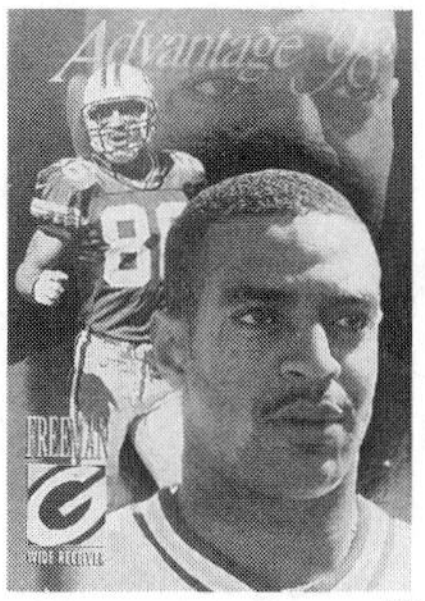

	MT
Gold Cards:	5x

1998 Collector's Edge Advantage 50-Point

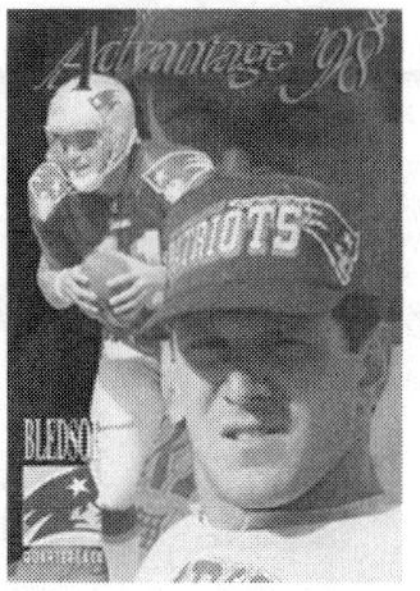

This parallel of the 180-card Advantage base set was printed on 50-point card stock and seeded one per pack.

	MT
50-Point Cards:	3x

1998 Collector's Edge Advantage Silver

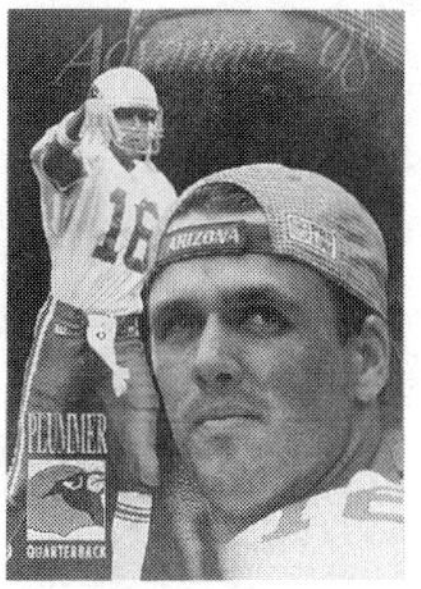

A parallel of the 180-card Advantage base set was printed on embossed silver stock and inserted 1:2.

	MT
Silver Cards:	4x

1998 Collector's Edge Advantage Livin' Large

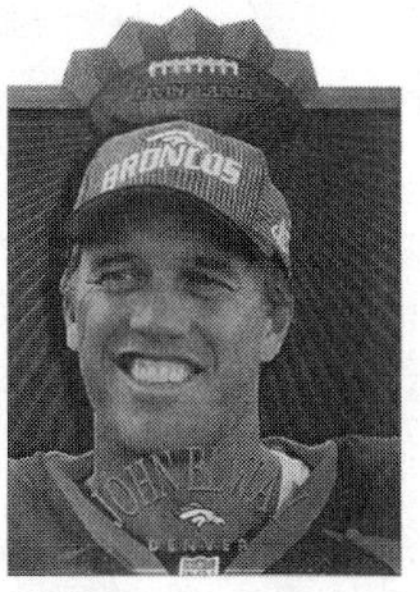

Livin' Large was a 22-card insert that was printed on plastic with a die-cut out of the top of the card. Inserted every 12 packs, these inserts featured a head shot of the player, with a football over his head with the insert name inside. The player's name, position and team logo was printed across the bottom, with the background colors related to that team. Holofoil versions of each card were also printed with a stated print run of 100 sets.

		MT
Complete Set (22):		150.00
Common Player:		2.00
Minor Stars:		4.00
Holofoil Cards:		5x-10x
1	Leeland McElroy	2.00
2	Jamal Anderson	4.00
3	Antowain Smith	8.00
4	Emmitt Smith	20.00
5	John Elway	12.00
6	Barry Sanders	20.00
7	Elvis Grbac	2.00
8	Dan Marino	20.00
9	Cris Carter	2.00
10	Drew Bledsoe	12.00
11	Curtis Martin	12.00
12	Troy Davis	4.00
13	Ike Hilliard	4.00
14	Adrian Murrell	2.00
15	Tim Brown	2.00
16	Kordell Stewart	12.00
17	Jerry Rice	12.00
18	Tony Banks	4.00
19	Mike Alstott	5.00
20	Trent Dilfer	4.00
21	Eddie George	12.00
22	Steve McNair	8.00

1998 Collector's Edge Advantage Personal Victory

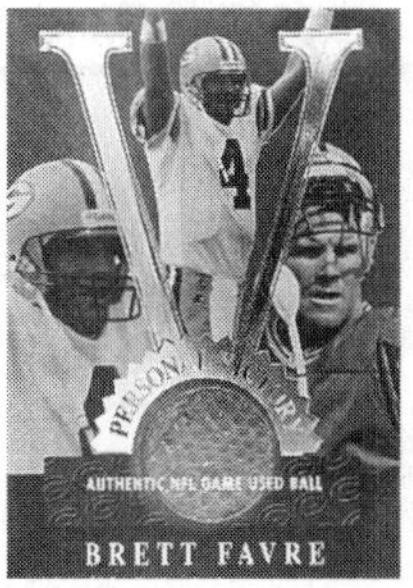

This six-card set was also individually numbered to 200 on the back and contained a piece of a game-used ball on the front. The front has three shots of the player - one on each side of a large gold foil "V" and another inside the "V." The player's name is stamped across the bottom, with the piece of game ball above it with the words "Personal Victory" over the game ball. A dull finish is used on the back of the card along with a shot of the game in which the featured player achieved his personal victory.

		MT
Complete Set (6):		800.00
Common Player:		150.00
1	John Elway	200.00
2	Barry Sanders	300.00
3	Brett Favre	400.00
4	Mark Brunell	150.00
5	Drew Bledsoe	150.00
6	Jerry Rice	200.00

1998 Collector's Edge Advantage Prime Connection

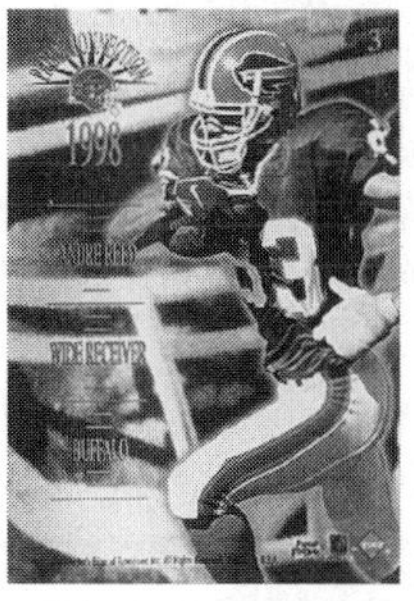

Prime Connection spotlights the top tandems of 25 NFL teams on a double-sided, metallic looking card. Each side has an action shot of a player on the right side, with the player's name, position and team on the left side, along with the Prime Connection's logo in the upper left corner. The cards are numbered on both sides in the upper right corner and were inserted every 36 packs of Advantage.

		MT
Complete Set (25):		500.00
Common Player:		5.00
1	LeShon Johnson, Leeland McElroy	5.00
2	Peter Boulware, Michael Jackson	5.00
3	Andre Reed, Antowain Smith	20.00
4	Rae Carruth, Anthony Johnson	10.00
5	Herschel Walker, Emmitt Smith	50.00
6	Terrell Davis, John Elway	40.00
7	Ed McCaffrey, Shannon Sharpe	5.00
8	Herman Moore, Barry Sanders	40.00
9	Brett Favre, Antonio Freeman	60.00
10	Mark Brunell, James Stewart	25.00
11	Marcus Allen, Elvis Grbac	10.00
12	Karim Abdul-Jabbar, Dan Marino	50.00
13	Drew Bledsoe, Ben Coates	25.00
14	Terry Glenn, Curtis Martin	25.00
15	Troy Davis, Danny Wuerffel	10.00
16	Ike Hilliard, Danny Kanell	10.00
17	Aaron Glenn, Adrian Murrell	5.00
18	Tim Brown, Napoleon Kaufman	10.00
19	Mark Bruener, Jerome Bettis	10.00
20	Jim Druckenmiller, Terrell Owens	20.00
21	Garrison Hearst, Steve Young	20.00
22	Tony Banks, Eddie Kennison	15.00
23	Mike Alstott, Reidel Anthony	15.00
24	Hardy Nickerson, Warrick Dunn	30.00
25	Eddie George, Steve McNair	30.00

1998 Collector's Edge Advantage Showtime

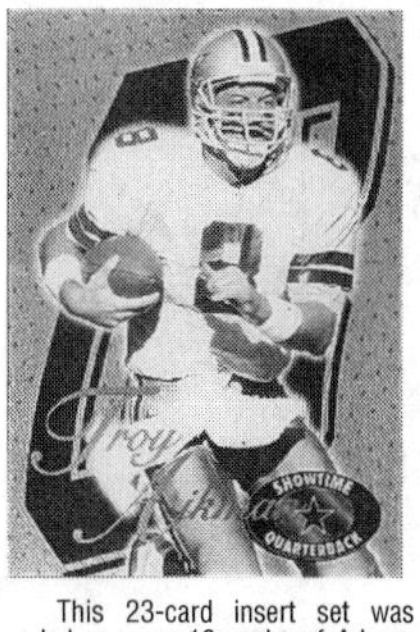

This 23-card insert set was seeded one per 18 packs of Advantage Football. Card fronts featured an action shot of the player, with his name written across the bottom. The background was printed in team colors and was supposed to look like jersey material, with the player's position in large letters behind him. Holofoil versions of these cards also exist and were limited in print run to 100 sets.

		MT
Complete Set (23):		250.00
Common Player:		3.00
Minor Stars:		6.00
Holofoils:		3x-6x
1	LeShon Johnson	3.00
2	Peter Boulware	3.00
3	Jim Kelly	6.00
4	Rae Carruth	6.00
5	Kerry Collins	10.00
6	Troy Aikman	20.00
7	Terrell Davis	20.00
8	Shannon Sharpe	3.00
9	Brett Favre	40.00
10	Mark Brunell	20.00
11	Keenan McCardell	3.00
12	Marcus Allen	6.00
13	Terry Glenn	8.00
14	Danny Wuerffel	6.00
15	Danny Kanell	3.00
16	Aaron Glenn	3.00
17	Napoleon Kaufman	8.00
18	Mark Bruener	3.00
19	Jim Druckenmiller	10.00
20	Terrell Owens	8.00
21	Steve Young	12.00
22	Reidel Anthony	8.00
23	Warrick Dunn	20.00

1998 Collector's Edge First Place

Singles from this base set feature large action shots of each of the 250 players in this set. Each single has a parallel 50-Point card that are found one per pack. Also, each player has a 50-Point Silver issue that is sequentially numbered to 125 and found 1:24 packs.

		MT
Complete Set (250):		70.00
Common Player:		.10
Minor Stars:		.20
50-Point Cards:		2x-4x
50-Point Rookies:		2x
Inserted 1:1		
50-Point Gold Cards:		15x-30x
50-Point Gold Rookies:		5x-10x
Inserted 1:24		
Production 125 Sets		
Pack (6):		5.00
Wax Box (24):		80.00
1	Karim Abdul-Jabbar	.50
2	*Flozell Adams*	.50
3	Troy Aikman	1.50
4	Robert Smith	.20
5	*Stephen Alexander*	1.00
6	*Harold Shaw*	.50
7	Marcus Allen	.20
8	Terry Allen	.20
9	Mike Alstott	.50
10	Jamal Anderson	.50
11	Reidel Anthony	.20
12	Jamie Asher	.10
13	Darnell Autry	.10
14	*Phil Savoy*	.50
15	*Jon Ritchie*	1.00
16	Tony Banks	.20
17	Tiki Barber	.20
18	Pat Barnes	.20
19	*Charlie Batch*	5.00
20	*Mikhael Ricks*	2.00
21	Jerome Bettis	.20
22	Tim Biakabutuka	.10
23	*Roosevelt Blackmon*	.50
24	Jeff Blake	.20
25	Drew Bledsoe	1.50
26	Tony Boselli	.10
27	Peter Boulware	.10
28	Tony Brackens	.10
29	*Corey Bradford*	4.00
30	*Michael Pittman*	1.00
31	*Keith Brooking*	1.00
32	Robert Brooks	.10
33	Derrick Brooks	.10
34	*Ken Oxendine*	1.50
35	*R.W. McQuarters*	1.00
36	Tim Brown	.20
37	Chad Brown	.10
38	Isaac Bruce	.20
39	Mark Brunell	1.50
40	Chris Canty	.10
41	Mark Carrier	.10
42	Rae Carruth	.10
43	Ki-Jana Carter	.10
44	Cris Carter	.20
45	Larry Centers	.10
46	*Corey Chavous*	.50
47	Mark Chmura	.10
48	*Cameron Cleeland*	2.00
49	Dexter Coakley	.10
50	Ben Coates	.10
51	*Jonathon Linton*	1.00
52	Todd Collins	.10
53	Kerry Collins	.20
54	*Tebucky Jones*	.50
55	Curtis Conway	.20
56	*Sam Cowart*	.50
57	Bryan Cox	.10
58	Randall Cunningham	.50
59	Terrell Davis	2.00
60	Troy Davis	.10
61	*Patrick Johnson*	.50
62	Trent Dilfer	.10
63	*Vonnie Holliday*	2.00
64	Corey Dillon	1.00
65	Hugh Douglas	.10
66	Jim Druckenmiller	.20
67	Warrick Dunn	1.50
68	*Robert Edwards*	3.00
69	*Greg Ellis*	1.00
70	John Elway	1.50
71	Bert Emanuel	.10
72	Bobby Engram	.10
73	*Curtis Enis*	4.00
74	Marshall Faulk	.50
75	Brett Favre	3.00
76	Doug Flutie	1.50
77	Glenn Foley	.10
78	Antonio Freeman	.50
79	Gus Frerotte	.10
80	John Friesz	.10
81	Irving Fryar	.10
82	Joey Galloway	.50
83	Rich Gannon	.10
84	Charlie Garner	.10
85	Jeff George	.20
86	Eddie George	1.25
87	Sean Gilbert	.10
88	Terry Glenn	.20
89	Aaron Glenn	.10
90	Tony Gonzalez	.10
91	Jeff Graham	.10
92	Elvis Grbac	.10
93	*Jacquez Green*	3.00
94	Kevin Greene	.10
95	*Brian Griese*	5.00
96	Byron Hanspard	.10
97	Jim Harbaugh	.10
98	Kevin Hardy	.10
99	Walt Harris	.10
100	Marvin Harrison	.20
101	Rodney Harrison	.10
102	Jeff Hartings	.10
103	Ken Harvey	.10
104	Garrison Hearst	.20
105	Ike Hilliard	.10
106	Jeff Hostetler	.10
107	Bobby Hoying	.20
108	Michael Jackson	.10
109	Anthony Johnson	.10
110	Brad Johnson	.50
111	Keyshawn Johnson	.20
112	Charles Johnson	.10
113	Daryl Johnston	.10
114	Chris Jones	.10
115	George Jones	.10
116	*Donald Hayes*	1.50
117	Danny Kanell	.10
118	Napoleon Kaufman	.50
119	Cortez Kennedy	.10
120	Eddie Kennison	.20
121	Levon Kirkland	.10
122	Jon Kitna	.10
123	Erik Kramer	.10
124	David LaFleur	.10
125	Lamar Lathon	.10
126	Ty Law	.10
127	*Ryan Leaf*	3.00
128	Dorsey Levens	.20
129	Ray Lewis	.10
130	Darryll Lewis	.10
131	*Matt Hasselbeck*	20.00
132	Greg Lloyd	.10
133	Kevin Lockett	.10
134	Keith Lyle	.10
135	*Peyton Manning*	12.00
136	Dan Marino	2.00
137	Wayne Martin	.10
138	*Ahman Green*	3.00
139	Tony Martin	.10
140	*E.G. Green*	1.50
141	Derrick Mayes	.10
142	Ed McCaffrey	.20
143	Keenan McCardell	.10
144	O.J. McDuffie	.10
145	Leeland McElroy	.10
146	Willie McGinest	.10
147	Chester McGlockton	.10
148	Steve McNair	.50
149	Natrone Means	.20
150	Eric Metcalf	.10
151	Anthony Miller	.10
152	Rick Mirer	.10
153	Scott Mitchell	.10
154	John Mobley	.10
155	Warren Moon	.50
156	Herman Moore	.50
157	*Randy Moss*	12.00
158	Eric Moulds	.20
159	Muhsin Muhammad	.10
160	Adrian Murrell	.10
161	*Marcus Nash*	3.00
162	Hardy Nickerson	.10
163	Ken Norton	.10
164	Neil O'Donnell	.10
165	Terrell Owens	.50
166	Orlando Pace	.10
167	*Jammi German*	1.50
168	Erric Pegram	.10
169	*Jason Peter*	.50
170	Carl Pickens	.20
171	Jake Plummer	1.50
172	John Randle	.10
173	Andre Reed	.10
174	Jake Reed	.10
175	Errict Rhett	.10
176	Simeon Rice	.10
177	Jerry Rice	1.50
178	Andre Rison	.20
179	Darrell Russell	.10
180	Rashaan Salaam	.10
181	Deion Sanders	.50
182	Barry Sanders	3.00
183	Chris Sanders	.10
184	Warren Sapp	.10
185	Junior Seau	.20
186	Jason Sehorn	.10
187	Shannon Sharpe	.20
188	Sedrick Shaw	.10
189	Heath Shuler	.10
190	*Chris Floyd*	.50
191	*Terry Fair*	1.50
192	*Kevin Dyson*	3.00
193	Torrance Small	.10
194	Antowain Smith	.75
195	Bruce Smith	.10
196	*Tarik Smith*	.50
197	Emmitt Smith	2.00
198	Neil Smith	.10
199	Jimmy Smith	.20
200	Chris Spielman	.10
201	Danny Wuerffel	.10
202	Irving Spikes	.10
203	Shawn Springs	.10
204	*Duane Starks*	.50
205	Kordell Stewart	1.50
206	J.J. Stokes	.20
207	Eric Swann	.10
208	Steve Tasker	.10
209	*Tim Dwight*	2.00
210	Jason Taylor	.10
211	Vinny Testaverde	.20
212	Thurman Thomas	.20
213	Broderick Thomas	.10
214	Derrick Thomas	.10
215	Zach Thomas	.10
216	*Germane Crowell*	2.50
217	Amani Toomer	.10
218	Tamarick Vanover	.10
219	Ross Verba	.10
220	*Andre Wadsworth*	1.50
221	Ray Zellars	.10
222	Chris Warren	.10
223	Steve Young	1.00
224	Tyrone Wheatley	.10
225	Reggie White	.50
226	*John Avery*	2.50
227	*Charles Woodson*	4.00
228	*Takeo Spikes*	1.50
229	Bryant Young	.10
230	*Tavian Banks*	2.50
231	*Fred Beasley*	.50
232	*Chris Ruhman*	.50

1998 Collector's Edge First Place Game Gear Jersey

Jerseys present at the NFL Draft Day Ceremonies and worn during the pre-season were used to make these cards. Singles were found 1:480 packs.

		MT
Complete Set (2):		300.00
Common Player:		100.00
Inserted 1:480		
1	Peyton Manning	200.00
2	Ryan Leaf	100.00

1998 Collector's Edge First Place Peyton Manning

Edge produced a five-card insert of Manning and inserted them 1:24 packs.

	MT
Complete Set (5):	40.00
Common Player:	8.00
Inserted 1:24	

1998 Collector's Edge First Place Rookie Ink

This set features autographed cards from the top 1998 rookies. Cards are enhanced with silver foil and each card back contains a certificate of authenticity. Singles are signed in blue ink and are found 1:24 packs. Red signatures also exist and are limited to 50 of each.

		MT
Complete Set (31):		750.00
Common Player:		8.00
Inserted 1:24		
Red Signatures:		3x
Production 50 Sets		
1	Brian Griese	45.00
2	Adrian Murrell	12.00
3	Marvin Harrison	20.00
4	Tavian Banks	25.00

5 Mike Alstott 18.00
6 Joe Jurevicius 12.00
7 Tim Dwight 18.00
8 Derrick Mayes 12.00
9 Kevin Greene 8.00
10 Marcus Nash 25.00
11 Charlie Batch 75.00
12 Cris Carter 25.00
13 Randy Moss 175.00
14 Tiki Barber 12.00
15 Ahman Green 25.00
16 Terrell Owens 20.00
17 Jim Druckenmiller 12.00
18 Reidel Anthony 12.00
19 Jacquez Green 25.00
20 Skip Hicks 20.00
21 Terry Allen 12.00
22 Fred Lane 12.00
23 Robert Holcombe 20.00
24 Jeremy Newberry 8.00
25 Fred Taylor 80.00
26 Mark Bruener 8.00
27 Hines Ward 20.00
28 Stephen Davis 12.00
29 Justin Armour 8.00
30 Peyton Manning 125.00
31 Ryan Leaf 50.00

1998 Collector's Edge First Place Rookie Markers

Each single in this 30-card set has a special embossed foil icon that recognizes the player's draft pick number. Singles were inserted 1:24 packs.

MT
Complete Set (30): 175.00
Common Player: 2.00
Minor Stars: 4.00
Inserted 1:24
1 Michael Pittman 2.00
2 Andre Wadsworth 4.00
3 Keith Brooking 2.00
4 Patrick Johnson 2.00
5 Jonathon Linton 2.00
6 Donald Hayes 4.00
7 Mark Chmura 2.00
8 Terry Allen 2.00
9 Brian Griese 8.00
10 Marcus Nash 8.00
11 Germane Crowell 8.00
12 Roosevelt Blackmon 2.00
13 Peyton Manning 30.00
14 Tavian Banks 8.00
15 Fred Taylor 20.00
16 Jim Druckenmiller 4.00
17 John Avery 8.00
18 Randy Moss 40.00
19 Robert Edwards 10.00
20 Cameron Cleeland 6.00
21 Joe Jurevicius 4.00
22 Charles Woodson 10.00
23 Terry Allen 2.00
24 Ryan Leaf 12.00
25 Chris Ruhman 2.00
26 Ahman Green 8.00
27 Jerome Pathon 4.00
28 Jacquez Green 8.00
29 Kevin Dyson 8.00
30 Skip Hicks 6.00

1998 Collector's Edge First Place Ryan Leaf

Edge produced a five-card insert set of Leaf and inserted them 1:24 packs.

MT
Complete Set (5): 25.00
Common Player: 5.00
Inserted 1:24

1998 Collector's Edge First Place Successors

Only the top players in the NFL are in this 25-card set. Singles are featured on mirror silver with gold foil. Cards were inserted 1:8 packs.

MT
Complete Set (25): 75.00
Common Player: 1.00
Minor Stars: 2.00
Inserted 1:8
1 Troy Aikman 4.00
2 Jerome Bettis 2.00
3 Drew Bledsoe 4.00
4 Tim Brown 1.00
5 Mark Brunell 4.00
6 Cris Carter 2.00
7 Terrell Davis 6.00
8 Robert Edwards 4.00
9 John Elway 4.00
10 Brett Favre 8.00
11 Eddie George 3.00
12 Brian Griese 3.00
13 Napoleon Kaufman 2.00
14 Ryan Leaf 5.00
15 Dorsey Levens 1.00
16 Peyton Manning 10.00
17 Dan Marino 6.00
18 Jim Druckenmiller 2.00
19 Herman Moore 2.00
20 Randy Moss 15.00
21 Jake Plummer 3.00
22 Barry Sanders 8.00
23 Emmitt Smith 6.00
24 Rod Smith 1.00
25 Fred Taylor 7.00

1998 Collector's Edge First Place Triple Threat

Three different levels to this 40-card insert. The first being Bronze that are found 1:12 packs. The next level is Silver that are inserted 1:24. The toughest is the Gold which are inserted 1:36.

MT
Complete Set (40): 185.00
Common Bronze: 1.50
Inserted 1:12
Common Silver: 2.50
Inserted 1:24
Common Gold: 4.00
Inserted 1:36
1 Robert Brooks 1.50
2 Troy Aikman 7.00
3 Randy Moss 20.00
4 Tim Brown 1.50
5 Brad Johnson 3.00
6 Kevin Dyson 4.00
7 Mark Chmura 1.50
8 Joey Galloway 3.00
9 Eddie George 6.00
10 Napoleon Kaufman 3.00
11 Dan Marino 12.00
12 Ed McCaffrey 3.00
13 Herman Moore 3.00
14 Carl Pickens 1.50
15 Emmitt Smith 12.00
16 Drew Bledsoe 7.00
17 Andre Wadsworth 3.00
18 Charles Woodson 7.00
19 Terrell Davis 12.00
20 Yancey Thigpen 2.50
21 Drew Bledsoe 7.00
22 Keith Brooking 2.50
23 Mark Brunell 7.00
24 Terrell Davis 12.00
25 Antonio Freeman 3.00
26 Peyton Manning 15.00
27 Jerry Rice 7.00
28 Takeo Spikes 3.00
29 Danny Wuerffel 1.50
30 Jerome Bettis 3.00
31 Cris Carter 4.00
32 Jim Druckenmiller 4.00
33 Warrick Dunn 8.00
34 John Elway 10.00
35 Brett Favre 20.00
36 Ryan Leaf 8.00
37 Dorsey Levens 4.00
38 Terrell Owens 6.00
39 Barry Sanders 20.00
40 Kordell Stewart 10.00

1998 Collector's Edge First Place Triumph

Each Triumph card is printed on clear acetate stock with a large action shot in the foreground with a head shot in the background. The 25 different singles were inserted 1:12 packs.

MT
Complete Set (25): 85.00
Common Player: 2.00
Inserted 1:12
1 Troy Aikman 5.00
2 Jerome Bettis 2.00
3 Drew Bledsoe 5.00
4 Tim Brown 2.00
5 Mark Brunell 4.00
6 Cris Carter 2.00
7 Terrell Davis 7.00
8 Jim Druckenmiller 2.00
9 Robert Edwards 4.00
10 John Elway 5.00
11 Brett Favre 10.00
12 Eddie George 4.00
13 Brian Griese 4.00
14 Napoleon Kaufman 2.00
15 Ryan Leaf 6.00
16 Dorsey Levens 2.00
17 Peyton Manning 10.00
18 Dan Marino 7.00
19 Herman Moore 2.00
20 Randy Moss 15.00
21 Jake Plummer 4.00
22 Barry Sanders 10.00
23 Emmitt Smith 7.00
24 Rod Smith 2.00
25 Fred Taylor 7.00

1998 Collector's Edge Masters

This is the first super-premium product that Edge has released. Every card in this set is sequentially numbered to 5,000, with double-thick parallel levels. The first being the 50-Point cards that are numbered to 3,000 and inserted one-per-pack. The 50-Point Gold singles are numbered to 150 and inserted 1:20 packs. HologGold cards are numbered to 10 and found 1:300 packs.

MT
Complete Set (199): 275.00
Common Player: .25
Minor Stars: .50
Common Rookie: 1.50
Production 5,000 Sets
50-Point Cards: 1.5x
Inserted 1:1
Production 3,000 Sets
50-Point Gold Cards: 7x-14x
50-Point Gold Rookies: 2x-4x
Inserted 1:20
Production 150 Sets
Hologold Cards: 50x-100x
Hologold Rookies: 8x-16x
Inserted 1:300
Production 10 Sets
Pack (3): 6.00
Wax Box (20): 110.00
1 Rob Moore .50
2 Adrian Murrell .25
3 Jake Plummer 3.00
4 *Michael Pittman* 1.50
5 Frank Sanders .50
6 *Andre Wadsworth* 3.00
7 Jamal Anderson 1.00
8 Chris Chandler .50
9 *Tim Dwight* 7.50
10 Tony Martin .25
11 Terance Mathis .25
12 *Ken Oxendine* 3.00
13 Jim Harbaugh .50
14 *Priest Holmes* 12.00
15 Michael Jackson .25
16 *Pat Johnson* 3.00
17 Jermaine Lewis .25
18 Eric Zeier .25
19 Doug Flutie 2.00
20 Rob Johnson .50
21 Eric Moulds 1.00
22 Andre Reed .50
23 Antowain Smith 1.00
24 Bruce Smith .25
25 Thurman Thomas .50
26 Steve Beuerlein .25
27 Kevin Greene .25
29 Raghib Ismail .25
30 Fred Lane .25
31 Muhsin Muhammad .25
32 Edgar Bennett .25
33 Curtis Conway .50
34 Bobby Engram .25
35 *Curtis Enis* 7.50
36 Erik Kramer .25
37 Chris Penn .25
38 Jeff Blake .50
39 Corey Dillon 2.00
40 Neil O'Donnell .25
41 Carl Pickens .50
42 Darnay Scott .25
43 *Damon Gibson* 1.50
44 Troy Aikman 3.00
45 Billy Davis .25
46 Michael Irvin .50
47 Ernie Mills .25
48 Deion Sanders 1.00
49 Emmitt Smith 4.50
50 Chris Warren .25
51 Bubby Brister .25
52 Terrell Davis 4.50
53 John Elway 4.50
54 *Brian Griese* 12.00
55 Ed McCaffrey .75
56 *Marcus Nash* 5.00
57 Shannon Sharpe .50
58 Rod Smith .50
59 *Charlie Batch* 10.00
60 *Germane Crowell* 7.00
61 Scott Mitchell .25
62 Johnnie Morton .25
63 Herman Moore .75
64 Barry Sanders 6.00
65 Robert Brooks .25
66 Brett Favre 6.00
67 Antonio Freeman 1.00
68 Raymont Harris .25
69 Dorsey Levens 1.00
70 Reggie White 1.00
71 Marshall Faulk 1.00
72 Marvin Harrison .50
73 *Peyton Manning* 25.00
74 *Jerome Pathon* 3.00
75 *Tavian Banks* 4.00
76 Mark Brunell 3.00
77 Keenan McCardell .25
78 Jimmy Smith .75
79 *Fred Taylor* 15.00
80 Derrick Alexander .25
81 Donnell Bennett .25
82 Rich Gannon .25
83 Elvis Grbac .50
84 Andre Rison .50
85 *Rashaan Shehee* 1.50
86 Karim Abdul .75
87 *John Avery* 5.00
88 *Oronde Gadsden* 5.00
89 Dan Marino 4.50
90 O.J. McDuffie .50
91 Zach Thomas .50
92 Cris Carter 1.00
93 Randall Cunningham 1.00
94 Brad Johnson .75
95 *Randy Moss* 25.00
96 Jake Reed .25
97 Robert Smith .50
98 Drew Bledsoe 3.00
99 Ben Coates .50
100 *Robert Edwards* 7.50
101 Terry Glenn .75
102 Shawn Jefferson .25
103 Ty Law .25
104 *Cameron Cleeland* 4.00
105 Kerry Collins .50
106 Sean Dawkins .25
107 Andre Hastings .25
108 Lamar Smith .25
109 Danny Wuerffel .25
110 Gary Brown .25
111 Chris Calloway .25
112 Ike Hilliard .25
113 *Joe Jurevicius* 3.00
114 Danny Kanell .25
115 Wayne Chrebet .75
116 Glenn Foley .50
117 Keyshawn Johnson 1.00
118 Leon Johnson .25
119 Curtis Martin 1.00
120 Vinny Testaverde .50
121 Tim Brown .50
122 Jeff George .50
123 James Jett .25
124 Napoleon Kaufman 1.00
125 *Charles Woodson* 7.50
126 Irving Fryar .25
127 Jeff Graham .25
128 Bobby Hoying .25
129 Duce Staley .25
130 Jerome Bettis .75
131 *Chris Fuamatu-Ma'afala* 3.00
132 Courtney Hawkins .25
133 Charles Johnson .25
134 Kordell Stewart 2.00
135 *Hines Ward* 3.00
136 Tony Banks .50
137 Isaac Bruce .50
138 *Robert Holcombe* 5.00
139 Eddie Kennison .50
140 *Ryan Leaf* 7.00
141 Natrone Means .50
142 *Mikhael Ricks* 3.00
143 Junior Seau .50
144 Bryan Still .25
145 Garrison Hearst .75
146 *R.W. McQuarters* 3.00
147 Terrell Owens 1.00
148 Jerry Rice 3.00
149 J.J. Stokes .50
150 Steve Young 2.00
151 Joey Galloway 1.00
152 *Ahman Green* 5.00
153 Warren Moon .50
154 Shawn Springs .25
155 Ricky Watters .50
156 Mike Alstott .50
157 Reidel Anthony .50
158 Trent Dilfer .50
159 Warrick Dunn 2.00
160 *Jacquez Green* 5.00
161 *Kevin Dyson* 5.00
162 Eddie George 2.00
163 Steve McNair 1.00
164 Yancy Thigpen .25
165 Frank Wycheck .25
166 Terry Allen .50
167 Gus Frerotte .25
168 Trent Green .50
169 *Skip Hicks* 5.00
170 Michael Westbrook .50
171 Jamal Anderson .50
172 Carl Pickens .25
173 Deion Sanders .50
174 Emmitt Smith 2.00
175 Terrell Davis 2.00
176 John Elway 2.00
177 Charlie Batch 7.50
178 Herman Moore .25
179 Barry Sanders 3.00
180 Brett Favre 3.00
181 Antonio Freeman .50
182 Marshall Faulk .50
183 Peyton Manning 15.00
184 Mark Brunell 1.50
185 Dan Marino 2.00
186 Randy Moss 15.00
187 Drew Bledsoe 1.50
188 Robert Edwards 3.00
189 Curtis Martin .50
190 Charles Woodson 3.00
191 Jerome Bettis .25
192 Robert Holcombe 2.00
193 Ryan Leaf 3.00
194 Natrone Means .50
195 Jerry Rice 1.50
196 Steve Young 1.00
197 Warrick Dunn 1.00
198 Eddie George 1.00
199 (Peyton Manning CL) 7.50
200 (Ryan Leaf CL) 4.00

1998 Collector's Edge Masters Legends

This 30-card set includes the top players from '98. Each card is sequentially numbered to 2,500 and inserted 1:8 packs.

MT
Complete Set (30): 85.00
Common Player: 1.50
Minor Stars: 3.00
Inserted 1:8
Production 2,500 Sets
1 Jake Plummer 6.00
2 Doug Flutie 4.00
3 Corey Dillon 3.00
4 Carl Pickens 1.50
5 Troy Aikman 6.00
6 Deion Sanders 3.00
7 Emmitt Smith 10.00
8 Terrell Davis 10.00
9 John Elway 10.00
10 Herman Moore 3.00
11 Barry Sanders 12.00
12 Brett Favre 12.00
13 Antonio Freeman 3.00
14 Marshall Faulk 3.00
15 Mark Brunell 5.00
16 Dan Marino 10.00
17 Cris Carter 5.00
18 Drew Bledsoe 5.00
19 Keyshawn Johnson 3.00
20 Curtis Martin 3.00
21 Napoleon Kaufman 3.00
22 Jerome Bettis 3.00
23 Kordell Stewart 5.00
24 Natrone Means 3.00
25 Jerry Rice 6.00
26 Steve Young 4.00
27 Joey Galloway 3.00
28 Warrick Dunn 4.00
29 Eddie George 5.00
30 Terry Allen 1.50

1998 Collector's Edge Masters Main Event

Main Event singles are sequentially numbered to 2,000 and inserted 1:16 packs.

MT
Complete Set (20): 160.00
Common Player: 2.50
Minor Stars: 5.00
Inserted 1:16
Production 2,000 Sets
1 Troy Aikman 8.00
2 Jamal Anderson 5.00
3 Charlie Batch 12.00
4 Jerome Bettis 2.50
5 Mark Brunell 6.00
6 Terrell Davis 12.00
7 Warrick Dunn 5.00
8 Robert Edwards 7.00
9 John Elway 12.00
10 Brett Favre 16.00
11 Doug Flutie 5.00
12 Eddie George 6.00
13 Dan Marino 12.00
14 Curtis Martin 5.00
15 Randy Moss 50.00
16 Carl Pickens 2.50
17 Jake Plummer 8.00
18 Barry Sanders 16.00
19 Emmitt Smith 12.00
20 Fred Taylor 25.00

1998 Collector's Edge Masters Rookie Masters

This 30-card set is made up of the top rookies from the class of '98. Each card is sequentially numbered to 2,500 and inserted 1:8 packs.

MT
Complete Set (30): 125.00
Common Player: 1.50
Minor Stars: 3.00
Inserted 1:8
Production 2,500 Sets
1 Peyton Manning 25.00
2 Ryan Leaf 10.00
3 Charlie Batch 12.00
4 Brian Griese 8.00
5 Randy Moss 40.00
6 Jacquez Green 4.00
7 Kevin Dyson 4.00
8 Mikhael Ricks 3.00
9 Jerome Pathon 3.00
10 Joe Jurevicius 3.00
11 Germane Crowell 4.00
12 Tim Dwight 6.00
13 Pat Johnson 3.00
14 Hines Ward 3.00
15 Marcus Nash 4.00
16 Damon Gibson 1.50
17 Robert Edwards 5.00
18 Robert Holcombe 4.00
19 Tavian Banks 3.00
20 Fred Taylor 20.00
21 Skip Hicks 4.00
22 Curtis Enis 6.00
23 Ahman Green 4.00
24 John Avery 4.00
25 Chris Fuamatu-Ma'afala 3.00
26 Rashaan Shehee 1.50
27 Cameron Cleeland 4.00
28 Charles Woodson 6.00
29 R.W. McQuarters 3.00
30 Andre Wadsworth 3.00

1998 Collector's Edge Masters Sentinels

This 10-card set is made up of the top 10 most collectible superstars in the NFL. Each card is sequentially numbered to 500 and found 1:120 packs.

MT
Complete Set (10): 275.00
Common Player: 15.00
Inserted 1:120
Production 500 Sets
1 John Elway 30.00
2 Brett Favre 40.00
3 Barry Sanders 40.00
4 Terrell Davis 30.00
5 Dan Marino 30.00
6 Emmitt Smith 30.00
7 Randy Moss 75.00
8 Peyton Manning 40.00
9 Robert Edwards 15.00
10 Fred Taylor 35.00

1998 Collector's Edge Masters Super Masters

We have the checklist at 23 players for a complete set. Ten of the players also have signed versions of their insert card. Insert odds are 1:10 packs for the regular insert and the Autographs vary.

MT
Complete Set (23): 75.00
Common Player: 1.50
Minor Stars: 3.00
Inserted 1:10
Production 2,000 Sets
Set Price Doesn't Include Autographs
Troy Aikman 8.00
Edgar Bennett 1.50
Robert Brooks 1.50
Dwight Clark 3.00
Dwight Clark AUTO 15.00
Roger Craig 3.00
Roger Craig AUTO 15.00
Terrell Davis 12.00
Len Dawson 3.00
Len Dawson AUTO 40.00
John Elway 12.00
Brett Favre 16.00
Antonio Freeman 3.00
Jack Ham 3.00
Jack Ham AUTO 15.00
Michael Irvin 3.00
Butch Johnson AUTO 10.00
Drew Pearson 3.00
Drew Pearson AUTO 15.00
Jerry Rice 8.00
Deion Sanders 5.00
Shannon Sharpe 3.00
Emmitt Smith 12.00
Rod Smith 3.00
John Stallworth 3.00
John Stallworth AUTO 15.00
Bart Starr 10.00
Bart Starr AUTO 325.00
Johnny Unitas 8.00
Johnny Unitas AUTO 300.00
Steve Young 5.00
Reggie White 3.00

1998 Collector's Edge Odyssey

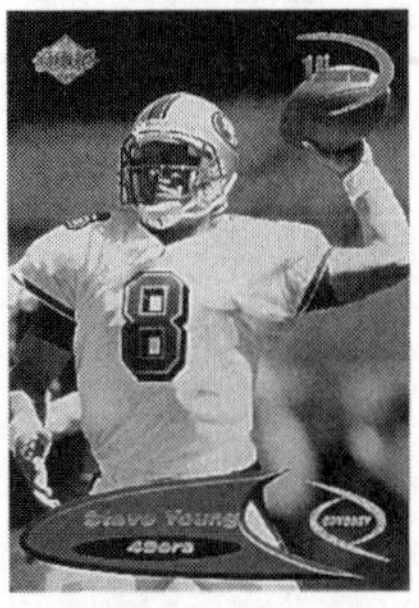

The base set is made up of 250 cards and is broken down into four tiers or quarters. The first 150 cards are from the 1st Quarter subset. Cards 151-200 are 2nd Quarter and are inserted 1:1.5 packs. Cards 201-230 are 3rd Quarter and are found 1:3 packs. Cards 231-250 are the 4th Quarter singles and are the toughest to find at 1:18 packs.

MT
Complete Set (250): 450.00
Common 1st Quarter: .10
Minor Stars: .20
Common Rookie: 1.50
Common 2nd Quarter: .50
Inserted 1:1.5
Common 3rd Quarter: .75
Inserted 1:3
Common 4th Quarter: 3.00
Inserted 1:18
Pack: 4.00
Wax Box (24): 85.00
1 Terance Mathis .10
2 Tony Martin .10
3 Chris Chandler .20
4 Jamal Anderson .50
5 Jake Plummer .75
6 Adrian Murrell .10
7 Rob Moore .10
8 Frank Sanders .10
9 Larry Centers .10
10 *Andre Wadsworth* 1.50
11 Jim Harbaugh .20
12 Errict Rhett .10
13 Jermaine Lewis .10
14 Michael Jackson .10
15 Eric Zeier .10
16 Rob Johnson .20
17 Antowain Smith .50
18 Andre Reed .10
19 Bruce Smith .10
20 Doug Flutie .50
21 Thurman Thomas .20
22 Kerry Collins .20
23 Fred Lane .20
24 Muhsin Mohammed .10
25 Rae Carruth .10
26 Raghib Islmail .10
27 Kevin Greene .10
28 *Curtis Enis* 3.00
29 Curtis Conway .20
30 Erik Kramer .10
31 Edgar Bennett .10
32 Neil O'Donnell .20
33 Jeff Blake .20
34 Carl Pickens .20
35 Corey Dillon .50
36 Troy Aikman 1.00
37 Jason Garrett .10
38 Emmitt Smith 1.50
39 Deion Sanders .50
40 Michael Irvin .20
41 Chris Warren .10
42 John Elway 1.00
43 Terrell Davis 1.50
44 Shannon Sharpe .20
45 Rod Smith .20
46 *Marcus Nash* 2.50
47 *Brian Griese* 4.00
48 Barry Sanders 2.00
49 Herman Moore .20
50 Scott Mitchell .10
51 Johnnie Morton .10
52 *Rashaan Shehee* 1.50
53 *Charlie Batch* 5.00
54 Brett Favre 2.00
55 Dorsey Levens .20
56 Antonio Freeman .50
57 Reggie White .50
58 Robert Brooks .10
59 Raymont Harris .10
60 *Peyton Manning* 12.00
61 Marshall Faulk .50
62 *Jerome Pathon* 2.00
63 Marvin Harrison .20
64 Mark Brunell .75
65 *Fred Taylor* 5.00
66 Jimmy Smith .20
67 James Stewart .20
68 Keenan McCardell .10
69 Andre Rison .10
70 Elvis Grbac .10
71 Donnell Bennett .10
72 Rich Gannon .10
73 Derrick Thomas .10
74 Dan Marino 1.50
75 Karim Abdul-Jabbar .50
76 *John Avery* 3.00
77 O.J. McDuffie .10
78 *Oronde Gadsden* 2.00
79 Zach Thomas .20
80 *Randy Moss* 12.00
81 Cris Carter .50
82 Jake Reed .10
83 Robert Smith .20
84 Brad Johnson .50
85 Drew Bledsoe 1.00
86 *Robert Edwards* 4.00
87 Terry Glenn .50
88 Troy Brown .10
89 Shawn Jefferson .10
90 Danny Wuerffel .10
91 Dana Stubblefield .10
92 Derrick Alexander .10
93 Ray Zellars .10
94 Andre Hastings .10
95 Danny Kanell .10
96 Tiki Barber .10
97 Ike Hilliard .10
98 Charles Way .10
99 Chris Calloway .10
100 Curtis Martin .50
101 Glenn Foley .20
102 Vinny Testaverde .20
103 Keyshawn Johnson .50
104 Wayne Chrebet .50
105 Leon Johnson .10
106 Jeff George .20
107 *Charles Woodson* 3.00
108 Tim Brown .20
109 James Jett .10
110 Napoleon Kaufman .50
111 Charlie Garner .10
112 Bobby Hoying .10
113 Duce Staley .75
114 Irving Fryar .10
115 Kordell Stewart .75
116 Jerome Bettis .50
117 Charles Johnson .10
118 Randall Cunningham .50
119 Courtney Hawkins .10

120	Tony Banks	.50
121	Isaac Bruce	.50
122	*Robert Holcombe*	2.50
123	Greg Hill	.10
124	*Ryan Leaf*	4.00
125	*Mikhael Ricks*	2.50
126	Natrone Means	.50
127	Junior Seau	.20
128	Jerry Rice	1.00
129	Terrell Owens	.75
130	Garrison Hearst	.20
131	Steve Young	.75
132	J.J. Stokes	.20
133	Warren Moon	.20
134	Joey Galloway	.50
135	Ricky Watters	.20
136	*Ahman Green*	2.50
137	Trent Dilfer	.20
138	Mike Alstott	.50
139	Warrick Dunn	.75
140	Reidel Anthony	.20
141	*Jacquez Green*	2.50
142	Steve McNair	.50
143	Eddie George	.75
144	Yancey Thigpen	.20
145	*Kevin Dyson*	2.50
146	Trent Green	.20
147	Gus Frerotte	.10
148	Terry Allen	.20
149	Michael Westbrook	.20
150	Jim Druckenmiller	.20
151	Jake Plummer	1.50
152	Adrian Murrell	.50
153	Rob Johnson	.50
154	Antowain Smith	.75
155	Kerry Collins	.50
156	Curtis Enis	5.00
157	Carl Pickens	.50
158	Corey Dillon	1.00
159	Troy Aikman	1.50
160	Emmitt Smith	2.00
161	Deion Sanders	.50
162	Michael Irvin	.50
163	John Elway	1.50
164	Terrell Davis	2.00
165	Shannon Sharpe	.50
166	Rod Smith	.50
167	Barry Sanders	3.00
168	Herman Moore	.50
169	Brett Favre	3.00
170	Dorsey Levens	.50
171	Antonio Freeman	.75
172	Peyton Manning	15.00
173	Marshall Faulk	.50
174	Mark Brunell	1.00
175	Fred Taylor	7.00
176	Dan Marino	2.00
177	Randy Moss	15.00
178	Cris Carter	.50
179	Drew Bledsoe	1.00
180	Robert Edwards	6.00
181	Curtis Martin	.50
182	Napoleon Kaufman	.50
183	Kordell Stewart	1.00
184	Jerome Bettis	.50
185	Tony Banks	.50
186	Isaac Bruce	.50
187	Ryan Leaf	6.00
188	Natrone Means	.50
189	Jerry Rice	1.50
190	Terrell Owens	.75
191	Garrison Hearst	.50
192	Steve Young	.75
193	Warren Moon	.50
194	Joey Galloway	.50
195	Trent Dilfer	.50
196	Mike Alstott	.50
197	Warrick Dunn	1.50
198	Steve McNair	.75
199	Eddie George	1.00
200	Terry Allen	.50
201	Jake Plummer	2.00
202	Curtis Enis	8.00
203	Carl Pickens	.75
204	Corey Dillon	1.00
205	Troy Aikman	2.00
206	Emmitt Smith	3.00
207	John Elway	2.00
208	Terrell Davis	3.00
209	Barry Sanders	4.00
210	Brett Favre	4.00
211	Antonio Freeman	.75
212	Peyton Manning	20.00
213	Mark Brunell	1.50
214	Fred Taylor	12.00
215	Dan Marino	3.00
216	Randy Moss	20.00
217	Drew Bledsoe	1.50
218	Robert Edwards	8.00
219	Curtis Martin	.75
220	Kordell Stewart	1.50
221	Jerome Bettis	.75
222	Tony Banks	.75
223	Ryan Leaf	8.00
224	Jerry Rice	2.00
225	Steve Young	1.00
226	Warren Moon	.75
227	Trent Dilfer	.75
228	Warrick Dunn	2.00
229	Steve McNair	1.00
230	Eddie George	1.50
231	Curtis Enis	10.00
232	Carl Pickens	3.00
233	Troy Aikman	6.00
234	Emmitt Smith	8.00
235	John Elway	6.00
236	Terrell Davis	10.00
237	Barry Sanders	12.00
238	Brett Favre	12.00
239	Peyton Manning	30.00
240	Fred Taylor	18.00
241	Dan Marino	8.00
242	Randy Moss	30.00
243	Drew Bledsoe	5.00
244	Kordell Stewart	5.00
245	Jerome Bettis	3.00
246	Ryan Leaf	12.00
247	Jerry Rice	6.00
248	Steve Young	4.00
249	Warren Moon	3.00
250	Eddie George	5.00

1998 Collector's Edge Odyssey Galvanized

Each base card has a parallel Galvanized single that is also tiered four ways. Each single has the letter "G" on the back and has a foil front. Cards 1-150 were inserted 1:3 packs, Cards 151-200 were found 1:15 packs, 201-230 at 1:29 and 231-250 at 1:59.

	MT
Complete Set (250):	1000.
1st Quarter Cards:	3x
1st Quarter Rookies:	1.5x
Inserted 1:3	
2nd Quarter Cards:	4x
2nd Quarter Rookies:	2x
Inserted 1:15	
3rd Quarter Cards:	3x
3rd Quarter Rookies:	1.5x
Inserted 1:29	
4th Quarter Cards:	4x
4th Quarter Rookies:	2x
Inserted 1:144	

1998 Collector's Edge Odyssey HoloGold

HoloGold is the second parallel set to the base and is also tiered four different ways. These singles have the letter "H" on the backs and also have foil fronts. Cards 1-150 are numbered to 150 and inserted 1:34 packs, cards 151-200 are numbered to 50 and found 1:307, cards 201-230 are limited to 30 and found 1:840 and the last tier are cards numbered 231-250 with a production run of 20 and inserted 1:1,920.

	MT
1st Quarter Cards: 20x-40x	
1st Quarter Rookies: 5x-10x	
Inserted 1:34	
Production 150 Sets	

1998 Collector's Edge Odyssey Leading Edge

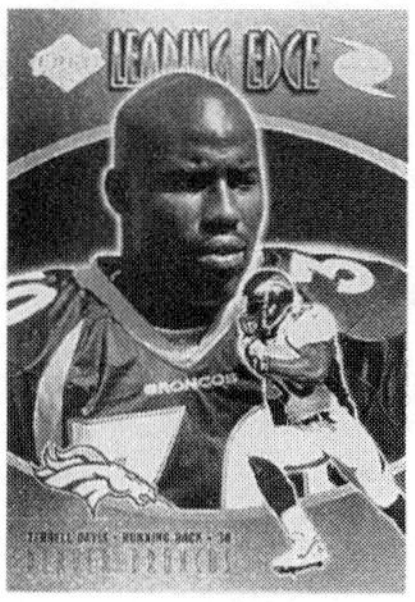

Leading Edge features 30 of the NFL's top stars in an attractive foil set. Singles were inserted 1:7 packs.

		MT
Complete Set (30):		75.00
Common Player:		1.00
Inserted 1:7		
1	Jake Plummer	2.00
2	Rob Johnson	1.00
3	Curtis Enis	3.00
4	Carl Pickens	1.00
5	Troy Aikman	3.00
6	Emmitt Smith	4.50
7	John Elway	3.00
8	Terrell Davis	4.50
9	Shannon Sharpe	1.00
10	Barry Sanders	6.00
11	Brett Favre	6.00
12	Antonio Freeman	1.50
13	Peyton Manning	10.00
14	Marshall Faulk	1.50
15	Mark Brunell	2.00
16	Dan Marino	4.50
17	Randy Moss	20.00
18	Cris Carter	1.50
19	Robert Edwards	4.00
20	Curtis Martin	1.50
21	Ryan Leaf	5.00
22	Terrell Owens	1.50
23	Garrison Hearst	1.00
24	Steve Young	1.50
25	Joey Galloway	1.50
26	Mike Alstott	1.50
27	Warrick Dunn	2.50
28	Eddie George	2.50
29	Kevin Dyson	2.00
30	Terry Allen	1.00

1998 Collector's Edge Odyssey Prodigies

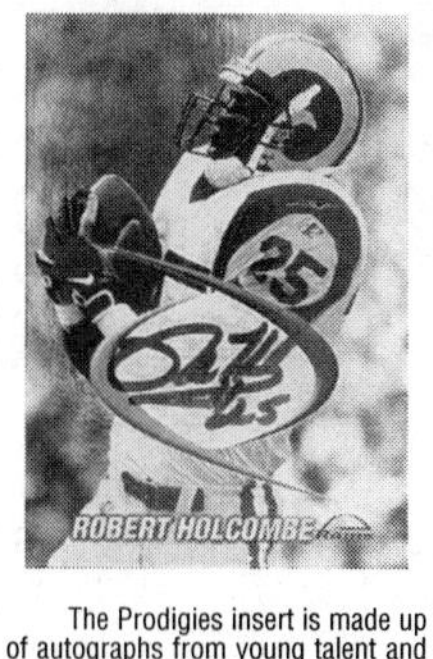

The Prodigies insert is made up of autographs from young talent and rookies from '98. Singles were inserted 1:24 packs. A parallel of Red Signatures exist with most signing between 50 to 80.

	MT
Complete Set (32):	1000.
Common Player:	10.00
Minor Stars:	20.00
Inserted 1:24	
John Avery	30.00
Tavian Banks	20.00
Charlie Batch	75.00
Blaine Bishop	10.00
Robert Brooks	30.00
Tim Brown	50.00
Mark Brunell	100.00
Wayne Chrebet	30.00
Jim Druckenmiller	20.00
Robert Edwards	45.00
Doug Flutie	60.00
Glenn Foley	10.00
Oronde Gadsden	30.00
Joey Galloway	20.00
Garrison Hearst	20.00
Robert Holcombe	20.00
Joey Kent	10.00
Jon Kitna	30.00
Herman Moore	30.00
Randy Moss	200.00
Terrell Owens	30.00
Mikhael Ricks	20.00
Rashaan Shehee	30.00
Antowain Smith	20.00
Emmitt Smith	180.00
Robert Smith	20.00
Rod Smith	20.00
J.J. Stokes	20.00
Fred Taylor	60.00
Derrick Thomas	20.00
Chris Warren	10.00
Eric Zeier	10.00

1998 Collector's Edge Odyssey S.L. Edge

Super Limited Edge singles includes 12 of the game's most collectible superstars and were found 1:99 packs.

		MT
Complete Set (12):		275.00
Common Player:		10.00
Inserted 1:99		
1	Emmitt Smith	45.00
2	Deion Sanders	15.00
3	John Elway	30.00
4	Brett Favre	60.00
5	Antonio Freeman	15.00
6	Peyton Manning	30.00
7	Mark Brunell	25.00
8	Dan Marino	45.00
9	Randy Moss	70.00
10	Joey Galloway	10.00
11	Mike Alstott	10.00
12	Eddie George	25.00

1998 Collector's Edge Supreme

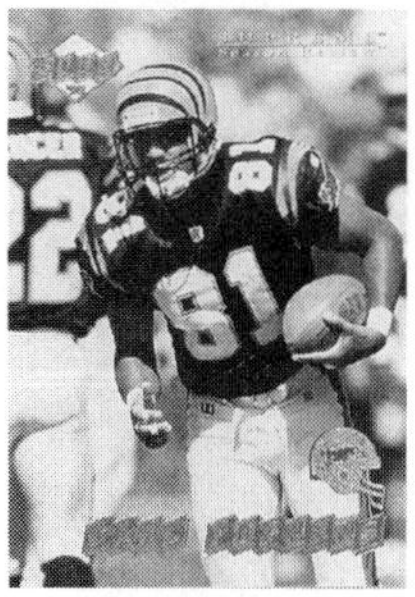

Supreme Season Review consists of a 200-card base set, with 170 veterans and 30 redmeption cards for the top draft pick from each NFL team. The player's name and Collector's Edge logo are printed in gold foil on the front. The base set is paralleled by Gold Ingots. Inserts include Markers, T-3 Triple Threat and Pro Signatures Authentic. Two 1-of-1 inserts were also created: Memorable Moments and the 200-card Personal Collection, which features photos from Super Bowl XXXII.

		MT
Complete Set (200):		75.00
Common Player:		.20
Minor Stars:		.40
Comp. Gold Ingot (200):		350.00
Gold Ingot Cards: 2x-4x		
Gold Ingot Rookies: 2x		
Pack (6):		4.00
Wax Box (24):		85.00
1	Larry Centers	.20
2	Jake Plummer	2.00
3	Simeon Rice	.20
4	Arizona Draft Pick	.20
4A	*(Andre Wadsworth)*	1.50
4B	*(Michael Pittman)*	2.00
5	Jamal Anderson	.40
6	Bert Emanuel	.20
7	Byron Hanspard	.40
8	Atlanta Draft Pick	.20
8A	*(Jammi German)*	1.50
8B	*(Keith Brooking)*	1.00
9	Derrick Alexander	.20
10	Peter Boulware	.20
11	Michael Jackson	.20
12	Ray Lewis	.20
13	Vinny Testaverde	.40
14	Baltimore Draft Pick	.20
14A	*(Duane Starks)*	1.00
14B	*(Patrick Johnson)*	1.50
15	Todd Collins	.20
16	Jim Kelly	.40
17	Andre Reed	.20
18	Antowain Smith	1.00
19	Bruce Smith	.20
20	Thurman Thomas	.40
21	Buffalo Draft Pick	.20
21A	*(Jonathan Linton)*	2.50
22	Tim Biakabutuka	.20
23	Rae Carruth	.40
24	Kerry Collins	.40
25	Anthony Johnson	.20
26	Lamar Lathon	.20
27	Carolina Draft Pick	.20
27A	*(Jason Peters)*	1.50
27B	*(Donald Hayes)*	3.00
28	Curtis Conway	.40
29	Bryan Cox	.20
30	Bobby Engram	.20
31	Erik Kramer	.20
32	Rick Mirer	.20
33	Rashaan Salaam	.40
34	Chicago Draft Pick	.20
34A	*(Curtis Enis)*	3.50
35	Jeff Blake	.40
36	Ki-Jana Carter	.20
37	Corey Dillon	1.50
38	Carl Pickens	.40
39	Cincinnati Draft Pick	.20
39A	*(Takeo Spikes)*	1.00
39B	*(Brian Simmons)*	1.00
40	Troy Aikman	2.00
41	Daryl Johnston	.20
42	David LaFleur	.40
43	Anthony Miller	.20
44	Deion Sanders	1.00
45	Emmitt Smith	3.00
46	Broderick Thomas	.20
47	Dallas Draft Pick	.20
47A	*(Greg Ellis)*	1.00
48	Terrell Davis	2.00
49	John Elway	2.00
50	Ed McCaffrey	.20
51	John Mobley	.20
52	Bill Romanowski	.20
53	Shannon Sharpe	.20
54	Neil Smith	.20
55	Rod Smith	.20
56	Maa Tanuvasa	.20
57	Denver Draft Pick	.20
57A	*(Marcus Nash)*	1.50
57B	*(Brian Griese)*	6.00
58	Scott Mitchell	.20
59	Herman Moore	.40
60	Barry Sanders	3.00
61	Detroit Draft Pick	.20
61A	*(Jamal Alexander)*	1.00
61B	*(Chris Liwienski)*	1.00
61C	*(Terry Fair)*	1.50
61D	*(Germane Crowell)*	4.00
61E	*(Charlie Batch)*	5.00
62	Robert Brooks	.40
63	Mark Chmura	.20
64	Brett Favre	4.00
65	Antonio Freeman	.40
66	Dorsey Levens	.40
67	Derrick Mayes	.20
68	Ross Verba	.20
69	Reggie White	.40
70	Green Bay Draft Pick	.20
70A	*(Vonnie Holliday)*	1.50
70B	*(Roosevelt Blackmon)*	1.00
71	Marshall Faulk	.40
72	Jim Harbaugh	.40
73	Marvin Harrison	.40
74	Indianapolis Draft Pick	.20
74A	*(E.G. Green)*	1.50
74B	*(Peyton Manning)*	15.00
75	Tony Brackens	.20
76	Mark Brunell	2.00
77	Rob Johnson	.40
78	Keenan McCardell	.20
79	Natrone Means	.40
80	Jimmy Smith	.20
81	Jacksonville Draft Pick	.20
81A	*(Tavian Banks)*	1.50
82	Marcus Allen	.40
83	Tony Gonzalez	.40
84	Elvis Grbac	.20
85	Derrick Thomas	.20
86	Tamarick Vanover	.20
87	Kansas City Draft Pick	.20
87A	*(Rashaan Shehee)*	1.50
88	Karim Abdul-Jabbar	.40
89	Fred Barnett	.20
90	Dan Marino	3.00
91	O.J. McDuffie	.20
92	Brett Perriman	.20
93	Irving Spikes	.20
94	Zach Thomas	.20
95	Miami Draft Pick	.20
95A	*(John Avery)*	1.50
96	Cris Carter	.20
97	Brad Johnson	.40
98	John Randle	.20
99	Jake Reed	.20
100	Robert Smith	.20
101	Minnesota Draft Pick	.20
101A	*(Randy Moss)*	15.00
102	Drew Bledsoe	2.00
103	Chris Canty	.20
104	Ben Coates	.20
105	Terry Glenn	.40
106	Curtis Martin	1.50
107	Willie McGinest	.20
108	Sedrick Shaw	.20
109	New England Draft Pick	.20
109A	*(Chris Floyd)*	1.00
109B	*(Tebucky Jones)*	1.00
109C	*(Harold Shaw)*	1.00
110	Mario Bates	.20
111	Heath Shuler	.20
112	Danny Wuerffel	.40
113	New Orleans Draft Pick	.20
113A	*(Cameron Cleeland)*	2.00
114	Ray Zellars	.20
115	Tiki Barber	.40
116	Dave Brown	.20
117	Ike Hilliard	.40
118	Danny Kanell	.20
119	Jason Sehorn	.20
120	Amani Toomer	.20
121	New York Giants Draft Pick	.20
121A	*(Shaun Williams)*	1.00
121B	*(Joe Jurevicius)*	2.00
121C	*(Brian Alford)*	1.00
122	Wayne Chrebet	.20
123	Hugh Douglas	.20
124	Jeff Graham	.20
125	Keyshawn Johnson	.40
126	Adrian Murrell	.40
127	Neil O'Donnell	.20
128	New York Jets Draft Pick	.20
128A	*(Scott Frost)*	1.50
129	Tim Brown	.40
130	Jeff George	.40
131	Desmond Howard	.20
132	Napoleon Kaufman	.40
133	Darrell Russell	.20
134	Oakland Draft Pick	.20
134A	*(Charles Woodson)*	3.50
135	Ty Detmer	.20
136	Irving Fryar	.20
137	Bobby Hoying	.40
138	Chris T. Jones	.20
139	Ricky Watters	.40
140	Philadelphia Draft Pick	.20
140A	*(Allen Rossum)*	2.00
141	Jerome Bettis	.40
142	Charles Johnson	.20
143	George Jones	.20
144	Greg Lloyd	.20
145	Kordell Stewart	2.00
146	Yancey Thigpen	.20
147	Pittsburgh Draft Pick	.20
147A	*(Chris Fuamatu-Ma'afala)*	2.00
148	Stan Humphries	.20
149	Tony Martin	.20
150	Eric Metcalf	.20
151	Junior Seau	.40
152	San Diego Draft Pick	.20
152A	*(Ryan Leaf)*	3.50
153	Jim Druckenmiller	.40
154	William Floyd	.40
155	Kevin Greene	.20
156	Garrison Hearst	.20
157	Ken Norton	.20
158	Terrell Owens	.40
159	Jerry Rice	2.00
160	J.J. Stokes	.20

1998 Collector's Edge Supreme Gold Ingots

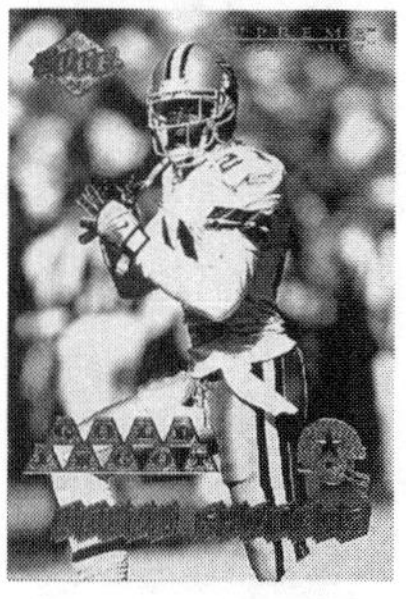

Gold Ingots is a full parallel of the Supreme Season Review base set. The cards are printed on 48-point card stock and have "Gold Ingots" printed in gold foil on the front.

	MT
Gold Ingots Cards:	2x-4x
Gold Ingots Rookies:	2x

1998 Collector's Edge Supreme Markers

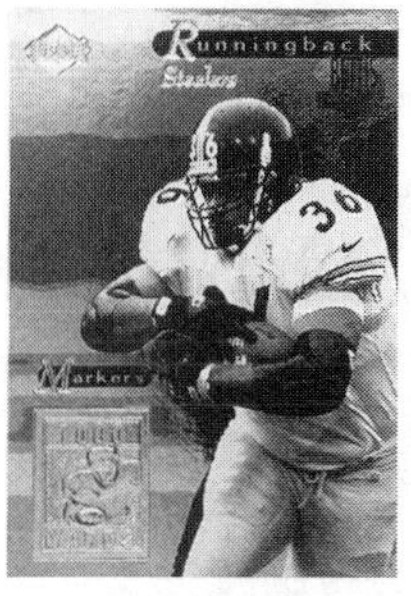

Markers is a 30-card insert seeded one per 24 packs. The cards are printed on 48-point stock. The player's last name, position and team are listed at the top. An embossed gold-foil logo denotes which statistical "marker" the player has acheived.

		MT
Complete Set (30):		375.00
Common Player:		5.00
Minor Stars:		10.00
1	Jamal Anderson	5.00
2	Corey Dillon	20.00
3	Emmitt Smith	40.00
4	Terrell Davis	25.00
5	John Elway	25.00
6	Rod Smith	5.00
7	Herman Moore	10.00
8	Barry Sanders	40.00
9	Robert Brooks	5.00
10	Brett Favre	50.00
11	Antonio Freeman	10.00
12	Dorsey Levens	10.00
13	Marshall Faulk	10.00
14	Mark Brunell	20.00
15	Karim Abdul-Jabbar	10.00
16	Dan Marino	40.00
17	Cris Carter	5.00
18	Drew Bledsoe	20.00
19	Curtis Martin	15.00
20	Adrian Murrell	5.00
21	Tim Brown	5.00
22	Jeff George	5.00
23	Napoleon Kaufman	10.00
24	Jerome Bettis	10.00
25	Kordell Stewart	20.00
26	Yancey Thigpen	5.00
27	Garrison Hearst	5.00
28	Steve Young	15.00
29	Joey Galloway	10.00
30	Eddie George	25.00

1998 Collector's Edge Supreme Pro Signatures Authentic

Seven players signed cards for the Pro Signatures Authentic insert (1:800). Collector's Edge also obtained rookie draft-day jerseys and put swatches on Draft Day Jersey cards.

		MT
Common Player:		100.00
TA	Troy Aikman	450.00
DH	Desmond Howard	100.00
JR	Jerry Rice	500.00
MA	Marcus Allen	200.00
TD	Terrell Davis	500.00
RL	Ryan Leaf	150.00
PM	Peyton Manning	150.00

1998 Collector's Edge Supreme T-3 Triple Threat

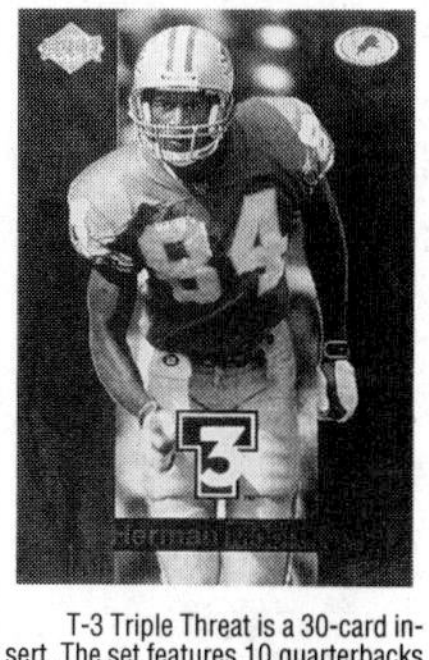

T-3 Triple Threat is a 30-card insert. The set features 10 quarterbacks (1:36), 10 running backs (1:24) and 10 wide receivers (1:12). The front has a color player image which is repeated on the left and right. The team's logo is in the upper right and the player's name and T-3 logo are at the bottom.

		MT
Complete Set (29):		225.00
Common WR:		2.50
Common RB:		4.00
Common QB:		6.00
Card #18 Never Issued		
1	Rae Carruth	2.50
2	Carl Pickens	2.50
3	Troy Aikman	15.00
4	Emmitt Smith	20.00
5	Terrell Davis	12.00
6	John Elway	15.00
7	Herman Moore	5.00
8	Barry Sanders	20.00
9	Robert Brooks	2.50
10	Brett Favre	30.00
11	Antonio Freeman	5.00
12	Dorsey Levens	4.00
13	Rob Johnson	6.00
14	Jerry Rice	10.00
15	Dan Marino	25.00
16	Cris Carter	2.50
17	Drew Bledsoe	15.00
19	Adrian Murrell	4.00
20	Tim Brown	2.50
21	Napoleon Kaufman	4.00
22	Jerome Bettis	4.00
23	Kordell Stewart	15.00
24	Joey Galloway	5.00
25	Jim Druckenmiller	6.00
26	Terrell Owens	2.50
27	Jake Plummer	12.00
28	Warrick Dunn	12.00
29	Eddie George	12.00
30	Steve McNair	8.00

1999 Collector's Edge Advantage

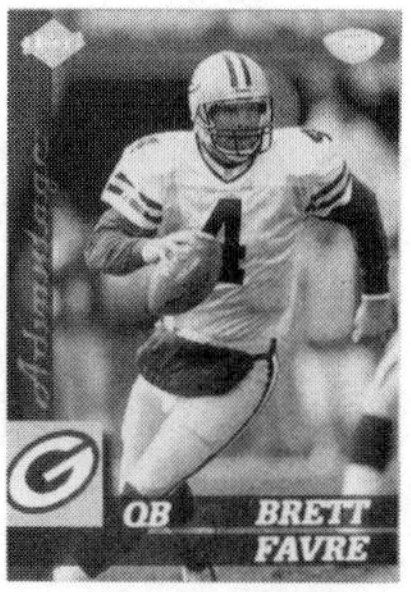

Edge Advantage is a 190-card set that is made up of 150 veterans, 38 draft pick rookies and 2 checklists. Each card has three different parallels that include Gold Ingot, Galvanized and HoloGold. Other inserts in the product include Rookie Autographs,

Jumpstarters, Memorable Moments, Overture, Prime Connection, Shockwaves and Showtime.

		MT
Complete Set (190):		65.00
Common Player:		.15
Minor Stars:		.30
Common Rookie:		.50
Pack (8):		5.00
Wax Box (24):		90.00
1	Larry Centers	.15
2	Rob Moore	.30
3	Adrian Murrell	.15
4	Jake Plummer	1.25
5	Frank Sanders	.15
6	Jamal Anderson	.50
7	Chris Chandler	.30
8	Tim Dwight	.50
9	Tony Martin	.15
10	Terance Mathis	.15
11	O.J. Santiago	.15
12	Jim Harbaugh	.30
13	Priest Holmes	.75
14	Jermaine Lewis	.30
15	Rod Woodson	.15
16	Eric Zeier	.15
17	Doug Flutie	.75
18	Sam Gash	.15
19	Rob Johnson	.30
20	Eric Moulds	.50
21	Andre Reed	.30
22	Antowain Smith	.50
23	Bruce Smith	.15
24	Thurman Thomas	.30
25	Steve Beuerlein	.15
26	Kevin Greene	.15
27	Raghib Ismail	.15
28	Fred Lane	.15
29	Muhsin Muhammad	.15
30	Edgar Bennett	.15
31	Curtis Conway	.30
32	Bobby Engram	.15
33	Curtis Enis	.50
34	Erik Kramer	.15
35	Jeff Blake	.30
36	Corey Dillon	.75
37	Neil O'Donnell	.30
38	Carl Pickens	.30
39	Takeo Spikes	.15
40	Troy Aikman	1.25
41	Billy Davis	.15
42	Michael Irvin	.30
43	Deion Sanders	.50
44	Emmitt Smith	1.75
45	Darren Woodson	.15
46	Bubby Brister	.30
47	Terrell Davis	1.75
48	John Elway	1.75
49	Ed McCaffrey	.30
50	Bill Romanowski	.15
51	Shannon Sharpe	.30
52	Rod Smith	.30
53	Charlie Batch	1.00
54	Germane Crowell	.30
55	Herman Moore	.50
56	Johnnie Morton	.15
57	Barry Sanders	2.50
58	Robert Brooks	.15
59	Brett Favre	2.50
60	Antonio Freeman	.50
61	Darick Holmes	.15
62	Dorsey Levens	.50
63	Roell Preston	.15
64	Marshall Faulk	.50
65	E.G. Green	.15
66	Marvin Harrison	.30
67	Peyton Manning	2.00
68	Jerome Pathon	.15
69	Mark Brunell	1.00
70	Kevin Hardy	.15
71	Keenan McCardell	.15
72	Jimmy Smith	.30
73	Fred Taylor	1.25
74	Alvis Whitted	.15
75	Kimble Anders	.15
76	Donnell Bennett	.15
77	Rich Gannon	.15
78	Elvis Grbac	.15
79	Bam Morris	.15
80	Andre Rison	.30
81	Karim Abdul	.30
82	John Avery	.30
83	Oronde Gadsden	.30
84	Sam Madison	.15
85	Dan Marino	1.75
86	O.J. McDuffie	.30
87	Zach Thomas	.30
88	Cris Carter	.50
89	Randall Cunningham	.50
90	Brad Johnson	.50
91	Randy Moss	3.00
92	John Randle	.30
93	Jake Reed	.15
94	Robert Smith	.50
95	Drew Bledsoe	1.00
96	Ben Coates	.30
97	Robert Edwards	.50
98	Terry Glenn	.50
99	Ty Law	.15
100	Cam Cleeland	.30
101	Kerry Collins	.30
102	Gary Brown	.15
103	Kent Graham	.15
104	Ike Hilliard	.30
105	Joe Jurevicius	.30
106	Danny Kanell	.15
107	Wayne Chrebet	.50
108	Aaron Glenn	.15
109	Keyshawn Johnson	.50
110	Curtis Martin	.50
111	Vinny Testaverde	.30
112	Tim Brown	.30
113	Jeff George	.30
114	James Jett	.15
115	Napoleon Kaufman	.50
116	Charles Woodson	.50
117	Koy Detmer	.15
118	Duce Staley	.15
119	Jerome Bettis	.50
120	Charles Johnson	.15
121	Kordell Stewart	.75
122	Tony Banks	.30
123	Isaac Bruce	.30
124	June Henley	.15
125	Ryan Leaf	.75
126	Natrone Means	.15
127	Mikhael Ricks	.15
128	Craig Whelihan	.15
129	Garrison Hearst	.30
130	Terrell Owens	.75
131	Jerry Rice	1.25
132	J.J. Stokes	.30
133	Steve Young	1.00
134	Joey Galloway	.50
135	Ahman Green	.30
136	Jon Kitna	.75
137	Ricky Watters	.30
138	Mike Alstott	.50
139	Reidel Anthony	.30
140	Trent Dilfer	.30
141	Warrick Dunn	.75
142	Jacquez Green	.30
143	Kevin Dyson	.30
144	Eddie George	.75
145	Steve McNair	.75
146	Yancy Thigpen	.30
147	Terry Allen	.30
148	Trent Green	.50
149	Skip Hicks	.30
150	Michael Westbrook	.30
151	*Rahim Abdullah*	1.00
152	*Champ Bailey*	2.00
153	*Marlon Barnes*	1.00
154	*D'Wayne Bates*	1.00
155	*Michael Bishop*	2.00
156	*Dre' Bly*	1.00
157	*David Boston*	2.00
158	*Chris Claiborne*	1.50
159	*Tim Couch*	6.00
160	*Daunte Culpepper*	10.00
161	*Autrey Denson*	1.75
162	*Jared DeVries*	1.00
163	*Troy Edwards*	2.00
164	*Kris Farris*	.50
165	*Kevin Faulk*	2.00
166	*Martin Gramatica*	1.50
167	*Torry Holt*	3.00
168	*Brock Huard*	2.00
169	*Sedrick Irvin*	1.75
170	*Edgerrin James*	15.00
171	*James Johnson*	2.00
172	*Kevin Johnson*	2.00
173	*Andy Katzenmoyer*	1.50
174	*Jevon Kearse*	2.00
175	*Shaun King*	3.00
176	*Rob Konrad*	1.00
177	*Chris McAlister*	1.00
178	*Darnell McDonald*	2.00
179	*Donovan McNabb*	6.00
180	*Cade McNown*	2.50
181	*Dat Nguyen*	1.50
182	*Peerless Price*	2.00
183	*Akili Smith*	3.00
184	*Tai Streets*	2.00
185	*Cuncho Brown*	1.00
186	*Ricky Williams*	6.00
187	*Craig Yeast*	1.00
188	*Amos Zereoue*	2.00
189	Checklist	.15
190	Checklist	.15

1999 Collector's Edge Advantage Galvanized Parallel

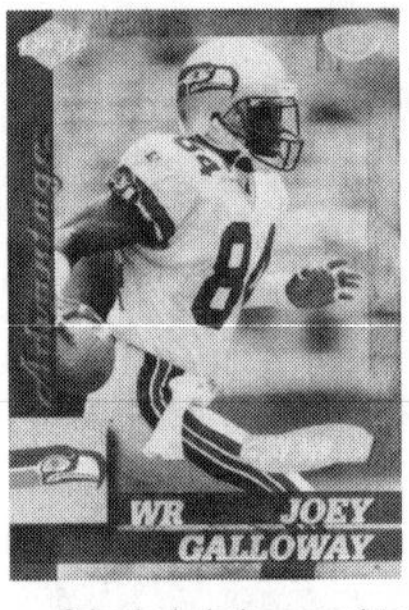

Galvanized singles are printed on silver foil board with gold foil stamping. Each has a Galvanized stamp on the front and are sequentially numbered on the back. Veterans are numbered to 500 and rookies to 200.

	MT
Galvanized Cards:	4x-8x
Production 500 Sets	
Galvanized Rookies:	3x-6x
Production 200 Sets	

1999 Collector's Edge Advantage Gold Ingot Parallel

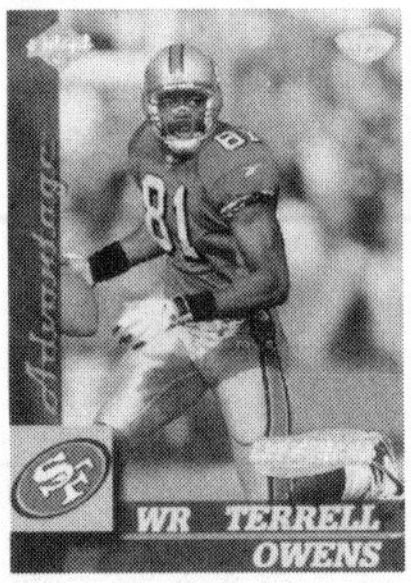

Each Gold Ingot single is identical to the base card except for the foil is in gold rather than silver and each has a Gold Ingot stamp on the fronts of the cards. It is a parallel to the base and singles were inserted 1:1 packs.

	MT
Complete Set (190):	100.00
Gold Ingot Cards:	2x
Gold Ingot Rookies:	1.5x
Inserted 1:1	

1999 Collector's Edge Advantage HoloGold Parallel

HoloGold singles are printed on holographic foil board with veterans numbered to 50 and rookies to 20.

	MT
HoloGold Cards:	40x-80x
Production 50 Sets	
HoloGold Rookies:	20x-40x
Production 20 Sets	

1999 Collector's Edge Advantage Jumpstarters

Each of the singles in this set are printed on clear acetate and offer commentary of each player from Peyton Manning. Each card was sequentially numbered to 500.

		MT
Complete Set (10):		75.00
Common Player:		5.00
Production 500 Sets		
1	Champ Bailey	5.00
2	David Boston	10.00
3	Tim Couch	25.00
4	Daunte Culpepper	12.00
5	Torry Holt	10.00
6	Donovan McNabb	12.00
7	Cade McNown	12.00
8	Peerless Price	7.00
9	Brock Huard	5.00
10	Ricky Williams	25.00

1999 Collector's Edge Advantage Memorable Moments

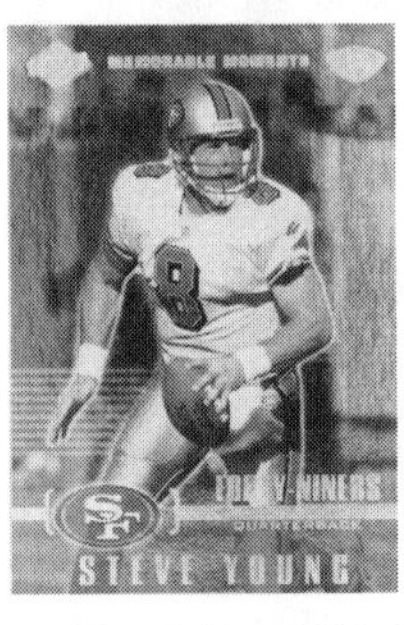

Each card in this set highlights a memorable moment from 1998. Each is printed on silver foil and they were found 1:24 packs.

		MT
Complete Set (10):		85.00
Common Player:		5.00
Inserted 1:24		
1	Terrell Davis	12.00
2	Randy Moss	15.00
3	Peyton Manning	12.00
4	Emmitt Smith	12.00
5	Keyshawn Johnson	5.00
6	Dan Marino	12.00
7	John Elway	12.00
8	Doug Flutie	7.00
9	Jerry Rice	10.00
10	Steve Young	8.00

1999 Collector's Edge Advantage Overture

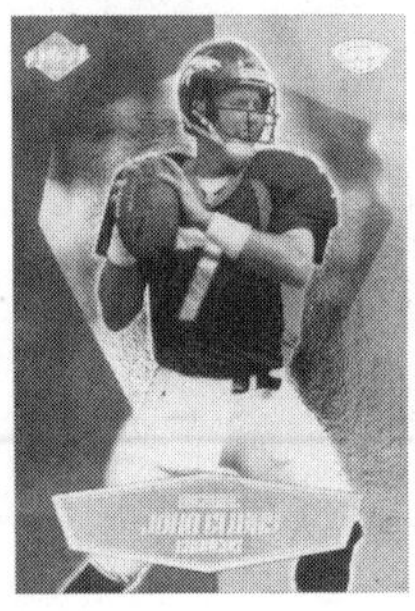

Ten of the NFL's superstars are featured in this foil set with gold foil stamping. Singles were inserted 1:24 packs.

		MT
Complete Set (10):		100.00
Common Player:		5.00
Inserted 1:24		
1	Jamal Anderson	5.00
2	Terrell Davis	12.00
3	John Elway	12.00
4	Brett Favre	15.00
5	Peyton Manning	12.00
6	Dan Marino	12.00
7	Randy Moss	15.00
8	Jerry Rice	10.00
9	Barry Sanders	15.00
10	Emmitt Smith	12.00

1999 Collector's Edge Advantage Prime Connection

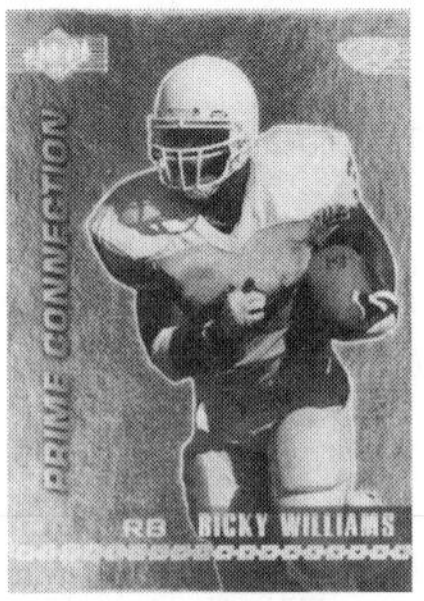

Current and future NFL stars were included in this 20-card set. Singles were inserted 1:4 packs.

		MT
Complete Set (20):		65.00
Common Player:		1.50
Minor Stars:		3.00
Inserted 1:4		
1	Ricky Williams	12.00
2	Fred Taylor	4.00
3	Tim Couch	12.00
4	Peyton Manning	5.00
5	Daunte Culpepper	5.00
6	Drew Bledsoe	3.50
7	Torry Holt	4.00
8	Keyshawn Johnson	1.50
9	Champ Bailey	1.50
10	Charles Woodson	1.50
11	Brock Huard	1.50
12	Jake Plummer	4.00
13	Donovan McNabb	6.00
14	Steve Young	3.50
15	Edgerrin James	7.00
16	Jamal Anderson	1.50
17	Cade McNown	6.00
18	Mark Brunell	3.50
19	Peerless Price	3.50
20	Randy Moss	6.00

1999 Collector's Edge Advantage Rookie Autographs

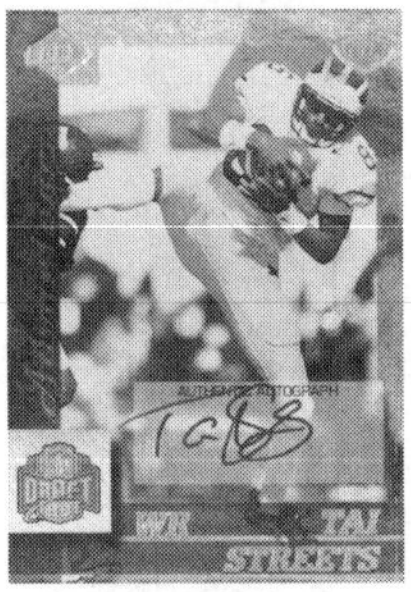

Each of the autographs are printed on holographic foil board with the signature found on the fronts of each card. Singles were inserted an average of 1:24 packs.

		MT
Common Player:		6.00
Minor Stars:		12.00
Inserted 1:24		
151	Rahim Abdullah	12.00
152	Champ Bailey	15.00
153	Marlon Barnes	12.00
154	D'Wayne Bates	12.00
155	Michael Bishop	20.00
156	Dre Bly	6.00
157	David Boston	30.00
158	Cuncho Brown	6.00
159	Chris Claiborne	12.00
160	Tim Couch	100.00
161	Daunte Culpepper	45.00
162	Autry Denson	12.00
163	Jared DeVries	12.00
164	Troy Edwards	20.00
165	Kris Farris	6.00
166	Kevin Faulk	30.00
167	Martin Gramatica	6.00
168	Torry Holt	25.00
169	Brock Huard	15.00
170	Sedrick Irvin	15.00
171	Edgerrin James	60.00
172	James Johnson	15.00
173	Kevin Johnson	15.00
174	Andy Katzenmoyer	15.00
175	Jevon Kearse	18.00
176	Shaun King	15.00
177	Rob Konrad	12.00
178	Chris McAlister	12.00
179	Darnell McDonald	15.00
180	Donovan McNabb	45.00
181	Cade McNown	45.00
182	Dat Nguyen	12.00
183	Peerless Price	20.00
184	Akili Smith	40.00
185	Tai Streets	15.00
186	Ricky Williams	100.00
187	Craig Yeast	12.00
188	Amos Zereoue	20.00

1999 Collector's Edge Advantage Shockwaves

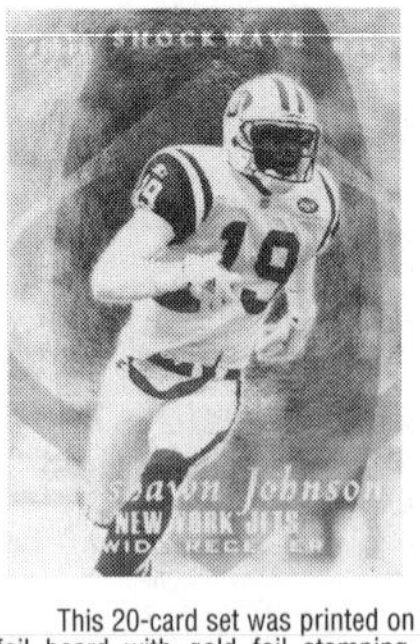

This 20-card set was printed on foil board with gold foil stamping. They were inserted 1:12 packs.

		MT
Complete Set (20):		120.00
Common Player:		3.50
Inserted 1:12		
1	Jamal Anderson	3.50
2	Jake Plummer	8.00
3	Eric Moulds	3.50
4	Troy Aikman	8.00
5	Emmitt Smith	12.00
6	Marshall Faulk	3.50
7	Jerome Bettis	3.50
8	Barry Sanders	16.00
9	Brett Favre	16.00
10	Peyton Manning	12.00
11	Mark Brunell	6.00
12	Fred Taylor	8.00
13	Randall Cunningham	3.50
14	Randy Moss	16.00
15	Drew Bledsoe	6.00
16	Keyshawn Johnson	3.50
17	Curtis Martin	3.50
18	Steve Young	5.00
19	Warrick Dunn	5.00
20	Eddie George	5.00

1999 Collector's Edge Advantage Showtime

Each of the 15 cards in this insert are printed on clear acetate with gold foil stamping. Each was sequentially numbered to 500.

		MT
Complete Set (15):		125.00
Common Player:		5.00
Production 500 Sets		
1	Troy Aikman	10.00
2	Jamal Anderson	5.00
3	Mark Brunell	8.00
4	Terrell Davis	15.00
5	Warrick Dunn	7.00
6	Brett Favre	20.00
7	Doug Flutie	7.00
8	Eddie George	7.00
9	Keyshawn Johnson	5.00
10	Peyton Manning	15.00
11	Dan Marino	15.00
12	Randy Moss	20.00
13	Jake Plummer	10.00
14	Jerry Rice	10.00
15	Barry Sanders	20.00

1999 Collector's Edge First Place

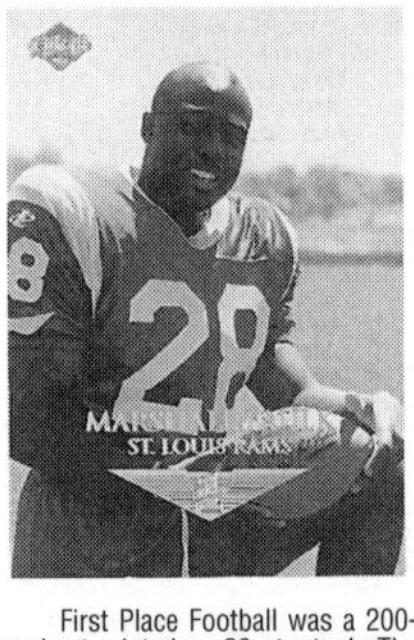

First Place Football was a 200-card set printed on 20-pt. stock. The set included 148 veterans, 50 rookies and 2 checklists. The Kurt Warner #201 was added late to the print run and each was hand-numbered to 500. Parallel sets included Galvanized, Gold Ingot and HoloGold. Other insert sets included: Adrenalin, Excalibur, Future Legends, Loud & Proud, Pro Signature Authentics, Rookie Game Gear and Successors. SRP was $3.99 for 12-card packs.

		MT
Complete Set (200):		60.00
Common Player:		.15
Minor Stars:		.30
Common Rookie:		.50
Pack (12):		3.00
Wax Box (24):		60.00
1	Adrian Murrell	.15
2	Rob Moore	.30
3	Jake Plummer	1.25
4	Simeon Rice	.15
5	Frank Sanders	.15
6	Jamal Anderson	.75
7	Chris Calloway	.15
8	Chris Chandler	.30
9	Tim Dwight	.75
10	Terance Mathis	.15
11	Jessie Tuggle	.15
12	Tony Banks	.30
13	Priest Holmes	.50
14	Jermaine Lewis	.15
15	Scott Mitchell	.15
16	Doug Flutie	1.00
17	Eric Moulds	.75
18	Andre Reed	.30
19	Antowain Smith	.50
20	Bruce Smith	.15
21	Thurman Thomas	.30
22	Steve Beuerlein	.30
23	Tim Biakabutuka	.30
24	Kevin Greene	.15
25	Muhsin Muhammad	.30
26	Edgar Bennett	.15
27	Curtis Conway	.30
28	Bobby Engram	.15
29	Curtis Enis	.75
30	Erik Kramer	.15
31	Jeff Blake	.30
32	Corey Dillon	.75
33	Carl Pickens	.30
34	Darnay Scott	.30
35	Takeo Spikes	.15
36	Ty Detmer	.15
37	Terry Kirby	.15
38	Leslie Shepherd	.15
39	Chris Spielman	.15
40	Troy Aikman	1.50
41	Michael Irvin	.30
42	Raghib Ismail	.15
43	Ernie Mills	.15
44	Deion Sanders	.75
45	Emmitt Smith	2.00
46	Chris Warren	.15
47	Bubby Brister	.30
48	Terrell Davis	2.00
49	Brian Griese	1.25
50	Ed McCaffrey	.50
51	Shannon Sharpe	.30
52	Rod Smith	.50
53	Charlie Batch	1.00
54	Terry Fair	.15
55	Herman Moore	.75
56	Johnnie Morton	.15
57	Barry Sanders	3.00
58	Robert Brooks	.15
59	Brett Favre	3.00
60	Mark Chmura	.30
61	Antonio Freeman	.75
62	Dorsey Levens	.75
63	Derrick Mayes	.30
64	Marvin Harrison	.75
65	Peyton Manning	2.00
66	Jerome Pathon	.15
67	Mark Brunell	1.25
68	Keenan McCardell	.30
69	Jimmy Smith	.75
70	Fred Taylor	1.50
71	Derrick Alexander	.15
72	Kimble Anders	.15
73	Elvis Grbac	.30
74	Warren Moon	.30
75	Bam Morris	.15
76	Andre Rison	.30
77	Karim Abdul	.30
78	Dan Marino	2.00
79	Tony Martin	.15
80	O.J. McDuffie	.30
81	Zach Thomas	.30
82	Cris Carter	.75
83	Randall Cunningham	.75
84	Jeff George	.75
85	Randy Moss	3.00
86	Jake Reed	.30
87	Robert Smith	.75
88	Drew Bledsoe	1.25
89	Ben Coates	.30
90	Terry Glenn	.75
91	Ty Law	.15
92	Shawn Jefferson	.15
93	Cameron Cleeland	.30
94	Andre Hastings	.15
95	Billy Joe Hobert	.15
96	Eddie Kennison	.15
97	Gary Brown	.15
98	Kerry Collins	.30
99	Kent Graham	.15
100	Ike Hilliard	.30
101	Joe Jurevicius	.15
102	Wayne Chrebet	.75
103	Aaron Glenn	.15
104	Keyshawn Johnson	.75
105	Mo Lewis	.15
106	Curtis Martin	.75
107	Vinny Testaverde	.50
108	Tim Brown	.30
109	Rich Gannon	.30
110	James Jett	.15
111	Napoleon Kaufman	.75
112	Charles Woodson	.75
113	Koy Detmer	.15
114	Charles Johnson	.15
115	Duce Staley	.50
116	Jerome Bettis	.75
117	Courtney Hawkins	.15
118	Levon Kirkland	.15
119	Kordell Stewart	.75
120	Isaac Bruce	.75
121	Marshall Faulk	.75
122	Trent Green	.50
123	Amp Lee	.15
124	Jim Harbaugh	.30
125	Charlie Jones	.15
126	Freddie Jones	.30
127	Ryan Leaf	.75
128	Natrone Means	.50
129	Junior Seau	.30
130	Garrison Hearst	.50
131	Terrell Owens	.75
132	Jerry Rice	1.50
133	J.J. Stokes	.30
134	Steve Young	1.00
135	Joey Galloway	.75
136	Jon Kitna	.75
137	Ricky Watters	.50
138	Mike Alstott	.75
139	Reidel Anthony	.30
140	Trent Dilfer	.50
141	Warrick Dunn	.75
142	Kevin Dyson	.30
143	Eddie George	1.00
144	Steve McNair	1.00
145	Frank Wycheck	.30
146	Skip Hicks	.30
147	Brad Johnson	.50

148 Michael Westbrook .30
149 Checklist .15
150 Checklist .15
151 *David Boston* 2.50
152 *Patrick Kerney* .50
153 *Chris McAlister* 1.00
154 *Peerless Price* 2.00
155 *Antoine Winfield* 1.00
156 *D'Wayne Bates* 1.00
157 *Cade McNown* 2.00
158 *Akili Smith* 4.00
159 *Rahim Abdullah* .50
160 *Tim Couch* 7.00
161 *Kevin Johnson* 4.00
162 *Ebenezer Ekuban* 1.00
163 *Dat Nguyen* .50
164 *Al Wilson* .50
165 *Chris Claiborne* 1.00
166 *Sedrick Irvin* 1.50
167 *Antwan Edwards* 1.00
168 *Aaron Brooks* 3.00
169 *De'Mond Parker* 1.50
170 *Edgerrin James* 10.00
171 *Fernando Bryant* .50
172 *Michael Cloud* 1.00
173 *John Tait* .50
174 *Cecil Collins* 2.50
175 *J.J. Johnson* 1.50
176 *Rob Konrad* 1.00
177 *Daunte Culpepper* 8.00
178 *Jim Kleinsasser* 1.00
179 *Dimitrius Underwood* 1.00
180 *Michael Bishop* 1.75
181 *Kevin Faulk* 1.75
182 *Andy Katzenmoyer* 1.00
183 *Ricky Williams* 7.00
184 *Joe Montgomery* 1.50
185 *Donovan McNabb* 4.00
186 *Troy Edwards* 2.50
187 *Amos Zereoue* 1.50
188 *Joe Germaine* 1.00
189 *Torry Holt* 2.50
190 *Jermaine Fazande* 1.00
191 *Reggie McGrew* .50
192 *Karsten Bailey* 1.00
193 *Lamar King* .50
194 *Autry Denson* 1.00
195 *Martin Gramatica* 1.00
196 *Shaun King* 4.00
197 *Darnell McDonald* 1.00
198 *Anthony McFarland* .50
199 *Jevon Kearse* 2.00
200 *Champ Bailey* 1.50
201 *Kurt Warner/500* 400.00

1999 Collector's Edge First Place Galvanized Parallel

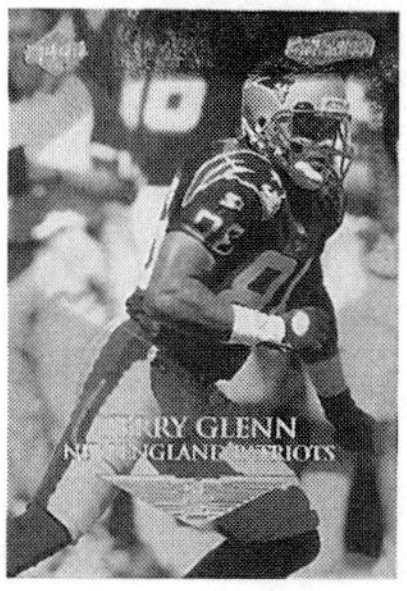

This was a 200-card parallel to the base set. Each single had the Galvanized stamp on the front of the card. Veterans were sequentially numbered to 500 and rookies to 100.

MT
Galvanized Cards: 3x-6x
Production 500 Sets
Galvanized Rookies: 5x-10x
Production 100 Sets

1 Adrian Murrell .15
2 Rob Moore .30
3 Jake Plummer 1.25
4 Simeon Rice .15
5 Frank Sanders .15
6 Jamal Anderson .75
7 Chris Calloway .15
8 Chris Chandler .30
9 Tim Dwight .75
10 Terance Mathis .15
11 Jessie Tuggle .15
12 Tony Banks .30
13 Priest Holmes .50
14 Jermaine Lewis .15
15 Scott Mitchell .15
16 Doug Flutie 1.00
17 Eric Moulds .75
18 Andre Reed .30
19 Antowain Smith .50
20 Bruce Smith .15
21 Thurman Thomas .30
22 Steve Beuerlein .30
23 Tim Biakabutuka .30
24 Kevin Greene .15
25 Muhsin Muhammad .30
26 Edgar Bennett .15
27 Curtis Conway .30
28 Bobby Engram .15
29 Curtis Enis .75
30 Erik Kramer .15
31 Jeff Blake .30
32 Corey Dillon .75
33 Carl Pickens .30
34 Darnay Scott .30
35 Takeo Spikes .15
36 Ty Detmer .15
37 Terry Kirby .15
38 Leslie Shepherd .15
39 Chris Spielman .15
40 Troy Aikman 1.50
41 Michael Irvin .30
42 Raghib Ismail .15
43 Ernie Mills .15
44 Deion Sanders .75
45 Emmitt Smith 2.00
46 Chris Warren .15
47 Bubby Brister .30
48 Terrell Davis 2.00
49 Brian Griese 1.25
50 Ed McCaffrey .50
51 Shannon Sharpe .30
52 Rod Smith .30
53 Charlie Batch 1.00
54 Terry Fair .15
55 Herman Moore .75
56 Johnnie Morton .15
57 Barry Sanders 3.00
58 Robert Brooks .15
59 Brett Favre 3.00
60 Mark Chmura .30
61 Antonio Freeman .75
62 Dorsey Levens .75
63 Derrick Mayes .30
64 Marvin Harrison .75
65 Peyton Manning 2.00
66 Jerome Pathon .15
67 Mark Brunell 1.25
68 Keenan McCardell .30
69 Jimmy Smith .75
70 Fred Taylor 1.50
71 Derrick Alexander .15
72 Kimble Anders .15
73 Elvis Grbac .30
74 Warren Moon .30
75 Bam Morris .15
76 Andre Rison .30
77 Karim Abdul .30
78 Dan Marino 2.00
79 Tony Martin .15
80 O.J. McDuffie .30
81 Zach Thomas .30
82 Cris Carter .75
83 Randall Cunningham .75
84 Jeff George .75
85 Randy Moss 3.00
86 Jake Reed .30
87 Robert Smith .75
88 Drew Bledsoe 1.25
89 Ben Coates .30
90 Terry Glenn .75
91 Ty Law .15
92 Shawn Jefferson .15
93 Cameron Cleeland .30
94 Andre Hastings .15
95 Billy Joe Hobert .15
96 Eddie Kennison .15
97 Gary Brown .15
98 Kerry Collins .30
99 Kent Graham .15
100 Ike Hilliard .30
101 Joe Jurevicius .15
102 Wayne Chrebet .75
103 Aaron Glenn .15
104 Keyshawn Johnson .75
105 Mo Lewis .15
106 Curtis Martin .75
107 Vinny Testaverde .50
108 Tim Brown .30
109 Rich Gannon .30
110 James Jett .15
111 Napoleon Kaufman .75
112 Charles Woodson .75
113 Koy Detmer .15
114 Charles Johnson .15
115 Duce Staley .50
116 Jerome Bettis .75
117 Courtney Hawkins .15
118 Levon Kirkland .15
119 Kordell Stewart .75
120 Isaac Bruce .75
121 Marshall Faulk .75
122 Trent Green .50
123 Amp Lee .15
124 Jim Harbaugh .30
125 Charlie Jones .15
126 Freddie Jones .30
127 Ryan Leaf .75
128 Natrone Means .50
129 Junior Seau .30
130 Garrison Hearst .50
131 Terrell Owens .75
132 Jerry Rice 1.50
133 J.J. Stokes .30
134 Steve Young 1.00
135 Joey Galloway .75
136 Jon Kitna .75
137 Ricky Watters .50
138 Mike Alstott .75
139 Reidel Anthony .30
140 Trent Dilfer .50
141 Warrick Dunn .75
142 Kevin Dyson .30
143 Eddie George 1.00
144 Steve McNair 1.00
145 Frank Wycheck .30
146 Skip Hicks .30
147 Brad Johnson .50
148 Michael Westbrook .30
149 Checklist .15
150 Checklist .15
151 *David Boston* 2.50
152 *Patrick Kerney* .50
153 *Chris McAlister* 1.00
154 *Peerless Price* 2.00
155 *Antoine Winfield* 1.00
156 *D'Wayne Bates* 1.00
157 *Cade McNown* 4.00
158 *Akili Smith* 4.00
159 *Rahim Abdullah* .50
160 *Tim Couch* 7.00
161 *Kevin Johnson* 4.00
162 *Ebenezer Ekuban* 1.00
163 *Dat Nguyen* .50
164 *Al Wilson* .50
165 *Chris Claiborne* 1.00
166 *Sedrick Irvin* 1.50
167 *Antwan Edwards* 1.00
168 *Aaron Brooks* 1.00
169 *De'Mond Parker* 1.50
170 *Edgerrin James* 10.00
171 *Fernando Bryant* .50
172 *Michael Cloud* 1.00
173 *John Tait* .50
174 *Cecil Collins* 2.50
175 *J.J. Johnson* 1.50
176 *Rob Konrad* 1.00
177 *Daunte Culpepper* 4.00
178 *Jim Kleinsasser* 1.00
179 *Dimitrius Underwood* 1.00
180 *Michael Bishop* 1.75
181 *Kevin Faulk* 1.75
182 *Andy Katzenmoyer* 1.00
183 *Ricky Williams* 7.00
184 *Joe Montgomery* 1.50
185 *Donovan McNabb* 4.00
186 *Troy Edwards* 2.50
187 *Amos Zereoue* 1.50
188 *Joe Germaine* 1.00
189 *Torry Holt* 2.50
190 *Jermaine Fazande* 1.00
191 *Reggie McGrew* .50
192 *Karsten Bailey* 1.00
193 *Lamar King* .50
194 *Autry Denson* 1.00
195 *Martin Gramatica* 1.00
196 *Shaun King* 4.00
197 *Darnell McDonald* 1.00
198 *Anthony McFarland* .50
199 *Jevon Kearse* 1.75
200 *Champ Bailey* 1.50
201 *Kurt Warner/500* 200.00

1999 Collector's Edge First Place Gold Ingot Parallel

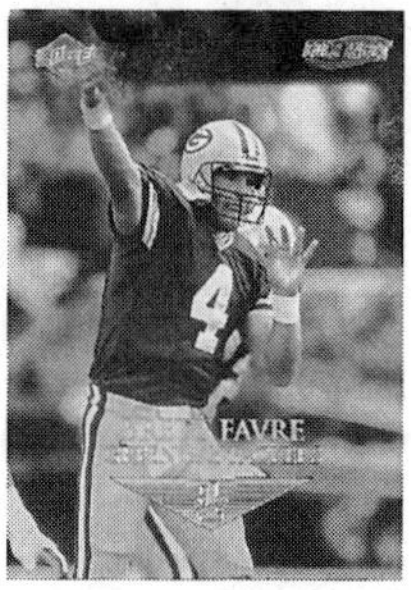

This was a 200-card parallel to the base set. Each single had the Gold Ingot stamp on the front of the card. Singles were found one- per-pack.

MT
Gold Ingot Cards: 2x
Gold Ingot Rookies: 1.5x
Inserted 1:1

1999 Collector's Edge First Place HoloGold Parallel

This was a 200-card parallel to the base set. Each single had the HoloGold stamp on the front of the card. Veterans were sequentially numbered to 50 and rookies to 10.

MT
HoloGold Cards: 30x-60x
Production 50 Sets
HoloGold Rookies: 25x-50x
Production 10 Sets

1999 Collector's Edge First Place Adrenalin

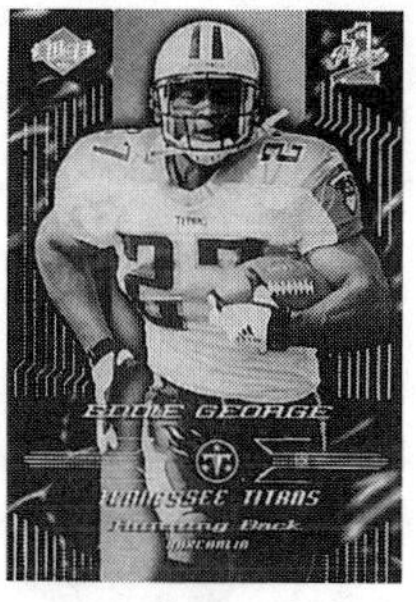

This 20-card insert set included high impact players. Each single was sequentially numbered to 1,000 and printed on clear vinyl stock.

MT
Complete Set (20): 100.00
Common Player: 4.00
Production 1,000 Sets
1 Jake Plummer 6.00
2 Jamal Anderson 4.00
3 Eric Moulds 4.00
4 Emmitt Smith 10.00
5 Terrell Davis 10.00
6 Barry Sanders 15.00
7 Brett Favre 15.00
8 Antonio Freeman 4.00
9 Peyton Manning 10.00
10 Mark Brunell 6.00
11 Fred Taylor 8.00
12 Dan Marino 10.00
13 Cris Carter 4.00
14 Randy Moss 15.00
15 Keyshawn Johnson 4.00
16 Curtis Martin 4.00
17 Jerome Bettis 4.00
18 Terrell Owens 4.00
19 Joey Galloway 4.00
20 Eddie George 4.00

1999 Collector's Edge First Place Excalibur

Excalibur was a 25-card set that was a cross-brand program. Singles were found in First Place, Odyssey and Masters. Nine of the singles appeared in First Place and were found 1:24 packs.

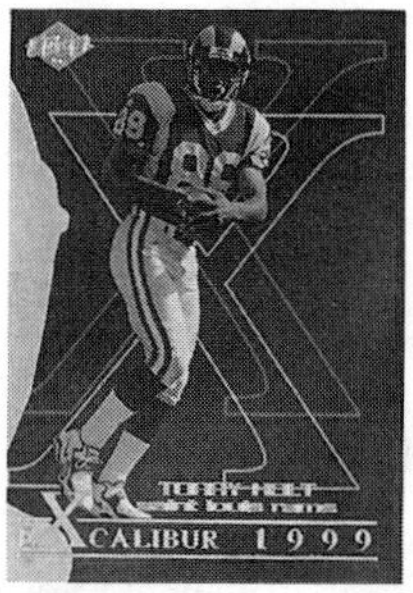

MT
Complete Set (9): 50.00
Common Player: 3.00
Inserted 1:24
2 Torry Holt 6.00
5 Edgerrin James 15.00
6 Brett Favre 12.00
13 Peyton Manning 10.00
17 Randy Moss 12.00
19 Terrell Davis 10.00
20 Mark Brunell 5.00
22 Eddie George 3.00
24 Doug Flutie 5.00

1999 Collector's Edge First Place Future Legends

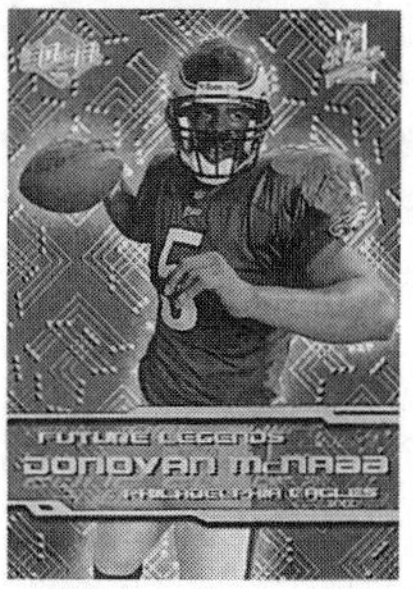

This 20-card insert set included all of the top rookies from 1999. Singles were found 1:6 packs.

MT
Complete Set (20): 45.00
Common Player: .75
Minor Stars: 1.50
Inserted 1:6
1 Tim Couch 10.00
2 Donovan McNabb 5.00
3 Akili Smith 5.00
4 Edgerrin James 12.00
5 Ricky Williams 10.00
6 Torry Holt 3.00
7 Champ Bailey 1.50
8 David Boston 3.00
9 Daunte Culpepper 5.00
10 Cade McNown 5.00
11 Troy Edwards 3.00
12 Chris Claiborne 1.50
13 Jevon Kearse 2.50
14 Shaun King 5.00
15 Kevin Faulk 2.00
16 James Johnson 1.50
17 Peerless Price 2.00
18 Kevin Johnson 3.00
19 Brock Huard 1.50
20 Joe Germaine .75

1999 Collector's Edge First Place Loud and Proud

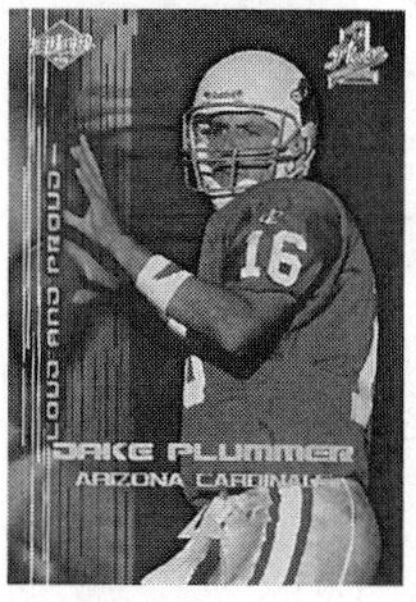

This 20-card insert set included the top stars in the NFL. Singles were found 1:12 packs.

MT
Complete Set (20): 45.00
Common Player: 2.00
Inserted 1:12
1 Jamal Anderson 2.00
2 Emmitt Smith 6.00
3 Terrell Davis 6.00
4 Barry Sanders 8.00
5 Fred Taylor 4.00
6 Randy Moss 8.00
7 Antonio Freeman 2.00
8 Curtis Martin 2.00
9 Terrell Owens 2.00
10 Eddie George 2.00
11 Dan Marino 6.00
12 Brett Favre 8.00
13 Jerry Rice 4.00
14 Steve Young 3.00
15 Doug Flutie 3.00
16 Jake Plummer 3.00
17 Troy Aikman 4.00
18 Mark Brunell 3.00
19 Jon Kitna 2.00
20 Charlie Batch 3.00

1999 Collector's Edge First Place Pro Signatures

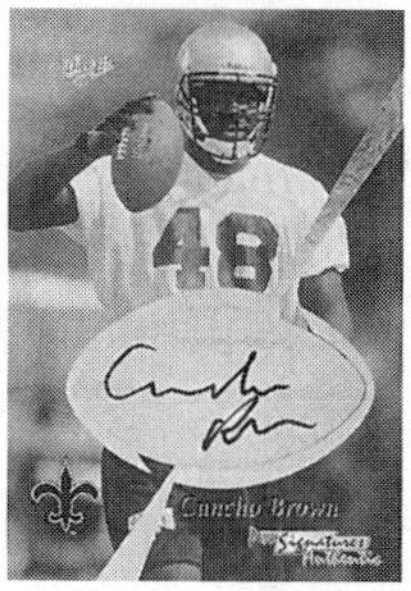

This 29-card insert set included autographed cards from both rookies and veterans. Singles were found 1:24 packs. A parallel Blue version was made with each single sequentially numbered to 40. A Red version was also made with each single numbered to 10.

MT
Complete Set (29): 425.00
Common Player: 6.00
Minor Stars: 12.00
Inserted 1:24
Blue Cards: 3x
Production 40 Sets
Red Cards:
Production 10 Sets
Rahim Abdullah 6.00
Kimble Anders 6.00
Dre Bly 12.00
David Boston 25.00
Cuncho Brown 6.00
Gary Brown 6.00
Ray Buchanan 6.00
Tim Couch 75.00
Autry Denson 12.00
Jared DeVries 6.00
Bobby Engram 6.00
Terry Fair 6.00
Kevin Faulk 20.00
Joey Galloway 20.00
Rich Gannon 12.00
Marvin Harrison 20.00
Andre Hastings 6.00
Courtney Hawkins 6.00
Brock Huard 15.00
Edgerrin James 100.00
Shaun King 40.00
Chris McAlister 12.00
Keenan McCardell 12.00
Dat Nguyen 12.00
Andre Reed 12.00
Jimmy Smith 20.00
Akili Smith 35.00
Duce Staley 20.00
Craig Yeast 12.00

1999 Collector's Edge First Place Rookie Game Gear

This 10-card insert set included only rookies from 1999. Each single was sequentially numbered to 500.

MT
Complete Set (10): 220.00
Common Player: 10.00
Production 500 Sets
1 Tim Couch 60.00
2 Donovan McNabb 30.00
3 Akili Smith 30.00
4 Daunte Culpepper 30.00
5 Ricky Williams 60.00
6 Kevin Johnson 20.00
7 Cade McNown 30.00
8 Torry Holt 20.00
9 Champ Bailey 10.00
10 David Boston 20.00

1999 Collector's Edge First Place Successors

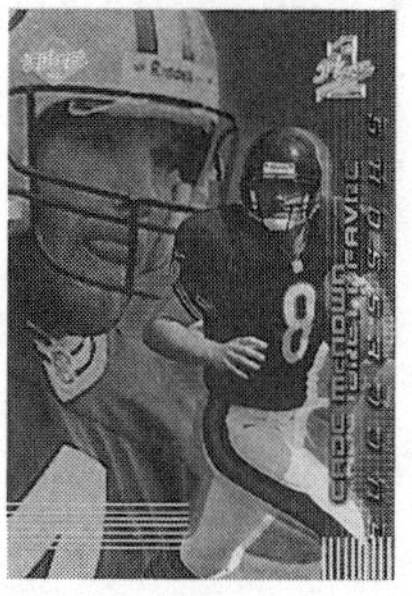

This 15-card insert set included a top rookie and a top NFL star from the same position and matched them up on the same card. Singles were found 1:12 packs.

MT
Complete Set (15): 65.00
Common Player: 2.00
Minor Stars: 4.00
Inserted 1:12
1 David Boston, Cris Carter 4.00
2 Peerless Price, Eric Moulds 2.00
3 Cade McNown, Brett Favre 8.00
4 Akili Smith, Charlie Batch 5.00
5 Tim Couch, Peyton Manning 10.00
6 Keyshawn Johnson, Joey Galloway 2.00
7 Edgerrin James, Emmitt Smith 12.00
8 James Johnson, Curtis Martin 2.00
9 Daunte Culpepper, Dan Marino 6.00
10 Kevin Faulk, Barry Sanders 8.00
11 Ricky Williams, Marshall Faulk 8.00
12 Donovan McNabb, Steve Young 5.00
13 Troy Edwards, Kevin Johnson 4.00
14 Torry Holt, Jerry Rice 5.00
15 Shaun King, Jake Plummer 5.00

1999 Collector's Edge Fury

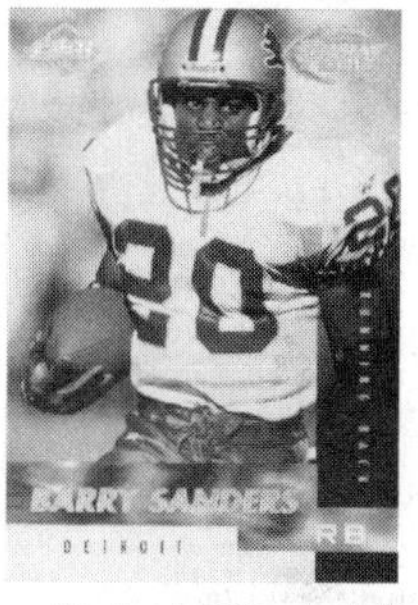

Edge Fury is a 200-card set with 148 veteran players, two checklists and 50 seeded rookies found one-per-pack. The product includes three parallel sets with Gold Ingot, Galvanized and HoloGold inserts. Other inserts include: Extreme Team, Fast and Furious, Forerunners, Game Ball, Heir Force and Xplosive.

MT
Complete Set (200): 70.00
Common Player: .15
Minor Stars: .30
Common Rookie: .50
Inserted 1:1
Pack (10): 3.25
Wax Box (24): 70.00
1 Checklist .15
2 Checklist .15
3 Karim Abdul .30
4 Troy Aikman 1.50
5 Derrick Alexander .15
6 Mike Alstott .50
7 Jamal Anderson .50
8 Reidel Anthony .30
9 Tiki Barber .15
10 Charlie Batch 1.00
11 Edgar Bennett .15
12 Jerome Bettis .50
13 Steve Beuerlein .15
14 Tim Biakabutuka .30
15 Jeff Blake .30
16 Drew Bledsoe 1.00
17 Bubby Brister .30
18 Robert Brooks .15
19 Gary Brown .15
20 Tim Brown .30
21 Isaac Bruce .30
22 Mark Brunell 1.00
23 Chris Calloway .15
24 Cris Carter .50
25 Larry Centers .15
26 Chris Chandler .30
27 Wayne Chrebet .50
28 Cam Cleeland .30
29 Kerry Collins .30
30 Curtis Conway .30
31 Germane Crowell .30
32 Randall Cunningham .50
33 Terrell Davis 2.00
34 Koy Detmer .15
35 Ty Detmer .30
36 Trent Dilfer .50
37 Corey Dillon .50
38 Warrick Dunn .75
39 Tim Dwight .50
40 Kevin Dyson .30
41 John Elway 2.00
42 Bobby Engram .15
43 Curtis Enis .50
44 Terry Fair .15
45 Marshall Faulk .50
46 Brett Favre 3.00
47 Doug Flutie .75
48 Antonio Freeman .50
49 Joey Galloway .50
50 Rich Gannon .15
51 Eddie George .75
52 Jeff George .30
53 Terry Glenn .50
54 Elvis Grbac .15
55 Ahman Green .30
56 Jacquez Green .30
57 Trent Green .50

58	Kevin Greene	.15
59	Brian Griese	1.00
60	Az-Zahir Hakim	.30
61	Jim Harbaugh	.30
62	Marvin Harrison	.30
63	Courtney Hawkins	.15
64	Garrison Hearst	.50
65	Ike Hilliard	.30
66	Billy Joe Hobert	.15
67	Priest Holmes	.50
68	Michael Irvin	.30
69	Raghib Ismail	.15
70	Shawn Jefferson	.15
71	James Jett	.15
72	Brad Johnson	.50
73	Charles Johnson	.15
74	Keyshawn Johnson	.50
75	Pat Johnson	.15
76	Joe Jurevicius	.15
77	Napoleon Kaufman	.50
78	Eddie Kennison	.30
79	Terry Kirby	.15
80	Jon Kitna	.75
81	Erik Kramer	.15
82	Fred Lane	.15
83	Ty Law	.15
84	Ryan Leaf	.75
85	Amp Lee	.15
86	Dorsey Levens	.50
87	Jermaine Lewis	.30
88	Sam Madison	.15
89	Peyton Manning	2.00
90	Dan Marino	2.00
91	Curtis Martin	.75
92	Tony Martin	.15
93	Terance Mathis	.15
94	Ed McCaffrey	.30
95	Keenan McCardell	.15
96	O.J. McDuffie	.30
97	Steve McNair	.75
98	Natrone Means	.30
99	Herman Moore	.50
100	Rob Moore	.30
101	Bam Morris	.30
102	Johnnie Morton	.15
103	Randy Moss	3.50
104	Eric Moulds	.50
105	Muhsin Muhammad	.15
106	Adrian Murrell	.30
107	Terrell Owens	.50
108	Jerome Pathon	.15
109	Carl Pickens	.30
110	Jake Plummer	1.25
111	Andre Reed	.15
112	Jake Reed	.15
113	Jerry Rice	1.50
114	Mikhael Ricks	.15
115	Andre Rison	.30
116	Barry Sanders	3.00
117	Deion Sanders	.50
118	Frank Sanders	.30
119	O.J. Santiago	.15
120	Darnay Scott	.15
121	Junior Seau	.30
122	Shannon Sharpe	.30
123	Leslie Shepherd	.15
124	Antowain Smith	.50
125	Bruce Smith	.15
126	Emmitt Smith	2.00
127	Jimmy Smith	.30
128	Robert Smith	.50
129	Rod Smith	.30
130	Chris Spielman	.15
131	Takeo Spikes	.15
132	Duce Staley	.30
133	Kordell Stewart	.75
134	Bryan Still	.15
135	J.J. Stokes	.30
136	Fred Taylor	1.50
137	Vinny Testaverde	.30
138	Yancey Thigpen	.30
139	Thurman Thomas	.30
140	Zach Thomas	.30
141	Amani Toomer	.15
142	Hines Ward	.30
143	Chris Warren	.30
144	Ricky Watters	.30
145	Michael Westbrook	.30
146	Alvis Whitted	.15
147	Charles Woodson	.50
148	Rod Woodson	.15
149	Frank Wycheck	.15
150	Steve Young	1.00
151	*Rabih Abdullah*	.50
152	*Champ Bailey*	2.00
153	*D'Wayne Bates*	1.00
154	*Michael Bishop*	2.00
155	*Dre' Bly*	1.00
156	*David Boston*	2.00
157	*Fernando Bryant*	.50
158	*Chris Claiborne*	1.00
159	Mike Cloud	1.00
160	*Cecil Collins*	1.50
161	*Tim Couch*	6.00
162	*Daunte Culpepper*	10.00
163	*Antwan Edwards*	1.00
164	*Troy Edwards*	2.00
165	*Ebenezer Ekuban*	1.00
166	*Kevin Faulk*	2.00
167	*Joe Germaine*	1.50
168	*Aaron Gibson*	.50
169	*Martin Gramatica*	1.00
170	*Torry Holt*	2.50
171	*Brock Huard*	2.00
172	*Sedrick Irvin*	1.50
173	*Edgerrin James*	12.00
174	*James Johnson*	1.50
175	*Kevin Johnson*	2.00
176	*Andy Katzenmoyer*	1.00
177	*Jevon Kearse*	2.50
178	*Patrick Kerney*	.50
179	*Lamar King*	.50
180	*Shaun King*	3.00
181	*Jim Kleinsasser*	1.00
182	*Rob Konrad*	1.00
183	*Chris McAlister*	1.00
184	*Anthony McFarland*	1.00
185	*Karsten Bailey*	1.00
186	*Donovan McNabb*	6.00
187	*Cade McNown*	2.50
188	*Joe Montgomery*	1.50
189	*Dat Nguyen*	1.00
190	*Luke Petitgout*	.50
191	*Peerless Price*	2.00
192	*Akili Smith*	3.00
193	*Matt Stinchcomb*	.50
194	*John Tait*	.50
195	*Jermaine Fazande*	1.50
196	*Ricky Williams*	6.00
197	*Al Wilson*	1.00
198	*Antoine Winfield*	1.00
199	*Damien Woody*	.50
200	*Amos Zereoue*	1.50

1999 Collector's Edge Fury Galvanized Parallel

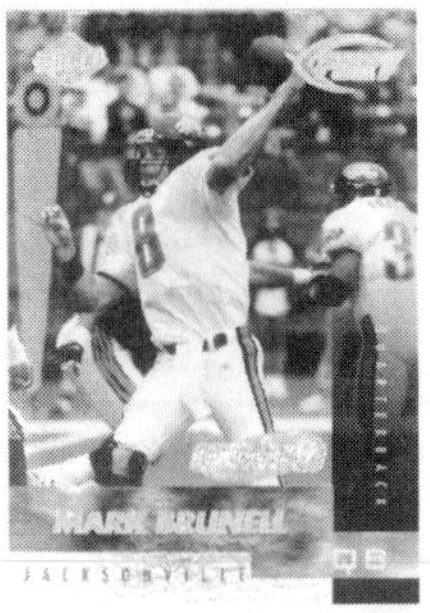

This 200-card parallel is identical to the Gold Ingot parallel except for the Galvanized stamp on the front of the card in silver and each card is sequentially numbered on the back. Veterans are numbered to 500 and rookies to 100.

	MT
Complete Set (200):	550.00
Galvanized Cards:	3x-6x
Production 500 Sets	
Galvanized Rookies:	5x-10x
Production 100 Sets	

1999 Collector's Edge Fury Gold Ingot Parallel

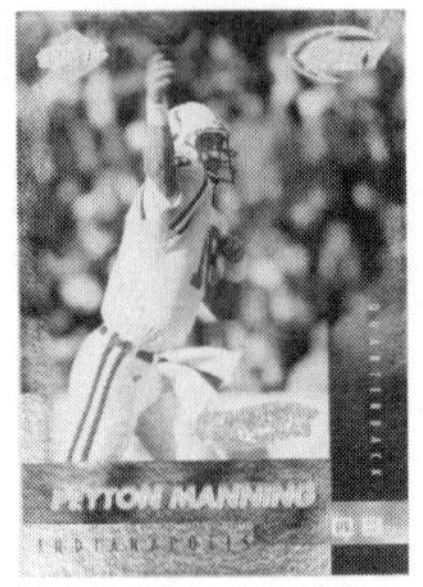

This is a 200-card parallel to the base set that was inserted 1:1 packs. The photo is the same as the base except for it's printed on foil board and the foil on the front is gold rather than silver. Each also has a Gold Ingot gold stamp on the fronts of the cards.

	MT
Complete Set (200):	140.00
Gold Ingot Cards:	2x
Gold Ingot Rookies:	1.5x
Inserted 1:1	

1999 Collector's Edge Fury HoloGold Parallel

Each card in this 200-card parallel set are printed on prismatic silver foil board. Each card front has the HoloGold stamp in gold foil. Veterans are printed to 50 and rookies to 10.

	MT
HoloGold Cards:	40x-80x
Production 50 Sets	
HoloGold Rookies:	25x-50x
Production 10 Sets	

1999 Collector's Edge Fury Extreme Team

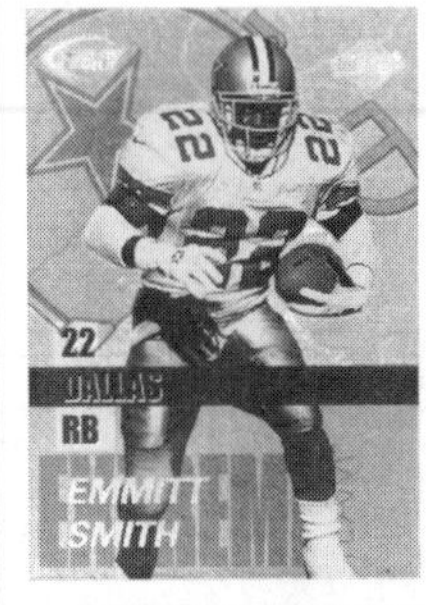

Each card in this 10-card set is printed on micro-etched gold holographic foil board. Singles were inserted 1:24 packs.

		MT
Complete Set (10):		60.00
Common Player:		4.00
Inserted 1:24		
1	Keyshawn Johnson	4.00
2	Emmitt Smith	12.00
3	John Elway	12.00
4	Terrell Davis	12.00
5	Barry Sanders	15.00
6	Brett Favre	15.00
7	Peyton Manning	12.00
8	Fred Taylor	8.00
9	Dan Marino	12.00
10	Randy Moss	15.00

1999 Collector's Edge Fury Fast and Furious

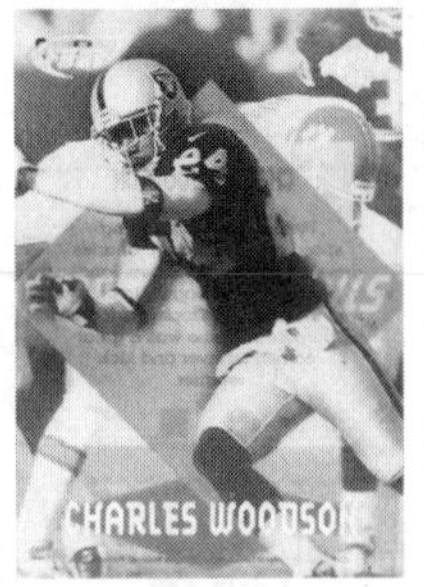

This 25-card insert is sequentially numbered to 500 and is printed on plastic card stock with gold foil stamping.

		MT
Complete Set (25):		100.00
Common Player:		2.00
Minor Stars:		4.00
Production 500 Sets		
1	Jake Plummer	8.00
2	Jamal Anderson	4.00
3	Eric Moulds	4.00
4	Curtis Enis	4.00
5	Emmitt Smith	12.00
6	Deion Sanders	4.00
7	Terrell Davis	12.00
8	Barry Sanders	15.00
9	Herman Moore	4.00
10	Charlie Batch	5.00
11	Marshall Faulk	4.00
12	Mark Brunell	6.00
13	Fred Taylor	8.00
14	Randy Moss	15.00
15	Cris Carter	4.00
16	Robert Edwards	2.00
17	Keyshawn Johnson	4.00
18	Curtis Martin	4.00
19	Charles Woodson	4.00
20	Jerome Bettis	4.00
21	Kordell Stewart	5.00
22	Steve Young	6.00
23	Jerry Rice	8.00
24	Warrick Dunn	5.00
25	Eddie George	5.00

1999 Collector's Edge Fury Forerunners

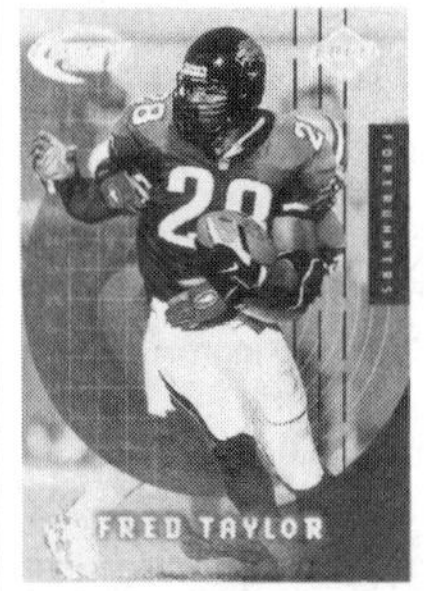

This 15-card set includes the top running backs in the NFL. Each card is printed on holographic foil board with gold foil stamping. Singles were inserted 1:8 packs.

		MT
Complete Set (15):		40.00
Common Player:		1.00
Minor Stars:		2.00
Inserted 1:8		
1	Jamal Anderson	2.00
2	Curtis Enis	2.00
3	Corey Dillon	2.00
4	Emmitt Smith	8.00
5	Barry Sanders	10.00
6	Terrell Davis	8.00
7	Marshall Faulk	2.00
8	Fred Taylor	6.00
9	Robert Smith	2.00
10	Curtis Martin	2.00
11	Jerome Bettis	2.00
12	Garrison Hearst	2.00
13	Warrick Dunn	4.00
14	Eddie George	4.00
15	Ricky Watters	1.00

1999 Collector's Edge Fury Game Ball

Each card in this 43-card set includes a piece of a game-used football that the player used. Singles were found 1:24 packs.

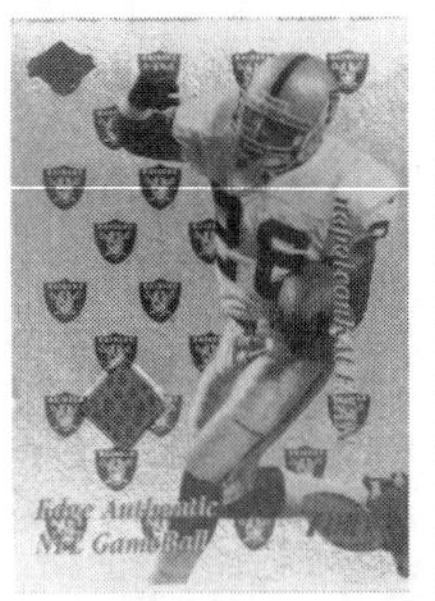

	MT
Complete Set (43):	600.00
Common Player:	6.00
Minor Stars:	12.00
Inserted 1:24	
Troy Aikman	25.00
Mike Alstott	12.00
Charlie Batch	20.00
Jerome Bettis	12.00
Mark Brunell	20.00
Cris Carter	12.00
Terrell Davis	40.00
Corey Dillon	12.00
Warrick Dunn	15.00
John Elway	40.00
Curtis Enis	12.00
Marshall Faulk	12.00
Brett Favre	50.00
Antonio Freeman	12.00
Joey Galloway	12.00
Eddie George	15.00
Garrison Hearst	12.00
Michael Irvin	6.00
Rob Johnson	12.00
Napoleon Kaufman	12.00
Ryan Leaf	15.00
Dorsey Levens	12.00
Peyton Manning	40.00
Curtis Martin	12.00
Steve McNair	15.00
Natrone Means	12.00
Warren Moon	12.00
Herman Moore	12.00
Randy Moss	50.00
Adrian Murrell	6.00
Terrell Owens	12.00
Carl Pickens	6.00
Jake Plummer	25.00
Jerry Rice	25.00
Barry Sanders	50.00
Deion Sanders	12.00
Shannon Sharpe	6.00
Antowain Smith	12.00
Emmitt Smith	35.00
Rod Smith	6.00
Kordell Stewart	15.00
Fred Taylor	25.00
Steve Young	20.00

1999 Collector's Edge Fury Heir Force

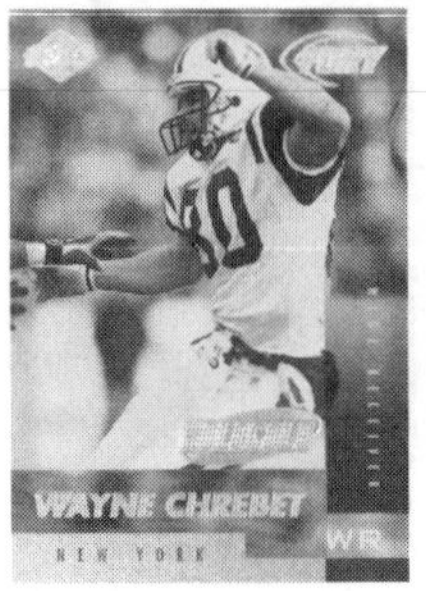

This 20-card set includes the top rookies and were inserted 1:6 packs. Each card was printed on holographic foil board with gold foil stamping.

		MT
Complete Set (20):		45.00
Common Player:		1.00
Inserted 1:6		
1	Rahim Abdullah	1.00
2	Champ Bailey	2.00
3	D'Wayne Bates	1.00
4	Michael Bishop	2.50
5	David Boston	3.00
6	Chris Claiborne	1.50
7	Tim Couch	12.00
8	Daunte Culpepper	5.00
9	Kevin Faulk	3.00
10	Torry Holt	2.50
11	Brock Huard	2.00
12	Edgerrin James	8.00
13	Andy Katzenmoyer	1.50
14	Shaun King	1.75
15	Rob Konrad	1.00
16	Donovan McNabb	5.00
17	Cade McNown	5.00
18	Peerless Price	2.00
19	Akili Smith	4.00
20	Ricky Williams	12.00

1999 Collector's Edge Fury X-Plosive

Each card is printed on explosive micro-etched holofoil with foil stamping. Singles from this 20-card set were found 1:12 packs.

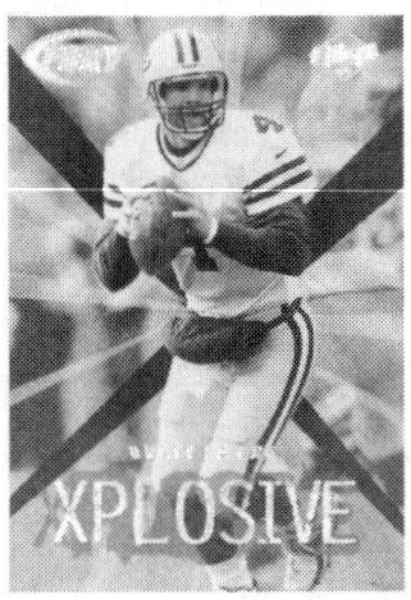

		MT
Complete Set (20):		100.00
Common Player:		1.50
Minor Stars:		3.00
Inserted 1:12		
1	Jake Plummer	8.00
2	Doug Flutie	5.00
3	Eric Moulds	3.00
4	Troy Aikman	8.00
5	John Elway	12.00
6	Charlie Batch	6.00
7	Herman Moore	3.00
8	Brett Favre	15.00
9	Antonio Freeman	3.00
10	Peyton Manning	12.00
11	Mark Brunell	6.00
12	Dan Marino	12.00
13	Randy Moss	15.00
14	Drew Bledsoe	6.00
15	Keyshawn Johnson	3.00
16	Vinny Testaverde	1.50
17	Kordell Stewart	4.00
18	Terrell Owens	3.00
19	Jerry Rice	8.00
20	Steve Young	6.00

1999 Collector's Edge Masters

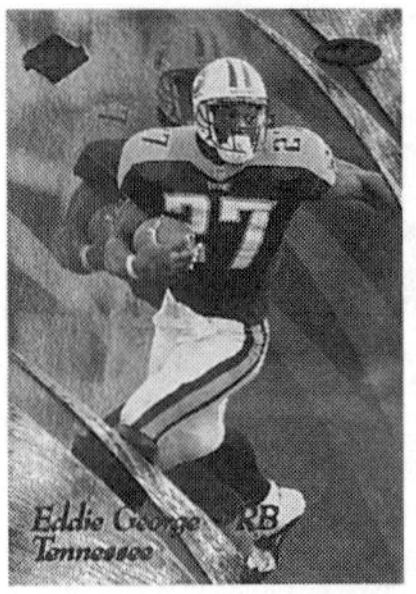

Edge Masters was a 200-card set that had every single card sequentially numbered. Veterans were numbered to 5,000 and rookies to 2,000. Each card was printed on micro-etched holographic foil board. Two parallel sets were issued as HoloSilver and HoloGold. Insert sets included Excalibur, Master Legends, Main Event, Majestic, Pro Signature Authentics, Quest, Rookie Masters and Sentinels. Three-card packs had an SRP of $5.59.

		MT
Complete Set (200):		500.00
Common Player:		.25
Minor Stars:		.50
Production 5,000 Sets		
Common Rookie:		3.00
Production 2,000 Sets		
Pack (3):		6.00
Wax Box (20):		100.00
1	*David Boston*	10.00
2	*Marc Cody*	6.00
3	*Chris Griesen*	4.00
4	*Joel Makovicka*	4.00
5	Adrian Murrell	.25
6	Jake Plummer	1.50
7	Frank Sanders	.50
8	Jamal Anderson	1.00
9	Chris Chandler	.50
10	*Reggie Kelly*	3.00
11	*Patrick Kerney*	3.00
12	Terance Mathis	.25
13	*Jeff Paulk*	4.00
14	Stoney Case	.50
15	Qadry Ismail	.25
16	*Chris McAlister*	5.00
17	Errict Rhett	.50
18	*Brandon Stokley*	6.00
19	Doug Flutie	1.50
20	*Kamil Loud*	4.00
21	Eric Moulds	.50
22	*Peerless Price*	10.00
23	Andre Reed	.50
24	Antowain Smith	1.00
25	*Antoine Winfield*	5.00
26	Steve Beuerlein	.50
27	Tim Biakabutuka	.50
28	*Dameyune Craig*	6.00
29	*Patrick Jeffers*	15.00
30	Muhsin Muhammad	.50
31	*D'Wayne Bates*	4.00
32	*Marty Booker*	4.00
33	Bobby Engram	.25
34	Curtis Enis	1.00
35	*Ty Hallock*	4.00
36	Shane Matthews	1.00
37	*Cade McNown*	10.00
38	Marcus Robinson	2.00
39	*Scott Covington*	4.00
40	Corey Dillon	1.00
41	*Damon Griffin*	4.00
42	Carl Pickens	.50
43	Darnay Scott	.50
44	*Akili Smith*	12.00
45	*Craig Yeast*	4.00
46	*Darrin Chiaverini*	5.00
47	*Tim Couch*	40.00
48	*Phil Dawson*	3.00
49	*Kevin Johnson*	10.00
50	Terry Kirby	.25
51	*Wali Ranier*	3.00
52	Troy Aikman	2.00
53	*Ebenezer Ekuban*	4.00
54	Michael Irvin	.50
55	Raghib Ismail	.25
56	*Wane McGarity*	4.00
57	*Dat Nguyen*	4.00
58	Deion Sanders	1.00
59	Emmitt Smith	3.00
60	Byron Chamberlain	.50
61	*Andre Cooper*	3.00
62	Terrell Davis	3.00
63	*Olandis Gary*	15.00
64	Brian Griese	2.00
65	Ed McCaffrey	.50
66	*Travis McGriff*	4.00
67	Shannon Sharpe	.50
68	Rod Smith	.50
69	*Al Wilson*	4.00
70	Charlie Batch	1.50
71	*Chris Claiborne*	4.00
72	Germane Crowell	.50
73	Greg Hill	.25
74	*Sedrick Irvin*	5.00
75	Herman Moore	1.00
76	Johnnie Morton	.25
77	Barry Sanders	4.00
78	*Aaron Brooks*	25.00
79	*Antwan Edwards*	4.00
80	Brett Favre	4.00
81	Antonio Freeman	1.00
82	Dorsey Levens	1.00
83	Bill Schroeder	.25
84	E.G. Green	.25
85	Marvin Harrison	1.00
86	*Edgerrin James*	35.00
87	Peyton Manning	3.00
88	Mark Brunell	1.50
89	Jay Fiedler	.50
90	Keenan McCardell	.50
91	Jimmy Smith	1.00
92	James Stewart	.50
93	Fred Taylor	2.00
94	Derrick Alexander	.25
95	*Michael Cloud*	5.00
96	Elvis Grbac	.50
97	Bam Morris	.25
98	Andre Rison	.50
99	*Cecil Collins*	5.00
100	Damon Huard	1.50
101	*J.J. Johnson*	5.00
102	*Rob Konrad*	4.00
103	Dan Marino	3.00
104	O.J. McDuffie	.50
105	Cris Carter	1.00
106	*Daunte Culpepper*	30.00
107	Randall Cunningham	1.00
108	Jeff George	1.00
109	*Jim Kleinsasser*	5.00
110	Randy Moss	4.00
111	Robert Smith	1.00
112	Terry Allen	.50
113	*Michael Bishop*	10.00
114	Drew Bledsoe	1.50
115	*Kevin Faulk*	10.00
116	Terry Glenn	1.00
117	*Andy Katzenmoyer*	5.00
118	Billy Joe Hobert	.25
119	Eddie Kennison	.25
120	*Ricky Williams*	25.00
121	Tiki Barber	.50
122	*Sean Bennett*	5.00
123	Gary Brown	.25
124	Kent Graham	.25
125	Ike Hilliard	.25
126	*Joe Montgomery*	5.00
127	Amani Toomer	.50
128	Wayne Chrebet	1.00
129	Keyshawn Johnson	1.00
130	Curtis Martin	1.00
131	*Ray Lucas*	10.00
132	Vinny Testaverde	1.00
133	Tim Brown	.50
134	*Tony Bryant*	3.00
135	*Scott Dreisbach*	4.00
136	Rich Gannon	.25
137	Tyrone Wheatley	.50
138	Charles Woodson	1.00
139	*Na Brown*	3.00
140	Charles Johnson	.25
141	*Cecil Martin*	4.00
142	*Donovan McNabb*	25.00
143	Doug Pederson	.25
144	Duce Staley	1.00
145	Jerome Bettis	1.00
146	*Kris Brown*	5.00
147	*Troy Edwards*	10.00
148	Kordell Stewart	1.00
149	Hines Ward	.50
150	*Amos Zereoue*	5.00
151	*Dre Bly*	4.00
152	Isaac Bruce	1.00
153	Marshall Faulk	1.00
154	*Joe Germaine*	5.00
155	Az-Zahir Hakim	.50
156	*Torry Holt*	15.00
157	*Kurt Warner*	65.00
158	*Justin Watson*	6.00
159	*Jermaine Fazande*	8.00
160	Jeff Graham	.25
161	Jim Harbaugh	.50
162	*Steve Heiden*	3.00
163	Erik Kramer	.25
164	Natrone Means	.50
165	Mikhael Ricks	.50
166	Junior Seau	.50
167	*Jeff Garcia*	35.00
168	Charlie Garner	.50
169	*Terry Jackson*	5.00
170	Terrell Owens	1.00
171	Jerry Rice	2.00
172	Steve Young	1.25
173	*Karsten Bailey*	4.00
174	Joey Galloway	1.00
175	*Brock Huard*	8.00
176	Jon Kitna	.50
177	Derrick Mayes	.50
178	*Charlie Rogers*	4.00
179	Ricky Watters	.50
180	*Rabih Abdullah*	3.00
181	Mike Alstott	1.00
182	Reidel Anthony	.50
183	Trent Dilfer	.50
184	Warrick Dunn	1.00
185	*Martin Gramatica*	6.00
186	*Shaun King*	15.00

187	*Darnell McDonald*	5.00
188	*Yo Murphy*	3.00
189	*Kevin Daft*	4.00
190	Kevin Dyson	.50
191	Eddie George	1.25
192	*Jevon Kearse*	12.00
193	Steve McNair	1.25
194	Yancey Thigpen	.50
195	*Champ Bailey*	8.00
196	Albert Connell	.50
197	Stephen Davis	1.00
198	Skip Hicks	.50
199	Brad Johnson	1.00
200	Michael Westbrook	.50

1999 Collector's Edge Masters HoloSilver Parallel

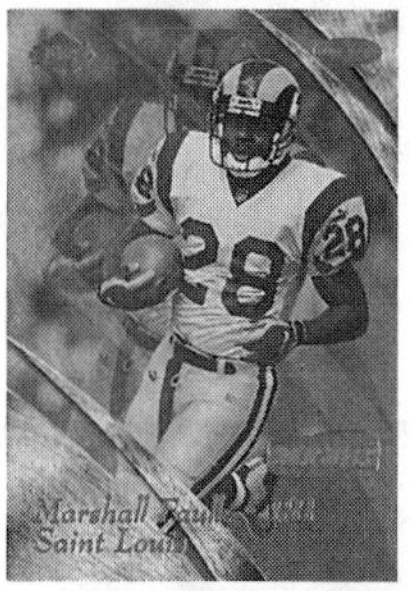

This was a 200-card parallel to the base set. Each card was sequentially numbered to 3,500.

	MT
HoloSilver Cards:	2x
Production 3,500 Sets	

1999 Collector's Edge Masters HoloGold Parallel

This was a 200-card parallel to the base set. Each single was sequentially numbered to 25.

	MT
HoloGold Cards:	25x-50x
Production 25 Sets	

1999 Collector's Edge Masters Excalibur

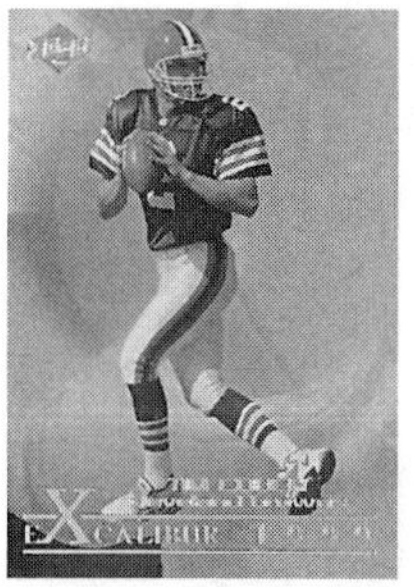

Excalibur was a 25-card set that was a cross-brand program. Singles were found in First Place, Odyssey and Masters. Eight of the singles were inserted into Masters and were sequentially numbered to 5,000.

		MT
Complete Set (8):		35.00
Common Player:		2.00
Production 5,000 Sets		
3	Dan Marino	8.00
6	Champ Bailey	2.00
9	Barry Sanders	10.00
10	Brett Favre	10.00
12	Tim Couch	10.00
14	Akili Smith	5.00
18	Steve Young	4.00
21	Curtis Martin	2.00

1999 Collector's Edge Masters Main Event

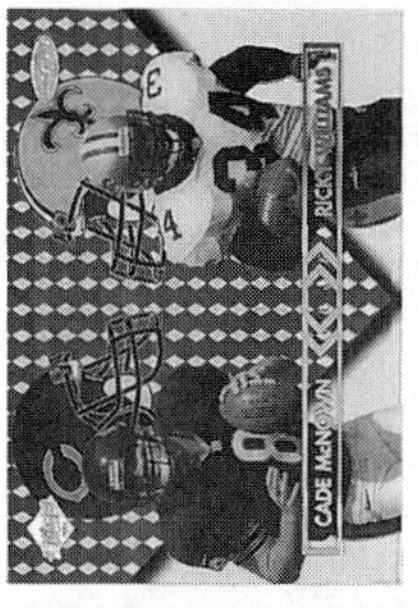

This 10-card insert set included the key matchups from the 1999 NFL season. Each card included two players whose teams went head-to-head in big games. Each single was printed on clear plastic and was sequentially numbered to 1,000.

		MT
Complete Set (10):		45.00
Common Player:		3.00
Production 1,000 Sets		
1	Randy Moss, Jamal Anderson	15.00
2	Mark Brunell, Eddie George	6.00
3	Terrell Davis, Cecil Collins	8.00
4	Rocket Ismail, Stephen Davis	3.00
5	Troy Edwards, Kevin Johnson	7.00
6	Antonio Freeman, Charlie Batch	5.00
7	Terry Glenn, Marvin Harrison	3.00
8	Keyshawn Johnson, Doug Flutie	6.00
9	Cade McNown, Ricky Williams	15.00
10	Steve Young, Marshall Faulk	6.00

1999 Collector's Edge Masters Majestic

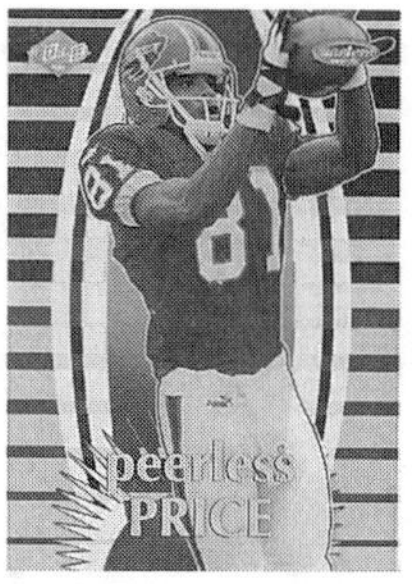

This 30-card insert set included the most popular and collectible stars and featured them on a clear vinyl card. Singles were sequentially numbered to 3,000.

		MT
Complete Set (30):		100.00
Common Player:		1.00
Minor Stars:		2.00
Production 3,000 Sets		
1	Jake Plummer	4.00
2	David Boston	4.00
3	Doug Flutie	4.00
4	Eric Moulds	2.00
5	Peerless Price	2.50
6	Tim Biakabutuka	1.00
7	Troy Aikman	6.00
8	Olandis Gary	8.00
9	Brian Griese	4.00
10	Charlie Batch	3.00
11	Antonio Freeman	2.00
12	Peyton Manning	8.00
13	Edgerrin James	15.00
14	Marvin Harrison	2.00
15	Fred Taylor	6.00
16	Daunte Culpepper	6.00
17	Terry Glenn	2.00
18	Keyshawn Johnson	2.00
19	Curtis Martin	2.00
20	Donovan McNabb	6.00
21	Kordell Stewart	2.00
22	Torry Holt	4.00
23	Marshall Faulk	2.00
24	Kurt Warner	25.00
25	Jerry Rice	6.00
26	Jon Kitna	2.50
27	Eddie George	3.00
28	Champ Bailey	2.00
29	Brad Johnson	2.00
30	Stephen Davis	2.00

1999 Collector's Edge Masters Master Legends

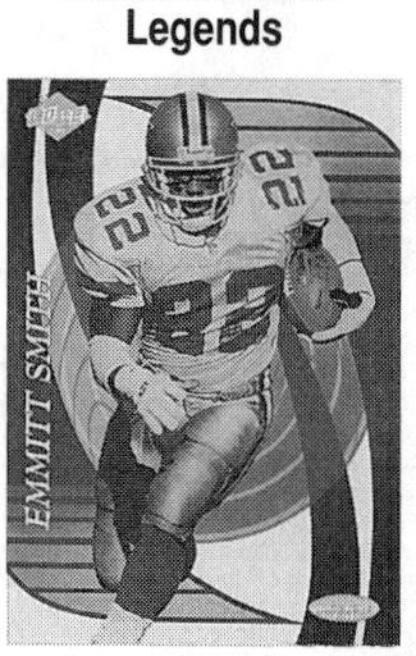

This 20-card insert set included the best players in football and pictured them on a clear card. Singles were sequentially numbered to 3,000.

		MT
Complete Set (20):		150.00
Common Player:		3.00
Production 1,000 Sets		
1	Doug Flutie	6.00
2	Troy Aikman	8.00
3	Emmitt Smith	10.00
4	Terrell Davis	10.00
5	Charlie Batch	5.00
6	Barry Sanders	15.00
7	Brett Favre	15.00
8	Antonio Freeman	3.00
9	Peyton Manning	10.00
10	Mark Brunell	6.00
11	Fred Taylor	8.00
12	Dan Marino	10.00
13	Randy Moss	15.00
14	Drew Bledsoe	6.00
15	Kurt Warner	35.00
16	Marshall Faulk	3.00
17	Steve Young	6.00
18	Jerry Rice	8.00
19	Jon Kitna	4.00
20	Eddie George	4.00

1999 Collector's Edge Masters Pro Signature Authentics

This 3-card insert set included some of the top names in the NFL. Each single was numbered to 500. The Manning 1B was a mail-in redemption and was numbered to 445.

		MT
Complete Set (3):		300.00
Common Player:		20.00
Production 500 Sets		
--	Stephen Davis	20.00
1A	Peyton Manning 500	100.00
1B	Peyton Manning 445	125.00
--	Kurt Warner	200.00

1999 Collector's Edge Masters Quest

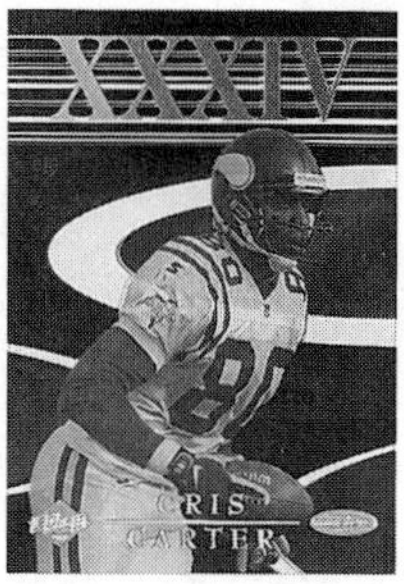

This 20-card insert set included players who had the Super Bowl in their sights. Each single had a vinyl background and was sequentially numbered to 3,000.

		MT
Complete Set (20):		40.00
Common Player:		1.00
Minor Stars:		2.00
Production 3,000 Sets		
1	Jake Plummer	4.00
2	Eric Moulds	2.00
3	Curtis Enis	2.00
4	Emmitt Smith	7.00
5	Brian Griese	4.00
6	Dorsey Levens	2.00
7	Marvin Harrison	2.00
8	Mark Brunell	4.00
9	Fred Taylor	6.00
10	Cris Carter	2.00
11	Terry Glenn	2.00
12	Keyshawn Johnson	2.00
13	Isaac Bruce	2.00
14	Terrell Owens	2.00
15	Jon Kitna	2.50
16	Natrone Means	1.00
17	Warrick Dunn	2.00
18	Steve McNair	2.00
19	Brad Johnson	2.00
20	Stephen Davis	2.00

1999 Collector's Edge Masters Rookie Masters

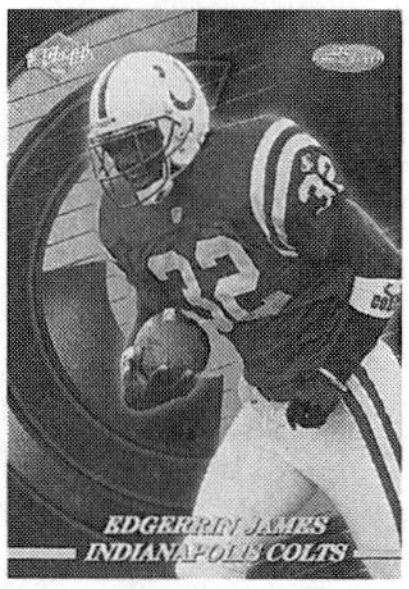

This 30-card insert set included the hottest rookies from the 1999 Draft. Each single was sequentially numbered to 3,000.

		MT
Complete Set (30):		75.00
Common Player:		1.00
Minor Stars:		2.00
Production 3,000 Sets		
1	David Boston	4.00
2	Chris McAlister	1.00
3	Peerless Price	3.00
4	D'Wayne Bates	2.00
5	Cade McNown	6.00
6	Akili Smith	5.00
7	Tim Couch	10.00
8	Kevin Johnson	4.00
9	Wane McGarity	1.00
10	Chris Claiborne	1.00
11	Sedrick Irvin	2.00
12	Edgerrin James	15.00
13	Michael Cloud	2.00
14	Cecil Collins	3.00
15	J.J. Johnson	2.50
16	Rob Konrad	2.00
17	Daunte Culpepper	6.00
18	Kevin Faulk	2.50
19	Andy Katzenmoyer	2.00
20	Ricky Williams	10.00
21	Donovan McNabb	6.00
22	Troy Edwards	4.00
23	Amos Zereoue	2.00
24	Joe Germaine	2.00
25	Torry Holt	4.00
26	Karsten Bailey	2.00
27	Brock Huard	2.50
28	Shaun King	6.00
29	Jevon Kearse	4.00
30	Champ Bailey	2.50

1999 Collector's Edge Masters Sentinels

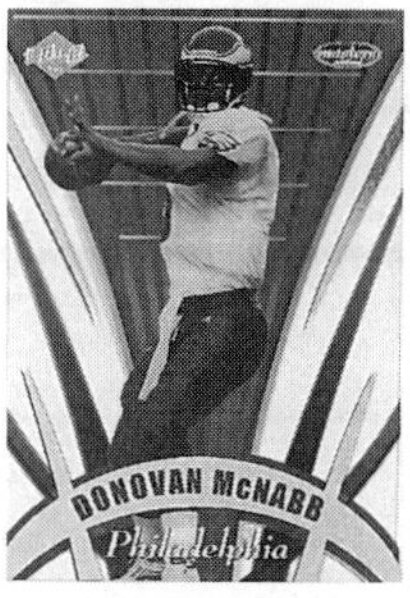

This 20-card set included the 10 hottest veterans and the 10 hottest rookies from 1999. Each single was sequentially numbered to 500.

		MT
Complete Set (20):		250.00
Common Player:		5.00
Production 500 Sets		
1	Troy Aikman	15.00
2	Emmitt Smith	20.00
3	Terrell Davis	20.00
4	Barry Sanders	30.00
5	Brett Favre	30.00
6	Peyton Manning	20.00
7	Dan Marino	20.00
8	Randy Moss	30.00
9	Drew Bledsoe	10.00
10	Isaac Bruce	5.00
11	Kurt Warner	50.00
12	David Boston	5.00
13	Cade McNown	12.00
14	Akili Smith	10.00
15	Tim Couch	20.00
16	Edgerrin James	30.00
17	Ricky Williams	20.00
18	Donovan McNabb	12.00
19	Troy Edwards	5.00
20	Torry Holt	8.00

1999 Collector's Edge Odyssey

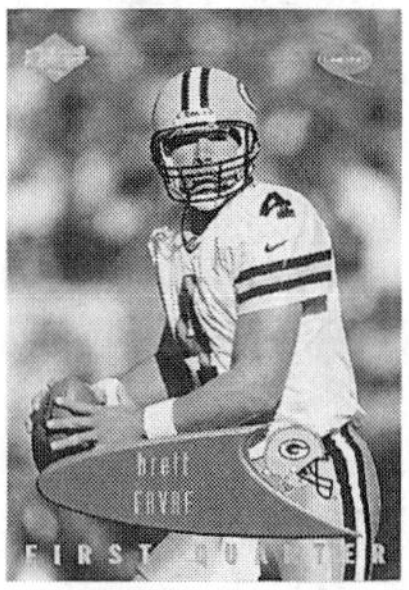

This 193-card set was supposed to be a 195-card set, but cards #21 and #55 were never produced. The first 150 cards were 1st Quarter singles. Cards #151-170 were 2nd Quarter singles and were inserted 1:4 packs. Cards #171-185 were 3rd Quarter singles and they were found 1:8 packs. Cards #186-195 were 4th Quarter singles and they were found 1:24 packs. Insert sets included: Two Minute Warning, Overtime, Cut 'n' Ripped, Cutting Edge, Excalibur, End Zone, Game Gear, Old School, Pro Signature Authentics and Super Limited Edge. Ten-card packs had an SRP of $3.99.

		MT
Complete Set (193):		175.00
Common Player:		.15
Minor Stars:		.30
Common Rookie:		.50
Common Player (151-170):		1.00
Inserted 1:4		
Common Player (171-185):		2.50
Inserted 1:8		
Common Player (186-195):		5.00
Inserted 1:24		
#21 and 55 never produced		
Wax Box:		55.00
1	Checklist	.15
2	Checklist	.15
3	*David Boston*	1.75
4	Rob Moore	.30
5	Adrian Murrell	.30
6	Jake Plummer	1.00
7	Frank Sanders	.30
8	Jamal Anderson	.50
9	Chris Calloway	.15
10	Chris Chandler	.30
11	Tim Dwight	.50
12	Terance Mathis	.15
13	Tony Banks	.30
14	Priest Holmes	.50
15	Jermaine Lewis	.15
16	*Chris McAlister*	.50
17	Scott Mitchell	.15
18	Doug Flutie	.75
19	Eric Moulds	.50
20	*Peerless Price*	1.25
22	Antowain Smith	.50
23	*Antoine Winfield*	.50
24	Steve Beuerlein	.30
25	Tim Biakabutuka	.30
26	Rae Carruth	.15
27	Muhsin Muhammad	.30
28	*D'Wayne Bates*	1.00
29	Bobby Engram	.15
30	Curtis Enis	.50
31	Shane Matthews	.30
32	*Cade McNown*	1.50
33	Jeff Blake	.30
34	Corey Dillon	.50
35	Carl Pickens	.30
36	Darnay Scott	.30
37	*Akili Smith*	2.50
38	*Tim Couch*	5.00
39	*Kevin Johnson*	2.00
40	Terry Kirby	.15
41	Leslie Shepherd	.15
42	Troy Aikman	1.25
43	Michael Irvin	.30
44	Raghib Ismail	.15
45	Deion Sanders	.50
46	Emmitt Smith	1.75
47	Bubby Brister	.30
48	Terrell Davis	1.75
49	Brian Griese	1.00
50	Ed McCaffrey	.50
51	Shannon Sharpe	.30
52	Rod Smith	.50
53	Charlie Batch	.75
54	*Chris Claiborne*	.50
56	Herman Moore	.50
57	Johnnie Morton	.15
58	Ron Rivers	.15
59	Brett Favre	2.50
60	Mark Chmura	.30
61	Antonio Freeman	.50
62	Dorsey Levens	.50
63	E.G. Green	.15
64	Marvin Harrison	.50
65	*Edgerrin James*	8.00
66	Peyton Manning	1.75
67	Mark Brunell	1.00
68	Keenan McCardell	.30
69	Jimmy Smith	.50
70	Fred Taylor	1.25
71	Derrick Alexander	.15
72	Kimble Anders	.15
73	*Michael Cloud*	.50
74	Elvis Grbac	.30
75	Andre Rison	.30
76	Karim Abdul	.30
77	*Cecil Collins*	1.00
78	*J.J. Johnson*	1.00
79	*Rob Konrad*	.50
80	Dan Marino	1.75
81	O.J. McDuffie	.30
82	Cris Carter	.50
83	*Daunte Culpepper*	5.00
84	Randall Cunningham	.50
85	Randy Moss	2.50
86	Jake Reed	.30
87	Robert Smith	.50
88	Terry Allen	.30
89	Drew Bledsoe	1.00
90	Ben Coates	.30
91	*Kevin Faulk*	1.25
92	Terry Glenn	.50
93	*Andy Katzenmoyer*	.50
94	Cameron Cleeland	.30
95	Billy Joe Hobert	.15
96	Eddie Kennison	.15
97	*Ricky Williams*	5.00
98	*Sean Bennett*	.75
99	Gary Brown	.15
100	Kerry Collins	.30
101	Kent Graham	.15
102	Ike Hilliard	.15
103	Wayne Chrebet	.50
104	Keyshawn Johnson	.50
105	Curtis Martin	.50
106	Rick Mirer	.30
107	Tim Brown	.30
108	Rich Gannon	.30
109	Napoleon Kaufman	.50
110	Charles Woodson	.50
111	Charles Johnson	.15
112	*Donovan McNabb*	3.00
113	Doug Pederson	.15
114	Duce Staley	.50
115	Jerome Bettis	.50
116	*Troy Edwards*	1.75
117	Kordell Stewart	.50
118	*Amos Zereoue*	.75
119	Isaac Bruce	.50
120	Marshall Faulk	.50
121	*Joe Germaine*	1.00
122	*Torry Holt*	1.75
123	*Kurt Warner*	20.00
124	Jim Harbaugh	.30
125	Erik Kramer	.15
126	Natrone Means	.30
127	Junior Seau	.30
128	Terrell Owens	.50
129	Lawrence Phillips	.30
130	Jerry Rice	1.25
131	J.J. Stokes	.30
132	Steve Young	.75
133	*Karsten Bailey*	.50
134	Joey Galloway	.50
135	*Brock Huard*	1.25
136	Jon Kitna	.50
137	Ricky Watters	.30
138	Reidel Anthony	.30
139	Trent Dilfer	.30
140	Warrick Dunn	.50
141	*Shaun King*	3.00
142	*Jevon Kearse*	2.00
143	Kevin Dyson	.30
144	Eddie George	.75
145	Steve McNair	.75
146	*Champ Bailey*	1.25
147	Stephen Davis	.50
148	Skip Hicks	.30
149	Brad Johnson	.50
150	Michael Westbrook	.30
151	Chris McAlister	1.00
152	Peerless Price	1.75
153	Antoine Winfield	1.00
154	D'Wayne Bates	1.00
155	Kevin Johnson	3.00
156	Chris Claiborne	1.00
157	Sedrick Irvin	1.00
158	Michael Cloud	1.00
159	Cecil Collins	1.50
160	J.J. Johnson	1.50
161	Rob Konrad	1.00
162	Daunte Culpepper	3.50
163	Andy Katzenmoyer	1.00
164	Amos Zereoue	1.00
165	Joe Germaine	1.00
166	Karsten Bailey	1.00
167	Brock Huard	1.50
168	Shaun King	4.00
169	Jevon Kearse	2.50
170	Champ Bailey	1.50
171	Jake Plummer	2.50
172	Doug Flutie	2.50
173	Troy Aikman	4.00
174	Emmitt Smith	5.00
175	Terrell Davis	5.00
176	Barry Sanders	7.00
177	Brett Favre	7.00
178	Peyton Manning	7.00
179	Mark Brunell	2.50
180	Fred Taylor	4.00
181	Dan Marino	5.00
182	Randy Moss	7.00
183	Drew Bledsoe	2.50
184	Jerry Rice	5.00
185	Steve Young	2.50
186	David Boston	6.00
187	Cade McNown	12.00
188	Akili Smith	10.00
189	Tim Couch	20.00
190	Edgerrin James	30.00
191	Kevin Faulk	5.00
192	Ricky Williams	20.00
193	Donovan McNabb	12.00
194	Troy Edwards	6.00
195	Torry Holt	8.00

1999 Collector's Edge Odyssey Two Minute Warning

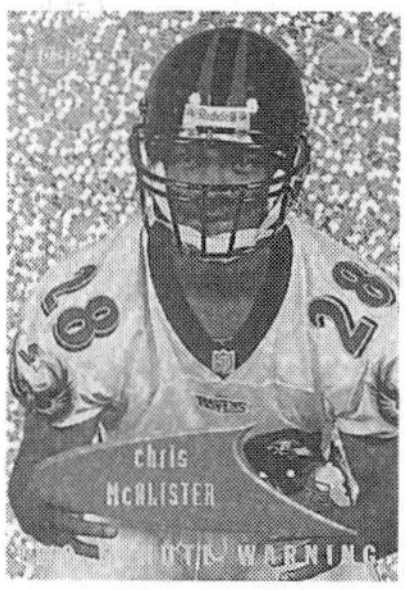

This insert was a 45-card partial parallel to the base set. Cards #151-170 were sequentially numbered to 600. Cards #171-185 were numbered to 300 and cards #186-195 were numbered to 100.

	MT
Common Player (151-170):	3.50
Rookies:	4x
Production 600 Sets	
Common Player (171-185):	7.50
Stars:	3x
Production 300 Sets	
Common Player (186-195):	20.00
Rookies:	4x
Production 100 Sets	

1999 Collector's Edge Odyssey Overtime

This was a 45-card partial set parallel to the base set. Cards #151-170 were sequentially numbered to 60. Cards #171-185 were numbered to 30 and cards #186-195 were numbered to 10.

	MT
Common Player (151-170):	25.00
Rookies:	12x-24x
Production 60 Sets	
Common Player (171-185):	75.00
Stars:	15x-30x
Production 30 Sets	
Common Player (186-195):	100.00
Rookies:	10x-20x
Production 10 Sets	

Values quoted in this guide reflect the retail price of a card — the price a collector can expect to pay when buying a card from a dealer. The wholesale price — that which a collector can expect to receive from a dealer when selling cards — will be significantly lower, depending on desirability and condition.

1999 Collector's Edge Odyssey Cut'n'Ripped

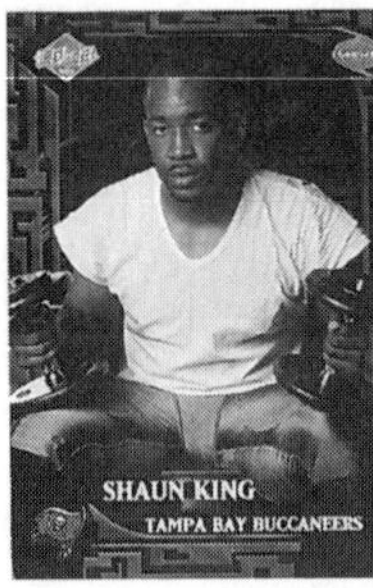

This 15-card insert set included the top rookies from the 1999 class. Each was photographed in the weight room and singles were found 1:12 packs.

		MT
Complete Set (15):		20.00
Common Player:		1.00
Inserted 1:12		
1	Chris McAlister	1.00
2	Kevin Johnson	2.00
3	Chris Claiborne	1.00
4	Sedrick Irvin	1.00
5	Edgerrin James	8.00
6	Michael Cloud	1.00
7	J.J. Johnson	1.50
8	Rob Konrad	1.00
9	Daunte Culpepper	4.00
10	Andy Katzenmoyer	1.00
11	Amos Zereoue	1.00
12	Torry Holt	2.00
13	Shaun King	4.00
14	Jevon Kearse	2.50
15	Champ Bailey	1.50

1999 Collector's Edge Odyssey Cutting Edge

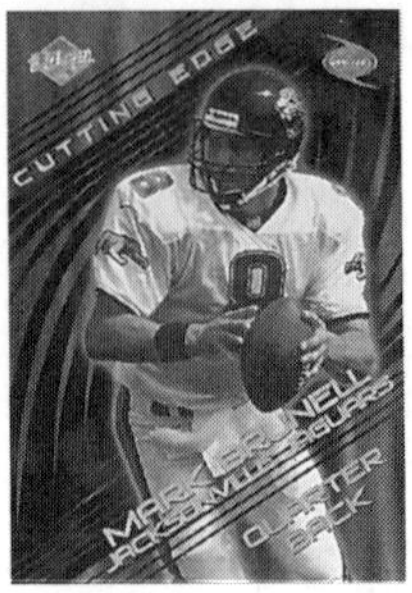

This 10-card set had each single printed on holographic foil with foil stamping. Singles were found 1:18 packs.

		MT
Complete Set (10):		30.00
Common Player:		2.50
Inserted 1:18		
1	Akili Smith	4.00
2	Tim Couch	7.00
3	Brian Griese	3.50
4	Charlie Batch	2.50
5	Brett Favre	8.00
6	Peyton Manning	6.00
7	Mark Brunell	2.50
8	Dan Marino	6.00
9	Drew Bledsoe	2.50
10	Steve Young	2.50

1999 Collector's Edge Odyssey End Zone

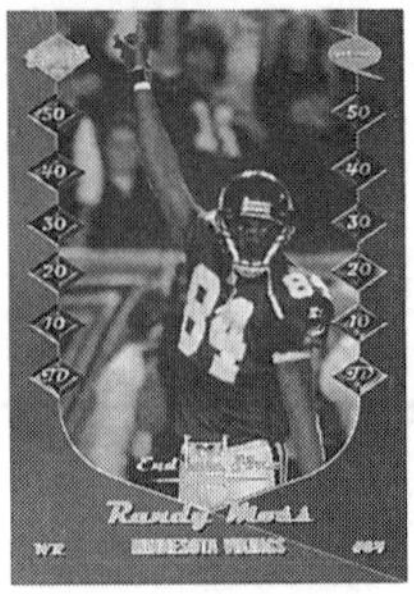

This 20-card insert set included the top players in the NFL. Singles were inserted 1:9 packs.

		MT
Complete Set (20):		30.00
Common Player:		1.00
Minor Stars:		2.00
Inserted 1:9		
1	Jamal Anderson	2.00
2	Priest Holmes	2.00
3	Doug Flutie	3.00
4	Eric Moulds	2.00
5	Charlie Batch	3.00
6	Barry Sanders	8.00
7	Antonio Freeman	2.00
8	Fred Taylor	4.00
9	Cris Carter	2.00
10	Randy Moss	8.00
11	Keyshawn Johnson	2.00
12	Curtis Martin	2.00
13	Vinny Testaverde	1.00
14	Kordell Stewart	2.00
15	Jerry Rice	4.00
16	Terrell Owens	2.00
17	Jon Kitna	2.00
18	Warrick Dunn	2.00
19	Eddie George	2.50
20	Steve McNair	2.50

1999 Collector's Edge Odyssey Excalibur

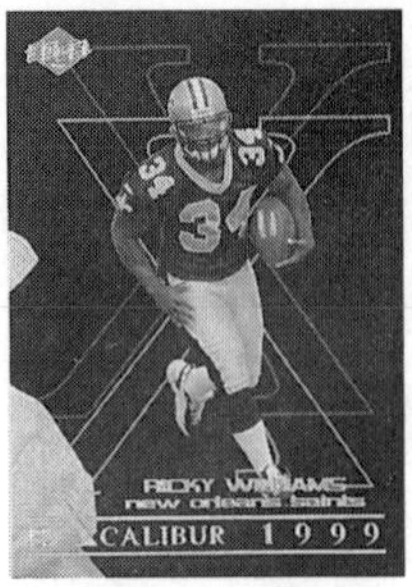

Excalibur was a 25-card set that was a cross-brand program. Singles were inserted into First Place, Odyssey and Masters. Eight of the singles were found in Odyssey at 1:24 packs.

		MT
Complete Set (8):		35.00
Common Player:		5.00
Inserted 1:24		
2	Cade McNown	7.00
5	David Boston	5.00
7	Daunte Culpepper	6.00
8	Troy Edwards	5.00
11	Donovan McNabb	7.00
15	Ricky Williams	10.00
20	Troy Aikman	6.00
25	Emmitt Smith	8.00

1999 Collector's Edge Odyssey Game Gear

This 8-card insert set included a swatch of a game-used football. Each card is sequentially numbered and odds were 1:360 packs.

		MT
Complete Set (8):		300.00
Common Player:		25.00
Inserted 1:360		
1	Terrell Davis 500	40.00
2	Curtis Enis 338	25.00
3	Marshall Faulk 247	35.00
4	Brian Griese 500	25.00
5	Skip Hicks 315	25.00
6	Randy Moss 415	60.00
7	Lawrence Phillips 406	25.00
8	Fred Taylor 85	85.00

1999 Collector's Edge Odyssey Old School

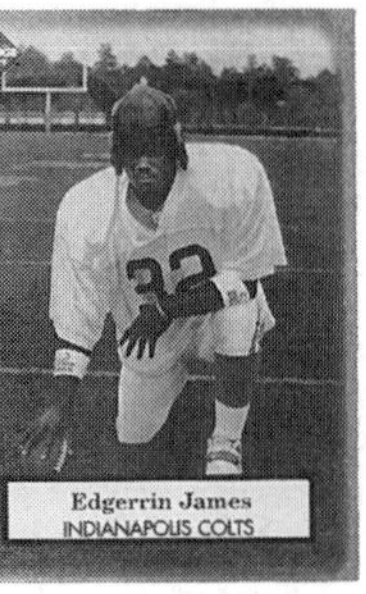

Each card in this 25-card set is in black and white and has an Old School theme to it. Players are photographed in throwback jerseys, leather helmets and in Heisman-style poses. Singles were inserted 1:8 packs.

		MT
Complete Set (25):		45.00
Common Player:		1.00
Minor Stars:		2.00
Inserted 1:8		
1	David Boston	3.00
2	Chris McAlister	1.00
3	Peerless Price	2.00
4	D'Wayne Bates	2.00
5	Cade McNown	5.00
6	Akili Smith	4.00
7	Tim Couch	8.00
8	Kevin Johnson	4.00
9	Chris Claiborne	1.00
10	Sedrick Irvin	2.00
11	Edgerrin James	12.00
12	Michael Cloud	1.00
13	J.J. Johnson	2.50
14	Rob Konrad	1.00
15	Daunte Culpepper	4.00
16	Kevin Faulk	2.50
17	Donovan McNabb	5.00
18	Troy Edwards	3.00
19	Amos Zereoue	2.00
20	Joe Germaine	2.00
21	Torry Holt	3.00
22	Karsten Bailey	2.00
23	Shaun King	5.00
24	Jevon Kearse	3.50
25	Champ Bailey	2.00

1999 Collector's Edge Odyssey Pro Signature Authentics

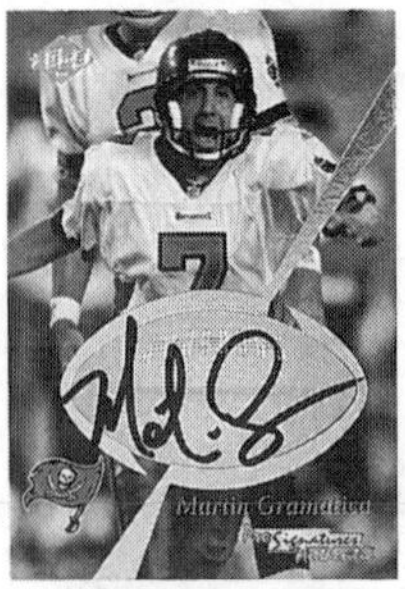

This 18-card set included autographs from the rookies of 1999. Each player had signed a different amount of cards and each was sequentially numbered. They were inserted 1:36 packs.

		MT
Complete Set (18):		425.00
Common Player:		8.00
Minor Stars:		16.00
Inserted 1:36		
DB	D'Wayne Bates 1450	16.00
MB	Michael Bishop 2200	16.00
CC	Chris Claiborne 1120	8.00
DC	Daunte Culpepper 450	45.00
JD	Jared DeVries 290	16.00
JG	Jeff Garcia 2110	25.00
MG	Martin Gramatica 1950	16.00
TH	Torry Holt 1115	25.00
BH	Brock Huard 350	20.00
SI	Sedrick Irvin 1240	16.00
EJ	Edgerrin James 435	125.00
KJ	Kevin Johnson 1920	25.00
SK	Shaun King 920	45.00
RK	Rob Konrad 1420	8.00
DM	Darnell McDonald 2435	8.00
PP	Peerless Price 825	20.00
AS	Akili Smith 111	100.00
AZ	Amos Zereoue 1450	8.00

1999 Collector's Edge Odyssey Super Limited Edge

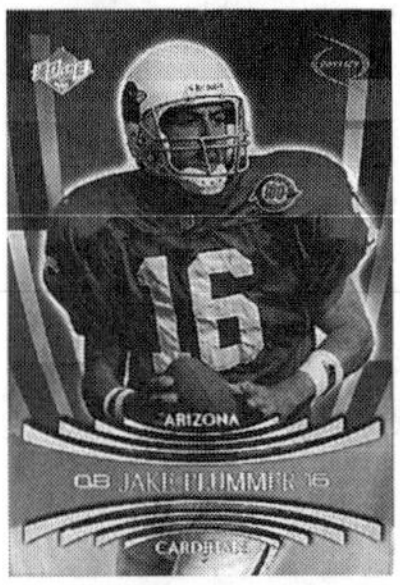

This 30-card insert set included football's biggest stars and featured them on a clear, vinyl card with foil stamping. Each single was sequentially numbered to 1,000.

		MT
Complete Set (30):		100.00
Common Player:		3.00
Production 1,000 Sets		
1	Jake Plummer	5.00
2	Jamal Anderson	3.00
3	Doug Flutie	4.00
4	Eric Moulds	3.00
5	Troy Aikman	8.00
6	Emmitt Smith	10.00
7	Terrell Davis	10.00
8	Charlie Batch	4.00
9	Herman Moore	3.00
10	Barry Sanders	12.00
11	Brett Favre	12.00
12	Antonio Freeman	3.00
13	Dorsey Levens	3.00
14	Peyton Manning	10.00
15	Mark Brunell	4.00
16	Fred Taylor	8.00
17	Dan Marino	10.00
18	Cris Carter	3.00
19	Randall Cunningham	3.00
20	Randy Moss	12.00
21	Drew Bledsoe	4.00
22	Ricky Williams	12.00
23	Keyshawn Johnson	3.00
24	Curtis Martin	3.00
25	Jerome Bettis	3.00
26	Jerry Rice	8.00
27	Terrell Owens	3.00
28	Jon Kitna	4.00
29	Eddie George	4.00
30	Steve Young	4.00

1999 Collector's Edge Supreme

The 170-card base set includes 40 rookie cards. A few errors in the set with two different Tim Couch cards #141. The error is the rarest to find without stats on the back. The corrected versions are numbered TC and include stats. Michael Wiley was suppose to be #166, but chose to stay in college and they had to be pulled from the set. Some still found their way into packs. The #166B Edgerrin James Trade card was inserted late and tough to find. Two parallel sets with Gold Ingot and Galvanized. Other inserts include: Future, Homecoming, Markers, PSA 10 Redemptions, Route XXXIII, Supremacy and T3.

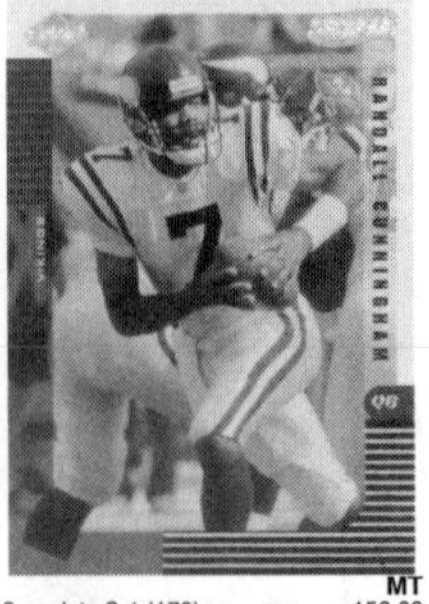

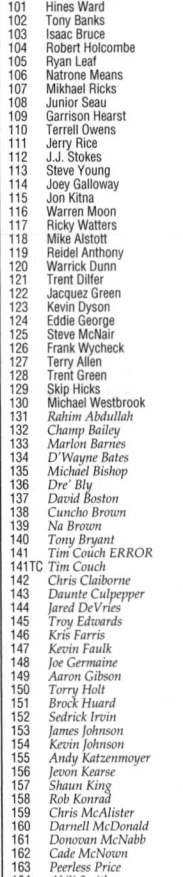

		MT
Complete Set (170):		150.00
Common Player:		.20
Minor Stars:		.40
Common Rookie:		1.00
Card #166A not part of set price		
Gold Ingot Cards:		2x
Gold Ingot Rookies:		1x
Inserted 1:1		
Galvanized Cards:		3x-6x
Production 500 Sets		
Galvanized Rookies:		5x
Production 250 Sets		
Pack (8):		5.00
Wax Box (24):		115.00
1	(Randy Moss CL)	1.50
2	(Peyton Manning CL)	.75
3	Rob Moore	.40
4	Adrian Murrell	.20
5	Jake Plummer	1.50
6	Andre Wadsworth	.20
7	Jamal Anderson	.75
8	Chris Chandler	.40
9	Tony Martin	.20
10	Terance Mathis	.20
11	Jim Harbaugh	.40
12	Priest Holmes	.75
13	Jermaine Lewis	.20
14	Eric Zeier	.20
15	Doug Flutie	.75
16	Eric Moulds	.75
17	Andre Reed	.40
18	Antowain Smith	.75
19	Steve Beuerlein	.20
20	Kevin Greene	.20
21	Raghib Ismail	.20
22	Fred Lane	.20
23	Edgar Bennett	.20
24	Curtis Conway	.40
25	Curtis Enis	.75
26	Erik Kramer	.20
27	Corey Dillon	.75
28	Neil O'Donnell	.20
29	Carl Pickens	.40
30	Darnay Scott	.20
31	Troy Aikman	1.50
32	Michael Irvin	.40
33	Deion Sanders	.75
34	Emmitt Smith	2.00
35	Chris Warren	.40
36	Terrell Davis	2.00
37	John Elway	2.00
38	Ed McCaffrey	.75
39	Shannon Sharpe	.40
40	Rod Smith	.40
41	Charlie Batch	1.25
42	Herman Moore	.40
43	Johnnie Morton	.20
44	Barry Sanders	3.00
45	Robert Brooks	.20
46	Brett Favre	3.00
47	Antonio Freeman	.75
48	Darick Holmes	.20
49	Dorsey Levens	.75
50	Reggie White	.40
51	Marshall Faulk	.75
52	Marvin Harrison	.40
53	Peyton Manning	2.50
54	Jerome Pathon	.40
55	Tavian Banks	.40
56	Mark Brunell	1.25
57	Keenan McCardell	.20
58	Fred Taylor	2.00
59	Derrick Alexander	.20
60	Donnell Bennett	.20
61	Rich Gannon	.20
62	Andre Rison	.40
63	Karim Abdul	.40
64	John Avery	.40
65	Oronde Gadsden	.40
66	Dan Marino	2.00
67	O.J. McDuffie	.20
68	Cris Carter	.75
69	Randall Cunningham	.75
70	Brad Johnson	.40
71	Randy Moss	5.00
72	Jake Reed	.20
73	Robert Smith	.40
74	Drew Bledsoe	1.25
75	Ben Coates	.40
76	Robert Edwards	.75
77	Terry Glenn	.40
78	Cameron Cleeland	.40
79	Kerry Collins	.40
80	Sean Dawkins	.20
81	Lamar Smith	.20
82	Gary Brown	.20
83	Chris Calloway	.20
84	Ike Hilliard	.20
85	Danny Kanell	.20
86	Wayne Chrebet	.75
87	Keyshawn Johnson	.75
88	Curtis Martin	.75
89	Vinny Testaverde	.40
90	Tim Brown	.40
91	Jeff George	.40
92	Napoleon Kaufman	.75
93	Charles Woodson	.75
94	Irving Fryar	.20
95	Bobby Hoying	.20
96	Duce Staley	.20
97	Jerome Bettis	.40
98	Courtney Hawkins	.20
99	Charles Johnson	.20
100	Kordell Stewart	1.00
101	Hines Ward	.40
102	Tony Banks	.40
103	Isaac Bruce	.40
104	Robert Holcombe	.40
105	Ryan Leaf	1.00
106	Natrone Means	.40
107	Mikhael Ricks	.40
108	Junior Seau	.40
109	Garrison Hearst	.40
110	Terrell Owens	.75
111	Jerry Rice	1.50
112	J.J. Stokes	.40
113	Steve Young	1.00
114	Joey Galloway	.75
115	Jon Kitna	1.00
116	Warren Moon	.40
117	Ricky Watters	.40
118	Mike Alstott	.40
119	Reidel Anthony	.40
120	Warrick Dunn	1.00
121	Trent Dilfer	.40
122	Jacquez Green	.40
123	Kevin Dyson	.40
124	Eddie George	1.00
125	Steve McNair	.75
126	Frank Wycheck	.20
127	Terry Allen	.40
128	Trent Green	.40
129	Skip Hicks	.40
130	Michael Westbrook	.20
131	*Rahim Abdullah*	1.00
132	*Champ Bailey*	3.00
133	*Marlon Barnes*	1.00
134	*D'Wayne Bates*	2.00
135	*Michael Bishop*	3.00
136	*Dre' Bly*	1.00
137	*David Boston*	3.00
138	*Cuncho Brown*	1.00
139	*Na Brown*	1.00
140	*Tony Bryant*	1.00
141	*Tim Couch ERROR*	70.00
141TC	*Tim Couch*	20.00
142	*Chris Claiborne*	2.00
143	*Daunte Culpepper*	15.00
144	*Jared DeVries*	1.00
145	*Troy Edwards*	3.00
146	*Kris Farris*	1.00
147	*Kevin Faulk*	3.00
148	*Joe Germaine*	2.50
149	*Aaron Gibson*	1.00
150	*Torry Holt*	4.00
151	*Brock Huard*	3.00
152	*Sedrick Irvin*	2.00
153	*James Johnson*	2.00
154	*Kevin Johnson*	3.00
155	*Andy Katzenmoyer*	2.00
156	*Jevon Kearse*	5.00
157	*Shaun King*	4.00
158	*Rob Konrad*	2.00
159	*Chris McAlister*	2.00
160	*Darnell McDonald*	2.00
161	*Donovan McNabb*	7.00
162	*Cade McNown*	3.00
163	*Peerless Price*	3.00
164	*Akili Smith*	5.00
165	*Matt Stinchcomb*	1.00
166A	Michael Wiley	200.00
166B	*Edgerrin James Trade*	75.00
167	*Ricky Williams*	8.00
168	*Antoine Winfield*	2.00
169	*Craig Yeast*	2.00
170	*Amos Zereoue*	2.00

1999 Collector's Edge Supreme Galvanized Parallel

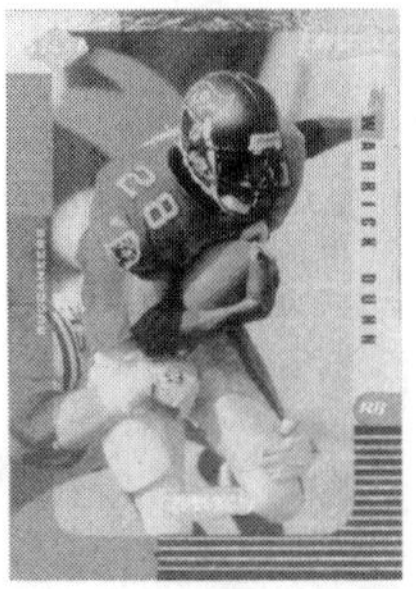

This 169-card set is a parallel to the base minus the cards of Michael Wiley and Edgerrin James #166. Each card is printed on silver foil board and is sequentially numbered. Veterans are printed to 500 and rookies to 250.

		MT
Complete Set (169):		800.00
Galvanized Cards:		3x-6x
Production 500 Sets		
Galvanized Rookies:		5x
Production 250 Sets		

1999 Collector's Edge Supreme Gold Ingot Parallel

The 169-card set is a parallel to the base minus the Michael Wiley and Edgerrin James cards #166. The cards are the same as the base except for the foil is in gold and the Gold Ingot stamp on the fronts. They were inserted one-per-pack.

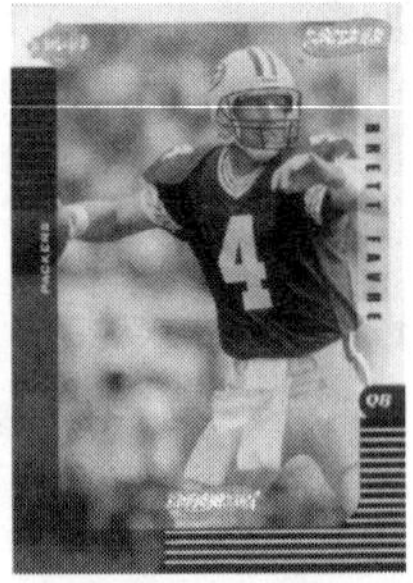

		MT
Complete Set (169):		300.00
Gold Ingot Cards:		2x
Gold Ingot Rookies:		1x
Inserted 1:1		

1999 Collector's Edge Supreme Future

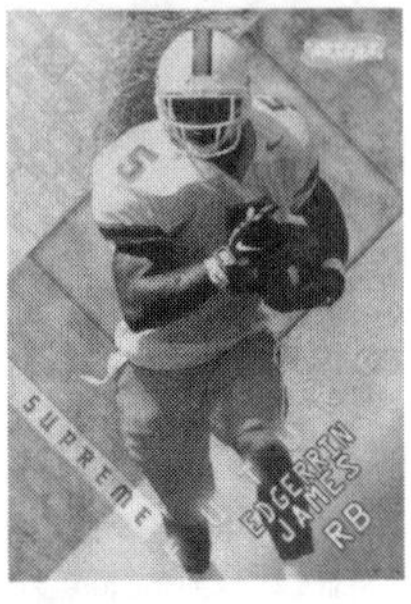

Each card in this 10-card set is printed on micro-etched foil board and was inserted 1:24 packs.

		MT
Complete Set (10):		60.00
Common Player:		2.00
Inserted 1:24		
1	Ricky Williams	20.00
2	Tim Couch	20.00
3	Daunte Culpepper	7.00
4	Torry Holt	5.00
5	Edgerrin James	10.00
6	Brock Huard	2.00
7	Donovan McNabb	7.00
8	Joe Germaine	4.00
9	Cade McNown	7.00
10	Michael Bishop	4.00

1999 Collector's Edge Supreme Homecoming

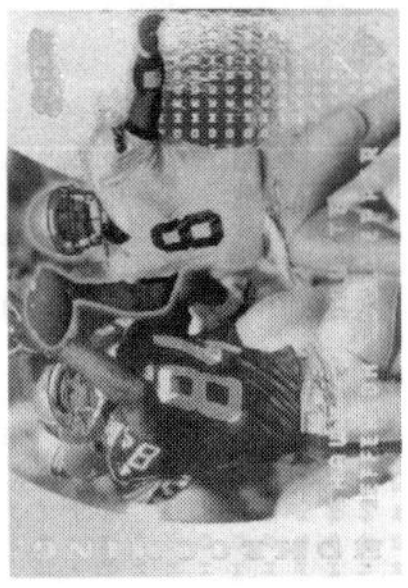

Each card in this 20-card set includes two players on the front who went to the same college. A rookie from the 1999 draft and a veteran. Singles were inserted 1:12 packs.

		MT
Complete Set (20):		60.00
Common Player:		1.50
Inserted 1:12		
1	Ricky Williams, Priest Holmes	15.00
2	Andy Katzenmoyer, Eddie George	4.00
3	Daunte Culpepper, Shawn Jefferson	5.00
4	Torry Holt, Erik Kramer	4.00
5	Edgerrin James, Vinny Testaverde	8.00
6	Chris Claiborne, Junior Seau	1.50
7	Brock Huard, Mark Brunell	4.00
8	Champ Bailey, Terrell Davis	8.00
9	Donovan McNabb, Rob Moore	6.00
10	David Boston, Joey Galloway	4.00
11	Cade McNown, Troy Aikman	6.00
12	Kevin Faulk, Eddie Kennison	1.50
13	Sedrick Irvin, Andre Rison	1.50
14	Rob Konrad, Darryl Johnston	1.50

15	Amos Zereoue, Adrian Murrell	1.50
16	Peerless Price, Peyton Manning	10.00
17	Kevin Johnson, Marvin Harrison	3.00
18	Jevon Kearse, Emmitt Smith	7.00
19	Antoine Winfield, Shawn Springs	1.50
20	Tony Bryant, Andre Wadsworth	1.50

1999 Collector's Edge Supreme Markers

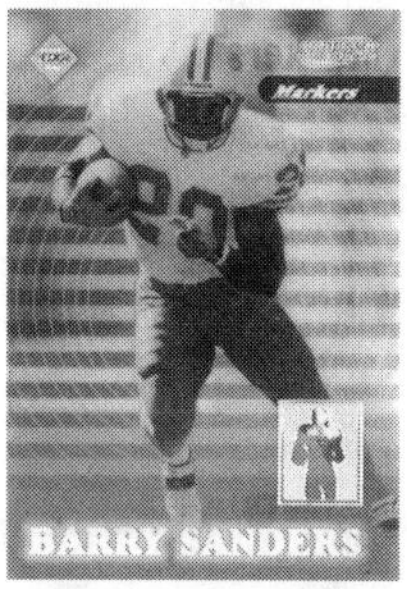
Markers
BARRY SANDERS

The cards are printed on clear vinyl stock with foil stamping. The set features 15 NFL stars and focuses on record-setting performances and milestones reached in the 1998 NFL season. They were sequentially numbered to 5,000.

		MT
	Complete Set (15):	60.00
	Common Player:	1.00
	Minor Stars:	2.00
	Production 5,000 Sets	
1	Terrell Davis	6.00
2	John Elway	5.00
3	Dan Marino	6.00
4	Peyton Manning	7.00
5	Barry Sanders	8.00
6	Emmitt Smith	6.00
7	Randy Moss	12.00
8	Jake Plummer	4.00
9	Cris Carter	1.00
10	Brett Favre	8.00
11	Drew Bledsoe	3.00
12	Charlie Batch	4.00
13	Curtis Martin	1.00
14	Mark Brunell	3.00
15	Jamal Anderson	2.00

1999 Collector's Edge Supreme PSA 10 Redemptions

Each card in this set was a redemption card for the player that was on it. You could then redeem it for a PSA 10 graded rookie of that player. The redemption cards were limited to 1,999.

		MT
	Complete Set (3):	250.00
	Common Player:	75.00
	Production 1,999 Sets	
1	Ricky Williams	100.00
2	Tim Couch	100.00
3	Daunte Culpepper	75.00

1999 Collector's Edge Supreme Route XXXIII

This set includes the top stars from the 1998 NFL playoffs. Each player in the 10-card set is sequentially numbered to 1,000.

		MT
	Complete Set (10):	150.00
	Common Player:	8.00
	Production 1,000 Sets	
1	Randy Moss	55.00
2	Jamal Anderson	8.00
3	Jake Plummer	15.00
4	Steve Young	12.00
5	Fred Taylor	20.00
6	Dan Marino	20.00
7	Keyshawn Johnson	8.00
8	Curtis Martin	12.00
9	John Elway	20.00
10	Terrell Davis	20.00

1999 Collector's Edge Supreme Supremacy

This set features 5 players from Super Bowl XXXIII. Each is printed on foil board with foil stamping and is sequentially numbered to 500.

		MT
	Complete Set (5):	75.00
	Common Player:	10.00
	Production 500 Sets	
1	John Elway	25.00
2	Terrell Davis	25.00
3	Ed McCaffrey	10.00
4	Jamal Anderson	15.00
5	Chris Chandler	10.00

1999 Collector's Edge Supreme T3

This 30-card set is tiered into three levels with 10 wide receivers (foil board with bronze foil stamping), running backs (foil board with silver foil stamping) and quarterbacks (foil board with gold foil stamping). The receivers were the easiest to find at 1:8, running backs at 1:12 and the quarterbacks the toughest to get at 1:24.

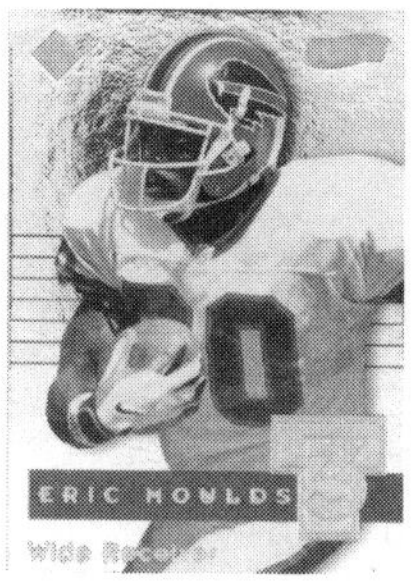
ERIC MOULDS

		MT
	Complete Set (30):	180.00
	Common WR:	1.50
	Inserted 1:8	
	Common RB:	2.50
	Inserted 1:12	
	Common QB:	5.00
	Inserted 1:24	
1	Doug Flutie (QB)	5.00
2	Troy Aikman (QB)	10.00
3	John Elway (QB)	15.00
4	Jake Plummer (QB)	10.00
5	Brett Favre (QB)	20.00
6	Mark Brunell (QB)	8.00
7	Peyton Manning (QB)	15.00
8	Dan Marino (QB)	15.00
9	Drew Bledsoe (QB)	8.00
10	Steve Young (QB)	7.00
11	Jamal Anderson (RB)	3.00
12	Emmitt Smith (RB)	8.00
13	Terrell Davis (RB)	10.00
14	Barry Sanders (RB)	10.00
15	Robert Smith (RB)	2.50
16	Robert Edwards (RB)	3.00
17	Curtis Martin (RB)	3.00
18	Jerome Bettis (RB)	2.50
19	Fred Taylor (RB)	10.00
20	Eddie George (RB)	5.00
21	Michael Irvin (WR)	1.50
22	Eric Moulds (WR)	3.00
23	Herman Moore (WR)	1.50
24	Reidel Anthony (WR)	1.50
25	Randy Moss (WR)	12.00
26	Cris Carter (WR)	1.50
27	Keyshawn Johnson (WR)	3.00
28	Jacquez Green (WR)	1.50
29	Jerry Rice (WR)	7.00
30	Terrell Owens (WR)	4.00

1999 Collector's Edge Triumph

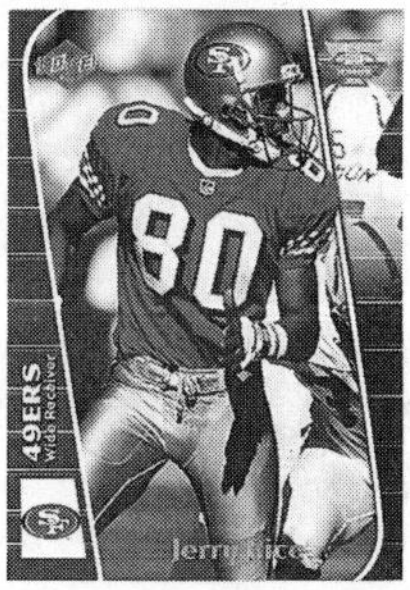
49ERS
Jerry Rice

Triumph was a 180-card set that included 40 rookie cards found one-per-pack. Insert sets included: Commissioner's Choice, Fantasy Team, Future Fantasy Team, Heir Supply, K-Klub Y3K, Pack Warriors and Signed, Sealed, Delivered. Packs contained eight cards.

		MT
	Complete Set (180):	55.00
	Common Player:	.15
	Minor Stars:	.30
	Common Rookie:	.50
	Inserted 1:1	
	Pack (8):	3.50
	Wax Box (32):	100.00
1	Jamal Anderson	.50
2	Jerome Bettis	.50
3	Terrell Davis	1.75
4	Corey Dillon	.50
5	Warrick Dunn	.50
6	Marshall Faulk	.50
7	Eddie George	.75
8	Garrison Hearst	.30
9	Skip Hicks	.30
10	Napoleon Kaufman	.50
11	Dorsey Levens	.50
12	Curtis Martin	.50
13	Natrone Means	.30
14	Adrian Murrell	.30
15	Barry Sanders	2.50
16	Antowain Smith	.50
17	Emmitt Smith	1.75
18	Robert Smith	.50
19	Fred Taylor	1.25
20	Ricky Watters	.30
21	Cameron Cleeland	.30
22	Ben Coates	.30
23	Shannon Sharpe	.30
24	Frank Wycheck	.15
25	Derrick Alexander	.15
26	Reidel Anthony	.30
27	Robert Brooks	.15
28	Tim Brown	.30
29	Cris Carter	.50
30	Wayne Chrebet	.50
31	Curtis Conway	.30
32	Tim Dwight	.50
33	Kevin Dyson	.30
34	Antonio Freeman	.50
35	Joey Galloway	.50
36	Terry Glenn	.50
37	Marvin Harrison	.30
38	Ike Hilliard	.30
39	Michael Irvin	.30
40	Keyshawn Johnson	.50
41	Jermaine Lewis	.15
42	Terance Mathis	.15
43	Ed McCaffrey	.50
44	Keenan McCardell	.30
45	O.J. McDuffie	.30
46	Herman Moore	.50
47	Rob Moore	.30
48	Randy Moss	2.50
49	Eric Moulds	.50
50	Muhsin Muhammad	.30
51	Terrell Owens	.50
52	Jerome Pathon	.15
53	Carl Pickens	.30
54	Andre Reed	.30
55	Jake Reed	.30
56	Jerry Rice	1.25
57	Andre Rison	.30
58	Jimmy Smith	.50
59	Rod Smith	.50
60	Michael Westbrook	.30
61	Morten Andersen	.15
62	Gary Anderson	.15
63	Doug Brien	.15
64	Chris Boniol	.15
65	John Carney	.15
66	Steve Christie	.15
67	Richie Cunningham	.15
68	Brad Daluiso	.15
69	Al Del Greco	.15
70	Jason Elam	.15
71	John Hall	.15
72	Jason Hanson	.15
73	Mike Hollis	.15
74	Norm Johnson	.15
75	Olindo Mare	.15
76	Doug Pelfrey	.15
77	Wade Richey	.15
78	Pete Stoyanovich	.15
79	Mike Vanderjagt	.15
80	Adam Vinatieri	.15
81	Ray Buchanan	.15
82	Jim Flanigan	.15
83	Darrell Green	.15
84	Kevin Greene	.15
85	Ty Law	.15
86	Ken Norton Jr.	.15
87	John Randle	.15
88	Bill Romanowski	.15
89	Deion Sanders	.50
90	Junior Seau	.30
91	Michael Sinclair	.15
92	Bruce Smith	.15
93	Takeo Spikes	.15
94	Michael Strahan	.15
95	Derrick Thomas	.30
96	Zach Thomas	.30
97	Andre Wadsworth	.30
98	Charles Woodson	.50
99	Checklist	.15
100	Checklist	.15
101	Troy Aikman	1.25
102	Tony Banks	.30
103	Charlie Batch	.75
104	Steve Beuerlein	.30
105	Jeff Blake	.30
106	Drew Bledsoe	1.00
107	Bubby Brister	.30
108	Mark Brunell	1.00
109	Chris Chandler	.30
110	Kerry Collins	.30
111	Randall Cunningham	.50
112	Koy Detmer	.15
113	Ty Detmer	.15
114	Trent Dilfer	.30
115	John Elway	1.75
116	Brett Favre	2.50
117	Doug Flutie	.75
118	Rich Gannon	.30
119	*Jeff Garcia*	6.00
120	Jeff George	.30
121	Kent Graham	.15
122	Elvis Grbac	.30
123	Brian Griese	1.00
124	Trent Green	.30
125	Jim Harbaugh	.30
126	Billy Joe Hobert	.15
127	Brad Johnson	.50
128	Rob Johnson	.30
129	Jon Kitna	.50
130	Erik Kramer	.15
131	Ryan Leaf	.50
132	Peyton Manning	1.75
133	Dan Marino	1.75
134	Steve McNair	.75
135	Scott Mitchell	.15
136	Warren Moon	.30
137	Jake Plummer	1.00
138	Kordell Stewart	.50
139	Vinny Testaverde	.30
140	Steve Young	.75
141	*Champ Bailey*	2.00
142	*Karsten Bailey*	1.00
143	*D'Wayne Bates*	1.00
144	*David Boston*	3.00
145	*Cuncho Brown*	.50
146	*Dat Nguyen*	.50
147	*Chris Claiborne*	1.00
148	*Michael Cloud*	1.00
149	*Cecil Collins*	1.50
150	*Tim Couch*	8.00
151	*Daunte Culpepper*	10.00
152	*Autry Denson*	1.00
153	*Troy Edwards*	3.00
154	*Ebenezer Ekuban*	.50
155	*Kevin Faulk*	2.00
156	*Jermaine Fazande*	1.00
157	*Joe Germaine*	1.00
158	*Martin Gramatica*	1.00
159	*Torry Holt*	3.50
160	*Brock Huard*	2.00
161	*Sedrick Irvin*	1.00
162	*Edgerrin James*	12.00
163	*James Johnson*	2.00
164	*Kevin Johnson*	3.50
165	*Andy Katzenmoyer*	1.00
166	*Jevon Kearse*	3.00
167	*Patrick Kerney*	.50
168	*Shaun King*	5.00
169	*Jim Kleinsasser*	1.00
170	*Rob Konrad*	1.00
171	*Chris McAlister*	1.00
172	*Donovan McNabb*	5.00
173	*Cade McNown*	2.50
174	*Joe Montgomery*	1.00
175	*Peerless Price*	2.00
176	*Akili Smith*	4.00
177	*Ricky Williams*	8.00
178	*Larry Parker*	.50
179	*Antoine Winfield*	.50
180	*Amos Zereoue*	1.00

1999 Collector's Edge Triumph Commissioner's Choice

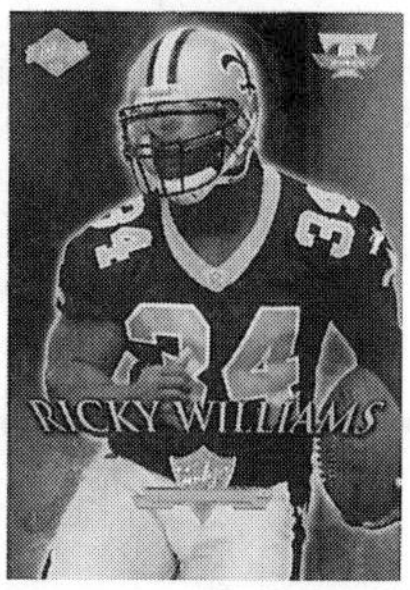
RICKY WILLIAMS

This 10-card insert set included the top rookies from the 1999 Draft. Singles were inserted 1:15 packs. A parallel Gold version was also made and each card was sequentially numbered to 500.

		MT
	Complete Set (10):	45.00
	Common Player:	2.00
	Inserted 1:15	
	Gold Cards:	2x
	Production 500 Sets	
1	Tim Couch	8.00
2	Donovan McNabb	5.00
3	Cade McNown	5.00
4	Daunte Culpepper	5.00
5	Akili Smith	4.00
6	Ricky Williams	8.00
7	Edgerrin James	12.00
8	Torry Holt	3.50
9	David Boston	3.50
10	Champ Bailey	2.00

1999 Collector's Edge Triumph Fantasy Team

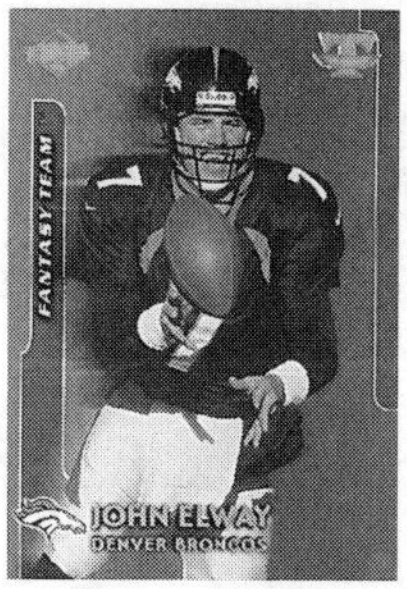
FANTASY TEAM
JOHN ELWAY
DENVER BRONCOS

This 10-card insert set included the top players in the NFL and inserted them 1:10 packs.

		MT
	Complete Set (10):	45.00
	Common Player:	3.50
	Inserted 1:10	
1	Terrell Davis	6.00
2	John Elway	6.00
3	Brett Favre	8.00
4	Peyton Manning	6.00
5	Dan Marino	6.00
6	Randy Moss	8.00
7	Jake Plummer	3.50
8	Barry Sanders	8.00
9	Emmitt Smith	6.00
10	Fred Taylor	3.50

1999 Collector's Edge Triumph Future Fantasy Team

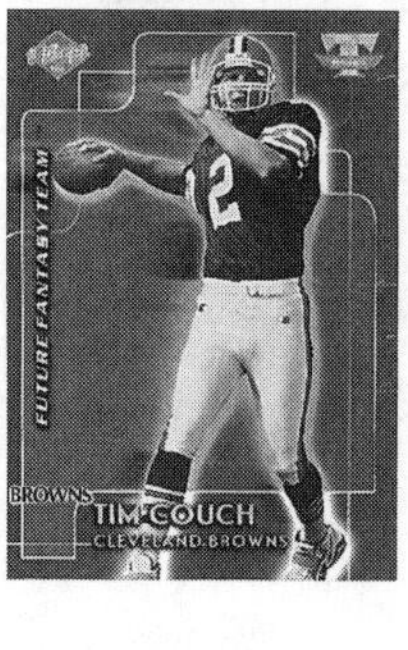
FUTURE FANTASY TEAM
BROWNS
TIM COUCH
CLEVELAND BROWNS

This 20-card insert set included the top rookies from 1999. Singles were inserted 1:6 packs.

		MT
	Complete Set (20):	45.00
	Common Player:	1.00
	Inserted 1:6	
1	Champ Bailey	1.50
2	D'Wayne Bates	1.00
3	David Boston	2.00
4	Tim Couch	6.00
5	Daunte Culpepper	6.00
6	Troy Edwards	2.00
7	Kevin Faulk	1.50
8	Torry Holt	3.50
9	Brock Huard	1.50
10	Sedrick Irvin	1.50
11	Edgerrin James	10.00
12	James Johnson	1.50
13	Kevin Johnson	3.00
14	Rob Konrad	1.00
15	Donovan McNabb	5.00
16	Cade McNown	3.00
17	Peerless Price	2.00
18	Akili Smith	2.00
19	Ricky Williams	6.00
20	Amos Zereoue	1.50

1999 Collector's Edge Triumph Heir Supply

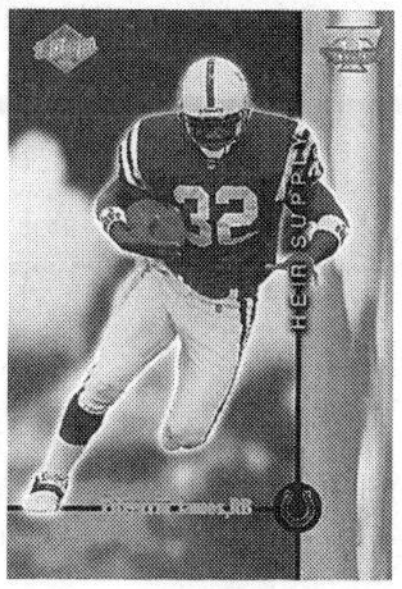
HEIR SUPPLY

This 15-card insert set included the top rookies from the 1999 Draft. Singles were inserted 1:3 packs.

		MT
	Complete Set (15):	25.00
	Common Player:	.75
	Minor Stars:	1.50
	Inserted 1:3	
1	Ricky Williams	5.00
2	Tim Couch	5.00
3	Cade McNown	3.00
4	Donovan McNabb	3.00
5	Akili Smith	2.50
6	Daunte Culpepper	3.00
7	Torry Holt	2.00
8	Edgerrin James	7.00
9	David Boston	2.00
10	Troy Edwards	2.00
11	Peerless Price	1.50
12	Champ Bailey	1.50
13	D'Wayne Bates	.75
14	Kevin Faulk	.75
15	Amos Zereoue	.75

1999 Collector's Edge Triumph K-Klub Y3K

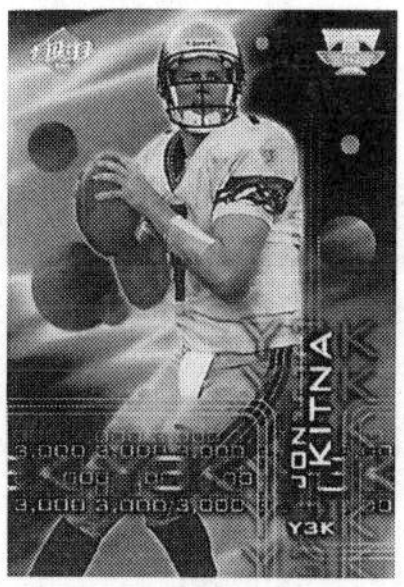
JON KITNA

This 50-card insert set included both young and veteran players. Singles were sequentially numbered to 1,000.

		MT
	Complete Set (50):	100.00
	Common Player:	1.50
	Minor Stars:	3.00
	Production 1,000 Sets	
1	Kareem Abdul-Jabbar	1.50
2	Jamal Anderson	3.00
3	Jerome Bettis	3.00
4	Isaac Bruce	3.00
5	Cris Carter	3.00
6	Terrell Davis	8.00
7	Corey Dillon	3.00
8	Warrick Dunn	3.00
9	Curtis Enis	3.00
10	Marshall Faulk	3.00
11	Antonio Freeman	3.00
12	Joey Galloway	3.00
13	Eddie George	4.00
14	Terry Glenn	3.00
15	Garrison Hearst	1.50
16	Keyshawn Johnson	3.00
17	Napoleon Kaufman	1.50
18	Curtis Martin	3.00
19	Rob Moore	1.50
20	Herman Moore	3.00
21	Eric Moulds	3.00
22	Randy Moss	12.00
23	Adrian Murrell	1.50
24	Carl Pickens	1.50
25	Jerry Rice	6.00
26	Barry Sanders	12.00
27	Antowain Smith	1.50
28	Emmitt Smith	8.00
29	Fred Taylor	6.00
30	Ricky Watters	1.50
31	Troy Aikman	6.00
32	Charlie Batch	4.00
33	Drew Bledsoe	5.00
34	Mark Brunell	5.00
35	Chris Chandler	1.50
36	Randall Cunningham	3.00
37	Trent Dilfer	1.50
38	John Elway	8.00
39	Brett Favre	12.00
40	Doug Flutie	4.00
41	Brad Johnson	3.00
42	Jon Kitna	3.00
43	Ryan Leaf	3.00
44	Peyton Manning	8.00
45	Dan Marino	8.00
46	Steve McNair	4.00
47	Jake Plummer	5.00
48	Kordell Stewart	3.00
49	Vinny Testaverde	1.50
50	Steve Young	4.00

1999 Collector's Edge Triumph Pack Warriors

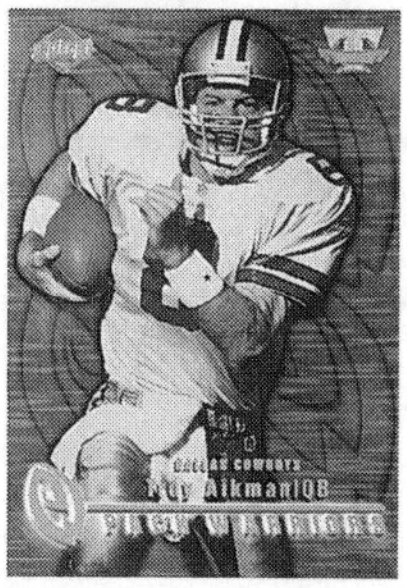

This 15-card insert set included veteran players. Singles were inserted 1:4 packs.

		MT
	Complete Set (15):	30.00
	Common Player:	1.00
	Inserted 1:4	
1	Jamal Anderson	1.00
2	Jake Plummer	2.00
3	Emmitt Smith	3.50
4	Troy Aikman	3.00
5	Terrell Davis	3.50
6	John Elway	3.50
7	Barry Sanders	5.00
8	Brett Favre	5.00
9	Peyton Manning	3.50
10	Randy Moss	5.00
11	Dan Marino	3.50
12	Keyshawn Johnson	1.00
13	Fred Taylor	3.00
14	Jerry Rice	3.00
15	Jerome Bettis	1.00

1999 Collector's Edge Triumph Signed, Sealed, Delivered

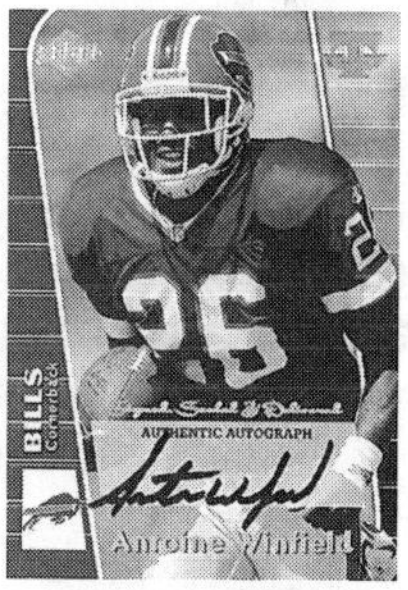
BILLS
AUTHENTIC AUTOGRAPH
Antoine Winfield

This was a 40-card set that included autographs from the top rookies of 1999. Singles were inserted 1:32 packs. A parallel Blue version was issued and each was sequentially numbered to 40. A parallel Red version was also made and each of those singles was numbered to 10.

	MT
Complete Set (40):	550.00
Common Player:	5.00
Minor Stars:	10.00
Inserted 1:32	
Blue Cards:	4x
Production 40 Sets	
Red Cards:	
Production 10 Sets	
Champ Bailey	15.00
Karsten Bailey	10.00
D'Wayne Bates	10.00
David Boston	20.00
Cuncho Brown	5.00
Dat Nguyen	5.00
Chris Claiborne	10.00
Michael Cloud	10.00
Cecil Collins	15.00
Tim Couch	70.00
Daunte Culpepper	30.00
Autry Denson	10.00
Troy Edwards	20.00
Ebenezer Ekuban	5.00
Kevin Faulk	15.00
Jermaine Fazande	10.00
Joe Germaine	10.00

Martin Gramatica	10.00
Torry Holt	20.00
Brock Huard	15.00
Sedrick Irvin	15.00
Edgerrin James	100.00
James Johnson	15.00
Kevin Johnson	20.00
Andy Katzenmoyer	10.00
Jevon Kearse	20.00
Patrick Kerney	5.00
Shaun King	30.00
Jim Kleinsasser	10.00
Rob Konrad	10.00
Chris McAlister	10.00
Donovan McNabb	30.00
Cade McNown	30.00
Joe Montgomery	10.00
Peerless Price	15.00
Akili Smith	25.00
Ricky Williams	60.00
Larry Parker	5.00
Antoine Winfield	5.00
Amos Zereoue	10.00

2000 Collector's Edge Graded

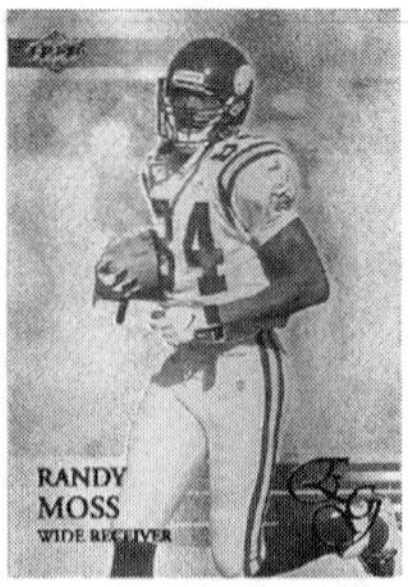

		MT
Complete Set (148):		125.00
Common Player:		.25
Minor Stars:		.50
Common Rookie:		1.25
Pack (10 + PSA Graded Card):		23.00
Wax Box (12):		225.00
Cards #93 & 110 Never Released		
1	Marcus Robinson	1.00
2	Adrian Murrell	.25
3	Qadry Ismail	.25
4	Tim Biakabutuka	.50
5	Jamal Anderson	1.00
6	Dorsey Levens	1.00
7	Robert Smith	1.00
8	Tony Banks	.50
9	Yancey Thigpen	.50
10	Elvis Grbac	.50
11	Sedrick Irvin	.50
12	Rob Johnson	.50
13	Frank Sanders	.50
14	Rich Gannon	.50
15	Steve Beuerlein	.50
16	James Stewart	.50
17	Ricky Watters	.50
18	Curtis Enis	.75
19	Eddie Kennison	.50
20	Kerry Collins	.50
21	Ray Lucas	.75
22	Carl Pickens	.50
23	Natrone Means	.50
24	Daunte Culpepper	1.75
25	Karim Abdul	.50
26	David Boston	1.00
27	Raghib Ismail	.25
28	Jacquez Green	.50
29	Kevin Dyson	.50
30	Chris Chandler	.50
31	Brian Griese	1.25
32	Charlie Garner	.50
33	Wayne Chrebet	.75
34	Mike Alstott	1.00
35	Germane Crowell	1.00
36	Michael Cloud	.25
37	Antowain Smith	.50
38	Jeff George	.75
39	Antonio Freeman	1.00
40	Champ Bailey	.75
41	Terrence Wilkins	1.00
42	Junior Seau	.50
43	Jimmy Smith	1.00
44	Greg Hill	.25
45	Tyrone Wheatley	.50
46	Tony Gonzalez	.75
47	Rod Smith	.75
48	Damon Huard	1.00
49	Jerome Bettis	1.00
50	Cris Carter	1.00
51	Darnay Scott	.50
52	Ike Hilliard	.25
53	Errict Rhett	.50
54	Tim Brown	.75
55	Terry Glenn	1.00
56	Jeff Blake	.50
57	Terance Mathis	.25
58	Duce Staley	1.00
59	Amani Toomer	.25
60	Terry Allen	.25
61	Corey Dillon	1.00
62	Kordell Stewart	1.00
63	Az-Zahir Hakim	.50
64	Jim Harbaugh	.50
65	Bill Schroeder	.25
66	O.J. McDuffie	.50
67	Keenan McCardell	.50
68	Terrell Owens	1.00
69	Joey Galloway	1.00
70	Derrick Alexander	.25
71	Ed McCaffrey	.75
72	Reidel Anthony	.50
73	Michael Irvin	.50
74	Herman Moore	.50
75	Joe Montgomery	.25
76	Muhsin Muhammad	.50
77	Charles Johnson	.25
78	Michael Westbrook	.50
79	Jevon Kearse	1.00
80	*Courtney Brown*	3.50
81	*Shaun Alexander*	6.00
82	*R. Jay Soward*	2.50
83	*Sylvester Morris*	4.00
84	*Giovanni Carmazzi*	3.50
85	*J.R. Redmond*	3.00
86	*Sherrod Gideon*	1.25
87	*Tee Martin*	2.50
88	*Dennis Northcutt*	3.00
89	*Troy Walters*	1.25
90	*Joe Hamilton*	2.00
91	*Reuben Droughns*	2.00
92	*Trung Canidate*	2.00
94	*Tim Rattay*	3.00
95	*Jerry Porter*	2.50
96	*Michael Wiley*	2.50
97	*Anthony Lucas*	1.25
98	*Danny Farmer*	1.25
99	*Travis Prentice*	4.00
100	*Dez White*	2.50
101	*Chad Pennington*	8.00
102	*Chris Redman*	4.00
103	*Thomas Jones*	6.00
104	*Ron Dayne*	10.00
105	*Jamal Lewis*	6.00
106	*Shyrone Stith*	2.00
107	*Peter Warrick*	10.00
108	*Plaxico Burress*	5.00
109	*Travis Taylor*	4.00
111	Terrell Davis	3.00
112	Dan Marino	3.00
113	Brad Johnson	1.00
114	Isaac Bruce	1.00
115	Eric Moulds	1.00
116	Olandis Gary	1.25
117	Drew Bledsoe	1.50
118	Steve Young	1.50
119	Keyshawn Johnson	1.00
120	Emmitt Smith	3.00
121	Warrick Dunn	1.00
122	Doug Flutie	1.25
123	Troy Edwards	1.00
124	Brett Favre	4.00
125	Charlie Batch	1.00
126	Curtis Martin	1.00
127	Stephen Davis	1.00
128	Troy Aikman	2.50
129	Fred Taylor	1.50
130	Jerry Rice	2.50
131	Jon Kitna	1.00
132	Steve McNair	1.00
133	Jake Plummer	1.00
134	Donovan McNabb	1.50
135	Ricky Williams	2.50
136	Torry Holt	1.00
137	J.J. Johnson	1.00
138	Kevin Johnson	1.00
139	Akili Smith	1.25
140	Cade McNown	1.50
141	Eddie George	1.25
142	Shaun King	1.50
143	Marshall Faulk	1.00
144	Kurt Warner	5.00
145	Randy Moss	4.00
146	Mark Brunell	1.50
147	Marvin Harrison	1.00
148	Edgerrin James	4.00
149	Tim Couch	2.50
150	Peyton Manning	4.00

2000 Collector's Edge Graded Brilliant

		MT
Common Gem Mint:		40.00
Common Mint:		20.00
Production 500 Sets		
101	Chad Pennington Gem	200.00
101	Chad Pennington Mint	100.00
102	Chris Redman Gem	60.00
102	Chris Redman Mint	30.00
103	Thomas Jones Gem	100.00
103	Thomas Jones Mint	50.00
104	Ron Dayne Gem	200.00
104	Ron Dayne Mint	100.00
105	Jamal Lewis Gem	100.00
105	Jamal Lewis Mint	50.00
106	Shyrone Stith Gem	50.00
106	Shyrone Stith Mint	25.00
107	Peter Warrick Gem	200.00
107	Peter Warrick Mint	100.00
108	Plaxico Burress Gem	150.00
108	Plaxico Burress Mint	75.00
109	Travis Taylor Gem	70.00
109	Travis Taylor Mint	35.00
111	Terrell Davis Gem	70.00
111	Terrell Davis Mint	35.00
112	Dan Marino Gem	70.00
112	Dan Marino Mint	35.00
113	Brad Johnson Gem	40.00
113	Brad Johnson Mint	20.00
114	Isaac Bruce Gem	40.00
114	Isaac Bruce Mint	20.00
115	Eric Moulds Gem	40.00
115	Eric Moulds Mint	20.00
116	Olandis Gary Gem	40.00
116	Olandis Gary Mint	20.00
117	Drew Bledsoe Gem	50.00
117	Drew Bledsoe Mint	25.00
118	Steve Young Gem	50.00
118	Steve Young Mint	25.00
119	Keyshawn Johnson Gem	40.00
119	Keyshawn Johnson Mint	20.00
120	Emmitt Smith Gem	70.00
120	Emmitt Smith Mint	35.00
121	Warrick Dunn Gem	40.00
121	Warrick Dunn Mint	20.00
122	Doug Flutie Gem	50.00
122	Doug Flutie Mint	25.00
123	Troy Edwards Gem	40.00
123	Troy Edwards Mint	20.00
124	Brett Favre Gem	80.00
124	Brett Favre Mint	40.00
125	Charlie Batch Gem	40.00
125	Charlie Batch Mint	20.00
126	Curtis Martin Gem	40.00
126	Curtis Martin Mint	20.00
127	Stephen Davis Gem	40.00
127	Stephen Davis Mint	20.00
128	Troy Aikman Gem	60.00
128	Troy Aikman Mint	30.00
129	Fred Taylor Gem	50.00
129	Fred Taylor Mint	25.00
130	Jerry Rice Gem	60.00
130	Jerry Rice Mint	30.00
131	Jon Kitna Gem	40.00
131	Jon Kitna Mint	20.00
132	Steve McNair Gem	40.00
132	Steve McNair Mint	20.00
133	Jake Plummer Gem	40.00
133	Jake Plummer Mint	20.00
134	Donovan McNabb Gem	50.00
134	Donovan McNabb Mint	25.00
135	Ricky Williams Gem	60.00
135	Ricky Williams Mint	30.00
136	Torry Holt Gem	40.00
136	Torry Holt Mint	20.00
137	J.J. Johnson Gem	40.00
137	J.J. Johnson Mint	20.00
138	Kevin Johnson Gem	40.00
138	Kevin Johnson Mint	20.00
139	Akili Smith Gem	40.00
139	Akili Smith Mint	20.00
140	Cade McNown Gem	50.00
140	Cade McNown Mint	25.00
141	Eddie George Gem	40.00
141	Eddie George Mint	20.00
142	Shaun King Gem	50.00
142	Shaun King Mint	25.00
143	Marshall Faulk Gem	40.00
143	Marshall Faulk Mint	20.00
144	Kurt Warner Gem	100.00
144	Kurt Warner Mint	50.00
145	Randy Moss Gem	80.00
145	Randy Moss Mint	40.00
146	Mark Brunell Gem	50.00
146	Mark Brunell Mint	25.00
147	Marvin Harrison Gem	40.00
147	Marvin Harrison Mint	20.00
148	Edgerrin James Gem	80.00
148	Edgerrin James Mint	40.00
149	Tim Couch Gem	60.00
149	Tim Couch Mint	30.00
150	Peyton Manning Gem	80.00
150	Peyton Manning Mint	40.00

2000 Collector's Edge Graded Edge Gems

		MT
Complete Set (49):		375.00
Common Player:		3.50
Production 500 Sets		
E1	Doug Flutie	4.00
E2	Cade McNown	5.00
E3	Akili Smith	4.00
E4	Tim Couch	8.00
E5	Kevin Johnson	3.50
E6	Troy Aikman	8.00
E7	Emmitt Smith	10.00
E8	Terrell Davis	10.00
E9	Brett Favre	15.00
E10	Marvin Harrison	3.50
E11	Edgerrin James	15.00
E12	Peyton Manning	15.00
E13	Mark Brunell	6.00
E14	Dan Marino	10.00
E15	Randy Moss	15.00
E16	Drew Bledsoe	6.00
E17	Ricky Williams	8.00
E18	Keyshawn Johnson	3.50
E19	Curtis Martin	3.50
E20	Donovan McNabb	5.00
E21	Marshall Faulk	3.50
E22	Torry Holt	3.50
E23	Kurt Warner	15.00
E24	Jerry Rice	8.00
E25	Steve Young	6.00
E26	Jon Kitna	3.50
E27	Shaun King	5.00
E28	Eddie George	4.00
E29	Stephen Davis	3.50
E30	Brad Johnson	3.50
E31	Chad Pennington	20.00
E32	Chris Redman	10.00
E33	Tim Rattay	8.00
E34	Tee Martin	7.00
E35	Thomas Jones	15.00
E36	Ron Dayne	25.00
E37	Jamal Lewis	15.00
E38	J.R. Redmond	10.00
E39	Travis Prentice	12.00
E40	Shaun Alexander	15.00
E41	Michael Wiley	7.00
E42	Quinton Spotwood	7.00
E43	Peter Warrick	25.00
E44	Plaxico Burress	20.00
E45	Travis Taylor	12.00
E46	Troy Walters	5.00
E47	R. Jay Soward	8.00
E48	Dez White	7.00
E50	Courtney Brown	10.00

2000 Collector's Edge Graded Golden Edge

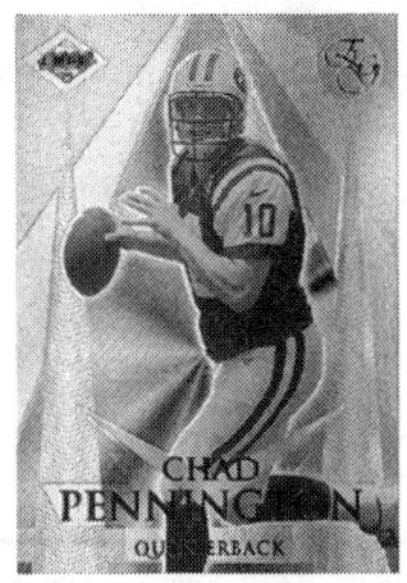

		MT
Complete Set (49):		185.00
Common Player:		1.25
Minor Stars:		2.50
Production 2,000 Sets		
GE1	Jake Plummer	2.50
GE2	Qadry Ismail	1.25
GE3	Doug Flutie	3.00
GE4	Muhsin Muhammad	1.25
GE5	Cade McNown	3.50
GE6	Marcus Robinson	2.50
GE7	Akili Smith	3.00
GE8	Tim Couch	5.00
GE9	Kevin Johnson	2.50
GE10	Troy Aikman	5.00
GE11	Emmitt Smith	7.00
GE12	Terrell Davis	7.00
GE13	Charlie Batch	2.50
GE14	Brett Favre	10.00
GE15	Marvin Harrison	2.50
GE16	Edgerrin James	10.00
GE17	Peyton Manning	10.00
GE18	Mark Brunell	4.00
GE19	Fred Taylor	4.00
GE20	Dan Marino	7.00
GE21	Randy Moss	10.00
GE22	Drew Bledsoe	4.00
GE23	Ricky Williams	5.00
GE24	Curtis Martin	2.50
GE25	Donovan McNabb	3.50
GE26	Isaac Bruce	2.50
GE27	Marshall Faulk	2.50
GE28	Torry Holt	2.50
GE29	Kurt Warner	10.00
GE30	Jerry Rice	5.00
GE31	Jon Kitna	2.50
GE32	Eddie George	3.00
GE33	Steve McNair	2.50
GE34	Stephen Davis	2.50
GE35	Brad Johnson	2.50
GE36	Travis Prentice	6.00
GE37	Dez White	4.00
GE38	Chad Pennington	12.00
GE39	Chris Redman	5.00
GE40	Thomas Jones	10.00
GE41	Ron Dayne	15.00
GE42	Jamal Lewis	10.00
GE43	Shyrone Stith	2.50
GE44	Peter Warrick	15.00
GE45	Plaxico Burress	12.00
GE46	Travis Taylor	6.00
GE48	Shaun Alexander	10.00
GE49	R. Jay Soward	4.00
GE50	Sylvester Morris	6.00

2000 Collector's Edge Graded Impeccable

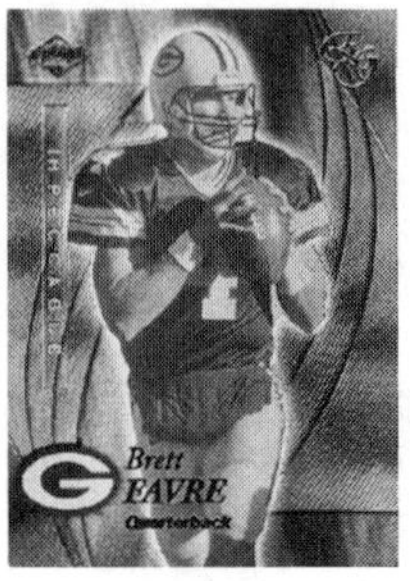

		MT
Complete Set (20):		85.00
Common Player:		2.50
Production 2,000 Sets		
I1	Cade McNown	3.00
I2	Tim Couch	5.00
I3	Troy Aikman	5.00
I4	Emmitt Smith	8.00
I5	Terrell Davis	8.00
I6	Brett Favre	10.00
I7	Edgerrin James	10.00
I8	Peyton Manning	10.00
I9	Mark Brunell	4.00
I10	Fred Taylor	4.00
I11	Dan Marino	8.00
I12	Randy Moss	10.00
I13	Drew Bledsoe	4.00
I14	Ricky Williams	5.00
I15	Curtis Martin	2.50
I16	Marshall Faulk	2.50
I17	Kurt Warner	10.00
I18	Eddie George	3.00
I19	Steve McNair	2.50
I20	Stephen Davis	2.50

2000 Collector's Edge Graded Making the Grade

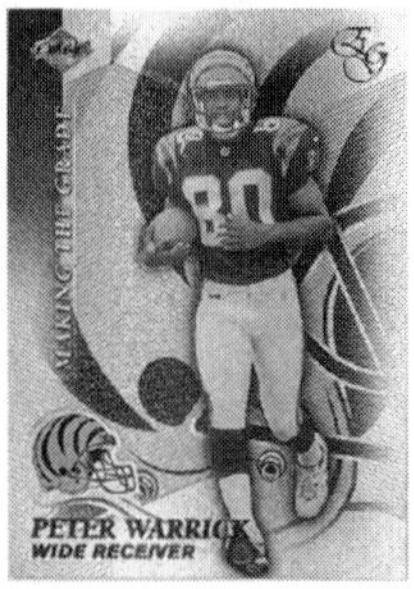

		MT
Complete Set (29):		100.00
Common Player:		2.00
Production 2,000 Sets		
M1	Shaun Alexander	10.00
M2	R. Jay Soward	4.00
M3	Sylvester Morris	6.00
M4	Giovanni Carmazzi	5.00
M5	J.R. Redmond	5.00
M6	Bubba Franks	2.00
M7	Tee Martin	4.00
M8	Dennis Northcutt	5.00
M9	Troy Walters	2.00
M10	Joe Hamilton	4.00
M11	Reuben Droughns	3.00
M12	Trung Canidate	2.00
M13	Laveranues Coles	3.00
M14	Tim Rattay	4.00
M15	Jerry Porter	4.00
M16	Ron Dugans	3.00
M17	Anthony Becht	2.00
M18	Danny Farmer	2.00
M19	Travis Prentice	6.00
M20	Dez White	4.00
M21	Chad Pennington	12.00
M22	Chris Redman	5.00
M23	Thomas Jones	10.00
M24	Ron Dayne	15.00
M25	Jamal Lewis	10.00
M26	Todd Pinkston	3.00
M27	Peter Warrick	15.00
M28	Plaxico Burress	12.00
M29	Travis Taylor	6.00

2000 Collector's Edge Graded Rookie Leatherbacks

		MT
Common Player:		150.00
Production 12 Sets		
SA	Shaun Alexander	350.00
AB	Anthony Becht	150.00
PB	Plaxico Burress	450.00
TC	Trung Canidate	200.00
LC	Laveranues Coles	200.00
RD	Ron Dayne	600.00
RD	Reuben Droughns	150.00
RD	Ron Dugans	200.00
DF	Danny Farmer	150.00
BF	Bubba Franks	200.00
JH	Joe Hamilton	225.00
TJ	Thomas Jones	350.00
CK	Curtis Keaton	150.00
JL	Jamal Lewis	350.00
TM	Tee Martin	250.00
SM	Sylvester Morris	300.00
DN	Dennis Northcutt	225.00
CP	Chad Pennington	450.00
TP	Todd Pinkston	200.00
JP	Jerry Porter	200.00
TP	Travis Prentice	300.00
CR	Chris Redman	275.00
JR	J.R. Redmond	275.00
CS	Corey Simon	150.00
RS	R. Jay Soward	225.00
TT	Travis Taylor	300.00
BU	Brian Urlacher	275.00
PW	Peter Warrick	600.00
DW	Dez White	200.00

2000 Collector's Edge Graded Uncirculated

		MT
Common Gem Mint:		12.00
Common Mint:		6.00
Production 5,000 Sets		
101	Chad Pennington Gem	50.00
101	Chad Pennington Mint	25.00
102	Chris Redman Gem	25.00
102	Chris Redman Mint	12.00
103	Thomas Jones Gem	40.00
103	Thomas Jones Mint	20.00
104	Ron Dayne Gem	60.00
104	Ron Dayne Mint	30.00
105	Jamal Lewis Gem	40.00
105	Jamal Lewis Mint	20.00
106	Shyrone Stith Gem	15.00
106	Shyrone Stith Mint	8.00
107	Peter Warrick Gem	60.00
107	Peter Warrick Mint	30.00
108	Plaxico Burress Gem	50.00
108	Plaxico Burress Mint	25.00
109	Travis Taylor Gem	30.00
109	Travis Taylor Mint	15.00
111	Terrell Davis Gem	30.00
111	Terrell Davis Mint	15.00
112	Dan Marino Gem	30.00
112	Dan Marino Mint	15.00
113	Brad Johnson Gem	12.00
113	Brad Johnson Mint	6.00
114	Isaac Bruce Gem	12.00
114	Isaac Bruce Mint	6.00
115	Eric Moulds Gem	12.00
115	Eric Moulds Mint	6.00
116	Olandis Gary Gem	12.00
116	Olandis Gary Mint	6.00
117	Drew Bledsoe Gem	20.00
117	Drew Bledsoe Mint	10.00
118	Steve Young Gem	20.00
118	Steve Young Mint	10.00
119	Keyshawn Johnson Gem	12.00
119	Keyshawn Johnson Mint	6.00
120	Emmitt Smith Gem	30.00
120	Emmitt Smith Mint	15.00
121	Warrick Dunn Gem	12.00
121	Warrick Dunn Mint	6.00
122	Doug Flutie Gem	20.00
122	Doug Flutie Mint	10.00
123	Troy Edwards Gem	12.00
123	Troy Edwards Mint	6.00
124	Brett Favre Gem	40.00
124	Brett Favre Mint	20.00
125	Charlie Batch Gem	12.00
125	Charlie Batch Mint	6.00
126	Curtis Martin Gem	12.00
126	Curtis Martin Mint	6.00
127	Stephen Davis Gem	12.00
127	Stephen Davis Mint	6.00
128	Troy Aikman Gem	25.00
128	Troy Aikman Mint	12.00
129	Fred Taylor Gem	20.00
129	Fred Taylor Mint	10.00
130	Jerry Rice Gem	25.00
130	Jerry Rice Mint	12.00
131	Jon Kitna Gem	12.00
131	Jon Kitna Mint	6.00
132	Steve McNair Gem	12.00
132	Steve McNair Mint	6.00
133	Jake Plummer Gem	12.00
133	Jake Plummer Mint	6.00
134	Donovan McNabb Gem	16.00
134	Donovan McNabb Mint	8.00
135	Ricky Williams Gem	30.00
135	Ricky Williams Mint	15.00
136	Torry Holt Gem	12.00
136	Torry Holt Mint	6.00
137	J.J. Johnson Gem	12.00
137	J.J. Johnson Mint	6.00
138	Kevin Johnson Gem	12.00
138	Kevin Johnson Mint	6.00
139	Akili Smith Gem	12.00
139	Akili Smith Mint	6.00
140	Cade McNown Gem	16.00
140	Cade McNown Mint	8.00
141	Eddie George Gem	16.00
141	Eddie George Mint	8.00
142	Shaun King Gem	16.00
142	Shaun King Mint	8.00
143	Marshall Faulk Gem	12.00
143	Marshall Faulk Mint	6.00
144	Kurt Warner Gem	40.00
144	Kurt Warner Mint	20.00
145	Randy Moss Gem	40.00
145	Randy Moss Mint	20.00
146	Mark Brunell Gem	20.00
146	Mark Brunell Mint	10.00
147	Marvin Harrison Gem	12.00
147	Marvin Harrison Mint	6.00
148	Edgerrin James Gem	40.00
148	Edgerrin James Mint	20.00
149	Tim Couch Gem	30.00
149	Tim Couch Mint	15.00
150	Peyton Manning Gem	40.00
150	Peyton Manning Mint	20.00

2000 Collector's Edge Masters

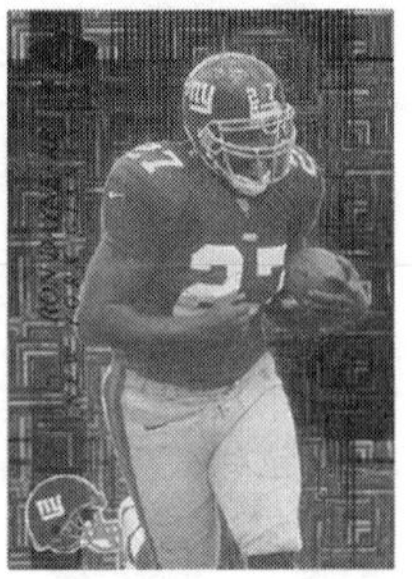

		MT
Complete Set (250):		375.00
Common Player:		.50
Minor Stars:		1.00
Production 2,000 Sets		
Common Rookies:		2.00
Production 1,000 Sets		
Retail Box (3 packs + 2 PSA):		35.00
1	David Boston	1.50
2	Michael Pittman	.50
3	Jake Plummer	1.50
4	Frank Sanders	1.00
5	Jamal Anderson	1.50
6	Chris Chandler	1.00
7	Tim Dwight	1.50
8	Shawn Jefferson	.50
9	Terance Mathis	.50
10	Tony Banks	1.00
11	Trent Dilfer	1.00
12	Priest Holmes	1.00
13	Qadry Ismail	.50
14	Jermaine Lewis	.50
15	Shannon Sharpe	1.00
16	Doug Flutie	2.00
17	Rob Johnson	1.00
18	Jeremy McDaniel	.50
19	Eric Moulds	1.50
20	Peerless Price	1.00
21	Antowain Smith	1.00
22	Steve Beuerlein	1.00
23	Tim Biakabutuka	1.00
24	Dialleo Burks	.50
25	Dameyune Craig	.50
26	Donald Hayes	1.00
27	Patrick Jeffers	1.50
28	Muhsin Muhammad	1.00
29	Reggie White	1.00
30	Bobby Engram	.50
31	Curtis Enis	1.00
32	Eddie Kennison	.50
33	Cade McNown	1.50
34	Marcus Robinson	1.50
35	Corey Dillon	1.50
36	James Hundon	.50
37	Scott Mitchell	.50
38	Tony McGee	.50
39	Akili Smith	1.50
40	Craig Yeast	.50
41	Darrin Chiaverini	.50
42	Tim Couch	3.00
43	Kevin Johnson	1.50
44	Errict Rhett	1.00
45	Troy Aikman	3.50
46	Randall Cunningham	1.00
47	Joey Galloway	1.50
48	Raghib Ismail	.50
49	James McKnight	.50
50	Dat Nguyen	.50
51	Emmitt Smith	4.50
52	Chris Warren	1.00
53	Robert Brooks	.50
54	Terrell Davis	4.50
55	Gus Frerotte	.50
56	Olandis Gary	1.75
57	Brian Griese	2.00
58	Ed McCaffrey	1.00
59	Rod Smith	1.50
60	Charlie Batch	1.50
61	Germane Crowell	1.50
62	Sedrick Irvin	.50
63	Herman Moore	1.00
64	Johnnie Morton	1.00
65	James Stewart	1.50
66	Corey Bradford	.50
67	Brett Favre	6.00
68	Antonio Freeman	1.50
69	Matt Hasselbeck	1.00
70	Dorsey Levens	1.00
71	Bill Schroeder	.50
72	Ken Dilger	.50
73	E.G. Green	.50
74	Marvin Harrison	1.50
75	Edgerrin James	6.00
76	Peyton Manning	5.00
77	Jerome Pathon	.50
78	Terrence Wilkins	1.00
79	Kyle Brady	.50
80	Mark Brunell	2.50
81	Kevin Hardy	.50
82	Stacey Mack	.50
83	Keenan McCardell	1.00
84	Jimmy Smith	1.50
85	Fred Taylor	2.00
86	Derrick Alexander	.50
87	Michael Cloud	.50
88	Tony Gonzalez	1.00
89	Elvis Grbac	1.00
90	Kevin Lockett	.50
91	Tony Richardson	.50

92	Jay Fiedler	1.00
93	Oronde Gadsden	.50
94	Damon Huard	1.00
95	Rob Konrad	.50
96	J.J. Johnson	1.00
97	Tony Martin	.50
98	O.J. McDuffie	1.00
99	Lamar Smith	1.00
100	Thurman Thomas	1.00
101	Todd Bouman	.50
102	Bubby Brister	1.00
103	Cris Carter	1.50
104	Daunte Culpepper	3.00
105	Matthew Hatchette	.50
106	Randy Moss	5.00
107	Robert Smith	1.50
108	Moe Williams	.50
109	Michael Bishop	1.50
110	Drew Bledsoe	2.50
111	Troy Brown	.50
112	Kevin Faulk	1.00
113	Terry Glenn	1.50
114	Andy Katzenmoyer	.50
115	Tony Simmons	1.00
116	Jeff Blake	1.00
117	Aaron Brooks	2.00
118	Jake Delhomme	1.50
119	Joe Horn	1.00
120	Jake Reed	.50
121	Ricky Williams	4.00
122	Tiki Barber	1.50
123	Kerry Collins	1.50
124	Ike Hilliard	1.00
125	Amani Toomer	1.00
126	Wayne Chrebet	1.50
127	Ray Lucas	1.50
128	Curtis Martin	1.50
129	Vinny Testaverde	1.00
130	Dedric Ward	1.00
131	Tim Brown	1.50
132	Rickey Dudley	.50
133	Rich Gannon	1.00
134	James Jett	.50
135	Napoleon Kaufman	1.50
136	Tyrone Wheatley	1.00
137	Charles Woodson	1.50
138	Charles Johnson	.50
139	Donovan McNabb	2.50
140	Torrance Small	.50
141	Duce Staley	1.50
142	Jerome Bettis	1.50
143	Troy Edwards	1.00
144	Kent Graham	.50
145	Richard Huntley	1.00
146	Kordell Stewart	1.75
147	Amos Zereoue	1.00
148	Isaac Bruce	1.50
149	Kevin Carter	.50
150	Marshall Faulk	1.50
151	Trent Green	1.00
152	Az-Zahir Hakim	1.00
153	Robert Holcombe	1.00
154	Torry Holt	1.50
155	Kurt Warner	7.00
156	Kenny Bynum	.50
157	Robert Chancey	.50
158	Curtis Conway	1.00
159	Jermaine Fazande	1.00
160	Jeff Graham	.50
161	Jim Harbaugh	1.00
162	Ryan Leaf	1.50
163	Junior Seau	1.00
164	Jeff Garcia	1.50
165	Charlie Garner	1.00
166	Terrell Owens	1.50
167	Jerry Rice	3.50
168	J.J. Stokes	1.00
169	Karsten Bailey	.50
170	Sean Dawkins	.50
171	Brock Huard	1.50
172	Jon Kitna	1.50
173	Derrick Mayes	1.00
174	Ricky Watters	1.00
175	Rabih Abdullah	.50
176	Mike Alstott	1.50
177	Reidel Anthony	.50
178	Warrick Dunn	1.50
179	Jacquez Green	.50
180	Keyshawn Johnson	1.50
181	Shaun King	2.50
182	Warren Sapp	1.00
183	Kevin Dyson	.50
184	Eddie George	1.75
185	Jevon Kearse	1.50
186	Steve McNair	1.50
187	Neil O'Donnell	.50
188	Carl Pickens	1.00
189	Yancey Thigpen	1.00
190	Frank Wycheck	.50
191	Champ Bailey	1.50
192	Larry Centers	.50
193	Albert Connell	1.00
194	Stephen Davis	1.50
195	Jeff George	1.00
196	Brad Johnson	1.00
197	Deion Sanders	1.50
198	Bruce Smith	.50
199	James Thrash	1.00
200	Michael Westbrook	1.00
201	*Thomas Jones*	7.50
202	*Jamal Lewis*	25.00
203	*Chris Redman*	7.50
204	*Travis Taylor*	5.00
205	*Avion Black*	2.00
206	*Kwame Cavil*	2.00
207	*Sammy Morris*	5.00
208	*Brian Urlacher*	12.50
209	*Dez White*	3.00
210	*Ron Dugans*	3.00
211	*Danny Farmer*	3.00
212	*Curtis Keaton*	2.00
213	*Peter Warrick*	17.50
214	*Courtney Brown*	4.00
215	*JaJuan Dawson*	2.00
216	*Dennis Northcutt*	4.00
217	*Travis Prentice*	6.00
218	*Spergon Wynn*	3.00
219	*Michael Wiley*	3.00
220	*Mike Anderson*	20.00
221	*Chris Cole*	2.00
222	*Deltha O'Neal*	2.00
223	*Reuben Droughns*	2.00
224	*Bubba Franks*	3.00
225	*Charles Lee*	2.00
226	*Rob Morris*	2.00
227	*R. Jay Soward*	2.00
228	*Shyrone Stith*	2.00
229	*Frank Moreau*	3.00
230	*Sylvester Morris*	10.00
231	*J.R. Redmond*	5.00
232	*Chad Morton*	3.00
233	*Ron Dayne*	20.00
234	*Ron Dixon*	4.00
235	*Anthony Becht*	3.00
236	*Laveranues Coles*	4.00
237	*Chad Pennington*	15.00
238	*Sebastian Janikowski*	4.00
239	*Jerry Porter*	3.00
240	*Todd Pinkston*	3.00
241	*Gari Scott*	2.00
242	*Corey Simon*	3.00
243	*Plaxico Burress*	10.00
244	*Tee Martin*	4.00
245	*Trung Canidate*	3.00
246	*Trevor Gaylor*	3.00
247	*Giovanni Carmazzi*	4.00
248	*Tim Rattay*	4.00
249	*Shaun Alexander*	12.50
250	*Joe Hamilton*	4.00

2000 Collector's Edge Masters HoloGold Parallel

	MT
HoloGold Cards:	6x-12x
HoloGold Rookies:	3x
Production 50 Sets	

2000 Collector's Edge Masters HoloSilver Parallel

	MT
HoloSilver Cards:	2x
Production 1,000 Sets	

2000 Collector's Edge Masters Domain

		MT
Complete Set (20):		20.00
Common Player:		.75
Minor Stars:		1.50
Production 5,000 Sets		
D1	Qadry Ismail	.75
D2	Muhsin Muhammad	.75
D3	Marcus Robinson	1.50
D4	Akili Smith	1.50
D5	Tim Couch	3.00
D6	Kevin Johnson	1.50
D7	Troy Aikman	4.50
D8	Brian Griese	2.00
D9	James Stewart	.75
D10	Dorsey Levens	1.50
D11	Marvin Harrison	1.50
D12	Cris Carter	1.50
D13	Daunte Culpepper	3.00
D14	Donovan McNabb	2.50
D15	Duce Staley	1.50
D16	Isaac Bruce	1.50
D17	Torry Holt	1.50
D18	Kurt Warner	6.00
D19	Jeff Garcia	1.50
D20	Jerry Rice	4.50

2000 Collector's Edge Masters Future Masters

		MT
Complete Set (30):		75.00
Common Player:		1.00
Minor Stars:		2.00
Production 2,000 Sets		
FM1	Thomas Jones	4.00
FM2	Jamal Lewis	12.00
FM3	Chris Redman	4.00
FM4	Travis Taylor	2.50
FM5	Brian Urlacher	6.00
FM6	Dez White	2.00
FM7	Ron Dugans	2.00
FM8	Danny Farmer	2.00
FM9	Curtis Keaton	1.00
FM10	Peter Warrick	8.50
FM11	Courtney Brown	2.00
FM12	JaJuan Dawson	2.00
FM13	Dennis Northcutt	2.00
FM14	Travis Prentice	3.00
FM15	Spergon Wynn	2.00
FM16	Reuben Droughns	2.00
FM17	R. Jay Soward	2.00
FM18	J.R. Redmond	2.50
FM19	Ron Dayne	10.00
FM20	Anthony Becht	2.00
FM21	Laveranues Coles	2.50
FM22	Chad Pennington	7.50
FM23	Jerry Porter	2.00
FM24	Todd Pinkston	2.00
FM25	Plaxico Burress	4.50
FM26	Tee Martin	2.50
FM27	Trung Canidate	2.00
FM28	Giovanni Carmazzi	2.50
FM29	Tim Rattay	2.50
FM30	Joe Hamilton	2.00

2000 Collector's Edge Masters Game Gear Leatherbacks

		MT
Common Player:		150.00
Production 12 Sets		
TC	Tim Couch	300.00
DC	Daunte Culpepper	325.00
RD	Ron Dayne	450.00
EJ	Edgerrin James	400.00
PM	Peyton Manning	400.00
SM	Sylvester Morris	250.00
RM	Randy Moss	400.00
TT	Travis Taylor	150.00
KW	Kurt Warner	450.00
PW	Peter Warrick	400.00

2000 Collector's Edge Masters Hasta La Vista

		MT
Complete Set (20):		50.00
Common Player:		1.50
Minor Stars:		3.00
Production 2,000 Sets		
H1	Eric Moulds	3.00
H2	Cade McNown	3.00
H3	Emmitt Smith	7.00
H4	Terrell Davis	7.00
H5	Charlie Batch	3.00
H6	Marvin Harrison	3.00
H7	Edgerrin James	8.00
H8	Peyton Manning	8.00
H9	Mark Brunell	4.00
H10	Fred Taylor	3.50
H11	Daunte Culpepper	4.50
H12	Torry Holt	1.50
H13	Marshall Faulk	3.00
H14	Kurt Warner	10.00
H15	Ryan Leaf	1.50
H16	Keyshawn Johnson	3.00
H17	Shaun King	3.50
H18	Steve McNair	3.00
H19	Stephen Davis	3.00
H20	Brad Johnson	1.50

2000 Collector's Edge Masters K-Klub

		MT
Complete Set (50):		50.00
Common Player:		.75
Minor Stars:		1.50
Production 3,000 Sets		
K1	David Boston	1.50
K2	Frank Sanders	.75
K3	Jamal Anderson	1.50
K4	Terance Mathis	.75
K5	Qadry Ismail	.75
K6	Eric Moulds	1.50
K7	Antowain Smith	1.50
K8	Patrick Jeffers	1.50
K9	Muhsin Muhammad	.75
K10	Curtis Enis	1.50
K11	Marcus Robinson	1.50
K12	Corey Dillon	1.50
K13	Kevin Johnson	1.50
K14	Joey Galloway	1.50
K15	Raghib Ismail	.75
K16	Emmitt Smith	5.00
K17	Olandis Gary	1.50
K18	Ed McCaffrey	1.50
K19	Germane Crowell	1.50
K20	Herman Moore	1.50
K21	Antonio Freeman	1.50
K22	Dorsey Levens	1.50
K23	Marvin Harrison	1.50
K24	Edgerrin James	6.00
K25	Keenan McCardell	.75
K26	Jimmy Smith	1.50
K27	Fred Taylor	2.00
K28	Cris Carter	1.50
K29	Randy Moss	6.00
K30	Robert Smith	1.50
K31	Terry Glenn	1.50
K32	Ricky Williams	4.00
K33	Curtis Martin	1.50
K34	Tim Brown	1.50
K35	Duce Staley	1.50
K36	Jerome Bettis	1.50
K37	Isaac Bruce	1.50
K38	Marshall Faulk	1.50
K39	Torry Holt	1.50
K40	Charlie Garner	.75
K41	Terrell Owens	1.50
K42	Ricky Watters	.75
K43	Warrick Dunn	1.50
K44	Keyshawn Johnson	1.50
K45	Kevin Dyson	.75
K46	Eddie George	1.75
K47	Carl Pickens	.75
K48	Albert Connell	.75
K49	Stephen Davis	1.50
K50	Michael Westbrook	1.50

2000 Collector's Edge Masters Legends

		MT
Complete Set (30):		35.00
Common Player:		.50
Minor Stars:		1.00
Production 5,000 Sets		
ML1	Jake Plummer	1.00
ML2	Eric Moulds	1.00
ML3	Cade McNown	1.00
ML4	Marcus Robinson	1.00
ML5	Akili Smith	1.00
ML6	Tim Couch	2.00
ML7	Troy Aikman	3.50
ML8	Emmitt Smith	4.00
ML9	Terrell Davis	4.00
ML10	Brett Favre	6.00
ML11	Antonio Freeman	1.00
ML12	Dorsey Levens	.50
ML13	Mark Brunell	2.00
ML14	Fred Taylor	1.75
ML15	Cris Carter	1.00
ML16	Randy Moss	5.00
ML17	Drew Bledsoe	2.50
ML18	Curtis Martin	1.00
ML19	Donovan McNabb	2.00
ML20	Ricky Williams	2.50
ML21	Jerome Bettis	1.00
ML22	Isaac Bruce	1.00
ML23	Marshall Faulk	1.00
ML24	Jerry Rice	3.50
ML25	Jon Kitna	1.00
ML26	Keyshawn Johnson	1.00
ML27	Shaun King	1.50
ML28	Steve McNair	1.00
ML29	Stephen Davis	1.00
ML30	Brad Johnson	1.00

2000 Collector's Edge Masters Majestic

		MT
Complete Set (30):		45.00
Common Player:		.50
Minor Stars:		1.00
Production 5,000 Sets		
M1	Thomas Jones	3.00
M2	Jamal Lewis	10.00
M3	Travis Taylor	2.00
M4	Brian Urlacher	5.00
M5	Dez White	1.00
M6	Danny Farmer	1.00
M7	Curtis Keaton	.50
M8	Peter Warrick	7.00
M9	Courtney Brown	1.50
M10	JaJuan Dawson	1.50
M11	Spergon Wynn	1.50
M12	Michael Wiley	1.00
M13	Reuben Droughns	.50
M14	Bubba Franks	1.50
M15	Rob Morris	.50
M16	Sylvester Morris	3.50
M17	Ron Dayne	8.50
M18	Ron Dixon	1.50
M19	Anthony Becht	1.00
M20	Chad Pennington	6.00
M21	Sebastian Janikowski	1.00
M22	Todd Pinkston	1.00
M23	Corey Simon	1.00
M24	Plaxico Burress	3.50
M25	Tee Martin	1.00
M26	Trevor Gaylor	1.00
M27	Giovanni Carmazzi	1.50
M28	Tim Rattay	1.50
M29	Shaun Alexander	5.00
M30	Joe Hamilton	1.50

2000 Collector's Edge Masters Rookie Masters

		MT
Complete Set (30):		75.00
Common Player:		1.00
Minor Stars:		2.00
Production 2,000 Sets		
MR1	Thomas Jones	3.00
MR2	Jamal Lewis	10.00
MR3	Chris Redman	3.00
MR4	Travis Taylor	2.50
MR5	Dez White	2.00
MR6	Ron Dugans	2.00
MR7	Curtis Keaton	1.00
MR8	Peter Warrick	7.00
MR9	Brian Urlacher	5.00
MR10	JaJuan Dawson	2.00
MR11	Dennis Northcutt	2.00
MR12	Travis Prentice	2.50
MR13	Spergon Wynn	2.00
MR14	Reuben Droughns	1.00
MR15	Bubba Franks	2.00
MR16	Sylvester Morris	3.50
MR17	J.R. Redmond	2.50
MR18	Ron Dayne	8.50
MR19	Anthony Becht	2.00
MR20	Laveranues Coles	2.00
MR21	Chad Pennington	6.00
MR22	Jerry Porter	2.00
MR23	Todd Pinkston	2.00
MR24	Plaxico Burress	3.50
MR25	Tee Martin	2.00
MR26	Trung Canidate	1.00
MR27	Giovanni Carmazzi	2.00
MR28	Tim Rattay	2.00
MR29	Shaun Alexander	5.00
MR30	Joe Hamilton	2.00

2000 Collector's Edge Masters Rookie Sentinels

		MT
Complete Set (30):		120.00
Common Player:		1.50
Minor Stars:		3.00
Production 1,000 Sets		
RS1	Thomas Jones	4.50
RS2	Jamal Lewis	15.00
RS3	Chris Redman	4.50
RS4	Travis Taylor	3.50
RS5	Ron Dugans	3.00
RS6	Peter Warrick	10.00
RS7	Courtney Brown	3.00
RS8	Dennis Northcutt	3.00
RS9	Travis Prentice	4.00
RS10	Bubba Franks	3.00
RS11	R. Jay Soward	3.00
RS12	Sylvester Morris	5.00
RS13	J.R. Redmond	3.50
RS14	Ron Dayne	12.50
RS15	Laveranues Coles	3.00
RS16	Chad Pennington	8.00
RS17	Jerry Porter	3.00
RS18	Plaxico Burress	5.00
RS19	Trung Canidate	3.00
RS20	Shaun Alexander	7.50
RS21	Mike Anderson	12.50
RS22	Danny Farmer	3.00
RS23	Brian Urlacher	7.50
RS24	Michael Wiley	1.50
RS25	Rob Morris	1.50
RS26	Corey Simon	3.00
RS27	Sebastian Janikowski	3.00
RS28	Sammy Morris	3.00
RS29	Keith Bulluck	1.50
RS30	Frank Moreau	3.00

2000 Collector's Edge Masters Sentinels

		MT
Complete Set (20):		75.00
Common Player:		3.00
Production 1,000 Sets		
S1	Jake Plummer	3.00
S2	Eric Moulds	3.00
S3	Cade McNown	3.00
S4	Akili Smith	3.00
S5	Tim Couch	5.00
S6	Kevin Johnson	3.00
S7	Troy Aikman	7.00
S8	Terrell Davis	8.00
S9	Brett Favre	12.00
S10	Edgerrin James	10.00
S11	Peyton Manning	10.00
S12	Daunte Culpepper	5.00
S13	Randy Moss	10.00
S14	Curtis Martin	3.00
S15	Donovan McNabb	4.00
S16	Ricky Williams	6.00
S17	Kurt Warner	12.00
S18	Jon Kitna	3.00
S19	Eddie George	4.00
S20	Brad Johnson	3.00

A player's name in *italic* type indicates a rookie card.

2000 Collector's Edge Odyssey

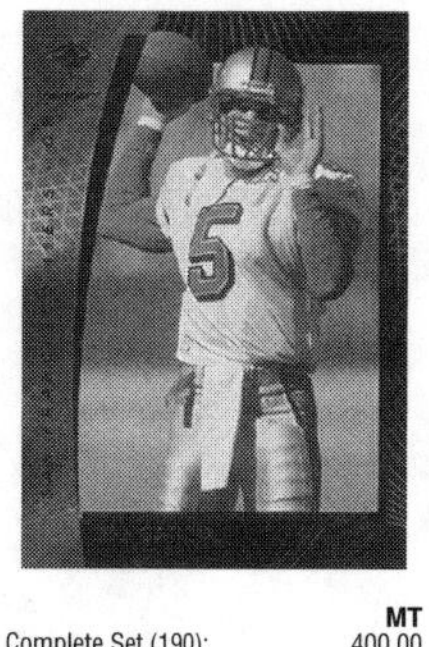

		MT
Complete Set (190):		400.00
Common Player:		.15
Minor Stars:		.30
Common Rookie:		3.50
Production 999 Sets		
Common Survivor/Last Man Standing:		1.50
Production 2,500 Sets		
Pack (5):		5.00
Wax Box (20):		70.00
1	David Boston	.50
2	Jake Plummer	.50
3	Frank Sanders	.30
4	Jamal Anderson	.50
5	Chris Chandler	.30
6	Terance Mathis	.15
7	Tony Banks	.30
8	Qadry Ismail	.15
9	Doug Flutie	.75
10	Rob Johnson	.30
11	Eric Moulds	.50
12	Peerless Price	.50
13	Antowain Smith	.30
14	Steve Beuerlein	.30
15	Tim Biakabutuka	.30
16	Muhsin Muhammad	.30
17	Curtis Enis	.50
18	Cade McNown	.75
19	Marcus Robinson	.50
20	Corey Dillon	.50
21	Akili Smith	.50
22	Tim Couch	1.25
23	Kevin Johnson	.50
24	Errict Rhett	.30
25	Troy Aikman	1.25
26	Joey Galloway	.50
27	Raghib Ismail	.30
28	Emmitt Smith	1.75
29	Terrell Davis	1.75
30	Olandis Gary	.60
31	Brian Griese	.75
32	Ed McCaffrey	.50
33	Charlie Batch	.50
34	Germane Crowell	.30
35	Herman Moore	.30
36	James Stewart	.30
37	Brett Favre	2.50
38	Antonio Freeman	.50
39	Dorsey Levens	.50
40	Marvin Harrison	.50
41	Edgerrin James	2.50
42	Peyton Manning	2.50
43	Terrence Wilkins	.50
44	Mark Brunell	1.00
45	Keenan McCardell	.30
46	Jimmy Smith	.50
47	Fred Taylor	1.00
48	Michael Cloud	.15
49	Tony Gonzalez	.30
50	Elvis Grbac	.30
51	Damon Huard	.50
52	J.J. Johnson	.30
53	Tony Martin	.15
54	Cris Carter	.50
55	Daunte Culpepper	1.25
56	Randy Moss	2.50
57	Robert Smith	.50
58	Drew Bledsoe	1.00
59	Terry Glenn	.50
60	Jeff Blake	.50
61	Ricky Williams	1.25
62	Kerry Collins	.30
63	Ike Hilliard	.30
64	Amani Toomer	.30
65	Wayne Chrebet	.50
66	Curtis Martin	.50
67	Vinny Testaverde	.30
68	Tim Brown	.50
69	Rich Gannon	.30
70	Donovan McNabb	1.00
71	Duce Staley	.50
72	Jerome Bettis	.50
73	Troy Edwards	.30
74	Kordell Stewart	.60
75	Isaac Bruce	.50
76	Marshall Faulk	.50
77	Torry Holt	.50
78	Kurt Warner	3.00
79	Jermaine Fazande	.30
80	Jim Harbaugh	.30
81	Jeff Garcia	.50
82	Charlie Garner	.30
83	Terrell Owens	.50
84	Jerry Rice	1.25
85	Jon Kitna	.50
86	Derrick Mayes	.30
87	Ricky Watters	.50
88	Mike Alstott	.50
89	Warrick Dunn	.50
90	Keyshawn Johnson	.50
91	Shaun King	1.00
92	Kevin Dyson	.30
93	Eddie George	.75
94	Jevon Kearse	.50
95	Steve McNair	.50
96	Carl Pickens	.30
97	Champ Bailey	.30
98	Stephen Davis	.50
99	Brad Johnson	.50
100	Michael Westbrook	.30
101	*Thomas Jones*	15.00
102	*Doug Johnson*	8.00
103	*Mareno Philyaw*	3.50
104	*Jamal Lewis*	35.00
105	*Chris Redman*	15.00
106	*Travis Taylor*	10.00
107	*Kwame Cavil*	5.00
108	*Sammy Morris*	8.00
109	*Frank Murphy*	3.50
110	*Brian Urlacher*	15.00
111	*Dez White*	6.00
112	*Ron Dugans*	6.00
113	*Curtis Keaton*	3.50
114	*Peter Warrick*	30.00
115	*Courtney Brown*	10.00
116	*JaJuan Dawson*	10.00
117	*Dennis Northcutt*	8.00
118	*Travis Prentice*	10.00
119	*Michael Wiley*	7.00
120	*Mike Anderson*	25.00
121	*Chris Cole*	5.00
122	*Jarious Jackson*	6.00
123	*Deltha O'Neal*	5.00
124	*Reuben Droughns*	7.00
125	*Bubba Franks*	10.00
126	*Anthony Lucas*	3.50
127	*Rondell Mealey*	5.00
128	*Rob Morris*	5.00
129	*R. Jay Soward*	7.00
130	*Shyrone Stith*	5.00
131	*Frank Moreau*	7.00
132	*Sylvester Morris*	15.00
133	*Doug Chapman*	6.00
134	*J.R. Redmond*	10.00
135	*Marc Bulger*	6.00
136	*Sherrod Gideon*	3.50
137	*Terrelle Smith*	5.00
138	*Ron Dayne*	35.00
139	*Anthony Becht*	7.00
140	*Laveranues Coles*	10.00
141	*Shaun Ellis*	5.00
142	*Chad Pennington*	25.00
143	*Sebastian Janikowski*	7.00
144	*Jerry Porter*	7.00
145	*Todd Pinkston*	7.00
146	*Gari Scott*	5.00
147	*Corey Simon*	7.00
148	*Plaxico Burress*	20.00
149	*Danny Farmer*	7.00
150	*Tee Martin*	10.00
151	*Trung Canidate*	7.00
152	*Trevor Gaylor*	5.00
153	*Giovanni Carmazzi*	10.00
154	*John Engelberger*	3.50
155	*Ahmed Plummer*	6.00
156	*Tim Rattay*	10.00
157	*Shaun Alexander*	20.00
158	*Joe Hamilton*	8.00
159	*Keith Bulluck*	3.50
160	*Todd Husak*	7.00
161	Cade McNown	2.00
162	Tim Couch	3.00
163	Terrell Davis	4.50
164	Brett Favre	6.00
165	Edgerrin James	6.00
166	Peyton Manning	6.00
167	Daunte Culpepper	3.00
168	Randy Moss	6.00
169	Ricky Williams	4.00
170	Kurt Warner	6.00
171	Cade McNown	2.00
172	Akili Smith	1.50
173	Tim Couch	3.00
174	Troy Aikman	3.50
175	Emmitt Smith	4.50
176	Terrell Davis	4.50
177	Brett Favre	6.00
178	Edgerrin James	6.00
179	Peyton Manning	6.00
180	Mark Brunell	2.50
181	Daunte Culpepper	3.00
182	Randy Moss	6.00
183	Drew Bledsoe	2.50
184	Ricky Williams	4.00
185	Donovan McNabb	2.00
186	Torry Holt	1.50
187	Kurt Warner	6.00
188	Shaun King	2.00
189	Eddie George	1.75
190	Steve McNair	1.50

2000 Collector's Edge Odyssey Hologold Rookies

	MT
Complete Set (60):	325.00
Hologold Rookies:	1x
Production 500 Sets	

2000 Collector's Edge Odyssey GameGear

		MT
Common Player:		20.00
SA	Shaun Alexander	160.00
AB	Anthony Becht	20.00
PB	Plaxico Burress	75.00
TC	Trung Canidate	20.00
LC	Laveranues Coles	75.00
RD	Ron Dayne	75.00
RD	Reuben Droughns	20.00
RD	Ron Dugans	20.00
DF	Danny Farmer	20.00
BF	Bubba Franks	60.00
JH	Joe Hamilton	20.00
TJ	Thomas Jones	50.00
CK	Curtis Keaton	25.00
JL	Jamal Lewis	140.00
TM	Tee Martin	40.00
SM	Sylvester Morris	40.00
DN	Dennis Northcutt	20.00
CP	Chad Pennington	125.00
TP	Todd Pinkston	20.00
JP	Jerry Porter	40.00
TP	Travis Prentice	20.00
CR	Chris Redman	60.00
JR	J.R. Redmond	20.00
CS	Corey Simon	20.00
RS	R. Jay Soward	20.00
TT	Travis Taylor	50.00
BU	Brian Urlacher	160.00
PW	Peter Warrick	100.00
DW	Dez White	50.00

A card number in parentheses ( ) indicates the set is unnumbered.

2000 Collector's Edge Odyssey Old School

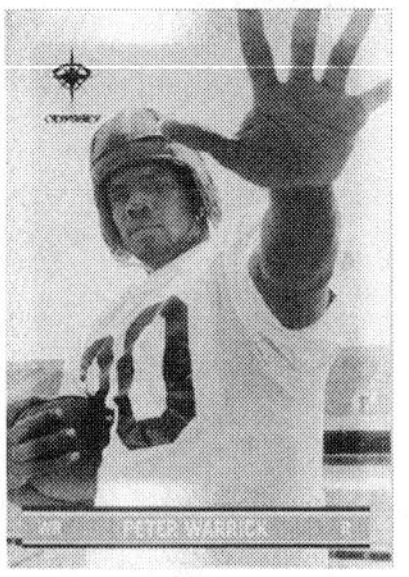

		MT
Complete Set (30):		30.00
Common Player:		.50
Minor Stars:		1.00
Inserted 1:6		
OS1	Thomas Jones	2.00
OS2	Jamal Lewis	4.00
OS3	Chris Redman	1.75
OS4	Travis Taylor	1.50
OS5	Brian Urlacher	2.00
OS6	Dez White	1.00
OS7	Ron Dugans	1.00
OS8	Curtis Keaton	.50
OS9	Peter Warrick	4.00
OS10	Courtney Brown	1.25
OS11	Dennis Northcutt	1.25
OS12	Travis Prentice	1.50
OS13	Reuben Droughns	1.00
OS14	Bubba Franks	1.25
OS15	R. Jay Soward	1.00
OS16	Sylvester Morris	1.50
OS17	J.R. Redmond	1.25
OS18	Ron Dayne	5.00
OS19	Anthony Becht	1.00
OS20	Laveranues Coles	1.25
OS21	Chad Pennington	3.50
OS22	Jerry Porter	1.00
OS23	Todd Pinkston	1.00
OS24	Corey Simon	1.00
OS25	Plaxico Burress	2.50
OS26	Danny Farmer	1.00
OS27	Tee Martin	1.50
OS28	Trung Canidate	1.00
OS29	Shaun Alexander	3.00
OS30	Joe Hamilton	1.25

2000 Collector's Edge Odyssey Restaurant Quality

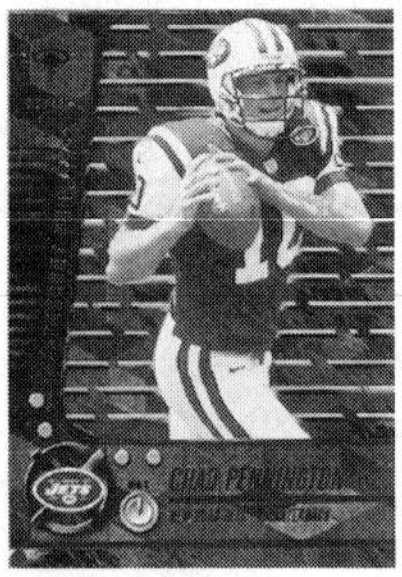

		MT
Complete Set (10):		20.00
Common Player:		1.50
Inserted 1:20		
RQ1	Thomas Jones	2.50
RQ2	Jamal Lewis	5.00
RQ3	Travis Taylor	2.00
RQ4	Peter Warrick	4.00
RQ5	Bubba Franks	1.50
RQ6	Sylvester Morris	2.00
RQ7	Ron Dayne	5.00
RQ8	Chad Pennington	3.50
RQ9	Plaxico Burress	3.00
RQ10	Shaun Alexander	3.50

2000 Collector's Edge Odyssey Rookie Ink

		MT
Common Player:		10.00
Inserted 1:99		
PB	Plaxico Burress	40.00
TC	Trung Canidate	10.00
LC	Laveranues Coles	20.00
TJ	Thomas Jones	40.00
CK	Curtis Keaton	10.00
JL	Jamal Lewis	65.00
SM	Sylvester Morris	35.00
DN	Dennis Northcutt	10.00
CP	Chad Pennington	50.00
TP	Todd Pinkston	10.00
TP	Travis Prentice	25.00
CR	Chris Redman	35.00
JR	J.R. Redmond	30.00
TT	Travis Taylor	30.00
BU	Brian Urlacher	30.00

Post-1980 cards in Near Mint condition will generally sell for about 75% of the quoted Mint value. Excellent-condition cards bring no more than 40%.

2000 Collector's Edge Odyssey Tight

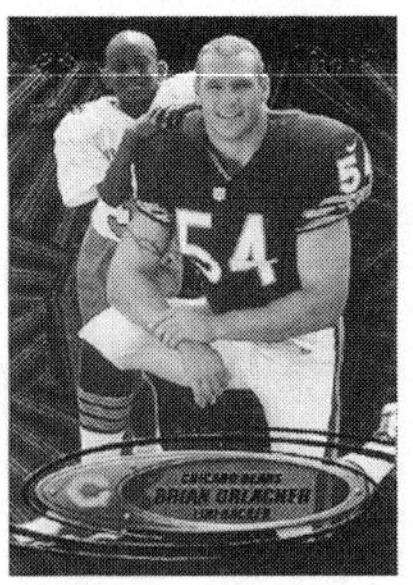

		MT
Complete Set (30):		40.00
Common Player:		.75
Minor Stars:		1.50
Inserted 1:10		
T1	Thomas Jones	3.00
T2	Jamal Lewis	6.00
T3	Chris Redman	3.00
T4	Travis Taylor	2.50
T5	Brian Urlacher	3.00
T6	Dez White	1.50
T7	Ron Dugans	1.50
T8	Curtis Keaton	.75
T9	Peter Warrick	5.00
T10	Courtney Brown	1.75
T11	Dennis Northcutt	1.75
T12	Travis Prentice	2.50
T13	Reuben Droughns	1.50
T14	Bubba Franks	1.75
T15	R. Jay Soward	1.50
T16	Sylvester Morris	2.50
T17	J.R. Redmond	2.00
T18	Ron Dayne	6.00
T19	Anthony Becht	1.50
T20	Laveranues Coles	1.75
T21	Chad Pennington	4.50
T22	Jerry Porter	1.50
T23	Todd Pinkston	1.50
T24	Corey Simon	1.50
T25	Plaxico Burress	3.50
T26	Danny Farmer	1.50
T27	Tee Martin	2.00
T28	Trung Canidate	1.50
T29	Shaun Alexander	4.00
T30	Joe Hamilton	1.75

2000 Collector's Edge Odyssey Wasssuppp

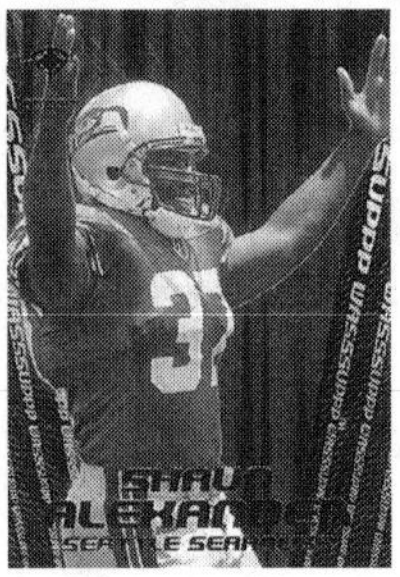

		MT
Complete Set (20):		25.00
Common Player:		1.00
Inserted 1:10		
W1	Thomas Jones	2.50
W2	Jamal Lewis	5.00
W3	Travis Taylor	1.50
W4	Ron Dugans	1.00
W5	Peter Warrick	4.00
W6	Dez White	1.00
W7	Dennis Northcutt	1.25
W8	Travis Prentice	1.50
W9	Bubba Franks	1.50
W10	R. Jay Soward	1.00
W11	Sylvester Morris	1.75
W12	J.R. Redmond	1.50
W13	Ron Dayne	5.00
W14	Laveranues Coles	1.25
W15	Chad Pennington	3.50
W16	Jerry Porter	1.00
W17	Todd Pinkston	1.00
W18	Plaxico Burress	3.00
W19	Danny Farmer	1.00
W20	Shaun Alexander	3.00

2000 Collector's Edge Supreme

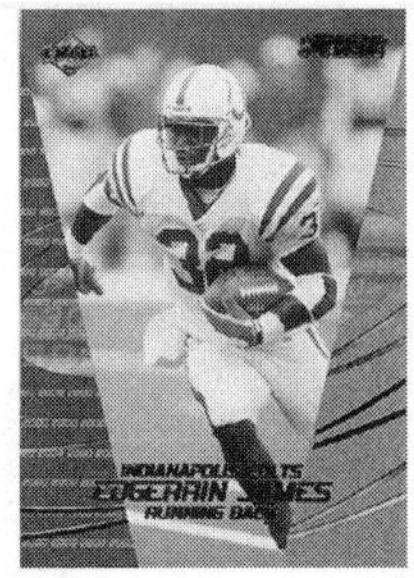

		MT
Complete Set (190):		175.00
Common Player:		.10
Minor Stars:		.20
Common Rookie:		4.00
Production 2,000 Sets		
Pack (10):		3.00
Wax Box (24):		60.00
1	David Boston	.50
2	Adrian Murrell	.20
3	Michael Pittman	.10
4	Jake Plummer	.50
5	Frank Sanders	.10
6	Jamal Anderson	.30
7	Chris Chandler	.20
8	Terance Mathis	.10
9	Justin Armour	.10
10	Tony Banks	.20
11	Qadry Ismail	.10
12	Errict Rhett	.20
13	Doug Flutie	.75
14	Eric Moulds	.50
15	Peerless Price	.50
16	Andre Reed	.20
17	Antowain Smith	.30
18	Steve Beuerlein	.20
19	Tim Biakabutuka	.20
20	Muhsin Muhammad	.20
21	Wesley Walls	.20
22	Bobby Engram	.10
23	Curtis Enis	.30
24	Shane Matthews	.10
25	Cade McNown	.75
26	Jim Miller	.10
27	Marcus Robinson	.50
28	Corey Dillon	.50
29	Carl Pickens	.20
30	Darnay Scott	.20
31	Akili Smith	.75
32	Karim Abdul	.20
33	Tim Couch	1.25
34	Kevin Johnson	.50
35	Troy Aikman	1.25
36	Michael Irvin	.20
37	Raghib Ismail	.10
38	Deion Sanders	.30
39	Emmitt Smith	1.50
40	Terrell Davis	1.50
41	Olandis Gary	.75
42	Brian Griese	.50
43	Ed McCaffrey	.20
44	Rod Smith	.20
45	Charlie Batch	.50
46	Germane Crowell	.20
47	Greg Hill	.10
48	Sedrick Irvin	.20
49	Herman Moore	.30
50	Johnnie Morton	.10
51	Corey Bradford	.20
52	Brett Favre	2.50
53	Antonio Freeman	.30
54	Dorsey Levens	.30
55	Bill Schroeder	.10
56	E.G. Green	.10
57	Marvin Harrison	.50
58	Edgerrin James	2.50
59	Peyton Manning	1.50
60	Terrence Wilkins	.10
61	Mark Brunell	.75
62	Keenan McCardell	.20
63	Jimmy Smith	.30
64	James Stewart	.20
65	Fred Taylor	.75
66	Derrick Alexander	.10
67	Donnell Bennett	.10
68	Michael Cloud	.10
69	Tony Gonzalez	.30
70	Elvis Grbac	.20
71	Damon Huard	.20
72	J.J. Johnson	.10
73	Rob Konrad	.10
74	Dan Marino	1.50
75	Tony Martin	.10
76	O.J. McDuffie	.20
77	Cris Carter	.50
78	Daunte Culpepper	.75
79	Jeff George	.50
80	Randy Moss	2.00
81	Robert Smith	.30
82	Terry Allen	.20
83	Drew Bledsoe	.75
84	Kevin Faulk	.30
85	Terry Glenn	.30
86	Shawn Jefferson	.10
87	Billy Joe Hobert	.10
88	Eddie Kennison	.20
89	Billy Joe Tolliver	.10
90	Ricky Williams	1.25
91	Tiki Barber	.20
92	Gary Brown	.10
93	Kent Graham	.10
94	Ike Hilliard	.20
95	Amani Toomer	.20
96	Wayne Chrebet	.30
97	Keyshawn Johnson	.50
98	Ray Lucas	.30
99	Curtis Martin	.50
100	Vinny Testaverde	.30
101	Tim Brown	.30
102	Rich Gannon	.20
103	James Jett	.10
104	Napoleon Kaufman	.30
105	Tyrone Wheatley	.20
106	Charles Johnson	.10
107	Donovan McNabb	.75
108	Duce Staley	.30
109	Jerome Bettis	.30
110	Troy Edwards	.50
111	Kordell Stewart	.50
112	Hines Ward	.20
113	Isaac Bruce	.50
114	Marshall Faulk	.50
115	Az-Zahir Hakim	.20
116	Torry Holt	.50
117	Kurt Warner	2.50
118	Jeff Graham	.10
119	Jim Harbaugh	.20
120	Freddie Jones	.10
121	Natrone Means	.20
122	Junior Seau	.20
123	Jeff Garcia	.50
124	Charlie Garner	.20
125	Terrell Owens	.50
126	Jerry Rice	1.25
127	Steve Young	.75
128	Sean Dawkins	.10
129	Joey Galloway	.50
130	Jon Kitna	.50
131	Derrick Mayes	.30
132	Ricky Watters	.20
133	Mike Alstott	.50
134	Reidel Anthony	.20
135	Trent Dilfer	.20
136	Warrick Dunn	.50
137	Jacquez Green	.20
138	Shaun King	.75
139	Kevin Dyson	.20
140	Eddie George	.50
141	Jevon Kearse	.50
142	Steve McNair	.50
143	Yancey Thigpen	.20
144	Champ Bailey	.30
145	Albert Connell	.20
146	Stephen Davis	.50
147	Brad Johnson	.50
148	Michael Westbrook	.30
149	Checklist	.10
150	Checklist	.10
151	Redemption	8.00
152	*Peter Warrick*	20.00
153	*Chad Pennington*	18.00
154	*Courtney Brown*	8.00
155	*Thomas Jones*	12.00
156	*Chris Redman*	12.00
157	*R. Jay Soward*	6.00
158	*Jamal Lewis*	30.00
159	*Shaun Alexander*	15.00
160	*Travis Taylor*	8.00
161	*Ron Dayne*	25.00
162	*Travis Prentice*	10.00
163	*Plaxico Burress*	12.50
164	*J.R. Redmond*	8.00
165	*Sherrod Gideon*	4.00
166	*Dez White*	6.00
167	*Chafie Fields*	4.00
168	*(Brandon Short)*	8.00
169	*Reuben Droughns*	6.00
170	*Trung Canidate*	6.00
171	Redemption	8.00
172	Redemption	8.00
173	*Shyrone Stith*	4.00
174	*Michael Wiley*	6.00
175	*Bubba Franks*	8.00
176	*Tom Brady*	6.00
177	*Anthony Lucas*	4.00
178	*Danny Farmer*	6.00
179	*Rob Morris*	4.00
180	*Dennis Northcutt*	8.00
181	*Troy Walters*	6.00
182	*Giovanni Carmazzi*	8.00
183	*Tee Martin*	8.00
184	*Joe Hamilton*	6.00
185	*Tim Rattay*	8.00
186	*Sebastian Janikowski*	6.00
187	*Na'il Diggs*	4.00
188	*Todd Husak*	4.00
189	*Jerry Porter*	6.00
190	Redemption	8.00

2000 Collector's Edge Supreme Hologold Parallel

	MT
Hologold Cards:	5x-10x
Production 200 Sets	
Hologold Rookies:	3x-6x
Production 20 Sets	

2000 Collector's Edge Supreme Edge Tech

		MT
Common Player:		7.00
Production 100 Sets		
ET1	Doug Flutie	10.00
ET2	Cade McNown	10.00
ET3	Akili Smith	10.00
ET4	Tim Couch	15.00
ET5	Kevin Johnson	7.00
ET6	Troy Aikman	15.00
ET7	Emmitt Smith	20.00
ET8	Terrell Davis	20.00
ET9	Brett Favre	30.00
ET10	Marvin Harrison	7.00
ET11	Edgerrin James	30.00
ET12	Peyton Manning	25.00
ET13	Mark Brunell	10.00
ET14	Dan Marino	25.00
ET15	Randy Moss	30.00
ET16	Drew Bledsoe	10.00
ET17	Ricky Williams	15.00
ET18	Keyshawn Johnson	7.00
ET19	Curtis Martin	7.00
ET20	Donovan McNabb	10.00
ET21	Marshall Faulk	7.00
ET22	Torry Holt	7.00
ET23	Kurt Warner	40.00
ET24	Jerry Rice	15.00
ET25	Steve Young	10.00
ET26	Jon Kitna	7.00
ET27	Shaun King	10.00
ET28	Eddie George	10.00
ET29	Stephen Davis	7.00
ET30	Brad Johnson	7.00
ET31	Chad Pennington	30.00
ET32	Chris Redman	20.00
ET33	Tim Rattay	12.00
ET34	Tee Martin	15.00
ET35	Thomas Jones	30.00
ET36	Ron Dayne	40.00
ET37	Jamal Lewis	30.00
ET38	J.R. Redmond	15.00
ET39	Travis Prentice	12.00
ET40	Shaun Alexander	25.00
ET41	Michael Wiley	12.00
ET42	Shyrone Stith	7.00
ET43	Peter Warrick	50.00
ET44	Plaxico Burress	30.00
ET45	Travis Taylor	20.00
ET46	Jerry Porter	15.00
ET47	R. Jay Soward	15.00
ET48	Dez White	12.00
ET49	TBA	7.00
ET50	Courtney Brown	20.00

2000 Collector's Edge Supreme Future

		MT
Common Player:		10.00
Production 100 Sets		
SF1	Peter Warrick	50.00
SF2	Plaxico Burress	30.00
SF3	R. Jay Soward	10.00
SF4	Ron Dayne	40.00
SF5	Thomas Jones	30.00
SF6	Shaun Alexander	25.00
SF7	Chad Pennington	30.00
SF8	Chris Redman	20.00
SF9	Travis Prentice	10.00
SF10	TBA	10.00

2000 Collector's Edge Supreme Monday Knights

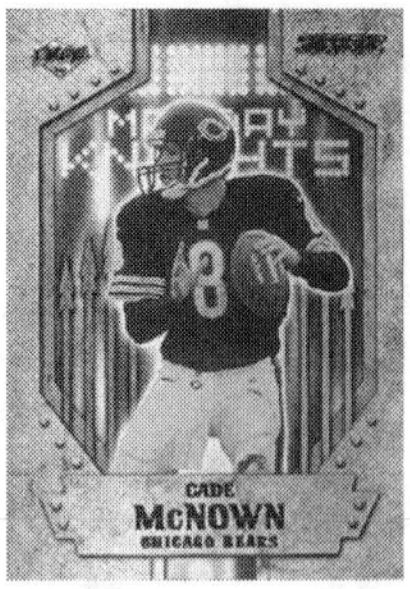

		MT
Complete Set (20):		25.00
Common Player:		1.00
Inserted 1:8		
MK1	Jake Plummer	1.50
MK2	Doug Flutie	1.50
MK3	Cade McNown	1.50
MK4	Akili Smith	1.00
MK5	Tim Couch	2.50
MK6	Kevin Johnson	1.00
MK7	Troy Aikman	2.50
MK8	Emmitt Smith	3.50
MK9	Terrell Davis	3.50
MK10	Charlie Batch	1.00
MK11	Brett Favre	5.00
MK12	Cris Carter	1.00
MK13	Drew Bledsoe	2.00
MK14	Ricky Williams	2.50
MK15	Curtis Martin	1.00
MK16	Jerry Rice	2.50
MK17	Jon Kitna	1.00
MK18	Shaun King	1.50
MK19	Eddie George	1.25
MK20	Brad Johnson	1.00

2000 Collector's Edge Supreme Pro Signature Authentics

		MT
Complete Set (7):		
Common Player:		
TC	Tim Couch	
JJ	J.J. Johnson	
DM	Darnell McDonald	
PM	Peyton Manning	
CM	Cade McNown	
RM	Randy Moss	
RW	Ricky Williams	

2000 Collector's Edge Supreme PSA Redemption

		MT
Common Player:		50.00
Production 100 Sets		
1	Peter Warrick	150.00
2	Plaxico Burress	100.00
3	R. Jay Soward	50.00
4	Ron Dayne	125.00
5	Thomas Jones	100.00
6	Shaun Alexander	85.00
7	Chad Pennington	100.00
8	Chris Redman	75.00
9	Travis Prentice	50.00
10	TBA	50.00

2000 Collector's Edge Supreme Route XXXIV

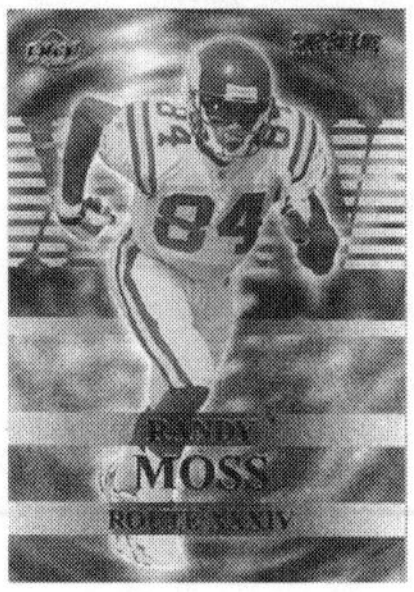

		MT
Complete Set (10):		20.00
Common Player:		1.00
Inserted 1:16		
R1	Peyton Manning	3.50
R2	Edgerrin James	4.00
R3	Warrick Dunn	1.00
R4	Dan Marino	3.50
R5	Steve McNair	1.00
R6	Mark Brunell	1.50
R7	Kurt Warner	6.00
R8	Marshall Faulk	1.00
R9	Randy Moss	4.00
R10	Stephen Davis	1.00

A player's name in *italic type* indicates a rookie card.

2000 Collector's Edge Supreme Team

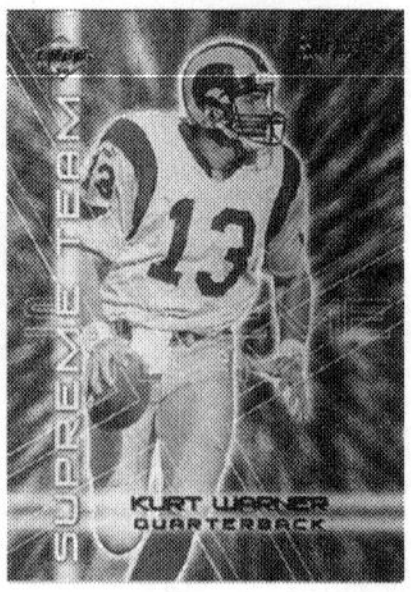

		MT
Complete Set (20):		30.00
Common Player:		1.00
Inserted 1:8		
ST1	Peyton Manning	3.50
ST2	Kurt Warner	6.00
ST3	Tim Couch	2.50
ST4	Cade McNown	1.50
ST5	Akili Smith	1.00
ST6	Donovan McNabb	1.50
ST7	Edgerrin James	4.00
ST8	Stephen Davis	1.00
ST9	Mark Brunell	1.50
ST10	Brett Favre	5.00
ST11	Marvin Harrison	1.00
ST12	Isaac Bruce	1.00
ST13	Terrell Davis	3.50
ST14	Ricky Williams	2.50
ST15	Keyshawn Johnson	1.00
ST16	Randy Moss	4.00
ST17	Kevin Johnson	1.00
ST18	Torry Holt	1.00
ST19	Dan Marino	3.50
ST20	Troy Aikman	2.50

2000 Collector's Edge T-3

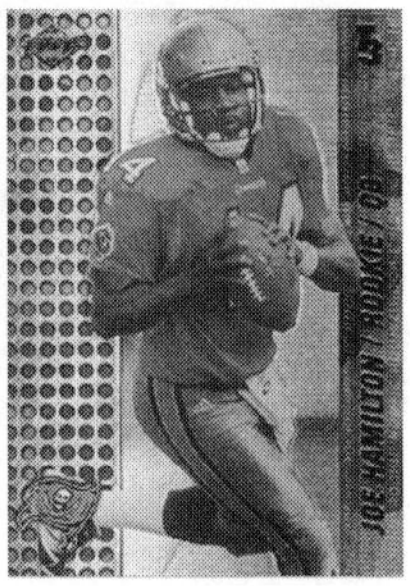

		MT
Complete Set (225):		850.00
Common Player:		.15
Minor Stars:		.30
Common Rookie:		6.00
Production 999 Sets		
Pack (5):		5.00
Wax Box (20):		80.00
1	David Boston	.50
2	Rob Moore	.30
3	Michael Pittman	.15
4	Jake Plummer	.50
5	Frank Sanders	.30
6	Jamal Anderson	.50
7	Chris Chandler	.30
8	Tim Dwight	.50
9	Shawn Jefferson	.15
10	Terance Mathis	.15
11	Tony Banks	.30
12	Priest Holmes	.50
13	Qadry Ismail	.15
14	Shannon Sharpe	.30
15	Doug Flutie	.75
16	Rob Johnson	.30
17	Eric Moulds	.50
18	Peerless Price	.50
19	Antowain Smith	.30
20	Steve Beuerlein	.30
21	Tim Biakabutuka	.30
22	Muhsin Muhammad	.30
23	Patrick Jeffers	.50
24	Wesley Walls	.15
25	Bobby Engram	.15
26	Curtis Enis	.30
27	Cade McNown	1.00
28	Marcus Robinson	.50
29	Corey Dillon	.50
30	Carl Pickens	.30
31	Darnay Scott	.30
32	Akili Smith	.50
33	Tim Couch	1.50
34	Kevin Johnson	.50
35	Errict Rhett	.30
36	Troy Aikman	1.25
37	Joey Galloway	.50
38	Raghib Ismail	.15
39	Emmitt Smith	1.75
40	Chris Warren	.15
41	Terrell Davis	1.75
42	Olandis Gary	.60
43	Brian Griese	.75
44	Ed McCaffrey	.30
45	Rod Smith	.30
46	Charlie Batch	.50
47	Germane Crowell	.50
48	Sedrick Irvin	.15
49	Herman Moore	.50
50	Johnnie Morton	.30
51	James Stewart	.30
52	Brett Favre	2.50
53	Antonio Freeman	.50
54	Dorsey Levens	.50

55 Bill Schroeder .30
56 Ken Dilger .15
57 Marvin Harrison .50
58 Edgerrin James 2.50
59 Peyton Manning 2.00
60 Terrence Wilkins .30
61 Mark Brunell 1.00
62 Keenan McCardell .30
63 Jimmy Smith .50
64 Fred Taylor 1.00
65 Derrick Alexander .15
66 Donnell Bennett .15
67 Michael Cloud .15
68 Tony Gonzalez .30
69 Elvis Grbac .30
70 Tony Richardson .15
71 Damon Huard .30
72 J.J. Johnson .30
73 Rob Konrad .15
74 Tony Martin .15
75 O.J. McDuffie .30
76 Cris Carter .50
77 Daunte Culpepper 1.25
78 Randy Moss 2.00
79 Robert Smith .50
80 Drew Bledsoe 1.00
81 Kevin Faulk .50
82 Terry Glenn .50
83 Willie McGinest .15
84 Tony Simmons .15
85 Jeff Blake .30
86 Jake Reed .15
87 Ricky Williams 1.50
88 Kerry Collins .30
89 Ike Hilliard .15
90 Joe Montgomery .15
91 Amani Toomer .15
92 Wayne Chrebet .30
93 Ray Lucas .30
94 Curtis Martin .50
95 Vinny Testaverde .50
96 Tim Brown .30
97 Rich Gannon .30
98 James Jett .15
99 Napoleon Kaufman .30
100 Tyrone Wheatley .30
101 Charles Woodson .30
102 Charles Johnson .15
103 Donovan McNabb 1.00
104 Duce Staley .50
105 Jerome Bettis .50
106 Troy Edwards .50
107 Kent Graham .15
108 Kordell Stewart .50
109 Hines Ward .30
110 Isaac Bruce .50
111 Kevin Carter .15
112 Marshall Faulk .50
113 Trent Green .30
114 Az-Zahir Hakim .30
115 Torry Holt .50
116 Kurt Warner 3.00
117 Curtis Conway .30
118 Jermaine Fazande .30
119 Jeff Graham .15
120 Jim Harbaugh .30
121 Junior Seau .30
122 Jeff Garcia .50
123 Charlie Garner .30
124 Garrison Hearst .30
125 Terrell Owens .50
126 Jerry Rice 1.25
127 Steve Young 1.00
128 Sean Dawkins .15
129 Jon Kitna .50
130 Derrick Mayes .30
131 Ricky Watters .30
132 Mike Alstott .50
133 Warrick Dunn .50
134 Jacquez Green .30
135 Keyshawn Johnson .50
136 Shaun King 1.00
137 Warren Sapp .30
138 Kevin Dyson .30
139 Eddie George .75
140 Jevon Kearse .50
141 Steve McNair .60
142 Yancey Thigpen .30
143 Frank Wycheck .15
144 Champ Bailey .30
145 Larry Centers .15
146 Albert Connell .30
147 Stephen Davis .50
148 Jeff George .50
149 Brad Johnson .50
150 Michael Westbrook .30
151 *Thomas Jones* 35.00
152 *Doug Johnson* 6.00
153 *Mareno Philyaw* 6.00
154 *Jamal Lewis* 75.00
155 *Chris Redman* 30.00
156 *Travis Taylor* 20.00
157 *Kwame Cavil* 6.00
158 *Sammy Morris* 18.00
159 *Deon Grant* 6.00
160 *Frank Murphy* 6.00
161 *Brian Urlacher* 40.00
162 *Dez White* 12.00
163 *Ron Dugans* 12.00
164 *Curtis Keaton* 12.00
165 *Peter Warrick* 50.00
166 *Courtney Brown* 15.00
167 *JaJuan Dawson* 12.00
168 *Dennis Northcutt* 12.00
169 *Travis Prentice* 20.00
170 *Michael Wiley* 10.00
171 *Mike Anderson* 75.00
172 *Chris Cole* 6.00
173 *Jarious Jackson* 10.00
174 *Deltha O'Neal* 6.00
175 *Reuben Droughns* 10.00
176 *Na'il Diggs* 6.00
177 *Bubba Franks* 12.00
178 *Anthony Lucas* 10.00
179 *Rondell Mealey* 10.00
180 *Dan Kendra* 6.00
181 *Rob Morris* 10.00
182 *R. Jay Soward* 12.00
183 *Shyrone Stith* 10.00
184 *Frank Moreau* 12.00
185 *Sylvester Morris* 35.00
186 *Deon Dyer* 6.00
187 *Quinton Spotwood* 10.00
188 *Doug Chapman* 6.00
189 *Troy Walters* 10.00
190 *J.R. Redmond* 20.00
191 *Marc Bulger* 6.00
192 *Sherrod Gideon* 10.00
193 *Darren Howard* 6.00
194 *Chad Morton* 10.00
195 *Terrelle Smith* 6.00
196 *Ron Dayne* 50.00
197 *John Abraham* 6.00
198 *Anthony Becht* 10.00
199 *Laveranues Coles* 20.00
200 *Shaun Ellis* 6.00
201 *Chad Pennington* 40.00
202 *Sebastian Janikowski* 12.00
203 *Jerry Porter* 12.00
204 *Todd Pinkston* 12.00
205 *Corey Simon* 12.00
206 *Plaxico Burress* 35.00
207 *Danny Farmer* 10.00
208 *Tee Martin* 12.00
209 *Hank Poteat* 6.00
210 *Trung Canidate* 10.00
211 *Jacoby Shepherd* 6.00
212 *Trevor Gaylor* 12.00
213 *Giovanni Carmazzi* 15.00
214 *John Engelberger* 6.00
215 *Chafie Fields* 6.00
216 *Julian Peterson* 6.00
217 *Ahmed Plummer* 10.00
218 *Tim Rattay* 15.00
219 *Paul Smith* 6.00
220 *Shaun Alexander* 40.00
221 *Joe Hamilton* 12.00
222 *Keith Bulluck* 6.00
223 *Erron Kinney* 6.00
224 *Todd Husak* 10.00
225 *Chris Samuels* 10.00

2000 Collector's Edge T-3 HoloPlatinum Parallel

MT
Platinum Cards: 3x-6x
Platinum Rookies: 1x
Production 500 Sets

2000 Collector's Edge T-3 HoloRed Parallel

MT
Red Cards: 15x-30x
Red Rookies: 2x
Production 50 Sets

2000 Collector's Edge T-3 Adrenaline

MT
Complete Set (20): 20.00
Common Player: 1.00
Inserted 1:10
A1 Doug Flutie 1.50
A2 Troy Aikman 2.50
A3 Emmitt Smith 3.00
A4 Terrell Davis 3.00
A5 Brett Favre 5.00
A6 Mark Brunell 2.00
A7 Fred Taylor 2.00
A8 Daunte Culpepper 2.00
A9 Drew Bledsoe 2.00
A10 Donovan McNabb 1.50
A11 Troy Edwards 1.00
A12 Isaac Bruce 1.00
A13 Marshall Faulk 1.00
A14 Jerry Rice 2.50
A15 Jon Kitna 1.00
A16 Shaun King 1.50
A17 Keyshawn Johnson 1.00
A18 Eddie George 1.50
A19 Steve McNair 1.00
A20 Stephen Davis 1.00

2000 Collector's Edge T-3 EdgeQuest

MT
Complete Set (25): 65.00
Common Player: 2.00
Production 1,000 Sets
EQ1 Marcus Robinson 2.00
EQ2 Kevin Johnson 2.00
EQ3 Randy Moss 10.00
EQ4 Troy Edwards 2.00
EQ5 Torry Holt 2.00
EQ6 Keyshawn Johnson 2.00
EQ7 Emmitt Smith 7.00
EQ8 Terrell Davis 7.00
EQ9 Edgerrin James 12.00
EQ10 Fred Taylor 4.00
EQ11 Ricky Williams 5.00
EQ12 Curtis Martin 2.00
EQ13 Marshall Faulk 2.00
EQ14 Eddie George 3.00
EQ15 Stephen Davis 2.00
EQ16 Cade McNown 3.50
EQ17 Akili Smith 2.00
EQ18 Tim Couch 5.00
EQ19 Brett Favre 12.00
EQ20 Peyton Manning 10.00
EQ21 Daunte Culpepper 4.00
EQ22 Donovan McNabb 3.50
EQ23 Kurt Warner 12.00
EQ24 Jon Kitna 2.00
EQ25 Shaun King 3.50

2000 Collector's Edge T-3 Future Legends

MT
Complete Set (20): 40.00
Common Player: 1.00
Inserted 1:10
FL1 Thomas Jones 4.00
FL2 Jamal Lewis 4.00
FL3 Travis Taylor 2.50
FL4 Peter Warrick 7.00
FL5 Ron Dayne 7.00
FL6 Chad Pennington 5.00
FL7 Plaxico Burress 5.00
FL8 Bubba Franks 1.50
FL9 Shaun Alexander 4.00
FL10 Sylvester Morris 3.00
FL11 Laveranues Coles 1.00
FL12 Jerry Porter 1.00
FL13 Todd Pinkston 1.00
FL14 Dennis Northcutt 1.50
FL15 Travis Prentice 2.50
FL16 R. Jay Soward 1.50
FL17 Chris Redman 2.50
FL18 Trung Canidate 1.00
FL19 Dez White 1.00
FL20 J.R. Redmond 2.00

2000 Collector's Edge T-3 Heir Force

MT
Complete Set (30): 80.00
Common Player: 2.00
Production 1,000 Sets
HF1 Thomas Jones 8.00
HF2 Jamal Lewis 8.00
HF3 Chris Redman 5.00
HF4 Travis Taylor 5.00
HF5 Brian Urlacher 3.00
HF6 Dez White 3.00
HF7 Ron Dugans 3.00
HF8 Curtis Keaton 2.00
HF9 Peter Warrick 12.00
HF10 Courtney Brown 4.00
HF11 Dennis Northcutt 3.00
HF12 Travis Prentice 5.00
HF13 Reuben Droughns 2.00
HF14 Bubba Franks 3.00
HF15 R. Jay Soward 3.00
HF16 Sylvester Morris 6.00
HF17 J.R. Redmond 4.00
HF18 Ron Dayne 12.00
HF19 Anthony Becht 2.00
HF20 Laveranues Coles 3.00
HF21 Chad Pennington 10.00
HF22 Jerry Porter 3.00
HF23 Todd Pinkston 3.00
HF24 Corey Simon 3.00
HF25 Plaxico Burress 10.00
HF26 Danny Farmer 2.00
HF27 Tee Martin 3.00
HF28 Trung Canidate 2.00
HF29 Shaun Alexander 8.00
HF30 Joe Hamilton 3.00

2000 Collector's Edge T-3 JerseyBacks

MT
Common Player: 150.00
Production 20 Sets
GG1 Thomas Jones 350.00
GG2 Jamal Lewis 350.00
GG3 Travis Taylor 250.00
GG4 Peter Warrick 500.00
GG5 R. Jay Soward 150.00
GG6 Sylvester Morris 300.00
GG7 Ron Dayne 500.00
GG8 Chad Pennington 400.00
GG9 Plaxico Burress 400.00
GG10 Shaun Alexander 350.00

2000 Collector's Edge T-3 LeatherBacks

MT
Common Player: 150.00
Production 12 Sets
GG1 Cade McNown 200.00
GG2 Marcus Robinson 150.00
GG3 Akili Smith 175.00
GG4 Tim Couch 300.00
GG5 Troy Aikman 325.00
GG6 Emmitt Smith 350.00
GG7 Terrell Davis 350.00
GG8 Brett Favre 450.00
GG9 Edgerrin James 450.00
GG10 Peyton Manning 450.00
GG11 Randy Moss 450.00
GG12 Ricky Williams 300.00
GG13 Donovan McNabb 200.00
GG14 Torry Holt 150.00
GG15 Kurt Warner 450.00
GG16 Jon Kitna 150.00
GG17 Shaun King 200.00
GG18 Eddie George 175.00
GG19 Steve McNair 150.00
GG20 Stephen Davis 150.00

2000 Collector's Edge T-3 Overture

MT
Complete Set (10): 20.00
Common Player: 1.50
Inserted 1:20
O1 Cade McNown 2.00
O2 Akili Smith 1.50
O3 Tim Couch 3.00
O4 Edgerrin James 5.00
O5 Peyton Manning 5.00
O6 Daunte Culpepper 2.50
O7 Randy Moss 5.00
O8 Ricky Williams 3.00
O9 Torry Holt 1.50
O10 Kurt Warner 5.00

2000 Collector's Edge T-3 Rookie Excalibur

MT
Complete Set (20): 70.00
Common Player: 2.00
Production 1,000 Sets
RE1 Thomas Jones 8.00
RE2 Jamal Lewis 8.00
RE3 Chris Redman 5.00
RE4 Travis Taylor 5.00
RE5 Dez White 2.00
RE6 Peter Warrick 12.00
RE7 Dennis Northcutt 3.00
RE8 Travis Prentice 5.00
RE9 R. Jay Soward 3.00
RE10 Sylvester Morris 6.00
RE11 Ron Dayne 12.00
RE12 Chad Pennington 10.00
RE13 Laveranues Coles 3.00
RE14 Jerry Porter 3.00
RE15 Todd Pinkston 3.00
RE16 Plaxico Burress 10.00
RE17 Trung Canidate 2.00
RE18 Bubba Franks 3.00
RE19 Shaun Alexander 8.00
RE20 J.R. Redmond 4.00

2000 Collector's Edge T-3 Rookie Ink

MT
Complete Set (9): 275.00
Common Player: 10.00
Inserted 1:99
Blue Cards: 2x-4x
Production 24-40 Sets
Red Cards: 6x
Production 10 Sets
Plaxico Burress 440 60.00
Giovanni Carmazzi 1455 20.00
Thomas Jones 915 35.00
Jamal Lewis 485 60.00
Sylvester Morris 1000 30.00
Chad Pennington 470 70.00
Chris Redman 480 35.00
J.R. Redmond 1610 10.00
R. Jay Soward 1350 15.00

1961 Colts Jay Publishing

Measuring 5" x 7", the 12-card set showcases black-and-white posed photos on the front. The 12 cards were included in a package and sold for 25 cents. The backs are blank and unnumbered.

NM
Complete Set (12): 80.00
Common Player: 5.00
1 Raymond Berry 14.00
2 Art Donovan 12.00
3 Weeb Ewbank (CO) 5.00
4 Alex Hawkins 5.00
5 Gino Marchetti 10.00
6 Lenny Moore 12.00
7 Jim Mutscheller 5.00
8 Steve Myhra 5.00
9 Jimmy Orr 5.00
10 Jim Parker 7.00
11 Joe Perry 10.00
12 Johnny Unitas 25.00

1967 Colts Johnny Pro

Measuring 4-1/8" x 2-7/8", each player punchout featured a color photo, with the player's name, number and position inside a white box near the bottom. By inserting the punchout into a stand, which was included with each punchout, the player punchout stood upright. The punchouts are unnumbered.

NM
Complete Set (41): 750.00
Common Player: 15.00
1 Sam Ball 15.00
2 Raymond Berry 40.00
3 Bob Boyd 15.00
4 Ordell Braase 15.00
5 Barry Brown 15.00
6 Bill Curry 20.00
7 Mike Curtis 20.00
8 Norman Davis 15.00
9 Jim Detwiler 15.00
10 Dennis Gaubatz 15.00
11 Alvin Haymond 15.00
12 Jerry Hill 15.00
13 Roy Hilton 15.00
14 David Lee 15.00
15 Jerry Logan 15.00
16 Tony Lorick 15.00
17 Lenny Lyles 15.00
18 John Mackey 30.00
19 Tom Matte 20.00
20 Lou Michaels 15.00
21 Fred Miller 15.00
22 Lenny Moore 40.00
23 Jimmy Orr 20.00
24 Jim Parker 30.00
25 Ray Perkins 20.00
26 Glenn Ressler 15.00
27 Willie Richardson 20.00
28 Don Shinnick 15.00
29 Billy Ray Smith 20.00
30 Bubba Smith 40.00
31 Charlie Stukes 15.00
32 Andy Stynchula 15.00
33 Dan Sullivan 15.00
34 Dick Szymanski 15.00
35 Johnny Unitas 75.00
36 Bob Vogel 15.00
37 Rick Volk 20.00
38 Bob Wade 15.00
39 Jim Ward 15.00
40 Jim Welch 15.00
41 Butch Wilson 15.00

1978 Colts Team Issue

Measuring 5" x 7", the 28-photo set featured a player photo on the front, with the player's name, team and position listed under the photo. The blank backs are also unnumbered.

NM
Complete Set (28): 45.00
Common Player: 1.50
1 Mack Alston 2.00
2 Ron Baker 1.50
3 Mike Barnes 1.50
4 Tim Baylor 1.50
5 Randy Burke 1.50
6 Glenn Doughty 2.00
7 Joe Ehrmann 2.00
8 Wade Griffin 1.50
9 Don Hardeman 1.50
10 Dwight Harrison 1.50
11 Ken Huff 1.50
12 Marshall Johnson 1.50
13 Bert Jones 8.00
14 Bruce Laird 1.50
15 Roosevelt Leaks 2.50
16 David Lee 1.50
17 Ron Lee 1.50
18 Toni Linhart 1.50
19 Derrel Luce 1.50
20 Reese McCall 1.50
21 Ken Mendenhall 1.50
22 Don Morrison 1.50
23 Lloyd Mumphord 1.50
24 Calvin O'Neal 1.50
25 Robert Pratt 1.50
26 Mike Siani 1.50
27 Bill Troup 1.50
28 Stan White 1.50

1985 Colts Kroger

Measuring 5-1/2" x 8-1/2", the 17-photo set spotlighted a large photo on the front, with the Colts' helmet, player name, position, number and Kroger logo underneath from left to right. The card backs have the Indianapolis Colts at the top, with the player's name, position, number and bio underneath. The NFL logo and Kroger logos are also printed on the backs. The cards are unnumbered.

MT
Complete Set (17): 30.00
Common Player: 1.00
1 Karl Baldischwiler 1.00
2 Pat Beach 1.00
3 Albert Bentley 2.00
4 Duane Bickett 3.00
5 Matt Bouza 1.00
6 Nesby Glasgow 1.00
7 Chris Hinton 2.00
8 Lamonte Hunley 1.00
9 Barry Krauss 1.00
10 Orlando Lowry 1.00
11 Tate Randle 1.00
12 Tim Sherwin 1.00
13 Ron Solt 1.00
14 Rohn Stark 1.50
15 Ben Utt 1.00
16 Brad White 1.00
17 Anthony Young 1.50

1988 Colts Police

Measuring 2-5/8" x 4-1/8", the eight-card set boasts a large photo, with the photo credit, player's name, number, position and bio beneath it. The Colts' helmet and name are at the bottom of the card front. The card backs feature two cartoon drawings - - one is a Colts Tip, while the other is a Crime Stoppers Tip. The card backs are numbered "of 8." Oscar Mayer and WTHR-TV logos are printed at the bottom of the card backs.

MT
Complete Set (8): 8.00
Common Player: 1.00
1 Eric Dickerson 3.00
2 Barry Krauss 1.00
3 Bill Brooks 1.50
4 Duane Bickett 1.00
5 Chris Hinton 1.00
6 Eugene Daniel 1.00
7 Jack Trudeau 1.00
8 Ron Meyer (CO) 1.00

1989 Colts Police

Measuring 2-5/8" x 4-1/8", the nine-card set showcases a photo on the front, with a photo credit, player's name, number, position, bio, Colts' helmet and "Indianapolis Colts" printed beneath the photo. The card backs feature two cartoon drawings -- one being a Colts Tip and the other a Crime Stoppers Tip. The cards are numbered. The Indiana Law Enforcement, Louis Rich and WTHR logos are at the bottom of the card backs.

MT
Complete Set (9): 8.00
Common Player: .50
1 Colts Team Card .50
2 Dean Biasucci .50
3 Andre Rison 1.75
4 Chris Chandler 1.25
5 O'Brien Alston .50
6 Ray Donaldson .75
7 Donnell Thompson .50
8 Fredd Young .50
9 Eric Dickerson 1.50

1990 Colts Police

Measuring 2-5/8" x 4-1/8", the eight-card set features a large photo on the front, with a photo credit, player's name, position, bio, Colts' helmet and "Indianapolis Colts" printed underneath. The card backs have a Colts Tip and a Crime Stoppers Tip. The Indiana Law Enforcement, Louis Rich and WTHR logos are printed at the bottom of the card backs.

MT
Complete Set (8): 6.00
Common Player: .50
1 Harvey Armstrong .50
2 Pat Beach .50
3 Albert Bentley .75
4 Kevin Call .50
5 Jeff George 3.00
6 Mike Prior .50
7 Rohn Stark .50
8 Clarence Verdin .50

1991 Colts Police

Measuring 2-5/8" x 4-1/4", the eight-card set showcases a photo on the front, with a photo credit, player's name, Colts' helmet, "Indianapolis Colts" and Indiana Law Enforcement logo beneath it. The card backs feature the player's name, number, position and bio at the top and Colts quiz in the center. An anti-drug message, WTHR and Coke logos are printed at the bottom. The cards are numbered in the lower right corner.

MT
Complete Set (8): 5.00
Common Player: .75
1 Jeff George 1.75
2 Jack Trudeau 1.00
3 Jeff Herrod .75
4 Eric Dickerson 1.50
5 Bill Brooks 1.25
6 Jon Hand .75
7 Keith Taylor .75
8 Randy Dixon .75

1994 Costacos Brothers Poster Cards

Measuring 4-1/4" x 6-1/4", the 12 mini-poster cards were packaged in cello packs. A cardboard sleeve in the packs pictured the set on the front, while the back was numbered of 25,000. The poster was bordered in white on the front, while the backs have the standard postcard look, with the team's logo in the center. The cards are numbered at the bottom center.

MT
Complete Set (12): 15.00
Common Player: .50
1 Troy Aikman (Strong Arm of the Law) 2.00
2 Barry Sanders (The Silver Streak) 2.00
3 Steve Young (Run and Gun) 1.00
4 Rick Mirer (Natural Wonder) .75
5 John Elway (The Rifleman) 1.00
6 Dan Marino (Tropical Storm) 3.00
7 Drew Bledsoe (Patriot Games) 2.00
8 Emmitt Smith (Catch 22) 3.00
9 Warren Moon (Moonshine) .50
10 Jerry Rice (Elite) 2.00
11 Michael Irvin (Playmaker) .50
12 Jim Kelly (Machine Gun Kelly) .50

1992 Courtside Draft Pix Promos

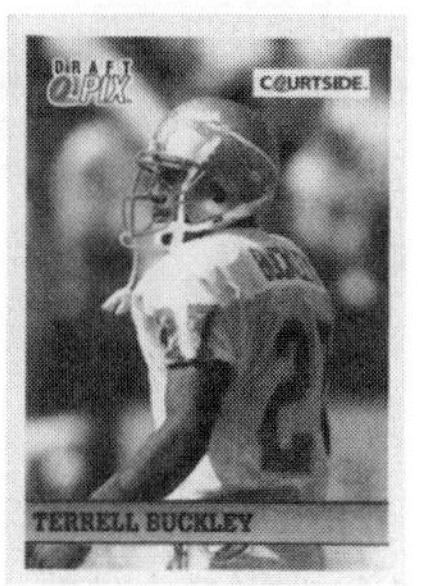

These eight cards were produced to preview Courtside's 1992 Draft Pix set. The cards are similar in design to those in the regular set, but are labeled on the back as being "Promotion - Not For Sale." A card number appears on the back; two #20 cards were made. Some of the cards were given away at card shows and may be stamped on the back in red indicating what show they were given away at.

MT
Complete Set (8): 15.00
Common Player: 2.00
20A Tony Brooks 2.00
20B Amp Lee 3.00
22 Terrell Buckley 2.50
30 Tommy Vardell 2.00
40 Carl Pickens 3.00
44 Quentin Coryatt 2.00
50 Mike Gaddis 2.00
60 Steve Emtman 2.00

1992 Courtside Fb

Courtside's 1992 set had an abundance of insert cards, each of which had a limited print run. The main set's cards are glossy and have a color action photo on the front. A gold stripe at the bottom of the card has the player's name and position inside. The card back has another photo on the top half, with biographical and collegiate statistics under the picture. A card number and the set's logo are also on the back. Special bronze, silver and gold foil versions were also made for each regular card; they were random inserts in limited quantities and command higher prices. There were also autographed cards inserted into the packs; these cards also command premium values, based on the value of the player's regular card. Short printed insert cards were also randomly included in packs. These cards, five each for Award Winners and All-Americans, are numbered using an "AW" or "AA" prefix. In addition, there were 50,000 Steve Emt-

man foilgram cards randomly inserted in packs.

		MT
Complete Set (140):		6.00
Common Player:		.05
Bronze Cards:		2x
Silver Cards:		2x
Gold Cards:		2x
Common Autograph:		4.00
Autograph Cards: 15x-30x		
1	Steve Emtman	.10
2	Quentin Coryatt	.30
3	Ken Swilling	.10
4	Jay Leeuwenburg	.05
5	Mazio Royster	.05
6	Matt Veatch	.05
7	Scott Lockwood	.05
8	Todd Collins	.05
9	Gene McGuire	.05
10	Dale Carter	.10
11	Michael Bankston	.05
12	Jeremy Lincoln	.10
13	Troy Auzenne	.05
14	Rod Smith	.05
15	Andy Kelly	.05
16	Chris Holder	.05
17	Rico Smith	.05
18	Chris Pedersen	.05
19	Brian Treggs	.05
20	Eugene Chung	.05
21	Joel Steed	.05
22	Ricardo McDonald	.05
23	Nate Turner	.05
24	Sean Lumpkin	.05
25	Ty Detmer	.25
26	Matt Darby	.05
27	Michael Warfield	.05
28	Tracy Scroggins	.10
29	Carl Pickens	1.50
30	Chris Mims	.10
31	Mark D'Onofrio	.05
32	Dwight Hollier	.05
33	Siupeli Malamala	.05
34	Mark Barsotti	.05
35	Charles Davenport	.05
36	Brian Bollinger	.05
37	Willie McClendon	.05
38	Calvin Holmes	.05
39	Phillippi Sparks	.05
40	Darryl Williams	.05
41	Greg Skrepenak	.05
42	Larry Webster	.05
43	Dion Lambert	.05
44	Sam Gash	.10
45	Patrick Rowe	.05
46	Scottie Graham	.15
47	Darian Hagan	.05
48	Arthur Marshall	.05
49	Amp Lee	.25
50	Tommy Vardell	.10
51	Robert Porcher	.10
52	Reggie Dwight	.05
53	Torrance Small	.05
54	Ronnie West	.05
55	Tony Brooks	.05
56	Anthony McDowell	.05
57	Chris Haskel	.05
58	Ed Cunningham	.05
59	Ashley Ambrose	.05
60	Alonzo Spellman	.15
61	Harold Heath	.05
62	Ron Lopez	.05
63	Bill Johnson	.05
64	Kent Graham	.05
65	Aaron Pierce	.05
66	Bucky Richardson	.05
67	Todd Kinchen	.10
68	Ken Ealy	.05
69	Carlos Snow	.05
70	Dana Hall	.05
71	Matt Rodgers	.05
72	Howard Dinkins	.05
73	Tim Lester	.05
74	Mark Chmura	.75
75	Johnny Mitchell	.25
76	Mirko Jurkovic	.05
77	Anthony Lynn	.05
78	Roosevelt Collins	.05
79	Tony Sands	.05
80	Kevin Smith	.05
81	Tony Brown	.05
82	Bobby Fuller	.05
83	Darryl Ashmore	.05
84	Tyrone Legette	.05
85	Mike Gaddis	.05
86	Gerald Dixon	.05
87	T.J. Rubley	.05
88	Mark Thomas	.05
89	Corey Widmer	.05
90	Robert Jones	.05
91	Eddie Robinson	.05
92	Rob Tomlinson	.05
93	Russ Campbell	.05
94	Keith Goganious	.05
95	Rod Moore	.05
96	Jerry Ostroski	.05
97	Tyji Armstrong	.10
98	Ronald Humphrey	.05
99	Corey Harris	.05
100	Terrell Buckley	.15
101	Cal Dixon	.05
102	Tyrone Williams	.05
103	Joe Bowden	.05
104	Santana Dotson	.10
105	Jeff Blake	1.50
106	Erick Anderson	.05
107	Steve Israel	.05
108	Chad Roghair	.05
109	Todd Harrison	.05
110	Chester McGlockton	.10
111	Marquez Pope	.10
112	George Rooks	.05
113	Dion Johnson	.05
114	Tim Simpson	.05
115	Chris Walsh	.05
116	Marc Boutte	.05
117	Jamie Gill	.05
118	Willie Clay	.05
119	Tim Paulk	.05
120	Ray Roberts	.05
121	Jeff Thomason	.05
122	Leodis Flowers	.05
123	Robert Brooks	.75
124	Jeff Ellis	.05
125	John Fina	.05
126	Michael Smith	.05
127	Mike Saunders	.05
128	John Brown III	.05
129	Reggie Yarbrough	.05
130	Leon Searcy	.05
131	Marcus Woods	.05
132	Shane Collins	.05
133	Chuck Smith	.05
134	Keith Hamilton	.05
135	Rodney Blackshear	.05
136	Corey Barlow	.05
137	Robert Harris	.05
138	Tony Smith	.05
139	Checklist 1	.05
140	Checklist 2	.05

1992 Courtside Foilgrams

1992 Courtside Draft Pix wrappers offered these foilgram cards as a mail-in offer; collectors could receive one by sending in 10 wrappers. There were 15,000 foilgram cards produced for each card; which is numbered #1 of 5 limited edition foilgram cards.

		MT
Complete Set (5):		5.00
Common Player:		1.00
1	Steve Emtman	1.00
2	Tommy Vardell	1.25
3	Terrell Buckley	1.25
4	Ty Detmer	1.00
5	Amp Lee	1.00

1992 Courtside Inserts

These short-printed foilgram cards, random inserts in 1992 Courtside Draft Pix foil cases, feature glossy color action photos on the front, bordered with a white frame. Five Award Winners and Five All-Americans are featured in the set; the football logo on the card front indicates if the player is an Award Winner or All-American. The card back, which features a color photo on one side and player profile on the other, also distinguishes which type of card it is by using a corresponding "AW" or "AA" prefix for the card number.

		MT
Complete Set (10):		10.00
Common Player:		.50
Award Winners		
1	Outland Trophy (Steve Emtman)	2.00
2	'90 Heisman Trophy (Ty Detmer)	3.00
3	Lombardi Award (Steve Emtman)	2.00
4	Jim Thorpe Award (Terrell Buckley)	2.00
5	Dick Butkus Award (Erick Anderson)	.50
All-America		
1	Carl Pickens	4.00
2	Dale Carter	2.00
3	Tommy Vardell	2.00
4	Amp Lee	2.00
5	Leon Searcy	.50

1993 Courtside Sean Dawkins

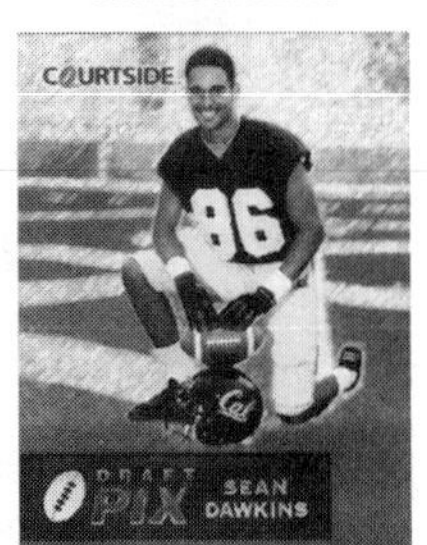

Indiana Colts first-round draft pick Sean Dawkins is featured in this five-card insert set. There were 20,000 sets produced; the complete set value below does not include an autographed card. Dawkins signed 5,000 cards, which were randomly inserted within the sets. Each card front has a color action photo against a blurred background. Gold foil stamping is used to incorporate the player's name, a football and "Draft Pix" into the design. A promotional card was also produced, similar to card #3, except it has "Promotional - Not For Sale" and "Authentic Signature" written on the card front.

		MT
Complete Set (5):		10.00
Common Player:		2.00
1	Sean Dawkins (Ball cradles in right arm, running up field)	2.00
2	Sean Dawkins (Hands outstretched to catch ball)	2.00
3	Sean Dawkins (Being handchecked by cornerback)	2.00
4	Sean Dawkins (Kneeling pose)	2.00
5	Sean Dawkins (Dressed in tuxedo)	2.00
----	Sean Dawkins (AU 5000, certified autograph)	15.00

A player's name in *italic type* indicates a rookie card.

1993 Courtside Russell White

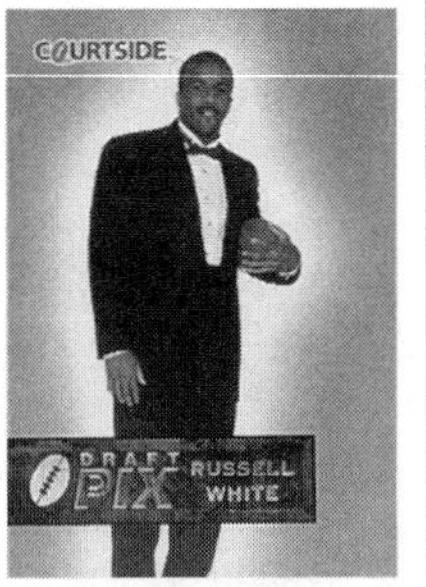

Los Angeles Rams' third-round draft pick Russell White is featured in this five-card insert set. Each card front has a full-bleed color, glossy action photo against a blurred background. Gold foil is used to incorporate the player's name, Draft Pix and football logo into the design of the card. The card back has a color photo of the player, plus either statistics, biographical or player profile information, or highlights. A card number is also included. There were 20,000 sets produced. White autographed 5,000 cards, which were randomly inserted within the set. (The complete set price does not include an autographed card.) Promo cards were also issued for #s 3-5. They can be distinguished from the regular cards by the words "Promotional - Not For Sale," which appear on the card front, and the words "Authentic Signature," which also appear on the front.

		MT
Complete Set (5):		10.00
Common White:		2.00
1	Russell White (Running almost straight head)	2.00
2	Russell White (Running toward the right)	2.00
3	Russell White (Running toward defensive player number 78)	2.00
4	Russell White (Running upfield; side view)	2.00
5	Russell White (Dressed in tuxedo)	2.00
----	Russell White (AU/5000, certified autograph)	12.00

1969 Cowboys Team Issue

Measuring 7" x 10", the card fronts showcase color action shots of players. The photos have black rounded-corner borders. The player's name and team are printed below the photo. The unnumbered backs are blank.

		NM
Complete Set (5):		35.00
Common Player:		5.00
1	Walt Garrison	5.00
2	Lee Roy Jordan	7.00
3	Bob Lilly	10.00
4	Dave Manders	5.00
5	Mel Renfro	8.00

1971 Cowboys Team Issue

Measuring 5" x 6-1/2", the 40-card set showcases black-and-white posed shots on the front, bordered in white. The player's name and team are printed below the photo. The cards are unnumbered and have blank backs.

		NM
Complete Set (40):		150.00
Common Player:		2.00
1	Herb Adderley	5.00
2	Lance Alworth	12.00
3	George Andrie	2.00
4	Mike Clark	2.00
5	Larry Cole	2.00
6	Mike Ditka	16.00
7	Dave Edwards	2.00
8	John Fitzgerald	2.00
9	Toni Fritsch	2.00
10	Walt Garrison	2.00
11	Cornell Green	2.00
12	Bill Gregory	2.00
13	Cliff Harris	3.00
14	Bob Hayes	6.00
15	Calvin Hill	5.00
16	Chuck Howley	3.00
17	Lee Roy Jordan	4.00
18	D.D. Lewis	2.00
19	Bob Lilly	10.00
20	Tony Liscio	2.00
21	Dave Manders	2.00
22	Craig Morton	5.00
23	Ralph Neely	2.00
24	John Niland	2.00
25	Jethro Pugh	2.00
26	Dan Reeves	12.00
27	Mel Renfro	8.00
28	Gloster Richardson	2.00
29	Tody Smith	2.00
30	Roger Staubach	30.00
31	Don Talbert	2.00
32	Duane Thomas	2.00
33	Isaac Thomas	2.00
34	Pat Toomay	2.00
35	Billy Truax	2.00
36	Rodney Wallace	2.00
37	Mark Washington	2.00
38	Charlie Waters	3.00
39	Claxton Welch	2.00
40	Ron Widby	2.00

1972 Cowboys Team Issue

Measuring 4-1/4" x 5-1/2", the 13-card set showcases black-and-white photos on the front, bordered in white. The player's name is printed underneath the photo. The cards are unnumbered and have blank backs.

		NM
Complete Set (13):		50.00
Common Player:		2.00
1	Herb Adderley	4.00
2	Mike Ditka	15.00
3	Toni Fritsch	2.00
4	Walt Garrison	2.00
5	Cornell Green	2.00
6	Cliff Harris	3.00
7	Bob Hayes	6.00
8	Calvin Hill	5.00
9	Robert Newhouse	2.00
10	Billy Parks	2.00
11	Mel Renfro	6.00
12	Dan Reeves	10.00
13	Charlie Waters	3.00

1979 Cowboys Police

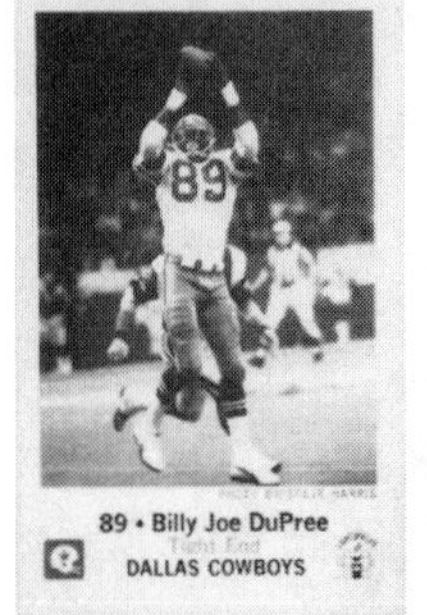

Measuring 2-5/8" x 4-1/8", the 15-card set showcases a player photo on the front, with a photo credit, player's name, number, position and team listed below. The Cowboys logo is in the lower left. The card backs have Cowboys Tips in a box, with the Cowboys' helmet at the top. The sponsors are listed at the bottom of the card back. D.D. Lewis replaced Thomas "Hollywood" Henderson during the season, which means lesser amounts were printed of both cards.

		NM
Complete Set (15):		25.00
Common Player:		.50
12	Roger Staubach	6.00
33	Tony Dorsett	4.00
41	Charlie Waters	.75
43	Cliff Harris	.50
44	Robert Newhouse	.50
50	D.D. Lewis (SP)	2.00
53	Bob Breunig	.50
54	Randy White	2.00
56	Thomas Henderson (SP)	2.00
67	Pat Donovan	.50
79	Harvey Martin	.50
80	Tony Hill	.50
88	Drew Pearson	1.00
89	Billy Joe DuPree	.50
NNO	Tom Landry (CO)	2.50

1980 Cowboys Police

Measuring 2-5/8" x 4-1/8", the 14-card set is anchored by a large photo on the front, with the player's name, number, position and team printed under the photo. A photo credit is also listed beneath the photo. The Cowboys' helmet is printed in the lower left, while a Kiwanis logo is located in the lower right. The card backs feature Cowboys Tips inside a box, which features the Cowboys' helmet at the top. The sponsor names are printed at the bottom of the card backs. The cards are numbered by the player's jersey numbers.

		NM
Complete Set (14):		10.00
Common Player:		.50
1	Rafael Septien	.50
11	Danny White	2.00
25	Aaron Kyle	.50
26	Preston Pearson	1.00
31	Benny Barnes	.75
35	Scott Laidlaw	.50
42	Randy Hughes	.50
62	John Fitzgerald	.75
63	Larry Cole	.75
64	Tom Rafferty	.75
68	Herbert Scott	.50
70	Rayfield Wright	.75
78	John Dutton	.75
87	Jay Saldi	.75

1981 Cowboys Police

Measuring 2-5/8" x 4-1/8", the 14-card set showcases a photo on the front, with a photo credit, player's name, jersey number, position and team printed beneath the photo. The Cowboys' helmet is in the lower left corner, while the Kiwanis' logo is in the lower right. The card backs feature Cowboys Tips inside, a box with the Cowboys helmet at the top. The cards are numbered with the player's jersey number.

		MT
Complete Set (14):		10.00
Common Player:		.50
18	Glenn Carano	.75
20	Ron Springs	1.00
23	James Jones	.50
26	Michael Downs	.75
32	Dennis Thurman	.75
45	Steve Wilson	.50
51	Anthony Dickerson	.50
52	Robert Shaw	.50
58	Mike Hegman	.50
59	Guy Brown	.50
61	Jim Cooper	.50
72	Ed "Too Tall" Jones	2.00
84	Doug Cosbie	1.00
86	Butch Johnson	1.00

1981 Cowboys Thousand Oaks Police

Measuring 2-5/8" x 4-1/8", the 14-card set is anchored by a photo on the front. A photo credit, player's name, jersey number, position and team are printed below the photo. The Cowboys' helmet is in the lower left, while a sponsor's logo is in the lower right. The card backs feature Cowboys Tips inside a box, with the Cowboys' helmet at the top. The sponsors, including the Thousand Oaks Police Dept., are listed at the bottom of the card backs.

		MT
Complete Set (14):		42.00
Common Player:		1.50
11	Danny White	4.00
31	Benny Barnes	1.50
33	Tony Dorsett	8.00
41	Charlie Waters	3.00
42	Randy Hughes	1.50
44	Robert Newhouse	2.00
54	Randy White	6.00
55	D.D. Lewis	1.50
78	John Dutton	1.50
79	Harvey Martin	3.00
80	Tony Hill	3.00
88	Drew Pearson	4.00
89	Billy Joe DuPree	2.00
NNO	Tom Landry (CO)	7.00

1982 Cowboys Carrollton Park

Measuring 3" x 4", the six-card set showcases a large photo on the front, with "Carrollton Park Mall" printed below it inside a white border. The card backs spotlight the card's number at the top inside a circle. The player's name, position and stats are printed below the number. The Cowboys' 1982-83 scheduled takes up the bottom 2/3 of the card back. The set is also available in uncut sheets.

		MT
Complete Set (6):		5.00
Common Player:		.50
1	Roger Staubach	2.00
2	Danny White	.75
3	Tony Dorsett	1.00
4	Randy White	.75
5	Charlie Waters	.50
6	Billy Joe DuPree	.50

1983 Cowboys Police

Measuring 2-5/8" x 4-1/8", the 28-card set is anchored by a large photo on the front, with a photo credit, player's name, number, position and team printed underneath the photo. The Cowboys' helmet is printed in the lower right, while the Kiwanis' logo is in the lower right. The card backs have Cowboys Tips inside a box, with the Cowboys' helmet at the top. The sponsors are listed at the bottom of the card back.

		MT
Complete Set (28):		25.00
Common Player:		.50
1	Rafael Septien	.50
11	Danny White	1.50
20	Ron Springs	.50
24	Everson Walls	.50
26	Michael Downs	.50
30	Timmy Newsome	.50
32	Dennis Thurman	.50
33	Tony Dorsett	3.00
47	Dexter Clinkscale	.50
53	Bob Breunig	.50
54	Randy White	3.00
65	Kurt Petersen	.50
67	Pat Donovan	.50
70	Howard Richards	.50
72	Ed "Too Tall" Jones	2.00
78	John Dutton	.50
79	Harvey Martin	1.00
80	Tony Hill	.75
83	Doug Donley	.50
84	Doug Cosbie	.50
86	Butch Johnson	.50
88	Drew Pearson	1.75
89	Billy Joe DuPree	.50
NNO	Tom Landry (CO)	2.00
NNO	Melinda May (CHEER)	.50
NNO	Dana Presley (CHEER)	.50
NNO	Judy Trammell (CHEER)	.50
NNO	Toni Washington (CHEER)	.50

1985 Cowboys Frito Lay

Measuring 4" x 5-1/2", this 41 card set is anchored on the front by a large black-and-white photo. The player's name, jersey number, position and bio are listed beneath the photo on the front. The Cowboys' helmet is printed in the lower left, with the Frito Lay logo in the lower right. The backs are unnumbered and blank.

		MT
Complete Set (41):		50.00
Common Player:		1.00
1	Vince Albritton	1.00
2	Brian Baldinger	1.00
3	Dexter Clinkscale	1.00
4	Jim Cooper	1.00
5	Fred Cornwell	1.00
6	Doug Crosbie	1.50
7	Steve DeOssie	1.00
8	John Dutton	1.00
9	Ricky Easmon	1.00
10	Ron Fellows	1.00
11	Leon Gonzalez	1.00
12	Gary Hogeboom	1.50
13	Jim Jeffcoat	2.50
14	Ed "Too Tall" Jones	3.00
15	James Jones	1.00
16	Crawford Ker	1.00
17	Robert Lavette	1.00
18	Eugene Lockhart	1.00
19	Timmy Newsome	1.00
20	Drew Pearson (ACO)	2.00
21	Steve Pelluer	1.50
22	Jesse Penn	1.00
23	Kurt Petersen	1.00
24	Karl Powe	1.00
25	Phil Pozderac	1.00
26	Tom Rafferty	1.00
27	Mike Renfro	1.00
28	Howard Richards	1.00
29	Jeff Rohrer	1.00
30	Mike Saxon	1.00
31	Victor Scott	1.00
32	Rafael Septien	1.00
33	Don Smerek	1.00
34	Roger Staubach	10.00
35	Broderick Thompson	1.00
36	Dennis Thurman	1.00
37	Glen Titensor	1.00
38	Mark Tuinei	1.50
39	Everson Walls	1.50
40	John Williams	1.00
41	Team Photo	3.00

1994 Cowboys ProLine Live Kroger Stickers

Each sticker measures 3-5/8 inches and is part of a three-sticker strip which measures 2-1/2" x 12". The sticker fronts showcase the same design as the 1994 Pro Line card series, with the player's name printed in large letters at the bottom of the sticker and his team printed inside a stripe beneath his name. The Classic Pro Line logo is located in the upper right corner. The sticker backs feature $1 off Fuji Film coupons or a team poster sweepstakes form. The strips were sold at Kroger stores for 99 cents for seven weeks. The sticker strips are numbered by their respective weeks.

		MT
Complete Set (7):		5.00
Common Player:		.50
1	Troy Aikman, Darren Woodson, Erik Williams	1.50
2	Emmitt Smith, James Washington, Mark Stepnoski	2.00
3	Michael Irvin, Kenneth Gant, Tony Tolbert	.75
4	Daryl Johnston, Kevin Williams WR, Leon Lett	.50
5	Nate Newton, Shante Carver, Charles Haley	.50
6	Russell Maryland, Mark Tuinei, Kevin Smith	.50
7	Alvin Harper, Willie Jackson, Jay Novacek	.50

1976 Crane Discs

These circular cards measure 3-3/8" in diameter and were produced by Michael Schechter Associates, as noted by the MSA letters on the card back. Each card front has a black-and-white mug shot of a player, along with his team, name and position. The card has a colored border with the word "Crane" at the top, representing Crane Potato Chips, which offered the cards as a mail-in offer. The Crane logo appears on the card back, but there are a few other sponsors which may also appear on the back; these are slightly more valuable than their Crane counterparts. The cards are unnumbered.

		NM
Complete Set (30):		15.00
Common Player:		.10
(1)	Ken Anderson	.50
(2)	Otis Armstrong	.15
(3)	Steve Bartkowski	.35
(4)	Terry Bradshaw	2.00
(5)	John Brockington	.25
(6)	Doug Buffone	.10
(7)	Wally Chambers	.10
(8)	Isaac Curtis	.25
(9)	Chuck Foreman	.20
(10)	Roman Gabriel	.75
(11)	Mel Gray	.15
(12)	Joe Greene	.65
(13)	James Harris	.25
(14)	Jim Hart	.25

(15)	Billy Kilmer	.25
(16)	Greg Landry	.25
(17)	Ed Marinaro	.50
(18)	Lawrence McCutcheon	.25
(19)	Terry Metcalf	.15
(20)	Lydell Mitchell	.25
(21)	Jim Otis	.15
(22)	Alan Page	.35
(23)	Walter Payton	10.00
(24)	Greg Pruitt	.40
(25)	Charlie Sanders	.25
(26)	Ron Shanklin	.25
(27)	Roger Staubach	2.00
(28)	Jan Stenerud	.40
(29)	Charley Taylor	.40
(30)	Roger Wehrli	.25

1992 Crown Pro Dogtags Fb

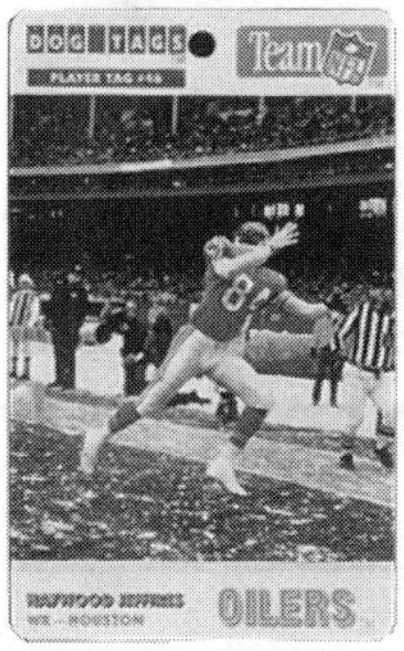

Measuring 2-1/8" x 3-3/8", the 81 dog tags were manufactured by Chris Martin Enterprises Inc., which later became Crown Pro. Produced of plastic, the tags are similar to credit cards. The tag fronts include a color photo in the center, with the "Dog Tags," NFL logo and tag number inside a white border at the top. The player's name, position and team, along with the team's logo, are printed inside a white border at the bottom. The backs have the player's name, headshot, bio, highlights and a team logo area that could be autographed. The top center of each tag had a hole in it, which allowed collectors to wear the tags on a chain. The team tags were horizontal and featured a photo of the team's stadium on the front. The rookie tags resemble the regular tags, however, they have a gold-foil border at the top. An Emmitt Smith promo tag was also released and it has "promo tag" printed on the back. Chris Martin autographed tags were also produced.

		MT
Complete Set (81):		70.00
Common Player:		.50
1	Atlanta Falcons	.50
2	Buffalo Bills	.50
3	Chicago Bears	.50
4	Cincinnati Bengals	.50
5	Cleveland Browns	.50
6	Dallas Cowboys	.50
7	Denver Broncos	.50
8	Detroit Lions	.50
9	Green Bay Packers	.50
10	Houston Oilers	.50
11	Indianapolis Colts	.50
12	Kansas City Chiefs	.50
13	Los Angeles Raiders	.50
14	Los Angeles Rams	.50
15	Miami Dolphins	.50
16	Minnesota Vikings	.50
17	New England Patriots	.50
18	New Orleans Saints	.50
19	New York Giants	.50
20	New York Jets	.50
21	Philadelphia Eagles	.50
22	Phoenix Cardinals	.50
23	Pittsburgh Steelers	.50
24	San Diego Chargers	.50
25	San Francisco 49ers	.50
26	Seattle Seahawks	.50
27	Tampa Bay Buccaneers	.50
28	Washington Redskins	.50
29A	Chris Martin (Reg.)	1.00
29B	Chris Martin (Gold)	2.00
29AU	Chris Martin (Autograph)	10.00
30	Dan Marino	10.00
31	Chris Miller	.50
32	Deion Sanders	3.00
33	Jim Kelly	1.00
34	Thurman Thomas	1.00
35	Jim Harbaugh	1.00
36	Mike Singletary	.50
37	Boomer Esiason	.50
38	Anthony Munoz	.50
39	Bernie Kosar	.50
40	Troy Aikman	5.00
41	Michael Irvin	2.00
42	Emmitt Smith	10.00
43	John Elway	3.00
44	Rodney Peete	.50
45	Sterling Sharpe	1.00
46	Haywood Jeffires	.50
47	Warren Moon	1.00
48	Jeff George	1.00
49	Christian Okoye	.50
50	Derrick Thomas	1.00
51	Howie Long	.50
52	Ronnie Lott	.50
53	Jim Everett	.50
54	Mark Clayton	.50
55	Anthony Carter	.50
56A	Chris Doleman	.50
56B	Chris Doleman (Autograph)	.50
57	Andre Tippett	.50
58A	Pat Swilling	.50
58B	Pat Swilling (Autograph)	.50
59	Jeff Hostetler	.50
60	Lawrence Taylor	1.00
61	Robert Moore	.50
62	Ken O'Brien	.50
63	Keith Byars	.50
64	Randall Cunningham	.50
65	Keith Byars	.50
66	Timm Rosenbach	.50
67	Bubby Brister	.50
68	John Friesz	1.00
69	Jerry Rice	5.00
70	Steve Young	4.00
71	Dan McGwire	.50
72	Broderick Thomas	.50
73	Vinny Testaverde	1.00
74	Gary Clark	.50
75	Mark Rypien	.50

1993 Crown Pro Dogtags Fb

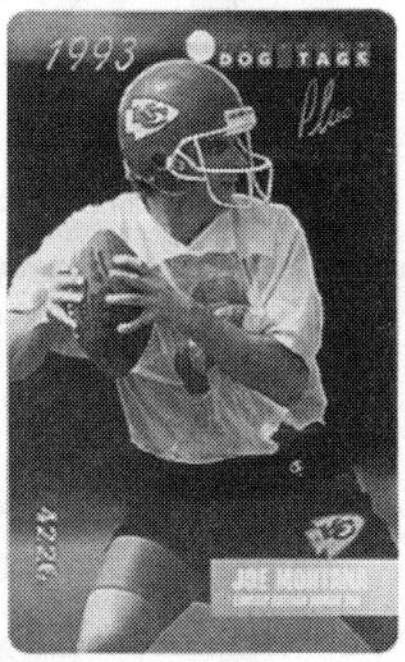

Measuring 2-1/8" x 3-3/8", the tags were produced by Chris Martin Enterprises, which later became Crown Pro. The 138-plastic tag set featured a full-bleed photo on the front with "1993" gold-foil stamped in the upper left and the Dog Tags logo printed in the upper right. The player's name is printed in white inside a stripe in the lower right. The tag backs have the number in the upper left, with the player's headshot, name, number, bio, highlights and stats listed along the right side. An autograph strip is located along the left border. Overall, 50,000 of each tag was produced. Tag Nos. 48 and 138 were not printed for the set. Originally, the tags were sold in packs, however, complete team sets were sold later in the season. Atlanta and the Raiders were not distributed as team sets. In addition, 25,000 Joe Montana bonus tags were available through a mail-in offer. A contest offered collectors the chance to win a 14K gold bead chain or a seven-point diamond tag.

		MT
Complete Set (140):		80.00
Common Player:		.50
1	Atlanta Falcons	.50
2	Buffalo Bills	.50
3	Chicago Bears	.50
4	Cincinnati Bengals	.50
5	Cleveland Browns	.50
6	Dallas Cowboys	.50
7	Denver Broncos	.50
8	Detroit Lions	.50
9	Green Bay Packers	.50
10	Houston Oilers	.50
11	Indianapolis Colts	.50
12	Kansas City Chiefs	.50
13	Los Angeles Raiders	.50
14	Los Angeles Rams	.50
15	Miami Dolphins	.50
16	Minnesota Vikins	.50
17	New England Patriots	.50
18	New Orleans Saints	.50
19	New York Giants	.50
20	New York Jets	.50
21	Philadelphia Eagles	.50
22	Phoenix Cardinals	.50
23	Pittsburgh Steelers	.50
24	San Diego Chargers	.50
25	San Francisco 49ers	.50
26	Seattle Seahawks	.50
27	Tampa Bay Buccaneers	.50
28	Washington Redskins	.50
29	Steve Broussard	.50
30	Chris Miller	.50
31	Andre Rison	1.00
32	Deion Sanders	3.00
33	Cornelius Bennett	.50
34	Jim Kelly	1.00
35	Bruce Smith	.50
36	Thurman Thomas	1.00
37	Neal Anderson	.50
38	Mark Carrier	.50
39	Jim Harbaugh	1.00
40	Alonzo Spellman	1.00
41	David Fulcher	.50
42	Harold Green	.50
43	David Klingler	.50
44	Carl Pickens	2.00
45	Bernie Kosar	.50
46	Clay Matthews	.50
47	Eric Metcalf	.50
49	Troy Aikman	4.00
50	Michael Irvin	2.00
51	Russell Maryland	.50
52	Emmitt Smith	8.00
53	Steve Atwater	.50
54	John Elway	3.00
55	Tommy Maddox	.50
56	Shannon Sharpe	1.00
57	Herman Moore	2.00
58	Rodney Peete	.50
59	Barry Sanders	4.00
60	Andre Ware	.50
61	Terrell Buckley	.50
62	Brett Favre	10.00
63	Sterling Sharpe	1.00
64	Reggie White	2.00
65	Ray Childress	.50
66	Haywood Jeffires	.50
67	Warren Moon	1.00
68	Lorenzo White	.50
69	Duane Bickett	.50
70	Quentin Coryatt	.50
71	Steve Emtman	.50
72	Jeff George	.50
73	Dale Carter	.50
74	Neil Smith	.50
75	Derrick Thomas	1.00
76	Harvey Williams	.50
77	Eric Dickerson	.50
78	Howie Long	.50
79	Todd Marinovich	.50
80	Alexander Wright	.50
81A	Flipper Anderson	.50
81B	Flipper Anderson (Autograph)	.50
82A	Jim Everett	.50
82B	Jim Everett (Autograph)	.50
83	Cleveland Gary	.50
84A	Chris Martin	.50
84B	Chris Martin (Autograph)	.50
85	Irving Fryer	.50
86	Keith Jackson	.50
87	Dan Marino	8.00
88	Louis Oliver	.50
89	Terry Allen	2.00
90	Anthony Carter	.50
91	Chris Doleman	.50
92	Rich Gannon	.50
93	Eugene Chung	.50
94	Marv Cook	.50
95	Leonard Russell	.50
96	Andre Tippett	.50
97	Morten Anderson	.50
98	Vaughn Dunbar	.50
99	Rickey Jackson	.50
100	Sam Mills	.50
101	Derek Brown	.50
102	Lawrence Taylor	1.00
103	Rodney Hampton	1.00
104	Phil Simms	.50
105	Johnny Mitchell	.50
106	Rob Moore	.50
107	Blair Thomas	.50
108	Browning Nagle	.50
109	Eric Allen	.50
110	Fred Barnett	.50
111	Randall Cunningham	.50
112	Herschel Walker	.50
113	Chris Chandler	.50
114	Randal Hill	.50
115	Ricky Proehl	.50
116	Eric Swann	.50
117	Barry Foster	.50
118	Eric Green	.50
119	Neil O'Donnell	.50
120	Rod Woodson	.50
121	Marion Butts	.50
122	Stan Humphries	.50
123	Anthony Miller	.50
124	Junior Seau	1.00
125	Amp Lee	.50
126	Jerry Rice	4.00
127	Ricky Watters	2.00
128	Steve Young	3.00
129	Brian Blades	.50
130	Cortez Kennedy	.50
131	Dan McGwire	.50
132	John L. Williams	.50
133	Reggie Cobb	.50
134	Steve Deberg	.50
135	Keith McCants	.50
136	Broderick Thomas	.50
137	Earnest Byner	.50
138	Mark Rypien	.50
140	Ricky Sanders	.50

1994-95 Crown Pro Tags Fb

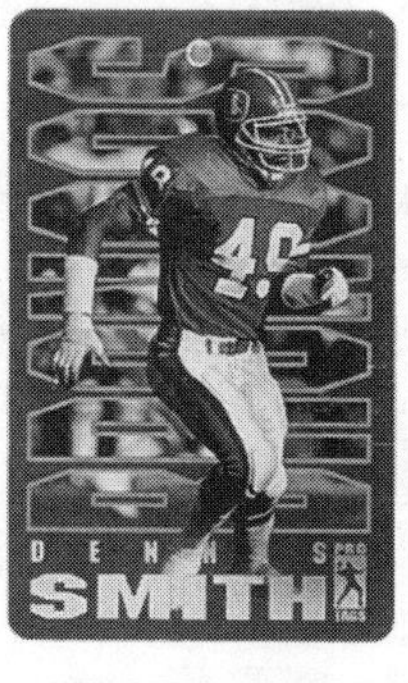

While the first two sets of these tags were known as Dog Tags, this 168-card issue was called Pro Tags, and was sold in six-card packs. Like Dog Tags, this set was made of plastic and measured 2-1/8" x 3-3/8". Autographed tags were available of Jerome Bettis, J.J. Birden, Dale Carter, Keith Cash, Willie Davis, Sean Gilbert, Chris Martin, Roman Phifer, Todd Lyght and Neil Smith. Pro Tags offered a chance to receive six AFC or six NFC Super Rookie Pro Tags for three proofs of purchase and $10.99 per set, or all 12 for five proofs of purchase and $15.99. The set also exists in a Super Bowl XXIX version, with no premium in price.

		MT
Complete Set (168):		70.00
Common Player:		.50
1	Steve Beuerlein	.50
2	Chuck Cecil	.50
3	Randal Hill	.50
4	Garrison Hearst	.50
5	Ricky Proehl	.50
6	Eric Swann	.50
7	Jeff George	.50
8	Drew Hill	.50
9	Erric Pegram	.50
10	Andre Rison	.50
11	Deion Sanders	1.50
12	Jessie Tuggle	.50
13	Cornelius Bennett	.50
14	Kenneth Davis	.50
15	Jim Kelly	1.00
16	Andre Reed	.50
17	Darryl Talley	.50
18	Steve Tasker	.50
19	Trace Armstrong	.50
20	Curtis Conway	1.00
21	Dante Jones	.50
22	Donnell Woolford	.50
23	Tim Worley	.50
24	Chris Zorich	.50
25	Derrick Fenner	.50
26	Harold Green	.50
27	David Klingler	.50
28	Tony McGee	.50
29	Carl Pickens	1.00
30	Jeff Query	.50
31	Mark Carrier	.50
32	Michael Jackson	.50
33	Eric Metcalf	.50
34	Michael Dean Perry	.50
35	Vinny Testaverde	.50
36	Tommy Vardell	.50
37	Troy Aikman	3.00
38	Alvin Harper	.50
39	Michael Irvin	1.00
40	Russell Maryland	.50
41	Jay Novacek	.50
42	Emmitt Smith	6.00
43	Rod Bernstine	.50
44	Mike Croel	.50
45	John Elway	1.50
46	Glyn Milburn	.50
47	Shannon Sharpe	.50
48	Dennis Smith	.50
49	Jason Hanson	.50
50	Herman Moore	1.00
51	Brett Perriman	.50
52	Barry Sanders	3.00
53	Chris Spielman	.50
54	Pat Swilling	.50
55	Edgar Bennett	.50
56	Terrell Buckley	.50
57	Brett Favre	8.00
58	Chris Jacke	.50
59	Sterling Sharpe	1.00
60	Reggie White	1.00
61	Gary Brown	.50
62	Cody Carlson	.50
63	Ernest Givins	.50
64	Haywood Jeffires	.50
65	Bruce Matthews	.50
66	Webster Slaughter	.50
67	Jason Belser	.50
68	Roosevelt Potts	.50
69	Rodney Culver	.50
70	Jim Harbaugh	1.00
71	Scott Radecic	.50
72	Kerry Cash	.50
73	Marcus Allen	1.00
74	J.J. Birden	.50
75	Dale Carter	.50
76	Keith Cash	.50
77	Willie Davis	.50
78	Neil Smith	.50
79	Eddie Anderson	.50
80	Tim Brown	1.00
81	Jeff Hostetler	.50
82	Raghib Ismail	.50
83	James Jett	.50
84	Terry McDaniel	.50
85	Willie Anderson	.50
86	Jerome Bettis	1.50
87	Todd Drayton	.50
88	Sean Gilbert	.50
89	Todd Lyght	.50
90	Chris Martin	.50
91	Keith Byars	.50
92	Bryan Cox	.50
93	Irving Fryar	.50
94	Terry Kirby	.50
95	Dan Marino	6.00
96	O.J. McDuffie	.50
97	Terry Allen	.50
98	Cris Carter	.50
99	Qadry Ismail	.50
100	Randall McDaniel	.50
101	Warren Moon	1.00
102	Robert Smith	1.00
103	Drew Bledsoe	3.00
104	Vincent Brisby	.50
105	Vincent Brown	.50
106	Marv Cook	.50
107	Leonard Russell	.50
108	Reyna Thompson	.50
109	Morten Andersen	.50
110	Quinn Early	.50
111	Tyrone Hughes	.50
112	Sam Mills	.50
113	William Roaf	.50
114	Renaldo Turnbull	.50
115	Stephen Baker	.50
116	John Elliott	.50
117	Rodney Hampton	.50
118	Mark Jackson	.50
119	David Meggett	.50
120	Kenyon Rasheed	.50
121	Brad Baxter	.50
122	Boomer Esiason	.50
123	Johnny Johnson	.50
124	Ronnie Lott	.50
125	Johnny Mitchell	.50
126	Rob Moore	.50
127	Fred Barnett	.50
128	Mark Bavaro	.50
129	Bubby Brister	.50
130	Randall Cunningham	.50
131	Tim Harris	.50
132	Herschel Walker	.50
133	Gary Anderson	.50
134	Barry Foster	.50
135	Kevin Greene	.50
136	Greg Lloyd	.50
137	Neil O'Donnell	1.00
138	Rod Woodson	.50
139	Eric Bieniemy	.50
140	Ronnie Harmon	.50
141	Stan Humphries	.50
142	Natrone Means	1.50
143	Leslie O'Neal	.50
144	Junior Seau	1.00
145	Tim McDonald	.50
146	Jerry Rice	3.00
147	Dana Stubblefield	.50
148	John Taylor	.50
149	Ricky Watters	1.00
150	Steve Young	2.00
151	Brian Blades	.50
152	Cortez Kennedy	.50
153	Rick Mirer	.50
154	Rufus Porter	.50
155	Eugene Robinson	.50
156	Chris Warren	.50
157	Santana Dotson	.50
158	Craig Erickson	.50
159	Hardy Nickerson	.50
160	Dan Stryzinski	.50
161	Charles Wilson	.50
162	Thomas Everett	.50
163	Reggie Brooks	.50
164	Darryl Green	.50
165	Ricky Ervins	.50
166	John Friesz	.50
167	Brian Mitchell	.50
168	Sterling Palmer	.50

1994-95 Crown Pro Mags Fb

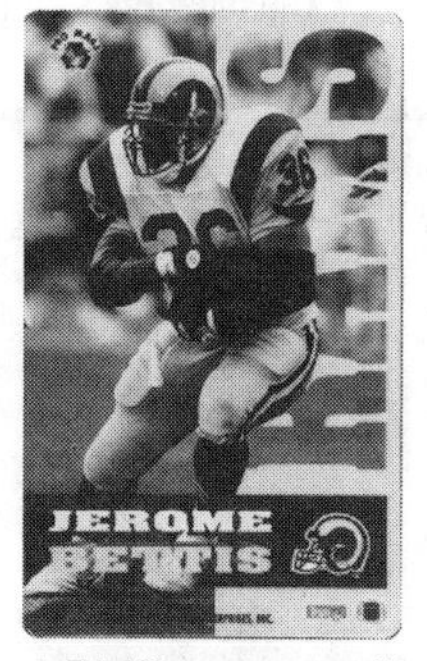

This 168-magnet set was sold in five-magnet packs that included a team magnet. It included 140 players and 28 team magnets, which all measure 2-1/8" x 3-3/8". A Warren Moon magnet was also available by mailing in a redemption card and three proofs of purchase along with $6. The magnets display the player's name at the bottom in team colors, with the team name running up the right side. A parallel Super Bowl XXIX set was also issued, but carries no premium in price. The player magnets are numbered on the front, but the team magnets were unnumbered and checklisted in alphabetical order. In addition, a Troy Aikman promo magnet is also listed below.

		MT
Complete Set (140):		75.00
Common Player:		.50
1	Rod Bernstine	.50
2	John Elway	2.00
3	Glyn Milburn	.50
4	Shannon Sharpe	.50
5	Dennis Smith	.50
6	Cody Carlson	.50
7	Ernest Givins	.50
8	Haywood Jeffires	.50
9	Bruce Matthews	.50
10	Webster Slaughter	.50
11	O.J. McDuffie	1.00
12	Keith Byars	.50
13	Bryan Cox	.50
14	Irving Fryar	.50
15	Dan Marino	6.00
16	Barry Foster	.50
17	Kevin Greene	1.00
18	Greg Lloyd	1.00
19	Neil O'Donnell	.50
20	Rod Woodson	.50
21	Steve Beuerlein	.50
22	Chuck Cecil	.50
23	Randal Hill	.50
24	Ricky Proehl	.50
25	Eric Swann	.50
26	Troy Aikman	3.00
27	Emmitt Smith	6.00
28	Michael Irvin	1.00
29	Russell Maryland	.50
30	Jay Novacek	.50
31	Jerome Bettis	2.00
32	Sean Gilbert	.50
33	Todd Lyght	.50
34	Chris Martin	.50
35	Roman Phifer	.50
36	Neal Anderson	.50
37	Quinn Early	.50
38	Rickey Jackson	.50
39	Sam Mills	.50
40	William Roaf	.50
41	Cornelius Bennett	.50
42	Jim Kelly	1.00
43	Kenneth Davis	.50
44	Darryl Tallfy	.50
45	Andre Reed	.50
46	Cris Carter	1.00
47	Warren Moon	1.00
48	Terry Allen	1.00
49	Raghib Ismail	.50
50	Robert Smith	1.00
51	Erric Pegram	.50
52	Andre Rison	1.00
53	Deion Sanders	2.00
54	Jessie Tuggle	.50
55	Jeff George	.50
56	Brian Blades	.50
57	Rick Mirer	1.00
58	Cortez Kennedy	.50
59	Chris Warren	1.00
60	Eugene Robinson	.50
61	Reggie Brooks	.50
62	Ricky Ervins	.50
63	Brian Mitchell	.50
64	Ricky Sanders	.50
65	Sterling Palmer	.50
66	Tim Brown	1.00
67	Jeff Hostetler	.50
68	Raghib Ismail	.50
69	Terry McDaniel	.50
70	James Jett	.50
71	Sterling Sharpe	1.00
72	Brett Favre	8.00
73	Reggie White	1.00
74	Terrell Buckley	.50
75	Edgar Bennett	.50
76	Jerry Rice	3.00
77	Steve Young	2.00
78	Ricky Watters	1.00
79	Dana Stubblefield	1.00
80	John Taylor	.50
81	Ronnie Harmon	.50
82	Stan Humphries	.50
83	Natrone Means	1.50
84	Junior Seau	1.00
85	Eric Bieniemy	.50
86	Dean Biasucci	.50
87	Jim Harbaugh	1.00
88	Roosevelt Potts	.50
89	Scott Radecic	.50
90	Rohn Stark	.50
91	Eric Metcalf	.50
92	Michael Dean Perry	.50
93	Vinny Testaverde	.50
94	Mark Carrier	.50
95	Michael Jackson	.50
96	Marcus Allen	1.00
97	Dale Carter	.50
98	Neil Smith	.50
99	J.J. Birden	.50
100	Willie Davis	.50
101	Rodney Hampton	.50
102	Mark Jackson	.50
103	David Meggett	.50
104	John Elliott	.50
105	Kenyon Rasheed	.50
106	Boomer Esiason	.50
107	Johnny Johnson	.50
108	Johnny Mitchell	.50
109	Brad Baxter	.50
110	Ronnie Lott	.50
111	Derrick Fenner	.50
112	David Klingler	.50
113	Bruce Pickens	.50
114	Harold Green	.50
115	Jeff Query	.50
116	Leonard Russell	.50
117	Drew Bledsoe	3.00
118	Marv Cook	.50
119	Vincent Brisby	.50
120	Vincent Brown	.50
121	Trace Armstrong	.50
122	Curtis Conway	1.00
123	Dante Jones	.50
124	Tim Worley	.50
125	Chris Zorich	.50
126	Ron Moore	.50
127	Barry Sanders	3.00
128	Pat Swilling	.50
129	Brett Perriman	.50
130	Chris Spielman	.50
131	Keith Byars	.50
132	Fred Barnett	.50
133	Randall Cunningham	.50
134	Herschel Walker	.50
135	Bubby Brister	.50
136	Craig Erickson	.50
137	Hardy Nickerson	.50
138	Demetrius Dubose	.50
139	Dan Stryzinski	.50
140	Charles Wilson	.50

1995 Crown Pro Magnets Fb

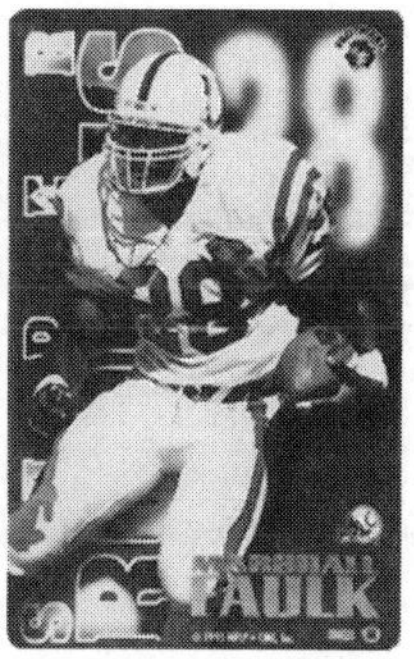

This 150-card set was produced by Chris Martin Enterprises and was sold in five-card packs. The magnets are grouped alphabetically according to team below. There were three insert sets available, called By The Zone, Classics and Die-cuts, as well as a Superhero Jumbos redemption set.

		MT
Complete Set (150):		70.00
Common Player:		.50
1	Larry Centers	.50
2	Garrison Hearst	1.00
3	Seth Joyner	.50
4	Ron Moore	.50
5	Eric Swann	.50
6	Chris Doleman	.50
7	Jeff George	.50
8	Craig Heyward	.50
9	Terrance Mathis	.50
10	Jessie Tuggle	.50
11	Cornelius Bennett	.50
12	Jim Kelly	1.00
13	Andre Reed	.50
14	Bruce Smith	.50
15	Darryl Talley	.50
16	Trace Armstrong	.50
17	Dante Jones	.50

18 Steve Walsh .50
19 Donnell Woolford .50
20 Tim Worley .50
21 Jeff Blake 2.00
22 Harold Green .50
23 Carl Pickens 1.00
24 Danny Scott 1.00
25 Dan Wilkinson .50
26 Derrick Alexander .50
27 Leroy Hoard .50
28 Antonio Langham .50
29 Vinny Testaverde .50
30 Eric Turner .50
31 Troy Aikman 2.00
32 Michael Irvin 1.00
33 Darryl Johnston .50
34 Russell Maryland .50
35 Emmitt Smith 4.00
36 Rod Bernstine .50
37 John Elway 1.50
38 Anthony Miller .50
39 Glyn Milburn .50
40 Shannon Sharpe .50
41 Scott Mitchell 1.00
42 Herman Moore 1.00
43 Brett Perriman .50
44 Barry Sanders 2.00
45 Chris Spielman .50
46 Edgar Bennett .50
47 Robert Brooks .50
48 Brett Favre 6.00
49 Sean Jones .50
50 Reggie White 1.00
51 Gary Brown .50
52 Cody Carlson .50
53 Ernest Givins .50
54 Haywood Jeffires .50
55 Bruce Matthews .50
56 Quentin Coryatt .50
57 Steve Emtman .50
58 Marshall Faulk 1.50
59 Jim Harbaugh 1.00
60 Roosevelt Potts .50
61 Marcus Allen 1.00
62 Steve Bono .50
63 Willie Davis .50
64 Lake Dawson .50
65 Neil Smith .50
66 Tim Brown .50
67 Jeff Hostetler .50
68 Raghib Ismail .50
69 James Jett .50
70 Harvey Williams .50
71 Jerome Bettis 1.00
72 Troy Drayton .50
73 Wayne Gandy .50
74 Sean Gilbert .50
75 Todd Lyght .50
76 Tim Bowens .50
77 Bryan Cox .50
78 Irving Fryar .50
79 Dan Marino 4.00
80 Bernie Parmalee .50
81 Terry Allen 1.00
82 Cris Carter .50
83 Qadry Ismail .50
84 Warren Moon 1.00
85 John Randle .50
86 Bruce Armstrong .50
87 Drew Bledsoe 2.00
88 Vincent Brisby .50
89 Marion Butts .50
90 Ben Coates .50
91 Morten Andersen .50
92 Quinn Early .50
93 Jim Everett .50
94 Tyrone Hughes .50
95 Renaldo Turnbull .50
96 Michael Brooks .50
97 Dave Brown .50
98 John Elliott .50
99 Rodney Hampton .50
100 Mike Sherrard .50
101 Boomer Esiason .50
102 Johnny Johnson .50
103 Nick Lowery .50
104 Johnny Mitchell .50
105 Aaron Glenn .50
106 Fred Barnett .50
107 Bubby Brister .50
108 Randall Cunningham .50
109 Charlie Garner .50
110 Calvin Williams .50
111 Byron "Bam" Morris .50
112 Barry Foster .50
113 Kevin Greene .50
114 Neil O'Donnell .50
115 Rod Woodson .50
116 Ronnie Harmon .50
117 Stan Humphries .50
118 Tony Martin .50
119 Natrone Means 1.00
120 Junior Seau 1.00
121 William Floyd 1.00
122 Jerry Rice 2.00
123 Deion Sanders 1.50
124 Dana Stubblefield .50
125 Steve Young 1.50
126 Brian Blades .50
127 Cortez Kennedy .50
128 Rick Mirer .50
129 Eugene Robinson .50
130 Chris Warren .50
131 Trent Dilfer 1.00
132 Santana Dotson .50
133 Craig Erickson .50
134 Thomas Everett .50
135 Errict Rhett 1.00
136 Reggie Brooks .50
137 Ricky Ervins .50
138 Darryl Green .50
139 Brian Mitchell .50
140 Heath Shuler 1.00
141 Frank Ricci .50
142 Tim McKyer .50
143 Tyrone Poole .50
144 Derrick Lassic .50
145 Bob Christian .50
146 Steve Beuerlein .50
147 Cedric Tillman .50
148 Reggie Cobb .50
149 Eugene Chung .50
150 Desmond Howard .50

A player's name in *italic type* indicates a rookie card.

1995 Crown Pro Magnets In The Zone Fb

By the Zone was a 12-card magnet insert in 1995 Pro Mags. The magnets feature a borderless color action shot of a player, and were inserted every three packs.

MT
Complete Set (12): 15.00
Common Player: .75
1 Troy Aikman 2.00
2 Drew Bledsoe 2.00
3 John Elway 1.50
4 Brett Favre 4.00
5 Jeff Hostetler .75
6 Stan Humphries .75
7 Dan Marino 4.00
8 Jim Kelly .75
9 Warren Moon .75
10 Neil O'Donnell .75
11 Rick Mirer .75
12 Steve Young 1.50

1995 Crown Pro Magnets Magnetic Classics Fb

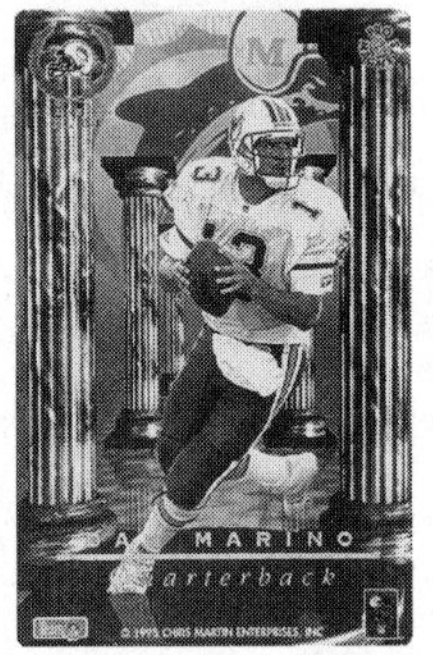

Classics features 12 players in front of a column background with the team logo. Classics were inserted into every three packs of 1995 Pro Mags.

MT
Complete Set (12): 15.00
Common Player: .75
1 Barry Sanders 2.00
2 Deion Sanders 1.50
3 Dan Marino 4.00
4 Drew Bledsoe 2.00
5 Marcus Allen .75
6 Jerome Bettis 1.00
7 John Elway 1.50
8 Jerry Rice 2.00
9 Emmitt Smith 4.00
10 Steve Young 1.50
11 Troy Aikman 2.00
12 Marshall Faulk 1.00

1995 Crown Pro Mags Rookies

This 12-magnet set features players taken in the 1994 NFL Draft. The magnets measure 2-1/8" x 3-3/8" and include a color photo and the player's name printed in gold foil.

MT
Complete Set (12): 12.00
Common Player: .75
1 Trent Dilfer 1.50
2 Heath Shuler 1.00
3 John Thierry .75
4 Wayne Gandy .75
5 Errict Rhett 1.00
6 David Palmer 1.00
7 Andre Coleman .75
8 Lake Dawson 1.00
9 Marshall Faulk 1.50
10 Dan Wilkinson .75
11 Greg Hill .75
12 Willie McGinest 1.00

1995 Crown Pro Superhero Jumbos

Chris Martin Enterprises offered this three oversized magnet set through the mail. With details on 1995 Pro Mag packs, collectors received the set for $6. Each card, measuring 3-3/4" x 7", features fantasy art of either Jerome Bettis, John Elway or Warren Moon.

MT
Complete Set (3): 20.00
Common Player: 6.00
1 Jerome Bettis 7.00
2 John Elway 8.00
3 Warren Moon 6.00

1995 Crown Pro Mags Teams

Each magnet in this set features three top players from an NFL team and the embossed team logo. The unnumbered magnets were originally released as a promo set.

MT
Complete Set (5): 20.00
Common Player: 3.00
1 Chargers (Junior Seau, Stan Humphries, Natrone Means) 3.00
2 Cowboys (Michael Irvin, Troy Aikman, Emmitt Smith) 6.00
3 Dolphins (Dan Marino, O.J. McDuffie, Bernie Parmalee) 6.00
4 49ers (Ricky Watters, Steve Young, Jerry Rice) 5.00
5 Steelers (Barry Foster, Neil O'Donnell, Rod Woodson) 3.00

1995 Crown Pro Stamps

This 140-stamp set was sold in 12-stamp sheets. The stamps measure 1-1/2" x 2".

MT
Complete Set (140): 40.00
Common Player: .25
1 Steve Young DP .50
2 Jerry Rice 1.00
3 Deion Sanders .75
4 Dana Stubblefield .25
5 William Floyd .40
6 Troy Aikman DP .75
7 Michael Irvin .50
8 Emmitt Smith DP 1.50
9 Russell Maryland .25
10 Daryl Johnston .40
11 Dan Marino DP 1.50
12 Bernie Parmalee .25
13 Tim Bowens .25
14 Irving Fryar .25
15 Bryan Cox .25
16 Drew Bledsoe 1.00
17 Bruce Armstrong .25
18 Vincent Brisby .25
19 Marion Butts .25
20 Ben Coates .25
21 Dave Brown .25
22 Michael Brooks .25
23 Jumbo Elliott .25
24 Rodney Hampton .25
25 Mike Sherrard .25
26 Jeff Hostetler .25
27 Tim Brown .60
28 Rocket Ismail .25
29 James Jett .25
30 Harvey Williams .25
31 Heath Shuler .50
32 Reggie Brooks .25
33 Ricky Ervins .25
34 Darrell Green UER (Darryl on front) .25
35 Brian Mitchell .25
36 Trace Armstrong .25
37 Dante Jones .25
38 Steve Walsh .25
39 Donnell Woolford .25
40 Tim Worley .25
41 Boomer Esiason .25
42 Aaron Glenn .25
43 Johnny Johnson .25
44 Nick Lowery .25
45 Johnny Mitchell .25
46 Neil O'Donnell .25
47 Barry Foster .25
48 Byron "Bam" Morris .25
49 Rod Woodson .25
50 Kevin Greene .25
51 Randall Cunningham .25
52 Bubby Brister .25
53 Fred Barnett .25
54 Charlie Garner .25
55 Calvin Williams .25
56 Brett Favre 2.00
57 Reggie White .60
58 Edgar Bennett .25
59 Robert Brooks .25
60 Sean Jones .25
61 Ronnie Harmon .25
62 Stan Humphries .25
63 Natrone Means .60
64 Tony Martin .25
65 Junior Seau .25
66 John Elway .75
67 Glyn Milburn .25
68 Rod Bernstine .25
69 Anthony Miller .25
70 Shannon Sharpe .60
71 Barry Sanders 1.00
72 Scott Mitchell .40
73 Herman Moore .60
74 Brett Perriman .40
75 Chris Spielman .40
76 Marcus Allen .60
77 Steve Bono .40
78 Willie Davis .25
79 Lake Dawson .25
80 Neil Smith .25
81 Vinny Testaverde .60
82 Eric Turner .25
83 Antonio Langham .25
84 Leroy Hoard .25
85 Derrick Alexander WR .25
86 Jim Kelly .60
87 Cornelius Bennett .25
88 Andre Reed .25
89 Bruce Smith .25
90 Darryl Talley .25
91 Warren Moon .60
92 Qadry Ismail .25
93 Terry Allen .60
94 Cris Carter .60
95 John Randle .25
96 Jeff George .60
97 Chris Doleman .25
98 Craig Heyward .25
99 Terance Mathis .25
100 Jessie Tuggle .25
101 Jerome Bettis .60
102 Sean Gilbert .25
103 Troy Drayton .25
104 Wayne Gandy .25
105 Todd Lyght .25
106 Jeff Blake .75
107 Harold Green .25
108 Carl Pickens .60
109 Dan Wilkinson .25
110 Darnay Scott .40
111 Cody Carlson .25
112 Gary Brown .25
113 Ernest Givins .25
114 Haywood Jeffires .25
115 Bruce Matthews .25
116 Jim Everett .25
117 Morten Andersen .25
118 Quinn Early .25
119 Tyrone Hughes .25
120 Renaldo Turnbull .25
121 Larry Centers .25
122 Garrison Hearst .60
123 Seth Joyner .25
124 Ronald Moore .25
125 Eric Swann .25
126 Rick Mirer .60
127 Chris Warren .40
128 Brian Blades .25
129 Cortez Kennedy .25
130 Eugene Robinson .25
131 Marshall Faulk .60
132 Quentin Coryatt .25
133 Jim Harbaugh .60
134 Roosevelt Potts .25
135 Steve Emtman .25
136 Trent Dilfer .60
137 Santana Dotson .25
138 Errict Rhett .60
139 Thomas Everett .25
140 Craig Erickson .25

1996 Crown Pro Retail Mags

Not to be confused with the 1996 Pro Magnets, this 12-magnet set was sold in one-magnet cello packs. A cut-out action photo of the player is placed over a team-colored foil background. "Compacted" ghosted images of the action shot are also included in the foil background. The player's name is printed in gold foil along the left side of the magnet. The team logo is in foil in the lower left, while a larger team logo is located in the lower right. The magnet's number is printed in gold foil in the lower right. A 1996 Chris Martin Enterprises copyright tag line is printed at the bottom of the magnet in black. The backs are blank.

MT
Complete Set (12): 30.00
Common Player: 1.00
1 Tim Brown 1.00
2 John Elway 4.00
3 Marshall Faulk 2.00
4 Dan Marino 6.00
5 Curtis Martin 3.00
6 Rashaan Salaam 1.00
7 Barry Sanders 6.00
8 Emmitt Smith 6.00
9 Neil Smith 1.00
10 Reggie White 2.00
11 Rod Woodson 1.00
12 Steve Young 3.00

1996 Crown Pro Magnets Fb

The 100-card set features a cut-out action photo of a player placed over a team-colored foil background. A marble-type 3-D box is behind the cut-out photo. The player's name is in gold-foil along the left side, with the team's logo in gold-foil near the bottom right. The fronts include the magnet number in the lower left in gold-foil. The team name is printed in all capital letters at the top right of the magnet. The Pro Magnets logo is in the upper left. NFL and NFL Players Inc. logos, along with the Chris Martin Enterprises tag line, are printed at the bottom. The backs are blank.

MT
Complete Set (100): 70.00
Common Player: .50
1 Troy Aikman 2.00
2 Michael Irvin 1.00
3 Emmitt Smith 4.00
4 Deion Sanders 1.50
5 Jay Novacek .50
6 Jerry Rice 2.00
7 Steve Young 1.50
8 J.J. Stokes .50
9 William Floyd .50
10 Merton Hanks .50
11 Greg Lloyd .50
12 Rod Woodson .50
13 Kordell Stewart 3.00
14 Yancey Thigpen .50
15 Charles Johnson .50
16 Richmond Webb .50
17 Eric Green .50
18 Bernie Parmalee .50
19 Dan Marino 4.00
20 O.J. McDuffie .50
21 Brett Favre 5.00
22 Reggie White 1.00
23 Robert Brooks .50
24 Edgar Bennett .50
25 Marcus Allen 1.00
26 Tamarick Vanover 1.00
27 Lake Dawson .50
28 Neil Smith .50
29 Steve Bono .50
30 Harvey Williams .50
31 Tim Brown .50
32 Jeff Hostetler .50
33 Drew Bledsoe 2.00
34 Vincent Brisby .50
35 Curtis Martin 3.00
36 Rashaan Salaam 1.00
37 Erik Kramer .50
38 Curtis Conway 1.00
39 Kerry Collins 2.00
40 Sam Mills .50
41 Mark Carrier .50
42 Dave Brown .50
43 Rodney Hampton .50
44 Tyrone Wheatley .50
45 Vinny Testaverde .50
46 Andre Rison .50
47 Eric Turner .50
48 Michael Jackson .50
49 Mark Brunell 1.50
50 Jeff Lageman .50
51 Roman Phifer .50
52 Isaac Bruce 1.00
53 Rodney Peete .50
54 Ricky Watters 1.00
55 Calvin Williams .50
56 Warren Moon .50
57 Cris Carter .50
58 David Palmer .50
59 Scott Mitchell .50
60 Barry Sanders 2.00
61 Herman Moore 1.00
62 Brett Perriman .50
63 Jim Kelly .50
64 Bruce Smith .50
65 Bryce Paup .50
66 Junior Seau 1.00
67 Stan Humphries .50
68 Andre Coleman .50
69 Tony Martin .50
70 Terry Allen .50
71 Heath Shuler .50
72 John Elway 1.50
73 Terrell Davis 2.00
74 Mike Pritchard .50
75 Neil O'Donnell .50
76 Kyle Brady .50
77 Jim Harbaugh .50
78 Marshall Faulk 1.00
79 Zack Crockett .50
80 Quentin Coryatt .50
81 Jeff George .50
82 Morten Anderson .50
83 Eric Metcalf .50
84 Joey Galloway 1.00
85 Rick Mirer .50
86 Chris Warren .50
87 Ray Zellars .50
88 Eric Allen .50
89 Jim Everett .50
90 Jeff Blake 1.00
91 Carl Pickens .50
92 Ki-Jana Carter .50
93 Larry Centers .50
94 Garrison Hearst .50
95 Trent Dilfer .50
96 Errict Rhett 1.00
97 Hardy Nickerson .50
98 Alvin Harper .50
99 Steve McNair 2.00
100 Haywood Jeffires .50

1996 Crown Pro Destination All-Pro Fb

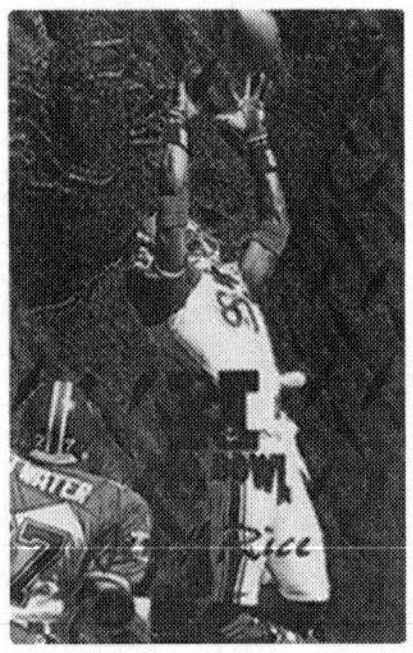

This six-magnet set was randomly inserted one per four Pro Magnets packs. The magnets have a cut-out action photo of the player placed over an etched-foil background, which is red and silver for the AFC and blue and silver for the NFC Pro Bowlers. A ghosted image of the player is included in the background at the upper left. The Pro Magnets logo is in the upper right. The AFC or NFC Pro Bowl logo, along with the player's name, are printed in gold foil at the bottom center of the magnet. The magnets are numbered in the lower left with a prefix of "PB". The backs are blank.

MT
Complete Set (6): 20.00
Common Player: 1.00
1 Jim Harbaugh 1.00
2 Curtis Martin 3.00
3 Yancey Thigpen 1.00
4 Brett Favre 8.00
5 Jerry Rice 4.00
6 Barry Sanders 6.00

1996 Crown Pro Die-Cuts

This 16-magnet set includes a cut-out action shot of the player placed over a die-cut background of the team's logo and player name. The player's first name is printed in gold foil over the top left portion of his last name, which is printed in team colors. "Die-Cut Magnets" is printed in gold foil to the right of the NFL and NFL Players Inc. logos at the bottom. The team's logo is printed in team colors over the upper right portion of the player's last name. A 1996 Chris Martin Enterprises Inc. copyright tag line is printed in black at the bottom center of the magnets. The magnets were sold in one-magnet cello packs.

MT
Complete Set (16): 50.00
Common Player: 1.00
1 Troy Aikman 4.00
2 Deion Sanders 3.00
3 Emmitt Smith 6.00
4 Jerry Rice 4.00
5 Steve Young 3.00
6 Kordell Stewart 4.00
7 Dan Marino 6.00
8 Brett Favre 8.00
9 Marcus Allen 2.00
10 Drew Bledsoe 4.00
11 Barry Sanders 6.00
12 Marshall Faulk 2.00
13 John Elway 4.00
14 Rashaan Salaam 1.00
15 Jeff Hostetler 1.00
16 Keyshawn Johnson 1.00

1996 Crown Pro Draft Day Future Stars Fb

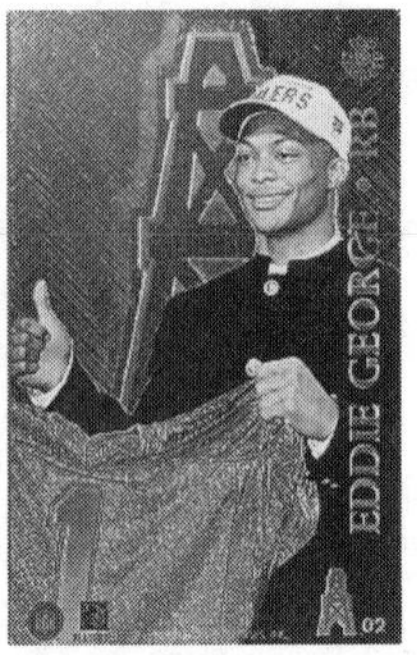

This six-card chase set included NFL rookies on randomly inserted magnets. The magnets are the same size as the other magnets in the Pro Magnets set.

MT
Complete Set (6): 15.00
Common Player: 1.00
1 Kevin Hardy 1.00
2 Eddie George 8.00
3 Keyshawn Johnson 5.00
4 Tim Biakabutuka 1.00
5 Lawrence Phillips 3.00
6 Alex Molden 1.00

1996 Crown Pro Stamps

This 144-stamp set is similar to the 1995 series. They are the same size and utilize the same design and many of the same player photos. They were also sold in 12-stamp packs.

MT
Complete Set (144): 35.00
Common Player: .25
1 Steve Young .75
2 Jerry Rice 1.00
3 Merton Hanks .25
4 J.J. Stokes .40
5 William Floyd .40
6 Troy Aikman 1.00
7 Michael Irvin .50
8 Emmitt Smith 2.00
9 Deion Sanders .60
10 Daryl Johnston .40
11 Dan Marino 2.00
12 Bernie Parmalee .25
13 O.J. McDuffie .40
14 Richmond Webb .25
15 Eric Green .25
16 Drew Bledsoe 1.00
17 Bruce Armstrong .25
18 Dave Meggett .25
19 Curtis Martin 1.00
20 Ben Coates .40
21 Dave Brown .25
22 Michael Brooks .25
23 Tyrone Wheatley .40
24 Rodney Hampton .40
25 Jeff Hostetler .25
26 Tim Brown .50
27 Rocket Ismail .40
28 James Jett .25
29 Harvey Williams .40
30 Heath Shuler .50
31 Michael Westbrook .50
32 Terry Allen .50
33 Darrell Green .40
34 Brian Mitchell .25
35 Rashaan Salaam .50
36 Erik Kramer UER 37 .25
37 Donnell Woolford .25
38 Alonzo Spellman .25
39 Kyle Brady .40
40 Aaron Glenn .25
41 Adrian Murrell .40
42 Nick Lowery .25
43 Charles Johnson .40
44 Kordell Stewart 1.00
45 Yancey Thigpen .40
46 Rod Woodson .40
47 Greg Lloyd .50
48 Randall Cunningham .40
49 Rodney Peete .25
50 Ricky Watters .50
51 Charlie Garner .25
52 Calvin Williams .25
53 Brett Favre 2.50
54 Reggie White .50
55 Edgar Bennett .40
56 Robert Brooks .50
57 Sean Jones .25
58 Ronnie Harmon .25
59 Stan Humphries .40
60 Andre Coleman .25
61 Tony Martin .40
62 Junior Seau .50
63 John Elway .75
64 Mike Pritchard .25
65 Terrell Davis 1.00
66 Anthony Miller .40

67	Shannon Sharpe	.50
68	Barry Sanders	1.25
69	Scott Mitchell	.40
70	Herman Moore	.50
71	Brett Perriman	.40
72	Johnnie Morton	.40
73	Marcus Allen	.50
74	Steve Bono	.40
75	Tamarick Vanover	.25
76	Lake Dawson	.25
77	Neil Smith	.25
78	Vinny Testaverde	.40
79	Eric Turner	.25
80	Michael Jackson	.40
81	Leroy Hoard	.25
82	Andre Rison	.50
83	Jim Kelly	.50
84	Carwell Gardner	.25
85	Andre Reed	.40
86	Bruce Smith	.50
87	Bryce Paup	.40
88	Warren Moon	.50
89	Qadry Ismail	.40
90	Robert Smith	.40
91	Cris Carter	.50
92	David Palmer	.25
93	Jeff George	.50
94	Morten Andersen	.25
95	Craig Heyward	.25
96	Eric Metcalf	.40
97	Jessie Tuggle	.25
98	Roman Phifer	.25
99	Todd Lyght	.25
100	Troy Drayton	.25
101	Isaac Bruce	.50
102	Sean Gilbert	.25
103	Jeff Blake	.60
104	Harold Green	.25
105	Carl Pickens	.50
106	Dan Wilkinson	.25
107	Ki-Jana Carter	.40
108	Steve McNair	.75
109	Gary Brown	.25
110	Haywood Jeffires	.25
111	Bruce Matthews	.25
112	Jim Everett	.25
113	Mario Bates	.25
114	Ray Zellars	.25
115	Tyrone Hughes	.25
116	Eric Allen	.25
117	Larry Centers	.40
118	Garrison Hearst	.50
119	Aeneas Williams	.25
120	Rob Moore	.25
121	Neil O'Donnell	.40
122	Rick Mirer	.25
123	Chris Warren	.40
124	Eric Swann	.25
125	Cortez Kennedy	.25
126	Joey Galloway	.50
127	Marshall Faulk	.50
128	Quentin Coryatt	.25
129	Jim Harbaugh	.50
130	Trev Alberts	.25
131	Zack Crockett	.25
132	Trent Dilfer	.40
133	Hardy Nickerson	.25
134	Errict Rhett	.50
135	Alvin Harper	.25
136	Sam Mills	.25
137	Tyrone Poole	.40
138	Kerry Collins	.75
139	Bob Christian	.25
140	Randy Baldwin	.25
141	Steve Beuerlein	.25
142	Mark Brunell	1.00
143	Tony Boselli	.40
144	Jeff Lageman	.25

D

1986 DairyPak Cartons

These cards were sponsored by various brands of milk across the country in 1986; different colors (purple, green, lavender, aqua, orange, red, light blue, dark blue, black and brown) were used for different sponsors. Each card is perforated and features a black-and-white head shot of the player, plus a facsimilie autograph and card number. Cards which have been cut from the milk carton measure 3-1/4" x 4-7/16", but generally are more valuable if they are left intact as a complete carton. The set was not licensed by the NFL, so no team logos are shown; the NFLPA, however, licensed the set. Below each card was an offer to receive a 24" x 32" poster featuring the 24 cards.

		MT
Complete Set (24):		65.00
Common Player:		1.25
1	Joe Montana	10.00
2	Marcus Allen	3.00
3	Art Monk	2.00
4	Mike Quick	1.25
5	John Elway	5.00
6	Eric Hipple	1.25
7	Louis Lipps	1.25
8	Dan Fouts	2.00
9	Phil Simms	2.00
10	Mike Rozier	1.25
11	Greg Bell	1.25
12	Ottis Anderson	1.50
13	Dave Krieg	1.75
14	Anthony Carter	1.25
15	Freeman McNeil	1.25
16	Doug Cosbie	1.25
17	James Lofton	6.00
18	Dan Marino	8.00
19	James Wilder	1.25
20	Cris Collinsworth	1.50
21	Eric Dickerson	4.00
22	Walter Payton	6.00
23	Ozzie Newsome	2.00
24	Chris Hinton	1.25

1971-72 Dell

This 48-player set, which measures 8-1/4" x 10-3/4", from the 1971-72 Dell Pro Football Guide includes a center insert that unfolds to show 48 color photos. The photos, bordered in black and yellow, each measure 1-3/4" x 3". The player's name and team name are located inside a rectangle under the photo. The backs boast action photos, which are bordered in black and white. The football guide includes bios on each of the players offered in the set. The photos are not numbered. A complete set which is still intact in the guides are valued at 25 percent over what is listed here.

		NM
Complete Set (48):		100.00
Common Player:		1.00
1	Dan Abramowicz	1.00
2	Herb Adderley	2.00
3	Lem Barney	1.00
4	Bobby Bell	1.00
5	George Blanda	3.00
6	Terry Bradshaw	15.00
7	John Brodie	2.00
8	Larry Brown	1.00
9	Dick Butkus	10.00
10	Fred Carr	1.00
11	Virgil Carter	1.00
12	Mike Curtis	1.00
13	Len Dawson	2.50
14	Carl Eller	1.00
15	Mel Farr	1.00
16	Roman Gabriel	1.50
17	Gary Garrison	1.00
18	Dick Gordon	1.00
19	Bob Griese	5.00
20	Bob Hayes	1.50
21	Rich Jackson	1.00
22	Charlie Johnson	1.00
23	Ron Johnson	1.00
24	Deacon Jones	2.50
25	Sonny Jurgensen	2.50
26	Leroy Kelly	1.50
27	Daryle Lamonica	1.50
28	MacArthur Lane	1.00
29	Willie Lanier	1.50
30	Bob Lilly	3.00
31	Floyd Little	1.00
32	Mike Lucci	1.00
33	Don Maynard	2.50
34	Joe Namath	16.00
35	Tommy Nobis	1.50
36	Merlin Olsen	3.00
37	Alan Page	2.00
38	Gerry Philbin	1.00
39	Jim Plunkett	2.00
40	Tim Rossovich	1.00
41	Gale Sayers	10.00
42	Dennis Shaw	1.00
43	O.J. Simpson	14.00
44	Fran Tarkenton	7.00
45	Johnny Unitas	12.00
46	Paul Warfield	3.00
47	Gene Washington	1.00
48	Larry Wilson	1.50

1933 Diamond Matchbooks Silver

With covers measuring 1-1/2" x 4-1/2" when folded out, the 95-matchbook set has a photo of the player over a pink or green background, bordered in silver. Prices listed here are with the matches removed. The player's name and team are listed at the bottom of the cover fronts. The cover backs showcase the player's name and highlights inside a box. The matchbooks are not numbered. Matchbooks with the matches intact are worth 1-1/2 to 2 times more than what is listed.

		NM
Complete Set (95):		1100.
Common Player:		10.00
1	All-American Board of Football Seal	15.00
2	Gene Alford	10.00
3	Marger Apsit	10.00
4	Morris (Red) Badgro	25.00
5	Cliff Battles	35.00
6	Morris (Maury) Bodenger	10.00
7	Jimmy Bowdoin	10.00
8	John Boylan	10.00
9	Hank Bruder	10.00
10	Carl Brumbaugh	15.00
11	Bill Buckler	10.00
12	Jerome Buckley	10.00
13	Dale Burnett	10.00
14	Ernie Caddel	12.00
15	Red Cagle	12.00
16	Glen Campbell	10.00
17	John Cannella	10.00
18	Zuck Carlson	10.00
19	George Christensen	15.00
20	Stu Clancy	10.00
21	Paul (Rip) Collins	10.00
22	John F. Connell	10.00
23	George Corbett	10.00
24	Orien Crow	10.00
25	Ed Danowski	12.00
26	Sylvester (Red) Davis	10.00
27	John Isola	12.00
28	John Doehring	10.00
29	Glen Edwards	20.00
30	Earl Elser	10.00
31	Ox Emerson	15.00
32	Tiny Feather	10.00
33	Ray Flaherty	20.00
34	Ike Frankian	10.00
35	Red Grange	290.00
36	Len Grant	10.00
37	Ace Gutowsky	12.00
38	Mel Hein	20.00
39	Arnie Herber	20.00
40	Bill Hewitt	20.00
41	Herman Hickman	20.00
42	Clarke Hinkle	20.00
43	Cal Hubbard	20.00
44	George Hurley	10.00
45	Herman Hussey	10.00
46	Cecil (Tex) Irvin	10.00
47	Luke Johnson	12.00
48	Bruce Jones	10.00
49	Tom Jones	10.00
50	Thacker Kay	10.00
51	John Kelly	12.00
52	Joe (Doc) Kopcha	12.00
53	Joe Kurth	10.00
54	Milo Lubratevich	10.00
55	Father Lumpkin	12.00
56	Jim MacMurdo	10.00
57	Joe Maniaci	10.00
58	Jack McBride	10.00
59	Ookie Miller	10.00
60	Granville Mitchell	10.00
61	Keith Molesworth	12.00
62	Bob Monnett	10.00
63	Hap Moran	10.00
64	Bill Morgan	10.00
65	Maynard (Doc) Morrison	10.00
66	Mathew Murray	10.00
67	Jim Musick	10.00
68	Bronko Nagurski	290.00
69	Dick Nesbitt	10.00
70	Harry Newman	12.00
71	Steve Owen	15.00
72	Bill (Red) Owen	10.00
73	Andy Pavlicovic	10.00
74	Bert Pearson	10.00
75	William Pendergast	10.00
76	Jerry Pepper	10.00
77	Stan Piawlock	10.00
78	Ernie Pinckert	12.00
79	Glenn Presnell	10.00
80	Jess Quatse	10.00
81	Hank Reese	10.00
82	Dick Richards	10.00
83	Tony Sarausky	10.00
84	Elmer (Dutch) Schaake	10.00
85	John Schneller	10.00
86	Johnny Sisk	10.00
87	Mike Steponovich	10.00
88	Ken Strong	30.00
89	Charles Tackwell	10.00
90	Harry Thayer	15.00
91	Walt Uzdavinis	10.00
92	John Welch	10.00
93	William Whelan	10.00
94	Fay (Mule) Wilson	12.00
95	Frank (Babe) Wright	10.00

1934 Diamond Matchbooks

Measuring 1-1/2" x 4-1/2", each matchbook showcases four different colored borders, including blue, red, tan and green. Many players have each of the four color combinations. Other players have one or two variations of borders. The player's name and team are printed above the photo on the front. The backs spotlight the player's name and highlights. This set features "The Diamond Match Co., N.Y.C" above the striking strip on the matchbook backs. As a note, the 1935 matchbooks resemble this set, but do not have the "Diamond Match" tag line at the bottom. The books are unnumbered. If matches are intact in the book, they are worth 1-1/2 times more.

		NM
Complete Set (121):		1500.
Common Player:		10.00
1	Arvo Antilla	10.00
2	Morris (Red) Badgro	20.00
3	Norbert Bartell	10.00
4	Cliff Battles	25.00
5	Chuck Bennis	10.00
6	Jack Beynon	10.00
7	Morris (Maury) Bodenger	10.00
8	John Bond	10.00
9	John Brown	10.00
10	Carl Brumbaugh	10.00
11	Dale Burnett	10.00
12	Ernie Caddel	10.00
13	Red Cagle	10.00
14	Glen Campbell	10.00
15	John Cannella	10.00
16	Joe Carter	10.00
17	Les Caywood	10.00
18	George (Buck) Chapman	10.00
19	Frank Christensen	10.00
20	Stu Clancy	10.00
21	Algy Clark	10.00
22	Paul (Rip) Collins	10.00
23	Jack Connell	10.00
24	Orien Crow	10.00
25	Lone Star Dietz (CO)	10.00
26	John Doehring	10.00
27	Glen Edwards	20.00
28	Ox Emerson	10.00
29	Tiny Feather	10.00
30	Ray Flaherty	20.00
31	Frank Froschauer	10.00
32	Chuck Galbreath	10.00
33	Elbert (Red) Gragg	10.00
34	Red Grange	210.00
35	Cy Grant	10.00
36	Len Grant	10.00
37	Ross Grant	10.00
38	Jack Griffith	10.00
39	Ed Gryboski	10.00
40	Ace Gutowsky	10.00
41	Thomas (Swede) Hanson	10.00
42	Mel Hein	25.00
43	Warren Heller	10.00
44	Bill Hewitt	20.00
45	Cecil (Tex) Irvin	10.00
46	Frank Johnson	10.00
47	Jack Johnson	10.00
48	Bob Jones	10.00
49	Tom Jones	10.00
50	Carl Jorgensen	10.00
51	John Karcis	10.00
52	Eddie Kawal	10.00
53	John Kelly	10.00
54	George Kenneally	10.00
55	Walt Kiesling	20.00
56	Jack Knapper	10.00
57	Frank Knox	10.00
58	Joe (Doc) Kopcha	10.00
59	Joe Kresky	10.00
60	Joe Laws	10.00
61	Russ Lay	10.00
62	Biff Lee	10.00
63	Gil LeFebvre	10.00
64	Jim Leonard	10.00
65	Les Lindberg	10.00
66	John Lipski	10.00
67	Milo Lubratevich	10.00
68	Father Lumpkin	10.00
69	Jim MacMurdo	10.00
70	Ed Matesic	10.00
71	Dave McCollough	10.00
72	John McKnight	10.00
73	Johnny (Blood) McNally	30.00
74	Al Minot	10.00
75	Keith Molesworth	10.00
76	Jim Mooney	10.00
77	Leroy Moorehead	10.00
78	Bill Morgan	10.00
79	Bob Moser	10.00
80	Lee Mulleneaux	10.00
81	George Munday	10.00
82	George Musso	20.00
83	Harry Newman	10.00
84	Al Norgard	10.00
85	John (Cap) Oehler	10.00
86	Charlie Opper	10.00
87	Bill (Red) Owen	10.00
88	Steve Owen	20.00
89	Bert Pearson	10.00
90	Tom Perkinson	10.00
91	Mace Pike	10.00
92	Joe Pilconis	10.00
93	Lew Pope	10.00
94	Crain Portman	10.00
95	Glenn Presnell	10.00
96	Jess Quatse	10.00
97	Clare Randolph	10.00
98	Hank Reese	10.00
99	Paul Riblett	10.00
100	Dick Richards	10.00
101	Jack Roberts	10.00
102	John Rogers	10.00
103	Gene Ronzani	10.00
104	John Schueller	10.00
105	Bob Rowe	10.00
106	Alolph Schwammel	10.00
107	Earl (Red) Seick	10.00
108	Allen Shi	10.00
109	Ben Smith	10.00
110	Ken Strong	30.00
111	Elmer Taber	10.00
112	Charles Tackwell	10.00
113	Ray Tesser	10.00
114	John (Stumpy) Thomason	10.00
115	Charlie Turbyville	10.00
116	Claude Urevig	10.00
117	John (Harp) Vaughan	10.00
118	Henry Wagnon	10.00
119	John West	10.00
120	Lee Woodruff	10.00
121	Jim Zyntell	10.00

1934 Diamond Matchbooks College Rivals

The 12-matchbook set honors a college rivalry with text about the recent history of the games. Bordered in black or tan, matchbooks could be found in either variation. Matchbooks which still have the matches intact are worth 1-1/2 times more than what is listed here.

		NM
Complete Set (12):		100.00
Common Player:		10.00
1	Alabama vs. Fordham 1933	10.00
2	Army vs. Navy start to finish	10.00
3	Fordham vs. St. Mary's lose by a 13-6 score	10.00
4	Georgia vs. Georgia Tech Bulldog Alumni and followers	10.00
5	Holy Cross vs. Boston College in atoning for this one defeat	10.00
6	Lafayette vs. Lehigh victory for Lafayette	10.00
7	Michigan vs. Ohio State Champions	10.00
8	Notre Dame vs. Army leader of men, Knute Rockne	12.00
9	Penn vs. Cornell pass	10.00
10	USC vs. Notre Dame year	12.00
11	Yale vs. Harvard Harvard	10.00
12	Yale vs. Princeton scoring 27	10.00

1935 Diamond Matchbooks

In 1935, three different colored borders were used for this set, including tan, green and red. However, this time players were only printed with one color border. Resembling the 1934 set, this set can be identified by the "Made in U.S.A./The Diamond Match Co., N.Y.C." tag line. The unnumbered matchbooks measure 1-1/2" x 4-1/2". The player photo is not bordered and a player position is not listed. Matchbooks with the matches intact are valued at 1-1/2 times the values listed here.

		NM
Complete Set (96):		1000.
Common Player:		10.00
1	Alf Anderson	10.00
2	Alec Ashford	10.00
3	Gene Augusterfer	10.00
4	Morris (Red) Badgro	20.00
5	Cliff Battles	25.00
6	Harry Benson	10.00
7	Tony Blazine	10.00
8	John Bond	10.00
9	Maurice (Mule) Bray	10.00
10	Dale Burnett	10.00
11	Charles (Cocky) Bush	10.00
12	Ernie Caddel	10.00
13	Zuck Carlson	10.00
14	Joe Carter	10.00
15	Cy Casper	10.00
16	Paul Causey	10.00
17	Frank Christensen	10.00
18	Stu Clancy	10.00
19	Earl "Dutch" Clark	30.00
20	Paul (Rip) Collins	10.00
21	Dave Cook (Chicago Cardinals)	10.00
22	Fred Crawford	10.00
23	Paul Cuba	10.00
24	Harry Ebding	10.00
25	Glen Edwards	20.00
26	Marvin (Swede) Ellstrom	10.00
27	Beattie Feathers	20.00
28	Ray Flaherty	20.00
29	John Gildea	10.00
30	Tom Graham	10.00
31	Len Grant	10.00
32	Maurice Green	10.00
33	Norman Greeney	10.00
34	Ace Gutowsky	10.00
35	Julius Hall	10.00
36	Thomas (Swede) Hanson	10.00
37	Charles Harold	10.00
38	Tom Haywood	10.00
39	Mel Hein	20.00
40	Bill Hewitt	20.00
41	Cecil (Tex) Irvin	10.00
42	Frank Johnson	10.00
43	Jack Johnson	10.00
44	Luke Johnson	10.00
45	Tom Jones	10.00
46	Carl Jorgensen	10.00
47	George Kenneally	10.00
48	Roger Kirkman	10.00
49	Frank Knox	10.00
50	Joe (Doc) Kopcha	10.00
51	Rick Lackman	10.00
52	Jim Leonard	10.00
53	Joe (Hunk) Malkovich	10.00
54	Ed Manske	10.00
55	Bernie Masterson	10.00
56	James McMillen	10.00
57	Mike Mikulak	10.00
58	Ookie Miller	10.00
59	Milford (Dub) Miller	10.00
60	Al Minot	10.00
61	Buster Mitchell	10.00
62	Bill Morgan	10.00
63	George Musso	20.00
64	Harry Newman	10.00
65	Al Nichelini	10.00
66	Bill (Red) Owen	10.00
67	Steve Owen	20.00
68	Max Padlow	10.00
69	Hal Pangle	10.00
70	Melvin Pittman	10.00
71	William Pollock	10.00
72	Glenn Presnell	10.00
73	George Rado	10.00
74	Clare Randolph	10.00
75	Hank Reese	10.00
76	Ray Richards	10.00
77	Doug Russell	10.00
78	Sandy Sandberg	10.00
79	John Schneller	10.00
80	Michael Sebastian	10.00
81	Allen Shi	10.00
82	Johnny Sisk	10.00
83	Phil Sarboe	10.00
84	James Stacy	10.00
85	Ed Storm	10.00
86	Ken Strong	25.00
87	Art Strutt	10.00
88	Frank Sullivan	10.00
89	Charles Treadaway	10.00
90	John Turley	10.00
91	Claude Urevig	10.00
92	Charles Vaughan	10.00
93	Izzy Weinstock	10.00
94	Henry Wiesenbaugh	10.00
95	Joe Zeller	10.00
96	Vince Zizak	10.00

1935 Diamond Matchbooks College Rivals

With all the variations available, this set goes from 12 matchbooks to 36. Covers include highlights on recent games in the rivalry. The Diamond name is printed in tan with a double-lined company name or the Diamond name is printed on a single line with a tan or black border. Matchbooks with the matches intact are valued at 1-1/2 times more than what is listed here.

		NM
Complete Set (12):		100.00
Common Player:		10.00
1	Alabama vs. Fordham once championship	10.00
2	Army vs. Navy over the Cadets since 1921	10.00
3	Fordham vs. St. Mary's the gamely fighting "Rams"	10.00
4	Georgia vs. Georgia Tech 7-0 defeat	10.00
5	Holy Cross vs. Boston College defeat	10.00
6	Lafayette vs. Lehigh in a 13-7 victory for Lehigh	10.00
7	Michigan vs. Ohio State tory for State	10.00
8	Notre Dame vs. Army Cadets 12-6	12.00
9	Penn vs. Cornell from start to finish	10.00
10	USC vs. Notre Dame carries of Elmer Layden	12.00
11	Yale vs. Harvard set back	10.00
12	Yale vs. Princeton ed still led 7-0	10.00

1936 Diamond Matchbooks

Chicago Bears and Philadelphia Eagles players were featured in this matchbook set. The matchbooks, when folded out, measure 1-1/2" x 4-1/2". The words were printed in black or brown, while borders were in three different colors, tan, red and green. Ray Nolting is the lone exception to the rule, as matchbooks featuring him were printed with black and brown ink. The front of the books include a player picture, his name and team. The backs showcase his name and his highlights. With the different variations available, a complete set totals 96 matchbooks, which are unnumbered. Books with matches intact are worth 1-1/2 times more than what is listed here.

		NM
Complete Set (47):		500.00
Common Player:		10.00
1	Carl Brumbaugh	10.00
2	Zuck Carlson	10.00
3	George Corbett (last line - Sigma Alpha Epsilon.)	10.00
4	John Doehring (last line - is a bachelor.)	10.00
5	Beattie Feathers (first line - ...will be 28 years)	15.00
6	Dan Fortmann (first line - ...April 11, 1916, at)	15.00
7	George Grosvenor	10.00
8	Bill Hewitt	15.00
9	Luke Johnson	10.00
10	William Karr (first line - ...in Ripley,)	10.00
11	Eddie Kawal	10.00
12	Jack Manders (last line - 200, Height 6 ft. 1 in.)	10.00
13	Bernie Masterson (last line - Alpha Epsilon, Single.)	10.00
14	Eddie Michaels	10.00
15	Ookie Miller	10.00
16	Keith Molesworth (last line - 5 ft. 9 1/2 in. Weight 168.)	10.00
17	George Musso (last line - Science degree, Is single.)	20.00
18	Bronko Nagurski	210.00
19	Ray Nolting (first line - ...three years of Cin-)	10.00
20	Vernon Oech	10.00
21	William Pollock	10.00
22	Gene Ronzani (last line - is married.)	10.00
23	Ted Rosequist	10.00
24	Johnny Sisk	10.00
25	Joe Stydahar (last line - is single.)	15.00
26	Frank Sullivan (first line - ...Loyola U.) (New)	10.00
27	Russell Thompson (last line - Sigma Nu fraternity.)	10.00
28	Milt Trost (last line - is single.)	10.00
29	Joe Zeller (last line - and is single, Sigma Nu.)	10.00
30	Bill Brian	10.00
31	Art Buss	10.00
32	Joe Carter	10.00
33	Thomas (Swede) Hanson	10.00
34	Don Jackson	10.00
35	John Kusko	10.00
36	Jim Leonard	10.00
37	Jim MacMurdo	10.00
38	Ed Manske	10.00
39	George McPherson	10.00
40	George Mulligan	10.00
41	Joe Pilconis	10.00
42	Hank Reese	10.00
43	Jim Russell	10.00
44	Dave Smukler	10.00
45	Pete Stevens	10.00
46	John Thomason	10.00
47	Vince Zizak	10.00

1937 Diamond Matchbooks

This time only Chicago Bears players were featured. Measuring 1-1/2" x 4-1/2" when folded out, the matchbooks resemble the 1936 set, however, this 1937 set has a smaller type size. With text printed in gray or black, the 24-matchbook set showcases three different colored borders - red, green and tan. The cover fronts feature a player photo, with his name and team printed above the photo. The backs of the matchbooks have the player's name and highlights inside a box. Matchbooks with the matches intact are valued at 1-1/2 times the prices listed here.

		NM
Complete Set (24):		225.00
Common Player:		7.00
1	Frank Bausch	7.00
2	Delbert Bjork	7.00
3	William Conkright	7.00
4	George Corbett (last line - ion.)	7.00
5	John Doehring (last line - baseball.)	7.00
6	Beattie Feathers (first line - ...turned 29 years)	15.00
7	Dan Fortmann (first line - April 11, 1916, in)	15.00
8	Harrison Francis	7.00
9	Henry Hammond	7.00

10 William Karr (first line - in Ripley, W.) 7.00
11 Jack Manders (last line - height 6 ft. 1 in.) 12.00
12 Ed Manske 7.00
13 Bernie Masterson (last line - single.) 10.00
14 Keith Molesworth (last line - 9 1/2 in. Weight 168.) 10.00
15 George Musso (last line - married.) 20.00
16 Ray Nolting (first line - ... three years for) 7.00
17 Richard Plasman 7.00
18 Gene Ronzani (last line - married.) 12.00
19 Joe Stydahar (last line - ing. Is single.) 18.00
20 Frank Sullivan (first line - Loyola U. New) 7.00
21 Russell Thompson (last line - year.) 7.00
22 Milt Trost (last line - pounds. Is single.) 7.00
23 George Wilson 12.00
24 Joe Zeller (last line - Nu.) 7.00

1938 Diamond Matchbooks

Showcasing players from the Chicago Bears and Detroit Lions, the 24-matchbook set measures 1-1/2" x 4-1/2" when folded out. They are bordered in silver. The player's highlights feature different colored backgrounds for the two teams - Bears have red backgrounds, while the Lions have blue. No variations are known for this set. The unnumbered matchbooks are listed alphabetically. As always, matchbooks with the matches intact are valued at 1-1/2 times the values listed here.

NM
Complete Set (24): 225.00
Common Player: 7.00
1 Delbert Bjork 7.00
2 Raymond Buivid 7.00
3 Gary Famiglietti 2.50
4 Dan Fortmann 15.00
5 Bert Johnson 7.00
6 Jack Manders 12.00
7 Joe Maniaci 12.00
8 Lester McDonald 7.00
9 Frank Sullivan 7.00
10 Robert Swisher 7.00
11 Russell Thompson 7.00
12 Gus Zarnas 7.00
13 Ernie Caddel 12.00
14 Lloyd Cardwell 7.00
15 Earl "Dutch" Clark 30.00
16 Jack Johnson 7.00
17 Ed Klewicki 7.00
18 James McDonald 7.00
19 James (Monk) Moscrip 7.00
20 Maurice (Babe) Patt 7.00
21 Bob Reynolds 7.00
22 Kent Ryan 7.00
23 Fred Vanzo 7.00
24 Alex Wojciechowicz 20.00

1967 Dolphins Royal Castle

Measuring 3" x 4-3/8", the 27-card set was released by Royal Castle restaurants in South Florida. The fronts showcase a large black-and-white photo, with his facsimile signature under the photo in a white area. The card fronts are bordered in orange. Each card back includes the player's name, position and bio, along with the Royal Castle and Miami Dolphins' logos. A 28th card in the set, featuring George Wilson Jr., may have also been produced.

NM
Complete Set (27): 2700.
Common Player: 25.00
Common Player (SP): 100.00
1 Joe Auer (SP) 100.00
2 Tom Beier 25.00
3 Mel Branch 25.00
4 Jon Brittenum 35.00
5 George Chesser 25.00
6 Edward Cooke 25.00
7 Frank Emanuel (SP) 125.00
8 Tom Erlandson (SP) 100.00
9 Norm Evans (SP) 150.00
10 Bob Griese (SP) 800.00
11 Abner Haynes (SP) 175.00
12 Jerry Hopkins (SP) 100.00
13 Frank Jackson 25.00
14 Billy Joe 25.00
15 Wahoo McDaniel 150.00
16 Robert Neff 25.00
17 Billy Neighbors 25.00
18 Rick Norton 25.00
19 Bob Petrich 25.00
20 Jim Riley 25.00
21 John Stofa (SP) 150.00
22 Lavern Torczon 25.00
23 Howard Twilley 80.00
24 Jimmy Warren (SP) 100.00
25 Richard Westmoreland 25.00
26 Maxie Williams (SP) 150.00
27 George Wilson, Sr. (SP) (Head Coach) 150.00

1974 Dolphins All-Pro Graphics

Measuring 8-1/4" x 10-3/4", the 10-photo set showcases color action shots on the front, surrounded by a white border. The player's name, position and team are printed in the top left corner. The unnumbered photos have blank backs.

NM
Complete Set (10): 100.00
Common Player: 5.00
1 Dick Anderson 8.00
2 Nick Buoniconti 14.00
3 Larry Csonka 18.00
4 Manny Fernandez 6.00
5 Bob Griese 25.00
6 Jim Kiick 8.00
7 Earl Morrall 12.00
8 Mercury Morris 8.00
9 Jake Scott 6.00
10 Garo Yepremian 5.00

1980 Dolphins Police

Measuring 2-5/8" x 4-1/8", the 16-card set features a photo on the front, with the player's name and position under the photo. The Kiwanis logo appears in the lower right. The unnumbered card backs feature Miami Dolphins Tips inside a box, which has the Dolphins' logo at the top. Sponsors are listed at the bottom of the card backs.

NM
Complete Set (16): 75.00
Common Player: 2.50
5 Uwe Von Schamann 2.50
10 Don Strock 5.00
12 Bob Griese 12.00
22 Tony Nathan 5.00
24 Delvin Williams 5.00
25 Tim Foley 4.00
50 Larry Gordon 2.50
58 Kim Bokamper 2.50
64 Ed Newman 2.50
66 Larry Little (SP) 20.00
67 Bob Kuechenberg 5.00
73 Bob Baumhower 4.00
77 A.J. Duhe 5.00
82 Duriel Harris 4.00
89 Nat Moore 5.00
NNO Don Shula (CO) 15.00

1981 Dolphins Police

Measuring 2-5/8" x 4-1/8", the 16-card set features a photo, with the player's name, number, position and bio under the photo. The Dolphins and Kiwanis logos appear on the lower left and right, respectively. The card backs, numbered in the upper left corner, have Dolphins Tips in a box, with the Dolphins logo at the top. The sponsors are listed at the bottom of the card backs.

MT
Complete Set (16): 25.00
Common Player: 1.00
1 Duriel Harris 1.00
2 Bob Kuechenberg 1.00
3 Don Bessillieu 1.00
4 Gerald Small 1.00
5 David Woodley 1.50
6 Don McNeal 1.00
7 Nat Moore 2.00
8 A.J. Duhe 1.75
9 Glenn Blackwood 1.00
10 Don Strock 2.00
11 Doug Betters 1.00
12 George Roberts 1.00
13 Bob Baumhower 1.75
14 Kim Bokamper 1.00
15 Tony Nathan 2.00
16 Don Shula (CO) 6.00

1982 Dolphins Police

Measuring 2-5/8" x 4-1/8", the 16-card set is anchored by a color photo on the front, with the player's name and number in the upper left corner. His position and college are located in a stripe above the photo. The Kiwanis logo is in the lower right. The card fronts are bordered in orange and aqua. The card backs, numbered in the lower right, showcase Dolphins Tips inside a box, with the Dolphins logo in the upper right. The sponsors names are listed in the lower left.

MT
Complete Set (16): 25.00
Common Player: 1.00
1 Don Shula (CO) (SP) 10.00
2 Uwe Von Schamann (SP) 5.00
3 Jimmy Cefalo 1.50
4 Andra Franklin 1.50
5 Larry Gordon 1.00
6 Nat Moore 1.75
7 Bob Baumhower 1.25
8 A.J. Duhe 1.25
9 Tony Nathan 1.75
10 Glenn Blackwood 1.00
11 Don Strock 2.00
12 David Woodley 1.25
13 Kim Bokamper 1.00
14 Bob Kuechenberg 1.25
15 Duriel Harris 1.25
16 Ed Newman 1.00

1983 Dolphins Police

Measuring 2-5/8" x 4-1/8", the 16-card set is anchored by a photo on the front, with the player's name in the upper left and his position near the bottom of the photo. The cards are bordered in aqua and orange. The card backs, numbered in the lower right, feature Dolphins Tips, with the Dolphins logo in the upper right. The sponsors are listed at the bottom of the card back. The Kiwanis and Burger King logos both are printed inside the photo on the front of the cards.

MT
Complete Set (16): 15.00
Common Player: .50
1 Earnie Rhone .50
2 Andra Franklin .75
3 Eric Laakso .50
4 Joe Rose .50
5 David Woodley 1.00
6 Uwe Von Schamann .50
7 Eddie Hill .50
8 Bruce Hardy .50
9 Woody Bennett .50
10 Fulton Walker .50
11 Lyle Blackwood .50
12 A.J. Duhe .75
13 Bob Baumhower .75
14 Duriel Harris .50
15 Bob Brudzinski .50
16 Don Shula (CO) 3.00

1984 Dolphins Police

Measuring 2-5/8" x 4-1/8", the 17-card set is anchored by a photo on the front, with the player's number and name in the upper left and his position at the bottom center. Sponsor logos are printed in the two lower corners. The card backs, which are unnumbered, have a "Dolphins Say" safety tip, with the Dolphins logo in the upper right. The sponsors are listed at the bottom of the card backs. The Mark Clayton card was added to the set after it was released.

MT
Complete Set (17): 30.00
Common Player: .50
1 Bob Baumhower .75
2 Doug Betters .50
3 Glenn Blackwood .50
4 Kim Bokamper .50
5 Dolfan Denny (Mascot) .50
6 A.J. Duhe .75
7 Mark Duper 1.75
8 Jim Jensen .50
9 Dan Marino 25.00
10 Don McNeal .50
11 Nat Moore 1.00
12 Tony Nathan 1.00
13 Ed Newman .50
14 Don Shula (CO) 2.00
15 Dwight Stephenson .75
16 Fulton Walker .50
17 Mark Clayton (SP) 4.00

1985 Dolphins Police

Measuring 2-5/8" x 4-1/8", the 16-card set is anchored by a large photo on the front, with the player's name, number and position listed at the bottom center. The Dolphins and Kiwanis logos are in the lower left and right, respectively. The card backs, which are numbered in the lower right, have a "Dolphins Say" safety tip, with the Dolphins logo in the upper right. The sponsors are printed at the bottom of the card backs.

MT
Complete Set (16): 20.00
Common Player: .50
1 William Judson .50
2 Fulton Walker .50
3 Mark Clayton 1.25
4 Lyle & Glenn Blackwood, Glenn Blackwood (Bruise Brothers) .50
5 Dan Marino 12.00
6 Reggie Roby .75
7 Doug Betters .50
8 Jay Brophy .50
9 Dolfan Denny (Mascot) .50
10 Kim Bokamper .50
11 Mark Duper 1.00
12 Nat Moore .75
13 Mike Kozlowski .50
14 Don Shula (CO) 1.50
15 Don McNeal .50
16 Tony Nathan .75

1986 Dolphins Police

Measuring 2-5/8" x 4-1/8", the 16-card set is anchored by a large photo on the front, with the player's name printed inside a stripe on the right, his number printed inside a helmet in the lower left and his position located inside a stripe in the lower right. Anon Anew and the Kiwanis logos are printed in the lower right, too. The card backs, which are numbered in the lower right, have a "Dolphins Say" safety tip, along with the sponsors names.

MT
Complete Set (16): 15.00
Common Player: .50
1 Dwight Stephenson .75
2 Bob Baumhower .75
3 Dolfan Denny (Mascot) .50
4 Don Shula (CO) 1.50
5 Dan Marino 8.00
6 Tony Nathan .75
7 Mark Duper 1.00
8 John Offerdahl 1.00
9 Fuad Reveiz .50
10 Hugh Green .50
11 Lorenzo Hampton .50
12 Mark Clayton 1.50
13 Nat Moore .75
14 Bob Brudzinski .50
15 Reggie Roby .50
16 T.J. Turner .50

1987 Dolphins Holsum

The cards in this Miami Dolphins' set were available in Holsum Bread packages. The fronts have a color photo inside a green border and the backs feature basic player information.

MT
Complete Set (22): 60.00
Common Player: 2.00
1 Bob Baumhower 3.00
2 Mark Brown 2.00
3 Mark Clayton 6.00
4 Mark Duper 4.00
5 Roy Foster 2.00
6 Hugh Green 3.00
7 Lorenzo Hampton 2.00
8 William Judson 2.00
9 George Little 2.00
10 Dan Marino 40.00
11 Nat Moore 3.00
12 Tony Nathan 3.00
13 John Offerdahl 4.00
14 James Pruitt 2.00
15 Fuad Reveiz 2.00
16 Dwight Stephenson 3.00
17 Glenn Blackwood 2.00
18 Bruce Hardy 2.00
19 Reggie Roby 2.00
20 Bob Brudzinski 2.00
21 Ron Jaworski 3.00
22 T.J. Turner 2.00

1987 Dolphins Police

Measuring 2-5/8" x 4-1/8", the 16-card set resembles the 1986 set in design. This time, however, the player's name is printed in a stripe on the left, with his position printed inside a stripe under the photo. The player's number is located inside a helmet on the lower right. The Kiwanis and Fair Oaks Hospital logos appear in the lower left. The card backs, which are numbered in the lower right, have a "Dolphins Say" safety message and the sponsors listed.

MT
Complete Set (16): 20.00
Common Player: .50
1 Joe Robbie (OWN) .50
2 Glenn Blackwood .50
3 Mark Duper 1.00
4 Fuad Reveiz .50
5 Dolfan Denny (Mascot) .50
6 Dwight Stephenson (SP) 5.00
7 Hugh Green .50
8 Larry Csonka (All-Time Great) 3.00
9 Bud Brown .50
10 Don Shula (CO) 1.50
11 T.J. Turner .50
12 Reggie Roby .50
13 Dan Marino 10.00
14 John Offerdahl .75
15 Bruce Hardy .50
16 Lorenzo Hampton .50

1988 Dolphins Holsum

The standard sized cards in this 12-card set showcase the Holsum logo in the upper left corner, with "1988 Annual Collectors' Edition" printed in the upper right. The player's name and team are printed inside a rectangle at the bottom of the card, beneath the player's photo. The card backs, numbered "of 12," have the player's facsimile autograph at the top and his number, bio and stats printed underneath inside a box. Cards were available in specially marked packages of Holsum Bread.

MT
Complete Set (12): 30.00
Common Player: 1.50
1 Mark Clayton 3.00
2 Dwight Stephenson 2.00
3 Mark Duper 2.00
4 John Offerdahl 2.00
5 Dan Marino 20.00
6 T.J. Turner 1.50
7 Lorenzo Hampton 1.50
8 Bruce Hardy 1.50
9 Fuad Reveiz 1.50
10 Reggie Roby 1.50
11 William Judson 1.50
12 Bob Brudzinski 1.50

1995 Dolphins Chevron Pin Cards

Each 3" x 5" card in this eight-card set features a pin at the bottom. The unnumbered cards were part of a Chevron promotion. The card fronts have the player's name and position at the top, with his photo and Dolphins logo underneath. The Chevron logo is next to the pin at the bottom of the card. The card backs have the player's name, number, bio, highlights and a checklist.

MT
Complete Set (8): 20.00
Common Player: 2.00
1 Miami Dolphins 2.00
2 Dan Marino 10.00
3 Bryan Cox 2.00
4 Troy Vincent 2.00
5 Irving Fryar 2.00
6 Eric Green 2.00
7 Team '95 2.00
8 Hall of Famers 3.00

1996 Dolphins AT&T Set

Fans who attended the Miami Dolphins home season finale were rewarded for their fan appreciation by receiving a photo album card set of the team, sponsored by AT&T. The booklet features Zach Thomas, Dan Marino and the team picture on the cover. The 24-card perforated set, which is standard size, has the player's name vertically along the left side and position along the bottom. The player's number and Dolphins logo appear along the side of the position. The AT&T logo is printed in the top left corner. The backs feature a color profile, as well as personal and career stats. The cards are numbered with the player's jersey numbers.

MT
Complete Set (24): 15.00
Common Player: .25
--- Jimmy Johnson 1.00
13 Dan Marino 6.00
17 Jason Kidd .25
22 Shawn Wooden .25
25 Louis Oliver .25
27 Terrell Buckley .25
33 Karim Abdul-Jabbar 2.00
36 Stanley Pritchett .25
38 Calvin Jackson .25
50 Dwight Hollier .25
54 Zach Thomas 1.00
55 Chris Singleton .25
61 Tim Ruddy .25
62 Chris Gray .25
69 Keith Sims .25
76 James Brown .25
78 Richmond Webb .25
80 Fred Barnett .50
81 O.J. McDuffie 1.00
84 Troy Drayton .50
92 Daryl Gardner .25
93 Trace Armstrong .25
95 Tim Bowens .25
96 Daniel Stubbs .25

1996 Dolphins Miami Subs Cards/Coins

The Dolphins and Miami Subs Restaurants produced this 9-card, 9-coin set. The cards front features a color player photo and the backs have the card set checklist. The coins have the player's likeness on one side and the Dolphins logo on the other. The coins are unnumbered. A cardboard holder featuring five Dolphins was produced to hold the set.

MT
Complete Set (18): 20.00
Complete Card Set (9): 10.00
Complete Coin Set (9): 10.00
Common Card (CA1-CA9): .75
Common Coin (CO1-CO9): .75
CA1 (Dan Marino) 6.00
CA2 Larry Csonka 1.50
CA3 Pete Stoyanovich .75
CA4 Paul Warfield 1.50
CA5 Bernie Kosar .75
CA6 Mark Clayton .75
CA7 Fred Barnett .75
CA8 Nat Moore 1.00
CA9 Super Bowl VII (Don Shula, George Allen) 2.00
CO1 Fred Barnett .75
CO2 Mark Clayton .75
CO3 Larry Csonka 1.50
CO4 Bernie Kosar .75
CO5 Dan Marino 6.00
CO6 Nat Moore 1.00
CO7 Pete Stoyanovich .75
CO8 Paul Warfield 1.50
CO9 Super Bowl VII Trophy gold coin 1.25
--- Display Holder (Dan Marino, Jimmy Johnson, Bernie Kosar, Mark Clayton, Fred Barnett, Pete Stoyanovich) 1.50

2000 Dominion

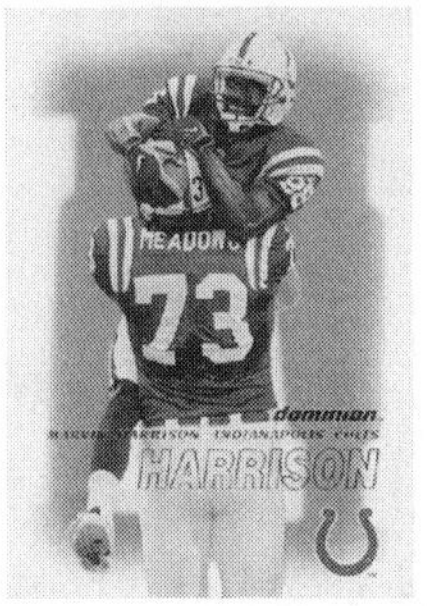

MT
Complete Set (243): 25.00
Common Player: .10
Minor Stars: .20
Common Rookie: .30
Pack (10): 2.00
Wax Box (36): 55.00
Cards #214 & #226 Never Released
1 Tim Couch 1.00
2 Byron Hanspard .10
3 Jay Riemersma .10
4 Cade McNown .75
5 Darnay Scott .20
6 Emmitt Smith 1.25
7 Rod Smith .20
8 James Stewart .20
9 Marvin Harrison .30
10 Keenan McCardell .20
11 Andre Rison .20
12 Jeff George .30
13 Terry Glenn .30
14 Cameron Cleeland .30
15 Curtis Martin .30
16 Troy Edwards .30
17 Mikhael Ricks .10
18 Joey Galloway .30
19 Az-Zahir Hakim .20
20 Mike Alstott .30
21 Samari Rolle .10
22 Michael Pittman .10
23 Tony Banks .20
24 Bruce Smith .20
25 Curtis Enis .30
26 Jake Plummer .50
27 Darren Woodson .10
28 Bill Romanowski .10
29 Antonio Freeman .30
30 Terrence Wilkins .10
31 Kevin Hardy .10
32 Peerless Price .30
33 Cris Carter .30
34 Willie McGinest .10
35 Kerry Collins .20
36 Bryan Cox .10
37 Tyrone Wheatley .10
38 Jason Sehorn .10
39 Jerry Rice 1.00
40 Christian Fauria .10
41 Kevin Carter .10
42 John Lynch .10
43 Brad Johnson .30
44 David Boston .30
45 Peter Boulware .10
46 Muhsin Muhammad .30
47 Bobby Engram .10
48 Kevin Johnson .40
49 Charlie Batch .40
50 Dorsey Levens .30
51 Cornelius Bennett .10
52 Kyle Brady .10
53 Damon Huard .20
54 Robert Smith .30
55 Ty Law .10
56 Amani Toomer .20
57 Aaron Glenn .10
58 Donovan McNabb .75
59 Levon Kirkland .10
60 Terrell Owens .30
61 Sam Adams .10
62 London Fletcher .10
63 Steve McNair .40
64 Stephen Davis .30
65 Daunte Culpepper .75
66 Andre Wadsworth .10
67 Priest Holmes .30
68 Patrick Jeffers .20
69 Walt Harris .10
70 Darrin Chiaverini .20
71 Dat Nguyen .10
72 Robert Porcher .10
73 Bill Schroeder .20
74 Tyrone Poole .10
75 Bryce Paup .10
76 O.J. McDuffie .20
77 Jake Reed .20
78 Ike Hilliard .20
79 Victor Green .10
80 Duce Staley .30
81 Amos Zereoue .20
82 Charlie Garner .20
83 Shawn Springs .10
84 Shaun King .75
85 Eddie George .40
86 Michael Westbrook .20
87 Ricky Williams 1.00
88 Chris Chandler .20
89 Chris McAlister .10
90 Steve Beuerlein .20
91 Marty Booker .10
92 Karim Abdul .20
93 Brian Griese .50
94 Germane Crowell .30
95 Mark Chmura .20
96 E.G. Green .10
97 Elvis Grbac .20
98 Tony Martin .20
99 John Randle .20
100 Michael Strahan .10
101 Tim Brown .30
102 Torrance Small .10
103 Junior Seau .20
104 Bryant Young .10
105 Kurt Warner 1.75
106 Trent Dilfer .20
107 Kevin Dyson .20
108 Stephen Alexander .10
109 Tim Dwight .30
110 Rob Johnson .20
111 Tim Biakabutuka .20
112 Akili Smith .50
113 Terry Kirby .10
114 Terrell Davis 1.25
115 Herman Moore .30
116 Vonnie Holliday .10
117 Mark Brunell .60
118 Derrick Alexander .20
119 Oronde Gadsden .20
120 Ed McDaniel .10
121 Eddie Kennison .10
122 Jessie Armstead .10
123 Charles Woodson .20
124 Troy Vincent .10
125 Jeff Garcia .20
126 Marshall Faulk .40
127 Jacquez Green .20
128 Frank Wycheck .10
129 Champ Bailey .20
130 Natrone Means .20
131 Jamal Anderson .30
132 Doug Flutie .50
133 Michael Bates .10
134 Corey Dillon .40
135 Corey Fuller .10
136 Olandis Gary .50
137 Johnnie Morton .10
138 Peyton Manning 1.25
139 Fred Taylor .75
140 Tony Gonzalez .30
141 Zach Thomas .20
142 Drew Bledsoe .60
143 Keith Poole .10
144 Vinny Testaverde .30
145 Rich Gannon .20
146 Jeremiah Trotter .10
147 Freddie Jones .10
148 Jon Kitna .30
149 Isaac Bruce .20
150 Warrick Dunn .40
151 Yancey Thigpen .20
152 Darrell Green .10
153 Terance Mathis .10
154 Eric Moulds .30
155 Wesley Walls .10
156 Carl Pickens .20
157 Troy Aikman 1.00
158 Dwayne Carswell .10
159 David Sloan .10
160 Edgerrin James 1.50

161 Jimmy Smith .30
162 Tamarick Vanover .10
163 Sam Madison .10
164 Tony Simmons .20
165 Andre Hastings .10
166 Keyshawn Johnson .30
167 Napoleon Kaufman .30
168 Hines Ward .20
169 Jeff Graham .10
170 Derrick Mayes .20
171 Torry Holt .40
172 Blaine Bishop .10
173 Rob Moore .20
174 Patrick Johnson .10
175 Antowain Smith .30
176 Marcus Robinson .50
177 Takeo Spikes .10
178 Raghib Ismail .10
179 Ed McCaffrey .30
180 Brett Favre 1.50
181 Ken Dilger .10
182 Carnell Lake .10
183 Cris Dishman .10
184 Randy Moss 1.50
185 Lawyer Milloy .10
186 *Jake Delhomme* 1.00
187 Wayne Chrebet .30
188 Darrell Russell .10
189 Jerome Bettis .20
190 Steve Young .60
191 Ricky Watters .30
192 Grant Wistrom .10
193 Warren Sapp .10
194 Jevon Kearse .40
195 James Jett .10
196 *Courtney Brown* 1.00
197 *Peter Warrick* 3.00
198 *Thomas Jones* 2.00
199 *Sylvester Morris* 1.00
200 *Chad Pennington* 2.50
201 *Ron Dayne* 3.00
202 *Todd Pinkston* .50
203 *Deon Dyer* .50
204 *Chris Redman* 1.00
205 *Jerry Porter* 1.00
206 *Michael Wiley* .75
207 *J.R. Redmond* 1.00
208 *Dennis Northcutt* .75
209 *Gari Scott* .50
210 *Anthony Lucas* .50
211 *Danny Farmer* .50
212 *Marcus Knight* .30
213 *Plaxico Burress* 1.75
215 *Bubba Franks* 1.00
216 *Shaun Alexander* 1.75
217 *Dez White* .75
218 *Mareno Philyaw* .30
219 *Travis Taylor* 1.50
220 *Kwame Cavil* .30
221 *Jamal Lewis* 2.00
222 *Sebastian Janikowski* .60
223 *Shyrone Stith* .30
224 *Ron Dugans* .50
225 *Darrell Jackson* .50
227 *Tee Martin* 1.00
228 *Tim Rattay* 1.00
229 *Marc Bulger* .50
230 *Doug Johnson* .75
231 *Joe Hamilton,Todd Husak* .75
232 *Travis Prentice,R. Jay Soward* 1.00
233 *Trung Canidate,Reuben Droughns* .75
234 *Giovanni Carmazzi,Tom Brady* 2.00
235 *Laveranues Coles,Chafie Fields* .50
236 *Jarious Jackson,Sherrod Gideon* .50
237 *Troy Walters,Erron Kinney* .50
238 *Rondell Mealey,Joey Goodspeed* .75
239 *Anthony Becht,Quinton Spotwood* .50
240 *Deltha O'Neal,Na'il Diggs* .30
241 *Corey Simon,Chris Hovan* .50
242 *Brian Urlacher,Corey Moore* .75
243 *Keith Bulluck,Rob Morris* .30
244 *Raynoch Thompson,Deon Grant* .30
245 *Shaun Ellis,John Abraham* .30

2000 Dominion Extra Parallel

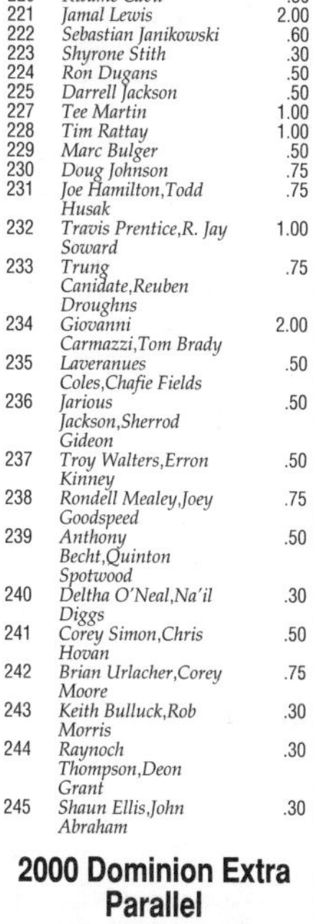

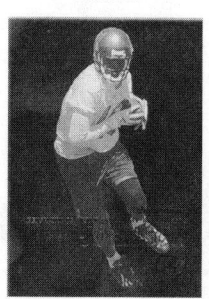

	MT
Complete Set (243):	100.00
Extra Cards:	3x
Extra Rookies:	1.5x
Inserted 1:2	

A player's name in *italic type* indicates a rookie card.

2000 Dominion Autographics

	MT
Common Player:	10.00
Minor Stars:	20.00
Inserted 1:192	

1 Karim Abdul 20.00
2 Troy Aikman 65.00
3 Terry Allen 10.00
4 Champ Bailey 20.00
5 Charlie Batch 20.00
6 Tim Biakabutuka 10.00
7 Peter Boulware 10.00
8 Tom Brady 10.00
9 Cris Carter 30.00
10 Wayne Chrebet 20.00
11 Germane Crowell 10.00
12 Ron Dayne 85.00
13 Danny Farmer 10.00
14 Christian Fauria 10.00
15 Jermaine Fazande 10.00
16 Rich Gannon 10.00
17 Charlie Garner 10.00
18 Olandis Gary 30.00
19 Sherrod Gideon 10.00
20 Az-Zahir Hakim 20.00
21 Torry Holt 30.00
22 Darrell Jackson 10.00
23 Brad Johnson 20.00
24 Kevin Johnson 25.00
25 Ed McCaffrey 20.00
26 Rondell Mealey 10.00
27 Sylvester Morris 25.00
28 Chad Pennington 65.00
29 John Randle 10.00
30 Jon Ritchie 10.00
31 Chris Watson 10.00
32 Frank Wycheck 10.00

2000 Dominion Characteristics

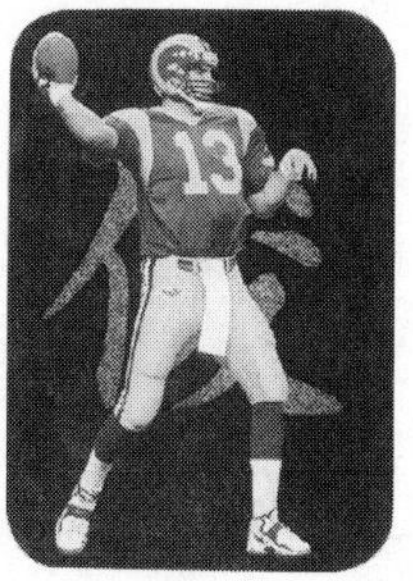

	MT
Complete Set (10):	35.00
Common Player:	2.00
Inserted 1:35	

1 Brett Favre 7.00
2 Troy Aikman 5.00
3 Terrell Davis 6.00
4 Emmitt Smith 5.00
5 Peyton Manning 6.00
6 Randy Moss 6.00
7 Tim Couch 3.00
8 Eddie George 2.00
9 Kurt Warner 7.00
10 Edgerrin James 7.00

2000 Dominion Genuine Coverage

	MT
Complete Set (10):	325.00
Common Player:	25.00
Inserted 1:720	

1 Charlie Batch 25.00
2 Isaac Bruce 30.00
3 Chris Chandler 25.00
4 Tim Couch 75.00
5 Marvin Harrison 30.00
6 Ed McCaffrey 25.00
7 Herman Moore 25.00
8 Marcus Robinson 40.00
9 Troy Aikman 75.00
10 Cade McNown 60.00

2000 Dominion Go-To Guys

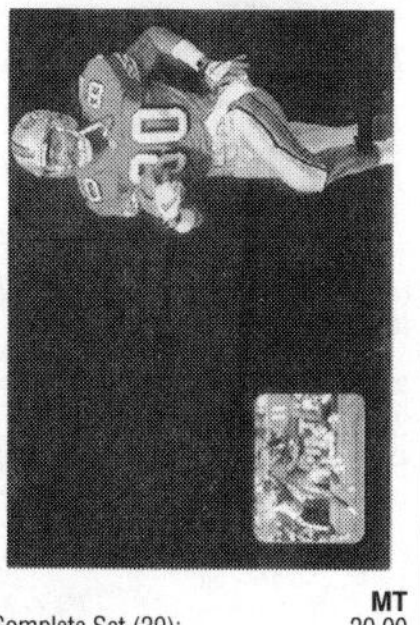

	MT
Complete Set (20):	20.00
Common Player:	.75
Minor Stars:	1.50
Inserted 1:12	

1 Peyton Manning 4.00
2 Brett Favre 5.00
3 Troy Aikman 3.00
4 Kurt Warner 5.00
5 Randy Moss 4.00
6 Germane Crowell .75
7 Marvin Harrison 1.50
8 Jerry Rice 3.00
9 Muhsin Muhammad .75
10 Marcus Robinson 1.50
11 Isaac Bruce 1.50
12 Tim Brown 1.50
13 Stephen Davis 1.50
14 Cris Carter 1.50
15 Tim Couch 2.50
16 Ricky Williams 3.00
17 Dorsey Levens 1.50
18 Keyshawn Johnson 1.50
19 Mark Brunell 1.50
20 Jimmy Smith 1.50

2000 Dominion Hard Corps

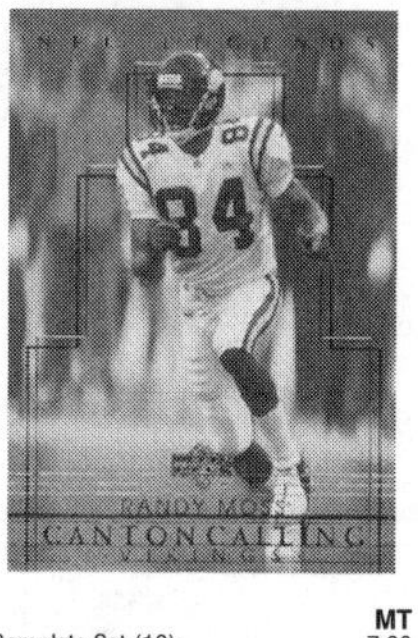

	MT
Complete Set (10):	7.00
Common Player:	.50
Inserted 1:6	

1 Brett Favre 2.00
2 Eddie George .75
3 Terrell Davis 1.25
4 Randy Moss 2.00
5 Marshall Faulk .50
6 Ricky Williams 1.00
7 Keyshawn Johnson .50
8 Fred Taylor .75
9 Steve Young .75
10 Edgerrin James 1.50

2000 Dominion Turf's Up

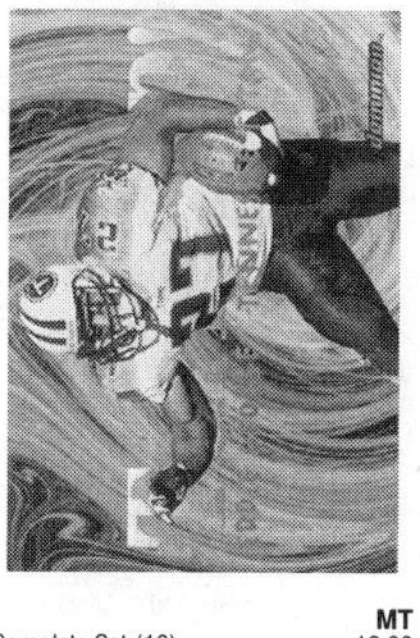

	MT
Complete Set (10):	18.00
Common Player:	1.50
Inserted 1:18	

1 Terrell Davis 4.00
2 Ricky Williams 3.00
3 Jamal Anderson 1.50
4 Marshall Faulk 1.50
5 Emmitt Smith 4.00
6 Eddie George 1.75
7 Fred Taylor 2.00
8 Edgerrin James 5.00
9 Warrick Dunn 1.50
10 Stephen Davis 1.50

1991 Domino's Quarterbacks

Upper Deck produced 50-card sets of NFL Quarterback cards in conjunction with a national promotion kicked off during the Aug. 3 NBC telecast of "NFL Quarterback Challenge". The set was sponsored by Dominos, sold in foil packs and feature 32 active quarterbacks, 14 retired quarterbacks and three multi-player cards. Cards were produced especially for this promotion and were distributed through the 5,000 Domino's stores across the country. Each franchise initially received 2,500 packs or two cases of 1,250. Stores could order additional packs in cases of 1,250 or 500. Stores could also order sets.

	MT
Complete Set (50):	6.00
Common Player:	.05

1 Chris Miller .05
2 Jim Kelly .20
3 Jim Harbaugh .10
4 Boomer Esiason .10
5 Bernie Kosar .10
6 Troy Aikman 1.00
7 John Elway .50
8 Rodney Peete .05
9 Andre Ware .05
10 Anthony Dilweg .05
11 Warren Moon .10
12 Jeff George .10
13 Jim Everett .05
14 Jay Schroeder .05
15 Dave Wilson .05
16 Dan Marino 1.50
17 Phil Simms .05
18 Jeff Hostetler .05
19 Ken O'Brien .05
20 Timm Rosenbach .05
21 Bubby Brister .05
22 Steve DeBerg .05
23 Randall Cunningham .10
24 Steve Walsh .10
25 Billy Joe Tolliver .05
26 Steve Young .50
27 Dave Krieg .05
28 Dan McGwire .05
29 Vinny Testaverde .10
30 Stan Humphries .10
31 Mark Rypien .05
32 Terry Bradshaw .75
33 John Brodie .10
34 Len Dawson .10
35 Dan Fouts .25
36 Otto Graham .50
37 Bob Griese .25
38 Sonny Jurgensen .20
39 Daryle Lamonica .20
40 Archie Manning .20
41 Jim Plunkett .10
42 Bart Starr .40
43 Roger Staubach .75
44 Joe Theismann .25
45 Y.A. Tittle .20
46 Johnny Unitas .50
47 Cowboy Gunslingers (Troy Aikman, Roger Staubach) .75
48 Cajun Connection (Bubby Brister, Terry Bradshaw) .30
49 Dolphin Duo (Dan Marino, Bob Griese) .75
50 Checklist Card .05

1995 Donruss Red Zone

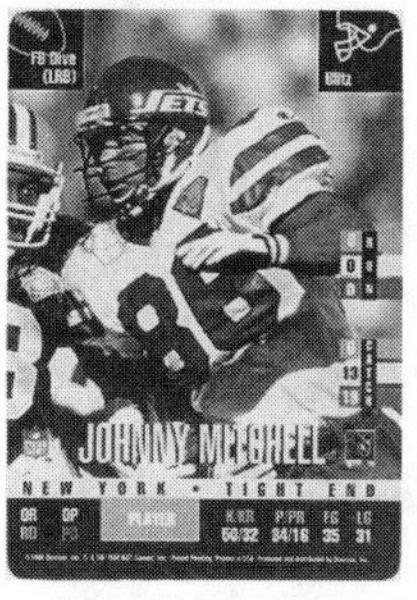

Cards for this game were available in both 80-card starter decks and 12-card booster packs. The 336-card set has the game logo in red on the backs of the cards. The cards were unnumbered.

	MT
Complete Set (336):	225.00
Common DP Player:	.05
Common Player:	.30
Common SP Player:	1.50

1 Michael Bankston .30
2 Larry Centers .30
3 Ben Coleman (DP) .05
4 Ed Cunningham (DP) .05
5 Garrison Hearst .75
6 Eric Hill .30
7 Lorenzo Lynch (DP) .05
8 Clyde Simmons (DP) .05
9 Eric Swann .30
10 Aeneas Williams (SP) 1.50
11 Chris Doleman .30
12 Bert Emanuel (DP) .30
13 Roman Fortin (DP) .05
14 Jeff George (SP) 2.50
15 Craig Heyward (DP) .05
16 D.J. Johnson (SP) 1.50
17 Terance Mathis (SP) 2.00
18 Clay Matthews (DP) .05
19 Kevin Ross (DP) .05
20 Jessie Tuggle (DP) .05
21 Bob Whitfield (SP) 1.50
22 Cornelius Bennett (SP) 1.50
23 Russell Copeland (DP) .05
24 John Fina (SP) 1.50
25 Carwell Gardner (DP) .05
26 Henry Jones (DP) .05
27 Jim Kelly (SP) 3.00
28 Mark Maddox (DP) .05
29 Glenn Parker .30
30 Andre Reed (SP) 2.00
31 Bruce Smith (SP) 2.00
32 Thomas Smith (DP) .05
33 Joe Cain (DP) .05
34 Mark Carrier .30
35 Curtis Conway (DP) .30
36 Al Fontenot (DP) .05
37 Jeff Graham (DP) .05
38 Raymont Harris (DP) .05
39 Andy Heck .30
40 Erik Kramer (DP) .10
41 Vinson Smith .30
42 Lewis Tillman (DP) .05
43 Steve Walsh .30
44 James Williams (DP) .05
45 Donnell Woolford (SP) 1.50
46 Mike Brim (DP) .05
47 Tony McGee (DP) .05
48 Carl Pickens 1.00
49 Keith Rucker (DP) .05
50 Darnay Scott (SP) 3.00
51 Dan Wilkinson (DP) .10
52 Darryl Williams (DP) .05
53 Derrick Alexander (WR) .50
54 Carl Banks (DP) .05
55 Rob Burnett (SP) 1.50
56 Earnest Byner .30
57 Steve Everitt (DP) .05
58 Leroy Hoard (SP) 1.50
59 Michael Jackson (DP) .10
60 Pepper Johnson .30
61 Tony Jones .30
62 Antonio Langham .30
63 Anthony Pleasant (DP) .05
64 Vinny Testaverde (DP) .10
65 Eric Turner (SP) 1.50
66 Tommy Vardell .30
67 Troy Aikman (SP) 12.00
68 Larry Brown .30
69 Dixon Edwards (DP) .05
70 Charles Haley (SP) 2.00
71 Michael Irvin (SP) 3.00
72 Daryl Johnston (DP) .10
73 Leon Lett .30
74 Nate Newton .30
75 Jay Novacek (SP) 2.00
76 Darrin Smith .30
77 Kevin Smith .30
78 Tony Tolbert (DP) .05
79 Mark Tuinei (SP) 1.50
80 Kevin Williams (DP) .10
81 Darren Woodson .30
82 Elijah Alexander .30
83 Steve Atwater .30
84 Rod Bernstine (SP) 1.50
85 Ray Crockett .30
86 Shane Dronett (DP) .05
87 John Elway (SP) 8.00
88 Simon Fletcher .30
89 Brian Habib (DP) .05
90 Glyn Milburn .30
91 Anthony Miller (SP) 3.00
92 Mike Pritchard (DP) .10
93 Shannon Sharpe .60
94 Gary Zimmerman (DP) .05
95 Bennie Blades .30
96 Lomas Brown (SP) 1.50
97 Mike Johnson (DP) .05
98 Robert Massey (DP) .05
99 Scott Mitchell (DP) .10
100 Herman Moore (SP) 5.00
101 Brett Perriman .60
102 Barry Sanders (SP) 12.00
103 Tracy Scroggins (DP) .05
104 Chris Spielman .30
105 Doug Widell (SP) 1.50
106 Edgar Bennett (SP) 3.00
107 LeRoy Butler (DP) .05
108 Harry Galbreath (DP) .05
109 Sean Jones (SP) 1.50
110 George Koonce (DP) .05
111 Anthony Morgan (DP) .05
112 Ken Ruettgers (DP) .05
113 Fred Strickland (DP) .05
114 George Teague .30
115 Reggie White (SP) 4.00
116 Michael Barrow .30
117 Blaine Bishop (DP) .05
118 Gary Brown .30
119 Ray Childress .30
120 Kenny Davidson (SP) 1.50
121 Cris Dishman (SP) 1.50
122 Brad Hopkins (SP) 1.50
123 Haywood Jeffires (DP) .05
124 Eddie Robinson (DP) .05
125 Al Smith (DP) .05
126 David Williams (SP) 1.50
127 Tony Bennett (SP) 1.50
128 Ray Buchanan (SP) 1.50
129 Quentin Coryatt (DP) .05
130 Eugene Daniel (DP) .05
131 Sean Dawkins (DP) .05
132 Marshall Faulk (SP) 5.00
133 Jim Harbaugh .60
134 Jeff Herrod (DP) .05
135 Kirk Lowdermilk (DP) .05
136 Tony Siragusa (DP) .05
137 Floyd Turner (DP) .05
138 Will Wolford (SP) 1.50
139 Marcus Allen .75
140 Kimble Anders (SP) 1.50
141 Steve Bono (DP) .40
142 Dale Carter (DP) .05
143 Mark Collins (DP) .05
144 Willie Davis .30
145 Lake Dawson (DP) .20
146 Tim Grunhard (DP) .05
147 Greg Hill (DP) .10
148 George Jamison (DP) .05
149 Darren Mickell (DP) .05
150 Will Shields (DP) .05
151 Tracy Simien (DP) .05
152 Neil Smith (SP) 2.00
153 Tim Bowens (DP) .05
154 J.B. Brown (DP) .05
155 Keith Byars .30
156 Bryan Cox .30
157 Jeff Cross .30
158 Irving Fryar (SP) 2.00
159 Ron Heller .30
160 Terry Kirby (SP) 1.50
161 Dan Marino (SP) 24.00
162 O.J. McDuffie .60
163 Bernie Parmalee (DP) .05
164 Chris Singleton (DP) .05
165 Troy Vincent (SP) 1.50
166 Richmond Webb (SP) 1.50
167 Roy Barker (DP) .05
168 Cris Carter (DP) .10
169 Jack Del Rio (SP) 1.50
170 Chris Hinton (DP) .05
171 Qadry Ismail .60
172 Amp Lee .30
173 Ed McDaniel .30
174 Randall McDaniel (DP) .05
175 Warren Moon (SP) 3.00
176 John Randle (SP) 1.50
177 Jake Reed (DP) .10
178 Robert Smith (DP) .10
179 Todd Steussie (DP) .05
180 DeWayne Washington (DP) .05
181 Bruce Armstrong (DP) .05
182 Drew Bledsoe 3.00
183 Vincent Brisby (DP) .05
184 Vincent Brown (DP) .05
185 Ben Coates (SP) 3.00
186 Sam Gash (DP) .05
187 Myron Guyton (DP) .05
188 Maurice Hurst (SP) 1.50
189 Mike Jones (DP) .05
190 Bob Kratch (DP) .05
191 Chris Slade (SP) 1.50
192 Derek Brown (DP) .05
193 Vince Buck (DP) .05
194 Jim Dombrowski (DP) .05
195 Quinn Early (DP) .05
196 Jim Everett .30
197 Michael Haynes (DP) .05
198 Wayne Martin (SP) 1.50
199 Lorenzo Neal (DP) .05
200 William Roaf (SP) 1.50
201 Irv Smith (DP) .05
202 Jimmy Spencer (DP) .05
203 Winfred Tubbs (DP) .05
204 Renaldo Turnbull (SP) 1.50
205 Michael Brooks (DP) .05
206 Dave Brown (DP) .05
207 Chris Calloway .30
208 Jesse Campbell (DP) .05
209 John Elliott (DP) .05
210 Keith Hamilton (DP) .05
211 Rodney Hampton (DP) .10
212 Corey Miller (DP) .05
213 Doug Riesenberg (DP) .05
214 Mike Sherrard .30
215 Phillippi Sparks .30
216 Michael Strahan (DP) .05
217 Richie Anderson (DP) .05
218 Brad Baxter (DP) .05
219 Tony Casillas (DP) .05
220 Roger Duffy .30
221 Boomer Esiason (DP) .10
222 Aaron Glenn (DP) .05
223 Bobby Houston (DP) .05
224 Mo Lewis (SP) 1.50
225 Siupeli Malamala (DP) .05
226 Johnny Mitchell (DP) .05
227 Eddie Anderson (DP) .05
228 Jerry Ball (DP) .05
229 Greg Biekert .30
230 Tim Brown (SP) 3.00
231 Rob Fredrickson (DP) .05
232 Nolan Harrison .30
233 Jeff Hostetler (DP) .10
234 Rocket Ismail (SP) 2.00
235 Terry McDaniel (SP) 1.50
236 Chester McGlockton (SP) 1.50
237 Don Mosebar .30
238 Anthony Smith .30
239 Harvey Williams (DP) .05
240 Steve Wisniewski (DP) .05
241 Fred Barnett .30
242 Randall Cunningham .30
243 William Fuller (SP) 1.50
244 Charlie Garner .30
245 Vaughn Hebron (DP) .05
246 Lester Holmes .30
247 Greg Jackson (SP) 1.50
248 Bill Romanowski (DP) .05
249 William Thomas (SP) 1.50
250 Bernard Williams .30
251 Calvin Williams (DP) .05
252 Michael Zordich (SP) 1.50
253 Chad Brown (SP) 3.00
254 Dermontti Dawson (DP) .05
255 Kevin Greene (SP) 3.00
256 Charles Johnson .60
257 Carnell Lake .30
258 Greg Lloyd (SP) 3.00
259 Neil O'Donnell (DP) .10
260 Ray Seals (DP) .05
261 Leon Searcy (SP) 1.50
262 Yancey Thigpen (DP) 1.00
263 John L. Williams (DP) .05
264 Rod Woodson (SP) 3.00
265 Stan Brock .30
266 Courtney Hall .30
267 Ronnie Harmon .30
268 Dwayne Harper (DP) .05
269 Rodney Harrison (DP) .05
270 Stan Humphries (DP) .20
271 Shawn Jefferson .30
272 Shawn Lee .30
273 Tony Martin .75
274 Natrone Means (SP) 5.00
275 Chris Mims (SP) 1.50
276 Leslie O'Neal (SP) 1.50
277 Junior Seau (SP) 3.00
278 Mark Seay (DP) .10
279 Harry Swayne (DP) .05
280 Eric Davis .30
281 William Floyd .75
282 Merton Hanks (SP) 1.50
283 Brent Jones .30
284 Tim McDonald (DP) .05
285 Ken Norton (SP) 1.50
286 Gary Plummer (DP) .05
287 Jerry Rice (SP) 12.00
288 Dana Stubblefield (SP) 3.00
289 John Taylor (SP) 1.50
290 Bryant Young (DP) .10
291 Steve Young (SP) 8.00
292 Steve Wallace (SP) 1.50
293 Sam Adams (DP) .05
294 Robert Blackmon (DP) .05
295 Jeff Blackshear (DP) .05
296 Brian Blades .30
297 Howard Ballard (SP) 1.50
298 Cortez Kennedy (DP) .05
299 Rick Mirer .75
300 Eugene Robinson (DP) .05
301 Chris Warren (SP) 3.00
302 Terry Wooden (SP) 1.50
303 Johnny Bailey .30
304 Isaac Bruce (DP) .75
305 Shane Conlan (DP) .05
306 Troy Drayton (DP) .05
307 Sean Gilbert (DP) .05
308 Leo Goeas (DP) .05
309 Jessie Hester .30
310 Clarence Jones .30
311 Todd Lyght .30
312 Chris Miller (DP) .05
313 Toby Wright (DP) .05
314 Robert Young (DP) .05
315 Eric Curry (DP) .05
316 Trent Dilfer .75
317 Thomas Everett (DP) .05
318 Paul Gruber (DP) .05
319 Jackie Harris (DP) .05
320 Courtney Hawkins (DP) .05
321 Lonnie Marts (DP) .05
322 Tony Mayberry (DP) .05
323 Martin Mayhew (DP) .05
324 Hardy Nickerson (DP) .05
325 Errict Rhett (DP) .50
326 Reggie Brooks (DP) .05
327 Tom Carter (DP) .05
328 Henry Ellard (SP) 1.50
329 Darrell Green (SP) 1.50
330 Ken Harvey (SP) 1.50
331 James Jenkins (DP) .05
332 Tim Johnson (DP) .05
333 Jim Lachey .30
334 Brian Mitchell .30
335 Heath Shuler 1.00
336 Tony Woods (DP) .05

1996 Donruss

This 250-card set marks the debut of Donruss football cards. The base brand includes 10 Rated Rookies, a subset made popular in the

Donruss baseball sets. Each card front has a full-bleed color action photo, with a banner at the top in the team's primary color containing the player's name. The Donruss logo is stamped in silver in the upper left corner. A football, using team colors, is at the bottom of the card, with the position along the top and the team name below. A star in the middle of the football contains a team logo. The horizontal back has the player's position in the upper left corner, with the player's name running in a team-colored banner along the top. Career totals and stats from 1995 are below this information, followed by a brief recap of the player's accomplishments underneath. The background is a team logo. The right side of the card has a number in the upper corner, with a photograph below. Biographical information is in a stripe along the bottom. There were 240 of the cards also produced as a parallel Press Proof set. Each card, numbered 1 of 2,000, has a helmet die-cut in it. The Donruss logo is stamped at the top in gold foil, which is also used for the words "First 2,000 Printed" and "Press Proof" toward the bottom. Insert sets include Hit List, Stop Action, What If?, Will to Win and Silver and Gold Elite cards.

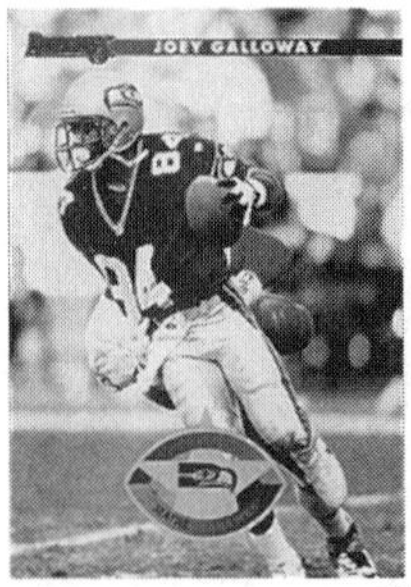

		MT
Complete Set (240):		20.00
Common Player:		.05
Minor Stars:		.10
Comp. Gold Press Proof (240):		600.00
Gold Press Proof Cards:		12x-24x
Hobby Pack (11):		2.00
Hobby Wax Box (18):		32.00
Retail Pack (16):		2.50
Retail Wax Box (24):		45.00
Magazine Pack (5):		1.50
Magazine Wax Box (48):		65.00
1	Barry Sanders	1.25
2	Flipper Anderson	.05
3	Ben Coates	.05
4	Rob Johnson	.05
5	Rodney Hampton	.05
6	Desmond Howard	.05
7	Craig Heyward	.05
8	Alvin Harper	.05
9	Todd Collins	.05
10	Ken Norton Jr.	.05
11	Stan Humphries	.05
12	Aeneas Williams	.05
13	Jeff Hostetler	.05
14	Frank Sanders	.05
15	J.J. Birden	.05
16	Bryce Paup	.05
17	Bill Brooks	.05
18	Kevin Williams	.05
19	Boomer Esiason	.05
20	O.J. McDuffie	.05
21	Eric Swann	.05
22	Neil Smith	.05
23	Charlie Garner	.05
24	Greg Lloyd	.05
25	Willie Jackson	.05
26	Shawn Jefferson	.05
27	Rodney Peete	.05
28	Michael Westbrook	.50
29	J.J. Stokes	.50
30	Troy Aikman	1.00
31	Sean Dawkins	.05
32	Larry Centers	.05
33	Herschel Walker	.05
34	Stoney Case	.05
35	Kevin Greene	.05
36	Quinn Early	.05
37	Fred Barnett	.05
38	Andre Coleman	.05
39	Mark Chmura	.25
40	Adrian Murrell	.05
41	Roosevelt Potts	.05
42	Jay Novacek	.05
43	Derrick Alexander	.05
44	Ken Dilger	.05
45	Rob Moore	.05
46	Cris Carter	.05
47	Jeff Blake	.50
48	Derek Loville	.05
49	Tyrone Wheatley	.05
50	Terrell Fletcher	.05
51	Sherman Williams	.05
52	Justin Armour	.05
53	Kordell Stewart	1.00
54	Tim Brown	.05
55	Kevin Carter	.05
56	Andre Rison	.05
57	James Stewart	.05
58	Brent Jones	.05
59	Erik Kramer	.05
60	Floyd Turner	.05
61	Ricky Watters	.05
62	Hardy Nickerson	.05
63	Aaron Craver	.05
64	Dave Krieg	.05
65	Warren Moon	.05
66	Wayne Chrebet	.05
67	Napoleon Kaufman	.10
68	Terance Mathis	.05
69	Chad May	.05
70	Andre Reed	.05
71	Reggie White	.10
72	Brett Favre	2.00
73	Chris Zorich	.05
74	Kerry Collins	.30
75	Herman Moore	.30
76	Yancey Thigpen	.50
77	Glenn Foley	.05
78	Quentin Coryatt	.05
79	Terry Kirby	.05
80	Edgar Bennett	.05
81	Mark Brunell	.75
82	Heath Shuler	.05
83	Gus Frerotte	.05
84	Deion Sanders	.50
85	Calvin Williams	.05
86	Junior Seau	.10
87	Jim Kelly	.10
88	Daryl Johnston	.05
89	Irving Fryar	.05
90	Brian Blades	.05
91	Willie Davis	.05
92	Jerome Bettis	.10
93	Marcus Allen	.10
94	Jeff Graham	.05
95	Rick Mirer	.05
96	Harvey Williams	.05
97	Steve Atwater	.05
98	Carl Pickens	.10
99	Darick Holmes	.05
100	Bruce Smith	.05
101	Vinny Testaverde	.05
102	Thurman Thomas	.10
103	Drew Bledsoe	.75
104	Bernie Parmalee	.05
105	Greg Hill	.05
106	Steve McNair	.50
107	Andre Hastings	.05
108	Eric Metcalf	.05
109	Kimble Anders	.05
110	Steve Tasker	.05
111	Mark Carrier	.05
112	Jerry Rice	1.00
113	Joey Galloway	.75
114	Robert Smith	.05
115	Hugh Douglas	.05
116	Willie McGinest	.05
117	Terrell Davis	.75
118	Cortez Kennedy	.05
119	Marshall Faulk	.50
120	Michael Haynes	.05
121	Isaac Bruce	.50
122	Brian Mitchell	.05
123	Bryan Cox	.05
124	Tamarick Vanover	.50
125	William Floyd	.05
126	Chris Chandler	.05
127	Carnell Lake	.05
128	Aaron Bailey	.05
129	Darnay Scott	.20
130	Darren Woodson	.05
131	Ernie Mills	.05
132	Charles Haley	.05
133	Rocket Ismail	.05
134	Bert Emanuel	.05
135	Lake Dawson	.05
136	Jake Reed	.05
137	Dave Brown	.05
138	Steve Bono	.05
139	Terry Allen	.05
140	Errict Rhett	.20
141	Rod Woodson	.05
142	Charles Johnson	.05
143	Emmitt Smith	2.00
144	Ki-Jana Carter	.40
145	Garrison Hearst	.05
146	Rashaan Salaam	.50
147	Tony Boselli	.05
148	Derrick Thomas	.05
149	Mark Seay	.05
150	Derrick Alexander	.05
151	Christian Fauria	.05
152	Aaron Hayden	.05
153	Chris Warren	.10
154	Dave Meggett	.05
155	Jeff George	.10
156	Jackie Harris	.05
157	Michael Irvin	.10
158	Scott Mitchell	.05
159	Trent Dilfer	.05
160	Kyle Brady	.05
161	Dan Marino	2.00
162	Curtis Martin	1.50
163	Mario Bates	.05
164	Erric Pegram	.05
165	Eric Zeier	.05
166	Rodney Thomas	.05
167	Neil O'Donnell	.05
168	Warren Sapp	.05
169	Jim Harbaugh	.10
170	Henry Ellard	.05
171	Anthony Miller	.05
172	Derrick Moore	.05
173	John Elway	.50
174	Vincent Brisby	.05
175	Antonio Freeman	.05
176	Chris Sanders	.30
177	Steve Young	.75
178	Shannon Sharpe	.05
179	Brett Perriman	.05
180	Orlando Thomas	.05
181	Eric Bjornson	.05
182	Natrone Means	.05
183	Jim Everett	.05
184	Curtis Conway	.05
185	Robert Brooks	.10
186	Tony Martin	.05
187	Mark Carrier	.05
188	LeShon Johnson	.05
189	Bernie Kosar	.05
190	Ray Zellars	.05
191	Steve Walsh	.05
192	Craig Erickson	.05
193	Tommy Maddox	.05
194	Leslie O'Neal	.05
195	Harold Green	.05
196	Steve Beuerlein	.05
197	Ron Moore	.05
198	Leslie Shepherd	.05
199	Leroy Hoard	.05
200	Michael Jackson	.05
201	Will Moore	.05
202	Ricky Ervins	.05
203	Keith Jennings	.05
204	Eric Green	.05
205	Mark Rypien	.05
206	Torrance Small	.05
207	Sean Gilbert	.05
208	*Mike Alstott*	1.50
209	Willie Anderson	.05
210	Alex Molden	.05
211	Jonathan Ogden	.05
212	Stepfret Williams	.05
213	*Jeff Lewis*	.50
214	Regan Upshaw	.05
215	Daryl Gardener	.05
216	*Danny Kanell*	.50
217	John Mobley	.05
218	Reggie Brown	.05
219	*Mushin Muhammad*	.75
220	*Kevin Hardy*	.25
221	*Stanley Pritchett*	.40
222	Cedric Jones	.05
223	Marco Battaglia	.05
224	Duane Clemons	.05
225	Jerald Moore	.05
226	*Simeon Rice*	.30
227	Chris Darkins	.10
228	*Bobby Hoying*	.50
229	*Stephen Davis*	3.00
230	*Walt Harris*	.30
231	Jermain Mayberry	.05
232	(Tony Brackens)	.05
233	*(Eric Moulds)*	2.00
234	*(Alex Van Dyke)*	.50
235	*(Marvin Harrison)*	2.50
236	*Rickey Dudley*	.50
237	*Terrell Owens*	3.00
238	Checklist (Jerry Rice CL)	.25
239	Checklist (Dan Marino CL)	.30
240	Checklist	.05

1996 Donruss Press Proofs

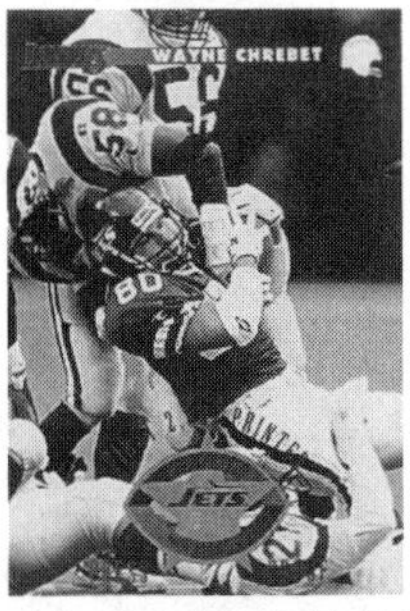

Press Proofs paralleled the 240-card regular-issue set, and included the words "Press Proof" in gold foil on the front of the card, along with a die-cut. Each Gold Press Proof was numbered 1 of 2,000.

	MT
Complete Set (240):	300.00
Press Proof Cards:	6x-12x

1996 Donruss Elite

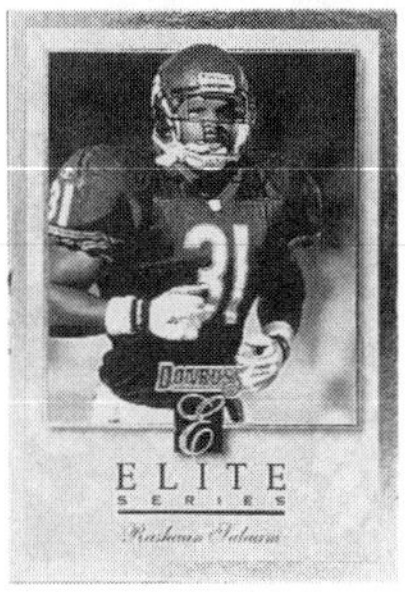

Donruss' initial football set continues the legacy of an Elite insert set, which debuted in the company's baseball line in 1991. Ten of the NFL's premiere running backs are featured on two versions of the foil-enhanced card - Silver Elite and Gold Elite. The Silver cards are limited to 10,000 each; the Gold ones are sequentially numbered to 2,000. The card front uses the corresponding color for the foiled borders around the picture, plus the Donruss and Elite logos. The card back uses the appropriate color for the background, which has a scripted Elite "E" and a short player profile on the left side. The right side has a color photo with a team logo underneath. The card number is along the top of the card.

		MT
Complete Set (20):		125.00
Common Player:		1.00
Comp. Gold Set (20):		900.00
Gold Cards:		3x
1	Emmitt Smith	15.00
2	Barry Sanders	20.00
3	Marshall Faulk	3.00
4	Curtis Martin	5.00
5	Junior Seau	1.00
6	Troy Aikman	10.00
7	Steve Young	6.00
8	Dan Marino	15.00
9	Brett Favre	20.00
10	John Elway	15.00
11	Kerry Collins	2.00
12	Drew Bledsoe	10.00
13	Jerry Rice	15.00
14	Keyshawn Johnson	6.00
15	Deion Sanders	3.00
16	Isaac Bruce	3.00
17	Rashaan Salaam	1.00
18	Tim Biakabutuka	1.00
19	Lawrence Phillips	2.00
20	Robert Brooks	1.00

1996 Donruss Elite Gold

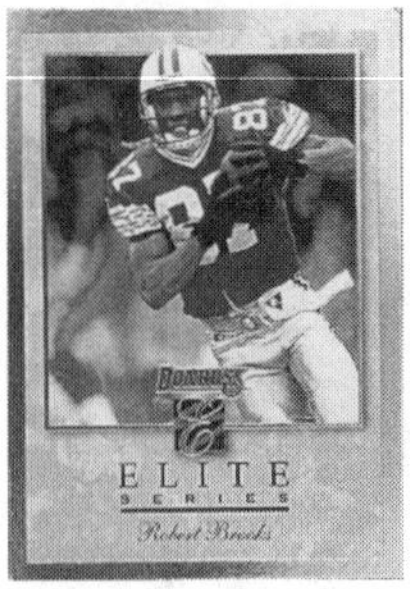

Donruss Elite Golds run parallel with the Elite Silvers, but are numbered up to 2,000. In this insert, the silver foil is replaced by gold foil.

	MT
Complete Set (20):	250.00
Gold Cards:	2x

1996 Donruss Hit List

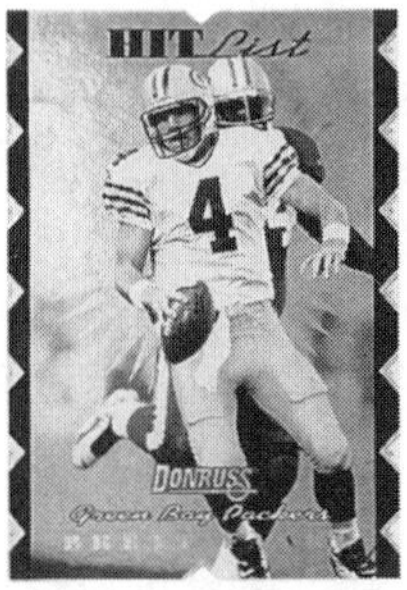

These 1996 Donruss insert cards feature the NFL's most physical players on cards which use silver holographic foil and die-cutting for the design. The front has a color photo, with a holographic background. "Hit List" is written at the top of the card; Donruss and the player's team name are below the photo. The sides of the card are die-cut, with foiled rivets in them. The card back has a color photo on it, with most of it, except for the player's face, ghosted as the background. The player's face is in full color, highlighted by a sunburst around it. There's a paragraph below which details a moment when the player survived, or delivered, a devastating hit. A serial number appears in a white rectangle along the bottom. The card number is in the upper right corner.

		MT
Complete Set (20):		100.00
Common Player:		.50
1	Bruce Smith	.50
2	Barry Sanders	12.00
3	Kevin Hardy	.50
4	Greg Lloyd	.50
5	Brett Favre	12.00
6	Emmitt Smith	8.00
7	Kerry Collins	1.00
8	Ken Norton Jr.	.50
9	Steve Atwater	.50
10	Curtis Martin	4.00
11	Chris Warren	.50
12	Steve Young	4.00
13	Marshall Faulk	2.00
14	Junior Seau	.50
15	Lawrence Phillips	6.00
16	Troy Aikman	6.00
17	Jerry Rice	6.00
18	Dan Marino	8.00
19	Reggie White	1.00
20	John Elway	8.00

1996 Donruss Rated Rookies

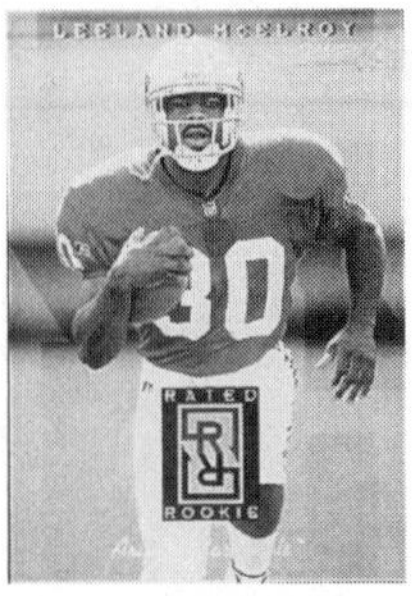

In a concept first made popular with its baseball line, Donruss has issued this 10-card insert set honoring 10 of the top NFL newcomers.

		MT
Complete Set (10):		40.00
Common Player:		2.00
1	Keyshawn Johnson	5.00
2	Terry Glenn	7.00
3	Tim Biakabutuka	4.00
4	Bobby Engram	2.00
5	Leeland McElroy	2.00
6	Eddie George	8.00
7	Lawrence Phillips	4.00
8	Derrick Mayes	2.00
9	Karim Abdul-Jabbar	5.00
10	Eddie Kennison	4.00

1996 Donruss What If?

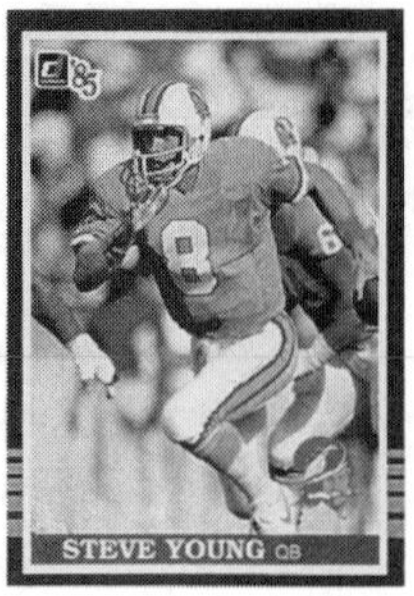

These 1996 Donruss inserts go back in time to chronicle the NFL's top talents with a post-dated rookie card. Each card uses rookie photography, with a design that fits the era that the player entered the league. Each card also has a sequential serial number. Cards were in hobby packs only.

		MT
Complete Set (10):		100.00
Common Player:		3.00
1	Troy Aikman	10.00
2	Jerry Rice	10.00
3	Barry Sanders	15.00
4	Drew Bledsoe	8.00
5	Deion Sanders	3.00
6	Brett Favre	15.00
7	Dan Marino	12.00
8	Steve Young	7.00
9	Emmitt Smith	12.00
10	John Elway	10.00

1996 Donruss Stop Action

1996 Donruss football magazine packs have these Stop Action inserts, which feature some of the best action photos in the sport. Each shot is enhanced by holographic foil and die-cutting. Each card is serial numbered to 5,000.

		MT
Complete Set (10):		85.00
Common Player:		2.00
1	Deion Sanders	3.00
2	Troy Aikman	10.00
3	Brett Favre	15.00
4	Steve Young	7.00
5	Joey Galloway	2.00
6	Dan Marino	12.00
7	Jerry Rice	10.00
8	Emmitt Smith	12.00
9	Isaac Bruce	3.00
10	Barry Sanders	15.00

1996 Donruss Will to Win

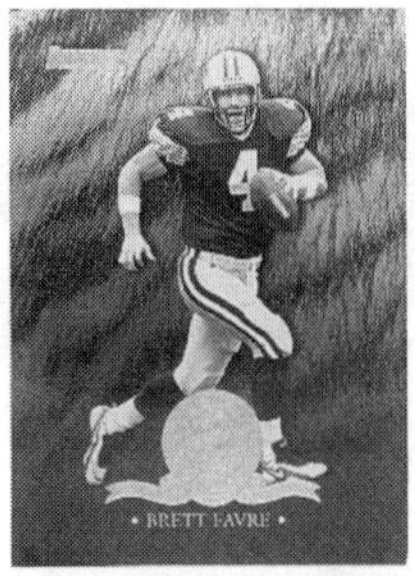

These inserts are exclusive to 1996 Donruss retail packs only. The cards, having sequential numbering to 5,000, are one of the scarcest inserts in the product. They feature some of the NFL's grittiest competitors.

		MT
Complete Set (10):		85.00
Common Player:		3.00
1	Emmitt Smith	12.00
2	Brett Favre	15.00
3	Curtis Martin	6.00
4	Jerry Rice	10.00
5	Barry Sanders	15.00
6	Errict Rhett	3.00
7	Troy Aikman	10.00
8	Dan Marino	12.00
9	Steve Young	7.00
10	John Elway	12.00

A player's name in *italic type* indicates a rookie card.

1997 Donruss

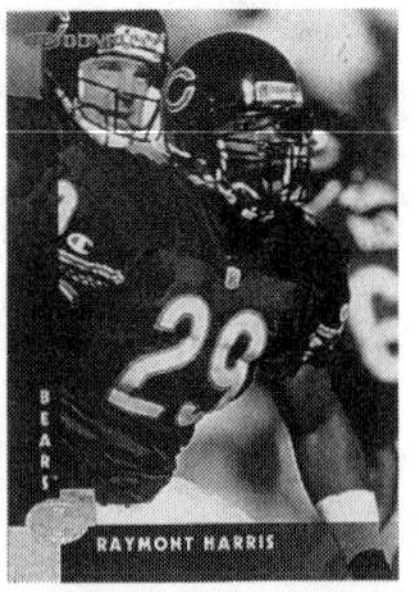

The 230-card set features a full-bleed photo on the front. The Donruss logo is in the upper left. The team name is printed vertically in the lower left, while the team logo and player position are in the lower left corner. The player's name is to the right of the team logo. The base set is paralleled with a Press Proofs set, which are numbered "1 of 1,500," and Press Proofs - First 500, which are numbered "1 of 500" and die-cut with gold foil.

		MT
Complete Set (230):		20.00
Common Player:		.05
Minor Stars:		.10
Silvers:		20x-40x
Golds:		25x-50x
Pack (10):		2.00
Wax Box (24):		42.00
1	Dan Marino	1.50
2	Brett Favre	1.75
3	Emmitt Smith	1.50
4	Eddie George	1.25
5	Karim Abdul-Jabbar	.50
6	Terrell Davis	1.00
7	Curtis Martin	1.00
8	Drew Bledsoe	.75
9	Jerry Rice	.75
10	Troy Aikman	.75
11	Barry Sanders	1.25
12	Mark Brunell	.75
13	Kerry Collins	.30
14	Steve Young	.50
15	Kordell Stewart	.75
16	Eddie Kennison	.40
17	Terry Glenn	.75
18	John Elway	.50
19	Joey Galloway	.30
20	Deion Sanders	.40
21	Keyshawn Johnson	.40
22	Lawrence Phillips	.10
23	Ricky Watters	.10
24	Marvin Harrison	.40
25	Bobby Engram	.10
26	Marshall Faulk	.10
27	Carl Pickens	.10
28	Isaac Bruce	.15
29	Herman Moore	.15
30	Jerome Bettis	.10
31	Rashaan Salaam	.10
32	Errict Rhett	.10
33	Tim Biakabutuka	.10
34	Robert Brooks	.10
35	Antonio Freeman	.30
36	Steve McNair	.50
37	Jeff Blake	.10
38	Tony Banks	.30
39	Terrell Owens	.50
40	Eric Moulds	.05
41	Leeland McElroy	.10
42	Chris Sanders	.05
43	Thurman Thomas	.10
44	Bruce Smith	.05
45	Reggie White	.10
46	Chris Warren	.05
47	J.J. Stokes	.05
48	Ben Coates	.05
49	Tim Brown	.05
50	Marcus Allen	.10
51	Michael Irvin	.10
52	William Floyd	.05
53	Ken Dilger	.05
54	Bobby Taylor	.05
55	Keenan McCardell	.05
56	Raymont Harris	.05
57	Keith Byars	.05
58	O.J. McDuffie	.05
59	Robert Smith	.05
60	Bert Emanuel	.05
61	Rick Mirer	.05
62	Vinny Testaverde	.05
63	Kyle Brady	.05
64	Mark Bruener	.05
65	Neil O'Donnell	.05
66	Anthony Johnson	.05
67	Ken Norton	.05
68	Warren Sapp	.05
69	Amani Toomer	.05
70	Simeon Rice	.05
71	Kevin Hardy	.05
72	Junior Seau	.05
73	Neil Smith	.05
74	LeShon Johnson	.05
75	Quinn Early	.05
76	Andre Reed	.05
77	Jake Reed	.05
78	Elvis Grbac	.05
79	Tyrone Wheatley	.05
80	Adrian Murrell	.05
81	Fred Barnett	.05
82	Darrell Green	.05
83	Stan Humphries	.05
84	Troy Drayton	.05
85	Steve Atwater	.05
86	Quentin Coryatt	.05
87	Dan Wilkinson	.05
88	Scott Mitchell	.05
89	Willie McGinest	.05
90	Kevin Smith	.05
91	Gus Frerotte	.05
92	Bam Morris	.05
93	Darick Holmes	.05
94	Zach Thomas	.20
95	Tom Carter	.05
96	Cortez Kennedy	.05
97	Kevin Williams	.05

98	Michael Haynes	.05
99	Lamont Warren	.05
100	Jeff Graham	.05
101	Alex Van Dyke	.05
102	Jim Everett	.05
103	Chris Chandler	.05
104	Qadry Ismail	.05
105	Ray Zellars	.05
106	Chris T. Jones	.05
107	Charlie Garner	.05
108	Bobby Hoying	.05
109	Mark Chmura	.05
110	Cris Carter	.05
111	Darnay Scott	.05
112	Anthony Miller	.05
113	Desmond Howard	.05
114	Terance Mathis	.05
115	Rodney Hampton	.05
116	Napoleon Kaufman	.05
117	Jim Harbaugh	.05
118	Shannon Sharpe	.05
119	Irving Fryar	.05
120	Garrison Hearst	.05
121	Terry Allen	.05
122	Larry Centers	.05
123	Sean Dawkins	.05
124	Jeff George	.05
125	Tony Martin	.05
126	Mike Alstott	.10
127	Rickey Dudley	.05
128	Kevin Carter	.05
129	Derrick Alexander	.05
130	Greg Lloyd	.05
131	Bryce Paup	.05
132	Derrick Thomas	.05
133	Greg Hill	.05
134	Jamal Anderson	.05
135	Curtis Conway	.05
136	Frank Sanders	.05
137	Brett Perriman	.05
138	Edgar Bennett	.05
139	Wayne Chrebet	.05
140	Natrone Means	.05
141	Eric Metcalf	.05
142	Trent Dilfer	.05
143	Terry Kirby	.05
144	Johnnie Morton	.05
145	Dale Carter	.05
146	Michael Westbrook	.05
147	Stanley Pritchett	.05
148	Todd Collins	.05
149	Tamarick Vanover	.05
150	Kevin Greene	.05
151	Lamar Lathon	.05
152	Muhsin Muhammad	.05
153	Dorsey Levens	.10
154	Rod Woodson	.05
155	Brent Jones	.05
156	Michael Jackson	.05
157	Shawn Jefferson	.05
158	Kimble Anders	.05
159	Sean Gilbert	.05
160	Carnell Lake	.05
161	Darren Woodson	.05
162	Dave Meggett	.05
163	Henry Ellard	.05
164	Eric Swann	.05
165	Tony Boselli	.05
166	Daryl Johnston	.05
167	Willie Jackson	.05
168	Wesley Walls	.05
169	Mario Bates	.05
170	Lake Dawson	.05
171	Mike Mamula	.05
172	Ed McCaffrey	.05
173	Tony Brackens	.05
174	Craig Heyward	.05
175	Harvey Williams	.05
176	Dave Brown	.05
177	Aaron Glenn	.05
178	Jeff Hostetler	.05
179	Alvin Harper	.05
180	Ty Detmer	.05
181	James Jett	.05
182	James Stewart	.05
183	Warren Moon	.05
184	Herschel Walker	.05
185	Ki-Jana Carter	.05
186	Leslie O'Neal	.05
187	Danny Kanell	.05
188	Eric Bjornson	.05
189	Alex Molden	.05
190	Bryant Young	.05
191	Merton Hanks	.05
192	Heath Shuler	.05
193	Brian Blades	.05
194	Steve Bono	.05
195	Wayne Simmons	.05
196	*Warrick Dunn*	1.25
197	*Peter Boulware*	.10
198	*David LaFleur*	.50
199	*Shawn Springs*	.40
200	*Reidel Anthony*	1.00
201	*Jim Druckenmiller*	1.00
202	*Orlando Pace*	.40
203	*Yatil Green*	.50
204	*Bryant Westbrook*	.10
205	*Tiki Barber*	1.00
206	*James Farrior*	.10
207	*Rae Carruth*	.25
208	*Danny Wuerffel*	.50
209	*Corey Dillon*	2.50
210	*Ike Hilliard*	1.00
211	*Tony Gonzalez*	1.00
212	*Antowain Smith*	1.25
213	*Pat Barnes*	.50
214	*Troy Davis*	.50
215	*Byron Hanspard*	.50
216	*Joey Kent*	.40
217	*Jake Plummer*	2.50
218	*Kenny Holmes*	.10
219	*Darnell Autry*	.25
220	*Darrell Russell*	.10
221	*Walter Jones*	.10
222	*Dwayne Rudd*	.10
223	*Tom Knight*	.10
224	*Kevin Lockett*	.20
225	*Will Blackwell*	.20
226	(Dan Marino CL)	.75
227	(Brett Favre CL)	1.00
228	(Emmitt Smith CL)	.75
229	(Barry Sanders CL)	.50
230	(Jerry Rice CL)	.30

1997 Donruss Press Proof Silvers

Silver Press Proofs were a parallel set to the 230-card Donruss set in 1997. Silver Press Proofs have silver foil added to the front in streaks throughout the card, which originate from the bottom left corner. The words "Press Proof" are printed up the right side in silver foil. Card backs contain a "1 of 1,500" line printed just below the player's name.

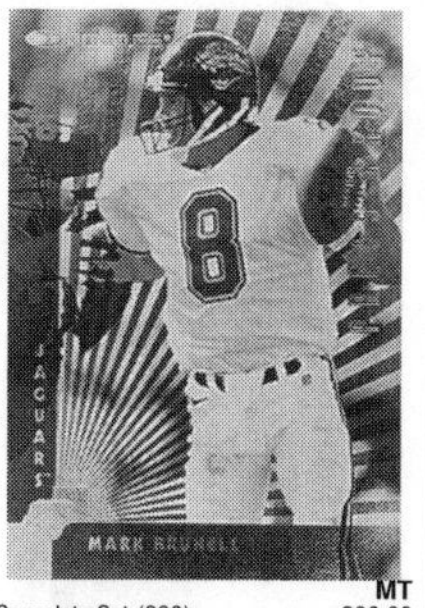

	MT
Complete Set (230):	200.00
Silver Cards:	5x-10x

1997 Donruss Press Proof Golds

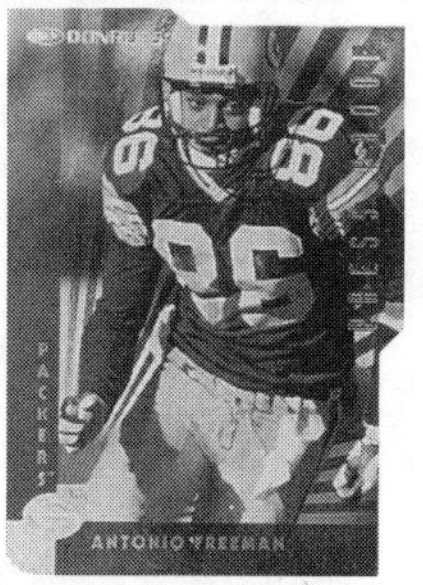

Gold Press Proofs were a parallel to the 230-card Donruss set in 1997. Gold Press Proofs were die-cut across the top and right side and had rounded corners in the bottom left corner. Fronts featured gold foil streaks across the front that originated in the bottom left corner. The words "Press Proof" are printed in gold up the right side of the card, while the backs are numbered "1 of 500" under the player's name.

	MT
Complete Set (230):	400.00
Gold Cards:	10x-20x

1997 Donruss Elite

The 20-card chase set is featured on Silver and Gold foil cards. The Silver Elite is numbered to 5,000, while the Gold version was produced in an edition of 2,000 sets.

		MT
Complete Set (20):		200.00
Common Player:		5.00
Minor Stars:		10.00
Production 5,000 Sets		
Gold Cards:		2x
Production 2,000 Sets		
1	Emmitt Smith	20.00
2	Dan Marino	20.00
3	Brett Favre	30.00
4	Curtis Martin	10.00
5	Terrell Davis	25.00
6	Barry Sanders	30.00
7	Drew Bledsoe	15.00
8	Mark Brunell	15.00
9	Troy Aikman	15.00
10	Jerry Rice	15.00
11	Steve McNair	10.00
12	Kerry Collins	10.00
13	John Elway	20.00
14	Eddie George	15.00
15	Karim Abdul-Jabbar	10.00
16	Kordell Stewart	15.00
17	Jerome Bettis	5.00
18	Terry Glenn	10.00
19	Errict Rhett	5.00
20	Carl Pickens	5.00

1997 Donruss Legends of the Fall

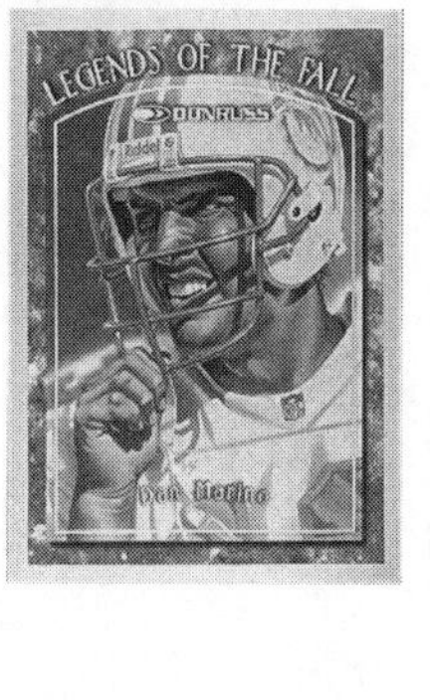

The 10-card chase set is numbered to 10,000 and features artwork from artist Dan Gardiner. The first 500 of the cards were printed directly on actual canvas.

		MT
Complete Set (10):		125.00
Common Player:		5.00
Canvas Cards:		3x-6x
1	Troy Aikman	16.00
2	Barry Sanders	20.00
3	John Elway	10.00
4	Dan Marino	30.00
5	Emmitt Smith	30.00
6	Jerry Rice	16.00
7	Deion Sanders	10.00
8	Brett Favre	35.00
9	Marcus Allen	5.00
10	Steve Young	10.00

1997 Donruss Passing Grade

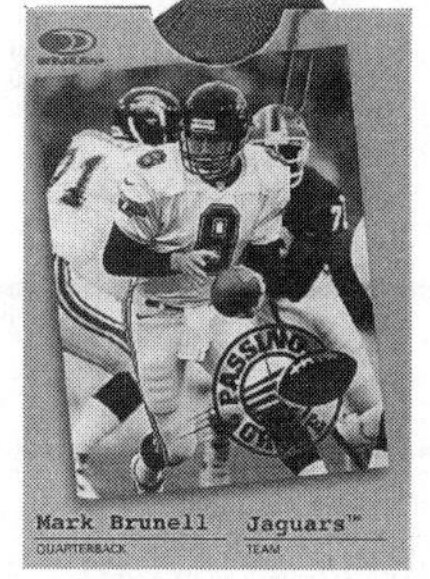

The 16-card hobby-exclusive set is styled like a report card. The die-cut insert showcases the talents of the top quarterbacks. It utilizes a card-within-a-card design with red-foil stamping. Each football shaped, die-cut card came in its own envelope. The cards are numbered to 3,000.

		MT
Complete Set (16):		150.00
Common Player:		4.00
Minor Stars:		8.00
Production 3,000 Sets		
1	Steve Young	10.00
2	Drew Bledsoe	15.00
3	Mark Brunell	15.00
4	Kerry Collins	8.00
5	Steve McNair	10.00
6	John Elway	20.00
7	Ty Detmer	4.00
8	Jeff Blake	4.00
9	Dan Marino	20.00
10	Kordell Stewart	12.00
11	Tony Banks	8.00
12	Brett Favre	30.00
13	Gus Frerotte	4.00
14	Troy Aikman	15.00
15	Jeff George	4.00
16	Brad Johnson	8.00

1997 Donruss Rated Rookies

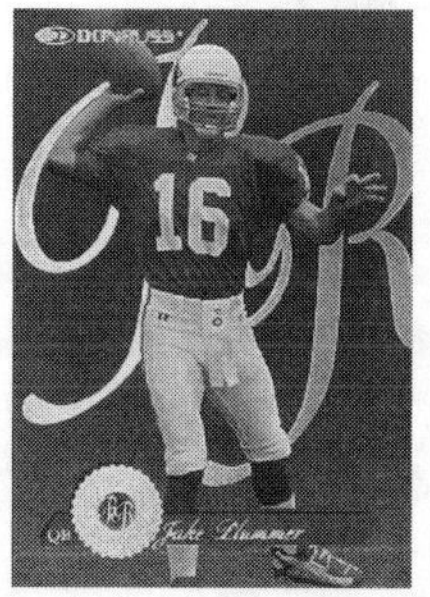

The 10-card chase set features a rookie player, with the Rated Rookies logo in the lower left corner. The set was paralleled by a Medalist micro-etched, all foil set with gold-foil holographic stamping.

		MT
Complete Set (10):		45.00
Common Player:		3.00
Medalist Cards: 5x-10x		
1	Ike Hilliard	4.00
2	Warrick Dunn	10.00
3	Yatil Green	3.00
4	Jim Druckenmiller	6.00
5	Rae Carruth	4.00
6	Antowain Smith	8.00
7	Tiki Barber	4.00
8	Byron Hanspard	3.00
9	Reidel Anthony	5.00
10	Jake Plummer	20.00

1997 Donruss Zoning Commission

The 20-card retail-exclusive set is printed on micro-etched, holographic foil card stock, with gold-foil stamping. The cards are numbered to 5,000.

		MT
Complete Set (20):		200.00
Common Player:		5.00
Minor Stars:		10.00
1	Brett Favre	40.00
2	Jerry Rice	20.00
3	Jerome Bettis	10.00
4	Troy Aikman	20.00
5	Drew Bledsoe	20.00
6	Natrone Means	10.00
7	Steve Young	15.00
8	John Elway	15.00
9	Barry Sanders	25.00
10	Emmitt Smith	35.00
11	Curtis Martin	20.00
12	Terry Allen	5.00
13	Dan Marino	35.00
14	Mark Brunell	20.00
15	Terry Glenn	10.00
16	Herman Moore	5.00
17	Ricky Watters	5.00
18	Terrell Davis	20.00
19	Isaac Bruce	10.00
20	Curtis Conway	5.00

1997 Donruss Preferred

The inaugural issue of Donruss Preferred Football contained 150 cards which were divided into four different tiers, with 80 Bronze, 40 Silver, 20 Gold and 10 Platinum cards. The cards are printed on all-foil, micro-etched surfaces and contain an action shot of the player, with his name and team across the bottom and "Donruss Preferred" and the word bronze, silver, gold or platinum across the top. There is also a white star in each corner of the card within the color border. Preferred also had a Cut to the Chase parallel set, as well as Chain Reaction, Staremaster and Precious Metals insert sets. Another interesting facet of this product is that it arrived in collectible tins, of which, there were 24 different players featured. The tins were packed into larger Hobby Master Tins for hobby accounts and came in boxes to retail accounts.

		MT
Complete Set (150):		425.00
Complete Bronze (80):		35.00
Common Bronze:		.25
Minor Bronze Star:		.50
Common Silver:		2.00
Minor Silver Star:		4.00
Inserted 1:5		
Common Gold:		4.00
Minor Gold Star:		8.00
Inserted 1:17		
Common Platinum:		10.00
1	Emmitt Smith P	30.00
2	Steve Young G	10.00
3	Cris Carter S	4.00
4	Tim Biakabutuka B	.25
5	Brett Favre P	30.00
6	Troy Aikman G	12.00
7	Eddie Kennison S	2.00
8	Ben Coates B	.25
9	Dan Marino P	30.00
10	Deion Sanders G	8.00
11	Curtis Conway S	2.00
12	Jeff George S	2.00
13	Barry Sanders P	30.00
14	Kerry Collins G	8.00
15	Marvin Harrison S	4.00
16	Bobby Engram B	.25
17	Jerry Rice P	20.00
18	Kordell Stewart G	10.00
19	Tony Banks S	4.00
20	Jim Harbaugh B	.25
21	Mark Brunell P	15.00
22	Steve McNair G	10.00
23	Terrell Owens S	8.00
24	Raymont Harris B	.25
25	Curtis Martin P	12.00
26	Karim Abdul-Jabbar G	4.00
27	Joey Galloway S	4.00
28	Bobby Hoying B	.25
29	Terrell Davis P	30.00
30	Terry Glenn G	8.00
31	Antonio Freeman S	4.00
32	Brad Johnson B	1.00
33	Drew Bledsoe P	15.00
34	John Elway G	25.00
35	Herman Moore G	8.00
36	Robert Brooks S	2.00
37	Rod Smith B	.50
38	Eddie George P	15.00
39	Keyshawn Johnson G	8.00
40	Greg Hill S	2.00
41	Scott Mitchell B	.25
42	Muhsin Muhammad B	.75
43	Isaac Bruce G	10.00
44	Jeff Blake S	4.00
45	Neil O'Donnell B	.25
46	Jimmy Smith B	.75
47	Jerome Bettis G	8.00
48	Terry Allen S	2.00
49	Andre Reed B	.50
50	Frank Sanders B	.50
51	Tim Brown G	8.00
52	Thurman Thomas S	4.00
53	Heath Shuler B	.25
54	Vinny Testaverde B	.75
55	Marcus Allen S	4.00
56	Napoleon Kaufman B	.75
57	Derrick Alexander B	.25
58	Carl Pickens G	4.00
59	Marshall Faulk S	5.00
60	Mike Alstott B	1.00
61	Jamal Anderson B	2.00
62	Ricky Watters G	8.00
63	Dorsey Levens S	4.00
64	Todd Collins B	.25
65	Trent Dilfer B	.50
66	Natrone Means S	4.00
67	Gus Frerotte B	.25
68	Irving Fryar B	.25
69	Adrian Murrell S	2.00
70	Rodney Hampton B	.25
71	Garrison Hearst B	.50
72	Reggie White S	4.00
73	Anthony Johnson B	.25
74	Tony Martin B	.25
75	Chris Sanders S	2.00
76	O.J. McDuffie B	.50
77	Leeland McElroy B	.25
78	Ki-Jana Carter S	2.00
79	Anthony Miller B	.25
80	Johnnie Morton B	.25
81	Robert Smith S	4.00
82	Brett Perriman B	.25
83	Errict Rhett B	.50
84	Michael Irvin S	4.00
85	Darnay Scott B	.50
86	Shannon Sharpe B	.50
87	Lawrence Phillips S	2.00
88	Bruce Smith B	.25
89	James Stewart B	1.00
90	J.J. Stokes B	.50
91	Chris Warren B	.25
92	Daryl Johnston B	.25
93	Andre Rison B	.50
94	Rashaan Salaam B	.25
95	Amani Toomer B	.50
96	*Warrick Dunn G*	20.00
97	*Tiki Barber S*	8.00
98	*Peter Boulware B*	1.00
99	*Ike Hilliard G*	12.00
100	*Antowain Smith S*	8.00
101	*Yatil Green S*	2.00
102	*Tony Gonzalez B*	5.00
103	*Reidel Anthony G*	12.00
104	*Troy Davis S*	2.00
105	*Rae Carruth S*	2.00
106	*David LaFleur B*	1.00
107	*Jim Druckenmiller G*	10.00
108	*Joey Kent S*	2.00
109	*Byron Hanspard S*	5.00
110	*Darrell Russell B*	1.00
111	*Danny Wuerffel S*	4.00
112	*Jake Plummer S*	15.00
113	*Jay Graham B*	1.00
114	*Corey Dillon S*	12.00
115	*Orlando Pace B*	1.00
116	*Pat Barnes S*	4.00
117	*Shawn Springs B*	1.00
118	Troy Aikman B (National Treasures)	2.00
119	Drew Bledsoe B (National Treasures)	2.00
120	Mark Brunell B (National Treasures)	2.00
121	Kerry Collins B (National Treasures)	.50
122	Terrell Davis B (National Treasures)	3.00
123	Jerome Bettis B (National Treasures)	.50
124	Brett Favre B (National Treasures)	4.00
125	Eddie George B (National Treasures)	2.00
126	Terry Glenn B (National Treasures)	.50
127	Karim Abdul-Jabbar B (National Treasures)	.25
128	Keyshawn Johnson B (National Treasures)	.50
129	Dan Marino B (National Treasures)	4.00
130	Curtis Martin B (National Treasures)	1.00
131	Natrone Means B (National Treasures)	.25
132	Herman Moore S (National Treasures)	2.00
133	Jerry Rice B (National Treasures)	2.00
134	Barry Sanders B (National Treasures)	4.00
135	Deion Sanders B (National Treasures)	.50
136	Emmitt Smith B (National Treasures)	3.00
137	Kordell Stewart B (National Treasures)	1.00
138	Steve Young B (National Treasures)	1.50
139	Carl Pickens S (National Treasures)	2.00
140	Isaac Bruce S (National Treasures)	3.00
141	Steve McNair S (National Treasures)	5.00
142	John Elway S (National Treasures)	8.00
143	Cris Carter B (National Treasures)	.50
144	Tim Brown B (National Treasures)	.50
145	Ricky Watters S (National Treasures)	.50
146	Robert Brooks B (National Treasures)	.25
147	Jeff Blake B (National Treasures)	.25
148	(Tiki Barber CL B)	.50
149	(Jim Druckenmiller CL B)	.50
150	(Warrick Dunn CL B)	1.00

1997 Donruss Preferred Tins

Each pack of Donruss Preferred arrived for sale in a collectible tin, with 24 different players each featured on their own tin. The 24 tins arrived in five different varieties: smaller blue pack tins were the "base" tins; silver pack tins were in hobby exclusive boxes and numbered to 1,200; gold pack tins were also available in hobby box tins and numbered to 300; blue box tins were hobby exclusive and contained 24 smaller tins - these were numbered to 1,200 and essentially the same as the smaller blue tins except in size; and gold box tins, which were parallel to the larger blue box tins, but printed in gold and numbered to 300. The larger box tins were only available to hobby accounts. Retail accounts received the tins packed in cardboard boxes.

		MT
Complete Blue Pack (24):		20.00
Common Pack:		.25
Complete Silver Pack (24):		200.00
Silver Pack Tins:		5x-10x
Complete Silver Box (24):		150.00
Blue Box Tins:		4x-8x
Complete Gold Pack (24):		400.00
Gold Pack Tins:		10x-20x
Complete Gold Box (24):		300.00
Gold Box Tins:		8x-16x
1	Mark Brunell	1.00
2	Karim Abdul-Jabbar	.50
3	Terry Glenn	.75
4	Brett Favre	2.00
5	Troy Aikman	1.00
6	Eddie George	1.50
7	John Elway	.75
8	Steve Young	.75
9	Terrell Davis	1.00
10	Kordell Stewart	1.00
11	Drew Bledsoe	1.00
12	Kerry Collins	.75
13	Dan Marino	2.00
14	Tim Brown	.25
15	Carl Pickens	.25
16	Warrick Dunn	1.50
17	Herman Moore	.25
18	Curtis Martin	.75
19	Ike Hilliard	.50
20	Barry Sanders	1.25
21	Deion Sanders	.50
22	Emmitt Smith	2.00
23	Keyshawn Johnson	.25
24	Jerry Rice	1.00

1997 Donruss Preferred Chain Reaction

This 24-card insert set captured 12 different offensive teammates on die-cut cards that linked together in order to display them side by side. The insert was printed on thick plastic stock with holographic treatments and sequentially numbered to 3,000.

		MT
Complete Set (24):		350.00
Common Player:		5.00
Minor Stars:		10.00
1a	Dan Marino	40.00
1b	Karim Abdul-Jabbar	10.00
2a	Troy Aikman	20.00
2b	Emmitt Smith	40.00
3a	Steve McNair	15.00
3b	Eddie George	30.00
4a	Brett Favre	45.00
4b	Robert Brooks	5.00
5a	John Elway	15.00
5b	Terrell Davis	20.00
6a	Drew Bledsoe	20.00
6b	Curtis Martin	15.00
7a	Steve Young	15.00
7b	Jerry Rice	20.00
8a	Mark Brunell	20.00
8b	Natrone Means	5.00
9a	Barry Sanders	30.00
9b	Herman Moore	10.00
10a	Kordell Stewart	20.00
10b	Jerome Bettis	10.00
11a	Jeff Blake	10.00
11b	Carl Pickens	5.00
12a	Lawrence Phillips	5.00
12b	Isaac Bruce	10.00

1997 Donruss Preferred Cut To The Chase

Cut to the Chase paralleled the full 150-card set from Donruss Preferred. The base set was fractured into different colors corresponding to the base set and was also die-cut around the perimeter. Cut to the Chase bronze cards are one per seven packs, silvers are one per 63, golds are one per 189 and platinums are one per 756.

	MT
Complete Set (150):	2500.
Complete Bronze (80):	300.00
Bronze Stars:	4x-8x
Bronze Rookies:	2x-4x
Complete Silver (40):	500.00
Silver Stars:	2x-4x
Silver Rookies:	1x-2x
Complete Gold (20):	600.00
Gold Cards:	1x-2x
Complete Platinum (10):	1100.
Platinum Cards:	2x-3x

1997 Donruss Preferred Precious Metals

Precious Metals was a 15-card partial parallel set that was printed on actual silver, gold or platinum corresponding to which color subset the base card was from. Only 100 individually numbered Precious Metals sets were produced.

		MT
Complete Set (15):		4000.
Common Player:		100.00
1	Drew Bledsoe	250.00
2	Curtis Martin	225.00
3	Troy Aikman	250.00
4	Eddie George	300.00
5	Warrick Dunn	300.00
6	Brett Favre	500.00
7	John Elway	200.00
8	Barry Sanders	350.00
9	Emmitt Smith	400.00
10	Terrell Davis	250.00
11	Mark Brunell	250.00
12	Jerry Rice	250.00
13	Dan Marino	400.00
14	Terry Glenn	125.00
15	Tiki Barber	100.00

A player's name in *italic* type indicates a rookie card.

1997 Donruss Preferred Staremasters

These horizontal cards were printed on all-foil card stock with holographic foil stamping. Card fronts featured two close-up photos of the player, with one in full color and the other within the foil background. There were 1,500 sequentially numbered sets of Staremaster produced.

		MT
Complete Set (24):		750.00
Common Player:		6.00
Minor Stars:		12.00
1	Tim Brown	6.00
2	Mark Brunell	40.00
3	Kerry Collins	30.00
4	Brett Favre	80.00
5	Eddie George	60.00
6	Terry Glenn	25.00
7	Dan Marino	70.00
8	Curtis Martin	30.00
9	Jerry Rice	40.00
10	Barry Sanders	50.00
11	Deion Sanders	20.00
12	Emmitt Smith	70.00
13	Drew Bledsoe	40.00
14	Troy Aikman	40.00
15	Tiki Barber	12.00
16	Terrell Davis	40.00
17	Karim Abdul-Jabbar	12.00
18	Warrick Dunn	40.00
19	John Elway	30.00
20	Yatil Green	12.00
21	Ike Hilliard	12.00
22	Kordell Stewart	40.00
23	Ricky Watters	6.00
24	Steve Young	30.00

1997 Studio

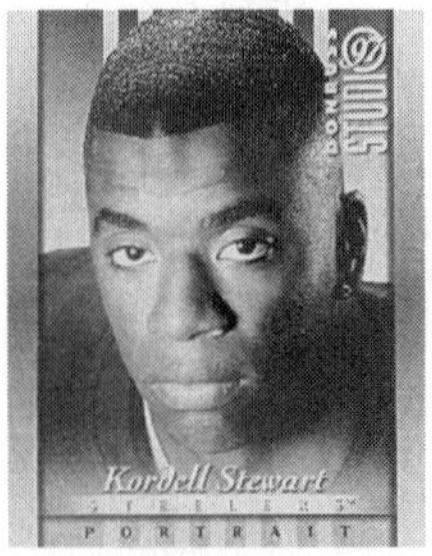

1997 Studio Football is a special Quarterback Club edition. The 36-card base set features the NFL Quarterback Club stars on 8x10 cards. Each player is captured in full-color portrait photography. The base set features 24 Studio Portraits and 12 Class of Distinction cards. Class of Distinction highlights 12 of the stars in an action shot. The parallel sets include Silver Portrait Proof (individually numbered to 4,000) and Gold Portrait Proof (numbered to 1,000). The insert sets were Red Zone Masterpieces and Stained Glass Stars.

		MT
Complete Set (36):		50.00
Common Player:		.50
Minor Stars:		1.00
Silver Proof Cards:		2x-4x
Gold Proof Cards:		5x-10x
Pack (2):		4.00
Wax Box (18):		65.00
1	Troy Aikman	3.00
2	Tony Banks	1.00
3	Jeff Blake	1.00
4	Drew Bledsoe	3.00
5	Mark Brunell	3.00
6	Kerry Collins	1.00
7	Trent Dilfer	1.00
8	John Elway	2.00
9	Brett Favre	6.00
10	Gus Frerotte	.50
11	Jeff George	.50
12	Neil O'Donnell	.50
13	Jim Harbaugh	.50
14	Michael Irvin	1.00
15	Dan Marino	5.00
16	Steve McNair	2.00
17	Rick Mirer	.50
18	Jerry Rice	3.00
19	Barry Sanders	3.00
20	Junior Seau	.50
21	Heath Shuler	.50
22	Emmitt Smith	5.00
23	Kordell Stewart	3.00
24	Steve Young	2.00
25	Troy Aikman (Class of Distinction)	1.50
26	Drew Bledsoe (Class of Distinction)	1.50
27	Mark Brunell (Class of Distinction)	1.50
28	Kerry Collins (Class of Distinction)	1.00
29	John Elway (Class of Distinction)	1.00
30	Brett Favre (Class of Distinction)	3.00
31	Dan Marino (Class of Distinction)	2.50
32	Jerry Rice (Class of Distinction)	1.50
33	Barry Sanders (Class of Distinction)	2.00
34	Emmitt Smith (Class of Distinction)	2.50
35	Kordell Stewart (Class of Distinction)	1.50
36	Steve Young (Class of Distinction)	1.00

1997 Studio Red Zone Masterpiece

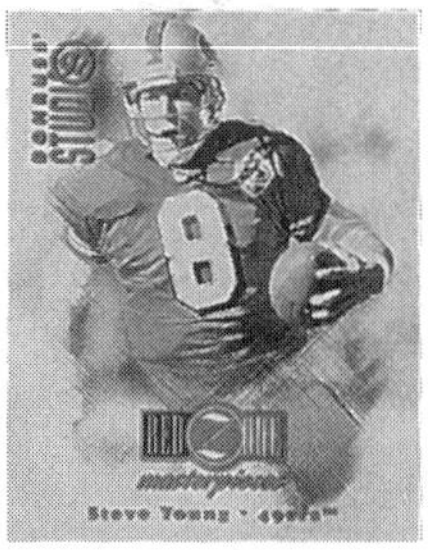

Red Zone Masterpieces features the 24 players in the base set on a canvas material card. Each card is individually numbered to 3,500.

		MT
Complete Set (24):		300.00
Common Player:		5.00
Minor Stars:		10.00
1	Troy Aikman	20.00
2	Tony Banks	10.00
3	Jeff Blake	10.00
4	Drew Bledsoe	20.00
5	Mark Brunell	20.00
6	Kerry Collins	15.00
7	Trent Dilfer	10.00
8	John Elway	15.00
9	Brett Favre	40.00
10	Gus Frerotte	5.00
11	Jeff George	5.00
12	Elvis Grbac	5.00
13	Neil O'Donnell	5.00
14	Michael Irvin	10.00
15	Dan Marino	35.00
16	Steve McNair	15.00
17	Rick Mirer	5.00
18	Jerry Rice	20.00
19	Barry Sanders	25.00
20	Warren Moon	5.00
21	Heath Shuler	5.00
22	Emmitt Smith	35.00
23	Kordell Stewart	20.00
24	Steve Young	15.00

1997 Studio Stained Glass Stars

This 24-card insert features the QB Club stars on a die-cut plastic 8x10 card. Multi-color ink is used to give the appearance of stained glass. Stained Glass Stars are numbered to 1,000.

		MT
Complete Set (24):		650.00
Common Player:		10.00
Minor Stars:		20.00
1	Troy Aikman	40.00
2	Tony Banks	20.00
3	Jeff Blake	20.00
4	Drew Bledsoe	40.00
5	Mark Brunell	40.00
6	Kerry Collins	20.00
7	Trent Dilfer	20.00
8	John Elway	25.00
9	Brett Favre	100.00
10	Gus Frerotte	10.00
11	Jeff George	10.00
12	Elvis Grbac	10.00
13	Jim Harbaugh	10.00
14	Michael Irvin	20.00
15	Dan Marino	80.00
16	Steve McNair	30.00
17	Rick Mirer	10.00
18	Jerry Rice	40.00
19	Barry Sanders	60.00
20	Junior Seau	10.00
21	Vinny Testaverde	10.00
22	Emmitt Smith	80.00
23	Kordell Stewart	40.00
24	Steve Young	25.00

1999 Donruss

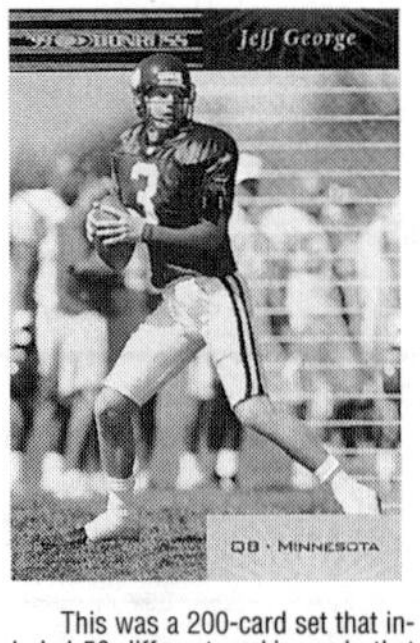

This was a 200-card set that included 50 different rookie cards that were inserted 1:4 packs. Parallel sets included Career Stat Line and Season Stat Line. Other insert sets included: All-Time Gridiron Kings, All-Time Gridiron Kings Autographs, Elite Inserts, Executive Producers, Fan Club, Gridiron Kings, Private Signings, Rated Rookies, Rookie Gridiron Kings, Zoning Commission and Zoning Commission Red. Packs contained seven cards.

		MT
Complete Set (200):		180.00
Common Player:		.15
Minor Stars:		.30
Common Rookie:		1.50
Inserted 1:4		
Pack (7):		2.50
Wax Box (24):		50.00
1	Jake Plummer	.75
2	Rob Moore	.30
3	Adrian Murrell	.15
4	Frank Sanders	.15
5	Jamal Anderson	.50
6	Tim Dwight	.50
7	Terance Mathis	.15
8	Chris Chandler	.30
9	Byron Hanspard	.15
10	Priest Holmes	.15
11	Jermaine Lewis	.15
12	Errict Rhett	.15
13	Doug Flutie	.75
14	Eric Moulds	.50
15	Antowain Smith	.50
16	Thurman Thomas	.30
17	Andre Reed	.30
18	Bruce Smith	.15
19	Tim Biakabutuka	.30
20	Rae Carruth	.15
21	Muhsin Muhammad	.30
22	Curtis Enis	.50
23	Curtis Conway	.30
24	Bobby Engram	.15
25	Corey Dillon	.50
26	Carl Pickens	.30
27	Jeff Blake	.30
28	Darnay Scott	.30
29	Ty Detmer	.15
30	Leslie Shepherd	.15
31	Emmitt Smith	1.50
32	Troy Aikman	1.00
33	Michael Irvin	.30
34	Deion Sanders	.50
35	Raghib Ismail	.15
36	John Elway	1.50
37	Terrell Davis	1.50
38	Ed McCaffrey	.50
39	Shannon Sharpe	.30
40	Rod Smith	.30
41	Bubby Brister	.30
42	Brian Griese	1.00
43	Barry Sanders	2.00
44	Charlie Batch	.75
45	Herman Moore	.50
46	Germane Crowell	.30
47	Johnnie Morton	.15
48	Ron Rivers	.15
49	Brett Favre	2.00
50	Antonio Freeman	.50
51	Dorsey Levens	.50
52	Mark Chmura	.30
53	Corey Bradford	.30
54	Bill Schroeder	.30
55	Peyton Manning	1.50
56	Marvin Harrison	.50
57	E.G. Green	.15
58	Fred Taylor	1.00
59	Mark Brunell	.75
60	Tavian Banks	.30
61	Jimmy Smith	.50
62	Keenan McCardell	.30
63	Warren Moon	.30
64	Derrick Alexander	.15
65	Bam Morris	.15
66	Elvis Grbac	.30
67	Andre Rison	.30
68	Dan Marino	1.50
69	Karim Abdul	.30
70	O.J. McDuffie	.30
71	Tony Martin	.15
72	Randy Moss	2.00
73	Cris Carter	.50
74	Randall Cunningham	.50
75	Robert Smith	.50
76	Jeff George	.50
77	Jake Reed	.30
78	Terry Allen	.30
79	Drew Bledsoe	.75
80	Terry Glenn	.50
81	Ben Coates	.30
82	Tony Simmons	.30
83	Cameron Cleeland	.30
84	Eddie Kennison	.15
85	Kerry Collins	.30
86	Ike Hilliard	.30
87	Gary Brown	.15
88	Joe Jurevicius	.15
89	Kent Graham	.15
90	Wayne Chrebet	.50
91	Keyshawn Johnson	.50
92	Curtis Martin	.50
93	Vinny Testaverde	.50
94	Tim Brown	.50
95	Napoleon Kaufman	.50
96	Charles Woodson	.50
97	Tyrone Wheatley	.30
98	Rich Gannon	.15
99	Charles Johnson	.15
100	Duce Staley	.50
101	Kordell Stewart	.50
102	Jerome Bettis	.50
103	Hines Ward	.30
104	Ryan Leaf	.30
105	Natrone Means	.30
106	Jim Harbaugh	.30
107	Junior Seau	.30
108	Mikhael Ricks	.15
109	Jerry Rice	1.00
110	Steve Young	.75
111	Garrison Hearst	.50
112	Terrell Owens	.75
113	Lawrence Phillips	.30
114	J.J. Stokes	.30
115	Sean Dawkins	.15
116	Derrick Mayes	.30
117	Joey Galloway	.50
118	Jon Kitna	.50
119	Ahman Green	.30
120	Ricky Watters	.30
121	Isaac Bruce	.50
122	Marshall Faulk	.50
123	Az-Zahir Hakim	.30
124	Warrick Dunn	.50
125	Mike Alstott	.50
126	Trent Dilfer	.30
127	Reidel Anthony	.30
128	Jacquez Green	.30
129	Warren Sapp	.15
130	Eddie George	.60
131	Steve McNair	.60
132	Kevin Dyson	.30
133	Yancey Thigpen	.30
134	Frank Wycheck	.15
135	Stephen Davis	.50
136	Brad Johnson	.50
137	Skip Hicks	.30
138	Michael Westbrook	.30
139	Darrell Green	.15
140	Albert Connell	.15
141	*Tim Couch*	15.00
142	*Donovan McNabb*	8.00
143	*Akili Smith*	8.00
144	*Edgerrin James*	25.00
145	*Ricky Williams*	15.00
146	*Torry Holt*	5.00
147	*Champ Bailey*	3.00
148	*David Boston*	5.00
149	*Andy Katzenmoyer*	2.00
150	*Chris McAlister*	2.00
151	*Daunte Culpepper*	20.00
152	*Cade McNown*	5.00
153	*Troy Edwards*	5.00
154	*Kevin Johnson*	5.00
155	*James Johnson*	3.00
156	*Rob Konrad*	2.00
157	*Jim Kleinsasser*	2.00
158	*Kevin Faulk*	3.00
159	*Joe Montgomery*	2.00
160	*Shaun King*	8.00
161	*Peerless Price*	3.50
162	*Michael Cloud*	2.00
163	*Jermaine Fazande*	3.00
164	*D'Wayne Bates*	2.00
165	*Brock Huard*	3.00
166	*Marty Booker*	2.00
167	*Karsten Bailey*	2.00
168	*Shawn Bryson*	1.50
169	*Jeff Paulk*	2.00
170	*Travis McGriff*	2.00
171	*Amos Zereoue*	3.00
172	*Craig Yeast*	1.50
173	*Joe Germaine*	2.00
174	*Dameane Douglas*	1.50
175	*Brandon Stokley*	1.50
176	*Larry Parker*	1.50
177	*Joel Makovicka*	2.00
178	*Wane McGarity*	1.50
179	*Na Brown*	1.50
180	*Cecil Collins*	5.00
181	*Nick Williams*	1.50
182	*Charlie Rogers*	1.50
183	*Darrin Chiaverini*	2.00
184	*Terry Jackson*	2.00
185	*De'Mond Parker*	3.00
186	*Sedrick Irvin*	3.00
187	*Mar Tay Jenkins*	2.00
188	*Kurt Warner*	40.00
189	*Michael Bishop*	3.00
190	*Sean Bennett*	2.00
191	Jamal Anderson CL	.30
192	Eric Moulds CL	.30
193	Terrell Davis CL	.75
194	John Elway CL	.75
195	Barry Sanders CL	1.00
196	Peyton Manning CL	.75
197	Fred Taylor CL	.50
198	Dan Marino CL	.75
199	Randy Moss CL	1.00
200	Terrell Owens CL	.30

1999 Donruss All-Time Gridiron Kings

This insert included five NFL legends. Each card was sequentially numbered to 1,000 and accented with bronze foil. The first 500 of each card was printed on canvas and was autographed.

		MT
Complete Set (5):		70.00
Common Player:		10.00
Production 1,000 Sets		
1	Bart Starr	20.00
2	Johnny Unitas	20.00
3	Earl Campbell	10.00
4	Walter Payton	30.00
5	Jim Brown	25.00

1999 Donruss All-Time Gridiron Kings Autographs

This was a parallel to the All-Time Gridiron Kings insert. Each of these singles was printed on canvas and was autographed. Each single was sequentially numbered to 500.

		MT
Complete Set (5):		600.00
Common Player:		60.00
Production 500 Sets		
1	Bart Starr	125.00
2	Johnny Unitas	125.00
3	Earl Campbell	60.00
4	Walter Payton	250.00
5	Jim Brown	150.00

1999 Donruss Elite Inserts

This 20-card insert set included the NFL's cream of the crop and featured them on foil board with microetching and silver foil stamping. Each card was sequentially numbered to 2,500.

		MT
Complete Set (20):		85.00
Common Player:		2.00
Production 2,500 Sets		
1	Cris Carter	2.00
2	Jerry Rice	6.00
3	Mark Brunell	4.00
4	Brett Favre	10.00
5	Keyshawn Johnson	2.00
6	Eddie George	3.00
7	John Elway	8.00
8	Troy Aikman	6.00
9	Marshall Faulk	2.00
10	Antonio Freeman	2.00
11	Drew Bledsoe	4.00
12	Steve Young	3.00
13	Dan Marino	8.00
14	Emmitt Smith	8.00
15	Fred Taylor	6.00
16	Jake Plummer	4.00
17	Terrell Davis	8.00
18	Peyton Manning	8.00
19	Randy Moss	10.00
20	Barry Sanders	10.00

1999 Donruss Executive Producers

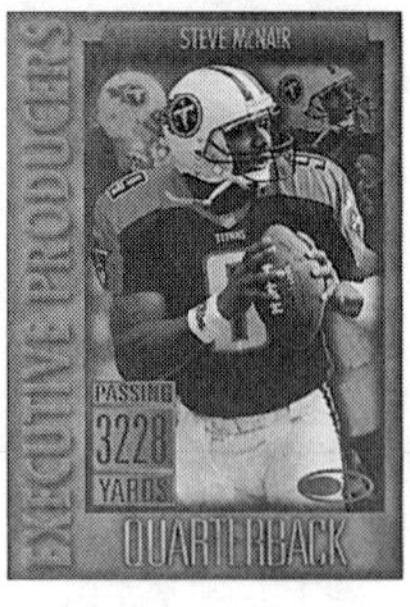

This 45-card insert set included the top producers at quarterback, running back and wide receiver and highlighted each position on a different colored, holographic foil board. Each card was sequentially numbered to the player's specific 1998 stat.

		MT
Complete Set (45):		125.00
Common Player:		2.00
1	Dan Marino 3497	5.00
2	John Elway 2806	7.00
3	Kordell Stewart 2560	2.00
4	Troy Aikman 2330	5.00
5	Steve Young 4170	2.00
6	Doug Flutie 2711	3.00
7	Drew Bledsoe 3633	2.00
8	Jon Kitna 1177	3.00
9	Steve McNair 3228	2.00
10	Mark Brunell 2601	3.00
11	Randall Cunningham 3704	2.00
12	Jake Plummer 3737	3.00
13	Charlie Batch 2178	3.00
14	Peyton Manning 3739	5.00
15	Brett Favre 4212	6.00
16	Terrell Davis 2008	5.00
17	Fred Taylor 1223	5.00
18	Eddie George 1294	2.00
19	Corey Dillon 1130	2.00
20	Jamal Anderson 1846	2.00
21	Curtis Martin 1287	2.00
22	Dorsey Levens 378	3.00
23	Karim Abdul 960	2.00
24	Curtis Enis 497	3.00
25	Mike Alstott 846	2.00
26	Natrone Means 883	2.00
27	Jerome Bettis 1185	2.00
28	Warrick Dunn 1026	2.00
29	Emmitt Smith 1332	6.00
30	Barry Sanders 1491	10.00
31	Jerry Rice 1157	6.00
32	Randy Moss 1313	10.00
33	Keyshawn Johnson 1131	2.00
34	Isaac Bruce 457	3.00
35	Antonio Freeman 1424	2.00
36	Eric Moulds 1368	2.00
37	Tim Dwight 94	12.00
38	Herman Moore 983	2.00
39	Tim Brown 1012	2.00
40	Marshall Faulk 1319	2.00
41	Terry Glenn 792	2.00
42	Joey Galloway 1047	2.00
43	Carl Pickens 1023	2.00
44	Terrell Owens 1097	2.00
45	Cris Carter 1011	2.00

1999 Donruss Fan Club

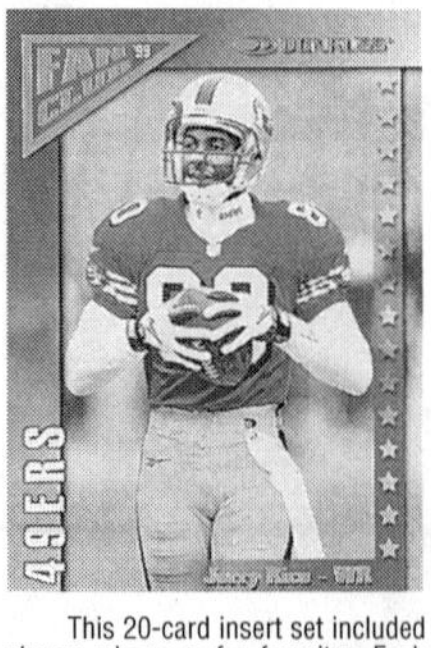

This 20-card insert set included players who were fan favorites. Each single was sequentially numbered to 5,000.

		MT
Complete Set (20):		60.00
Common Player:		1.00
Minor Stars:		2.00
Production 5,000 Sets		
1	Troy Aikman	5.00
2	Ricky Williams	10.00
3	Jerry Rice	5.00
4	Brett Favre	10.00
5	Terrell Davis	7.00
6	Doug Flutie	3.00
7	John Elway	7.00
8	Steve Young	3.00
9	Steve McNair	2.00
10	Kordell Stewart	2.00
11	Drew Bledsoe	3.00
12	Donovan McNabb	5.00
13	Dan Marino	7.00
14	Cade McNown	5.00
15	Vinny Testaverde	1.00
16	Jake Plummer	3.00
17	Randall Cunningham	2.00
18	Peyton Manning	7.00
19	Keyshawn Johnson	2.00
20	Barry Sanders	10.00

1999 Donruss Gridiron Kings

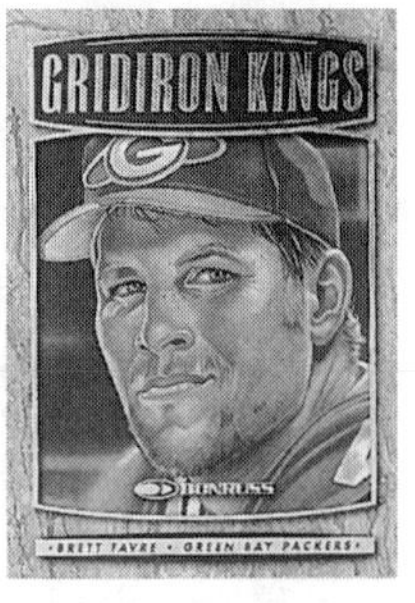

This 20-card insert set showcased artwork of each player. Singles were sequentially numbered to 5,000. A parallel Canvas version was also made with each of those singles numbered to 500.

		MT
Complete Set (20):		100.00
Common Player:		3.00
Production 5,000 Sets		
Canvas Cards:		3x
Production 500 Sets		
1	Randy Moss	12.00
2	Fred Taylor	6.00
3	Doug Flutie	5.00
4	Brett Favre	12.00
5	Mark Brunell	5.00
6	Troy Aikman	6.00
7	John Elway	8.00
8	Jerry Rice	6.00
9	Drew Bledsoe	5.00
10	Eddie George	3.00
11	Randall Cunningham	3.00
12	Emmitt Smith	8.00
13	Dan Marino	8.00
14	Jake Plummer	5.00
15	Jamal Anderson	3.00
16	Terrell Davis	8.00
17	Steve Young	5.00
18	Peyton Manning	8.00
19	Jerome Bettis	3.00
20	Barry Sanders	12.00

1999 Donruss Gridiron Kings Canvas Parallel

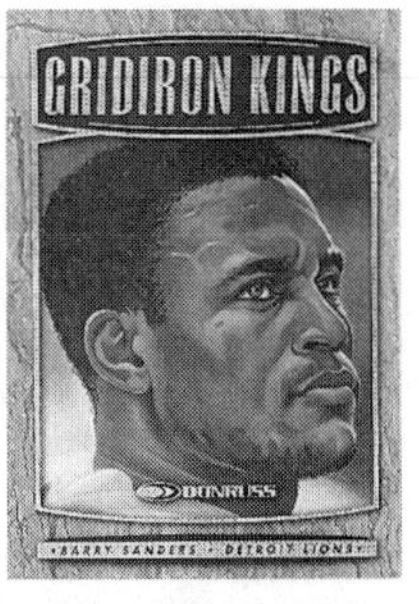

This 20-card insert set was a parallel to the Gridiron Kings insert. Each of these singles was printed on canvas and was sequentially numbered to 500.

	MT
Canvas Cards:	3x
Production 500 Sets	

1999 Donruss Private Signings

This 32-card insert set included autographs from some of the top players in the NFL. More than 10,000 autographs were randomly inserted into packs. The print runs were between 50 and 600, depending on the player.

		MT
Complete Set (32):		1200.
Common Player:		12.50
Minor Stars:		25.00
1	Terrell Davis	75.00
2	Cris Carter	30.00
3	Thurman Thomas	25.00
4	Derrick Thomas	12.50
5	Priest Holmes	12.50
6	Corey Dillon	25.00
7	Antonio Freeman	25.00
8	Duce Staley	12.50
9	Jerome Bettis	12.50
10	Natrone Means	12.50
11	Mike Alstott	30.00
12	Eddie George	45.00
13	Terrell Owens	25.00

14	Curtis Enis	25.00
15	Wesley Walls	12.50
16	Neil Smith	12.50
17	Doug Flutie	45.00
18	Tim Brown	25.00
19	Randy Moss	150.00
20	Ricky Williams	100.00
21	Skip Hicks	12.50
22	Isaac Bruce	30.00
23	Barry Sanders	125.00
24	Fred Taylor	50.00
25	Steve Young	50.00
26	Vinny Testaverde	12.50
27	Randall Cunningham	25.00
28	Jake Plummer	50.00
29	Jerry Rice	100.00
30	Eric Moulds	25.00
31	Kordell Stewart	30.00
32	Brian Griese	35.00

1999 Donruss Rated Rookies

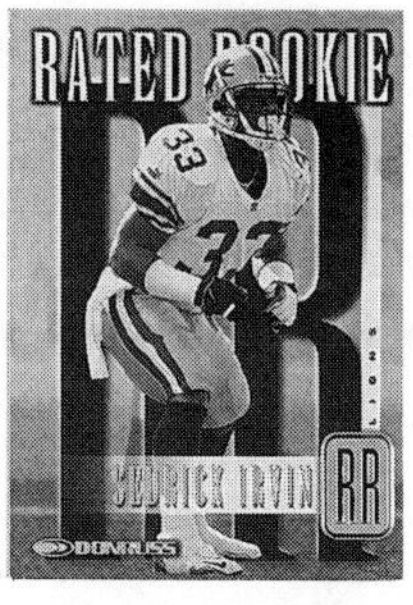

This 20-card insert set included rookies from 1999 and featured them on silver foil board. Each was sequentially numbered to 5,000. A parallel Medalist version was made in which the first 250 singles were sequentially numbered. Each was printed with gold foil instead of silver.

		MT
Complete Set (20):		75.00
Common Player:		2.00
Production 5,000 Sets		
Medalists Cards:		3x
Production 250 Sets		
1	Tim Couch	12.00
2	Peerless Price	4.00
3	Ricky Williams	10.00
4	Torry Holt	5.00
5	Champ Bailey	3.00
6	Rob Konrad	2.00
7	Donovan McNabb	8.00
8	Edgerrin James	20.00
9	David Boston	5.00
10	Akili Smith	8.00
11	Cecil Collins	4.00
12	Troy Edwards	5.00
13	Daunte Culpepper	8.00
14	Kevin Faulk	3.00
15	Kevin Johnson	5.00
16	Cade McNown	8.00
17	Shaun King	8.00
18	Brock Huard	3.00
19	James Johnson	3.00
20	Sedrick Irvin	3.00

1999 Donruss Rated Rookies Medalists Parallel

This was a 20-card insert set that paralleled the Rated Rookies set. Each of these singles was sequentially numbered to 250 and had gold foil stamping, rather than the silver foil on the regular cards.

	MT
Medalists Cards:	3x
Production 250 Sets	

1999 Donruss Rookie Gridiron Kings

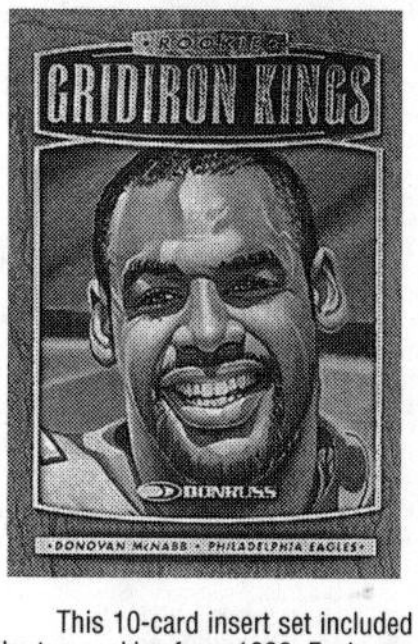

This 10-card insert set included the top rookies from 1999. Each was sequentially numbered to 5,000 and included gold foil on the front of each card. The first 500 singles were printed on canvas stock.

		MT
Complete Set (10):		65.00
Common Player:		2.50
Production 5,000 Sets		
Canvas Cards:		3x
Production 500 Sets		
1	Ricky Williams	10.00
2	Donovan McNabb	8.00
3	Daunte Culpepper	8.00
4	Edgerrin James	18.00
5	David Boston	5.00
6	Champ Bailey	2.50
7	Torry Holt	5.00
8	Cade McNown	8.00
9	Akili Smith	8.00
10	Tim Couch	12.00

1999 Donruss Rookie Gridiron Kings Canvas Parallel

This was a 10-card insert set that paralleled the Rookie Gridiron Kings insert. Each of these singles was printed on canvas stock and was sequentially numbered to 500.

	MT
Canvas Cards:	3x
Production 500 Sets	

1999 Donruss Zoning Commission

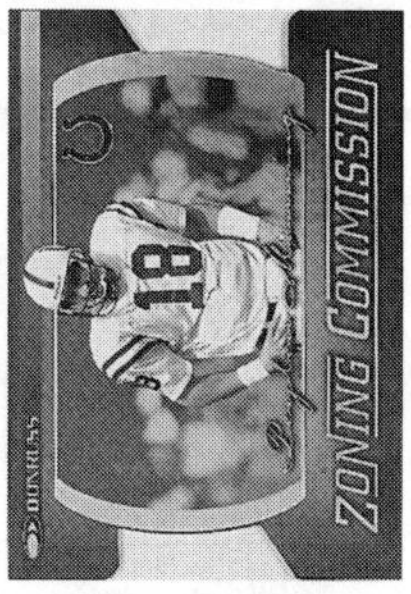

This 25-card insert set included star players who patrol the end zone. Each die-cut single was sequentially numbered to 1,000. A parallel Red version was made in which each single was sequentially numbered to the player's 1998 touchdown total.

		MT
Complete Set (25):		70.00
Common Player:		2.00
Production 1,000 Sets		
1	Eric Moulds	2.00
2	Steve Young	3.00
3	Brad Johnson	2.00
4	Peyton Manning	7.00
5	Randy Moss	10.00
6	Brett Favre	10.00
7	Emmitt Smith	7.00
8	Mark Brunell	3.00
9	Keyshawn Johnson	2.00
10	Dan Marino	7.00
11	Eddie George	2.00
12	Drew Bledsoe	3.00
13	Terrell Davis	7.00
14	Terrell Owens	2.00
15	Barry Sanders	10.00
16	Curtis Martin	2.00
17	John Elway	7.00
18	Jake Plummer	3.00
19	Jerry Rice	5.00
20	Fred Taylor	5.00
21	Antonio Freeman	2.00
22	Marshall Faulk	2.00
23	Dorsey Levens	2.00
24	Steve McNair	2.00
25	Cris Carter	2.00

1999 Donruss Elite

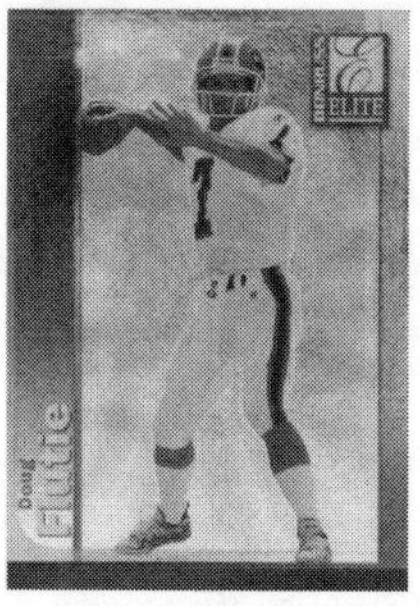

This is a 200-card base set that includes 40 rookies. Cards #1-100 are printed on 20 point foil board with a foil stamped logo in red and full UV coating on both sides. They were inserted four-per-pack. Cards #101-200 are also printed on 20 point foil board with full UV coating and platinum blue tint on each side. They are found one-per-pack. Inserts include Common Threads, Field of Vision, Passing the Torch, Power Formulas and Primary Colors.

		MT
Complete Set (200):		250.00
Common Player (1-100):		.25
Minor Stars (1-100):		.50
Common Player (101-200):		.50
Minor Stars (101-200):		1.00
Common Rookie (161-200):		3.00
#101-200 Inserted 1:1		
Pack (5):		8.00
Wax Box (18):		125.00
1	Warren Moon	.50
2	Terry Allen	.50
3	Jeff George	.50
4	Brett Favre	3.00
5	Rob Moore	.50
6	Bubby Brister	.25
7	John Elway	2.50
8	Troy Aikman	1.50
9	Steve McNair	.75
10	Charlie Batch	1.00
11	Elvis Grbac	.25
12	Trent Dilfer	.25
13	Kerry Collins	.50
14	Neil O'Donnell	.25
15	Tony Simmons	.50
16	Ryan Leaf	1.00
17	Bobby Hoying	.25
18	Marvin Harrison	.50
19	Keyshawn Johnson	.75
20	Cris Carter	.75
21	Deion Sanders	.75
22	Emmitt Smith	2.50
23	Antowain Smith	.75
24	Terry Fair	.25
25	Robert Holcombe	.50
26	Napoleon Kaufman	.75
27	Eddie George	1.00
28	Corey Dillon	.75
29	Adrian Murrell	.25
30	Charles Way	.25
31	Amp Lee	.25
32	Ricky Watters	.50
33	Gary Brown	.25
34	Thurman Thomas	.50
35	Patrick Johnson	.25
36	Jerome Bettis	.75
37	Muhsin Muhammad	.25
38	Kimble Anders	.25
39	Curtis Enis	.75
40	Mike Alstott	.75
41	Charles Johnson	.25
42	Chris Warren	.25
43	Tony Banks	.50
44	Leroy Hoard	.25
45	Chris Fuamatu-Ma'afala	.25
46	Michael Irvin	.75
47	Robert Edwards	.75
48	Hines Ward	.50
49	Trent Green	.50
50	Eric Zeier	.25
51	Sean Dawkins	.25
52	Yancey Thigpen	.25
53	Jacquez Green	.50
54	Zach Thomas	.50
55	Junior Seau	.50
56	Darnay Scott	.25
57	Kent Graham	.25
58	O.J. Santiago	.25
59	Tony Gonzalez	.25
60	Ty Detmer	.25
61	Albert Connell	.25
62	James Jett	.25
63	Bert Emanuel	.25
64	Derrick Alexander	.25
65	Wesley Walls	.25
66	Jake Reed	.25
67	Randall Cunningham	.75
68	Leslie Shepherd	.25
69	Mark Chmura	.25
70	Bobby Engram	.25
71	Rickey Dudley	.25
72	Darick Holmes	.25
73	Andre Reed	.50
74	Az-Zahir Hakim	.50
75	Cameron Cleeland	.25
76	Lamar Thomas	.25
77	Oronde Gadsden	.50
78	Ben Coates	.50
79	Bruce Smith	.25
80	Jerry Rice	1.50
81	Tim Brown	.50
82	Michael Westbrook	.50
83	J.J. Stokes	.50
84	Shannon Sharpe	.50
85	Reidel Anthony	.50
86	Antonio Freeman	.75
87	Keenan McCardell	.50
88	Terry Glenn	.75
89	Andre Rison	.50
90	Neil Smith	.25
91	Terrance Mathis	.25
92	Raghib Ismail	.25
93	Bam Morris	.25
94	Ike Hillard	.25
95	Eddie Kennison	.25
96	Tavian Banks	.50
97	Yatil Green	.25
98	Frank Wycheck	.25
99	Warren Sapp	.25
100	Germane Crowell	1.00
101	Curtis Martin	2.00
102	John Avery	1.00
103	Eric Moulds	2.00
104	Randy Moss	12.00
105	Terrell Owens	2.00
106	Vinny Testaverde	1.00
107	Doug Flutie	2.50
108	Mark Brunell	3.00
109	Isaac Bruce	1.00
110	Kordell Stewart	2.50
111	Drew Bledsoe	3.00
112	Chris Chandler	.50
113	Dan Marino	6.00
114	Brian Griese	4.00
115	Carl Pickens	.50
116	Jake Plummer	4.00
117	Natrone Means	1.00
118	Peyton Manning	8.00
119	Garrison Hearst	1.00
120	Barry Sanders	8.00
121	Steve Young	3.00
122	Rashaan Shehee	.50
123	Ed McCaffrey	1.50
124	Charles Woodson	2.00
125	Dorsey Levens	1.50
126	Robert Smith	1.50
127	Greg Hill	.50
128	Fred Taylor	5.00
129	Marcus Nash	1.00
130	Terrell Davis	6.00
131	Ahman Green	1.00
132	Jamal Anderson	2.00
133	Karim Abdul	1.00
134	Jermaine Lewis	.50
135	Jerome Pathon	.50
136	Brad Johnson	1.00
137	Herman Moore	1.50
138	Tim Dwight	2.00
139	Johnnie Morton	.50
140	Marshall Faulk	2.00
141	Frank Sanders	1.00
142	Kevin Dyson	1.00
143	Curtis Conway	1.00
144	Derrick Mayes	.50
145	O.J. McDuffie	1.00
146	Joe Jurevicius	.50
147	Jon Kitna	2.00
148	Joey Galloway	1.50
149	Jimmy Smith	1.00
150	Skip Hicks	1.00
151	Rod Smith	1.00
152	Duce Staley	.50
153	James O. Stewart	.50
154	Rob Johnson	1.00
155	Mikhael Ricks	.50
156	Wayne Chrebet	1.50
157	Robert Brooks	.50
158	Tim Biakabutuka	.50
159	Priest Holmes	2.00
160	Warrick Dunn	2.00
161	*Champ Bailey*	5.00
162	*D'Wayne Bates*	3.00
163	*Michael Bishop*	5.00
164	*David Boston*	6.00
165	*Na Brown*	3.00
166	*Chris Claiborne*	3.00
167	*Joe Montgomery*	3.00
168	*Mike Cloud*	3.00
169	*Travis McGriff*	3.00
170	*Tim Couch*	15.00
171	*Daunte Culpepper*	20.00
172	*Autry Denson*	3.00
173	*Jermaine Fazande*	4.00
174	*Troy Edwards*	5.00
175	*Kevin Faulk*	6.00
176	*Dee Miller*	3.00
177	*Brock Huard*	6.00
178	*Torry Holt*	10.00
179	*Sedrick Irvin*	4.00
180	*Edgerrin James*	25.00
181	*Joe Germaine*	4.00
182	*James Johnson*	4.00
183	*Kevin Johnson*	6.00
184	*Andy Katzenmoyer*	4.00
185	*Jevon Kearse*	8.00
186	*Shaun King*	8.00
187	*Rob Konrad*	3.00
188	*Jim Kleinsasser*	4.00
189	*Chris McAlister*	4.00
190	*Donovan McNabb*	12.00
191	*Cade McNown*	5.00
192	*De'Mond Parker*	3.00
193	*Craig Yeast*	3.00
194	*Shawn Bryson*	3.00
195	*Peerless Price*	5.00
196	*Darnell McDonald*	3.00
197	*Akili Smith*	8.00
198	*Tai Streets*	4.00
199	*Ricky Williams*	15.00
200	*Amos Zereoue*	4.00

1999 Donruss Elite Common Threads

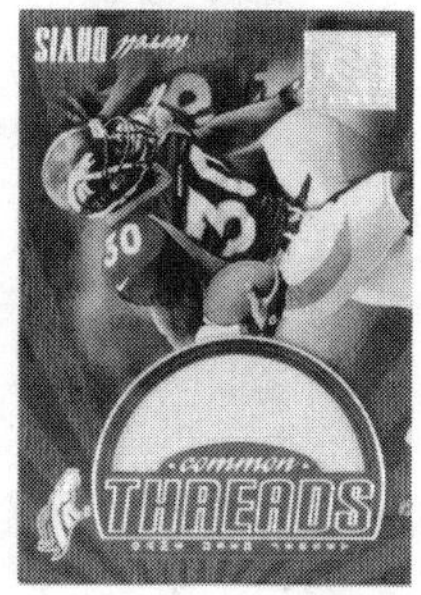

Each card is printed on conventional board with foil and game-used jersey swatches. Twelve players are featured with six cards with one player on it and the other six are combo cards. Each is sequentially numbered to 150.

		MT
Complete Set (18):		3000.
Common Player:		100.00
Production 150 Sets		
1	Randy Moss, Randall Cunningham	400.00
2	Randy Moss	350.00
3	Randall Cunningham	125.00
4	John Elway, Terrell Davis	350.00
5	John Elway	275.00
6	Terrell Davis	225.00
7	Jerry Rice, Steve Young	300.00
8	Jerry Rice	250.00
9	Steve Young	150.00
10	Mark Brunell, Fred Taylor	175.00
11	Mark Brunell	125.00
12	Fred Taylor	150.00
13	Kordell Stewart, Jerome Bettis	150.00
14	Kordell Stewart	125.00
15	Jerome Bettis	100.00
16	Dan Marino, Karim Abdul	300.00
17	Dan Marino	300.00
18	Karim Abdul	100.00

1999 Donruss Elite Field of Vision

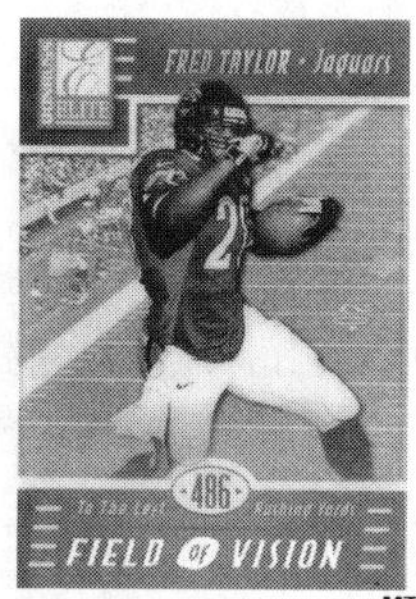

Each card is printed on clear plastic with holo-foil stamping. Twelve players are featured on three seperate cards, with each representing a section of the playing field (left-middle-right). Each card is then sequentially numbered to the yards the player gained in that area of the field in 1998.

		MT
Common Player:		5.00
Production #'d to a Season Stat		
1A	Dan Marino 1712	12.00
1B	Dan Marino 834	20.00
1C	Dan Marino 951	20.00
2A	Emmitt Smith 640	20.00
2B	Emmitt Smith 202	35.00
2C	Emmitt Smith 490	20.00
3A	Jake Plummer 1165	10.00
3B	Jake Plummer 624	15.00
3C	Jake Plummer 1948	5.00
4A	Brett Favre 1408	14.00
4B	Brett Favre 983	25.00
4C	Brett Favre 1820	12.00
5A	Fred Taylor 486	10.00
5B	Fred Taylor 400	12.00
5C	Fred Taylor 337	15.00
6A	Drew Bledsoe 1355	5.00
6B	Drew Bledsoe 689	10.00
6C	Drew Bledsoe 1589	5.00
7A	Terrell Davis 1283	12.00
7B	Terrell Davis 306	25.00
7C	Terrell Davis 419	20.00
8A	Jerry Rice 611	10.00
8B	Jerry Rice 234	25.00
8C	Jerry Rice 312	20.00
9A	Randy Moss 639	30.00
9B	Randy Moss 16	350.00
9C	Randy Moss 658	30.00
10A	John Elway 1320	12.00
10B	John Elway 615	25.00
10C	John Elway 871	20.00
11A	Peyton Manning 1141	15.00
11B	Peyton Manning 1020	15.00
11C	Peyton Manning 1578	12.00
12A	Barry Sanders 556	20.00
12B	Barry Sanders 373	30.00
12C	Barry Sanders 562	20.00

1999 Donruss Elite Field of Vision Die Cuts

This is similar to the Field of Vision cards except each card is die-cut and sequentially numbered to the number of attempts, receptions or completions of that particular player.

		MT
Common Player:		25.00
Production #'d to a Season Stat		
1A	Dan Marino 164	45.00
1B	Dan Marino 56	100.00
1C	Dan Marino 90	70.00
2A	Emmitt Smith 158	30.00
2B	Emmitt Smith 64	75.00
2C	Emmitt Smith 97	45.00
3A	Jake Plummer 89	35.00
3B	Jake Plummer 44	60.00
3C	Jake Plummer 191	25.00
4A	Brett Favre 112	60.00
4B	Brett Favre 67	100.00
4C	Brett Favre 168	40.00
5A	Fred Taylor 103	35.00
5B	Fred Taylor 79	45.00
5C	Fred Taylor 82	45.00
6A	Drew Bledsoe 90	30.00
6B	Drew Bledsoe 48	45.00
6C	Drew Bledsoe 125	25.00
7A	Terrell Davis 217	35.00
7B	Terrell Davis 66	70.00
7C	Terrell Davis 109	50.00
8A	Jerry Rice 50	70.00
8B	Jerry Rice 11	325.00
8C	Jerry Rice 21	200.00
9A	Randy Moss 34	225.00
9B	Randy Moss 2	
9C	Randy Moss 33	225.00
10A	John Elway 98	50.00
10B	John Elway 35	150.00
10C	John Elway 77	75.00
11A	Peyton Manning 110	45.00
11B	Peyton Manning 79	60.00
11C	Peyton Manning 137	35.00
12A	Barry Sanders 137	45.00
12B	Barry Sanders 83	85.00
12C	Barry Sanders 123	45.00

1999 Donruss Elite Passing the Torch

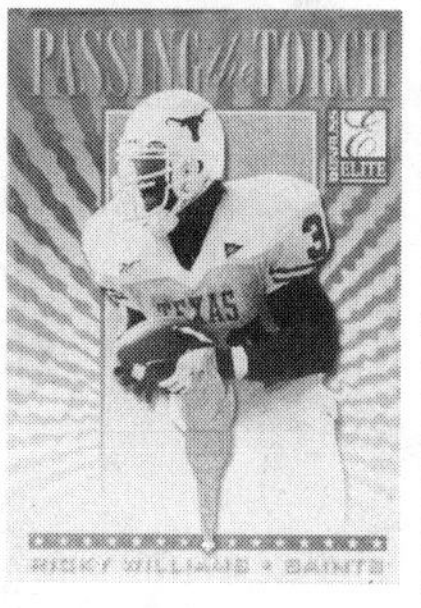

Each card is printed with holo-foil board on the front and back with UV coating on both sides and sequentially numbered to 1,500. Twelve players were used with each having an individual card as well as six cards pairing two players together. The first 100 of each card are autographed.

		MT
Complete Set (18):		175.00
Common Player:		5.00
Production 1,500 Sets		
1	Johnny Unitas, Peyton Manning	15.00
2	Johnny Unitas	8.00
3	Peyton Manning	12.00
4	Walter Payton, Barry Sanders	20.00
5	Walter Payton	10.00
6	Barry Sanders	15.00
7	Earl Campbell, Ricky Williams	20.00
8	Earl Campbell	5.00
9	Ricky Williams	25.00
10	Jim Brown, Terrell Davis	15.00
11	Jim Brown	10.00
12	Terrell Davis	15.00
13	Emmitt Smith, Fred Taylor	15.00
14	Emmitt Smith	10.00
15	Fred Taylor	10.00
16	Cris Carter, Randy Moss	20.00
17	Cris Carter	5.00
18	Randy Moss	20.00

1999 Donruss Elite Passing the Torch Autographs

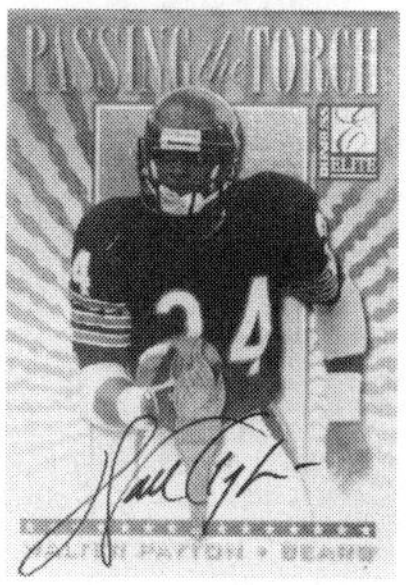

This is the same as the regular Passing the Torch cards except for each one of these are autographed. They are each sequentially numbered to 100.

		MT
Complete Set (18):		5000.
Common Player:		85.00
Production 100 Sets		
1	Johnny Unitas, Peyton Manning	400.00
2	Johnny Unitas	150.00
3	Peyton Manning	200.00
4	Walter Payton, Barry Sanders	1000.
5	Walter Payton	275.00
6	Barry Sanders	400.00
7	Earl Campbell, Ricky Williams	350.00
8	Earl Campbell	100.00
9	Ricky Williams	250.00
10	Jim Brown, Terrell Davis	400.00
11	Jim Brown	200.00
12	Terrell Davis	250.00
13	Emmitt Smith, Fred Taylor	350.00
14	Emmitt Smith	300.00
15	Fred Taylor	125.00
16	Cris Carter, Randy Moss	325.00
17	Cris Carter	85.00
18	Randy Moss	325.00

1999 Donruss Elite Power Formulas

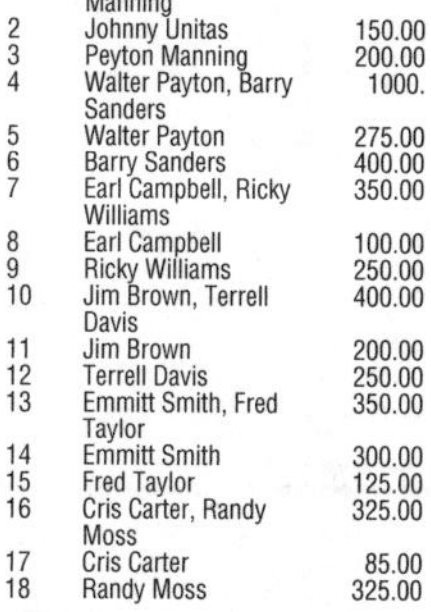

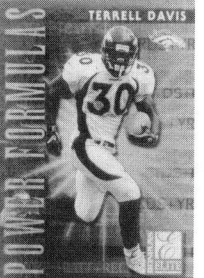

This 30-card set spotlights the NFL's most powerful players and the statistical formulas behind their greatness. Each is sequentially numbered to 3,500.

		MT
Complete Set (30):		120.00
Common Player:		1.50
Minor Stars:		4.00
Production 3,500 Sets		
1	Randy Moss	15.00
2	Terrell Davis	10.00

3 Brett Favre 12.00
4 Dan Marino 8.00
5 Barry Sanders 12.00
6 Peyton Manning 8.00
7 John Elway 8.00
8 Fred Taylor 6.00
9 Emmitt Smith 8.00
10 Steve Young 5.00
11 Jerry Rice 6.00
12 Jake Plummer 5.00
13 Kordell Stewart 5.00
14 Mark Brunell 5.00
15 Drew Bledsoe 5.00
16 Eddie George 5.00
17 Troy Aikman 6.00
18 Warrick Dunn 4.00
19 Keyshawn Johnson 3.00
20 Jamal Anderson 3.00
21 Randall Cunningham 3.00
22 Doug Flutie 4.00
23 Jerome Bettis 3.00
24 Garrison Hearst 1.50
25 Curtis Martin 3.00
26 Corey Dillon 3.00
27 Antowain Smith 3.00
28 Antonio Freeman 3.00
29 Terrell Owens 3.00
30 Carl Pickens 1.50

1999 Donruss Elite Primary Colors

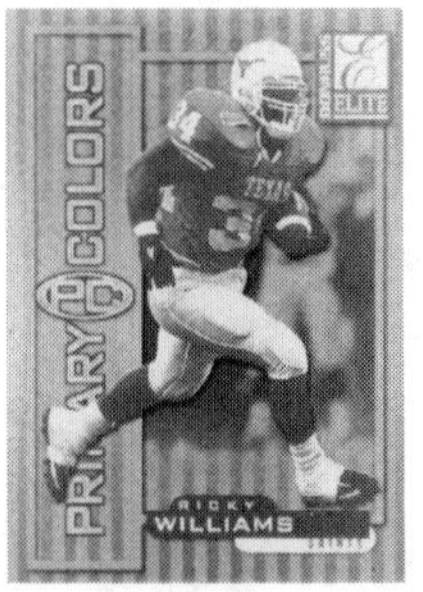

The 40-card set is printed on holo-foil board and is sequentially numbered to 1,875. This insert has five different parallel sets with a Blue (#'d to 950), Red (#'d to 25), Blue Die-Cut (#'d to 50), Red Die-Cut (#'d to 75) and a Yellow Die-Cut (#'d to 25) version.

MT
Complete Set (40): 160.00
Common Yellow: 3.00
Production 1,875 Sets
Blue Cards: 1.5x
Production 950 Sets
Red Cards: 15x-30x
Red Rookies: 7x-14x
Production 25 Sets
Blue Die-Cut Cards: 10x-20x
Blue Die-Cut Rookies: 5x-10x
Production 50 Sets
Red Die-Cut Cards: 7x-14x
Red Die-Cut Rookies: 3x-6x
Production 75 Sets
Yellow Die-Cut Cards: 15x-30x
Yellow Die-Cut Rookies: 7x-14x
Production 25 Sets
1 Herman Moore 3.00
2 Marshall Faulk 3.00
3 Dorsey Levens 3.00
4 Napoleon Kaufman 3.00
5 Jamal Anderson 3.00
6 Edgerrin James 10.00
7 Troy Aikman 6.00
8 Cris Carter 3.00
9 Eddie George 4.00
10 Donovan McNabb 10.00
11 Drew Bledsoe 5.00
12 Daunte Culpepper 8.00
13 Mark Brunell 5.00
14 Corey Dillon 3.00
15 Kordell Stewart 5.00
16 Curtis Martin 3.00
17 Jake Plummer 5.00
18 Charlie Batch 4.00
19 Jerry Rice 6.00
20 Antonio Freeman 3.00
21 Steve Young 4.00
22 Steve McNair 3.00
23 Emmitt Smith 8.00
24 Terrell Owens 3.00
25 Fred Taylor 6.00
26 Joey Galloway 3.00
27 John Elway 8.00
28 Ryan Leaf 3.00
29 Barry Sanders 12.00
30 Ricky Williams 20.00
31 Dan Marino 8.00
32 Tim Couch 20.00
33 Brett Favre 12.00
34 Eric Moulds 3.00
35 Peyton Manning 8.00
36 Deion Sanders 3.00
37 Terrell Davis 8.00
38 Tim Brown 3.00
39 Randy Moss 15.00
40 Mike Alstott 3.00

1999 Donruss Preferred QBC

This was a 120-card set that was divided into four levels. The first 45 cards were in Bronze and cards #46-#80 were in Silver and found one-per-pack. Cards #81-#105 were in Gold and inserted 1:4 packs and cards #106-#120 were Platinum singles and found 1:8 packs. The set featured all 44 members of the Quarterback Club. Insert sets included: Power (parallel), Autographs, Chain Reaction, Hard Hats, Materials, National Treasures, Passing Grade, Precious Metals, Staremasters and X-Ponential Power. SRP was $3.99 for four-card packs.

MT
Complete Set (120): 250.00
Common Bronze: .15
Minor Stars Bronze: .30
Common Silver: .50
Minor Stars Silver: 1.00
Inserted 1:1
Common Gold: 1.00
Minor Stars Gold: 2.00
Inserted 1:4
Common Platinum: 2.50
Inserted 1:8
Pack (4): 5.50
Wax Box (20): 100.00
1 Troy Aikman B 1.50
2 Tony Banks B .30
3 Jeff Blake B .30
4 Drew Bledsoe B 1.00
5 Bubby Brister B .15
6 Chris Chandler B .15
7 Kerry Collins B .30
8 Randall Cunningham B .50
9 Terrell Davis B 2.00
10 Trent Dilfer B .30
11 John Elway B 2.00
12 Boomer Esiason B .30
13 Jim Everett B .15
14 Brett Favre B 3.00
15 Doug Flutie B .75
16 Gus Frerotte B .15
17 Jeff George B .50
18 Elvis Grbac B .15
19 Jim Harbaugh B .30
20 Michael Irvin B .30
21 Brad Johnson B .50
22 Keyshawn Johnson B .50
23 Danny Kanell B .15
24 Jim Kelly B .50
25 Bernie Kosar B .15
26 Erik Kramer B .15
27 Ryan Leaf B .50
28 Peyton Manning B 2.00
29 Dan Marino B 2.00
30 *Donovan McNabb B* 4.00
31 Steve McNair B .50
32 *Cade McNown B* 2.50
33 Scott Mitchell B .15
34 Warren Moon B .30
35 Neil O'Donnell B .15
36 Jake Plummer B 1.50
37 Jerry Rice B 1.50
38 Barry Sanders B 3.00
39 Junior Seau B .30
40 Phil Simms B .30
41 Kordell Stewart B .50
42 Vinny Testaverde B .30
43 *Ricky Williams B* 8.00
44 Steve Young B .75
45 Dan Marino, Brett Favre, John Elway B 2.00
46 Troy Aikman S 2.50
47 Tony Banks S .50
48 Drew Bledsoe S 1.75
49 Bubby Brister S .50
50 Chris Chandler S .50
51 Kerry Collins S .50
52 Randall Cunningham S 1.00
53 Terrell Davis S 3.50
54 Trent Dilfer S 1.00
55 John Elway S 3.50
56 Boomer Esiason S 1.00
57 Brett Favre S 5.00
58 Doug Flutie S 1.50
59 Elvis Grbac S .50
60 Jim Harbaugh S .50
61 Michael Irvin S 1.00
62 Brad Johnson S 1.00
63 Keyshawn Johnson S 1.00
64 Jim Kelly S 1.00
65 Ryan Leaf S 1.00
66 Peyton Manning S 3.50
67 Dan Marino S 3.50
68 Donovan McNabb S 6.00
69 Steve McNair S 1.25
70 Cade McNown S 6.00
71 Warren Moon S 1.00
72 Jake Plummer S 2.50
73 Jerry Rice S 2.50
74 Barry Sanders S 5.00
75 Junior Seau S 1.00
76 Phil Simms S 1.00
77 Kordell Stewart S 1.25
78 Vinny Testaverde S 1.00
79 Ricky Williams S 12.00
80 Steve Young S 1.75
81 Troy Aikman G 4.00
82 Drew Bledsoe G 3.00
83 Bubby Brister G 1.00
84 Chris Chandler G 1.00
85 Randall Cunningham G 2.00
86 Terrell Davis G 6.00
87 John Elway G 6.00
88 Brett Favre G 8.00
89 Doug Flutie G 2.50
90 Brad Johnson G 2.00
91 Keyshawn Johnson G 2.00
92 Ryan Leaf G 2.00
93 Peyton Manning G 6.00
94 Dan Marino G 6.00
95 Donovan McNabb G 12.00
96 Steve McNair G 2.00
97 Cade McNown G 12.00
98 Warren Moon G 2.00
99 Jake Plummer G 4.00
100 Jerry Rice G 4.00
101 Barry Sanders G 8.00
102 Kordell Stewart G 2.00
103 Vinny Testaverde G 2.00
104 Ricky Williams G 25.00
105 Steve Young G 2.50
106 Troy Aikman P 8.00
107 Drew Bledsoe P 6.00
108 Terrell Davis P 10.00
109 John Elway P 10.00
110 Brett Favre P 15.00
111 Keyshawn Johnson P 2.50
112 Peyton Manning P 10.00
113 Dan Marino P 10.00
114 Donovan McNabb P 15.00
115 Cade McNown P 15.00
116 Jake Plummer P 8.00
117 Jerry Rice P 8.00
118 Barry Sanders P 15.00
119 Kordell Stewart P 2.50
120 Ricky Williams P 30.00

1999 Donruss Preferred QBC Power Parallel

This was a 120-card parallel to the base set. Each single was printed on holographic-foil board. The Bronze singles were numbered to 500, Silver singles to 300, Gold singles to 150 and Platinum singles to 50.

MT
Bronze Cards: 3x-6x
Bronze Rookies: 3x
Production 500 Sets
Silver Cards: 3x-6x
Silver Rookies: 3x
Production 300 Sets
Gold Cards: 3x-6x
Gold Rookies: 3x
Production 150 Sets
Platinum Cards: 4x-8x
Platinum Rookies: 4x
Production 50 Sets

1999 Donruss Preferred QBC Autographs

This was a 15-card insert set that included autographs of the top players in the NFL. Cards were randomly inserted into packs.

MT
Complete Set (15): 850.00
Common Player: 25.00
1 Steve Young 700 50.00
2 Ricky Williams 700 125.00
3 Jerry Rice 350 100.00
4 Jake Plummer 700 70.00
5 Peyton Manning 650 100.00
6 Michael Irvin 500 35.00
7 Dan Marino 600 125.00
8 Randall Cunningham 700 40.00
9 Troy Aikman 600 85.00
10 Terrell Davis 500 90.00
11 Vinny Testaverde 700 25.00
12 Chris Chandler 600 25.00
13 Bubby Brister 500 25.00
14 Steve McNair 700 50.00
15 Kordell Stewart 700 50.00

1999 Donruss Preferred QBC Chain Reaction

This was a 20-card insert set that included players who know how to move the chains. Each single was sequentially numbered to 5,000 and was printed on prismatic-foil board stock.

MT
Complete Set (20): 65.00
Common Player: 1.00
Minor Stars: 2.00
Production 5,000 Sets
1A Terrell Davis 7.00
1B Ricky Williams 10.00
2A Donovan McNabb 5.00
2B Cade McNown 5.00
3A Brett Favre 10.00
3B Barry Sanders 10.00
4A Jerry Rice 5.00
4B Steve Young 3.00
5A John Elway 7.00
5B Chris Chandler 1.00
6A Dan Marino 7.00
6B Drew Bledsoe 4.00
7A Keyshawn Johnson 2.00
7B Vinny Testaverde 2.00
8A Warren Moon 2.00
8B Steve McNair 2.00
9A Jake Plummer 5.00
9B Kordell Stewart 2.00
10A Troy Aikman 5.00
10B Peyton Manning 7.00

1999 Donruss Preferred QBC Hard Hats

This was a 30-card insert set that pictured each player on a helmet-shaped die-cut card. Each single was printed on clear plastic and was sequentially numbered to 3,000.

MT
Complete Set (30): 125.00
Common Player: 1.50
Minor Stars: 3.00
Production 3,000 Sets
1 Brett Favre 12.00
2 Keyshawn Johnson 3.00
3 John Elway 8.00
4 Drew Bledsoe 5.00
5 Chris Chandler 1.50
6 Terrell Davis 8.00
7 Ryan Leaf 3.00
8 Ricky Williams 15.00
9 Cade McNown 8.00
10 Barry Sanders 12.00
11 Donovan McNabb 8.00
12 Peyton Manning 8.00
13 Troy Aikman 6.00
14 Steve Young 4.00
15 Vinny Testaverde 1.50
16 Dan Marino 8.00
17 Steve McNair 3.00
18 Kordell Stewart 3.00
19 Michael Irvin 3.00
20 Jake Plummer 6.00
21 Jerry Rice 6.00
22 Brad Johnson 3.00
23 Phil Simms 3.00
24 Jim Kelly 3.00
25 Trent Dilfer 3.00
26 Kerry Collins 1.50
27 Warren Moon 3.00
28 Bubby Brister 1.50
29 Randall Cunningham 3.00
30 Doug Flutie 4.00

1999 Donruss Preferred QBC Materials

This was a 21-card insert set that included either a piece of game-used helmet, jersey or cleats. Jersey and cleat singles were numbered to 300 and helmet singles were numbered to 120. Singles were randomly inserted into packs.

MT
Common Player: 75.00
#13 never produced
1 Dan Marino Jersey 300 150.00
2 John Elway Jersey 300 150.00
3 Drew Bledsoe Jersey 300 100.00
4 Jake Plummer Jersey 300 100.00
5A Doug Flutie White Jersey 150 100.00
5B Doug Flutie Blue Jersey 150 100.00
6 Peyton Manning Jersey 300 150.00
7A Jerry Rice White Jersey 150 175.00
7B Jerry Rice Red Jersey 150 175.00
8 Brett Favre Jersey 300 200.00
9 Jim Kelly Jersey 300 75.00
10 Barry Sanders Jersey 300 200.00
11 Keyshawn Johnson Shoes 200 75.00
12 Brett Favre Shoes 100 250.00
14 Troy Aikman Shoes 300 125.00
15 Terrell Davis Shoes 300 125.00
16 Dan Marino Helmets 125 250.00
17 Troy Aikman Helmets 125 200.00
18 Brett Favre Helmets 125 300.00
19 Jerry Rice Helmets 125 200.00
20 Terrell Davis Helmets 125 200.00

1999 Donruss Preferred QBC National Treasures

This 44-card insert set included the top stars in the NFL. Each single was sequentially numbered to 2,000.

MT
Complete Set (44): 150.00
Common Player: 1.50
Minor Stars: 3.00
Production 2,000 Sets
1 Jake Plummer 10.00
2 Chris Chandler 1.50
3 Danny Kanell 1.50
4 Tony Banks 1.50
5 Scott Mitchell 1.50
6 Doug Flutie 6.00
7 Jim Kelly 3.00
8 Erik Kramer 1.50
9 Cade McNown 10.00
10 Jeff Blake 3.00
11 Boomer Esiason 3.00
12 Bernie Kosar 1.50
13 Troy Aikman 10.00
14 Michael Irvin 3.00
15 Bubby Brister 3.00
16 Terrell Davis 15.00
17 John Elway 15.00
18 Gus Frerotte 1.50
19 Barry Sanders 20.00
20 Brett Favre 20.00
21 Peyton Manning 15.00
22 Elvis Grbac 1.50
23 Warren Moon 3.00
24 Dan Marino 15.00
25 Randall Cunningham 3.00
26 Jeff George 3.00
27 Drew Bledsoe 8.00
28 Ricky Williams 20.00
29 Kerry Collins 3.00
30 Phil Simms 3.00
31 Keyshawn Johnson 3.00
32 Vinny Testaverde 3.00
33 Donovan McNabb 10.00
34 Kordell Stewart 4.00
35 Jim Harbaugh 3.00
36 Ryan Leaf 3.00
37 Junior Seau 3.00
38 Jerry Rice 10.00
39 Steve Young 6.00
40 Jim Everett 1.50
41 Trent Dilfer 3.00
42 Steve McNair 4.00
43 Brad Johnson 3.00
44 Neil O'Donnell 1.50

1999 Donruss Preferred QBC Passing Grade

This 20-card insert set included the top Quarterbacks in the NFL. Each single was a two-piece card that included a football-shaped die-cut inside a conventional card envelope. Each was sequentially numbered to 1,500.

MT
Complete Set (20): 150.00
Common Player: 2.00
Minor Stars: 4.00
Production 1,500 Sets
1 Steve Young 6.00
2 Dan Marino 15.00
3 Kordell Stewart 5.00
4 Trent Dilfer 4.00
5 Doug Flutie 6.00
6 Vinny Testaverde 4.00
7 Donovan McNabb 10.00
8 Brad Johnson 4.00
9 Troy Aikman 10.00
10 Brett Favre 20.00
11 Steve McNair 5.00
12 Peyton Manning 15.00
13 John Elway 15.00
14 Chris Chandler 2.00
15 Randall Cunningham 4.00
16 Cade McNown 10.00
17 Ryan Leaf 4.00
18 Drew Bledsoe 8.00
19 Jake Plummer 10.00
20 Warren Moon 4.00

1999 Donruss Preferred QBC Staremasters

This was a 20-card insert set that included the most intense players in the game today. Each single was sequentially numbered to 1,000.

MT
Complete Set (20): 230.00
Common Player: 3.00
Minor Stars: 6.00
Production 1,000 Sets
1 Jake Plummer 15.00
2 Doug Flutie 10.00
3 Cade McNown 15.00
4 Troy Aikman 15.00
5 Michael Irvin 3.00
6 Terrell Davis 20.00
7 John Elway 20.00
8 Barry Sanders 30.00
9 Brett Favre 30.00
10 Peyton Manning 20.00
11 Dan Marino 20.00
12 Randall Cunningham 6.00
13 Drew Bledsoe 12.00
14 Ricky Williams 30.00
15 Keyshawn Johnson 6.00
16 Donovan McNabb 15.00
17 Kordell Stewart 8.00
18 Ryan Leaf 6.00
19 Steve Young 10.00
20 Jerry Rice 15.00

1999 Donruss Preferred QBC X-Ponential Power

This 20-card insert set matched fellow stars from the same position. Each was printed on die-cut plastic with foil highlights and each was numbered to 2,500.

MT
Complete Set (20): 150.00
Common Player: 5.00
Production 2,500 Sets
1A Troy Aikman 10.00
1B Cade McNown 10.00
2A Kordell Stewart 5.00
2B Steve McNair 5.00
3A Donovan McNabb 10.00
3B Ricky Williams 20.00
4A Barry Sanders 20.00
4B Terrell Davis 15.00
5A Dan Marino 15.00
5B Peyton Manning 15.00
6A Jerry Rice 10.00
6B Keyshawn Johnson 5.00
7A Doug Flutie 7.00
7B Jim Kelly 5.00
8A Brett Favre 20.00
8B Steve Young 7.00
9A Drew Bledsoe 8.00
9B Ryan Leaf 5.00
10A John Elway 15.00
10B Jake Plummer 10.00

2000 Donruss

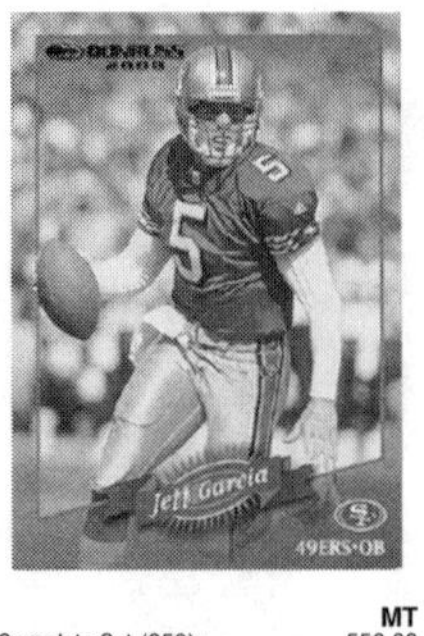

MT
Complete Set (250): 550.00
Common Player: .15
Minor Stars: .30
Common Rookie: 3.00
Production 1,325 Sets
Pack (16): 4.00
Wax Box (18): 55.00
1 Jake Plummer .50
2 Frank Sanders .30
3 Rob Moore .30
4 David Boston .50
5 Tim Dwight .50
6 Jamal Anderson .50
7 Chris Chandler .30
8 Terance Mathis .15
9 Tony Banks .30
10 Jermaine Lewis .15
11 Shannon Sharpe .30
12 Trent Dilfer .30
13 Qadry Ismail .15
14 Eric Moulds .50
15 Doug Flutie .75
16 Antowain Smith .30
17 Jonathon Linton .30
18 Peerless Price .50
19 Rob Johnson .30
20 Natrone Means .30
21 Muhsin Muhammad .30
22 Wesley Walls .30
23 Tim Biakabutuka .30
24 Steve Beuerlein .30
25 Patrick Jeffers .50
26 Curtis Enis .30
27 Cade McNown .50
28 Bobby Engram .15
29 Marcus Robinson .50
30 Marty Booker .15
31 Corey Dillon .50
32 Darnay Scott .30
33 Carl Pickens .30
34 Akili Smith .50
35 Michael Basnight .15
36 Tim Couch 1.00
37 Kevin Johnson .50
38 Karim Abdul .15
39 Errict Rhett .30
40 Darrin Chiaverini .15
41 Emmitt Smith 1.50
42 Troy Aikman 1.25
43 Joey Galloway .50
44 Randall Cunningham .30
45 Michael Irvin .30
46 Raghib Ismail .15
47 Jason Tucker .30
48 Terrell Davis 1.50
49 John Elway 1.50
50 Olandis Gary .50
51 Ed McCaffrey .30
52 Rod Smith .50
53 Brian Griese .75
54 Charlie Batch .50
55 Barry Sanders 1.75
56 Herman Moore .50
57 Johnnie Morton .30
58 Germane Crowell .50
59 James Stewart .30
60 Brett Favre 2.50
61 Dorsey Levens .50
62 Antonio Freeman .50
63 Corey Bradford .15
64 Bill Schroeder .15
65 E.G. Green .30
66 Peyton Manning 2.00
67 Edgerrin James 2.00
68 Marvin Harrison .50
69 Terrence Wilkins .50
70 Mark Brunell .75
71 Fred Taylor .75
72 Keenan McCardell .30
73 Jimmy Smith .50
74 Warren Moon .30
75 Elvis Grbac .30
76 Tony Gonzalez .30
77 Dan Marino 1.50
78 O.J. McDuffie .30
79 Tony Martin .15
80 James Johnson .30
81 Thurman Thomas .30
82 Randy Moss 2.00
83 Daunte Culpepper 1.00
84 Cris Carter .50
85 Robert Smith .50
86 John Randle .30
87 Drew Bledsoe .75
88 Terry Glenn .50
89 Kevin Faulk .30
90 Ricky Williams 1.00
91 Jeff Blake .30
92 Jake Reed .30
93 Amani Toomer .30
94 Kerry Collins .30
95 Tiki Barber .30
96 Ike Hilliard .30
97 Curtis Martin .50
98 Vinny Testaverde .30
99 Wayne Chrebet .50
100 Ray Lucas .30
101 Charles Woodson .50
102 Napoleon Kaufman .50
103 Tim Brown .50
104 Tyrone Wheatley .50
105 Rich Gannon .30
106 Duce Staley .30
107 Donovan McNabb .75
108 Amos Zereoue .30
109 Kordell Stewart .50
110 Jerome Bettis .50
111 Troy Edwards .30
112 Ryan Leaf .50
113 Junior Seau .30
114 Jim Harbaugh .30
115 Jermaine Fazande .30
116 Curtis Conway .30
117 Steve Young .75
118 Jerry Rice 1.25
119 Terrell Owens .50
120 Charlie Garner .30
121 Jeff Garcia .50
122 Jon Kitna .50
123 Derrick Mayes .30
124 Ricky Watters .30
125 Kurt Warner 2.50
126 Marshall Faulk .50
127 Torry Holt .50
128 Az-Zahir Hakim .30
129 Isaac Bruce .50
130 Mike Alstott .50
131 Warrick Dunn .50
132 Shaun King .50
133 Keyshawn Johnson .50
134 Jacquez Green .30
135 Reidel Anthony .30
136 Warren Sapp .30
137 Eddie George .75
138 Steve McNair .50
139 Yancey Thigpen .30
140 Kevin Dyson .30
141 Frank Wycheck .30
142 Jevon Kearse .50
143 Stephen Davis .50
144 Skip Hicks .30
145 Brad Johnson .30
146 Bruce Smith .30
147 Michael Westbrook .30
148 Albert Connell .30
149 Jeff George .30
150 Deion Sanders .50
151 *Courtney Brown* 6.00
152 *Corey Simon* 6.00
153 *Brian Urlacher* 20.00
154 *Shaun Ellis* 3.00
155 *John Abraham* 3.00
156 *Deltha O'Neal* 3.00
157 *Ahmed Plummer* 4.00
158 *Chris Hovan* 4.00

159	Rob Morris	3.00
160	Keith Bulluck	3.00
161	Darren Howard	3.00
162	John Engelberger	3.00
163	Raynoch Thompson	3.00
164	Cornelius Griffin	3.00
165	William Bartee	3.00
166	Fred Robbins	3.00
167	Micheal Boireau	3.00
168	Brandon Short	3.00
169	Jacoby Shepherd	3.00
170	Peter Warrick	30.00
171	Jamal Lewis	40.00
172	Thomas Jones	12.00
173	Plaxico Burress	15.00
174	Travis Taylor	8.00
175	Ron Dayne	30.00
176	Bubba Franks	5.00
177	Sebastian Janikowski	4.00
178	Chad Pennington	25.00
179	Shaun Alexander	20.00
180	Sylvester Morris	15.00
181	Anthony Becht	4.00
182	R. Jay Soward	5.00
183	Trung Canidate	5.00
184	Dennis Northcutt	6.00
185	Todd Pinkston	6.00
186	Jerry Porter	5.00
187	Travis Prentice	10.00
188	Giovanni Carmazzi	6.00
189	Ron Dugans	4.00
190	Erron Kinney	3.00
191	Dez White	5.00
192	Chris Cole	5.00
193	Ron Dixon	8.00
194	Chris Redman	12.00
195	J.R. Redmond	8.00
196	Laveranues Coles	8.00
197	JaJuan Dawson	7.00
198	Darrell Jackson	8.00
199	Reuben Droughns	4.00
200	Doug Chapman	4.00
201	Terrelle Smith	3.00
202	Curtis Keaton	4.00
203	Gari Scott	3.00
204	Danny Farmer	5.00
205	Hank Poteat	4.00
206	Ben Kelly	3.00
207	Corey Moore	3.00
208	Na'il Diggs	3.00
209	Aaron Shea	3.00
210	Trevor Gaylor	5.00
211	Julian Peterson	3.00
212	Frank Moreau	6.00
213	Deon Dyer	3.00
214	Avion Black	3.00
215	Paul Smith	3.00
216	Michael Wiley	6.00
217	Dante Hall	3.00
218	Mike Brown	3.00
219	Sammy Morris	3.00
220	Billy Volek	4.00
221	Tee Martin	6.00
222	Troy Walters	5.00
223	Chad Morton	5.00
224	Erik Flowers	3.00
225	Ronney Jenkins	3.00
226	Thomas Hamner	3.00
227	Mareno Philyaw	3.00
228	James Williams	3.00
229	Mike Anderson	35.00
230	Tom Brady	5.00
231	Mike Green	3.00
232	Todd Husak	4.00
233	Tim Rattay	6.00
234	Jarious Jackson	5.00
235	Joe Hamilton	5.00
236	Shyrone Stith	4.00
237	Rondell Mealey	4.00
238	Demario Brown	3.00
239	Chris Coleman	3.00
240	Dwayne Goodrich	3.00
241	Drew Haddad	3.00
242	Doug Johnson	5.00
243	Windrell Hayes	4.00
244	Charles Lee	4.00
245	Kevin McDougal	3.00
246	Spergon Wynn	5.00
247	Shockmain Davis	4.00
248	Jamel White	4.00
249	Bashir Yamini	3.00
250	Kwame Cavil	3.00

2000 Donruss Stat Line Career

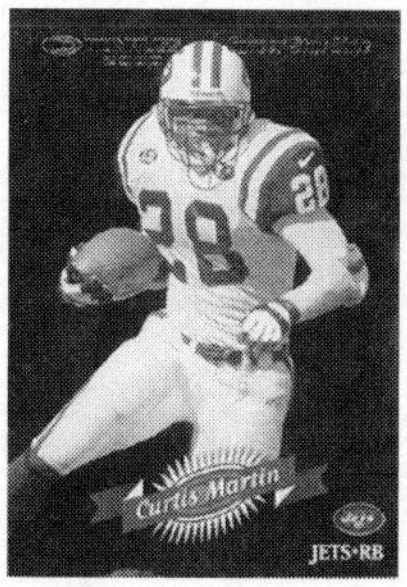

		MT
Common Player (131-300):		2.50
Common Player (65-130):		5.00
Common Player (30-64):		12.00
Common Player (10-29):		25.00
Production to a career stat.		
Inserted 1:25		
1	Jake Plummer 129	10.00
2	Frank Sanders 70	10.00
3	Rob Moore 153	2.50
4	David Boston 52	25.00
5	Tim Dwight 80	10.00
6	Jamal Anderson 47	25.00
7	Chris Chandler 300	5.00
8	Terance Mathis 81	5.00
9	Tony Banks 80	10.00
10	Jermaine Lewis 96	5.00
11	Shannon Sharpe 44	12.00
12	Trent Dilfer 70	10.00
13	Qadry Ismail 186	2.50
14	Eric Moulds 84	12.00
15	Doug Flutie 205	7.00
16	Antowain Smith 22	25.00
17	Jonathon Linton 250	5.00
18	Peerless Price 45	12.00
19	Rob Johnson 65	5.00
20	Natrone Means 72	5.00
21	Muhsin Muhammad 216	5.00
22	Wesley Walls 42	12.00
23	Tim Biakabutuka 67	5.00
24	Steve Beurlein 120	10.00
25	Patrick Jeffers 84	10.00
26	Curtis Enis 51	12.00
27	Cade McNown 235	6.00
28	Bobby Engram 230	2.50
29	Marcus Robinson 80	12.00
30	Marty Booker 57	12.00
31	Corey Dillon 71	12.00
32	Darnay Scott 93	5.00
33	Carl Pickens 63	12.00
34	Akili Smith 153	6.00
35	Michael Basnight 62	12.00
36	Tim Couch 15	85.00
37	Kevin Johnson 66	10.00
38	Karim Abdul 33	12.00
39	Errict Rhett 52	12.00
40	Darrin Chiaverini 44	12.00
41	Emmitt Smith 155	25.00
42	Troy Aikman 158	20.00
43	Randall Cunningham 95	12.00
44	Joey Galloway 283	5.00
45	Michael Irvin 65	10.00
46	Raghib Ismail 76	5.00
47	Jason Tucker 90	5.00
48	Terrell Davis 58	50.00
49	John Elway 300	20.00
50	Olandis Gary 276	7.00
51	Ed McCaffrey 78	10.00
52	Rod Smith 257	5.00
53	Brian Griese 262	6.00
54	Charlie Batch 98	10.00
55	Barry Sanders 99	45.00
56	Herman Moore 93	5.00
57	Johnnie Morton 98	5.00
58	Germane Crowell 106	5.00
59	James Stewart 119	5.00
60	Brett Favre 129	45.00
61	Dorsey Levens 52	12.00
62	Antonio Freeman 42	12.00
63	Corey Bradford 74	5.00
64	Bill Schroeder 74	5.00
65	E.G. Green 50	12.00
66	Peyton Manning 52	70.00
67	Edgerrin James 72	60.00
68	Marvin Harrison 61	15.00
69	Terrence Wilkins 42	12.00
70	Mark Brunell 297	6.00
71	Fred Taylor 78	12.00
72	Keenan McCardell 99	5.00
73	Jimmy Smith 28	25.00
74	Warren Moon 290	5.00
75	Elvis Grbac 260	5.00
76	Tony Gonzalez 168	5.00
77	Dan Marino 240	20.00
78	O.J. McDuffie 2	50.00
79	Tony Martin 99	5.00
80	James Johnson 100	5.00
81	Thurman Thomas 74	10.00
82	Randy Moss 28	125.00
83	Daunte Culpepper 6	125.00
84	Cris Carter 93	15.00
85	Robert Smith 78	10.00
86	John Randle 105	8.00
87	Drew Bledsoe 147	12.00
88	Terry Glenn 86	10.00
89	Kevin Faulk 98	10.00
90	Ricky Williams 253	10.00
91	Jeff Blake 88	10.00
92	Jake Reed 82	10.00
93	Amani Toomer 101	5.00
94	Kerry Collins 149	5.00
95	Tiki Barber 250	5.00
96	Ike Hilliard 125	5.00
97	Curtis Martin 70	12.00
98	Vinny Testaverde 205	5.00
99	Wayne Chrebet 21	30.00
100	Ray Lucas 279	5.00
101	Charles Woodson 6	40.00
102	Napoleon Kaufman 83	10.00
103	Tim Brown 176	5.00
104	Tyrone Wheatley 21	25.00
105	Rich Gannon 90	5.00
106	Duce Staley 64	25.00
107	Donovan McNabb 216	8.00
108	Amos Zereoue 48	12.00
109	Kordell Stewart 279	5.00
110	Jerome Bettis 41	12.00
111	Troy Edwards 234	5.00
112	Ryan Leaf 245	5.00
113	Junior Seau 224	2.50
114	Jim Harbaugh 139	2.50
115	Jermaine Fazande 54	12.00
116	Curtis Conway 85	5.00
117	Steve Young 96	20.00
118	Jerry Rice 180	15.00
119	Terrell Owens 222	5.00
120	Charlie Garner 23	25.00
121	Jeff Garcia 225	6.00
122	Jon Kitna 132	5.00
123	Derrick Mayes 116	5.00
124	Ricky Watters 123	10.00
125	Kurt Warner 41	100.00
126	Marshall Faulk 63	25.00
127	Torry Holt 63	15.00
128	Az-Zahir Hakim 75	5.00
129	Isaac Bruce 41	25.00
130	Mike Alstott 137	5.00
131	Warrick Dunn 76	10.00
132	Shaun King 89	10.00
133	Keyshawn Johnson 31	25.00
134	Jacquez Green 53	12.00
135	Reidel Anthony 79	5.00
136	Warren Sapp 160	5.00
137	Eddie George 114	12.00
138	Steve McNair 292	6.00
139	Yancey Thigpen 298	2.50
140	Kevin Dyson 75	5.00
141	Frank Wycheck 42	12.00
142	Jevon Kearse 48	20.00
143	Stephen Davis 22	30.00
144	Skip Hicks 200	2.50
145	Brad Johnson 82	10.00
146	Bruce Smith 281	5.00
147	Michael Westbrook 211	5.00
148	Albert Connell 99	5.00
149	Jeff George 147	5.00
150	Deion Sanders 21	35.00
151	Courtney Brown 106	12.00
152	Corey Simon 14	50.00
153	Brian Urlacher 3	175.00
154	Shaun Ellis 12	25.00
155	John Abraham 60	20.00
156	Deltha O'Neal 5	50.00
157	Ahmed Plummer 14	30.00
158	Chris Hovan 148	5.00
159	Rob Morris 223	5.00
160	Keith Bulluck 3	45.00
161	Darren Howard 84	5.00
162	John Engelberger 26	25.00
163	Raynoch Thompson 4	45.00
164	Cornelius Griffin 6	45.00
165	William Bartee 41	20.00
166	Fred Robbins 132	5.00
167	Micheal Boireau 62	15.00
168	Deon Grant 14	30.00
169	Jacoby Shepherd 2	50.00
170	Peter Warrick 31	100.00
171	Jamal Lewis 17	250.00
172	Thomas Jones 36	60.00
173	Plaxico Burress 131	20.00
174	Travis Taylor 15	65.00
175	Ron Dayne 63	75.00
176	Bubba Franks 77	25.00
177	Sebastian Janikowski 66	12.00
178	Chad Pennington 123	45.00
179	Shaun Alexander 41	85.00
180	Sylvester Morris 34	75.00
181	Anthony Becht 11	30.00
182	R. Jay Soward 179	6.00
183	Trung Canidate 25	40.00
184	Dennis Northcutt 225	8.00
185	Todd Pinkston 22	35.00
186	Jerry Porter 38	25.00
187	Travis Prentice 73	30.00
188	Giovanni Carmazzi 71	25.00
189	Ron Dugans 105	10.00
190	Erron Kinney 5	30.00
191	Dez White 14	35.00
192	Chris Cole 8	30.00
193	Ron Dixon 89	20.00
194	Chris Redman 84	35.00
195	J.R. Redmond 28	60.00
196	Laveranues Coles 7	65.00
197	JaJuan Dawson 29	35.00
198	Darrell Jackson 97	30.00
199	Reuben Droughns 19	30.00
200	Doug Chapman 55	15.00
201	Terrelle Smith 126	8.00
202	Curtis Keaton 33	25.00
203	Gari Scott 18	30.00
204	Danny Farmer 159	7.00
205	Hank Poteat 10	30.00
206	Ben Kelly 11	30.00
207	Corey Moore 166	6.00
208	Na'il Diggs 18	30.00
209	Aaron Shea 27	25.00
210	Trevor Gaylor 128	6.00
211	Anthony Lucas 134	5.00
212	Frank Moreau 233	5.00
213	Deon Dyer 9	35.00
214	Avion Black 11	35.00
215	Paul Smith 16	30.00
216	Michael Wiley 27	35.00
217	Dante Hall 22	30.00
218	Muneer Moore 144	5.00
219	Sammy Morris 169	12.00
220	James Whalen 120	5.00
221	Tee Martin 32	50.00
222	Troy Walters 244	5.00
223	Chad Morton 24	40.00
224	Marc Bulger 59	15.00
225	Frank Murphy 8	35.00
226	Thomas Hamner 21	30.00
227	Mareno Philyaw 59	15.00
228	James Williams 17	30.00
229	Mike Anderson 22	200.00
230	Tom Brady 298	6.00
231	Sherrod Gideon 193	2.50
232	Todd Husak 41	25.00
233	Tim Rattay 112	25.00
234	Jarious Jackson 34	25.00
235	Joe Hamilton 203	8.00
236	Shyrone Stith 21	30.00
237	Rondell Mealey 29	30.00
238	Demario Brown 37	15.00
239	Chris Coleman 122	10.00
240	Chafie Fields 8	35.00
241	Drew Haddad 124	5.00
242	Doug Johnson 62	20.00
243	Windrell Hayes 176	5.00
244	Charles Lee 162	5.00
245	Marcus Knight 82	8.00
246	Spergon Wynn 24	40.00
247	Leon Murray 56	15.00
248	Quinton Spotwood 105	10.00
249	Bashir Yamini 10	35.00
250	Kwame Cavil 174	5.00

2000 Donruss Stat Line Season

		MT
Common Player (80-175):		4.00
Common Player (45-79):		7.00
Common Player (20-44):		18.00
Common Player (10-19):		25.00
Production to a 1999 season stat.		
Inserted 1:192		
1	Jake Plummer 57	15.00
2	Frank Sanders 79	7.00
3	Rob Moore 37	18.00
4	David Boston 53	15.00
5	Tim Dwight 80	8.00
6	Jamal Anderson 32	25.00
7	Chris Chandler 42	18.00
8	Terance Mathis 98	4.00
9	Tony Banks 24	18.00
10	Jermaine Lewis 57	7.00
11	Shannon Sharpe 86	4.00
12	Trent Dilfer 25	30.00
13	Qadry Ismail 3	50.00
14	Eric Moulds 10	50.00
15	Doug Flutie 50	25.00
16	Antowain Smith 30	18.00
17	Jonathon Linton 96	4.00
18	Peerless Price 62	7.00
19	Rob Johnson 32	18.00
20	Natrone Means 79	7.00
21	Muhsin Muhammad 11	35.00
22	Wesley Walls 96	4.00
23	Tim Biakabutuka 31	18.00
24	Steve Beurlein 5	45.00
25	Patrick Jeffers 8	45.00
26	Curtis Enis 79	7.00
27	Cade McNown 4	60.00
28	Bobby Engram 13	25.00
29	Marcus Robinson 3	85.00
30	Marty Booker 19	25.00
31	Corey Dillon 3	85.00
32	Darnay Scott 8	35.00
33	Carl Pickens 7	35.00
34	Akili Smith 42	25.00
35	Michael Basnight 62	7.00
36	Tim Couch 46	35.00
37	Kevin Johnson 90	8.00
38	Karim Abdul 84	4.00
39	Errict Rhett 27	18.00
40	Darrin Chiaverini 10	25.00
41	Emmitt Smith 9	125.00
42	Troy Aikman 5	125.00
43	Randall Cunningham 47	10.00
44	Joey Galloway 15	35.00
45	Michael Irvin 3	45.00
46	Raghib Ismail 8	30.00
47	Jason Tucker 27	20.00
48	Terrell Davis 67	45.00
49	John Elway 26	150.00
50	Olandis Gary 95	10.00
51	Ed McCaffrey 3	45.00
52	Rod Smith 9	40.00
53	Brian Griese 3	80.00
54	Charlie Batch 74	10.00
55	Barry Sanders 8	150.00
56	Herman Moore 16	35.00
57	Johnnie Morton 10	30.00
58	Germane Crowell 99	8.00
59	James Stewart 30	18.00
60	Brett Favre 50	85.00
61	Dorsey Levens 99	8.00
62	Antonio Freeman 8	40.00
63	Corey Bradford 94	4.00
64	Bill Schroeder 93	4.00
65	E.G. Green 21	18.00
66	Peyton Manning 54	70.00
67	Edgerrin James 3	200.00
68	Marvin Harrison 14	35.00
69	Terrence Wilkins 81	8.00
70	Mark Brunell 3	85.00
71	Fred Taylor 27	30.00
72	Keenan McCardell 9	25.00
73	Jimmy Smith 14	30.00
74	Warren Moon 20	20.00
75	Elvis Grbac 49	10.00
76	Tony Gonzalez 90	15.00
77	Dan Marino 52	85.00
78	O.J. McDuffie 85	4.00
79	Tony Martin 10	30.00
80	James Johnson 86	4.00
81	Thurman Thomas 36	18.00
82	Randy Moss 12	150.00
83	Daunte Culpepper 3	275.00
84	Cris Carter 3	80.00
85	Robert Smith 70	15.00
86	John Randle 27	18.00
87	Drew Bledsoe 49	30.00
88	Terry Glenn 13	25.00
89	Kevin Faulk 43	18.00
90	Ricky Williams 99	30.00
91	Jeff Blake 4	50.00
92	Jake Reed 50	7.00
93	Amani Toomer 99	4.00
94	Kerry Collins 51	7.00
95	Tiki Barber 66	10.00
96	Ike Hilliard 8	35.00
97	Curtis Martin 38	20.00
98	Vinny Testaverde 15	25.00
99	Wayne Chrebet 88	10.00
100	Ray Lucas 4	50.00
101	Charles Woodson 52	10.00
102	Napoleon Kaufman 76	10.00
103	Tim Brown 11	35.00
104	Tyrone Wheatley 66	10.00
105	Rich Gannon 4	50.00
106	Duce Staley 93	8.00
107	Donovan McNabb 3	85.00
108	Amos Zereoue 17	25.00
109	Kordell Stewart 32	20.00
110	Jerome Bettis 99	8.00
111	Troy Edwards 86	4.00
112	Ryan Leaf 2	70.00
113	Junior Seau 75	10.00
114	Jim Harbaugh 46	15.00
115	Jermaine Fazande 30	20.00
116	Curtis Conway 9	30.00
117	Steve Young 93	35.00
118	Jerry Rice 9	100.00
119	Terrell Owens 9	50.00
120	Charlie Garner 53	10.00
121	Jeff Garcia 11	45.00
122	Jon Kitna 3	60.00
123	Derrick Mayes 7	50.00
124	Ricky Watters 99	8.00
125	Kurt Warner 5	175.00
126	Marshall Faulk 7	70.00
127	Torry Holt 87	10.00
128	Az-Zahir Hakim 4	35.00
129	Isaac Bruce 4	50.00
130	Mike Alstott 4	50.00
131	Warrick Dunn 11	40.00
132	Shaun King 23	30.00
133	Keyshawn Johnson 11	40.00
134	Jacquez Green 96	4.00
135	Reidel Anthony 94	4.00
136	Warren Sapp 12	30.00
137	Eddie George 31	40.00
138	Steve McNair 5	60.00
139	Yancey Thigpen 84	4.00
140	Kevin Dyson 79	7.00
141	Frank Wycheck 87	4.00
142	Jevon Kearse 14	10.00
143	Stephen Davis 6	60.00
144	Skip Hicks 52	7.00
145	Brad Johnson 32	25.00
146	Bruce Smith 3	50.00
147	Michael Westbrook 5	50.00
148	Albert Connell 97	4.00
149	Jeff George 45	10.00
150	Deion Sanders 3	60.00
151	Courtney Brown 16	60.00
152	Corey Simon 59	25.00
153	Brian Urlacher 90	40.00
154	Shaun Ellis 30	20.00
155	John Abraham 6	35.00
156	Deltha O'Neal 9	35.00
157	Ahmed Plummer 48	15.00
158	Chris Hovan 11	35.00
159	Rob Morris 6	45.00
160	Keith Bulluck 90	5.00
161	Darren Howard 2	50.00
162	John Engelberger 31	20.00
163	Raynoch Thompson 49	12.00
164	Cornelius Griffin 30	25.00
165	William Bartee 1	60.00
166	Fred Robbins 5	45.00
167	Micheal Boireau 3	45.00
168	Deon Grant 49	15.00
169	Jacoby Shepherd 12	30.00
170	Peter Warrick 71	60.00
171	Jamal Lewis 15	250.00
172	Thomas Jones 16	150.00
173	Plaxico Burress 12	150.00
174	Travis Taylor 34	45.00
175	Ron Dayne 19	175.00
176	Bubba Franks 5	65.00
177	Sebastian Janikowski 54	15.00
178	Chad Pennington 38	85.00
179	Shaun Alexander 19	125.00
180	Sylvester Morris 69	45.00
181	Anthony Becht 35	25.00
182	R. Jay Soward 4	50.00
183	Trung Canidate 11	45.00
184	Dennis Northcutt 8	50.00
185	Todd Pinkston 48	25.00
186	Jerry Porter 4	50.00
187	Travis Prentice 17	75.00
188	Giovanni Carmazzi 11	60.00
189	Ron Dugans 3	55.00
190	Erron Kinney 16	40.00
191	Dez White 44	25.00
192	Chris Cole 22	30.00
193	Ron Dixon 19	60.00
194	Chris Redman 29	85.00
195	J.R. Redmond 78	25.00
196	Laveranues Coles 12	75.00
197	JaJuan Dawson 78	10.00
198	Darrell Jackson 9	45.00
199	Reuben Droughns 10	35.00
200	Doug Chapman 12	35.00
201	Terrelle Smith 22	25.00
202	Curtis Keaton 20	25.00
203	Gari Scott 30	20.00
204	Danny Farmer 3	50.00
205	Hank Poteat 31	20.00
206	Ben Kelly 27	20.00
207	Corey Moore 60	15.00
208	Na'il Diggs 64	15.00
209	Aaron Shea 31	20.00
210	Trevor Gaylor 11	35.00
211	Anthony Lucas 5	40.00
212	Frank Moreau 17	40.00
213	Deon Dyer 73	10.00
214	Avion Black 47	15.00
215	Paul Smith 12	30.00
216	Michael Wiley 10	45.00
217	Dante Hall 53	15.00
218	Muneer Moore 7	40.00
219	Sammy Morris 3	65.00
220	James Whalen 10	30.00
221	Tee Martin 12	65.00
222	Troy Walters 10	35.00
223	Chad Morton 15	40.00
224	Marc Bulger 145	4.00
225	Frank Murphy 11	35.00
226	Thomas Hamner 10	35.00
227	Mareno Philyaw 4	45.00
228	James Williams 47	12.00
229	Mike Anderson 10	275.00
230	Tom Brady 20	30.00
231	Sherrod Gideon 7	35.00
232	Todd Husak 18	40.00
233	Tim Rattay 32	50.00
234	Jarious Jackson 17	45.00
235	Joe Hamilton 29	45.00
236	Shyrone Stith 13	40.00
237	Rondell Mealey 8	40.00
238	Demario Brown 14	35.00
239	Chris Coleman 41	20.00
240	Chafie Fields 39	20.00
241	Drew Haddad 6	35.00
242	Doug Johnson 20	35.00
243	Windrell Hayes 4	35.00
244	Charles Lee 5	35.00
245	Marcus Knight 36	20.00
246	Spergon Wynn 14	30.00
247	Leon Murray 18	25.00
248	Quinton Spotwood 3	40.00
249	Bashir Yamini 31	20.00
250	Kwame Cavil 6	35.00

2000 Donruss All-Time Gridiron Kings

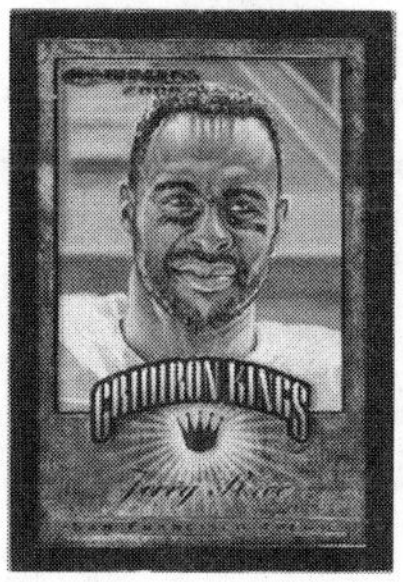

		MT
Complete Set (10):		35.00
Common Player:		2.50
Production 2,500 Sets		
Studio Autographs:		12x
Fouts Autograph never released.		
Production 250 Sets		
1	Joe Montana	12.00
2	Terry Bradshaw	7.00
3	Fran Tarkenton	6.00
4	Dan Fouts	5.00
5	Sammy Baugh	4.00
6	Eric Dickerson	2.50
7	Bob Griese	5.00
8	Ken Stabler	5.00
9	Joe Namath	8.00
10	Lawrence Taylor	4.00

Post-1980 cards in Near Mint condition will generally sell for about 75% of the quoted Mint value. Excellent-condition cards bring no more than 40%.

2000 Donruss Dominators

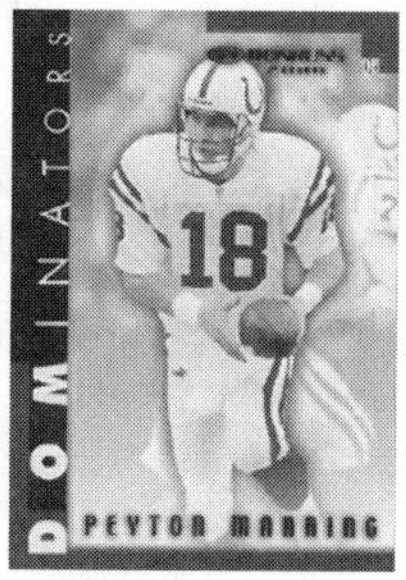

		MT
Complete Set (60):		30.00
Common Player:		.50
Minor Stars:		1.00
Production 5,000 Sets		
1	Jake Plummer	1.00
2	Tim Couch	1.50
3	Emmitt Smith	2.50
4	Troy Aikman	2.00
5	John Elway	2.50
6	Terrell Davis	2.50
7	Charlie Batch	1.00
8	Barry Sanders	2.50
9	Brett Favre	3.50
10	Peyton Manning	3.00
11	Edgerrin James	3.00
12	Mark Brunell	1.50
13	Fred Tayor	1.25
14	Dan Marino	2.50
15	Randy Moss	3.00
16	Drew Bledsoe	1.50
17	Ricky Williams	1.75
18	Jerry Rice	2.00
19	Steve Young	1.50
20	Kurt Warner	3.50
21	Eddie George	1.25
22	Jamal Anderson	1.00
23	Eric Moulds	1.00
24	Cade McNown	1.00
25	Corey Dillon	1.00
26	Kevin Johnson	.50
27	Joey Galloway	1.00
28	Olandis Gary	1.00
29	Dorsey Levens	1.00
30	Antonio Freeman	1.00
31	Marvin Harrison	1.00
32	Daunte Culpepper	1.75
33	Cris Carter	1.00
34	Robert Smith	1.00
35	Curtis Martin	1.00
36	Tim Brown	1.00
37	Duce Staley	1.00
38	Donovan McNabb	1.25
39	Jerome Bettis	1.00
40	Terrell Owens	1.00
41	Jon Kitna	1.00
42	Marshall Faulk	1.25
43	Warrick Dunn	1.00
44	Shaun King	1.00
45	Keyshawn Johnson	1.00
46	Steve McNair	1.00
47	Stephen Davis	1.00
48	Brad Johnson	.50
49	Muhsin Muhammad	.50
50	Marcus Robinson	1.00
51	Akili Smith	1.00
52	Brian Griese	1.25
53	Germane Crowell	1.00
54	Jimmy Smith	1.00
55	Ricky Watters	1.00
56	Isaac Bruce	1.00
57	Warren Sapp	.50
58	Jevon Kearse	1.00
59	Michael Westbrook	1.00
60	Ed McCaffrey	1.00

2000 Donruss Elite Series

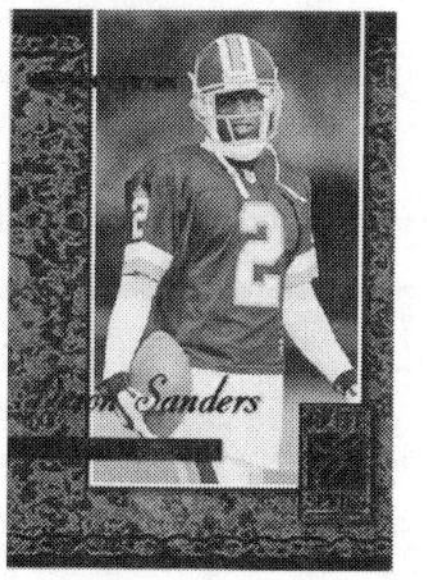

		MT
Complete Set (40):		60.00
Common Player:		.75
Minor Stars:		1.50
Production 2,500 Sets		
1	Jake Plummer	1.50
2	Emmitt Smith	5.00
3	Tim Couch	2.50
4	Troy Aikman	4.00
5	John Elway	5.00
6	Terrell Davis	5.00
7	Barry Sanders	5.00
8	Brett Favre	7.00
9	Peyton Manning	5.00
10	Mark Brunell	2.50
11	Edgerrin James	5.00
12	Fred Taylor	2.00
13	Dan Marino	5.00
14	Randy Moss	5.00
15	Drew Bledsoe	2.50
16	Ricky Williams	3.00

17 Jerry Rice 4.00
18 Steve Young 2.50
19 Kurt Warner 7.00
20 Eddie George 2.00
21 Deion Sanders 1.50
22 Cade McNown 1.50
23 Joey Galloway 1.50
24 Dorsey Levens 1.50
25 Antonio Freeman 1.50
26 Marvin Harrison 1.50
27 Daunte Culpepper 3.00
28 Cris Carter 1.50
29 Curtis Martin 1.50
30 Tim Brown 1.50
31 Donovan McNabb 2.00
32 Jerome Bettis 1.50
33 Marshall Faulk 1.75
34 Jon Kitna 1.50
35 Keyshawn Johnson 1.50
36 Steve McNair 1.50
37 Stephen Davis 1.50
38 Jimmy Smith 1.50
39 Brad Johnson .75
40 Isaac Bruce 1.50

2000 Donruss Gridiron Kings

MT
Complete Set (10): 35.00
Common Player: 3.00
Production 2,500 Sets
Studio Cards: 5x
Production 250 Sets
Studio Autographs: 30x
Production 50 Sets
1 Emmitt Smith 5.00
2 John Elway 5.00
3 Barry Sanders 5.00
4 Brett Favre 7.00
5 Peyton Manning 5.00
6 Dan Marino 5.00
7 Randy Moss 5.00
8 Jerry Rice 4.00
9 Steve Young 3.00
10 Kurt Warner 7.00

2000 Donruss Jersey King Autographs

MT
Complete Set (10): 2000.
Common Player: 85.00
Production 50 Sets
1 John Elway 200.00
2 Barry Sanders 225.00
3 Dan Marino 250.00
4 Jerry Rice 200.00
5 Kurt Warner 250.00
6 Joe Montana 250.00
7 Terry Bradshaw 175.00
8 Fran Tarkenton 175.00
9 Eric Dickerson 85.00
10 Joe Namath 250.00

2000 Donruss Rated Rookies

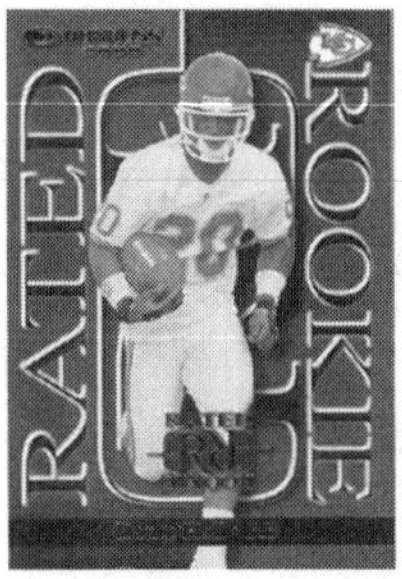

MT
Complete Set (40): 60.00
Common Player: 1.00
Minor Stars: 2.00
Production 2,500 Sets
Medalist Cards: 5x
Production 100 Sets
1 Peter Warrick 7.00
2 Jamal Lewis 10.00
3 Thomas Jones 3.00
4 Plaxico Burress 4.00
5 Travis Taylor 2.50
6 Ron Dayne 7.00
7 Bubba Franks 2.00
8 Chad Pennington 6.00
9 Shaun Alexander 5.00
10 Sylvester Morris 4.00
11 R. Jay Soward 2.00
12 Trung Canidate 1.00
13 Dennis Northcutt 2.00
14 Todd Pinkston 2.00
15 Jerry Porter 2.00
16 Travis Prentice 2.50
17 Giovanni Carmazzi 2.00
18 Ron Dugans 2.00
19 Dez White 2.00
20 Chris Cole 1.00
21 Ron Dixon 2.50
22 Chris Redman 3.00
23 J.R. Redmond 2.50
24 Laveranues Coles 2.50
25 JaJuan Dawson 2.00
26 Darrell Jackson 2.50
27 Reuben Droughns 1.00
28 Doug Chapman 1.00
29 Curtis Keaton 1.00
30 Gari Scott 1.00
31 Danny Farmer 1.00
32 Trevor Gaylor 1.00
33 Anthony Lucas 1.00
34 Frank Moreau 2.00
35 Avion Black 1.00
36 Michael Wiley 1.00
37 Dante Hall 1.00
38 Tim Rattay 2.00
39 Tee Martin 2.00
40 Courtney Brown 2.00

2000 Donruss Rookie Gridiron Kings

MT
Complete Set (10): 25.00
Common Player: 2.00
Production 2,500 Sets
Studio Cards: 4x
Production 250 Sets
Studio Autographs: 15x
Production 50 Sets
1 Peter Warrick 7.00
2 Jamal Lewis 10.00
3 Thomas Jones 3.00
4 Plaxico Burress 4.00
5 Travis Taylor 2.00
6 Ron Dayne 7.00
7 Chad Pennington 6.00
8 Shaun Alexander 5.00
9 Sylvester Morris 4.00
10 Chris Redman 3.00

2000 Donruss Signature Series Red

MT
Common Player: 10.00
1 Troy Aikman 25 100.00
2 Tony Banks 325 10.00
3 Jeff Blake 125 15.00
4 Drew Bledsoe 35 50.00
5 Isaac Bruce 25 25.00
6 Trung Canidate 75 15.00
7 Giovanni Carmazzi 175 15.00
8 Kwame Cavil 375 10.00
9 Doug Chapman 375 10.00
10 Laveranues Coles 175 20.00
11 Kerry Collins 125 15.00
12 Albert Connell 750 10.00
13 Tim Couch 25 50.00
14 Germane Crowell 350 10.00
15 Daunte Culpepper 375 40.00
16 Reuben Droughns 375 10.00
17 Ron Dugans 175 15.00
18 Tim Dwight 350 15.00
19 Troy Edwards 350 10.00
20 Kevin Faulk 750 10.00
21 Danny Farmer 175 15.00
22 Marshall Faulk 25 40.00
23 Jermaine Fazande 750 10.00
24 Antonio Freeman 175 15.00
25 Charlie Garner 750 10.00
26 Olandis Gary 350 15.00
27 Trevor Gaylor 175 10.00
28 Eddie George 25 50.00
29 Marvin Harrison 75 25.00
30 Torry Holt 75 25.00
31 Darrell Jackson 175 20.00
32 Edgerrin James 25 125.00
33 Patrick Jeffers 750 10.00
34 Brad Johnson 25 30.00
35 Kevin Johnson 350 10.00
36 Curtis Martin 75 25.00
37 Tee Martin 275 15.00
38 Derrick Mayes 750 10.00
39 Cade McNown 75 35.00
40 Sylvester Morris 125 30.00
41 Randy Moss 75 150.00
42 Eric Moulds 100 20.00
43 Dennis Northcutt 175 15.00
44 Todd Pinkston 175 15.00
45 Jake Plummer 25 25.00
46 Jerry Porter 175 15.00
47 Travis Prentice 175 20.00
48 Tim Rattay 375 20.00
49 J.R. Redmond 175 15.00
50 Corey Simon 175 15.00
51 Akili Smith 75 10.00
52 Antowain Smith 75 15.00
53 Jimmy Smith 75 15.00
54 R. Jay Soward 175 15.00
55 Shyrone Stith 175 10.00
56 Fred Taylor 75 45.00
57 Thurman Thomas 75 20.00
58 Kurt Warner 75 125.00
59 Ricky Williams 25 65.00
60 Tyrone Wheatley 350 10.00

2000 Donruss Signature Series Blue

MT
Common Player: 12.50
Production 100 Sets
2 Tony Banks 12.50
3 Jeff Blake 12.50
7 Giovanni Carmazzi 20.00
8 Kwame Cavil 12.50
9 Doug Chapman 12.50
10 Laveranues Coles 25.00
11 Kerry Collins 12.50
12 Albert Connell 12.50
14 Germane Crowell 12.50
15 Daunte Culpepper 65.00
16 Reuben Droughns 12.50
17 Ron Dugans 20.00
18 Tim Dwight 20.00
19 Troy Edwards 12.50
20 Kevin Faulk 12.50
21 Danny Farmer 12.50
23 Jermaine Fazande 12.50
24 Antonio Freeman 20.00
25 Charlie Garner 12.50
26 Olandis Gary 20.00
27 Trevor Gaylor 12.50
31 Darrell Jackson 25.00
33 Patrick Jeffers 15.00
35 Kevin Johnson 15.00
37 Tee Martin 20.00
38 Derrick Mayes 12.50
40 Sylvester Morris 40.00
43 Dennis Northcutt 20.00
44 Todd Pinkston 20.00
46 Jerry Porter 20.00
47 Travis Prentice 30.00
48 Tim Rattay 25.00
49 J.R. Redmond 25.00
50 Corey Simon 25.00
54 R. Jay Soward 20.00
55 Shyrone Stith 12.50
60 Tyrone Wheatley 12.50

2000 Donruss Signature Series Gold

MT
Common Player: 20.00
Production 25 Sets
1 Troy Aikman 100.00
2 Tony Banks 20.00
3 Jeff Blake 20.00
4 Drew Bledsoe 60.00
5 Isaac Bruce 25.00
6 Trung Canidate 25.00
7 Giovanni Carmazzi 35.00
8 Kwame Cavil 20.00
9 Doug Chapman 20.00
10 Laveranues Coles 40.00
11 Kerry Collins 20.00
12 Albert Connell 20.00
13 Tim Couch 60.00
14 Germane Crowell 25.00
15 Daunte Culpepper 80.00
16 Reuben Droughns 20.00
17 Ron Dugans 20.00
18 Tim Dwight 40.00
19 Troy Edwards 20.00
20 Kevin Faulk 20.00
21 Danny Farmer 20.00
22 Marshall Faulk 45.00
23 Jermaine Fazande 20.00
24 Antonio Freeman 40.00
25 Charlie Garner 20.00
26 Olandis Gary 40.00
27 Trevor Gaylor 20.00
28 Eddie George 50.00
29 Marvin Harrison 40.00
30 Torry Holt 35.00
31 Darrell Jackson 40.00
32 Edgerrin James 125.00
33 Patrick Jeffers 35.00
34 Brad Johnson 30.00
35 Kevin Johnson 30.00
36 Curtis Martin 30.00
37 Tee Martin 30.00
38 Derrick Mayes 20.00
39 Cade McNown 35.00
40 Sylvester Morris 50.00
41 Randy Moss 150.00
42 Eric Moulds 30.00
43 Dennis Northcutt 25.00
44 Todd Pinkston 25.00
45 Jake Plummer 35.00
46 Jerry Porter 35.00
47 Travis Prentice 45.00
48 Tim Rattay 35.00
49 J.R. Redmond 30.00
50 Corey Simon 35.00
51 Akili Smith 30.00
52 Antowain Smith 25.00
53 Jimmy Smith 30.00
54 R. Jay Soward 30.00
55 Shyrone Stith 25.00
56 Fred Taylor 50.00
57 Thurman Thomas 35.00
58 Kurt Warner 120.00
59 Ricky Williams 60.00
60 Tyrone Wheatley 20.00

2000 Donruss Zoning Commission

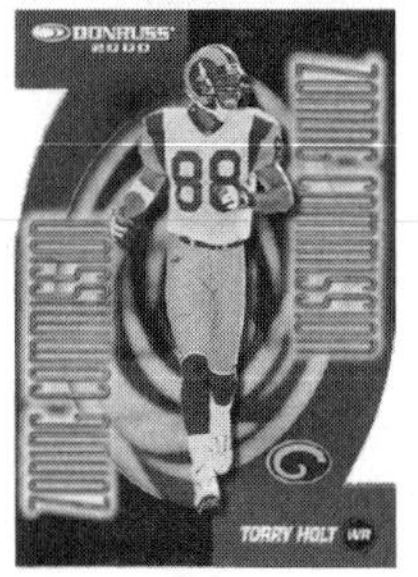

MT
Complete Set (60): 85.00
Common Player: 1.00
Minor Stars: 2.00
Production 1,000 Sets
1 Jake Plummer 2.00
2 Tim Couch 3.00
3 Emmitt Smith 6.00
4 Troy Aikman 5.00
5 Charlie Batch 2.00
6 Brett Favre 10.00
7 Peyton Manning 8.00
8 Edgerrin James 8.00
9 Mark Brunell 3.00
10 Fred Taylor 2.50
11 Dan Marino 8.00
12 Randy Moss 8.00
13 Drew Bledsoe 3.00
14 Ricky Williams 4.00
15 Jerry Rice 5.00
16 Steve Young 3.00
17 Kurt Warner 10.00
18 Eddie George 2.50
19 Eric Moulds 2.00
20 Doug Flutie 2.50
21 Antowain Smith 1.00
22 Cade McNown 2.00
23 Corey Dillon 2.00
24 Kevin Johnson 1.00
25 Joey Galloway 2.00
26 Olandis Gary 2.00
27 Dorsey Levens 2.00
28 Antonio Freeman 2.00
29 Marvin Harrison 2.00
30 Cris Carter 2.00
31 Robert Smith 2.00
32 Curtis Martin 2.00
33 Tim Brown 2.00
34 Duce Staley 2.00
35 Donovan McNabb 2.50
36 Kordell Stewart 2.00
37 Jerome Bettis 2.00
38 Terrell Owens 2.00
39 Jon Kitna 2.00
40 Marshall Faulk 2.50
41 Torry Holt 2.00
42 Mike Alstott 2.00
43 Shaun King 2.50
44 Keyshawn Johnson 2.00
45 Steve McNair 2.00
46 Stephen Davis 2.00
47 Brad Johnson 1.00
48 Qadry Ismail 1.00
49 Muhsin Muhammad 1.00
50 Patrick Jeffers 2.00
51 Marcus Robinson 2.00
52 Akili Smith 2.00
53 Germane Crowell 2.00
54 James Stewart 2.00
55 Jimmy Smith 2.00
56 Amani Toomer 1.00
57 Charlie Garner 2.00
58 Isaac Bruce 2.00
59 Albert Connell 1.00
60 Jeff George 2.00

2000 Donruss Zoning Commission Red

MT
Common Player: 20.00
Minor Stars: 40.00
Production to 1999 TD total.
1 Jake Plummer 9 40.00
2 Tim Couch 15 65.00
3 Emmitt Smith 11 120.00
4 Troy Aikman 17 100.00
5 Charlie Batch 13 40.00
6 Brett Favre 22 125.00
7 Peyton Manning 26 100.00
8 Edgerrin James 13 125.00
9 Mark Brunell 14 65.00
10 Fred Taylor 6 65.00
11 Dan Marino 12 150.00
12 Randy Moss 11 130.00
13 Drew Bledsoe 19 65.00
14 Ricky Williams 2 100.00
15 Jerry Rice 5 125.00
16 Steve Young 3 75.00
17 Kurt Warner 41 70.00
18 Eddie George 9 65.00
19 Eric Moulds 7 50.00
20 Doug Flutie 19 50.00
21 Antowain Smith 6 40.00
22 Cade McNown 8 50.00
23 Corey Dillon 5 50.00
24 Kevin Johnson 8 50.00
25 Joey Galloway 1 80.00
26 Olandis Gary 7 50.00
27 Dorsey Levens 9 50.00
28 Antonio Freeman 6 50.00
29 Marvin Harrison 12 40.00
30 Cris Carter 13 40.00
31 Robert Smith 2 50.00
32 Curtis Martin 5 50.00
33 Tim Brown 6 50.00
34 Duce Staley 4 60.00
35 Donovan McNabb 8 80.00
36 Kordell Stewart 6 60.00
37 Jerome Bettis 7 50.00
38 Terrell Owens 4 50.00
39 Jon Kitna 23 20.00
40 Marshall Faulk 7 60.00
41 Torry Holt 6 50.00
42 Mike Alstott 7 50.00
43 Shaun King 7 50.00
44 Keyshawn Johnson 8 50.00
45 Steve McNair 12 50.00
46 Stephen Davis 17 40.00
47 Brad Johnson 24 40.00
48 Qadry Ismail 6 40.00
49 Muhsin Muhammad 8 40.00
50 Patrick Jeffers 12 50.00
51 Marcus Robinson 9 50.00
52 Akili Smith 2 60.00
53 Germane Crowell 7 50.00
54 James Stewart 13 40.00
55 Jimmy Smith 6 50.00
56 Amani Toomer 6 50.00
57 Charlie Garner 4 50.00
58 Isaac Bruce 12 50.00
59 Albert Connell 7 40.00
60 Jeff George 23 20.00

2000 Donruss Elite

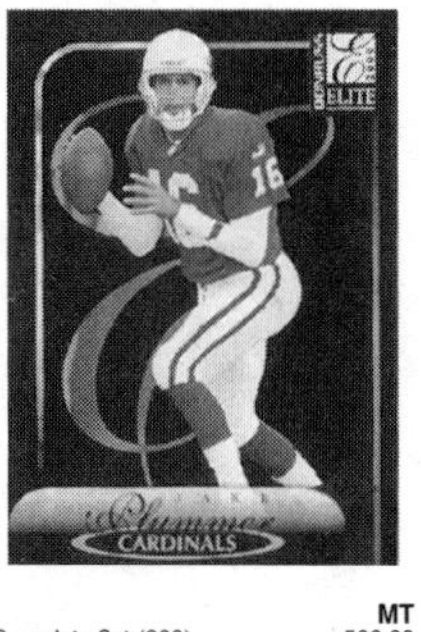

MT
Complete Set (200): 500.00
Common Player: .20
Minor Stars: .40
Common Player (101-125): 1.00
Minor Stars (101-125): 2.00
Common Rookie: 4.00
Production 2,000 Sets
Pack (5): 6.00
Wax Box (18): 85.00
1 Jake Plummer 1.00
2 David Boston .75
3 Rob Moore .40
4 Chris Chandler .40
5 Tim Dwight .75
6 Terance Mathis .20
7 Jamal Anderson .75
8 Priest Holmes .75
9 Tony Banks .40
10 Shannon Sharpe .40
11 Qadry Ismail .20
12 Eric Moulds .75
13 Doug Flutie 1.00
14 Antowain Smith .40
15 Peerless Price .50
16 Muhsin Muhammad .40
17 Tim Biakabutuka .40
18 Patrick Jeffers .75
19 Steve Beuerlein .40
20 Wesley Walls .40
21 Curtis Enis .50
22 Marcus Robinson .75
23 Carl Pickens .40
24 Corey Dillon .50
25 Akili Smith 1.00
26 Darnay Scott .40
27 Kevin Johnson .75
28 Errict Rhett .40
29 Emmitt Smith 2.00
30 Deion Sanders .75
31 Troy Aikman 1.50
32 Joey Galloway .75
33 Michael Irvin .40
34 Raghib Ismail .20
35 Jason Tucker .75
36 Ed McCaffrey .50
37 Rod Smith .50
38 Brian Griese 1.00
39 Terrell Davis 2.00
40 Olandis Gary 1.00
41 Charlie Batch .75
42 Johnnie Morton .20
43 Herman Moore .50
44 James Stewart .50
45 Dorsey Levens .50
46 Antonio Freeman .50
47 Brett Favre 3.00
48 Bill Schroeder .20
49 Peyton Manning 2.00
50 Keenan McCardell .40
51 Fred Taylor 1.25
52 Jimmy Smith .50
53 Elvis Grbac .40
54 Tony Gonzalez .50
55 Derrick Alexander .20
56 Dan Marino 2.00
57 Tony Martin .20
58 James Johnson .20
59 Damon Huard .40
60 Thurman Thomas .40
61 Robert Smith .50
62 Randall Cunningham .50
63 Jeff George .50
64 Terry Glenn .50
65 Drew Bledsoe 1.00
66 Jeff Blake .40
67 Amani Toomer .40
68 Kerry Collins .40
69 Joe Montgomery .20
70 Vinny Testaverde .50
71 Ray Lucas .40
72 Keyshawn Johnson .75
73 Wayne Chrebet .50
74 Napoleon Kaufman .50
75 Tim Brown .50
76 Rich Gannon .40
77 Duce Staley .75
78 Kordell Stewart .75
79 Jerome Bettis .50
80 Troy Edwards .75
81 Natrone Means .40
82 Curtis Conway .40
83 Jim Harbaugh .40
84 Junior Seau .40
85 Jermaine Fazande .40
86 Terrell Owens .75
87 Charlie Garner .40
88 Steve Young 1.00
89 Jeff Garcia .50
90 Derrick Mayes .40
91 Ricky Watters .40
92 Az-Zahir Hakim .40
93 Torry Holt .75
94 Warren Sapp .40
95 Mike Alstott .75
96 Warrick Dunn .75
97 Kevin Dyson .40
98 Bruce Smith .20
99 Albert Connell .40
100 Michael Westbrook 1.00
101 Cade McNown 3.00
102 Tim Couch 5.00
103 John Elway 6.00
104 Barry Sanders 6.00
105 Germane Crowell 1.00
106 Marvin Harrison 2.00
107 Edgerrin James 8.00
108 Mark Brunell 3.00
109 Randy Moss 6.00
110 Cris Carter 2.00
111 Daunte Culpepper 3.00
112 Ricky Williams 5.00
113 Curtis Martin 2.00
114 Donovan McNabb 3.00
115 Jerry Rice 4.00
116 Jon Kitna 2.00
117 Isaac Bruce 2.00
118 Marshall Faulk 2.00
119 Kurt Warner 10.00
120 Shaun King 3.00
121 Eddie George 2.00
122 Steve McNair 2.00
123 Jevon Kearse 2.00
124 Stephen Davis 2.00
125 Brad Johnson 2.00
126 *(Mike Anderson)* 50.00
127 *Peter Warrick* 30.00
128 *Courtney Brown* 10.00
129 *Plaxico Burress* 15.00
130 *Corey Simon* 4.00
131 *Thomas Jones* 15.00
132 *Travis Taylor* 10.00
133 *Shaun Alexander* 20.00
134 *Deon Grant* 4.00
135 *Chris Redman* 12.50
136 *Chad Pennington* 25.00
137 *Jamal Lewis* 50.00
138 *Brian Urlacher* 20.00
139 *Keith Bulluck* 8.00
140 *Bubba Franks* 10.00
141 *Dez White* 8.00
142 *Na'il Diggs* 4.00
143 *Ahmed Plummer* 4.00
144 *Ron Dayne* 40.00
145 *Shaun Ellis* 10.00
146 *Sylvester Morris* 15.00
147 *Delthea O'Neal* 4.00
148 *Raynoch Thompson* 4.00
149 *R. Jay Soward* 8.00
150 *Mario Edwards* 4.00
151 *John Engelberger* 4.00
152 Redemption 4.00
153 *Sherrod Gideon* 4.00
154 *John Abraham* 4.00
155 Redemption 4.00
156 *Travis Prentice* 12.00
157 *Darrell Jackson* 10.00
158 *Giovanni Carmazzi* 12.00
159 *Anthony Lucas* 8.00
160 *Danny Farmer* 8.00
161 *Dennis Northcutt* 10.00
162 *Troy Walters* 8.00
163 *Laveranues Coles* 12.00
164 *Tee Martin* 12.00
165 *J.R. Redmond* 12.00
166 *Tim Rattay* 12.00
167 *Jerry Porter* 10.00
168 *Sebastian Janikowski* 8.00
169 *Michael Wiley* 8.00
170 *Reuben Droughns* 8.00
171 *Trung Canidate* 8.00
172 *Shyrone Stith* 8.00
173 *Chris Hovan* 4.00
174 Redemption Card 4.00
175 Redemption Card 4.00
176 *Trevor Gaylor* 8.00
177 *Chris Cole* 8.00
178 *Hank Poteat* 8.00
179 *Darren Howard* 8.00
180 *Rob Morris* 8.00
181 Redemption Card 4.00
182 *Marc Bulger* 4.00
183 *Tom Brady* 8.00
184 *Todd Husak* 8.00
185 *Gari Scott* 8.00
186 *Erron Kinney* 8.00
187 Redemption Card 4.00
188 *Sammy Morris* 12.00
189 *Rondell Mealey* 8.00
190 Redemption Card 4.00
191 *Ron Dugans* 8.00
192 *Deon Dyer* 8.00
193 *Fred Robbins* 4.00
194 Redemption Card 4.00
195 *Mareno Philyaw* 4.00
196 Redemption Card 4.00
197 *Jarious Jackson* 8.00
198 *Anthony Becht* 8.00
199 *Joe Hamilton* 10.00
200 *Todd Pinkston* 10.00

2000 Donruss Elite Aspirations

MT
Common Player 65-99: 5.00
Common Player 45-64: 10.00
Common Player 20-29: 15.00
Common Player 10-19: 20.00
Cards #'d 9 And Under Not Priced 4.00
1 Jake Plummer 84 15.00
2 David Boston 11 40.00
3 Rob Moore 15 20.00
4 Chris Chandler 88 10.00
5 Tim Dwight 17 40.00
6 Terance Mathis 19 20.00
7 Jamal Anderson 68 15.00
8 Priest Holmes 67 15.00
9 Tony Banks 88 10.00
10 Shannon Sharpe 16 40.00
11 Qadry Ismail 13 20.00
12 Eric Moulds 20 45.00
13 Doug Flutie 93 20.00
14 Antowain Smith 77 10.00
15 Peerless Price 19 35.00
16 Muhsin Muhammad 13 35.00
17 Tim Biakabutuka 79 10.00
18 Patrick Jeffers 17 40.00
19 Steve Beuerlein 93 5.00
20 Wesley Walls 15 20.00
21 Curtis Enis 56 20.00
22 Marcus Robinson 12 50.00
23 Carl Pickens 19 35.00
24 Corey Dillon 72 10.00
25 Akili Smith 89 12.00
26 Darnay Scott 14 30.00
27 Kevin Johnson 14 50.00
28 Errict Rhett 68 5.00
29 Emmitt Smith 78 60.00
30 Deion Sanders 79 10.00
31 Troy Aikman 92 40.00
32 Joey Galloway 16 35.00
33 Michael Irvin 12 30.00
34 Raghib Ismail 19 20.00
35 Jason Tucker 13 35.00
36 Ed McCaffrey 13 35.00
37 Rod Smith 20 25.00
38 Brian Griese 86 20.00
39 Terrell Davis 70 60.00
40 Olandis Gary 78 12.00
41 Charlie Batch 90 12.00
42 Johnnie Morton 13 25.00
43 Herman Moore 16 35.00
44 James Stewart 67 10.00
45 Dorsey Levens 75 10.00
46 Antonio Freeman 14 45.00
47 Brett Favre 96 70.00
48 Bill Schroeder 16 20.00
49 Peyton Manning 82 60.00
50 Keenan McCardell 13 30.00
51 Fred Taylor 72 35.00
52 Jimmy Smith 18 35.00
53 Elvis Grbac 82 5.00
54 Tony Gonzalez 12 35.00
55 Derrick Alexander 18 20.00
56 Dan Marino 87 60.00
57 Tony Martin 20 30.00
58 James Johnson 68 5.00
59 Damon Huard 89 12.00
60 Thurman Thomas 66 10.00
61 Robert Smith 74 10.00
62 Randall Cunningham 93 12.00
63 Jeff George 97 12.00
64 Terry Glenn 12 50.00
65 Drew Bledsoe 89 25.00
66 Jeff Blake 92 10.00
67 Amani Toomer 19 20.00
68 Kerry Collins 95 5.00
69 Joe Montgomery 75 5.00
70 Vinny Testaverde 84 5.00
71 Ray Lucas 94 10.00
72 Keyshawn Johnson 81 10.00
73 Wayne Chrebet 20 25.00
74 Napoleon Kaufman 74 10.00
75 Tim Brown 19 40.00
76 Rich Gannon 85 5.00
77 Duce Staley 78 10.00
78 Kordell Stewart 90 12.00
79 Jerome Bettis 64 15.00
80 Troy Edwards 19 40.00
81 Natrone Means 80 10.00
82 Curtis Conway 20 30.00
83 Jim Harbaugh 96 5.00
84 Junior Seau 45 10.00
85 Jermaine Fazande 65 10.00

86	Terrell Owens 19	40.00
87	Charlie Garner 75	5.00
88	Steve Young 92	25.00
89	Jeff Garcia 95	10.00
90	Derrick Mayes 13	30.00
91	Ricky Watters 68	10.00
92	Az-Zahir Hakim 19	35.00
93	Torry Holt 12	45.00
94	Warren Sapp 1	
95	Mike Alstott 60	15.00
96	Warrick Dunn 72	12.00
97	Kevin Dyson 13	30.00
98	Bruce Smith 22	20.00
99	Albert Connell 17	30.00
100	Michael Westbrook 18	30.00
101	Cade McNown 92	20.00
102	Tim Couch 98	30.00
103	John Elway 93	60.00
104	Barry Sanders 80	70.00
105	Germane Crowell 18	30.00
106	Marvin Harrison 12	45.00
107	Edgerrin James 68	60.00
108	Mark Brunell 92	25.00
109	Randy Moss 16	150.00
110	Cris Carter 20	45.00
111	Daunte Culpepper 88	20.00
112	Ricky Williams 66	40.00
113	Curtis Martin 72	10.00
114	Donovan McNabb 95	20.00
115	Jerry Rice 20	125.00
116	Jon Kitna 93	12.00
117	Isaac Bruce 20	50.00
118	Marshall Faulk 72	12.00
119	Kurt Warner 87	85.00
120	Shaun King 90	20.00
121	Eddie George 73	25.00
122	Steve McNair 91	15.00
123	Jevon Kearse 10	50.00
124	Stephen Davis 52	15.00
125	Brad Johnson 86	10.00
127	Peter Warrick 91	120.00
128	Courtney Brown 14	100.00
129	Plaxico Burress 96	75.00
130	Corey Simon 47	30.00
131	Thomas Jones 94	60.00
132	Travis Taylor 81	40.00
133	Shaun Alexander 63	50.00
134	Deon Grant 93	15.00
135	Chris Redman 93	30.00
136	Chad Pennington 90	85.00
137	Jamal Lewis 69	75.00
138	Brian Urlacher 56	45.00
139	Keith Bulluck 67	20.00
140	Bubba Franks 12	75.00
141	Dez White 78	25.00
142	Na'il Diggs 68	20.00
143	Ahmed Plummer 81	15.00
144	Ron Dayne 67	120.00
145	Shaun Ellis 7	
146	Sylvester Morris 15	100.00
147	Delthea O'Neal 92	15.00
148	Raynoch Thompson 54	20.00
149	R. Jay Soward 82	35.00
150	Mario Edwards 85	10.00
151	John Engelberger 4	
153	Sherrod Gideon 89	15.00
154	John Abraham 5	
156	Travis Prentice 59	40.00
157	Darrell Jackson 91	20.00
158	Giovanni Carmazzi 81	45.00
159	Anthony Lucas 20	45.00
160	Danny Farmer 13	40.00
161	Dennis Northcutt 92	25.00
162	Troy Walters 95	20.00
163	Laveranues Coles 93	20.00
164	Tee Martin 83	30.00
165	J.R. Redmond 79	40.00
166	Tim Rattay 87	25.00
167	Jerry Porter 99	30.00
168	Sebastian Janikowski 62	20.00
169	Michael Wiley 95	25.00
170	Reuben Droughns 78	25.00
171	Trung Canidate 70	25.00
172	Shyrone Stith 62	25.00
173	Chris Hovan 5	
176	Trevor Gaylor 91	12.00
177	Chris Cole 20	40.00
178	Hank Poteat 69	20.00
179	Darren Howard 51	20.00
180	Rob Morris 56	20.00
182	Marc Bulger 90	15.00
183	Tom Brady 90	20.00
184	Todd Husak 93	20.00
185	Gari Scott 14	35.00
186	Erron Kinney 12	35.00
188	Sammy Morris 95	20.00
189	Rondell Mealey 93	20.00
191	Ron Dugans 20	50.00
192	Deon Dyer 62	20.00
193	Fred Robbins 10	40.00
195	Mareno Philyaw 92	12.00
197	Jarious Jackson 93	25.00
198	Anthony Becht 18	35.00
199	Joe Hamilton 86	25.00
200	Todd Pinkston 20	50.00

2000 Donruss Elite Rookie Die Cuts

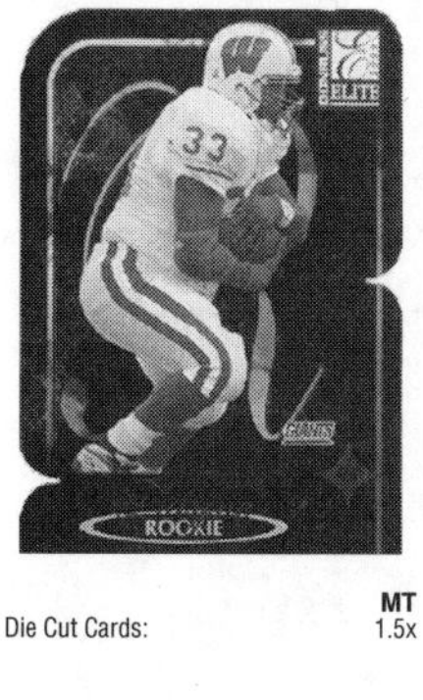

	MT
Die Cut Cards:	1.5x

2000 Donruss Elite Status

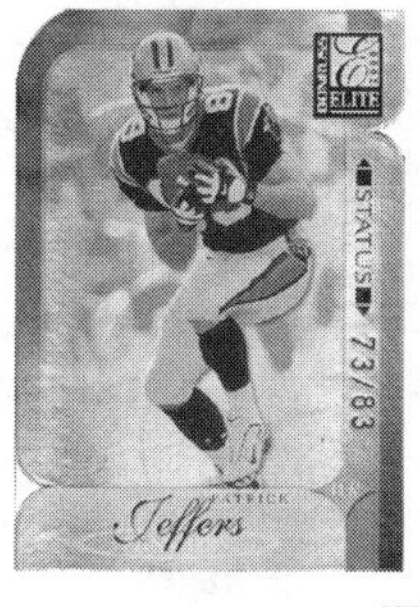

		MT
Common Player 65-99:		5.00
Common Player 20-64:		10.00
Common Player 10-19:		30.00
Cards #'d 9 And Under Not Priced		2.00
1	Jake Plummer 16	60.00
2	David Boston 89	12.00
3	Rob Moore 85	5.00
4	Chris Chandler 12	30.00
5	Tim Dwight 83	10.00
6	Terance Mathis 81	5.00
7	Jamal Anderson 32	30.00
8	Priest Holmes 33	25.00
9	Tony Banks 12	30.00
10	Shannon Sharpe 84	10.00
11	Qadry Ismail 87	5.00
12	Eric Moulds 80	12.00
13	Doug Flutie 7	
14	Antowain Smith 23	40.00
15	Peerless Price 81	10.00
16	Muhsin Muhammad 87	10.00
17	Tim Biakabutuka 21	20.00
18	Patrick Jeffers 83	12.00
19	Steve Beuerlein 7	
20	Wesley Walls 85	8.00
21	Curtis Enis 44	30.00
22	Marcus Robinson 88	12.00
23	Carl Pickens 81	8.00
24	Corey Dillon 28	40.00
25	Akili Smith 11	65.00
26	Darnay Scott 86	5.00
27	Kevin Johnson 86	10.00
28	Errict Rhett 32	15.00
29	Emmitt Smith 22	120.00
30	Deion Sanders 21	40.00
31	Troy Aikman 8	
32	Joey Galloway 84	10.00
33	Michael Irvin 88	10.00
34	Raghib Ismail 81	5.00
35	Jason Tucker 87	8.00
36	Ed McCaffrey 87	10.00
37	Rod Smith 80	8.00
38	Brian Griese 14	70.00
39	Terrell Davis 30	85.00
40	Olandis Gary 22	40.00
41	Charlie Batch 10	65.00
42	Johnnie Morton 87	5.00
43	Herman Moore 84	10.00
44	James Stewart 33	20.00
45	Dorsey Levens 25	30.00
46	Antonio Freeman 86	10.00
47	Brett Favre 4	
48	Bill Schroeder 84	5.00
49	Peyton Manning 18	200.00
50	Keenan McCardell 87	5.00
51	Fred Taylor 28	75.00
52	Jimmy Smith 82	10.00
53	Elvis Grbac 18	30.00
54	Tony Gonzalez 88	8.00
55	Derrick Alexander 82	5.00
56	Dan Marino 13	225.00
57	Tony Martin 80	5.00
58	James Johnson 32	15.00
59	Damon Huard 11	50.00
60	Thurman Thomas 34	25.00
61	Robert Smith 26	25.00
62	Randall Cunningham 7	
63	Jeff George 3	
64	Terry Glenn 88	10.00
65	Drew Bledsoe 11	120.00
66	Jeff Blake 8	
67	Amani Toomer 81	5.00
68	Kerry Collins 5	
69	Joe Montgomery 25	15.00
70	Vinny Testaverde 16	45.00
71	Ray Lucas 6	
72	Keyshawn Johnson 19	60.00
73	Wayne Chrebet 80	10.00
74	Napoleon Kaufman 26	35.00
75	Tim Brown 81	8.00
76	Rich Gannon 12	30.00
77	Duce Staley 22	40.00
78	Kordell Stewart 10	60.00
79	Jerome Bettis 36	20.00
80	Troy Edwards 81	10.00
81	Natrone Means 20	20.00
82	Curtis Conway 80	5.00
83	Jim Harbaugh 4	
84	Junior Seau 55	10.00
85	Jermaine Fazande 35	20.00
86	Terrell Owens 81	10.00
87	Charlie Garner 25	15.00
88	Steve Young 8	
89	Jeff Garcia 5	
90	Derrick Mayes 87	8.00
91	Ricky Watters 32	25.00
92	Az-Zahir Hakim 81	5.00
93	Torry Holt 88	10.00
94	Warren Sapp 99	5.00
95	Mike Alstott 40	25.00
96	Warrick Dunn 28	25.00
97	Kevin Dyson 87	8.00
98	Bruce Smith 78	5.00
99	Albert Connell 83	5.00
100	Michael Westbrook 82	10.00
101	Cade McNown 8	
102	Tim Couch 2	
103	John Elway 7	
104	Barry Sanders 20	175.00
105	Germane Crowell 82	8.00
106	Marvin Harrison 88	10.00
107	Edgerrin James 32	125.00
108	Mark Brunell 8	
109	Randy Moss 84	60.00
110	Cris Carter 80	10.00
111	Daunte Culpepper 12	85.00
112	Ricky Williams 34	70.00
113	Curtis Martin 28	25.00
114	Donovan McNabb 5	
115	Jerry Rice 80	45.00
116	Jon Kitna 7	
117	Isaac Bruce 80	10.00
118	Marshall Faulk 28	45.00
119	Kurt Warner 13	300.00
120	Shaun King 10	85.00
121	Eddie George 27	35.00
122	Steve McNair 9	
123	Jevon Kearse 90	12.00
124	Stephen Davis 48	20.00
125	Brad Johnson 14	45.00
127	Peter Warrick 9	
128	Courtney Brown 86	35.00
129	Plaxico Burress 4	
130	Corey Simon 53	25.00
131	Thomas Jones 6	
132	Travis Taylor 19	125.00
133	Shaun Alexander 37	125.00
134	Deon Grant 7	
135	Chris Redman 7	
136	Chad Pennington 10	300.00
137	Jamal Lewis 31	150.00
138	Brian Urlacher 44	50.00
139	Keith Bulluck 33	40.00
140	Bubba Franks 88	30.00
141	Dez White 22	60.00
142	Na'il Diggs 32	25.00
143	Ahmed Plummer 19	45.00
144	Ron Dayne 33	250.00
145	Shaun Ellis 93	12.00
146	Sylvester Morris 85	30.00
147	Delthea O'Neal 8	
148	Raynoch Thompson 46	25.00
149	R. Jay Soward 18	85.00
150	Mario Edwards 15	50.00
151	John Engelberger 96	10.00
153	Sherrod Gideon 11	50.00
154	John Abraham 95	15.00
156	Travis Prentice 41	60.00
157	Darrell Jackson 9	
158	Giovanni Carmazzi 19	125.00
159	Anthony Lucas 80	20.00
160	Danny Farmer 87	20.00
161	Dennis Northcutt 8	
162	Troy Walters 5	
163	Laveranues Coles 7	
164	Tee Martin 17	85.00
165	J.R. Redmond 21	85.00
166	Tim Rattay 13	80.00
167	Jerry Porter 1	
168	Sebastian Janikowski 38	25.00
169	Michael Wiley 5	
170	Reuben Droughns 22	50.00
171	Trung Canidate 30	40.00
172	Shyrone Stith 38	25.00
173	Chris Hovan 95	12.00
175	(Mark Roman 8)	
177	Chris Cole 80	12.00
178	Hank Poteat 31	25.00
179	Darren Howard 49	25.00
180	Rob Morris 44	15.00
182	Marc Bulger 10	45.00
183	Tom Brady 10	60.00
184	Todd Husak 7	
185	Gari Scott 86	15.00
186	Erron Kinney 88	15.00
188	Sammy Morris 5	
189	Rondell Mealey 7	
191	Ron Dugans 80	15.00
192	Deon Dyer 38	25.00
193	Fred Robbins 90	10.00
195	Mareno Philyaw 8	
197	Jarious Jackson 7	
198	Anthony Becht 82	15.00
199	Joe Hamilton 14	60.00
200	Todd Pinkston 80	20.00

2000 Donruss Elite Craftsmen

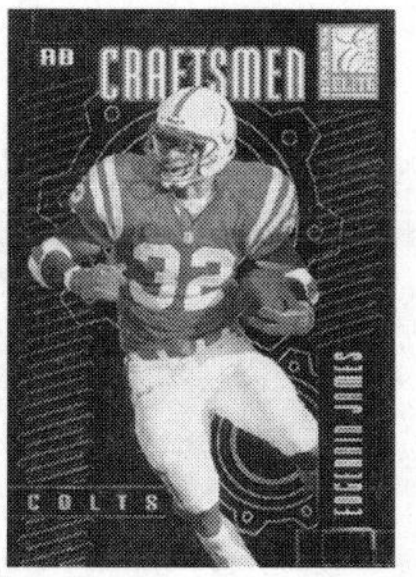

		MT
Complete Set (40):		85.00
Common Player:		1.50
Production 2,500 Sets		
Master Cards:		6x-12x
Production 50 Sets		
C1	Dan Marino	5.00
C2	Edgerrin James	5.00
C3	Peyton Manning	5.00
C4	Drew Bledsoe	2.50
C5	Doug Flutie	2.00
C6	Curtis Martin	1.50
C7	Eddie George	2.00
C8	Steve McNair	2.00
C9	Fred Taylor	2.50
C10	Mark Brunell	2.50
C11	Tim Couch	3.00
C12	Corey Dillon	1.50
C13	Terrell Davis	4.00
C14	Jon Kitna	1.50
C15	Emmitt Smith	4.00
C16	Troy Aikman	3.50
C17	Stephen Davis	1.50
C18	Brad Johnson	1.50
C19	Jake Plummer	2.00
C20	Brett Favre	6.00
C21	Barry Sanders	6.00
C22	Marshall Faulk	1.50
C23	Kurt Warner	8.00
C24	Ricky Williams	3.00
C25	Steve Young	2.50
C26	Randy Moss	6.00
C27	John Elway	5.00
C28	Jerry Rice	3.50
C29	Tim Brown	1.50
C30	Cris Carter	1.50
C31	Antonio Freeman	1.50
C32	Joey Galloway	1.50
C33	Terry Glenn	1.50
C34	Marvin Harrison	1.50
C35	Keyshawn Johnson	1.50
C36	Eric Moulds	1.50
C37	Isaac Bruce	1.50
C38	Peter Warrick	10.00
C39	Plaxico Burress	8.00
C40	Thomas Jones	7.00

2000 Donruss Elite Down and Distance

		MT
Common Player:		5.00
Production #'d To A Season Stat		
Cards #'d 9 And Under Not Priced		
1A	Randy Moss 611	10.00
1B	Randy Moss 493	15.00
1C	Randy Moss 263	20.00
1D	Randy Moss 46	45.00
2A	Brett Favre 1386	10.00
2B	Brett Favre 1543	10.00
2C	Brett Favre 1139	15.00
2D	Brett Favre 23	125.00
3A	Dan Marino 1023	10.00
3B	Dan Marino 855	15.00
3C	Dan Marino 505	20.00
3D	Dan Marino 65	60.00
4A	Peyton Manning 1857	10.00
4B	Peyton Manning 1219	15.00
4C	Peyton Manning 1029	15.00
4D	Peyton Manning 30	85.00
5A	Emmitt Smith 832	10.00
5B	Emmitt Smith 506	15.00
5C	Emmitt Smith 55	40.00
5D	Emmitt Smith 4	
6A	Jerry Rice 391	15.00
6B	Jerry Rice 238	20.00
6C	Jerry Rice 176	25.00
6D	Jerry Rice 25	60.00
7A	Mark Brunell 1066	5.00
7B	Mark Brunell 1112	5.00
7C	Mark Brunell 878	5.00
7D	Mark Brunell 4	
8A	Eddie George 716	5.00
8B	Eddie George 487	7.00
8C	Eddie George 98	15.00
8D	Eddie George 3	
9A	Marshall Faulk 762	5.00
9B	Marshall Faulk 512	6.00
9C	Marshall Faulk 101	10.00
9D	Marshall Faulk 6	
10A	Kurt Warner 1682	12.00
10B	Kurt Warner 1336	15.00
10C	Kurt Warner 1307	15.00
10D	Kurt Warner 28	150.00
11A	Edgerrin James 894	12.00
11B	Edgerrin James 531	15.00
11C	Edgerrin James 126	30.00
11D	Edgerrin James 2	
12A	Tim Couch 940	10.00
12B	Tim Couch 908	10.00
12C	Tim Couch 564	15.00
12D	Tim Couch 35	65.00

2000 Donruss Elite Down and Distance Die-Cuts

		MT
Common Player:		7.00
Production #'d To A Season Stat		
Cards #'d 9 And Under Not Priced		
1A	Randy Moss 34	85.00
1B	Randy Moss 30	85.00
1C	Randy Moss 14	125.00
1D	Randy Moss 2	
2A	Brett Favre 133	35.00
2B	Brett Favre 119	35.00
2C	Brett Favre 88	45.00
2D	Brett Favre 1	
3A	Dan Marino 82	40.00
3B	Dan Marino 77	40.00
3C	Dan Marino 42	50.00
3D	Dan Marino 3	
4A	Peyton Manning 121	25.00
4B	Peyton Manning 118	25.00
4C	Peyton Manning 91	30.00
4D	Peyton Manning 3	
5A	Emmitt Smith 175	20.00
5B	Emmitt Smith 121	20.00
5C	Emmitt Smith 29	75.00
5D	Emmitt Smith 4	
6A	Jerry Rice 24	65.00
6B	Jerry Rice 24	65.00
6C	Jerry Rice 16	85.00
6D	Jerry Rice 3	
7A	Mark Brunell 81	15.00
7B	Mark Brunell 100	10.00
7C	Mark Brunell 77	15.00
7D	Mark Brunell 1	
8A	Eddie George 171	7.00
8B	Eddie George 119	10.00
8C	Eddie George 29	30.00
8D	Eddie George 1	
9A	Marshall Faulk 138	7.00
9B	Marshall Faulk 94	10.00
9C	Marshall Faulk 20	25.00
9D	Marshall Faulk 1	
10A	Kurt Warner 129	45.00
10B	Kurt Warner 106	45.00
10C	Kurt Warner 87	55.00
10D	Kurt Warner 3	
11A	Edgerrin James 220	20.00
11B	Edgerrin James 130	30.00
11C	Edgerrin James 17	150.00
11D	Edgerrin James 2	
12A	Tim Couch 83	25.00
12B	Tim Couch 81	25.00
12C	Tim Couch 56	35.00
12D	Tim Couch 3	

Post-1980 cards in Near Mint condition will generally sell for about 75% of the quoted Mint value. Excellent-condition cards bring no more than 40%.

2000 Donruss Elite Passing the Torch

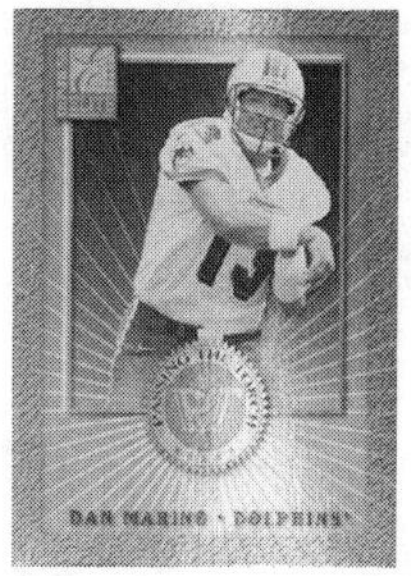

		MT
Complete Set (18):		200.00
Common Player:		5.00
#1-#12 Production 1,500 Sets		
#13-#18 Production 500 Sets		
PT1	Jerry Rice	7.00
PT2	Randy Moss	12.00
PT3	Dan Marino	10.00
PT4	Kurt Warner	15.00
PT5	Joe Montana	15.00
PT6	Steve Young	5.00
PT7	Bart Starr	10.00
PT8	Brett Favre	12.00
PT9	Roger Staubach	10.00
PT10	Troy Aikman	8.00
PT11	Gale Sayers	8.00
PT12	Edgerrin James	12.00
PT13	Jerry Rice, Randy Moss	12.00
PT14	Dan Marino, Kurt Warner	20.00
PT15	Joe Montana, Steve Young	20.00
PT16	Bart Starr, Brett Favre	15.00
PT17	Roger Staubach, Troy Aikman	12.00
PT18	Gale Sayers, Edgerrin James	15.00

2000 Donruss Elite Passing the Torch Autographs

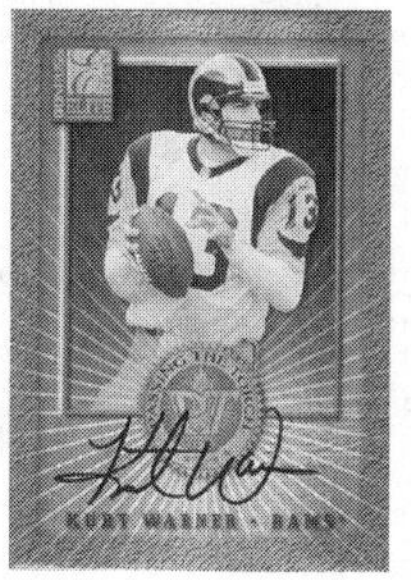

		MT
Common Player:		50.00
#1-#12 Production 150 Sets		
#13-#18 Production 50 Sets		
PT1	Jerry Rice	125.00
PT2	Randy Moss	175.00
PT3	Dan Marino	200.00
PT4	Kurt Warner	225.00
PT5	Joe Montana	250.00
PT6	Steve Young	100.00
PT7	Bart Starr	175.00
PT8	Brett Favre	250.00
PT9	Roger Staubach	150.00
PT10	Troy Aikman	125.00
PT11	Gale Sayers	50.00
PT12	Edgerrin James	175.00
PT13	Jerry Rice, Randy Moss	250.00
PT14	Dan Marino, Kurt Warner	350.00
PT15	Joe Montana, Steve Young	450.00
PT16	Bart Starr, Brett Favre	400.00
PT17	Roger Staubach, Troy Aikman	250.00
PT18	Gale Sayers, Edgerrin James	325.00

2000 Donruss Elite Throwback Threads

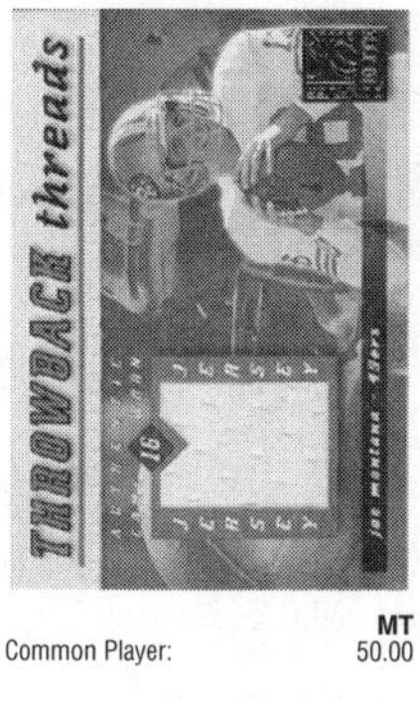

		MT
Common Player:		50.00
Single Jerseys Production #'d To 100		
Dual Jerseys Production #'d To 50		
TT1	Joe Namath AUTO	450.00
TT2	Dan Marino	150.00
TT3	Walter Payton	275.00
TT4	Barry Sanders	150.00
TT5	Joe Montana 50	300.00
TT5A	Joe Montana AUTO 50	450.00
TT6	Steve Young	85.00
TT7	Eric Dickerson 50	50.00
TT7A	Eric Dickerson AUTO 50	150.00
TT8	Edgerrin James	175.00
TT9	Johnny Unitas 75	175.00
TT10	Peyton Manning	175.00
TT11	Bart Starr	175.00
TT12	Brett Favre	150.00
TT13	Terry Bradshaw 50	175.00
TT13A	Terry Bradshaw AUTO 50	450.00
TT14	Kurt Warner	150.00
TT15	Dan Fouts 50	75.00
TT15A	Dan Fouts AUTO 50	150.00
TT16	Drew Bledsoe	85.00
TT17	Earl Campbell 75	125.00
TT17A	Earl Campbell AUTO 25	200.00
TT18	Eddie George	75.00
TT19	Jim Brown	175.00
TT20	Terrell Davis	125.00
TT21	Marcus Allen	75.00
TT22	Emmitt Smith	125.00
TT23	Bob Griese 75	75.00
TT24	Brian Griese	75.00
TT25	Don Meredith AUTO	150.00
TT26	Troy Aikman	100.00
TT27	Ken Stabler 75	100.00
TT27A	Ken Stabler AUTO 25	275.00
TT28	Jake Plummer	50.00
TT29	Fran Tarkenton 75	150.00
TT29A	Fran Tarkenton AUTO 25	275.00
TT30	Mark Brunell	85.00
TT31	Joe Namath, Dan Marino AUTO	1000.
TT32	Walter Payton, Barry Sanders	550.00
TT33	Joe Montana, Steve Young	500.00
TT34	Eric Dickerson, Edgerrin James	250.00
TT35	Johnny Unitas, Peyton Manning	400.00
TT36	Bart Starr, Brett Favre	400.00
TT37	Terry Bradshaw, Kurt Warner	275.00
TT38	Dan Fouts, Drew Bledsoe	125.00
TT39	Earl Campbell, Eddie George	150.00
TT40	Jim Brown, Terrell Davis	300.00
TT41	Marcus Allen, Emmitt Smith	175.00
TT42	Bob Griese, Brian Griese	150.00
TT43	Don Meredith, Troy Aikman AUTO	225.00
TT44	Ken Stabler, Jake Plummer	150.00
TT45	Fran Tarkenton, Mark Brunell	200.00

2000 Donruss Elite Turn of the Century

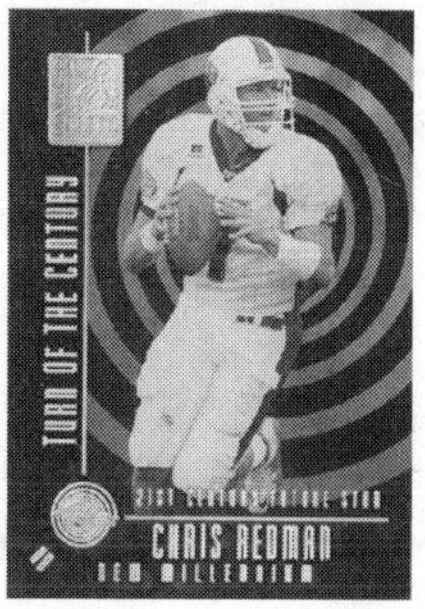

		MT
Complete Set (60):		200.00
Common Player:		1.50
Minor Stars:		3.00
Production 1,000 Sets		
Die Cut Cards:		8x-16x
Production 21 Sets		
TC1	Dan Marino	10.00
TC2	Edgerrin James	10.00
TC3	Peyton Manning	10.00
TC4	Drew Bledsoe	5.00
TC5	Doug Flutie	3.50
TC6	Curtis Martin	3.00
TC7	Eddie George	3.00
TC8	Steve McNair	3.00
TC9	Fred Taylor	3.50
TC10	Mark Brunell	3.50
TC11	Tim Couch	6.00
TC12	Peter Warrick	15.00
TC13	Terrell Davis	8.00
TC14	Jon Kitna	3.00
TC15	Emmitt Smith	8.00
TC16	Troy Aikman	6.00
TC17	Stephen Davis	3.00
TC18	Brad Johnson	3.00
TC19	Jake Plummer	3.00
TC20	Brett Favre	10.00
TC21	Barry Sanders	10.00
TC22	Marshall Faulk	3.00
TC23	Kurt Warner	12.00
TC24	Ricky Williams	6.00
TC25	Steve Young	4.00
TC26	Randy Moss	10.00
TC27	John Elway	10.00
TC28	Jerry Rice	6.00
TC29	Plaxico Burress	10.00
TC30	Cris Carter	3.00
TC31	Antonio Freeman	1.50
TC32	Thomas Jones	8.00
TC33	Travis Taylor	6.00
TC34	Marvin Harrison	3.00
TC35	Keyshawn Johnson	3.00

TC36	Shaun Alexander	7.00
TC37	Isaac Bruce	3.00
TC38	Ricky Watters	1.50
TC39	Ron Dayne	15.00
TC40	Brian Griese	3.50
TC41	Charlie Batch	3.00
TC42	Jamal Lewis	8.00
TC43	Jamal Anderson	3.00
TC44	Dorsey Levens	3.00
TC45	Chris Redman	5.00
TC46	Robert Smith	1.50
TC47	Chad Pennington	10.00
TC48	Terrell Owens	3.00
TC49	Deion Sanders	3.00
TC50	Duce Staley	3.00
TC51	Dez White	4.00
TC52	Jimmy Smith	3.00
TC53	Cade McNown	4.00
TC54	Daunte Culpepper	4.00
TC55	Akili Smith	3.00
TC56	Torry Holt	3.00
TC57	Kevin Johnson	3.00
TC58	Shaun King	4.00
TC59	Olandis Gary	3.00
TC60	Donovan McNabb	4.00

2000 Donruss Preferred

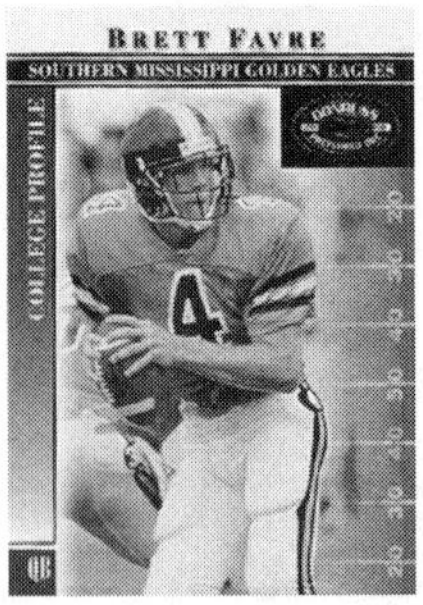
BRETT FAVRE
SOUTHERN MISSISSIPPI GOLDEN EAGLES
COLLEGE PROFILE
QB

		MT
Complete Set (100):		20.00
Common Player:		.20
Minor Stars:		.40
Pack (4plus Graded):		16.00
Wax Box (10):		140.00
1	Jake Plummer	.40
2	Chris Chandler	.20
3	Trent Dilfer	.20
4	Doug Flutie	.50
5	Cade McNown	.40
6	Michael Irvin	.40
7	Troy Aikman	1.00
8	Terrell Davis	1.25
9	John Elway	1.50
10	Brett Favre	1.50
11	Peyton Manning	1.25
12	Warren Moon	.20
13	Randall Cunningham	.20
14	Drew Bledsoe	.60
15	Ricky Williams	.75
16	Kerry Collins	.20
17	Vinny Testaverde	.20
18	Donovan McNabb	.60
19	Jim Harbaugh	.20
20	Jerry Rice	1.00
21	Steve Young	.60
22	Keyshawn Johnson	.40
23	Neil O'Donnell	.20
24	Steve McNair	.50
25	Brad Johnson	.40
26	Jeff George	.40
27	Dan Marino	1.50
28	Jim Kelly	.40
29	Barry Sanders	1.50
30	Phil Simms	.20
31	Gus Frerotte	.20
32	Elvis Grbac	.40
33	Jeff Blake	.20
34	Kordell Stewart	.40
35	Tony Banks	.20
36	Doug Flutie	.50
37	Cade McNown	.40
38	Troy Aikman	1.00
39	Terrell Davis	1.25
40	John Elway	1.50
41	Brett Favre	1.50
42	Peyton Manning	1.25
43	Drew Bledsoe	.60
44	Ricky Williams	.75
45	Kerry Collins	.20
46	Vinny Testaverde	.20
47	Donovan McNabb	.60
48	Kordell Stewart	.40
49	Ryan Leaf	.20
50	Jerry Rice	1.00
51	Steve Young	.60
52	Keyshawn Johnson	.40
53	Steve McNair	.40
54	Jeff George	.40
55	Dan Marino	1.50
56	Jim Kelly	.40
57	Barry Sanders	1.50
58	Bernie Kosar	.20
59	Chris Chandler	.20
60	Jim Everett	.20
61	Jake Plummer	.40
62	Cade McNown	.40
63	Troy Aikman	1.00
64	Ricky Williams	.75
65	Donovan McNabb	.60
66	Steve Young	.60
67	Brad Johnson	.40
68	Kerry Collins	.20
69	Ryan Leaf	.20
70	Drew Bledsoe	.60
71	Jake Plummer	.40
72	Chris Chandler	.20
73	Michael Irvin	.20
74	Troy Aikman	1.00
75	Terrell Davis	1.25
76	John Elway	1.50
77	Brett Favre	1.50
78	Peyton Manning	1.25
79	Drew Bledsoe	.60
80	Junior Seau	.20
81	Jerry Rice	1.00
82	Steve Young	.60
83	Keyshawn Johnson	.40
84	Steve McNair	.40
85	Brad Johnson	.40
86	Dan Marino	1.50
87	Jim Kelly	.40
88	Barry Sanders	1.50
89	Phil Simms	.20
90	Boomer Esiason	.20
91	Jake Plummer	.40
92	Chris Chandler	.20
93	Bubby Brister	.20
94	Cade McNown	.20
95	Jim Harbaugh	.20
96	Peyton Manning	1.25
97	Donovan McNabb	.60
98	Jim Kelly	.40
99	Brad Johnson	.40
100	Kordell Stewart	.40

2000 Donruss Preferred Graded Series

		MT
Common BGS 9.5:		12.00
Common BGS 9:		8.00
Common BGS 8.5:		5.00
Common BGS 8:		5.00
1	Jake Plummer 9.5	15.00
1	Jake Plummer 9.0	10.00
1	Jake Plummer 8.5	6.00
1	Jake Plummer 8.0	6.00
2	Chris Chandler 9.5	12.00
2	Chris Chandler 9.0	8.00
2	Chris Chandler 8.5	5.00
2	Chris Chandler 8.0	5.00
3	Trent Dilfer 9.5	12.00
3	Trent Dilfer 9.0	8.00
3	Trent Dilfer 8.5	5.00
3	Trent Dilfer 8.0	5.00
4	Doug Flutie 9.5	15.00
4	Doug Flutie 9.0	10.00
4	Doug Flutie 8.5	6.00
4	Doug Flutie 8.0	6.00
5	Cade McNown 9.5	12.00
5	Cade McNown 9.0	8.00
5	Cade McNown 8.5	5.00
5	Cade McNown 8.0	5.00
6	Michael Irvin 9.5	12.00
6	Michael Irvin 9.0	8.00
6	Michael Irvin 8.5	5.00
6	Michael Irvin 8.0	5.00
7	Troy Aikman 9.5	20.00
7	Troy Aikman 9.0	13.00
7	Troy Aikman 8.5	8.00
7	Troy Aikman 8.0	8.00
8	Terrell Davis 9.5	25.00
8	Terrell Davis 9.0	15.00
8	Terrell Davis 8.5	10.00
8	Terrell Davis 8.0	10.00
9	John Elway 9.5	25.00
9	John Elway 9.0	15.00
9	John Elway 8.5	10.00
9	John Elway 8.0	10.00
10	Brett Favre 9.5	35.00
10	Brett Favre 9.0	18.00
10	Brett Favre 8.5	12.00
10	Brett Favre 8.0	12.00
11	Peyton Manning 9.5	25.00
11	Peyton Manning 9.0	15.00
11	Peyton Manning 8.5	10.00
11	Peyton Manning 8.0	10.00
12	Warren Moon 9.5	12.00
12	Warren Moon 9.0	8.00
12	Warren Moon 8.5	5.00
12	Warren Moon 8.0	5.00
13	Randall Cunningham 9.5	12.00
13	Randall Cunningham 9.0	8.00
13	Randall Cunningham 8.5	5.00
13	Randall Cunningham 8.0	5.00
14	Drew Bledsoe 9.5	15.00
14	Drew Bledsoe 9.0	10.00
14	Drew Bledsoe 8.5	6.00
14	Drew Bledsoe 8.0	6.00
15	Ricky Williams 9.5	20.00
15	Ricky Williams 9.0	12.00
15	Ricky Williams 8.5	8.00
15	Ricky Williams 8.0	8.00
16	Kerry Collins 9.5	12.00
16	Kerry Collins 9.0	8.00
16	Kerry Collins 8.5	5.00
17	Vinny Testaverde 9.5	12.00
17	Vinny Testaverde 9.0	8.00
17	Vinny Testaverde 8.5	5.00
17	Vinny Testaverde 8.0	5.00
18	Donovan McNabb 9.5	20.00
18	Donovan McNabb 9.0	10.00
18	Donovan McNabb 8.5	6.00
18	Donovan McNabb 8.0	6.00
18	Donovan McNabb 7.5	6.00
19	Jim Harbaugh 9.5	12.00
19	Jim Harbaugh 9.0	8.00
19	Jim Harbaugh 8.5	5.00
19	Jim Harbaugh 8.0	5.00
20	Jerry Rice 9.5	20.00
20	Jerry Rice 9.0	12.00
20	Jerry Rice 8.5	8.00
20	Jerry Rice 8.0	8.00
20	Jerry Rice 7.5	7.00
21	Steve Young 9.5	15.00
21	Steve Young 9.0	10.00
21	Steve Young 8.5	6.00
21	Steve Young 8.0	6.00
22	Keyshawn Johnson 9.5	12.00
22	Keyshawn Johnson 9.0	8.00
22	Keyshawn Johnson 8.5	5.00
22	Keyshawn Johnson 8.0	5.00
23	Neil O'Donnell 9.5	12.00
23	Neil O'Donnell 9.0	8.00
23	Neil O'Donnell 8.5	5.00
23	Neil O'Donnell 8.0	5.00
24	Steve McNair 9.5	12.00
24	Steve McNair 9.0	8.00
24	Steve McNair 8.5	5.00
24	Steve McNair 8.0	5.00
25	Brad Johnson 9.0	12.00
25	Brad Johnson 8.5	8.00
25	Brad Johnson 8.0	5.00
26	Jeff George 9.5	12.00
26	Jeff George 9.0	8.00
26	Jeff George 8.5	5.00
26	Jeff George 8.0	5.00
27	Dan Marino 9.5	25.00
27	Dan Marino 9.0	15.00
27	Dan Marino 8.5	10.00
27	Dan Marino 8.0	10.00
28	Jim Kelly 9.5	12.00
28	Jim Kelly 9.0	8.00
28	Jim Kelly 8.5	5.00
28	Jim Kelly 8.0	5.00
29	Barry Sanders 9.5	25.00
29	Barry Sanders 9.0	15.00
29	Barry Sanders 8.5	10.00
29	Barry Sanders 8.0	10.00
30	Phil Simms 9.5	12.00
30	Phil Simms 9.0	8.00
30	Phil Simms 8.5	5.00
30	Phil Simms 8.0	5.00
31	Gus Frerotte 9.5	12.00
31	Gus Frerotte 9.0	8.00
31	Gus Frerotte 8.5	5.00
31	Gus Frerotte 8.0	5.00
32	Elvis Grbac 9.0	8.00
32	Elvis Grbac 8.5	5.00
32	Elvis Grbac 8.0	5.00
33	Jeff Blake 9.5	12.00
33	Jeff Blake 9.0	8.00
33	Jeff Blake 8.5	5.00
33	Jeff Blake 8.0	5.00
34	Kordell Stewart 9.5	12.00
34	Kordell Stewart 9.0	8.00
34	Kordell Stewart 8.5	5.00
34	Kordell Stewart 8.0	5.00
34	Kordell Stewart 7.5	5.00
35	Tony Banks 9.5	12.00
35	Tony Banks 9.0	8.00
35	Tony Banks 8.5	5.00
35	Tony Banks 8.0	5.00
36	Doug Flutie 9.5	15.00
36	Doug Flutie 9.0	10.00
36	Doug Flutie 8.5	6.00
36	Doug Flutie 8.0	6.00
37	Cade McNown 9.5	12.00
37	Cade McNown 9.0	8.00
37	Cade McNown 8.5	5.00
37	Cade McNown 8.0	5.00
38	Troy Aikman 9.5	20.00
38	Troy Aikman 9.0	12.00
38	Troy Aikman 8.5	8.00
38	Troy Aikman 8.0	8.00
39	Terrell Davis 9.5	25.00
39	Terrell Davis 9.0	15.00
39	Terrell Davis 8.5	10.00
39	Terrell Davis 8.0	10.00
40	John Elway 9.5	25.00
40	John Elway 9.0	15.00
40	John Elway 8.5	10.00
40	John Elway 8.0	10.00
41	Brett Favre 9.5	35.00
41	Brett Favre 9.0	18.00
41	Brett Favre 8.5	12.00
41	Brett Favre 8.0	12.00
41	Brett Favre 7.5	10.00
42	Peyton Manning 9.5	25.00
42	Peyton Manning 9.0	15.00
42	Peyton Manning 8.5	10.00
42	Peyton Manning 8.0	10.00
43	Drew Bledsoe 9.5	15.00
43	Drew Bledsoe 9.0	10.00
43	Drew Bledsoe 8.5	6.00
43	Drew Bledsoe 8.0	6.00
44	Ricky Williams 9.5	20.00
44	Ricky Williams 9.0	12.00
44	Ricky Williams 8.5	8.00
44	Ricky Williams 8.0	8.00
45	Kerry Collins 9.5	12.00
45	Kerry Collins 9.0	8.00
45	Kerry Collins 8.5	5.00
45	Kerry Collins 8.0	5.00
46	Vinny Testaverde 9.5	12.00
46	Vinny Testaverde 9.0	8.00
46	Vinny Testaverde 8.5	5.00
46	Vinny Testaverde 8.0	5.00
47	Donovan McNabb 9.5	20.00
47	Donovan McNabb 9.0	10.00
47	Donovan McNabb 8.5	6.00
47	Donovan McNabb 8.0	6.00
48	Kordell Stewart 9.5	12.00
48	Kordell Stewart 9.0	8.00
48	Kordell Stewart 8.5	5.00
48	Kordell Stewart 8.0	5.00
49	Ryan Leaf 9.5	12.00
49	Ryan Leaf 9.0	8.00
49	Ryan Leaf 8.5	5.00
50	Jerry Rice 9.5	20.00
50	Jerry Rice 9.0	12.00
50	Jerry Rice 8.5	8.00
50	Jerry Rice 8.0	8.00
51	Steve Young 9.5	15.00
51	Steve Young 9.0	10.00
51	Steve Young 8.5	6.00
51	Steve Young 8.0	6.00
52	Keyshawn Johnson 9.5	12.00
52	Keyshawn Johnson 9.0	8.00
52	Keyshawn Johnson 8.5	5.00
52	Keyshawn Johnson 8.0	5.00
53	Steve McNair 9.5	12.00
53	Steve McNair 9.0	8.00
53	Steve McNair 8.5	5.00
53	Steve McNair 8.0	5.00
54	Jeff George 9.5	12.00
54	Jeff George 9.0	8.00
54	Jeff George 8.5	5.00
55	Dan Marino 9.5	25.00
55	Dan Marino 9.0	15.00
55	Dan Marino 8.5	10.00
55	Dan Marino 8.0	10.00
56	Jim Kelly 9.5	12.00
56	Jim Kelly 9.0	8.00
56	Jim Kelly 8.5	5.00
56	Jim Kelly 8.0	5.00
57	Barry Sanders 9.5	25.00
57	Barry Sanders 9.0	15.00
57	Barry Sanders 8.5	10.00
57	Barry Sanders 8.0	10.00
58	Bernie Kosar 9.5	12.00
58	Bernie Kosar 9.0	8.00
58	Bernie Kosar 8.5	5.00
58	Bernie Kosar 8.0	5.00
59	Chris Chandler 9.5	12.00
59	Chris Chandler 9.0	8.00
59	Chris Chandler 8.5	5.00
59	Chris Chandler 8.0	5.00
60	Jim Everett 9.5	12.00
60	Jim Everett 9.0	8.00
60	Jim Everett 8.5	5.00
60	Jim Everett 8.0	5.00
61	Jake Plummer 9.5	15.00
61	Jake Plummer 9.0	10.00
61	Jake Plummer 8.5	6.00
61	Jake Plummer 8.0	6.00
62	Cade McNown 9.5	12.00
62	Cade McNown 9.0	8.00
62	Cade McNown 8.5	5.00
62	Cade McNown 8.0	5.00
62	Cade McNown 7.5	5.00
63	Troy Aikman 9.5	20.00
63	Troy Aikman 9.0	12.00
63	Troy Aikman 8.5	8.00
63	Troy Aikman 8.0	8.00
64	Ricky Williams 9.5	20.00
64	Ricky Williams 9.0	12.00
64	Ricky Williams 8.5	8.00
64	Ricky Williams 8.0	8.00
65	Donovan McNabb 9.5	20.00
65	Donovan McNabb 9.0	10.00
65	Donovan McNabb 8.5	6.00
66	Steve Young 9.5	15.00
66	Steve Young 9.0	10.00
66	Steve Young 8.5	6.00
66	Steve Young 8.0	6.00
67	Brad Johnson 9.5	12.00
67	Brad Johnson 9.0	8.00
67	Brad Johnson 8.5	5.00
67	Brad Johnson 8.0	5.00
68	Kerry Collins 9.0	8.00
68	Kerry Collins 8.5	5.00
68	Kerry Collins 8.0	5.00
69	Ryan Leaf 9.5	12.00
69	Ryan Leaf 9.0	8.00
69	Ryan Leaf 8.5	5.00
69	Ryan Leaf 8.0	5.00
70	Drew Bledsoe 9.5	15.00
70	Drew Bledsoe 9.0	10.00
70	Drew Bledsoe 8.5	6.00
70	Drew Bledsoe 8.0	6.00
71	Jake Plummer 9.5	15.00
71	Jake Plummer 9.0	10.00
71	Jake Plummer 8.5	6.00
71	Jake Plummer 8.0	6.00
72	Chris Chandler 9.5	12.00
72	Chris Chandler 9.0	8.00
72	Chris Chandler 8.5	5.00
72	Chris Chandler 8.0	5.00
73	Michael Irvin 9.5	12.00
73	Michael Irvin 9.0	8.00
73	Michael Irvin 8.5	5.00
73	Michael Irvin 8.0	5.00
74	Troy Aikman 9.5	20.00
74	Troy Aikman 9.0	12.00
74	Troy Aikman 8.5	8.00
74	Troy Aikman 8.0	8.00
75	Terrell Davis 9.5	25.00
75	Terrell Davis 9.0	15.00
75	Terrell Davis 8.5	10.00
75	Terrell Davis 8.0	10.00
76	John Elway 9.5	25.00
76	John Elway 9.0	15.00
76	John Elway 8.5	10.00
76	John Elway 8.0	10.00
77	Brett Favre 9.5	35.00
77	Brett Favre 9.0	18.00
77	Brett Favre 8.5	12.00
77	Brett Favre 8.0	12.00
78	Peyton Manning 9.5	15.00
78	Peyton Manning 9.0	10.00
78	Peyton Manning 8.5	7.00
78	Peyton Manning 8.0	7.00
79	Drew Bledsoe 9.5	15.00
79	Drew Bledsoe 9.0	10.00
79	Drew Bledsoe 8.5	6.00
79	Drew Bledsoe 8.0	6.00
80	Junior Seau 9.5	12.00
80	Junior Seau 9.0	8.00
80	Junior Seau 8.5	5.00
80	Junior Seau 8.0	5.00
81	Jerry Rice 9.5	20.00
81	Jerry Rice 9.0	12.00
81	Jerry Rice 8.5	8.00
81	Jerry Rice 8.0	8.00
82	Steve Young 9.5	15.00
82	Steve Young 9.0	10.00
82	Steve Young 8.5	6.00
82	Steve Young 8.0	6.00
82	Steve Young 7.5	6.00
83	Keyshawn Johnson 9.5	12.00
83	Keyshawn Johnson 9.0	8.00
83	Keyshawn Johnson 8.5	5.00
83	Keyshawn Johnson 8.0	5.00
84	Steve McNair 9.5	12.00
84	Steve McNair 9.0	8.00
84	Steve McNair 8.5	5.00
84	Steve McNair 8.0	5.00
85	Brad Johnson 9.5	12.00
85	Brad Johnson 9.0	8.00
85	Brad Johnson 8.5	5.00
85	Brad Johnson 8.0	5.00
86	Dan Marino 9.5	25.00
86	Dan Marino 9.0	15.00
86	Dan Marino 8.5	10.00
86	Dan Marino 8.0	10.00
87	Jim Kelly 9.5	12.00
87	Jim Kelly 9.0	8.00
87	Jim Kelly 8.5	5.00
87	Jim Kelly 8.0	5.00
88	Barry Sanders 9.5	25.00
88	Barry Sanders 9.0	15.00
88	Barry Sanders 8.5	10.00
88	Barry Sanders 8.0	10.00
89	Phil Simms 9.5	12.00
89	Phil Simms 9.0	8.00
89	Phil Simms 8.5	5.00
89	Phil Simms 8.0	5.00
90	Boomer Esiason 9.5	12.00
90	Boomer Esiason 9.0	8.00
90	Boomer Esiason 8.5	5.00
90	Boomer Esiason 8.0	5.00
91	Jake Plummer 9.5	15.00
91	Jake Plummer 9.0	10.00
91	Jake Plummer 8.5	6.00
91	Jake Plummer 8.0	6.00
92	Chris Chandler 9.5	12.00
92	Chris Chandler 9.0	8.00
92	Chris Chandler 8.5	5.00
92	Chris Chandler 8.0	5.00
93	Bubby Brister 9.5	12.00
93	Bubby Brister 9.0	8.00
93	Bubby Brister 8.5	5.00
93	Bubby Brister 8.0	5.00
94	Cade McNown 9.5	15.00
94	Cade McNown 9.0	10.00
94	Cade McNown 8.5	6.00
94	Cade McNown 8.0	6.00
95	Jim Harbaugh 9.5	12.00
95	Jim Harbaugh 9.0	8.00
95	Jim Harbaugh 8.5	5.00
95	Jim Harbaugh 8.0	5.00
96	Peyton Manning 9.5	25.00
96	Peyton Manning 9.0	15.00
96	Peyton Manning 8.5	10.00
96	Peyton Manning 8.0	10.00
97	Donovan McNabb 9.5	20.00
97	Donovan McNabb 9.0	10.00
97	Donovan McNabb 8.5	7.00
97	Donovan McNabb 8.0	7.00
98	Jim Kelly 9.5	15.00
98	Jim Kelly 9.0	10.00
98	Jim Kelly 8.5	6.00
98	Jim Kelly 8.0	6.00
99	Brad Johnson 9.5	12.00
99	Brad Johnson 9.0	8.00
99	Brad Johnson 8.5	5.00
99	Brad Johnson 8.0	5.00
100	Kordell Stewart 9.5	15.00
100	Kordell Stewart 9.0	10.00
100	Kordell Stewart 8.5	6.00
100	Kordell Stewart 8.0	6.00
101	Rob Johnson 9.5	12.00
101	Rob Johnson 9.0	8.00
101	Rob Johnson 8.5	5.00
101	Rob Johnson 8.0	5.00
102	Jevon Kearse 9.5	12.00
102	Jevon Kearse 9.0	8.00
102	Jevon Kearse 8.5	5.00
103	Rich Gannon 9.5	12.00
103	Rich Gannon 9.0	8.00
103	Rich Gannon 8.5	5.00
103	Rich Gannon 8.0	5.00

2000 Donruss Preferred Power Parallel

	MT
#1-20 Power:	3x-6x
Production 750 Sets	
#21-40 Power:	4x-8x
Production 500 Sets	
#41-60 Power:	5x-10x
Production 300 Sets	
#61-80 Power:	6x-12x
Production 150 Sets	
#81-103 Power:	15x-30x
Production 50 Sets	

2000 Donruss Preferred Materials

		MT
Common Player 125:		40.00
Common Player 300:		20.00
Inserted 1:34		
1	Jerry Rice H 125	120.00
2	John Elway H 125	150.00
3	Doug Flutie H 125	85.00
4	Barry Sanders H 125	125.00
5	Dan Marino P 250	100.00
6	Jerry Rice P 250	75.00
7	Steve McNair S 50	60.00
9	Peyton Manning S 125	120.00
10	Steve Young S 125	50.00
11	John Elway S 125	125.00
12	Dan Marino S 125	125.00
14	Kordell Stewart	20.00
15	Brett Favre S 125	120.00
16	Barry Sanders S 125	120.00
17	Randall Cunningham	20.00
18	Bernie Kosar	20.00
19	Boomer Esiason	20.00
20	Brett Favre J 100	120.00
21	Barry Sanders J 200	75.00
22	Cade McNown	20.00
23	Dan Marino J 300	75.00
24	Drew Bledsoe J 100	50.00
25	Doug Flutie Wh. J 300	25.00
26	Doug Flutie Bl. J 300	25.00
27	Donovan McNabb J 300	30.00
28	Jerry Rice J 300	50.00
29	Jim Harbaugh	20.00
30	Jim Kelly	40.00
31	John Elway J 100	100.00
32	Jake Plummer	20.00
33	Junior Seau	20.00
34	Kordell Stewart	30.00
35	Phil Simms	30.00
36	Peyton Manning J 100	100.00
37	Randall Cunningham	20.00
38	Ricky Williams Wh. J 100	70.00
39	Ricky Williams Bl. J 100	70.00
40	Steve McNair J 100	45.00
41	Steve Young J 300	30.00
42	Troy Aikman J 100	85.00
43	Vinny Testaverde	20.00
44	Warren Moon	20.00

2000 Donruss Preferred National Treasures

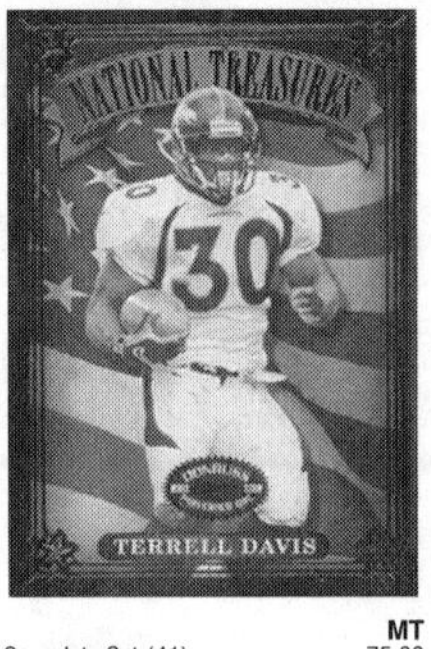
NATIONAL TREASURES
TERRELL DAVIS

		MT
Complete Set (41):		75.00
Common Player:		1.50
Minor Stars:		3.00
Inserted 1:8		
Production 1,000 Sets		
1	Warren Moon	1.50
2	Steve Young	4.00
3	Jeff Blake	1.50
4	Brett Favre	12.00
5	Donovan McNabb	3.50
6	Bubby Brister	1.50
7	John Elway	8.00
8	Troy Aikman	6.00
9	Steve McNair	3.00
10	Kordell Stewart	3.00
11	Drew Bledsoe	4.00
12	Chris Chandler	1.50
13	Dan Marino	8.00
14	Brad Johnson	1.50
15	Jim Kelly	3.00
16	Jake Plummer	3.00
17	Boomer Esiason	1.50
18	Peyton Manning	10.00
19	Keyshawn Johnson	3.00
20	Barry Sanders	10.00
21	Bernie Kosar	1.50
22	Cade McNown	3.00
23	Elvis Grbac	1.50
24	Junior Seau	1.50
25	Phil Simms	3.00
26	Jim Everett	1.50
27	Vinny Testaverde	3.00
28	Jerry Rice	6.00
29	Terrell Davis	8.00
30	Ryan Leaf	3.00
31	Neil O'Donnell	1.50
32	Ricky Williams	5.00
33	Michael Irvin	3.00
34	Jim Harbaugh	1.50
36	Jeff George	3.00
36	Gus Frerotte	1.50
37	Doug Flutie	3.50
38	Trent Dilfer	3.00
39	Randall Cunningham	3.00
40	Kerry Collins	3.00
41	Tony Banks	1.50

2000 Donruss Preferred Pass Time

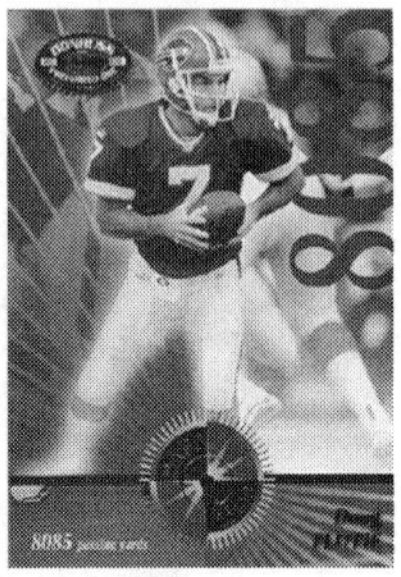

		MT
Complete Set (20):		70.00
Common Player:		2.50
Inserted 1:31		
Production 500 Sets		
1	John Elway	12.00
2	Jim Kelly	5.00
3	Steve McNair	2.50
4	Doug Flutie	5.00
5	Dan Marino	12.00
6	Brett Favre	15.00
7	Cade McNown	4.00
8	Elvis Grbac	2.50
9	Vinny Testaverde	2.50
10	Kordell Stewart	4.00
11	Donovan McNabb	5.00
12	Jake Plummer	4.00
13	Troy Aikman	8.00
14	Chris Chandler	2.50
15	Kerry Collins	2.50
16	Peyton Manning	10.00
17	Steve Young	5.00
18	Brad Johnson	2.50
19	Jeff Blake	2.50
20	Drew Bledsoe	5.00

2001 Donruss Classics

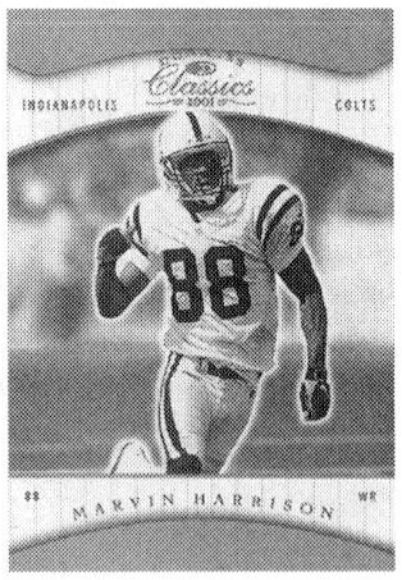
INDIANAPOLIS
COLTS
MARVIN HARRISON
WR

		MT
Complete Set (200):		450.00
Common Player:		.15
Minor Stars:		.30
Common Rookie:		4.00
Production 475 Sets		
Common Legends:		1.00
Production 1,425 Sets		
1	David Boston	.50
2	Jake Plummer	.50
3	Thomas Jones	.30
4	Jamal Anderson	.50
5	Chris Redman	.30
6	Elvis Grbac	.30
7	Jamal Lewis	1.50
8	Qadry Ismail	.30
9	Ray Lewis	.50
10	Shannon Sharpe	.30
11	Travis Taylor	.30
12	Eric Moulds	.50
13	Rob Johnson	.30
14	Muhsin Muhammad	.50
15	Brian Urlacher	1.25
16	Cade McNown	.50
17	Marcus Robinson	.50
18	Akili Smith	.50
19	Corey Dillon	.50
20	Peter Warrick	.75
21	Courtney Brown	.30
22	Tim Couch	.75
23	Emmitt Smith	1.50
24	Brian Griese	.60
25	Ed McCaffrey	.50

26 Olandis Gary .50
27 Mike Anderson 1.50
28 Rod Smith .50
29 Terrell Davis 1.25
30 Charlie Batch .50
31 James Stewart .30
32 Ahman Green .50
33 Antonio Freeman .40
34 Brett Favre 2.50
35 Edgerrin James 1.50
36 Marvin Harrison .50
37 Peyton Manning 2.00
38 Fred Taylor .75
39 Jimmy Smith .40
40 Keenan McCardell .30
41 Mark Brunell .75
42 Sylvester Morris .30
43 Tony Gonzalez .30
44 Zach Thomas .30
45 Jay Fiedler .30
46 Lamar Smith .30
47 Cris Carter .50
48 Daunte Culpepper 1.25
49 Randy Moss 2.00
50 Drew Bledsoe .75
51 Terry Glenn .40
52 Aaron Brooks .50
53 Joe Horn .30
54 Ricky Williams 1.00
55 Amani Toomer .30
56 Ike Hilliard .30
57 Kerry Collins .30
58 Ron Dayne 1.00
59 Tiki Barber .50
60 Chad Pennington .50
61 Curtis Martin .50
62 Laveranues Coles .30
63 Vinny Testaverde .30
64 Wayne Chrebet .50
65 Charles Woodson .50
66 Rich Gannon .40
67 Tim Brown .40
68 Tyrone Wheatley .30
69 Corey Simon .30
70 Donovan McNabb 1.00
71 Duce Staley .50
72 Jerome Bettis .50
73 Plaxico Burress .50
74 Doug Flutie .75
75 Junior Seau .40
76 Jeff Garcia .50
77 Jerry Rice 1.50
78 Giovanni Carmazzi .30
79 Terrell Owens .50
80 Darrell Jackson .30
81 Ricky Watters .40
82 Shaun Alexander .50
83 Isaac Bruce .50
84 Kurt Warner 3.00
85 Marshall Faulk .75
86 Torry Holt .50
87 Brad Johnson .40
88 Keyshawn Johnson .50
89 Mike Alstott .50
90 Shaun King .50
91 Warren Sapp .40
92 Warrick Dunn .50
93 Eddie George .75
94 Jevon Kearse .50
95 Steve McNair .50
96 Jeff George .30
97 Stephen Davis .50
98 Charlie Garner .40
99 Trent Dilfer .40
100 Troy Aikman 1.25
101 *Michael Vick* 40.00
102 *Drew Brees* 30.00
103 *Chris Weinke* 20.00
104 *Mike McMahon* 15.00
105 *Jesse Palmer* 8.00
106 *Quincy Carter* 20.00
107 *Josh Heupel* 12.00
108 *Tim Hasselbeck* 8.00
109 *LaDainian Tomlinson* 30.00
110 *Deuce McAllister* 20.00
111 *Michael Bennett* 20.00
112 *Anthony Thomas* 40.00
113 *LaMont Jordan* 10.00
114 *Travis Henry* 15.00
115 *Kevan Barlow* 12.00
116 *Travis Minor* 10.00
117 *Rudi Johnson* 8.00
118 *David Allen* 5.00
119 *Heath Evans* 4.00
120 *Moran Norris* 4.00
121 *David Terrell* 20.00
122 *Koren Robinson* 12.00
123 *Rod Gardner* 15.00
124 *Santana Moss* 15.00
125 *Freddie Mitchell* 15.00
126 *Reggie Wayne* 15.00
127 *Quincy Morgan* 10.00
128 *Chad Johnson* 10.00
129 *Robert Ferguson* 8.00
130 *Chris Chambers* 20.00
131 *Marvin "Snoop" Minnis* 12.00
132 *Eddie Berlin* 4.00
133 *Alex Bannister* 7.00
134 *Todd Heap* 7.00
135 *Alge Crumpler* 7.00
136 *Justin Smith* 7.00
137 *Andre Carter* 7.00
138 *Jamal Reynolds* 7.00
139 *Richard Seymour* 5.00
140 *Marcus Stroud* 6.00
141 *Casey Hampton* 5.00
142 *Gerard Warren* 10.00
143 *Torrance Marshall* 7.00
144 *Brian Allen* 4.00
145 *Morlon Greenwood* 5.00
146 *Keith Adams* 4.00
147 *Will Allen* 5.00
148 *Nate Clements* 5.00
149 *Adam Archuleta* 10.00
150 *Hakim Akbar* 4.00
151 James Lofton 1.00
152 Jim Kelly 2.00
154 Mike Singletary 1.50
155 Boomer Esiason 1.25
156 Charlie Joiner 1.00
157 Ken Anderson 1.50
158 Y.A. Tittle 2.00
159 Jim Brown 3.50
160 Otto Graham 2.00
161 Ozzie Newsome 1.25
162 Drew Pearson 1.50
163 Lance Alworth 1.50
164 Roger Staubach 4.00
165 Tony Dorsett 2.00
166 John Elway 5.00
167 Barry Sanders 3.50
168 Bart Starr 4.00
169 Paul Hornung 2.00
171 Warren Moon 1.50
172 Johnny Unitas 3.00
173 Deacon Jones 1.50
174 Eric Dickerson 1.50
175 Bob Griese 2.00
176 Dan Marino 5.00
177 Larry Csonka 1.75
178 Paul Warfield 1.75
179 Fran Tarkenton 2.50
180 Archie Manning 1.50
181 Frank Gifford 3.00
182 Lawrence Taylor 1.50
183 Dan Fouts 2.00
184 Don Maynard 1.50
185 Joe Namath 4.00
186 Fred Biletnikoff 2.00
187 Marcus Allen 2.00
188 Jim Plunkett 1.50
189 Franco Harris 2.00
190 Terry Bradshaw 4.00
191 Joe Montana 7.00
192 Roger Craig 1.50
193 Steve Young 2.50
194 Dwight Clark 1.00
195 Steve Largent 2.00
196 Art Monk 1.50
197 Charley Taylor 1.50
198 Joe Theismann 2.00
199 Sammy Baugh 2.00
200 Sonny Jurgensen 2.00

2001 Donruss Classics Combos

MT
Common Player: 30.00
Dual Cards #'d to 100
Quad Cards #'d to 25

1 Walter Payton, Gale Sayers 75 175.00
1A Walter Payton, Gale Sayers AUTO 25
2 Cade McNown, Jim McMahon 100.00
3 Roger Staubach, Tony Dorsett 75.00
4 Troy Aikman, Emmitt Smith 75.00
5 Terry Bradshaw, Franco Harris 75.00
6 Jack Ham, Joe Greene 100.00
7 Joe Montana, Jerry Rice 150.00
8 Steve Young, Terrell Owens 50.00
9 Jim Kelly, Thurman Thomas 50.00
10 Doug Flutie, Eric Moulds 50.00
11 Joe Namath, Don Maynard 100.00
12 Vinny Testaverde, Curtis Martin 25.00
13 Deacon Jones, Fred Dryer 50.00
14 Kurt Warner, Isaac Bruce 50.00
15 Joe Montana, Marcus Allen 100.00
16 Tony Gonzalez, Sylvester Morris 25.00
17 Phil Simms, Lawrence Taylor 100.00
18 Kerry Collins, Ron Dayne 25.00
19 Jim Plunkett, George Blanda 50.00
20 Ken Stabler, Daryle Lamonica 100.00
21 Earl Campbell, Warren Moon 50.00
22 Eddie George, Steve McNair 50.00
23 Dan Marino, John Elway 100.00
24 Brian Griese, Jay Fiedler 50.00
25 Barry Sanders, Eric Dickerson 50.00
26 Marshall Faulk, Terrell Davis 50.00
27 Peyton Manning, Edgerrin James 50.00
28 Mark Brunell, Fred Taylor 50.00
29 Daunte Culpepper, Randy Moss 75.00
30 Brett Favre, Antonio Freeman 50.00
31 Walter Payton, Gale Sayers, Cade McNown, Jim McMahon
32 Roger Staubach, Tony Dorsett, Troy Aikman, Emmitt Smith
33 Terry Bradshaw, Franco Harris, Jack Ham, Joe Greene
34 Joe Montana, Jerry Rice, Steve Young, Terrell Owens
35 Jim Kelly, Thurman Thomas, Doug Flutie, Eric Moulds
36 Joe Namath, Don Maynard, Vinny Testaverde, Curtis Martin
37 Deacon Jones, Fred Dryer, Kurt Warner, Isaac Bruce
38 Joe Montana, Marcus Allen, Tony Gonzalez, Sylvester Morris
39 Phil Simms, Lawrence Taylor, Kerry Collins, Ron Dayne
40 Jim Plunkett, George Blanda, Ken Stabler, Daryle Lamonica
41 Earl Campbell, Warren Moon, Eddie George, Steve McNair
42 Dan Marino, John Elway, Jay Fiedler, Brian Griese
43 Barry Sanders, Eric Dickerson, Marshall Faulk, Terrell Davis
44 Peyton Manning, Edgerrin James, Mark Brunell, Fred Taylor
45 Daunte Culpepper, Randy Moss, Brett Favre, Antonio Freeman

2001 Donruss Classics Hash Marks

MT
Complete Set (25): 280.00
Common Player: 15.00
Inserted 1:box

1 Jamal Lewis 20.00
2 Jim Kelly 20.00
3 Archie Griffin 15.00
4 Walter Payton 35.00
5 Emmitt Smith 25.00
6 Troy Aikman 20.00
7 John Elway 30.00
8 Barry Sanders 25.00
9 Bart Starr 20.00
10 Brett Favre 30.00
11 Reggie White 15.00
12 Edgerrin James 25.00
13 Dan Marino 30.00
14 Fran Tarkenton 15.00
15 Cris Carter 15.00
16 Cris Collinsworth 15.00
17 Fred Biletnikoff 15.00
18 George Blanda 15.00
19 Donovan McNabb 20.00
20 Jerry Rice 25.00
21 Steve Young 18.00
22 Steve Largent 15.00
23 Marshall Faulk 18.00
24 Eddie George 18.00
25 Joe Theismann 15.00

2001 Donruss Classics Hash Marks Autographs

MT
Common Player:

2 Jim Kelly 50.00
3 Archie Griffin 10.00
7 John Elway 100.00
8 Barry Sanders 100.00
9 Bart Starr 100.00
14 Fran Tarkenton 100.00
16 Cris Collinsworth 10.00
18 George Blanda 25.00

2001 Donruss Classics Significant Signatures

MT
Common Player: 12.00
Inserted 1:18

101 Michael Vick 25 125.00
102 Drew Brees 75.00
103 Chris Weinke 55.00
104 Mike McMahon 20.00
105 Jesse Palmer 15.00
106 Quincy Carter 40.00
107 Josh Heupel 20.00
108 Tim Hasselbeck 15.00
109 LaDainian Tomlinson 100.00
110 Deuce McAllister 25 35.00
111 Michael Bennett 45.00
112 Anthony Thomas 55.00
113 LaMont Jordan 15.00
114 Travis Henry 30.00
115 Kevan Barlow 25.00
116 Travis Minor 15.00
117 Rudi Johnson 15.00
118 David Allen 12.00
119 Heath Evans 12.00
120 Moran Norris 12.00
121 David Terrell 25 40.00
122 Koren Robinson 25 30.00
123 Rod Gardner 25 30.00
124 Santana Moss 30.00
125 Freddie Mitchell 25.00
126 Reggie Wayne 25.00
127 Quincy Morgan 25.00
128 Chad Johnson 20.00
129 Robert Ferguson 15.00
130 Chris Chambers 20.00
131 Marvin "Snoop" Minnis 20.00
132 Eddie Berlin 15.00
133 Alex Bannister 15.00
134 Todd Heap 15.00
135 Alge Crumpler 15.00
136 Justin Smith 12.00
137 Andre Carter 15.00
138 Jamal Reynolds 15.00
139 Richard Seymour 12.00
140 Marcus Stroud 12.00
141 Casey Hampton 12.00
142 Gerald Warren 20.00
143 Torrance Marshall 12.00
144 Brian Allen 12.00
145 Morlon Greenwood 12.00
146 Keith Adams 12.00
147 Will Allen 15.00
148 Nate Clements 12.00
149 Adam Archuleta 18.00
150 Hakim Akbar 12.00
151 James Lofton 15.00
152 Jim Kelly 45.00
153 Gale Sayers 35.00
154 Mike Singletary 15.00
155 Boomer Esiason 18.00
156 Charlie Joiner 12.00
157 Ken Anderson 15.00
158 Y.A. Tittle 18.00
159 Jim Brown 60.00
160 Otto Graham 20.00
161 Ozzie Newsome 12.00
162 Drew Pearson 12.00
163 Lance Alworth 30.00
164 Roger Staubach 50.00
165 Tony Dorsett 40.00
166 John Elway 50 125.00
167 Barry Sanders 125.00
168 Bart Starr 100.00
169 Paul Hornung 30.00
170 Earl Campbell 25.00
171 Warren Moon 25.00
172 Johnny Unitas 50.00
173 Deacon Jones 15.00
174 Eric Dickerson 25.00
175 Bob Griese 40.00
176 Dan Marino 50 125.00
177 Larry Csonka 35.00
178 Paul Warfield 15.00
179 Fran Tarkenton 25.00
180 Archie Manning 18.00
181 Frank Gifford 30.00
182 Lawrence Taylor 25.00
183 Dan Fouts 20.00
184 Don Maynard 15.00
185 Joe Namath 85.00
186 Fred Biletnikoff 20.00
187 Marcus Allen 35.00
188 Jim Plunkett 15.00
189 Franco Harris 25.00
190 Terry Bradshaw 65.00
191 Joe Montana 125.00
192 Roger Craig 12.00
193 Steve Young 35.00
194 Dwight Clark 12.00
195 Steve Largent 20.00
196 Art Monk 15.00
197 Charlie Taylor 12.00
198 Joe Theismann 20.00
199 Sammy Baugh 25.00
200 Sonny Jurgenson 25.00

2001 Donruss Classics Stadium Stars

MT
Complete Set (25): 225.00
Common Player: 10.00
Inserted 1:18
Card #12 Never Released

1 Johnny Unitas 20.00
2 Raymond Berry 10.00
3 Jamal Lewis 15.00
4 Ray Lewis 10.00
5 Eddie George 12.00
6 Jim Brown 25.00
7 Ozzie Newsome 10.00
8 Paul Warfield 10.00
9 Tim Couch 12.00
10 John Elway 25.00
11 Rocky Bleier 12.00
13 Jack Lambert 18.00
14 John Stallworth 15.00
15 Bernie Kosar 12.00
16 Jerome Bettis 12.00
17 Emmitt Smith 20.00
18 Troy Aikman 15.00
19 Barry Sanders 20.00
20 Brett Favre 25.00
21 Donovan McNabb 15.00
22 Corey Dillon 12.00
23 Jerry Rice 18.00
24 Steve Young 12.00
25 Dan Marino 25.00

2001 Donruss Classics Stadium Stars Autographs

MT
Common Player: 25.00
Randomly Inserted

1 Johnny Unitas 25.00
2 Raymond Berry 25.00
6 Jim Brown 25.00
7 Ozzie Newsome 25.00
8 Paul Warfield 25.00
11 Rocky Bleier 25.00
13 Jack Lambert 25.00
14 John Stallworth 25.00
24 Steve Young 25.00

2001 Donruss Classics Team Colors

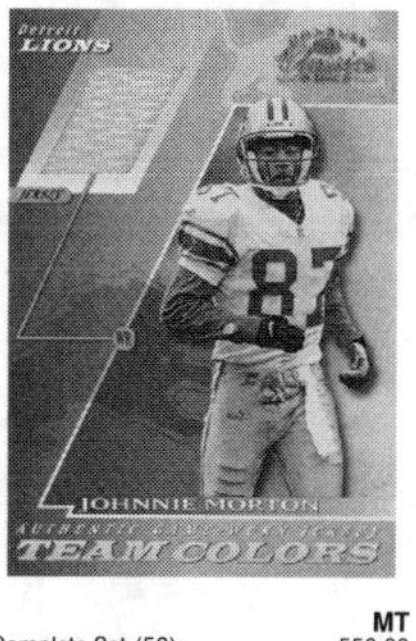

MT
Complete Set (50): 550.00
Common Player: 10.00
Inserted 1:18

1 John Elway 65.00
2 Brian Griese 20.00
3 Terrell Davis 30.00
4 Olandis Gary 10.00
5 Rod Smith 10.00
6 Ed McCaffrey 10.00
7 Allen Aldridge, Bill Romanowski, John Mobley, Keith Traylor, Neil Smith, Trevor Pryce 25.00
8 Dan Neil, Gary Zimmerman, Mark Schlereth 20.00
9 Kurt Warner 35.00
10 Marshall Faulk 20.00
11 Isaac Bruce 18.00
12 London Fletcher, Mike Jones, Todd Lyght 20.00
13 Az-Zahir Hakim, Isaac Bruce, Torry Holt 40.00
14 Marshall Faulk, Justin Watson, Robert Holcombe 30.00
15 Eddie George PANTS 20.00
16 Eddie George 20.00
17 Jevon Kearse PANTS 15.00
18 Jevon Kearse 15.00
19 Steve McNair 12.00
20 Brett Favre 35.00
21 Antonio Freeman 10.00
22 Dorsey Levens 10.00
23 LeRoy Butler 10.00
24 Daunte Culpepper 25.00
25 Warren Moon 15.00
26 Cris Carter, Jake Reed, Randy Moss 50.00
27 Mark Brunell 15.00
28 Fred Taylor 15.00
29 Jimmy Smith, Keenan McCardell, R. Jay Soward 20.00
30 Hardy Nickerson 10.00
31 Tony Boselli 10.00
32 Troy Aikman 30.00
33 Emmitt Smith 45.00
34 Daryl Johnston 20.00
35 Deion Sanders 25.00
36 Bill Bates 15.00
37 Michael Irvin 20.00
38 Barry Sanders 50.00
39 Sedrick Irvin 10.00
40 Charlie Batch 12.00
41 Herman Moore 10.00
42 Johnnie Morton 10.00
43 Donovan McNabb 15.00
44 Irving Fryar 10.00
45 Charles Johnson 10.00
46 Duce Staley 12.00
47 Curtis Martin 15.00
48 Bryan Cox 10.00
49 Vinny Testaverde 10.00
50 Ray Lucas, Keyshawn Johnson, Wayne Chrebet 20.00

2001 Donruss Classics Team Colors Autos

MT
Complete Set (5):
Common Player:

9 Kurt Warner
25 Warren Moon
34 Daryl Johnston
36 Bill Bates
44 Irving Fryar

2001 Donruss Classics Timeless Treasures

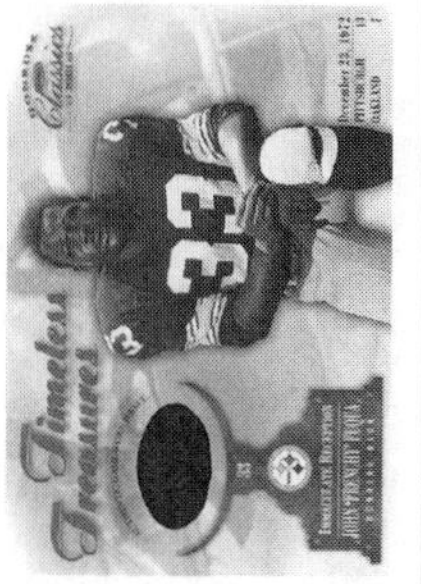

MT
Common Player: 25.00
Inserted 1:340

1 Mike Anderson 60.00
2 Frenchy Fuqua 25.00
3 Corey Dillon 25.00
4 Jamal Lewis 35.00
5 Drew Bledsoe 35.00

2001 Donruss Classics Timeless Tributes

MT
TT Cards: 6x-12x
TT Rookies: 2x
Production 100 Sets

2001 Donruss Elite

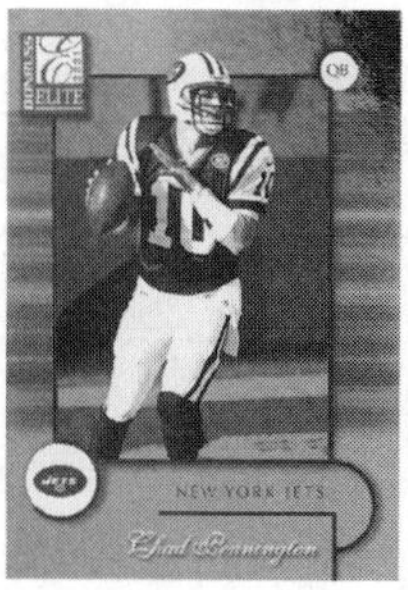

MT
Complete Set (200): 1500.
Common Player: .15
Minor Stars: .30
Common Rookie: 7.00
Production 500 Sets
Rookie Autographs: 2x
First 50 Rookies Signed
Pack (5): 4.00
Wax Box (18): 65.00

1 David Boston .50
2 Jake Plummer .50
3 Thomas Jones .50
4 Chris Redman .50
5 Jamal Anderson .50
6 Jamal Lewis 1.50
7 Shannon Sharpe .30
8 Travis Taylor .50
9 Trent Dilfer .30
10 Doug Flutie .50
11 Eric Moulds .50
12 Rob Johnson .30
13 Muhsin Muhammad .30
14 Steve Beuerlein .30
15 Brian Urlacher 1.00
16 Cade McNown .50
17 Marcus Robinson .50
18 Akili Smith .50
19 Corey Dillon .50
20 Peter Warrick 1.00
21 Kevin Johnson .30
22 Tim Couch .75
23 Emmitt Smith 1.50
24 Troy Aikman 1.00
25 Brian Griese .60
26 John Elway 1.75
27 Mike Anderson 1.50
28 Rod Smith .30
29 Terrell Davis 1.25
30 Barry Sanders 1.75
31 Charlie Batch .50
32 James Stewart .50
33 Ahman Green .50
34 Antonio Freeman .50
35 Brett Favre 2.00
36 Edgerrin James 1.50
37 Marvin Harrison .50
38 Peyton Manning 1.50
39 Fred Taylor .75
40 Jimmy Smith .50
41 Keenan McCardell .30
42 Mark Brunell .75
43 Derrick Alexander .15
44 Elvis Grbac .30
45 Sylvester Morris .50
46 Tony Gonzalez .30
47 Dan Marino 1.75
48 Jay Fiedler .50
49 Lamar Smith .50
50 Oronde Gadsden .30
51 Cris Carter .50
52 Daunte Culpepper 1.00
53 Randy Moss 1.50
54 Robert Smith .30
55 Drew Bledsoe .75
56 Terry Glenn .50
57 Aaron Brooks .75
58 Joe Horn .30
59 Ricky Williams .75
60 Amani Toomer .30
61 Ike Hilliard .30
62 Kerry Collins .30
63 Ron Dayne 1.00
64 Tiki Barber .30
65 Chad Pennington 1.00
66 Curtis Martin .50
67 Vinny Testaverde .50
68 Wayne Chrebet .50
69 Rich Gannon .50
70 Tim Brown .30
71 Tyrone Wheatley .30
72 Donovan McNabb .75
73 Jerome Bettis .50
74 Plaxico Burress .50
75 Junior Seau .30
76 Charlie Garner .30
77 Jeff Garcia .50
78 Jerry Rice 1.25
79 Terrell Owens .50
80 Darrell Jackson .30
81 Ricky Watters .30
82 Shaun Alexander .50
83 Isaac Bruce .50
84 Kurt Warner 2.00
85 Marshall Faulk .60
86 Torry Holt .50
87 Trent Green .50
88 Keyshawn Johnson .50
89 Shaun King .50
90 Warren Sapp .30
91 Warrick Dunn .50
92 Eddie George .60
93 Jevon Kearse .50
94 Steve McNair .50
95 Albert Connell .30
96 Jeff George .50
97 Brad Johnson .50
98 Bruce Smith .15
99 Michael Westbrook .30
100 Stephen Davis .50
101 *Michael Vick* 70.00
102 *Drew Brees* 50.00
103 *Chris Weinke* 30.00
105 *Sage Rosenfels* 18.00
106 *Josh Heupel* 15.00
107 *Tony Driver* 10.00
108 *Ben Leard* 10.00
109 *Marques Tuiasosopo* 30.00
110 *Tim Hasselbeck* 12.00
111 *Mike McMahon* 25.00
112 *Deuce McAllister* 25.00
113 *LaMont Jordan* 20.00
114 *LaDainian Tomlinson* 50.00
115 *James Jackson* 20.00
116 *Anthony Thomas* 70.00
117 *Travis Henry* 20.00
118 *DeAngelo Evans* 7.00
119 *Travis Minor* 15.00
120 *Rudi Johnson* 12.00
121 *Michael Bennett* 30.00
122 *Kevan Barlow* 25.00
123 *Dan Alexander* 15.00
124 *David Allen* 10.00
125 *Correl Buckhalter* 15.00
126 *David Rivers* 10.00
127 *Reggie White* 12.00
128 *Moran Norris* 7.00
129 *Ja'Mar Toombs* 10.00
130 *Jason McKinley* 10.00
131 *Scotty Anderson* 10.00
132 *Dustin McClintock* 12.00
133 *Heath Evans* 10.00
134 *David Terrell* 30.00
135 *Santana Moss* 25.00
136 *Rod Gardner* 25.00
137 *Quincy Morgan* 25.00
138 *Freddie Mitchell* 35.00
139 *Boo Williams* 7.00
140 *Reggie Wayne* 20.00
141 *Ronney Daniels* 7.00
142 *Bobby Newcombe* 12.00
143 *Reggie Germany 250* 25.00
144 *Jesse Palmer* 15.00
145 *Robert Ferguson* 20.00
146 *Ken-Yon Rambo* 12.00
147 *Alex Bannister* 18.00
148 *Koren Robinson* 20.00

149	*Chad Johnson*	12.00
150	*Chris Chambers*	30.00
151	*Javon Green*	7.00
152	*Marvin "Snoop" Minnis*	20.00
153	*Vinny Sutherland*	12.00
154	*Cedrick Wilson*	10.00
155	*John Capel 250*	20.00
156	*T.J. Houshmandzadeh*	10.00
157	*Todd Heap*	15.00
158	*Alge Crumpler*	12.00
159	*Jabari Holloway*	10.00
160	*Marcellus Rivers*	7.00
161	*Rashon Burns*	7.00
162	*Tony Stewart*	12.00
163	*Jevaris Johnson*	7.00
164	*Jamal Reynolds*	10.00
165	*Andre Carter*	12.00
166	*David Warren*	7.00
167	*Justin Smith*	15.00
168	*Josh Booty*	12.00
169	*Karon Riley*	7.00
170	*Cedric Scott*	7.00
171	*Kenny Smith*	7.00
172	*Richard Seymour*	10.00
173	*Willie Howard*	10.00
175	*Marcus Stroud*	12.00
176	*Damione Lewis*	10.00
177	*Casey Hampton*	10.00
178	*Ennis Davis*	7.00
179	*Gerard Warren*	20.00
180	*Tommy Polley*	10.00
181	*Kendrell Bell 250*	75.00
182	*Dan Morgan*	20.00
183	*Morlon Greenwood*	7.00
184	*Quinton Caver*	20.00
185	*Keith Adams*	7.00
186	*Brian Allen*	7.00
187	*Carlos Polk*	10.00
188	*Torrance Marshall*	12.00
189	*Jamie Winborn*	7.00
190	*Jamar Fletcher*	10.00
191	*Ken Lucas*	10.00
192	*Fred Smoot*	15.00
193	*Nate Clements*	10.00
194	*Will Allen*	10.00
195	*Willie Middlebrooks*	20.00
196	*Gary Baxter*	10.00
197	*Derrick Gibson*	7.00
198	*Robert Carswell*	15.00
199	*Hakim Akbar*	7.00
200	*Adam Archuleta*	15.00

2001 Donruss Elite Face to Face

		MT
	Common Player:	20.00
	Single Masks #'d to 100	
	Double Masks #'d to 50	
1	John Elway	125.00
2	Dan Marino	125.00
3	Brett Favre	125.00
4	Barry Sanders	100.00
5	Marshall Faulk	50.00
6	Edgerrin James	100.00
7	Troy Aikman	80.00
8	Steve Young	60.00
9	Terrell Davis	80.00
10	Jamal Anderson	20.00
11	Tim Brown	40.00
12	Jerry Rice	80.00
13	Isaac Bruce	30.00
14	Torry Holt	30.00
15	Warren Sapp	20.00
17	Jerome Bettis	25.00
18	Fred Taylor	35.00
19	Ray Lewis	30.00
20	Eddie George	50.00
21	Ryan Leaf	20.00
22	Peyton Manning	100.00
24	Phil Simms	35.00
27	Keyshawn Johnson	30.00
28	Wayne Chrebet	30.00
29	Shaun King	30.00
30	Donovan McNabb	60.00
31	Dan Marino, John Elway	300.00
32	Brett Favre, Barry Sanders	250.00
33	Edgerrin James, Marshall Faulk	125.00
34	Troy Aikman, Steve Young	100.00
35	Jamal Anderson, Terrell Davis	75.00
36	Jerry Rice, Tim Brown	120.00
37	Isaac Bruce, Torry Holt	50.00
38	Warren Sapp, Reggie White	40.00
39	Fred Taylor, Jerome Bettis	60.00
40	Ray Lewis, Eddie George	60.00
41	Peyton Manning, Ryan Leaf	100.00
42	Phil Simms, Lawrence Taylor	45.00
43	Joe Montana, Marcus Allen	150.00
44	Wayne Chrebet, Keyshawn Johnson	40.00
45	Donovan McNabb, Shaun King	100.00

2001 Donruss Elite Passing the Torch

		MT
	Complete Set (24):	100.00
	Common Player:	3.00
	Single Player #'d to 1,000	
	Double Player #'d to 500	
1	John Elway	10.00
2	Brian Griese	3.50
3	Dick Butkus	8.00
4	Brian Urlacher	4.00
5	Fran Tarkenton	5.00
6	Daunte Culpepper	5.00
7	Jim Brown	5.00
8	Jamal Lewis	6.00
9	Larry Csonka	4.00
10	Ron Dayne	4.00
11	Tony Dorsett	3.50
12	Emmitt Smith	6.00
13	Eric Dickerson	3.00
14	Marshall Faulk	3.00
15	Joe Namath	8.00
16	Chad Pennington	4.00
17	John Elway, Brian Griese	20.00
18	Brian Urlacher, Dick Butkus	20.00
19	Fran Tarkenton, Daunte Culpepper	10.00
20	Jamal Lewis, Jim Brown	12.00
21	Larry Csonka, Ron Dayne	7.00
22	Tony Dorsett, Emmitt Smith	12.00
23	Marshall Faulk, Eric Dickerson	6.00
24	Chad Pennington, Joe Namath	15.00

2001 Donruss Elite Passing the Torch Autographs

		MT
	Common Player:	40.00
	Single Player #'d to 100	
	Double Player #'d to 50	
1	John Elway	150.00
2	Brian Griese	75.00
3	Dick Butkus	100.00
4	Brian Urlacher	85.00
5	Fran Tarkenton	60.00
6	Daunte Culpepper	85.00
7	Jim Brown	125.00
8	Jamal Lewis	85.00
9	Larry Csonka	75.00
10	Ron Dayne	60.00
11	Tony Dorsett	75.00
12	Emmitt Smith	175.00
13	Eric Dickerson	40.00
14	Marshall Faulk	75.00
15	Joe Namath	150.00
16	Chad Pennington	60.00
17	John Elway, Brian Griese	225.00
18	Brian Urlacher, Dick Butkus	150.00
19	Fran Tarkenton, Daunte Culpepper	180.00
20	Jamal Lewis, Jim Brown	200.00
21	Larry Csonka, Ron Dayne	125.00
22	Tony Dorsett, Emmitt Smith	200.00
23	Marshall Faulk, Eric Dickerson	100.00
24	Chad Pennington, Joe Namath	300.00

2001 Donruss Elite Primary Colors

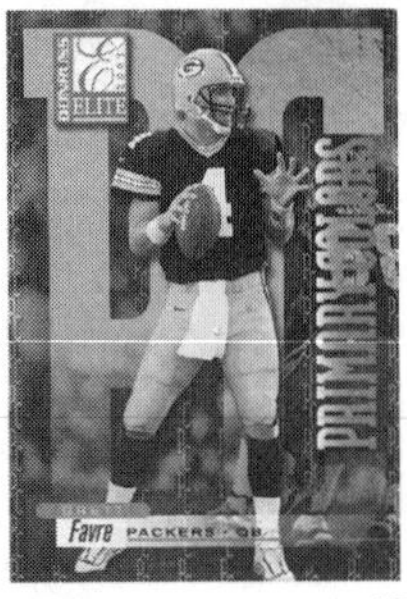

		MT
	Complete Set (40):	100.00
	Common Player:	1.50
	Production 975 Sets	
	Red Die-Cut Cards:	6x-12x
	Production 25 Sets	
	Blue Cards:	2x
	Production 200 Sets	
	Blue Die Cut Cards:	4x-8x
	Production 50 Sets	
	Yellow Cards:	6x-12x
	Production 25 Sets	
	Yellow Die Cut Cards:	3x-6x
	Production 75 Sets	
1	Peyton Manning	6.00
2	Edgerrin James	6.00
3	Marvin Harrison	2.00
4	Curtis Martin	2.00
5	Eric Moulds	1.50
6	Dan Marino	7.00
7	Drew Bledsoe	2.50
8	Drew Brees	8.00
9	Jamal Lewis	5.00
10	Michael Vick	18.00
11	Eddie George	2.00
12	Steve McNair	1.50
13	Jerome Bettis	1.50
14	Koren Robinson	5.00
15	Mark Brunell	2.50
16	Fred Taylor	2.50
17	Michael Bennett	7.00
18	David Terrell	7.00
19	Brian Griese	2.00
20	Mike Anderson	5.00
21	John Elway	7.00
22	Terrell Owens	2.00
23	Rudi Johnson	2.50
24	Jerry Rice	5.00
25	Ricky Williams	3.00
26	Aaron Brooks	2.00
27	Kurt Warner	7.00
28	Marshall Faulk	2.50
29	Isaac Bruce	2.00
30	Brett Favre	8.00
31	Santana Moss	7.00
32	Daunte Culpepper	4.00
33	Randy Moss	7.00
34	Cris Carter	2.00
35	Barry Sanders	6.00
36	Emmitt Smith	5.00
37	Stephen Davis	1.50
38	Ron Dayne	3.00
39	Donovan McNabb	3.00
40	Deuce McAllister	6.00

2001 Donruss Elite Prime Numbers

		MT
	Complete Set (10):	
	Common Player:	
1	Dan Marino	
2	John Elway	
3	Mike Anderson	
4	Randy Moss	
5	Daunte Culpepper	
6	Kurt Warner	
7	Jerry Rice	
8	Edgerrin James	
9	Peyton Manning	
10	Brett Favre	

2001 Donruss Elite Throwback Threads

		MT
	Common Player:	25.00
	Single Jerseys #'d to 100:	
	Double Jerseys #'d to 50:	
1	Art Monk	45.00
2	Joe Theismann	45.00
3	Jim Kelly	75.00
4	Thurman Thomas	25.00
5	Joe Namath	125.00
6	Don Maynard	25.00
7	Bob Griese	40.00
8	Larry Csonka	60.00
9	Joe Montana	125.00
10	Jerry Rice	85.00
11	Raymond Berry	25.00
12	Marvin Harrison	40.00
13	Warren Moon	35.00
14	Steve McNair	25.00
15	Terrell Davis	70.00
16	Mike Anderson	60.00
17	Frank Gifford	50.00
18	Ron Dayne	25.00
19	Walter Payton	150.00
20	Gale Sayers	60.00
21	Terry Bradshaw	100.00
22	Lynn Swann	50.00
23	Troy Aikman	80.00
24	Emmitt Smith	100.00
25	Fran Tarkenton	60.00
26	Daunte Culpepper	60.00
27	John Elway	100.00
28	Brian Griese	50.00
29	Eric Dickerson	25.00
30	Marshall Faulk	50.00
31	Joe Theismann, Art Monk	85.00
32	Thurman Thomas, Jim Kelly	100.00
33	Don Maynard, Joe Namath	120.00
34	Larry Csonka, Bob Griese	100.00
35	Jerry Rice, Joe Montana	250.00
36	Marvin Harrison, Raymond Berry	50.00
37	Warren Moon, Steve McNair	75.00
38	Terrell Davis, Mike Anderson	100.00
39	Ron Dayne, Frank Gifford	75.00
40	Walter Payton, Gale Sayers	250.00
41	Terry Bradshaw, Franco Harris	175.00
42	Troy Aikman, Emmitt Smith	200.00
43	Fran Tarkenton, Daunte Culpepper	175.00
44	John Elway, Brian Griese	180.00
45	Eric Dickerson, Marshall Faulk	100.00

2001 Donruss Elite Title Waves

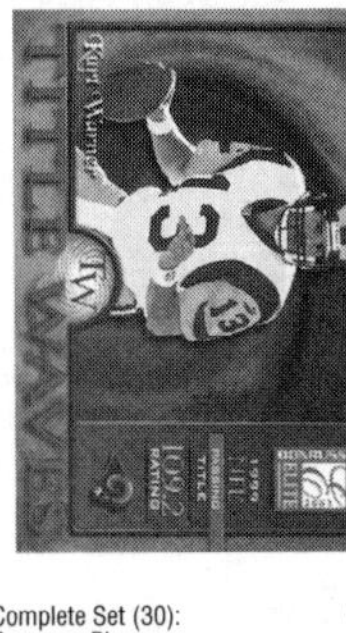

		MT
	Complete Set (30):	60.00
	Common Player:	1.50
	Numbered To Stat	
	Holofoil Cards:	4x-8x
	Production 100 Sets	
1	Kurt Warner 1999	5.00
2	Dan Marino 1994	5.00
3	Brett Favre 1995	6.00
4	Peyton Manning 2000	5.00
5	John Elway 1996	5.00
6	Steve Young 1997	2.50
7	Barry Sanders 1997	4.00
8	Emmitt Smith 1993	4.00
9	Terrell Davis 1998	3.50
10	Edgerrin James 2000	4.00
11	Stephen Davis 1999	1.50
12	Curtis Martin 1995	1.50
13	Marvin Harrison 1999	1.50
14	Antonio Freeman 1998	1.50
15	Jerry Rice 1995	3.00
16	Randy Moss 1999	5.00
17	Tim Brown 1997	1.50
18	Isaac Bruce 1996	1.50
19	Ricky Williams 2000	2.50
20	Peyton Manning 1999	5.00
21	Eddie George 2000	2.00
22	Barry Sanders 1993	4.00
23	Daunte Culpepper 2000	3.00
24	Dan Marino 1994	5.00
25	John Elway 1999	5.00
26	Marshall Faulk 2000	2.00
27	Brett Favre 1997	6.00
28	Steve Young 1995	2.50
29	Troy Aikman 1993	3.00
30	Jerry Rice 1990	3.00

E

1959 Eagles Jay Publishing

Measuring 5" x 7", the 12-card set is anchored by a black-and-white photo on the front, with the player's name and team printed in the white border underneath. The cards are blank-backed and unnumbered. The set was originally sold in 12-card packs for 25 cents.

		NM
	Complete Set (12):	75.00
	Common Player:	5.00
1	Bill Barnes	5.00
2	Chuck Bednarik	10.00
3	Tom Brookshier	5.00
4	Marion Campbell	5.00
5	Ted Dean	5.00
6	Tommy McDonald	8.00
7	Clarence Peaks	5.00
8	Pete Retzlaff	5.00
9	Jesse Richardson	5.00
10	Norm Van Brocklin	15.00
11	Bobby Walston	5.00
12	Chuck Weber	5.00

1960 Eagles White Border

Measuring 5" x 7", the 11-card set is anchored by a black-and-white photo on the front, wth the player's name and team printed in the white border underneath. The cards are blank-backed and unnumbered.

		NM
	Complete Set (11):	50.00
	Common Player:	5.00
1	Maxie Baughan	7.00
2	Chuck Bednarik	10.00
3	Don Burroughs	5.00
4	Jimmy Carr	5.00
5	Howard Keys	5.00
6	Ed Khayat	5.00
7	Jim McCusker	5.00
8	John Nocera	5.00
9	Nick Skorich	5.00
10	J.D. Smith	5.00
11	John Wittenborn	5.00

1961 Eagles Jay Publishing

Measuring 5" x 7", the 12-card set is anchored by a black-and-white photo on the front, with his name and team printed underneath in a white border. The backs are blank and unnumbered. Originally, the set was sold in packs for 25 cents.

		NM
	Complete Set (12):	50.00
	Common Player:	5.00
1	Maxie Baughan	7.00
2	Jim McCusker	5.00
3	Tommy McDonald	7.00
4	Bob Pellegrini	5.00
5	Pete Retzlaff	5.00
6	Jesse Richardson	5.00
7	Joe Robb	5.00
8	Theron Sapp	5.00
9	J.D. Smith	5.00
10	Bobby Walston	5.00
11	Jerry Williams (ACO)	5.00
12	John Wittenborn	5.00

1971 Eagles Team Issue

Measuring 4-1/4" x 5-1/2", the 16-card set showcases a posed black-and-white photo on the front, with the player's name and team printed inside the white border at the bottom of the card. The cards are unnumbered and the backs are blank.

		NM
	Complete Set (16):	45.00
	Common Player:	3.00
1	Gary Ballman	3.00
2	Lee Bouggess	3.00
3	Kent Kramer	3.00
4	Tom McNeill	3.00
5	Mark Nordquist	3.00
6	Ron Porter	3.00
7	Steve Preece	3.00
8	Tim Rossovich (Facing right edge of card)	3.00
9	Tim Rossovich (Facing left edge of card)	3.00
10	Jim Skaggs	3.00
11	Norm Snead	5.00
12	Jim Thrower	3.00
13	Mel Tom	3.00
14	Jim Ward	3.00
15	Adrian Young	3.00
16	Don Zimmerman	3.00

1983 Eagles Frito Lay

Measuring 4-1/4" x 5-1/2", the 37-card set is anchored by an action photo on the front, with the player's facsimile autograph on the photo. The player's name, position and Frito Lay logo are printed inside the white border under the photo. The top white margin features the "Philadelphia Eagles" and their logo on the card front. The set is unnumbered. The backs of Harold Carmichael, Max Runager and Jerry Sisemore's cards are done in a postcard format, while the others are blank.

		MT
	Complete Set (37):	45.00
	Common Player:	1.00
1	Harvey Armstrong	1.00
2	Ron Baker	1.00
3	Greg Brown	1.00
4	Marion Campbell (CO)	1.00
5	Harold Carmichael	3.00
6	Ken Clarke	1.00
7	Dennis DeVaughn	1.00
8	Herman Edwards	1.00
9	Ray Ellis	1.00
10	Major Everett	1.50
11	Anthony Griggs	1.00
12	Michael Haddix	1.50
13	Perry Harrington	1.00
14	Dennis Harrison	1.00
15	Wes Hopkins	1.50
16	Ron Jaworski	4.00
17	Ron Johnson	1.00
18	Vyto Kab	1.00
19	Steve Kenney	1.00
20	Dean Miraldi	1.00
21	Leonard Mitchell	1.00
22	Wilbert Montgomery	4.00
23	Hubie Oliver	1.00
24	Joe Pisarcik	1.50
25	Mike Quick	2.00
26	Jerry Robinson	1.50
27	Max Runager	1.00
28	Buddy Ryan (CO)	4.00
29	Lawrence Sampleton	1.00
30	Jody Schulz	1.00
31	Jerry Sisemore	1.00
32	John Spagnola	1.50
33	Reggie Wilkes	1.00
34	Mike Williams	1.00
35	Tony Woodruff	1.00
36	Glen Young	1.00
37	Roynell Young	1.00

1984 Eagles Police

Measuring 2-5/8" x 4-1/8", this eight-card set is anchored on the front with a photo, with the player's name, number, position, team and Eagles' logo inside a box at the bottom. The backs have the card number, player's name, number, position, bio, safety tip and sponsors.

		MT
	Complete Set (8):	6.00
	Common Player:	.50
1	Mike Quick	1.00
2	Dennis Harrison	.50
3	Jerry Robinson	.75
4	Wilbert Montgomery	1.50
5	Herman Edwards	.50
6	Kenny Jackson	1.00
7	Anthony Griggs	.50
8	Ron Jaworski	1.75

1985 Eagles Police

Measuring 2-5/8" x 4-1/8", the 16-card set is identical on the front to the 1984 set, with the large photo and the player's name, number, position, team and Eagles' logo in a box at the bottom. The backs have the card number, player's name, number, bio, highlights and a safety tip. The sponsors are listed at the bottom of the card back.

		MT
	Complete Set (16):	6.00
	Common Player:	.50
1	Ken Clarke	.50
2	Roynell Young	.50
3	Ray Ellis	.50
4	Ron Baker	.50
5	John Spagnola	.50
6	Reggie Wilkes	.50
7	Ron Jaworski	1.00
8	Steve Kenney	.50
9	Paul McFadden	.50
10	Mike Quick	1.00
11	Hubie Oliver	.50
12	Greg Brown	.50
13	Anthony Griggs	.50
14	Michael Haddix	.50
15	Kenny Jackson	.75
16	Vyto Kab	.50

1985 Eagles Team Issue

Measuring 2-15/16" x 3-7/8", the 53-card set is anchored by a glossy color photo on the front, with the player's name, position and number in the white margin under the photo. The backs have the player's name, position and number at the top, with his career highlights located inside a box. The cards are unnumbered.

		MT
	Complete Set (53):	50.00
	Common Player:	1.00
1	Harvey Armstrong	1.00
2	Ron Baker	1.00
3	Norman Braman (PRES)	1.00
4	Greg Brown	1.00
5	Marion Campbell (CO)	1.00
6	Jeff Christensen	1.00
7	Ken Clarke	1.00
8	Evan Cooper	1.00
9	Byron Darby	1.00
10	Mark Dennard	1.00
11	Herman Edwards	1.00
12	Ray Ellis	1.00
13	Major Everett	1.00
14	Gerry Feehery	1.00
15	Elbert Foules	1.00
16	Gregg Garrity	1.00
17	Anthony Griggs	1.00
18	Michael Haddix	1.00
19	Andre Hardy	1.00
20	Dennis Harrison	1.00
21	Joe Hayes	1.00
22	Melvin Hoover	1.00
23	Wes Hopkins	1.50
24	Mike Horan	1.00
25	Kenny Jackson	1.50
26	Ron Jaworski	4.00
27	Vyto Kab	1.00
28	Steve Kenney	1.00
29	Rich Kraynak	1.00
30	Dean May	1.00
31	Paul McFadden	1.00
32	Dean Miraldi	1.00
33	Leonard Mitchell	1.00
34	Wilbert Montgomery	3.00
35	Hubie Oliver	1.00
36	Mike Quick	2.00
37	Mike Reichenbach	1.00
38	Jerry Robinson	1.00
39	Rusty Russell	1.00
40	Lawrence Sampleton	1.00
41	Jody Schulz	1.00
42	John Spagnola	1.50
43	Tom Strauthers	1.00
44	Andre Waters	2.00
45	Reggie Wilkes	1.00
46	Joel Williams	1.00
47	Michael Williams	1.00
48	Brenard Wilson	1.00
49	Tony Woodruff	1.00
50	Roynell Young	1.00
51	Logo Card (Eagle holding football on both sides)	1.50
52	1985 Schedule Card (Both sides)	1.50
53	Title Card 1985-86 (Eagles' Helmet)	1.50

1986 Eagles Frito Lay

The cards in this set are 4-1/4" x 5-1/2". They can be distinguished from other Eagles Frito Lay sets by the Frito Lay logo in the lower right and the 3/8" borders on the sides. The cards are blank-backed and unnumbered.

		MT
	Complete Set (7):	12.00
	Common Player:	1.00
1	Wes Hopkins	1.50
2	Ron Jaworski	4.00
3	Ron Johnson WR	1.00
4	Mike Quick	2.00
5	Buddy Ryan CO	4.00
6	Tom Strauthers	1.00
7	Andre Waters	1.50

1986 Eagles Police

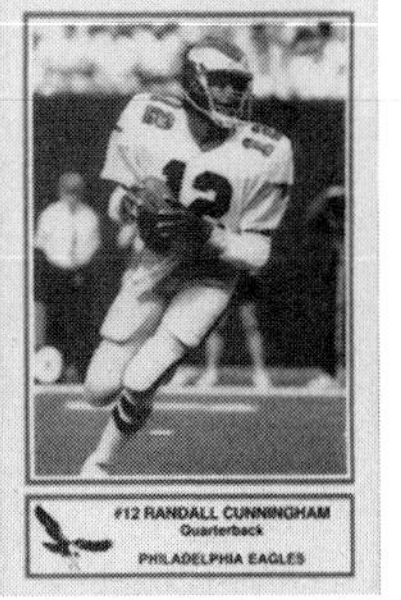

Measuring 2-5/8" x 4-1/8", the 16-card set is anchored by a large photo on the front, with the player's name, number, position, team and Eagles' logo in a box at the bottom. The backs have the card number, player's name, number, bio, position, highlights, safety tip and sponsors. The Eagles' and Frito Lay logos are also shown on the backs.

		MT
	Complete Set (16):	10.00
	Common Player:	.50
1	Greg Brown	.50
2	Reggie White	3.50
3	John Spagnola	.50
4	Mike Quick	.75
5	Ken Clarke	.50
6	Ken Reeves	.50
7	Mike Reichenbach	.50
8	Wes Hopkins	.75
9	Roynell Young	.50
10	Randall Cunningham	3.00
11	Paul McFadden	.50
12	Matt Cavanaugh	.50
13	Ron Jaworski	1.00
14	Byron Darby	.50
15	Andre Waters	.75
16	Buddy Ryan (CO)	1.00

1987 Eagles Police

Measuring 2-3/4" x 4-1/8", the 12-card set includes a photo on the front, along with the player's name, bio and position. The Eagles' helmet is printed in the bottom center. The backs have "Tips from the Eagles" printed at the top, with the New Jersey

police force logos printed directly underneath. A safety tip is also included on the unnumbered backs, which feature the sponsor names at the bottom. Overall, 10,000 sets were handed out by New Jersey police officers.

		MT
	Complete Set (12):	60.00
	Common Player:	3.00
1	Ron Baker	3.00
2	Keith Byars	7.00
3	Ken Clarke	3.00
4	Randall Cunningham	12.00
5	Paul McFadden	3.00
6	Mike Quick	5.00
7	Mike Reichenbach	3.00
8	Buddy Ryan (CO)	7.00
9	John Spagnola	3.00
10	Anthony Toney	5.00
11	Andre Waters	5.00
12	Reggie White	16.00

1988 Eagles Police

Measuring 2-3/4" x 4-1/8", the 12-card set is anchored on the front by a large photo. "Philadelphia Eagles" and two Eagles' helmets printed in each corner are at the top of the card fronts. Under the photo are the player's name, number, height, position and weight. The unnumbered backs feature "Tips from the Eagles" at the top, with the New Jersey police logos located directly underneath. The McGruff the Crime Dog logo is printed at the bottom, along with the sponsors.

		MT
	Complete Set (12):	60.00
	Common Player:	3.00
1	Jerome Brown	5.00
2	Keith Byars	5.00
3	Randall Cunningham	8.00
4	Matt Darwin	3.00
5	Keith Jackson	8.00
6	Seth Joyner	5.00
7	Mike Quick	4.00
8	Buddy Ryan (CO)	6.00
9	Clyde Simmons	5.00
10	John Teltschik	3.00
11	Anthony Toney	4.00
12	Reggie White	10.00

1989 Eagles Daily News

Measuring 5-9/16" x 4-1/4", the 24-card set features the Eagles logo in the upper left corner, with "Philadelphia Eagles" on the right side above the photo on the card front. Beneath the photo are the player's name and position, along with McDonald's, KYW radio and the Philadelphia News logos. The unnumbered cards have blank backs.

		MT
	Complete Set (24):	25.00
	Common Player:	1.00
1	Eric Allen	2.00
2	Jerome Brown	2.00
3	Keith Byars	2.00
4	Cris Carter (UER) (Name misspelled Chris on front)	5.00
5	Randall Cunningham	3.00
6	Matt Darwin	1.00
7	Gerry Feehery	1.00
8	Ron Heller	1.00
9A	Terry Hoage (Solid color jersey)	1.00
9B	Terry Hoage (With white collar or undershirt)	1.00
10	Wes Hopkins	1.50
11	Keith Jackson	3.00
12	Seth Joyner	2.00
13	Mike Pitts	1.00
14	Mike Quick	1.50
15	Mike Reichenbach	1.00
16	Clyde Simmons	2.00
17	John Spagnola	1.00
18	Junior Tautalatasi	1.00
19	John Teltschik	1.00
20	Anthony Toney	1.00
21	Andre Waters	1.50
22	Reggie White	6.00
23	Luis Zendejas	1.00

1989 Eagles Police

Measuring 8-1/2" x 11", the nine-card set is anchored by a photo on the front, with the player's name and bio underneath the photo between the New Jersey State Police Crime Prevention Resource Center and Security Savings Bank logos. The unnumbered backs have "Alcohol and Other Drugs: Facts and Myths" and five questions and answers. The team logo and sponsors' logos are on the back. This set was released after the season.

		MT
	Complete Set (9):	50.00
	Common Player:	3.00
1	Cris Carter	15.00
2	Gregg Garrity	3.00
3	Mike Golic	4.00
4	Keith Jackson	7.00
5	Clyde Simmons	6.00
6	John Teltschik	3.00
7	Anthony Toney	3.00
8	Andre Waters	4.00
9	Luis Zendejas	3.00

1989 Eagles Smokey

Measuring 3" x 5", the 49-card set features a full-bleed photo on the front, with the player's name, number and position in the lower right. The unnumbered card backs have the player's name, number, position and bio at the top, with a Smokey the Bear cartoon underneath. The Eagles' and sponsor logos appear at the bottom of the card backs. Some cards were produced with two versions, which can be differentiated by the home and away jerseys.

		MT
	Complete Set (49):	125.00
	Common Player:	1.50
6	Matt Cavanaugh	2.00
8	Luis Zendejas	1.50
9	Don McPherson	2.00
10	John Teltschik	1.50
12A	Randall Cunningham (White jersey)	8.00
12B	Randall Cunningham (Green jersey)	8.00
20	Andre Waters	3.00
21	Eric Allen	3.00
25	Anthony Toney	2.00
33	William Frizzell	1.50
34	Terry Hoage	1.50
35	Mark Konecny	1.50
41	Keith Byars	3.00
42	Eric Everett	1.50
43	Roynell Young	1.50
46	Izel Jenkins	1.50
48	Wes Hopkins	2.00
50	Dave Rimington	1.50
52	Todd Bell	1.50
53	Dwayne Jiles	1.50
55	Mike Reichenbach	1.50
56	Byron Evans	1.50
58	Ty Allert	1.50
59	Seth Joyner	3.00
61	Ben Tamburello	1.50
63	Ron Baker	1.50
66	Ken Reeves	1.50
68	Reggie Singletary	1.50
72	David Alexander	1.50
73	Ron Heller	1.50
74	Mike Pitts	1.50
78	Matt Darwin	1.50
80	Cris Carter	8.00
81	Kenny Jackson	2.00
82A	Mike Quick (White jersey)	2.50
82B	Mike Quick (Green jersey)	2.50
83	Jimmie Giles	1.50
85	Ron Johnson	1.50
86	Gregg Garrity	1.50
88	Keith Jackson	5.00
89	David Little	2.00
90	Mike Golic	2.00
91	Scott Curtis	1.50
92	Reggie White	14.00
96	Clyde Simmons	3.00
97	John Klingel	1.50
99	Jerome Brown	4.00
NNO	Buddy Ryan (CO) (Wearing white cap)	7.00
NNO	Buddy Ryan (CO) (Wearing green cap)	7.00

1990 Eagles Police

Measuring 2-5/8" x 4-1/8", the 12-card set has "Philadelphia Eagles" and two Eagles' helmets at the top of the card fronts above the photo. Beneath the photo are the player's name, position and bio. The unnumbered card backs have "Tips from the Eagles" and sponsor logos at the top, with a tip and McGruff the Crime Dog logo at the bottom.

		MT
	Complete Set (12):	30.00
	Common Player:	2.00
1	David Alexander	2.00
2	Eric Allen	3.00
3	Randall Cunningham	5.00
4	Keith Byars	3.00
5	James Feagles	2.00
6	Mike Golic	3.00
7	Keith Jackson	4.00
8	Rich Kotite (CO)	3.00
9	Roger Ruzek	2.00
10	Mickey Shuler	3.00
11	Clyde Simmons	4.00
12	Reggie White	8.00

1990 Eagles Sealtest

Measuring 2" x 8", the set of six bookmarks showcases the Sealtest logo at the top, with "The Reading Team" inside a scoreboard above the player photo. The Eagles' logo, player name, number, bio and highlights are printed inside a box at the bottom of the card. The backs are unnumbered and contain the sponsor logos and give information on two books that are available at the public library. This set is identical to the the 1990 Knudsen 49ers and Chargers sets.

		MT
	Complete Set (6):	15.00
	Common Player:	2.50
1	David Alexander	2.50
2	Eric Allen	3.50
3	Keith Byars	3.50
4	Randall Cunningham	4.00
5	Mike Pitts	2.50
6	Mike Quick	3.50

1991 Enor Pro Football HOF Promos

The six standard-sized cards were produced to show what the 1991 Enor set would look like. The cards are identical to the regular cards, except for the differences in numbering and color tones. To tell these cards apart from the regular cards, look at the Team NFL logo on the back. If the NFL logo is black and white it is a promo card. If it is red, white and blue, it is a card from the regular series.

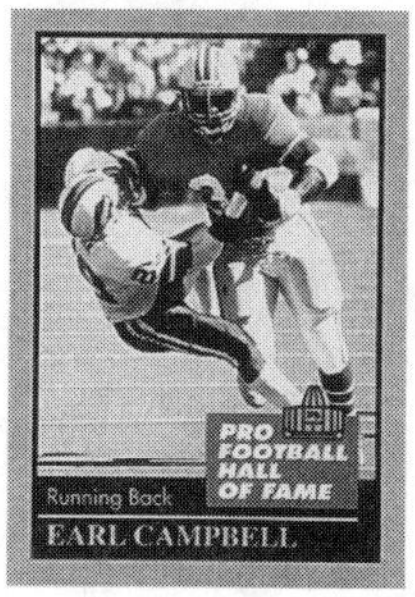

		MT
	Complete Set (6):	8.00
	Common Player:	1.00
1	Pro Football Hall of Fame (Building) (Regular issue card number is also 1)	1.00
2	Earl Campbell (Regular issue card number is 23)	3.50
3	John Hannah (Regular issue card number is 57)	1.00
4	Stan Jones (Regular issue card number is 74)	1.00
5	Jan Stenerud (Regular issue card number is 131)	1.00
6	Tex Schramm ADM (Regular issue card number is 127)	1.00

1991 Enor Pro Football Hall of Fame

Photos from the NFL's files were used for the card fronts for this 160-card set, which features a blend of color and black-and-white photos bordered by black and gold frames. The Pro Football Hall of Fame logo also appears on the card front, in a purple square. The player's name and position are in the lower left corner in a black panel. The card back has a photo of the Hall of Fame on the bottom half, along with a card number. Biographical information, a career summary and the year of induction comprise the rest of the back. Special cards randomly inserted in packs allowed the holder to redeem them for a special Hall of Fame card album and free admission to the museum. Six different promo cards were also produced for the set. The cards, which are numbered on the back, do not match the numbers assigned to their counterparts in the regular set. Also, the cards have a different shade of color and the NFL logo on the back is black-and-white, not in color like those on the regular cards.

		MT
	Complete Set (160):	12.00
	Common Player:	.10
1	Pro Football Hall of Fame	.15
1A	Free Admission Pro Football Hall of Fame (Canton, OH)	.15
2	Herb Adderley	.15
3	Lance Alworth	.20
4	Doug Atkins	.15
5	Morris (Red) Badgro	.10
6	Cliff Battles	.15
7	Sammy Baugh	.60
8	Chuck Bednarik	.25
9A	Bert Bell (FOUND/OWN) (Factory set version in coat and tie)	.20
9B	Bert Bell (FOUND/OWN) (Wax pack version in Steelers tee shirt)	.20
10	Bobby Bell	.10
11	Raymond Berry	.30
12	Charles W. Bidwill (OWN)	.10
13	Fred Biletnikoff	.25
14	George Blanda	.30
15	Mel Blount	.20
16	Terry Bradshaw	.75
17	Jim Brown	.75
18	Paul Brown (CO/OWN/FOUND)	.20
19	Roosevelt Brown	.10
20	Willie Brown	.15
21	Buck Buchanan	.15
22	Dick Butkus	.50
23	Earl Campbell	.75
24	Tony Canadeo	.10
25	Joe Carr (PRES)	.10
26	Guy Chamberlin	.10
27	Jack Christiansen	.10
28	Earl "Dutch" Clark	.15
29	George Connor	.15
30	Jimmy Conzelman	.10
31	Larry Csonka	.30
32	Willie Davis	.10
33	Len Dawson	.25
34	Mike Ditka	.30
35	Art Donovan	.25
36	John (Paddy) Driscoll	.10
37	Billy Dudley	.15
38	Turk Edwards	.10
39	Weeb Ewbank (CO)	.10
40	Tom Fears	.10
41	Ray Flaherty (CO)	.10
42	Len Ford	.10
43	Dan Fortmann	.10
44	Frank Gatski	.10
45	Bill George	.10
46	Frank Gifford	.50
47	Sid Gillman (CO)	.10
48	Otto Graham	.50
49	Harold (Red) Grange	.50
50	Joe Greene	.20
51	Forrest Gregg	.15
52	Bob Griese	.30
53	Lou Groza	.20
54	Joe Guyon	.10
55	George Halas (CO/OWN/FOUND)	.30
56	Jack Ham	.25
57	John Hannah	.10
58	Franco Harris	.30
59	Ed Healey	.10
60	Mel Hein	.10
61	Ted Hendricks	.15
62	Pete (Fats) Henry	.10
63	Arnie Herber	.10
64	Bill Hewitt	.10
65	Clarke Hinkle	.10
66	Elroy Hirsch	.20
67	Ken Houston	.15
68	Cal Hubbard	.10
69	Sam Huff	.20
70	Lamar Hunt (OWN/FOUND)	.10
71	Don Hutson	.20
72	John Henry Johnson	.15
73	Deacon Jones	.25
74	Stan Jones	.15
75	Sonny Jurgensen	.25
76	Walt Kiesling	.10
77	Frank (Bruiser) Kinard	.10
78	Earl (Curly) Lambeau (CO/FOUND/OWN)	.25
79	Jack Lambert	.30
80	Tom Landry (CO)	.30
81	Dick Lane	.15
82	Jim Langer	.10
83	Willie Lanier	.15
84	Yale Lary	.10
85	Dante Lavelli	.15
86	Bobby Layne	.50
87	Tuffy Leemans	.10
88	Bob Lilly	.25
89	Sid Luckman	.25
90	William Roy Lyman	.10
91	Tim Mara (FOUND/OWN)	.10
92	Gino Marchetti	.20
93	Geo. Preston Marshall (FOUND/OWN)	.10
94	Don Maynard	.20
95	George McAfee	.10
96	Mike McCormack	.10
97	Johnny (Blood) McNally	.10
98	Mike Michalske	.10
99	Wayne Millner	.10
100	Bobby Mitchell	.20
101	Ron Mix	.15
102	Lenny Moore	.20
103	Marion Motley (See also 130)	.20
104	George Musso	.10
105	Bronko Nagurski	.30
106	Earle (Greasy) Neale (CO)	.10
107	Ernie Nevers	.10
108	Ray Nitschke	.25
109	Leo Nomellini	.15
110	Merlin Olsen	.25
111	Jim Otto	.20
112	Steve Owen (CO)	.10
113	Alan Page	.15
114	Clarence (Ace) Parker	.10
115	Jim Parker	.10
116	1958 NFL Championship	.10
117	Pete Pihos	.10
118	Hugh (Shorty) Ray (OFF)	.10
119	Dan Reeves (OWN)	.10
120	Jim Ringo	.10
121	Andy Robustelli	.15
122	Art Rooney (FOUND/ADM)	.15
123	Pete Rozelle (COMM)	.20
124	Bob St. Clair	.15
125	Gale Sayers	.50
126	Joe Schmidt	.15
127	Tex Schramm (ADM)	.15
128	Art Shell	.20
129	Roger Staubach	.75
130	Ernie Stautner (UER) (Numbered as 103)	.20
131	Jan Stenerud	.15
132	Ken Strong	.15
133	Joe Stydahar	.10
134	Fran Tarkenton	.30
135	Charley Taylor	.15
136	Jim Taylor	.15
137	Jim Thorpe	.50
138	Y.A. Tittle	.40
139	George Trafton	.10
140	Charlie Trippi	.10
141	Emlen Tunnell	.10
142	Clyde "Bulldog" Turner	.20
143	Johnny Unitas	.50
144	Gene Upshaw	.15
145	Norm Van Brocklin	.20
146	Steve Van Buren	.20
147	Doak Walker	.20
148	Paul Warfield	.20
149	Bob Waterfield	.20
150	Arnie Weinmeister	.10
151	Bill Willis	.10
152	Larry Wilson	.10
153	Alex Wojciechowicz	.10
154	Willie Wood	.15
155	Enshrinement Day HOF Induction Ceremony	.10
156	Mementoes Exhibit Enshrinee Mementos Room	.10
157	Checklist 1 - The Beginning	.10
158	Checklist 2 - The Early Years	.10
159	Checklist 3 - The Modern Era	.10
160A	Checklist 4 - Evolution of Uniform (includes #133-160)	.10

1994 Enor Pro Football HOF

Having the identical design as the 1991 set, these six cards were inserted into ProGard protective sheet boxes. The cards are unnumbered. They feature each of the players and coach who were inducted into the Hall of Fame in 1994.

		MT
	Complete Set (6):	4.00
	Common Player:	.40
1	Tony Dorsett	1.25
2	Bud Grant (CO)	.40
3	Jim Johnson	.40
4	Leroy Kelly	.40
5	Jackie Smith	.40
6	Randy White	.75

1995 Enor Pro Football HOF

The company re-released its 1991 Hall of Fame series in a factory set in 1995. This includes the first 159 cards from the 1991 set, in addition to 21 new cards, which feature a 1995 copyright date. The original cards still carry the 1991 copyright. Card No. 160 carries a "B" suffix.

		MT
	Complete Set (21):	8.00
	Common Player:	.25
160B	Checklist 4 - Evolution of Uniform (includes #133-180)	.25
161	Lem Barney	.25
162	Al Davis	.40
163	John Mackey	.25
164	John Riggins	.50
165	Dan Fouts	.50
166	Larry Little	.25
167	Chuck Noll	.50
168	Bill Walsh	.50
169	Tony Dorsett	1.00
170	Bud Grant	.25
171	Jimmy Johnson	.25
172	Leroy Kelly	.25
173	Jackie Smith	.25
174	Randy White	.50
175	O.J. Simpson	1.00
176	Jim Finks	.25
177	Hank Jordan	.25
178	Steve Largent	.75
179	Lee Roy Selmon	.25
180	Kellen Winslow	.40

1969 Eskimo Pie

These 2-1/2" x 3" panels each feature two mug shot stickers of American Football League players. The panels are in color but are unnumbered. Card 14 (Len Dawson/Jim Otto) has the players' names reversed under their pictures. The bottom half of each panel explains that these cards were also on other Eskimo "take home cartons."

		NM
	Complete Set (15):	850.00
	Common Player:	50.00
(1)	Lance Alworth, John Charles	95.00
(2)	Al Atkinson, George Goeddeke	50.00
(3)	Marlin Briscoe, Billy Shaw	50.00
(4)	Gino Cappelletti, Dale Livingston	50.00
(5)	Eric Crabtree, Jim Dunaway	50.00
(6)	Ben Davidson, Bob Griese	130.00
(7)	Hewritt Dixon, Pete Beathard	60.00
(8)	Mike Garrett, Bob Hunt	50.00
(9)	Daryle Lamonica, Willie Frazier	60.00
(10)	Jim Lynch, John Hadl	60.00
(11)	Kent McCloughan, Tom Regner	50.00
(12)	Jim Nance, Billy Neighbors	50.00
(13)	Rick Norton, Paul Costa	50.00
(14)	Jim Otto, Len Dawson (Names reversed)	125.00
(15)	Matt Snell, Dick Post	50.00

1997 E-X2000

E-X2000 consists of a 60-card base set with one parallel and four inserts. The base cards feature "Sky-View" technology, with a die-cut image over a transparent window. The Essential Credentials parallel set consists of less than 100 numbered sets. The inserts include A Cut Above, Fleet of Foot, Star Date 2000 and Autographs.

		MT
	Complete Set (60):	100.00
	Common Player:	.40
	Minor Stars:	.75
	Credential Cards:	10x-20x
	Credential Rookies:	5x-10x
	Pack (2):	5.00
	Wax Box (24):	100.00
1	*Jake Plummer*	18.00
2	Jamal Anderson	.75
3	*Rae Carruth*	5.00
4	Kerry Collins	1.00
5	*Darnell Autry*	3.00
6	Rashaan Salaam	.75
7	Troy Aikman	5.00
8	Deion Sanders	2.50
9	Emmitt Smith	8.00
10	Herman Moore	.75
11	Barry Sanders	5.00
12	Mark Chmura	.75
13	Brett Favre	12.00
14	Antonio Freeman	.75
15	Reggie White	.75
16	Cris Carter	.40
17	Brad Johnson	.40
18	*Troy Davis*	.75
19	*Danny Wuerffel*	4.00
20	Dave Brown	.40
21	*Ike Hilliard*	5.00
22	Ty Detmer	.40
23	Ricky Watters	.75
24	Tony Banks	3.00
25	Eddie Kennison	2.50
26	*Jim Druckenmiller*	8.00
27	Jerry Rice	5.00
28	Steve Young	3.00
29	Trent Dilfer	.75
30	*Warrick Dunn*	8.00
31	Terry Allen	.40
32	Gus Frerotte	.40
33	Vinny Testaverde	.40
34	*Antowain Smith*	6.00
35	Thurman Thomas	.75
36	Jeff Blake	.75
37	Carl Pickens	.40
38	Terrell Davis	5.00
39	John Elway	3.00
40	Eddie George	7.00
41	Steve McNair	4.00
42	Marshall Faulk	.75
43	Marvin Harrison	2.50
44	Mark Brunell	5.00
45	Marcus Allen	.75
46	Elvis Grbac	.40
47	Karim Abdul-Jabbar	3.50
48	Dan Marino	10.00
49	Drew Bledsoe	5.00
50	Terry Glenn	4.00
51	Curtis Martin	5.00
52	Keyshawn Johnson	1.00
53	Tim Brown	.40
54	Jeff George	.40
55	Jerome Bettis	.75
56	Kordell Stewart	5.00
57	Stan Humphries	.40
58	Junior Seau	.75
59	Joey Galloway	.75
60	Chris Warren	.40

1997 E-X2000 Essential Credentials

Essential Credentials paralleled the 60-card E-X2000 set, but was reprinted with silver holofoil around the border. The cards contained the words "Essential Credentials" across the top and were numbered to 100 sets on the back.

	MT
Essential Credential Cards:	10x-20x
Essential Credential Rookies:	5x-10x
Production 100 Sets	

1997 E-X2000 Essential Creditials Parallel

	MT
Complete Set (60):	100.00
Common Player:	.40
Minor Stars:	.75
Credential Cards:	10x-20x
Credential Rookies:	5x-10x
Wax Box:	100.00

1997 E-X2000 A Cut Above

This 10-card insert features players on cards die-cut to look like saw blades. A Cut Above cards were inserted 1:288.

		MT
	Complete Set (10):	600.00
	Common Player:	15.00
1	Barry Sanders	75.00
2	Brett Favre	120.00
3	Dan Marino	100.00
4	Eddie George	80.00
5	Emmitt Smith	100.00
6	Jerry Rice	60.00
7	Joey Galloway	15.00
8	John Elway	40.00
9	Mark Brunell	60.00
10	Terrell Davis	60.00

1997 E-X2000 Fleet of Foot

The cards in this 20-card insert are die-cut to look like football cleats. They were inserted 1:20.

		MT
	Complete Set (20):	220.00
	Common Player:	3.00
1	Antonio Freeman	8.00
2	Barry Sanders	25.00
3	Carl Pickens	3.00
4	Chris Warren	3.00
5	Curtis Martin	20.00
6	Deion Sanders	12.00
7	Emmitt Smith	40.00
8	Jerry Rice	20.00
9	Joey Galloway	6.00
10	Karim Abdul-Jabbar	15.00
11	Kordell Stewart	20.00
12	Lawrence Phillips	3.00
13	Mark Brunell	20.00
14	Marvin Harrison	8.00
15	Rae Carruth	10.00
16	Ricky Watters	3.00
17	Steve Young	15.00
18	Terrell Davis	20.00
19	Terry Glenn	18.00
20	Shawn Springs	3.00

A player's name in *italic type* indicates a rookie card.

1997 E-X2000 Star Date 2000

This 15-card insert features young stars of the NFL. The cards were inserted 1:9.

		MT
Complete Set (15):		60.00
Common Player:		1.50
1	Curtis Martin	6.00
2	Darnell Autry	3.00
3	Darrell Russell	1.50
4	Eddie Kennison	3.00
5	Jim Druckenmiller	8.00
6	Karim Abdul-Jabbar	6.00
7	Kerry Collins	3.00
8	Keyshawn Johnson	3.00
9	Marvin Harrison	3.00
10	Orlando Pace	1.50
11	Pat Barnes	1.50
12	Reidel Anthony	5.00
13	Tim Biakabutuka	1.50
14	Warrick Dunn	12.00
15	Yatil Green	4.00

1998 E-X2001

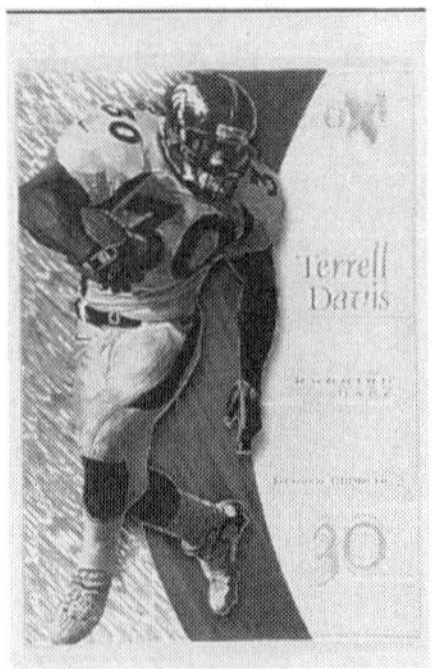

Each of the 60 base cards in this set are holographic and gold-foil stamped with player-specific die-cuts mounted on durable, see-thru plastic stock exposed along a large portion of the card. The Essential Credentials Now parallel cards differ from the base set in color, holo-foil and scarcity. Each card is sequentially numbered according to the player's card number in the base set. Card #1 has only one single and card #60 has cards numbered to 60. The Essential Credentials Future is similar to the Now set except in color, holo-foil and the sequentially numbering is opposite the player's card number. For example, card #1 has 60 cards and card #60 only has one.

		MT
Complete Set (60):		100.00
Common Player:		.30
Minor Stars:		.60
Pack (2):		5.00
Wax Box (24):		110.00
1	Kordell Stewart	3.00
2	Steve Young	2.50
3	Mark Brunell	3.00
4	Brett Favre	8.00
5	Barry Sanders	8.00
6	Warrick Dunn	3.00
7	Jerry Rice	4.00
8	Dan Marino	6.00
9	Emmitt Smith	6.00
10	John Elway	4.00
11	Eddie George	3.00
12	Jake Plummer	3.00
13	Terrell Davis	6.00
14	Curtis Martin	2.50
15	Troy Aikman	4.00
16	Terry Glenn	1.00
17	Mike Alstott	1.00
18	Drew Bledsoe	3.00
19	Keyshawn Johnson	.30
20	Dorsey Levens	.30
21	Elvis Grbac	.30
22	Ricky Watters	1.00
23	Robert Smith	1.00
24	Trent Dilfer	1.00
25	Joey Galloway	1.00
26	Rob Moore	.30
27	Steve McNair	1.50
28	Jim Harbaugh	.30
29	Troy Davis	.30
30	Rob Johnson	1.00
31	Shannon Sharpe	.30
32	Jerome Bettis	1.00
33	Tim Brown	.30
34	Kerry Collins	1.00
35	Garrison Hearst	.30
36	Antonio Freeman	1.00
37	Charlie Garner	.30
38	Glenn Foley	.30
39	Yatil Green	.30
40	Tiki Barber	.30
41	Bobby Hoying	.30
42	Corey Dillon	2.00
43	Antowain Smith	1.50
44	*Robert Edwards*	10.00
45	*Jammi German*	2.00
46	*Ahman Green*	8.00
47	*Hines Ward*	5.00
48	*Skip Hicks*	4.00
49	*Brian Griese*	12.00
50	*Charlie Batch*	10.00
51	*Jacquez Green*	6.00
52	*John Avery*	6.00
53	*Kevin Dyson*	6.00
54	*Peyton Manning*	25.00
55	*Randy Moss*	25.00
56	*Ryan Leaf*	12.00
57	*Curtis Enis*	10.00
58	*Charles Woodson*	10.00
59	*Robert Holcombe*	6.00
60	*Fred Taylor*	15.00

1998 E-X2001 Essential Credentials Future Parallel

		MT
Complete Set (60):		125.00
Common Player:		.30
Minor Stars:		.60
Wax Box:		110.00
1	Kordell Stewart (60)	3.00
2	Steve Young (59)	2.50
3	Mark Brunell (58)	3.00
4	Brett Favre (57)	8.00
5	Barry Sanders (56)	8.00
6	Warrick Dunn (55)	3.00
7	Jerry Rice (54)	4.00
8	Dan Marino (53)	6.00
9	Emmitt Smith (52)	6.00
10	John Elway (51)	4.00
11	Eddie George (50)	3.00
12	Jake Plummer (49)	3.00
13	Terrell Davis (48)	6.00
14	Curtis Martin (47)	2.50
15	Troy Aikman (46)	4.00
16	Terry Glenn (45)	1.00
17	Mike Alstott (44)	1.00
18	Drew Bledsoe (43)	3.00
19	Keyshawn Johnson (42)	.50
20	Dorsey Levens (41)	.50
21	Elvis Grbac (40)	.50
22	Ricky Watters (39)	1.00
23	Robert Smith (38)	1.00
24	Trent Dilfer (37)	1.00
25	Joey Galloway (36)	1.00
26	Rob Moore (35)	.50
27	Steve McNair (34)	1.50
28	Jim Harbaugh (33)	.50
29	Troy Davis (32)	.50
30	Rob Johnson (31)	1.00
31	Shannon Sharpe (30)	.50
32	Jerome Bettis (29)	1.00
33	Tim Brown (28)	.50
34	Kerry Collins (27)	1.00
35	Garrison Hearst (26)	.50
36	Antonio Freeman (25)	1.00
37	Charlie Garner (24)	.50
38	Glenn Foley (23)	.50
39	Yatil Green (22)	.50
40	Tiki Barber (21)	.50
41	Bobby Hoying (20)	.50
42	Corey Dillon (19)	2.00
43	Antowain Smith (18)	1.50
44	*Robert Edwards (17)*	10.00
45	*Jammi German (16)*	2.00
46	*Ahman Green (15)*	6.00
47	*Hines Ward (14)*	5.00
48	*Skip Hicks (13)*	4.00
49	*Brian Griese (12)*	6.00
50	*Charlie Batch (11)*	12.00
51	*Jacquez Green (10)*	6.00
52	*John Avery (9)*	6.00
53	*Kevin Dyson (8)*	6.00
54	*Peyton Manning (7)*	600.00
55	*Randy Moss (6)*	40.00
56	*Ryan Leaf (5)*	12.00
57	*Curtis Enis (4)*	10.00
58	*Charles Woodson (3)*	10.00
59	*Robert Holcombe (2)*	6.00
60	*Fred Taylor (1)*	18.00

1998 E-X2001 Essential Credentials Now Parallel

		MT
Complete Set (60):		125.00
Common Player:		.30
Minor Stars:		.60
Wax Box:		110.00
1	Kordell Stewart (1)	3.00
2	Steve Young (2)	2.50
3	Mark Brunell (3)	3.00
4	Brett Favre (4)	8.00
5	Barry Sanders (5)	8.00
6	Warrick Dunn (6)	3.00
7	Jerry Rice (7)	4.00
8	Dan Marino (8)	6.00
9	Emmitt Smith (9)	6.00
10	John Elway (10)	4.00
11	Eddie George (11)	3.00
12	Jake Plummer (12)	3.00
13	Terrell Davis (13)	6.00
14	Curtis Martin (14)	2.50
15	Troy Aikman (15)	4.00
16	Terry Glenn (16)	1.00
17	Mike Alstott (17)	1.00
18	Drew Bledsoe (18)	3.00
19	Keyshawn Johnson (19)	.50
20	Dorsey Levens (20)	.50
21	Elvis Grbac (21)	.50
22	Ricky Watters (22)	1.00
23	Robert Smith (23)	1.00
24	Trent Dilfer (24)	1.00
25	Joey Galloway (25)	1.00
26	Rob Moore (26)	.50
27	Steve McNair (27)	1.50
28	Jim Harbaugh (28)	.50
29	Troy Davis (29)	.50
30	Rob Johnson (30)	1.00
31	Shannon Sharpe (31)	.50
32	Jerome Bettis (32)	1.00
33	Jim Brown (33)	.50
34	Kerry Collins (34)	1.00
35	Garrison Hearst (35)	.50
36	Antonio Freeman (36)	1.00
37	Charlie Garner (37)	.50
38	Glenn Foley (38)	.50
39	Yatil Green (39)	.50
40	Tiki Barber (40)	.50
41	Bobby Hoying (41)	.50
42	Corey Dillon (42)	2.00
43	Antowain Smith (43)	1.50
44	*Robert Edwards (44)*	10.00
45	*Jammi German (45)*	2.00
46	*Ahman Green (46)*	6.00
47	*Hines Ward (47)*	5.00
48	*Skip Hicks (48)*	4.00
49	*Brian Griese (49)*	6.00
50	*Charlie Batch (50)*	12.00
51	*Jacquez Green (51)*	6.00
52	*John Avery (52)*	6.00
53	*Kevin Dyson (53)*	6.00
54	*Peyton Manning (54)*	250.00
55	*Randy Moss (55)*	400.00
56	*Ryan Leaf (56)*	12.00
57	*Curtis Enis (57)*	10.00
58	*Charles Woodson (58)*	10.00
59	*Robert Holcombe (59)*	6.00
60	*Fred Taylor (60)*	18.00

1998 E-X2001 Destination Honolulu

Hawaiian culture is celebrated on these wooden inserts, with five different statuesque die-cuts. Singles were inserted 1:720 packs.

		MT
Complete Set (10):		900.00
Common Player:		35.00
Inserted 1:720		
1	Peyton Manning	175.00
2	Terrell Davis	150.00
3	Corey Dillon	70.00
4	Eddie George	80.00
5	Emmitt Smith	150.00
6	Warrick Dunn	100.00
7	Brett Favre	200.00
8	Antowain Smith	35.00
9	Barry Sanders	200.00
10	Ryan Leaf	100.00

1998 E-X2001 Helmet Heroes

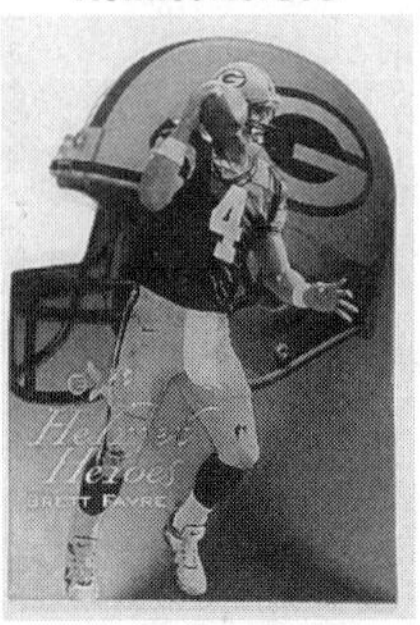

Each single is die-cut around the helmet at the top of the cards. These team color-coded, thick plastic inserts featured some of the NFL's most dynamic players. They were found 1:24 packs.

		MT
Complete Set (20):		200.00
Common Player:		3.00
Inserted 1:24		
1	Barry Sanders	25.00
2	Emmitt Smith	18.00
3	Brett Favre	25.00
4	Mark Brunell	10.00
5	Jerry Rice	12.00
6	Steve Young	8.00
7	Warrick Dunn	10.00
8	Kordell Stewart	10.00
9	John Elway	12.00
10	Troy Aikman	12.00
11	Dan Marino	18.00
12	Curtis Martin	8.00
13	Dorsey Levens	3.00
14	Jake Plummer	10.00
15	Corey Dillon	7.00
16	Yancey Thigpen	3.00
17	Randy Moss	35.00
18	Curtis Enis	10.00
19	Charles Woodson	10.00
20	Fred Taylor	18.00

1998 E-X2001 Star Date 2001

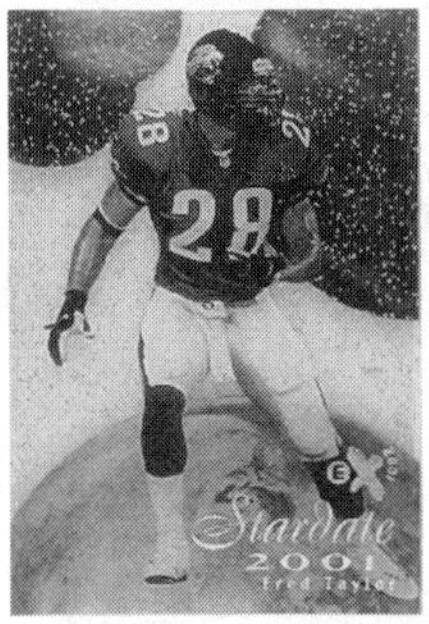

The idea behind this set was to include the stars of tomorrow on a thick, plastic stock with flecks of foil running through it and highlighted with etched silver foil stamping. Singles were inserted 1:12 packs.

		MT
Complete Set (15):		70.00
Common Player:		1.50
Minor Stars:		3.00
Inserted 1:12		
1	Randy Moss	20.00
2	Fred Taylor	10.00
3	Corey Dillon	6.00
4	Jake Plummer	8.00
5	Antowain Smith	4.00
6	Wilmont Perry	1.50
7	Donald Hayes	1.50
8	Tavian Banks	8.00
9	John Dutton	1.50
10	Kevin Dyson	6.00
11	Germane Crowell	3.00
12	Bobby Hoying	1.50
13	Jerome Pathon	3.00
14	Ryan Leaf	8.00
15	Peyton Manning	15.00

1999 E-X Century

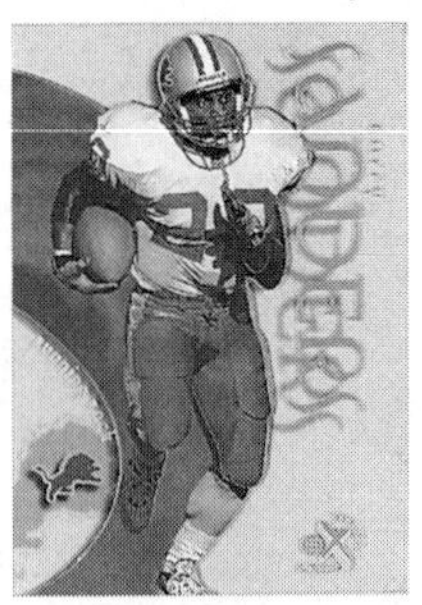

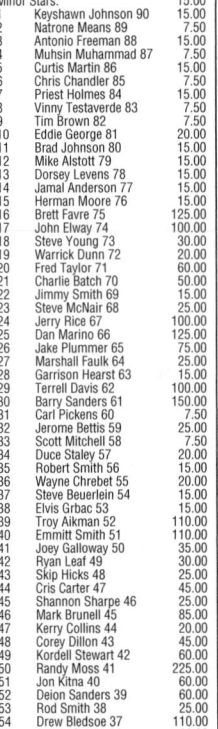

This was a 90-card set that included 30 rookie cards found 1:4 packs. Each base card was printed on clear plastic stock with holographic foil stamping. Parallel sets included Essential Credentials Future and Essential Credentials Now. Other inserts included: Authen-Kicks, Autographics, Bright Lites and E-Xtraordinary. SRP was $5.99 for three-card packs.

		MT
Complete Set (90):		175.00
Common Player:		.25
Minor Stars:		.50
Common Rookie:		1.50
Inserted 1:4		
Pack (3):		6.00
Wax Box (24):		125.00
1	Keyshawn Johnson	1.00
2	Natrone Means	.50
3	Antonio Freeman	1.00
4	Muhsin Muhammad	.50
5	Curtis Martin	1.00
6	Chris Chandler	.50
7	Priest Holmes	1.00
8	Vinny Testaverde	.50
9	Tim Brown	.50
10	Eddie George	1.25
11	Brad Johnson	1.00
12	Mike Alstott	1.00
13	Dorsey Levens	1.00
14	Jamal Anderson	1.00
15	Herman Moore	1.00
16	Brett Favre	4.00
17	John Elway	3.00
18	Steve Young	1.50
19	Warrick Dunn	1.00
20	Fred Taylor	2.00
21	Charlie Batch	1.75
22	Jimmy Smith	1.00
23	Steve McNair	1.25
24	Jerry Rice	2.00
25	Dan Marino	3.00
26	Jake Plummer	2.00
27	Marshall Faulk	1.00
28	Garrison Hearst	.50
29	Terrell Davis	3.00
30	Barry Sanders	4.00
31	Carl Pickens	.50
32	Jerome Bettis	1.00
33	Scott Mitchell	.25
34	Duce Staley	.75
35	Robert Smith	1.00
36	Wayne Chrebet	1.00
37	Steve Beuerlein	.50
38	Elvis Grbac	.50
39	Troy Aikman	2.00
40	Emmitt Smith	3.00
41	Joey Galloway	1.00
42	Ryan Leaf	1.00
43	Skip Hicks	.50
44	Cris Carter	1.00
45	Shannon Sharpe	.50
46	Mark Brunell	1.50
47	Kerry Collins	.50
48	Corey Dillon	1.00
49	Kordell Stewart	1.25
50	Randy Moss	4.00
51	Jon Kitna	1.25
52	Deion Sanders	1.00
53	Rod Smith	.50
54	Drew Bledsoe	1.50
55	Terrell Owens	1.00
56	Napoleon Kaufman	1.00
57	Trent Green	1.00
58	Ricky Watters	1.00
59	Randall Cunningham	1.00
60	Peyton Manning	3.00
61	*Tim Couch*	20.00
62	*Amos Zereoue*	5.00
63	*Cade McNown*	7.00
64	*Donovan McNabb*	10.00
65	*Ricky Williams*	25.00
66	*Daunte Culpepper*	20.00
67	*Troy Edwards*	7.00
68	*Peerless Price*	5.00
69	*Edgerrin James*	25.00
70	*Champ Bailey*	4.00
71	*Akili Smith*	10.00
72	*Kevin Johnson*	7.00
73	*Cecil Collins*	10.00
74	*David Boston*	7.00
75	*Torry Holt*	7.00
76	*J.J. Johnson*	6.00
77	*Na Brown*	1.50
78	*Rob Konrad*	3.00
79	*Michael Cloud*	3.00
80	*Craig Yeast*	1.50
81	*Brock Huard*	4.00
82	*Chris McAlister*	3.00
83	*Shaun King*	8.00
84	*Dee Miller*	1.50
85	*Joe Germaine*	4.00
86	*D'Wayne Bates*	3.00
87	*Kevin Faulk*	5.00
88	*Antoine Winfield*	3.00
89	*Reggie Kelly*	1.50
90	*Antwan Edwards*	1.50

A player's name in *italic type* indicates a rookie card.

1999 E-X Century Essential Credentials Future Parallel

This was a 90-card parallel set that was sequentially numbered opposite of the player's card number.

		MT
Common Player:		7.50
Minor Stars:		15.00
1	Keyshawn Johnson 90	15.00
2	Natrone Means 89	7.50
3	Antonio Freeman 88	15.00
4	Muhsin Muhammad 87	7.50
5	Curtis Martin 86	15.00
6	Chris Chandler 85	7.50
7	Priest Holmes 84	15.00
8	Vinny Testaverde 83	7.50
9	Tim Brown 82	7.50
10	Eddie George 81	20.00
11	Brad Johnson 80	15.00
12	Mike Alstott 79	15.00
13	Dorsey Levens 78	15.00
14	Jamal Anderson 77	15.00
15	Herman Moore 76	15.00
16	Brett Favre 75	125.00
17	John Elway 74	100.00
18	Steve Young 73	30.00
19	Warrick Dunn 72	20.00
20	Fred Taylor 71	60.00
21	Charlie Batch 70	50.00
22	Jimmy Smith 69	15.00
23	Steve McNair 68	25.00
24	Jerry Rice 67	100.00
25	Dan Marino 66	125.00
26	Jake Plummer 65	75.00
27	Marshall Faulk 64	25.00
28	Garrison Hearst 63	15.00
29	Terrell Davis 62	100.00
30	Barry Sanders 61	150.00
31	Carl Pickens 60	7.50
32	Jerome Bettis 59	25.00
33	Scott Mitchell 58	7.50
34	Duce Staley 57	20.00
35	Robert Smith 56	15.00
36	Wayne Chrebet 55	20.00
37	Steve Beuerlein 54	15.00
38	Elvis Grbac 53	15.00
39	Troy Aikman 52	110.00
40	Emmitt Smith 51	110.00
41	Joey Galloway 50	35.00
42	Ryan Leaf 49	30.00
43	Skip Hicks 48	25.00
44	Cris Carter 47	45.00
45	Shannon Sharpe 46	25.00
46	Mark Brunell 45	85.00
47	Kerry Collins 44	20.00
48	Corey Dillon 43	45.00
49	Kordell Stewart 42	60.00
50	Randy Moss 41	225.00
51	Jon Kitna 40	60.00
52	Deion Sanders 39	60.00
53	Rod Smith 38	25.00
54	Drew Bledsoe 37	110.00
55	Terrell Owens 36	60.00
56	Napoleon Kaufman 35	50.00
57	Trent Green 34	30.00
58	Ricky Watters 33	30.00
59	Randall Cunningham 32	50.00
60	Peyton Manning 31	160.00
61	Tim Couch 30	300.00
62	Amos Zereoue 29	75.00
63	Cade McNown 28	150.00
64	Donovan McNabb 27	150.00
65	Ricky Williams 26	300.00
66	Daunte Culpepper 25	150.00
67	Troy Edwards 24	100.00
68	Peerless Price 23	85.00
69	Edgerrin James 22	350.00
70	Champ Bailey 21	60.00
71	Akili Smith 20	125.00
72	Kevin Johnson 19	85.00
73	Cecil Collins 18	200.00
74	David Boston 17	125.00
75	Torry Holt 16	125.00
76	J.J. Johnson 15	100.00
77	Na Brown 14	75.00
78	Rob Konrad 13	75.00
79	Michael Cloud 12	80.00
80	Craig Yeast 11	80.00
81	Brock Huard 10	125.00
82	Chris McAlister 9	7.50
83	Shaun King 8	7.50
84	Dee Miller 7	7.50
85	Joe Germaine 6	7.50
86	D'Wayne Bates 5	7.50
87	Kevin Faulk 4	7.50
88	Antoine Winfield 3	7.50
89	Reggie Kelly 2	7.50
90	Antwan Edwards 1	7.50

1999 E-X Century Essential Credentials Now Parallel

This was a 90-card parallel set that was sequentially numbered to the player's card number.

		MT
Common Player:		7.50
Minor Stars:		15.00
1	Keyshawn Johnson 1	7.50
2	Natrone Means 2	7.50
3	Antonio Freeman 3	7.50
4	Muhsin Muhammad 4	7.50
5	Curtis Martin 5	7.50
6	Chris Chandler 6	7.50
7	Priest Holmes 7	7.50
8	Vinny Testaverde 8	7.50
9	Tim Brown 9	7.50
10	Eddie George 10	125.00
11	Brad Johnson 11	100.00
12	Mike Alstott 12	100.00
13	Dorsey Levens 13	85.00
14	Jamal Anderson 14	85.00
15	Herman Moore 15	85.00
16	Brett Favre 16	400.00
17	John Elway 17	350.00
18	Steve Young 18	175.00
19	Warrick Dunn 19	85.00
20	Fred Taylor 20	160.00
21	Charlie Batch 21	125.00
22	Jimmy Smith 22	50.00
23	Steve McNair 23	75.00
24	Jerry Rice 24	160.00
25	Dan Marino 25	250.00
26	Jake Plummer 26	130.00
27	Marshall Faulk 27	60.00
28	Garrison Hearst 28	40.00
29	Terrell Davis 29	175.00
30	Barry Sanders 30	275.00
31	Carl Pickens 31	30.00
32	Jerome Bettis 32	60.00
33	Scott Mitchell 33	25.00
34	Duce Staley 34	50.00
35	Robert Smith 35	35.00
36	Wayne Chrebet 36	45.00
37	Steve Beuerlein 37	20.00
38	Elvis Grbac 38	20.00
39	Troy Aikman 39	125.00
40	Emmitt Smith 40	140.00
41	Joey Galloway 41	45.00
42	Ryan Leaf 42	30.00
43	Skip Hicks 43	30.00
44	Cris Carter 44	45.00
45	Shannon Sharpe 45	25.00
46	Mark Brunell 46	80.00
47	Kerry Collins 47	20.00
48	Corey Dillon 48	45.00
49	Kordell Stewart 49	45.00
50	Randy Moss 50	175.00
51	Jon Kitna 51	35.00
52	Deion Sanders 52	35.00
53	Rod Smith 53	15.00
54	Drew Bledsoe 54	60.00
55	Terrell Owens 55	35.00
56	Napoleon Kaufman 56	25.00
57	Trent Green 57	20.00
58	Ricky Watters 58	15.00
59	Randall Cunningham 59	25.00
60	Peyton Manning 60	120.00
61	Tim Couch 61	200.00
62	Amos Zereoue 62	50.00
63	Cade McNown 63	100.00
64	Donovan McNabb 64	100.00
65	Ricky Williams 65	200.00
66	Daunte Culpepper 66	100.00
67	Troy Edwards 67	60.00
68	Peerless Price 68	50.00
69	Edgerrin James 69	200.00
70	Champ Bailey 70	40.00
71	Akili Smith 71	85.00
72	Kevin Johnson 72	50.00
73	Cecil Collins 73	75.00
74	David Boston 74	50.00
75	Torry Holt 75	50.00
76	J.J. Johnson 76	35.00
77	Na Brown 77	15.00
78	Rob Konrad 78	20.00
79	Michael Cloud 79	20.00
80	Craig Yeast 80	15.00
81	Brock Huard 81	35.00
82	Chris McAlister 82	15.00
83	Shaun King 83	35.00
84	Dee Miller 84	7.50
85	Joe Germaine 85	25.00
86	D'Wayne Bates 86	20.00
87	Kevin Faulk 87	35.00
88	Antoine Winfield 88	15.00
89	Reggie Kelly 89	7.50
90	Antwan Edwards 90	7.50

1999 E-X Century Authen-Kicks

This 12-card insert included swatches of game-worn shoes. Each player hand-numbered their cards with each to a different amount. Singles were randomly inserted.

		MT
Complete Set (12):		1000.
Common Player:		50.00
1	Travis McGriff 235	50.00
2	Trent Green 190	50.00
3	Brock Huard 280	50.00
4	Randall Cunningham 290	60.00
5	Donovan McNabb 210	125.00
6	Torry Holt 285	85.00
7	Joe Germaine 280	50.00
8	Cade McNown 260	125.00
9	Doug Flutie 215	85.00
10	O.J. McDuffie 285	50.00
11	Ricky Williams 215	225.00
12	Dan Marino 285	175.00

1999 E-X Century Bright Lites

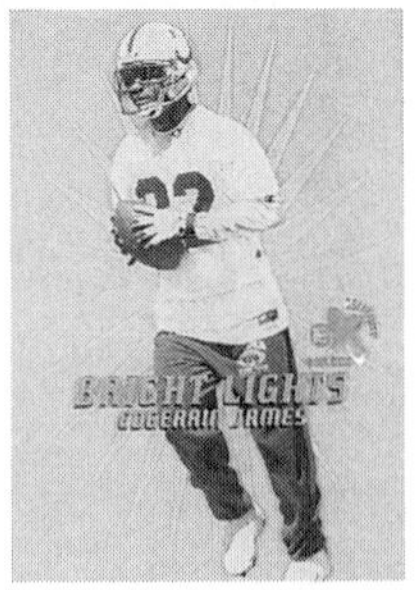

This was a 20-card insert that included the game's best and pictured them on a green plastic stock with a glowing star background. Singles were found 1:24 packs. A parallel Orange version was also issued.

		MT
Complete Set (20):		160.00
Common Player:		3.00
Inserted 1:24		
1	Randy Moss	15.00
2	Tim Couch	20.00
3	Eddie George	6.00
4	Brett Favre	15.00
5	Steve Young	7.00
6	Barry Sanders	15.00
7	Troy Aikman	10.00
8	Jake Plummer	10.00

9 Edgerrin James 20.00
10 Terrell Davis 12.00
11 Warrick Dunn 3.00
12 Jerry Rice 10.00
13 Fred Taylor 10.00
14 Mark Brunell 7.00
15 Emmitt Smith 12.00
16 Ricky Williams 20.00
17 Charlie Batch 6.00
18 Jamal Anderson 3.00
19 Peyton Manning 12.00
20 Dan Marino 12.00

1999 E-X Century E-Xtraordinary

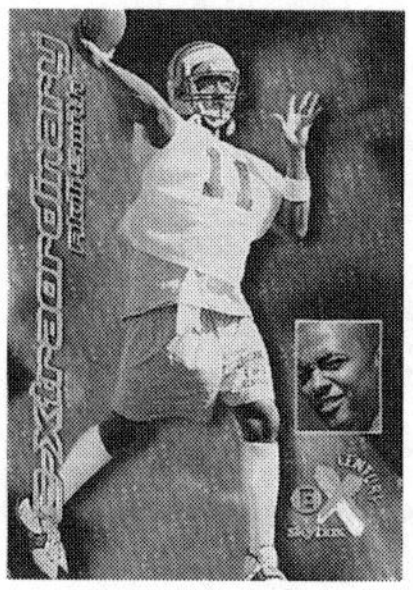

This 15-card insert included the top young players in the game and pictured them on lenticular stock with a team color coded background. Singles were inserted 1:9 packs.

MT
Complete Set (15): 75.00
Common Player: 2.00
Inserted 1:9
1 Ricky Williams 12.00
2 Corey Dillon 2.00
3 Charlie Batch 4.00
4 Terrell Davis 8.00
5 Edgerrin James 12.00
6 Jake Plummer 6.00
7 Tim Couch 12.00
8 Warrick Dunn 2.00
9 Akili Smith 6.00
10 Randy Moss 12.00
11 Cade McNown 6.00
12 Fred Taylor 5.00
13 Donovan McNabb 6.00
14 Torry Holt 4.00
15 Peyton Manning 8.00

2000 E-X

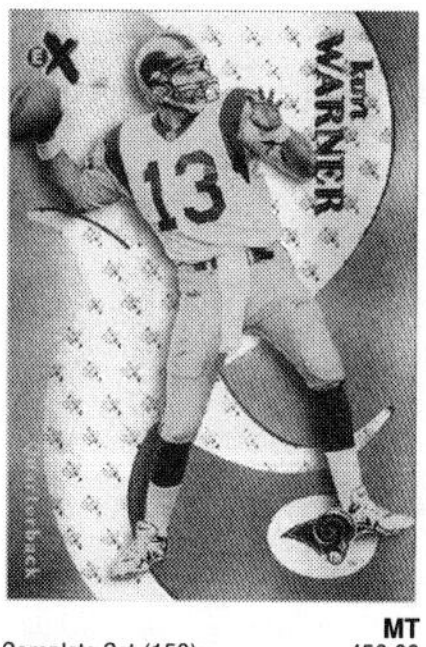

MT
Complete Set (150): 450.00
Common Player: .20
Minor Stars: .40
Common Rookie: 4.00
Production 1,500 Sets
Pack (5): 4.00
Wax Box (24): 70.00
1 Tim Couch 1.25
2 Daunte Culpepper 1.25
3 Jake Reed .40
4 Donovan McNabb 1.00
5 Terry Glenn .50
6 Vinny Testaverde .40
7 Michael Westbrook .40
8 Errict Rhett .40
9 Joey Galloway .50
10 O.J. McDuffie .20
11 Rob Johnson .40
12 Warren Sapp .40
13 Brian Griese .75
14 Derrick Mayes .40
15 Ike Hilliard .20
16 Kevin Dyson .40
17 Shannon Sharpe .40
18 Cade McNown .75
19 Damon Huard .50
20 James Stewart .40
21 Kevin Johnson .50
22 Muhsin Muhammad .40
23 Shaun King 1.00
24 Corey Dillon .50
25 Fred Taylor 1.00
26 Peyton Manning 2.50
27 Steve McNair .50
28 Tim Brown .50
29 Brad Johnson .50
30 Edgerrin James 2.50
31 Germane Crowell .40
32 Kordell Stewart .50
33 Randy Moss 2.50
34 Tony Banks .40
35 Akili Smith .50
36 Charlie Batch .50
37 Duce Staley .50
38 Jerome Bettis .50
39 Rich Gannon .40
40 Steve Young 1.00
41 Tony Gonzalez .40
42 Curtis Martin .50
43 Eddie George .75
44 Marshall Faulk .50
45 Troy Edwards .40
46 Curtis Enis .40
47 Jake Plummer .50
48 Jon Kitna .50
49 Qadry Ismail .20
50 Terrell Davis 1.75
51 Troy Aikman 1.25
52 Elvis Grbac .40
53 Jeff Blake .40
54 Kurt Warner 2.50
55 Ricky Watters .40
56 Torry Holt .50
57 Brett Favre 2.50
58 Chris Chandler .40
59 Eric Moulds .50
60 Jimmy Smith .50
61 Ricky Williams 1.50
62 Antonio Freeman .50
63 Curtis Conway .40
64 Emmitt Smith 1.75
65 Kerry Collins .40
66 Marvin Harrison .50
67 Tyrone Wheatley .40
68 Charlie Garner .40
69 Derrick Alexander .20
70 Jamal Anderson .50
71 Mike Alstott .50
72 Ryan Leaf .50
73 Tim Biakabutuka .40
74 Amani Toomer .20
75 Dorsey Levens .50
76 Frank Sanders .40
77 Junior Seau .40
78 Steve Beuerlein .40
79 Wayne Chrebet .50
80 Carl Pickens .40
81 Drew Bledsoe 1.00
82 Isaac Bruce .50
83 Marcus Robinson .50
84 Stephen Davis .50
85 Cris Carter .50
86 Ed McCaffrey .50
87 Jerry Rice 1.25
88 Mark Brunell 1.00
89 Peerless Price .40
90 Terance Mathis .20
91 Tony Martin .20
92 Jevon Kearse .50
93 Robert Smith .50
94 Rob Moore .40
95 Charles Johnson .20
96 Doug Flutie .75
97 Sean Dawkins .20
98 Keenan McCardell .20
99 Bill Schroeder .20
100 Rod Smith .40
101 *Peter Warrick* 35.00
102 *Corey Simon* 6.00
103 *Danny Farmer* 6.00
104 *Jamal Lewis* 50.00
105 *Jerry Porter* 6.00
106 *Joe Hamilton* 7.50
107 *Marc Bulger* 4.00
108 *R. Jay Soward* 7.50
109 *Ron Dugans* 6.00
110 *Shaun Alexander* 25.00
111 *Travis Prentice* 12.50
112 *Anthony Becht* 6.00
113 *Bubba Franks* 7.50
114 *Chris Redman* 15.00
115 *Dennis Northcutt* 7.50
116 *Dez White* 5.00
117 *Gari Scott* 4.00
118 *Mareno Philyaw* 4.00
119 *Ron Dayne* 40.00
120 *Shyrone Stith* 6.00
121 *Tee Martin* 6.00
122 *Tom Brady* 15.00
123 *Trung Canidate* 6.00
124 *Chad Pennington* 30.00
125 *Chris Cole* 4.00
126 *Courtney Brown* 7.50
127 *Doug Chapman* 4.00
128 *Giovanni Carmazzi* 7.50
129 *J.R. Redmond* 10.00
130 *Michael Wiley* 5.00
131 *Reuben Droughns* 5.00
132 *Terrelle Smith* 4.00
133 *Thomas Jones* 15.00
134 *Travis Taylor* 10.00
135 *Anthony Lucas* 4.00
136 *Curtis Keaton* 5.00
137 *Frank Moreau* 7.50
138 *Darrell Jackson* 7.50
139 *Laveranues Coles* 7.50
140 *Brian Urlacher* 25.00
141 *Plaxico Burress* 20.00
142 *Sammy Morris* 10.00
143 *Sylvester Morris* 20.00
144 *Tim Rattay* 7.50
145 *Todd Pinkston* 6.00
146 *Troy Walters* 6.00
147 *Sebastian Janikowski* 6.00
148 *JaJuan Dawson* 7.50
149 *Trevor Gaylor* 5.00
150 *Rondell Mealey* 5.00

2000 E-X Essential Credentials Parallel

MT
Essential Credential Cards: 15x-30x
Production 50 Sets
Essential Credential Rookies: 2x-4x
Production 25 Sets
1 Tim Couch 1.25
2 Daunte Culpepper 1.25
3 Jake Reed .40
4 Donovan McNabb 1.00
5 Terry Glenn .50
6 Vinny Testaverde .40
7 Michael Westbrook .40
8 Errict Rhett .40
9 Joey Galloway .50
10 O.J. McDuffie .20
11 Rob Johnson .40
12 Warren Sapp .40
13 Brian Griese .75
14 Derrick Mayes .40
15 Ike Hilliard .20
16 Kevin Dyson .40
17 Shannon Sharpe .40
18 Cade McNown .75
19 Damon Huard .50
20 James Stewart .40
21 Kevin Johnson .50
22 Muhsin Muhammad .40
23 Shaun King 1.00
24 Corey Dillon .50
25 Fred Taylor 1.00
26 Peyton Manning 2.50
27 Steve McNair .50
28 Tim Brown .50
29 Brad Johnson .50
30 Edgerrin James 2.50
31 Germane Crowell .40
32 Kordell Stewart .50
33 Randy Moss 2.50
34 Tony Banks .40
35 Akili Smith .50
36 Charlie Batch .50
37 Duce Staley .50
38 Jerome Bettis .50
39 Rich Gannon .40
40 Steve Young 1.00
41 Tony Gonzalez .40
42 Curtis Martin .50
43 Eddie George .75
44 Marshall Faulk .50
45 Troy Edwards .40
46 Curtis Enis .40
47 Jake Plummer .50
48 Jon Kitna .50
49 Qadry Ismail .20
50 Terrell Davis 1.75
51 Troy Aikman 1.25
52 Elvis Grbac .40
53 Jeff Blake .40
54 Kurt Warner 2.50
55 Ricky Watters .40
56 Torry Holt .50
57 Brett Favre 2.50
58 Chris Chandler .40
59 Eric Moulds .50
60 Jimmy Smith .50
61 Ricky Williams 1.50
62 Antonio Freeman .50
63 Curtis Conway .40
64 Emmitt Smith 1.75
65 Kerry Collins .40
66 Marvin Harrison .50
67 Tyrone Wheatley .40
68 Charlie Garner .40
69 Derrick Alexander .20
70 Jamal Anderson .50
71 Mike Alstott .50
72 Ryan Leaf .50
73 Tim Biakabutuka .40
74 Amani Toomer .20
75 Dorsey Levens .50
76 Frank Sanders .40
77 Junior Seau .40
78 Steve Beuerlein .40
79 Wayne Chrebet .50
80 Carl Pickens .40
81 Drew Bledsoe 1.00
82 Isaac Bruce .50
83 Marcus Robinson .50
84 Stephen Davis .50
85 Cris Carter .50
86 Ed McCaffrey .50
87 Jerry Rice 1.25
88 Mark Brunell 1.00
89 Peerless Price .40
90 Terance Mathis .20
91 Tony Martin .20
92 Jevon Kearse .50
93 Robert Smith .50
94 Rob Moore .40
95 Charles Johnson .20
96 Doug Flutie .75
97 Sean Dawkins .20
98 Keenan McCardell .20
99 Bill Schroeder .20
100 Rod Smith .40
101 *Peter Warrick* 35.00
102 *Corey Simon* 6.00
103 *Danny Farmer* 6.00
104 *Jamal Lewis* 50.00
105 *Jerry Porter* 6.00
106 *Joe Hamilton* 7.50
107 *Marc Bulger* 4.00
108 *R. Jay Soward* 7.50
109 *Ron Dugans* 6.00
110 *Shaun Alexander* 25.00
111 *Travis Prentice* 12.50
112 *Anthony Becht* 6.00
113 *Bubba Franks* 7.50
114 *Chris Redman* 15.00
115 *Dennis Northcutt* 7.50
116 *Dez White* 5.00
117 *Gari Scott* 4.00
118 *Mareno Philyaw* 4.00
119 *Ron Dayne* 40.00
120 *Shyrone Stith* 6.00
121 *Tee Martin* 6.00
122 *Tom Brady* 6.00
123 *Trung Canidate* 6.00
124 *Chad Pennington* 30.00
125 *Chris Cole* 4.00
126 *Courtney Brown* 7.50
127 *Doug Chapman* 4.00
128 *Giovanni Carmazzi* 7.50
129 *J.R. Redmond* 10.00
130 *Michael Wiley* 5.00
131 *Reuben Droughns* 5.00
132 *Terrelle Smith* 4.00
133 *Thomas Jones* 15.00
134 *Travis Taylor* 10.00
135 *Anthony Lucas* 4.00
136 *Curtis Keaton* 5.00
137 *Frank Moreau* 7.50
138 *Darrell Jackson* 7.50
139 *Laveranues Coles* 7.50
140 *Brian Urlacher* 25.00
141 *Plaxico Burress* 20.00
142 *Sammy Morris* 10.00
143 *Sylvester Morris* 20.00
144 *Tim Rattay* 7.50
145 *Todd Pinkston* 6.00
146 *Troy Walters* 6.00
147 *Sebastian Janikowski* 6.00
148 *JaJuan Dawson* 7.50
149 *Trevor Gaylor* 5.00
150 *Rondell Mealey* 5.00

Post-1980 cards in Near Mint condition will generally sell for about 75% of the quoted Mint value. Excellent-condition cards bring no more than 40%.

2000 E-X E-Xceptional Red

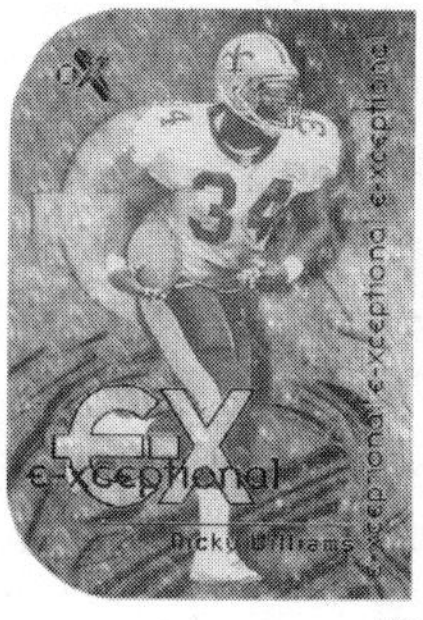

MT
Complete Set (15): 25.00
Common Player: 1.00
Minor Stars: 2.00
Inserted 1:12
Green Cards: 3x-6x
Inserted 1:288
Blue Cards: 5x-10x
Production 100 Sets
1 Kurt Warner 5.00
2 Peyton Manning 4.00
3 Brett Favre 4.00
4 Tim Couch 2.50
5 Keyshawn Johnson 1.00
6 Mark Brunell 2.00
7 Eddie George 2.00
8 Edgerrin James 4.00
9 Ricky Williams 2.50
10 Randy Moss 4.00
11 Jamal Lewis 5.00
12 Emmitt Smith 3.00
13 Thomas Jones 3.00
14 Fred Taylor 2.00
15 Chad Pennington 4.00

2000 E-X E-Xciting

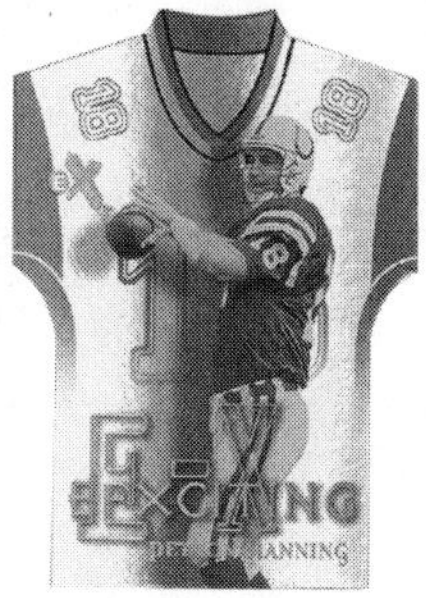

MT
Complete Set (10): 35.00
Common Player: 2.00
Inserted 1:24
1 Fred Taylor 3.00
2 Troy Aikman 4.00
3 Edgerrin James 7.00
4 Brett Favre 7.00
5 Peyton Manning 7.00
6 Emmitt Smith 5.00
7 Randy Moss 7.00
8 Kurt Warner 8.00
9 Marshall Faulk 2.00
10 Peter Warrick 8.00

2000 E-X E-Xplosive

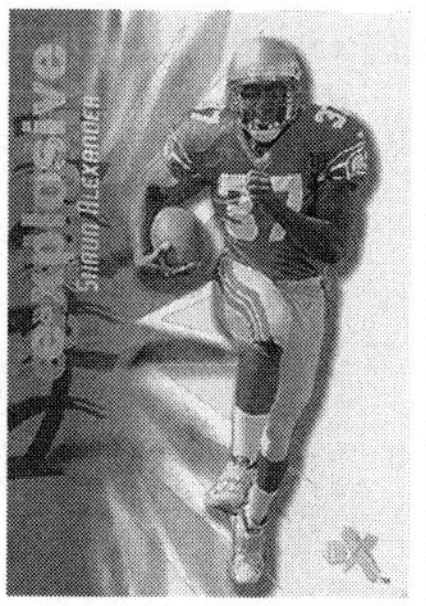

MT
Complete Set (20): 35.00
Common Player: 1.00
Inserted 1:8
1 Kurt Warner 5.00
2 Marvin Harrison 1.00
3 Ricky Williams 2.50
4 Eddie George 1.50
5 Emmitt Smith 3.00
6 Troy Aikman 2.50
7 Randy Moss 4.00
8 Edgerrin James 4.00
9 Keyshawn Johnson 1.00
10 Tim Couch 2.00
11 Fred Taylor 1.75
12 Brett Favre 4.00
13 Peyton Manning 4.00
14 Donovan McNabb 1.50
15 Ron Dayne 5.00
16 Jake Plummer 1.00
17 Marshall Faulk 1.00
18 Travis Taylor 2.00
19 Terrell Davis 3.00
20 Shaun Alexander 3.50

2000 E-X Generation E-X

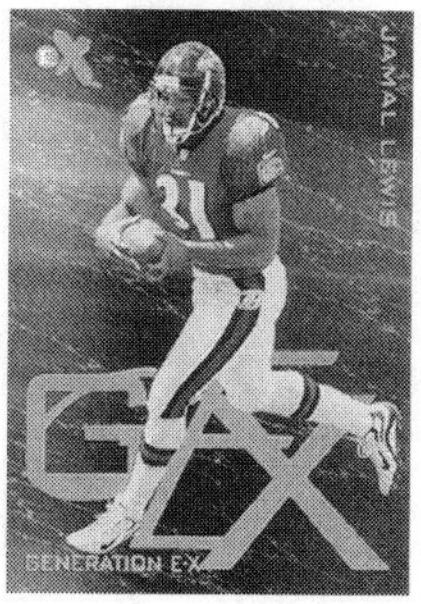

MT
Complete Set (15): 15.00
Common Player: .50
Minor Stars: 1.00
Inserted 1:4
1 Peter Warrick 3.50
2 Plaxico Burress 1.75
3 R. Jay Soward 1.00
4 Shaun Alexander 2.50
5 Chad Pennington 3.00
6 Giovanni Carmazzi 1.00
7 Thomas Jones 1.50
8 Todd Pinkston .50
9 Chris Redman 1.50
10 Jamal Lewis 5.00
11 Ron Dayne 4.00
12 Dez White .50
13 J.R. Redmond 1.25
14 Sylvester Morris 1.75
15 Travis Taylor 1.25

2000 E-X NFL Debut Postmarks

MT
Complete Set (15): 300.00
Common Player: 15.00
Inserted 1:288
1 Peter Warrick 50.00
2 Travis Taylor 25.00
3 Thomas Jones 30.00
4 Ron Dayne 50.00
5 Plaxico Burress 35.00
6 Sylvester Morris 35.00
7 Todd Pinkston 20.00
8 Jamal Lewis 60.00
9 Shaun Alexander 40.00
10 J.R. Redmond 25.00
11 Dennis Northcutt 20.00
12 Bubba Franks 15.00
13 R. Jay Soward 15.00
14 Jerry Porter 15.00
15 Chad Pennington 45.00

1948-52 Exhibit W468 Football

The 59-card set, which measures 3-1/4" x 5-3/8", was released by the Exhibit Supply Co. of Chicago in 1948-52. The thick cards were sold in vending machines. The cards, which have blank backs, were originally in black and white. In the following years they were released in sepia, blue, yellow and red. The cards that are colored carry a 3-4 times higher value than the black-and-white and sepia cards. Released in three groups of 32 in 1948, 1950 and 1951, the 1951 set is the easiest to find of the three. The 1951 cards were also reissued in sepia tone in 1952 and possibly 1953. A checklist card was produced in 1950. It was printed in black-and-white and green. It resembles the Bednarik card, however, it lists the 32 players from the 1950 set on the front. In addition, nine-card ad displays were produced, and feature the Bednarik checklist. In 1948, the words "Made in USA" measure 5/8 inch on the card. Also, 11 of the 1948 cards were single prints (Comp, Jacobs, Cifers, Horvath, Mastrangelo, LeForce, Johnson, Pritko, Wedemeyer, Coulter and Schlinkman). In 1950, the single-print cards were Bednarik, Hoerner, Davis, Perry, Ruby and Justice. When the 1950 cards went into a second printing, 11 new cards were issued to replace the original 11 single prints. On the new cards, "Made in USA" measures 7/16 of an inch. The 1951 printing featured only 16 cards, with the six single-print cards from 1950 and 10 cards from 1948 shelved. The 1951 cards feature "Made in USA" in 1/2-inch high letters.

NM
Complete Set (59): 4000.
Common Player DP: 10.00
Common Player: 40.00
Common Player SP48: 175.00
Common Player SP50: 50.00
1 Frankie Albert (DP) (48/50/51/52) 10.00
2 Dick Barwegan (DP) (51/52) 10.00
3 Sammy Baugh (DP) (48/50/51/52) 45.00
4 Chuck Bednarik (SP50) 125.00
5 Tony Canadeo (DP) (51/52) 15.00
6 Paul Christman (48/50) 40.00
7 Bob Cifers (SP48) 175.00
8 Irv Comp (SP48) 175.00
9 Charley Conerly (DP) (48/50/51/52) 20.00
10 George Connor (DP) (51/52) 15.00
11 Dewitt Coulter (SP50) 175.00
12 Glenn Davis (SP50) 100.00
13 Glenn Dobbs (48/50) 40.00
14 John Dottley (DP) (51/52) 10.00
15 Bill Dudley (48/50) 50.00
16 Tom Fears (DP) (51/52) 15.00
17 Joe Geri (DP) (51/52) 10.00
18 Otto Graham (DP) (48/50/51/52) 50.00
19 Pat Harder (48/50) 40.00
20 Elroy Hirsch (DP) (51/52) 20.00
21 Dick Hoerner (SP50) 60.00
22 Bob Hoernschemeyer (DP) (51/52) 10.00
23 Les Horvath (SP48) 200.00
24 Jack Jacobs (SP48) 175.00
25 Nate Johnson (SP48) 175.00
26 Charlie Justice (SP50) 75.00
27 Bobby Layne (DP) (48/50/51/52) 35.00
28 Clyde LeForce (SP48) 175.00
29 Sid Luckman (48/50) 75.00
30 John Lujack (48/50) 60.00
31 Bill McColl (DP) (51/52) 175.00
32 Ollie Matson (DP) (51/52) 20.00
33 Bill McColl (DP) (51/52) 10.00
34 Fred Morrison (DP) (50/51/52) 10.00
35 Marion Motley (DP) (48/50/51/52) 20.00
36 Chuck Ortmann (DP) (51/52) 10.00
37 Joe Perry (SP50) 100.00
38 Pete Pihos (48/50) 50.00
39 Steve Pritko (SP48) 175.00
40 George Ratterman (DP) (48/50/51/52) 10.00
41 Jay Rhodemyre (DP) (51/52) 10.00
42 Martin Ruby (SP50) 75.00
43 Julie Rykovich (DP) (51/52) 10.00
44 Walt Schlinkman (SP48) 185.00
45 Emil (Red) Sitko (DP) (51/52) 10.00
46 Vitamin Smith (DP) (50/51/52) 10.00
47 Norm Standlee (48/50) 40.00
48 George Taliaferro (DP) (50/51/52) 10.00
49 Y.A. Tittle (HOR) (48/50) 75.00
50 Charley Trippi (DP) (48/50/51/52) 15.00
51 Frank Tripucka (DP) (48/50/51/52) 12.00
52 Emlen Tunnell (DP) (51/52) 15.00
53 Bulldog Turner (DP) (48/50/51/52) 15.00
54 Steve Van Buren (48/50) 60.00
55 Bob Waterfield (DP) (48/50/51/52) 25.00
56 Herm Wedemeyer (SP48) 500.00
57 Bob Williams (DP) (51/52) 10.00
58 Claude Buddy Young (DP) (passing) (48/50/51/52) 10.00
59 Tank Younger (DP) (50/51/52) 10.00
NNO Checklist Card SP50 (Chuck Bednarik) 500.00

F

1990 FACT Pro Set Cincinnati

Produced for 29 schools in the Cincinnati school district, the set was used as an educational tool for grade school students. The promotion ran for 15 straight weeks, with 25-card cello packs handed out to the students. The card fronts are identical to 1990 Pro Set Series I cards, while the backs have math, grammar and science questions. The card backs carry the card numbers in the lower right. The missing numbers from the first series are 338, 376 and 377.

MT
Complete Set (375): 550.00
Common Player: 1.00
1 Barry Sanders (W1) 25.00
2 Joe Montana (W1) 20.00
3 Coach of the Year (Lindy Infante) (W1) (UER) (missing Coach next to Packers) 1.00
4 Man of the Year (Warren Moon) (W1) (UER) (missing R symbol) 2.00
5 Defensive Player of the Year (Keith Millard) (W1) 1.00
6 Defensive Rookie of the Year (Derrick Thomas) (W1) (UER) (no 1989 on front banner of card) 2.00

7	Comeback Player of the Year (Ottis Anderson) (W1)	1.50
8	Passing Leader (Joe Montana) (W2)	20.00
9	Rushing Leader (Christian Okoye) (W2)	1.00
10	Total Yardage Leader (Thurman Thomas) (W2)	3.00
11	Kick Scoring Leader (Mike Cofer) (W2)	1.00
12	TD Scoring Leader (Dalton Hilliard) (W2) (UER) (O.J. Simpson not listed in stats, but is mentioned in text)	1.00
13	Receiving Leader (Sterling Sharpe) (W2)	3.00
14	Punting Leader (Rich Camarillo) (W3)	1.00
15	Punt Return Leader (Walter Stanley) (W3)	1.00
16	Kickoff Return Leader (Rod Woodson) (W3)	2.00
17	Interception Leader (Felix Wright) (W3)	1.00
18	Sack Leader (Chris Doleman) (W3)	1.00
19	Heisman Trophy (Andre Ware) (W3)	1.00
20	Outland Trophy (Mohammed Elewonibi) (W4)	1.00
21	Lombardi Award (Percy Snow) (W4)	1.00
22	Maxwell Award (Anthony Thompson) (W4)	1.00
23	1990 HOF Selection (Buck Buchanan) (W4) (Sacking Bart Starr))	1.00
24	1990 HOF Selection (Bob Griese) (W4)	1.50
25	1990 HOF Selection (Franco Harris) (W5)	1.50
26	1990 HOF Selection (Ted Hendricks) (W4)	1.00
27	1990 HOF Selection (Jack Lambert) (W5)	1.00
28	1990 HOF Selection (Tom Landry) (W5)	1.50
29	1990 HOF Selection (Bob St. Clair) (W5)	1.00
30	Aundray Bruce (W5) (UER) (Stats say Falcons)	1.00
31	Tony Casillas (W5) (UER) (Stats say Falcons)	1.00
32	Shawn Collins (W5)	1.00
33	Marcus Cotton (W6)	1.00
34	Bill Fralic (W6)	1.00
35	Chris Miller (W6)	1.50
36	Deion Sanders (W6) (UER) (Stats say Falcons)	14.00
37	John Settle (W6)	1.00
38	Jerry Glanville (CO) (W6)	1.00
39	Cornelius Bennett (W7)	1.50
40	Jim Kelly (W7)	3.00
41	Mark Kelso (W7) (UER) (No fumble rec. in '88; mentioned in '89)	1.00
42	Scott Norwood (W7)	1.00
43	Nate Odomes (W7)	1.50
44	Scott Radecic (W7)	1.00
45	Jim Ritcher (W8)	1.00
46	Leonard Smith (W8)	1.00
47	Darryl Talley (W8)	1.00
48	Marv Levy (CO) (W8)	1.00
49	Neal Anderson (W8)	1.00
50	Kevin Butler (W8)	1.00
51	Jim Covert (W9)	1.00
52	Richard Dent (W9)	1.00
53	Jay Hilgenberg (W9)	1.00
54	Steve McMichael (W9)	1.00
55	Ron Morris (W9)	1.00
56	John Roper (W9)	1.00
57	Mike Singletary (W9)	1.50
58	Keith Van Horne (W10)	1.00
59	Mike Ditka (CO) (W10)	3.00
60	Lewis Billups (W10)	1.00
61	Eddie Brown (W10)	1.00
62	Jason Buck (W10)	1.00
63	Rickey Dixon (W10)	1.00
64	Tim McGee (W11)	1.00
65	Eric Thomas (W11)	1.00
66	Ickey Woods (W11)	1.00
67	Carl Zander (W11)	1.00
68	Sam Wyche (CO) (W11)	1.00
69	Paul Farren (W11)	1.00
70	Thane Gash (W12)	1.00
71	David Grayson (W12)	1.00
72	Bernie Kosar (W12)	1.50
73	Reggie Langhorne (W12)	1.00
74	Eric Metcalf (W12)	2.00
75	Ozzie Newsome (W12)	1.50
76	Felix Wright (W13)	1.00
77	Bud Carson (CO) (W13)	1.00
78	Troy Aikman (W13)	25.00
79	Michael Irvin (W13)	4.00
80	Jim Jeffcoat (W13)	1.00
81	Crawford Ker (W13)	1.00
82	Eugene Lockhart (W13)	1.00
83	Kelvin Martin (W14)	1.50
84	Ken Norton Jr.	1.50
85	Jimmy Johnson (CO) (W14)	2.00
86	Steve Atwater (W14)	1.00
87	Tyrone Braxton (W14)	1.00
88	John Elway (W14)	14.00
89	Simon Fletcher (W15)	1.00
90	Ron Holmes (W15)	1.00
91	Bobby Humphrey (W15)	1.00
92	Vance Johnson (W15)	1.00
93	Ricky Nattiel (W15)	1.00
94	Dan Reeves (CO) (W15)	1.50
95	Jim Arnold (W1)	1.00
96	Jerry Ball (W1)	1.00
97	Bennie Blades (W1)	1.00
98	Lomas Brown (W1)	1.00
99	Michael Cofer (W1)	1.00
100	Richard Johnson (W4)	1.00
101	Eddie Murray (W4)	1.00
102	Barry Sanders (W2)	25.00
103	Chris Spielman (W2)	1.00
104	William White (W2)	1.50
105	Eric Williams (W2)	1.00
106	Wayne Fontes (CO) (W3) (UER) (Says born in MO, actually born in MA)	1.00
107	Brent Fullwood (W3)	1.00
108	Ron Hallstrom (W3)	1.00
109	Tim Harris (W8)	1.00
110	Johnny Holland (W8)	1.00
111	Perry Kemp (W8)	1.00
112	Don Majkowski (W9)	1.00
113	Mark Murphy (W9)	1.00
114	Sterling Sharpe (W9)	4.00
115	Ed West (W9)	1.50
116	Lindy Infante (CO) (W9)	1.00
117	Steve Brown (W9)	1.00
118	Ray Childress (W10)	1.00
119	Ernest Givins (W10)	1.50
120	John Grimsley (W10)	1.00
121	Alonzo Highsmith (W10)	1.00
122	Drew Hill (W10)	1.50
123	Bubba McDowell (W10)	1.50
124	Dean Steinkuhler (W10)	1.00
125	Lorenzo White (W11)	1.00
126	Tony Zendejas (W11)	1.00
127	Jack Pardee (CO) (W11)	1.00
128	Albert Bentley (W11)	1.00
129	Dean Biasucci (W11)	1.00
130	Duane Bickett (W11)	1.00
131	Bill Brooks (W12)	1.50
132	Jon Hand (W12)	1.00
133	Mike Prior (W12)	1.00
134	Andre Rison (W12)	2.00
135	Rohn Stark (W12)	1.00
136	Donnell Thompson (W12)	1.00
137	Clarence Verdin (W13)	1.00
138	Fredd Young (W13)	1.00
139	Ron Meyer (CO) (W14)	1.00
140	John Alt (W14)	1.00
141	Steve DeBerg (W14)	1.50
142	Irv Eatman (W1)	1.00
143	Dino Hackett (W2)	1.00
144	Nick Lowery (W2)	1.00
145	Bill Maas (W2)	1.00
146	Stephone Paige (W5)	1.00
147	Neil Smith (W3)	2.00
148	Marty Schottenheimer (CO) (W3)	1.00
149	Steve Beuerlein (W3)	1.00
150	Tim Brown (W4)	3.00
151	Mike Dyal (W4)	1.00
152	Mervyn Fernandez (W4)	1.00
153	Willie Gault (W4)	1.00
154	Bob Golic (W5)	1.00
155	Bo Jackson (W5)	3.00
156	Don Mosebar (W5)	1.00
157	Steve Smith (W5)	1.00
158	Greg Townsend (W5)	1.00
159	Bruce Wilkerson (W6)	1.00
160	Steve Wisniewski (W6) (Blocking for Bo Jackson)	1.00
161	Art Shell (CO) (W6)	2.00
162	Flipper Anderson (W6)	1.00
163	Greg Bell (W6) (UER) (Stats have 5 catches, should be 9)	1.00
164	Henry Ellard (W6)	1.50
165	Jim Everett (W6)	1.50
166	Jerry Gray (W7)	1.00
167	Kevin Greene (W7)	2.00
168	Pete Holohan (W13)	1.00
169	Larry Kelm (W13)	1.00
170	Tom Newberry (W13)	1.00
171	Vince Newsome (W13)	1.00
172	Irv Pankey (W14)	1.00
173	Jackie Slater (W14)	1.00
174	Fred Strickland (W14)	1.00
175	Mike Wilcher (W14) (UER) (Fumble rec. number different from 1989 Pro Set card)	1.00
176	John Robinson (CO) (W7) (UER) (Stats say Rams, should says L.A. Rams)	1.00
177	Mark Clayton (W7)	1.50
178	Roy Foster (W7)	1.00
179	Harry Galbreath (W7)	1.00
180	Jim C. Jensen (W8)	1.00
181	Dan Marino (W15)	35.00
182	Louis Oliver (W15)	1.00
183	Sammie Smith (W15)	1.00
184	Brian Sochia (W15)	1.00
185	Don Shula (CO) (W15)	1.50
186	Joey Browner (W8)	1.00
187	Anthony Carter (W15)	1.50
188	Chris Doleman (W8)	1.00
189	Steve Jordan (W4)	1.00
190	Carl Lee (W4)	1.00
191	Randall McDaniel (W5)	1.00
192	Mike Merriweather (W5)	1.00
193	Keith Millard (W14)	1.00
194	Al Noga (W12)	1.00
195	Scott Studwell (W5)	1.00
196	Henry Thomas (W12)	1.50
197	Herschel Walker (W5)	1.50
198	Wade Wilson (W5)	1.50
199	Gary Zimmerman (W5)	1.00
200	Jerry Burns (CO) (W6)	1.00
201	Vincent Brown (W6)	1.50
202	Hart Lee Dykes (W14)	1.00
203	Sean Farrell (W6)	1.00
204	Fred Marion (W6)	1.00
205	Stanley Morgan (W15) (UER) (Text says he reached 10,000 yards fastest; 3 players did it in 10 seasons)	1.50
206	Eric Sievers (W6)	1.00
207	John Stephens (W15)	1.00
208	Andre Tippett (W15)	1.00
209	Rod Rust (CO) (W15)	1.00
210	Morten Andersen (W6)	1.00
211	Brad Edelman (W12)	1.00
212	John Fourcade (W12)	1.00
213	Dalton Hilliard (W13)	1.00
214	Rickey Jackson (W13) (Forcing Jim Kelly fumble)	1.00
215	Vaughan Johnson (W13)	1.00
216	Eric Martin (W13)	1.50
217	Sam Mills (W7)	1.00
218	Pat Swilling (W7) (UER) (Total fumble recoveries listed as 4, should be 5)	1.50
219	Frank Warren (W7)	1.00
220	Jim Wilks (W7)	1.00
221	Jim Mora (CO) (W7)	1.00
222	Raul Allegre (W2)	1.00
223	Carl Banks (W1)	1.00
224	John Elliott (W1)	1.00
225	Erik Howard (W7)	1.00
226	Pepper Johnson (W2)	1.00
227	Leonard Marshall (W7) (UER) (In Super Bowl XXI, George Martin had the safety)	1.00
228	Dave Meggett (W2)	1.50
229	Bart Oates (W3)	1.00
230	Phil Simms (W8)	1.50
231	Lawrence Taylor (W8)	2.00
232	Bill Parcells (CO) (W8)	1.50
233	Troy Benson (W8)	1.00
234	Kyle Clifton (W8) (UER) (Born: Onley, should be Olney)	1.00
235	Johnny Hector (W8)	1.00
236	Jeff Lageman (W9)	1.50
237	Pat Leahy (W9)	1.00
238	Freeman McNeil (W9)	1.00
239	Ken O'Brien (W9)	1.00
240	Al Toon (W9)	1.50
241	Jo Jo Townsell	1.00
242	Bruce Coslet (CO) (W10)	1.00
243	Eric Allen (W10)	1.00
244	Jerome Brown (W10)	1.50
245	Keith Byars (W10)	1.50
246	Cris Carter (W13)	4.00
247	Randall Cunningham (W13)	2.00
248	Keith Jackson (W14)	1.50
249	Mike Quick (W14)	1.50
250	Clyde Simmons (W14)	1.50
251	Andre Waters (W14)	1.00
252	Reggie White (W15)	2.00
253	Buddy Ryan (CO) (W15)	1.00
254	Rich Camarillo (W15)	1.00
255	Earl Ferrell (W10) (No mention of retirement on card front)	1.00
256	Roy Green (W10)	1.00
257	Ken Harvey (W3)	1.00
258	Ernie Jones	1.00
259	Tim McDonald (W11)	1.00
260	Timm Rosenbach (W11) (UER) (Born '67, should be '66)	1.50
261	Luis Sharpe (W3)	1.00
262	Vai Sikahema (W3)	1.00
263	J.T. Smith (W1)	1.00
264	Ron Wolfley (W1) (UER) (Born Blaisdel, should be Blasdel)	1.00
265	Joe Bugel (CO) (W11)	1.00
266	Gary Anderson (W11)	1.00
267	Bubby Brister (W1)	1.00
268	Merril Hoge (W11)	1.00
269	Carnell Lake (W2)	1.00
270	Louis Lipps (W11)	1.00
271	David Little (W3)	1.00
272	Greg Lloyd (W3)	2.00
273	Keith Willis (W11)	1.00
274	Tim Worley (W3)	1.00
275	Chuck Noll (CO) (W4)	1.50
276	Marion Butts (W4)	1.00
277	Gill Byrd (W2)	1.00
278	Vencie Glenn (W2) (UER) (Sack total should be 2, not 2.5)	1.00
279	Burt Grossman (W4)	1.00
280	Gary Plummer (W4)	1.00
281	Bill Ray Smith (W12)	1.00
282	Billy Joe Tolliver (W12)	1.00
283	Dan Henning (CO) (W1)	1.00
284	Harris Barton (W1)	1.00
285	Michael Carter (W1)	1.00
286	Mike Cofer (W1)	1.00
287	Roger Craig (W1)	1.50
288	Don Griffin (W1)	1.00
289	Charles Haley (W2)	1.50
290	Pierce Holt (W2)	1.00
291	Ronnie Lott (W2)	1.50
292	Guy McIntyre (W2)	1.00
293	Joe Montana (W2)	20.00
294	Tom Rathman (W2)	1.50
295	Jerry Rice (W3)	20.00
296	Jesse Sapolu (W3)	1.00
297	John Taylor (W3)	1.50
298	Michael Walter (W3)	1.00
299	George Seifert (CO) (W3)	2.00
300	Jeff Bryant (W3)	1.00
301	Jacob Green (W4)	1.00
302	Norm Johnson (UER) (W4) (Card shop not in Garden Grove, should say Fullerton)	1.00
303	Bryan Millard (W4)	1.00
304	Joe Nash (W4)	1.00
305	Eugene Robinson (W4)	1.00
306	John L. Williams (W14)	1.00
307	Dave Wyman (W14) (NFL EXP is in caps, inconsisten with rest of the set)	1.00
308	Chuck Knox (CO) (W14)	1.00
309	Mark Carrier (C14)	1.50
310	Paul Gruber (W14)	1.00
311	Harry Hamilton (W15)	1.00
312	Bruce Hill (W15)	1.00
313	Donald Igwebuike (W15)	1.00
314	Kevin Murphy (W15)	1.00
315	Ervin Randle (W12)	1.00
316	Mark Robinson (W12)	1.00
317	Lars Tate (W12)	1.00
318	Vinny Testaverde (W12)	2.00
319	Ray Perkins (CO) (W12)	1.00
320	Earnest Byner (W12)	1.00
321	Gary Clark (W12) (Randall Cunningham looking on from sidelines)	2.00
322	Darryl Grant (W13)	1.00
323	Darrell Green (W13)	1.00
324	Jim Lachey (W13)	1.00
325	Charles Mann (W13)	1.00
326	Wilber Marshall (W13)	1.00
327	Ralf Mojsiejenko (W13)	1.00
328	Art Monk (W15)	2.00
329	Gerald Riggs (W15)	1.00
330	Mark Rypien (W14)	1.00
331	Ricky Sanders (W14)	1.00
332	Alvin Walton (W4)	1.00
333	Joe Gibbs (CO) (W5)	2.00
334	Aloha Stadium (W5) (Site of Pro Bowl)	1.00
335	Brian Blades (PB) (W5)	1.50
336	James Brooks (PB) (W5)	1.00
337	Shane Conlan (PB) (W5)	1.00
339	Ray Donaldson (PB) (W5)	1.00
340	Ferrell Edmunds (PB) (W6)	1.00
341	Boomer Esiason (PB) (W6)	1.50
342	David Fulcher (PB) (W6)	1.00
343	Chris Hinton (PB) (W6)	1.00
344	Rodney Holman (PB) (W6)	1.00
345	Kent Hull (PB) (W6)	1.00
346	Tunch Ilkin (PB) (W7)	1.00
347	Mike Johnson (PB) (W7)	1.00
348	Greg Kragen (PB) (W7)	1.00
349	Dave Krieg (PB) (W7)	1.00
350	Albert Lewis (PB) (W7)	1.00
351	Howie Long (PB) (W7)	1.50
352	Bruce Matthews (PB) (W8)	1.00
353	Clay Matthews (PB) (W8)	1.00
354	Erik McMillan (PB) (W8)	1.00
355	Karl Mecklenburg (PB) (W8)	1.00
356	Anthony Miller (PB) (W8)	2.00
357	Frank Minnifield (PB) (W8)	1.00
358	Max Montoya (PB) (W8)	1.00
359	Warren Moon (PB) (W10)	2.00
360	Mike Munchak (PB) (W9)	1.00
361	Anthony Munoz (PB) (W9)	1.00
362	John Offerdahl (PB) (W9)	1.00
363	Christian Okoye (PB) (W9)	1.00
364	Leslie O'Neal (PB) (W9)	1.00
365	Rufus Porter (PB) (W9) (UER) (TM logo missing)	1.00
366	Andre Reed (PB) (W10)	1.50
367	Johnny Rembert (PB) (W10)	1.00
368	Reggie Roby (PB) (W10)	1.00
369	Kevin Ross (PB) (W10)	1.00
370	Webster Slaughter (PB) (W10)	1.00
371	Bruce Smith (PB) (W11)	1.50
372	Dennis Smith (PB) (W11)	1.00
373	Derrick Thomas (PB) (W11)	2.00
374	Thurman Thomas (PB) (W11)	2.00
375	David Treadwell (PB) (W11)	1.00
376	Lee Williams (PB) (W11)	1.00

1991 FACT Pro Set Mobil

Each of the NFL cities received these cards, sponsored by Mobil Oil and Pro Set, to use as an educational tool for fourth grade students. The cards are identical to the 1990 Pro Set Series I cards, while the backs have questions for the students. Six different sets were issued throughout the program, each with a header card.

		MT
Complete Set (108):		130.00
Common Player:		.75
3	Joe Montana (S1)	10.00
5	Mike Singletary (S2)	1.00
12	Jay Novacek (S3)	1.50
20	Ottis Anderson (S2)	1.00
40	Tim Brown (S1)	1.50
44	Herschel Walker (S1)	1.00
59	Eric Dorsey (S3)	.75
60	John Elliott (S1)	.75
63	Jeff Hostetler (S2)	1.00
69	Eric Moore (S4)	.75
70	Bart Oates (S3)	.75
71	Gary Reasons (S4)	.75
75	Shane Conlan (S3)	.75
78	Jim Kelly (S4)	2.50
84	Darryl Talley (S4)	.75
90	Marv Levy (CO) (S1)	.75
94	Tim Green (S2)	.75
99	Jerry Glanville (CO) (S3)	.75
101	Mark Carrier (S3)	.75
104	Jim Harbaugh (S6)	1.50
105	Brad Muster (S4)	.75
107	Keith Van Horne (S6)	.75
111	Boomer Esiason (S1)	1.00
116	Anthony Munoz (S2)	1.00
117	Sam Wyche (CO) (S4)	.75
118	Paul Farren (S6)	.75
119	Thane Gash (S3)	.75
122	Clay Matthews (S2)	.75
123	Eric Metcalf (S6)	1.25
127	Tommie Agee (S6)	.75
128	Troy Aikman (S6)	12.00
132	Michael Irvin (S6)	3.00
134	Daniel Stubbs (S6)	.75
136	Steve Atwater (S1)	.75
138	John Elway (S2)	8.00
141	Mark Jackson (S6)	.75
142	Karl Mecklenburg (S3)	.75
143	Doug Widell (S2)	.75
153	Wayne Fontes (CO) (S2)	.75
156	Don Majkowski (S1)	.75
157	Tony Mandarich (S6)	.75
158	Mark Murphy (S6)	.75
161	Sterling Sharpe (S4)	2.00
162	Lindy Infante (CO) (S3)	.75
163	Ray Childress (S6)	.75
166	Bruce Matthews (S3)	.75
167	Warren Moon (S6)	2.50
168	Mike Munchak (S4)	.75
169	Al Smith (S6)	.75
174	Bill Brooks (S1)	1.00
179	Clarence Verdin (S3)	.75
182	Steve DeBerg (S1)	1.00
185	Christian Okoye (S3)	.75
189	Marty Schottenheimer (CO) (S1)	.75
191	Howie Long (S2)	1.00
194	Steve Smith (S4)	.75
196	Lionel Washington (S6)	.75
198	Art Shell (CO) (S3)	1.00
203	Buford McGee (S2)	.75
204	Tom Newberry (S6)	.75
205	Frank Stams (S1)	.75
210	Dan Marino (S4)	18.00
212	John Offerdahl (S1)	.75
216	Don Shula (S4)	1.00
217	Darrell Fullington (S6)	.75
218	Tim Irwin (S2)	.75
219	Mike Merriweather (S3)	.75
231	Ed Reynolds (S3)	.75
238	Robert Massey (S4)	.75
246	James Hasty (S1)	.75
247	Erik McMillan (S2)	.75
249	Ken O'Brien (S4)	.75
260	Andre Waters (S2)	.75
270	Joe Bugel (CO) (S2)	.75
271	Gary Anderson (S1)	.75
272	Dermontti Dawson (S4)	.75
275	Tunch Ilkin (S2)	.75
282	Gill Byrd (S4)	.75
290	Michael Carter (S2)	.75
292	Pierce Holt (S3)	.75
297	George Seifert (CO) (S1)	1.25
306	Chuck Knox (CO) (S3)	.75
310	Harry Hamilton (S4)	.75
321	Martin Mayhew (S4)	.75
322	Mark Rypien (S1)	.75
NNO	Title Card - Stay Fit (S1)	.75
NNO	Title Card - Eat Smart (S2)	.75
NNO	Title Card - Stay Off Drugs (S3)	.75
NNO	Title Card - Stay In Tune (S4)	.75
NNO	Title Card - Stay True to Yourself (S5)	.75
NNO	Title Card - Stay In School (S6)	.75
NNO	Title Card - Stay In School (S6)	.75

1992 FACT NFL Properties

The 18-card set was produced by NFL Properties. It showcases a photo of the player, with the NFL shield and "It's A Fact" printed at the top and a slogan at the bottom. The card is bordered in black at the top and bottom. The backs include a quote, with "Think about it..." printed in the lower right. The card number is printed in a black stripe in the lower right.

		MT
Complete Set (18):		35.00
Common Player:		1.00
1	Crack Kills (Warren Moon)	1.50
2	Think Before You Drink (Boomer Esiason)	1.00
3	Play It Straight (Troy Aikman)	8.00
4	Quedate en la Escuela (Anthony Munoz)	1.00
5	Steroids Destroy (Charles Mann)	1.00
6	Never Give Up (Earnest Byner)	1.00
7	Don't Pollute (Joe Jacoby)	1.00
8	Aids Kills (Howie Long)	1.00
9	School's The Ticket (Dan Marino)	12.00
10	Be The Best (Mike Singletary)	1.50
11	Chill (Cornelius Bennett)	1.00
12	Turn It Off (Chris Doleman)	1.00
13	Eat To Win (Jim Harbaugh)	1.50
14	Say It Don't Spray It (Chris Hinton)	1.00
15	Heal The Planet (Nick Lowery)	1.00
16	Respect The Law (Rodney Peete)	1.00
17	Vote (Pat Swilling)	1.00
18	Study (Jim Everett)	1.00

1993 FACT Fleer Shell

Fleer, Shell Oil and Russell Athletic sponsored this 108-card set. The cards were used as educational materials for teachers throughout the country. A set of 18 cards were released each month. The card fronts were identical to the regular 1993 Fleer cards. The backs, however, featured educational questions and player bios.

		MT
Complete Set (108):		50.00
Common Player:		.25
1	Stay in School - Scorecard	.25
2	Andre Rison	.50
3	Jim Kelly	.50
4	Mark Carrier (DB)	.25
5	David Fulcher	.25
6	Eric Metcalf	.25
7	Emmitt Smith	5.00
8	John Elway	2.00
9	Rodney Peete	.25
10	Brett Favre	5.00
11	Houson Oilers (Warren Moon)	.50
12	Reggie Langhorne	.25
13	Christian Okoye	.25
14	Nick Bell	.25
15	Jim Everett	.25
16	Dan Marino	5.00
17	Chris Doleman	.25
18	Leonard Russell	.25
19	Stay Fit - Scoreboard	.25
20	Sam Mills	.25
21	Rodney Hampton	.50
22	Rob Moore	.25
23	Seth Joyner	.25
24	Chris Chandler	.25
25	Barry Foster	.25
26	Stan Humphries	.50
27	Steve Young	2.00
28	Cortez Kennedy	.25
29	Reggie Cobb	.25
30	Mark Rypien	.25
31	Michael Haynes	.25
32	Thurman Thomas	.50
33	Tom Waddle	.25
34	Harold Green	.25
35	Tommy Vardell	.25
36	Michael Irvin	.50
37	Eat Smart - Scorecard	.25
38	Mike Croel	.25
39	Barry Sanders	3.00
40	Sterling Sharpe	.50
41	Haywood Jeffires	.25
42	Duane Bickett	.25
43	Nick Lowery	.25
44	Greg Townsend	.25
45	Todd Lyght	.25
46	Richmond Webb	.25
47	Cris Carter	.50
48	Marv Cook	.25
49	Vaughan Johnson	.25
50	Pepper Johnson	.25
51	Kyle Clifton	.25
52	Fred Barnett	.25
53	Ken Harvey	.25
54	Rod Woodson	.50
55	Stay In Tune - Scorecard	.25
56	Marion Butts	.25
57	Ricky Watters	.50
58	Brian Blades	.25
59	Broderick Thomas	.25
60	Charles Mann	.25
61	Chris Hinton	.25
62	Cornelius Bennett	.25
63	Jim Harbaugh	.50
64	Tim Krumrie	.25
65	Bernie Kosar	.50
66	Troy Aikman	3.00
67	Shannon Sharpe	.50
68	Chris Spielman	.25
69	Brian Noble	.25
70	Curtis Duncan	.25
71	Quentin Coryatt	.50
72	Derrick Thomas	.50
73	Stay Off Drugs - Scorecard	.25
74	Tim Brown	.50
75	Jackie Slater	.25
76	Keith Jackson	.25
77	Terry Allen	.50
78	Andre Tippett	.25
79	Morten Andersen	.25
80	Phil Simms	.25
81	Jeff Lageman	.25
82	Randall Cunningham	.25
83	Randal Hill	.25
84	Neil O'Donnell	.50
85	Gill Byrd	.25
86	John Taylor	.25
87	Eugene Robinson	.25
88	Paul Gruber	.25
89	Andre Collins	.25
90	Chris Miller	.25
91	Stay True To Yourself - Scorecard	.25
92	Andre Reed	.50
93	Richard Dent	.25
94	David Klingler	.25
95	Jay Novacek	.50
96	Steve Atwater	.25
97	Bennie Blades	.25
98	Terrell Buckley	.25
99	Ray Childress	.25
100	Harvey Williams	.25
101	Howie Long	.25
102	Lawrence Taylor	.50
103	Johnny Mitchell	.25
104	Carnell Lake	.25
105	Junior Seau	.50
106	Kevin Fagan	.25
107	Lawrence Dawsey	.25
108	Art Monk	.50

1994 FACT Fleer Shell

This 108-card set was sponsored by Fleer and Shell Oil. The educational sets were broken up into six 18-card subsets which showcased 17 player cards and one header card. The fronts feature the same design as the 1994 Fleer set. The card backs include a head shot and an action photo, with questions printed over the top. The card number is printed in the lower left corner, with the player's name and facsimile autograph in the upper left.

		MT
Complete Set (108):		35.00
Common Player:		.10
1	Cover Card - Stay In School	.10
2	Steve Beuerlein	.10
3	Erric Pegram	.10
4	Darryl Talley	.10
5	Tom Waddle	.10
6	Darryl Williams	.10
7	Tony Jones	.10
8	Jay Novacek	.20

9	Simon Fletcher	.10
10	Jason Hanson	.10
11	Reggie White	.30
12	Ernest Givins	.10
13	Kerry Cash	.10
14	Joe Montana	1.75
15	Anthony Smith	.10
16	Jackie Slater	.10
17	Terry Kirby	.10
18	John Randle	.10
19	Cover Card - Stay Fit	.10
20	Drew Bledsoe	1.75
21	Vaughan Johnson	.10
22	Greg Jackson	.10
23	Rob Moore	.10
24	Byron Evans	.10
25	Rod Woodson	.20
26	Junior Seau	.20
27	Steve Young	1.25
28	Cortez Kennedy	.10
29	Paul Gruber	.10
30	Darrell Green	.10
31	Tyronne Stowe	.10
32	Pierce Holt	.10
33	Steve Tasker	.10
34	Chris Zorich	.10
35	Ricardo McDonald	.10
36	Mark Carrier (WR)	.10
37	Cover Card - Eat Smart	.10
38	Emmitt Smith	3.50
39	Shannon Sharpe	.20
40	Chris Spielman	.10
41	Ken Ruettgers	.10
42	Bubba McDowell	.10
43	Rohn Stark	.10
44	Derrick Thomas	.20
45	Tim Brown	.20
46	Shane Conlan	.10
47	Marco Coleman	.10
48	Steve Jordan	.10
49	Ben Coates	.20
50	Willie Roaf	.10
51	Carlton Bailey	.10
52	Ronnie Lott	.20
53	Eric Allen	.10
54	Dermontti Dawson	.10
55	Cover Card - Stay In Tune	.10
56	Ronnie Harmon	.10
57	Dana Stubblefield	.20
58	Rick Mirer	.30
59	Santana Dotson	.10
60	Jim Lachey	.10
61	Ricky Proehl	.10
62	Jessie Tuggle	.10
63	Jim Kelly	.20
64	Mark Carrier (DB)	.10
65	David Klingler	.10
66	Eric Turner	.10
67	Darrin Smith	.10
68	Glyn Milburn	.20
69	Herman Moore	.30
70	Sterling Sharpe	.20
71	Ray Childress	.10
72	Quentin Coryatt	.10
73	Cover Card - Stay Off Drugs	.10
74	Marcus Allen	.20
75	Jeff Hostetler	.10
76	Jerome Bettis	.40
77	Richmond Webb	.10
78	Randall McDaniel	.10
79	Maurice Hurst	.10
80	Morten Andersen	.10
81	Dave Meggett	.10
82	Brian Washington	.10
83	Randall Cunningham	.10
84	Kevin Greene	.20
85	Leslie O'Neal	.10
86	Tim McDonald	.10
87	Eugene Robinson	.10
88	Hardy Nickerson	.10
89	Chip Lohmiller	.10
90	Jeff George	.20
91	Cover Card - Stay True To Yourself	.10
92	Cornelius Bennett	.10
93	Erik Kramer	.10
94	Tommy Vardell	.10
95	Troy Aikman	1.75
96	John Elway	1.25
97	Barry Sanders	1.75
98	Dan Saleaumua	.10
99	Dan Marino	3.50
100	Jack Del Rio	.10
101	Bruce Armstrong	.10
102	Renaldo Turnbull	.10
103	Phil Simms	.10
104	Boomer Esiason	.10
105	Fred Barnett	.10
106	Greg Lloyd	.20
107	John Carney	.10
108	Jerry Rice	1.75

1994 FACT NFL Properties

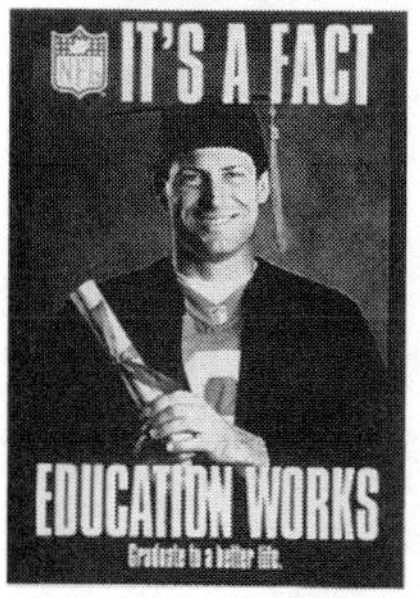

The 18-card NFL Properties set has the NFL shield and "It's A Fact" printed at the top and a slogan at the bottom. The top and bottom are bordered with a black stripe. The backs include a quote, with "Think About It..." printed in the bottom right. The card number is located in a black stripe in the lower right.

		MT
Complete Set (18):		30.00
Common Player:		.75
1	Play It Straight (Troy Aikman)	4.00
2	Chill (Cornelius Bennett)	.75
3	Aim High (Lesley Visser) (ANN)	.75
4	Eat Smart (Junior Seau)	1.50
5	Clean Up Your Act (Chris Hinton)	.75
6	Plan Ahead (Howie Long)	1.00
7	Heal The Planet (Nick Lowery)	.75
8	Guns Are For Foods (Tony Casillas)	.75
9	School's The Ticket (Dan Marino)	7.00
10	Make A Difference (Warren Moon)	1.25
11	Jim Kelly - We're the Same Inside (Rod Bernstine)	.75
12	Smoking Is Stupid (Rohn Stark)	.75
13	Respect The Law (Michael Irvin)	1.00
14	Education Works (Steve Young)	3.00
15	Kids Deserve Love (Bart Oates)	.75
16	Be Fit! (Erik Kramer)	.75
17	Don't Quit (Emmitt Smith)	7.00
18	Think (Steve Beuerlein)	.75

1994 FACT NFL Properties Artex

The three-card set carries the same design as the NFL Properties set, except it is numbered 1-3 and the Artex logo is printed on the back. The cards were distributed through K-Mart.

		MT
Complete Set (3):		7.00
Common Player:		1.50
1	Play It Straight (Troy Aikman)	1.50
2	School's The Ticket (Dan Marino)	3.00
3	Don't Quit (Emmitt Smith)	3.00

1995 FACT Fleer Shell

The 108-card set, sponsored by Fleer and Shell Oil, was used as an educational tool by elementary school teachers. The set was broken up into six subsets of 18 cards each. The card fronts are identical to the 1995 Fleer set, while the backs carry the same design, except for educational questions instead of player stats.

		MT
Complete Set (108):		20.00
Common Player:		.10
1	Cover Card - Stay In School	.10
2	Seth Joyner	.10
3	J.J. Birden	.10
4	Jim Kelly	.20
5	Pete Metzelaars	.10
6	Joe Cain	.10
7	Carl Pickens	.20
8	Leroy Hoard	.10
9	Troy Aikman	1.50
10	Steve Atwater	.10
11	Bennie Blades	.10
12	Brett Favre	3.00
13	Mel Gray	.10
14	Tony Bennett	.10
15	Steve Beuerlein	.10
16	Marcus Allen	.20
17	Tim Brown	.20
18	Tim Bowens	.10
19	Cover Card - Stay Fit	.10
20	Jack Del Rio	.10
21	Drew Bledsoe	1.50
22	Jim Everett	.10
23	Michael Brooks	.10
24	Tony Casillas	.10
25	Fred Barnett	.10
26	Kevin Greene	.10
27	Jerome Bettis	.40
28	John Carney	.10
29	Ken Norton	.10
30	Cortez Kennedy	.10
31	Alvin Harper	.10
32	Henry Ellard	.10
33	Aeneas Williams	.10
34	Jeff George	.20
35	Bryce Paup	.20
36	Sam Mills	.10
37	Cover Card - Eat Smart	.10
38	Mark Carrier	.10
39	Darnay Scott	.20
40	Pepper Johnson	.10
41	Michael Irvin	.20
42	John Elway	1.00
43	Herman Moore	.30
44	John Jurkovic	.10
45	Al Smith	.10
46	Steve Emtman	.10
47	Darren Carrington	.10
48	Kimble Anders	.10
49	Jeff Hostetler	.10
50	Eric Green	.10
51	Cris Carter	.20
52	Ben Coates	.10
53	Michael Haynes	.10
55	Cover Card - Stay In Tune (Dave Brown)	.10
56	Boomer Esiason	.10
57	Randall Cunningham	.10
58	Byron "Bam" Morris	.10
59	Sean Gilbert	.10
60	Stan Humphries	.20
61	Jerry Rice	1.50
62	Rick Mirer	.40
63	Hardy Nickerson	.10
64	Ricky Ervins	.10
65	Eric Swann	.10
66	Craig Heyward	.10
67	Andre Reed	.10
68	Frank Reich	.10
69	Steve Walsh	.10
70	Dan Wilkinson	.10
71	Vinny Testaverde	.10
72	Russell Maryland	.10
73	Cover Card - Stay Off Drugs	.10
74	Shannon Sharpe	.10
75	Brett Perriman	.10
76	Reggie White	.25
77	Mark Stepnoski	.10
78	Marshall Faulk	.75
79	Reggie Cobb	.10
80	Lake Dawson	.10
81	Rocket Ismail	.10
82	Dan Marino	3.00
83	Warren Moon	.20
84	Willie McGinest	.10
85	William Roaf	.10
86	Rodney Hampton	.20
87	Marvin Washington	.10
88	Charlie Garner	.10
89	Neil O'Donnell	.20
90	Todd Lyght	.10
91	Cover Card - Stay True To Yourself	.10
92	Natrone Means	.40
93	Deion Sanders	1.00
94	Chris Warren	.20
95	Errict Rhett	1.00
96	Ken Harvey	.10
97	Bruce Smith	.10
98	Chris Zorich	.10
99	Eric Turner	.10
100	Emmitt Smith	3.00
101	Barry Sanders	1.50
102	Neil Smith	.10
103	Chester McGlockton	.10
104	Fuad Reveiz	.10
105	Thomas Lewis	.10
106	Rod Woodson	.10
107	Junior Seau	.20
108	Steve Young	1.00

1995 FACT NFL Properties

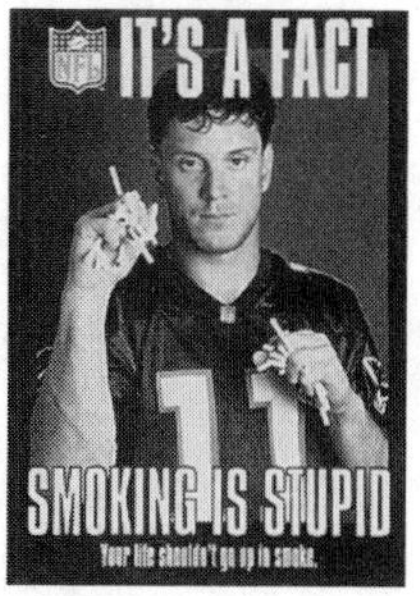

Produced by NFL Properties, the 18-card set had the NFL shield and "It's A Fact" printed at the top on the card fronts. A slogan was printed at the bottom. The card fronts are bordered with black stripes on the top and bottom. The backs have a quote and "Think About It..." printed in the lower right. The card number is printed in a black stripe on the bottom right.

		MT
Complete Set (18):		20.00
Common Player:		.50
1	Troy Aikman	2.50
2	Rocket Ismail, Qadry Ismail	.75
3	Robin Roberts	.50
4	Junior Seau	1.00
5	Chris Hinton	.50
6	Sean Jones	.50
7	Thurman Thomas	1.00
8	Neil Smith	.50
9	Dan Marino	5.00
10	Reggie Williams	.50
11	(Rod Bernstine, Jim Kelly)	1.00
12	Drew Bledsoe	2.50
13	Michael Irvin	1.00
14	Steve Young	1.75
15	Jerry Rice	2.50
16	Herschel Walker	.75
17	Emmitt Smith	5.00
18	Barry Sanders	2.50

1968 Falcons Team Issue

Measuring 7-1/2" x 9-1/2", the fronts feature a black-and-white photo, with the player's name and team printed in the white border at the bottom. The only card not using a posed action photo is Bob Berry's, which features a portrait. The cards are unnumbered and the backs are blank.

		NM
Complete Set (14):		65.00
Common Player:		4.00
1	Bob Berry	4.00
2	Carlton Dabney	4.00
3	Bob Etter	4.00
4	Bill Harris	4.00
5	Ralph Heck	4.00
6	Claude Humphrey	4.00
7	Randy Johnson	4.00
8	George Kunz (White jersey 78)	6.00
9	George Kunz (Dark jersey 75)	6.00
10	Errol Linden	4.00
11	Billy Lothridge	4.00
12	Ken Reaves	4.00
13	Jerry Shay	4.00
14	Tommy Nobis	15.00

1978 Falcons Kinnett Dairies

Measuring 4-1/4" x 6", this six-card set showcases four black-and-white player head shots on the front. The Kinnett logo appears in the middle left, while "Atlanta Player Cards" and the NFLPA logo are printed to the right. The unnumbered cards have blank backs.

		NM
Complete Set (6):		35.00
Common Player:		5.00
1	William Andrews, Jeff Yeates, Wilson Faumuina, Phil McKinnely	5.00
2	Warren Bryant, R.C. Thielemann, Steve Bartkowski, Frank Reed	10.00
3	Wallace Francis, Jim Mitchell, Jeff Van Note, Ray Easterling	5.00
4	Dewey McClain, Billy Ryckman, Paul Ryczek, Bubba Bean	5.00
5	Robert Pennywell, Dave Scott, Jim Bailey, John James	5.00
6	Haskel Stanback, Rick Byas, Mike Esposito, Tom Moriarty	5.00

1980 Falcons Police

Measuring 2-5/8" x 4-1/8", the 30-card set boasts a player photo on the front, with the Falcons' logo in the upper left and the player's name, number, position and bio under the photo on the left. Below the photo on the right is the Falcons' logo. The unnumbered card backs include "Tips from the Falcons" at the top, with the Atlanta Police Athletic League and Atlanta Jaycees logos underneath. A safety tip is printed in the center of the card, with the Coca-Cola logo at the bottom center of the card back.

		NM
Complete Set (30):		30.00
Common Player:		.90
1	William Andrews	3.75
2	Steve Bartkowski	7.50
3	Bubba Bean	2.00
4	Warren Bryant	.90
5	Rick Byas	.90
6	Lynn Cain	2.25
7	Buddy Curry	.90
8	Edgar Fields	.90
9	Wallace Francis	2.75
10	Alfred Jackson	2.25
11	John James	.90
12	Alfred Jenkins	3.00
13	Kenny Johnson	.90
14	Mike Kenn	2.25
15	Fulton Kuykendall	1.50
16	Rolland Lawrence	1.50
17	Tim Mazzetti	.90
18	Dewey McLean	.90
19	Jeff Merrow	1.50
20	Junior Miller	2.25
21	Tom Pridemore	.90
22	Frank Reed	.90
23	Al Richardson	.90
24	Dave Scott	.90
25	Don Smith	.90
26	Reggie Smith	.90
27	R.C. Thielemann	1.50
28	Jeff Van Note	2.25
29	Joel Williams	.90
30	Jeff Yeates	.90

1981 Falcons Police

Measuring 2-5/8" x 4-1/8", the 30-card set is anchored with a large photo on the front. The Atlanta Police Athletic League logo is printed in the upper left of the card front, while "NFC Western Division Champions 1980" is located in the upper right. Beneath the photo are the player's name, number, position, bio and Falcons' logo. The unnumbered card backs boast a Coca-Cola logo in the upper left and a Chevron logo in the upper right. The player's name and a highlight are printed in the center of the back, with a safety tip located beneath it. Photo and printing credits appear on the bottom of the card backs.

		MT
Complete Set (30):		12.00
Common Player:		.50
6	John James	.50
10	Steve Bartkowski	3.00
16	Reggie Smith	.50
18	Mick Luckhurst	.50
21	Lynn Cain	1.00
23	Bobby Butler	.50
27	Tom Pridemore	.50
30	Scott Woerner	.50
31	William Andrews	1.25
36	Bob Glazebrook	.50
37	Kenny Johnson	.50
50	Buddy Curry	.50
51	Jim Laughlin	.50
54	Fulton Kuykendall	.50
56	Al Richardson	.50
57	Jeff Van Note	.50
58	Joel Williams	.50
65	Don Smith	.50
66	Warren Bryant	.50
68	R.C. Thielemann	.50
70	Dave Scott	.50
74	Wilson Faumuina	.50
75	Jeff Merrow	.50
78	Mike Kenn	.50
79	Jeff Yeates	.50
80	Junior Miller	.50
84	Alfred Jenkins	1.00
85	Alfred Jackson	.50
89	Wallace Francis	1.00
NNO	(Leeman Bennett) (CO)	.50

1993 FCA Super Bowl

Showcased on the front of these six standard-sized cards is the Fellowship of Christian Athletes' logo in the upper left, with "professional football" located along the left border. The player photo, which is bordered in a screen that goes from light blue to dark blue, is featured on the left side of the card, with the player's name and position printed on the bottom right. The card backs, which are numbered in the upper right, have a player headshot in the upper left, with his name and bio printed along the right. A Christian message from the player is printed in yellow in the center. The FCA's toll-free number is printed at the bottom right.

		MT
Complete Set (6)		8.00
Common Player:		.75
1	Alfred Anderson	.75
2	Bob Lilly	1.50
3	Tom Landry (CO)	2.00
4	Brent Jones	1.00
5	Bruce Matthews	.75
6	Title Card	.75

1992 Finest

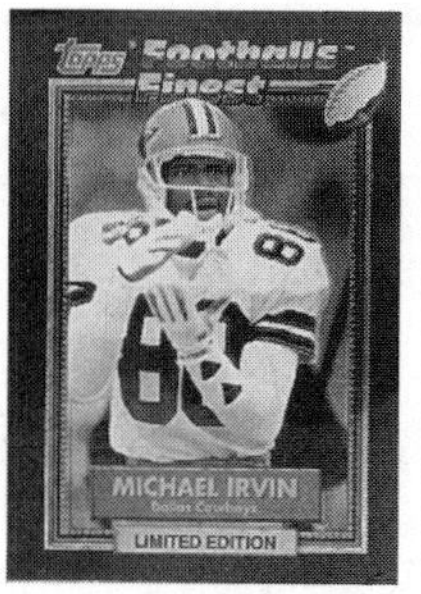

Produced in a print run of 3,000 cases, with 20 sets per case, the 44-card set showcases a player photo in foil on the front of the card, with the Topps Football's Finest logo at the top. The player's name and team are listed under the photo in a blue rectangle. "Limited Edition" is printed inside a gold stripe at the bottom. The 33 veteran cards are bordered in blue, gold and black. The 11 rookie cards are bordered in gold and red. The card backs have "Topps Football's Finest" at the top, with the player's name printed in large letters, overlapping a football helmet on the left. The cards are numbered "of 44" and feature the player's bio and position at the bottom.

		MT
Complete Set (45):		25.00
Common Player:		.25
1	Neal Anderson	.25
2	Cornelius Bennett	.25
3	Marion Butts	.25
4	Anthony Carter	.25
5	Mike Croel	.25
6	John Elway	10.00
7	Jim Everett	.25
8	Ernest Givins	.25
9	Rodney Hampton	.50
10	Alvin Harper	.50
11	Michael Irvin	.75
12	Rickey Jackson	.25
13	Seth Joyner	.25
14	James Lofton	.25
15	Ronnie Lott	.50
16	Eric Metcalf	.25
17	Chris Miller	.25
18	Art Monk	.50
19	Warren Moon	.50
20	Rob Moore	.25
21	Anthony Munoz	.25
22	Christian Okoye	.25
23	Andre Rison	.50
24	Leonard Russell	.25
25	Mark Rypien	.25
26	Barry Sanders	10.00
27	Emmitt Smith	10.00
28	Pat Swilling	.25
29	John Taylor	.25
30	Derrick Thomas	1.00
31	Thurman Thomas	1.00
32	Reggie White	1.00
33	Rod Woodson	.25
34	Edgar Bennett	.50
35	Terrell Buckley	.25
36	Keith Hamilton	.25
37	Amp Lee	.25
38	Ricardo McDonald	.25
39	Chris Mims	.25
40	Robert Porcher	.25
41	Leon Searcy	.25
42	Siran Stacy	.25
43	Tommy Vardell	.25
44	Bob Whitfield	.25
NNO	Checklist	.25

Post-1980 cards in Near Mint condition will generally sell for about 75% of the quoted Mint value. Excellent-condition cards bring no more than 40%.

1994 Finest

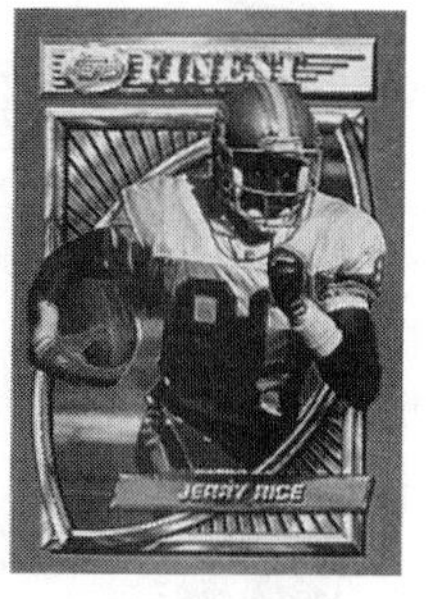

Topps created its 1994 Finest set using its chromium technology to give the cards a high-tech metallic look. Each front has a full-color player action shot, with a color bar at the bottom which has his name; the Topps Finest logo is at the top of the card. The back is horizontal. One side has a full-color photo bordered by a picture frame. Stats, biographical information and a summary of the player's finest moment in football are on the opposite side. A parallel set featuring refracting foil cards for each regular card was also made. These refractors were randomly inserted into every ninth pack. In addition, super size versions of 37 specially-designed rookie cards from the main were made in a 4" x 6" format. One of these cards was put into every 24-count box of packs. One in every six of these cards is enhanced with refracting foil.

		MT
Complete Set (220):		80.00
Common Player:		.50
Minor Stars:		1.00
Refractor Cards:		4x-8x
Pack (6):		7.00
Wax Box (24):		150.00
1	Emmitt Smith	10.00
2	Calvin Williams	.50
3	Mark Collins	.50
4	Steve McMichael	.50
5	Jim Kelly	1.00
6	Michael Dean Perry	.50
7	Wayne Simmons	.50
8	Raghib Ismail	.50
9	Mark Rypien	.50
10	Brian Blades	.50
11	Barry Word	.50
12	Jerry Rice	8.00
13	Derrick Fenner	.50
14	Karl Mecklenburg	.50
15	Reggie Cobb	.50
16	Eric Swann	.50
17	Neil Smith	.50
18	Barry Foster	.50
19	Willie Roaf	.50
20	Troy Drayton	.50
21	Warren Moon	1.00
22	Richmond Webb	.50
23	Anthony Miller	.50
24	Chris Slade	.50
25	Mel Gray	.50
26	Ronnie Lott	.50
27	Andre Rison	1.00
28	Jeff George	1.00
29	John Copeland	.50
30	Derrick Thomas	1.00
31	Sterling Sharpe	1.00
32	Chris Doleman	.50
33	Monte Coleman	.50
34	Mark Bavaro	.50
35	Kevin Williams	1.00
36	Eric Metcalf	.50
37	Brent Jones	.50
38	Steve Tasker	.50
39	Dave Meggett	.50
40	Howie Long	.50
41	Rick Mirer	2.00
42	Jerome Bettis	4.00
43	Marion Butts	.50
44	Barry Sanders	12.00
45	Jason Elam	.50
46	Broderick Thomas	.50
47	Derek Brown	.50
48	Lorenzo White	.50
49	Neil O'Donnell	1.00
50	Chris Burkett	.50
51	John Offerdahl	.50
52	Rohn Stark	.50
53	Neal Anderson	.50
54	Steve Beuerlein	.50
55	Bruce Armstrong	.50
56	Lincoln Kennedy	.50
57	Darrell Green	.50
58	Ricardo McDonald	.50
59	Chris Warren	1.00
60	Mark Jackson	.50
61	Pepper Johnson	.50
62	Chris Spielman	.50
63	Marcus Allen	1.00
64	Jim Everett	.50
65	Greg Townsend	.50
66	Cris Carter	1.00
67	Don Beebe	.50
68	Reggie Langhorne	.50
69	Randall Cunningham	.50
70	Johnny Holland	.50
71	Morten Andersen	.50
72	Leonard Marshall	.50
73	Keith Jackson	.50
74	Leslie O'Neal	.50
75	Hardy Nickerson	.50
76	Dan Williams	.50
77	Steve Young	6.00
78	Deon Figures	.50
79	Michael Irvin	2.00
80	Luis Sharpe	.50
81	Andre Tippett	.50
82	Ricky Sanders	.50
83	Erric Pegram	.50
84	Albert Lewis	.50

85	Anthony Blaylock	.50
86	Pat Swilling	.50
87	Duane Bickett	.50
88	Myron Guyton	.50
89	Clay Matthews	.50
90	Jim McMahon	.50
91	Bruce Smith	.50
92	Reggie White	1.00
93	Shannon Sharpe	.50
94	Rickey Jackson	.50
95	Ronnie Harmon	.50
96	Terry McDaniel	.50
97	Bryan Cox	.50
98	Webster Slaughter	.50
99	Boomer Esiason	.50
100	Tim Krumrie	.50
101	Cortez Kennedy	.50
102	Henry Ellard	.50
103	Clyde Simmons	.50
104	Craig Erickson	.50
105	Eric Green	.50
106	Gary Clark	.50
107	Jay Novacek	.50
108	Dana Stubblefield	.50
109	Mike Johnson	.50
110	Ray Crockett	.50
111	Leonard Russell	.50
112	Robert Smith	3.00
113	Art Monk	1.00
114	Ray Childress	.50
115	O.J. McDuffie	2.00
116	Tim Brown	.50
117	Kevin Ross	.50
118	Richard Dent	.50
119	John Elway	10.00
120	James Hasty	.50
121	Gary Plummer	.50
122	Pierce Holt	.50
123	Eric Martin	.50
124	Brett Favre	12.00
125	Cornelius Bennett	.50
126	Jessie Hester	.50
127	Lewis Tillman	.50
128	Quadry Ismail	.50
129	Jay Schroeder	.50
130	Curtis Conway	3.00
131	Santana Dotson	.50
132	Nick Lowery	.50
133	Lomas Brown	.50
134	Reggie Roby	.50
135	John L. Williams	.50
136	Vinny Testaverde	.50
137	Seth Joyner	.50
138	Ethan Horton	.50
139	Jackie Slater	.50
140	Rod Bernstine	.50
141	Rob Moore	.50
142	Dan Marino	10.00
143	Ken Harvey	.50
144	Ernest Givins	.50
145	Russell Maryland	.50
146	Drew Bledsoe	6.00
147	Kevin Greene	.50
148	Bobby Hebert	.50
149	Junior Seau	1.00
150	Tim McDonald	.50
151	Thurman Thomas	1.00
152	Phil Simms	.50
153	Terrell Buckley	.50
154	Sam Mills	.50
155	Anthony Carter	.50
156	Kelvin Martin	.50
157	Shane Conlan	.50
158	Irving Fryar	.50
159	Demetrius DuBose	.50
160	David Klingler	.50
161	Herman Moore	2.00
162	Jeff Hostetler	1.00
163	Tommy Vardell	.50
164	Craig Heyward	.50
165	Wilber Marshall	.50
166	Quentin Coryatt	.50
167	Glyn Milburn	1.00
168	Fred Barnett	.50
169	Charles Haley	.50
170	Carl Banks	.50
171	Ricky Proehl	.50
172	Joe Montana	8.00
173	Johnny Mitchell	.50
174	Andre Reed	1.00
175	Marco Coleman	.50
176	Vaughan Johnson	.50
177	Carl Pickens	1.00
178	Dwight Stone	.50
179	Ricky Watters	1.00
180	Michael Haynes	.50
181	Roger Craig	.50
182	Cleveland Gary	.50
183	Steve Emtman	.50
184	Patrick Bates	.50
185	Mark Carrier	.50
186	Brad Hopkins	.50
187	Dennis Smith	.50
188	Natrone Means	3.00
189	Michael Jackson	.50
190	Ken Norton	.50
191	Carlton Gray	.50
192	Edgar Bennett	.50
193	Lawrence Taylor	1.00
194	Marv Cook	.50
195	Eric Curry	.50
196	Victor Bailey	.50
197	Ryan McNeil	.50
198	Rod Woodson	1.00
199	Ernest Byner	.50
200	Marvin Jones	.50
201	Thomas Smith	.50
202	Troy Aikman	8.00
203	Audray McMillian	.50
204	Wade Wilson	.50
205	George Teague	.50
206	Deion Sanders	4.00
207	Will Shields	.50
208	John Taylor	.50
209	Jim Harbaugh	.50
210	Michael Barrow	.50
211	Harold Green	.50
212	Steve Everitt	.50
213	Flipper Anderson	.50
214	Rodney Hampton	1.00
215	Steve Atwater	.50
216	James Trapp	.50
217	Terry Kirby	.50
218	Garrison Hearst	4.00
219	Jeff Bryant	.50
220	Roosevelt Potts	.50

1994 Finest Refractors

Refractors paralleled the 220-card regular-issue set with a holographic, rainbow finish on each card. Refractors were inserted every nine packs of Finest.

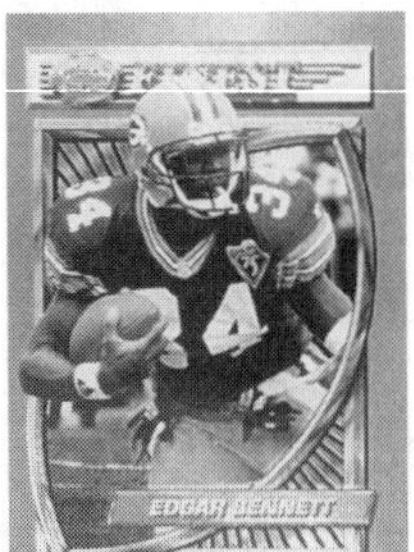

		MT
Complete Set (220):		1700.
Common Player:		4.00
Minor Stars:		8.00
Unlisted Stars:		5x-10x
1	Emmitt Smith	85.00
2	Calvin Williams	4.00
3	Mark Collins	4.00
4	Steve McMichael	4.00
5	Jim Kelly	10.00
6	Michael Dean Perry	4.00
7	Wayne Simmons	4.00
8	Raghib Ismail	4.00
9	Mark Rypien	4.00
10	Brian Blades	4.00
11	Barry Word	4.00
12	Jerry Rice	50.00
13	Derrick Fenner	4.00
14	Karl Mecklenburg	4.00
15	Reggie Cobb	4.00
16	Eric Swann	4.00
17	Neil Smith	4.00
18	Barry Foster	4.00
19	Willie Roaf	4.00
20	Troy Drayton	4.00
21	Warren Moon	8.00
22	Richmond Webb	4.00
23	Anthony Miller	4.00
24	Chris Slade	4.00
25	Mel Gray	4.00
26	Ronnie Lott	4.00
27	Andre Rison	8.00
28	Jeff George	8.00
29	John Copeland	4.00
30	Derrick Thomas	8.00
31	Sterling Sharpe	8.00
32	Chris Doleman	4.00
33	Monte Coleman	4.00
34	Mark Bavaro	4.00
35	Kevin Williams	10.00
36	Eric Metcalf	4.00
37	Brent Jones	4.00
38	Steve Tasker	4.00
39	Dave Meggett	4.00
40	Howie Long	4.00
41	Rick Mirer	8.00
42	Jerome Bettis	25.00
43	Marion Butts	4.00
44	Barry Sanders	100.00
45	Jason Elam	4.00
46	Broderick Thomas	4.00
47	Derek Brown	4.00
48	Lorenzo White	4.00
49	Neil O'Donnell	8.00
50	Chris Burkett	4.00
51	John Offerdahl	4.00
52	Rohn Stark	4.00
53	Neal Anderson	4.00
54	Steve Beuerlein	4.00
55	Bruce Armstrong	4.00
56	Lincoln Kennedy	4.00
57	Darrell Green	4.00
58	Ricardo McDonald	4.00
59	Chris Warren	8.00
60	Mark Jackson	4.00
61	Pepper Johnson	4.00
62	Chris Spielman	4.00
63	Marcus Allen	10.00
64	Jim Everett	4.00
65	Greg Townsend	4.00
66	Cris Carter	8.00
67	Don Beebe	4.00
68	Reggie Langhorne	4.00
69	Randall Cunningham	8.00
70	Johnny Holland	4.00
71	Morten Andersen	4.00
72	Leonard Marshall	4.00
73	Keith Jackson	4.00
74	Leslie O'Neal	4.00
75	Hardy Nickerson	4.00
76	Dan Williams	4.00
77	Steve Young	40.00
78	Deon Figures	4.00
79	Michael Irvin	10.00
80	Luis Sharpe	4.00
81	Andre Tippett	4.00
82	Ricky Sanders	4.00
83	Eric Pegram	4.00
84	Albert Lewis	4.00
85	Anthony Blaylock	4.00
86	Pat Swilling	4.00
87	Duane Bickett	4.00
88	Myron Guyton	4.00
89	Clay Matthews	4.00
90	Jim McMahon	4.00
91	Bruce Smith	4.00
92	Reggie White	10.00
93	Shannon Sharpe	4.00
94	Rickey Jackson	4.00
95	Ronnie Harmon	4.00
96	Terry McDaniel	4.00
97	Bryan Cox	4.00
98	Webster Slaughter	4.00
99	Boomer Esiason	4.00
100	Tim Krumrie	4.00
101	Cortez Kennedy	4.00
102	Henry Ellard	4.00
103	Clyde Simmons	4.00
104	Craig Erickson	4.00
105	Eric Green	4.00
106	Gary Clark	4.00
107	Jay Novacek	4.00
108	Dana Stubblefield	8.00
109	Mike Johnson	4.00
110	Ray Crockett	4.00
111	Leonard Russell	4.00
112	Robert Smith	30.00
113	Art Monk	8.00
114	Ray Childress	4.00
115	O.J. McDuffie	8.00
116	Tim Brown	8.00
117	Kevin Ross	4.00
118	Richard Dent	4.00
119	John Elway	80.00
120	James Hasty	4.00
121	Gary Plummer	4.00
122	Pierce Holt	4.00
123	Eric Martin	4.00
124	Brett Favre	100.00
125	Cornelius Bennett	4.00
126	Jessie Hester	4.00
127	Lewis Tillman	4.00
128	Qadry Ismail	4.00
129	Jay Schroeder	4.00
130	Curtis Conway	30.00
131	Santana Dotson	4.00
132	Nick Lowery	4.00
133	Lomas Brown	4.00
134	Reggie Roby	4.00
135	John L. Williams	4.00
136	Vinny Testaverde	4.00
137	Seth Joyner	4.00
138	Ethan Horton	4.00
139	Jackie Slater	4.00
140	Rod Bernstine	4.00
141	Rob Moore	4.00
142	Dan Marino	85.00
143	Ken Harvey	4.00
144	Ernest Givins	4.00
145	Russell Maryland	4.00
146	Drew Bledsoe	60.00
147	Kevin Greene	4.00
148	Bobby Hebert	4.00
149	Junior Seau	8.00
150	Tim McDonald	4.00
151	Thurman Thomas	10.00
152	Phil Simms	4.00
153	Terrell Buckley	4.00
154	Sam Mills	4.00
155	Anthony Carter	4.00
156	Kelvin Martin	4.00
157	Shane Conlan	4.00
158	Irving Fryar	4.00
159	Demetrius DuBose	4.00
160	David Klingler	4.00
161	Herman Moore	10.00
162	Jeff Hostetler	8.00
163	Tommy Vardell	4.00
164	Craig Heyward	4.00
165	Wilber Marshall	4.00
166	Quentin Coryatt	4.00
167	Glyn Milburn	4.00
168	Fred Barnett	4.00
169	Charles Haley	4.00
170	Carl Banks	4.00
171	Ricky Proehl	4.00
172	Joe Montana	100.00
173	Johnny Mitchell	4.00
174	Andre Reed	8.00
175	Marco Coleman	4.00
176	Vaughan Johnson	4.00
177	Carl Pickens	10.00
178	Dwight Stone	4.00
179	Ricky Watters	8.00
180	Michael Haynes	4.00
181	Roger Craig	4.00
182	Cleveland Gary	4.00
183	Steve Emtman	4.00
184	Patrick Bates	4.00
185	Mark Carrier	4.00
186	Brad Hopkins	4.00
187	Dennis Smith	4.00
188	Natrone Means	25.00
189	Michael Jackson	4.00
190	Ken Norton	4.00
191	Carlton Gray	4.00
192	Edgar Bennett	4.00
193	Lawrence Taylor	8.00
194	Marv Cook	4.00
195	Eric Curry	4.00
196	Victor Bailey	4.00
197	Ryan McNeil	4.00
198	Rod Woodson	8.00
199	Ernest Byner	4.00
200	Marvin Jones	4.00
201	Thomas Smith	4.00
202	Troy Aikman	50.00
203	Audray McMillian	4.00
204	Wade Wilson	4.00
205	George Teague	4.00
206	Deion Sanders	25.00
207	Will Shields	4.00
208	John Taylor	4.00
209	Jim Harbaugh	8.00
210	Michael Barrow	4.00
211	Harold Green	4.00
212	Steve Everitt	4.00
213	Flipper Anderson	4.00
214	Rodney Hampton	8.00
215	Steve Atwater	4.00
216	James Trapp	4.00
217	Terry Kirby	4.00
218	Garrison Hearst	25.00
219	Jeff Bryant	4.00
220	Roosevelt Potts	4.00

1994 Finest Rookie Jumbos

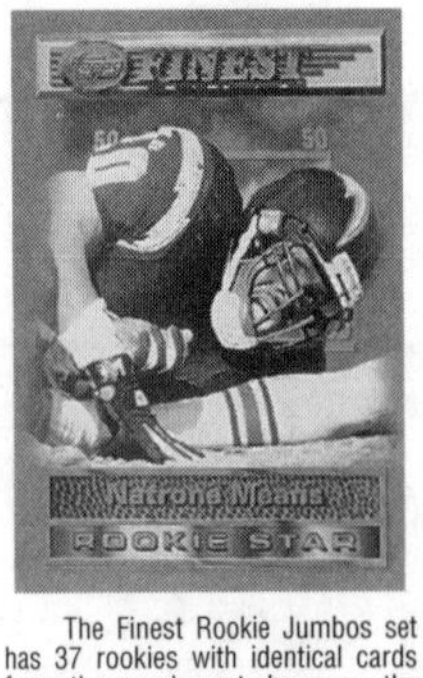

The Finest Rookie Jumbos set has 37 rookies with identical cards from the regular set; however, the jumbos measure 4-1/2" x 6". These oversized cards were found at a rate of one per 24-count box.

		MT
Complete Set (37):		180.00
Common Player:		3.00
Minor Stars:		6.00
1:Box		
7	Wayne Simmons	3.00
19	Willie Roaf	3.00
20	Troy Drayton	3.00
24	Chris Slade	3.00
29	John Copeland	3.00
35	Kevin Williams	6.00
41	Rick Mirer	6.00
42	Jerome Bettis	12.00
45	Jason Elam	6.00
47	Derek Brown (RB)	3.00
56	Lincoln Kennedy	3.00
78	Deon Figures	3.00
108	Dana Stubblefield	6.00
112	Robert Smith	10.00
115	O.J. McDuffie	8.00
128	Qadry Ismail	3.00
130	Curtis Conway	8.00
146	Drew Bledsoe	30.00
159	Demetrius DuBose	3.00
167	Glyn Milburn	6.00
184	Patrick Bates	3.00
186	Brad Hopkins	3.00
188	Natrone Means	8.00
191	Carlton Gray	3.00
195	Eric Curry	3.00
196	Victor Bailey	3.00
197	Ryan McNeil	3.00
200	Marvin Jones	3.00
201	Thomas Smith	3.00
205	George Teague	3.00
207	Will Shields	3.00
210	Michael Barrow	3.00
212	Steve Everitt	3.00
216	James Trapp	3.00
217	Terry Kirby	6.00
218	Garrison Hearst	10.00
220	Roosevelt Potts	3.00

1995 Finest

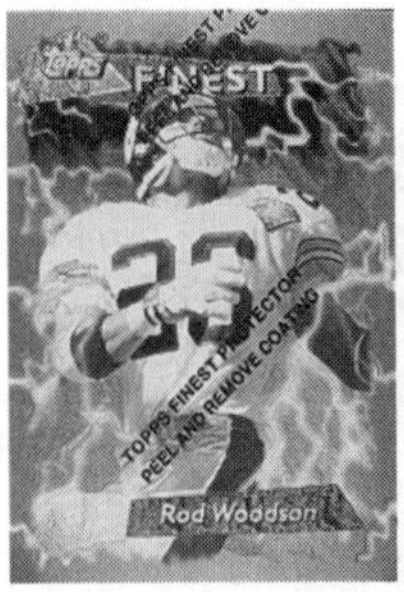

The regular issue 1995 Topps Finest set was released in two series - Series I had 165 cards, while Series II had 110. Each card comes with the standard Finest Protector, a peel-off laminate, to assure its Mint condition out of the pack. A 1994 Draft Picks subset was included in Series I; it features a different design from the regular cards. A 275-card parallel set of Finest Refractor cards was also made; cards were seeded one per every 12 packs. Series I inserts, titled Fan Favorites, feature impact players on clear cut cards. Series II inserts were Boosters, numbered B166-B187.

		MT
Complete Set (275):		170.00
Complete Series 1 (165):		70.00
Complete Series 2 (110):		100.00
Common Player:		.50
Minor Stars:		1.00
Series 1 Pack (7):		5.00
Series 1 Wax Box (24):		90.00
Series 2 Pack (7):		4.50
Series 2 Wax Box (24):		90.00
1	Natrone Means	1.50
2	David Meggett	.50
3	*Tim Bowens*	1.00
4	Jay Novacek	.50
5	Michael Jackson	.50
6	Eric Allen	.50
7	Neil Smith	.50
8	Chris Gardocki	.50
9	*Jeff Burris*	1.00
10	Warren Moon	1.00
11	Gary Anderson	.50
12	*Bert Emanuel*	1.50
13	Rick Tuten	.50
14	Steve Wallace	.50
15	Marion Butts	.50
16	*Johnnie Morton*	1.50
17	Art Monk	1.00
18	*Wayne Gandy*	.50
19	Quentin Coryatt	.50
20	Richmond Webb	.50
21	*Errict Rhett*	1.00
22	*Joe Johnson*	.50
23	Gary Brown	.50
24	Jeff Hostetler	.50
25	Larry Centers	.50
26	Tom Carter	.50
27	Steve Atwater	.50
28	Doug Pelfrey	.50
29	Bryce Paup	.50
30	Erik Williams	.50
31	Henry Jones	.50
32	Stanley Richard	.50
33	Marcus Allen	1.00
34	*Antonio Langham*	1.00
35	Lewis Tillman	.50
36	*Thomas Randolph*	.50
37	*Byron Morris*	1.00
38	*David Palmer*	1.00
39	Ricky Watters	1.00
40	Brett Perriman	.50
41	Will Wolford	.50
42	Burt Grossman	.50
43	Vincent Brisby	.50
44	Ronnie Lott	.50
45	Brian Blades	.50
46	Brent Jones	.50
47	Anthony Newman	.50
48	William Roaf	.50
49	Paul Gruber	.50
50	Jeff George	1.00
51	*Jamir Miller*	1.00
52	Anthony Miller	.50
53	Darrell Green	.50
54	Steve Wisniewski	.50
55	*Dan Wilkinson*	1.00
56	Brett Favre	10.00
57	Leslie O'Neal	.50
58	Keith Byars	.50
59	James Washington	.50
60	Andre Reed	.50
61	Ken Norton	.50
62	John Randle	.50
63	*Lake Dawson*	1.00
64	Greg Montgomery	.50
65	Erric Pegram	.50
66	Steve Everitt	.50
67	*Chris Brantley*	.50
68	Rod Woodson	1.00
69	Eugene Robinson	.50
70	Dave Brown	.50
71	Ricky Reynolds	.50
72	Rohn Stark	.50
73	Randal Hill	.50
74	Brian Washington	.50
75	*Heath Shuler*	1.50
76	Darion Conner	.50
77	Terry McDaniel	.50
78	Al Del Greco	.50
79	*Allen Aldridge*	.50
80	Trace Armstrong	.50
81	*Darnay Scott*	2.00
82	Charlie Garner	2.00
83	*Harold Bishop*	.50
84	Reggie White	1.00
85	Shawn Jefferson	.50
86	Irving Spikes	1.00
87	Mel Gray	.50
88	D.J. Johnson	.50
89	Daryl Johnston	.50
90	Joe Montana	7.00
91	Michael Strahan	.50
92	Robert Blackmon	.50
93	*Ryan Yarborough*	.50
94	Terry Allen	.50
95	Michael Haynes	.50
96	Jim Harbaugh	.50
97	Michael Barrow	.50
98	*John Thierry*	.50
99	Seth Joyner	.50
100	Deion Sanders	3.00
101	Eric Turner	.50
102	*LeShon Johnson*	1.00
103	John Copeland	.50
104	Cornelius Bennett	.50
105	Sean Gilbert	.50
106	Herschel Walker	.50
107	Henry Ellard	.50
108	Neil O'Donnell	1.00
109	Charles Wilson	.50
110	*Willie McGinest*	1.00
111	Tim Brown	1.00
112	Simon Fletcher	.50
113	Broderick Thomas	.50
114	Tom Waddle	.50
115	Jessie Tuggle	.50
116	Maurice Hurst	.50
117	*Aubrey Beavers*	.50
118	*Donnell Bennett*	.50
119	*Shante Carver*	.50
120	Eric Metcalf	.50
121	John Carney	.50
122	*Thomas Lewis*	.50
123	Johnny Mitchell	.50
124	Trent Dilfer	4.00
125	Marshall Faulk	4.00
126	Ernest Givins	.50
127	Aeneas Williams	.50
128	*Bucky Brooks*	1.00
129	*Todd Steussie*	1.00
130	Randall Cunningham	1.00
131	Reggie Brooks	.50
132	Morten Andersen	.50
133	James Jett	.50
134	George Teague	.50
135	John Taylor	.50
136	*Charles Johnson*	1.50
137	Isaac Bruce	4.00
138	Jason Elam	.50
139	Carl Pickens	1.00
140	Chris Warren	1.00
141	Bruce Armstrong	.50
142	Mark Carrier	.50
143	Irving Fryar	.50
144	*Van Malone*	.50
145	Charles Haley	.50
146	Chris Calloway	.50
147	J.J. Birden	.50
148	Tony Bennett	.50
149	Lincoln Kennedy	.50
150	Stan Humphries	1.00
151	Hardy Nickerson	.50
152	Randall McDaniel	.50
153	Marcus Robertson	.50
154	Ronald Moore	.50
155	Thurman Thomas	1.00
156	Tommy Vardell	.50
157	Ken Ruettgers	.50
158	*Rob Fredrickson*	.50
159	Johnny Bailey	.50
160	Greg Lloyd	.50
161	David Alexander	.50
162	*Kevin Mawae*	.50
163	Derek Brown	.50
164	*William Floyd*	1.50
165	*Aaron Glenn*	1.00
166	*Joey Galloway*	12.00
167	Troy Drayton	.50
168	Dermontti Dawson	.50
169	Ronald Moore	.50
170	Dan Marino	8.00
171	Dennis Gibson	.50
172	Raymont Harris	.50
173	Shannon Sharpe	.50
174	Kevin Williams	.50
175	Jim Everett	.50
176	Raghib Ismail	.50
177	Mark Fields	.50
178	George Koonce	.50
179	Chris Hudson	.50
180	Jerry Rice	5.00
181	DeWayne Washington	.50
182	Dale Carter	.50
183	Pete Stoyanovich	.50
184	Blake Brockermeyer	.50
185	Troy Aikman	5.00
186	*Jeff Blake*	2.00
187	Troy Vincent	.50
188	Lamar Lathon	.50
189	*Tony Boselli*	1.00
190	Emmitt Smith	8.00
191	Bobby Houston	.50
192	Edgar Bennett	.50
193	Derrick Brooks	.50
194	Ricky Proehl	.50
195	Rodney Hampton	.50
196	Dave Krieg	.50
197	Vinny Testaverde	.50
198	Erik Kramer	.50
199	Ben Coates	.50
200	Steve Young	4.00
201	Glyn Milburn	.50
202	Bryan Cox	.50
203	Luther Elliss	.50
204	Mark McMillian	.50
205	Jerome Bettis	1.50
206	Craig Heyward	.50
207	Ray Buchanan	.50
208	Kimble Anders	.50
209	Kevin Greene	.50
210	Eric Allen	.50
211	Ricardo McDonald	.50
212	Ruben Brown	.50
213	Harvey Williams	.50
214	Broderick Thomas	.50
215	Frank Reich	.50
216	*Frank Sanders*	5.00
217	Craig Newsome	.50
218	Merton Hanks	.50
219	Chris Miller	.50
220	John Elway	4.00
221	Ernest Givins	.50
222	Boomer Esiason	.50
223	Reggie Roby	.50
224	Qadry Ismail	.50
225	*Ki-Jana Carter*	2.00
226	Leon Lett	.50
227	Eric Hill	.50
228	Scott Mitchell	.50
229	Craig Erickson	.50
230	Drew Bledsoe	5.00
231	Sean Landeta	.50
232	Barrett Brooks	.50
233	Brian Mitchell	.50
234	Tyrone Poole	.50
235	Desmond Howard	.50
236	Wayne Simmons	.50
237	*Michael Westbrook*	4.00
238	Quinn Early	.50
239	Willie Davis	.50
240	*Rashaan Salaam*	2.00
241	Devin Bush	.50
242	Dana Stubblefield	.50
243	Dexter Carter	.50
244	Shane Conlan	.50
245	Keith Elias	.50
246	Robert Brooks	1.50
247	Garrison Hearst	1.50
248	*Eric Zeier*	3.00
249	Nate Newton	.50
250	Barry Sanders	10.00
251	David Meggett	.50
252	Courtney Hawkins	.50
253	Cortez Kennedy	.50
254	Mario Bates	2.50
255	Junior Seau	1.00
256	Brian Washington	.50
257	Darius Holland	.50
258	Jeff Graham	.50
259	Rob Moore	.50
260	Andre Rison	.50
261	*Kerry Collins*	8.00
262	Roosevelt Potts	.50
263	Cris Carter	1.00
264	*Curtis Martin*	15.00
265	Rick Mirer	1.50
266	Mo Lewis	.50
267	Mike Sherrard	.50
268	Herman Moore	2.00
269	Eric Metcalf	.50
270	Ray Childress	.50
271	Chris Slade	.50
272	Michael Irvin	1.00
273	Jim Kelly	1.00
274	Terance Mathis	.50
275	LeRoy Butler	.50

1995 Finest Refractors

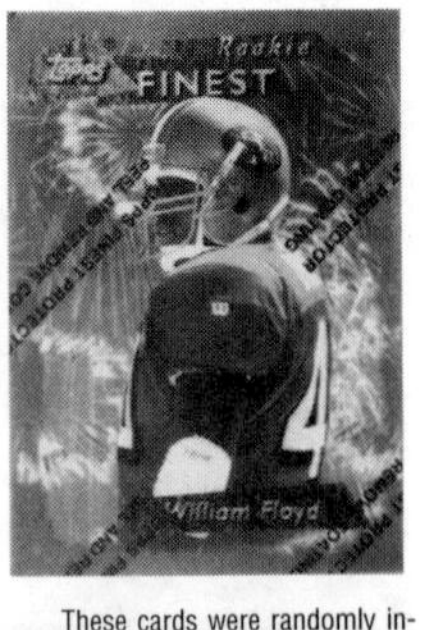

These cards were randomly inserted into Series I and II packs of 1995 Topps Finest, one per every 12 packs. The cards, a parallel set to the regular issue, have a shiny, rainbow effect when viewed.

		MT
Complete Set (275):		1800.
Complete Series 1 (165):		800.00
Complete Series 2 (110):		1000.
Common Player:		3.00
Minor Stars:		6.00
Unlisted Stars:		5x-10x
1	Natrone Means	15.00
2	David Meggett	3.00
3	Tim Bowens	6.00
4	Jay Novacek	3.00
5	Michael Jackson	3.00
6	Eric Allen	3.00
7	Neil Smith	3.00
8	Chris Gardocki	3.00
9	Jeff Burris	6.00
10	Warren Moon	6.00

11 Gary Anderson 3.00
12 Bert Emanuel 25.00
13 Rick Tuten 3.00
14 Steve Wallace 3.00
15 Marion Butts 3.00
16 Johnnie Morton 10.00
17 Art Monk 6.00
18 Wayne Gandy 3.00
19 Quentin Coryatt 3.00
20 Richmond Webb 3.00
21 Errict Rhett 10.00
22 Joe Johnson 3.00
23 Gary Brown 3.00
24 Jeff Hostetler 3.00
25 Larry Centers 3.00
26 Tom Carter 3.00
27 Steve Atwater 3.00
28 Doug Pelfrey 3.00
29 Bryce Paup 3.00
30 Erik Williams 3.00
31 Henry Jones 3.00
32 Stanley Richard 3.00
33 Marcus Allen 6.00
34 Antonio Langham 6.00
35 Lewis Tillman 3.00
36 Thomas Randolph 3.00
37 Byron Morris 10.00
38 David Palmer 6.00
39 Ricky Watters 6.00
40 Brett Perriman 3.00
41 Will Wolford 3.00
42 Burt Grossman 3.00
43 Vincent Brisby 3.00
44 Ronnie Lott 3.00
45 Brian Blades 3.00
46 Brent Jones 3.00
47 Anthony Newman 3.00
48 William Roaf 3.00
49 Paul Gruber 3.00
50 Jeff George 6.00
51 Jamir Miller 6.00
52 Anthony Miller 3.00
53 Darrell Green 3.00
54 Steve Wisniewski 3.00
55 Dan Wilkinson 6.00
56 Brett Favre 100.00
57 Leslie O'Neal 3.00
58 Keith Byars 3.00
59 James Washington 3.00
60 Andre Reed 3.00
61 Ken Norton 3.00
62 John Randle 3.00
63 Lake Dawson 10.00
64 Greg Montgomery 3.00
65 Erric Pegram 3.00
66 Steve Everitt 3.00
67 Chris Brantley 3.00
68 Rod Woodson 6.00
69 Eugene Robinson 3.00
70 Dave Brown 3.00
71 Ricky Reynolds 3.00
72 Rohn Stark 3.00
73 Randal Hill 3.00
74 Brian Washington 3.00
75 Heath Shuler 15.00
76 Darion Conner 3.00
77 Terry McDaniel 3.00
78 Al Del Greco 3.00
79 Allen Aldridge 3.00
80 Trace Armstrong 3.00
81 Darnay Scott 10.00
82 Charlie Garner 20.00
83 Harold Bishop 3.00
84 Reggie White 6.00
85 Shawn Jefferson 3.00
86 Irving Spikes 6.00
87 Mel Gray 3.00
88 D.J. Johnson 3.00
89 Daryl Johnston 3.00
90 Joe Montana 75.00
91 Michael Strahan 3.00
92 Robert Blackmon 3.00
93 Ryan Yarborough 3.00
94 Terry Allen 3.00
95 Michael Haynes 3.00
96 Jim Harbaugh 3.00
97 Michael Barrow 3.00
98 John Thierry 3.00
99 Seth Joyner 3.00
100 Deion Sanders 40.00
101 Eric Turner 3.00
102 LeShon Johnson 6.00
103 John Copeland 3.00
104 Cornelius Bennett 3.00
105 Sean Gilbert 3.00
106 Herschel Walker 3.00
107 Henry Ellard 3.00
108 Neil O'Donnell 6.00
109 Charles Wilson 3.00
110 Willie McGinest 6.00
111 Tim Brown 6.00
112 Simon Fletcher 3.00
113 Broderick Thomas 3.00
114 Tom Waddle 3.00
115 Jessie Tuggle 3.00
116 Maurice Hurst 3.00
117 Aubrey Beavers 3.00
118 Donnell Bennett 3.00
119 Shante Carver 3.00
120 Eric Metcalf 3.00
121 John Carney 3.00
122 Thomas Lewis 3.00
123 Johnny Mitchell 3.00
124 Trent Dilfer 30.00
125 Marshall Faulk 40.00
126 Ernest Givins 3.00
127 Aeneas Williams 3.00
128 Bucky Brooks 6.00
129 Todd Steussie 6.00
130 Randall Cunningham 6.00
131 Reggie Brooks 3.00
132 Morten Andersen 3.00
133 James Jett 3.00
134 George Teague 3.00
135 John Taylor 3.00
136 Charles Johnson 15.00
137 Isaac Bruce 35.00
138 Jason Elam 3.00
139 Carl Pickens 6.00
140 Chris Warren 6.00
141 Bruce Armstrong 3.00
142 Mark Carrier 3.00
143 Irving Fryar 3.00
144 Van Malone 3.00
145 Charles Haley 3.00
146 Chris Calloway 3.00
147 J.J. Birden 3.00
148 Tony Bennett 3.00
149 Lincoln Kennedy 3.00
150 Stan Humphries 6.00
151 Hardy Nickerson 3.00
152 Randall McDaniel 3.00
153 Marcus Robertson 3.00
154 Ronald Moore 3.00
155 Thurman Thomas 6.00
156 Tommy Vardell 3.00
157 Ken Ruettgers 3.00
158 Rob Fredrickson 3.00
159 Johnny Bailey 3.00
160 Greg Lloyd 3.00
161 David Alexander 3.00
162 Kevin Mawae 3.00
163 Derek Brown 3.00
164 William Floyd 8.00
165 Aaron Glenn 6.00
166 Joey Galloway 75.00
167 Troy Drayton 3.00
168 Dermontti Dawson 3.00
169 Ronald Moore 3.00
170 Dan Marino 85.00
171 Dennis Gibson 3.00
172 Raymont Harris 3.00
173 Shannon Sharpe 3.00
174 Kevin Williams 3.00
175 Jim Everett 3.00
176 Raghib Ismail 3.00
177 Mark Fields 3.00
178 George Koonce 3.00
179 Chris Hudson 3.00
180 Jerry Rice 60.00
181 DeWayne Washington 3.00
182 Dale Carter 3.00
183 Pete Stoyanovich 3.00
184 Blake Brockermeyer 3.00
185 Troy Aikman 60.00
186 Jeff Blake 8.00
187 Troy Vincent 3.00
188 Lamar Lathon 3.00
189 Tony Boselli 6.00
190 Emmitt Smith 85.00
191 Bobby Houston 3.00
192 Edgar Bennett 3.00
193 Derrick Brooks 3.00
194 Ricky Proehl 3.00
195 Rodney Hampton 3.00
196 Dave Krieg 3.00
197 Vinny Testaverde 3.00
198 Erik Kramer 3.00
199 Ben Coates 3.00
200 Steve Young 45.00
201 Glyn Milburn 3.00
202 Bryan Cox 3.00
203 Luther Elliss 3.00
204 Mark McMillian 3.00
205 Jerome Bettis 25.00
206 Craig Heyward 3.00
207 Ray Buchanan 3.00
208 Kimble Anders 3.00
209 Kevin Greene 3.00
210 Eric Allen 3.00
211 Ricardo McDonald 3.00
212 Ruben Brown 3.00
213 Harvey Williams 3.00
214 Broderick Thomas 3.00
215 Frank Reich 3.00
216 Frank Sanders 25.00
217 Craig Newsome 3.00
218 Merton Hanks 3.00
219 Chris Miller 3.00
220 John Elway 60.00
221 Ernest Givins 3.00
222 Boomer Esiason 3.00
223 Reggie Roby 3.00
224 Qadry Ismail 3.00
225 Ki-Jana Carter 20.00
226 Leon Lett 3.00
227 Eric Hill 3.00
228 Scott Mitchell 3.00
229 Craig Erickson 3.00
230 Drew Bledsoe 60.00
231 Sean Landeta 3.00
232 Barrett Brooks 3.00
233 Brian Mitchell 3.00
234 Tyrone Poole 3.00
235 Desmond Howard 3.00
236 Wayne Simmons 3.00
237 Michael Westbrook 20.00
238 Quinn Early 3.00
239 Willie Davis 3.00
240 Rashaan Salaam 15.00
241 Devin Bush 3.00
242 Dana Stubblefield 3.00
243 Dexter Carter 3.00
244 Shane Conlan 3.00
245 Keith Elias 3.00
246 Robert Brooks 8.00
247 Garrison Hearst 15.00
248 Eric Zeier 20.00
249 Nate Newton 3.00
250 Barry Sanders 100.00
251 David Meggett 3.00
252 Courtney Hawkins 3.00
253 Cortez Kennedy 3.00
254 Mario Bates 8.00
255 Junior Seau 6.00
256 Brian Washington 3.00
257 Darius Holland 3.00
258 Jeff Graham 3.00
259 Rob Moore 3.00
260 Andre Rison 3.00
261 Kerry Collins 30.00
262 Roosevelt Potts 3.00
263 Cris Carter 3.00
264 Curtis Martin 100.00
265 Rick Mirer 10.00
266 Mo Lewis 3.00
267 Mike Sherrard 3.00
268 Herman Moore 15.00
269 Eric Metcalf 3.00
270 Ray Childress 3.00
271 Chris Slade 3.00
272 Michael Irvin 15.00
273 Jim Kelly 6.00
274 Terance Mathis 3.00
275 LeRoy Butler 3.00

1995 Finest Fan Favorite

These cards, random inserts in 1995 Topps Finest football packs, feature impact players on clear cut cards. The back, numbered using an "FF" prefix, has biographical information and a list of where the player played in college and in the NFL. Cards were included in every 12th pack.

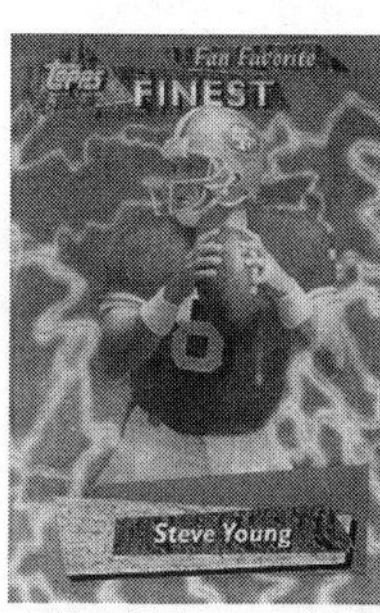

MT
Complete Set (25): 160.00
Common Player: 1.00
Minor Stars: 2.00
1 Drew Bledsoe 10.00
2 Jerome Bettis 6.00
3 Rick Mirer 6.00
4 Andre Rison 1.00
5 Troy Aikman 10.00
6 Cortez Kennedy 1.00
7 Emmitt Smith 15.00
8 Sterling Sharpe 6.00
9 Junior Seau 6.00
10 Michael Irvin 6.00
11 Jim Kelly 6.00
12 Steve Young 7.00
13 John Elway 10.00
14 Jerry Rice 10.00
15 Barry Sanders 20.00
16 Dan Marino 15.00
17 Dan Wilkinson 1.00
18 Reggie White 6.00
19 Deion Sanders 6.00
20 Willie McGinest 1.00
21 Stan Humphries 1.00
22 Heath Shuler 6.00
23 Natrone Means 6.00
24 Warren Moon 6.00
25 Marshall Faulk 3.00

1995 Topps Finest Landmark

This four-card set was available only through Topps direct mailers ($99 plus shipping), and utilizes Finest technology on metal cards overlaid on a four-ounce ingot of solid bronze.

MT
Complete Set (4): 170.00
Common Player: 25.00
1 Troy Aikman 40.00
2 Jerry Rice 40.00
3 Emmitt Smith 70.00
4 Steve Young 25.00

1995-96 Topps Finest Pro Bowl Jumbos

This 22-card set was distributed at the 1996 NFL Experience Pro Bowl show in Hawaii, and is almost identical to the 1995 Finest cards, except for its 4" x 5-5/8" measurement. The only difference is in addition to the cards' original number, each also carries a new 1-22 card number. A larger, poster-sized Steve Young card was also produced for promotional purposes and for distribution at the Pro Bowl show. Parallel Refractor versions are also available, but with a reduced print run.

MT
Complete Set (22): 70.00
Common Player: 1.00
1 Troy Aikman 7.00
2 Tim Brown 2.00
3 Cris Carter 2.00
4 Marshall Faulk 5.00
5 Brett Favre 14.00
6 Merton Hanks 1.00
7 Michael Irvin 2.00
8 Greg Lloyd 1.00
9 Dan Marino 14.00
10 Curtis Martin 10.00
11 Herman Moore 3.00
12 Terry McDaniel 1.00
13 Ken Norton 1.00
14 Bryce Paup 1.00
15 John Randle 1.00
16 Jerry Rice 7.00
17 Barry Sanders 7.00
18 Junior Seau 3.00
19 Steve Young 5.00
20 Reggie White 3.00
21 Chris Warren 2.00
22 Emmitt Smith 14.00
P1 Steve Young (20" by 14" poster Promo) 45.00

1995-96 Topps Finest Pro Bowl Jumbos Refractors

Refractor versions of the Pro Bowl Jumbo Refractors were also available at the 1996 NFL Experience Show in Hawaii. Odds for the Refractor versions are not known.

MT
Complete Set (22): 1400.
Common Player: 20.00
1 Troy Aikman 140.00
2 Tim Brown 40.00
3 Cris Carter 40.00
4 Marshall Faulk 100.00
5 Brett Favre 275.00
6 Merton Hanks 20.00
7 Michael Irvin 40.00
8 Greg Lloyd 20.00
9 Dan Marino 275.00
10 Curtis Martin 200.00
11 Herman Moore 60.00
12 Terry McDaniel 20.00
13 Ken Norton 20.00
14 Bryce Paup 20.00
15 John Randle 20.00
16 Jerry Rice 140.00
17 Barry Sanders 140.00
18 Junior Seau 60.00
19 Steve Young 100.00
20 Reggie White 60.00
21 Chris Warren 40.00
22 Emmitt Smith 275.00

1996 Finest

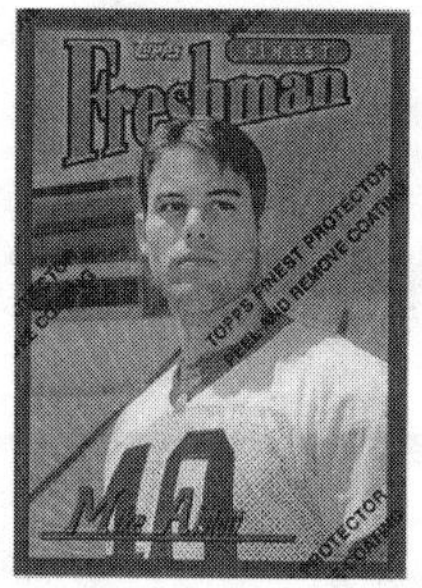

Topps' 1996 Finest football has 359 cards, split into five different subsets - 113 Destroyers, 43 Future, 34 Freshman, 115 Playmakers and 52 Sterling cards. Cards are numbered within the regular issue set from 1-359, and also within the subset, using a "D", "F", "P" or "S" prefix. Within the regular issue set there are three types of cards. There are 220 common cards, 91 uncommon cards (one per every four packs) and 47 rare cards (one per every 24 packs). Commons have a bronze border, uncommons have a silver border, and rares have a gold border. Refractors of every card were also made. Commons are seeded one per every 12 packs, uncommons are one per every 48, and rares are one every 288. Fewer than 150 Refractor sets were produced.

MT
Complete Set (359): 1700.
Comp. Bronze Ser.1 (110): 40.00
Comp. Bronze Ser.2 (110): 50.00
Common Bronze Player: .25
Comp. Silver Ser.1 (55): 200.00
Comp. Silver Ser.2 (36): 150.00
Common Silver Player: 2.00
Comp. Gold Ser.1 (26): 800.00
Comp. Gold Ser.2 (22): 500.00
Common Gold Player: 15.00
Series 1 Pack (6): 5.50
Series 1 Wax Box (24): 120.00
Series 2 Pack (6): 5.50
Series 2 Wax Box (24): 120.00
1 Kordell Stewart G 50.00
2 Jay Novacek .25
3 Ray Buchanan .25
4 Brett Favre S 25.00
5 Phil Hansen .25
6 Mike Mamula .25
7 Kimble Anders G 15.00
8 Merton Hanks G 15.00
9 Bernie Parmalee .25
10 Herman Moore 1.50
11 Shawn Jefferson .25
12 Chris Doleman .25
13 Erik Kramer .25
14 Chester McGlockton S 2.00
15 Orlando Thomas .25
16 Terrell Davis 10.00
17 Rick Mirer G 25.00
18 Roman Phifer .25
19 Trent Dilfer .50
20 Tyrone Hughes S 2.00
21 Darnay Scott .25
22 Steve McNair 3.00
23 Lamar Lathon .25
24 Ty Law S 2.00
25 Brian Mitchell S 2.00
26 Thomas Randolph .25
27 Michael Jackson .25
28 Seth Joyner .25
29 Jeff Lageman .25
30 Darryl Williams .25
31 Darren Woodson S 2.00
32 Erric Pegram .25
33 Craig Newsome G 15.00
34 Sean Dawkins .25
35 Brian Mitchell S 2.00
36 Bryce Paup G 15.00
37 Dana Stubblefield S 2.00
38 Dan Saleaumua .25
39 Henry Thomas .25
40 Dan Marino G 75.00
41 Kerry Collins S 10.00
42 Andre Coleman G 15.00
43 Pat Swilling .25
44 Marty Carter .25
45 Anthony Miller .25
46 Orlando Thomas S 2.00
47 Kevin Carter G 15.00
48 Chris Warren .50
49 Derek Brown .25
50 Jerry Rice S 12.00
51 Blaine Bishop .25
52 Jake Reed .25
53 Willie McGinest S 2.00
54 Blake Brockermeyer S 2.00
55 Vencie Glenn .25
56 Michael Westbrook S 10.00
57 Garrison Hearst S 4.00
58 Derrick Alexander .25
59 Kyle Brady S 2.00
60 Mark Brunell G 45.00
61 David Palmer G 15.00
62 Tim Brown S 4.00
63 Jeff Graham S 2.00
64 Jessie Tuggle .25
65 Terrance Shaw .25
66 David Sloan .25
67 Dan Marino S 25.00
68 Brent Jones .25
69 Tamarick Vanover S 10.00
70 William Thomas .25
71 Robert Smith .25
72 Wayne Simmons .25
73 Jim Harbaugh .25
74 Daryl Johnston S 2.00
75 Carnell Lake G 15.00
76 Wayne Chrebet .25
77 Chris Hudson .25
78 Frank Sanders S 5.00
79 Stevon Moore .25
80 Chris Calloway .25
81 Tom Carter .25
82 David Meggett .25
83 Sam Mills .25
84 Darryll Lewis S 2.00
85 Carl Pickens S 4.00
86 Renaldo Turnbull .25
87 Derrick Brooks .25
88 Jerome Bettis S 4.00
89 Eugene Robinson .25
90 Terrell Davis S 25.00
91 Rodney Thomas 2.00
92 Dan Wilkinson .25
93 Mark Fields .25
94 Warren Sapp .25
95 Curtis Martin 5.00
96 Joey Galloway G 30.00
97 Ray Crockett .25
98 Ed McDaniel .25
99 Napoleon Kaufman S 10.00
100 Rashaan Salaam S 10.00
101 Craig Heyward .25
102 Ellis Johnson .25
103 Barry Sanders S 25.00
104 O.J. McDuffie .25
105 J.J. Stokes 2.50
106 Mo Lewis .25
107 Tony Boselli S 2.00
108 Rob Moore .25
109 Eric Zeier S 2.00
110 Tyrone Wheatley .50
111 Ken Harvey .25
112 Melvin Tuten G 15.00
113 Willie Green .25
114 Willie Davis .25
115 Andy Harmon .25
116 Bruce Smith S 2.00
117 Bryan Cox .25
118 Zack Crockett S 2.00
119 Bert Emanuel .25
120 Greg Lloyd .25
121 Aaron Glenn G 15.00
122 Willie Jackson .25
123 Lorenzo Lynch .25
124 Pepper Johnson .25
125 Joey Galloway S 14.00
126 Heath Shuler S 6.00
127 Curtis Martin S 12.00
128 Tyrone Poole .25
129 Neil Smith .25
130 Eddie Robinson .25
131 Bryce Paup .25
132 Brett Favre G 80.00
133 Ken Dilger G 15.00
134 Troy Aikman 5.00
135 Greg Lloyd S 4.00
136 Chris Sanders 2.00
137 Marshall Faulk S 15.00
138 Jim Everett .25
139 Frank Sanders .50
140 Barry Sanders G 80.00
141 Cortez Kennedy .25
142 Glyn Milburn G 15.00
143 Derrick Alexander .25
144 Rob Fredrickson .25
145 Chris Zorich .25
146 Devin Bush .25
147 Tyrone Poole S 2.00
148 Brett Perriman G 15.00
149 Troy Vincent .25
150 J.J. Stokes S 10.00
151 Deion Sanders 4.00
152 James Stewart .25
153 Drew Bledsoe S 15.00
154 Terry McDaniel S 2.00
155 Terrell Fletcher S 2.00
156 Lawrence Dawsey .25
157 Robert Brooks .50
158 Rashaan Salaam 2.50
159 Dave Brown S 2.00
160 Kerry Collins G 35.00
161 Tim Brown .50
162 Brendan Stai .25
163 Sean Gilbert .25
164 Lee Woodall G 15.00
165 Jim Harbaugh S 4.00
166 Larry Brown S 2.00
167 Neil Smith S 2.00
168 Herman Moore S 5.00
169 Calvin Williams .25
170 Deion Sanders S 10.00
171 Ruben Brown .25
172 Eric Green .25
173 Marshall Faulk G 30.00
174 Mark Chmura S 4.00
175 Jerry Rice 5.00
176 Bruce Smith .25
177 Mark Bruener .25
178 Troy Aikman G 50.00
179 Lamont Warren .25
180 Tamarick Vanover 2.50
181 Chris Warren S 4.00
182 Scott Mitchell .25
183 Robert Brooks S 4.00
184 Steve McNair S 10.00
185 Kordell Stewart S 15.00
186 Terry Wooden .25
187 Ken Norton .25
188 Jeff Herrod .25
189 Charlie Garner S 2.00
190 Drew Bledsoe G 50.00
191 Checklist .25
192 Gus Frerotte .25
193 Michael Irvin G 20.00
194 Brett Maxie .25
195 Harvey Williams S 2.00
196 Warren Moon G 20.00
197 Jeff George S 2.00
198 *Eddie Kennison* 4.00
199 Ricky Watters S 4.00
200 Steve Young G 35.00
201 Marcus Jones .25
202 Terry Allen .50
203 Leroy Hoard .25
204 Steve Bono S 2.00
205 Reggie White .50
206 Larry Centers .25
207 *Alex Van Dyke G* 25.00
208 Vincent Brisby .25
209 Michael Timpson .25
210 Jeff Blake S 6.00
211 John Mobley .25
212 Clay Matthews .25
213 Shannon Sharpe .25
214 Tony Bennett .25
215 Phillippi Sparks S 2.00
216 Mickey Washington .25
217 Fred Barnett .25
218 Michael Haynes .25
219 Stan Humphries .25
220 Cris Carter G 15.00
221 Winston Moss .25
222 *Tim Biakabutuka* 4.00
223 *Leeland McElroy* 1.50
224 Vinnie Clark .25
225 *Keyshawn Johnson* 10.00
226 William Floyd S 4.00
227 Troy Drayton S 2.00
228 Tony Woods .25
229 Rodney Hampton S 2.00
230 John Elway G 50.00
231 Anthony Pleasant .25
232 Jeff George .25
233 Curtis Conway .50
234 Charles Haley G 15.00
235 *Jeff Lewis* 2.50
236 Edgar Bennett .25
237 Regan Upshaw .25
238 William Fuller .25
239 Duane Clemons S 2.00
240 Jim Kelly G 20.00
241 Willie Anderson .25
242 Derrick Thomas .25
243 *Marvin Harrison* 15.00
244 Darion Conner .25
245 Antonio Langham .25
246 Rodney Peete .25
247 Tim McDonald .25
248 Robert Jones .25
249 Curtis Conway S 4.00
250 Rodney Hampton G 15.00
251 Mark Carrier .25
252 Steve Grant .25
253 John Mobley S 2.00
254 Jeff Hostetler .25
255 Darrell Green .25
256 Errict Rhett G 30.00
257 *Alex Molden G* 15.00
258 Chris Slade S 2.00
259 Derrick Thomas S 2.00
260 *Kevin Hardy G* 25.00
261 Eric Swann .25
262 Eric Metcalf S 2.00
263 Irv Smith .25
264 Tim McKyer .25
265 Emmitt Smith S 20.00
266 Sean Jones .25
267 Bryant Young G 15.00
268 Jeff Blake G 30.00
269 Jeff Hostetler S 2.00
270 *Keyshawn Johnson G* 30.00
271 Yancey Thigpen 1.00
272 Thurman Thomas S 4.00
273 Quentin Coryatt .25
274 Hardy Nickerson .25
275 Ricardo McDonald .25
276 Steve Atwater S 2.00
277 Robert Blackmon .25
278 Junior Seau G 20.00
279 Alonzo Spellman .25
280 Isaac Bruce S 8.00
281 *Rickey Dudley* 3.00
282 Joe Cain .25
283 Neil O'Donnell S 2.00
284 John Randle .25
285 Terry Kirby G 15.00
286 Vinny Testaverde .25
287 Jim Kelly S 4.00
288 *Lawrence Phillips S* 15.00
289 Henry Jones .25
290 *Simeon Rice* 1.50
291 Terance Mathis S 2.00
292 Errict Rhett S 6.00
293 Hugh Douglas G 15.00
294 Santo Stephens S 2.00
295 Leslie O'Neal .25
296 Reggie White G 20.00
297 Greg Hill .25
298 Elvis Grbac G 15.00
299 *Walt Harris S* 4.00
300 Emmitt Smith G 75.00
301 Eric Metcalf .25
302 Jamir Miller S 2.00
303 Jerome Woods .25
304 Ben Coates S 2.00
305 Marcus Allen S 4.00
306 Anthony Smith .25
307 Darren Perry .25
308 *Jonathan Ogden S* 6.00
309 Ricky Watters G 20.00
310 John Elway S 12.00
311 James Hasty .25
312 Cris Carter .50
313 Irving Fryar S 2.00
314 *Lawrence Phillips* 3.00
315 Junior Seau S 4.00
316 *Alex Molden S* 1.50
317 Aeneas Williams .25
318 Eric Hill .25
319 *Kevin Hardy* 1.50
320 Steve Young S 10.00
321 Chris Chandler .25
322 Raghib Ismail .25
323 Anthony Parker .25
324 John Thierry .25
325 Michael Barrow .25
326 Henry Ford .25
327 Aaron Hayden .25
328 Terance Mathis .25
329 Kirk Pointer .25
330 *Ray Mickens* .75
331 Jermaine Mayberry .25
332 Mario Bates .25
333 Carlton Gray .25
334 Derek Loville .25
335 *Mike Alstott* 6.00
336 Eric Guliford .25
337 Marcus Patton .25
338 *Terrell Owens* 15.00
339 Lance Johnstone .25
340 Lake Dawson .25
341 Winslow Oliver .25

342	Adrian Murrell	.25
343	Jason Belser	.25
344	Brian Dawkins	.25
345	Reggie Brown	.25
346	Shaun Gayle	.25
347	*Tony Brackens*	1.00
348	Thomas Lewis	.25
349	Kelvin Pritchett	.25
350	*Bobby Engram*	3.00
351	Moe Williams	.25
352	Thomas Smith	.25
353	Dexter Carter	.25
354	Qadry Ismail	.25
355	Marco Battaglia	.25
356	Levon Kirkland	.25
357	Eric Allen	.25
358	*Bobby Hoying*	2.50
359	Checklist	.25

1996 Finest Refractors

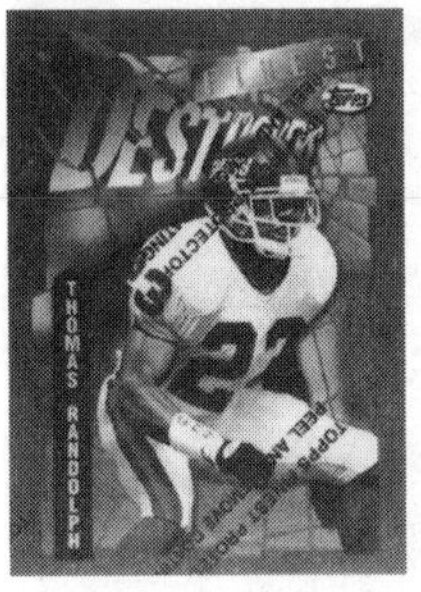

Each card in Topps' 1996 Finest set has a Refractor card made for it, as labeled on the back. Commons are seeded one per every 12 packs, uncommons are one every 48, and rares are one every 288 packs. Fewer than 150 rare Refractor sets were produced.

		MT
	Comp. Bronze Ser.1 (110):	550.00
	Comp. Bronze Ser.2 (110):	550.00
	Common Bronze Player:	3.00
	Comp. Silver Ser.1 (55):	1800.
	Comp. Silver Ser.2 (36):	1000.
	Common Silver Player:	12.00
	Comp. Gold Ser.1 (26):	2000.
	Comp. Gold Ser.2 (22):	1000.
	Common Gold Player:	25.00
1	Kordell Stewart G	150.00
2	Jay Novacek	3.00
3	Ray Buchanan	3.00
4	Brett Favre S	175.00
5	Phil Hansen	3.00
6	Mike Mamula	3.00
7	Kimble Anders G	25.00
8	Merton Hanks G	25.00
9	Bernie Parmalee	3.00
10	Herman Moore	6.00
11	Shawn Jefferson	3.00
12	Chris Doleman	3.00
13	Erik Kramer	3.00
14	Chester McGlockton S	12.00
15	Orlando Thomas	3.00
16	Terrell Davis	120.00
17	Rick Mirer G	75.00
18	Roman Phifer	3.00
19	Trent Dilfer	6.00
20	Tyrone Hughes S	12.00
21	Darnay Scott	6.00
22	Steve McNair	40.00
23	Lamar Lathon	3.00
24	Ty Law S	12.00
25	Brian Mitchell S	12.00
26	Thomas Randolph	3.00
27	Michael Jackson	3.00
28	Seth Joyner	3.00
29	Jeff Lageman	3.00
30	Darryl Williams	3.00
31	Darren Woodson S	12.00
32	Eric Pegram	3.00
33	Craig Newsome G	25.00
34	Sean Dawkins	3.00
35	Brian Mitchell S	12.00
36	Bryce Paup G	25.00
37	Dana Stubblefield S	12.00
38	Dan Saleaumua	3.00
39	Henry Thomas	3.00
40	Dan Marino G	175.00
41	Kerry Collins S	60.00
42	Andre Coleman G	25.00
43	Pat Swilling	3.00
44	Marty Carter	3.00
45	Anthony Miller	3.00
46	Orlando Thomas S	12.00
47	Kevin Carter G	25.00
48	Chris Warren	6.00
49	Derek Brown	3.00
50	Jerry Rice S	80.00
51	Blaine Bishop	3.00
52	Jake Reed	3.00
53	Willie McGinest S	12.00
54	Blake Brockermeyer S	12.00
55	Vencie Glenn	3.00
56	Michael Westbrook S	75.00
57	Garrison Hearst S	24.00
58	Derrick Alexander	3.00
59	Kyle Brady S	12.00
60	Mark Brunell G	125.00
61	David Palmer G	25.00
62	Tim Brown S	24.00
63	Jeff Graham S	12.00
64	Jessie Tuggle	3.00
65	Terrance Shaw	3.00
66	David Sloan	3.00
67	Dan Marino S	160.00
68	Brent Jones	3.00
69	Tamarick Vanover S	75.00
70	William Thomas	3.00
71	Robert Smith	3.00
72	Wayne Simmons	3.00
73	Jim Harbaugh	6.00
74	Daryl Johnston S	12.00
75	Carnell Lake G	25.00
76	Wayne Chrebet	3.00
77	Chris Hudson	3.00
78	Frank Sanders S	24.00
79	Stevon Moore	3.00
80	Chris Calloway	3.00
81	Tom Carter	3.00
82	David Meggett	3.00
83	Sam Mills	3.00
84	Darryll Lewis S	12.00
85	Carl Pickens S	24.00
86	Renaldo Turnbull	3.00
87	Derrick Brooks	3.00
88	Jerome Bettis S	30.00
89	Eugene Robinson	3.00
90	Terrell Davis S	150.00
91	Rodney Thomas	8.00
92	Dan Wilkinson	3.00
93	Mark Fields	3.00
94	Warren Sapp	3.00
95	Curtis Martin	50.00
96	Joey Galloway G	60.00
97	Ray Crockett	3.00
98	Ed McDaniel	3.00
99	Napoleon Kaufman S	24.00
100	Rashaan Salaam S	60.00
101	Craig Heyward	3.00
102	Ellis Johnson	3.00
103	Barry Sanders S	175.00
104	O.J. McDuffie	3.00
105	J.J. Stokes	20.00
106	Mo Lewis	3.00
107	Tony Boselli S	12.00
108	Rob Moore	3.00
109	Eric Zeier S	12.00
110	Tyrone Wheatley	6.00
111	Ken Harvey	3.00
112	Melvin Tuten G	25.00
113	Willie Green	3.00
114	Willie Davis	3.00
115	Andy Harmon	3.00
116	Bruce Smith S	12.00
117	Bryan Cox	3.00
118	Zack Crockett S	12.00
119	Bert Emanuel	3.00
120	Greg Lloyd	3.00
121	Aaron Glenn G	25.00
122	Willie Jackson	3.00
123	Lorenzo Lynch	3.00
124	Pepper Johnson	3.00
125	Joey Galloway S	80.00
126	Heath Shuler S	24.00
127	Curtis Martin S	60.00
128	Tyrone Poole	3.00
129	Neil Smith	3.00
130	Eddie Robinson	3.00
131	Bryce Paup	3.00
132	Brett Favre G	180.00
133	Ken Dilger G	25.00
134	Troy Aikman	60.00
135	Greg Lloyd S	12.00
136	Chris Sanders	6.00
137	Marshall Faulk S	60.00
138	Jim Everett	3.00
139	Frank Sanders	6.00
140	Barry Sanders G	180.00
141	Cortez Kennedy	3.00
142	Glyn Milburn G	25.00
143	Derrick Alexander	3.00
144	Rob Fredrickson	3.00
145	Chris Zorich	3.00
146	Devin Bush	3.00
147	Tyrone Poole S	12.00
148	Brett Perriman G	25.00
149	Troy Vincent	3.00
150	J.J. Stokes S	75.00
151	Deion Sanders	30.00
152	James Stewart	3.00
153	Drew Bledsoe S	80.00
154	Terry McDaniel S	12.00
155	Terrell Fletcher S	12.00
156	Lawrence Dawsey	3.00
157	Robert Brooks	6.00
158	Rashaan Salaam	30.00
159	Dave Brown S	12.00
160	Kerry Collins G	100.00
161	Tim Brown	6.00
162	Brendan Stai	3.00
163	Sean Gilbert	3.00
164	Lee Woodall G	25.00
165	Jim Harbaugh S	24.00
166	Larry Brown S	12.00
167	Neil Smith S	12.00
168	Herman Moore S	30.00
169	Calvin Williams	3.00
170	Deion Sanders S	50.00
171	Ruben Brown	3.00
172	Eric Green	3.00
173	Marshall Faulk G	60.00
174	Mark Chmura S	24.00
175	Jerry Rice	60.00
176	Bruce Smith	3.00
177	Mark Bruener	3.00
178	Troy Aikman G	125.00
179	Lamont Warren	3.00
180	Tamarick Vanover	30.00
181	Chris Warren S	24.00
182	Scott Mitchell	3.00
183	Robert Brooks S	24.00
184	Steve McNair S	60.00
185	Kordell Stewart S	80.00
186	Terry Wooden	3.00
187	Ken Norton	3.00
188	Jeff Herrod	3.00
189	Charlie Garner S	12.00
190	Drew Bledsoe G	125.00
191	Checklist	100.00
192	Gus Frerotte	3.00
193	Michael Irvin G	50.00
194	Brett Maxie	3.00
195	Harvey Williams S	12.00
196	Warren Moon G	50.00
197	Jeff George S	12.00
198	Eddie Kennison	25.00
199	Ricky Watters S	24.00
200	Steve Young G	200.00
201	Marcus Jones	3.00
202	Terry Allen	6.00
203	Leroy Hoard	3.00
204	Steve Bono S	12.00
205	Reggie White	6.00
206	Larry Centers	3.00
207	Alex Van Dyke G	75.00
208	Vincent Brisby	3.00
209	Michael Timpson	3.00
210	Jeff Blake S	50.00
211	John Mobley	3.00
212	Clay Matthews	3.00
213	Shannon Sharpe	3.00
214	Tony Bennett	3.00
215	Phillippi Sparks S	12.00
216	Mickey Washington	3.00
217	Fred Barnett	3.00
218	Michael Haynes	3.00
219	Stan Humphries	3.00
220	Cris Carter G	25.00
221	Winston Moss	3.00
222	Tim Biakabutuka	20.00
223	Leeland McElroy	20.00
224	Vinnie Clark	3.00
225	Keyshawn Johnson	50.00
226	William Floyd S	24.00
227	Troy Drayton S	12.00
228	Tony Woods	3.00
229	Rodney Hampton S	12.00
230	John Elway G	125.00
231	Anthony Pleasant	3.00
232	Jeff George	3.00
233	Curtis Conway	6.00
234	Charles Haley G	25.00
235	Jeff Lewis	3.00
236	Edgar Bennett	3.00
237	Regan Upshaw	3.00
238	William Fuller	3.00
239	Duane Clemons S	12.00
240	Jim Kelly G	80.00
241	Willie Anderson	3.00
242	Derrick Thomas	3.00
243	Marvin Harrison	60.00
244	Darion Conner	3.00
245	Antonio Langham	3.00
246	Rodney Peete	3.00
247	Tim McDonald	3.00
248	Robert Jones	3.00
249	Curtis Conway S	24.00
250	Rodney Hampton G	25.00
251	Mark Carrier	3.00
252	Steve Grant	3.00
253	John Mobley S	12.00
254	Jeff Hostetler	3.00
255	Darrell Green	3.00
256	Errict Rhett G	75.00
257	Alex Molden G	25.00
258	Chris Slade S	12.00
259	Derrick Thomas S	12.00
260	Kevin Hardy G	75.00
261	Eric Swann	3.00
262	Eric Metcalf S	12.00
263	Irv Smith	3.00
264	Tim McKyer	3.00
265	Emmitt Smith S	125.00
266	Sean Jones	3.00
267	Bryant Young G	25.00
268	Jeff Blake G	50.00
269	Jeff Hostetler S	12.00
270	Keyshawn Johnson G	75.00
271	Yancey Thigpen	12.00
272	Thurman Thomas S	24.00
273	Quentin Coryatt	3.00
274	Hardy Nickerson	3.00
275	Ricardo McDonald	3.00
276	Steve Atwater S	12.00
277	Robert Blackmon	3.00
278	Junior Seau G	50.00
279	Alonzo Spellman	3.00
280	Isaac Bruce S	50.00
281	Rickey Dudley	15.00
282	Joe Cain	3.00
283	Neil O'Donnell S	12.00
284	John Randle	3.00
285	Terry Kirby G	25.00
286	Vinny Testaverde	3.00
287	Jim Kelly S	24.00
288	Lawrence Phillips S	70.00
289	Henry Jones	3.00
290	Simeon Rice	3.00
291	Terance Mathis S	12.00
292	Errict Rhett S	60.00
293	Hugh Douglas G	25.00
294	Santo Stephens S	12.00
295	Leslie O'Neal	3.00
296	Reggie White G	80.00
297	Greg Hill	3.00
298	Elvis Grbac G	60.00
299	Walt Harris S	24.00
300	Emmitt Smith G	150.00
301	Eric Metcalf	3.00
302	Jamir Miller S	12.00
303	Jerome Woods	3.00
304	Ben Coates S	12.00
305	Marcus Allen S	24.00
306	Anthony Smith	3.00
307	Darren Perry	3.00
308	Jonathan Ogden S	35.00
309	Ricky Watters G	50.00
310	John Elway S	80.00
311	James Hasty	3.00
312	Cris Carter	6.00
313	Irving Fryar S	12.00
314	Lawrence Phillips	30.00
315	Junior Seau S	24.00
316	Alex Molden S	12.00
317	Aeneas Williams	3.00
318	Eric Hill	3.00
319	Kevin Hardy	12.00
320	Steve Young S	60.00
321	Chris Chandler	3.00
322	Raghib Ismail	3.00
323	Anthony Parker	3.00
324	John Thierry	3.00
325	Michael Barrow	3.00
326	Henry Ford	3.00
327	Aaron Hayden	3.00
328	Terance Mathis	3.00
329	Kirk Pointer	3.00
330	Ray Mickens	7.50
331	Jermaine Mayberry	3.00
332	Mario Bates	3.00
333	Carlton Gray	3.00
334	Derek Loville	3.00
335	Mike Alstott	30.00
336	Eric Guliford	3.00
337	Marvcus Patton	3.00
338	Terrell Owens	90.00
339	Lance Johnstone	3.00
340	Lake Dawson	3.00
341	Winslow Oliver	3.00
342	Adrian Murrell	3.00
343	Jason Belser	3.00
344	Brian Dawkins	3.00
345	Reggie Brown	3.00
346	Shaun Gayle	3.00
347	Tony Brackens	3.00
348	Thomas Lewis	3.00
349	Kelvin Pritchett	3.00
350	Bobby Engram	20.00
351	Moe Williams	3.00
352	Thomas Smith	3.00
353	Dexter Carter	3.00
354	Qadry Ismail	3.00
355	Marco Battaglia	3.00
356	Levon Kirkland	3.00
357	Eric Allen	3.00
358	Bobby Hoying	40.00
359	Checklist	3.00

1997 Finest

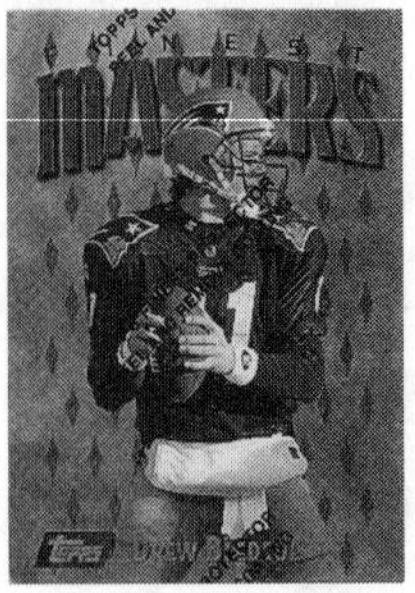

The 175-card Series I set has a numbering format that features card No. 1-100 labeled as Common, cards No. 101-150 as Uncommon and No. 151-175 as Rare. Each card also has a different number corresponding to its theme. The Finest themes are Masters, Bulldozers, Hitmen, Dynamos and Field Generals. The numbering box on each card back indicates both sets of numbers, and which type of card it is, either Common, Uncommon or Rare. The card's theme is printed at the top of each card. Uncommon cards were seeded 1:4 packs, while Rare cards were inserted 1:24. Embossed Uncommon cards were seeded 1:16, while Embossed Die-Cut Rare cards were inserted 1:96. Embossed Die-Cut Rare cards were found 1:96. Series II was numbered 176-350. It consisted of 100 commons, 50 uncommons and 25 rares. The themes in Series II were Champions, Dominators, Impact, Masters and Stalwarts. Insertion rates for Series II were identical to Series I.

		MT
	Complete Set (350):	1000.
	Comp. Bronze Ser.1 (100):	30.00
	Comp. Bronze Ser.2 (100):	60.00
	Common Bronze Player:	.25
	Comp. Silver Ser.1 (50):	150.00
	Comp. Silver Ser.2 (50):	150.00
	Common Silver Player:	2.00
	Embossed Silvers:	2x
	Comp. Gold Ser.1 (25):	400.00
	Comp. Gold Ser.2 (25):	300.00
	Common Gold Player:	7.50
	Embossed Die-Cut Golds:	1.5x
	Series 1 Pack (6):	5.00
	Series 1 Wax Box (24):	100.00
	Series 2 Pack (6):	5.00
	Series 2 Wax Box (24):	100.00
1	Mark Brunell	3.00
2	Chris Slade	.25
3	Chris Doleman	.25
4	Chris Hudson	.25
5	Karim Abdul-Jabbar	2.00
6	Darren Perry	.25
7	Daryl Johnston	.25
8	Rob Moore	.25
9	Robert Smith	.25
10	Terry Allen	.25
11	Jason Dunn	.25
12	Henry Thomas	.25
13	Rod Stephens	.25
14	Ray Mickens	.25
15	Ty Detmer	.25
16	Fred Barnett	.25
17	Derrick Alexander	.25
18	Marcus Robertson	.25
19	Robert Blackmon	.25
20	Isaac Bruce	.75
21	Chester McGlockton	.25
22	Stan Humphries	.25
23	Lonnie Marts	.25
24	Jason Sehorn	.25
25	Bobby Engram	.25
26	Brett Perriman	.25
27	Stevon Moore	.25
28	Jamal Anderson	2.00
29	Wayne Martin	.25
30	Michael Irvin	.50
31	Thomas Smith	.25
32	Tony Brackens	.25
33	Eric Davis	.25
34	James Stewart	.25
35	Ki-Jana Carter	.25
36	Ken Norton	.25
37	William Thomas	.25
38	Tim Brown	.25
39	Lawrence Phillips	.50
40	Ricky Watters	.50
41	Tony Boselli	.25
42	Jesse Armstead	.25
43	Trent Dilfer	.25
44	Rodney Hampton	.25
45	Sam Mills	.25
46	Rodney Harrison	.25
47	Rob Fredrickson	.25
48	Eric Hill	.25
49	Bennie Blades	.25
50	Eddie George	4.00
51	Dave Brown	.25
52	Raymont Harris	.25
53	Steve Tovar	.25
54	Thurman Thomas	.50
55	Leeland McElroy	.25
56	Brian Mitchell	.25
57	Eric Allen	.25
58	Vinny Testaverde	.25
59	Marvin Washington	.25
60	Junior Seau	.25
61	Bert Emanuel	.25
62	Kevin Carter	.25
63	Mark Carrier	.25
64	Andre Coleman	.25
65	Chris Warren	.25
66	Aeneas Williams	.25
67	Eugene Robinson	.25
68	Darren Woodson	.25
69	Anthony Johnson	.25
70	Terry Glenn	2.50
71	Troy Vincent	.25
72	John Copeland	.25
73	Warren Sapp	.25
74	Bobby Hebert	.25
75	Jeff Hostetler	.25
76	Willie Davis	.25
77	Mickey Washington	.25
78	Cortez Kennedy	.25
79	Michael Strahan	.25
80	Jerome Bettis	.50
81	Andre Hastings	.25
82	Simeon Rice	.25
83	Cornelius Bennett	.25
84	Napoleon Kaufman	2.00
85	Jim Harbaugh	.25
86	Aaron Hayden	.25
87	Gus Frerotte	.25
88	Jeff Blake	.50
89	Anthony Miller	.25
90	Deion Sanders	1.75
91	Curtis Conway	.25
92	William Floyd	.25
93	Eric Moulds	.25
94	Mel Gray	.25
95	Andre Rison	.25
96	Eugene Daniel	.25
97	Jason Belser	.25
98	Mike Mamula	.25
99	Jim Everett	.25
100	Checklist	.25
101	Drew Bledsoe S	12.00
102	Shannon Sharpe S	2.00
103	Ken Harvey S	2.00
104	Isaac Bruce S	4.00
105	Terry Allen S	2.00
106	Lawyer Milloy S	2.00
107	Ashley Ambrose S	2.00
108	Alfred Williams S	2.00
109	Hugh Douglas S	2.00
110	Junior Seau S	3.00
111	Kordell Stewart S	12.00
112	Adrian Murrell S	2.00
113	Byron Morris S	2.00
114	Terrell Buckley S	2.00
115	Dan Marino S	20.00
116	Willie Clay S	2.00
117	Neil Smith S	2.00
118	Blaine Bishop S	2.00
119	John Mobley S	2.00
120	Herman Moore S	3.00
121	Keyshawn Johnson S	6.00
122	Boomer Esiason S	2.00
123	Marshall Faulk S	3.00
124	Keith Jackson S	2.00
125	Ricky Watters S	3.00
126	Carl Pickens S	3.00
127	Cris Carter S	2.00
128	Mike Alstott S	6.00
129	Simeon Rice S	2.00
130	Troy Aikman S	12.00
131	Tamarick Vanover S	3.00
132	Marquez Pope S	2.00
133	Winslow Oliver S	2.00
134	Edgar Bennett S	2.00
135	David Meggett S	2.00
136	Marcus Allen S	3.00
137	Jerry Rice S	12.00
138	Steve Atwater S	2.00
139	Tim McDonald S	2.00
140	Barry Sanders S	20.00
141	Eddie George S	15.00
142	Wesley Walls S	2.00
143	Jerome Bettis S	3.00
144	Kevin Greene S	2.00
145	Terrell Davis S	15.00
146	Gus Frerotte S	2.00
147	Joey Galloway S	3.00
148	Vinny Testaverde S	2.00
149	Hardy Nickerson S	2.00
150	Brett Favre S	30.00
151	Desmond Howard G	7.50
152	Keyshawn Johnson G	12.00
153	Tony Banks G	15.00
154	Chris Spielman G	7.50
155	Reggie White G	12.00
156	Zach Thomas G	12.00
157	Carl Pickens G	7.50
158	Karim Abdul-Jabbar G	12.00
159	Chad Brown G	7.50
160	Kerry Collins G	15.00
161	Marvin Harrison G	12.00
162	Steve Young G	25.00
163	Deion Sanders G	20.00
164	Trent Dilfer G	12.00
165	Barry Sanders G	50.00
166	Cris Carter G	7.50
167	Keenan McCardell G	7.50
168	Terry Glenn G	20.00
169	Emmitt Smith G	40.00
170	John Elway G	30.00
171	Jerry Rice G	30.00
172	Troy Aikman G	30.00
173	Curtis Martin G	25.00
174	Darrell Green G	7.50
175	Mark Brunell G	30.00
176	*Corey Dillon*	10.00
177	Tyrone Poole	.25
178	Anthony Pleasant	.25
179	Frank Sanders	.25
180	Troy Aikman	4.00
181	Bill Romanowski	.25
182	Ty Law	.25
183	Orlando Thomas	.25
184	Quentin Coryatt	.25
185	Kenny Holmes	.25
186	Bryant Young	.25
187	Michael Sinclair	.25
188	Mike Tomczak	.25
189	Bobby Taylor	.25
190	Brett Favre	7.00
191	Kent Graham	.25
192	Jessie Tuggle	.25
193	Jimmy Smith	.25
194	Greg Hill	.25
195	*Yatil Green*	2.00
196	Mark Fields	.25
197	Phillippi Sparks	.25
198	Aaron Glenn	.25
199	Pat Swilling	.25
200	Barry Sanders	7.00
201	Mark Chmura	.50
202	Marco Coleman	.25
203	Merton Hanks	.25
204	Brian Blades	.25
205	Errict Rhett	.50
206	Henry Ellard	.25
207	Andre Reed	.25
208	Bryan Cox	.25
209	Darnay Scott	.25
210	John Elway	3.00
211	Glyn Milburn	.25
212	Don Beebe	.25
213	Kevin Lockett	.25
214	Dorsey Levens	.50
215	Kordell Stewart	4.00
216	Larry Centers	.25
217	Cris Carter	.50
218	Willie McGinest	.25
219	Renaldo Wynn	.25
220	Jerry Rice	4.00
221	*Reidel Anthony*	5.00
222	Mark Carrier	.25
223	Quinn Early	.25
224	Chris Sanders	.25
225	*Shawn Springs*	.50
226	Kevin Smith	.25
227	Ben Coates	.25
228	Tyrone Wheatley	.25
229	Antonio Freeman	1.50
230	Dan Marino	6.00
231	Dwayne Rudd	.50
232	Leslie O'Neal	.25
233	Brent Jones	.25
234	*Jake Plummer*	12.00
235	Kerry Collins	2.00
236	Rashaan Salaam	.50
237	Tyrone Braxton	.25
238	Herman Moore	.50
239	Keyshawn Johnson	.50
240	Drew Bledsoe	4.00
241	Rickey Dudley	.25
242	*Antowain Smith*	6.00
243	Jeff Lageman	.25
244	Chris T. Jones	.25
245	Steve Young	3.00
246	Eddie Robinson	.25
247	Chad Cota	.25
248	Michael Jackson	.25
249	Robert Porcher	.25
250	Reggie White	.50
251	Carnell Lake	.25
252	Chris Calloway	.25
253	Terance Mathis	.25
254	Carl Pickens	.50
255	Curtis Martin	3.00
256	Jeff Graham	.25
257	Regan Upshaw	.25
258	Sean Gilbert	.25
259	*Will Blackwell*	1.00
260	Emmitt Smith	6.00
261	*Reinard Wilson*	.50
262	*Darrell Russell*	.50
263	Wayne Chrebet	.25
264	Kevin Hardy	.25
265	Shannon Sharpe	.25
266	Harvey Williams	.25
267	John Randle	.25
268	Tim Bowens	.25
269	*Tony Gonzalez*	6.00
270	*Warrick Dunn*	6.00
271	Sean Dawkins	.25
272	Darryll Lewis	.25
273	Alonzo Spellman	.25
274	Mark Collins	.25
275	Checklist 2	.25
276	*Pat Barnes S*	4.00
277	Dana Stubblefield S	2.00
278	Dan Wilkinson S	2.00
279	Bryce Paup S	2.00
280	Kerry Collins S	8.00
281	Derrick Brooks S	2.00
282	Walter Jones S	2.00
283	Terry McDaniel S	2.00
284	James Farrior S	2.00
285	Curtis Martin S	10.00
286	O.J. McDuffie S	2.00
287	Natrone Means S	3.00
288	*Bryant Westbrook S*	3.00
289	*Peter Boulware S*	3.00
290	Emmitt Smith S	15.00
291	*Joey Kent S*	4.00
292	Eddie Kennison S	4.00
293	LeRoy Butler S	2.00
294	Dale Carter S	2.00
295	*Jim Druckenmiller S*	15.00
296	*Byron Hanspard S*	8.00
297	Jeff Blake S	3.00
298	Levon Kirkland S	2.00
299	Michael Westbrook S	2.00
300	John Elway S	12.00
301	Lamar Lathon S	2.00
302	Ray Lewis S	2.00
303	Steve McNair S	7.00
304	*Shawn Springs S*	3.00
305	Karim Abdul-Jabbar S	4.00
306	*Orlando Pace S*	3.00
307	Scott Mitchell S	2.00
308	Walt Harris S	2.00
309	Bruce Smith S	2.00
310	Reggie White S	3.00
311	Eric Swann S	2.00
312	Derrick Thomas S	2.00
313	Tony Martin S	2.00
314	Darrell Russell S	2.00
315	Mark Brunell S	12.00
316	Trent Dilfer S	3.00
317	Irving Fryar S	2.00
318	Amani Toomer S	2.00
319	Jake Reed S	2.00
320	Steve Young S	8.00
321	*Troy Davis S*	4.00
322	Jim Harbaugh S	2.00
323	Neil O'Donnell S	2.00
324	Terry Glenn S	6.00
325	Deion Sanders S	6.00
326	Gus Frerotte G	7.50
327	Tom Knight G	7.50
328	*Peter Boulware G*	7.50
329	Jerome Bettis G	12.00
330	*Orlando Pace G*	12.00
331	*Darnell Autry G*	15.00
332	*Ike Hilliard G*	25.00
333	*David LaFleur G*	25.00
334	Jim Harbaugh G	7.50
335	Eddie George G	45.00
336	Vinny Testaverde G	7.50
337	Terry Allen G	7.50
338	*Jim Druckenmiller G*	30.00
339	Ricky Watters G	15.00
340	Brett Favre G	60.00
341	Simeon Rice G	7.50
342	Shannon Sharpe G	7.50
343	Kordell Stewart G	30.00
344	Isaac Bruce G	15.00
345	Drew Bledsoe G	30.00
346	Jeff Blake G	12.00
347	Herman Moore G	12.00
348	Junior Seau G	7.50
349	*Rae Carruth G*	20.00
350	Dan Marino G	50.00

1997 Finest Refractors

Each of the 350 base cards has a parallel Refractor. Refractor Common cards were inserted 1:12 packs, while Refractor Uncommon were seeded 1:48. Refractor Rare could be found 1:288 packs. In addition, Refractors of the Embossed and Embossed Die-Cut cards were also randomly seeded. An Embossed Uncommon Refractor was inserted 1:192 packs, while an Embossed Die-Cut Refractor was seeded 1:1,152 packs.

	MT
Complete Set (350):	7200.
Comp. Bronze Ser.1 (100):	500.00
Comp. Bronze Ser.2 (100):	850.00
Common Bronze Player:	3.00
Comp. Silver Ser.1 (50):	900.00
Comp. Silver Ser.2 (50):	900.00
Common Silver Player:	10.00
Embossed Silver Refractors:	2x
Comp. Gold Ser.1 (25):	2000.
Comp. Gold Ser.2 (25):	2000.
Common Gold Player:	40.00
Embossed DC Gold Refractors:	2x

1	Mark Brunell	30.00
2	Chris Slade	3.00
3	Chris Doleman	3.00
4	Chris Hudson	3.00
5	Karim Abdul-Jabbar	10.00
6	Darren Perry	3.00
7	Daryl Johnston	3.00
8	Rob Moore	3.00
9	Robert Smith	3.00
10	Terry Allen	3.00
11	Jason Dunn	3.00
12	Henry Thomas	3.00
13	Rod Stephens	3.00
14	Ray Mickens	3.00
15	Ty Detmer	3.00
16	Fred Barnett	3.00
17	Derrick Alexander	3.00
18	Marcus Robertson	3.00
19	Robert Blackmon	3.00
20	Isaac Bruce	10.00
21	Chester McGlockton	3.00
22	Stan Humphries	3.00
23	Lonnie Marts	3.00
24	Jason Sehorn	3.00
25	Bobby Engram	3.00
26	Brett Perriman	3.00
27	Stevon Moore	3.00
28	Jamal Anderson	20.00
29	Wayne Martin	3.00
30	Michael Irvin	6.00
31	Thomas Smith	3.00
32	Tony Brackens	3.00
33	Eric Davis	3.00
34	James Stewart	3.00
35	Ki-Jana Carter	3.00
36	Ken Norton	3.00
37	William Thomas	3.00
38	Tim Brown	3.00
39	Lawrence Phillips	6.00
40	Ricky Watters	6.00
41	Tony Bennett	3.00
42	Jesse Armstead	3.00
43	Trent Dilfer	3.00
44	Rodney Hampton	3.00
45	Sam Mills	3.00
46	Rodney Harrison	3.00
47	Rob Fredrickson	3.00
48	Eric Hill	3.00
49	Bennie Blades	3.00
50	Eddie George	40.00
51	Dave Brown	3.00
52	Raymont Harris	3.00
53	Steve Tovar	3.00
54	Thurman Thomas	6.00
55	Leeland McElroy	3.00
56	Brian Mitchell	3.00
57	Eric Allen	3.00
58	Vinny Testaverde	3.00
59	Marvin Washington	3.00
60	Junior Seau	3.00
61	Bert Emanuel	3.00
62	Kevin Carter	3.00
63	Mark Carrier	3.00
64	Andre Coleman	3.00
65	Chris Warren	3.00
66	Aeneas Williams	3.00
67	Eugene Robinson	3.00
68	Darren Woodson	3.00
69	Anthony Johnson	3.00
70	Terry Glenn	10.00
71	Troy Vincent	3.00
72	John Copeland	3.00
73	Warren Sapp	3.00
74	Bobby Hebert	3.00
75	Jeff Hostetler	3.00
76	Willie Davis	3.00
77	Mickey Washington	3.00
78	Cortez Kennedy	3.00
79	Michael Strahan	3.00
80	Jerome Bettis	6.00
81	Andre Hastings	3.00
82	Simeon Rice	3.00
83	Cornelius Bennett	3.00
84	Napoleon Kaufman	20.00
85	Jim Harbaugh	3.00
86	Aaron Hayden	3.00
87	Gus Frerotte	3.00
88	Jeff Blake	6.00
89	Anthony Miller	3.00
90	Deion Sanders	15.00
91	Curtis Conway	3.00
92	William Floyd	3.00
93	Eric Moulds	3.00
94	Mel Gray	3.00
95	Andre Rison	3.00
96	Eugene Daniel	3.00
97	Jason Belser	3.00
98	Mike Mamula	3.00
99	Jim Everett	3.00
100	Checklist	3.00
101	Drew Bledsoe S	60.00
102	Shannon Sharpe S	10.00
103	Ken Harvey S	10.00
104	Isaac Bruce S	20.00
105	Terry Allen S	10.00
106	Lawyer Milloy S	10.00
107	Ashley Ambrose S	10.00
108	Alfred Williams S	10.00
109	Hugh Douglas S	10.00
110	Junior Seau S	20.00
111	Kordell Stewart S	60.00
112	Adrian Murrell S	10.00
113	Byron Morris S	10.00
114	Terrell Buckley S	10.00
115	Dan Marino S	100.00
116	Willie Clay S	10.00
117	Neil Smith S	10.00
118	Blaine Bishop S	10.00
119	John Mobley S	10.00
120	Herman Moore S	20.00
121	Keyshawn Johnson S	20.00
122	Boomer Esiason S	10.00
123	Marshall Faulk S	15.00
124	Keith Jackson S	10.00
125	Ricky Watters S	20.00
126	Carl Pickens S	20.00
127	Cris Carter S	10.00
128	Mike Alstott S	20.00
129	Simeon Rice S	10.00
130	Troy Aikman S	60.00
131	Tamarick Vanover S	20.00
132	Marquez Pope S	10.00
133	Winslow Oliver S	10.00
134	Edgar Bennett S	10.00
135	David Meggett S	10.00
136	Marcus Allen S	20.00
137	Jerry Rice S	60.00
138	Steve Atwater S	10.00
139	Tim McDonald S	10.00
140	Barry Sanders S	100.00
141	Eddie George S	70.00
142	Wesley Walls S	10.00
143	Jerome Bettis S	20.00
144	Kevin Greene S	10.00
145	Terrell Davis S	75.00
146	Gus Frerotte S	10.00
147	Joey Galloway S	15.00
148	Vinny Testaverde S	10.00
149	Hardy Nickerson S	10.00
150	Brett Favre S	100.00
151	Desmond Howard G	40.00
152	Keyshawn Johnson G	60.00
153	Tony Banks G	80.00
154	Chris Spielman G	40.00
155	Reggie White G	60.00
156	Zach Thomas G	60.00
157	Carl Pickens G	40.00
158	Karim Abdul-Jabbar G	60.00
159	Chad Brown G	40.00
160	Kerry Collins G	75.00
161	Marvin Harrison G	60.00
162	Steve Young G	125.00
163	Deion Sanders G	100.00
164	Trent Dilfer G	60.00
165	Barry Sanders G	300.00
166	Cris Carter G	40.00
167	Keenan McCardell G	40.00
168	Terry Glenn G	100.00
169	Emmitt Smith G	250.00
170	John Elway G	175.00
171	Jerry Rice G	175.00
172	Troy Aikman G	175.00
173	Curtis Martin G	100.00
174	Darrell Green G	40.00
175	Mark Brunell G	175.00
176	Corey Dillon	60.00
177	Tyrone Poole	3.00
178	Anthony Pleasant	3.00
179	Frank Sanders	3.00
180	Troy Aikman	30.00
181	Bill Romanowski	3.00
182	Ty Law	3.00
183	Orlando Thomas	3.00
184	Quentin Coryatt	3.00
185	Kenny Holmes	3.00
186	Bryant Young	3.00
187	Michael Sinclair	3.00
188	Mike Tomczak	3.00
189	Bobby Taylor	3.00
190	Brett Favre	60.00
191	Kent Graham	3.00
192	Jessie Tuggle	3.00
193	Jimmy Smith	3.00
194	Greg Hill	3.00
195	Yatil Green	10.00
196	Mark Fields	3.00
197	Phillippi Sparks	3.00
198	Aaron Glenn	3.00
199	Pat Swilling	3.00
200	Barry Sanders	60.00
201	Mark Chmura	6.00
202	Marco Coleman	3.00
203	Merton Hanks	3.00
204	Brian Blades	3.00
205	Errict Rhett	6.00
206	Henry Ellard	3.00
207	Andre Reed	3.00
208	Bryan Cox	3.00
209	Darnay Scott	3.00
210	John Elway	30.00
211	Glyn Milburn	3.00
212	Don Beebe	3.00
213	Kevin Lockett	3.00
214	Dorsey Levens	6.00
215	Kordell Stewart	30.00
216	Larry Centers	3.00
217	Cris Carter	6.00
218	Willie McGinest	3.00
219	Renaldo Wynn	3.00
220	Jerry Rice	20.00
221	Reidel Anthony	225.00
222	Mark Carrier	3.00
223	Quinn Early	3.00
224	Chris Sanders	3.00
225	Shawn Springs	6.00
226	Kevin Smith	3.00
227	Ben Coates	3.00
228	Tyrone Wheatley	3.00
229	Antonio Freeman	20.00
230	Dan Marino	50.00
231	Dwayne Rudd	6.00
232	Leslie O'Neal	3.00
233	Brent Jones	3.00
234	Jake Plummer	75.00
235	Kerry Collins	20.00
236	Rashaan Salaam	6.00
237	Tyrone Braxton	3.00
238	Herman Moore	6.00
239	Keyshawn Johnson	6.00
240	Drew Bledsoe	30.00
241	Rickey Dudley	3.00
242	Antowain Smith	35.00
243	Jeff Lageman	3.00
244	Chris T. Jones	3.00
245	Steve Young	20.00
246	Eddie Robinson	3.00
247	Chad Cota	3.00
248	Michael Jackson	3.00
249	Robert Porcher	3.00
250	Reggie White	6.00
251	Carnell Lake	3.00
252	Chris Galloway	3.00
253	Terance Mathis	3.00
254	Carl Pickens	6.00
255	Curtis Martin	25.00
256	Jeff Graham	3.00
257	Regan Upshaw	3.00
258	Sean Gilbert	3.00
259	Will Blackwell	8.00
260	Emmitt Smith	50.00
261	Reinard Wilson	6.00
262	Darrell Russell	6.00
263	Wayne Chrebet	3.00
264	Kevin Hardy	3.00
265	Shannon Sharpe	3.00
266	Harvey Williams	3.00
267	John Randle	3.00
268	Tim Bowens	3.00
269	Tony Gonzalez	20.00
270	Warrick Dunn	75.00
271	Sean Dawkins	3.00
272	Darryll Lewis	3.00
273	Alonzo Spellman	3.00
274	Mark Collins	3.00
275	Checklist 2	3.00
276	Pat Barnes S	20.00
277	Dana Stubblefield S	10.00
278	Dan Wilkinson S	10.00
279	Bryce Paup S	10.00
280	Kerry Collins S	30.00
281	Derrick Brooks S	10.00
282	Walter Jones S	10.00
283	Terry McDaniel S	10.00
284	James Farrior S	10.00
285	Curtis Martin S	40.00
286	O.J. McDuffie S	10.00
287	Natrone Means S	20.00
288	Bryant Westbrook S	20.00
289	Peter Boulware S	20.00
290	Emmitt Smith S	75.00
291	Joey Kent S	20.00
292	Eddie Kennison S	20.00
293	LeRoy Butler S	10.00
294	Dale Carter S	10.00
295	Jim Druckenmiller S	50.00
296	Byron Hanspard S	35.00
297	Jeff Blake S	20.00
298	Levon Kirkland S	10.00
299	Michael Westbrook S	10.00
300	John Elway S	50.00
301	Lamar Lathon S	10.00
302	Ray Lewis S	10.00
303	Steve McNair S	30.00
304	Shawn Springs S	20.00
305	Karim Abdul-Jabbar S	20.00
306	Orlando Pace S	20.00
307	Scott Mitchell S	10.00
308	Walt Harris S	10.00
309	Bruce Smith S	10.00
310	Reggie White S	20.00
311	Eric Swann S	10.00
312	Derrick Thomas S	10.00
313	Tony Martin S	10.00
314	Darrell Russell S	10.00
315	Mark Brunell S	60.00
316	Trent Dilfer S	20.00
317	Irving Fryar S	10.00
318	Amani Toomer S	10.00
319	Jake Reed S	10.00
320	Steve Young S	40.00
321	Troy Davis S	20.00
322	Jim Harbaugh S	10.00
323	Neil O'Donnell S	10.00
324	Terry Glenn S	25.00
325	Deion Sanders S	30.00
326	Gus Frerotte G	40.00
327	Tom Knight G	40.00
328	Peter Boulware G	40.00
329	Jerome Bettis G	60.00
330	Orlando Pace G	60.00
331	Darnell Autry G	60.00
332	Ike Hilliard G	75.00
333	David LaFleur G	60.00
334	Jim Harbaugh G	40.00
335	Eddie George G	150.00
336	Vinny Testaverde G	40.00
337	Terry Allen G	40.00
338	Jim Druckenmiller G	100.00
339	Ricky Watters G	80.00
340	Brett Favre G	300.00
341	Simeon Rice G	40.00
342	Shannon Sharpe G	40.00
343	Kordell Stewart G	150.00
344	Isaac Bruce G	80.00
345	Drew Bledsoe G	150.00
346	Jeff Blake G	60.00
347	Herman Moore G	60.00
348	Junior Seau G	40.00
349	Rae Carruth G	75.00
350	Dan Marino G	250.00

1998 Finest

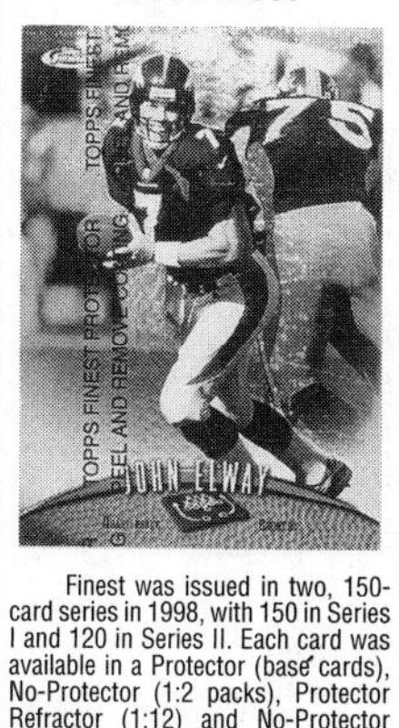

Finest was issued in two, 150-card series in 1998, with 150 in Series I and 120 in Series II. Each card was available in a Protector (base cards), No-Protector (1:2 packs), Protector Refractor (1:12) and No-Protector Refractor (1:24) version. An interesting twist to the releases was that the 30 rookies (121-150) were available in Protector and No-Protector Refractor versions in Series I, but the No-Protector and Protector Refractor versions were only issued in Series II packs. Series I inserts were: Double-Sided Mystery Finest, Centurions, Undergrads and Jumbos, while Series II inserts included Mystery Finest, Stadium Stars, Future's Finest, Jumbos (base cards), Jumbo Stadium Stars and Jumbo Mystery.

	MT
Complete Set (270):	170.00
Complete Series 1 (150):	130.00
Complete Series 2 (120):	40.00
Common Player:	.25
Minor Stars:	.50
Common Rookie:	1.50
Refractor Set (270):	1100.
Refractor Cards:	5x-10x
Refractor Rookies:	2x-4x
Inserted 1:12	
No-Protector Set (270):	600.00
No-Protector Cards:	2x-4x
No-Protector Rookies:	2x
Inserted 1:2	
NP Refractor Set (270):	2000.
NP Refractor Cards:	10x-20x
NP Refractor Rookies:	3x-6x
Inserted 1:24	
Series 1 Pack (6):	5.00
Series 1 Wax Box (24):	110.00
Series 2 Pack (6):	2.50
Series 2 Wax Box (24):	55.00

1	John Elway	3.00
2	Terance Mathis	.25
3	Jermaine Lewis	.25
4	Fred Lane	.50
5	Bryan Cox	.25
6	David Dunn	.25
7	Dexter Coakley	.25
8	Carl Pickens	.50
9	Antonio Freeman	.75
10	Herman Moore	.75
11	Kevin Hardy	.25
12	Tony Gonzalez	.50
13	O.J. McDuffie	.25
14	David Palmer	.25
15	Lawyer Milloy	.25
16	Danny Kanell	.25
17	Randal Hill	.25
18	Keyshawn Johnson	.75
19	Charlie Garner	.25
20	Mark Brunell	2.00
21	Donnell Woolford	.25
22	Freddie Jones	.25
23	Ken Norton	.25
24	Tony Banks	.50
25	Isaac Bruce	.50
26	Willie Davis	.25
27	Cris Dishman	.25
28	Aeneas Williams	.25
29	Michael Booker	.25
30	Cris Carter	.75
31	Michael McCrary	.25
32	Eric Moulds	.50
33	Rae Carruth	.25
34	Bobby Engram	.25
35	Jeff Blake	.50
36	Deion Sanders	1.00
37	Rod Smith	.50
38	Bryant Westbrook	.25
39	Mark Chmura	.50
40	Tim Brown	.50
41	Bobby Taylor	.25
42	James Stewart	.25
43	Kimble Anders	.25
44	Karim Abdul-Jabbar	.75
45	Willie McGinest	.25
46	Jessie Armstead	.25
47	Aaron Glenn	.25
48	Greg Lloyd	.25
49	Stephen Davis	.25
50	Jerome Bettis	.75
51	Warren Sapp	.25
52	Horace Copeland	.25
53	Chad Brown	.25
54	Chris Canty	.25
55	Robert Smith	.50
56	Pete Mitchell	.25
57	Aaron Bailey	.25
58	Robert Porcher	.25
59	John Mobley	.25
60	Tony Martin	.25
61	Michael Irvin	.50
62	Charles Way	.25
63	Raymont Harris	.25
64	Chuck Smith	.25
65	Larry Centers	.25
66	Greg Hill	.25
67	Kenny Holmes	.25
68	John Lynch	.25
69	Michael Sinclair	.25
70	Steve Young	1.50
71	Michael Strahan	.25
72	Levon Kirkland	.25
73	Rickey Dudley	.25
74	Marcus Allen	.50
75	John Randle	.25
76	Erik Kramer	.25
77	Neil Smith	.25
78	Byron Hanspard	.50
79	Quinn Early	.25
80	Warren Moon	.50
81	William Thomas	.25
82	Ben Coates	.25
83	Lake Dawson	.25
84	Steve McNair	1.00
85	Gus Frerotte	.25
86	Rodney Harrison	.25
87	Reggie White	.75
88	Derrick Thomas	.25
89	Dale Carter	.25
90	Warrick Dunn	2.00
91	Will Blackwell	.25
92	Troy Vincent	.25
93	Johnnie Morton	.25
94	David LaFleur	.25
95	Tony McGee	.25
96	Lonnie Johnson	.25
97	Thurman Thomas	.50
98	Chris Chandler	.50
99	Jamal Anderson	1.00
100	Checklist	.25
101	Marshall Faulk	1.00
102	Chris Calloway	.25
103	Chris Spielman	.25
104	Zach Thomas	.50
105	Jeff George	.50
106	Darrell Russell	.25
107	Darryll Lewis	.25
108	Reidel Anthony	.50
109	Terrell Owens	1.00
110	Rob Moore	.50
111	Darrell Green	.25
112	Merton Hanks	.25
113	Shawn Jefferson	.25
114	Chris Sanders	.25
115	Scott Mitchell	.50
116	Vaughn Hebron	.25
117	Ed McCaffrey	.50
118	Bruce Smith	.25
119	Peter Boulware	.25
120	Brett Favre	5.00
121	*Peyton Manning*	30.00
122	*Brian Griese*	12.00
123	*Tavian Banks*	6.00
124	*Duane Starks*	1.50
125	*Robert Holcombe*	5.00
126	*Brian Simmons*	1.50
127	*Skip Hicks*	6.00
128	*Keith Brooking*	1.50
129	*Ahman Green*	10.00
130	*Jerome Pathon*	3.00
131	*Curtis Enis*	8.00
132	*Grant Wistrom*	2.00
133	*Germane Crowell*	6.00
134	*Jacquez Green*	6.00
135	*Randy Moss*	30.00
136	*Jason Peter*	2.00
137	*John Avery*	6.00
138	*Takeo Spikes*	2.00
139	*Patrick Johnson*	2.00
140	*Andre Wadsworth*	3.00
141	*Fred Taylor*	15.00
142	*Charles Woodson*	10.00
143	*Marcus Nash*	6.00
144	*Robert Edwards*	8.00
145	*Kevin Dyson*	6.00
146	*Joe Jurevicius*	3.00
147	*Anthony Simmons*	2.00
148	*Hines Ward*	4.00
149	*Greg Ellis*	2.00
150	*Ryan Leaf*	10.00
151	Jerry Rice	2.50
152	Tony Martin	.25
153	Billy Joe Hobert	.25
154	Rob Johnson	.50
155	Shannon Sharpe	.50
156	Bert Emanuel	.25
157	Curtis Metcalf	.25
158	Natrone Means	.75
159	Derrick Alexander	.25
160	Emmitt Smith	3.50
161	Jeff Burris	.25
162	Chris Warren	.25
163	Corey Fuller	.25
164	Courtney Hawkins	.25
165	James McKnight	.25
166	Shawn Springs	.25
167	Wayne Martin	.25
168	Michael Westbrook	.25
169	Michael Jackson	.25
170	Dan Marino	3.50
171	Amp Lee	.25
172	James Jett	.25
173	Ty Law	.25
174	Kerry Collins	.50
175	Robert Brooks	.50
176	Blaine Bishop	.25
177	Stephen Boyd	.25
178	Keyshawn Johnson	.75
179	Deon Figures	.25
180	Allen Aldridge	.25
181	Corey Miller	.25
182	Chad Lewis	.25
183	Derrick Rodgers	.25
184	Troy Drayton	.25
185	Darren Woodson	.25
186	Ken Dilger	.25
187	Elvis Grbac	.50
188	Terrell Fletcher	.25
189	Frank Sanders	.25
190	Curtis Martin	1.00
191	Derrick Brooks	.25
192	Darrien Gordon	.25
193	Andre Reed	.50
194	Darnay Scott	.25
195	Curtis Conway	.50
196	Tim McDonald	.25
197	Sean Dawkins	.25
198	Napoleon Kaufman	1.00
199	Willie Clay	.25
200	Terrell Davis	4.00
201	Wesley Walls	.25
202	Santana Dotson	.25
203	Frank Wycheck	.25
204	Wayne Chrebet	.75
205	Andre Rison	.50
206	Jason Sehorn	.25
207	Jessie Tuggle	.25
208	Kevin Turner	.25
209	Jason Taylor	.25
210	Yancey Thigpen	.25
211	Jake Reed	.50
212	Carnell Lake	.25
213	Joey Galloway	.75
214	Andre Hastings	.25
215	Terry Allen	.50
216	Jim Harbaugh	.50
217	Tony Banks	.50
218	Greg Clark	.25
219	Corey Dillon	1.25
220	Troy Aikman	2.50
221	Antowain Smith	1.00
222	Steve Atwater	.25
223	Trent Dilfer	.75
224	Junior Seau	.50
225	Garrison Hearst	.75
226	Eric Allen	.25
227	Chad Cota	.25
228	Vinny Testaverde	.50
229	Chris T. Jones	.25
230	Drew Bledsoe	2.00
231	Charles Johnson	.25
232	Jake Plummer	2.00
233	Errict Rhett	.25
234	Doug Evans	.25
235	Phillippi Sparks	.25
236	Ashley Ambrose	.25
237	Bryan Cox	.25
238	Kevin Smith	.25
239	Hardy Nickerson	.25
240	Terry Glenn	.75
241	Lee Woodall	.25
242	Andre Coleman	.25
243	Michael Bates	.25
244	Mark Fields	.25
245	Eddie Kennison	.50
246	Dana Stubblefield	.25
247	Bobby Hoying	.50
248	Mo Lewis	.25
249	Derrick Mayes	.25
250	Eddie George	2.00
251	Mike Alstott	1.00
252	J.J. Stokes	.50
253	Adrian Murrell	.50
254	Kevin Greene	.25
255	LeRoy Butler	.25
256	Glenn Foley	.50
257	Jimmy Smith	.50
258	Tiki Barber	.25
259	Irving Fryar	.25
260	Ricky Watters	.50
261	Jeff Graham	.25
262	Kordell Stewart	2.00
263	Rod Woodson	.25
264	Leslie Shepherd	.25
265	Ryan McNeil	.25
266	Ike Hilliard	.25
267	Keenan McCardell	.50
268	Marvin Harrison	.75
269	Dorsey Levens	.75
270	Barry Sanders	5.00

1998 Finest Refractors

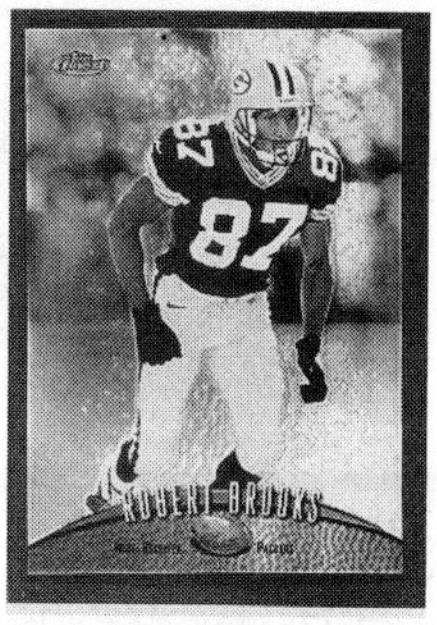

Both Protector and No-Protector versions had parallel Refractor versions for all 270 cards. Protector Refractors were inserted one per 12 packs and had only the front of the card with a Refractor finish, while No-Protector Refractors were inserted one per 24 packs and were basically a double-sided Refractor. No-Protector Refractor versions of the 30 rookies (121-150) were inserted into Series I packs, while Protector Refractor versions were only in Series II packs.

	MT
Refractors:	6x-12x

1998 Finest Centurions

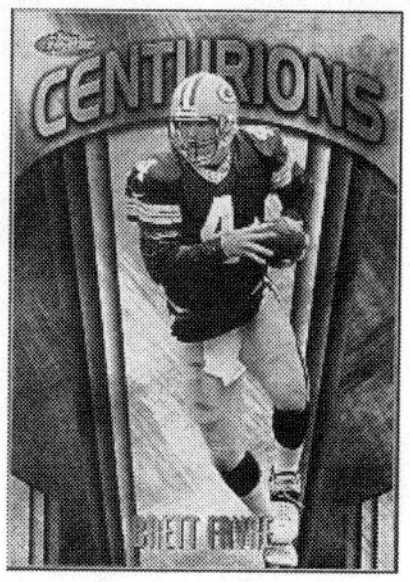

This 20-card insert set was found in packs of Series I. Regular versions were numbered to 500, while Refractors were numbered to only 75. Centurions inserts were numbered with a "C" prefix.

	MT
Complete Set (20):	550.00
Common Player:	12.00
Minor Stars:	24.00
Inserted 1:125	
Production 500 Sets	
Refractor Set (20):	1100.
Refractors:	2x
Inserted 1:831	
Production 75 Sets	

C1	Brett Favre	100.00
C2	Eddie George	45.00
C3	Antonio Freeman	24.00
C4	Napoleon Kaufman	24.00
C5	Terrell Davis	60.00
C6	Keyshawn Johnson	24.00
C7	Peter Boulware	12.00
C8	Mike Alstott	24.00
C9	Jake Plummer	50.00
C10	Mark Brunell	45.00
C11	Marvin Harrison	12.00
C12	Antowain Smith	24.00
C13	Dorsey Levens	24.00
C14	Terry Glenn	24.00
C15	Warrick Dunn	40.00
C16	Joey Galloway	24.00
C17	Steve McNair	30.00
C18	Corey Dillon	30.00
C19	Drew Bledsoe	45.00
C20	Kordell Stewart	45.00

1998 Finest Future's Finest

This insert set features 20 players taking America's game into the next century. Singles were sequentially numbered to 500 and inserted 1:83 packs. Each card also had a parallel Refractor that was numbered to 75 and found 1:557 packs.

	MT
Complete Set (20):	325.00
Common Player:	7.00
Minor Stars:	14.00
Inserted 1:83	
Production 500 Sets	

Refractors: 2x-3x
Inserted 1:557
Production 75 Sets
F1 Peyton Manning 40.00
F2 Napoleon Kaufman 14.00
F3 Jake Plummer 25.00
F4 Terry Glenn 14.00
F5 Ryan Leaf 20.00
F6 Drew Bledsoe 25.00
F7 Dorsey Levens 14.00
F8 Andre Wadsworth 7.00
F9 Joey Galloway 14.00
F10 Curtis Enis 18.00
F11 Warrick Dunn 25.00
F12 Kordell Stewart 25.00
F13 Randy Moss 80.00
F14 Robert Edwards 15.00
F15 Eddie George 25.00
F16 Fred Taylor 25.00
F17 Corey Dillon 14.00
F18 Brett Favre 60.00
F19 Kevin Dyson 14.00
F20 Terrell Davis 45.00

1998 Finest Jumbos 1

Eight different Jumbo Finest cards were inserted as box toppers in both Series I and II. The 16-card set was inserted 1:3 boxes (1:2 hobby collector boxes), with Refractors every 12 boxes (1:6 hobby collector boxes).

MT
Complete Set (8): 125.00
Common Player: 5.00
Inserted 1:3 Boxes
Refractors: 2x
Inserted 1:12 Boxes
1 John Elway 20.00
2 Peyton Manning 35.00
3 Mark Brunell 15.00
4 Curtis Enis 15.00
5 Jerome Bettis 5.00
6 Ryan Leaf 20.00
7 Warrick Dunn 15.00
8 Brett Favre 30.00

1998 Finest Jumbos 2

Eight different Jumbo Finest cards were inserted as box toppers in both Series I and II. The 16-card set was inserted 1:3 boxes (1:2 hobby collector boxes), with Refractors every 12 boxes (1:6 hobby collector boxes).

MT
Complete Set (7): 100.00
Common Player: 5.00
Inserted 1:3 Boxes
Refractors: 2x
Inserted 1:12 Boxes
151 Jerry Rice 15.00
160 Emmitt Smith 25.00
170 Dan Marino 25.00
213 Joey Galloway 5.00
230 Drew Bledsoe 12.00
250 Eddie George 12.00
270 Barry Sanders 30.00

1998 Finest Mystery Finest 1

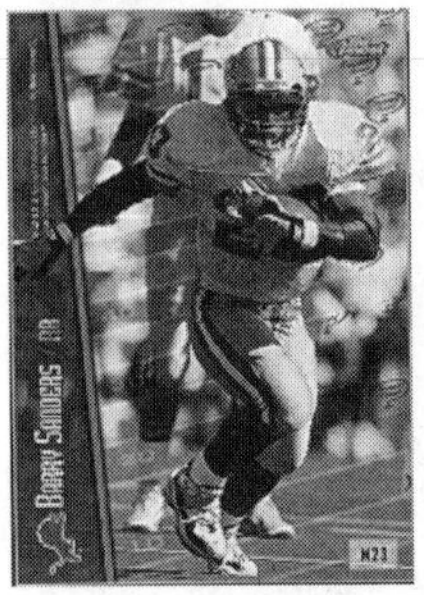

Twenty different players were displayed either with one of three other players on the back, or by themselves on both sides in Mystery Finest. Each side has a Finest Opaque protector and is numbered with a "M" prefix. Regular versions are seeded one per 36 packs, while Refractors are found every 144 packs.

MT
Complete Set (50): 1100.
Common Player: 10.00
Inserted 1:36
Refractor Set (50): 1650.
Refractors: 1.5x
Inserted 1:144
M1 Brett Favre, Mark Brunell 45.00
M2 Brett Favre, Jake Plummer 45.00
M3 Brett Favre, Steve Young 45.00
M4 Brett Favre, Brett Favre 50.00
M5 Mark Brunell, Steve Young 15.00
M6 Mark Brunell, Mark Brunell 15.00
M7 Jake Plummer, Mark Brunell 15.00
M8 Jake Plummer, Jake Plummer 20.00
M9 Steve Young, Jake Plummer 15.00
M10 Steve Young, Steve Young 15.00
M11 John Elway, Drew Bledsoe 25.00
M12 John Elway, Troy Aikman 25.00
M13 John Elway, Dan Marino 40.00
M14 John Elway, John Elway 30.00
M15 Drew Bledsoe, Troy Aikman 25.00
M16 Drew Bledsoe, Drew Bledsoe 20.00
M17 Troy Aikman, Dan Marino 40.00
M18 Troy Aikman, Troy Aikman 20.00
M19 Dan Marino, Drew Bledsoe 40.00
M20 Dan Marino, Dan Marino 45.00
M21 Kordell Stewart, Corey Dillon 15.00
M22 Kordell Stewart, Tim Brown 15.00
M23 Kordell Stewart, Barry Sanders 40.00
M24 Kordell Stewart, Kordell Stewart 18.00
M25 Corey Dillon, Tim Brown 10.00
M26 Corey Dillon, Corey Dillon 10.00
M27 Tim Brown, Barry Sanders 40.00
M28 Tim Brown, Tim Brown 10.00
M29 Barry Sanders, Corey Dillon 40.00
M30 Barry Sanders, Barry Sanders 50.00
M31 Terrell Davis, Emmitt Smith 35.00
M32 Terrell Davis, Jerome Bettis 30.00
M33 Terrell Davis, Eddie George 30.00
M34 Terrell Davis, Terrell Davis 35.00
M35 Emmitt Smith, Eddie George 30.00
M36 Emmitt Smith, Emmitt Smith 35.00
M37 Jerome Bettis, Emmitt Smith 30.00
M38 Jerome Bettis, Jerome Bettis 10.00
M39 Eddie George, Jerome Bettis 15.00
M40 Eddie George, Eddie George 15.00
M41 Herman Moore, Jerry Rice 20.00
M42 Herman Moore, Herman Moore 10.00
M43 Warrick Dunn, Herman Moore 15.00
M44 Warrick Dunn, Jerry Rice 25.00
M45 Warrick Dunn, Dorsey Levens 15.00
M46 Warrick Dunn, Warrick Dunn 20.00
M47 Jerry Rice, Dorsey Levens 20.00
M48 Jerry Rice, Jerry Rice 25.00
M49 Dorsey Levens, Herman Moore 10.00
M50 Dorsey Levens, Dorsey Levens 10.00

1998 Finest Mystery Finest 2

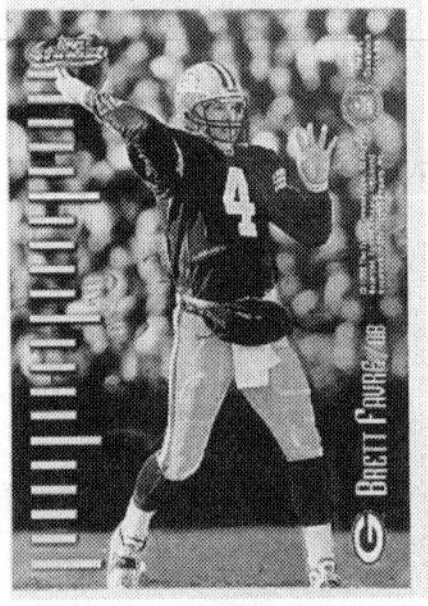

Twenty different players were displayed either with one of three other players on the back, or by themselves on both sides in Mystery Finest. Each side has a Finest Opaque protector and is numbered with an "M" prefix. Regular versions are seeded one per 36 packs, while Refractors are found every 144 packs.

MT
Complete Set (40): 550.00
Common Player: 7.00
Inserted 1:36
Refractors: 1.5x
Inserted 1:144
M1 Brett Favre, Dan Marino 30.00
M2 Brett Favre, Peyton Manning 35.00
M3 Brett Favre, Ryan Leaf 25.00
M4 Dan Marino, Peyton Manning 30.00
M5 Dan Marino, Ryan Leaf 25.00
M6 Peyton Manning, Ryan Leaf 25.00
M7 Barry Sanders, Emmitt Smith 30.00
M8 Barry Sanders, Curtis Enis 20.00
M9 Barry Sanders, Fred Taylor 30.00
M10 Emmitt Smith, Curtis Enis 15.00
M11 Emmitt Smith, Fred Taylor 20.00
M12 Curtis Enis, Fred Taylor 15.00
M13 John Elway, Jerry Rice 20.00
M14 John Elway, Randy Moss 40.00
M15 John Elway, Charles Woodson 20.00
M16 Jerry Rice, Randy Moss 40.00
M17 Jerry Rice, Charles Woodson 15.00
M18 Randy Moss, Charles Woodson 35.00
M19 Terrell Davis, Kordell Stewart 20.00
M20 Terrell Davis, Ricky Watters 15.00
M21 Terrell Davis, Kevin Dyson 15.00
M22 Kordell Stewart, Ricky Watters 12.00
M23 Kordell Stewart, Kevin Dyson 12.00
M24 Ricky Watters, Kevin Dyson 7.00
M25 Warrick Dunn, Eddie George 15.00
M26 Warrick Dunn, Curtis Martin 12.00
M27 Warrick Dunn, Robert Edwards 12.00
M28 Eddie George, Curtis Martin 12.00
M29 Eddie George, Robert Edwards 12.00
M30 Curtis Martin, Robert Edwards 12.00
M31 Peyton Manning, Peyton Manning 25.00
M32 Ryan Leaf, Ryan Leaf 15.00
M33 Curtis Enis, Curtis Enis 12.00
M34 Fred Taylor, Fred Taylor 15.00
M35 Randy Moss, Randy Moss 50.00
M36 Charles Woodson, Charles Woodson 12.00
M37 Ricky Watters, Ricky Watters 7.00
M38 Kevin Dyson, Kevin Dyson 10.00
M39 Curtis Martin, Curtis Martin 10.00
M40 Robert Edwards, Robert Edwards 12.00

1998 Finest Mystery Finest Jumbos 2

These singles measured 3-1/2" x 5", were inserted as box toppers and found 1:4 boxes. Refractor versions for each single were also produced and found 1:17 boxes.

MT
Complete Set (3): 50.00
Common Player: 15.00
Inserted 1:4 Boxes
Refractors: 2x
Inserted 1:17 Boxes
M3 Brett Favre, Ryan Leaf 15.00
M8 Barry Sanders, Curtis Enis 15.00
M16 Jerry Rice, Randy Moss 30.00

1998 Finest Stadium Stars

Only 20 of the top players in the game were included in this 1:45 pack insert. Each single has the letter "S" prefixed to the card number.

MT
Complete Set (20): 160.00
Common Player: 5.00
Inserted 1:45
S1 Barry Sanders 30.00
S2 Steve Young 10.00
S3 Emmitt Smith 20.00
S4 Mark Brunell 10.00
S5 Curtis Martin 5.00
S6 Kordell Stewart 10.00
S7 Jerry Rice 15.00
S8 Warrick Dunn 10.00
S9 Peyton Manning 20.00
S10 Brett Favre 30.00
S11 Terrell Davis 25.00
S12 Cris Carter 5.00
S13 Herman Moore 5.00
S14 Troy Aikman 15.00
S15 Tim Brown 5.00
S16 Dan Marino 20.00
S17 Drew Bledsoe 10.00
S18 Jerome Bettis 5.00
S19 Ryan Leaf 10.00
S20 John Elway 15.00

1998 Finest Stadium Stars Jumbos

These cards were inserted as box toppers at 1:12 boxes. Each single measures 3-1/2" x 5".

MT
Complete Set (6): 85.00
Common Player: 5.00
Inserted 1:12 Boxes
9 Peyton Manning 25.00
10 Brett Favre 30.00
11 Terrell Davis 25.00
18 Jerome Bettis 5.00
19 Ryan Leaf 10.00
20 John Elway 20.00

1998 Finest Undergrads

This 20-card insert showcased top rookies and second-year players. Undergrads were numbered with a "U" prefix and inserted one per 72 packs, with Refractor versions one per 216 packs.

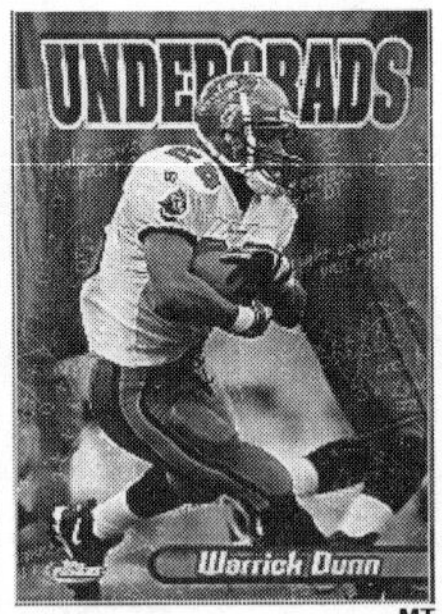

MT
Complete Set (20): 250.00
Common Player: 8.00
Inserted 1:72
Refractor Set (20): 375.00
Refractors: 1.5x
Inserted 1:216
U1 Warrick Dunn 20.00
U2 Tony Gonzalez 8.00
U3 Antowain Smith 12.00
U4 Jake Plummer 25.00
U5 Peter Boulware 8.00
U6 Derrick Rodgers 8.00
U7 Freddie Jones 8.00
U8 Reidel Anthony 10.00
U9 Bryant Westbrook 8.00
U10 Corey Dillon 15.00
U11 Curtis Enis 15.00
U12 Andre Wadsworth 8.00
U13 Fred Taylor 30.00
U14 Greg Ellis 8.00
U15 Ryan Leaf 20.00
U16 Robert Edwards 15.00
U17 Germane Crowell 12.00
U18 Brian Griese 14.00
U19 Kevin Dyson 10.00
U20 Peyton Manning 50.00

1999 Finest

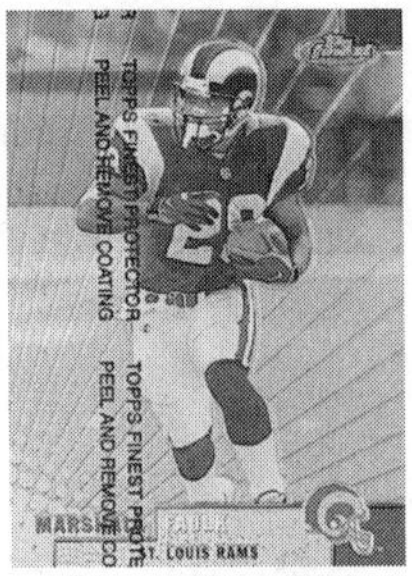

This was a 175-card set that included 51 bonus base cards found 1:1. The bonus cards were divided into three subsets: Rookies, Gems and Sensations. Each base card was printed on 27-point stock. Two parallel sets were issued with Refractors and Gold Refractors. Other inserts included: Double Team, Future's Finest, Leading Indicators, Main Attractions, Prominent Figures, Salute and Team Finest. SRP was $5.00 for six-card packs.

MT
Complete Set (175): 225.00
Common Player: .25
Minor Stars: .50
Common Rookie: 2.00
Inserted 1:1
Pack (6): 5.00
Wax Box (24): 110.00
1 Peyton Manning 3.00
2 Priest Holmes .75
3 Kordell Stewart 1.00
4 Shannon Sharpe .50
5 Andre Rison .50
6 Rickey Dudley .25
7 Duce Staley .50
8 Randall Cunningham .75
9 Warrick Dunn 1.00
10 Dan Marino 3.00
11 Kevin Greene .25
12 Garrison Hearst .50
13 Eric Moulds .75
14 Marvin Harrison 1.00
15 Eddie George 1.00
16 Vinny Testaverde .50
17 Darrell Green .25
18 Derrick Thomas .25
19 Chris Chandler .50
20 Troy Aikman 2.00
21 Terance Mathis .25
22 Terrell Owens .75
23 Junior Seau .50
24 Cris Carter .75
25 Fred Taylor 2.00
26 Adrian Murrell .25
27 Terry Glenn .75
28 Rod Smith .50
29 Darnay Scott .25
30 Brett Favre 4.00
31 Cameron Cleeland .50
32 Ricky Watters .50
33 Derrick Alexander .25
34 Bruce Smith .25
35 Steve McNair 1.00
36 Wayne Chrebet .75
37 Herman Moore .75
38 Bert Emanuel .25
39 Michael Irvin .50
40 Steve Young 1.50
41 Napoleon Kaufman .75
42 Tim Biakabutuka .25
43 Isaac Bruce .75
44 J.J. Stokes .50
45 Antonio Freeman .75
46 John Randle .25
47 Frank Sanders .50
48 O.J. McDuffie .25
49 Keenan McCardell .25
50 Randy Moss 4.00
51 Ed McCaffrey .75
52 Yancey Thigpen .50
53 Curtis Conway .50
54 Mike Alstott .75
55 Deion Sanders 1.00
56 Dorsey Levens .75
57 Joey Galloway .75
58 Natrone Means .50
59 Tim Brown .50
60 Jerry Rice 2.00
61 Robert Smith .75
62 Carl Pickens .50
63 Ben Coates .50
64 Jerome Bettis .75
65 Corey Dillon .75
66 Curtis Martin .75
67 Jimmy Smith .50
68 Keyshawn Johnson .75
69 Charlie Batch 1.25
70 Jamal Anderson .75
71 Mark Brunell 1.50
72 Antowain Smith .75
73 Aeneas Williams .25
74 Wesley Walls .25
75 Jake Plummer 2.00
76 Oronde Gadsden .50
77 Gary Brown .25
78 Peter Boulware .25
79 Stephen Alexander .25
80 Barry Sanders 4.00
81 Warren Sapp .25
82 Michael Sinclair .25
83 Freddie Jones .25
84 Ike Hilliard .25
85 Jake Reed .25
86 Tim Dwight .75
87 Johnnie Morton .25
88 Robert Brooks .25
89 Frank Wycheck .25
90 Emmitt Smith 3.00
91 Ricky Proehl .25
92 James Jett .25
93 Karim Abdul .50
94 Mark Chmura .50
95 Andre Reed .50
96 Michael Westbrook .50
97 Michael Strahan .25
98 Chad Brown .25
99 Trent Dilfer .50
100 Terrell Davis 3.00
101 Aaron Glenn .25
102 Skip Hicks .50
103 Tony Gonzalez .50
104 Ty Law .25
105 Jermaine Lewis .50
106 Ray Lewis .25
107 Zach Thomas .50
108 Reidel Anthony .25
109 Levon Kirkland .25
110 Drew Bledsoe 2.00
111 Bobby Engram .25
112 Jerome Pathon .25
113 Muhsin Muhammed .50
114 Vonnie Holliday .50
115 Bill Romanowski .25
116 Marshall Faulk 1.00
117 Jessie Armstead .25
118 Mo Lewis .25
119 Charles Woodson 1.00
120 Doug Flutie 1.25
121 Jon Kitna 1.00
122 Courtney Hawkins .25
123 Stephen Boyd .25
124 John Elway 3.00
125 Gems (Barry Sanders) 4.00
126 Gems (Brett Favre) 4.00
127 Gems (Curtis Martin) .75
128 Gems (Dan Marino) 3.00
129 Gems (Eddie George) 1.00
130 Gems (Emmitt Smith) 3.00
131 Gems (Jamal Anderson) .75
132 Gems (Jerry Rice) 2.00
133 Gems (John Elway) 3.00
134 Gems (Terrell Davis) 3.00
135 Gems (Troy Aikman) 2.00
136 Sensations (Skip Hicks) .75
137 Sensations (Charles Woodson) .75
138 Sensations (Charlie Batch) 1.25
139 Sensations (Curtis Enis) .75
140 Sensations (Fred Taylor) 2.00
141 Sensations (Jake Plummer) 2.00
142 Sensations (Peyton Manning) 3.00
143 Sensations (Randy Moss) 4.00
144 Sensations (Corey Dillon) 1.00
145 Sensations (Priest Holmes) .75
146 Sensations (Warrick Dunn) .75
147 *Jevon Kearse* 7.00
148 *Chris Claiborne* 4.00
149 *Akili Smith* 8.00
150 *Brock Huard* 5.00
151 *Daunte Culpepper* 20.00
152 *Edgerrin James* 30.00
153 *Cecil Collins* 4.00
154 *Kevin Faulk* 6.00
155 *Amos Zereoue* 5.00
156 *James Johnson* 5.00
157 *Sedrick Irvin* 5.00
158 *Ricky Williams* 25.00
159 *Michael Cloud* 2.00
160 *Chris McAlister* 2.00
161 *Rob Konrad* 4.00
162 *Champ Bailey* 5.00
163 *Ebenezer Ekuban* 2.00
164 *Tim Couch* 20.00
165 *Cade McNown* 7.00
166 *Donovan McNabb* 12.00
167 *Joe Germaine* 5.00
168 *Shaun King* 12.00
169 *Peerless Price* 6.00
170 *Kevin Johnson* 8.00
171 *Troy Edwards* 8.00
172 *Karsten Bailey* 2.00
173 *David Boston* 8.00
174 *D'Wayne Bates* 4.00
175 *Torry Holt* 10.00

1999 Finest Refractors Parallel

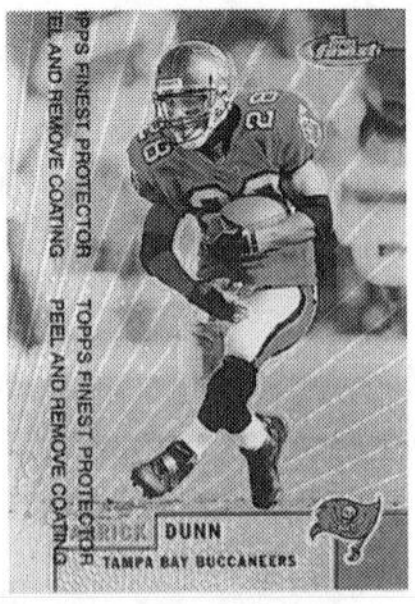

This was a 175-card set that paralleled the base set. Each of these singles used the Refractor technology on the fronts of the cards. Singles were found 1:12 packs.

MT
Refractor Cards: 5x-10x
Refractor Gems/Sensations: 3x-6x
Refractor Rookies: 2x-4x
Inserted 1:12

1999 Finest Gold Refractors Parallel

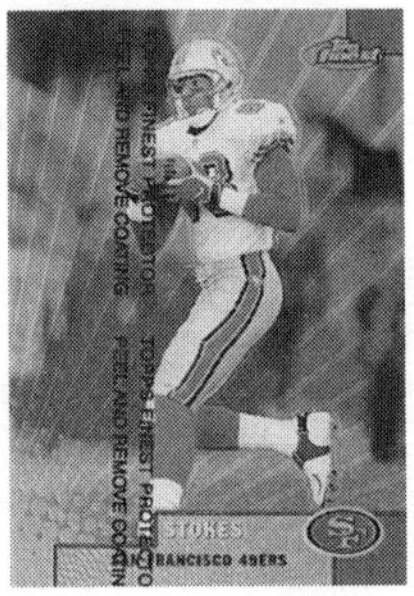

This was a 175-card parallel to the base set. Each single was die cut and printed with a gold background. They were found 1:72 packs and were sequentially numbered to 100.

MT
Refractor Cards: 20x-40x
Refractor Gems/Sensations: 10x-20x
Refractor Rookies: 5x-10x
Inserted 1:72
Production 100 Sets

1999 Finest Double Team

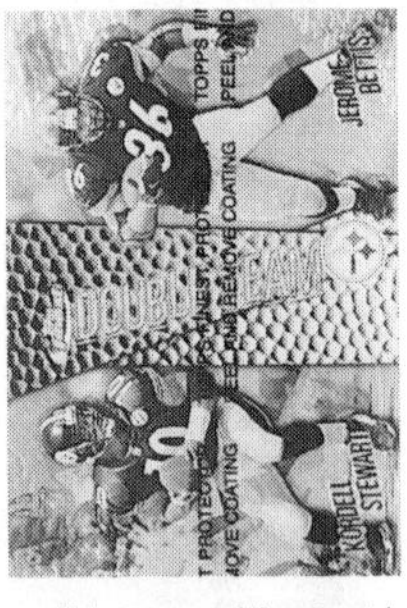

This seven-card insert set included a pair of teammates on the same card and pictured each on the fronts of the cards. Singles were inserted 1:50 packs. Partial Refractor versions were also issued with half the card a Refractor and the other half normal. They were also found 1:50 packs. A complete Refractor version was issued and found 1:150 packs.

MT
Complete Set (7): 25.00
Common Player: 2.50
Inserted 1:50
Dual Refractors: 2x
Inserted 1:150
1 Akili Smith, Carl Pickens 8.00
2 Cade McNown, Curtis Enis 10.00
3 Doug Flutie, Eric Moulds 5.00
4 Mark Brunell, Fred Taylor 5.00
5 Kordell Stewart, Jerome Bettis 2.50
6 Jon Kitna, Joey Galloway 2.50
7 Warrick Dunn, Mike Alstott 2.50

1999 Finest Future's Finest

This 10-card insert set included the top rookies from 1999. Singles were inserted 1:253 packs and sequentially numbered to 500. A parallel Refractor version was also released. Each of those singles was sequentially numbered to 100 and found 1:1,262 packs.

		MT
	Complete Set (10):	175.00
	Common Player:	10.00
	Inserted 1:253	
	Production 500 Sets	
	Refractors:	3x
	Inserted 1:1,264	
	Production 100 Sets	
1	Akili Smith	20.00
2	Cade McNown	20.00
3	Champ Bailey	10.00
4	Daunte Culpepper	20.00
5	David Boston	15.00
6	Donovan McNabb	20.00
7	Edgerrin James	40.00
8	Ricky Williams	45.00
9	Tim Couch	45.00
10	Torry Holt	15.00

1999 Finest Leading Indicators

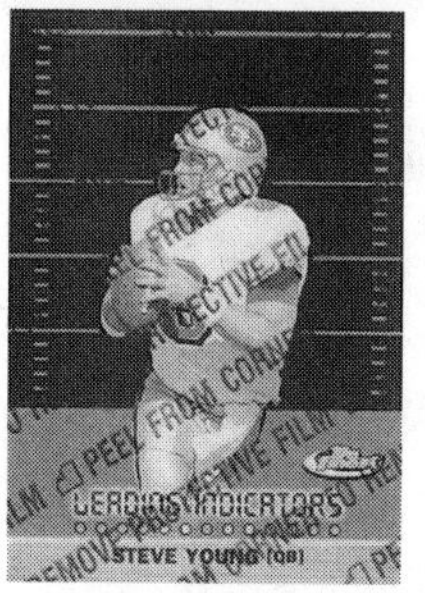

Each of the singles in this 10-card set utilized an innovative, heat-sensitive, thermal ink technology with each star in this insert set. Collectors touched points of the field behind each player image and the player's statistics appeared. Singles were inserted 1:30 packs.

		MT
	Complete Set (10):	40.00
	Common Player:	2.00
	Minor Stars:	4.00
	Inserted 1:30	
1	Jamal Anderson	4.00
2	Doug Flutie	5.00
3	Drew Bledsoe	6.00
4	Eddie George	5.00
5	Emmitt Smith	10.00
6	John Elway	10.00
7	Keyshawn Johnson	4.00
8	Steve Young	5.00
9	Terrell Owens	4.00
10	Vinny Testaverde	2.00

1999 Finest Main Attractions

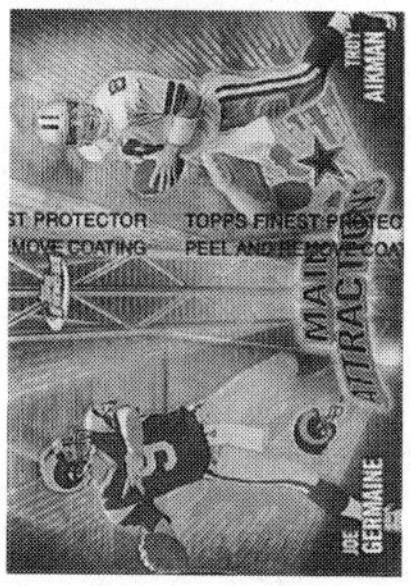

This seven-card insert set included 14 different players with two per card. Singles were found 1:50 packs. A parallel version with half the card a Refractor and the other a non-Refractor was issued at 1:50 packs. The Refractor version with the whole card as a Refractor was issued 1:150 packs.

		MT
	Complete Set (7):	35.00
	Common Player:	2.50
	Inserted 1:50	
	Dual Refractors:	2x
	Inserted 1:150	
1	Champ Bailey, Deion Sanders	5.00
2	Daunte Culpepper, Steve McNair	8.00
3	Donovan McNabb, Kordell Stewart	8.00
4	Edgerrin James, Marshall Faulk	12.00
5	Kevin Faulk, Warrick Dunn	5.00
6	Joe Germaine, Troy Aikman	7.00
7	Rob Konrad, Mike Alstott	2.50

1999 Finest Prominent Figures

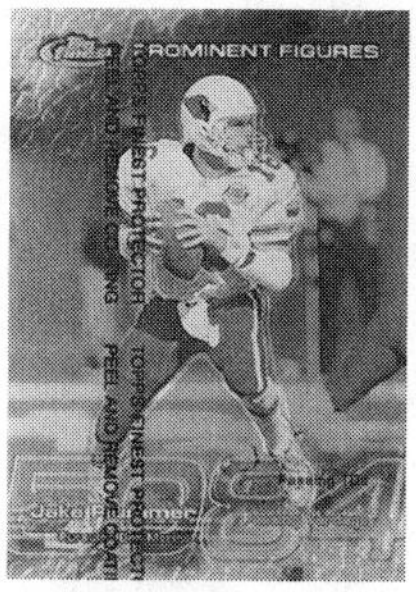

This 60-card insert set included players who were chasing records and the set was divided into six statistical categories. Each of these singles was sequentially numbered to the all-time single season record. Passing Yards were numbered to 5,084 and inserted 1:25 packs. Touchdown Passes were numbered to 48 and inserted 1:2,634. Rushing Yards were numbered to 2,105 and found 1:60 packs. Rushing Touchdowns were numbered to 25 and inserted 1:5,099. Receiving Yards were numbered to 1,848 and found 1:68 packs. Touchdown Receptions were numbered to 22 and found 1:5,779.

		MT
	Common QB (1-10):	1.00
	Inserted 1:25	
	Production 5,084 Sets	
	Common QB (11-20):	25.00
	Inserted 1:2,634	
	Production 48 Sets	
	Common RB (21-30):	50.00
	Inserted 1:5,099	
	Production 25 Sets	
	Common RB (31-40):	5.00
	Inserted 1:60	
	Production 2,105 Sets	
	Common WR (41-50):	50.00
	Inserted 1:5,779	
	Production 22 Sets	
	Common WR (51-60):	3.00
	Inserted 1:68	
	Production 1,848 Sets	
1	Brett Favre	10.00
2	Dan Marino	7.00
3	Drew Bledsoe	4.00
4	Jake Plummer	5.00
5	Mark Brunell	4.00
6	Peyton Manning	7.00
7	Randall Cunningham	2.00
8	Steve Young	3.00
9	Tim Couch	15.00
10	Vinny Testaverde	1.00
11	Brett Favre	150.00
12	Dan Marino	120.00
13	Drew Bledsoe	50.00
14	Jake Plummer	75.00
15	Mark Brunell	50.00
16	Peyton Manning	120.00
17	Randall Cunningham	35.00
18	Steve Young	50.00
19	Tim Couch	200.00
20	Vinny Testaverde	25.00
21	Barry Sanders	250.00
22	Curtis Martin	50.00
23	Eddie George	75.00
24	Emmitt Smith	175.00
25	Fred Taylor	125.00
26	Garrison Hearst	50.00
27	Jamal Anderson	50.00
28	Marshall Faulk	50.00
29	Ricky Williams	300.00
30	Terrell Davis	175.00
31	Barry Sanders	20.00
32	Curtis Martin	5.00
33	Eddie George	6.00
34	Emmitt Smith	15.00
35	Fred Taylor	10.00
36	Garrison Hearst	5.00
37	Jamal Anderson	5.00
38	Marshall Faulk	5.00
39	Ricky Williams	30.00
40	Terrell Davis	15.00
41	Antonio Freeman	50.00
42	David Boston	75.00
43	Cris Carter	50.00
44	Jerry Rice	125.00
45	Joey Galloway	50.00
46	Keyshawn Johnson	50.00
47	Randy Moss	250.00
48	Terrell Owens	50.00
49	Tim Brown	50.00
50	Torry Holt	75.00
51	Antonio Freeman	4.00
52	David Boston	8.00
53	Eric Moulds	4.00
54	Jerry Rice	10.00
55	Joey Galloway	4.00
56	Keyshawn Johnson	4.00
57	Randy Moss	20.00
58	Terrell Owens	4.00
59	Jimmy Smith	3.00
60	Torry Holt	8.00

1999 Finest Salute

One card was made for this set with two parallel versions. The card included the three 1998 season award winners with the NFL Rookie of the Year Randy Moss, NFL MVP Terrell Davis and Super Bowl XXXIII MVP John Elway. The single was found 1:53 packs. A parallel Refractor was made and inserted 1:1,900 packs. Also, a parallel Gold Refractor was found 1:12,384 packs and was sequentially numbered to 100.

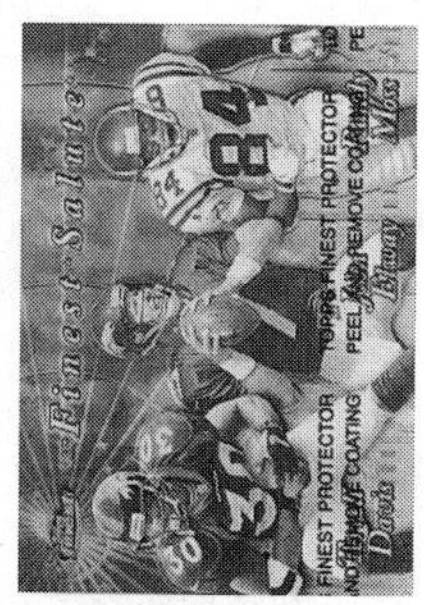

		MT
	Complete Set (3):	275.00
	Inserted 1:53	
	Refractor Inserted 1:1,900	
	Gold Ref. Inserted 1:12,384	
	Production 100 Sets	
	Terrell Davis, John Elway, Randy Moss	10.00
	Terrell Davis, John Elway, Randy Moss GR	250.00
	Terrell Davis, John Elway, Randy Moss REF	75.00

1999 Finest Team Finest

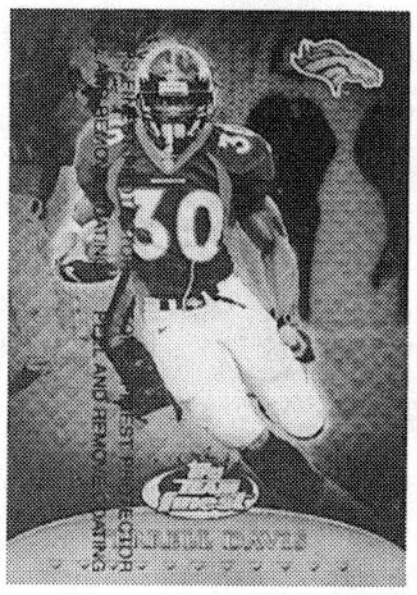

This was a 10-card set that included top NFL stars and pictured them on a prismatic card. The base set was in Blue, inserted 1:84 packs and numbered to 1,500. A Gold parallel was made and inserted 1:57 packs and numbered to 250. A Red version was issued at 1:29 packs and numbered to 500. Each had a parallel Refractor version. The Blue singles were found 1:843 packs and numbered to 150. The Red singles were inserted 1:285 packs and numbered to 50. While the Gold singles were issued 1:573 packs and numbered to 25.

		MT
	Complete Set (10):	100.00
	Common Player:	5.00
	Inserted 1:84	
	Production 1,500 Sets	
	Blue Refractors:	4x
	Inserted 1:843	
	Production 150 Sets	
	Gold Cards:	3x
	Inserted 1:57	
	Production 250 Sets	
	Gold Refractors:	8x-16x
	Inserted 1:573	
	Production 25 Sets	
	Red Cards:	2x
	Inserted 1:29	
	Production 500 Sets	
	Red Refractors:	4x-8x
	Inserted 1:285	
	Production 50 Sets	
1	Barry Sanders	15.00
2	Brett Favre	15.00
3	Dan Marino	12.00
4	Drew Bledsoe	7.00
5	Jamal Anderson	5.00
6	John Elway	12.00
7	Peyton Manning	12.00
8	Randy Moss	15.00
9	Terrell Davis	12.00
10	Troy Aikman	8.00

2000 Finest

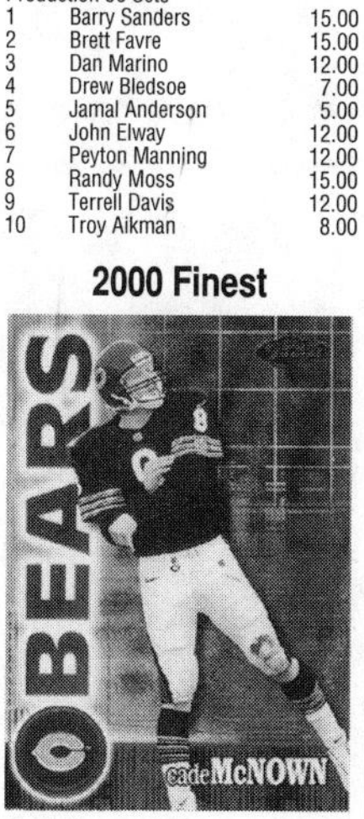

		MT
	Complete Set (205):	550.00
	Common Player:	.15
	Minor Stars:	.30
	Common Rookie:	6.00
	Production 2,400 Sets	
	Inserted 1:11	
	Common Inherent Fire:	2.00
	Inserted 1:8	
	Common Gems:	2.00
	Inserted 1:24	
	Pack (5):	5.00
	Wax Box (24):	85.00
1	Tim Dwight	.50
2	Cade McNown	1.00
3	Drew Bledsoe	1.00
4	Torry Holt	.50
5	Derrick Mayes	.30
6	Vinny Testaverde	.30
7	Patrick Jeffers	.50
8	Dorsey Levens	.30
9	James Johnson	.30
10	Champ Bailey	.30
11	Jeff George	.50
12	Shawn Jefferson	.15
13	Terrence Wilkins	.15
14	J.J. Stokes	.30
15	Doug Flutie	.75
16	Corey Dillon	.50
17	Rod Smith	.30
18	Jimmy Smith	.50
19	Amani Toomer	.15
20	Curtis Conway	.15
21	Brad Johnson	.50
22	Edgerrin James	2.50
23	Derrick Alexander	.15
24	Terrell Owens	.50
25	Kurt Warner	3.00
26	Frank Sanders	.30
27	Tony Banks	.30
28	Troy Aikman	1.25
29	Curtis Enis	.30
30	Eddie George	.75
31	Bill Schroeder	.15
32	Kent Graham	.15
33	Mike Alstott	.50
34	Steve Young	1.00
35	Jacquez Green	.30
36	Frank Wycheck	.15
37	Kerry Collins	.30
38	Stephen Davis	.50
39	Tony Gonzalez	.30
40	Tyrone Wheatley	.30
41	Brett Favre	2.50
42	Joey Galloway	.50
43	Terrell Davis	1.75
44	Marvin Harrison	.50
45	Zach Thomas	.30
46	Jerry Rice	1.25
47	Keyshawn Johnson	.50
48	Rob Johnson	.30
49	Raghib Ismail	.15
50	Elvis Grbac	.30
51	Warrick Dunn	.50
52	Jevon Kearse	.60
53	Albert Connell	.30
54	Muhsin Muhammad	.30
55	Carl Pickens	.30
56	Peyton Manning	2.00
57	Daunte Culpepper	1.25
58	Ike Hilliard	.15
59	Steve McNair	.50
60	Sean Dawkins	.15
61	Steve Beuerlein	.30
62	Priest Holmes	.50
63	Jim Harbaugh	.30
64	Germane Crowell	.50
65	Cris Carter	.50
66	Jamal Anderson	.50
67	Kevin Johnson	.50
68	Herman Moore	.30
69	Ricky Williams	1.50
70	Rich Gannon	.30
71	Isaac Bruce	.50
72	Peerless Price	.50
73	Az-Zahir Hakim	.30
74	Mark Brunell	1.00
75	Rob Moore	.30
76	Antowain Smith	.30
77	Tim Biakabutuka	.30
78	Ed McCaffrey	.30
79	Tony Martin	.15
80	Marcus Robinson	.50
81	Kevin Dyson	.30
82	Wesley Walls	.30
83	Chris Chandler	.30
84	Keenan McCardell	.30
85	Napoleon Kaufman	.30
86	Emmitt Smith	1.75
87	James Stewart	.30
88	Tim Brown	.30
89	Ricky Watters	.30
90	Johnnie Morton	.15
91	Jake Plummer	.50
92	Olandis Gary	.60
93	Jerome Bettis	.50
94	Terry Glenn	.50
95	Kordell Stewart	.50
96	Charlie Garner	.30
97	Yancey Thigpen	.15
98	Michael Westbrook	.30
99	Bobby Engram	.15
100	Eric Moulds	.50
101	Darnay Scott	.30
102	Antonio Freeman	.50
103	Wayne Chrebet	.30
104	Akili Smith	.50
105	Jeff Blake	.30
106	Curtis Martin	.50
107	Errict Rhett	.30
108	Damon Huard	.50
109	Jeff Graham	.15
110	Terance Mathis	.15
111	Jon Kitna	.50
112	Tim Couch	1.50
113	Fred Taylor	1.00
114	Qadry Ismail	.15
115	Donovan McNabb	1.00
116	Charles Johnson	.15
117	Troy Edwards	.50
118	Shaun King	1.00
119	Charlie Batch	.50
120	Robert Smith	.50
121	Marshall Faulk	.50
122	Brian Griese	.75
123	O.J. McDuffie	.30
124	Randy Moss	2.00
125	Duce Staley	.30
126	*Peter Warrick*	30.00
127	*Dez White*	8.00
128	*Ron Dayne*	40.00
129	*J.R. Redmond*	12.00
130	*Thomas Jones*	20.00
131	*Plaxico Burress*	25.00
132	*Reuben Droughns*	8.00
133	*Shaun Alexander*	30.00
134	*Ron Dugans*	10.00
135	*Travis Prentice*	15.00
136	*Joe Hamilton*	10.00
137	*Curtis Keaton*	6.00
138	*Chris Redman*	15.00
139	*Chad Pennington*	35.00
140	*Travis Taylor*	15.00
141	*Bubba Franks*	10.00
142	*Dennis Northcutt*	10.00
143	*Jerry Porter*	10.00
144	*Sylvester Morris*	20.00
145	*Anthony Becht*	8.00
146	*Trung Canidate*	8.00
147	*Jamal Lewis*	50.00
148	*R. Jay Soward*	10.00
149	*Tee Martin*	8.00
150	*Courtney Brown*	10.00
151	*Brian Urlacher*	25.00
152	*Danny Farmer*	8.00
153	*Laveranues Coles*	12.00
154	*Todd Pinkston*	10.00
155	*Corey Simon*	8.00
156	*Spergon Wynn*	6.00
157	*Tim Rattay*	12.00
158	*Todd Husak*	8.00
159	*Aaron Shea*	6.00
160	*Giovanni Carmazzi*	12.00
161	*Trevor Gaylor*	8.00
162	*JuJuan Dawson*	10.00
163	*Jarious Jackson*	8.00
164	*Chris Samuels*	8.00
165	*Rob Morris*	8.00
166	Peter Warrick, Randy Moss	6.00
167	Randy Moss, Peter Warrick	6.00
168	Travis Prentice, Stephen Davis	2.00
169	Stephen Davis, Travis Prentice	2.00
170	Chris Redman, Kurt Warner	5.00
171	Kurt Warner, Chris Redman	5.00
172	Sylvester Morris, Jimmy Smith	2.00
173	Jimmy Smith, Sylvester Morris	2.00
174	Chad Pennington, Peyton Manning	5.00
175	Peyton Manning, Chad Pennington	5.00
176	R. Jay Soward, Marvin Harrison	2.00
177	Marvin Harrison, R. Jay Soward	2.00
178	Ron Dayne, Jamal Anderson	4.00
179	Jamal Anderson, Ron Dayne	4.00
180	Shaun Alexander, Eddie George	3.00
181	Eddie George, Shaun Alexander	3.00
182	Courtney Brown, Bruce Smith	2.00
183	Bruce Smith, Courtney Brown	2.00
184	Jamal Lewis, Edgerrin James	5.00
185	Edgerrin James, Jamal Lewis	5.00
186	Trung Canidate, Emmitt Smith	3.00
187	Emmitt Smith, Trung Canidate	3.00
188	Travis Taylor, Cris Carter	2.00
189	Cris Carter, Travis Taylor	2.00
190	Curtis Keaton, Marshall Faulk	2.00
191	Marshall Faulk, Curtis Keaton	2.00
192	Plaxico Burress, Jerry Rice	3.00
193	Jerry Rice, Plaxico Burress	3.00
194	Thomas Jones, Terrell Davis	3.00
195	Terrell Davis, Thomas Jones	3.00
196	Peyton Manning	5.00
197	Randy Moss	5.00
198	Terrell Davis	4.00
199	Marshall Faulk	2.00
200	Edgerrin James	6.00
201	Emmitt Smith	4.00
202	Ricky Williams	3.00
203	Kurt Warner	7.00
204	Eddie George	2.00
205	Brett Favre	6.00

2000 Finest Gold Refractors Parallel

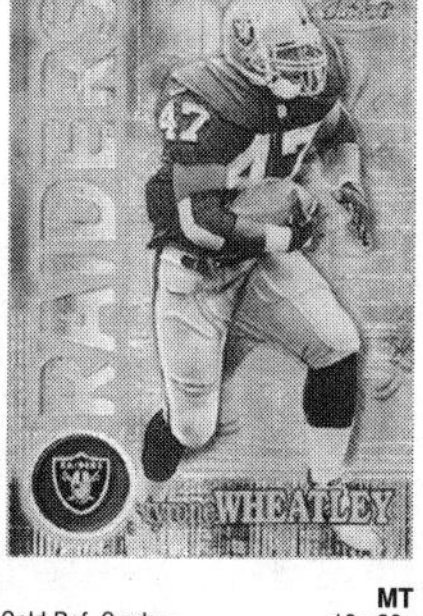

	MT
Gold Ref. Cards:	10x-20x
Production #1-125 300 Sets	
Gold Ref. Rookies:	3x
Production 200 Sets	
Inserted 1:132	
Gold Ref. Inherent Fire:	8x-16x
Production 100 Sets	
Inserted 1:365	
Gold Ref. Gems:	10x-20x
Production 50 Sets	
Inserted 1:2,372	

2000 Finest Moments

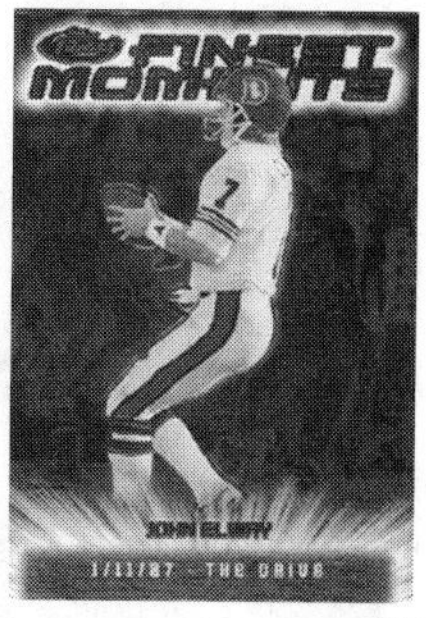

		MT
	Complete Set (25):	25.00
	Common Player:	.50
	Minor Stars:	1.00
	Inserted 1:8	
	Refractor Cards:	2x
	Inserted 1:18	
1	Bart Starr	2.00
2	Phil Simms	1.00
3	John Elway	6.00
4	Dan Marino	6.00
5	Kellen Winslow	1.00
6	Franco Harris	2.00
7	Stephen Davis	1.00
8	Isaac Bruce	1.00
9	Edgerrin James	5.00
10	Marshall Faulk	1.00
11	Patrick Jeffers	1.00
12	Kurt Warner	6.00
13	Joe Montana	10.00
14	Kevin Carter	.50
15	Andre Reed	.50
16	Torry Holt	1.00
17	Frank Wycheck, Kevin Dyson	1.00
18	Jason Elam	.50
19	Mike Jones	.50
20	Cade McNown	2.00
21	Germane Crowell	1.00
22	Bruce Matthews	.50
23	Champ Bailey	1.00
24	Qadry Ismail	.50
25	Tony Brackens	.50

2000 Finest Moments Refractor Autographs

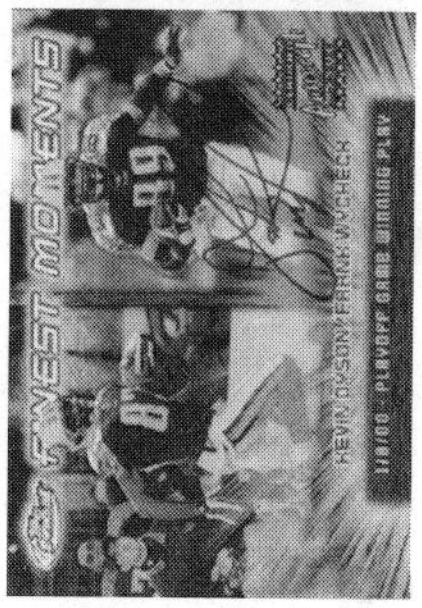

		MT
	Common Player:	15.00
	Minor Stars:	30.00
	Inserted 1:48	
1	Bart Starr	150.00
2	Phil Simms	30.00
3	John Elway	175.00
4	Dan Marino	175.00
5	Kellen Winslow	30.00
6	Franco Harris	50.00
7	Stephen Davis	30.00
8	Isaac Bruce	30.00
9	Edgerrin James	100.00
10	Marshall Faulk	30.00
11	Patrick Jeffers	30.00
12	Kurt Warner	125.00
13	Joe Montana	300.00
14	Kevin Carter	15.00
15	Andre Reed	15.00
16	Torry Holt	30.00
17	Frank Wycheck, Kevin Dyson	30.00
18	Jason Elam	15.00
19	Mike Jones	15.00
20	Cade McNown	50.00
21	Germane Crowell	30.00
22	Bruce Matthews	15.00
23	Champ Bailey	30.00
24	Qadry Ismail	15.00
25	Tony Brackens	15.00

2000 Finest Moments Jumbos

		MT
	Complete Set (7):	30.00
	Common Player:	2.00
	Inserted 1:Box	
1	Bart Starr	6.00
2	Phil Simms	2.00
3	John Elway	8.00
4	Dan Marino	8.00
5	Edgerrin James	6.00
6	Marshall Faulk	2.00
7	Joe Montana	10.00

A player's name in *italic type* indicates a rookie card.

2000 Finest NFL Europe's Finest

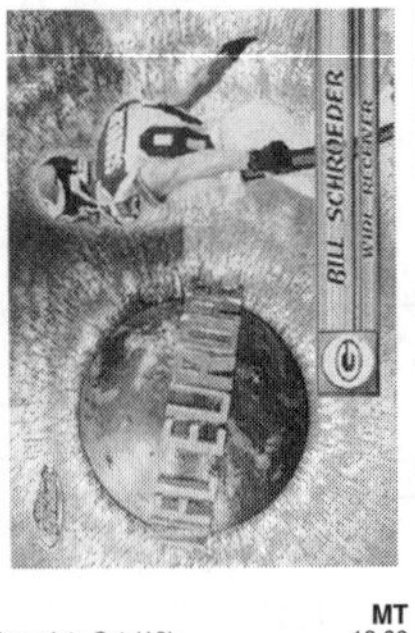

		MT
Complete Set (10):		12.00
Common Player:		1.00
Inserted 1:24		
1	Kurt Warner	7.00
2	Bill Schroeder	1.50
3	Andy McCullough	1.00
4	Dameyune Craig	1.00
5	Marcus Robinson	2.00
6	La'Roi Glover	1.00
7	Damon Huard	2.00
8	Brad Johnson	2.00
9	Jake Delhomme	1.50
10	Jon Kitna	1.50

2000 Finest Out of the Blue

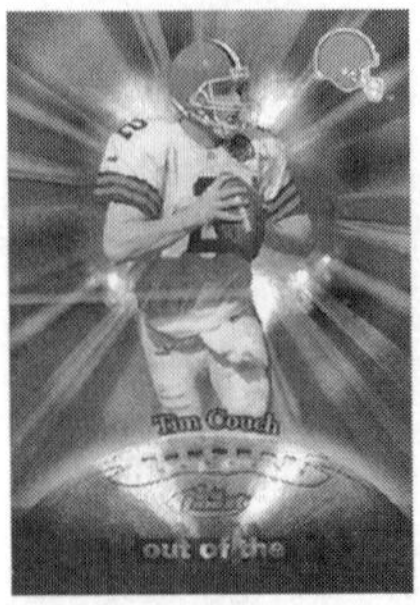

		MT
Complete Set (15):		25.00
Common Player:		.75
Minor Stars:		1.50
Inserted 1:24		
1	Kurt Warner	7.00
2	Patrick Jeffers	1.50
3	Stephen Davis	1.50
4	Amani Toomer	.75
5	Marcus Robinson	1.50
6	Tyrone Wheatley	.75
7	Kevin Johnson	1.50
8	Tony Gonzalez	.75
9	Olandis Gary	1.50
10	Brad Johnson	1.50
11	Germane Crowell	1.50
12	Ricky Williams	3.50
13	Edgerrin James	6.00
14	Tim Couch	3.50
15	Steve Beuerlein	.75

2000 Finest Pro Bowl Jerseys

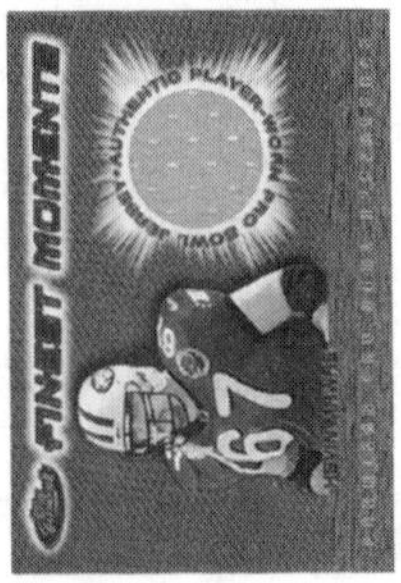

		MT
Common Player:		20.00
Minor Stars:		40.00
Inserted 1:77		
MB	Mitch Berger	20.00
SB	Steve Beuerlein	40.00
SB	Stephen Boyd	20.00
TB	Tony Brackens	20.00
KC	Kevin Carter	20.00
DC	Dexter Coakley	20.00
SD	Stephen Davis	40.00
BD	Brian Dawkins	20.00
CD	Corey Dillon	40.00
LE	Luther Ellis	20.00
RG	Rich Gannon	40.00
TG	Tony Gonzalez	40.00
KH	Kevin Hardy	20.00
MH	Marvin Harrison	50.00
EJ	Edgerrin James	100.00
BJ	Brad Johnson	40.00
TJ	Tre' Johnson	20.00
JK	Jevon Kearse	50.00
TL	Todd Lyght	20.00
TM	Tremain Mack	20.00
SM	Sam Madison	20.00
OM	Olindo Mare	20.00
KM	Kevin Mawae	20.00
MM	Muhsin Muhammad	40.00
OP	Orlando Pace	20.00
TP	Trevor Pryce	20.00
LS	Lance Schulters	20.00
LS	Leon Searcy	20.00
DS	David Sloan	20.00
DS	Detron Smith	20.00
ZT	Zach Thomas	20.00
TT	Tom Tupa	20.00
KW	Kurt Warner	125.00

2000 Finest Superstars

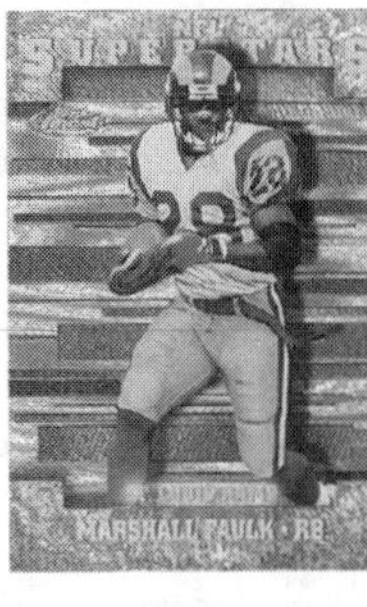

		MT
Complete Set (15):		25.00
Common Player:		1.00
Inserted 1:16		
1	Dan Marino	4.00
2	Eddie George	1.50
3	Marshall Faulk	1.00
4	Stephen Davis	1.00
5	Jerry Rice	2.50
6	Emmitt Smith	3.00
7	Terrell Davis	3.00
8	Jimmy Smith	1.00
9	Cris Carter	1.00
10	Troy Aikman	2.50
11	Curtis Martin	1.00
12	Brett Favre	5.00
13	Kurt Warner	6.00
14	Marvin Harrison	1.00
15	Steve Young	1.75

2001 Finest

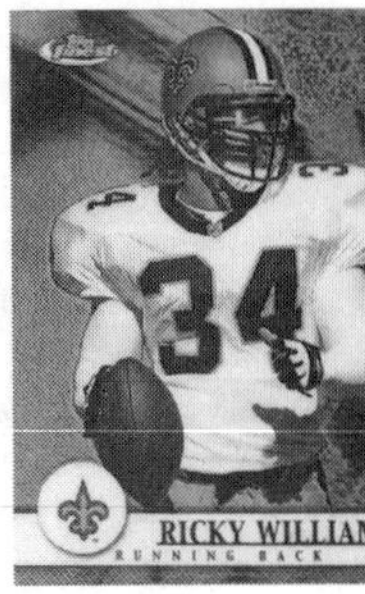

		MT
Complete Set (140):		400.00
Common Player:		.25
Minor Stars:		.50
Common Rookie:		5.00
Production 1,000 Sets		
Inserted 1:4		
Wax Box (10):		150.00
1	Eddie George	1.25
2	Jay Fiedler	1.00
3	Peter Warrick	1.25
4	Vinny Testaverde	.50
5	Charles Johnson	.25
6	Ahman Green	.75
7	Isaac Bruce	1.00
8	Junior Seau	.50
9	Daunte Culpepper	2.00
10	Ike Hilliard	.50
11	Tony Banks	.50
12	Steve Beuerlein	.50
13	Jamal Anderson	1.00
14	Tyrone Wheatley	.50
15	Sylvester Morris	.75
16	Edgerrin James	2.50
17	Shaun King	1.00
18	Terrell Owens	1.00
19	Donovan McNabb	1.50
20	Cade McNown	1.00
21	Elvis Grbac	.75
22	James Stewart	.75
23	Joe Horn	.75
24	Randy Moss	3.00
25	Matt Hasselbeck	.75
26	Jerome Bettis	1.00
27	Bill Schroeder	.50
28	Jake Plummer	1.00
29	Rod Smith	1.00
30	Akili Smith	1.00
31	Jimmy Smith	.75
32	Oronde Gadsden	.50
33	Kerry Collins	.75
34	Warrick Dunn	1.00
35	Jeff Graham	.25
36	Ray Lewis	.75
37	Joey Galloway	1.00
38	Tim Brown	1.00
39	Derrick Alexander	.25
40	Jerry Rice	2.50
41	Muhsin Muhammad	1.00
42	Shawn Jefferson	.50
43	Curtis Martin	1.00
44	Terry Glenn	.75
45	Marvin Harrison	1.00
46	Mike Anderson	2.50
47	Stephen Davis	1.00
48	Chad Lewis	.75
49	Fred Taylor	1.25
50	Corey Dillon	1.00
51	Charlie Batch	1.00
52	Kevin Johnson	.75
53	Brett Favre	4.00
54	Marshall Faulk	1.25
55	Kordell Stewart	1.00
56	Steve McNair	1.00
57	Jeff Blake	.50
58	Eric Moulds	1.00
59	Emmitt Smith	2.50
60	David Boston	1.00
61	Cris Carter	1.00
62	Peyton Manning	3.00
63	Keyshawn Johnson	1.00
64	Doug Flutie	1.25
65	Drew Bledsoe	1.25
66	Ricky Williams	1.50
67	Keenan McCardell	.50
68	Brian Urlacher	2.00
69	Jamal Lewis	2.50
70	Ed McCaffrey	1.00
71	Antonio Freeman	1.00
72	Darrell Jackson	.75
73	Jeff George	.75
74	Chris Chandler	.50
75	Germane Crowell	.75
76	Tim Biakabutuka	.75
77	Jon Kitna	.75
78	Troy Brown	.50
79	Lamar Smith	1.00
80	Derrick Mason	.75
81	Hines Ward	.50
82	Mark Brunell	1.25
83	Trent Dilfer	.75
84	Tim Couch	1.25
85	Donald Hayes	.50
86	Amani Toomer	.50
87	Tony Gonzalez	.75
88	Rich Gannon	.75
89	Rob Johnson	.50
90	Torry Holt	1.00
91	Jeff Garcia	1.00
92	Kurt Warner	3.00
93	Aaron Brooks	1.00
94	Brian Griese	1.25
95	James Allen	.75
96	Wayne Chrebet	1.00
97	Tiki Barber	1.00
98	Brad Johnson	.75
99	Ricky Watters	.75
100	Charlie Garner	.75
101	*Andre Carter*	7.00
102	*Dan Morgan*	7.00
103	*Gerard Warren*	8.00
104	*Jesse Palmer*	8.00
105	*Josh Heupel*	12.00
106	*Justin Smith*	7.00
107	*LaMont Jordan*	10.00
108	*Leonard Davis*	5.00
109	*Marques Tuiasosopo*	15.00
110	*Marvin "Snoop" Minnis*	12.00
111	*Quincy Carter*	20.00
112	*Quincy Morgan*	15.00
113	*Richard Seymour*	5.00
114	*Rudi Johnson*	8.00
115	*Sage Rosenfels*	10.00
116	*Todd Heap*	8.00
117	*Travis Minor*	8.00
118	*Will Allen*	5.00
119	*Jamal Reynolds*	7.00
120	*Scotty Anderson*	5.00
121	*Anthony Thomas*	40.00
122	*Chad Johnson*	10.00
123	*Chris Chambers*	20.00
124	*Chris Weinke*	20.00
125	*David Terrell*	25.00
126	*Deuce McAllister*	20.00
127	*Drew Brees*	30.00
128	*Freddie Mitchell*	15.00
129	*James Jackson*	12.00
130	*Kevan Barlow*	12.00
131	*Koren Robinson*	18.00
132	*LaDainian Tomlinson*	30.00
133	*Michael Bennett*	20.00
134	*Michael Vick*	40.00
135	*Mike McMahon*	10.00
136	*Reggie Wayne*	15.00
137	*Robert Ferguson*	8.00
138	*Rod Gardner*	15.00
139	*Santana Moss*	15.00
140	*Travis Henry*	15.00

2001 Finest Refractor Autographs

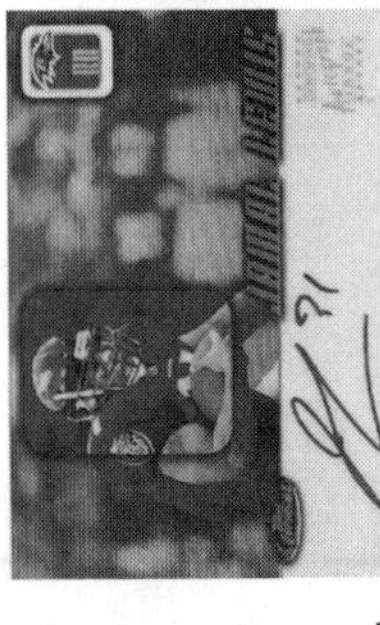

		MT
Common Player:		8.00
Inserted 1:5		
FA-DA	Dan Alexander	8.00
FA-MB	Michael Bennett	45.00
FA-AB	Aaron Brooks	20.00
FA-DC	Daunte Culpepper	45.00
FA-JG	Jeff Garcia	20.00
FA-EG	Eddie George	30.00
FA-DH	Donald Hayes	8.00
FA-TH	Travis Henry	15.00
FA-JH	Joe Horn	8.00
FA-JJ	James Jackson	15.00
FA-EJ	Edgerrin James	60.00
FA-JL	Jamal Lewis	25.00
FA-TM	Travis Minor	12.00
FA-SCM	Sammy Morris	8.00
FA-SM	Sylvester Morris	15.00
FA-SMO	Santana Moss	20.00
FA-EM	Eric Moulds	12.00
FA-BN	Bobby Newcombe	8.00
FA-MR	Marcus Robinson	10.00
FA-BS	Bill Schroeder	15.00
FA-ES	Emmitt Smith	100.00
FA-JS	Jimmy Smith	10.00
FA-LS	Lamar Smith	12.00
FA-CW	Chris Weinke	40.00

2001 Finest Jersey Relics

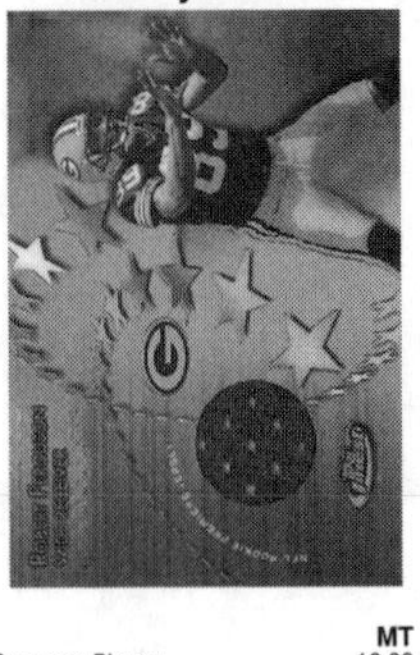

		MT
Common Player:		10.00
Inserted 1:5		
RPJ-KB	Kevan Barlow	12.00
RPJ-AC	Andre Carter	10.00
RPJ-LD	Leonard Davis	10.00
RPJ-RF	Robert Ferguson	10.00
RPJ-RG	Rod Gardner	12.00
RPJ-TH	Todd Heap	10.00
RPJ-CJ	Chad Johnson	10.00
RPJ-RJ	Rudi Johnson	12.00
RPJ-MM	Mike McMahon	10.00
RPJ-MMI	Marvin "Snoop" Minnis	12.00
RPJ-TM	Travis Minor	10.00
RPJ-SM	Santana Moss	15.00
RPJ-JP	Jesse Palmer	10.00
RPJ-KR	Koren Robinson	12.00
RPJ-SR	Sage Rosenfels	10.00
RPJ-JS	Justin Smith	10.00
RPJ-AT	Anthony Thomas	35.00
RPJ-MT	Marques Tuiasosopo	12.00
RPJ-RW	Reggie Wayne	12.00
RPJ-CW	Chris Weinke	20.00

2001 Finest Moments Relics

		MT
Complete Set (10):		120.00
Common Player:		10.00
Inserted 1:176		
FMR-DA	Dan Alexander	10.00
FMR-KB	Kevan Barlow	15.00
FMR-DC	Daunte Culpepper	20.00
FMR-RG	Rich Gannon	15.00
FMR-RGA	Rod Gardner	15.00
FMR-EJ	Edgerrin James	30.00
FMR-CJ	Chad Johnson	10.00
FMR-LJ	LaMont Jordan	12.00
FMR-LT	LaDainian Tomlinson	50.00
FMR-RW	Reggie Wayne	15.00

2001 Finest Moments Refractor Autographs

		MT
Common Player:		15.00
Inserted 1:160		
FMA-DC	Daunte Culpepper	45.00
FMA-JG	Jeff Garcia	25.00
FMA-EM	Eric Moulds	15.00
FMA-MV	Michael Vick	85.00
FMA-CW	Chris Weinke	45.00

2001 Finest Stadium Throwback Relics

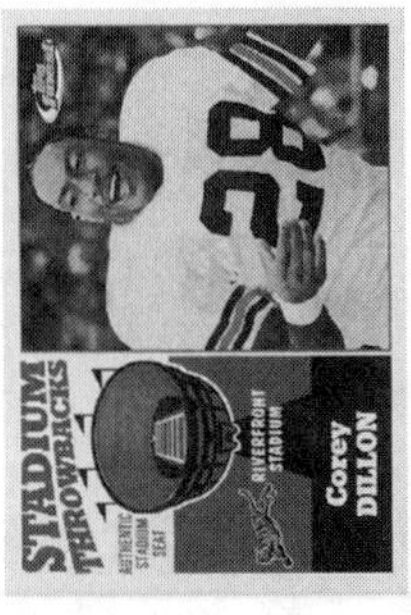

		MT
Complete Set (20):		185.00
Common Player:		10.00
Inserted 1:10		
FS DB	Drew Brees	25.00
FS CC	Cris Carter	12.00
FS TC	Tim Couch	15.00
FS DC	Daunte Culpepper	15.00
FS CD	Corey Dillon	12.00
FS MF	Marshall Faulk	15.00
FS BF	Brett Favre	25.00
FS RG	Rod Gardner	10.00
FS TG	Tony Gonzalez	10.00
FS MH	Marvin Harrison	12.00
FS EJ	Edgerrin James	25.00
FS PM	Peyton Manning	25.00
FS DM	Donovan McNabb	15.00
FS MM	Marvin "Snoop" Minnis	10.00
FS RM	Randy Moss	25.00
FS KR	Koren Robinson	10.00
FS LT	LaDainian Tomlinson	30.00
FS KW	Kurt Warner	30.00

2001 Finest Team Topps Legends

		MT
Complete Set (8):		
Common Player:		
TTR10	Chuck Foreman	8.00
TTF16	Cliff Branch	8.00
TTR15	Mike Singletary	10.00
TTR22	Barry Sanders	20.00
TTR18	Fred Biletnikoff	8.00
TTF14	Charlie Joiner	8.00
TTF4	Tommy McDonald	8.00
TTR5	John Hannah	8.00

1995 Flair

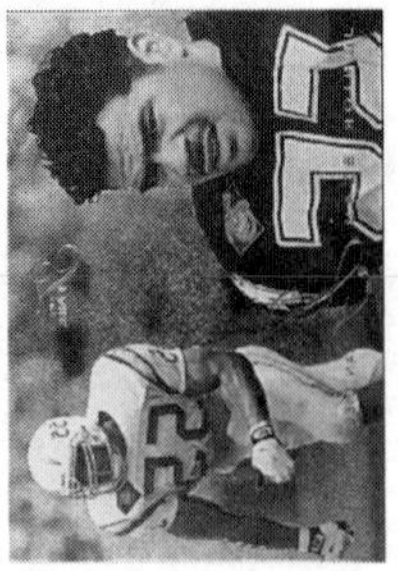

Each of the regular 220 cards in this set features a player on a horizontal card with a foil-etched background. Two photos appear on each front - one is a mug shot of the player without his helmet on, the other is an action photo. The Flair logo is stamped in gold at the top of the card; the player's name and team are stamped at the bottom. The player's initials are scripted in silver foil at the bottom. The card back has a full-bleed action photo, with the player's name and team helmet stamped in the center in gold foil. The player's statistics are also listed. Insert sets include Hot Numbers, TD Power and Wave of the Future.

		MT
Complete Set (220):		40.00
Common Player:		.20
Minor Stars:		.40
Pack (11):		1.50
Pack (9):		2.50
Wax Box (36):		75.00
1	Larry Centers	.20
2	Garrison Hearst	.50
3	Seth Joyner	.20
4	Dave Krieg	.20
5	Rob Moore	.20
6	*Frank Sanders*	2.00
7	Eric Swann	.20
8	Devin Bush	.20
9	Chris Coleman	.20
10	Bert Emanuel	.50
11	Jeff George	.50
12	Craig Heyward	.20
13	Terance Mathis	.20
14	Eric Metcalf	.20
15	Cornelius Bennett	.20
16	Jeff Burris	.20
17	*Todd Collins*	.50
18	Russell Copeland	.20
19	Jim Kelly	.75
20	Andre Reed	.40
21	Bruce Smith	.40
22	Don Beebe	.20
23	Mark Carrier	.20
24	*Kerry Collins*	2.50
25	Barry Foster	.20
26	Pete Metzelaars	.20
27	Tyrone Poole	.20
28	Frank Reich	.20
29	Curtis Conway	.40
30	Chris Gedney	.20
31	Jeff Graham	.20
32	Raymont Harris	.20
33	Erik Kramer	.20
34	*Rashaan Salaam*	.50
35	Lewis Tillman	.20
36	Michael Timpson	.20
37	*Jeff Blake*	2.00
38	*Ki-Jana Carter*	.75
39	Tony McGee	.20
40	Carl Pickens	.40
41	Corey Sawyer	.20
42	Darnay Scott	.40
43	Dan Wilkinson	.20
44	Derrick Alexander	.40
45	Leroy Hoard	.20
46	Michael Jackson	.20
47	Antonio Langham	.20
48	Andre Rison	.40
49	Vinny Testaverde	.75
50	Eric Turner	.20
51	Troy Aikman	2.00
52	Charles Haley	.20
53	Michael Irvin	.40
54	Daryl Johnston	.20
55	Leon Lett	.20
56	Jay Novacek	.20
57	Emmitt Smith	4.00
58	Kevin Williams	.20
59	Steve Atwater	.20
60	Rod Bernstine	.20
61	John Elway	3.00
62	Glyn Milburn	.20
63	Anthony Miller	.20
64	Mike Pritchard	.20
65	Shannon Sharpe	.40
66	Scott Mitchell	.40
67	Herman Moore	.75
68	Johnnie Morton	.20
69	Brett Perriman	.20
70	Barry Sanders	4.00
71	Chris Spielman	.20
72	Edgar Bennett	.20
73	Robert Brooks	.40
74	Brett Favre	4.00
75	LeShon Johnson	.20
76	Sean Jones	.20
77	George Teague	.20
78	Reggie White	.50
79	Micheal Barrow	.20
80	Gary Brown	.20
81	Mel Gray	.20
82	Haywood Jeffires	.20
83	*Steve McNair*	5.00
84	*Rodney Thomas*	.40
85	Trev Alberts	.20
86	Flipper Anderson	.20
87	Tony Bennett	.20
88	Quentin Coryatt	.20
89	Sean Dawkins	.20
90	Craig Erickson	.20
91	Marshall Faulk	.75
92	Steve Beuerlein	.40
93	*Tony Boselli*	.75
94	Reggie Cobb	.20
95	Ernest Givens	.20
96	Desmond Howard	.20
97	Jeff Lageman	.20
98	*James Stewart*	3.00
99	Marcus Allen	.50
100	Steve Bono	.40
101	Dale Carter	.20
102	Willie Davis	.20
103	Lake Dawson	.40
104	Greg Hill	.40
105	Neil Smith	.20
106	Tim Bowens	.20
107	Bryan Cox	.20
108	Irving Fryar	.20
109	Eric Green	.20
110	Terry Kirby	.20
111	Dan Marino	3.00
112	O.J. McDuffie	.40
113	Bernie Parmalee	.20
114	Derrick Alexander	.20
115	Cris Carter	.75
116	Qadry Ismail	.40
117	Warren Moon	.40
118	Jake Reed	.20
119	Robert Smith	.75
120	DeWayne Washington	.20
121	Drew Bledsoe	2.00
122	Vincent Brisby	.20
123	Ben Coates	.40
124	*Curtis Martin*	5.00
125	Willie McGinest	.20
126	Dave Meggett	.20
127	Chris Slade	.20
128	Eric Allen	.20
129	Mario Bates	.40
130	Jim Everett	.40
131	Michael Haynes	.20
132	Tyrone Hughes	.20
133	Renaldo Turnbull	.20
134	*Ray Zellars*	.40
135	Michael Brooks	.20
136	Dave Brown	.20
137	Rodney Hampton	.20
138	Thomas Lewis	.20
139	Mike Sherrard	.20
140	Herschel Walker	.40
141	*Tyrone Wheatley*	2.50
142	*Kyle Brady*	.75
143	Boomer Esiason	.40
144	Aaron Glenn	.20
145	Mo Lewis	.20
146	Johnny Mitchell	.20
147	Ronald Moore	.20
148	*Joe Aska*	.40
149	Tim Brown	.75
150	Jeff Hostetler	.20
151	Raghib Ismail	.20
152	*Napoleon Kaufman*	2.50
153	Chester McGlockton	.20
154	Harvey Williams	.20
155	Fred Barnett	.20
156	Randall Cunningham	.75
157	Charlie Garner	.20
158	*Mike Mamula*	.40
159	Kevin Turner	.20
160	Ricky Watters	.75
161	Calvin Williams	.20
162	*Mark Bruener*	.75
163	Kevin Greene	.20
164	Charles Johnson	.50
165	Greg Lloyd	.20
166	Bam Morris	.40
167	Neil O'Donnell	.40
168	*Kordell Stewart*	3.50
169	John L. Williams	.20
170	Rod Woodson	.20
171	Jerome Bettis	.75
172	Isaac Bruce	1.50
173	*Kevin Carter*	.50
174	Troy Drayton	.20
175	Sean Gilbert	.20
176	Carlos Jenkins	.20
177	Todd Lyght	.20
178	Chris Miller	.20
179	Andre Coleman	.20
180	Stan Humphries	.40
181	Shawn Jefferson	.20
182	Natrone Means	.40
183	Leslie O'Neal	.20
184	Junior Seau	.40
185	Mark Seay	.20
186	William Floyd	.40
187	Merton Hanks	.20
188	Brent Jones	.20
189	Ken Norton	.20
190	Jerry Rice	2.00
191	Deion Sanders	1.00
192	*J.J. Stokes*	1.00
193	Dana Stubblefield	.20
194	Steve Young	1.50
195	Sam Adams	.20
196	Brian Blades	.20
197	*Joey Galloway*	3.00
198	Cortez Kennedy	.20
199	Rick Mirer	.40
200	Chris Warren	.40
201	Derrick Brooks	.20
202	Lawrence Dawsey	.20
203	Trent Dilfer	.40
204	Alvin Harper	.20
205	Jackie Harris	.20
206	Courtney Hawkins	.20
207	Hardy Nickerson	.20
208	Errict Rhett	.50
209	*Warren Sapp*	1.50
210	Terry Allen	.40
211	Tom Carter	.20
212	Henry Ellard	.20
213	Darrell Green	.20
214	Brian Mitchell	.20

215	Heath Shuler	.40
216	*Michael Westbrook*	2.00
217	Tydus Winans	.20
218	Checklist	.20
219	Checklist	.20
220	Checklist	.20

1995 Flair Hot Numbers

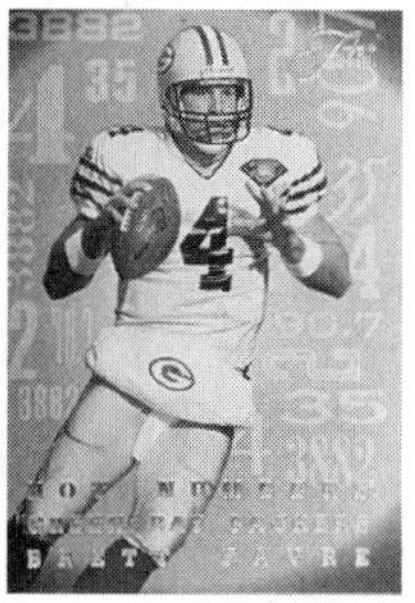

These 1995 Fleer Flair inserts feature 10 top statistical leaders for the 1994-95 season. Cards, numbered 1 of 10, etc., were were randomly included one per every six packs. The card front has gold foil stamping for the player's name, position and Flair and insert set logos. The key numbers from the player's season statistics are in the background of the card. The horizontal back has another photo of the player, with a box next to it containing a brief summary of his accomplishments. Gold foil stamping is used for his name, team name and "Hot Numbers," which are at the top of the box.

		MT
Complete Set (10):		40.00
Common Player:		1.00
1	Jeff Blake	2.00
2	Drew Bledsoe	7.00
3	Tim Brown	1.00
4	Ben Coates	1.00
5	Trent Dilfer	2.00
6	Brett Favre	14.00
7	Dan Marino	14.00
8	Bam Morris	1.00
9	Ricky Watters	2.00
10	Steve Young	5.00

1995 Flair TD Power

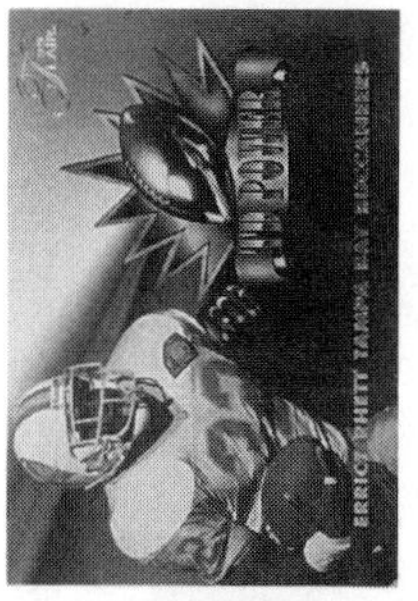

These horizontally-designed insert cards could be found one per every 12 packs of 1995 Fleer Flair. The cards feature 10 of the top touchdown scorers from the previous season. The TD Power logo appears on the front, along with a player action photo and the Flair logo, which is stamped in gold. The player's name and team name are stamped in gold and are at the bottom of the card. The card back has another photo on one side, with a box containing a brief player profile. The insert set logo is included inside the box, at the top. Cards are numbered 1 of 10, etc.

		MT
Complete Set (10):		40.00
Common Player:		2.00
1	Marshall Faulk	5.00
2	William Floyd	2.00
3	Natrone Means	3.00
4	Bam Morris	2.00
5	Errict Rhett	4.00
6	Jerry Rice	7.00
7	Andre Rison	2.00
8	Barry Sanders	7.00
9	Emmitt Smith	14.00
10	Chris Warren	2.00

1995 Flair Wave of the Future

These 1995 Fleer Flair insert cards, randomly included one per every 37 packs, feature nine top rookies. The cards, which use gold foil stamping on the front, offer a unique die-cut that is actually cut around the player's face. The back, numbered 1 of 9, etc., also uses gold foil stamping and includes another action photo. A brief summary of the player's collegiate accomplishments, plus his potential as a pro, is also given.

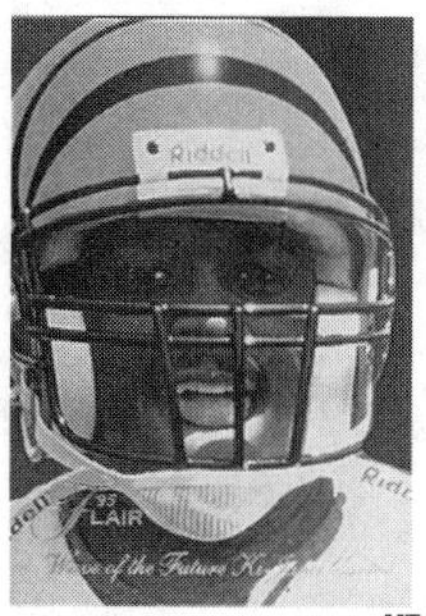

		MT
Complete Set (9):		175.00
Common Player:		10.00
1	Kyle Brady	10.00
2	Ki-Jana Carter	20.00
3	Kerry Collins	50.00
4	Joey Galloway	30.00
5	Steve McNair	40.00
6	Rashaan Salaam	20.00
7	James Stewart	10.00
8	Michael Westbrook	15.00
9	Tyrone Wheatley	10.00

1997 Flair Showcase

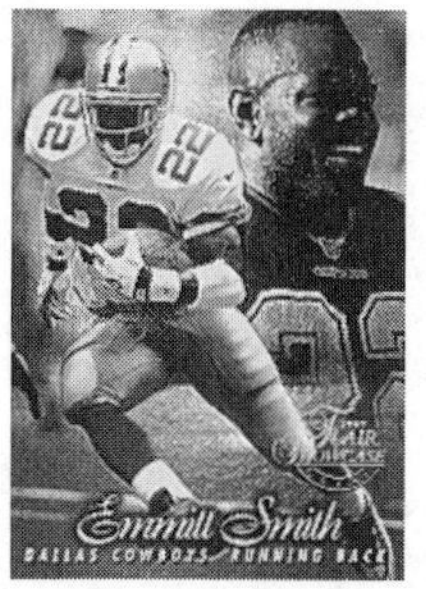

Flair Showcase NFL is a 360-card set featuring 120 players. Each player has three base cards: Style, Grace and Showcase. The fronts feature distinct action and headshots with a holographic foil background on 24 pt card stock. The backs have another photo and complete career statistics. The basic card types have a tiered insertion ratio. Two parallel sets were issued: Legacy, with less than 100 cards per player, and the one-of-a-kind Legacy Masterpiece. Four insert sets were included: Wave of the Future, Hot Hands, Midas Touch and Then & Now.

		MT
Complete Set (360):		1700.
Comp. Style Set (120):		75.00
Common Style (A1-A120):		.25
Comp. Grace Set (120):		150.00
Common Grace (B1-B120):		.50
Comp. Showcase Set (120):		1500.
Common Showcase (C1-C120):		2.00
Pack (5):		7.00
Wax Box (24):		145.00
A1	Jerry Rice STY	4.00
A2	Mark Brunell STY	4.00
A3	Eddie Kennison STY	.50
A4	Brett Favre STY	8.00
A5	Karim Abdul-Jabbar STY	.75
A6	*David LaFleur STY*	1.50
A7	John Elway STY	3.00
A8	Troy Aikman STY	4.00
A9	Steve McNair STY	3.00
A10	Kordell Stewart STY	4.00
A11	Drew Bledsoe STY	4.00
A12	Kerry Collins STY	.50
A13	Dan Marino STY	6.00
A14	Steve Young STY	3.00
A15	Marvin Harrison STY	1.00
A16	Lawrence Phillips STY	.50
A17	Jeff Blake STY	.50
A18	*Yatil Green STY*	1.50
A19	*Jake Plummer STY*	8.00
A20	Barry Sanders STY	4.00
A21	Deion Sanders STY	2.50
A22	Emmitt Smith STY	6.00
A23	*Rae Carruth STY*	2.00
A24	Chris Warren STY	.25
A25	Terry Glenn STY	1.00
A26	*Jim Druckenmiller STY*	4.00
A27	Eddie George STY	5.00
A28	Curtis Martin STY	4.00
A29	*Warrick Dunn STY*	4.00
A30	Terrell Davis STY	4.00
A31	Rashaan Salaam STY	.25
A32	Marcus Allen STY	.50
A33	Jeff George STY	.50
A34	Thurman Thomas STY	.50
A35	Keyshawn Johnson STY	1.00
A36	Jerome Bettis STY	.50
A37	Larry Centers STY	.25
A38	Tony Banks STY	1.00
A39	Marshall Faulk STY	.50
A40	Mike Alstott STY	.50
A41	Elvis Grbac STY	.25
A42	Errict Rhett STY	.50
A43	Edgar Bennett STY	.25
A44	Jim Harbaugh STY	.25
A45	Antonio Freeman STY	1.00
A46	*Tiki Barber STY*	3.00
A47	Tim Biakabutuka STY	.25
A48	Joey Galloway STY	.50
A49	*Tony Gonzalez STY*	1.50
A50	Keenan McCardell STY	.25
A51	Darnay Scott STY	.25
A52	Brad Johnson STY	.25
A53	Herman Moore STY	.50
A54	*Reidel Anthony STY*	3.00
A55	Junior Seau STY	.50
A56	Ricky Watters STY	.50
A57	Amani Toomer STY	.25
A58	Andre Reed STY	.25
A59	*Antowain Smith STY*	5.00
A60	*Ike Hilliard STY*	2.50
A61	*Byron Hanspard STY*	1.50
A62	Robert Smith STY	.25
A63	Gus Frerotte STY	.25
A64	Charles Way STY	.25
A65	Trent Dilfer STY	.50
A66	Adrian Murrell STY	.50
A67	Stan Humphries STY	.25
A68	Robert Brooks STY	.25
A69	Jamal Anderson STY	.50
A70	Natrone Means STY	.50
A71	John Friesz STY	.25
A72	Ki-Jana Carter STY	.25
A73	Marc Edwards STY	.25
A74	Michael Westbrook STY	.25
A75	Neil O'Donnell STY	.25
A76	Scott Mitchell STY	.25
A77	Wesley Walls STY	.25
A78	Bruce Smith STY	.25
A79	*Corey Dillon STY*	7.00
A80	Wayne Chrebet STY	.25
A81	Tony Martin STY	.25
A82	Jimmy Smith STY	.25
A83	Terry Allen STY	.25
A84	Shannon Sharpe STY	.25
A85	Derrick Alexander STY	.25
A86	Garrison Hearst STY	.25
A87	Tamarick Vanover STY	.25
A88	Michael Irvin STY	.50
A89	Mark Chmura STY	.50
A90	Bert Emanuel STY	.25
A91	Eric Metcalf STY	.25
A92	Reggie White STY	.50
A93	Carl Pickens STY	.25
A94	Chris Sanders STY	.25
A95	Frank Sanders STY	.25
A96	Desmond Howard STY	.25
A97	Michael Jackson STY	.25
A98	Tim Brown STY	.50
A99	O.J. McDuffie STY	.25
A100	Mario Bates STY	.25
A101	Warren Moon STY	.25
A102	Curtis Conway STY	.25
A103	Irving Fryar STY	.25
A104	Isaac Bruce STY	.50
A105	Cris Carter STY	.50
A106	Chris Chandler STY	.25
A107	Charles Johnson STY	.25
A108	Kevin Lockett STY	.25
A109	Rob Moore STY	.25
A110	Napoleon Kaufman STY	.75
A111	Henry Ellard STY	.25
A112	Vinny Testaverde STY	.25
A113	Rick Mirer STY	.25
A114	Ty Detmer STY	.25
A115	Todd Collins STY	.25
A116	Jake Reed STY	.25
A117	Dave Brown STY	.25
A118	*Dedric Ward STY*	1.50
A119	Heath Shuler STY	.25
A120	Ben Coates STY	.25
B1	Jerry Rice GRA	6.00
B2	Mark Brunell GRA	6.00
B3	Eddie Kennison GRA	1.00
B4	Brett Favre GRA	12.00
B5	Karim Abdul-Jabbar GRA	1.50
B6	David LaFleur GRA	2.00
B7	John Elway GRA	4.50
B8	Troy Aikman GRA	6.00
B9	Steve McNair GRA	4.50
B10	Kordell Stewart GRA	6.00
B11	Drew Bledsoe GRA	6.00
B12	Kerry Collins GRA	1.50
B13	Dan Marino GRA	9.00
B14	Steve Young GRA	4.50
B15	Marvin Harrison GRA	2.00
B16	Lawrence Phillips GRA	.75
B17	Jeff Blake GRA	.75
B18	Yatil Green GRA	2.50
B19	Jake Plummer GRA	10.00
B20	Barry Sanders GRA	6.00
B21	Deion Sanders GRA	4.00
B22	Emmitt Smith GRA	9.00
B23	Rae Carruth GRA	3.00
B24	Chris Warren GRA	.50
B25	Terry Glenn GRA	2.50
B26	Jim Druckenmiller GRA	6.00
B27	Eddie George GRA	7.50
B28	Curtis Martin GRA	6.00
B29	Warrick Dunn GRA	5.00
B30	Terrell Davis GRA	6.00
B31	Rashaan Salaam GRA	.50
B32	Marcus Allen GRA	.75
B33	Jeff George GRA	.75
B34	Thurman Thomas GRA	.75
B35	Keyshawn Johnson GRA	2.00
B36	Jerome Bettis GRA	.75
B37	Larry Centers GRA	.50
B38	Tony Banks GRA	2.00
B39	Marshall Faulk GRA	.75
B40	Mike Alstott GRA	.75
B41	Elvis Grbac GRA	.50
B42	Errict Rhett GRA	.75
B43	Edgar Bennett GRA	.50
B44	Jim Harbaugh GRA	.50
B45	Antonio Freeman GRA	1.50
B46	Tiki Barber GRA	4.50
B47	Tim Biakabutuka GRA	.50
B48	Joey Galloway GRA	.75
B49	Tony Gonzalez GRA	2.00
B50	Keenan McCardell GRA	.50
B51	Darnay Scott GRA	.50
B52	Brad Johnson GRA	.50
B53	Herman Moore GRA	.75
B54	Reidel Anthony GRA	4.50
B55	Junior Seau GRA	.75
B56	Ricky Watters GRA	.75
B57	Amani Toomer GRA	.50
B58	Andre Reed GRA	.50
B59	Antowain Smith GRA	8.00
B60	Ike Hilliard GRA	4.00
B61	Byron Hanspard GRA	1.50
B62	Robert Smith GRA	.50
B63	Gus Frerotte GRA	.50
B64	Charles Way GRA	.50
B65	Trent Dilfer GRA	.75
B66	Adrian Murrell GRA	.75
B67	Stan Humphries GRA	.50
B68	Robert Brooks GRA	.50
B69	Jamal Anderson GRA	.75
B70	Natrone Means GRA	.75
B71	John Friesz GRA	.50
B72	Ki-Jana Carter GRA	.50
B73	Marc Edwards GRA	.50
B74	Michael Westbrook GRA	.50
B75	Neil O'Donnell GRA	.50
B76	Scott Mitchell GRA	.50
B77	Wesley Walls GRA	.50
B78	Bruce Smith GRA	.50
B79	Corey Dillon GRA	8.00
B80	Wayne Chrebet GRA	.50
B81	Tony Martin GRA	.50
B82	Jimmy Smith GRA	.50
B83	Terry Allen GRA	.50
B84	Shannon Sharpe GRA	.50
B85	Derrick Alexander GRA	.50
B86	Garrison Hearst GRA	.50
B87	Tamarick Vanover GRA	.50
B88	Michael Irvin GRA	.75
B89	Mark Chmura GRA	.75
B90	Bert Emanuel GRA	.50
B91	Eric Metcalf GRA	.50
B92	Reggie White GRA	.75
B93	Carl Pickens GRA	.50
B94	Chris Sanders GRA	.50
B95	Frank Sanders GRA	.50
B96	Desmond Howard GRA	.50
B97	Michael Jackson GRA	.50
B98	Tim Brown GRA	.75
B99	O.J. McDuffie GRA	.50
B100	Mario Bates GRA	.50
B101	Warren Moon GRA	.50
B102	Curtis Conway GRA	.50
B103	Irving Fryar GRA	.50
B104	Isaac Bruce GRA	.75
B105	Cris Carter GRA	.75
B106	Chris Chandler GRA	.50
B107	Charles Johnson GRA	.50
B108	Kevin Lockett GRA	.50
B109	Rob Moore GRA	.50
B110	Napoleon Kaufman GRA	1.00
B111	Henry Ellard GRA	.50
B112	Vinny Testaverde GRA	.50
B113	Rick Mirer GRA	.50
B114	Ty Detmer GRA	.50
B115	Todd Collins GRA	.50
B116	Jake Reed GRA	.50
B117	Dave Brown GRA	.50
B118	Dedric Ward GRA	.50
B119	Heath Shuler GRA	.50
B120	Ben Coates GRA	.50
C1	Jerry Rice SHOW	60.00
C2	Mark Brunell SHOW	60.00
C3	Eddie Kennison SHOW	6.00
C4	Brett Favre SHOW	125.00
C5	Karim Abdul-Jabbar SHOW	6.00
C6	David LaFleur SHOW	15.00
C7	John Elway SHOW	50.00
C8	Troy Aikman SHOW	60.00
C9	Steve McNair SHOW	50.00
C10	Kordell Stewart SHOW	60.00
C11	Drew Bledsoe SHOW	60.00
C12	Kerry Collins SHOW	6.00
C13	Dan Marino SHOW	100.00
C14	Steve Young SHOW	50.00
C15	Marvin Harrison SHOW	8.00
C16	Lawrence Phillips SHOW	6.00
C17	Jeff Blake SHOW	4.00
C18	Yatil Green SHOW	6.00
C19	Jake Plummer SHOW	75.00
C20	Barry Sanders SHOW	70.00
C21	Deion Sanders SHOW	40.00
C22	Emmitt Smith SHOW	100.00
C23	Rae Carruth SHOW	25.00
C24	Chris Warren SHOW	2.00
C25	Terry Glenn SHOW	8.00
C26	Jim Druckenmiller SHOW	60.00
C27	Eddie George SHOW	75.00
C28	Curtis Martin SHOW	60.00
C29	Warrick Dunn SHOW	50.00
C30	Terrell Davis SHOW	60.00
C31	Rashaan Salaam SHOW	2.00
C32	Marcus Allen SHOW	6.00
C33	Jeff George SHOW	6.00
C34	Thurman Thomas SHOW	6.00
C35	Keyshawn Johnson SHOW	8.00
C36	Jerome Bettis SHOW	6.00
C37	Larry Centers SHOW	2.00
C38	Tony Banks SHOW	6.00
C39	Marshall Faulk SHOW	6.00
C40	Mike Alstott SHOW	7.50
C41	Elvis Grbac SHOW	2.00
C42	Errict Rhett SHOW	4.00
C43	Edgar Bennett SHOW	2.00
C44	Jim Harbaugh SHOW	2.00
C45	Antonio Freeman SHOW	8.00
C46	Tiki Barber SHOW	25.00
C47	Tim Biakabutuka SHOW	2.00
C48	Joey Galloway SHOW	7.50
C49	Tony Gonzalez SHOW	15.00
C50	Keenan McCardell SHOW	2.00
C51	Darnay Scott SHOW	2.00
C52	Brad Johnson SHOW	2.00
C53	Herman Moore SHOW	7.50
C54	Reidel Anthony SHOW	25.00
C55	Junior Seau SHOW	4.00
C56	Ricky Watters SHOW	4.00
C57	Amani Toomer SHOW	2.00
C58	Andre Reed SHOW	2.00
C59	Antowain Smith SHOW	25.00
C60	Ike Hilliard SHOW	25.00
C61	Byron Hanspard SHOW	6.00
C62	Robert Smith SHOW	2.00
C63	Gus Frerotte SHOW	2.00
C64	Charles Way SHOW	2.00
C65	Trent Dilfer SHOW	6.00
C66	Adrian Murrell SHOW	4.00
C67	Stan Humphries SHOW	2.00
C68	Robert Brooks SHOW	2.00
C69	Jamal Anderson SHOW	7.50
C70	Natrone Means SHOW	6.00
C71	John Friesz SHOW	2.00
C72	Ki-Jana Carter SHOW	2.00
C73	Marc Edwards SHOW	2.00
C74	Michael Westbrook SHOW	2.00
C75	Neil O'Donnell SHOW	2.00
C76	Scott Mitchell SHOW	2.00
C77	Wesley Walls SHOW	2.00
C78	Bruce Smith SHOW	2.00
C79	Corey Dillon SHOW	30.00
C80	Wayne Chrebet SHOW	2.00
C81	Tony Martin SHOW	2.00
C82	Jimmy Smith SHOW	2.00
C83	Terry Allen SHOW	2.00
C84	Shannon Sharpe SHOW	2.00
C85	Derrick Alexander SHOW	2.00
C86	Garrison Hearst SHOW	2.00
C87	Tamarick Vanover SHOW	2.00
C88	Michael Irvin SHOW	5.00
C89	Mark Chmura SHOW	4.00
C90	Bert Emanuel SHOW	2.00
C91	Eric Metcalf SHOW	2.00
C92	Reggie White SHOW	5.00
C93	Carl Pickens SHOW	2.00
C94	Chris Sanders SHOW	2.00
C95	Frank Sanders SHOW	2.00
C96	Desmond Howard SHOW	2.00
C97	Michael Jackson SHOW	2.00
C98	Tim Brown SHOW	4.00
C99	O.J. McDuffie SHOW	2.00
C100	Mario Bates SHOW	2.00
C101	Warren Moon SHOW	2.00
C102	Curtis Conway SHOW	2.00
C103	Irving Fryar SHOW	2.00
C104	Isaac Bruce SHOW	4.00
C105	Cris Carter SHOW	4.00
C106	Chris Chandler SHOW	2.00
C107	Charles Johnson SHOW	2.00
C108	Kevin Lockett SHOW	2.00
C109	Rob Moore SHOW	2.00
C110	Napoleon Kaufman SHOW	6.00
C111	Henry Ellard SHOW	2.00
C112	Vinny Testaverde SHOW	2.00
C113	Rick Mirer SHOW	2.00
C114	Ty Detmer SHOW	2.00
C115	Todd Collins SHOW	2.00
C116	Jake Reed SHOW	2.00
C117	Dave Brown SHOW	2.00
C118	Dedric Ward SHOW	2.00
C119	Heath Shuler SHOW	2.00
C120	Ben Coates SHOW	2.00

1997 Flair Showcase Legacy

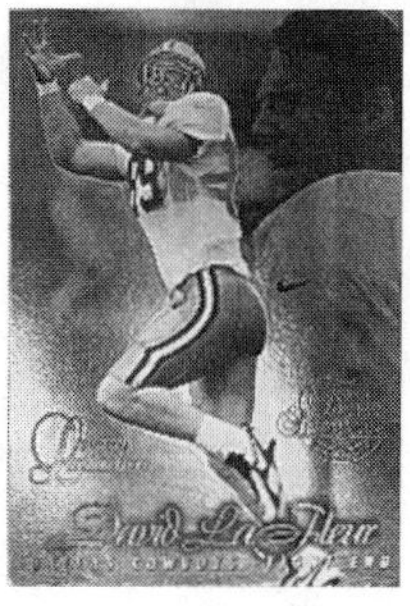

Legacy parallels the 360-base cards in Flair Showcase. The cards feature blue-foil stamping and are sequentially numbered to 100. The backs are done in matte finish. The Legacy Masterpiece versions are a one-of-one parallel of each base card. The cards are stamped to signify their distinctness.

		MT
Common Player:		10.00
Minor Stars:		20.00
Production 100 Sets		
1	Jerry Rice	75.00
2	Mark Brunell	75.00
3	Eddie Kennison	10.00
4	Brett Favre	150.00
5	Karim Abdul-Jabbar	20.00
6	David LaFleur	10.00
7	John Elway	120.00
8	Troy Aikman	75.00
9	Steve McNair	45.00
10	Kordell Stewart	60.00
11	Drew Bledsoe	75.00
12	Kerry Collins	20.00
13	Dan Marino	120.00
14	Steve Young	45.00
15	Marvin Harrison	25.00
16	Lawrence Phillips	20.00
17	Jeff Blake	20.00
18	Yatil Green	10.00
19	Jake Plummer	125.00
20	Barry Sanders	150.00
21	Deion Sanders	20.00
22	Emmitt Smith	120.00
23	Rae Carruth	10.00
24	Chris Warren	10.00
25	Terry Glenn	20.00
26	Jim Druckenmiller	20.00
27	Eddie George	75.00
28	Curtis Martin	45.00
29	Warrick Dunn	60.00
30	Terrell Davis	120.00
31	Rashaan Salaam	10.00
32	Marcus Allen	20.00
33	Jeff George	20.00
34	Thurman Thomas	20.00
35	Keyshawn Johnson	25.00
36	Jerome Bettis	20.00
37	Larry Centers	10.00
38	Tony Banks	20.00
39	Marshall Faulk	25.00
40	Mike Alstott	25.00
41	Elvis Grbac	10.00
42	Errict Rhett	20.00
43	Edgar Bennett	10.00
44	Jim Harbaugh	10.00
45	Antonio Freeman	40.00
46	Tiki Barber	35.00
47	Tim Biakabutuka	20.00
48	Joey Galloway	25.00
49	Tony Gonzalez	35.00
50	Keenan McCardell	10.00
51	Darnay Scott	20.00
52	Brad Johnson	30.00
53	Herman Moore	20.00
54	Reidel Anthony	35.00
55	Junior Seau	20.00
56	Ricky Watters	20.00
57	Amani Toomer	10.00
58	Andre Reed	10.00
59	Antowain Smith	75.00
60	Ike Hilliard	35.00
61	Byron Hanspard	50.00
62	Robert Smith	20.00
63	Gus Frerotte	10.00
64	Charles Way	10.00
65	Trent Dilfer	20.00
66	Adrian Murrell	20.00
67	Stan Humphries	10.00
68	Robert Brooks	10.00
69	Jamal Anderson	40.00
70	Natrone Means	20.00
71	John Friesz	10.00
72	Ki-Jana Carter	10.00
73	Marc Edwards	10.00
74	Michael Westbrook	20.00
75	Neil O'Donnell	10.00
76	Scott Mitchell	10.00
77	Wesley Walls	10.00
78	Bruce Smith	10.00
79	Corey Dillon	85.00
80	Wayne Chrebet	20.00
81	Tony Martin	10.00
82	Jimmy Smith	20.00
83	Terry Allen	20.00
84	Shannon Sharpe	20.00
85	Derrick Alexander	10.00
86	Garrison Hearst	20.00
87	Tamarick Vanover	10.00
88	Michael Irvin	20.00
89	Mark Chmura	20.00
90	Bert Emanuel	10.00
91	Eric Metcalf	10.00
92	Reggie White	20.00
93	Carl Pickens	20.00
94	Chris Sanders	10.00
95	Frank Sanders	10.00
96	Desmond Howard	10.00
97	Michael Jackson	10.00
98	Tim Brown	20.00
99	O.J. McDuffie	10.00
100	Mario Bates	10.00
101	Warren Moon	20.00
102	Curtis Conway	20.00
103	Irving Fryar	10.00
104	Isaac Bruce	20.00
105	Cris Carter	25.00
106	Chris Chandler	20.00
107	Charles Johnson	10.00
108	Kevin Lockett	10.00
109	Rob Moore	10.00
110	Napoleon Kaufman	20.00
111	Henry Ellard	10.00
112	Vinny Testaverde	20.00
113	Rick Mirer	10.00
114	Ty Detmer	10.00
115	Todd Collins	10.00
116	Jake Reed	10.00
117	Dave Brown	10.00
118	Dedric Ward	20.00
119	Heath Shuler	10.00
120	Ben Coates	20.00

1997 Flair Showcase Hot Hands

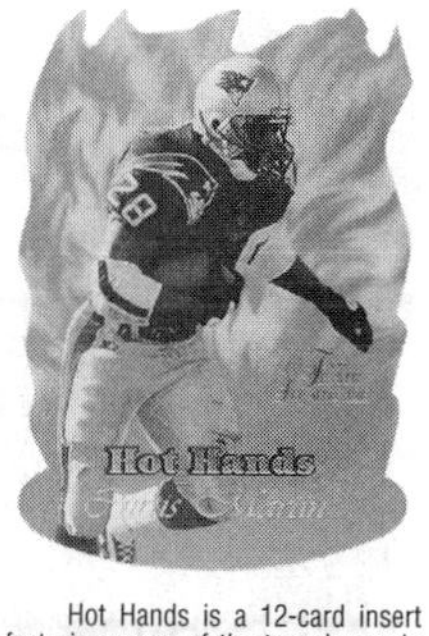

Hot Hands is a 12-card insert featuring some of the top players in the NFL. The cards are die-cut in the shape of flames and have a fiery background. They are inserted once in every 90 packs. The cards are numbered with the "HH" prefix.

		MT
Complete Set (12):		700.00
Common Player:		10.00
1	Kerry Collins	50.00
2	Emmitt Smith	100.00
3	Terrell Davis	60.00
4	Brett Favre	125.00
5	Eddie George	80.00
6	Marvin Harrison	10.00
7	Mark Brunell	60.00
8	Dan Marino	100.00
9	Curtis Martin	60.00
10	Terry Glenn	45.00
11	Keyshawn Johnson	10.00
12	Jerry Rice	60.00

Post-1980 cards in Near Mint condition will generally sell for about 75% of the quoted Mint value. Excellent-condition cards bring no more than 40%.

1997 Flair Showcase Midas Touch

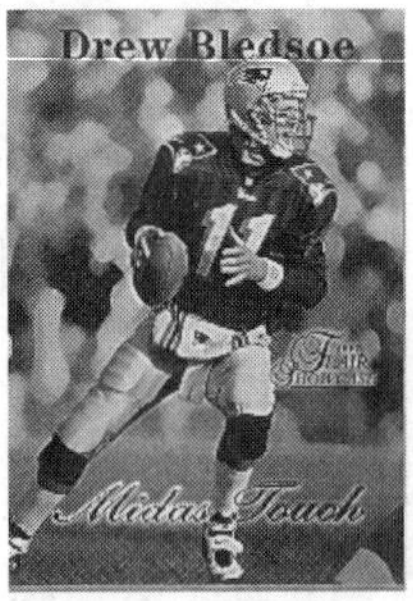

Midas Touch is a 12-card insert featuring superstars with a "golden touch." The cards have a gold-colored background and were inserted once in every 20 packs. The cards are numbered with the "MT" prefix.

		MT
Complete Set (12):		150.00
Common Player:		3.00
Minor Stars:		6.00
1	Troy Aikman	25.00
2	John Elway	20.00
3	Barry Sanders	25.00
4	Marshall Faulk	6.00
5	Karim Abdul-Jabbar	15.00
6	Drew Bledsoe	25.00
7	Ricky Watters	6.00
8	Kordell Stewart	25.00
9	Tony Martin	3.00
10	Steve Young	20.00
11	Joey Galloway	3.00
12	Isaac Bruce	6.00

1997 Flair Showcase Now & Then

A four-card insert set, Then & Now features 12 NFL players as they looked when they entered the league. Each card highlights a particular draft year and three of the top players who were picked. The cards were inserted once in every 288 packs. The cards are numbered with the "NT" prefix.

		MT
Complete Set (4):		800.00
Common Player:		175.00
1	Marino, Elway, D. Green (1983)	225.00
2	Aikman, B. Sanders, D. Sanders (1989)	175.00
3	E. Smith, C. Warren, J. Seau (1990)	225.00
4	Favre, H. Moore, R. Watters (1991)	275.00

1997 Flair Showcase Wave of the Future

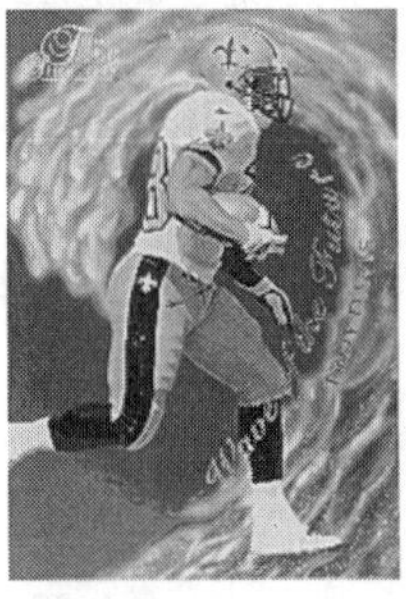

Wave of the Future showcases 25 top rookies entering the 1997 season. The fronts and backs feature a tidal wave design. Inserted once in every four packs. The cards are numbered with the "WF" prefix.

		MT
Complete Set (25):		30.00
Common Player:		1.00
Minor Stars:		2.00
1	Mike Adams	1.00
2	John Allred	1.00
3	Pat Barnes	2.00
4	Kenny Bynum	1.00
5	Will Blackwell	2.00
6	Peter Boulware	2.00
7	Greg Clark	2.00
8	Troy Davis	2.00
9	Albert Connell	2.00
10	Jay Graham	2.00
11	Leon Johnson	1.00
12	Damon Jones	1.00
13	Freddie Jones	3.00
14	George Jones	2.00
15	Chad Levitt	1.00
16	Joey Kent	2.00
17	Danny Wuerffel	2.00
18	Orlando Pace	2.00
19	Darnell Autry	1.00
20	Sedrick Shaw	2.00
21	Shawn Springs	2.00
22	Duce Staley	10.00
23	Darrell Russell	2.00
24	Bryant Westbrook	2.00
25	Antowuan Wyatt	1.00

1998 Flair Showcase Row 3

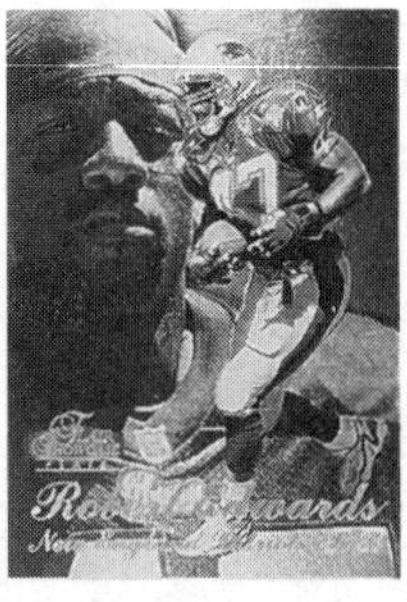

Row 3 is made up of 80 base cards with four different tiers. Cards 1-20 were inserted 1:0.9 packs, cards 21-40 at 1:1.1, cards 41-60 at 1:1.4 and cards 61-80 at 1:1.8.

		MT
Complete Set (80):		75.00
Common Player:		.25
Minor Stars:		.50
Common Rookie:		1.00
1-20 Inserted 1:0.9		
21-40 Inserted 1:1.1		
41-60 Inserted 1:1.4		
61-80 Inserted 1:1.8		
Pack (5):		4.50
Wax Box (24):		100.00
1	Brett Favre	3.00
2	Emmitt Smith	2.00
3	*Peyton Manning*	12.00
4	Mark Brunell	1.00
5	*Randy Moss*	12.00
6	Jerry Rice	1.50
7	John Elway	1.50
8	Troy Aikman	1.50
9	Warrick Dunn	1.00
10	Kordell Stewart	1.00
11	Drew Bledsoe	1.00
12	Eddie George	1.00
13	Dan Marino	2.00
14	Antowain Smith	.75
15	*Curtis Enis*	3.00
16	Jake Plummer	1.00
17	Steve Young	1.00
18	*Ryan Leaf*	4.00
19	Terrell Davis	2.00
20	Barry Sanders	3.00
21	Corey Dillon	1.00
22	*Fred Taylor*	8.00
23	Herman Moore	.50
24	Marshall Faulk	.75
25	*John Avery*	2.50
26	Terry Glenn	.50
27	Keyshawn Johnson	.50
28	*Charles Woodson*	3.00
29	Garrison Hearst	.50
30	Steve McNair	.75
31	Deion Sanders	.75
32	*Robert Holcombe*	2.50
33	Jerome Bettis	.50
34	*Robert Edwards*	3.00
35	*Skip Hicks*	2.50
36	*Marcus Nash*	2.50
37	Fred Lane	.25
38	*Kevin Dyson*	2.50
39	Dorsey Levens	.50
40	*Jacquez Green*	2.50
41	Shannon Sharpe	.50
42	Michael Irvin	.75
43	Jim Harbaugh	.25
44	Curtis Martin	.75
45	Bobby Hoying	.25
46	Trent Dilfer	.50
47	Yancey Thigpen	.25
48	Warren Moon	.50
49	Danny Kanell	.25
50	Rob Johnson	.50
51	Carl Pickens	.50
52	Scott Mitchell	.25
53	Tim Brown	.50
54	Tony Banks	.50
55	Jamal Anderson	1.00
56	Kerry Collins	.50
57	Elvis Grbac	.25
58	Mike Alstott	.75
59	Glenn Foley	.25
60	Brad Johnson	.75
61	Robert Brooks	.25
62	Irving Fryar	.25
63	Natrone Means	1.00
64	Rae Carruth	.25
65	Isaac Bruce	.75
66	Andre Rison	.50
67	Jeff George	.50
68	Charles Way	.25
69	Derrick Alexander	.25
70	Michael Jackson	.25
71	Rob Moore	.50
72	Ricky Watters	.50
73	Curtis Conway	.50
74	Antonio Freeman	1.25
75	Jimmy Smith	.75
76	Troy Davis	.25
77	Robert Smith	1.25
78	Terry Allen	.50
79	Joey Galloway	1.25
80	Charles Johnson	.25

1998 Flair Showcase Row 2

Row 2 is set up the same way that Row 3 is with 80 base cards and four tiers. It has different insert odds with cards 1-20 found 1:3 packs, cards 21-40 at 1:2.5 packs, cards 41-60 at 1:4 packs and cards 61-80 at 1:3.4 packs.

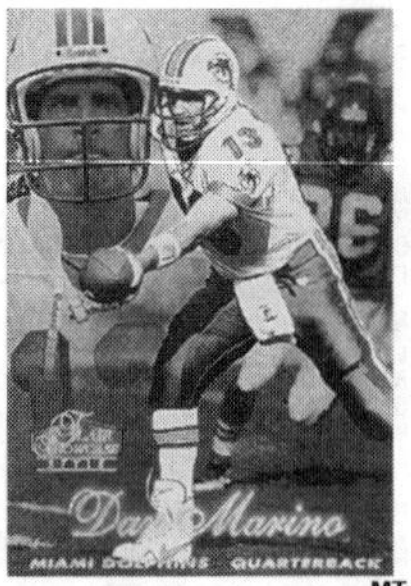

		MT
Complete Set (80):		150.00
Common Player:		.50
Minor Stars:		1.00
Common Rookie:		1.50
1-20 Inserted 1:3		
21-40 Inserted 1:2.5		
41-60 Inserted 1:4		
61-80 Inserted 1:3.4		
1	Brett Favre	6.00
2	Emmitt Smith	4.00
3	Peyton Manning	18.00
4	Mark Brunell	2.00
5	Randy Moss	35.00
6	Jerry Rice	3.00
7	John Elway	3.00
8	Troy Aikman	3.00
9	Warrick Dunn	2.00
10	Kordell Stewart	2.00
11	Drew Bledsoe	2.00
12	Eddie George	2.00
13	Dan Marino	4.00
14	Antowain Smith	1.50
15	Curtis Enis	6.00
16	Jake Plummer	2.00
17	Steve Young	2.00
18	Ryan Leaf	10.00
19	Terrell Davis	4.00
20	Barry Sanders	6.00
21	Corey Dillon	2.00
22	Fred Taylor	10.00
23	Herman Moore	1.00
24	Marshall Faulk	1.50
25	John Avery	4.00
26	Terry Glenn	1.00
27	Keyshawn Johnson	1.00
28	Charles Woodson	5.00
29	Garrison Hearst	1.00
30	Steve McNair	1.50
31	Deion Sanders	1.50
32	Robert Holcombe	4.00
33	Jerome Bettis	1.00
34	Robert Edwards	4.00
35	Skip Hicks	4.00
36	Marcus Nash	4.00
37	Fred Lane	.50
38	Kevin Dyson	4.00
39	Dorsey Levens	1.00
40	Jacquez Green	4.00
41	Shannon Sharpe	1.00
42	Michael Irvin	1.50
43	Jim Harbaugh	.50
44	Curtis Martin	1.50
45	Bobby Hoying	.50
46	Trent Dilfer	1.00
47	Yancey Thigpen	.50
48	Warren Moon	1.00
49	Danny Kanell	.50
50	Rob Johnson	1.00
51	Carl Pickens	1.00
52	Scott Mitchell	.50
53	Tim Brown	1.00
54	Tony Banks	1.00
55	Jamal Anderson	2.00
56	Kerry Collins	1.00
57	Elvis Grbac	.50
58	Mike Alstott	1.50
59	Glenn Foley	.50
60	Brad Johnson	1.50
61	Robert Brooks	.50
62	Irving Fryar	.50
63	Natrone Means	1.50
64	Rae Carruth	.50
65	Isaac Bruce	1.25
66	Andre Rison	1.00
67	Jeff George	1.00
68	Charles Way	.50
69	Derrick Alexander	.50
70	Michael Jackson	.50
71	Rob Moore	1.00
72	Ricky Watters	1.00
73	Curtis Conway	.50
74	Antonio Freeman	2.50
75	Jimmy Smith	1.50
76	Troy Davis	.50
77	Robert Smith	2.50
78	Terry Allen	1.00
79	Joey Galloway	2.50
80	Charles Johnson	.50

1998 Flair Showcase Row 1

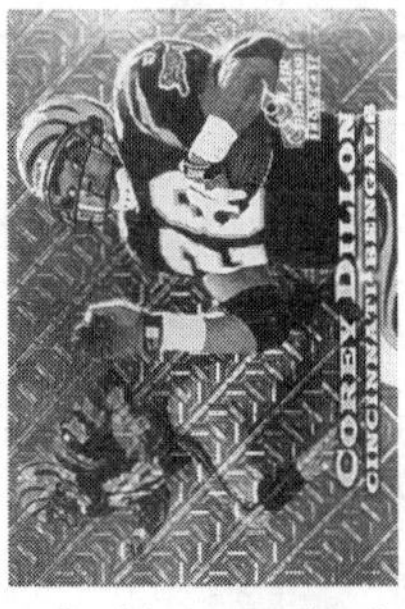

Row 1 singles are much tougher than the previous Row 3 and 2 because of tougher insert odds. Same setup with 80 cards and four tiers. Cards 1-20 were inserted 1:16 packs, cards 21-40 at 1:24, cards 41-60 at 1:6 and the last tier of cards 61-80 at 1:9.6.

		MT
Complete Set (80):		600.00
Common Player:		1.50
Minor Stars:		3.00
Common Rookie:		4.00
1-20 Inserted 1:16		
21-40 Inserted 1:24		
41-60 Inserted 1:6		
61-80 Inserted 1:9.6		
1	Brett Favre	25.00
2	Emmitt Smith	16.00
3	Peyton Manning	45.00
4	Mark Brunell	8.00
5	Randy Moss	100.00
6	Jerry Rice	12.00
7	John Elway	12.00
8	Troy Aikman	12.00
9	Warrick Dunn	8.00
10	Kordell Stewart	8.00
11	Drew Bledsoe	8.00
12	Eddie George	8.00
13	Dan Marino	16.00
14	Antowain Smith	6.00
15	Curtis Enis	15.00
16	Jake Plummer	8.00
17	Steve Young	8.00
18	Ryan Leaf	25.00
19	Terrell Davis	16.00
20	Barry Sanders	25.00
21	Corey Dillon	8.00
22	Fred Taylor	25.00
23	Herman Moore	3.00
24	Marshall Faulk	6.00
25	John Avery	10.00
26	Terry Glenn	3.00
27	Keyshawn Johnson	3.00
28	Charles Woodson	12.00
29	Garrison Hearst	3.00
30	Steve McNair	6.00
31	Deion Sanders	6.00
32	Robert Holcombe	10.00
33	Jerome Bettis	3.00
34	Robert Edwards	12.00
35	Skip Hicks	10.00
36	Marcus Nash	10.00
37	Fred Lane	1.50
38	Kevin Dyson	10.00
39	Dorsey Levens	3.00
40	Jacquez Green	10.00
41	Shannon Sharpe	3.00
42	Michael Irvin	3.00
43	Jim Harbaugh	1.50
44	Curtis Martin	4.00
45	Bobby Hoying	1.50
46	Trent Dilfer	3.00
47	Yancey Thigpen	1.50
48	Warren Moon	3.00
49	Danny Kanell	1.50
50	Rob Johnson	3.00
51	Carl Pickens	3.00
52	Scott Mitchell	1.50
53	Tim Brown	3.00
54	Tony Banks	3.00
55	Jamal Anderson	5.00
56	Kerry Collins	3.00
57	Elvis Grbac	1.50
58	Mike Alstott	3.00
59	Glenn Foley	1.50
60	Brad Johnson	3.00
61	Robert Brooks	1.50
62	Irving Fryar	1.50
63	Natrone Means	4.00
64	Rae Carruth	1.50
65	Isaac Bruce	3.00
66	Andre Rison	3.00
67	Jeff George	3.00
68	Charles Way	1.50
69	Derrick Alexander	1.50
70	Michael Jackson	1.50
71	Rob Moore	3.00
72	Ricky Watters	3.00
73	Curtis Conway	1.50
74	Antonio Freeman	5.00
75	Jimmy Smith	3.00
76	Troy Davis	1.50
77	Robert Smith	5.00
78	Terry Allen	1.50
79	Joey Galloway	5.00
80	Charles Johnson	1.50

1998 Flair Showcase Row 0

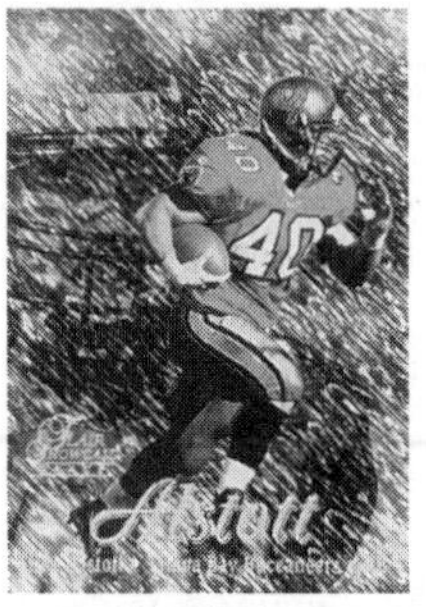

The Row 0 set is made up of 80 cards and is tiered at four different levels. The first level includes cards 1-20 and each is sequentially numbered to 250. The next level includes cards 21-40 and are numbered to 500. Cards 41-60 are numbered to 1,000 and the last level of cards 61-80 are numbered to 2,000.

		MT
Complete Set (80):		3500.
Common Player (1-20):		7.00
Production 250 Sets		
Common Player (21-40):		5.00
Production 500 Sets		
Common Player (41-60):		3.00
Production 1000 Sets		
Common Player (61-80):		2.00
Production 2000 Sets		
1	Brett Favre	100.00
2	Emmitt Smith	70.00
3	Peyton Manning	120.00
4	Mark Brunell	35.00
5	Randy Moss	250.00
6	Jerry Rice	50.00
7	John Elway	50.00
8	Troy Aikman	50.00
9	Warrick Dunn	35.00
10	Kordell Stewart	35.00
11	Drew Bledsoe	35.00
12	Eddie George	35.00
13	Dan Marino	70.00
14	Antowain Smith	20.00
15	Curtis Enis	40.00
16	Jake Plummer	35.00
17	Steve Young	35.00
18	Ryan Leaf	60.00
19	Terrell Davis	70.00
20	Barry Sanders	100.00
21	Corey Dillon	20.00
22	Fred Taylor	50.00
23	Herman Moore	10.00
24	Marshall Faulk	15.00
25	John Avery	20.00
26	Terry Glenn	10.00
27	Keyshawn Johnson	10.00
28	Charles Woodson	25.00
29	Garrison Hearst	10.00
30	Steve McNair	15.00
31	Deion Sanders	15.00
32	Robert Holcombe	20.00
33	Jerome Bettis	10.00
34	Robert Edwards	20.00
35	Skip Hicks	20.00
36	Marcus Nash	20.00
37	Fred Lane	5.00
38	Kevin Dyson	20.00
39	Dorsey Levens	10.00
40	Jacquez Green	20.00
41	Shannon Sharpe	6.00
42	Michael Irvin	8.00
43	Jim Harbaugh	3.00
44	Curtis Martin	8.00
45	Bobby Hoying	3.00
46	Trent Dilfer	6.00
47	Yancey Thigpen	3.00
48	Warren Moon	6.00
49	Danny Kanell	3.00
50	Rob Johnson	6.00
51	Carl Pickens	6.00
52	Scott Mitchell	3.00
53	Tim Brown	6.00
54	Tony Banks	6.00
55	Jamal Anderson	15.00
56	Kerry Collins	6.00
57	Elvis Grbac	3.00
58	Mike Alstott	8.00
59	Glenn Foley	3.00
60	Brad Johnson	8.00
61	Robert Brooks	2.00
62	Irving Fryar	2.00
63	Natrone Means	10.00
64	Rae Carruth	2.00
65	Isaac Bruce	7.50
66	Andre Rison	4.00
67	Jeff George	4.00
68	Charles Way	2.00
69	Derrick Alexander	2.00
70	Michael Jackson	2.00
71	Rob Moore	4.00
72	Ricky Watters	4.00
73	Curtis Conway	4.00
74	Antonio Freeman	12.50
75	Jimmy Smith	7.50
76	Troy Davis	2.00
77	Robert Smith	12.50
78	Terry Allen	4.00
79	Joey Galloway	12.50
80	Charles Johnson	2.00

1998 Flair Showcase Legacy

Each of the 320 cards in this set has a parallel Legacy card. Each card has a foil front and is sequentially numbered to 100.

		MT
Common Player:		15.00
Minor Stars:		30.00
Production 100 Sets		
Each Player Has Four Different Cards		
1	Brett Favre	200.00
2	Emmitt Smith	150.00
3	Peyton Manning	175.00
4	Mark Brunell	85.00
5	Randy Moss	325.00
6	Jerry Rice	100.00
7	John Elway	100.00
8	Troy Aikman	100.00
9	Warrick Dunn	85.00
10	Kordell Stewart	85.00
11	Drew Bledsoe	85.00
12	Eddie George	85.00
13	Dan Marino	150.00
14	Antowain Smith	50.00
15	Curtis Enis	50.00
16	Jake Plummer	85.00
17	Steve Young	75.00
18	Ryan Leaf	90.00
19	Terrell Davis	150.00
20	Barry Sanders	200.00
21	Corey Dillon	60.00
22	Fred Taylor	100.00
23	Herman Moore	30.00
24	Marshall Faulk	40.00
25	John Avery	40.00
26	Terry Glenn	30.00
27	Keyshawn Johnson	30.00
28	Charles Woodson	50.00
29	Garrison Hearst	30.00
30	Steve McNair	40.00
31	Deion Sanders	40.00
32	Robert Holcombe	40.00
33	Jerome Bettis	30.00
34	Robert Edwards	50.00
35	Skip Hicks	45.00
36	Marcus Nash	45.00
37	Fred Lane	15.00
38	Kevin Dyson	40.00
39	Dorsey Levens	30.00
40	Jacquez Green	45.00
41	Shannon Sharpe	30.00
42	Michael Irvin	40.00
43	Jim Harbaugh	15.00
44	Curtis Martin	40.00
45	Bobby Hoying	15.00
46	Trent Dilfer	30.00
47	Yancey Thigpen	15.00
48	Warren Moon	30.00
49	Danny Kanell	15.00
50	Rob Johnson	30.00
51	Carl Pickens	30.00
52	Scott Mitchell	15.00
53	Tim Brown	30.00
54	Tony Banks	30.00
55	Jamal Anderson	40.00
56	Kerry Collins	30.00
57	Elvis Grbac	15.00
58	Mike Alstott	40.00
59	Glenn Foley	15.00
60	Brad Johnson	30.00
61	Robert Brooks	15.00
62	Irving Fryar	15.00
63	Natrone Means	30.00
64	Rae Carruth	15.00
65	Isaac Bruce	30.00
66	Andre Rison	15.00
67	Jeff George	30.00
68	Charles Way	15.00
69	Derrick Alexander	15.00
70	Michael Jackson	15.00
71	Rob Moore	30.00
72	Ricky Watters	30.00
73	Curtis Conway	15.00
74	Antonio Freeman	40.00
75	Jimmy Smith	30.00
76	Troy Davis	15.00
77	Robert Smith	30.00
78	Terry Allen	30.00
79	Joey Galloway	30.00
80	Charles Johnson	15.00

1998 Flair Showcase Feature Film

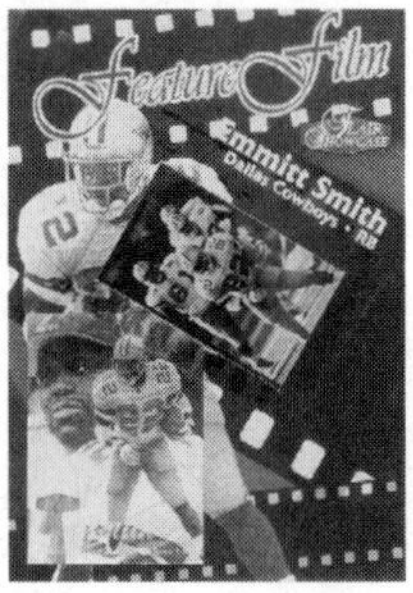

Each card in this set has an actual slide from the Showcase set mounted on it. Singles were inserted 1:60 packs.

		MT
Complete Set (10):		230.00
Common Player:		10.00
Inserted 1:60		
1	Terrell Davis	35.00
2	Brett Favre	50.00
3	Antowain Smith	10.00
4	Emmitt Smith	35.00
5	Dan Marino	35.00
6	Kordell Stewart	20.00
7	Warrick Dunn	15.00
8	Barry Sanders	50.00
9	Peyton Manning	40.00
10	Ryan Leaf	20.00

1999 Flair Showcase

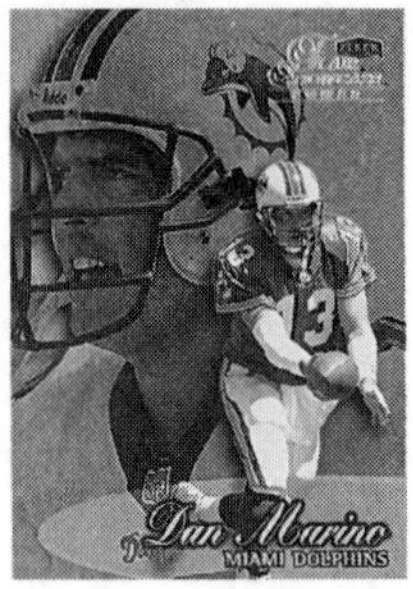

This was a 192-card set that included three levels of scarcity. The Power subset included 32 veterans, the Passion subset was made up of 64 veterans and the Showcase subset included the last 96 cards with 21 of them being rookies and 11 of them being veterans, sequentially numbered to 1,999. Two parallel sets were issued with the Legacy Collection and Masterpieces. Other inserts included: Class of '99, Feel the Game, First Rounders and Shrine Time. SRP was $4.99 for five-card packs.

		MT
Complete Set (192):		850.00
Common Player:		.25
Minor Stars:		.50
Common Rookie:		10.00
Production 1,999 Sets		
Pack (5):		6.00
Wax Box (24):		130.00
1	Troy Aikman	2.00
2	Jamal Anderson	.75
3	Charlie Batch	1.25
4	Jerome Bettis	.75
5	Drew Bledsoe	1.50
6	Mark Brunell	1.50
7	Randall Cunningham	.75
8	Terrell Davis	3.00

9 Corey Dillon .75
10 Warrick Dunn .75
11 Curtis Enis .75
12 Marshall Faulk .75
13 Brett Favre 4.00
14 Doug Flutie 1.25
15 Eddie George 1.00
16 Brian Griese 1.50
17 Keyshawn Johnson .75
18 Peyton Manning 3.00
19 Dan Marino 3.00
20 Curtis Martin .75
21 Steve McNair 1.00
22 Randy Moss 4.00
23 Terrell Owens .75
24 Jake Plummer 1.50
25 Jerry Rice 2.00
26 Barry Sanders 4.00
27 Antowain Smith .75
28 Emmitt Smith 3.00
29 Kordell Stewart .75
30 J.J. Stokes .50
31 Fred Taylor 2.00
32 Steve Young 1.25
33 Troy Aikman 2.00
34 Mike Alstott .75
35 Jamal Anderson .75
36 Charlie Batch 1.25
37 Jerome Bettis .75
38 Drew Bledsoe 1.50
39 Mark Brunell 1.50
40 Cris Carter .75
41 Mark Chmura .50
42 Wayne Chrebet .75
43 Kerry Collins .50
44 Randall Cunningham .75
45 Terrell Davis 3.00
46 Trent Dilfer .50
47 Corey Dillon .75
48 Warrick Dunn .75
49 Kevin Dyson .25
50 Curtis Enis .75
51 Marshall Faulk .75
52 Brett Favre 4.00
53 Doug Flutie 1.25
54 Antonio Freeman .75
55 Eddie George 1.00
56 Terry Glenn .75
57 Tony Gonzalez .50
58 Elvis Grbac .50
59 Jacquez Green .50
60 Brian Griese 1.50
61 Marvin Harrison .75
62 Garrison Hearst .50
63 Skip Hicks .50
64 Priest Holmes .75
65 Michael Irvin .50
66 Brad Johnson .75
67 Keyshawn Johnson .75
68 Napoleon Kaufman .75
69 Dorsey Levens .75
70 Peyton Manning 3.00
71 Dan Marino 3.00
72 Curtis Martin .75
73 Ed McCaffrey .75
74 Keenan McCardell .50
75 O.J. McDuffie .25
76 Steve McNair 1.00
77 Scott Mitchell .25
78 Randy Moss 4.00
79 Eric Moulds .75
80 Terrell Owens .75
81 Lawrence Phillips .25
82 Jake Plummer 1.50
83 Jerry Rice 2.00
84 Andre Rison .50
85 Barry Sanders 4.00
86 Shannon Sharpe .75
87 Antowain Smith .75
88 Emmitt Smith 3.00
89 Rod Smith .75
90 Duce Staley .75
91 Kordell Stewart .75
92 J.J. Stokes .50
93 Fred Taylor 3.00
94 Vinny Testaverde .50
95 Ricky Watters .50
96 Steve Young 1.25
97 Mike Alstott .75
98 Jamal Anderson .75
99 Charlie Batch 1.25
100 Jerome Bettis .75
101 Tim Biakabutuka .50
102 Drew Bledsoe 1.50
103 Tim Brown .50
104 Mark Brunell 1.25
105 Cris Carter .75
106 Chris Chandler .50
107 Mark Chmura .50
108 Wayne Chrebet .75
109 Ben Coates .50
110 Kerry Collins .50
111 Randall Cunningham .75
112 Trent Dilfer .50
113 Corey Dillon .75
114 Warrick Dunn .75
115 Kevin Dyson .25
116 Curtis Enis .75
117 Marshall Faulk .75
118 Doug Flutie 1.25
119 Antonio Freeman .75
120 Joey Galloway .75
121 Rich Gannon .50
122 Eddie George 1.00
123 Terry Glenn .75
124 Tony Gonzalez .50
125 Elvis Grbac .50
126 Jacquez Green .50
127 Brian Griese 1.50
128 Marvin Harrison .75
129 Garrison Hearst .50
130 Skip Hicks .50
131 Priest Holmes .75
132 Michael Irvin .50
133 Brad Johnson .75
134 Napoleon Kaufman .75
135 Terry Kirby .25
136 Dorsey Levens .75
137 Curtis Martin .75
138 Ed McCaffrey .75
139 Keenan McCardell .50
140 O.J. McDuffie .25
141 Steve McNair 1.00
142 Natrone Means .50
143 Scott Mitchell .25
144 Herman Moore .75
145 Eric Moulds .75
146 Terrell Owens .75
147 Lawrence Phillips .25
148 Jerry Rice 2.00
149 Andre Rison .50
150 Deion Sanders .50
151 Shannon Sharpe .50
152 Antowain Smith .75
153 Rod Smith .75
154 Duce Staley .75
155 Kordell Stewart .75
156 J.J. Stokes .50
157 Vinny Testaverde .50
158 Yancey Thigpen .25
159 Ricky Watters .50
160 Steve Young 1.25
161 Troy Aikman SP 10.00
162 *Champ Bailey* 20.00
163 *Karsten Bailey* 10.00
164 *D'Wayne Bates* 10.00
165 *David Boston* 30.00
166 *Michael Cloud* 15.00
167 *Cecil Collins* 20.00
168 *Tim Couch* 85.00
169 *Daunte Culpepper* 125.00
170 Terrell Davis SP 15.00
171 *Troy Edwards* 30.00
172 *Kevin Faulk* 20.00
173 Brett Favre SP 20.00
174 *Torry Holt* 30.00
175 *Sedrick Irvin* 20.00
176 *Edgerrin James* 150.00
177 *J.J. Johnson* 20.00
178 *Kevin Johnson* 30.00
179 Keyshawn Johnson SP 5.00
180 Peyton Manning SP 15.00
181 Dan Marino SP 15.00
182 *Donovan McNabb* 75.00
183 *Cade McNown* 35.00
184 *Joe Montgomery* 15.00
185 Randy Moss SP 20.00
186 Jake Plummer SP 10.00
187 *Peerless Price* 20.00
188 Barry Sanders SP 20.00
189 *Akili Smith* 30.00
190 Emmitt Smith SP 15.00
191 Fred Taylor SP 15.00
192 *Ricky Williams* 85.00

1999 Flair Showcase Legacy Collection Parallel

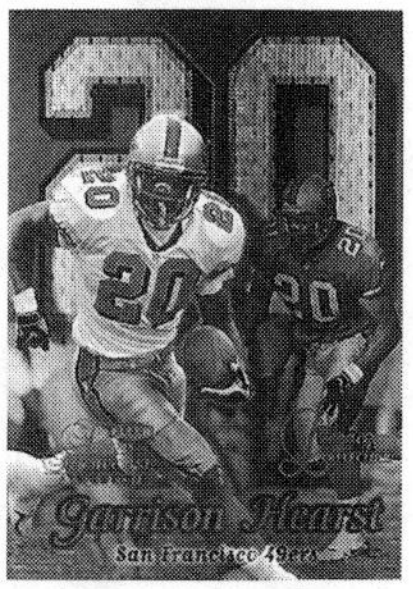

This was a 192-card parallel to the base set. Each single was sequentially numbered to 99.

	MT
Legacy Cards:	15x-30x
Legacy Rookies:	1.5x
Production 99 Sets	

1999 Flair Showcase Class of '99

This 15-card insert set included the top rookies from 1999. Each was sequentially numbered to 500.

	MT
Complete Set (15):	275.00
Common Player:	10.00
Production 500 Sets	
1 Tim Couch	50.00
2 Donovan McNabb	25.00
3 Akili Smith	25.00
4 Cade McNown	25.00
5 Daunte Culpepper	25.00
6 Ricky Williams	50.00
7 Edgerrin James	70.00
8 Kevin Faulk	12.00
9 Torry Holt	15.00
10 David Boston	15.00
11 Sedrick Irvin	10.00
12 Peerless Price	12.00
13 Joe Germaine	10.00
14 Brock Huard	10.00
15 Shaun King	15.00

1999 Flair Showcase Feel The Game

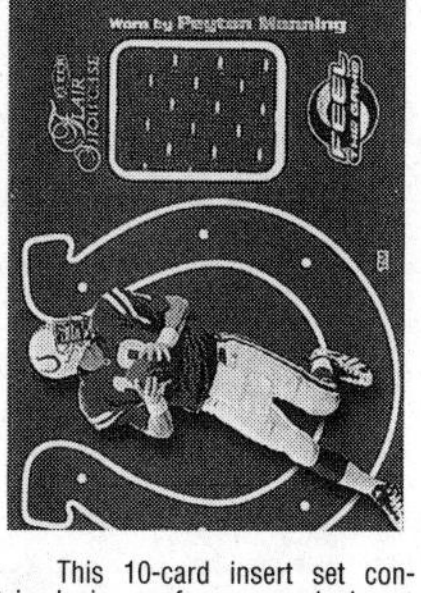

This 10-card insert set contained pieces of game-used gloves, shorts, jerseys or shoes. Each single was hand-numbered and inserted 1:168 packs.

	MT
Complete Set (10):	800.00
Common Player:	25.00
Cecil Collins shoes	60.00
Sean Dawkins shoes	25.00
Marshall Faulk jersey	75.00
Brett Favre jersey	150.00
Torry Holt shoes	50.00
Edgerrin James gloves	175.00
Peyton Manning jersey	150.00
Dan Marino jersey	125.00
Jake Plummer shoes	75.00
Antowain Smith shorts	50.00

1999 Flair Showcase First Rounders

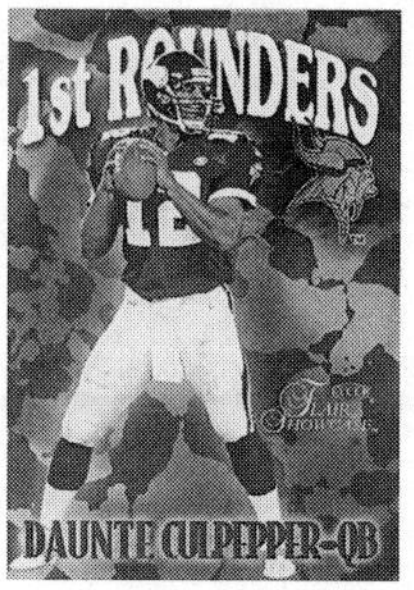

This 10-card set included the top skilled position players selected in the 1999 NFL Draft. Singles were inserted 1:10 packs.

	MT
Complete Set (10):	45.00
Common Player:	2.50
Inserted 1:10	
1 Tim Couch	10.00
2 Donovan McNabb	5.00
3 Akili Smith	5.00
4 Cade McNown	5.00
5 Daunte Culpepper	5.00
6 David Boston	2.50
7 Torry Holt	2.50
8 Ricky Williams	10.00
9 Edgerrin James	12.00
10 Troy Edwards	2.50

1999 Flair Showcase Shrine Time

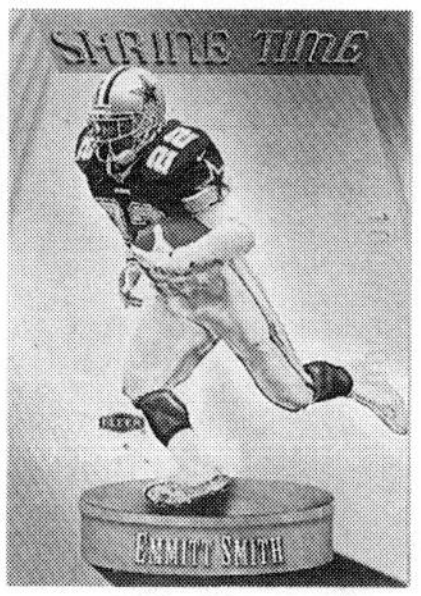

This 15-card insert set included players who could be on their way to the Hall of Fame. Each single was sequentially numbered to 1,500.

	MT
Complete Set (15):	100.00
Common Player:	3.00
Production 1,500 Sets	
1 Peyton Manning	12.00
2 Fred Taylor	8.00
3 Terrell Owens	3.00
4 Charlie Batch	5.00
5 Jerry Rice	8.00
6 Randy Moss	15.00
7 Warrick Dunn	3.00
8 Mark Brunell	6.00
9 Emmitt Smith	12.00
10 Eddie George	5.00
11 Barry Sanders	15.00
12 Terrell Davis	12.00
13 Dan Marino	12.00
14 Troy Aikman	8.00
15 Brett Favre	15.00

2000 Fleer Showcase

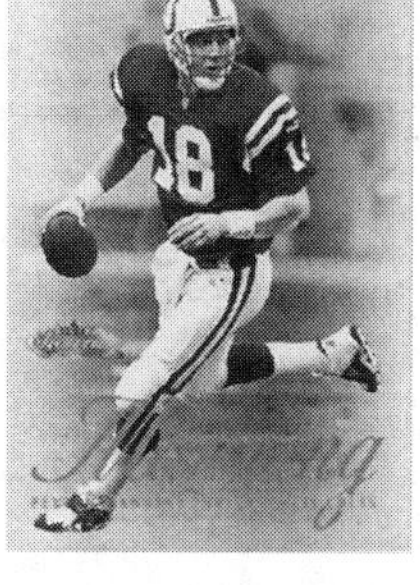

	MT
Complete Set (160):	400.00
Common Player:	.15
Minor Stars:	.30
Common Rookie (101-120):	8.00
Production 1,000 Sets	
Common Rookie (121-160):	3.00
Production 2,000 Sets	
Pack (5):	5.00
Wax Box (24):	80.00

1 Tim Couch 1.25
2 Deion Sanders .50
3 Darnay Scott .30
4 Brett Favre 2.50
5 Mark Brunell 1.00
6 Randy Moss 2.00
7 Tyrone Wheatley .30
8 Isaac Bruce .50
9 Eddie George .75
10 Troy Aikman 1.50
11 Charlie Batch .50
12 Marvin Harrison .50
13 Terry Glenn .50
14 Charles Johnson .15
15 Jerry Rice 1.50
16 Kurt Warner 3.00
17 Kevin Johnson .50
18 Jay Fiedler .50
19 Vinny Testaverde .50
20 Curtis Enis .50
21 Elvis Grbac .30
22 Kordell Stewart .50
23 Jamal Anderson .50
24 Dorsey Levens .50
25 Derrick Mayes .30
26 Marcus Robinson .50
27 Cam Cleeland .30
28 Charlie Garner .30
29 Germane Crowell .30
30 Cade McNown .75
31 Tony Gonzalez .30
32 Shaun King 1.00
33 Wayne Chrebet .50
34 Muhsin Muhammad .30
35 Olandis Gary .50
36 Ray Lewis .15
37 Terrell Davis 1.75
38 Steve Beuerlein .30
39 James Stewart .30
40 Jon Kitna .50
41 Tim Biakabutuka .30
42 Ryan Leaf .50
43 Mike Alstott .50
44 Yancey Thigpen .30
45 Champ Bailey .50
46 Peerless Price .50
47 Ken Dilger .15
48 Derrick Alexander .15
49 Drew Bledsoe 1.00
50 Jerome Bettis .50
51 Jermaine Fazande .30
52 Joey Galloway .50
53 Jeff Blake .30
54 Emmitt Smith 1.75
55 Ricky Williams 1.50
56 Marshall Faulk .50
57 Stephen Davis .50
58 Rob Johnson .30
59 Brian Griese .75
60 Damon Huard .50
61 Jevon Kearse .50
62 Doug Flutie .75
63 Curtis Martin .50
64 Torry Holt .50
65 David Boston .50
66 Cris Carter .50
67 Jason Sehorn .15
68 Keyshawn Johnson .50
69 Chris Chandler .30
70 Antonio Freeman .50
71 Kerry Collins .30
72 Akili Smith .50
73 Troy Edwards .50
74 Tim Dwight .50
75 Donovan McNabb 1.00
76 Tony Banks .30
77 Ed McCaffrey .50
78 Errict Rhett .30
79 Fred Taylor 1.00
80 Terrell Owens .50
81 Steve McNair .60
82 Rob Moore .30
83 Jimmy Smith .50
84 Daunte Culpepper 1.25
85 Carl Pickens .30
86 Moses Moreno .15
87 Brad Johnson .50
88 Jake Plummer .50
89 Edgerrin James 2.50
90 Zach Thomas .30
91 Rich Gannon .30
92 Warrick Dunn .50
93 Shannon Sharpe .30
94 Peyton Manning 2.00
95 Keenan McCardell .30
96 Tony Simmons .15
97 Duce Staley .50
98 Corey Dillon .50
99 Tim Brown .50
100 Ricky Watters .30
101 *Peter Warrick* 45.00
102 *Shaun Alexander* 30.00
103 *Anthony Becht* 8.00
104 *Courtney Brown* 10.00
105 *Plaxico Burress* 20.00
106 *Trung Canidate* 8.00
107 *Giovanni Carmazzi* 12.00
108 *Laveranues Coles* 10.00
109 *Ron Dayne* 50.00
110 *Reuben Droughns* 8.00
111 *Danny Farmer* 10.00
112 *Bubba Franks* 12.00
113 *Thomas Jones* 18.00
114 *Jamal Lewis* 60.00
115 *Sylvester Morris* 20.00
116 *Chad Pennington* 40.00
117 *Travis Prentice* 15.00
118 *J.R. Redmond* 15.00
119 *R. Jay Soward* 12.00
120 *Dez White* 10.00
121 *Sebastian Janikowski* 6.00
122 *Todd Pinkston* 6.00
123 *Spergon Wynn* 5.00
124 *Ron Dugans* 6.00
125 *Joe Hamilton* 8.00
126 *Curtis Keaton* 5.00
127 *Tee Martin* 10.00
128 *Dennis Northcutt* 8.00
129 *Corey Simon* 8.00
130 *Chris Redman* 12.00
131 *Brian Urlacher* 15.00
132 *Travis Taylor* 8.00
133 *Michael Wiley* 6.00
134 *Tim Rattay* 10.00
135 *Jerry Porter* 6.00
136 *Tom Brady* 10.00
137 *Deon Dyer* 3.00
138 *Mareno Philyaw* 3.00
139 *Shaun Ellis* 3.00
140 *John Abraham* 3.00
141 *Ahmed Plummer* 5.00
142 *Chris Hovan* 5.00
143 *Rob Morris* 5.00
144 *Keith Bulluck* 3.00
145 *JaJuan Dawson* 7.00
146 *Chris Cole* 5.00
147 *Chafie Fields* 3.00
148 *Darrell Jackson* 10.00
149 *Marcus Knight* 3.00
150 *Gari Scott* 3.00
151 *Kwame Cavil* 3.00
152 *Frank Moreau* 7.00
153 *Doug Chapman* 5.00
154 *Erron Kinney* 3.00
155 *Ron Dixon* 8.00
156 *Ben Kelly* 3.00
157 *Bashir Yamini* 3.00
158 *Anthony Lucas* 3.00
159 *Avion Black* 3.00
160 *Ian Gold* 5.00

2000 Fleer Showcase Legacy Parallel

	MT
Legacy Cards:	25x-50x
Legacy Rookies (#101-120):	2.5x
Legacy Rookies (#121-160):	4x-8x
Production 20 Sets	

2000 Fleer Showcase Rookie Showcase Firsts Parallel

	MT
#1-20 Firsts:	1x
#21-60 Firsts:	2x
Production 250 Sets	

2000 Fleer Showcase Air to the Throne

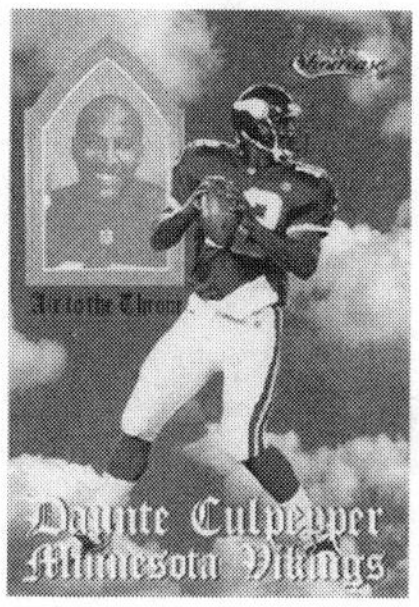

	MT
Complete Set (10):	12.00
Common Player:	1.00
Inserted 1:10	
1 Peyton Manning	5.00
2 Charlie Batch	1.00
3 Giovanni Carmazzi	1.50
4 Brian Griese	1.50
5 Daunte Culpepper	2.50
6 Steve McNair	1.50
7 Brad Johnson	1.00
8 Rob Johnson	1.00
9 Cade McNown	1.50
10 Chad Pennington	3.50

2000 Fleer Showcase Autographics

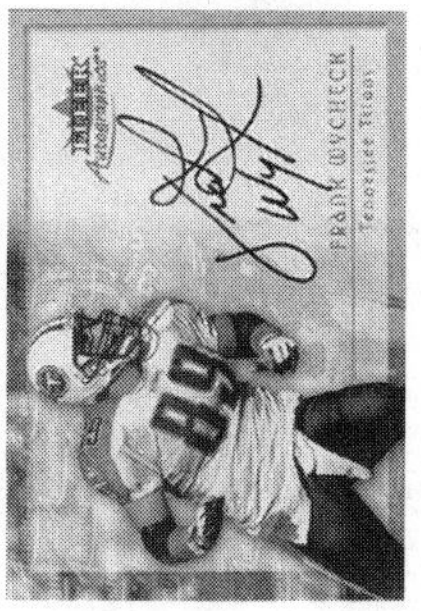

	MT
Common Player:	10.00
Minor Stars:	20.00
Inserted 1:24	
Silver Cards:	1.2x
Production 250 Sets	
1 Champ Bailey	20.00
2 Donnell Bennett	10.00
3 Jerome Bettis	20.00
4 Drew Bledsoe	40.00
5 David Boston	20.00
6 Tom Brady	10.00
7 Trung Canidate	10.00
8 Giovanni Carmazzi	30.00
9 Darren Chiaverini	10.00
10 Laveranues Coles	20.00
11 Kerry Collins	20.00
12 Daunte Culpepper	65.00
13 Stephen Davis	25.00
14 Ron Dayne	65.00
15 Corey Dillon	25.00
16 Tim Dwight	20.00
17 Deon Dyer	10.00
18 Kevin Dyson	10.00
19 Danny Farmer	20.00
20 Kevin Faulk	10.00
21 Marshall Faulk	25.00
22 Christian Fauria	10.00
23 Olandis Gary	25.00
24 Trevor Gaylor	10.00
25 Tony Gonzalez	20.00
26 Az-Zahir Hakim	20.00
27 Joe Hamilton	20.00
28 Marvin Harrison	25.00
29 Priest Holmes	20.00
30 Torry Holt	20.00
31 Damon Huard	20.00
32 Raghib Ismail	10.00
33 Patrick Jeffers	20.00
34 Curtis Keaton	10.00
35 Curtis Martin	25.00
36 Tee Martin	25.00
37 Shane Matthews	10.00
38 Derrick Mayes	10.00
39 Ed McCaffrey	20.00
40 Cade McNown	25.00
41 Herman Moore	20.00
42 Sylvester Morris	30.00
43 Johnnie Morton	10.00
45 Muhsin Muhammad	10.00
46 Dennis Northcutt	20.00
47 Terrell Owens	25.00
48 Chad Pennington	50.00
49 Jake Plummer	25.00
50 Travis Prentice	20.00
51 Peerless Price	20.00
52 John Randle	10.00
53 Tim Rattay	20.00
54 Chris Redmond	45.00
55 Jay Riemersma	10.00
56 Marcus Robinson	20.00
57 Warren Sapp	20.00
58 Gari Scott	10.00
59 Jason Sehorn	10.00
60 Shannon Sharpe	20.00
61 David Sloan	10.00
62 Akili Smith	25.00
63 Rod Smith	20.00
64 R. Jay Soward	20.00
65 Shawn Springs	10.00
66 Duce Staley	25.00
67 Kordell Stewart	25.00
68 Michael Strahan	10.00
69 Amani Toomer	10.00
70 Kurt Warner	80.00
71 Peter Warrick	50.00
72 Tyrone Wheatley	20.00
73 Frank Wycheck	10.00

2000 Fleer Showcase Feel the Game

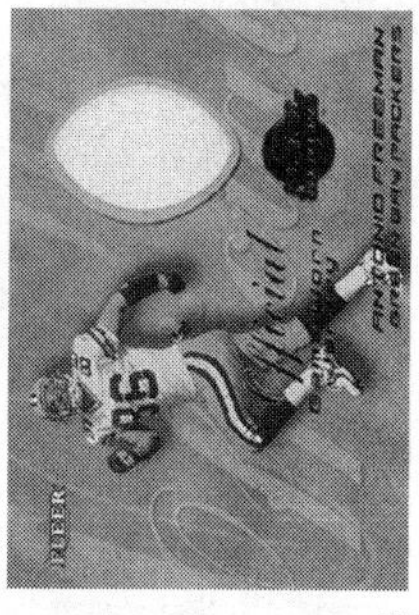

	MT
Common Player:	15.00
Inserted 1:72	
Gold Cards:	2x
Production 50 Sets	
1 Troy Aikman	50.00
2 Jamal Anderson	20.00
3 David Boston	20.00
4 Curtis Conway	15.00
5 Tim Couch	50.00
6 Germane Crowell	20.00
7 Kevin Dyson	15.00
8 Curtis Enis Pants	20.00
9 Brett Favre	60.00
10 Eddie George	40.00
11 Rob Johnson	15.00
12 Jevon Kearse	30.00
13 Peyton Manning	75.00
14 Steve McNair	40.00
15 Rob Moore	15.00
16 Johnnie Morton	15.00
17 Jake Plummer	25.00
18 Jerry Rice	50.00
19 Deion Sanders	25.00
20 Frank Sanders	15.00
21 Emmitt Smith	50.00
22 Jimmy Smith	20.00
23 J.J. Stokes	15.00
24 Fred Taylor	35.00
25 Kurt Warner Pants	100.00
26 Charles Woodson	15.00

Values quoted in this guide reflect the retail price of a card — the price a collector can expect to pay when buying a card from a dealer. The wholesale price — that which a collector can expect to receive from a dealer when selling cards — will be significantly lower, depending on desirability and condition.

2000 Fleer Showcase License to Skill

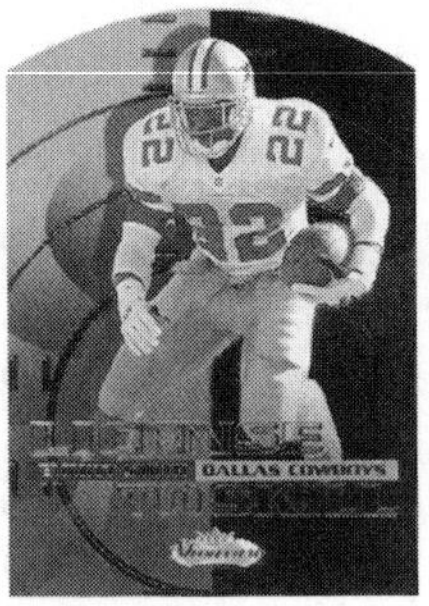

		MT
Complete Set (10):		25.00
Common Player:		2.00
Inserted 1:20		
1	Tim Couch	3.00
2	Keyshawn Johnson	2.00
3	Peyton Manning	8.00
4	Brett Favre	10.00
5	Terrell Davis	6.00
6	Cade McNown	2.00
7	Marvin Harrison	2.00
8	Eddie George	2.50
9	Randy Moss	8.00
10	Emmitt Smith	6.00

2000 Fleer Showcase Mission Possible

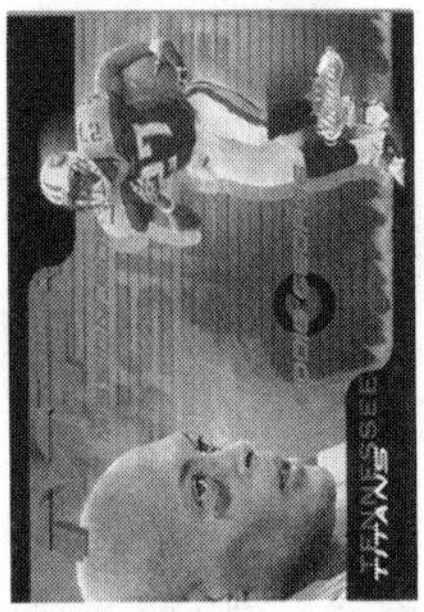

		MT
Complete Set (10):		10.00
Common Player:		.50
Inserted 1:5		
1	Tim Couch	1.25
2	Brett Favre	3.00
3	Ricky Williams	1.50
4	Akili Smith	.75
5	Shaun King	1.00
6	Marvin Harrison	.75
7	Vinny Testaverde	.50
8	Terrell Davis	2.00
9	Edgerrin James	3.00
10	Eddie George	1.00

2000 Fleer Showcase Next

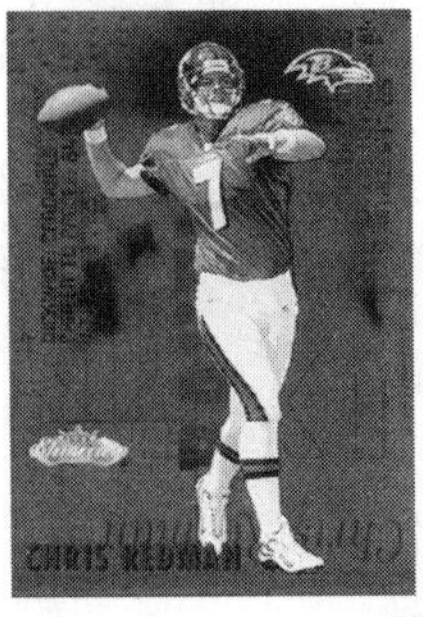

		MT
Complete Set (20):		18.00
Common Player:		.50
Inserted 1:2.5		
1	Peter Warrick	3.50
2	Bubba Franks	.75
3	Jamal Lewis	5.00
4	Anthony Becht	.50
5	R. Jay Soward	.75
6	Courtney Brown	.75
7	Plaxico Burress	2.00
8	Trung Canidate	.50
9	Chris Redman	1.50
10	Laveranues Coles	1.00
11	Ron Dayne	4.00
12	Reuben Droughns	.50
13	Danny Farmer	.50
14	Travis Prentice	1.50
15	Dez White	.50
16	Shaun Alexander	2.50
17	Thomas Jones	1.50
18	J.R. Redmond	1.00
19	Sylvester Morris	2.00
20	Chad Pennington	3.00

A player's name in *italic type* indicates a rookie card.

2000 Fleer Showcase Super Natural

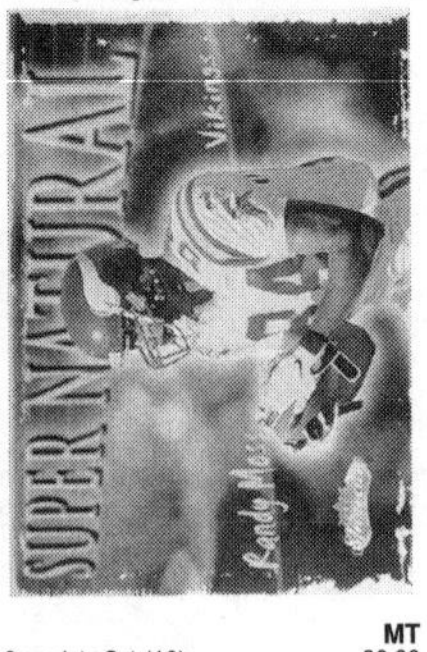

		MT
Complete Set (10):		30.00
Common Player:		2.00
Inserted 1:20		
1	Randy Moss	8.00
2	Marshall Faulk	2.00
3	Edgerrin James	8.00
4	Terrell Davis	6.00
5	Kurt Warner	10.00
6	Fred Taylor	3.00
7	Peyton Manning	8.00
8	Brett Favre	10.00
9	Brad Johnson	2.00
10	Warrick Dunn	2.00

2000 Fleer Showcase Touch Football

		MT
Complete Set (30):		625.00
Common Player:		8.00
Inserted 1:150		
1	Trung Canidate	8.00
2	Thomas Jones	25.00
3	Curtis Keaton	8.00
4	Anthony Becht	10.00
5	Courtney Brown	12.00
6	Chris Redman	25.00
7	Dennis Northcutt	12.00
8	Sylvester Morris	30.00
9	Shaun Alexander	40.00
10	Todd Pinkston	10.00
11	Danny Farmer	10.00
12	Dez White	10.00
13	Laveranues Coles	12.00
14	R. Jay Soward	12.00
15	Jamal Lewis	80.00
16	J.R. Redmond	16.00
17	Travis Taylor	16.00
18	Plaxico Burress	30.00
19	Peter Warrick	60.00
20	Joe Hamilton	12.00
21	Ron Dugans	8.00
22	Tee Martin	12.00
23	Brian Urlacher	40.00
24	Ron Dayne	70.00
25	Travis Prentice	20.00
26	Chad Pennington	50.00
27	Bubba Franks	12.00
28	Reuben Droughns	8.00
29	Corey Simon	10.00
30	Jerry Porter	10.00

1960 Fleer

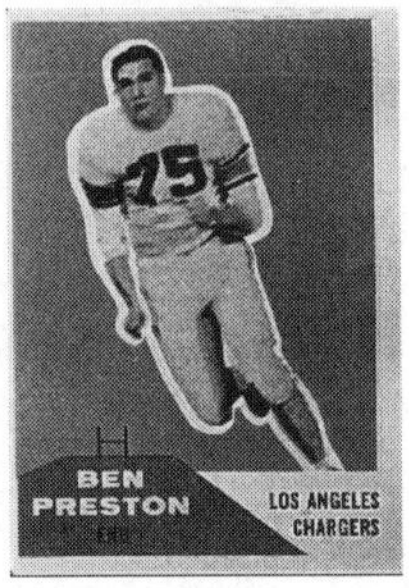

Fleer's first venture into football depicted cards of players from the newly-formed American Football League. Outside of George Blanda, Sammy Baugh and several rookie cards detailed below, the set basically features a lot of no-names, many of whom appeared on their only card with this issue. It's not surprising that this set includes the most rookie cards of any other set issued since football cards were issued. (Not coincidentally, Topps' 1984 USFL set ranks second because of the amount of rookies who played in that league.) Rookie cards in this set include Sid Gillman (as a coach - this was his only card), Lou Saban (only card), Hank Stram (only card until Pro Set announcer cards), Abner Haynes, and Ron Mix. The card that carries the set is Jack Kemp's rookie card.

		NM
Complete Set (132):		750.00
Common Player:		3.00
Wax Pack (6):		225.00
1	*Harvey White*	20.00
2	Tom "Corky" Tharp	3.00
3	Dan McGrew	3.00
4	Bob White	3.25
5	Dick Jamieson	3.00
6	Sam Salerno	3.00
7	*Sid Gillman*	15.00
8	Ben Preston	3.00
9	George Blanch	3.00
10	Bob Stransky	3.00
11	Fran Curci	3.00
12	George Shirkey	3.00
13	Paul Larson	3.00
14	John Stolte	3.00
15	*Serafino Frazio*	3.50
16	Tom Dimitroff	3.00
17	*Elbert Dubenion*	7.50
18	Hogan Wharton	3.00
19	Tom O'Connell	3.00
20	Sammy Baugh	40.00
21	Tony Sardisco	3.00
22	Alan Cann	3.00
23	Mike Hudock	3.00
24	Bill Atkins	3.00
25	Charlie Jackson	3.00
26	Frank Tripucka	4.00
27	Tony Teresa	3.00
28	Joe Amstutz	3.00
29	Bob Fee	3.00
30	Jim Baldwin	3.00
31	Jim Yates	3.00
32	Don Flynn	3.00
33	Ken Adamson	3.00
34	Ron Drzewiecki	3.00
35	J.W. Slack	3.00
36	Bob Yates	3.00
37	Gary Cobb	3.00
38	*Jacky Lee*	4.00
39	*Jack Spikes*	3.50
40	Jim Padgett	3.00
41	Jack Larsheid	3.00
42	Bob Reifsnyder	3.00
43	Fran Rogel	3.00
44	Ray Moss	3.00
45	Tony Banfield	3.25
46	George Herring	3.00
47	Willie Smith	3.00
48	Buddy Allen	3.00
49	Bill Brown	3.00
50	Ken Ford	3.00
51	Billy Kinard	3.00
52	Buddy Mayfield	3.00
53	Bill Krisher	3.25
54	Frank Bernardi	3.00
55	*Lou Saban*	3.50
56	Gene Cockrell	3.00
57	Sam Sanders	3.00
58	George Blanda	40.00
59	*Sherrill Headrick*	5.50
60	Carl Larpenter	3.00
61	Gene Prebola	3.00
62	Dick Chorovich	3.00
63	Bob McNamara	3.00
64	Tom Saidock	3.00
65	Willie Evans	3.00
66	*Billy Cannon*	16.00
67	Sam McCord	3.00
68	Mike Simmons	3.00
69	*Jim Swink*	3.50
70	Don Hitt	3.00
71	Gerhard Schwedes	3.00
72	Thurlow Cooper	3.00
73	*Abner Haynes*	16.00
74	Billy Shoemaker	3.00
75	Marv Lasater	3.00
76	*Paul Lowe*	15.00
77	Bruce Hartman	3.00
78	Blanche Martin	3.00
79	Gene Grabosky	3.00
80	Lou Rymkus	3.00
81	*Chris Burford*	5.50
82	Don Allen	3.00
83	Bob Nelson	3.00
84	Jim Woodard	3.00
85	Tom Rychlec	3.00
86	Bob Cox	3.00
87	Jerry Cornelison	3.00
88	Jack Work	3.00
89	Sam DeLuca	3.00
90	Rommie Loudd	3.00
91	Teddy Edmondson	3.00
92	Buster Ramsey	3.00
93	Doug Asad	3.00
94	Jimmy Harris	3.00
95	Lary Cundiff	3.00
96	*Richie Lucas*	3.50
97	Don Norwood	3.00
98	*Larry Grantham*	4.00
99	*Bill Mathis*	4.00
100	*Mel Branch*	4.00
101	Marvin Terrell	3.00
102	Charlie Flowers	3.25
103	John McMullan	3.00
104	Charlie Kaaihue	3.00
105	Joe Schaffer	3.00
106	Al Day	3.00
107	Johnny Carson	3.00
108	Alan Goldstein	3.00
109	Doug Cline	3.00
110	Al Carmichael	3.00
111	Bob Dee	3.00
112	John Bredice	3.00
113	Don Floyd	3.00
114	Ronnie Cain	3.00
115	Stan Flowers	3.00
116	*Hank Stram*	45.00
117	Bob Dougherty	3.00
118	*Ron Mix*	35.00
120	Elvin Caldwell	3.00
121	Bill Kimber	3.00
122	Jim Matheny	3.00
123	*Curley Johnson*	3.00
124	*Jack Kemp*	350.00
125	Ed Denk	3.00
126	Jerry McFarland	3.00
127	Dan Lamphear	3.00
128	*Paul Maguire*	16.00
129	Ray Collins	3.00
130	*Ron Burton*	5.00
131	Eddie Erdelatz	3.00
132	*Ron Beagle*	16.00

1960 Fleer Decals

This group of eight American Football League inserts was inserted in wax packs of Fleer football. The decals, which measure about 1-1/2" x 3-1/2", depict the logo of each AFL team. The decals were unnumbered.

		NM
Complete Set (8):		50.00
Common Team:		4.00
1	Boston Patriots	4.00
2	Buffalo Bills	5.00
3	Dallas Texans	5.00
4	Denver Broncos	5.00
5	Houston Oilers	5.00
6	Los Angeles Chargers	4.00
7	New York Titans	5.00
8	Oakland Raiders	5.00

1960 Fleer College Pennant Decals

This 19-decal set was also inserted into packs of 1960 Fleer Football along with the AFL Team Decals. These decals measured approximately 2-1/4" x 3" and included two colleges per card.

		NM
Complete Set (19):		180.00
Common Player:		8.00
1	Alabama/Yale	10.00
2	Army/Mississippi	8.00
3	California/Indiana	8.00
4	Duke/Notre Dame	18.00
5	Florida St./Kentucky	10.00
6	Georgia/Oklahoma	10.00
7	Houston/Iowa	8.00
8	Idaho St./Penn.	8.00
9	Iowa St./Penn State	14.00
10	Kansas/UCLA	12.00
11	Marquette/New Mexico	8.00
12	Maryland/Missouri	8.00
13	Miss.South./N.Carolina	8.00
14	Navy/Stanford	10.00
15	Nebraska/Purdue	12.00
16	Pittsburgh/Utah	8.00
17	SMU/West Virginia	8.00
18	So.Carolina/USC	10.00
19	Wake Forest/Wisconsin	10.00

1961 Fleer

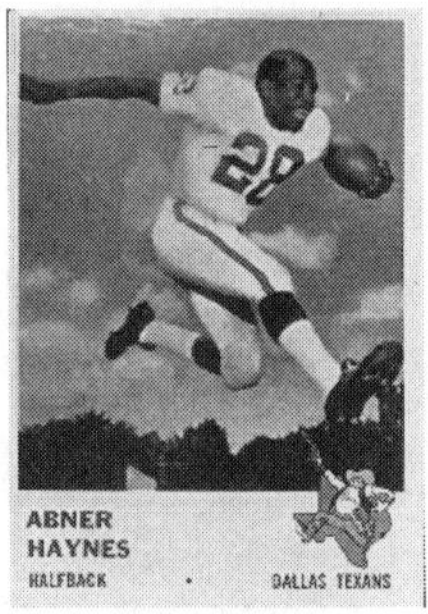

This 220-card set by Fleer - its biggest of the four it produced was the last to include NFL players (future sets would include only AFL players). Cards 1-132 showcase NFL players; 133-up depict AFLers. Cards are again grouped alphabetically by city name. A number of cards in this set are short-printed, and are indicated by (SP) in the following checklist. Rookies in the '61 Fleer issue include Don Meredith, Tom Flores, Don Maynard, and Jim Otto. Second-year cards include Night Train Lane (his rookie card was in '57), Forrest Gregg, Jerry Kramer, Jack Kemp and Ron Mix. (Key: SP meads short-printed).

		NM
Complete Set (220):		1600.
Common Player (1-132):		3.50
Common Player (133-220):		5.50
Series 1 Wax Pack (5):		215.00
Series 2 Wax Pack (5):		230.00
1	Ed Brown	12.00
2	Rick Casares	3.50
3	Willie Galimore	5.50
4	Jim Dooley	3.50
5	Harlon Hill	3.50
6	Stan Jones	5.00
7	J.C. Caroline	3.50
8	Joe Fortunato	3.50
9	Doug Atkins	6.25
10	Milt Plum	3.50
11	Jim Brown	130.00
12	Bobby Mitchell	8.00
13	Ray Renfro	3.50
14	Gern Nagler	3.50
15	Jim Shofner	3.50
16	Vince Costello	3.50
17	Galen Fiss	3.50
18	Walt Michaels	3.50
19	Bob Gain	3.50
20	Mal Hammack	3.50
21	Frank Mestnick	3.50
22	Bobby Joe Conrad	3.50
23	John David Crow	4.00
24	*Sonny Randle*	4.00
25	Don Gillis	3.50
26	Jerry Norton	3.50
27	Bill Stacy	3.50
28	Leo Sugar	3.50
29	Frank Fuller	3.50
30	John Unitas	70.00
31	Alan Ameche	8.00
32	Lenny Moore	12.00
33	Raymond Berry	12.00
34	Jim Mutscheller	3.50
35	Jim Parker	6.50
36	Bill Pellington	3.50
37	Gino Marchetti	6.00
38	Gene Lipscomb	5.50
39	Art Donovan	12.00
40	Eddie LeBaron	4.00
41	*Don Meredith*	140.00
42	Don McIlhenny	3.50
43	L.G. Dupre	3.50
44	Fred Dugan	3.50
45	Bill Howton	3.50
46	Duane Putnam	3.50
47	Gene Cronin	3.50
48	Jerry Tubbs	3.50
49	Clarence Peaks	3.50
50	*Ted Dean*	4.00
51	Tommy McDonald	3.50
52	Bill Barnes	3.50
53	Pete Retzlaff	3.50
54	Bobby Walston	3.50
55	Chuck Bednarik	12.00
56	Maxie Baughan	5.50
57	Bob Pellegrini	3.50
58	Jesse Richardson	3.50
59	*John Brodie*	50.00
60	J.D. Smith	3.50
61	*Ray Norton*	3.50
62	Monty Stickles	3.50
63	Bob St. Clair	5.00
64	Dave Baker	3.50
65	Abe Woodson	3.50
66	Matt Hazeltine	3.50
67	Leo Nomellini	7.00
68	Charley Conerly	13.00
69	Kyle Rote	5.50
70	Jack Stroud	3.50
71	Roosevelt Brown	5.00
72	Jim Patton	3.50
73	Erich Barnes	3.50
74	Sam Huff	12.00
75	Andy Robustelli	6.00
76	Dick Modzelewski	3.50
77	Roosevelt Grier	4.00
78	Earl Morrall	4.50
79	Jim Ninowski	3.50
80	*Nick Pietrosante*	4.00
81	Howard Cassady	3.50
82	Jim Gibbons	3.50
83	*Gail Cogdill*	3.50
84	Dick Lane	6.00
85	Yale Lary	6.00
86	Joe Schmidt	6.50
87	Darris McCord	3.50
88	Bart Starr	50.00
89	Jim Taylor	30.00
90	Paul Hornung	45.00
91	*Tom Moore*	5.00
92	*Boyd Dowler*	8.00
93	Max McGee	3.50
94	*Forrest Gregg*	8.50
95	Jerry Kramer	7.50
96	Jim Ringo	6.50
97	Bill Forester	3.50
98	Frank Ryan	3.50
99	Ollie Matson	9.50
100	Jon Arnett	3.50
101	*Dick Bass*	4.00
102	Jim Phillips	3.50
103	Del Shofner	3.50
104	Art Hunter	3.50
105	Lindon Crow	3.50
106	Les Richter	4.00
107	Lou Michaels	3.50
108	Ralph Guglielmi	4.00
109	Don Bosseler	3.50
110	John Olszewski	3.50
111	Bill Anderson	3.50
112	Joe Walton	4.00
113	Jim Schrader	3.50
114	Gary Glick	3.50
115	Ralph Felton	3.50
116	Bob Toneff	3.50
117	Bobby Layne	25.00
118	John Henry Johnson	8.00
119	Tom Tracy	3.50
120	*Jimmy Orr*	6.50
121	John Nisby	3.50
122	Dean Derby	3.50
123	John Reger	3.50
124	George Tarsovic	3.50
125	Ernie Stautner	6.00
126	George Shaw	3.50
127	Hugh McElhenny	9.00
128	Dick Haley	3.50
129	Dave Middleton	3.50
130	Perry Richards	3.50
131	Gene Johnson	3.50
132	Don Joyce	3.50
133	John "Chuck" Green	5.50
134	*Wray Carlton*	5.50
135	Richie Lucas	5.50
136	Elbert Dubenion	5.50
137	Tom Rychlec (SP)	5.50
138	Mark Yoho (SP)	5.50
139	Phil Blazer (SP)	5.50
140	Dan McGrew (SP)	5.50
141	Bill Atkins	5.50
142	*Archie Matsos*	5.50
143	Gene Grabosky	5.50
144	Frank Tripucka	6.00
145	Al Carmichael (SP)	6.00
146	Bob McNamara (SP)	6.00
147	*Lionel Taylor* (SP)	12.00
148	Eldon Danenhauer (SP)	6.00
149	Willie Smith	5.50
150	Carl Larpenter	5.50
151	Ken Adamson	5.50
152	*Goose Gonsoulin*	5.50
153	Joe Young (SP)	4.00
154	Gordy Molz (SP)	4.00
155	Jack Kemp (SP)	230.00
156	Charlie Flowers (SP)	6.00
157	Paul Lowe	7.00
158	Don Norton	5.50
159	Howard Clark	5.50
160	Paul Maguire	15.00
161	*Ernie Wright* (SP)	6.00
162	Ron Mix (SP)	16.00
163	Fred Cole (SP)	6.00
164	Jim Sears (SP)	6.00
165	Volney Peters	5.50
166	George Blanda	45.00
167	Jacky Lee	5.50
168	Bob White	5.50
169	Doug Cline (SP)	6.00
170	Dave Smith (SP)	6.00
171	Billy Cannon (SP)	8.00
172	Bill Groman (SP)	6.00
173	Al Jamison	5.50
174	Jim Norton	5.50
175	Dennit Morris	5.50
176	Don Floyd	5.50
177	Butch Songin (SP)	6.00
178	Billy Lott (SP)	6.00
179	Ron Burton (SP)	6.00
180	Jim Colchough (SP)	6.00
181	Charley Leo	5.50
182	Walt Cudzik	5.50
183	Fred Bruney	5.50
184	Ross O'Hanley	5.50
185	Tony Sardisco (SP)	6.00
186	Harry Jacobs (SP)	6.00
187	Bob Dee (SP)	6.00
188	*Tom Flores* (SP)	35.00
189	Jack Larsheid	5.50
190	Dick Christy	5.50
191	Alan Miller	5.50
192	Jim Smith	5.50
193	Gerald Burch (SP)	6.00
194	Gene Prebola (SP)	6.00
195	Alan Goldstein (SP)	6.00
196	Don Manoukian (SP)	6.00
197	*Jim Otto*	60.00
198	Wayne Crow	5.50
199	*Cotton Davidson*	5.50
200	*Randy Duncan*	5.50
201	Jack Spikes (SP)	6.00
202	*Johnny Robinson* (SP)	12.00
203	Abner Haynes (SP)	6.00
204	Chris Burford (SP)	6.00
205	Bill Krisher	5.50
206	Marvin Terrell	5.50
207	Jimmy Harris	5.50
208	Mel Branch (SP)	6.00
209	Paul Miller (SP)	6.00
210	Al Dorow (SP)	6.00
211	Dick Jamieson (SP)	6.00
212	Pete Hart	5.50
213	Bill Shockley	5.50
214	Dewey Bohling	5.50
215	*Don Maynard*	90.00
216	Bob Mischak	5.50
217	Mike Hudock (SP)	6.00
218	Bob Reifsnyder (SP)	6.00
219	Tom Saidock (SP)	6.00
220	Sid Youngelman (SP)	22.00

1961 Fleer Magic Message Blue Inserts

These 40 cards, which pose a trivia question on the front, instruct collectors to turn and wet the card to determine the answer. A line drawing also appears on the front, as does a card number, which is located in the lower right corner. Along the bottom of the card is a tag line which indicates the cards were printed by Business Service of Long Island, N.Y. The blank-backed cards, measuring 3" x 2-1/8", were inserts in 1961 Fleer football packs.

		NM
Complete Set (40):		125.00
Common Player:		4.00
1	First Sugar Bowl game	4.00
2	Point-A-Minute team	4.00
3	Gloomy Gil	4.00
4	College record for years coached	4.00
5	Two Platoon System	4.00
6	The only Sudden Death playoff	4.00
7	Sudden Death playoff	4.00
8	Longest field goal	4.00
9	Colorado All-American	5.00
10	Michigan All-American sportscaster	5.00
11	First North-South game	4.00
12	First Army-Navy game	4.00
13	Outfielder/All-American back	5.00
14	All-American Mr. Inside & Mr. Outside	5.00
15	The Thundering Herd	4.00
16	First NFL Championship playoff	4.00
17	Record for field goals dropkicked	4.00
18	Longest college winning streak	4.00
19	First collegian drafted	4.00
20	First team to use the huddle	4.00
21	The first Intercollegiate Champion	4.00
22	The first broadcast	4.00
23	The longest field goal	4.00
24	The tackling dummy	4.00
25	Greatest player in teh half-century	5.00
26	The most touchdowns in a game	4.00
27	Who ran the wrong way?	4.00
28	The first college field goal	4.00
29	The first All-American team	4.00
30	The forward pass	4.00
31	The first college to use numbers	4.00
32	The first professional football game	4.00
33	Where is the Football Hall of Fame?	4.00
34	The Four Horsemen	5.00
35	The first Rose Bowl	4.00
36	Record for forward passes in a prof gam	4.00
37	Galloping Ghost	5.00
38	Rose Bowl in California	4.00
39	Seven Blocks of Granite	4.00
40	First game in the U.S.	4.00

1962 Fleer

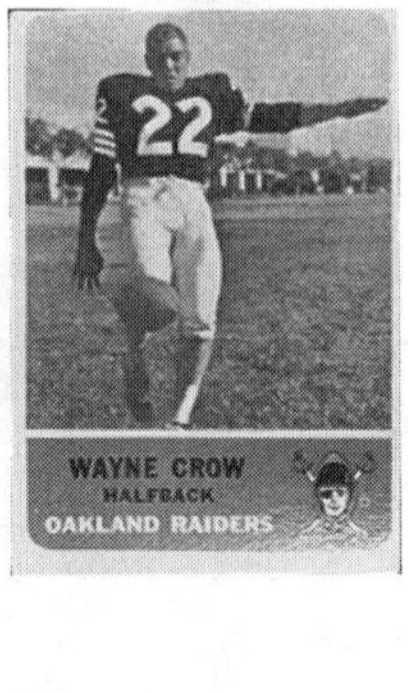

Fleer's third of four early '60s sets included only AFL players this time around. Cards are again grouped by team, alphabetically by city. The only rookie card of note in this set is Gino Cappelletti; second-year cards in this issue are Don Maynard, Tom Flores and Jim Otto.

		NM
Complete Set (88):		800.00
Common Player:		6.00
Wax Pack (6):		375.00
1	Billy Lott	15.00
2	Ron Burton	7.00
3	*Gino Cappelletti*	17.00
4	Babe Parilli	7.00
5	Jim Colclough	6.00
6	Tony Sardisco	6.00
7	Walt Cudzik	6.00
8	Bob Dee	6.00
9	Tommy Addison	6.50
10	Harry Jacobs	6.00
11	Ross O'Hanley	6.00
12	Art Baker	6.00
13	John "Chuck" Green	6.00
14	Elbert Dubenion	3.00
15	Tom Rychlec	6.00
16	*Billy Shaw*	8.50
17	Ken Rice	6.00
18	Bill Atkins	6.00
19	Richie Lucas	6.00
20	Archie Matsos	6.00
21	Lavern Torczon	6.00
22	Warren Rabb	6.00
23	Jack Spikes	6.00
24	Cotton Davidson	6.00
25	*Abner Haynes*	9.00
26	Jimmy Saxton	6.00
27	Chris Burford	6.00
28	Bill Miller	6.00
29	Sherrill Headrick	6.00
30	*E.J. Holub*	9.50
31	*Jerry Mays*	9.00
32	Mel Branch	6.00
33	Paul Rochester	6.00
34	Frank Tripucka	8.00
35	Gene Mingo	6.00
36	Lionel Taylor	9.50
37	Ken Adamson	6.00
38	Eldon Danenhauer	6.00
39	Goose Gonsoulin	6.00
40	Gordy Holz	6.00
41	Bud McFadin	6.00
42	Jim Stinnette	6.00
43	Bob Hudson	6.00
44	George Herring	6.00
45	*Charley Tolar*	7.50
46	George Blanda	55.00
47	Billy Cannon	10.00
48	*Charlie Hennigan*	16.00
49	Bill Groman	6.00
50	Al Jamison	6.00
51	Tony Banfield	6.00
52	Jim Norton	6.00
53	Dennit Morris	6.00
54	Don Floyd	6.00
55	Ed Husmann	6.00
56	Robert Brooks	6.00
57	Al Dorow	6.00
58	Dick Christy	6.00
59	Don Maynard	35.00
60	Art Powell	10.00
61	Mike Hudock	6.00
62	Bill Mathis	6.00
63	Butch Songin	6.00
64	Larry Grantham	6.50
65	Nick Mumley	6.00
66	Tom Saidock	6.00
67	Alan Miller	6.00
68	Tom Flores	10.00
69	Bob Coolbaugh	6.00
70	George Fleming	6.00
71	*Wayne Hawkins*	6.00
72	Jim Otto	25.00
73	Wayne Crow	6.00
74	*Fred Willamson*	20.00
75	Tom Lauderback	6.00
76	Volney Peters	6.00
77	Charley Powell	6.00
78	Don Norton	6.00
79	Jack Kemp	250.00
80	Paul Lowe	9.00
81	Dave Kocourek	6.00
82	Ron Mix	13.00
83	Ernie Wright	6.00
84	Dick Harris	6.00
85	Bill Hudson	6.00
86	*Ernie Ladd*	30.00
87	Earl Faison	7.00
88	*Ron Nery*	15.00

1963 Fleer

After a four-year run, this 89-card set (88 player cards plus an unnumbered checklist) was the company's football farewell. (Fleer printed football "Teams in Action" sets in the '70s and '80s that featured NFL offenses and defenses, but apparently was unable to obtain a contract allowing the production of individual player cards. The 1963 Fleer football set showcases three of the most sought-after and rarest cards of the '60s - the checklist card (almost impossible to find in Mint condition), and cards #6 (Charles Long) and #64 (Bob Dougherty). The latter two cards were short-printed; it's believed both were pulled to make room for the checklist. The set includes AFL players only. Rookies featured in the set are Nick Buoniconti, Cookie Gilchrist, Keith Lincoln, Len Dawson and Lance Alworth. Gino Cappelletti's second-year card is in the set as well. (Key: SP means short-printed).

		NM
Complete Set (88):		1900.
Common Player:		8.00
Checklist:		350.00
Wax Pack (5):		430.00
1	*Larry Garron*	17.00
2	Babe Parilli	9.00
3	Ron Burton	8.00
4	Jim Colclough	8.00
5	Gino Cappelletti	11.00
6	*Charles Long (SP)*	180.00
7	*Bill Neighbors*	10.00
8	Dick Felt	8.00
9	Tommy Addison	8.00
10	*Nick Buoniconti*	75.00
11	Larry Eisenhauer	10.00
12	Bill Mathis	8.00
13	*Lee Grosscup*	10.00
14	Dick Christy	8.00
15	Don Maynard	45.00
16	*Alex Kroll*	8.00
17	Bob Mischak	8.00
18	Dainard Paulson	8.00
19	Lee Riley	8.00
20	Larry Grantham	8.00
21	Hubert Bobo	8.00
22	Nick Mumley	8.00
23	*Cookie Gilchrist*	40.00
24	Jack Kemp	250.00
25	Wray Carlton	8.00
26	Elbert Dubenion	8.00
27	Ernie Warlick	8.00
28	Billy Shaw	8.00
29	Ken Rice	8.00
30	Booker Edgerson	8.00
31	Ray Abbruzzese	8.00
32	Mike Stratton	9.00
33	Tom Sestak	10.00
34	Charlie Tolar	8.00
35	Dave Smith	8.00
36	George Blanda	55.00
37	Billy Cannon	9.00
38	Charlie Hennegan	13.00
39	*Bob Talamini*	10.00
40	Jim Norton	8.00
41	Tony Banfield	8.00
42	Doug Cline	8.00
43	Don Floyd	8.00
44	Ed Husmann	8.00
45	*Curtis McClinton*	12.00
46	Jack Spikes	8.00
47	*Len Dawson*	250.00
48	Abner Haynes	10.00
49	Chris Burford	8.00
50	*Fred Arbanas*	12.00
51	Johnny Robinson	9.00
52	E.J. Holub	8.00
53	Sherrill Headrick	8.00
54	Mel Branch	8.00
55	Jerry Mays	8.00
56	Cotton Davidson	8.00
57	*Clem Daniels*	15.00
58	Bo Roberson	8.00
59	Art Powell	10.00
60	Bob Coolbaugh	8.00
61	Wayne Hawkins	8.00
62	Jim Otto	30.00
63	Fred Williamson	9.00
64	Bob Dougherty (SP)	230.00
65	Dalva Allen	8.00
66	Chuck McMutry	8.00
67	Gerry McDougall	8.00
68	Tobin Rote	9.00
69	Paul Lowe	10.00
70	*Keith Lincoln*	25.00
71	Dave Kocourek	8.00
72	*Lance Alworth*	250.00
73	Ron Mix	22.00
74	*Charles McNeil*	10.00
75	Emil Karas	8.00
76	Ernie Ladd	15.00
77	Earl Faison	8.00
78	Jim Stinnette	8.00
79	Frank Tripucka	9.50
80	Don Stone	8.00
81	Bob Scarpitto	8.00
82	Lionel Taylor	10.50
83	Jerry Tarr	8.00
84	Eldon Danehauer	8.00
85	Goose Gonsoulin	8.00
86	Jim Fraser	8.00
87	Chuck Gavin	10.00
88	Bud McFadin	16.00

1972 Fleer Quiz

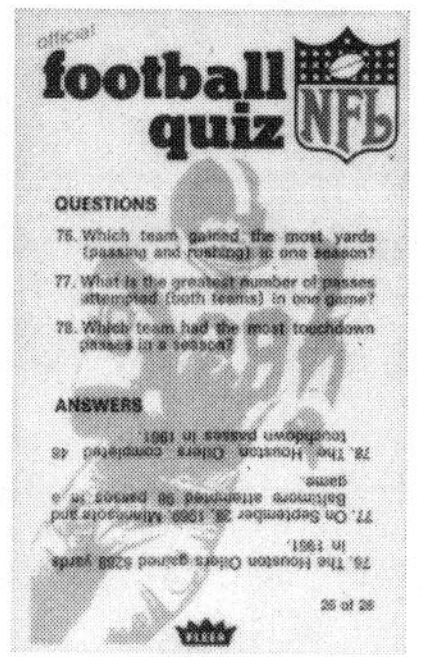

This 28-card set was issued at a rate of one per pack with Fleer cloth team patches. Cards measure 2-1/2" x 4" and feature three questions about players and events, with answers upside down. Each card has the words "Official Football Quiz" across the top, a card number in the lower right hand corner and a blank back.

		NM
Complete Set (28):		45.00
Common Player:		2.50
1	Questions 1-3	2.50
2	Questions 4-6	2.50
3	Questions 7-9	2.50
4	Questions 10-12	2.50
5	Questions 13-15	2.50
6	Questions 16-18	2.50
7	Questions 19-21	2.50
8	Questions 22-24	2.50
9	Questions 25-27	2.50
10	Questions 28-30	2.50
11	Questions 31-33	2.50
12	Questions 34-36	2.50
13	Questions 37-39	2.50
14	Questions 40-42	2.50
15	Questions 43-45	2.50
16	Questions 46-48	2.50
17	Questions 49-51	2.50
18	Questions 52-54	2.50
19	Questions 55-57	2.50
20	Questions 58-60	2.50
21	Questions 61-63	2.50
22	Questions 64-66	2.50
23	Questions 67-69	2.50
24	Questions 70-72	2.50
25	Questions 73-75	2.50
26	Questions 76-78	2.50
27	Questions 79-81	2.50
28	Questions 82-84	2.50

1973 Fleer Pro Bowl Scouting Report

The 14-card, blank backed set explains the ideal responsibilities and assignments of each player on an NFL team. These unnumbered cards were found at a rate of one per pack with two cloth football logos from 1972.

		NM
Complete Set (14):		35.00
Common Player:		3.00
1	Center	3.00
2	Cornerback	3.00
3	Defensive End	3.00
4	Defensive Tackle	3.00
5	Guard	3.00
6	Kicker	3.00
7	Linebacker	3.00
8	Offensive Tackle	3.00
9	Punter	3.00
10	Quarterback	3.00
11	Running Back	3.00
12	Safety	3.00
13	Tight End	3.00
14	Wide Receiver	3.00

1974 Fleer Big Signs

The 1974 version of Big Signs is generally considered a Series II issue, but is credited to 1968 in roman numerals on the back. The cards measure 7-3/4" x 11-1/2" and have blank backs that are unnumbered. The 1974 set was issued in a brown box, while the fronts contain generic, faceless color drawings. Two 26-card Big Signs sets were produced by Fleer that carry a 1968 copyright on them, but one released in 1970 with this series releasing in 1974. The former version was issued in a green box and contains the team name in small letters across the top, while the 1974 version has the team name in bold letters across the card bottom.

		NM
Complete Set (26):		45.00
Common Player:		2.50
1	Atlanta Falcons	2.50
2	Baltimore Colts	2.50
3	Buffalo Bills	2.50
4	Chicago Bears	4.00
5	Cincinnati Bengals	2.50
6	Cleveland Browns	2.50
7	Dallas Cowboys	4.00
8	Denver Broncos	2.50
9	Detroit Lions	2.50
10	Green Bay Packers	4.00
11	Houston Oilers	2.50
12	Kansas City Chiefs	2.50
13	Los Angeles Rams	2.50
14	Miami Dolphins	4.00
15	Minnesota Vikings	2.50
16	New England Patriots	2.50
17	New Orleans Saints	2.50
18	New York Giants	2.50
19	New York Jets	2.50
20	Oakland Raiders	4.00
21	Philadelphia Eagles	2.50
22	Pittsburgh Steelers	4.00
23	St. Louis Cardinals	2.50
24	San Diego Chargers	2.50
25	San Francisco 49ers	4.00
26	Washington Redskins	4.00

1974 Fleer Hall of Fame

These cards were issued one per pack, along with two cloth stickers featuring team logos. Each card front has a black- and-white player action photo, with a set logo and "The Immortal Role" at the bottom of the card. The cards, which are unnumbered, are listed below alphabetically and feature 50 players who have been enshrined in the Pro Football Hall of Fame in Canton, Ohio. The Hall of Fame logo appears on the back of the card, along with biographical information about the player. Each card measures 2-1/2" x 4".

		NM
Complete Set (50):		50.00
Common Player:		1.00
(1)	Cliff Battles	1.00
(2)	Sammy Baugh	1.50
(3)	Chuck Bednarik	1.00
(4)	Bert Bell	1.00
(5)	Paul Brown	1.00
(6)	Joe Carr	1.00
(7)	Guy Chamberlin	1.00
(8)	Earl "Dutch" Clark	1.00
(9)	Jimmy Conzelman	1.00
(10)	Art Donovan	1.00
(11)	John (Paddy) Driscoll	1.00
(12)	Billy Dudley	1.00
(13)	Dan Fortmann	1.00
(14)	Otto Graham	1.00
(15)	Red Grange	2.00
(16)	George Halas	1.00
(17)	Mel Hein	1.00
(18)	Fats Henry	1.25
(19)	Bill Hewitt	1.00
(20)	Clarke Hinkle	1.25
(21)	Elroy (Crazylegs) Hirsch	1.00
(22)	Robert (Cal) Hubbard	1.00
(23)	Lamar Hunt	1.00
(24)	Don Hutson	1.00
(25)	Earl (Curly) Lambeau	1.25
(26)	Bobby Layne	1.00
(27)	Vince Lombardi	2.00
(28)	Sid Luckman	1.00
(29)	Gino Marchetti	1.25
(30)	Ollie Matson	1.00
(31)	George McAfee	1.00
(32)	Hugh McElhenny	1.00
(33)	Johnny (Blood) McNally	1.00
(34)	Marion Motley	1.00
(35)	Bronko Nagurski	1.50
(36)	Ernie Nevers	1.00
(37)	Leo Nomellini	1.25
(38)	Steve Owen	1.00
(39)	Joe Perry	1.00
(40)	Pete Pihos	1.25
(41)	Andy Robustelli	1.00
(42)	Ken Strong	1.00
(43)	Jim Thorpe	2.00
(44)	Y.A. Tittle	1.00
(45)	Charlie Trippi	1.00
(46)	Emlen Tunnell	1.25
(47)	Clyde "Bulldog" Turner	1.00
(48)	Norm Van Brocklin	1.00
(49)	Steve Van Buren	1.00
(50)	Bob Waterfield	1.25

1975 Fleer Hall of Fame

These 84 cards, which feature players who have been inducted into the Football Hall of Fame, can be distinguished from the 1974 cards by the card numbers which appear on the card backs. Fifty of the cards in the set are similar to the 1974 cards, except the fronts have brown borders, not white ones like the 1974 cards have. Each card measures 2-1/2" x 4". They were issued in wax packs along with cloth team logo stickers.

		NM
Complete Set (84):		30.00
Common Player:		.35
1	Jim Thorpe	1.00
2	Cliff Battles	.35
3	Bronko Nagurski	.75
4	Harold Grange	1.00
5	Guy Chamberlin	.35
6	Joe Carr	.35
7	George Halas	.50
8	Jimmy Conzelman	.35
9	George McAfee	.35
10	Clarke Hinkle	.35
11	John Driscoll	.35
12	Mel Hein	.35
13	Johnny McNally	.35
14	Earl Clark	.35
15	Steve Owen	.35
16	Bill Hewitt	.35
17	Robert Hubbard	.35
18	Don Hutson	.50
19	Ernie Nevers	.50
20	Dan Fortmann	.35
21	Ken Strong	.35
22	Chuck Bednarik	.50
23	Bert Bell	.50
24	Paul Brown	.50
25	Art Donovan	.50
26	Bill Dudley	.35
27	Otto Graham	1.00
28	Fats Henry	.35
29	Elroy Hirsch	.50
30	Lamar Hunt	.50
31	Earl Lambeau	.75
32	Vince Lombardi	.75
33	Sid Luckman	.75
34	Gino Marchetti	.50
35	Ollie Matson	.50
36	Hugh McElhenny	.50
37	Marion Motley	.50
38	Leo Nomellini	.35
39	Joe Perry	.50
40	Andy Robustelli	.35
41	Pete Pihos	.35
42	Y.A. Tittle	.50
43	Charlie Trippi	.35
44	Emlen Tunnell	.35
45	Clyde Turner	.35
46	Norm Van Brocklin	.50
47	Steve Van Buren	.50
48	Bob Waterfield	.75
49	Bobby Layne	.50
50	Sammy Baugh	1.00
51	Joe Guyon	.35
52	William Roy Lyman	.35
53	George Trafton	.35
54	Albert G. Edwards	.35
55	Ed Healey	.35
56	Mike Michalske	.35
57	Alex Wojciechowicz	.35
58	Dante Lavelli	.35
59	George Connor	.35
60	Wayne Millner	.35
61	Jack Christiansen	.35
62	Roosevelt Brown	.35
63	Joe Stydahar	.35
64	Ernie Stautner	.35
65	Jim Parker	.50
66	Raymond Berry	.50
67	George Preston Marshall	.35
68	Clarence Parker	.50
69	Earle Neale	.35
70	Tim Mara	.35
71	Hugh Ray	.35
72	Tom Fears	.50
73	Arnie Herber	.35
74	Walt Kiesling	.35
75	Frank Kinard	.35
76	Tony Canadeo	.35
77	Bill George	.35
78	Art Rooney	.50
79	Joe Schmidt	.50
80	Dan Reeves	.35
81	Lou Groza	.50
82	Charles W. Bidwill	.35
83	Lenny Moore	.50
84	Dick Lane	.50

1976 Fleer Team Action

Beginning in 1976, and continuing through 1988, Fleer produced a series of "Team Action" cards showing football action shots but not identifying the individual players. All cards measure the standard 2-1/2" x 3-1/2". Because the sets did not contain individual player cards they have held little interest for collectors, and very few cards have any premium value. Generally, only the cards priced above common price are those with recognizable superstars prominently displayed in the action scene. The various years of issue can be determined by the border color on the front and the copyright date on the back. Sets from 1976 through 1984 and 1987 and 1988 feature an odd-numbered offensive card and an even-numbered defensive card for each NFL team. The backs list statistics from the previous year. In 1985 and 1986 each team had a third "In Action" card added - the backs of which show team schedules for the upcoming season. All sets (except 1988) are essentially numbered to correspond to team-city alphabetical order. The 1976 set is actually comprised of 66 stickercards and is quite scarce. For each subsequent year (up through 1980) the number of cards in the set was increased by one, adding a card for the most recent Super Bowl. Beginning in 1981, all sets were enlarged to 88 cards. Fleer's initial set in 1976 has two cards per team, plus 10 Super Bowl cards. The cards were issued in four-card wax packs, without inserts. It includes a Jack Lambert "rookie", a Joe Namath (not found in Topps) and the only team action card of O.J. Simpson.

		NM
Complete Set (66):		375.00
Common Card:		5.00
Common SB Card:		7.50
1	Baltimore Colts (High Scorers)	5.25
2	Baltimore Colts (Effective Tackle)	5.00
3	Buffalo Bills (Perfect Blocking)	5.00
4	Buffalo Bills (The Sack)	5.00
5	Cincinnati Bengals (Being Hit Behind The Runner)	5.00
6	Cincinnati Bengals (Franco Harris) (A Little Help)	9.00
7	Cleveland Browns (Blocking Tight End)	5.00
8	Cleveland Browns (Stopping the Double Threat)	5.00
9	Denver Broncos (The Swing Pass)	5.00
10	Denver Broncos (The Gang Tackle)	5.00
11	Houston Oilers (Dan Pastorini) (Short Zone Flooded)	6.00
12	Houston Oilers (Franco Harris) (Run Stoppers)	9.00
13	Kansas City Chiefs (Off On the Ball)	5.00
14	Kansas City Chiefs (Forcing the Scramble)	5.00
15	Miami Dolphins (Bob Griese) (Pass Protection)	10.00
16	Miami Dolphins (Natural Turf)	6.00
17	New England Patriots (Quicker Than the Eye)	5.00
18	New England Patriots (The Rugby Touch)	5.00
19	New York Jets (John Riggins, Joe Namath) (They Run, Too)	16.50
20	New York Jets (O.J. Simpson) (The Buck Stops Here)	15.00
21	Oakland Raiders (A Strong Offense)	6.00
22	Oakland Raiders (High and Low)	6.00
23	Pittsburgh Steelers (Terry Bradshaw, Franco Harris, Rocky Bleier) (The Pitch-Out)	14.00
24	Pittsburgh Steelers (Jack Lambert) (The Takeaway)	15.00
25	San Diego Chargers (Run to Daylight)	5.00
26	San Diego Chargers (The Swarm)	5.00
27	Tampa Bay Buccaneers (Stadium)	5.00
28	Tampa Bay Bucaneers (Buccaneers Uniform)	5.00
29	Atlanta Falcons (A Key Block)	5.00
30	Atlanta Falcons (Robert Newhouse) (Breakthrough)	5.00
31	Chicago Bears (An Inside Look)	5.00
32	Chicago Bears (Defensive Emphasis)	5.00
33	Dallas Cowboys (Robert Newhouse) (Eight-Yard Burst)	6.00
34	Dallas Cowboys (The Big Return)	6.00
35	Detroit Lions (Power Sweep)	5.00
36	Detroit Lions (A Tough Defense)	5.00
37	Green Bay Packers (Tearaway Gain)	5.00
38	Green Bay Packers (Good Support)	5.00
39	Los Angeles Rams	5.00
40	Los Angeles Rams (Low-Point Defense)	5.00
41	Minnesota Vikings (Fran Tarkenton, Chuck Foreman) (The Running Guards)	10.00
42	Minnesota Vikings (A Stingy Defense)	5.00
43	New York Giants (The Quick Opener)	5.00
44	New York Giants (Defending a Tradition)	5.00
45	New Orleans Saints (Archie Manning) (Head for the Hole)	6.00
46	New Orleans Saints (The Contain Man)	5.00
47	Philadelphia Eagles (Line Signals)	5.00
48	Philadelphia Eagles (Don't Take Sides)	5.00
49	San Francisco 49ers (The Clues)	5.00
50	San Francisco 49ers (Goal-Line Stand)	5.00
51	St. Louis Cardinals (Jim Hart) (Nonskid Handoff)	6.00
52	St. Louis Cardinals (Strong Pursuit)	5.00
53	Seattle Seahawks (Stadium)	5.25
54	Seattle Seahawks (Uniform)	5.25
55	Washington Redskins (Billy Kilmer) (A Fancy Passing)	6.00
56	Washington Redskins (Chris Hanburger) (Let's Go Defense)	5.00
57	Super Bowl I (Jim Taylor) (Green Bay vs. Kansas City)	7.50
58	Super Bowl II (Ben Davidson) (Green Bay vs. Oakland)	7.50
59	Super Bowl III (New York vs. Baltimore)	7.50
60	Super Bowl IV (Kansas City vs. Minnesota)	7.50
61	Super Bowl V (Baltimore vs. Dallas)	7.50
62	Super Bowl VI (Roger Staubach, Walt Garrison) (Dallas vs. Miami)	16.00
63	Super Bowl VII (Larry Csonka) (Miami vs. Washington)	9.50
64	Super Bowl VIII (Larry Csonka) (Miami vs. Minnesota)	9.50
65	Super Bowl IX (Pittsburgh vs. Minnesota)	7.50
66	Super Bowl X (Terry Bradshaw, Franco Harris) (Pittsburgh vs. Dallas)	19.00

1977 Fleer Team Action

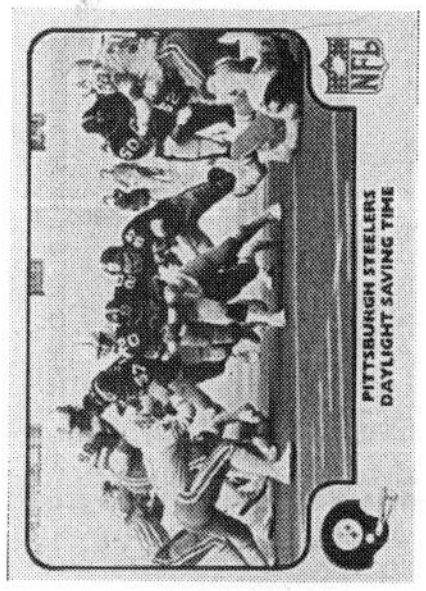

The 1977 set Fleer set has white borders and is complete at 67 cards, two for each NFL team and one for each Super Bowl. Odd-numbered cards picture offensive teams; defensive squads are on even-numbered cards. The set features Joe Namath (not found in 1977 Topps) and two different first-year Fleer Walter Payton cards. The packs had four cards and four team logo stickers.

		NM
Complete Set (67):		80.00
Common Card:		1.00
Common SB Card:		1.50
1	Baltimore Colts (Bert Jones) (The Easy Chair)	1.75
2	Baltimore Colts (A Handy Solution)	1.00
3	Buffalo Bills (Blocking Tight End)	1.00
4	Buffalo Bills (Search and Destroy)	1.00
5	Cincinnati Bengals (Ken Anderson) (Cutting on a Rug)	1.50
6	Cincinnati Bengals (Strength in the Middle)	1.00
7	Cleveland Browns (Brian Sipe) (Snap, Drop, Set)	1.25
8	Cleveland Browns (High and Low)	1.00
9	Denver Broncos (Green Light)	1.25
10	Denver Broncos (Help From Behind)	1.25

11 Houston Oilers (Room to Move) 1.00
12 Houston Oilers (For The Defense) 1.00
13 Kansas City Chiefs (Chance to Motor) 1.00
14 Kansas City Chiefs (From the Ground Up) 1.00
15 Miami Dolphins (Eye of the Storm) 1.25
16 Miami Dolphins (When Man Takes Flight) 1.25
17 New England Patriots (Turning the Corner) 1.00
18 New England Patriots (A Matter of Inches) 1.00
19 New York Jets (Joe Namath) (Keeping Him Clean) 7.25
20 New York Jets (Plugging the Leaks) 1.00
21 Oakland Raiders (On Solid Ground) 1.25
22 Oakland Raiders (3-4 and Shut the Door) 1.25
23 Pittsburgh Steelers (Rocky Bleier) (Daylight Saving Time) 1.25
24 Pittsburgh Steelers (A Controlled Swarm) 1.25
25 San Diego Chargers (Dan Fouts) (Youth on the Move) 3.75
26 San Diego Chargers (A Rude Housewarming) 1.00
27 Seattle Seahawks (Jim Zorn) (Play Action Pass) 2.00
28 Seattle Seahawks (Birds of Prey) 1.25
29 Atlanta Falcons (Ad-Libbing on Defense) 1.00
30 Atlanta Falcons (A Futile Chase) 1.00
31 Chicago Bears (Walter Payton) (Follow Me) 6.75
32 Chicago Bears (A Nose for the Ball) 1.00
33 Dallas Cowboys (The Plunge) 1.25
34 Dallas Cowboys (Ed "Too Tall" Jones) (Unassisted Sack) 3.00
35 Detroit Lions (Motor City Might) 1.00
36 Detroit Lions (Block Party) 1.00
37 Green Bay Packers (Another Era) 1.00
38 Green Bay Packers (Walter Payton) (Face-to-Face) 6.50
39 Los Angeles Rams (Personal Escort) 1.00
40 Los Angeles Rams (A Closed Case) 1.00
41 Minnesota Vikings (Nothing Fancy) 1.00
42 Minnesota Vikings (Lending a Hand) 1.00
43 New Orleans Saints (Ample Protection) 1.00
44 New Orleans Saints (Well-Timed Contact) 1.00
45 New York Giants (Quick Pitch) 1.00
46 New York Giants (In a Pinch) 1.00
47 Philadelphia Eagles (When to Fly) 1.00
48 Philadelphia Eagles (Swooping Defense) 1.00
49 St. Louis Cardinals (Jim Hart) (Speed Outside) 1.25
50 St. Louis Cardinals (The Circle Tightens) 1.00
51 San Francisco 49ers (Gene Washington) (Sideline Route) 1.25
52 San Francisco 49ers (The Gold Rush) 1.00
53 Tampa Bay Buccaneers (A Rare Occasion) 1.00
54 Tampa Bay Buccaneers (Expansion Blues) 1.00
55 Washington Redskins (Joe Theismann) (Splitting the Seam) 2.75
56 Washington Redskins (The Hands of Time) 1.00
57 Super Bowl I (Green Bay vs. Kansas City) 1.50
58 Super Bowl II (Green Bay vs. Oakland) 1.50
59 Super Bowl III (Tom Matte) (New York vs. Baltimore) 1.50
60 Super Bowl IV (Kansas City vs. Minnesota) 1.50
61 Super Bowl V (Baltimore vs. Dallas) 1.50
62 Super Bowl VI (Walt Garrison, Roger Staubach) (Dallas vs. Miami) 4.25
63 Super Bowl VII (Larry Csonka) (Miami vs. Washington) 2.25
64 Super Bowl VIII (Larry Csonka) (Miami vs. Minnesota) 2.25
65 Super Bowl IX (Pittsburgh vs. Minnesota) 1.50
66 Super Bowl X (Terry Bradshaw, Franco Harris) (Pittsburgh vs. Dallas) 3.75
67 Super Bowl XI (Ken Stabler) (Oakland vs. Minnesota) 3.75

1978 Fleer Team Action

The 1978 Fleer set contains 68 cards, two for each team and for each Super Bowl. The borders are yellow. Fleer continued with its odd-for-offense and even-for-defense numbering scheme. The set is highlighted by a Tony Dorsett "rookie" card. Seven cards and four team logo stickers were in each pack.

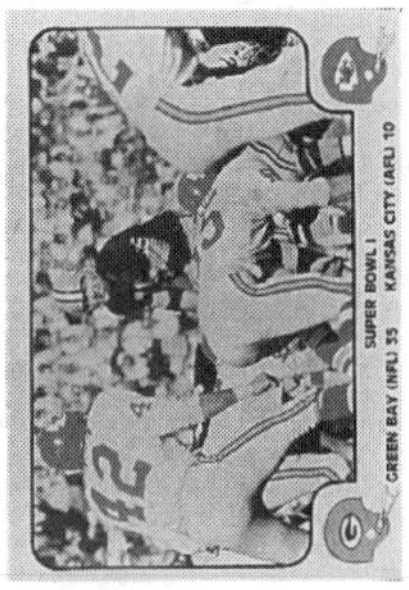

	NM
Complete Set (68):	50.00
Common Card:	.55
Common SB Card:	.70

1 Atlanta Falcons (Sticking to Basics) .60
2 Atlanta Falcons (In Pursuit) .55
3 New England Colts (Foward Plunge) .55
4 New England Colts (Stacking It Up) .55
5 Buffalo Bills (Daylight Breakers) .55
6 Buffalo Bills (Swarming Defense) .55
7 Chicago Bears (Walter Payton) (Up the Middle) 6.75
8 Chicago Bears (Rejuvenated Defense) .55
9 Cincinnati Bengals (Ken Anderson) (Poise and Execution) 1.25
10 Cincinnati Bengals (Down-to-Earth) .55
11 Cleveland Browns (Greg Pruitt) (Breakaway) .80
12 Cleveland Browns (Ken Anderson) (Red Dogs) 1.00
13 Dallas Cowboys (Dorsett) (Up and Over) 7.50
14 Dallas Cowboys (Doomsday II) .75
15 Denver Broncos (Mile-Hile Offense) .75
16 Denver Broncos (Walter Payton) (Orange Crush) 5.25
17 Detroit Lions (End-Around) .55
18 Detroit Lions (Special Teams) .55
19 Green Bay Packers (Running Strong) .55
20 Green Bay Packers (Tearin' em Down) .55
21 Houston Oilers (Goal-Line Drive) .55
22 Houston Oilers (Interception) .55
23 Kansas City Chiefs (Ed Podolak) (Running Wide) .60
24 Kansas City Chiefs (Armed Defense) .55
25 Los Angeles Rams (Rushing Power) .55
26 Los Angeles Rams (Backing the Line) .55
27 Miami Dolphins (Bob Griese) (Protective Pocket) 2.50
28 Miami Dolphins (Life in the Pit) .75
29 Minnesota Vikings (Chuck Foreman) (Storm Breakers) .80
30 Minnesota Vikings (Blocking the Kick) .55
31 New England Patriots (Clearing the Way) .55
32 New England Patriots (One-on-One) .55
33 New Orleans Saints (Extra Yardage) .55
34 New Orleans Saints (Drag-Down Defense) .55
35 New York Giants (Ready, Aim, Fire) .55
36 New York Giants (Meeting of Minds) .55
37 New York Jets (Take-Off) .55
38 New York Jets (Ambush) .55
39 Oakland Raiders (Power 31 Left) .75
40 Oakland Raiders (Welcoming Committee) .75
41 Philadelphia Eagles (Taking Flight) .55
42 Philadelphia Eagles (Soaring High) .55
43 Pittsburgh Steelers (Ironclad Offense) .75
44 Pittsburgh Steelers (Jack Lambert) (Curtain Closes) 2.00
45 St. Louis Cardinals (A Good Bet) .55
46 St. Louis Cardinals (Gang Tackle) .55
47 San Diego Chargers (Circus Catch) .55
48 San Diego Chargers (Charge) .55
49 San Francisco 49ers (Follow the Block) .55
50 San Francisco 49ers (Goal-Line Stand) .55
51 Seattle Seahawks (Finding Daylight) .60
52 Seattle Seahawks (Rushing the Pass) .60
53 Tampa Bay Buccaneers (Play Action) .55
54 Tampa Bay Buccaneers (Youth on the Move) .55
55 Washington Redskins (Renegade Runners) .55
56 Washington Redskins (Dual Action) .55
57 Super Bowl I (Bart Starr) (Green Bay vs. Kansas City) 2.25
58 Super Bowl II (Green Bay vs. Oakland) .70
59 Super Bowl III (New York vs. Baltimore) .70
60 Super Bowl IV (Kansas City vs. Minnesota) .70
61 Super Bowl V (Baltimore vs. Dallas) .70
62 Super Bowl VI (Dallas vs. Miami) .70
63 Super Bowl VII (Miami vs. Washington) .70
64 Super Bowl VIII (Larry Csonka) (Miami vs. Minnesota) 1.75
65 Super Bowl IX (Terry Bradshaw, Franco Harris) (Pittsburgh vs. Minnesota) 3.00
66 Super Bowl X (Pittsburgh vs. Dallas) .70
67 Super Bowl XI (Ken Stabler) (Oakland vs. Minnesota) 2.00
68 Super Bowl XII (Roger Staubach, Tony Dorsett) (Dallas vs. Denver) 5.75

1979 Fleer Team Action

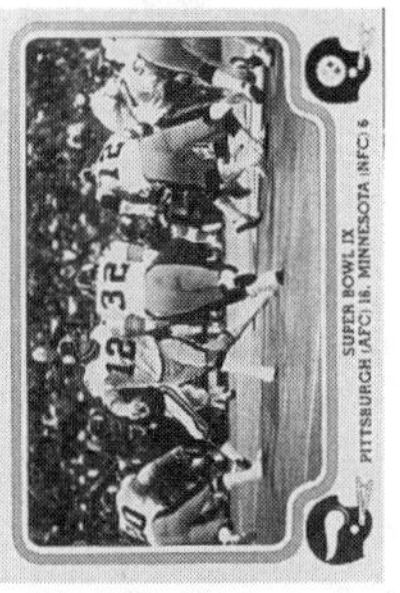

The 1979 white-bordered set contains 69 cards, two for each team plus one for each Super Bowl. The cards are numbered to correspond to team-city alphabetical order, followed by a chronological series of all 13 Super Bowls. An odd-offensive and even-defensive numbering format is used again. Earl Campbell's rookie card is the set's most significant. Packs were distributed with seven cards and three logo stickers.

	NM
Complete Set (69):	40.00
Common Card:	.50
Common SB Card:	.60

1 Atlanta Falcons (What's Up Front Counts) .80
2 Atlanta Falcons (Following the Bouncing Ball) .50
3 Baltimore Colts (Big Enough to Drive a Truck Through) .50
4 Baltimore Colts (When the Defense Becomes the Offense) .50
5 Buffalo Bills (Full Steam Ahead) .50
6 Buffalo Bills (Three's a Crowd) .50
7 Chicago Bears (Moving Out as One) .50
8 Chicago Bears (Stack' Em Up) .50
9 Cincinnati Bengals (Out in the Open Field) .50
10 Cincinnati Bengals (Sandwiched) .50
11 Cleveland Browns (Protective Pocket) .50
12 Cleveland Browns (Shake Rattle and Roll) .50
13 Dallas Cowboys (Tony Dorsett) (Paving the Way) 3.75
14 Dallas Cowboys (The Right Place at the Right Time) .65
15 Denver Broncos (A Stable of Runners) .65
16 Denver Broncos (Orange Crush) .65
17 Detroit Lions (Through the Line) .50
18 Detroit Lions (Tracked Down) .50
19 Green Bay Packers (Power Play) .50
20 Green Bay Packers (Four-To-One Odds) .50
21 Houston Oilers (Earl Campbell) (Offensive Gusher) 7.00
22 Houston Oilers (Gotcha) .50
23 Kansas Chiefs (Get Wings) .50
24 Kansas City Chiefs (Ambushed) .50
25 Los Angeles Rams (Men in the Middle) .50
26 Los Angeles Rams (Nowhere To Go But Down) .50
27 Miami Dolphins (Escort Service) .65
28 Miami Dolphins (All For One) .65
29 Minnesota Vikings (Up and Over) .50
30 Minnesota Vikings (The Purple Gang) .50
31 New England Patriots (Prepare For Takeoff) .50
32 New England Patriots (Dept. of Defense) .50
33 New Orleans Saints (Archie Manning) (Bombs Away) .85
34 New Orleans Saints (Duel in the Dome) .50
35 New York Giants (Battle of the Line of Scrimmage) .50
36 New York Giants (Piled Up) .50
37 New York Jets (Hitting the Hole) .50
38 New York Jets (Making Sure) .50
39 Oakland Raiders (Ken Stabler) (Left-Handed Strength) 2.00
40 Oakland Raiders (Black Sunday) .85
41 Philadelphia Eagles (Ready Aim Fire) .50
42 Philadelphia Eagles (Closing In) .50
43 Pittsburgh Steelers (Anchor Man) .65
44 Pittsburgh Steelers (The Steel Curtain) .85
45 St. Louis Cardinals (Jim Hart) (High Altitude Bomber) .85
46 St. Louis Cardinals (Three On One) .50
47 San Diego Chargers (Charge) .50
48 San Diego Chargers (Special Teams Shot) .50
49 San Francisco 49ers (In For the Score) .50
50 San Francisco 49ers (Nothing But Red Shirts) .50
51 Seattle Seahawks (North-South Runner) .65
52 Seattle Seahawks (The Sting) .65
53 Tampa Bay Buccaneers (Hitting Paydirt) .50
54 Tmpa Bay Buccaneers (Making' Em Pay the Price) .50
55 Washington Redskins (On the Warpath) .50
56 Washington Redskins (Drawing a Crowd) .50
57 Super Bowl I (Jim Taylor) (Green Bay vs. Kansas City) .85
58 Super Bowl II (Bart Starr) (Green Bay vs. Oakland) 2.00
59 Super Bowl III (New York vs. Baltimore) .65
60 Super Bowl IV (Kansas City vs. Minnesota) .65
61 Super Bowl V (Baltimore vs. Dallas) .65
62 Super Bowl VI (Bob Griese, Bob Lilly) (Dallas vs. Miami) 2.00
63 Super Bowl VII (Miami vs. Washington) .65
64 Super Bowl VIII (Bob Griese, Larry Csonka) (Miami vs. Minnesota) 2.00
65 Super Bowl IX (Terry Bradshaw, Franco Harris) (Pittsburgh vs. Minnesota) 3.00
66 Super Bowl X (Pittsburgh vs. Dallas) .65
67 Super Bowl XI (Oakland vs. Minnesota) .65
68 Super Bowl XII (Dallas vs. Denver) .65
69 Super Bowl XIII (Pittsburgh vs Dallas) 1.25

1980 Fleer Team Action

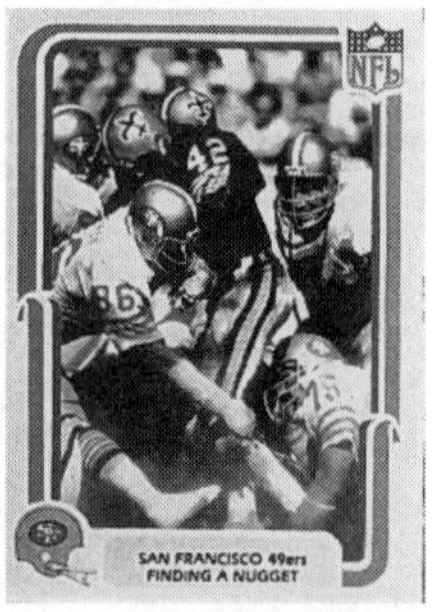

The 1980 Fleer set has white borders and is complete at 70 cards, two for each NFL team and one for each Super Bowl. The cards are numbered to correspond to team-city alphabetical order. Odds are offensive cards, evens are defensive plays. The last 14 picture Super Bowl action. A key card in the set is the Phil Simms "rookie" card. Seven cards and three logo stickers were in each pack.

	NM
Complete Set (70):	38.00
Common Card:	.40
Common SB Card:	.50

1 Atlanta Falcons (Getting the Extra Yards) .70
2 Atlanta Falcons (Falcons Get Their Prey) .40
3 Baltimore Colts (Looking for Daylight) .45
4 Baltimore Colts (Ready If Needed) .40
5 Buffalo Bills (You Block For Me, I'll Block For You) .40
6 Buffalo Bills (Stand 'Em Up and Push 'Em Back) .40
7 Chicago Bears (Walter Payton) (Coming Through) 4.00
8 Chicago Bears (Four On One) .40
9 Cincinnati Bengals (Power Running) .40
10 Cincinnati Bengals (Out Of Running Room) .40
11 Cleveland Browns (Ozzie Newsome) (End Around) 2.00
12 Cleveland Browns (Rubber Band Defense) .40
13 Dallas Cowboys (Tony Dorsett) (Point of Attack) 3.00
14 Dallas Cowboys (Bob Breunig) (Man in the Middle) .60
15 Denver Broncos (Strong and Steady) .45
16 Denver Broncos (Orange Power) .45
17 Detroit Lions (On the March) .40
18 Detroit Lions (The Silver Rush) .40
19 Green Bay Packers (Getting Underway) .40
20 Green Bay Packers (The Best Offense is a Good Defense) .40
21 Houston Oilers (Airborne) .40
22 Houston Oilers (Search and Destroy) .40
23 Kansas City Chiefs (Blazing the Trail) .40
24 Kansas City Chiefs (Making Sure) .40
25 Los Angeles Rams (One Good Turn Deserves Another) .40
26 Los Angeles Rams (Shedding the Block) .40
27 Miami Dolphins (Sweeping the Flanks) .50
28 Miami Dolphins (Keep 'Em Busy) .50
29 Minnesota Vikings (One Man To Beat) .40
30 Minnesota Vikings (Purple People Eaters II) .40
31 New England Patriots (Hitting the Hole) .40
32 New England Patriots (Getting to the Ball) .40
33 New Orleans Saints (Splitting the Defenders) .40
34 New Orleans Saints (Joe Theismann) (Don't Let Him Get Outside) 1.00
35 New York Giants (Phil Simms) (Audible) 4.00
36 New York Giants (Wrong Side Up) .40
37 New York Jets (Make Him Miss) .40
38 New York Jets (Mark Gastineau) (The Only Way To Play) .45
39 Oakland Raiders (Pulling Out All the Stops) .60
40 Oakland Raiders (Right On) .60
41 Philadelphia Eagles (Not Pretty, But Still Points) .40
42 Philadelphia Eagles (Applying the Clamps) .40
43 Pittsburgh Steelers (Franco Harris) (All Systems Go) 1.75
44 Pittsburgh Steelers (Still the Steal Curtain) .70
45 St. Louis Cardinals (Ottis Anderson) (On the Move) 2.00
46 St. Louis Cardinals (Long Gone) .40
47 San Diego Chargers (Short-Range Success) .40
48 San Diego Chargers (Pursuit) .40
49 San Francisco 49ers (Getting Field Position) .40
50 San Francisco 49ers (Finding a Nugget) .40
51 Seattle Seahawks (They'll Try Anything Once) .45
52 Seattle Seahawks (Paying the Price) .45
53 Tampa Bay Buccaneers (Coming of Age) .40
54 Tampa Bay Buccaneers (Walter Payton) (3-4 Shut the Door) 3.00
55 Washington Redskins (Wide Open) .40
56 Washington Redskins (Rude Reception) .40
57 Super Bowl I (Green Bay vs. Kansas City) .50
58 Super Bowl II (Bart Starr) (Green Bay vs. Oakland) 1.75
59 Super Bowl III (Joe Namath) (New York vs. Baltimore) 3.75
60 Super Bowl IV (Kansas City vs. Minnesota) .50
61 Super Bowl V (Baltimore vs. Dallas) .50
62 Super Bowl VI (Roger Staubach) (Dallas vs. Miami) 3.00
63 Super Bowl VII (Miami vs. Washington) .50
64 Super Bowl VIII (Miami vs. Minnesota) .50
65 Super Bowl IX (Terry Bradshaw, Rocky Bleier) (Pittsburgh vs. Minnesota) 1.75
66 Super Bowl X (Jack Lambert) (Pittsburgh vs. Dallas) .70
67 Super Bowl XI (Chuck Foreman) (Oakland vs. Minnesota) .60
68 Super Bowl XII (Dallas vs. Denver) .50
69 Super Bowl XIII (Terry Bradshaw) (Pittsburgh vs. Dallas) 2.00
70 Super Bowl XIV (Franco Harris) (Pittsburgh vs. Los Angeles) 2.00

1981 Fleer Team Action

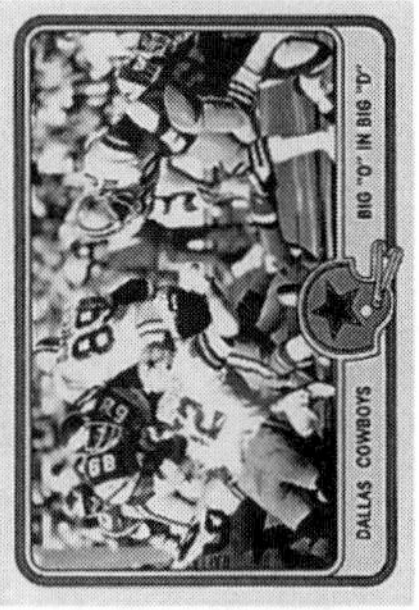

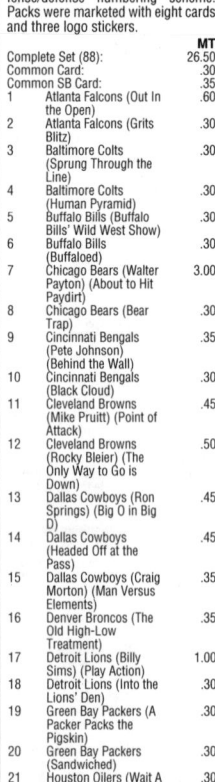

The 1981 Fleer football set is complete at 88 cards, including two cards for each team, one for each Super Bowl, plus a series of extra cards at the end to round out the set. The front borders are white, while the backs are designed around a red, white and blue color scheme. Once again, Fleer used its alphabetical, offense/defense numbering scheme. Packs were marketed with eight cards and three logo stickers.

	MT
Complete Set (88):	26.50
Common Card:	.30
Common SB Card:	.35

1 Atlanta Falcons (Out In the Open) .60
2 Atlanta Falcons (Grits Blitz) .30
3 Baltimore Colts (Sprung Through the Line) .30
4 Baltimore Colts (Human Pyramid) .30
5 Buffalo Bills (Buffalo Bills' Wild West Show) .30
6 Buffalo Bills (Buffaloed) .30
7 Chicago Bears (Walter Payton) (About to Hit Paydirt) 3.00
8 Chicago Bears (Bear Trap) .30
9 Cincinnati Bengals (Pete Johnson) (Behind the Wall) .35
10 Cincinnati Bengals (Black Cloud) .30
11 Cleveland Browns (Mike Pruitt) (Point of Attack) .45
12 Cleveland Browns (Rocky Bleier) (The Only Way to Go is Down) .50
13 Dallas Cowboys (Ron Springs) (Big O in Big D) .45
14 Dallas Cowboys (Headed Off at the Pass) .45
15 Dallas Cowboys (Craig Morton) (Man Versus Elements) .35
16 Denver Broncos (The Old High-Low Treatment) .35
17 Detroit Lions (Billy Sims) (Play Action) 1.00
18 Detroit Lions (Into the Lions' Den) .30
19 Green Bay Packers (A Packer Packs the Pigskin) .30
20 Green Bay Packers (Sandwiched) .30
21 Houston Oilers (Wait A Minute) .30
22 Houston Oilers (3-4 Shut the Door) .30

23 Kansas City Chiefs (On the Ball) .30
24 Kansas City Chiefs (Seeing Red) .30
25 Los Angeles Rams (The Point of Attack) .30
26 Los Angeles Rams (Get Your Hands Up) .30
27 Miami Dolphins (David Woodley) (Plenty of Time) .45
28 Miami Dolphins (Pursuit) .35
29 Minnesota Vikings (Tough Yardage) .30
30 Minnesota Vikings (Pete Johnson) (Purple Avalanche) .35
31 New England Patriots (In High Gear) .30
32 New England Patriots (Ken Stabler) (Keep 'Em Covered) 1.50
33 New Orleans Saints (Archie Manning) (Setting Up) .45
34 New Orleans Saints (Air Ball) .30
35 New York Giants (Off Tackle) .30
36 New York Giants (In the Land of the Giants) .30
37 New York Jets (Richard Todd) (Cleared for Launching) .35
38 New York Jets (Airborne) .30
39 Oakland Raiders (Off and Running) .45
40 Oakland Raiders (Block that Kick) .45
41 Philadelphia Eagles (About to Take Flight) .30
42 Philadelphia Eagles (Robert Newhouse) (Birds of Prey) .45
43 Pittsburgh Steelers (Franco Harris) (Here Comes the Infantry) 1.25
44 Pittsburgh Steelers (Like a Steel Trap) .35
45 St. Louis Cardinals (Run to Daylight) .30
46 St. Louis Cardinals (Stacked Up and Up) .30
47 San Diego Chargers (Straight-Ahead Power) .30
48 San Diego Chargers (Stonewalled) .30
49 San Francisco 49ers (Follow the Leader) .30
50 San Francisco 49ers (Search and Destroy) .30
51 Seattle Seahawks (Short-Range Success) .30
52 Seattle Seahawks (Take Down) .30
53 Tampa Bay Buccaneers (Jerry Eckwood) (Orange Blossom Special) .35
54 Tampa Bay Buccaneers (Tropical Storm Buc) .30
55 Washington Redskins (Alone for a Moment) .30
56 Washington Redskins (Ambushed) .30
57 Super Bowl I (Jim Taylor) (Green Bay vs. Kansas City) .50
58 Super Bowl II (Green Bay vs. Oakland) .30
59 Super Bowl III (New York vs. Baltimore) .30
60 Super Bowl IV (Kansas City vs. Minnesota) .30
61 Super Bowl V (Baltimore vs. Dallas) .30
62 Super Bowl VI (Dallas vs. Miami) .30
63 Super Bowl VII (Miami vs. Washington) .30
64 Super Bowl VIII (Larry Csonka) (Miami vs. Minnesota) 1.00
65 Super Bowl IX (Franco Harris) (Pittsburgh vs. Minnesota) 1.00
66 Super Bowl X (Franco Harris) (Pittsburgh vs. Dallas) .35
67 Super Bowl XI (Kenny Stabler) (Oakland vs. Minnesota) 1.50
68 Super Bowl XII (Roger Staubach, Tony Dorsett) (Dallas vs. Denver) 2.25
69 Super Bowl XIII (Roger Staubach, Tony Dorsett) (Pittsburgh vs. Dallas) 2.25
70 Super Bowl XIV (Franco Harris) (Pittsburgh vs. Los Angeles) 1.00
71 Super Bowl XV (Jim Plunkett) (Oakland vs. Philadelphia) .50
72 Steeler Training Camp (Chuck Noll) .50
73 Practice Makes Perfect .30
74 Airborn Carrier .30
75 The National Anthem Chargers .30
76 Filling Up .30
77 Terry Bradshaw (Away in Time) 2.00
78 Flat Out .30
79 Halftime (Band playing) .30
80 Warm Ups Patriots .30
81 Getting to the Bottom of It .30
82 Souvenir (Crowd) .30
83 A Game of Inches (Officials measuring) .30
84 The Overview .30
85 The Dropback .30
86 Pregame Huddle (Washington Redskins) .30
87 Every Way But Loose .30
88 Mudders .50

1982 Fleer Team Action

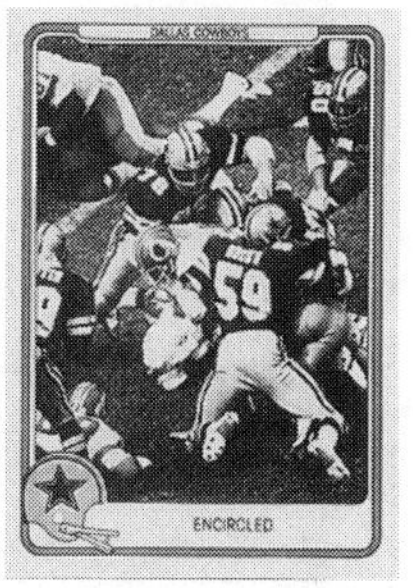

The 1982 Fleer set is again complete at 88 cards, but is slightly more valuable than other Fleer sets from this period, because it contains a couple of cards featuring Joe Montana. The same numbering scheme is used, but 16 NFL Team Highlight cards are included and added at the end. Seven cards and three logo stickers were in each pack.

MT
Complete Set (88): 45.00
Common Card: .25
Common SB Card: .30
1 Atlanta Falcons (Running to Daylight) .50
2 Atlanta Falcons (Airborne Falcons) .25
3 Baltimore Colts (Mark Gastineau, Bert Jones) (Plenty of Time to Throw) .45
4 Baltimore Colts (Lassoing the Opponent) .25
5 Buffalo Bills (Joe Ferguson) (Point of Attack) .45
6 Buffalo Bills (Capturing the Enemy) .25
7 Chicago Bears (Walter Payton) (Three on One) 2.50
8 Chicago Bears (Stretched Out) .25
9 Cincinnati Bengals (Pete Johnson) (About to Hit Paydirt) .30
10 Cincinnati Bengals (Tiger-Striped Attack) .25
11 Cleveland Browns (Brian Sipe) (Reading the Field) .45
12 Cleveland Browns (Covered From All Angles) .25
13 Dallas Cowboys (Tony Dorsett) (Blocking Convoy) 1.50
14 Dallas Cowboys (Encircled) .45
15 Denver Broncos (Craig Morton) (Springing into Action) .45
16 Denver Broncos (High and Low) .30
17 Detroit Lions (Setting Up the Screen Pass) .25
18 Detroit Lions (Doug Williams) (Poised and Ready to Attack) .30
19 Green Bay Packers (Flying Through the Air) .25
20 Green Bay Packers (Hitting the Pack) .25
21 Houston Oilers (Earl Campbell) (Waiting for the Hole to Open) 3.25
22 Houston Oilers (Biting the Dust) .25
23 Kansas City Chiefs (Going in Untouched) .25
24 Kansas City Chiefs (No Place to Go) .25
25 Los Angeles Rams (Wendell Tyler) (Getting to the Outside) .30
26 Los Angeles Rams (John Riggins) (Double Team, Double Trouble) .70
27 Miami Dolphins (Tony Nathan) (Cutting Back Against the Grain) .45
28 Miami Dolphins (Taking Two Down) .30
29 Minnesota Vikings (Running Inside for Tough Yardage) .25
30 Minnesota Vikings (Bowling Over the Oppenent) .25
31 New England Patriots (Leaping for the First Down) .25
32 New England Patriots (Gang Tackling) .25
33 New Orleans Saints (Breaking Into the Clear) .45
34 New Orleans Saints (Double Jeopardy) .25
35 New York Giants (Getting Ready to Hit the Opening) .25
36 New York Giants (Tony Dorsett) (Negative Yardage) 1.25
37 New York Jets (Freeman McNeil) (Off to the Races) 1.00
38 New York Jets (Sandwiched) .25
39 Oakland Raiders (Marc Wilson) (Throwing the Down and Out) .45
40 Oakland Raiders (The Second Wave is on the Way) .45
41 Philadelphia Eagles (Ron Jaworski) (Blasting Up the Middle) .45
42 Philadelphia Eagles (Carl Hairston, John Riggins) (Triple Teaming) .70
43 Pittsburgh Steelers (Stretching for the Score) .30
44 Pittsburgh Steelers (Rising Above the Crowd) .30
45 St. Louis Cardinals (Jim Hart) (Sweeping to the Right) .45
46 St. Louis Cardinals (No Plave to go but Down) .25
47 San Diego Chargers (Looking for Someone to Block) .25
48 San Diego Chargers (Being in the Right Place) .25
49 San Francisco 49ers (Joe Montana) (Giving Second Effort) 17.50
50 San Francisco 49ers (Steve Bartkowski) (In Your Face) .50
51 Seattle Seahawks (Jack Lambert) (Nothing But Open Space) .70
52 Seattle Seahawks (Brian Sipe) (Attacking From the Blind Side) .45
53 Tampa Bay Buccaneers (Doug Williams) (Everyone in Motion) .30
54 Tampa Bay Buccaneers (Ring Around the Running Back) .25
55 Washington Redskins (Joe Theismann) (Knocking Them Down One-By-One) .70
56 Washington Redskins (Coming From All Directions) .25
57 Super Bowl I (Jim Taylor) (Green Bay vs. Kansas City) .50
58 Super Bowl II (Green Bay vs. Oakland) .25
59 Super Bowl III (New York vs. Baltimore) .25
60 Super Bowl IV (Kansas City vs. Minnesota) .25
61 Super Bowl V (Baltimore vs. Dallas) .25
62 Super Bowl VI (Bob Griese, Bob Lilly) (Dallas vs. Miami) .80
63 Super Bowl VII (Larry Csonka) (Miami vs. Washington) .70
64 Super Bowl VIII (Larry Csonka, Paul Warfield) (Miami vs. Minnesota) 1.00
65 Super Bowl IX (Pittsburgh vs. Minnesota) .25
66 Super Bowl X (Roger Staubach) (Pittsburgh vs. Dallas) 2.00
67 Super Bowl XI (Mark Van Eeghen) (Oakland vs. Minnesota) .30
68 Super Bowl XII (Roger Staubach) (Dallas vs. Denver) 2.00
69 Super Bowl XIII (Lynn Swann) (Pittsburgh vs. Dallas) 1.00
70 Super Bowl XIV (Pittsburgh vs. Los Angeles) .25
71 Super Bowl XV (Jim Plunkett) (Oakland vs. Philadelphia) .45
72 Super Bowl XVI (Dwight Clark) (San Francisco vs. Cincinnati) .85
73 NFL Team Highlights (Joe Montana) (Pro Bowl) 12.00
74 NFL Team Highlights (Ken Anderson, Anthony Munoz) (Pro Bowl) 2.50
75 NFL Team Highlights (Aloha Stadium) .75
76 NFL Team Highlights (On the Field Meeting) .25
77 NFL Team Highlights (Joe Theismann) (First Down) .70
78 NFL Team Highlights (Jerry Markbright) (The Man in Charge) .25
79 NFL Team Highlights (Coming Onto the Field) .25
80 NFL Team Highlights (In the Huddle) .30
81 NFL Team Highlights (Lying In Wait) .25
82 NFL Team Highlights (Celebration) .25
83 NFL Team Highlights (Men in Motion) .25
84 NFL Team Highlights (Shotgun Formation) .25
85 NFL Team Highlights (Training Camp) .25
86 NFL Team Highlights (Bill Walsh) (Halftime Instructions) .75
87 NFL Team Highlights (Rolf Bernirschke) (Field Goal Attempt) .30
88 NFL Team Highlights (Free Kick) .50

1983 Fleer Team Action

The 1983 Fleer football set is again complete at 88 cards, including two cards for each team, one for each Super Bowl, plus a series of "Highlights" cards at the end of the set. There is a numbering error in the set that was not corrected. The card depicting Super Bowl X, which should have been card number "66," was erroneously numbered "67," meaning there are two cards numbered "67" in the set and no card numbered "66." Collectors should be aware that the premium value attached to the Super Bowl X card is because it pictures Terry Bradshaw, and not because of the numbering error. The set follows all of Fleer's usual numbering formats. A Jim McMahon "rookie" card highlights the set. Packs had seven cards and three logo stickers.

MT
Complete Set (88): 26.00
Common Card: .25
Common SB Card: .30
1 Atlanta Falcons (Ronnie Lott) (Breaking Away to Daylight) 2.50
2 Atlanta Falcons (Piles Up) .25
3 Baltimore Colts (Cutting Back to Daylight) .25
4 Baltimore Colts (Joe Ferguson) (Pressuring the QB) .30
5 Buffalo Bills (Moving to the Outside) .30
6 Buffalo Bills (Buffalo Stampede) .25
7 Chicago Bears (Jim McMahon, Walter Payton) (Ready to Let it Fly) 2.25
8 Chicago Bears (Jump Ball) .25
9 Cincinnati Bengals (Hurdling Into Open) .25
10 Cincinnati Bengals (Hands Up) .25
11 Cleveland Browns (Mike Pruitt) (An Open Field Ahead) .30
12 Cleveland Browns (Reacting to the Ball Carrier) .25
13 Dallas Cowboys (Tony Dorsett) (Mid-Air Ballet) 1.50
14 Dallas Cowboys (3, 2, 1 Takeoff) .30
15 Denver Broncos (Clear Sailing) .30
16 Denver Broncos (Stacking Up Offense) .30
17 Detroit Lions (Hitting the Wall) .25
18 Detroit Lions (Snapping into Action) .25
19 Green Bay Packers (Ed "Too Tall" Jones) (Fingertip Control) .60
20 Green Bay Packers (QB Sack) .25
21 Houston Oilers (Sweeping to Outside) .25
22 Houston Oilers (Freeman McNeil) (Halting Forward Progress) .45
23 Kansas City Chiefs (Waiting for the Key Block) .25
24 Kansas City Chiefs (John Hannah) (Going Head to Head) .50
25 Los Angeles Raiders (Jim Plunkett) (Bowms Away) .45
26 Los Angeles Raiders (Caged Bengal) .45
27 Los Angeles Rams (Clearing Out Middle) .25
28 Los Angeles Rams (One on One Tackle) .25
29 Miami Dolphins (Skating Through Hole) .30
30 Miami Dolphins (Follow the Bouncing Ball) .30
31 Minnesota Vikings (Tommy Kramer) (Dropping into Pocket) .30
32 Minnesota Vikings (Attacking from All Angles) .25
33 New England Patriots (Touchdown) .25
34 New England Patriots (Walter Payton) (Pouncing Patroits) 2.00
35 New Orleans Saints (Only One Man to Beat) .25
36 New Orleans Saints (Tony Dorsett) (Closing In) 1.25
37 New York Giants (Setting Up to Pass) .25
38 New York Giants (In Pursuit) .25
39 New York Jets (Just Enough Room) .25
40 New York Jets (Warpping Up Runner) .25
41 Philadelphia Eagles (Ron Jarowski, Harry Carson) (Play Action Fakers) .30
42 Philadelphia Eagles (Archie Manning) (Step Away From Sack) .45
43 Pittsburgh Steelers (Franco Harris, Terry Bradshaw) (Exploding Through a Hole) 1.50
44 Pittsburgh Steelers (Jack Lambert) (Outnumbered) .60
45 St. Louis Cardinals (Keeping His Balance) .25
46 St. Louis Cardinals (Waiting for the Reinforcements) .25
47 San Diego Chargers (Supercharged Charger) .25
48 San Diego Chargers (Triple Team Tackle) .25
49 San Francisco 49ers (There's No Stopping Him Now) .25
50 San Francisco 49ers (Heading 'Em Off at the Pass) .30
51 Seattle Seahawks (Jim Zorn) (Calling the Signals) .45
52 Seattle Seahawks (The Hands Have it) .30
53 Tampa Bay Buccaneers (Off to the Races) .25
54 Tampa Bay Buccaneers (Buccaneer Sandwich) .25
55 Washington Redskins (Looking for Daylight) .25
56 Washington Redskins (Smothering the Ball Carrier) .25
57 Super Bowl I (Jim Taylor) (Green Bay vs. Kansas City) .60
58 Super Bowl II (Green Bay vs. Oakland) .30
59 Super Bowl III (New York vs. Baltimore) .30
60 Super Bowl IV (Kansas City vs. Minnesota) .30
61 Super Bowl V (Johnny Unitas) (Baltimore vs. Dallas) 1.50
62 Super Bowl VI (Bob Griese, Bob Lilly) (Dallas vs. Miami) .75
63 Super Bowl VII (Manny Fernandez) (Miami vs. Washington) .30
64 Super Bowl VIII (Larry Csonka) (Miami vs. Minnesota) .60
65 Super Bowl IX (Franco Harris) (Pittsburgh vs. Minnesota) 1.00
66 Super Bowl X (Terry Bradshaw) (Pittsburgh vs. Dallas) 1.75
67 Super Bowl XI (Oakland vs. Minnesota) .45
68 Super Bowl XII (Dallas vs. Denver) .30
69 Super Bowl XIII (Terry Bradshaw) (Pittsburgh vs. Dallas) 1.50
70 Super Bowl XIV (Vince Ferragamo) (Pittsburgh vs. Los Angeles) .30
71 Super Bowl XV (Oakland vs. Philadelphia) .30
72 Super Bowl XVI (San Francisco vs. Cincinnati) .30
73 Super Bowl XVII (John Riggins) (Washington vs. Miami) .60
74 NFL Team Highlights (Dan Fouts) (Pro Bowl) 1.00
75 NFL Team Highlights (Super Bowl XVII Spectacular) .30
76 NFL Team Highlights (Tampa Stadium: Super Bowl XVIII) .30
77 NFL Team Highlights (Up, Up, and Away) .30
78 NFL Team Highlights (Steve Bartkowski) (Sideline Conference) .30
79 NFL Team Highlights (Mike Lansford) (Barefoot Follow-Through) .30
80 NFL Team Highlights (Fourth and Long) .30
81 NFL Team Highlights (Blocked Punt) .30
82 NFL Team Highlights (Fumble) .30
83 NFL Team Highlights (National Anthem) .30
84 NFL Team Highlights (Tony Franklin) (Concentrating on the Ball) .30
85 NFL Team Highlights (Splashing Around) .30
86 NFL Team Highlights (Loading in Shotgun) .30
87 NFL Team Highlights (Taking the Snap) .30
88 NFL Team Highlights (Line of Scrimmage) .45

1984 Fleer Team Action

The 1984 Fleer football set is again complete at 88 cards, using Fleer's typical numbering arrangement. However, the newly-relocated Indianapolis Colts are placed in Baltimore's usual position. A series of 18 Super Bowl and 14 NFL Team Highlight cards are included. The most signigicant cards are two of Earl Campbell, which are not found in the 1984 Topps set, a first-year Marcus Allen, and a Howie Long "rookie." Seven cards and three logo stickers were in each pack. Cards green borders.

MT
Complete Set (88): 23.50
Common Card: .25
1 Atlanta Falcons .50
2 Atlanta Falcons (Gang Tackle) .25
3 Indianapolis Colts (About to Break Free) .25
4 Indianapolis Colts (Cutting Off All the Angles) .25
5 Buffalo Bills (Cracking the First Line of Defense) .25
6 Buffalo Bills (Getting Help from a Friend) .25
7 Chicago Bears (Jim McMahon, Walter Payton) (Over the Top) 1.75
8 Chicago Bears (You Grab Him High I'll Grab Him Low) .25
9 Cincinnati Bengals (Skipping Through an Opening) .25
10 Cincinnati Bengals (Joe Ferguson) (Saying Hello to a QB) .40
11 Cleveland Browns (Greg Pruitt) (Free Sailing into the End Zone) .40
12 Cleveland Browns (Making Sure of the Tackle) .25
13 Dallas Cowboys (Danny White) .50
14 Dallas Cowboys (Ed "Too Tall" Jones) (Cowboy's Corral) .60
15 Denver Broncos (Sprinting into the Open) .40
16 Denver Broncos (Curt Warner) (Ready to Pounce) .50
17 Detroit Lions (Billy Sims) (Lion on the Prowl) .50
18 Detroit Lions (John Riggins) (Stacking Up the Ball Carrier) .60
19 Green Bay Packers (Waiting for the Hole to Open) .25
20 Green Bay Packers (Packing Up Your Opponent) .25
21 Houston Oilers (Earl Campbell) (Nothing but Open Spaces Ahead) 2.50
22 Houston Oilers (Meeting Him Head On) .25
23 Kansas City Chiefs (Going Outside for Extra Yardage) .25
24 Kansas City Chiefs (A Running Back in Trouble) .25
25 Los Angeles Raiders (Marcus Allen) (No Defenders in Sight) 2.75
26 Los Angeles Raiders (Howie Long, John Riggins) (Rampaging Raiders) 2.25
27 Los Angeles Rams (Making the Cut) .25
28 Los Angeles Rams (Caught From Behind) .25
29 Miami Dolphins (Sliding Down the Line) .40
30 Miami Dolphins (Making Sure) .40
31 Minnesota Vikings (Stretching For Touchdown) .25
32 Minnesota Vikings (Hitting the Wall) .25
33 New England Patriots (Steve Grogan) (Straight Up the Middle) .50
34 New England Patriots (Earl Campbell) (Come Here an Give Me a Hug) 2.00
35 New Orleans Saints (One Defender to Beat) .25
36 New Orleans Saints (Saints Sandwich) .25
37 New York Giants (A Six Point Landing) .25
38 New York Giants (Leaping to the Aid of a Teammate) .25
39 New York Jets (Galloping Through Untouched) .25
40 New York Jets (Capturing the Enemy) .25
41 Philadelphia Eagles (One More Block and He's Gone) .25
42 Philadelphoa Ealges (Meeting an Oppenent With Open Arms) .25
43 Pittsburgh Steelers (The Play Begins to Develop) .40
44 Pittsburgh Steelers (Rally Around the Ball Carrier) .40
45 St. Louis Cardinals (Sprinting Around the Corner) .25
46 St. Louis Cardinals (Overmatched) .25
47 San Diego Chargers (Up, Up and Away) .25
48 San Diego Chargers (Engulfing the Oppenent) .25
49 San Francisco 49ers (Wendell Tyler) (Tunneling Up the Middle) .40
50 San Francisco 49ers (John Riggins) (Nowhere to Go but Down) .60

51	Seattle Seahawks (Jim Zorn) (Letting the Ball Fly)	.50
52	Seattle Seahawks (Handing Out Some Punishment)	.40
53	Tampa Bay Buccaneers (When He Hits the Ground He's Gone)	.25
54	Tampa Bay Buccaneers (One Leg Takedown)	.25
55	Washington Redskins (John Riggins) (Plenty of Room to Run)	.60
56	Washington Redskins (Squashing the Oppenent)	.25
57	Super Bowl I (Jim Taylor) (Green Bay vs. Kansas City)	.60
58	Super Bowl II (Bart Starr) (Green Bay vs. Oakland)	.80
59	Super Bowl III (New York vs. Baltimore)	.25
60	Super Bowl IV (Kansas City vs. Minnesota)	.25
61	Super Bowl V (Earl Morrall) (Baltimore vs. Dallas)	.75
62	Super Bowl VI (Roger Staubach) (Dallas vs. Miami)	1.50
63	Super Bowl VII (Jim Kiick, Bob Griese) (Miami vs. Washington)	.50
64	Super Bowl VIII (Larry Csonka) (Miami vs. Minnesota)	.75
65	Super Bowl IX (Terry Bradshaw) (Pittsburgh vs. Minnesota)	1.25
66	Super Bowl X (Franco Harris) (Pittsburgh vs. Dallas)	.75
67	Super Bowl XI (Oakland vs. Minnesota)	.25
68	Super Bowl XII (Tony Dorsett) (Dallas vs. Denver)	1.00
69	Super Bowl XIII (Franco Harris) (Pittsburgh vs. Dallas)	.75
70	Super Bowl XIV (Franco Harris) (Pittsburgh vs. Los Angeles)	.75
71	Super Bowl XV (Jim Plunkett) (Oakland vs. Philadelphia)	.40
72	Super Bowl XVI (San Francisco vs. Cincinnati)	.25
73	Super Bowl XVII (Washington vs. Miami)	.25
74	Super Bowl XVIII (Howie Long) (Los Angeles vs. Washington)	1.75
75	NFL Team Highlights (Official's Conference)	.25
76	NFL Team Highlights (Leaping for the Ball Carrier)	.25
77	NFL Team Highlights (Jim Plunkett) (Setting Up in the Passing Pocket)	.40
78	NFL Team Highlights (Field Goal Block)	.25
79	NFL Team Highlights (Steve Grogan) (Stopped for No Gain)	.40
80	NFL Team Highlights (Double Team Block)	.25
81	NFL Team Highlights (Kickoff)	.25
82	NFL Team Highlights (Punt Block)	.25
83	NFL Team Highlights (Coaches Signals)	.25
84	NFL Team Highlights (Training Camp)	.25
85	NFL Team Highlights (Dwight Stephenson) (Fumble)	.50
86	NFL Team Highlights (1984 AFC-NFC Pro Bowl)	.25
87	NFL Team Highlights (Cheerleaders)	.50
88	NFL Team Highlights (Joe Theismann) (In the Huddle)	.80

1985 Fleer Team Action

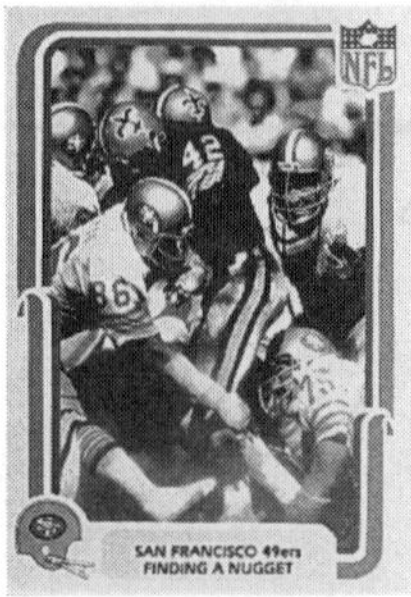

Fleer changed its format slightly for its 1985 set. The set is still complete at 88 cards, but there are three cards for each team this year and fewer Super Bowl cards. The "In Action" cards for each team have a team schedule. Three cards for Super Bowl XIX and a 1985 Pro Bowl card are also included. A first-year Fleer Dan Marino card and a Warren Moon "rookie" card highlight the set. Packs had 15 cards and one logo sticker.

		MT
	Complete Set (88):	30.00
	Common Card:	.25
1	Atlanta Falcons (Nothing But Open Spaces Ahead)	.50
2	Atlanta Falcons (Leveling Ball Carrier)	.25
3	Atlanta Falcons (Joe Theismann, John Riggins) (Flying Falcon)	.60
4	Buffalo Bills (Ducking Under the Pressure)	.25
5	Buffalo Bills (Swallowing Up the Oppenent)	.25
6	Buffalo Bills (Avoiding Late Hits)	.25
7	Chicago Bears (Walter Payton) (Picking His Spot)	1.50
8	Chicago Bears (C'Mon Guys, Give Me Some Room to Breath e)	.25
9	Chicago Bears (Richard Dent) (Just Hanging Around in Case They're Needed)	2.25
10	Cincinnati Bengals (Struggling for Every Extra Yard)	.25
11	Cincinnati Bengals (Making Opponent Pay)	.25
12	Cincinnati Bengals (Just Out of the Reach of the Defender)	.25
13	Cleveland Browns (Plenty of Time to Fire the Ball)	.25
14	Cleveland Browns (Hitting the Wall)	.25
15	Cleveland Browns (Look What We Found)	.25
16	Dallas Cowboys (Tony Dorsett, Wilbur Marshall) (Waiting for the Right Moment to Burst Upfield)	1.25
17	Dallas Cowboys (Walter Payton, Ed "Too Tall" Jones) (Sorry Buddy, This is the End of the Line)	1.50
18	Dallas Cowboys (Ed "Too Tall" Jones) (Following Through for Three Points)	.60
19	Denver Broncos (Blasting Up the Middle)	.40
20	Denver Broncos (Finishing Off the Tackle)	.40
21	Denver Broncos (About to Hit Paydirt)	.40
22	Detroit Lions (Dexter Manley) (Waiting to Throw Until the Last Second)	.40
23	Detroit Lions (Double Trouble on the Tackle)	.25
24	Detroit Lions (Quick Pitch)	.25
25	Green Bay Packers (Steve McMichael) (Unleashing the Long Bomb)	.90
26	Green Bay Packers (Marcus Allen) (Encircling the Ball Carrier)	1.50
27	Green Bay Packers (Piggy-Back Ride)	.25
28	Houston Oilers (Warren Moon, Earl Campbell) (Retreating into the Pocket)	5.75
29	Houston Oilers (Punishing the Enemy)	.25
30	Houston Oilers (No Chance to Block This One)	.25
31	Indianapolis Colts (Getting Ready to Let It Fly)	.25
32	Indianapolis Colts (Pushing the Ball Carrier Backward)	.25
33	Indianapolis Colts (Nowhere to Go)	.25
34	Kansas City Chiefs (Cutting Back for Extra Yardage)	.25
35	Kansas City Chiefs (Reaching for the Deflection)	.25
36	Kansas City Chiefs (Rising to the Occasion)	.25
37	Los Angeles Raiders (Howie Long) (Hurdling into the Open Field)	.40
38	Los Angeles Raiders (No Place to Go)	.25
39	Los Angeles Raiders (Standing Tall in the Pocket)	.25
40	Los Angeles Rams (Eric Dickerson) (One More Barrier and He's Off to the Races)	1.50
41	Los Angeles Rams (Driving a Shoulder into the Opponent)	.25
42	Los Angeles Rams (The Kickoff)	.25
43	Miami Dolphins (Tony Nathan) (Sidestepping Trouble)	.50
44	Miami Dolphins (Hold On, We're Coming)	.40
45	Miami Dolphins (Dan Marino) (The Release Point)	7.25
46	Minnesota Vikings (Tommy Kramer) (Putting as Much as He Has into the Pass)	.40
47	Minnesota Vikings (Gang Tackling)	.25
48	Minnesota Vikings (You're Not Getting Away From Me This Time)	.25
49	New England Patriots (Tony Eason) (Throwing on the Run)	.40
50	New England Patriots (The Only Place to Go is Down)	.25
51	New England Patriots (Standing the Ball Carrier Up)	.25
52	New Orleans Saints (Going Up the Middle)	.25
53	New Orleans Saints (Putting Everything They've Got into the Tackle)	.25
54	New Orleans Saints (Getting Off the Ground to Block the Kick)	.25
55	New York Giants (Over the Top)	.25
56	New York Giants (Rallying Around the Opposition)	.25
57	New York Giants (Phil Simms) (The Huddle)	.60
58	New York Jets (Following His Blockers)	.25
59	New York Jets (This is as Far as You Go)	.25
60	New York Jets (Looking Over the Defense)	.25
61	Philadelphia Eagles (Going Through the Opening Untouched)	.25
62	Philadelphia Eagles (Squashing the Enemy)	.25
63	Philadelphia Eagles (There's No Room Here, So Let's Go Outside)	.25
64	Pittsburgh Steelers (Sprinting Around the End)	.40
65	Pittsburgh Steelers (Mismatch)	.40
66	Pittsburgh Steelers (About to Be Thrown Back)	.40
67	St. Louis Cardinals (In for Six)	.25
68	St. Louis Cardinals (Piling Ip the Ball Carrier)	.25
69	St. Louis Cardinals (Joe Theismann) (Causing the Fumble)	.75
70	San Diego Chargers (Plenty of Open Space Ahead)	.25
71	San Diego Chargers (Ready to Be Swallowed Up)	.25
72	San Diego Chargers (A Quarterback in Serious Trouble)	.25
73	San Francisco 49ers (Reading the Hole and Exploding Through)	.25
74	San Francisco 49ers (Burying the Opponent)	.25
75	San Francisco 49ers (Joe Montana, Russ Francis) (Waiting to Throw Until His Receiver Breaks Free)	4.25
76	Seattle Seahawks (Dave Krieg) (Getting Just Enough Time to Pass)	.50
77	Seattle Seahawks (Craig James) (Capturing the Enemy)	.50
78	Seattle Seahawks (It's Going to be a Fottrace Now)	.40
79	Tampa Bay Buccaneers (Heading Outside Away From Trouble)	.25
80	Tampa Bay Buccaneers (One-On-One Tackle)	.25
81	Tampa Bay Buccaneers (Eric Dickerson) (A Buccaneers Sandwich)	1.25
82	Washington Redskins (John Riggins) (Just Enough Room to Get Through)	.60
83	Washington Redskins (Wrapping Up the Opponent)	.25
84	Washington Redskins (Mark Moseley) (Field-Goal Attempt)	.40
85	Super Bowl XIX (Roger Craig) (San Francisco vs. Miami)	.90
86	Super Bowl XIX (Joe Montana) (San Francisco vs. Miami)	3.75
87	Super Bowl XIX (Tony Nathan) (San Francisco vs. Miami)	.40
88	1985 Pro Bowl	.50

1986 Fleer Team Action

The 1986 Fleer football set is again complete at 88 cards and is organized in an identical fashion to the previous year's set. These cards, which have a light blue border, include three for Super Bowl XX and a 1986 Pro Bowl card. Other highlights include a first-year Fleer John Elway, a Bernie Kosar "rookie" and a pre-Topps Keith Byars "rookie." Packs had seven cards and three logo stickers.

		MT
	Complete Set (88):	23.00
	Common Card:	.25
1	Atlanta Falcons (Preparing to Make Cut)	.50
2	Atlanta Falcons (Everybody Gets Into the Act)	.25
3	Atlanta Falcons (Where Do You Think You're Going)	.25
4	Buffalo Bills (Turning On the After-Burners)	.25
5	Buffalo Bills (Running Into a Wall of Blue)	.25
6	Buffalo Bills (Up and Over)	.25
7	Chicago Bears (Jim McMahon, Walter Payton) (Pocket Forms Around Passer)	1.25
8	Chicago Bears (Richard Dent, Dan Hampton) (Monsters of the Midway II)	1.00
9	Chicago Bears (Mike Singletary) (Blitz in a Blizzard)	.85
10	Cincinnati Bengals (Dave Rimington, Anthony Munoz) (Plowing Trough Defense)	.60
11	Cincinnati Bengals (Zeroing in for the Hit)	.25
12	Cincinnati Bengals (Marcus Allen) (Oh, No You Don't)	1.25
13	Cleveland Browns (Bernie Kosar, Kevin Mack) (Looking for a Hole to Develop)	2.25
14	Cleveland Browns (Buried by the Browns)	.25
15	Cleveland Browns (Another Runner Pounded Into the Turf)	.25
16	Dallas Cowboys (Tony Dorsett) (Hole You Could Drive Truck Through)	.85
17	Dallas Cowboys (We've Got You Surrounded)	.50
18	Dallas Cowboys (Randy White) (Giving the Referee Some Help)	.75
19	Denver Broncos (John Elway) (The Blockers Spring into Action)	3.75
20	Denver Broncos (The Orange Crush Shows Its Stuff)	.50
21	Denver Broncos (A Stampede to Block the Kick)	.40
22	Detroit Lions (A Runner's Eye View of the Situation)	.25
23	Detroit Lions (Leveling the Ball Carrier)	.25
24	Detroit Lions (Going All Out to Get the Quarterback)	.25
25	Green Bay Packers (Sweeping Around the Corner)	.25
26	Green Bay Packers (Not Afraid to Go Head to Head)	.25
27	Green Bay Packers (Taking the Snap)	.25
28	Houston Oilers (Plunging for That Extra Yard)	.25
29	Houston Oilers (Tightening the Vise)	.25
30	Houston Oilers (Launching a Field Goal)	.25
31	Indianapolis Colts (Galloping Out of an Arm-Tackle)	.25
32	Indianpolis Colts (Ball is Knocked Loose)	.25
33	Indianapolis Colts (Busting Out of the Backfield)	.25
34	Kansas City Chiefs (About to Head Upfield)	.25
35	Kansas City Chiefs (One the Warpath)	.25
36	Kansas City Chiefs (Getting the Point Across)	.25
37	Los Angeles Raiders (Looks Like Clear Sailing Ahead)	.40
38	Los Angeles Raiders (Surrounded by Unfriendly Faces)	.40
39	Los Angeles Raiders (Vaulting for Six Points)	.40
40	Los Angeles Rams (Eric Dickerson) (Breaking into an Open Field)	.85
41	Los Angeles Rams (Swept Away by a Wave of Rams)	.25
42	Los Angeles Rams (Alertly Scooping Up a Fumble)	.25
43	Miami Dolphins (Clearing a Path for the Running Bacj)	.40
44	Miami Dolphins (Teaching a Painful Lesson)	.40
45	Miami Dolphins (Trying for a Piece of the Ball)	.40
46	Minnesota Vikings (Tommy Kramer) (All Day to Throw)	.50
47	Minnesota Vikings (Walter Payton) (The Moment Before Impact)	1.00
48	Minnesota Vikings (Leaving the Competition Behind)	.25
49	New England Patriots (Solid Line of Blockers)	.25
50	New England Patriots (Surprise Attack From the Rear)	.25
51	New England Patriots (Getting a Grip on the Opponent)	.25
52	New Orleans Saints (Look Out, I'm Coming Through)	.25
53	New Orleans Saints (A Furious Assault)	.25
54	New Orleans Saints (Line of Scrimmage)	.25
55	New York Giants (Phil Simms, Joe Morris) (Pass Play Develops)	.75
56	New York Giants (Putting Squeeze on Offense)	.25
57	New York Giants (Using a Great Block to Turn Corner)	.25
58	New York Jets (The Runner Spots Lane)	.25
59	New York Jets (About to Deliver a Headache)	.25
60	New York Jets (Flying Formation)	.25
61	Philadelphia Eagles (Keith Byars) (Slipping a Tackle)	1.50
62	Philadelphia Ealges (Airborne Eagles Break Up Pass)	.25
63	Philadelphia Eagles (Ron Jaworski) (Connecting On Toss Over Middle)	.50
64	Pittsburgh Steelers (Letting Big Guy Lead the Way)	.25
65	Pittsburgh Steelers (Converging From Every Direction)	.25
66	Pittsburgh Steelers (Gary Anderson) (All Eyes are on the Football)	.40
67	St. Louis Cardinals (Neil Lomax, Jim Burt) (Calmly Dropping Back to Pass)	.40
68	St. Louis Cardinals (Applying Some Bruises)	.25
69	St. Louis Cardinals (Looking for Yardage on Interception Return)	.25
70	San Diego Chargers (Human Cannonball)	.50
71	San Diego Chargers (Dave Krieg) (Another One Bites the Dust)	.50
72	San Diego Chargers (A Clean Steel by the Defense)	.25
73	San Francisco 49ers (Joe Montana) (Looking for Safe Passage)	4.00
74	San Francisco 49ers (An Uplifting Experience)	.25
75	San Francisco 49ers (Danny White) (In Hot Pursuit)	.50
76	Seattle Seahawks (Perparing for Collision)	.40
77	Seattle Seahawks (A Group Effort)	.40
78	Seattle Seahawks (Dan Fouts) (Forcing a Hurried Throw)	.75
79	Tamps Bay Buccaneers (Protecting Quarterback at All Costs)	.25
80	Tampa Bay Buccaneers (Dishing Out Some Punishment)	.25
81	Tampa Bay Buccaneers (No Trespassing)	.25
82	Washington Redskins (Squaring Off in the Trenches)	.25
83	Washington Redskins (Danny White) (Pouncing on the Passer)	.50
84	Washington Redskins (Two Hits Are Better Than One)	.25
85	Super Bowl XX (Walter Payton) (Chicago vs. New England)	1.25
86	Super Bowl XX (Jim McMahon) (Chicago vs. New England)	.75
87	Super Bowl XX (Chicago vs. New England)	.40
88	Pro Bowl 1986 (Marcus Allen)	1.50

1987 Fleer Team Action

Again complete at 88 cards, the 1987 Fleer football set contains two cards for each team, one card representing each Super Bowl and eight cards depicting the previous season's playoff games. The cards have a yellow and black border. The set features a first-year Fleer Steve Young and two pre-Topps Bo Jackson "rookies." Each pack had seven cards and three logo stickers.

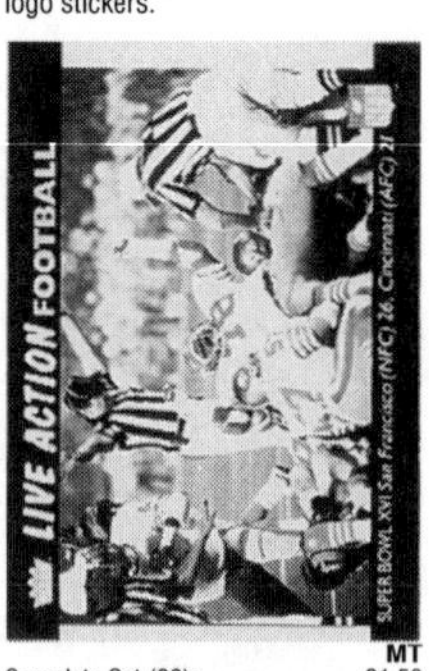

		MT
	Complete Set (88):	21.50
	Common Card:	.20
1	Atlanta Falcons (A Clear View Downfield)	.45
2	Atlanta Falcons (Roger Craig) (Pouncing on a Runner)	.45
3	Buffalo Bills (Buffalo Stampede)	.20
4	Buffalo Bills (Double Bill)	.20
5	Chicago Bears (Walter Payton) (Stay Out of Our Way)	1.00
6	Chicago Bears (Dan Hampton) (Quarterback's Nightmare)	.45
7	Cincinnati Bengals (Eddie Brown) (Irresistible Force)	.45
8	Cincinnati Bengals (Bengals on the Prowl)	.20
9	Cleveland Browns (Following the Lead Blocker)	.20
10	Cleveland Browns (Block That Kick)	.20
11	Dallas Cowboys (Next Stop...End Zone)	.30
12	Dallas Cowboys (Ride 'Em Cowboys)	.30
13	Denver Broncos (John Elway) (Pitchout in Progress)	2.25
14	Denver Broncos (Broncos' Busters)	.30
15	Detroit Lions (Off to the Races)	.20
16	Detroit Lions (Entering the Lions' Den)	.20
17	Green Bay Packers (Setting the Wheels in Motion)	.20
18	Green Bay Packers (Stack of Packers)	.20
19	Houston Oilers (Making a Cut at the Line of Scrimmage)	.20
20	Houston Oilers (Hit Parade)	.20
21	Indianapolis Colts (The Horses Up Front)	.20
22	Indianapolis Colts (Stopping the Runner in His Tracks)	.20
23	Kansas City Chiefs (It's A Snap)	.20
24	Kansas City Chiefs (Bo Jackson) (Nowhere to Hide)	1.50
25	Los Angeles Raiders (Bo Jackson) (Looking For Daylight)	2.00
26	Los Angeles Raiders (Wrapped Up by Raiders)	.30
27	Los Angeles Rams (Jim Everett) (Movers and Shakers)	2.00
28	Los Angeles Rams (In the Quarterback's Face)	.20
29	Miami Dolphins (Full Speed Ahead)	.30
30	Miami Dolphins (Acrobatic Interception)	.30
31	Minnesota Vikings (Tommy Kramer) (Solid Line of Protection)	.30
32	Minnesota Vikings (Bearing a Heavy Load)	.20
33	New England Patriots (Craig James) (The Blockers Fan Out)	.45
34	New England Patriots (Converging Linebackers)	.20
35	New Orleans Saints (Dalton Hilliard, Jim Burt) (Saints Go Diving In)	.45
36	New Orleans Saints (Crash Course)	.20
37	New York Giants (Phil Simms) (Armed and Dangerous)	.45
38	New York Giants (Lawrence Taylor) (A Giant-sized Hit)	.75
39	New York Jets (Ken O'Brien) (Jets Prepare for Takeoff)	.30
40	New York Jets (Showing No Mercy)	.20
41	Philadelphia Eagles (Taking It Straight Up the Middle)	.20
42	Philadelphia Eagles (Reggie White) (The Strong Arm of the Defense)	1.25
43	Pittsburgh Steelers (Double-Team Trouble)	.20

44	Pittsburgh Steelers (Caught in a Steel Trap)	.20
45	St. Louis Cardinals (The Kick is Up and...It's Good)	.20
46	St. Louis Cardinals (Seeing Red)	.20
47	San Diego Chargers (Blast Off)	.20
48	San Diego Chargers (Todd Christensen) (Lightning Strikes)	.45
49	San Francisco 49ers (The Rush Is On)	.75
50	San Francisco 49ers (Shoulder to Shoulder)	.20
51	Seattle Seahawks (Curt Warner) (Not a Defender in Sight)	.30
52	Seattle Seahawks (Hard Knocks)	.20
53	Tampa Bay Bucaneers (Steve Young) (Rolling Out Against the Grain)	3.75
54	Tampa Bay Buccaneers (Crunch Time)	.20
55	Washington Redskins (Jay Schroeder) (Getting the Drop on the Defense)	.45
56	Washington Redskins (The Blitz Claims Another Victim)	.20
57	AFC Championship Game (Denver vs. Cleveland)	.20
58	AFC Divisional Playoff (Cleveland vs. New York Jets)	.20
59	AFC Divisional Playoff (Andre Tippett) (Denver vs. New England)	.30
60	AFC Wild Card Game (New York Jets vs. Kansas City)	.20
61	NFC Championship (Lawrence Taylor) (New York Giants vs. Washington)	.60
62	NFC Divisional Playoff (William Perry) (Chicago vs. Washington)	.30
63	NFC Divisional Playoff (Joe Morris) (New York Giants vs. San Francisco)	.30
64	NFC Wild Card Game (Eric Dickerson) (Washington vs. Los Angeles Rams)	.65
65	Super Bowl I (Green Bay vs. Kansas City)	.30
66	Super Bowl II (Bart Starr) (Green Bay vs. Oakland)	.50
67	Super Bowl III (Matt Snell) (New York vs. Baltimore)	.30
68	Super Bowl IV (Kansas City vs. Minnesota)	.20
69	Super Bowl V (Duane Thomas) (Baltimore vs. Dallas)	.45
70	Super Bowl VI (Roger Staubach) (Dallas vs. Miami)	.85
71	Super Bowl VII (Bob Griese, Jim Kiick) (Miami vs. Washington)	.60
72	Super Bowl VIII (Larry Csonka) (Miami vs. Minnesota)	.60
73	Super Bowl IX (Fran Tarkenton) (Pittsburgh vs. Minnesota)	.75
74	Super Bowl X (Franco Harris) (Pittsburgh vs. Dallas)	.75
75	Super Bowl XI (Chuck Foreman) (Oakland vs. Minnesota)	.30
76	Super Bowl XII (Tony Dorsett) (Dallas vs. Denver)	.60
77	Super Bowl XIII (Terry Bradshaw) (Pittsburgh vs. Dallas)	1.00
78	Super Bowl XIV (Cullen Bryant) (Pittsburgh vs. Los Angeles)	.30
79	Super Bowl XV (Jim Plunkett) (Oakland vs. Philadelphia)	.30
80	Super Bowl XVI (San Francisco vs. Cincinnati)	.20
81	Super Bowl XVII (Washington vs. Miami)	.20
82	Super Bowl XVIII (Los Angeles vs. Washington)	.20
83	Super Bowl XIX (R. Craig, Joe Montana) (San Francisco vs. Miami)	2.50
84	Super Bowl XX (Wilber Marshall, Richard Dent) (Chicago vs. New England)	.45
85	Super Bowl XXI (Lawrence Taylor) (New York vs. Denver)	.70
86	Super Bowl XXI (Phil Simms) (New York vs. Denver)	.45
87	Super Bowl XXI (Lawrence Taylor, Carl Banks) (Giants erupt in 3rd, Score 17 Points)	.50
88	Super Bowl XXI (Giants Outrun Broncos by only 27 yards)	.50

A player's name in *italic type* indicates a rookie card.

1988 Fleer Team Action

The final Fleer Team Action set contained 88 cards, including two for each team, 11 Super Bowl cards, special playoff cards and a few league-leader cards at the end of the set. The set was basically structured alphabetically by team nicknames within each conference. There are three subsets: Super Bowls of the Decade (#s 57-67); Playoff Games (#s 68-75) and "League Leading Teams" (#s 76-88). Other highlights are two cards each for Dan Marino, Joe Montana, John Elway and Bo Jackson. Cards were sold in packs of seven, plus three logo stickers.

		MT
Complete Set (88):		18.50
Common Card:		.18
1	Cincinnati Bengals (Boomer Esiason) (A Great Wall)	.80
2	Cincinnati Bengals (Stacking the Odds)	.18
3	Buffalo Bills (Jim Kelly) (Play-Action)	1.25
4	Buffalo Bills (Buffalo Soldiers)	.18
5	Denver Broncos (John Elway) (Sneak Attack)	1.25
6	Denver Broncos (Crushing the Opposition)	.18
7	Cleveland Browns (Bernie Kosar, Kevin Mack) (On the Run)	.50
8	Cleveland Browns (Eric Dickerson) (Dogs' Day)	.65
9	San Diego Chargers (Gary Anderson) (A Bolt of Blue)	.25
10	San Diego Chargers (That's a Wrap)	.18
11	Kansas City Chiefs (Last Line of Offense)	.18
12	Kansas City Chiefs (Hard-Hitting in the Heartland)	.18
13	Indianapolis Colts (An Eye to the End Zone)	.18
14	Indianapolis Colts (Free Ball)	.18
15	Miami Dolphins (Dan Marino) (Miami Scoring Machine)	2.00
16	Miami Dolphins (No Mercy)	.25
17	New York Jets (Ken O'Brien) (On a Roll)	.25
18	New York Jets (Jets Win a Dogfight)	.18
19	Houston Oilers (Warren Moon) (Well-Oiled Machine)	.85
20	Houston Oilers (Hard Shoulder)	.18
21	New England Patriots (Craig James) (A Clean Sweep)	.25
22	New England Patriots (Bo Jackson) (A Fall in New England)	1.00
23	Los Angeles Raiders (Bo Jackson) (Rush Hour in Los Angeles)	1.50
24	Los Angeles Raiders (Howie Long) (Cut Me Some Slack)	.30
25	Seattle Seahawks (Curt Warner) (Follow the Leader)	.25
26	Seattle Seahawks (Brian Bosworth) (Pain, But No Gain)	.30
27	Pittsburgh Steelers (Life in the Fast Lane)	.18
28	Pittsburgh Steelers (No Exit)	.18
29	Chicago Bears (Bearly Audible)	.18
30	Chicago Bears (Here, Kitty, Kitty)	.18
31	Tampa Bay Buccaneers (Vinny Testaverde) (Letting Loose)	1.00
32	Tampa Bay Buccaneers (In the Grasp)	.18
33	St. Louis Cardinals (Neil Lomax) (You've Gotta Hand it to Him)	.25
34	St. Louis Cardinals (Roger Craig) (Stack of Cards)	.35
35	Dallas Cowboys (Herschel Walker) (Take it Away)	.50
36	Dallas Cowboys (Randy White) (Howdy, Partner)	.40
37	Philadelphia Eagles (Randall Cunningham) (Eagle in Flight)	1.25
38	Philadelphia Eagles (Reggie White) (Buffalo Sandwich)	.75
39	Atlanta Falcons (Rumbling Runner)	.18
40	Atlanta Falcons (The Brink of Disaster)	.18
41	San Francisco 49ers (Roger Craig) (Move Aside)	.40
42	San Francisco 49ers (Ronnie Lott) (Bullies By the Bay)	.50
43	New York Giants (Phil Simms) (Firing a Fastball)	.40
44	New York Giants (A Giant Headache)	.18
45	Detroit Lions (Charge Up the Middle)	.18
46	Detroit Lions (Rocking and Rolling in Motown)	.18
47	Green Bay Packers (Carl Lee) (Gaining Attitude)	.18
48	Green Bay Packers (This Play is a Hit)	.18
49	Los Angeles Rams (Jim Everett) (Rams Lock Horns)	.40
50	Los Angeles Rams (Greetings from L.A.)	.18
51	Washington Redskins (Capital Gains)	.18
52	Washington Redskins (No More Mr. Nice Guy)	.18
53	New Orleans Saints (Roamin' in the Dome)	.18
54	New Orleans Saints (He'll Feel This One Tomorrow)	.18
55	Minnesota Vikings (Wade Wilson) (Passing Fancy)	.45
56	Minnesota Vikings (A Vikings' Siege)	.18
57	Super Bowl XXII (Timmy Smith) (Washington vs. Denver)	.25
58	Super Bowl Checklist (Timmy Smith)	.25
59	Super Bowl Checklist (John Elway)	1.00
60	Super Bowl XXI (Lawrence Taylor, Carl Banks) (New York vs. Denver)	.75
61	Super Bowl XX (Walter Payton) (Chicago vs. New England)	.75
62	Super Bowl XIX (Roger Craig) (San Francisco vs. Miami)	.30
63	Super Bowl XVIII (Marcus Allen) (Los Angeles Raiders vs. Washington)	.50
64	Super Bowl XVII (Washington vs. Miami)	.18
65	Super Bowl XVI (Joe Montana) (San Francisco vs. Cincinnati)	1.75
66	Super Bowl XV (Jim Plunkett) (Oakland vs. Philadelphia)	.25
67	Super Bowl XIV (Pittsburgh vs. Los Angeles Rams)	.18
68	NFC Championship (Washington vs. Minnesota)	.18
69	AFC Championship (John Elway) (Denver vs. Cleveland)	1.00
70	NFC Playoff Game (Joe Montana) (Minnesota vs. San Francisco)	1.75
71	NFC Playoff Game (Washington vs. Chicago)	.18
72	AFC Playoff Game (Ozzie Newsome, Kevin Mack) (Cleveland vs. Indianapolis)	.30
73	AFC Playoff Game (Denver vs. Houston)	.18
74	NFC Wild Card Game (Minnesota vs. New Orleans)	.18
75	AFC Wild Card Game (Houston vs. Seattle)	.18
76	League Leading Team Rushing (Roger Craig) (San Francisco 49ers)	.25
77	League Leading Team Passing (Dan Marino) (Miami Dolphins)	1.50
78	League Leading Team Interceptions (New Orleans Saints)	.18
79	League Leading Team Fumble Recovery (Philadelphia Eagles)	.18
80	League Leading Team Sacks (Richard Dent) (Chicago Bears)	.40
81	League Leading Team Defense Against Kickoff Reurns (Buffalo Bills)	.18
82	League Leading Team Defense Against Punt Returns (New York Jets)	.18
83	League Leading Teams Punt Returns (St. Louis Cardinals)	.18
84	League Leading Team Kickoff Returns (Atlanta Falcons)	.18
85	League Leading Team Fewest Fumbles (Pittsburgh Steelers)	.18
86	League Leading Team Fewest Interceptions (Bernie Kosar) (Cleveland Browns)	.50
87	League Leading Team Fewest Points Allowed (Indianapolis Colts)	.18
88	League Leading Team TD's on Returns (Henry Ellard) (Los Angeles Rams)	.40

1990 Fleer

The 1990 "Premier Edition" football card series, Fleer's first player card issue since 1963, was issued in mid-June. Cards were available in 15- and 43-count packs and 45-count three-pack strips. The cards carry full-color printing on the fronts and backs. Card fronts show full-figure action photography, while backs highlight a head shot, stats and text. The 25 cards in the All-Pro subset are different than the other Premier Edition cards. The All-Pro cards contain two photos on each card front - a large facial close-up and a smaller full-figure shot against a silver background. Special metallic links are used for graphic design effect. Jeff George, Andre Ware, Blair Thomas and Percy Snow are featured within the set as first-round draft choices by their respective teams. With the introduction of this football card set, Fleer was the only manufacturer offering a full line of football, baseball and basketball cards.

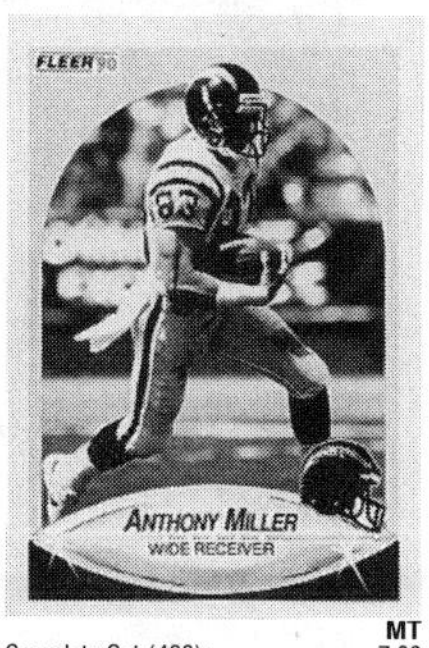

		MT
Complete Set (400):		7.00
Common Player:		.03
Wax Pack (15):		.45
Wax Box (36):		7.00
1	Harris Barton	.03
2	Chet Brooks	.03
3	Michael Carter	.03
4	Mike Cofer	.03
5	Roger Craig	.03
6	*Kevin Fagan*	.06
7	Charles Haley	.03
8	*Pierce Holt*	.15
9	Ronnie Lott	.03
10	Joe Montana (stats reversed on back)	1.00
11	Bubba Paris	.03
12	Tom Rathman	.03
13	Jerry Rice	.75
14	John Taylor	.20
15	Keena Turner	.03
16	Mike Walter	.03
17	Steve Young	.75
18	Steve Atwater	.03
19	Tyrone Braxton	.03
20	*Michael Brooks*	.15
21	John Elway	.50
22	Simon Fletcher	.03
23	Bobby Humphrey	.03
24	Mark Jackson	.03
25	Vance Johnson	.03
26	Greg Kragen	.03
27	Ken Lanier	.03
28	Karl Mecklenburg	.03
29	Orson Mobley	.03
30	Steve Sewell	.03
31	Dennis Smith	.03
32	David Treadwell	.03
33	Willie Anderson	.03
34	Greg Bell	.03
35	Henry Ellard	.03
36	Jim Everett	.03
37	Jerry Gray	.03
38	Kevin Greene	.03
39	Pete Holohan	.03
40	LeRoy Irvin	.03
41	Mike Lansford	.03
42	*Buford McGee*	.08
43	Tom Newberry	.03
44	Vince Newsome	.03
45	Jackie Slater	.03
46	Mike Wilcher	.03
47	Matt Bahr	.03
48	Brian Brennan	.03
49	Thane Gash	.03
50	Mike Johnson	.03
51	Bernie Kosar	.03
52	Reggie Langhorne	.03
53	Tim Manoa	.03
54	Clay Matthews	.03
55	Eric Metcalf	.08
56	Frank Minnifield	.03
57	Gregg Rakoczy	.03
58	Webster Slaughter	.03
59	Bryan Wagner	.03
60	Felix Wright	.03
61	Raul Allegre	.03
62	Ottis Anderson	.03
63	Carl Banks	.03
64	Mark Bavaro	.03
65	Maurice Carthon	.03
66	Mark Collins	.03
67	*Jeff Hostetler*	.50
68	Erik Howard	.03
69	Pepper Johnson	.03
70	Sean Landeta	.03
71	Lionel Manuel	.03
72	Leonard Marshall	.03
73	Dave Meggett	.08
74	Bart Oates	.03
75	Doug Riesenberg	.03
76	Phil Simms	.10
77	Lawrence Taylor	.10
78	Eric Allen	.03
79	Jerome Brown	.03
80	Keith Byars	.03
81	Cris Carter	.30
82	Randall Cunningham, Byron Evans (error)	.20
83	Ron Heller, Byron Evans (error)	.10
84	Ron Heller	.03
85	Terry Hoage	.03
86	Keith Jackson	.20
87	Seth Joyner	.03
88	Mike Quick	.03
89	Mike Schad	.03
90	Clyde Simmons	.03
91	John Teltschik	.03
92	Anthony Toney	.03
93	Reggie White	.15
94	Ray Berry	.03
95	Joey Browner	.03
96	Anthony Carter	.03
97	Chris Doleman	.03
98	Rick Fenney	.03
99	*Rich Gannon*	1.50
100	Hassan Jones	.03
101	Steve Jordan	.03
102	Rich Karlis	.03
103	*Andre Ware*	.20
104	Kirk Lowdermilk	.03
105	Keith Millard	.03
106	Scott Studwell	.03
107	Herschel Walker	.03
108	Wade Wilson	.03
109	Gary Zimmerman	.03
110	Don Beebe	.10
111	Cornelius Bennett	.03
112	Shane Conlan	.03
113	Jim Kelly	.20
114	Scott Norwood	.03
115	Mark Kelso	.03
116	Larry Kinnebrew	.03
117	Pete Metzelaars	.03
118	Scott Radecic	.03
119	Andre Reed	.20
120	Jim Richter	.03
121	Bruce Smith	.03
122	Leonard Smith	.03
123	Art Still	.03
124	Thurman Thomas	.50
125	Steve Brown	.03
126	Ray Childress	.03
127	Ernest Givins	.03
128	John Grimsley	.03
129	Alonzo Highsmith	.03
130	Drew Hill	.03
131	Bruce Matthews	.03
132	Johnny Meads	.03
133	Warren Moon	.20
134	Mike Munchak	.03
135	Mike Rozier	.03
136	Dean Steinkuhler	.03
137	Lorenzo White	.15
138	Tony Zendejas	.03
139	Gary Anderson	.03
140	Bubby Brister	.08
141	Thomas Everett	.03
142	Derek Hill	.03
143	Merril Hoge	.03
144	Tim Johnson	.03
145	Louis Lipps	.03
146	David Little	.03
147	Greg Lloyd	.03
148	Mike Mularkey	.03
149	John Rienstra	.03
150	Gerald Williams	.08
151	Keith Willis	.03
152	Rod Woodson	.10
153	Tim Worley	.03
154	Gary Clark	.10
155	Darryl Grant	.03
156	Darrell Green	.03
157	Joe Jacoby	.03
158	Jim Lachey	.03
159	Chip Lohmiller	.03
160	Charles Mann	.03
161	Wilber Marshall	.03
162	Mark May	.03
163	Ralf Mojsiejenko	.03
164	Art Monk	.06
165	Gerald Riggs	.03
166	Mark Rypien	.15
167	Ricky Sanders	.03
168	Don Warren	.03
169	Robert Brown	.03
170	Blair Bush	.03
171	Brent Fullwood	.03
172	Tim Harris	.03
173	Chris Jacke	.03
174	Perry Kemp	.03
175	Don Majkowski	.03
176	Tony Mandarich	.03
177	Mark Murphy	.03
178	Brian Noble	.03
179	Ken Ruettgers	.03
180	Sterling Sharpe	.20
181	Ed West	.03
182	Keith Woodside	.03
183	Morten Andersen	.03
184	Stan Brock	.03
185	*Jim Dombrowski*	.10
186	John Fourcade	.03
187	Bobby Hebert	.10
188	Craig Heyward	.03
189	Dalton Hilliard	.03
190	Rickey Jackson	.03
191	Buford Jordan	.03
192	Eric Martin	.03
193	Robert Massey	.03
194	Sam Mills	.03
195	Pat Swilling	.03
196	Jim Wilks	.03
197	*John Alt*	.10
198	Walker Lee Ashley	.03
199	Steve DeBerg	.03
200	Leonard Griffin	.03
201	Albert Lewis	.03
202	Nick Lowery	.03
203	Bill Maas	.03
204	Pete Mandley	.03
205	*Chris Martin*	.10
206	Christian Okoye	.03
207	Stephone Paige	.03
208	*Kevin Porter*	.10
209	Derrick Thomas	.20
210	Lewis Billups	.03
211	James Brooks	.03
212	Jason Buck	.03
213	*Rickey Dixon*	.10
214	Boomer Esiason	.10
215	David Fulcher	.03
216	Rodney Holman	.03
217	Lee Johnson	.03
218	Tim Krumrie	.03
219	Tim McGee	.03
220	Anthony Munoz	.03
221	Bruce Reimers	.03
222	Leon White	.03
223	Ickey Woods	.03
224	Harvey Armstrong	.03
225	Michael Ball	.03
226	Chip Banks	.03
227	Pat Beach	.03
228	Duane Bickett	.03
229	Bill Brooks	.03
230	Jon Hand	.03
231	Andre Rison	.25
232	Rohn Stark	.03
233	Donnell Thompson	.03
234	Jack Trudeau	.03
235	Clarence Verdin	.03
236	Mark Clayton	.03
237	Jeff Cross	.03
238	*Jeff Dellenbach*	.10
239	Mark Duper	.03
240	Ferrell Edmunds	.03
241	Hugh Green	.03
242	E.J. Junior	.03
243	Marc Logan	.03
244	Dan Marino	1.00
245	John Offerdahl	.03
246	Reggie Roby	.03
247	Sammie Smith	.03
248	Pete Stoyanovich	.03
249	Marcus Allen	.08
250	*Eddie Anderson*	.10
251	Steve Beuerlein	.15
252	Mike Dyal	.03
253	Mervyn Fernandez	.03
254	Bob Golic	.03
255	Mike Harden	.03
256	Bo Jackson	.40
257	Howie Long	.03
258	Don Mosebar	.03
259	Jay Schroeder	.03
260	Steve Smith	.03
261	Greg Townsend	.03
262	Lionel Washington	.03
263	Brian Blades	.10
264	Jeff Bryant	.03
265	Grant Feasel	.03
266	Jacob Green	.03
267	James Jefferson	.03
268	Norm Johnson	.03
269	Dave Krieg	.03
270	Travis McNeal	.03
271	Joe Nash	.03
272	Rufus Porter	.03
273	Kelly Stouffer	.03
274	John L. Williams	.03
275	Jim Arnold	.03
276	Jerry Ball	.03
277	Bennie Blades	.03
278	Lomas Brown	.03
279	Mike Cofer	.03
280	Bob Gagliano	.03
281	Richard Johnson	.03
282	Eddie Murray	.03
283	Rodney Peete	.10
284	Barry Sanders	1.25
285	Eric Sanders	.03
286	Chris Spielman	.03
287	*Eric Williams*	.10
288	Neal Anderson	.08
289	Kevin Butler (placekicker/PK placekicker/P punter/P punter/PK)	.08
290	Jim Covert	.03
291	Richard Dent	.03
292	Dennis Gentry	.03
293	Jim Harbaugh	.15
294	Jay Hilgenberg	.03
295	Vestee Jackson	.03
296	Steve McMichael	.03
297	Ron Morris	.03
298	Brad Muster	.03
299	Mike Singletary	.03
300	James Thornton	.03
301	Mike Tomczak	.03
302	Keith Van Horne	.03
303	Chris Bahr	.03
304	*Martin Bayless*	.10
305	Marion Butts	.10
306	Gill Byrd	.03
307	Arthur Cox	.03
308	Burt Grossman	.03
309	Jamie Holland	.03
310	Jim McMahon	.03
311	Anthony Miller	.30
312	Leslie O'Neal	.03
313	Billy Ray Smith	.03
314	Tim Spencer	.03
315	*Broderick Thompson*	.10
316	Lee Williams	.03
317	Bruce Armstrong	.03
318	Tim Goad	.03
319	Steve Grogan	.03
320	Roland James	.03
321	Cedric Jones	.03
322	Fred Marion	.03
323	Stanley Morgan	.03
324	Robert Perryman	.03
325	Johnny Rembert	.03
326	Ed Reynolds	.03
327	Kenneth Sims	.03
328	John Stephens	.03
329	*Danny Villa*	.06
330	Robert Awalt	.03
331	Anthony Bell	.03
332	Rich Camarillo	.03
333	Earl Ferrell	.03
334	Roy Green	.03
335	Gary Hogeboom	.03
336	Cedric Mack	.03
337	Freddie Joe Nunn	.03
338	Luis Sharpe	.03
339	Vai Sikahema	.03
340	J.T. Smith	.03
341	*Tom Tupa*	.08
342	*Percy Snow*	.10
343	Mark Carrier (TB)	.03
344	Randy Grimes	.03
345	Paul Gruber	.03
346	Ron Hall	.03
347	*Jeff George*	1.25
348	Bruce Hill	.03
349	William Howard	.03
350	Donald Igwebuike	.03
351	*Chris Mohr*	.08
352	*Winston Moss*	.08
353	Ricky Reynolds	.03
354	Mark Robinson	.03
355	Lars Tate	.03
356	Vinny Testaverde	.10
357	Broderick Thomas	.03
358	Troy Benson	.03
359	*Jeff Criswell*	.10
360	Tony Eason	.03
361	James Hasty	.03
362	Johnny Hector	.03
363	Bobby Humphery	.03
364	Pat Leahy	.03
365	Erik McMillan	.03
366	Freeman McNeil	.03
367	Ken O'Brien	.03
368	Ron Stallworth	.03
369	Al Toon	.03
370	*Blair Thomas*	.15
371	Aundray Bruce	.03
372	Tony Casillas	.03
373	Shawn Collins	.03
374	Evan Cooper	.03
375	Bill Fralic	.03

376 Scott Fulhage .03
377 Mike Gann .03
378 Ron Heller .03
379 Keith Jones .03
380 Mike Kenn .03
381 Chris Miller .10
382 Deion Sanders .35
383 John Settle .03
384 Troy Aikman .75
385 Bill Bates .03
386 Willie Broughton .03
387 Steve Folsom .03
388 Ray Horton .03
389 Michael Irvin .25
390 Jim Jeffcoat .03
391 Eugene Lockhart .03
392 *Kelvin Martin* .15
393 Nate Newton .03
394 Mike Saxon .03
395 Derrick Shepard .03
396 Steve Walsh .03
397 Joe Montana, Jerry Rice .70
398 Checklist .03
399 Checklist .03
400 Checklist .03

1990 Fleer All-Pro

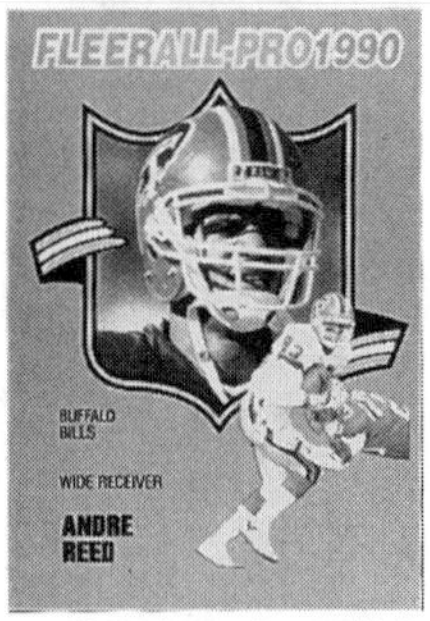

These silver cards were distributed randomly in Fleer wax and cello packs. Cards were prone to damage, since the silver coating easily suffered scratches and dings. Cards were issued approximately one to every six to 10 packs.

MT
Complete Set (25): 7.50
Common Player: .25
1 Joe Montana 3.00
2 Jerry Rice 2.00
3 Keith Jackson .50
4 Barry Sanders 3.00
5 Christian Okoye .25
6 Tom Newberry .25
7 Jim Covert .25
8 Anthony Munoz .25
9 Mike Munchak .25
10 Jay Hilgenberg .25
11 Chris Doleman .25
12 Keith Millard .25
13 Derrick Thomas 1.00
14 Lawrence Taylor .75
15 Karl Mecklenburg .25
16 Reggie White .60
17 Tim Harris .25
18 David Fulcher .25
19 Ronnie Lott .50
20 Eric Allen .50
21 Steve Atwater .25
22 Rich Camarillo .25
23 Morten Anderson .25
24 Andre Reed 1.00
25 Rod Woodson .50

1990 Fleer Stars 'n Stripes

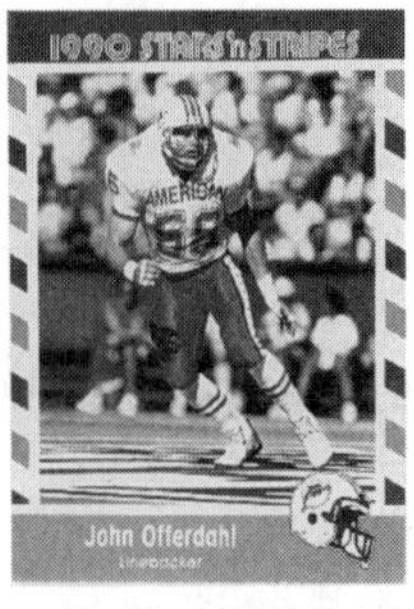

Issued in eight-card boxes by the Asher Candy Co., a subsidiary of Fleer, these cards were considered by the parent company to be little more than a test set. Collation was bad, and the set was riddled with basic errors. The first edition of Stars 'N Stripes features 80 players from the 1990 Pro Bowl plus 10 college stars selected in the first round of the 1990 NFL draft. All 90 cards carry full-color printing on both sides, with action photography on the front and a head shot of the player on the back. Pro Bowlers are shown in their all-conference uniforms while first-round picks are shown in collegiate action. Front borders have red, white and blue striping. Each package is shrink-wrapped. A full checklist is on the back of each pack.

MT
Complete Set (90): 25.00
Common Player: .05
1 Warren Moon .35
2 Reggie Roby .05
3 David Treadwell .05
4 Dave Krieg .05
5 James Brooks .20
6 Erik McMillan .05
7 Rod Woodson .10
8 Albert Lewis .05
9 Kevin Ross .05
10 Frank Minnifield .05
11 David Fulcher .07
12 Thurman Thomas .75
13 Christian Okoye .25
14 Dennis Smith .05
15 Johnny Rembert .05
16 Ray Donaldson .05
17 John Offerdahl .15
18 Clay Matthews .05
19 Shane Conlan .10
20 Derrick Thomas .30
21 Tunch Ilken .05
22 Mike Munchak .07
23 Max Montoya .05
24 Kent Hull .07
25 Greg Kragen .05
26 Bruce Matthews .70
27 Howie Long .10
28 Chris Hinton .10
29 Anthony Munoz .10
30 Bruce Smith .20
31 Ferrell Edmunds .05
32 Rodney Holman .05
33 Andre Reed .50
34 Webster Slaughter .05
35 Anthony Miller .20
36 Brian Blades .10
37 Leslie O'Neal .10
38 Rufus Porter .10
39 Lee Williams .05
40 Ed Murray .05
41 Mark Rypien .20
42 Randall Cunningham .35
43 Rich Camarillo .10
44 Barry Sanders 2.50
45 Dalton Hilliard .10
46 Eric Allen .10
47 Brent Fullwood .05
48 Ron Wolfley .05
49 Jerry Gray .05
50 Dave Meggett .50
51 Roger Craig .35
52 Carl Lee .10
53 Ronnie Lott .20
54 Tim McDonald .05
55 Joey Browner .10
56 Mike Singletary .20
57 Vaughan Johnson .05
58 Chris Spielman .05
59 Doug Smith .05
60 Lawrence Taylor .50
61 Chris Doleman .10
62 Guy McIntyre .05
63 Jay Hilgenberg .07
64 Randall McDaniel .05
65 Gary Zimmerman .05
66 Luis Sharpe .05
67 Charles Mann .05
68 Keith Millard .10
69 Jackie Slater .05
70 Bill Fralic .05
71 Henry Ellard .10
72 Jerry Rice .65
73 Steve Jordan .05
74 Sterling Sharpe .50
75 Keith Jackson .25
76 Mark Carrier (TB) .10
77 Kevin Greene .10
78 Reggie White .20
79 Jerry Ball .10
80 Tim Harris .10
81 Jeff George 2.50
82 Blair Thomas 3.00
83 Cortez Kennedy .75
84 Junior Seau .75
85 Mark Carrier 1.25
86 Andre Ware 1.25
87 Chris Singleton .50
88 Percy Snow .75
89 Steve Broussard .90
90 Rodney Hampton 1.75

1990 Fleer Update

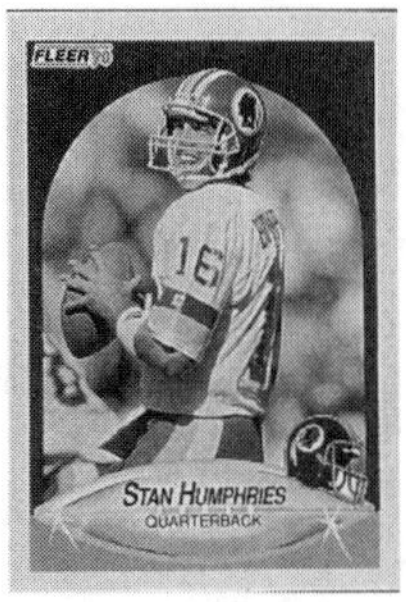

Fleer's 1990 update football set of 120 cards was sold to hobby shops in boxed form. Cards are arranged alphabetically by teams and are the same style as 1990 Fleer football.

MT
Complete Set (120): 35.00
Common Player: .10
Minor Stars: .20
1 Albert Bentley .10
2 Dean Biasucci .10
3 Ray Donaldson .10
4 Jeff George 2.00
5 *Ray Agnew* .10
6 Greg McMurtry .10
7 *Chris Singleton* .10
8 *James Francis* .10
9 *Harold Green* .20
10 John Elliott .10
11 *Rodney Hampton* .75
12 Gary Reasons .10
13 *Lewis Tillman* .20
14 Everson Walls .10
15 *David Alexander* .10
16 Jim McMahon .20
17 *Ben Smith* .10
18 Andre Waters .10
19 *Calvin Williams* .20
20 Earnest Byner .10
21 *Andre Collins* .10
22 Russ Grimm .10
23 *Stan Humphries* .50
24 *Martin Mayhew* .10
25 *Barry Foster* .20
26 *Eric Green* .30
27 Tunch Ilkin .10
28 Hardy Nickerson .10
29 Jerrol Williams .10
30 Mike Baab .10
31 *Leroy Hoard* 1.50
32 Eddie Johnson .10
33 William Fuller .10
34 *Haywood Jeffires* .30
35 *Don Maggs* .10
36 Allen Pinkett .10
37 Robert Awalt .10
38 Dennis McKinnon .10
39 *Ken Norton Jr.* .30
40 *Emmitt Smith* 30.00
41 *Alexander Wright* .20
42 Eric Hill .10
43 *Johnny Johnson* .20
44 Timm Rosenbach .10
45 *Anthony Thompson* .20
46 *Dexter Carter* .20
47 Eric Davis .10
48 Keith DeLong .10
49 *Brent Jones* .30
50 *Darryl Pollard* .10
51 *Steve Wallace* .10
52 *Bern Brostek* .10
53 Aaron Cox .10
54 Cleveland Gary .10
55 *Fred Strickland* .20
56 *Pat Terrell* .10
57 Steve Broussard .10
58 Scott Case .10
59 *Brian Jordan* .30
60 Andre Rison .30
61 Kevin Haverdink .10
62 Reuben Mayes .10
63 Steve Walsh .20
64 Greg Bell .10
65 Tim Brown .30
66 Willie Gault .10
67 *Vance Mueller* .10
68 Bill Pickel .10
69 Aaron Wallace .10
70 Glenn Parker .10
71 Frank Reich .20
72 *Leon Seals* .10
73 Darryl Talley .10
74 *Brad Baxter* .10
75 Jeff Causwell .10
76 Jeff Lageman .10
77 *Rob Moore* 3.00
78 Blair Thomas .20
79 Louis Oliver .10
80 Tony Paige .10
81 *Richmond Webb* .20
82 *Robert Blackmon* .10
83 *Derrick Fenner* .20
84 Andy Heck .10
85 *Cortez Kennedy* .30
86 *Terry Wooden* .10
87 Jeff Donaldson .10
88 *Tim Grunhard* .10
89 Emile Harry .10
90 *Dan Saleaumua* .20
91 Percy Snow .10
92 Andre Ware .20
93 *Darrell Fullington* .10
94 Mike Merriweather .10
95 Henry Thomas .10
96 Robert Brown .10
97 *Leroy Butler* .10
98 Anthony Dilweg .10
99 *Darrel Thompson* .10
100 Keith Woodside .10
101 Gary Plummer .10
102 *Junior Seau* 3.00
103 Billy Joe Tolliver .20
104 Mark Vlasic .10
105 Gary Anderson .10
106 *Ian Beckles* .10
107 *Reggie Cobb* .20
108 *Keith McCants* .20
109 *Mark Bortz* .10
110 Maury Buford .10
111 *Mark Carrier* .20
112 Dan Hampton .10
113 William Perry .10
114 Ron Rivera .10
115 Lemuel Stinson .10
116 *Melvin Bratton* .10
117 *Gary Kubiak* .10
118 *Alton Montgomery* .10
119 Ricky Nattiel .10
120 Checklist .10

1991 Fleer

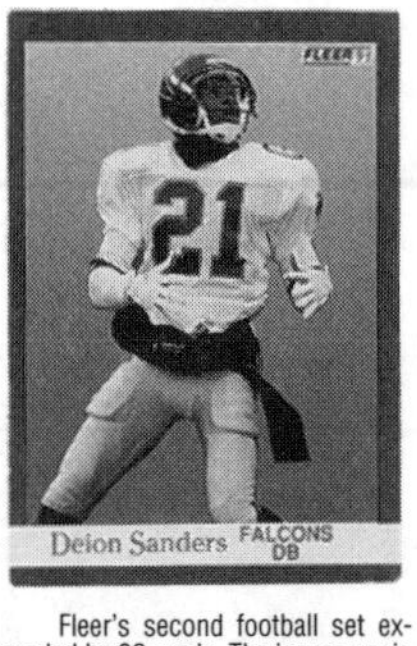

Fleer's second football set expanded by 32 cards. The issues again included randomly-packed all-star cards. New features included a league leaders subset, a hitters subset, and Pro Visions and All-Pros randomly-packed insert sets.

MT
Complete Set (432): 6.00
Common Player: .03
Pack (14): .10
Wax Box (36): 3.00
1 Shane Conlan .07
2 John Davis .03
3 Kent Hull .03
4 James Lofton .10
5 Keith McKeller .07
6 Scott Norwood .03
7 Nate Odomes .03
8 Andre Reed .20
9 Jim Ritcher .03
10 Leon Seals .03
11 Bruce Smith .15
12 Leonard Smith .07
13 Steve Tasker .05
14 Thurman Thomas .40
15 Lewis Billups .03
16 James Brooks .15
17 Eddie Brown .07
18 Carl Carter .03
19 Boomer Esiason .15
20 James Francis .10
21 David Fulcher .10
22 Harold Green .15
23 Rodney Holman .07
24 Bruce Kozerski .03
25 Tim McGee .07
26 Anthony Munoz .07
27 Bruce Reimers .03
28 Ickey Woods .10
29 Carl Zander .10
30 Mike Baab .03
31 Brian Brennan .05
32 Rob Burnett .03
33 Paul Farren .03
34 Thane Gash .03
35 David Grayson .03
36 Mike Johnson .03
37 Reggie Langhorne .05
38 Kevin Mack .05
39 Eric Metcalf .07
40 Frank Minnifield .03
41 Gregg Rakoczy .03
42 Felix Wright .03
43 Steve Atwater .05
44 Michael Brooks .03
45 John Elway .35
46 Simon Fletcher .03
47 Bobby Humphrey .20
48 Mark Jackson .05
49 Keith Kartz .03
50 Clarence Kay .03
51 Greg Kragen .03
52 Karl Mecklenburg .10
53 Warren Powers .03
54 Dennis Smith .05
55 Jim Szymanski .03
56 David Treadwell .03
57 Michael Young .03
58 Ray Childress .05
59 Curtis Duncan .05
60 William Fuller .05
61 Ernest Givins .07
62 Drew Hill .10
63 Haywood Jeffires .15
64 Richard Johnson .03
65 Sean Jones .03
66 Don Maggs .03
67 Bruce Matthews .05
68 Johnny Meads .03
69 Greg Montgomery .05
70 Warren Moon .20
71 Mike Munchak .05
72 Allen Pinkett .05
73 Lorenzo White .05
74 Pat Beach .03
75 Albert Bentley .05
76 Dean Biasucci .05
77 Duane Bickett .03
78 Bill Brooks .03
79 Sam Clancy .03
80 Ray Donaldson .03
81 Jeff George .30
82 Alan Grant .03
83 Jessie Hester .03
84 Jeff Herrod .03
85 Rohn Stark .03
86 Jack Trudeau .03
87 Clarence Verdin .05
88 John Alt .03
89 Steve DeBerg .15
90 Tim Grunhard .03
91 Dino Hackett .03
92 Jonathan Hayes .03
93 Albert Lewis .07
94 Nick Lowery .03
95 Bill Maas .03
96 Christian Okoye .15
97 Stephone Paige .07
98 Kevin Porter .03
99 David Szott .03
100 Derrick Thomas .25
101 Barry Word .20
102 Marcus Allen .15
103 Tom Benson .03
104 Tim Brown .07
105 Riki Ellison .03
106 Mervyn Fernandez .07
107 Willie Gault .07
108 Bob Golic .03
109 Ethan Horton .03
110 Bo Jackson .35
111 Howie Long .10
112 Don Mosebar .03
113 Jerry Robinson .03
114 Jay Schroeder .10
115 Steve Smith .05
116 Greg Townsend .05
117 Steve Wisniewski .05
118 Mark Clayton .07
119 Mark Duper .07
120 Ferrell Edmunds .03
121 Hugh Green .03
122 David Griggs .03
123 Jim Jensen .03
124 Dan Marino .75
125 Tim McKyer .03
126 John Offerdahl .07
127 Louis Oliver .05
128 Tony Paige .03
129 Reggie Roby .03
130 Keith Sims .03
131 Sammie Smith .07
132 Pete Stoyanovich .03
133 Richmond Webb .07
134 Bruce Armstrong .05
135 Vincent Brown .03
136 Hart Lee Dykes .05
137 Irving Fryar .05
138 Tim Goad .03
139 Tom Hodson .10
140 Maurice Hurst .03
141 Ronnie Lippett .03
142 Greg McMurtry .03
143 Ed Reynold .03
144 John Stephens .10
145 Andre Tippett .05
146 Danny Villa .03
147 Brad Baxter .15
148 Kyle Clifton .03
149 Jeff Criswell .03
150 James Hasty .03
151 Jeff Lageman .03
152 Pat Leahy .03
153 Rob Moore .20
154 Al Toon .10
155 Gary Anderson .03
156 Bubby Brister .10
157 Chris Calloway .03
158 Donald Evans .03
159 Eric Green .15
160 Bryan Hinkle .03
161 Merril Hoge .07
162 Tunch Ilkin .03
163 Louis Lipps .05
164 David Little .05
165 Mike Mularkey .03
166 Gerald Williams .03
167 Warren Williams .03
168 Rod Woodson .10
169 Tim Worley .07
170 Martin Bayless .03
171 Marion Butts .20
172 Gill Byrd .03
173 Frank Cornish .03
174 Arthur Cox .03
175 Burt Grossman .07
176 Anthony Miller .15
177 Leslie O'Neal .05
178 Gary Plummer .03
179 Junior Seau .25
180 Billy Joe Tolliver .07
181 Derrick Walker .03
182 Lee Williams .07
183 Robert Blackmon .03
184 Brian Blades .10
185 Grant Feasel .03
186 Derrick Fenner .25
187 Andy Heck .03
188 Norm Johnson .03
189 Tommy Kane .10
190 Cortez Kennedy .20
191 Dave Krieg .10
192 Travis McNeal .03
193 Eugene Robinson .03
194 Chris Warren .50
195 John L. Williams .10
196 Steve Broussard .10
197 Scott Case .03
198 Shawn Collins .05
199 Darion Conner .03
200 Tory Epps .03
201 Bill Fralic .05
202 Michael Haynes .25
203 Chris Hinton .05
204 Keith Jones .03
205 Brian Jordan .03
206 Mike Kenn .03
207 Chris Miller .15
208 Andre Rison .25
209 Mike Rozier .07
210 Deion Sanders .25
211 Gary Wilkins .03
212 Neal Anderson .20
213 Trace Armstrong .05
214 Mark Bortz .03
215 Kevin Butler .03
216 Mark Carrier .10
217 Wendell Davis .07
218 Richard Dent .07
219 Dennis Gentry .05
220 Jim Harbaugh .15
221 Jay Hilgenberg .05
222 Steve McMichael .05
223 Ron Morris .03
224 Brad Muster .07
225 Mike Singletary .05
226 James Thornton .03
227 Tommie Agee .07
228 Troy Aikman 1.50
229 Jack Del Rio .03
230 Issiac Holt .03
231 Ray Horton .03
232 Jim Jeffcoat .03
233 Eugene Lockhart .03
234 Kelvin Martin .07
235 Nate Newton .03
236 Mike Saxon .03
237 Emmitt Smith 2.00
238 Danny Stubbs .03
239 Jim Arnold .03
240 Jerry Ball .05
241 Benny Blades .03
242 Lomas Brown .03
243 Robert Clark .03
244 Mike Cofer .03
245 Mel Gray .03
246 Rodney Peete .15
247 Barry Sanders 1.25
248 Andre Ware .15
249 *Matt Brock* .05
250 Robert Brown .03
251 Anthony Dilweg .07
252 Johnny Holland .03
253 Tim Harris .07
254 Chris Jacke .03
255 Perry Kemp .05
256 Don Majkowski .15
257 Tony Mandarich .05
258 Mark Murphy .03
259 Brian Noble .03
260 Jeff Query .07
261 Sterling Sharpe .10
262 Ed West .03
263 Keith Woodside .03
264 Willie Anderson .10
265 Aaron Cox .05
266 Henry Ellard .07
267 Jim Everett .15
268 Cleveland Gary .05
269 Kevin Greene .07
270 Pete Holohan .03
271 Mike Lansford .03
272 Duval Love .03
273 Buford McGee .05
274 Tom Newberry .05
275 Jackie Slater .05
276 Frank Stams .05
277 Alfred Anderson .05
278 Joey Browner .07
279 Anthony Carter .07
280 Chris Doleman .10
281 Rick Fenney .05
282 Rich Gannon .07
283 Hassan Jones .05
284 Steve Jordan .05
285 Carl Lee .05
286 Randall McDaniel .05
287 Keith Millard .10
288 Herschel Walker .15
289 Wade Wilson .05
290 Gary Zimmerman .05
291 Morten Andersen .05
292 Jim Dombrowski .03
293 Gill Fenerty .07
294 Craig Heyward .07
295 Dalton Hilliard .10
296 Rickey Jackson .05
297 Vaughan Johnson .05
298 Eric Martin .05
299 Robert Massey .05
300 Rueben Mayes .05
301 Sam Mills .05
302 Brett Perriman .03
303 Pat Swilling .05
304 Steve Walsh .10
305 Ottis Anderson .03
306 Matt Bahr .03
307 Mark Bavaro .03
308 Maurice Carthon .03
309 Mark Collins .03
310 John Elliott .03
311 Rodney Hampton .10
312 Jeff Hostetler .10
313 Erik Howard .10
314 Pepper Johnson .03
315 Sean Landeta .03
316 Dave Meggett .03
317 Bart Oates .03
318 Phil Simms .08
319 Lawrence Taylor .10
320 Reyna Thompson .03
321 Everson Walls .03
322 Eric Allen .03
323 Fred Barnett .15
324 Jerome Brown .03
325 Keith Byars .03
326 Randall Cunningham .10
327 Byran Evans .03
328 Ron Heller .03
329 Keith Jackson .06
330 Seth Joyner .03
331 Heath Sherman .03
332 Clyde Simmons .03
333 Ben Smith .03
334 Anthony Toney .03
335 Andre Waters .03
336 Reggie White .15
337 Calvin Williams .20
338 Anthony Bell .03
339 Rich Camarillo .03
340 Roy Green .03
341 Tim Jorden .03
342 Cedric Mack .03
343 Dexter Manley .03
344 Freddie Joe Nunn .03
345 Ricky Proehl .03
346 Tootie Robbins .03
347 Timm Rosenbach .10
348 Luis Sharpe .03
349 Vai Sikahema .03
350 Anthony Thompson .03
351 Lonnie Young .03
352 Dexter Carter .03
353 Mike Cofer .03
354 Kevin Fagan .03
355 Don Griffin .03
356 Charles Haley .03
357 Pierce Holt .03
358 Brent Jones .03
359 Guy McIntyre .03
360 Joe Montana 1.00
361 Darryl Pollard .03
362 Tom Rathman .03
363 Jerry Rice .75
364 Bill Romanowski .03
365 John Taylor .10
366 Steve Wallace .03
367 Steve Young .40
368 Gary Anderson .03
369 Ian Beckles .03
370 Mark Carrier (TB) .03
371 Reggie Cobb .25
372 Reuben Davis .03
373 Randy Grimes .03
374 Wayne Haddix .03
375 Ron Hall .03
376 Harry Hamilton .03
377 Bruce Hill .03
378 Keith McCants .03
379 Bruce Perkins .03
380 Vinny Testaverde .10
381 Broderick Thomas .04
382 Jeff Bostic .03
383 Earnest Byner .03
384 Gary Clark .06
385 Darryl Grant .03
386 Darrell Green .05
387 Stan Humphries .35
388 Jim Lachey .03
389 Charles Mann .03
390 Wilber Marshall .03
391 Art Monk .06
392 Gerald Riggs .03
393 Mark Rypien .15
394 Ricky Sanders .03
395 Don Warren .03
396 Bruce Smith (H) .03
397 Reggie White (H) .08
398 Lawrence Taylor (H) .08
399 David Fulcher (H) .03
400 Derrick Thomas (H) .08
401 Mark Carrier (H) .05
402 Mike Singletary (H) .05
403 Charles Haley (H) .04
404 Jeff Cross (H) .03
405 Leslie O'Neal (H) .03
406 Tim Harris (H) .03
407 Steve Atwater (H) .03
408 Joe Montana (LL) .50
409 Randall Cunningham (LL) .08
410 Warren Moon (LL) .08
411 Andre Rison (LL) .08
412 Haywood Jeffires (LL) .06
413 Stephone Paige (LL) .03
414 Phil Simms (LL) .08
415 Barry Sanders (LL) .50
416 Bo Jackson (LL) .20
417 Thurman Thomas (LL) .20

418 Emmitt Smith (LL) 1.00
419 John L. Williams (LL) .03
420 *Nick Bell* (R) .10
422 *Eric Bienemy* .10
423 *Russell Maryland* .45
424 *Derek Russel* .20
425 Chris Smith .08
426 *Michael Stonebreaker* .08
427 Patrick Tyrance .04
428 Kenny Walker .08
429 Checklist 1 .03
430 Checklist 2 .03
431 Checklist 3 .03
432 Checklist 4 .03

1991 Fleer All-Pro

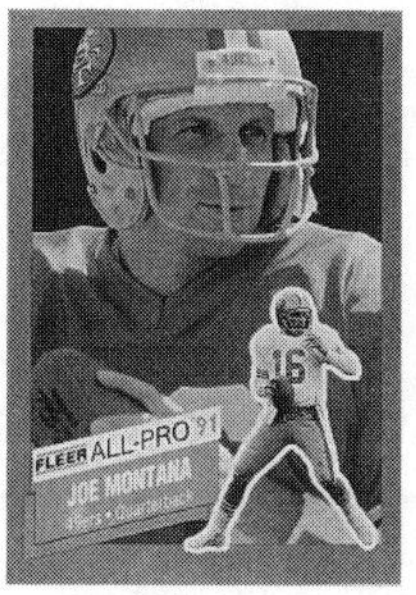

These standard-size cards were random inserts in 1991 Fleer football packs. The card front has a full-color portrait and a smaller picture of the player in action. Card backs contain the card number and a career summary.

MT
Complete Set (26): 5.00
Common Player: .10
1 Andre Reed .35
2 Bobby Humphrey .10
3 Kent Hull .10
4 Mark Bortz .10
5 Bruce Smith .10
6 Greg Townsend .10
7 Ray Childress .10
8 Andre Rison .40
9 Barry Sanders 1.50
10 Bo Jackson .50
11 Neal Anderson .10
12 Keith Jackson .30
13 Derrick Thomas .40
14 John Offerdahl .10
15 Lawrence Taylor .40
16 Darrell Green .10
17 Mark Carrier .10
18 David Fulcher .10
19 Joe Montana 1.00
20 Jerry Rice 1.50
21 Charles Haley .10
22 Mike Singletary .10
23 Nick Lowery .10
24 Jim Lachey .10
25 Anthony Munoz .10
26 Thurman Thomas 1.00

1991 Fleer Pro Visions

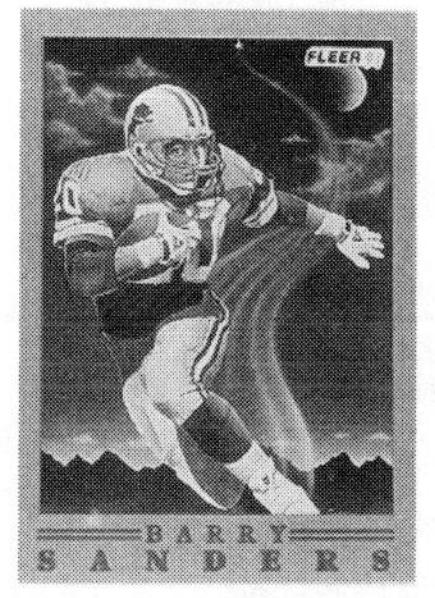

These 1991 Fleer inserts feature artwork from artist Terry Smith. The cards are similar to Fleer's baseball Pro Vision counterparts. The card front has a drawing of the player and his name at the bottom. The back, numbered 1 of 10, etc., has a career summary.

MT
Complete Set (10): 5.00
Common Player: .25
1 Joe Montana 1.00
2 Barry Sanders 1.50
3 Lawrence Taylor .40
4 Mike Singletary .25
5 Dan Marino 2.00
6 Bo Jackson .50
7 Randall Cunningham .40
8 Bruce Smith .25
9 Derrick Thomas .50
10 Howie Long .25

1991 Fleer Stars 'n Stripes

This 140-card set was produced by Fleer in conjunction with Asher Candy, which sold the set with cherry-flavored candy sticks. Each card front has a color action photo, with the set logo in the upper left corner. The card back has biographical information, statistics and a card number, plus a circle which contains a player mug shot.

MT
Complete Set (140): 14.00
Common Player: .10
1 Shane Conlan .15
2 Kent Hull .10
3 Andre Reed .35
4 Bruce Smith .30
5 Thurman Thomas .75
6 James Brooks .15
7 Boomer Esiason .35
8 David Fulcher .10
9 Rodney Holman .10
10 Anthony Munoz .15
11 Reggie Langhorne .10
12 Clay Matthews .10
13 Eric Metcalf .20
14 Gregg Rakoczy .10
15 Steve Atwater .15
16 John Elway .50
17 Bobby Humphrey .15
18 Karl Mecklenburg .15
19 Dennis Smith .10
20 Ray Childress .15
21 Ernest Givins .20
22 Haywood Jeffires .25
23 Warren Moon .60
24 Mike Munchak .10
25 Albert Bentley .10
26 Jeff George .25
27 Rohn Stark .10
28 Clarence Verdin .10
29 Albert Lewis .10
30 Nick Lowery .10
31 Christian Okoye .10
32 Stephone Paige .10
33 Derrick Thomas .25
34 Barry Word .10
35 Albert Lewis .50
36 Howie Long .15
37 Greg Townsend .10
38 Steve Wisniewski .10
39 Mark Clayton .10
40 Dan Marino 1.50
41 John Offerdahl .10
42 Richmond Webb .10
43 Irving Fryar .15
44 Ed Reynolds .10
45 John Stephens .10
46 Rob Moore .25
47 Ken O'Brien .15
48 Al Toon .20
49 Bubby Brister .20
50 Eric Green .15
51 Merril Hoge .10
52 David Little .10
53 Rod Woodson .20
54 Marion Butts .15
55 Leslie O'Neal .10
56 Junior Seau .20
57 Billy Joe Tolliver .15
58 Cortez Kennedy .20
59 Dave Krieg .15
60 John L. Williams .10
61 Steve Broussard .10
62 Bill Fralic .15
63 Andre Rison .35
64 Neal Anderson .15
65 Mark Carrier .15
66 Richard Dent .15
67 Jim Harbaugh .15
68 Mike Singletary .20
69 Troy Aikman 2.00
70 Emmitt Smith 3.00
71 Mel Gray .10
72 Rodney Peete .20
73 Barry Sanders 2.00
74 Tim Harris .15
75 Perry Kemp .10
76 Sterling Sharpe .40
77 Henry Ellard .15
78 Jim Everett .20
79 Kevin Greene .15
80 Jackie Slater .15
81 Joey Browner .15
82 Chris Doleman .15
83 Steve Jordan .10
84 Carl Lee .10
85 Herschel Walker .25
86 Morten Andersen .15
87 Dalton Hilliard .10
88 Vaughan Johnson .10
89 Steve Walsh .15
90 Ottis Anderson .15
91 John Elliott .10
92 Rodney Hampton .50
93 Sean Landeta .10
94 Dave Meggett .15
95 Phil Simms .25
96 Lawrence Taylor .35
97 Randall Cunningham .25
98 Keith Jackson .20
99 Seth Joyner .15
100 Reggie White .35
101 Roy Green .15
102 Johnny Johnson .20
103 Ricky Proehl .15
104 Tootie Robbins .10
105 Kevin Fagan .10
106 Charles Haley .15
107 Guy McIntyre .10
108 Joe Montana 3.00
109 Tom Rathman .15
110 Jerry Rice 1.50
111 John Taylor .20
112 Wayne Haddix .10
113 Vinny Testaverde .20
114 Earnest Byner .15
115 Gary Clark .20
116 Darrell Green .15
117 Jim Lachey .10
118 Art Monk .25
119 Mark Rypien .20
120 Nick Bell .15
121 Eric Bieniemy .10
122 Jarrod Bunch .15
123 Aaron Craver .10
124 Lawrence Dawsey .25
125 Mike Dumas .15
126 Jeff Graham .15
127 Paul Justin .10
128 Darryll Lewis .15
129 Todd Marinovich .20
130 Russell Maryland .20
131 Kanavis McGhee .10
132 Ernie Mills .10
133 Herman Moore .20
134 Godfrey Myles .15
135 Browning Nagle .15
136 Esera Tuaolo .10
137 Mark Vander Poel .10
138 Harvey Williams .15
139 Chris Zorich .15
140 Checklist Card .10

1992 Fleer Prototypes

These standard-size cards were distributed as two- and three-card panels to promote Fleer's 1992 cards. Each card back clearly identifies it as a prototype card; "1992 Pre-Production Sample" is written on the card back. Otherwise, the cards are identical in design to the regular 1992 Fleer cards.

MT
Complete Set (6): 10.00
Common Player: 1.00
93 Mike Croel 1.00
191 Tim Brown 1.50
428 Mark Rypien 1.50
435 Terrell Buckley 1.00
457 Barry Sanders (LL) 3.00
475 Emmitt Smith (PV) 4.00

1992 Fleer

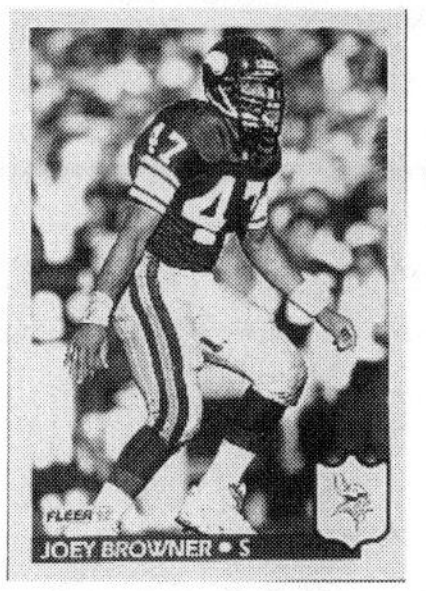

Fleer increased its 1992 set to 480 cards and this time used a glossy format. The player's name, position and team logo are at the bottom, along with "Fleer 92". The back has a close-up shot, with career stats and a biography. The cards are numbered alphabetically by team, beginning with Atlanta and ending with Washington. Subsets include Prospects (#s 432-451), League Leaders (#s 452-470), Pro-Visions (#s 471-476) and checklists (#s 477-480). Insert sets include All-Pro (24 cards, in wax packs), Mark Rypien (12, in wax, rack and cellos), Rookie Sensations (20, in cello packs) and Team Leaders (24, in rack packs).

MT
Complete Set (480): 8.00
Common Player: .03
Pack (17): .30
Wax Box (36): 9.00
1 Steve Broussard .03
2 Rick Bryan .03
3 Scott Case .03
4 Tony Epps .03
5 Bill Fralic .03
6 Moe Gardner .03
7 Michael Haynes .25
8 Chris Hinton .03
9 Brian Jordan .03
10 Mike Kenn .03
11 Tim McKyer .03
12 Chris Miller .03
13 Erric Pegram .20
14 Mike Pritchard .20
15 Andre Rison .25
16 Jessie Tuggle .03
17 Carlton Bailey .03
18 Howard Ballard .03
19 Don Beebe .03
20 Cornelius Bennett .03
21 Shane Conlan .03
22 Kent Hull .03
23 Mark Kelso .03
24 James Lofton .03
25 Keith McKeller .03
26 Scott Norwood .03
27 Nate Odomes .03
28 Frank Reich .03
29 Jim Ritcher .03
30 Leon Seals .03
31 Darryl Talley .03
32 Steve Tasker .03
33 Thurman Thomas .50
34 Will Wolford .03
35 Neal Anderson .10
36 Trace Armstrong .03
37 Mark Carrier .03
38 Richard Dent .03
39 Shaun Gayle .03
40 Jim Harbaugh .03
41 Jay Hilgenberg .03
42 Darren Lewis .03
43 Steve McMichael .03
44 Brad Muster .03
45 William Perry .03
46 John Roper .03
47 Lemuel Stinson .03
48 Stan Thomas .03
49 Keith Van Horne .03
50 Tom Waddle .10
51 Donnell Woolford .03
52 Chris Zorich .10
53 Eddie Brown .03
54 James Francis .03
55 David Fulcher .03
56 David Grant .03
57 Harold Green .03
58 Rodney Holman .03
59 Lee Johnson .03
60 Tim Krumrie .03
61 Anthony Munoz .03
62 *Joe Walter* .10
63 Mike Baab .03
64 Stephen Braggs .04
65 *Richard Brown* .10
66 Dan Fike .03
67 *Scott Galbraith* .10
68 *Randy Hilliard* .10
69 Michael Jackson .15
70 Tony Jones .03
71 Ed King .03
72 Kevin Mack .03
73 Clay Matthews .03
74 Eric Metcalf .03
75 Vince Newsome .03
76 John Rienstra .03
77 Steve Beuerlein .15
78 Larry Brown .03
79 Tony Casillas .03
80 Alvin Harper .10
81 Issiac Holt .03
82 Ray Horton .03
83 Michael Irvin .40
84 Daryl Johnston .08
85 Kelvin Martin .03
86 Nate Newton .03
87 Ken Norton .03
88 Jay Novacek .15
89 Emmitt Smith 2.00
90 Vinson Smith .03
91 Mark Stepnoski .03
92 Steve Atwater .03
93 Mike Croel .03
94 John Elway .50
95 Simon Fletcher .03
96 Gaston Green .03
97 Mark Jackson .03
98 Keith Kartz .03
99 Greg Kragen .03
100 Greg Lewis .03
101 Karl Mecklenburg .03
102 Derek Russell .15
103 Steve Sewell .03
104 Dennis Smith .03
105 David Treadwell .03
106 Kenny Walker .03
107 Doug Widell .03
108 Michael Young .03
109 Jerry Ball .03
110 Bennie Blades .03
111 Lomas Brown .03
112 *Scott Conover* .10
113 Ray Crockett .03
114 Mike Farr .03
115 Mel Gray .03
116 Willie Green .15
117 *Tracy Hayworth* .15
118 Erik Kramer .03
119 Herman Moore .50
120 Dan Owens .03
121 Rodney Peete .03
122 Brett Perriman .03
123 Barry Sanders 1.25
124 Chris Spielman .03
125 Marc Spindler .03
126 Tony Bennett .03
127 Matt Brock .03
128 LeRoy Butler .06
129 Johnny Holland .03
130 Perry Kemp .03
131 Don Majkowski .03
132 Mark Murphy .03
133 Brian Noble .03
134 Bryce Paup .03
135 Sterling Sharpe .10
136 Scott Stephen .03
137 Darrell Thompson .03
138 Mike Tomczak .03
139 Esera Tuaolo .03
140 Keith Woodside .03
141 Ray Childress .03
142 Cris Dishman .03
143 Curtis Duncan .03
144 John Flannery .03
145 William Fuller .03
146 Ernest Givins .03
147 Haywood Jeffires .15
148 Sean Jones .03
149 Lamar Lathon .03
150 Bruce Matthews .03
151 Bubba McDowell .03
152 Johnny Meads .03
153 Warren Moon .20
154 Mike Munchak .03
155 Al Smith .03
156 Doug Smith .25
157 Lorenzo White .03
158 Michael Ball .03
159 Chip Banks .03
160 Duane Bickett .03
161 Bill Brooks .03
162 Ken Clark .03
163 Jon Hand .03
164 Jeff Herrod .03
165 Jessie Hester .03
166 Scott Radecic .03
167 Rohn Stark .03
168 Clarence Verdin .03
169 John Alt .03
170 Tim Barnett .03
171 Tim Grunhard .03
172 Dino Hackett .03
173 Jonathan Hayes .03
174 Bill Maas .03
175 Chris Martin .03
176 Christian Okoye .03
177 Stephone Paige .03
178 *Jayice Pearson* .10
179 Kevin Porter .03
180 Kevin Ross .03
181 Dan Saleaumua .03
182 *Tracy Simien* .10
183 Neil Smith .03
184 Derrick Thomas .15
185 Robb Thomas .03
186 Mark Vlasic .03
187 Barry Word .15
188 Marcus Allen .08
189 Eddie Anderson .03
190 Nick Bell .10
191 Tim Brown .10
192 Scott Davis .03
193 Riki Ellison .03
194 Mervyn Fernandez .03
195 Willie Gault .03
196 Jeff Gossett .03
197 Ethan Horton .03
198 Jeff Jaeger .03
199 Howie Long .03
200 Ronnie Lott .03
201 Todd Marinovich .10
202 Don Mosebar .03
203 Jay Schroeder .03
204 Greg Townsend .03
205 Lionel Washington .03
206 Steve Wisniewski .03
207 Flipper Anderson .03
208 Bern Brostek .03
209 Robert Delpino .03
210 Henry Ellard .03
211 Jim Everett .03
212 Cleveland Gary .03
213 Kevin Greene .03
214 Darryl Henely .03
215 Damone Johnson .03
216 Larry Kelm .03
217 Todd Lyght .03
218 Jackie Slater .03
219 Michael Stewart .03
220 Pat Terrell .03
221 Robert Young .03
222 Mark Clayton .03
223 Bryan Cox .03
224 Aaron Craver .03
225 Jeff Cross .03
226 Mark Duper .03
227 Harry Galbreath .03
228 David Griggs .03
229 Mark Higgs .15
230 Vestee Jackson .03
231 John Offerdahl .03
232 Louis Oliver .03
233 Tony Paige .03
234 Reggie Roby .03
235 Sammie Smith .03
236 Pete Stoyanovich .03
237 Richmond Webb .03
238 Terry Allen .20
239 Ray Berry .03
240 Joey Browner .03
241 Anthony Carter .03
242 Cris Carter .03
243 Chris Doleman .03
244 Rich Gannon .10
245 Tim Irwin .03
246 Steve Jordan .03
247 Carl Lee .03
248 Randall Cunningham .03
249 Mike Merriweather .03
250 Harry Newsome .03
251 John Randle .03
252 Henry Thomas .03
253 Herschel Walker .03
254 Ray Agnew .03
255 Bruce Armstrong .03
256 Vincent Brown .03
257 Marv Cook .03
258 Irving Fryar .03
259 Pat Harlow .03
260 Tommy Hodson .03
261 Maurice Hurst .03
262 Ronnie Lippett .03
263 Eugene Lockhart .03
264 Greg McMurty .03
265 Hugh Millen .03
266 Leonard Russell .25
267 Andre Tippett .03
268 Brent Williams .03
269 Morten Andersen .03
270 Gene Atkins .03
271 Wesley Carroll .03
272 Jim Dombrowski .03
273 Quinn Early .03
274 Gill Fenerty .03
275 Bobby Hebert .03
276 Joel Hilgenberg .03
277 Rickey Jackson .03
278 Vaughan Johnson .03
279 Eric Martin .03
280 Brett Maxie .03
281 *Fred McAfee* .10
282 Sam Mills .03
283 Pat Swilling .03
284 Floyd Turner .03
285 Steve Walsh .03
286 Frank Warren .03
287 Stephen Baker .03
288 Maurice Carthon .03
289 Mark Collins .03
290 John Elliott .03
291 Myron Guyton .03
292 Rodney Hampton .10
293 Jeff Hostetler .10
294 Mark Ingram .03
295 Pepper Johnson .03
296 Sean Landeta .03
297 Leonard Marshall .03
298 Dave Meggett .03
299 Bart Oates .03
300 Phil Simms .10
301 Reyna Thompson .03
302 Lewis Tillman .03
303 Brad Baxter .03
304 Kyle Clifton .03
305 James Hasty .03
306 Joe Kelly .03
307 Jeff Lageman .03
308 Mo Lewis .03
309 Erik McMillan .03
310 Rob Moore .10
311 Tony Stargell .03
312 Jim Sweeney .03
313 Marvin Washington .03
314 Lonnie Young .03
315 Eric Allen .03
316 Fred Barnett .10
317 Jerome Brown .03
318 Keith Byars .03
319 Wes Hopkins .03
320 Keith Jackson .10
321 James Joseph .03
322 Seth Joyner .03
323 Jeff Kemp .03
324 Roger Ruzek .03
325 Clyde Simmons .03
326 William Thomas .03
327 Reggie White .15
328 Calvin Williams .15
329 Rich Camarillo .03
330 Ken Harvey .03
331 Eric Hill .03
332 Johnny Johnson .15
333 Ernie Jones .03
334 Tim Jorden .03
335 Tim McDonald .03
336 Freddie Joe Nunn .03
337 Luis Sharpe .03
338 Eric Swann .03
339 Aeneas Williams .03
340 Gary Anderson .03
341 Bubby Brsiter .03
342 Adrian Cooper .03
343 Barry Foster .10
344 Eric Green .03
345 Bryan Hinkle .03
346 Tunch Ilkin .03
347 Carnell Lake .03
348 Louis Lipps .03
349 David Little .03
350 Greg Lloyd .03
351 Neil O'Donnell .25
352 Dwight Stone .03
353 Rod Woodson .03
354 Rod Bernstine .03
355 Eric Bieniemy .03
356 Marion Butts .03
357 Gill Byrd .03
358 John Friesz .03
359 Burt Grossman .03
360 Courtney Hall .03
361 Ronnie Harmon .03
362 Shawn Jefferson .03
363 Nate Lewis .03
364 *Craig McEwen* .10
365 Eric Moten .03
366 Joe Phillips .03
367 Gary Plummer .03
368 Henry Rolling .03
369 Broderick Thompson .03
370 Harris Barton .03
371 *Steve Bono* 1.00
372 Todd Bowles .03
373 Dexter Carter .03
374 Michael Carter .03
375 Mike Cofer .03
376 Keith DeLong .03
377 Charles Haley .03
378 Menton Hanks .03
379 Tim Harris .03
380 Brent Jones .03
381 Guy McIntyre .03
382 Tom Rathman .03
383 Bill Romanowski .03
384 Jesse Sapolu .03
385 John Taylor .03
386 Steve Young 1.00
387 Robert Blackmon .03
388 Brian Blades .03
389 Jacob Green .03
390 Dwayne Harper .03
391 Andy Heck .03
392 Tommy Kane .03
393 John Kasay .03
394 Cortez Kennedy .15
395 Bryan Millard .03
396 Rufus Porter .03
397 Eugene Robinson .03
398 John L. Williams .03
399 Terry Wooden .03
400 Gary Anderson .03
401 Ian Beckles .03
402 Mark Carrier .03
403 Reggie Cobb .15
404 Lawrence Dawsey .03
405 Ron Hall .03
406 Keith McCants .03
407 Charles McRae .03
408 Tim Newton .03
409 Jesse Solomon .03
410 Vinny Testaverde .03
411 Broderick Thomas .03
412 Robert Wilson .03
413 Jeff Bostic .03
414 Earnest Byner .03
415 Gary Clark .03
416 Andre Collins .03
417 Brad Edwards .03
418 Kurt Gouveia .03
419 Darrell Green .03
420 Joe Jacoby .03
421 Jim Lachey .03
422 Chip Lohmiller .03
423 Charles Mann .03
424 Wilber Marshall .03
425 *Ron Middleton* .10
426 Brian Mitchell .03
427 Art Monk .03
428 Mark Rypien .10
429 Ricky Sanders .03
430 *Mark Schlereth* .10
431 Fred Stokes .03
432 *Edgar Bennett* .75
433 *Brian Bollinger* .08
434 *Joe Bowden* .08
435 *Terrell Buckley* .35
436 *Willie Clay* .10
437 Steve Gordon .03
438 *Keith Hamilton* .10
439 Carlos Huerta .03
440 Matt LaBounty .03
441 *Amp Lee* .40
442 *Ricardo McDonald* .10
443 *Chris Mims* .20
444 *Michael Mooney* .10
445 *Patrick Rowe* .10
446 *Leon Searcy* .10
447 *Siran Stacy* .10
448 *Kevin Turner* .15
449 *Tommy Vardell* .30
450 *Bob Whitfield* .10
451 *Darryl Williams* .10
452 Thurman Thomas (LL) .25
453 Emmitt Smith (LL) 1.00
454 Haywood Jeffires (LL) .08
455 Michael Irvin (LL) .20
456 Mark Clayton (LL) .03
457 Barry Sanders (LL) .50
458 Pete Stoyanovich (LL) .03
459 Chip Lohmiller (LL) .03
460 William Fuller (LL) .03
461 Pat Swilling (LL) .03
462 Ronnie Lott (LL) .03
463 Ray Crockett (LL) .03
464 Tim McKyer (LL) .03
465 Aeneas Williams (LL) .03
466 Rod Woodson (LL) .03
467 Mel Gray (LL) .03
468 Nate Lewis (LL) .03
469 Steve Young (LL) .03
470 Reggie Roby (LL) .03
471 John Elway (PV) .10
472 Ronnie Lott (PV) .03
473 Art Monk (PV) .03
474 Warren Moon (PV) .10
475 Emmitt Smith (PV) 1.00
476 Thurman Thomas (PV) .20
477 Checklist Card .03
478 Checklist Card .03
479 Checklist Card .03
480 Checklist Card .03

A player's name in *italic type* indicates a rookie card.

1992 Fleer All-Pro

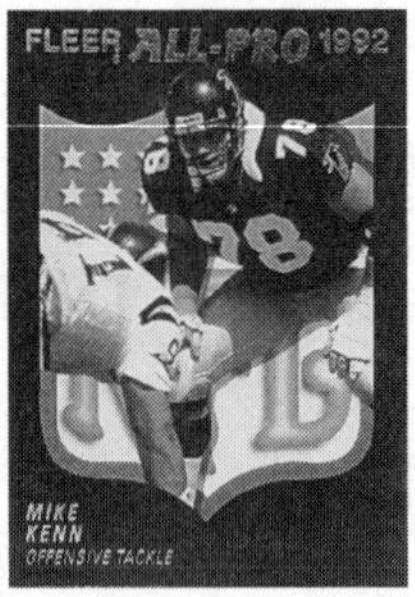

These 24 inserts were randomly included in 1992 Fleer wax packs. The card front has a red-white-and-blue NFL emblem with a cutout player photo superimposed on it. The card background is blue. The player's name and position are also given in gold foil letters. The back has a pink background with a career summary and color portrait. Cards are numbered 1 of 24, etc.

		MT
Complete Set (24):		7.00
Common Player:		.25
1	Marv Cook	.25
2	Mike Kenn	.25
3	Steve Wisniewski	.25
4	Jim Ritcher	.25
5	Jim Lachey	.25
6	Michael Irvin	.75
7	Andre Rison	.50
8	Thurman Thomas	.75
9	Barry Sanders	3.00
10	Bruce Matthews	.25
11	Mark Rypien	.25
12	Jeff Jaeger	.25
13	Reggie White	.75
14	Clyde Simmons	.25
15	Pat Swilling	.25
16	Sam Mills	.25
17	Ray Childress	.25
18	Jerry Ball	.25
19	Derrick Thomas	.50
20	Darrell Green	.25
21	Ronnie Lott	.50
22	Steve Atwater	.25
23	Mark Carrier	.25
24	Jeff Gossett	.25

1992 Fleer Rookie Sensations

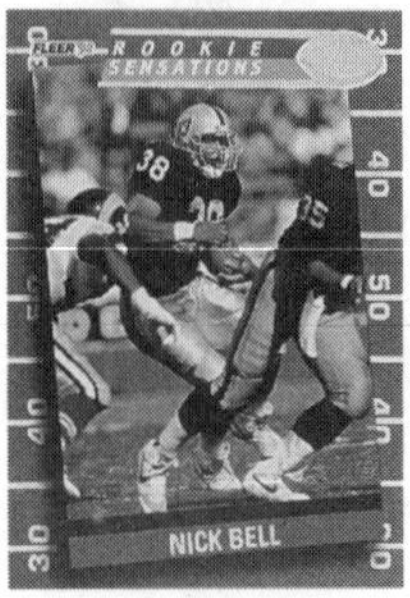

These 20 cards, featuring some of the NFL's top rookies in 1991, were random inserts in Fleer cello packs. Each card front is designed like a football field, containing a player photo which slants to the left with shadow borders on the left and bottom. "Rookie Sensations" appears at the top of the card, highlighted by gold foil stripes simulating the flight of a football. The player's name is in gold foil at the bottom. The back, which is designed similar to the front, has a career summary and card number.

		MT
Complete Set (20):		25.00
Common Player:		1.00
Minor Stars:		2.00
1	Moe Gardner	1.00
2	Mike Pritchard	2.00
3	Stan Thomas	1.00
4	Larry Brown	1.00
5	Todd Lyght	2.00
6	James Joseph	1.00
7	Aeneas Williams	3.00
8	Michael Jackson	4.00
9	Ed King	1.00
10	Mike Croel	1.00
11	Kenny Walker	1.00
12	Tim Barnett	1.00
13	Nick Bell	1.00
14	Todd Marinovich	1.00
15	Leonard Russell	2.00
16	Pat Harlow	1.00
17	Mo Lewis	1.00
18	John Kasay	1.00
19	Lawrence Dawsey	1.00
20	Charles McRae	1.00

1992 Fleer Mark Rypien

Mark Rypien is featured in this 15-card "Performance Highlight" insert set. Cards were randomly included in 1992 Fleer Football packs. Each card front has a dark blue background with a player action photo outlined in the team's colors. Rypien's name and "Performance Highlights" are in gold-foil lettering at the top. Each back has a summary of a different stage of Rypien's career. Cards are numbered on the back. Rypien, the MVP of Super Bowl XXVI, autographed more than 2,000 cards, which were then randomly inserted. Collectors could also get three extra Rypien cards by mailing in 10 Fleer pack proofs of purchase. These cards are numbered 13-15.

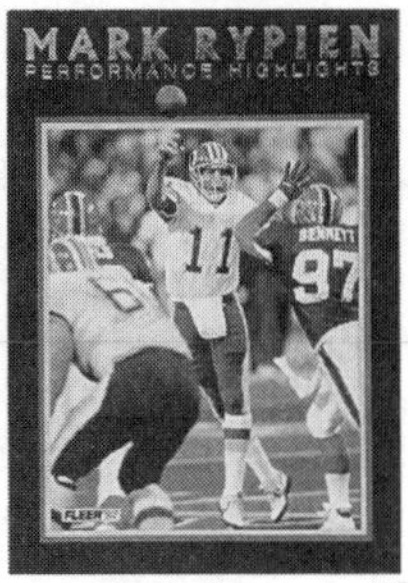

		MT
Complete Set (12):		4.00
Common Rypien:		.40
1	A Matter of Faith (Mark Rypien)	.40
2	Mr. Everything (Mark Rypien)	.40
3	Great Expectations (Mark Rypien)	.40
4	Hill and Valleys (Mark Rypien)	.40
5	Breakout Season (Mark Rypien)	.40
6	The End of the Beginning (Mark Rypien)	.40
7	Bowled Over (Mark Rypien)	.40
8	Watching and Waiting (Mark Rypien)	.40
9	QB Controversy (Mark Rypien)	.40
10	Redemption (Mark Rypien)	.40
11	Pain and Pressure (Mark Rypien)	.40
12	Jubilation (Mark Rypien)	.40

1992 Fleer Team Leaders

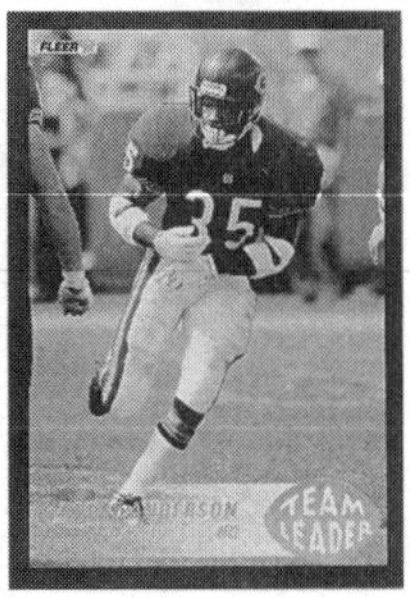

These 24 inserts were randomly included in 1992 Fleer rack packs. Each color photo on the front has a black border. The player's name, position, team and "Team Leader" logo are at the bottom of the card in green foil lettering. Each back has a player portrait in an oval frame in the upper left corner, plus a career summary. The background is grayish-blue. A card number is also included on the card back.

		MT
Complete Set (24):		50.00
Common Player:		1.50
Minor Stars:		3.00
1	Chris Miller	1.50
2	Neal Anderson	1.50
3	Emmitt Smith	20.00
4	Chris Spielman	1.50
5	Brian Noble	1.50
6	Jim Everett	3.00
7	Joey Browner	1.50
8	Sam Mills	1.50
9	Rodney Hampton	3.00
10	Reggie White	4.00
11	Tim McDonald	1.50
12	Charles Haley	3.00
13	Mark Rypien	1.50
14	Cornelius Bennett	1.50
15	Clay Matthews	1.50
16	John Elway	15.00
17	Warren Moon	3.00
18	Derrick Thomas	3.00
19	Greg Townsend	1.50
20	Bruce Armstrong	1.50
21	Brad Baxter	1.50
22	Rod Woodson	1.50
23	Marion Butts	1.50
24	Rufus Porter	1.50

A player's name in *italic type* indicates a rookie card.

1992 Fleer GameDay Draft Day Promos

These 2-1/2" x 4-11/16" cards feature six players who were projected to be top selections in the 1992 NFL draft. Some of the players have more than one card, to cover various draft day scenarios. The card front has a full-color action photo with a white border. The team name and GameDay logo are at the bottom of the card. The back has a mug shot of the player, plus a summary of his collegiate accomplishments. Each card has an NFL Draft logo, and the same card number, #1. NFL Properties produced the set. An ad in a May 1992 issue of USA Today offered the 13-card set for $50. Proceeds went to NFL Charities. Dealers and members of the hobby press also received promo sets.

		MT
Complete Set (13):		30.00
Common Player:		2.00
1	Quentin Coryatt (Los Angeles Rams)	4.00
2	Vaughn Dunbar (Atlanta Falcons)	2.00
3	Vaughn Dunbar (San Francisco 49ers)	2.00
4	Vaughn Dunbar (Seattle Seahawks)	2.00
5	Steve Emtman (Indianapolis Colts)	3.00
6	Steve Emtman (Los Angeles Rams)	3.00
7	Desmond Howard (Indianapolis Colts)	4.00
8	Desmond Howard (Washington Redskins)	4.00
9	David Klingler (Kansas City Chiefs)	3.00
10	David Klingler (New York Giants)	3.00
11	Troy Vincent (Cincinnati Bengals)	2.00
12	Troy Vincent (Indianapolis Colts)	2.00
13	Troy Vincent (Green Bay Packers)	2.00

1992 Fleer GameDay

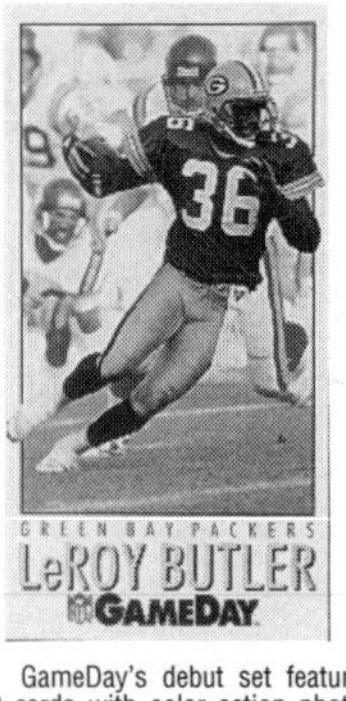

GameDay's debut set features 500 cards with color action photos against a black-and-white background. Each card is bordered with the player's corresponding team color, and team colors are used for the player's name and GameDay, which are printed at the bottom. Card backs are printed horizontally, and contain a close-up photo, biography, statistics and career highlights. The numbered card backs feature the player's name, team name, position and team logo in his team's colors. What distinguishes these cards from other sets is the size - they are 2-1/2" x 4-11/16", which makes them the same size as Topps' 1965 football issue.

		MT
Complete Set (500):		25.00
Common Player:		.10
Wax Box:		20.00
1	Jim Kelly	.75
2	Mark Ingram	.12
3	Travis McNeal	.10
4	Ricky Ervins	.20
5	Joe Montana	3.50
6	Broderick Thompson	.10
7	Darion Conner	.10
8	Jim Harbaugh	.15
9	Harvey Williams	.35
10	Chip Banks	.10
11	Henry Thomas	.10
12	*Derek Brown*	.20
13	James Joseph	.15
14	Kevin Fagan	.10
15	*Chuck Klingbell*	.20
16	Harlon Barnett	.10
17	Jim Price	.10
18	*Terrell Buckley*	.40
19	*Paul McJulien*	.15
20	James Hasty	.10
21	James Francis	.12
22	Andre Tippett	.12
23	John Elway	1.00
24	Eric Dickerson	.40
25	James Jefferson	.10
26	Danny Noonan	.10
27	Warren Moon	.40
28	Gene Atkins	.10
29	Jessie Hester	.10
30	*Mike Mooney,Kevin Smith,Ron Humphrey,Tracy Boyd*	.25
31	*Toby Caston*	.15
32	*Howard Dinkins*	.15
33	*James Patton*	.15
34	Walter Reeves	.10
35	*Johnny Mitchell*	1.25
36	*Michael Brim*	.20
37	Irving Fryar	.12
38	Lewis Billups	.10
39	*Alonzo Spellman*	.50
40	John Friesz	.12
41	Patrick Hunter	.10
42	Reuben Davis	.10
43	*Tom Myslinski,Shawn Harper,Mark Thomas,Mike Frier*	.15
44	*Siran Stacy*	.15
45	Stephone Paige	.12
46	*Eddie Robinson*	.15
47	*Tracy Scroggins*	.35
48	*David Klingler*	.50
49a	Deion Sanders	.75
49b	Deion Sanders (Last line of card says plays outfield)	.40
50	Tom Waddle	.20
51	Gary Anderson	.12
52	Kevin Butler	.10
53	Bruce Smith	.12
54	Steve Sewell	.10
55	Wesley Walls	.10
56	Lawrence Taylor	.20
57	Mike Merriweather	.12
58	Roman Phifer	.10
59	Shaun Gayle	.10
60	*Marc Boutte*	.15
61	*Tony Mayberry*	.15
62	Antone Davis (Card has 9th pick in 91 draft, was 8th)	.10
63	Rod Bernstine	.12
64	*Shane Collins*	.25
65	Martin Bayless	.10
66	*Corey Harris*	.15
67	*Jason Hanson*	.25
68	*John Fina*	.15
69	Cornelius Bennett	.12
70	Mark Bortz	.10
71	Gary Anderson	.10
72	*Paul Siever*	.20
73	Flipper Anderson	.12
74	*Shane Dronett*	.30
75	Brian Noble	.10
76	Tim Green	.10
77	Percy Snow	.10
78	Greg McMurty	.10
79	*Dana Hall*	.30
80	*Tyji Armstrong*	.20
81	Gary Clark	.25
82	*Steve Emtman*	.30
83	Eric Moore	.10
84	Brent Jones	.12
85	*Ray Seals*	.20
86	James Jones	.10
87	Jeff Hostetler	.25
88	Keith Jackson	.15
89	Gary Plummer	.10
90	Robert Blackmon	.10
91	*Larry Tharpe,Mike Brandon,Anthony Hamlet,Mike Pawlawski*	.15
92	*Greg Skrepenak*	.20
93	Kevin Call	.10
94	Clarence Kay	.10
95	William Fuller	.10
96	*Troy Auzenne*	.15
97	*Carl Pickens*	3.50
98	Lorenzo White	.25
99	Doug Smith	.10
100	*Dale Carter*	.40
101	*Fred McAfee*	.20
102	Jack Del Rio	.10
103	*Vaugn Dunbar*	.20
104	J.J. Birden	.12
105	Harris Barton	.10
106	*Ray Ethridge*	.15
107	John Gesek	.10
108	Mike Singletary	.12
109	Mark Rypien	.15
110	Robb Thomas	.10
111	Joe Kelly	.10
112	Ben Smith	.10
113	Neil O'Donnell	.50
114	John L. Williams	.12
115	Mike Sherrard	.12
116	*Chad Hennings*	.15
117	Henry Ellard	.12
118	Jay Hilgenberg	.12
119	Charles Dimry	.10
120	*Chuck Smith*	.15
121	Brian Mitchell	.12
122	Eric Allen	.12
123	Nate Lewis	.20
124	Kevin Ross	.12
125	*Jimmy Smith*	3.50
126	*Kevin Smith*	.60
127	*Larry Webster*	.25
128	Marv Cook	.12
129	Calvin Williams	.10
130	*Harry Swayne*	.15
131	Jimmie Jones	.10
132	Ethan Horton	.10
133	*Chris Mims*	.20
134	Derrick Thomas	.20
135	*Gerald Dixon*	.25
136	Gary Zimmerman	.10
137	*Robert Jones*	.20
138	Steve Broussard	.12
139	David Wyman	.10
140	Ian Beckles	.10
141	*Steve Bono*	2.00
142	Cris Carter	.10
143	Anthony Cater	.12
144	Greg Townsend	.10
145	Al Smith	.10
146	*Troy Vincent*	.25
147	Jessie Tuggle	.10
148	David Fulcher	.10
149	Johnny Rembert	.10
150	Ernie Jones	.10
151	Mark Royals	.10
152	Jeff Bryant	.10
153	Vai Sikahema	.12
154	Tony Woods	.10
155	*Joe Bowden,Doug Rigby,Marcus Dowdell,Ostell Miles*	.15
156	Mark Carrier	.12
157	Joe Nash	.10
158	Keith Van Horne	.10
159	Kelvin Martin	.12
160	Peter Tom Willis	.12
161	Richard Johnson	.10
162	Louis Oliver	.12
163	Nick Lowery	.12
164	Ricky Proehl	.12
165	Terance Mathis	.10
166	Keith Sims	.10
167	E.J. Junior	.10
168	Scott Mersereau	.10
169	Tom Rathman	.12
170	*Robert Harris*	.15
171	*Ashley Ambrose*	.15
172	David Treadwell	.10
173	Mark Green	.10
174	*Clayton Holmes*	.15
175	*Tony Sacca*	.25
176	Wes Hopkins	.10
177	*Mark Wheeler*	.15
178	Robert Clark	.10
179	Eugene Daniel	.10
180	Rob Burnett	.10
181	Al Edwards	.10
182	Clarence Verdin	.10
183	Tom Newberry	.10
184	Mike Jones	.10
185	Roy Foster	.10
186	Leslie O'Neal	.12
187	Izel Jenkins	.10
188	*Willie Clay,Ty Detmer,Mike Evans,Ed McDaniel*	1.00
189	Mike Tomczak	.12
190	*Leonard Wheeler*	.15
191	Gaston Green	.15
192	Maury Buford	.10
193	*Jeremy Lincoln*	.15
194	*Todd Collins*	.15
195	Billy Ray Smith	.10
196	Renaldo Turnbull	.10
197	Michael Carter	.10
198	*Rod Milstead,Dion Lambert,Hesham Ismail,Reggie E. White*	.15
199	Shawn Collins	.10
200	Issiac Holt	.10
201	Irv Eatman	.10
202	Anthony Thompson	.12
203	*Chester McGlockton*	.25
204	*Greg Biggs,Chris Crooms,Ephesians Bartley,Curtis Whitley*	.15
205	*James Brown*	.15
206	Marvin Washington	.10
207	*Richard Cooper*	.15
208	Jim C. Jensen	.10
209	Sam Seale	.10
210	Andre Reed	.15
211	Thane Gash	.10
212	Randal Hill	.20
213	Brad Baxter	.12
214	Michael Cofer	.10
215	Ray Crockett	.10
216	Tony Mandarich	.10
217	Warren Williams	.10
218	Erik Kramer	.25
219	Bubby Brister	.12
220	Steve Young	1.50
221	Jeff George	.35
222	James Washington	.10
223	*Bruce Alexander*	.15
224	Broderick Thomas	.12
225	Bern Brostek	.10
226	Brian Blades	.12
227	Troy Aikman	4.00
228	Aaron Wallace	.10
229	*Tommy Jeter*	.15
230	Russell Maryland	.30
231	Charles Haley	.12
232	James Lofton	.20
233	William White	.10
234	Tim McGee	.10
235	Haywood Jeffires	.15
236	Charles Mann	.12
237	Robert Lyles	.10
238	Rohn Stark	.10
239	Jim Morrissey	.10
240	Mel Gray	.12
241	Barry Word	.20
242	*Dave Widell*	.15
243	*Sean Gilbert*	.40
244	*Tommy Maddox*	.50
245	Bernie Kosar	.15
246	John Roper	.10
247	Mark Higgs	.20
248	Rob Moore	.20
249	Dan Fike	.10
250	Dan Saleaumua	.10
251	Tim Krumrie	.10
252	Tony Casillas	.10
253	*Jayice Pearson*	.12
254	Dan Marino	4.00
255	Tony Marty	.10
256	Mike Fox	.10
257	*Courtney Hawkins*	.75
258	Leonard Marshall	.12
259	Willie Gault	.12
260	Al Toon	.12
261	Browning Nagle	.20
262	Ronnie Lott	.12
263	Sean Jones	.10
264	Ernest Givins	.20
265	Ray Donaldson	.10
266	Vaughan Johnson	.12
267	Tom Hodson	.12
268	Chris Doleman	.12
269	Pat Swilling	.10
270	Merril Hoge	.12
271	Bill Maas	.10
272	Sterling Sharpe	1.00
273	Mitchell Price	.10
274	*Richard Brown*	.15
275	Randall Cunningham	.25
276	Chris Martin	.10
277	Courtney Hall	.10
278	Michael Walter	.10
279	*Ricardo McDonald,David Wilson,Sean Lumpkin,Tony Brooks*	.10
280	Bill Brooks	.12
281	Jay Schroeder	.12
282	John Stephens	.12
283	William Perry	.12
284	Floyd Turner	.10
285	Carnell Lake	.10
286	*Joel Steed*	.15
287	Vinnie Clark	.10
288	Ken Norton	.12
289	Eric Thomas	.10
290	Derrick Fenner	.12
291	*Tony Smith*	.20
292	Eric Metcalf	.12
293	Roger Craig	.12
294	*Leon Searcy*	.15
295	*Tyrone Legette*	.15
296	Rob Taylor	.10
297	Eric Williams	.10
298	David Little	.10
299	Wayne Martin	.10
300	Eric Martin	.12
301	Jim Everett	.20
302	Michael Dean Perry	.20
303	*Dwayne White*	.12
304	Greg Lloyd	.10
305	Ricky Reynolds	.10
306	Anthony Smith	.10
307	Robert Delpino	.12
308	Ken Clark	.10
309	Chris Jacke	.10
310	*Reggie Dwight,Anthony McCoy,Craig Thompson,Klaus Wilmsmeyer*	.15
311	Doug Widell	.10
312	Sammie Smith	.12
313	Ken O'Brien	.12
314	Timm Rosenbach	.10
315	Jesse Sapolu	.10
316	Ronnie Harmon	.10
317	Bill Pickel	.10
318	Lonnie Young	.10
319	Chris Burkett	.10
320	Ervin Randle	.10
321	Ed West	.10
322	Tom Thayer	.10
323	Keith McKeller	.10
324	Webster Slaughter	.12
325	Duane Bickett	.10
326	Howie Long	.12
327	Sam Mills	.12
328	Mike Golic	.10
329	Bruce Armstrong	.10
330	Pat Terrell	.10
331	Mike Pritchard	.45
332	Audray McMillian	.10
333	*Marquez Pope*	.12
334	Pierce Holt	.10
335	Erik Howard	.10
336	Jerry Rice	2.25
337	Vinny Testaverde	.12
338	Bart Oates	.10
339	*Nolan Harrison*	.12
340	Chris Goode	.10
341	Ken Ruettgers	.10
342	Brad Muster	.12
343	Paul Farren	.10
344	*Corey Miller*	.20
345	Brian Washington	.10
346	Jim Sweeney	.10
347	Keith McCants	.10
348	Louis Lipps	.12
349	Keith Byars	.12
350	Steve Walsh	.12
351	Jeff Jaeger	.10
352	Christian Okoye	.12
353	Cris Dishman	.12
354	Keith Kartz	.10
355	Harold Green	.10
356	*Richard Shelton*	.15
357	Jacob Green	.12
358	Al Noga	.10
359	Dean Biasucci	.10
360	Jeff Herrod	.10
361	Bennie Blades	.10
362	Mark Vlasic	.12
363	Chris Miller	.15
364	Bubba McDowell	.10
365	*Tyrone Stowe*	.15
366	Jon Vaughn	.15
367	Winston Moss	.10
368	*Levon Kirkland*	.15
369	Ted Washington	.10
370	Cortez Kennedy	.25
371	Jeff Feagles	.10
372	Aundray Bruce	.10
373	Michael Irvin	.30
374	Lemuel Stinson	.10
375	Billy Joe Tolliver	.12
376	Anthony Munoz	.12
377	Nate Newton	.10
378	Steve Smith	.12
379	*Eugene Chung*	.15
380	Bryan Hinkle	.10
381	Dan McGwire	.30
382	Jeff Cross	.10
383	Ferrell Edmunds	.10
384	Craig Heyward	.12
385	Shannon Sharpe	.50
386	Anthony Miller	.12
387	Eugene Lockhart	.10
388	Darryl Henley	.10
389	LeRoy Butler	.10
390	Scott Fulhage	.10
391	Andre Ware	.35
392	Lionel Washington	.10
393	Rick Fenney	.10
394	John Taylor	.20
395	Chris Singleton	.10
396	Monte Coleman	.10
397	Brett Perriman	.12
398	Hugh Millen	.35
399	Dennis Gentry	.10
400	Eddie Anderson	.10
401	*Lance Olberding,Eddie Miller,Dwayne Sabb,Corey Widmer*	.15
402	Brent Williams	.10
403	Tony Zendejas	.10
404	Donnell Woolford	.10
405	Boomer Esiason	.20
406	Gill Fenerty	.12
407	*Kurt Barber*	.12
408	William Thomas	.10
409	Keith Henderson	.10
410	Paul Gruber	.12
411	Alfred Oglesby	.10
412	Wendell Davis	.20
413	*Robert Brooks*	2.00
414	Ken Willis	.10
415	Aaron Cox	.10
416	Thurman Thomas	.50
417	Alton Montgomery	.10
418	Mike Prior	.10
419	Albert Bentley	.10
420	John Randle	.10
421	Dermontti Dawson	.10
422	*Phillippi Sparks*	.15
423	Michael Jackson	.30
424	Carl Banks	.12

425	Chris Zorich	.10
426	Dwight Stone	.10
427	Bryan Millard	.10
428	Neal Anderson	.20
429	Michael Haynes	.15
430	Michael Young	.10
431	Dennis Byrd	.12
432	Fred Barnett	.15
433	Junior Seau	.50
434	Mark Clayton	.12
435	*Marco Coleman*	.50
436	Lee Williams	.12
437	Stan Thomas	.10
438	Lawrence Dawsey	.15
439	*Tommy Vardell*	.60
440	*Steve Israel*	.20
441	Ray Childress	.12
442	*Darren Woodson*	.20
443	Lamar Lathon	.10
444	Reggie Roby	.12
445	Eric Green	.12
446	Mark Carrier	.12
447	Kevin Walker	.10
448	Vince Workman	.20
449	Leonard Griffin	.10
450	*Robert Porcher*	.40
451	Hart Lee Dykes	.10
452	*Thomas McLemore*	.15
453	*Jamie Dukes*	.15
454	Bill Romanowski	.10
455	Deron Cherry	.10
456	Burt Grossman	.10
457	Lance Smith	.10
458	Jay Novacek	.15
459	Erric Pegram	.20
460	Reggie Rutland	.10
461	Rickey Jackson	.12
462	Dennis Brown	.10
463	Neil Smith	.12
464	Rich Gannon	.15
465	Herman Moore	1.00
466	Rodney Peete	.25
467	Alvin Harper	.50
468	Andre Rison	.50
469	Rufus Porter	.10
470	Robert Wilson	.10
471	Phil Simms	.15
472	Art Monk	.15
473	Mike Tice	.10
474	*Quentin Coryatt*	.60
475	Chris Hinton	.10
476	Vance Johnson	.12
477	Kyle Clifton	.10
478	Garth Jax	.10
479	Ray Agnew	.10
480	*Patrick Rowe*	.15
481	Joe Jacoby	.10
482	Bruce Pickens	.10
483	Keith DeLong	.10
484	Eric Swann	.12
485	Steve McMichael	.12
486	Leroy Hoard	.12
487	Rickey Dixon	.10
488	Robert Perryman	.10
489	*Darryl Williams*	.30
490	Emmitt Smith	6.00
491	Dino Hackett	.10
492	Earnest Byner	.12
493	*Bucky Richardson,Bernard Dafney,Anthony Davis,Tony Brown*	.50
494	*Bill Johnson*	.20
495	*Darryl Ashmore,Joe Campbell,Kelvin Harris,Tim Lester*	.15
496	Nick Bell	.20
497	Jerry Ball	.12
498	*Edgar Bennett,Mark Chmura,Chris Holder,Mazio Royster*	4.00
499	Steve Christie	.10
500	Kenneth Davis	.12

1992 Fleer GameDay Box Tops

Display boxes from 1992 GameDay featured four different box tops, all of which have blank backs and are unnumbered. Although most photos are different than the player's card in the regular-issue set, Randall Cunningham is on all four tops.

		MT
Complete Set (4):		2.00
Common Player:		.50
1	Randall Cunningham, Anthony Munoz, Earnest Byner, Jim Everett	.50
2	Haywood Jeffires, Randall Cunningham, Mark Carrier, Vinny Testaverde	.50
3	Howie Long, Thurman Thomas, Randall Cunningham, Jerry Rice	.75
4	Christian Okoye, Pat Swilling, Steve Emtman, Randall Cunningham	.50

1992 Fleer GameDay National

Persons attending the 13th National Sports Card Convention in Atlanta, Ga., were given this 46-card set, which was contained in a black vinyl binder. The convention logo is printed on the card back, thereby distinguishing the card from GameDay's regular cards. The card front has a color action photo against a black-and-white background. The back has a card number, biographical information, stats and a mug shot. Each card measures 2-1/2" x 4-11/16".

		MT
Complete Set (46):		40.00
Common Player:		1.00
1	Deion Sanders	2.50
2	Jim Kelly	2.00
3	Jim Harbaugh	1.25
4	Boomer Esiason	1.50
5	Bernie Kosar	1.50
6	Troy Aikman	7.00
7	John Elway	3.00
8	Rodney Peete	1.00
9	Sterling Sharpe	2.50
10	Warren Moon	2.00
11	Jeff George	2.00
12	Derrick Thomas	2.00
13	Howie Long	1.25
14	Jim Everett	1.50
15	Dan Marino	5.00
16	Chris Doleman	1.00
17	Irving Fryar	1.25
18	Pat Swilling	1.25
19	Lawrence Taylor	2.00
20	Ken O'Brien	1.00
21	Randall Cunningham	2.00
22	Timm Rosenbach	1.00
23	Bubby Brister	1.25
24	John Friesz	2.00
25	Joe Montana	6.00
26	Dan McGwire	1.00
27	Vinny Testaverde	1.25
28	Mark Rypien	1.25
29	Ronnie Lott	2.00
30	Marco Coleman	1.50
31	Rob Moore	2.00
32	Bill Pickel	1.00
33	Brad Baxter	1.25
34	Steve Broussard	1.00
35	Darion Conner	1.00
36	Chris Hinton	1.00
37	Erric Pegram	1.25
38	Jessie Tuggle	1.00
39	Billy Joe Tolliver	1.00
40	David Klingler	2.00
41	Michael Irvin	3.00
42	Emmitt Smith	8.00
43	Quentin Coryatt	1.50
44	Steve Emtman	1.25
45	Deron Cherry	1.00
46	Ricky Ervins	1.00

1992-93 Fleer GameDay Gamebreakers

This 14-card set previewed the 1993 GameDay design and was available at the Super Bowl show. According to the checklist card, there are 5,000 sets produced.

		MT
Complete Set (14):		7.00
Common Player:		.20
1	Marco Coleman	.20
2	Bill Cowher (CO)	.20
3	John Elway	1.50
4	Barry Foster	.20
5	Cortez Kennedy	.20
6	James Lofton	.30
7	Art Monk	.30
8	Jerry Rice	2.00
9	Sterling Sharpe	.40
10	Emmitt Smith	4.00
11	Thurman Thomas	.50
12	Gino Torretta	.20
13	Steve Young	1.75
14	Checklist Card	.20

1992-93 Fleer GameDay SB Program

This six-card set was available through 1993 Super Bowl programs (one card per program). The cards are unnumbered and preview the 1993 GameDay set.

		MT
Complete Set (6):		10.00
Common Player:		1.00
1	Troy Aikman	5.00
2	Terry Allen	1.75
3	Ray Childress	1.00
4	Marco Coleman	1.00
5	Barry Foster	1.00
6	Sterling Sharpe	1.50

1993 Fleer

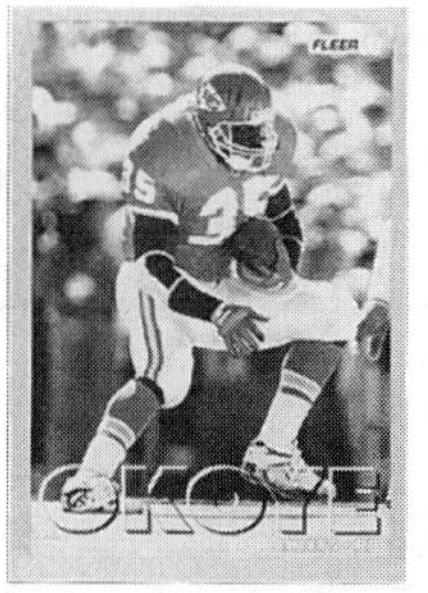

This 500-card set features color action photos and UV coating. The card front has a silver metallic border. The player's name is at the bottom in an embossed, transparent lettering. His team and position are at the lower right. The back has a color-coded panel which includes a close-up photo, stats, profile, biography and team logo. Subsets include Award Winners (#s 236-240, 253-257), League Leaders (#s 241-243, 258-262) and Pro Visions (#s 246-248, 263-264). Insert sets include NFL Prospects (30 cards, randomly in foil packs), All-Pro (25, in foil), Rookie Sensations (20, in jumbo packs), Team Leaders (5, in foil) and Steve Young (10, in foil). A nine-card promo sheet was also produced. It measures 7-1/2" x 10-1/2" and previews the 1993 Fleer card design. The nine players are: Steve Young, Kenny Walker, Chip Lohmiller, Kevin Greene, Craig Heyward, Ernie Jones, Emmitt Smith, Keith Byars and a promotional Fleer card.

		MT
Complete Set (500):		25.00
Common Player:		.05
Minor Stars:		.10
Pack (15):		.75
Wax Box (36):		20.00
1	Dan Saleaumua	.05
2	Bryan Cox	.05
3	Dermontti Dawson	.05
4	Michael Jackson	.05
5	Calvin Williams	.05
6	Terry McDaniel	.05
7	Jack Del Rio	.05
9	Ernie Jones	.05
10	Brad Muster	.05
11	Harold Green	.05
12	Eric Bieniemy	.05
13	Eric Dorsey	.05
14	Fred Barnett	.05
15	Cleveland Gary	.05
16	Darion Conner	.05
17	Jerry Ball	.05
18	Tony Casillas	.05
19	Brian Blades	.05
20	Tony Bennett	.05
21	Reggie Cobb	.05
22	Kurt Gouveia	.05
23	Greg McMurty	.05
24	Kyle Clifton	.05
25	Trace Armstrong	.05
26	Terry Allen	.05
27	Steve Bono	.50
28	Barry Word	.05
29	Mark Duper	.05
30	Nate Newton	.05
31	Will Wolford	.05
32	Curtis Duncan	.05
33	Nick Bell	.05
34	Don Beebe	.05
36	Rich Camarillo	.05
37	Wade Wilson	.05
38	John Taylor	.05
39	Marion Butts	.05
40	Rodney Hampton	.10
41	Seth Joyner	.05
42	Wilber Marshall	.05
43	Bobby Hebert	.05
44	Bennie Blades	.05
45	Thomas Everett	.05
46	Ricky Sanders	.05
47	Matt Brock	.05
48	Lawrence Dawsey	.05
49	Brad Edwards	.05
50	Vincent Brown	.05
51	Jeff Lageman	.05
52	Mark Carrier	.05
53	Cris Carter	.50
54	Brent Jones	.05
55	Barry Foster	.05
56	Derrick Thomas	.10
57	Scott Zolak	.05
58	Mark Stepnoski	.05
59	Eric Metcalf	.05
60	Al Smith	.05
61	Ronnie Harmon	.05
62	Cornelius Bennett	.05
64	Chris Chandler	.05
65	Toi Cook	.05
66	Tim Krumrie	.05
67	Gill Byrd	.05
68	Mark Jackson	.05
69	Tim Harris	.05
70	Shane Conlan	.05
71	Moe Gardner	.05
72	Lomas Brown	.05
73	Charles Haley	.05
74	Mark Rypien	.05
75	LeRoy Butler	.05
76	Steve DeBerg	.05
77	Darrell Green	.05
78	Marv Cook	.05
79	Chris Burkett	.05
80	Richard Dent	.05
81	Roger Craig	.05
82	Amp Lee	.05
83	Eric Green	.05
84	Willie Davis	.05
85	Mark Higgs	.05
86	Carlton Haselrig	.05
87	Tommy Vardell	.05
88	Haywood Jeffires	.05
89	Tim Brown	.10
90	Randall McDaniel	.05
91	John Elway	1.00
92	Ken Harvey	.05
93	Joel Hilgenberg	.05
94	Steve Wallace	.05
95	Stan Humphries	.10
96	Greg Jackson	.05
97	Clyde Simmons	.05
98	Jim Everett	.05
99	Michael Hayes	.05
100	Mel Gray	.05
101	Alvin Harper	.10
102	Art Monk	.10
103	Brett Favre	2.00
104	Keith McCants	.05
105	Charles Mann	.05
106	Leonard Russell	.05
107	Mo Lewis	.05
108	Shaun Gayle	.05
109	Chris Doleman	.05
110	Tim McDonald	.05
111	Louis Oliver	.05
112	Greg Lloyd	.10
113	Chip Banks	.05
114	Sean Jones	.05
115	Ethan Horton	.05
116	Kenneth Davis	.05
118	Johnny Johnson	.05
119	Vaughan Johnson	.05
120	Derrick Fenner	.05
121	Nate Lewis	.05
122	Pepper Johnson	.05
123	Heath Sherman	.05
124	Darryl Henley	.05
125	Pierce Holt	.05
126	Herman Moore	.50
127	Michael Irvin	.30
128	Tommy Kane	.05
129	Jackie Harris	.05
130	Hardy Nickerson	.05
131	Chip Lohmiller	.05
132	Andre Tippett	.05
133	Leonard Marshall	.05
134	Craig Heyward	.05
135	Anthony Carter	.05
136	Tom Rathman	.05
137	Lorenzo White	.05
138	Nick Lowery	.05
139	John Offerdahl	.05
140	Neil O'Donnell	.10
141	Clarence Verdin	.05
142	Ernest Givins	.05
143	Todd Marinovich	.05
144	Jeff Wright	.05
146	Freddie Joe Nunn	.05
147	William Perry	.05
148	Daniel Stubbs	.05
149	Morten Anderson	.05
150	David Meggett	.05
151	Andre Waters	.05
152	Todd Lyght	.05
153	Chris Miller	.05
154	Rodney Peete	.05
155	Jim Jeffcoat	.05
156	Cortez Kennedy	.05
157	Johnny Holland	.05
158	Ricky Reynolds	.05
159	Kevin Greene	.05
160	Jeff Herrod	.05
161	Bruce Matthews	.05
162	Anthony Smith	.05
163	Henry Jones	.05
164	Rob Burnett	.05
165	Eric Swann	.05
166	Tom Waddle	.05
167	Alfred Williams	.05
168	*Darren Carrington*	.05
169	Mike Sherrard	.05
170	Frank Reich	.05
171	*Anthony Newman*	.05
172	Mike Pritchard	.05
173	Andre Ware	.05
174	Daryl Johnston	.05
175	Rufus Porter	.05
176	Reggie White	.10
177	*Charles Mincy*	.05
178	Pete Stoyanovich	.05
179	Rod Woodson	.10
180	Anthony Johnson	.05
181	Cody Carlson	.05
182	Gaston Green	.05
183	Audray McMillian	.05
184	Mike Johnson	.05
185	Aeneas Williams	.05
186	Jarrod Bunch	.05
188	Quinn Early	.05
189	James Hasty	.05
190	Darryl Talley	.05
191	Jon Vaughn	.05
192	Andre Rison	.10
193	Kelvin Pritchett	.05
194	Ken Norton	.05
195	Chris Warren	.25
196	Sterling Sharpe	.10
197	Christian Okoye	.05
198	Richmond Webb	.05
199	James Francis	.05
200	Reggie Langhorne	.05
201	J.J. Birden	.05
202	Aaron Wallace	.05
203	Henry Thomas	.05
204	Clay Matthews	.05
205	Robert Massey	.05
206	Donnell Woolford	.05
207	Ricky Watters	.20
208	Wayne Martin	.05
209	Rob Moore	.05
210	Steve Tasker	.05
211	Jackie Slater	.05
212	Steve Young	1.00
213	Barry Sanders	1.25
214	Jay Novacek	.05
215	Eugene Robinson	.05
216	Duane Bickett	.05
217	Broderick Thomas	.05
218	David Fulcher	.05
219	Rohn Stark	.05
220	Warren Moon	.10
221	Steve Wisniewski	.05
222	Nate Odomes	.05
224	Byron Evans	.05
225	Mark Collins	.05
227	Sam Mills	.05
228	Marvin Washington	.05
229	Thurman Thomas	.15
230	Brent Williams	.05
231	Jesse Tuggle	.05
232	Chris Spielman	.05
233	Emmitt Smith	2.00
234	John L. Williams	.05
235	Jeff Cross	.05
236	Chris Doleman	.05
237	John Elway (AW)	.20
238	Barry Foster (AW)	.05
239	Cortez Kennedy (AW)	.05
240	Steve Young (AW)	.50
241	Barry Foster (LL)	.05
242	Warren Moon (LL)	.05
243	Sterling Sharpe (LL)	.05
244	Emmitt Smith (LL)	1.00
245	Thurman Thomas (LL)	.10
246	Michael Irvin (PV)	.15
247	Steve Young (PV)	.50
248	Barry Foster (PV)	.05
249	Checklist	.05
250	Checklist	.05
251	Checklist	.05
252	Checklist	.05
253	Troy Aikman (AW)	.40
254	Jason Hanson (AW)	.05
255	Carl Pickens (AW)	.20
256	Santana Doleman	.05
257	Dale Carter	.05
258	Clyde Simmons	.05
259	Audray McMillian	.05
260	Henry Jones	.05
261	Deion Sanders	.20
262	Haywood Foster	.05
263	Deion Sanders	.20
264	Andre Reed	.05
265	Vince Workman	.05
266	Robert Brown	.05
267	Ray Agnew	.05
268	Ronnie Lott	.05
269	Wesley Carroll	.05
270	John Randle	.05
271	Rodney Culver	.05
272	David Alexander	.05
273	Troy Aikman	1.00
274	Bernie Kosar	.05
275	Scott Case	.05
276	Dan McGwire	.05
277	John Alt	.05
278	Dan Marino	2.00
279	Santana Dotson	.05
280	Johnny Mitchell	.05
281	Alonzo Spellman	.05
282	Adrian Cooper	.05
283	Gary Clark	.05
285	Eric Martin	.05
286	Jesse Solomon	.05
287	Carl Banks	.05
288	Harris Barton	.05
289	Jim Harbaugh	.10
290	Bubba McDowell	.05
291	*Anthony McDowell*	.05
292	Terrell Buckley	.05
293	Bruce Armstrong	.05
294	Kurt Barber	.05
295	Reginald Jones	.05
296	Steve Jordan	.05
297	Kerry Cash	.05
298	Ray Crockett	.05
299	Keith Byars	.05
300	Russell Maryland	.05
301	Johnny Bailey	.05
302	Vinnie Clark	.05
303	Terry Wooden	.05
304	Harvey Williams	.05
305	Marco Coleman	.05
306	Mark Wheeler	.05
307	Greg Townsend	.05
308	Tim McGee	.05
309	Donald Evans	.05
310	Randal Hill	.05
312	Dalton Hilliard	.05
313	Howard Ballard	.05
314	Phil Simms	.05
315	Jerry Rice	1.00
316	Courtney Hall	.05
317	Darren Lewis	.05
318	Greg Montgomery	.05
319	Paul Gruber	.05
320	*George Koonce*	.05
321	Eugene Chung	.05
322	Mike Brim	.05
323	Patrick Hunter	.05
324	Todd Scott	.05
325	Steve Emtman	.05
326	*Andy Harmon*	.05
327	Larry Brown	.05
328	Chuck Cecil	.05
329	Tim McKyer	.05
330	Jeff Bryant	.05
331	Tim Barnett	.05
332	Irving Fryar	.05
333	Tyji Armstrong	.05
334	Brad Baxter	.05
335	Shane Collins	.05
336	Jeff Graham	.05
337	Ricky Proehl	.05
338	Tommy Maddox	.05
339	Jim Dombrowski	.05
340	Bill Brooks	.05
341	*Dave Brown*	.30
342	Eric Davis	.05
345	Mike Munchak	.05
346	Ron Hall	.05
347	Brian Noble	.05
348	Chris Singleton	.05
349	Boomer Esiason	.05
350	Ray Roberts	.05
351	Gary Zimmerman	.05
352	Quentin Coryatt	.05
353	Willie Green	.05
354	Randall Cunningham	.05
355	Kevin Smith	.05
356	Michael Dean Perry	.05
357	Tim Green	.05
358	Dwayne Harper	.05
359	Dale Carter	.05
360	Keith Jackson	.05
361	Martin Mayhew	.05
362	Brian Washington	.05
363	Earnest Byner	.05
364	David Johnson	.05
365	Timm Rosenbach	.05
367	Vaughn Dunbar	.05
368	Phil Hansen	.05
369	Mike Fox	.05
370	Dana Hall	.05
371	Junior Seau	.10
373	Eddie Robinson	.05
374	*Milton Mack*	.05
375	Mike Prior	.05
376	Jerome Henderson	.05
377	Scott Mersereau	.05
378	Neal Anderson	.05
379	Harry Newsome	.05
380	John Baylor	.05
381	Bill Fralic	.05
382	Mark Bavaro	.05
383	Robert Jones	.05
384	Tyronne Stowe	.05
385	Deion Sanders	.50
386	Robert Blackman	.05
387	Neil Smith	.05
388	Mark Ingram	.05
389	Mark Carrier	.05
390	Browning Nagle	.05
391	Ricky Evans	.05
392	Carnell Lake	.05
393	Luis Sharpe	.05
395	Tommy Barnhardt	.05
396	Mark Kelso	.05
397	*Kent Graham*	.10
398	Bill Romanowski	.05
399	Anthony Miller	.05
400	John Roper	.05
401	Lamar Rogers	.05
402	Troy Auzenne	.05
403	Webster Slaughter	.05
404	David Brandon	.05
405	Chris Hinton	.05
406	Andy Heck	.05
407	Tracy Simien	.05
408	Troy Vincent	.05
409	Jason Hanson	.05
410	*Rod Jones*	.05
411	Al Noga	.05
412	Ernie Mills	.05
413	Willie Gault	.05
414	Henry Ellard	.05
415	Rickey Jackson	.05
416	Bruce Smith	.05
417	Derek Brown	.05
418	Kevin Fagan	.05
419	Gary Plummer	.05
420	Wendell Davis	.05
421	Craig Thompson	.05
422	Wes Hopkins	.05
423	Ray Childress	.05
424	Pat Harlow	.05
425	Howie Long	.05
427	Sean Salisbury	.05
428	*Dwight Hollier*	.05
429	Brett Perriman	.10
430	Donald Hollas	.05
431	Jim Lachey	.05
432	Darren Perry	.05
433	Lionel Washington	.05
434	Sean Gilbert	.05
435	Gene Atkins	.05
436	Jim Kelly	.15
437	Ed McCaffrey	.05
438	Don Griffin	.05
439	Jerrol Williams	.05
440	Bryce Paup	.10
441	Darryl Williams	.05
442	Vai Sikahema	.05
443	Cris Dishman	.05
444	Kevin Mack	.05
445	Winston Moss	.05
447	Mike Merriweather	.05
448	Tony Paige	.05
449	Robert Porcher	.05
450	Ricardo McDonald	.05
451	Danny Copeland	.05
452	Tony Tolbert	.05
453	Eric Dickerson	.05
454	Willie Anderson	.05
455	Dave Krieg	.05
456	*Brad Lamb*	.05
457	Bart Oates	.05
458	Guy McIntyre	.05
459	Stanley Richard	.05
460	Edgar Bennett	.05
461	Pat Carter	.05
462	Eric Allen	.05
463	William Fuller	.05
464	James Jones	.05
465	Chester McGlockton	.05
467	Tim Grunhard	.05
468	Jarvis Williams	.05
469	Tracy Scroggins	.05
470	David Klingler	.05
471	Andre Collins	.05
472	Erik Williams	.05
473	Eddie Anderson	.05
474	Marc Boutte	.05
475	Joe Montana	1.00
476	Andre Reed	.10
477	Lawrence Taylor	.10
478	Jeff George	.15
479	Chris Mims	.05
480	Ken Ruettgers	.05
481	Roman Phifer	.05
482	William Thomas	.05
483	Lamar Lathon	.05
484	Vinny Testaverde	.05
485	Mike Kenn	.05
487	Chris Martin	.05
488	Maurice Hurst	.05
489	Pat Swilling	.05
490	Carl Pickens	.75
491	Tony Smith	.05
492	James Washington	.05
493	Jeff Hostetler	.10
494	Jeff Chadwick	.05
495	Kevin Ross	.05
496	Jim Ritcher	.05
497	Jessie Hester	.05
498	Burt Grossman	.05
499	Keith Van Horne	.05
500	Gerald Robinson	.05

1993 Fleer All-Pros

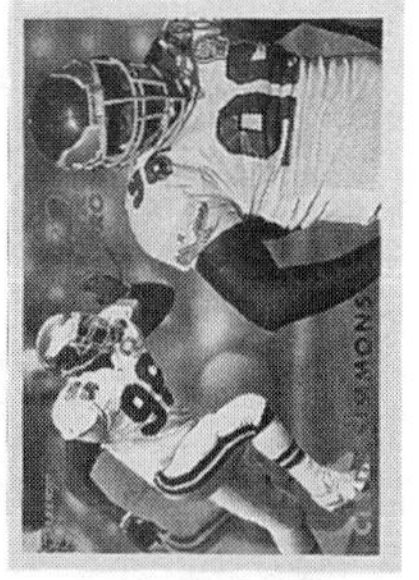

Twenty-five of the NFL's best are featured on these cards, which were randomly inserted into 1993 Fleer foil packs. Each card front is horizontal with white borders and features a color photo of the player superimposed against a black-and-white action photo. The "All-Pro" logo and player's name are in gold foil at the bottom. Each card back is numbered and includes a career summary on a background of team color-coded panels.

		MT
Complete Set (25):		40.00
Common Player:		1.00
Minor Stars:		2.00
1	Steve Atwater	1.00
2	Rich Camarillo	1.00
3	Ray Childress	1.00
4	Chris Doleman	1.00
5	Barry Foster	1.00
6	Henry Jones	1.00
7	Cortez Kennedy	1.00
8	Nick Lowery	1.00
9	Wilber Marshall	1.00
10	Bruce Matthews	1.00
11	Randall McDaniel	1.00
12	Audray McMillian	1.00
13	Sam Mills	1.00
14	Jay Novacek	1.00
15	Jerry Rice	8.00
16	Junior Seau	2.00
17	Sterling Sharpe	2.00
18	Clyde Simmons	1.00
19	Emmitt Smith	20.00
20	Derrick Thomas	2.00
21	Steve Wallace	1.00
22	Richmond Webb	1.00
23	Steve Wisniewski	1.00
24	Rod Woodson	1.00
25	Steve Young	8.00

1993 Fleer Prospects

Thirty players from the 1993 NFL draft are featured on these cards, which were randomly inserted in 1993 Fleer foil packs. Each card front has a color cut-out photo of the player on a gold background with blue borders. The "1993 NFL Prospect" logo, player's name, round he was drafted in and team name are in gold foil on the front, too. The back has a close-up shot and a career summary, plus a card number.

		MT
Complete Set (30):		70.00
Common Player:		1.50
1	Drew Bledsoe	25.00
2	Garrison Hearst	10.00
3	John Copeland	1.50
4	Eric Curry	1.50
5	Curtis Conway	7.00
6	Lincoln Kennedy	1.50
7	Jerome Bettis	10.00
8	Patrick Bates	1.50
9	Brad Hopkins	1.50
10	Tom Carter	1.50
11	Irv Smith	1.50
12	Robert Smith	7.00
13	Deon Figures	1.50
14	Leonard Renfro	1.50
15	O.J. McDuffie	5.00
16	Dana Stubblefield	3.00
17	Todd Kelly	1.50
18	George Teague	1.50
19	Demetrius DeBose	1.50
20	Coleman Rudolph	1.50
21	Carlton Gray	1.50
22	Troy Drayton	1.50
23	Natrone Means	8.00
24	Qadry Ismail	4.00
25	Gino Torretta	1.50
26	Carl Simpson	1.50
27	Glyn Milburn	3.00
28	Chad Brown	3.00
29	Reggie Brooks	1.50
30	Billy Joe Hobert	1.50

1993 Fleer Rookie Sensations

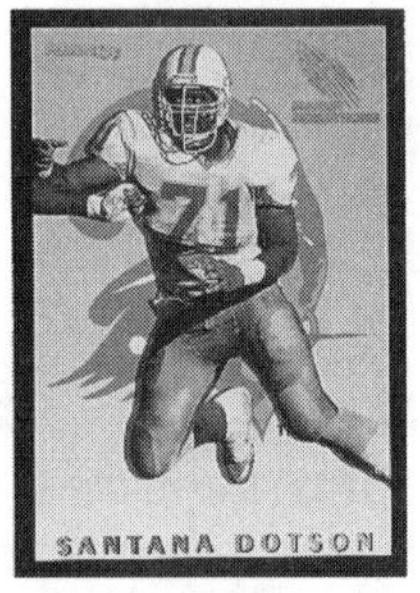

These cards feature 20 of the NFL's top players beginning their NFL careers. The cards have the player's name and "Rookie Sensations" logo in gold foil on the front. The backs have a player profile and card number, 1 of 20, etc. Cards were random inserts in 1993 Fleer football jumbo packs.

		MT
Complete Set (20):		100.00
Common Player:		5.00
1	Dale Carter	5.00
2	Eugene Chung	5.00
3	Marco Coleman	5.00
4	Quentin Coryatt	7.00
5	Santana Dotson	7.00
6	Vaughn Dunbar	5.00
7	Steve Emtman	5.00
8	Sean Gilbert	7.00
9	Dana Hall	5.00
10	Jason Hanson	5.00
11	Robert Jones	5.00
12	David Klingler	5.00
13	Amp Lee	7.00
14	Troy Auzenne	5.00
15	Ricardo McDonald	5.00
16	Chris Mims	5.00
17	Johnny Mitchell	7.00
18	Carl Pickens	20.00
19	Darren Perry	5.00
20	Troy Vincent	5.00

1993 Fleer Team Leaders

Five premiere players in the NFL are featured in this insert set; cards were randomly inserted into 1993 Fleer foil packs. The card front features a player action photo against a blue background with lightning streaks. "Team Leader" and the player's name are in gold foil at the bottom. The backs have a blue background with gold border and contain another color photo and career summary, plus a card number (1 of 5 etc.).

		MT
Complete Set (5):		35.00
Common Player:		3.00
1	Brett Favre	15.00
2	Derrick Thomas	3.00
3	Steve Young	7.00
4	John Elway	10.00
5	Cortez Kennedy	3.00

1993 Fleer Steve Young

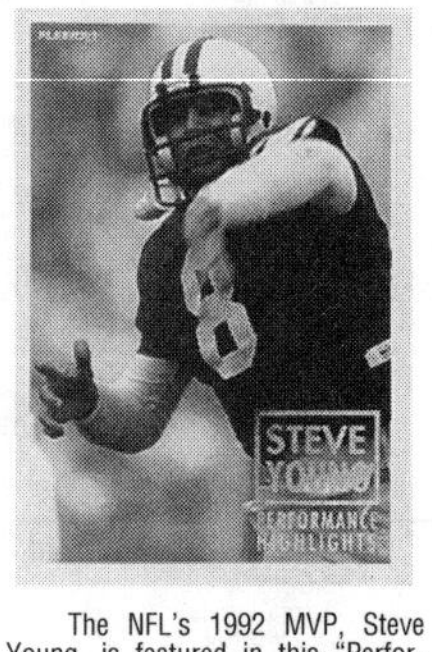

The NFL's 1992 MVP, Steve Young, is featured in this "Performance Highlights" issue from Fleer. Each card front has an action photo with a white border, plus the set and player's name stamped in gold foil. The back has a close-up shot and player profile against a red background with white borders. The cards are numbered on the backs. Cards 11-13 were available through Fleer through a mail-in offer only, for 10 wrappers and $1. Young also signed more than 2,000 cards, which were randomly inserted.

	MT
Complete Set (10):	10.00
Common Young:	1.00
Autograph:	120.00
Mail-In Young (11-13):	2.00

1993 Fleer Fruit of the Loom

Specially-marked packages of Fruit of the Loom underwear contained six of these cards, which were produced by Fleer. The cards are similar in design to Fleer's regular 1993 set, except a Fruit of the Loom logo appears on the card front. The photos are the same, but the card number, which is on the back, indicates the card is x of 50, etc.

		MT
Complete Set (50):		100.00
Common Player:		1.50
1	Andre Rison	4.00
2	Deion Sanders	6.00
3	Neal Anderson	2.00
4	Jim Harbaugh	2.00
5	Bernie Kosar	2.50
6	Eric Metcalf	3.00
7	John Elway	7.00
8	Karl Mecklenburg	1.50
9	Sterling Sharpe	5.00
10	Reggie White (Traded to Green Bay Packers)	4.00
11	Steve Emtman	2.00
12	Jeff George	3.00
13	Willie Gault	2.00
14	Jim Kelly	5.00
15	Thurman Thomas	5.00
16	Harold Green	2.00
17	Carl Pickens	1.50
18	Troy Aikman	17.00
19	Emmitt Smith	20.00
20	Barry Sanders	10.00
21	Pat Swilling (Traded to Detroit Lions)	2.00
22	Haywood Jeffires	2.50
23	Warren Moon	3.00
24	Derrick Thomas	3.00
25	Christian Okoye	2.00
26	Flipper Anderson	1.50
27	Jim Everett	2.50
28	Keith Jackson	2.50
29	Dan Marino	15.00
30	Andre Tippett	1.50
31	Lawrence Taylor	2.50
32	Randall Cunningham	2.50
33	Barry Foster	4.00
34	Rod Woodson	3.00
35	Jerry Rice	8.00
36	Steve Young	6.00
37	Reggie Cobb	1.50
38	Roger Craig	2.00
39	Chris Doleman	1.50
40	Morten Andersen	1.50
41	Dalton Hilliard	1.50
42	Ronnie Lott (Traded to New York Jets)	2.50
43	Chris Chandler	1.50
44	Stan Humphries	3.00
45	Junior Seau	4.00
46	Brian Blades	2.00
47	Cortez Kennedy	2.00
48	Wilber Marshall	1.50
49	Art Monk	2.50
50	Checklist Card	1.50

1993 Fleer GameDay

GameDay used the same format as its 1992 debut set - oversized cards which measure 2-1/2" x 4-11/16" - but cut back the number of cards by 20. However, the 1993 set included three insert sets - "Game-Breakers" (20 cards of impact players), "Rookie Standouts" (16 of the top 1993 NFL draft picks), and "Second-Year Stars" (16 of the game's top sophomores). All three types were randomly inserted in packs.

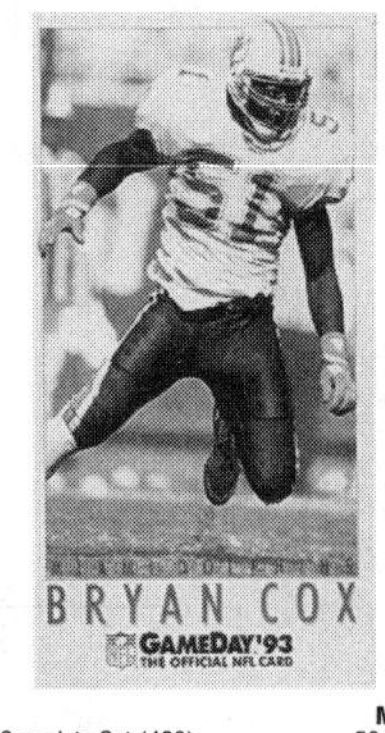

		MT
Complete Set (480):		50.00
Common Player:		.10
Minor Stars:		.20
Wax Box:		35.00
1	Troy Aikman	2.00
2	Terry Allen	.10
3	Ray Childress	.10
4	Marco Coleman	.10
5	Barry Foster	.20
6	Sterling Sharpe	.30
7	Steve McMichael	.10
8	Steve Young	2.00
9	Derrick Thomas	.20
10	John Elway	1.00
11	*Drew Bledsoe*	7.00
12	Jim Kelly	.30
13	Dan Marino	3.00
14	Mo Lewis	.10
15	David Klingler	.20
16	Darrell Green	.10
17	James Francis	.10
18	*John Copeland*	.30
19	Terry McDaniel	.10
20	Barry Sanders	2.00
21	Deion Sanders	1.00
22	Emmitt Smith	4.00
23	Marion Butts	.10
24	Darryl Talley	.10
25	Randall Cunningham	.20
26	Rod Woodson	.20
27	Terrell Buckley	.10
28	Michael Haynes	.10
29	Tony Jones	.10
30	Santana Dotson	.10
31	Lomas Brown	.10
32	Eric Metcalf	.10
33	Morten Andersen	.10
34	Reggie Cobb	.10
35	Ferrell Edmunds	.10
36	Joe Montana	3.00
37	Ken Harvey	.10
38	Rodney Hampton	.30
39	Kurt Gouveia	.10
40	Ken Norton	.10
41	Frank Reich	.10
42	Kevin Greene	.10
43	Cleveland Gary	.10
44	Maurice Hurst	.10
45	Troy Vincent	.10
46	*Eric Curry*	.30
47	*Curtis Conway*	1.25
48	Christian Okoye	.10
49	Tunch Ilkin	.10
50	Michael Irvin	.50
51	Bart Oates	.10
52	Pepper Johnson	.10
53	Vaughan Johnson	.10
54	Lawrence Taylor	.20
55	Junior Seau	.40
56	Michael Brooks	.10
57	Neal Anderson	.10
58	D.J. Johnson	.10
59	Seth Joyner	.10
60	Marvin Washington	.10
61	Ernest Givins	.10
62	*Jaime Feilds*	.10
63	Vincent Brown	.10
64	Randall McDaniel	.10
65	Tommy Maddox	.10
66	*Steve Everitt*	.30
67	Brian Noble	.10
68	Bryce Paup	.10
69	Brad Baxter	.10
70	*Demetrius DuBose*	.20
71	Duane Bickett	.10
72	Mark Rypien	.10
73	Harris Barton	.10
74	Bruce Matthews	.10
75	Irving Fryar	.10
76	Steve Wisniewski	.10
77	*Will Shields*	.10
78	*Tom Carter*	.40
79	Steve Emtman	.10
80	Jerry Rice	2.00
81	Art Monk	.20
82	Tony Tolbert	.10
83	Johnny Mitchell	.10
84	*Deon Figures*	.30
85	Marv Cook	.10
86	Darion Conner	.10
87	Ricky Proehl	.10
88	Tony Bennett	.10
89	Jay Schroeder	.10
90	Neil Smith	.10
91	Jarvis Williams	.10
92	James Hasty	.10
93	Anthony Miller	.20
94	*Thomas Smith*	.10
95	Richard Dent	.10
96	Henry Jones	.10
97	Renaldo Turnbull	.10
98	Jason Hanson	.10
99	Cortez Kennedy	.20
100	Brett Favre	3.00
101	Anthony Carter	.10
102	Cris Carter	.20
103	*Dana Stubblefield*	1.00
104	Nick Bell	.10
105	Marcus Allen	.20
106	Neil O'Donnell	.40
107	Steve DeBerg	.10
108	Leonard Russell	.10
109	Ethan Horton	.10
110	William Perry	.10
111	Don Griffin	.10
112	Clarence Verdin	.10
113	Amp Lee	.10
114	Earnest Byner	.10
115	Ricky Reynolds	.10
116	Tom Waddle	.10
117	Robert Jones	.10
118	Willie Davis	.10
119	Chris Miller	.10
120	Drew Hill	.10
121	Warren Moon	.30
122	Willie Anderson	.10
123	*George Teague*	.30
124	John L. Williams	.10
125	Ed McCaffrey	.10
126	Eric Green	.10
127	Scott Mersereau	.10
128	Charles Mann	.10
129	Todd Lyght	.10
130	Rodney Culver	.10
131	Richmond Webb	.10
132	*John Parrella*	.10
133	*Reggie Brooks*	.50
134	*Lincoln Kennedy*	.20
135	Tim Johnson	.10
136	Robert Massey	.10
137	Keith Jackson	.20
138	Alfred Williams	.10
139	Leroy Hoard	.10
140	Jessie Tuggle	.10
141	Chris Mims	.10
142	Herschel Walker	.10
143	Clyde Simmons	.10
144	Dana Hall	.10
145	Nate Newton	.10
146	Dennis Smith	.10
147	Rich Camarillo	.10
148	Chris Spielman	.10
149	Jim Dombrowski	.10
150	Steve Beuerlein	.10
151	Mark Clayton	.10
152	Lee Williams	.10
153	*Robert Smith*	1.50
154	Greg Jackson	.10
155	Jay Hilgenberg	.10
156	Howard Ballard	.10
157	*Mike Compton*	.10
158	Brent Williams	.10
159	Tommy Kane	.10
160	Barry Word	.10
161	Darren Lewis	.10
162	Steve Atwater	.10
163	Gary Clark	.10
164	Donnell Woolford	.10
165	Henry Thomas	.10
166	Tim Brown	.25
167	Andre Ware	.10
168	Jackie Harris	.20
169	Browning Nagle	.10
170	Chris Singleton	.10
171	Ronnie Lott	.10
172	Leonard Marshall	.10
173	Dale Carter	.10
174	Bruce Armstrong	.10
175	Tommy Vardell	.10
176	Bubba McDowell	.10
177	*Patrick Bates*	.20
178	Tyji Armstrong	.10
179	Keith Sims	.10
180	Boomer Esiason	.20
181	Ricky Watters	.40
182	Keith Sims	.10
183	Burt Grossman	.10
184	Richard Cooper	.10
185	Marc Boutte	.10
186	Shane Conlan	.10
187	Luis Sharpe	.10
188	*O.J. McDuffie*	2.00
189	Harvey Williams	.10
190	Blair Thomas	.10
191	Charles Haley	.10
192	Chip Lohmiller	.10
193	Vinny Testaverde	.20
194	Desmond Howard	.20
195	Johnny Johnson	.10
196	Bennie Blades	.10
197	Jeff Wright	.10
198	Cody Carlson	.10
199	*Michael Barrow*	.10
200	Pat Swilling	.10
201	*Willie Roaf*	.25
202	Mike Walter	.10
203	Kevin Fagan	.10
204	Nate Odomes	.10
205	Michael Dean Perry	.10
206	Bruce Pickens	.10
207	Mel Gray	.10
208	Jack Trudeau	.10
209	Ricky Sanders	.10
210	Bobby Hebert	.10
211	Craig Heyward	.10
212	Eric Bieniemy	.10
213	Andre Rison	.20
214	Bernie Kosar	.10
215	*Lester Holmes*	.10
216	*Marcus Buckley*	.20
217	Tony Casillas	.10
218	Cornelius Bennett	.10
219	Kyle Clifton	.10
220	Kirk Lowdermilk	.10
221	Leon Searcy	.10
222	Gary Anderson	.10
223	Tim Barnett	.10
224	Gene Atkins	.10
225	Jeff Cross	.10
226	*Darrin Smith*	.25
227	Rohn Stark	.10
228	Chris Warren	.50
229	Eric Allen	.10
230	*Wayne Simmons*	.10
231	Al Smith	.10
232	*Reggie Rivers*	.10
233	Kevin Smith	.10
234	Vince Workman	.10
235	Thurman Thomas	.30
236	*Kevin Williams*	1.50
237	Dan McGwire	.10
238	Greg Lloyd	.10
239	*Ray Buchanan*	.25
240	Shannon Sharpe	.20
241	Ricardo McDonald	.10
242	Aaron Wallace	.10
243	Chris Hinton	.10
244	Bill Romanowski	.10
245	Randal Hill	.10
246	Ray Agnew	.10
247	*Todd Kelly*	.10
248	John Stephens	.10
249	Sean Salisbury	.10
250	Roger Craig	.10
251	Dave Krieg	.10
252	Brian Blades	.10
253	Jerrod Bunch	.10
254	Phil Simms	.10
255	Keith Van Horne	.10
256	Jim Price	.10
257	*Garrison Hearst*	3.00
258	Derrick Walker	.10
259	Mike Pritchard	.10
260	*Leonard Renfro*	.10
261	Rodney Peete	.10
262	Jeff Bryant	.10
263	Dermontti Dawson	.10
264	Greg McMurty	.10
265	Wendell Davis	.10
266	Kerry Cash	.10
267	Jackie Slater	.10
268	Sam Mills	.10
269	Carlton Bailey	.10
270	Mark Wheeler	.10
271	Darren Perry	.10
272	Todd Scott	.10
273	John Holland	.10
274	Mike Croel	.10
275	Shane Dronett	.10
276	Andre Collins	.10
277	Eric Swann	.10
278	Jessie Hester	.10
279	Bryan Cox	.10
280	Mark Jackson	.10
281	Thomas Everett	.10
282	James Lofton	.10
283	Carl Pickens	1.00
284	Mark Carrier (Cleve)	.10
285	Heath Sherman	.10
286	Chris Burkett	.10
287	*Coleman Rudolph*	.10
288	Todd Marinovich	.10
289	Nate Lewis	.10
290	Fred Barnett	.10
291	Jim Lachey	.10
292	Jerry Ball	.10
293	Jeff George	.50
294	William Fuller	.10
295	Courtney Hawkins	.10
296	Kelvin Martin	.10
297	Trace Armstrong	.10
298	Carl Banks	.10
299	*Terry Kirby*	.75
301	John Offerdahl	.10
302	Wilber Marshall	.10
303	Guy McIntyre	.10
304	Steve Wallace	.10
305	*Chris Slade*	.50
306	*Anthony Newman*	.10
307	Chip Banks	.10
308	*Carlton Gray*	.10
309	Wayne Martin	.10
310	Tom Rathman	.10
311	Shaun Gayle	.10
312	*Billy Joe Hobert*	.50
313	Matt Brock	.10
314	*Arthur Marshall*	.25
315	Wade Wilson	.10
316	Michael Jackson	.10
317	Bruce Kozerski	.10
318	Reggie Langhorne	.10
319	Jerrol Williams	.10
320	Aeneas Williams	.10
321	*Tony McGee*	.50
322	*Carl Simpson*	.10
323	Russell Maryland	.10
324	Nick Lowery	.10
325	Steve Tasker	.10
326	Alvin Harper	.40
327	Haywood Jeffires	.10
328	Hardy Nickerson	.10
329	Alonzo Spellman	.10
330	Eric Dickerson	.10
331	Scott Zolak	.10
332	Darryl Henley	.10
333	Daniel Stubbs	.10
334	Andy Heck	.10
335	Mark May	.10
336	*Roosevelt Potts*	.25
337	Erik Howard	.10
338	Sean Gilbert	.10
339	*Jerome Bettis*	3.00
340	*Darren Carrington*	.20
341	Gill Byrd	.10
342	John Friesz	.10
343	*Roger Harper*	.10
344	Fred Stokes	.10
345	Stanley Richard	.10
346	Johnny Bailey	.10
347	David Wyman	.10
348	Merril Hoge	.10
349	Brett Perriman	.10
350	Kelvin Pritchett	.10
351	Rod Bernstine	.10
352	Jim Ritcher	.10
353	Mark Stepnoski	.10
354	Jeff Lageman	.10
355	*Darrin Gordon*	.50
356	Don Mosebar	.10
357	Simon Fletcher	.10
358	*Charles Mincy*	.20
359	Ron Hall	.10
360	Brent Jones	.10
361	Byron Evans	.10
362	*Dan Footman*	.20
363	Mark Higgs	.10
364	Brian Washington	.10
365	*Brad Hopkins*	.10
366	Tracy Simien	.10
367	Derrick Fenner	.10
368	Lorenzo White	.10
369	*Marvin Jones*	.25
370	Chris Doleman	.10
371	Jeff Harrod	.10
372	Jim Harbaugh	.10
373	Jim Jeffcoat	.10
374	*Michael Strahan*	.10
375	Ricky Ervins	.10
376	Joel Hilgenberg	.10
377	Curtis Duncan	.10
378	*Glyn Milburn*	.75
379	Jack Del Rio	.10
380	Eric Martin	.10
381	David Meggett	.10
382	Jeff Hostetler	.20
383	Greg Townsend	.10
384	Brad Muster	.10
385	*Irv Smith*	.50
386	Chris Jacke	.10
387	*Ernest Dye*	.20
388	Henry Ellard	.10
389	John Taylor	.10
390	Chris Chandler	.10
391	*Larry Centers*	.50
392	Henry Rolling	.10
393	Dan Saleaumua	.10
394	Moe Gardner	.10
395	Darryl Williams	.10
396	Paul Gruber	.10
397	Dwayne Harper	.10
398	Pat Harlow	.10
399	Rickey Jackson	.10
400	Quentin Coryatt	.10
401	Steve Jordan	.10
402	*Rick Mirer*	.75
403	Howard Cross	.10
404	Mike Johnson	.10
405	Broderick Thomas	.10
406	Stan Humphries	.40
407	Ronnie Harmon	.10
408	*Andy Harmon*	.10
409	*Troy Drayton*	.75
410	*Dan Williams*	.10
411	Mark Bavaro	.10
412	Bruce Smith	.10
413	*Elbert Shelley*	.20
414	Tim McGee	.10
415	Tim Harris	.10
416	Rob Moore	.10
417	Rob Burnett	.10
418	Howie Long	.10
419	Chuck Cecil	.10
420	Carl Lee	.10
421	Anthony Smith	.10
422	Jeff Graham	.20
423	Clay Matthews	.10
424	Jay Novacek	.10
425	Phil Hansen	.10
426	*Andre Hastings*	.75
427	Toi Cook	.10
428	Rufus Porter	.10
429	Mike Pitts	.10
430	Eddie Robinson	.10
431	Herman Moore	1.00
432	Erik Kramer	.10
433	Mark Carrier (Chi.)	.10
434	*Natrone Means*	3.00
435	Carnell Lake	.10
436	Carlton Haselrig	.10
437	John Randle	.10
438	Louis Oliver	.10
439	Ray Roberts	.10
440	Leslie O'Neal	.10
441	Reggie White	.25
442	Dalton Hilliard	.10
443	Tim Krumrie	.10
444	Leroy Butler	.10
445	Greg Kragen	.10
446	Anthony Johnson	.10
447	Aydrey McMillian	.10
448	Lawrence Dawsey	.10
449	Pierce Holt	.10
450	Brad Edwards	.10
451	J.J. Birden	.10
452	Mike Munchak	.10
453	Tracy Scroggins	.10
454	Mike Tomczak	.10
455	Harold Green	.10
456	Vaughn Dunbar	.10
457	Calvin Williams	.10
458	Pete Stoyanovich	.10
459	Willie Gault	.10
460	Ken Ruettgers	.10
461	Eugene Robinson	.10
462	Larry Brown	.10
463	*Antonio London*	.10
464	Andre Reed	.10
465	Daryl Johnston	.10
466	Karl Mecklenburg	.10
467	David Lang	.10
468	Bill Brooks	.10
469	Jim Everett	.20
470	*Qadry Ismail*	1.00
471	Vai Sikahema	.10
472	Andre Tippett	.10
473	Eugene Chung	.10
474	Cris Dishman	.10
475	Tim McDonald	.10
476	Freddie Joe Nunn	.10
477	Checklist #1	.10
478	Checklist #2	.10
479	Checklist #3	.10
480	Checklist #4	.10

1993 Fleer GameDay Game Breakers

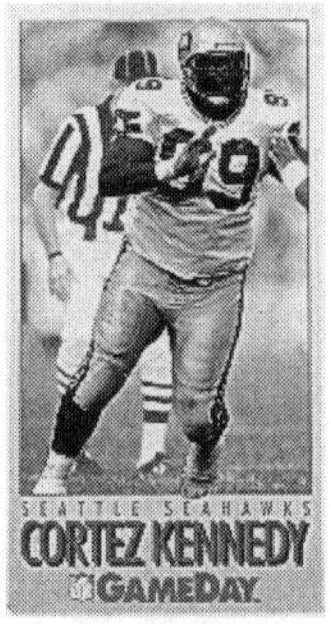

These 2-1/2" x 4-3/4" cards were randomly inserted in 1993 GameDay packs. Twenty top offensive players are represented. The card front has a color action photo against a black-and-white game action photo, with a black border. The player's and set's name are stamped in gold foil at the bottom. Each back has a closeup picture of the player, his name, his jersey number and a recap of his 1992 season. The backs are borderless and are numbered 1 of 20, etc.

		MT
Complete Set (20):		30.00
Common Player:		.50
Minor Stars:		1.00
1	Troy Aikman	4.00
2	Brett Favre	4.00
3	Steve Young	4.00
4	Dan Marino	6.00
5	Joe Montana	4.00

6 Jim Kelly 1.00
7 Emmitt Smith 7.00
8 Ricky Watters 1.00
9 Barry Foster .50
10 Barry Sanders 4.00
11 Michael Irvin 1.50
12 Thurman Thomas 1.00
13 Sterling Sharpe 1.00
14 Jerry Rice 4.00
15 Andre Rison .50
16 Deion Sanders 2.00
17 Harold Green .50
18 Lorenzo White .50
19 Terry Allen .50
20 Haywood Jeffires .50

1993 Fleer GameDay Rookie Standouts

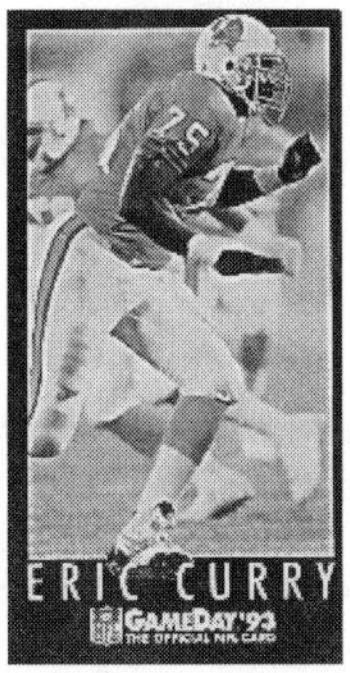

These cards are devoted to the top 16 players chosen in the 1993 NFL Draft. Cards, which measure 2-1/2" x 4-3/4", were random inserts in 1993 GameDay packs. Each card front is dark blue and features a color action photo against a black-and-white action background. The player's and set's name are stamped in gold foil at the bottom. The card back, numbered 1 of 16, etc., is white and includes the player's name and uniform number, plus a color photo and recap of his 1992 season.

MT
Complete Set (16): 25.00
Common Player: .50
Minor Stars: 1.00
1 Drew Bledsoe 7.00
2 Rick Mirer 3.00
3 Garrison Hearst 3.00
4 Jerome Bettis 4.00
5 Marvin Jones .50
6 Reggie Brooks .50
7 O.J. McDuffie 2.00
8 Qadry Ismail 1.00
9 Glyn Milburn 1.00
10 Andre Hastings .50
11 Curtis Conway 2.00
12 Eric Curry .50
13 John Copeland .50
14 Kevin Williams 2.00
15 Patrick Bates .50
16 Lincoln Kennedy .50

1993 Fleer GameDay Second-Year Stars

Sixteen top rookies from the 1992 NFL season are featured on these cards, which were random inserts in 1993 GameDay packs. Each card is 2-1/2" x 4-3/4" and has a green-bordered front which includes a color action photo against a black-and-white action background. The set's and player's name are stamped in gold foil at the bottom. The back has a shot of the player, his name and jersey number and a recap of his 1992 season. Each is numbered 1 of 16, etc.

MT
Complete Set (16): 10.00
Common Player: .25
1 Carl Pickens 2.00
2 David Klingler .50
3 Santana Dotson .25
4 Chris Mims .25
5 Steve Emtman .25
6 Marco Coleman .25
7 Robert Jones .25
8 Dale Carter .25
9 Troy Vincent .25
10 Tracy Scroggins .25
11 Vaughn Dunbar .25
12 Quentin Coryatt .25
13 Dana Hall .25
14 Terrell Buckley .25
15 Tommy Vardell .25
16 Johnny Mitchell .25

1994 Fleer

Fleer's 1994 set includes 474 player cards and six checklist cards. There were also 137 different insert cards produced; one was randomly included in every pack. The regular cards have a color-enhanced photo and gold-foil stamped player signature on the front, plus his team logo, position and name. Card backs have two large photos with a screened-back action shot and a closeup player portrait. Insert cards have full-bleed photos; the regular cards have a white frame around the photo on the card front.

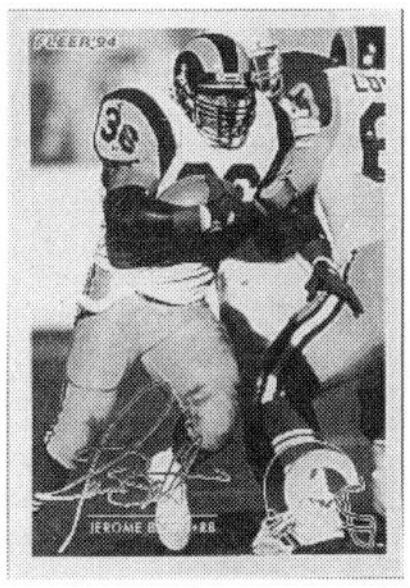

MT
Complete Set (480): 20.00
Common Player: .05
Minor Stars: .10
Pack (15): 1.50
Wax Box (36): 40.00
1 Michael Bankston .05
2 Steve Beuerlein .05
3 John Booty .05
4 Rich Camarillo .05
5 Chuck Cecil .05
6 Larry Centers .10
7 Gary Clark .05
8 Garrison Hearst .50
9 Eric Hill .05
10 Randal Hill .05
11 Ron Moore .10
12 Ricky Proehl .05
13 Luis Sharpe .05
14 Clyde Simmons .05
15 Tyronne Stow .05
16 Eric Swann .05
17 Aeneas Williams .05
18 Darion Conner .05
19 Moe Gardner .05
20 Jumpy Geathers .05
21 Jeff George .10
22 Roger Harper .05
23 Bobby Hebert .10
24 Pierce Holt .05
25 David Johnson .05
26 Mike Kenn .05
27 Lincoln Kennedy .05
28 Erric Pegram .05
29 Mike Pritchard .10
30 Andre Rison .15
31 Deion Sanders .40
32 Tony Smith .05
33 Jesse Solomon .05
34 Jessie Tuggle .05
35 Don Beebe .05
36 Cornelius Bennett .05
37 Bill Brooks .05
38 Kenneth Davis .05
39 John Fina .05
40 Phil Hansen .05
41 Kent Hull .05
42 Henry Jones .05
43 Jim Kelly .15
44 Pete Metzelaars .05
45 Marvcus Patton .05
46 Andre Reed .10
47 Frank Reich .05
48 Bruce Smith .05
49 Thomas Smith .05
50 Darryl Talley .05
51 Steve Tasker .05
52 Thurman Thomas .20
53 Jeff Wright .05
54 Neal Anderson .05
55 Trace Armstrong .05
56 Troy Auzenne .05
57 Joe Cain .15
58 Mark Carrier .05
59 Curtis Conway .10
60 Richard Dent .05
61 Shaun Gayle .05
62 Andy Heck .05
63 Dante Jones .05
64 Erik Kramer .05
65 Steve McMichael .05
66 Terry Obee .05
67 Vinson Smith .05
68 Alonzo Spellman .05
69 Tom Waddle .05
70 Donnell Woolford .05
71 Tim Worley .05
72 Chris Zorich .05
73 Mike Brim .05
74 John Copeland .05
75 Derrick Fenner .05
76 James Francis .05
77 Harold Green .05
78 Rod Jones .05
79 David Klingler .10
80 Bruce Kozerski .05
81 Tim Krumrie .05
82 Ricardo McDonald .05
83 Tim McGee .05
84 Tony McGee .05
85 Louis Oliver .05
86 Carl Pickens .30
87 Jeff Query .05
88 Daniel Stubbs .05
89 Steve Tovar .05
90 Alfred Williams .05
91 Darryl Williams .05
92 Rob Burnett .05
93 Mark Carrier .05
94 Leroy Hoard .05
95 Michael Jackson .05
96 Mike Johnson .05
97 Pepper Johnson .05
98 Tony Jones .05
99 Clay Matthews .05
100 Eric Metcalf .05
101 Stevon Moore .05
102 Michael Dean Perry .05
103 Anthony Pleasant .05
104 Vinny Testaverde .10
105 Eric Turner .05
106 Tommy Vardell .05
107 Troy Aikman .75
108 Larry Brown .05
109 Dixon Edwards .05
110 Charles Haley .05
111 Alvin Harper .15
112 Michael Irvin .25
113 Jim Jeffcoat .05
114 Daryl Johnston .05
115 Leon Lett .05
116 Russell Maryland .05
117 Nate Newton .05
118 Ken Norton Jr. .05
119 Jay Novacek .05
120 Darrin Smith .05
121 Emmitt Smith 2.00
122 Kevin Smith .05
123 Mark Stepnoski .05
124 Tony Tolbert .05
125 Erik Williams .05
126 Kevin Williams .40
127 Darren Woodson .05
128 Steve Atwater .05
129 Rod Bernstine .05
130 Ray Crockett .05
131 Mike Croel .05
132 Robert Delpino .05
133 Shane Dronett .05
134 Jason Elam .05
135 John Elway .40
136 Simon Fletcher .05
137 Greg Kragen .05
138 Karl Mecklenburg .05
139 Glyn Milburn .10
140 Anthony Miller .10
141 Derek Russell .05
142 Shannon Sharpe .10
143 Dennis Smith .05
144 Dan Williams .05
145 Gary Zimmerman .05
146 Bennie Blades .05
147 Lomas Brown .05
148 Bill Fralic .05
149 Mel Gray .05
150 Willie Green .05
151 Jason Hanson .05
152 Robert Massey .05
153 Ryn McNeil .05
154 Scott Mitchell .15
155 Derrick Moore .05
156 Herman Moore .30
157 Brett Perriman .05
158 Robert Porcher .05
159 Kelvin Pritchett .05
160 Barry Sanders 1.25
161 Tracy Scroggins .05
162 Chris Spielman .05
163 Pat Swilling .05
164 Edgar Bennett .05
165 Robert Brooks .05
166 Terrell Buckley .05
167 LeRoy Butler .05
168 Brett Favre 2.00
169 Harry Galbreath .05
170 Jackie Harris .05
171 Johnny Holland .05
172 Chris Jacke .05
173 George Koonce .05
174 Bryce Paup .05
175 Ken Ruettgers .05
176 Sterling Sharpe .15
177 Wayne Simmons .05
178 George Teague .05
179 Darrell Thompson .05
180 Reggie White .15
181 Gary Brown .05
182 Cody Carlson .10
183 Ray Childress .05
184 Cris Dishman .05
185 Ernest Givins .05
186 Haywood Jeffires .05
187 Sean Jones .05
188 Lamar Lathon .05
189 Bruce Matthews .05
190 Bubba McDowell .05
191 Glenn Montgomery .05
192 Greg Montgomery .05
193 Warren Moon .15
194 Bo Orlando .05
195 Marcus Robertson .05
196 Eddie Robinson .05
197 Webster Slaughter .05
198 Lorenzo White .05
199 John Baylor .05
200 Jason Belser .05
201 Tony Bennett .05
202 Dean Biasucci .05
203 Ray Buchanan .05
204 Kerry Cash .05
205 Quentin Coryatt .05
206 Eugene Daniel .05
207 Steve Emtman .05
208 Jon Hand .05
209 Jim Harbaugh .05
210 Jeff Herrod .05
211 Anthony Johnson .05
212 Roosevelt Potts .05
213 Rohn Stark .05
214 Will Wolford .05
215 Marcus Allen .10
216 John Alt .05
217 Kimble Anders .05
218 J.J. Birden .05
219 Dale Carter .05
220 Keith Cash .05
221 Tony Casillas .05
222 Willie Davis .05
223 Tim Grunhard .05
224 Nick Lowery .05
225 Charles Mincy .05
226 Joe Montana 1.50
227 Dan Saleaumua .05
228 Travy Simien .05
229 Neil Smith .05
230 Derrick Thomas .10
231 Eddie Anderson .05
232 Tim Brown .10
233 Nolan Harrison .05
234 Jeff Hostetler .10
235 Raghib Ismail .10
236 Jeff Jaeger .05
237 James Jett .05
238 Joe Kelly .05
239 Albert Lewis .05
240 Terry McDaniel .05
241 Chester McGlockton .05
242 Winston Moss .05
243 Gerald Perry .05
244 Greg Robinson .05
245 Anthony Smith .05
246 Steve Smith .05
247 Greg Townsend .05
248 Lionel Washington .05
249 Steve Wisniewski .05
250 Alexander Wright .05
251 Willie Anderson .05
252 Jerome Bettis .50
253 Marc Boutte .05
254 Shane Conlan .05
255 Troy Drayton .20
256 Henry Ellard .05
257 Sean Gilbert .10
258 Nate Lewis .05
259 Todd Lyght .05
260 Chris Miller .10
261 Anthony Newman .05
262 Roman Phifer .05
263 Henry Rolling .05
264 T.J. Rubley .05
265 Jackie Slater .05
266 Fred Stokes .05
267 Robert Young .05
268 Gene Atkins .05
269 J.B. Brown .05
270 Keith Byars .05
271 Marco Coleman .05
272 Bryan Cox .05
273 Jeff Cross .05
274 Irving Fryar .05
275 Mark Higgs .05
276 Dwight Hollier .05
277 Mark Ingram .05
278 Keith Jackson .05
279 Terry Kirby .10
280 Bernie Kosar .05
281 Dan Marino 2.00
282 O.J. McDuffie .20
283 Keith Sims .05
284 Pete Stoyanovich .05
285 Troy Vincent .05
286 Richmond Webb .05
287 Terry Allen .05
288 Anthony Carter .05
289 Cris Carter .10
290 Jack Del Rio .05
291 Chris Doleman .05
292 Vencie Glenn .05
293 Scottie Graham .20
294 Chris Hinton .05
295 Qadry Ismail .10
296 Carlos Jenkins .05
297 Steve Jordan .05
298 Carl Lee .05
299 Randall McDaniel .05
300 John Randle .05
301 Todd Scott .05
302 Robert Smith .15
303 Fred Strickland .05
304 Henry Thomas .05
305 Bruce Armstrong .05
306 Harlon Barnett .05
307 Drew Bledsoe 1.25
308 Vincent Brown .05
309 Ben Coates .20
310 Todd Collins .05
311 Myron Guyton .05
312 Pat Harlow .05
313 Maurice Hurst .05
314 Leonard Russell .05
315 Chris Slade .10
316 Michael Thompson .05
317 Andre Tippett .05
318 Morten Andersen .05
319 Derek Brown .05
320 Vince Buck .05
321 Toi Cook .05
322 Quinn Early .05
323 Jim Everett .10
324 Michael Haynes .05
325 Tyrone Hughes .05
326 Rickey Jackson .05
327 Vaughan Johnson .05
328 Eric Martin .05
329 Wayne Martin .05
330 Sam Mills .05
331 William Roaf .05
332 Irv Smith .05
333 Keith Taylor .05
334 Renaldo Turnbull .05
335 Carlton Bailey .05
336 Michael Brooks .05
337 Jarrod Bunch .05
338 Chris Calloway .05
339 Mark Collins .05
340 Howard Cross .05
341 Stacey Dillard .05
342 John Elliot .05
343 Rodney Hampton .10
344 Greg Jackson .05
345 Mark Jackson .05
346 David Meggett .05
347 Corey Miller .05
348 Mike Sherrard .05
349 Phil Simms .05
350 Lewis Tillman .05
351 Brad Baxter .05
352 Kyle Clifton .05
353 Boomer Esiason .10
354 James Hasty .05
355 Bobby Houston .05
356 Johnny Johnson .05
357 Jeff Lageman .05
358 Mo Lewis .05
359 Ronnie Lott .05
360 Leonard Marshall .05
361 Johnny Mitchell .05
362 Rob Moore .05
363 Eric Thomas .05
364 Brian Washington .05
365 Marvin Washington .05
366 Eric Allen .05
367 Fred Barnett .05
368 Bubby Brister .05
369 Randall Cunningham .15
370 Byron Evans .05
371 William Fuller .05
372 Andy Harmon .05
373 Seth Joyner .05
374 William Perry .05
375 Leonard Renfro .05
376 Heath Sherman .05
377 Ben Smith .05
378 William Thomas .05
379 Herschel Walker .05
380 Calvin Williams .05
381 Chad Brown .10
382 Dermontti Dawson .05
383 Deon Figures .05
384 Barry Foster .10
385 Jeff Graham .05
386 Eric Green .05
387 Kevin Greene .05
388 Carlton Haselrig .05
389 Levon Kirkland .05
390 Carnell Lake .05
391 Greg Lloyd .05
392 Neil O'Donnell .10
393 Darren Perry .05
394 Dwight Stone .05
395 Leroy Thompson .05
396 Rod Woodson .10
397 Marion Butts .05
398 John Carney .05
399 Darren Carrington .05
400 Burt Grossman .05
401 Courtney Hall .05
402 Ronnie Harmon .05
403 Stan Humphries .20
404 Shawn Jefferson .05
405 Vance Johnson .05
406 Chris Mims .05
407 Leslie O'Neal .05
408 Stanley Richard .05
409 Junior Seau .15
410 Harris Barton .05
411 Dennis Brown .05
412 Eric Davis .05
413 Merton Hanks .05
414 John Johnson .05
415 Brent Jones .05
416 Marc Logan .05
417 Tim McDonald .05
418 Gary Plummer .05
419 Tom Rathman .05
420 Jerry Rice 1.00
421 Bill Romanowski .05
422 Jesse Sapolu .05
423 Dana Stubblefield .10
424 John Taylor .05
425 Steve Wallace .05
426 Ted Washington .05
427 Ricky Watters .10
428 Troy Wilson .05
429 Steve Young 1.00
430 Howard Ballard .05
431 Michael Bates .05
432 Robert Blackmon .05
433 Brian Blades .05
434 Ferrell Edmunds .05
435 Carlton Gray .05
436 Patrick Hunter .05
437 Cortez Kennedy .10
438 Kelvin Martin .05
439 Rick Mirer .10
440 Nate Odomes .05
441 Ray Roberts .05
442 Eugene Robinson .05
443 Rod Stephens .05
444 Chris Warren .10
445 John L. Williams .05
446 Terry Wooden .05
447 Marty Carter .05
448 Reggie Cobb .05
449 Lawrence Dawsey .05
450 Santana Dotson .05
451 Craig Erickson .05
452 Thomas Everett .05
453 Paul Gruber .05
454 Courtney Hawkins .05
455 Martin Mayhew .05
456 Hardy Nickerson .05
457 Ricky Reynolds .05
458 Vince Workman .05
459 Reggie Brooks .10
460 Earnest Byner .05
461 Andre Collins .05
462 Brad Edwards .05
463 Kurt Gouveia .05
464 Darrell Green .05
465 Ken Harvey .05
466 Ethan Horton .05
467 A.J. Johnson .05
468 Tim Johnson .05
469 Jim Lachey .05
470 Chip Lohmiller .05
471 Art Monk .10
472 Sterling Palmer .05
473 Mark Rypien .05
474 Ricky Sanders .05
475 Checklist .05
476 Checklist .05
477 Checklist .05
478 Checklist .05
479 Checklist .05
480 Checklist .05

1994 Fleer All-Pros

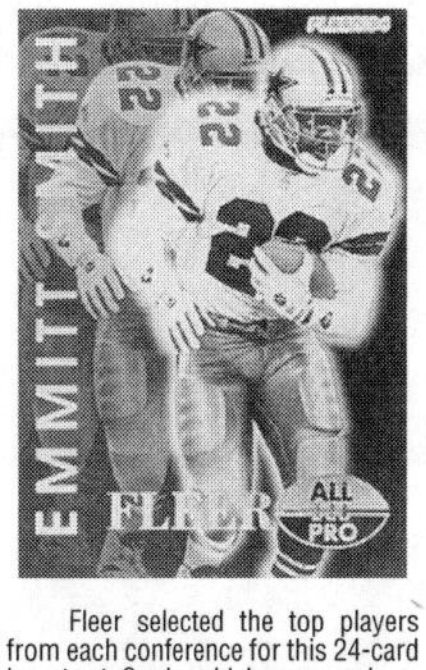

Fleer selected the top players from each conference for this 24-card insert set. Cards, which were randomly inserted in packs, feature borderless color action photos on the front, with ghosted images behind the main picture. The player's name is in gold foil running vertical on the left side of the card. The back is borderless and includes a career summary and a photo of the player with a glowing aura about him. Cards are numbered 1 of 24, etc.

MT
Complete Set (24): 25.00
Common Player: .25
Minor Stars: .50
1 Troy Aikman 3.00
2 Eric Allen .25
3 Jerome Bettis 1.00
4 Barry Foster .50
5 Michael Irvin .50
6 Cortez Kennedy .50
7 Joe Montana 4.00
8 Hardy Nickerson .25
9 Jerry Rice 3.00
10 Andre Rison .50
11 Barry Sanders 4.00
12 Deion Sanders 2.00
13 Junior Seau .50
14 Shannon Sharpe .50
15 Sterling Sharpe .50
16 Bruce Smith .25
17 Emmitt Smith 5.00
18 Neil Smith .25
19 Derrick Thomas .50
20 Thurman Thomas .50
21 Renaldo Turnbull .25
22 Reggie White .50
23 Rod Woodson .50
24 Steve Young 3.00

1994 Fleer Award Winners

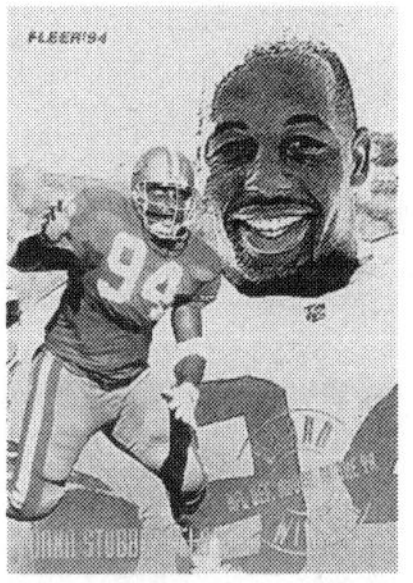

Five award-winning performers from the 1993 season are featured on these insert cards randomly available in 1994 packs. Each card front has a smaller cutout photo of the player against a larger black-and-white closeup photo. The player's name is in gold foil in the lower left corner; the set logo is to the right. The backs have a background which fades from black to white and features a color action photo. A color-screened box contains a summary of the player's career. The cards are numbered 1 of 5, etc. The Super Bowl MVP, AFC and NFC Offensive Rookies of the Year, the NFL Defensive Player of the Year, and the NFL Rookie of the Year are represented in the set.

MT
Complete Set (5): 4.00
Common Player: .25
1 Jerome Bettis 1.00
2 Rick Mirer .50
3 Deion Sanders 1.00
4 Emmitt Smith 2.00
5 Dana Stubblefield .25

1994 Fleer Jerome Bettis

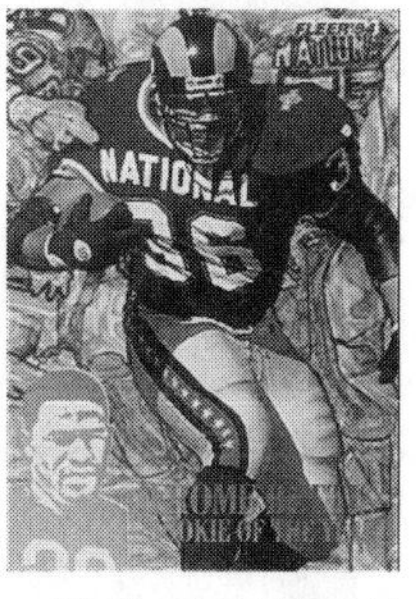

This 12-card set is devoted to former Notre Dame and Los Angeles Rams running back Jerome Bettis, a Rookie of the Year. Each card has a color action photo on the front against an abstract background. A player head shot and Fleer and Bettis' name are stamped in gold foil at the bottom. The horizontal back includes a color photo, career highlights and a card number. Three cards in the set could be obtained only through the mail for ten 1994 Fleer Football wrappers and $1.50.

MT
Complete Set (12): 6.00
Common Bettis: .50
Mail-In Bettis (13-15): 1.00

1994 Fleer League Leaders

The top quarterbacks, running backs and receivers from 1993 are featured in this 10-card insert set devoted to statistical leaders. The card front has a color photo of the player emerging from a blurred background. The "League Leader" logo and player's name are on the front, while the back has a small color photo and a summary of the player's 1993 accomplishments. Cards were randomly inserted in Fleer packs.

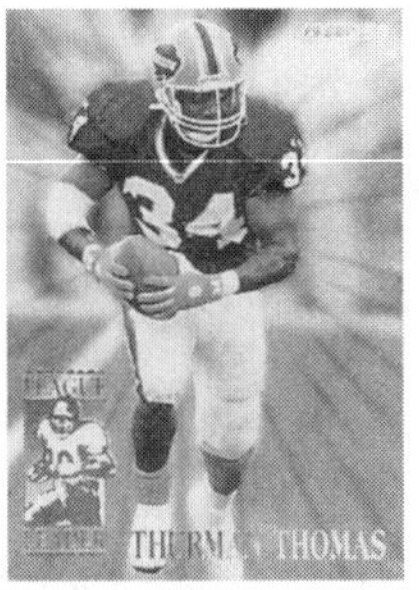

		MT
Complete Set (10):		10.00
Common Player:		.50
1	Marcus Allen	.50
2	Tim Brown	.50
3	John Elway	1.50
4	Tyrone Huges	.50
5	Jerry Rice	2.50
6	Sterling Sharpe	.50
7	Emmitt Smith	4.00
8	Neil Smith	.50
9	Thurman Thomas	.50
10	Steve Young	2.00

1994 Fleer Living Legends

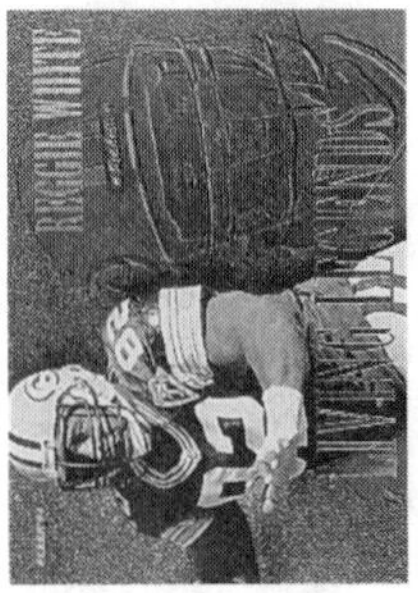

Six legendary active players are featured in this insert set; cards were randomly inserted in 1994 packs. The horizontally-arranged card front uses a metallic design for the photo, while the player's and set's name are stamped in foil. The card back is numbered 1 of 6, etc., and has a color photo and career highlights.

		MT
Complete Set (6):		75.00
Common Player:		5.00
1	Marcus Allen	5.00
2	John Elway	10.00
3	Joe Montana	15.00
4	Jerry Rice	15.00
5	Emmitt Smith	30.00
6	Reggie White	5.00

1994 Fleer Pro-Vision

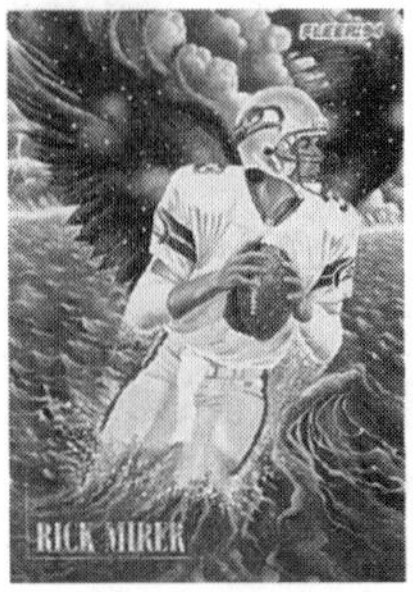

This set continues Fleer's tradition of using artwork on the card fronts. The player is featured against a background with a landmark from his team's city. The backs, numbered 1 of 9, etc., have a career summary. Cards were standard size (2-1/2" x 3-1/2") and were random inserts in Fleer packs, but jumbo versions were also made for each card. One nine-card jumbo set was included in every hobby case. Jumbo cards are generally worth two to four times more than the standard-size cards.

		MT
Complete Set (9):		5.00
Common Player:		.25
Minor Stars:		.50
1	Rodney Hampton	.25
2	Ricky Watters	.50
3	Rick Mirer	.50
4	Brett Favre	3.00
5	Troy Aikman	1.25
6	Jerome Bettis	.50
7	Joe Montana	2.00
8	Cornelius Bennett	.25
9	Rod Woodson	.25

1994 Fleer Prospects

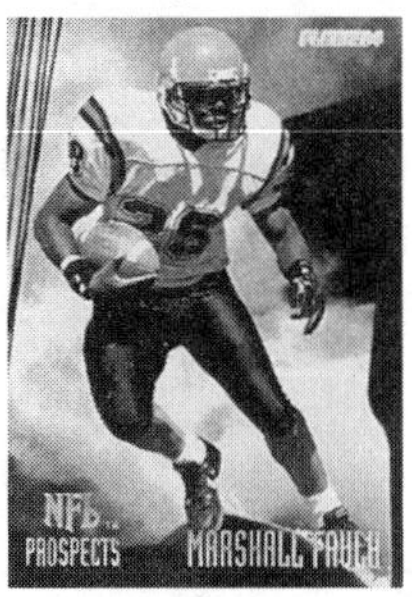

This insert set features 25 top collegiate prospects who have a chance to shine in the NFL. The card front shows the player in his collegiate uniform, superimposed against a background of a steel mill. The backs have a card number (1 of 25, etc.), a photo and a summary of the player's collegiate achievements.

		MT
Complete Set (25):		30.00
Common Player:		.50
Minor Stars:		1.00
1	Sam Adams	.50
2	Trev Alberts	.50
3	Derrick Alexander	2.00
4	Mario Bates	1.00
5	Jeff Buris	.50
6	Shante Carver	.50
7	Marshall Faulk	6.00
8	William Floyd	3.00
9	Rob Fredrickson	.50
10	Wayne Gandy	.50
11	Charlie Garner	1.00
12	Aaron Glenn	.50
13	Charles Johnson	2.00
14	Joe Johnson	.50
15	Tre Johnson	.50
16	Antonio Langham	1.00
17	Chuck Levy	1.00
18	Willie McGinest	1.00
19	David Palmer	1.00
20	Errict Rhett	4.00
21	Jason Sehorn	.50
22	Heath Shuler	1.00
23	Charlie Ward	1.00
24	DeWayne Washington	.50
25	Bryant Young	1.00

1994 Fleer Rookie Exchange

This 12-card Rookie Exchange set featured the same design as the 1994 Fleer set and was available by sending in a Rookie Exchange card found in packs.

		MT
Complete Set (12):		40.00
Common Player:		1.00
Minor Stars:		2.00
1	Derrick Alexander	3.50
2	Trent Dilfer	6.00
3	Marshall Faulk	25.00
4	Charlie Garner	7.00
5	Greg Hill	1.00
6	Charles Johnson	4.00
7	Antonio Langham	1.00
8	Willie McGinest	1.00
9	Heath Shuler	4.00
10	DeWayne Washington	1.00
11	Dan Wilkinson	2.00
12	Bryant Young	2.00
NNO	Rookie Exchange Exp.	1.00

1994 Fleer Rookie Sensations

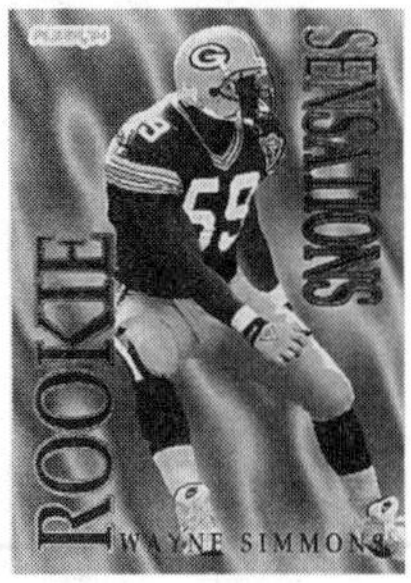

These cards were randomly inserted in 1994 21-card jumbo packs. Players who were rookies during the 1993 NFL season are featured. The card front shows a picture of the player against a wavy background design that is primarily in his team's dominant color. The back also features his team's colors, with a smaller photo and biography. The set name is stamped in foil on the card front; the back has the card number, 1 of 20, etc.

		MT
Complete Set (20):		175.00
Common Player:		4.50
1	Jerome Bettis	20.00
2	Drew Bledsoe	65.00
3	Reggie Brooks	7.00
4	Tom Carter	7.00
5	John Copeland	7.00
6	Jason Elam	7.00
7	Garrison Hearst	20.00
8	Tyrone Hughes	7.00
9	James Jett	7.00
10	Lincoln Kennedy	7.00
11	Terry Kirby	7.00
12	Glyn Milburn	7.00
13	Rick Mirer	10.00
14	Ron Moore	7.00
15	William Roaf	7.00
16	Wayne Simmons	7.00
17	Chris Slade	7.00
18	Darrin Smith	4.50
19	Dana Stubblefield	7.00
20	George Teague	4.50

1994 Fleer Scoring Machines

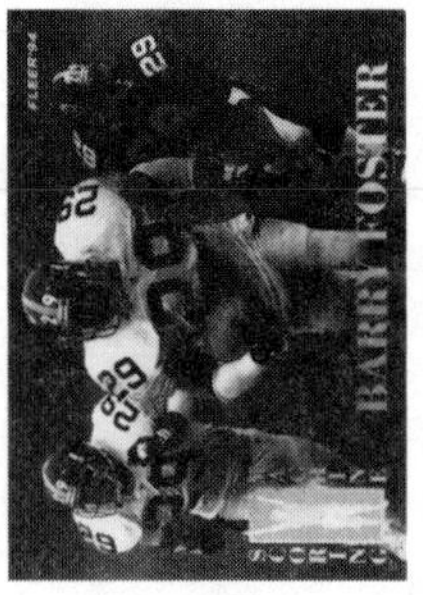

These cards, inserted only in 15-card 1994 Fleer packs, feature some of the leading point producers in the NFL who play running back, quarterback and receiver. Card fronts have three photos of the player, plus his name and set logo stamped in foil. The back has a color photo and career summary, plus a card number (1of 10, etc.).

		MT
Complete Set (20):		250.00
Common Player:		5.00
1	Marcus Allen	5.00
2	Natrone Means	10.00
3	Jerome Bettis	10.00
4	Tim Brown	5.00
5	Barry Foster	5.00
6	Rodney Hampton	5.00
7	Michael Irvin	5.00
8	Nick Lowery	5.00
9	Dan Marino	40.00
10	Joe Montana	25.00
11	Warren Moon	5.00
12	Andre Rison	5.00
13	Jerry Rice	25.00
14	Andre Rison	5.00
15	Barry Sanders	25.00
16	Shannon Sharpe	5.00
17	Sterling Sharpe	5.00
18	Emmitt Smith	40.00
19	Thurman Thomas	5.00
20	Ricky Watters	5.00

1994 Fleer GameDay

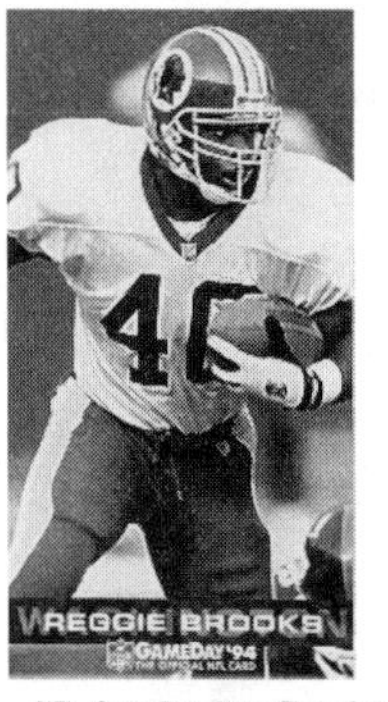

NFL GameDay from Fleer feature an all-new design in a supersized format. The cards are 35 percent larger than a normal card, measuring 4-11/16" x 2-1/2". UV coating and team color-coding are used on the cards, which feature "up-close-and-personal" photos on the fronts. Card backs have another player photo, with statistics and a player profile. Four insert sets were also made: GameBreakers, 2nd Year Stars, Rookie Standouts, and Flashing Stars.

		MT
Complete Set (420):		42.00
Common Player:		.10
Wax Box:		40.00
1	Michael Bankston	.10
2	Steve Beuerlein	.10
3	Gary Clark	.10
4	Garrison Hearst	1.00
5	Eric Hill	.10
6	Randal Hill	.10
7	Seth Joyner	.10
8	Jim McMahon	.10
9	*Jamir Miller*	.40
10	Ron Moore	.45
11	Ricky Proehl	.10
12	Luis Sharpe	.10
13	Clyde Simmons	.10
14	Eric Swann	.10
15	Aeneas Williams	.10
16	Chris Doleman	.10
17	*Bert Emanuel*	1.50
18	Moe Gardner	.10
19	Jeff George	.10
20	Roger Harper	.10
21	Pierce Holt	.10
22	Lincoln Kennedy	.12
23	Erric Pegram	.10
24	Andre Rison	.20
25	Deion Sanders	1.00
26	Tony Smith	.10
27	Jessie Tuggle	.10
28	Don Beebe	.10
29	Cornelius Bennett	.10
30	Bill Brooks	.10
31	*Bucky Brooks*	.50
32	*Jeff Burris*	.75
33	Kenneth Davis	.10
34	Phil Hansen	.10
35	Kent Hull	.10
36	Henry Jones	.10
37	Jim Kelly	.30
38	Pete Metzelaars	.10
39	Marvcus Patton	.10
40	Andre Reed	.10
41	Bruce Smith	.10
42	Thomas Smith	.10
43	Darryl Talley	.10
44	Steve Tasker	.10
45	Thurman Thomas	.45
46	Jeff Wright	.10
47	Trace Armstrong	.10
48	Joe Cain	.10
49	Mark Carrier	.10
50	Curtis Conway	.25
51	Shaun Gayle	.10
52	Dante Jones	.10
53	Erik Kramer	.10
54	Terry Obee	.10
55	Vinson Smith	.10
56	Alonzo Spellman	.10
57	*John Thierry*	.35
58	Tom Waddle	.10
59	Donnell Woolford	.10
60	Tim Worley	.10
61	Chris Zorich	.10
62	Mike Brim	.10
63	John Copeland	.10
64	Derrick Fenner	.10
65	James Francis	.10
66	Harold Green	.10
67	David Klingler	.10
68	Ricardo McDonald	.10
69	Tony McGee	.10
70	Carl Pickens	.10
71	Jeff Query	.10
72	*Darnay Scott*	2.25
73	Steve Tovar	.10
74	*Dan Wilkinson*	.60
75	Alfred Williams	.10
76	Darryl Williams	.10
77	*Derrick Alexander*	.50
78	Rob Burnett	.10
79	Steve Everitt	.10
80	Michael Jackson	.10
81	Pepper Johnson	.10
82	Tony Jones	.10
83	*Antonio Langham*	.60
84	Eric Metcalf	.10
85	Stevon Moore	.10
86	Michael Dean Perry	.10
87	Anthony Pleasant	.10
88	Vinny Testaverde	.10
89	Eric Turner	.12
90	Tommy Vardell	.10
91	Troy Aikman	2.75
92	Larry Brown	.10
93	*Shante Carver*	.25
94	Charles Haley	.10
95	Alvin Harper	.10
96	Michael Irvin	.50
97	Daryl Johnston	.10
98	Leon Lett	.10
99	Russell Maryland	.10
100	Nate Newton	.10
101	Jay Novacek	.10
102	Darrin Smith	.10
103	Emmitt Smith	3.00
104	Kevin Smith	.10
105	Mark Stepnoski	.10
106	Tony Tolbert	.10
107	Erik Williams	.10
108	Kevin Williams	.25
109	Darren Woodson	.10
110	*Allen Aldridge*	.25
111	Steve Atwater	.10
112	Rod Bernstine	.10
113	Ray Crockett	.10
114	Mike Croel	.10
115	Robert Delpino	.10
116	Shane Dronett	.10
117	Jason Elam	.10
118	John Elway	1.00
119	Simon Fletcher	.10
120	Glyn Milburn	.30
121	Anthony Miller	.10
122	Mike Pritchard	.10
123	Shannon Sharpe	.10
124	Dan Williams	.10
125	Bennie Blades	.10
126	Lomas Brown	.10
127	Anthony Carter	.10
128	Mel Gray	.10
129	Jason Hanson	.10
130	Robert Massey	.10
131	Ryan McNeil	.10
132	Scott Mitchell	.15
133	Herman Moore	1.00
134	*Johnnie Morton*	.90
135	Brett Perriman	.10
136	Robert Porcher	.10
137	Barry Sanders	1.50
138	Tracy Scroggins	.10
139	Chris Spielman	.10
140	Pat Swilling	.10
141	Edgar Bennett	.10
142	Robert Brooks	.10
143	Terrell Buckley	.10
144	LeRoy Butler	.10
145	Reggie Cobb	.10
146	Curtis Duncan	.10
147	Brett Favre	2.00
148	Sean Jones	.10
149	George Koonce	.10
150	Ken Ruettgers	.10
151	Sterling Sharpe	.50
152	Wayne Simmons	.10
153	*Aaron Taylor*	.25
154	George Teague	.10
155	Reggie White	.10
156	Michael Barrow	.10
157	Gary Brown	.10
158	Rich Camarillo	.10
159	Cody Carlson	.10
160	Ray Childress	.10
161	Cris Dishman	.10
162	*Henry Ford*	.30
163	Ernest Givins	.10
164	Steve Jackson	.10
165	Haywood Jeffires	.10
166	Bruce Matthews	.10
167	Bubba McDowell	.10
168	Marcus Robertson	.10
169	Eddie Robinson	.10
170	Webster Slaughter	.10
171	*Trev Alberts*	.50
172	Tony Bennett	.10
173	Ray Buchanan	.10
174	Kerry Cash	.10
175	Quentin Coryatt	.10
176	Eugene Daniel	.10
177	*Sean Dawkins*	1.00
178	Steve Emtman	.10
179	*Marshall Faulk*	6.00
180	John Hand	.10
181	Jim Harbaugh	.10
182	Jeff Herrod	.10
183	Roosevelt Potts	.20
184	Rohn Stark	.10
185	Marcus Allen	.10
186	*Donnell Bennett*	.45
187	J.J. Birden	.10
188	Dale Carter	.10
189	Mark Collins	.10
190	Willie Davis	.10
191	*Lake Dawson*	1.50
192	Tim Grunhard	.10
193	*Greg Hill*	.50
194	Joe Montana	2.50
195	Tracy Simion	.10
196	Neil Smith	.10
197	Derrick Thomas	.15
198	Tim Brown	.12
199	*James Folston*	.25
200	*Rob Fredrickson*	.25
201	Nolan Harrison	.10
202	Jeff Hostetler	.10
203	Raghib Ismail	.25
204	Jeff Jaeger	.10
205	James Jett	.20
206	Terry McDaniel	.10
207	Chester McGlockton	.10
208	Winston Moss	.10
209	Tom Rathman	.10
210	Anthony Smith	.10
211	Harvey Williams	.10
212	Steve Wisniewski	.10
213	Alexander Wright	.10
214	Willie Anderson	.10
215	Jerome Bettis	1.00
216	*Isaac Bruce*	4.00
217	Troy Drayton	.20
218	*Wayne Gandy*	.20
219	Sean Gilbert	.15
220	Nate Lewis	.10
221	Todd Lyght	.10
222	Chris Miller	.10
223	Anthony Newman	.10
224	Roman Phifer	.10
225	Henry Rolling	.10
226	Jackie Slater	.10
227	Fred Stokes	.10
228	Gene Atkins	.10
229	*Aubrey Beavers*	.30
230	*Tim Bowens*	.30
231	J.B. Brown	.10
232	Keith Byars	.10
233	Marco Coleman	.10
234	Bryan Cox	.10
235	Jeff Cross	.10
236	Irving Fryar	.10
237	Mark Ingram	.10
238	Keith Jackson	.10
239	Terry Kirby	.25
240	Dan Marino	1.25
241	Michael Stewart	.10
242	Troy Vincent	.10
243	Richmond Webb	.10
244	Terry Allen	.12
245	Cris Carter	.12
246	Jack Del Rio	.10
247	Vencie Glenn	.10
248	Chris Hinton	.10
249	Qadry Ismail	.25
250	Carlos Jenkins	.10
251	Randall McDaniel	.10
252	Warren Moon	.10
253	*David Palmer*	.50
254	John Randle	.10
255	Jake Reed	.10
256	Todd Scott	.10
257	*Todd Steussie*	.25
258	Henry Thomas	.10
259	*DeWayne Washington*	.25
260	Bruce Armstrong	.10
261	Drew Bledsoe	2.00
262	Vincent Brisby	.20
263	Vincent Brown	.10
264	Marion Butts	.10
265	Ben Coates	.20
266	Pat Harlow	.10
267	Maurice Hurst	.10
268	*Willie McGinest*	.75
269	Chris Slade	.10
270	Michael Timpson	.10
271	Morten Andersen	.10
272	*Mario Bates*	2.00
273	Derek Brown	.25
274	Quinn Early	.10
275	Jim Everett	.10
276	Michael Haynes	.10
277	Tyrone Hughes	.10
278	*Joe Johnson*	.25
279	Eric Martin	.10
280	Wayne Martin	.10
281	Sam Mills	.10
282	William Roaf	.15
283	Irv Smith	.10
284	Renaldo Turnbull	.10
285	Carlton Bailey	.10
286	Michael Brooks	.10
287	*Dave Brown*	.30
288	Jarrod Bunch	.10
289	Howard Cross	.10
290	John Elliott	.10
291	Keith Hamilton	.10
292	Rodney Hampton	.40
293	Mark Jackson	.10
294	*Thomas Lewis*	.80
295	David Meggett	.10
296	Corey Miller	.10
297	Mike Sherrard	.10
298	Brad Baxter	.10
299	Kyle Clifton	.10
300	Boomer Esiason	.10
301	*Aaron Glenn*	.25
302	James Hasty	.10
303	Johnny Johnson	.10
304	Jeff Lageman	.10
305	Mo Lewis	.10
306	Ronnie Lott	.10
307	Johnny Mitchell	.10
308	Art Monk	.10
309	Rob Moore	.10
310	Brian Washington	.10
311	Marvin Washington	.10
312	*Ryan Yarborough*	.45
313	Eric Allen	.10
314	Victor Bailey	.10
315	Fred Barnett	.10
316	Mark Bavaro	.10
317	Randall Cunningham	.20
318	Byron Evans	.10
319	William Fuller	.10
320	*Charlie Garner*	1.50
321	Andy Harmon	.10
322	Vaughn Hebron	.10
323	Mark McMillan	.10
324	Bill Romanowski	.10
325	William Thomas	.10
326	Greg Townsend	.10
327	Herschel Walker	.10
328	*Bernard Williams*	.25
329	Calvin Williams	.10
330	Dermontti Dawson	.10
331	Deon Figures	.10
332	Barry Foster	.25
333	Eric Green	.10
334	Kevin Greene	.10
335	Carlton Haselrig	.10
336	*Charles Johnson*	1.00
337	Levon Kirkland	.10
338	Carnell Lake	.10
339	Greg Lloyd	.10
340	Neil O'Donnell	.10
341	Darren Perry	.10
342	Dwight Stone	.10
343	John L. Williams	.10
344	Rod Woodson	.10
345	John Carney	.10
346	Darren Carrington	.10
347	*Isaac Davis*	.25
348	Courtney Hall	.10
349	Ronnie Harmon	.10
350	Dwayne Harper	.10
351	Stan Humphries	.10
352	Shawn Jefferson	.10
353	Vance Johnson	.10
354	Natrone Means	.75
355	Chris Mims	.10
356	Leslie O'Neal	.10
357	Stanley Richard	.10
358	Junior Seau	.12
359	Harris Barton	.10
360	Eric Davis	.10
361	Richard Dent	.10
362	*William Floyd*	2.00
363	Merton Hanks	.10
364	Brent Jones	.10
365	Marc Logan	.10
366	Tim McDonald	.10
367	Ken Norton	.10
368	Jerry Rice	1.00
369	Jesse Sapolu	.10
370	Dana Stubblefield	.15
371	John Taylor	.10
372	Ricky Watters	.10
373	*Bryant Young*	.50
374	Steve Young	1.50
375	*Sam Adams*	.35
376	Michael Bates	.10
377	Robert Blackmon	.10
378	Brian Blades	.10
379	Ferrell Edmunds	.10
380	John Kasay	.10
381	Cortez Kennedy	.10
382	Kelvin Martin	.10
383	Rick Mirer	.75
384	Rufus Porter	.10
385	Eugene Robinson	.10
386	Rod Stephens	.10
387	Chris Warren	.10
388	Marty Carter	.10
389	Horace Copeland	.10
390	Eric Curry	.10
391	Lawrence Dawsey	.10
392	*Trent Dilfer*	1.00
393	Santana Dotson	.10
394	Craig Erickson	.10
395	Thomas Everett	.10
396	Paul Gruber	.10
397	Jackie Harris	.10
398	Courtney Hawkins	.10
399	Martin Mayhew	.10
400	Hardy Nickerson	.10
401	*Errict Rhett*	4.00
402	Vince Workman	.10
403	Reggie Brooks	.75
404	Tom Carter	.10
405	Andre Collins	.10
406	Henry Ellard	.10
407	Kurt Gouveia	.10
408	Darrell Green	.10
409	Ken Harvey	.10
410	Ethan Horton	.15
411	Desmond Howard	.10
412	Jim Lachey	.10
413	Sterling Palmer	.10
414	*Heath Shuler*	3.00
415	Tyronne Stowe	.10
416	Tony Woods	.10
417	Checklist	.10
418	Checklist	.10
419	Checklist	.10
420	Checklist	.10

1994 Fleer GameDay Flashing Stars

These cards, the scarcest of all inserts in the 1994 Fleer GameDay set, were randomly included in 1994 packs. The set features four of the NFL's outstanding younger players on 100 percent etched foil. Card backs, numbered 1 of 4, etc., include information about the player and a color photo of the player. Each card measures 4-11/16" x 2-1/2."

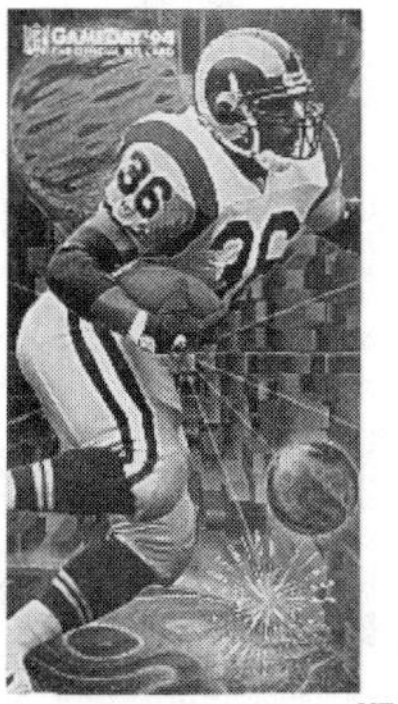

		MT
Complete Set (4):		60.00
Common Player:		10.00
1	Jerome Bettis	10.00
2	Rick Mirer	10.00
3	Jerry Rice	20.00
4	Emmitt Smith	40.00

1994 Fleer GameDay Game Breakers

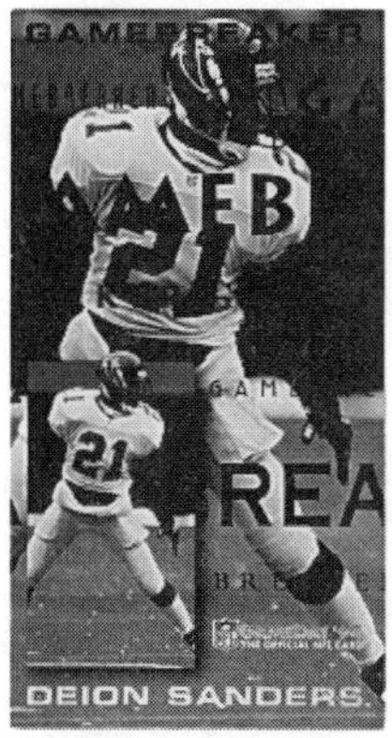

Top running backs, quarterbacks and receivers who can break the game wide open are featured in this 1994 GameDay insert set. The cards, which measure 4-11/16" x 2-1/2" inches, were random inserts in GameDay packs. The card front has a large sepia-toned photo, along with a smaller, color photo of the same picture. The player's name and GameDay logo are stamped in gold foil; "Gamebreaker" is written across the card front in different type sizes and styles. The card back has a color photo against a sepia background, with a card number, too (1 of 16, etc.). A summary of the player's career is also given.

		MT
Complete Set (16):		30.00
Common Player:		.50
1	Troy Aikman	4.00
2	Marcus Allen	.50
3	Tim Brown	.50
4	John Elway	1.50
5	Michael Irvin	.75
6	Dan Marino	6.00
7	Joe Montana	4.00
8	Jerry Rice	4.00
9	Andre Rison	.50
10	Barry Sanders	4.00
11	Deion Sanders	2.00
12	Sterling Sharpe	.75
13	Emmitt Smith	6.00
14	Thurman Thomas	.75
15	Rod Woodson	.50
16	Steve Young	3.00

1994 Fleer GameDay Rookie Standouts

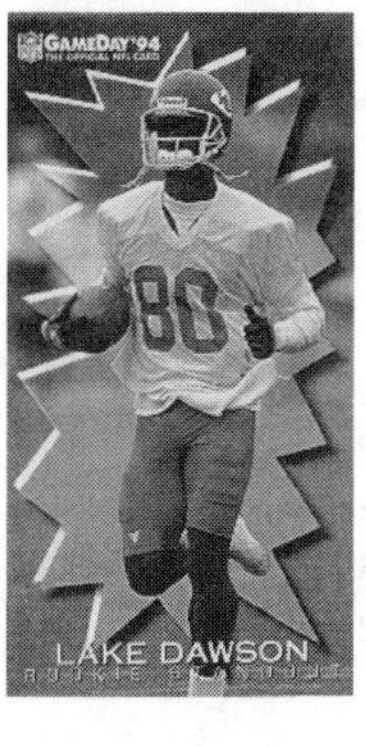

Sixteen "can't-miss" rookies are featured on these cards, which were randomly inserted in 1994 Fleer GameDay packs. The card front shows a color action photo of the player on a 3-D embossed design. Unlike the other inserts in this set, the "Rookie Standouts" insert set does not use any foil stamping. The card back has a player mug shot and provides a scouting report on the player as he enters his first year in the NFL. Cards are numbered 1 of 16, etc., and measure 4-11/16" x 2-1/2."

		MT
Complete Set (16):		25.00
Common Player:		.65
1	Sam Adams	.65
2	Trev Alberts	1.00
3	Lake Dawson	2.00
4	Trent Dilfer	3.00
5	Marshall Faulk	6.00
6	Aaron Glenn	1.00
7	Charles Johnson	3.00
8	Willie McGinest	1.25
9	Jamir Miller	.65
10	Johnnie Morton	2.00
11	David Palmer	4.00
12	Errict Rhett	3.00
13	Heath Shuler	3.00
14	John Thierry	.65
15	Dan Wilkinson	1.50
16	Bryant Young	1.00

1994 Fleer GameDay Second-Year Stars

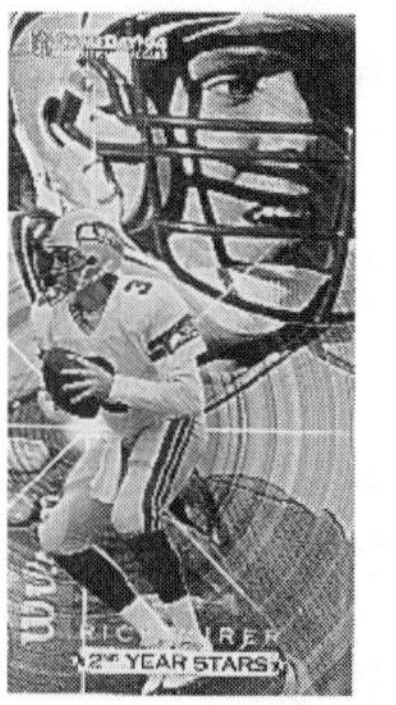

These cards, randomly inserted in 1994 Fleer GameDay packs, feature 16 of the top rookies in 1993 who are beginning their second year in the NFL in 1994. The "GameDay," the set name and player name are stamped in gold foil on the card front. A small action shot appears against a larger, full-bleed profile shot, which has a swirl effect to it. The card back also has a swirl effect, which is used to present information about the player's first NFL season. Cards, numbered 1 of 16, etc., have an action photo on the back. Cards are 35 percent larger than a standard size card; they measure 4-11/16" x 2-1/2".

		MT
Complete Set (16):		18.00
Common Player:		.50
1	Jerome Bettis	2.00
2	Drew Bledsoe	5.00
3	Reggie Brooks	1.00
4	Tom Carter	.60
5	Eric Curry	.60
6	Steve Everitt	.60
7	Tyrone Hughes	.50
8	James Jett	1.50
9	Terry Kirby	1.00
10	Natrone Means	4.00
11	Rick Mirer	4.00
12	Ron Moore	1.00
13	William Roaf	.50
14	Chris Slade	.50
15	Darrin Smith	.60
16	Dana Stubblefield	1.00

1995 Fleer

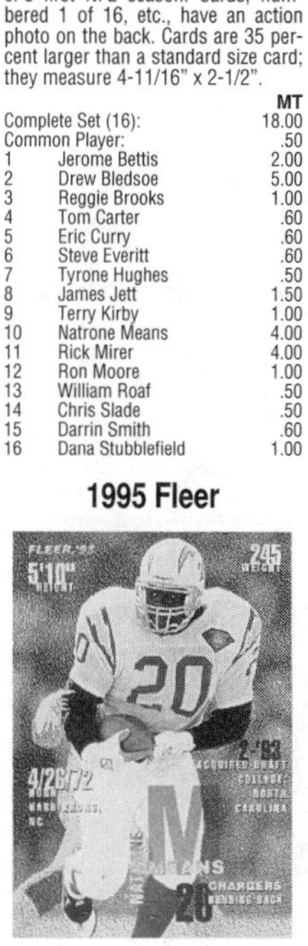

Fleer's 1995 set includes 400 cards, using the "Different by Design" concept it has used for baseball issues; different styles are used for different divisions. Several insert sets were randomly included in packs: Pro-Visions (1 in 6 packs); Rookie Sensations (1 in 3 17-card packs); Aerial Attack (1 in 37); Gridiron Leaders (1 in 4); TD Sensations (1 in 3 11-card packs); NFL Prospects (1 in 6); and Flair Preview (1 in each pack). Fleer products were sold in 11-card and 17-card packs. The cards are numbered alphabetically by team names, with the players numbered alphabetically within the team subsets.

		MT
Complete Set (400):		20.00
Common Player:		.05
Minor Stars:		.10
Wax Box:		25.00
1	Michael Bankston	.05
2	Larry Centers	.05
3	Gary Clark	.05
4	Eric Hill	.05
5	Seth Joyner	.05
6	Dave Krieg	.05
7	Lorenzo Lynch	.05
8	Jamir Miller	.05
9	Ron Moore	.05
10	Ricky Proehl	.05
11	Clyde Simmons	.05
12	Eric Swann	.05
13	Aeneas Williams	.05
14	J.J. Birden	.05
15	Chris Doleman	.05
16	Bert Emanuel	.20
17	Jumpy Geathers	.05
18	Jeff George	.10
19	Roger Harper	.05
20	Craig Heyward	.05
21	Pierce Holt	.05
22	D.J. Johnson	.05
23	Terance Mathis	.05
24	Clay Mathews	.05
25	Andre Rison	.10
26	Chuck Smith	.05
27	Jessie Tuggle	.05
28	Cornelius Bennett	.05
29	Bucky Brooks	.05
30	Jeff Burris	.05
31	Russell Copeland	.05
32	Matt Darby	.05
33	Phil Hansen	.05
34	Henry Jones	.05
35	Jim Kelly	.10
36	Mark Maddox	.10
37	Bryce Paup	.05
38	Andre Reed	.10
39	Bruce Smith	.05
40	Darryl Talley	.05
41	Dewell Brewer	.10
42	Mike Fox	.05
43	Eric Guliford	.05
44	Lamar Lathon	.05
45	Pete Metzelaars	.05
46	Sam Mills	.05
47	Frank Reich	.05
48	Rod Smith	.05
49	Jack Trudeau	.05
50	Trace Armstrong	.05
51	Joe Cain	.05
52	Mark Carrier	.05
53	Curtis Conway	.05
54	Shaun Gayle	.05
55	Jeff Graham	.05
56	Raymont Harris	.15
57	Erik Kramer	.05
58	Lewis Tillman	.05
59	Tom Waddle	.05
60	Steve Walsh	.05
61	Donnell Woolford	.05
62	Chris Zorich	.05
63	*Jeff Blake*	.50
64	Mike Brim	.05
65	Steve Broussard	.05
66	James Francis	.05
67	Ricardo McDonald	.05
68	Tony McGee	.05
69	Carl Pickens	.05
70	Darnay Scott	.40
71	Steve Tovar	.05
72	Dan Wilkinson	.05
73	Alfred Williams	.05
74	Darryl Williams	.05
75	Derrick Alexander	.20
76	Randy Baldwin	.05
77	Carl Banks	.05
78	Rob Burnett	.05
79	Steve Everitt	.05
80	Leroy Hoard	.05
81	Michael Jackson	.05
82	Pepper Johnson	.05
83	Tony Jones	.05
84	Antonio Langham	.05
85	Eric Metcalf	.05
86	Stevon Moore	.05
87	Anthony Pleasant	.05
88	Vinny Testaverde	.05
89	Eric Turner	.05
90	Troy Aikman	.60
91	Charles Haley	.05
92	Michael Irvin	.20
93	Daryl Johnston	.05
94	Robert Jones	.05
95	Leon Lett	.05
96	Russell Maryland	.05
97	Nate Newton	.05
98	Jay Novacek	.05
99	Darrin Smith	.05
100	Emmitt Smith	1.50
101	Kevin Smith	.05
102	Erik Williams	.05
103	Kevin Williams	.05
104	Darren Woodson	.05
105	Elijah Alexander	.05
106	Steve Atwater	.05
107	Ray Crockett	.05
108	Shane Dronett	.05
109	Jason Elam	.05
110	John Elway	.25
111	Simon Fletcher	.05
112	Glyn Milburn	.05
113	Anthony Miller	.05
114	Michael Dean Perry	.05
115	Mike Pritchard	.05
116	Derek Russell	.05
117	Leonard Russell	.05
118	Shannon Sharpe	.05
119	Gary Zimmerman	.05
120	Bennie Blades	.05
121	Lomas Brown	.05
122	Willie Clay	.05
123	Mike Johnson	.05
124	Robert Massey	.05
125	Scott Mitchell	.05
126	Herman Moore	.05
127	Brett Perriman	.05
128	Robert Porcher	.05
129	Barry Sanders	1.25
130	Chris Spielman	.05
131	Henry Thomas	.05
132	Edgar Bennett	.05
133	Robert Brooks	.05
134	LeRoy Butler	.05
135	Brett Favre	1.50
136	Sean Jones	.05
137	John Jurkovic	.05
138	George Koonce	.05
139	Wayne Simmons	.05
140	George Teague	.05
141	Reggie White	.10
142	Michael Barrow	.05
143	Gary Brown	.05
144	Cody Carlson	.05
145	Ray Childress	.05
146	Cris Dishman	.05
147	Ernest Givins	.05
148	Mel Gray	.05
149	Darryl Lewis	.05
150	Bruce Matthews	.05
151	Marcus Robertson	.05
152	Webster Slaughter	.05
153	Al Smith	.05
154	Mark Stepnoski	.05
155	Trev Alberts	.05
156	Willie Anderson	.05
157	Jason Belser	.05
158	Tony Bennett	.05
159	Ray Buchanan	.05
160	Quentin Coryatt	.05
161	Sean Dawkins	.15
162	Steve Emtman	.05
163	Marshall Faulk	1.00
164	Steve Grant	.05
165	Jim Harbaugh	.05
166	Jeff Herrod	.05
167	Tony Siragusa	.05
168	Steve Beuerlein	.05
169	Darren Carrington	.05
170	Reggie Cobb	.05
171	Kelvin Martin	.05
172	Kelvin Pritchett	.05
173	Joel Smeenge	.05
174	James Williams	.05
175	Marcus Allen	.10
176	Kimble Anders	.05
177	Dale Carter	.05
178	Mark Collins	.05
179	Willie Davis	.05
180	Lake Dawson	.20
181	Greg Hill	.20
182	Darren Mickell	.05
183	Joe Montana	1.00
184	Tracy Simien	.05
185	Neil Smith	.05
186	William White	.05
187	Greg Biekert	.05
188	Tim Brown	.10
189	Rob Fredrickson	.05
190	*Andrew Glover*	.10
191	Nolan Harrison	.05
192	Jeff Hostetler	.05
193	Raghib Ismail	.05
194	Terry McDaniel	.05
195	Chester McGlockton	.05
196	Winston Moss	.05
197	Anthony Smith	.05
198	Harvey Williams	.05
199	Steve Wisniewski	.05
200	Johnny Bailey	.05
201	Jerome Bettis	.25
202	Isaac Bruce	.50
203	Shane Conlan	.05
204	Troy Drayton	.05
205	Sean Gilbert	.05
206	Jessie Hester	.05
207	Jimmie Jones	.05
208	Todd Lyght	.05
209	Chris Miller	.05
210	Roman Phifer	.05
211	Marquez Pope	.05
212	Robert Young	.05
213	Gene Atkins	.05
214	Aubrey Beavers	.05
215	Tim Bowens	.05
216	Bryan Cox	.05
217	Jeff Cross	.05
218	Irving Fryar	.05
219	Eric Green	.05
220	Mark Ingram	.05
221	Terry Kirby	.05
222	Dan Marino	1.50
223	O.J. McDuffie	.05
224	Bernie Parmalee	.25
225	Keith Sims	.05
226	Irving Spikes	.10
227	Michael Stewart	.05
228	Troy Vincent	.05
229	Richmond Webb	.05
230	Terry Allen	.05
231	Cris Carter	.10
232	Jack Del Rio	.05
233	Vencie Glenn	.05
234	Quadry Ismail	.05
235	Carlos Jenkins	.05
236	Ed McDaniel	.05
237	Randall McDaniel	.05
238	Warren Moon	.10
239	Anthony Parker	.05
240	John Randle	.05
241	Jake Reed	.05
242	Fuad Reveiz	.05
243	Broderick Thomas	.05
244	DeWayne Washington	.05
245	Bruce Armstrong	.05
246	Drew Bledsoe	1.00
247	Vincent Brisby	.05
248	Vincent Brown	.05
249	Marion Butts	.05
250	Ben Coates	.05
251	Tim Goad	.05
252	Myron Guyton	.05
253	Maurice Hurst	.05
254	Mike Jones	.05
255	Willie McGinest	.05
256	David Meggett	.05
257	Ricky Reynolds	.05
258	Chris Slade	.05
259	Michael Timpson	.05
260	Mario Bates	.20
261	Derek Brown	.05
262	Darion Connor	.05
263	Quinn Early	.05
264	Jim Everett	.05
265	Michael Haynes	.05
266	Tyrone Hughes	.05
267	Joe Johnson	.05
268	Wayne Martin	.05
269	William Roaf	.05
270	Irv Smith	.05
271	Jimmy Spencer	.05
272	Winfred Tubbs	.05
273	Renaldo Turnbull	.05
274	Michael Brooks	.05
275	Dave Brown	.05
276	Chris Calloway	.05
277	Jesse Campbell	.05
278	Howard Cross	.05
279	John Elliott	.05
280	Keith Hamilton	.05
281	Rodney Hampton	.05
282	Thomas Lewis	.05
283	Thomas Randolph	.05
284	Mike Sherrard	.05
285	Michael Strahan	.05
286	Brad Baxter	.05
287	Tony Casillas	.05
288	Kyle Clifton	.05
289	Boomer Esiason	.05
290	Aaron Glenn	.05
291	Bobby Houston	.05
292	Johnny Johnson	.05
293	Jeff Lageman	.05
294	Mo Lewis	.05
295	Johnny Mitchell	.05
296	Rob Moore	.05
297	Marcus Turner	.05
298	Marvin Washington	.05
299	Eric Allen	.05
300	Fred Barnett	.05
301	Randall Cunningham	.10
302	Byron Evans	.05
303	William Fuller	.05
304	Charlie Garner	.10
305	Andy Harmon	.05
306	Greg Jackson	.05
307	Bill Romanowski	.05
308	William Thomas	.05
309	Herschel Walker	.10
310	Calvin Williams	.05
311	Michael Zordich	.05
312	Chad Brown	.05
313	Dermontti Dawson	.05
314	Barry Foster	.10
315	Kevin Greene	.05
316	Charles Johnson	.20
317	Levon Kirkland	.05
318	Carnell Lake	.05
319	Greg Lloyd	.05
320	Bam Morris	.40
321	Neil O'Donnell	.10
322	Darren Perry	.05
323	Ray Seals	.05
324	John L. Williams	.05
325	Rod Woodson	.05
326	John Carney	.05
327	Andre Coleman	.05
328	Courtney Hall	.05
329	Ronnie Harmon	.05
330	Dwayne Harper	.05
331	Stan Humphries	.10
332	Shawn Jefferson	.05
333	Tony Martin	.05
334	Natrone Means	.40
335	Chris Mims	.05
336	Leslie O'Neal	.05
337	Alfred Pupunu	.15
338	Junior Seau	.10
339	Mark Seay	.05
340	Eric Davis	.05
341	William Floyd	.25
342	Merton Hanks	.05
343	Rickey Jackson	.05
344	Brent Jones	.05
345	Tim McDonald	.05
346	Ken Norton	.05
347	Gary Plummer	.05
348	Jerry Rice	.50
349	Deion Sanders	.50
350	Jesse Sapolu	.05
351	Dana Stubblefield	.05
352	John Taylor	.05
353	Steve Wallace	.05
354	Ricky Watters	.10
355	Lee Woodall	.05
356	Bryant Young	.05
357	Steve Young	.40
358	Sam Adams	.05
359	Howard Ballard	.05
360	Robert Blackmon	.05
361	Brian Blades	.05
362	Carlton Gray	.05
363	Cortez Kennedy	.05
364	Rick Mirer	.35
365	Eugene Robinson	.05
366	Chris Warren	.05
367	Terry Wooden	.05
368	Brad Culpepper	.05
369	Lawrence Dawsey	.05
370	Trent Dilfer	.40
371	Santana Dotson	.05
372	Craig Erickson	.05
373	Thomas Everett	.05
374	Paul Gruber	.05
375	Alvin Harper	.05
376	Jackie Harris	.05
377	Courtney Hawkins	.05
378	Martin Mayhew	.05
379	Hardy Nickerson	.05
380	Errict Rhett	.50
381	Charles Wilson	.05
382	Reggie Brooks	.05
383	Tom Carter	.05
384	Andre Collins	.05
385	Henry Ellard	.05
386	Ricky Ervins	.05
387	Darrell Green	.05
388	Ken Harvey	.05
389	Brian Mitchell	.05
390	Stanley Richard	.05
391	Heath Shuler	.50
392	Rod Stephens	.05
393	Tyronne Stowe	.05
394	Tydus Winans	.05
395	Tony Woods	.05
396	Checklist	.05
397	Checklist	.05
398	Checklist	.05
399	Checklist	.05
400	Checklist	.05

1995 Fleer Aerial Attack

This 6-card insert set features two top NFL quarterbacks and four top wide receivers. Cards, which were included one per every 37 packs, use 100 percent foil-etched designs, with an "Aerial Attack" football logo on the front. An action photo is also featured, against a background of footballs. The card back is numbered 1 of 6, etc.

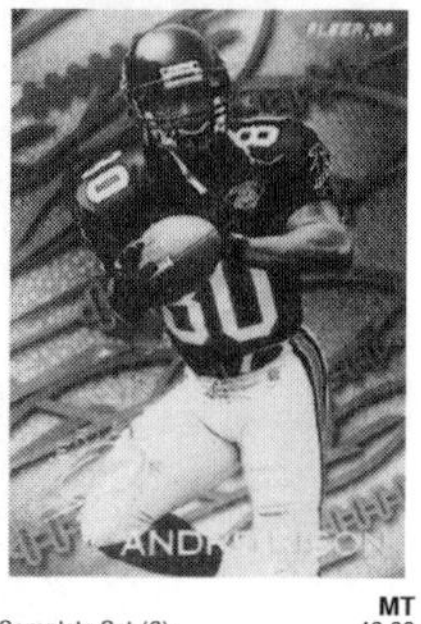

		MT
Complete Set (6):		40.00
Common Player:		3.00
1	Tim Brown	3.00
2	Dan Marino	20.00
3	Joe Montana	10.00
4	Jerry Rice	10.00
5	Andre Rison	3.00
6	Sterling Sharpe	3.00

1995 Fleer Flair Preview

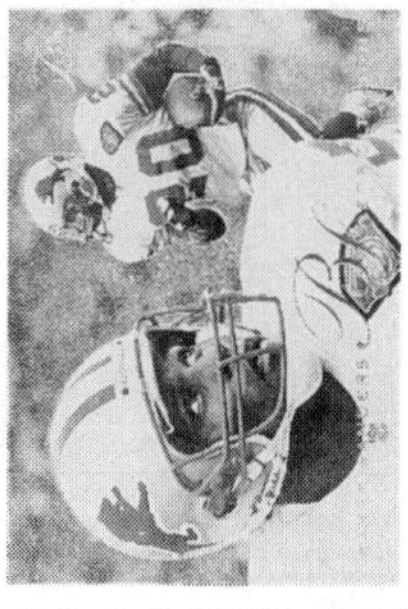

Every pack of 1995 Fleer football included one of these 1995 Fleer Flair preview cards, showcasing the company's 100 percent etched-foil Flair product. The card front uses a horizontal format, with a player mug shot and an action shot. The player's initials are stamped in silver in a scripted typeface. The card back, numbered 1 of 30, etc., has a brief summary of the player's 1994 season. It also indicates the card backs of the regular Flair set will feature statistics and a player photo on them. Cards are glossy poly-laminated and are double in thickness.

		MT
Complete Set (30):		20.00
Common Player:		.25
Minor Stars:		.50
1	Aeneas Williams	.25
2	Jeff George	.50
3	Andre Reed	.25
4	Kerry Collins	.50
5	Mark Carrier	.25
6	Jeff Blake	.50
7	Leroy Hoard	.25
8	Emmitt Smith	3.00
9	Shannon Sharpe	.50
10	Barry Sanders	2.50
11	Reggie White	.50
12	Bruce Matthews	.25
13	Marshall Faulk	2.00
14	Tony Boselli	.75
15	Joe Montana	2.00
16	Tim Brown	.25
17	Jerome Bettis	.75
18	Dan Marino	3.00
19	Cris Carter	.50
20	Drew Bledsoe	2.00
21	William Roaf	.25
22	Rodney Hampton	.25
23	Rob Moore	.25
24	Fred Barnett	.25
25	Rod Woodson	.25
26	Natrone Means	1.50
27	Jerry Rice	1.75
28	Chris Warren	.50
29	Errict Rhett	.75
30	Henry Ellard	.25

1995 Fleer Gridiron Leaders

Ten of the NFL's top statistical leaders from 1994 are shown on these 1995 Fleer insert cards. Cards were randomly included one per every four packs. The card front has the player photo against a grid-like background, with "Gridiron Leader" running along the left side. The back has another color photo and a summary of the player's 1994 accomplishments, plus the categories he led the league in. Cards are numbered 1 of 10, etc.

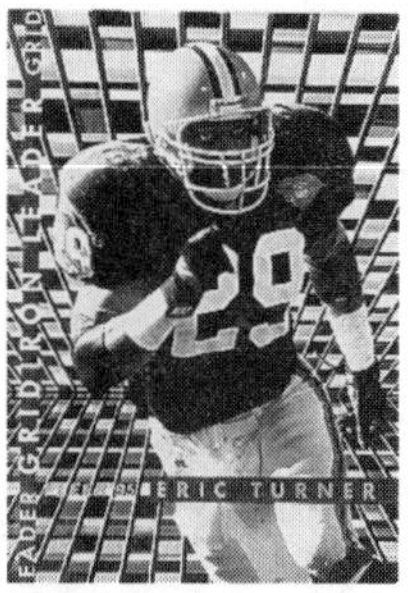

		MT
Complete Set (10):		8.00
Common Player:		.25
Minor Stars:		.50
1	Cris Carter	.50
2	Ben Coates	.25
3	Marshall Faulk	.50
4	Jerry Rice	1.00
5	Barry Sanders	1.50
6	Deion Sanders	.75
7	Emmitt Smith	2.00
8	Eric Turner	.25
9	Chris Warren	.25
10	Steve Young	1.00

1995 Fleer Prospects

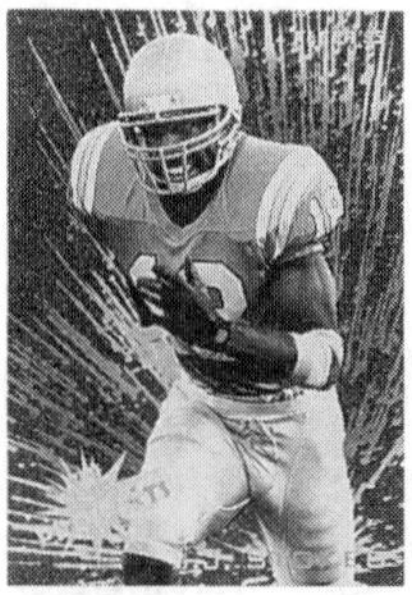

Twenty of the top 1995 NFL draft picks with promising futures are featured on these 1995 insert cards. Cards, numbered on the back 1 of 20, etc., feature a color action photo of the player on the front; he is wearing his collegiate uniform. The background is a metallic-like burst. The player's name and the "NFL Prospects" logo are in gold. The card back has another photo of the player, plus a summary of the player's collegiate achievements.

		MT
Complete Set (20):		30.00
Common Player:		.50
Minor Stars:		1.00
1	Tony Boselli	.75
2	Kyle Brady	1.00
3	Ruben Brown	.50
4	Kevin Carter	1.00
5	Ki-Jana Carter	1.00
6	Kerry Collins	2.00
7	Luther Elliss	.50
8	Jimmy Hitchcock	.50
9	Jack Jackson	.50
10	Ellis Johnson	.50
11	Rob Johnson	2.00
12	Steve McNair	5.00
13	Rashaan Salaam	1.00
14	Warren Sapp	1.00
15	J.J. Stokes	2.00
16	Bobby Taylor	.50
17	John Walsh	.50
18	Michael Westbrook	1.50
19	Tyrone Wheatley	1.00
20	Sherman Williams	1.00

1995 Fleer Pro-Visions

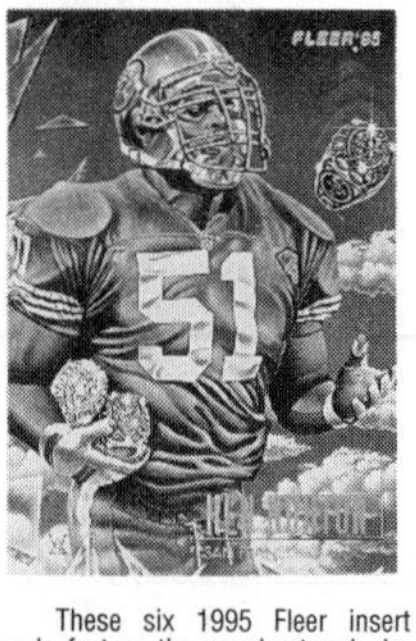

These six 1995 Fleer insert cards feature the usual artwork design which has been used for previous Pro Visions sets. Cards were randomly included one per every six packs. The fronts of the six cards combine to form an interlocking design. Card backs, numbered 1 of 6, etc., have a summary of the player's career, but no photo or artwork.

		MT
Complete Set (6):		5.00
Common Player:		.25
1	Natrone Means	.50
2	Sterling Sharpe	.25
3	Ken Norton	.25
4	Drew Bledsoe	1.00
5	Marshall Faulk	1.00
6	Tim Brown	.50

1995 Fleer Rookie Sensations

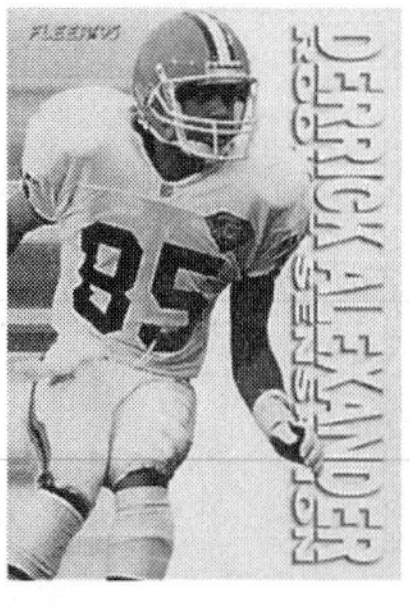

Twenty top rookies from 1994 are featured on these insert cards, included one per every three 17-card packs. The card front has a color action photo, with the player's name and "Rookie Sensations" running down the side of the card. Card backs are numbered 1 of 20, etc.

		MT
Complete Set (20):		70.00
Common Player:		2.00
Minor Stars:		4.00
1	Derrick Alexander	3.00
2	Mario Bates	4.00
3	Tim Bowens	2.00
4	Lake Dawson	4.00
5	Bert Emanuel	4.00
6	Marshall Faulk	10.00
7	William Floyd	5.00
8	Rob Frederickson	2.00
9	Greg Hill	4.00
10	Charles Johnson	4.00
11	Antonio Langham	2.00
12	Willie McGinest	2.00
13	Bam Morris	4.00
14	Errict Rhett	4.00
15	Darnay Scott	5.00
16	Heath Shuler	5.00
17	DeWayne Washington	2.00
18	Dan Wilkinson	2.00
19	Lee Woodall	2.00
20	Bryant Young	2.00

1995 Fleer TD Sensations

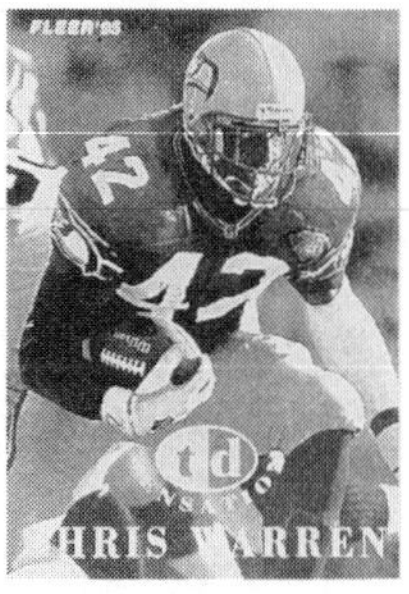

Ten top NFL scorers are featured on these 1995 Fleer insert cards, issued one per every three 11-card packs. Card fronts have a color action photo, with the "TD Sensation" logo stamped in green and gold. The player's name is also in gold. The card back has another color photo, plus a brief player profile running down one side of the card. Cards are numbered 1 of 10, etc..

		MT
Complete Set (10):		8.00
Common Player:		.25
Minor Stars:		.50
1	Marshall Faulk	1.00
2	Dan Marino	2.00
3	Natrone Means	.50
4	Herman Moore	.25
5	Jerry Rice	1.00
6	Sterling Sharpe	.25
7	Emmitt Smith	2.00
8	Chris Warren	.25
9	Ricky Watters	.50
10	Steve Young	1.00

1995 Fleer Bettis/Mirer Sheet

These sheets feature 10 cards of Jerome Bettis on one side and 10 cards of Rick Mirer on the other and were distributed at the Super Bowl show in Miami. The sheets could be purchased for five wrappers and $1. There were also 400 sheets signed by one of the players that were sold for $25.

		MT
Complete Set (1):		2.50
1	Jerome Bettis, Rick Mirer	2.50

1995 Fleer Shell

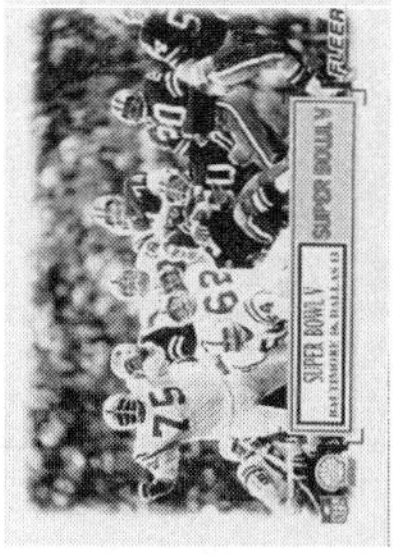

This 10-card set was produced by Fleer and issued by Shell in its "Drive for the Super Bowl XXX" sweepstakes. The cards are standard sized and were originally attached to a rub-off tab card of equal size and divided by a perforated line.

		MT
Complete Set (10):		10.00
Common Player:		1.00
1	Super Bowl XXIII (Joe Montana's drive)	1.50
2	1967 NFL Championship (Bart Starr's TD)	1.00
3	1986 AFC Championship (The Drive, Mark Jackson)	1.00
4	Super Bowl XIII (Steeler's drive, Terry Bradshaw)	1.00
5	1975 NFC Divisional Playoffs (Cowboy's drive, Doug Dennison featured)	1.00
6	1968 AFL Championship (Jet's drive)	1.00
7	1981 NFC Championship (49ers team shot)	1.00
8	1983 NFC Championship (Redskin's drive, John Riggins' TD)	1.00
9	1969 AFL Divisional Playoffs (Len Dawson in huddle)	1.00
10	Super Bowl V (Colts' field goal, Bob Lilly and Mel Renfro pictured)	1.00

1996 Fleer

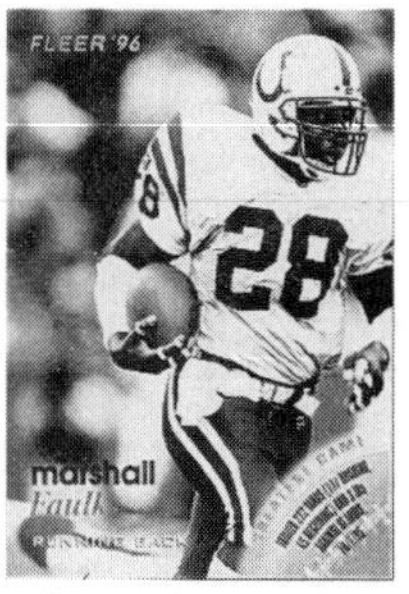

Fleer's 1996 football card set contains 200 cards, many of which are from subsets in the main set. The best players from the 1996 draft are featured on 40 cards, while the top 20 from 1995 have their own subset. Key match-ups for 1996's biggest games, as selected by Pro Football Weekly, are spotlighted on 17 other subset cards. Pro Football Weekly writers have also written the card backs. Each basic card design includes a "Greatest Game" note on the front, plus career statistics, basic statistics and the player's "Triangle Numbers" - his height, weight and time in the 40-yard dash. Six insert sets were created - Rookie Sensations, Breakthrough, RAC Pack, Statistically Speaking, Rookie Write Up and Signature Series. The Signature Series cards are autographed cards by Eddie George, Leeland McElroy and Tim Biakabutuka. Fleer also offered Rookie Sensation Hot Packs, which contained specially-marked versions of all 11 cards from that insert set. These packs were seeded one per every 960 packs.

		MT
Complete Set (200):		20.00
Common Player:		.05
Minor Stars:		.10
Pack (11):		1.50
Wax Box (24):		34.00
1	Garrison Hearst	.10
2	Rob Moore	.05
3	Frank Sanders	.05
4	Eric Swann	.05
5	Aeneas Williams	.05
6	Jeff George	.10
7	Craig Heyward	.05
8	Terance Mathis	.05
9	Eric Metcalf	.05
10	Michael Jackson	.05
11	Andre Rison	.05
12	Vinny Testaverde	.05
13	Eric Turner	.05
14	Darick Holmes	.05
15	Jim Kelly	.10
16	Bryce Paup	.05
17	Bruce Smith	.05
18	Thurman Thomas	.10
19	Kerry Collins	.30
20	Lamar Lathon	.05
21	Derrick Moore	.05
22	Tyrone Poole	.05
23	Curtis Conway	.05
24	Bryan Cox	.05
25	Erik Kramer	.05
26	Rashaan Salaam	.60
27	Jeff Blake	.60
28	Ki-Jana Carter	.25
29	Carl Pickens	.10
30	Darnay Scott	.05
31	Troy Aikman	1.00
32	Charles Haley	.05
33	Michael Irvin	.10
34	Daryl Johnston	.05
35	Jay Novacek	.05
36	Deion Sanders	.60
37	Emmitt Smith	2.00
38	Steve Atwater	.05
39	Terrell Davis	.60
40	John Elway	.50
41	Anthony Miller	.05
42	Shannon Sharpe	.05
43	Scott Mitchell	.05
44	Herman Moore	.30
45	Johnnie Morton	.05
46	Brett Perriman	.05
47	Barry Sanders	1.00
48	Edgar Bennett	.05
49	Robert Brooks	.05
50	Mark Chmura	.30
51	Brett Favre	2.00
52	Reggie White	.10
53	Mel Gray	.05
54	Steve McNair	.60
55	Chris Sanders	.30
56	Rodney Thomas	.05
57	Quentin Coryatt	.05
58	Sean Dawkins	.05
59	Ken Dilger	.05
60	Marshall Faulk	.75
61	Jim Harbaugh	.05
62	Tony Boselli	.05
63	Mark Brunell	.50
64	Natrone Means	.10
65	James Stewart	.05
66	Marcus Allen	.05
67	Steve Bono	.05
68	Neil Smith	.05
69	Derrick Thomas	.05
70	Tamarick Vanover	.60
71	Fred Barnett	.05
72	Eric Green	.05
73	Dan Marino	2.00
74	O.J. McDuffie	.05
75	Bernie Parmalee	.05
76	Cris Carter	.05
77	Qadry Ismail	.05
78	Warren Moon	.05
79	Jake Reed	.05
80	Robert Smith	.05
81	Drew Bledsoe	.75
82	Vincent Brisby	.05
83	Ben Coates	.05
84	Curtis Martin	1.50
85	David Meggett	.05
86	Mario Bates	.05
87	Jim Everett	.05
88	Michael Haynes	.05
89	Renaldo Turnbull	.05
90	Dave Brown	.05
91	Rodney Hampton	.05
92	Thomas Lewis	.05
93	Tyrone Wheatley	.05
94	Kyle Brady	.05
95	Hugh Douglas	.05
96	Aaron Glenn	.05
97	Jeff Graham	.05
98	Adrian Murrell	.05
99	Neil O'Donnell	.05
100	Tim Brown	.05
101	Jeff Hostetler	.05
102	Napoleon Kaufman	.30
103	Chester McGlockton	.05
104	Harvey Williams	.05
105	William Fuller	.05
106	Charlie Garner	.05
107	Ricky Watters	.05
108	Calvin Williams	.05
109	Jerome Bettis	.05
110	Greg Lloyd	.05
111	Bam Morris	.05
112	Kordell Stewart	1.00
113	Yancey Thigpen	.40
114	Rod Woodson	.05
115	Isaac Bruce	.50
116	Troy Drayton	.05
117	Leslie O'Neal	.05
118	Steve Walsh	.05
119	Marco Coleman	.05
120	Aaron Hayden	.05
121	Stan Humphries	.05
122	Junior Seau	.10
123	William Floyd	.05
124	Brent Jones	.05
125	Ken Norton	.05
126	Jerry Rice	1.00
127	J.J. Stokes	.10
128	Steve Young	.75
129	Brian Blades	.05
130	Joey Galloway	.60
131	Rick Mirer	.05
132	Chris Warren	.10
133	Trent Dilfer	.05
134	Alvin Harper	.05
135	Hardy Nickerson	.05
136	Errict Rhett	.50
137	Terry Allen	.05
138	Henry Ellard	.05
139	Heath Shuler	.30
140	Michael Westbrook	.10
141	*Karim Abdul-Jabbar*	.50
142	*Mike Alstott*	1.00
143	*Marco Battaglia*	.05
144	*Tim Biakabutuka*	.75
145	*Tony Brackens*	.05
146	*Duane Clemons*	.05
147	*Ernie Conwell*	.05
148	*Chris Darkins*	.25
149	*Stephen Davis*	3.00
150	*Brian Dawkins*	.05
151	*Rickey Dudley*	.50
152	*Jason Dunn*	.05
153	*Bobby Engram*	.50
154	*Daryl Gardener*	.05
155	*Eddie George*	3.00
156	*Terry Glenn*	1.50
157	*Kevin Hardy*	.40
158	*Walt Harris*	.05
159	*Marvin Harrison*	2.00
160	*Bobby Hoying*	.50
161	*Keyshawn Johnson*	2.00
162	*Cedric Jones*	.05
163	*Marcus Jones*	.05
164	*Eddie Kennison*	.30
165	*Ray Lewis*	5.00
166	*Derrick Mayes*	.75
167	*Leeland McElroy*	.20
168	*Johnny McWilliams*	.05
169	*John Mobley*	.05
170	*Alex Molden*	.05
171	*Eric Moulds*	1.50
172	*Muhsin Muhammad*	.75
173	*Jonathan Ogden*	.05
174	*Lawrence Phillips*	.50
175	*Stanley Pritchett*	.25
176	*Simeon Rice*	.30
177	*Bryan Still*	.05
178	*Amani Toomer*	.50
179	*Regan Upshaw*	.05
180	*Alex Van Dyke*	.25
181	Minnesota/Detroit (PFW Weekly Matchups)	.05
182	Oakland/Kansas City (PFW Weekly Matchups)	.05
183	Buffalo/Pittsburgh (PFW Weekly Matchups)	.05
184	Atlanta/San Francisco (PFW Weekly Matchups)	.05
185	Carolina/Jacksonville (PFW Weekly Matchups)	.05
186	Philadelphia/Dallas (PFW Weekly Matchups)	.05
187	Green Bay/Chicago (PFW Weekly Matchups)	.05
188	Pittsburgh/Kansas City (PFW Weekly Matchups)	.05
189	Cincinnati/Pittsburgh (PFW Weekly Matchups)	.05
190	Dallas/Miami (PFW Weekly Matchups)	.05
191	Denver/Oakland (PFW Weekly Matchups)	.05
192	Kansas City/Minnesota (PFW Weekly Matchups)	.05
193	San Diego/Indianapolis (PFW Weekly Matchups)	.05
194	Dallas/San Francisco (PFW Weekly Matchups)	.05
195	Miami/Oakland (PFW Weekly Matchups)	.05
196	San Francisco/Pittsburgh (PFW Weekly Matchups)	.05
197	Kansas City/Buffalo (PFW Weekly Matchups)	.05
198	Checklist	.05
199	Checklist	.05
200	Checklist	.05

1996 Fleer Rookie Sensations

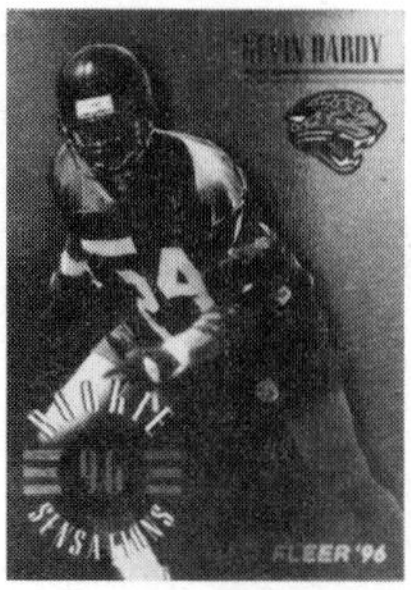

Eleven of the NFL's top rookies entering the 1996 season are featured on these 1996 Fleer football plastic card inserts. The cards were seeded one per every 72 packs. Each front has an action photo on it, with the player's name and a team logo in the upper right corner. The Fleer logo is at the bottom of the card, with the Rookie Sensations logo in the bottom left corner. The card back has a card number (1 of 11, etc.) in the upper right corner; the set's logo is also at the top. A brief career write-up is in the middle, with a Pro Football Weekly logo and the player's name and position underneath. Special Rookie Sensation Hot Packs were also created; these packs contained all 11 cards, each with a special Hot Packs logo on it. Hot Packs were seeded one per every 960 packs.

		MT
Complete Set (11):		125.00
Common Player:		6.00
Comp. Hot Pack Set (11):		60.00
Hot Pack Cards: Half Price		
1	Karim Abdul-Jabbar	15.00
2	Tim Biakabutuka	8.00
3	Rickey Dudley	6.00
4	Eddie George	40.00
5	Terry Glenn	15.00
6	Kevin Hardy	6.00
7	Marvin Harrison	12.00
8	Keyshawn Johnson	20.00
9	Jon Ogden	6.00
10	Lawrence Phillips	15.00
11	Simeon Rice	6.00

1996 Fleer Rookie Sensations Hot Packs

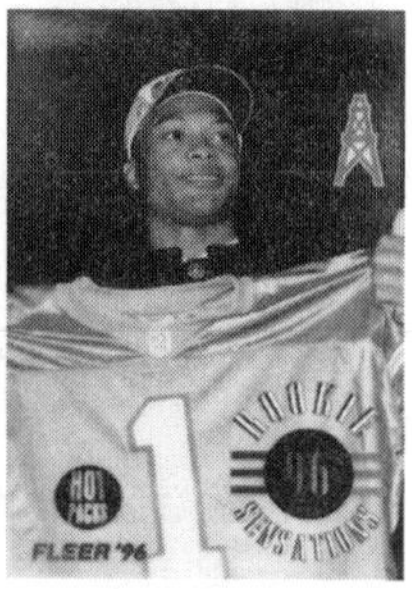

This 11-card insert parallels the Rookie Sensations insert, but was found as a complete set in every 960 packs of Fleer Football. The cards are exactly like regular Rookie Sensations, except for a red foil Hot Packs logo on the front.

	MT
Complete Set (11):	75.00
Hot Pack Cards: 50%	

1996 Fleer Rookie Signatures

Three top rookie running backs have autographed cards for this 1996 Fleer insert set. The cards were seeded one per every 288 hobby packs only.

		MT
Complete Set (3):		100.00
Common Player:		10.00
Inserted 1:288 Hobby		
Blue Signatures:		1.5x
A1	Tim Biakabutuka	20.00
A2	Eddie George	70.00
A3	Leeland McElroy	10.00

1996 Fleer Breakthroughs

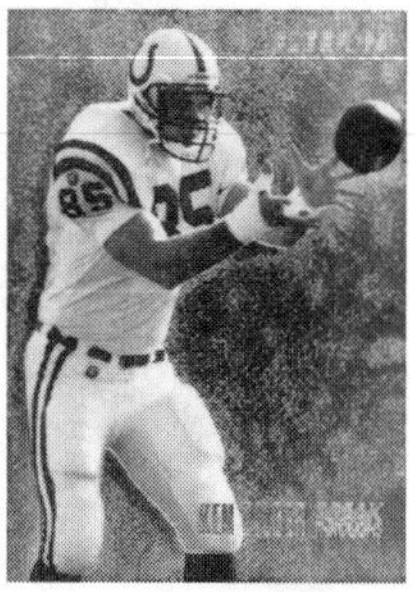

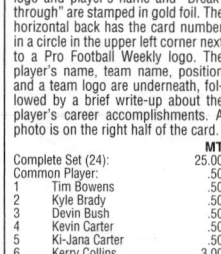

These players were chosen by Pro Football Weekly to have career seasons in 1996, including rookies who are predicted to have breakthrough campaigns in their first NFL season. The cards, seeded one per every three packs of 1996 Fleer football product, feature a 100% etched foil design for the card front. The Fleer logo and player's name and "Breakthrough" are stamped in gold foil. The horizontal back has the card number in a circle in the upper left corner next to a Pro Football Weekly logo. The player's name, team name, position and a team logo are underneath, followed by a brief write-up about the player's career accomplishments. A photo is on the right half of the card.

		MT
Complete Set (24):		25.00
Common Player:		.50
1	Tim Bowens	.50
2	Kyle Brady	.50
3	Devin Bush	.50
4	Kevin Carter	.50
5	Ki-Jana Carter	.50
6	Kerry Collins	3.00
7	Trent Dilfer	.50
8	Ken Dilger	.50
9	Joey Galloway	2.00
10	Aaron Hayden	.50
11	Napoleon Kaufman	.50
12	Craig Newsome	.50
13	Tyrone Poole	.50
14	Jake Reed	.50
15	Rashaan Salaam	.50
16	Chris Sanders	.50
17	Frank Sanders	.50
18	Kordell Stewart	5.00

19	J.J. Stokes	.50
20	Bobby Taylor	.50
21	Orlando Thomas	.50
22	Michael Timpson	.50
23	Tamarick Vanover	.50
24	Michael Westbrook	.50

1996 Fleer RAC Pack

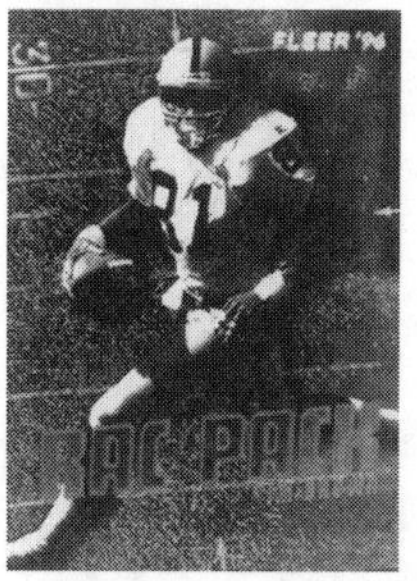

These 10 cards showcase receivers who rack up yards after the catch (Run After Catch yards). The cards, seeded one every 18th pack of 1996 Fleer product, feature an etched foil and color-foil stamped design for the card front's background (a football field design) and set/brand logos and player's name. The horizontal back has a bull's-eye in the upper left corner, with a player photo against it. The player's name, Pro Football Weekly logo and an explanation of the player's run-after-catch skills are on the opposite side.

		MT
Complete Set (10):		25.00
Common Player:		1.00
1	Robert Brooks	1.00
2	Tim Brown	1.00
3	Isaac Bruce	6.00
4	Cris Carter	1.00
5	Curtis Conway	1.00
6	Michael Irvin	2.00
7	Eric Metcalf	1.00
8	Herman Moore	3.00
9	Carl Pickens	2.00
10	Jerry Rice	10.00

1996 Fleer Statistically Speaking

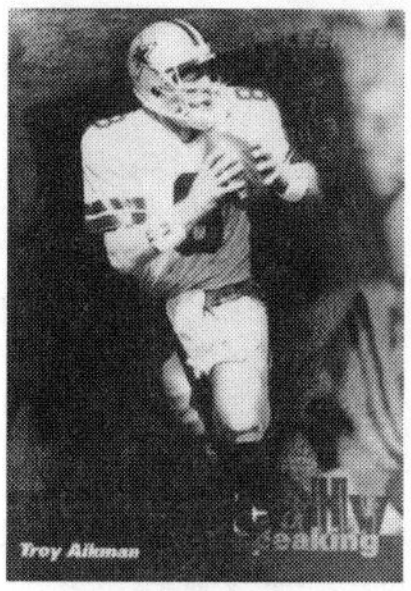

The NFL's statistical standouts are featured on these plastic cards using hot colors. These 1996 Fleer inserts are some of the tougher to find; they are seeded one per every 37 packs. Each card front has an action photo against a box filled with stats. The set's logo and player's name are along the bottom of the card. The background is a ghosted action scene. The horizontal back has a photo of the player on one side, against a ghosted action background which also contains a stat box. The card number (1 of 20, etc.) is in the upper left corner. The right side has a colored panel which has his name, position, team logo, Pro Football Weekly logo and a write-up of his accomplishments.

		MT
Complete Set (20):		100.00
Common Player:		1.50
1	Troy Aikman	10.00
2	Larry Centers	1.50
3	Ben Coates	1.50
4	Brett Favre	20.00
5	Joey Galloway	8.00
6	Rodney Hampton	1.50
7	Dan Marino	20.00
8	Curtis Martin	15.00
9	Anthony Miller	1.50
10	Brian Mitchell	1.50
11	Herman Moore	1.50
12	Errict Rhett	1.50
13	Rashaan Salaam	1.50
14	Barry Sanders	10.00
15	Deion Sanders	6.00
16	Emmitt Smith	20.00
17	Kordell Stewart	10.00
18	Chris Warren	1.50
19	Ricky Watters	1.50
20	Steve Young	8.00

A card number in parentheses ( ) indicates the set is unnumbered.

1996 Fleer Rookie Write-Ups

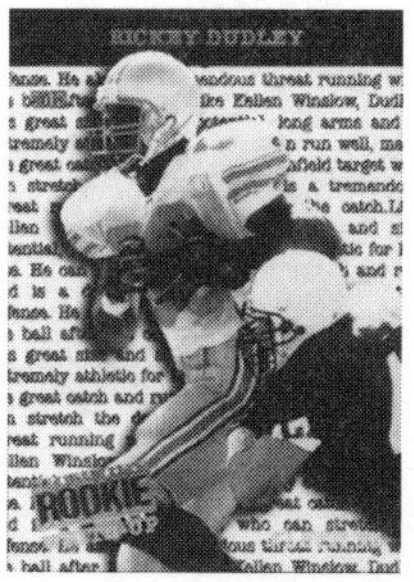

These hobby-exclusive insert cards feature 10 rookies entering the 1996 NFL season with scouting reports similar to those of previous rookies. Cards were inserted at a ratio of one per every 12 packs of 1996 Fleer hobby packs. The card front has a black band at the top with the player's name stamped in gold foil. His position and the set/brand logos are also stamped in gold. The middle of the card has an action shot of the player, against a written scouting report. The back has the player's name at the top, along with a card number (1 of 10, etc.). The background is white, with a brief write-up of the player and a colored/ghosted photo on it. The Pro Football Weekly Logo is also on the back.

		MT
Complete Set (10):		40.00
Common Player:		1.50
1	Tim Biakabutuka	1.50
2	Rickey Dudley	1.50
3	Eddie George	8.00
4	Terry Glenn	7.00
5	Kevin Hardy	1.50
6	Marvin Harrison	4.00
7	Keyshawn Johnson	5.00
8	Leeland McElroy	1.50
9	Lawrence Phillips	1.50
10	Simeon Rice	1.50

1997 Fleer

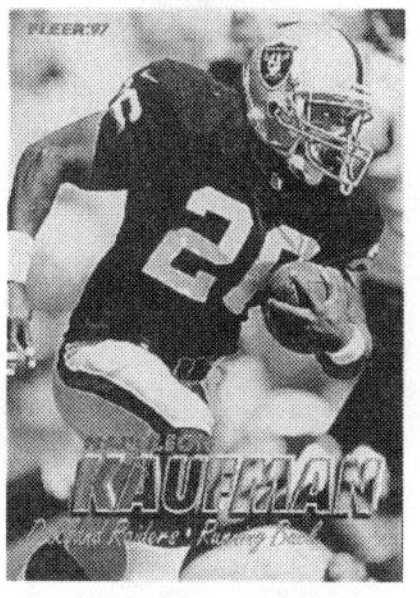

The 450-card set includes 415 player cards, five checklists and 30 Something Special subset cards. The matte-finish cards have full-bleed photos on the front, with his last name in large block letters at the bottom. His first name is printed in small letters above, while his team and position appear directly below the player's last name. The backs have the name in the upper left, with the card number in the upper right. Rounding out the backs are a player head shot, team name and logo, highlights, bio and career stats. Two parallels are randomly seeded in hobby packs. Crystal Collection cards were seeded 1:2, while Tiffany Collection cards were 1:20.

		MT
Complete Set (450):		40.00
Common Player:		.05
Minor Stars:		.10
Crystal Collection:		2x-4x
Tiffany Collection:		15x-30x
Pack (10):		1.50
Wax Box (36):		45.00
1	Mark Brunell	1.00
2	Andre Reed	.05
3	Darrell Green	.05
4	Mario Bates	.05
5	Eddie George	1.50
6	Cris Carter	.05
7	Terrell Owens	1.00
8	Bill Romanowski	.05
9	Isaac Bruce	.20
10	Eric Curry	.05
11	Danny Kanell	.05
12	Ki-Jana Carter	.10
13	Antonio Freeman	.30
14	Ricky Watters	.10
15	Ty Law	.05
16	Alonzo Spellman	.05
17	Kordell Stewart	.75
18	Jerry Rice	1.00
19	Derrick Alexander	.05
20	Barry Sanders	2.00
21	Keyshawn Johnson	.75
22	Emmitt Smith	2.00
23	Ricky Proehl	.05
24	Daryl Gardner	.05
25	Dan Saleaumua	.05
26	Kevin Greene	.05
27	Junior Seau	.10
28	Randall McDaniel	.05
29	Marshall Faulk	.25
30	Lorenzo Lynch	.05
31	Terance Mathis	.05
32	Warren Sapp	.05
33	Chris Sanders	.05
34	Tom Carter	.05
35	Aeneas Williams	.05
36	Lawrence Phillips	.10
37	John Elway	.75
38	Stanley Richard	.05
39	Darryl Williams	.05
40	Phillippi Sparks	.05
41	Tedy Bruschi	.05
42	Merton Hanks	.05
43	Ray Lewis	.05
44	Erik Williams	.05
45	Jason Gildon	.05
46	George Koonce	.05
47	Louis Oliver	.05
48	Muhsin Muhammad	.30
49	Daryl Hobbs	.05
50	Terry Glenn	1.25
51	Marvin Harrison	.75
52	Brian Dawkins	.05
53	Dale Carter	.05
54	Alex Molden	.05
55	Raymont Harris	.05
56	Jeff Burris	.05
57	Don Beebe	.05
58	Jamir Miller	.05
59	Carl Pickens	.10
60	Antonio London	.05
61	Courtney Hall	.05
62	Derrick Brooks	.05
63	Chris Boniol	.05
64	Jeff Lageman	.05
65	Roy Barker	.05
66	Devin Bush	.05
67	Aaron Glenn	.05
68	Wayne Simmons	.05
69	Steve Atwater	.05
70	Jimmie Jones	.05
71	Mark Carrier	.05
72	Chris.Chandler	.05
73	Andy Harmon	.05
74	John Friesz	.05
75	Karim Abdul-Jabbar	1.00
76	Levon Kirkland	.05
77	Torrance Small	.05
78	Harvey Williams	.05
79	Chris Calloway	.05
80	Vinny Testaverde	.05
81	Bryant Young	.05
82	Ray Buchanan	.05
83	Robert Smith	.05
84	Robert Brooks	.10
85	Ray Crockett	.05
86	Bennie Blades	.05
87	Mark Carrier	.05
88	Mike Tomczak	.05
89	Darick Holmes	.05
90	Drew Bledsoe	1.00
91	Darren Woodson	.05
92	Dan Wilkinson	.05
93	Charles Way	.05
94	Ray Farmer	.05
95	Marcus Allen	.10
96	Marco Coleman	.05
97	Zach Thomas	.30
98	Wesley Walls	.05
99	Frank Wycheck	.05
100	Troy Aikman	1.00
101	Clyde Simmons	.05
102	Courtney Hawkins	.05
103	Chuck Smith	.05
104	Neil O'Donnell	.05
105	Kevin Carter	.05
106	Chris Slade	.05
107	Jessie Armstead	.05
108	Sean Dawkins	.05
109	Robert Blackmon	.05
110	Kevin Smith	.05
111	Lonnie Johnson	.05
112	Craig Newsome	.05
113	Jonathan Ogden	.05
114	Chris Zorich	.05
115	Tim Brown	.05
116	Fred Barnett	.05
117	Michael Haynes	.05
118	Eric Hill	.05
119	Ronnie Harmon	.05
120	Sean Gilbert	.05
121	Derrick Alexander	.05
122	Derrick Thomas	.10
123	Tyrone Wheatley	.10
124	Cortez Kennedy	.05
125	Jeff George	.05
126	Chad Cota	.05
127	Gary Zimmerman	.05
128	Johnnie Morton	.05
129	Chad Brown	.05
130	Marvcus Patton	.05
131	James Stewart	.05
132	Terry Kirby	.05
133	Chris Mims	.05
134	William Thomas	.05
135	Steve Tasker	.05
136	Jason Belser	.05
137	Bryan Cox	.05
138	Jessie Tuggle	.05
139	Ashley Ambrose	.05
140	Mark Chmura	.05
141	Jeff Hostetler	.05
142	Rich Owens	.05
143	Willie Davis	.05
144	Hardy Nickerson	.05
145	Curtis Martin	1.25
146	Ken Norton	.05
147	Victor Green	.05
148	Anthony Miller	.05
149	John Kasay	.05
150	O.J. McDuffie	.05
151	Darren Perry	.05
152	Luther Elliss	.05
153	Greg Hill	.05
154	John Randle	.05
155	Stephen Grant	.05
156	Leon Lett	.05
157	Darrien Gordon	.05
158	Ray Zellars	.05
159	Michael Jackson	.05
160	Leslie O'Neal	.05
161	Bruce Smith	.05
162	Santana Dotson	.05
163	Bobby Hebert	.05
164	Keith Hamilton	.05
165	Tony Boselli	.05
166	Alfred Williams	.05
167	Ty Detmer	.05
168	Chester McGlockton	.05
169	William Floyd	.05
170	Bruce Matthews	.05
171	Simeon Rice	.05
172	Scott Mitchell	.05
173	Ricardo McDonald	.05
174	Tyrone Poole	.05
175	Greg Lloyd	.05
176	Bruce Armstrong	.05
177	Erik Kramer	.05
178	Kimble Anders	.05
179	Lamar Smith	.05
180	Tony Tolbert	.05
181	Joe Aska	.05
182	Eric Allen	.05
183	Eric Turner	.05
184	Brad Johnson	.05
185	Tony Martin	.05
186	Mike Mamula	.05
187	Irving Spikes	.05
188	Keith Jackson	.05
189	Carlton Bailey	.05
190	Tyrone Braxton	.05
191	Chad Bratzke	.05
192	Adrian Murrell	.05
193	Roman Phifer	.05
194	Todd Collins	.05
195	Chris Warren	.05
196	Kevin Hardy	.05
197	Rick Mirer	.10
198	Cornelius Bennett	.05
199	Jimmy Hitchcock	.05
200	Michael Irvin	.10
201	Quentin Coryatt	.05
202	Reggie White	.10
203	Larry Centers	.05
204	Rodney Thomas	.05
205	Dana Stubblefield	.05
206	Rod Woodson	.05
207	Rhett Hall	.05
208	Steve Tovar	.05
209	Michael Westbrook	.10
210	Steve Wisniewski	.05
211	Carlester Crumpler	.05
212	Elvis Grbac	.10
213	Tim Bowens	.05
214	Kevin Porcher	.05
215	John Carney	.05
216	Anthony Newman	.05
217	Ernest Byner	.05
218	DeWayne Washington	.05
219	Willie Green	.05
220	Terry Allen	.10
221	William Fuller	.05
222	Al Del Greco	.05
223	Trent Dilfer	.10
224	Michael Dean Perry	.05
225	Larry Allen	.05
226	Mark Bruener	.05
227	Clay Matthews	.05
228	Ruben Brown	.05
229	Edgar Bennett	.05
230	Neil Smith	.05
231	Ken Harvey	.05
232	Kyle Brady	.05
233	Corey Miller	.05
234	Tony Siragusa	.05
235	Todd Sauerbrun	.05
236	Daniel Stubbs	.05
237	Robb Thomas	.05
238	Jimmy Smith	.05
239	Marquez Pope	.05
240	Tim Biakabutuka	.10
241	Jamie Asher	.05
242	Steve McNair	.75
243	Harold Green	.05
244	Frank Sanders	.05
245	Joe Johnson	.05
246	Eric Bieniemy	.05
247	Kevin Turner	.05
248	Rickey Dudley	.10
249	Orlando Thomas	.05
250	Dan Marino	2.00
251	Deion Sanders	.50
252	Dan Williams	.05
253	Sam Gash	.05
254	Lonnie Marts	.05
255	Mo Lewis	.05
256	Charles Johnson	.05
257	Chris Jacke	.05
258	Keenan McCardell	.05
259	Donnell Woolford	.05
260	Terrance Shaw	.05
261	Jason Dunn	.05
262	Willie McGinest	.05
263	Ken Dilger	.05
264	Keith Lyle	.05
265	Antonio Langham	.05
266	Carlton Gray	.05
267	LeShon Johnson	.05
268	Thurman Thomas	.10
269	Jesse Campbell	.05
270	Carnell Lake	.05
271	Cris Dishman	.05
272	Kevin Williams	.05
273	Troy Brown	.05
274	William Roaf	.05
275	Terrell Davis	1.25
276	Herman Moore	.20
277	Walt Harris	.05
278	Mark Collins	.05
279	Bert Emanuel	.05
280	Qadry Ismail	.05
281	Phil Hansen	.05
282	Steve Young	.75
283	Michael Sinclair	.05
284	Jeff Graham	.05
285	Sam Mills	.05
286	Terry McDaniel	.05
287	Eugene Robinson	.05
288	Tony Bennett	.05
289	Daryl Johnston	.05
290	Eric Swann	.05
291	Bam Morris	.05
292	Thomas Lewis	.05
293	Terrell Fletcher	.05
294	Gus Frerotte	.05
295	Stanley Pritchett	.05
296	Mike Alstott	.10
297	Will Shields	.05
298	Errict Rhett	.10
299	Garrison Hearst	.05
300	Kerry Collins	.25
301	Darryll Lewis	.05
302	Chris T. Jones	.05
303	Yancey Thigpen	.05
304	Jackie Harris	.05
305	Steve Christie	.05
306	Gilbert Brown	.05
307	Terry Wooden	.05
308	Pete Mitchell	.05
309	Tim McDonald	.05
310	Jake Reed	.05
311	Ed McCaffrey	.05
312	Chris Doleman	.05
313	Eric Metcalf	.05
314	Ricky Reynolds	.05
315	David Sloan	.05
316	Marvin Washington	.05
317	Herschel Walker	.05
318	Michael Timpson	.05
319	Blaine Bishop	.05
320	Irv Smith	.05
321	Seth Joyner	.05
322	Terrell Buckley	.05
323	Michael Strahan	.05
324	Sam Adams	.05
325	Leslie Shepherd	.05
326	James Jett	.05
327	Anthony Pleasant	.05
328	Lee Woodall	.05
329	Shannon Sharpe	.05
330	Jamal Anderson	.20
331	Andre Hastings	.05
332	Troy Vincent	.05
333	Sean LaChapelle	.05
334	Winslow Oliver	.05
335	Sean Jones	.05
336	Darnay Scott	.05
337	Todd Lyght	.05
338	Leonard Russell	.05
339	Nate Newton	.05
340	Zack Crockett	.05
341	Amp Lee	.05
342	Bobby Engram	.05
343	Mike Hollis	.05
344	Rodney Hampton	.05
345	Mel Gray	.05
346	Van Malone	.05
347	Aaron Craver	.05
348	Jim Everett	.05
349	Trace Armstrong	.05
350	Pat Swilling	.05
351	Brent Jones	.05
352	Chris Spielman	.05
353	Brett Perriman	.05
354	Brian Kinchen	.05
355	Joey Galloway	.30
356	Henry Ellard	.05
357	Ben Coates	.05
358	Dorsey Levens	.20
359	Charlie Garner	.05
360	Erric Pegram	.05
361	Anthony Johnson	.05
362	Rashaan Salaam	.10
363	Jeff Blake	.20
364	Kent Graham	.05
365	Broderick Thomas	.05
366	Richmond Webb	.05
367	Alfred Pupunu	.05
368	Mark Stepnoski	.05
369	David Dunn	.05
370	Bobby Houston	.05
371	Anthony Parker	.05
372	Quinn Early	.05
373	LeRoy Butler	.05
374	Kurt Gouveia	.05
375	Greg Biekert	.05
376	Jim Harbaugh	.05
377	Eric Bjornson	.05
378	Craig Heyward	.05
379	Steve Bono	.05
380	Tony Banks	.30
381	John Mobley	.05
382	Irving Fryar	.05
383	Dermontti Dawson	.05
384	Eric Davis	.05
385	Natrone Means	.10
386	Jason Sehorn	.05
387	Michael McCrary	.05
388	Corwin Brown	.05
389	Kevin Glover	.05
390	Jerris McPhail	.05
391	Bobby Taylor	.05
392	Tony McGee	.05
393	Curtis Conway	.05
394	Napoleon Kaufman	.05
395	Brian Blades	.05
396	Richard Dent	.05
397	Dave Brown	.05
398	Stan Humphries	.05
399	Stevon Moore	.05
400	Brett Favre	2.00
401	Jerome Bettis	.10
402	Darrin Smith	.05
403	Chris Penn	.05
404	Rob Moore	.05
405	Michael Barrow	.05
406	Tony Brackens	.05
407	Wayne Martin	.05
408	Warren Moon	.05
409	Jason Elam	.05
410	J.J. Birden	.05
411	Hugh Douglas	.05
412	Lamar Lathon	.05
413	John Kidd	.05
414	Bryce Paup	.05
415	Shawn Jefferson	.05
416	Leeland McElroy	.10
417	Elbert Shelley	.05
418	Jermaine Lewis	.05
419	Eric Moulds	.10
420	Michael Bates	.05
421	John Mangum	.05
422	Corey Sawyer	.05
423	Jim Schwantz	.05
424	Rod Smith	.05
425	Glyn Milburn	.05
426	Desmond Howard	.10
427	John Henry Mills	.05
428	Cary Blanchard	.05
429	Chris Hudson	.05
430	Tamarick Vanover	.10
431	Kirby Dar Dar	.05
432	David Palmer	.05
433	Dave Meggett	.05
434	Tyrone Hughes	.05
435	Amani Toomer	.10
436	Wayne Chrebet	.05
437	Carl Kidd	.05
438	Derrick Witherspoon	.05
439	Jahine Arnold	.05
440	Andre Coleman	.05
441	Jeff Wilkins	.05
442	Jay Bellamy	.05
443	Eddie Kennison	.50
444	Nilo Silvan	.05
445	Brian Mitchell	.05
446	Checklist	.05
447	Checklist	.05
448	Checklist	.05
449	Checklist	.05
450	Checklist	.05

1997 Fleer All-Pro

This 24-card set was inserted 1:36 retail packs. All-Pros from the previous season were commemorated.

		MT
Complete Set (24):		160.00
Common Player:		2.00
Minor Stars:		4.00
1	Troy Aikman	15.00
2	Larry Allen	2.00
3	Drew Bledsoe	15.00
4	Terrell Davis	18.00
5	Dermontti Dawson	2.00
6	John Elway	12.00
7	Brett Favre	30.00
8	Herman Moore	4.00
9	Jerry Rice	15.00
10	Barry Sanders	25.00
11	Shannon Sharpe	2.00
12	Erik Williams	2.00
13	Ashley Ambrose	2.00
14	Chad Brown	2.00
15	LeRoy Butler	2.00
16	Kevin Greene	2.00
17	Sam Mills	2.00
18	John Randle	2.00
19	Deion Sanders	8.00
20	Junior Seau	4.00
21	Bruce Smith	2.00
22	Alfred Williams	2.00
23	Darren Woodson	2.00
24	Bryant Young	2.00

1997 Fleer Crystal Silver

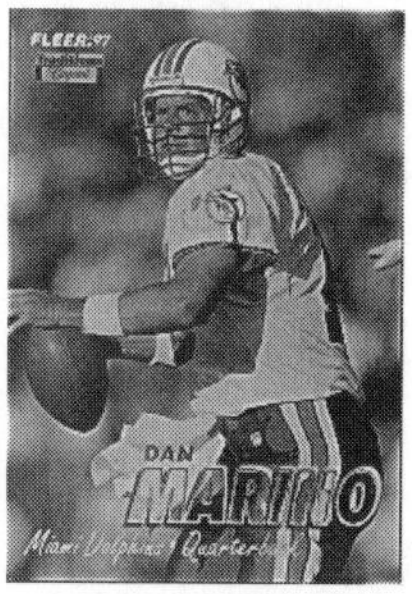

This set paralleled the 445 cards included in Fleer Football (minus five checklist cards) and was seeded one per pack. Each card was distinguished by a "Traditions Crystal" logo on one of the upper corners. This parallel also contained a glossy finish, whereas the base cards had a matte finish, and silver foil instead of the gold foil used on the base cards.

	MT
Complete Set (445):	160.00
Crystal Silver Cards:	2x-4x

1997 Fleer Decade of Excellence

Inserted 1:36 hobby packs, this 12-card set featured photography from 10 years prior. Ten percent of the cards were printed with holographic foil and were inserted 1:360 hobby packs.

		MT
Complete Set (12):		60.00
Common Player:		1.50
1	Marcus Allen	3.00
2	Cris Carter	3.00
3	John Elway	12.00
4	Irving Fryar	1.50
5	Darrell Green	1.50
6	Dan Marino	12.00
7	Jerry Rice	8.00
8	Bruce Smith	1.50
9	Herschel Walker	1.50
10	Reggie White	3.00
11	Rod Woodson	1.50
12	Steve Young	6.00

1997 Fleer Game Breakers

Inserted 1:2 retail packs, this 20-card set showcased players who have the ability to break a game open. A Game Breakers Supreme parallel was inserted 1:18 of all pack types.

		MT
Complete Set (20):		20.00
Common Player:		.30
Minor Stars:		.60
Supreme Cards:		2x-4x
1	Troy Aikman	2.50
2	Jerome Bettis	.60
3	Drew Bledsoe	2.50
4	Isaac Bruce	.75
5	Mark Brunell	2.50
6	Kerry Collins	2.00
7	Terrell Davis	2.50
8	Marshall Faulk	.30
9	Antonio Freeman	.60
10	Joey Galloway	1.00
11	Terry Glenn	.75
12	Desmond Howard	.30
13	Keyshawn Johnson	1.00
14	Eddie Kennison	1.00
15	Curtis Martin	2.50

16	Herman Moore	.30
17	Lawrence Phillips	.60
18	Barry Sanders	3.00
19	Shannon Sharpe	.30
20	Emmitt Smith	5.00

1997 Fleer Goudey

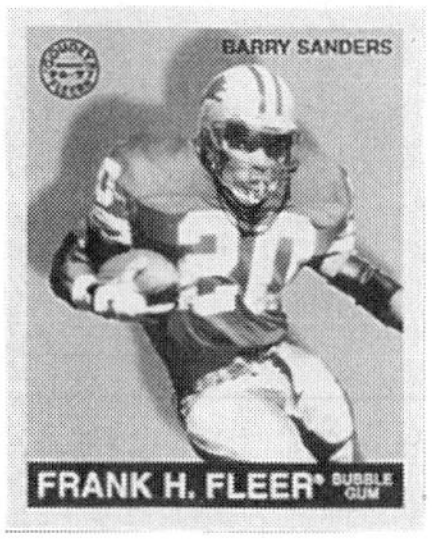

Goudey included 150 cards that adopted the old-time look of the Goudey brand from the 1930s. The cards measure 2-3/8" x 2-7/8", with player pictures appearing as illustrations. Backs include a player synopsis "old-time" text. Also included in the regular-issue set were cards of Chuck Bednarik and Y.A. Tittle, as well as two checklists and a History of Goudey card. Insert sets found in Goudey were Gridiron Greats (parallel set), Heads Up, Concrete Chuck Bednarik Says, Y.A.Tittle Says and Pigskin 2000.

		MT
Complete Set (150):		18.00
Common Player:		.05
Minor Stars:		.10
Pack (10):		1.50
Wax Box (36):		45.00
1	Michael Jackson	.05
2	Ray Lewis	.05
3	Vinny Testaverde	.05
4	Eric Turner	.05
5	Jim Kelly	.10
6	Bryce Paup	.05
7	Andre Reed	.05
8	Bruce Smith	.05
9	Thurman Thomas	.10
10	Jeff Blake	.10
11	Ki-Jana Carter	.10
12	Carl Pickens	.05
13	Darnay Scott	.05
14	Terrell Davis	1.25
15	John Elway	.75
16	Anthony Miller	.05
17	John Mobley	.05
18	Shannon Sharpe	.05
19	Chris Chandler	.05
20	Eddie George	1.50
21	Steve McNair	.50
22	Chris Sanders	.05
23	Quentin Coryatt	.05
24	Sean Dawkins	.05
25	Ken Dilger	.05
26	Marshall Faulk	.30
27	Jim Harbaugh	.05
28	Marvin Harrison	.75
29	Tony Brackens	.05
30	Mark Brunell	1.00
31	Kevin Hardy	.10
32	Keenan McCardell	.05
33	James Stewart	.05
34	Marcus Allen	.10
35	Steve Bono	.05
36	Dale Carter	.05
37	Neil Smith	.05
38	Derrick Thomas	.05
39	Tamarick Vanover	.10
40	Karim Abdul-Jabbar	.25
41	Dan Marino	2.00
42	O.J. McDuffie	.05
43	Stanley Pritchett	.05
44	Zach Thomas	.50
45	Drew Bledsoe	1.00
46	Ben Coates	.05
47	Terry Glenn	.25
48	Shawn Jefferson	.05
49	Curtis Martin	1.50
50	David Meggett	.05
51	Hugh Douglas	.05
52	Keyshawn Johnson	.75
53	Adrian Murrell	.05
54	Tim Brown	.05
55	Rickey Dudley	.05
56	Jeff Hostetler	.05
57	Napoleon Kaufman	.05
58	Chester McGlockton	.05
59	Jerome Bettis	.10
60	Andre Hastings	.05
61	Greg Lloyd	.05
62	Kordell Stewart	1.00
63	Yancey Thigpen	.05
64	Rod Woodson	.05
65	Andre Coleman	.05
66	Stan Humphries	.05
67	Tony Martin	.05
68	Leonard Russell	.05
69	Junior Seau	.05
70	Brian Blades	.05
71	Joey Galloway	.50
72	Chris Warren	.05
73	Larry Centers	.05
74	Leeland McElroy	.10
75	Simeon Rice	.10
76	Frank Sanders	.05
77	Eric Swann	.05
78	Jamal Anderson	.40
79	Bert Emanuel	.05
80	Terance Mathis	.05
81	Eric Metcalf	.05
82	Tim Biakabutuka	.40
83	Kerry Collins	.25
84	Kevin Greene	.05
85	Muhsin Muhammad	.10
86	Wesley Walls	.05
87	Curtis Conway	.05
88	Bryan Cox	.05
89	Walt Harris	.05
90	Erik Kramer	.05
91	Rashaan Salaam	.10
92	Troy Aikman	1.00
93	Michael Irvin	.10
94	Daryl Johnston	.05
95	Leon Lett	.05
96	Deion Sanders	.50
97	Emmitt Smith	2.00
98	Scott Mitchell	.05
99	Herman Moore	.10
100	Johnnie Morton	.05
101	Brett Perriman	.05
102	Barry Sanders	1.25
103	Edgar Bennett	.05
104	Robert Brooks	.05
105	Brett Favre	2.00
106	Antonio Freeman	.05
107	Keith Jackson	.05
108	Reggie White	.10
109	Cris Carter	.05
110	Warren Moon	.10
111	John Randle	.05
112	Jake Reed	.05
113	Robert Smith	.05
114	Jim Everett	.05
115	Michael Haynes	.05
116	Alex Molden	.05
117	Ray Zellars	.05
118	Chris Calloway	.05
119	Rodney Hampton	.05
120	Phillippi Sparks	.05
121	Amani Toomer	.10
122	Ty Detmer	.05
123	Jason Dunn	.05
124	Irving Fryar	.05
125	Chris T. Jones	.05
126	Ricky Watters	.10
127	Tony Banks	.25
128	Isaac Bruce	.25
129	Eddie Kennison	.20
130	Lawrence Phillips	.10
131	Merton Hanks	.05
132	Terry Kirby	.05
133	Ken Norton	.05
134	Jerry Rice	1.00
135	J.J. Stokes	.10
136	Steve Young	.75
137	Alvin Harper	.05
138	Jackie Harris	.05
139	Hardy Nickerson	.05
140	Errict Rhett	.20
141	Terry Allen	.05
142	Henry Ellard	.05
143	Gus Frerotte	.05
144	Brian Mitchell	.05
145	Michael Westbrook	.10
146	Chuck Bednarik	.10
147	Y.A. Tittle	.10
148	Checklist	.05
149	Checklist	.05
150	Checklist	.05

1997 Fleer Goudey Bednarik Says

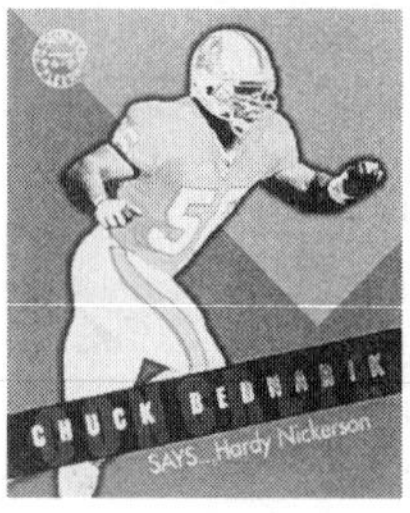

This insert highlighted 15 of the top defensive players in the league, with Bednarik's assessment of each player on the card back. Cards in this insert are identified by a large solid block pattern in the back featuring the team's colors, with a black strip near the bottom with the words "Concrete Chuck Bednarik" in it. These inserts were found every 60 hobby packs and every 72 retail packs.

		MT
Complete Set (15):		100.00
Common Player:		3.00
1	Kevin Greene	3.00
2	Ray Lewis	3.00
3	Greg Lloyd	3.00
4	Chester McGlockton	3.00
5	Hardy Nickerson	3.00
6	Bryce Paup	3.00
7	Simeon Rice	3.00
8	Deion Sanders	14.00
9	Junior Seau	3.00
10	Bruce Smith	3.00
11	Derrick Thomas	3.00
12	Zach Thomas	12.00
13	Eric Turner	3.00
14	Reggie White	10.00
15	Rod Woodson	3.00

1997 Fleer Goudey Gridiron Greats

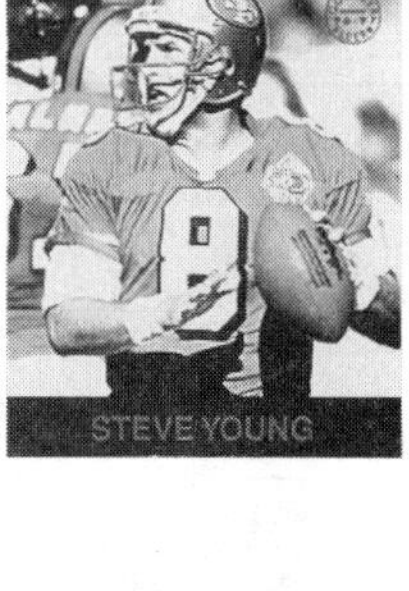

Gridiron Greats was a 147-card parallel set (150 minus the two checklists and one History of Goudey card) that was found at a rate of one per three packs in Goudey Football. Each card contains a solid black strip across the bottom with the player's name in red foil. Unlike the regular-issue cards, these are actual photos instead of illustrations.

	MT
Complete Set (147):	100.00
Gridiron Greats Cards:	3x-6x

1997 Fleer Goudey Heads Up

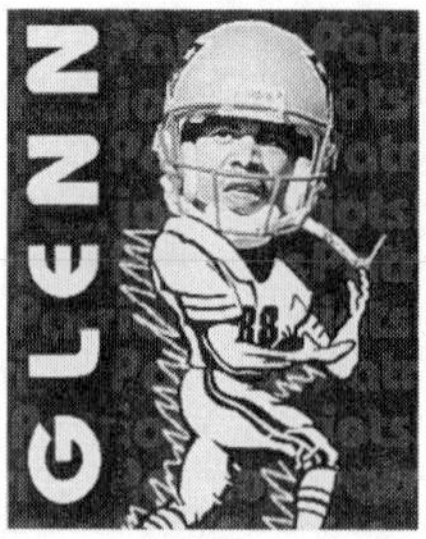

Heads Up contained 20 players in a cartoon format, with the player's head larger and in color, compared to the small black and white body. The player's last name runs up the left side in white letters. Heads Up cards were found in every 30 hobby packs and every 36 retail packs.

		MT
Complete Set (20):		150.00
Common Player:		3.00
1	Troy Aikman	15.00
2	Marcus Allen	3.00
3	Tim Biakabutuka	6.00
4	Robert Brooks	3.00
5	Isaac Bruce	6.00
6	Kerry Collins	6.00
7	Terrell Davis	18.00
8	Brett Favre	30.00
9	Terry Glenn	6.00
10	Rodney Hampton	3.00
11	Michael Irvin	6.00
12	Chris T. Jones	3.00
13	Carl Pickens	3.00
14	Barry Sanders	18.00
15	Kordell Stewart	15.00
16	Thurman Thomas	3.00
17	Tamarick Vanover	8.00
18	Chris Warren	3.00
19	Ricky Watters	3.00
20	Steve Young	10.00

1997 Fleer Goudey II

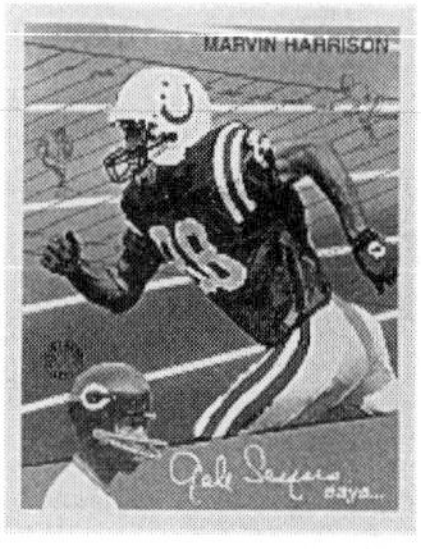

Goudey Series II is a 150-card set. It contians 145 player cards, all of which feature "Gale Sayers Says" on the backs. There are also two checklist cards and a three card Gale Sayers subset (1:9). The parallel sets are Gridiron Greats (1:3) and Goudey Greats (numbered to 150). Sayers has autographed 40 of each subset card and each card #40 of the Goudey Greats parallel set. The insert sets included Rookie Classics, Glory Days, Vintage Goudey, Big Time Backs and Million Dollar Moments.

		MT
Complete Set (150):		25.00
Common Player:		.05
Minor Stars:		.10
Gridiron Greats:		2x-4x
Goudey Greats Cards:		20x-40x
Goudey Greats Rookies:		10x-20x
Pack (8):		1.00
Wax Box (36):		35.00
1	Gale Sayers	1.25
2	Vinny Testaverde	.05
3	Jeff George	.10
4	Brett Favre	2.25
5	Eddie Kennison	.50
6	Ken Norton	.05
7	John Elway	.75
8	Troy Aikman	1.00
9	Steve McNair	.75
10	Kordell Stewart	1.00
11	Drew Bledsoe	1.00
12	Kerry Collins	.25
13	Dan Marino	2.00
14	Brad Johnson	.05
15	Todd Collins	.05
16	Ki-Jana Carter	.10
17	*Pat Barnes*	.50
18	Aeneas Williams	.05
19	Keyshawn Johnson	.20
20	Barry Sanders	1.25
21	*Tiki Barber*	1.00
22	Emmitt Smith	2.00
23	Kevin Hardy	.05
24	Mario Bates	.05
25	Ricky Watters	.10
26	Chris Canty	.05
27	Eddie George	1.50
28	Curtis Martin	1.00
29	Adrian Murrell	.10
30	Terrell Davis	1.00
31	Rashaan Salaam	.10
32	Marcus Allen	.10
33	Karim Abdul-Jabbar	.50
34	Thurman Thomas	.10
35	Marvin Harrison	.50
36	Jerome Bettis	.10
37	Larry Centers	.05
38	Stan Humphries	.05
39	Lawrence Phillips	.10
40	Gale Sayers	1.25
41	Henry Ellard	.05
42	Chris Warren	.05
43	Robert Brooks	.10
44	*Sedrick Shaw*	.50
45	Muhsin Muhammad	.05
46	Napoleon Kaufman	.20
47	*Reidel Anthony*	1.00
48	Jamal Anderson	.10
49	Scott Mitchell	.05
50	Mark Brunell	1.00
51	William Thomas	.05
52	Bryan Cox	.05
53	Carl Pickens	.10
54	Chris Spielman	.05
55	Junior Seau	.10
56	Hardy Nickerson	.05
57	*Dwayne Rudd*	.10
58	*Peter Boulware*	.10
59	*Jim Druckenmiller*	2.00
60	Michael Westbrook	.10
61	*Shawn Springs*	.25
62	Zach Thomas	.10
63	*David LaFleur*	.50
64	*Darrell Russell*	.10
65	*Jake Plummer*	1.50
66	Tim Biakabutuka	.10
67	Tyrone Wheatley	.05
68	Elvis Grbac	.05
69	Antonio Freeman	.30
70	Wayne Chrebet	.05
71	*Walter Jones*	.10
72	Marshall Faulk	.10
73	Jason Dunn	.05
74	Darnay Scott	.05
75	Errict Rhett	.10
76	*Orlando Pace*	.25
77	Natrone Means	.10
78	Bruce Smith	.05
79	Jamie Sharper	.05
80	Jerry Rice	1.00
81	Tim Brown	.10
82	Brian Mitchell	.05
83	Andre Reed	.05
84	Herman Moore	.10
85	Rob Moore	.05
86	*Rae Carruth*	.75
87	Bert Emanuel	.05
88	Michael Irvin	.10
89	Mark Chmura	.10
90	Tony Brackens	.05
91	Kevin Greene	.05
92	Reggie White	.10
93	Derrick Thomas	.05
94	*Troy Davis*	.25
95	Greg Lloyd	.05
96	Cortez Kennedy	.05
97	Simeon Rice	.05
98	Terrell Owens	.50
99	Hugh Douglas	.05
100	Terry Glenn	.25
101	Jim Harbaugh	.05
102	Shannon Sharpe	.05
103	*Joey Kent*	.30
104	Jeff Blake	.10
105	Terry Allen	.05
106	Cris Carter	.05
107	Amani Toomer	.05
108	Derrick Alexander	.05
109	*Darnell Autry*	.50
110	Irving Fryar	.05
111	*Bryant Westbrook*	.10
112	Tony Banks	.50
113	Michael Booker	.05
114	*Yatil Green*	.40
115	*James Farrior*	.10
116	*Warrick Dunn*	1.50
117	Greg Hill	.05
118	Tony Martin	.05
119	Chris Sanders	.05
120	Charles Johnson	.05
121	John Mobley	.05
122	Keenan McCardell	.05
123	Willie McGinest	.05
124	O.J. McDuffie	.05
125	Deion Sanders	.50
126	Curtis Conway	.05
127	Desmond Howard	.05
128	Johnnie Morton	.05
129	*Ike Hilliard*	1.00
130	Gus Frerotte	.05
131	*Tom Knight*	.10
132	Sean Dawkins	.05
133	Isaac Bruce	.10
134	Wesley Walls	.05
135	*Danny Wuerffel*	1.00
136	*Tony Gonzalez*	.50
137	Ben Coates	.05
138	Joey Galloway	.10
139	Michael Jackson	.05
140	Steve Young	.10
141	*Corey Dillon*	2.00
142	Jake Reed	.05
143	Edgar Bennett	.05
144	Ty Detmer	.05
145	Darrell Green	.05
146	*Antowain Smith*	1.50
147	Mike Alstott	.10
148	Checklist	.05
149	Checklist	.05
150	Gale Sayers (Commemorative Card)	1.25

1997 Fleer Goudey II Big Time Backs

This 10-card insert features top quarterbacks and running backs on a die-cut, embossed card designed as a clipboard. The cards were inserted 1:72.

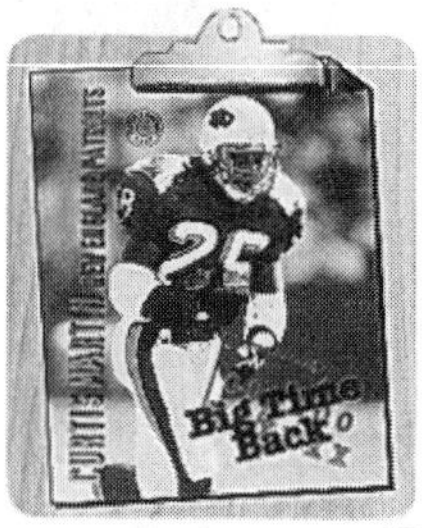

		MT
Complete Set (10):		150.00
Common Player:		3.00
1	Karim Abdul-Jabbar	10.00
2	Marcus Allen	3.00
3	Jerome Bettis	3.00
4	Terrell Davis	15.00
5	Brett Favre	30.00
6	Eddie George	20.00
7	Dan Marino	25.00
8	Curtis Martin	15.00
9	Barry Sanders	30.00
10	Emmitt Smith	25.00

1997 Fleer Goudey II Glory Days

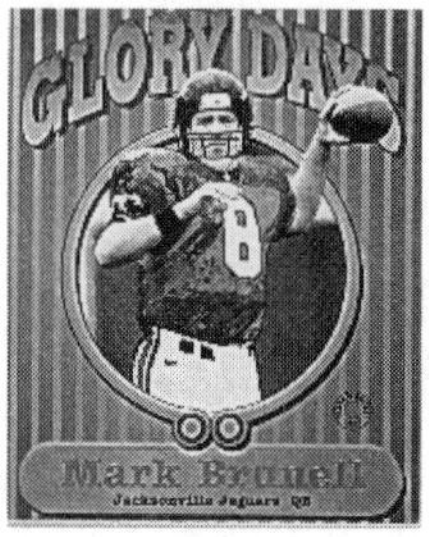

This 18-card insert features top players on an embossed card. Glory Days was inserted once per 18 retail packs.

		MT
Complete Set (15):		70.00
Common Player:		2.00
1	Troy Aikman	8.00
2	Isaac Bruce	2.00
3	Mark Brunell	8.00
4	Cris Carter	2.00
5	Joey Galloway	4.00
6	Terry Glenn	6.00
7	Marvin Harrison	4.00
8	Dan Marino	15.00
9	Deion Sanders	4.00
10	Shannon Sharpe	2.00
11	Emmitt Smith	15.00
12	Bruce Smith	2.00
13	Kordell Stewart	8.00
14	Ricky Watters	2.00
15	Reggie White	2.00

1997 Fleer Goudey II Rookie Classics

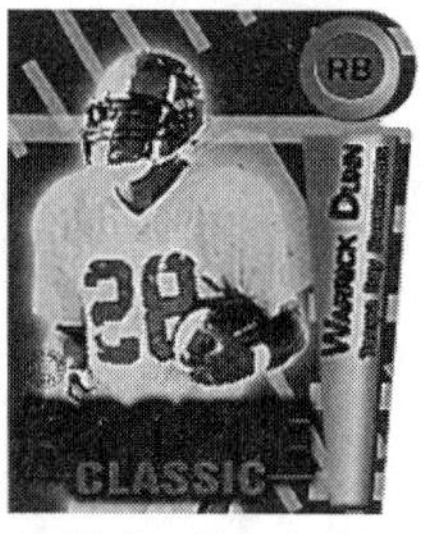

This 20-card insert features top 1997 rookies on a die-cut card. The first down marker is die-cut on the right side of the card. This set was inserted 1:3.

		MT
Complete Set (20):		18.00
Common Player:		.25
1	Reidel Anthony	1.50
2	Pat Barnes	.50
3	Peter Boulware	.25
4	Rae Carruth	.75
5	Troy Davis	.50
6	Corey Dillon	2.50
7	Jim Druckenmiller	2.00
8	Warrick Dunn	3.00
9	Tony Gonzalez	.75
10	Yatil Green	.50
11	Ike Hilliard	1.00
12	Walter Jones	.25
13	David LaFleur	.75
14	Orlando Pace	.50
15	Jake Plummer	5.00
16	Darrell Russell	.25
17	Antowain Smith	2.00
18	Shawn Springs	.25
19	Bryant Westbrook	.25
20	Danny Wuerffel	1.00

1997 Fleer Goudey II Vintage Goudey

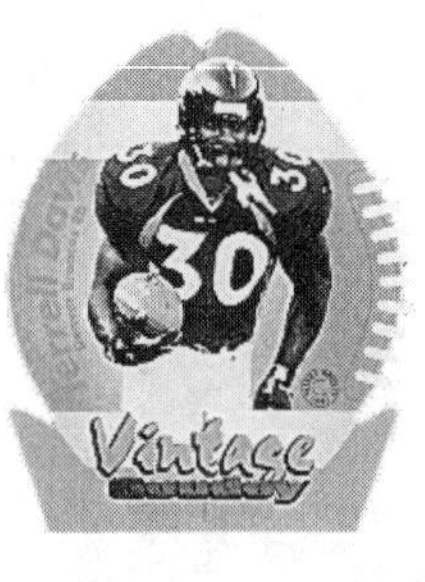

This 15-card insert features players who are throwbacks to old-time football. The players are featured on cards die-cut into a football shape. This set also contained redemption cards for an original 1933 Sport Kings Football card of Red Grange, Jim Thorpe and Knute Rockne. This set was inserted 1:36 in hobby packs.

		MT
Complete Set (15):		120.00
Common Player:		4.00
1	Karim Abdul-Jabbar	8.00
2	Kerry Collins	8.00
3	Terrell Davis	12.00
4	John Elway	8.00
5	Brett Favre	25.00
6	Eddie George	18.00
7	Terry Glenn	8.00
8	Keyshawn Johnson	4.00
9	Curtis Martin	12.00
10	Herman Moore	4.00
11	Jerry Rice	12.00
12	Barry Sanders	20.00
13	Deion Sanders	6.00
14	Zach Thomas	4.00
15	Steve Young	8.00

1997 Fleer Goudey Pigskin 2000

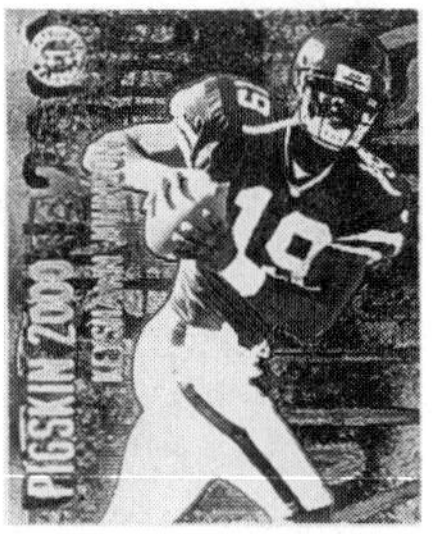

Pigskin 2000 was a 15-card foil-etched insert that highlighted some of the NFL's elite. The insert name and player's name are included in gold foil along the left side, with the Fleer Goudey logo in the top left corner. Pigskin 2000 cards are found every 360 hobby packs.

		MT
Complete Set (15):		400.00
Common Player:		10.00
1	Karim Abdul-Jabbar	40.00
2	Jeff Blake	10.00
3	Drew Bledsoe	40.00
4	Robert Brooks	10.00
5	Terrell Davis	40.00
6	Marshall Faulk	20.00
7	Joey Galloway	10.00
8	Eddie George	40.00
9	Terry Glenn	20.00
10	Keyshawn Johnson	20.00
11	Chris T. Jones	10.00
12	Curtis Martin	40.00
13	Steve McNair	25.00
14	Lawrence Phillips	10.00
15	Kordell Stewart	30.00

1997 Fleer Goudey Tittle Says

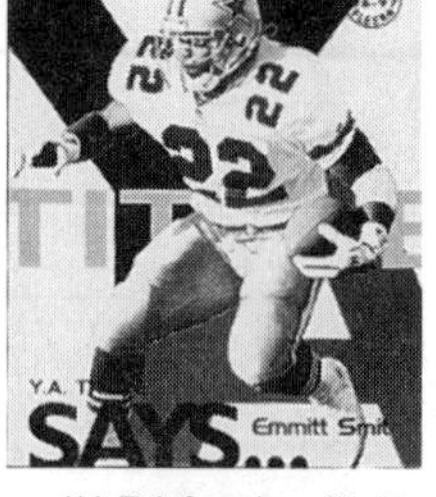

Y.A. Tittle Says shows 20 of the top offensive stars, with Tittle providing insight on each card back. Each card has a color photo of the player over a color background with the insert's name scattered across it. They

were found every 72 hobby and every 85 retail packs.

		MT
Complete Set (20):		225.00
Common Player:		5.00
1	Karim Abdul-Jabbar	8.00
2	Jerome Bettis	5.00
3	Tim Brown	5.00
4	Isaac Bruce	8.00
5	Cris Carter	5.00
6	Curtis Conway	5.00
7	John Elway	12.00
8	Marshall Faulk	10.00
9	Brett Favre	30.00
10	Joey Galloway	5.00
11	Eddie George	25.00
12	Keyshawn Johnson	12.00
13	Dan Marino	30.00
14	Curtis Martin	25.00
15	Herman Moore	5.00
16	Jerry Rice	15.00
17	Barry Sanders	15.00
18	Emmitt Smith	30.00
19	Thurman Thomas	5.00
20	Ricky Watters	5.00

1997 Fleer Million Dollar Moments

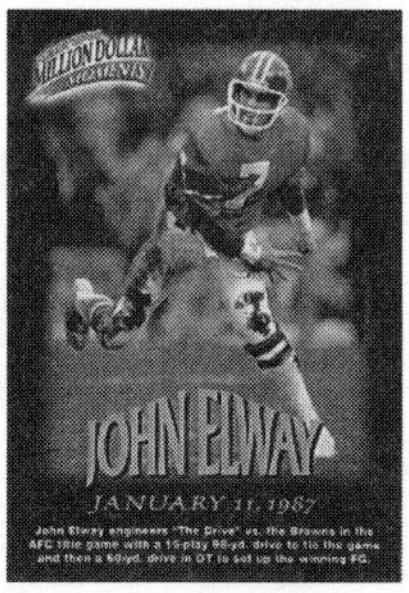

The 50-card set was part of a season-long multi-sport promotion which was available in all 1997 packs of Fleer, Fleer Ultra and Flair Showcase football products released after June, 1997. Each pack contained one of 50 different Million Dollar Moments cards. The fronts of the cards had the Million Dollar Moments logo in the upper left. The player's name, date of his highlight and highlight are included at the bottom front. The backs include the contest details. Cards numbered 1-45 are common, while 46-50 are difficult to find. Those who collected cards 1-45 plus any one of 46-49 won up to a $1,000 shopping spree. The grand prize of $1 million was awarded to the collector of all 50 cards. To reward collectors who complete the "common" 45-card set, Fleer offered the opportunity to redeem the 45-card set (with $5.99 for shipping) for a complete parallel 50-card set.

		MT
Complete Set (45):		5.00
Common Player:		.05
Minor Stars:		.10
1	Checklist	.05
2	Troy Aikman	.50
3	Sid Luckman	.10
4	Barry Sanders	.50
5	Tom Fears	.05
6	Reggie White	.10
7	Lou Groza	.05
8	John Elway	.35
9	Raymond Berry	.05
10	Marcus Allen	.10
11	Paul Hornung	.10
12	Herschel Walker	.05
13	Norm Van Brocklin	.05
14	Bruce Smith	.05
15	Billy Wade	.05
16	Andre Reed	.05
17	Gale Sayers	.10
18	Terrell Davis	.50
19	Jim Bakken	.05
20	Marshall Faulk	.10
21	Tom Dempsey	.05
22	Dan Marino	1.00
23	Garo Yepremian	.05
24	Jerry Rice	.50
25	Herman Edwards	.05
26	Derrick Thomas	.05
27	Kellen Winslow	.05
28	Steve Young	.35
29	Tony Dorsett	.10
30	Desmond Howard	.05
31	Roger Craig	.05
32	Drew Bledsoe	.50
33	Doug Williams	.05
34	Jerome Bettis	.10
35	Bobby Layne	.05
36	Junior Seau	.10
37	Roman Gabriel	.05
38	Cris Carter	.10
39	Drew Pearson	.05
40	Warren Moon	.05
41	Wesley Walker	.05
42	Ricky Watters	.10
43	Carl Eller	.05
44	Kordell Stewart	.50
45	John Mackey	.05
46	Thurman Thomas	
47	Ken Stabler	
48	Emmitt Smith	
49	Jim Brown	
50	Eddie George	

1997 Fleer Prospects

The 10-card set was inserted 1:6 packs. It featured the top prospects from the 1997 NFL Draft.

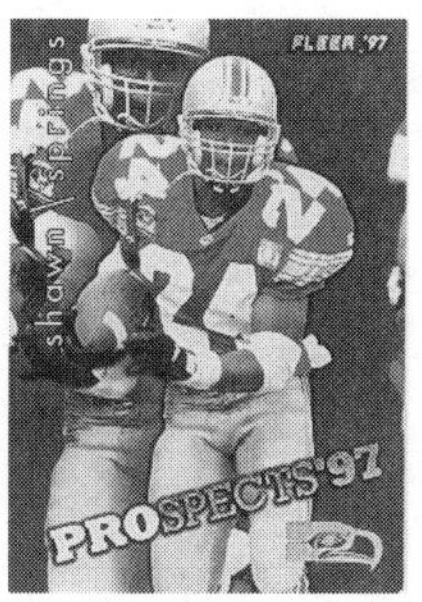

		MT
Complete Set (10):		20.00
Common Player:		.75
1	Peter Boulware	.75
2	Rae Carruth	3.00
3	Jim Druckenmiller	5.00
4	Warrick Dunn	7.00
5	Tony Gonzalez	1.50
6	Yatil Green	4.00
7	Ike Hilliard	4.00
8	Orlando Pace	1.50
9	Darrell Russell	.75
10	Shawn Springs	1.50

1997 Fleer Rookie Sensations

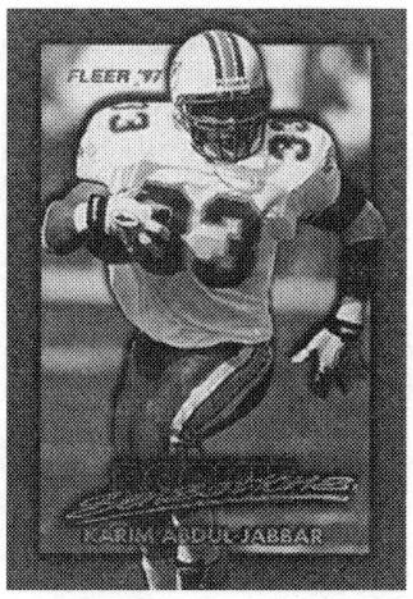

Inserted 1:4 packs, the 20-card set focused on rookies who had positive impacts on their team in 1996.

		MT
Complete Set (20):		25.00
Common Player:		.50
Minor Stars:		1.00
1	Karim Abdul-Jabbar	3.00
2	Mike Alstott	1.00
3	Tony Banks	2.00
4	Tony Brackens	.50
5	Rickey Dudley	.50
6	Bobby Engram	.50
7	Eddie George	7.00
8	Terry Glenn	4.00
9	Kevin Hardy	.50
10	Marvin Harrison	2.00
11	Keyshawn Johnson	2.00
12	Eddie Kennison	2.00
13	Jermaine Lewis	.50
14	Ray Lewis	.50
15	John Mobley	.50
16	Eric Moulds	.50
17	Jonathan Ogden	.50
18	Lawrence Phillips	1.00
19	Simeon Rice	.50
20	Zach Thomas	1.50

1997 Fleer Thrill Seekers

Inserted 1:288 packs, the 12-card set looks at players known for making the big play.

		MT
Complete Set (12):		500.00
Common Player:		15.00
1	Karim Abdul-Jabbar	40.00
2	Jerome Bettis	15.00
3	Terrell Davis	50.00
4	John Elway	35.00
5	Brett Favre	90.00
6	Eddie George	65.00
7	Terry Glenn	20.00
8	Keyshawn Johnson	30.00
9	Dan Marino	80.00
10	Curtis Martin	50.00
11	Deion Sanders	20.00
12	Emmitt Smith	80.00

1997 Fleer Tiffany Blue

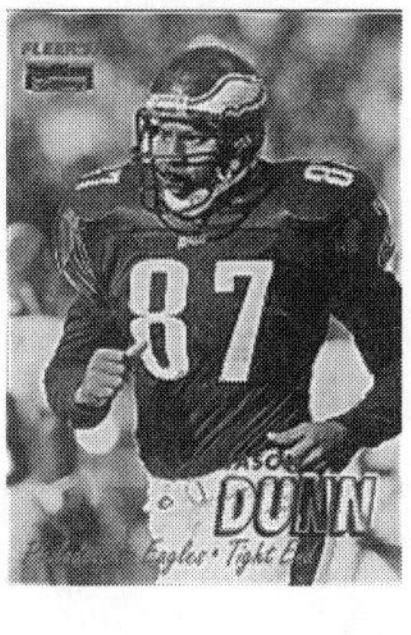

This parallel reprinted 445 cards from Fleer Football and was seeded one per 20 packs. The fronts featured a glossy silver finish versus the matte finish on the base cards, and featured blue foil stamping on the front versus gold foil on the base cards. Card fronts also had a "Traditions Tiffany" logo in either top corner.

		MT
Complete Set (445):		1200.
Tiffany Blue Cards:		15x-30x

1998 Fleer

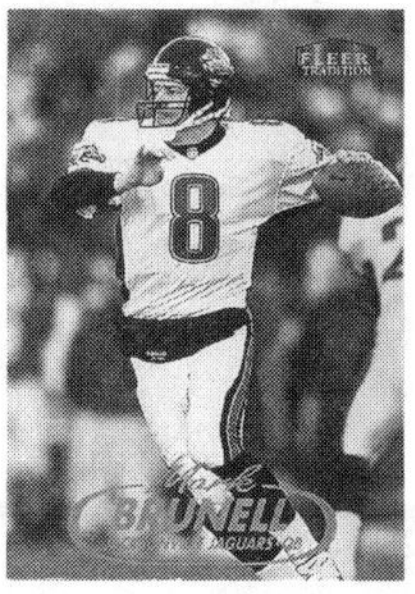

Fleer scrapped its matte finish and produced Tradtion in 1998. This 250-card set, including 247 player cards and three checklists, is printed on a borderless design with the player's name, position and team printed across the bottom in gold foil. Tradition arrived with a parallel set called Heritage, which was numbered to 125 sets, and four different inserts, including Big Numbers, Rookie Sensations, Red Zone Rockers and Playmakers Theatre.

		MT
Complete Set (250):		45.00
Common Player:		.15
Minor Stars:		.30
Heritage Cards:		30x-60x
Heritage Rookies:		10x-20x
Production 125 Sets		
Pack (10):		1.75
Wax Box (36):		55.00
1	Brett Favre	3.00
2	Barry Sanders	2.50
3	John Elway	1.50
4	Emmitt Smith	2.50
5	Dan Marino	2.50
6	Eddie George	1.50
7	Jerry Rice	1.50
8	Jake Plummer	1.50
9	Joey Galloway	.50
10	Mike Alstott	.50
11	Brian Mitchell	.15
12	Keyshawn Johnson	.30
13	Jerald Moore	.15
14	Randal Hill	.15
15	Byron Hanspard	.15
16	Jeff George	.30
17	Terry Glenn	.30
18	Jerome Bettis	.30
19	Curtis Conway	.30
20	Fred Lane	.30
21	Isaac Bruce	.30
22	Tiki Barber	.30
23	Bobby Hoying	.15
24	Marcus Allen	.30
25	Dana Stubblefield	.15
26	Peter Boulware	.15
27	John Randle	.15
28	Jason Sehorn	.15
29	Rod Smith	.30
30	Michael Sinclair	.15
31	Marshall Faulk	.30
32	Karl Williams	.15
33	Kordell Stewart	1.50
34	Corey Dillon	1.00
35	Bryant Young	.15
36	Charlie Garner	.15
37	Andre Reed	.15
38	Ray Buchanan	.15
39	Brett Perriman	.15
40	Leon Lett	.15
41	Keenan McCardell	.15
42	Eric Swann	.15
43	Leslie Shepherd	.15
44	Curtis Martin	1.00
45	Andre Rison	.30
46	Keith Lyle	.15
47	Rae Carruth	.15
48	William Henderson	.15
49	Sean Dawkins	.15
50	Terrell Davis	1.50
51	Tim Brown	.30
52	Willie McGinest	.15
53	Jermaine Lewis	.15
54	Ricky Watters	.30
55	Freddie Jones	.15
56	Robert Smith	.30
57	Reidel Anthony	.15
58	James Stewart	.15
59	Earl Holmes	.15
60	Dale Carter	.15
61	Michael Irvin	.30
62	Jason Taylor	.15
63	Eric Metcalf	.15
64	LeRoy Butler	.15
65	Jamal Anderson	.30
66	Jamie Asher	.15
67	Chris Sanders	.15
68	Warren Sapp	.15
69	Ray Zellars	.15
70	Carl Pickens	.30
71	Garrison Hearst	.30
72	Eddie Kennison	.30
73	John Mobley	.15
74	Rob Johnson	.30
75	William Thomas	.15
76	Drew Bledsoe	1.50
77	Michael Barrow	.15
78	Jim Harbaugh	.30
79	Terry McDaniel	.15
80	Johnnie Morton	.15
81	Danny Kanell	.15
82	Larry Centers	.15
83	Courtney Hawkins	.15
84	Tony Brackens	.15
85	Tony Gonzalez	.15
86	Aaron Glenn	.15
87	Cris Carter	.30
88	Chuck Smith	.15
89	Tamarick Vanover	.15
90	Karim Abdul-Jabbar	.30
91	Bryant Westbrook	.15
92	Mike Pritchard	.15
93	Darren Woodson	.15
94	Wesley Walls	.15
95	Tony Banks	.30
96	Michael Westbrook	.15
97	Shannon Sharpe	.30
98	Jeff Blake	.30
99	Terrell Owens	.30
100	Warrick Dunn	1.50
101	Levon Kirkland	.15
102	Frank Wycheck	.15
103	Gus Frerotte	.15
104	Simeon Rice	.15
105	Shawn Jefferson	.15
106	Irving Fryar	.15
107	Michael McCrary	.15
108	Robert Brooks	.15
109	Chris Chandler	.15
110	Junior Seau	.30
111	O.J. McDuffie	.15
112	Glenn Foley	.15
113	Darryl Williams	.15
114	Elvis Grbac	.15
115	Napoleon Kaufman	.50
116	Anthony Miller	.15
117	Troy Davis	.15
118	Charles Way	.15
119	Scott Mitchell	.15
120	Ken Harvey	.15
121	Tyrone Hughes	.15
122	Mark Brunell	1.25
123	David Palmer	.15
124	Rob Moore	.15
125	Kerry Collins	.75
126	Will Blackwell	.15
127	Ray Crockett	.15
128	Leslie O'Neal	.15
129	Antowain Smith	.75
130	Carlester Crumpler	.15
131	Michael Jackson	.15
132	Trent Dilfer	.30
133	Dan Williams	.15
134	Dorsey Levens	.30
135	Ty Law	.15
136	Rickey Dudley	.15
137	Jessie Tuggle	.15
138	Darrien Gordon	.15
139	Kevin Turner	.15
140	Willie Davis	.15
141	Zach Thomas	.15
142	Tony McGee	.15
143	Dexter Coakley	.15
144	Troy Brown	.15
145	Leeland McElroy	.15
146	Michael Strahan	.15
147	Ken Dilger	.15
148	Bryce Paup	.15
149	Herman Moore	.30
150	Reggie White	.30
151	DeWayne Washington	.15
152	Natrone Means	.30
153	Ben Coates	.15
154	Bert Emanuel	.15
155	Steve Young	1.00
156	Jimmy Smith	.15
157	Darrell Green	.15
158	Troy Aikman	1.50
159	Greg Hill	.15
160	Raymont Harris	.15
161	Troy Drayton	.15
162	Stevon Moore	.15
163	Warren Moon	.30
164	Wayne Martin	.15
165	Jason Gildon	.15
166	Chris Calloway	.15
167	Aeneas Williams	.15
168	Michael Bates	.15
169	Hugh Douglas	.15
170	Brad Johnson	.30
171	Bruce Smith	.15
172	Neil Smith	.15
173	James McKnight	.15
174	Robert Porcher	.15
175	Merton Hanks	.15
176	Ki-Jana Carter	.15
177	Mo Lewis	.15
178	Chester McGlockton	.15
179	Zack Crockett	.15
180	Derrick Thomas	.15
181	J.J. Stokes	.15
182	Derrick Rodgers	.15
183	Daryl Johnston	.15
184	Chris Penn	.15
185	Steve Atwater	.15
186	Amp Lee	.15
187	Frank Sanders	.15
188	Chris Slade	.15
189	Mark Chmura	.30
190	Kimble Anders	.15
191	Charles Johnson	.15
192	William Floyd	.15
193	Jay Graham	.15
194	Hardy Nickerson	.15
195	Terry Allen	.15
196	James Jett	.15
197	Jessie Armstead	.15
198	Yancey Thigpen	.15
199	Terance Mathis	.15
200	Steve McNair	.75
201	Wayne Chrebet	.15
202	Jamir Miller	.15
203	Duce Staley	.15
204	Deion Sanders	.75
205	Carnell Lake	.15
206	Ed McCaffrey	.15
207	Shawn Springs	.15
208	Tony Martin	.15
209	Jerris McPhail	.15
210	Darnay Scott	.15
211	Jake Reed	.15
212	Adrian Murrell	.30
213	Quinn Early	.15
214	Marvin Harrison	.30
215	Ryan McNeil	.15
216	Derrick Alexander	.15
217	Ray Lewis	.15
218	Antonio Freeman	.30
219	Dwayne Rudd	.15
220	Muhsin Muhammad	.15
221	Kevin Hardy	.15
222	Andre Hastings	.15
223	*John Avery*	2.00
224	*Keith Brooking*	1.00
225	*Kevin Dyson*	1.50
226	*Robert Edwards*	2.50
227	*Greg Ellis*	.15
228	*Curtis Enis*	3.00
229	*Terry Fair*	1.00
230	*Ahman Green*	2.00
231	*Jacquez Green*	2.00
232	*Brian Griese*	4.00
233	*Skip Hicks*	2.00
234	*Ryan Leaf*	4.00
235	*Peyton Manning*	10.00
236	*R.W. McQuarters*	.15
237	*Randy Moss*	10.00
238	*Marcus Nash*	2.00
239	*Anthony Simmons*	.50
240	*Brian Simmons*	1.00
241	*Takeo Spikes*	1.00
242	*Duane Starks*	.15
243	*Fred Taylor*	5.00
244	*Andre Wadsworth*	1.00
245	*Shaun Williams*	.15
246	*Grant Wistrom*	1.00
247	*Charles Woodson*	2.50
248	Checklist	.15
249	Checklist	.15
250	Checklist	.15

1998 Fleer Big Numbers

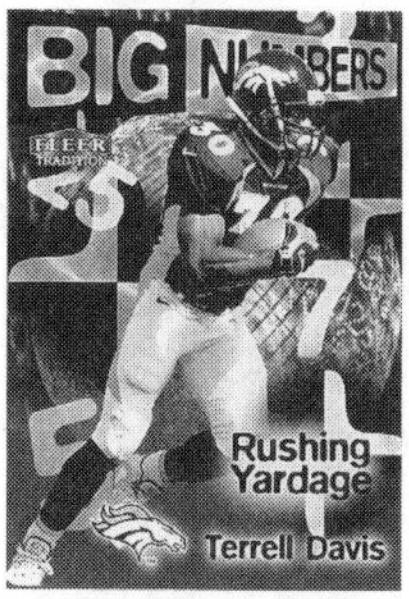

Big Numbers was a nine-card interactive set featuring top players at each skill position, with nine total players each featured on 11 different versions (0-9 and a wild card). The goal was to collect four cards, whereby the overprinted numbers, when combined, make out the players total yards through all games of Dec. 1, 1998. Winners were eligible to enter a contest for a chance to win a trip to the 2000 Pro Bowl. Big Numbers inserts were seeded one per four packs.

		MT
Common Player:		.25
BN1	Tim Brown	.25
BN2	Cris Carter	.25
BN3	Terrell Davis	1.00
BN4	John Elway	1.00
BN5	Brett Favre	2.00
BN6	Eddie George	1.00
BN7	Dorsey Levens	.50
BN8	Herman Moore	.50
BN9	Steve Young	.75

1998 Fleer Brilliants

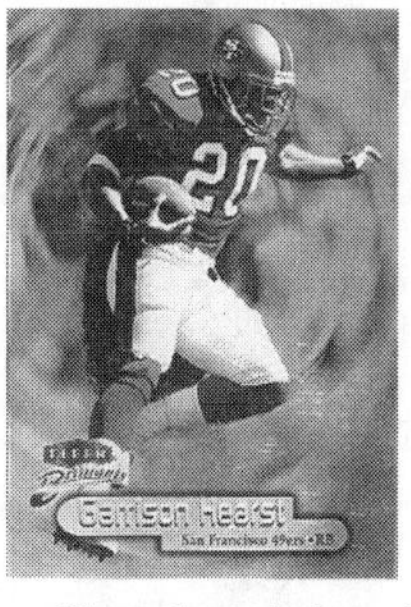

This was the premier issue of Brilliants by Fleer. The 150-card set is made up of 100 veterans and 50 rookies (inserted 1:2 packs). The product also included three parallel sets. The easiest being the Brilliant Blues with veterans found 1:3 packs and the rookies 1:6. Each single from this series has a blue background with the letter "B" prefix on the card number. The Brilliant Golds have a sparkling gold background on super bright mirror foil and the letter "G" prefix on the card number. Each single is sequentially numbered to 99. The rarest parallel is the 24-Karat Gold set. Each single has a sparkling gold background on rainbow holographic reflective mirror foil with an actual 24-kt. gold logo. Each single is sequentially numbered to 24.

		MT
Complete Set (150):		200.00
Common Player:		.15
Minor Stars:		.30
Common Rookie:		3.00
Inserted 1:2		
Blue Veterans:		2x-3x
Inserted 1:3		
Blue Rookies:		1.2x
Inserted 1:6		
Brilliant Gold Cards:		20x-40x
Brilliant Gold Rookies:		3x-5x
Production 99 Sets		
24-Karat Gold Cards:		40x-80x
24-Karat Gold Rookies:		5x-10x
Production 24 Sets		
Pack (5):		5.00
Wax Box (24):		100.00
1	John Elway	3.00
2	Curtis Conway	.30
3	Danny Wuerffel	.15
4	Emmitt Smith	4.50
5	Marvin Harrison	.30
6	Antowain Smith	.75
7	James Stewart	.15
8	Junior Seau	.30
9	Herman Moore	.50
10	Drew Bledsoe	2.00
11	Rae Carruth	.15
12	Trent Dilfer	.30
13	Derrick Alexander	.15
14	Ike Hilliard	.15
15	Bruce Smith	.15
16	Warren Moon	.30
17	Jermaine Lewis	.15
18	Mike Alstott	.50
19	Robert Brooks	.15
20	Jerome Bettis	.50
21	Brett Favre	6.00
22	Garrison Hearst	.50
23	Neil O'Donnell	.15
24	Joey Galloway	.50
25	Barry Sanders	6.00
26	Donnell Bennett	.15
27	Jamal Anderson	.75
28	Isaac Bruce	.30
29	Chris Chandler	.30
30	Kordell Stewart	2.00
31	Corey Dillon	1.75
32	Troy Aikman	3.00
33	Frank Sanders	.15
34	Cris Carter	.50
35	Greg Hill	.15
36	Tony Martin	.15
37	Shannon Sharpe	.30
38	Wayne Chrebet	.30
39	Trent Green	.30
40	Warrick Dunn	2.00
41	Michael Irvin	.30
42	Eddie George	2.00
43	Carl Pickens	.30
44	Wesley Walls	.15
45	Steve McNair	.75
46	Bert Emanuel	.15
47	Terry Glenn	.30
48	Elvis Grbac	.15
49	Charles Way	.15
50	Steve Young	1.75
51	Deion Sanders	.75
52	Keyshawn Johnson	.50
53	Kerry Collins	.30
54	O.J. McDuffie	.15
55	Ricky Watters	.30
56	Scott Mitchell	.15
57	Antonio Freeman	.50
58	Jake Plummer	2.00
59	Andre Reed	.15
60	Jerry Rice	3.00
61	Dorsey Levens	.50
62	Eddie Kennison	.30
63	Marshall Faulk	.50
64	Michael Jackson	.15
65	Karim Abdul-Jabbar	.30
66	Andre Rison	.15
67	Glenn Foley	.30
68	Jake Reed	.15
69	Tony Banks	.30
70	Dan Marino	4.50
71	Bryan Still	.15
72	Tim Brown	.30
73	Charles Johnson	.30
74	Jeff George	.30
75	Jimmy Smith	.30
76	Ben Coates	.30
77	Rob Moore	.15
78	Johnnie Morton	.15
79	Peter Boulware	.15
80	Curtis Martin	.75
81	James McKnight	.15
82	Danny Kanell	.15
83	Brad Johnson	.30
84	Amani Toomer	.15
85	Terry Allen	.30
86	Rod Smith	.30
87	Keenan McCardell	.30
88	Leslie Shepherd	.15
89	Irving Fryar	.15
90	Terrell Davis	4.50
91	Robert Smith	.50
92	Duce Staley	.15
93	Rickey Dudley	.15
94	Bobby Hoying	.15
95	Terrell Owens	.75
96	Fred Lane	.30
97	Natrone Means	.30
98	Yancey Thigpen	.15
99	Reggie White	.50
100	Mark Brunell	2.00
101	*Ahman Green*	10.00
102	*Skip Hicks*	5.00
103	*Hines Ward*	5.00
104	*Marcus Nash*	6.00
105	*Terry Hardy*	3.00
106	*Patrick Johnson*	4.00
107	*Tremayne Stephens*	3.00
108	*Joe Jurevicius*	4.00
109	*Moses Moreno*	4.00
110	*Charles Woodson*	10.00
111	*Kevin Dyson*	6.00
112	*Alvis Whitted*	3.00
113	*Michael Pittman*	3.00
114	*Stephen Alexander*	4.00
115	*Tavian Banks*	6.00
116	*John Avery*	6.00
117	*Keith Brooking*	3.00
118	*Jerome Pathon*	5.00
119	*Terry Fair*	4.00
120	*Peyton Manning*	30.00
121	*R.W. McQuarters*	4.00
122	*Charlie Batch*	10.00
123	*Jonathan Quinn*	5.00
124	*Chris Fuamatu-Ma'afala*	5.00
125	*Jacquez Green*	6.00
126	*Germane Crowell*	8.00
127	*Oronde Gadsden*	5.00
128	*Koy Detmer*	4.00

129	*Robert Holcombe*	8.00
130	*Curtis Enis*	3.00
131	*Brian Griese*	12.00
132	*Tony Simmons*	5.00
133	*Vonnie Holliday*	4.00
134	*Alonzo Mayes*	3.00
135	*Jon Ritchie*	4.00
136	*Robert Edwards*	12.00
137	*Mike Vanderjagt*	3.00
138	*Jonathon Linton*	3.00
139	*Fred Taylor*	15.00
140	*Randy Moss*	30.00
141	*Rod Rutledge*	3.00
142	*Andre Wadsworth*	4.00
143	*Rashaan Shehee*	4.00
144	*Shaun Williams*	3.00
145	*Mikhael Ricks*	5.00
146	*Wade Richey*	3.00
147	*Carlos King*	3.00
148	*Tim Dwight*	6.00
149	*Scott Frost*	4.00
150	*Ryan Leaf*	8.00

1998 Fleer Brilliants Illuminators

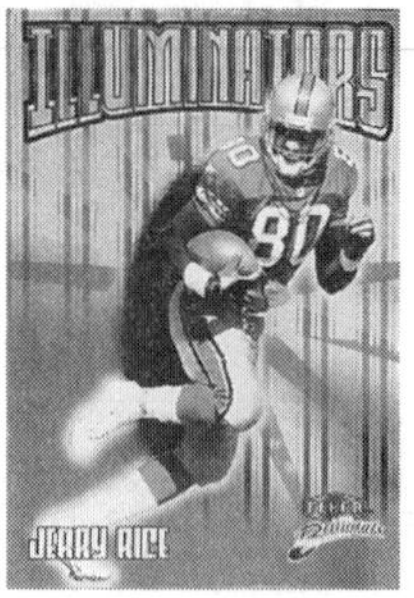
ILLUMINATORS
JERRY RICE

Each card in this 15-card set has the players team color in super bright mirror foil on the front. Singles can be found 1:10 packs.

		MT
Complete Set (15):		70.00
Common Player:		1.50
Minor Stars:		3.00
Inserted 1:10		
1	Robert Edwards	6.00
2	Fred Taylor	10.00
3	Kordell Stewart	10.00
4	Troy Aikman	15.00
5	Curtis Enis	6.00
6	Drew Bledsoe	10.00
7	Curtis Martin	4.00
8	Joey Galloway	3.00
9	Jerome Bettis	3.00
10	Glenn Foley	1.50
11	Karim Abdul-Jabbar	3.00
12	Jake Plummer	8.00
13	Jerry Rice	15.00
14	Charlie Batch	12.00
15	Jacquez Green	4.00

1998 Fleer Brilliants Shining Stars

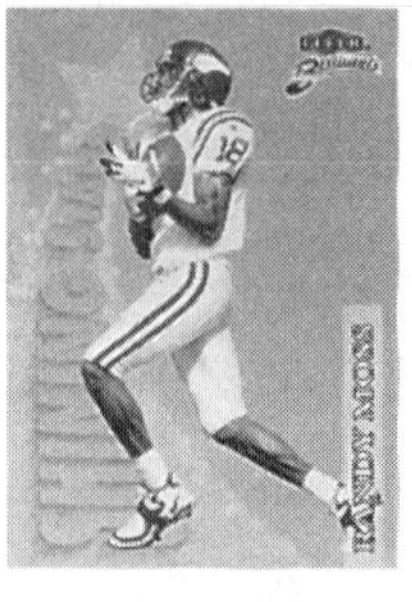
RANDY MOSS

Singles in this insert are two-sided with super bright mirror foil and includes the top 15 players from the NFL. Singles were inserted 1:20 packs. A parallel version called Pulsars can also be found 1:400 packs.

		MT
Complete Set (15):		120.00
Common Player:		2.00
Inserted 1:20		
Pulsar Cards:		5x-10x
Inserted 1:400		
1	Terrell Davis	15.00
2	Emmitt Smith	15.00
3	Barry Sanders	20.00
4	Mark Brunell	8.00
5	Brett Favre	20.00
6	Ryan Leaf	10.00
7	Randy Moss	30.00
8	Warrick Dunn	8.00
9	Peyton Manning	20.00
10	Corey Dillon	4.00
11	Dan Marino	15.00
12	Keyshawn Johnson	2.00
13	John Elway	10.00
14	Eddie George	8.00
15	Antowain Smith	5.00

1998 Fleer Heritage

This parallel set was exclusive to hobby packs and was sequentially numbered to 125 sets. Heritage cards added a special foil treatment on the front and sequential numbering on the back.

	MT
Heritage Cards:	30x-60x
Heritage Rookies:	10x-20x

1998 Fleer Playmakers Theatre

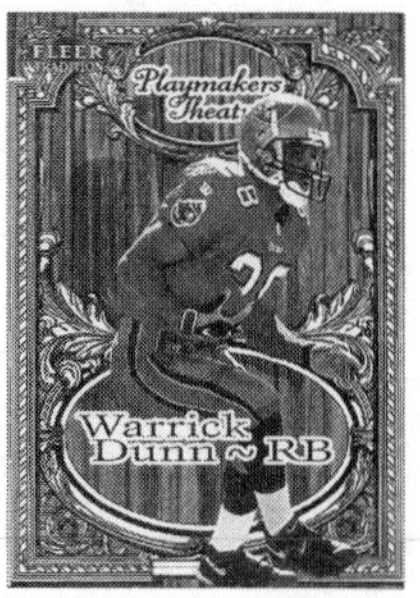
Playmakers Theatre
Warrick Dunn ~ RB

This 15-card insert set included the game's elite players on silver holofoil and sculpture embossing. Playmakers Theatre cards were sequentially numbered to 100 sets.

		MT
Complete Set (15):		1000.
Common Player:		30.00
Production 100 Sets		
PT1	Terrell Davis	100.00
PT2	Corey Dillon	60.00
PT3	Warrick Dunn	85.00
PT4	John Elway	100.00
PT5	Brett Favre	200.00
PT6	Antonio Freeman	30.00
PT7	Joey Galloway	30.00
PT8	Eddie George	85.00
PT9	Terry Glenn	30.00
PT10	Dan Marino	175.00
PT11	Curtis Martin	60.00
PT12	Jake Plummer	85.00
PT13	Barry Sanders	200.00
PT14	Deion Sanders	50.00
PT15	Kordell Stewart	85.00

1998 Fleer Red Zone Rockers

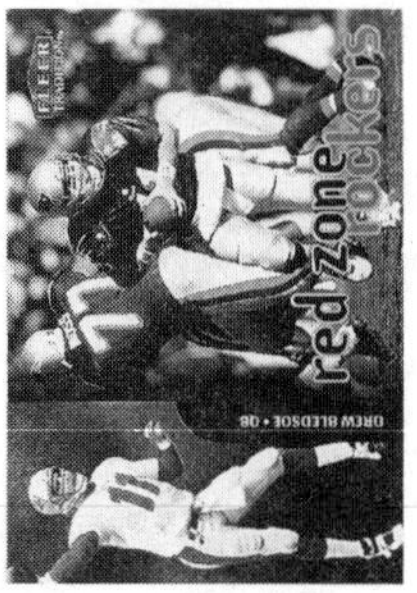
red zone rockers
DREW BLEDSOE • QB

Red Zone Rockers were printed on a horizontal red laser holofoil and inserted one per 32 packs. The insert included 10 players who are best in the clutch.

		MT
Complete Set (10):		70.00
Common Player:		2.00
RZ1	Jerome Bettis	2.00
RZ2	Drew Bledsoe	10.00
RZ3	Mark Brunell	8.00
RZ4	Corey Dillon	6.00
RZ5	Joey Galloway	2.00
RZ6	Keyshawn Johnson	2.00
RZ7	Dorsey Levens	2.00
RZ8	Dan Marino	15.00
RZ9	Barry Sanders	20.00
RZ10	Emmitt Smith	15.00

1998 Fleer Rookie Sensations

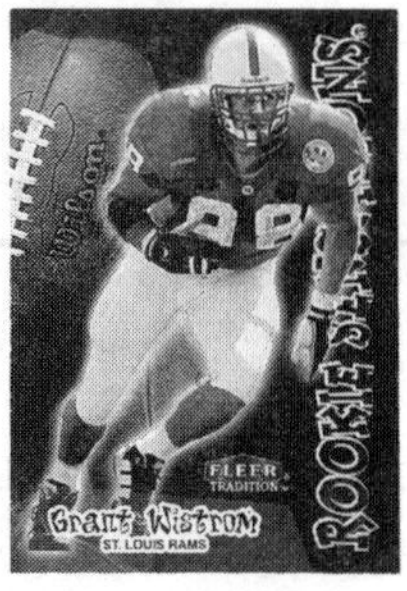
ROOKIE SENSATIONS
Grant Wistrom
ST. LOUIS RAMS

This 15-card insert displayed the top rookies in 1998. Cards were embossed with spot UV coating and inserted one per 16 packs.

		MT
Complete Set (15):		60.00
Common Player:		2.00
RS1	John Avery	4.00
RS2	Keith Brooking	2.00
RS3	Kevin Dyson	4.00
RS4	Robert Edwards	5.00
RS5	Greg Ellis	2.00
RS6	Curtis Enis	7.00
RS7	Terry Fair	2.00
RS8	Ryan Leaf	7.00
RS9	Peyton Manning	15.00
RS10	Randy Moss	20.00
RS11	Marcus Nash	4.00
RS12	Fred Taylor	7.00
RS13	Andre Wadsworth	2.00
RS14	Grant Wistrom	2.00
RS15	Charles Woodson	5.00

1999 Fleer

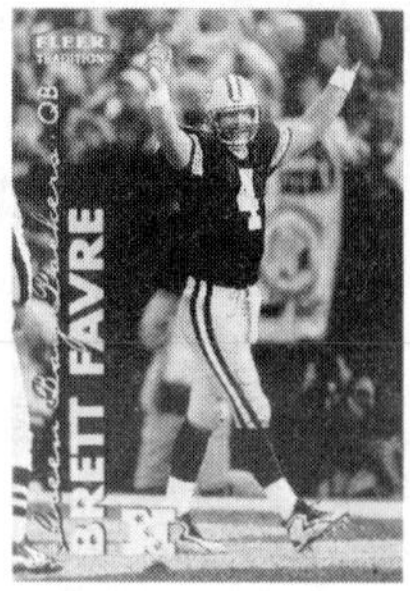
BRETT FAVRE

The 300-card set includes 50 unseeded rookies. The card fronts include the player's name and conference logo in blue foil for the NFC and red for the AFC. Inserts include: Trophy Case, Aerial Assault, Rookie Sensations, Under Pressure and Unsung Heroes.

		MT
Complete Set (300):		50.00
Common Player:		.10
Minor Stars:		.20
Common Rookie:		.40
Pack (10):		2.00
Wax Box (36):		65.00
1	Randy Moss	2.00
2	Peyton Manning	1.50
3	Barry Sanders	2.00
4	Terrell Davis	1.50
5	Brett Favre	2.00
6	Fred Taylor	1.00
7	Jake Plummer	1.00
8	John Elway	1.50
9	Emmitt Smith	1.50
10	Kerry Collins	.20
11	Peter Boulware	.10
12	Jamal Anderson	.50
13	Doug Flutie	.75
14	Michael Bates	.10
15	Corey Dillon	.50
16	Curtis Conway	.20
17	Ty Detmer	.20
18	Robert Brooks	.10
19	Dale Carter	.10
20	Charlie Batch	.75
21	Ken Dilger	.10
22	Troy Aikman	1.00
23	Tavian Banks	.20
24	Cris Carter	.50
25	Derrick Alexander	.10
26	Chris Bordano	.10
27	Karim Abdul	.30
28	Jessie Armstead	.10
29	Drew Bledsoe	.75
30	Brian Dawkins	.10
31	Wayne Chrebet	.50
32	Garrison Hearst	.30
33	Eric Allen	.10
34	Tony Banks	.20
35	Jerome Bettis	.50
36	Stephen Alexander	.10
37	Rodney Harrison	.10
38	Mike Alstott	.50
39	Chad Brown	.10
40	Johnny McWilliams	.10
41	Kevin Dyson	.20
42	Keith Brooking	.10
43	Jim Harbaugh	.20
44	Bobby Engram	.10
45	John Holecek	.10
46	Steve Beuerlein	.10
47	Tony McGee	.10
48	Greg Ellis	.10
49	Corey Fuller	.10
50	Stephen Boyd	.10
51	Marshall Faulk	.50
52	Leroy Butler	.10
53	Reggie Barlow	.10
54	Randall Cunningham	.50
55	Aeneas Williams	.10
56	Kimble Anders	.10
57	Cameron Cleeland	.20
58	John Avery	.20
59	Gary Brown	.10
60	Ben Coates	.20
61	Koy Detmer	.10
62	Bryan Cox	.10
63	Edgar Bennett	.10
64	Tim Brown	.20
65	Isaac Bruce	.30
66	Eddie George	.75
67	Reidel Anthony	.20
68	Charlie Jones	.10
69	Terry Allen	.20
70	Joey Galloway	.50
71	Jamir Miller	.10
72	Will Blackwell	.10
73	Ray Buchanan	.10
74	Priest Holmes	.50
75	Michael Irvin	.20
76	Jonathon Linton	.10
77	Curtis Enis	.50
78	Neil O'Donnell	.20
79	Tim Biakabutuka	.20
80	Terry Kirby	.10
81	Germane Crowell	.20
82	Jason Elam	.10
83	Mark Chmura	.20
84	Marvin Harrison	.30
85	Jimmy Hitchcock	.10
86	Tony Brackens	.10
87	Sean Dawkins	.10
88	Tony Gonzalez	.20
89	Kent Graham	.10
90	Oronde Gadsden	.20
91	Hugh Douglas	.10
92	Robert Edwards	.30
93	R.W. McQuarters	.10
94	Aaron Glenn	.10
95	Kevin Carter	.10
96	Rickey Dudley	.10
97	Derrick Brooks	.10
98	Mark Bruener	.10
99	Darrell Green	.10
100	Jessie Tuggle	.10
101	Freddie Jones	.10
102	Rob Moore	.20
103	Ahman Green	.20
104	Chris Chandler	.20
105	Steve McNair	.50
106	Kevin Greene	.10
107	Jermaine Lewis	.20
108	Erik Kramer	.10
109	Eric Moulds	.50
110	Terry Fair	.10
111	Carl Pickens	.20
112	La'Roi Glover	.10
113	Chris Spielman	.10
114	Leroy Hoard	.10
115	Mark Brunell	.75
116	*Patrick Jeffers*	2.50
117	Elvis Grbac	.20
118	Ike Hilliard	.20
119	Sam Madison	.10
120	Terrell Owens	.50
121	Rich Gannon	.10
122	Skip Hicks	.50
123	Eric Green	.10
124	Trent Dilfer	.50
125	Terry Glenn	.30
126	Trent Green	.50
127	Charles Johnson	.10
128	Adrian Murrell	.20
129	Jason Gildon	.10
130	Tim Dwight	.50
131	Ryan Leaf	.50
132	Raghib Ismail	.20
133	Jon Kitna	.50
134	Alonzo Mayes	.10
135	Yancey Thigpen	.20
136	David LaFleur	.10
137	Ray Lewis	.10
138	Herman Moore	.50
139	Brian Griese	.30
140	Antonio Freeman	.50
141	Darnay Scott	.10
142	Ed McDaniel	.10
143	Andre Reed	.10
144	Andre Hastings	.10
145	Chris Warren	.10
146	Kevin Hardy	.10
147	Joe Jurevicius	.10
148	Jerome Pathon	.10
149	Duce Staley	.20
150	Dan Marino	1.50
151	Jerry Rice	1.00
152	Bam Morris	.20
153	Az-Zahir Hakim	.20
154	Ty Law	.10
155	Warrick Dunn	.50
156	Keyshawn Johnson	.50
157	Brian Mitchell	.10
158	James Jett	.10
159	Fred Lane	.10
160	Courtney Hawkins	.10
161	Andre Wadsworth	.20
162	Natrone Means	.30
163	Andrew Glover	.10
164	Anthony Simmons	.10
165	Leon Lett	.10
166	Frank Wycheck	.10
167	Barry Minter	.10
168	Michael McCrary	.10
169	Johnnie Morton	.10
170	Jay Riemersma	.10
171	Vonnie Holliday	.20
172	Brian Simmons	.10
173	Joe Johnson	.10
174	Ed McCaffrey	.30
175	Jason Sehorn	.10
176	Keenan McCardell	.10
177	Bobby Taylor	.10
178	Andre Rison	.20
179	Greg Hill	.10
180	O.J. McDuffie	.20
181	Darren Woodson	.10
182	Willie McGinest	.10
183	J.J. Stokes	.20
184	Leon Johnson	.10
185	Bert Emanuel	.10
186	Napoleon Kaufman	.50
187	Leslie Shepherd	.10
188	Levon Kirkland	.10
189	Simeon Rice	.10
190	Mikhael Ricks	.10
191	Robert Smith	.50
192	Michael Sinclair	.10
193	Muhsin Muhammad	.10
194	Duane Starks	.10
195	Terance Mathis	.10
196	Antowain Smith	.50
197	Tony Parrish	.10
198	Takeo Spikes	.10
199	Ernie Mills	.10
200	John Mobley	.10
201	Robert Porcher	.10
202	Pete Mitchell	.10
203	Darick Holmes	.10
204	Derrick Thomas	.20
205	David Palmer	.10
206	Jason Taylor	.10
207	Sammy Knight	.10
208	Dwayne Rudd	.10
209	Lawyer Milloy	.10
210	Michael Strahan	.10
211	Mo Lewis	.10
212	William Thomas	.10
213	Darrell Russell	.10
214	Brad Johnson	.50
215	Kordell Stewart	.50
216	Robert Holcombe	.20
217	Junior Seau	.20
218	Jacquez Green	.20
219	Shawn Springs	.10
220	Michael Westbrook	.20
221	Rod Woodson	.10
222	Frank Sanders	.10
223	Bruce Smith	.10
224	Eugene Robinson	.10
225	Bill Romanowski	.10
226	Wesley Walls	.10
227	Jimmy Smith	.20
228	Deion Sanders	.50
229	Lamar Thomas	.10
230	Dorsey Levens	.50
231	Tony Simmons	.20
232	John Randle	.10
233	Curtis Martin	.50
234	Bryant Young	.10
235	Charles Woodson	.50
236	Charles Way	.10
237	Zack Thomas	.20
238	Ricky Proehl	.10
239	Ricky Watters	.20
240	Hardy Nickerson	.10
241	Shannon Sharpe	.20
242	O.J. Santiago	.10
243	Vinny Testaverde	.20
244	Preston Roell	.10
245	James Stewart	.10
246	Jake Reed	.10
247	Steve Young	.75
248	Shaun Williams	.10
249	Rod Smith	.20
250	Warren Sapp	.10
251	*Champ Bailey*	1.50
252	*Karsten Bailey*	.40
253	*D'Wayne Bates*	.75
254	*Michael Bishop*	1.50
255	*David Boston*	3.00
256	*Na Brown*	.40
257	*Fernando Bryant*	.40
258	*Shawn Bryson*	.40
259	*Darrin Chiaverini*	.40
260	*Chris Claiborne*	1.00
261	*Mike Cloud*	.40
262	*Cecil Collins*	2.50
263	*Tim Couch*	8.00
264	*Scott Covington*	.40
265	*Daunte Culpepper*	7.00
266	*Antwan Edwards*	.40
267	*Troy Edwards*	2.50
268	*Ebenezer Ekuban*	.75
269	*Kevin Faulk*	3.00
270	*Jermaine Fazande*	.40
271	*Joe Germaine*	1.25
272	*Martin Gramatica*	.40
273	*Torry Holt*	2.50
274	*Brock Huard*	1.50
275	*Sedrick Irvin*	1.50
276	*Sheldon Jackson*	.40
277	*Edgerrin James*	10.00
278	*James Johnson*	1.50
279	*Kevin Johnson*	1.50
280	*Malcolm Johnson*	.40
281	*Andy Katzenmoyer*	1.00
282	*Jevon Kearse*	2.00
283	*Patrick Kerney*	.40
284	*Shaun King*	3.00
285	*Jim Kleinsasser*	.40
286	*Rob Konrad*	.75
287	*Chris McAlister*	.75
288	*Donovan McNabb*	4.00
289	*Cade McNown*	3.00
290	*Dee Miller*	.40
291	*Joe Montgomery*	1.00
292	*De'Mond Parker*	.40
293	*Peerless Price*	2.00
294	*Akili Smith*	4.00
295	*Justin Swift*	.40
296	*Jerame Tuman*	.40
297	*Ricky Williams*	8.00
298	*Antoine Winfield*	.75
299	*Craig Yeast*	.40
300	*Amos Zereoue*	2.00

1999 Fleer Aerial Assault

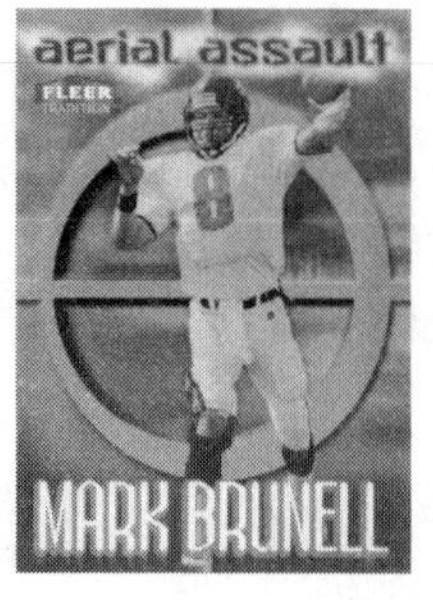
aerial assault
MARK BRUNELL

Each card is printed on plastic with silver holofoil featuring the NFL's top throwers and their targets. The 15 different singles were inserted 1:24 packs.

		MT
Complete Set (15):		85.00
Common Player:		2.00
Minor Stars:		4.00
Inserted 1:24		
1	Troy Aikman	8.00
2	Jamal Anderson	2.00
3	Charlie Batch	5.00
4	Mark Brunell	6.00
5	Terrell Davis	10.00
6	John Elway	10.00
7	Brett Favre	15.00
8	Keyshawn Johnson	4.00
9	Jon Kitna	5.00
10	Peyton Manning	10.00
11	Dan Marino	10.00
12	Randy Moss	15.00
13	Eric Moulds	2.00
14	Jake Plummer	8.00
15	Jerry Rice	8.00

1999 Fleer Focus

This 175-card set included 75 rookie cards found at four different levels. The 10 defensive rookies were found 1:4 packs. The 25 wide receiver rookies were sequentially numbered to 3,850. The 25 running backs were numbered to 2,500 and the 15 quarterbacks were numbered to 2,250. The Stealth insert was a parallel to the base and each was sequentially numbered to 300. Other inserts include: Feel the Game, Fresh Ink, Glimmer Men, Reflexions, Sparklers and Wondrous. SRP was $2.99 for five-card packs.

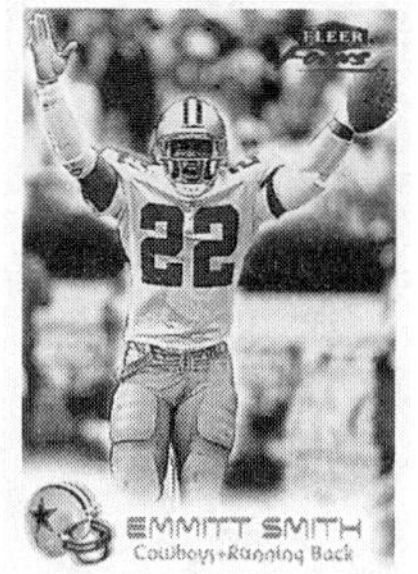
EMMITT SMITH
Cowboys • Running Back

		MT
Complete Set (175):		425.00
Common Player:		.20
Minor Stars:		.40
Common Rookie (101-110):		1.00
Inserted 1:4		
Common Rookie (111-135):		3.00
Production 3,850 Sets		
Common Rookie (136-160):		4.00
Production 2,500 Sets		
Common Rookie (161-175):		6.00
Production 2,250 Sets		
Pack (5):		3.00
Wax Box (24):		60.00
1	Randy Moss	4.00
2	Andre Rison	.40
3	Ed McCaffrey	.50
4	Jerry Rice	2.00
5	Tim Biakabutuka	.40
6	Wayne Chrebet	.75
7	Deion Sanders	.75
8	Ricky Watters	.50
9	Skip Hicks	.40
10	Charlie Batch	1.25
11	Joey Galloway	.75
12	Stephen Alexander	.20
13	Curtis Conway	.40
14	Garrison Hearst	.40
15	Kerry Collins	.40
16	Cris Carter	.75
17	Eddie George	1.00
18	Eric Moulds	.75
19	Vinny Testaverde	.40
20	Curtis Enis	.75
21	Gary Brown	.20
22	Junior Seau	.40
23	Kevin Dyson	.40
24	Jeff Blake	.40
25	Herman Moore	.75
26	Natrone Means	.50
27	Terry Glenn	.75
28	Fred Taylor	2.00
29	Ben Coates	.40
30	Corey Dillon	.75
31	Eddie Kennison	.20
32	Bam Morris	.20
33	Doug Pederson	.20
34	Jamal Anderson	.75
35	Michael Westbrook	.50
36	Peyton Manning	3.00
37	Carl Pickens	.40
38	Drew Bledsoe	1.50
39	Jim Harbaugh	.40
40	*Kurt Warner*	15.00
41	Mark Chmura	.40
42	Hines Ward	.40
43	Terry Kirby	.20
44	Brett Favre	4.00
45	Kordell Stewart	.75
46	Leslie Shepherd	.20
47	Marshall Faulk	.75
48	Troy Aikman	2.00
49	Isaac Bruce	.75
50	Michael Irvin	.40
51	Robert Smith	.75
52	Dorsey Levens	.75
53	Duce Staley	.50
54	Jake Plummer	1.50
55	Adrian Murrell	.40
56	Antonio Freeman	.75
57	Jerome Bettis	.75
58	Elvis Grbac	.40
59	Keyshawn Johnson	.75
60	Steve Beuerlein	.40
61	Yancey Thigpen	.20
62	Doug Flutie	1.25
63	Jacquez Green	.40
64	Jimmy Smith	.75
65	Tim Brown	.50
66	Jason Sehorn	.20
67	Muhsin Muhammad	.40
68	Shannon Sharpe	.40
69	Terrell Owens	.75
70	Keenan McCardell	.40
71	Rich Gannon	.40
72	Scott Mitchell	.20
73	Warrick Dunn	.75
74	Brad Johnson	.75
75	Charles Johnson	.20
76	Chris Chandler	.40
77	Marcus Pollard	.20
78	Mike Alstott	.75
79	Bubby Brister	.40
80	Jon Kitna	1.00
81	Randall Cunningham	.75
82	Antowain Smith	.75
83	Curtis Martin	.75
84	Steve McNair	1.00
85	Tony Gonzalez	.40
86	O.J. McDuffie	.40
87	Steve Young	1.25
88	Terrell Davis	3.00
89	Mark Brunell	1.50
90	Napoleon Kaufman	.75
91	Priest Holmes	.75
92	Trent Dilfer	.50
93	Brian Griese	1.50
94	J.J. Stokes	.40
95	Karim Abdul	.40
96	Barry Sanders	4.00
97	Dan Marino	3.00
98	Emmitt Smith	3.00

99	Marvin Harrison	.75
100	Rod Smith	.50
101	Champ Bailey	4.00
102	Fernando Bryant	2.00
103	Chris Claiborne	2.00
104	Antwan Edwards	2.00
105	Martin Gramatica	1.00
106	Andy Katzenmoyer	2.50
107	Jevon Kearse	5.00
108	Chris McAlister	2.00
109	Al Wilson	2.00
110	Antoine Winfield	2.00
111	Karsten Bailey	4.00
112	D'Wayne Bates	4.00
113	Marty Booker	4.00
114	David Boston	10.00
115	Na Brown	3.00
116	Desmond Clark	3.00
117	Dameane Douglas	3.00
118	Donald Driver	3.00
119	Troy Edwards	6.00
120	Torry Holt	10.00
121	Kevin Johnson	10.00
122	Reggie Kelly	3.00
123	Jim Kleinsasser	4.00
124	Jeremy McDaniel	3.00
125	Darnell McDonald	4.00
126	Travis McGriff	3.00
127	Billy Miller	3.00
128	Dee Miller	3.00
129	Peerless Price	8.00
130	Troy Smith	3.00
131	Brandon Stokley	3.00
132	Wane McGarity	3.00
133	Mark Campbell	3.00
134	Jerame Tuman	3.00
135	Craig Yeast	3.00
136	Jerry Azumah	5.00
137	Marlon Barnes	4.00
138	Michael Basnight	5.00
139	Shawn Bryson	5.00
140	Michael Cloud	7.00
141	Cecil Collins	12.00
142	Autry Denson	7.00
143	Kevin Faulk	10.00
144	Jermaine Fazande	7.00
145	Jim Finn	4.00
146	Madre Hill	5.00
147	Sedrick Irvin	10.00
148	Terry Jackson	6.00
149	Edgerrin James	50.00
150	J.J. Johnson	6.00
151	Rob Konrad	6.00
152	Joel Makovicka	6.00
153	Cecil Martin	5.00
154	Joe Montgomery	6.00
155	Demonn Parker	5.00
156	Sirr Parker	5.00
157	Jeff Paulk	6.00
158	Nick Williams	5.00
159	Ricky Williams	35.00
160	Amos Zereoue	8.00
161	Michael Bishop	10.00
162	Aaron Brooks	30.00
163	Tim Couch	35.00
164	Scott Covington	8.00
165	Daunte Culpepper	40.00
166	Kevin Daft	7.00
167	Joe Germaine	8.00
168	Chris Greisen	8.00
169	Brock Huard	10.00
170	Shaun King	15.00
171	Cory Sauter	6.00
172	Donovan McNabb	30.00
173	Cade McNown	15.00
174	Chad Plummer	6.00
175	Akili Smith	25.00

1999 Fleer Focus Feel the Game

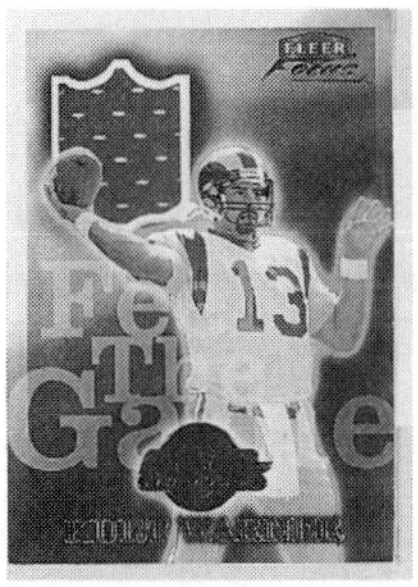

This 10-card insert set included pieces of game-used jerseys except for the Brett Favre single which included a piece of game-worn shoes. Singles were inserted 1:192 packs.

		MT
Complete Set (10):		600.00
Common Player:		40.00
Inserted 1:192		
1	Vinny Testaverde	40.00
2	Mark Brunell	60.00
3	Brett Favre Shoes	125.00
4	Fred Taylor	70.00
5	Jeff Blake	40.00
6	Emmitt Smith	100.00
7	Joe Germaine	40.00
8	Cecil Collins	50.00
9	Charles Woodson	50.00
10	Kurt Warner	200.00

Post-1980 cards in Near Mint condition will generally sell for about 75% of the quoted Mint value. Excellent-condition cards bring no more than 40%.

1999 Fleer Focus Fresh Ink

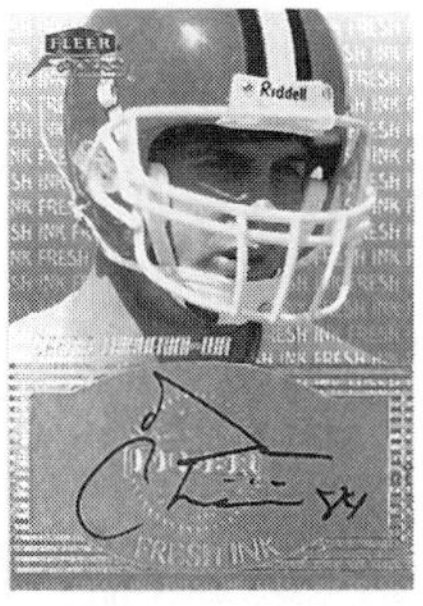

This 37-card insert set included autographs of both veterans and rookies. Each single was hand-numbered and found 1:48 packs.

	MT
Complete Set (37):	1250.
Common Player:	10.00
Minor Stars:	20.00
Inserted 1:48	
Reidel Anthony	10.00
Charlie Batch	30.00
Jeff Blake	10.00
Darrin Chiaverini	20.00
Wayne Chrebet	20.00
Daunte Culpepper	45.00
Terrell Davis	120.00
Koy Detmer	10.00
Corey Dillon	30.00
Troy Edwards	30.00
Doug Flutie	40.00
Eddie George	30.00
Trent Green	10.00
Marvin Harrison	25.00
Torry Holt	30.00
Sedrick Irvin	20.00
Edgerrin James	200.00
Brad Johnson	20.00
Charles Johnson	10.00
Jon Kitna	30.00
Jim Kleinsasser	10.00
Peyton Manning	120.00
O.J. McDuffie	10.00
Travis McGriff	10.00
Donovan McNabb	45.00
Cade McNown	45.00
Joe Montgomery	20.00
Randy Moss	125.00
Jake Plummer	50.00
Akili Smith	45.00
Antowain Smith	20.00
Duce Staley	20.00
Brandon Stokley	10.00
Fred Taylor	50.00
Vinny Testaverde	20.00
Ricky Williams	150.00
Steve Young	50.00

1999 Fleer Focus Glimmer Men

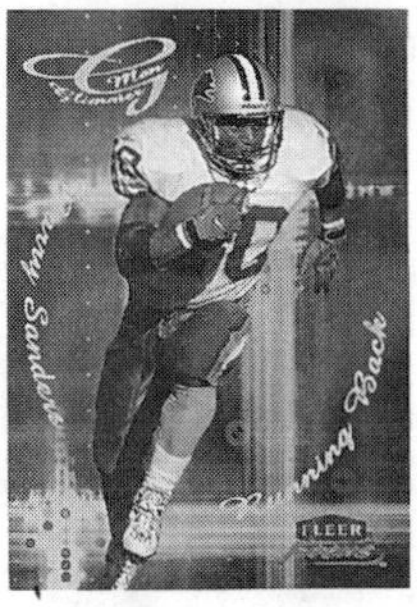

This 10-card insert set included stars from the NFL and were printed with silver and gold foil. Singles were inserted 1:20 packs.

		MT
Complete Set (10):		45.00
Common Player:		4.00
Inserted 1:20		
1	Tim Couch	8.00
2	Barry Sanders	8.00
3	Terrell Davis	6.00
4	Dan Marino	6.00
5	Troy Aikman	5.00
6	Brett Favre	8.00
7	Randy Moss	8.00
8	Emmitt Smith	6.00
9	Edgerrin James	10.00
10	Fred Taylor	4.00

1999 Fleer Focus Reflexions

This 10-card insert set was a parallel to the Glimmer Men insert. Each single was sequentially numbered to 100.

		MT
Complete Set (10):		350.00
Common Player:		20.00
Production 100 Sets		
1	Tim Couch	75.00
2	Barry Sanders	50.00
3	Terrell Davis	35.00
4	Dan Marino	35.00
5	Troy Aikman	25.00
6	Brett Favre	50.00
7	Randy Moss	50.00
8	Emmitt Smith	35.00
9	Edgerrin James	125.00
10	Fred Taylor	20.00

1999 Fleer Focus Sparklers

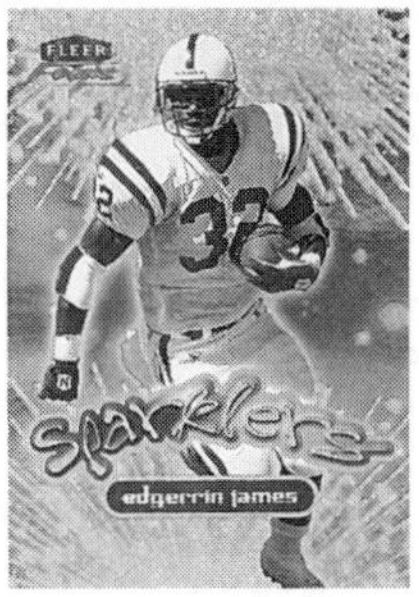

This 15-card insert set highlighted the top rookies from 1999. Singles were found 1:10 packs.

		MT
Complete Set (15):		30.00
Common Player:		1.50
Inserted 1:10		
1	Tim Couch	7.00
2	Donovan McNabb	4.00
3	Akili Smith	4.00
4	Cade McNown	4.00
5	Daunte Culpepper	4.00
6	Ricky Williams	7.00
7	Edgerrin James	10.00
8	Kevin Faulk	1.50
9	Torry Holt	3.00
10	David Boston	3.00
11	Sedrick Irvin	1.50
12	Peerless Price	2.00
13	Troy Edwards	3.00
14	Brock Huard	1.50
15	Shaun King	4.00

1999 Fleer Focus Stealth Parallel

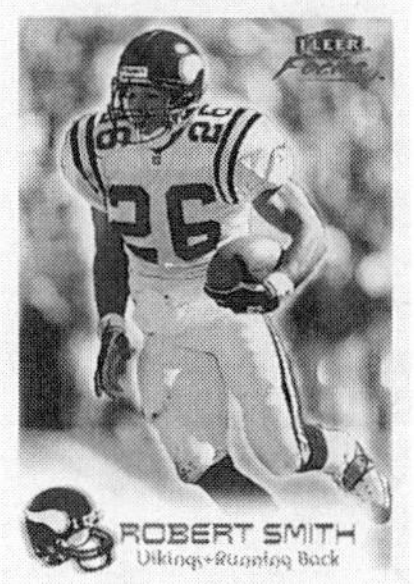

This was a 175-card parallel to the base set. Each single was sequentially numbered to 300.

	MT
Complete Set (175):	1000.
Stealth Cards:	5x-10x
Stealth Rookies:	2x
#40 Kurt Warner	100.00
Production 300 Sets	

1999 Fleer Focus Wondrous

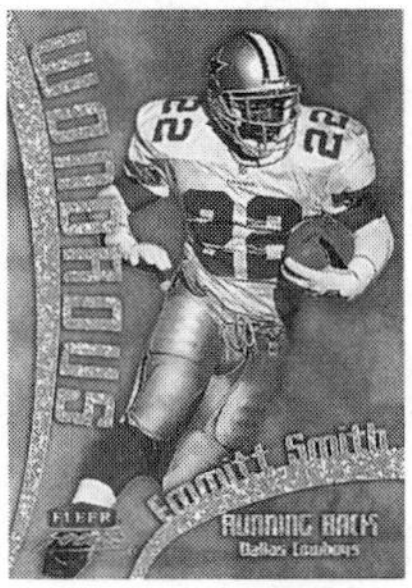

This was a 20-card insert set that pictured each star on silver holo foil with gold foil stamping. Singles were found 1:20 packs.

		MT
Complete Set (20):		65.00
Common Player:		2.00
Inserted 1:20		
1	Peyton Manning	6.00
2	Fred Taylor	4.00
3	Tim Couch	8.00
4	Charlie Batch	3.00
5	Jerry Rice	4.00
6	Randy Moss	8.00
7	Warrick Dunn	2.00
8	Mark Brunell	3.00
9	Emmitt Smith	6.00
10	Eddie George	2.00
11	Brian Griese	3.00
12	Terrell Davis	6.00
13	Dan Marino	6.00
14	Ricky Williams	8.00
15	Brett Favre	8.00
16	Jake Plummer	3.00
17	Troy Aikman	4.00
18	Drew Bledsoe	3.00
19	Edgerrin James	12.00
20	Cade McNown	5.00

1999 Fleer Mystique

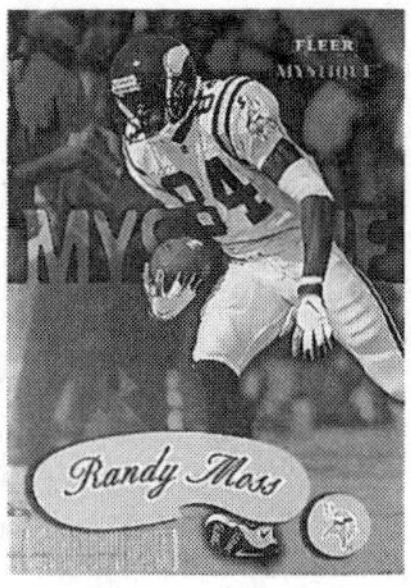

The 160-card set included 50 short-printed rookie cards that were sequentially numbered to 2,999 and 10 veteran stars numbered to 2,500. Parallel sets of Gold and Masterpieces were made for the first 100 cards in the base set. Other insert sets included: Feel the Game, Fresh Ink, NFL 2000, Protential and Star Power. SRP was $4.99 for four-card packs.

		MT
Complete Set (160):		650.00
Common Player:		.25
Minor Stars:		.50
Common SP (1-100):		1.50
Common Rookie:		5.00
Production 2,999 Sets		
Common Player (151-160):		5.00
Production 2,500 Sets		
Pack (4):		6.00
Wax Box (24):		120.00
1	Terrell Davis SP	4.00
2	Jerome Bettis SP	1.50
3	J.J. Stokes	.50
4	Frank Wycheck	.25
5	O.J. McDuffie	.25
6	Johnnie Morton	.25
7	Marshall Faulk SP	1.50
8	Ryan Leaf	.75
9	Sean Dawkins	.25
10	Brett Favre SP	6.00
11	Steve Young SP	2.50
12	Jimmy Smith	.75
13	Isaac Bruce	.75
14	Trent Dilfer	.50
15	Brian Mitchell	.25
16	Kordell Stewart SP	1.50
17	Herman Moore	.75
18	Troy Aikman SP	3.00
19	Cris Carter	.75
20	Barry Sanders SP	6.00
21	Tony Gonzalez	.50
22	Skip Hicks	.50
23	Steve McNair SP	1.50
24	Brad Johnson	.75
25	Mark Chmura	.50
26	Randall Cunningham SP	1.50
27	Jerry Rice SP	3.00
28	Jamie Asher	.25
29	Brian Griese SP	2.50
30	Peyton Manning SP	4.00
31	Keith Poole	.25
32	Wayne Chrebet	.75
33	Rich Gannon	.50
34	Michael Irvin	.50
35	Yancey Thigpen	.50
36	Corey Dillon	.75
37	Steve Beuerlein	.50
38	Terry Kirby	.25
39	Jacquez Green	.50
40	Mark Brunell SP	2.50
41	Rickey Dudley	.50
42	Shannon Sharpe	.75
43	Andre Rison	.50
44	Chris Chandler	.50
45	Fred Taylor SP	3.00
46	Kerry Collins	.50
47	Antowain Smith SP	1.50
48	Wesley Walls	.50
49	Rob Moore	.50
50	Dan Marino SP	4.00
51	Robert Smith	.75
52	Keenan McCardell	.50
53	Joey Galloway	.75
54	Fred Lane	.50
55	Napoleon Kaufman	.75
56	Curtis Martin	.75
57	Rod Smith	.75
58	Curtis Conway	.50
59	Kevin Dyson	.25
60	Warrick Dunn SP	1.50
61	Ahman Green	.50
62	Duce Staley	.50
63	Emmitt Smith SP	4.00
64	Adrian Murrell	.25
65	Dorsey Levens	.75
66	Drew Bledsoe SP	2.50
67	Ed McCaffery	.75
68	Natrone Means	.50
69	Deion Sanders	.50
70	Keyshawn Johnson SP	1.50
71	Antonio Freeman	.75
72	James Stewart	.50
73	Ben Coates	.50
74	Priest Holmes	.75
75	Jake Reed	.50
76	Mike Alstott	.75
77	Vinny Testaverde	.50
78	Ricky Watters	.50
79	Garrison Hearst	.50
80	Junior Seau	.50
81	Tim Brown	.50
82	Jamal Anderson	.75
83	Robert Brooks	.25
84	Marc Edwards	.25
85	Curtis Enis	.75
86	Doug Flutie	1.25
87	Terry Glenn	.75
88	Charlie Batch SP	2.00
89	Marvin Harrison	.75
90	Jake Plummer SP	3.00
91	Terrell Owens	.75
92	Scott Mitchell	.25
93	Tim Dwight	.75
94	Eddie George SP	1.50
95	Ike Hilliard	.50
96	Robert Holcombe	.25
97	Charles Johnson	.25
98	Eric Moulds	.75
99	Michael Westbrook	.75
100	Randy Moss SP	6.00
101	Tim Couch	30.00
102	Donovan McNabb	25.00
103	Akili Smith	12.00
104	Cade McNown	12.00
105	Daunte Culpepper	50.00
106	Ricky Williams	30.00
107	Edgerrin James	60.00
108	Kevin Faulk	12.00
109	Torry Holt	15.00
110	David Boston	12.00
111	Chris Claiborne	7.00
112	Mike Cloud	7.00
113	Joe Germaine	8.00
114	Cecil Collins	7.00
115	Tim Alexander	5.00
116	Brandon Stokley	5.00
117	Lamarr Glenn	5.00
118	Shawn Bryson	5.00
119	Jeff Paulk	5.00
120	Kevin Johnson	12.00
121	Charlie Rogers	5.00
122	Joe Montgomery	10.00
123	Travis McGriff	7.00
124	Dee Miller	5.00
125	Rob Konrad	8.00
126	Peerless Price	10.00
127	D'Wayne Bates	7.00
128	Craig Yeast	5.00
129	Malcolm Johnson	5.00
130	Brock Huard	10.00
131	Sedrick Irvin	10.00
132	Troy Smith	5.00
133	Troy Edwards	12.00
134	Al Wilson	5.00
135	Terry Jackson	7.00
136	Dameane Douglas	5.00
137	Amos Zereoue	8.00
138	Shaun King	12.00
139	James Johnson	8.00
140	Jermaine Fazande	8.00
141	Autry Denson	7.00
142	Darren Hall	5.00
143	Na Brown	5.00
144	Mike Lucky	5.00
145	Karsten Bailey	6.00
146	Kevin Daft	5.00
147	Sean Bennett	8.00
148	Madre Hill	5.00
149	Michael Bishop	12.00
150	Scott Covington	7.00
151	Randy Moss STAR	20.00
152	Fred Taylor STAR	10.00
153	Brett Favre STAR	20.00
154	Dan Marino STAR	15.00
155	Terrell Davis STAR	15.00
156	Barry Sanders STAR	20.00
157	Emmitt Smith STAR	15.00
158	Jake Plummer STAR	8.00
159	Warrick Dunn STAR	5.00
160	Troy Aikman STAR	10.00

1999 Fleer Mystique Feel The Game

This 10-card insert set featured a piece of game-used memorabilia. Each single was hand-numbered and randomly inserted.

	MT
Complete Set (10):	550.00
Common Player:	25.00
Terrell Davis jersey 510	100.00
Charles Johnson shoes 325	25.00
Jon Kitna shorts 640	50.00
Dorsey Levens jersey 515	50.00
Dan Marino socks 220	150.00
Curtis Martin jersey 690	50.00
Johnnie Morton jersey 580	25.00
Randy Moss jersey 510	175.00
Brandon Stokley gloves 85	50.00
Steve Young jersey 580	85.00

1999 Fleer Mystique Fresh Ink

This 30-card insert set ncluded autographs of both veterans and rookies. Each single was hand-numbered and randomly inserted.

		MT
Complete Set (30):		1850.
Common Player:		10.00
Minor Stars:		20.00
1	Charlie Batch 250	50.00
2	Mark Brunell 45	125.00
3	Shawn Bryson 650	10.00
4	Cecil Collins 725	35.00
5	Daunte Culpepper 300	60.00
6	Randall Cunningham 200	35.00
7	Terrell Davis 50	200.00
8	Sean Dawkins 700	10.00
9	Corey Dillon 250	30.00
10	Dameane Douglas 750	10.00
11	Tim Dwight 725	20.00
12	Troy Edwards 200	50.00
13	Doug Flutie 250	50.00
14	Eddie George 250	35.00
15	Joe Germaine 575	20.00
16	Trent Green 350	20.00
17	Torry Holt 350	40.00
18	Brock Huard 700	20.00
19	Edgerrin James 150	300.00
20	Brad Johnson 300	25.00
21	Jon Kitna 350	40.00
22	Peyton Manning 250	150.00
23	Randy Moss 150	200.00
24	Doug Peterson 750	10.00
25	Jake Plummer 300	40.00
26	Peerless Price 675	20.00
27	Akili Smith 100	120.00
28	Antowain Smith 150	45.00
29	Emmitt Smith 125	200.00
30	Ricky Williams 150	250.00

1999 Fleer Mystique Gold Parallel

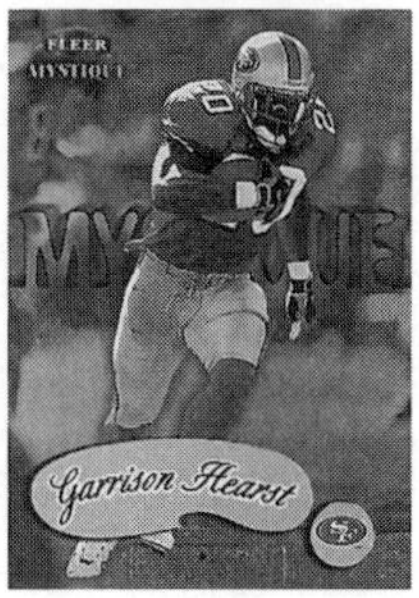

This was a parallel to the first 100 cards in the set. The name is in gold foil rather than silver as in the base set. Singles were randomly inserted.

	MT
Complete Set (100):	300.00
Gold Cards:	3x-6x

1999 Fleer Mystique NFL 2000

This 10-card insert set included players who are ready for super-stardom. Each single was sequentially numbered to 999.

		MT
Complete Set (10):		45.00
Common Player:		3.00
Production 999 Sets		
1	Peyton Manning	15.00
2	Ryan Leaf	5.00
3	Charlie Batch	7.00
4	Fred Taylor	10.00
5	Keyshawn Johnson	5.00
6	J.J. Stokes	3.00
7	Jake Plummer	8.00
8	Brian Griese	8.00
9	Antowain Smith	5.00
10	Jamal Anderson	5.00

1999 Fleer Mystique Pro-Tential

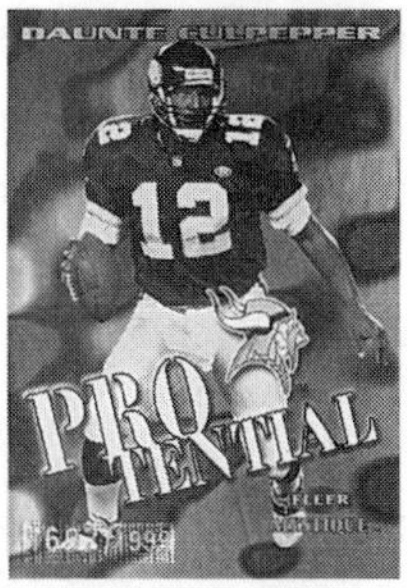

This 10-card insert set included the top rookies from 1999. Each of these singles was sequentially numbered to 1,999.

		MT
Complete Set (10):		65.00
Common Player:		5.00
Production 1,999 Sets		
1	Tim Couch	20.00
2	Donovan McNabb	10.00
3	Akili Smith	10.00
4	Cade McNown	10.00
5	Daunte Culpepper	10.00
6	Ricky Williams	20.00
7	Edgerrin James	25.00
8	Kevin Faulk	5.00
9	Torry Holt	7.00
10	David Boston	7.00

1999 Fleer Mystique Star Power

This 10-card insert set included the superstars from the NFL and featured them on a plastic card with a full silver-metallic holofoil background. Each single was sequentially numbered to 100.

		MT
Complete Set (10):		350.00
Common Player:		15.00
Production 100 Sets		
1	Randy Moss	70.00
2	Warrick Dunn	15.00
3	Mark Brunell	30.00
4	Emmitt Smith	50.00
5	Eddie George	15.00
6	Barry Sanders	70.00
7	Terrell Davis	50.00
8	Dan Marino	50.00
9	Troy Aikman	35.00
10	Brett Favre	70.00

1999 Fleer Rookie Sensations

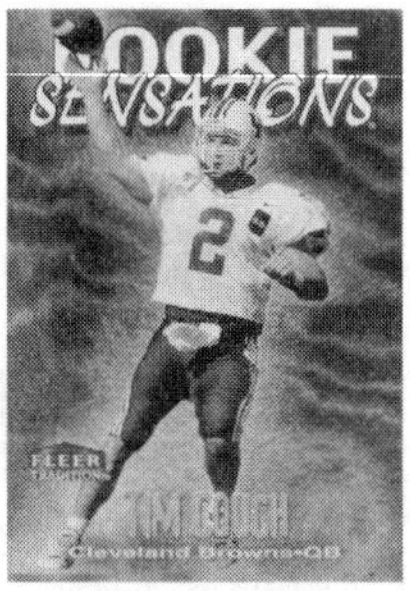

Rookies from the 1999 season are featured against team color backgrounds and glistening on silver foil fronts. The 20 different singles can be found 1:6 packs.

		MT
Complete Set (20):		50.00
Common Player:		1.00
Inserted 1:6		
1	Champ Bailey	2.00
2	Michael Bishop	2.50
3	David Boston	3.00
4	Chris Claiborne	1.00
5	Tim Couch	10.00
6	Daunte Culpepper	4.00
7	Troy Edwards	3.00
8	Kevin Faulk	3.00
9	Torry Holt	3.00
10	Brock Huard	2.00
11	Edgerrin James	6.00
12	Kevin Johnson	2.00
13	Shaun King	2.00
14	Rob Konrad	1.00
15	Chris McAlister	1.00
16	Donovan McNabb	4.00
17	Cade McNown	4.00
18	Peerless Price	2.50
19	Akili Smith	4.00
20	Ricky Williams	10.00

1999 Fleer Under Pressure

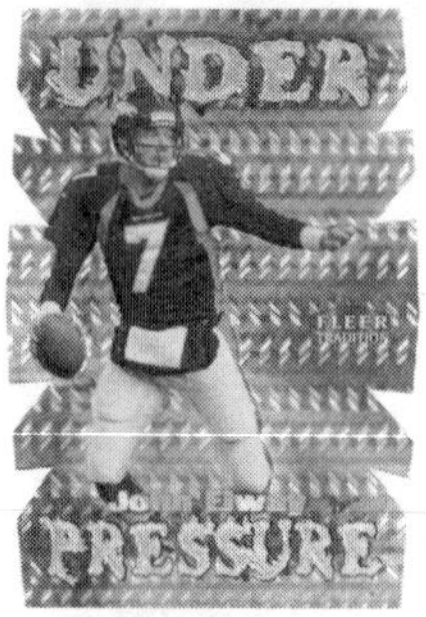

This 15-card set spotlights a sculpture embossed player image on patterned holofoil. Each is die- cut and found 1:96 packs.

		MT
Complete Set (15):		250.00
Common Player:		8.00
Inserted 1:96		
1	Charlie Batch	12.00
2	Terrell Davis	30.00
3	Warrick Dunn	12.00
4	John Elway	30.00
5	Brett Favre	40.00
6	Keyshawn Johnson	8.00
7	Peyton Manning	30.00
8	Dan Marino	30.00
9	Curtis Martin	12.00
10	Randy Moss	40.00
11	Jake Plummer	20.00
12	Barry Sanders	40.00
13	Emmitt Smith	30.00
14	Fred Taylor	20.00
15	Charles Woodson	8.00

1999 Fleer Unsung Heroes

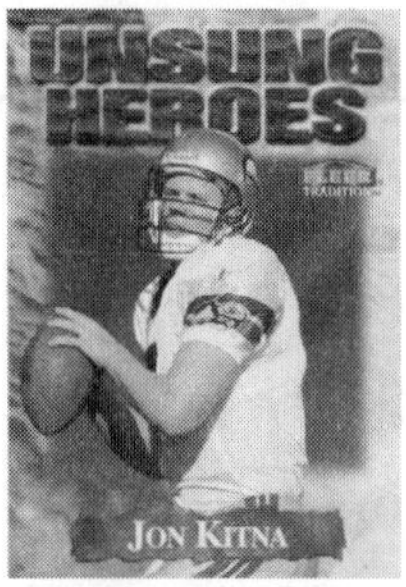

This 30-card set picks one under-recognized star from each team and highlights him on cardboard. Singles were inserted 1:3 packs.

		MT
Complete Set (30):		7.00
Common Player:		.25
Minor Stars:		.50
Inserted 1:3		
1	Tommy Bennett	.25
2	Lester Archambeau	.25
3	James Jones	.25
4	Phil Hansen	.25
5	Anthony Johnson	.25
6	Bobby Engram	.25
7	Eric Bieniemy	.25
8	Daryl Johnston	.25
9	Maa Tanuvasa	.25
10	Stephen Boyd	.25
11	Adam Timmerman	.25
12	Ken Dilger	.25
13	Bryan Barker	.25
14	Rich Gannon	.25
15	O.J. Brigance	.25
16	Jeff Christy	.25
17	Shawn Jefferson	.25
18	Aaron Craver	.25
19	Chris Calloway	.25
20	Pepper Johnson	.25
21	Greg Biekert	.25
22	Duce Staley	.50
23	Courtney Hawkins	.25
24	Rodney Harrison	.25
25	Ray Brown	.25
26	Jon Kitna	1.50
27	D'Marco Farr	.25
28	Brad Culpepper	.25
29	Steve Jackson	.25
30	Brian Mitchell	.25

2000 Fleer

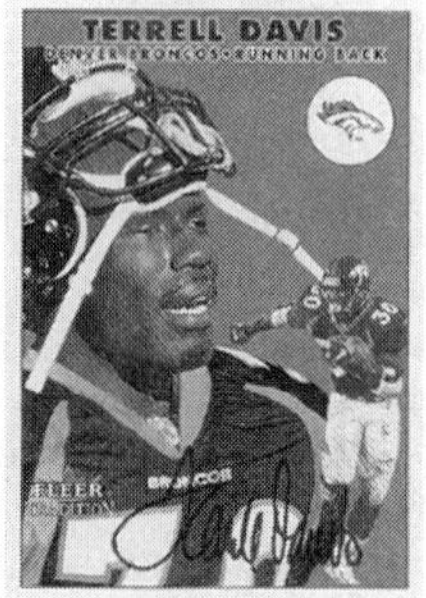

		MT
Complete Set (400):		50.00
Common Player:		.10
Minor Stars:		.20
Common Rookie:		.30
Pack (10):		1.50
Wax Box (36):		40.00
1	Kevin Johnson	.30
2	Chris Chandler	.20
3	Peerless Price	.30
4	Andre Rison	.20
5	Curtis Enis	.20
6	Tim Couch	1.00
7	Brian Dawkins	.10
8	Akili Smith	.40
9	Kevin Faulk	.30
10	Joey Galloway	.40
11	Bill Romanowski	.10
12	Charlie Batch	.40
13	Terence Wilkins	.30
14	Kevin Hardy	.10
15	Cade McNown	.75
16	Elvis Grbac	.20
17	Cris Carter	.40
18	Willie McGinest	.10
19	Michael Bishop	.30
20	Lee Woodall	.10
21	Jake Reed	.20
22	Bryan Cox	.10
23	Chris Sanders	.10
24	Tavian Banks	.20
25	Levon Kirkland	.10
26	James Hundon	.10
27	Junior Seau	.20
28	Darren Woodson	.10
29	Kevin Carter	.10
30	Joe Jurevicius	.10
31	John Lynch	.10
32	Steve McNair	.40
33	Jake Plummer	.40
34	Antonio Freeman	.40
35	Peter Boulware	.10
36	Brad Johnson	.40
37	Bobby Engram	.10
38	David Boston	.40
39	Jason Tucker	.20
40	Troy Brown	.10
41	Brian Griese	.50
42	Dorsey Levens	.40
43	Cornelius Bennett	.10
44	Donovan McNabb	.75
45	Rob Johnson	.30
46	Robert Smith	.40
47	Stanley Pritchett	.10
48	Tedy Bruschi	.10
49	Dan Marino	1.25
50	Amani Toomer	.20
51	Aaron Glenn	.10
52	Rickey Dudley	.20
53	Tim Brown	.30
54	Jim Harbaugh	.20
55	Terrell Owens	.40
56	Jason Sehorn	.10
57	Cortez Kennedy	.10
58	London Fletcher	.10
59	Simeon Rice	.10
60	Shaun King	.75
61	Stephen Davis	.40
62	Andre Wadsworth	.10
63	Kyle Brady	.10
64	Priest Holmes	.30
65	Patrick Jeffers	.40
66	Barry Minter	.10
67	Curtis Martin	.40
68	Darrin Chiaverini	.10
69	Robert Thomas	.10
70	Samari Rolle	.10
71	Robert Porcher	.10
72	Jerry Rice	1.00
73	Bill Schroeder	.20
74	Chad Bratzke	.10
75	Tony Brackens	.10
76	O.J. McDuffie	.20
77	John Randle	.20
78	Michael Pittman	.20
79	Drew Bledsoe	.75
80	Ike Hilliard	.20
81	Victor Green	.10
82	Duce Staley	.40
83	Bruce Smith	.10
84	Amos Zereoue	.20
85	Charlie Garner	.30
86	Shawn Springs	.10
87	Kurt Warner	2.00
88	Eddie George	.50
89	Michael Westbrook	.30
90	Dexter Coakley	.10
91	Rob Moore	.20
92	Duane Starks	.10
93	Steve Beuerlein	.20
94	Marty Booker	.10
95	Karim Abdul	.10
96	Troy Aikman	1.00
97	Germane Crowell	.40
98	Matt Hasselbeck	.20
99	E.G. Green	.10
100	Mark Brunell	.75
101	Tony Martin	.10
102	Darrell Green	.10
103	Ricky Williams	1.00
104	Michael Strahan	.10
105	Vinny Testaverde	.30
106	Charles Johnson	.10
107	Hines Ward	.30
108	Bryant Young	.10
109	Mo Lewis	.10
110	Greg Clark	.10
111	Jon Kitna	.30
112	Jacquez Green	.20
113	Kevin Dyson	.20
114	Stephen Alexander	.10
115	Cameron Cleeland	.20
116	Keith Poole	.10
117	Az-Zahir Hakim	.20
118	Tim Dwight	.30
119	Corey Bradford	.20
120	Carlos Emmons	.10
121	Trent Dilfer	.20
122	Lance Schulters	.10
123	Byron Hanspard	.10
124	Tim Biakabutuka	.20
125	Eddie Kennison	.10
126	Terry Kirby	.10
127	Mike McKenzie	.10
128	Fred Beasley	.10
129	Chad Brown	.10
130	Terrell Davis	1.25
131	Herman Moore	.30
132	Vonnie Holliday	.10
133	Jim Miller	.10
134	Peyton Manning	1.25
135	Derrick Alexander	.10
136	Oronde Gadsden	.20
137	Robert Griffith	.10
138	Troy Edwards	.30
139	Damon Huard	.40
140	Jessie Armstead	.10
141	Charles Woodson	.30
142	Troy Vincent	.10
143	Natrone Means	.20
144	Jeff Garcia	.50
145	Terry Glenn	.40
146	Marshall Faulk	.40
147	Patrick Johnson	.20
148	Frank Wycheck	.10
149	Champ Bailey	.30
150	Jamal Anderson	.40
151	Doug Flutie	.50
152	Michael Bates	.10
153	Corey Dillon	.40
154	Keith McKenzie	.10
155	Orpheus Roye	.10
156	Olandis Gary	.50
157	Johnnie Morton	.20
158	Brett Favre	1.50
159	Adrian Murrell	.20
160	Fred Taylor	.60
161	Tony Gonzalez	.30
162	Zach Thomas	.30
163	Randy Moss	1.25
164	Marcus Robinson	.40
165	Tiki Barber	.30
166	Rich Gannon	.30
167	Jeremiah Trotter	.10
168	Jermaine Fazande	.20
169	Steve Young	.75
170	Isaac Bruce	.40
171	Warrick Dunn	.40
172	Yancey Thigpen	.20
173	Rod Smith	.30
174	Albert Connell	.20
175	Freddie Jones	.20
176	Terance Mathis	.10
177	Eric Moulds	.40
178	Brian Mitchell	.10
179	Wesley Walls	.20
180	Carl Pickens	.20
181	Errict Rhett	.20
182	Madre Hill	.10
183	Jason Elam	.10
184	Greg Ellis	.10
185	David Sloan	.10
186	Edgerrin James	1.50
187	Jimmy Smith	.40
188	Tony Richardson	.10
189	James Hasty	.10
190	Sam Madison	.10
191	Tony Simmons	.10
192	Andre Hastings	.10
193	Keyshawn Johnson	.40
194	Na Brown	.10
195	Napoleon Kaufman	.30
196	Torrance Small	.10
197	Curtis Conway	.20
198	Jeff Graham	.10
199	Jason Hanson	.10
200	Derrick Mayes	.20
201	Torry Holt	.40
202	Warren Sapp	.20
203	Kimble Anders	.10
204	Blaine Bishop	.10
205	Leroy Hoard	.10
206	Larry Centers	.10
207	O.J. Santiago	.10
208	Antowain Smith	.20
209	Chuck Smith	.10
210	Takeo Spikes	.10
211	Raghib Ismail	.10
212	Ed McCaffrey	.30
213	Karsten Bailey	.10
214	Terry Fair	.10
215	Ken Dilger	.10
216	Jamie Martin	.10
217	Cris Dishman	.10
218	Jay Fiedler	.40
219	Lawyer Milloy	.10
220	*Jake Delhomme*	1.00
221	Wayne Chrebet	.30
222	Darrell Russell	.10
223	Christian Fauria	.10
224	Jerome Bettis	.40
225	Ryan Leaf	.40
226	Ricky Watters	.30
227	Keenan McCardell	.20
228	Grant Wistrom	.10
229	Jevon Kearse	.40
230	Frank Sanders	.20
231	Shannon Sharpe	.20
232	Jonathon Linton	.20
233	Alonzo Mayes	.10
234	Jason Garrett	.10
235	Kordell S5.03.30	.40
339	*Deon Grant,Alvin McKinley*	
340	*Dez White,Frank Murphy*	.75
341	*Ron Dugans,Curtis Keaton*	.75
342	*Dennis Northcutt,Travis Prentice*	1.25
343	*Dwayne Goodrich,Orantes Grant*	.30
344	*Deltha O'Neal,Ian Gold*	.30
345	*Stockar McDougle,Barrett Green*	.30
346	*Na'il Diggs,Anthony Lucas*	.30
347	*Marcus Washington,Dan Kendra*	.30
348	*T.J. Slaughter,Shyrone Stith*	.50
349	*William Bartee,Frank Moreau*	.50
350	*Deon Dyer,Todd Wade*	.30
351	*Chris Hovan,Troy Walters*	.30
352	*David Stachelski,Tom Brady*	1.50
353	*Terrelle Smith,Marc Bulger*	.30
354	*Ron Dixon,Cornelius Griffin*	.75
355	*Laveranues Coles,Anthony Becht*	.75
356	*Sebastian Janikowski,Shane Lechler*	.75
357	*Todd Pinkston,Gari Scott*	.75
358	*Danny Farmer,Tee Martin*	1.00
359	*Jacoby Shepherd,Brian Young*	.30
360	*Trevor Gaylor,JaJuan Seider*	.50
361	*Chafie Fields,Tim Rattay*	1.00
362	*Darrell Jackson,James Williams*	.75
363	*Nate Webster,James Whalen*	.30
364	*Erron Kinney,Chris Coleman*	.30
365	*Chris Samuels,Leon Murray*	.50
366	Arizona Cardinals Team	.20
367	Atlanta Falcons Team	.10
368	Baltimore Ravens Team	.10
369	Buffalo Bills Team	.20
370	Carolina Panthers Team	.10
371	Chicago Bears Team	.20
372	Cincinnati Bengals Team	.20
373	Cleveland Browns Team	.20
374	Dallas Cowboys Team	.50
375	Denver Broncos Team	.10
376	Detroit Lions Team	.10
377	Green Bay Packers Team	.10
378	Indianapolis Colts Team	.75
379	Jacksonville Jaguars Team	.10
380	Kansas City Chiefs Team	.10
381	Miami Dolphins Team	.50
382	Minnesota Vikings Team	.10
383	New England Patriots Team	.30
384	New Orleans Saints Team	.10
385	New York Giants Team	.10
386	New York Jets Team	.20
387	Oakland Raiders Team	.10
388	Philadelphia Eagles Team	.20
389	Pittsburgh Steelers Team	.10
390	St. Louis Rams Team	.20
391	San Diego Chargers Team	.10
392	San Francisco 49ers Team	.10
393	Seattle Seahawks Team	.10
394	Tampa Bay Buccaneers Team	.10
395	Tennessee Titans Team	.20
396	Washington Redskins Team	.20
397	Tim Couch CL	.50
398	Peyton Manning CL	.75
399	Kurt Warner CL	.75
400	Randy Moss CL	.75

2000 Fleer Autographics

		MT
Common Player:		10.00
Minor Stars:		20.00
Inserted 1:144		
Silver Cards:		1.2x
Production 250 Sets		
1	Shaun Alexander	45.00
2	Mike Alstott	20.00
3	Charlie Batch	20.00
4	Donnell Bennett	10.00
5	Peter Boulware	10.00
6	Tom Brady	20.00
7	Isaac Bruce	25.00
8	Marc Bulger	10.00
9	Trung Canidate	20.00
10	Giovanni Carmazzi	35.00
11	Darren Chiaverini	10.00
12	Laveranues Coles	20.00
13	Tim Couch	50.00
14	Daunte Culpepper	45.00
15	Stephen Davis	25.00
16	Jake Delhomme	20.00
17	Corey Dillon	25.00
18	Reuben Droughns	10.00
19	Deon Dyer	10.00
20	Kevin Dyson	10.00
21	Kevin Faulk	10.00
22	Jay Fiedler	20.00
23	Bubba Franks	25.00
24	Jason Garrett	10.00
25	Trevor Gaylor	10.00
26	Jeff Graham	10.00
27	Az-Zahir Hakim	20.00
28	Joe Hamilton	20.00
29	Tony Hartley	10.00
30	Priest Holmes	20.00
31	Raghib Ismail	10.00
32	Edgerrin James	85.00
33	Thomas Jones	35.00
34	Keyshawn Johnson	25.00
35	Curtis Keaton	10.00
36	Dorsey Levens	20.00
37	Curtis Martin	20.00
38	Derrick Mayes	10.00
39	O.J. McDuffie	10.00
40	Cade McNown	30.00
41	Johnnie Morton	10.00
42	Randy Moss Silver	100.00
43	Eric Moulds	25.00
44	Dennis Northcutt	20.00
45	Terrell Owens	25.00
46	Mareno Philyaw	10.00
47	Peerless Price	20.00
48	Chris Redman	45.00
49	J.R. Redmond	35.00
51	Warren Sapp	20.00
52	Gari Scott	10.00
53	Jason Sehorn	10.00
54	Akili Smith	25.00
55	Quinton Spotwood	10.00
56	Duce Staley	25.00
57	Michael Strahan	10.00
58	Amani Toomer	10.00
59	Peter Warrick	80.00
60	Tyrone Wheatley	20.00

2000 Fleer Focus

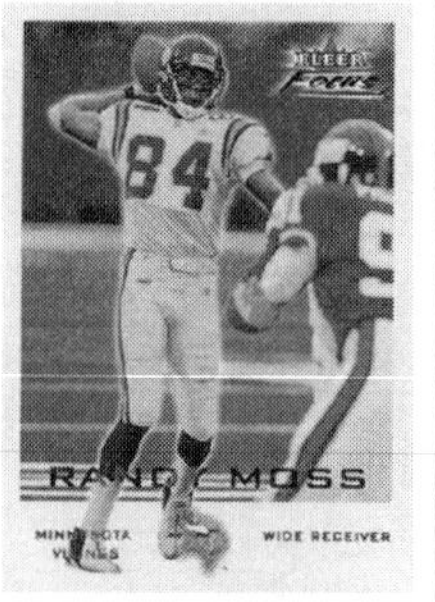

		MT
Complete Set (260):		425.00
Common Player:		.15
Minor Stars:		.30
Common Rookie (201-211):		3.00
Production 3,999 Sets		
Common Rookie (212-233):		6.00
Production 1,999 Sets		
Common Rookie (234-250):		4.00
Production 2,499 Sets		
Common Rookie (251-260):		5.00
Production 2,999 Sets		
Pack (10):		3.00
Wax Box (24):		55.00
1	Tim Couch	1.25
2	Germane Crowell	.30
3	Curtis Martin	.50
4	Samari Rolle	.15
5	Brian Griese	.50
6	Kerry Collins	.30
7	Jevon Kearse	.50
8	Raghib Ismail	.15
9	Cameron Cleeland	.30
10	Warrick Dunn	.50
11	Carl Pickens	.30
12	Cris Carter	.50
13	Mike Pritchard	.15
14	Corey Dillon	.50
15	Randy Moss	2.00
16	Derrick Mayes	.30
17	Marcus Robinson	.50
18	Thurman Thomas	.30
19	J.J. Stokes	.15
20	Muhsin Muhammad	.30
21	Derrick Alexander	.15
22	Curtis Conway	.15
23	Qadry Ismail	.15
24	Ken Dilger	.15
25	Troy Edwards	.50
26	Shawn Jefferson	.15
27	Terrence Wilkins	.30
28	Duce Staley	.50
29	Aeneas Williams	.15
30	Antonio Freeman	.50
31	Tim Brown	.30
32	Darrell Green	.15
33	Herman Moore	.30
34	Vinny Testaverde	.30
35	Yancey Thigpen	.15
36	Emmitt Smith	1.50
37	Ricky Williams	1.25
38	Keyshawn Johnson	.15
39	Eddie Kennison	.15
40	Zach Thomas	.30
41	Shawn Springs	.15
42	Wesley Walls	.15
43	Andre Rison	.15
44	Jerry Rice	1.25
45	Rob Johnson	.30
46	Keenan McCardell	.30
47	Ryan Leaf	.50
48	Mike McCrary	.15
49	Marvin Harrison	.50
50	Donovan McNabb	.75
51	Curtis Enis	.50
52	Tony Martin	.15
53	Jeff Garcia	.50
54	Tim Biakabutuka	.30
55	Tony Gonzalez	.30
56	Jim Harbaugh	.15
57	Peerless Price	.50
58	Fred Taylor	.75
59	Kordell Stewart	.50
60	Chris Chandler	.30
61	Bill Schroeder	.15
62	Charles Woodson	.30
63	Terance Mathis	.15
64	Brett Favre	2.00
65	Rickey Dudley	.15
66	Rob Moore	.30
67	Charlie Batch	.50
68	Wayne Chrebet	.30
69	Jeff George	.30
70	Olandis Gary	.50
71	Amani Toomer	.30
72	Kevin Dyson	.30
73	Darrin Chiaverini	.15
74	Willie McGinest	.15
75	Ricky Proehl	.15
76	Craig Yeast	.15
77	Dwayne Rudd	.15
78	Marshall Faulk	.50
79	Bobby Engram	.15
80	Jay Fiedler	.50
81	Jon Kitna	.50
82	Patrick Jeffers	.50
83	J.J. Johnson	.30
84	Charlie Garner	.30
85	Eric Moulds	.30
86	Mark Brunell	.75
87	Richard Huntley	.30
88	Frank Sanders	.15
89	Robert Porcher	.15
90	Aaron Glenn	.15
91	Stephen Davis	.50
92	Ed McCaffrey	.30
93	Pete Mitchell	.15
94	Frank Wycheck	.15
95	David LaFleur	.15
96	*Jake Delhomme*	1.50
97	John Lynch	.15
98	Michael Pittman	.15
99	Andy Katzenmoyer	.15
100	Isaac Bruce	.50
101	Terry Kirby	.15
102	Kevin Faulk	.30
103	Kevin Carter	.15
104	Darnay Scott	.30
105	Robert Smith	.50
106	Brian Mitchell	.15
107	Shane Matthews	.15
108	O.J. McDuffie	.30
109	Bryant Young	.15
110	Jay Riemersma	.15
111	Elvis Grbac	.30
112	Jermaine Fazande	.30
113	Jonathon Linton	.30
114	Kyle Brady	.15
115	Junior Seau	.30
116	Shannon Sharpe	.30
117	Jerome Pathon	.15
118	Jerome Bettis	.50
119	O.J. Santiago	.15
120	Ahman Green	.15
121	Troy Vincent	.15
122	David Boston	.50
123	James Stewart	.30
124	Ray Lucas	.50
125	Brad Johnson	.50
126	Rod Smith	.30
127	Joe Jurevicius	.15
128	Eddie George	.60
129	Darren Woodson	.15
130	Jake Reed	.15
131	Mike Alstott	.50
132	Leslie Shepherd	.15
133	Terry Glenn	.50
134	Az-Zahir Hakim	.30
135	Alonzo Mayes	.15
136	Sam Madison	.15
137	Ricky Watters	.30
138	Antowain Smith	.50
139	Jimmy Smith	.50
140	Hines Ward	.15
141	Priest Holmes	.30
142	Edgerrin James	2.00
143	Charles Johnson	.15
144	Jamal Anderson	.50
145	Dorsey Levens	.50
146	Rich Gannon	.30
147	Champ Bailey	.30
148	Bill Romanowski	.15
149	Jason Sehorn	.15
150	Steve McNair	.50
151	Jermaine Lewis	.15
152	Cornelius Bennett	.15
153	Torrance Small	.15
154	Tim Dwight	.50
155	Corey Bradford	.15
156	Napoleon Kaufman	.50
157	Jake Plummer	.50
158	David Sloan	.15
159	Dedric Ward	.15
160	Michael Westbrook	.30
161	Terrell Davis	1.50
162	Ike Hilliard	.30
163	Derrick Brooks	.15
164	Greg Ellis	.15
165	Keith Poole	.15
166	Jacquez Green	.30
167	Joey Galloway	.50
168	Lawyer Milloy	.15
169	Warren Sapp	.15
170	Takeo Spikes	.15
171	John Randle	.15
172	Torry Holt	.50
173	Cade McNown	.75
174	Damon Huard	.30
175	Terrell Owens	.50
176	Steve Beuerlein	.30
177	Tony Richardson	.15
178	Jeff Graham	.15
179	Doug Flutie	.50
180	Kevin Hardy	.15
181	Mark Bruener	.15

182 Tony Banks .30
183 Peyton Manning 1.75
184 Hugh Douglas .15
185 Simeon Rice .15
186 Terry Fair .15
187 James Jett .15
188 Albert Connell .30
189 Troy Aikman 1.25
190 Jeff Blake .30
191 Shaun King .75
192 Kevin Johnson .50
193 Drew Bledsoe .75
194 Kurt Warner 2.50
195 Akili Smith .50
196 Daunte Culpepper .75
197 Sean Dawkins .15
198 Natrone Means .30
199 Kimble Anders .15
200 Steve Young .75
201 *Courtney Brown* 7.00
202 *Chris Samuels* 3.00
203 *Corey Simon* 4.00
204 *Deon Grant* 3.00
205 *Darren Howard* 3.00
206 *Rob Morris* 3.00
207 *Ahmed Plummer* 3.00
208 *Anthony Becht* 4.00
209 *Brian Urlacher* 10.00
210 *Shaun Ellis* 3.00
211 *Bubba Franks* 5.00
212 *Plaxico Burress* 25.00
213 *R. Jay Soward* 12.00
214 *Dez White* 10.00
215 *Peter Warrick* 35.00
216 *Jerry Porter* 10.00
217 *Ron Dugans* 10.00
218 *Laveranues Coles* 12.00
219 *Travis Taylor* 20.00
220 *Anthony Lucas* 8.00
221 *Sylvester Morris* 20.00
222 *Dennis Northcutt* 10.00
223 *Chafie Fields* 6.00
224 *Danny Farmer* 6.00
225 *Chris Cole* 6.00
226 *Sherrod Gideon* 6.00
227 *Todd Pinkston* 8.00
228 *Gari Scott* 6.00
229 *Darrell Jackson* 8.00
230 *JaJuan Dawson* 12.00
231 *Trevor Gaylor* 6.00
232 *Bashir Yamini* 6.00
233 *Quinton Spotwood* 6.00
234 *Michael Wiley* 8.00
235 *Ron Dayne* 40.00
236 *Thomas Jones* 15.00
237 *Jamal Lewis* 50.00
238 *Travis Prentice* 12.00
239 *J.R. Redmond* 10.00
240 *Trung Canidate* 6.00
241 *Shaun Alexander* 20.00
242 *Frank Murphy* 4.00
243 *Shyrone Stith* 4.00
244 *Rondell Mealey* 4.00
245 *Terrelle Smith* 4.00
246 *Reuben Droughns* 6.00
247 *Chad Morton* 6.00
248 *Mike Anderson* 50.00
249 *Paul Smith* 4.00
250 *Curtis Keaton* 4.00
251 *Jarious Jackson* 5.00
252 *Marc Bulger* 5.00
253 *Tee Martin* 7.00
254 *Todd Husak* 5.00
255 *Joe Hamilton* 6.00
256 *Doug Johnson* 7.00
257 *Giovanni Carmazzi* 7.00
258 *Chris Redman* 10.00
259 *Tim Rattay* 8.00
260 *Chad Pennington* 20.00

2000 Fleer Focus Autographics

MT
Common Player: 10.00
Minor Stars: 20.00
Inserted 1:72
Silver Cards: 1.2x
Production 250 Sets
1 Troy Aikman 60.00
2 Shaun Alexander 50.00
3 Mike Alstott 25.00
4 Kimble Anders 10.00
5 Tim Biakabutuka 10.00
6 Peter Boulware 10.00
7 Trung Canidate 20.00
8 Giovanni Carmazzi 35.00
9 Darren Chiaverini 10.00
10 Germane Crowell 10.00
11 Stephen Davis 25.00
12 Jake Delhomme 20.00
13 Reuben Droughns 20.00
14 Kevin Dyson 10.00
15 Marshall Faulk 30.00
16 Jay Fiedler 20.00
17 Bubba Franks 25.00
18 Jeff Garcia 25.00
19 Olandis Gary 30.00
20 Sherrod Gideon 10.00
21 Tony Graziani 10.00
22 Marvin Harrison 30.00
23 Priest Holmes 20.00
24 Torry Holt 20.00
25 Damon Huard 20.00
26 Darrell Jackson 20.00
27 Edgerrin James 85.00
28 Jon Kitna 20.00
29 Marcus Knight 10.00
30 Dorsey Levens 20.00
31 Tee Martin 25.00
32 Shane Matthews 20.00
33 O.J. McDuffie 10.00
34 Cade McNown 30.00
35 Rondell Mealey 20.00
36 Sylvester Morris 25.00
37 Johnnie Morton 10.00
38 Dennis Northcutt 20.00
39 Chad Pennington 60.00
40 Travis Prentice 25.00
41 Peerless Price 20.00
42 Jon Ritchie 10.00
43 Marcus Robinson 25.00
44 Warren Sapp 10.00
45 Jason Sehorn 10.00
46 Jimmy Smith 20.00
47 Rod Smith 20.00
48 Amani Toomer 10.00
49 Troy Walters 10.00
50 Kurt Warner 100.00
51 Peter Warrick 80.00
52 Dez White 20.00

2000 Fleer Focus Feel the Game

MT
Common Player: 20.00
Inserted 1:144
1 Troy Aikman Blue 50.00
2 Tim Brown 20.00
3 Curtis Conway Jersey 20.00
4 Curtis Conway Pants 20.00
5 Germane Crowell 25.00
6 Terrell Davis 65.00
7 Kevin Dyson Jersey 20.00
8 Kevin Dyson Pants 20.00
9 Curtis Enis Pants 25.00
10 Antonio Freeman 25.00
11 Eddie George Jersey 45.00
12 Eddie George Pants 45.00
13 Edgerrin James 100.00
14 Rob Johnson 25.00
15 Jevon Kearse 30.00
16 Peyton Manning 100.00
17 Terance Mathis 20.00
18 Steve McNair Jersey 40.00
19 Steve McNair Pants 40.00
20 Cade McNown Pants 50.00
21 Herman Moore 20.00
22 Johnnie Morton White 20.00
23 Marcus Robinson Pants 40.00
24 Deion Sanders 35.00
25 Emmitt Smith Blue 75.00

2000 Fleer Focus Good Hands

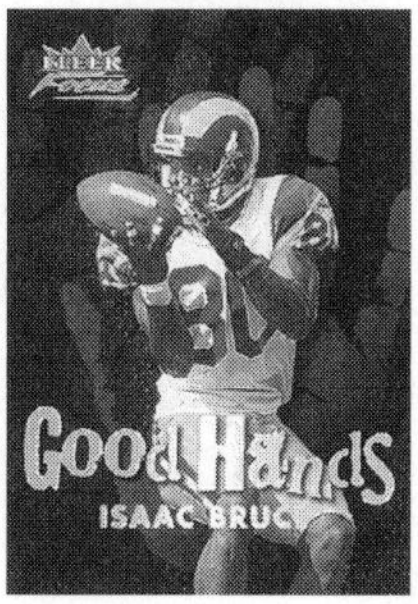

MT
Complete Set (15): 30.00
Common Player: .75
Minor Stars: 1.50
Inserted 1:18
1 Keyshawn Johnson 1.50
2 Joey Galloway 1.50
3 Jerry Rice 4.00
4 Cris Carter 1.50
5 Randy Moss 6.00
6 Marvin Harrison 1.50
7 Marcus Robinson 1.50
8 Edgerrin James 5.00
9 Tim Brown .75
10 Jimmy Smith 1.50
11 Isaac Bruce 1.50
12 Peter Warrick 7.00
13 Marshall Faulk 1.50
14 Germane Crowell .75
15 Plaxico Burress 5.00

2000 Fleer Focus Good Hands TD Edition Paralell

MT
Numbered to 1999 TD total
Cards numbered under 10 not priced
1 Keyshawn Johnson 8
2 Joey Galloway 1
3 Jerry Rice 5
4 Cris Carter 13 50.00
5 Randy Moss 12 125.00
6 Marvin Harrison 12 50.00
7 Marcus Robinson 9
8 Edgerrin James 17 125.00
9 Tim Brown 6
10 Jimmy Smith 6
11 Isaac Bruce 12 50.00
12 Peter Warrick 12 125.00
13 Marshall Faulk 12 50.00
14 Germane Crowell 7
15 Plaxico Burress 12 125.00

2000 Fleer Focus Last Man Standing

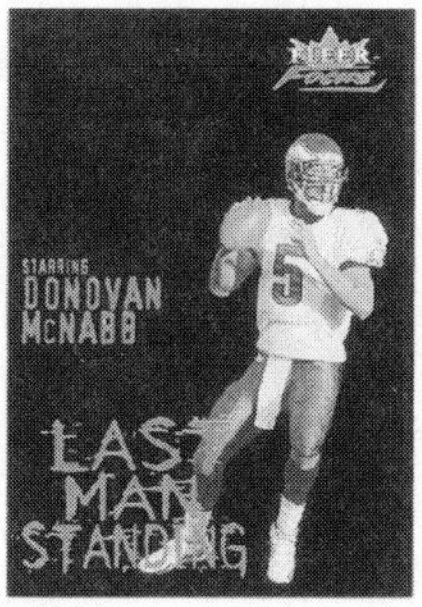

MT
Complete Set (25): 65.00
Common Player: 1.50
Inserted 1:12
1 Tim Couch 3.00
2 Randy Moss 5.00
3 Akili Smith 1.50
4 Peyton Manning 5.00
5 Kurt Warner 6.00
6 Ricky Williams 3.00
7 Edgerrin James 5.00
8 Eddie George 2.00
9 Emmitt Smith 4.00
10 Terrell Davis 4.00
11 Brett Favre 6.00
12 Brian Griese 2.00
13 Donovan McNabb 2.00
14 Charlie Batch 1.50
15 Shaun King 2.00
16 Marshall Faulk 1.50
17 Jake Plummer 1.50
18 Cade McNown 2.00
19 Jerry Rice 4.00
20 Troy Aikman 4.00
21 Keyshawn Johnson 1.50
22 Peter Warrick 7.00
23 Ron Dayne 7.00
24 Mark Brunell 2.50
25 Fred Taylor 3.00

2000 Fleer Focus Last Man Standing TD Edition Parallel

MT
Numbered to 1999 TD total
Cards numbered under 10 not priced
1 Tim Couch 16 85.00
2 Randy Moss 12 125.00
3 Akili Smith 3
4 Peyton Manning 28 100.00
5 Kurt Warner 42 85.00
6 Ricky Williams 2
7 Edgerrin James 17 125.00
8 Eddie George 13 60.00
9 Emmitt Smith 13 100.00
10 Terrell Davis 2
11 Brett Favre 22 125.00
12 Brian Griese 16 50.00
13 Donovan McNabb 18 50.00
14 Charlie Batch 15 50.00
15 Shaun King 7
16 Marshall Faulk 12 50.00
17 Jake Plummer 11 50.00
18 Cade McNown 8
19 Jerry Rice 5
20 Troy Aikman 18 90.00
21 Keyshawn Johnson 8
22 Peter Warrick 12 150.00
23 Ron Dayne 20 125.00
24 Mark Brunell 15 60.00
25 Fred Taylor 6

2000 Fleer Focus Sparklers

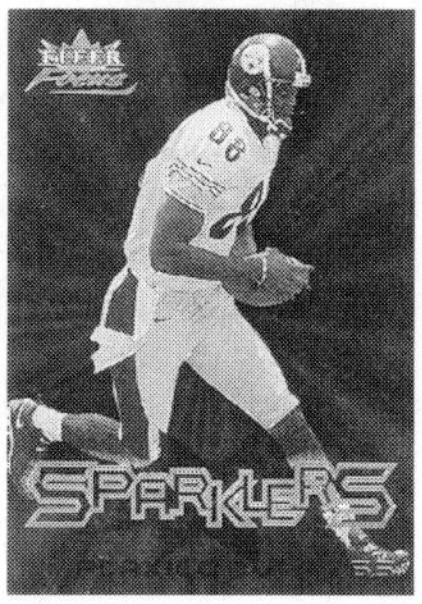

MT
Complete Set (15): 30.00
Common Player: 1.00
Inserted 1:6
1 Chad Pennington 4.00
2 Ron Dayne 5.00
3 Shaun Alexander 3.00
4 Plaxico Burress 4.00
5 Peter Warrick 5.00
6 Thomas Jones 3.00
7 Chris Redman 2.00
8 Sylvester Morris 1.50
9 J.R. Redmond 1.50
10 Dez White 1.00
11 Jamal Lewis 3.00
12 Travis Taylor 2.00
13 R. Jay Soward 1.00
14 Todd Pinkston 1.00
15 Dennis Northcutt 1.00

2000 Fleer Focus Sparklers TD Edition Parallel

MT
Numbered to 1999 TD total
Cards numbered under 10 not priced
1 Chad Pennington 40 60.00
2 Ron Dayne 20 125.00
3 Shaun Alexander 26 65.00
4 Plaxico Burress 12 125.00
5 Peter Warrick 12 150.00
6 Thomas Jones 18 80.00
7 Chris Redman 32 30.00
8 Sylvester Morris 13 40.00
9 J.R. Redmond 13 40.00
10 Dez White 5
11 Jamal Lewis 8
12 Travis Taylor 6
13 R. Jay Soward 5
14 Todd Pinkston 11 25.00
15 Dennis Northcutt 8

A player's name in *italic* type indicates a rookie card.

2000 Fleer Focus Star Studded

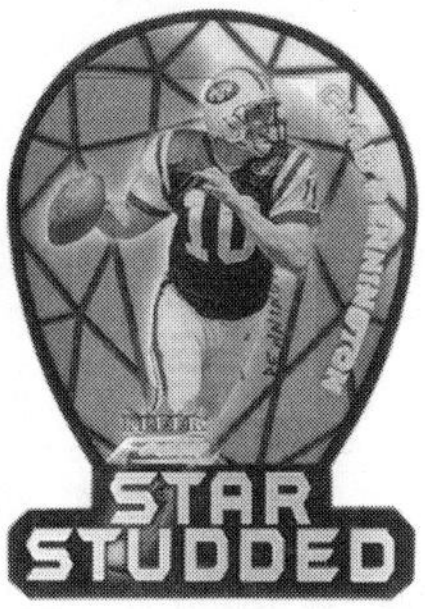

MT
Complete Set (25): 125.00
Common Player: 3.00
Inserted 1:24
1 Peyton Manning 10.00
2 Fred Taylor 5.00
3 Tim Couch 6.00
4 Charlie Batch 3.00
5 Jerry Rice 7.00
6 Randy Moss 10.00
7 Ron Dayne 15.00
8 Mark Brunell 5.00
9 Emmitt Smith 8.00
10 Thomas Jones 10.00
11 Brian Griese 4.00
12 Terrell Davis 8.00
13 Brad Johnson 3.00
14 Ricky Williams 6.00
15 Brett Favre 10.00
16 Jake Plummer 3.00
17 Troy Aikman 7.00
18 Drew Bledsoe 5.00
19 Edgerrin James 10.00
20 Steve McNair 3.00
21 Doug Flutie 3.00
22 Chad Pennington 12.00
23 Jamal Lewis 10.00
24 Plaxico Burress 12.00
25 Kurt Warner 12.00

2000 Fleer Focus Star Studded TD Edition Parallel

MT
Numbered to 1999 TD total
Cards numbered under 10 not priced
1 Peyton Manning 28 100.00
2 Fred Taylor 6
3 Tim Couch 16 85.00
4 Charlie Batch 15 50.00
5 Jerry Rice 5
6 Randy Moss 12 125.00
7 Ron Dayne 20 125.00
8 Mark Brunell 15 60.00
9 Emmitt Smith 13 100.00
10 Thomas Jones 18 75.00
11 Brian Griese 16 50.00
12 Terrell Davis 2
13 Brad Johnson 26 40.00
14 Ricky Williams 2
15 Brett Favre 22 125.00
16 Jake Plummer 11 50.00
17 Troy Aikman 18 90.00
18 Drew Bledsoe 19 60.00
19 Edgerrin James 17 125.00
20 Steve McNair 20 40.00
21 Doug Flutie 20 45.00
22 Chad Pennington 40 65.00
23 Jamal Lewis 8
24 Plaxico Burress 12 125.00
25 Kurt Warner 42 85.00

2000 Fleer Gamers

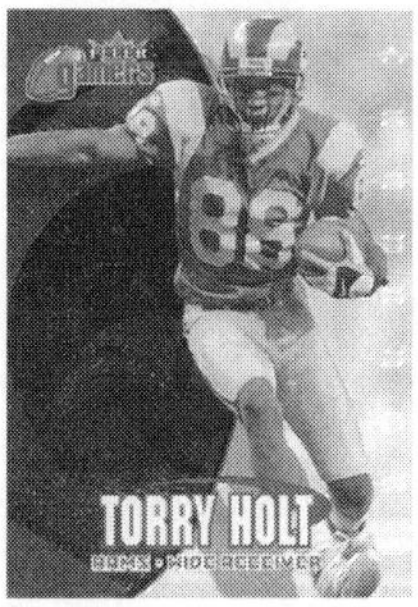

MT
Complete Set (145): 130.00
Common Player: .15
Minor Stars: .30
Common Rookie: 2.50
Inserted 1:8
Pack (5): 4.00
Wax Box (24): 70.00
1 Edgerrin James 2.50
2 Tim Couch 1.50
3 Cris Carter .50
4 Rich Gannon .30
5 Akili Smith .50
6 Muhsin Muhammad .30
7 Dorsey Levens .50
8 Dedric Ward .30
9 Jevon Kearse .50
10 Peerless Price .30
11 Mike Alstott .50
12 Michael Strahan .15
13 Stephen Davis .50
14 Rob Moore .30
15 James Stewart .30
16 Robert Smith .50
17 Napoleon Kaufman .30
18 Peyton Manning 2.00
19 Keyshawn Johnson .50
20 Tony Martin .15
21 Jermaine Fazande .30
22 Jamal Anderson .50
23 Ed McCaffrey .30
24 Drew Bledsoe 1.00
25 Duce Staley .50
26 Warrick Dunn .50
27 Chris Chandler .30
28 Olandis Gary .60
29 Terry Glenn .50
30 Donovan McNabb 1.00
31 Torry Holt .50
32 Tim Dwight .30
33 Terrell Davis 1.75
34 Tony Simmons .15
35 Jerome Bettis .50
36 Az-Zahir Hakim .30
37 Darrin Chiaverini .30
38 Fred Taylor .75
39 Jon Kitna .30
40 Tony Banks .30
41 Brian Griese .75
42 Jeff Blake .30
43 Kordell Stewart .50
44 Isaac Bruce .50
45 Shannon Sharpe .30
46 Raghib Ismail .15
47 Ricky Williams 1.50
48 Marshall Faulk .50
49 Qadry Ismail .15
50 Joey Galloway .50
51 Jake Reed .15
52 Kurt Warner 3.00
53 Cade McNown 1.00
54 Herman Moore .30
55 Curtis Martin .50
56 Steve McNair .50
57 Tim Biakabutuka .30
58 Brett Favre 2.50
59 Wayne Chrebet .30
60 Eddie George .75
61 Troy Aikman 1.25
62 Jimmy Smith .50
63 Derrick Mayes .30
64 Emmitt Smith 1.75
65 Mark Brunell 1.00
66 Ricky Watters .30
67 Marcus Robinson .50
68 Randy Moss 2.50
69 Troy Edwards .50
70 Carl Pickens .30
71 Damon Huard .50
72 Mikhael Ricks .15
73 David Boston .50
74 Charlie Batch .50
75 Randall Cunningham .50
76 Tim Brown .30
77 Shaun King 1.00
78 Darnay Scott .30
79 Derrick Alexander .15
80 Steve Young 1.00
81 Kevin Johnson .50
82 Elvis Grbac .30
83 Tai Streets .30
84 Steve Beuerlein .30
85 Antonio Freeman .50
86 Vinny Testaverde .30
87 Brad Johnson .50
88 Curtis Enis .30
89 Jay Fiedler .50
90 Junior Seau .30
91 Eric Moulds .50
92 Jake Plummer .50
93 Amani Toomer .15
94 Champ Bailey .30
95 Germane Crowell .30
96 Tony Gonzalez .30
97 Jerry Rice 1.25
98 Rob Johnson .30
99 Marvin Harrison .50
100 Kerry Collins .30
101 *Thomas Jones* 8.00
102 *Jarious Jackson* 3.00
103 *R. Jay Soward* 3.50
104 *Trung Canidate* 3.00
105 *Travis Taylor* 5.00
106 *Giovanni Carmazzi* 4.00
107 *Jerry Porter* 3.00
108 *Chris Redman* 5.00
109 *Tee Martin* 3.50
110 *Dez White* 3.00
111 *Danny Farmer* 2.50
112 *Brian Urlacher* 3.50
113 *Reuben Droughns* 2.50
114 *Marc Bulger* 2.50
115 *Peter Warrick* 15.00
116 *Plaxico Burress* 6.00
117 *Ron Dugans* 3.00
118 *Gari Scott* 2.50
119 *Curtis Keaton* 2.50
120 *Corey Simon* 3.00
121 *Rob Morris* 2.50
122 *Chad Morton* 2.50
123 *Hank Poteat* 2.50
124 *Ahmed Plummer* 2.50
125 *Bashir Yamini* 2.50
126 *J.R. Redmond* 5.00
127 *Travis Prentice* 5.00
128 *Todd Pinkston* 3.00
129 *Courtney Brown* 3.50
130 *Laveranues Coles* 3.50
131 *Jamal Lewis* 10.00
132 *Tim Rattay* 4.00
133 *Anthony Becht* 3.00
134 *Chris Cole* 2.50
135 *Ron Dayne* 15.00
136 *Sylvester Morris* 7.00
137 *Joe Hamilton* 3.00
138 *Dennis Northcutt* 3.50
139 *Doug Johnson* 2.50
140 *Shyrone Stith* 2.50
141 *Darrell Jackson* 3.50
142 *Michael Wiley* 3.00
143 *Chad Pennington* 12.00
144 *Bubba Franks* 3.50
145 *Shaun Alexander* 10.00

2000 Fleer Gamers Autographics

MT
Common Player: 10.00
Minor Stars: 20.00
Inserted 1:287
Silver Cards: 1.2x
Production 250 Sets
1 Shaun Alexander 45.00
2 Charlie Batch 20.00
3 Drew Bledsoe 35.00
4 Tim Brown 20.00
5 Isaac Bruce 25.00
6 Giovanni Carmazzi 35.00
7 Laveranues Coles 20.00
8 Tim Couch 55.00
9 Ron Dayne 85.00
10 Danny Farmer 10.00
11 Bubba Franks 20.00
12 Tony Gonzalez 20.00
13 Thomas Jones 35.00
14 Cade McNown 35.00
15 Dennis Northcutt 20.00
16 J.R. Redmond 25.00
17 Peter Warrick 85.00

2000 Fleer Gamers Change the Game

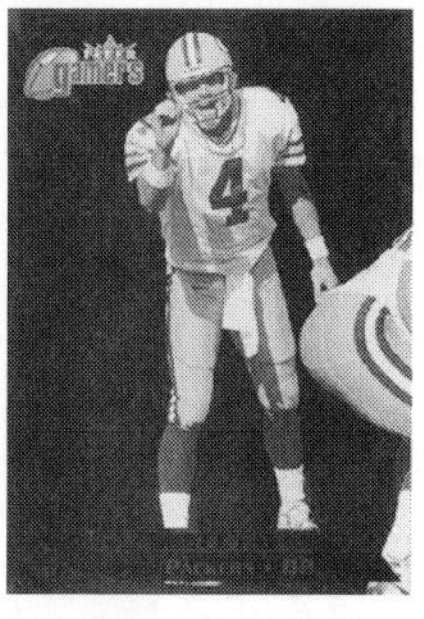

MT
Complete Set (15): 65.00
Common Player: 2.50
Inserted 1:24
1 Kurt Warner 10.00
2 Brett Favre 8.00
3 Eddie George 3.00
4 Keyshawn Johnson 2.50
5 Randy Moss 8.00
6 Tim Couch 4.00
7 Ricky Williams 4.00
8 Peyton Manning 8.00
9 Terrell Davis 6.00
10 Troy Aikman 4.00
11 Fred Taylor 3.50
12 Cade McNown 3.50
13 Edgerrin James 8.00
14 Peter Warrick 10.00
15 Jamal Lewis 6.00

2000 Fleer Gamers Contact Sport

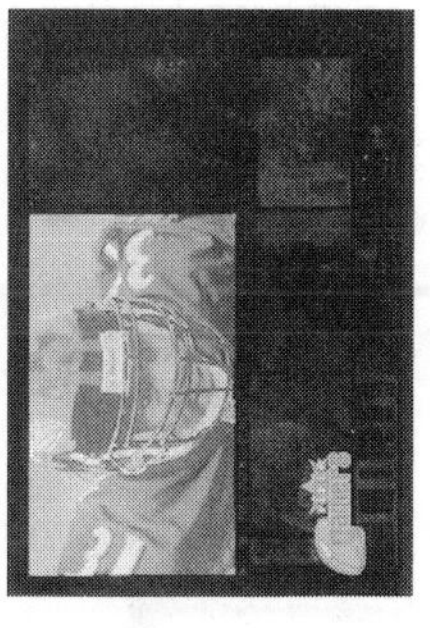

MT
Complete Set (20): 25.00
Common Player: 1.00
Inserted 1:4
1 Peter Warrick 6.00
2 Jamal Lewis 4.00
3 Thomas Jones 3.00
4 Plaxico Burress 3.00
5 Travis Taylor 2.00
6 Ron Dayne 6.00
7 Bubba Franks 1.50
8 Chad Pennington 5.00
9 Shaun Alexander 4.00
10 Sylvester Morris 2.50
11 R. Jay Soward 1.00
12 Trung Canidate 1.00
13 Dennis Northcutt 1.00
14 Todd Pinkston 1.00
15 Jerry Porter 1.00
16 Travis Prentice 2.00
17 Courtney Brown 1.50
18 Ron Dugans 1.00
19 Dez White 1.00
20 Chris Redman 2.00

A card number in parentheses ( ) indicates the set is unnumbered.

2000 Fleer Gamers Extra Parallel

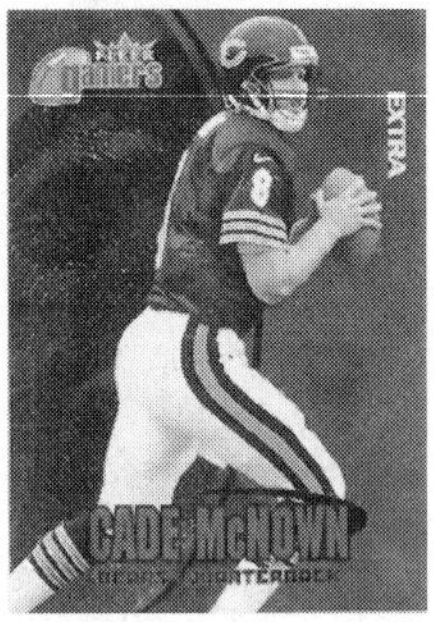

	MT
Complete Set (145):	275.00
Extra Cards:	3x-6x
Inserted 1:8	
Extra Rookies:	2x
Inserted 1:24	

2000 Fleer Gamers Uniformity

		MT
Complete Set (34):		750.00
Common Player:		15.00
Inserted 1:44		
1	Kurt Warner	100.00
2	Az-Zahir Hakim	15.00
3	Marshall Faulk	35.00
4	Bruce Smith	15.00
5	Curtis Enis	15.00
6	Mark Brunell	45.00
7	Troy Aikman	55.00
8	Emmitt Smith	65.00
9	Ed McCaffrey	25.00
10	Jerry Rice	55.00
11	Stephen Davis	30.00
12	Tim Brown	25.00
13	Randall Cunningham	30.00
14	Steve Young	45.00
15	John Lynch	15.00
16	Isaac Bruce	35.00
17	Torry Holt	35.00
18	Jake Plummer	35.00
19	David Boston	30.00
20	Charlie Batch	35.00
21	Germane Crowell	25.00
22	Herman Moore	25.00
23	Johnnie Morton	15.00
24	Peyton Manning	85.00
25	Edgerrin James	75.00
26	Marvin Harrison	35.00
27	Tim Couch	55.00
28	Kevin Johnson	25.00
29	Rob Moore	15.00
30	Frank Sanders	15.00
31	Chris Chandler	15.00
32	Jamal Anderson	30.00
33	Tim Dwight	30.00
34	Terry Kirby	15.00

2000 Fleer Gamers Yard Chargers

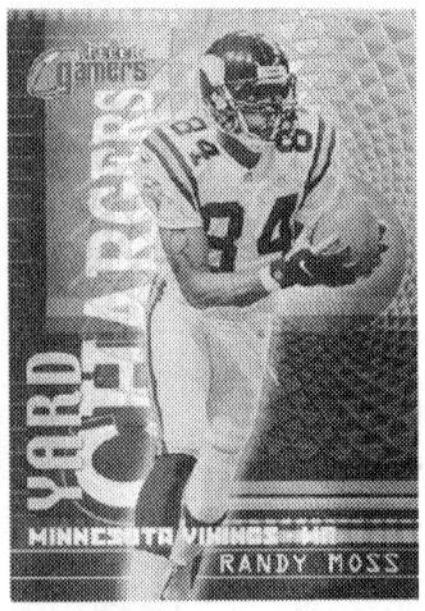

		MT
Complete Set (15):		75.00
Common Player:		1.50
#1-5 Inserted 1:9		
#6-10 Inserted 1:24		
#11-15 Inserted 1:144		
1	Marvin Harrison	1.50
2	Randy Moss	3.00
3	Keyshawn Johnson	1.50
4	Tim Brown	1.50
5	Jerry Rice	2.00
6	Terrell Davis	4.50
7	Emmitt Smith	4.50
8	Eddie George	2.50
9	Edgerrin James	6.00
10	Marshall Faulk	2.00
11	Tim Couch	12.00
12	Kurt Warner	20.00
13	Peyton Manning	20.00
14	Brett Favre	20.00
15	Troy Aikman	12.00

2000 Fleer Genuine Coverage Nostalgic

		MT
Complete Set (9):		220.00
Common Player:		20.00
Inserted 1:360		
1	Chad Pennington	50.00
2	Ron Dayne	65.00
3	Plaxico Burress	40.00
4	Brian Urlacher	35.00
5	Bubba Franks	25.00
6	Jerry Porter	25.00
7	Trung Canidate	20.00
8	Dez White	25.00
9	Courtney Brown	30.00

2000 Fleer Glossy

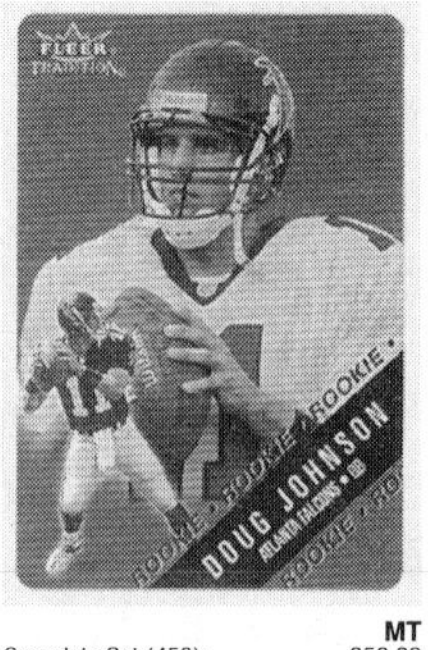

		MT
Complete Set (450):		350.00
Complete Set (400):		125.00
Complete Factory Set:		175.00
Factory set includes cards #1-400, 5 rookies (#401-450) & Threads card.		
Common Player:		.25
Minor Stars:		.50
Common Rookie (#304-365):		1.00
Common Rookie (#401-450):		2.00
Production for Rookies (#401-450) 750 Sets		
Total of 7,500 Factory Sets Released		
1	Kevin Johnson	.75
2	Chris Chandler	.50
3	Peerless Price	.75
4	Andre Rison	.50
5	Curtis Enis	.50
6	Tim Couch	1.50
7	Brian Dawkins	.25
8	Akili Smith	.75
9	Kevin Faulk	.50
10	Joey Galloway	.75
11	Bill Romanowski	.25
12	Charlie Batch	.75
13	Terrence Wilkins	.50
14	Kevin Hardy	.25
15	Cade McNown	.75
16	Elvis Grbac	.50
17	Cris Carter	.75
18	Willie McGinest	.25
19	Michael Bishop	.75
20	Lee Woodall	.25
21	Jake Reed	.50
22	Bryan Cox	.25
23	Chris Sanders	.25
24	Tavian Banks	.50
25	Levon Kirkland	.25
26	James Hundon	.25
27	Junior Seau	.50
28	Darren Woodson	.25
29	Kevin Carter	.25
30	Joe Jurevicius	.50
31	John Lynch	.25
32	Steve McNair	.75
33	Jake Plummer	.75
34	Antonio Freeman	.75
35	Peter Boulware	.25
36	Brad Johnson	.75
37	Bobby Engram	.25
38	David Boston	.75
39	Jason Tucker	.50
40	Troy Brown	.25
41	Brian Griese	1.00
42	Dorsey Levens	.75
43	Cornelius Bennett	.25
44	Donovan McNabb	1.25
45	Rob Johnson	.75
46	Robert Smith	.75
47	Stanley Pritchett	.25
48	Tedy Bruschi	.25
49	Dan Marino	2.50
50	Amani Toomer	.25
51	Aaron Glenn	.25
52	Rickey Dudley	.25
53	Tim Brown	.75
54	Jim Harbaugh	.50
55	Terrell Owens	.75
56	Jason Sehorn	.25
57	Cortez Kennedy	.25
58	London Fletcher	.25
59	Simeon Rice	.25
60	Shaun King	1.25
61	Stephen Davis	.75
62	Andre Wadsworth	.25
63	Kyle Brady	.25
64	Priest Holmes	.75
65	Patrick Jeffers	.75
66	Barry Minter	.25
67	Curtis Martin	.75
68	Darrin Chiaverini	.25
69	Robert Thomas	.25
70	Samari Rolle	.25
71	Robert Porcher	.25
72	Jerry Rice	1.75
73	Bill Schroeder	.50
74	Chad Bratzke	.25
75	Tony Brackens	.25
76	O.J. McDuffie	.50
77	John Randle	.50
78	Michael Pittman	.50
79	Drew Bledsoe	1.25
80	Ike Hilliard	.50
81	Victor Green	.25
82	Duce Staley	.75
83	Bruce Smith	.50
84	Amos Zereoue	.50
85	Charlie Garner	.50
86	Shawn Springs	.25
87	Kurt Warner	3.00
88	Eddie George	.75
89	Michael Westbrook	.50
90	Dexter Coakley	.25
91	Rob Moore	.50
92	Duane Starks	.25
93	Steve Beuerlein	.50
94	Marty Booker	.25
95	Karim Abdul	.25
96	Troy Aikman	1.75
97	Germane Crowell	.75
98	Matt Hasselbeck	.50
99	E.G. Green	.50
100	Mark Brunell	1.25
101	Tony Martin	.25
102	Darrell Green	.25
103	Ricky Williams	2.00
104	Michael Strahan	.25
105	Vinny Testaverde	.75
106	Charles Johnson	.50
107	Hines Ward	.50
108	Bryant Young	.25
109	Mo Lewis	.25
110	Greg Clark	.25
111	Jon Kitna	.75
112	Jacquez Green	.50
113	Kevin Dyson	.50
114	Stephen Alexander	.25
115	Cameron Cleeland	.50
116	Keith Poole	.25
117	Az-Zahir Hakim	.50
118	Tim Dwight	.75
119	Corey Bradford	.50
120	Carlos Emmons	.25
121	Trent Dilfer	.50
122	Lance Schulters	.25
123	Byron Hanspard	.50
124	Tim Biakabutuka	.50
125	Eddie Kennison	.50
126	Terry Kirby	.25
127	Mike McKenzie	.25
128	Fred Beasley	.25
129	Chad Brown	.25
130	Terrell Davis	2.50
131	Herman Moore	.75
132	Vonnie Holliday	.25
133	Jim Miller	.25
134	Peyton Manning	3.00
135	Derrick Alexander	.25
136	Oronde Gadsden	.50
137	Robert Griffith	.25
138	Troy Edwards	.50
139	Damon Huard	.50
140	Jessie Armstead	.25
141	Charles Woodson	.75
142	Troy Vincent	.25
143	Natrone Means	.50
144	Jeff Garcia	.75
145	Terry Glenn	.75
146	Marshall Faulk	1.00
147	Patrick Johnson	.50
148	Frank Wycheck	.25
149	Champ Bailey	.50
150	Jamal Anderson	.75
151	Doug Flutie	1.00
152	Michael Bates	.25
153	Corey Dillon	1.00
154	Keith McKenzie	.25
155	Orpheus Roye	.25
156	Olandis Gary	.75
157	Johnnie Morton	.50
158	Brett Favre	3.50
159	Adrian Murrell	.25
160	Fred Taylor	1.25
161	Tony Gonzalez	.75
162	Zach Thomas	.50
163	Randy Moss	3.00
164	Marcus Robinson	.75
165	Tiki Barber	.75
166	Rich Gannon	.50
167	Jeremiah Trotter	.25
168	Jermaine Fazande	.50
169	Steve Young	1.25
170	Isaac Bruce	.75
171	Warrick Dunn	.75
172	Yancey Thigpen	.50
173	Rod Smith	.75
174	Albert Connell	.50
175	Freddie Jones	.50
176	Terance Mathis	.25
177	Eric Moulds	.75
178	Brian Mitchell	.25
179	Wesley Walls	.50
180	Carl Pickens	.50
181	Errict Rhett	.50
182	Madre Hill	.25
183	Jason Elam	.25
184	Greg Ellis	.25
185	David Sloan	.25
186	Edgerrin James	3.00
187	Jimmy Smith	.75
188	Tony Richardson	.50
189	James Hasty	.25
190	Sam Madison	.25
191	Tony Simmons	.50
192	Andre Hastings	.25
193	Keyshawn Johnson	.75
194	Na Brown	.25
195	Napoleon Kaufman	.75
196	Torrance Small	.25
197	Curtis Conway	.50
198	Jeff Graham	.25
199	Jason Hanson	.25
200	Derrick Mayes	.50
201	Torry Holt	.75
202	Warren Sapp	.50
203	Kimble Anders	.25
204	Blaine Bishop	.25
205	Leroy Hoard	.25
206	Larry Centers	.25
207	O.J. Santiago	.25
208	Antowain Smith	.50
209	Chuck Smith	.25
210	Takeo Spikes	.25
211	Raghib Ismail	.25
212	Ed McCaffrey	.75
213	Karsten Bailey	.25
214	Terry Fair	.25
215	Ken Dilger	.25
216	Jamie Martin	.25
217	Cris Dishman	.25
218	Jay Fiedler	.50
219	Lawyer Milloy	.25
220	*Jake Delhomme*	2.00
221	Wayne Chrebet	.75
222	Darrell Russell	.25
223	Christian Fauria	.25
224	Jerome Bettis	.75
225	Ryan Leaf	.75
226	Ricky Watters	.75
227	Keenan McCardell	.50
228	Grant Wistrom	.25
229	Jevon Kearse	.75
230	Frank Sanders	.50
231	Shannon Sharpe	.50
232	Jonathon Linton	.50
233	Alonzo Mayes	.25
234	Jason Garrett	.25
235	Kordell Stewart	.75
236	David LaFleur	.25
237	Kenny Bynum	.25
238	Byron Chamberlain	.25
239	Tyrone Davis	.25
240	Jerome Pathon	.25
241	Alvis Whitted	.25
242	Kevin Lockett	.25
243	Matthew Hatchette	.50
244	Rod Woodson	.25
245	Joe Horn	.75
246	Ronnie Powell	.25
247	Dedric Ward	.50
248	J.J. Johnson	.50
249	James Jett	.25
250	*Bobby Shaw*	1.50
251	J.J. Stokes	.50
252	Paul Shields	.25
253	Sean Dawkins	.25
254	Hardy Nickerson	.25
255	Stephen Boyd	.25
256	Chris Warren	.50
257	Kerry Collins	.75
258	Isaac Byrd	.25
259	Bobby Hoying	.50
260	Daunte Culpepper	1.75
261	Moe Williams	.25
262	Kamil Loud	.25
263	Derrick Brooks	.25
264	Jay Riemersma	.50
265	Ray Lucas	.50
266	Jason Gildon	.25
267	James Stewart	.50
268	Marcelius Wiley	.25
269	Craig Yeast	.25
270	Michael Basnight	.25
271	Tyrone Wheatley	.50
272	Martin Gramatica	.50
273	Phillip Daniels	.25
274	Richard Huntley	.50
275	Muhsin Muhammad	.50
276	Todd Lyght	.25
277	Carlester Crumpler	.50
278	Jeff Lewis	.50
279	Jeff George	.50
280	Jeff Blake	.50
281	Mike McCrary	.25
282	Shawn Jefferson	.25
283	Mark Bruener	.25
284	Donnie Abraham	.25
285	Yatil Green	.25
286	Jermaine Lewis	.50
287	Rob Fredrickson	.25
288	Thurman Thomas	.50
289	Kent Graham	.25
290	Darnay Scott	.50
291	Tony Graziani	.50
292	Qadry Ismail	.50
293	Aeneas Williams	.25
294	Marvin Harrison	.75
295	Jimmy Hitchcock	.25
296	Bob Christian	.25
297	Pete Mitchell	.25
298	Mike Alstott	.75
299	Emmitt Smith	2.50
300	Trevor Pryce	.25
301	Tony Banks	.50
302	Mikhael Ricks	.25
303	Randall Cunningham	.50
304	*Thomas Jones*	3.00
305	*Mark Simoneau*	1.00
306	*Jamal Lewis*	10.00
307	*Kwame Cavil*	1.00
308	*Rashard Anderson*	1.50
309	*Brian Urlacher*	5.00
310	*Peter Warrick*	7.00
311	*Courtney Brown*	1.50
312	*Michael Wiley*	1.50
313	*Chris Cole*	1.00
314	*Reuben Droughns*	1.00
315	*Bubba Franks*	1.50
316	*Rob Morris*	1.00
317	*R. Jay Soward*	1.50
318	*Sylvester Morris*	4.00
319	*Ben Kelly*	1.00
320	*Doug Chapman*	1.00
321	*J.R. Redmond*	2.00
322	*Darren Howard*	1.00
323	*Ron Dayne*	8.00
324	*Chad Pennington*	6.00
325	*Jerry Porter*	1.50
326	*Corey Simon*	1.50
327	*Plaxico Burress*	4.00
328	*Trung Canidate*	1.50
329	*Rogers Beckett*	1.00
330	*Giovanni Carmazzi*	1.50
331	*Shaun Alexander*	5.00
332	*Joe Hamilton*	1.50
333	*Keith Bulluck*	1.50
334	*Todd Husak*	1.00
335	*Raynoch Thompson,Darwin Walker*	1.00
336	*Anthony Midget,Mareno Philyaw*	1.00
337	*Travis Taylor,Chris Redman*	3.00
338	*Avion Black,Sammy Morris*	2.50
339	*Deon Grant,Alvin McKinley*	1.00
340	*Dez White,Frank Murphy*	1.00
341	*Ron Dugans,Curtis Keaton*	1.50
342	*Dennis Northcutt,Travis Prentice*	2.50
343	*Dwayne Goodrich,Orantes Grant*	1.00
344	*Deltha O'Neal,Ian Gold*	1.00
345	*Stockar McDougle,Barrett Green*	1.00
346	*Na'il Diggs,Anthony Lucas*	1.00
347	*Marcus Washington,Dan Kendra*	1.00
348	*T.J. Slaughter,Shyrone Stith*	1.50
349	*William Bartee,Frank Moreau*	1.50
350	*Deon Dyer,Todd Wade*	1.00
351	*Chris Hovan,Troy Walters*	1.50
352	*David Stachelski,Tom Brady*	1.50
353	*Terrelle Smith,Marc Bulger*	1.00
354	*Ron Dixon,Cornelius Griffin*	2.00
355	*Laveranues Coles,Anthony Becht*	2.00
356	*Sebastian Janikowski,Shane Lechler*	1.50
357	*Todd Pinkston,Gari Scott*	1.50
358	*Danny Farmer,Tee Martin*	1.50
359	*Jacoby Shepherd,Brian Young*	1.00
360	*Trevor Gaylor,JaJuan Seider*	1.50
361	*Chafie Fields,Tim Rattay*	1.50
362	*Darrell Jackson,James Williams*	2.00
363	*Nate Webster,James Whalen*	1.00
364	*Erron Kinney,Chris Coleman*	1.00
365	*Chris Samuels,Leon Murray*	1.00
366	Arizona Cardinals Team	.50
367	Atlanta Falcons Team	.25
368	Baltimore Ravens Team	.50
369	Buffalo Bills Team	.50
370	Carolina Panthers Team	.25
371	Chicago Bears Team	.50
372	Cincinnati Bengals Team	.50
373	Cleveland Browns Team	.75
374	Dallas Cowboys Team	1.50
375	Denver Broncos Team	.50
376	Detroit Lions Team	.25
377	Green Bay Packers Team	.50
378	Indianapolis Colts Team	1.50
379	Jacksonville Jaguars Team	.50
380	Kansas City Chiefs Team	.25
381	Miami Dolphins Team	1.50
382	Minnesota Vikings Team	.50
383	New England Patriots Team	.50
384	New Orleans Saints Team	.75
385	New York Giants Team	.25
386	New York Jets Team	.25
387	Oakland Raiders Team	.25
388	Philadelphia Eagles Team	.50
389	Pittsburgh Steelers Team	.25
390	St. Louis Rams Team	.50
391	San Diego Chargers Team	.25
392	San Francisco 49ers Team	.50
393	Seattle Seahawks Team	.25
394	Tampa Bay Buccaneers Team	.25
395	Tennessee Titans Team	.50
396	Washington Redskins Team	.25
397	Tim Couch CL	.75
398	Peyton Manning CL	1.50
399	Kurt Warner CL	1.50
400	Randy Moss CL	1.50
401	*JaJuan Dawson*	7.00
402	*Mike Anderson*	50.00
403	*Windrell Hayes*	4.00
404	*Shockmain Davis*	4.00
405	*Dante Hall*	4.00
406	*Charles Lee*	4.00
407	*Maurice Smith*	20.00
408	*Obafemi Ayanbadejo*	6.00
409	Travis Taylor	5.00
410	Dez White	3.00
411	Sammy Morris	4.00
412	Darrell Jackson	7.00
413	Todd Pinkston	5.00
414	Ron Dixon	5.00
415	Frank Moreau	5.00
416	James Williams	2.00
417	*Lenzie Jackson*	5.00
418	*Chad Morton*	7.00
419	*Matt Lytle*	5.00
420	Travis Prentice	5.00
421	Laveranues Coles	5.00
422	*Clint Stoerner*	12.00
423	*KaRon Coleman*	4.00
424	Ron Dugans	3.00
425	Dennis Northcutt	5.00
426	*Herbert Goodman*	5.00
427	*Dane Looker*	4.00
428	*Mike Brown*	5.00
429	*Derrius Thompson*	4.00
430	Danny Farmer	3.00
431	*Bashir Yamini*	5.00
432	Trevor Gaylor	3.00
433	*Erron Kinney*	6.00
434	*James Hodgins*	4.00
435	*Aaron Shea*	5.00
436	*Patrick Pass*	5.00
437	Terrelle Smith	5.00
438	Avion Black	3.00
439	Deltha O'Neal	3.00
440	Chris Coleman	2.00
441	*Reggie Jones*	3.00
442	Shyrone Stith	3.00
443	*Aaron Stecker*	8.00
444	Chris Redman	8.00
445	Curtis Keaton	8.00
446	*Jamel White*	7.00
447	Troy Walters	3.00
448	Spergon Wynn	4.00
449	*Ronney Jenkins*	5.00
450	*Doug Johnson*	8.00

2000 Fleer Glossy Traditional Threads

		MT
Common Player:		15.00
Inserted 1:Factory Set		
1	Troy Aikman 140	40.00
2	Jamal Anderson 225	15.00
3	Charlie Batch 55	20.00
4	Drew Bledsoe 325	20.00
5	David Boston 55	25.00
6	Tim Brown 81	20.00
7	Mark Brunell 700	18.00
8	Chris Chandler 12	30.00
9	Tim Couch 430	25.00
10	Germane Crowell 82	20.00
11	Stephen Davis 155	20.00
12	Terrell Davis 100	40.00
13	Ron Dayne 27	100.00
14	Curtis Enis 44	35.00
15	Marshall Faulk 275	30.00
16	Brett Favre 585	50.00
17	Doug Flutie 7	60.00
18	Antonio Freeman 86	20.00
19	Brian Griese 165	30.00
20	Marvin Harrison 250	20.00
21	Torry Holt 55	35.00
22	Edgerrin James 285	60.00
23	Dorsey Levens 25	45.00
24	Peyton Manning 345	60.00
25	Dan Marino 14	100.00
26	Curtis Martin 90	25.00
27	Steve McNair 200	20.00
28	Herman Moore 15	45.00
29	Johnnie Morton 25	35.00
30	Jake Plummer 250	25.00
31	Junior Seau 55	35.00
32	Antowain Smith 26	25.00
33	Emmitt Smith 750	45.00
34	Rod Smith 25	35.00
35	Fred Taylor 325	30.00
36	Vinny Testaverde 225	15.00
37	Amani Toomer 25	30.00
38	Kurt Warner 700	50.00
39	Charles Woodson 24	35.00
40	Steve Young 125	35.00

2000 Fleer Greats of the Game

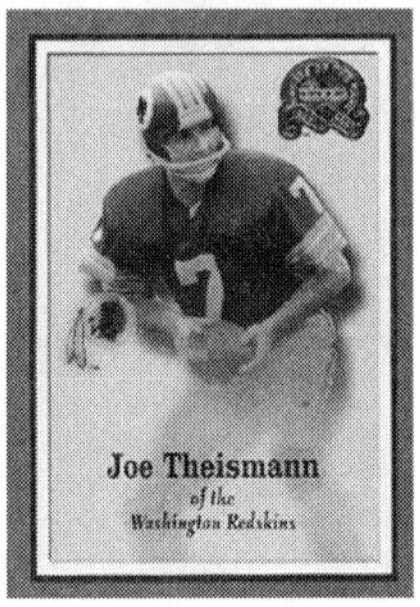

		MT
Complete Set (130):		350.00
Common Player:		.15
Minor Stars:		.30
Common Rookie:		5.00
Production 1,500 Sets		
Cards #131-134 are Redemptions		
Production 500 Sets		
Wax Box (24):		100.00
Pack (5):		5.00
1	Terry Bradshaw	2.50
2	Paul Hornung	.50
3	Tony Dorsett	.50
4	L.C. Greenwood	.15
5	Ozzie Newsome	.30
6	Michael Irvin	.30
7	Art Donovan	.30
8	Don Maynard	.30
9	Bobby Mitchell	.15
10	Bob Lilly	.30
11	Earl Morrall	.15
12	Harvey Martin	.15
13	Dan Fouts	.50
14	Joe Theismann	.30
15	Roger Staubach	2.50
16	Otto Graham	.50
17	Cliff Branch	.30
18	Sonny Jurgensen	.30
19	Eric Dickerson	.30
20	Lee Roy Selmon	.15
21	Roger Craig	.30
22	Raymond Berry	.15
23	Bob Hayes	.15
24	Steve Largent	.50
25	Lenny Moore	.15
26	Chuck Bednarik	.15
27	Ken Stabler	2.00
28	William Perry	.30
29	Joe Greene	.30
30	Joe Namath	2.50
31	Jim Kelly	.50
32	Steve Young	.75
33	Randy White	.30
34	Lawrence Taylor	.30
35	Franco Harris	.50
36	Marcus Allen	.50
37	Mike Singletary	.30
38	Fran Tarkenton	1.00
39	Mel Renfro	.15
40	Len Dawson	.50
41	Carl Eller	.15
42	Chuck Foreman	.15
43	Gino Marchetti	.15
44	Jim Marshall	.15
45	Jack Ham	.15
46	Mercury Morris	.15
47	Anthony Munoz	.15
48	Herschel Walker	.30
49	Drew Pearson	.15
50	John Elway	2.50
51	George Blanda	.30
52	Earl Campbell	.50
53	Bart Starr	2.00
54	Dan Marino	2.50
55	Johnny Unitas	2.00
56	Sammy Baugh	.50
57	Steve Van Buren	.15
58	Mel Blount	.15
59	Fred Biletnikoff	.30
60	John Brodie	.15
61	Daryle Lamonica	.15
62	James Lofton	.30
63	Ronnie Lott	.30
64	Gale Sayers	1.00
65	Art Monk	.30
66	Jim Plunkett	.30
67	Charlie Joiner	.30
68	Deacon Jones	.30
69	Paul Warfield	.50

70	Jim Otto	.15
71	Billy Kilmer	.15
72	Archie Manning	.30
73	Alex Karras	.30
74	Tom Matte	.15
75	Jay Novacek	.15
76	Charley Taylor	.15
77	Sam Huff	.15
78	Jack Lambert	.15
79	Mike Ditka	1.00
80	Frank Gifford	.75
81	Jim Thorpe	.50
82	Walter Payton	3.00
83	Doak Walker	.15
84	Sid Luckman	.15
85	Bronko Nagurski	.50
86	Alan Ameche	.15
87	Merlin Olsen	.30
88	Dick Butkus	1.00
89	Elroy Hirsch	.30
90	Max McGee	.30
91	Ray Nitschke	.30
92	Phil Simms	.30
93	Vince Lombardi	1.50
94	Tom Landry	1.00
95	Bill Walsh	.30
96	Mike Ditka	.75
97	Jimmy Johnson	.30
98	Chuck Noll	.15
99	Dan Reeves	.30
100	Don Shula	.50
101	*Peter Warrick*	30.00
102	*Thomas Jones*	12.00
103	*Jamal Lewis*	40.00
104	*Chad Pennington*	25.00
105	*Chris Redman*	12.00
106	*Ron Dayne*	30.00
107	*Trung Canidate*	6.00
108	*Shaun Alexander*	20.00
109	*Plaxico Burress*	15.00
110	*J.R. Redmond*	8.00
111	*Travis Taylor*	8.00
112	*Dez White*	6.00
113	*Todd Pinkston*	7.00
114	*Laveranues Coles*	8.00
115	*Dennis Northcutt*	7.00
116	*Jerry Porter*	6.00
117	*R. Jay Soward*	6.00
118	*Sylvester Morris*	15.00
119	*Ron Dugans*	5.00
120	*Travis Prentice*	10.00
121	*Tee Martin*	6.00
122	*James Williams*	5.00
123	*Trevor Gaylor*	6.00
124	*Shyrone Stith*	6.00
125	*Frank Moreau*	7.00
126	*Kwame Cavil*	5.00
127	*Ron Dixon*	8.00
128	*Darrell Jackson*	8.00
129	*Sammy Morris*	8.00
130	*JuJuan Dawson*	7.00
131	*Doug Johnson*	35.00
132	*Brian Urlacher*	60.00
133	*Brad Hoover*	45.00
134	*Mike Anderson AUTO*	150.00

2000 Fleer Greats of the Game Autographs

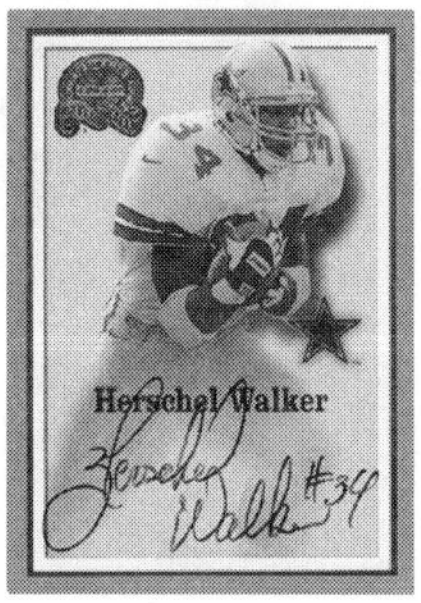

		MT
Common Player:		10.00
Minor Stars:		20.00
Inserted 1:24		
1	Marcus Allen	25.00
2	Sammy Baugh	150.00
3	Chuck Bednarik	10.00
4	Raymond Berry	10.00
5	Fred Biletnikoff	20.00
6	George Blanda	30.00
7	Mel Blount	20.00
8	Terry Bradshaw	125.00
9	Cliff Branch	20.00
10	John Brodie	250.00
11	Earl Campbell	40.00
12	Roger Craig	20.00
13	Len Dawson	25.00
14	Eric Dickerson	20.00
15	Mike Ditka	200.00
16	Mike Ditka CC	200.00
17	Art Donovan	20.00
18	Tony Dorsett	50.00
19	Carl Eller	100.00
20	John Elway	150.00
21	Chuck Foreman	20.00
22	Dan Fouts	20.00
23	Frank Gifford	250.00
24	Otto Graham	30.00
25	Joe Greene	40.00
26	L.C. Greenwood	20.00
27	Jack Ham	20.00
28	Franco Harris	50.00
29	Bob Hayes	30.00
30	Paul Hornung	50.00
31	Sam Huff	20.00
32	Michael Irvin	175.00
33	Jimmy Johnson	200.00
34	Charlie Joiner	10.00
35	Deacon Jones	25.00
36	Sonny Jurgensen	40.00
37	Alex Karras	30.00
38	Jim Kelly	50.00
39	Billy Kilmer	25.00
40	Jack Lambert	50.00
41	Daryle Lamonica	25.00
42	Steve Largent	30.00
43	Bob Lilly	20.00
44	James Lofton	20.00
45	Ronnie Lott	25.00
46	Archie Manning	30.00
47	Gino Marchetti	20.00
48	Dan Marino	200.00
49	Jim Marshall	25.00
50	Harvey Martin	10.00
51	Tom Matte	10.00
52	Don Maynard	20.00
53	Bobby Mitchell	10.00
54	Art Monk	150.00
55	Lenny Moore	10.00
56	Earl Morrall	10.00
57	Mercury Morris	20.00
58	Anthony Munoz	20.00
59	Joe Namath	85.00
60	Ozzie Newsome	20.00
61	Chuck Noll	75.00
62	Jay Novacek	20.00
63	Jim Otto	20.00
64	Drew Pearson	20.00
65	William Perry	20.00
66	Jim Plunkett	30.00
67	Dan Reeves	35.00
68	Mel Renfro	10.00
69	Gale Sayers	40.00
70	Lee Roy Selmon	10.00
71	Don Shula	100.00
72	Mike Singletary	20.00
73	Ken Stabler	30.00
74	Bart Starr	250.00
75	Roger Staubach	100.00
76	Fran Tarkenton	50.00
77	Charley Taylor	10.00
78	Lawrence Taylor	250.00
79	Joe Theismann	30.00
80	Johnny Unitas	175.00
81	Steve Van Buren	150.00
82	Herschel Walker	30.00
83	Bill Walsh	100.00
84	Paul Warfield	20.00
85	Randy White	20.00
86	Steve Young	60.00

2000 Fleer Greats of the Game Cowboys Clippings

		MT
Complete Set (9):		600.00
Common Player:		25.00
Inserted 1:72		
Card #3 Bob Hayes was never issued		
CCL1	Troy Aikman	50.00
CCL2	Tony Dorsett	50.00
CCL4	Michael Irvin	25.00
CCL5	Tom Landry SP	425.00
CCL6	Bob Lilly	25.00
CCL7	Harvey Martin Shoes	75.00
CCL8	Jay Novacek	25.00
CCL9	Mel Renfro	25.00
CCL10	Roger Staubach	75.00

2000 Fleer Greats of the Game Feel The Game Classics

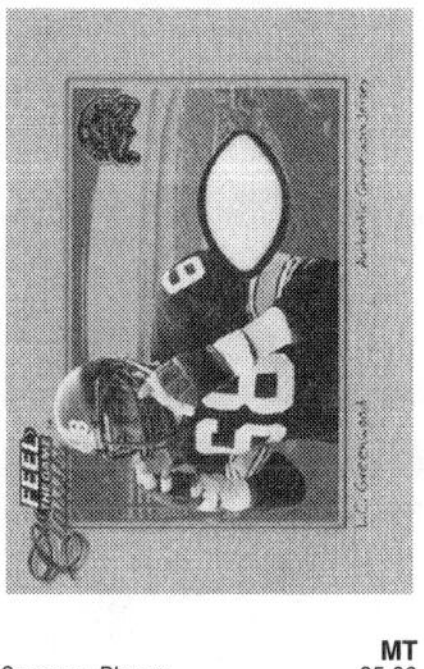

		MT
Common Player:		25.00
Inserted 1:36		
1	Marcus Allen	25.00
2	Fred Biletnikoff	25.00
3	Terry Bradshaw	50.00
4	Eric Dickerson	25.00
5	John Elway	75.00
6	L.C. Greenwood Jersey	25.00
7	L.C. Greenwood Shoe	35.00
8	Paul Hornung Pants	35.00
9	Jim Kelly	35.00
10	James Lofton	25.00
11	Ronnie Lott	25.00
12	Dan Marino White	75.00
13	Dan Marino Teal	75.00
14	Joe Namath	80.00
15	Walter Payton	100.00
16	Jim Plunkett Black	25.00
17	Jim Plunkett White	25.00
18	Mike Singletary	25.00
19	Bart Starr Pants	50.00
20	Fran Tarkenton	35.00
21	Lawrence Taylor	35.00
22	Johnny Unitas	50.00
23	Steve Young	30.00

Post-1980 cards in Near Mint condition will generally sell for about 75% of the quoted Mint value. Excellent-condition cards bring no more than 40%.

2000 Fleer Greats of the Game Retrospection Collection

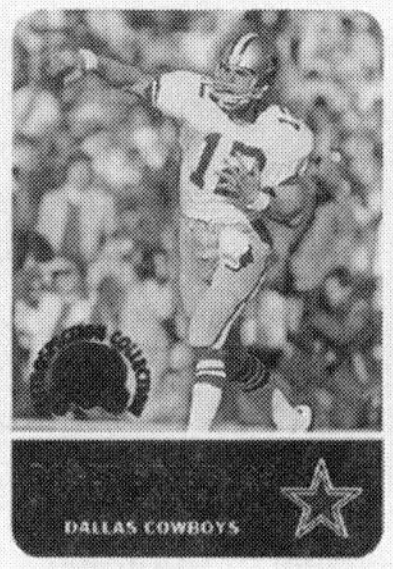

		MT
Complete Set (10):		18.00
Common Player:		1.00
Inserted 1:6		
RC1	Terry Bradshaw	3.00
RC2	John Elway	3.00
RC3	Roger Staubach	2.50
RC4	Franco Harris	1.00
RC5	Paul Hornung	1.00
RC6	Dan Marino	3.00
RC7	Fran Tarkenton	1.50
RC8	Joe Namath	3.00
RC9	Walter Payton	4.00
RC10	Jim Thorpe	1.00

2000 Fleer Mystique

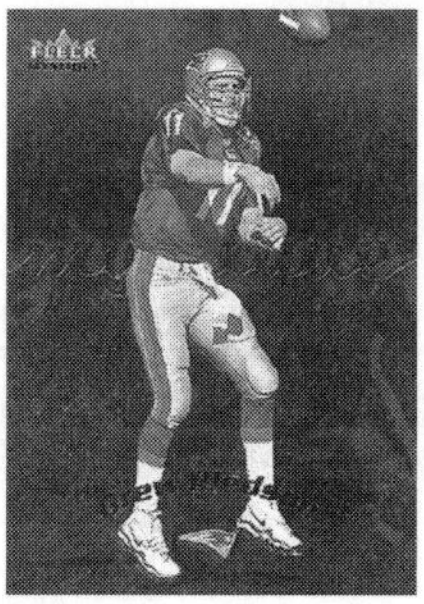

		MT
Complete Set (145):		275.00
Common Player:		.25
Minor Stars:		.50
Common Rookie:		2.50
Production 2,000 Sets		
Pack (5):		4.00
Wax Box (20):		60.00
1	Tim Couch	1.50
2	Edgerrin James	3.50
3	Terrell Davis	2.50
4	Eddie George	1.00
5	Jevon Kearse	.75
6	Mike Alstott	.75
7	Tony Martin	.25
8	Jermaine Fazande	.50
9	Akili Smith	.75
10	Damon Huard	.75
11	Kordell Stewart	.75
12	Peyton Manning	3.50
13	Michael Westbrook	.50
14	Tim Biakabutuka	.50
15	Curtis Martin	.75
16	Shaun King	1.25
17	Jamal Anderson	.75
18	Terry Allen	.50
19	Sean Dawkins	.25
20	Muhsin Muhammad	.50
21	Vinny Testaverde	.75
22	Warren Sapp	.25
23	Wesley Walls	.50
24	Mark Brunell	1.25
25	Tim Brown	.75
26	Kevin Dyson	.50
27	Curtis Enis	.50
28	Keenan McCardell	.50
29	Rich Gannon	.50
30	Jermaine Lewis	.25
31	Johnnie Morton	.50
32	Kerry Collins	.50
33	Az-Zahir Hakim	.50
34	Cade McNown	1.00
35	Jimmy Smith	.75
36	Tyrone Wheatley	.50
37	Marcus Robinson	.75
38	Fred Taylor	1.25
39	Donovan McNabb	1.25
40	Steve McNair	.75
41	Corey Dillon	.75
42	Tony Gonzalez	.50
43	Duce Staley	.75
44	Albert Connell	.50
45	Isaac Bruce	.75
46	Troy Aikman	1.75
47	Charlie Garner	.50
48	Kevin Johnson	.50
49	Cris Carter	.75
50	Ryan Leaf	.75
51	Doug Flutie	1.00
52	Brett Favre	3.50
53	Joe Montgomery	.25
54	Torry Holt	.75
55	Jonathon Linton	.50
56	Antonio Freeman	.75
57	Amani Toomer	.50
58	Kurt Warner	4.00
59	Jake Plummer	1.00
60	Rob Johnson	.50
61	Randy Moss	3.50
62	Jerry Rice	1.75
63	Chris Chandler	.50
64	Joey Galloway	.75
65	Olandis Gary	1.00
66	Drew Bledsoe	1.25
67	Steve Beuerlein	.50
68	Marvin Harrison	.75
69	Keyshawn Johnson	.75
70	Warrick Dunn	.75
71	Tim Dwight	.75
72	Brian Griese	1.00
73	Terry Glenn	.75
74	Jon Kitna	.75
75	Qadry Ismail	.25
76	Germane Crowell	.75
77	Ricky Williams	2.00
78	Marshall Faulk	.75
79	Karim Abdul	.25
80	J.J. Johnson	.50
81	Hines Ward	.50
82	Frank Sanders	.50
83	Emmitt Smith	2.50
84	Robert Smith	.75
85	Steve Young	1.25
86	Darnay Scott	.50
87	Tamarick Vanover	.25
88	Troy Edwards	.75
89	Brad Johnson	.75
90	Tony Banks	.50
91	Charlie Batch	.75
92	Jeff Blake	.50
93	Ricky Watters	.50
94	Carl Pickens	.50
95	Elvis Grbac	.50
96	Jerome Bettis	.75
97	Eric Moulds	.75
98	Dorsey Levens	.75
99	Wayne Chrebet	.75
100	Stephen Davis	.75
101	*Shaun Alexander*	15.00
102	*Sebastian Janikowski*	4.00
103	*Tom Brady*	8.00
104	*Courtney Brown*	5.00
105	*Marc Bulger*	2.50
106	*Plaxico Burress*	10.00
107	*Trung Canidate*	4.00
108	*Giovanni Carmazzi*	5.00
109	*Trevor Gaylor*	3.00
110	*Laveranues Coles*	5.00
111	*Ron Dayne*	25.00
112	*Reuben Droughns*	3.00
113	*Danny Farmer*	4.00
114	*Chafie Fields*	2.50
115	*Bubba Franks*	5.00
116	*Sherrod Gideon*	2.50
117	*Joe Hamilton*	5.00
118	*Chris Cole*	2.50
119	*Darrell Jackson*	5.00
120	*Thomas Jones*	8.00
121	*Jamal Lewis*	30.00
122	*Anthony Lucas*	2.50
123	*Tee Martin*	4.00
124	*Frank Murphy*	2.50
125	*Rondell Mealey*	3.00
126	*Sylvester Morris*	10.00
127	*Dennis Northcutt*	5.00
128	*Chad Pennington*	18.00
129	*Travis Prentice*	7.00
130	*Tim Rattay*	5.00
131	*Chris Redman*	8.00
132	*J.R. Redmond*	6.00
133	*R. Jay Soward*	5.00
134	*Quinton Spotwood*	2.50
135	*Shyrone Stith*	4.00
136	*Travis Taylor*	6.00
137	*Troy Walters*	5.00
138	*Peter Warrick*	20.00
139	*Dez White*	3.00
140	*Michael Wiley*	3.00
141	*Jerry Porter*	4.00
142	*Mareno Philyaw*	2.50
143	*Anthony Becht*	4.00
144	*JaJuan Dawson*	5.00
145	*Ron Dugans*	4.00

2000 Fleer Mystique Big Buzz

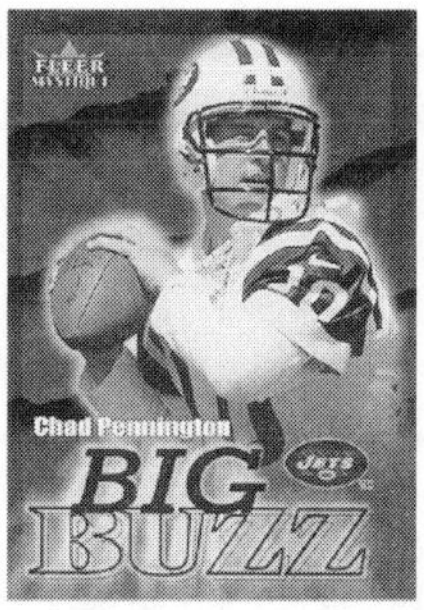

		MT
Complete Set (10):		20.00
Common Player:		1.50
Inserted 1:10		
1	Peter Warrick	4.00
2	Shaun Alexander	3.00
3	Ron Dayne	5.00
4	Joe Hamilton	1.50
5	Thomas Jones	2.00
6	Jamal Lewis	6.00
7	Chad Pennington	3.50
8	Tim Rattay	1.75
9	Chris Redman	2.00
10	Plaxico Burress	2.50

Post-1980 cards in Near Mint condition will generally sell for about 75% of the quoted Mint value. Excellent-condition cards bring no more than 40%.

2000 Fleer Mystique Canton Calling

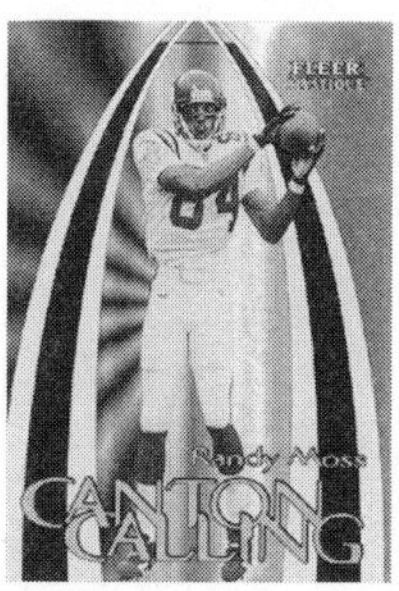

		MT
Complete Set (10):		30.00
Common Player:		1.00
Minor Stars:		2.00
Inserted 1:20		
1	Jerry Rice	4.00
2	Troy Aikman	4.00
3	Dan Marino	6.00
4	Brett Favre	8.00
5	Peyton Manning	8.00
6	Emmitt Smith	6.00
7	Randy Moss	8.00
8	Marvin Harrison	2.00
9	Marshall Faulk	2.00
10	Thurman Thomas	1.00

2000 Fleer Mystique Destination Tampa

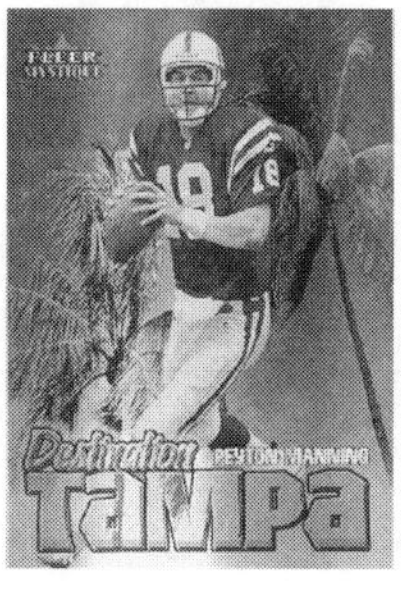

		MT
Complete Set (10):		15.00
Common Player:		1.00
Inserted 1:10		
1	Kurt Warner	5.00
2	Peyton Manning	4.00
3	Brett Favre	4.00
4	Tim Couch	1.75
5	Keyshawn Johnson	1.00
6	Mark Brunell	1.50
7	Eddie George	1.25
8	Edgerrin James	4.00
9	Ricky Williams	2.00
10	Randy Moss	4.00

2000 Fleer Mystique Gold Parallel

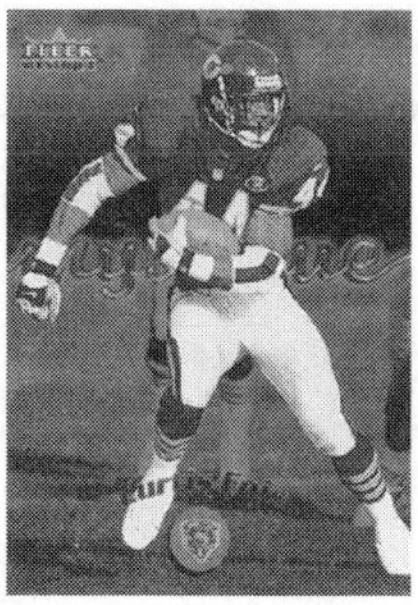

	MT
Gold Cards:	2x-4x
Gold Rookies:	1.5x
Inserted 1:20	

Values quoted in this guide reflect the retail price of a card — the price a collector can expect to pay when buying a card from a dealer. The wholesale price — that which a collector can expect to receive from a dealer when selling cards — will be significantly lower, depending on desirability and condition.

2000 Fleer Mystique Numbers Game

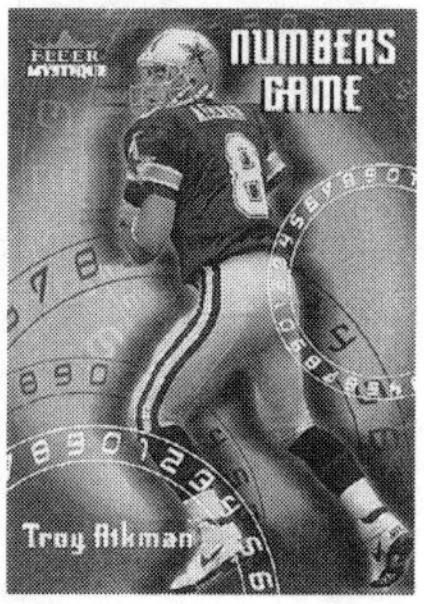

		MT
Complete Set (10):		45.00
Common Player:		3.00
Inserted 1:40		
Red Zone cards:		4x
Production 100 Sets		
1	Kurt Warner	12.00
2	Peyton Manning	10.00
3	Keyshawn Johnson	3.00
4	Terrell Davis	7.00
5	Brett Favre	10.00
6	Jevon Kearse	3.00
7	Troy Aikman	6.00
8	Edgerrin James	10.00
9	Eddie George	4.00
10	Marshall Faulk	3.00

2000 Fleer Mystique Running Men

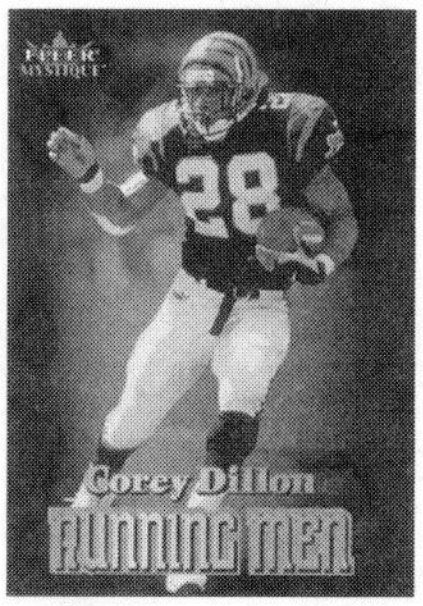

		MT
Complete Set (20):		15.00
Common Player:		.50
Minor Stars:		1.00
Inserted 1:5		
1	Antowain Smith	1.00
2	Corey Dillon	1.00
3	Terrell Davis	2.50
4	Edgerrin James	3.50
5	Fred Taylor	1.50
6	Kevin Faulk	.50
7	Jerome Bettis	1.00
8	Ricky Watters	1.00
9	Eddie George	1.25
10	Jamal Anderson	1.00
11	Tim Biakabutuka	.50
12	Curtis Enis	.50
13	Emmitt Smith	2.50
14	James Stewart	.50
15	Dorsey Levens	1.00
16	Robert Smith	1.00
17	Duce Staley	1.00
18	Marshall Faulk	1.00
19	Stephen Davis	1.00
20	Mike Alstott	1.00

2000 Fleer Rookie Retro

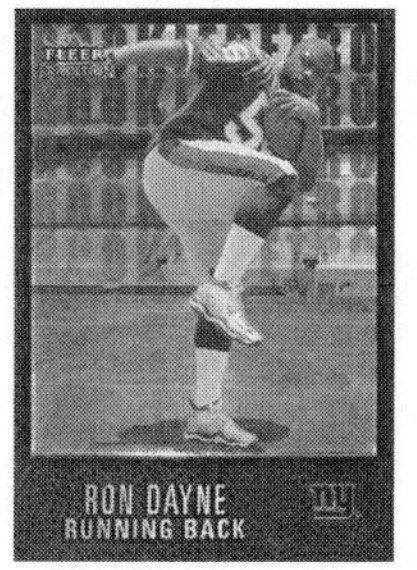

		MT
Complete Set (10):		30.00
Common Player:		2.00
Inserted 1:36		
1	Chad Pennington	8.00
2	Ron Dayne	12.00
3	Plaxico Burress	6.00
4	Brian Urlacher	4.00
5	Bubba Franks	3.00
6	Jerry Porter	2.00
7	Trung Canidate	2.00
8	Dez White	2.00
9	Courtney Brown	3.00
10	Shaun Alexander	5.00

2000 Fleer Throwbacks

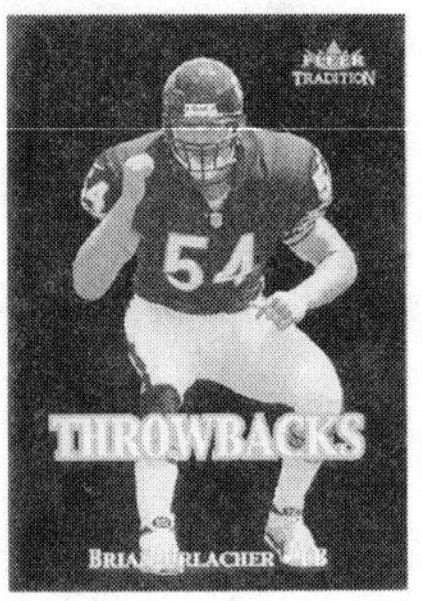

		MT
Complete Set (20):		10.00
Common Player:		.25
Minor Stars:		.50
Inserted 1:3		
1	Troy Aikman	1.00
2	Junior Seau	.25
3	Ron Dayne	3.00
4	Steve Young	.75
5	Wesley Walls	.25
6	Duce Staley	.50
7	Brian Urlacher	.75
8	Jerome Bettis	.50
9	Marshall Faulk	.50
10	Doug Flutie	.75
11	Brett Favre	2.00
12	Warren Sapp	.50
13	Charlie Batch	.50
14	Mike Alstott	.50
15	Cade McNown	.75
16	Jon Kitna	.50
17	Emmitt Smith	1.50
18	Tony Gonzalez	.50
19	Zach Thomas	.25
20	Cris Carter	.50

2000 Fleer Tradition of Excellence

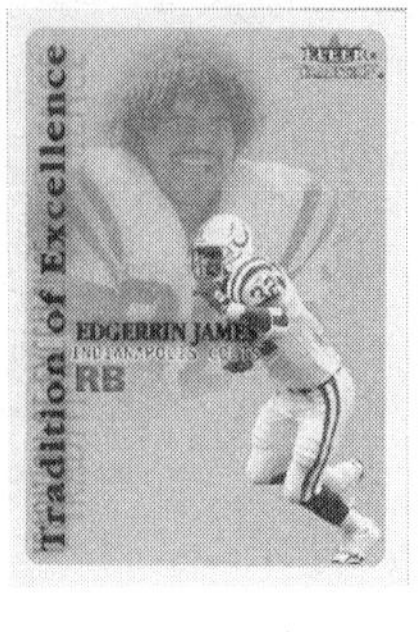

		MT
Complete Set (20):		40.00
Common Player:		.75
Inserted 1:9		
1	Brett Favre	4.00
2	Randy Moss	4.00
3	Tim Couch	2.00
4	Peter Warrick	6.00
5	Ron Dayne	6.00
6	Kurt Warner	5.00
7	Jevon Kearse	.75
8	Ricky Williams	2.00
9	Keyshawn Johnson	.75
10	Emmitt Smith	2.50
11	Donovan McNabb	1.50
12	Jamal Lewis	3.50
13	Jerry Rice	2.00
14	Eddie George	1.25
15	Peyton Manning	4.00
16	Stephen Davis	.75
17	Thomas Jones	3.00
18	Plaxico Burress	3.00
19	Troy Aikman	2.00
20	Edgerrin James	4.00

2000 Fleer Whole Ten Yards

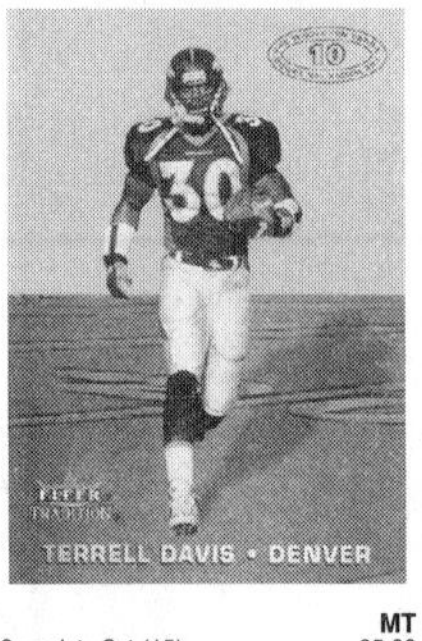

		MT
Complete Set (15):		35.00
Common Player:		1.00
Inserted 1:18		
1	Edgerrin James	5.00
2	Stephen Davis	1.00
3	Kurt Warner	6.00
4	Keyshawn Johnson	1.00
5	Mark Brunell	2.00
6	Peyton Manning	5.00
7	Emmitt Smith	3.50
8	Peter Warrick	10.00
9	Brett Favre	5.00
10	Marshall Faulk	1.00
11	Fred Taylor	1.75
12	Shaun Alexander	4.00
13	Terrell Davis	3.50
14	Eddie George	1.25
15	Randy Moss	5.00

2001 Fleer Authority

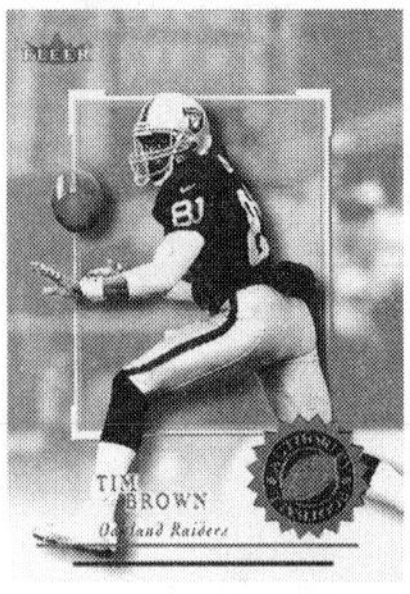

		MT
Complete Set (155):		300.00
Common Player:		.15
Minor Stars:		.30
Common Rookie:		3.00
Production 1,350 Sets		
Pack (5):		4.00
Box (20):		75.00
1	Brian Urlacher	1.25
2	James Stewart	.30
3	Lamar Smith	.30
4	Curtis Martin	.40
5	Shannon Sharpe	.30
6	Germane Crowell	.15
7	Daunte Culpepper	1.25
8	Charlie Garner	.30
9	Jake Plummer	.40
10	Eric Moulds	.40
11	Brett Favre	2.50
12	Robert Smith	.15
13	Tim Brown	.50
14	David Boston	.60
15	Cade McNown	.15
16	Ahman Green	.60
17	Terry Glenn	.30
18	Wayne Chrebet	.30
19	Jamal Lewis	1.25
20	Peter Warrick	.50
21	Peyton Manning	2.00
22	Ricky Williams	1.00
23	Donovan McNabb	1.25
24	Isaac Bruce	.60
25	Tim Couch	.75
26	Marvin Harrison	.60
27	Kerry Collins	.30
28	Kordell Stewart	.50
29	Keyshawn Johnson	.50
30	Kevin Johnson	.30
31	Mark Brunell	.75
32	Ron Dayne	.40
33	Doug Flutie	.75
34	Warrick Dunn	.30
35	Emmitt Smith	1.50
36	Jimmy Smith	.30
37	Amani Toomer	.15
38	Chad Pennington	.60
39	Steve McNair	.50
40	Brian Griese	.75
41	Derrick Alexander	.30
42	Vinny Testaverde	.40
43	Terrell Owens	.60
44	Derrick Mason	.30
45	Mike Anderson	1.00
46	Michael Westbrook	.30
47	Rich Gannon	.50
48	Shaun Alexander	1.00
49	Jevon Kearse	.30
50	Ed McCaffrey	.30
51	Tony Gonzalez	.30
52	Tyrone Wheatley	.15
53	Kurt Warner	2.00
54	Stephen Davis	.40
55	Rod Smith	.50
56	Deion Sanders	.50
57	Brad Johnson	.50
58	Ike Hilliard	.15
59	Trent Green	.40
60	Terrell Davis	1.25
61	Warren Sapp	.30
62	Marshall Faulk	.75
63	Tiki Barber	.30
64	Keenan McCardell	.15
65	Joey Galloway	.30
66	Frank Wycheck	.15
67	Ricky Watters	.30
68	Joe Horn	.15
69	Fred Taylor	.75
70	Troy Aikman	1.25
71	Mike Alstott	.40
72	Matt Hasselbeck	.40
73	Aaron Brooks	.75
74	Terrence Wilkins	.15
75	Travis Prentice	.15
76	Eddie George	.75
77	Jeff Garcia	.50
78	Randy Moss	2.00
79	Edgerrin James	1.50
80	Corey Dillon	.50
81	Torry Holt	.60
82	Todd Pinkston	.30
83	Drew Bledsoe	.75
84	Antonio Freeman	.50
85	Marcus Robinson	.40
86	Muhsin Muhammad	.15
87	Junior Seau	.30
88	Zach Thomas	.15
89	Dorsey Levens	.30
90	Tim Biakabutuka	.30
91	Elvis Grbac	.50
92	Jerome Bettis	.50
93	Cris Carter	.50
94	Jerry Rice	1.50
95	Rob Johnson	.30
96	Thomas Jones	.15
97	Duce Staley	.30
98	Ray Lucas	.15
99	Charlie Batch	.15
100	Jamal Anderson	.30
101	*Michael Vick*	25.00
102	*Drew Brees*	20.00
103	*Andre Carter*	3.00
104	*David Terrell*	15.00
105	*Koren Robinson*	10.00
106	*Rod Gardner*	10.00
107	*Santana Moss*	10.00
108	*Deuce McCallister*	12.00
109	*Freddie Mitchell*	10.00
110	*Michael Bennett*	12.00
111	*Reggie Wayne*	10.00
112	*Todd Heap*	3.00
113	*LaDainian Tomlinson*	20.00
114	*Chad Johnson*	5.00
115	*Anthony Thomas*	25.00
116	*Robert Ferguson*	5.00
117	*LaMont Jordan*	5.00
118	*Chris Chambers*	12.00
119	*Travis Henry*	8.00
120	*Marques Tuiasosopo*	10.00
121	*James Jackson*	6.00
122	*Heath Evans*	3.00
123	*Travis Minor*	6.00
124	*Rudi Johnson*	4.00
125	*Chris Weinke*	10.00
126	*Sage Rosenfels*	6.00
127	*Fred Smoot*	4.00
128	*Correll Buckhalter*	8.00
129	*Justin McCareins*	3.00
130	*Jesse Palmer*	6.00
131	*Scotty Anderson*	4.00
132	*Kevan Barlow*	8.00
133	*John Capel*	4.00
134	*Mike McMahon*	10.00
135	*Marvin "Snoop" Minnis*	8.00
136	*Quincy Morgan*	6.00
137	*Vinny Sutherland*	5.00
138	*Dan Alexander*	5.00
139	*Cedrick Wilson*	4.00
140	*Josh Booty*	4.00
141	*Bobby Newcombe*	4.00
142	*Josh Heupel*	6.00
143	*Ken-Yon Rambo*	5.00
144	*Eddie Berlin*	3.00
145	*Reggie Germany*	4.00
146	*Quincy Carter*	12.00
147	*Steve Smith*	4.00
148	*Dan Morgan*	3.00
149	*Chris Barnes*	4.00
150	*Alex Bannister*	4.00
151	*A.J. Feeley*	4.00
152	*Jason Brookins*	5.00
153	*Kevin Kasper*	5.00
154	*Nick Goings*	4.00
155	*Gerard Warren*	3.00

2001 Fleer Authority Prominence 75

	MT
Veterans:	10x-20x
Rookies:	3x
Production 75 Sets	

2001 Fleer Authority Prominence 125

	MT
Veterans:	6x-12x
Production 125 Sets	

2001 Fleer Authority Autographs

		MT
Complete Set (31):		
Common Player:		8.00
1	Shaun Alexander	15.00
2	Drew Brees	25.00
3	Isaac Bruce	15.00
4	Chris Chambers	25.00
5	Wayne Chrebet	8.00
6	Daunte Culpepper	100.00
7	Stephen Davis	10.00
8	Corey Dillon	10.00
9	Marshall Faulk	100.00
10	Eddie George	100.00
11	Travis Henry	8.00
12	Josh Heupel	8.00
13	Torry Holt	10.00
14	Edgerrin James	100.00
15	Jamal Lewis	15.00
16	Donovan McNabb	30.00
17	Travis Minor	8.00
18	Quincy Morgan	10.00
19	Randy Moss	20.00
20	Santana Moss	25.00
21	Ken-Yon Rambo	10.00
22	Koren Robinson	10.00
23	Sage Rosenfels	10.00
24	Jimmy Smith	10.00
25	Duce Staley	10.00
26	David Terrell	10.00
27	Anthony Thomas	25.00
28	LaDainian Tomlinson	25.00
29	Marques Tuiasosopo	10.00
30	Michael Vick	100.00
31	Chris Weinke	15.00

2001 Fleer Authority Authority Figures

		MT
Complete Set (20):		35.00
Common Player:		1.00
Production 1,750 Sets		
1AF	Michael Vick, Jamal Anderson	6.00
2AF	Drew Brees, Doug Flutie	2.00
3AF	David Terrell, Marcus Robinson	3.00
4AF	Koren Robinson, Matt Hasselbeck	1.00
5AF	Rod Gardner, Stephen Davis	1.00
6AF	Santana Moss, Wayne Chrebet	1.00
7AF	Deuce McAllister, Ricky Williams	3.00
8AF	Dan Morgan, Brian Urlacher	2000001.
9AF	Reggie Wayne, Marvin Harrison	2.00
10AF	Marques Tuiasosopo, Tim Brown	2.00
11AF	Freddie Mitchell, Donovan McNabb	2.00
12AF	Quincy Morgan, Tim Couch	1.00
13AF	Chad Johnson, Peter Warrick	1.00
14AF	Robert Ferguson, Brett Favre	5.00
15AF	Josh Heupel, Chris Weinke	2.00
16AF	Anthony Thomas, Cade McNown	4.00
17AF	Quincy Carter, Emmitt Smith	3.00
18AF	Kevan Barlow, Jeff Garcia	1.00
19AF	James Jackson, Edgerrin James	2.00
20AF	Michael Bennett, Randy Moss	4.00

2001 Fleer Authority Seal of Approval

		MT
Complete Set (15):		75.00
Common Player:		3.00
Inserted 1:80		
1SA	Donovan McNabb	6.00
2SA	Emmitt Smith	8.00
3SA	Edgerrin James	8.00
4SA	Brett Favre	12.00
5SA	Michael Vick	12.00
6SA	Daunte Culpepper	6.00
7SA	Eddie George	3.00
8SA	LaDainian Tomlinson	10.00
9SA	Jamal Lewis	6.00
10SA	Marshall Faulk	3.00
11SA	Peyton Manning	10.00
12SA	Randy Moss	10.00
13SA	Ricky Williams	4.00
14SA	Fred Taylor	3.00
15SA	Kurt Warner	10.00

2001 Fleer Authority We're No. 1

	MT
Complete Set (14):	30.00
Common Player:	1.50
Inserted 1:20	
Troy Aikman	5.00
Drew Bledsoe	3.00
Terry Bradshaw	5.00
Earl Campbell	3.00
Tim Couch	3.00
John Elway	8.00
Irving Fryar	1.50
Paul Hornung	3.00
Bo Jackson	4.00
Keyshawn Johnson	2.00
Jim Plunkett	3.00
George Rogers	1.50
Billy Sims	2.00
Michael Vick	8.00

2001 Fleer Authority We're No. 1 Autographs

	MT
Common Player:	
Troy Aikman	50.00
Drew Bledsoe	30.00
Terry Bradshaw	100.00
Earl Campbell	40.00
Irving Fryar	25.00
Paul Hornung	30.00
Bo Jackson	100.00
Jim Plunkett	25.00
George Rogers	25.00
Michael Vick	100.00

2001 Fleer Authority We're No. 1 Jerseys

	MT
Common Player:	20.00
Inserted 1:100	
Drew Bledsoe	20.00
Terry Bradshaw	40.00
Tim Couch	20.00
John Elway	50.00
Bo Jackson	40.00
Jim Plunkett	20.00

2001 Fleer E-X

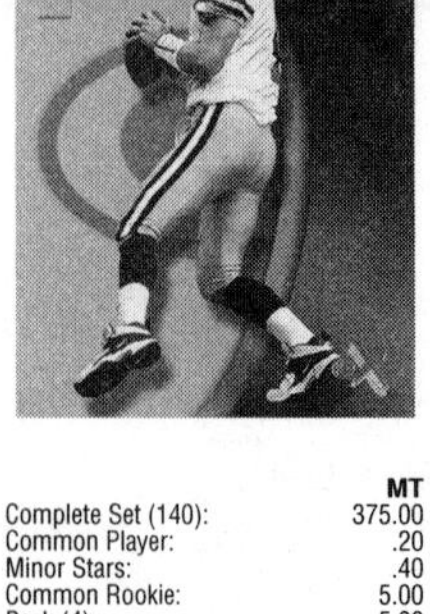

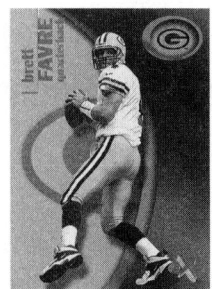

		MT
Complete Set (140):		375.00
Common Player:		.20
Minor Stars:		.40
Common Rookie:		5.00
Pack (4):		5.00
Wax Box (24):		80.00
1	Jamal Anderson	.50
2	Tim Couch	.75
3	Jeff Garcia	.50
4	Brett Favre	2.75
5	Donovan McNabb	1.00
6	Kerry Collins	.40
7	Doug Flutie	.50
8	Steve McNair	.50
9	Kordell Stewart	.50
10	Daunte Culpepper	1.25
11	Rich Gannon	.40
12	Kurt Warner	2.75
13	Brian Griese	.60
14	Brad Johnson	.40
15	Jake Plummer	.50
16	Mark Brunell	.60
17	Peyton Manning	2.00
18	Keyshawn Johnson	.50
19	Derrick Alexander	.20
20	Emmitt Smith	1.75
21	Rob Johnson	.40
22	Aaron Brooks	.50
23	Charlie Garner	.30
24	Lamar Smith	.40
25	Eddie George	.60
26	Marshall Faulk	.75
27	Tiki Barber	.40
28	Terrell Davis	1.50
29	Jamal Lewis	1.50
30	Edgerrin James	2.00
31	Duce Staley	.50
32	Ricky Williams	1.00
33	Dorsey Levens	.40
34	Jerome Bettis	.50
35	Ron Dayne	1.25
36	Mike Anderson	1.25
37	Peter Warrick	.50
38	Mike Alstott	.50
39	Fred Taylor	.60
40	Curtis Martin	.50
41	Warrick Dunn	.50
42	Vinny Testaverde	.40
43	Stephen Davis	.50
44	Ahman Green	.50
45	James Stewart	.40
46	Ricky Watters	.40
47	Ray Lewis	.40
48	Thomas Jones	.40
49	Zach Thomas	.40
50	Junior Seau	.40
51	Brian Urlacher	1.25
52	Isaac Bruce	.50
53	Corey Dillon	.50
54	Cris Carter	.50
55	Terrell Owens	.50
56	Drew Bledsoe	.60
57	Torry Holt	.50
58	Charlie Batch	.50
59	Germane Crowell	.40
60	Jimmy Smith	.40
61	Tim Biakabutuka	.30
62	Jay Fiedler	.40
63	Joey Galloway	.40
64	Michael Westbrook	.30
65	Shaun Alexander	.50
66	Matt Hasselbeck	.40
67	Elvis Grbac	.50
68	Derrick Mason	.40
69	Trent Green	.40
70	Wayne Chrebet	.40
71	Rod Smith	.40
72	Jerry Rice	1.50
73	Tim Brown	.50
74	Shannon Sharpe	.40
75	Joe Horn	.50
76	Randy Moss	2.00
77	Amani Toomer	.30
78	Antonio Freeman	.40
79	Ed McCaffrey	.40
80	Marvin Harrison	.50
81	Muhsin Muhammad	.40
82	Chad Pennington	1.00
83	Kevin Johnson	.40
84	Tony Gonzalez	.40
85	Terry Glenn	.40
86	David Boston	.50
87	Jevon Kearse	.40
88	Marcus Robinson	.50
89	Warren Sapp	.30
90	Eric Moulds	.50
91	*Andre Carter 1250*	8.00
92	*Kevan Barlow 1250*	12.00
93	*Michael Bennett 1000*	25.00
94	*Josh Booty 1500*	8.00
95	*Drew Brees 1000*	35.00
96	*Correll Buckhalter 1500*	15.00
97	*Quincy Carter 1250*	20.00
98	*Chris Chambers 1000*	20.00
99	*Nick Goings 1500*	8.00
100	*Kevin Kasper 1500*	8.00
101	*Dave Dickenson 1500*	12.00
102	*Robert Ferguson 1250*	8.00
103	*Jamar Fletcher 1250*	5.00
104	*Rod Gardner 1250*	15.00
105	*Justin McCareins 1250*	5.00
106	*Jason Brookins 1500*	12.00
107	*Todd Heap 1500*	8.00
108	*Travis Henry 1000*	18.00
109	*Gerard Warren 1500*	8.00
110	*James Jackson 1250*	8.00
111	*Chad Johnson 1250*	10.00
112	*Rudi Johnson 1500*	10.00
113	*LaMont Jordan 1250*	10.00
114	*Deuce McAllister 1250*	15.00
115	*Mike McMahon 1250*	15.00
116	*Marvin "Snoop" Minnis 1000*	15.00
117	*Travis Minor 1500*	8.00
118	*Freddie Mitchell 1000*	15.00
119	*Quincy Morgan 1250*	12.00
120	*Santana Moss 1250*	15.00
121	*Cedrick Wilson 1500*	5.00
122	*Jesse Palmer 1500*	8.00
123	*Ken-Yon Rambo 1500*	5.00
124	*Jamal Reynolds 1500*	7.00
125	*Koren Robinson 1250*	15.00
126	*Sage Rosenfels 1500*	10.00
127	*Dan Morgan 1250*	7.00
128	*Justin Smith 1500*	7.00
129	*Fred Smoot 1500*	7.00
130	*Vinny Sutherland 1500*	8.00
131	*David Terrell 1000*	25.00
132	*Anthony Thomas 1250*	35.00
133	*LaDainian Tomlinson 1000*	30.00
134	*Dan Alexander 1500*	8.00
135	*Marques Tuiasosopo 1250*	15.00
136	*Michael Vick 1000*	35.00
137	*Steve Smith 1250*	5.00
138	*Reggie Wayne 1250*	12.00
139	*Chris Weinke 1000*	20.00
140	*Alex Bannister 1250*	7.00

2001 Fleer E-X Essential Credentials

	MT
Ess.Cred. Cards:	6x-12x
Production 299 Sets	
Ess.Cred. Rookies:	5x
Production 29 Sets	

2001 Fleer E-X Behind the Numbers

		MT
Common Player:		10.00
Minor Stars:		15.00
Inserted 1:24		
1BN	Mike Alstott	15.00
2BN	Mark Brunell	15.00
3BN	Cris Carter	15.00
4BN	Daunte Culpepper	20.00
5BN	Stephen Davis	10.00
6BN	Terrell Davis	25.00
7BN	Ron Dayne	18.00
8BN	Corey Dillon	15.00
9BN	Marshall Faulk	20.00
10BN	Brett Favre	35.00
11BN	Eddie George	20.00
12BN	Brian Griese	18.00
13BN	Marvin Harrison	15.00
14BN	Edgerrin James	25.00
15BN	Curtis Martin	10.00
16BN	Donovan McNabb	20.00
17BN	Randy Moss	30.00
18BN	Emmitt Smith	25.00
19BN	Fred Taylor	18.00
20BN	Ricky Williams	20.00
21BN	Jamal Anderson	12.00
22BN	Tim Brown	12.00
23BN	Isaac Bruce	15.00
24BN	Antonio Freeman	12.00
25BN	Jeff Garcia	15.00

2001 Fleer E-X Constant Threads

		MT
Common Player:		10.00
Minor Stars:		15.00
Inserted 1:40		
1CT	Tim Brown	12.00
2CT	Mark Brunell	16.00
3CT	Germane Crowell	10.00
4CT	Tim Dwight	10.00
5CT	Torry Holt	15.00
6CT	Dan Marino	40.00
7CT	Fred Taylor	16.00
8CT	Edgerrin James	25.00
9CT	Kevin Johnson	10.00
10CT	Herman Moore	10.00
11CT	Eddie George	25.00
12CT	Steve McNair	10.00
13CT	Jake Plummer	15.00
14CT	Brett Favre	30.00
15CT	Jerry Rice	25.00
16CT	Brad Johnson	10.00
17CT	Doug Flutie	10.00

2001 Fleer E-X Turf Team

		MT
Common Player:		15.00
Inserted 1:240		
1TT	Jake Plummer	15.00
2TT	Troy Aikman	40.00
3TT	Stephen Davis	15.00
4TT	Duce Staley	15.00
5TT	Peyton Manning	45.00
6TT	Edgerrin James	30.00
7TT	Marvin Harrison	20.00
8TT	Drew Bledsoe	20.00
9TT	Kurt Warner	50.00
10TT	Torry Holt	15.00
11TT	Marshall Faulk	25.00
12TT	Ron Dayne	20.00
13TT	Donovan McNabb	25.00
14TT	Emmitt Smith	40.00
15TT	Eddie George	20.00
16TT	Steve McNair	15.00
17TT	Keyshawn Johnson	15.00
18TT	Peter Warrick	20.00
19TT	Corey Dillon	20.00
20TT	Jamal Anderson	15.00

Values quoted in this guide reflect the retail price of a card — the price a collector can expect to pay when buying a card from a dealer. The wholesale price — that which a collector can expect to receive from a dealer when selling cards — will be significantly lower, depending on desirability and condition.

2001 Fleer Focus

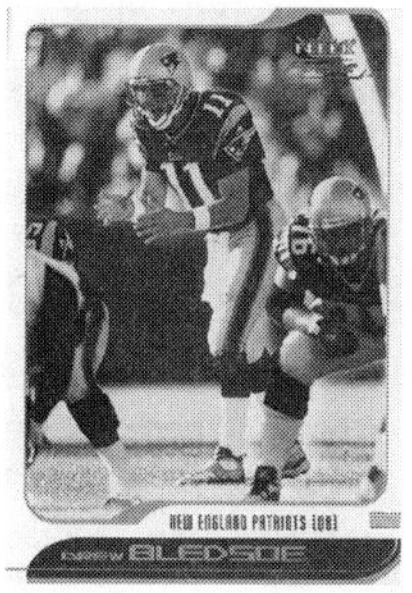

	MT
Complete Set (230):	235.00
Common Player:	.15
Minor Stars:	.30
Common Rookie:	2.50
Production 1,850 Sets	
Pack (8):	3.00
Wax Box (24):	55.00

1	Marshall Faulk	.60
2	Randy Moss	1.50
3	Cade McNown	.50
4	Jeff Graham	.15
5	Donovan McNabb	.75
6	Shannon Sharpe	.30
7	Todd Pinkston	.30
8	Terrence Wilkins	.30
9	Michael Strahan	.30
10	Rich Gannon	.30
11	Germane Crowell	.30
12	Warren Sapp	.30
13	La'Roi Glover	.15
14	Peter Warrick	.60
15	Shaun Alexander	.50
16	Ray Lucas	.30
17	Muhsin Muhammad	.30
18	Curtis Conway	.30
19	R. Jay Soward	.30
20	Jamal Lewis	1.25
21	Tony Gonzalez	.30
22	Bill Schroeder	.30
23	Frank Sanders	.30
24	Charles Woodson	.30
25	Johnnie Morton	.30
26	Frank Wycheck	.15
27	Ron Dayne	.75
28	Travis Prentice	.30
29	Isaac Bruce	.50
30	Drew Bledsoe	.60
31	James Allen	.30
32	Matt Hasselbeck	.50
33	Zach Thomas	.30
34	Shawn Bryson	.15
35	Jerry Rice	1.00
36	Michael Cloud	.15
37	Sammy Morris	.30
38	Corey Simon	.15
39	Peyton Manning	1.50
40	Thomas Jones	.30
41	Tyrone Wheatley	.30
42	Herman Moore	.30
43	Jeff George	.30
44	Kerry Collins	.30
45	Raghib Ismail	.30
46	Andre Rison	.30
47	David Sloan	.15
48	Michael Westbrook	.30
49	Ron Dixon	.15
50	Randall Cunningham	.30
51	Keyshawn Johnson	.50
52	Aaron Brooks	.60
53	Corey Dillon	.50
54	John Randle	.30
55	Cris Carter	.50
56	Donald Hayes	.30
57	Hines Ward	.30
58	Edgerrin James	1.25
59	Terance Mathis	.15
60	Doug Johnson	.30
61	Rod Smith	.50
62	Kevin Dyson	.30
63	Amani Toomer	.30
64	Courtney Brown	.30
65	Mike Alstott	.50
66	Kevin Faulk	.30
67	Shane Matthews	.30
68	Ricky Watters	.30
69	Peter Boulware	.15
70	Tim Biakabutuka	.30
71	Troy Aikman	1.00
72	Keenan McCardell	.30
73	Priest Holmes	.30
74	Duce Staley	.50
75	Antonio Freeman	.50
76	David Boston	.50
77	Chad Pennington	.50
78	Brian Griese	.60
79	Stephen Davis	.50
80	Curtis Martin	.50
81	Tony Banks	.30
82	Warrick Dunn	.50
83	Willie McGinest	.15
84	Marty Booker	.30
85	James Williams	.15
86	Oronde Gadsden	.30
87	Patrick Jeffers	.30
88	Junior Seau	.30
89	Frank Moreau	.15
90	Ray Lewis	.50
91	Doug Flutie	.60
92	Jimmy Smith	.50
93	Qadry Ismail	.30
94	Jeremiah Trotter	.15
95	Dorsey Levens	.30
96	Michael Pittman	.30
97	Wayne Chrebet	.50
98	Mike Anderson	1.25
99	Derrick Mason	.30
100	Jason Sehorn	.15
101	Kevin Johnson	.50
102	Terrell Owens	.50
103	Lamar Smith	.50
104	Eric Moulds	.50
105	Jerome Bettis	.50
106	Marvin Harrison	.50
107	Shawn Jefferson	.15
108	Rickey Dudley	.30
109	James Stewart	.50
110	Bruce Smith	.30
111	Matthew Hatchette	.15
112	Emmitt Smith	1.25
113	Steve McNair	.50
114	Ricky Williams	.75
115	Tim Couch	.60
116	Darrell Jackson	.50
117	Doug Chapman	.30
118	Jeff Lewis	.30
119	Freddie Jones	.30
120	Sylvester Morris	.50
121	Elvis Grbac	.50
122	Plaxico Burress	.50
123	Marcus Pollard	.15
124	Chris Chandler	.30
125	James Thrash	.30
126	Brett Favre	2.00
127	Jake Plummer	.30
128	Vinny Testaverde	.30
129	Terrell Davis	1.00
130	Jevon Kearse	.50
131	Albert Connell	.30
132	Dennis Northcutt	.30
133	Az-Zahir Hakim	.30
134	J.R. Redmond	.30
135	Marcus Robinson	.50
136	Eddie George	.60
137	Ike Hilliard	.30
138	Hugh Douglas	.15
139	Kurt Warner	1.75
140	Terry Glenn	.30
141	Brian Urlacher	1.00
142	Charlie Garner	.50
143	Jay Fiedler	.50
144	Rob Johnson	.30
145	Kordell Stewart	.50
146	Mark Brunell	.60
147	Travis Taylor	.50
148	Laveranues Coles	.50
149	Ed McCaffrey	.50
150	Jacquez Green	.15
151	Joe Horn	.30
152	Darnay Scott	.30
153	Torry Holt	.50
154	Daunte Culpepper	1.00
155	Wesley Walls	.30
156	Jeff Garcia	.50
157	Derrick Alexander	.30
158	Peerless Price	.50
159	Bobby Shaw	.15
160	Fred Taylor	.60
161	Chris Redman	.50
162	Tim Brown	.50
163	Charlie Batch	.50
164	Champ Bailey	.30
165	Tiki Barber	.50
166	Joey Galloway	.30
167	Brad Johnson	.50
168	Jeff Blake	.30
169	Jon Kitna	.30
170	Trent Green	.30
171	Troy Brown	.15
172	Eddie Kennison	.15
173	J.J. Stokes	.30
174	James McKnight	.15
175	Jeremy McDaniel	.15
176	Richard Huntley	.15
177	Kyle Brady	.15
178	Jamal Anderson	.50
179	Chad Lewis	.30
180	Ahman Green	.50
181	*Michael Vick*	20.00
182	*Deuce McAllister*	8.00
183	*David Terrell*	12.00
184	*Koren Robinson*	8.00
185	*LaDainian Tomlinson*	15.00
186	*Michael Bennett*	10.00
187	*Chris Chambers*	10.00
188	*Chad Johnson*	5.00
189	*Santana Moss*	7.00
190	*Todd Heap*	5.00
191	*Freddie Mitchell*	7.00
192	*Quincy Morgan*	6.00
193	*Rod Gardner*	10.00
194	*Kevan Barlow*	5.00
195	*Drew Brees*	15.00
196	*Robert Ferguson*	4.00
197	*Ken-Yon Rambo*	4.00
198	*Travis Henry*	8.00
199	*LaMont Jordan*	7.00
200	*Chris Weinke*	12.00
201	*Sage Rosenfels*	4.00
202	*Josh Heupel*	7.00
203	*Quincy Carter*	10.00
204	*Jesse Palmer*	4.00
205	*Mike McMahon*	5.00
206	*Rudi Johnson*	5.00
207	*Anthony Thomas*	20.00
208	*James Jackson*	5.00
209	*Marvin "Snoop" Minnis*	6.00
210	*Derek Combs*	2.50
211	*Ronney Daniels*	2.50
212	*Alex Bannister*	4.00
213	*Cedrick Wilson*	4.00
214	*Travis Minor*	3.00
215	*Marques Tuiasosopo*	8.00
216	*Reggie Wayne*	7.00
217	*Josh Booty*	3.00
218	*Jamal Reynolds*	3.00
219	*Gerard Warren*	4.00
220	*Justin Smith*	3.00
221	*Andre Carter*	4.00
222	*Milton Wynn*	2.50
223	*Fred Smoot*	4.00
224	*Jamar Fletcher*	3.00
225	*Dan Morgan*	4.00
226	*Jon Carter*	2.50
227	*Correll Buckhalter*	6.00
228	*Kevin Kasper*	4.00
229	*Derrick Blaylock*	2.50
230	*Justin McCareins*	2.50

2001 Fleer Focus Certified Cuts

	MT
Common Player:	15.00
Inserted 1:72	

1CC	Freddie Mitchell	15.00
2CC	James Jackson	20.00
3CC	Josh Heupel	25.00
4CC	Kevan Barlow	20.00
5CC	LaMont Jordan	15.00
6CC	Chris Chambers	20.00
7CC	Chris Weinke	50.00
8CC	David Terrell	30.00
9CC	Deuce McAllister	30.00
10CC	Drew Brees	60.00
11CC	Jesse Palmer	15.00
12CC	Koren Robinson	20.00
13CC	LaDainian Tomlinson	60.00
14CC	Michael Vick	100.00
15CC	Michael Bennett	50.00
16CC	Quincy Morgan	15.00
17CC	Reggie Wayne	20.00
18CC	Rod Gardner	15.00
19CC	Rudi Johnson	15.00
20CC	Santana Moss	25.00
21CC	Donovan McNabb	70.00

2001 Fleer Focus Numbers

	MT
Common Player:	2.00

1	Marshall Faulk 253	6.00
2	Randy Moss 187	20.00
3	Cade McNown 154	5.00
4	Jeff Graham 165	2.00
5	Donovan McNabb 330	6.00
6	Shannon Sharpe 121	4.00
7	Todd Pinkston 181	3.00
8	Terrence Wilkins 132	8.00
9	Michael Strahan 51	6.00
10	Rich Gannon 284	2.50
11	Germane Crowell 126	5.00
12	Warren Sapp 43	10.00
13	La'Roi Glover 53	5.00
14	Peter Warrick 116	8.00
15	Shaun Alexander 64	15.00
16	Ray Lucas 21	20.00
17	Muhsin Muhammad 116	4.00
18	Curtis Conway 134	2.50
19	R. Jay Soward 110	3.00
20	Jamal Lewis 309	7.00
21	Tony Gonzalez 129	4.00
22	Bill Schroeder 154	2.00
23	Frank Sanders 139	4.00
24	Charles Woodson 16	25.00
25	Johnnie Morton 129	4.00
26	Frank Wycheck 91	4.00
27	Ron Dayne 228	7.00
28	Travis Prentice 16	20.00
29	Isaac Bruce 169	7.00
30	Drew Bledsoe 312	4.00
31	James Allen 290	2.50
32	Matt Hasselbeck 10	25.00
33	Zach Thomas 56	8.00
34	Shawn Bryson 161	2.00
35	Jerry Rice 107	20.00
36	Michael Cloud 30	6.00
37	Sammy Morris 93	5.00
38	Corey Simon 38	8.00
39	Peyton Manning 357	10.00
40	Thomas Jones 112	3.00
41	Tyrone Wheatley 232	2.50
42	Herman Moore 109	4.00
43	Jeff George 113	4.00
44	Kerry Collins 311	1.50
45	Raghib Ismail 140	3.00
46	Andre Rison 148	2.00
47	David Sloan 118	2.50
48	Michael Westbrook 114	4.00
49	Ron Dixon 153	2.50
50	Randall Cunningham 74	10.00
51	Keyshawn Johnson 123	7.00
52	Aaron Brooks 113	10.00
53	Corey Dillon 315	4.00
54	John Randle 25	15.00
55	Cris Carter 133	7.00
56	Donald Hayes 140	3.00
57	Hines Ward 140	2.00
58	Edgerrin James 387	10.00
59	Terance Mathis 119	2.50
60	Doug Johnson 93	6.00
61	Rod Smith 160	4.00
62	Kevin Dyson 173	3.00
63	Amani Toomer 140	3.00
64	Courtney Brown 62	5.00
65	Mike Alstott 131	7.00
66	Kevin Faulk 164	3.00
67	Shane Matthews 102	3.00
68	Ricky Watters 278	3.00
69	Peter Boulware 33	6.00
70	Tim Biakabutuka 173	3.00
71	Troy Aikman 156	10.00
72	Keenan McCardell 128	2.50
73	Priest Holmes 137	3.00
74	Duce Staley 79	10.00
75	Antonio Freeman 147	6.00
76	David Boston 163	6.00
77	Chad Pennington 2	
78	Brian Griese 216	7.00
79	Stephen Davis 332	4.00
80	Curtis Martin 316	4.00
81	Tony Banks 150	3.00
82	Warrick Dunn 248	5.00
83	Willie McGinest 45	5.00
84	Marty Booker 104	4.00
85	James Williams 24	12.00
86	Oronde Gadsden 140	3.00
87	Patrick Jeffers 1	
88	Junior Seau 102	4.00
89	Frank Moreau 67	4.00
90	Ray Lewis 108	8.00
91	Doug Flutie 132	10.00
92	Jimmy Smith 133	4.00
93	Qadry Ismail 134	2.50
94	Jeremiah Trotter 100	2.50
95	Dorsey Levens 77	5.00
96	Michael Pittman 184	2.00
97	Wayne Chrebet 136	4.00
98	Mike Anderson 297	10.00
99	Derrick Mason 142	3.00
100	Jason Sehorn 59	5.00
101	Kevin Johnson 117	8.00
102	Terrell Owens 150	7.00
103	Lamar Smith 309	3.00
104	Eric Moulds 141	4.00
105	Jerome Bettis 355	3.00
106	Marvin Harrison 139	8.00
107	Shawn Jefferson 137	2.50
108	Rickey Dudley 121	2.50
109	James Stewart 339	1.50
110	Bruce Smith 46	5.00
111	Matthew Hatchette 119	2.50
112	Emmitt Smith 294	12.00
113	Steve McNair 248	5.00
114	Ricky Williams 248	8.00
115	Tim Couch 137	10.00
116	Darrell Jackson 135	60.00
117	Doug Chapman 1	
118	Jeff Lewis 16	15.00
119	Freddie Jones 108	3.00
120	Sylvester Morris 141	4.00
121	Elvis Grbac 326	2.00
122	Plaxico Burress 124	6.00
123	Marcus Pollard 146	2.00
124	Chris Chandler 192	3.00
125	James Thrash 131	2.50
126	Brett Favre 338	12.00
127	Jake Plummer 270	5.00
128	Vinny Testaverde 328	1.50
129	Terrell Davis 78	25.00
130	Jevon Kearse 36	20.00
131	Albert Connell 195	2.00
132	Dennis Northcutt 108	3.00
133	Az-Zahir Hakim 138	4.00
134	J.R. Redmond 125	3.00
135	Marcus Robinson 134	8.00
136	Eddie George 403	4.00
137	Ike Hilliard 143	3.00
138	Hugh Douglas 44	6.00
139	Kurt Warner 235	20.00
140	Terry Glenn 122	4.00
141	Brian Urlacher 98	20.00
142	Charlie Garner 258	3.00
143	Jay Fiedler 204	4.00
144	Rob Johnson 175	3.00
145	Kordell Stewart 151	6.00
146	Mark Brunell 311	4.00
147	Travis Taylor 99	5.00
148	Laveranues Coles 168	5.00
149	Ed McCaffrey 130	8.00
150	Jacquez Green 152	2.00
151	Joe Horn 143	3.00
152	Darnay Scott 1	
153	Torry Holt 199	6.00
154	Daunte Culpepper 297	10.00
155	Wesley Walls 136	2.50
156	Jeff Garcia 355	4.00
157	Derrick Alexander 178	3.00
158	Peerless Price 147	3.00
159	Bobby Shaw 168	2.00
160	Fred Taylor 292	5.00
161	Chris Redman 2	
162	Tim Brown 148	6.00
163	Charlie Batch 221	5.00
164	Champ Bailey 57	8.00
165	Tiki Barber 213	3.00
166	Joey Galloway 155	6.00
167	Brad Johnson 228	5.00
168	Jeff Blake 184	3.00
169	Jon Kitna 259	2.50
170	Trent Green 145	6.00
171	Troy Brown 114	2.50
172	Eddie Kennison 100	4.00
173	J.J. Stokes 175	3.00
174	James McKnight 178	3.00
175	Jeremy McDaniel 162	2.00
176	Richard Huntley 46	5.00
177	Kyle Brady 114	2.50
178	Jamal Anderson 282	5.00
179	Chad Lewis 107	2.50
180	Ahman Green 263	4.00
181	Michael Vick 87	100.00
182	Deuce McAllister 159	20.00
183	David Terrell 169	20.00
184	Koren Robinson 171	15.00
185	LaDainian Tomlinson 369	25.00
186	Michael Bennett 310	20.00
187	Chris Chambers 156	15.00
188	Chad Johnson 218	7.00
189	Santana Moss 166	12.00
190	Todd Heap 134	8.00
191	Freddie Mitchell 194	12.00
192	Quincy Morgan 182	10.00
193	Rod Gardner 181	15.00
194	Kevan Barlow 197	12.00
195	Drew Brees 309	20.00
196	Robert Ferguson 153	7.00
197	Ken-Yon Rambo 150	4.00
198	Travis Henry 253	12.00
199	LaMont Jordan 213	7.00
200	Chris Weinke 266	20.00
201	Sage Rosenfels 172	8.00
202	Josh Heupel 280	10.00
203	Quincy Carter 91	30.00
204	Jesse Palmer 116	10.00
205	Mike McMahon 169	8.00
206	Rudi Johnson 324	5.00
207	Anthony Thomas 319	8.00
208	James Jackson 201	8.00
209	Marvin "Snoop" Minnis 213	10.00
210	Derek Combs 175	6.00
211	Ronney Daniels 111	6.00
212	Alex Bannister 158	6.00
213	Cedrick Wilson 110	8.00
214	Travis Minor 181	6.00
215	Marques Tuiasosopo 176	12.00
216	Reggie Wayne 176	10.00
217	Josh Booty 145	6.00
218	Jamal Reynolds 58	15.00
219	Gerard Warren 76	15.00
220	Justin Smith 97	12.00
221	Andre Carter 59	15.00
222	Milton Wynn 185	5.00
223	Fred Smoot 55	15.00
224	Jamar Fletcher 34	15.00
225	Dan Morgan 138	8.00
226	Jon Carter 158	5.00
227	Correll Buckhalter 196	10.00
228	Kevin Kasper 123	10.00
229	Derrick Blaylock 202	4.00
230	Justin McCareins 177	5.00

2001 Fleer Focus Property Of

	MT
Common Player:	15.00
Inserted 1:192	
Shirts/Skins Cards:	4x
Production 50 Sets	

1PO	Brett Favre	45.00
2PO	Dan Marino	50.00
3PO	Jerry Rice	35.00
4PO	Wayne Chrebet	15.00
5PO	Marshall Faulk	20.00
6PO	Kurt Warner	35.00
7PO	Ray Lewis	15.00
8PO	Rod Smith	15.00
9PO	Corey Dillon	15.00
10PO	Kordell Stewart	15.00

2001 Fleer Focus Rookie Premiere Jersey

	MT
Common Player:	12.00
Inserted 1:65	
Shirts/Skins Cards:	3x
Production 50 Sets	

1RP	Leonard Davis	12.00
2RP	Michael Vick	60.00
3RP	Todd Heap	12.00
4RP	Travis Henry	15.00
5RP	Dan Morgan	12.00
6RP	Chris Weinke	30.00
7RP	David Terrell	20.00
8RP	Anthony Thomas	15.00
9RP	Chad Johnson	12.00
10RP	Justin Smith	12.00
11RP	Rudi Johnson	12.00
12RP	James Jackson	20.00
13RP	Quincy Morgan	12.00
14RP	Gerard Warren	12.00
15RP	Quincy Carter	20.00
16RP	Mike McMahon	12.00
17RP	Robert Ferguson	12.00
18RP	Reggie Wayne	12.00
19RP	Marvin "Snoop" Minnis	12.00
20RP	Chris Chambers	12.00
21RP	Travis Minor	12.00
22RP	Rod Gardner	15.00
23RP	Michael Bennett	30.00
24RP	Richard Seymour	12.00
25RP	Deuce McAllister	20.00
26RP	Jesse Palmer	12.00
27RP	Santana Moss	15.00
28RP	Marques Tuiasosopo	20.00
29RP	Freddie Mitchell	15.00
30RP	Drew Brees	35.00
31RP	LaDainian Tomlinson	40.00
32RP	Kevan Barlow	12.00
33RP	Andre Carter	12.00
34RP	Koren Robinson	15.00

2001 Fleer Focus Tag Team

	MT
Common Player:	20.00
Inserted 1:140	

1TGT	Paul Hornung	30.00
2TGT	Brett Favre	50.00
3TGT	Troy Aikman	35.00
4TGT	Roger Staubach	60.00
5TGT	Bo Jackson	30.00
6TGT	Marcus Allen	20.00
7TGT	Daunte Culpepper	30.00
8TGT	Warren Moon	20.00
9TGT	John Elway	50.00
10TGT	Terrell Davis	30.00
11TGT	Marshall Faulk	25.00
12TGT	Eric Dickerson	20.00
13TGT	George Rogers	20.00
14TGT	Deuce McAllister	25.00
15TGT	Randy Moss	45.00
16TGT	Dan Marino	50.00
17TGT	Joe Montana	150.00
18TGT	Steve Young	30.00
19TGT	Steve McNair	20.00
20TGT	Eddie George	25.00
21TGT	Johnny Unitas	50.00
22TGT	Edgerrin James	45.00
23TGT	Emmitt Smith	45.00
24TGT	Tony Dorsett	30.00
25TGT	Walter Payton	125.00
26TGT	Gale Sayers	20.00
27TGT	Jerry Rice	40.00
28TGT	William Perry	20.00
29TGT	Brian Urlacher	30.00
30TGT	Donovan McNabb	25.00
31TGT	Randall Cunningham	25.00

2001 Fleer Focus Tag Team Tandems

	MT
Common Player:	50.00
Production 50 Sets	

1TGTT	Paul Hornung, Brett Favre	150.00
2TGTT	Troy Aikman, Roger Staubach	150.00
3TGTT	Bo Jackson, Marcus Allen	85.00
4TGTT	Daunte Culpepper, Warren Moon	100.00
5TGTT	John Elway, Terrell Davis	150.00
6TGTT	Marshall Faulk, Eric Dickerson	65.00
7TGTT	Deuce McAllister, Ricky Williams	65.00
8TGTT	Randy Moss, Daunte Culpepper	100.00
9TGTT	Joe Montana, Steve Young	200.00
10TGTT	Steve McNair, Eddie George	75.00
11TGTT	Johnny Unitas, Edgerrin James	100.00
12TGTT	Emmitt Smith, Tony Dorsett	150.00
14TGTT	Jerry Rice, Steve Young	100.00
15TGTT	William Perry, Brian Urlacher	50.00
16TGTT	Donovan McNabb, Randall Cunningham	85.00

2001 Fleer Focus Toast of the Town

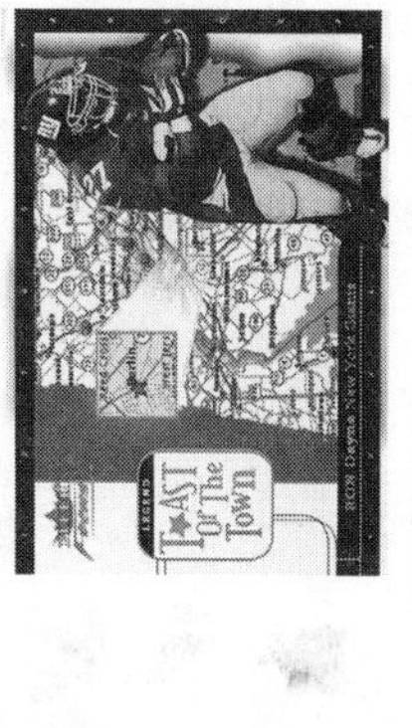

	MT
Complete Set (20):	45.00
Common Player:	.75
Minor Stars:	1.50
Inserted 1:6	

1TT	Donovan McNabb	2.50
2TT	Brett Favre	6.00
3TT	Jerome Bettis	1.50
4TT	Stephen Davis	1.50
5TT	Emmitt Smith	4.00
6TT	Cris Carter	1.50
7TT	Peyton Manning	5.00
8TT	Eddie George	2.00
9TT	Edgerrin James	4.00
10TT	Daunte Culpepper	3.00
11TT	Kurt Warner	6.00
12TT	Mark Brunell	2.00
13TT	Randy Moss	5.00
14TT	Marvin Harrison	1.50
15TT	Jamal Lewis	3.50
16TT	Warren Sapp	.75
17TT	Jerry Rice	4.00
18TT	Ricky Williams	2.50
19TT	Ron Dayne	2.50
20TT	Brian Griese	2.00

2001 Fleer Focus Ultra Rookie Update

	MT
Complete Set (10):	10.00
Common Player:	1.00

1	Quincy Carter	3.00
2	Derrick Blaylock	1.00
3	Correll Buckhalter	2.00
4	Henry Burris	1.00
5	Cedric James	1.00
6	Kevin Kasper	1.00
7	Justin McCareins	1.00
8	Dave Dickenson	1.00
9	Steve Smith	1.00
10	Moran Norris	1.00

2001 Fleer Focus Vision Tunnel

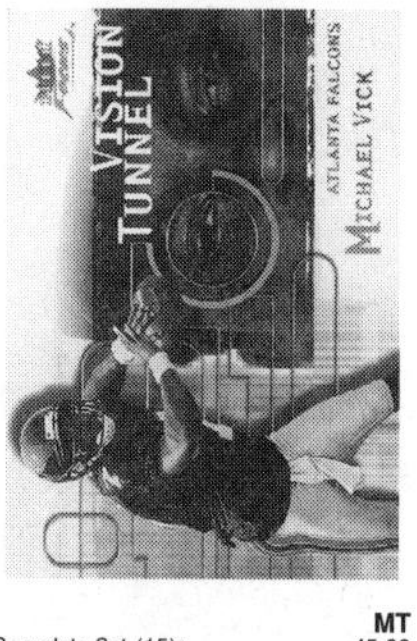

	MT
Complete Set (15):	45.00
Common Player:	1.00
Minor Stars:	2.00
Inserted 1:12	

1TV	Peyton Manning	6.00
2TV	Jamal Lewis	4.00
3TV	Emmitt Smith	5.00
4TV	Eddie George	2.50
5TV	Michael Vick	12.00
6TV	Brett Favre	8.00
7TV	Ricky Williams	3.00
8TV	Edgerrin James	5.00
9TV	Ron Dayne	2.50
10TV	Eric Moulds	2.00
11TV	Tim Brown	2.00
12TV	Terrell Davis	4.00
13TV	Jevon Kearse	2.00
14TV	Peter Warrick	2.00
15TV	Ray Lewis	1.00

2001 Fleer Game Time

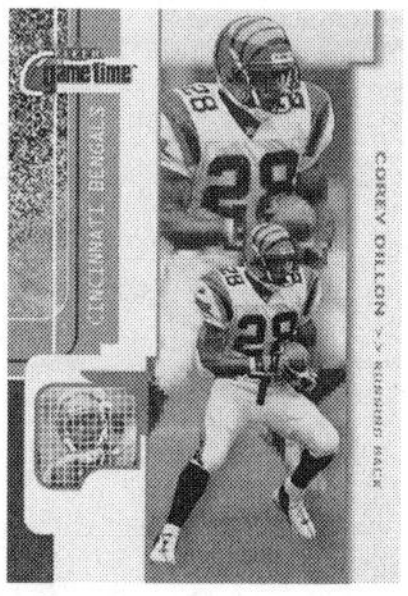

	MT
Complete Set (150):	200.00
Common Player:	.15
Minor Stars:	.30
Common Rookie:	1.00
Production 2001 Sets	
Pack (5):	4.00
Wax Box (24)	65.00

1	Donovan McNabb	.75
2	Travis Prentice	.30
3	Keenan McCardell	.15
4	Kurt Warner	1.75
5	Ray Lewis	.30
6	Terrell Davis	1.00
7	Kevin Faulk	.30
8	Terrell Owens	.50
9	Jeff George	.30
10	Dennis Northcutt	.30
11	Fred Taylor	.60
12	Cris Carter	.50
13	Aaron Brooks	.50
14	Marshall Faulk	.60
15	David Boston	.50

16	Raghib Ismail	.15
17	Jerome Bettis	.50
18	Warrick Dunn	.50
19	Corey Dillon	.50
20	Mark Brunell	.60
21	Torry Holt	.50
22	Michael McCrary	.15
23	Rod Smith	.30
24	Charlie Garner	.30
25	Bruce Smith	.15
26	Doug Johnson	.30
27	Brian Griese	.60
28	Jeff Garcia	.50
29	Eddie George	.60
30	Shawn Bryson	.30
31	Marvin Harrison	.50
32	Hugh Douglas	.15
33	Terance Mathis	.15
34	Emmitt Smith	1.25
35	Lamar Smith	.50
36	Junior Seau	.30
37	Steve McNair	.50
38	Jake Plummer	.50
39	Tim Couch	.75
40	Jay Fiedler	.50
41	Plaxico Burress	.50
42	Keyshawn Johnson	.50
43	Trent Dilfer	.30
44	Charlie Batch	.50
45	Terry Glenn	.50
46	Laveranues Coles	.50
47	Darrell Jackson	.50
48	Jamal Lewis	1.50
49	Ed McCaffrey	.30
50	Vinny Testaverde	.50
51	Ricky Watters	.50
52	Champ Bailey	.50
53	Peter Warrick	1.00
54	Eric Moulds	.50
55	Michael Strahan	.15
56	Warren Sapp	.30
57	Tony Gonzalez	.30
58	Kerry Collins	.50
59	Shaun King	.50
60	Jason Sehorn	.15
61	Marcus Robinson	.50
62	James Stewart	.50
63	Curtis Martin	.50
64	Brian Urlacher	1.00
65	Germane Crowell	.50
66	Wesley Walls	.30
67	Antonio Freeman	.50
68	Ron Dayne	1.00
69	Tyrone Wheatley	.30
70	Zach Thomas	.30
71	Shannon Sharpe	.30
72	Mike Anderson	1.50
73	Wayne Chrebet	.30
74	Shaun Alexander	.50
75	Stephen Davis	.50
76	Steve Beuerlein	.30
77	Dorsey Levens	.50
78	Jessie Armstead	.15
79	Rich Gannon	.30
80	Muhsin Muhammad	.30
81	Brett Favre	2.00
82	Randy Moss	1.50
83	Joe Horn	.50
84	Charles Woodson	.30
85	Brad Hoover	.30
86	Terrence Wilkins	.30
87	Sylvester Morris	.50
88	Tim Brown	.30
89	Jamal Anderson	.50
90	Joey Galloway	.50
91	Drew Bledsoe	.60
92	Rodney Harrison	.15
93	Jevon Kearse	.50
94	Rob Johnson	.30
95	Edgerrin James	1.50
96	Thomas Jones	.50
97	Courtney Brown	.30
98	Jimmy Smith	.50
99	Ricky Williams	.75
100	Isaac Bruce	.50
101	Akili Smith	.50
102	Derrick Alexander	.15
103	Daunte Culpepper	1.00
104	Amani Toomer	.30
105	Mike Alstott	.50
106	Sam Cowart	.15
107	Peyton Manning	1.50
108	Robert Smith	.30
109	Duce Staley	.50
110	Cade McNown	.50
111	*Michael Vick*	20.00
112	*David Terrell*	12.00
113	*Deuce McAllister*	10.00
114	*Koren Robinson*	10.00
115	*Rod Gardner*	10.00
116	*Chris Chambers*	10.00
117	*Santana Moss*	10.00
118	*Reggie Wayne*	7.00
119	*Quincy Morgan*	4.00
120	*Rudi Johnson*	4.00
121	*Robert Ferguson*	4.00
122	*Ja'Mar Toombs*	2.00
123	*Michael Bennett*	12.00
124	*Ronney Daniels*	2.00
125	*Drew Brees*	15.00
126	*Josh Heupel*	6.00
127	*Chris Weinke*	10.00
128	*LaDainian Tomlinson*	15.00
129	*Chad Johnson*	4.00
130	*LaMont Jordan*	4.00
131	*Freddie Mitchell*	5.00
132	*Anthony Thomas*	20.00
133	*Ben Leard*	2.00
134	*Sage Rosenfels*	4.00
135	*Marques Tuiasosopo*	6.00
136	*Gerard Warren*	3.00
137	*Jamar Fletcher*	3.00
138	*Justin Smith*	3.00
139	*Dan Morgan*	4.00
140	*Jamal Reynolds*	2.00
141	*Shaun Rogers*	1.00
142	*Todd Heap*	3.00
143	*Travis Minor*	5.00
144	*Mike McMahon*	4.00
145	*Travis Henry*	6.00
146	*Kevan Barlow*	4.00
147	*Javon Green*	2.00
148	*Ken-Yon Rambo*	3.00
149	*Tim Hasselbeck*	3.00
150	*Marvin "Snoop" Minnis*	5.00

A player's name in *italic* type indicates a rookie card.

2001 Fleer Game Time Extra

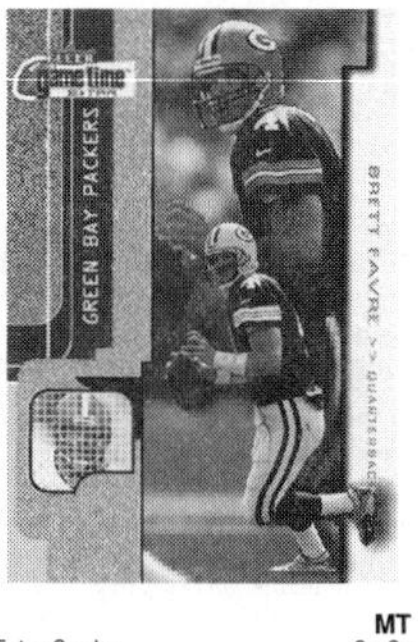

	MT
Extra Cards:	3x-6x
Inserted 1:8	
Extra Rookies:	3x
Production 201 Sets	

2001 Fleer Game Time CrunchTime

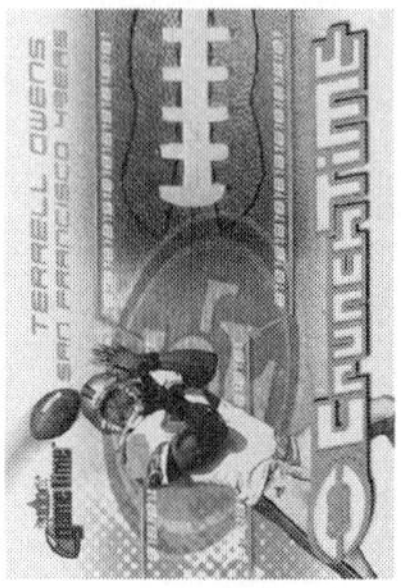

		MT
Complete Set (20):		15.00
Common Player:		.50
Minor Stars:		1.00
Inserted 1:4		
1CT	Emmitt Smith	3.50
2CT	Isaac Bruce	1.00
3CT	James Stewart	.50
4CT	Warrick Dunn	1.00
5CT	Jake Plummer	1.00
6CT	Shannon Sharpe	.50
7CT	Robert Smith	1.00
8CT	Jamal Anderson	1.00
9CT	Terrell Owens	1.00
10CT	Marcus Robinson	1.00
11CT	Ed McCaffrey	.50
12CT	Jamal Lewis	.50
13CT	Amani Toomer	.50
14CT	Jerome Bettis	1.00
15CT	Cris Carter	1.00
16CT	Stephen Davis	1.00
17CT	Marvin Harrison	1.00
18CT	Joe Horn	1.00
19CT	Tim Couch	2.00
20CT	Drew Bledsoe	1.75

2001 Fleer Game Time Double Trouble

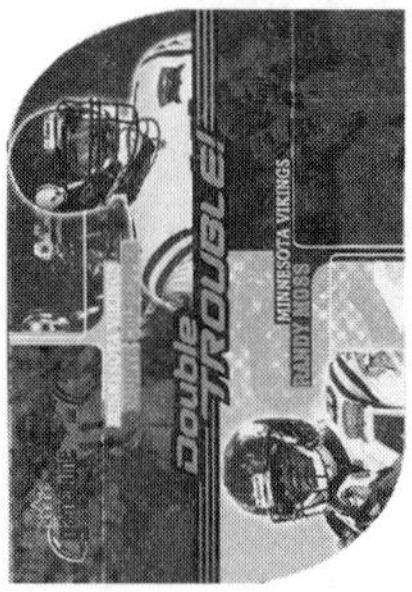

		MT
Complete Set (15):		35.00
Common Player:		1.00
Minor Stars:		2.00
Inserted 1:24		
1DT	Daunte Culpepper, Randy Moss	8.00
2DT	Kurt Warner, Marshall Faulk	8.00
3DT	Peyton Manning, Edgerrin James	8.00
4DT	Warrick Dunn, Keyshawn Johnson	2.00
5DT	Brett Favre, Antonio Freeman	8.00
6DT	Tiki Barber, Ron Dayne	3.00
7DT	Corey Dillon, Peter Warrick	4.00
8DT	Donovan McNabb, Duce Staley	3.00
9DT	Fred Taylor, Jimmy Smith	2.50
10DT	Rich Gannon, Tim Brown	2.00
11DT	Steve McNair, Eddie George	2.50
12DT	Curtis Martin, Wayne Chrebet	2.00
13DT	Ricky Williams, Aaron Brooks	3.50
14DT	Derrick Alexander, Tony Gonzalez	1.00
15DT	Brian Griese, Terrell Davis	4.00

2001 Fleer Game Time Eleven Up

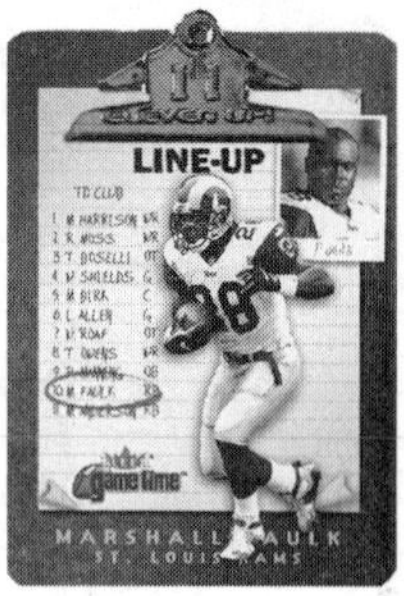

		MT
Complete Set (15):		30.00
Common Player:		1.50
Inserted 1:12		
1EU	Jamal Lewis	5.00
2EU	Randy Moss	6.00
3EU	Ricky Williams	3.00
4EU	Terrell Davis	4.00
5EU	Donovan McNabb	3.00
6EU	Curtis Martin	1.50
7EU	Brett Favre	8.00
8EU	Aaron Brooks	1.50
9EU	Kurt Warner	7.00
10EU	Eddie George	2.00
11EU	Daunte Culpepper	4.00
12EU	Jamal Anderson	1.50
13EU	Marshall Faulk	2.00
14EU	Ray Lewis	1.50
15EU	Ron Dayne	3.00

2001 Fleer Game Time Fame Time

		MT
Common Player:		35.00
Production 100 Sets		
1	Terry Bradshaw	100.00
2	Eric Dickerson	35.00
3	Tony Dorsett	50.00
4	Paul Hornung	60.00
5	Howie Long	50.00
6	Joe Montana	150.00
7	Walter Payton	150.00
8	Roger Staubach	100.00
9	Fran Tarkenton	45.00
10	Lawrence Taylor	50.00
11	Johnny Unitas	60.00

2001 Fleer Game Time In the Zone

	MT
Complete Set (14):	200.00
Common Player:	10.00
Inserted 1:73	
Drew Bledsoe	20.00
Daunte Culpepper	30.00
Oronde Gadsden	10.00
Rich Gannon	10.00
Marvin Harrison	15.00
Edgerrin James	40.00
Peyton Manning	50.00
Curtis Martin	15.00
Randy Moss	50.00
Peerless Price	10.00
J.R. Redmond	10.00
Jimmy Smith	10.00
James Stewart	10.00
Tyrone Wheatley	10.00

2001 Fleer Game Time Uniformity

	MT
Common Player:	10.00
Inserted 1:19	
Jessie Armstead	10.00
Champ Bailey	15.00
David Boston	15.00
Kyle Brady Pants	10.00
Courtney Brown	12.00
Isaac Bruce	15.00
Mark Brunell	20.00
Plaxico Burress	15.00
Trung Canidate Pants	10.00
Wayne Chrebet	12.00
Tim Couch Pants	20.00
Marshall Faulk Pants	30.00
Marvin Harrison	15.00
Torry Holt	15.00
Kevin Johnson Pants	10.00
Jevon Kearse	15.00
Shaun King	15.00
Dorsey Levens	12.00
Dan Marino	50.00
Keenan McCardell	10.00
Donovan McNabb	25.00
Cade McNown	15.00
Jake Plummer	15.00
Travis Prentice	15.00
Peerless Price	12.00
Chris Redman	15.00
Jerry Rice	35.00
Marcus Robinson	15.00
Corey Simon	12.00
Jimmy Smith	12.00
Duce Staley	15.00
Kordell Stewart	15.00
Michael Strahan Pants	10.00
Fred Taylor	20.00
Kurt Warner	45.00

2001 Fleer Genuine

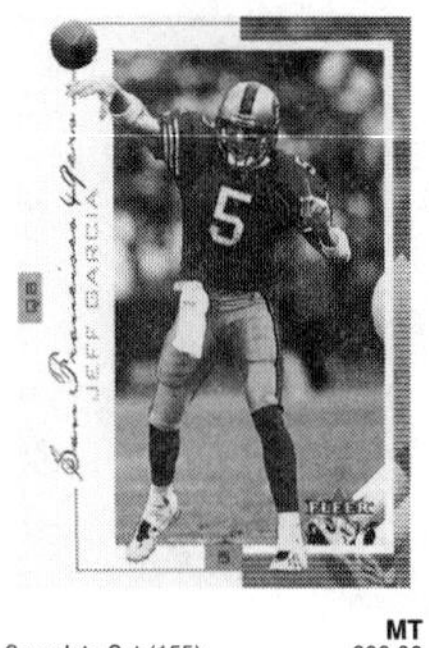

		MT
Complete Set (155):		600.00
Common Player:		.20
Minor Stars:		.40
Common Rookie:		10.00
Production 1000 Sets		
Pack (5):		6.00
Wax Box (24):		100.00
1	Donovan McNabb	1.25
2	Daunte Culpepper	1.50
3	Derrick Alexander	.20
4	Jessie Armstead	.20
5	Hines Ward	.40
6	Peter Warrick	1.50
7	Jay Fiedler	.50
8	Cris Carter	.75
9	Az-Zahir Hakim	.40
10	Michael Westbrook	.50
11	Akili Smith	.75
12	Lamar Smith	.75
13	Eric Moulds	.75
14	Shaun Alexander	1.00
15	Jeff George	.75
16	Brad Hoover	.75
17	Brian Griese	1.00
18	Keenan McCardell	.50
19	Freddie Jones	.40
20	Brian Urlacher	1.50
21	Thomas Jones	.75
22	Charlie Batch	.75
23	Aaron Brooks	.75
24	Hugh Douglas	.20
25	Mike Alstott	.75
26	Darrell Russell	.20
27	Muhsin Muhammad	.40
28	Raghib Ismail	.20
29	Fred Taylor	1.00
30	Tyrone Wheatley	.40
31	Rodney Harrison	.20
32	Curtis Martin	.75
33	Jason Sehorn	.20
34	James McKnight	.20
35	Jimmy Smith	.50
36	Laveranues Coles	.75
37	Jeff Garcia	.75
38	Sam Cowart	.20
39	Joey Galloway	.75
40	Mark Brunell	1.00
41	Vinny Testaverde	.50
42	Terrell Owens	.75
43	Ray Lewis	.50
44	Ahman Green	.50
45	Ron Dayne	1.50
46	Samari Rolle	.20
47	Shawn Bryson	.20
48	Emmitt Smith	2.00
49	Terrence Wilkins	.40
50	Charlie Garner	.40
51	Rob Johnson	.40
52	Courtney Brown	.40
53	Edgerrin James	2.50
54	Kurt Warner	3.00
55	Michael McCrary	.20
56	Dennis Northcutt	.40
57	Marvin Harrison	.75
58	Rich Gannon	.75
59	Marshall Faulk	1.00
60	Travis Prentice	.75
61	Terrell Davis	2.00
62	Charles Woodson	.50
63	Isaac Bruce	.75
64	Tim Couch	1.25
65	Oronde Gadsden	.40
66	Randy Moss	2.50
67	Torry Holt	.75
68	Shannon Sharpe	.40
69	Antonio Freeman	.75
70	Michael Strahan	.20
71	Jevon Kearse	.75
72	Jamal Lewis	2.00
73	Peyton Manning	2.50
74	Amani Toomer	.40
75	Derrick Mason	.75
76	Jake Plummer	.75
77	Rod Smith	.50
78	Terry Glenn	.50
79	Plaxico Burress	.75
80	Warren Sapp	.40
81	Jamal Anderson	.50
82	James Stewart	.50
83	Ricky Williams	1.25
84	Chad Lewis	.50
85	Shaun King	.50
86	Wesley Walls	.50
87	Mike Anderson	2.00
88	Corey Simon	.40
89	Wayne Chrebet	.50
90	Junior Seau	.40
91	Terance Mathis	.20
92	Germane Crowell	.75
93	Joe Horn	.75
94	Duce Staley	.75
95	Keyshawn Johnson	.75
96	Qadry Ismail	.20
97	Dorsey Levens	.75
98	Kerry Collins	.50
99	Corey Dillon	.75
100	Zach Thomas	.40
101	Chad Pennington	1.50
102	Ricky Watters	.50
103	Bruce Smith	.20
104	David Boston	.75
105	Ed McCaffrey	.50
106	Kevin Faulk	.50
107	Jerome Bettis	.50
108	Warrick Dunn	.50
109	Tim Brown	.50
110	Marcus Robinson	.75
111	Tony Gonzalez	.50
112	Drew Bledsoe	1.00
113	Darrell Jackson	.40
114	Stephen Davis	.75
115	Doug Johnson	.40
116	Brett Favre	3.00
117	Darren Howard	.20
118	Cade McNown	.75
119	Steve McNair	.75
120	James Allen	.50
121	Sylvester Morris	.75
122	J.R. Redmond	.50
123	Jacquez Green	.20
124	Champ Bailey	.40
125	Eddie George	1.00
126	*Michael Vick*	60.00
127	*David Terrell*	40.00
128	*Deuce McAllister*	25.00
129	*Koren Robinson*	25.00
130	*Rod Gardner*	25.00
131	*Chris Chambers*	30.00
132	*Santana Moss*	25.00
133	*Reggie Wayne*	25.00
134	*Quincy Morgan*	20.00
135	*Rudi Johnson*	15.00
136	*Robert Ferguson*	15.00
137	*Todd Heap*	10.00
138	*Michael Bennett*	30.00
139	*Jesse Palmer*	10.00
140	*Drew Brees*	50.00
141	*James Jackson*	15.00
142	*Chris Weinke*	40.00
143	*LaDainian Tomlinson*	50.00
144	*Chad Johnson*	15.00
145	*Quincy Carter*	35.00
146	*Freddie Mitchell*	30.00
147	*Anthony Thomas*	60.00
148	*Travis Henry*	25.00
149	*Marvin "Snoop" Minnis*	20.00
150	*Marques Tuiasosopo*	25.00
151	*Travis Minor*	20.00
152	*Mike McMahon*	15.00
153	*Josh Heupel*	40.00
154	*Sage Rosenfels*	15.00
155	*Kevan Barlow*	15.00

2001 Fleer Genuine Autographs

		MT
Too Uncommon to Price		
Complete Set (74):		
Common Player:		
1A	Troy Aikman	
2A	Derrick Alexander	
3A	Shaun Alexander	
4A	Mike Anderson	
5A	Drew Brees	
6A	Koren Robinson	
7A	Isaac Bruce	
8A	Mark Brunell	
9A	Cris Carter	
10A	Chris Chambers	
11A	Wayne Chrebet	
12A	Daunte Culpepper	
13A	Stephen Davis	
14A	Terrell Davis	
15A	Ron Dayne	
16A	Corey Dillon	
17A	Marshall Faulk	
18A	Jeff Garcia	
19A	Eddie George	
20A	Tony Gonzalez	
21A	Brian Griese	
22A	Marvin Harrison	
23A	Travis Henry	
24A	Josh Heupel	
25A	Torry Holt	
26A	Edgerrin James	
27A	LaMont Jordan	
28A	Jamal Lewis	
29A	Deuce McAllister	
30A	Donovan McNabb	
31A	Travis Minor	
32A	Quincy Morgan	
33A	Randy Moss	
34A	Santana Moss	
35A	Terrell Owens	
36A	Ken-Yon Rambo	
37A	Marcus Robinson	
38A	Sage Rosenfels	
39A	Jimmy Smith	
40A	Duce Staley	
41A	Fred Taylor	
42A	David Terrell	
43A	Anthony Thomas	
44A	LaDainian Tomlinson	
45A	Marques Tuiasosopo	
46A	Michael Vick	
47A	Kurt Warner	
48A	Reggie Wayne	
49A	Chris Weinke	
50A	Ricky Williams	
51A	Troy Aikman	
52A	Jamal Anderson	
53A	Charlie Batch	
54A	David Boston	
55A	Isaac Bruce	
56A	Tim Couch	
57A	Terrell Davis	
58A	Kevin Dyson	
59A	L.C. Greenwood	
60A	Marvin Harrison	
61A	Edgerrin James	
62A	Rob Johnson	
63A	Jevon Kearse	
64A	Jim Kelly	
65A	James Lofton	
66A	Ed McCaffrey	
67A	Rob Moore	
68A	Johnnie Morton	
69A	Jake Plummer	
70A	Jerry Rice	
71A	Mike Singletary	
72A	Emmitt Smith	
73A	Charles Woodson	
74A	Steve Young	

Post-1980 cards in Near Mint condition will generally sell for about 75% of the quoted Mint value. Excellent-condition cards bring no more than 40%.

2001 Fleer Genuine Coverage Plus

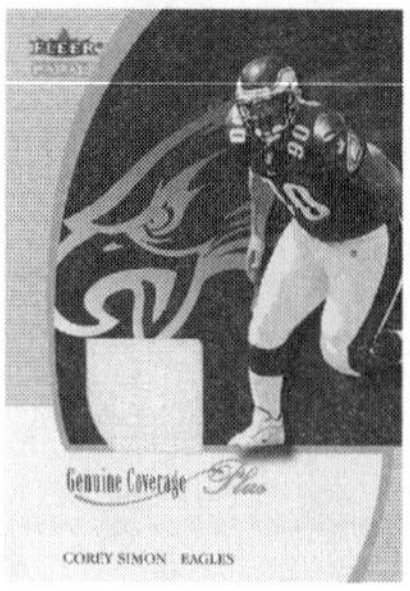

		MT
Complete Set (27):		225.00
Common Player:		8.00
Inserted 1:24		
1GC	Isaac Bruce	12.00
2GC	Mark Brunell	15.00
3GC	Az-Zahir Hakim	8.00
4GC	Marvin Harrison	12.00
5GC	Edgerrin James	35.00
6GC	Kevin Johnson	8.00
7GC	Fred Taylor	15.00
8GC	Kurt Warner	45.00
9GC	Brian Urlacher	25.00
10GC	Duce Staley	12.00
11GC	Jimmy Smith	8.00
12GC	Corey Simon	8.00
13GC	Marcus Robinson	12.00
14GC	Travis Prentice	12.00
15GC	Jake Plummer	12.00
16GC	Cade McNown	12.00
17GC	Peyton Manning	35.00
18GC	Thomas Jones	12.00
19GC	Keenan McCardell	8.00
20GC	Dez White	8.00
21GC	Ed McCaffrey	8.00
22GC	Eric Moulds	12.00
23GC	Brad Johnson	12.00
24GC	Rob Johnson	8.00
25GC	Warren Sapp	8.00
26GC	Courtney Brown	8.00
27GC	Torry Holt	12.00

2001 Fleer Genuine Final Cut

		MT
Complete Set (24):		275.00
Common Player:		8.00
Inserted 1:24		
1FC	Troy Aikman	35.00
2FC	Jamal Anderson	12.00
3FC	Charlie Batch	12.00
4FC	David Boston	12.00
5FC	Isaac Bruce	12.00
6FC	Tim Couch	20.00
7FC	Terrell Davis	30.00
8FC	Kevin Dyson	8.00
9FC	L.C. Greenwood	12.00
10FC	Marvin Harrison	12.00
11FC	Edgerrin James	35.00
12FC	Rob Johnson	8.00
13FC	Jevon Kearse	12.00
14FC	Jim Kelly	25.00
15FC	James Lofton	12.00
16FC	Ed McCaffrey	12.00
17FC	Rob Moore	8.00
18FC	Johnnie Morton	8.00
19FC	Jake Plummer	12.00
20FC	Jerry Rice	35.00
21FC	Mike Singletary	15.00
22FC	Emmitt Smith	40.00
23FC	Charles Woodson	12.00
24FC	Steve Young	20.00

2001 Fleer Genuine Future Swatch Tandems

		MT
Complete Set (5):		475.00
Common Player:		75.00
Production 50 Sets		
1FST	Michael Vick, Drew Brees	225.00
2FST	David Terrell, Anthony Thomas	100.00
3FST	Santana Moss, Reggie Wayne	75.00
4FST	Deuce McAllister, LaDainian Tomlinson	180.00
5FST	Koren Robinson, Rod Gardner	75.00

2001 Fleer Genuine Hawaii Live "O"

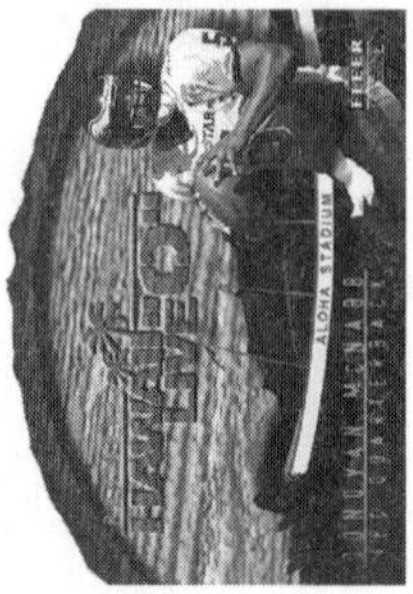

		MT
Complete Set (15):		35.00
Common Player:		1.50
Minor Stars:		3.00
Inserted 1:23		
1HL	Daunte Culpepper	6.00
2HL	Donovan McNabb	4.50
3HL	Torry Holt	3.00
4HL	Terrell Owens	3.00
5HL	Jimmy Smith	1.50
6HL	Jeff Garcia	3.00
7HL	Rich Gannon	1.50
8HL	Peyton Manning	10.00
9HL	Joe Horn	3.00
10HL	Tony Gonzalez	1.50
11HL	Edgerrin James	7.50
12HL	Eddie George	3.50
13HL	Corey Dillon	3.00
14HL	Warrick Dunn	3.00
15HL	Marvin Harrison	3.00

2001 Fleer Genuine Names of the Game

		MT
Common Player:		20.00
Production 100 Sets		
1NG	Daunte Culpepper	50.00
2NG	Terrell Davis	40.00
3NG	Ron Dayne	25.00
4NG	Eric Dickerson	35.00
5NG	Tony Dorsett	50.00
6NG	Edgerrin James	65.00
7NG	Jevon Kearse	25.00
8NG	Curtis Martin	20.00
9NG	Steve McNair	20.00
10NG	Joe Montana	150.00
11NG	Randy Moss	85.00
12NG	Walter Payton	150.00
13NG	William Perry	20.00
14NG	Deion Sanders	50.00
15NG	Roger Staubach	75.00
16NG	Lawrence Taylor	45.00
17NG	Johnny Unitas	75.00

2001 Fleer Genuine Pennant Aggression

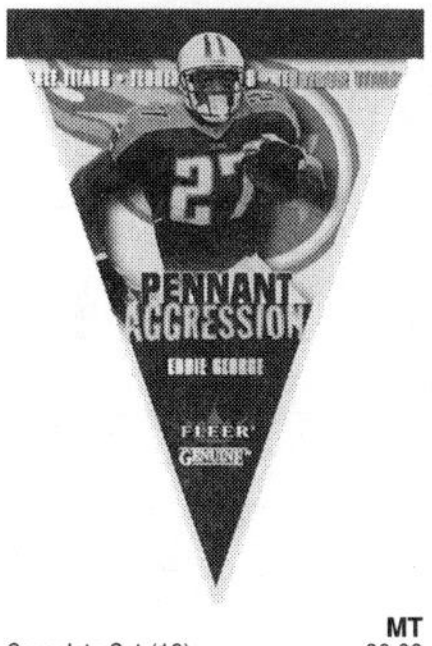

		MT
Complete Set (10):		30.00
Common Player:		3.00
Inserted 1:23		
1PA	Kurt Warner	8.00
2PA	Brett Favre	10.00
3PA	Emmitt Smith	6.00
4PA	Daunte Culpepper	4.50
5PA	Terrell Davis	5.00
6PA	Peyton Manning	8.00
7PA	Eddie George	3.50
8PA	Donovan McNabb	4.00
9PA	Ricky Williams	4.00
10PA	Tim Couch	3.50

2001 Fleer Genuine Seek and Deploy

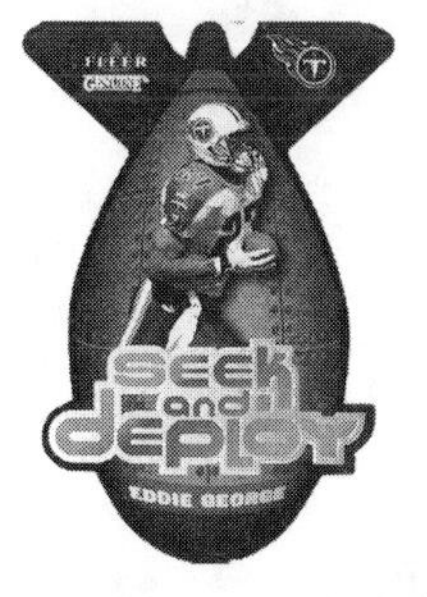

		MT
Complete Set (15):		40.00
Common Player:		3.00
Inserted 1:23		
1SD	Jamal Lewis	6.00
2SD	Randy Moss	8.00
3SD	Ricky Williams	4.50
4SD	Terrell Davis	6.00
5SD	Donovan McNabb	4.50
6SD	Curtis Martin	3.00
7SD	Brett Favre	12.00
8SD	Aaron Brooks	3.50
9SD	Kurt Warner	10.00
10SD	Eddie George	3.50
11SD	Daunte Culpepper	6.00
12SD	Jamal Anderson	3.00
13SD	Marshall Faulk	3.50
14SD	Ray Lewis	3.00
15SD	Ron Dayne	4.50

A card number in parentheses ( ) indicates the set is unnumbered.

2001 Fleer Genuine Donovan McNabb Uncut Sheet

		MT
Complete Set (1):		
1US	Donovan McNabb	

2001 Fleer Glossy

		MT
Complete Set (450):		275.00
Common Player:		.20
Minor Stars:		.40
Common Rookie (401-450):		2.50
Pack (10):		1.50
Box (24):		30.00
1	Thomas Jones	.40
2	Bruce Smith	.20
3	Marvin Harrison	.60
4	Darrell Jackson	.40
5	Trent Green	.50
6	Wesley Walls	.20
7	Jimmy Smith	.50
8	Isaac Bruce	.50
9	Jamal Anderson	.50
10	Marty Booker	.40
11	Elvis Grbac	.60
12	Joe Jurevicius	.20
13	Reidel Anthony	.20
14	Darnay Scott	.40
15	Oronde Gadsden	.40
16	Shawn Bryson	.20
17	Jonathan Ogden	.20
18	Aaron Shea	.20
19	Randy Moss	2.00
20	Eddie George	.75
21	Stephen Davis	.40
22	Emmitt Smith	1.50
23	Willie McGinest	.20
24	Trent Dilfer	.40
25	Peter Boulware	.20
26	Rod Smith	.50
27	Ricky Williams	1.00
28	Albert Connell	.20
29	Robert Porcher	.20
30	Jessie Armstead	.20
31	Shane Matthews	.20
32	Eric Moulds	.50
33	Kurt Schulz	.20
34	Richie Anderson	.20
35	Ron Dugans	.40
36	Steve Beuerlein	.40
37	Darren Sharper	.40
38	Andre Rison	.40
39	Courtney Brown	.40
40	Eddie Kennison	.40
41	Ken Dilger	.20
42	Charles Johnson	.20
43	Dexter Coakley	.20
44	Akili Smith	.40
45	R. Jay Soward	.20
46	Danny Farmer	.40
47	Dez White	.40
48	Olandis Gary	.60
49	Wali Rainer	.20
50	Derrick Alexander	.40
51	Donnie Abraham	.20
52	David Sloan	.20
53	Larry Allen	.20
54	Sam Madison	.40
55	Troy Edwards	.50
56	Ryan Longwell	.20
57	Brian Griese	.75
58	John Randle	.20
59	Reggie Jones	.20
60	Mike Peterson	.20
61	Bill Romanowski	.20
62	Kevin Faulk	.40
63	Tai Streets	.40
64	Tony Brackens	.20
65	James Stewart	.40
66	Joe Horn	.40
67	Kurt Warner	2.00
68	Eric Hicks	.20
69	Bryant Westbrook	.20
70	Tiki Barber	.50
71	Frank Sanders	.40
72	Olindo Mare	.20
73	Bill Schroeder	.40
74	Anthony Becht	.40
75	Rob Johnson	.50
76	Troy Brown	.40
77	Chad Bratzke	.20
78	Rickey Dudley	.40
79	Doug Johnson	.20
80	Joe Johnson	.20
81	Keenan McCardell	.40
82	Tim Brown	.60
83	Blaine Bishop	.20
84	Ron Dixon	.40
85	Mike Cloud	.20
86	Todd Pinkston	.50
87	Shannon Sharpe	.50
88	Marvin Jones	.20
89	Zach Thomas	.50
90	Kordell Stewart	.75
91	Champ Bailey	.50
92	Jacquez Green	.40
93	Daunte Culpepper	1.25
94	Freddie Jones	.20
95	Donald Hayes	.40
96	Rich Gannon	.60
97	Ty Law	.50
98	Grant Wilstrom	.20
99	James Allen	.20
100	Corey Simon	.20
101	Jeff Blake	.40
102	Bryant Young	.40
103	Craig Yeast	.20
104	Bobby Shaw	.20
105	Kerry Collins	.50
106	Brock Huard	.50
107	JaJuan Dawson	.40
108	Jeff Graham	.20
109	Chad Pennington	1.25
110	Jake Plummer	.50
111	James McKnight	.20
112	Terrell Owens	.60
113	Mo Lewis	.20
114	Jeremy McDaniel	.20
115	Ed McCaffrey	.50
116	Ricky Watters	.50
117	Jerry Porter	.60
118	Shawn Jefferson	.20
119	Charlie Batch	.40
120	Justin Watson	.20
121	Donovan McNabb	1.25
122	Shaun King	.40
123	Brett Favre	2.50
124	Ronald McKinnon	.20
125	Richard Huntley	.20
126	Ray Lewis	.60
127	Jerome Pathon	.20
128	Sam Cowart	.20
129	Ryan Leaf	.40
130	Greg Clark	.20
131	Tony Boselli	.20
132	Frank Wycheck	.20
133	Charlie Garner	.40
134	Tony Siragusa	.20
135	Sylvester Morris	.50
136	Qadry Ismail	.40
137	Jon Kitna	.40
138	James Thrash	.40
139	Lamar Smith	.40
140	Brad Johnson	.60
141	London Fletcher	.20
142	Tim Biakabutuka	.40
143	Ed McDaniel	.20
144	Tony Parrish	.20
145	David Boston	.60
146	Brian Urlacher	1.25
147	Drew Bledsoe	.75
148	David Patten	.20
149	Marcellus Wiley	.20
150	Peter Warrick	.60
151	La'Roi Glover	.20
152	Troy Aikman	1.25
153	Chris Chandler	.20
154	Travis Prentice	.40
155	Ike Hilliard	.40
156	John Mobley	.20
157	Warren Sapp	.40
158	Joey Galloway	.50
159	Laveranues Coles	.50
160	Germane Crowell	.40
161	Jamal Lewis	1.25
162	Mike Anderson	1.00
163	Charles Woodson	.40
164	Antonio Freeman	.50
165	Derrick Mason	.50
166	Chris Claiborne	.20
167	Brian Mitchell	.20
168	Mike Vanderjagt	.20
169	Rod Woodson	.40
170	Doug Chapman	.40
171	John Lynch	.20
172	Kevin Hardy	.20
173	Sam Shade	.20
174	Edgerrin James	1.50
175	Brian Dawkins	.20
176	Donnie Edwards	.20
177	Patrick Jeffers	.20
178	Mark Brunell	.50
179	Junior Seau	.40
180	Trace Armstrong	.20
181	Marcus Robinson	.50
182	Tony Gonzalez	.60
183	J.J. Stokes	.50
184	Jake Reed	.20
185	Corey Dillon	.40
186	Jay Fiedler	.60
187	Christian Fauria	.20
188	Sammy Knight	.20
189	Kevin Johnson	.50
190	Matthew Hatchette	.20
191	Az-Zahir Hakim	.40
192	Keith Hamilton	.20
193	Darren Woodson	.20
194	Terry Glenn	.40
195	Simeon Rice	.20
196	Keyshawn Johnson	.60
197	Terrell Davis	1.25
198	Willie Roaf	.20
199	Doug Flutie	.75
200	Kevin Carter	.20
201	Stephen Boyd	.20
202	Michael Strahan	.40
203	Ray Buchanan	.20
204	Tyrone Wheatley	.40
205	Jason Hanson	.20
206	Wayne Chrebet	.50
207	Samari Rolle	.20
208	Duce Staley	.50
209	Dorsey Levens	.40
210	Sebastian Janikowski	.40
211	Duane Starks	.20
212	Jason Gildon	.20
213	Terrence Wilkins	.20
214	Eric Allen	.20
215	Deion Sanders	.50
216	Curtis Conway	.20
217	Fred Taylor	.75
218	Troy Vincent	.20
219	Mike Minter	.20
220	Jeff Garcia	.75
221	Tony Richardson	.20
222	Jerome Bettis	.50
223	Chad Morton	.20
224	Tony Horne	.20
225	Dave Moore	.20
226	Victor Green	.20
227	Chris Sanders	.20
228	Marshall Faulk	.75
229	Cris Carter	.60
230	Rodney Harrison	.20
231	Tim Couch	.75
232	Antowain Smith	.60
233	Lawyer Milloy	.20
234	Lance Schulters	.20
235	Michael Wiley	.20
236	Steve McNair	.50
237	Aaron Brooks	.75
238	Anthony Simmons	.20
239	Dwayne Carswell	.20
240	Priest Holmes	.50
241	Amani Toomer	.50
242	Aeneas Williams	.40
243	MarTay Jenkins	.20
244	Jeff George	.40
245	Vinny Testaverde	.50
246	Peerless Price	.40
247	Bubba Franks	.40
248	Randall Cunningham	.40
249	Aaron Glenn	.20
250	Terance Mathis	.20
251	Peyton Manning	2.00
252	Terrell Buckley	.20
253	Greg Biekert	.20
254	Martin Gramatica	.40
255	Kyle Brady	.40
256	Johnnie Morton	.40
257	Jeremiah Trotter	.20
258	Travis Taylor	.50
259	Frank Moreau	.20
260	LeRoy Butler	.40
261	Plaxico Burress	.60
262	Randall Godfrey	.20
263	Jason Taylor	.20
264	Jeff Burris	.20
265	Jim Harbaugh	.40
266	Marco Coleman	.20
267	Robert Smith	.40
268	Mike Hollis	.20
269	Jerry Rice	1.50
270	Muhsin Muhammad	.40
271	J.R. Redmond	.40
272	Brian Walker	.20
273	Orlando Pace	.20
274	Cade McNown	.40
275	Darren Howard	.20
276	Ron Dayne	.50
277	Shaun Alexander	1.00
278	Brandon Bennett	.20
279	Jason Sehorn	.20
280	Matt Hasselbeck	.40
281	Michael Pittman	.20
282	Dennis Northcutt	.20
283	Dedric Ward	.40
284	Curtis Martin	.50
285	Sammy Morris	.20
286	Raghib Ismail	.20
287	Jon Ritchie	.20
288	Shaun Ellis	.20
289	Tim Dwight	.40
290	Trevor Pryce	.20
291	Warrick Dunn	.60
292	Napoleon Kaufman	.20
293	Mike Alstott	.50
294	Herman Moore	.40
295	Chad Lewis	.20
296	Hugh Douglas	.20
297	Chris Redman	.40
298	Ahman Green	.50
299	Hines Ward	.50
300	Mark Bruener	.20
301	Jevon Kearse	.20
302	Jermaine Fazande	.20
303	Terrell Fletcher	.20
304	Torry Holt	.60
305	Chris McAlister	.20
306	Jason Elam	.20
307	Fred Beasley	.20
308	Frank Wycheck	.20
309	Michael McCrary	.20
310	Mark Brunell	.20
311	Tim Couch	.40
312	Takeo Spikes	.20
313	Jerome Bettis	.20
314	Zach Thomas	.20
315	Drew Bledsoe	40.00
316	Wayne Chrebet	.20
317	Jay Riemersma	.20
318	Marvin Harrison	.20
319	Ed McCaffrey	.20
320	Tony Gonzalez	.20
321	Tim Brown	.20
322	Junior Seau	.20
323	Shawn Springs	.20
324	Troy Aikman	.60
325	Pat Tilman	.20
326	David Akers	.20
327	Michael Strahan	.20
328	Darrell Green	.20
329	Kurt Warner	1.00
330	Jeff Garcia	.40
331	Aaron Brooks	.40
332	Jamal Anderson	.20
333	Brad Hoover	.20
334	Cris Carter	.20
335	Derrick Brooks	.20
336	Antonio Freeman	.20
337	Luther Elliss	.20
338	James Allen	.20
339	Cardinals	.20
340	Falcons	.20
341	Ravens	.20
342	Bills	.20
343	Panthers	.20
344	Bears	.20
345	Bengals	.20
346	Browns	.20
347	Cowboys	.60
348	Broncos	.20
349	Lions	.20
350	Packers	1.25
351	Colts	.60
352	Jaguars	.20
353	Chiefs	.20
354	Dolphins	.20
355	Vikings	.40
356	Patriots	.20
357	Saints	.20
358	Giants	.20
359	Jets	.20
360	Raiders	.20
361	Eagles	.40
362	Steelers	.40
363	Chargers	.20
364	49ers	.40
365	Seahawks	.20
366	Rams	1.00
367	Buccaneers	.20
368	Titans	.20
369	Redskins	.20
370	Bills	.20
371	Colts	.40
372	Dolphins	.20
373	Patriots	.20
374	Jets	.20
375	Ravens	.20
376	Bengals	.20
377	Browns	.20
378	Jaguars	.20
379	Steelers	.40
380	Titans	.40
381	Broncos	.40
382	Chiefs	.20
383	Raiders	.40
384	Chargers	.20
385	Seahawks	.20
386	Cardinals	.20
387	Cowboys	.60
388	Giants	.20
389	Eagles	.20
390	Redskins	.20
391	Bears	.20
392	Lions	.20
393	Packers	.60
394	Vikings	.40
395	Buccaneers	.20
396	Falcons	.20
397	Panthers	.20
398	Saints	.20
399	49ers	.40
400	Rams	.60
401	*Michael Vick*	20.00
402	*Drew Brees*	15.00
403	*Michael Bennett*	10.00
404	*David Terrell*	12.00
405	*Deuce McAllister*	8.00
406	*Santana Moss*	8.00
407	*Koren Robinson*	8.00
408	*Chris Weinke*	8.00
409	*Reggie Wayne*	8.00
410	*Rod Gardner*	8.00
411	*James Jackson*	5.00
412	*Travis Henry*	6.00
413	*Josh Heupel*	5.00
414	*LaDainian Tomlinson*	15.00
415	*Chad Johnson*	4.00
416	*Sage Rosenfels*	5.00
417	*Quincy Morgan*	5.00
418	*Ken-Yon Rambo*	3.00
419	*LaMont Jordan*	4.00
420	*Anthony Thomas*	20.00
421	*Dave Dickenson*	3.00
422	*Travis Minor*	5.00
423	*Kevan Barlow*	6.00
424	*Chris Chambers*	10.00
425	*Richard Seymour*	2.50
426	*Gerard Warren*	2.50
427	*Jamar Fletcher*	2.50
428	*Freddie Mitchell*	8.00
429	*Jamal Reynolds*	2.50
430	*Marques Tuiasosopo*	8.00
431	*Marvin "Snoop" Minnis*	6.00
432	*Mike McMahon*	8.00
433	*Robert Ferguson*	3.00
434	*Ronney Daniels*	2.50
435	*Rudi Johnson*	3.00
436	*Vinny Sutherland*	3.00
437	*Josh Booty*	4.00
438	*Reggie White*	2.50
439	*Todd Heap*	3.00
440	*Justin Smith*	2.50
441	*Andre Carter*	2.50
442	*Bobby Newcombe*	2.50
443	*Alex Bannister*	3.00
444	*Correll Buckhalter*	6.00
445	*Quincy Carter*	10.00
446	*Jesse Palmer*	5.00
447	*Heath Evans*	2.50
448	*Dan Morgan*	2.50
449	*Justin McCareins*	2.50
450	*Alge Crumpler*	3.00

2001 Fleer Glossy Nameplates

		MT
Common Player:		15.00
1NP	Ron Dayne	15.00
2NP	Kurt Warner	60.00
3NP	Curtis Martin	25.00
4NP	Jake Plummer	15.00
5NP	Mark Brunell	20.00
6NP	Drew Bledsoe	30.00
7NP	Kevin Johnson	15.00
8NP	Brian Griese	50.00
9NP	Terrell Owens	20.00
10NP	Brian Urlacher	60.00
11NP	Jamal Anderson	15.00
12NP	Isaac Bruce	20.00
13NP	Jerome Bettis	25.00
14NP	Fred Taylor	25.00
15NP	Tim Couch	40.00
16NP	Stephen Davis	15.00
17NP	Warrick Dunn	20.00
18NP	Rod Smith	20.00
19NP	Marshall Faulk	50.00
20NP	Thomas Jones	15.00
21NP	Emmitt Smith	75.00
22NP	Marcus Robinson	20.00
23NP	Daunte Culpepper	60.00
24NP	Antonio Freeman	25.00
25NP	Marvin Harrison	30.00
26NP	Dan Marino	100.00
27NP	Steve Young	60.00
28NP	Deion Sanders	60.00
29NP	Edgerrin James	60.00
30NP	Jerry Rice	75.00

2001 Fleer Glossy Rookie Mini

		MT
Mini Cards:		1x-1.5x
Production 350 Sets		
1RM	Michael Vick	
2RM	Drew Brees	
3RM	Michael Bennett	
4RM	David Terrell	
5RM	Deuce McAllister	
6RM	Santana Moss	
7RM	Koren Robinson	
8RM	Chris Weinke	
9RM	Reggie Wayne	
10RM	Rod Gardner	
11RM	James Jackson	
12RM	Travis Henry	
13RM	Josh Heupel	
14RM	LaDainian Tomlinson	
15RM	Chad Johnson	
16RM	Sage Rosenfels	
17RM	Quincy Morgan	
18RM	Ken-Yon Rambo	
19RM	LaMont Jordan	
20RM	Anthony Thomas	
21RM	Dave Dickenson	
22RM	Travis Minor	
23RM	Kevan Barlow	
24RM	Chris Chambers	
25RM	Richard Seymour	
26RM	Gerard Warren	
27RM	Jamar Fletcher	
28RM	Freddie Mitchell	
29RM	Jamal Reynolds	
30RM	Marques Tuiasosopo	
31RM	Marvin "Snoop" Minnis	
32RM	Mike McMahon	
33RM	Robert Ferguson	
34RM	Ronney Daniels	
35RM	Rudi Johnson	
36RM	Vinny Sutherland	
37RM	Josh Booty	
38RM	Reggie White	
39RM	Todd Heap	
40RM	Justin Smith	
41RM	Andre Carter	
42RM	Bobby Newcombe	
43RM	Alex Bannister	
44RM	Correll Buckhalter	
45RM	Quincy Carter	
46RM	Jesse Palmer	
47RM	Heath Evans	
48RM	Dan Morgan	
49RM	Justin McCareins	
50RM	Alge Crumpler	

2001 Fleer Glossy Rookie Sticker

		MT
Stickers:		.5-1x
Production 699 Sets		
1RS	Michael Vick	
2RS	Drew Brees	
3RS	Michael Bennett	
4RS	David Terrell	
5RS	Deuce McAllister	
6RS	Santana Moss	
7RS	Koren Robinson	
8RS	Chris Weinke	
9RS	Reggie Wayne	
10RS	Rod Gardner	
11RS	James Jackson	
12RS	Travis Henry	
13RS	Josh Heupel	
14RS	LaDainian Tomlinson	
15RS	Chad Johnson	
16RS	Sage Rosenfels	
17RS	Quincy Morgan	
18RS	Ken-Yon Rambo	
19RS	LaMont Jordan	
20RS	Anthony Thomas	
21RS	Dave Dickenson	
22RS	Travis Minor	
23RS	Kevan Barlow	
24RS	Chris Chambers	
25RS	Richard Seymour	
26RS	Gerard Warren	
27RS	Jamar Fletcher	
28RS	Freddie Mitchell	
29RS	Jamal Reynolds	
30RS	Marques Tuiasosopo	
31RS	Marvin "Snoop" Minnis	
32RS	Mike McMahon	
33RS	Robert Ferguson	
34RS	Ronney Daniels	
35RS	Rudi Johnson	
36RS	Vinny Sutherland	
37RS	Josh Booty	
38RS	Reggie White	
39RS	Todd Heap	
40RS	Justin Smith	
41RS	Andre Carter	
42RS	Bobby Newcombe	
43RS	Alex Bannister	
44RS	Correll Buckhalter	
45RS	Quincy Carter	
46RS	Jesse Palmer	
47RS	Heath Evans	
48RS	Dan Morgan	
49RS	Justin McCareins	
50RS	Alge Crumpler	

2001 Fleer Glossy Throwbacks

		MT
Complete Set (20):		75.00
Common Player:		2.00
Inserted 1:12 Glossy		
Inserted 1:20 Tradition		
1TB	Jamal Lewis	5.00
2TB	Eddie George	3.00
3TB	Marvin Harrison	2.00
4TB	Brett Favre	10.00
5TB	Donovan McNabb	5.00
6TB	Troy Aikman	5.00
7TB	Edgerrin James	6.00
8TB	Brian Urlacher	5.00
9TB	Stephen Davis	2.00
10TB	Daunte Culpepper	5.00
11TB	Jerry Rice	6.00
12TB	Emmitt Smith	6.00
13TB	Kurt Warner	8.00
14TB	Ricky Williams	4.00
15TB	Cris Carter	2.00
16TB	Mark Brunell	3.00
17TB	Ron Dayne	2.00
18TB	Peyton Manning	8.00
19TB	Randy Moss	8.00
20TB	Brian Griese	3.00

2001 Fleer Glossy Traditional Threads

		MT
Common Player:		10.00
1TT	Troy Aikman	30.00
2TT	Jamal Anderson	10.00
3TT	Jerome Bettis	15.00
4TT	Drew Bledsoe	15.00
5TT	Isaac Bruce	12.00
6TT	Mark Brunell	12.00
7TT	Tim Couch	15.00
8TT	Daunte Culpepper	30.00
9TT	Stephen Davis	10.00
10TT	Ron Dayne	10.00
11TT	Warrick Dunn	12.00
12TT	Marshall Faulk	20.00
13TT	Brett Favre	50.00
14TT	Antonio Freeman	15.00
15TT	Eddie George	15.00
16TT	Brian Griese	15.00
17TT	Marvin Harrison	15.00
18TT	Edgerrin James	30.00
19TT	Kevin Johnson	10.00
20TT	Thomas Jones	10.00
21TT	Jevon Kearse	10.00
22TT	Ray Lewis	15.00
23TT	Dan Marino	60.00
24TT	Curtis Martin	15.00
25TT	Randy Moss	40.00
26TT	Terrell Owens	15.00
27TT	Jake Plummer	10.00
28TT	Jerry Rice	30.00
29TT	Rod Smith	12.00
30TT	Jimmy Smith	12.00
31TT	Kordell Stewart	15.00
32TT	Fred Taylor	12.00
33TT	Brian Urlacher	25.00
34TT	Kurt Warner	40.00
35TT	Steve Young	20.00

A player's name in *italic type* indicates a rookie card.

2001 Fleer Hot Prospects

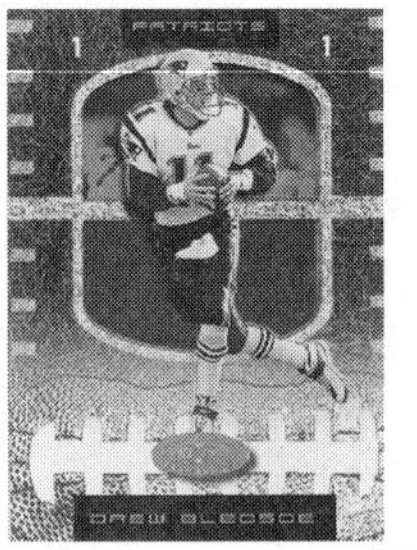

		MT
Complete Set (100):		25.00
Common Player:		.20
Minor Stars:		.40
Pack (5):		10.00
Wax Box (15):		110.00
1	Aaron Brooks	.75
2	Tim Couch	1.00
3	Jeff George	.40
4	Brett Favre	3.00
5	Donovan McNabb	1.25
6	Ray Lucas	.20
7	Doug Flutie	1.00
8	Mark Brunell	1.00
9	Steve McNair	.75
10	Trent Green	.40
11	Daunte Culpepper	1.50
12	Rich Gannon	.40
13	Kurt Warner	3.00
14	Brian Griese	1.00
15	Kerry Collins	.40
16	Vinny Testaverde	.40
17	David Boston	.75
18	Peyton Manning	2.50
19	Keyshawn Johnson	.75
20	Tim Biakabutuka	.40
21	J.R. Redmond	.40
22	Emmitt Smith	2.00
23	Terry Glenn	.50
24	Tony Gonzalez	.50
25	Charlie Garner	.40
26	Lamar Smith	.50
27	Eddie George	1.00
28	Fred Taylor	1.00
29	Marvin Harrison	.75
30	Terrell Davis	1.50
31	Marcus Robinson	.75
32	Edgerrin James	2.50
33	Ed McCaffrey	.50
34	Ricky Williams	1.25
35	Todd Pinkston	.40
36	Jerome Bettis	.75
37	Shaun Alexander	.75
38	Mike Anderson	2.00
39	Keenan McCardell	.40
40	Mike Alstott	.75
41	Terrell Fletcher	.20
42	Kevin Johnson	.50
43	Wesley Walls	.20
44	Derrick Mason	.20
45	Sammy Morris	.40
46	Joey Galloway	.75
47	Sylvester Morris	.75
48	Stephen Davis	.75
49	Terrell Owens	.75
50	Troy Edwards	.50
51	Amani Toomer	.40
52	Ray Lewis	.50
53	Terance Mathis	.20
54	Brian Urlacher	1.50
55	Junior Seau	.50
56	Raghib Ismail	.40
57	Wayne Chrebet	.50
58	Peter Warrick	1.50
59	Andre Rison	.20
60	Desmond Howard	.20
61	Eric Moulds	.75
62	Jerry Rice	1.75
63	Stephen Alexander	.20
64	Isaac Bruce	.75
65	Travis Prentice	.50
66	James Stewart	.50
67	Jamal Anderson	.50
68	Ricky Watters	.50
69	Jamal Lewis	2.00
70	Priest Holmes	.40
71	Ahman Green	.50
72	Marshall Faulk	1.00
73	Warrick Dunn	.75
74	Curtis Martin	.75
75	Corey Dillon	.75
76	Ron Dayne	1.50
77	Thomas Jones	.50
78	Duce Staley	.75
79	Tiki Barber	.75
80	Cris Carter	.75
81	Tim Brown	.50
82	Jimmy Smith	.50
83	Elvis Grbac	.50
84	Randy Moss	2.50
85	Tim Dwight	.50
86	Antonio Freeman	.50
87	Muhsin Muhammad	.50
88	Torry Holt	.75
89	Frank Wycheck	.20
90	Jake Plummer	.75
91	Brad Johnson	.50
92	Chris Chandler	.40
93	Drew Bledsoe	1.00
94	Rob Johnson	.50
95	Matt Hasselbeck	.75
96	Jon Kitna	.50
97	Kordell Stewart	.75
98	Charlie Batch	.75
99	Cade McNown	.75
100	Jeff Garcia	.75

2001 Fleer Hot Prospects Draft Day Postmarks

	MT
Common Player:	12.00
Kevan Barlow	20.00
Michael Bennett	45.00
Drew Brees	50.00
Rod Gardner	20.00
Josh Heupel	20.00
James Jackson	20.00
Chad Johnson	15.00
Rudi Johnson	15.00
Deuce McAllister	25.00
Freddie Mitchell	20.00
Quincy Morgan	20.00
Santana Moss	25.00
Jesse Palmer	12.00
Koren Robinson	25.00
David Terrell	30.00
Anthony Thomas	20.00
LaDainian Tomlinson	50.00
Marques Tuiasosopo	20.00
Michael Vick	75.00
Reggie Wayne	20.00
Chris Weinke	45.00

2001 Fleer Hot Prospects Draft Day Postmarks Autographs

	MT
Common Player:	20.00
Kevan Barlow	25.00
Michael Bennett	75.00
Drew Brees	150.00
Rod Gardner	30.00
Josh Heupel	25.00
James Jackson	20.00
Chad Johnson	20.00
Rudi Johnson	20.00
Deuce McAllister	40.00
Freddie Mitchell	30.00
Quincy Morgan	30.00
Santana Moss	60.00
Jesse Palmer	20.00
Koren Robinson	30.00
David Terrell	40.00
Anthony Thomas	30.00
LaDainian Tomlinson	150.00
Marques Tuiasosopo	30.00
Michael Vick	250.00
Reggie Wayne	25.00
Chris Weinke	85.00

2001 Fleer Hot Prospects Honor Guard

		MT
Complete Set (49):		75.00
Common Player:		1.00
Minor Stars:		2.00
Inserted 1:5		
1HG	Troy Aikman	4.00
2HG	Marcus Allen	2.00
3HG	Mike Alstott	2.00
4HG	Jerome Bettis	2.00
5HG	Drew Bledsoe	2.25
6HG	Isaac Bruce	2.00
7HG	Mark Brunell	2.25
8HG	Wayne Chrebet	1.00
9HG	Daunte Culpepper	3.00
10HG	Randall Cunningham	1.00
11HG	Terrell Davis	3.00
12HG	Stephen Davis	2.00
13HG	Corey Dillon	2.00
14HG	Warrick Dunn	2.00
15HG	Marshall Faulk	2.25
16HG	Brett Favre	6.00
17HG	Doug Flutie	2.25
18HG	Jeff Garcia	2.00
19HG	Eddie George	2.25
20HG	Brian Griese	2.25
21HG	Bo Jackson	3.00
22HG	Jamal Lewis	4.50
23HG	Dan Marino	8.00
24HG	Donovan McNabb	2.50
25HG	Steve McNair	2.00
26HG	Joe Montana	10.00
27HG	Randy Moss	5.00
28HG	Jerry Rice	3.50
29HG	Jerry Rice	3.50
30HG	Deion Sanders	2.00
31HG	Emmitt Smith	4.50
32HG	Fred Taylor	2.25
33HG	John Elway	8.00
34HG	Kurt Warner	6.00
35HG	Ricky Williams	2.50
36HG	Marvin Harrison	2.00
37HG	Edgerrin James	5.00
38HG	Curtis Martin	2.00
39HG	Vinny Testaverde	1.00
40HG	Rod Smith	1.00
41HG	Warren Moon	2.00
42HG	Steve Young	2.50
43HG	Jamal Anderson	2.00
44HG	Tim Brown	2.00
45HG	Plaxico Burress	2.00
46HG	Tim Couch	2.25
47HG	Az-Zahir Hakim	1.00
48HG	Ed McCaffrey	2.00
49HG	Ron Dayne	2.50

2001 Fleer Hot Prospects Pigskin Prospects

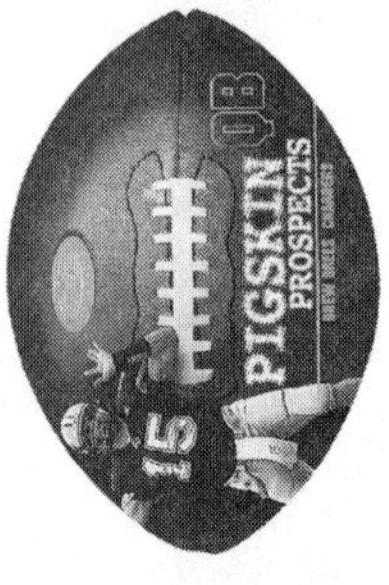

		MT
Complete Set (15):		50.00
Common Player:		2.50
Inserted 1:15		
1PP	Drew Brees	10.00
2PP	Koren Robinson	4.00
3PP	Robert Ferguson	2.50
4PP	Rod Gardner	4.00
5PP	Chad Johnson	2.50
6PP	Reggie Wayne	3.00
7PP	Chris Weinke	6.00
8PP	Deuce McAllister	5.00
9PP	Chris Chambers	2.50
10PP	Freddie Mitchell	3.50
11PP	Quincy Carter	5.00
12PP	LaDainian Tomlinson	8.00
13PP	Santana Moss	4.00
14PP	David Terrell	5.00
15PP	Michael Vick	15.00

2001 Fleer Hot Prospects Pigskin Prospects Jersey

		MT
Common Player:		15.00
Inserted 1:51		
1PPJ	Drew Brees	45.00
2PPJ	Robert Ferguson	20.00
3PPJ	Rod Gardner	25.00
4PPJ	Chad Johnson	15.00
5PPJ	Reggie Wayne	20.00
6PPJ	Chris Weinke	30.00

2001 Fleer Hot Prospects Rookie Premiere Postmarks

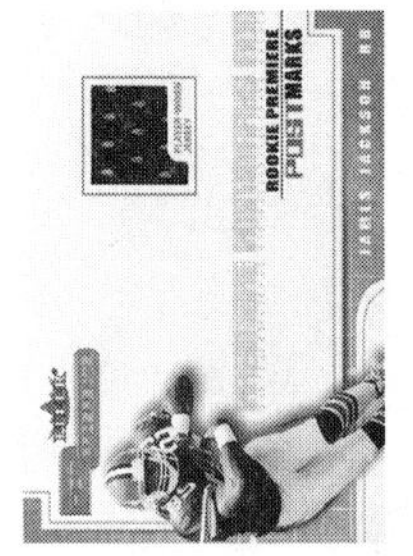

	MT
Complete Set (35):	450.00
Common Player:	8.00
Kevan Barlow	20.00
Michael Bennett	35.00
Drew Brees	50.00
Quincy Carter	25.00
Chris Chambers	25.00
Leonard Davis	8.00
Robert Ferguson	10.00
Rod Gardner	15.00
Todd Heap	10.00
Travis Henry	20.00
Josh Heupel	15.00
James Jackson	15.00
Chad Johnson	10.00
Rudi Johnson	10.00
Deuce McAllister	25.00
Mike McMahon	10.00
Marvin Minnis	20.00
Travis Minor	15.00
Freddie Mitchell	20.00
Dan Morgan	10.00
Quincy Morgan	15.00
Santana Moss	25.00
Jesse Palmer	10.00
Koren Robinson	20.00
Sage Rosenfels	10.00
Richard Seymour	8.00
Justin Smith	8.00
David Terrell	25.00
Anthony Thomas	15.00
LaDainian Tomlinson	50.00
Marques Tuiasosopo	20.00
Michael Vick	75.00
Gerard Warren	10.00
Reggie Wayne	20.00
Chris Weinke	40.00

2001 Fleer Hot Prospects TD Fever

		MT
Complete Set (15):		150.00
Common Player:		10.00
Inserted 1:21		
1TDF	Daunte Culpepper	25.00
2TDF	James Stewart	10.00
3TDF	Jimmy Smith	10.00
4TDF	Marvin Harrison	12.00
5TDF	Drew Bledsoe	15.00
6TDF	Randy Moss	35.00
7TDF	Oronde Gadsden	10.00
8TDF	Peyton Manning	35.00
9TDF	J.R. Redmond	10.00
10TDF	Rich Gannon	12.00
11TDF	Edgerrin James	30.00
12TDF	Peerless Price	10.00
13TDF	Tyrone Wheatley	10.00
14TDF	Curtis Martin	12.00

Post-1980 cards in Near Mint condition will generally sell for about 75% of the quoted Mint value. Excellent-condition cards bring no more than 40%.

2001 Fleer Legacy

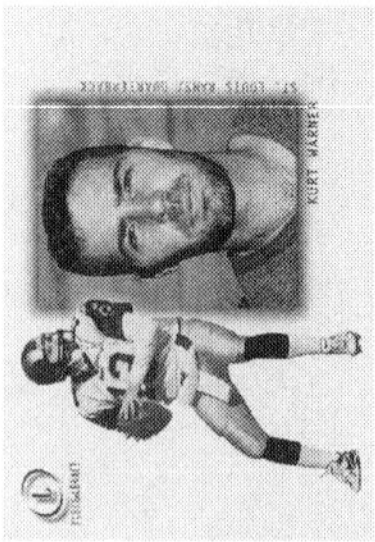

		MT
Complete Set (120):		300.00
Common Player:		.25
Minor Stars:		.40
Common Rookie:		5.00
Production 999 Sets		
First 300 Are Rookie Postmarks		
Pack (5):		3.50
Box (24):		70.00
1	Donovan McNabb	1.50
2	Doug Flutie	1.00
3	Amani Toomer	.40
4	Jay Fiedler	.40
5	Antonio Freeman	.75
6	Jon Kitna	.40
7	Jake Plummer	.75
8	Ricky Watters	.40
9	Jerry Rice	2.00
10	Troy Brown	.40
11	Jimmy Smith	.40
12	Edgerrin James	2.00
13	Todd Pinkston	.25
14	Eric Moulds	.40
15	Stephen Davis	.75
16	Matt Hasselbeck	.40
17	Vinny Testaverde	.40
18	Priest Holmes	.75
19	Mike Anderson	1.25
20	Shane Matthews	.25
21	Qadry Ismail	.25
22	Torry Holt	.75
23	Duce Staley	.75
24	Ahman Green	.75
25	Corey Dillon	.75
26	Peerless Price	.40
27	Steve McNair	.75
28	Junior Seau	.40
29	Doug Chapman	.25
30	Mark Brunell	1.00
31	Joey Galloway	.40
32	James Allen	.25
33	David Boston	.75
34	Marshall Faulk	1.00
35	Shaun Alexander	1.00
36	Wayne Chrebet	.40
37	Randy Moss	2.50
38	Marvin Harrison	.75
39	Tim Couch	1.00
40	Jamal Anderson	.75
41	Warren Sapp	.40
42	Brad Johnson	.75
43	Kerry Collins	.40
44	Derrick Alexander	.25
45	Terrell Davis	1.50
46	Tiki Barber	.25
47	Trent Green	.40
48	James Stewart	.25
49	Kevin Johnson	.40
50	Ray Lewis	.75
51	Warrick Dunn	.75
52	Tim Brown	.75
53	Daunte Culpepper	1.50
54	Fred Taylor	1.00
55	Brian Griese	1.00
56	Wesley Walls	.25
57	Rob Johnson	.40
58	Jeff George	.25
59	Jeff Garcia	.75
60	Rich Gannon	.40
61	Cris Carter	.75
62	Peyton Manning	2.50
63	Peter Warrick	.75
64	Terance Mathis	.25
65	Kurt Warner	2.50
66	Kordell Stewart	.75
67	Aaron Brooks	.75
68	JaJuan Dawson	.25
69	Elvis Grbac	.40
70	Keyshawn Johnson	.75
71	Terrell Owens	.75
72	Curtis Martin	.75
73	Lamar Smith	.40
74	Rod Smith	.40
75	Tim Biakabutuka	.25
76	Thomas Jones	.40
77	Isaac Bruce	.75
78	Joe Horn	.40
79	Drew Bledsoe	1.00
80	Oronde Gadsden	.25
81	Brett Favre	3.00
82	Emmitt Smith	2.00
83	Muhsin Muhammad	.40
84	Eddie George	1.00
85	Jerome Bettis	.75
86	Ricky Williams	1.25
87	Tony Gonzalez	.40
88	Germane Crowell	.40
89	Brian Urlacher	1.50
90	Shawn Jefferson	.25
91	*Michael Vick*	30.00
92	*David Terrell*	20.00
93	*Chris Chambers*	15.00
94	*Freddie Mitchell*	12.00
95	*Drew Brees*	25.00
96	*LaMont Jordan*	6.00
97	*Quincy Carter*	15.00
98	*Anthony Thomas*	30.00
99	*LaDainian Tomlinson*	25.00
100	*Santana Moss*	12.00
101	*Rod Gardner*	12.00
102	*Nick Goings*	5.00
103	*Sage Rosenfels*	8.00
104	*Mike McMahon*	12.00
105	*Marvin "Snoop" Minnis*	10.00
106	*Michael Bennett*	15.00
107	*Todd Heap*	5.00
108	*Kevan Barlow*	10.00
109	*Travis Henry*	10.00
110	*Jason Brookins*	6.00
111	*Rudi Johnson*	5.00
112	*Reggie Wayne*	10.00
113	*Koren Robinson*	12.00
114	*Chad Johnson*	6.00
115	*Quincy Morgan*	8.00
116	*Robert Ferguson*	6.00
117	*Chris Weinke*	12.00
118	*Jesse Palmer*	8.00
119	*James Jackson*	8.00
120	*Deuce McAllister*	12.00

2001 Fleer Legacy Hall of Fame Material

	MT
Common Player:	20.00
Inserted 1:288	
Troy Aikman	30.00
Marcus Allen	30.00
John Elway	60.00
Marshall Faulk	30.00
Brett Favre	60.00
Bo Jackson	40.00
Dan Marino	75.00
Jerry Rice	50.00
Junior Seau	20.00
Emmitt Smith	60.00

2001 Fleer Legacy Rookie Postmarks

		MT
Common Player:		8.00
Production 300 Sets		
First 300 Are Autographs		
91	Michael Vick	40.00
92	David Terrell	25.00
93	Chris Chambers	20.00
94	Freddie Mitchell	15.00
95	Drew Brees	30.00
96	LaMont Jordan	8.00
97	Quincy Carter	20.00
98	Anthony Thomas	40.00
99	LaDainian Tomlinson	40.00
100	Santana Moss	15.00
101	Rod Gardner	15.00
102	Nick Goings	8.00
103	Sage Rosenfels	10.00
104	Mike McMahon	15.00
105	Marvin "Snoop" Minnis	12.00
106	Michael Bennett	20.00
107	Todd Heap	8.00
108	Kevan Barlow	12.00
109	Travis Henry	12.00
110	Jason Brookins	8.00
111	Rudi Johnson	8.00
112	Reggie Wayne	12.00
113	Koren Robinson	15.00
114	Chad Johnson	8.00
115	Quincy Morgan	10.00
116	Robert Ferguson	8.00
117	Chris Weinke	15.00
118	Jesse Palmer	10.00
119	James Jackson	10.00
120	Deuce McAllister	15.00

2001 Fleer Legacy NFL Game Issue

	MT
Common Player:	6.00
2nd Quarter:	2x
Production 100 Sets	
3rd Quarter:	2.5x
Production 50 Sets	
4th Quarter:	3x-6x
Production 25 Sets	
David Boston	10.00
Mark Brunell	12.00
Cris Carter	12.00
Germane Crowell	6.00
Daunte Culpepper	15.00
Ron Dayne	8.00
Brett Favre	20.00
Rich Gannon	10.00
Jeff Garcia	12.00
Brian Griese	15.00
Bo Jackson	20.00
Edgerrin James	15.00
Kevin Johnson	6.00
Rob Johnson	6.00
Ray Lewis	12.00
Donovan McNabb	15.00
Jake Plummer	6.00
Kordell Stewart	12.00
Vinny Testaverde	8.00
Kurt Warner	20.00

2001 Fleer Legacy Triple Threads

		MT
Complete Set (30):		
Common Player:		40.00
1	Chris Weinke, Drew Brees, Quincy Carter	40.00
2	Michael Vick, Drew Brees, Quincy Carter	50.00
3	Jesse Palmer, Drew Brees, Sage Rosenfels	30.00
4	Josh Heupel, Quincy Carter, Michael Vick	40.00
5	LaDainian Tomlinson, Deuce McAllister, Michael Bennett	40.00
6	Anthony Thomas, James Jackson, Kevan Barlow	30.00
7	Reggie Wayne, Santana Moss, Koren Robinson	20.00
8	David Terrell, Freddie Mitchell, Rod Gardner	25.00
9	Rudi Johnson, James Jackson, Travis Minor	15.00
10	Chris Chambers, Marvin "Snoop" Minnis, Robert Ferguson	25.00
11	Chad Johnson, Todd Heap, Santana Moss	15.00
12	Mike McMahon, Chris Weinke, Marques Tuiasosopo	25.00
13	Travis Minor, Travis Henry, Michael Bennett	30.00
14	Michael Vick, LaDainian Tomlinson, David Terrell	60.00
15	Santana Moss, Freddie Mitchell, Chad Johnson	20.00
16	Kevan Barlow, Michael Bennett, Rudi Johnson	20.00
17	Koren Robinson, Freddie Mitchell, Quincy Morgan	20.00
18	Josh Heupel, Jesse Palmer, Marques Tuiasosopo	20.00
19	Mike McMahon, Jesse Palmer, Chris Weinke	25.00
20	Deuce McAllister, Travis Minor, Anthony Thomas	40.00
21	Robert Ferguson, Reggie Wayne, Marvin "Snoop" Minnis	20.00
22	Chris Chambers, Rod Gardner, Koren Robinson	30.00
23	Todd Heap, Quincy Morgan, Chris Chambers	20.00
24	LaDainian Tomlinson, Kevan Barlow, Travis Henry	20.00
25	Mike McMahon, Marques Tuiasosopo, Sage Rosenfels	25.00
26	David Terrell, Rod Gardner, Reggie Wayne	25.00
27	Josh Heupel, Sage Rosenfels, Todd Heap	15.00
28	Travis Henry, Anthony Thomas, James Jackson	30.00
29	Deuce McAllister, Rudi Johnson, Chad Johnson	15.00
30	Quincy Morgan, Robert Ferguson, Marvin "Snoop" Minnis	15.00

2001 Fleer Legacy 1,000 Yard Club

		MT
Common Player:		12.00
Inserted 1:69		
1YC	Stephen Davis	12.00
2YC	Warrick Dunn	12.00
3YC	Barry Sanders	50.00
4YC	Randy Moss	40.00
5YC	Marvin Harrison	15.00
6YC	Duce Staley	12.00
7YC	Jamal Lewis	15.00
8YC	Isaac Bruce	15.00
9YC	Wayne Chrebet	15.00
10YC	Terrell Owens	20.00
11YC	Rod Smith	15.00
12YC	Ed McCaffrey	12.00
13YC	Jerome Bettis	15.00
14YC	Fred Taylor	15.00
15YC	Edgerrin James	25.00
16YC	Curtis Martin	20.00
17YC	Eric Moulds	15.00
18YC	Corey Dillon	15.00
19YC	Marcus Robinson	15.00
20YC	Tiki Barber	15.00
21YC	Jamal Anderson	15.00
22YC	Torry Holt	20.00
23YC	Frank Sanders	12.00

2001 Fleer Legacy 1,000 Yard Club Dual Swatch

		MT
Common Player:		15.00
Production 400 Sets		
1IB	Stephen Davis, Warrick Dunn	15.00
2IB	Stephen Davis, Duce Staley	15.00
3IB	Stephen Davis, Terrell Davis	25.00
4IB	Jamal Anderson, Barry Sanders	40.00
5IB	Barry Sanders, Randy Moss	60.00
6IB	Marvin Harrison, Isaac Bruce	25.00
7IB	Marvin Harrison, Rod Smith	20.00
8IB	Isaac Bruce, Terrell Owens	25.00
9IB	Isaac Bruce, Marcus Robinson	20.00
10IB	Wayne Chrebet, Curtis Martin	25.00
11IB	Wayne Chrebet, Jimmy Smith	20.00
12IB	Rod Smith, Ed McCaffrey	15.00
13IB	Ed McCaffrey, Jimmy Smith	15.00
14IB	Jerome Bettis, Fred Taylor	20.00
15IB	Jerome Bettis, Edgerrin James	30.00
16IB	Corey Dillon, Terrell Davis	25.00
17IB	Marcus Robinson, Marvin Harrison	20.00
18IB	Tiki Barber, Warrick Dunn	15.00
19IB	Tiki Barber, Eddie George	20.00
20IB	Eddie George, Warrick Dunn	20.00

A card number in parentheses ( ) indicates the set is unnumbered.

2001 Fleer Premium

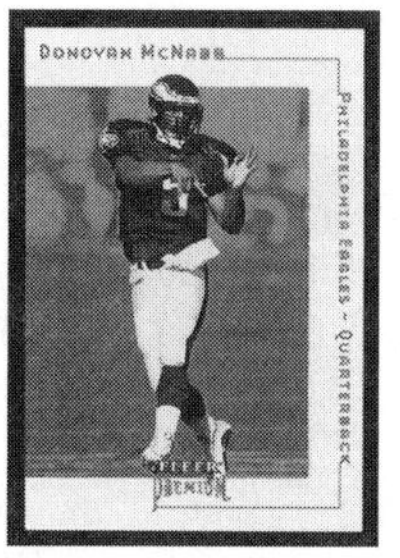

		MT
Complete Set (250):		225.00
Common Player:		.15
Minor Stars:		.30
Common Rookies:		1.50
Production 2,001 Sets		
Pack (8):		4.00
Wax Box (24):		70.00
1	Ricky Williams	.75
2	Dez White	.15
3	Jay Riemersma	.15
4	Derrick Mason	.30
5	Chad Lewis	.15
6	Shaun King	.50
7	Jevon Kearse	.50
8	Bobby Engram	.15
9	Warrick Dunn	.50
10	Randall Cunningham	.30
11	Stephen Alexander	.15
12	Jimmy Smith	.50
13	Az-Zahir Hakim	.30
14	Antonio Freeman	.50
15	Curtis Conway	.30
16	Tim Biakabutuka	.30
17	Peter Warrick	1.00
18	Kurt Warner	1.75
19	Brian Urlacher	1.00
20	Rod Smith	.30
21	Frank Sanders	.30
22	Trevor Pryce	.15
23	Sammy Morris	.15
24	Cade McNown	.50
25	Keyshawn Johnson	.50
26	Tim Couch	.75
27	Dedric Ward	.15
28	Bill Schroeder	.15
29	John Randle	.30
30	Donovan McNabb	.75
31	Marvin Harrison	.50
32	Trent Dilfer	.30
33	David Boston	.50
34	Donnell Bennett	.15
35	Trace Armstrong	.15
36	Sam Adams	.15
37	Jeremiah Trotter	.15
38	Zach Thomas	.15
39	Shaun Jefferson	.15
40	J.J. Stokes	.30
41	Akili Smith	.50
42	Tony Siragusa	.15
43	William Roaf	.15
44	Muhsin Muhammad	.30
45	Terance Mathis	.15
46	Tee Martin	.30
47	Ray Lewis	.50
48	Matt Hasselbeck	.50
49	Todd Pinkston	.30
50	Rob Johnson	.30
51	Edgerrin James	1.25
52	Raghib Ismail	.15
53	Trent Green	.30
54	Tim Dwight	.50
55	Anthony Becht	.15
56	Jessie Armstead	.15
57	Mike Anderson	1.25
58	Jamal Anderson	.50
59	Anthony Wright	.15
60	Regan Upshaw	.15
61	John Holecek	.15
62	Shaun Alexander	.50
63	Troy Aikman	1.00
64	Peter Boulware	.15
65	Hines Ward	.15
66	Michael Strahan	.15
67	Herman Moore	.30
68	Rich Gannon	.30
69	Ken Dilger	.15
70	Terrell Davis	1.25
71	Terrence Wilkins	.30
72	Fred Taylor	.75
73	Napoleon Kaufman	.15
74	Tony Horne	.15
75	Ahman Green	.30
76	Jay Fiedler	.50
77	Albert Connell	.15
78	Charlie Batch	.50
79	James Allen	.30
80	Sylvester Morris	.30
81	Isaac Bruce	.50
82	Charles Woodson	.30
83	Lamar Smith	.30
84	Peyton Manning	1.50
85	Sam Madison	.15
86	Olandis Gary	.50
87	Kevin Faulk	.30
88	Jeff Garcia	.50
89	JaJuan Dawson	.15
90	Sam Cowart	.15
91	David Sloan	.15
92	Bobby Shaw	.15
93	Travis Prentice	.30
94	Terrell Owens	.50
95	John Lynch	.15
96	Jim Harbaugh	.15
97	Brian Griese	.60
98	Jeff Graham	.15
99	La'Roi Glover	.15
100	Joey Galloway	.50
101	Wesley Walls	.15
102	Vinny Testaverde	.30
103	Jason Taylor	.15
104	Darnay Scott	.15
105	Samari Rolle	.15
106	Adrian Murrell	.15
107	Eric Moulds	.30
108	Keenan McCardell	.30
109	Donald Hayes	.15
110	Brett Favre	2.00
111	Troy Edwards	.30
112	Ron Dayne	1.00
113	Daunte Culpepper	1.00
114	Chris Chandler	.30
115	Mark Brunell	.60
116	Courtney Brown	.30
117	Aaron Brooks	.60
118	Fred Beasley	.15
119	Mike Alstott	.50
120	Tyrone Wheatley	.30
121	R. Jay Soward	.30
122	Deion Sanders	.50
123	Jake Reed	.15
124	Jamal Lewis	1.50
125	Tony Gonzalez	.30
126	Terrell Fletcher	.15
127	Wayne Chrebet	.30
128	Cris Carter	.50
129	Drew Bledsoe	.60
130	Tiki Barber	.30
131	Derrick Alexander	.15
132	Frank Wycheck	.15
133	Jerome Pathon	.15
134	Warren Sapp	.30
135	Joe Horn	.30
136	Ricky Watters	.30
137	Amani Toomer	.30
138	Bruce Smith	.30
139	Andre Rison	.15
140	J.R. Redmond	.15
141	Steve McNair	.50
142	Michael McCrary	.15
143	Ike Hillard	.30
144	Charlie Garner	.30
145	Mark Bruener	.15
146	Emmitt Smith	1.25
147	Darren Sharper	.15
148	Peerless Price	.30
149	Johnnie Morton	.30
150	Curtis Martin	.50
151	Joe Johnson	.15
152	MarTay Jenkins	.15
153	Priest Holmes	.15
154	Terry Glenn	.30
155	Oronde Gadsden	.30
156	Germane Crowell	.50
157	Steve Beuerlein	.15
158	Champ Bailey	.50
159	Troy Vincent	.15
160	James Stewart	.30
161	Jerry Rice	1.25
162	Randy Moss	1.75
163	Dave Moore	.15
164	Ed McCaffrey	.30
165	Thomas Jones	.30
166	Rickey Dudley	.15
167	Hugh Douglas	.15
168	Stephen Davis	.50
169	Kerry Collins	.30
170	Cam Cleeland	.30
171	Stephen Boyd	.15
172	Jerome Bettis	.50
173	Aeneas Williams	.15
174	Chad Pennington	.75
175	Dorsey Levens	.30
176	Desmond Howard	.15
177	Torry Holt	.50
178	Plaxico Burress	.50
179	Kevin Johnson	.30
180	Kyle Brady	.15
181	Jake Plummer	.50
182	Brad Johnson	.50
183	Eddie George	.60
184	Corey Dillon	.50
185	Curtis Enis	.15
186	Tim Brown	.30
187	Tony Boselli	.15
188	Duce Staley	.30
189	Junior Seau	.30
190	Marshall Faulk	.60
191	Kordell Stewart	.50
192	Corey Simon	.30
193	Shannon Sharpe	.30
194	Marcus Robinson	.50
195	Carl Pickens	.15
196	Doug Flutie	.60
197	Freddie Jones	.15
198	Patrick Jeffers	.30
199	Shawn Bryson	.15
200	Kevin Dyson	.30
201	*David Terrell*	12.00
202	*Dan Morgan*	3.00
203	*Chris Weinke*	12.00
204	*Correl Buckhalter*	4.00
205	*Chad Johnson*	4.00
206	*LaDainian Tomlinson*	20.00
207	*Reggie Wayne*	10.00
208	*Tim Hasselbeck*	4.00
209	*Michael Vick*	25.00
210	*Heath Evans*	1.50
211	*Damione Lewis*	3.00
212	*Richard Seymour*	1.50
213	*Quincy Morgan*	6.00
214	*Drew Brees*	20.00
215	*Freddie Mitchell*	10.00
216	*Moran Norris*	3.00
217	*Mike McMahon*	4.00
218	*Derrick Gibson*	1.50
219	*Rudi Johnson*	5.00
220	*Todd Heap*	5.00
221	*Josh Booty*	3.00
222	*Justin Smith*	4.00
223	*Marcus Stroud*	3.00
224	*Rod Gardner*	10.00
225	*Vinny Sutherland*	3.00
226	*Marques Tuiasosopo*	8.00
227	*Anthony Thomas*	20.00
228	*Bobby Newcombe*	3.00
229	*Michael Bennett*	12.00
230	*Marvin "Snoop" Minnis*	6.00
231	*Travis Minor*	5.00
232	*Travis Henry*	10.00
233	*Kevan Barlow*	5.00
234	*Gerard Warren*	4.00
235	*Sage Rosenfels*	4.00
236	*Chris Chambers*	4.00
237	*James Jackson*	4.00
238	*Deuce McAllister*	12.00
239	*Koren Robinson*	10.00
240	*Andre Carter*	4.00
241	*Santana Moss*	10.00
242	*LaMont Jordan*	4.00
243	*Ken-Yon Rambo*	3.00
244	*Jamal Reynolds*	3.00
245	*Fred Smoot*	3.00
246	*Robert Ferguson*	4.00
247	*Ken Lucas*	4.00
248	*Dan Alexander*	3.00
249	*Nate Clements*	3.00
250	*Quincy Carter*	12.00

2001 Fleer Premium Clothes to the Game

		MT
Common Player:		8.00
Inserted 1:59		
1CG	Jessie Armstead	8.00
2CG	Todd Pinkston	8.00
3CG	R. Jay Soward	8.00
4CG	Travis Prentice	8.00
5CG	Courtney Brown	8.00
6CG	Ken Dilger	8.00
7CG	Curtis Enis	8.00
8CG	E.G. Green	8.00
9CG	Torry Holt	12.00
10CG	David Boston	12.00
11CG	Michael Pittman	8.00
12CG	Edgerrin James	25.00
13CG	Marvin Harrison	12.00
14CG	Johnnie Morton	8.00
15CG	Cade McNown	12.00
16CG	Isaac Bruce	12.00
17CG	Jake Plummer	12.00
18CG	Jerry Rice	25.00
19CG	Champ Bailey	8.00
20CG	Kordell Stewart	8.00
21CG	Kurt Warner	35.00

2001 Fleer Premium Commanding Respect

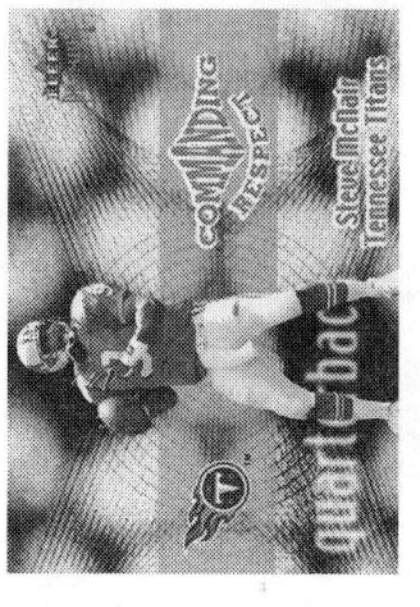

		MT
Complete Set (15):		18.00
Common Player:		1.50
Inserted 1:20		
Patch Cards:		8x-16x
Production 80 Sets		
1CR	Brian Griese	2.00
2CR	Jamal Lewis	4.00
3CR	Fred Taylor	2.00
4CR	Stephen Davis	1.50
5CR	Marcus Robinson	1.50
6CR	Marvin Harrison	1.50
7CR	Marshall Faulk	2.00
8CR	Doug Flutie	2.00
9CR	Jamal Anderson	1.50
10CR	Donovan McNabb	3.00
11CR	Steve McNair	1.50
12CR	Jeff Garcia	1.50
13CR	Daunte Culpepper	3.50
14CR	Isaac Bruce	1.50
15CR	Jimmy Smith	1.50

2001 Fleer Premium Greatest Plays

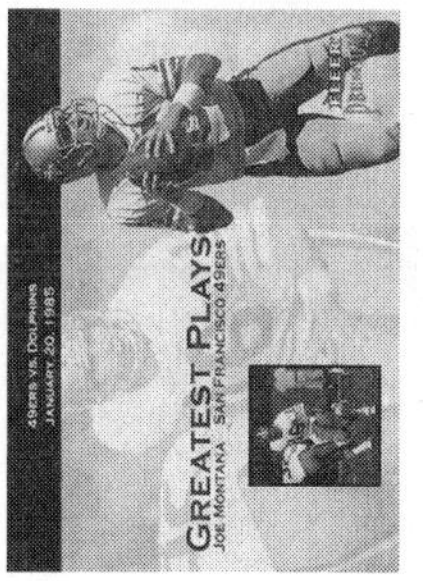

		MT
Complete Set (21):		20.00
Common Player:		.75
Inserted 1:10		
#1 & #7 never released		
2GP	Emmitt Smith	3.00
3GP	Roger Staubach	3.00
4GP	Jerry Rice	3.00
5GP	Doug Flutie	1.25
6GP	Earl Campbell	1.50
8GP	John Elway	5.00
9GP	Joe Montana	5.00
10GP	Dan Marino	5.00
11GP	Dwight Clark	.75
12GP	Franco Harris	1.50
13GP	Gale Sayers	1.50
14GP	Ken Stabler	2.00
15GP	Steve Young	2.00
16GP	William Perry	.75
17GP	Michael Westbrook	.75
18GP	Kordell Stewart	1.50
19GP	Terry Bradshaw	4.00
20GP	Tony Dorsett	2.00
21GP	Eric Dickerson	1.50

2001 Fleer Premium Home Field Advantage

		MT
Complete Set (12):		60.00
Common Player:		3.00
Inserted 1:72		
Turf Cards: 2x-4x		
Production 314 Sets		
1HA	Eddie George	6.00
2HA	Edgerrin James	12.00
3HA	Ricky Williams	8.00
4HA	Jeff Garcia	4.00
5HA	Brett Favre	15.00
6HA	Warrick Dunn	3.00
7HA	Donovan McNabb	7.00
8HA	Brian Urlacher	7.00
9HA	Kurt Warner	15.00
10HA	Emmitt Smith	10.00
11HA	Rich Gannon	3.00
12HA	Cris Carter	4.00

2001 Fleer Premium Premium Advantage

		MT
Common Player:		8.00
Inserted 1:109		
1SU	Jessie Armstead	8.00
2SU	Todd Pinkston	8.00
3SU	R. Jay Soward	8.00
4SU	Travis Prentice	12.00
5SU	Courtney Brown	8.00
6SU	Ken Dilger	8.00
7SU	Curtis Enis	8.00
8SU	E.G. Green	8.00
9SU	Torry Holt	8.00
10SU	David Boston	12.00
11SU	Michael Pittman	8.00
12SU	Edgerrin James	30.00
13SU	Marvin Harrison	12.00
14SU	Johnnie Morton	8.00
15SU	Cade McNown	12.00
16SU	Isaac Bruce	12.00
17SU	Jake Plummer	12.00
18SU	Jerry Rice	20.00
19SU	Champ Bailey	8.00

2001 Fleer Premium Rookie Revolution

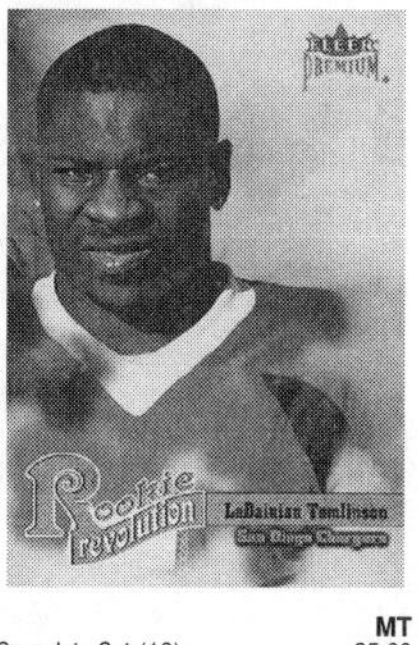

		MT
Complete Set (10):		25.00
Common Player:		1.00
Inserted 1:10		
Autographs:		20x
Production 50 Sets		
1RR	Deuce McAllister	3.00
2RR	David Terrell	3.00
3RR	Drew Brees	6.00
4RR	Chad Johnson	1.00
5RR	LaDainian Tomlinson	5.00
6RR	Marques Tuiasosopo	2.00
7RR	Michael Vick	10.00
8RR	Michael Bennett	5.00
9RR	Anthony Thomas	2.50
10RR	Santana Moss	2.50

2001 Fleer Premium Solid Performers

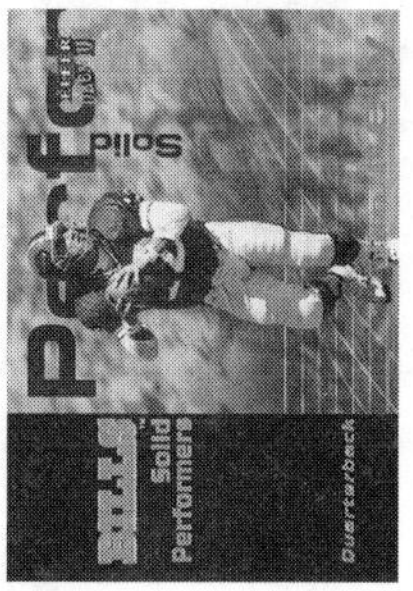

		MT
Complete Set (20):		30.00
Common Player:		1.00
Minor Stars:		2.00
Inserted 1:20		
Jersey Cards: 5x		
Production 900 Sets		
1SP	Jerome Bettis	2.00
2SP	David Boston	2.00
3SP	Cade McNown	2.00
4SP	Keenan McCardell	1.00
5SP	Thomas Jones	1.00
6SP	Edgerrin James	5.00
7SP	Torry Holt	2.00
8SP	Az-Zahir Hakim	1.00
9SP	Jake Plummer	2.00
10SP	Travis Prentice	1.00
11SP	Marcus Robinson	2.00
12SP	Duce Staley	2.00
13SP	Kurt Warner	7.00
14SP	Kordell Stewart	2.00
15SP	Rob Johnson	1.00
16SP	Jamal Lewis	5.00
17SP	Donovan McNabb	3.00
18SP	Kevin Johnson	2.00
19SP	Jim Kelly	2.00
20SP	Jerry Rice	4.00

2001 Fleer Showcase

		MT
Complete Set (160):		550.00
Common Player:		.20
Minor Stars:		.40
Common Rookie:		5.00
Pack (5):		5.00
Wax Box (24):		85.00
1	Cris Carter	.75
2	Sylvester Morris	.75
3	Vinny Testaverde	.50
4	Jevon Kearse	.75
5	Terance Mathis	.20
6	Mike Anderson	2.00
7	Aaron Brooks	.75
8	Jerry Rice	2.00
9	Mike Alstott	.75
10	Jon Kitna	.40
11	Derrick Alexander	.40
12	Shaun Alexander	.75
13	Thomas Jones	.75
14	James Stewart	.50
15	Ron Dayne	1.25
16	Az-Zahir Hakim	.40
17	Terrell Owens	.75
18	Travis Prentice	.50
19	Lamar Smith	.75
20	James Thrash	.40
21	Doug Flutie	1.00
22	Derrick Mason	.75
23	Ray Lewis	.75
24	Ed McCaffrey	.75
25	Ricky Williams	1.25
26	Tyrone Wheatley	.50
27	Chris Chandler	.50
28	Rod Smith	.75
29	Joe Horn	.50
30	Jerome Bettis	.75
31	Brian Urlacher	1.50
32	Dorsey Levens	.50
33	Kordell Stewart	.75
34	Michael Westbrook	.50
35	Jamal Anderson	.75
36	Charlie Batch	.75
37	Kerry Collins	.50
38	Jake Plummer	.75
39	Robert Porcher	.20
40	Jason Sehorn	.40
41	Junior Seau	.50
42	Warren Sapp	.50
43	Champ Bailey	.50
44	Jamal Lewis	2.00
45	Tony Banks	.40
46	Doug Chapman	.40
47	Stephen Davis	.75
48	Elvis Grbac	.75
49	Joey Galloway	.75
50	Terry Glenn	.50
51	Todd Pinkston	.50
52	JaJuan Dawson	.40
53	Zach Thomas	.50
54	Tim Couch	1.00
55	Cade McNown	.75
56	Charlie Garner	.50
57	Jeff George	.40
58	Peerless Price	.50
59	Tony Gonzalez	.50
60	Rob Johnson	.50
61	Keenan McCardell	.40
62	Eric Moulds	.75
63	Jimmy Smith	.75
64	Jeff Garcia	.75
65	Rod Woodson	.50
66	Brian Griese	1.00
67	Kevin Faulk	.40
68	Plaxico Burress	.75
69	Isaac Bruce	.75
70	Keyshawn Johnson	.75
71	Tim Biakabutuka	.40
72	Mark Brunell	1.00
73	Wesley Walls	.40
74	Jerome Pathon	.20
75	Wayne Chrebet	.75
76	Muhsin Muhammad	.50
77	Marvin Harrison	.75
78	David Boston	.75
79	Germane Crowell	.75
80	Tiki Barber	.50
81	Laveranues Coles	.50
82	Tim Brown	.50
83	Matt Hasselbeck	.75
84	Brad Johnson	.50
85	Marcus Robinson	.75
86	Ahman Green	.75
87	Curtis Martin	.75
88	Peter Warrick	1.00
89	Ray Lucas	.40
90	Duce Staley	.75
91	Darrell Jackson	.50
92	Steve McNair	.75
93	Rickey Dudley	.40
94	Jason Taylor	.40
95	Rich Gannon	.50
96	Torry Holt	.75
97	James Allen	.75
98	Antonio Freeman	.75
99	Trent Green	.75
100	Ricky Watters	.50
101	Corey Dillon	3.00
102	Emmitt Smith	8.00
103	Terrell Davis	7.00
104	Brett Favre	12.00
105	Peyton Manning	10.00
106	Edgerrin James	8.00
107	Fred Taylor	4.00
108	Daunte Culpepper	6.00
109	Randy Moss	10.00
110	Drew Bledsoe	4.00
111	Donovan McNabb	5.00
112	Kurt Warner	12.00
113	Marshall Faulk	4.00
114	Warrick Dunn	3.00
115	Eddie George	4.00
116	*Michael Vick*	100.00
117	*David Terrell*	30.00
118	*Deuce McAllister*	30.00
119	*Koren Robinson*	30.00
120	*Rod Gardner*	30.00
121	*Santana Moss*	25.00
122	*Drew Brees*	50.00
123	*Chris Weinke*	30.00
124	*LaDainian Tomlinson*	75.00
125	*Freddie Mitchell*	25.00
126	*Chris Chambers*	15.00
127	*Reggie Wayne*	10.00
128	*Quincy Morgan*	10.00
129	*Rudi Johnson*	8.00
130	*Robert Ferguson*	6.00
131	*Todd Heap*	6.00
132	*Michael Bennett*	20.00
133	*Jesse Palmer*	6.00
134	*James Jackson*	10.00
135	*Chad Johnson*	8.00
136	*LaMont Jordan*	7.00
137	*Anthony Thomas*	30.00
138	*Travis Henry*	15.00
139	*Marvin "Snoop" Minnis*	10.00
140	*Marques Tuiasosopo*	12.00
141	*Travis Minor*	6.00
142	*Mike McMahon*	7.00
143	*Josh Heupel*	10.00
144	*Sage Rosenfels*	7.00
145	*Quincy Carter*	15.00
146	*Alge Crumpler*	5.00
147	*Kevan Barlow*	8.00
148	*Heath Evans*	3.00
149	*Correll Buckhalter*	8.00
150	*Justin McCareins*	3.00
151	*Reggie Germany*	4.00
152	*Vinny Sutherland*	4.00
153	*Scotty Anderson*	3.00
154	*Tim Hasselbeck*	5.00
155	*Alex Bannister*	5.00
156	*Andre Carter*	5.00
157	*Adam Archuleta*	6.00
158	*Ken-Yon Rambo*	5.00
159	*Gerard Warren*	5.00
160	*Justin Smith*	5.00
NNO	Donovan McNabb AU/300	75.00

2001 Fleer Showcase Awards Showcase

		MT
Common Player:		35.00
1ASB	Randy Moss	85.00
2ASB	Marvin Harrison	35.00
3ASB	Tony Gonzalez	35.00
4ASB	Rich Gannon	35.00
5ASB	Marshall Faulk	45.00
6ASB	Edgerrin James	65.00
7ASB	Warren Sapp	35.00
8ASB	Ray Lewis	35.00
9ASB	Brian Urlacher	60.00
10ASB	Chris Weinke	65.00
11ASB	Eric Moulds	35.00
12ASB	Isaac Bruce	35.00
13ASB	Daunte Culpepper	35.00
14ASB	Curtis Martin	35.00
15ASB	Kurt Warner	35.00
16ASB	Mike Anderson	35.00
17ASB	Robert Smith	35.00
18ASB	Jamal Lewis	35.00
19ASB	Rod Smith	35.00
20ASB	Junior Seau	35.00

2001 Fleer Showcase Awards Showcase Memorabilia

		MT
Common Player:		45.00
Production 100 Sets		
1AS	Marcus Allen	45.00
2AS	Terry Bradshaw	60.00
3AS	Terrell Davis	60.00
4AS	Eric Dickerson	45.00
5AS	Tony Dorsett	65.00
6AS	Marshall Faulk	50.00
7AS	Brett Favre	85.00
8AS	Eddie George	50.00
9AS	Edgerrin James	70.00
10AS	Joe Montana	150.00
11AS	Randy Moss	85.00
12AS	Walter Payton	150.00
13AS	Jerry Rice	60.00
14AS	Emmitt Smith	60.00
15AS	Fran Tarkenton	60.00
16AS	Lawrence Taylor	45.00
17AS	Johnny Unitas	80.00
18AS	Steve Young	45.00

2001 Fleer Showcase Awards Showcase Mem. Autograph

		MT
Complete Set (15):		
Common Player:		
1ASMA	Marcus Allen	50.00
2ASMA	Terry Bradshaw	150.00
3ASMA	Earl Campbell	
4ASMA	Eric Dickerson	
5ASMA	Tony Dorsett	75.00
6ASMA	Marshall Faulk	75.00
7ASMA	Eddie George	75.00
8ASMA	Edgerrin James	100.00
9ASMA	Joe Montana	200.00
10ASMA	Randy Moss	150.00
11ASMA	Jerry Rice	150.00
12ASMA	Emmitt Smith	200.00
13ASMA	Fran Tarkenton	75.00
14ASMA	Lawrence Taylor	75.00
15ASMA	Johnny Unitas	75.00

2001 Fleer Showcase Patchwork

		MT
Common Player:		10.00
Inserted 1:20:		
1PW	Bruce Smith	10.00
2PW	Lawrence Taylor	20.00
3PW	Brian Urlacher	25.00
4PW	Warren Sapp	10.00
5PW	Deion Sanders	20.00
6PW	Dan Marino	60.00
7PW	Junior Seau	10.00
8PW	Jerry Rice	30.00
9PW	Brian Griese	20.00
10PW	Mark Brunell	15.00
11PW	Ronnie Lott	15.00
12PW	Marvin Harrison	15.00
13PW	Edgerrin James	30.00
14PW	Marshall Faulk	20.00
15PW	Todd Pinkston	15.00
16PW	Troy Aikman	25.00
17PW	Charlie Batch	10.00
18PW	Johnnie Morton	10.00
19PW	Steve Young	20.00
20PW	Terrell Davis	25.00
21PW	Torry Holt	15.00

22PW	Charles Woodson	15.00
23PW	Steve McNair	15.00
24PW	Rod Smith	15.00
25PW	Jamal Anderson	15.00
26PW	Drew Bledsoe	20.00
27PW	Dorsey Levens	15.00
28PW	Chris Chandler	10.00
29PW	Kurt Warner	30.00
30PW	Fred Taylor	15.00
31PW	Chris Redman	15.00
32PW	Travis Prentice	15.00
33PW	Peerless Price	15.00

2001 Fleer Showcase Stitches

		MT
Common Player:		15.00
Inserted 1:20		
1SS	Cris Carter	20.00
2SS	Daunte Culpepper	25.00
3SS	Corey Dillon	15.00
4SS	John Elway	50.00
5SS	Steve McNair	15.00
6SS	Todd Pinkston	15.00
7SS	Steve Young	20.00
8SS	Marvin Harrison	15.00
9SS	Fred Taylor	15.00
10SS	Peter Warrick	15.00
11SS	Ricky Williams	20.00
12SS	Brett Favre	45.00
13SS	Kurt Warner	30.00
14SS	Marshall Faulk	20.00
15SS	Robert Smith	15.00
16SS	Dan Marino	50.00
17SS	Joe Montana	100.00

2001 Fleer Showcase Signed Avant Card

		MT
Complete Set (1):		
1SAC	Donovan McNabb	50.00

2001 Fleer Tradition

		MT
Complete Set (450):		60.00
Common Player:		.15
Minor Stars:		.30
Common Rookie (401-450):		.50
1	Thomas Jones	.30
2	Bruce Smith	.30
3	Marvin Harrison	.50
4	Darrell Jackson	.30
5	Trent Green	.30
6	Wesley Walls	.30
7	Jimmy Smith	1.50
8	Isaac Bruce	.50
9	Jamal Anderson	.40
10	Marty Booker	.15
11	Elvis Grbac	.50
12	Joe Jurevicius	.15
13	Reidel Anthony	.15
14	Darnay Scott	.30
15	Oronde Gadsden	.30
16	Shawn Bryson	.15
17	Jonathan Ogden	.15
18	Aaron Shea	.15
19	Randy Moss	1.50
20	Eddie George	.60
21	Stephen Davis	.30
22	Emmitt Smith	1.25
23	Willie McGinest	.15
24	Trent Dilfer	.30
25	Peter Boulware	.15
26	Rod Smith	.40
27	Ricky Williams	.75
28	Albert Connell	.15
29	Robert Porcher	.15
30	Jessie Armstead	.15
31	Shane Matthews	.15
32	Eric Moulds	.40
33	Kurt Schulz	.15
34	Richie Anderson	.15
35	Ron Dugans	.30
36	Steve Beuerlein	.30
37	Darren Sharper	.30
38	Andre Rison	.30
39	Courtney Brown	.30
40	Eddie Kennison	.30
41	Ken Dilger	.15
42	Charles Johnson	.15
43	Dexter Coakley	.15
44	Akili Smith	.30
45	R. Jay Soward	.15
46	Danny Farmer	.30
47	Dez White	.30
48	Olandis Gary	.50
49	Wali Rainer	.15
50	Derrick Alexander	.30
51	Donnie Abraham	.15
52	David Sloan	.15
53	Larry Allen	.15
54	Sam Madison	.30
55	Troy Edwards	.40
56	Ryan Longwell	.15
57	Brian Griese	.60
58	John Randle	.15
59	Reggie Jones	.15
60	Mike Peterson	.15
61	Bill Romanowski	.15
62	Kevin Faulk	.30
63	Tai Streets	.30
64	Tony Brackens	.15
65	James Stewart	.15
66	Joe Horn	.15
67	Kurt Warner	.15
68	Eric Hicks	.15
69	Bryant Westbrook	.15
70	Tiki Barber	.40
71	Frank Sanders	.30
72	Olindo Mare	.15
73	Bill Schroeder	.30
74	Anthony Becht	.30
75	Rob Johnson	.40
76	Troy Brown	.30
77	Chad Bratzke	.15
78	Rickey Dudley	.15
79	Doug Johnson	.15
80	Joe Johnson	.15
81	Keenan McCardell	.30
82	Tim Brown	.50
83	Blaine Bishop	.15
84	Ron Dixon	.30
85	Mike Cloud	.15
86	Todd Pinkston	.40
87	Shannon Sharpe	.40
88	Marvin Jones	.15
89	Zach Thomas	.40
90	Kordell Stewart	.60
91	Champ Bailey	.30
92	Jacquez Green	.30
93	Daunte Culpepper	1.00
94	Freddie Jones	.15
95	Donald Hayes	.30
96	Rich Gannon	.50
97	Ty Law	.40
98	Grant Wilstrom	.15
99	James Allen	.15
100	Corey Simon	.15
101	Jeff Blake	.30
102	Bryant Young	.30
103	Craig Yeast	.15
104	Bobby Shaw	.15
105	Kerry Collins	.40
106	Brock Huard	.40
107	JaJuan Dawson	.30
108	Jeff Graham	.15
109	Chad Pennington	1.00
110	Jake Plummer	.40
111	James McKnight	.15
112	Terrell Owens	.50
113	Mo Lewis	.15
114	Jeremy McDaniel	.15
115	Ed McCaffrey	.40
116	Ricky Watters	.40
117	Jerry Porter	.50
118	Shawn Jefferson	.15
119	Charlie Batch	.30
120	Justin Watson	.15
121	Donovan McNabb	1.00
122	Shaun King	.30
123	Brett Favre	2.00
124	Ronald McKinnon	.15
125	Richard Huntley	.15
126	Ray Lewis	.50
127	Jerome Pathon	.15
128	Sam Cowart	.15
129	Ryan Leaf	.30
130	Greg Clark	.15
131	Tony Boselli	.15
132	Frank Wycheck	.15
133	Charlie Garner	.30
134	Tony Siragusa	.15
135	Sylvester Morris	.40
136	Qadry Ismail	.30
137	Jon Kitna	.30
138	James Thrash	.30
139	Lamar Smith	.30
140	Brad Johnson	.50
141	London Fletcher	.15
142	Tim Biakabutuka	.30
143	Ed McDaniel	.15
144	Tony Parrish	.15
145	David Boston	.50
146	Brian Urlacher	1.00
147	Drew Bledsoe	.60
148	David Patten	.15
149	Marcellus Wiley	.15
150	Peter Warrick	.50
151	La'Roi Glover	.15
152	Troy Aikman	1.00
153	Chris Chandler	.15
154	Travis Prentice	.30
155	Ike Hilliard	.30
156	John Mobley	.15
157	Warren Sapp	.30
158	Joey Galloway	.40
159	Laveranues Coles	.40
160	Germane Crowell	.30
161	Jamal Lewis	1.00
162	Mike Anderson	.75
163	Charles Woodson	.30
164	Antonio Freeman	.40
165	Derrick Mason	.40
166	Chris Claiborne	.15
167	Brian Mitchell	.15
168	Mike Vanderjagt	.15
169	Rod Woodson	.30
170	Doug Chapman	.30
171	John Lynch	.15
172	Kevin Hardy	.15
173	Sam Shade	.15
174	Edgerrin James	1.25
175	Brian Dawkins	.15
176	Donnie Edwards	.15
177	Patrick Jeffers	.15
178	Mark Brunell	.40
179	Junior Seau	.30
180	Trace Armstrong	.15
181	Marcus Robinson	.40
182	Tony Gonzalez	.50
183	J.J. Stokes	.40
184	Jake Reed	.15
185	Corey Dillon	.30
186	Jay Fiedler	.50
187	Christian Fauria	.15
188	Sammy Knight	.15
189	Kevin Johnson	.40
190	Matthew Hatchette	.15
191	Az-Zahir Hakim	.30
192	Keith Hamilton	.15
193	Darren Woodson	.15
194	Terry Glenn	.30
195	Simeon Rice	.15
196	Keyshawn Johnson	.50
197	Terrell Davis	1.00
198	Willie Roaf	.15
199	Doug Flutie	.60
200	Kevin Carter	.15
201	Stephen Boyd	.15
202	Michael Strahan	.30
203	Ray Buchanan	.15
204	Tyrone Wheatley	.30
205	Jason Hanson	.15
206	Wayne Chrebet	.40
207	Samari Rolle	.15
208	Duce Staley	.40
209	Dorsey Levens	.30
210	Sebastian Janikowski	.30
211	Duane Starks	.15
212	Jason Gildon	.15
213	Terrence Wilkins	.15
214	Eric Allen	.15
215	Deion Sanders	.40
216	Curtis Conway	.15
217	Fred Taylor	.60
218	Troy Vincent	.15
219	Mike Minter	.15
220	Jeff Garcia	.60
221	Tony Richardson	.15
222	Jerome Bettis	.40
223	Chad Morton	.15
224	Tony Horne	.15
225	Dave Moore	.15
226	Victor Green	.15
227	Chris Sanders	.15
228	Marshall Faulk	.60
229	Cris Carter	.50
230	Rodney Harrison	.15
231	Tim Couch	.60
232	Antowain Smith	.50
233	Lawyer Milloy	.15
234	Lance Schulters	.15
235	Michael Wiley	.15
236	Steve McNair	.40
237	Aaron Brooks	.60
238	Anthony Simmons	.15
239	Dwayne Carswell	.15
240	Priest Holmes	.40
241	Amani Toomer	.40
242	Aeneas Williams	.30
243	MarTay Jenkins	.15
244	Jeff George	.30
245	Vinny Testaverde	.40
246	Peerless Price	.30
247	Bubba Franks	.30
248	Randall Cunningham	.30
249	Aaron Glenn	.15
250	Terance Mathis	.15
251	Peyton Manning	1.50
252	Terrell Buckley	.15
253	Greg Biekert	.15
254	Martin Gramatica	.30
255	Kyle Brady	.30
256	Johnnie Morton	.30
257	Jeremiah Trotter	.15
258	Travis Taylor	.40
259	Frank Moreau	.15
260	LeRoy Butler	.30
261	Plaxico Burress	.50
262	Randall Godfrey	.15
263	Jason Taylor	.15
264	Jeff Burris	.15
265	Jim Harbaugh	.30
266	Marco Coleman	.15
267	Robert Smith	.30
268	Mike Hollis	.15
269	Jerry Rice	1.25
270	Muhsin Muhammad	.30
271	J.R. Redmond	.30
272	Brian Walker	.15
273	Orlando Pace	.15
274	Cade McNown	.30
275	Darren Howard	.15
276	Ron Dayne	.40
277	Shaun Alexander	.75
278	Brandon Bennett	.15
279	Jason Sehorn	.15
280	Matt Hasselbeck	.30
281	Michael Pittman	.15
282	Dennis Northcutt	.15
283	Dedric Ward	.30
284	Curtis Martin	.40
285	Sammy Morris	.15
286	Raghib Ismail	.15
287	Jon Ritchie	.15
288	Shaun Ellis	.15
289	Tim Dwight	.30
290	Trevor Pryce	.15
291	Warrick Dunn	.50
292	Napoleon Kaufman	.15
293	Mike Alstott	.40
294	Herman Moore	.30
295	Chad Lewis	.15
296	Hugh Douglas	.15
297	Chris Redman	.30
298	Ahman Green	.40
299	Hines Ward	.40
300	Mark Bruener	.15
301	Jevon Kearse	.15
302	Jermaine Fazande	.15
303	Terrell Fletcher	.15
304	Torry Holt	.50
305	Chris McAlister	.15
306	Jason Elam	.15
307	Fred Beasley	.15
308	Frank Wycheck	.15
309	Michael McCrary	.15
310	Mark Brunell	.15
311	Tim Couch	.30
312	Takeo Spikes	.15
313	Jerome Bettis	.15
314	Zach Thomas	.15
315	Drew Bledsoe	.30
316	Wayne Chrebet	.15
317	Jay Riemersma	.15
318	Marvin Harrison	.15
319	Ed McCaffrey	.15
320	Tony Gonzalez	.15
321	Tim Brown	.15
322	Junior Seau	.15
323	Shawn Springs	.15
324	Troy Aikman	.50
325	Pat Tilman	.15
326	David Akers	.15
327	Michael Strahan	.15
328	Darrell Green	.15
329	Kurt Warner	.75
330	Jeff Garcia	.30
331	Aaron Brooks	.30
332	Jamal Anderson	.15
333	Brad Hoover	.15
334	Cris Carter	.15
335	Derrick Brooks	.15
336	Antonio Freeman	.15
337	Luther Elliss	.15
338	James Allen	.15
339	Cardinals	.15
340	Falcons	.15
341	Ravens	.15
342	Bills	.15
343	Panthers	.15
344	Bears	.15
345	Bengals	.15
346	Browns	.15
347	Cowboys	.50
348	Broncos	.15
349	Lions	.15
350	Packers	1.00
351	Colts	.50
352	Jaguars	.15
353	Chiefs	.15
354	Dolphins	.15
355	Vikings	.30
356	Patriots	.15
357	Saints	.15
358	Giants	.15
359	Jets	.15
360	Raiders	.15
361	Eagles	.30
362	Steelers	.30
363	Chargers	.15
364	49ers	.30
365	Seahawks	.15
366	Rams	.75
367	Buccaneers	.15
368	Titans	.15
369	Redskins	.15
370	Bills	.15
371	Colts	.30
372	Dolphins	.15
373	Patriots	.15
374	Jets	.15
375	Ravens	.15
376	Bengals	.15
377	Browns	.15
378	Jaguars	.15
379	Steelers	.30
380	Titans	.30
381	Broncos	.30
382	Chiefs	.15
383	Raiders	.30
384	Chargers	.15
385	Seahawks	.15
386	Cardinals	.15
387	Cowboys	.50
388	Giants	.15
389	Eagles	.15
390	Redskins	.15
391	Bears	.15
392	Lions	.15
393	Packers	.50
394	Vikings	.30
395	Buccaneers	.15
396	Falcons	.15
397	Panthers	.15
398	Saints	.15
399	49ers	.30
400	Rams	.50
401	*Michael Vick*	5.00
402	*Drew Brees*	4.00
403	*Michael Bennett*	2.50
404	*David Terrell*	3.00
405	*Deuce McAllister*	2.00
406	*Santana Moss*	2.00
407	*Koren Robinson*	2.00
408	*Chris Weinke*	2.00
409	*Reggie Wayne*	2.00
410	*Rod Gardner*	2.00
411	*James Jackson*	1.25
412	*Travis Henry*	1.50
413	*Josh Heupel*	1.25
414	*LaDainian Tomlinson*	4.00
415	*Chad Johnson*	1.00
416	*Sage Rosenfels*	1.25
417	*Quincy Morgan*	1.25
418	*Ken-Yon Rambo*	.75
419	*LaMont Jordan*	1.00
420	*Anthony Thomas*	5.00
421	*Dave Dickenson*	.75
422	*Travis Minor*	1.25
423	*Kevan Barlow*	1.50
424	*Chris Chambers*	2.50
425	*Richard Seymour*	.50
426	*Gerard Warren*	.50
427	*Jamar Fletcher*	.50
428	*Freddie Mitchell*	2.00
429	*Jamal Reynolds*	.50
430	*Marques Tuiasosopo*	2.00
431	*Marvin "Snoop" Minnis*	1.50
432	*Mike McMahon*	2.00
433	*Robert Ferguson*	.75
434	*Ronney Daniels*	.50
435	*Rudi Johnson*	.75
436	*Vinny Sutherland*	.75
437	*Josh Booty*	1.00
438	*Reggie White*	.50
439	*Todd Heap*	.75
440	*Justin Smith*	.50
441	*Andre Carter*	.50
442	*Bobby Newcombe*	.50
443	*Alex Bannister*	.75
444	*Correll Buckhalter*	1.50
445	*Quincy Carter*	2.50
446	*Jesse Palmer*	1.25
447	*Heath Evans*	.50
448	*Dan Morgan*	.50
449	*Justin McCareins*	.50
450	*Alge Crumpler*	.75

2001 Fleer Autographics

		MT
Common Player:		10.00
Inserted 1:96		
1	Shaun Alexander	20.00
2	Mike Anderson	30.00
3	Drew Brees	70.00
4	Isaac Bruce	25.00
6	Chris Chambers	20.00
7	Wayne Chrebet	15.00
8	Daunte Culpepper	50.00
9	Stephen Davis	10.00
10	Ron Dayne	25.00
11	Corey Dillon	20.00
12	Marshall Faulk	35.00
13	Eddie George	30.00
14	Brian Griese	25.00
15	Travis Henry	15.00
16	Josh Heupel	15.00
17	Torry Holt	15.00
18	Edgerrin James	50.00
19	LaMont Jordan	15.00
20	Deuce McAllister	25.00
21	Donovan McNabb	50.00
22	Travis Minor	10.00
23	Randy Moss	60.00
24	Santana Moss	25.00
25	Ken-Yon Rambo	15.00
26	Koren Robinson	25.00
27	Marcus Robinson	20.00
28	Sage Rosenfels	15.00
29	Jimmy Smith	15.00
30	Duce Staley	15.00
31	David Terrell	25.00
32	Anthony Thomas	50.00
33	LaDainian Tomlinson	50.00
34	Marques Tuiasosopo	20.00
35	Michael Vick	100.00
36	Kurt Warner	60.00
37	Reggie Wayne	20.00
38	Chris Weinke	45.00

Post-1980 cards in Near Mint condition will generally sell for about 75% of the quoted Mint value. Excellent-condition cards bring no more than 40%.

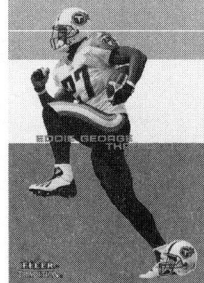

2001 Fleer Tradition Throwbacks

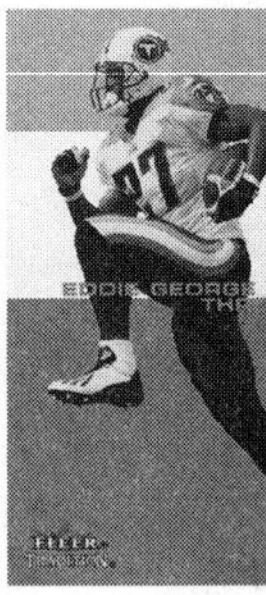

		MT
Complete Set (20):		75.00
Common Player:		2.00
Inserted 1:12 Glossy		
Inserted 1:20 Tradition		
1TB	Jamal Lewis	5.00
2TB	Eddie George	3.00
3TB	Marvin Harrison	2.00
4TB	Brett Favre	10.00
5TB	Donovan McNabb	5.00
6TB	Troy Aikman	5.00
7TB	Edgerrin James	6.00
8TB	Brian Urlacher	5.00
9TB	Stephen Davis	2.00
10TB	Daunte Culpepper	5.00
11TB	Jerry Rice	6.00
12TB	Emmitt Smith	6.00
13TB	Kurt Warner	8.00
14TB	Ricky Williams	4.00
15TB	Cris Carter	2.00
16TB	Mark Brunell	3.00
17TB	Ron Dayne	2.00
18TB	Peyton Manning	8.00
19TB	Randy Moss	8.00
20TB	Brian Griese	3.00

2001 Fleer Tradition Keeping Pace

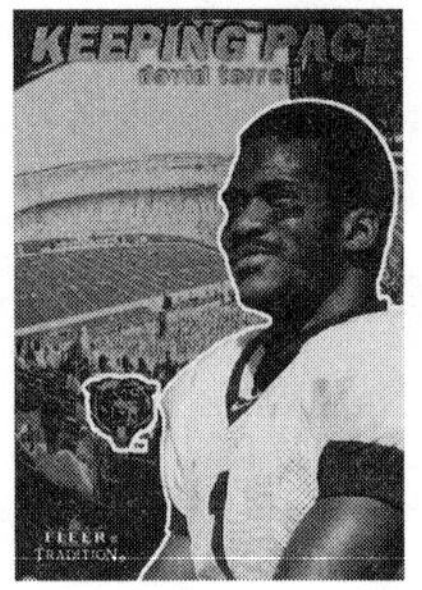

		MT
Complete Set (15):		30.00
Common Player:		1.00
Inserted 1:12 Glossy		
Inserted 1:20 Tradition		
1KP	Michael Vick	5.00
2KP	Drew Brees	4.00
3KP	Michael Bennett	2.50
4KP	David Terrell	3.00
5KP	Deuce McAllister	2.50
6KP	Santana Moss	2.50
7KP	Koren Robinson	2.50
8KP	Chris Weinke	2.50
9KP	Reggie Wayne	2.50
10KP	Rod Gardner	2.50
11KP	James Jackson	1.50
12KP	Travis Henry	2.00
13KP	Josh Heupel	1.50
14KP	LaDainian Tomlinson	4.00
15KP	Chad Johnson	1.00

A card number in parentheses ( ) indicates the set is unnumbered.

2001 Fleer Tradition Grass Roots

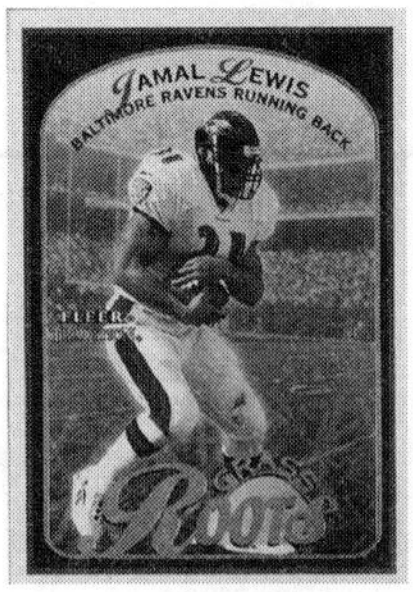

		MT
Complete Set (10):		40.00
Common Player:		3.00
Inserted 1:24 Glossy		
Inserted 1:40 Tradition		
1GR	Donovan McNabb	5.00
2GR	Edgerrin James	8.00
3GR	Ricky Williams	4.00
4GR	Fred Taylor	3.00
5GR	Terrell Davis	5.00
6GR	Eddie George	3.00
7GR	Jamal Lewis	5.00
8GR	Marshall Faulk	3.00
9GR	Daunte Culpepper	5.00
10GR	Emmitt Smith	8.00

2001 Fleer Tradition Grass Roots Turf

		MT
Common Player:		20.00
1GR	Donovan McNabb	30.00
2GR	Edgerrin James	50.00
3GR	Ricky Williams	25.00
4GR	Fred Taylor	20.00
5GR	Terrell Davis	30.00
6GR	Eddie George	20.00
7GR	Jamal Lewis	30.00
8GR	Marshall Faulk	25.00
9GR	Daunte Culpepper	30.00
10GR	Emmitt Smith	50.00

2001 Fleer Tradition Art of a Champion

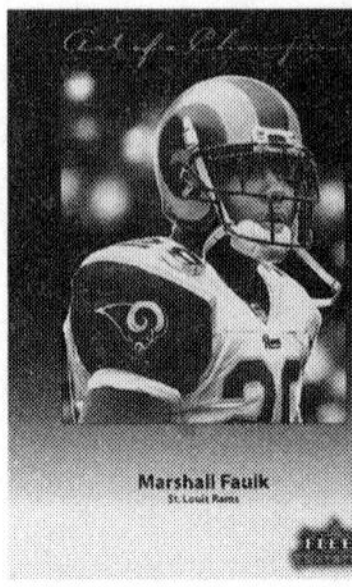

		MT
Complete Set (10):		25.00
Common Player:		6.00
Inserted 1:120 Glossy		
Inserted 1:240 Tradition		
1AC	Drew Brees	20.00
2AC	Daunte Culpepper	15.00
3AC	Ron Dayne	6.00
4AC	Marshall Faulk	10.00
5AC	Eddie George	10.00
6AC	Edgerrin James	20.00
7AC	Jamal Lewis	15.00
8AC	Randy Moss	25.00
9AC	Fred Taylor	10.00
10AC	Michael Vick	25.00

2001 Fleer Tradition Art of a Champion Autographs

		MT
Common Player:		15.00
1AC	Drew Brees	100.00
2AC	Daunte Culpepper	50.00
3AC	Ron Dayne	25.00
4AC	Marshall Faulk	50.00
5AC	Eddie George	40.00
6AC	Edgerrin James	50.00
7AC	Jamal Lewis	40.00
8AC	Randy Moss	15.00
9AC	Fred Taylor	60.00
10AC	Michael Vick	125.00

1996 FlickBall Team Sets

These three team sets were regionally distributed. Each set consisted of five player cards and one team helmet card.

		MT
Complete Set (18):		17.00
Comp. Cowboys Set (6):		7.00
Comp. Vikings Set (6):		3.50
Comp. Packers Set (6):		7.00
Common Player:		.50
DC1	Troy Aikman	2.00
DC2	Deion Sanders	1.25
DC3	Emmitt Smith	4.00
DC4	Daryl Johnston	.75
DC5	Cowboys Helmet	.50
DC6	Darren Woodson	.50
MV1	Warren Moon	.75
MV2	Cris Carter	.75
MV3	Robert Smith	.75
MV4	Qadry Ismail	.50
MV5	Vikings Helmet	.50
MV6	David Palmer	.50
GBP1	Brett Favre	5.00
GBP2	Edgar Bennett	.75
GBP3	Reggie White	1.00
GBP4	Robert Brooks	1.00
GBP5	Packers Helmet	.50
GBP6	George Teague	.50

1995 Flickball NFL Helmets

Flickball debuted in 1995 and featured team helmets and Super Bowl logos. They arrived in six-card packs and featured two expansion team helmets, cards 61 and 62, that were found every 48 packs.

		MT
Complete Set (60):		12.00
Common Player:		.25
1	Dallas Cowboys	.50
2	New York Giants	.25
3	Arizona Cardinals	.25

4	Philadelphia Eagles	.25
5	Washington Redskins	.35
6	Minnesota Vikings	.25
7	Chicago Bears	.35
8	Green Bay Packers	.50
9	Detroit Lions	.25
10	Tampa Bay Buccaneers	.25
11	San Francisco 49ers	.50
12	New Orleans Saints	.25
13	Atlanta Falcons	.25
14	Carolina Panthers	.35
15	St. Louis Rams	.25
16	New England Patriots	.25
17	Miami Dolphins	.35
18	Buffalo Bills	.25
19	Indianapolis Colts	.25
20	New York Jets	.25
21	Pittsburgh Steelers	.35
22	Cleveland Browns	.25
23	Cincinnati Bengals	.25
24	Jacksonville Jaguars	.35
25	Houston Oilers	.25
26	San Diego Chargers	.25
27	Oakland Raiders	.35
28	Kansas City Chiefs	.25
29	Denver Broncos	.25
30	Seattle Seahawks	.25
31	Super Bowl I	.25
32	Super Bowl II	.25
33	Super Bowl III	.25
34	Super Bowl IV	.25
35	Super Bowl V	.25
36	Super Bowl VI	.25
37	Super Bowl VII	.25
38	Super Bowl VIII	.25
39	Super Bowl IX	.25
40	Super Bowl X	.25
41	Super Bowl XI	.25
42	Super Bowl XII	.25
43	Super Bowl XIII	.25
44	Super Bowl XIV	.25
45	Super Bowl XV	.25
46	Super Bowl XVI	.25
47	Super Bowl XVII	.25
48	Super Bowl XVIII	.25
49	Super Bowl XIX	.25
50	Super Bowl XX	.25
51	Super Bowl XXI	.25
52	Super Bowl XXII	.25
53	Super Bowl XXIII	.25
54	Super Bowl XXIV	.25
55	Super Bowl XXV	.25
56	Super Bowl XXVI	.25
57	Super Bowl XXVII	.25
58	Super Bowl XXVIII	.25
59	Super Bowl XXIX	.25
60	Super Bowl XXX Logo	.25
61	Carolina Panthers Inaugural Season	1.25
62	Jacksonville Jaguars Inaugural Season	1.25

1995 Flickball Prototypes

This unnumbered 10-card set was a prelude to the 1996 Flickball release. Each card arrived in the shape of a football and featured a finger-sized cut-out space to flick the card as part of a game. Card No. 7 included a different player on each side and was called a "Double Flick". Each card in this prototype set contained the words "Pre-Production" on its back.

		MT
Complete Set (10):		5.00
Common Player:		.25
1	Bill Bates	.25
2	Jeff Blake	.50
3	Drew Bledsoe	1.00
4	Brett Favre	2.00
5	Kevin Greene	.25
6	Daryl Johnston	.25
7	Steve McNair, Kerry Collins	1.00
8	Jerry Rice	1.00
9	Tamarick Vanover	.50
10	Chris Warren	.25

1996 Flickball

The first Flickball set to feature players contained 100 top stars and arrived in seven-card packs. Inserts included in the release were: Commemoratives, DoubleFlicks, Hawaiian Flicks, PreviewFlick Cowboys and Rookies.

		MT
Complete Set (100):		20.00
Common Player:		.10
1	Troy Aikman	1.00
2	Emmitt Smith	2.00
3	Neil O'Donnell (UER, name spelled Niel)	.10
4	Deion Sanders	.50
5	Bill Bates	.10
6	Rodney Peete	.10
7	Ricky Watters	.20
8	Fred Barnett	.10
9	Dave Krieg	.10
10	Larry Centers	.10
11	Garrison Hearst	.20
12	Dave Brown	.10
13	Rodney Hampton	.20
14	Mike Sherrard	.10
15	Gus Frerotte	.20
16	Henry Ellard	.10
17	Darrell Green	.10
18	Scott Mitchell	.20
19	Barry Sanders	1.00
20	Herman Moore	.35
21	Erik Kramer	.10
22	Curtis Conway	.20
23	Jeff Graham	.10
24	Brett Favre	2.00
25	Edgar Bennett	.20
26	Robert Brooks	.30
27	Reggie White	.25
28	Warren Moon	.20
29	Robert Smith	.20
30	Cris Carter	.20
31	Trent Dilfer	.30
32	Errict Rhett	.75
33	Santana Dotson	.10
34	Steve Young	.75
35	Jerry Rice	1.00
36	Merton Hanks	.10
37	Ken Norton	.10
38	Jesse Sapolu	.10
39	Jim Everett	.10
40	Willie Roaf	.10
41	Tyrone Hughes	.10
42	Chris Miller	.10
43	Isaac Bruce	.75
44	Shane Conlan	.10
45	Jeff George	.20
46	Eric Metcalf	.10
47	Craig Heyward	.10
48	Sam Mills	.10
49	Mark Carrier (WR)	.10
50	Brett Maxie	.10
51	Jim Kelly	.20
52	Andre Reed	.20
53	Bruce Smith	.10
54	Bryce Paup	.10
55	Jim Harbaugh	.20
56	Marshall Faulk	.75
57	Sean Dawkins	.10
58	Dan Marino	2.00
59	Terry Kirby	.10
60	O.J. McDuffie	.20
61	Bernie Parmalee	.10
62	Wayne Chrebet	.20
63	Adrian Murrell	.20
64	Ron Moore	.10
65	Drew Bledsoe	1.00
66	Vincent Brisby	.10
67	Vincent Brown	.10
68	Neil O'Donnell	.20
69	Erric Pegram	.10
70	Rohn Stark	.10
71	Kevin Greene	.20
72	Greg Lloyd	.20
73	Todd McNair	.10
74	Mark Stepnoski	.10
75	Bruce Matthews	.10
76	Jeff Blake	.75
77	Carl Pickens	.20
78	John Copeland	.10
79	Vinny Testaverde	.10
80	Andre Rison	.10
81	Leroy Hoard	.10
82	Mark Brunell	1.00
83	Cedric Tillman	.10
84	Desmond Howard	.20
85	Stan Humphries	.20
86	Natrone Means	.30
87	Junior Seau	.20
88	Steve Bono	.20
89	Marcus Allen	.20
90	Derrick Thomas	.20
91	Neil Smith	.10
92	Rick Mirer	.30
93	Chris Warren	.10
94	Cortez Kennedy	.10
95	Jeff Hostetler	.10
96	Tim Brown	.20
97	Terry McDaniel	.10
98	John Elway	.75
99	Shannon Sharpe	.20
100	Steve Atwater	.10

1996 Flickball Commemoratives

This four-card Flickball insert was inserted every 357 packs, with each card being hand-numbered to 700.

		MT
Complete Set (4):		75.00
Common Player:		15.00
C1	Emmitt Smith (25 Touchdowns)	20.00
C2	Dan Marino (Most passing yards)	20.00
C3	Brett Favre (MVP)	20.00
C4	Curtis Martin (Rookie of the Year)	15.00

1996 Flickball DoubleFlicks

This 12-card, double-sided insert set was inserted in every three packs. Cards feature a player on each side from the same position. The cards are numbered with the "DF" prefix.

		MT
Complete Set (12):		18.00
Common Player:		.75
1	Dan Marino, Drew Bledsoe	5.00
2	Troy Aikman, Steve Young	2.50
3	Kerry Collins, Steve McNair	2.50
4	Eric Zeier, Kordell Stewart	2.50
5	Emmitt Smith, Marshall Faulk	5.00
6	Barry Sanders, Errict Davis	2.50
7	Curtis Martin, Terrell Davis	3.50
8	Rashaan Salaam, Napoleon Kaufman	1.50
9	Michael Irvin, Jerry Rice	2.50
10	Tim Brown, Cris Carter	.75
11	Joey Galloway, J.J. Stokes	1.50
12	Frank Sanders, Michael Westbrook	1.25

> Post-1980 cards in Near Mint condition will generally sell for about 75% of the quoted Mint value. Excellent-condition cards bring no more than 40%.

1996 Flickball Hawaiian Flicks

Four different players that are native to Hawaii are featured in Hawaiian Flicks. These were found every eight packs.

		MT
Complete Set (4):		4.00
Common Player:		1.00
H1	Mark Tuinei	1.00
H2	Jesse Sapolu	1.00
H3	Jason Elam	1.00
H4	Junior Seau	1.50

1996 Flickball PreviewFlick Cowboys

PreviewFlick Cowboys were included in every four packs. The set includes eight Cowboys, with cards carrying a "P" prefix on the card number.

		MT
Complete Set (8):		6.00
Common Player:		.50
1	Daryl Johnston	1.00
2	Jay Novacek	1.00
3	Kevin Williams (WR)	1.50
4	Charles Haley	1.00
5	Darren Woodson	.50
6	Leon Lett	.75
7	Chad Hennings	.50
8	Mark Tuinei	.50

1996 Flickball Rookies

This 20-card insert captured the top rookies from the 1995 season, and was inserted every two packs.

		MT
Complete Set (20):		18.00
Common Player:		.25
R1	Sherman Williams	.25
R2	Mike Mamula	.25
R3	Frank Sanders	.50
R4	Steve Stenstrom	.25
R5	Michael Westbrook	1.00
R6	Warren Sapp	.50
R7	Rashaan Salaam	1.50
R8	J.J. Stokes	1.00
R9	Kevin Carter	.25
R10	Kerry Collins	2.50
R11	Curtis Martin	3.00
R12	Kordell Stewart	2.50
R13	Steve McNair	2.00
R14	Rodney Thomas	.25
R15	Eric Zeier	.25
R16	Tony Boselli	.25
R17	Tamarick Vanover	1.00
R18	Joey Galloway	1.75
R19	Napoleon Kaufman	.75
R20	Terrell Davis	2.00

1988 Football Heroes Sticker Book

This 20-page booklet served as an introduction to American football, with a discussion of how the game is played and a glossary. The sticker book measures 9-1/4" x 12-1/2", while the stickers measure three inches in height. Stickers were issued on two sheets of 15 and were to be stuck in a glossy Football Heroes poster.

		MT
Complete Set (30):		30.00
Common Player:		.20
1	Marcus Allen	.50
2	Gary Anderson	.20
3	Brian Bosworth	.20
4	Anthony Carter	.20
5	Deron Cherry	.20
6	Eric Dickerson	.50
7	John Elway	2.00
8	Bo Jackson	1.00
9	Rich Karlis	.20
10	Bernie Kosar	.40
11	Steve Largent	.50
12	Mick Luckhurst	.20
13	Dexter Manley	.20
14	Dan Marino	6.00
15	Jim McMahon	.40
16	Joe Montana	3.00
17	Joe Morris	.20
18	Anthony Munoz	.20
19	Ozzie Newsome	.40
20	Walter Payton	4.00
21	William Perry	.40
22	Jerry Rice	3.00
23	Ricky Sanders	.20
24	Phil Simms	.40
25	Mike Singletary	.50
26	Dwight Stephenson	.20
27	Lawrence Taylor	.50
28	Herschel Walker	.50
29	Doug Williams	.20
30	Kellen Winslow	.40

1985-87 Football Immortals

FOOTBALL IMMORTALS

JOHN (Blood) McNALLY
Charter Enshrinee, 1963

Although this set was produced in both 1985 and 1987, they are similar enough to group together. The 1985 set had 135 cards, while the 1987 set featured 142 Hall of Famers, with their induction year on the front and back of each card. The first 45 cards feature a red border, while cards 46-90 feature a blue border, 91-135 have a green border and 136-142 have a yellow border.

		MT
Complete Set (147):		75.00
Common Player:		.35
1	Pete Rozelle	.70
2	Joe Namath	1.50
3	Frank Gatski	.35
4	O.J. Simpson	1.50
5	Roger Staubach	1.25
6	Herb Adderley	.70
7	Lance Alworth	.70
8	Doug Atkins	.35
9	Morris (Red) Badgro	.35
10	Cliff Battles	.35
11	Sammy Baugh	1.00
12	Raymond Berry	.70
13	Charles W. Bidwill	.35
14	Chuck Bednarik	.70
15	Bert Bell	.35
16	Bobby Bell	.50
17	George Blanda	.70
18	Jim Brown	1.25
19	Paul Brown	.75
20	Roosevelt Brown	.50
21	Ray Flaherty	.50
22	Len Ford	.35
23	Dan Fortmann	.35
24	Bill George	.35
25	Art Donovan	.75
26	John (Paddy) Driscoll	.35
27	Jimmy Conzelman	.35
28	Willie Davis	.35
29	Earl "Dutch" Clark	.50
30	George Connor	.35
31	Guy Chamberlain	.35
32	Jack Christiansen	.50
33	Tony Canadeo	.50
34	Joe Carr	.35
35	Willie Brown	.50
36	Dick Butkus	1.25
37	Bill Dudley	.50
38	Glen Edwards	.50
39	Weeb Ewbank	.50
40	Tom Fears	.50
41	Otto Graham	1.25
42	Red Grange	1.25
43	Frank Gifford	1.25
44	Sid Gillman	.35
45	Forrest Gregg	.50
46	Lou Groza	.75
47	Joe Guyon	.35
48	George Halas	.50
49	Ed Healy	.35
50	Mel Hein	.35
51	Fats Henry	.35
52	Arnie Herber	.35
53	Bill Hewitt	.35
54	Clarke Hinkle	.50
55	Elroy Hirsch	.60
56	Robert (Cal) Hubbard	.35
57	Sam Huff	.50
58	Lamar Hunt	.50
59	Don Hutson	.50
60	Deacon Jones	.50
61	Sonny Jurgensen	.50
62	Walt Kiesling	.35
63	Frank (Bruiser) Kinard	.35
64	Earl (Curly) Lambeau	.50
65	Dick "Night Train" Lane	.50
66	Yale Lary	.50
67	Dante Lavelli	.50
68	Bobby Layne	1.00
69	Tuffy Leemans	.50
70	Bob Lilly	.50
71	Vince Lombardi	1.00
72	Sid Luckman	1.00
73	Link Lyman	.35
74	Tim Mara	.35
75	Gino Marchetti	.50
76	Geo. Preston Marshall	.35
77	Ollie Matson	.50
78	George McAfee	.50
79	Mike McCormack	.50
80	Hugh McElhenny	.60
81	Johnny (Blood) McNally	.60
82	Mike Michalske	.35
83	Wayne Millner	.35
84	Bobby Mitchell	.50
85	Ron Mix	.50
86	Lenny Moore	.60
87	Marion Motley	.50
88	George Musso	.35
89	Bronko Nagurski	.70
90	Earl (Greasy) Neale	.50
91	Ernie Nevers	.50
92	Ray Nitschke	.50
93	Leo Nomellini	.50
94	Merlin Olsen	.75
95	Jim Otto	.35
96	Steve Owen	.35
97	Clarence (Ace) Parker	.35
98	Jim Parker	.35
99	Joe Perry	.60
100	Pete Pihos	.50
101	Hugh (Shorty) Ray	.35
102	Dan Reeves (OWN)	.35
103	Jim Ringo	.50
104	Andy Robustelli	.50
105	Art Rooney	.35
106	Gale Sayers	1.25
107	Joe Schmidt	.50
108	Bart Starr	1.25
109	Ernie Stautner	.50
110	Ken Strong	.50
111	Joe Stydahar	.35
112	Charley Taylor	.50
113	Jim Taylor	.60
114	Jim Thorpe	1.25
115	Y.A. Tittle	1.25
116	George Trafton	.35
117	Charley Trippi	.50
118	Emlen Tunnell	.50
119	Clyde "Bulldog" Turner	.50
120	Johnny Unitas	1.50
121	Norm Van Brocklin	.75
122	Steve Van Buren	.60
123	Paul Warfield	.50
124	Bob Waterfield	.75
125	Arnie Weinmeister	.35
126	Bill Willis	.35
127	Larry Wilson	.50
128	Alex Wojciechowicz	.35
129	Pro Football Hall of Fame (Entrance pictured)	.35
130A	Jim Thorpe Statue	1.00
130B	Doak Walker	3.00
131A	Enshrinement Galleries	.75
131B	Willie Lanier	1.75
132	Pro Football HOF on Enshrinement Day (Aerial shot of crowd)	.35
133A	Eric Dickerson (Display)	1.00
133B	Paul Hornung	5.00
134A	Walter Payton (Display)	1.50
134B	Ken Houston	1.75
135A	Super Bowl Display	1.00
135B	Fran Tarkenton	5.00
136	Don Maynard	2.50
137	Larry Csonka	5.00
138	Joe Greene	5.00
139	Len Dawson	4.00
140	Gene Upshaw	2.00
141	Jim Langer	1.25
142	John Henry Johnson	1.50

1955 49ers White Border

This 38-card set was available direct from the team as part of a package to fans. Cards are unnumbered and very similar to other issues, except for the text on the back. The fronts feature a black and white posed photo, with the player's signature across the bottom.

		NM
Complete Set (38):		185.00
Common Player:		3.00
1	Frankie Albert (CO One of Red)	3.00
2	Joe Arenas (The All-Time)	3.00
3	Harry Babcock	3.00
4	Ed Beatty (After searching)	3.00
5	Phil Bengston (An All-America)	3.00
6	Rex Berry (One of the)	3.00
7	Hardy Brown	7.00
8	Marion Campbell	5.00
9	Al Carapella	3.00
10	Paul Carr (Drafted by)	3.00
11	Maury Duncan	3.00
12	Bob Hantla	3.00
13	Carroll Hardy	3.00
14	Matt Hazeltine (Won a)	4.00
15	Red Hickey (CO After 14 years)	4.00
16	Doug Hogland	3.00
17	Bill Johnson (Here's one..with ten lines of text)	3.00
18	John Henry Johnson	18.00
19	Eldred Kraemer	3.00
20	Bob Laughlin	3.00
21	Bobby Luna	3.00
22	George Maderos (The greatest..)	3.00
23	Clay Matthews	4.00
24	Hugh McElhenny (NFL Commissioner)	18.00
25	Dick Moegle (25 text lines)	4.00
26	Leo Nomellini (Leo was..)	14.00
27	Lou Palatella (Like Eldred)	3.00
28	Joe Perry (First man)	18.00
29	Charley Powell (Charley..)	4.00
30	Gordy Soltau (One of the..)	3.00
31	Bob St. Clair (In two years)	14.00
32	Tom Stolhandske	3.00
33	Roy Storey (ANN Bob Fouts ANN and Red Strader Co)	3.00
34	Red Strader (CO)	3.00
35	Y.A. Tittle (Jinxed by..)	20.00
36	Bob Toneff (Rated the..)	3.00
37	Billy Wilson (Named the..)	5.00
38	Sid Youngelman	3.00

1956 49ers White Border

This 29-card set was available direct from the team as part of a package to fans. Many of the cards are similar to other early issues, and are only distinguishable by the text on the back. Cards are black and white posed photos with the player's signature across the bottom.

		NM
Complete Set (29):		125.00
Common Player:		3.00
1	Frankie Albert (Frank Culling Albert, who..)	3.00
2	Ed Beatty (Traded by..)	3.00
3	Phil Bengston (Phil is known..)	3.00
4	Rex Berry (Unanimously..)	3.00
5	Bruce Bosley (Bosley was..)	4.00
6	Fred Bruney	3.00
7	Paul Carr (A redshirt..)	3.00
8	Clyde Conner (One of the..)	3.00
9	Paul Goad	3.00
10	Matt Hazeltine (Matt reported..)	3.00
11	Ed Henke (After attending)	3.00
12	Bill Herchman (Bill was..)	3.00
13	Red Hickey (Red Hickey..)	3.00
14	Bill Jessup (Bill is one..)	3.00
15	Bill Johnson (Here's one..with nine lines of text)	3.00
16	George Maderos (A 21st..)	3.00
17	Dick Moegle (San..with 11 lines of text)	4.00
18	George Morris	3.00
19	Leo Nomellini (A 49er standby..)	14.00
20	Lou Palatella (Most..same as 1957)	3.00
21	Joe Perry (Joe is..)	18.00
22	Charley Powell	4.00
23	Leo Rucka	3.00
24	Ed Sharkey	3.00
25	Charles Smith	3.00
26	Gordy Soltau (No all-time..)	3.00
27	Bob St. Clair (Tallest man)	10.00
28	Bob Toneff (Another..)	3.00
29	Billy Wilson (Billy is..)	4.00

1957 49ers White Border

As with many other early 49ers issues, this 43-card set is very similar to previous issues, except for the text on the card backs. For the players that were included in the 1956 set, the photos are the same. This issue features the first John Brodie card, which predates his Topps and Fleer rookies by four years.

		NM
Complete Set (43):		180.00
Common Player:		3.00
1	Frankie Albert (CO Frank Culling Albert played..same as 1958)	3.00
2	Joe Arenas (Again in 1956..)	3.00
3	Gene Babb (Drafted 19th..)	3.00
4	Larry Barnes	3.00
5	Phil Bengston (CO Beginning his eighth..)	3.00
6	Bruce Bosley (After a same as 1958)	3.00
7	John Brodie (According to..)	30.00
8	Paul Carr (Versatile on..)	3.00
9	Clyde Conner (Football)	3.00
10	Ted Connolly (The 49er..)	3.00
11	Bob Cross	3.00
12	Mark Duncan (CO Mark..same as 1958)	3.00
13	Bob Fouts (ANN Lon Simmons ANN and Frankie Albert CO same as 1958)	3.00
14	John Gonzaga (One of the)	3.00
15	Tom Harmon (Kids' ages are 11, 8 and 5)	5.00
16	Matt Hazeltine (An All-American)	3.00
17	Ed Henke (Studious-looking)	3.00
18	Bill Herchman (The 49ers)	3.00
19	Red Hickey (CO After 14 campaigns same as 1958)	3.00
20	Bobby Holladay	3.00
21	Bill Jessup (One of the)	3.00
22	Bill Johnson (CO No all-time same as 1958)	3.00
23	Marv Matuszak (Traded to)	3.00
24	Hugh McElhenny (Sidelined)	14.00
25	Dick Moegle (An with 11 lines of text)	3.00
26	Frank Morze (The 49ers, used)	3.00
27	Leo Nomellini (He was)	10.00
28	R.C. Owens (If the)	5.00
29	Lou Palatella (Most..same as 1956)	3.00
30	Joe Perry (The greatest)	14.00
31	Charley Powell (Name almost)	3.00
32	Jim Ridlon (Teaming with)	3.00
33	Karl Rubke (The 16th)	3.00
34	J.D. Smith (J.D.'s football)	3.00
35	Gordy Soltau (Already listed)	3.00
36	Bob St. Clair (A born leader)	8.00

37 Bill Stits (An All-American) 3.00
38 Y.A. Tittle (For sheer) 18.00
39 Bob Toneff (After a) 3.00
40 Lynn Waldorf (Director of Personnel Vertical text, same as 1958) 3.00
41 Val Walker 3.00
42 Billy Wilson (Born on) 4.00
43 49ers Coaches (Bill Johnson, Phil Bengtson, Frankie Albert, Mark Duncan, Red Hickey) (Blank back, same as 1958) 3.00

1958 49ers White Border

This 44-card set is very similar to other issues and is only distinguishable by the text on the card backs. The cards are in black and white, with posed photos and a signature across the bottom.

NM
Complete Set (44): 185.00
Common Player: 3.00
1 Frankie Albert (Frank culling Albert played same as 1957) 3.00
2 Bill Atkins (Alabama) 3.00
3 Gene Babb (A great) 3.00
4 Phil Bengtson (CO Beginning his 9th) 3.00
5 Bruce Bosley (After a same as 1957) 3.00
6 John Brodie (With John) 18.00
7 Clyde Conner (In signing running pose) 3.00
8 Ted Connolly (When Santa Clara) 3.00
9 Fred Dugan (Butch Dugan) 3.00
10 Mark Duncan (CO Mark same as 1957) 3.00
11 Bob Fouts (Lon Simmons ANN and Frankie Albert CO same as 1957) 3.00
12 John Gonzaga (Recommended) 3.00
13 Tom Harmon (ANN Kids' ages are 12, 9 and 6) 4.00
14 Matt Hazeltine (Improved) 4.00
15 Ed Henke (The Frank Buck) 3.00
16 Bill Herchman (A lineman's) 3.00
17 Red Hickey (CO After 14 campaigns same as 1957) 3.00
18 Bill Jessup (Hard luck) 3.00
19 Bill Johnson (No all-time same as 1957) 3.00
20 Marv Matuszak (The best) 4.00
21 Hugh McElhenny (More people) 14.00
22 Jerry Mertens (A 20th draft selection, Jerry) 3.00
23 Dick Moegle (13 text lines) 3.00
24 Dennit Morris 3.00
25 Frank Morze (The 49ers drafted) 3.00
26 Leo Nomellini (Defensive) 10.00
27 R.C. Owens (There's always) 5.00
28 Jim Pace 3.00
29 Lou Palatella (When) 3.00
30 Joe Perry (The all-time) 12.00
31 Jim Ridlon (After a) 3.00
32 Karl Rubke (Desperately) 3.00
33 J.D. Smith (Used mainly) 3.00
34 Gordy Soltau (In the eight) 3.00
35 Bob St. Clair (The only) 8.00
36 Bill Stits (When the) 3.00
37 John Thomas (This is) 3.00
38 Y.A. Tittle (His real) 18.00
39 Bob Toneff (A chronic) 3.00
40 Lynn Waldorf (Director of Personnel Vertical text same as 1957) 3.00
41 Billy Wilson (Em Tunnell, great) 3.00
42 John Wittenborn (John) 3.00
43 Abe Woodson (The 49ers) 5.00
44 49ers Coachers (Bill Johnson, Phil Bengtson, Frankie Albert, Mark Duncan, Red Hickey) (Blank back, same as 1957) 3.00

1959 49ers White Border

This 45-card set is very similar to other team issues around this time and can only be distinguished by the text on the back. Sets were available as part of a package available to fans. Fronts feature a black and white posed photo with a signature across the bottom.

NM
Complete Set (45): 185.00
Common Player: 3.00
1 Bill Atkins (Played defensive) 3.00
2 Dave Baker 3.00
3 Bruce Bosley (Starred as) 3.00
4 John Brodie (Led NFL) 18.00
5 Jack Christiansen (CO) 8.00
6 Monte Clark 4.00
7 Clyde Conner (Standing pose, uniform number 88) 3.00
8 Ted Connolly (Realized his) 3.00
9 Tommy Davis 4.00
10 Eddie Dove 3.00
11 Fred Dugan (Made) 3.00
12 Mark Duncan (CO A versatile) 3.00
13 Bob Fouts (ANN) 3.00
14 John Gonzaga (One of few) 3.00
15 Bob Harrison 3.00
16 Matt Hazeltine (One of the) 3.00
17 Ed Henke (Suffered a) 3.00
18 Bill Herchman (Starting) 3.00
19 Red Hickey (Baseball) 3.00
20 Russ Hodges (ANN) 4.00
21 Bill Johnson (CO Bill Johnson) 3.00
22 Charlie Krueger 3.00
23 Lenny Lyles 3.00
24 Hugh McElhenny (One of the) 14.00
25 Jerry Mertens (A 20th draft selection last) 3.00
26 Dick Moegle (7 text lines) 4.00
27 Frank Morze (Transferred) 3.00
28 Leo Nomellini (Has never) 10.00
29 Clancy Osborne 3.00
30 R.C. Owens (Have football) 5.00
31 Joe Perry (Football's) 14.00
32 Jim Ridlon (Showed) 3.00
33 Karl Rubke (Started his) 3.00
34 Bob St. Clair (Tallest player) 8.00
35 Henry Schmidt 3.00
36 Bob Shaw (CO) 3.00
37 Lon Simmons (ANN) 3.00
38 J.D. Smith (One of the) 3.00
39 John Thomas (Didn't make) 3.00
40 Y.A. Tittle (In 11 years) 18.00
41 Jerry Tubbs 4.00
42 Lynn Waldorf (Director of Personnel Horizontal text) 3.00
43 Billy Wilson (Emlen Tunnell, 12-year) 4.00
44 John Wittenborn (Handy) 3.00
45 Abe Woodson (Received) 4.00

1960 49ers White Border

This 44-card set was available through a package offered to fans and is similar to other issues in that time span, and can be distinguished by the text on the back. Players are featured in black and white posed photos, with a facsimile signature across the photo.

NM
Complete Set (44): 185.00
Common Player: 3.00
1 Dave Baker (David Lee Baker) 3.00
2 Bruce Bosley (Born in Fresno) 3.00
3 John Brodie (This could be) 14.00
4 Jack Christiansen (ACO) 8.00
5 Monte Clark (A special chapter) 5.00
6 Dan Colchico (Big Dan) 3.00
7 Clyde Conner (Clyde Raymond) 3.00
8 Ted Connolly (When Theodore) 3.00
9 Tommy Davis (San Francisco) 4.00
10 Eddie Dove (Edward Everett) 3.00
11 Mark Duncan (ACO A versatile) 3.00
12 Bob Fouts (ANN) 3.00
13 Bob Harrison (There is no more) 3.00
14 Matt Hazeltine (Matthew Hazeltine) 3.00
15 Ed Henke (Desire and) 3.00
16 Red Hickey (CO Baseball) 3.00
17 Russ Hodges (ANN) 3.00
18 Bill Johnson (CO Bill Johnson) 3.00
19 Gordon Kelley (This Southern) 3.00
20 Charlie Krueger (The 49ers) 4.00
21 Lenny Lyles (Leonard Lyles) 3.00
22 Hugh McElhenny (San Francisco's) 14.00
23 Mike Magac (Mike was) 3.00
24 Jerry Mertens (Jerome William) 3.00
25 Frank Morze (Anyone with) 3.00
26 Leo Nomellini (Leo Joseph) 10.00
27 Clancy Osborne (Desire) 4.00
28 R.C. Owens (Few players) 5.00
29 Jim Ridlon (James Ridlon) 3.00
30 C.R. Roberts (After trials) 3.00
31 Len Rohde (Len, a three) 3.00
32 Karl Rubke (Only 20 years) 3.00
33 Bob St. Clair (Robert Bruce) 8.00
34 Henry Schmidt (After two years) 3.00
35 Lon Simmons (ANN) 3.00
36 J.D. Smith (In J.D. Smith) 4.00
37 Gordy Soltau (ANN) 3.00
38 Monty Stickles (The football) 3.00
39 John Thomas (Noted more) 3.00
40 Y.A. Tittle (When Yelberton) 18.00
41 Lynn Waldorf (Director of Personnel) 3.00
42 Bobby Waters (A smart) 5.00
43 Billy Wilson (Only Don Hutson) 4.00
44 Abe Woodson (A Big 10) 4.00

1968 49ers White Border

This 35-card oversized set measures 8-1/2" x 11" and displays different 49ers players in posed, black and white photos. Card backs are blank, with no card numbers listed either. In addition, Steve Spurrier's card in this set predates his rookie by four years.

NM
Complete Set (35): 125.00
Common Player: 2.50
1 Kermit Alexander 2.50
2 Cas Banaszek 2.50
3 Ed Beard 2.50
4 Forrest Blue 4.00
5 Bruce Bosley 4.00
6 John Brodie 10.00
7 Elmer Collett 2.50
8 Doug Cunningham 2.50
9 Tommy Davis 4.00
10 Kevin Hardy 2.50
11 Matt Hazeltine 4.00
12 Stan Hindman 2.50
13 Tom Holzer 2.50
14 Jim Johnson 8.00
15 Charlie Krueger 4.00
16 Roland Lakes 2.50
17 Gary Lewis 2.50
18 Kay McFarland 2.50
19 Clifton McNeil 4.00
20 George Mira 5.00
21 Howard Mudd 2.50
22 Dick Nolan (CO) 4.00
23 Frank Nunley 2.50
24 Don Parker 2.50
25 Mel Phillips 4.00
26 Al Randolph 2.50
27 Len Rohde 2.50
28 Steve Spurrier 28.00
29 John Thomas 2.50
30 Bill Tucker 2.50
31 Dave Wilcox 4.00
32 Ken Willard 4.00
33 Bob Windsor 4.00
34 Dick Witcher 4.00
35 Team Photo 10.00

1972 49ers Redwood City Tribune

This six-card set measures 3" x 5-1/2" and contains a head shot of the featured player in black and white with white borders. There is a large white space below the photo that contains a facsimile autograph. Cards are unnumbered and listed below in alphabetical order.

NM
Complete Set (6): 50.00
Common Player: 8.00
1 Frank Edwards 8.00
2 Frank Nunley 8.00
3 Len Rohde 8.00
4 Larry Schrieber 8.00
5 Steve Spurrier 30.00
6 Gene Washington 12.00

1982 49ers Team Issue

This 5" x 8" set has 44 cards in black and white with white borders. The backs of the cards are blank and unnumbered.

MT
Complete Set (44): 55.00
Common Player: 1.00
1 Dan Audick 1.00
2 John Ayers 1.00
3 Guy Benjamin 1.00
4 Dwaine Board 1.00
5 Ken Bungarda 1.00
6 Dan Bunz 1.00
7 Dwight Clark 4.00
8 Ricky Churchman 1.00
9 Earl Cooper 1.00
10 Randy Cross 1.50
11 Johnny Davis 1.00
12 Fred Dean 1.00
13 Walt Downing 1.00
14 Walt Easley 1.00
15 Lenvil Elliott 1.00
16 Keith Fahnhorst 1.00
17 Rick Gervais 1.00
18 Willie Harper 1.00
19 John Harty 1.00
20 Pete Kugler 1.00
21 Amos Lawrence 1.00
22 Bobby Leopold 1.00
23 Saladin Martin 1.00
24 Milt McColl 1.00
25 Jim Miller 1.00
26 Joe Montana 22.00
27 Ricky Patton 1.00
28 Lawrence Pillers 1.00
29 Craig Puki 1.00
30 Fred Quillan 1.00
31 Eason Ramson 1.00
32 Archie Reese 1.00
33 Jack Reynolds 1.00
34 Mike Shumann 1.00
35 Freddie Solomon 1.50
36 Scott Stauch 1.00
37 Jim Stuckey 1.00
38 Lynn Thomas 1.00
39 Keena Turner 1.25
40 Ray Wersching 1.00
41 Carlton Williamson 1.00
42 Mike Wilson 1.00
43 Eric Wright 1.00
44 Charlie Young 1.00

1984 49ers Police

This 12-card set was issued in three panels of four cards each and measures 2-1/2" x 4". The set is unnumbered and sponsored by 7-Eleven, Dr. Pepper and KCB's.

MT
Complete Set (12): 25.00
Common Player: 1.00
1 Dwaine Board 1.00
2 Roger Craig 3.50
3 Riki Ellison 1.00
4 Keith Fahnhorst 1.00
5 Joe Montana, Dwight Clark 10.00
6 Jack Reynolds 1.00
7 Freddie Solomon 1.00
8 Keena Turner 1.00
9 Wendall Tyler 1.00
10 Bill Walsh (CO) 3.00
11 Ray Wersching 1.00
12 Eric Wright 1.00

1985 49ers Police

This 16-card set was issued in four panels of four cards each, and is very similar to the 1984 set except its sponsored only by Dr. Pepper and 7-Eleven. The cards are unnumbered and measure 2-1/2" x 4".

MT
Complete Set (16): 18.00
Common Player: .50
1 John Ayers .50
2 Roger Craig 2.00
3 Fred Dean .75
4 Riki Ellison .50
5 Keith Fahnhorst .50
6 Russ Francis .75
7 Dwight Hicks .50
8 Ronnie Lott 1.75
9 Dana McLemore .50
10 Joe Montana 10.00
11 Todd Shell .50
12 Freddie Solomon .75
13 Keena Turner .50
14 Bill Walsh (CO) 1.50
15 Ray Wersching .50
16 Eric Wright .50

1985 49ers Smokey

This seven-card oversized set measures approximately 3" x 4-3/8". It was issued by the 49ers and Smokey Bear, and features a cartoon fire safety tip and a facsimile signature of the player on the back.

MT
Complete Set (7): 30.00
Common Player: 2.00
1 Group Picture with (Smokey Player list on back of card) 6.00
2 Joe Montana 18.00
3 Jack Reynolds 3.00
4 Eric Wright 2.00
5 Dwight Hicks 2.00
6 Dwight Clark 4.00
7 Keena Turner 2.00

1988 49ers Police

This 20-card set included 19 players and one coach card and was sponsored by 7-Eleven and Oscar Mayer. The fronts are almost full-bleed photos with a thin white border. Backs have a football tip and a McGruff crime tip.

MT
Complete Set (20): 20.00
Common Player: .50
1 Harris Barton .75
2 Dwaine Board .50
3 Michael Carter .75
4 Roger Craig 1.50
5 Randy Cross .75
6 Riki Ellison .50
7 John Frank .50
8 Jeff Fuller .50
9 Pete Kugler .50
10 Ronnie Lott 2.00
11 Joe Montana 8.00
12 Tom Rathman 1.75
13 Jerry Rice 8.00
14 Jeff Stover .50
15 Keena Turner .75
16 Bill Walsh (CO) 1.50
17 Michael Walter .50
18 Mike Wilson .50
19 Eric Wright .75
20 Steve Young 8.00

1988 49ers Smokey

This 35-card set was printed on a 5" x 8" format and is unnumbered, except for the uniform number. Fronts feature a full-bleed shot with a thin white border around the inside of the card. Backs have a fire safety cartoon usually featuring Smokey the Bear.

MT
Complete Set (35): 100.00
Common Player: 1.00
1 Harris Barton 1.50
2 Dwaine Board (SP) 8.00
3 Michael Carter 1.50
4 Bruce Collie 1.00
5 Roger Craig 3.50
6 Randy Cross 1.75
7 Eddie DeBartolo (Jr Owner, President) 2.50
8 Riki Ellison 1.00
9 Kevin Fagan 1.00
10 Jim Fahnhorst 1.00
11 John Frank 1.00
12 Jeff Fuller 1.00
13 Don Griffin 1.50
14 Charles Haley 3.00
15 Ron Heller 1.00
16 Tom Holmoe 1.00
17 Pete Kugler 1.00
18 Ronnie Lott 4.00
19 Tim McKyer 1.50
20 Joe Montana 20.00
21 Tory Nixon 1.00
22 Bubba Paris 1.00
23 John Paye 1.00
24 Tom Rathman 3.00
25 Jerry Rice 20.00
26 Jeff Stover 1.00
27 Harry Sydney 1.00
28 John Taylor 4.00
29 Keena Turner 1.50
30 Steve Wallace 1.50
31 Bill Walsh (CO) 3.00
32 Michael Walter 1.00
33 Mike Wilson 1.00
34 Eric Wright 1.50
35 Steve Young 20.00

1990-91 49ers SF Examiner

This 16-card set was issued on two unperforated sheets measuring 14" x 11", and was issued by the San Francisco Examiner. Eight-card panels included a newspaper headline across the top reading "San Francisco Examiner Salutes the 49ers' Finest." Card fronts are in color with a thin orange border on the red-face card. Backs are horizontal and black and white with a head shot and stats.

MT
Complete Set (16): 10.00
Common Player: .50
1 Harris Barton .75
2 Michael Carter .50
3 Mike Cofer .50
4 Roger Craig 1.00
5 Kevin Fagan .50
6 Don Griffin .50
7 Charles Haley 1.25
8 Pierce Holt .50
9 Brent Jones 1.25
10 Ronnie Lott 1.25
11 Guy McIntyre .50
12 Matt Millen .75
13 Joe Montana 4.00
14 Tom Rathman 1.00
15 Jerry Rice 4.00
16 John Taylor 1.50

1992 49ers FBI

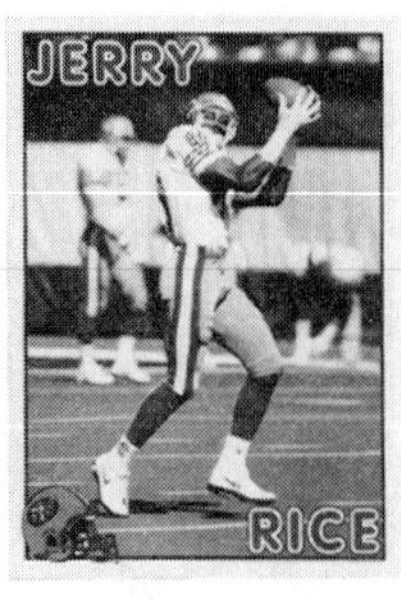

This 40-card set was available in different packs for free with 49ers' edition of GameDay Magazine at regular-season home games each week at Candlestick Park. The set was sponsored by the 49ers and the FBI and contains a public service message on the back in the form of a player quote.

MT
Complete Set (40): 45.00
Common Player: .50
1 Michael Carter .50
2 Kevin Fagan .50
3 Charles Haley 1.00
4 Guy McIntyre .50
5 George Seifert (CO) 1.00
6 Harry Sydney .50
7 John Taylor 1.00
8 Mike Walter .50
9 Steve Young 10.00
10 Mike Cofer .50
11 Keith DeLong .50
12 Don Griffin .50
13 Pierce Holt .50
14 Mike Sherrard .75
15 Larry Roberts .50
16 Bill Romanowski .50
17 Tom Rathman 1.00
18 Jesse Sapolu .75
19 Brent Jones 1.25
20 Brian Bollinger .50
21 Eric Davis .50
22 Antonio Goss .50
23 Alan Grant .50
24 Harris Barton .75
25 Ricky Watters 4.00
26 Darin Jordan .50
27 Odessa Turner .50
28 David Wilkins .50
29 Merton Hanks 1.00
30 David Whitmore .50
31 Joe Montana 10.00
32 Klaus Wilmsmeyer .50
33 Tim Harris .75
34 Roy Foster .50
35 Bill Musgrave .75
36 Dana Hall .75
37 Steve Wallace .75
38 Steve Bono 4.00
39 Jerry Rice 10.00
NNO Title Card 1.00

1994 49ers Pro Mags/Pro Tags

49ers Pro Mags and Pro Tags were each a six-card set issued in a black cardboard box and numbered out of 750. Each card is borderless and contains a gold-foil Super Bowl XXIX logo printed in the lower right corner. The tags feature Roman numerals XXIX in back of a superimposed shot of the player. Magnet backs are black and blank, Tags backs have a color close-up photo, an autograph strip and a player profile. The magnets are listed 1-6, while the tags are 7-12.

MT
Complete Set (12): 20.00
Common Player: 1.00
1 Ken Norton 1.00
2 Jerry Rice 4.00
3 Deion Sanders 2.50
4 John Taylor 1.00
5 Ricky Watters 1.50
6 Steve Young 3.00
7 Ken Norton 1.00
8 Jerry Rice 4.00
9 Deion Sanders 2.50
10 John Taylor 1.00
11 Ricky Watters 1.50
12 Steve Young 3.00

1996 49ers Save Mart

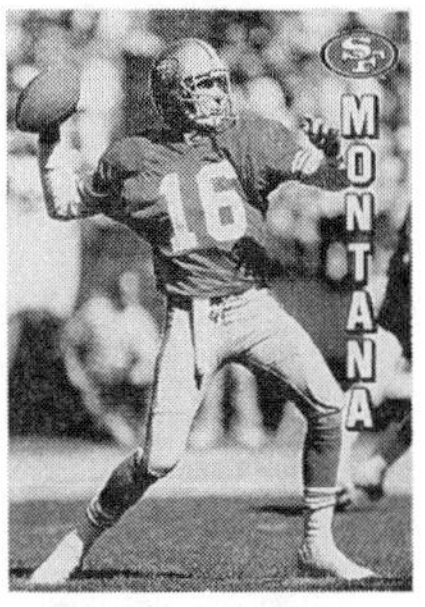

This nine-card set celebrates the 49ers' star Super Bowl players. Each full-bleed card front includes an action shot of the player, with his last name and San Francisco logo appearing along the right border. Each card back includes the 50-year anniversary and 49ers' logos along with the checklist. The Save Mart and UPI Marketing Inc. logos appear at the bottom, with the card number located in the lower right. One card and one coin were sold in each cello pack. The coins feature the player's likeness, name, team, years with the team and his jersey number on the front. The reverse side of the coin boasts the 49ers' 50-year logo. A coin holder was also given away.

MT
Complete Set (9): 12.00
Common Player: .50
1 Steve Young 3.00
2 Roger Craig 1.00
3 Jerry Rice 4.00
4 Ronnie Lott 1.00
5 Ken Norton Jr. .50
6 Dwight Clark .50
7 Brent Jones .50
8 Joe Montana 5.00
9 Super Bowl 1.00

1989 Franchise Game

The 1989 Franchise Game is modeled after Monopoly, with players beginning with a sum of money and traveling around the board acquiring different players to fill out a 23-man roster. There are 304 players depicted and 28 different NFL teams. Fronts have the player's name, team, point value and salary. Backs contain the player's position written at the top, as well as a large acronym for the position in the middle of the player's city. Franchise was produced by Rohrwood Enterprises.

MT
Complete Set (332): 200.00
Common Player: .60
1 Neal Anderson .60
2 Kevin Butler .60
3 Jimbo Covert .60
4 Dave Duerson .60
5 Dan Hampton 1.00
6 Jay Hilgenberg .60
7 Mike Richardson .60
8 Ron Rivera .60
9 Mike Singletary 1.00
10 Mike Tomczak 1.00
11 Keith Van Horne .60
12 Lewis Billups .60
13 Jim Breech .60
14 James Brooks .75
15 Eddie Brown .60
16 Ross Browner .60
17 Jason Buck .60
18 Cris Collinsworth .75

19	Eddie Edwards	.60
20	Boomer Esiason	.75
21	David Fulcher	.60
22	Ray Horton	.60
23	Tim Krumrie	.60
24	Max Montoya	.60
25	Anthony Munoz	1.50
26	Jim Skow	.60
27	Reggie Williams	.60
28	Ickey Woods	.60
29	Cornelius Bennett	1.00
30	Shane Conlan	1.00
31	Joe Devlin	.60
32	Nate Odomes	.60
33	Scott Norwood	.60
34	Andre Reed	1.50
35	Jim Ritcher	.60
36	Fred Smerlas	.60
37	Bruce Smith	1.50
38	Art Still	.60
39	Keith Bishop	.60
40	Bill Bryan	.60
41	Tony Dorsett	3.00
42	Simon Fletcher	.60
43	Mike Harden	.60
44	Mark Haynes	.60
45	Mike Horan	.60
46	Vance Johnson	.75
47	Rulon Jones	.60
48	Rich Karlis	.60
49	Karl Mecklenburg	1.00
50	Dennis Smith	.60
51	Dave Studdard	.60
52	Andre Townsend	.60
53	Steve Watson	.60
54	Sammy Winder	.60
55	Matt Bahr	.60
56	Rickey Bolden	.60
57	Earnest Byner	.75
58	Sam Clancy	.60
59	Hanford Dixon	.60
60	Bob Golic	.60
61	Carl Hairston	.60
62	Eddie Johnson	.60
63	Kevin Mack	.60
64	Clay Matthews	.75
65	Frank Minnifield	.60
66	Ozzie Newsome	1.00
67	Cody Risien	.60
68	John Cannon	.60
69	Ron Holmes	.60
70	Winston Moss	.60
71	Rob Taylor	.60
72	Joe Bostic	.60
73	Roy Green	.75
74	Ricky Hunley	.60
75	E.J. Junior	.60
76	Neil Lomax	.60
77	Tim McDonald	.60
78	Cedric Mack	.60
79	Freddie Joe Nunn	.60
80	Gary Anderson	.75
81	Keith Baldwin	.60
82	Gill Byrd	.60
83	Elvis Patterson	.60
84	Gary Plummer	.60
85	Billy Ray Smith	.60
86	Lee Williams	.60
87	Mike Bell	.60
88	Lloyd Burruss	.60
89	Carlos Carson	.60
90	Deron Cherry	.60
91	Jack Del Rio	.60
92	Irv Eatman	.60
93	Dino Hackett	.60
94	Bill Kenney	.60
95	Albert Lewis	.60
96	David Lutz	.60
97	Bill Maas	.60
98	Stephone Paige	.75
99	Neil Smith	1.50
100	Dean Biasucci	.60
101	Duane Bickett	.60
102	Chris Chandler	1.50
103	Eugene Daniel	.60
104	Ray Donaldson	.60
105	Jon Hand	.60
106	Chris Hinton	.60
107	Joe Klecko	.60
108	Cliff Odom	.60
109	Rohn Stark	.60
110	Donnell Thompson	.60
111	Willie Tullis	.60
112	Freddie Young	.60
113	Michael Downs	.60
114	Michael Irvin	3.00
115	Jim Jeffcoat	.60
116	Ed "Too Tall" Jones	1.00
117	Tom Rafferty	.60
118	Herschel Walker	1.25
119	Everson Walls	.60
120	Danny White	.75
121	Randy White	1.50
122	Bob Brudzinski	.60
123	Mark Clayton	.75
124	Mark Duper	1.00
125	Ron Jaworski	1.00
126	Paul Lankford	.60
127	Dan Marino	14.00
128	John Offerdahl	.60
129	Reggie Roby	.60
130	Dwight Stephenson	.60
131	Randall Cunningham	.75
132	Ron Heller	.60
133	Mike Quick	.75
134	Ken Reeves	.60
135	Dave Rimington	.60
136	Reggie Singletary	.60
137	Andre Waters	.60
138	Reggie White	2.00
139	Roynell Young	.60
140	Aundray Bruce	.60
141	Bobby Butler	.60
142	Bill Fralic	.60
143	Mike Kenn	.60
144	Chris Miller	.60
145	John Settle	.60
146	George Yarno	.60
147	Michael Carter	.60
148	Wes Chandler	1.00
149	Roger Craig	1.50
150	Randy Cross	.60
151	Riki Ellison	.60
152	Jim Fahnhorst	.60
153	Charles Haley	1.50
154	Barry Helton	.60
155	Guy McIntyre	.75
156	Tim McKyer	.60
157	Joe Montana	10.00
158	Jerry Rice	10.00
159	Keena Turner	.60
160	Eric Wright	.60
161	Steve Young	10.00
162	Raul Allegre	.60
163	Ottis Anderson	.75
164	Billy Ard	.60
165	Carl Banks	.60
166	Mark Bavaro	.75
167	Jim Burt	.75
168	Harry Carson	.75
169	John Elliott	.60
170	Terry Kinard	.60
171	Sean Landeta	.60
172	Lionel Manuel	.60
173	Joe Morris	.75
174	Bart Oates	.60
175	Phil Simms	1.00
176	Pat Leahy	.60
177	Marty Lyons	.60
178	Erik McMillan	.60
179	Freeman McNeil	1.00
180	Scott Mersereau	.60
181	Ken O'Brien	.60
182	Jim Sweeney	.60
183	Al Toon	.75
184	Wesley Walker	.75
185	Jim Arnold	.60
186	Bennie Blades	.60
187	Mike Cofer	.60
188	Keith Ferguson	.60
189	Steve Mott	.60
190	Eddie Murray	.60
191	Harvey Salem	.60
192	Bobby Watkins	.60
192	Keith Bostic	.60
194	Richard Byrd	.60
195	Ray Childress	.75
196	Ernest Givins	.75
197	Kenny Johnson	.60
198	Sean Jones	.75
199	Robert Lyles	.60
200	Bruce Matthews	.75
201	Johnny Meads	.60
202	Warren Moon	2.00
203	Mike Munchak	.75
204	Mike Rozier	.60
205	Dean Steinkuhler	.60
206	Tony Zendejas	.60
207	Mark Cannon	.60
208	Alphonso Carreker	.60
209	Phillip Epps	.60
210	Tim Harris	.75
211	Brian Noble	.60
212	Raymond Clayborn	.60
213	Steve Grogan	.75
214	Roland James	.60
215	Fred Marion	.60
216	Stanley Morgan	.75
217	Kenneth Sims	.60
218	Andre Tippett	.75
219	Marcus Allen	2.00
220	Chris Bahr	.60
221	Steve Beuerlein	.75
222	Tim Brown	4.00
223	Todd Christensen	.75
224	Ron Fellows	.60
225	Willie Gault	.75
226	Mike Haynes	.75
227	Bo Jackson	2.00
228	James Lofton	1.50
229	Howie Long	1.50
230	Vann McElroy	.60
231	Rod Martin	.60
232	Matt Millen	.75
233	Bill Pickel	.60
234	Jay Schroeder	.75
235	Stacey Toran	.60
236	Greg Townsend	.75
237	Greg Bell	.60
238	Henry Ellard	1.25
239	Jerry Gray	.60
240	Leroy Irvin	.60
241	Gary Jeter	.60
242	Johnnie Johnson	.60
243	Larry Kelm	.60
244	Mike Lansford	.60
245	Shawn Miller	.60
246	Mel Owens	.60
247	Jackie Slater	.60
248	Charles White	.60
249	Jeff Bostic	.60
250	Kelvin Bryant	.60
251	Dave Butz	.60
252	Gary Clark	1.50
253	Steve Cox	.60
254	Darryl Grant	.60
255	Darrell Green	.75
256	Joe Jacoby	.60
257	Mel Kaufman	.60
258	Jim Lachey	.60
259	Dexter Manley	.60
260	Charles Mann	.60
261	Mark May	.60
262	Art Monk	1.50
263	Ricky Sanders	.75
264	Alvin Walton	.60
265	Doug Williams	.75
266	Morten Andersen	.60
267	Bruce Clark	.60
268	Jim Dombrowski	.60
269	Mel Gray	.75
270	Bobby Hebert	.75
271	Rickey Jackson	.60
272	Van Jakes	.60
273	Steve Korte	.60
274	Rueben Mayes	.60
275	Sam Mills	.75
276	Dave Waymer	.60
277	Jeff Bryant	.60
278	Blair Bush	.60
279	Jacob Green	.60
280	Melvin Jenkins	.60
281	Norm Johnson	.60
282	Dave Krieg	.75
283	Bryan Millard	.60
284	Ruben Rodriguez	.60
285	Terry Taylor	.60
286	Curt Warner	1.00
287	Tony Woods	.60
288	Gary Anderson	.60
289	Tunch Ilkin	.60
290	Earnest Jackson	.60
291	Louis Lipps	.60
292	Mike Webster	.75
293	Rod Woodson	3.00
294	Joey Browner	.60
295	Anthony Carter	1.25
296	Chris Doleman	.75
297	Tim Irwin	.60
298	Tommy Kramer	.75
299	Carl Lee	.60
300	Kirk Lowdermilk	.60
301	Keith Millard	.60
302	Scott Studwell	.60
303	Wade Wilson	.75
304	Gary Zimmerman	.60
T1	Atlanta Falcons Team Helmet	.60
T2	Buffalo Bills	.60
T3	Chicago Bears	.60
T4	Cincinnati Bengals	.60
T5	Cleveland Browns	.60
T6	Dallas Cowboys	.75
T7	Denver Broncos	.60
T8	Detroit Lions	.60
T9	Green Bay Packers	.60
T10	Houston Oilers	.60
T11	Indianapolis Colts	.60
T12	Kansas City Chiefs	.60
T13	Los Angeles Raiders	.75
T14	Los Angeles Rams	.60
T15	Miami Dolphins	.75
T16	Minnesota Vikings	.60
T17	New England Patriots	.60
T18	New Orleans Saints	.60
T19	New York Giants	.60
T20	New York Jets	.60
T21	Philadelphia Eagles	.60
T22	Phoenix Cardinals	.60
T23	Pittsburgh Steelers	.60
T24	San Diego Chargers	.60
T25	San Francisco 49ers	.60
T26	Seattle Seahawks	.60
T27	Tampa Bay Buccaneers	.60
T28	Washington Redskins	.60

1993 Front Row Gold Collection

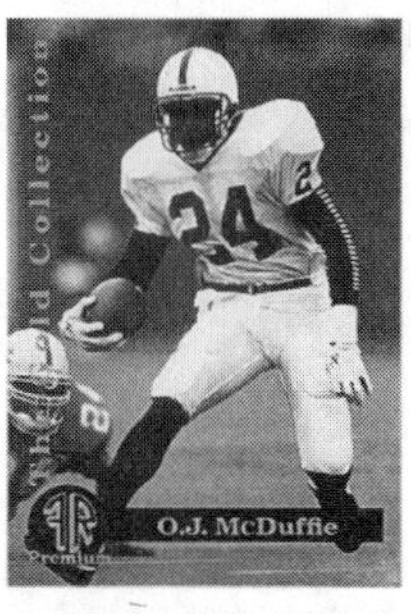

The 10-card, standard-size set features "Gold Collection" in gold foil on the card front over the color action photo. The card backs have another borderless color photo with a brief player summary (odd-numbered) and bio and stat information (even-numbered). Each of the 5,000 sets produced came with a certificate of authenticity.

		MT
Complete Set (10):		5.00
Common Player:		.50
1	Eric Curry	.75
2	Eric Curry	.75
3	Lincoln Kennedy	.50
4	Lincoln Kennedy	.50
5	O.J. McDuffie	1.00
6	O.J. McDuffie	1.00
7	Qadry Ismail	1.00
8	Qadry Ismail	1.00
9	Andre Hastings	1.00
10	Andre Hastings	1.00

G

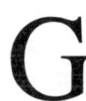

1956 Giants Team Issue

This 36-card, black and white set contains posed player shots on the front surrounded by a white border and a facsimile signature. Backs are unnumbered, while each card measures approximately 5" x 7".

		NM
Complete Set (36):		200.00
Common Player:		4.00
1	Bill Austin	4.00
2	Ray Beck	4.00
3	Roosevelt Brown	10.00
4	Hank Burnine	4.00
5	Don Chandler	4.00
6	Bobby Clatterbuck	4.00
7	Charley Conerly	20.00
8	Frank Gifford	30.00
9	Roosevelt Grier	10.00
10	Don Heinrich	5.00
11	John Hermann	4.00
12	Jim Lee Howell (CO)	5.00
13	Sam Huff	16.00
14	Ed Hughes	4.00
15	Gerald Huth	4.00
16	Jim Katcavage	6.00
17	Gene Kirby (ANN)	4.00
18	Ken MacAfee	5.00
19	Dick Modzelewski (Misspelled Modelewski on the reverse)	5.00
20	Henry Moore	4.00
21	Dick Nolan	5.00
22	Jimmy Patton	5.00
23	Andy Robustelli	10.00
24	Kyle Rote	10.00
25	Chris Schenkel (ANN)	5.00
26	Bob Schnelker	4.00
27	Jack Stroud	4.00
28	Harland Svare	5.00
29	Bill Svoboda	4.00
30	Bob Topp	4.00
31	Mel Triplett	5.00
32	Emlen Tunnell	10.00
33	Alex Webster	5.00
34	Ray Wietecha	4.00
35	Dick Yelvington	4.00
36	Walt Yowarsky	4.00

1957 Giants Team Issue

This 1957 Giants team set measures approximately 5" x 7", with black and white photos and a glossy finish. The set contains 40 unnumbered cards that are listed below in alphabetical order.

		NM
Complete Set (40):		250.00
Common Player:		4.00
1	Ben Agajanian	4.00
2	Bill Austin	4.00
3	Ray Beck	4.00
4	John Bookman	4.00
5	Roosevelt Brown	8.00
6	Don Chandler	5.00
7	Bobby Clatterbuck	4.00
8	Charley Conerly	15.00
9	John Dell Isola (CO)	4.00
10	Gene Filipski	5.00
11	Frank Gifford	25.00
12	Don Heinrich	5.00
13	Jim Lee Howell (CO)	5.00
14	Sam Huff	10.00
15	Ed Hughes	4.00
16	Gerald Huth	4.00
17	Jim Katcavage	5.00
18	Ken Kavanaugh (CO)	5.00
19	Les Keiter (ANN)	4.00
20	Tom Landry (CO)	45.00
21	Cliff Livingston	4.00
22	Vince Lombardi (CO)	50.00
23	Ken MacAfee	5.00
24	Dennis Mendyk	4.00
25	Dick Modzelewski	5.00
26	Dick Nolan	5.00
27	Jim Patton	5.00
28	Andy Robustelli	10.00
29	Kyle Rote	10.00
30	Chris Schenkel (ANN)	5.00
31	Jack Spinks	4.00
32	Jack Stroud	4.00
33	Harland Svare	4.00
34	Bill Svoboda	4.00
35	Mel Triplett	5.00
36	Emlen Tunnell	8.00
37	Alex Webster	5.00
38	Ray Wietecha	5.00
39	Dick Yelvington	4.00
40	Walt Yowarsky	4.00

1960 Giants Jay Publishing

This 12-card set shows players in black and white on 5" x 7" cards. Cards were sold in 12-card packs and have blank, unnumbered backs.

		NM
Complete Set (12):		85.00
Common Player:		4.00
1	Roosevelt Brown	8.00
2	Don Chandler	4.00
3	Charley Conerly	8.00
4	Frank Gifford	20.00
5	Roosevelt Grier	8.00
6	Sam Huff	10.00
7	Phil King	4.00
8	Andy Robustelli	6.00
9	Kyle Rote	6.00
10	Bob Schnelker	4.00
11	Pat Summerall	6.00
12	Alex Webster	5.00

1960 Giants Shell/Riger Posters

This set features 10 black and white posters by Robert Siger and distributed by Shell Oil in 1960. Each poster measures approximately 11-3/4" x 13-3/4".

		NM
Complete Set (10):		150.00
Common Player:		10.00
1	Charley Conerly	25.00
2	Frank Gifford	45.00
3	Sam Huff	20.00
4	Dick Modzelewski	10.00
5	Jim Patton	10.00
6	Andy Robustelli	16.00
7	Kyle Rote	16.00
8	Bob Schnelker	10.00
9	Pat Summerall	20.00
10	Alex Webster, Roosevelt Brown	16.00

1961 Giants Jay Publishing

Similar to the 1960 issue, this 12-card set is composed of black and white, 5" x 7" photos. It features traditional players and was available in 12-card packs.

		NM
Complete Set (12):		65.00
Common Player:		4.00
1	Roosevelt Brown	10.00
2	Don Chandler	4.00
3	Charley Conerly	10.00
4	Roosevelt Grier	8.00
5	Sam Huff	10.00
6	Dick Modzelewski	4.00
7	Jimmy Patton	5.00
8	Jim Podoley	4.00
9	Andy Robustelli	8.00
10	Allie Sherman (CO)	4.00
11	Del Shofner	5.00
12	Y.A. Tittle	15.00

1973 Giants Color Litho

Measuring 8-1/2" x 11", the eight-card set showcased color lithographs on the front. A facsimile player signature is printed at the bottom right inside a white triangle. The unnumbered cards are not bordered and have blank backs.

		NM
Complete Set (8):		50.00
Common Player:		5.00
1	Jim Files	5.00
2	Jack Gregory	5.00
3	Ron Johnson	7.50
4	Greg Larson	5.00
5	Spider Lockhart	7.50
6	Norm Snead	12.00
7	Bob Tucker	7.50
8	Brad Van Pelt	7.50

1987 Giants Police

Measuring 2-3/4" x 4-1/8", the 12-card set is anchored by a large photo on the front, with "New York Giants" printed at the top. Beneath the photo are the player's name and position printed between Giants' helmets. The card backs, which are unnumbered, have "Tips from the Giants" at the top, with two New Jersey law enforcement logos printed below. A safety tip and a McGruff the Crime Dog logo round out the backs. Overall, 10,000 sets were printed.

		MT
Complete Set (12):		75.00
Common Player:		3.00
1	Carl Banks	5.00
2	Mark Bavaro	5.00
3	Brad Benson	3.00
4	Jim Burt	3.00
5	Harry Carson	5.00
6	Maurice Carthon	3.00
7	Sean Landeta	3.00
8	Leonard Marshall	5.00
9	George Martin	3.00
10	Joe Morris	6.00
11	Bill Parcells (CO)	8.00
12	Phil Simms	25.00

1988 Giants Police

Measuring 2-3/4" x 4-1/8", the card fronts are anchored by a large photo. A Giants' helmet is printed in both corners at the top, with "New York Giants" located at the top center. Beneath the photo are the player's name, number, position and bio. The unnumbered backs have "Tips from the Giants" at the top, with two New Jersey law enforcement logos located underneath. A safety tip and a McGruff the Crime Dog logo round out the card backs.

		MT
Complete Set (12):		55.00
Common Player:		3.00
1	Billy Ard	3.00
2	Jim Burt	3.00
3	Harry Carson	5.00
4	Maurice Carthon	3.00
5	Leonard Marshall	5.00
6	George Martin	3.00
7	Phil McConkey	3.00
8	Joe Morris	6.00
9	Karl Nelson	3.00
10	Bart Oates	5.00
11	Bill Parcells (CO)	8.00
12	Phil Simms	16.00

1990 Giants Police

Measuring 2-3/4" x 4-1/8", the 12-card set is anchored by a large photo on the front, with a Giants' helmet in each of the top corners, with "New York Giants" printed at the top center. The player's name, position and bio are printed under the photo. The card backs, which are unnumbered, have "Tips from the Giants" at the top, with two New Jersey law enforcement logos beneath it. A safety tip and a McGruff the Crime Dog logo round out the card backs.

		MT
Complete Set (12):		45.00
Common Player:		2.50
1	Ottis Anderson	5.00
2	Matt Bahr	2.50
3	Eric Dorsey	2.50
4	John Elliott	2.50
5	Ray Handley (CO)	2.50
6	Jeff Hostetler	7.00
7	Erik Howard	2.50
8	Pepper Johnson	4.00
9	Leonard Marshall	4.00
10	Bart Oates	4.00
11	Gary Reasons	2.50
12	Phil Simms	8.00

1992 Giants Police

Measuring 2-3/4" x 4-1/8", the 12-card set is anchored on the front by a large photo and the player's name and bio beneath the photo. "New York Giants" is printed above the photo. The unnumbered card backs have "Tips from the Giants" at the top, a safety tip and a McGruff the Crime Dog logo at the bottom.

		MT
Complete Set (12):		20.00
Common Player:		1.00
1	Ottis Anderson	2.00
2	Matt Bahr	1.00
3	Eric Dorsey	1.00
4	John Elliott	1.00
5	Ray Handley (CO)	1.00
6	Jeff Hostetler	3.00
7	Erik Howard	1.00
8	Pepper Johnson	1.50
9	Leonard Marshall	1.50
10	Bart Oates	1.50
11	Gary Reasons	1.00
12	Phil Simms	5.00

1969 Glendale Stamps

These unnumbered stamps, which measure 1-13/16" x 3-15/16", feature a color player photo on the front; the back has his name, team and instructions on how to apply the stamp to the corresponding album which was produced. "Dampen strip and affix in ablum" is on the back. The album measures 9" x 12" and is arranged alphabetically by team city.

		NM
Complete Set (312):		200.00
Common Player:		.25
(1)	Bob Berry	.40
(2)	Clark Miller	.25
(3)	Jim Butler	.25
(4)	Junior Coffey	.25
(5)	Paul Flatley	.40
(6)	Randy Johnson	.45
(7)	Charlie Bryant	.25
(8)	Billy Lothridge	.25
(9)	Tommy Nobis	2.00
(10)	Claude Humphrey	.40
(11)	Ken Reaves	.25
(12)	Jerry Simmons	.40
(13)	Mike Curtis	.75
(14)	Dennis Gaubatz	.25
(15)	Jerry Logan	.25
(16)	Lenny Lyles	.25
(17)	John Mackey	2.00
(18)	Tom Matte	.50
(19)	Lou Michaels	.35
(20)	Jimmy Orr	.50
(21)	Willie Richardson	.35
(22)	Don Shinnick	.25
(23)	Dan Sullivan	.25
(24)	Johnny Unitas	15.00
(25)	Houston Antwine	.25
(26)	John Bramlett	.25
(27)	Aaron Marsh	.25
(28)	R.C. Gamble	.25
(29)	Gino Cappelletti	.75
(30)	John Charles	.25
(31)	Larry Eisenhauer	.35
(32)	Jon Morris	.25
(33)	Jim Nance	.50
(34)	Len St. Jean	.25
(35)	Mike Taliaferro	.25
(36)	Jim Whalen	.25
(37)	Stew Barber	.35
(38)	Al Bemiller	.25
(39)	George (Butch) Byrd	.35
(40)	Booker Edgerson	.25
(41)	Harry Jacobs	.35
(42)	Jack Kemp	18.00
(43)	Ron McDole	.35
(44)	Joe O'Donnell	.25
(45)	John Pitts	.25
(46)	George Saimes	.35
(47)	Mike Stratton	.35
(48)	O.J. Simpson	35.00
(49)	Ronnie Bull	.35
(50)	Dick Butkus	8.00
(51)	Jim Cadile	.25
(52)	Jack Concannon	.35
(53)	Dick Evey	.25
(54)	Bennie McRae	.25
(55)	Ed O'Bradovich	.25
(56)	Brian Piccolo	10.00
(57)	Mike Pyle	.25
(58)	Gale Sayers	10.00
(59)	Dick Gordon	.35
(60)	Roosevelt Taylor	.35
(61)	Al Beauchamp	.25
(62)	Dave Middendorf	.25
(63)	Harry Gunner	.25
(64)	Bobby Hunt	.25
(65)	Bob Johnson	.40
(66)	Charley King	.25
(67)	Andy Rice	.25
(68)	Paul Robinson	.35
(69)	Bill Staley	.25
(70)	Pat Matson	.25
(71)	Bob Trumpy	2.00
(72)	Sam Wyche	5.00
(73)	Erich Barnes	.35
(74)	Gary Collins	.35
(75)	Ben Davis	.25
(76)	John Demarie	.25
(77)	Gene Hickerson	.35
(78)	Jim Houston	.35
(79)	Ernie Kellerman	.25
(80)	Leroy Kelly	3.00
(81)	Dale Lindsey	.25
(82)	Bill Nelsen	.75
(83)	Jim Kanicki	.25
(84)	Dick Schafrath	.35
(85)	George Andrie	.75
(86)	Mike Clark	.25
(87)	Cornell Green	.50
(88)	Bob Hayes	1.50
(89)	Chuck Howley	.75
(90)	Lee Roy Jordan	1.25
(91)	Bob Lilly	3.00
(92)	Craig Morton	1.00
(93)	John Niland	.25
(94)	Dan Reeves	5.00
(95)	Mel Renfro	1.00
(96)	Lance Rentzel	.50
(97)	Tom Beer	.25
(98)	Billy Van Heusen	.25
(99)	Mike Current	.25
(100)	Al Denson	.25
(101)	Pete Duranko	.25
(102)	George Goeddeke	.25
(103)	John Huard	.25
(104)	Richard Jackson	.25
(105)	Pete Jaquess	.35
(106)	Fran Lynch	.25
(107)	Floyd Little	2.00
(108)	Steve Tensi	.50
(109)	Lem Barney	3.00
(110)	Nick Eddy	.50

(111) Mel Farr .75
(112) Ed Flanagan .25
(113) Larry Hand .25
(114) Alex Karras 2.50
(115) Dick LeBeau .35
(116) Mike Lucci .35
(117) Earl McCullouch .35
(118) Bill Munson .40
(119) Jerry Rush .25
(120) Wayne Walker .35
(121) Herb Adderley 2.00
(122) Donny Anderson .50
(123) Lee Roy Caffey .25
(124) Carroll Dale .35
(125) Willie Davis 1.50
(126) Boyd Dowler .35
(127) Marv Fleming .50
(128) Bob Jeter .35
(129) Henry Jordan .35
(130) Dave Robinson .35
(131) Bart Starr 10.00
(132) Willie Wood 1.50
(133) Pete Beathard .75
(134) Jim Beirne .25
(135) Garland Boyette .25
(136) Woody Campbell .25
(137) Miller Farr .25
(138) Hoyle Granger .25
(139) Mac Haik .25
(140) Ken Houston 3.00
(141) Bobby Maples .35
(142) Alvin Reed .25
(143) Don Trull .35
(144) George Webster .50
(145) Bobby Bell 2.00
(146) Aaron Brown .25
(147) Buck Buchanan 2.00
(148) Len Dawson 5.00
(149) Mike Garrett .50
(150) Robert Holmes .35
(151) Willie Lanier 3.00
(152) Frank Pitts .25
(153) Johnny Robinson .75
(154) Jan Stenerud 3.00
(155) Otis Taylor .75
(156) Jim Tyrer .50
(157) Dick Bass .35
(158) Maxie Baughan .50
(159) Rich Petitbon .50
(160) Roger Brown .35
(161) Roman Gabriel 1.50
(162) Bruce Gossett .25
(163) David (Deacon) Jones 1.50
(164) Tom Mack 1.25
(165) Tommy Mason .50
(166) Ed Meador .35
(167) Merlin Olsen 3.00
(168) Pat Studstill .35
(169) Jack Clancy .25
(170) Maxie Williams .25
(171) Larry Csonka 10.00
(172) Jimmy Warren .25
(173) Norm Evans .35
(174) Rick Norton .25
(175) Bob Griese 7.50
(176) Howard Twilley .50
(177) Billy Neighbors .35
(178) Nick Buoniconti 1.25
(179) Tom Goode .25
(180) Dick Westmoreland .25
(181) Grady Alderman .25
(182) Bill Brown .75
(183) Fred Cox .35
(184) Clint Jones .35
(185) Joe Kapp 1.00
(186) Paul Krause 1.00
(187) Gary Larsen .25
(188) Jim Marshall 1.50
(189) Dave Osborn .25
(190) Alan Page 4.00
191 Mike Tingelhoff .75
(192) Roy Winston .35
(193) Dan Abramowicz .50
(194) Doug Atkins 1.50
(195) Bo Burris .25
(196) John Douglas .25
(197) Don Shy .25
(198) Bill Kilmer .75
(199) Tony Lorick .25
(200) David Parks .50
(201) Dave Rowe .25
(202) Monty Stickles .25
(203) Steve Stonebreaker .25
(204) Del Williams .25
(205) Pete Case .25
(206) Tommy Crutcher .35
(207) Scott Eaton .25
(208) Tucker Frederickson .75
(209) Peter Gogolak .35
(210) Homer Jones .35
(211) Ernie Koy .35
(212) Carl (Spider) Lockhart .35
(213) Bruce Maher .25
(214) Aaron Thomas .35
(215) Fran Tarkenton 12.00
(216) Jim Katcavage .35
(217) Al Atkinson .25
(218) Emerson Boozer .35
(219) John Elliott .25
(220) Dave Herman .25
(221) Winston Hill .35
(222) Jim Hudson .25
(223) Pete Lammons .35
(224) Gerry Philbin .35
(225) George Sauer .50
(226) Joe Namath 20.00
(227) Matt Snell .50
(228) Jim Turner .35
(229) Fred Biletnikoff 3.00
(230) Willie Brown 1.50
(231) Billy Cannon .50
(232) Dan Conners .25
(233) Ben Davidson .75
(234) Hewritt Dixon .35
(235) Daryle Lamonica 1.00
(236) Ike Lassiter .25
(237) Ken McCloughan .25
(238) Jim Otto 1.50
(239) Harry Schuh .25
(240) Gene Upshaw 3.00
(241) Gary Ballman .35
(242) Joe Carollo .25
(243) Dave Lloyd .25
(244) Fred Hill .25
(245) Al Nelson .25
(246) Joe Scarpati .25
(247) Sam Baker .35
(248) Fred Brown .25
(249) Floyd Peters .50
(250) Nate Ramsey .25
(251) Norman Snead .50
(252) Tom Woodeshick .25
(253) John Hilton .25
(254) Kent Nix .25
(255) Paul Martha .50
(256) Ben McGee .25
(257) Andy Russell .50
(258) Dick Shiner .25
(259) J.R. Wilburn .25
(260) Marv Woodson .25
(261) Earl Gros .25
(262) Dick Hoak .50
(263) Roy Jefferson .50
(264) Larry Gagner .25
(265) Johnny Roland .75
(266) Jackie Smith 3.00
(267) Jim Bakken .50
(268) Don Brumm .25
(269) Bob DeMarco .35
(270) Irv Goode .25
(271) Ken Gray .35
(272) Charlie Johnson 1.00
(273) Ernie McMillan .35
(274) Larry Stallings .35
(275) Jerry Stovall .50
(276) Larry Wilson 1.50
(277) Chuck Allen .25
(278) Lance Alworth 3.00
(279) Kenny Graham .25
(280) Steve DeLong .35
(281) Willie Frazier .35
(282) Gary Garrison .35
(283) Sam Gruniesen .25
(284) John Hadl .75
(285) Brad Hubbert .25
(286) Ron Mix 2.00
(287) Dick Post .35
(288) Walt Sweeney .35
(289) Kermit Alexander .50
(290) Ed Beard .25
(291) Bruce Bosley .35
(292) John Brodie 3.00
(293) Stan Hindman .25
(294) Jim Johnson 1.50
(295) Charlie Krueger .35
(296) Clifton McNeil .35
(297) Gary Lewis .25
(298) Howard Mudd .25
(299) Dave Wilcox .50
(300) Ken Willard .50
(301) Charlie Gogolak .35
(302) Len Hauss .50
(303) Sonny Jurgensen 3.50
(304) Carl Kammerer .25
(305) Walt Rock .25
(306) Ray Schoenke .25
(307) Chris Hanburger .75
(308) Tom Brown .50
(309) Sam Huff 2.00
(310) Bob Long .25
(311) Vince Promuto .25
(312) Pat Richter .50

1989 Goal Line Hall of Fame

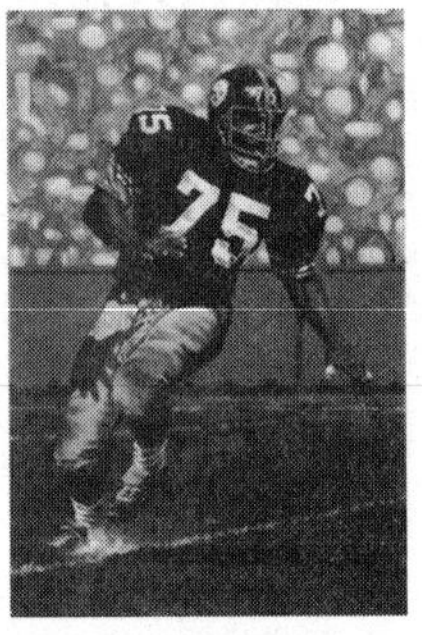

These postcard-size cards (4" x 6") feature full-color action paintings of inductees into the Pro Football Hall of Fame. The cards were part of an art series done by artist Gary Thomas and were offered by subscription. Each set was packaged in a custom box and was given a serial number (Set No. x of 5,000), which appears on each card, too. The border of the card is white and uses black ink. The player's name, college, position, biographical information, years he played, teams he played with and the year he was inducted are all listed, as well as a set and card number. A Football Hall of Fame logo is also given. Each of the first five series contains 30 cards; series 6 has 25. However, a card for Johnny Unitas (#174) was never issued. Series I was issued in 1989; a new series has followed each year since then. The cards are numbered alphabetically within each series.

		MT
	Complete Set (175):	400.00
	Common Player:	2.00
1	Lance Alworth	6.00
2	Morris (Red) Badgro	2.50
3	Cliff Battles	2.50
4	Mel Blount	2.50
5	Terry Bradshaw	10.00
6	Jim Brown	12.00
7	George Connor	2.50
8	Turk Edwards	2.50
9	Tom Fears	2.50
10	Frank Gifford	10.00
11	Otto Graham	6.00
12	Red Grange	5.00
13	George Halas	4.00
14	Clarke Hinkle	2.50
15	Robert (Cal) Hubbard	2.50
16	Sam Huff	2.50
17	Frank (Bruiser) Kinard	2.50
18	Dick "Night Train" Lane	2.50
19	Sid Luckman	6.00
20	Bobby Mitchell	2.50
21	Merlin Olsen	4.00
22	Jim Parker	2.50
23	Joe Perry	3.00
24	Pete Rozelle	3.00
25	Art Shell	3.00
26	Fran Tarkenton	9.00
27	Jim Thorpe	6.00
28	Paul Warfield	3.00
29	Larry Wilson	2.50
30	Willie Wood	2.50
31	Doug Atkins	2.00
32	Bobby Bell	2.00
33	Raymond Berry	3.00
34	Paul Brown	2.00
35	Guy Chamberlin	2.00
36	Earl "Dutch" Clark	2.00
37	Jimmy Conzelman	2.00
38	Len Dawson	3.00
39	Mike Ditka	8.00
40	Dan Fortmann	2.00
41	Frank Gatski	2.00
42	Bill George	2.00
43	Elroy Hirsch	3.00
44	Paul Hornung	4.00
45	John Henry Johnson	2.00
46	Walt Kiesling	2.00
47	Yale Lary	2.00
48	Bobby Layne	3.00
49	Tuffy Leemans	2.00
50	Geo. Preston Marshall	2.00
51	George McAfee	2.00
52	Wayne Millner	2.00
53	Bronko Nagurski	4.00
54	Joe Namath	12.00
55	Ray Nitschke	3.00
56	Jim Ringo	2.00
57	Art Rooney	2.00
58	Joe Stydahar	2.00
59	Charley Taylor	2.00
60	Charlie Trippi	2.00
61	Fred Biletnikoff	3.00
62	Buck Buchanan	2.00
63	Dick Butkus	6.00
64	Earl Campbell	8.00
65	Tony Canadeo	2.00
66	Art Donovan	3.00
67	Ray Flaherty	2.00
68	Forrest Gregg	2.50
69	Lou Groza	3.00
70	John Hannah	2.00
71	Don Hutson	2.50
72	David (Deacon) Jones	2.00
73	Stan Jones	2.00
74	Sonny Jurgensen	3.00
75	Vince Lombardi	3.00
76	Tim Mara	2.00
77	Ollie Matson	2.00
78	Mike McCormack	2.00
79	John (Blood) McNally	2.00
80	Marion Motley	2.00
81	George Musso	2.00
82	Earle (Greasy) Neale	2.00
83	Clarence (Ace) Parker	2.00
84	Pete Pihos	2.00
85	Tex Schramm	2.00
86	Roger Staubach	12.00
87	Jan Stenerud	2.00
88	Y.A. Tittle	3.00
89	Clyde "Bulldog" Turner	2.00
90	Steve Van Buren	2.00
91	Herb Adderley	2.00
92	Lem Barney	2.00
93	Sammy Baugh	5.00
94	Chuck Bednarik	3.00
95	Charles W. Bidwill	2.00
96	Willie Brown	2.00
97	Al Davis	4.00
98	Bill Dudley	2.00
99	Weeb Ewbank	2.00
100	Len Ford	2.00
101	Sid Gillman	2.00
102	Jack Ham	2.00
103	Mel Hein	2.00
104	Bill Hewitt	2.00
105	Dante Lavelli	2.00
106	Bob Lilly	3.00
107	John Mackey	2.00
108	Hugh McElhenny	3.00
109	Mike Michalske	2.00
110	Ron Mix	2.00
111	Leo Nomenllini	2.00
112	Steve Owen	2.00
113	Alan Page	2.50
114	Dan Reeves	2.00
115	John Riggins	3.00
116	Gale Sayers	6.00
117	Ken Strong	2.00
118	Gene Upshaw	3.00
119	Norm Van Brocklin	4.00
120	Alex Wojciechowicz	2.00
121	Bert Bell	2.00
122	George Blanda	4.00
123	Joe Carr	2.00
124	Larry Csonka	4.00
125	John (Paddy) Driscoll	2.00
126	Dan Fouts	3.00
127	Bob Griese	4.00
128	Ed Healy	2.00
129	Wilbur (Fats) Henry	2.00
130	Ken Houston	2.00
131	Lamar Hunt	2.00
132	Jack Lambert	2.50
133	Tom Landry	4.00
134	Willie Lanier	2.00
135	Larry Little	2.00
136	Don Maynard	3.00
137	Lenny Moore	3.00
138	Chuck Noll	3.00
139	Jim Otto	2.00
140	Walter Payton	10.00
141	Hugh (Shorty) Ray	2.00
142	Andy Robustelli	2.00
143	Bob St. Clair	2.00
144	Joe Schmidt	3.00
145	Jim Taylor	3.00
146	Doak Walker	3.00
147	Bill Walsh	3.00
148	Bob Waterfield	3.00
149	Arnie Weinmeister	2.00
150	Bill Willis	2.00
151	Roosevelt Brown	2.00
152	Jack Christiansen	2.00
153	Willie Davis	3.00
154	Tony Dorsett	6.00
155	Bud Grant	2.00
156	Joe Greene	5.00
157	Joe Guyon	2.00
158	Franco Harris	4.00
159	Ted Hendricks	2.00
160	Arnie Herber	2.00
161	Jimmy Johnson	2.00
162	Leroy Kelly	2.00
163	Curly Lambeau	2.00
164	Jim Langer	2.00
165	Link Lyman	2.00
166	Gino Marchetti	3.00
167	Ernie Nevers	3.00
168	O.J. Simpson	12.00
169	Jackie Smith	2.00
170	Bart Starr	6.00
171	Ernie Stautner	2.50
172	George Trafton	2.00
173	Emlen Tunnell	2.00
174	Johnny Unitas (not issued)	
175	Randy White	2.00
176	Jim Finks	2.00
177	Henry Jordan	2.00
178	Steve Largent	4.00
179	Lee Roy Selmon	2.00
180	Kellen Winslow	2.00

1939 Gridiron Greats Blotters

The 12-card, 3-7/8" x 9" blotter set was sponsored by Louis F. Dow Company. The blotter card fronts feature a headshot on the left side, superimposed over a football, with the collegiate player's school letter appearing in a pennant below. The right side of the card blotters feature a player profile and a monthly calendar, as each of the 12 blotter cards have a different month. The backs are blank. The cards are numbered with the "B" prefix.

		NM
	Complete Set (12):	3500.
	Common Player:	150.00
3941	Jim Thorpe	700.00
3942	Walter Eckersall	150.00
3943	Edward Mahan	150.00
3944	Sammy Baugh	550.00
3945	Thomas Shevlin	150.00
3946	Red Grange	600.00
3947	Ernie Nevers	325.00
3948	George Gipp	525.00
3949	Pudge Heffelfinger	150.00
3950	Bronko Nagurski	600.00
3951	Willie Heston	150.00
3952	Jay Berwanger	150.00

1992 Gridiron Promos

The four-card, standard-size promo set was issued to show the design of the 1992 regular set. The cards are similar in design to the base set and each card has a "P" prefix.

		MT
	Complete Set (4):	5.00
	Common Player:	.50
1	Siran Stacy	.50
2	Casey Weldon	.75
3	Mike Saunders	.50
4	Jeff Blake	5.00

1992 Gridiron

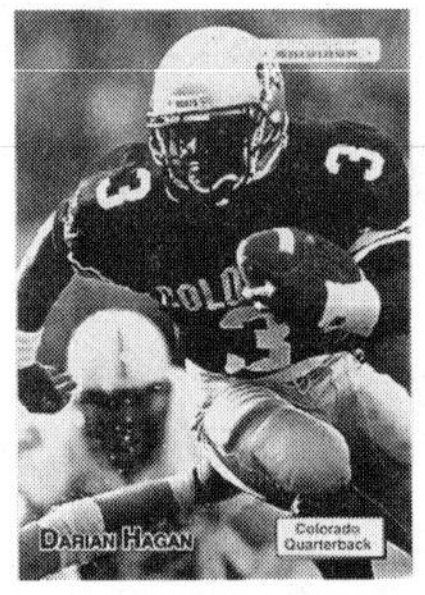

The 110-card, standard-size set, produced by Lafayette Sportscard Corporation, features the top players and coaches from the top 25 college teams. Three players and one coach represent each team. Production was limited to 50,000 sets. The card fronts feature a glossy color action shot while the back contains bio and stat information.

		MT
	Complete Set (110):	25.00
	Common Player:	.10
1	Robert Perez	.20
2	Jason Jones	.10
3	Jason Christ	.10
4	Fisher DeBerry (CO)	.20
5	Danny Woodson	.10
6	Siran Stacy	.20
7	Robert Stewart	.10
8	Gene Stallings (CO)	.75
9	Santana Dotson	.50
10	Curtis Hafford	.10
11	John Turnpaugh	.10
12	Grant Teaff (CO)	.30
13B	Desmond Howard	.50
14	Brian Treggs	.10
15	Troy Auzenne	.20
16	Bruce Snyder (CO)	.10
17	DeChane Cameron	.10
18	Levon Kirkland	.35
19	*Ed McDaniel*	.25
20	Ken Hatfield (CO)	.25
21	Darian Hagan	.20
22	Rico Smith	.20
23	Joel Steed	.20
24	Bill McCartney (CO)	.75
25	Jeff Blake	4.00
26	David Daniels	.10
27	Robert Jones	.20
28	Bill Lewis (CO)	.20
29	Tim Paulk	.10
30	Arden Czyzewski	.10
31	Cal Dixon	.10
32	Steve Spurrier (CO)	2.00
33B	Desmond Howard	.50
34	Casey Weldon	.35
35	Kirk Carruthers	.10
36	Bobby Bowden (CO)	2.00
37	Mark Barsotti	.10
38	Kelvin Means	.10
39	Marquez Pope	.20
40	Jim Sweeney (CO)	.25
41	Kameno Bell	.10
42	Elbert Turner	.10
43	Marlin Primous	.10
44	John Mackovic (CO)	.50
45	Matt Rodgers	.20
46	Mike Saunders	.20
47	John Derby	.10
48	Hayden Fry (CO)	.75
49	Carlos Huerta	.20
50	Leon Searcy	.20
51	Claude Jones	.10
52	Dennis Erickson (CO)	.75
53	Erick Anderson	.10
54	J.D. Carlson	.10
55	Greg Skrepenak	.35
56	Gary Moeller	.20
57	Keithen McCant	.20
58	Nate Turner	.10
59	Pat Englebert	.10
60	Tom Osborne (CO)	2.00
61	Charles Davenport	.10
62	Mark Thomas	.10
63	Clyde Hawley	.10
64	Dick Sheridan (CO)	.20
65	Derek Brown (TE)	.20
66	Rodney Culver	.20
67	Tony Smith	.20
68	Lou Holtz (CO)	2.00
69	Kent Graham	.35
70	Scottie Graham	1.25
71	John Kacherski	.10
72	John Cooper (CO)	.50
73	Mike Gaddis	.20
74	Joe Bowden	.20
75	Mike McKinley	.10
76	Gary Gibbs (CO)	.20
77	Sam Gash	.20
78	Keith Goganious	.20
79	Darren Perry	.35
80	Joe Paterno (CO)	3.00
81	Steve Israel	.20
82	Eric Seaman	.10
83	Glen Deveaux	.10
84	Paul Hackett (CO)	.35
85	Tommy Vardell	.35
86	Chris Walsh	.10
87	Jason Palumbis	.10
88	Dennis Green (CO)	.75
89	Andy Kelly	.10
90	Dale Carter	.75
91	Shon Walker	.10
92	Johnny Majors	.50
93	Bucky Richardson	.20
94	Quentin Coryatt	1.25
95	Kevin Smith	.75
96	R.C. Slocum (CO)	.75
97	Ed Cunningham	.20
98	Mario Bailey	.20
99	Donald Jones	.10
100	Don James (CO)	.75
101	Vaughn Dunbar	.35
102	Reggie Yarbrough	.10
103	Matt Blundin	.35
104	Tony Sands	.10
105B	Desmond Howard	.50
106	Ty Detmer	.50
107B	Desmond Howard	.50
NNO	Mario Bates CL, Jeff Blake	1.00
NNO	Mike Gaddis CL, Tommy Vardell	.20
NNO	Title Card	.10

1991 GTE Super Bowl Theme Art

The 25-card, 4-5/8" x 6" set was distributed by GTE in correlation with the 25th anniversary of the Super Bowl. The card fronts feature the Super Bowl program art while the backs contain game summaries and a GTE Telefact.

		MT
	Complete Set (25):	5.00
	Common Player:	.30
1	Super Bowl I	.50
2	Super Bowl II	.30
3	Super Bowl III	.30
4	Super Bowl IV	.30
5	Super Bowl V	.30
6	Super Bowl VI	.30
7	Super Bowl VII	.30
8	Super Bowl VIII	.30
9	Super Bowl IX	.30
10	Super Bowl X	.30
11	Super Bowl XI	.30
12	Super Bowl XII	.30
13	Super Bowl XIII	.30
14	Super Bowl XIV	.30
15	Suepr Bowl XV	.30
16	Super Bowl XVI	.30
17	Super Bowl XVII	.30
18	Super Bowl XVIII	.30
19	Super Bowl XIX	.30
20	Super Bowl XX	.30
21	Super Bowl XXI	.30
22	Super Bowl XXII	.30
23	Super Bowl XXIII	.30
24	Super Bowl XXIV	.30
25	Super Bowl XXV	.30

Post-1980 cards in Near Mint condition will generally sell for about 75% of the quoted Mint value. Excellent-condition cards bring no more than 40%.

H

1990 Hall of Fame Stickers

These 80 stickers feature members of the Pro Football Hall of Fame. Each sticker measures 1-7/8" x 2-1/8" and was created for inclusion in a book titled "The Official Pro Football Hall of Fame Fun and Fact Sticker Book." Artist Mark Rucker did the original artwork which appears on each sticker. The player's name, position and sticker number are given on the front.

		MT
	Complete Set (80):	12.00
	Common Player:	.15
1	Wilbur Henry	.20
2	George Trafton	.15
3	Mike Michalske	.15
4	Turk Edwards	.15
5	Bill Hewitt	.20
6	Mel Hein	.15
7	Joe Stydahar	.15
8	Dan Fortmann	.15
9	Alex Wojciechowicz	.15
10	George Connor	.20
11	Jim Thorpe	.75
12	Ernie Nevers	.35
13	John McNally	.25
14	Ken Strong	.15
15	Bronko Nagurski	.50
16	Clarke Hinkle	.15
17	Ace Parker	.15
18	Billy Dudley	.20
19	Don Hutson	.30
20	Dante Lavelli	.15
21	Elroy Hirsch	.25
22	Raymond Berry	.25
23	Bobby Mitchell	.15
24	Don Maynard	.25
25	Mike Ditka	.50
26	Lance Alworth	.25
27	Charley Taylor	.15
28	Paul Warfield	.30
29	Lou Groza	.35
30	Art Donovan	.25
31	Leo Nomellini	.15
32	Andy Robustelli	.20
33	Gino Marchetti	.15
34	Forrest Gregg	.15
35	Jim Otto	.20
36	Ron Mix	.15
37	Deacon Jones	.15
38	Bob Lilly	.25
39	Merlin Olsen	.25
40	Alan Page	.20
41	Joe Greene	.25
42	Art Shell	.25
43	Sammy Baugh	.35
44	Sid Luckman	.45
45	Bob Waterfield	.40
46	Bobby Layne	.25
47	Norm Van Brocklin	.25
48	Y.A. Tittle	.25
49	Johnny Unitas	.50
50	Bart Starr	.35
51	Sonny Jurgensen	.25
52	Joe Namath	.75
53	Roger Staubach	.75
54	Terry Bradshaw	.50
55	Steve Van Buren	.25
56	Marion Motley	.25
57	Joe Perry	.25
58	Hugh McElhenny	.25
59	Frank Gifford	.50
60	Jim Brown	1.00
61	Jim Taylor	.25
62	Gale Sayers	.35
63	Larry Csonka	.25
64	Emlen Tunnell	.15
65	Jack Christiansen	.15
66	Dick "Night Train" Lane	.15
67	Sam Huff	.25
68	Ray Nitschke	.15
69	Larry Wilson	.15
70	Willie Wood	.20
71	Bobby Bell	.15
72	Willie Brown	.20
73	Dick Butkus	.35
74	Jack Ham	.15
75	George Halas	.25
76	Steve Owen	.15
77	Art Rooney	.20
78	Bert Bell	.15
79	Paul Brown	.15
80	Pete Rozelle	.20

1993 Heads and Tails SB XXVII

The 25-card, regular-sized set, produced by Heads and Tails Inc., honored players from Super Bowl XXVII (Dallas vs. Buffalo), as well as past Super Bowl stars and current Pro Bowl players. The card fronts feature the player's name printed down one side with a silver foil "Rose Bowl" emblem along the bottom border. The card backs feature a filled Rose Bowl with Cowboys and Bills air-brushed end zones and player highlights. Gold-foil versions were randomly inserted (10,000) in the entire run (200,000).

		MT
	Complete Set (25):	10.00
	Common Player:	.25
1	Title Card CL	.25

2	Lawrence Taylor, Mike Singletary	.50
3	Dennis Byrd	.25
4	Junior Seau	.50
5	Steve Young	1.00
6	Sterling Sharpe	.50
7	Cortez Kennedy	.25
8	Terry Bradshaw	.75
9	Fred Biletnikoff	.25
10	John Riggins	.25
11	Phil Simms	.25
12	Cornelius Bennett	.50
13	Jim Kelly	.75
14	Bruce Smith	.50
15	Andre Reed	.50
16	Keith McKeller	.25
17	James Lofton	.25
18	Thurman Thomas	.75
19	Emmitt Smith	3.00
20	Kelvin Martin	.25
21	Troy Aikman	1.50
22	Charles Haley	.25
23	Alvin Harper	.25
24	Michael Irvin	.50
25	Jay Novacek	.25

1991 Heisman Collection I

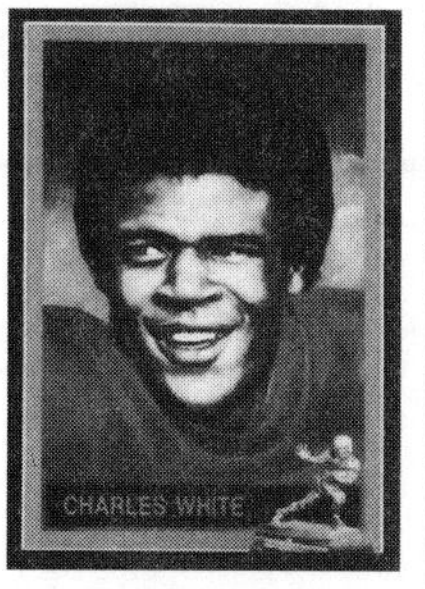
CHARLES WHITE

The 20-card, regular-sized set, produced by College Classics in association with The Downtown Athletic Club of New York, features 20 Heisman winners in skip-numbered order (based on chronological order). The card fronts feature a color posed shot of the player with a Heisman trophy in the lower right corner. The card back informs collectors of the year the player won the award, player summary and a larger Heisman Trophy image. The production total was 100,000 sets and each case (1,000 sets) contained two player autograph cards. The set also had a serially numbered header card and a sample Bo Jackson card was also distributed.

		MT
Complete Set (21):		5.00
Common Player:		.15
1	Jay Berwanger	.15
6	Tom Harmon	.25
9	Angelo Bertelli	.15
11	Doc Blanchard	.25
13	John Lujack	.25
15	Leon Hart	.25
16	Vic Janowicz	.25
19	John Lattner	.25
23	John David Crow	.15
26	Joe Bellino	.15
30	John Huarte	.15
32	Steve Spurrier	1.00
36	Jim Plunkett	.40
40	Archie Griffin	.25
42	Tony Dorsett	1.00
43	Earl Campbell	1.00
45	Charles White	.15
48	Herschel Walker	.50
51	Bo Jackson	1.00
53	Tim Brown	.40
NNO	Title Card	.15
SAM	Bo Jackson (Sample Promo)	3.00

1992 Heisman Collection II

The 20-card, standard-size set is a continuation of the 1991 Hesiman Collection set, as the set is skip-numbered in chronological order. The card fronts and backs are identical in design with the 1991 set. As with the previous set, 100,000 sets were produced by College Classics and each set comes with a serially numbered header card. Sample cards of Barry Sanders and Roger Staubach were also available in 3-1/2" x 7-1/2" strips.

		MT
Complete Set (21):		10.00
Common Player:		.50
2	Larry Kelley	.50
3	Clint Frank	.50
5	Niles Kinnick	.75
7	Bruce Smith	.50
10	Les Horvath	.50
14	Doak Walker	.75
17	Dick Kazmaier	.50
20	Alan Ameche	.50
21	Howard Cassady	.50
25	Billy Cannon	.75
27	Ernie Davis	1.75
29	Roger Staubach	2.00
31	Mike Garrett	.50
35	Steve Owens	.50
38	Johnny Rodgers	.75
39	John Cappelletti	.50
44	Billy Sims	.75
50	Doug Flutie	1.50
52	Vinny Testaverde	.50
54	Barry Sanders	2.50
NNO	Title Card	.50
SAM	Barry Sanders (Sample Promo)	10.00
SAM	Roger Staubach (Sample Promo)	12.00

1970 Hi-C Posters

These posters were featured on the insides of Hi-C drink can labels. The featured players were statistical leaders at their positions during the 1969 season. Each poster measures 6-5/8" x 13-3/4" and is numbered below the player photo.

		NM
Complete Set (10):		700.00
Common Player:		75.00
(1)	Greg Cook	80.00
(2)	Fred Cox	75.00
(3)	Sonny Jurgensen	125.00
(4)	David Lee	75.00
(5)	Dennis Partee	75.00
(6)	Dick Post	75.00
(7)	Mel Renfro	90.00
(8)	Gale Sayers	175.00
(9)	Emmitt Thomas	80.00
(10)	Jim Turner	75.00

1991 Homers

In 1991, boxes of QB's Cookies contained one of six different cards featuring Hall of Fame football players. Each standard-size card has a sepia-toned photograph on the front, with a bronze frame. The player's name is in a bronze panel in the lower left. The numbered back has a checklist for the set, plus information about the player's accomplishments, biographical information and the year he was inducted into the Hall of Fame. The set was sponsored by Legend Food Products.

		MT
Complete Set (6):		10.00
Common Player:		1.00
1	Vince Lombardi	2.00
2	Hugh McElhenny	2.00
3	Elroy Hirsch	2.00
4	Jim Thorpe	4.00
5	Dick Lane	1.00
6	Bart Starr	3.00

I

2000 Impact

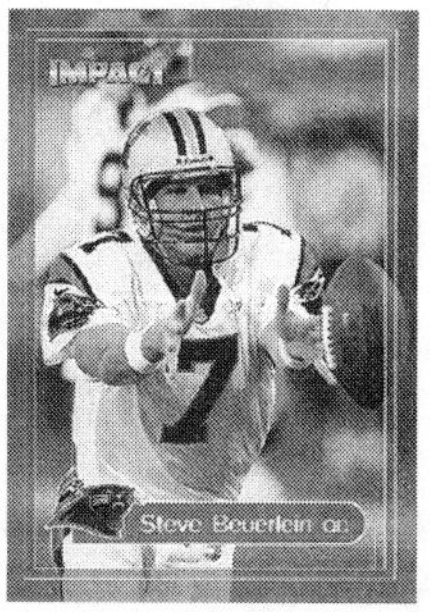
IMPACT
Steve Beuerlein

		MT
Complete Set (199):		25.00
Common Player:		.10
Minor Stars:		.20
Common Rookie:		.30
Card #137 Never Issued		
Pack (10):		1.00
Wax Box (36):		26.00
1	Kurt Warner	2.00
2	Dan Marino	1.50
3	Sedrick Irvin	.20
4	*Chris Redman*	1.00
5	Robert Smith	.30
6	Amani Toomer	.10
7	Richard Huntley	.10
8	Ahman Green	.20
9	Fred Lane	.10
10	Eddie George	.50
11	Raghib Ismail	.10
12	Shannon Sharpe	.20
13	Shawn Jefferson	.10
14	*Michael Wiley*	.75
15	Jeff Graham	.10
16	Steve Beuerlein	.20
17	Tim Biakabutuka	.20
18	Chris Watson	.10
19	Kevin Faulk	.20
20	Emmitt Smith	1.50
21	*Plaxico Burress*	1.75
22	Hines Ward	.20
23	Jacquez Green	.20
24	Doug Flutie	.50
25	Leslie Shepherd	.10
26	Johnnie Morton	.20
27	*Tom Brady*	1.00
28	Jeff George	.20
29	Derrick Mason	.10
30	Marshall Faulk	.50
31	Derrick Mayes	.20
32	Jerome Bettis	.30
33	Adrian Murrell	.20
34	Curtis Enis	.30
35	Kimble Anders	.10
36	*Travis Prentice*	.75
37	Curtis Martin	.30
38	*Ronnie Powell*	.30
39	Steve Christie	.10
40	Brett Favre	1.75
41	Michael Bates	.10
42	*Rondell Mealey*	.50
43	Randall Cunningham	.30
44	Kerry Collins	.20
45	William Thomas	.20
46	Ricky Watters	.30
47	Marvin Harrison	.50
48	Corey Bradford	.20
49	Terry Kirby	.10
50	Troy Aikman	1.25
51	Cris Carter	.50
52	*Jamal Lewis*	2.00
53	Duce Staley	.30
54	Isaac Bruce	.50
55	Yancey Thigpen	.20
56	*R. Jay Soward*	1.00
57	Jermaine Lewis	.20
58	Zach Thomas	.20
59	*Sylvester Morris*	1.25
60	Steve McNair	.50
61	Tiki Barber	.20
62	Torrance Small	.10
63	Champ Bailey	.20
64	Tim Dwight	.30
65	Willie Jackson	.20
66	Edgerrin James	1.75
67	*Ron Dayne*	3.00
68	Rich Gannon	.20
69	Junior Seau	.20
70	Warren Sapp	.20
71	Rob Johnson	.20
72	Antonio Freeman	.50
73	O.J. McDuffie	.20
74	Tamarick Vanover	.10
75	*Courtney Brown*	1.25
76	Donovan McNabb	.75
77	Az-Zahir Hakim	.20
78	Albert Connell	.20
79	Qadry Ismail	.20
80	Terrell Davis	1.50
81	Dorsey Levens	.10
82	Tony Martin	.50
83	*Laveranues Coles*	.10
84	Karim Abdul	.20
85	Charles Johnson	.10
86	Torry Holt	.50
87	Stephen Davis	.20
88	Tony Banks	.20
89	Akili Smith	.50
90	Tim Couch	1.00
91	Bill Schroeder	.10
92	Andre Hastings	.10
93	Eddie Kennison	.10
94	Randy Moss	1.75
95	Tony Horne	.10
96	*Sherrod Gideon*	.30
97	Wesley Walls	.20
98	Brian Griese	.50
99	*Jake Delhomme*	1.50
100	Peyton Manning	1.50
101	Brad Johnson	.50
102	*Trung Canidate*	.50
103	Freddie Jones	.10
104	Muhsin Muhammad	.20
105	Eric Moulds	.50
106	Ed McCaffrey	.30
107	Joe Montgomery	.10
108	Olandis Gary	.50
109	J.J. Stokes	.20
110	Ricky Williams	1.00
111	Jim Harbaugh	.20
112	Mike Alstott	.50
113	Errict Rhett	.20
114	Terance Mathis	.10
115	Kevin Johnson	.50
116	Tremain Mack	.10
117	*Peter Warrick*	3.00
118	Lamont Warren	.10
119	Damon Huard	.30
120	Cade McNown	.75
121	Natrone Means	.20
122	Ken Oxendine	.10
123	*J.R. Redmond*	1.00
124	Ken Dilger	.10
125	J.J. Johnson	.20
126	Napoleon Kaufman	.30
127	Ryan Leaf	.30
128	Michael Westbrook	.20
129	Mario Bates	.10
130	Jake Plummer	.75
131	James Jett	.10
132	Darnay Scott	.20
133	Curtis Conway	.20
134	Fred Taylor	.75
135	Wayne Chrebet	.30
136	Sean Dawkins	.10
138	Keenan McCardell	.20
139	Donnell Bennett	.10
140	Jerry Rice	1.25
141	Vinny Testaverde	.30
142	*Chad Pennington*	2.50
143	Jonathon Linton	.10
144	Herman Moore	.30
145	David Patten	.10
146	Troy Edwards	.50
147	Jon Kitna	.50
148	Jimmy Smith	.30
149	*Tee Martin*	1.00
150	Jevon Kearse	.50
151	Frank Sanders	.20
152	Marcus Robinson	.50
153	Mike Hollis	.10
154	Frank Wycheck	.10
155	*Tim Rattay*	.75
156	Dedric Ward	.10
157	Terrell Owens	.50
158	Chris Chandler	.20
159	Damon Griffin	.10
160	Mike Vanderjagt	.10
161	Elvis Grbac	.20
162	Rickey Dudley	.20
163	Jeff Garcia	.20
164	*Thomas Jones*	2.00
165	Tyrone Wheatley	.20
166	Rod Smith	.30
167	*Bubba Franks*	.75
168	Chris Warren	.20
169	*Anthony Lucas*	.50
170	Terry Glenn	.50
171	John Carney	.10
172	Warrick Dunn	.50
173	*Shaun Alexander*	1.50
174	David Boston	.50
175	Bobby Engram	.10
176	*Travis Taylor*	1.25
177	Derrick Alexander	.10
178	Keyshawn Johnson	.50
179	Steve Young	.75
180	Deion Sanders	.50
181	Charlie Batch	.50
182	Drew Bledsoe	.75
183	*Reuben Droughns*	.75
184	Ray Lucas	.50
185	Shaun King	.75
186	Jamal Anderson	.20
187	Corey Dillon	.20
188	*Joe Hamilton*	.75
189	Terrence Wilkins	.20
190	Mark Brunell	.75
191	Tony Gonzalez	.20
192	Tim Brown	.30
193	Charlie Garner	.20
194	Antowain Smith	.30
195	David LaFleur	.10
196	Germane Crowell	.20
197	Terry Allen	.20
198	Marc Bulger	.20
199	Kevin Dyson	.20
200	Kordell Stewart	.20

2000 Impact Hat's Off

		MT
Common Player:		25.00
Inserted 1:720		
1	Karim Abdul	25.00
2	Jamal Anderson	50.00
3	David Boston	35.00
4	Isaac Bruce	50.00
5	Chris Chandler	25.00
6	Curtis Conway	25.00
7	Tim Couch	85.00
8	Tim Dwight	35.00
9	Curtis Enis	35.00
10	Marshall Faulk	60.00
11	Az-Zahir Hakim	25.00
12	Torry Holt	40.00
13	Kevin Johnson	50.00
14	Terry Kirby	25.00
15	Terance Mathis	25.00
16	Shane Matthews	25.00
17	Cade McNown	75.00
18	Rob Moore	25.00
19	Jake Plummer	60.00
20	Marcus Robinson	60.00
21	Frank Sanders	25.00

2000 Impact Point of Impact

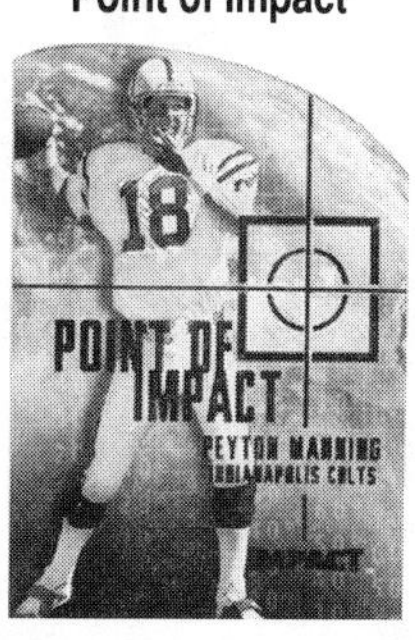
POINT OF IMPACT
PEYTON MANNING
INDIANAPOLIS COLTS
IMPACT

		MT
Complete Set (10):		30.00
Common Player:		1.50
Inserted 1:30		
PI1	Peyton Manning	6.00
PI2	Edgerrin James	8.00
PI3	Brett Favre	8.00
PI4	Marshall Faulk	1.50
PI5	Fred Taylor	3.00
PI6	Tim Couch	4.00
PI7	Emmitt Smith	6.00
PI8	Eddie George	3.00
PI9	Randy Moss	8.00
PI10	Terrell Davis	6.00

2000 Impact Rewind '99

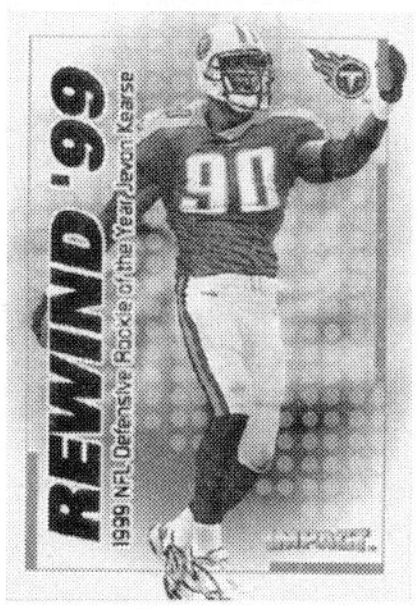
REWIND '99
1999 NFL Defensive Rookie of the Year Jevon Kearse
IMPACT

		MT
Complete Set (40):		15.00
Common Player:		.15
Minor Stars:		.30
Inserted 1:1		
1	Jake Plummer	.50
2	Tim Dwight	.30
3	Tony Banks	.15
4	Doug Flutie	.50
5	Tim Biakabutuka	.15
6	Marcus Robinson	.50
7	Corey Dillon	.50
8	Tim Couch	1.00
9	Troy Aikman	1.25
10	Olandis Gary	.50
11	Germane Crowell	.15
12	Brett Favre	2.00
13	Peyton Manning	1.50
14	Mark Brunell	.75
15	Tony Gonzalez	.30
16	Dan Marino	1.50
17	Randy Moss	2.00
18	Drew Bledsoe	.75
19	Ricky Williams	1.00
20	Amani Toomer	.15
21	Keyshawn Johnson	.50
22	Rich Gannon	.15
23	Duce Staley	.30
24	Jerome Bettis	.30
25	Kenny Bynum	.15
26	Charlie Garner	.30
27	Jon Kitna	.50
28	Kurt Warner	2.50
29	Mike Alstott	.50
30	Eddie George	.50
31	Stephen Davis	.50
32	Kurt Warner	2.50
33	Edgerrin James	1.50
34	Jevon Kearse	.50
35	Marshall Faulk	.50
36	Edgerrin James	1.50
37	Marvin Harrison	.50
38	Jimmy Smith	.30
39	Steve Beuerlein	.15
40	Kurt Warner	2.50

2000 Impact Tattoos

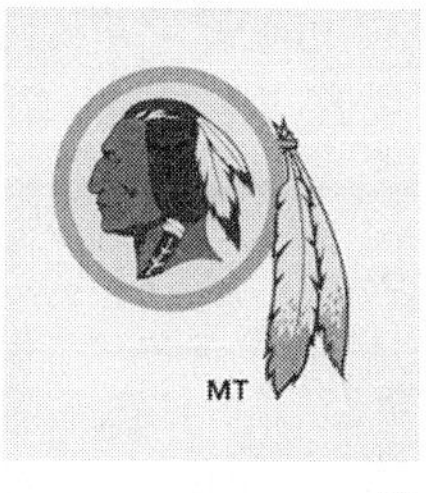
MT

		MT
Complete Set (31):		15.00
Common Tattoo:		.50
Inserted 1:4		

1992-93 Intimidator Bio Sheets

The 36-card, 8-1/2" x 11" set features color action shots on the glossy card fronts with the player's name printed in gold foil down the right side, along wih his team name and uniform number. The card backs contain college and pro summaries, as well as biographical information.

		MT
Complete Set (36):		65.00
Common Player:		1.00
1	Troy Aikman	8.00
2	Jerry Ball	1.00
3	Cornelius Bennett	1.00
4	Earnest Byner	1.00
5	Randall Cunningham	1.00
6	Chris Doleman	1.00
7	John Elway	5.00
8	Jim Everett	1.00
9	Michael Irvin	2.50
10	Jim Kelly	2.50
11	James Lofton	1.00
12	Howie Long	1.50
13	Ronnie Lott	1.50
14	Nick Lowery	1.00
15	Charles Mann	1.00
16	Dan Marino	12.00
17	Art Monk	1.50
18	Joe Montana	8.00
19	Warren Moon	2.50
20	Christian Okoye	1.00
21	Leslie O'Neal	1.00
22	Andre Reed	2.50
23	Jerry Rice	8.00
24	Andre Rison	2.50
25	Deion Sanders	5.00
26	Junior Seau	2.50
27	Mike Singletary	1.50
28	Bruce Smith	2.50
29	Emmitt Smith	12.00
30	Neil Smith	2.50
31	Pat Swilling	1.00
32	Lawrence Taylor	2.50
33	Broderick Thomas	1.00
34	Derrick Thomas	2.50
35	Thurman Thomas	2.50
36	Lorenzo White	1.00

1984 Invaders Smokey

The five-card, 5" x 7" set featured four players and Smokey The Bear in a forestry promotion set. The card fronts feature a posed player shot with Smokey, as well as the player's signature. The card backs contain bio information. Notable in the set is future NFL linebacker Gary Plummer, who went on to play with San Diego and San Francisco.

		MT
Complete Set (5):		65.00
Common Player:		10.00
1	Dupre Marshall	10.00
2	Gary Plummer	20.00
3	David Shaw	10.00
4	Kevin Shea	10.00
5	Smokey Bear (With players above)	10.00

A player's name in *italic type* indicates a rookie card.

J

1986 Jeno's Pizza

Two players from each of the 28 NFL teams were selected for this 58-card set offered by Jeno's Pizza. Specially- marked Jeno's Pizza boxes each contained one card inside, sealed in plastic. Current and former stars are represented in the set. Each card back has a number which corresponds to the location in a Terry Bradshaw Action Play Book which was created to display the cards. The Play Book was available through a mail-in coupon. Each card back also has a summary of the player's career accomplishments.

		MT
Complete Set (56):		25.00
Common Player:		.40
1	Duane Thomas	.75
2	Butch Johnson	.40
3	Andy Headen	.40
4	Joe Morris	.60
5	Wilbert Montgomery	.50
6	Harold Carmichael	.75
7	Ottis Anderson	.60
8	Roy Green	.50
9	Mark Murphy	.40
10	Joe Theismann	1.50
11	Jim McMahon	1.00
12	Walter Payton	3.00
13	Billy Sims	.75
14	James Jones	.40
15	Willie Davis	.75
16	Eddie Lee Ivery	.40
17	Fran Tarkenton	2.00
18	Alan Page	.75
19	Ricky Bell	.60
20	Cecil Johnson	.40
21	Bubba Bean	.40
22	Gerald Riggs	.50
23	Eric Dickerson, Barry Redden	1.00
24	Jack Reynolds	.50
25	Archie Manning	1.00
26	Wayne Wilson	.60
27	Dan Bunz, Pete Johnson	.40
28	Roger Craig	1.00
29	O.J. Simpson	6.00
30	Joe Cribbs	.50
31	Rick Volk, Leroy Kelly	.60
32	Earl Morrall	.75
33	Jim Klick	.50
34	Dan Marino	5.00
35	Craig James	1.00
36	Julius Adams	.40
37	Joe Namath	4.00
38	Freeman McNeil	.60
39	Pete Johnson	.40
40	Larry Kinnebrew	.40
41	Brian Sipe	.50
42	Kevin Mack, Earnest Byner	.60
43	Dan Pastorini	.60
44	Elvin Bethea, Carter Hartwig	.40
45	Fran Tarkenton, Jack Lambert	1.00
46	Terry Bradshaw	3.00
47	Randy Gradishar, Steve Foley	.50
48	Sammy Winder	.40
49	Robert Holmes	.40
50	Buck Buchanan	.75
51	Willie Jones, Cedrick Hardman	.40
52	Marcus Allen	1.50
53	Dan Fouts, Don Macek	.75
54	Dan Fouts	1.50
55	Blair Bush	.40
56	Steve Largent	2.50
----	Play Book (Terry Bradshaw)	3.00

1966 Jets Team Issue

The nine-card, 5" x 7" set features black and white player photos on the fronts with blank backs.

		NM
Complete Set (9):		80.00
Common Player:		4.00
1	Ralph Baker	4.00
2	Larry Grantham	5.00
3	Bill Mathis	4.00
4	Don Maynard	15.00
5	Joe Namath	40.00
6	Gerry Philbin	5.00
7	Mark Smolinski	4.00
8	Matt Snell	8.00
9	Bake Turner	4.00

1969 Jets Tasco Prints

The six-card, 11" x 16" set, produced by Tasco Associates, features an artist's depiction of the players with blank backs.

		NM
Complete Set (6):		100.00
Common Player:		10.00
1	Winston Hill	10.00
2	Joe Namath	50.00
3	Gerry Philbin	15.00
4	Johnny Sample	10.00
5	Matt Snell	18.00
6	Jim Turner	10.00

1981 Jets Police

The 10-card, 2-5/8" x 4-1/8" set have green-bordered fronts and were

sponsored by Frito-Lay, Kiwanis, local law enforcement and the Jets. The card backs contain a safety tip in red print. Apparently, four of the cards were short-printed and thus are more scarce.

		MT
Complete Set (10):		20.00
Common Player:		1.00
14	Richard Todd (SP)	4.00
42	Bruce Harper	1.00
51	Greg Buttle	1.00
73	Joe Klecko	2.50
79	Marvin Powell	2.00
80	Johnny Lam Jones (SP)	3.50
85	Wesley Walker (SP)	5.00
93	Marty Lyons	2.50
99	Mark Gastineau	2.50
xx0	Team Effort (SP)	2.50

1997 John Elway Convenience Store News

This 7" x 10" Elway card was rubber cemented inside the April 7, 1997 issue of Convenience Store News. The front features Elway in a posed shot of him passing the ball, with the words "Trading Cards" in bold white letters across the top, with the NFL logo in the middle. The back is split, with half containing facts and the other half featuring a comic.

		MT
Complete Set (1):		8.00
Common Player:		8.00
	John Elway	8.00

K

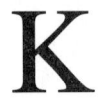

1959 Kahn's

Kahn's Wieners produced this set, which features members of the Cleveland Indians and Pittsburgh Steelers. The card front contains the Kahn's slogan (The Wiener the World Awaited), plus a black-and-white photograph and a facsimile autograph. Each back has biographical and statistical information. Each unnumbered card measures 3-1/4" x 3-15/16".

		NM
Complete Set (31):		1250.
Common Player:		30.00
(1)	Dick Alban	30.00
(2)	Jim Brown	375.00
(3)	Jack Butler	30.00
(4)	Lew Carpenter	35.00
(5)	Preston Carpenter	30.00
(6)	Vince Costello	30.00
(7)	Dale Dodrill	30.00
(8)	Bob Gain	30.00
(9)	Gary Glick	30.00
(10)	Lou Groza	75.00
(11)	Gene Hickerson	30.00
(12)	Billy Howton	35.00
(13)	Art Hunter	30.00
(14)	Joe Kruppa	30.00
(15)	Bobby Layne	65.00
(16)	Joe Lewis	30.00
(17)	Jack McClairen	30.00
(18)	Mike McCormack	45.00
(19)	Walt Michaels	40.00
(20)	Bobby Mitchell	75.00
(21)	Jim Ninowski	35.00
(22)	Chuck Noll	110.00
(23)	Jimmy Orr	35.00
(24)	Milt Plum	35.00
(25)	Ray Renfro	35.00
(26)	Mike Sandusky	30.00
(27)	Billy Ray Smith	30.00
(28)	Jim Ray Smith	30.00
(29)	Ernie Stautner	50.00
(30)	Tom Tracy	30.00
(31)	Frank Varrichione	30.00

1960 Kahn's

Kahn's once again featured members of the Pittsburgh Steelers and Cleveland Browns in this 38-card set. The 3-1/4" x 3-15/16" cards had black-and-white photos on the front, along with the Kahn's slogan. The back has statistical and biographical information, plus an offer for collectors to send in for a free album and instructional booklet. The cards are not numbered and are listed alphabetically.

		NM
Complete Set (38):		1200.
Common Player:		25.00
(1)	Sam Baker	25.00
(2)	Jim Brown	230.00
(3)	Ray Campbell	25.00
(4)	Preston Carpenter	25.00
(5)	Vince Costello	25.00
(6)	Willie Davis	65.00
(7)	Galen Fiss	25.00
(8)	Bob Gain	30.00
(9)	Lou Groza	50.00
(10)	Gene Hickerson	25.00
(11)	John Henry Johnson	55.00
(12)	Rich Kreitling	25.00
(13)	Joe Krupa	25.00
(14)	Bobby Layne	50.00
(15)	Jack McClairen	25.00
(16)	Mike McCormack	35.00
(17)	Walt Michaels	25.00
(18)	Bobby Mitchell	40.00
(19)	Dicky Moegle	25.00
(20)	John Morrow	25.00
(21)	Gern Nagler	25.00
(22)	John Nisby	25.00
(23)	Jimmy Orr	30.00
(24)	Bernie Parrish	25.00
(25)	Milt Plum	30.00
(26)	John Reger	25.00
(27)	Ray Renfro	30.00
(28)	Will Renfro	25.00
(29)	Mike Sandusky	30.00
(30)	Dick Schafrath	25.00
(31)	Jim Ray Smith	25.00
(32)	Billy Ray Smith	25.00
(33)	Ernie Stautner	40.00
(34)	George Tarasovic	25.00
(35)	Tom Tracy	30.00
(36)	Frank Varrichione	25.00
(37)	John Wooten	25.00
(38)	Lowe W. Wren	25.00

1961 Kahn's

In addition to featuring Cleveland Browns and Pittsburgh Steelers, as Kahn's sets from the two years before did, the 1961 set included players from the Baltimore Colts, Los Angeles Rams and Philadelphia Eagles. The cards are slightly larger than previous years' issues, measuring 3-1/4" x 4-1/16". The backs are similar to the 1961 backs, except the offer for the album and instructional booklet is slightly different. (The 1960 cards required two labels to be sent in for the album; the 1961 cards only required one.) The fronts are black-and-white and have a facsimile autograph and the Kahn's slogan. Once again, the cards are unnumbered.

		NM
Complete Set (36):		1000.
Common Player:		20.00
(1)	Sam Baker	20.00
(2)	Jim Brown	225.00
(3)	Preston Carpenter	20.00
(4)	Vince Costello	20.00
(5)	Buddy Dial	20.00
(6)	Dean Derby	25.00
(7)	Don Fleming	25.00
(8)	Bob Gain	20.00
(9)	Bobby Joe Green	20.00
(10)	Gene Hickerson	25.00
(11)	Jim Houston	25.00
(12)	Dan James	20.00
(13)	John Henry Johnson	40.00
(14)	Rich Kreitling	20.00
(15)	Joe Krupa	20.00
(16)	Larry Krutko (photo actually Tom Tracy)	20.00
(17)	Bobby Layne	60.00
(18)	Joe Lewis	20.00
(19)	Gene Lipscomb	40.00
(20)	Mike McCormack	30.00
(21)	Bobby Mitchell	45.00
(22)	John Morrow	20.00
(23)	John Nisby	20.00
(24)	Jimmy Orr	25.00
(25)	Milt Plum	25.00
(26)	John Reger	20.00
(27)	Ray Renfro	30.00
(28)	Will Renfro	20.00
(29)	Mike Sandusky	20.00
(30)	Dick Schafrath	20.00
(31)	Jim Ray Smith	20.00
(32)	Ernie Stautner	45.00
(33)	George Tarasovic	20.00
(34)	Tom Tracy (photo actually Larry Krutko)	20.00
(35)	Frank Varrichione	20.00
(36)	John Wooten	20.00

1962 Kahn's

This Kahn's set adds three new teams to the mix - the Chicago Bears, Detroit Lions and Minnesota Vikings. The unnumbered cards are 3-1/4" x 4-3/16" and can be identified from previous issues by the player's name on the back, which is in bold. The stats on the back are also double-spaced. Basically, the card design is similar to previous issues.

		NM
Complete Set (38):		1000.
Common Player:		20.00
(1)	Maxie Baughan	22.00
(2)	Charley Britt	20.00
(3)	Jim Brown	185.00
(4)	Preston Carpenter	20.00
(5)	Pete Case	22.00
(6)	Howard Cassady	25.00
(7)	Vince Costello	20.00
(8)	Buddy Dial	22.00
(9)	Gene Hickerson	20.00
(10)	Jim Houston	22.00
(11)	Dan James	20.00
(12)	Rich Kreitling	20.00
(13)	Joe Krupa	20.00
(14)	Bobby Layne	50.00
(15)	Ray Lemek	20.00
(16)	Gene Lipscomb	30.00
(17)	David Lloyd	20.00
(18)	Lou Michaels	22.00
(19)	Larry Morris	20.00
(20)	John Morrow	20.00
(21)	Jim Ninowski	20.00
(22)	Buzz Nutter	20.00
(23)	Jimmy Orr	25.00
(24)	Bernie Parrish	22.00
(25)	Milt Plum	22.00
(26)	Myron Pottios	22.00
(27)	John Reger	20.00
(28)	Ray Renfro	22.00
(29)	Frank Ryan	25.00
(30)	John Sample	22.00
(31)	Mike Sandusky	25.00
(32)	Dick Schafrath	20.00
(33)	Jim Shofner	22.00
(34)	Jim Ray Smith	20.00
(35)	Ernie Stautner	35.00
(36)	Fran Tarkenton	250.00
(37)	Paul Wiggin	22.00
(38)	John Wooten	20.00

1963 Kahn's

Kahn's included players from all 14 NFL teams this year, by adding players from the Dallas Cowboys, Green Bay Packers, New York Giants, St. Louis Cardinals, San Francisco 49ers and Washington Redskins to its 1963 lineup of eight teams. Although the backs are generally similar to those from previous sets, these cards can be distinguished from prior sets by the card front, which, for the first time, uses a white border around the black-and-white photo. Once again, the cards are unnumbered and measure 3-1/4" x 4-3/16".

		NM
Complete Set (92):		2300.
Common Player:		18.00
(1)	Bill Barnes	18.00
(2)	Erich Barnes	20.00
(3)	Dick Bass	20.00
(4)	Don Bosseler	18.00
(5)	Jim Brown	200.00
(6)	Roger Brown	20.00
(7)	Roosevelt Brown	25.00
(8)	Ron Bull	20.00
(9)	Preston Carpenter	18.00
(10)	Frank Clarke	18.00
(11)	Gail Cogdill	18.00
(12)	Bobby Joe Conrad	18.00
(13)	John David Crow	30.00
(14)	Dan Currie	18.00
(15)	Buddy Dial	20.00
(16)	Mike Ditka	70.00
(17)	Fred Dugan	18.00
(18)	Galen Fiss	18.00
(19)	Bill Forester	20.00
(20)	Bob Gain	18.00
(21)	Willie Gailmore	20.00
(22)	Bill George	25.00
(23)	Frank Gifford	125.00
(24)	Bill Glass	22.00
(25)	Forrest Gregg	25.00
(26)	Fred Hageman	18.00
(27)	Jimmy Hill	18.00
(28)	Sam Huff	30.00
(29)	Dan James	18.00
(30)	John Henry Johnson	25.00
(31)	Sonny Jurgensen	35.00
(32)	Jim Katcavage	20.00
(33)	Ron Kostelnik	18.00
(34)	Jerry Kramer	25.00
(35)	Ron Kramer	22.00
(36)	Dick Lane	25.00
(37)	Yale Lary	25.00
(38)	Eddie LeBaron	25.00
(39)	Dick Lynch	18.00
(40)	Tommy Mason	20.00
(41)	Tommy McDonald	20.00
(42)	Lou Michaels	18.00
(43)	Bobby Mitchell	30.00
(44)	Dick Modzelewski	18.00
(45)	Lenny Moore	30.00
(46)	John Morrow	18.00
(47)	John Nisby	18.00
(48)	Ray Nitschke	40.00
(49)	Leo Nomellini	25.00
(50)	Jimmy Orr	20.00
(51)	John Paluck	18.00
(52)	Jim Parker	25.00
(53)	Bernie Parrish	18.00
(54)	Jim Patton	18.00
(55)	Don Perkins	20.00
(56)	Richie Petitbon	18.00
(57)	Jim Phillips	18.00
(58)	Nick Pietrosante	18.00
(59)	Milt Plum	20.00
(60)	Myron Pottios	18.00
(61)	Sonny Randle	18.00
(62)	John Reger	18.00
(63)	Ray Renfro	22.00
(64)	Pete Retzlaff	20.00
(65)	Pat Richter	22.00
(66)	Jim Ringo	25.00
(67)	Andy Robustelli	25.00
(68)	Joe Rutgens	18.00
(69)	Bob St. Clair	25.00
(70)	John Sample	18.00
(71)	Lonnie Sanders	18.00
(72)	Dick Schafrath	18.00
(73)	Joe Schmidt	30.00
(74)	Del Shofner	20.00
(75)	J.D. Smith	18.00
(76)	Norm Snead	20.00
(77)	Billy Stacy	18.00
(78)	Bart Starr	60.00
(79)	Ernie Stautner	30.00
(80)	Jim Steffen	18.00
(81)	Andy Stynchula	18.00
(82)	Fran Tarkenton	110.00
(83)	Jim Taylor	40.00
(84)	Clendon Thomas	18.00
(85)	Fred (Fuzzy) Thurston	25.00
(86)	Y.A. Tittle	50.00
(87)	Bob Toneff	18.00
(88)	Jerry Tubbs	18.00
(89)	John Unitas	130.00
(90)	Billy Wade	18.00
(91)	Willie Wood	25.00
(92)	Abe Woodson	18.00

1964 Kahn's

Kahn's introduced color to its 1964 set, making it distinctively different from its prior black-and-white efforts. The Kahn's slogan has also been removed from the card fronts; it has been placed on the card back instead. The card backs are generally the same as those in previous issues. The unnumbered cards measure 3" x 3-5/8".

		NM
Complete Set (53):		1400.
Common Player:		15.00
(1)	Doug Atkins	25.00
(2)	Terry Barr	15.00
(3)	Dick Bass	20.00
(4)	Ordell Braase	15.00
(5)	Ed Brown	20.00
(6)	Jimmy Brown	160.00
(7)	Gary Collins	20.00
(8)	Bobby Joe Conrad	20.00
(9)	Mike Ditka	45.00
(10)	Galen Fiss	15.00
(11)	Paul Flatley	22.00
(12)	Joe Fortunato	18.00
(13)	Bill George	25.00
(14)	Bill Glass	18.00
(15)	Ernie Green	18.00
(16)	Dick Hoak	18.00
(17)	Paul Hornung	45.00
(18)	Sam Huff	35.00
(19)	Charlie Johnson	20.00
(20)	John Henry Johnson	30.00
(21)	Alex Karras	35.00
(22)	Jim Katcavage	18.00
(23)	Joe Krupa	15.00
(24)	Dick Lane	25.00
(25)	Tommy Mason	18.00
(26)	Don Meredith	60.00
(27)	Bobby Mitchell	30.00
(28)	Larry Morris	15.00
(29)	Jimmy Orr	18.00
(30)	Jim Parker	25.00
(31)	Bernie Parrish	20.00
(32)	Don Perkins	18.00
(33)	Jim Phillips	15.00
(34)	Sonny Randle	
(35)	Pete Retzlaff	18.00
(36)	Jim Ringo	25.00
(37)	Frank Ryan	20.00
(38)	Dick Schafrath	20.00
(39)	Joe Schmidt	25.00
(40)	Del Shofner	18.00
(41)	J.D. Smith	15.00
(42)	Norm Snead	18.00
(43)	Bart Starr	60.00
(44)	Fran Tarkenton	75.00
(45)	Jim Taylor	30.00
(46)	Clendon Thomas	15.00
(47)	Y.A. Tittle	50.00
(48)	Jerry Tubbs	18.00
(49)	John Unitas	80.00
(50)	Billy Wade	18.00
(51)	Paul Warfield	65.00
(52)	Alex Webster	18.00
(53)	Abe Woodson	15.00

1970 Kellogg's

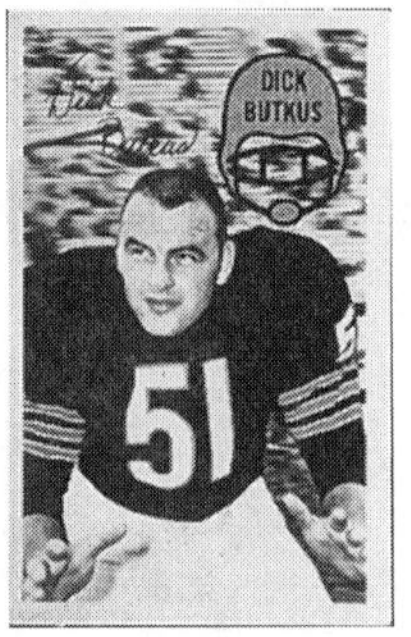

Kellogg's cereal entered the football card market in 1970 with a set of 60 cards featuring the 3D effect utilized for many of its baseball card issues from the same period. The cards, which measure approximately 2-1/4" x 3-1/2", could be obtained inside cereal boxes or through a mail-in offer. Because of the process used to make the 3D effect, the cards are susceptible to cracking and curling, making perfect condition somewhat difficult.

		NM
Complete Set (60):		50.00
Common Player:		.40
1	Carl Eller	1.25
2	Jim Otto	1.25
3	Tom Matte	.60
4	Bill Nelson	.50
5	Travis Williams	.40
6	Len Dawson	2.00
7	Gene Washington	.60
8	Jim Nance	.50
9	Norm Snead	.60
10	Dick Butkus	4.00
11	George Sauer	.50
12	Billy Kilmer	.75
13	Alex Karras	3.00
14	Larry Wilson	1.25
15	Dave Robinson	.50
16	Bill Brown	.50
17	Bob Griese	4.00
18	Al Denson	.40
19	Dick Post	.40
20	Jan Stenerud	.60
21	Paul Warfield	1.50
22	Mel Farr	.50
23	Mel Renfro	.60
24	Roy Jefferson	.40
25	Mike Garrett	.50
26	Harry Jacobs	.40
27	Carl Garrett	.40
28	Dave Wilcox	.50
29	Matt Snell	.60
30	Tom Woodeshick	.40
31	Leroy Kelly	.75
32	Floyd Little	.75
33	Ken Willard	.60
34	John Mackey	1.25
35	Merlin Olsen	3.50
36	David Grayson	.40
37	Lem Barney	2.00
38	Deacon Jones	1.25
39	Bob Hayes	.75
40	Lance Alworth	2.00
41	Larry Csonka	2.00
42	Bobby Bell	1.25
43	George Webster	.50
44	John Roland	.50
45	Dick Shiner	.40
46	Charles (Bubba) Smith	2.00
47	Daryle Lamonica	.75
48	O.J. Simpson	20.00
49	Calvin Hill	1.00
50	Fred Biletnikoff	1.50
51	Gale Sayers	5.00
52	Homer Jones	.50
53	Sonny Jurgensen	2.50
54	Bob Lilly	2.00
55	Johnny Unitas	6.00
56	Tommy Nobis	.75
57	Ed Meador	.50
58	Carl Lockhart	.40
59	Don Maynard	1.25
60	Greg Cook	.50

1971 Kellogg's

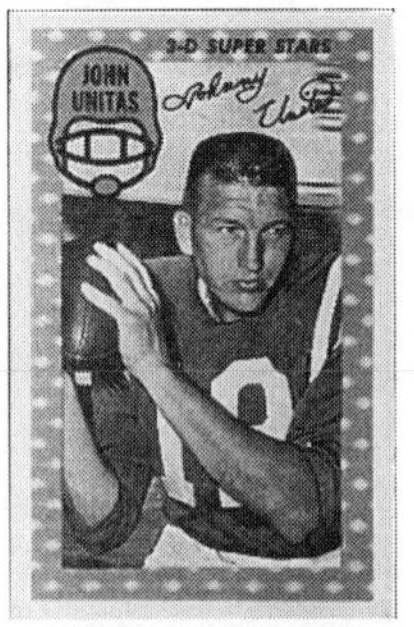

The 1971 Kellogg's football set was again complete at 60 cards and featured the 3D effect. The cards measure approximately 2-1/4" x 3-1/2", and again, because of the process used to achieve the 3D effect, are susceptible to cracking and curling. Cards from the 1971 set were available only in boxes of cereal. Because sets were not available through a mail-in offer, the '71 Kellogg's set is considerably scarcer and more valuable than the '70 set.

		NM
Complete Set (60):		360.00
Common Player:		4.50
1	Tom Barrington	4.50
2	Chris Hanburger	5.00
3	Frank Nunley	4.50
4	Houston Antwine	4.50
5	Ron Johnson	5.00
6	Craig Morton	6.50
7	Jack Snow	5.00
8	Mel Renfro	5.00
9	Les Josephson	4.50
10	Gary Garrison	4.50
11	Dave Herman	4.50
12	Fred Dryer	6.50
13	Larry Brown	5.00
14	Gene Washington	4.50
15	Joe Greene	25.00
16	Marlin Briscoe	4.50
17	Bob Grant	4.50
18	Dan Conners	4.50
19	Mike Curtis	5.00
20	Harry Schuh	4.50
21	Rich Jackson	4.50
22	Clint Jones	4.50
23	Hewritt Dixon	4.50
24	Jess Phillips	4.50
25	Gary Cuozzo	4.50
26	Bo Scott	4.50
27	Glen Ray Hines	4.50
28	Johnny Unitas	27.00
29	John Gilliam	4.50
30	Harmon Wages	4.50
31	Walt Sweeney	4.50
32	Bruce Taylor	4.50
33	George Blanda	17.00
34	Ken Bowman	4.50
35	Johnny Robinson	5.00
36	Ed Podolak	4.50
37	Curley Culp	4.50
38	Jim Hart	6.50
39	Dick Butkus	20.00
40	Floyd Little	6.50
41	Nick Buoniconti	6.50
42	Larry Smith	4.50
43	Wayne Walker	4.50
44	MacArthur Lane	5.00
45	John Brodie	15.00
46	Dick LeBeau	4.50
47	Claude Humphrey	4.50
48	Jerry LeVias	4.50
49	Erich Barnes	4.50
50	Andy Russell	5.00
51	Donny Anderson	5.00
52	Mike Reid	7.50
53	Al Atkinson	4.50
54	Tom Dempsey	5.00
55	Bob Griese	18.00
56	Dick Gordon	4.50
57	Charlie Sanders	5.00
58	Doug Cunningham	4.50
59	Cyril Pinder	4.50
60	Dave Osborn	5.00

1978 Kellogg's Stickers

Measuring 2-1/2" x 2-5/8", the sticker fronts showcase the team's name beneath the team helmets. Spotlighted on the back are a brief history on each team and a referee's signals quiz. Each sticker is numbered on the back.

		NM
Complete Set (28):		30.00
Common Player:		1.00
1	Atlanta Falcons	1.00
2	Baltimore Colts	1.00
3	Buffalo Bills	1.00
4	Chicago Bears	1.00
5	Cincinnati Bengals	1.00
6	Cleveland Browns	1.00
7	Dallas Cowboys	2.00
8	Denver Broncos	1.00
9	Detroit Lions	1.00
10	Green Bay Packers	1.50
11	Houston Oilers	1.00
12	Kansas City Chiefs	1.00
13	Los Angeles Rams	1.00
14	Miami Dolphins	2.00
15	Minnesota Vikings	1.00
16	New England Patriots	1.00
17	New Orleans Saints	1.00
18	New York Giants	1.00
19	New York Jets	1.00
20	Oakland Raiders	2.00
21	Philadelphia Eagles	1.00
22	Pittsburgh Steelers	2.00
23	St. Louis Cardinals	1.00
24	San Diego Chargers	1.00
25	San Francisco 49ers	2.00
26	Seattle Seahawks	1.00
27	Tampa Bay Buccaneers	1.00
28	Washington Redskins	2.00

1982 Kellogg's

After a hiatus of more than a decade, Kellogg's returned in 1982 with a small (24-card) set that appeared in three-card panels on the backs of Raisin Bran boxes. The individual cards measure the standard 2-1/2" x 3-1/2", but the set is usually collected in panel-form, so it has little value cut into individual cards. The prices below, therefore, are for complete panels. The cards are unnumbered and are checklisted here in alphabetical order based on the last name of the first player on each panel. Each panel measures approximately 4-1/8" x 7-1/2". Card fronts have the player's name, position and team on the bottom left, with the Kellogg's logo inside a football on the bottom right. Card backs feature the player's name and bio at the top, with his stats in the middle. His honors received are printed at the bottom, along with the team helmet and NFLPA and NFL logos. Billy Joe DuPree's photo is mistakenly labeled Harvey Martin, while Martin's is labeled DuPree.

		MT
Complete Set (8):		5.00
Common Panel:		.60
1	Ken Anderson, Frank Lewis, Gifford Nielsen	.75
2	Ottis Anderson, Chris Collinsworth, Franco Harris	1.75
3	William Andrews, Brian Sipe, Fred Smerlas	.60
4	Steve Bartkowski, Robert Brazile, Jack Rudnay	.60
5	Tony Dorsett, Eric Hipple, Pat McInally	1.25
6	Billy Joe DuPree, David Hill, John Stallworth	.75
7	Harvey Martin, Mike Pruitt, Joe Senser	.60
8	Art Still, Mel Gray, Tommy Kramer	.60

1982 Kellogg's Teams

Inserted into specially marked boxes of Kellogg's Raisin Bran cereal, this 28-poster set measures 8" x 10-1/2". Inside a black border, color artwork of generic players is featured, with a smaller color painting inset on one side. The team name, helmet and NFL shield are located inside an oval at the bottom. The backs include the official rules and an entry form for the "Raisin Bran Super Bowl Sweepstakes." If the team showcased on the front won the 1983 Super Bowl, the collector had to fill out the form and mail the poster to Kellogg's to win various prizes.

		MT
Complete Set (28):		100.00
Common Player:		5.00
1	Atlanta Falcons	5.00
2	Buffalo Bills	5.00
3	Chicago Bears	5.00
4	Cincinnati Bengals	5.00
5	Cleveland Browns	5.00
6	Dallas Cowboys	8.00
7	Denver Broncos	5.00
8	Detroit Lions	5.00
9	Green Bay Packers	8.00
10	Houston Oilers	5.00
11	Indianapolis Colts	5.00
12	Kansas City Chiefs	5.00
13	Los Angeles Raiders	8.00
14	Los Angeles Rams	5.00
15	Miami Dolphins	8.00
16	Minnesota Vikings	5.00
17	New England Patriots	5.00
18	New Orleans Saints	5.00
19	New York Giants	5.00
20	New York Jets	5.00
21	Philadelphia Eagles	5.00
22	Pittsburgh Steelers	5.00
23	St. Louis Cardinals	5.00
24	San Diego Chargers	5.00
25	San francisco 49ers	8.00
26	Seattle Seahawks	5.00
27	Tampa Bay Buccaneers	5.00
28	Washington Redskins	8.00

1989 King B Discs

These red-bordered discs, which feature 24 NFL stars, were included in specially-marked cans of King B beef jerky, one per can. The front has a color head shot of the player, along with the King B logo. "1st Annual Collectors Edition" is also written on the front. The back includes the King B and NFLPA logos, plus biographical information and

1988 and career statistics. A ring of stars runs along the border. The cards, produced by Michael Schechter Associates, are numbered on the back.

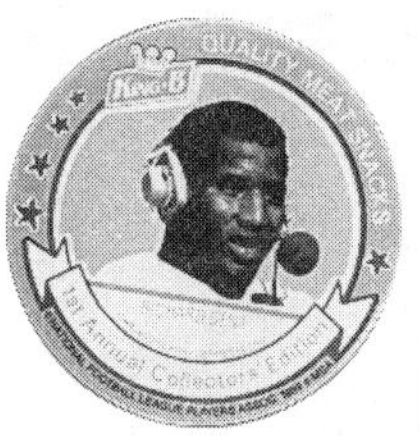

		MT
Complete Set (24):		50.00
Common Player:		1.00
1	Chris Miller	2.50
2	Shane Conlan	1.25
3	Richard Dent	1.75
4	Boomer Esiason	1.75
5	Frank Minnifield	1.00
6	Herschel Walker	2.00
7	Karl Mecklenburg	1.50
8	Mike Cofer	1.00
9	Warren Moon	3.00
10	Chris Chandler	1.50
11	Deron Cherry	1.00
12	Bo Jackson	2.00
13	Jim Everett	1.50
14	Dan Marino	12.00
15	Anthony Carter	1.25
16	Andre Tippett	1.50
17	Bobby Hebert	1.50
18	Phil Simms	1.75
19	Al Toon	1.50
20	Gary Anderson	1.50
21	Joe Montana	14.00
22	Dave Krieg	1.50
23	Randall Cunningham	2.50
24	Bubby Brister	1.00

1990 King B Discs

Once again, these discs were available in specially-marked cans of King B beef jerky, one per can. The front has a color mug shot of the player, surrounded by a red border with a yellow background. The year 1990 appears at the bottom of the card in green; the King B logo is underneath the year. Each card back is numbered and has a border of stars around it. Biographical information and a comment about the player's accomplishments are also given on the back, along with the King B and NFLPA logos.

		MT
Complete Set (24):		45.00
Common Player:		1.00
1	Jim Everett	2.00
2	Marcus Allen	2.00
3	Brian Blades	1.50
4	Bubby Brister	1.00
5	Mark Carrier	1.50
6	Steve Jordan	1.00
7	Barry Sanders	7.00
8	Ronnie Lott	2.00
9	Howie Long	2.00
10	Steve Atwater	1.50
11	Dan Marino	8.00
12	Boomer Esiason	2.00
13	Dalton Hilliard	1.00
14	Phil Simms	2.50
15	Jim Kelly	3.00
16	Mike Singletary	1.50
17	John Stephens	1.50
18	Christian Okoye	1.50
19	Art Monk	2.00
20	Chris Miller	2.50
21	Roger Craig	2.00
22	Duane Bickett	1.00
23	Don Majkowski	1.00
24	Eric Metcalf	2.50

1991 King B Discs

Specially-marked cans of King B beef jerky each contained a disc featuring one of 24 NFL stars. The front has a color mug shot of the player surrounded by a purple border. His name, team and position are printed in gold. The King B logo and 1991 are printed at the bottom of the disc. The back is numbered and includes 1990 and career statistics, plus brief biographical information, all in red ink. A ring of stars comprises the border. An NFLPA and King B logo are also included on the back. The discs were produced by Michael Schechter Associates.

		MT
Complete Set (24):		35.00
Common Player:		1.00
1	Mark Rypien	1.25
2	Art Monk	2.00
3	Sean Jones	1.00
4	Bubby Brister	1.00
5	Warren Moon	3.00
6	Andre Rison	2.00
7	Emmitt Smith	9.00
8	Mervyn Fernandez	1.00
9	Rickey Jackson	1.00
10	Bruce Armstrong	1.00
11	Neal Anderson	1.25
12	Christian Okoye	1.00
13	Thurman Thomas	3.00
14	Bruce Smith	1.25
15	Jeff Hostetler	1.50
16	Barry Sanders	6.00
17	Andre Reed	1.25
18	Derrick Thomas	2.50
19	Jim Everett	1.25
20	Boomer Esiason	1.50
21	Merril Hoge	1.00
22	Steve Atwater	1.25
23	Dan Marino	8.00
24	Mark Collins	1.00

1992 King B Discs

This fourth annual collectors' edition features 24 NFL stars on discs available in specially-marked cans of King B beef jerky. The front of each disc, which is black with a yellow border, has a color mug shot of the player. His name, team and position are written in white at the top of the card. A yellow King B logo and the year, 1992, are at the bottom. The back is numbered and includes 1991 and career statistics, plus brief biographical information. King B and NFLPA logos also appear. An alternating ring of white and black stars runs along the border of the back. Michael Schechter Associates again produced the set.

		MT
Complete Set (24):		30.00
Common Player:		1.00
1	Derrick Thomas	2.00
2	Wilber Marshall	1.50
3	Andre Rison	2.00
4	Thurman Thomas	2.50
5	Emmitt Smith	8.00
6	Charles Mann	1.00
7	Michael Irvin	3.00
8	Jim Everett	1.50
9	Gary Anderson	1.00
10	Trace Armstrong	1.00
11	John Elway	3.50
12	Chip Lohmiller	1.00
13	Bobby Hebert	1.00
14	Cornelius Bennett	1.25
15	Chris Miller	1.50
16	Warren Moon	2.00
17	Charles Haley	1.50
18	Mark Rypien	1.00
19	Darrell Green	1.25
20	Barry Sanders	5.00
21	Rodney Hampton	2.50
22	Shane Conlan	1.00
23	Jerry Ball	1.00
24	Morten Andersen	1.50

1993 King B Discs

These 2-3/8" discs were included one per specially-marked can of King B beef jerky. Twenty-four NFL stars are featured. The front of the card uses a green football field motif and features a color mug shot of the player. A black panel at the top includes the player's name, team and position, written in orange and white letters. A blue King B logo and the year appear at the bottom of the disc. The back is numbered and uses black ink to present brief biographical information, plus a brief career summary. King B and NFLPA logos are also included on the back, which has black and white stars along the rim. Each disc, produced by Michael Schechter Associates, measures 2-3/8". An uncut sheet, measuring 17-1/4" x 12-3/4", was also issued.

		MT
Complete Set (24):		30.00
Common Player:		1.00
1	Luis Sharpe	1.00
2	Erik McMillan	1.00
3	Chris Doleman	1.25
4	Cortez Kennedy	1.50
5	Howie Long	1.25
6	Bill Romanowski	1.00
7	Andre Tippett	1.00
8	Simon Fletcher	1.50
9	Derrick Thomas	2.00
10	Rodney Peete	1.00
11	Ronnie Lott	1.50
12	Duane Bickett	1.00
13	Steve Walsh	1.25
14	Stan Humphries	1.50
15	Jeff George	2.75
16	Jay Novacek	2.00
17	Andre Reed	2.00
18	Andre Rison	2.00
19	Emmitt Smith	8.00
20	Neal Anderson	1.00
21	Ricky Sanders	1.25
22	Thurman Thomas	2.50
23	Lorenzo White	1.00
24	Barry Foster	1.00

1994 King B Discs

The sixth edition of this set, issued by Michael Schechter Associates, was inserted one disc per specially marked can of King B beef jerky. Each disc measures 2-3/8" in diameter. Color headshots of the player are showcased over a green background. The player's name, position and team name are included in a yellow rectangle at the bottom of the photo. The white backs have the player's name with his team, position and bio listed at the top, along with the NFLPA logo. His stats are listed in the center. All print on the backs is in green. The back is bordered with stars.

		MT
Complete Set (24):		25.00
Common Player:		.75
1	Marcus Allen	1.50
2	Jerome Bettis	2.00
3	Terrell Buckley	.75
4	Craig Erickson	.75
5	Brett Favre	6.00
6	Barry Foster	.75
7	Irving Fryar	.75
8	Gary Brown	.75
9	Rodney Hampton	.75
10	Qadry Ismail	.75
11	Jim Jeffcoat	.75
12	Jim Lachey	.75
13	Natrone Means	2.00
14	Tony Meola	.75
15	Pete Metzelaars	.75
16	Scott Mitchell	1.00
17	Ronald Moore	.75
18	Andre Rison	.75
19	Jay Schroeder	.75
20	Junior Seau	1.25
21	Shannon Sharpe	1.00
22	Sterling Sharpe	1.00
23	Tim Brown	1.00
24	Chris Warren	1.00

1995 King B Discs

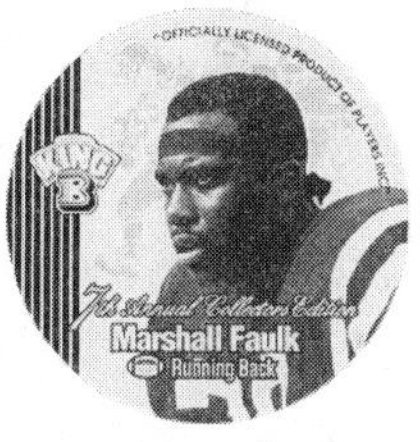

Labeled on the disc front as the "7th Annual Collectors Edition," these discs measure 2-5/8". A color headshot of the player is featured, with a background drawing of a running back chased by two defensive players. A brown and gold vertical striped background borders the left side of the disc. The King B logo also is printed at the left. The player's name and position are located at the bottom. The disc backs feature the player's name, team and bio at the top. His stats are in the middle, with the King B logo and the disc number at the bottom. Text is housed inside a circle of alternating stars and footballs. The discs were available either one disc per shredded beef jerky can or as a 17-1/4" x 12-1/2" collector sheet.

		MT
Complete Set (24):		18.00
Common Player:		.50
1	Errict Rhett	1.00
2	Andre Reed	.50
3	Rodney Hampton	.75
4	Kevin Greene	.50
5	Merton Hanks	.50
6	Jerome Bettis	1.50
7	Johnny Johnson	.50
8	Ricky Watters	1.00
9	Harvey Williams	.50
10	Mel Gray	.50
11	Craig Erickson	.50
12	Stan Humphries	.50
13	Natrone Means	1.50
14	Terance Mathis	.50
15	Ken Harvey	.50
16	Brian Mitchell	.50
17	Cris Carter	.50
18	Tim Brown	1.00
19	Marshall Faulk	2.00
20	Eric Turner	.50
21	Terry Allen	1.00
22	Chris Warren	1.00
23	Randy Baldwin	.50
24	Ben Coates	.50

1996 All King B Sack Attack Team

Measuring 2-3/8" in diameter, the 24-disc set focused on defensive players. The front of the disc includes a headshot of the player, his name at the top and a "Sack-It-To-'Em" logo at the bottom. A drawing of a defensive player is included along the left border. The disc backs feature the player's career sacks. One disc was included in each specially marked King B beef jerky canister.

		MT
Complete Set (24):		15.00
Common Player:		.50
1	Reggie White	2.00
2	Rickey Jackson	.50
3	Kevin Greene	1.00
4	Tony Bennett	.50
5	Bryce Paup	1.00
6	John Copeland	.50
7	Pat Swilling	.50
8	Willie McGinest	.50
9	Charles Haley	.50
10	Chris Doleman	.50
11	Clyde Simmons	.50
12	Hugh Douglas	.50
13	Henry Thomas	.50
14	John Randle	1.00
15	Phil Hansen	.50
16	Bruce Smith	1.00
17	Jim Flanigan	1.00
18	D'Marco Farr	.50
19	Ray Seals	.50
20	Neil Smith	1.00
21	Andy Harmon	.50
22	William Fuller	.50
23	Tracy Scoggins	.50
24	Leslie O'Neal	.50

1997 King B Discs

This 24-disc set includes only rookies from the 1997 season and were distributed one per specially marked package of the beef jerky snack. The discs contain the player's portrait over a purple background which features diagrammed plays. The King B logo is in the lower left portion of the photo, while "Rookies Collector Edition," the player's name and position are included inside a purple area at the bottom of the disc front.

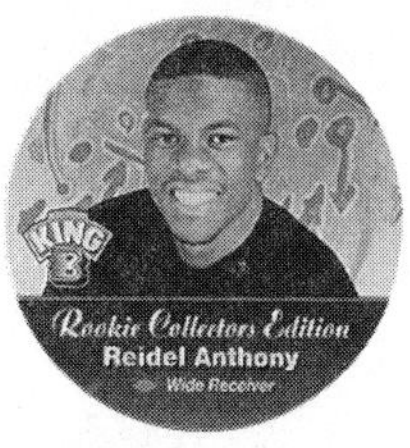

		MT
Complete Set (24):		20.00
Common Player:		.50
1	Orlando Pace	1.00
2	Darrell Russell	.50
3	Shawn Springs	1.00
4	Peter Boulware	.50
5	Bryant Westbrook	.50
6	Walter Jones	.50
7	Ike Hilliard	1.50
8	James Farrior	.50
9	Tom Knight	.50
10	Chris Naeole	.50
11	Warrick Dunn	3.00
12	Tony Gonzalez	1.25
13	Reinard Wilson	.50
14	Yatil Green	.50
15	Reidel Anthony	1.50
16	Dwayne Rudd	1.50
17	Renaldo Wynn	.50
18	David LaFleur	1.00
19	Antowain Smith	2.00
20	Chad Scott	.50
21	Jim Druckenmiller	2.00
22	Rae Carruth	1.50
23	Jake Plummer	3.00
24	Ronnie McAda	.50

1989 Knudsen Raiders

Measuring 2" x 8", this bookmark set of 12 was introduced by Knudsen's Dairy of California. The bookmarks were available to children who checked out books from the Los Angeles Public Library during the 1989 season. The fronts featured a photo of a Raiders player, with "Knudsen presents Raiders Readers" at the top. The Raiders' logo, the player's name, position and bio, along with his highlights are listed below the photo. The unnumbered backs feature reading tips, the player's name, L.A. Public Library, MCLS, Knudsen and Raiders' logos. The Mike Shanahan card is a tough one to locate, as it was not distributed or pulled after he left the Raiders for a position with another NFL team.

		MT
Complete Set (14):		30.00
Common Player:		1.50
6	Jeff Gossett	1.50
13	Jay Schroeder	2.00
26	Vann McElroy	1.50
35	Steve Smith	2.00
36	Terry McDaniel	2.00
70	Scott Davis	1.50
72	Don Mosebar	1.50
75	Howie Long	2.50
76	Steve Wisniewski	2.00
81	Tim Brown	6.00
83	Willie Gault	2.00
NNO	Mike Shanahan (SP) (CO)	16.00
NNO	Raiders/Super Bowl	1.50
NNO	Raiderettes (SP)	2.00

1990 Knudsen Chargers

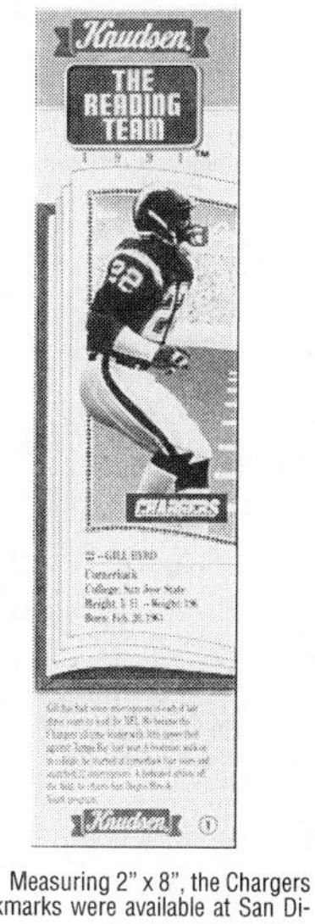

Measuring 2" x 8", the Chargers bookmarks were available at San Diego libraries. The fronts showcase the Knudsen logo at the top, with "The Reading Team" below it. The player photo is shown in the middle, with the Chargers' logo, player's name, uniform number and bio in a box under the photo. The unnumbered backs contain the Knudsen, American Library Association and San Diego libraries' logos.

		MT
Complete Set (6):		10.00
Common Player:		1.50
1	Marion Butts	2.50
2	Anthony Miller	3.50
3	Leslie O'Neal	2.50
4	Gary Plummer	1.50
5	Billy Ray Smith	1.50
6	Billy Joe Tolliver	2.00

1990 Knudsen 49ers

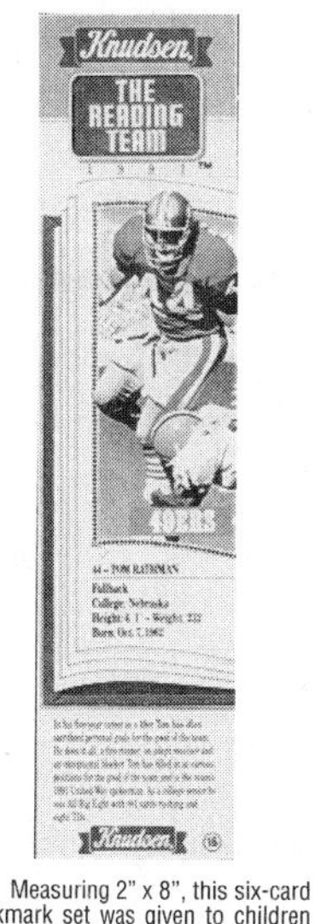

Measuring 2" x 8", this six-card bookmark set was given to children under 15 years of age at libraries in the San Francisco metro area. The design is basically the same as the Chargers set, with the Knudsen logo at the top and "The Reading Team" below it. The player's photo is in the center, above a box which contains the 49ers' logo and the player's name, uniform number and bio. The unnumbered backs have the Knudsen logo at the top and the San Francisco Public Library logo at the bottom. Two books are listed on the back of each bookmark.

		MT
Complete Set (6):		25.00
Common Player:		1.50
1	Roger Craig	2.50
2	Ronnie Lott	4.00
3	Joe Montana	12.00
4	Jerry Rice	12.00
5	George Siefert (CO)	3.00
6	Michael Walter	1.50

1990 Knudsen/Sealtest Patriots

Measuring 2" x 8", this six-card bookmark set was sponsored by Knudsen's and Sealtest. Those children under 15 years of age in the New England area received the bookmarks at their local libraries. The Knudsen or Sealtest logos were located at the top of the front, with "The Reading Team" below it. The player's photo is showcased above a box which contains the Patriots' logo, player's name, uniform number and bio. The backs have the sponsor logos and information on two books.

		MT
Complete Set (6):		25.00
Common Player:		4.00
1	Steve Grogan	6.00
2	Ronnie Lippett	4.00
3	Eric Sievers	4.00
4	Mosi Tatupu	4.00
5	Andre Tippett	6.00
6	Garin Veris	4.00

Values quoted in this guide reflect the retail price of a card — the price a collector can expect to pay when buying a card from a dealer. The wholesale price — that which a collector can expect to receive from a dealer when selling cards — will be significantly lower, depending on desirability and condition.

1990 Knudsen Rams

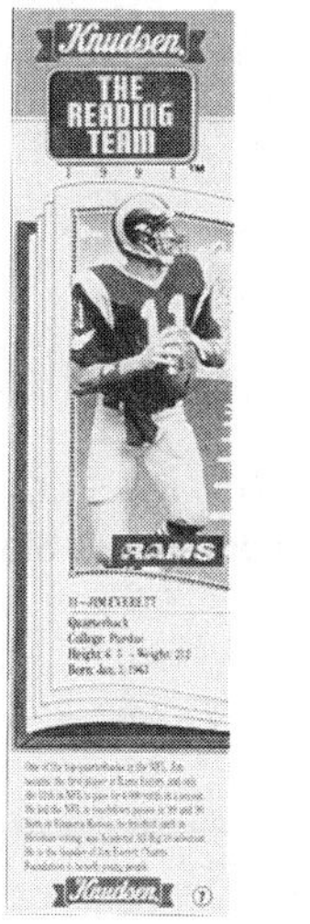

Measuring 2" x 8", the six-bookmark set promoted reading to children under 15 years of age in the Los Angeles area. The front design is the same as the Chargers, 49ers and Patriots sets of 1990.

		MT
Complete Set (6):		25.00
Common Player:		4.00
1	Henry Ellard	8.00
2	Jim Everett	6.00
3	Jerry Gray	4.00
4	Pete Holohan	4.00
5	Mike Lansford	4.00
6	Irv Pankey	4.00

1991 Knudsen

Measuring 2" x 8", the 18-bookmark set was available to children who checked out books at San Diego, Los Angeles and San Francisco public libraries. The fronts have the Knudsen logo at the top, with "The Reading Team" printed below it. A photo of a player is included on a page of a book. The player's team name is superimposed over the photo. His name, position and bio are printed under the photo. The backs have the Knudsen and public library logos, along with information on two books. Each team's bookmarks were available only in its area. Nos. 1-6 are Chargers, Nos. 7-12 are Rams and Nos. 13-18 are 49ers.

		MT
Complete Set (18):		30.00
Common Player:		1.50
1	Gill Byrd	1.50
2	Courtney Hall	1.50
3	Ronnie Harmon	2.00
4	Anthony Miller	3.00
5	Joe Phillips	1.50
6	Junior Seau	5.00
7	Jim Everett	2.50
8	Kevin Greene	2.50
9	Damone Johnson	1.50
10	Tom Newberry	1.50
11	John Robinson (CO)	2.00
12	Michael Stewart	1.50
13	Michael Carter	1.50
14	Charles Haley	2.50
15	Joe Montana	10.00
16	Tom Rathman	2.00
17	Jerry Rice	10.00
18	George Seifert (CO)	3.00

L

1983 Latrobe Police

The black-and-white or sepia-toned standard sized cards were issued in Latrobe, Pa. Titled "Birthplace of Pro Football," the 30-card set featured a photo of the player in an oval, with his name and position in a box at the bottom of the card. The card backs, which came in two versions, have the 1895 "Birthplace of Pro Football" logo in the upper left, with the player's name and position at the right. A write-up of his career highlights also is included on the horizontal card backs. The cards were produced by Chess Promotions Inc. of Latrobe, Pa. The variation backs include safety tips.

		MT
Complete Set (30):		8.00
Common Player:		.30
1	John Brallier	1.00

2	John K. Brallier	.50
3	Latrobe YMCA Team 1895	.50
4	Brallier and Team at W and J 1895	.50
5	Latrobe A.A. Team 1896	.50
6	Latrobe A.A. 1897	.50
7	1st All Pro Team 1897	.50
8	David Berry (Mgr.)	.30
9	Harry Ryan (RT)	.30
10	Walter Okeson (LE)	.30
11	Edward Wood (RE)	.30
12	E. Hammer (C)	.30
13	Marcus Saxman (LH)	.30
14	Charles Shumaker (SUB)	.30
15	Charles McDyre (LE)	.30
16	Edward Abbatticchio (FB)	.30
17	George Flickinger (C/LT)	.30
18	Walter Howard (RH)	.30
19	Thomas Trenchard	.50
20	John Kinport Brallier (QB)	.75
21	Jack Gass (LH)	.30
22	Dave Campbell (LT)	.30
23	Edward Blair (RH)	.30
24	John Johnston (RG)	.30
25	Sam Johnston (LG)	.30
26	Alex Laird (SUB)	.30
27	Latrobe A.A. 1897 Team	.50
28	Pro Football Memorial Plaque	.30
29	Commemorative Medallion	.30
30	Birth of Pro Football Checklist Card	.50

1975 Laughlin Flaky Football

Artist R.G. Laughlin created this 26-card set in 1975 as a parody to the NFL. Measuring 2-1/2" x 3-3/8", the card fronts have the city name and a parody NFL nickname, such as the Green Bay Porkers, with artwork relating to the nickname. "Flaky Football" is printed at the top of the cards, with the card number in a white circle in one of the corners of the horizontal fronts. The backs of the cards are blank.

		NM
Complete Set (27):		125.00
Common Player:		4.50
1	Pittsburgh Stealers	8.00
2	Minnesota Spikings	6.00
3	Cincinnati Bungles	6.00
4	Chicago Bares	6.00
5	Miami Dullfins	8.00
6	Philadelphia Eggles	6.00
7	Cleveland Brawns	4.50
8	New York Gianuts	4.50
9	Buffalo Bulls	4.50
10	Dallas Plowboys	8.00
11	New England Pastry Nuts	4.50
12	Green Bay Porkers	8.00
13	Denver Bongos	4.50
14	St. Louis Cigardinals	4.50
15	New York Jests	4.50
16	Washington Redshins	8.00
17	Oakland Waders	8.00
18	Los Angeles Yams	4.50
19	Baltimore Kilts	4.50
20	New Orleans Scents	4.50
21	San Diego Charges	4.50
22	Detroit Loins	4.50
23	Kansas City Chefs	4.50
24	Atlanta Fakin's	4.50
25	Houston Owlers	4.50
26	San Francisco 40 Miners	8.00
NNO	Title Card Flaky Football	8.00

1948 Leaf

This 98-card set, the first of two Leaf sets to be issued in the late 1940s, features players posed in front of solid backgrounds (player hands and faces are in black and white). Cards measure 2-3/8" x 2-7/8", and the final 49 cards are more difficult to find than the first 49. Rookies in this set include Sid Luckman, Bulldog Turner, Doak Walker, Bobby Lane, Pete Pihos, George McAfee, Steve Van Buren, Bob Waterfield, Charlie Trippi, Sammy Baugh, Bill Dudley, George Connor, Frank Tripucka, Leo Nomellini, Charley Conerly, Leo Nomellini, Chuck Bednarik, and Jackie Jensen.

		NM
Complete Set (98):		5800.
Common Player (1-49):		20.00
Common Player (50-98):		100.00
1	*Sid Luckman*	300.00
2	Steve Suhey	20.00
3	*Bulldog Turner*	90.00
4	*Doak Walker*	125.00
5	Levi Jackson	20.00
6	*Bobby Layne*	300.00
7	Bill Fischer	20.00
8	Vice Banonis	20.00
9	*Tommy Thompson*	20.00
10	Perry Moss	20.00
11	*Terry Brennan*	20.00
12	*William Swiacki*	20.00
13	*Johnny Lujack*	125.00
14	Mal Kutner	20.00
15	*Charlie Justice*	60.00
16	*Pete Pihos*	95.00
17	*Kenny Washington*	55.00
18	*Harry Gilmer*	30.00
19	*George McAfee*	100.00
20	*George Taliaferro*	25.00
21	*Paul Christman*	40.00
22	*Steve Van Buren*	140.00
23	*Ken Kavanaugh*	25.00
24	*Jim Martin*	25.00
25	Bud Angsman	20.00
26	*Bob Waterfield*	200.00
27	Fred Davis	20.00
28	*Whitey Wistert*	20.00
29	*Charlie Trippi*	100.00
30	Paul Governali	20.00
31	Tom McWilliams	20.00
32	Larry Zimmerman	20.00
33	Pat Harder	40.00
34	*Sammy Baugh*	425.00
35	Ted Fritsch Sr.	20.00
36	*Bill Dudley*	85.00
37	*George Connor*	65.00
38	Frank Dancewicz	20.00
39	Billy Dewell	20.00
40	John Nolan	20.00
41	Harry Szulborski	20.00
42	Tex Coulter	20.00
43	Robert Nussbaumer	20.00
44	Bob Mann	20.00
45	Jim White	20.00
46	Jack Jacobs	20.00
47	John Clement	20.00
48	Frank Reagan	20.00
49	*Frank Tripucka*	30.00
50	*John Rauch*	100.00
51	Mike Dimitrio	100.00
52	*Leo Nomellini*	250.00
53	*Charlie Conerly*	250.00
54	*Chuck Bednarik*	400.00
55	Chick Jagade	100.00
56	*Bob Folsom*	100.00
57	*Eugene Rossides*	100.00
58	Art Weiner	100.00
59	Alex Sarkistian	100.00
60	Dick Harris	100.00
61	Len Younce	100.00
62	Gene Derricotte	100.00
63	Roy Steiner	100.00
64	Frank Seno	100.00
65	Bob Hendreen	100.00
66	Jack Cloud	100.00
67	Harrell Collins	100.00
68	Clyde LeForce	100.00
69	Larry Joe	100.00
70	Phil O'Reilly	100.00
71	Paul Campbell	100.00
72	Ray Evans	100.00
73	*Jackie Jensen*	300.00
74	Russ Steger	100.00
75	Tony Minisi	100.00
76	Clayton Tonnemaker	100.00
77	George Savitsky	100.00
78	Clarence Self	100.00
79	Rod Franz	100.00
80	Jim Youle	100.00
81	Billy Bye	100.00
82	Fred Enke	100.00
83	Fred Folger	100.00
84	Jug Girard	100.00
85	Joe Scott	100.00
86	Bob Demoss	100.00
87	Dave Templeton	100.00
88	Herb Siegert	100.00
89	Bucky O'Conner	100.00
90	Joe Whisler	100.00
91	*Leon Hart*	175.00
92	Earl Banks	100.00
93	Frank Aschenbrenner	100.00
94	John Golddsberry	100.00
95	Porter Payne	100.00
96	Pete Perini	100.00
97	Jay Rhodemyre	100.00
98	*Al DiMarco*	175.00

1949 Leaf

The 1949 Leaf issue is quite possibly the stupidest of what is considered the "major" football issues. There are but 49 cards in the set, but numerically the set jumps around until it reaches a 150 count. There are several gaps in the numbering sequence. Even less appealing is the fact that there is exactly one rookie card in the set - that of #1, Bob Hendren. Cards, which measure 2-3/8" x 2-7/8", bear close resemblance to the 1948 Leaf football set, as well as to the Leaf baseball sets of the era. The second-year cards in the set include those of Hall of Famers Sid Luckman, Charley Trippi, Bill Dudley, Sammy Baugh, Pete Pihos, George Connor, Ken McAfee (last card), Bobby Lane, Steve Van Buren, Bob Waterfield, Chuck Bednarik, and Bulldog Turner. Other sophomore cards include Charley Conerly, Johnny Lujack, and Frank Tripucka.

		NM
Complete Set (49):		2000.
Common Player:		25.00
1	Bob Hendren	75.00
2	Joe Scott	25.00
3	Frank Reagan	25.00
4	John Rauch	25.00
7	Bill Fischer	25.00
9	Bud Angsman	25.00
10	Billy Dewell	25.00
13	Tommy Thompson	25.00
15	Sid Luckman	100.00
16	Charlie Trippi	45.00
17	Bob Mann	25.00
19	Paul Christman	25.00
22	Bill Dudley	45.00
23	Clyde LeForce	25.00
26	Sammy Baugh	250.00
28	Pete Pihos	45.00
31	Tex Coulter	25.00
32	Mal Kutner	25.00
35	Whitey Wistert	25.00
37	Ted Fritsch Sr.	25.00
38	Vince Banonis	25.00
39	Jim White	25.00
40	George Connor	45.00
41	George McAfee	45.00
43	Frank Tripucka	25.00
47	Fred Enke	25.00
49	Charlie Conerly	80.00
51	Ken Kavanaugh	25.00
56	John Lujack	80.00
57	Jim Youle	25.00
62	Harry Gilmer	25.00
65	Robert Nussbaumer	25.00
67	Bobby Layne	140.00
70	Herb Siegert	25.00
74	Tony Minisi	25.00
79	Steve Van Buren	80.00
81	Perry Moss	25.00
89	Bob Waterfield	90.00
90	Jack Jacobs	25.00
95	Kenny Washington	30.00
101	Pat Harder	25.00
110	William Swiacki	25.00
118	Fred Davis	25.00
126	Jay Rhodemyre	25.00
134	Chuck Bednarik	100.00
144	George Savitsky	25.00
150	Bulldog Turner	125.00

1996 Leaf

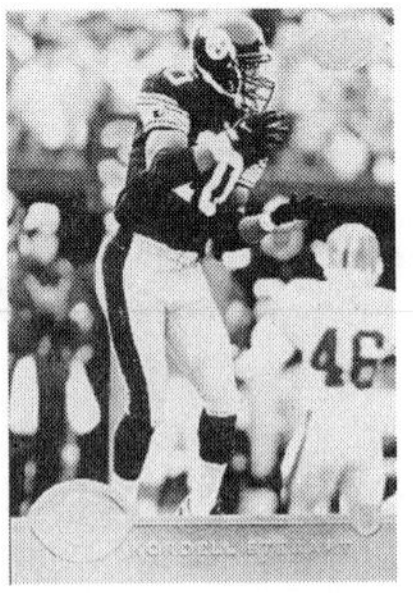

Leaf Football contained 190 cards in the regular-issue set, plus 10 Gold Leaf Rookies that were numbered like inserts, but considered part of the regular-issue set. Leaf arrived for the first time since 1949, and was packaged in 10-card packs. The 190 players from the base set were also available in factory sets receiving special foil treatment and limited to 1,996 sets. The factory sets also included one of 25 different autographed future stars. Inserts found in Leaf Football included: 190-card Press Proof parallel set, Statistical Standouts, Grass Roots, Gold Leaf Stars, American All-Stars and Shirt Off My Back. Cards from regular packs had the bottom strip of the card in the player's team colors, with no foil, while pre- priced packs featured red foil and Collector's Edition cards had gold foil.

		MT
Complete Set (190):		20.00
Common Player:		.10
Minor Stars:		.20
Gold Press Proof Cards:		15x-30x
Hobby Pack (10):		3.00
Hobby Wax Box (18):		40.00
1	Troy Aikman	1.50
2	Ricky Watters	.20
3	Robert Brooks	.10
4	Ki-Jana Carter	.20
5	Drew Bledsoe	1.25
6	Eric Swann	.10
7	Hardy Nickerson	.10
8	Tony Martin	.10
9	Garrison Hearst	.10
10	Bernie Parmalee	.10
11	Neil Smith	.10
12	Aaron Craver	.10
13	Rashaan Salaam	.20
14	Greg Hill	.10
15	Charlie Garner	.10
16	Kimble Anders	.10
17	Steve McNair	1.00
18	Neil O'Donnell	.10
19	Greg Lloyd	.10
20	Warren Moon	.10
21	Bernie Kosar	.10
22	Derrick Thomas	.10
23	Andre Hastings	.10
24	Wayne Chrebet	.10
25	Mark Seay	.10
26	Eric Metcalf	.10
27	Shawn Jefferson	.10
28	Napoleon Kaufman	.10
29	Steve Walsh	.10
30	Derrick Alexander	.10
31	Rodney Peete	.10
32	Terance Mathis	.10
33	Michael Westbrook	.20
34	Kevin Carter	.10
35	Aaron Hayden	.10
36	J.J. Stokes	.20
37	Andre Reed	.10
38	Chris Warren	.20
39	Jerry Rice	1.50
40	Ben Coates	.10
41	Reggie White	.20
42	Joey Galloway	1.25
43	Sean Dawkins	.10
44	Brett Favre	3.00
45	Jeff George	.10
46	Robert Smith	.10
47	Ken Dilger	.10
48	Larry Centers	.10
49	Jackie Harris	.10
50	Hugh Douglas	.10
51	Herschel Walker	.10
52	Kerry Collins	.30
53	Michael Irvin	.20
54	Willie McGinest	.10
55	Herman Moore	.20
56	Leroy Hoard	.10
57	Scott Mitchell	.10
58	Terrell Davis	1.50
59	Kevin Greene	.10
60	Yancey Thigpen	.20
61	Kevin Smith	.10
62	Trent Dilfer	.10
63	Cortez Kennedy	.10
64	Carnell Lake	.10
65	Quinn Early	.10
66	Kyle Brady	.10
67	Marshall Faulk	.30
68	Fred Barnett	.10
69	Quentin Coryatt	.10
70	Dan Marino	3.00
71	Junior Seau	.10
72	Andre Coleman	.10
73	Terry Kirby	.10
74	Curtis Martin	2.00
75	Isaac Bruce	.75
76	Mark Chmura	.10
77	Edgar Bennett	.10
78	Mario Bates	.10
79	Eric Zeier	.10
80	Adrian Murrell	.10
81	Mark Brunell	1.00
82	Mark Rypien	.10
83	Erric Pegram	.10
84	Bryan Cox	.10
85	Heath Shuler	.10
86	Lake Dawson	.10
87	O.J. McDuffie	.10
88	Emmitt Smith	3.00
89	Jim Harbaugh	.10
90	Aaron Bailey	.10
91	Jim Kelly	.20
92	Rodney Hampton	.10
93	Cris Carter	.10
94	Henry Ellard	.10
95	Darnay Scott	.20
96	Daryl Johnston	.10
97	Tamarick Vanover	.20
98	Jeff Blake	.75
99	Anthony Miller	.10
100	Darren Woodson	.10
101	Irving Fryar	.10
102	Craig Heyward	.10
103	Derek Loville	.10
104	Ernie Mills	.10
105	Brian Blades	.10
106	Gus Frerotte	.10
107	Alvin Harper	.10
108	Tyrone Wheatley	.10
109	John Elway	1.00
110	Charles Haley	.10
111	Terrell Fletcher	.10
112	Vincent Brisby	.10
113	Jerome Bettis	.20
114	Barry Sanders	1.50
115	Ken Norton Jr.	.10
116	Sherman Williams	.10
117	Antonio Freeman	.10
118	Bert Emanuel	.10
119	Marcus Allen	.20
120	Stan Humphries	.10
121	Chris Sanders	.10
122	Jeff Graham	.10
123	Jay Novacek	.10
124	Aeneas Williams	.10
125	Kordell Stewart	1.25
126	Steve Young	1.00
127	Jake Reed	.10
128	Rick Mirer	.10
129	Jeff Hostetler	.10
130	Tim Brown	.10
131	Shannon Sharpe	.10
132	Dave Brown	.10
133	Harvey Williams	.10
134	Rodney Thomas	.10
135	Frank Sanders	.10
136	Brett Perriman	.10
137	Steve Bono	.10
138	Steve Atwater	.10
139	Andre Rison	.10
140	Orlando Thomas	.10
141	Terry Allen	.10
142	Carl Pickens	.20
143	William Floyd	.20
144	Bryce Paup	.10
145	James Stewart	.10
146	Eric Bjornson	.10
147	Errict Rhett	.20
148	Darick Holmes	.10
149	Bill Brooks	.10
150	Brent Jones	.10
151	Natrone Means	.10
152	Rod Woodson	.10
153	Bruce Smith	.10
154	Deion Sanders	.75
155	Kevin Williams	.10
156	Erik Kramer	.10
157	Jim Everett	.10
158	Vinny Testaverde	.10
159	Boomer Esiason	.10
160	Floyd Turner	.10
161	Curtis Conway	.20
162	Thurman Thomas	.20
163	Tony Brackens	.10
164	Stepfret Williams	.10
165	Alex Van Dyke	.75
166	Cedric Jones	.10
167	Stanley Pritchett	.10
168	Willie Anderson	.10
169	Regan Upshaw	.10
170	Daryl Gardener	.10
171	Alex Molden	.10
172	John Mobley	.10
173	*Danny Kanell*	.50
174	Marco Battaglia	.10
175	Simeon Rice	.10
176	*Tony Banks*	.75
177	*Stephen Davis*	3.00
178	Walt Harris	.30
179	Amani Toomer	.30
180	*Derrick Mayes*	1.00
181	*Jeff Lewis*	.50
182	Chris Darkins	.10
183	*Rickey Dudley*	.75
184	Jonathan Ogden	.10
185	*Mike Alstott*	1.75
186	*Eric Moulds*	2.00
187	*Karim Abdul-Jabbar*	.75
188	Checklist	.10
189	Checklist	.10
190	Checklist	.10

1996 Leaf Press Proofs

The first 190 cards in 1996 Leaf Football were die-cut and printed in gold foil to form this Press Proofs parallel set. Each Press Proof insert carried a 1 of 2,000 produced number.

	MT
Complete Set (190):	600.00
Press Proof Cards:	15x-30x

A card number in parentheses ( ) indicates the set is unnumbered.

1996 Leaf Gold Leaf Rookies

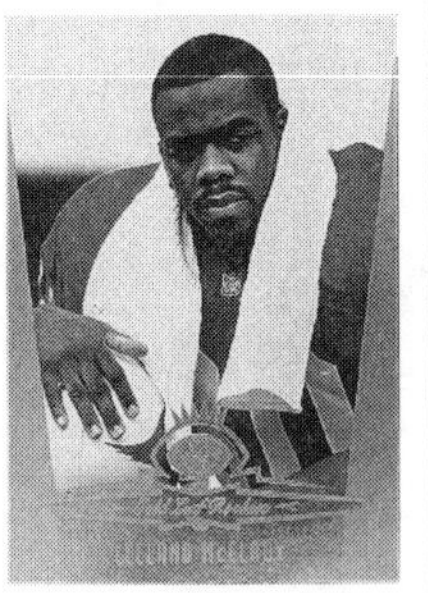

Gold Leaf Rookies were numbered as an insert set, but are actually considered part of the base set. It features 10 rookies on a distinctly different design than base cards.

		MT
Complete Set (10):		40.00
Common Player:		3.00
1	Leeland McElroy	3.00
2	Marvin Harrison	6.00
3	Lawrence Phillips	4.00
4	Bobby Engram	3.00
5	Kevin Hardy	3.00
6	Keyshawn Johnson	5.00
7	Eddie Kennison	5.00
8	Tim Biakabutuka	4.00
9	Eddie George	12.00
10	Terry Glenn	8.00

1996 Leaf American All-Stars

American All-Stars showcased 20 NFL players who were All-America selections in college. The cards were printed on a simulated sailcloth card stock that attempts to have the look and feel of an American flag. American All-Stars arrived in regular and Gold Team versions, with 5,000 regular sets and 1,000 Gold Team sets.

		MT
Complete Set (20):		300.00
Common Player:		4.00
Gold Cards:		2x-3x
1	Emmitt Smith	40.00
2	Drew Bledsoe	15.00
3	Jerry Rice	20.00
4	Kerry Collins	20.00
5	Eddie George	25.00
6	Keyshawn Johnson	15.00
7	Lawrence Phillips	4.00
8	Rashaan Salaam	4.00
9	Deion Sanders	10.00
10	Marshall Faulk	15.00
11	Steve Young	15.00
12	Ki-Jana Carter	4.00
13	Curtis Martin	30.00
14	Joey Galloway	18.00
15	Troy Aikman	20.00
16	Barry Sanders	30.00
17	Dan Marino	40.00
18	John Elway	15.00
19	Steve McNair	4.00
20	Tim Biakabutuka	4.00

1996 Leaf American All-Stars Gold

American All-Stars Gold featured the same 20 cards found in the All-Stars Silver set, but with upgraded cloth stock and gold enhancements. Gold versions are sequentially numbered up to 1,000.

	MT
Complete Set (20):	900.00
Gold Cards:	2x-3x

1996 Leaf Gold Leaf Stars

Fifteen of the top players in the NFL were included in Gold Leaf Stars. These were found in retail packs only and contain a 22kt. gold logo.

		MT
Complete Set (15):		550.00
Common Player:		10.00
1	Drew Bledsoe	30.00
2	Jerry Rice	40.00
3	Emmitt Smith	80.00
4	Dan Marino	80.00
5	Isaac Bruce	20.00
6	Kerry Collins	30.00
7	Barry Sanders	40.00
8	Keyshawn Johnson	40.00
9	Errict Rhett	10.00
10	Joey Galloway	20.00
11	Brett Favre	80.00
12	Curtis Martin	60.00
13	Steve Young	30.00
14	Troy Aikman	40.00
15	John Elway	20.00

1996 Leaf Grass Roots

Printed on a card stock that simulates artificial turf, Grass Roots highlighted 20 running backs that perform the best on artificial turf. This insert was limited to 5,000 sets produced.

		MT
Complete Set (20):		250.00
Common Player:		4.00
Minor Stars:		8.00
1	Thurman Thomas	8.00
2	Eddie George	25.00
3	Rodney Hampton	4.00
4	Rashaan Salaam	8.00
5	Natrone Means	4.00
6	Errict Rhett	8.00
7	Leeland McElroy	4.00
8	Emmitt Smith	40.00
9	Marshall Faulk	8.00
10	Ricky Watters	4.00
11	Chris Warren	4.00
12	Tim Biakabutuka	8.00
13	Barry Sanders	20.00
14	Karim Abdul-Jabbar	20.00
15	Darick Holmes	4.00
16	Terrell Davis	20.00
17	Lawrence Phillips	8.00
18	Ki-Jana Carter	8.00
19	Curtis Martin	30.00
20	Kordell Stewart	20.00

1996 Leaf Shirt Off My Back

Shirt Off My Back inserts were found only in special pre-priced retail packs. The cards were printed on stock that simulates jersey material and includes 10 of the top quarterbacks. Shirt Off My Back was limited to 2,500 sets.

		MT
Complete Set (10):		170.00
Common Player:		5.00
1	Steve Young	10.00
2	Jeff Blake	5.00
3	Drew Bledsoe	18.00
4	Kordell Stewart	10.00
5	Troy Aikman	15.00
6	Steve McNair	10.00
7	John Elway	25.00
8	Dan Marino	25.00
9	Kerry Collins	5.00
10	Brett Favre	30.00

1996 Leaf Statisical Standouts

Printed on simulated leather and inserted only in hobby packs, Statistical Standouts includes 15 top players. These cards have the feel of leather and are individually numbered to 2,500.

		MT
Complete Set (15):		425.00
Common Player:		10.00
1	John Elway	30.00
2	Jerry Rice	40.00
3	Reggie White	10.00
4	Drew Bledsoe	30.00
5	Chris Warren	10.00
6	Bruce Smith	10.00
7	Barry Sanders	40.00
8	Greg Lloyd	10.00
9	Emmitt Smith	80.00
10	Dan Marino	80.00
11	Steve Young	30.00
12	Steve Atwater	10.00
13	Isaac Bruce	20.00
14	Deion Sanders	20.00
15	Brett Favre	80.00

1996 Leaf Collector's Edition Autographs

This 12-card autographed set was found one per Collector's Edition in factory sets from Leaf. The autographed cards all carry the words "Authentic Signature" on the front. Autographs of Leeland McElroy, Marvin Harrison, Lawrence Phillips, Bobby Engram and Eddie Kennison were printed on Gold Leaf Rookies inserts. Autographs of Tony Banks and Karim Abdul-Jabbar were on rookie subset cards, while the remaining autographs were found on regular-issue cards.

		MT
Complete Set (12):		200.00
Common Player:		10.00
	Karim Abdul-Jabbar	15.00
	Tony Banks	15.00
	Isaac Bruce	20.00
	Terrell Davis	75.00
	Bobby Engram	10.00
	Joey Galloway	20.00
	Marvin Harrison	35.00
	Eddie Kennison	10.00
	Leeland McElroy	10.00
	Lawrence Phillips	15.00
	Rashaan Salaam	10.00
	Tamarick Vanover	10.00

Values quoted in this guide reflect the retail price of a card — the price a collector can expect to pay when buying a card from a dealer. The wholesale price — that which a collector can expect to receive from a dealer when selling cards — will be significantly lower, depending on desirability and condition.

1997 Leaf

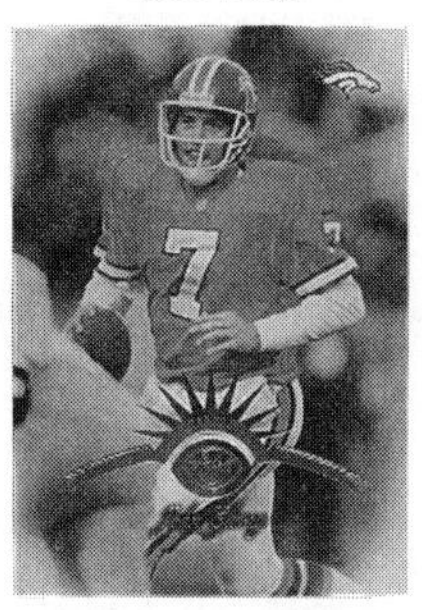

Leaf Football is a 200-card set featuring a player action shot on the front and a close-up on the back. The backs also include the past season's statistics. The Fractal Matrix chase set makes its Leaf Football debut. This base set parallel features three different color schemes and three different die-cuts. The breakdown of die-cuts and colors is 100 X-Axis (5 gold/20 silver/75 bronze), 60 Y-Axis (10 gold/30 silver/20 bronze) and 40 Z-Axis (25 gold/10 silver/5 bronze). Inserts in this set include 1948 Leaf Reproductions, Lettermen, Run & Gun and Hardwear.

		MT
Complete Set (200):		35.00
Common Player:		.15
Minor Stars:		.30
Signature Proof Cards:		20x-40x
Signature Proof Rookies:		10x-20x
Production 200 Sets		
Pack (10):		2.50
Wax Box (24):		65.00
1	Steve Young	1.00
2	Brett Favre	3.00
3	Barry Sanders	3.00
4	Drew Bledsoe	1.50
5	Troy Aikman	1.50
6	Kerry Collins	.30
7	Dan Marino	2.00
8	Jerry Rice	1.50
9	John Elway	1.50
10	Emmitt Smith	2.00
11	Tony Banks	.30
12	Gus Frerotte	.15
13	Elvis Grbac	.15
14	Neil O'Donnell	.15
15	Michael Irvin	.30
16	Marshall Faulk	.50
17	Todd Collins	.15
18	Scott Mitchell	.15
19	Trent Dilfer	.30
20	Rick Mirer	.15
21	Frank Sanders	.15
22	Larry Centers	.15
23	Brad Johnson	.30
24	Garrison Hearst	.30
25	Steve McNair	.75
26	Dorsey Levens	.30
27	Eric Metcalf	.15
28	Jeff George	.30
29	Rodney Hampton	.15
30	Michael Westbrook	.15
31	Cris Carter	.50
32	Heath Shuler	.15
33	Warren Moon	.30
34	Rod Woodson	.15
35	Ken Dilger	.15
36	Ben Coates	.15
37	Andre Reed	.15
38	Terrell Owens	.75
39	Jeff Blake	.30
40	Vinny Testaverde	.30
41	Robert Brooks	.15
42	Shannon Sharpe	.30
43	Terry Allen	.30
44	Terance Mathis	.15
45	Bobby Engram	.15
46	Rickey Dudley	.15
47	Alex Molden	.15
48	Lawrence Phillips	.15
49	Curtis Martin	.75
50	Jim Harbaugh	.30
51	Wayne Chrebet	.30
52	Quentin Coryatt	.15
53	Eddie George	1.50
54	Michael Jackson	.15
55	Greg Lloyd	.15
56	Natrone Means	.30
57	Marcus Allen	.30
58	Desmond Howard	.15
59	Stan Humphries	.15
60	Reggie White	.30
61	Brett Perriman	.15
62	Warren Sapp	.15
63	Adrian Murrell	.30
64	Mark Brunell	1.50
65	Carl Pickens	.30
66	Kordell Stewart	1.50
67	Ricky Watters	.30
68	Tyrone Wheatley	.15
69	Stanley Pritchett	.15
70	Kevin Greene	.15
71	Karim Abdul-Jabbar	.30
72	Ki-Jana Carter	.15
73	Rashaan Salaam	.15
74	Simeon Rice	.15
75	Napoleon Kaufman	.75
76	Muhsin Muhammad	.15
77	Bruce Smith	.15
78	Eric Moulds	.50
79	O.J. McDuffie	.15
80	Danny Kanell	.15
81	Harvey Williams	.15
82	Greg Hill	.15
83	Terrell Davis	2.00
84	Dan Wilkinson	.15
85	Yancey Thigpen	.15
86	Darrell Green	.15
87	Tamarick Vanover	.15
88	Mike Alstott	.50
89	Johnnie Morton	.15
90	Dale Carter	.15
91	Jerome Bettis	.30
92	James Stewart	.15
93	Irving Fryar	.15
94	Junior Seau	.30
95	Sean Dawkins	.15
96	J.J. Stokes	.30
97	Tim Biakabutuka	.30
98	Bert Emanuel	.15
99	Eddie Kennison	.30
100	Ray Zellars	.15
101	Dave Brown	.15
102	Leeland McElroy	.15
103	Chris Warren	.15
104	Bam Morris	.15
105	Thurman Thomas	.30
106	Kyle Brady	.15
107	Anthony Miller	.15
108	Derrick Thomas	.15
109	Mark Chmura	.30
110	Deion Sanders	.50
111	Eric Swann	.15
112	Amani Toomer	.15
113	Raymont Harris	.15
114	Jake Reed	.15
115	Bryant Young	.15
116	Keenan McCardell	.30
117	Herman Moore	.30
118	Errict Rhett	.15
119	Henry Ellard	.15
120	Bobby Hoying	.15
121	Robert Smith	.30
122	Keyshawn Johnson	.50
123	Zach Thomas	.30
124	Charlie Garner	.15
125	Terry Kirby	.15
126	Darren Woodson	.15
127	Darnay Scott	.15
128	Chris Sanders	.15
129	Charles Johnson	.15
130	Joey Galloway	.50
131	Curtis Conway	.30
132	Isaac Bruce	.30
133	Bobby Taylor	.15
134	Jamal Anderson	.75
135	Ken Norton	.15
136	Darick Holmes	.30
137	Tony Brackens	.15
138	Tony Martin	.15
139	Antonio Freeman	.75
140	Neil Smith	.15
141	Terry Glenn	.30
142	Marvin Harrison	.30
143	Daryl Johnston	.15
144	Tim Brown	.30
145	Kimble Anders	.15
146	Derrick Alexander	.15
147	LeShon Johnson	.15
148	Anthony Johnson	.15
149	Leslie Shepherd	.15
150	Chris T. Jones	.15
151	Edgar Bennett	.15
152	Ty Detmer	.15
153	*Ike Hilliard*	1.00
154	*Jim Druckenmiller*	1.50
155	*Warrick Dunn*	1.50
156	*Yatil Green*	.30
157	*Reidel Anthony*	1.50
158	*Antowain Smith*	1.50
159	*Rae Carruth*	.75
160	*Tiki Barber*	1.00
161	*Byron Hanspard*	.75
162	*Jake Plummer*	3.00
163	*Joey Kent*	.30
164	*Corey Dillon*	2.50
165	*Kevin Lockett*	.15
166	*Will Blackwell*	.15
167	*Troy Davis*	.30
168	*James Farrior*	.15
169	*Danny Wuerffel*	.75
170	*Pat Barnes*	.50
171	*Darnell Autry*	.30
172	*Tom Knight*	.15
173	*David LaFleur*	.30
174	*Tony Gonzalez*	.75
175	*Kenny Holmes*	.15
176	*Reinard Wilson*	.15
177	*Renaldo Wynn*	.15
178	*Bryant Westbrook*	.15
179	*Darrell Russell*	.30
180	*Orlando Pace*	.30
181	*Shawn Springs*	.30
182	*Peter Boulware*	.30
183	Dan Marino (Legacy)	1.00
184	Brett Favre (Legacy)	1.50
185	Emmitt Smith (Legacy)	1.00
186	Eddie George (Legacy)	.75
187	Curtis Martin (Legacy)	.50
188	Tim Brown (Legacy)	.15
189	Mark Brunell (Legacy)	.75
190	Isaac Bruce (Legacy)	.15
191	Deion Sanders (Legacy)	.30
192	John Elway (Legacy)	.75
193	Jerry Rice (Legacy)	.75
194	Barry Sanders (Legacy)	1.50
195	Herman Moore (Legacy)	.15
196	Carl Pickens (Legacy)	.15
197	Karim Abdul-Jabbar (Legacy)	.15
198	(Drew Bledsoe CL)	.75
199	(Troy Aikman CL)	.75
200	(Terrell Davis CL)	.75

1997 Leaf Fractal Matrix

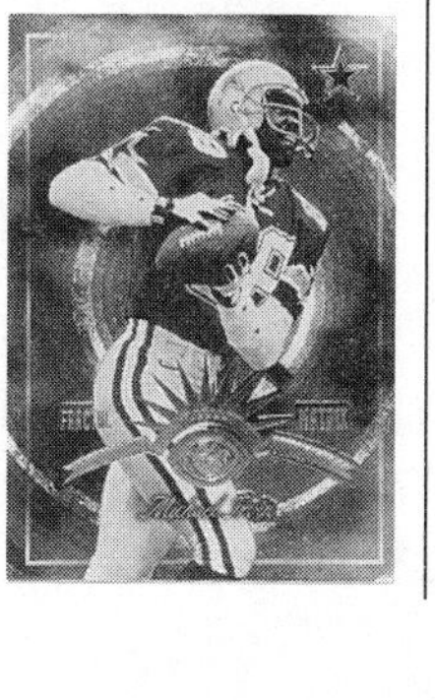

This 200-card parallel features multi-fractured technology. Each card is done in one of three colors: bronze (100 cards), silver (60 cards) or gold (40 cards).

		MT
Common Bronze X:		2.00
Common Bronze Y:		1.50
Common Bronze Z:		1.50
Common Silver X:		6.00
Common Silver Y:		5.00
Common Silver Z:		4.00
1	Steve Young GZ	70.00
2	Brett Favre GX	500.00
3	Barry Sanders GZ	100.00
4	Drew Bledsoe GZ	100.00
5	Troy Aikman GZ	100.00
6	Kerry Collins GZ	85.00
7	Dan Marino GX	450.00
8	Jerry Rice GZ	100.00
9	John Elway GZ	70.00
10	Emmitt Smith GX	450.00
11	Tony Banks GY	50.00
12	Gus Frerotte SX	6.00
13	Elvis Grbac SX	6.00
14	Neil O'Donnell BX	2.00
15	Michael Irvin SY	7.00
16	Marshall Faulk SY	7.00
17	Todd Collins SX	6.00
18	Scott Mitchell BX	2.00
19	Trent Dilfer SY	5.00
20	Rick Mirer SX	6.00
21	Frank Sanders SX	6.00
22	Larry Centers BX	2.00
23	Brad Johnson BX	2.00
24	Garrison Hearst SY	5.00
25	Steve McNair GZ	85.00
26	Dorsey Levens BX	4.00
27	Eric Metcalf BX	2.00
28	Jeff George SX	6.00
29	Rodney Hampton BX	2.00
30	Michael Westbrook SY	5.00
31	Cris Carter SY	5.00
32	Heath Shuler SX	6.00
33	Warren Moon BX	2.00
34	Rod Woodson SX	6.00
35	Ken Dilger BX	2.00
36	Ben Coates BX	2.00
37	Andre Reed BX	2.00
38	Terrell Owens SZ	25.00
39	Jeff Blake SY	5.00
40	Vinny Testaverde BX	2.00
41	Robert Brooks SY	5.00
42	Shannon Sharpe SX	6.00
43	Terry Allen SY	5.00
44	Terance Mathis BX	2.00
45	Bobby Engram BZ	3.00
46	Rickey Dudley BX	2.00
47	Alex Molden BX	2.00
48	Lawrence Phillips SY	5.00
49	Curtis Martin GZ	100.00
50	Jim Harbaugh BX	2.00
51	Wayne Chrebet BX	2.00
52	Quentin Coryatt BX	2.00
53	Eddie George GX	325.00
54	Michael Jackson BX	2.00
55	Greg Lloyd BX	2.00
56	Natrone Means SZ	7.00
57	Marcus Allen GY	30.00
58	Desmond Howard BX	2.00
59	Stan Humphries BX	2.00
60	Reggie White GY	30.00
61	Brett Perriman SY	5.00
62	Warren Sapp BX	2.00
63	Adrian Murrell SZ	4.00
64	Mark Brunell GZ	100.00
65	Carl Pickens GY	5.00
66	Kordell Stewart GZ	100.00
67	Ricky Watters GY	30.00
68	Tyrone Wheatley BX	2.00
69	Stanley Pritchett BX	2.00
70	Kevin Greene BX	2.00
71	Karim Abdul-Jabbar GZ	85.00
72	Ki-Jana Carter SY	5.00
73	Rashaan Salaam SY	5.00
74	Simeon Rice BX	2.00
75	Napoleon Kaufman SY	5.00
76	Muhsin Muhammad SZ	4.00
77	Bruce Smith GY	5.00
78	Eric Moulds SX	6.00
79	O.J. McDuffie BX	2.00
80	Danny Kanell BZ	1.50
81	Harvey Williams BX	2.00
82	Greg Hill SY	5.00
83	Terrell Davis GZ	100.00
84	Dan Wilkinson BX	2.00
85	Yancey Thigpen BX	2.00
86	Darrell Green SX	6.00
87	Tamarick Vanover SX	6.00
88	Mike Alstott BX	2.00
89	Johnnie Morton SX	6.00
90	Dale Carter BX	2.00
91	Jerome Bettis GY	30.00
92	James Stewart BX	2.00
93	Irving Fryar SX	6.00
94	Junior Seau SY	5.00
95	Sean Dawkins BX	2.00
96	J.J. Stokes BZ	1.50
97	Tim Biakabutuka SY	5.00
98	Bert Emanuel BX	2.00
99	Eddie Kennison GY	50.00
100	Ray Zellars BX	2.00
101	Dave Brown BX	2.00
102	Leeland McElroy SY	5.00
103	Chris Warren SY	5.00
104	Bam Morris BX	2.00
105	Thurman Thomas GY	30.00
106	Kyle Brady BX	2.00
107	Anthony Miller GY	10.00
108	Derrick Thomas SY	5.00
109	Mark Chmura BX	2.00
110	Deion Sanders GZ	50.00
111	Eric Swann BX	2.00
112	Amani Toomer SX	6.00
113	Raymont Harris BX	2.00
114	Jake Reed BX	2.00
115	Bryant Young BX	2.00
116	Keenan McCardell SX	6.00
117	Herman Moore GZ	20.00
118	Errict Rhett SZ	4.00
119	Henry Ellard BX	2.00
120	Bobby Hoying SX	6.00
121	Robert Smith BX	4.00
122	Keyshawn Johnson GZ	50.00
123	Zach Thomas BX	10.00
124	Charlie Garner BX	2.00
125	Terry Kirby BX	2.00
126	Darren Woodson BX	2.00
127	Darnay Scott SX	6.00
128	Chris Sanders SY	5.00
129	Charles Johnson SX	6.00
130	Joey Galloway SZ	8.00
131	Curtis Conway SY	5.00
132	Isaac Bruce GZ	20.00
133	Bobby Taylor BX	2.00
134	Jamal Anderson SY	5.00
135	Ken Norton BX	2.00
136	Darick Holmes BX	2.00
137	Tony Brackens BX	2.00
138	Tony Martin BX	2.00
139	Antonio Freeman SZ	15.00
140	Neil Smith BX	2.00
141	Terry Glenn GZ	85.00
142	Marvin Harrison SY	25.00
143	Daryl Johnston BX	2.00
144	Tim Brown GY	10.00
145	Kimble Anders BX	2.00
146	Derrick Alexander SX	6.00
147	LeShon Johnson BX	2.00
148	Anthony Johnson BX	2.00
149	Leslie Shepherd BX	2.00
150	Chris T. Jones BX	2.00
151	Edgar Bennett BX	2.00
152	Ty Detmer BX	2.00
153	*Ike Hilliard GX*	100.00
154	*Jim Druckenmiller SZ*	30.00
155	*Warrick Dunn GZ*	100.00
156	*Yatil Green GZ*	20.00
157	*Reidel Anthony GZ*	30.00
158	*Antowain Smith GZ*	15.00
159	*Rae Carruth SY*	10.00
160	*Tiki Barber GZ*	30.00
161	*Byron Hanspard SZ*	10.00
162	*Jake Plummer SY*	15.00
163	*Joey Kent SZ*	10.00
164	*Corey Dillon SY*	15.00
165	*Kevin Lockett BZ*	3.00
166	*Will Blackwell BY*	6.00
167	*Troy Davis GZ*	25.00
168	*James Farrior BX*	4.00
169	*Danny Wuerffel SY*	15.00
170	*Pat Barnes SY*	10.00
171	*Darnell Autry SY*	10.00
172	*Tom Knight BX*	4.00
173	*David LaFleur BY*	10.00
174	*Tony Gonzalez BY*	10.00
175	*Kenny Holmes BX*	4.00
176	*Reinard Wilson BX*	4.00
177	*Renaldo Wynn BX*	4.00
178	*Bryant Westbrook BX*	4.00
179	*Darrell Russell BX*	4.00
180	*Orlando Pace BX*	6.00
181	*Shawn Springs BX*	4.00
182	*Peter Boulware BX*	4.00
183	Dan Marino BY (Legacy)	20.00
184	Brett Favre BY (Legacy)	25.00
185	Emmitt Smith BY (Legacy)	20.00
186	Eddie George BY (Legacy)	18.00
187	Curtis Martin BY (Legacy)	15.00
188	Tim Brown BZ (Legacy)	3.00
189	Mark Brunell BY (Legacy)	15.00
190	Isaac Bruce BY (Legacy)	3.00
191	Deion Sanders BY (Legacy)	6.00
192	John Elway BY (Legacy)	10.00
193	Jerry Rice BY (Legacy)	15.00
194	Barry Sanders BY (Legacy)	20.00
195	Herman Moore BY (Legacy)	3.00
196	Carl Pickens BY (Legacy)	3.00
197	Karim Abdul-Jabbar BY (Legacy)	10.00
198	Checklist (Drew Bledsoe BY)	15.00
199	Checklist (Troy Aikman BY)	15.00
200	Checklist (Terrell Davis BY)	15.00

1997 Leaf Fractal Matrix Die-Cuts

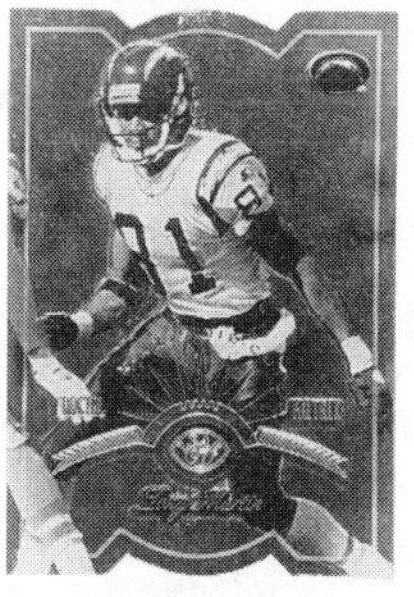

This insert adds die-cutting to the Fractal Matrix parallel. The breakdown of cards is 100 X-Axis (5 gold/20 silver/75 bronze), 60 Y-Axis (10 gold/30 silver/20 bronze) and 40 Z-Axis (25 gold/10 silver/5 bronze).

		MT
Common X-Axis:		5.00
Common Y-Axis:		8.00
Common Z-Axis:		12.00
1	Steve Young GZ	100.00
2	Brett Favre GX	120.00
3	Barry Sanders GZ	150.00
4	Drew Bledsoe GZ	150.00
5	Troy Aikman GZ	150.00
6	Kerry Collins GZ	125.00
7	Dan Marino GX	100.00
8	Jerry Rice GZ	150.00
9	John Elway GZ	100.00
10	Emmitt Smith GX	100.00
11	Tony Banks GY	60.00
12	Gus Frerotte SX	5.00
13	Elvis Grbac SX	5.00
14	Neil O'Donnell BX	5.00
15	Michael Irvin SY	15.00
16	Marshall Faulk SY	15.00
17	Todd Collins SX	5.00
18	Scott Mitchell BX	5.00
19	Trent Dilfer SY	8.00
20	Rick Mirer SX	5.00
21	Frank Sanders SX	5.00
22	Larry Centers BX	5.00
23	Brad Johnson BX	5.00
24	Garrison Hearst SY	8.00
25	Steve McNair GZ	125.00
26	Dorsey Levens BX	5.00
27	Eric Metcalf BX	5.00
28	Jeff George SX	5.00
29	Rodney Hampton BX	5.00
30	Michael Westbrook SY	8.00
31	Cris Carter SY	8.00
32	Heath Shuler SX	5.00
33	Warren Moon BX	5.00
34	Rod Woodson SX	5.00
35	Ken Dilger BX	5.00
36	Ben Coates BX	5.00
37	Andre Reed BX	5.00
38	Terrell Owens SZ	75.00
39	Jeff Blake SY	15.00
40	Vinny Testaverde BX	5.00
41	Robert Brooks SY	10.00
42	Shannon Sharpe SX	5.00
43	Terry Allen SY	8.00
44	Terance Mathis BX	5.00
45	Bobby Engram BZ	25.00
46	Rickey Dudley BX	5.00
47	Alex Molden BX	5.00
48	Lawrence Phillips SY	8.00
49	Curtis Martin GZ	150.00
50	Jim Harbaugh BX	5.00
51	Wayne Chrebet BX	5.00
52	Quentin Coryatt BX	5.00
53	Eddie George GX	75.00
54	Michael Jackson BX	5.00
55	Greg Lloyd BX	5.00
56	Natrone Means SZ	25.00
57	Marcus Allen GY	15.00
58	Desmond Howard BX	5.00
59	Stan Humphries BX	5.00
60	Reggie White GY	15.00
61	Brett Perriman SY	8.00
62	Warren Sapp BX	5.00
63	Adrian Murrell SZ	12.00
64	Mark Brunell GZ	150.00
65	Carl Pickens GY	8.00
66	Kordell Stewart GZ	150.00
67	Ricky Watters GY	15.00
68	Tyrone Wheatley BX	5.00
69	Stanley Pritchett BX	5.00
70	Kevin Greene BX	5.00
71	Karim Abdul-Jabbar GZ	100.00
72	Ki-Jana Carter SY	8.00
73	Rashaan Salaam SY	8.00
74	Simeon Rice BX	5.00
75	Napoleon Kaufman SY	15.00
76	Muhsin Muhammad SZ	12.00
77	Bruce Smith GY	8.00
78	Eric Moulds SX	5.00
79	O.J. McDuffie BX	5.00
80	Danny Kanell BZ	12.00
81	Harvey Williams BX	5.00
82	Greg Hill SY	8.00
83	Terrell Davis GZ	150.00
84	Dan Wilkinson BX	5.00
85	Yancey Thigpen BX	5.00
86	Darrell Green SX	5.00
87	Tamarick Vanover SX	5.00
88	Mike Alstott BX	5.00
89	Johnnie Morton SX	5.00
90	Dale Carter BX	5.00
91	Jerome Bettis GY	15.00
92	James Stewart BX	5.00
93	Irving Fryar SX	5.00
94	Junior Seau SY	8.00
95	Sean Dawkins BX	5.00
96	J.J. Stokes BZ	12.00
97	Tim Biakabutuka SY	8.00
98	Bert Emanuel BX	5.00
99	Eddie Kennison GY	60.00
100	Ray Zellars BX	5.00
101	Dave Brown BX	5.00
102	Leeland McElroy SY	8.00
103	Chris Warren SY	8.00
104	Bam Morris BX	5.00
105	Thurman Thomas GY	15.00
106	Kyle Brady BX	5.00
107	Anthony Miller GY	8.00
108	Derrick Thomas SY	8.00
109	Mark Chmura BX	5.00
110	Deion Sanders GZ	75.00
111	Eric Swann BX	5.00
112	Amani Toomer SX	5.00
113	Raymont Harris BX	5.00
114	Jake Reed BX	5.00
115	Bryant Young BX	5.00
116	Keenan McCardell SX	5.00
117	Herman Moore GZ	25.00
118	Errict Rhett SZ	25.00
119	Henry Ellard BX	5.00
120	Bobby Hoying SX	5.00
121	Robert Smith BX	5.00
122	Keyshawn Johnson GZ	75.00
123	Zach Thomas BX	20.00
124	Charlie Garner BX	5.00
125	Terry Kirby BX	5.00
126	Darren Woodson BX	5.00
127	Darnay Scott SX	5.00
128	Chris Sanders SY	8.00
129	Charles Johnson SX	5.00
130	Joey Galloway SZ	25.00
131	Curtis Conway SY	8.00
132	Isaac Bruce GZ	25.00
133	Bobby Taylor BX	5.00
134	Jamal Anderson SY	8.00
135	Ken Norton BX	5.00
136	Darick Holmes BX	5.00
137	Tony Brackens BX	5.00
138	Tony Martin BX	5.00
139	Antonio Freeman SZ	60.00
140	Neil Smith BX	5.00
141	Terry Glenn GZ	130.00
142	Marvin Harrison SY	60.00
143	Daryl Johnston BX	5.00
144	Tim Brown GY	8.00
145	Kimble Anders BX	5.00
146	Derrick Alexander SX	5.00
147	LeShon Johnson BX	5.00
148	Anthony Johnson BX	5.00
149	Leslie Shepherd BX	5.00
150	Chris T. Jones BX	5.00
151	Edgar Bennett BX	5.00
152	Ty Detmer BX	5.00
153	*Ike Hilliard GX*	20.00
154	*Jim Druckenmiller SZ*	100.00
155	*Warrick Dunn GZ*	150.00
156	*Yatil Green GZ*	40.00
157	*Reidel Anthony GZ*	60.00
158	*Antowain Smith GZ*	70.00
159	*Rae Carruth SY*	30.00
160	*Tiki Barber GZ*	40.00
161	*Byron Hanspard SZ*	20.00
162	*Jake Plummer SY*	30.00
163	*Joey Kent SZ*	15.00
164	*Corey Dillon SY*	45.00
165	*Kevin Lockett BZ*	12.00
166	*Will Blackwell BY*	15.00
167	*Troy Davis GZ*	40.00
168	*James Farrior BX*	5.00
169	*Danny Wuerffel SY*	60.00
170	*Pat Barnes SY*	20.00
171	*Darnell Autry SY*	15.00
172	*Tom Knight BX*	5.00
173	*David LaFleur BY*	20.00
174	*Tony Gonzalez BY*	20.00
175	*Kenny Holmes BX*	5.00
176	*Reinard Wilson BX*	5.00
177	*Renaldo Wynn BX*	5.00
178	*Bryant Westbrook BX*	5.00
179	*Darrell Russell BX*	5.00
180	*Orlando Pace BX*	10.00
181	*Shawn Springs BX*	5.00
182	*Peter Boulware BX*	5.00
183	Dan Marino BY (Legacy)	100.00
184	Brett Favre BY (Legacy)	100.00
185	Emmitt Smith BY (Legacy)	100.00
186	Eddie George BY (Legacy)	75.00
187	Curtis Martin BY (Legacy)	50.00
188	Tim Brown BZ (Legacy)	12.00
189	Mark Brunell BY (Legacy)	50.00
190	Isaac Bruce BY (Legacy)	15.00
191	Deion Sanders BY (Legacy)	25.00
192	John Elway BY (Legacy)	35.00
193	Jerry Rice BY (Legacy)	50.00
194	Barry Sanders BY (Legacy)	50.00
195	Herman Moore BY (Legacy)	8.00
196	Carl Pickens BY (Legacy)	8.00
197	Karim Abdul-Jabbar BY (Legacy)	40.00
198	Checklist (Drew Bledsoe BY)	50.00
199	Checklist (Troy Aikman BY)	50.00
200	Checklist (Terrell Davis BY)	50.00

1997 Leaf Hardwear

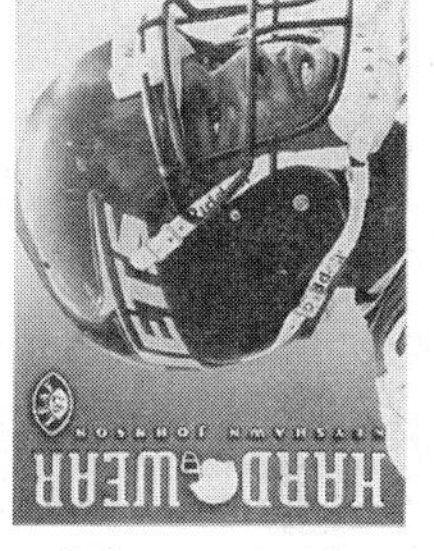

Hardwear is a 20-card insert featuring top players on a plastic card. The cards are die-cut into a helmet-shaped design and sequentially numbered to 3,500.

		MT
Complete Set (20):		250.00
Common Player:		4.00
Minor Stars:		8.00
Production 3,500 Sets		
1	Dan Marino	25.00
2	Brett Favre	30.00
3	Emmitt Smith	25.00
4	Jerry Rice	15.00
5	Barry Sanders	30.00
6	Deion Sanders	8.00
7	Reggie White	8.00
8	Tim Brown	4.00
9	Steve McNair	8.00
10	Steve Young	12.00
11	Mark Brunell	15.00
12	Ricky Watters	4.00
13	Eddie Kennison	4.00
14	Kordell Stewart	12.00
15	Kerry Collins	4.00
16	Joey Galloway	8.00
17	Terrell Owens	8.00
18	Terry Glenn	8.00
19	Keyshawn Johnson	8.00
20	Eddie George	15.00

1997 Leaf Letterman

The cards in this 15-card insert look and feel like a college letter. The cards are also embossed and foil stamped. Each card is sequentially numbered to 1,000.

		MT
Complete Set (15):		500.00
Common Player:		15.00
Production 1,000 Sets		
1	Brett Favre	60.00
2	Emmitt Smith	45.00
3	Dan Marino	45.00
4	Jerry Rice	30.00
5	Mark Brunell	30.00
6	Barry Sanders	60.00
7	John Elway	30.00
8	Eddie George	30.00
9	Troy Aikman	30.00
10	Curtis Martin	20.00
11	Karim Abdul-Jabbar	15.00
12	Terrell Davis	45.00

13 Ike Hilliard 15.00
14 Yatil Green 15.00
15 Drew Bledsoe 30.00

1997 Leaf Run & Gun

This 18-card insert features a top quarterback/running back combo from the same team, one on each side of the card. One side features holographic foil stock and the other is foil stamped. The cards are numbered to 3,500.

	MT
Complete Set (18):	250.00
Common Player:	5.00
Minor Stars:	10.00
Production 3,500 Sets	
1 Dan Marino, Karim Abdul-Jabbar	25.00
2 Troy Aikman, Emmitt Smith	25.00
3 John Elway, Terrell Davis	40.00
4 Drew Bledsoe, Curtis Martin	20.00
5 Kordell Stewart, Jerome Bettis	20.00
6 Mark Brunell, Natrone Means	15.00
7 Kerry Collins, Tim Biakabutuka	10.00
8 Rick Mirer, Rashaan Salaam	5.00
9 Scott Mitchell, Barry Sanders	30.00
10 Steve McNair, Eddie George	15.00
11 Trent Dilfer, Warrick Dunn	15.00
12 Jeff Blake, Ki-Jana Carter	5.00
13 Tony Banks, Lawrence Phillips	10.00
14 Steve Young, Garrison Hearst	15.00
15 Jim Harbaugh, Marshall Faulk	10.00
16 Elvis Grbac, Marcus Allen	5.00
17 Neil O'Donnell, Adrian Murrell	5.00
18 Gus Frerotte, Terry Allen	5.00

1997 Leaf Reproductions

Twelve current and 12 former NFL stars are featured in this 24-card set. The cards are a reproduction of Leaf's 1948 set design. The first 500 cards of each former great are autographed. Each insert card is numbered to 1,948.

	MT
Complete Set (24):	375.00
Common Player:	7.00
Minor Stars:	14.00
Production 1,948 Sets	
Complete Autograph Set (11):	300.00
Common Autograph (13-24):	20.00
Minor Autograph Stars:	40.00
Production 500 Sets	
1 Emmitt Smith	30.00
2 Brett Favre	40.00
3 Dan Marino	30.00
4 Barry Sanders	40.00
5 Jerry Rice	20.00
6 Terrell Davis	30.00
7 Curtis Martin	14.00
8 Troy Aikman	20.00
9 Drew Bledsoe	20.00
10 Herman Moore	7.00
11 Isaac Bruce	7.00
12 Carl Pickens	7.00
13 Len Dawson	14.00
14 Dan Fouts	14.00
15 Jim Plunkett	7.00
16 Ken Stabler	14.00
17 Joe Theismann	14.00
18 Billy Kilmer	14.00
19 Danny White	14.00
20 Archie Manning	7.00
21 Ron Jaworski	7.00
22 Y.A. Tittle	14.00
23 Sid Luckman	14.00
23a Sid Luckman AUTO	180.00

1997 Leaf Signature

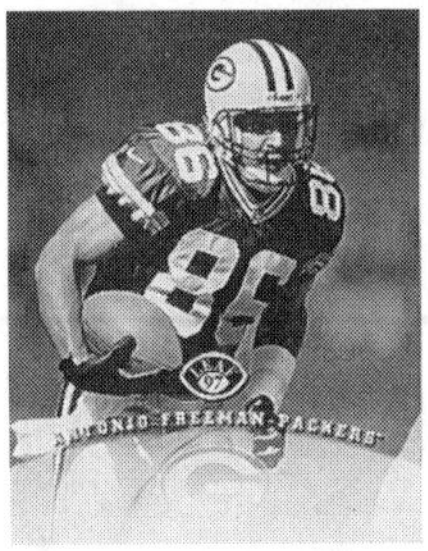

Leaf Signature Football consisted of 118 8" x 10" cards that featured top established players and rookies. The card fronts feature a large color shot of the player, with a large off-color oval taking up the bottom portion. The player's name is stamped in silver foil above this oval, with a Leaf '97 Football logo in silver and black above that. The backs are horizontal and unnumbered and contain a large close-up shot of the player on the left side with a brief biography on the right. Most of the players also arrive in an autographed version, which have the words "Authentic Signature" printed in black across the bottom. Also included in packs were Old School Draft Autographs, which featured 11 retired quarterbacks.

	MT
Complete Set (118):	150.00
Common Player:	.50
Minor Stars:	1.00
Pack (2):	14.00
Wax Box (8):	110.00
1 Karim Abdul-Jabbar	2.00
2 Troy Aikman	5.00
3 Derrick Alexander	.50
4 Terry Allen	1.00
5 Mike Alstott	2.00
6 Jamal Anderson	3.00
7 Reidel Anthony	2.50
8 Darnell Autry	1.00
9 Tony Banks	1.00
10 Tiki Barber	1.00
11 Pat Barnes	1.00
12 Jerome Bettis	1.00
13 Tim Biakabutuka	1.00
14 Will Blackwell	1.00
15 Jeff Blake	1.00
16 Drew Bledsoe	5.00
17 Peter Boulware	.50
18 Robert Brooks	.50
19 Dave Brown	.50
20 Tim Brown	1.00
21 Isaac Bruce	1.00
22 Mark Brunell	5.00
23 Rae Carruth	2.00
24 Cris Carter	2.00
25 Ki-Jana Carter	.50
26 Larry Centers	.50
27 Ben Coates	1.00
28 Kerry Collins	1.00
29 Todd Collins	.50
30 Albert Connell	.50
31 Curtis Conway	1.00
32 Terrell Davis	8.00
33 Troy Davis	1.00
34 Trent Dilfer	2.00
35 Corey Dillon	6.00
36 Jim Druckenmiller	5.00
37 Warrick Dunn	10.00
38 John Elway	5.00
39 Bert Emmanuel	.50
40 Bobby Engram	.50
41 Boomer Esiason	.50
42 Jim Everett	.50
43 Marshall Faulk	2.00
44 Brett Favre	10.00
45 Antonio Freeman	2.00
46 Gus Frerotte	.50
47 Irving Fryar	.50
48 Joey Galloway	2.00
49 Eddie George	6.00
50 Jeff George	1.00
51 Tony Gonzalez	2.00
52 Jay Graham	1.00
53 Elvis Grbac	1.00
54 Darrell Green	.50
55 Yatil Green	1.00
56 Rodney Hampton	.50
57 Byron Hanspard	2.00
58 Jim Harbaugh	1.00
59 Marvin Harrison	1.00
60 Garrison Hearst	2.00
61 Greg Hill	.50
62 Ike Hilliard	2.00
63 Jeff Hostetler	.50
64 Brad Johnson	2.00
65 Keyshawn Johnson	2.00
66 Darryl Johnston	.50
67 Napoleon Kaufman	3.00
68 Jim Kelly	1.00
69 Eddie Kennison	1.00
70 Joey Kent	1.00
71 Bernie Kosar	.50
72 Eric Kramer	.50
73 Dorsey Levens	1.00
74 Kevin Lockett	.50
75 Dan Marino	8.00
76 Curtis Martin	4.00
77 Tony Martin	.50
78 Leeland McElroy	.50
79 Steve McNair	4.00
80 Natrone Means	1.00
81 Eric Metcalf	.50
82 Anthony Miller	.50
83 Rick Mirer	.50
84 Scott Mitchell	.50
85 Warren Moon	1.00
86 Herman Moore	1.00
87 Muhsin Muhammad	.50
88 Adrian Murrell	1.00
89 Neil O'Donnell	.50
90 Terrell Owens	3.00
91 Brett Perriman	.50
92 Lawrence Phillips	.50
93 Jake Plummer	10.00
94 Andre Reed	.50
95 Jerry Rice	5.00
96 Darrell Russell	.50
97 Rashaan Salaam	.50
98 Barry Sanders	10.00
99 Deion Sanders	2.00
100 Frank Sanders	.50
101 Chris Sanders	.50
102 Junior Seau	.50
103 Darnay Scott	.50
104 Shannon Sharpe	1.00
105 Sedrick Shaw	.50
106 Heath Shuler	.50
107 Antowain Smith	5.00
108 Bruce Smith	.50
109 Emmitt Smith	8.00
110 Kordell Stewart	5.00
111 J.J. Stokes	1.00
112 Vinny Testaverde	1.00
113 Thurman Thomas	1.00
114 Tamarick Vanover	.50
115 Herschel Walker	.50
116 Michael Westbrook	.50
117 Danny Wuerffel	2.00
118 Steve Young	3.50

1997 Leaf Signature Autographs

All but 11 of the players included in Leaf Signature Series Football signed cards for the product. Signature cards are identified by the player's autograph, usually found in the large, off-color oval part of the card and the words "Authentic Signature" in black letters across the bottom. Signature cards were inserted at a rate of one per pack. Included below with the player listing is the number of cards that was reported that each player signed.

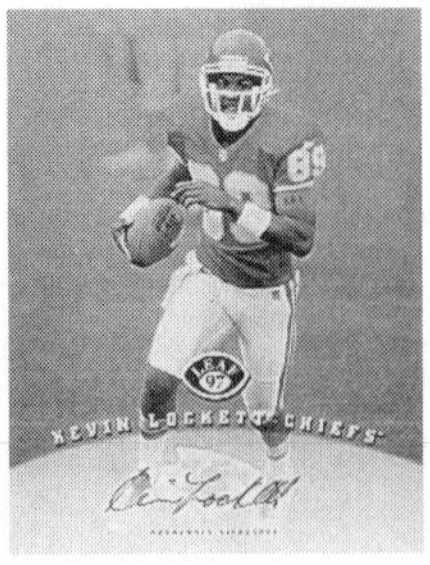

	MT
Common Player:	10.00
Minor Stars:	20.00
First Down Markers:	2x
Karim Abdul-Jabbar 2500	30.00
Derrick Alexander 4000	10.00
Terry Allen 3000	20.00
Mike Alstott 4000	30.00
Jamal Anderson 4000	20.00
Reidel Anthony 2000	30.00
Darnell Autry 4000	20.00
Tony Banks 500	45.00
Tiki Barber 4000	30.00
Pat Barnes 4000	20.00
Jerome Bettis 500	60.00
Tim Biakabutuka 3000	20.00
Will Blackwell 2500	20.00
Jeff Blake 500	45.00
Drew Bledsoe 500	150.00
Peter Boulware 4000	10.00
Robert Brooks 1000	30.00
Dave Brown 500	40.00
Tim Brown 2500	30.00
Isaac Bruce 2500	30.00
Mark Brunell 500	150.00
Rae Carruth 5000	20.00
Cris Carter 2500	20.00
Larry Centers 4000	10.00
Ben Coates 4000	10.00
Todd Collins 4000	10.00
Albert Connell 4000	10.00
Curtis Conway 3000	20.00
Terrell Davis 2500	100.00
Troy Davis 4000	20.00
Trent Dilfer 500	60.00
Corey Dillon 4000	60.00
Jim Druckenmiller 5000	50.00
Warrick Dunn 2000	120.00
John Elway 500	150.00
Bert Emmanuel 4000	10.00
Bobby Engram 3000	10.00
Boomer Esiason 500	50.00
Jim Everett 500	40.00
Marshall Faulk 3000	30.00
Antonio Freeman 2000	30.00
Gus Frerotte 500	40.00
Irving Fryar 3000	10.00
Joey Galloway 3000	30.00
Eddie George 300	180.00
Jeff George 500	40.00
Tony Gonzalez 3500	20.00
Jay Graham 1000	30.00
Elvis Grbac 500	40.00
Darrell Green 2500	10.00
Yatil Green 5000	30.00
Rodney Hampton 4000	10.00
Byron Hanspard 4000	20.00
Jim Harbaugh 500	40.00
Marvin Harrison 3000	30.00
Garrison Hearst 4000	10.00
Greg Hill 4000	10.00
Ike Hilliard 2000	20.00
Jeff Hostetler 500	40.00
Brad Johnson 2000	20.00
Keyshawn Johnson 900	45.00
Darryl Johnston 3000	10.00
Jim Kelly 500	75.00
Eddie Kennison 3000	20.00
Joey Kent 4000	10.00
Bernie Kosar 500	40.00
Eric Kramer 500	40.00
Dorsey Levens 3000	30.00
Kevin Lockett 4000	10.00
Tony Martin 4000	10.00
Leeland McElroy 4000	10.00
Natrone Means 3000	20.00
Eric Metcalf 4000	10.00
Anthony Miller 3000	10.00
Rick Mirer 500	40.00
Scott Mitchell 500	40.00
Warren Moon 500	50.00
Herman Moore 2500	20.00
Muhsin Muhammad 3000	10.00
Adrian Murrell 3000	20.00
Neil O'Donnell 500	40.00
Terrell Owens 3000	30.00
Brett Perriman 700	40.00
Lawrence Phillips 750	40.00
Jake Plummer 5000	60.00
Andre Reed 3000	10.00
Darrell Russell 2000	20.00
Rashaan Salaam 3000	10.00
Frank Sanders 3000	10.00
Chris Sanders 3000	10.00
Junior Seau 500	40.00
Darnay Scott 2000	20.00
Shannon Sharpe 1000	30.00
Sedrick Shaw 4000	20.00
Heath Shuler 500	40.00
Antowain Smith 5000	50.00
Kordell Stewart 500	150.00
J.J. Stokes 3000	10.00
Vinny Testaverde 250	80.00
Thurman Thomas 2500	20.00
Tamarick Vanover 4000	10.00
Herschel Walker 3000	10.00
Michael Westbrook 3000	10.00
Danny Wuerffel 3000	20.00
Steve Young 500	150.00

1997 Leaf Signature Old School Drafts Autographs

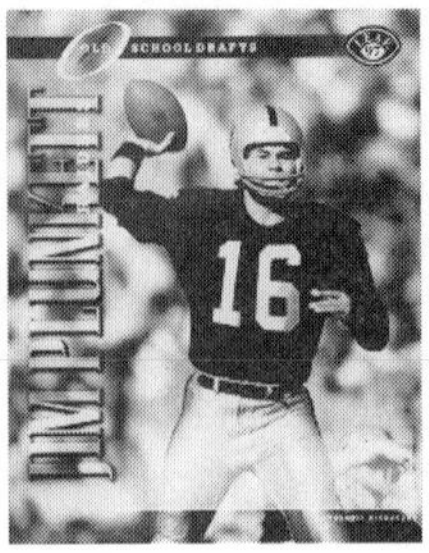

Old School Drafts Autographs included 11 former quarterbacks on 8" x 10" cards. The cards feature the insert name in large bold letters across the top and are individually numbered to 1,000. Card No. 10 is not available.

	MT
Complete Set (11):	500.00
Common Player:	25.00
Card #10 not included	
1 Joe Theismann	50.00
2 Archie Manning	50.00
3 Len Dawson	50.00
4 Sammy Baugh	120.00
5 Dan Fouts	75.00
6 Danny White	50.00
7 Ron Jaworski	25.00
8 Jim Plunkett	25.00
9 Y.A. Tittle	85.00
10 N/A	
11 Ken Stabler	85.00
12 Billy Kilmer	25.00

1998 Leaf Rookies & Stars

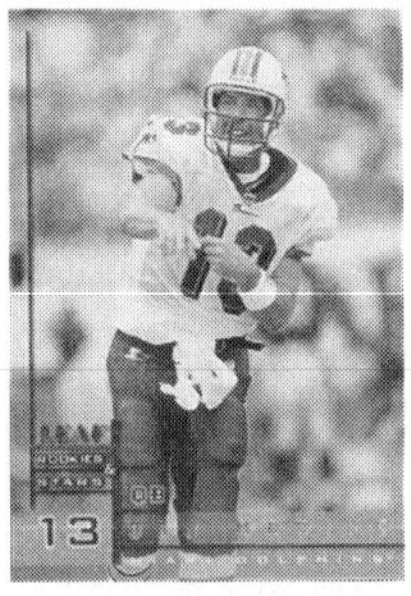

This is the first Leaf product released under Playoff. The 300-card set includes short-printed cards of 70 rookies and 30 Power Tools inserted 1:2 packs. Two parallel sets with the True Blue singles sequentially numbered to 500 and the Longevity parallel numbered to 50. The product also includes 13 other sequentially numbered inserts.

	MT
Complete Set (300):	450.00
Common Player:	.15
Minor Stars:	.30
Common Rookie (171-240):	2.00
Common Power Tool (241-270):	2.00
Inserted 1:2	
Longevity Cards:	50x-100x
Longevity Rookies:	2x
Longevity PT Cards:	10x-20x
Longevity PT Rookies:	2x-4x
Production 50 Sets	
True Blue Cards:	7x-14x
True Blue Rookies:	1x
True Blue PT:	2x
Production 500 Sets	
Pack (9):	5.50
Wax Box (24):	120.00
1 Keyshawn Johnson	.50
2 Marvin Harrison	.30
3 Eddie Kennison	.15
4 Bryant Young	.15
5 Darren Woodson	.15
6 Tyrone Wheatley	.15
7 Michael Westbrook	.15
8 Charles Way	.15
9 Ricky Watters	.30
10 Chris Warren	.15
11 Wesley Walls	.15
12 Tamarick Vanover	.15
13 Zach Thomas	.30
14 Derrick Thomas	.15
15 Yancey Thigpen	.15
16 Vinny Testaverde	.30
17 Dana Stubblefield	.15
18 J.J. Stokes	.30
19 James Stewart	.15
20 Jeff George	.30
21 John Randle	.15
22 Gary Brown	.15
23 Ed McCaffrey	.30
24 James Jett	.15
25 Rob Johnson	.30
26 Daryl Johnston	.15
27 Jermaine Lewis	.15
28 Tony Martin	.15
29 Derrick Mayes	.15
30 Keenan McCardell	.30
31 O.J. McDuffie	.30
32 Chris Chandler	.30
33 Doug Flutie	.75
34 Scott Mitchell	.30
35 Warren Moon	.30
36 Rob Moore	.30
37 Johnnie Morton	.15
38 Neil O'Donnell	.15
39 Rich Gannon	.15
40 Andre Reed	.15
41 Jake Reed	.15
42 Errict Rhett	.15
43 Simeon Rice	.15
44 Andre Rison	.30
45 Eric Moulds	.30
46 Frank Sanders	.15
47 Darnay Scott	.15
48 Junior Seau	.30
49 Shannon Sharpe	.30
50 Bruce Smith	.15
51 Jimmy Smith	.30
52 Robert Smith	.30
53 Derrick Alexander	.15
54 Kimble Anders	.15
55 Jamal Anderson	.75
56 Mario Bates	.15
57 Edgar Bennett	.15
58 Tim Biakabutuka	.15
59 Ki-Jana Carter	.15
60 Larry Centers	.15
61 Mark Chmura	.30
62 Wayne Chrebet	.30
63 Ben Coates	.30
64 Curtis Conway	.30
65 Randall Cunningham	.75
66 Rickey Dudley	.15
67 Bert Emanuel	.15
68 Bobby Engram	.15
69 William Floyd	.15
70 Irving Fryar	.15
71 Elvis Grbac	.15
72 Kevin Greene	.15
73 Jim Harbaugh	.30
74 Raymont Harris	.15
75 Garrison Hearst	.50
76 Greg Hill	.15
77 Desmond Howard	.15
78 Bobby Hoying	.30
79 Michael Jackson	.15
80 Terry Allen	.30
81 Jerome Bettis	.50
82 Jeff Blake	.30
83 Robert Brooks	.15
84 Tim Brown	.30
85 Isaac Bruce	.30
86 Cris Carter	.50
87 Ty Detmer	.30
88 Trent Dilfer	.30
89 Marshall Faulk	.50
90 Antonio Freeman	.75
91 Gus Frerotte	.30
92 Joey Galloway	.50
93 Michael Irvin	.50
94 Brad Johnson	.50
95 Danny Kanell	.15
96 Napoleon Kaufman	.50
97 Dorsey Levens	.50
98 Natrone Means	.50
99 Herman Moore	.50
100 Adrian Murrell	.30
101 Carl Pickens	.30
102 Rod Smith	.30
103 Thurman Thomas	.30
104 Reggie White	.50
105 Jim Druckenmiller	.30
106 Antowain Smith	.50
107 Reidel Anthony	.30
108 Ike Hilliard	.15
109 Rae Carruth	.15
110 Troy Davis	.15
111 Terrance Mathis	.15
112 Brett Favre	3.00
113 Dan Marino	2.00
114 Emmitt Smith	2.00
115 Barry Sanders	3.00
116 Eddie George	1.25
117 Drew Bledsoe	1.25
118 Troy Aikman	1.50
119 Terrell Davis	2.50
120 John Elway	1.75
121 Mark Brunell	1.25
122 Jerry Rice	1.50
123 Kordell Stewart	1.25
124 Steve McNair	.75
125 Curtis Martin	.75
126 Steve Young	1.00
127 Kerry Collins	.50
128 Terry Glenn	.50
129 Deion Sanders	.50
130 Mike Alstott	.50
131 Tony Banks	.30
132 Karim Abdul-Jabbar	.50
133 Terrell Owens	.75
134 Yatil Green	.30
135 Tony Gonzalez	.30
136 Byron Hanspard	.30
137 David LaFleur	.30
138 Danny Wuerffel	.30
139 Tiki Barber	.30
140 Peter Boulware	.15
141 Will Blackwell	.15
142 Warrick Dunn	1.00
143 Corey Dillon	.75
144 Jake Plummer	1.25
145 Neil Smith	.15
146 Charles Johnson	.30
147 Fred Lane	.30
148 Dan Wilkinson	.15
149 Ken Norton Jr.	.15
150 Stephen Davis	.15
151 Gilbert Brown	.15
152 Kenny Bynum	.15
153 Derrick Cullors	.15
154 Charlie Garner	.30
155 Jeff Graham	.15
156 Warren Sapp	.15
157 Jerald Moore	.15
158 Sean Dawkins	.15
159 Charlie Jones	.15
160 Kevin Lockett	.15
161 James McKnight	.15
162 Chris Penn	.15
163 Leslie Shepherd	.15
164 Karl Williams	.15
165 Mark Bruener	.15
166 Ernie Conwell	.15
167 Ken Dilger	.15
168 Troy Drayton	.15
169 Freddie Jones	.15
170 Dale Carter	.15
171 *Charles Woodson*	10.00
172 *Alonzo Mayes*	2.00
173 *Andre Wadsworth*	6.00
174 *Grant Winstrom*	4.00
175 *Greg Ellis*	4.00
176 *Chris Howard*	2.00
177 *Keith Brooking*	4.00
178 *Takeo Spikes*	6.00
179 *Anthony Simmons*	4.00
180 *Brian Simmons*	4.00
181 *Sam Cowart*	2.00
182 *Ken Oxendine*	8.00
183 *Vonnie Holliday*	6.00
184 *Terry Fair*	4.00
185 *Shaun Williams*	2.00
186 *Tremayne Stephens*	2.00
187 *Duane Starks*	6.00
188 *Jason Peter*	4.00
189 *Tebucky Jones*	2.00
190 *Donovin Darius*	2.00
191 *R.W. McQuarters*	4.00
192 *Corey Chavous*	4.00
193 *Cameron Cleeland*	8.00
194 *Stephen Alexander*	6.00
195 *Rod Rutledge*	2.00
196 *Scott Frost*	4.00
197 *Fred Beasley*	2.00
198 *Dorian Boose*	2.00
199 *Randy Moss*	60.00
200 *Jacquez Green*	12.00
201 *Marcus Nash*	15.00
202 *Hines Ward*	8.00
203 *Kevin Dyson*	12.00
204 *E.G. Green*	10.00
205 *Germane Crowell*	15.00
206 *Joe Jurevicius*	8.00
207 *Tony Simmons*	10.00
208 *Tim Dwight*	15.00
209 *Az-Zahir Hakim*	12.00
210 *Jerome Pathon*	8.00
211 *Patrick Johnson*	8.00
212 *Mikhael Ricks*	8.00
213 *Donald Hayes*	4.00
214 *Jammi German*	4.00
215 *Larry Shannon*	2.00
216 *Brian Alford*	4.00
217 *Curtis Enis*	15.00
218 *Fred Taylor*	22.00
219 *Robert Edwards*	5.00
220 *Ahman Green*	12.00
221 *Tavian Banks*	8.00
222 *Skip Hicks*	12.00
223 *Robert Holcombe*	8.00
224 *John Avery*	8.00
225 *Chris Fuamatu-Ma'afala*	8.00
226 *Michael Pittman*	6.00
227 *Rashaan Shehee*	6.00
228 *Jonathon Linton*	8.00
229 *Jon Ritchie*	4.00
230 *Chris Floyd*	4.00
231 *Wilmont Perry*	2.00
232 *Raymond Priester*	2.00
233 *Peyton Manning*	60.00
234 *Ryan Leaf*	15.00
235 *Brian Griese*	30.00
236 *Jeff Ogden*	4.00
237 *Charlie Batch*	12.00
238 *Moses Moreno*	4.00
239 *Jonathan Quinn*	6.00
240 *Flozell Adams*	2.00
241 Brett Favre PT	14.00
242 Dan Marino PT	10.00
243 Emmitt Smith PT	10.00
244 Barry Sanders PT	14.00
245 Eddie George PT	6.00
246 Drew Bledsoe PT	6.00
247 Troy Aikman PT	7.00
248 Terrell Davis PT	12.00
249 John Elway PT	8.00
250 Carl Pickens PT	2.00
251 Jerry Rice PT	7.00
252 Kordell Stewart PT	6.00
253 Steve McNair PT	4.00
254 Curtis Martin PT	4.00
255 Steve Young PT	5.00
256 Herman Moore PT	2.00
257 Dorsey Levens PT	2.00
258 Deion Sanders PT	3.00
259 Napoleon Kaufman PT	2.00
260 Warrick Dunn PT	5.00
261 Corey Dillon PT	4.00
262 Jerome Bettis PT	2.00
263 Tim Brown PT	2.00
264 Cris Carter PT	3.00
265 Antonio Freeman PT	3.00
266 Randy Moss PT	20.00
267 Curtis Enis PT	7.00
268 Fred Taylor PT	10.00
269 Robert Edwards PT	8.00
270 Peyton Manning PT	25.00
271 Barry Sanders TL	1.50
272 Eddie George TL	.50
273 Troy Aikman TL	.75
274 Mark Brunell TL	.50
275 Kordell Stewart TL	.50
276 Kerry Collins TL	.15
277 Terry Glenn TL	.30
278 Mike Alstott TL	.30
279 Tony Banks TL	.15
280 Karim Abdul TL	.30
281 Terrell Owens TL	.40
282 Byron Hanspard TL	.15
283 Jake Plummer TL	.50
284 Terry Allen TL	.15
285 Jeff Blake TL	.15
286 Brad Johnson TL	.30
287 Danny Kanell TL	.15
288 Natrone Means TL	.30
289 Rod Smith TL	.15
290 Thurman Thomas TL	.15
291 Reggie White TL	.30
292 Troy Davis TL	.15
293 Curtis Conway TL	.15
294 Irving Fryar TL	.15
295 Jim Harbaugh TL	.15
296 Andre Rison TL	.15
297 Ricky Watters TL	.15
298 Keyshawn Johnson TL	.30
299 Jeff George TL	.15
300 Marshall Faulk TL	.30

1998 Leaf Rookies & Stars Crosstraining

Each card in this 10-card set highlights the same player on front and back, demonstrating the different skills that make them great. All cards are printed on foil board and are sequentially numbered to 1,000.

		MT
Complete Set (10):		85.00
Common Player:		6.00
Production 1,000 Sets		
1	Brett Favre	30.00
2	Mark Brunell	12.00
3	Barry Sanders	30.00
4	John Elway	20.00
5	Jerry Rice	15.00
6	Kordell Stewart	12.00
7	Steve McNair	6.00
8	Deion Sanders	6.00
9	Jake Plummer	12.00
10	Steve Young	10.00

1998 Leaf Rookies & Stars Crusade

The 30-card set includes both stars and rookies from '98. Each of the Green singles are sequentially numbered to 250. A parallel Purple set is numbered to 100 and a parallel Red set is numbered to 25.

		MT
Complete Set (30):		650.00
Common Player:		10.00
Production 250 Sets		
Purple Cards:		2x
Production 100 Sets		
Red Cards:		2x-4x
Production 25 Sets		
1	Brett Favre	60.00
2	Dan Marino	45.00
3	Emmitt Smith	45.00
4	Barry Sanders	60.00
5	Eddie George	25.00
6	Drew Bledsoe	25.00
7	Troy Aikman	30.00
8	Terrell Davis	50.00
9	John Elway	40.00
10	Mark Brunell	25.00
11	Jerry Rice	30.00
12	Kordell Stewart	25.00
13	Steve McNair	10.00
14	Curtis Martin	10.00
16	Steve Young	20.00
18	Deion Sanders	10.00
22	Terrell Owens	10.00
23	Jamal Anderson	10.00
25	Jerome Bettis	10.00
30	Cris Carter	10.00
32	Marshall Faulk	10.00
33	Antonio Freeman	10.00
40	Dorsey Levens	10.00
49	Garrison Hearst	10.00
57	Warrick Dunn	20.00
59	Jake Plummer	25.00
66	Peyton Manning	50.00
69	Randy Moss	100.00
77	Fred Taylor	45.00
78	Robert Edwards	20.00

1998 Leaf Rookies & Stars Extreme Measures

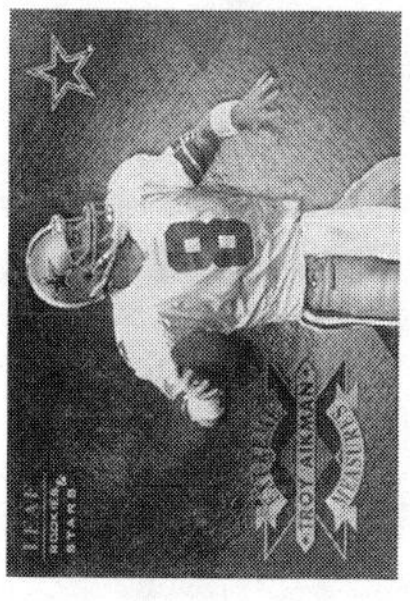

This 10-card set takes the top players in the game and highlights an outstanding but extreme statistic for each. These cards are each printed on foil board and sequentially numbered to 1,000.

		MT
Complete Set (10):		135.00
Common Player:		5.00
1	Barry Sanders/918	30.00
2	Warrick Dunn/941	10.00
3	Curtis Martin/930	5.00
4	Terrell Davis/419	35.00
5	Troy Aikman/929	15.00
6	Drew Bledsoe/972	10.00
7	Eddie George/191	30.00
8	Emmitt Smith/888	20.00
9	Dan Marino/615	25.00
10	Brett Favre/965	30.00

1998 Leaf Rookies & Stars Extreme Measures Die Cuts

Each single in this set is sequentially numbered to a stat that was picked by the manufacturer. Each player in this set has a different amount of cards printed. Cards are identical to their Extreme Measures card except for being die cut in this set.

		MT
Complete Set (10):		725.00
Common Player:		15.00
1	Barry Sanders/82	150.00
2	Warrick Dunn/59	60.00
3	Curtis Martin/70	35.00
4	Terrell Davis/581	25.00
5	Troy Aikman/71	75.00
6	Drew Bledsoe/28	175.00
7	Eddie George/809	15.00
8	Emmitt Smith/112	100.00
9	Dan Marino/385	60.00
10	Brett Favre/35	300.00

1998 Leaf Rookies & Stars Freshman Orientation

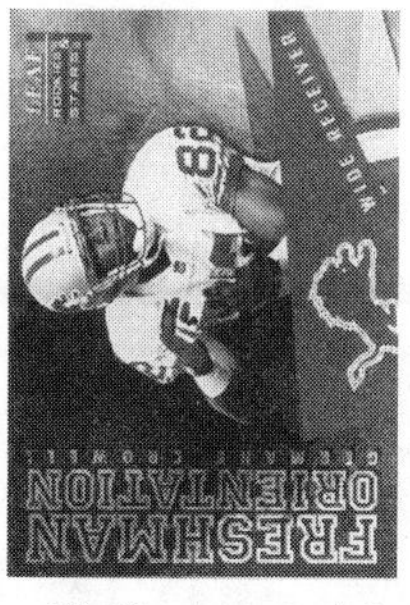

This 20-card set not only features the future stars of the game, but also highlights which round and overall number each player was selected in the NFL draft. Each card is sequentially numbered to 2,500 and printed on holographic foil.

		MT
Complete Set (20):		100.00
Common Player:		2.50
Minor Stars:		5.00
Production 2,500 Sets		
1	Peyton Manning	20.00
2	Kevin Dyson	5.00
3	Joe Jurevicius	2.50
4	Tony Simmons	5.00
5	Marcus Nash	5.00
6	Ryan Leaf	10.00
7	Curtis Enis	6.00
8	Skip Hicks	5.00
9	Brian Griese	7.00
10	Jerome Pathon	2.50
11	John Avery	5.00
12	Fred Taylor	18.00
13	Robert Edwards	7.00
14	Robert Holcombe	5.00
15	Ahman Green	5.00
16	Hines Ward	2.50
17	Jacquez Green	5.00
18	Germane Crowell	5.00
19	Randy Moss	40.00
20	Charles Woodson	7.00

1998 Leaf Rookies & Stars Game Plan

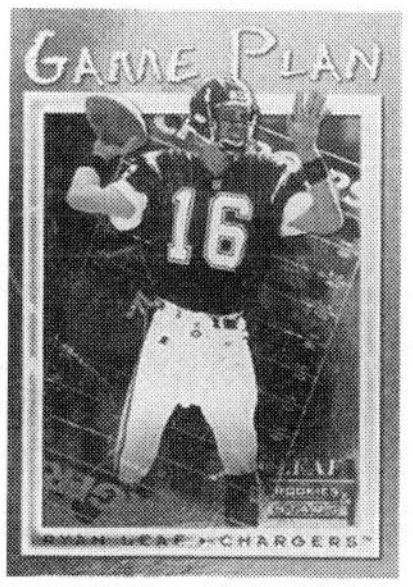

Each card in this inside the game set is printed on foil board and sequentially numbered to 5,000. The first 500 of each card is treated with a "Master Game Plan" logo and unique color coating.

		MT
Complete Set (20):		45.00
Common Player:		1.50
Minor Stars:		3.00
Production 5,000 Sets		
Master Cards:		3x
Production First 500 Sets		
1	Ryan Leaf	5.00
2	Peyton Manning	12.00
3	Brett Favre	8.00
4	Mark Brunell	4.00
5	Isaac Bruce	3.00
6	Dan Marino	6.00
7	Jerry Rice	4.00
8	Cris Carter	3.00
9	Emmitt Smith	6.00
10	Kordell Stewart	4.00
11	Corey Dillon	3.00
12	Barry Sanders	8.00
13	Curtis Martin	3.00
14	Carl Pickens	1.50
15	Eddie George	4.00
16	Warrick Dunn	3.00
17	Jake Plummer	4.00
18	Curtis Enis	4.00
19	Drew Bledsoe	4.00
20	Terrell Davis	6.00

1998 Leaf Rookies & Stars Great American Heroes

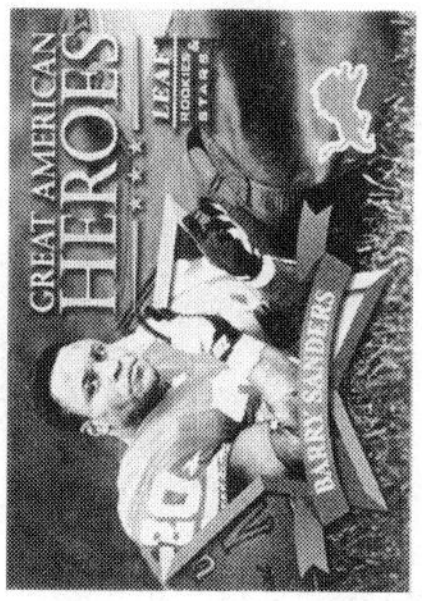

The theme to this insert is players that have helped make the great American game of football. Each card in this set is stamped with holographic foil and sequentially numbered to 2,500.

		MT
Complete Set (20):		85.00
Common Player:		2.00
Minor Stars:		4.00
Production 2,500 Sets		
1	Brett Favre	12.00
2	Dan Marino	8.00
3	Emmitt Smith	8.00
4	Barry Sanders	12.00
5	Eddie George	5.00
6	Drew Bledsoe	5.00
7	Troy Aikman	6.00
8	Terrell Davis	10.00
9	John Elway	7.00
10	Mark Brunell	5.00
11	Jerry Rice	6.00
12	Kordell Stewart	5.00
13	Steve McNair	4.00
14	Curtis Martin	4.00
15	Steve Young	4.00
16	Dorsey Levens	2.00
17	Herman Moore	2.00
18	Deion Sanders	2.00
19	Thurman Thomas	2.00
20	Peyton Manning	18.00

1998 Leaf Rookies & Stars Greatest Hits

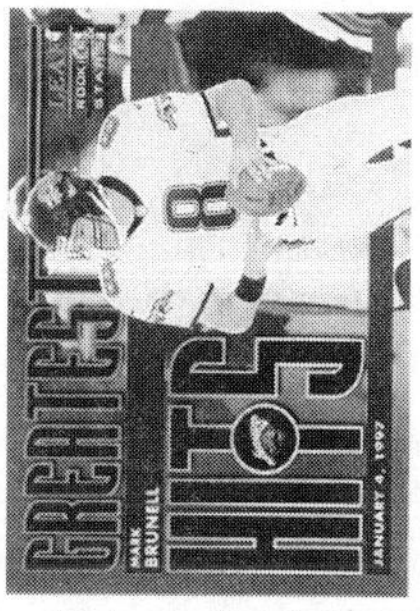

The top 20 players in the NFL are included in this insert and each card is sequentially numbered to 2,500.

		MT
Complete Set (20):		85.00
Common Player:		2.00
Minor Stars:		4.00
Production 2,500 Sets		
1	Brett Favre	12.00
2	Eddie George	5.00
3	John Elway	7.00
4	Steve Young	4.00
5	Napoleon Kaufman	2.00
6	Dan Marino	8.00
7	Drew Bledsoe	5.00
8	Mark Brunell	5.00
9	Warrick Dunn	4.00
10	Dorsey Levens	2.00
11	Emmitt Smith	8.00
12	Troy Aikman	6.00
13	Jerry Rice	6.00
14	Jake Plummer	5.00
15	Herman Moore	2.00
16	Barry Sanders	12.00
17	Terrell Davis	10.00
18	Kordell Stewart	5.00
19	Jerome Bettis	2.00
20	Isaac Bruce	2.00

1998 Leaf Rookies & Stars MVP Contenders

The set is made up of 20 of the league's top players who will contend for the MVP award. Each card is accented with holographic foil stamping and sequentially numbered to 2,500.

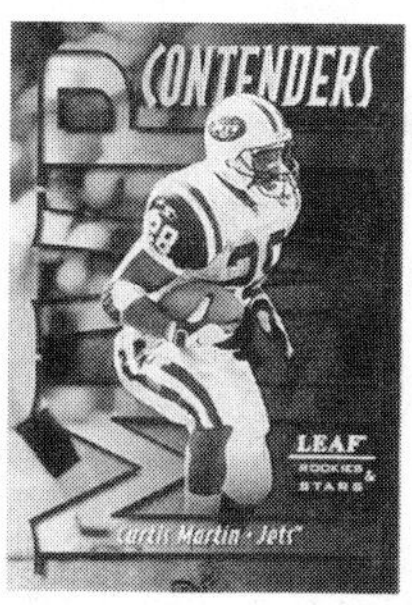

		MT
Complete Set (20):		85.00
Common Player:		2.00
Minor Stars:		4.00
Production 2,500 Sets		
1	Tim Brown	2.00
2	Herman Moore	2.00
3	Jake Plummer	5.00
4	Warrick Dunn	4.00
5	Dorsey Levens	2.00
6	Steve McNair	4.00
7	John Elway	7.00
8	Troy Aikman	6.00
9	Steve Young	5.00
10	Curtis Martin	4.00
11	Kordell Stewart	5.00
12	Jerry Rice	6.00
13	Mark Brunell	5.00
14	Terrell Davis	10.00
15	Drew Bledsoe	5.00
16	Eddie George	5.00
17	Barry Sanders	12.00
18	Emmitt Smith	8.00
19	Dan Marino	8.00
20	Brett Favre	12.00

1998 Leaf Rookies & Stars Standing Ovation

This 10-card set is printed with holographic foil stamping and sequentially numbered to 5,000. It features players who truly deserve a standing ovation for their accomplishments.

		MT
Complete Set (10):		40.00
Common Player:		1.50
Minor Stars:		3.00
Production 5,000 Sets		
1	Brett Favre	8.00
2	Dan Marino	6.00
3	Emmitt Smith	6.00
4	Barry Sanders	8.00
5	Terrell Davis	7.00
6	Jerry Rice	4.00
7	Steve Young	3.00
8	Reggie White	1.50
9	John Elway	5.00
10	Eddie George	3.00

1998 Leaf Rookies & Stars Ticket Masters

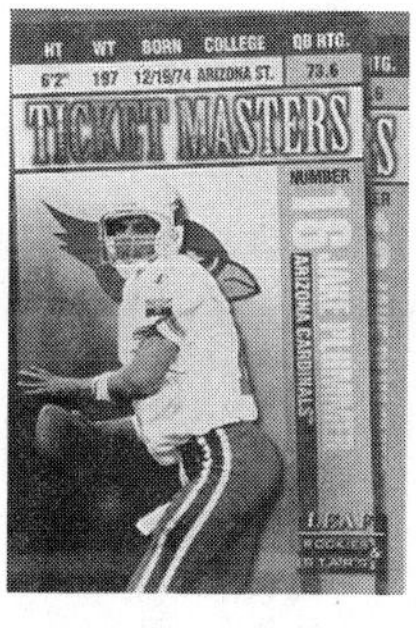

This double-sided 20-card set is printed on foil board and features players from the same team, like Terrell Davis and John Elway, that fill the seats for their franchise. Each card is sequentially numbered to 2,500 with the first 500 die-cut like a ticket.

		MT
Complete Set (20):		120.00
Common Player:		2.00
Minor Stars:		4.00
Production 2,500 Sets		
Die-Cut Cards:		3x
Production First 500 Sets		
1	Brett Favre, Dorsey Levens	12.00
2	Dan Marino, Karim Abdul	8.00
3	Troy Aikman, Deion Sanders	6.00
4	Barry Sanders, Herman Moore	12.00
5	Steve McNair, Eddie George	5.00
6	Drew Bledsoe, Robert Edwards	5.00
7	Terrell Davis, John Elway	10.00
8	Jerry Rice, Steve Young	6.00
9	Kordell Stewart, Jerome Bettis	5.00
10	Curtis Martin, Keyshawn Johnson	4.00
11	Warrick Dunn, Trent Dilfer	5.00
12	Corey Dillon, Carl Pickens	4.00
13	Tim Brown, Napoleon Kaufman	2.00
14	Jake Plummer, Frank Sanders	5.00
15	Ryan Leaf, Natrone Means	8.00
16	Peyton Manning, Marshall Faulk	15.00
17	Mark Brunell, Fred Taylor	10.00
18	Curtis Enis, Curtis Conway	5.00
19	Cris Carter, Randy Moss	30.00
20	Isaac Bruce, Tony Banks	2.00

1998 Leaf Rookies & Stars Touchdown Club

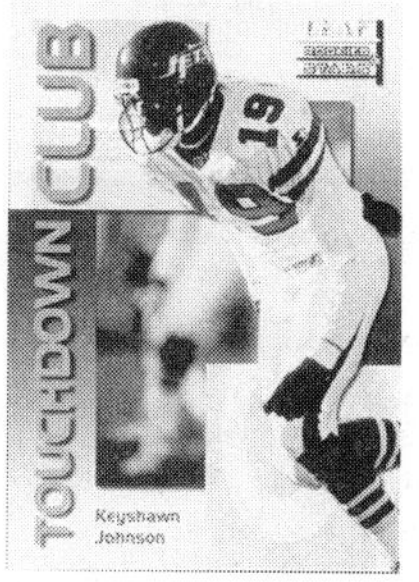

The 20 players showcased in this insert set are known for their ability to get into the end zone. Whether it's through the air, on the ground or both, these NFL stars get the job done. Each card is printed on foil board and sequentially numbered to 5,000.

		MT
Complete Set (20):		50.00
Common Player:		1.50
Minor Stars:		3.00
Production 5,000 Sets		
1	Brett Favre	8.00
2	Dan Marino	6.00
3	Emmitt Smith	6.00
4	Barry Sanders	8.00
5	Eddie George	3.00
6	Drew Bledsoe	4.00
7	Terrell Davis	7.00
8	Mark Brunell	4.00
9	Jerry Rice	4.00
10	Kordell Stewart	4.00
11	Curtis Martin	1.50
12	Karim Abdul	1.50
13	Warrick Dunn	3.00
14	Corey Dillon	3.00
15	Jerome Bettis	1.50
16	Antonio Freeman	1.50
17	Keyshawn Johnson	1.50
18	John Elway	5.00
19	Steve Young	3.00
20	Jake Plummer	4.00

1999 Leaf Certified

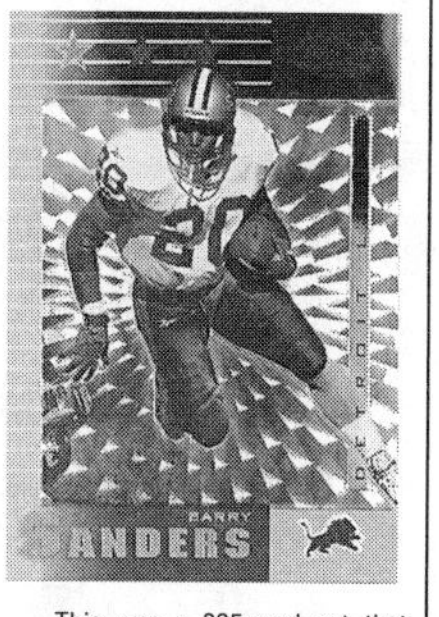

This was a 225-card set that was divided into four tiers. The first 100 cards contained one star and were found four to a pack. Two-star cards included #101-150 and they were inserted one-per-pack. Three-star cards included #151-175 and they were inserted 1:3 packs. The four-star singles were cards #176-225 and they were found 1:5 packs. Parallel sets included Mirror Red and Mirror Gold. Other inserts included: Certified Skills, Fabric of the Game, Gold Future, Gold Team and Gridiron Gear. SRP was $3.99 for five-card packs.

		MT
Complete Set (225):		350.00
Common Player (1-100):		.20
Minor Stars (1-100):		.40
Inserted 4:1		
Common Player (101-150):		.50
Minor Stars (101-150):		1.00
Inserted 1:1		
Common Player (151-175):		1.00
Minor Stars (151-175):		2.00
Inserted 1:3		
Common Player (176-225):		5.00
Inserted 1:5		
Pack (5):		8.00
Wax Box (18):		130.00
1	Simeon Rice	.20
2	Frank Sanders	.40
3	Andre Wadsworth	.20
4	Larry Centers	.20
5	Byron Hanspard	.20
6	Terance Mathis	.20
7	O.J. Santiago	.20
8	Chris Calloway	.20
9	Michael Jackson	.20
10	Rod Woodson	.20
11	Pat Johnson	.20
12	Rob Johnson	.40
13	Andre Reed	.20
14	Tim Biakabutuka	.20
15	Rae Carruth	.20
16	Fred Lane	.20
17	Muhsin Muhammad	.40
18	Wesley Walls	.20
19	Edgar Bennett	.20
20	Curtis Conway	.40
21	Bobby Engram	.20
22	Jeff Blake	.40
23	Darnay Scott	.40
24	Ty Detmer	.20
25	Sedrick Shaw	.20
26	Leslie Shepherd	.20
27	Keith Byars	.20
28	Chris Warren	.20
29	Raghib Ismail	.20
30	Marcus Nash	.20
31	Neil Smith	.20
32	Bubby Brister	.40
33	Brian Griese	1.50
34	Germane Crowell	.40
35	Johnnie Morton	.20
36	Gus Frerotte	.20
37	Robert Brooks	.20
38	Mark Chmura	.40
39	Derrick Mayes	.40
40	Jerome Pathon	.20
41	Jimmy Smith	.40
42	James Stewart	.20
43	Tavian Banks	.20
44	Derrick Alexander	.20
45	Kimble Anders	.20
46	Elvis Grbac	.40
47	Derrick Thomas	.20
48	Bam Morris	.20
49	Tony Gonzalez	.20
50	John Avery	.20
51	Tyrone Wheatley	.20
52	Zach Thomas	.40
53	Lamar Thomas	.20
54	Jeff George	.40
55	John Randle	.20
56	Jake Reed	.20
57	Leroy Hoard	.20
58	Robert Edwards	.40
59	Ben Coates	.40
60	Tony Simmons	.40
61	Shawn Jefferson	.20
62	Eddie Kennison	.20
63	Lamar Smith	.20
64	Tiki Barber	.20
65	Kerry Collins	.40
66	Ike Hilliard	.20
67	Gary Brown	.20
68	Joe Jurevicius	.20
69	Kent Graham	.20
70	Dedric Ward	.20
71	Terry Allen	.20
72	Neil O'Donnell	.40
73	Desmond Howard	.20
74	James Jett	.20
75	Jon Ritchie	.20
76	Rickey Dudley	.20
77	Charles Johnson	.20
78	Chris Fuamatu-Ma'afala	.20
79	Hines Ward	.40
80	Ryan Leaf	.50
81	Jim Harbaugh	.40
82	Junior Seau	.40
83	Mikhael Ricks	.20
84	J.J. Stokes	.40
85	Ahman Green	.40
86	Tony Banks	.40
87	Robert Holcombe	.20
88	Az-Zahir Hakim	.40
89	Greg Hill	.40
90	Trent Green	.40
91	Eric Zeier	.20
92	Reidel Anthony	.40
93	Bert Emmanuel	.20
94	Warren Sapp	.20
95	Kevin Dyson	.40
96	Yancey Thigpen	.20
97	Frank Wycheck	.20
98	Michael Westbrook	.40
99	Albert Connell	.20
100	Darrell Green	.20
101	Rob Moore	.50
102	Adrian Murrell	.50
103	Jake Plummer	3.00
104	Chris Chandler	1.00
105	Jamal Anderson	1.50
106	Tim Dwight	1.50
107	Jermaine Lewis	.50
108	Priest Holmes	1.50
109	Bruce Smith	.50
110	Eric Moulds	1.50
111	Antowain Smith	1.00
112	Curtis Enis	1.50
113	Corey Dillon	1.50
114	Michael Irvin	1.00
115	Ed McCaffrey	1.00
116	Shannon Sharpe	1.00
117	Terrell Davis	5.00
118	Charlie Batch	2.00
119	Antonio Freeman	1.50
120	Dorsey Levens	1.50
121	Marvin Harrison	1.50
122	Peyton Manning	5.00
123	Keenan McCardell	1.00
124	Fred Taylor	3.00
125	Andre Rison	.50
126	O.J. McDuffie	.50
127	Karim Abdul	1.00
128	Randy Moss	7.00
129	Terry Glenn	1.50
130	Vinny Testaverde	1.00
131	Keyshawn Johnson	1.50
132	Curtis Martin	1.50
133	Wayne Chrebet	1.00
134	Napoleon Kaufman	1.00
135	Charles Woodson	1.50
136	Duce Staley	1.00

137 Kordell Stewart 1.75
138 Terrell Owens 1.50
139 Ricky Watters 1.00
140 Joey Galloway 1.50
141 Jon Kitna 1.75
142 Isaac Bruce 1.00
143 Jacquez Green .50
144 Warrick Dunn 1.50
145 Mike Alstott 1.50
146 Trent Dilfer 1.00
147 Steve McNair 1.50
148 Eddie George 1.50
149 Skip Hicks 1.00
150 Brad Johnson 1.50
151 Doug Flutie 3.00
152 Thurman Thomas 2.00
153 Carl Pickens 2.00
154 Emmitt Smith 7.00
155 Troy Aikman 5.00
156 Deion Sanders 2.00
157 John Elway 7.00
158 Rod Smith 1.00
159 Barry Sanders 10.00
160 Herman Moore 2.00
161 Brett Favre 10.00
162 Mark Brunell 4.00
163 Warren Moon 2.00
164 Dan Marino 7.00
165 Randall Cunningham 2.00
166 Robert Smith 2.00
167 Cris Carter 2.00
168 Drew Bledsoe 4.00
169 Tim Brown 2.00
170 Jerome Bettis 2.00
171 Natrone Means 1.00
172 Jerry Rice 5.00
173 Steve Young 3.00
174 Garrison Hearst 2.00
175 Marshall Faulk 2.00
176 *David Boston* 10.00
177 *Jeff Paulk* 5.00
178 *Reginald Kelly* 5.00
179 *Brandon Stokely* 7.00
180 *Chris McAlister* 6.00
181 *Shawn Bryson* 5.00
182 *Peerless Price* 8.00
183 *Cade McNown* 12.00
184 *Jerry Azumah* 5.00
185 *D'Wayne Bates* 6.00
186 *Marty Booker* 5.00
187 *Akili Smith* 12.00
188 *Craig Yeast* 5.00
189 *Tim Couch* 20.00
190 *Kevin Johnson* 10.00
191 *Wane McGarity* 5.00
192 *Olandis Gary* 15.00
193 *Travis McGriff* 5.00
194 *Sedrick Irvin* 6.00
195 *Chris Claiborne* 6.00
196 *De'Mond Parker* 6.00
197 *Dee Miller* 5.00
198 *Edgerrin James* 35.00
199 *Michael Cloud* 6.00
200 *Larry Parker* 5.00
201 *Cecil Collins* 7.00
202 *James Johnson* 7.00
203 *Rob Konrad* 7.00
204 *Daunte Culpepper* 25.00
205 *Jim Kleinsasser* 6.00
206 *Kevin Faulk* 10.00
207 *Andy Katzenmoyer* 6.00
208 *Ricky Williams* 20.00
209 *Joe Montgomery* 6.00
210 *Sean Bennett* 6.00
211 *Dameane Douglas* 5.00
212 *Donovan McNabb* 15.00
213 *Na Brown* 5.00
214 *Amos Zereoue* 7.00
215 *Troy Edwards* 10.00
216 *Jermaine Fazande* 7.00
217 *Tai Streets* 8.00
218 *Brock Huard* 10.00
219 *Charlie Rogers* 5.00
220 *Karsten Bailey* 5.00
221 *Joe Germaine* 6.00
222 *Torry Holt* 12.00
223 *Shaun King* 12.00
224 *Jevon Kearse* 10.00
225 *Champ Bailey* 10.00

1999 Leaf Certified Mirror Gold Parallel

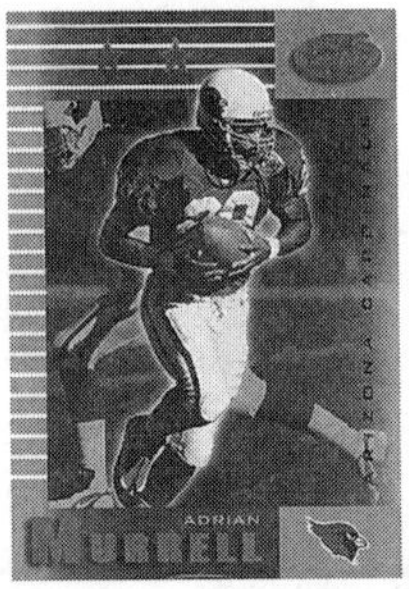

This was a 225-card parallel to the base set found at four different tiers. Each single was printed on holographic stock with gold tint. The first 100 cards were sequentially numbered to 45. Cards 101-150 were numbered to 35. Cards 151-175 were numbered to 25 and cards 176-225 were numbered to 30.

MT
Common Player (1-100): 10.00
1-Star Cards: 35x-70x
Production 45 Sets
Common Player (101-150): 20.00
2-Star Cards: 25x-50x
Production 35 Sets
Common Player (151-175): 35.00
3-Star Cards: 20x-40x
Production 25 Sets
Common Player (176-225): 25.00
4-Star Cards: 2x-4x
Production 30 Sets

1999 Leaf Certified Mirror Red Parallel

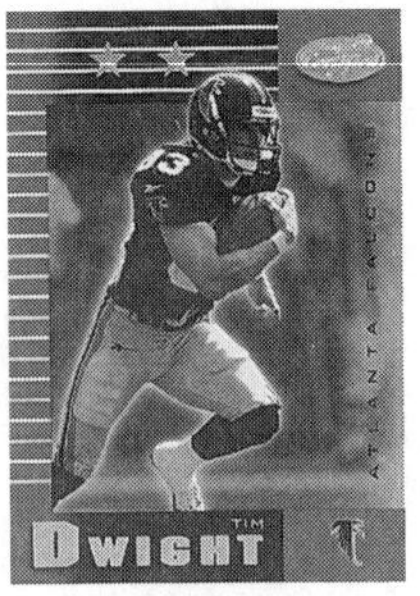

This was a 225-card parallel to the base set found at four different tiers. Each single was printed on holographic stock with red tint. The first 100 cards were found 1:17 packs. Cards 101-150 were inserted 1:53 packs. Cards 151-175 were found 1:125 and cards 176-225 were inserted 1:89 packs.

MT
Common Player (1-100): 3.00
1-Star Cards: 10x-20x
Inserted 1:17
Common Player (101-150): 5.00
2-Star Cards: 4x-8x
Inserted 1:53
Common Player (151-175): 10.00
3-Star Cards: 5x-10x
Inserted 1:125
Common Player (176-225): 10.00
4-Star Cards: 1.5x
Inserted 1:89

1999 Leaf Certified Fabric of the Game

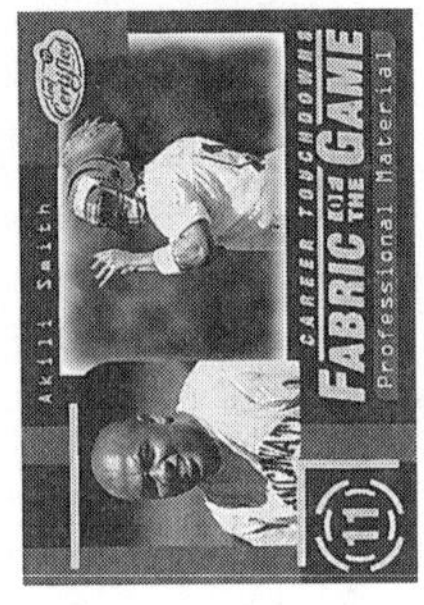

This was a 75-card insert set with the singles found at three levels. The three technologies used were nylon, leather and plastic. A total of 25 players were showcased according to Pro Bowl appearances, career TDs and career yards. Each level had five categories with different sequential numbering ranging from 100 to 1,000.

MT
Complete Set (75): 1650.
Common Player: 5.00
1 John Elway 100 120.00
2 Barry Sanders 100 120.00
3 Jerry Rice 100 60.00
4 Brett Favre 250 70.00
5 Steve Young 250 25.00
6 Troy Aikman 250 40.00
7 Deion Sanders 250 15.00
8 Terrell Davis 500 30.00
9 Mark Brunell 500 15.00
10 Drew Bledsoe 500 15.00
11 Randall Cunningham 500 10.00
12 Eddie George 500 12.00
13 Jamal Anderson 500 8.00
14 Doug Flutie 750 12.00
15 Robert Smith 750 8.00
16 Garrison Hearst 750 8.00
17 Keyshawn Johnson 750 8.00
18 Randy Moss 750 40.00
19 Eric Moulds 1000 8.00
20 Curtis Enis 1000 8.00
21 Ricky Williams 1000 50.00
22 Peyton Manning 1000 30.00
23 Tim Couch 1000 50.00
24 Cade McNown 1000 20.00
25 Akili Smith 1000 20.00
26 Dan Marino 100 100.00
27 Jerry Rice 100 60.00
28 Emmitt Smith 100 100.00
29 Cris Carter 250 15.00
30 Steve Young 250 25.00
31 Herman Moore 250 15.00
32 Tim Brown 250 15.00
33 Jerome Bettis 500 10.00
34 Natrone Means 500 5.00
35 Antonio Freeman 500 10.00
36 Terrell Davis 500 30.00
37 Carl Pickens 500 5.00
38 Karim Abdul 750 5.00
39 Mike Alstott 750 8.00
40 Jake Plummer 750 15.00
41 Steve McNair 750 8.00
42 Terrell Owens 750 8.00
43 Kordell Stewart 750 10.00
44 Randy Moss 1000 35.00
45 Fred Taylor 1000 20.00
46 Peyton Manning 1000 30.00
47 Tim Couch 1000 50.00
48 Akili Smith 1000 20.00
49 Torry Holt 1000 12.00
50 Donovan McNabb 1000 20.00
51 Barry Sanders 100 120.00
52 Dan Marino 100 100.00
53 Jerry Rice 100 60.00
54 John Elway 250 50.00
55 Brett Favre 250 70.00
56 Emmitt Smith 250 50.00
57 Mark Brunell 250 30.00
58 Jake Plummer 500 20.00
59 Ricky Watters 500 5.00
60 Dorsey Levens 500 10.00
61 Curtis Martin 500 10.00
62 Marshall Faulk 500 10.00
63 Eddie George 750 10.00
64 Corey Dillon 750 8.00
65 Warrick Dunn 750 10.00
66 Antowain Smith 750 8.00
67 Napoleon Kaufman 750 8.00
68 Joey Galloway 750 8.00
69 Fred Taylor 1000 20.00
70 Charlie Batch 1000 10.00
71 Ricky Williams 1000 50.00
72 Edgerrin James 1000 50.00
73 Jon Kitna 1000 10.00
74 Daunte Culpepper 1000 20.00
75 Skip Hicks 1000 5.00

1999 Leaf Certified Gold Future

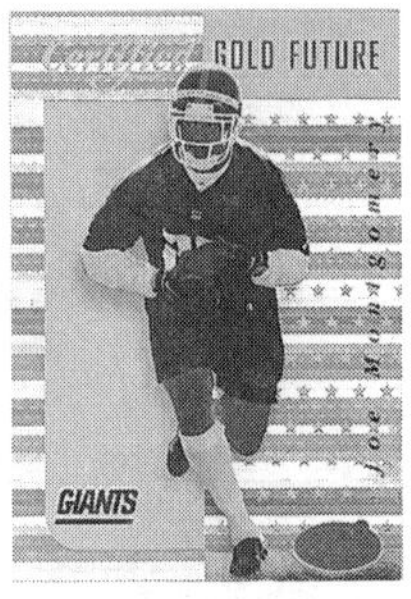

This 30-card insert set included the top rookies from the 1999 NFL Draft. Each single was printed on mirror Mylar with foil and micro-etching. Singles were found 1:17 packs. A parallel Mirror Black version was also made with each of those singles sequentially numbered to 25.

MT
Complete Set (30): 185.00
Common Player: 3.00
Inserted 1:17
Mirror Black Cards: 6x-12x
Production 25 Sets
1 Travis McGriff 4.00
2 Jermaine Fazande 3.00
3 Kevin Faulk 6.00
4 Edgerrin James 25.00
5 Ricky Williams 25.00
6 Tim Couch 25.00
7 Torry Holt 8.00
8 Kevin Johnson 8.00
9 Amos Zereoue 6.00
10 Joe Germaine 4.00
11 Shawn Bryson 3.00
12 D'Wayne Bates 3.00
13 Akili Smith 12.00
14 Shaun King 5.00
15 Joe Montgomery 4.00
16 Troy Edwards 8.00
17 Rob Konrad 4.00
18 David Boston 8.00
19 Reginald Kelly 3.00
20 Donovan McNabb 12.00
21 Champ Bailey 5.00
22 Craig Yeast 3.00
23 Daunte Culpepper 12.00
24 Peerless Price 6.00
25 Cecil Collins 15.00
26 Cade McNown 12.00
27 Karsten Bailey 3.00
28 James Johnson 5.00
29 Brock Huard 5.00
30 Michael Cloud 4.00

1999 Leaf Certified Gold Team

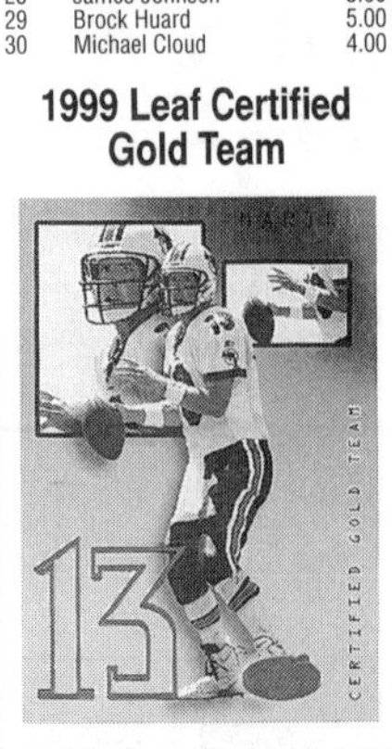

This 30-card insert set included the top veterans and pictured them on mirror Mylar board with foil. Singles were inserted 1:17 packs. A parallel Mirror Black version was also produced with each of those singles sequentially numbered to 25.

MT
Complete Set (30): 200.00
Common Player: 3.00
Inserted 1:17
Mirror Black Cards: 6x-12x
Production 25 Sets
1 Randy Moss 25.00
2 Terrell Davis 18.00
3 Peyton Manning 18.00
4 Fred Taylor 12.00
5 Jake Plummer 12.00
6 Drew Bledsoe 8.00
7 John Elway 18.00
8 Mark Brunell 8.00
9 Joey Galloway 3.00
10 Troy Aikman 12.00
11 Jerome Bettis 3.00
12 Tim Brown 3.00
13 Dan Marino 18.00
14 Antonio Freeman 3.00
15 Steve Young 7.00
16 Jamal Anderson 3.00
17 Brett Favre 25.00
18 Jerry Rice 12.00
19 Corey Dillon 3.00
20 Barry Sanders 25.00
21 Doug Flutie 7.00
22 Emmitt Smith 18.00
23 Curtis Martin 3.00
24 Dorsey Levens 3.00
25 Kordell Stewart 6.00
26 Eddie George 6.00
27 Terrell Owens 3.00
28 Keyshawn Johnson 3.00
29 Steve McNair 6.00
30 Cris Carter 3.00

1999 Leaf Certified Gridiron Gear

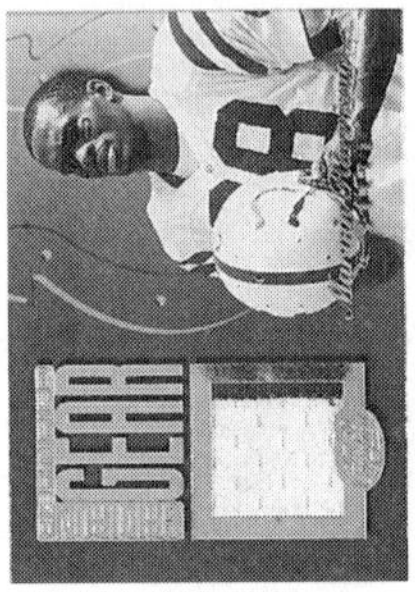

This 72-card insert set included pieces of game-used jerseys from the top veterans in the NFL. Each of the singles was sequentially numbered to 300.

MT
Common Player: 50.00
Multi-Colored Swatches: 1.5x
Production 300 Sets
KA33 Karim Abdul 50.00
TA8 Troy Aikman 150.00
JA32 Jamal Anderson 75.00
JB36 Jerome Bettis 75.00
DB11 Drew Bledsoe 125.00
TB71 Tony Boselli 50.00
RB87 Robert Brooks 50.00
TB81 Tim Brown 50.00
IB80 Isaac Bruce 75.00
MB8A Mark Brunell White 100.00
MB8H Mark Brunell Teal 100.00
MC89 Mark Chmura 50.00
BC87 Ben Coates 50.00
CC80 Curtis Conway 50.00
RC7 Randall Cunningham 75.00
TD30A Terrell Davis White 150.00
TD30H Terrell Davis Blue 150.00
TD12 Trent Dilfer 50.00
WD28 Warrick Dunn 75.00
JE7H John Elway Blue 175.00
JE7HC John Elway Orange 175.00
BF4A Brett Favre White 200.00
BF4H Brett Favre Green 200.00
DF7A Doug Flutie White 100.00
DF7H Doug Flutie Blue 100.00
AF86 Antonio Freeman 75.00
EG27 Eddie George 75.00
DG28 Darrell Green 50.00
MH88 Marvin Harrison 75.00
DH80 Desmond Howard 50.00
MI88 Michael Irvin 50.00
JJ82 James Jett 50.00
KJ19 Keyshawn Johnson 75.00
NK26A Napoleon Kaufman White 50.00
NK26H Napoleon Kaufman Black 50.00
JK12 Jim Kelly 75.00
RL16 Ryan Leaf 50.00
DL25A Dorsey Levens White 75.00
DL25H Dorsey Levens Green 75.00
PM18 Peyton Manning 175.00
DM13A Dan Marino White 175.00
DM13H Dan Marino Teal 175.00
CM28 Curtis Martin 50.00
KM87 Keenan McCardell 50.00
OM81 O.J. McDuffie 50.00
SM9 Steve McNair 75.00
NM20 Natrone Means 50.00
JM19 Joe Montana 200.00
WM1 Warren Moon 50.00
HMB4 Herman Moore 75.00
RM84A Randy Moss White 250.00
RM84H Randy Moss Purple 250.00
JP16 Jake Plummer 100.00
JR80A Jerry Rice White 150.00
JR80H Jerry Rice Red 150.00
BS20 Barry Sanders 200.00
CS81 Chris Sanders 50.00
DS21 Deion Sanders 75.00
WS99 Warren Sapp 50.00
JS55 Junior Seau 50.00
PH12 Phil Simms 50.00
ES22 Emmitt Smith 175.00
NS90 Neil Smith 50.00
JS82 Jimmy Smith 50.00
JS33 James Stewart 50.00
KS10 Kordell Stewart 75.00
VT12 Vinny Testaverde 50.00
DT58 Derrick Thomas 50.00
TT34 Thurman Thomas 50.00
ZT54 Zach Thomas 50.00
CW24 Charles Woodson 75.00
SY8 Steve Young 100.00

1999 Leaf Certified Skills

This 20-card insert set featured 20 pairs of NFL superstars back-to-back on dual-sided mirror Mylar board. Singles were inserted 1:35 packs. A parallel Mirror Black version was also produced and each of those singles was sequentially numbered to 25.

MT
Complete Set (20): 225.00
Common Player: 7.00
Inserted 1:35
Mirror Black Cards: 5x-10x
Production 25 Sets
1 Deion Sanders, Champ Bailey 7.00
2 John Elway, Cade McNown 25.00
3 Cris Carter, David Boston 7.00
4 Marshall Faulk, Edgerrin James 25.00
5 Jerry Rice, Randy Moss 30.00
6 Antonio Freeman, Terrell Owens 7.00
7 Terrell Davis, Ricky Williams 30.00
8 Drew Bledsoe, Doug Flutie 12.00
9 Eddie George, Jamal Anderson 10.00
10 Troy Aikman, Peyton Manning 25.00
11 Barry Sanders, Warrick Dunn 30.00
12 Randall Cunningham, Daunte Culpepper 12.00
13 Dan Marino, Tim Couch 30.00
14 Emmitt Smith, Fred Taylor 20.00
15 Keyshawn Johnson, Eric Moulds 7.00
16 Steve Young, Mark Brunell 12.00
17 Donovan McNabb, Akili Smith 10.00
18 Brett Favre, Jake Plummer 30.00
19 Kordell Stewart, Steve McNair 7.00
20 Torry Holt, Troy Edwards 7.00

1999 Leaf Rookies & Stars

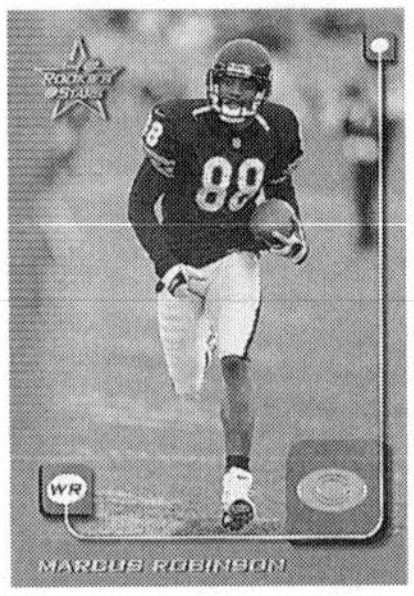

This was a 300-card base set that included 100 rookie cards found 1:2 packs. The Longevity insert was a parallel to the base with each card sequentially numbered. The first 200 cards were numbered to 50 and the 100 rookies were numbered to 30. Other inserts included: Cross Training, Dress for Success, John Elway Collection, Freshman Orientation, Game Plan, Great American Heroes, Greatest Hits, Prime Cuts, Signature Series, Slide Show, Statistical Standouts, Ticket Masters and Touchdown Club. SRP was $2.99 for 9-card packs.

MT
Complete Set (300): 325.00
Common Player: .15
Minor Stars: .30
Common Rookie: 2.00
Inserted 1:2
Pack (9): 4.00
Wax Box (24): 95.00
1 Frank Sanders .15
2 Adrian Murrell .15
3 Rob Moore .30
4 Simeon Rice .15
5 Michael Pittman .30
6 Jake Plummer .75
7 Chris Chandler .30
8 Tim Dwight .50
9 Chris Calloway .15
10 Terance Mathis .15
11 Jamal Anderson .50
12 Byron Hanspard .30
13 O.J. Santiago .15
14 Ken Oxendine .30
15 Priest Holmes .50
16 Scott Mitchell .15
17 Tony Banks .30
18 Patrick Johnson .15
19 Rod Woodson .15
20 Jermaine Lewis .15
21 Errict Rhett .30
22 Stoney Case .30
23 Andre Reed .30
24 Eric Moulds .50
25 Rob Johnson .30
26 Doug Flutie .75
27 Bruce Smith .15
28 Jay Riemersma .15
29 Antowain Smith .50
30 Thurman Thomas .30
31 Jonathon Linton .30
32 Muhsin Muhammad .30
33 Rae Carruth .15
34 Wesley Walls .30
35 Fred Lane .30
36 Kevin Greene .15
37 Tim Biakabutuka .30
38 Curtis Enis .50
39 Shane Matthews .30
40 Bobby Engram .15
41 Curtis Conway .30
42 Marcus Robinson 1.00
43 Darnay Scott .30
44 Carl Pickens .30
45 Corey Dillon .50
46 Jeff Blake .30
47 Terry Kirby .15
48 Ty Detmer .15
49 Leslie Shepherd .15
50 Karim Abdul .30
51 Emmitt Smith 1.50
52 Deion Sanders .50
53 Michael Irvin .30
54 Raghib Ismail .15
55 David LaFleur .15
56 Troy Aikman 1.00
57 Ed McCaffrey .50
58 Rod Smith .50
59 Shannon Sharpe .30
60 Brian Griese 1.00
61 John Elway 1.50
62 Bubby Brister .30
63 Neil Smith .15
64 Terrell Davis 1.50
65 John Avery .30
66 Derek Loville .15
67 Ron Rivers .15
68 Herman Moore .50
69 Johnnie Morton .15
70 Charlie Batch .75
71 Barry Sanders 2.00
72 Germane Crowell .30
73 Greg Hill .15
74 Gus Frerotte .30
75 Corey Bradford .30
76 Dorsey Levens .50
77 Antonio Freeman .50
78 Mark Chmura .30
79 Brett Favre 2.00
80 Bill Schroeder .30
81 Matt Hasselbeck .50
82 E.G. Green .30
83 Ken Dilger .15
84 Jerome Pathon .15
85 Marvin Harrison .50
86 Peyton Manning 1.50
87 Tavian Banks .30
88 Keenan McCardell .30
89 Mark Brunell .75
90 Fred Taylor 1.00
91 Jimmy Smith .75
92 James Stewart .50
93 Kyle Brady .15
94 Derrick Thomas .30
95 Rashaan Shehee .15
96 Derrick Alexander .15
97 Bam Morris .15
98 Andre Rison .30
99 Elvis Grbac .30
100 Tony Gonzalez .30
101 Donnell Bennett .15
102 Warren Moon .30
103 Zach Thomas .30
104 Oronde Gadsden .30
105 Dan Marino 1.50
106 O.J. McDuffie .30
107 Tony Martin .15
108 Randy Moss 2.00
109 Cris Carter .50
110 Robert Smith .50
111 Randall Cunningham .50
112 Jake Reed .30
113 John Randle .30
114 Leroy Hoard .15
115 Jeff George .50
116 Ty Law .15
117 Shawn Jefferson .15
118 Troy Brown .15
119 Robert Edwards .30
120 Tony Simmons .30
121 Terry Glenn .50
122 Ben Coates .30
123 Drew Bledsoe .75
124 Terry Allen .30
125 Cameron Cleeland .30
126 Eddie Kennison .15
127 Amani Toomer .15
128 Kerry Collins .30
129 Joe Jurevicius .15
130 Tiki Barber .15
131 Ike Hilliard .30
132 Michael Strahan .15
133 Gary Brown .15
134 Jason Sehorn .15
135 Curtis Martin .50
136 Vinny Testaverde .30
137 Dedric Ward .30
138 Keyshawn Johnson .50
139 Wayne Chrebet .50
140 Tyrone Wheatley .30
141 Napoleon Kaufman .50
142 Tim Brown .30
143 Rickey Dudley .30
144 Jon Ritchie .15
145 James Jett .15
146 Rich Gannon .30
147 Charles Woodson .50
148 Charles Johnson .15
149 Duce Staley .50
150 Will Blackwell .15
151 Kordell Stewart .50
152 Jerome Bettis .50
153 Hines Ward .30
154 Richard Huntley .30
155 Natrone Means .30
156 Mikhael Ricks .15
157 Junior Seau .30
158 Jim Harbaugh .30
159 Ryan Leaf .50
160 Erik Kramer .15
161 Terrell Owens .50
162 J.J. Stokes .30
163 Lawrence Phillips .30
164 Charlie Garner .30

165	Jerry Rice	1.00
166	Garrison Hearst	.50
167	Steve Young	.75
168	Derrick Mayes	.30
169	Ahman Green	.30
170	Joey Galloway	.50
171	Ricky Watters	.30
172	Jon Kitna	.50
173	Sean Dawkins	.15
174	Az-Zahir Hakim	.30
175	Robert Holcombe	.30
176	Isaac Bruce	.50
177	Amp Lee	.15
178	Marshall Faulk	.50
179	Trent Green	.30
180	Eric Zeier	.15
181	Bert Emanuel	.15
182	Jacquez Green	.30
183	Reidel Anthony	.30
184	Warren Sapp	.30
185	Mike Alstott	.50
186	Warrick Dunn	.50
187	Trent Dilfer	.30
188	Neil O'Donnell	.30
189	Eddie George	.60
190	Yancey Thigpen	.30
191	Steve McNair	.60
192	Kevin Dyson	.30
193	Frank Wycheck	.30
194	Stephen Davis	.50
195	Stephen Alexander	.15
196	Darrell Green	.15
197	Skip Hicks	.30
198	Brad Johnson	.50
199	Michael Westbrook	.30
200	Albert Connell	.15
201	*David Boston*	10.00
202	*Joel Makovicka*	3.00
203	*Chris Greisen*	3.00
204	*Jeff Paulk*	3.00
205	*Reginald Kelly*	2.00
206	*Chris McAlister*	3.00
207	*Brandon Stokley*	4.00
208	*Antoine Winfield*	3.00
209	*Bobby Collins*	3.00
210	*Peerless Price*	6.00
211	*Shawn Bryson*	2.00
212	*Sheldon Jackson*	2.00
213	*Kamil Loud*	2.00
214	*D'Wayne Bates*	3.00
215	*Jerry Azumah*	3.00
216	*Marty Booker*	3.00
217	*Cade McNown*	12.00
218	*James Allen*	8.00
219	*Nick Williams*	2.00
220	*Akili Smith*	12.00
221	*Craig Yeast*	2.00
222	*Damon Griffin*	3.00
223	*Scott Covington*	3.00
224	*Michael Basnight*	2.00
225	*Ronnie Powell*	2.00
226	*Rahim Abdullah*	2.00
227	*Tim Couch*	20.00
228	*Kevin Johnson*	10.00
229	*Darrin Chiaverini*	4.00
230	*Mark Campbell*	2.00
231	*Mike Lucky*	2.00
232	*Robert Thomas*	2.00
233	*Ebenezer Ekuban*	3.00
234	*Dat Nguyen*	3.00
235	*Wane McGarity*	3.00
236	*Jason Tucker*	8.00
237	*Olandis Gary*	12.00
238	*Al Wilson*	3.00
239	*Travis McGriff*	3.00
240	*Desmond Clark*	2.00
241	*Andre Cooper*	2.00
242	*Chris Watson*	3.00
243	*Sedrick Irvin*	5.00
244	*Chris Claiborne*	3.00
245	*Cory Sauter*	2.00
246	*Brock Olivo*	2.00
247	*De'Mond Parker*	5.00
248	*Aaron Brooks*	20.00
249	*Antwan Edwards*	3.00
250	*Basil Mitchell*	3.00
251	*Terrence Wilkins*	8.00
252	*Edgerrin James*	35.00
253	*Fernando Bryant*	2.00
254	*Michael Cloud*	3.00
255	*Larry Parker*	2.00
256	*Rob Konrad*	3.00
257	*Cecil Collins*	3.00
258	*James Johnson*	5.00
259	*Jim Kleinsasser*	3.00
260	*Daunte Culpepper*	30.00
261	*Michael Bishop*	7.00
262	*Andy Katzenmoyer*	4.00
263	*Kevin Faulk*	6.00
264	*Brett Bech*	2.00
265	*Ricky Williams*	20.00
266	*Sean Bennett*	3.00
267	*Joe Montgomery*	3.00
268	*Dan Campbell*	2.00
269	*Ray Lucas*	8.00
270	*Scott Dreisbach*	3.00
271	*Jed Weaver*	2.00
272	*Dameane Douglas*	3.00
273	*Cecil Martin*	3.00
274	*Donovan McNabb*	15.00
275	*Na Brown*	3.00
276	*Jerame Tuman*	2.00
277	*Amos Zereoue*	4.00
278	*Troy Edwards*	6.00
279	*Jermaine Fazande*	5.00
280	*Steve Heiden*	2.00
281	*Jeff Garcia*	25.00
282	*Terry Jackson*	3.00
283	*Charlie Rogers*	3.00
284	*Brock Huard*	6.00
285	*Karsten Bailey*	3.00
286	*Lamar King*	2.00
287	*Justin Watson*	3.00
288	*Kurt Warner*	60.00
289	*Torry Holt*	10.00
290	*Joe Germaine*	4.00
291	*Dre' Bly*	3.00
292	*Martin Gramatica*	3.00
293	*Rabih Abdullah*	2.00
294	*Shaun King*	12.00
295	*Anthony McFarland*	3.00
296	*Darnell McDonald*	4.00
297	*Kevin Daft*	3.00
298	*Jevon Kearse*	10.00
299	*Mike Sellers*	2.00
300	*Champ Bailey*	6.00

1999 Leaf Rookies & Stars Longevity Parallel

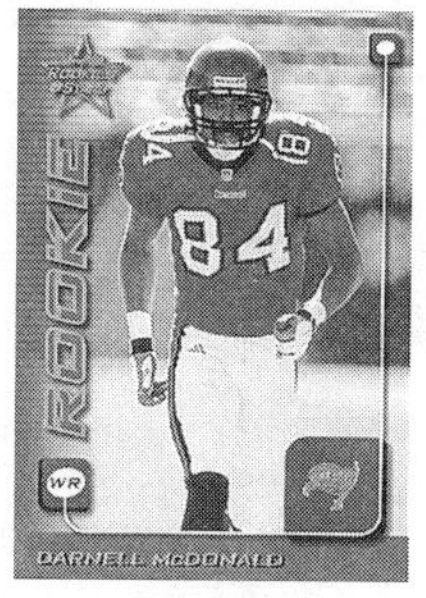

This was a 300-card parallel to the base set. Each single was printed on foil board with holographic foil stamping. The first 200 cards were sequentially numbered to 50 and the 100 rookies were numbered to 30.

	MT
Longevity Cards:	40x-80x
Production 50 Sets	
Longevity Rookies:	3x-6x
Production 30 Sets	

1999 Leaf Rookies & Stars Cross Training

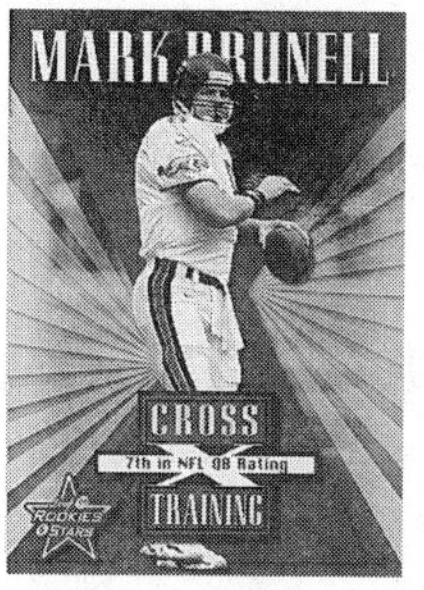

This 25-card insert set included the most versatile players in the NFL. Each card highlighted the player's different skills, one on each side of the card. Each card in the set was sequentially numbered to 1,250.

		MT
Complete Set (25):		125.00
Common Player:		3.00
Production 1,250 Sets		
1	Champ Bailey	3.00
2	Mark Brunell	6.00
3	Daunte Culpepper	10.00
4	Randall Cunningham	3.00
5	Terrell Davis	10.00
6	Charlie Batch	5.00
7	Dorsey Levens	3.00
8	John Elway	10.00
9	Marshall Faulk	3.00
10	Brett Favre	15.00
11	Doug Flutie	6.00
12	Edgerrin James	30.00
13	Curtis Martin	3.00
14	Donovan McNabb	10.00
15	Steve McNair	4.00
16	Cade McNown	10.00
17	Randy Moss	15.00
18	Jake Plummer	6.00
19	Barry Sanders	15.00
20	Deion Sanders	3.00
21	Akili Smith	10.00
22	Kordell Stewart	3.00
23	Ricky Williams	15.00
24	Charles Woodson	3.00
25	Steve Young	6.00

1999 Leaf Rookies & Stars Dress for Success

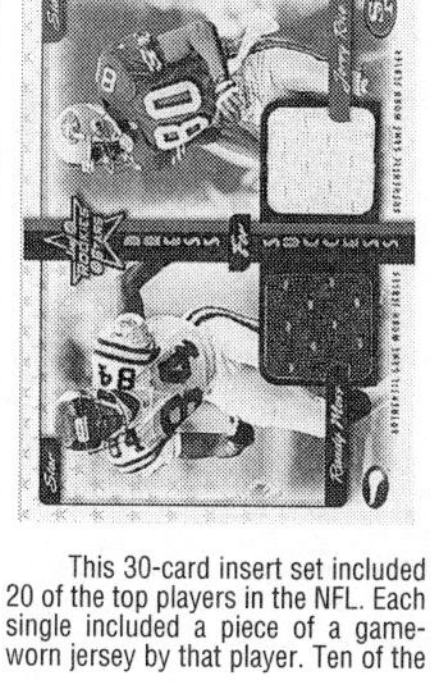

This 30-card insert set included 20 of the top players in the NFL. Each single included a piece of a game-worn jersey by that player. Ten of the cards included two players on the front of the cards. Single-jersey cards were numbered to 200 and dual-jersey cards were numbered to 100.

		MT
Complete Set (30):		3250.
Common Player:		50.00
Single Jersey 200 Sets		
Dual Jersey 100 Sets		
1	Barry Sanders	150.00
2	Emmitt Smith	125.00
3	Barry Sanders, Emmitt Smith	300.00
4	Eddie George	50.00
5	Terrell Davis	125.00
6	Eddie George, Terrell Davis	200.00
7	Tim Couch	150.00
8	Dan Marino	125.00
9	Tim Couch, Dan Marino	300.00
10	Brett Favre	150.00
11	Troy Aikman	100.00
12	Brett Favre, Troy Aikman	300.00
13	Drew Bledsoe	75.00
14	Mark Brunell	75.00
15	Drew Bledsoe, Mark Brunell	150.00
16	Randy Moss	150.00
17	Jerry Rice	120.00
18	Randy Moss, Jerry Rice	275.00
19	Antonio Freeman	50.00
20	Terry Glenn	50.00
21	Antonio Freeman, Terry Glenn	75.00
22	Steve Young	75.00
23	Kordell Stewart	50.00
24	Steve Young, Kordell Stewart	125.00
25	Fred Taylor	100.00
26	Dorsey Levens	50.00
27	Fred Taylor, Dorsey Levens	150.00
28	Keyshawn Johnson	50.00
29	Herman Moore	50.00
30	Keyshawn Johnson, Herman Moore	85.00

1999 Leaf Rookies & Stars John Elway Collection

This 5-card insert set included pieces of authentic game-worn jerseys, shoes and helmets. The helmet and shoe singles were sequentially numbered to 125 and the jersey singles were numbered to 300.

		MT
Complete Set (5):		850.00
Common Player:		125.00
Helmet/Shoes 125 Sets		
Jersey 300 Sets		
1	John Elway Home Jer.	125.00
2	John Elway Away Jer.	125.00
3	John Elway Shoe	200.00
4	John Elway Blue Hel.	250.00
5	John Elway Orange Hel.	250.00

1999 Leaf Rookies & Stars Freshman Orientation

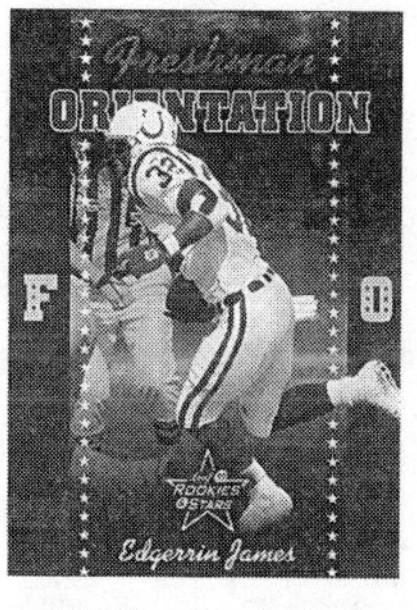

This 25-card insert set included the best rookies from the 1999 NFL Draft. Each card was printed on silver foil board and was sequentially numbered to 2,500.

		MT
Complete Set (25):		75.00
Common Player:		2.00
Production 2,500 Sets		
1	Champ Bailey	3.00
2	D'Wayne Bates	2.00
3	David Boston	4.00
4	Kurt Warner	25.00
5	Cecil Collins	4.00
6	Tim Couch	12.00
7	Daunte Culpepper	6.00
8	Troy Edwards	4.00
9	Kevin Faulk	3.00
10	Joe Germaine	3.00
11	Torry Holt	4.00
12	Brock Huard	3.00
13	Sedrick Irvin	3.00
14	Edgerrin James	20.00
15	Kevin Johnson	4.00
16	Shaun King	6.00
17	Rob Konrad	3.00
18	Sean Bennett	2.00
19	Donovan McNabb	6.00
20	Cade McNown	6.00
21	Peerless Price	3.00
22	Akili Smith	6.00
23	Ricky Williams	10.00
24	James Johnson	3.00
25	Olandis Gary	7.00

1999 Leaf Rookies & Stars Game Plan

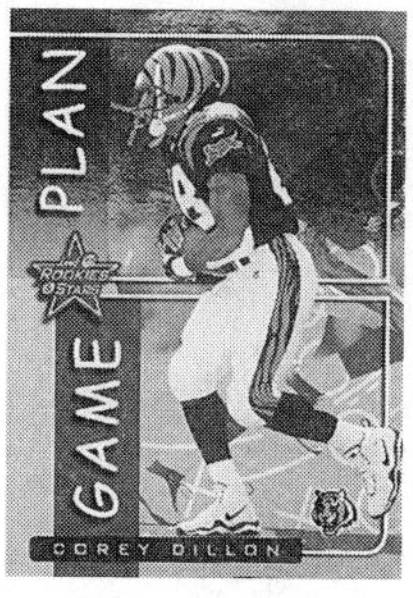

This 25-card insert set included a mix of veterans and rookies. Each card was printed on foil board and was sequentially numbered to 2,500. A Masters parallel was also produced on holographic foil board and each of those was numbered to 50.

		MT
Complete Set (25):		75.00
Common Player:		2.00
Production 2,500 Sets		
Masters Cards:		5x-10x
Production 50 Sets		
1	Jamal Anderson	2.00
2	Jerome Bettis	2.00
3	Drew Bledsoe	4.00
4	Tim Brown	2.00
5	Mark Brunell	4.00
6	Tim Couch	10.00
7	Terrell Davis	8.00
8	Corey Dillon	2.00
9	Warrick Dunn	2.00
10	Brad Johnson	2.00
11	Brett Favre	10.00
12	Doug Flutie	4.00
13	Joey Galloway	2.00
14	Eddie George	2.00
15	Keyshawn Johnson	2.00
16	Peyton Manning	8.00
17	Dan Marino	8.00
18	Donovan McNabb	6.00
19	Cade McNown	6.00
20	Randy Moss	10.00
21	Jake Plummer	4.00
22	Barry Sanders	10.00
23	Emmitt Smith	8.00
24	Ricky Williams	10.00
25	Steve Young	4.00

1999 Leaf Rookies & Stars Game Plan Masters Parallel

This was a 25-card parallel to the Game Plan insert. Each of these singles was printed on holographic foil board and was sequentially numbered to 50.

		MT
Masters Cards:		5x-10x
Production 50 Sets		
1	Jamal Anderson	2.00
2	Jerome Bettis	2.00
3	Drew Bledsoe	4.00
4	Tim Brown	2.00
5	Mark Brunell	4.00
6	Tim Couch	10.00
7	Terrell Davis	8.00
8	Corey Dillon	2.00
9	Warrick Dunn	2.00
10	Brad Johnson	2.00
11	Brett Favre	10.00
12	Doug Flutie	4.00
13	Joey Galloway	2.00
14	Eddie George	2.00
15	Keyshawn Johnson	2.00
16	Peyton Manning	8.00
17	Dan Marino	8.00
18	Donovan McNabb	6.00
19	Cade McNown	6.00
20	Randy Moss	10.00
21	Jake Plummer	4.00
22	Barry Sanders	10.00
23	Emmitt Smith	8.00
24	Ricky Williams	10.00
25	Steve Young	4.00

1999 Leaf Rookies & Stars Great American Heroes

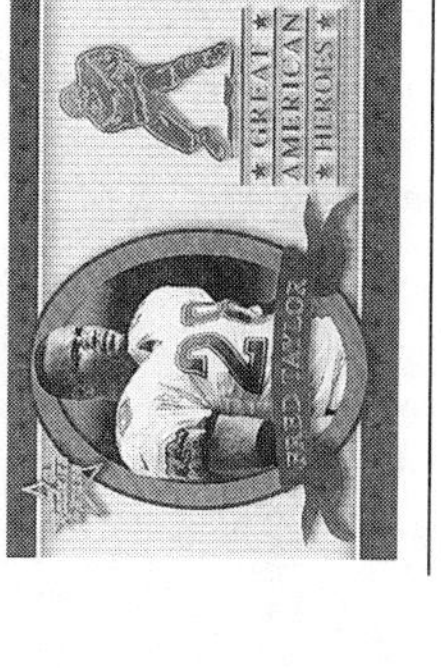

This 25-card insert set included mostly veterans. Singles were sequentially numbered to 2,500.

		MT
Complete Set (25):		75.00
Common Player:		2.00
Production 2,500 Sets		
1	Troy Aikman	6.00
2	Jamal Anderson	2.00
3	Drew Bledsoe	4.00
4	Mark Brunell	4.00
5	Cris Carter	2.00
6	Randall Cunningham	2.00
7	Terrell Davis	8.00
8	John Elway	8.00
9	Brett Favre	10.00
10	Doug Flutie	4.00
11	Antonio Freeman	2.00
12	Eddie George	3.00
13	Peyton Manning	8.00
14	Dan Marino	8.00
15	Curtis Martin	2.00
16	Warren Moon	2.00
17	Randy Moss	10.00
18	Jake Plummer	4.00
19	Jerry Rice	6.00
20	Barry Sanders	10.00
21	Deion Sanders	2.00
22	Emmitt Smith	8.00
23	Fred Taylor	6.00
24	Ricky Williams	10.00
25	Steve Young	4.00

1999 Leaf Rookies & Stars Greatest Hits

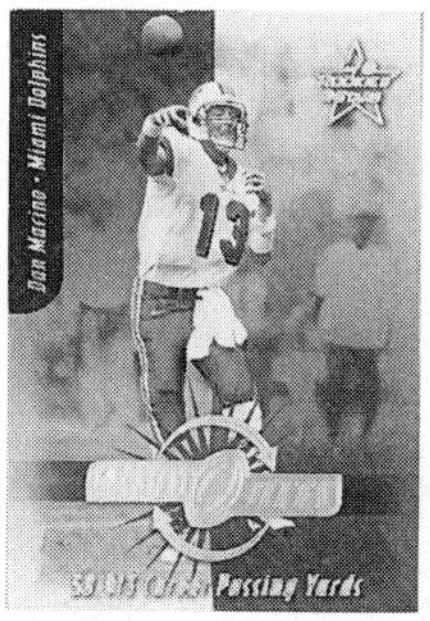

This 25-card insert set included the hottest superstars from the NFL. Singles were sequentially numbered to 2,500.

		MT
Complete Set (25):		70.00
Common Player:		2.00
Production 2,500 Sets		
1	Troy Aikman	6.00
2	Terry Glenn	2.00
3	Jamal Anderson	2.00
4	Drew Bledsoe	4.00
5	Cris Carter	2.00
6	Terrell Davis	8.00
7	John Elway	8.00
8	Brett Favre	10.00
9	Antonio Freeman	2.00
10	Eddie George	3.00
11	Priest Holmes	2.00
12	Keyshawn Johnson	2.00
13	Dorsey Levens	2.00
14	Dan Marino	8.00
15	Curtis Martin	2.00
16	Randy Moss	10.00
17	Eric Moulds	2.00
18	Terrell Owens	2.00
19	Carl Pickens	2.00
20	Jake Plummer	4.00
21	Jerry Rice	6.00
22	Barry Sanders	10.00
23	Marvin Harrison	2.00
24	Robert Smith	2.00
25	Fred Taylor	6.00

1999 Leaf Rookies & Stars Prime Cuts

This 15-card insert set included prime cuts from game-worn jerseys and incorporated them in this insert. Singles were randomly inserted.

		MT
Complete Set (15):		2500.
Common Player:		100.00
1	Tim Couch	300.00
2	Fred Taylor	150.00
3	Terry Glenn	100.00
4	Drew Bledsoe	125.00
5	Dan Marino	250.00
6	Jerry Rice	200.00
7	Barry Sanders	300.00
8	Mark Brunell	125.00
9	Brett Favre	300.00
10	Steve Young	125.00
11	Keyshawn Johnson	100.00
12	Antonio Freeman	100.00
13	Randy Moss	300.00
14	Troy Aikman	200.00
15	Emmitt Smith	250.00

1999 Leaf Rookies & Stars Signature Series

This 30-card insert set included signatures of the top veteran and rookies in the NFL. Single signed cards were sequentially numbered to 150 and dual signature cards were numbered to 50.

		MT
Common Player:		50.00
Singles 150 Sets		
Duals 50 Sets		
1	Terrell Davis	120.00
2	Edgerrin James	275.00
3	Terrell Davis, Edgerrin James	600.00
4	Eddie George	50.00
5	Ricky Williams	200.00
6	Eddie George, Ricky Williams	325.00
7	Jake Plummer	75.00
8	Donovan McNabb	125.00
9	Jake Plummer, Donovan McNabb	200.00
10	Randall Cunningham	50.00
11	Daunte Culpepper	125.00
12	Randall Cunningham, Daunte Culpepper	175.00
13	Fred Taylor	85.00
14	Cecil Collins	50.00
15	Fred Taylor, Cecil Collins	125.00
16	Randy Moss	150.00
17	Torry Holt	75.00
18	Randy Moss, Torry Holt	300.00
19	Steve Young	75.00
20	Cade McNown	125.00
21	Steve Young, Cade McNown	200.00
22	Jerry Rice	120.00
23	David Boston	75.00
24	Jerry Rice, David Boston	225.00
25	Doug Flutie	75.00
26	Akili Smith	120.00
27	Doug Flutie, Akili Smith	150.00
28	Dan Marino	150.00
29	Tim Couch	200.00
30	Dan Marino, Tim Couch	300.00

1999 Leaf Rookies & Stars Slide Show

This 25-card insert set included mostly veterans and a few rookies. Each single was printed on red foil board and was sequentially numbered to 100. A parallel Green set was made with each of those singles numbered to 50. The parallel Blue set was numbered to 25 and the parallel Studios only had one card of each.

		MT
Complete Set (25):		500.00
Common Player:		10.00
Production 100 Sets		
Green Cards:		2x
Production 50 Sets		
Blue Cards:		3x
Production 25 Sets		
Studio Cards:		
Production 1 Set		
1	Troy Aikman	30.00
2	Drew Bledsoe	20.00
3	Mark Brunell	20.00
4	Tim Couch	50.00
5	Terrell Davis	40.00
6	John Elway	40.00
7	Brett Favre	50.00
8	Antonio Freeman	10.00
9	Eddie George	10.00
10	Torry Holt	20.00
11	Edgerrin James	85.00
12	Keyshawn Johnson	10.00
13	Jon Kitna	10.00
14	Dorsey Levens	10.00
15	Peyton Manning	40.00
16	Dan Marino	40.00
17	Randy Moss	50.00
18	Jake Plummer	20.00
19	Jerry Rice	30.00
20	Barry Sanders	50.00
21	Marvin Harrison	10.00
22	Emmitt Smith	40.00
23	Fred Taylor	30.00
24	Ricky Williams	50.00
25	Steve Young	20.00

1999 Leaf Rookies & Stars Statistical Standouts

This 25-card insert set included the top producers in receiving, rushing and passing, and highlighted them on simulated leather with white foil. Each single was sequentially numbered to 1,250. A parallel Die Cut version was also produced with each of those singles numbered to a 1998 stat.

		MT
Complete Set (25):		100.00
Common Player:		2.00
Minor Stars:		4.00
Production 1,250 Sets		
1	Jamal Anderson	4.00
2	Jerome Bettis	4.00
3	Drew Bledsoe	6.00
4	Cris Carter	4.00
5	Randall Cunningham	4.00
6	Terrell Davis	10.00
7	John Elway	10.00
8	Marshall Faulk	4.00
9	Brett Favre	15.00
10	Antonio Freeman	4.00
11	Joey Galloway	4.00
12	Eddie George	4.00
13	Garrison Hearst	2.00
14	Keyshawn Johnson	4.00
15	Peyton Manning	10.00
16	Steve McNair	4.00
17	Randy Moss	15.00
18	Eric Moulds	4.00
19	Terrell Owens	4.00
20	Jake Plummer	6.00
21	Barry Sanders	15.00
22	Emmitt Smith	10.00
23	Fred Taylor	8.00
24	Vinny Testaverde	2.00
25	Steve Young	5.00

1999 Leaf Rookies & Stars Ticket Masters

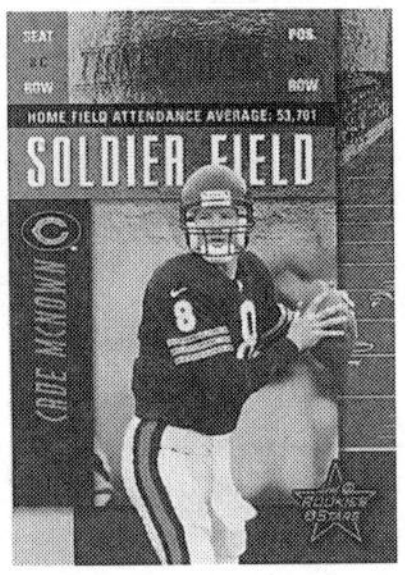

This 25-card insert set included the top NFL stars. Each single was sequentially numbered to 2,500. A parallel Executive Ticket Master set was also produced with each of those singles die cut and numbered to 50.

MT
Complete Set (25): 100.00
Common Player: 2.00
Production 2,500 Sets
Executive Cards: 5x-10x
Production 50 Sets
1 Randy Moss, Cris Carter 12.00
2 Brett Favre, Antonio Freeman 12.00
3 Cecil Collins, Dan Marino 10.00
4 Brian Griese, Terrell Davis 8.00
5 Edgerrin James, Peyton Manning 25.00
6 Emmitt Smith, Troy Aikman 10.00
7 Jerry Rice, Steve Young 8.00
8 Mark Brunell, Fred Taylor 7.00
9 David Boston, Jake Plummer 5.00
10 Terry Glenn, Drew Bledsoe 5.00
11 Charlie Batch, Herman Moore 5.00
12 Mike Alstott, Warrick Dunn 2.00
13 Eddie George, Steve McNair 3.00
14 Kordell Stewart, Jerome Bettis 2.00
15 Chris Chandler, Jamal Anderson 2.00
16 Akili Smith, Corey Dillon 4.00
17 Curtis Enis, Cade McNown 8.00
18 Isaac Bruce, Marshall Faulk 3.00
19 Eric Moulds, Doug Flutie 5.00
20 Joey Galloway, Ricky Watters 2.00
21 Michael Westbrook, Brad Johnson 2.00
22 Curtis Martin, Keyshawn Johnson 3.00
23 Napoleon Kaufman, Tim Brown 2.00
24 Kevin Johnson, Tim Couch 15.00
25 Duce Staley, Donovan McNabb 10.00

1999 Leaf Rookies & Stars Ticket Masters Executives Par

This was a parallel to the Ticket Master insert. Each of these singles was die cut and numbered to 50.

MT
Executive Cards: 5x-10x
Production 50 Sets
1 Randy Moss, Cris Carter 12.00
2 Brett Favre, Antonio Freeman 12.00
3 Cecil Collins, Dan Marino 10.00
4 Brian Griese, Terrell Davis 8.00
5 Edgerrin James, Peyton Manning 25.00
6 Emmitt Smith, Troy Aikman 10.00
7 Jerry Rice, Steve Young 8.00
8 Mark Brunell, Fred Taylor 7.00
9 David Boston, Jake Plummer 5.00
10 Terry Glenn, Drew Bledsoe 5.00
11 Charlie Batch, Herman Moore 5.00
12 Mike Alstott, Warrick Dunn 2.00
13 Eddie George, Steve McNair 3.00
14 Kordell Stewart, Jerome Bettis 2.00
15 Chris Chandler, Jamal Anderson 2.00
16 Akili Smith, Corey Dillon 4.00
17 Curtis Enis, Cade McNown 8.00
18 Isaac Bruce, Marshall Faulk 3.00
19 Eric Moulds, Doug Flutie 5.00
20 Joey Galloway, Ricky Watters 2.00
21 Michael Westbrook, Brad Johnson 2.00
22 Curtis Martin, Keyshawn Johnson 3.00
23 Napoleon Kaufman, Tim Brown 2.00
24 Kevin Johnson, Tim Couch 15.00
25 Duce Staley, Donovan McNabb 10.00

1999 Leaf Rookies & Stars Touchdown Club

This 20-card insert set included the players who see the end zone the most. Each of these singles was sequentially numbered to 1,000. A parallel Die Cut version was also produced with each of those singles numbered to 60.

MT
Complete Set (20): 150.00
Common Player: 4.00
Production 1,000 Sets
Die-Cut Cards: 3x-6x
Production 60 Sets
1 Randy Moss 20.00
2 Brett Favre 20.00
3 Dan Marino 15.00
4 Barry Sanders 20.00
5 John Elway 15.00
6 Terrell Davis 15.00
7 Peyton Manning 15.00
8 Emmitt Smith 15.00
9 Jerry Rice 12.00
10 Fred Taylor 12.00
11 Drew Bledsoe 8.00
12 Steve Young 8.00
13 Eddie George 5.00
14 Cris Carter 4.00
15 Antonio Freeman 4.00
16 Marvin Harrison 4.00
17 Kurt Warner 30.00
18 Stephen Davis 4.00
19 Terry Glenn 4.00
20 Brad Johnson 4.00

1999 Leaf Rookies & Stars Touchdown Club Die Cuts Para.

This was a parallel to the Touchdown Club insert. Each of these singles was sequentially numbered to 60 and was die cut.

MT
Die-Cut Cards 3x-6x
Production 60 Sets
1 Randy Moss 20.00
2 Brett Favre 20.00
3 Dan Marino 15.00
4 Barry Sanders 20.00
5 John Elway 15.00
6 Terrell Davis 15.00
7 Peyton Manning 15.00
8 Emmitt Smith 15.00
9 Jerry Rice 12.00
10 Fred Taylor 12.00
11 Drew Bledsoe 8.00
12 Steve Young 8.00
13 Eddie George 5.00
14 Cris Carter 4.00
15 Antonio Freeman 4.00
16 Marvin Harrison 4.00
17 Kurt Warner 30.00
18 Stephen Davis 4.00
19 Terry Glenn 4.00
20 Brad Johnson 4.00

2000 Leaf Certified

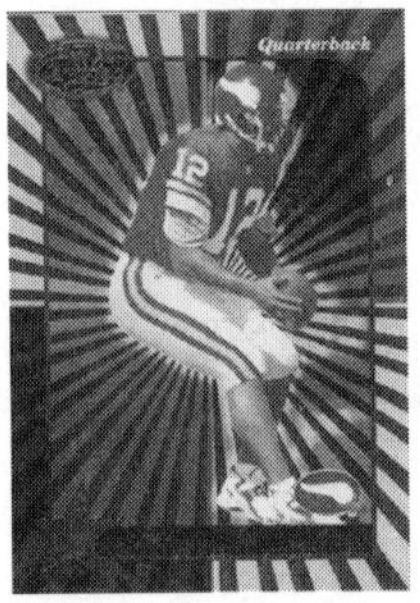

MT
Complete Set (250): 950.00
Common Player (1-100): .20
Minor Stars: .40
Common Player (101-150): .30
Minor Stars: .60
Inserted 1:2
Common Rookie (151-190): 3.00
Production 2,000 Sets
Common Rookie (191-220): 4.00
Production 1,500 Sets
Common Rookie (221-250): 12.00
Production 1,000 Sets
Pack (5): 6.50
Wax Box (18): 90.00
1 Frank Sanders .40
2 Rob Moore .40
3 Simeon Rice .40
4 David Boston .75
5 Tim Dwight .75
6 Jamal Anderson .75
7 Chris Chandler .75
8 Terance Mathis .20
9 Priest Holmes .40
10 Rod Woodson .20
11 Tony Banks .40
12 Jermaine Lewis .20
13 Shannon Sharpe .40
14 Qadry Ismail .20
15 Doug Flutie .75
16 Antowain Smith .40
17 Peerless Price .40
18 Rob Johnson .40
19 Muhsin Muhammad .40
20 Wesley Walls .40
21 Tim Biakabutuka .40
22 Steve Beuerlein .40
23 Patrick Jeffers .75
24 Natrone Means .40
25 Curtis Enis .50
26 Bobby Engram .20
27 Marcus Robinson .75
28 Eddie Kennison .20
29 Marty Booker .20
30 Darnay Scott .40
31 Carl Pickens .40
32 Karim Abdul .20
33 Errict Rhett .20
34 Darrin Chiaverini .20
35 Randall Cunningham .40
36 Michael Irvin .40
37 Raghib Ismail .20
38 Ed McCaffrey .50
39 Rod Smith .50
40 Herman Moore .40
41 Johnnie Morton .40
42 James Stewart .40
43 Bill Schroeder .40
44 Ahman Green .40
45 Terrence Wilkins .40
46 Keenan McCardell .40
47 Derrick Alexander .40
48 Elvis Grbac .40
49 Tony Gonzalez .40
50 O.J. McDuffie .40
51 Tony Martin .20
52 James Johnson .20
53 Thurman Thomas .40
54 Jay Fiedler .40
55 Damon Huard .40
56 Leroy Hoard .20
57 Terry Glenn .75
58 Kevin Faulk .40
59 Jeff Blake .40
60 Jake Reed .40
61 Amani Toomer .20
62 Kerry Collins .40
63 Ike Hilliard .20
64 Joe Montgomery .20
65 Vinny Testaverde .40
66 Wayne Chrebet .40
67 Ray Lucas .50
68 Napoleon Kaufman .40
69 Charles Woodson .40
70 Tyrone Wheatley .40
71 Rich Gannon .40
72 Duce Staley .75
73 Kordell Stewart .75
74 Jerome Bettis .50
75 Troy Edwards .50
76 Junior Seau .40
77 Jim Harbaugh .40
78 Curtis Conway .20
79 Jermaine Fazande .40
80 Terrell Owens .75
81 Charlie Garner .40
82 Garrison Hearst .40
83 Jeff Garcia .75
84 Derrick Mayes .40
85 Az-Zahir Hakim .40
86 Mike Alstott .75
87 Warrick Dunn .75
88 Jacquez Green .20
89 Warren Sapp .20
90 Yancey Thigpen .20
91 Kevin Dyson .40
92 Frank Wycheck .20
93 Jevon Kearse .50
94 Adrian Murrell .40
95 Bruce Smith .20
96 Michael Westbrook .40
97 Albert Connell .40
98 Champ Bailey .40
99 Jeff George .50
100 Deion Sanders .75
101 Jake Plummer 1.25
102 Eric Moulds 1.25
103 Cade McNown 1.75
104 Corey Dillon 1.25
105 Akili Smith 1.50
106 Tim Couch 2.50
107 Kevin Johnson .60
108 Emmitt Smith 3.50
109 Troy Aikman 3.00
110 Joey Galloway 1.25
111 John Elway 4.00
112 Terrell Davis 3.50
113 Olandis Gary 1.25
114 Brian Griese 1.50
115 Charlie Batch 1.25
116 Barry Sanders 4.00
117 Germane Crowell 1.25
118 Brett Favre 5.00
119 Dorsey Levens 1.25
120 Antonio Freeman 1.25
121 Peyton Manning 4.00
122 Edgerrin James 5.00
123 Marvin Harrison 1.25
124 Mark Brunell 2.00
125 Fred Taylor 1.75
126 Jimmy Smith 1.25
127 Dan Marino 4.00
128 Randy Moss 5.00
129 Daunte Culpepper 2.50
130 Cris Carter 1.25
131 Robert Smith 1.25
132 Drew Bledsoe 2.00
133 Ricky Williams 3.00
134 Curtis Martin 1.25
135 Tim Brown 1.00
136 Donovan McNabb 2.00
137 Jerry Rice 3.00
138 Steve Young 1.75
139 Jon Kitna 1.00
140 Ricky Watters .75
141 Kurt Warner 6.00
142 Marshall Faulk 1.25
143 Torry Holt 1.25
144 Isaac Bruce 1.25
145 Shaun King 2.00
146 Keyshawn Johnson 1.25
147 Eddie George 1.50
148 Steve McNair 1.25
149 Stephen Davis 1.25
150 Brad Johnson 1.00
151 *Rogers Beckett* 3.00
152 *Erik Flowers* 3.00
153 *Demario Brown* 3.00
154 *Doug Johnson* 3.00
155 *Deon Grant* 3.00
156 *Ian Gold* 3.00
157 *Brian Urlacher* 12.00
158 *Frank Murphy* 3.00
159 *James Whalen* 3.00
160 *JaJuan Dawson* 8.00
161 *William Bartee* 3.00
162 *Aaron Shea* 3.00
163 *Deltha O'Neal* 6.00
164 *Jarious Jackson* 6.00
165 *Muneer Moore* 3.00
166 *Hank Poteat* 3.00
167 *Jacoby Shepherd* 3.00
168 *Ben Kelly* 3.00
169 *Orantes Grant* 3.00
170 *Chris Hovan* 3.00
171 *Leon Murray* 3.00
172 *Marc Bulger* 3.00
173 *Chad Morton* 8.00
174 *Na'il Diggs* 3.00
175 *Shaun Ellis* 3.00
176 *John Abraham* 3.00
177 *Fred Robbins* 3.00
178 *Marcus Knight* 3.00
179 *Thomas Hamner* 3.00
180 *Cornelius Griffin* 3.00
181 *Raynoch Thompson* 3.00
182 *Paul Smith* 3.00
183 *Ahmed Plummer* 6.00
184 *John Engelberger* 3.00
185 *Darren Howard* 3.00
186 *Corey Moore* 3.00
187 *Joe Hamilton* 8.00
188 *Rob Morris* 6.00
189 *Keith Bulluck* 3.00
190 *Todd Husak* 6.00
191 *Mareno Philyaw* 4.00
192 *Kwame Cavil* 4.00
193 *Sammy Morris* 12.00
194 *Avion Black* 4.00
195 *Bashir Yamini* 4.00
196 *Curtis Keaton* 6.00
197 *Mike Anderson* 40.00
198 *Bubba Franks* 12.00
199 *Anthony Lucas* 10.00
200 *Rondell Mealey* 10.00
201 *Terrelle Smith* 8.00
202 *Frank Moreau* 10.00
203 *Deon Dyer* 4.00
204 *Quinton Spotwood* 8.00
205 *Troy Walters* 8.00
206 *Doug Chapman* 4.00
207 *Tom Brady* 15.00
208 *Sherrod Gideon* 8.00
209 *Ron Dixon* 10.00
210 *Anthony Becht* 8.00
211 *James Williams* 4.00
212 *Sebastian Janikowski* 10.00
213 *Corey Simon* 10.00
214 *Gari Scott* 4.00
215 *Dante Hall* 4.00
216 *Tim Rattay* 15.00
217 *Chafie Fields* 4.00
218 *Trung Canidate* 10.00
219 *Chris Coleman* 4.00
220 *Erron Kinney* 4.00
221 *Thomas Jones* 30.00
222 *Travis Taylor* 20.00
223 *Chris Redman* 30.00
224 *Jamal Lewis* 75.00
225 *Dez White* 15.00
226 *Peter Warrick* 45.00
227 *Ron Dugans* 15.00
228 *Courtney Brown* 20.00
229 *Travis Prentice* 30.00
230 *Dennis Northcutt* 20.00
231 *Michael Wiley* 12.00
232 *Chris Cole* 12.00
233 *Reuben Droughns* 12.00
234 *R. Jay Soward* 20.00
235 *Shyrone Stith* 20.00
236 *Sylvester Morris* 40.00
237 *J.R. Redmond* 25.00
238 *Ron Dayne* 70.00
239 *Chad Pennington* 50.00
240 *Laveranues Coles* 25.00
241 *Jerry Porter* 20.00
242 *Todd Pinkston* 20.00
243 *Plaxico Burress* 35.00
244 *Danny Farmer* 12.00
245 *Tee Martin* 20.00
246 *Trevor Gaylor* 20.00
247 *Giovanni Carmazzi* 25.00
248 *Darrell Jackson* 25.00
249 *Shaun Alexander* 45.00
250 *Chris Samuels* 20.00

2000 Leaf Certified Mirror Gold Parallel

MT
One Star Cards: 30x-60x
Production 20 Sets
Two Star Cards: 20x-40x
Production 25 Sets
Three Star Cards: 4x-8x
Production 30 Sets
Four Star Cards: 2x-4x
Production 35 Sets
Five Star Cards: 2x
Production 40 Sets

2000 Leaf Certified Mirror Red Parallel

MT
One Star Cards: 3x-6x
Inserted 1:17
Two Star Cards: 3x-6x
Inserted 1:53
Three Star Cards: 2x
Inserted 1:89
Four Star Cards: 1.5x
Inserted 1:125
Five Star Cards: 1x
Inserted 1:161

2000 Leaf Certified Rookie Die Cuts

MT
Three Star Cards: 3x
Four Star Cards: 2x
Five Star Cards: 1.5x
Production 250 Sets

2000 Leaf Certified Fabric of the Game

MT
Complete Set (75): 700.00
Common Player: 5.00
Production 100 to 1,000 Sets
FG1 Barry Sanders 100 45.00
FG2 John Elway 100 45.00
FG3 Jerry Rice 100 30.00
FG4 Cris Carter 250 10.00
FG5 Emmitt Smith 250 25.00
FG6 Troy Aikman 250 20.00
FG7 Deion Sanders 250 5.00
FG8 Terrell Davis 500 20.00
FG9 Marshall Faulk 500 5.00
FG10 Mark Brunell 500 10.00
FG11 Randy Moss 500 25.00
FG12 Peyton Manning 500 25.00
FG13 Kurt Warner 750 20.00
FG14 Jamal Anderson 750 5.00
FG15 Edgerrin James 750 15.00
FG16 Isaac Bruce 750 5.00
FG17 Jimmy Smith 750 5.00
FG18 Keyshawn Johnson 750 5.00
FG19 Brian Griese 1000 5.00
FG20 Cade McNown 1000 5.00
FG21 Shaun King 1000 5.00
FG22 Chad Pennington 1000 12.00
FG23 Plaxico Burress 1000 10.00
FG24 Thomas Jones 1000 8.00
FG25 Peter Warrick 1000 15.00
FG26 Dan Marino 100 50.00
FG27 John Elway 100 50.00
FG28 Emmitt Smith 100 35.00
FG29 Brett Favre 250 30.00
FG30 Steve Young 250 10.00
FG31 Cris Carter 250 5.00
FG32 Michael Irvin 250 5.00
FG33 Eddie George 500 7.00
FG34 Drew Bledsoe 500 10.00
FG35 Antonio Freeman 500 5.00
FG36 Steve McNair 500 5.00
FG37 Randy Moss 500 20.00
FG38 Kurt Warner 750 15.00
FG39 Eric Moulds 750 5.00
FG40 Fred Taylor 750 5.00
FG41 Charlie Batch 750 5.00
FG42 Marvin Harrison 750 5.00
FG43 Joey Galloway 750 5.00
FG44 Tim Couch 1000 7.00
FG45 Ricky Williams 1000 8.00
FG46 Donovan McNabb 1000 5.00
FG47 Akili Smith 1000 5.00
FG48 Kevin Johnson 1000 5.00
FG49 Thomas Jones 1000 8.00
FG50 Ron Dayne 1000 20.00
FG51 Dan Marino 100 50.00
FG52 Barry Sanders 100 50.00
FG53 Jerry Rice 100 35.00
FG54 Brett Favre 250 30.00
FG55 Tim Brown 250 5.00
FG56 Steve Young 250 10.00
FG57 Thurman Thomas 250 5.00
FG58 Jeff George 500 5.00
FG59 Curtis Martin 500 5.00
FG60 Terrell Davis 500 20.00
FG61 Peyton Manning 500 25.00
FG62 Ricky Watters 500 5.00
FG63 Edgerrin James 750 15.00
FG64 Fred Taylor 750 5.00
FG65 Stephen Davis 750 5.00
FG66 Jake Plummer 750 5.00
FG67 Brad Johnson 750 5.00
FG68 Jon Kitna 750 5.00
FG69 Tim Couch 1000 7.00
FG70 Daunte Culpepper 1000 7.00
FG71 Olandis Gary 1000 5.00
FG72 Jamal Lewis 1000 12.00
FG73 Peter Warrick 1000 15.00
FG74 Shaun Alexander 1000 10.00
FG75 Travis Taylor 1000 8.00

2000 Leaf Certified Gold Future

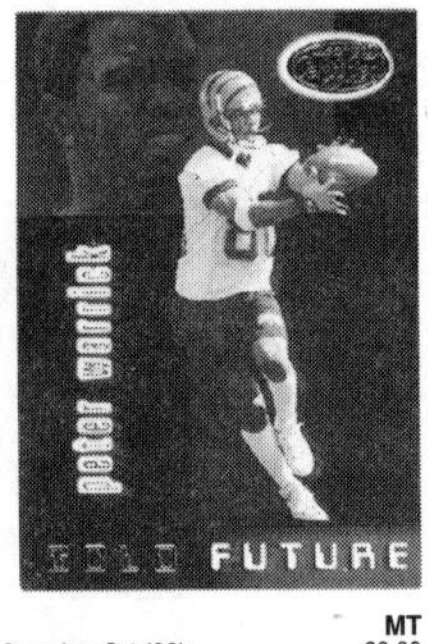

MT
Complete Set (30): 60.00
Common Player: 2.00
Inserted 1:17
Mirror Black Cards: 10x-20x
Production 25 Sets
CGF1 Peter Warrick 10.00
CGF2 Chad Pennington 8.00
CGF3 Thomas Jones 4.00
CGF4 Plaxico Burress 5.00
CGF5 Jamal Lewis 6.00
CGF6 Travis Taylor 3.00
CGF7 Chris Redman 4.00
CGF8 Dez White 2.00
CGF9 Shaun Alexander 5.00
CGF10 Sylvester Morris 4.00
CGF11 Ron Dayne 10.00
CGF12 R. Jay Soward 2.00
CGF13 Travis Prentice 3.00
CGF14 Giovanni Carmazzi 3.00
CGF15 Todd Pinkston 2.00
CGF16 J.R. Redmond 3.00
CGF17 Trevor Gaylor 2.00
CGF18 Trung Canidate 2.00
CGF19 Danny Farmer 2.00
CGF20 Tee Martin 2.00
CGF21 Darrell Jackson 2.00
CGF22 Gari Scott 2.00
CGF23 Dennis Northcutt 2.00
CGF24 Jerry Porter 2.00
CGF25 Reuben Droughns 2.00
CGF26 Laveranues Coles 3.00
CGF27 Bubba Franks 3.00
CGF28 Doug Chapman 2.00
CGF29 Chris Cole 2.00
CGF30 Ron Dugans 2.00

2000 Leaf Certified Gold Team

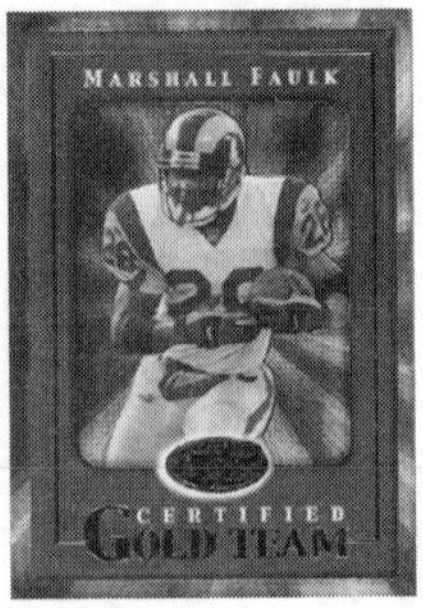

MT
Complete Set (40): 100.00
Common Player: 3.00
Inserted 1:17
Mirror Black Cards: 10x-20x
Production 25 Sets
CGT1 Randy Moss 10.00
CGT2 Brett Favre 10.00
CGT3 Dan Marino 8.00
CGT4 Barry Sanders 8.00
CGT5 John Elway 8.00
CGT6 Peyton Manning 10.00
CGT7 Terrell Davis 7.00
CGT8 Emmitt Smith 7.00
CGT9 Troy Aikman 6.00
CGT10 Jerry Rice 6.00
CGT11 Fred Taylor 3.50
CGT12 Jake Plummer 3.00
CGT13 Charlie Batch 3.00
CGT14 Drew Bledsoe 4.00
CGT15 Mark Brunell 4.00
CGT16 Steve Young 4.00
CGT17 Eddie George 3.50
CGT18 Tim Brown 3.00
CGT19 Cris Carter 3.00
CGT20 Stephen Davis 3.00
CGT21 Marshall Faulk 3.00
CGT22 Antonio Freeman 3.00
CGT23 Marvin Harrison 3.00
CGT24 Brad Johnson 3.00
CGT25 Keyshawn Johnson 3.00
CGT26 Jon Kitna 3.00
CGT27 Curtis Martin 3.00
CGT28 Steve McNair 3.00
CGT29 Isaac Bruce 3.00
CGT30 Kurt Warner 12.00
CGT31 Edgerrin James 10.00
CGT32 Tim Couch 5.00
CGT33 Ricky Williams 5.00
CGT34 Donovan McNabb 3.50
CGT35 Cade McNown 3.00
CGT36 Daunte Culpepper 4.50
CGT37 Torry Holt 3.00
CGT38 Robert Smith 3.00
CGT39 Mike Alstott 3.00
CGT40 Dorsey Levens 3.00

2000 Leaf Certified Gridiron Gear

MT
Common Jersey 300: 20.00
Common Jersey 100: 30.00
Century 300: 3x
Century 100: 2x
Production 21 Sets
Troy Aikman 100 100.00
Mike Alstott 300 30.00
Champ Bailey 300 20.00
Charlie Batch 300 20.00
Jerome Bettis 100 30.00
Drew Bledsoe 100 50.00
Tim Brown White 300 25.00
Tim Brown Black 300 25.00
Isaac Bruce White 100 40.00
Isaac Bruce Blue 300 30.00
Mark Brunell White 100 65.00
Mark Brunell Teal 300 40.00
Cris Carter 100 40.00
Wayne Chrebet 300 20.00
Tim Couch 100 85.00
Randall Cunningham 300 20.00
Terrell Davis 100 85.00
Corey Dillon 300 20.00
Warrick Dunn 300 20.00
John Elway 100 100.00
Curtis Enis White 300 20.00
Curtis Enis Blue 300 20.00
Marshall Faulk White 100 50.00
Marshall Faulk Blue 300 30.00
Brett Favre White 300 60.00
Brett Favre Green 100 100.00
Doug Flutie 300 30.00
Antonio Freeman 300 20.00
Olandis Gary 100 35.00
Eddie George 100 50.00
Brian Griese 100 45.00
Jim Harbaugh 300 20.00
Marvin Harrison 300 30.00
Damon Huard 300 20.00
Edgerrin James Blue 100 100.00
Edgerrin James PB 300 75.00
Napoleon Kaufman 100 30.00
Jevon Kearse 300 30.00
Shaun King 100 50.00
Dorsey Levens White 300 20.00
Dorsey Levens Green 300 20.00
Ray Lucas 100 30.00
Peyton Manning 100 125.00

Dan Marino White 300 100.00
Dan Marino Teal 100 150.00
Curtis Martin 100 40.00
Ed McCaffrey 300 20.00
Keenan McCardell 300 20.00
Donovan McNabb 300 30.00
Steve McNair 100 45.00
Cade McNown 300 30.00
Johnnie Morton 300 20.00
Randy Moss 100 125.00
Eric Moulds 300 30.00
Terrell Owens 300 30.00
Jake Plummer 300 30.00
Jerry Rice White 100 85.00
Jerry Rice Red 300 60.00
Barry Sanders 100 100.00
Deion Sanders 300 30.00
Emmitt Smith 100 100.00
Jimmy Smith White 100 40.00
Jimmy Smith Teal 300 25.00
Rod Smith 300 25.00
Kordell Stewart 300 30.00
Fred Taylor White 300 35.00
Fred Taylor Teal 100 50.00
Kurt Warner White 300 85.00
Kurt Warner Blue 100 150.00
Ricky Watters 300 20.00
Tyrone Wheatley 300 20.00
Ricky Williams White 100 65.00
Ricky Williams Black 100 65.00
Charles Woodson 300 20.00
Steve Young 100 75.00

2000 Leaf Certified Heritage Collection

MT
Production 100 Sets
Century Autographs: 3x
Century Non Auto: 2x
Marcus Allen White 50.00
Marcus Allen Red 50.00
Raymond Berry 35.00
Terry Bradshaw White 125.00
Terry Bradshaw PB 125.00
John Brodie 35.00
Jim Brown 125.00
Earl Campbell 50.00
Eric Dickerson White 50.00
Eric Dickerson Blue 50.00
Tony Dorsett 75.00
Boomer Esiason 35.00
Dan Fouts White 60.00
Dan Fouts Blue 60.00
Frank Gifford 85.00
Bob Griese 60.00
Ted Hendricks 35.00
Keith Jackson 35.00
Craig James 35.00
Bert Jones 35.00
Sonny Jurgensen 50.00
Jim Kelly 85.00
Bernie Kosar 35.00
Steve Largent 85.00
Howie Long 75.00
Ronnie Lott 35.00
Don Maynard 35.00
Joe Montana SF 200.00
Joe Montana KC 200.00
Warren Moon 35.00
Joe Namath 150.00
Ozzie Newsome 35.00
Ray Nitschke 100.00
Merlin Olsen 35.00
Walter Payton White 200.00
Walter Payton Blue 200.00
Jim Plunkett 50.00
Gale Sayers 100.00
Phil Simms 50.00
Ken Stabler 100.00
Bart Starr 150.00
Fran Tarkenton 100.00
Joe Theismann 50.00
Derrick Thomas 75.00
Johnny Unitas 150.00
Herschel Walker 35.00
Reggie White 35.00

2000 Leaf Certified Skills

MT
Complete Set (30): 125.00
Common Player: 2.50
Inserted 1:35:
Mirror Black Cards: 5x-10x
Production 25 Sets
CS1 Jamal Anderson, Thomas Jones 5.00
CS2 Randy Moss, Germane Crowell 10.00
CS3 Brett Favre, Donovan McNabb 10.00
CS4 Dan Marino, Tim Couch 8.00
CS5 Barry Sanders, James Stewart 8.00
CS6 John Elway, Brian Griese 8.00
CS7 Peyton Manning, Chad Pennington 10.00
CS8 Terrell Davis, Olandis Gary 7.00
CS9 Emmitt Smith, Duce Staley 7.00
CS10 Troy Aikman, Cade McNown 6.00
CS11 Jerry Rice, Isaac Bruce 6.00
CS12 Fred Taylor, Stephen Davis 3.50
CS13 Drew Bledsoe, Brad Johnson 4.00
CS14 Mark Brunell, Shaun King 4.00
CS15 Steve Young, Akili Smith 4.00
CS16 Eddie George, Ricky Williams 5.00
CS17 Kurt Warner, Jon Kitna 10.00
CS18 Edgerrin James, Corey Dillon 10.00
CS19 Cris Carter, Tim Brown 2.50
CS20 Keyshawn Johnson, Plaxico Burress 7.00
CS21 Marshall Faulk, Robert Smith 2.50
CS22 Antonio Freeman, Travis Taylor 5.00
CS23 Marvin Harrison, Kevin Johnson 2.50
CS24 Dorsey Levens, Jamal Lewis 8.00
CS25 Curtis Martin, Shaun Alexander 7.00
CS26 Steve McNair, Daunte Culpepper 3.50
CS27 Jimmy Smith, Peter Warrick 10.00
CS28 Jerome Bettis, Ron Dayne 10.00
CS29 Joey Galloway, Torry Holt 2.50
CS30 Eric Moulds, Terrell Owens 2.50

2000 Leaf Limited

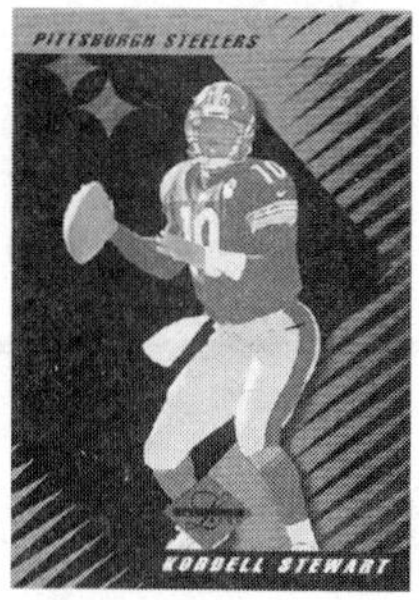

MT
Complete Set (425): 3000.
Common Player (1-50): .50
Minor Stars (1-50): 1.00
Production 5,000 Sets
Common Player (51-100): .75
Minor Stars (51-100): 1.50
Production 4,000 Sets
Common Player (101-150): 1.00
Minor Stars (101-150): 2.00
Production 3,000 Sets
Common Player (151-200): 1.25
Minor Stars (151-200): 2.50
Production 2,000 Sets
Common Rookie (201-250): 3.50
Production 1,500 Sets
Common Rookie (251-300): 5.00
Production 1,000 Sets
Common Rookie (301-350): 7.50
Production 500 Sets
Common Rookie (351-400): 10.00
Production 350 Sets
Common Rookie (401-425): 20.00
Production 250,500,750 or 1,000 Sets
Pack (3): 10.00
Wax Box (18): 150.00
1 Ben Coates .50
2 Joe Horn .50
3 Jonathon Linton .50
4 Derrick Mason 1.00
5 Ray Lucas 1.00
6 Brock Huard 1.00
7 Frank Wycheck .50
8 Michael Strahan .50
9 Jessie Armstead .50
10 Stephen Alexander .50
11 Larry Centers .50
12 Michael Pittman .50
13 Priest Holmes 1.00
14 Jermaine Lewis .50
15 Jay Riemersma .50
16 Wesley Walls .50
17 Curtis Enis .50
18 Bobby Engram .50
19 Jim Miller .50
20 Eddie Kennison .50
21 Errict Rhett .50
22 Chris Warren .50
23 Byron Chamberlain .50
24 Desmond Howard .50
25 Lamar Smith .50
26 Robert Porcher .50
27 Corey Bradford .50
28 Donald Driver .50
29 Ahman Green 1.00
30 Ken Dilger .50
31 James McKnight .50
32 Kimble Anders .50
33 Zach Thomas .50
34 James Johnson .50
35 Lawyer Milloy .50
36 Ty Law .50
37 Willie McGinest .50
38 Jason Sehorn .50
39 Andre Rison .50
40 Rickey Dudley .50
41 Patrick Jeffers 1.00
42 Darrell Russell .50
43 Charles Johnson .50
44 Michael Westbrook .50
45 Levon Kirkland .50
46 Ryan Leahy .50
47 Sean Dawkins .50
48 Todd Lyght .50
49 Kevin Carter .50
50 Neil O'Donnell .50
51 Randall Cunningham 1.50
52 Oronde Gadsden .75
53 O.J. McDuffie .75
54 Jake Reed .75
55 Brian Mitchell .75
56 Kordell Stewart 1.75
57 Derrick Mayes .75
58 Az-Zahir Hakim 1.50
59 Jacquez Green .75
60 Andre Reed .75
61 Deion Sanders 1.75
62 Frank Sanders .75
63 Rob Moore .75
64 Shawn Jefferson .75
65 Patrick Johnson .75
66 Peter Boulware .75
67 Donald Hayes .75
68 Marty Booker .75
69 Leslie Shepherd .75
70 Jason Tucker .75
71 Johnnie Morton .75
72 Germane Crowell 1.50
73 Herman Moore 1.50
74 Bill Schroeder .75
75 E.G. Green .75
76 Jerome Pathon .75
77 Tony Brackens .75
78 Tony Richardson .75
79 Sam Madison .75
80 Jeff George 1.50
81 Matthew Hatchette .75
82 Kevin Faulk 1.50
83 Jeff Blake 1.50
84 Ike Hilliard 1.50
85 Napoleon Kaufman 1.50
86 Charles Woodson 1.50
87 Na Brown .75
88 Hines Ward 1.50
89 Troy Edwards 1.50
90 Curtis Conway .75
91 Junior Seau 1.50
92 Jim Harbaugh .75
93 J.J. Stokes .75
94 Jon Kitna 1.50
95 Reidel Anthony .75
96 Warrick Dunn 1.50
97 Carl Pickens 1.50
98 Yancey Thigpen .75
99 Albert Connell .75
100 Irving Fryar .75
101 Qadry Ismail 1.00
102 Shannon Sharpe 1.00
103 Joey Galloway 2.00
104 Ed McCaffrey 2.00
105 Rod Smith 2.00
106 Terrell Owens 2.00
107 Warren Sapp 1.00
108 Jevon Kearse 2.00
109 Bruce Smith 1.00
110 Champ Bailey 2.00
111 David Boston 2.00
112 Tim Dwight 2.00
113 Terance Mathis 1.00
114 Tony Banks 1.00
115 Shawn Bryson 1.00
116 Peerless Price 1.00
117 Muhsin Muhammad 1.00
118 Tim Biakabutuka 1.00
119 Steve Beuerlein 1.00
120 Corey Dillon 2.00
121 Kevin Johnson 2.00
122 Raghib Ismail 1.00
123 Charlie Batch 2.00
124 James Stewart 1.00
125 Terrence Wilkins 1.00
126 Keenan McCardell 1.00
127 Mark Brunell 3.00
128 Fred Taylor 3.00
129 Derrick Alexander 1.00
130 Tony Gonzalez 2.00
131 Warren Moon 1.00
132 Thurman Thomas 1.00
133 Tony Martin 1.00
134 Jay Fiedler 2.00
135 John Randle 1.00
136 Troy Brown 1.00
137 Amani Toomer 2.00
138 Kerry Collins 2.00
139 Tiki Barber 2.00
140 Wayne Chrebet 2.00
141 Tyrone Wheatley 1.00
142 Duce Staley 2.00
143 Jermaine Fazande 1.00
144 Charlie Garner 2.00
145 Torry Holt 2.00
146 Mike Alstott 2.00
147 Shaun King 2.50
148 Darrell Green 1.00
149 Brad Johnson 2.00
150 Olandis Gary 2.00
151 Jake Plummer 2.50
152 Chris Chandler 1.25
153 Jamal Anderson 2.50
154 Eric Moulds 2.50
155 Doug Flutie 3.00
156 Rob Johnson 1.25
157 Marcus Robinson 2.50
158 Cade McNown 2.50
159 Akili Smith 2.50
160 Tim Couch 4.00
161 Emmitt Smith 6.00
162 Troy Aikman 5.00
163 Brian Griese 3.00
164 John Elway 7.00
165 Terrell Davis 6.00
166 Dorsey Levens 2.50
167 Antonio Freeman 2.50
168 Brett Favre 10.00
169 Marvin Harrison 2.50
170 Peyton Manning 8.00
171 Edgerrin James 8.00
172 Jimmy Smith 2.50
173 Elvis Grbac 1.25
174 Dan Marino 7.00
175 Randy Moss 8.00
176 Cris Carter 2.50
177 Robert Smith 2.50
178 Daunte Culpepper 4.00
179 Terry Glenn 2.50
180 Drew Bledsoe 3.50
181 Ricky Williams 5.00
182 *Jake Delhomme* 4.00
183 Curtis Martin 2.50
184 Vinny Testaverde 1.25
185 Tim Brown 2.50
186 Rich Gannon 1.25
187 Donovan McNabb 3.50
188 Jerome Bettis 2.50
189 *Bobby Shaw* 5.00
190 Jerry Rice 5.00
191 Steve Young 3.50
192 Jeff Garcia 2.50
193 Ricky Watters 1.25
194 Isaac Bruce 2.50
195 Marshall Faulk 3.00
196 Kurt Warner 10.00
197 Keyshawn Johnson 2.50
198 Eddie George 3.00
199 Steve McNair 2.50
200 Stephen Davis 2.50
201 *Bobby Brooks* 3.50
202 *Cornelius Griffin* 3.50
203 *Danny Clark* 3.50
204 *Pat Dennis* 3.50
205 *Tommy Hendricks* 3.50
206 *Fred Jones* 3.50
207 *Isaiah Kacyvenski* 3.50
208 *Keith Miller* 3.50
209 *Andre O'Neal* 3.50
210 *Justin Snow* 3.50
211 *Armegis Spearman* 3.50
212 *Lester Towns* 3.50
213 *Antonio Wilson* 3.50
214 *Greg Wesley* 3.50
215 *Jabari Issa* 3.50
216 *Darwin Walker* 3.50
217 *Reggie Grimes* 3.50
218 *Rian Lindell* 3.50
219 *Chris Combs* 3.50
220 *Rashard Anderson* 5.00
221 *Erik Flowers* 5.00
222 *Corey Moore* 5.00
223 *Rob Meier* 3.50
224 *John Milem* 3.50
225 *Jeremiah Parker* 3.50
226 *Neil Rackers* 3.50
227 *Josh Taves* 5.00
228 *Mao Tosi* 3.50
229 *Gary Berry* 3.50
230 *Matt Bowen* 3.50
231 *Ralph Brown* 3.50
232 *Tony Darden* 3.50
233 *Arturo Freeman* 3.50
234 *David Gibson* 3.50
235 *Demario Brown* 5.00
236 *Deveron Harper* 3.50
237 *Johnnie Harris* 3.50
238 *Marcus Knight* 3.50
239 *Ronnie Heard* 3.50
240 *Eric Johnson* 3.50
241 *John Keith* 3.50
242 *Anthony Malbrough* 3.50
243 *Anthony Mitchell* 3.50
244 *Aric Morris* 3.50
245 *Bobby Myers* 3.50
246 *Erik Olson* 5.00
247 *Lewis Sanders* 3.50
248 *Tony Scott* 3.50
249 *David Terrell* 3.50
250 *Travares Tillman* 3.50
251 *Dave Stachelski* 5.00
252 *Darren Howard* 5.00
253 *Frank Chamberlin* 5.00
254 *Na'il Diggs* 8.00
255 *Orantes Grant* 6.00
256 *Barrett Green* 5.00
257 *Kory Minor* 5.00
258 *Deon Grant* 5.00
259 *Mark Simoneau* 8.00
260 *Raynoch Thompson* 5.00
261 *Kenyatta Wright* 5.00
262 *Marcus Bell* 5.00
263 *Jack Golden* 5.00
264 *Thomas Hamner* 5.00
265 *Sekou Sanyika* 5.00
266 *Marcus Washington* 5.00
267 *Tim Seder* 7.00
268 *Paul Edinger* 7.00
269 *Micheal Boireau* 5.00
270 *Byron Frisch* 5.00
271 *Ketric Sanford* 5.00
272 *Frank Murphy* 5.00
273 *Robaire Smith* 5.00
274 *Adalius Thomas* 5.00
275 *William Bartee* 5.00
276 *Robert Bean* 5.00
277 *Tyrone Carter* 5.00
278 *Ike Charlton* 5.00
279 *Mario Edwards* 5.00
280 *Dwayne Goodrich* 5.00
281 *Michael Hawthorne* 5.00
282 *Kareem Larrimore* 5.00
283 *Mark Roman* 5.00
284 *Jacoby Shepherd* 5.00
285 *Jason Webster* 5.00
286 *Jimmy Wyrick* 5.00
287 *Rashidi Barnes* 5.00
288 *David Barrett* 5.00
289 *Ainsley Battles* 5.00
290 *Lamar Chapman* 5.00
291 *Todd Franz* 5.00
292 *Michael Green* 5.00
293 *Antwan Harris* 5.00
294 *Brandon Jennings* 5.00
295 *Darrick Vaughn* 5.00
296 *David Macklin* 5.00
297 *Bobby Brown* 5.00
298 *Reggie Stephens* 5.00
299 *Kenoy Kennedy* 5.00
300 *Raion Hill* 5.00
301 *Windrell Hayes* 10.00
302 *DaShon Polk* 7.50
303 *Tywan Mitchell* 7.50
304 *Casey Crawford* 7.50
305 *Hank Poteat* 10.00
306 *Mondriel Fulcher* 7.50
307 *Cory Geason* 7.50
308 *James Hill* 7.50
309 *Brian Jennings* 7.50
310 *John Jones* 7.50
311 *Anthony Lucas* 7.50
312 *Mike Leach* 7.50
313 *Dustin Lyman* 7.50
314 *Derek Rackley* 7.50
315 *Sebastian Janikowski* 12.00
316 *Brad St. Louis* 7.50
317 *Jay Tant* 7.50
318 *Austin Wheatley* 7.50
319 *Jermaine Wiggins* 7.50
320 *Todd Yoder* 7.50
321 *Deon Dyer* 7.50
322 *Jim Finn* 7.50
323 *Herbert Goodman* 10.00
324 *Mike Green* 7.50
325 *Dante Hall* 10.00
326 *Thabiti Davis* 7.50
327 *Kevin Houser* 7.50
328 *Jonas Lewis* 7.50
329 *Chad Morton* 12.00
330 *Patrick Pass* 10.00
331 *Maurice Smith* 40.00
332 *Paul Smith* 7.50
333 *Terrelle Smith* 7.50
334 *Craig Walendy* 7.50
335 *Jamel White* 10.00
336 *Jarious Jackson* 12.00
337 *Matt Lytle* 7.50
338 *Ron Powlus* 15.00
339 *Ian Gold* 10.00
340 *Brandon Short* 7.50
341 *T.J. Slaughter* 10.00
342 *Nate Webster* 7.50
343 *John Engelberger* 7.50
344 *Rogers Beckett* 7.50
345 *Mike Brown* 7.50
346 *Anthony Wright* 25.00
347 *Danny Farmer* 12.00
348 *Clint Stoerner* 15.00
349 *Julian Peterson* 7.50
350 *Ahmed Plummer* 10.00
351 *Avion Black* 10.00
352 *Kwame Cavil* 10.00
353 *Chris Cole* 10.00
354 *Chris Coleman* 10.00
355 *Trevor Gaylor* 12.00
356 *Damon Hodge* 10.00
357 *Darrell Jackson* 45.00
358 *Reggie Jones* 15.00
359 *Charles Lee* 10.00
360 *Jerry Porter* 15.00
361 *Bobby Shaw* 15.00
362 *Ron Dugans* 15.00
363 *James Williams* 10.00
364 *Bashir Yamini* 10.00
365 *Anthony Becht* 12.00
366 *Erron Kinney* 10.00
367 *Aaron Shea* 12.00
368 *Chris Samuels* 12.00
369 *Trung Canidate* 15.00
370 *Obafemi Ayanbadejo* 12.00
371 *Doug Chapman* 30.00
372 *Ronney Jenkins* 12.00
373 *Curtis Keaton* 12.00
374 *Kevin McDougal* 10.00
375 *Frank Moreau* 15.00
376 *Aaron Stecker* 15.00
377 *Shyrone Stith* 12.00
378 *Tom Brady* 60.00
379 *Giovanni Carmazzi* 20.00
380 *Joe Hamilton* 15.00
381 *Todd Husak* 15.00
382 *Doug Johnson* 15.00
383 *Tee Martin* 20.00
384 *Chad Pennington* 100.00
385 *Tim Rattay* 30.00
386 *Chris Redman* 60.00
387 *Billy Volek* 15.00
388 *Spergon Wynn* 15.00
389 *John Abraham* 12.00
390 *Keith Bulluck* 10.00
391 *Rob Morris* 12.00
392 *JaJuan Dawson* 15.00
393 *Chris Hovan* 12.00
394 *Shaun Ellis* 10.00
395 *Deltha O'Neal* 10.00
396 *Gari Scott* 10.00
397 *Dialleo Burks* 10.00
398 *Shockmain Davis* 12.00
399 *Brad Hoover* 35.00
400 *Brian Finneran* 10.00
401 *Sylvester Morris 750* 35.00
402 *Dennis Northcutt 500* 25.00
403 *Todd Pinkston 1000* 25.00
404 *Larry Foster 500* 20.00
405 *R. Jay Soward 1000* 25.00
406 *Travis Taylor 250* 60.00
407 *Peter Warrick 1000* 70.00
408 *Dez White 1000* 20.00
409 *Ron Dayne 1000* 70.00
410 *Thomas Jones 500* 40.00
411 *Jamal Lewis 1000* 100.00
412 *Sammy Morris 500* 30.00
413 *Travis Prentice 500* 35.00
414 *J.R. Redmond 250* 75.00
415 *Michael Wiley 1000* 20.00
416 *Laveranues Coles 250* 60.00
417 *Bubba Franks 500* 35.00
418 *Mike Anderson 250* 200.00
419 *Plaxico Burress 250* 100.00
420 *Ron Dixon 1000* 20.00
421 *Troy Walters 1000* 20.00
422 *Shaun Alexander 1000* 50.00
423 *Brian Urlacher 1000* 60.00
424 *Corey Simon 1000* 20.00
425 *Courtney Brown 500* 40.00

2000 Leaf Limited Limited Series Parallel

MT
LS 1-50 Cards: 15x-30x
LS 51-100 Cards: 12x-24x
LS 101-150 Cards: 10x-20x
LS 151-200 Cards: 8x-16x
LS 151-200 Rookies: 4x
Production 35 Sets
LS 201-250 Rookies: 6x
LS 251-300 Rookies: 5x
LS 301-350 Rookies: 3x
LS 351-400 Rookies: 2x
Production 50 Sets
LS 401-425 Rookies: 2.5x
Production 25 Sets

2000 Leaf Limited Piece of the Game Previews

MT
Complete Set (25): 550.00
Common Player: 20.00
3rd Down Cards: 1.5x
Production 300 Sets
2nd Down Cards: 2x
Production 100 Sets
1st Down Cards: 4x
Production 25 Sets
JB36-B Jerome Bettis 20.00
IB80-W Isaac Bruce 20.00
MB8-W Mark Brunell 30.00
TC2-B Tim Couch 30.00
DC11-P Daunte Culpepper 30.00
SD48-W Stephen Davis 20.00
JE7-W John Elway 45.00
BF4-G Brett Favre 50.00
DF7-W Doug Flutie 25.00
BG14-N Brian Griese 25.00
EJ32-R Edgerrin James 45.00
JK12-W Jim Kelly 25.00
DM13-W Dan Marino 45.00
EM87-N Ed McCaffrey 20.00
DM5-W Donovan McNabb 25.00
RM84-P Randy Moss 40.00
JP16-W Jake Plummer 20.00
JR80-R Jerry Rice 40.00
45.00
JS82-B Jimmy Smith 20.00
RS26-P Robert Smith 20.00
DS22-G Duce Staley 20.00
FT28-W Fred Taylor 25.00
KW13-W Kurt Warner 50.00
SY8-R Steve Young 30.00

2000 Leaf Rookies & Stars

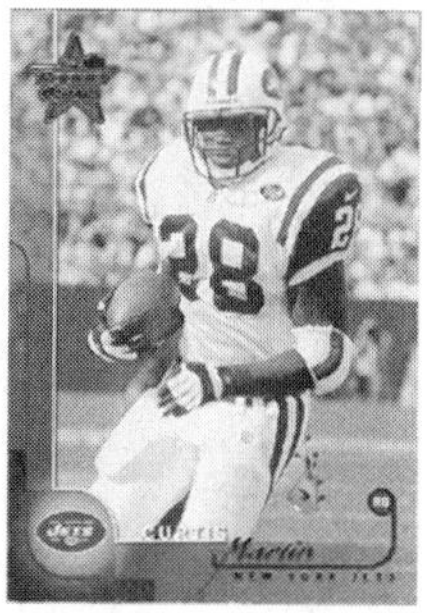

MT
Complete Set (300): 1250.
Common Player: .15
Minor Stars: .30
Common Rookie: 5.00
Production 1,000 Sets
Rookie Autographs: 2x
Production 200 Sets
Common Europe Prospect: 1.50
Production 3,000 Sets
Europe Autographs: 3x
Production 200 Sets
Pack (5): 3.50
Wax Box (24): 70.00
1 Jake Plummer .50
2 David Boston .50
3 Tim Dwight .50
4 Jamal Anderson .50
5 Chris Chandler .30
6 Tony Banks .30
7 Qadry Ismail .15
8 Eric Moulds .50
9 Doug Flutie .75
10 Lamar Smith .30
11 Peerless Price .30
12 Rob Johnson .30
13 Reggie White .30
14 Muhsin Muhammad .30
15 Steve Beuerlein .30
16 Cade McNown .50
17 Derrick Alexander .15
18 Marcus Robinson .50
19 Corey Dillon .50
20 Akili Smith .50
21 Tim Couch 1.00
22 Kevin Johnson .30
23 Emmitt Smith 1.50
24 Troy Aikman 1.25
25 Joey Galloway .50
26 Raghib Ismail .15
27 John Elway 1.75
28 Terrell Davis 1.50
29 Brian Griese .75
30 Olandis Gary .50
31 Ed McCaffrey .30
32 Rod Smith .30
33 Barry Sanders 1.75
34 Charlie Batch .50
35 Germane Crowell .50
36 James Stewart .30
37 Brett Favre 2.00
38 Dorsey Levens .50
39 Antonio Freeman .50
40 Peyton Manning 1.75
41 Edgerrin James 2.00
42 Marvin Harrison .50
43 Fred Taylor .75
44 Mark Brunell .75
45 Jimmy Smith .50
46 Elvis Grbac .30
47 Tony Gonzalez .30
48 Dan Marino 1.75
49 Joe Horn .30
50 Jay Fiedler .30
51 James Allen .30
52 Randy Moss 1.75
53 Daunte Culpepper 1.00
54 Cris Carter .50
55 Robert Smith .50
56 Drew Bledsoe .75
57 Terry Glenn .50
58 Ricky Williams 1.25
59 Amani Toomer .30
60 Kerry Collins .30
61 Curtis Martin .50
62 Vinny Testaverde .30
63 Wayne Chrebet .30
64 Tim Brown .50
65 Tyrone Wheatley .30
66 Rich Gannon .30
67 Donovan McNabb .75
68 Duce Staley .50
69 Jerome Bettis .50
70 Donald Hayes .30
71 Junior Seau .30
72 Jermaine Fazande .30
73 Jerry Rice 1.25
74 Steve Young .75
75 Terrell Owens .50
76 Charlie Garner .30
77 Jeff Garcia .50
78 Tim Biakabutuka .30
79 Tiki Barber .50
80 Ricky Watters .30
81 Kurt Warner 2.50
82 Marshall Faulk .50
83 Isaac Bruce .50
84 Torry Holt .50
85 Mike Alstott .50
86 Warrick Dunn .50
87 Shaun King .75
88 Keyshawn Johnson .50
89 Warren Sapp .30
90 Eddie George .75
91 Jevon Kearse .50
92 Steve McNair .50
93 Carl Pickens .30
94 Deion Sanders .50
95 Stephen Davis .50
96 Brad Johnson .30
97 Bruce Smith .30
98 Michael Westbrook .30
99 Albert Connell .30
100 Jeff George .30

101	*Thomas Jones*	20.00
102	*Bashir Yamini*	5.00
103	*Jamal Lewis*	70.00
104	*Travis Taylor*	10.00
105	*Chris Redman*	20.00
106	*Avion Black*	5.00
107	*Sammy Morris*	10.00
108	*Dez White*	6.00
109	*Peter Warrick*	50.00
110	*Ron Dugans*	6.00
111	*Curtis Keaton*	6.00
112	*Danny Farmer*	7.00
113	*Courtney Brown*	8.00
114	*Dennis Northcutt*	8.00
115	*Travis Prentice*	15.00
116	*JaJuan Dawson*	8.00
117	*Spergon Wynn*	7.00
118	*Michael Wiley*	7.00
119	*Chris Cole*	5.00
120	*Mike Anderson*	60.00
121	*Muneer Moore*	5.00
122	*Reuben Droughns*	5.00
123	*Bubba Franks*	8.00
124	*Anthony Lucas*	5.00
125	*Charles Lee*	6.00
126	*R. Jay Soward*	8.00
127	*Shyrone Stith*	6.00
128	*Sylvester Morris*	25.00
129	*Frank Moreau*	8.00
130	*Dante Hall*	5.00
131	*Doug Chapman*	5.00
132	*Troy Walters*	6.00
133	*J.R. Redmond*	10.00
134	*Tom Brady*	25.00
135	*Terrelle Smith*	5.00
136	*Chad Morton*	7.00
137	*Ron Dayne*	50.00
138	*Ron Dixon*	6.00
139	*Chad Pennington*	45.00
140	*Anthony Becht*	6.00
141	*Laveranues Coles*	8.00
142	*Windrell Hayes*	5.00
143	*Sebastian Janikowski*	7.00
144	*Jerry Porter*	8.00
145	*Corey Simon*	8.00
146	*Todd Pinkston*	8.00
147	*Gari Scott*	8.00
148	*Plaxico Burress*	25.00
149	*Tee Martin*	8.00
150	*Trevor Gaylor*	7.00
151	*Ronney Jenkins*	5.00
152	*Giovanni Carmazzi*	8.00
153	*Tim Rattay*	8.00
154	*Shaun Alexander*	35.00
155	*Darrell Jackson*	8.00
156	*James Williams*	5.00
157	*Trung Canidate*	7.00
158	*Joe Hamilton*	8.00
159	*Erron Kinney*	5.00
160	*Todd Husak*	7.00
161	*Raynoch Thompson*	5.00
162	*Darwin Walker*	5.00
163	*Jay Tant*	5.00
164	*Doug Johnson*	7.00
165	*Robert Bean*	5.00
166	*Mark Simoneau*	5.00
167	*John Jones*	5.00
168	*Obafemi Ayanbadejo*	5.00
169	*Mike Brown*	5.00
170	*Shockmain Davis*	5.00
171	*Erik Flowers*	5.00
172	*Corey Moore*	5.00
173	*Drew Haddad*	5.00
174	*Kwame Cavil*	5.00
175	*Pat Dennis*	5.00
176	*Rashard Anderson*	6.00
177	*Brian Finneran*	5.00
178	*Na'il Diggs*	5.00
179	*Marc Bulger*	5.00
180	*Mark Fulcher*	5.00
181	*Dwayne Carswell*	5.00
182	*Brian Urlacher*	35.00
183	*Paul Edinger*	6.00
184	*KaRon Coleman*	5.00
185	*Aaron Shea*	5.00
186	*Fabien Bownes*	6.00
187	*Damon Hodge*	5.00
188	*Dwayne Goodrich*	5.00
189	*Clint Stoerner*	20.00
190	*James Whalen*	5.00
191	*Deltha O'Neal*	5.00
192	*Ian Gold*	6.00
193	*Kenoy Kennedy*	5.00
194	*Jarious Jackson*	7.00
195	*Leroy Fields*	5.00
196	*Barrett Green*	5.00
197	*Joey Jamison*	5.00
198	*Rondell Mealey*	7.00
199	*Rob Morris*	5.00
200	*Marcus Washington*	5.00
201	*Trevor Insley*	5.00
202	*Jamel White*	5.00
203	*Kevin McDougal*	5.00
204	*Ibn Green*	5.00
205	*T.J. Slaughter*	5.00
206	*Emanuel Smith*	5.00
207	*Herbert Goodman*	5.00
208	*William Bartee*	5.00
209	*Rashidi Barnes*	5.00
210	*Brad Hoover*	25.00
211	*Deon Dyer*	5.00
212	*Jonas Lewis*	5.00
213	*Chris Hovan*	5.00
214	*Fred Robbins*	5.00
215	*Micheal Boireau*	5.00
216	*Giles Cole*	5.00
217	*Dave Stachelski*	5.00
218	*Patrick Pass*	6.00
219	*Darren Howard*	5.00
220	*Austin Wheatley*	5.00
221	*Kevin Houser*	5.00
222	*Rian Lindell*	5.00
223	*Jake Delhomme*	8.00
224	*Cornelius Griffin*	5.00
225	*Shaun Ellis*	5.00
226	*John Abraham*	5.00
227	*Travares Tillman*	5.00
228	*Julian Peterson*	5.00
229	*Marcus Knight*	5.00
230	*Thomas Hamner*	5.00
231	*Hank Poteat*	5.00
232	*Neil Rackers*	5.00
233	*Bobby Shaw*	5.00
234	*Rogers Beckett*	5.00
235	*Reggie Jones*	8.00
236	*Tim Seder*	6.00
237	*Durell Price*	5.00
238	*Ahmed Plummer*	6.00
239	*John Engelberger*	5.00
240	*Paul Smith*	5.00
241	*Chafie Fields*	5.00
242	*Kevin Feterik*	5.00
243	*Jacoby Shepherd*	5.00
244	*Nate Webster*	5.00
245	*Ketric Sanford*	5.00
246	*Tavarus Hogans*	5.00
247	*Keith Bulluck*	5.00
248	*Mike Green*	5.00
249	*Chris Coleman*	5.00
250	*Demario Brown*	5.00
251	*Billy Volek*	5.00
252	*Mareno Philyaw*	5.00
253	*Ethan Howell*	5.00
254	*Chris Samuels*	7.00
255	*Brandon Short*	5.00
256	*Maurice Smith*	20.00
257	*Frank Murphy*	5.00
258	*Darrick Vaughn*	5.00
259	*Payton Williams*	5.00
260	*Jafuan Seider*	5.00
261	Antonio Banks	1.50
262	Jonathan Brown	1.50
263	Ontiwaun Carter	1.50
264	Jeremaine Copeland	1.50
265	Ralph Dawkins	1.50
266	Marques Douglas	1.50
267	Kevin Drake	1.50
268	Damon Dunn	1.50
269	Todd Floyd	1.50
270	Tony Graziani	2.00
271	Derrick Ham	1.50
272	Duane Hawthorne	1.50
273	Alonzo Johnson	1.50
274	Mark Kacmarynski	1.50
275	Eric Kresser	1.50
276	Jim Kubiak	1.50
277	Blaine McElmurry	1.50
278	Scott Milanovich	2.00
279	Norman Miller	1.50
280	Sean Morey	1.50
281	Jeff Ogden	2.50
282	Pepe Pearson	2.00
283	Ron Powlus	6.00
284	Jason Shelley	1.50
285	Ben Snell	1.50
286	Aaron Stecker	2.50
287	L.C. Stevens	1.50
288	Mike Sutton	1.50
289	Damian Vaughn	1.50
290	Ted White	1.50
291	Marcus Crandell	1.50
292	Darryl Daniel	1.50
293	Jesse Haynes	1.50
294	Matt Lytle	1.50
295	Deon Mitchell	1.50
296	Kendrick Nord	1.50
297	Ronnie Powell	1.50
298	Selucio Sanford	1.50
299	Corey Thomas	1.50
300	Vershan Jackson	1.50

2000 Leaf Rookies & Stars 2001 Draft Class

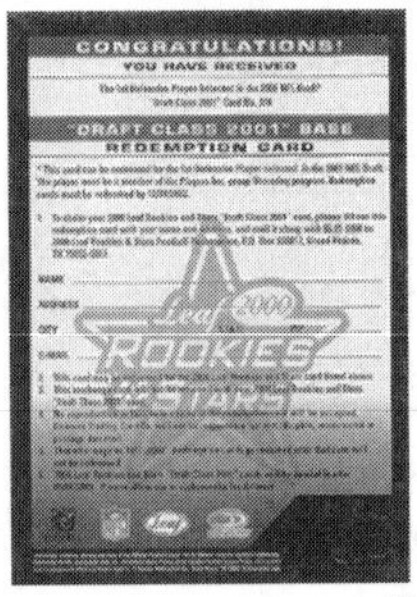

		MT
Common Draft:		10.00
Inserted 1:2 Boxes		
Redemptions expire 12/31/02		
301	First QB	150.00
302	Second QB	75.00
303	Third QB	25.00
304	Fourth QB	25.00
305	Fifth QB	25.00
306	First RB	75.00
307	Second RB	50.00
308	Third RB	30.00
309	Fourth RB	25.00
310	Fifth RB	25.00
311	First WR	45.00
312	Second WR	30.00
313	Third WR	25.00
314	Fourth WR	20.00
315	Fifth WR	20.00
316	First Def	25.00
317	Second Def	15.00
318	Third Def	10.00
319	Fourth Def	10.00
320	Fifth Def	10.00

2000 Leaf Rookies & Stars Longevity Parallel

	MT
Longevity Cards:	15x-30x
Production 50 Sets	
Longevity Rookies:	2x
Production 30 Sets	
Longevity Europe:	3x-6x
Production 30 Sets	

2000 Leaf Rookies & Stars Dress for Success

		MT
"Prices for most common Version"		
Complete Set (10):		
Common Player:		
1	Jerry Rice	50.00
2	Eddie George	25.00
3	Troy Aikman	50.00
4	Mark Brunell	25.00
5	Barry Sanders	50.00
6	Marshall Faulk	25.00
7	Dan Marino	75.00
8	Stephen Davis	25.00
9	Terrell Davis	25.00
10	Brett Favre	100.00

2000 Leaf Rookies & Stars Freshman Orientation

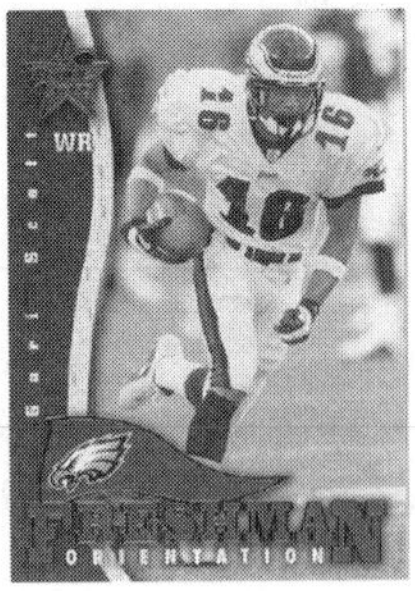

		MT
Complete Set (30):		100.00
Common Player:		1.50
Minor Stars:		3.00
Production 2,000 Sets		
FO1	Peter Warrick	10.00
FO2	Jamal Lewis	15.00
FO3	Thomas Jones	5.00
FO4	Plaxico Burress	6.00
FO5	Travis Taylor	4.00
FO6	Ron Dayne	12.00
FO7	Bubba Franks	3.00
FO8	Chad Pennington	8.00
FO9	Shaun Alexander	7.00
FO10	Sylvester Morris	6.00
FO11	R. Jay Soward	3.00
FO12	Trung Canidate	3.00
FO13	Dennis Northcutt	3.00
FO14	Todd Pinkston	3.00
FO15	Jerry Porter	3.00
FO16	Travis Prentice	4.00
FO17	Giovanni Carmazzi	3.50
FO18	Ron Dugans	3.00
FO19	Dez White	3.00
FO20	Mike Anderson	12.00
FO21	Ron Dixon	3.00
FO22	Chris Redman	5.00
FO23	J.R. Redmond	3.50
FO24	Laveranues Coles	3.50
FO25	JaJuan Dawson	3.00
FO26	Darrell Jackson	3.00
FO27	Sammy Morris	3.00
FO28	Doug Chapman	1.50
FO29	Tim Rattay	4.00
FO30	Gari Scott	1.50

2000 Leaf Rookies & Stars Game Plan

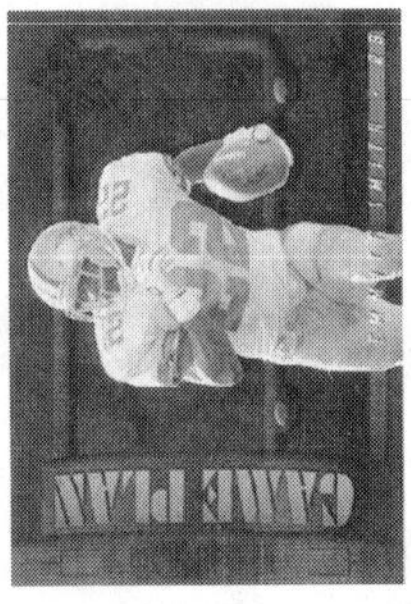

		MT
Complete Set (30):		75.00
Common Player:		1.50
Production 2,000 Sets		
Master Cards:		3x-6x
Production 50 Sets		
GP1	Jerome Bettis	1.50
GP2	Charlie Garner	1.50
GP3	Jamal Lewis	15.00
GP4	Eric Moulds	1.50
GP5	Cade McNown	2.50
GP6	Peter Warrick	10.00
GP7	Tim Couch	3.50
GP8	Emmitt Smith	7.00
GP9	Troy Aikman	5.00
GP10	Terrell Davis	7.00
GP11	Brett Favre	10.00
GP12	Peyton Manning	10.00
GP13	Edgerrin James	10.00
GP14	Fred Taylor	3.00
GP15	Randy Moss	10.00
GP16	Daunte Culpepper	4.00
GP17	Drew Bledsoe	3.00
GP18	Ricky Williams	4.00
GP19	Ron Dayne	12.00
GP20	Curtis Martin	1.50
GP21	Donovan McNabb	2.50
GP22	Plaxico Burress	6.00
GP23	Jerry Rice	5.00
GP24	Shaun Alexander	7.00
GP25	Kurt Warner	12.00
GP26	Marshall Faulk	2.50
GP27	Keyshawn Johnson	1.50
GP28	Eddie George	2.50
GP29	Steve McNair	1.50
GP30	Stephen Davis	1.50

A player's name in *italic type* indicates a rookie card.

2000 Leaf Rookies & Stars Great American Heroes

		MT
Complete Set (10):		45.00
Common Player:		4.00
Production 1,000 Sets		
Signatures:		20x
Production 100 Sets		
Treasures:		20x
Production 100 Sets		
Treasures Autographs:		30x
Production 25 Sets		
GAH1	John Elway	7.00
GAH2	Terrell Davis	6.00
GAH3	Barry Sanders	7.00
GAH4	Edgerrin James	8.00
GAH5	Dan Marino	7.00
GAH6	Randy Moss	8.00
GAH7	Ricky Williams	5.00
GAH8	Jerry Rice	6.00
GAH9	Steve Young	4.00
GAH10	Kurt Warner	8.00

2000 Leaf Rookies & Stars Joe Montana Collection

		MT
Randomly Inserted		
Autographed:		2x
Production 25 Sets		
MC1	(Joe Montana SF Jer/300)	150.00
MC2	(Joe Montana KC Jer/300)	150.00
MC3	(Joe Montana KC Helmet/125)	225.00
MC4	(Joe Montana Shoes/125)	225.00
MC5	(Joe Montana FB/125)	225.00

2000 Leaf Rookies & Stars Prime Cuts

		MT
Common Player:		50.00
Production 25 Sets		
PC1	Eric Moulds	50.00
PC2	Cade McNown	60.00
PC3	Tim Couch	80.00
PC4	Emmitt Smith	150.00
PC5	John Elway	175.00
PC6	Terrell Davis	125.00
PC8	Barry Sanders	175.00
PC9	Brett Favre	200.00
PC10	Antonio Freeman	50.00
PC11	Peyton Manning	150.00
PC12	Edgerrin James	150.00
PC13	Marvin Harrison	50.00
PC14	Fred Taylor	60.00
PC15	Mark Brunell	60.00
PC16	Jimmy Smith	50.00
PC17	Dan Marino	175.00
PC18	Randy Moss	150.00
PC19	Cris Carter	50.00
PC20	Ricky Williams	100.00
PC21	Curtis Martin	50.00
PC22	Donovan McNabb	75.00
PC23	Jerry Rice	125.00
PC24	Steve Young	75.00
PC25	Kurt Warner	175.00
PC26	Marshall Faulk	60.00
PC27	Isaac Bruce	60.00
PC28	Shaun King	50.00
PC29	Eddie George	60.00
PC30	Steve McNair	50.00

2000 Leaf Rookies & Stars Slideshow

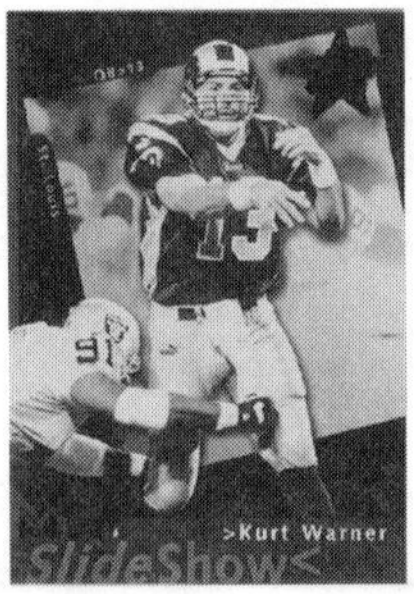

		MT
Complete Set (60):		150.00
Common Player:		2.00
Production 1,000 Sets		
Studio Cards:		6x-12x
Production 25 Sets		
S1	Jake Plummer	3.00
S2	Thomas Jones	6.00
S3	Jamal Anderson	3.00
S4	Jamal Lewis	15.00
S5	Travis Taylor	4.00
S6	Eric Moulds	3.00
S7	Cade McNown	3.00
S8	Marcus Robinson	3.00
S9	Corey Dillon	3.00
S10	Akili Smith	3.00
S11	Peter Warrick	10.00
S12	Tim Couch	4.50
S13	Travis Prentice	4.50
S14	Emmitt Smith	8.00
S15	Troy Aikman	6.00
S16	Mike Anderson	12.50
S17	John Elway	8.00
S18	Terrell Davis	7.00
S19	Brian Griese	4.00
S20	Terrell Owens	3.00
S21	Barry Sanders	8.00
S22	Charlie Batch	3.00
S23	Brett Favre	10.00
S24	Dorsey Levens	2.00
S25	Antonio Freeman	3.00
S26	Peyton Manning	8.00
S27	Edgerrin James	8.00
S28	Marvin Harrison	3.00
S29	Fred Taylor	4.50
S30	Mark Brunell	4.50
S31	Jimmy Smith	2.00
S32	Sylvester Morris	6.00
S33	Dan Marino	10.00
S34	Randy Moss	8.00
S35	Daunte Culpepper	4.50
S36	Cris Carter	3.00
S37	Robert Smith	3.00
S38	Drew Bledsoe	4.50
S39	Ricky Williams	4.50
S40	Ron Dayne	12.00
S41	Curtis Martin	3.00
S42	Chad Pennington	8.00
S43	Tim Brown	3.00
S44	Donovan McNabb	4.00
S45	Torry Holt	3.00
S46	Plaxico Burress	6.00
S47	Jerry Rice	6.00
S48	Steve Young	4.50
S49	Shaun Alexander	7.00
S50	Kurt Warner	10.00
S51	Marshall Faulk	3.00
S52	Isaac Bruce	3.00
S53	Shaun King	3.50
S54	Keyshawn Johnson	3.00
S55	Mike Alstott	3.00
S56	Eddie George	3.50
S57	Steve McNair	3.00
S58	Jevon Kearse	3.00
S59	Stephen Davis	3.00
S60	Brad Johnson	3.00

2000 Leaf Rookies & Stars Statistical Standouts

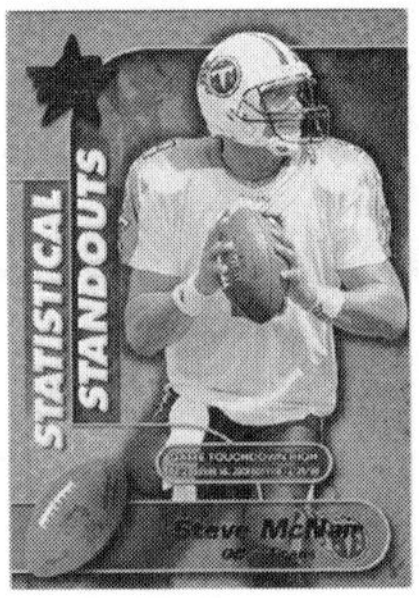

		MT
Complete Set (40):		200.00
Common Player:		3.00
Production 500 Sets		
SS1	Thomas Jones	6.00
SS2	Jamal Lewis	20.00
SS3	Travis Taylor	4.00
SS4	Cade McNown	3.00
SS5	Corey Dillon	3.00
SS6	Akili Smith	3.00
SS7	Peter Warrick	15.00
SS8	Tim Couch	6.00
SS9	Emmitt Smith	10.00
SS10	Troy Aikman	8.00
SS11	John Elway	10.00
SS12	Terrell Davis	10.00
SS13	Barry Sanders	12.00
SS14	Brett Favre	15.00
SS15	Dorsey Levens	3.00
SS16	Antonio Freeman	3.00
SS17	Peyton Manning	12.00
SS18	Edgerrin James	12.00
SS19	Marvin Harrison	3.00
SS20	Fred Taylor	5.00
SS21	Dan Marino	10.00
SS22	Randy Moss	12.00
SS23	Daunte Culpepper	7.00
SS24	Cris Carter	3.00
SS25	Drew Bledsoe	6.00
SS26	Ricky Williams	6.00
SS27	Ron Dayne	17.00
SS28	Curtis Martin	3.00
SS29	Chad Pennington	12.00
SS30	Plaxico Burress	7.00
SS31	Jerry Rice	8.00
SS32	Steve Young	6.00
SS33	Shaun Alexander	10.00
SS34	Kurt Warner	15.00
SS35	Marshall Faulk	3.00
SS36	Isaac Bruce	3.00
SS37	Eddie George	4.00
SS38	Steve McNair	3.00
SS39	Stephen Davis	3.00
SS40	Brad Johnson	3.00

Values quoted in this guide reflect the retail price of a card — the price a collector can expect to pay when buying a card from a dealer. The wholesale price — that which a collector can expect to receive from a dealer when selling cards — will be significantly lower, depending on desirability and condition.

2000 Leaf Rookies & Stars Ticket Masters

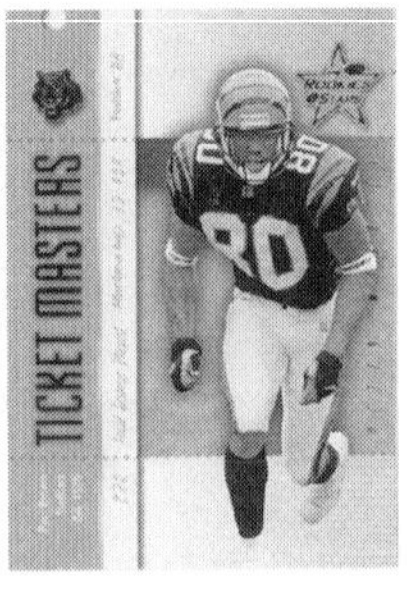

		MT
Complete Set (30):		70.00
Common Player:		1.00
Minor Stars:		2.00
Production 2,000 Sets		
TM1	Thomas Jones, Jake Plummer	3.00
TM2	Jamal Anderson, Chris Chandler	2.00
TM3	Travis Taylor, Jamal Lewis	10.00
TM4	Eric Moulds, Rob Johnson	2.00
TM5	Muhsin Muhammad, Steve Beuerlein	1.00
TM6	Cade McNown, Marcus Robinson	2.00
TM7	Peter Warrick, Akili Smith	7.00
TM8	Tim Couch, Kevin Johnson	2.50
TM9	Emmitt Smith, Troy Aikman	4.00
TM10	Terrell Davis, Brian Griese	5.00
TM11	Charlie Batch, James Stewart	2.00
TM12	Brett Favre, Antonio Freeman	8.00
TM13	Peyton Manning, Edgerrin James	7.00
TM14	Mark Brunell, Fred Taylor	3.00
TM15	Jay Fiedler, Lamar Smith	2.00
TM16	Randy Moss, Daunte Culpepper	7.00
TM17	Drew Bledsoe, Terry Glenn	3.00
TM18	Ricky Williams, Jeff Blake	3.00
TM19	Kerry Collins, Ron Dayne	8.00
TM20	Chad Pennington, Curtis Martin	6.00
TM21	Tim Brown, Rich Gannon	2.00
TM22	Donovan McNabb, Duce Staley	2.50
TM23	Plaxico Burress, Jerome Bettis	3.50
TM24	Ryan Leaf, Jermaine Fazande	1.00
TM25	Jerry Rice, Terrell Owens	4.00
TM26	Shaun Alexander, Ricky Watters	5.00
TM27	Kurt Warner, Marshall Faulk	7.00
TM28	Shaun King, Keyshawn Johnson	2.50
TM29	Eddie George, Steve McNair	2.50
TM30	Stephen Davis, Brad Johnson	2.00

2000 Quantum Leaf

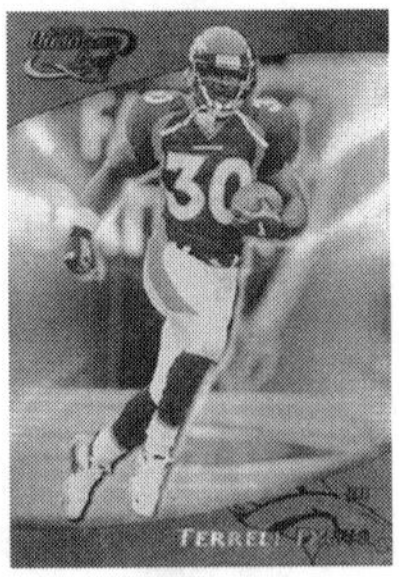

		MT
Complete Set (350):		200.00
Common Player:		.20
Minor Stars:		.40
Common Rookie:		1.50
Inserted 1:2		
Pack (4):		3.50
Wax Box (24):		80.00
1	Frank Sanders	.40
2	Adrian Murrell	.40
3	Rob Moore	.40
4	Simeon Rice	.20
5	Michael Pittman	.20
6	Jake Plummer	1.00
7	David Boston	.75
8	Mario Bates	.20
9	Chris Chandler	.40
10	Tim Dwight	.75
11	Chris Calloway	.20
12	Terance Mathis	.20
13	Jamal Anderson	.75

(base set, continued)

14 Byron Hanspard .40
15 Ken Oxendine .20
16 Tony Graziani .20
17 Bob Christian .20
18 Priest Holmes .40
19 Tony Banks .40
20 Patrick Johnson .40
21 Rod Woodson .20
22 Jermaine Lewis .40
23 Errict Rhett .40
24 Stoney Case .20
25 Peter Boulware .20
26 Qadry Ismail .20
27 Brandon Stokley .40
28 Andre Reed .40
29 Eric Moulds .75
30 Doug Flutie 1.25
31 Bruce Smith .20
32 Jay Riemersma .20
33 Antowain Smith .75
34 Thurman Thomas .40
35 Jonathon Linton .40
36 Peerless Price .75
37 Rob Johnson .40
38 Sam Gash .20
39 Muhsin Muhammad .40
40 Wesley Walls .40
41 Fred Lane .20
42 Kevin Greene .20
43 Tim Biakabutuka .40
44 Steve Beuerlein .40
45 Donald Hayes .20
46 Patrick Jeffers 1.00
47 Curtis Enis .75
48 Bobby Engram .20
49 Curtis Conway .40
50 Marcus Robinson 1.00
51 Marty Booker .20
52 Cade McNown 1.50
53 Shane Matthews .40
54 Jim Miller .40
55 Darnay Scott .40
56 Carl Pickens .40
57 Corey Dillon .75
58 Jeff Blake .40
59 Akili Smith 1.25
60 Michael Basnight .20
61 Karim Abdul .20
62 Tim Couch 3.00
63 Kevin Johnson 1.00
64 Terry Kirby .20
65 Ty Detmer .20
66 Leslie Shepherd .20
67 Darrin Chiaverini .20
68 Emmitt Smith 2.50
69 Deion Sanders .75
70 Michael Irvin .20
71 Raghib Ismail .20
72 Troy Aikman 2.00
73 Daryl Johnston .20
74 Chris Warren .40
75 Jason Garrett .20
76 Jason Tucker 1.00
77 Lawyer Milloy .20
78 Dexter Coakley .20
79 Greg Ellis .20
80 David LaFleur .20
81 Todd Lyght .20
82 Ernie Mills .20
83 Wane McGarity .20
84 Chris Brazzell .20
85 Ed McCaffrey .40
86 Rod Smith .40
87 Shannon Sharpe .40
88 Brian Griese 1.00
89 John Elway 3.00
90 Neil Smith .20
91 Terrell Davis 3.00
92 Olandis Gary 1.50
93 Derek Loville .20
94 John Avery .20
95 Bubby Brister .40
96 Byron Chamberlain .20
97 Dale Carter .20
98 Johnnie Morton .20
99 Charlie Batch 1.00
100 Barry Sanders 3.00
101 Germane Crowell .40
102 Gus Frerotte .20
103 Desmond Howard .20
104 Terry Fair .20
105 Ron Rivers .20
106 Greg Hill .20
107 Sedrick Irvin .40
108 David Sloan .20
109 Herman Moore .75
110 Robert Porcher .20
111 Corey Bradford .20
112 Dorsey Levens 1.00
113 Antonio Freeman 1.00
114 Brett Favre 4.00
115 De'Mond Parker .40
116 Bill Schroeder .40
117 Matt Hasselbeck .40
118 Donald Driver .40
119 Basil Mitchell .20
120 E.G. Green .20
121 Ken Dilger .20
122 Marvin Harrison 1.00
123 Peyton Manning 3.00
124 Terrence Wilkins 1.00
125 Edgerrin James 4.00
126 Jerome Pathon .20
127 Marcus Pollard .20
128 Keenan McCardell .40
129 Mark Brunell 1.50
130 Fred Taylor 1.50
131 Jimmy Smith .75
132 James Stewart .75
133 Kyle Brady .20
134 Tony Brackens .20
135 Derrick Thomas .40
136 Rashaan Shehee .20
137 Derrick Alexander .20
138 Bam Morris .20
139 Andre Rison .40
140 Elvis Grbac .20
141 Tony Gonzalez .40
142 Donnell Bennett .20
143 Warren Moon .75
144 Tamarick Vanover .20
145 Kimble Anders .20
146 Tony Richardson .20
147 Zach Thomas .40
148 Oronde Gadsden .40
149 Dan Marino 3.00
150 O.J. McDuffie .40
151 Tony Martin .20
152 Cecil Collins .40
153 James Johnson .20
154 Rob Konrad .20
155 Yatil Green .20
156 Damon Huard .75
157 Nate Jacquet .20
158 Stanley Pritchett .20
159 Sam Madison .20
160 Randy Moss 3.00
161 Cris Carter 1.00
162 Robert Smith 1.00
163 Randall Cunningham .75
164 Jake Reed .40
165 John Randle .40
166 Leroy Hoard .20
167 Jeff George .75
168 Daunte Culpepper 1.50
169 Matthew Hatchette .20
170 Robert Tate .20
171 Ty Law .20
172 Troy Brown .20
173 Tony Simmons .40
174 Terry Glenn .75
175 Ben Coates .40
176 Drew Bledsoe 1.50
177 Terry Allen .40
178 Kevin Faulk .40
179 Shawn Jefferson .20
180 Andy Katzenmoyer .20
181 Willie McGinest .20
182 Cameron Cleeland .40
183 Eddie Kennison .40
184 Ricky Williams 3.00
185 Danny Wuerffel .20
186 Brett Bech .20
187 Billy Joe Hobert .20
188 Jake Delhomme 4.00
189 Wilmont Perry .20
190 Keith Poole .20
191 Ashley Ambrose .20
192 Amani Toomer .40
193 Kerry Collins .40
194 Tiki Barber .40
195 Ike Hilliard .40
196 Jason Sehorn .20
197 Joe Montgomery .20
198 Joe Jurevicius .20
199 Michael Strahan .20
200 Sean Bennett .20
201 Jessie Armstead .20
202 Pete Mitchell .20
203 Curtis Martin .75
204 Vinny Testaverde .40
205 Keyshawn Johnson 1.00
206 Wayne Chrebet .75
207 Ray Lucas 1.00
208 Tyrone Wheatley .40
209 Napoleon Kaufman .75
210 Tim Brown .75
211 Rickey Dudley .20
212 James Jett .20
213 Rich Gannon .40
214 Charles Woodson 1.00
215 Zack Crockett .20
216 Darrell Russell .20
217 Duce Staley 1.00
218 Donovan McNabb 1.50
219 Charles Johnson .20
220 Dameane Douglas .20
221 Doug Pederson .20
222 Torrance Small .20
223 Troy Vincent .20
224 Na Brown .20
225 Kordell Stewart 1.00
226 Jerome Bettis 1.00
227 Hines Ward .40
228 Troy Edwards 1.00
229 Richard Huntley .40
230 Mark Bruener .20
231 Pete Gonzalez .40
232 Levon Kirkland .20
233 Bobby Shaw 1.00
234 Amos Zereoue .40
235 Natrone Means .40
236 Junior Seau .40
237 Jim Harbaugh .40
238 Ryan Leaf 1.00
239 Mikhael Ricks .20
240 Jermaine Fazande .20
241 Jeff Graham .20
242 Tremayne Stephens .20
243 Terrell Owens 1.00
244 J.J. Stokes .40
245 Charlie Garner .40
246 Jerry Rice 2.00
247 Garrison Hearst .40
248 Steve Young 1.50
249 Jeff Garcia 1.00
250 Fred Beasley .20
251 Bryant Young .20
252 Derrick Mayes .40
253 Ahman Green .40
254 Joey Galloway 1.00
255 Ricky Watters 1.00
256 Jon Kitna 1.00
257 Sean Dawkins .20
258 Sam Adams .20
259 Christian Fauria .20
260 Shawn Springs .20
261 Az-Zahir Hakim .40
262 Isaac Bruce 1.00
263 Marshall Faulk 1.00
264 Trent Green .40
265 Kurt Warner 6.00
266 Torry Holt 1.00
267 Robert Holcombe .20
268 Kevin Carter .20
269 Amp Lee .20
270 Roland Williams .20
271 Jacquez Green .40
272 Reidel Anthony .40
273 Warren Sapp .20
274 Mike Alstott 1.00
275 Warrick Dunn 1.00
276 Shaun King 1.50
277 Bert Emanuel .20
278 Eric Zeier .20
279 Neil O'Donnell .20
280 Eddie George 1.00
281 Yancey Thigpen .20
282 Steve McNair 1.00
283 Kevin Dyson .20
284 Frank Wycheck .20
285 Jevon Kearse 1.50
286 Bruce Matthews .20
287 Lorenzo Neal .20
288 Stephen Davis .75
289 Stephen Alexander .20
290 Darrell Green .20
291 Skip Hicks .40
292 Brad Johnson .75
293 Michael Westbrook .40
294 Albert Connell .40
296 Irving Fryar .20
297 Champ Bailey 1.00
298 Larry Centers .20
299 Brian Mitchell .20
300 James Thrash .20
301 LaVar Arrington 8.00
302 Peter Warrick 8.00
303 Courtney Brown 3.00
304 Plaxico Burress 5.00
305 Corey Simon 2.00
306 Thomas Jones 5.00
307 Travis Taylor 3.50
308 Shaun Alexander 6.00
309 Chris Redman 5.00
310 Chad Pennington 8.00
311 Jamal Lewis 12.00
312 Brian Urlacher 6.00
313 Keith Bullock 1.50
314 Daniel Franks 3.00
315 Dez White 2.00
316 Ahmed Plummer 1.50
317 Ron Dayne 10.00
318 Shaun Ellis 1.50
319 Sylvester Morris 5.00
320 Delthea O'Neal 1.50
321 R. Jay Soward 2.50
322 Sherrod Gideon 1.50
323 John Abraham 1.50
324 Travis Prentice 4.00
325 Darrell Jackson 3.00
326 Giovanni Carmazzi 4.00
327 Anthony Lucas 1.50
328 Danny Farmer 2.50
329 Dennis Northcutt 3.00
330 Troy Walters 2.00
331 Laveranues Coles 3.00
332 Tee Martin 3.00
333 J.R. Redmond 3.00
334 Jerry Porter 2.00
335 Sebastian Janikowski 2.00
336 Michael Wiley 2.50
337 Reuben Droughns 2.00
338 Trung Candidate 2.00
339 Shyrone Stith 1.50
340 Trevor Gaylor 2.00
341 Rob Morris 1.50
342 Marc Bulger 1.50
343 Tom Brady 5.00
344 Todd Husak 1.50
345 Gari Scott 1.50
346 Erron Kinney 1.50
347 Julian Peterson 1.50
348 Doug Chapman 1.50
349 Ron Dugans 1.50
350 Todd Pinkston 2.50
351 Deon Grant .20
352 Na'il Diggs .20
353 Raynoch Thompson .20
354 Mario Edwards .20
355 John Engelberger .20
356 Dwayne Goodrich .20
357 Ben Kelly .20
358 Sekou Sanyika .20
359 Brandon Short .20
360 Jabari Issa .20
361 Darwin Walker .20
362 Jerry Johnson .20
363 Robaire Smith .20
364 Mark Roman .20
365 Leonardo Carson .20
366 Mark Simoneau .20
367 Hank Poteat .20
368 Darren Howard .20
369 David Macklin .20
370 Adalius Thomas .20
371 Ralph Brown .20
372 Mondriel Fulcher .20
373 Sammy Morris 2.50
374 Rondell Mealey .50
375 Deon Dyer .50
376 Mareno Philyaw .20
377 Thomas Hamner .20
378 Jarious Jackson .50
379 Joe Hamilton 2.50
380 Tim Rattay 3.00
381 Chris Hovan .20

2000 Quantum Leaf Infinity Green Parallel

	MT
Cards #1-100:	10x-20x
Production 100 Sets	
Cards #101-200:	20x-40x
Production 2 Sets	
Cards #201-300:	15x-30x
Production 50 Sets	
Cards #301-350:	4x-8x
Production 15 Sets	

1 Frank Sanders .40
2 Adrian Murrell .40
3 Rob Moore .40
4 Simeon Rice .20
5 Michael Pittman .20
6 Jake Plummer 1.00
7 David Boston .75
8 Mario Bates .20
9 Chris Chandler .40
10 Tim Dwight .75
11 Chris Calloway .20
12 Terance Mathis .20
13 Jamal Anderson .75
14 Byron Hanspard .40
15 Ken Oxendine .20
16 Tony Graziani .40
17 Bob Christian .40
18 Priest Holmes .40
19 Tony Banks .40
20 Patrick Johnson .40
21 Rod Woodson .40
22 Jermaine Lewis .40
23 Errict Rhett .40
24 Stoney Case .20
25 Peter Boulware .20
26 Qadry Ismail .40
27 Brandon Stokley .40
28 Andre Reed .40
29 Eric Moulds .75
30 Doug Flutie 1.25
31 Bruce Smith .20
32 Jay Riemersma .20
33 Antowain Smith .75
34 Thurman Thomas .40
35 Jonathon Linton .40
36 Peerless Price .75
37 Rob Johnson .40
38 Sam Gash .20
39 Muhsin Muhammad .40
40 Wesley Walls .40
41 Fred Lane .20
42 Kevin Greene .20
43 Tim Biakabutuka .40
44 Steve Beuerlein .20
45 Donald Hayes .20
46 Patrick Jeffers 1.00
47 Curtis Enis .75
48 Bobby Engram .20
49 Curtis Conway .40
50 Marcus Robinson 1.00
51 Marty Booker .20
52 Cade McNown 1.50
53 Shane Matthews .40
54 Jim Miller .40
55 Darnay Scott .40
56 Carl Pickens .40
57 Corey Dillon .75
58 Jeff Blake .40
59 Akili Smith 1.25
60 Michael Basnight .20
61 Karim Abdul .20
62 Tim Couch 3.00
63 Kevin Johnson 1.00
64 Terry Kirby .20
65 Ty Detmer .20
66 Leslie Shepherd .20
67 Darrin Chiaverini .20
68 Emmitt Smith 2.50
69 Deion Sanders .75
70 Michael Irvin .40
71 Raghib Ismail .20
72 Troy Aikman 2.00
73 Daryl Johnston .20
74 Chris Warren .40
75 Jason Garrett .20
76 Jason Tucker 1.00
77 Lawyer Milloy .20
78 Dexter Coakley .20
79 Greg Ellis .20
80 David LaFleur .20
81 Todd Lyght .20
82 Ernie Mills .20
83 Wane McGarity .20
84 Chris Brazzell .20
85 Ed McCaffrey .40
86 Rod Smith .40
87 Shannon Sharpe .40
88 Brian Griese 1.00
89 John Elway 3.00
90 Neil Smith .20
91 Terrell Davis 3.00
92 Olandis Gary 1.50
93 Derek Loville .20
94 John Avery .20
95 Bubby Brister .40
96 Byron Chamberlain .20
97 Dale Carter .20
98 Johnnie Morton .20
99 Charlie Batch 1.00
100 Barry Sanders 3.00
101 Germane Crowell .40
102 Gus Frerotte .20
103 Desmond Howard .20
104 Terry Fair .20
105 Ron Rivers .20
106 Greg Hill .20
107 Sedrick Irvin .40
108 David Sloan .20
109 Herman Moore .75
110 Robert Porcher .20
111 Corey Bradford .20
112 Dorsey Levens 1.00
113 Antonio Freeman 1.00
114 Brett Favre 4.00
115 De'Mond Parker .40
116 Bill Schroeder .40
117 Matt Hasselbeck .40
118 Donald Driver .40
119 Basil Mitchell .20
120 E.G. Green .20
121 Ken Dilger .20
122 Marvin Harrison 1.00
123 Peyton Manning 3.00
124 Terrence Wilkins 1.00
125 Edgerrin James 4.00
126 Jerome Pathon .20
127 Marcus Pollard .20
128 Keenan McCardell .40
129 Mark Brunell 1.50
130 Fred Taylor 1.50
131 Jimmy Smith .75
132 James Stewart .75
133 Kyle Brady .20
134 Tony Brackens .20
135 Derrick Thomas .40
136 Rashaan Shehee .20
137 Derrick Alexander .20
138 Bam Morris .20
139 Andre Rison .40
140 Elvis Grbac .20
141 Tony Gonzalez .40
142 Donnell Bennett .20
143 Warren Moon .75
144 Tamarick Vanover .20
145 Kimble Anders .20
146 Tony Richardson .20
147 Zach Thomas .40
148 Oronde Gadsden .40
149 Dan Marino 3.00
150 O.J. McDuffie .40
151 Tony Martin .20
152 Cecil Collins .40
153 James Johnson .20
154 Rob Konrad .20
155 Yatil Green .20
156 Damon Huard .75
157 Nate Jacquet .20
158 Stanley Pritchett .20
159 Sam Madison .20
160 Randy Moss 3.00
161 Cris Carter 1.00
162 Robert Smith 1.00
163 Randall Cunningham .75
164 Jake Reed .40
165 John Randle .40
166 Leroy Hoard .20
167 Jeff George .75
168 Daunte Culpepper 1.50
169 Matthew Hatchette .20
170 Robert Tate .20
171 Ty Law .20
172 Troy Brown .20
173 Tony Simmons .40
174 Terry Glenn .75
175 Ben Coates .40
176 Drew Bledsoe 1.50
177 Terry Allen .40
178 Kevin Faulk .40
179 Shawn Jefferson .20
180 Andy Katzenmoyer .20
181 Willie McGinest .20
182 Cameron Cleeland .40
183 Eddie Kennison .40
184 Ricky Williams 3.00
185 Danny Wuerffel .20
186 Brett Bech .20
187 Billy Joe Hobert .20
188 Jake Delhomme 4.00
189 Wilmont Perry .20
190 Keith Poole .20
191 Ashley Ambrose .20
192 Amani Toomer .40
193 Kerry Collins .40
194 Tiki Barber .40
195 Ike Hilliard .40
196 Jason Sehorn .20
197 Joe Montgomery .20
198 Joe Jurevicius .20
199 Michael Strahan .20
200 Sean Bennett .20
201 Jessie Armstead .20
202 Pete Mitchell .20
203 Curtis Martin .75
204 Vinny Testaverde .40
205 Keyshawn Johnson 1.00
206 Wayne Chrebet .75
207 Ray Lucas 1.00
208 Tyrone Wheatley .40
209 Napoleon Kaufman .75
210 Tim Brown .75
211 Rickey Dudley .20
212 James Jett .20
213 Rich Gannon .40
214 Charles Woodson 1.00
215 Zack Crockett .20
216 Darrell Russell .20
217 Duce Staley 1.00
218 Donovan McNabb 1.50
219 Charles Johnson .20
220 Dameane Douglas .20
221 Doug Pederson .20
222 Torrance Small .20
223 Troy Vincent .20
224 Na Brown .20
225 Kordell Stewart 1.00
226 Jerome Bettis 1.00
227 Hines Ward .40
228 Troy Edwards 1.00
229 Richard Huntley .40
230 Mark Bruener .20
231 Pete Gonzalez .40
232 Levon Kirkland .20
233 Bobby Shaw 1.00
234 Amos Zereoue .40
235 Natrone Means .40
236 Junior Seau .40
237 Jim Harbaugh .40
238 Ryan Leaf 1.00
239 Mikhael Ricks .20
240 Jermaine Fazande .20
241 Jeff Graham .20
242 Tremayne Stephens .20
243 Terrell Owens 1.00
244 J.J. Stokes .40
245 Charlie Garner .40
246 Jerry Rice 2.00
247 Garrison Hearst .40
248 Steve Young 1.50
249 Jeff Garcia 1.00
250 Fred Beasley .20
251 Bryant Young .20
252 Derrick Mayes .40
253 Ahman Green .40
254 Joey Galloway 1.00
255 Ricky Watters 1.00
256 Jon Kitna 1.00
257 Sean Dawkins .20
258 Sam Adams .20
259 Christian Fauria .20
260 Shawn Springs .20
261 Az-Zahir Hakim .40
262 Isaac Bruce 1.00
263 Marshall Faulk 1.00
264 Trent Green .40
265 Kurt Warner 6.00
266 Torry Holt 1.00
267 Robert Holcombe .20
268 Kevin Carter .20
269 Amp Lee .20
270 Roland Williams .20
271 Jacquez Green .40
272 Reidel Anthony .40
273 Warren Sapp .20
274 Mike Alstott 1.00
275 Warrick Dunn 1.00
276 Shaun King 1.50
277 Bert Emanuel .20
278 Eric Zeier .20
279 Neil O'Donnell .20
280 Eddie George 1.00
281 Yancey Thigpen .20
282 Steve McNair 1.00
283 Kevin Dyson .20
284 Frank Wycheck .20
285 Jevon Kearse 1.50
286 Bruce Matthews .20
287 Lorenzo Neal .20
288 Stephen Davis .75
289 Stephen Alexander .20
290 Darrell Green .20
291 Skip Hicks .40
292 Brad Johnson .75
293 Michael Westbrook .40
294 Albert Connell .40
296 Irving Fryar .20
297 Champ Bailey 1.00
298 Larry Centers 1.00
299 Brian Mitchell .20
300 James Thrash .20
301 Lavar Arrington 7.00
302 Peter Warrick 12.00
303 Courtney Brown 4.00
304 Plaxico Burress 8.00
305 Corey Simon 1.50
306 Thomas Jones 8.00
307 Travis Taylor 3.50
308 Shaun Alexander 6.00
309 Chris Redman 6.00
310 Chad Pennington 8.00
311 Jamal Lewis 8.00
312 Brian Urlacher 6.00
313 Keith Bullock 1.50
314 Daniel Franks 2.00
315 Dez White 2.00
316 Ahmed Plummer 1.50
317 Ron Dayne 10.00
318 Shaun Ellis 1.50
319 Sylvester Morris 4.00
320 Delthea O'Neal 1.50
321 R. Jay Soward 4.00
322 Sherrod Gideon 1.50
323 John Abraham 1.50
324 Travis Prentice 4.00
325 Darrell Jackson 1.50
326 Giovanni Carmazzi 5.00
327 Anthony Lucas 2.50
328 Danny Farmer 2.50
329 Dennis Northcutt 3.50
330 Troy Walters 2.00
331 Laveranues Coles 2.50
332 Tee Martin 4.00
333 J.R. Redmond 4.00
334 Jerry Porter 4.00
335 Sebastian Janikowski 1.50
336 Michael Wiley 2.50
337 Reuben Droughns 2.50
338 Trung Candidate 2.50
339 Shyrone Stith 1.50
340 Trevor Gaylor 1.50
341 Rob Morris 1.50
342 Marc Bulger 1.50
343 Tom Brady 2.50
344 Todd Husak 1.50
345 Gari Scott 1.50
346 Erron Kinney 1.50
347 Julian Peterson 1.50
348 Doug Chapman 1.50
349 Ron Dugans 1.50
350 Todd Pinkston 3.00
351 Deon Grant .20
352 Na'il Diggs .20
353 Raynoch Thompson .20
354 Mario Edwards .20
355 John Engelberger .20
356 Dwayne Goodrich .20
357 Ben Kelly .20
358 Sekou Sanyika .20
359 Brandon Short .20
360 Jabari Issa .20
361 Darwin Walker .20
362 Jerry Johnson .20
363 Robaire Smith .20
364 Mark Roman .20
365 Leonardo Carson .20
366 Mark Simoneau .20
367 Hank Poteat .20
368 Darren Howard .20
369 David Macklin .20
370 Adalius Thomas .20
371 Ralph Brown .20
372 Mondriel Fulcher .20
373 Sammy Morris 2.50
374 Rondell Mealey .50
375 Deon Dyer .50
376 Mareno Philyaw .20
377 Thomas Hamner .20
378 Jarious Jackson .50
379 Joe Hamilton 2.50
380 Tim Rattay 3.00
381 Chris Hovan .20

2000 Quantum Leaf Infinity Purple Parallel

	MT
Cards #1-100:	20x-40x
Production 25 Sets	
Cards #101-200:	15x-30x
Production 50 Sets	
Cards #201-300:	10x-20x
Production 100 Sets	
Cards #301-350:	10x-20x
Production 15 Sets	

1 Frank Sanders .40
2 Adrian Murrell .40
3 Rob Moore .40
4 Simeon Rice .20
5 Michael Pittman .20
6 Jake Plummer 1.00
7 David Boston .75
8 Mario Bates .20
9 Chris Chandler .40
10 Tim Dwight .75
11 Chris Calloway .20
12 Terance Mathis .20
13 Jamal Anderson .75
14 Byron Hanspard .20
15 Ken Oxendine .20
16 Tony Graziani .20
17 Bob Christian .20
18 Priest Holmes .40
19 Tony Banks .40
20 Patrick Johnson .40
21 Rod Woodson .20
22 Jermaine Lewis .40
23 Errict Rhett .40
24 Stoney Case .20
25 Peter Boulware .20
26 Qadry Ismail .20
27 Brandon Stokley .40
28 Andre Reed .40
29 Eric Moulds .75
30 Doug Flutie 1.25
31 Bruce Smith .20
32 Jay Riemersma .20
33 Antowain Smith .75
34 Thurman Thomas .40
35 Jonathon Linton .40
36 Peerless Price .75
37 Rob Johnson .40
38 Sam Gash .20
39 Muhsin Muhammad .40
40 Wesley Walls .40
41 Fred Lane .20
42 Kevin Greene .20
43 Tim Biakabutuka .40
44 Steve Beuerlein .40
45 Donald Hayes .20
46 Patrick Jeffers 1.00
47 Curtis Enis .75
48 Bobby Engram .20
49 Curtis Conway 1.00
50 Marcus Robinson 1.00
51 Marty Booker .20
52 Cade McNown 1.50
53 Shane Matthews .40
54 Jim Miller .40
55 Darnay Scott .40
56 Carl Pickens .40
57 Corey Dillon .75
58 Jeff Blake .40
59 Akili Smith 1.25
60 Michael Basnight .20
61 Karim Abdul .20
62 Tim Couch 3.00
63 Kevin Johnson 1.00
64 Terry Kirby .20
65 Ty Detmer .20
66 Leslie Shepherd .20
67 Darrin Chiaverini .20
68 Emmitt Smith 2.50
69 Deion Sanders .75

#	Player	MT
70	Michael Irvin	.40
71	Raghib Ismail	.20
72	Troy Aikman	2.00
73	Daryl Johnston	.20
74	Chris Warren	.40
75	Jason Garrett	.20
76	Jason Tucker	1.00
77	Lawyer Milloy	.20
78	Dexter Coakley	.20
79	Greg Ellis	.20
80	David LaFleur	.20
81	Todd Lyght	.20
82	Ernie Mills	.20
83	Wane McGarity	.20
84	Chris Brazzell	.20
85	Ed McCaffrey	.40
86	Rod Smith	.40
87	Shannon Sharpe	.40
88	Brian Griese	1.00
89	John Elway	3.00
90	Neil Smith	.20
91	Terrell Davis	3.00
92	Olandis Gary	1.50
93	Derek Loville	.20
94	John Avery	.20
95	Bubby Brister	.40
96	Byron Chamberlain	.20
97	Dale Carter	.20
98	Johnnie Morton	.20
99	Charlie Batch	1.00
100	Barry Sanders	3.00
101	Germane Crowell	.40
102	Gus Frerotte	.20
103	Desmond Howard	.20
104	Terry Fair	.20
105	Ron Rivers	.20
106	Greg Hill	.20
107	Sedrick Irvin	.40
108	David Sloan	.20
109	Herman Moore	.75
110	Robert Porcher	.40
111	Corey Bradford	.20
112	Dorsey Levens	1.00
113	Antonio Freeman	1.00
114	Brett Favre	4.00
115	De'Mond Parker	.20
116	Bill Schroeder	.20
117	Matt Hasselbeck	.20
118	Donald Driver	.40
119	Basil Mitchell	.20
120	E.G. Green	.20
121	Ken Dilger	.20
122	Marvin Harrison	1.00
123	Peyton Manning	3.00
124	Terrence Wilkins	1.00
125	Edgerrin James	4.00
126	Jerome Pathon	.20
127	Marcus Pollard	.20
128	Keenan McCardell	.40
129	Mark Brunell	1.50
130	Fred Taylor	1.50
131	Jimmy Smith	.75
132	James Stewart	.75
133	Kyle Brady	.20
134	Tony Brackens	.20
135	Derrick Thomas	.40
136	Rashaan Shehee	.20
137	Derrick Alexander	.20
138	Bam Morris	.20
139	Andre Rison	.40
140	Elvis Grbac	.40
141	Tony Gonzalez	.40
142	Donnell Bennett	.20
143	Warren Moon	.75
144	Tamarick Vanover	.20
145	Kimble Anders	.20
146	Tony Richardson	.20
147	Zach Thomas	.40
148	Oronde Gadsden	.40
149	Dan Marino	3.00
150	O.J. McDuffie	.40
151	Tony Martin	.20
152	Cecil Collins	.40
153	James Johnson	.20
154	Rob Konrad	.20
155	Yatil Green	.20
156	Damon Huard	.75
157	Nate Jacquet	.20
158	Stanley Pritchett	.20
159	Sam Madison	.20
160	Randy Moss	3.00
161	Cris Carter	1.00
162	Robert Smith	1.00
163	Randall Cunningham	.75
164	Jake Reed	.40
165	John Randle	.40
166	Leroy Hoard	.20
167	Jeff George	.75
168	Daunte Culpepper	1.50
169	Matthew Hatchette	.20
170	Robert Tate	.20
171	Ty Law	.20
172	Troy Brown	.20
173	Tony Simmons	.40
174	Terry Glenn	.75
175	Ben Coates	.40
176	Drew Bledsoe	1.50
177	Terry Allen	.40
178	Kevin Faulk	.40
179	Shawn Jefferson	.20
180	Andy Katzenmoyer	.20
181	Willie McGinest	.20
182	Cameron Cleeland	.20
183	Eddie Kennison	.40
184	Ricky Williams	3.00
185	Danny Wuerffel	.20
186	Brett Bech	.20
187	Billy Joe Hobert	.20
188	Jake Delhomme	4.00
189	Wilmont Perry	.20
190	Keith Poole	.20
191	Ashley Ambrose	.20
192	Amani Toomer	.40
193	Kerry Collins	.40
194	Tiki Barber	.40
195	Ike Hilliard	.40
196	Jason Sehorn	.20
197	Joe Montgomery	.20
198	Joe Jurevicius	.20
199	Michael Strahan	.20
200	Sean Bennett	.20
201	Jessie Armstead	.20
202	Pete Mitchell	.20
203	Curtis Martin	.75
204	Vinny Testaverde	.40
205	Keyshawn Johnson	1.00
206	Wayne Chrebet	.75
207	Ray Lucas	.20
208	Tyrone Wheatley	.40
209	Napoleon Kaufman	.75
210	Tim Brown	.75
211	Rickey Dudley	.20
212	James Jett	.20
213	Rich Gannon	.40
214	Charles Woodson	1.00
215	Zack Crockett	.20
216	Darrell Russell	.20
217	Duce Staley	1.00
218	Donovan McNabb	1.50
219	Charles Johnson	.20
220	Dameane Douglas	.20
221	Doug Pederson	.20
222	Torrance Small	.20
223	Troy Vincent	.20
224	Na Brown	.20
225	Kordell Stewart	1.00
226	Jerome Bettis	1.00
227	Hines Ward	.40
228	Troy Edwards	1.00
229	Richard Huntley	.40
230	Mark Bruener	.20
231	Pete Gonzalez	.20
232	Levon Kirkland	.20
233	Bobby Shaw	.20
234	Amos Zereoue	.40
235	Natrone Means	.40
236	Junior Seau	.40
237	Jim Harbaugh	.20
238	Ryan Leaf	1.00
239	Mikhael Ricks	.20
240	Jermaine Fazande	.40
241	Jeff Graham	.20
242	Tremayne Stephens	.40
243	Terrell Owens	1.00
244	J.J. Stokes	.40
245	Charlie Garner	.20
246	Jerry Rice	2.00
247	Garrison Hearst	.40
248	Steve Young	1.50
249	Jeff Garcia	1.00
250	Fred Beasley	.20
251	Bryant Young	.20
252	Derrick Mayes	.40
253	Ahman Green	.20
254	Joey Galloway	1.00
255	Ricky Watters	1.00
256	Jon Kitna	1.00
257	Sean Dawkins	.20
258	Sam Adams	.20
259	Christian Fauria	.20
260	Shawn Springs	.40
261	Az-Zahir Hakim	.40
262	Isaac Bruce	1.00
263	Marshall Faulk	1.00
264	Trent Green	.40
265	Kurt Warner	6.00
266	Torry Holt	1.00
267	Robert Holcombe	.20
268	Kevin Carter	.20
269	Amp Lee	.20
270	Roland Williams	.20
271	Jacquez Green	.40
272	Reidel Anthony	.40
273	Warren Sapp	.20
274	Mike Alstott	1.00
275	Warrick Dunn	.40
276	Trent Dilfer	.40
277	Shaun King	1.50
278	Bert Emanuel	.20
279	Eric Zeier	.20
280	Neil O'Donnell	.40
281	Eddie George	1.00
282	Yancey Thigpen	.40
283	Steve McNair	1.00
284	Kevin Dyson	.40
285	Frank Wycheck	.20
286	Jevon Kearse	1.00
287	Bruce Matthews	.20
288	Lorenzo Neal	.20
289	Stephen Davis	.75
290	Stephen Alexander	.20
291	Darrell Green	.20
292	Skip Hicks	.40
293	Brad Johnson	.40
294	Michael Westbrook	.75
295	Albert Connell	.40
296	Irving Fryar	.20
297	Champ Bailey	1.00
298	Larry Centers	.20
299	Brian Mitchell	.20
300	James Thrash	.20
301	Lavar Arrington	7.00
302	Peter Warrick	12.00
303	Courtney Brown	4.00
304	Plaxico Burress	8.00
305	Corey Simon	1.50
306	Thomas Jones	8.00
307	Travis Taylor	5.00
308	Shaun Alexander	6.00
309	Chris Redman	5.00
310	Chad Pennington	8.00
311	Jamal Lewis	8.00
312	Brian Urlacher	3.00
313	Keith Bullock	1.50
314	Daniel Franks	3.00
315	Dez White	2.00
316	Ron Dayne	10.00
317	Shaun Ellis	1.50
318	Sylvester Morris	4.00
319	Delthea O'Neal	1.50
320	R. Jay Soward	1.50
321	Sherrod Gideon	1.50
322	Travis Prentice	1.50
323	John Abraham	1.50
324	Darrell Jackson	1.50
325	Giovanni Carmazzi	5.00
326	Anthony Lucas	2.50
327	Danny Farmer	2.50
328	Dennis Northcutt	3.50
329	Troy Walters	2.00
330	Laveranues Coles	2.50
331	Tee Martin	4.00
332	J.R. Redmond	4.00
333	Jerry Porter	4.00
334	Michael Wiley	1.50
335	Sebastian Janikowski	2.50
336	Michael Wiley	2.50
337	Reuben Droughns	2.50
338	Trung Canidate	2.50
339	Shyrone Stith	1.50
340	Trevor Gaylor	1.50
341	Rob Morris	1.50
342	Marc Bulger	1.50
343	Tom Brady	2.50
344	Todd Husak	1.50
345	Gari Scott	1.50
346	Erron Kinney	1.50
347	Julian Peterson	1.50
348	Doug Chapman	1.50
349	Ron Dugans	1.50
350	Todd Pinkston	3.00
351	Deon Grant	1.50
352	Na'il Diggs	.20
353	Raynoch Thompson	.20
354	Mario Edwards	.20
355	John Engelberger	.20
356	Dwayne Goodrich	.20
357	Ben Kelly	.20
358	Sekou Sanyika	.20
359	Brandon Short	.20
360	Jabari Issa	.20
361	Darwin Walker	.20
362	Jerry Johnson	.20
363	Robaire Smith	.20
364	Mark Roman	.20
365	Leonardo Carson	.20
366	Mark Simoneau	.20
367	Hank Poteat	.20
368	Darren Howard	.20
369	David Macklin	.20
370	Adalius Thomas	.20
371	Ralph Brown	.20
372	Mondriel Fulcher	.20
373	Sammy Morris	.20
374	Rondell Mealey	.20
375	Deon Dyer	.20
376	Mareno Philyaw	.20
377	Thomas Hamner	.20
378	Jarious Jackson	.20
379	Joe Hamilton	.20
380	Tim Rattay	.20
381	Chris Hovan	.20

2000 Quantum Leaf Infinity Red Parallel

	MT
Cards #1-100:	15x-30x
Production 50 Sets	
Cards #101-200:	10x-20x
Production 100 Sets	
Cards #201-300:	20x-40x
Production 25 Sets	
Cards #301-350:	5x-10x
Production 35 Sets	

#	Player	MT
1	Frank Sanders	.40
2	Adrian Murrell	.20
3	Rob Moore	.40
4	Simeon Rice	.20
5	Michael Pittman	.20
6	Jake Plummer	1.00
7	David Boston	.75
8	Mario Bates	.20
9	Chris Chandler	.40
10	Tim Dwight	.75
11	Chris Calloway	.20
12	Terance Mathis	.20
13	Jamal Anderson	.75
14	Byron Hanspard	.40
15	Ken Oxendine	.20
16	Tony Graziani	.20
17	Bob Christian	.20
18	Priest Holmes	.40
19	Tony Banks	.40
20	Patrick Johnson	.40
21	Rod Woodson	.40
22	Jermaine Lewis	.40
23	Errict Rhett	.40
24	Stoney Case	.20
25	Peter Boulware	.20
26	Qadry Ismail	.40
27	Brandon Stokley	.20
28	Andre Reed	.40
29	Eric Moulds	.75
30	Doug Flutie	1.25
31	Bruce Smith	.40
32	Jay Riemersma	.20
33	Antowain Smith	.40
34	Thurman Thomas	.40
35	Jonathon Linton	.20
36	Peerless Price	.75
37	Rob Johnson	.20
38	Sam Gash	.20
39	Muhsin Muhammad	.40
40	Wesley Walls	.40
41	Fred Lane	.20
42	Kevin Greene	.20
43	Tim Biakabutuka	.20
44	Steve Beuerlein	.40
45	Donald Hayes	.20
46	Patrick Jeffers	1.00
47	Curtis Enis	.75
48	Bobby Engram	.20
49	Curtis Conway	.20
50	Marcus Robinson	1.00
51	Marty Booker	.20
52	Cade McNown	1.50
53	Shane Matthews	.20
54	Jim Miller	.40
55	Darnay Scott	.20
56	Carl Pickens	.40
57	Corey Dillon	.75
58	Jeff Blake	.40
59	Akili Smith	1.25
60	Michael Basnight	.20
61	Karim Abdul	.40
62	Tim Couch	3.00
63	Kevin Johnson	1.00
64	Terry Kirby	.20
65	Ty Detmer	.20
66	Leslie Shepherd	.20
67	Darrin Chiaverini	.20
68	Emmitt Smith	2.50
69	Deion Sanders	.75
70	Michael Irvin	.40
71	Raghib Ismail	.20
72	Troy Aikman	2.00
73	Daryl Johnston	.20
74	Chris Warren	.40
75	Jason Garrett	.20
76	Jason Tucker	1.00
77	Lawyer Milloy	.20
78	Dexter Coakley	.20
79	Greg Ellis	.20
80	David LaFleur	.20
81	Todd Lyght	.20
82	Ernie Mills	.20
83	Wane McGarity	.20
84	Chris Brazzell	.20
85	Ed McCaffrey	.40
86	Rod Smith	.40
87	Shannon Sharpe	.40
88	Brian Griese	1.00
89	John Elway	3.00
90	Neil Smith	.20
91	Terrell Davis	3.00
92	Olandis Gary	1.50
93	Derek Loville	.20
94	John Avery	.20
95	Bubby Brister	.40
96	Byron Chamberlain	.20
97	Dale Carter	.20
98	Johnnie Morton	.20
99	Charlie Batch	1.00
100	Barry Sanders	3.00
101	Germane Crowell	.40
102	Gus Frerotte	.20
103	Desmond Howard	.20
104	Terry Fair	.20
105	Ron Rivers	.20
106	Greg Hill	.20
107	Sedrick Irvin	.40
108	David Sloan	.20
109	Herman Moore	.75
110	Robert Porcher	.40
111	Corey Bradford	.20
112	Dorsey Levens	1.00
113	Antonio Freeman	1.00
114	Brett Favre	4.00
115	De'Mond Parker	.20
116	Bill Schroeder	.20
117	Matt Hasselbeck	.20
118	Donald Driver	.40
119	Basil Mitchell	.20
120	E.G. Green	.20
121	Ken Dilger	.20
122	Marvin Harrison	1.00
123	Peyton Manning	3.00
124	Terrence Wilkins	1.00
125	Edgerrin James	4.00
126	Jerome Pathon	.20
127	Marcus Pollard	.20
128	Keenan McCardell	.40
129	Mark Brunell	1.50
130	Fred Taylor	1.50
131	Jimmy Smith	.75
132	James Stewart	.75
133	Kyle Brady	.20
134	Tony Brackens	.20
135	Derrick Thomas	.40
136	Rashaan Shehee	.20
137	Derrick Alexander	.20
138	Bam Morris	.20
139	Andre Rison	.40
140	Elvis Grbac	.40
141	Tony Gonzalez	.40
142	Donnell Bennett	.20
143	Warren Moon	.75
144	Tamarick Vanover	.20
145	Kimble Anders	.20
146	Tony Richardson	.20
147	Zach Thomas	.40
148	Oronde Gadsden	.40
149	Dan Marino	3.00
150	O.J. McDuffie	.40
151	Tony Martin	.20
152	Cecil Collins	.40
153	James Johnson	.20
154	Rob Konrad	.20
155	Yatil Green	.20
156	Damon Huard	.75
157	Nate Jacquet	.20
158	Stanley Pritchett	.20
159	Sam Madison	.20
160	Randy Moss	3.00
161	Cris Carter	1.00
162	Robert Smith	1.00
163	Randall Cunningham	.75
164	Jake Reed	.40
165	John Randle	.40
166	Leroy Hoard	.20
167	Jeff George	.75
168	Daunte Culpepper	1.50
169	Matthew Hatchette	.20
170	Robert Tate	.20
171	Ty Law	.20
172	Troy Brown	.20
173	Tony Simmons	.40
174	Terry Glenn	.75
175	Ben Coates	.40
176	Drew Bledsoe	1.50
177	Terry Allen	.40
178	Kevin Faulk	.40
179	Shawn Jefferson	.20
180	Andy Katzenmoyer	.20
181	Willie McGinest	.20
182	Cameron Cleeland	.20
183	Eddie Kennison	.40
184	Ricky Williams	3.00
185	Danny Wuerffel	.20
186	Brett Bech	.20
187	Billy Joe Hobert	.20
188	Jake Delhomme	4.00
189	Wilmont Perry	.20
190	Keith Poole	.20
191	Ashley Ambrose	.20
192	Amani Toomer	.40
193	Kerry Collins	.40
194	Tiki Barber	.40
195	Ike Hilliard	.40
196	Jason Sehorn	.20
197	Joe Montgomery	.20
198	Joe Jurevicius	.20
199	Michael Strahan	.20
200	Sean Bennett	.20
201	Jessie Armstead	.20
202	Pete Mitchell	.20
203	Curtis Martin	.75
204	Vinny Testaverde	.40
205	Keyshawn Johnson	1.00
206	Wayne Chrebet	.75
207	Ray Lucas	.20
208	Tyrone Wheatley	.40
209	Napoleon Kaufman	.75
210	Tim Brown	.75
211	Rickey Dudley	.20
212	James Jett	.20
213	Rich Gannon	.40
214	Charles Woodson	1.00
215	Zack Crockett	.20
216	Darrell Russell	.20
217	Duce Staley	1.00
218	Donovan McNabb	1.50
219	Charles Johnson	.20
220	Dameane Douglas	.20
221	Doug Pederson	.20
222	Torrance Small	.20
223	Troy Vincent	.20
224	Na Brown	.20
225	Kordell Stewart	1.00
226	Jerome Bettis	1.00
227	Hines Ward	.40
228	Troy Edwards	1.00
229	Richard Huntley	.40
230	Mark Bruener	.20
231	Pete Gonzalez	.20
232	Levon Kirkland	.20
233	Bobby Shaw	.20
234	Amos Zereoue	.40
235	Natrone Means	.40
236	Junior Seau	.40
237	Jim Harbaugh	.20
238	Ryan Leaf	1.00
239	Mikhael Ricks	.20
240	Jermaine Fazande	.40
241	Jeff Graham	.20
242	Tremayne Stephens	.40
243	Terrell Owens	1.00
244	J.J. Stokes	.40
245	Charlie Garner	.20
246	Jerry Rice	2.00
247	Garrison Hearst	.40
248	Steve Young	1.50
249	Jeff Garcia	1.00
250	Fred Beasley	.20
251	Bryant Young	.20
252	Derrick Mayes	.40
253	Ahman Green	.20
254	Joey Galloway	1.00
255	Ricky Watters	1.00
256	Jon Kitna	1.00
257	Sean Dawkins	.20
258	Sam Adams	.20
259	Christian Fauria	.20
260	Shawn Springs	.40
261	Az-Zahir Hakim	.40
262	Isaac Bruce	1.00
263	Marshall Faulk	1.00
264	Trent Green	.40
265	Kurt Warner	6.00
266	Torry Holt	1.00
267	Robert Holcombe	.20
268	Kevin Carter	.20
269	Amp Lee	.20
270	Roland Williams	.20
271	Jacquez Green	.40
272	Reidel Anthony	.40
273	Warren Sapp	.20
274	Mike Alstott	1.00
275	Warrick Dunn	.40
276	Trent Dilfer	.40
277	Shaun King	1.50
278	Bert Emanuel	.20
279	Eric Zeier	.20
280	Neil O'Donnell	.40
281	Eddie George	1.00
282	Yancey Thigpen	.40
283	Steve McNair	1.00
284	Kevin Dyson	.40
285	Frank Wycheck	.20
286	Jevon Kearse	1.00
287	Bruce Matthews	.20
288	Lorenzo Neal	.20
289	Stephen Davis	.75
290	Stephen Alexander	.20
291	Darrell Green	.20
292	Skip Hicks	.40
293	Brad Johnson	.40
294	Michael Westbrook	.75
295	Albert Connell	.40
296	Irving Fryar	.20
297	Champ Bailey	1.00
298	Larry Centers	.20
299	Brian Mitchell	.20
300	James Thrash	.20
301	Lavar Arrington	7.00
302	Peter Warrick	12.00
303	Courtney Brown	4.00
304	Plaxico Burress	8.00
305	Corey Simon	1.50
306	Thomas Jones	8.00
307	Travis Taylor	5.00
308	Shaun Alexander	6.00
309	Chris Redman	5.00
310	Chad Pennington	8.00
311	Jamal Lewis	8.00
312	Brian Urlacher	3.00
313	Keith Bullock	1.50
314	Daniel Franks	3.00
315	Dez White	2.00
316	Ron Dayne	10.00
317	Shaun Ellis	1.50
318	Sylvester Morris	4.00
319	Delthea O'Neal	1.50
320	R. Jay Soward	1.50
321	Sherrod Gideon	1.50
322	Travis Prentice	1.50
323	John Abraham	1.50
324	Darrell Jackson	1.50
325	Giovanni Carmazzi	5.00
326	Anthony Lucas	2.50
327	Danny Farmer	2.50
328	Dennis Northcutt	3.50
329	Troy Walters	2.00
330	Laveranues Coles	2.50
331	Tee Martin	4.00
332	J.R. Redmond	4.00
333	Jerry Porter	4.00
334	Michael Wiley	1.50
335	Sebastian Janikowski	2.50
336	Michael Wiley	2.50
337	Reuben Droughns	2.50
338	Trung Canidate	2.50
339	Shyrone Stith	1.50
340	Trevor Gaylor	1.50
341	Rob Morris	1.50
342	Marc Bulger	1.50
343	Tom Brady	2.50
344	Todd Husak	1.50
345	Gari Scott	1.50
346	Erron Kinney	1.50
347	Julian Peterson	1.50
348	Doug Chapman	1.50
349	Ron Dugans	1.50
350	Todd Pinkston	3.00
351	Deon Grant	1.50
352	Na'il Diggs	.20
353	Raynoch Thompson	.20
354	Mario Edwards	.20
355	John Engelberger	.20
356	Dwayne Goodrich	.20
357	Ben Kelly	.20
358	Sekou Sanyika	.20
359	Brandon Short	.20
360	Jabari Issa	.20
361	Darwin Walker	.20
362	Jerry Johnson	.20
363	Robaire Smith	.20
364	Mark Roman	.20
365	Leonardo Carson	.20
366	Mark Simoneau	.20
367	Hank Poteat	.20
368	Darren Howard	.20
369	David Macklin	.20
370	Adalius Thomas	.20
371	Ralph Brown	.20
372	Mondriel Fulcher	.20
373	Sammy Morris	.20
374	Rondell Mealey	.20
375	Deon Dyer	.20
376	Mareno Philyaw	.20
377	Thomas Hamner	.20
378	Jarious Jackson	.20
379	Joe Hamilton	.20
380	Tim Rattay	.20
381	Chris Hovan	.20

2000 Quantum Leaf All-Millennium Team

	MT
Complete Set (28):	125.00
Common Player:	2.00
Minor Stars:	4.00
Production 1,000 Sets	
DM Dan Marino	12.00
JE John Elway	12.00
SB Sammy Baugh	4.00
JU Johnny Unitas	10.00
JM Joe Montana	15.00
PH Paul Hornung	4.00
JB Jim Brown	12.00
TD Tony Dorsett	6.00
EC Earl Campbell	6.00
BS Barry Sanders	12.00
ES Emmitt Smith	10.00
GS Gale Sayers	8.00
TD Terrell Davis	10.00
ED Eric Dickerson	2.00
MA Marcus Allen	4.00
JR Jerry Rice	8.00
LA Lance Alworth	2.00
KW Kellen Winslow	2.00
FB Fred Biletnikoff	6.00
RB Raymond Berry	4.00
JL James Lofton	2.00
RM Randy Moss	12.00
PW Paul Warfield	4.00
CC Cris Carter	4.00
TB Terry Bradshaw	10.00
RS Roger Staubach	10.00
SL Steve Largent	6.00
BST Bart Starr	10.00

2000 Quantum Leaf All-Millennium Team Autographs

	MT
Complete Set (28):	2800.
Common Player:	35.00
Minor Stars:	70.00
Production 100 Sets	
DM Dan Marino	200.00
JE John Elway	200.00
SB Sammy Baugh	70.00
JU Johnny Unitas	175.00
JM Joe Montana	250.00
PH Paul Hornung	70.00
JB Jim Brown	175.00
TD Tony Dorsett	100.00
EC Earl Campbell	85.00
BS Barry Sanders	200.00
ES Emmitt Smith	175.00
GS Gale Sayers	100.00
TD Terrell Davis	125.00
ED Eric Dickerson	35.00
MA Marcus Allen	70.00
JR Jerry Rice	150.00
LA Lance Alworth	35.00
KW Kellen Winslow	35.00
FB Fred Biletnikoff	75.00
RB Raymond Berry	35.00
JL James Lofton	35.00
RM Randy Moss	150.00
PW Paul Warfield	70.00
CC Cris Carter	70.00
TB Terry Bradshaw	150.00
RS Roger Staubach	150.00
SL Steve Largent	75.00
BST Bart Starr	175.00

2000 Quantum Leaf Banner Season

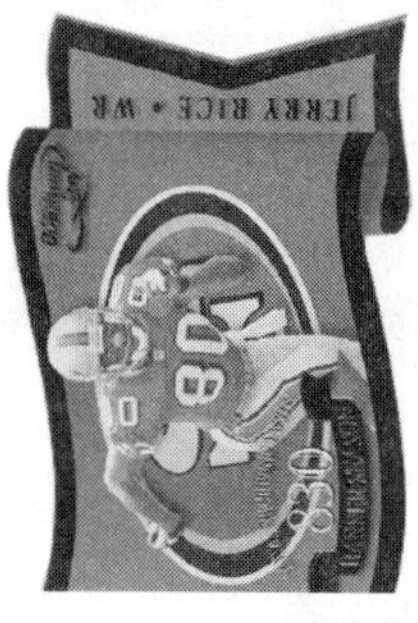

		MT
Complete Set (40):		85.00
Common Player:		1.50
Minor Stars:		3.00
Production #'d to 1999 Season Stat		
BS1	Brett Favre 4091	6.00
BS2	Marvin Harrison 1663	3.00
BS3	Tim Brown 1344	3.00
BS4	Randy Moss 1413	10.00
BS5	Edgerrin James 2139	8.00
BS6	Kurt Warner 4353	8.00
BS7	Marshall Faulk 2429	1.50
BS8	Dan Marino 2448	6.00
BS9	Tim Couch 2447	6.00
BS10	Ricky Williams 884	8.00
BS11	Eddie George 1304	4.00
BS12	Jerry Rice 830	8.00
BS13	Troy Aikman 2964	5.00
BS14	Emmitt Smith 1397	8.00
BS15	Antonio Freeman 1074	3.00
BS16	Jimmy Smith 1636	1.50
BS17	Charlie Batch 4857	1.50
BS18	Jake Plummer 2111	1.50
BS19	Drew Bledsoe 3985	3.00
BS20	Germane Crowell 1338	3.00
BS21	Cris Carter 1241	3.00
BS22	Deion Sanders 334	5.00
BS23	Donovan McNabb 948	5.00
BS24	Mark Brunell 3060	3.00
BS25	Fred Taylor 732	5.00
BS26	Stephen Davis 1405	3.00
BS27	Brad Johnson 4005	1.50
BS28	Jon Kitna 3346	1.50
BS29	Curtis Martin 1464	1.50
BS30	Keyshawn Johnson 1170	3.00
BS31	Shaun King 875	5.00
BS32	Isaac Bruce 1165	3.00
BS33	Kevin Johnson 986	3.00
BS34	Steve McNair 2179	1.50
BS35	Eric Moulds 994	3.00
BS36	Peyton Manning 4136	5.00
BS37	Dorsey Levens 1607	1.50
BS38	Olandis Gary 1159	3.00
BS39	James Stewart 931	1.50
BS40	Terry Glenn 1147	3.00

2000 Quantum Leaf Banner Season Century

		MT
Complete Set (40):		475.00
Common Player:		5.00
Minor Stars:		10.00
Production 99 Sets		
BS1	Brett Favre	40.00
BS2	Marvin Harrison	10.00
BS3	Tim Brown	10.00
BS4	Randy Moss	40.00
BS5	Edgerrin James	40.00
BS6	Kurt Warner	50.00
BS7	Marshall Faulk	12.00
BS8	Dan Marino	30.00
BS9	Tim Couch	25.00
BS10	Ricky Williams	25.00
BS11	Eddie George	12.00
BS12	Jerry Rice	25.00
BS13	Troy Aikman	25.00
BS14	Emmitt Smith	30.00
BS15	Antonio Freeman	10.00
BS16	Jimmy Smith	5.00
BS17	Charlie Batch	10.00
BS18	Jake Plummer	10.00
BS19	Drew Bledsoe	18.00
BS20	Germane Crowell	5.00
BS21	Cris Carter	10.00
BS22	Deion Sanders	10.00
BS23	Donovan McNabb	15.00
BS24	Mark Brunell	18.00
BS25	Fred Taylor	20.00
BS26	Stephen Davis	10.00
BS27	Brad Johnson	10.00
BS28	Jon Kitna	10.00
BS29	Curtis Martin	10.00
BS30	Keyshawn Johnson	10.00
BS31	Shaun King	15.00
BS32	Isaac Bruce	10.00
BS33	Kevin Johnson	10.00
BS34	Steve McNair	10.00
BS35	Eric Moulds	10.00
BS36	Peyton Manning	30.00
BS37	Dorsey Levens	10.00
BS38	Olandis Gary	10.00
BS39	James Stewart	5.00
BS40	Terry Glenn	10.00

Post-1980 cards in Near Mint condition will generally sell for about 75% of the quoted Mint value. Excellent-condition cards bring no more than 40%.

2000 Quantum Leaf Double Team

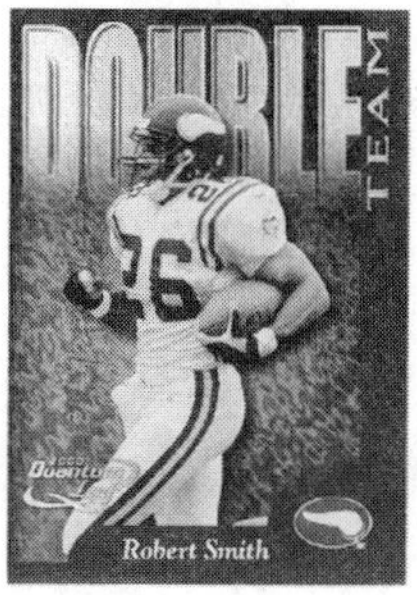

		MT
Complete Set (30):		50.00
Common Player:		1.00
Minor Stars:		2.00
Production 1,500 Sets		
DT1	J.J. Johnson, Dan Marino	6.00
DT2	Edgerrin James, Peyton Manning	8.00
DT3	Kevin Faulk, Drew Bledsoe	3.00
DT4	Antowain Smith, Doug Flutie	2.00
DT5	Curtis Martin, Vinny Testaverde	2.00
DT6	Jerome Bettis, Kordell Stewart	2.00
DT7	Eddie George, Steve McNair	3.00
DT8	Fred Taylor, Mark Brunell	3.00
DT9	Errict Rhett, Tony Banks	1.00
DT10	Karim Abdul, Tim Couch	4.00
DT11	Corey Dillon, Akili Smith	2.00
DT12	Terrell Davis, Brian Griese	5.00
DT13	Donnell Bennett, Elvis Grbac	1.00
DT14	Ricky Watters, Jon Kitna	2.00
DT15	Tyrone Wheatley, Rich Gannon	1.00
DT16	Natrone Means, Jim Harbaugh	1.00
DT17	Emmitt Smith, Troy Aikman	6.00
DT18	Stephen Davis, Brad Johnson	2.00
DT19	Duce Staley, Donovan McNabb	3.00
DT20	Michael Pittman, Jake Plummer	2.00
DT21	Dorsey Levens, Brett Favre	6.00
DT22	Robert Smith, Jeff George	2.00
DT23	Mike Alstott, Shaun King	3.00
DT24	Curtis Enis, Cade McNown	3.00
DT25	Barry Sanders, Charlie Batch	6.00
DT26	Marshall Faulk, Kurt Warner	10.00
DT27	Ricky Williams, Jeff Blake	4.00
DT28	Charlie Garner, Steve Young	2.00
DT29	Tim Biakabutuka, Steve Beuerlein	1.00
DT30	Jamal Anderson, Chris Chandler	2.00

2000 Quantum Leaf Gamers

		MT
Complete Set (20):		3200.
Common Player:		100.00
Production 25 Sets		
G1	Brett Favre	450.00
G2	Dan Marino	400.00
G3	Barry Sanders	350.00
G4	John Elway	300.00
G5	Peyton Manning	350.00
G6	Terrell Davis	200.00
G7	Fred Taylor	175.00
G8	Drew Bledsoe	175.00
G9	Mark Brunell	175.00
G10	Eddie George	150.00
G11	Isaac Bruce	100.00
G12	Jerry Rice	225.00
G13	Ray Lucas	100.00
G14	Olandis Gary	125.00
G15	Emmitt Smith	275.00
G16	Shaun King	175.00
G17	Edgerrin James	300.00
G18	Cris Carter	100.00
G19	Jimmy Smith	100.00
G20	Brian Griese	100.00

2000 Quantum Leaf Hardwear

		MT
Complete Set (15):		750.00
Common Player:		30.00
Production 125 Sets		
HW1	Brett Favre	100.00
HW2	Dan Marino	100.00
HW3	Barry Sanders	100.00
HW4	John Elway	100.00
HW5	Terrell Davis	75.00
HW6	Troy Aikman	75.00
HW7	Steve Young	60.00
HW8	Eddie George	50.00
HW9	Brad Johnson	30.00
HW10	Herman Moore	30.00
HW11	Antowain Smith	30.00
HW12	Kordell Stewart	50.00
HW13	Dorsey Levens	30.00
HW14	Peyton Manning	100.00
HW15	Jerry Rice	75.00

2000 Quantum Leaf Millennium Moments

		MT
Complete Set (20):		75.00
Common Player:		2.00
Production 1,000 Sets		
MM1	Drew Bledsoe	4.00
MM2	Emmitt Smith	7.00
MM3	Mark Brunell	4.00
MM4	Brett Favre	10.00
MM5	Randy Moss	8.00
MM6	Kurt Warner	10.00
MM7	John Elway	8.00
MM8	Steve Young	4.00
MM9	Eddie George	3.00
MM10	Marshall Faulk	2.00
MM11	Edgerrin James	8.00
MM12	Antonio Freeman	2.00
MM13	Dan Marino	8.00
MM14	Terrell Davis	6.00
MM15	Doug Flutie	3.00
MM16	Jerry Rice	5.00
MM17	Fred Taylor	4.00
MM18	Peyton Manning	8.00
MM19	Troy Aikman	5.00
MM20	Barry Sanders	8.00

2000 Quantum Leaf Rookie Revolution

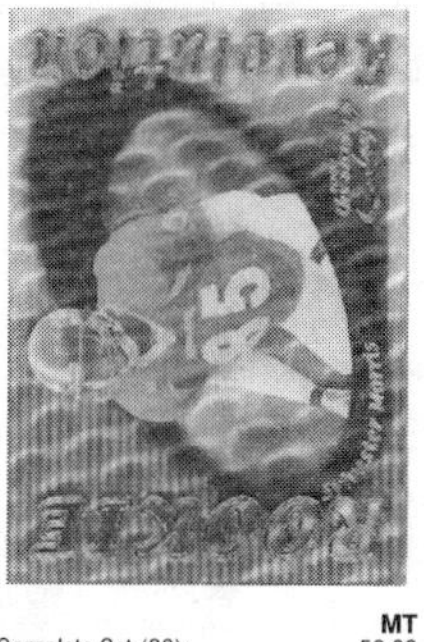

		MT
Complete Set (20):		50.00
Common Player:		1.50
Production 5,000 Sets		
First Strike Cards:		5x-10x
Production 50 Sets		
RR1	Peter Warrick	10.00
RR2	J.R. Redmond	3.00
RR3	Chris Redman	4.00
RR4	R. Jay Soward	3.00
RR5	Ron Dayne	8.00
RR6	Chad Pennington	7.00
RR7	Anthony Lucas	1.50
RR8	Tim Rattay	2.00
RR9	Shaun Alexander	6.00
RR10	Dez White	2.00
RR11	Tee Martin	3.00
RR12	Travis Taylor	4.00
RR13	Travis Prentice	3.00
RR14	Sylvester Morris	3.00
RR15	Jamal Lewis	7.00
RR16	Plaxico Burress	7.00
RR17	Sherrod Gideon	1.50
RR18	Shyrone Stith	1.50
RR19	Thomas Jones	7.00
RR20	Kwame Cavil	1.50

2000 Quantum Leaf Rookie Revolution First Strike Para.

		MT
First Strike Cards:		5x-10x
Production 50 Cards		
1	Peter Warrick	
2	J.R. Redmond	
3	Chris Redman	
4	R. Jay Soward	
5	Ron Dayne	
6	Chad Pennington	
7	Anthony Lucas	
8	Tim Rattay	
9	Shaun Alexander	
10	Dez White	
11	Tee Martin	
12	Travis Taylor	
13	Travis Prentice	
14	Sylvester Morris	
15	Jamal Lewis	
16	Plaxico Burress	
17	Sherrod Gideon	
18	Shyrone Stith	
19	Thomas Jones	
20	Kwame Cavil	

2000 Quantum Leaf Shirt Off My Back

		MT
Complete Set (20):		1250.
Common Player:		40.00
Production 100 Sets		
SB1	Brett Favre	150.00
SB2	Dan Marino	125.00
SB3	Barry Sanders	125.00
SB4	John Elway	125.00
SB5	Peyton Manning	150.00
SB6	Terrell Davis	100.00
SB7	Fred Taylor	85.00
SB8	Drew Bledsoe	75.00
SB9	Mark Brunell	75.00
SB10	Eddie George	60.00
SB11	Isaac Bruce	40.00
SB12	Jerry Rice	100.00
SB13	Ray Lucas	40.00
SB14	Olandis Gary	60.00
SB15	Emmitt Smith	125.00
SB16	Shaun King	85.00
SB17	Edgerrin James	150.00
SB18	Cris Carter	40.00
SB19	Jimmy Smith	40.00
SB20	Brian Griese	60.00

2000 Quantum Leaf Star Factor

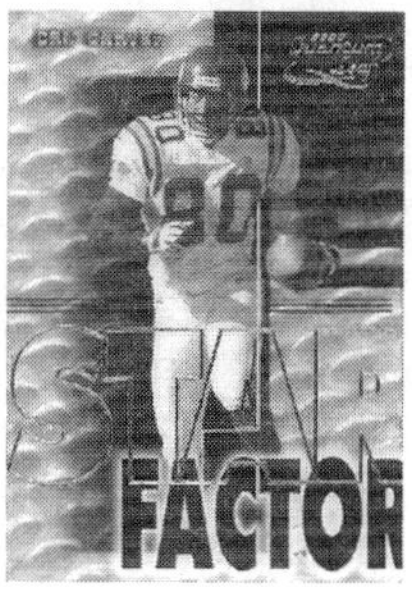

		MT
Complete Set (40):		70.00
Common Player:		1.00
Minor Stars:		2.00
Production 2,500 Sets		
Quasar Cards:		8x-16x
Production 50 Sets		
SF1	Edgerrin James	5.00
SF2	Cris Carter	1.00
SF3	Terrell Owens	1.00
SF4	Brett Favre	5.00
SF5	Tim Couch	3.00
SF6	Terry Glenn	1.00
SF7	John Elway	5.00
SF8	Troy Aikman	4.00
SF9	Charlie Batch	1.00
SF10	Steve McNair	1.00
SF11	Drew Bledsoe	2.50
SF12	Joey Galloway	1.00
SF13	Dan Marino	5.00
SF14	Marshall Faulk	1.00
SF15	Jamal Anderson	1.00
SF16	Jake Plummer	2.00
SF17	Curtis Martin	1.00
SF18	Peyton Manning	5.00
SF19	Keyshawn Johnson	1.00
SF20	Barry Sanders	5.00
SF21	Jerry Rice	4.00
SF22	Emmitt Smith	4.00
SF23	Daunte Culpepper	2.00
SF24	Brad Johnson	1.00
SF25	Kurt Warner	7.00
SF26	Steve Young	2.50
SF27	Eddie George	2.00
SF28	Fred Taylor	3.00
SF29	Randy Moss	5.00
SF30	Terrell Davis	4.00
SF31	Eric Moulds	1.00
SF32	Antonio Freeman	1.00
SF33	Isaac Bruce	1.00
SF34	Ricky Williams	3.00
SF35	Donovan McNabb	2.00
SF36	Stephen Davis	1.00
SF37	Jon Kitna	1.00
SF38	Marvin Harrison	1.00
SF39	Doug Flutie	2.00
SF40	Mark Brunell	2.50

2000 Quantum Leaf Star Factor Quasar Parallel

		MT
Quasar Cards:		8x-16x
Production 50 Sets		
1	Edgerrin James	
2	Cris Carter	
3	Terrell Owens	
4	Brett Favre	
5	Tim Couch	
6	Terry Glenn	
7	John Elway	
8	Troy Aikman	
9	Charlie Batch	
10	Steve McNair	
11	Drew Bledsoe	
12	Joey Galloway	
13	Dan Marino	
14	Marshall Faulk	
15	Jamal Anderson	
16	Jake Plummer	
17	Curtis Martin	
18	Peyton Manning	
19	Keyshawn Johnson	
20	Barry Sanders	
21	Jerry Rice	
22	Emmitt Smith	
23	Daunte Culpepper	
24	Brad Johnson	
25	Kurt Warner	
26	Steve Young	
27	Eddie George	
28	Fred Taylor	
29	Randy Moss	
30	Terrell Davis	
31	Eric Moulds	
32	Antonio Freeman	
33	Isaac Bruce	
34	Ricky Williams	
35	Donovan McNabb	
36	Stephen Davis	
37	Jon Kitna	
38	Marvin Harrison	
39	Doug Flutie	
40	Mark Brunell	

2000 Quantum Leaf Kurt Warner MVP

		MT
Complete Set (2):		30.00
Production 1,000 Sets		
Autographs:		10x
Production 100 Sets		
	Kurt Warner MVP	15.00
	Kurt Warner S.B. MVP	15.00

2001 Leaf Certified Materials

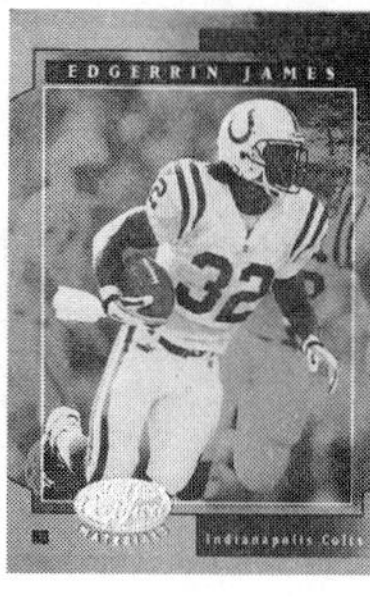

		MT
Complete Set (145):		600.00
Common Player:		.25
Minor Stars:		.50
Common Rookie (101-110):		6.00
Common Rookie Fabric (111-145):		10.00
Production 400 Sets		
Pack (4):		12.00
Box (8):		75.00
1	Aaron Brooks	1.00
2	Ahman Green	.75
3	Akili Smith	.25
4	Amani Toomer	.25
5	Antonio Freeman	.50
6	Barry Sanders	3.00
7	Brad Johnson	.50
8	Brett Favre	3.00
9	Brian Griese	1.00
10	Brian Urlacher	1.50
11	Bruce Smith	.50
12	Cade McNown	.25
13	Chad Pennington	.60
14	Charlie Batch	.50
15	Charlie Garner	.50
16	Corey Dillon	.60
17	Cris Carter	.60
18	Curtis Martin	.60
19	Dan Marino	4.00
20	Darrell Jackson	.25
21	Daunte Culpepper	1.50
22	David Boston	.75
23	Derrick Alexander	.50
24	Donovan McNabb	1.50
25	Dorsey Levens	.50
26	Doug Flutie	1.00
27	Drew Bledsoe	1.00
28	Ed McCaffery	.50
29	Eddie George	1.00
30	Edgerrin James	2.00
31	Elvis Grbac	.50
32	Emmitt Smith	2.00
33	Eric Moulds	.60
34	Frank Wycheck	.25
35	Fred Taylor	1.00
36	Ike Hilliard	.50
37	Isaac Bruce	.75
38	Jacquez Green	.25
39	Jake Plummer	.50
40	Jamal Anderson	.50
41	Jamal Lewis	1.50
42	James Stewart	.25
43	Jay Fiedler	.60
44	Jeff Garcia	.75
45	Jeff George	.50
46	Jerome Bettis	.60
47	Jerry Rice	2.00
48	Jevon Kearse	.50
49	Jimmy Smith	.50
50	Joe Horn	.25
51	Joey Galloway	.50
52	John Elway	3.50
53	Junior Seau	.50
54	Keenan McCardell	.25
55	Kerry Collins	.75
56	Keyshawn Johnson	.75
57	Kurt Warner	2.50
58	Lamar Smith	.50
59	Laveranues Coles	.60
60	Marcus Robinson	.50
61	Mark Brunell	1.00
62	Marshall Faulk	1.00
63	Marvin Harrison	.75
64	Matt Hasselbeck	.50
65	Mike Alstott	.50
66	Mike Anderson	1.25
67	Muhsin Muhammad	.50
68	Peter Warrick	.60
69	Peyton Manning	2.50
70	Plaxico Burress	.60
71	Randy Moss	2.50
72	Ray Lewis	.50
73	Rich Gannon	.50
74	Ricky Watters	.50
75	Ricky Williams	1.25
76	Rob Johnson	.50
77	Rod Smith	.50
78	Ron Dayne	.50
79	Shannon Sharpe	.50
80	Shaun Alexander	1.25
81	Stephen Davis	.50
82	Steve McNair	.60
83	Steve Young	1.50
84	Sylvester Morris	.50
85	Terrell Davis	1.50
86	Terrell Owens	.75
87	Terry Glenn	.50
88	Thomas Jones	.25
89	Tiki Barber	.50
90	Tim Brown	.60
91	Tim Couch	1.00
92	Tony Gonzalez	.50
93	Torry Holt	.75
94	Travis Taylor	.50
95	Troy Aikman	1.50
96	Tyrone Wheatley	.25
97	Vinny Testaverde	.50
98	Warren Sapp	.50
99	Warrick Dunn	.60
100	Wayne Chrebet	.50
101	Chris Taylor	6.00
102	Ken-Yon Rambo	8.00
103	Correll Buckhalter	15.00
104	A.J. Feeley	10.00
105	Josh Booty	8.00
106	LaMont Jordan	8.00
107	Alge Crumpler	6.00
108	Jamal Reynolds	6.00
109	Nate Clements	6.00
110	Will Allen	6.00
111	Santana Moss	30.00
112	Chad Johnson	15.00
113	Chris Chambers	40.00
114	David Terrell	50.00
115	Freddie Mitchell	30.00
116	Koren Robinson	30.00
117	Quincy Morgan	20.00
118	Reggie Wayne	30.00
119	Robert Ferguson	15.00
120	Rod Gardner	30.00
121	Marvin "Snoop" Minnis	25.00
122	Josh Heupel	20.00
123	Anthony Thomas	75.00
124	Deuce McCallister	30.00
125	James Jackson	20.00
126	Travis Minor	20.00
127	Kevan Barlow	25.00
128	LaDainian Tomlinson	60.00
129	Todd Heap	12.00
130	Michael Bennett	40.00
131	Rudi Johnson	12.00
132	Travis Henry	25.00
133	Michael Vick	75.00
134	Drew Brees	60.00
135	Chris Weinke	30.00
136	Quincy Carter	40.00
137	Mike McMahon	30.00
138	Jesse Palmer	20.00
139	Marques Tuiasosopo	30.00
140	Dan Morgan	10.00
141	Gerard Warren	10.00
142	Leonard Davis	10.00
143	Andre Carter	10.00
144	Justin Smith	10.00
145	Sage Rosenfels	20.00

2001 Leaf Rookies & Stars

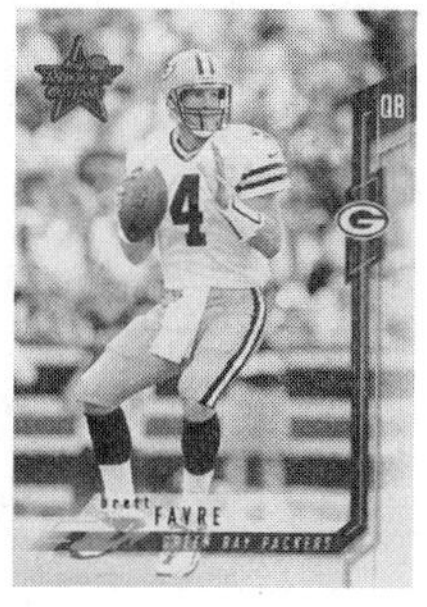

		MT
Complete Set (100):		25.00
Common Player:		.15
Mirror Stars:		.30
Common Rookie (101-200):		2.00
Inserted 1:4		
Common Rookie (201-300):		4.00
Inserted 1:24		
Pack (5):		3.00
Box (24):		55.00
1	Aaron Brooks	.60
2	Ahman Green	.50
3	Antonio Freeman	.40
4	Brad Johnson	.30
5	Brett Favre	2.00
6	Brian Griese	.60
7	Brian Urlacher	1.00
8	Bruce Smith	.30
9	Cade McNown	.15
10	Chad Pennington	.40
11	Champ Bailey	.30
12	Charles Woodson	.30
13	Charlie Batch	.30
14	Charlie Garner	.30
15	Corey Dillon	.50
16	Cris Carter	.50
17	Curtis Martin	.40
18	Dan Marino	3.00
19	Daunte Culpepper	1.00
20	David Boston	.60
21	Deion Sanders	.40
22	Donovan McNabb	1.00
23	Doug Flutie	.60
24	Drew Bledsoe	.60
25	Duce Staley	.30
26	Ed McCaffrey	.30
27	Eddie George	.60
28	Edgerrin James	1.25
29	Elvis Grbac	.30
30	Emmitt Smith	1.25
31	Eric Moulds	.50
32	Fred Taylor	.50
33	Germane Crowell	.30
34	Ike Hilliard	.15
35	Isaac Bruce	.50
36	Jake Plummer	.40
37	Jamal Anderson	.40
38	Jamal Lewis	1.00
39	James Allen	.15
40	James Stewart	.30
41	Jay Fiedler	.30
42	Jeff Garcia	.50
43	Jeff George	.30
44	Jeff Lewis	.30
45	Jerome Bettis	.30
46	Jerry Rice	1.25
47	Jevon Kearse	.30
48	Jimmy Smith	.30
49	Joey Galloway	.40
50	John Elway	2.50
51	Junior Seau	.30
52	Keenan McCardell	.30
53	Kerry Collins	.40
54	Kevin Johnson	.30
55	Keyshawn Johnson	.50
56	Kordell Stewart	.50
57	Kurt Warner	1.50
58	Lamar Smith	.30

59 Marcus Robinson .30
60 Mark Brunell .60
61 Marshall Faulk .60
62 Marvin Harrison .50
63 Matt Hasselbeck .15
64 Mike Alstott .30
65 Mike Anderson .75
66 Muhsin Muhammad .30
67 Peter Warrick .40
68 Peyton Manning 1.50
69 Priest Holmes .30
70 Randy Moss 1.50
71 Ray Lewis .40
72 Rich Gannon .40
73 Ricky Watters .40
74 Ricky Williams .75
75 Rob Johnson .30
76 Rod Smith .40
77 Ron Dayne .30
78 Shannon Sharpe .30
79 Shaun Alexander .75
80 Stephen Davis .30
81 Steve McNair .60
82 Steve Young 1.00
83 Sylvester Morris .30
84 Terrell Davis 1.00
85 Terrell Owens .50
86 Thomas Jones .30
87 Tim Brown .40
88 Tim Couch .60
89 Tony Banks .30
90 Tony Gonzalez .30
91 Torry Holt .40
92 Travis Taylor .30
93 Trent Green .30
94 Troy Aikman 1.00
95 Tyrone Wheatley .30
96 Vinny Testaverde .30
97 Warren Sapp .30
98 Warrick Dunn .40
99 Wayne Chrebet .30
100 Zach Thomas .15
101 *A.J. Feeley* 4.00
102 *Josh Booty* 4.00
103 *Roderick Robinson* 2.00
104 *Renaldo Hill* 2.00
105 *Harold Blackmon* 2.00
106 *Rudi Johnson* 5.00
107 *Curtis Fuller* 2.00
108 *Dan Alexander* 4.00
109 *Anthony Thomas* 15.00
110 *Travis Minor* 4.00
111 *Heath Evans* 2.00
112 *Joe Walker* 2.00
113 *Moran Norris* 2.00
114 *Quincy Carter* 8.00
115 *Michael Vick* 15.00
116 *Vinny Sutherland* 4.00
117 *Scotty Anderson* 2.00
118 *Eddie Berlin* 2.00
119 *Jonathan Carter* 2.00
120 *Monty Beisel* 2.00
121 *T.J. Houshmandzadeh* 2.00
122 *Rodney Bailey* 2.00
123 *Reggie Germany* 4.00
124 *Ellis Wyms* 2.00
125 *Koren Robinson* 6.00
126 *Antonio Pierce* 2.00
127 *Arnold Jackson* 2.00
128 *Andre Rone* 2.00
129 *Richard Newsome* 2.00
130 *Ifeanyi Ohalete* 2.00
131 *Dan O'Leary* 2.00
132 *Shad Meier* 2.00
133 *Jay Feeley* 2.00
134 *Brandon Manumaleuna* 2.00
135 *Riall Johnson* 2.00
136 *Marvin "Snoop" Minnis* 5.00
137 *Jermaine Hampton* 2.00
138 *Johnny Huggins* 2.00
139 *Marcellus Rivers* 2.00
140 *Andre Carter* 2.00
141 *Michael Stone* 2.00
142 *Tony Dixon* 2.00
143 *Bhawoh Jue* 2.00
144 *Will Peterson* 2.00
145 *Anthony Henry* 6.00
146 *Marques Tuiasosopo* 6.00
147 *Reggie Swinton* 4.00
148 *Robert Carswell* 2.00
149 *Freddie Mitchell* 6.00
150 *Idrees Bashir* 2.00
151 *James Boyd* 2.00
152 *Chris Chambers* 8.00
153 *Aaron Schobel* 2.00
154 *Dominic Rajola* 2.00
155 *Derrick Burgess* 2.00
156 *DeLawrence Grant* 2.00
157 *Karon Riley* 2.00
158 *Cedric Scott* 2.00
159 *David Warren* 2.00
160 *Eric Johnson* 5.00
161 *Tevita Ofahengaue* 2.00
162 *Chris Cooper* 2.00
163 *Fred Wakefield* 2.00
164 *Kenny Smith* 2.00
165 *Marcus Bell* 2.00
166 *Mario Fatafehi* 2.00
167 *Anthony Herron* 2.00
168 *Joe Tafoya* 2.00
169 *Morlon Greenwood* 2.00
170 *Orlando Huff* 2.00
171 *Carlos Polk* 2.00
172 *Edgerton Hartwell* 2.00
173 *Zeke Moreno* 2.00
174 *Alex Lincoln* 2.00
175 *Quinton Caver* 2.00
176 *Matt Stewart* 2.00
177 *Markus Steele* 2.00
178 *Dwight Smith* 2.00
179 *Reggie Wayne* 6.00
180 *Jerametrius Butler* 2.00
181 *Jason Doering* 2.00
182 *John Howell* 2.00
183 *Alvin Porter* 2.00
184 *Eric Downing* 2.00
185 *John Nix* 2.00
186 *Tim Baker* 2.00
187 *Robert Garza* 2.00
188 *Randy Chevrier* 2.00
189 *Drew Brees* 12.00
190 *Shawn Worthen* 2.00
191 *Drew Bennett* 12.00
192 *Marlon McCree* 2.00
193 *David Terrell* 10.00
194 *Jeff Backus* 2.00
195 *Otis Leverette* 2.00
196 *Jason Glenn* 2.00
197 *Rashad Holman* 2.00
198 *T.J. Turner* 2.00
199 *Lynn Scott* 2.00
200 *Bill Gramatica* 4.00
201 *Michael Vick* 40.00
202 *Drew Brees* 30.00
203 *Quincy Carter* 20.00
204 *Jesse Palmer* 10.00
205 *Mike McMahon* 15.00
206 *Dave Dickerson* 15.00
207 *Jameel Cook* 6.00
208 *Marques Tuiasosopo* 15.00
209 *Chris Weinke* 15.00
210 *Sage Rosenfels* 10.00
211 *Josh Heupel* 10.00
212 *LaDainian Tomlinson* 30.00
213 *Michael Bennett* 20.00
214 *Anthony Thomas* 40.00
215 *Travis Henry* 12.00
216 *James Jackson* 10.00
217 *Correll Buckhalter* 12.00
218 *Derrick Blaylock* 6.00
219 *Dadrian Brown* 6.00
220 *LaVar Woods* 4.00
221 *Deuce McAllister* 15.00
222 *LaMont Jordan* 10.00
223 *Kevan Barlow* 12.00
224 *Travis Minor* 10.00
225 *David Terrell* 25.00
226 *Koren Robinson* 15.00
227 *Rod Gardner* 15.00
228 *Santana Moss* 15.00
229 *Freddie Mitchell* 15.00
230 *Reggie Wayne* 15.00
231 *Quincy Morgan* 10.00
232 *Chris Chambers* 20.00
233 *Steve Smith* 8.00
234 *Marvin "Snoop" Minnis* 12.00
235 *Justin McCareins* 6.00
236 *Onome Ojo* 6.00
237 *Darnerian McCants* 6.00
238 *Bobby Newcombe* 10.00
239 *Cedrick Wilson* 6.00
240 *Kevin Kasper* 8.00
241 *Chris Taylor* 6.00
242 *Ken-Yon Rambo* 8.00
243 *Richmond Flowers* 6.00
244 *Andre King* 6.00
245 *Jabari "Boo" Williams* 6.00
246 *Adrian Wilson* 4.00
247 *Cory Bird* 4.00
248 *Alex Bannister* 8.00
249 *Elvis Joseph* 6.00
250 *Chad Johnson* 10.00
251 *Robert Ferguson* 10.00
252 *David Martin* 8.00
253 *Quentin McCord* 6.00
254 *Todd Heap* 6.00
255 *Alge Crumpler* 6.00
256 *Nate Clements* 6.00
257 *Will Allen* 6.00
258 *Willie Middlebrooks* 6.00
259 *Fred Smoot* 6.00
260 *Andre Dyson* 6.00
261 *Gary Baxter* 4.00
262 *Jamar Fletcher* 6.00
263 *Ken Lucas* 4.00
264 *Tay Cody* 4.00
265 *Eric Kelly* 4.00
266 *Adam Archuleta* 8.00
267 *Derrick Gibson* 6.00
268 *Jarrod Cooper* 4.00
269 *Hakim Akbar* 4.00
270 *Tony Driver* 4.00
271 *Justin Smith* 6.00
272 *Andre Carter* 6.00
273 *Jamal Reynolds* 6.00
274 *Gerard Warren* 8.00
275 *Richard Seymour* 8.00
276 *Damione Lewis* 6.00
277 *Casey Hampton* 4.00
278 *Marcus Stroud* 4.00
279 *Benjamin Gay* 8.00
280 *Shaun Rogers* 4.00
281 *Dan Morgan* 4.00
282 *Kendrell Bell* 20.00
283 *Tommy Polley* 10.00
284 *Jamie Winborn* 4.00
285 *Sedrick Hodge* 4.00
286 *Torrance Marshall* 4.00
287 *Eric Westmoreland* 4.00
288 *Brian Allen* 4.00
289 *Brandon Spoon* 4.00
290 *Henry Burris* 10.00
291 *Leonard Davis* 4.00
292 *Kenyatta Walker* 4.00
293 *Cedric James* 6.00
294 *Sean Brewer* 4.00
295 *Jason Brookins* 8.00
296 *Kyle Vanden Bosch* 8.00
297 *Nick Goings* 6.00
298 *Kris Jenkins* 4.00
299 *Dominic Rhodes* 20.00
300 *Leonard Myers* 4.00

2001 Leaf Rookies & Stars Crosstraining

MT
Common Player: 20.00
Production 100 Sets
1 Terrell Davis, Michael Bennett 30.00
2 Troy Aikman, Quincy Carter 50.00
3 Donovan McNabb, Michael Vick 75.00
4 Randy Moss, Rod Gardner 50.00
5 Corey Dillon, Kevan Barlow 20.00
6 Warren Sapp, Gerard Warren 20.00
7 Marshall Faulk, Deuce McAllister 40.00
8 Edgerrin James, James Jackson 30.00
9 Cris Carter, Reggie Wayne 30.00
10 Barry Sanders, LaDainian Tomlinson 100.00
11 Tim Couch, Drew Brees 50.00
12 Peter Warrick, Marvin "Snoop" Minnis 25.00
13 Torry Holt, Koren Robinson 25.00
14 Isaac Bruce, Santana Moss 25.00
15 Jerry Rice, David Terrell 50.00
16 Tim Brown, Chris Chambers 30.00
17 Emmitt Smith, Travis Henry 60.00
18 Eddie George, Anthony Thomas 50.00
19 Drew Bledsoe, Chris Weinke 25.00
20 Dan Marino, Josh Heupel 100.00
21 Jerome Bettis, Rudi Johnson 20.00
22 Keyshawn Johnson, Chad Johnson 20.00
23 Mark Brunell, Marques Tuiasosopo 25.00
24 Jevon Kearse, Andre Carter 20.00
25 Steve Young, Mike McMahon 50.00

2001 Leaf Rookies & Stars Dress For Success

MT
Common Player: 12.00
Inserted 1:96
Prime Cuts: 1x-2x
Production 50 Sets
1 Tim Brown 25.00
2 Lamar Smith 12.00
3 Boomer Esiason 12.00
4 Dan Marino 100.00
5 Lawrence Taylor 25.00
6 Marshall Faulk 40.00
7 Isaac Bruce 25.00
8 Stephen Davis 20.00
9 Marvin Harrison 20.00
10 Michael Strahan 12.00
11 Jerome Bettis 25.00
12 Cris Carter 25.00
13 Emmitt Smith 75.00
14 Jevon Kearse 12.00
15 Eric Moulds 20.00
16 Curtis Martin 25.00
17 Randy Moss 75.00
18 Peyton Manning 75.00
19 John Elway 100.00
20 Warrick Dunn 25.00
21 Steve Young 50.00
22 Donovan McNabb 40.00
23 Keyshawn Johnson 30.00
24 Ron Dayne 20.00
25 Rich Gannon 12.00

2001 Leaf Rookies & Stars Dress for Success Auto.

MT
"Too Uncommon to Price"
Common Player:
Production 25 Sets
1 Tim Brown
3 Boomer Esiason
4 Dan Marino
6 Marshall Faulk
7 Isaac Bruce
8 Stephen Davis
9 Marvin Harrison
12 Cris Carter
13 Emmitt Smith
15 Eric Moulds
19 John Elway
21 Steve Young
24 Ron Dayne

2001 Leaf Rookies & Stars Freshman Orientation

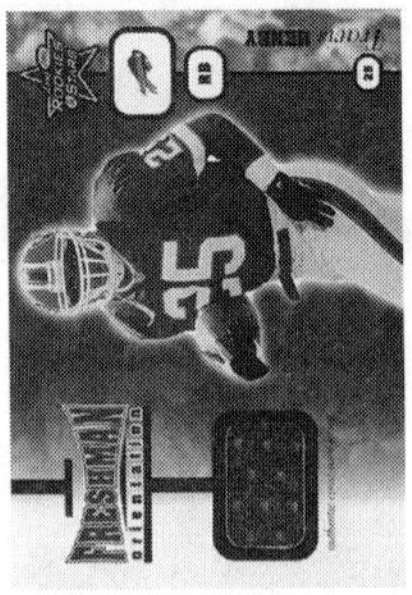

MT
Common Player: 12.00
Inserted 1:96
Class Officers: 2x-4x
Production 50 Sets
1 Michael Vick 50.00
2 Drew Brees 40.00
3 Quincy Carter 25.00
4 Chris Weinke 20.00
5 Santana Moss 20.00
6 Mike McMahon 20.00
7 Jesse Palmer 15.00
8 Deuce McAllister 20.00
9 LaDainian Tomlinson 40.00
10 Anthony Thomas 50.00
11 Michael Bennett 25.00
12 Travis Henry 15.00
13 James Jackson 15.00
14 Kevan Barlow 15.00
15 Rudi Johnson 12.00
16 Travis Minor 15.00
17 David Terrell 25.00
18 Rod Gardner 20.00
19 Quincy Morgan 12.00
20 Freddie Mitchell 20.00
21 Reggie Wayne 20.00
22 Koren Robinson 20.00
23 Chris Chambers 25.00
24 Marvin "Snoop" Minnis 15.00
25 Chad Johnson 15.00

2001 Leaf Rookies & Stars Freshman Orientation Auto.

MT
"Too Uncommon to Price"
Common Player:
Production 25 Sets
4 Chris Weinke
9 LaDainian Tomlinson
19 Quincy Morgan
24 Marvin "Snoop" Minnis
25 Chad Johnson

2001 Leaf Rookies & Stars Player's Collection

MT
Common Player: 25.00
Production 100 Sets
Combo Production 25 Sets
1 Eddie George gloves 25.00
2 Eddie George jersey 25.00
3 Eddie George helmet 25.00
4 Eddie George shoes 25.00
5 Eddie George combo
6 Troy Aikman ball 30.00
7 Troy Aikman jersey 50.00
8 Troy Aikman helmet 50.00
9 Troy Aikman shoes 50.00
10 Troy Aikman combo
11 Kurt Warner pants 50.00
12 Kurt Warner jersey 50.00
13 Kurt Warner helmet 50.00
14 Kurt Warner shoes 50.00
15 Kurt Warner combo

2001 Leaf Rookies & Stars Rookie Autographs

MT
Common Player: 10.00
Production 230 Sets
106 Rudi Johnson 15.00
111 Heath Evans 10.00
113 Moran Norris 10.00
118 Eddie Berlin 10.00
119 Jonathan Carter 10.00
121 T.J. Houshmandzadeh 10.00
123 Reggie Germany 12.00
201 Michael Vick 100.00
202 Drew Brees 80.00
204 Jesse Palmer 20.00
205 Mike McMahon 40.00
206 Dave Dickenson 20.00
209 Chris Weinke 40.00
212 LaDainian Tomlinson 80.00
213 Michael Bennett 40.00
214 Anthony Thomas 100.00
215 Travis Henry 20.00
216 James Jackson 20.00
217 Correll Buckhalter 25.00
218 Derrick Blaylock 12.00
219 Dadrian Brown 10.00
221 Deuce McAllister 40.00
222 LaMont Jordan 15.00
223 Kevan Barlow 15.00
224 Travis Minor 20.00
225 David Terrell 50.00
226 Koren Robinson 30.00
228 Santana Moss 30.00
229 Freddie Mitchell 30.00
231 Quincy Morgan 20.00
233 Steve Smith 15.00
234 Marvin "Snoop" Minnis 25.00
235 Justin McCareins 10.00
236 Onome Ojo 10.00
239 Cedrick Wilson 10.00
240 Kevin Kasper 15.00
242 Ken-Yon Rambo 20.00
248 Alex Bannister 15.00
250 Chad Johnson 20.00
251 Robert Ferguson 20.00
254 Todd Heap 15.00
255 Alge Crumpler 15.00
256 Nate Clements 12.00
257 Will Allen 12.00
271 Justin Smith 12.00
273 Jamal Reynolds 10.00
275 Richard Seymour 12.00
276 Damione Lewis 10.00
277 Casey Hampton 10.00
280 Shaun Rogers 10.00

2001 Leaf Rookies & Stars Slideshow

MT
Common Player: 15.00
Production 100 Sets
View Masters: 4x-8x
Production 25 Sets
1 Barry Sanders 60.00
2 Brett Favre 75.00
3 Brian Griese 20.00
4 Cris Carter 20.00
5 Dan Marino 100.00
6 Daunte Culpepper 30.00
7 Donovan McNabb 30.00
8 Drew Bledsoe 20.00
9 Eddie George 25.00
10 Edgerrin James 40.00
11 Emmitt Smith 60.00
12 Fred Taylor 15.00
13 John Elway 100.00
14 Kurt Warner 60.00
15 Marshall Faulk 30.00
16 Peyton Manning 60.00
17 Randy Moss 60.00
18 Ricky Williams 30.00
19 Ron Dayne 15.00
20 Steve McNair 15.00
21 Steve Young 40.00
22 Terrell Davis 30.00
23 Tim Brown 25.00
24 Tim Couch 25.00
25 Troy Aikman 40.00

2001 Leaf Rookies & Stars Slideshow Auto.

MT
"Too Uncommon to Price"
Common Player:
Production 25 Sets
3 Brian Griese
4 Cris Carter
18 Ricky Williams
21 Steve Young
23 Tim Brown

2001 Leaf Rookies & Stars Statistical Standouts

MT
Common Player: 10.00
Inserted 1:96
Supers: 1x-2x
Production 50 Sets
1 Peyton Manning 25.00
2 Jeff Garcia 15.00
3 Donovan McNabb 20.00
4 Daunte Culpepper 20.00
5 Kurt Warner 25.00
6 Vinny Testaverde 12.00
7 Mark Brunell 12.00
8 Edgerrin James 20.00
9 Eddie George 15.00
10 Mike Anderson 15.00
11 Corey Dillon 12.00
12 Fred Taylor 15.00
13 Marshall Faulk 20.00
14 Stephen Davis 10.00
15 Torry Holt 15.00
16 Rod Smith 12.00
17 Isaac Bruce 15.00
18 Terrell Owens 15.00
19 Randy Moss 30.00
20 Marvin Harrison 15.00
21 Kerry Collins 12.00
22 Junior Seau 10.00
23 Warren Sapp 10.00
24 Donnie Abraham 10.00
25 Dexter McCleon 10.00

2001 Leaf Rookies & Stars Statistical Standouts Auto.

MT
"Too Uncommon to Price"
Common Player:
Production 25 Sets
4 Daunte Culpepper
5 Kurt Warner
6 Vinny Testaverde
7 Mark Brunell
8 Edgerrin James
10 Mike Anderson
11 Corey Dillon
13 Marshall Faulk
14 Stephen Davis
15 Torry Holt
17 Isaac Bruce
18 Terrell Owens
20 Marvin Harrison

2001 Leaf Rookies & Stars Triple Threads

MT
Common Player: 30.00
Production 100 Sets
1 Cris Carter, Daunte Culpepper, Randy Moss 75.00
2 Fred Taylor, Jimmy Smith, Mark Brunell 30.00
3 Edgerrin James, Marvin Harrison, Peyton Manning 100.00
4 Antonio Freeman, Brett Favre, Dorsey Levens 100.00
5 Brian Griese, Ed McCaffrey, Terrell Davis 50.00
6 Isaac Bruce, Kurt Warner, Marshall Faulk 100.00
7 Troy Aikman, Emmitt Smith, Michael Irvin 100.00
8 Keyshawn Johnson, Warren Sapp, Warrick Dunn 30.00
9 Jim Kelly, Thurman Thomas, Andre Reed 50.00
10 Eddie George, Jevon Kearse, Steve McNair 50.00

2001 Leaf Rookies & Stars View Masters Auto.

MT
"Too Uncommon to Price"
Common Player:
Production 5 Sets
1 Barry Sanders
2 Brett Favre
5 Dan Marino
6 Daunte Culpepper
11 Emmitt Smith

A card number in parentheses ( ) indicates the set is unnumbered.

2001 Quantum Leaf

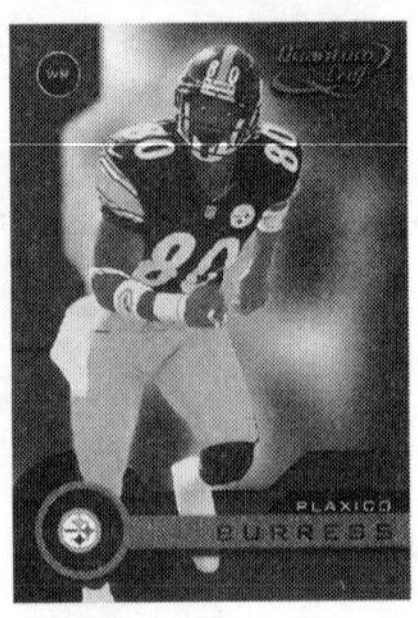

MT
Complete Set (260): 600.00
Common Player: .25
Minor Stars: .50
Common Rookie: 2.00
Inserted 1:2
Common Rookie SP: 70.00
Inserted 1:720
Pack (5): 4.00
Wax Box (24): 75.00
1 David Boston .75
2 Frank Sanders .50
3 Jake Plummer .75
4 Michael Pittman .25
5 Rob Moore .25
6 Thomas Jones .75
7 Chris Chandler .50
8 Doug Johnson .50
9 Jamal Anderson .50
10 Tim Dwight .50
11 Chris Redman .75
12 Jamal Lewis 1.50
13 Qadry Ismail .25
14 Ray Lewis .50
15 Rod Woodson .25
16 Shannon Sharpe .50
17 Travis Taylor .75
18 Trent Dilfer .50
19 Doug Flutie 1.00
20 Eric Moulds .75
21 Jay Riemersma .25
22 Peerless Price .50
23 Rob Johnson .50
24 Sammy Morris .50
25 Shawn Bryson .25
26 Donald Hayes .25
27 Muhsin Muhammad .50
28 Patrick Jeffers .50
29 Reggie White .50
30 Steve Beuerlein .50
31 Tim Biakabutuka .25
32 Wesley Walls .25
33 Brian Urlacher 1.00
34 Cade McNown .75
35 Dez White .25
36 James Allen .50
37 Marcus Robinson .75
38 Marty Booker .25
39 Akili Smith .75
40 Corey Dillon .75
41 Danny Farmer .50
42 Peter Warrick 1.25
43 Ron Dugans .25
44 Courtney Brown .50
45 Dennis Northcutt .50
46 JaJuan Dawson .50
47 Kevin Johnson .50
48 Tim Couch 1.00
49 Travis Prentice .75
50 Anthony Wright .50
51 Emmitt Smith 1.25
52 James McKnight .25
53 Joey Galloway .75
54 Raghib Ismail .25
55 Randall Cunningham .50
56 Troy Aikman 1.25
57 Brian Griese .75
58 Ed McCaffrey .50
59 Gus Frerotte .25
60 John Elway 1.50
61 Mike Anderson 1.50
62 Olandis Gary .75
63 Rod Smith .50
64 Terrell Davis 1.50
65 Barry Sanders 2.00
66 Charlie Batch .75
67 Germane Crowell .75
68 Herman Moore .50
69 James Stewart .50
70 Johnnie Morton .50
71 Ahman Green .50
72 Antonio Freeman .50
73 Bill Schroeder .25
74 Brett Favre 2.50
75 Dorsey Levens .50
76 Matt Hasselbeck .75
77 Edgerrin James 1.75
78 Jerome Pathon .25
79 Ken Dilger .25
80 Marvin Harrison .75
81 Peyton Manning 1.75
82 Fred Taylor 1.00
83 Hardy Nickerson .25
84 Jimmy Smith .50
85 Keenan McCardell .50
86 Mark Brunell 1.00
87 Tony Brackens .25
88 Derrick Alexander .25
89 Elvis Grbac .50
90 Sylvester Morris .75
91 Tony Gonzalez .50
92 Tony Richardson .25
93 Warren Moon .50
94 Dan Marino 1.50
95 Jay Fiedler .50
96 Lamar Smith .50
97 Oronde Gadsden .25
98 Sam Madison .25
99 Thurman Thomas .50
100 Tony Martin .25
101 Zach Thomas .25
102 Cris Carter .75
103 Daunte Culpepper 1.00
104 John Randle .25
105 Randy Moss 1.75
106 Robert Smith .50

107 Drew Bledsoe 1.00
108 J.R. Redmond .50
109 Kevin Faulk .50
110 Michael Bishop .75
111 Terry Glenn .75
112 Troy Brown .25
113 Aaron Brooks .75
114 Jake Reed .50
115 Jeff Blake .50
116 Joe Horn .50
117 La'Roi Glover .25
118 Ricky Williams 1.25
119 Willie Jackson .25
120 Amani Toomer .25
121 Ike Hilliard .25
122 Jason Sehorn .25
123 Kerry Collins .50
124 Michael Strahan .25
125 Ron Dayne 1.25
126 Ron Dixon .50
127 Tiki Barber .50
128 Chad Pennington 1.00
129 Curtis Martin .75
130 Dedric Ward .25
131 Laveranues Coles .75
132 Vinny Testaverde .50
133 Wayne Chrebet .50
134 Charles Woodson .50
135 Napoleon Kaufman .50
136 Rich Gannon .50
137 Tim Brown .50
138 Tyrone Wheatley .50
139 Charles Johnson .25
140 Donovan McNabb 1.00
141 Duce Staley .75
142 Hugh Douglas .25
143 Na Brown .25
144 Todd Pinkston .50
145 Bobby Shaw .25
146 Hines Ward .50
147 Jerome Bettis .50
148 Kordell Stewart .75
149 Levon Kirkland .25
150 Plaxico Burress 1.00
151 Richard Huntley .50
152 Troy Edwards .50
153 Jim Harbaugh .25
154 Junior Seau .50
155 Ryan Leaf .50
156 Charlie Garner .50
157 Jeff Garcia .75
158 Jerry Rice 1.25
159 Steve Young 1.00
160 Terrell Owens .75
161 Brock Huard .75
162 Darrell Jackson .50
163 Derrick Mayes .25
164 Ricky Watters .50
165 Shaun Alexander 1.00
166 Az-Zahir Hakim .50
167 Isaac Bruce .75
168 Kurt Warner 2.00
169 Marshall Faulk .75
170 Torry Holt .50
171 Trent Green .50
172 Derrick Brooks .25
173 Jacquez Green .25
174 John Lynch .25
175 Keyshawn Johnson .75
176 Mike Alstott .50
177 Reidel Anthony .25
178 Shaun King .75
179 Warren Sapp .25
180 Warrick Dunn .50
181 Carl Pickens .50
182 Derrick Mason .50
183 Eddie George .75
184 Frank Wycheck .25
185 Jevon Kearse .50
186 Neil O'Donnell .25
187 Steve McNair .75
188 Yancey Thigpen .25
189 Albert Connell .25
190 Andre Reed .25
191 Brad Johnson .50
192 Bruce Smith .25
193 Champ Bailey .50
194 Darrell Green .25
195 Deion Sanders .75
196 Irving Fryar .25
197 James Thrash .50
198 Jeff George .50
199 Michael Westbrook .50
200 Stephen Davis .50
201 *Michael Vick* 15.00
202 *Drew Brees* 10.00
203 *Chris Weinke* 6.00
204 *Sage Rosenfels* 3.00
205 *Josh Heupel* 4.00
206 *Marques Tuiasosopo* 4.00
207 *Mike McMahon SP* 75.00
208 *Deuce McAllister SP* 75.00
209 *LaMont Jordan* 3.00
210 *LaDainian Tomlinson* 7.00
211 *James Jackson* 2.00
212 *Anthony Thomas* 3.00
213 *Travis Henry* 3.00
214 *Travis Minor* 2.00
215 *Rudi Johnson* 3.00
216 *Michael Bennett* 7.00
217 *Kevan Barlow* 2.00
218 *Dan Alexander* 2.00
219 *Correll Buckhelter SP* 85.00
220 *Moran Norris* 2.00
221 *Jesse Palmer* 3.00
222 *Heath Evans* 2.00
223 *David Terrell SP* 100.00
224 *Santana Moss* 6.00
225 *Rod Gardner* 5.00
226 *Quincy Morgan SP* 50.00
227 *Freddie Mitchell* 3.00
228 *Reggie Wayne* 4.00
229 *Bobby Newcombe* 3.00
230 *Reggie Germany* 2.00
231 *Robert Ferguson* 3.00
232 *Ken-Yon Rambo* 3.00
233 *Alex Bannister* 3.00
234 *Koren Robinson* 5.00
235 *Chad Johnson* 4.00
236 *Chris Chambers* 3.00
237 *Marvin "Snoop" Minnis* 3.00
238 *Vinny Sutherland* 3.00
239 *Cedrick Wilson* 2.00
240 *T.J. Houshmandzadeh* 2.00
241 *Todd Heap* 2.00
242 *Alge Crumpler* 3.00
243 *Jabari Holloway* 3.00
244 *Tony Stewart* 2.00
245 *Jamal Reynolds* 2.00
246 *Andre Carter SP* 75.00
247 *Justin Smith SP* 40.00
248 *Richard Seymour* 2.00
249 *Marcus Stroud* 2.00
250 *Damione Lewis* 2.00
251 *Gerard Warren SP* 60.00
252 *Tommy Polley SP* 50.00
253 *Dan Morgan* 2.00
254 *Jamar Fletcher* 3.00
255 *Ken Lucas* 2.00
256 *Fred Smoot SP* 75.00
257 *Nate Clements* 3.00
258 *Will Allen* 2.00
259 *Derrick Gibson* 3.00
260 *Adam Archuleta* 3.00

2001 Quantum Leaf All-Millennium Marks

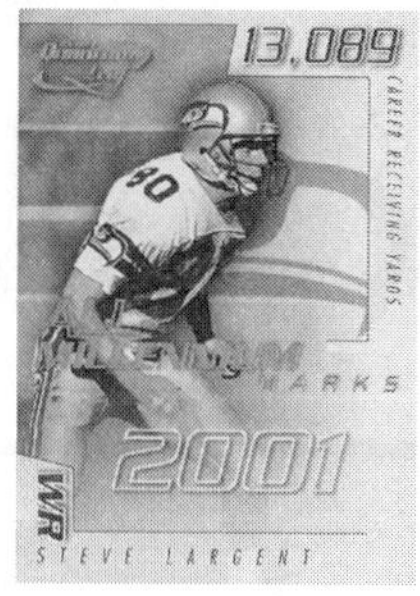

MT
Complete Set (30): 100.00
Common Player: 2.50
Production 1,000 Sets
Autograph Cards: 6x-12x
Production 100 Sets
1 Walter Payton 20.00
2 Barry Sanders 12.00
3 Emmitt Smith 10.00
4 Eric Dickerson 2.50
5 Ricky Watters 2.50
6 Jim Brown 10.00
7 Marcus Allen 4.00
8 Jerome Bettis 2.50
9 Thurman Thomas 2.50
10 Earl Campbell 4.00
11 Jerry Rice 8.00
12 Ozzie Newsome 2.50
13 Henry Ellard 2.50
14 Charlie Taylor 2.50
15 Steve Largent 4.00
16 Cris Carter 4.00
17 Art Monk 2.50
18 Irving Fryar 2.50
19 Michael Irvin 4.00
20 Tim Brown 4.00
21 Dan Marino 10.00
22 John Elway 10.00
23 Warren Moon 2.50
24 Fran Tarkenton 4.00
25 Dan Fouts 4.00
26 Joe Montana 20.00
27 Johnny Unitas 12.00
28 Boomer Esiason 2.50
29 Jim Kelly 5.00
30 Vinny Testaverde 2.50

2001 Quantum Leaf All-Millennium Materials

MT
Common Player: 25.00
Production 100 Sets
Autograph Cards: 2x-3x
Production 25 Sets
1 Walter Payton 150.00
2 Barry Sanders 100.00
3 Emmitt Smith 85.00
4 Eric Dickerson 25.00
5 Ricky Watters 25.00
6 Jim Brown 75.00
7 Marcus Allen 35.00
8 Jerome Bettis 25.00
9 Thurman Thomas 25.00
10 Earl Campbell 40.00
11 Jerry Rice 75.00
12 Ozzie Newsome 25.00
13 Henry Ellard 25.00
14 Charlie Taylor 25.00
15 Steve Largent 35.00
16 Cris Carter 35.00
17 Art Monk 25.00
18 Irving Fryar 25.00
19 Michael Irvin 35.00
20 Tim Brown 35.00
21 Dan Marino 85.00
22 John Elway 85.00
23 Warren Moon 25.00
24 Fran Tarkenton 35.00
25 Dan Fouts 35.00
26 Joe Montana 150.00
27 Johnny Unitas 100.00
28 Boomer Esiason 25.00
29 Jim Kelly 40.00
30 Vinny Testaverde 25.00

2001 Quantum Leaf All-Millennium Milestones

MT
Complete Set (4): 75.00
Common Player: 15.00
Production 1,000 Sets
Autograph Cards: 10x
Production 25 Sets
1 Dan Marino, John Elway 25.00
2 Jerry Rice, Cris Carter 15.00
3 Emmitt Smith, Barry Sanders, Walter Payton 25.00
5 Jerry Rice, Dan Marino, Emmitt Smith 25.00

2001 Quantum Leaf Century Season

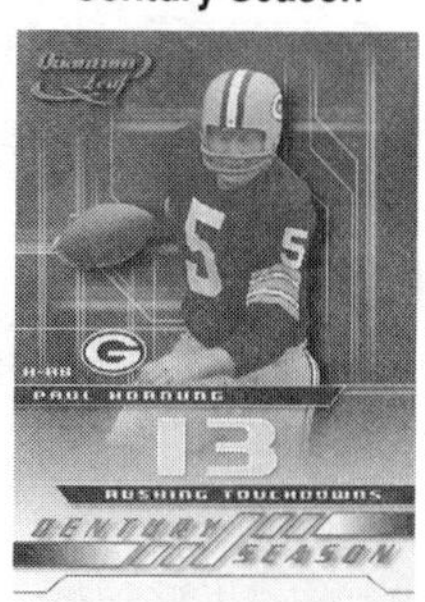

MT
Complete Set (65): 200.00
Common Player: 1.50
Minor Stars: 3.00
Production 1,000 Sets
Autograph Cards: 10x-20x
Production 21 Sets
1 Eric Dickerson 1.50
2 Barry Sanders 12.00
3 John Elway 10.00
4 Jim Brown 12.00
5 Sammy Baugh 1.50
6 Marcus Allen 3.00
7 Tony Gonzalez 1.50
8 Franco Harris 4.00
9 Dan Marino 10.00
10 Mike Singletary 1.50
11 Fred Biletnikoff 1.50
12 Warren Moon 1.50
13 Steve Largent 5.00
14 Fran Tarkenton 3.00
15 Lawrence Taylor 3.00
16 Roger Staubach 8.00
17 Roger Craig 1.50
18 Bart Starr 10.00
19 Gale Sayers 6.00
20 Steve Young 6.00
21 Don Maynard 1.50
22 Joe Montana 18.00
23 Tony Dorsett 4.00
24 Joe Namath 15.00
25 Johnny Unitas 10.00
26 Paul Hornung 5.00
27 Bob Griese 4.00
28 Isaac Bruce 3.00
29 Dan Fouts 3.00
30 Earl Campbell 4.00
31 Terry Bradshaw 8.00
32 Larry Csonka 3.00
33 Jim Kelly 4.00
34 Lance Alworth 1.50
35 Dick Butkus 4.00
36 Sonny Jurgensen 3.00
37 Ozzie Newsome 1.50
38 Kellen Winslow 1.50
39 Stephen Davis 3.00
40 Frank Gifford 5.00
41 Terrell Davis 7.00
42 Reggie White 3.00
43 Edgerrin James 10.00
44 Jerry Rice 8.00
45 Marshall Faulk 4.00
46 Kurt Warner 12.00
47 Cris Carter 3.00
48 Bruce Smith 1.50
49 Emmitt Smith 10.00
50 Ray Lewis 1.50
51 Jamal Lewis 8.00
52 Marvin Harrison 3.00
53 Eric Moulds 3.00
54 Eddie George 4.00
55 Ricky Williams 5.00
56 Mark Brunell 5.00
57 Brian Griese 3.00
58 Brett Favre 12.00
59 Daunte Culpepper 6.00
60 Mike Anderson 7.00
61 Donovan McNabb 5.00
62 Randall Cunningham 1.50
63 Drew Bledsoe 5.00
64 Troy Aikman 8.00
65 Randy Moss 10.00

2001 Quantum Leaf Gamers

MT
Common Player: 100.00
Production 25 Sets
1 Akili Smith 100.00
2 Corey Dillon 130.00
3 Donovan McNabb 175.00
4 Edgerrin James 250.00
5 Fred Taylor 150.00
6 Isaac Bruce 140.00
7 Shaun King 100.00
8 Tim Couch 200.00
9 Dan Marino, John Elway, Jim Kelly 400.00
10a Tim Couch, Daunte Culpepper, Donovan McNabb, Akili Smith, Cade McNown, Shaun King 500.00

2001 Quantum Leaf Hardwear

MT
Common Player: 25.00
Production 100 Sets
1 Akili Smith 35.00
2 Charlie Garner 25.00
3 Corey Dillon 35.00
4 Dan Marino 125.00
5 Donovan McNabb 70.00
6 Duce Staley 35.00
7 Edgerrin James 100.00
8 Fred Taylor 40.00
9 Isaac Bruce 40.00
10 Jamal Anderson 35.00
11 Jason Sehorn 25.00
12 Jay Fiedler 35.00
13 Jerome Bettis 35.00
14 Jerry Rice 85.00
15 John Elway 125.00
16 Junior Seau 25.00
17 Ray Lewis 35.00
18 Reggie White 35.00
19 Ricky Watters 25.00
20 Ryan Leaf 35.00
21 Shaun King 35.00
22 Steve Young 70.00
23 Terrell Davis 85.00
24 Terry Glenn 35.00
25 Tim Couch 75.00
26 Torry Holt 35.00
27 Vinny Testaverde 35.00
28 Warren Sapp 35.00
29 Wayne Chrebet 35.00
30 Zach Thomas 35.00

2001 Quantum Leaf Rookie Revolution

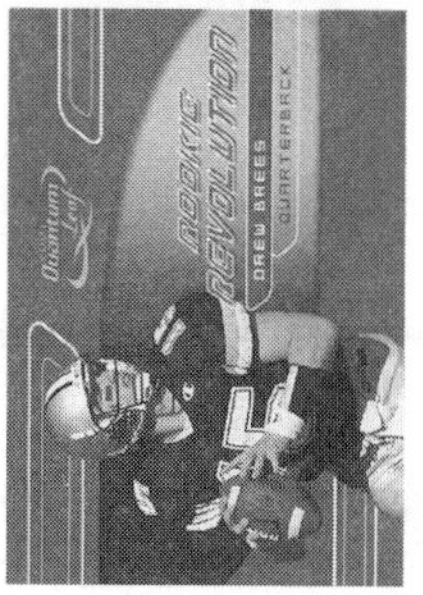

MT
Complete Set (20): 45.00
Common Player: 1.50
Minor Stars: 3.00
Production 4,000 Sets
Autograph Cards: 10x-20x
1 Michael Vick 12.00
2 David Terrell 7.00
3 Deuce McAllister 6.00
4 Drew Brees 10.00
5 Santana Moss 7.00
6 Anthony Thomas 4.00
7 Chris Weinke 5.00
8 Rod Gardner 4.00
9 LaDainian Tomlinson 8.00
10 Quincy Carter 1.50
11 Koren Robinson 6.00
12 Travis Henry 3.50
13 Quincy Morgan 3.00
14 LaMont Jordan 3.50
15 Rudi Johnson 3.50
16 Reggie Wayne 4.00
17 Michael Bennett 6.00
18 Freddie Mitchell 3.50
19 Chris Chambers 3.00
20 Chad Johnson 1.50

2001 Quantum Leaf Shirt Off My Back

MT
Common Player: 30.00
Production 100 Sets
1 Jamal Lewis 100.00
2 Mike Anderson 100.00
3 Ron Dayne 70.00
4 Peter Warrick 70.00
5 Shaun Alexander 60.00
6 Warrick Dunn 30.00
7 Shaun King 30.00
8 Tim Couch 60.00
9 Cade McNown 35.00
10 Akili Smith 35.00
11 Rich Gannon 30.00
12 Daunte Culpepper 100.00
13 Randy Moss 150.00
14 Cris Carter 35.00
15 Robert Smith 30.00
16 Kurt Warner 150.00
17 Marshall Faulk 60.00
18 Ricky Williams 70.00
19 Terrell Owens 30.00
20 Corey Dillon 35.00
21 Fred Taylor 40.00
22 Edgerrin James 150.00
23 Curtis Martin 35.00
24 Donovan McNabb 50.00
25 Steve McNair 40.00
26 Peyton Manning 150.00
27 Eric Moulds 35.00
28 Stephen Davis 35.00
29 Brian Griese 40.00
30 Isaac Bruce 35.00

2001 Quantum Leaf Star Factor

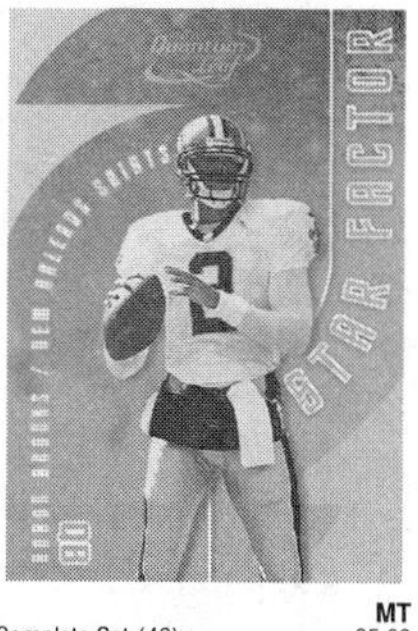

MT
Complete Set (40): 85.00
Common Player: 1.50
Production 2,000 Sets
X-Factor Cards: 5x-10x
Production 25 Sets
1 Peyton Manning 10.00
2 Edgerrin James 10.00
3 Marvin Harrison 1.50
4 Curtis Martin 1.50
5 Eric Moulds 1.50
6 Dan Marino 8.00
7 Jake Plummer 1.50
8 Troy Aikman 6.00
9 Jamal Lewis 8.00
10 Eddie George 2.50
11 Steve McNair 1.50
12 Steve Young 3.00
13 Jerome Bettis 1.50
14 Tim Couch 4.00
15 Mark Brunell 3.00
16 Fred Taylor 3.00
17 Corey Dillon 1.50
18 Chad Pennington 6.00
19 Brian Griese 2.50
20 Mike Anderson 8.00
21 John Elway 8.00
22 Terrell Owens 1.50
23 Rich Gannon 1.50
24 Jerry Rice 6.00
25 Ricky Williams 4.00
26 Aaron Brooks 3.00
27 Kurt Warner 10.00
28 Marshall Faulk 3.00
29 Isaac Bruce 2.50
30 Brett Favre 10.00
31 Antonio Freeman 1.50
32 Daunte Culpepper 4.00
33 Randy Moss 10.00
34 Cris Carter 1.50
35 Barry Sanders 10.00
36 Emmitt Smith 7.00
37 Stephen Davis 1.50
38 Ron Dayne 6.00
39 Donovan McNabb 3.00
40 Peter Warrick 6.00

2001 Quantum Leaf Touchdown Club

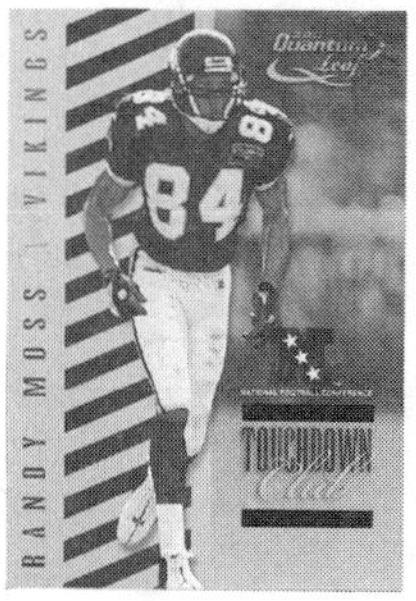

MT
Complete Set (40):
Common Player: 1.50
Production 2,000 Sets
1 Marshall Faulk 3.00
2 Edgerrin James 6.00
3 Randy Moss 6.00
4 Eddie George 2.50
5 Terrell Owens 2.00
6 Mike Anderson 5.00
7 Stephen Davis 2.00
8 Marvin Harrison 2.00
9 Robert Smith 1.50
10 Fred Taylor 2.50
11 Daunte Culpepper 3.50
12 Curtis Martin 1.50
13 Emmitt Smith 5.00
14 Jamal Lewis 5.00
15 Ricky Williams 3.50
16 John Elway 5.00
17 Jerry Rice 5.00
18 Peyton Manning 6.00
19 Kurt Warner 7.00
20 Tim Brown 1.50
21 Brett Favre 8.00
22 Jimmy Smith 1.50
23 Cris Carter 2.00
24 Terrell Davis 5.00
25 Jeff Garcia 2.00
26 Peter Warrick 3.00
27 Ron Dayne 3.00
28 Tony Gonzalez 1.50
29 Isaac Bruce 2.00
30 Drew Bledsoe 2.50
31 Marcus Robinson 2.00
32 Ricky Watters 1.50
33 Ahman Green 1.50
34 Dan Marino 5.00
35 Donovan McNabb 2.50
36 Eric Moulds 1.50
37 Aaron Brooks 2.00
38 Steve McNair 1.50
39 Barry Sanders 7.00
40 Brian Griese 2.50

2001 Quantum Leaf X-Ponential Power

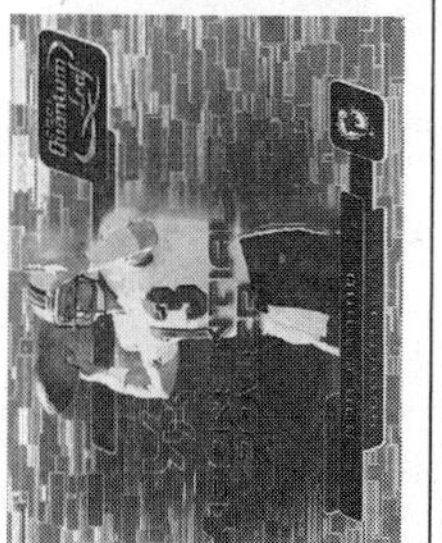

MT
Complete Set (10):
Common Player:
1 Kurt Warner 6.00
2 Peyton Manning 6.00
3 Steve Young 6.00
4 Dan Marino 10.00
5 Jerry Rice 6.00
6 John Elway 10.00
7 Barry Sanders 10.00
8 Steve McNair 6.00
9 Brett Favre 10.00
10 Terrell Davis 6.00

1961 Lions Jay Publishing

Measuring approximately 5" x 7", the 12-card set showcases black-and-white photos of players in the vintage football card poses. The blank-backed cards were sold in 12-card packs for 25 cents. The cards were unnumbered.

NM
Complete Set (12): 65.00
Common Player: 5.00
1 Carl Brettschneider 5.00
2 Howard Cassady 6.00
3 Gail Cogdill 5.00
4 Jim Gibbons 6.00
5 Alex Karras 12.00
6 Yale Lary 10.00
7 Jim Martin 5.00
8 Earl Morrall 8.00
9 Jim Ninowski 6.00
10 Nick Pietrosante 6.00
11 Joe Schmidt 10.00
12 George Wilson 5.00

1964 Lions White Border

Measuring 7-3/8" x 9-3/8", the 24-card set includes black-and-white photos that are bordered in white. The player's name and position, along with the Detroit Lions, are printed under the photo. The unnumbered cards could have been released in many series, as later cards have a date stamped on the otherwise blank backs.

NM
Complete Set (24): 90.00
Common Player: 4.00
1 Dick Compton 4.00
2 Larry Ferguson 4.00
3 Dennis Gaubatz 4.00
4 Jim Gibbons 5.00
5 John Gonzaga 4.00
6 John Gordy 5.00
7 Tom Hall 4.00
8 Roger LaLonde 4.00
9 Dan LaRose 4.00
10 Yale Lary 10.00
11 Dan Lewis 5.00
12 Gary Lowe 4.00
13 Bruce Maher 5.00
14 Hugh McInnis 4.00
15 Max Messner 4.00
16 Floyd Peters 6.00
17 Daryl Sanders 4.00
18 Joe Schmidt 12.00
19 Bob Scholtz 4.00
20 James Simon 4.00
21 J.D. Smith 5.00
22 Bill Quinlan 4.00
23 Bob Whitlow 4.00
24 Sam Williams 4.00

1966 Lions Marathon Oil

The 5" x 7" photos showcase black-and-white photos on the front, surrounded by white borders. The player's name, position and Detroit Lions are printed under the photo. The backs are unnumbered and blank.

NM
Complete Set (7): 42.00
Common Player: 5.00
1 Gail Cogdill 5.00
2 John Gordy 5.00
3 Alex Karras 15.00
4 Ron Kramer 6.00
5 Milt Plum 8.00
6 Wayne Rasmussen 5.00
7 Daryl Sanders 5.00

1986 Lions Police

Measuring 2-5/8" x 4-1/8", this 14-card police set is sponsored by Oscar Mayer, WJR/WHYT, Detroit Lions, Claussen, Pontiac Police Athletic League and the Detroit Crime Prevention Section. Card fronts have the player's name, uniform number and position in a box at the bottom center, while the Lions' logo is at the top center. A white border surrounds the photo. The card backs have the player's name, bio and highlights in a box on the left of the horizontal backed cards. A safety tip is located on the right.

MT
Complete Set (14): 5.00
Common Player: .50
1 William Gay .50
2 Pontiac Silverdome .60
3 Leonard Thompson .60
4 Eddie Murray 1.00
5 Eric Hipple 1.00
6 James Jones .75
7 Darryl Rogers (CO) .50
8 Chuck Long .75
9 Garry James .60
10 Michael Cofer .60
11 Jeff Chadwick .60

12	Jimmy Williams	.50
13	Keith Dorney	.50
14	Bobby Watkins	.50

1987 Lions Police

Measuring 2-5/8" x 4-1/8", the 14-card set is sponsored by Oscar Mayer, WJR/WHYT, Claussen, Detroit Lions, Pontiac Police Athletic League and the Detroit Crime Prevention Section. The card fronts have the Lions and NFL logos at the top, with the photo in the center. The player's name, uniform number and position are printed inside a box at the bottom center. The Oscar Mayer and Claussen logos are in the lower corners of the card front. The card backs include a cartoon in the upper left, with the player's highlights. The upper left has a safety tip.

		MT
Complete Set (14):		5.00
Common Player:		.40
1	Michael Cofer, Vernon Maxwell, William Gay	.50
2	Rich Strenger	.40
3	Keith Ferguson	.40
4	James Jones	.50
5	Jeff Chadwick	.50
6	Devon Mitchell	.40
7	Eddie Murray	.75
8	Reggie Rogers	.50
9	Chuck Long	.60
10	Jimmie Giles	.60
11	Eric Williams	.40
12	Lomas Brown	.50
13	Jimmy Williams	.40
14	Garry James	.50

1988 Lions Police

Measuring 2-5/8" x 4-1/8", the 14-card set boasts 13 single-player cards which feature veterans. The remaining card has three of the Lions' top three 1988 draft picks. The card fronts have the Lions logo under the photo, which is opposite the 1987 Lions Police set. The card backs have the standard career highlights and safety tips.

		MT
Complete Set (14):		5.00
Common Player:		.50
1	Rob Rubick	.50
2	Paul Butcher	.50
3	Pete Mandley	.60
4	Jimmy Williams	.50
5	Harvey Salem	.50
6	Chuck Long	.60
7	Pat Carter, Bennie Blades, Chris Spielman	1.00
8	Jerry Ball	.75
9	Lomas Brown	.60
10	Dennis Gibson	.50
11	Jim Arnold	.50
12	Michael Cofer	.50
13	James Jones	.60
14	Steve Mott	.50

1989 Lions Police

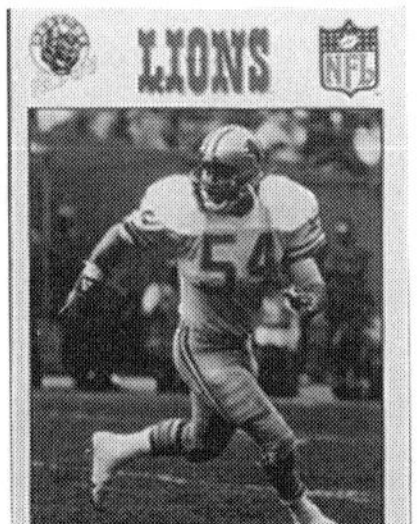

Measuring 2-5/8" x 4-1/8", the 12-card set has the Lions logo and NFL shields at the top. The player's name, uniform number and position are printed in a box at the bottom, sandwiched between Oscar Mayer and Claussen logos. The backs feature a cartoon in the upper left, with a highlight directly under it. The horizontal backs also include a safety tip in the upper right. A WWJ logo is printed at the bottom left, with the card number located at bottom center. The cards are printed on thin paper stock. These cards were distributed in Michigan and Ontario.

		MT
Complete Set (12):		14.00
Common Player:		.35
1	George Jamison	.35
2	Wayne Fontes (CO)	.75
3	Kevin Glover	.35
4	Chris Spielman	1.00
5	Eddie Murray	.75
6	Bennie Blades	.75
7	Joe Milinichik	.35
8	Michael Cofer	.35
9	Jerry Ball	.50
10	Dennis Gibson	.35
11	Barry Sanders	10.00
12	Jim Arnold	.35

1990 Lions Police

Measuring 2-5/8" x 4-1/8", the 12-card set includes the player's name and position at the bottom center, with his uniform number printed in much larger type. The Oscar Mayer and Claussen logos are in the lower left and right corners, respectively. The card backs have the player's name at the top, with a drawing of him and highlight directly under. A "Little Oscar" safety tip is included in the lower left. The card number is in the lower right, along with the WWJ Radio logo.

		MT
Complete Set (12):		5.00
Common Player:		.35
1	William White	.35
2	Chris Spielman	.75
3	Rodney Peete	.75
4	Jimmy Williams	.35
5	Bennie Blades	.50
6	Barry Sanders	3.00
7	Jerry Ball	.50
8	Richard Johnson	.50
9	Michael Cofer	.35
10	Lomas Brown	.50
11	Joe Schmidt, Andre Ware, Wayne Fontes	.50
12	Eddie Murray	.50

1991 Lions Police

Measuring 2-5/8" x 4-1/8", the 12-card set was available through Michigan police officers. The yellow-bordered cards feature a color action photo, with the Oscar Mayer logo in the lower left, the player's name in the lower center and Lions helmet in the lower right. Above and below the player's name are blue horizontal lines. Card backs include a player photo at the top, with his position and name below it. A Little Oscar safety tip is in the lower left. The cards are numbered and are located in the lower right. The WWJ Radio logo is in the lower right.

		MT
Complete Set (12):		5.00
Common Player:		.35
1	Mel Gray	.50
2	Ken Dallafior	.35
3	Chris Spielman	.50
4	Bennie Blades	.50
5	Robert Clark	.50
6	Eric Andolsek	.50
7	Rodney Peete	.75
8	William White	.35
9	Lomas Brown	.50
10	Jerry Ball	.50
11	Michael Cofer	.35
12	Barry Sanders	3.00

1993 Lions 60th Season Commemorative

After years of odd-sized cards, the Lions finally introduced a standard-sized set. The 16-card set features full-bleed photos on the front, with the Lions' 60th anniversary logo in one of the upper corners. The player's name or, in some cases, the card's caption are printed in a rectangle at the bottom. The horizontal card backs feature the player's name and the years he played with the team in the upper left. His career highlights are printed along the left side, with a black-and-white headshot of the player in the upper right. The Lions' 60th anniversary logo is in the lower right, along with the card number. The cards were housed in a 6" x 8" black binder.

		MT
Complete Set (16):		10.00
Common Player:		.50
1	Barry Sanders	5.00
2	Joe Schmidt	1.00
3	The Fearsome Foursome (Sam Williams, Roger Brown, Alex Karras, Darris McCord)	.75
4	Chris Spielman	.75
5	Billy Sims	.75
6	'40s Phenoms (Alex Wojciechowicz, Byron White)	.75
7	Thunder and Lightning (Bennie Blades, Mel Gray)	.50
8	Bobby Layne	1.50
9	Dutch Clark	.75
10	Great Games, Thanksgiving 1962	.50
11	Charlie Sanders	.75
12	Lomas Brown	.50
13	Doug English	.75
14	Doak Walker	1.50
15	Roaring 20's (Lem Barney, Billy Sims, Barry Sanders)	2.00
16	Anniversary Card	.50

1990 Little Big Leaguers

Boyhood photos and the highlights of the player's early athletic career are included in this 45-card set. The book, published by Simon and Schuster, included five 8-1/2" x 11" sheets, which included nine perforated cards. The card fronts included a black-and-white photo of the athlete as a child. A white border surrounds the card, with the player's name printed in a blue band at the top and "Little Football Big Leaguers" printed in a blue band at the bottom. The backs include the player's name, position, team, bio and write-up. The cards are unnumbered.

		MT
Complete Set (45):		40.00
Common Player:		.50
1	Troy Aikman	10.00
2	Morten Andersen	.50
3	Jerry Ball	.50
4	Carl Banks	.75
5	Bennie Blades	.50
6	Brian Blades	.75
7	Joey Browner	.50
8	Keith Byars	.75
9	Anthony Carter	.75
10	Deron Cherry	.50
11	Roger Craig	.75
12	John Elway	7.00
13	Doug Flutie	1.00
14	Tim Goad	.50
15	Bob Golic	.50
16	Dino Hackett	.50
17	Dan Hampton	.75
18	Bobby Hebert	.75
19	Darryl Henley	.50
20	Wes Hopkins	.50
21	Hank Ilesic	.50
22	Tunch Ilkin	.50
23	Perry Kemp	.50
24	Bernie Kosar	.75
25	Mike Lansford	.50
26	Shawn Lee	.50
27	Charles Mann	.75
28	Dan Marino	14.00
29	Bruce Matthews	.75
30	Clay Matthews	.75
31	Freeman McNeil	.75
32	Warren Moon	2.00
33	Anthony Munoz	.75
34	Andre Reed	1.00
35	Andre Rison	.75
36	Phil Simms	.75
37	Mike Singletary	.75
38	Rohn Stark	.50
39	Kelly Stouffer	.50
40	Vinny Testaverde	.75
41	Doug Williams	.50
42	Marc Wilson	.50
43	Craig Wolfley	.50
44	Ron Wolfley	.50
45	Steve Young	7.00

M

1977 Marketcom Test

With posters measuring approximately 5-1/2" x 8-1/2", the set boasts only two confirmed mini-posters. The unnumbered posters each have folds in them. They are blank-backed, except for a Marketcom 1977 copyright tag line at the bottom.

		NM
Complete Set (2):		100.00
Common Player:		50.00
1	Greg Pruitt	50.00
2	Jack Youngblood	50.00

1978 Marketcom Test

These unnumbered posters, featuring 32 NFL stars, measure 5-1/2" x 8-1/2". The fronts feature full-color photos, along with the player's name in the upper left corner. Marketcom, which produced the set, is listed in the lower right corner. The backs are blank.

		NM
Complete Set (32):		225.00
Common Player:		4.00
(1)	Otis Armstrong	6.00
(2)	Steve Bartkowski	9.00
(3)	Terry Bradshaw	25.00
(4)	Earl Campbell	25.00
(5)	Dave Casper	5.00
(6)	Dan Dierdorf	10.00
(7)	Dan Fouts	15.00
(8)	Tony Galbreath	4.00
(9)	Randy Gradishar	7.00
(10)	Bob Griese	12.00
(11)	Steve Grogan	5.00
(12)	Ray Guy	6.00
(13)	Pat Haden	8.00
(14)	Jack Ham	7.00
(15)	Cliff Harris	7.00
(16)	Franco Harris	8.00
(17)	Jim Hart	5.00
(18)	Ron Jaworski	5.00
(19)	Bert Jones	10.00
(20)	Jack Lambert	10.00
(21)	Reggie McKenzie	4.00
(22)	Karl Mecklenburg	7.00
(23)	Craig Morton	5.00
(24)	Dan Pastorini	4.00
(25)	Walter Payton	25.00
(26)	Lee Roy Selmon	5.00
(27)	Roger Staubach	25.00
(28)	Joe Theismann (misspelled Theisman)	9.00
(29)	Wesley Walker	7.00
(30)	Randy White	7.00
(31)	Jack Youngblood	12.00
(32)	Jim Zorn	5.00

A player's name in *italic type* indicates a rookie card.

1980 Marketcom

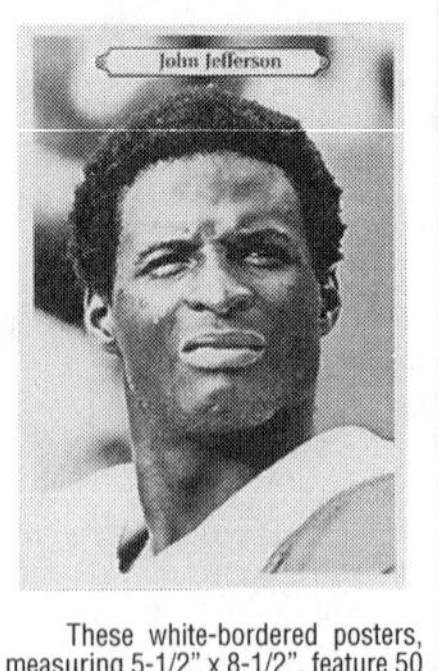

These white-bordered posters, measuring 5-1/2" x 8-1/2", feature 50 NFL stars. The player's name appears at the top of the card; Marketcom, the set's producer, is credited in the bottom lower right corner. A white facsimile autograph also appears on the card front. The back has the player's name at the top, and a card number on the bottom (Mini-Poster 1 of 50, etc.). Marketcom, of St. Louis, sold the posters in packs of five.

		NM
Complete Set (50):		25.00
Common Player:		.50
1	Ottis Anderson	1.00
2	Brian Sipe	.60
3	Lawrence McCutcheon	.60
4	Ken Anderson	1.25
5	Roland Harper	.50
6	Chuck Foreman	.75
7	Gary Danielson	.50
8	Wallace Francis	.50
9	John Jefferson	.75
10	Charlie Waters	.75
11	Jack Ham	1.00
12	Jack Lambert	1.25
13	Walter Payton	5.00
14	Bert Jones	1.00
15	Harvey Martin	.75
16	Jim Hart	.60
17	Craig Morton	.75
18	Reggie McKenzie	.50
19	Keith Wortman	.50
20	Otis Armstrong	.75
21	Steve Grogan	.75
22	Jim Zorn	.75
23	Bob Griese	2.00
24	Tony Dorsett	2.00
25	Wesley Walker	.75
26	Dan Fouts	2.00
27	Dan Dierdorf	1.00
28	Steve Bartkowski	.75
29	Archie Manning	1.00
30	Randy Gradishar	.75
31	Randy White	1.25
32	Joe Theismann	2.00
33	Tony Galbreath	.50
34	Cliff Harris	.75
35	Ray Guy	1.00
36	Dave Casper	.75
37	Ron Jaworski	.75
38	Greg Pruitt	.75
39	Ken Burrough	.60
40	Robert Brazile	.60
41	Pat Haden	1.00
42	Dan Pastorini	.60
43	Lee Roy Selmon	.75
44	Franco Harris	2.00
45	Jack Youngblood	1.25
46	Terry Bradshaw	5.00
47	Roger Staubach	6.00
48	Earl Campbell	5.00
49	Phil Simms	3.00
50	Delvin Williams	.50

1981 Marketcom

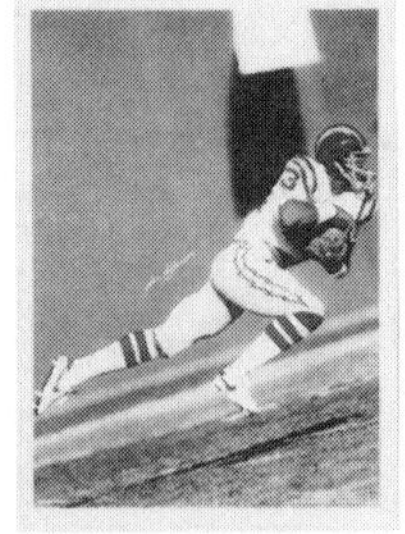

The 1981 Marketcom posters are the first set to include detailed information on the back of the poster. Along with biographical and statistical information for 1980 and for the player's career, a comprehensive summary of the player's accomplishments is provided. A poster number is also given. Each poster, measuring 5-1/2" x 8-1/2", has a full-color action photo of the player on the front, along with his facsimile signature. His name is listed in the upper left corner.

		MT
Complete Set (50):		32.00
Common Player:		.50
1	Ottis Anderson	.75
2	Brian Sipe	.60
3	Rocky Bleier	.75
4	Ken Anderson	1.00
5	Roland Harper	.50
6	Steve Furness	.50
7	Gary Danielson	.50
8	Wallace Francis	.60
9	John Jefferson	.60
10	Charlie Waters	.75
11	Jack Ham	.75
12	Jack Lambert	1.25
13	Walter Payton	5.00
14	Bert Jones	1.00
15	Harvey Martin	.75
16	Jim Hart	.75
17	Craig Morton	.50
18	Reggie McKenzie	.50
19	Keith Wortman	.50
20	Joe Greene	1.50
21	Steve Grogan	.75
22	Jim Zorn	.75
23	Bob Griese	2.00
24	Tony Dorsett	2.50
25	Wesley Walker	.75
26	Dan Fouts	2.00
27	Dan Dierdorf	1.00
28	Steve Bartkowski	.75
29	Archie Manning	1.00
30	Randy Gradishar	.75
31	Randy White	1.25
32	Joe Theismann	2.00
33	Tony Galbreath	.50
34	Cliff Harris	.75
35	Ray Guy	1.00
36	Joe Ferguson	.75
37	Ron Jaworski	.75
38	Greg Pruitt	.75
39	Ken Burrough	.60
40	Robert Brazile	.50
41	Pat Haden	1.00
42	Ken Stabler	2.00
43	Lee Roy Selmon	.75
44	Franco Harris	2.00
45	Jack Youngblood	1.25
46	Terry Bradshaw	6.00
47	Roger Staubach	6.00
48	Earl Campbell	4.00
49	Phil Simms	1.50
50	Delvin Williams	.50

1982 Marketcom

These 50 mini-posters from Marketcom are similar in design to the previous year's issue. Each poster is 5-1/2" x 8-1/2" and has a full-color action photo on the front, along with a facsimile signature in white letters. The backs are similar to the backs of the 1981 posters - they have a detailed career summary and biographical information, plus statistics for the player's career and 1981 season. In addition to a number, the back also says "St. Louis - Marketcom - Series C".

		MT
Complete Set (48):		175.00
Common Player:		2.00
1	Joe Ferguson	2.50
2	Kellen Winslow	3.00
3	Jim Hart	2.50
4	Archie Manning	4.00
5	Earl Campbell	15.00
6	Wallace Francis	2.00
7	Randy Gradishar	2.50
8	Ken Stabler	5.00
9	Danny White	3.00
10	Jack Ham	4.00
11	Lawrence Taylor	20.00
12	Eric Hipple	2.00
13	Ron Jaworski	2.50
14	George Rogers	2.00
15	Jack Lambert	5.00
16	Randy White	5.00
17	Terry Bradshaw	20.00
18	Ray Guy	3.00
19	Rob Carpenter	2.00
20	Reggie McKenzie	2.00
21	Tony Dorsett	7.50
22	Wesley Walker	2.50
23	Tommy Kramer	2.50
24	Dwight Clark	3.00
25	Franco Harris	5.00
26	Craig Morton	2.50
27	Harvey Martin	2.50
28	Jim Zorn	2.50
29	Steve Bartkowski	2.50
30	Joe Theismann	5.00
31	Dan Dierdorf	3.00
32	Walter Payton	25.00
33	John Jefferson	2.50
34	Phil Simms	5.00
35	Lee Roy Selmon	2.50
36	Joe Montana	40.00
37	Robert Brazile	2.00
38	Steve Grogan	2.50
39	Dave Logan	2.00
40	Ken Anderson	4.00
41	Richard Todd	2.50
42	Jack Youngblood	3.00
43	Ottis Anderson	3.00
44	Brian Sipe	2.50
45	Mark Gastineau	2.50
46	Mike Pruitt	2.00
47	Cris Collinsworth	2.50
48	Dan Fouts	5.00

1982 Marketcom Cowboys

Measuring 5-1/2" x 8-1/2", these nine NFL mini-posters feature the player's name at the top left, with a color photo dominating the white-bordered fronts. The player's facsimile autograph also appears on the photo. The unnumbered card backs showcase the player's name at the top, with his bio directly underneath. His career highlights are also included. "St. Louis Marketcom" is printed in the lower right of the back. Some experts say a 10th card may exist.

		MT
Complete Set (9):		50.00
Common Player:		5.00
1	Bob Breunig	5.00
2	Pat Donovan	5.00
3	Michael Downs	5.00
4	Butch Johnson	6.00
5	Harvey Martin	6.00
6	Timmy Newsome	5.00
7	Drew Pearson	6.00
8	Danny White	8.00
9	Randy White	10.00

1971 Mattel Mini-Records

Measuring approximately 2-1/2" in diameter, each of the 17 discs in the set were to be played on a specially made Mattel mini-record player. Some discs were packaged four to a pack, like Olsen, Hayes, Sayers and Brodie or Mackey, Lamonica, Simpson and Butkus. Other packs showcased eight discs and a Joe Namath or Bart Starr booklet. The discs have color artwork on one side and the recording on the reverse. The recording side has the player's name and "Instant Replay."

		NM
Complete Set (17):		200.00
Common Player:		4.00
1	Donny Anderson	4.00
2	Lem Barney	6.00
3	John Brodie (DP)	6.00
4	Dick Butkus (DP)	15.00
5	Bob Hayes (DP)	6.00
6	Sonny Jurgensen	10.00
7	Alex Karras	10.00
8	Leroy Kelly	9.00
9	Daryle Lamonica (DP)	4.00
10	John Mackey (DP)	6.00
11	Earl Morrall	4.00
12	Joe Namath	50.00
13	Merlin Olsen (DP)	6.00
14	Alan Page	9.00
15	Gale Sayers (DP)	20.00
16	O.J. Simpson (DP)	25.00
17	Bart Starr	30.00
NNO	Record Player	100.00

1894 Mayo

Thirty-five Ivy League college football players are included in this 35-card set. The card fronts include a sepia-toned photo and a black border. The player's name, college and Mayo Cut Plug advertisement are listed at the bottom. The unnumbered cards measure 1-5/8" x 2-7/8".

		NM
Complete Set (35):		32500.
Common Player:		750.00
1	R Acton (Harvard)	1000.
2	George Adee (Yale AA94)	1500.
3	R. Armstrong (Yale)	1000.
4	H.W. Barnett (Princeton)	1200.
5	A.M. Beale (Harvard)	825.00
6	Anson Beard (Yale)	1600.
7	Charles Brewer (Harvard AA92/93/95)	750.00
8	Brown (Princeton)	1200.
9	Burt (Princeton)	1000.
10	Frank Butterworth (Yale AA93/94)	750.00
11	Eddie Crowdis (Princeton)	900.00
12	Robert Emmons (Harvard)	1000.
13	M.G. Gonterman (UER Harvard) (Misspelled Gouterman)	1000.
14	G.A. Grey (Harvard)	750.00
15	John Greenway (Yale)	900.00
16	William Hickok (Yale AA93/94)	1000.
17	Frank Hinkey (Yale AA91/92/93/94)	4500.
18	Augustus Holly (Princeton)	1000.
19	Langdon Lea (Princeton AA93/94/95)	900.00
20	W.C. Mackie (Harvard)	1000.
21	T.J. Manahan (Harvard)	1000.
22	Jim McCrea (Yale)	1000.
23	Frank Morse (Princeton AA93)	750.00
24	Fred Murphy (Yale AA95/96)	1000.
25	Poe (Princeton thought to be Neilson or Arthur)	3500.
26	Dudley Riggs (Princeton AA95)	1200.
27	Phillip Stillman (Yale AA94)	1200.
28	Knox Taylor (Princeton)	1500.
29	Brinck Thorne (Yale AA95)	800.00
30	Thomas Trenchard (Princeton AA93)	750.00
31	William Ward (Princeton)	800.00
32	Bert Waters (Harvard AA92/94)	1000.
33	Arthur Wheeler (Princeton AA92/93/94)	1000.
34	Edgar Wrightington (Harvard AA96)	1000.
35	Anonymous (reportedly John Dunlop-Harvard)	3000.

1975 McDonald's Quarterbacks

Measuring 2-1/2" x 3-7/16", this four-card set was a McDonald's promotion. The yellow-bordered card fronts showcase the player's name and team at the top, with a photo in the center. Printed below the photo is "Get a quarter back..." The Mc-

Donald's logo is in the lower right. The backs of each card have different colors. The unnumbered card backs have the player's name, position and team at the top, with his stats below. The perforated coupon below explains the promotion. Each card was good for one week. Prices are for cards which have the coupons intact.

		NM
Complete Set (4):		10.00
Common Player:		.50
1	Terry Bradshaw	6.00
2	Joe Ferguson	1.00
3	Ken Stabler	4.00
4	Al Woodall	.50

1985 McDonald's Bears

This 32-card set picturing only Chicago Bears was issued by McDonald's in the Chicago area, apparently to test the concept of using football cards as a promotion. The full-color cards have three different tab colors (blue, orange, yellow), each referring to a specific week in the playoffs or Super Bowl. The cards measure approximately 4-1/2" x 5-7/8" with the tab intact. The prices below are for cards with the tab intact. Cards without the tabs have little collector value and are worth considerably less. Because of space limitations, only players with a significant value over common price are listed individually. Players not listed are worth approximately the common price (or perhaps slightly above for minor stars). The individual values listed are for the least expensive color tabs (yellow or orange). Cards with blue tabs are worth about twice as much as values listed. Card numbers refer to a player's uniform number.

		MT
Complete Set (Blue):		45.00
Complete Set (Orange):		25.00
Complete Set (Yellow):		20.00
Common Player:		.50
4	Steve Fuller	.75
6	Kevin Butler	1.00
8	Maury Buford	.50
9	Jim McMahon	2.50
21	Leslie Frazier	.50
22	Dave Duerson	.50
26	Matt Suhey	.75
27	Mike Richardson	.50
29	Dennis Gentry	.50
33	Calvin Thomas	.50
34	Walter Payton	7.00
45	Gary Fencik	.75
50	Mike Singletary	2.50
55	Otis Wilson	.50
58	Wilber Marshall	1.00
62	Mark Bortz	.50
63	Jay Hilgenberg	.75
72	William Perry	1.25
73	Mike Hartenstine	.50
74	Jim Covert	.75
75	Stefan Humphries	.50
76	Steve McMichael	1.00
78	Keith Van Horne	.50
80	Tim Wrightman	.50
82	Ken Margerum	.50
83	Willie Gault	1.00
85	Dennis McKinnon	.75
87	Emery Moorehead	.50
95	Richard Dent	2.00
99	Dan Hampton	2.00
	Mike Ditka (CO)	2.50
	Buddy Ryan (ACO)	1.50

1986 McDonald's All-Stars

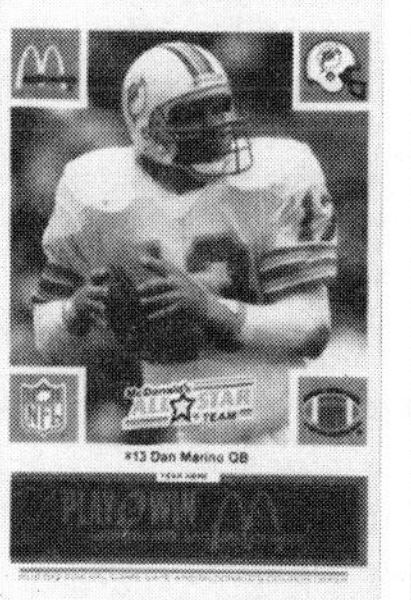

Measuring 3-1/16" x 4-11/16" with the tab intact or 3-1/16" x 3-5/8" without, this 30-card set was for participating McDonald's outside of an NFL market. Released over four weeks, the set featured different colored tabs -- with blue (first week), black or gray (second week), gold or orange (third week) and green (fourth week). The backs feature McDonald's All-Star Team printed at the top. Also included on the backs are the player's name, jersey number, career and 1985 highlights and a 1986 copyright date.

		MT
Complete Set (Blue):		6.00
Complete Set (Black):		6.00
Complete Set (Gold):		6.00
Complete Set (Green):		6.00
Common Player:		.15
9	Jim McMahon	.35
11	Phil Simms	.35
13	Dan Marino	2.50
14	Dan Fouts	.35
16	Joe Montana	2.00
20A	Deron Cherry	.15
20B	Joe Morris	.15
32	Marcus Allen	.35
33	Roger Craig	.25
34A	Kevin Mack	.15
35B	Walter Payton	1.75
42	Gerald Riggs	.15
45	Kenny Easley	.15
47A	Joey Browner	.15
47B	LeRoy Irvin	.15
52	Mike Webster	.25
54A	E.J. Junior	.15
54B	Randy White	.25
56	Lawrence Taylor	.35
63	Mike Munchak	.15
66	Joe Jacoby	.15
73	John Hannah	.25
75A	Chris Hinton	.15
75B	Rulon Jones	.15
75C	Howie Long	.25
78	Anthony Munoz	.25
81	Art Monk	.35
82A	Ozzie Newsome	.35
82B	Mike Quick	.15
99	Mark Gastineau	.15

1986 McDonald's Chicago Bears

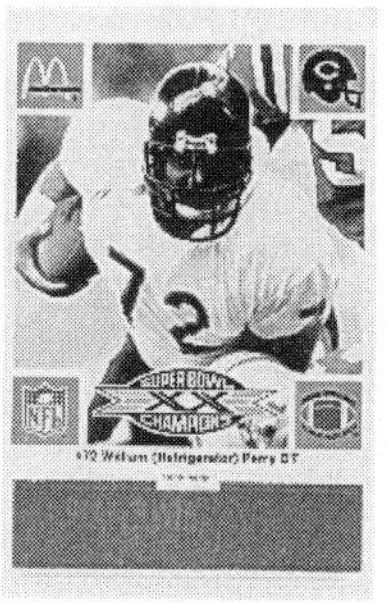

Released in the Chicago area, the 24-card set was released over four weeks at participating McDonald's. The tab colors were as follows: blue (first week), black or gray (second), gold or orange (third) and green (fourth). With the tab intact, the cards measure 3-1/16" x 4-11/16" and 3-1/16" x 3-5/8" without. The card fronts have the McDonald's logo in the upper left, Bears helmet in the upper right, NFL shield in the lower left and the NFLPA logo in the lower right. The card backs have "Super Bowl Collectors Edition" at the top. The player's name, uniform number, bio and 1986 and career highlights are also listed on the backs.

		MT
Complete Set (Blue):		15.00
Complete Set (Black):		7.50
Complete Set (Gold):		7.50
Complete Set (Green):		7.50
Common Player:		.30
6	Kevin Butler (DP)	.40
8	Maury Buford	.30
9	Jim McMahon (DP)	1.25
22	Dave Duerson	.30
26	Matt Suhey	.40
27	Mike Richardson	.30
34	Walter Payton (DP)	1.75
45	Gary Fencik	.40
50	Mike Singletary (DP)	1.25
55	Otis Wilson	.30
57	Tom Thayer	.30
58	Wilber Marshall	.50
62	Mark Bortz (DP)	.30
63	Jay Hilgenberg	.40
72	William Perry (DP)	.50
74	Jim Covert	.40
76	Steve McMichael	.50
78	Keith Van Horne	.30
80	Tim Wrightman	.30
82	Ken Margerum	.30
83	Willie Gault	.50
87	Emery Moorehead	.30
95	Richard Dent	1.00
99	Dan Hampton	1.00

1986 McDonald's Cincinnati Bengals

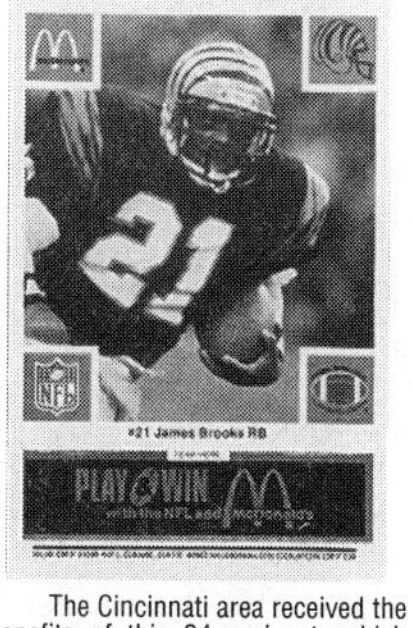

The Cincinnati area received the benefits of this 24-card set, which was part of the McDonald's promotion of 1986. The card fronts showcase the McDonald's logo in the upper left, with the Cincinnati helmet in the upper right. The NFL shield and NFLPA logos appear in the bottom left and right, respectively, of the color action photo. Card backs feature the player's number, name, bio, stats and highlights. The cards measure 3-1/16" x 4-11/16" with the tab and 3-1/16" x 3-5/8" without. Released over four weeks, the first week's cards had blue tabs, second had black or gray, third had gold or orange and the fourth week tabs were green.

		MT
Complete Set (Blue):		25.00
Complete Set (Black):		12.50
Complete Set (Gold):		12.50
Complete Set (Green):		12.50
Common Player:		.50
7	Boomer Esiason	2.50
14	Ken Anderson (DP)	1.00
20	Ray Horton	.60
21	James Brooks (DP)	1.00
22	James Griffin	.50
28	Larry Kinnebrew	.60
34	Louis Breeden (DP)	.50
37	Robert Jackson	.50
40	Charles Alexander (DP)	.50
52	Dave Rimington	.60
57	Reggie Williams	.75
65	Max Montoya	.60
69	Tim Krumrie	.75
73	Eddie Edwards	.60
74	Brian Blados (DP)	.50
77	Mike Wilson	.50
78	Anthony Munoz	1.25
79	Ross Browner	.60
80	Cris Collinsworth	1.00
81	Eddie Brown (DP)	.75
82	Rodney Holman	.60
83	M.L. Harris	.50
90	Emanuel King	.50
91	Carl Zander	.50

1986 McDonald's Buffalo Bills

Measuring 3-1/16" x 4-11/16" with the tab and 3-1/16" x 3-5/8" without, the 24-card set was distributed over four weeks of the 1986 season in the Buffalo area. In the top corners of the color action photo on the card front were the McDonald's logo and Bills helmet. At the bottom corners of the photo were the NFL shield and NFLPA logo. The player's name, number and position appear under the photo. The card backs have the player's name, jersey number and highlights. Each week featured a different colored tab: blue (first), black or gray (second), gold or orange (third) and green (fourth).

		MT
Complete Set (Blue):		150.00
Complete Set (Black):		30.00
Complete Set (Gold):		15.00
Complete Set (Green):		15.00
Common Player:		.75
4	John Kidd	.75
7	Bruce Mathison	.75
11	Scott Norwood	1.00
22	Steve Freeman	.75
26	Charles Romes	.75
28	Greg Bell (DP)	1.00
29	Derrick Burroughs (DP)	.75
43	Martin Bayless (DP)	.75
51	Jim Ritcher	1.00
54	Eugene Marve	.75
55	Jim Haslett	.75
57	Lucius Sanford	.75
63	Justin Cross	.75
65	Tim Vogler	.75
70	Joe Devlin	.75
72	Ken Jones	.75
76	Fred Smerlas	1.00
77	Ben Williams	1.00
78	Bruce Smith	5.00
80	Jerry Butler (DP)	1.00
83	Andre Reed	5.00
85	Chris Burkett (DP)	1.00
87	Eason Ramson	.75
95	Sean McNanie	.75

1986 McDonald's Denver Broncos

Released over four weeks in the Denver area during the 1986 season, this 24-card set measured 3-1/16" x 4-11/16" with the tab and 3-1/16" x 3-5/8" without. The card fronts and backs followed the same format as the other McDonald's sets of that season. Each week's cards featured a different colored tab: blue (first), black or gray (second), gold or orange (third) and green (fourth).

		MT
Complete Set (Blue):		25.00
Complete Set (Black):		8.00
Complete Set (Gold):		8.00
Complete Set (Green):		8.00
Common Player:		.30
3	Rich Karlis	.30
7	John Elway	3.50
20	Louis Wright	.40
22	Tony Lily	.30
23	Sammy Winder	.40
30	Steve Sewell	.40
31	Mike Harden	.40
43	Steve Foley	.40
47	Gerald Wilhite	.40
49	Dennis Smith	.50
50	Jim Ryan	.30
54	Keith Bishop (DP)	.30
55	Rick Dennison (DP)	.30
57	Tom Jackson	1.25
60	Paul Howard	.30
64	Bill Bryan (DP)	.30
68	Rubin Carter (DP)	.30
70	Dave Studdard	.30
75	Rulon Jones	.40
77	Karl Mecklenburg	.60
79	Barney Chavous (DP)	.30
81	Steve Watson	.40
82	Vance Johnson	.60
84	Clint Sampson	.30

1986 McDonald's Cleveland Browns

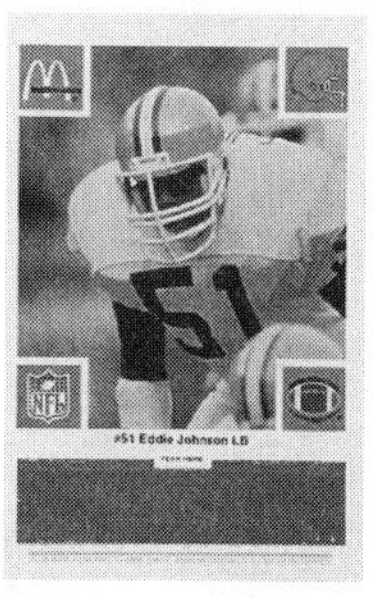

Issued over four weeks of the 1986 season in the Cleveland area, the 24-card set measure 3-1/16" x 4-11/16" with the tab and 3-1/16" x 3-5/8" without. The card fronts feature a color photo, with the McDonald's logo in the upper left and Browns helmet in the upper right. The NFL shields and NFLPA logo are on the bottom corners, left and right respectively. The card backs have the player's name, jersey number, bio and highlights. Each week's cards featured different colored tabs: blue (first), black or gray (second), gold or orange (third) and green (fourth).

		MT
Complete Set (Blue):		10.00
Complete Set (Black):		6.00
Complete Set (Gold):		6.00
Complete Set (Green):		6.00
Common Player:		.25
9	Matt Bahr (DP)	.25
18	Gary Danielson	.25
19	Bernie Kosar (DP)	1.75
27	Al Gross	.25
29	Hanford Dixon	.35
31	Frank Minnifield	.35
34	Kevin Mack	.50
37	Chris Rockins	.25
44	Earnest Byner	.75
51	Eddie Johnson	.25
55	Curtis Weathers	.25
56	Chip Banks (DP)	.25
57	Clay Matthews	.50
60	Tom Cousineau	.25
61	Mike Baab (DP)	.25
63	Cody Risien	.35
77	Rickey Bolden (DP)	.25
78	Carl Hairston	.25
79	Bob Golic	.35
82	Ozzie Newsome	1.00
84	Glen Young	.25
85	Clarence Weathers	.25
86	Brian Brennan (DP)	.35
96	Reggie Camp	.25

1986 McDonald's Tampa Bay Buccaneers

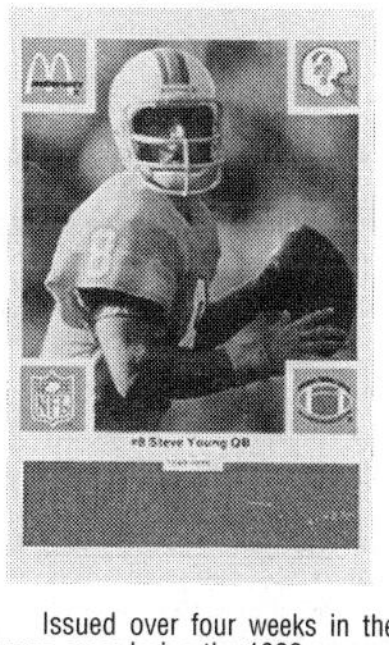

Issued over four weeks in the Tampa area during the 1986 season, the 24-card set measures 3-1/16" x 4-11/16" with the tab and 3-1/16" x 3-5/8" without. The card fronts have a color photo, with the McDonald's logo in the upper left and Tampa Bay helmet in the upper right. The NFL shield and NFLPA logo are in the bottom corners, left and right respectively. The card backs have the player's name, jersey number, bio and highlights. Each week's cards had different colored tabs: blue (first), black or gray (second), gold or orange (third) and green (fourth).

		MT
Complete Set (Blue):		15.00
Complete Set (Black):		15.00
Complete Set (Gold):		15.00
Complete Set (Green):		15.00
Common Player:		.30
1	Donald Igwebuike	.30
8	Steve Young	8.00
17	Steve DeBerg	.75
21	John Holt	.30
23	Jeremiah Castille (DP)	.30
30	David Greenwood	.30
32	James Wilder	.50
44	Ivory Sully	.30
51	Chris Washington	.30
52	Scot Brantley (DP)	.30
54	Ervin Randle	.30
58	Jeff Davis (DP)	.30
60	Randy Grimes	.30
62	Sean Farrell	.40
66	George Yarno	.30
73	Ron Heller	.30
76	David Logan	.30
78	John Cannon (DP)	.30
82	Jerry Bell (DP)	.30
86	Calvin Magee	.30
87	Gerald Carter	.30
88	Jimmie Giles	.50
89	Kevin House	.50
90	Ron Holmes	.40

1986 McDonald's St. Louis Cardinals

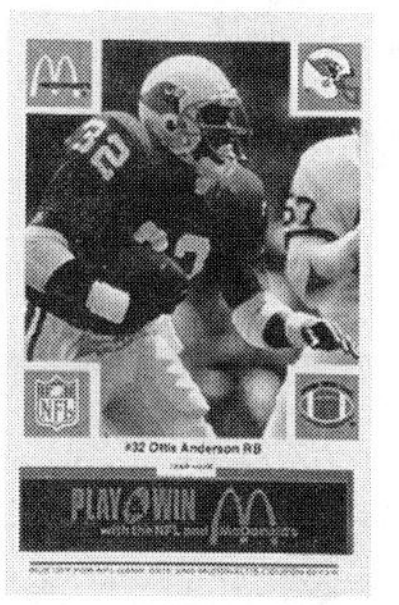

Released over four weeks in the St. Louis area during the 1986 season, the 24-card set measures 3-1/16" x 4-11/16" with the tabs and 3-1/16" x 3-5/8" without. The card fronts showcase a color photo, with the McDonald's logo in the upper left and the Cardinals' helmet in the upper right. The NFL shield and NFLPA logo appear at the bottom, left and right respectively. The player's name, jersey number and position are printed under the photo. The card backs showcase the player's name, jersey number, bio and highlights. Each week's card had a different colored tab: blue (first), black or gray (second), gold or orange (third) and green (fourth).

		MT
Complete Set (Blue):		10.00
Complete Set (Black):		6.00
Complete Set (Gold):		6.00
Complete Set (Green):		6.00
Common Player:		.25
15	Neil Lomax	.50
18	Carl Birdsong (DP)	.25
30	Stump Mitchell	.35
32	Ottis Anderson (DP)	.75
43	Lonnie Young	.25
45	Leonard Smith	.25
47	Cedric Mack	.25
48	Lionel Washington	.25
53	Freddie Joe Nunn	.35
54	E.J. Junior	.35
57	Niko Noga	.25
60	Al "Bubba" Baker (DP)	.35
63	Tootie Robbins	.25
65	David Galloway	.25
66	Doug Dawson (DP)	.25
67	Luis Sharpe	.25
71	Joe Bostic (DP)	.25
73	Mark Duda (DP)	.25
75	Curtis Greer	.25
80	Doug Marsh	.25
81	Roy Green	.50
83	Pat Tilley	.25
84	J.T. Smith	.35
89	Greg Lafleur	.25

1986 McDonald's San Diego Chargers

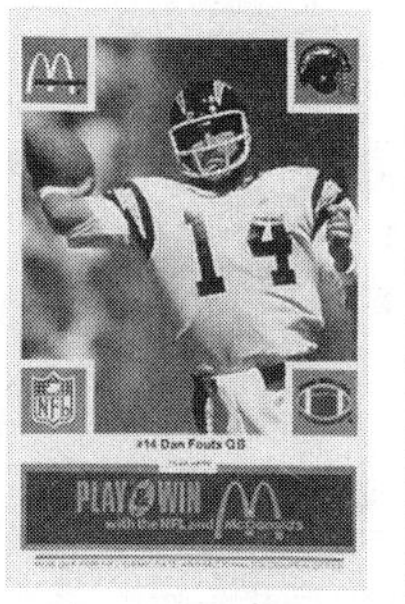

Released over four weeks in the San Diego area, the 24-card set measures 3-1/16" x 4-11/16" with the tab and 3-1/16" x 3-5/8" without. The card fronts showcase a color photo, with the McDonald's logo in the upper left, Chargers' helmet in the upper right, NFL shield in the bottom left and NFLPA logo in the lower right. The player's name, jersey number and position are printed under the photo. The card backs include the player's name, number, position, bio and highlights. Each week's cards had a different colored tab: blue (first), black or gray (second), gold or orange (third) and green (fourth).

		MT
Complete Set (Blue):		20.00
Complete Set (Black):		15.00
Complete Set (Gold):		10.00
Complete Set (Green):		10.00
Common Player:		.40
9	Mark Herrmann	.40
14	Dan Fouts	1.50
18	Charlie Joiner	1.25
21	Buford McGee	.40
22	Gill Byrd (DP)	.50
26	Lionel James	.50
29	John Hendy	.40
37	Jeff Dale (DP)	.40
40	Gary Anderson (RB) (DP)	.75
43	Tim Spencer	.40
51	Woodrow Lowe	.40
54	Bill Ray Smith	.50
60	Dennis McKnight	.40
62	Don Macek	.40
67	Ed White	.40
74	Jim Lachey	.50
78	Chuck Ehin (DP)	.40
80	Kellen Winslow	1.50
83	Trumaine Johnson	.40
85	Eric Sievers	.40
88	Pete Holohan	.50
89	Wes Chandler (DP)	.50
93	Earl Wilson	.40
99	Lee Williams	.50

1986 McDonald's Kansas City Chiefs

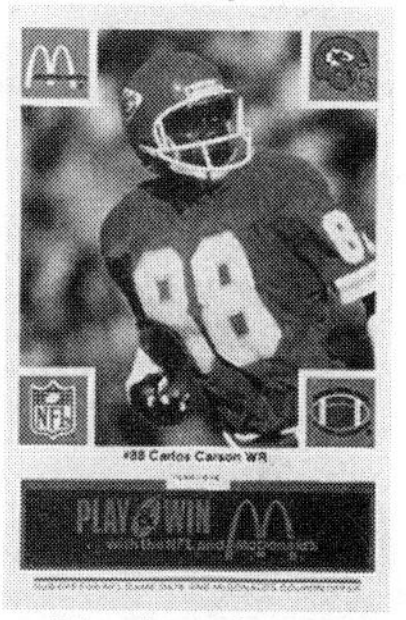

Released over a four-week time span at Kansas City area McDonald's, the 24-card set measures 3-1/16" x 4-11/16" with the tab and 3-1/16" x 3-5/8" without. Anchored with a color photo on the card front, the McDonald's logo is in the upper left and Chiefs' helmet in the upper right. The NFL shield and NFLPA logo are in the bottom corners, left and right respectively. The player's name, jersey number and position are located under the photo. The card backs have the player's name, jersey number, position, bio and career highlights. Each week's cards had different colored tabs: blue (first), black or gray (second), gold or orange (third) and green (fourth).

		MT
Complete Set (Blue):		20.00
Complete Set (Black):		40.00
Complete Set (Gold):		20.00
Complete Set (Green):		20.00
Common Player:		.75
6	Jim Arnold (DP)	.75
8	Nick Lowery	1.00
9	Bill Kenney	.75
14	Todd Blackledge (DP)	1.00
20	Deron Cherry (DP)	1.25
29	Albert Lewis	1.50
31	Kevin Ross	1.25
34	Lloyd Burruss (DP)	.75
41	Garcia Lane	.75
42	Jeff Smith	.75
43	Mike Pruitt	1.00
44	Herman Heard	.75
50	Calvin Daniels	.75
59	Gary Spani	.75
63	Bill Maas	.75
64	Bob Olderman	.75
66	Brad Budde (DP)	.75
67	Art Still	.75
72	David Lutz	.75
83	Stephone Paige	1.25
85	Jonathan Hayes	1.00
88	Carlos Carson (DP)	1.00
89	Henry Marshall	.75
97	Scott Radecic	.75

1986 McDonald's Indianapolis Colts

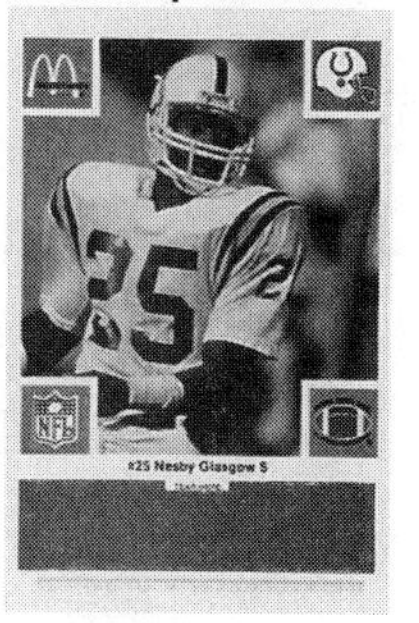

Released during a four-week time span at Indianapolis McDonald's, the 24-card set measures 3-1/16" x 4-11/16" with the tab and 3-1/16" x 3-5/8" without. Anchored with a color photo, the card fronts have a McDonald's logo in the upper left and a Colts' helmet in the upper right. The NFL shield and NFLPA logo are in the bottom corners, left and right respectively. The player's name, number and position are printed below the photo. The card backs showcase the player's name, number, bio and highlights. Each week's cards featured different colored tabs: blue (first), black or gray (second), gold or orange (third) and green (fourth).

		MT
Complete Set (Blue):		100.00
Complete Set (Black):		20.00
Complete Set (Gold):		15.00
Complete Set (Green):		20.00
Common Player:		.60
2	Raul Allegre (DP)	.60
3	Rohn Stark	.75
25	Nesby Glasgow	.60
27	Preston Davis	.60
32	Randy McMillian	.75
34	George Wonsley	.60
38	Eugene Daniel	.75
44	Owen Gill	.60
47	Leonard Coleman	.60
50	Duane Bickett (DP)	1.00
53	Ray Donaldson	.75
55	Barry Krauss	.60
64	Ben Utt	.60
66	Ron Solt	.60
72	Karl Baldischwiler (DP)	.60
75	Chris Hinton	.75
81	Pat Beach (DP)	.60
85	Matt Bouza (DP)	.60
87	Wayne Capers (DP)	.60
88	Robbie Martin	.60
92	Brad White	.60
93	Cliff Odom	.60
96	Blaise Winter	.60
98	Johnie Cooks	.60

1986 McDonald's Dallas Cowboys

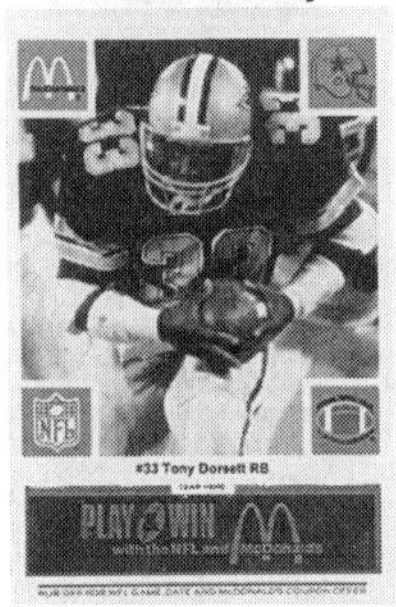

Issued over four weeks at Dallas-area McDonald's, the 25-card set measures 3-1/16" x 4-11/16" with the tab and 3-1/16" x 3-5/8" without. The card fronts boast a color photo, with the McDonald's logo in the upper left and Dallas helmet in the upper right. The NFL shield and NFLPA logo are located in the lower corners, left and right respectively. The player's name, number and position are printed under the photo. The card backs feature the player's name, number, bio and highlights. Each week's cards featured a different colored tab: blue (first), black or gray (second), gold or orange (third) and green (fourth).

		MT
Complete Set (Blue):		10.00
Complete Set (Black):		10.00
Complete Set (Gold):		10.00
Complete Set (Green):		10.00
Common Player:		.25
1	Rafael Septien	.25
11	Danny White	.50
24	Everson Walls	.35
26	Michael Downs (DP)	.25
27	Ron Fellows	.25
30	Timmy Newsome	.25
33	Tony Dorsett (DP)	1.50
34	Herschel Walker	2.00
40	Bill Bates (DP)	.50
47	Dexter Clinkscale (DP)	.25
50	Jeff Rohrer	.25
54	Randy White	.75
56	Eugene Lockhart	.35
58	Mike Hegman	.25
61	Jim Cooper (DP)	.25
63	Glen Titensor	.25
64	Tom Rafferty	.25
65	Kurt Peterson	.25
72	Ed "Too Tall" Jones	.75
75	Phil Pozderac	.25
77	Jim Jeffcoat	.50
78	John Dutton	.35
80	Tony Hill	.35
82	Mike Renfro	.25
84	Doug Cosbie (DP)	.25

1986 McDonald's Miami Dolphins

Issued over four weeks at Miami-area McDonald's, the 25-card set measure 3-1/16" x 4-11/16" with the tab and 3-1/16" x 3-5/8" without. Each card front is anchored with a color photo, with the McDonald's logo in the upper left and Miami helmet in the upper right. The NFL shield and NFLPA logo are in the bottom corners, left and right respectively. Below the photo are the player's name, number and position. The card backs showcase the player's name, number, position and highlights. Each week's cards featured a different colored tab: blue (first), black or gray (second), gold or orange (third) and green (fourth).

		MT
Complete Set (Blue):		40.00
Complete Set (Black):		20.00
Complete Set (Gold):		20.00
Complete Set (Green):		20.00
Common Player:		.50
4	Reggie Roby	.75
7	Fuad Reveiz	.75
10	Don Strock	.75
13	Dan Marino	10.00
22	Tony Nathan	.75
23A	Joe Carter (ERR) (Photo actually Tony Nathan 22)	.75
23B	Joe Carter (COR)	.50
27	Lorenzo Hampton	.50
30	Ron Davenport	.50
43	Bud Brown (DP)	.50
47	Glenn Blackwood (DP)	.50
49	William Judson	.50
55	Hugh Green	.75
57	Dwight Stephenson	.75
58	Kim Bokamper (DP)	.50
59	Bob Brudzinski (DP)	.50
61	Roy Foster	.50
71	Mike Charles	.50
75	Doug Betters (DP)	.50
79	Jon Giesler	.50
83	Mark Clayton	2.00
84	Bruce Hardy	.50
85	Mark Duper	1.00
89	Nat Moore	.75
91	Mack Moore	.50

1986 McDonald's Philadelphia Eagles

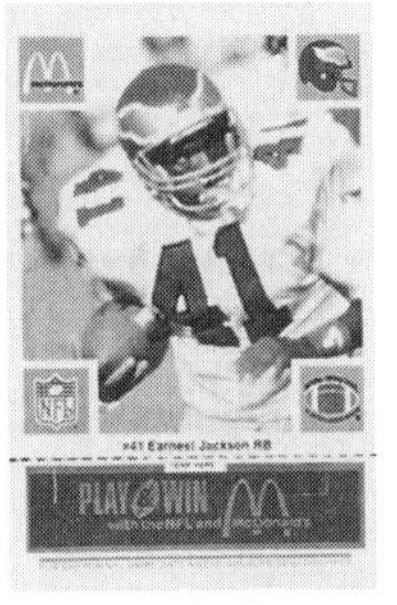

Issued over a four-week time span at Philadelphia-area McDonald's, the 24-card set measures 3-1/16" x 4-11/16" with the tab and 3-1/16" x 3-5/8" without. A color photo anchors the card front, with the McDonald's logo in the upper left and the Eagles' helmet in the upper right. The NFL shield and NFLPA logos are in the bottom corners, left and right respectively. The player's name, number and position are printed under the photo. The card backs have the player's name, number, bio and highlights. Each week's cards featured a different colored tab: blue (first), black or gray (second), gold or orange (third) and green (fourth).

		MT
Complete Set (Blue):		60.00
Complete Set (Black):		20.00
Complete Set (Gold):		10.00
Complete Set (Green):		10.00
Common Player:		.25
7	Ron Jaworski	.50
8	Paul McFadden	.25
12	Randall Cunningham (DP)	2.00
22	Brenard Wilson	.25
24	Ray Ellis	.25
29	Elbert Foules	.25
36	Herman Hunter	.35
41	Earnest Jackson	.35
43	Roynell Young	.35
48	Wes Hopkins	.25
50	Garry Cobb (DP)	.25
63	Ron Baker (DP)	.25
66	Ken Reeves	.25
71	Ken Clarke (DP)	.25
73	Steve Kenney	.25
74	Leonard Mitchell	.25
81	Kenny Jackson	.35
82	Mike Quick	.35
85	Ron Johnson	.25
88	John Spagnola	.25
91	Reggie White	4.00
93	Thomas Strauthers	.25
94	Byron Darby (DP)	.25
98	Greg Brown (DP)	.25

1986 McDonald's Atlanta Falcons

Released over a four-week time span at Atlanta-area McDonald's, the 24-card set measures 3-1/16" x 4-11/16" with the tab and 3-1/16" x 3-5/8" without. The card fronts are anchored with a color photo, with the McDonald's logo in the upper left and Falcons' helmet in the upper right. The NFL shield and NFLPA logo are located at the bottom, left and right respectively. The player's name, number and position are printed below the photo. The card backs include the player's name, number, position, bio and highlights. Each week featured a different colored tab: blue (first), black or gray (second), gold or orange (third) and green (fourth). The values listed are for cards with the tabs intact.

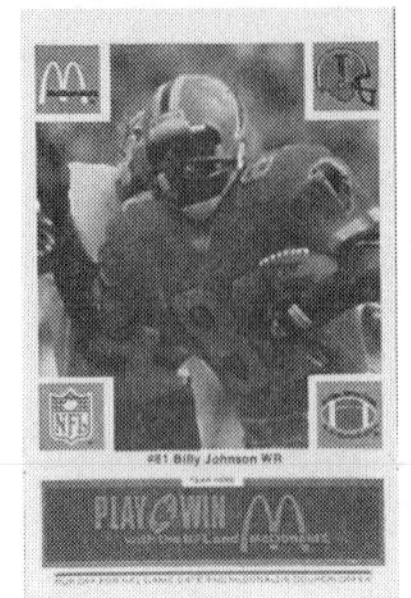

		MT
Complete Set (Blue):		60.00
Complete Set (Black):		200.00
Complete Set (Gold):		40.00
Complete Set (Green):		15.00
Common Player:		.60
3	Rick Donnelly	.60
16	Dave Archer (DP)	1.00
18	Mick Luckhurst	.60
23	Bobby Butler	.60
26	James Britt (DP)	.60
37	Kenny Johnson	.60
39	Cliff Austin	.60
42	Gerald Riggs	.75
50	Buddy Curry	.60
56	Al Richardson	.60
57	Jeff Van Note	.75
58	David Frye	.60
61	John Scully	.60
62	Brett Miller	.60
74	Mike Pitts	.60
76	Mike Gann	.60
77	Rick Bryan	.60
78	Mike Kenn	.75
79	Bill Fralic	1.00
81	Billy Johnson	.75
82	Stacey Bailey (DP)	.60
87	Cliff Benson (DP)	.60
88	Arthur Cox	.60
89	Charlie Brown (DP)	.75

1986 McDonald's San Francisco 49ers

Released over a four-week time span at San Francisco-area McDonald's, the 24-card set measures 3-1/16" x 4-11/16" with the tab and 3-1/16" x 3-5/8" without. The card fronts are anchored with a color photo, with the McDonald's logo in the upper left and 49ers' helmet in the upper right. The NFL shield and NFLPA logo are located at the bottom, left and right respectively. The player's name, number and position are printed below the photo. The card backs include the player's name, number, position, bio and highlights. Each week featured a different colored tab: blue (first), black or gray (second), gold or orange (third) and green (fourth). The values listed are for cards with the tabs intact.

		MT
Complete Set (Blue):		50.00
Complete Set (Black):		25.00
Complete Set (Gold):		25.00
Complete Set (Green):		25.00
Common Player:		.75
16	Joe Montana	12.00
21	Eric Wright	1.00
26	Wendell Tyler	1.00
27	Carlton Williamson	.75
33	Roger Craig (DP)	1.25
42	Ronnie Lott	2.00
49	Jeff Fuller	.75
50	Riki Ellison	.75
51	Randy Cross (DP)	1.00
56	Fred Quillan	.75
58	Keena Turner	.75
62	Guy McIntyre	.75
68	John Ayers (DP)	.75
71	Keith Fahnhorst	.75
72	Jeff Stover	.75
76	Dwaine Board (DP)	.75
77	Bubba Paris	.75
78	Manu Tuiasosopo	.75
80	Jerry Rice	12.00
81	Russ Francis	1.00
86	John Frank	.75
87	Dwight Clark (DP)	1.00
90	Todd Shell	.75
95	Michael Carter (DP)	1.00

1986 McDonald's New York Giants

Released over a four-week time span at New York-area McDonald's, the 24-card set measures 3-1/16" x 4-11/16" with the tab and 3-1/16" x 3-5/8" without. The card fronts are anchored with a color photo, with the McDonald's logo in the upper left and Giants' helmet in the upper right. The NFL shield and NFLPA logo are located at the bottom, left and right respectively. The player's name, number and position are printed below the photo. The card backs include the player's name, number, position, bio and highlights. Each week featured a different colored tab: blue (first), black or gray (second), gold or orange (third) and green (fourth). The values listed are for cards with the tabs in-tact.

		MT
Complete Set (Blue):		12.00
Complete Set (Black):		10.00
Complete Set (Gold):		6.00
Complete Set (Green):		6.00
Common Player:		.25
5	Sean Landeta	.35
11	Phil Simms	1.00
20	Joe Morris	.50
23	Perry Williams	.25
26	Rob Carpenter (DP)	.25
33	George Adams (DP)	.25
34	Elvis Patterson	.35
43	Terry Kinard	.25
44	Maurice Carthon	.25
48	Kenny Hill	.25
53	Harry Carson	.35
54	Andy Headen	.25
56	Lawrence Taylor	1.50
60	Brad Benson (DP)	.25
63	Karl Nelson	.25
64	Jim Burt (DP)	.35
67	Billy Ard (DP)	.25
70	Leonard Marshall	.35
75	George Martin	.35
80	Phil McConkey	.35
84	Zeke Mowatt	.25
85	Don Hasselbeck	.25
86	Lionel Manuel	.35
89	Mark Bavaro (DP)	.35

1986 McDonald's New York Jets

Released over a four-week time span at New York-area McDonald's, the 24-card set measures 3-1/16" x 4-11/16" with the tab and 3-1/16" x 3-5/8" without. The card fronts are anchored with a color photo, with the McDonald's logo in the upper left and Jets' helmet in the upper right. The NFL shield and NFLPA logo are located at the bottom, left and right respectively. The player's name, number and position are printed below the photo. The card backs include the player's name, number, position, bio and highlights. Each week featured a different colored tab: blue (first), black or gray (second), gold or orange (third) and green (fourth). The values listed are for cards with the tabs in-tact.

		MT
Complete Set (Blue):		150.00
Complete Set (Black):		150.00
Complete Set (Gold):		25.00
Complete Set (Green):		25.00
Common Player:		1.00
5	Pat Leahy	1.00
7	Ken O'Brien	1.50
21	Kirk Springs	1.00
24	Freeman McNeil	2.00
27	Russell Carter (DP)	1.00
29	Johnny Lynn	1.00
34	Johnny Hector	1.00
39	Harry Hamilton	1.00
49	Tony Paige	1.00
53	Jim Sweeney	1.00
56	Lance Mehl	1.00
59	Kyle Clifton (DP)	1.00
60	Dan Alexander (DP)	1.00
65	Joe Fields (DP)	1.00
73	Joe Klecko	1.25
78	Barry Bennett (DP)	1.00
80	Johnny Lam Jones	1.00
82	Mickey Shuler	1.00
85	Wesley Walker	1.25
87	Kurt Sohn	1.00
88	Al Toon	2.00
89	Rocky Klever	1.00
93	Marty Lyons	1.00
99	Mark Gastineau (DP)	1.50

1986 McDonald's Detroit Lions

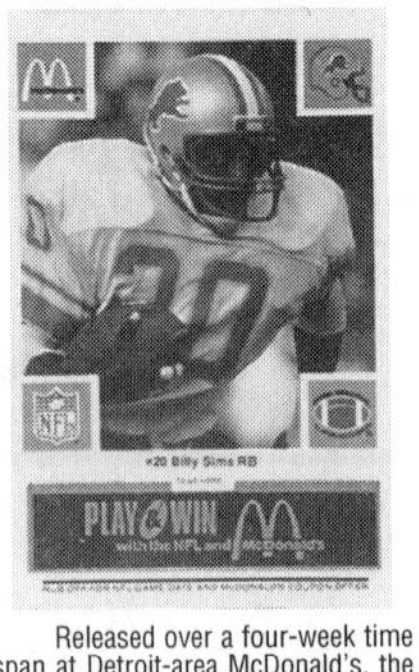

Released over a four-week time span at Detroit-area McDonald's, the 24-card set measures 3-1/16" x 4-11/16" with the tab and 3-1/16" x 3-5/8" without. The card fronts are anchored with a color photo, with the McDonald's logo in the upper left and Lions' helmet in the upper right. The NFL shield and NFLPA logo are located at the bottom, left and right respectively. The player's name, number and position are printed below the photo. The card backs include the player's name, number, position, bio and highlights. Each week featured a different colored tab: blue (first), black or gray (second), gold or orange (third) and green (fourth). The values listed are for cards which have the tabs intact.

		MT
Complete Set (Blue):		6.00
Complete Set (Black):		6.00
Complete Set (Gold):		6.00
Complete Set (Green):		6.00
Common Player:		.25
3	Eddie Murray	.35
11	Michael Black (DP)	.25
17	Eric Hipple	.35
20	Billy Sims	.50
21	Demetrious Johnson	.25
27	Bobby Watkins	.25
29	Bruce McNorton	.25
30	James Jones	.35
33	William Graham	.25
35	Alvin Hall	.25
39	Leonard Thompson	.35
50	August Curley (DP)	.25
52	Steve Mott	.25
55	Mike Cofer (DP)	.35
59	Jimmy Williams	.25
70	Keith Dorney (DP)	.25
71	Rich Strenger	.25
75	Lomas Brown (DP)	.35
76	Eric Williams	.25
79	William Gay	.25
82	Pete Mandley	.25
86	Mark Nichols	.25
87	David Lewis	.25
89	Jeff Chadwick (DP)	.25

1986 McDonald's Houston Oilers

Released over a four-week time span at Houston-area McDonald's, the 24-card set measures 3-1/16" x 4-11/16" with the tab and 3-1/16" x 3-5/8" without. The card fronts are anchored with a color photo, with the McDonald's logo in the upper left and Oilers' helmet in the upper right. The NFL shield and NFLPA logo are located at the bottom, left and right respectively. The player's name, number and position are printed below the photo. The card backs include the player's name, number, position, bio and highlights. Each week featured a different colored tab: blue (first), black or gray (second), gold or orange (third) and green (fourth). The values listed are for cards which have the tabs intact.

		MT
Complete Set (Blue):		12.00
Complete Set (Black):		8.00
Complete Set (Gold):		8.00
Complete Set (Green):		8.00
Common Player:		.30
1	Warren Moon	4.00
7	Tony Zendejas	.30
10	Oliver Luck	.40
21	Bo Eason	.30
23	Richard Johnson	.30
24	Steve Brown (DP)	.30
25	Keith Bostic (DP)	.30
29	Patrick Allen (DP)	.30
33	Mike Rozier	.50
40	Butch Woolfolk	.30
53	Avon Riley	.30
56	Robert Abraham (DP)	.30
63	Mike Munchak	.40
67	Mike Stensrud	.30
70	Dean Steinkuhler	.40
71	Richard Byrd (DP)	.30
73	Harvey Salem	.30
74	Bruce Matthews	.75
79	Ray Childress	.75
83	Tim Smith	.30
85	Drew Hill	.75
87	Jamie Williams	.30
91	Johnny Meads	.30
94	Frank Bush (DP)	.30

1986 McDonald's Green Bay Packers

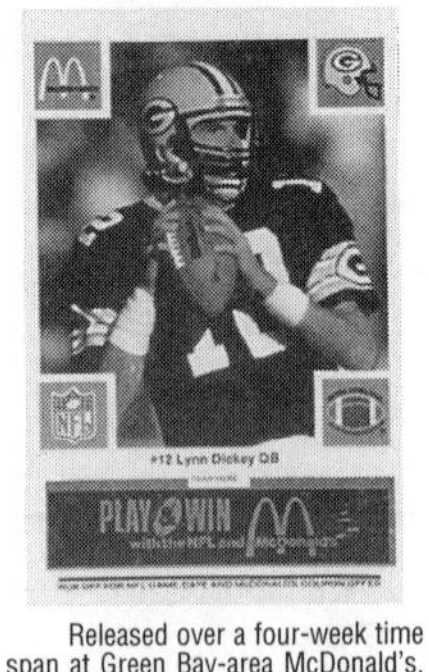

Released over a four-week time span at Green Bay-area McDonald's, the 24-card set measures 3-1/16" x 4-11/16" with the tab and 3-1/16" x 3-5/8" without. The card fronts are anchored with a color photo, with the McDonald's logo in the upper left and Packers' helmet in the upper right. The NFL shield and NFLPA logo are located at the bottom, left and right respectively. The player's name, number and position are printed below the photo. The card backs include the player's name, number, position, bio and highlights. Each week featured a different colored tab: blue (first), black or gray (second), gold or orange (third) and green (fourth). The values listed are for cards which have the tabs intact.

		MT
Complete Set (Blue):		6.00
Complete Set (Black):		6.00
Complete Set (Gold):		6.00
Complete Set (Green):		6.00
Common Player:		.25
10	Al Del Greco (DP)	.25
12	Lynn Dickey	.35
16	Randy Wright	.35
18	Jim Zorn	.35
22	Mark Lee	.25
26	Tim Lewis	.25
31	Gerry Ellis	.25
33	Jessie Clark (DP)	.25
37	Mark Murphy	.35
41	Tom Flynn	.25
42	Gary Ellerson	.25
53	Mike Douglass	.25
55	Randy Scott	.25
59	John Anderson (DP)	.25
67	Karl Swanke	.25
75	Ken Ruettgers	.25
76	Alphonso Carreker (DP)	.25
77	Mike Butler (DP)	.25
79	Donnie Humphrey	.25
82	Paul Coffman (DP)	.25
85	Phillip Epps	.35
90	Ezra Johnson	.25
91	Brian Noble	.35
94	Charles Martin	.25

1986 McDonald's New England Patriots

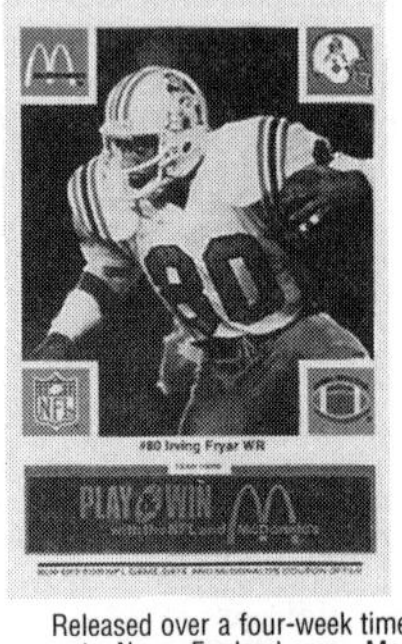

Released over a four-week time span at New England-area McDonald's, the 24-card set measures 3-1/16" x 4-11/16" with the tab and 3-1/16" x 3-5/8" without. The card fronts are anchored with a color photo, with the McDonald's logo in the upper left and Patriots' helmet in the upper right. The NFL shield and NFLPA logo are located at the bottom, left and right respectively. The player's name, number and position are printed below the photo. The card backs include the player's name, number, position, bio and highlights. Each week featured a different colored tab: blue (first), black or gray (second), gold or orange (third) and green (fourth). The values listed are for cards which have the tabs intact.

		MT
Complete Set (Blue):		6.00
Complete Set (Black):		6.00
Complete Set (Gold):		6.00
Complete Set (Green):		6.00
Common Player:		.25
3	Rich Camarillo (DP)	.25
11	Tony Eason (DP)	.35
14	Steve Grogan	.50
24	Robert Weathers	.25
26	Raymond Clayborn (DP)	.25
30	Mosi Tatupu	.25
31	Fred Marion	.25
32	Craig James	.50
33	Tony Collins (DP)	.35
38	Roland James	.25
42	Ronnie Lippett	.25
50	Larry McGrew	.25
55	Don Blackmon (DP)	.25
56	Andre Tippett	.50
57	Steve Nelson	.25
58	Pete Brock (DP)	.25
60	Garin Veris	.25
61	Ron Wooten	.25
73	John Hannah	.50
77	Kenneth Sims	.25
80	Irving Fryar	1.00
81	Stephen Starring	.25
83	Cedric Jones	.25
86	Stanley Morgan	.50

1986 McDonald's Los Angeles Raiders

Released over a four-week time span at Los Angeles-area McDonald's, the 24-card set measures 3-1/16" x 4-11/16" with the tab and 3-1/16" x 3-5/8" without. The card fronts are anchored with a color photo, with the McDonald's logo in the upper left and Raiders' helmet in the upper right. The NFL shield and NFLPA logo are located at the bottom, left and right respectively. The player's name, number and position are printed below the photo. The card backs include the player's name, number, position, bio and highlights. Each week featured a different colored tab: blue (first), black or gray (second), gold or orange (third) and green

(fourth). The values listed are for cards which have the tabs intact.

		MT
Complete Set (Blue):		20.00
Complete Set (Black):		10.00
Complete Set (Gold):		6.00
Complete Set (Green):		6.00
Common Player:		.25
1	Marc Wilson	.35
8	Ray Guy (DP)	.50
10	Chris Bahr (DP)	.25
16	Jim Plunkett	.50
22	Mike Haynes	.35
26	Vann McElroy	.25
27	Frank Hawkins	.25
32	Marcus Allen (DP)	1.50
36	Mike Davis (DP)	.25
37	Lester Hayes	.35
46	Todd Christensen (DP)	.50
53	Rod Martin	.35
54	Reggie McKenzie	.25
55	Matt Millen	.35
70	Henry Lawrence	.25
71	Bill Pickel	.25
72	Don Mosebar	.35
73	Charley Hannah	.25
75	Howie Long	1.00
79	Bruce Davis (DP)	.25
84	Jessie Hester	.50
85	Dokie Williams	.25
91	Brad Van Pelt	.25
99	Sean Jones	.50

1986 McDonald's Los Angeles Rams

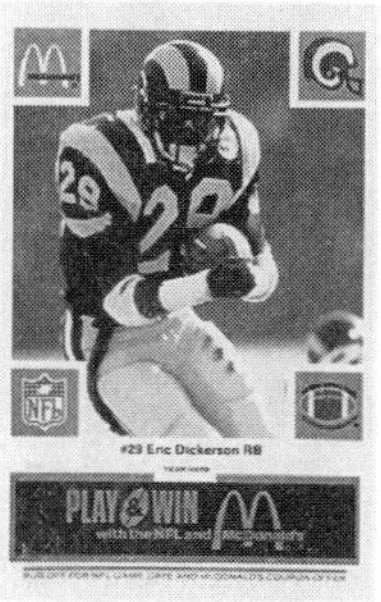

Released over a four-week time span at Los Angeles-area McDonald's, the 24-card set measures 3-1/16" x 4-11/16" with the tab and 3-1/16" x 3-5/8" without. The card fronts are anchored with a color photo, with the McDonald's logo in the upper left and Rams' helmet in the upper right. The NFL shield and NFLPA logo are located at the bottom, respectively. The player's name, number and position are printed below the photo. The card backs include the player's name, number, position, bio and highlights. Each week featured a different colored tab: first week (blue), second (black or gray), third (gold or orange) and fourth (green). The values listed are for cards which have the tabs intact.

		MT
Complete Set (Blue):		9.00
Complete Set (Black):		6.00
Complete Set (Gold):		6.00
Complete Set (Green):		6.00
Common Player:		.25
1	Mike Lansford	.25
3	Dale Hatcher	.25
5	Dieter Brock (DP)	.25
20	Johnnie Johnson	.25
21	Nolan Cromwell (DP)	.35
22	Vince Newsome	.25
27	Gary Green	.25
29	Eric Dickerson (DP)	1.00
44	Mike Guman	.25
47	LeRoy Irvin	.35
50	Jim Collins (DP)	.25
54	Mike Wilcher	.25
55	Carl Ekern	.25
56	Doug Smith	.25
58	Mel Owens	.25
60	Dennis Harrah	.25
71	Reggie Doss (DP)	.25
72	Kent Hill	.25
75	Irv Pankey	.25
78	Jackie Slater	.50
80	Henry Ellard	.75
81	David Hill	.25
87	Tony Hunter	.25
89	Ron Brown (DP)	.35

1986 McDonald's Washington Redskins

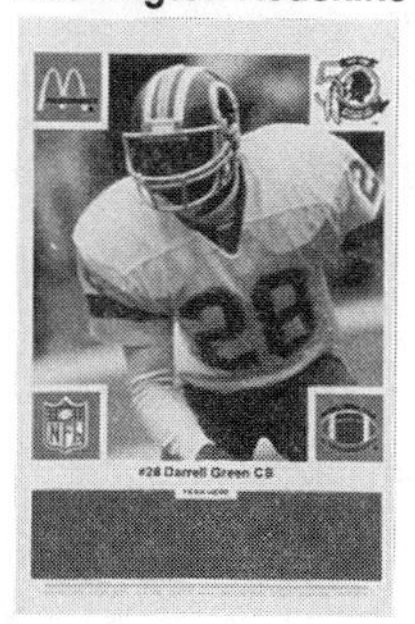

Released over a four-week time span at Washington, D.C.- area McDonald's, the 24-card set measures 3-1/16" x 4-11/16" with the tab and 3-1/16" x 3-5/8" without. The card fronts are anchored with a color photo, with the McDonald's logo in the upper left and Redskins' helmet in the upper right. The NFL shield and NFLPA logo are located at the bottom, left and right respectively. The player's name, number and position are printed below the photo. The card backs include the player's name, number, position, bio and highlights. Each week featured a different colored tab: blue (first), black or gray (second), gold or orange (third) and green (fourth). The values listed are for cards which have the tabs intact.

		MT
Complete Set (Blue):		6.00
Complete Set (Black):		6.00
Complete Set (Gold):		6.00
Complete Set (Green):		6.00
Common Player:		.25
3	Mark Moseley	.25
10	Jay Schroeder	.50
22	Curtis Jordan	.25
28	Darrell Green	.50
32	Vernon Dean (DP)	.25
35	Keith Griffin	.25
37	Raphel Cherry (DP)	.25
38	George Rogers	.35
51	Monte Coleman (DP)	.25
52	Neal Olkewicz	.25
53	Jeff Bostic (DP)	.25
55	Mel Kaufman	.25
57	Rich Milot	.25
65	Dave Butz (DP)	.35
66	Joe Jacoby	.35
68	Russ Grimm	.35
71	Charles Mann	.50
72	Dexter Manley	.35
73	Mark May	.35
77	Darryl Grant	.25
81	Art Monk	1.00
84	Gary Clark (DP)	1.00
85	Don Warren	.35
86	Clint Didier	.25

1986 McDonald's New Orleans Saints

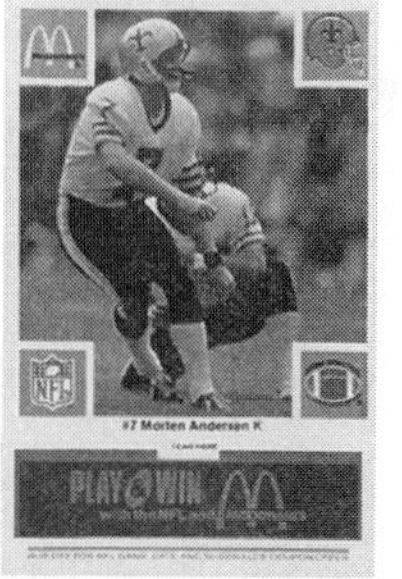

Released over a four-week time span at New Orleans-area McDonald's, the 24-card set measures 3-1/16" x 4-11/16" with the tab and 3-1/16" x 3-5/8" without. The card fronts are anchored with a color photo, with the McDonald's logo in the upper left and Saints' helmet in the upper right. The NFL shield and NFLPA logo are located at the bottom, left and right respectively. The player's name, number and position are printed below the photo. The card backs include the player's name, number, position, bio and highlights. Each week featured a different colored tab: blue (first), black or gray (second), gold or orange (third) and green (fourth). The values listed are for cards which have the tabs intact.

		MT
Complete Set (Blue):		150.00
Complete Set (Black):		30.00
Complete Set (Gold):		20.00
Complete Set (Green):		25.00
Common Player:		.75
3	Bobby Hebert	2.00
7	Morten Andersen (DP)	1.00
10	Brian Hansen	.75
18	Dave Wilson	.75
20	Russell Gary	.75
25	Johnnie Poe	.75
30	Wayne Wilson	.75
44	Dave Waymer	.75
46	Hokie Gajan	.75
49	Frank Wattelett	.75
50	Jack Del Rio (DP)	1.00
57	Rickey Jackson	1.00
60	Steve Korte	.75
61	Joel Hilgenberg	.75
63	Brad Edelman (DP)	.75
64	Dave Lafary	.75
67	Stan Brock (DP)	.75
73	Frank Warren	.75
75	Bruce Clark (DP)	.75
84	Eric Martin	1.50
85	Hoby Brenner (DP)	.75
88	Eugene Goodlow	.75
89	Tyrone Young	.75
99	Tony Elliott	.75

1986 McDonald's Seattle Seahawks

Released over a four-week time span at Seattle-area McDonald's, the 24-card set measures 3-1/16" x 4-11/16" with the tab and 3-1/16" x 3-5/8" without. The card fronts are anchored with a color photo, with the McDonald's logo in the upper left and Seahawks' helmet in the upper right. The NFL shield and NFLPA logo are located at the bottom, left and right respectively. The player's name, number and position are printed below the photo. The card backs include the player's name, number, position, bio and highlights. Each week featured a different colored tab: blue (first), black or gray (second), gold or orange (third) and green (fourth). The values listed are for cards which have the tabs intact.

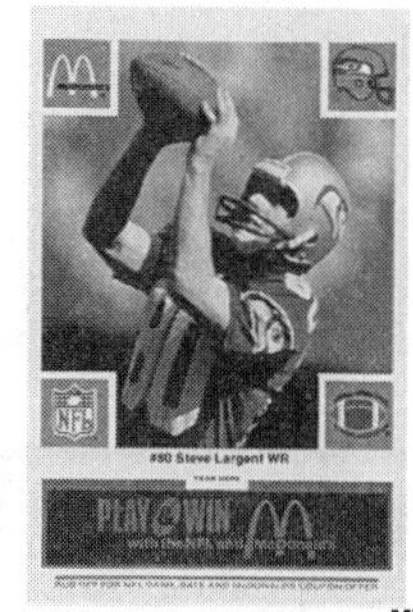

		MT
Complete Set (Blue):		10.00
Complete Set (Black):		7.00
Complete Set (Gold):		7.00
Complete Set (Green):		7.00
Common Player:		.25
9	Norm Johnson	.35
17	Dave Krieg	.50
20	Terry Taylor	.25
22	Dave Brown (DP)	.25
28	Curt Warner (DP)	.50
33	Dan Doornink	.25
44	John Harris	.25
45	Kenny Easley	.35
46	David Hughes	.25
50	Fredd Young	.25
53	Keith Butler (DP)	.25
55	Michael Jackson	.25
58	Bruce Scholtz	.25
59	Blair Bush (DP)	.25
61	Robert Pratt	.25
64	Ron Essink	.25
65	Edwin Bailey (DP)	.25
72	Joe Nash	.25
77	Jeff Bryant (DP)	.25
78	Bob Cryder (DP)	.25
79	Jacob Green	.35
80	Steve Largent	2.00
81	Daryl Turner	.25
82	Paul Skansi	.25

1986 McDonald's Pittsburgh Steelers

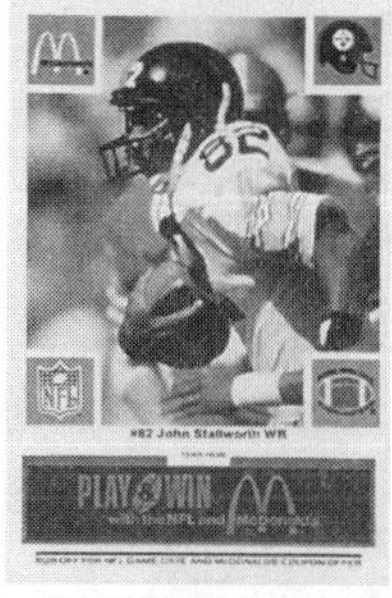

Released over a four-week time span at Pittsburgh-area McDonald's, the 24-card set measures 3-1/16" x 4-11/16" with the tab and 3-1/16" x 3-5/8" without. The card fronts are anchored with a color photo, with the McDonald's logo in the upper left and Steelers' helmet in the upper right. The NFL shield and NFLPA logo are located at the bottom, left and right respectively. The player's name, number and position are printed below the photo. The card backs include the player's name, number, position, bio and highlights. Each week featured a different colored tab: blue (first), black or gray (second), gold or orange (third) and green (fourth). The values listed are for cards which have the tabs intact.

		MT
Complete Set (Blue):		50.00
Complete Set (Black):		25.00
Complete Set (Gold):		10.00
Complete Set (Green):		10.00
Common Player:		.40
1	Gary Anderson (K) (DP)	.50
16	Mark Malone	.50
21	Eric Williams	.40
24	Rich Erenberg (DP)	.40
30	Frank Pollard	.40
31	Donnie Shell	.50
34	Walter Abercrombie (DP)	.40
49	Dwayne Woodruff	.40
50	David Little	.40
52	Mike Webster	.50
53	Bryan Hinkle	.50
56	Robin Cole (DP)	.40
57	Mike Merriweather	.50
62	Tunch Ilkin	.40
65	Ray Pinney	.40
67	Gary Dunn (DP)	.40
73	Craig Wolfley	.40
74	Terry Long	.40
82	John Stallworth	.75
83	Louis Lipps	.75
87	Weegie Thompson	.40
92	Keith Gary (DP)	.40
93	Keith Willis	.40
99	Darryl Sims	.40

1986 McDonald's Minnesota Vikings

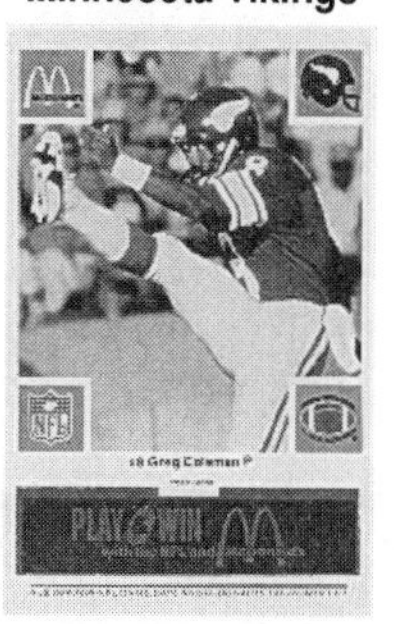

Released over a four-week time span at Minneapolis-area McDonald's, the 24-card set measures 3-1/16" x 4-11/16" with the tab and 3-1/16" x 3-5/8" without. The card fronts are anchored with a color photo, with the McDonald's logo in the upper left and Vikings' helmet in the upper right. The NFL shield and NFLPA logo are located at the bottom, left and right respectively. The player's name, number and position are printed below the photo. The card backs include the player's name, number, position, bio and highlights. Each week featured a different colored tab: blue (first), black or gray (second), gold or orange (third) and green (fourth). The values listed are for cards which have the tabs intact.

		MT
Complete Set (Blue):		45.00
Complete Set (Black):		30.00
Complete Set (Gold):		15.00
Complete Set (Green):		15.00
Common Player:		.60
8	Greg Coleman (DP)	.60
9	Tommy Kramer	.75
11	Wade Wilson	.75
20	Darrin Nelson	.75
23	Ted Brown (DP)	.60
37	Willie Teal	.60
39	Carl Lee	.75
46	Alfred Anderson (DP)	.60
47	Joey Browner (DP)	.75
55	Scott Studwell	.60
56	Chris Doleman	.75
59	Matt Blair (DP)	.75
67	Dennis Swilley	.60
68	Curtis Rouse	.60
75	Keith Millard	.75
76	Tim Irwin	.60
77	Mark Mullaney	.60
79	Doug Martin	.60
81	Anthony Carter (DP)	1.25
83	Steve Jordan	.75
87	Leo Lewis	.75
89	Mike Jones	.60
96	Tim Newton	.60
99	David Howard	.60

1993 McDonald's GameDay

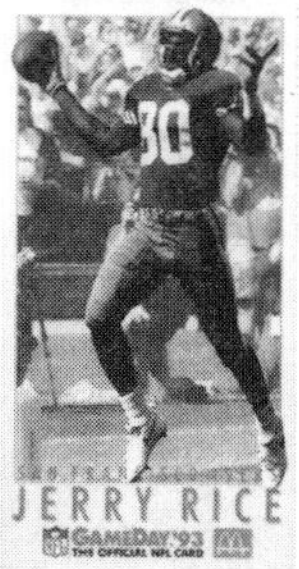

These cards were issued as part of the McDonald's/NFL Kickoff Playoff promotion. With a certain food combination purchase, customers received a game piece which offered prizes ranging from a trip to the Super Bowl to food. Or, the game piece had a point value on it - 6 (touchdown), 3 (field goal) or 1 (extra point). For 10 points, a collector could obtain a six-card panel featuring players from the NFL team in that participating McDonald's market. A different six-player sheet was given away in each of three weeks, making a complete set three panels, or 18 cards. The cards are identical in size to the regular issues (2-1/2" x 4-3/4"), but have a McDonald's logo on each side. Cards are also numbered using a McD prefix. Some restaurants also offered three sheets featuring 18 different All-Stars.

		MT
Complete Set:		35.00
Common Player:		1.50
1	All-Stars A (Deion Sanders, Thurman Thomas, Troy Aikman, John Elway, Barry Sanders, Sterling Sharpe)	1.50
2	All-Stars B (Derrick Thomas, Howie Long, Dan Marino, Chris Doleman, Vaughan Johnson, Phil Simms)	1.50
3	All-Stars C (Randall Cunningham, Barry Foster, Jerry Rice, Junior Seau, Cortez Kennedy, Mark Rypien)	1.00
4	Atlanta Falcons A (Deion Sanders, Moe Gardner, Tim Green, Michael Haynes, Chris Hinton, Tim McKyer)	1.50
5	Atlanta Falcons B (Chris Miller, Bruce Pickens, Mike Pritchard, Andre Rison, Chris Miller, Bruce Pickens, Mike Pritchard, Andre Rison, Darion Conner, Jessie Tuggle)	1.00
6	Atlanta Falcons C (Drew Hill, Pierce Holt, Elbert Shelley, Jesse Solomon, Bobby Hebert, Lincoln Kennedy)	.75
7	Buffalo Bills A (Howard Ballard, Don Beebe, Cornelius Bennett, Phil Hansen, Henry Jones, Jim Kelly)	1.00
8	Buffalo Bills B (Nate Odomes, Andre Reed, Frank Reich, Bruce Smith, Darryl Talley, Steve Tasker)	.75
9	Buffalo Bills C (Bill Brooks, Jim Ritcher, Thurman Thomas, Kenneth Davis, Jeff Wright, Thomas Smith)	1.25
10	Chicago Bears A (Neal Anderson, Trace Armstrong, Mark Carrier DB, Wendell Davis, Richard Dent, Shaun Gayle)	.75
11	Chicago Bears B (Jim Harbaugh, Darren Lewis, Jim Morrissey, William Perry, Alonzo Spellman, Tom Waddle)	.75
12	Chicago Bears C (Steve McMichael, Craig Heyward, Lemuel Stinson, Keith Van Horne, Donnell Woolford, Curtis Conway)	1.00
13	Cincinnati Bengals A (Derrick Fenner, James Francis, David Fulcher, Harold Green, Rod Jones CB, David Klingler)	.75
14	Cincinnati Bengals B (Bruce Kozerski, Tim Krumrie, Ricardo McDonald, Carl Pickens, Reggie Rembert, Daniel Stubbs)	.75
15	Cincinnati Bengals C (Eddie Brown, Gary Reasons, Lamar Rogers, Alfred Williams, Darryl Williams, John Copeland)	.75
16	Cleveland Browns A (Rob Burnett, Jay Hilgenberg, Leroy Hoard, Michael Jackson, Mike Johnson, Bernie Kosar)	1.00
17	Cleveland Browns B (Eric Metcalf, Michael Dean Perry, Clay Matthews, Lawyer Tillman, Eric Turner, Tommy Vardell)	1.00
18	Cleveland Browns C (David Brandon, Tony Jones T, Scott Galbraith, James Jones DT, Vinny Testaverde, Steve Everitt)	.75
19	Dallas Cowboys A (Troy Aikman, Tony Casillas, Thomas Everett, Charles Haley, Alvin Harper, Michael Irvin)	1.75
20	Dallas Cowboys B (Jim Jeffcoat, Daryl Johnston, Robert Jones, Nate Newton, Ken Norton Jr., Jay Novacek)	1.00
21	Dallas Cowboys C (Russell Maryland, Emmitt Smith, Kevin Smith, Mark Stepnoski, Tony Tolbert, Larry Brown DB)	2.00
22	Denver Broncos A (Steve Atwater, Mike Croel, Shane Dronett, John Elway, Simon Fletcher, Reggie Rivers)	1.50
23	Denver Broncos B (Vance Johnson, Greg Lewis, Tommy Maddox, Arthur Marshall, Shannon Sharpe, Dennis Smith)	.75
24	Denver Broncos C (Rod Bernstine, Michael Brooks, Wymon Henderson, Greg Kragen, Karl Mecklenburg, Dan Williams)	.75
25	Detroit Lions A (Bennie Blades, Michael Cofer, Ray Crockett, Mel Gray, Willie Green, Jason Hanson)	.75
26	Detroit Lions B (Herman Moore, Rodney Peete, Brett Perriman, Kelvin Pritchett, Barry Sanders, Tracy Scroggins)	1.50
27	Detroit Lions C (Pat Swilling, Lomas Brown, Erik Kramer, Chris Spielman, Andre Ware, William White)	1.00
28	Green Bay Packers A (Tony Bennett, Matt Brock, Terrell Buckley, LeRoy Butler, Chris Jacke, Brett Favre)	2.00
29	Green Bay Packers B (Jackie Harris, Brian Noble, Bryce Paup, Sterling Sharpe, Ed West, Johnny Holland)	1.00
30	Green Bay Packers C (Tunch Ilkin, George Teague, Reggie White, Ken O'Brien, John Stephens, Wayne Simmons)	1.50
31	Houston Oilers A (Cody Carlson, Ray Childress, Curtis Duncan, William Fuller, Haywood Jeffires, Lamar Lathon)	.75
32	Houston Oilers B (Bruce Matthews, Bubba McDowell, Warren Moon, Mike Munchak, Eddie Robinson, Webster Slaughter)	1.00
33	Houston Oilers C (Ernest Givins, Cris Dishman, Al Smith, Lorenzo White, Lee Williams, Brad Hopkins)	.75
34	Indianapolis Colts A (Chip Banks, Kerry Cash, Quentin Coryatt, Rodney Culver, Steve Emtman, Reggie Langhorne)	.75
35	Indianapolis Colts B (Jeff Herrod, Anthony Johnson, Jeff George, Rohn Stark, Jack Trudeau, Clarence Verdin)	1.00
36	Indianapolis Colts C (Duane Bickett, Eugene Daniel, Jessie Hester, Chris Goode, Kirk Lowdermilk, Sean Dawkins)	.75
37	Kansas City Chiefs A (Dale Carter, Willie Davis, Dave Krieg, Albert Lewis, Nick Lowery, J.J. Birden)	.75
38	Kansas City Chiefs B (Charles Mincy, Christian Okoye, Kevin Ross, Dan Saleaumua, Tracy Simien, Harvey Williams)	.75
39	Kansas City Chiefs C (Todd McNair, Neil Smith, Derrick Thomas, Leonard Griffin, Barry Word, Joe Montana)	1.50
40	Los Angeles Raiders A (Eddie Anderson, Jeff Gossett, Ethan Horton, Jeff Jaeger, Howie Long, Todd Marinovich)	.75
41	Los Angeles Raiders B (Terry McDaniel, Don Mosebar, Anthony Smith, Greg Townsend, Aaron Wallace, Steve Wisniewski)	.75
42	Los Angeles Raiders C (Nick Bell, Tim Brown, Eric Dickerson, James Lofton, Jeff Hostetler, Patrick Bates)	1.00
43	Los Angeles Rams A (Flipper Anderson, Marc Boutte, Henry Ellard, Bill Hawkins, Cleveland Gary, David Lang)	.75
44	Los Angeles Rams B (Jim Everett, Darryl Henley, Todd Lyght, Anthony Newman, Roman Phifer, Jim Price)	1.00
45	Los Angeles Rams C (Shane Conlan, Henry Rolling, Larry Kelm, Jackie Slater, Fred Stokes, Jerome Bettis)	1.25
46	Miami Dolphins A (Marco Coleman, Bryan Cox, Jeff Cross, Mark Duper, Keith Sims, Mark Higgs)	.75
47	Miami Dolphins B (Keith Jackson, Dan Marino, John Offerdahl, Louis Oliver, Tony Paige, Pete Stoyanovich)	2.00

48	Miami Dolphins C (Tony Martin, Irving Fryar, Troy Vincent, Richmond Webb, Jarvis Williams, O.J. McDuffie)	1.00
49	Minnesota Vikings A (Terry Allen, Anthony Carter, Cris Carter, Jack Del Rio, Chris Doleman, Rich Gannon)	1.00
50	Minnesota Vikings B (Steve Jordan, Carl Lee, Randall McDaniel, John Randle, Sean Salisbury, Todd Scott)	.75
51	Minnesota Vikings C (Jim McMahon, Audray McMillian, Mike Merriweather, Henry Thomas, Gary Zimmerman, Robert Smith)	.75
52	New England Patriots A (Ray Agnew, Bruce Armstrong, Vincent Brown, Eugene Chung, Marv Cook, Maurice Hurst)	.75
53	New England Patriots B (Pat Harlow, Eugene Lockhart, Greg McMurtry, Scott Zolak, Leonard Russell, Andre Tippett)	1.00
54	New England Patriots C (David Howard, Johnny Rembert, Jon Vaughn, Brent Williams, Scott Secules, Drew Bledsoe)	1.50
55	New Orleans Saints A (Morten Andersen, Gene Atkins, Toi Cook, Richard Cooper, Jim Dombrowski, Vaughn Dunbar)	.75
56	New Orleans Saints B (Joel Hilgenberg, Rickey Jackson, Vaughan Johnson, Wayne Martin, Renaldo Turnbull, Frank Warren)	.75
57	New Orleans Saints C (Irv Smith, Brad Muster, Dalton Hilliard, Eric Martin, Sam Mills, Willie Roaf)	.75
58	New York Giants A (Jarrod Bunch, Mark Collins, Howard Cross, Rodney Hampton, Erik Howard, Greg Jackson)	1.00
59	New York Giants B (Pepper Johnson, Sean Landeta, Ed McCaffrey, Dave Meggett, Bart Oates, Phil Simms)	1.00
60	New York Giants C (Carlton Bailey, Carl Banks, John Elliott, Eric Dorsey, Lawrence Taylor, Mike Sherrard)	1.00
61	New York Jets A (Brad Baxter, Scott Mersereau, Chris Burkett, Kyle Clifton, Jeff Lageman, Mo Lewis)	.75
62	New York Jets B (Johnny Mitchell, Rob Moore, Browning Nagle, Blair Thomas, Brian Washington, Marvin Washington)	.75
63	New York Jets C (Boomer Esiason, James Hasty, Ronnie Lott, Leonard Marshall, Terance Mathis, Marvin Jones)	1.00
64	Philadelphia Eagles A (Eric Allen, Fred Barnett, Randall Cunningham, Byron Evans, Andy Harmon, Seth Joyner)	1.00
65	Philadelphia Eagles B (Heath Sherman, Vai Sikahema, Clyde Simmons, Herschel Walker, Andre Waters, Calvin Williams)	1.00
66	Philadelphia Eagles C (Keith Byars, Mike Golic, Leonard Renfro, William Thomas, Antone Davis, Lester Holmes)	.75
67	Phoenix Cardinals A (Johnny Bailey, Rich Camarillo, Larry Centers, Chris Chandler, Ken Harvey, Randal Hill)	.75
68	Phoenix Cardinals B (Mark May, Robert Massey, Freddie Joe Nunn, Ricky Proehl, Eric Hill, Eric Swann)	1.00
69	Phoenix Cardinals C (Gary Clark, John Booty, Chuck Cecil, Steve Beuerlein, Ernest Dye, Garrison Hearst)	1.00
70	Pittsburgh Steelers A (Dermontti Dawson, Barry Foster, Jeff Graham, Eric Green, Carlton Haselrig, Bryan Hinkle)	1.00
71	Pittsburgh Steelers B (Merril Hoge, D.J. Johnson, Carnell Lake, David Little, Neil O'Donnell, Darren Perry)	1.00
72	Pittsburgh Steelers C (Bubby Brister, Kevin Greene, Greg Lloyd, Leon Searcy, Rod Woodson, Deon Figures)	1.00
73	San Diego Chargers A (Eric Bieniemy, Marion Butts, Burt Grossman, Ronnie Harmon, Stan Humphries, Nate Lewis)	1.00
74	San Diego Chargers B (Chris Mims, Leslie O'Neal, Stanley Richard, Junior Seau, Harry Swayne, Derrick Walker)	1.00
75	San Diego Chargers C (Jerrol Williams, Gill Byrd, John Friesz, Anthony Miller, Gary Plummer, Darrien Gordon)	1.00
76	San Francisco 49ers A (Ricky Watters, Michael Carter, Don Griffin, Dana Hall, Brent Jones, Harris Barton)	1.00
77	San Francisco 49ers B (Tom Rathman, Jerry Rice, Bill Romanowski, John Taylor, Steve Wallace, Mike Walter)	1.50
78	San Francisco 49ers C (Kevin Fagan, Todd Kelly, Guy McIntyre, Tim McDonald, Steve Young, Dana Stubblefield)	1.50
79	Seattle Seahawks A (Robert Blackmon, Brian Blades, Jeff Bryant, Dwayne Harper, Andy Heck, Tommy Kane)	.75
80	Seattle Seahawks B (Cortez Kennedy, Dan McGwire, Rufus Porter, Ray Roberts, Eugene Robinson, Chris Warren)	1.00
81	Seattle Seahawks C (Ferrell Edmunds, Kelvin Martin, John L. Williams, Tony Woods, David Wyman, Rick Mirer)	1.25
82	Tampa Bay Buccaneers A (Gary Anderson RB, Tyji Armstrong, Reggie Cobb, Lawrence Dawsey, Steve DeBerg, Santana Dotson)	.75
83	Tampa Bay Buccaneers B (Ron Hall, Courtney Hawkins, Keith McCants, Charles McRae, Ricky Reynolds, Broderick Thomas)	.75
84	Tampa Bay Buccaneers C (Vince Workman, Paul Gruber, Hardy Nickerson, Marty Carter, Mark Wheeler, Eric Curry)	.75
85	Washington Redskins A (Earnest Byner, Andre Collins, Brad Edwards, Ricky Ervins, Darrell Green, Desmond Howard)	1.00
86	Washington Redskins B (Tim Johnson, Jim Lachey, Chip Lohmiller, Mark Rypien, Ricky Sanders, Mark Schlereth)	1.00
87	Washington Redskins C (Al Noga, Kurt Gouveia, Charles Mann, Wilber Marshall, Art Monk, Tom Carter)	1.00

1996 McDonald's Looney Tunes Cups

These four cups were available at McDonalds during the 1996 NFL season. Each cup featured a player and a Looney Tunes character.

		MT
Complete Set (4):		6.00
Common Cup:		1.00
1	Wile E. Coyote (Drew Bledsoe)	1.00
2	Daffy Duck (Dan Marino)	2.00
3	Tazmanian Devil (Barry Sanders)	1.50
4	Bugs Bunny (Emmitt Smith)	2.00

1995 Metal

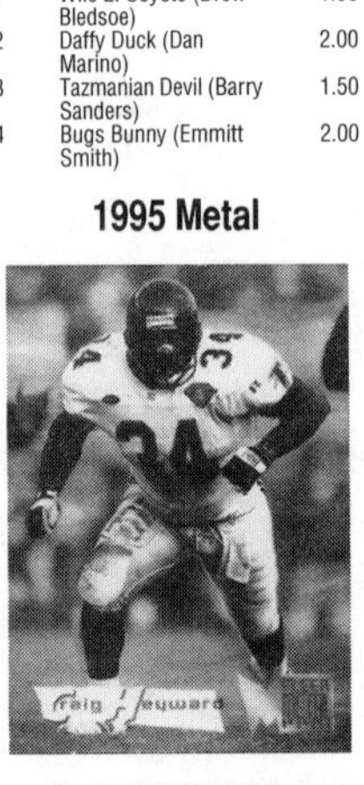

Fleer's 1995 Metal features the set's computer-generated metallic, hand foil-etched fronts with a color action photo. The player's name is written in a foil panel at the bottom of the card, next to the brand logo. The cards have a triangle in the lower left which has the card number; cards are numbered as subsets by team, alphabetically by city name and then by player name. An action photo comprises the top part of the card, with a bar graph depicting 1994 and career totals. Biographical information is also included. The team name is written along the right side of the card. Three insert sets were created: Silver Flashers, Gold Blasters and Platinum Portraits. As an added bonus, a Super Bowl XXX instant win card was randomly included in a pack; the finder was entitled to a trip to Super Bowl XXX in Phoenix.

		MT
Complete Set (200):		50.00
Common Player:		.10
Minor Stars:		.20
Pack (8):		2.50
Wax Box (36):		65.00
1	Garrison Hearst	.25
2	Seth Joyner	.10
3	Dave Krieg	.10
4	Lorenzo Lynch	.10
5	Rob Moore	.10
6	Eric Swann	.10
7	Aeneas Williams	.10
8	Chris Doleman	.10
9	Bert Emanuel	.50
10	Jeff George	.25
11	Craig Heyward	.10
12	Terance Mathis	.10
13	Eric Metcalf	.10
14	Cornelius Bennett	.10
15	Bucky Brooks	.10
16	Jeff Burris	.10
17	Jim Kelly	.20
18	Andre Reed	.20
19	Bruce Smith	.10
20	Don Beebe	.10
21	*Kerry Collins*	1.50
22	Barry Foster	.20
23	Lamar Lathon	.10
24	Sam Mills	.10
25	*Tyrone Poole*	.20
26	Frank Reich	.10
27	Joe Cain	.10
28	Curtis Conway	.10
29	Jeff Graham	.10
30	Erik Kramer	.10
31	*Rashaan Salaam*	.50
32	Lewis Tillman	.10
33	Chris Zorich	.10
34	*Jeff Blake*	.75
35	*Ki-Jana Carter*	.50
36	Carl Pickens	.50
37	Corey Sawyer	.10
38	Darnay Scott	.75
39	Dan Wilkinson	.10
40	Darryl Williams	.10
41	Derrick Alexander	.30
42	Leroy Hoard	.10
43	Michael Jackson	.10
44	Antonio Langham	.10
45	Andre Rison	.20
46	Vinny Testaverde	.10
47	Eric Turner	.10
48	Troy Aikman	1.50
49	Charles Haley	.10
50	Michael Irvin	.50
51	Daryl Johnston	.10
52	Jay Novacek	.10
53	Emmitt Smith	3.00
54	Kevin Williams	.10
55	Steve Atwater	.10
56	Rod Bernstine	.10
57	John Elway	.75
58	Glyn Milburn	.10
59	Anthony Miller	.10
60	Mike Pritchard	.10
61	Shannon Sharpe	.10
62	Mike Johnson	.10
63	Scott Mitchell	.10
64	Herman Moore	1.00
65	Brett Perriman	.10
66	Barry Sanders	2.50
67	Chris Spielman	.10
68	Edgar Bennett	.10
69	Robert Brooks	.10
70	Brett Favre	3.00
71	LeShon Johnson	.10
72	George Koonce	.10
73	Reggie White	.20
74	Gary Brown	.10
75	Cris Dishman	.10
76	Mel Gray	.10
77	*Steve McNair*	4.50
78	Webster Slaughter	.10
79	*Rodney Thomas*	.20
80	Trev Alberts	.10
81	Quentin Coryatt	.10
82	Sean Dawkins	.10
83	Craig Erickson	.10
84	Marshall Faulk	2.00
85	Stephen Grant	.20
86	Steve Beuerlein	.10
87	*Tony Boselli*	.50
88	Desmond Howard	.10
89	*James Stewart*	1.50
90	Marcus Allen	.20
91	Kimble Anders	.10
92	Steve Bono	.30
93	Lake Dawson	.40
94	Greg Hill	.40
95	Neil Smith	.10
96	Derrick Thomas	.20
97	Tim Bowens	.10
98	Brian Cox	.10
99	Irving Fryar	.10
100	Eric Green	.10
101	Dan Marino	3.00
102	O.J. McDuffie	.10
103	Bernie Parmalee	.40
104	Cris Carter	.20
105	Jack Del Rio	.10
106	Quadry Ismail	.10
107	Warren Moon	.20
108	Jake Reed	.10
109	DeWayne Washington	.10
110	Bruce Armstrong	.10
111	Drew Bledsoe	2.00
112	Vincent Brisby	.10
113	Ben Coates	.10
114	Willie McGinnest	.10
115	David Meggett	.10
116	Chris Slade	.10
117	Mario Bates	.50
118	Quinn Early	.10
119	Jim Everett	.20
120	Michael Haynes	.10
121	Tyrone Hughes	.10
122	Renaldo Turnbull	.10
123	*Ray Zellers*	.50
124	Dave Brown	.10
125	Chris Calloway	.10
126	Rodney Hampton	.20
127	Thomas Lewis	.10
128	Phillippi Sparks	.10
129	*Tyrone Wheatley*	.50
130	*Kyle Brady*	.75
131	Boomer Esiason	.10
132	Aaron Glenn	.10
133	Bobby Houston	.10
134	Mo Lewis	.10
135	Johnny Mitchell	.10
136	Ron Moore	.10
137	Greg Biekert	.10
138	Tim Brown	.20
139	Jeff Hostetler	.20
140	Raghib Ismail	.10
141	*Napoleon Kaufman*	4.00
142	Chester McGlockton	.10
143	Harvey Williams	.10
144	Fred Barnett	.10
145	Randall Cunningham	.10
146	William Fuller	.10
147	Charlie Garner	.10
148	Andy Harmon	.10
149	Ricky Watters	.20
150	Calvin Williams	.10
151	Kevin Greene	.10
152	Charles Johnson	.40
153	Greg Lloyd	.10
154	Bam Morris	.75
155	Neil O'Donnell	.10
156	Darren Perry	.10
157	Rod Woodson	.10
158	Jerome Bettis	.50
159	Isaac Bruce	.50
160	Troy Drayton	.10
161	Sean Gilbert	.10
162	Todd Lyght	.10
163	Chris Miller	.10
164	Andre Coleman	.10
165	Stan Humphries	.20
166	Shawn Jefferson	.10
167	Natrone Means	1.25
168	Leslie O'Neal	.10
169	Junior Seau	.30
170	Mark Seay	.10
171	William Floyd	.60
172	Merton Hanks	.10
173	Brent Jones	.10
174	Jerry Rice	2.00
175	Deion Sanders	1.25
176	*J.J. Stokes*	2.00
177	Lee Woodall	.10
178	Bryant Young	.10
179	Steve Young	1.50
180	Brian Blades	.10
181	*Joey Galloway*	4.00
182	Cortez Kennedy	.10
183	Kevin Mawae	.10
184	Rick Mirer	.50
185	Chris Warren	.20
186	Lawrence Dawsey	.10
187	Trent Dilfer	.75
188	Paul Gruber	.10
189	Hardy Nickerson	.10
190	Errict Rhett	.20
191	*Warren Sapp*	.75
192	Tom Carter	.10
193	Henry Ellard	.10
194	Darrell Green	.10
195	Brian Mitchell	.10
196	Heath Shuler	.30
197	*Michael Westbrook*	1.50
198	Checklist	.10
199	Checklist	.10
200	Checklist	.10

1995 Metal Gold Blasters

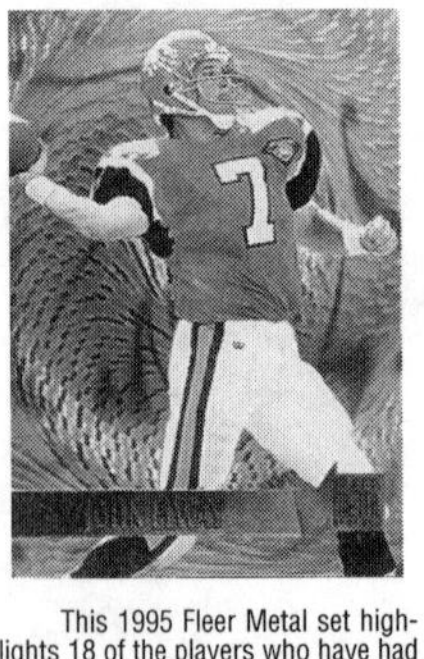

This 1995 Fleer Metal set highlights 18 of the players who have had a major impact on the NFL. Cards were randomly inserted into every fifth pack of 1995 Fleer Metal football. The card front has color action photo against a swirled, gold metallic background. The player's name is in a bar at the bottom of the card, next to the brand logo. The card back, numbered 1 of 18, etc., at the bottom, has the insert set icon in the lower left corner. A player profile is in the upper right corner.

		MT
Complete Set (18):		70.00
Common Player:		2.00
1	Troy Aikman	7.00
2	Jerome Bettis	3.00
3	Tim Brown	2.00
4	Ben Coates	2.00
5	John Elway	5.00
6	Brett Favre	12.00
7	William Floyd	2.00
8	Joey Galloway	5.00
9	Rodney Hampton	2.00
10	Dan Marino	12.00
11	Steve McNair	6.00
12	Herman Moore	2.00
13	Errict Rhett	2.00
14	Rashaan Salaam	2.00
15	Chris Warren	2.00
16	Michael Westbrook	3.00
17	Rod Woodson	2.00
18	Steve Young	7.00

1995 Metal Platinum Portraits

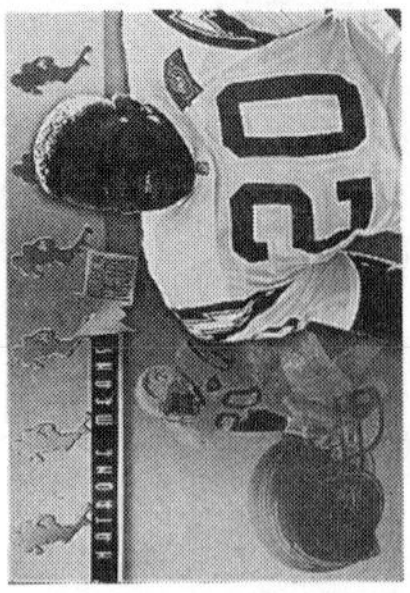

Twelve of the NFL's elite players are featured on these 1995 Fleer Metal insert football cards. Cards, numbered on the back "number x of 12!", were random inserts, one in every ninth pack. The horizontal card front has a color closeup of the player on the left, with ghosted images of his team logo and him in action on the right. The metallic background features his team's primary uniform color. Along the upper top of the card are several player icons, with the player's name and brand logo just below in the right corner. The back has a player profile written towards the top, with small and large icons from the front incorporated into the design.

		MT
Complete Set (12):		60.00
Common Player:		3.00
1	Drew Bledsoe	7.00
2	Ki-Jana Carter	3.00
3	Marshall Faulk	7.00
4	Natrone Means	5.00
5	Bam Morris	3.00
6	Jerry Rice	7.00
7	Andre Rison	3.00
8	Barry Sanders	8.00
9	Deion Sanders	6.00
10	Emmitt Smith	15.00
11	J.J. Stokes	8.00
12	Ricky Watters	3.00

1995 Metal Silver Flashers

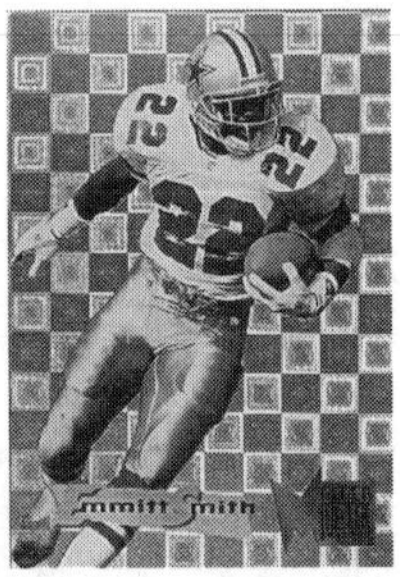

This 50-card set features some of the NFL's flashiest performers. Cards were random inserts, one every two packs of 1995 Fleer Metal football. The card front has a silver metallic background, with a color action photo superimposed in the forefront. The player's name is in a silver foil panel at the bottom, next to the brand logo in the lower right corner. The back's design has the brand logo incorporated into its design at the top, with a written player profile also included. A card number is in a triangle in the lower left corner.

		MT
Complete Set (50):		70.00
Common Player:		.50
Minor Stars:		1.00
1	Troy Aikman	4.00
2	Marcus Allen	.50
3	Jerome Bettis	1.00
4	Drew Bledsoe	4.00
5	Tim Brown	.50
6	Cris Carter	.50
7	Ki-Jana Carter	1.00
8	Ben Coates	.50
9	Kerry Collins	1.50
10	Randall Cunningham	1.00
11	Lake Dawson	.50
12	Trent Dilfer	1.00
13	John Elway	2.00
14	Jim Everett	.50
15	Marshall Faulk	2.00
16	Brett Favre	8.00
17	William Floyd	1.00
18	Jeff George	.50
19	Rodney Hampton	.50
20	Jeff Hostetler	.50
21	Stan Humphries	.50
22	Michael Irvin	1.00
23	Cortez Kennedy	.50
24	Dan Marino	8.00
25	Terance Mathis	.50
26	Willie McGinnest	.50
27	Natrone Means	1.25
28	Rick Mirer	1.00
29	Warren Moon	.50
30	Herman Moore	.50
31	Bam Morris	1.00
32	Carl Pickens	1.00
33	Errict Rhett	1.50
34	Jerry Rice	4.00
35	Andre Rison	.50
36	Rashaan Salaam	2.00
37	Barry Sanders	5.00
38	Deion Sanders	2.50
39	Junior Seau	.50
40	Shannon Sharpe	.50
41	Heath Shuler	1.00
42	Emmitt Smith	8.00
43	J.J. Stokes	2.00
44	Chris Warren	.50
45	Ricky Watters	.50
46	Michael Westbrook	1.50
47	Tyrone Wheatley	1.00
48	Reggie White	.50
49	Rod Woodson	.50
50	Steve Young	2.00

1996 Metal

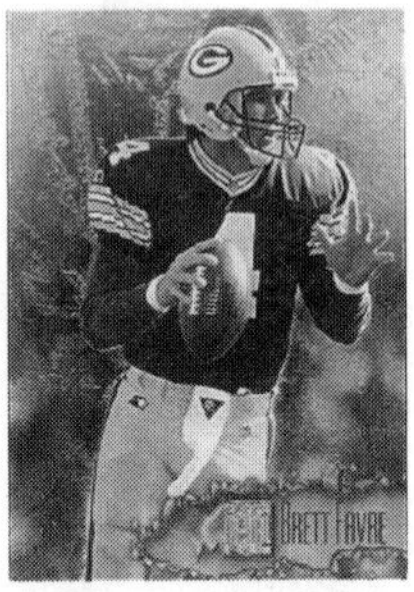

Fleer's 1996 Metal set has an all-new look for 1996 - metalized foil engraved by hand on each card front, meaning no two player cards are alike. The basic set includes 123 regular cards, 25 rookies and two checklists. The card front has a full-bleed color photograph, with the player's name "tearing through" the lower right-hand corner of the card. The back has another photo, a close-cropped headshot bursting through the card, 1995 and career statistics, and biographical information. An extra-rare parallel set - Precious Metal - was also produced. These cards, seeded one per box, feature an all-silver front and were limited to less than 550 each. They are numbered on the back using a PM prefix. There were five other insert sets included in packs - Goldfingers, Goldflingers, Platinum Portraits, Molten Metal and Freshly Forged.

		MT
Complete Set (150):		30.00
Common Player:		.10
Minor Stars:		.20
Comp. Precious Metal (148):		800.00
Precious Metal Cards:		15x-30x
Pack (8):		2.25
Wax Box (24):		52.00
1	Garrison Hearst	.10
2	Rob Moore	.10
3	Frank Sanders	.10
4	Eric Swann	.10
5	Jeff George	.20
6	Craig Heyward	.10
7	Terance Mathis	.10
8	Eric Metcalf	.10
9	Derrick Alexander	.10
10	Andre Rison	.10
11	Vinny Testaverde	.10
12	Eric Turner	.10
13	Jim Kelly	.10
14	Bryce Paup	.10
15	Bruce Smith	.10
16	Thurman Thomas	.20
17	Bob Christian	.10
18	Kerry Collins	.40
19	Lamar Lathon	.10
20	Tyrone Poole	.10
21	Curtis Conway	.10
22	Bryan Cox	.10
23	Erik Kramer	.10
24	Rashaan Salaam	.50
25	Jeff Blake	.20
26	Ki-Jana Carter	.50
27	Carl Pickens	.20
28	Darnay Scott	.30
29	Troy Aikman	1.50
30	Michael Irvin	.20
31	Daryl Johnston	.10
32	Deion Sanders	.75
33	Emmitt Smith	3.00
34	Terrell Davis	1.25
35	John Elway	.75
36	Anthony Miller	.10
37	Shannon Sharpe	.10
38	Scott Mitchell	.10
39	Herman Moore	.75
40	Brett Perriman	.10
41	Barry Sanders	2.00
42	Edgar Bennett	.10
43	Robert Brooks	.20
44	Mark Chmura	.30
45	Brett Favre	3.00
46	Reggie White	.20
47	Mel Gray	.10
48	Steve McNair	1.00

49	Chris Sanders	.30
50	Rodney Thomas	.20
51	Quentin Coryatt	.10
52	Sean Dawkins	.10
53	Ken Dilger	.10
54	Marshall Faulk	.75
55	Jim Harbaugh	.20
56	Tony Boselli	.10
57	Mark Brunell	1.00
58	Natrone Means	.20
59	James Stewart	.10
60	Marcus Allen	.20
61	Steve Bono	.20
62	Neil Smith	.10
63	Tamarick Vanover	.20
64	Eric Green	.10
65	Terry Kirby	.10
66	Dan Marino	3.00
67	O.J. McDuffie	.10
68	Cris Carter	.10
69	Qadry Ismail	.10
70	Warren Moon	.10
71	Jake Reed	.10
72	Drew Bledsoe	1.25
73	Ben Coates	.10
74	Curtis Martin	2.50
75	David Meggett	.10
76	Mario Bates	.10
77	Jim Everett	.10
78	Michael Haynes	.10
79	Tyrone Hughes	.10
80	Dave Brown	.10
81	Rodney Hampton	.10
82	Thomas Lewis	.10
83	Tyrone Wheatley	.10
84	Kyle Brady	.10
85	Hugh Douglas	.10
86	Adrian Murrell	.10
87	Neil O'Donnell	.10
88	Tim Brown	.10
89	Jeff Hostetler	.10
90	Napoleon Kaufman	.30
91	Harvey Williams	.10
92	Charlie Garner	.10
93	Rodney Peete	.10
94	Ricky Watters	.10
95	Calvin Williams	.10
96	Jerome Bettis	.20
97	Greg Lloyd	.10
98	Kordell Stewart	1.00
99	Yancey Thigpen	.30
100	Rod Woodson	.10
101	Isaac Bruce	.30
102	Kevin Carter	.10
103	Steve Walsh	.10
104	Aaron Hayden	.10
105	Stan Humphries	.10
106	Junior Seau	.10
107	William Floyd	.10
108	Brent Jones	.10
109	Jerry Rice	1.50
110	J.J. Stokes	.20
111	Steve Young	1.00
112	Brian Blades	.10
113	Joey Galloway	1.00
114	Rick Mirer	.10
115	Chris Warren	.20
116	Trent Dilfer	.10
117	Alvin Harper	.10
118	Hardy Nickerson	.10
119	Errict Rhett	.30
120	Terry Allen	.10
121	Brian Mitchell	.10
122	Heath Shuler	.10
123	Michael Westbrook	.20
124	*Karim Abdul-Jabbar*	.75
125	*Tim Biakabutuka*	1.00
126	*Duane Clemons*	.10
127	*Stephen Davis*	4.00
128	*Rickey Dudley*	.75
129	*Bobby Engram*	.50
130	*Daryl Gardener*	.10
131	*Eddie George*	4.00
132	*Terry Glenn*	2.00
133	*Kevin Hardy*	.20
134	*Walt Harris*	.20
135	*Marvin Harrison*	3.00
136	*Keyshawn Johnson*	2.50
137	*Cedric Jones*	.10
138	*Eddie Kennison*	.30
139	*Sam Manuel,Sean Manuel*	.10
140	*Leeland McElroy*	.30
141	*Ray Mickens*	.10
142	*Jonathan Ogden*	.10
143	*Lawrence Phillips*	.75
144	*Kavika Pittman*	.10
145	*Simeon Rice*	.20
146	*Regan Upshaw*	.10
147	*Alex Van Dyke*	.20
148	*Stepfret Williams*	.10
149	Checklist	.10
150	Checklist	.10

1996 Metal Precious Metal

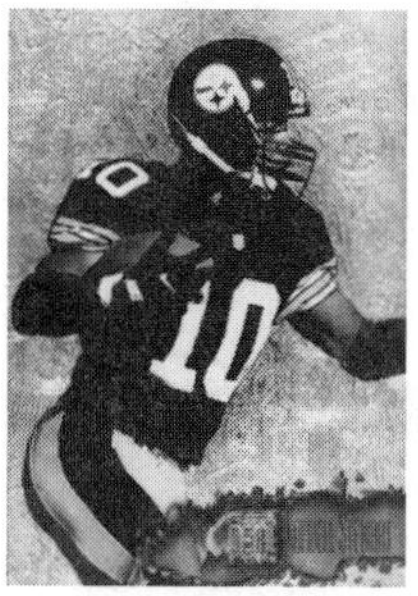

One Precious Metals parallel card was found in each box of Metal Football in 1996. The set included each card in the regular-issue set (minus the two checklists), but featured all-silver fronts and the letters "PM" preceding the card number on the back.

	MT
Complete Set (148):	800.00
Precious Metal Cards:	15x-30x

1996 Metal Goldfingers

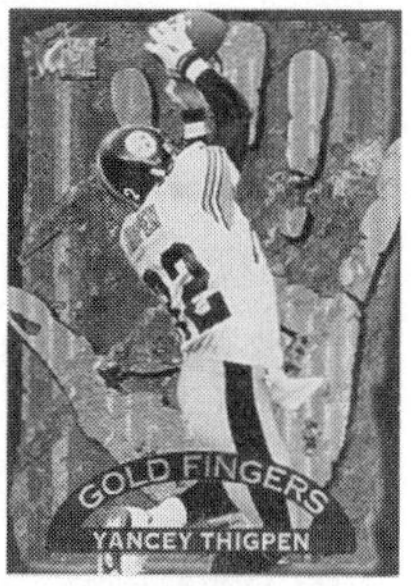

These 24-karat etched gold foil-stamped inserts feature some of the NFL's top-flight receivers. Each card front has a color action photo against a metallic background with an image of a gold hand. The Fleer logo is in the upper left corner. The player's name and "Goldfingers" are in gold foil in an arch at the bottom. The card back, numbered 1 of 10, etc., has a color photo on one side, with the player's name in the upper left corner. A brief player profile is below. Cards were seeded one per every eight packs.

		MT
Complete Set (12):		40.00
Common Player:		2.00
1	Isaac Bruce	5.00
2	Joey Galloway	7.00
3	Michael Irvin	3.00
4	Herman Moore	4.00
5	Carl Pickens	2.00
6	Jerry Rice	10.00
7	Chris Sanders	3.00
8	Frank Sanders	2.00
9	J.J. Stokes	4.00
10	Yancey Thigpen	4.00
11	Tamarick Vanover	2.00
12	Michael Westbrook	4.00

1996 Metal Goldflingers

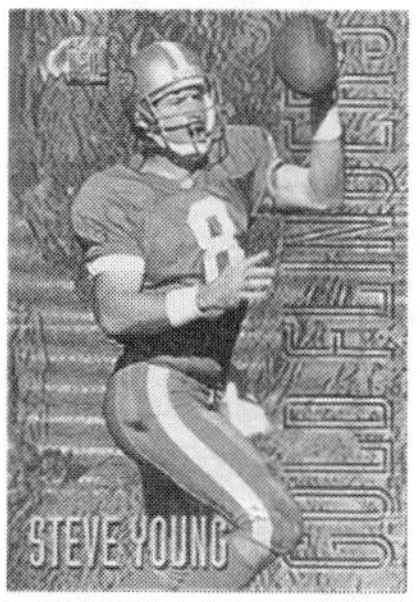

Twelve of the top quarterbacks in football were included in the Goldflingers insert, not to be confused with Goldfingers, which were both out of Metal. Goldflingers was a retail exclusive insert found every 12 packs.

		MT
Complete Set (12):		50.00
Common Player:		2.00
1	Troy Aikman	7.00
2	Steve Bono	2.00
3	Kerry Collins	4.00
4	Trent Dilfer	2.00
5	Brett Favre	14.00
6	Gus Frerotte	2.00
7	Stan Humphries	2.00
8	Dan Marino	14.00
9	Steve McNair	5.00
10	Scott Mitchell	2.00
11	Steve Young	5.00
12	Eric Zeier	2.00

1996 Metal Platinum Portraits

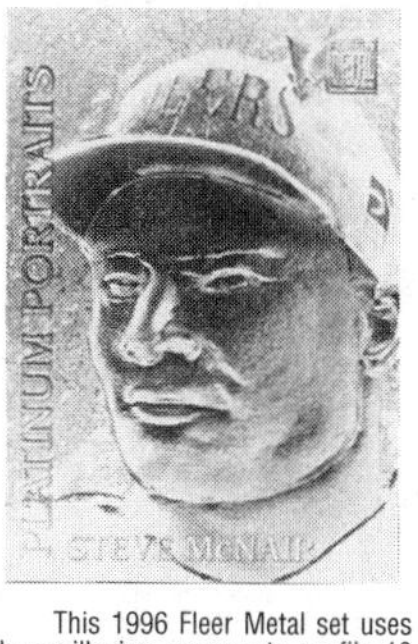

This 1996 Fleer Metal set uses the serillusion process to profile 10 NFL stars. The front shows a closeup head shot of the player, using a silvery embossed effect to create depth. The Fleer Metal logo is in the upper left corner; "Platinum Portraits" is written along the right side of the card. The player's name is along the bottom. The horizontal card back shows an image of the photo from the front as a background, with a brief writeup over it. One side of the card has a color action photo on it. The card number, 1 of 12, etc., is in the upper left corner, with the player's name next to it.

		MT
Complete Set (10):		100.00
Common Player:		5.00
1	Isaac Bruce	5.00
2	Terrell Davis	16.00
3	John Elway	12.00
4	Joey Galloway	16.00
5	Steve McNair	15.00
6	Errict Rhett	10.00
7	Rashaan Salaam	10.00
8	Barry Sanders	25.00
9	Chris Warren	5.00
10	Steve Young	18.00

1996 Metal Molten Metal

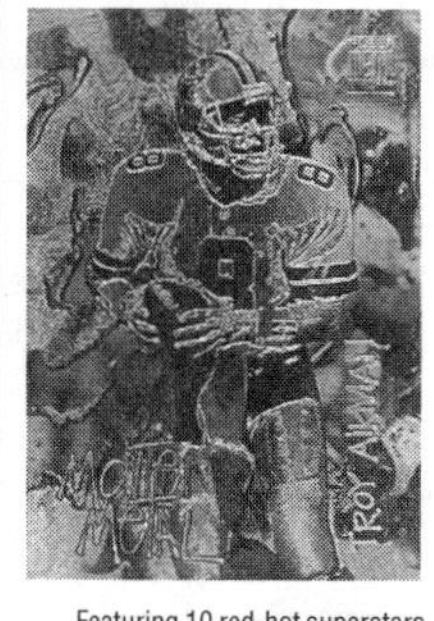

Featuring 10 red-hot superstars, these 1996 Fleer inserts use foil embossing on the front. The Fleer Metal logo is in an upper corner; Molten Metal, in gold foil, is in the lower left corner. The player's name is in gold foil, too, along the right side of the card. The card back, numbered 1 of 10, etc., has a photo on one side. The other side has a white rectangle which includes a brief player profile. The player's name is above the box. These cards were the scarcest of the Fleer Metal inserts; they were seeded one per every 120 packs.

		MT
Complete Set (10):		250.00
Common Player:		10.00
1	Troy Aikman	25.00
2	Ki-Jana Carter	10.00
3	Kerry Collins	15.00
4	Terrell Davis	35.00
5	Marshall Faulk	15.00
6	Brett Favre	50.00
7	Keyshawn Johnson	15.00
8	Curtis Martin	35.00
9	Deion Sanders	15.00
10	Emmitt Smith	50.00

1996 Metal Freshly Forged

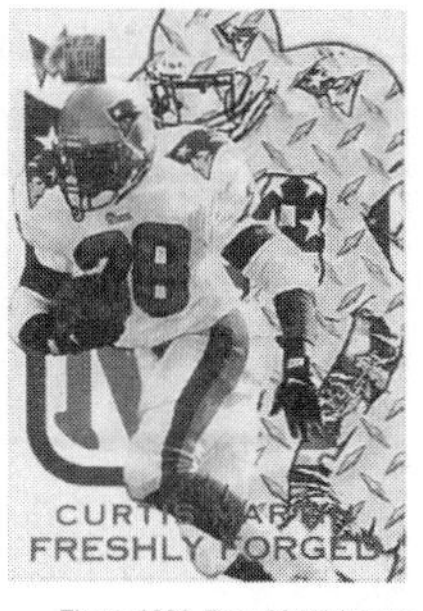

These 1996 Fleer Metal inserts highlight second-year NFL standouts and flashy rookies. The cards, seeded one per every 30 hobby packs only, are acrylic. The card front has a color action photo on it, with an NFL logo and line drawing of the photo as the background. The Fleer Metal logo is in an upper corner. The player's name and "Freshly Forged" are stamped in gold foil along the bottom. The card back shows the entire NFL logo, with a description of the player's skills inside. A card number, 1 of 10, etc., is also on the back.

		MT
Complete Set (10):		125.00
Common Player:		4.00
1	Tim Biakabutuka	4.00
2	Jeff Blake	10.00
3	Ki-Jana Carter	4.00
4	Eddie George	25.00
5	Terry Glenn	20.00
6	Keyshawn Johnson	12.00
7	Curtis Martin	20.00
8	Leeland McElroy	8.00
9	Lawrence Phillips	12.00
10	Kordell Stewart	18.00

1997 Metal

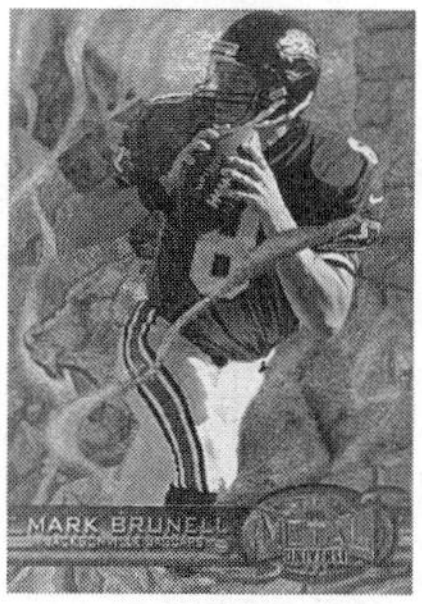

The 200-card set contains 173 player cards, two checklists and 25 rookies. Each card featured all etched foil. The players are presented in original Marvel comic illustrations on full-bleed backgrounds, with the player's name, team, position and Metal Universe logo located near the bottom of the card. Card backs contain another player photo and stats.

		MT
Complete Set (200):		30.00
Common Player:		.10
Minor Stars:		.20
Precious Metal Stars: 40x-80x		
Precious Metal Rookies: 20x-40x		
Pack (8):		2.50
Wax Box (24):		50.00
1	Terry Glenn	.30
2	Terry Kirby	.10
3	Thomas Lewis	.10
4	Tim Biakabutuka	.20
5	Tim Brown	.10
6	Todd Collins	.10
7	Tony Banks	.40
8	Tony Brackens	.10
9	Tony Martin	.10
10	Trent Dilfer	.20
11	Troy Aikman	1.00
12	Ty Detmer	.10
13	Tyrone Wheatley	.10
14	Vinny Testaverde	.10
15	Wayne Chrebet	.10
16	Wesley Walls	.10
17	William Floyd	.10
18	Willie McGinest	.10
19	Yancey Thigpen	.10
20	Zach Thomas	.30
21	Terry Allen	.10
22	Terrell Owens	.50
23	Terrell Davis	1.25
24	Terance Mathis	.10
25	Ted Johnson	.10
26	Tamarick Vanover	.20
27	Steve Young	.50
28	Steve McNair	.75
29	Stan Humphries	.10
30	Simeon Rice	.10
31	Shannon Sharpe	.10
32	Sean Jones	.10
33	Scott Mitchell	.10
34	Sam Mills	.10
35	Rodney Hampton	.10
36	Rod Woodson	.10
37	Robert Smith	.10
38	Rob Moore	.10
39	Ricky Watters	.20
40	Rickey Dudley	.10
41	Rick Mirer	.10
42	Reggie White	.20
43	Ray Zellars	.10
44	Ray Lewis	.10
45	Rashaan Salaam	.20
46	Quentin Coryatt	.10
47	Qadry Ismail	.10
48	O.J. McDuffie	.10
49	Nilo Silvan	.10
50	Neil Smith	.10
51	Neil O'Donnell	.10
52	Natrone Means	.20
53	Napoleon Kaufman	.10
54	Mike Tomczak	.10
55	Mike Alstott	.20
56	Michael Westbrook	.10
57	Michael Jackson	.10
58	Michael Irvin	.20
59	Michael Haynes	.10
60	Michael Bates	.10
61	Mel Gray	.10
62	Marvin Harrison	.50
63	Marshall Faulk	.30
64	Mark Brunell	1.00
65	Mario Bates	.10
66	Marcus Allen	.20
67	Lorenzo Neal	.10
68	Levon Kirkland	.10
69	Leonard Russell	.10
70	Leeland McElroy	.10
71	Lawyer Milloy	.10
72	Lawrence Phillips	.20
73	Larry Centers	.10
74	Lamar Lathon	.10
75	Kordell Stewart	.75
76	Kimble Anders	.10
77	Ki-Jana Carter	.10
78	Keyshawn Johnson	.50
79	Kevin Turner	.10
80	Jermaine Lewis	.10
81	Jerome Bettis	.20
82	Jerris McPhail	.10
83	Joey Galloway	.40
84	Jerry Rice	1.00
85	Jim Everett	.10
86	Jimmy Smith	.10
87	Jim Harbaugh	.10
88	John Elway	.75
89	John Friez	.10
90	John Mobley	.10
91	Johnnie Morton	.10
92	Junior Seau	.10
93	Karim Abdul-Jabbar	.30
94	Keenan McCardell	.10
95	Ken Dilger	.10
96	Ken Norton	.10
97	Kent Graham	.10
98	Kerry Collins	.30
99	Kevin Greene	.10
100	Kevin Hardy	.10
101	Jeff Lewis	.10
102	Jeff George	.10
103	Jeff Graham	.10
104	Jeff Blake	.30
105	Jason Sehorn	.10
106	Jason Dunn	.10
107	Jamie Asher	.10
108	Jamal Anderson	.30
109	Jake Reed	.10
110	Isaac Bruce	.30
111	Irving Fryar	.10
112	Iheanyi Uwaezuoke	.10
113	Hugh Douglas	.10
114	Herman Moore	.20
115	Harvey Williams	.10
116	Hardy Nickerson	.10
117	Gus Frerotte	.10
118	Greg Hill	.10
119	Glyn Milburn	.10
120	Frank Wycheck	.10
121	Frank Sanders	.10
122	Errict Rhett	.20
123	Erik Kramer	.10
124	Eric Moulds	.10
125	Eric Metcalf	.10
126	Emmitt Smith	2.00
127	Edgar Bennett	.10
128	Eddie Kennison	.50
129	Eddie George	1.50
130	Drew Bledsoe	1.00
131	Dorsey Levens	.20
132	Desmond Howard	.10
133	Derrick Thomas	.10
134	Derrick Alexander	.10
135	Deion Sanders	.50
136	Dave Brown	.10
137	Daryl Johnston	.10
138	Darnay Scott	.10
139	Darick Holmes	.10
140	Dan Marino	2.00
141	Curtis Martin	1.25
142	Curtis Conway	.10
143	Cris Carter	.10
144	Chris Warren	.10
145	Chris T. Jones	.10
146	Chris Slade	.10
147	Chris Sanders	.10
148	Chester McGlockton	.10
149	Charlie Jones	.10
150	Charles Way	.10
151	Carl Pickens	.10
152	Bryan Still	.10
153	Bruce Smith	.10
154	Brian Mitchell	.10
155	Brett Perriman	.10
156	Brett Favre	2.50
157	Brad Johnson	.10
158	Thurman Thomas	.20
159	Bobby Engram	.10
160	Bert Emanuel	.10
161	Ben Coates	.10
162	Barry Sanders	1.50
163	Bam Morris	.10
164	Ashley Ambrose	.10
165	Antonio Freeman	.30
166	Anthony Miller	.10
167	Anthony Johnson	.10
168	Andre Rison	.10
169	Andre Reed	.10
170	Alex Molden	.10
171	Aeneas Williams	.10
172	Adrian Murrell	.10
173	Aaron Hayden	.10
174	*Darnell Autry*	.20
175	*Orlando Pace*	.30
176	*Darrell Russell*	.10
177	*Peter Boulware*	.10
178	*Shawn Springs*	.30
179	*Bryant Westbrook*	.10
180	*Dwayne Rudd*	.10
181	*Rae Carruth*	.25
182	*Troy Davis*	.50
183	*Antowain Smith*	2.50
184	*James Farrior*	.10
185	*Walter Jones*	.10
186	*Sam Madison*	.10
187	*Tom Knight*	.10
188	*Reidel Anthony*	2.00
189	*Warrick Dunn*	2.00
190	*Reinard Wilson*	.10
191	*Tyrus McCloud*	.10
192	*Michael Booker*	.10
193	*Tony Gonzalez*	1.25
194	*Pat Barnes*	.30
195	*Tiki Barber*	1.00
196	*Sedrick Shaw*	.50
197	*Corey Dillon*	4.00
198	*Danny Wuerffel*	1.00
199	Checklist	.10
200	Checklist	.10

1997 Metal Precious Metal Gems

The 198-card parallel of the base set, not including the two checklists, was randomly seeded in packs. SkyBox produced 150 serial numbered sets. The first 15 cards of the print run were printed with green foil.

	MT
Precious Metal Stars:	40x-80x
Precious Metal Rookies:	20x-40x

1997 Metal Autographics Previews

Inserted 1:500 packs, autographed cards of 10 of the 75 NFL players appearing in the debut of the Autographics program are found here.

	MT
Complete Set (12):	800.00
Common Player:	25.00
Karim Abdul-Jabbar	100.00
Mike Alstott	50.00
Darnell Autry	40.00
Rae Carruth	60.00
Ty Detmer	25.00
Eddie Kennison	75.00
Brian Manning	25.00
Ed McCaffrey	25.00
Jerry Rice	350.00
Shannon Sharpe	40.00
Mike Vrabel	25.00
Chris Warren	25.00

1997 Metal Body Shop

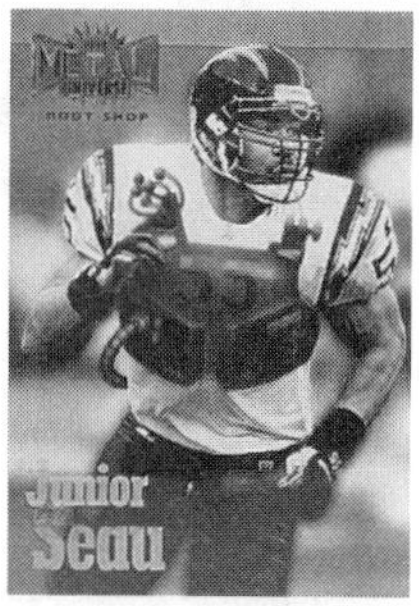

Inserted 1:96 packs, the 15-card set mixes photography and technology. Drew Bledsoe's arm and Jamal Anderson's legs turn bionic on these cards. The cards are numbered with a "BS" prefix.

		MT
Complete Set (15):		220.00
Common Player:		10.00
Minor Stars:		20.00
1	Zach Thomas	20.00
2	Steve Young	25.00
3	Steve McNair	35.00
4	Simeon Rice	10.00
5	Shannon Sharpe	10.00
6	Napoleon Kaufman	10.00
7	Mike Alstott	10.00
8	Michael Westbrook	10.00
9	Kordell Stewart	35.00
10	Kevin Hardy	10.00
11	Kerry Collins	20.00
12	Junior Seau	10.00
13	Jamal Anderson	10.00
14	Drew Bledsoe	35.00
15	Deion Sanders	25.00

1997 Metal Gold Universe

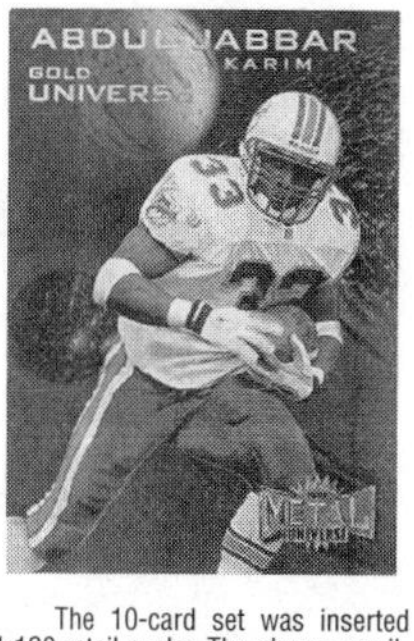

The 10-card set was inserted 1:120 retail packs. The players are illustrated in space on the card fronts. The cards are numbered with a "GU" prefix.

		MT
Complete Set (10):		200.00
Common Player:		10.00
1	Dan Marino	75.00
2	Deion Sanders	25.00
3	Drew Bledsoe	40.00
4	Isaac Bruce	15.00
5	Joey Galloway	15.00
6	Karim Abdul-Jabbar	25.00
7	Lawrence Phillips	10.00
8	Marshall Faulk	15.00
9	Marvin Harrison	15.00
10	Steve Young	25.00

1997 Metal Iron Rookies

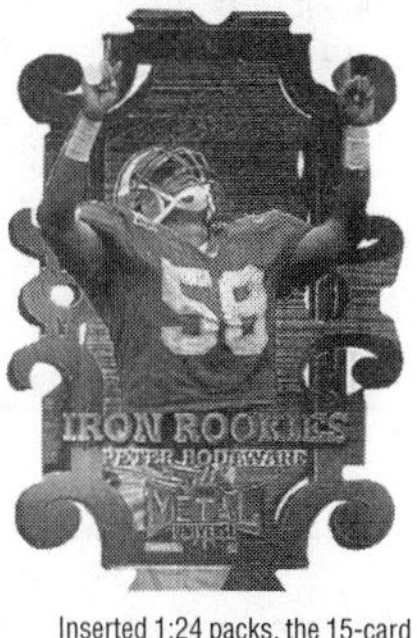

Inserted 1:24 packs, the 15-card set features the top players who were chosen in the 1997 NFL Draft. The

cards are numbered with an "IC" prefix.

		MT
Complete Set (15):		70.00
Common Player:		2.50
Minor Stars:		5.00
1	Darnell Autry	6.00
2	Orlando Pace	5.00
3	Peter Boulware	2.50
4	Shawn Springs	5.00
5	Bryant Westbrook	2.50
6	Rae Carruth	8.00
7	Troy Davis	12.00
8	Antowain Smith	10.00
9	James Farrior	2.50
10	Dwayne Rudd	2.50
11	Darrell Russell	2.50
12	Warrick Dunn	20.00
13	Sedrick Shaw	5.00
14	Danny Wuerffel	5.00
15	Sam Madison	2.50

1997 Metal Marvel Metal

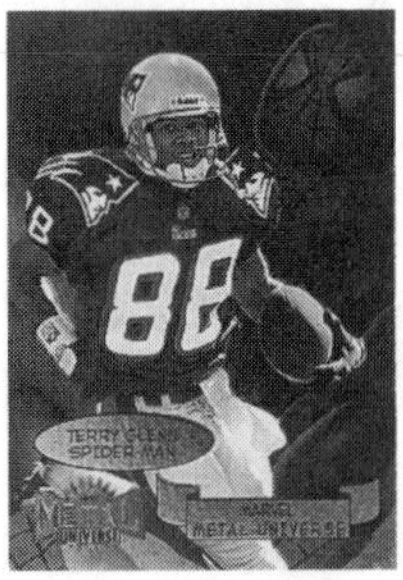

Inserted 1:6 packs, the 20-card set compares the players with Marvel Superheroes. For example, Isaac Bruce is pictured with Spider-Man. The cards are numbered with the "MM" prefix.

		MT
Complete Set (20):		40.00
Common Player:		1.00
Minor Stars:		2.00
1	Barry Sanders	7.00
2	Bruce Smith	1.00
3	Desmond Howard	1.00
4	Eddie George	6.00
5	Eddie Kennison	2.50
6	Jerry Rice	5.00
7	Joey Galloway	2.00
8	John Elway	3.00
9	Karim Abdul-Jabbar	2.00
10	Kerry Collins	2.00
11	Kevin Hardy	1.00
12	Kordell Stewart	4.00
13	Mark Brunell	5.00
14	Marshall Faulk	2.00
15	Michael Westbrook	1.00
16	Simeon Rice	1.00
17	Steve McNair	4.00
18	Terry Glenn	2.00
19	Tony Brackens	1.00
20	Tony Martin	1.00

1997 Metal Platinum Portraits

Inserted 1:288 packs, the 10-card set features the players on the card fronts with an etched-foil look. This was the third year for the chase set. The cards are numbered with a "PP" prefix.

		MT
Complete Set (10):		450.00
Common Player:		20.00
1	Troy Aikman	45.00
2	Terrell Davis	45.00
3	Marvin Harrison	20.00
4	Keyshawn Johnson	20.00
5	Jerry Rice	45.00
6	Emmitt Smith	80.00
7	Dan Marino	80.00
8	Curtis Martin	45.00
9	Brett Favre	90.00
10	Barry Sanders	75.00

1997 Metal Titanium

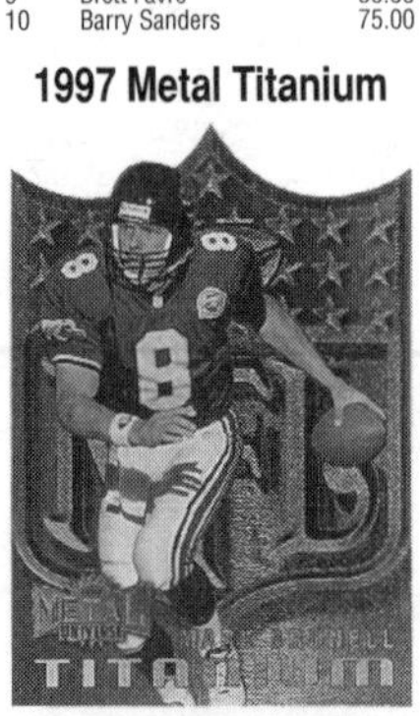

Inserted 1:72 hobby packs, the 20-card set featured a titanium background on die-cut cards. The cards are numbered with a "TT" prefix.

		MT
Complete Set (20):		400.00
Common Player:		7.00
Minor Stars:		14.00
1	Barry Sanders	45.00
2	Brett Favre	60.00
3	Curtis Martin	30.00
4	Eddie George	35.00
5	Eddie Kennison	7.00
6	Emmitt Smith	50.00
7	Herman Moore	7.00
8	Isaac Bruce	7.00
9	Jerry Rice	30.00
10	John Elway	25.00
11	Keyshawn Johnson	14.00
12	Lawrence Phillips	7.00
13	Mark Brunell	30.00
14	Mike Alstott	7.00
15	Steve McNair	25.00
16	Steve Young	25.00
17	Terrell Davis	30.00
18	Terry Glenn	14.00
19	Tony Banks	7.00
20	Troy Aikman	30.00

1998 Metal Universe

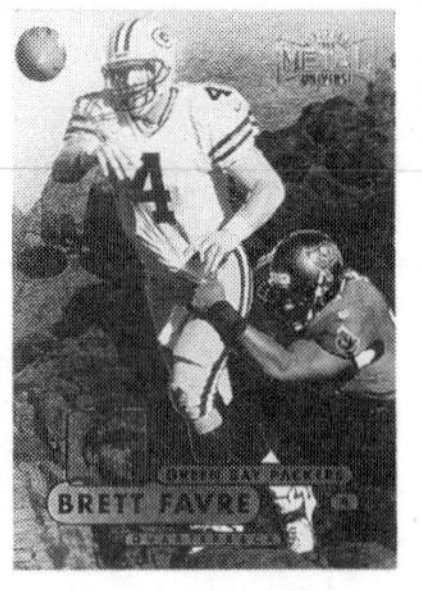

Metal Universe was released in a single series, 200-card set for 1998. The cards featured foil-etched designs in the background pertaining to the player or the city they play in. The set was paralleled in a Precious Metal Gems set. Inserts in Metal Universe include: Decided Edge, E-X2001 Previews, Planet Football, Quasars and Titanium.

		MT
Complete Set (200):		35.00
Common Player:		.10
Minor Stars:		.20
Precious Metal Gem Cards:		100x-200x
Precious Metal Gem Rookies:		15x-30x
Pack (8):		3.00
Wax Box (24):		60.00
1	Jerry Rice	1.00
2	Muhsin Muhammad	.10
3	Ed McCaffrey	.10
4	Brett Favre	2.50
5	Troy Brown	.10
6	Brad Johnson	.20
7	John Elway	1.00
8	Herman Moore	.20
9	O.J. McDuffie	.10
10	Tim Brown	.20
11	Byron Hanspard	.10
12	Rae Carruth	.10
13	Rod Smith	.10
14	John Randle	.10
15	Karim Abdul-Jabbar	.20
16	Bobby Hoying	.10
17	Steve Young	.50
18	Andre Hastings	.10
19	Chidi Ahanotu	.10
20	Barry Sanders	2.00
21	Bruce Smith	.10
22	Kimble Anders	.10
23	Troy Davis	.10
24	Jamal Anderson	.10
25	Curtis Conway	.20
26	Mark Chmura	.20
27	Reggie White	.20
28	Jake Reed	.10
29	Willie McGinest	.10
30	Terrell Davis	1.00
31	Joey Galloway	.20
32	Leslie Shepherd	.10
33	Peter Boulware	.10
34	Chad Lewis	.10
35	Marcus Allen	.20
36	Randal Hill	.10
37	Jerome Bettis	.20
38	William Floyd	.10
39	Warren Moon	.20
40	Mike Alstott	.40
41	Jay Graham	.10
42	Emmitt Smith	2.00
43	James Stewart	.10
44	Charlie Garner	.10
45	Merton Hanks	.10
46	Shawn Springs	.10
47	Chris Calloway	.10
48	Larry Centers	.10
49	Michael Jackson	.10
50	Deion Sanders	.50
51	Jimmy Smith	.10
52	Jason Sehorn	.10
53	Charles Johnson	.10
54	Garrison Hearst	.10
55	Chris Warren	.10
56	Warren Sapp	.10
57	Corey Dillon	.75
58	Marvin Harrison	.20
59	Chris Sanders	.10
60	Jamie Asher	.10
61	Yancey Thigpen	.10
62	Freddie Jones	.10
63	Rob Moore	.10
64	Jermaine Lewis	.10
65	Michael Irvin	.20
66	Natrone Means	.20
67	Charles Way	.10
68	Terry Kirby	.10
69	Tony Banks	.20
70	Steve McNair	.50
71	Vinny Testaverde	.10
72	Dexter Coakley	.10
73	Keenan McCardell	.10
74	Glenn Foley	.10
75	Isaac Bruce	.20
76	Terry Allen	.10
77	Todd Collins	.10
78	Troy Aikman	1.00
79	Damon Jones	.10
80	Leon Johnson	.10
81	James Jett	.10
82	Frank Wycheck	.10
83	Andre Reed	.10
84	Derrick Alexander	.10
85	Jason Taylor	.10
86	Wayne Chrebet	.10
87	Napoleon Kaufman	.50
88	Eddie George	1.00
89	Ernie Conwell	.10
90	Antowain Smith	.50
91	Johnnie Morton	.10
92	Jerris McPhail	.10
93	Cris Carter	.10
94	Danny Kanell	.10
95	Stan Humphries	.10
96	Terrell Owens	.10
97	Willie Davis	.10
98	David Dunn	.10
99	Tony Brackens	.10
100	Kordell Stewart	1.00
101	Rodney Thomas	.10
102	Keyshawn Johnson	.20
103	Carl Pickens	.10
104	Mark Brunell	.75
105	Jeff George	.20
106	Bert Emanuel	.10
107	Wesley Walls	.10
108	Bryant Westbrook	.10
109	Dorsey Levens	.20
110	Drew Bledsoe	1.00
111	Adrian Murrell	.20
112	Aeneas Williams	.10
113	Raymont Harris	.10
114	Tony Gonzalez	.20
115	Sean Dawkins	.10
116	Billy Joe Hobert	.10
117	James McKnight	.10
118	Reidel Anthony	.10
119	Terance Mathis	.10
120	Darrien Gordon	.10
121	Dale Carter	.10
122	Duce Staley	.10
123	Jerald Moore	.10
124	Eric Swann	.10
125	Antonio Freeman	.20
126	Chris Penn	.10
127	Ken Dilger	.10
128	Robert Smith	.20
129	Tiki Barber	.30
130	Mark Bruener	.10
131	Junior Seau	.20
132	Trent Dilfer	.20
133	Gus Frerotte	.10
134	Jake Plummer	1.00
135	Jeff Blake	.20
136	Jim Harbaugh	.20
137	Michael Strahan	.10
138	Gary Brown	.10
139	Tony Martin	.10
140	Stephen Davis	.10
141	Thurman Thomas	.20
142	Scott Mitchell	.10
143	Dan Marino	2.00
144	David Palmer	.10
145	J.J. Stokes	.10
146	Chris Chandler	.10
147	Darnell Autry	.20
148	Robert Brooks	.10
149	Derrick Mayes	.10
150	Curtis Martin	.75
151	Steve Broussard	.10
152	Eddie Kennison	.20
153	Kerry Collins	.30
154	Shannon Sharpe	.20
155	Andre Rison	.20
156	Dwayne Rudd	.10
157	Orlando Pace	.10
158	Terry Glenn	.20
159	Frank Sanders	.10
160	Ricky Proehl	.10
161	Marshall Faulk	.20
162	Irving Fryar	.10
163	Courtney Hawkins	.10
164	Eric Metcalf	.10
165	Warrick Dunn	1.00
166	Cris Dishman	.10
167	Fred Lane	.10
168	John Mobley	.10
169	Elvis Grbac	.10
170	Ben Coates	.10
171	Rickey Dudley	.10
172	Ricky Watters	.20
173	*Alonzo Mayes*	.30
174	*Andre Wadsworth*	.50
175	*Brian Simmons*	1.00
176	*Charles Woodson*	3.00
177	*Curtis Enis*	3.00
178	*Fred Taylor*	5.00
179	*Germane Crowell*	2.00
180	*Greg Ellis*	.30
181	*Jacquez Green*	2.00
182	*Jason Peter*	.30
183	*John Dutton*	.30
184	*Kevin Dyson*	2.00
185	*Kivuusama Mays*	.10
186	*Marcus Nash*	.75
187	*Michael Myers*	.10
188	*Ahman Green*	1.00
189	*Peyton Manning*	10.00
190	*Randy Moss*	10.00
191	*Robert Edwards*	1.00
192	*Robert Holcombe*	1.00
193	*Ryan Leaf*	2.00
194	*Takeo Spikes*	.50
195	*Tavian Banks*	1.00
196	*Tim Dwight*	2.00
197	*Vonnie Holliday*	.50
198	Dorsey Levens	.10
199	Jerry Rice	.50
200	Dan Marino	1.00

1998 Metal Universe Precious Metal Gems

Precious Metal Gems was a 200-card parallel set found only in hobby packs. Cards were sequentially numbered to 50 sets on the back.

	MT
Metal Gem Cards:	100x-200x
Metal Gem Rookies:	15x-30x

A player's name in *italic type* indicates a rookie card.

1998 Metal Universe Decided Edge

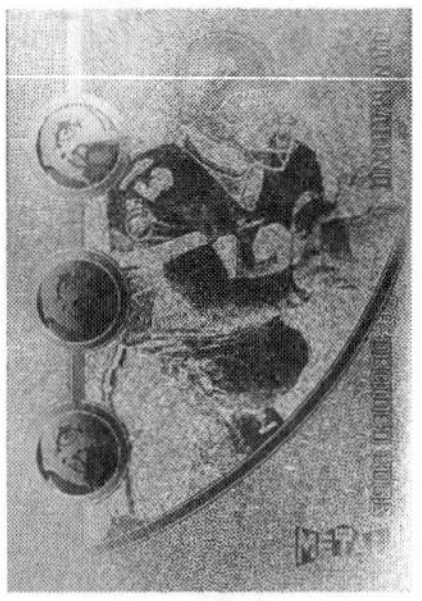

Decided Edge was a 10-card insert that was seeded one per 288 packs. The outside of these cards was silver foil with the player's image etched into it, while the inside could be pulled out to reveal another card of the player. Three circles were cut into the outside of the front, and one circle was on the back - each allowed you to see the inner card. When lined up, the player's face could be seen through each of the circles. Decided Edge inserts were numbered with a "CE" prefix on the inside card.

		MT
Complete Set (10):		450.00
Common Player:		20.00
1	Terrell Davis	45.00
2	Brett Favre	90.00
3	John Elway	45.00
4	Barry Sanders	80.00
5	Eddie George	45.00
6	Jerry Rice	45.00
7	Emmitt Smith	75.00
8	Dan Marino	75.00
9	Troy Aikman	45.00
10	Marcus Allen	20.00

1998 Metal Universe E-X2001 Previews

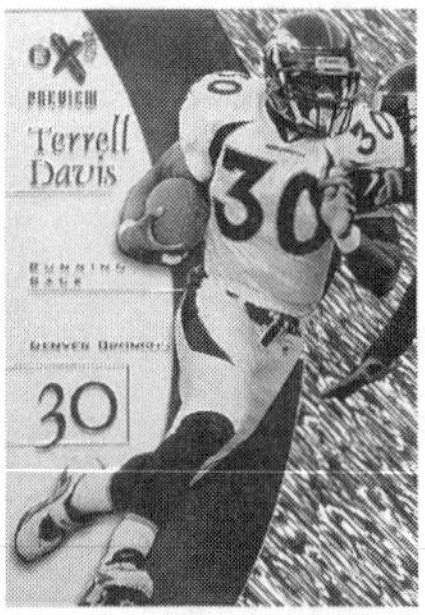

This 15-card insert previewed the upcoming E-X2001 set. Cards featured the two layered, plastic design, but added the word "Preview" in gold foil under the E-X2001 logo. The Metal Universe logo does not appear anywhere on the card. Preview inserts were seeded one per 144 packs. Cards are numbered with a "EX" prefix.

		MT
Complete Set (15):		300.00
Common Player:		6.00
Minor Stars:		12.00
1	Barry Sanders	50.00
2	Brett Favre	60.00
3	Corey Dillon	15.00
4	John Elway	30.00
5	Drew Bledsoe	30.00
6	Eddie George	30.00
7	Emmitt Smith	50.00
8	Joey Galloway	6.00
9	Karim Abdul-Jabbar	12.00
10	Kordell Stewart	30.00
11	Mark Brunell	20.00
12	Mike Alstott	15.00
13	Warrick Dunn	30.00
14	Antonio Freeman	6.00
15	Terrell Davis	30.00

1998 Metal Universe Planet Football

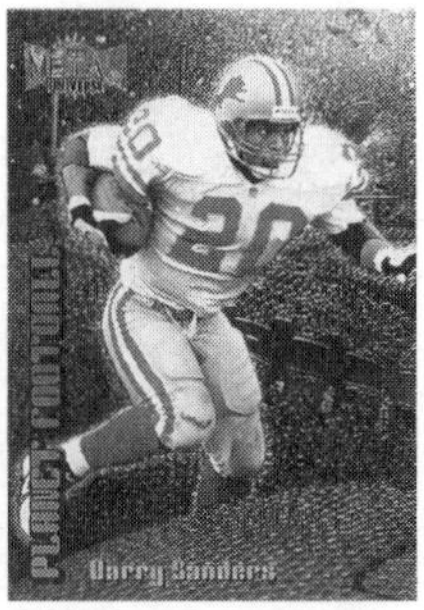

Planet Football was a 15-card insert that was seeded one per eight packs. The player's color image was shown over a foil etched background that contained a large football in space. Cards are numbered with a "PF" prefix.

		MT
Complete Set (15):		50.00
Common Player:		1.00
1	Barry Sanders	8.00
2	Corey Dillon	3.00
3	Warrick Dunn	5.00
4	Jake Plummer	5.00
5	John Elway	5.00
6	Kordell Stewart	5.00
7	Curtis Martin	3.00
8	Mark Brunell	4.00
9	Dorsey Levens	1.00
10	Troy Aikman	5.00
11	Terry Glenn	1.00
12	Eddie George	5.00
13	Keyshawn Johnson	1.00
14	Steve McNair	3.00
15	Jerry Rice	5.00

1998 Metal Universe Quasars

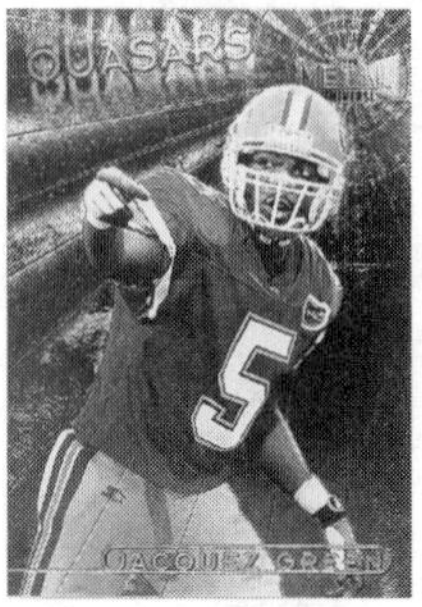

This 15-card set showcased the top rookies from the 1998 NFL Draft. Cards had a color shot of the player in his college uniform over a etched foil background. These were inserted one per 20 packs. Cards are numbered with a "QS" prefix.

		MT
Complete Set (15):		100.00
Common Player:		2.00
1	Peyton Manning	20.00
2	Ryan Leaf	14.00
3	Charles Woodson	10.00
4	Randy Moss	30.00
5	Curtis Enis	10.00
6	Tavian Banks	6.00
7	Germane Crowell	2.00
8	Kevin Dyson	6.00
9	Robert Edwards	8.00
10	Jacquez Green	8.00
11	Alonzo Mayes	3.00
12	Brian Simmons	2.50
13	Takeo Spikes	2.00
14	Andre Wadsworth	3.00
15	Ahman Green	8.00

1998 Metal Universe Titanium

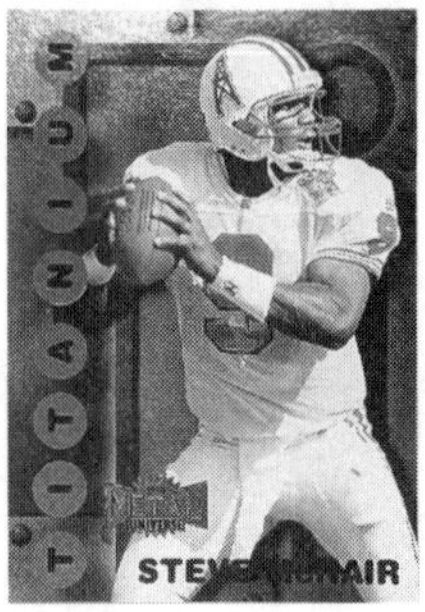

Titanium was a 10-card insert printed on a silver holofoil background. The insert name runs up the left side with the letters in circles. These were inserted one per 96 packs. Cards are numbered with a "TM" prefix.

		MT
Complete Set (10):		140.00
Common Player:		8.00
1	Corey Dillon	8.00
2	Emmitt Smith	30.00
3	Terrell Davis	30.00
4	Brett Favre	40.00
5	Mark Brunell	15.00
6	Dan Marino	30.00
7	Curtis Martin	12.00
8	Kordell Stewart	15.00
9	Warrick Dunn	15.00
10	Steve McNair	8.00

1999 Metal Universe

The 250-card base set features each player's name stamped in a steel-look foil across the top and stats laid into another steel motif on the card backs. The 182 player cards are joined by the 25 all-foil "N.F.L.P.D." subset. The base set also includes forty non-seeded rookies and three checklists. Top inserts include: Precious Metal, Gem Masters, Autographics, Linchpins, Planet Metal, Quasars and Starchild.

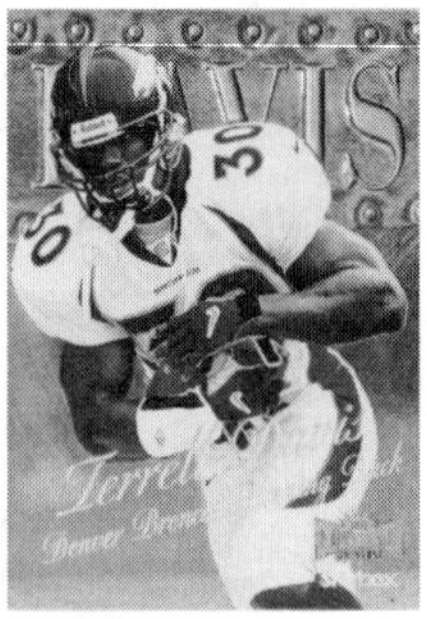

		MT
Complete Set (250):		50.00
Common Player:		.10
Minor Stars:		.20
Common Rookie:		.50
Hobby Pack (8):		3.25
Hobby Wax Box (24):		68.00
1	Eric Moulds	.50
2	David Palmer	.10
3	Ricky Watters	.20
4	Antonio Freeman	.50
5	Hugh Douglas	.10
6	Johnnie Morton	.10
7	Corey Fuller	.10
8	J.J. Stokes	.20
9	Keith Poole	.10
10	Steve Beuerlein	.10
11	Keenan McCardell	.10
12	Carl Pickens	.20
13	Mark Bruener	.10
14	Warren Sapp	.10
15	Rich Gannon	.10
16	Bruce Smith	.10
17	Mark Chmura	.20
18	Drew Bledsoe	.75
19	Charles Woodson	.50
20	Ahman Green	.20
21	Ricky Proehl	.10
22	Corey Dillon	.50
23	Terry Fair	.10
24	Mark Brunell	.75
25	Leroy Hoard	.10
26	La'Roi Glover	.10
27	Tim Brown	.20
28	Kevin Turner	.10
29	Terrell Owens	.50
30	Mike Alstott	.50
31	Rob Moore	.20
32	Troy Aikman	1.00
33	Derrick Alexander	.10
34	Chris Calloway	.10
35	Kordell Stewart	.75
36	Reidel Anthony	.20
37	Michael Westbrook	.20
38	Ray Lewis	.10
39	Alonzo Mayes	.10
40	Rod Smith	.20
41	Reggie Barlow	.10
42	Sean Dawkins	.10
43	Duce Staley	.10
44	R.W. McQuarters	.10
45	Robert Holcombe	.10
46	Priest Holmes	.50
47	Erik Kramer	.10
48	Shannon Sharpe	.20
49	Mike Vanderjagt	.10
50	Cris Carter	.50
51	Billy Joe Tolliver	.10
52	Vinny Testaverde	.20
53	Antonio Langham	.10
54	Damon Gibson	.10
55	Garrison Hearst	.30
56	Brad Johnson	.50
57	Randall Cunningham	.50
58	Jim Harbaugh	.20
59	Curtis Enis	.50
60	Bill Romanowski	.10
61	Marcus Pollard	.10
62	Zach Thomas	.20
63	Cameron Cleeland	.20
64	Curtis Martin	.50
65	Charlie Garner	.10
66	Jerris McPhail	.10
67	Jon Kitna	.75
68	Chris Chandler	.20
69	Emmitt Smith	1.50
70	Andre Rison	.20
71	Wayne Chrebet	.50
72	Mikhael Ricks	.10
73	Yancey Thigpen	.20
74	Peter Boulware	.10
75	Bobby Engram	.10
76	John Mobley	.10
77	Peyton Manning	1.50
78	O.J. McDuffie	.20
79	Tony Simmons	.20
80	Mo Lewis	.10
81	Bryan Still	.10
82	Eugene Robinson	.10
83	Curtis Conway	.20
84	Ed McCaffrey	.30
85	Marvin Harrison	.30
86	Dan Marino	1.50
87	Ty Law	.10
88	Leon Johnson	.10
89	Junior Seau	.20
90	Terance Mathis	.10
91	Wesley Walls	.10
92	John Elway	1.50
93	Marshall Faulk	.50
94	Oronde Gadsden	.20
95	Keyshawn Johnson	.50
96	Muhsin Muhammad	.10
97	Dorsey Levens	.50
98	Shawn Jefferson	.10
99	Rocket Ismail	.10
100	Vonnie Holliday	.20
101	Terry Glenn	.30
102	Shawn Springs	.10
103	Tim Dwight	.50
104	Terrell Davis	1.50
105	Karim Abdul	.30
106	Bryan Cox	.10

107	Steve McNair	.75
108	Tony Martin	.10
109	Jason Elam	.10
110	John Avery	.20
111	Aaron Glenn	.10
112	Eddie George	.75
113	Larry Centers	.10
114	Darnay Scott	.10
115	Jimmy Smith	.20
116	Tiki Barber	.10
117	Charles Johnson	.10
118	Mike Archie	.10
119	Adrian Murrell	.10
120	Dexter Coakley	.10
121	Dale Carter	.10
122	Kent Graham	.10
123	Hines Ward	.20
124	Greg Hill	.10
125	Skip Hicks	.50
126	Doug Flutie	.75
127	Leslie Shepherd	.10
128	Neil O'Donnell	.20
129	Herman Moore	.50
130	Kevin Hardy	.10
131	Randy Moss	2.00
132	Andre Hastings	.10
133	Rickey Dudley	.10
134	Jerome Bettis	.50
135	Jerry Rice	1.00
136	Jake Plummer	1.00
137	Billy Davis	.10
138	Tony Gonzalez	.20
139	Ike Hilliard	.20
140	Freddie Jones	.10
141	Isaac Bruce	.30
142	Darrell Green	.10
143	Trent Green	.50
144	Jamal Anderson	.50
145	Deion Sanders	.50
146	Bam Morris	.20
147	Charles Way	.10
148	Natrone Means	.30
149	Frank Wycheck	.10
150	Brett Favre	2.00
151	Michael Bates	.10
152	Ben Coates	.20
153	Koy Detmer	.10
154	Eddie Kennison	.10
155	Eric Metcalf	.10
156	Takeo Spikes	.10
157	Fred Taylor	1.00
158	Gary Brown	.10
159	Levon Kirkland	.10
160	Trent Dilfer	.30
161	Antowain Smith	.50
162	Robert Brooks	.10
163	Robert Smith	.50
164	Napoleon Kaufman	.50
165	Chad Brown	.10
166	Warrick Dunn	.75
167	Joey Galloway	.50
168	Frank Sanders	.20
169	Michael Irvin	.20
170	Elvis Grbac	.20
171	Michael Strahan	.10
172	Ryan Leaf	.50
173	Stephen Alexander	.10
174	Andre Reed	.10
175	Barry Sanders	2.00
176	Jake Reed	.10
177	James Jett	.10
178	Steve Young	.75
179	Jermaine Lewis	.20
180	Charlie Batch	.75
181	Jacquez Green	.20
182	Kevin Dyson	.20
183	Roell Preston	.10
184	Randall Cunningham	.20
185	Charlie Batch	.20
186	Kordell Stewart	.20
187	Bennie Thompson	.10
188	Deion Sanders	.20
189	Jake Plummer	.50
190	Eric Moulds	.20
191	Derrick Brooks	.10
192	Steve McNair	.20
193	Ryan Leaf	.20
194	Keyshawn Johnson	.20
195	Eddie George	.20
196	Warrick Dunn	.20
197	Jessie Tuggle	.10
198	Rodney Harrison	.10
199	Vinny Testaverde	.10
200	Marshall Faulk	.20
201	Ray Buchanon	.10
202	Garrison Hearst	.10
203	John Randle	.10
204	Drew Bledsoe	.50
205	Sam Gash	.10
206	Troy Aikman	.50
207	Michael McCrary	.10
208	*Chris Claiborne*	1.00
209	*Ricky Williams*	7.00
210	*Tim Couch*	7.00
211	*Champ Bailey*	1.50
212	*Torry Holt*	3.00
213	*Donovan McNabb*	4.00
214	*David Boston*	3.00
215	*Chris McAlister*	.75
216	*Aaron Gibson*	.50
217	*Daunte Culpepper*	6.00
218	*Matt Stinchcomb*	.50
219	*Edgerrin James*	10.00
220	*Jevon Kearse*	4.00
221	*Ebenezer Ekuban*	.50
222	*Kris Farris*	.50
223	*Chris Terry*	.50
224	*Cecil Collins*	1.00
225	*Akili Smith*	4.00
226	*Shaun King*	4.00
227	*Rahim Abdullah*	.50
228	*Peerless Price*	1.50
229	*Antoine Winfield*	.50
230	*Antwan Edwards*	.50
231	*Rob Konrad*	.75
232	*Troy Edwards*	2.00
233	*John Thornton*	.50
234	*Fred Vinson*	.50
235	*Gary Stills*	.50
236	*Desmond Clark*	.50
237	*Lamar King*	.50
238	*Jared DeVries*	.50
239	*Martin Gramatica*	.50
240	*Montae Reagor*	.50
241	*Andy Katzenmoyer*	1.00
242	*Rufus French*	.50
243	*D'Wayne Bates*	.75
244	*Amos Zereoue*	1.00
245	*Dre' Bly*	.75
246	*Kevin Johnson*	3.00
247	*Cade McNown*	2.00
248	Kordell Stewart	.20
249	Deion Sanders	.20
250	Vinny Testaverde	.10

1999 Metal Universe Precious Metal Gem Parallel

This is a 250-card parallel to the base that is sequentially numbered to 50.

	MT
Precious Metal Cards:	75x-150x
Precious Metal Rookies: 15x-30x	
Production 50 Sets	

1999 Metal Universe Linchpins

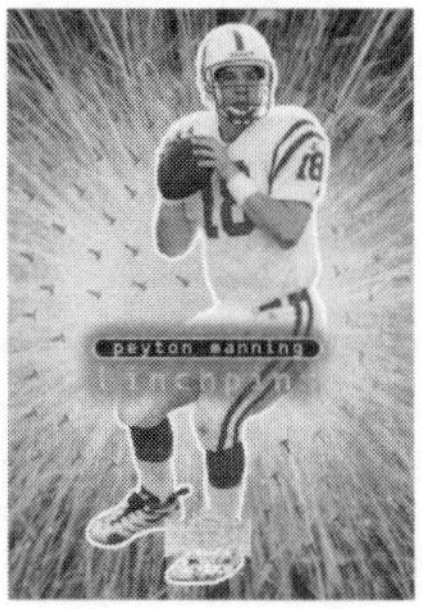

This 10-card set spotlights a laser die-cut design and highlights key players who hold their teams together on the field and in the clubhouse. Singles were found 1:360 packs.

		MT
Complete Set (10):		400.00
Common Player:		25.00
Inserted 1:360		
1	Emmitt Smith	60.00
2	Charlie Batch	25.00
3	Fred Taylor	60.00
4	Jake Plummer	40.00
5	Brett Favre	80.00
6	Barry Sanders	80.00
7	Mark Brunell	35.00
8	Peyton Manning	60.00
9	Randy Moss	80.00
10	Terrell Davis	60.00

1999 Metal Universe Planet Metal

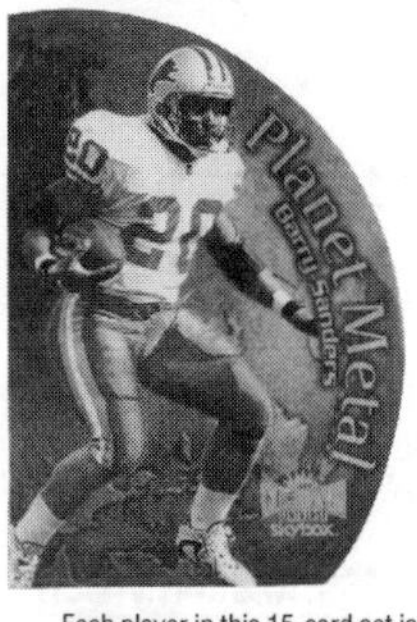

Each player in this 15-card set is printed on a die-cut card that features a metallic view of the planet. Singles were inserted 1:36 packs.

		MT
Complete Set (15):		135.00
Common Player:		4.00
Inserted 1:36		
1	Terrell Davis	15.00
2	Troy Aikman	10.00
3	Peyton Manning	15.00
4	Mark Brunell	8.00
5	John Elway	15.00
6	Doug Flutie	8.00
7	Dan Marino	15.00
8	Brett Favre	20.00
9	Barry Sanders	20.00
10	Emmitt Smith	15.00
11	Fred Taylor	10.00
12	Jerry Rice	10.00
13	Jamal Anderson	4.00
14	Randall Cunningham	4.00
15	Randy Moss	20.00

Values quoted in this guide reflect the retail price of a card — the price a collector can expect to pay when buying a card from a dealer. The wholesale price — that which a collector can expect to receive from a dealer when selling cards — will be significantly lower, depending on desirability and condition.

1999 Metal Universe Quasars

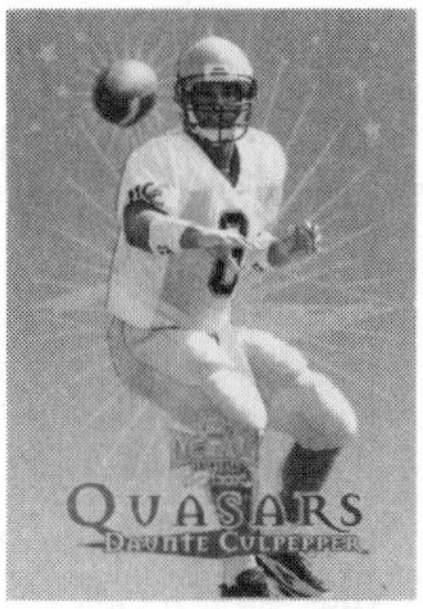

This 15-card set features the top rookies from 1999 and puts them on a silver rainbow holofoil card. They were inserted 1:18 packs.

		MT
Complete Set (15):		85.00
Common Player:		2.00
Inserted 1:18		
1	Ricky Williams	25.00
2	Tim Couch	25.00
3	Shaun King	3.00
4	Champ Bailey	3.00
5	Torry Holt	5.00
6	Donovan McNabb	8.00
7	David Boston	6.00
8	Andy Katzenmoyer	2.00
9	Daunte Culpepper	8.00
10	Edgerrin James	15.00
11	Cade McNown	8.00
12	Troy Edwards	4.00
13	Akili Smith	8.00
14	Peerless Price	4.00
15	Amos Zereoue	4.00

1999 Metal Universe Starchild

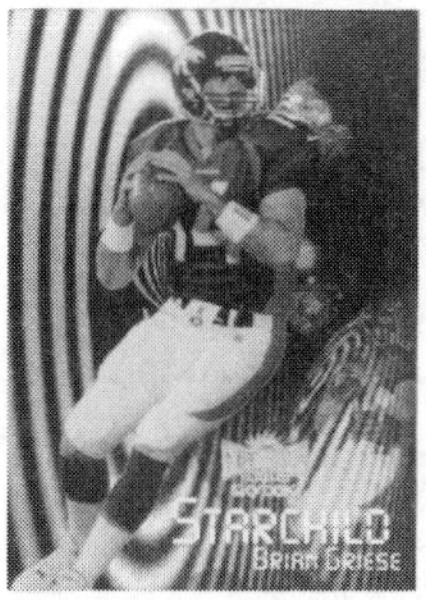

This 20-card insert has a young star theme to it and prints each player on a silver rainbow holofoil background. Singles were found 1:6 packs.

		MT
Complete Set (20):		30.00
Common Player:		1.00
Minor Stars:		2.00
Inserted 1:6		
1	Skip Hicks	2.00
2	Mike Alstott	2.00
3	Joey Galloway	2.00
4	Tony Simmons	1.00
5	Jamal Anderson	2.00
6	John Avery	1.00
7	Charles Woodson	2.00
8	Jon Kitna	3.00
9	Marshall Faulk	2.00
10	Eric Moulds	2.00
11	Keyshawn Johnson	3.00
12	Ryan Leaf	3.00
13	Curtis Enis	2.00
14	Steve McNair	2.00
15	Corey Dillon	2.00
16	Tim Dwight	2.00
17	Brian Griese	4.00
18	Drew Bledsoe	5.00
19	Eddie George	4.00
20	Terrell Owens	3.00

2000 Metal

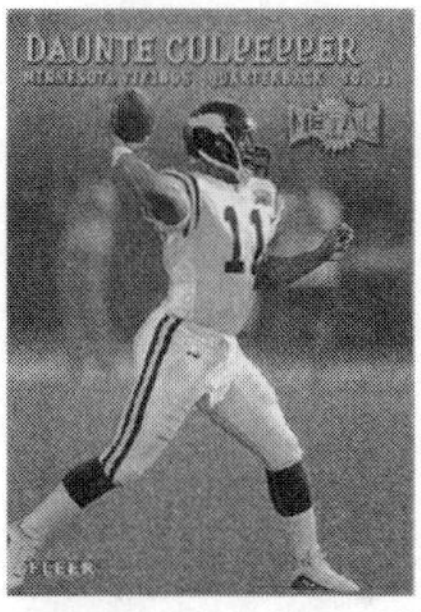

		MT
Complete Set (300):		100.00
Common Player:		.15
Minor Stars:		.30
Common Rookie (#201-250):		.50
Common Rookie (#251-300):		1.00
Inserted 1:2		
Pack (10):		2.00
Wax Box (24):		35.00
1	Tim Couch	.75
2	Olandis Gary	.50
3	Andre Hastings	.15
4	Donovan McNabb	.75
5	Bobby Engram	.15
6	Bert Emanuel	.15
7	Levon Kirkland	.15
8	Chris Chandler	.30
9	Herman Moore	.30
10	Jeff Blake	.30
11	Cortez Kennedy	.15
12	Antowain Smith	.30
13	Marvin Harrison	.50
14	Bryant Young	.15
15	Peerless Price	.30
16	Peyton Manning	1.75
17	Darrell Russell	.15
18	Darrell Green	.15
19	James Allen	.30
20	Tedy Bruschi	.15
21	Jon Kitna	.50
22	Doug Flutie	.75
23	Bill Schroeder	.15
24	Curtis Martin	.50
25	Kevin Lockett	.15
26	Errict Rhett	.30
27	Kevin Faulk	.30
28	J.J. Stokes	.30
29	Jonathon Linton	.30
30	Jimmy Smith	.50
31	Brian Dawkins	.15
32	Michael Westbrook	.30
33	Randall Cunningham	.30
34	Oronde Gadsden	.30
35	Shawn Springs	.15
36	Shannon Sharpe	.30
37	Terrence Wilkins	.30
38	Aaron Glenn	.15
39	Torrance Small	.15
40	Sean Dawkins	.15
41	Terrell Davis	1.25
42	Ike Hilliard	.30
43	Warrick Dunn	.50
44	Jeremiah Trotter	.15
45	O.J. McDuffie	.30
46	Richard Huntley	.30
47	Aeneas Williams	.15
48	Raghib Ismail	.15
49	Terry Glenn	.50
50	Derrick Mayes	.30
51	Wayne Chrebet	.50
52	Kevin Dyson	.30
53	Takeo Spikes	.15
54	Matthew Hatchette	.30
55	Shawn Bryson	.15
56	Qadry Ismail	.15
57	Jerome Pathon	.15
58	Rich Gannon	.30
59	Stephen Davis	.50
60	Marcus Robinson	.50
61	Damon Huard	.30
62	Junior Seau	.30
63	Curtis Enis	.30
64	Tony Richardson	.15
65	Troy Edwards	.30
66	Robert Brooks	.15
67	Antonio Freeman	.50
68	Kerry Collins	.30
69	Jacquez Green	.15
70	Akili Smith	.50
71	Zach Thomas	.30
72	Kordell Stewart	.60
73	Deion Sanders	.50
74	David Patten	.15
75	Drew Bledsoe	.75
76	Shaun King	.50
77	Eddie Kennison	.15
78	Stacey Mack	.15
79	Jim Harbaugh	.30
80	Shawn Jefferson	.15
81	James Stewart	.50
82	Pete Mitchell	.15
83	Mike Alstott	.50
84	Marty Booker	.15
85	Hardy Nickerson	.15
86	Charles Johnson	.15
87	Jeff George	.30
88	Jermaine Lewis	.15
89	Edgerrin James	1.50
90	Rickey Dudley	.15
91	Eddie George	.60
92	Darren Woodson	.15
93	Willie McGinest	.15
94	Jeff Garcia	.50
95	Eric Moulds	.50
96	Tony Brackens	.15
97	Charles Woodson	.50
98	Warren Sapp	.30
99	Corey Dillon	.50
100	Tony Martin	.15
101	Bruce Smith	.15
102	Troy Aikman	1.00
103	Daunte Culpepper	1.00
104	Christian Fauria	.15
105	Steve Beuerlein	.30
106	Fred Taylor	.75
107	Ricky Watters	.30
108	Brian Mitchell	.15
109	Emmitt Smith	1.25
110	Robert Smith	.50
111	Jerry Rice	1.00
112	Priest Holmes	.50
113	Jay Fiedler	.30
114	Curtis Conway	.30
115	Jamal Anderson	.50
116	E.G. Green	.15
117	Kent Graham	.15
118	Frank Wycheck	.15
119	Jake Plummer	.50
120	Randy Moss	1.25
121	Charlie Garner	.30
122	Frank Sanders	.30
123	Germane Crowell	.50
124	Jason Sehorn	.15
125	Marshall Faulk	.50
126	David Sloan	.15
127	Cris Carter	.50
128	Robert Chancey	.15
129	Tony Banks	.30
130	Ken Dilger	.15
131	Dedric Ward	.30
132	Yancey Thigpen	.30
133	Jeremy McDaniel	.15
134	John Randle	.30
135	Jerome Bettis	.50
136	Tim Dwight	.50
137	Charlie Batch	.50
138	Mark Brunell	.75
139	Tyrone Wheatley	.30
140	Champ Bailey	.30
141	Brian Griese	.60
142	Keith Poole	.15
143	Kurt Warner	1.75
144	Tim Biakabutuka	.30
145	Elvis Grbac	.30
146	Cade McNown	.50
147	Albert Connell	.30
148	Donald Driver	.30
149	Donald Hayes	.30
150	Terrell Owens	.50
151	Johnnie Morton	.30
152	Tiki Barber	.50
153	Keyshawn Johnson	.50
154	Carl Pickens	.30
155	Thurman Thomas	.30
156	Jeff Graham	.15
157	Peter Boulware	.15
158	Brett Favre	2.00
159	Vinny Testaverde	.30
160	Derrick Brooks	.15
161	Wesley Walls	.30
162	Derrick Alexander	.15
163	Duce Staley	.50
164	Troy Brown	.15
165	Keenan McCardell	.30
166	James Jett	.15
167	Simeon Rice	.15
168	Rod Smith	.50
169	Ricky Williams	1.25
170	Az-Zahir Hakim	.30
171	Muhsin Muhammad	.30
172	Andre Rison	.30
173	Tim Brown	.50
174	Brad Johnson	.30
175	Darrin Chiaverini	.15
176	Jake Reed	.30
177	Kevin Carter	.15
178	Jay Riemersma	.15
179	Tony Gonzalez	.30
180	Hines Ward	.30
181	David Boston	.50
182	Ed McCaffrey	.30
183	Amani Toomer	.30
184	Torry Holt	.50
185	Rob Johnson	.30
186	Kevin Hardy	.15
187	Napoleon Kaufman	.50
188	Jevon Kearse	.50
189	Terance Mathis	.15
190	Dorsey Levens	.50
191	Kyle Brady	.15
192	Steve McNair	.50
193	Kevin Johnson	.50
194	Lamar Smith	.30
195	Ryan Leaf	.50
196	Rod Woodson	.15
197	Corey Bradford	.15
198	Joe Horn	.30
199	Isaac Bruce	.50
200	Steve Young, Dan Marino	1.50
201	*Demario Brown*	.50
202	*Chad Morton*	1.50
203	*Quinton Spotwood*	.50
204	*Mike Anderson*	7.00
205	*Jarious Jackson*	1.25
206	*Hank Poteat*	.75
207	*Rogers Beckett*	.50
208	*Deon Dyer*	.50
209	*Charles Lee*	.75
210	*Barrett Green*	.50
211	*T.J. Slaughter*	.75
212	*Chris Hovan*	.75
213	*Mark Simoneau*	.50
214	*Rashard Anderson*	1.25
215	*Trevor Insley*	.50
216	*Paul Smith*	.75
217	*Doug Johnson*	1.50
218	*Dwayne Goodrich*	.50
219	*Julian Peterson*	.75
220	*Keith Bulluck*	.50
221	*Chris Samuels*	1.00
222	*Shaun Ellis*	.75
223	*Na'il Diggs*	1.00
224	*William Bartee*	.50
225	*John Abraham*	.50
226	*Trevor Gaylor*	1.25
227	*Dante Hall*	.50
228	*Marcus Knight*	.50
229	*Patrick Pass*	.75
230	*Bashir Yamini*	.50
231	*Deltha O'Neal*	.75
232	*Vaughn Sanders*	.50
233	*Todd Husak*	1.50
234	*Thomas Hamner*	.50
235	*Chafie Fields*	1.00
236	*Orantes Grant*	.50
237	*Muneer Moore*	.50
238	*Kwame Cavil*	.75
239	*Spergon Wynn*	1.25
240	*Leon Murray*	.50
241	*Rob Morris*	1.00
242	*Ben Kelly*	.50
243	*Darren Howard*	.75
244	*Raynoch Thompson*	1.00
245	*Mike Green*	.50
246	*Sammy Morris*	1.75
247	*Ahmed Plummer*	1.00
248	*Ian Gold*	.75
249	*Chris Coleman*	.50
250	*Ron Dixon*	1.75
251	*Peter Warrick*	7.00
252	*Joe Hamilton*	1.50
253	*Dennis Northcutt*	1.50
254	*Laveranues Coles*	1.50
255	*Michael Wiley*	1.50
256	*Plaxico Burress*	3.50
257	*Danny Farmer*	1.50
258	*Aaron Shea*	1.00
259	*Sebastian Janikowski*	1.50
260	*Corey Simon*	1.50
261	*Frank Murphy*	1.00
262	*JaJuan Dawson*	1.50
263	*Ron Dayne*	8.50
264	*Tim Rattay*	1.50
265	*Troy Walters*	1.25
266	*J.R. Redmond*	2.00
267	*Tom Brady*	1.25
268	*Jamal Lewis*	10.00
269	*Anthony Lucas*	1.00
270	*Reuben Droughns*	1.00
271	*James Williams*	1.00
272	*Shyrone Stith*	1.00
273	*Jerry Porter*	1.50
274	*Brian Urlacher*	5.00
275	*Avion Black*	1.00
276	*Thomas Jones*	5.00
277	*Chad Pennington*	6.00
278	*Travis Prentice*	2.50
279	*Chris Redman*	3.00
280	*Travis Taylor*	2.00
281	*Giovanni Carmazzi*	1.50
282	*Sherrod Gideon*	1.00
283	*Bubba Franks*	1.50
284	*Sylvester Morris*	3.50
285	*Curtis Keaton*	1.00
286	*Frank Moreau*	1.25
287	*Terrelle Smith*	1.00
288	*Shaun Alexander*	5.00
289	*Tee Martin*	1.50
290	*R. Jay Soward*	1.50
291	*Dez White*	1.25
292	*Trung Canidate*	1.25
293	*Darrell Jackson*	1.50
294	*Marc Bulger*	1.00
295	*Courtney Brown*	1.50
296	*Todd Pinkston*	1.50
297	*Anthony Becht*	1.25
298	*Doug Chapman*	1.00
299	*Gari Scott*	1.00
300	*Chris Cole*	1.00

2000 Metal Emerald Parallel

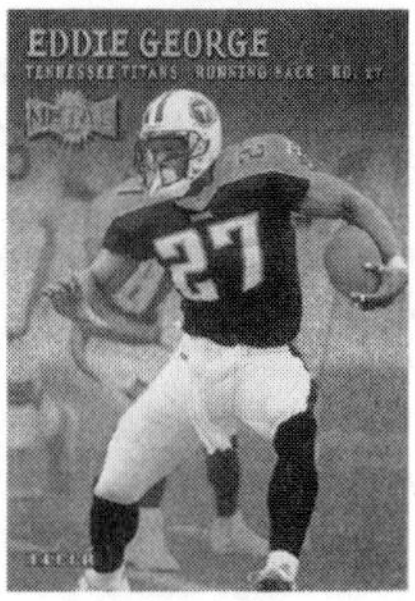

	MT
Emerald Cards:	2x-4x
Inserted 1:4	
Emerald Rookies (#201-250):	2x
Emerald Rookies (#251-300):	1x.
Inserted 1:7	

2000 Metal Heavy Metal

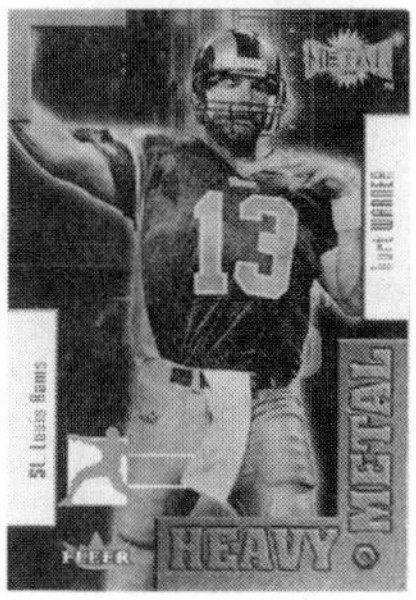

		MT
Complete Set (10):		30.00
Common Player:		1.50
Inserted 1:20		
1	Emmitt Smith	5.00
2	Randy Moss	6.00
3	Kurt Warner	7.00
4	Keyshawn Johnson	1.50
5	Ricky Williams	3.00
6	Peyton Manning	6.00
7	Edgerrin James	6.00
8	Peter Warrick	6.00
9	Brett Favre	7.00
10	Tim Couch	2.50

2000 Metal Hot Commodities

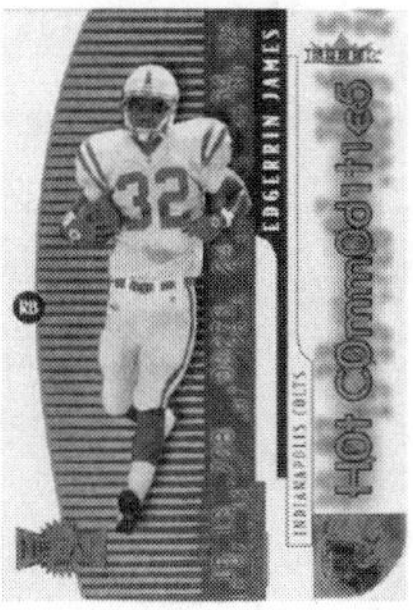

		MT
Complete Set (10):		20.00
Common Player:		1.25
Inserted 1:14		
1	Kurt Warner	5.00
2	Jerry Rice	3.00
3	Terrell Davis	4.00
4	Peyton Manning	4.00
5	Stephen Davis	1.25
6	Brett Favre	5.00
7	Ron Dayne	5.00
8	Troy Aikman	3.00
9	Edgerrin James	4.00
10	Eddie George	1.75

2000 Metal Steel of the Draft

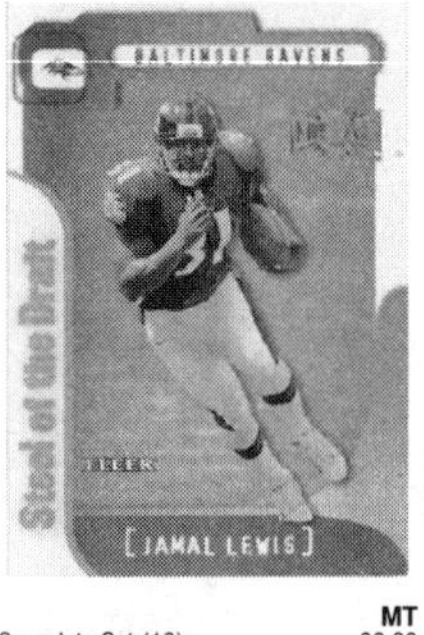

		MT
Complete Set (10):		30.00
Common Player:		2.00
Inserted 1:28		
1	Peter Warrick	7.00
2	Ron Dayne	8.50
3	Plaxico Burress	3.50
4	Thomas Jones	3.00
5	Jamal Lewis	10.00
6	Shaun Alexander	5.00
7	Chad Pennington	6.00
8	Travis Taylor	2.00
9	Chris Redman	3.00
10	J.R. Redmond	2.00

2000 Metal Sunday Showdown

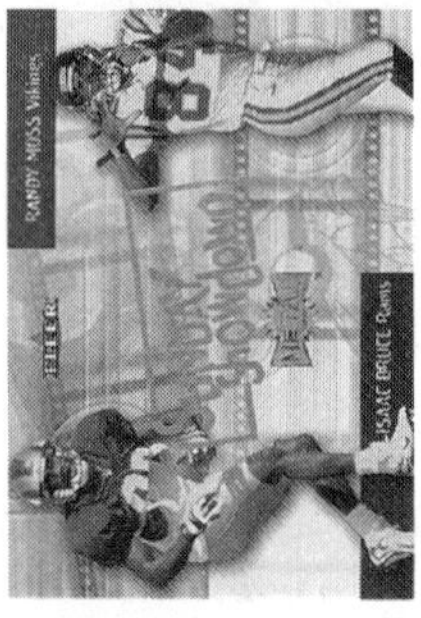

		MT
Complete Set (15):		18.00
Common Player:		1.00
Inserted 1:4		
1	Emmitt Smith, Stephen Davis	2.25
2	Mark Brunell, Tim Couch	1.50
3	Randy Moss, Isaac Bruce	3.00
4	Shaun King, Akili Smith	1.00
5	Peter Warrick, Plaxico Burress	3.00
6	Chad Pennington, Peyton Manning	2.50
7	Ricky Williams, Edgerrin James	3.00
8	Marshall Faulk, Jamal Anderson	1.00
9	Troy Aikman, Donovan McNabb	2.00
10	Daunte Culpepper, Cade McNown	1.75
11	Terrell Davis, Shaun Alexander	2.25
12	Brett Favre, Brad Johnson	3.00
13	Jevon Kearse, Fred Taylor	1.25
14	Thomas Jones, Ron Dayne	3.50
15	Jerry Rice, Keyshawn Johnson	2.00

1992 Metallic Images Tins

These collector's tins were used to package two decks of playing cards. Two active quarterbacks and two Hall of Famers were selected for the tins. The Marino and Moon tins have playing cards which incorporate the Quarterback Club logo into the design; the other two use a Quarterback Legends emblem on the card front. The unnumbered tins were produced by Metallic Images Inc. and were sold in 7-Eleven stores to benefit the Children's Miracle Network.

		MT
Complete Set (4):		15.00
Common Player:		3.00
1	Dan Marino	10.00
2	Warren Moon	4.00
3	Y.A. Tittle	3.00
4	Johnny Unitas	5.00

1993 Metallic Images QB Legends

These metal cards, honoring 20 star NFL quarterbacks, each measures 2-9/16" x 3-9/16" and was included inside a special collectors tin. Metallic Images produced the cards; each has a color action shot against a team color-coded background with gold stripes running through it. The player's team logo, uniform number and mug shot are also featured on the front. The back is numbered and gives a career summary of the player, framed by a team color-coded border. There were 49,000 numbered sets produced; each includes a certificate of authenticity.

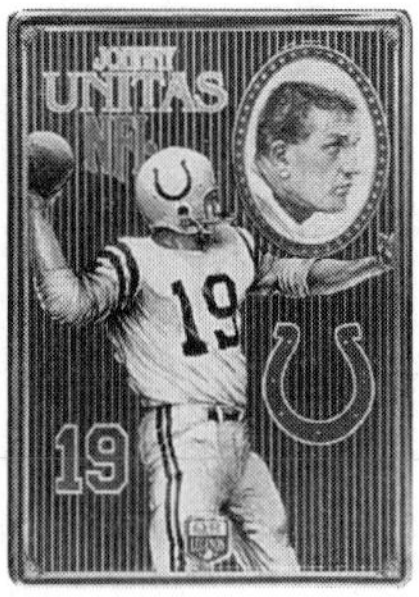

		MT
Complete Set (20):		35.00
Common Player:		1.50
1	Steve Bartkowski	1.50
2	John Brodie	2.50
3	Charley Conerly	2.50
4	Lynn Dickey	1.50
5	Tom Flores	2.00
6	Roman Gabriel	2.00
7	Bob Griese	5.00
8	Steve Grogan	1.50
9	James Harris	1.50
10	Jim Hart	1.50
11	Sonny Jurgensen	3.00
12	Billy Kilmer	2.00
13	Daryle Lamonica	2.50
14	Archie Manning	3.00
15	Craig Morton	1.50
16	Dan Pastorini	1.50
17	Jim Plunkett	2.50
18	Y.A. Tittle	5.00
19	Johnny Unitas	7.50
20	Danny White	2.00

1985 Miller Lite Beer

Measuring 4-3/4" x 7", the eight-card set is anchored on the front with a large player photo. The player's name, position, team helmet, player bio and NFL/Lite logo are beneath the photo. The card backs, which are unnumbered, have the Lite logo in the upper left, with the player's name and position on the upper right. The player's highlights on the field and off the field are printed at the bottom of the card.

		MT
Complete Set (6):		150.00
Common Player:		15.00
1	Larry Csonka	35.00
2	John Hadl (CO)	15.00
3	Freeman McNeil (NFL Man of the Year)	15.00
4	Jack Reynolds (Lite Beer All-Stars)	15.00
5	Steve Young (USFL Man of the Year)	80.00
6	1985 LA Express (Cheerleaders)	15.00

1988 Monte Gum

Monte Gum, in Europe, produced these 100 cards along with an album to hold them. The cards, 1-15/16" x 2-3/4", feature a generic team action photo and caption describing the play on the front. A card number is also included on the front, which has a yellow border around the photo. The backs are blank.

		MT
Complete Set (100):		85.00
Common Player:		1.00
1	Atlanta Falcons	1.75
2	Atlanta Falcons	1.00
3	Atlanta Falcons	1.00
4	Buffalo Bills	1.00
5	Chicago Bears	1.25
6	Chicago Bears	1.00
7	Cincinnati Bengals	1.00
8	Cincinnati Bengals	1.00
9	Cincinnato Bengals	5.00
10	Cincinnati Bengals	1.00
11	Cincinnati Bengals	1.50
12	Cleveland Browns	1.00
13	Cleveland Browns	2.50
14	Cleveland Browns	1.00
15	Cleveland Browns	1.00
16	Dallas Cowboys	1.00
17	Dallas Cowboys	1.25
18	Dallas Cowboys	1.25
19	Denver Broncos	1.00
20	Denver Broncos	1.00
21	Denver Broncos	2.00
22	Detroit Lions	1.00
23	Green Bay Packers	1.00
24	Green Bay Packers	1.00
25	Houston Oilers	1.00
26	Houston Oilers	1.00
27	Indianapolis Colts	1.00
28	Kansas City Chiefs	1.00
29	Kansas City Chiefs	1.00
30	Kansas City Chiefs	1.25
31	Los Angeles Raiders	1.00
32	Los Angeles Raiders	1.00
33	Los Angeles Raiders	1.00
34	Los Angeles Raiders	2.00
35	Los Angeles Rams	1.00
36	Los Angeles Rams	2.00
37	Los Angeles Rams	1.00
38	Miami Dolphins	1.25
39	Miami Dolphins	1.25
40	Minnesota Vikings	1.00
41	Minnesota Vikings	1.00
42	New England Patriots	1.00
43	New England Patriots	1.25
44	New England Patriots	3.00
45	New Orleans Saints	1.50
46	New Orleans Saints (photo actually shows Washington and Michigan in '81 Rose Bowl game)	1.25
47	New York Giants	1.25
48	New York Giants	1.00
49	New York Jets	1.00
50	New York Jets	1.00
51	Philadelphia Eagles	1.00
52	Philadelphia Eagles	1.00
53	Philadelphia Eagles	1.00
54	Philadelphia Eagles	1.00
55	Pittsburgh Steelers	1.00
56	Pittsburgh Steelers	1.50
57	Pittsburgh Steelers	1.00
58	St. Louis Cardinals	1.00
59	St. Louis Cardinals	1.00
60	St. Louis Cardinals	1.00
61	St. Louis Cardinals	1.00
62	San Diego Chargers	1.00
63	San Diego Chargers	1.00
64	San Diego Chargers	1.25
65	San Diego Chargers	1.00
66	San Francisco 49ers	1.00
67	San Francisco 49ers	1.25
68	San Francisco 49ers	10.00
69	San Francisco 49ers	1.25
70	Seattle Seahawks	1.00
71	Seattle Seahawks	1.00
72	Tampa Bay Buccaneers	1.00
73	Tampa Bay Buccaneers	1.00
74	Tampa Bay Buccaneers	1.00
75	Tampa Bay Buccaneers	1.00
76	Washington Redskins	1.00
77	Washington Redskins	1.00
78	Washington Redskins	1.00
79	Washington Redskins	1.00
80	Official NFL Football	1.00
81	Helmets: Falcons/Bills	1.00
82	Helmets: Bears/Bengals	1.00
83	Helmets: Browns/Cowboys	1.00
84	Helmets: Broncos/Lions	1.00
85	Helmets: Packers/Oilers	1.00
86	Helmets: Colts/Chiefs	1.00
87	Helmets: Raiders/Rams	1.00
88	Helmets: Dolphins/Vikings	1.00
89	Helmets: Patriots/Saints	1.00
90	Helmets: Giants/Jets	1.00
91	Philadelphia Eagles Helmet	1.00
92	Pittsburgh Steelers Helmet	1.00
93	St. Louis Cardinals Helmet	1.00
94	San Diego Chargers Helmet	1.00
95	San Francisco 49ers Helmet	1.00
96	Seattle Seahawks Helmet	1.00
97	Tampa Bay Buccaneers Helmet	1.00
98	Washington Redskins Helmet	1.00
99	National Football League Logo	1.00
100	American Football Fans	1.50

1996 Motion Vision

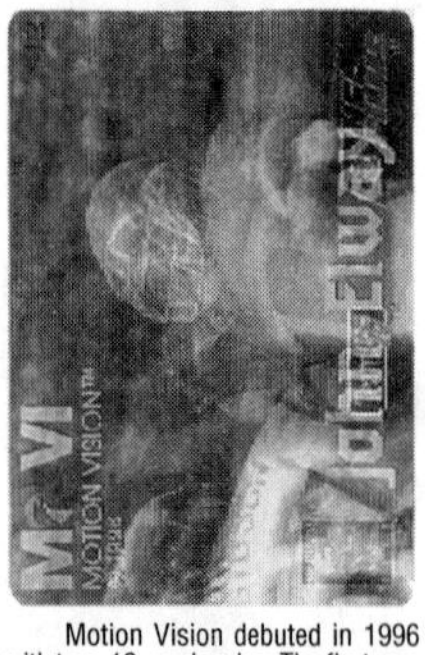

Motion Vision debuted in 1996 with two, 12-card series. The first was called Motion Vision, the second carried a 2.0 suffix. This product arrived in one card "packs" that actually resembled a compact disk case, with the cards inside a poly-sleeve. Motion Vision used Kodak technology to simulate actual game footage with tremendous clarity. The cards carried a Movi Motion Vision logo in the upper left-hand corner and the card number in the upper right- hand corner. The bottom of the card has the player's name, with nothing on the back. The card is best viewed by holding the plastic card up to light and rotating it to see game action. Motion Vision also had a 10-card Limited Digital Replay insert that was differentiated by having 25,000 produced.

		MT
Complete Set (24):		150.00
Comp. Series 1 (12):		75.00
Comp. Series 2 (12):		75.00
Common Player:		4.00
Series 1 Pack (1):		7.00
Series 1 Wax Box (25):		160.00
Series 2 Pack (1):		7.00
Series 2 Wax Box (25):		160.00
1	Troy Aikman	10.00
2	Dan Marino	15.00
3	Steve Young	7.00
4	Emmitt Smith	15.00
5	Drew Bledsoe	10.00
6	Kordell Stewart	10.00
7	Jerry Rice	10.00
8	Warren Moon	4.00
9	Junior Seau	4.00
10	Barry Sanders	12.00
11	Jim Harbaugh	4.00
12	John Elway	10.00
13	Brett Favre	17.00
14	Brett Favre	17.00
15	Troy Aikman	10.00
16	Emmitt Smith	15.00
17	Dan Marino	15.00
18	Kordell Stewart	10.00
19	John Elway	10.00
20	Kerry Collins	6.00
21	Jim Kelly	4.00
22	Drew Bledsoe	10.00
23	Mark Brunell	10.00
24	Jerry Rice	10.00

1996 Motion Vision Limited Digital Replays

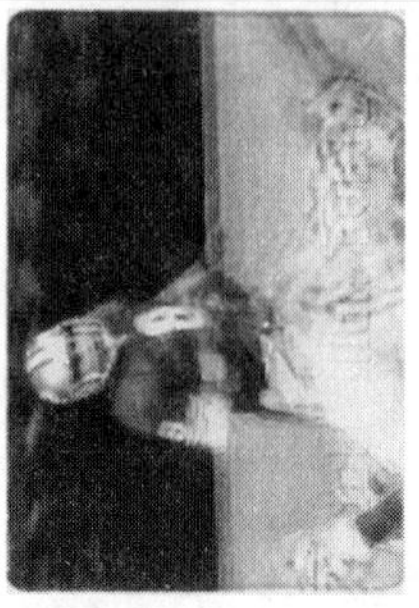

Limited Digital Replays were the only insert set in 1996 Motion Vision. The first six cards were inserted every 25 packs of Series I, with only 2,500 sets produced, while the last four were found in Series 2.0 at a rate of one per 22 packs, with 3,500 sets produced. LDRs are distinguished by having a card back that features another shot of the player and statistics (regular-issue cards have no backs). LDR fronts also carry no logos on the front and instead of a phrase at the bottom describing the play, LDRs have only the player's name. Cards are numbered LDR1-LDR10.

		MT
Complete Set (10):		400.00
Comp. Series 1 (6):		200.00
Comp. Series 2 (4):		200.00
Autographs of Aikman,Bledsoe, Stewart and Young: 10x		
1	Troy Aikman	30.00
2	Dan Marino	60.00
3	Steve Young	25.00
4	Emmitt Smith	60.00
5	Drew Bledsoe	30.00
6	Kordell Stewart	25.00
7	Brett Favre	60.00
8	Brett Favre	60.00
9	Emmitt Smith	60.00
10	Kerry Collins	20.00

1996 Motion Vision LDR Autographs

Limted Digital Replays Autographs consisted of four players who signed their LDR insert in 1996 Motion Vision. Drew Bledsoe, Kordell Stewart and Steve Young were inserted in Series I, while Troy Aikman and the remaining Steve Young cards were in Series 2.0. Fronts of these were the same, with the autograph on the back along with a seal to prove its autheticity.

		MT
Complete Set (4):		1000.
Common Player:		250.00
1	Troy Aikman AUTO	300.00
3	Steve Young AUTO	250.00
5	Drew Bledsoe AUTO	300.00
6	Kordell Stewart AUTO	275.00

1997 Motion Vision

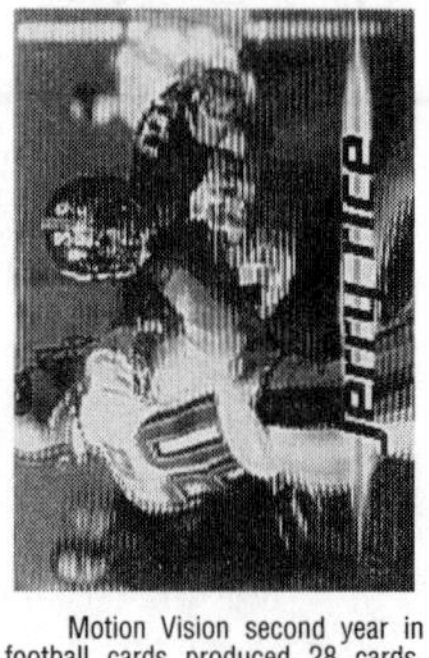

Motion Vision second year in football cards produced 28 cards, with 20 cards in Series I and eight in Series II. Packs consisted of compact disc-like cases that could be opened to expose the card, which is more like a video shown on thick plastic. The card is best viewed when held up to light and moved slightly with the hand. Each series had four insert cards, which were inserted one per 25, with Series I containing LDR1-4 and a Terrell Davis autograph version, while Series II had LDR5-6 and two redemption cards.

		MT
Complete Set (28):		150.00
Complete Series 1 (20):		90.00
Complete Series 2 (8):		60.00
Common Player:		3.00
Pack (1):		5.00
Wax Box (25):		100.00
1	Terrell Davis	10.00
2	Curtis Martin	7.00
3	Joey Galloway	3.00
4	Eddie George	10.00
5	Isaac Bruce	3.00
6	Antonio Freeman	3.00
7	Terry Glenn	4.00
8	Deion Sanders	5.00
9	Jerome Bettis	3.00
10	Reggie White	3.00
11	Brett Favre	15.00
12	Dan Marino	12.00
13	Emmitt Smith	12.00
14	Mark Brunell	8.00
15	John Elway	8.00
16	Drew Bledsoe	8.00
17	Barry Sanders	10.00
18	Jeff Blake	3.00
19	Kerry Collins	3.00
20	Jerry Rice	8.00
21	Dan Marino	12.00
22	Troy Aikman	8.00
23	Brett Favre	15.00
24	Emmitt Smith	12.00
25	Kordell Stewart	8.00
26	Terrell Davis	8.00
27	Eddie George	8.00
28	Drew Bledsoe	8.00

1997 Motion Vision Box Toppers

Five different box toppers were offered with boxes of Motion Vision Series II Football. The cards measure 4" x 6" and were included at a rate of one per box.

		MT
Complete Set (4):		50.00
Common Player:		7.00
	John Elway	10.00
	Brett Favre	20.00
	Dan Marino	15.00
	Steve Young	7.00

1997 Motion Vision Limited Digital Replays

Each series of Motion Vision included four inserts at a rate of one per 25 packs. The Limited Digital Replays are numbered LDR1-6, with numbers 5 and 6 being trade cards for Warrick Dunn and Antoine Smith. Also included are Dunn and Smith XVRR cards. In addition, a autographed version of Terrell Davis' LDR was available.

		MT
Complete Set (8):		140.00
Complete Series 1 (4):		100.00
Complete Series 2 (4):		40.00
Common Player:		10.00
1	Terrell Davis	30.00
1A	Terrell Davis AUTO	200.00
2	Curtis Martin	25.00
3	Brett Favre	45.00
4	Barry Sanders	30.00
5	Warrick Dunn	10.00

1997 Motion Vision Super Bowl XXXI

This four-card set was available through a redemption offer in 1996 MotionVision Series Two packs. The cards commemorate the Conference Championships and Super Bowl XXXI. The fourth card is jumbo format (5-5/8" x 3-3/4"). Each card is numbered one of 5,000.

		MT
Complete Set (4):		75.00
Common Player:		15.00
1	AFC Championship Game (Drew Bledsoe)	15.00
2	NFC Championship Game (Brett Favre)	20.00
3	Super Bowl XXXI (Brett Favre)	20.00
4	Super Bowl XXXI (Brett Favre Jumbo)	20.00

1981 Michael Schechter Associates Test Discs

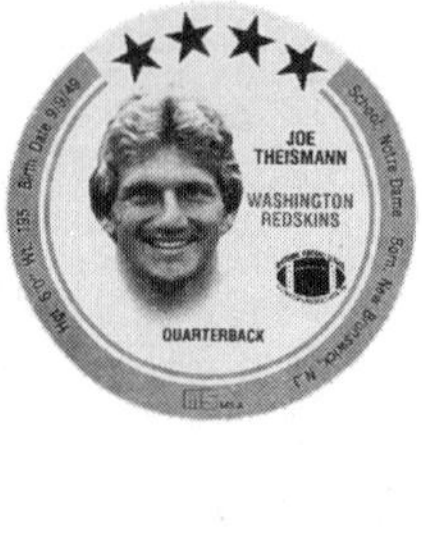

These discs, produced by Michael Schecter Associates, were included in specially-marked packages of bread. The front shows a head shot of the player, but team logos have been airbrushed off the helmets. An NFLPA logo appears on the card front, along with the player's name, team, position and biographical information. Four stars appear at the top of the card. The unnumbered cards have blank backs. Holsum and Gardner's are among the brands of bread which included the cards inside packages. These two companies also made different posters which were intended to be used to display the discs.

		MT
Complete Set (32):		175.00
Common Player:		2.50
(1)	Ken Anderson	4.00
(2)	Ottis Anderson	6.00
(3)	Steve Bartkowski	3.00
(4)	Ricky Bell	3.00
(5)	Terry Bradshaw	17.50
(6)	Harold Carmichael	3.00
(7)	Joe Cribbs	2.50
(8)	Gary Danielson	2.50
(9)	Lynn Dickey	2.50
(10)	Dan Doornink	2.50
(11)	Vince Evans	3.00
(12)	Joe Ferguson	3.00
(13)	Vagas Ferguson	2.50
(14)	Dan Fouts	8.00
(15)	Steve Fuller	2.50
(16)	Archie Griffin	3.00
(17)	Steve Grogan	3.00
(18)	Bruce Harper	2.50
(19)	Jim Hart	3.00
(20)	Jim Jensen	2.50
(21)	Bert Jones	3.00
(22)	Archie Manning	4.00
(23)	Ted McKnight	2.50
(24)	Joe Montana	85.00
(25)	Craig Morton	3.00
(26)	Robert Newhouse	3.00
(27)	Phil Simms	9.00
(28)	Billy Taylor	2.50
(29)	Joe Theismann	5.00
(30)	Mark Van Eeghen	2.50
(31)	Delvin Williams	2.50
(32)	Tim Wilson	2.50

1990 Michael Schechter Associates Superstars

These unnumbered cards, produced by Michael Schechter Associates, were included two per box of Ralston Purina's Staff and Food Club Frosted Flakes cereal. Each card front has a color closeup shot of the player, with "Superstars" written at the top, and the player's name and team at the bottom. Three footballs are in different corners; an NFLPA logo is in the fourth corner. The card back also has the NFLPA logo, plus biographical information and statistics.

		MT
Complete Set (12):		15.00
Common Player:		.75
(1)	Carl Banks	.75
(2)	Cornelius Bennett	.75
(3)	Roger Craig	1.50
(4)	Jim Everett	1.00
(5)	Bo Jackson	2.00
(6)	Ronnie Lott	1.50
(7)	Don Majkowski	.75
(8)	Dan Marino	8.00
(9)	Karl Mecklenburg	.75
(10)	Christian Okoye	.75
(11)	Mike Singletary	1.00
(12)	Herschel Walker	1.00

N

1994 Nabisco A.1. "Masters of the Grill"

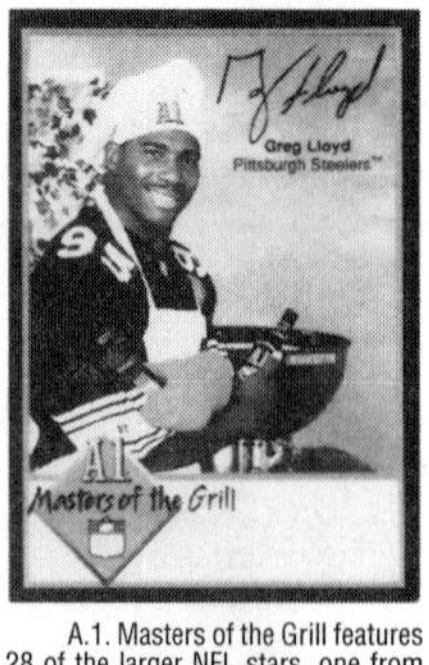

A.1. Masters of the Grill features 28 of the larger NFL stars, one from each team, equipped with all the necessary grill utensils and A.1. clothing, from chef hats to aprons. All the cards present grill recipes on the back; each recipe has A.1. as a key ingredient. The cards are surrounded by a black

border and have an A.1. Masters of the Grill logo.

		MT
Complete Set (28):		7.00
Common Player:		.25
(1)	Harris Barton	.25
(2)	Jerome Bettis	1.50
(3)	Ray Childress	.25
(4)	Eugene Chung	.25
(5)	Jamie Dukes	.25
(6)	Steve Emtman	.25
(7)	Burt Grossman	.25
(8)	Courney Hall	.25
(9)	Ken Harvey	.35
(10)	Chris Hinton	.35
(11)	Kent Hull	.25
(12)	Keith Jackson	.50
(13)	Rickey Jackson	.30
(14)	Cortez Kennedy	.35
(15)	Tim Krumrie	.25
(16)	Jeff Lageman	.25
(17)	Greg Lloyd	.35
(18)	Howie Long	.35
(19)	Hardy Nickerson	.30
(20)	Bart Oates	.25
(21)	Ken Ruettgers	.25
(22)	Dan Saleaumua	.25
(23)	Alonzo Spellman	.30
(24)	Eric Swann	.25
(25)	Pat Swilling	.25
(26)	Tommy Vardell	.25
(27)	Erik Williams	.25
(28)	Gary Zimmerman	.25

1935 National Chicle

The granddaddy of all football card sets, the 36-card National Chicle set was the first to be circulated nationally and the first set to feature only football players (all were pro football players except for Notre Dame coach Knute Rockne). Cards measure 2-3/8" x 2-7/8". The first 24 cards are easier to obtain than the final 12. Rookie cards in this set include Hall of Famers Earl "Dutch" Clark, Cliff Battles, Ken Strong, Turk Edwards, Clarke Hinkle and Bronko Nagurski. Nagurski's card is the most valuable football card in existence.

		NM
Complete Set (36):		17500.
Common Player (1-24):		110.00
Common Player (25-36):		375.00
1	*Earl "Dutch" Clark*	950.00
2	Bo Molenda	110.00
3	George Kenneally	110.00
4	Ed Matesic	110.00
5	Glenn Presnell	110.00
6	Pug Rentner	110.00
7	Ken Strong	225.00
8	Jim Zyntell	110.00
9	Knute Rockne	3000.
10	*Cliff Battles*	220.00
11	*Turk Edwards*	220.00
12	Tom Hupke	110.00
13	Homer Griffiths	110.00
14	Phil Sorboe	110.00
15	Ben Ciccone	110.00
16	Ben Smith	110.00
17	Tom Jones	110.00
18	Mike Mikulak	110.00
19	Ralph Kercheval	110.00
20	Warren Heller	110.00
21	Cliff Montgomery	110.00
22	Shipwreck Kelley	110.00
23	Beattie Feathers	220.00
24	Clarke Hinkle	200.00
25	Dale Burnett	375.00
26	John Isola	375.00
27	Bill Tosi	375.00
28	Stan Kosta	375.00
29	Jim MacMurdo	375.00
30	Ernie Caddel	375.00
31	Nic Niccola	375.00
32	Swede Johnston	375.00
33	Ernie Smith	375.00
34	*Bronko Nagurski*	6500.
35	Luke Johnson	375.00
36	Bernie Masterson	1300.

1992 NewSport

NewSport was issued exclusively in France, with four cards being distributed each month from November 1991 to June 1992. The 32-card glossy set was either issued in individual cards or in four-card strips. Each card measures 4" x 6", with card backs written in French.

		MT
Complete Set (32):		200.00
Common Player:		6.00
1	Bubby Brister	6.00
2	James Brooks	6.00
3	Joey Browner	6.00
4	Gill Byrd	6.00
5	Eric Dickerson	8.00
6	Henry Ellard	6.00
7	John Elway	20.00
8	Mervyn Fernandez	6.00
9	David Fulcher	6.00
10	Ernest Givins	6.00
11	Jay Hilgenberg	6.00
12	Michael Irvin	10.00
13	Dave Krieg	6.00
14	Albert Lewis	6.00
15	James Lofton	6.00
16	Dan Marino	45.00
17	Wilber Marshall	6.00
18	Freeman McNeil	6.00
19	Karl Mecklenberg	6.00
20	Joe Montana	35.00
21	Christian Okoye	6.00
22	Michael Dean Perry	6.00
23	Tom Rathman	6.00
24	Mark Rypien	6.00
25	Barry Sanders	30.00
26	Deion Sanders	20.00
27	Sterling Sharpe	8.00
28	Pat Swilling	6.00
29	Lawrence Taylor	10.00
30	Vinny Testaverde	6.00
31	Andre Tippett	6.00
32	Reggie White	10.00

1991 NFL Experience

These oversized cards feature artwork highlights from the first 25 Super Bowls. The black-bordered cards, which measure 2-1/2" x 4-3/4", were produced by the NFL, so each has an NFL Experience logo on the front. The back is in a horizontal format, with a pink bar at the top which has "The NFL Experience" written in it, plus the card number. A pink bar at the bottom carries a description of the action on the front. Sandwiched between the two bars is a brief comment about life in the NFL, plus a sponsor logo.

		MT
Complete Set (28):		4.00
Common Player:		.20
1	NFL Experience Theme Art	.20
2	Super Bowl I (Max McGee)	.20
3	Super Bowl II (Vince Lombardi, Bart Starr)	.50
4	Super Bowl III (Don Shula, Joe Namath)	.75
5	Super Bowl IV	.20
6	Super Bowl V - Colts vs. Cowboys	.20
7	Super Bowl VI (Duane Thomas, Bob Lily, Roger Staubach, Tom Landry, Tex Schramm)	.60
8	Super Bowl VII	.20
9	Super Bowl VIII (Larry Csonka)	.30
10	Super Bowl IX	.20
11	Super Bowl X (Lynn Swann, Jack Lambert)	.30
12	Super Bowl XI - Raiders vs. Vikings (John Madden)	.30
13	Super Bowl XII (Randy White, Harvey Martin, Craig Morton)	.30
14	Super Bowl XIII - Steelers vs. Cowboys	.20
15	Super Bowl XIV (Terry Bradshaw)	.60
16	Super Bowl XV - Raiders vs. Eagles	.20
17	Super Bowl XVI - 49ers vs. Bengals	.20
18	Super Bowl XVII (John Riggins)	.30
19	Super Bowl XVIII (Marcus Allen)	.30
20	Super Bowl XIX - 49ers vs. Dolphins	.20
21	Super Bowl XX (Richard Dent)	.30
22	Super Bowl XXI	.20
23	Super Bowl XXII (John Elway, Doug Williams)	.30
24	Super Bowl XXIII - 49ers vs. Bengals	.20
25	Super Bowl XXIV (Joe Montana)	1.00
26	Super Bowl XXV Collage of 25 Super Bowls	.20
27	Super Bowl XXVI - Lombardi Trophy	.20
28	Joe Theismann	.30

1993 NFL Properties Santa Claus

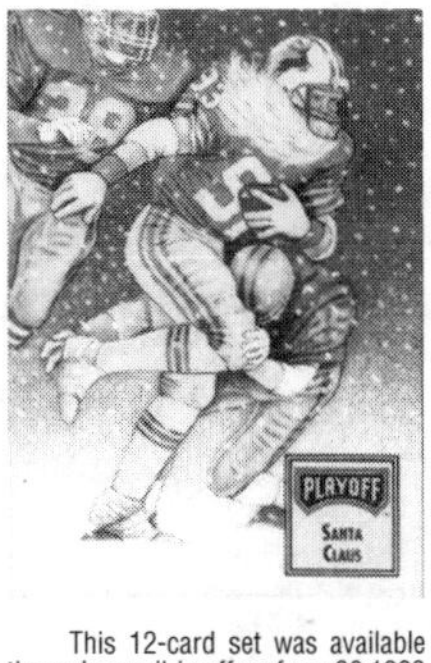

This 12-card set was available through a mail-in offer of any 30 1993 NFL trading card wrappers and $1.50 for postage and handling. In addition, sets were sent out to dealers with a season's greeting card. All 12 NFL trading card licensees produced a Santa Claus card, and there was a checklist card issued by NFL Properties included.

		MT
Complete Set (13):		15.00
Common Player:		1.50
1	Santa Claus Action Packed (Action Packed)	1.50
2	Santa Claus Classic	1.50
3	Santa Claus Collector's Edge	1.50
4	Santa Claus Fleer	1.50
5	Santa Claus Pacific	1.50
6	Santa Claus Pinnacle	1.50
7	Santa Claus Playoff	1.50
8	Santa Claus Pro Set	1.50
9	Santa Claus SkyBox	1.50
10	Santa Claus Topps	1.50
11	Santa Claus Upper Deck	1.50
12	Santa Claus Wild Card	1.50
13	Checklist Card NFL Properties	1.50

1993-95 NFL Properties Show Redemption Cards

This NFL Properties product was handed out to attendees at card shows over a three-year span, with a banner at the top of each card showing the city and dates that the show was held. The first card was issued at Chicago and is the only unnumbered card (others have roman numerals on the back). Card No. 2 was given out at a Labor Day Weekend Show in San Francisco and is the only card in the set to show the team's schedule on the back (others have text about players on the front). Card No. 4B was limited to 3,000 total cards, and replaced card No. 4A, which was done to commemorate the St. Louis Stallions NFL franchise that never materalized so it was not issued. Card No. 6A was issued at the Cocktail Reception sponsored by NFL Properties at the 15th National Sports Collectors Convention, with the three players autographing the card in blue ink. Card No. 6B was issued as part of the Back-to- School promotion, with collectors redeeming two proof of purchases for the oversized Elway NFL FACT card.

		MT
Complete Set (9):		750.00
Common Player:		10.00
1	Chicago Bears Saluting Hall of Famers (Dick Butkus, Mike Ditka, Gale Sayers) (7/24/93) (200) (Signed in silver ink)	100.00
2	San Francisco 49ers Labor Day Weekend (NFL Kickoff '93, Ricky Watters, Steve Young, Keith DeLong, Jerry Rice, John Taylor, Tim McDonald) (9/93) (1,000) (1993 49er schedule on card back)	20.00
3	San Francisco 49ers Labor Day Weekend (Y.A. Tittle, Ken Stabler) (9/93, 1,000) Saluting Bay Area Legends, (Career summaries on back)	15.00
3AU	San Francisco 49ers AUTO Labor Day Weekend (Y.A. Tittle, Ken Stabler) (9/93) (1,000) Saluting Bay Area Legends Signed by both players)	180.00
4B	St. Louis Cardinals Saluting Three Decades of Gateway City QBs (Jim Hart, Charlie Johnson, Neil Lomax) (10/29-31/93) (3000)	10.00
5	Dallas Cowboys Saluting the Super Bowl Champions (Michael Irvin, Troy Aikman, Emmitt Smith, Jay Novacek, Russell Maryland, Ken Norton) (11/19-21/93) 3000)	15.00
6A	Houston Oilers Saluting a Trio of Oilers Legends (Earl Campbell, Dan Pastorini, Ken Stabler) (Autographed) 8/4-7/94) (200)	180.00
6B	1995 Spokesman NFL Trading Cards (John Elway) (Autographed) (300)	100.00
7	Joe Namath, John Elway (Autographed) (300)	180.00

1994 NFL Back-to-School

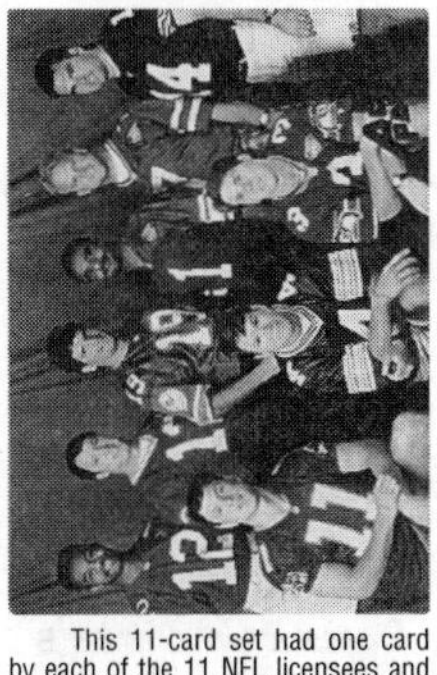

This 11-card set had one card by each of the 11 NFL licensees and was available to collectors who sent in 20 wrappers from NFL licensed products by the deadline of Nov. 30, 1994. Cards are unnumbered on the backs, except Action Packed (BS1) and Upper Deck (19) and are standard sized. At one point Pro Set had planned to do a Brett Favre card, however it went out of business before the card could be issued.

		MT
Complete Set (11):		15.00
Common Player:		.50
1	NFL Quarterback Club (Action Packed)	1.50
2	Emmitt Smith (Classic)	4.00
3	John Elway (Collector's Edge)	1.25
4	Jerome Bettis (Fleer)	1.00
5	Sterling Sharpe (Pacific)	.75
6	Drew Bledsoe (Pinnacle)	2.00
7	Dana Stubblefield (Playoff)	.75
8	Jim Kelly (SkyBox)	.75
9	Jerry Rice (Topps)	2.00
10	Joe Montana (Upper Deck)	2.50
11	Checklist NFL Properties	.50

1994 NFL Properties Santa Claus

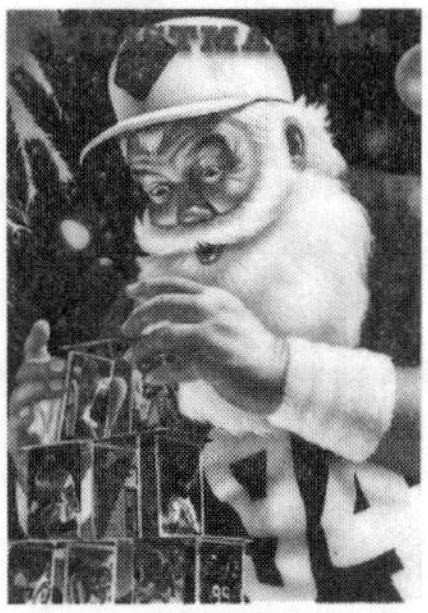

Each of the NFL's 10 card licensees printed a Santa card for the set, which was available through the mail in exchange for 20 NFL-licensed card wrappers and $1.50 postage. There is no consistent design throughout the set, as each company was allowed to create their own design. Some cards are numbered and others are not. The fronts each include Santa artwork, while the backs have holiday greetings.

		MT
Complete Set (10):		10.00
Common Player:		1.25
1	Santa Claus Action Packed	1.25
2	Santa Claus Classic	1.25
3	Santa Claus Collector's Edge	1.25
4	Santa Claus Fleer	1.25
5	Santa Claus Pacific	1.25
6	Santa Claus Pinnacle	1.25
7	Santa Claus Playoff	1.25
8	Santa Claus SkyBox	1.25
9	Santa Claus Upper Deck	1.25
10	Checklist Card, NFL Properties	1.25

1995 NFL Properties Santa Claus

Eight of the NFL's card licensees produced cards for this nine-card set. The fronts and backs do not have a consistent design. The set was available for 20 wrappers and $1.50 shipping.

		MT
Complete Set (9):		10.00
Common Player:		1.00
1	Title Card (Santa and friend)	1.00
2	Santa Claus Classic ProLine (Emmitt Smith, Drew Bledsoe)	2.00
3	Santa Claus Collector's Edge	1.00
4	Santa Claus Pacific	1.00
5	Santa Claus Pinnacle (Dan Marino, Emmitt Smith, Steve Young)	4.00
6	Santa Claus Playoff	1.00
7	Santa Claus SkyBox	1.00
8	Santa Claus Topps	1.00
9	Santa Claus Upper Deck	1.00

1996 NFL Properties 7-11

Fleer/SkyBox, Pinnacle, Topps and Upper Deck, along with NFL Properties, combined to produce this nine-card set. Each card front and back is designed identically to the companies' sets from 1996. The cards are numbered 1-9 on the backs. To receive the cards, collectors needed to send in two wrappers from any 1996 NFL trading card product, a 7-11 store receipt with the trading card purchase circled, completed entry form or 3 x 5 card and $1 for shipping had to be sent to a redemption house in Minnesota.

		MT
Complete Set (9):		20.00
Common Player:		1.00
1	John Elway	3.00
2	Jerry Rice	3.00
3	Dan Marino	4.00
4	Barry Sanders	5.00
5	Kordell Stewart	3.00
6	Steve Young	2.00
7	Joe Namath	3.00
8	Brett Favre	6.00
9	Trent Dilfer	1.00

1996 NFL Properties Back-to-School

One of each of the NFL's card licensees, along with NFL Properties, joined forces to produce this nine-card set. To receive the set, collectors needed to send in 20 wrappers from any 1996 NFL-licensed trading cards and $1.50 for shipping to a redemption house in Minnesota. The offer expired Nov. 30, 1996.

		MT
Complete Set (9):		10.00
Common Player:		.50
	Pacific (Chris Warren)	.50
	Pinnacle (Dan Marino, Steve Young)	2.00
	NFLP (John Elway)	1.50
	Topps (Steve Young)	1.00
	Fleer (Brett Favre)	3.00
	Collector's Edge (Steve Bono)	.50
	Upper Deck (Dan Marino)	2.00
	Classic (Emmitt Smith)	2.00
	Playoff (Deion Sanders)	1.00

1996 NFL Properties Santa Claus

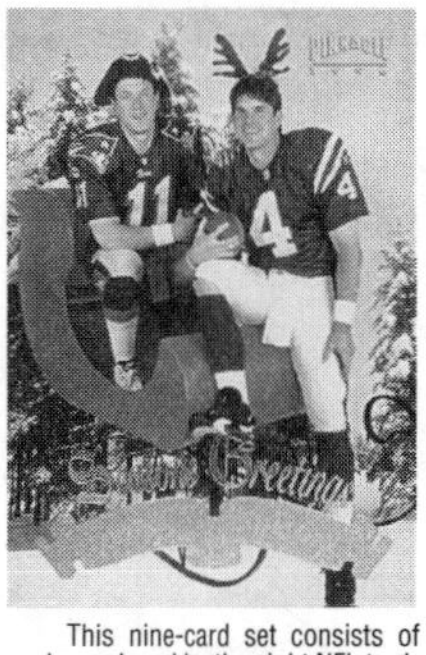

This nine-card set consists of cards produced by the eight NFL trading card licensees. All the cards feature Santa Claus and some have NFL players as well. The cards could be obtained via redemption of 20 wrappers of any participating manufacturers football products.

		MT
Complete Set (9):		8.00
Common Player:		1.00
1	Title Card - Santa Claus	1.00
2	Santa Claus (Collector's Edge with Jeff Blake and Steve Bono)	1.00
3	Santa Claus (Fleer/Skybox with Brett Favre on back)	1.00
4	Santa Claus (Pacific)	1.00
5	Santa Claus (Pinnacle with Drew Bledsoe and Jim Harbaugh)	1.00
6	Santa Claus (Playoff)	1.00
7	Santa Claus (Score Board with Troy Aikman)	1.00
8	Santa Claus (Topps)	1.00
9	Santa Claus (Upper Deck)	1.00

1972 NFLPA Wonderful World Stamps

These numbered stamps, which each measure 1-15/16" x 2-7/8", feature stars from each team in the NFL. The front of each stamp has a color photo of the player; the back has player's name, a stamp number and a place for it to be glued so it can be put into an accompanying album. The 30-page 9-1/2" x 13-1/4" album traces the history of pro football in the United States and provides short biographies of the players who are featured on the stamps. The NFLPA sponsored the album, which is titled "The Wonderful World of Pro Football USA." Stamps which are listed in the checklist with an A were issued in 1971.

		NM
Complete Set (390):		275.00
Common Player:		.35
1	Bob Berry	.50
2	Greg Brezina	.35
3	Ken Burrow	.35
4	Jim Butler	.40
5	Wes Chesson	.35
6	Claude Humphrey	.50
7	George Kunz	1.00
8	Tom McCauley	.35
9	Jim Mitchell	.50
10	Tommy Nobis	3.00
11	Ken Reaves	.35
12	Bill Sandeman	.35
13	John Small	.35
14	Harmon Wages	.35
15	John Zook	.50
16	Norm Bulaich	.60
17	Bill Curry	.75
18	Mike Curtis	.75
19	Ted Hendricks	3.00
20	Roy Hilton	.35
21	Eddie Hinton	.35
22	David Lee	.35
23	Jerry Logan	.35
24	John Mackey	2.00
25	Tom Matte	.75
26	Jim O'Brien	.50
27	Glenn Ressler	.35
28	Johnny Unitas	15.00
29	Bob Vogel	.50
30	Rick Volk	.50
31	Paul Costa	.35
32	Jim Dunaway	.50
33	Paul Guidry	.35
34	Jim Harris	.35
35	Robert James	.35
36	Mike McBath	.35
37	Haven Moses	1.00
38	Wayne Patrick	.35
39	John Pitts	.35
40	Jim Reilly	.35
41	Pete Richardson	.35
42	Dennis Shaw	.50
43	O.J. Simpson	25.00
44	Mike Stratton	.50
45	Bob Tatarek	.35
46	Dick Butkus	8.00
47	Jim Cadile	.35
48	Jack Concannon	.50
49	Bobby Douglass	.75
50	George Farmer	.50
51	Dick Gordon	.50
52	Bobby Joe Green	.35
53	Ed O'Bradovich	.35
54A	Bob Hyland	.35
54B	Mac Percival	.35
55A	Ed O'Bradovich	.50
55B	Gale Sayers	9.00
56A	Mac Percival	.35
56B	George Seals	.35
57	Jim Seymour	.35
58A	George Seals	.35
58B	Ron Smith	.50
59	Bill Staley	.35
60	Cecil Turner	.40
61	Al Beauchamp	.45
62	Virgil Carter	.50
63	Vernon Holland	.35
64	Bob Johnson	.50
65	Ron Lamb	.35
66	Dave Lewis	.35
67	Rufus Mayes	.50
68	Horst Muhlmann	.35
69	Lemar Parrish	.75
70	Jess Phillips	.35
71	Mike Reid	2.00
72	Ken Riley	1.00
73	Paul Robinson	.50
74	Bob Trumpy	2.25
75	Fred Willis	.35
76	Don Cockroft	.50
77	Gary Collins	.50
78	Gene Hickerson	.50
79	Fair Hooker	.75
80	Jim Houston	.50
81	Walter Johnson	.50
82	Joe Jones	.35
83	Leroy Kelly	3.00
84	Milt Morin	.50
85	Reece Morrison	.35
86	Bill Nelsen	.50
87	Mike Phipps	.75
88	Bo Scott	.50
89	Jerry Sherk	.50
90	Ron Snidow	.35
91	Herb Adderley	3.00
92	George Andrie	.75
93	Mike Clark	.35
94	Dave Edwards	.50
95	Walt Garrison	1.50
		.75
97	Bob Hayes	2.00
98	Calvin Hill	2.00
99	Chuck Howley	.75
100	Lee Roy Jordan	2.50
101	Dave Manders	.75
102	Craig Morton	1.25
103	Ralph Neely	.50
104	Mel Renfro	1.00
105	Roger Staubach	30.00
106	Bobby Anderson	.75
107	Sam Brunelli	.35
108	Dave Costa	.35
109	Mike Current	.35
110	Pete Duranko	.35
111	George Goeddeke	.35
112	Cornell Gordon	.35
113	Don Horn	.50
114	Rich Jackson	.35
115	Larry Kaminski	.35
116	Floyd Little	1.50
117	Marv Montgomery	.35
118	Steve Ramsey	.50
119	Paul Smith	.50
120	Billy Thompson	.75
121	Lem Barney	3.00
122	Nick Eddy	.50
123	Mel Farr	.75
124	Ed Flanagan	.35
125	Larry Hand	.35
126	Greg Landry	.75
127	Dick LeBeau	.50
128	Mike Lucci	.50
129	Earl McCullouch	.50
130	Bill Munson	.75
131	Wayne Rasmussen	.35
132	Joe Robb	.35
133	Jerry Rush	.35
134	Altie Taylor	.50
135	Wayne Walker	.50
136	Ken Bowman	.35
137	John Brockington	.75
138	Fred Carr	.50
139	Carroll Dale	.50
140	Ken Ellis	.35
141	Gale Gillingham	.50
142	Dave Hampton	.50
143	Doug Hart	.35
144A	John Hilton	.35
144B	MacArthur Lane	.35
145	Mike McCoy	.50
146	Ray Nitschke	2.50
147	Frank Patrick	.35
148	Francis Peay	.35
149	Dave Robinson	.75
150	Bart Starr	9.00
151	Bob Atkins	.35
152	Elvin Bethea	.75
153	Garland Boyette	.35
154	ken Burrough	.75
155	Woody Campbell	.35
156	John Charles	.35
157	Lynn Dickey	.75
158	Elbert Drungo	.35
159	Gene Ferguson	.35
160	Charlie Johnson	.75

161 Charlie Joyner 3.00
162 Dan Patorini .75
163 Ron Pritchard .35
164 Walt Suggs .35
165 Mike Tilleman .35
166 Bobby Bell 3.00
167 Aaron Brown .50
168 Buck Buchanan 2.00
169 Ed Buddle .75
170 Curley Culp 1.00
171 Len Dawson 6.00
172 Willie Lanier 2.50
173 Jim Lynch .50
174 Jim Marsalis .50
175 Mo Moorman .35
176 Ed Podolak .50
177 Johnny Robinson .75
178 Jan Stenerud 2.00
179 Otis Taylor 1.50
180 Jim Tyrer .75
181 Kermit Alexander .50
182 Coy Bacon .35
183 Dick Buzin .35
184 Roman Gabriel 1.00
185 Gene Howard .35
186 Ken Iman .35
187 Les Josephson .50
188 Marlin McKeever .50
189 Merlin Olsen 4.00
190A Richie Petitbon .75
190B Phil Olsen .35
191 David Ray .35
192 Lance Rentzel .75
193 Isiah Robertson .50
194 Larry Smith .35
195 Jack Snow .75
196 Nick Buoniconti 2.00
197 Doug Crusan .35
198 Larry Csonka 8.00
199 Bob DeMarco .50
200 Marv Fleming .50
201 Bob Griese 10.00
202 Jim Klick 1.00
203 Bob Kuechenberg 1.00
204 Mercury Morris 1.25
205A Jim Riley .35
205B John Richardson .35
206 Jim Riley .35
207 Jake Scott .75
208 Howard Twilley .75
209 Paul Warfield 5.00
210 Garo Yepremian .75
211 Grady Alderman .50
212 John Beasley .35
213 John Henderson .35
214 Wally Hilgenberg .50
215 Clinton Jones .50
216 Karl Kassulke .35
217 Paul Krause 1.25
218 Dave Osborn .50
219 Alan Page 2.00
220 Ed Sharockman .35
221 Fran Tarkenton 10.00
222 Mick Tingelhoff .75
223 Charlie West .35
224 Lonnie Warwick .35
225 Gene Washington .75
226 Hank Barton .35
227A Larry Carwell .35
227B Ron Berger .35
228 Larry Carwell .35
229A Carl Garrett .50
229B Jim Cheyunski .50
230A Jim Hunt .35
230B Carl Garrett .50
231 Rickie Harris .35
232 Daryl Johnson .35
233 Steve Kiner .35
234 Jon Morris .35
235 Jim Nance .75
236 Tom Neville .35
237 Jim Plunkett 4.00
238 Ron Sellers .50
239 Len St. Jean .35
240A Gerald Warren .35
240B Don Webb .35
241 Dan Abramowicz .75
242A Tony Baker .35
242B Dick Absher .35
243 Leo Carroll .35
244 Jim Duncan .35
245 Al Dodd .35
246 Jim Flanigan .35
247 Hoyle Granger .35
248 Edd Hargett .75
249 Glen Ray Hines .35
250 Hugo Hollas .35
251 Jake Kupp .35
252 Dave Long .35
253 Mike Morgan .35
254 Tom Roussel .35
255 Del Williams .35
256 Otto Brown .35
257 Bobby Duhon .50
258 Scott Eaton .35
259 Jim Flies .35
260 Tucker Fredrickson .75
261A Don Herrmann .35
261B Pete Gogolak .50
262 Bob Grim .50
263 Don Herrmann .35
264A Ernie Koy .75
264B Ron Johnson 1.00
265A Spider Lockhart .50
265B Jim Kanicki .50
266 Spider Lockhart .50
267 Joe Morrison .75
268 Bob Tucker 2.00
269 Willie Williams .35
270 Willie Young .35
271 Al Atkinson .35
272 Ralph Baker .35
273 Emerson Boozer .75
274 John Elliott .35
275 Dave Herman .35
276A Dave Herman .35
276B Winston Hill .50
277 Gus Hollomon .35
278 Bob Howfield .35
279 Pete Lammons .50
280 Joe Namath (numbered 281) 22.00
281 Gerry Philbin .50
282 Matt Snell .75
283 Steve Tannen .35
284 Earlie Thomas .35
285 Al Woodall .50
286 Fred Biletnikoff 4.00
287 George Blanda 6.00
288 Willie Brown 3.00
289 Ray Chester 1.00
290 Tony Cline .35
291 Dan Conners .35
292 Ben Davidson 1.50
293 Hewritt Dixon .50
294 Tom Keating .50
295 Daryle Lamonica 1.50
296 Gus Otto .35
297 Jim Otto 3.00
298 Rod Sherman .35
299 Bubba Smith .35
300A Warren Wells .50
300B Gene Upshaw 3.00
301 Rick Arrington .35
302 Gary Ballman .50
303 Lee Bouggess .35
304 Bill Bradley .75
305A Richard Harris .35
305B Happy Feller .75
306A Ben Hawkins .35
306B Richard Harris .35
307 Ben Hawkins .35
308 Harold Jackson 1.50
309 Pete Liske .75
310 Al Nelson .35
311 Gary Pettigrew .35
312 Tim Rossovich .75
313 Tom Woodeshick .50
314 Adrian Young .50
315 Steve Zabel .50
316 Chuck Allen .35
317 Warren Bankston .50
318 Chuck Beatty .35
319 Terry Bradshaw 20.00
320 John Fuqua .50
321 Terry Hanratty 1.00
322 Ray Mansfield .35
323 Ben McGee .35
324 John Rowser .35
325 Andy Russell 1.00
326 Ron Shanklin .50
327 Dave Smith .35
328 Bruce Van Dyke .35
329 Lloyd Voss .35
330 Bobby Walden .35
331 Donny Anderson .75
332 Jim Bakken .75
333 Pete Beathard .75
334A Mel Gray 2.00
334B Miller Farr .50
335A Jim Hart 1.00
335B Mel Gray 1.00
336 Jim Hart 1.00
337A Chuck Latourette .35
337B Rol Krueger .35
338 Chuck Latourette .35
339A Bob Reynolds .35
339B Ernie McMillan .50
340 Bob Reynolds .35
341 Jackie Smith 3.50
342 Larry Stallings .50
343 Chuck Walker .35
344 Roger Wehrli .75
345 Larry Wilson 2.00
346 Bob Babich .35
347 Pete Barnes .35
348A Marty Domres .50
348B Steve DeLong .50
349 Marty Domres .50
350 Gary Garrison .50
351A Walker Gillette .35
351B John Hadl 1.25
352 Kevin Hardy .35
353 Bob Howard .35
354A Jim Hill .35
354B Deacon Jones 1.75
355 Terry Owens .75
356 Dennis Partee .35
357A Dennis Partee .35
357B Jeff Queen .35
358 Jim Tolbert .35
359 Russ Washington .35
360 Doug Wilkerson .35
361 John Brodie 3.50
362 Doug Cunningham .35
363 Bruce Gossett .35
364 Stan Hindman .35
365 John Isenbarger .50
366 Charlie Krueger .50
367 Frank Nunley .35
368 Woody Peoples .35
369 Len Rohde .35
370 Steve Spurrier 6.50
371 Gene Washington 1.00
372 Dave Wilcox .75
373 Ken Willard 1.00
374 Bob Windsor .50
375 Dick Witcher .50
376 Verlon Biggs .75
377 Larry Brown 3.00
378 Speedy Duncan .50
379 Chris Hanburger 1.00
380 Charlie Harraway .50
381 Sonny Jurgensen 5.00
382 Bill Kilmer 1.50
383 Tommy Mason .50
384 Ron McDole .50
385 Brig Owens .35
386 Jack Pardee 2.00
387 Myron Pottios 1.00
388 Jerry Smith .50
389 Diron Talbert .50
390 Charley Taylor 4.00

1972 NFLPA Iron Ons

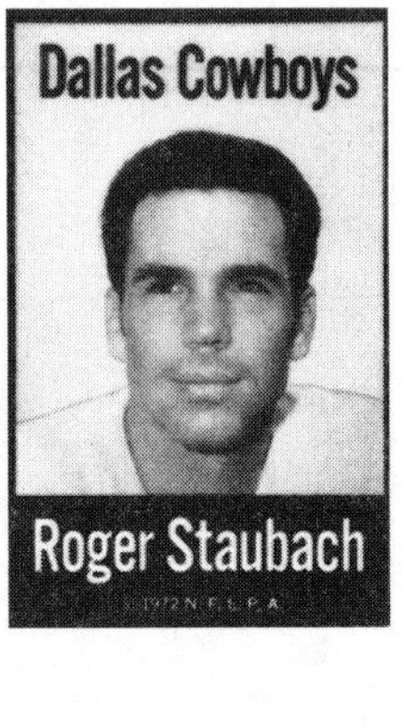

These 35 cards were created as cloth patches to be ironed onto clothes. Hence, the backs are blank. The front of the card has a full color head shot of the player, with his name and 1972 NFLPA copyright at the bottom. The player's name is above the photo, which is framed by a black border. The cards, which were sold through vending machines, measure 2-1/4" x 3-1/2" and are unnumbered.

NM
Complete Set (35): 175.00
Common Player: 2.00
(1) Donny Anderson 2.00
(2) George Blanda 7.50
(3) Terry Bradshaw 20.00
(4) John Brockington 2.00
(5) John Brodie 5.00
(6) Dick Butkus 10.00
(7) Larry Csonka 10.00
(8) Mike Curtis 2.00
(9) Len Dawson 6.00
(10) Carl Eller 3.00
(11) Mike Garrett 2.00
(12) Joe Greene 8.00
(13) Bob Griese 9.00
(14) Dick Gordon 2.00
(15) John Hadl 3.00
(16) Bob Hayes 3.00
(17) Ron Johnson 2.00
(18) Deacon Jones 3.00
(19) Sonny Jurgensen 6.00
(20) Leroy Kelly 3.00
(21) Jim Kiick 2.50
(22) Greg Landry 2.00
(23) Floyd Little 3.00
(24) Mike Lucci 2.00
(25) Archie Manning 5.00
(26) Joe Namath 35.00
(27) Tommy Nobis 3.00
(28) Alan Page 3.00
(29) Jim Plunkett 4.00
(30) Gale Sayers 10.00
(31) O.J. Simpson 35.00
(32) Roger Staubach 30.00
(33) Duane Thomas 2.00
(34) Johnny Unitas 25.00
(35) Paul Warfield 5.00

1972 NFLPA Vinyl Stickers

These stickers feature 20 of the NFL's stars and were sold through vending machines. Each sticker is 2-3/4" x 4-3/4" and is copyrighted on the front by the NFLPA. Each player's head appears on a caricature drawing of him in a football uniform; the outline of his body is what can actually be used as a sticker. Consequently, the backs are blank. The stickers are unnumbered.

NM
Complete Set (20): 95.00
Common Player: 2.00
(1) Donny Anderson 2.00
(2) George Blanda 5.00
(3) Terry Bradshaw 17.00
(4) John Brockington 2.00
(5) John Brodie 4.00
(6) Dick Butkus 8.00
(7) Dick Gordon 2.00
(8) Joe Greene 5.00
(9) John Hadl 2.00
(10) Bob Hayes 3.00
(11) Ron Johnson 9.00
(12) Floyd Little 3.00
(13) Joe Namath 25.00
(14) Tommy Nobis 3.00
(15) Alan Page 15.00
(16) Jim Plunkett 5.00
(17) Gale Sayers 10.00
(18) Roger Staubach 22.00
(19) Johnny Unitas 18.00
(20) Paul Warfield 4.00

1979 NFLPA Pennant Stickers

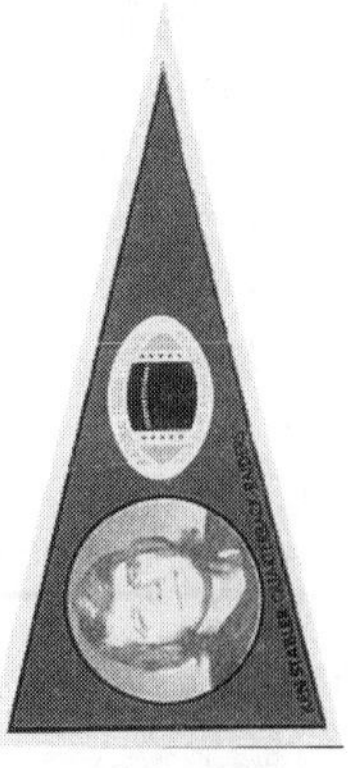

Each of these 50 stickers, sponsored by the NFLPA, is shaped like a pennant and features a black-and-white head shot of a player inside a circle. The NFLPA football logo is also on the front of the sticker. Different colors are used for the backgrounds of the stickers; some stickers can be found with various colors for a background, too. The stickers measure 2-1/2" x 5" and have the player's name, position and team on the front.

NM
Complete Set (50): 425.00
Common Player: 2.50
(1) Lyle Alzado 5.00
(2) Ken Anderson 7.50
(3) Steve Bartkowski 10.00
(4) Ricky Bell 4.00
(5) Elvin Bethea 2.50
(6) Tom Blanchard 2.50
(7) Terry Bradshaw 25.00
(8) Bob Breunig 4.00
(9) Greg Brezina 5.00
(10) Doug Buffone 9.00
(11) Earl Campbell 50.00
(12) John Cappelletti 3.00
(13) Harold Carmichael 4.00
(14) Chuck Crist 15.00
(15) Sam Cunningham 4.00
(16) Joe DeLamielleure 2.50
(17) Tom Dempsey 4.00
(18) Tony Dorsett 15.00
(19) Dan Fouts 20.00
(20) Roy Gerela 4.00
(21) Bob Griese (misspelled Greise) 12.00
(22) Franco Harris 15.00
(23) Jim Hart 12.00
(24) Charlie Joiner 6.00
(25) Paul Krause 4.00
(26) Bob Kuechenberg 4.00
(27) Greg Landry 2.50
(28) Archie Manning 6.00
(29) Chester Marcol 2.50
(30) Harvey Martin 4.00
(31) Lawrence McCutcheon 12.00
(32) Craig Morton 4.00
(33) Haven Moses 2.50
(34) Steve Odom 3.00
(35) Morris Owens 2.50
(36) Dan Pastorini 9.00
(37) Walter Payton 35.00
(38) Greg Pruitt 14.00
(39) John Riggins 9.00
(40) Jake Scott 3.00
(41) Ken Stabler 20.00
(42) Roger Staubach 30.00
(43) Jan Stenerud 6.00
(44) Art Still 9.00
(45) Mick Tingelhoff 4.00
(46) Richard Todd 2.50
(47) Phil Villapiano 9.00
(48) Wesley Walker 5.00
(49) Roger Werhli 9.00
(50) Jim Zorn 12.00

1995 NFLPA Super Bowl Party Giveaways

Produced as a premium for the NFLPA Super Bowl XXIX party, each NFL card licensee designed one card for the 10-card set. Overall, 500 of each card were printed. The cards are unnumbered. The NFL Players logo is included on the front of each card.

MT
Complete Set (10): 200.00
Common Player: 10.00
1 Marcus Allen (Pinnacle) 12.00
2 Jerome Bettis (Fleer) 12.00
3 Tim Brown (Collector's Edge) 10.00
4 Trent Dilfer (SkyBox) 12.00
5 Marshall Faulk (Pacific) 30.00
6 Ronnie Lott (Classic) 10.00
7 Dan Marino (Upper Deck) 80.00
8 Junior Seau (Stadium Club) 12.00
9 Sterling Sharpe (Action Packed) 10.00
10 Heath Shuler (Playoff) 20.00

1996 NFLPA Super Bowl Party Giveaways

Produced as a premium for the NFLPA Sega Sports Super Bowl XXX party, each NFL card licensee created one card for the 12-card set. The NFL Players' logo appears on the front and backs of the unnumbered cards.

MT
Complete Set (12): 15.00
Common Player: .75
1 Marcus Allen, Ronnie Lott (Collector's Edge) 1.00
2 Steve Beuerlein (Topps) .75
3 Jeff Blake (Pacific) 1.50
4 Tim Brown (Action Packed) 1.00
5 Kerry Collins (Classic) 3.00
6 Kevin Greene (Playoff) .75
7 Garrison Hearst (Fleer Metal) 1.00
8 Daryl Johnston (SkyBox Impact) .75
9 Joe Montana (Upper Deck) 3.00
10 Deion Sanders (Donruss Red Zone) 1.50
11 Herschel Walker (Pinnacle) .75
12 Logo Card (Checklist back) .75

1997 NFLPA Super Bowl Player's Party

This 11-card set was distributed at the NFLPA Super Bowl XXXI player's party. Cards were contributed by each NFL trading card licensee. The cards are unnumbered.

MT
Complete Set (11): 12.00
Common Player: .75
1 SkyBox (Morten Andersen) .75
2 Collector's Edge (Steve Bono) .75
3 Pacific (Robert Brooks) .75
4 Topps (Tony Dorsett) 1.50
5 Donruss (Gus Frerotte) .75
6 Pinnacle (Kevin Hardy) .75
7 Score Board (Tyrone Hughes) .75
8 Upper Deck (Dan Marino) 3.00
9 SkyBox (Curtis Martin) 2.00
10 Playoff (Deion Sanders) 1.50
11 Checklist Card - Upper Deck .75

O

1961 Oilers Jay Publishing

Measuring 5" x 7", the 24-card set is anchored by a black-and-white player photo on the front. The player's name and team appear in the white border beneath the photo. The player's facsimile signature is printed on the photo. The cards are unnumbered and have blank backs. Originally, the cards were sold in 12-card packs for 25 cents.

NM
Complete Set (24): 125.00
Common Player: 5.00
1 Dalva Allen 5.00
2 Tony Banfield 5.00
3 George Blanda 12.00
4 Billy Cannon 6.00
5 Doug Cline 5.00
6 Willard Dewveall 5.00
7 Mike Dukes 5.00
8 Don Floyd 5.00
9 Freddy Glick 6.00
10 Bill Groman 6.00
11 Charlie Hennigan 6.00
12 Ed Husmann 5.00
13 Al Jamison 5.00
14 Mark Johnston 5.00
15 Jacky Lee 6.00
16 Bob McLeod 5.00
17 Rich Michael 5.00
18 Dennit Morris 5.00
19 Jim Norton 6.00
20 Bob Schmidt 5.00
21 Dave Smith 5.00
22 Bob Talamini 6.00
23 Charles Tolar 6.00
24 Hogan Wharton 5.00

1964-65 Oilers Color Team Issue

Measuring 7-3/4" x 9-3/4", the 16-photo set is anchored by a color photo on the front, bordered in white. A facsimile signature is printed over the photo. The photos are unnumbered and have blank backs. The photos were sold in eight-photo packs for 50 cents.

NM
Complete Set (16): 80.00
Common Player: 5.00
1 Scott Appleton 6.00
2 Tony Banfield 6.00
3 Sonny Bishop 6.00
4 George Blanda 12.00
5 Sid Blanks 6.00
6 Danny Brabham 5.00
7 Ode Burrell 6.00
8 Doug Cline 5.00
9 Don Floyd 6.00
10 Freddy Glick 6.00
11 Charlie Hennigan 6.00
12 Ed Husmann 5.00
13 Walt Suggs 6.00
14 Bob Talamini 5.00
15 Charley Tolar 6.00
16 Don Trull 6.00

1967 Oilers Team Issue

Measuring 5-1/8" x 7", the 14-card set is anchored on the front with a black-and-white photo. The cards, which are unnumbered, have blank backs.

NM
Complete Set (14): 45.00
Common Player: 4.00
1 Pete Barnes 4.00
2 Sonny Bishop 5.00
3 Ode Burrell 5.00
4 Ronnie Caveness 4.00
5 Joe Childress (CO) 4.00
6 Glen Ray Hines 5.00
7 Pat Holmes 4.00
8 Bobby Jancik 5.00
9 Pete Johns 4.00
10 Jim Norton 5.00
11 Willie Parker 4.00
12 Bob Poole 4.00
13 Alvin Reed 4.00
14 Olen Underwood 4.00

1969 Oilers Team Issue

Measuring 8" x 10", the 39-photo set is anchored by a large black-and-white photo on the front, bordered in white. The player's name, team and position are located beneath the photo. The unnumbered photos have blank backs.

NM
Complete Set (39): 125.00
Common Player: 3.00
1 Jim Beirne (Wide receiver) 4.00
2 Jim Beirne (Split end) 4.00
3 Elvin Bethea 5.00
4 Sonny Bishop 4.00
5 Garland Boyette 4.00
6 Ode Burrell 4.00
7 Ed Carrington 3.00
8 Joe Childress (CO) 3.00
9 Bob Davis 3.00
10 Hugh Devore (CO) 3.00
11 Tom Domres 3.00
12 F.A. Dry 3.00
13 Miller Farr 4.00
14 Mac Haik (Action shot) 3.00
15 Mac Haik (Portrait) 3.00
16 W.K. Hicks 3.00
17 Glen Ray Hines 4.00
18 Pat Holmes 3.00
19 Roy Hopkins 3.00
20 Charlie Joiner 18.00
21 Jim LeMoine 3.00
22 Bobby Maples 4.00
23 Richard Marshall 3.00
24 Zeke Moore 4.00
25 Willie Parker 3.00
26 Johnny Peacock 3.00
27 Ron Pritchard (Back peddling) 3.00
28 Ron Pritchard (Cutting left) 3.00
29 Ron Pritchard (Preparing to fend off blocker) 3.00
30 Tom Regner 3.00
31 George Rice 3.00
32 George Rice 3.00
33 Bob Robertson 3.00
34 Walt Suggs 3.00
35 Don Trull 4.00
36 Olen Underwood 3.00
37 Loyd Wainscott 3.00
38 Wayne Walker 4.00
39 Glenn Woods 3.00

1971 Oilers Team Issue

Measuring 4" x 5-1/2", the 23-card set showcases a black-and-white photo on the front, with an Oilers' helmet in the upper left, "Houston Oilers" at the top center and the NFL shield in the upper right. The player's name and position are printed beneath the photo. The blank-backed cards are unnumbered.

NM
Complete Set (23): 50.00
Common Player: 2.00
1 Willie Alexander 2.50
2 Jim Beirne 2.50
3 Elvin Bethea 3.00
4 Ron Billingsley 2.00
5 Garland Boyette 2.50
6 Leo Brooks 2.00
7 Ken Burrough 4.00
8 Woody Campbell 2.00
9 Lynn Dickey 4.00
10 Elbert Drungo 2.00
11 Pat Holmes 2.00
12 Robert Holmes 2.50
13 Ken Houston 10.00
14 Charlie Johnson 4.00
15 Charlie Joiner 12.00
16 Zeke Moore 2.50
17 Mark Moseley 4.00
18 Dan Pastorini 5.00
19 Alvin Reed 2.00
20 Tom Regner 2.00
21 Floyd Rice 2.00
22 Mike Tilleman 2.00
23 George Webster 3.00

1972 Oilers Team Issue

Measuring 5" x 7", the 11-card set showcases full-bleed black-and-white photos on the front. The unnumbered backs are blank.

NM
Complete Set (11): 25.00
Common Player: 2.00
1 Ron Billingsley 2.00
2 Garland Boyette 2.00
3 Levert Carr 2.00
4 Walter Highsmith 2.00
5 Albert Johnson 2.00
6 Benny Johnson 2.00
7 Guy Murdock 2.00
8 Ron Saul 3.00
9 Mike Tilleman 2.00
10 Ward Walsh 2.00
11 George Webster 4.00

1973 Oilers McDonald's

Measuring 8" x 10", the three-photo card set is anchored by a color photo on the front, with the player's name and team beneath it. The fronts are bordered in white. The backs, which are unnumbered, have the player's name, bio, highlights and stats, along with the 1973 Oilers' schedule. The McDonald's logo is printed in the lower right.

NM
Complete Set (3): 25.00
Common Player: 6.00
1 John Matuszak 12.00
2 Zeke Moore 6.00
3 Dan Pastorini 12.00

1973 Oilers Team Issue

Measuring 5" x 8", the 17-card set is anchored by a large black-and-white photo on the front of the white-

bordered cards. The blank-backed cards are unnumbered.

		NM
Complete Set (17):		35.00
Common Player:		2.00
1	Mack Alston	2.00
2	Bob Atkins	2.00
3	Skip Butler	2.00
4	Al Cowlings	3.00
5	Lynn Dickey	3.00
6	Mike Fanucci	2.00
7	Edd Hargett	2.50
8	Lewis Jolley	2.00
9	Clifton McNeil	2.50
10	Ralph Miller	2.00
11	Zeke Moore	2.50
12	Dave Parks	2.50
13	Willie Rodgers	2.00
14	Greg Sampson	2.00
15	Finn Seemann	2.00
16	Jeff Severson	2.00
17	Fred Willis	2.50

1980 Oilers Police

The 14-card, 2-5/8" x 4-1/8" set, sponsored by Kiwanis, local law enforcement and the Oilers, features front color action photos with "Oilers Tips" appearing on the backs.

		NM
Complete Set (14):		12.00
Common Player:		.75
1	Gregg Bingham	1.00
2	Robert Brazile	.75
3	Ken Burrough	1.50
4	Rob Carpenter	1.00
5	Ronnie Coleman	1.00
6	Curley Culp	1.00
7	Carter Hartwig	.75
8	Billy Johnson	1.50
9	Carl Mauck	.75
10	Gifford Nielsen	1.00
11	Cliff Parsley	.75
12	Bum Phillips (CO)	1.00
13	Mike Renfro	1.00
14	Ken Stabler	4.00

P

1984 Pacific Legends

The 30-card, regular-size set features well-known athletes from the Pac 10 football conference, including John Wayne, Pop Warner, Jackie Robinson, Frank Gifford and Lynn Swann.

		MT
Complete Set (30):		20.00
Common Player:		.30
1	O.J. Simpson	5.00
2	Mike Garrett	.50
3	Pop Warner	.50
4	Bob Schloredt	.30
5	Pat Haden	.60
6	Ernie Nevers	.50
7	Jackie Robinson	2.50
8	Arnie Weinmeister	.50
9	Gary Beban	.50
10	Jim Plunkett	.60
11	Bobby Grayson	.30
12	Craig Morton	.50
13	Ben Davidson	.60
14	Jim Hardy	.30
15	Vern Burke	.30
16	Hugh McElhenny	.75
17	John Wayne	4.00
18	Ricky Bell (UER) (Name spelled Rickey on both sides)	.50
19	George Wildcat Wilson	.30
20	Bob Waterfield	.75
21	Charlie Mitchell	.30
22	Donn Moomaw	.30
23	Don Heinrich	.30
24	Terry Baker	.50
25	Jack Thompson	.50
26	Charles White	.50
27	Frank Gifford	1.50
28	Lynn Swann	1.75
29	Brick Muller	.30
30	Ron Yary	.50

1989 Pacific Steve Largent

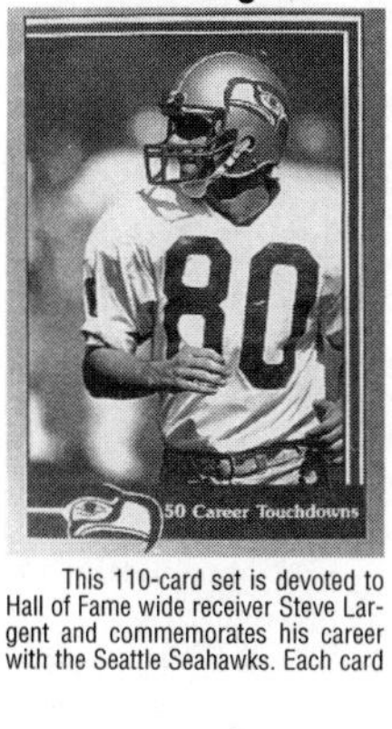

This 110-card set is devoted to Hall of Fame wide receiver Steve Largent and commemorates his career with the Seattle Seahawks. Each card front, with a silver border, captures an event in Largent's career. The horizontally-designed backs describe the action on the front and have light blue borders. There were 85 cards in the set which were numbered; the remaining 25 cards form a 12-1/2" x 17-1/2" poster of Largent. The entire set was available as a factory set or wax packs of 10 cards each. Pacific Trading Cards produced them.

		MT
Complete Set (110):		25.00
Common Player (1-85):		.25
1	Title Card (Steve Largent) (Checklist 1-42 On Back)	1.00
2	Santa, Can You Please (Steve Largent)	.25
3	Age 9 (Steve Largent)	.25
4	Junior High 1968 (Steve Largent)	.25
5	High School 1971 (Steve Largent)	.25
6	Baseball or Football (Steve Largent)	.25
7	Tulsa, Senior Bowl (Steve Largent)	.25
8	Led Nation in TD's (Steve Largent)	.25
9	Coach Patera, Coach Jerry Rhome	.40
10	Rookie 1976 (Steve Largent)	.50
11	First NFL TD (Steve Largent)	.25
12	Seahawk's First Win (Steve Largent)	.25
13	First Team All-Rookie (Steve Largent)	.40
14	Beats Buffalo 56-7 (Steve Largent)	.25
15	The Huddle (Steve Largent)	.25
16	Captains (Steve Largent, Norm Evans)	.40
17	First Win Against Raiders (Steve Largent)	.25
18	3000 Yards Receiving (Steve Largent)	.25
19	Jerry Rhome, Steve Largent	.50
20	Great Hands (Steve Largent)	.25
21	Climbs Mt. Rainier (Steve Largent)	.25
22	Zorn Connection (Steve Largent)	.40
23	Steve Largent, Jim Zorn	.40
24	First Team All-AFC (Steve Largent)	.25
25	Seahawks MVP 1981 (Steve Largent)	.40
26	Strike Season 1982 (Steve Largent)	.25
27	Training Camp 1983 (Steve Largent)	.25
28	Head Coach (Chuck Knox)	.40
29	50 Career TD's (Steve Largent)	.25
30	7000 Yards Receiving (Steve Largent)	.25
31	Tilley and Largent	.50
32	Cold Day in Cincy (Steve Largent)	.25
33	Catches 3 TD Passes (Steve Largent)	.25
34	Seahawks 12-4 in 1984 (Steve Largent)	.25
35	Defeated in AFC Championships (Steve Largent)	.25
36	Preparing for 1985 (Steve Largent)	.25
37	Career High 79 Catches (Steve Largent)	.25
38	Career High 1287 Yards (Steve Largent)	.25
39	10000 Yards Receiving (Steve Largent)	.25
40	Throws a Pass (Steve Largent)	.25
41	Game Day 1985 (Steve Largent)	.25
42	Seattle Sports Star of the Year (Steve Largent)	.40
43	A Very Sore Elbow (Steve Largent)	.25
44	The Concentration (Steve Largent)	.25
45	Steve Largent, Eugene Robinson	.40
46	Breaks Carmichael's Record (Steve Largent)	.35
47	Seahawks 37, Raiders 0 (Steve Largent)	.25
48	11000 Yards Receiving (Steve Largent)	.25
49	Rough Game (Steve Largent)	.25
50	Streak Continues (Steve Largent)	.25
51	Captains Lane, Brown and Largent	.40
52	Steve & Kyle Catch a Big One (Steve Largent)	.25
53	Krieg Connection (Steve Largent)	.40
54	Seahawk Camp (Steve Largent)	.25
55	NFL All-Time Leading Receiver (Steve Largent)	.40
56	Hall of Fame Bowl (Steve Largent)	.25
57	Steve Largent, Coach Knox	.40
58	1987 Seahawks MVP (Steve Largent)	.40
59	Largent at Quarterback (Steve Largent)	.50
60	NFL All-Time Great (Steve Largent)	.40
61	Travelers' NFL Man of the Year 1988 (Steve Largent)	.40
62	Steve Largent, Terry Largent	.25
63	Holding for Norm Johnson (Steve Largent)	.40
64	Great Moves (Steve Largent)	.25
65	Great Hands (Steve Largent)	.25
66	Seven-Time Pro Bowl Selection (Steve Largent)	.25
67	Agee, Steve Largent, Paul Skansi	.40
68	Signing for Fans (Steve Largent)	.25
69	Miller, Joe Nash, Steve Largent, Bryan Millard	.25
70	Pro Bowl Greats (Steve Largent, John Elway)	1.50
71	Hanging onto the Ball (Steve Largent)	.25
72	1618 Career Yards vs. Denver (Steve Largent)	.25
73	17 Pro Bowl Receptions (Steve Largent)	.25
74	Jim Zorn, Steve Largent	.40
75	Mr. Seahawk (Steve Largent)	.40
76	Sets NFL Career Yardage Record (Steve Largent)	.40
77	Two of the Greatest (Steve Largent)	.50
78	Steve Largent, Jerry Rhome, Charlie Joiner	.50
79	NFL All-Time Leader in Receptions (Steve Largent)	.40
80	Leader in Consecutive Game Receptions (Steve Largent)	.40
81	All-Time Leader 12686 Receiving Yards (Steve Largent)	.25
82	NFL All-Time Leader 1000 Yard Seasons (Steve Fulcher) (Steve Largent)	.40
83	First Recipient of the Bart Starr Trophy (Steve Largent)	.50
84	Steve Largent	.40
85	Future Hall of Famer (Steve Largent)	.75

1991 Pacific Prototypes

These cards were produced by Pacific Trading Cards to promote its 1991 set, its debut set. The cards, which are numbered on the back, use different numbers than their counterparts in the regular set, and can also be identified from the regulars by the statistics line on the card back. The prototype cards use zeroes to fill in the stats on the back. Approximately 5,000 sets were made and distributed to dealers.

		MT
Complete Set (5):		200.00
Common Player:		25.00
1	Joe Montana	75.00
2	Barry Sanders	50.00
3	Bo Jackson	25.00
4	Eric Metcalf	25.00
5	Troy Aikman	75.00

1991 Pacific

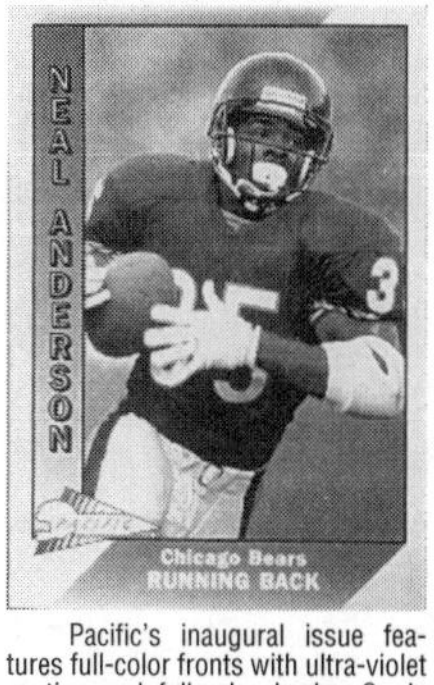

Pacific's inaugural issue features full-color fronts with ultra-violet coating and full-color backs. Cards began shipping in late June and were numbered alphabetically by city name and player name. Pacific's border colors echo the player's team colors.

		MT
Complete Set (660):		20.00
Complete Series 1 (550):		10.00
Complete Series 2 (110):		10.00
Common Player:		.04
Series 1 Pack (14):		.60
Series 1 Wax Box (36):		11.00
Series 2 Pack (14):		.90
Series 2 Wax Box (36):		17.00
1	Deion Sanders	.25
2	Steve Broussard	.04
3	Aundray Bruce	.04
4	Rick Bryant	.04
5	John Rade	.04
6	Scott Case	.04
7	Tony Casillas	.04
8	Shawn Collins	.04
9	Darion Conner	.04
10	Tory Epps	.04
11	Bill Fralic	.04
12	Mike Gann	.04
13	Tim Green	.04
14	Chris Hinton	.04
15	Houston Hoover	.04
16	Chris Miller	.04
17	Andre Rison	.25
18	Mike Rozier	.04
19	Jessie Tuggle	.04
20	Don Beebe	.04
21	Ray Bentley	.04
22	Shane Conlan	.04
23	Kent Hull	.04
24	Mark Kelso	.04
25	James Lofton	.04
26	Scott Norwood	.04
27	Andre Reed	.20
28	Leonard Smith	.04
29	Bruce Smith	.04
30	Leon Seals	.04
31	Darryl Talley	.04
32	Steve Tasker	.04
33	Thurman Thomas	.50
34	James Williams	.04
35	Will Wolford	.04
36	Frank Reich	.04
37	*Jeff Wright*	.12
38	Neal Anderson	.10
39	Trace Armstrong	.04
40	Johnny Bailey	.04
41	Mark Bortz	.04
42	Cap Boso	.04
43	Kevin Butler	.04
44	Mark Carrier	.04
45	Jim Covert	.04
46	Wendell Davis	.10
47	Richard Dent	.04
48	Shaun Gayle	.04
49	Jim Harbaugh	.10
50	Jay Hilgenberg	.04
51	Brad Muster	.04
52	William Perry	.04
53	Mike Singletary	.04
54	Peter Tom Willis	.04
55	Donnell Woolford	.04
56	Steve McMichael	.04
57	Eric Ball	.04
58	Lewis Billups	.04
59	Jim Breech	.04
60	James Brooks	.04
61	Eddie Brown	.04
62	Rickey Dixon	.04
63	Boomer Esiason	.15
64	James Francis	.04
65	David Fulcher	.04
66	David Grant	.04
67	Harold Green	.15
68	Rodney Holman	.04
69	Stanford Jennings	.04
70	Tim Krumrie	.04
71	Tim McGee	.04
72	Anthony Munoz	.04
73	Mitchell Price	.04
74	Eric Thomas	.04
75	Ickey Woods	.04
76	Mike Baab	.04
77	Thane Gash	.04
78	David Grayson	.04
79	Mike Johnson	.04
80	Reggie Langhorne	.04
81	Kevin Mack	.04
82	Clay Matthews	.04
83	Eric Metcalf	.04
84	Frank Minnifield	.04
85	Mike Oliphant	.04
86	Mike Pagel	.04
87	John Talley	.04
88	Lawyer Tillman	.04
89	Felix Wright	.04
90	Bryan Wagner	.04
91	*Bob Burnett*	.10
92	Tommie Agee	.04
93	Troy Aikman	1.00
94	Bill Bates	.04
95	Jack Del Rio	.04
96	Issiac Holt	.04
97	Michael Irvin	.50
98	Jim Jeffcoat	.04
99	Jimmy Jones	.04
100	Kelvin Martin	.04
101	Nate Newton	.04
102	Danny Noonan	.04
103	Ken Norton	.04
104	Jay Novacek	.15
105	Mike Saxon	.04
106	Derrick Sheppard	.04
107	Emmitt Smith	2.00
108	Daniel Stubbs	.04
109	Tony Tolbert	.04
110	Alexander Wright	.09
111	Steve Atwater	.04
112	Melvin Bratton	.04
113	Tyrone Braxton	.04
114	Alphonso Carreker	.04
115	John Elway	.35
116	Simon Fletcher	.04
117	Bobby Humphrey	.04
118	Mark Jackson	.04
119	Vance Johnson	.04
120	Greg Kragen	.04
121	Karl Mecklenburg	.04
122	Orson Mobley	.04
123	Alton Montgomery	.04
124	Rickey Nattiel	.04
125	Steve Sewell	.04
126	Shannon Sharpe	.50
127	Dennis Smith	.04
128	Andre Townsend	.50
129	Mike Horan	.04
130	Jerry Ball	.04
131	Bennie Blades	.04
132	Lomas Brown	.04
133	Jeff Campbell	.04
134	Robert Clark	.04
135	Michael Cofer	.04
136	Dennis Gibson	.04
137	Mel Gray	.04
138	LeRoy Irvin	.04
139	*George Jamison*	.12
140	Richard Johnson	.04
141	Eddie Murray	.04
142	Dan Owens	.04
143	Rodney Peete	.04
144	Barry Sanders	1.25
145	Chris Spielman	.04
146	Mark Spindler	.04
147	Andre Ware	.12
148	William White	.04
149	Tony Bennett	.04
150	Robert Brown	.04
151	LeRoy Butler	.04
152	Anthony Dilweg	.04
153	Michael Haddix	.04
154	Ron Hallstrom	.04
155	Tim Harris	.04
156	Johnny Holland	.04
157	Chris Jacke	.04
158	Perry Kemp	.04
159	Mark Lee	.04
160	Don Majkowski	.04
161	Tony Mandarich	.04
162	Mark Murphy	.04
163	Brian Noble	.04
164	Shawn Patterson	.04
165	Jeff Query	.04
166	Sterling Sharpe	.60
167	Darrell Thompson	.12
168	Ed West	.04
169	Ray Childress	.04
170	*Chris Dishman*	.35
171	Curtis Duncan	.04
172	William Fuller	.04
173	Ernest Givins	.04
174	Drew Hill	.04
175	Haywood Jeffires	.20
176	Sean Jones	.04
177	Lamar Lathon	.04
178	Bruce Matthews	.04
179	Bubba McDowell	.04
180	Johnny Meads	.04
181	Warren Moon	.15
182	Mike Munchak	.04
183	Allen Pinkett	.04
184	Dean Steinkuhler	.04
185	Lorenzo White	.25
186	John Grimsby	.04
187	Pat Beach	.04
188	Albert Bentley	.04
189	Dean Biasucci	.04
190	Duane Bickett	.04
191	Bill Brooks	.04
192	Eugene Daniel	.04
193	Jeff George	.30
194	Jon Hand	.04
195	Jeff Herrod	.04
196	Jesse Hester	.04
197	Mike Prior	.04
198	Stacey Simmons	.04
199	Rohn Stark	.04
200	Pat Tomberlin	.04
201	Clarence Verdin	.04
202	Keith Taylor	.04
203	Jack Trudeau	.04
204	Chip Banks	.04
205	John Alt	.04
206	Deron Cherry	.04
207	Steve DeBerg	.04
208	Tim Grunhard	.04
209	Albert Lewis	.04
210	Nick Lowery	.04
211	Bill Maas	.04
212	Chris Martin	.04
213	Todd McNair	.04
214	Christian Okoye	.04
215	Stephone Paige	.04
216	Steve Pelluer	.04
217	Kevin Porter	.04
218	Kevin Ross	.04
219	Dan Sealeaumua	.04
220	Neil Smith	.04
221	David Szott	.04
222	Derrick Thomas	.25
223	Barry Word	.12
224	Percy Snow	.04
225	Marcus Allen	.04
226	Eddie Anderson	.04
227	Steve Beuerlein	.25
228	Tim Brown	.20
229	Scott Davis	.04
230	Mike Dyal	.04
231	Mervyn Fernandez	.04
232	Willie Gault	.04
233	Ethan Horton	.04
234	Bo Jackson	.50
235	Howie Long	.04
236	Terry McDaniel	.04
237	Max Montoya	.04
238	Don Mosebar	.04
239	Jay Schroeder	.04
240	Steve Smith	.04
241	Greg Townsend	.04
242	Aaron Wallace	.04
243	Lionel Washington	.04
244	Steve Wisniewski	1.00
245	Willie Anderson	.04
246	Latin Berry	.04
247	Robert Delpino	.04
248	Marcus Dupree	.04
249	Henry Ellard	.04
250	Jim Everett	.04
251	Cleveland Gary	.04
252	Jerry Gray	.04
253	Kevin Greene	.04
254	Pete Holohan	.04
255	Buford McGee	.04
256	Tom Newberry	.04
257	Irv Pankey	.04
258	Jackie Slater	.04
259	Doug Smith	.04
260	Frank Stams	.04
261	Michael Stewart	.04
262	Fred Strickland	.04
263	J.D. Brown	.04
264	Mark Clayton	.04
265	Jeff Cross	.04
266	Mark Dennis	.08
267	Mark Duper	.04
268	Ferrell Edmunds	.04
269	Dan Marino	2.00
270	John Offerdahl	.04
271	Louis Oliver	.04
272	Tony Paige	.04
273	Reggie Roby	.04
274	Sammie Smith	.04
275	Keith Sims	.04
276	Brian Sochia	.04
277	Pete Stoyanovich	.04
278	Richmond Webb	.04
279	Jarvis Williams	.04
280	Tim McKyer	.04
281	Jim Jensen	.04
282	*Scott Secules*	.12
283	Ray Berry	.04
284	Joey Browner	.04
285	Anthony Carter	.04
286	Cris Carter	.25
287	Chris Doleman	.04
288	Mark Dusbabek	.04
289	Hassan Jones	.04
290	Steve Jordan	.04
291	Carl Lee	.04
292	Kirk Lowdermilk	.04
293	Randall McDaniel	.04
294	Mike Merriweather	.04
295	Keith Millard	.04
296	Al Noga	.04
297	Scott Studwell	.04
298	Henry Thomas	.04
299	Herschel Walker	.04
300	Gary Zimmerman	.04
301	Rich Gannon	.10
302	Wade Wilson	.04
303	Vincent Brown	.04
304	Marv Cook	.04
305	Hart Lee Dykes	.04
306	Irving Fryar	.04
307	Tom Hodson	.04
308	Maurice Hurst	.04
309	Ronnie Lippett	.04
310	Fred Marion	.04
311	Greg McMurty	.04
312	Johnny Rembert	.04
313	Chris Singleton	.04
314	Ed Reynolds	.04
315	Andre Tippett	.04
316	Garin Veris	.04
317	Brent Williams	.04
318	John Stephens	.75
319	Sammy Martin	.04
320	Bruce Armstrong	.04
321	Morten Andersen	.10
322	Gene Atkins	.04
323	Vince Buck	.04
324	John Fourcade	.04
325	Kevin Haverdink	.04
326	Bobby Hebert	.04
327	Craig Heyward	.04
328	Dalton Hilliard	.04
329	Rickey Jackson	.04
330	Vaughan Johnson	.04
331	Eric Martin	.04
332	Wayne Martin	.04
333	Rueben Mayes	.04
334	Sam Mills	.04
335	Brett Perriman	.04
336	Pat Swilling	.04
337	Renaldo Turnbull	.04
338	Lonzell Hill	.04
339	Steve Walsh	.04
340	Carl Banks	.04
341	Mark Bavaro	.04
342	Maurice Carthon	.04
343	*Pat Harlow*	.08
344	Eric Dorsey	.04
345	John Elliott	.04
346	Rodney Hampton	.50
347	Jeff Hostetler	.20
348	Erik Howard	.04
349	Pepper Johnson	.04
350	Sean Landeta	.50
351	Leonard Marshall	.04
352	David Meggett	.04
353	Bart Oates	.04
354	Gary Reasons	.04
355	Phil Simms	.10
356	Lawrence Taylor	.10
357	Reyna Thompson	.04
358	Brian Williams	.04
359	Matt Boyer	.04
360	Mark Ingram	.04
361	Brad Baxter	.15
362	Mark Boyer	.04
363	Dennis Byrd	.04
364	Dave Cadigan	.04
365	Kyle Clifton	.04
366	James Hasty	.04
367	Joe Kelly	.04
368	Jeff Lageman	.04
369	Pat Leahy	.04
370	Terance Mathis	.10
371	Erik McMillan	.04
372	Rob Moore	.25
373	Ken O'Brien	.04
374	Tony Stargell	.04
375	Jim Sweeney	.04
376	Al Toon	.04
377	Johnny Hector	.04
378	Jeff Criswell	.04
379	Mike Haight	.04
380	Troy Benson	.04
381	Eric Allen	.04
382	Fred Barnett	.15
383	Jerome Brown	.04
384	Keith Byars	.04
385	Randall Cunningham	.20
386	Byron Evans	.04
387	Wes Hopkins	.04
388	Keith Jackson	.20
389	Seth Joyner	.04
390	*Bobby Wilson*	.10
391	Heath Sherman	.10
392	Clyde Simmons	.04
393	Ben Smith	.04
394	Andre Waters	.04
395	Reggie White	.20
396	Calvin Williams	.15
397	Al Harris	.04
398	Anthony Toney	.04
399	Mike Quick	.04
400	Anthony Bell	.04
401	Rich Camarillo	.04
402	Roy Green	.04
403	Ken Harvey	.04
404	Eric Hill	.04
405	*Garth Jax*	.07
406	Ernie Jones	.04
407	Cedric Mack	.04
408	Dexter Manley	.04
409	Tim McDonald	.04
410	Freddie Joe Nunn	.04
411	Rickey Proehl	.10
412	*Moe Gardner*	.12
413	Timm Rosenbach	.04
414	Luis Sharpe	.04
415	Vai Sikahema	.04
416	Anthony Thompson	.04
417	Ron Wolfley	.04
418	Lonnie Young	.04
419	Gary Anderson	.04
420	Bubby Brister	.04
421	Thomas Everett	.04
422	Eric Green	.10
423	Delton Hall	.04
424	Bryan Hinkle	.04
425	Merril Hoge	.04
426	Carnell Lake	.04
427	Louis Lipps	.04
428	David Little	.04
429	Greg Lloyd	.04
430	Mike Mularkey	.04
431	Keith Willis	.04
432	Dwayne Woodruff	.04
433	Rod Woodson	.04
434	Tim Worley	.04
435	Warren Williams	.04

436	Terry Long	.04
437	Martin Bayless	.04
438	*Jarrod Bunch*	.15
439	Marion Butts	.04
440	Gill Byrd	.04
441	Arthur Cox	.04
442	John Friesz	.15
443	Leo Goeas	.04
444	Burt Grossman	.04
445	Courtney Hall	.04
446	Ronnie Harmon	.04
447	*Nate Lewis*	.25
448	Anthony Miller	.04
449	Leslie O'Neal	.04
450	Gary Plummer	.04
451	Junior Seau	.30
452	Billy Ray Smith	.04
453	Billy Joe Tolliver	.04
454	Broderick Thompson	.04
455	Lee Williams	.04
456	Michael Carter	.04
457	Mike Cofer	.04
458	Kevin Fagan	.04
459	Charles Haley	.04
460	Pierce Holt	.04
461	Johnny Jackson	.04
462	Brent Jones	.04
463	Guy McIntyre	.04
464	Joe Montana	1.00
465	Bubba Paris	.04
466	Tom Rathman	.04
467	Jerry Rice	1.00
468	Mike Sherrard	.04
469	John Taylor	.15
470	Steve Young	.75
471	Dennis Brown	.04
472	Dexter Carter	.04
473	Bill Romanowski	.04
474	Dave Waymer	.04
475	Robert Blackmon	.04
476	Derrick Fenner	.10
477	Nesby Glasgow	.04
478	Jacob Green	.04
479	Andy Heck	.04
480	Norm Johnson	.04
481	Tommy Kane	.04
482	Cortez Kennedy	.30
483	Dave Krieg	.04
484	Bryan Millard	.04
485	Joe Nash	.04
486	Rufus Porter	.04
487	Eugene Robinson	.04
488	*Mike Tice*	.10
489	Chris Warren	.50
490	John L. Williams	.04
491	Terry Wooden	.04
492	Tony Woods	.04
493	Brian Blades	.04
494	Paul Skansi	.04
495	Gary Anderson	.04
496	Mark Carrier	.04
497	Chris Chandler	.04
498	Steve Christie	.04
499	Reggie Cobb	.25
500	Reuben Davis	.04
501	Willie Drewery	.04
502	Randy Grimes	.04
503	Paul Gruber	.04
504	Wayne Haddix	.04
505	Ron Hall	.04
506	Harry Hamilton	.04
507	Bruce Hill	.04
508	Eugene Marve	.04
509	Keith McCants	.04
510	Winston Moss	.04
511	Kevin Murphy	.04
512	Mark Robinson	.04
513	Vinny Testaverde	.08
514	Broderick Thomas	.04
515	Jeff Bostic	.04
516	Todd Bowles	.04
517	Earnest Byner	.04
518	Gary Clark	.20
519	*Craig Erickson*	.50
520	Darryl Grant	.04
521	Darrell Green	.04
522	Russ Grimm	.04
523	Stan Humphries	.30
524	Joe Jacoby	.04
525	Jim Lachey	.04
526	Chip Lohmiller	.04
527	Charles Mann	.04
528	Wilber Marshall	.04
529	Art Monk	.04
530	Tracy Rocker	.04
531	Mark Rypien	.12
532	Ricky Sanders	.04
533	Alvin Walton	.04
534	*Todd Marinovich*	.15
535	Mike Dumas	.04
536	Russell Maryland	.50
537	*Eric Turner*	.20
538	*Ernie Mills*	.20
539	*Ed King*	.10
540	Michael Stonebreaker	.04
541	*Chris Zorich*	.25
542	Mike Croel	.35
543	*Eric Moten*	.10
544	*Dan McGwire*	.15
545	*Keith Cash*	.10
546	*Kenny Walker*	.12
547	Leroy Hoard	.08
548	Luis Chrisobol	.04
549	Stacy Danley	.04
550	*Todd Lyght*	.10
551	*Brett Favre*	5.00
552	*Mike Pritchard*	.50
553	Moe Gardner	.05
554	Tim McKyer	.05
555	*Erric Pegram*	.50
556	Norm Johnson	.05
557	*Bruce Pickens*	.10
558	*Henry Jones*	.35
559	*Phil Hansen*	.20
560	Cornelius Bennett	.05
561	Stan Thomas	.05
562	Chris Zorich	.10
563	*Anthony Morgan*	.15
564	*Darren Lewis*	.30
565	Mike Stonebreaker	.05
566	*Alfred Williams*	.15
567	Lamar Rogers	.05
568	*Erik Wilhelm*	.30
569	Ed King	.05
570	*Michael Jackson*	.75
571	*James Jones*	.15
572	Russell Maryland	.15
573	*Dixon Edwards*	.10
574	Derrick Brownlow	.05
575	*Larry Brown*	.50
576	Mike Croel	.20
577	*Keith Traylor*	.08
578	Kenny Walker	.05
579	*Reggie Johnson*	.12
580	*Herman Moore*	2.50
581	*Kelvin Pritchett*	.10
582	*Kevin Scott*	.10
583	*Vinnie Clark*	.10
584	*Esera Tuaolo*	.10
585	Don Davey	.05
586	*Blair Kiel*	.12
587	Mike Dumas	.05
588	*Darryll Lewis*	.10
589	*John Flannery*	.10
590	Kevin Donnally	.05
591	Shane Curry	.05
592	*Mark Vander Poel*	.08
593	Dave McCloughan	.05
594	*Mel Agee*	.10
595	*Kerry Cash*	.12
596	*Harvey Williams*	.50
597	Joe Valerio	.05
598	*Tim Barnett*	.30
599	Todd Marinovich	.05
600	*Nick Bell*	.20
601	Roger Craig	.05
602	Ronnie Lott	.10
603	*Mike Jones*	.10
604	Todd Lyght	.10
605	*Roman Phifer*	.10
606	*David Lang*	.15
607	*Aaron Craver*	.10
608	*Mark Higgs*	.75
609	Chris Green	.05
610	*Randy Baldwin*	.10
611	Pat Harlow	.05
612	*Leonard Russell*	.20
613	*Jerome Henderson*	.10
614	*Scott Zolak*	.20
615	*Jon Vaughn*	.15
616	*Harry Colon*	.12
617	*Wesley Carroll*	.15
618	Quinn Early	.05
619	*Reggie Jones*	.15
620	Jarrod Bunch	.10
621	*Kanavis McGhee*	.15
622	*Ed McCaffrey*	3.00
623	*Browning Nagle*	.35
624	*Mo Lewis*	.10
625	Blair Thomas	.10
626	Antone Davis	.10
627	Jim McMahon	.05
628	*Scott Kowalkowski*	.10
629	*Brad Goebel*	.15
630	*William Thomas*	.10
631	*Eric Swann*	.20
632	*Mike Jones*	.10
633	*Aeneas Williams*	.12
634	Dexter Davis	.05
635	Tom Tupa	.05
636	Johnny Johnson	.20
637	Randal Hill	.30
638	*Jeff Graham*	.75
639	Ernie Mills	.10
640	*Adrian Cooper*	.15
641	*Stanley Richard*	.35
642	*Eric Bieniemy*	.15
643	Eric Moten	.05
644	*Shawn Jefferson*	.35
645	*Ted Washington*	.10
646	*John Johnson*	.10
647	Dan McGwire	.10
648	*Doug Thomas*	.05
649	David Daniels	.05
650	*John Kasay*	.12
651	Jeff Kemp	.05
652	*Charles McRae*	.08
653	*Lawrence Dawsey*	.20
654	Robert Wilson	.05
655	Dexter Manley	.05
656	Chuck Weatherspoon	.05
657	Tim Ryan	.05
658	Bobby Wilson	.05
659	*Ricky Ervins*	.35
660	Matt Millen	.05

1991 Pacific Checklists

These checklists were issued for Pacific's first series of 1991 football cards and were randomly included in late-issue foil and wax packs. Pacific stated it only produced 10,000 checklist sets. Cards were numbered on the back.

		MT
Complete Set (5):		10.00
Common Player:		2.50
1	Checklist 1	2.50
2	Checklist 2	2.50
3	Checklist 3	2.50
4	Checklist 4	2.50
5	Checklist 5	2.50

1991 Pacific Picks The Pros

Pacific produced a 25-card insert set, including its choice as the best player at each position offensively and defensively plus a card of 1991 #1 draft choice Russell Maryland. Cards were either bordered in silver or gold, with 10,000 of each type produced and randomly inserted (gold in foil packs, silver in cello).

		MT
Complete Set (25):		60.00
Common Player:		2.00
1	Russell Maryland	3.00
2	Andre Reed	3.00
3	Jerry Rice	12.00
4	Keith Jackson	3.00
5	Jim Lachey	2.00
6	Anthony Munoz	2.00
7	Randall McDaniel	2.00
8	Bruce Matthews	2.00
9	Kent Hull	2.00
10	Joe Montana	10.00
11	Barry Sanders	15.00
12	Thurman Thomas	8.00
13	Morten Anderson	3.00
14	Jerry Ball	3.00
15	Jerome Brown	3.00
16	Reggie White	6.00
17	Bruce Smith	7.50
18	Derrick Thomas	4.00
19	Lawrence Taylor	3.00
20	Charles Haley	3.00
21	Albert Lewis	3.00
22	Rod Woodson	3.00
23	David Fulcher	3.00
24	Joey Browner	3.00
25	Sean Landeta	3.00

1991 Pacific Flash Cards

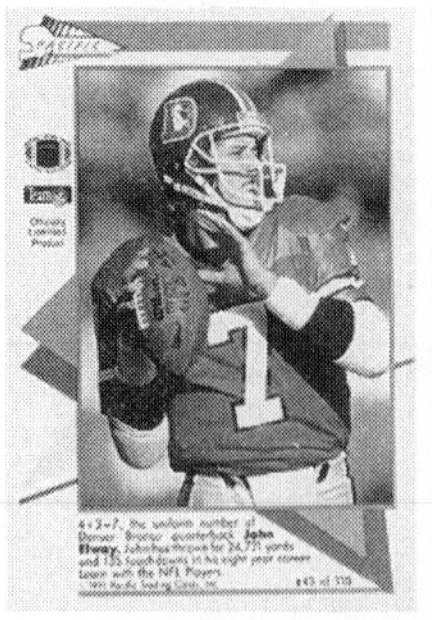

These mathematical flash cards contain a problem on the front which, when worked out correctly, equals the uniform number of the player pictured on the card back. The back of the card has a glossy picture of the player and either a career summary or highlights from the previous season. A card number also appears on the back. The cards are standard size.

		MT
Complete Set (110):		8.00
Common Player:		.05
1	Steve Young	.40
2	Hart Lee Dykes	.05
3	Timm Rosenbach	.05
4	Andre Collins	.05
5	Johnny Johnson	.20
6	Nick Lowery	.05
7	John Stephens	.05
8	Jim Arnold	.05
9	Steve DeBerg	.15
10	Christian Okoye	.05
11	Eric Swann	.10
12	Jerry Robinson	.05
13	Steve Wisniewski	.05
14	Jim Harbaugh	.10
15	Steve Broussard	.05
16	Mike Singletary	.15
17	Tim Green	.05
18	Roger Craig	.15
19	Maury Buford	.05
20	Marcus Allen	.25
21	Deion Sanders	.40
22	Chris Miller	.20
23	Joey Browner	.10
24	Bubby Brister	.10
25	Buford McGee	.05
26	Ed West	.05
27	Mark Murphy	.05
28	Tim Worley	.10
29	Keith Willis	.05
30	Rich Gannon	.05
31	Jim Everett	.15
32	Duval Love	.05
33	Bob Nelson	.05
34	Anthony Munoz	.15
35	Boomer Esiason	.20
36	Kenny Walker	.05
37	Mike Horan	.05
38	Gary Kubiak	.05
39	David Treadwell	.05
40	Robert Wilson	.05
41	Lewis Billups	.05
42	Kevin Mack	.05
43	John Elway	.50
44	Lee Johnson	.05
45	Ken Willis	.05
46	Herman Moore	.40
47	Eddie Murray	.05
48	Mike Saxon	.05
49	John L. Williams	.10
50	Barry Sanders	1.00
51	Andre Ware	.15
52	Dave Krieg	.10
53	Cortez Kennedy	.25
54	Bo Jackson	.50
55	Derrick Fenner	.05
56	Steve Walsh	.10
57	Brett Maxie	.05
58	Stan Brock	.05
59	DeMond Winston	.05
60	Sam Mills	.10
61	Eric Martin	.10
62	Michael Carter	.10
63	Steve Wallace	.05
64	Jesse Sapolu	.05
65	Bill Romanowski	.05
66	Joe Montana	2.00
67	Sean Landeta	.05
68	Doug Riesenberg	.05
69	Myron Guyton	.05
70	Andre Reed	.15
71	John Elliott	.05
72	Jeff Hostetler	.15
73	Rohn Stark	.05
74	Jeff George	.20
75	Duane Bickett	.05
76	Emmitt Smith	2.00
77	Michael Irvin	.50
78	Tony Stargell	.05
79	Kyle Clifton	.05
80	John Booty	.05
81	Fred Barnett	.20
82	Blair Thomas	.10
83	Erik McMillan	.05
84	Broderick Thomas	.10
85	Jim Skow	.05
86	Gary Anderson	.10
87	Mark Robinson	.05
88	Steve Christie	.05
89	Cody Carlson	.15
90	Warren Moon	.35
91	Lorenzo White	.10
92	Reggie Roby	.05
93	Jim C. Jensen	.05
94	Mark Clayton	.10
95	Willie Gault	.10
96	Don Mosebar	.05
97	Gary Plummer	.05
98	Leslie O'Neal	.10
99	Neal Anderson	.15
100	Derrick Thomas	.25
101	Luis Sharpe	.05
102	D.J. Dozier	.05
103	Jarrod Bunch	.05
104	Mark Ingram	.05
105	James Lofton	.15
106	Jay Schroeder	.10
107	Ronnie Lott	.15
108	Todd Marinovich	.10
109	Chris Zorich	.15
110	Charles McRae	.05

1992 Pacific Prototypes

These 1992 prototypes feature Pacific's new design for 1992. A full-color glossy photo is on the card front, framed by a white border. A color stripe, containing the player's name and team helmet, runs along the left side of the card. The back is numbered and includes a mug shot and career summary. Approximately 5,000 sets were produced; most were given away at the Super Bowl Card Show in Minneapolis.

		MT
Complete Set (6):		40.00
Common Player:		6.00
1	Warren Moon	10.00
2	Pat Swilling	6.00
3	Michael Irvin	12.00
4	Haywood Jeffires	8.00
5	Thurman Thomas	12.00
6	Leonard Russell	8.00

1992 Pacific

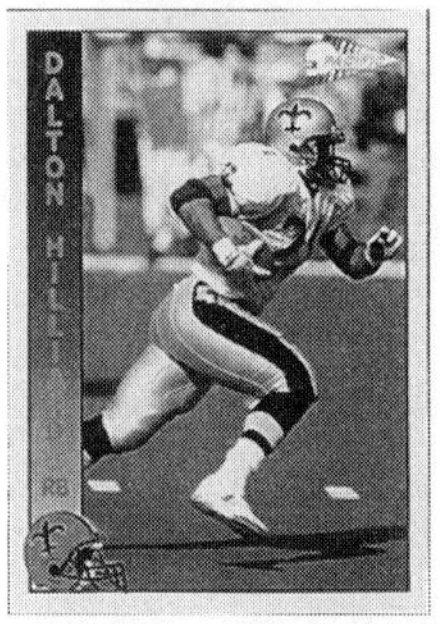

Pacific issued this set of 660 standard-sized cards in two series of 330 cards each. The glossy fronts feature color action shots framed by white borders. The player's name and team helmet run in a stripe down the left side. The backs are done in a horizontal format and also feature a color photo, plus statistics and a player profile. Cards are numbered alphabetically by player, by team, beginning with Atlanta and ending with Washington. Draft Picks are featured in a subset. Insert sets include Checklists (8 cards randomly inserted in packs); Bob Griese and Steve Largent (9 Legends of the Game cards for each, plus 1,000 autographed cards each; all are random inserts); Prisms (10 cards featuring top running backs, randomly inserted); Statistical Leaders (30 cards featuring the 28 statistical leaders from the 28 NFL teams, plus two cards devoted to the AFC and NFC rushing leaders; all were randomly inserted); and Pacific Picks the Pros (25 cards, Pacific's selection of the top players at each position). The Picks the Pros cards come in two versions - with gold foil or silver foil borders, and corresponding lettering.

		MT
Complete Set (660):		20.00
Complete Series 1 (330):		10.00
Complete Series 2 (330):		10.00
Complete Factory Set (690):		25.00
Common Player:		.05
Pack (17):		.25
Wax Box (36):		7.00
1	Steve Broussard	.05
2	Darion Connor	.05
3	Tory Epps	.05
4	Michael Haynes	.30
5	Chris Hinton	.05
6	Mike Kenn	.05
7	Tim McKyer	.05
8	Chris Miller	.05
9	Erric Pegram	.20
10	Mike Pritchard	.20
11	Moe Gardner	.05
12	Tim Green	.05
13	Norm Johnson	.05
14	Don Beebe	.05
15	Cornelius Bennett	.05
16	Al Edwards	.05
17	Mark Kelso	.05
18	James Lofton	.05
19	Frank Reich	.05
20	Leon Seals	.05
21	Darryl Talley	.05
22	Thurman Thomas	.40
23	Kent Hall	.05
24	Jeff Wright	.05
25	Nate Odomes	.05
26	Carwell Gardner	.05
27	Neal Anderson	.10
28	Mark Carrier	.05
29	Johnny Bailey	.05
30	Jim Harbaugh	.05
31	Jay Hilgenberg	.05
32	William Perry	.05
33	Wendell Davis	.05
34	Donnell Woolford	.05
35	Keith Van Horne	.05
36	Shaun Gayle	.05
37	Tom Waddle	.12
38	Chris Zorich	.05
39	Tom Thayer	.05
40	Rickey Dixon	.05
41	James Francis	.05
42	David Fulcher	.05
43	Reggie Rembert	.05
44	Anthony Munoz	.05
45	Harold Green	.05
46	Mitchell Price	.05
47	Rodney Holman	.05
48	Bruce Kozerski	.05
49	Bruce Reimers	.05
50	Erik Wilhelm	.05
51	Harlon Barnett	.05
52	Mike Johnson	.05
53	Brian Brennan	.05
54	Ed King	.05
55	Reggie Langhorne	.05
56	James Jones	.05
57	Mike Baab	.05
58	Dan Fike	.05
59	Frank Minnifield	.05
60	Clay Matthews	.05
61	Kevin Mack	.05
62	Tony Casillas	.05
63	Jay Novacek	.15
64	Larry Brown	.05
65	Michael Irvin	.25
66	Jack Del Rio	.05
67	Ken Willis	.05
68	Emmitt Smith	2.25
69	Alan Veingrad	.05
70	John Gesek	.05
71	Steve Beuerlein	.20
72	*Vinson Smith*	.08
73	Steve Atwater	.05
74	Mike Croel	.05
75	John Elway	.35
76	Gaston Green	.05
77	Mike Horan	.05
78	Vance Johnson	.05
79	Karl Mecklenburg	.05
80	Shannon Sharpe	.05
81	David Treadwell	.05
82	Kenny Walker	.05
83	Greg Lewis	.05
84	Shawn Moore	.05
85	Alton Montgomery	.05
86	Michael Young	.05
87	Jerry Ball	.05
88	Bennie Blades	.05
89	Mel Gray	.05
90	Herman Moore	.50
91	Erik Kramer	.05
92	Willie Green	.12
93	George Jamison	.05
94	Chris Spielman	.05
95	Kelvin Pritchett	.05
96	William White	.05
97	Mike Utley	.12
98	Tony Bennett	.05
99	LeRoy Butler	.05
100	Vinnie Clark	.05
101	Ron Hallstrom	.05
102	Chris Jacke	.05
103	Tony Mandarich	.05
104	Sterling Sharpe	.45
105	Don Maikowski	.05
106	Johnny Holland	.05
107	Esera Tuaolo	.05
108	Darrell Thompson	.05
109	Bubba McDowell	.05
110	Curtis Duncan	.05
111	Lamar Lathon	.05
112	Drew Hill	.05
113	Bruce Matthews	.05
114	*Bo Orlando*	.15
115	Don Maggs	.05
116	Lorenzo White	.05
117	Ernest Givins	.05
118	Tony Jones	.05
119	Dean Steinkuhler	.05
120	Dean Biasucci	.05
121	Duane Bickett	.05
122	Bill Brooks	.05
123	Ken Clark	.05
124	Jessie Hester	.05
125	Anthony Johnson	.05
126	Chip Banks	.05
127	Mike Prior	.05
128	Rohn Stark	.05
129	Jeff Herrod	.05
130	Clarence Verdin	.05
131	Tim Manoa	.05
132	*Brian Baldinger*	.05
133	Tim Barnett	.05
134	J.J. Birden	.05
135	Deron Cherry	.05
136	Steve DeBerg	.05
137	Nick Lowery	.05
138	Todd McNair	.05
139	Christian Okoye	.05
140	Mark Vlasic	.05
141	Dan Saleaumua	.05
142	Neil Smith	.05
143	Robb Thomas	.05
144	Eddie Anderson	.05
145	Nick Bell	.12
146	Tim Brown	.30
147	Roger Craig	.05
148	Jeff Gossett	.05
149	Ethan Horton	.05
150	Jamie Holland	.05
151	Jeff Jaeger	.05
152	Todd Marinovich	.05
153	Marcus Allen	.05
154	Steve Smith	.05
155	Flipper Anderson	.05
156	Robert Delpino	.05
157	Cleveland Gary	.05
158	Kevin Greene	.05
159	Dale Hatcher	.05
160	Duval Love	.05
161	Ron Brown	.05
162	Jackie Slater	.05
163	Doug Smith	.05
164	Aaron Cox	.05
165	Larry Kelm	.05
166	Mark Clayton	.05
167	Louis Oliver	.05
168	Mark Higgs	.15
169	Aaron Craver	.05
170	Sammie Smith	.05
171	Tony Paige	.05
172	Jeff Cross	.05
173	David Griggs	.05
174	Richmond Webb	.05
175	Vestee Jackson	.05
176	Jim C. Jensen	.05
177	Anthony Carter	.05
178	Cris Carter	.05
179	Chris Doleman	.05
180	Rich Gannon	.10
181	Al Noga	.05
182	Randall McDaniel	.05
183	Todd Scott	.05
184	Henry Thomas	.05
185	Felix Wright	.05
186	Gary Zimmerman	.05
187	Herschel Walker	.05
188	Vincent Brown	.05
189	Harry Colon	.05
190	Irving Fryar	.05
191	Marv Cook	.05
192	Leonard Russell	.25
193	Hugh Millen	.05
194	Pat Harlow	.05
195	Jon Vaughn	.12
196	*Ben Coates*	2.00
197	Johnny Rembert	.05
198	Greg McMurtry	.05
199	Morten Andersen	.05
200	Tommy Barnhardt	.05
201	Bobby Hebert	.05
202	Dalton Hilliard	.05
203	Sam Mills	.05
204	Pat Swilling	.05
205	Rickey Jackson	.05
206	Stan Brock	.05
207	Reggie Jones	.05
208	Gill Fenerty	.05
209	Eric Martin	.05
210	Matt Bahr	.05
211	Rodney Hampton	.40
212	Jeff Hostetler	.15
213	Pepper Johnson	.05
214	Leonard Marshall	.05
215	Doug Riesenberg	.05
216	Stephen Baker	.05
217	Mike Fox	.05
218	Bart Oates	.05
219	Everson Walls	.05
220	Gary Reasons	.05
221	Jeff Lageman	.05
222	Joe Kelly	.05
223	Mo Lewis	.05
224	Tony Stargell	.05
225	Jim Sweeney	.05
226	Freeman McNeil	.05
227	Brian Washington	.05
228	Johnny Hector	.05
229	Terance Mathis	.05
230	Rob Moore	.20
231	Brad Baxter	.05
232	Eric Allen	.05
233	Fred Barnett	.20
234	Jerome Brown	.05
235	Keith Byars	.05
236	William Thomas	.05
237	Jessie Small	.05
238	Robert Drummond	.05
239	Reggie White	.15
240	James Joseph	.05
241	Brad Goebel	.08
242	Clyde Simmons	.05
243	Rich Camarillo	.05
244	Ken Harvey	.05
245	Garth Jax	.05
246	Johnny Johnson	.15
247	Mike Jones	.05
248	Ernie Jones	.05
249	Tom Tupa	.05
250	Ron Wolfley	.05
251	Luis Sharpe	.05
252	Eric Swann	.05
253	Anthony Thompson	.05
254	Gary Anderson	.05
255	Dermontti Dawson	.05
256	Jeff Graham	.12
257	Eric Green	.05
258	Louis Lipps	.05
259	Neil O'Donnell	.25
260	Rod Woodson	.05
261	Dwight Stone	.05
262	Aaron Jones	.05
263	Keith Willis	.05
264	Ernie Mills	.05
265	Martin Bayless	.05
266	Rod Bernstine	.05
267	John Carney	.05
268	John Friesz	.05
269	Nate Lewis	.05
270	Shawn Jefferson	.05
271	Burt Grossman	.05
272	Eric Moten	.05
273	Gary Plummer	.05
274	Henry Rolling	.05
275	*Steve Hendrickson*	.10
276	Michael Carter	.05
277	*Steve Bono*	1.00
278	Dexter Carter	.05
279	Mike Cofer	.05
280	Charles Haley	.05
281	Tom Rathman	.05
282	Guy McIntyre	.05
283	John Taylor	.05
284	Dave Waymer	.05
285	Steve Wallace	.05
286	Jamie Williams	.05
287	Brian Blades	.05
288	Jeff Bryant	.05
289	Grant Feasel	.05
290	Jacob Green	.05
291	Andy Heck	.05
292	Kelly Stouffer	.05
293	John Kasay	.05
294	Cortez Kennedy	.15
295	Bryan Millard	.05
296	Eugene Robinson	.05
297	Tony Woods	.05
298	Jesse Anderson	.05
299	Gary Anderson	.05
300	Mark Carrier	.05
301	Reggie Cobb	.12
302	Robert Wilson	.05
303	Jesse Solomon	.05
304	Broderick Thomas	.05
305	Lawrence Dawsey	.05
306	Charles McRae	.05
307	Paul Gruber	.05
308	Vinny Testaverde	.05
309	Brian Mitchell	.05
310	Darrell Green	.05

311	Art Monk	.05
312	Russ Grimm	.05
313	Mark Rypien	.20
314	Bobby Wilson	.05
315	Wilber Marshall	.05
316	Gerald Riggs	.05
317	Chip Lohmiller	.05
318	Joe Jacoby	.05
319	Martin Mayhew	.05
320	*Amp Lee*	.35
321	*Terrell Buckley*	.30
322	*Tommy Vardell*	.25
323	*Ricardo McDonald*	.10
324	*Joe Bowden*	.08
325	*Darryl Williams*	.20
326	Carlos Huerta	.05
327	*Patrick Rowe*	.10
328	*Siran Stacy*	.15
329	*Dexter McNabb*	.08
330	*Willie Clay*	.10
331	Oliver Barnett	.05
332	Aundray Bruce	.05
333	*Ken Tippins*	.10
334	Jessie Tuggle	.05
335	Brian Jordan	.06
336	Andre Rison	.30
337	Houston Hoover	.05
338	Bill Fralic	.05
339	*Pat Chaffey*	.15
340	Keith Jones	.05
341	*Jamie Dukes*	.08
342	Chris Mohr	.05
343	John Davis	.05
344	Ray Bentley	.05
345	Scott Norwood	.05
346	Shane Conlan	.06
347	Steve Tasker	.06
348	Will Wolford	.05
349	*Gary Baldinger*	.10
350	Kirby Jackson	.05
351	Jamie Mueller	.05
352	Pete Metzelaars	.05
353	Richard Dent	.05
354	Ron Rivera	.05
355	Jim Morrissey	.05
356	John Roper	.05
357	Steve McMichael	.05
358	Ron Morris	.05
359	Darren Lewis	.15
360	Anthony Morgan	.10
361	Stan Thomas	.05
362	James Thornton	.05
363	Brad Muster	.05
364	Tim Krumrie	.05
365	Lee Johnson	.05
366	Eric Ball	.05
367	Alonzo Mitz	.10
368	David Grant	.05
369	Lynn James	.05
370	Lewis Billups	.05
371	Jim Breech	.05
372	Alfred Williams	.05
373	Wayne Haddix	.05
374	Tim McGee	.05
375	Michael Jackson	.10
376	Leroy Hoard	.05
377	Tony Jones	.05
378	Vince Newsome	.05
379	*Todd Philcox*	.15
380	Eric Metcalf	.05
381	John Rienstra	.05
382	Matt Stover	.05
383	Brian Hansen	.05
384	Joe Morris	.05
385	Anthony Pleasant	.05
386	Mark Stepnoski	.05
387	Erik Williams	.05
388	Jimmie Jones	.05
389	Kevin Gogan	.05
390	Manny Hendrix	.10
391	Issiac Holt	.05
392	Ken Norton	.05
393	Tommie Agee	.05
394	Alvin Harper	.10
395	Alexander Wright	.05
396	Mike Saxon	.05
397	Michael Brooks	.05
398	Bobby Humphrey	.05
399	Ken Lanier	.05
400	Steve Sewell	.05
401	Robert Perryman	.05
402	Wymon Henderson	.05
403	Keith Kartz	.05
404	Clarence Kay	.05
405	Keith Traylor	.05
406	Doug Widell	.05
407	Dennis Smith	.05
408	Marc Spindler	.05
409	Lomas Brown	.05
410	Robert Clark	.05
411	Eric Andolsek	.05
412	Mike Farr	.05
413	Ray Crockett	.05
414	Jeff Campbell	.05
415	Dan Owens	.05
416	Jim Arnold	.05
417	Barry Sanders	1.25
418	Eddie Murray	.05
419	Vince Workman	.10
420	Ed West	.05
421	Charles Wilson	.05
422	Perry Kemp	.05
423	Chuck Cecil	.05
424	James Campen	.05
425	Robert Brown	.05
426	Brian Noble	.05
427	Rich Moran	.05
428	Vai Sikahema	.05
429	Allen Rice	.05
430	Haywood Jeffires	.15
431	Warren Moon	.20
432	Greg Montgomery	.05
433	Sean Jones	.05
434	Richard Johnson	.05
435	Al Smith	.05
436	Johnny Meads	.05
437	William Fuller	.05
438	Mike Munchak	.05
439	Ray Childress	.05
440	Cody Carlson	.05
441	Scott Radecic	.05
442	*Quintus McDonald*	.10
443	Eugene Daniel	.05
444	Mark Herrmann	.15
445	*John Baylor*	.12
446	Dave McCloughan	.05
447	Mark Vander Poel	.05
448	Randy Dixon	.05
449	Keith Taylor	.05
450	Alan Grant	.05
451	Tony Siragusa	.05
452	Rich Baldinger	.05
453	Derrick Thomas	.20
454	Bill Jones	.05
455	Troy Stradford	.05
456	Barry Word	.15
457	Tim Grunhard	.05
458	Chris Martin	.05
459	*Jayice Pearson*	.10
460	Dino Hackett	.05
461	David Lutz	.05
462	Albert Lewis	.06
463	*Fred Jones*	.12
464	Winston Moss	.05
465	*Sam Graddy*	.20
466	Steve Wisniewski	.05
467	Jay Schroeder	.05
468	Ronnie Loft	.05
469	Willie Gault	.05
470	Greg Townsend	.05
471	Max Montoya	.05
472	Howie Long	.05
473	Lionel Washington	.05
474	Riki Ellison	.05
475	Tom Newberry	.05
476	Damone Johnson	.05
477	Pat Terrell	.05
478	Marcus Dupree	.05
479	Todd Lyght	.10
480	Buford McGee	.05
481	Bern Brostek	.05
482	Jim Price	.05
483	Robert Young	.05
484	Tony Zendejas	.05
485	*Robert Bailey*	.10
486	Alvin Wright	.05
487	Pat Carter	.05
488	Pete Stoyanovich	.05
489	Reggie Roby	.05
490	Harry Galbreath	.05
491	*Michael McGruder*	.10
492	J.B. Brown	.05
493	E.J. Junior	.05
494	Ferrell Edmunds	.05
495	Scott Secules	.05
496	*Greg Baty*	.15
497	Mike Iaquaniello	.05
498	Keith Sims	.05
499	John Randle	.05
500	Joey Browner	.05
501	Steve Jordan	.08
502	Darrin Nelson	.05
503	Audray McMillian	.10
504	Harry Newsome	.05
505	Hassan Jones	.05
506	Ray Berry	.05
507	Mike Merriweather	.05
508	Leo Lewis	.05
509	Tim Irwin	.05
510	Kirk Lowdermilk	.05
511	Alfred Anderson	.05
512	*Michael Timpson*	.75
513	Jerome Henderson	.05
514	Andre Tippett	.05
515	Chris Singleton	.05
516	John Stephens	.05
517	Ronnie Lippett	.05
518	Bruce Armstrong	.05
519	*Marion Hobby*	.10
520	Tim Goad	.05
521	*Mickey Washington*	.08
522	Fred Smerlas	.05
523	Wayne Martin	.05
524	Frank Warren	.05
525	Floyd Turner	.05
526	Wesley Carroll	.05
527	Gene Atkins	.05
528	Vaughan Johnson	.05
529	Hoby Brenner	.05
530	Renaldo Turnbull	.05
531	Joel Hilgenberg	.05
532	Craig Heyward	.05
533	Vince Buck	.05
534	Jim Dombrowski	.05
535	*Fred McAfee*	.12
536	Phil Simms	.10
537	Lewis Tillman	.05
538	John Elliott	.05
539	Dave Meggett	.05
540	Mark Collins	.05
541	Ottis Anderson	.05
542	*Bobby Abrams*	.10
543	Sean Landeta	.05
544	Brian Williams	.05
545	Erik Howard	.05
546	Mark Ingram	.05
547	Kanavis McGhee	.05
548	Kyle Clifton	.05
549	Marvin Washington	.05
550	Jeff Criswell	.05
551	Dave Cadigan	.05
552	Chris Burkett	.05
553	Erik McMillan	.05
554	James Hasty	.05
555	*Louie Aguiar*	.10
556	*Troy Johnson*	.10
557	*Troy Taylor*	.10
558	*Pat Kelly*	.08
559	Heath Sherman	.05
560	Roger Ruzek	.05
561	Andre Waters	.05
562	Izel Jenkins	.05
563	Keith Jackson	.15
564	Byron Evans	.05
565	Wes Hopkins	.05
566	Rich Miano	.05
567	Seth Joyner	.05
568	Thomas Sanders	.05
569	David Alexander	.05
570	Jeff Kemp	.05
571	*Jock Jones*	.10
572	*Craig Patterson*	.10
573	Robert Massey	.05
574	Bill Lewis	.05
575	Freddie Joe Nunn	.05
576	Aeneas Williams	.05
577	John Jackson	.05
578	Tim McDonald	.05
579	*Michael Zordich*	.10
580	Eric Hill	.05
581	Lorenzo Lynch	.05
582	*Vernice Smith*	.10
583	Greg Lloyd	.05
584	Carnell Lake	.05
585	Hardy Nickerson	.05
586	Delton Hall	.05
587	Gerald Williams	.05
588	Bryan Hinkle	.05
589	Barry Foster	.45
590	Bubby Brister	.06
591	*Rick Strom*	.15
592	David Little	.05
593	*Leroy Thompson*	.40
594	Eric Bieniemy	.05
595	Courtney Hall	.05
596	George Thornton	.05
597	Donnie Elder	.05
598	Billy Ray Smith	.05
599	Gill Byrd	.05
600	Marion Butts	.10
601	Ronnie Harmon	.05
602	Anthony Shelton	.05
603	Mark May	.05
604	*Craig McEwen*	.10
605	Steve Young	1.00
606	Keith Henderson	.05
607	Pierce Holt	.05
608	Roy Foster	.05
609	Don Griffin	.05
610	Harry Sydney	.05
611	Todd Bowles	.05
612	Ted Washington	.05
613	Johnny Jackson	.05
614	Jesse Sapolu	.05
615	Brent Jones	.05
616	Travis McNeal	.05
617	*Darrick Brilz*	.10
618	Terry Wooden	.05
619	Tommy Kane	.05
620	Nesby Glasgow	.05
621	Dwayne Harper	.05
622	Rick Tuten	.05
623	Chris Warren	.30
624	John L. Williams	.05
625	Rufus Porter	.05
626	David Daniels	.05
627	Keith McCants	.05
628	Reuben Davis	.05
629	Mark Royals	.05
630	*Marty Carter*	.15
631	Ian Beckles	.05
632	Ron Hall	.05
633	Eugene Marve	.05
634	Willie Drewrey	.05
635	*Tom McHale*	.10
636	Kevin Murphy	.05
637	Robert Hardy	.10
638	Ricky Sanders	.05
639	Gary Clark	.10
640	Andre Collins	.05
641	Brad Edwards	.08
642	Monte Coleman	.05
643	*Clarence Vaughn*	.10
644	Fred Stokes	.05
645	Charles Mann	.05
646	Earnest Byner	.05
647	Jim Lachey	.05
648	Jeff Bostic	.05
649	*Chris Mims*	.30
650	*George Williams*	.10
651	Ed Cunningham	.08
652	*Tony Smith*	.10
653	*Will Furrer*	.15
655	*Mike Mooney*	.08
656	*Eddie Blake*	.10
657	*Leon Searcy*	.12
658	*Kevin Turner*	.20
659	*Keith Hamilton*	.15
660	*Alan Haller*	.10

1992 Pacific Checklists

These inserts were released in 1992 Pacific foil, jumbo and 25-cent packs. Each card is numbered on the back 1 of 8, etc. Cards 1-4 were in Series I packs; cards 5-8 were in Series II packs.

		MT
Complete Set (8):		3.00
Common Player:		.50
1	Checklist 1 - (1-110)	.50
2	Checklist 2 - (111-220)	.50
3	Checklist 3 - (221-330)	.50
4	Checklist 4 (Highlight Cards)	.50
5	Checklist 5 - (1-110)	.50
6	Checklist 6 - (111-220)	.50
7	Checklist 7 - (221-330)	.50
8	Checklist 8 (Highlight Cards)	.50

1992 Pacific Legends of the Game Bob Griese

Miami Dolphins Hall of Fame quarterback Bob Griese is featured on this nine-card insert set. The cards, subtitled "Legends of the Game," were random inserts in 1992 Pacific Series II foil and jumbo packs. Each white-bordered card front has a color action shot, along with a caption and Griese's name in a colorful stripe at the bottom next to the Pacific logo. The back is in a horizontal format and features another photo of the player, plus a career summary. The cards are a continuation of the "Legends of the Game" series, so they start at 10, where the 1992 Steve Largent set ended. The Griese cards were also randomly inserted in triple folder card packs and five-card change-maker packs. Griese also autographed 1,000 cards.

		MT
Complete Set (9):		5.00
Common Griese:		.50
10	Purdue Star (Bob Griese)	.50
11	AFL Star (Bob Griese)	.50
12	Super Bowl Star (Bob Griese)	.50
13	Thinking Man's QB (Bob Griese)	.50
14	349 Yards (Bob Griese)	.50
15	All Star (Bob Griese)	.50
16	The 25,000 Yard Club (Bob Griese)	.50
17	Number 12 Retired (Bob Griese)	.50
18	Hall of Fame (Bob Griese)	.50

1992 Pacific Legends of the Game Steve Largent

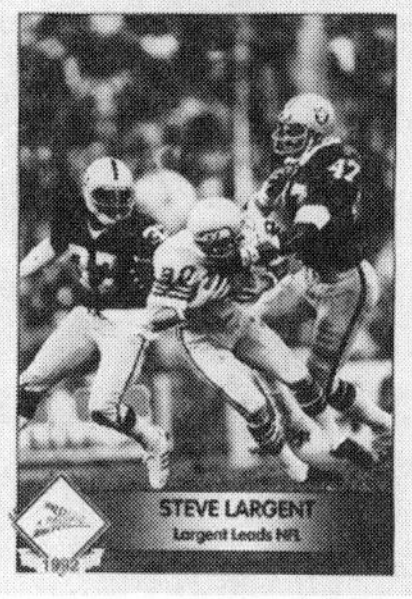

Seattle Seahawks Hall of Fame wide receiver Steve Largent is featured in this nine-card insert set. Cards were randomly inserted in Series I and jumbo packs. Fronts feature color action photos with white borders. The card title and Largent's name are in a colored panel at the bottom. The backs have a photo, career summary and card number, 1 of 9, etc. They are in a horizontal format. Largent autographed 1,000 cards.

		MT
Complete Set (9):		5.00
Common Player:		.50
1	Great Rookie Start	.50
2	Largent Leads NFL	.50
3	Hi-Steppin'	.50
4	NFL Leader	.50
5	Team Captain	.50
6	Pro Bowl	.50
7	Man of the Year	.50
8	The Final Season	.50
9	Retirement Celebration	.50

1992 Pacific Picks The Pros

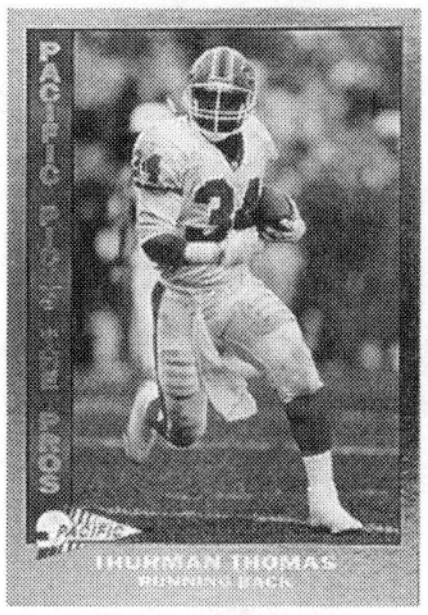

Pacific selected the best player at each position for this 25-card insert set. Gold foil versions of the cards, which say "Pacific Picks The Pros" in gold foil down the left side, were randomly inserted in Series I foil packs. Silver versions were also made and were random inserts in Series I jumbo packs. The backs present a career summary in a diagonal format with a red and yellow background. A card number is also included. The cards have the same value for both versions.

		MT
Complete Set (25):		40.00
Common Player:		1.00
1	Mark Rypien	1.00
2	Marv Cook	1.00
3	Jim Lachey	1.00
4	Darrell Green	1.00
5	Derrick Thomas	3.00
6	Thurman Thomas	6.00
7	Kent Hull	1.00
8	Tim McDonald	1.00
9	Mike Croel	1.00
10	Anthony Munoz	1.00
11	Jerome Brown	1.00
12	Reggie White	3.00
13	Gill Byrd	1.00
14	Jessie Tuggle	1.00
15	Randall McDaniel	1.00
16	Sam Mills	1.00
17	Pat Swilling	1.00
18	Eugene Robinson	1.00
19	Michael Irvin	6.00
20	Emmitt Smith	15.00
21	Jeff Gossett	1.00
22	Jeff Jaeger	1.00
23	William Fuller	1.00
24	Mike Munchak	1.00
25	Andre Rison	4.00

1992 Pacific Prism Inserts

The top 10 running backs in the NFL are featured in this set. Pacific stated it produced only 10,000 of each card and randomly inserted them in 1992 Pacific Series II foil packs and triple folder card packs. The front of each card features a player photo superimposed against a prism-patterned background. A color streak at the bottom contains the player's name. Each back has a green football field for a background and uses team-color bar graphics to give the back's rushing totals for each game in 1991. Backs are numbered 1 of 10, etc.

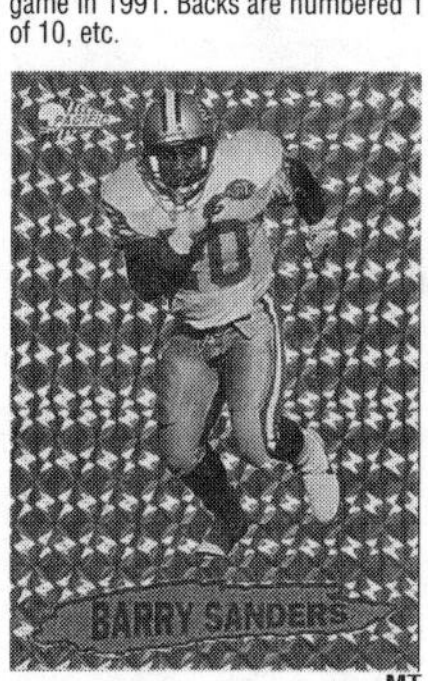

		MT
Complete Set (10):		25.00
Common Player:		1.50
1	Thurman Thomas	2.00
2	Gaston Green	1.50
3	Christian Okoye	2.75
4	Leonard Russell	2.50
5	Mark Higgs	2.50
6	Emmitt Smith	8.00
7	Barry Sanders	6.00
8	Rodney Hampton	2.00
9	Earnest Byner	2.50
10	Herschel Walker	1.50

1992 Pacific Statistical Leaders

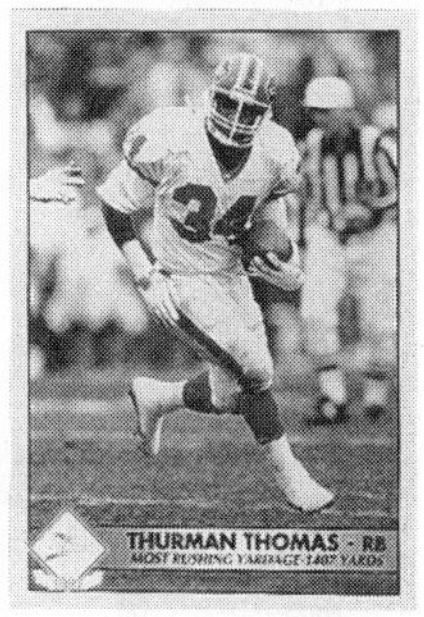

These cards, which feature statistical leaders from each NFL team, were random inserts in Series I foil packs. The front of the card has a glossy action photo bordered by a white frame. The player's name and category he lead are at the bottom in a multi-colored stripe. Three other team leaders are featured on each back, plus small photos of the player in action. The cards are also numbered on the back. Additional cards were made for the AFC and NFC rushing leaders.

		MT
Complete Set (30):		9.00
Common Player:		.25
1	Chris Miller	.25
2	Thurman Thomas	1.25
3	Jim Harbaugh	.25
4	Jim Breech	.25
5	Kevin Mack	.25
6	Emmitt Smith	4.00
7	Gaston Green	.25
8	Barry Sanders	2.50
9	Tony Bennett	.25
10	Warren Moon	.50
11	Bill Brooks	.25
12	Christian Okoye	.25
13	Jay Schroeder	.30
14	Robert Delpino	.25
15	Mark Higgs	.25
16	John Randle	.25
17	Leonard Russell	.25
18	Pat Swilling	.30
19	Rodney Hampton	.50
20	Terance Mathis	.40
21	Fred Barnett	.25
22	Aeneas Williams	.25
23	Neil O'Donnell	.35
24	Marion Butts	.25
25	Steve Young	1.25
26	John L. Williams	.25
27	Reggie Cobb	.25
28	Mark Rypien	.35
29	Thurman Thomas	.50
30	Emmitt Smith	1.50

1992 Pacific Triple Folders

One player from each NFL team was selected for this 28-card Pacific Trading Cards set. Each card front has two panels which, when closed, form a 3-1/2" x 5" glossy color action photo. The player's name and team helmet are on one side, while his position is on the other side. When opened up, the inside of the card reveals three smaller photos of the featured player. The cards use team color-coding for the background and have statistics and a player profile on the back, along with a card number. Each Triple Folder pack also included one card as an insert from the following sets: Steve Largent, Bob Griese, Statistical Leaders, Gold/Foil Prisms, Rushing Leaders Prisms, or checklists.

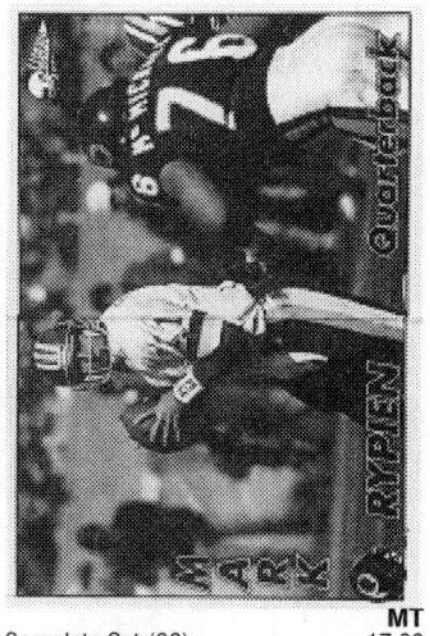

		MT
Complete Set (28):		17.00
Common Player:		.50
1	Chris Miller	1.00
2	Thurman Thomas	1.50
3	Neal Anderson	.50
4	Tim McGee	.50
5	Kevin Mack	.50
6	Emmitt Smith	5.00
7	John Elway	2.00
8	Barry Sanders	3.00
9	Sterling Sharpe	2.00
10	Warren Moon	1.25
11	Bill Brooks	.50
12	Christian Okoye	.50
13	Nick Bell	.50
14	Robert Delpino	.50
15	Mark Higgs	.75
16	Rich Gannon	.50
17	Leonard Russell	1.00
18	Pat Swilling	.75
19	Rodney Hampton	1.25
20	Rob Moore	1.25
21	Reggie White	1.50
22	Johnny Johnson	1.00
23	Neil O'Donnell	1.50
24	Marion Butts	1.00
25	Steve Young	3.00
26	John L. Williams	.50
27	Reggie Cobb	.50
28	Mark Rypien	1.00

1993 Pacific Protypes

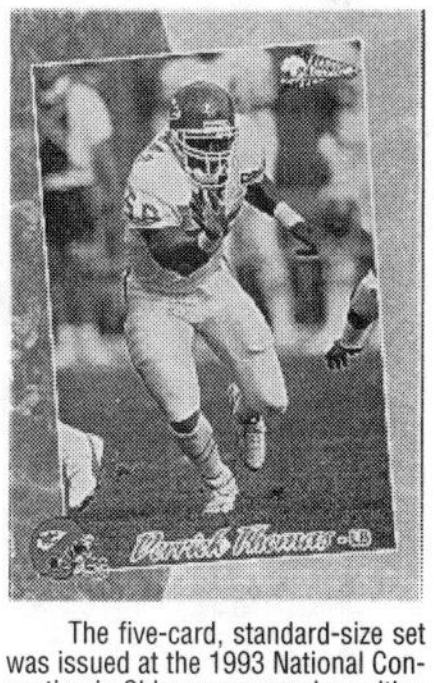

The five-card, standard-size set was issued at the 1993 National Convention in Chicago as samples, with a production total of 5,000 sets.

		MT
Complete Set (5):		20.00
Common Player:		1.50
1	Emmitt Smith	10.00
2	Barry Sanders	5.00
3	Derrick Thomas	1.50
4	Jim Everett	1.50
5	Steve Young	4.00

1993 Pacific

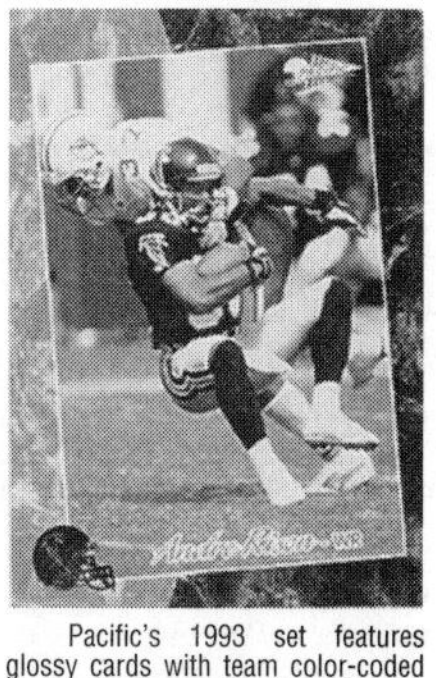

Pacific's 1993 set features glossy cards with team color-coded marble backgrounds. The 440-card set has two subsets - "NFL Stars" (#s 393-417) and "Rookies" (#s 418-440). Random inserts include Prism (20 cards) and Pacific Picks the Pros (25) cards. The five prototype cards are similar to the regular set, except they say "1993 Prototypes" on the back. Approximately 5,000 sets were made; many were given away at the 1993 National Sports Collectors Convention in Chicago in July.

		MT
Complete Set (440):		18.00
Common Player:		.05
Minor Stars:		.10
Checklist Set (4):		4.00
Pack (12):		.60
Wax Box (36):		20.00
1	Emmitt Smith	1.50
2	Troy Aikman	.75
3	Larry Brown	.05
4	Tony Castillas	.05
5	Thomas Everett	.05
6	Alvin Harper	.10
7	Michael Irvin	.30
8	Charles Haley	.05
9	*Leon Lett*	.30
10	Kevin Smith	.05
11	Robert Jones	.05
12	Jimmy Smith	.25
13	*Derrick Gainer*	.05
14	*Lin Elliott*	.05
15	William Thomas	.05
16	Clyde Simmons	.05
17	Seth Joyner	.05
18	Randall Cunningham	.10
19	Byron Evans	.05
20	Fred Barnett	.05
21	Calvin Williams	.05
22	James Joseph	.05
23	Heath Sherman	.05
24	Siran Stacy	.05
25	*Andy Harmon*	.05
26	Eric Allen	.05
27	Herschel Walker	.05
28	Vai Sikahema	.05
29	Ernest Byner	.05
30	Jeff Bostic	.05
31	Monte Coleman	.05
32	Ricky Ervins	.05
33	Darrell Green	.05
34	Mark Schlereth	.05
35	Mark Rypien	.05
36	Art Monk	.10
37	Brian Mitchell	.05
38	Chip Lohmiller	.05
39	Charles Mann	.05
40	Shane Collins	.05
41	Jim Lachey	.05
42	Joe Jacoby	.05
43	Rodney Hampton	.10
44	*Dave Brown*	.60
45	Mark Collins	.05
46	Jerrod Bunch	.05
47	William Roberts	.05
48	Sean Landetta	.05
49	Lawrence Taylor	.10
50	Ed McCaffrey	.05
51	Bart Oates	.05
52	Pepper Johnson	.05
53	Eric Dorsey	.05
54	Erik Howard	.05
55	Phil Simms	.10
56	Derek Brown	.05
57	Johnny Bailey	.05
58	Rich Camarillo	.05
59	*Larry Centers*	.50
60	Chris Chandler	.05
61	Randal Hill	.05
62	Rickey Proehl	.05
63	Freddie Joe Nunn	.05
64	Robert Massey	.05
65	Aeneas Williams	.05
66	Luis Sharpe	.05
67	Eric Swann	.05
68	Timm Rosenbach	.05
69	*Anthony Edwards*	.10
70	Greg Davis	.05
71	Terry Allen	.10
72	Anthony Carter	.05
73	Cris Carter	.10
74	Roger Craig	.05
75	Jack Del Rio	.05
76	Chris Doleman	.05
77	Rich Gannon	.05
78	Hassan Jones	.05
79	Steve Jordan	.05
80	Randall McDaniel	.05
81	Sean Salisbury	.05
82	Harry Newsome	.05
83	Carlos Jenkins	.05
84	Jake Reed	.05
85	Edgar Bennett	.10
86	Tony Bennett	.05
87	Terrell Buckley	.05
88	Ty Detmer	.05
89	Brett Favre	1.50
90	Chris Jackie (Jacke)	.05
91	Sterling Sharpe	.10
92	James Campen	.05
93	Brian Noble	.05
94	*Lester Archambeau*	.05
95	Harry Sydney	.05
96	Corey Harris	.05
97	Don Majkowski	.05
98	Ken Ruettgers	.05
99	Lomas Brown	.05
100	Jason Hanson	.05
101	Robert Porcher	.05
102	Chris Spielman	.05
103	Erik Kramer	.05
104	Tracy Scroggins	.05
105	Rodney Peete	.05
106	Barry Sanders	1.25
107	Herman Moore	.30
108	Brett Perriman	.05
109	Mel Gray	.05
110	Dennis Gibson	.05
111	Bennie Blades	.05
112	Andre Ware	.05
113	Gary Anderson	.05
114	Tyji Armstrong	.05
115	Reggie Cobb	.05
116	Marty Carter	.05
117	Lawrence Dawsey	.05
118	Steve DeBerg	.05
119	Ron Hall	.05
120	Courtney Hawkins	.05
121	Broderick Thomas	.05
122	Keith McCants	.05
123	Bruce Reimers	.05
124	Darrick Brownlow	.05
125	Mark Wheeler	.05
126	Ricky Reynolds	.05
127	Neal Anderson	.05
128	Trace Armstrong	.05
129	Mark Carrier	.05
130	Richard Dent	.05
131	Wendall Davis	.05
132	Darren Lewis	.05
133	Tom Waddle	.05
134	Jim Harbaugh	.05
135	Steve McMichael	.05
136	William Perry	.05
137	Alonzo Spellman	.05
138	John Roper	.05
139	Peter Tom Willis	.05
140	Dante Jones	.05
141	Harris Barton	.05
142	Michael Carter	.05
143	Eric Davis	.05
144	Dana Hall	.05
145	Amp Lee	.05
146	Don Griffin	.05
147	Jerry Rice	.75
148	Ricky Watters	.20
149	Steve Young	.75
150	Bill Romanowski	.05
151	Klaus Wilmsmeyer	.05
152	Steve Bono	.30
153	Tom Rathman	.05
154	Odessa Turner	.05
155	Morten Andersen	.05
156	Richard Cooper	.05
157	Toi Cook	.05
158	Quinn Early	.05
159	Vaughn Dunbar	.05
160	Rickey Jackson	.05
161	Wayne Mottin	.05
162	Hoby Brenner	.05
163	Joel Hilgenberg	.05
164	Mike Buck	.05
165	Torrance Small	.05
166	Eric Martin	.05
167	Vaughan Johnson	.05
168	Sam Mills	.05
169	Steve Broussard	.05
170	Darion Connel	.05
171	Drew Hill	.05
172	Chris Hinton	.05
173	Chris Miller	.05
174	Tim McKyer	.05
175	Norm Johnson	.05
176	Mike Pritchard	.05
177	Andre Rison	.10
178	Deion Sanders	.40
179	Tony Smith	.05
180	Bruce Pickens	.05
181	Michael Haynes	.05
182	Jessie Tuggle	.05
183	Makr Boutte	.05
184	Don Bracken	.05
185	Bern Brostek	.05
186	Henry Ellard	.05
187	Jim Everett	.10
188	Sean Gilbert	.05
189	Cleveland Gary	.05
190	Todd Kinchen	.10
191	Pat Terrell	.05
192	Jackie Slater	.05
193	David Lang	.05
194	Willie Anderson	.05
195	Tony Zendejas	.05
196	Roman Phifer	.05
197	Steve Christie	.05
198	Cornelius Bennett	.05
199	Phil Hansen	.05
200	Don Beebe	.05
201	Mark Kelso	.05
202	Bruce Smith	.05
203	Darryl Talley	.05
204	Andre Reed	.05
205	Mike Lodish	.05
206	Jim Kelly	.20
207	Thurman Thomas	.20
208	Kenneth Davis	.05
209	Frank Reich	.05
210	Kent Hall	.05
211	Marco Coleman	.05
212	Bryan Cox	.05
213	Jeff Cross	.05
214	Mark Higgs	.05
215	Keith Jackson	.05
216	Scott Miller	.05
217	John Offerdahl	.05
218	Dan Marino	1.50
219	Keith Sims	.05
220	Chuck Klingbell	.05
221	Troy Vincent	.05
222	*Mike Williams*	.05
223	Pete Stoyanovich	.05
224	J.B. Brown	.05
225	Ashley Ambrose	.05
226	*Jason Belser*	.05
227	Jeff George	.10
228	Quentin Coryatt	.05
229	Duane Bickett	.05
230	Steve Emtman	.05
231	Anthony Johnson	.05
232	Rohn Stark	.05
233	Jessie Hester	.05
234	Reggie Langhorne	.05
235	Clarence Verdin	.05
236	Dean Biasucci	.05
237	Jack Trudeau	.05
238	Tony Siragusa	.05
239	Chris Burkett	.05
240	Brad Baxter	.05
241	Rob Moore	.05
242	Browning Nagle	.05
243	Jim Sweeney	.05
244	Kent Barber	.05
245	*Siupeli Malamala*	.05
246	Mike Brim	.05
247	Mo Lewis	.05
248	Johnny Mitchell	.05
249	*Ken Whisenhunt*	.05
250	James Hasty	.05
251	Kyle Clifton	.05
252	Terance Mathis	.05
253	Ray Agnew	.05
254	Eugene Chung	.05
255	Marv Cook	.05
256	Johnny Rembert	.05
257	Maurice Hurst	.05
258	John Vaughn	.05
259	Leonard Russell	.05
260	Pat Harlow	.05
261	Andre Tippet	.05
262	Michael Timpson	.05
263	Greg McCarthy	.05
264	Chris Singleton	.05
265	*Reggie Redding*	.05
266	Walter Stanley	.05
267	Gary Anderson	.05
268	Merril Hoge	.05
269	Barry Foster	.10
270	Charles Davenport	.05
271	Jeff Graham	.05
272	Adrian Cooper	.05
273	David Little	.05
274	Neil O'Donnell	.10
275	Rod Woodson	.10
276	Ernie Mills	.05
277	Dwight Stone	.05
278	Darren Perry	.05
279	Dermontti Dawson	.05
280	Carlton Haselrig	.05
281	Pat Coleman	.05
282	Ernest Givins	.05
283	Warren Moon	.10
284	Haywood Jeffires	.05
285	Cody Carlson	.05
286	Ray Childress	.05
287	Bruce Matthews	.05
288	Webster Slaughter	.05
289	Bo Orlando	.05
290	Lorenzo White	.05
291	Eddie Robinson	.05
292	Bubba McDowell	.05
293	Bucky Richardson	.10
294	Sean Jones	.05
295	David Brandon	.05
296	Shawn Collins	.05
297	Lawyer Tillman	.05
298	Bob Dahl	.05
299	Kevin Mack	.05
300	Bernie Kosar	.05
301	Tommy Vardell	.05
302	Jay Hilgenberg	.05
303	Michael Dean Perry	.05
304	Michael Jackson	.05
305	Eric Metcalf	.05
306	*Rico Smith*	.05
307	*Stevon Moore*	.05
308	Leroy Hoard	.05
309	Eric Ball	.05
310	Derrick Fenner	.05
311	James Francis	.05
312	Ricardo McDonald	.05
313	Tim Krumrie	.05
314	Carl Pickens	.50
315	David Klingler	.10
316	Donald Hollas	.05
317	Harold Green	.05
318	Daniel Stubbs	.05
319	Alfred Williams	.05
320	Darryl Williams	.05
321	*Mike Arthur*	.05
322	Leonard Wheeler	.05
323	Gil Byrd	.05
324	Eric Bieniemy	.05
325	Marion Butts	.05
326	John Carney	.05
327	Stan Humphries	.10
328	Ronnie Harmon	.05
329	Junior Seau	.10
330	Nate Lewis	.05
331	Harry Swayne	.05
332	Leslie O'Neal	.05
333	Eric Moten	.05
334	*Blaise Winter*	.05
335	Anthony Miller	.05
336	Gary Plummer	.05
337	Willie Davis	.05
338	J.T. Birden	.05
339	Tim Barnett	.05
340	Dave Krieg	.05
341	Barry Word	.05
342	Tracy Simien	.05
343	Christian Okoye	.05
344	Todd McNair	.05
345	Dan Salesaumua	.05
346	Derrick Thomas	.10
347	Harvey Williams	.05
348	*Kimble Anders*	.10
349	Tim Grunhard	.05
350	*Tony Hargain*	.05
351	Simon Fletcher	.05
352	John Elway	.30
353	Mike Croel	.05
354	Steve Atwater	.05
355	Tommy Maddox	.05
356	Karl Mecklenberg	.05
357	Shane Dronett	.05
358	Kenny Walker	.05
359	*Reggie Rivers*	.05
360	*Cedric Tilman*	.05
361	*Arthur Marshall*	.10
362	Greg Lewis	.05
363	Shannon Sharpe	.10
364	Doug Widell	.05
365	Todd Marinovich	.05
366	Nick Bell	.05
367	Eric Dickerson	.05
368	Max Montoya	.05
369	Winston Moss	.05
370	Howie Long	.05
371	Willie Gault	.05
372	Tim Brown	.10
373	Steve Smith	.05
374	Steve Wisniewski	.05
375	Alexander Wright	.05
376	Ethan Horton	.05
377	Napoleon McCallum	.05
378	Terry McDaniel	.05
379	Patrick Hunter	.05
380	Robert Blackmon	.05
381	John Kasay	.05
382	Cortez Kennedy	.10
383	Andy Heck	.05
384	*Bill Hitchcock*	.05
385	*Rick Mirer*	.30
386	Jeff Bryant	.05
387	Eugene Robinson	.05
388	John L. Williams	.05
389	Chris Warren	.20
390	Rufus Porter	.05
391	*Joe Tofflemire*	.05
392	Dan McGwire	.05
393	Boomer Esiason	.10
394	Brad Muster	.05
395	James Lofton	.05
396	Tim McGee	.05
397	Steve Beurlein	.10
398	Gaston Green	.05
399	Bill Brooks	.05
400	Ronnie Lott	.05
401	Jay Schroeder	.05
402	Marcus Allen	.10
403	Kevin Green	.05
404	Kirk Lowdermilk	.05
405	Hugh Millen	.05
406	Pat Swilling	.05
407	Bobby Herbert	.05
408	Carl Banks	.05
409	Jeff Hostetler	.10
410	Leonard Marshall	.05
411	Ken O'Brien	.05
412	Joe Montana	1.00
413	Reggie White	.10
414	Gary Clark	.05
415	Johnny Johnson	.05
416	Tim McDonald	.05
417	Pierce Holt	.05
418	*Gino Torretta*	.10
419	*Glyn Milburn*	.30
420	*O.J. McDuffie*	.60
421	*Coleman Rudolph*	.10
422	*Reggie Brooks*	.10
423	*Garrison Hearst*	1.50
424	*Leonard Renfro*	.10
425	*Kevin Williams*	.30
426	*Demetrius DuBose*	.10
427	*Elvis Grbac*	1.50
428	*Lincoln Kennedy*	.10
429	*Carlton Gray*	.10
430	*Michael Barrow*	.10
431	*George Teague*	.25
432	*Curtis Conway*	1.00
433	*Natrone Means*	1.00
434	*Jerome Bettis*	1.00
435	*Drew Bledsoe*	3.00
436	*Robert Smith*	1.00
437	*Deon Figures*	.20
438	*Qadry Ismail*	.50
439	*Chris Slade*	.30
440	*Dana Stubblefield*	.50

1993 Pacific Picks the Pros Gold

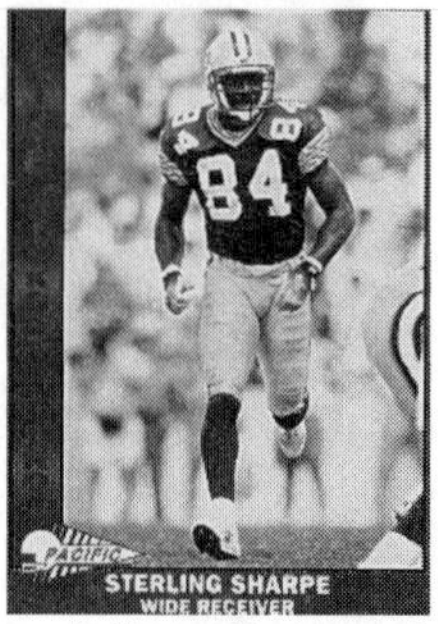

Pacific's top picks at each position are featured in this 25-card insert set. Cards were randomly included in packs and have a color action photo on the front with a gold-foil border. The player's name and position are at the bottom in a gold-foil panel. The back is in a horizontal format and includes the player's name, position, team name and season recap in black letters on a blue and gray background. A card number is also given. A silver version was also made for these cards; these cards were randomly included in 1993 Pacific Triple Folders.

		MT
Complete Set (25):		75.00
Common Player:		2.00
Minor Stars:		4.00
1	Jerry Rice	15.00
2	Sterling Sharpe	4.00
3	Richmond Webb	2.00
4	Harris Barton	2.00
5	Randall McDaniel	2.00
6	Steve Wisniewski	2.00
7	Mark Stepnoski	2.00
8	Steve Young	15.00
9	Emmitt Smith	20.00
10	Barry Foster	4.00
11	Nick Lowery	2.00
12	Reggie White	6.00
13	Leslie O'Neal	2.00
14	Cortez Kennedy	4.00
15	Ray Childress	2.00
16	Vaughan Johnson	2.00
17	Wilber Marshall	2.00
18	Junior Seau	6.00
19	Sam Mills	2.00
20	Rod Woodson	4.00
21	Ricky Reynolds	2.00
22	Steve Atwater	2.00
23	Chuck Cecil	2.00
24	Rich Camarillo	2.00
25	Dale Carter	2.00

1993 Pacific Silver Prism Inserts

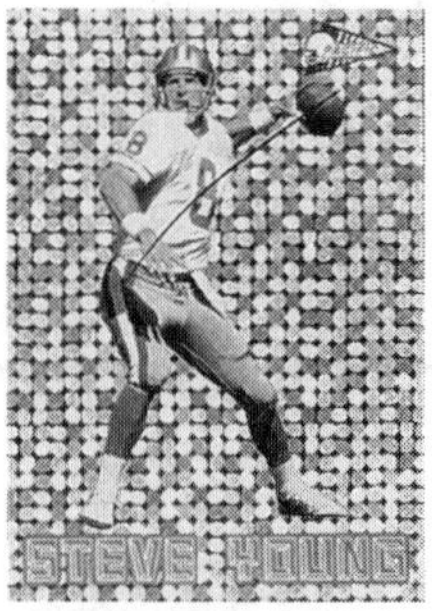

Pacific produced three versions of its 1993 Prism inserts. The first version, the regular prism inserts, have triangular prisms for a background. There were 8,000 of each of these cards made; they were randomly included in 1993 Pacific packs and 1993 Pacific Triple Folder packs. A circular version background was also made; these cards were randomly included in retail packs and were easier to find than the triangular versions. The third type of prism insert was limited to 1,000 per card and features a gold triangular prism background. They were randomly included in 1993 Pacific Triple Folder packs. Each card design is basically the same for all three versions. The front has a color action photo against the prism background; the player's name is at the bottom in block letters in team colors. The back has the same photo used for the front, except the entire background of the photo is also used. The player's name and position are given in scripted white letters. A card number is also given (1 of 20, etc.).

		MT
Complete Set (20):		100.00
Common Player:		2.00
Minor Stars:		4.00
Comp. Gold Set (20):		300.00
Gold Cards:		1.5x-3x
1	Troy Aikman	7.00
2	Jerome Bettis	4.00
3	Drew Bledsoe	10.00
4	Reggie Brooks	4.00
5	Brett Favre	15.00
6	Barry Foster	4.00
7	Garrison Hearst	4.00
8	Michael Irvin	4.00
9	Cortez Kennedy	2.00
10	David Klingler	2.00
11	Dan Marino	15.00
12	Rick Mirer	4.00
13	Joe Montana	10.00
14	Jay Novacek	2.00
15	Jerry Rice	8.00
16	Barry Sanders	10.00
17	Sterling Sharpe	4.00
18	Emmitt Smith	15.00
19	Thurman Thomas	4.00
20	Steve Young	8.00

1993 Pacific Prisms

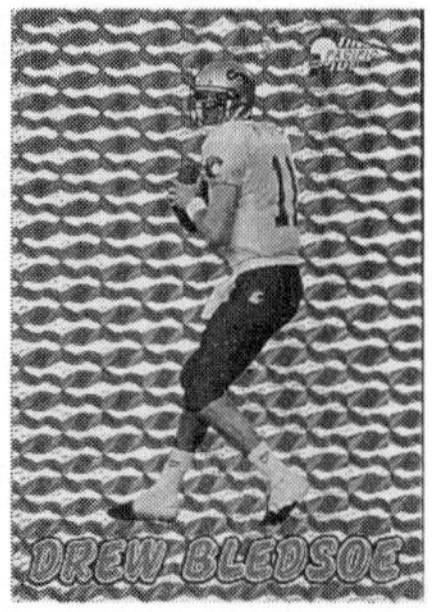

Approximately 17,000 of each card in this 108-card set were produced. Each card front has a player action photo against a prism-like foil background. The player's name is in team colors and appears at the bottom of the card. The back is numbered and includes a player profile, two photos, a team helmet and the Pacific logo. The card back is in a horizontal format and uses a gray background. There were also two promotional cards made for the set - (22) Emmitt Smith and (61) Drew Bledsoe. The cards, which were given away at the 1993 National Card Collectors Convention in Chicago, are similar in design to the regular set.

		MT
Complete Set (108):		130.00
Common Player:		.50
Minor Stars:		1.00
Checklist (NNO):		.25
Pack (1):		2.25
Wax Box (36):		70.00
1	Chris Miller	.50
2	Mike Pritchard	.50
3	Andre Rison	1.00
4	Deion Sanders	3.00
5	Tony Smith	.50
6	Jim Kelly	2.00
7	Andre Reed	1.00
8	Thurman Thomas	2.00
9	Neal Anderson	.50
10	Jim Harbaugh	.50
11	Donnell Woolford	.50
12	David Klingler	.50
13	Carl Pickens	3.00
14	Alfred Williams	.50
15	Michael Jackson	.50
16	Bernie Kosar	1.00
17	Tommy Vardell	.50
18	Troy Aikman	8.00
19	Alvin Harper	2.00
20	Michael Irvin	2.00
21	Russell Maryland	.50
22	Emmitt Smith	12.00
23	John Elway	5.00
24	Tommy Maddox	.50
25	Shannon Sharpe	1.00
26	Herman Moore	3.00
27	Rodney Peete	.50
28	Barry Sanders	10.00
29	Pat Swilling	.50
30	Terrell Buckley	.50
31	Brett Favre	12.00
32	Sterling Sharpe	2.00
33	Reggie White	1.00
34	Ernest Givins	.50
35	Haywood Jeffires	.50
36	Warren Moon	2.00
37	Lorenzo White	.50
38	Steve Emtman	.50
39	Jeff George	2.00
40	Reggie Langhorne	.50
41	Dale Carter	.50
42	Joe Montana	10.00
43	Derrick Thomas	1.00
44	Barry Word	.50
45	Nick Bell	.50
46	Eric Dickerson	1.00
47	Jeff Jaeger	.50
48	Jerome Bettis	5.00
49	Henry Ellard	.50
50	Jim Everett	1.00
51	Cleveland Gary	.50
52	Marco Coleman	.50
53	Mark Higgs	.50
54	Keith Jackson	.50
55	Dan Marino	15.00
56	Troy Vincent	.50
57	Terry Allen	.50
58	Jack Del Rio	.50
59	Sean Salisbury	.50
60	Robert Smith	5.00
61	Drew Bledsoe	16.00
62	Marv Cook	.50
63	Irving Fryar	.50
64	Leonard Russell	.50
65	Andre Tippett	.50
66	Morten Andersen	.50
67	Vaughn Dunbar	.50
68	Eric Martin	.50
69	David Brown	2.00
70	Rodney Hampton	2.00
71	Phil Simms	.50
72	Lawrence Taylor	1.00
73	Ronnie Lott	.50
74	Johnny Mitchell	.50
75	Rob Moore	.50
76	Browning Nagle	.50
77	Fred Barnett	.50
78	Randall Cunningham	1.00
79	Herschel Walker	.50
80	Gary Clark	.50
81	Ken Harvey	.50
82	Garrison Hearst	6.00
83	Ricky Proehl	.50
84	Barry Foster	1.00
85	Ernie Mills	.50
86	Neil O'Donnell	1.50
87	Stan Humpheries	1.50
88	Leslie O'Neil	.50
89	Junior Seau	2.00
90	Amp Lee	.50
91	Jerry Rice	7.00
92	Ricky Watters	2.00
93	Steve Young	7.00
94	Cortez Kennedy	.50
95	Rick Mirer	1.00
96	Eugene Robinson	.50
97	Chris Warren	1.00
98	John L. Williams	.50
99	Reggie Cobb	.50
100	Lawrence Dawsey	.50
101	Santana Dotson	.50
102	Courtney Hawkins	.50
103	Reggie Brooks	2.00
104	Ricky Ervins	.50
105	Desmond Howard	1.00
106	Art Monk	1.00
107	Mark Rypien	.50
108	Ricky Sanders	.50

1993 Pacific Triple Folders

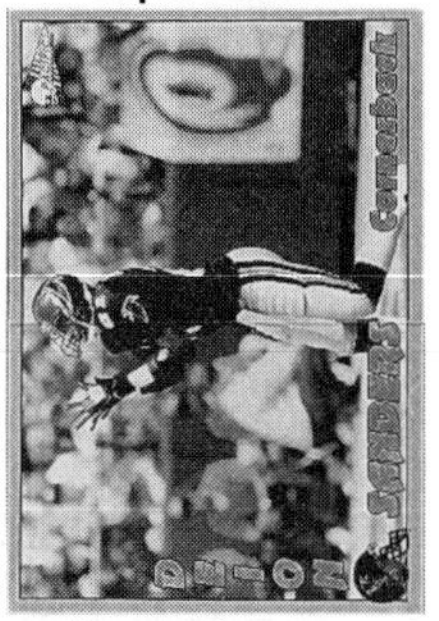

These cards feature two panels on the front which, when closed, form a color action photo of an NFL star player. The player's name and team helmet are on one panel; his position is printed on the other side. When opened up, the inside of the card panels reveal additional player photos. The card back is numbered and has 1992 statistics, a career summary, the player's name and team helmet, and position, all against a team color-coded marble-like background. Approximately 2,500 cases were produced.

		MT
Complete Set (30):		18.00
Common Player:		.45
1	Thurman Thomas	1.25
2	Carl Pickens	.75
3	Glyn Milburn	.75
4	Lorenzo White	.45
5	Anthony Johnson	.45
6	Joe Montana	3.50
7	Nick Bell	.45
8	Dan Marino	2.50
9	Anthony Carter	.45
10	Drew Bledsoe	3.00
11	Rob Moore	.75
12	Barry Foster	1.00
13	Stan Humphries	.75
14	Cortez Kennedy	.75
15	Rick Mirer	2.25
16	Deion Sanders	1.50
17	Curtis Conway	1.00
18	Tommy Vardell	.75
19	Emmitt Smith	4.50
20	Barry Sanders	2.50
21	Brett Favre	1.50
22	Cleveland Gary	.45
23	Morten Andersen	.45
24	Marcus Buckley	.45
25	Rodney Hampton	1.00
26	Herschel Walker	.75
27	Garrison Hearst	1.00
28	Jerry Rice	2.00
29	Lawrence Dawsey	.45
30	Desmond Howard	1.00

1993 Pacific Triple Folder Superstars

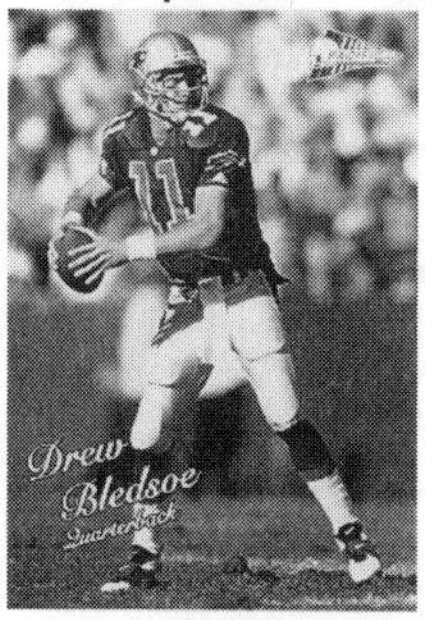

These 20 cards were randomly inserted into 1993 Pacific Triple Folder packs. Each card front has a borderless, full-color action photo, with the player's name in white letters at the bottom of the card. His position is also given. The back is numbered and has a player profile, along with the player's name, position and team helmet. The background uses the player's team colors. Some of the players featured in the set were rookies.

		MT
Complete Set (20):		20.00
Common Player:		.35
1	Troy Aikman	3.50
2	*Victor Bailey*	.50
3	*Jerome Bettis*	3.50
4	*Drew Bledsoe*	3.50
5	*Reggie Brooks*	1.25
6	*Derek Brown*	1.00
7	*Marcus Buckley*	.35
8	*Curtis Conway*	.75
9	Brett Favre	2.00
10	Barry Foster	.75
11	*Garrison Hearst*	.75
12	Cortez Kennedy	.50
13	*Rick Mirer*	.50
14	Joe Montana	4.00
15	Jerry Rice	2.50
16	Barry Sanders	2.50
17	Sterling Sharpe	1.50
18	Emmitt Smith	5.00
19	*Robert Smith*	.50
20	Thurman Thomas	1.00

1994 Pacific

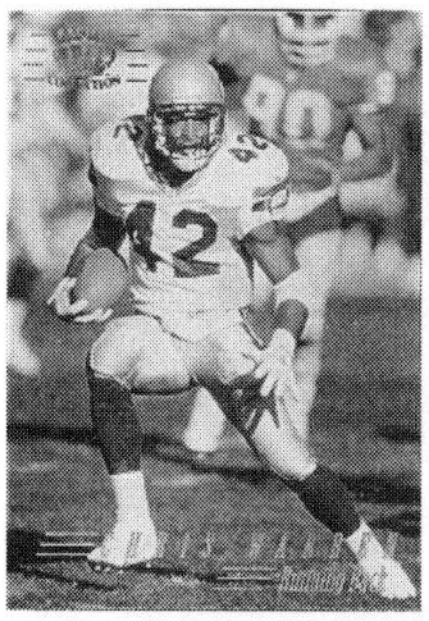

Crown Collection 1994 Football from Pacific Trading Cards contained 450 cards in the primary set, with three insert sets called Gems of the Crown, Crown Collection Crystalline and Knights of the Gridiron. There were only 7,000 of each insert set produced and a card from one of the three was inserted into each 12-card pack.

		MT
Complete Set (450):		28.00
Common Player:		.05
Pack (12):		1.25
Wax Box (36):		40.00
1	Troy Aikman	1.00
2	Charles Haley	.05
3	Alvin Harper	.05
4	Michael Irvin	.10
5	Jim Jeffcoat	.05
6	Daryl Johnston	.05
7	Robert Jones	.05
8	*Brock Marion*	.05
9	Russell Maryland	.05
10	Ken Norton	.05
11	Jay Novacek	.05
12	Emmitt Smith	2.00
13	Kevin Smith	.05
14	Tony Tolbert	.05
15	Kevin Williams	.40
16	Don Beebe	.05
17	Cornelius Bennett	.05
18	Bill Brooks	.05
19	Steve Christie	.05
20	Russell Copeland	.05
21	Kenneth Davis	.05
22	Kent Hull	.05
23	Jim Kelly	.10
24	Pete Metzelaars	.05
25	Andre Reed	.05
26	Frank Reich	.05
27	Bruce Smith	.05
28	Darryl Talley	.05
29	Steve Tasker	.05
30	Thurman Thomas	.10
31	Steve Bono	.20
32	Dexter Carter	.05
33	Kevin Fagan	.05
34	Dana Hall	.05
35	Brent Jones	.05
36	Amp Lee	.05
37	Marc Logan	.05
38	Tim McDonald	.05
39	Guy McIntyre	.05
40	Tom Rathman	.05
41	Jerry Rice	1.00
42	Dana Stubblefield	.05
43	Steve Wallace	.05
44	Ricky Watters	.10
45	Steve Young	1.00
46	Marcus Allen	.10
47	Kimble Anders	.05
48	Tim Barnett	.05
49	J.J. Birden	.05
50	Dale Carter	.05
51	Jonathan Hayes	.05
52	Dave Krieg	.05
53	Albert Lewis	.05
54	Nick Lowery	.05
55	Joe Montana	1.00
56	Neil Smith	.05
57	John Stephens	.05
58	Derrick Thomas	.10
59	Harvey Williams	.05
60	Michael Barrow	.05
61	Gary Brown	.05
62	Cody Carlson	.05
63	Ray Childress	.05
64	Curtis Duncan	.05
65	Ernest Givins	.05
66	Haywood Jeffires	.05
67	Wilber Marshall	.05
68	Bubba McDowell	.05
69	Warren Moon	.10
70	Mike Munchak	.05
71	Marcus Robertson	.05
72	Webster Slaughter	.05
73	*Gary Wellman*	.05
74	Lorenzo White	.05
75	Ray Crockett	.05
76	Jason Hanson	.05
77	Rodney Holman	.05
78	George Jamison	.05
79	Erik Kramer	.05
80	Ryan McNeil	.05
81	Derrick Moore	.05
82	Herman Moore	.50
83	Rodney Peete	.05
84	Brett Perriman	.05
85	Barry Sanders	1.25
86	Chris Spielman	.05
87	Pat Swilling	.05
88	Vernon Turner	.05
89	Andre Ware	.05
90	Michael Brooks	.05
91	Dave Brown	.05
92	Derek Brown	.05
93	Jarrod Bunch	.05
94	Chris Calloway	.05
95	Kent Graham	.05
96	Rodney Hampton	.10
97	Mark Jackson	.05
98	Ed McCaffrey	.05
99	Dave Meggett	.05
100	Aaron Pierce	.05
101	Mike Sherrard	.05
102	Phil Simms	.05
103	Lewis Tillman	.05
104	Eddie Anderson	.05
105	Patrick Bates	.05
106	Nick Bell	.05
107	Tim Brown	.10
108	Willie Gault	.05
109	Jeff Gossett	.05
110	Ethan Horton	.05
111	Jeff Hostetler	.05
112	Rocket Ismail	.05
113	Chester McGlockton	.05
114	Anthony Smith	.05
115	Steve Smith	.05
116	Greg Townsend	.05
117	Steve Wisniewski	.05
118	Alexander Wright	.05
119	Steve Atwater	.05
120	Rod Bernstine	.05
121	Mike Croel	.05
122	Shane Dronett	.05
123	Jason Elam	.05
124	John Elway	.30
125	Brian Habib	.05
126	Rondell Jones	.05
127	Tommy Maddox	.05
128	Karl Mecklenburg	.05
129	Glyn Milburn	.05
130	Derek Russell	.05
131	Shannon Sharpe	.05
132	Dennis Smith	.05
133	Edgar Bennett	.05
134	Tony Bennett	.05
135	Robert Brooks	.20
136	Terrell Buckley	.05
137	LeRoy Butler	.05
138	Mark Clayton	.05
139	Ty Detmer	.05
140	Brett Favre	2.00
141	*John Jurkovic*	.10
142	Bryce Paup	.05
143	Sterling Sharpe	.10
144	George Teague	.05
145	Darrell Thompson	.05
146	Ed West	.05
147	Reggie White	.10
148	Terry Allen	.05
149	Anthony Carter	.05
150	Cris Carter	.10
151	Roger Craig	.05
152	Jack Del Rio	.05
153	Chris Doleman	.05
154	*Scottie Graham*	.10
155	Eric Guliford	.05
156	Qadry Ismail	.10
157	Steve Jordan	.05
158	Randall McDaniel	.05
159	Jim McMahon	.05
160	Audray McMillian	.05
161	Sean Salisbury	.05
162	Robert Smith	.25
163	Henry Thomas	.05
164	Gary Anderson	.05
165	Deon Figures	.05
166	Barry Foster	.10
167	Jeff Graham	.05
168	Kevin Greene	.05
169	*Dave Hoffman*	.05
170	Merril Hoge	.05
171	Gary Jones	.05
172	Greg Lloyd	.05
173	Ernie Mills	.10
174	Neil O'Donnell	.10
175	Darren Perry	.05
176	Leon Searcy	.05
177	Leroy Thompson	.05
178	*Willie Williams*	.05
179	Rod Woodson	.05
180	Keith Byars	.05
181	Marco Coleman	.05
182	Bryan Cox	.05
183	Irving Fryar	.05
184	John Grimsley	.05
185	Mark Higgs	.05
186	Mark Ingram	.05
187	Keith Jackson	.05
188	Terry Kirby	.10
189	Dan Marino	2.00
190	O.J. McDuffie	.25
191	Scott Mitchell	.10
192	Pete Stoyanovich	.05
193	Troy Vincent	.05
194	Richmond Webb	.05
195	Brad Baxter	.05
196	Chris Burkett	.05
197	Rob Carpenter	.05
198	Boomer Esiason	.05
199	Johnny Johnson	.05
200	Jeff Lageman	.05
201	Mo Lewis	.05
202	Ronnie Lott	.05
203	Leonard Marshall	.05
204	Terance Mathis	.05
205	Johnny Mitchell	.05
206	Rob Moore	.05
207	Anthony Prior	.05
208	Blair Thomas	.05
209	Brian Washington	.05
210	Eric Bieniemy	.05
211	Marion Butts	.05
212	Gill Byrd	.05
213	John Carney	.05
214	Darren Carrington	.05
215	John Friesz	.05
216	Ronnie Harmon	.05
217	Stan Humphries	.05
218	Nate Lewis	.05
219	Natrone Means	.25
220	Anthony Miller	.05
221	Chris Mims	.05
222	Eric Moten	.05
223	Leslie O'Neal	.05
224	Junior Seau	.10
225	Morten Andersen	.05
226	Gene Atkins	.05
227	Derek Brown	.05
228	Toi Cook	.05
229	Vaughn Dunbar	.05
230	Quinn Early	.05
231	Reggie Freeman	.05
232	Tyrone Hughes	.05
233	Rickey Jackson	.05
234	Eric Martin	.05
235	Sam Mills	.05
236	Brad Muster	.05
237	Torrance Small	.05
238	Irv Smith	.05
239	Wade Wilson	.05
240	Eric Allen	.05
241	Victor Bailey	.05
242	Fred Barnett	.05
243	Mark Bavaro	.05
244	Bubby Brister	.05
245	Randall Cunningham	.05
246	Antone Davis	.05
247	*Britt Hager*	.05
248	Vaughn Hebron	.05
249	James Joseph	.05
250	Seth Joyner	.05
251	Rich Miano	.05
252	Heath Sherman	.05
253	Clyde Simmons	.05
254	Herschel Walker	.05
255	Calvin Williams	.05
256	Jerry Ball	.05
257	Mark Carrier	.05
258	Michael Jackson	.05
259	Mike Johnson	.05
260	James Jones	.05
261	Brian Kinchen	.05
262	Clay Matthews	.05
263	Eric Metcalf	.05
264	Stevon Moore	.05
265	Michael Dean Perry	.05
266	Todd Philcox	.05
267	Anthony Pleasant	.05
268	Vinny Testaverde	.05
269	Eric Turner	.05
270	Tommy Vardell	.05
271	Neal Anderson	.05
272	Trace Armstrong	.05
273	Mark Carrier	.05
274	Bob Christian	.05
275	Curtis Conway	.30
276	Richard Dent	.05
277	Robert Green	.05
278	Jim Harbaugh	.05
279	Craig Heyward	.05
280	Terry Obee	.05
281	Alonzo Spellman	.05
282	Tom Waddle	.05
283	Peter Tom Willis	.05
284	Donnell Woolford	.05
285	Tim Worley	.05
286	Chris Zorich	.05
287	Steve Broussard	.05
288	Darion Conner	.05
289	James Geathers	.05
290	Michael Haynes	.05
291	Bobby Hebert	.05
292	Lincoln Kennedy	.05
293	Chris Miller	.05
294	*David Mims*	.05
295	Erric Pegram	.05
296	Mike Pritchard	.05
297	Andre Rison	.10
298	Deion Sanders	.50
299	Chuck Smith	.05
300	Tony Smith	.05
301	Johnny Bailey	.05
302	Steve Beuerlein	.05
303	Chuck Cecil	.05
304	Chris Chandler	.05
305	Gary Clark	.05
306	*Rick Cunningham*	.05
307	Ken Harvey	.05
308	Garrison Hearst	.50
309	Randal Hill	.05
310	Robert Massey	.05
311	Ron Moore	.05
312	Ricky Proehl	.05
313	Eric Swann	.05
314	Aeneas Williams	.05
315	Michael Bates	.05
316	Brian Blades	.05
317	Carlton Gray	.05
318	*Paul Green*	.05
319	Patrick Hunter	.05
320	John Kasay	.05
321	Cortez Kennedy	.05
322	Kelvin Martin	.05
323	Dan McGwire	.05
324	Rick Mirer	.30
325	Eugene Robinson	.05
326	Rick Tuten	.05
327	Chris Warren	.15
328	John L. Williams	.05
329	Reggie Cobb	.05
330	Horace Copeland	.05
331	Lawrence Dawsey	.05
332	Santana Dotson	.05
333	Craig Erickson	.05
334	Ron Hall	.05
335	Courtney Hawkins	.05
336	Keith McCants	.05
337	Hardy Nickerson	.05
338	*Mazio Royster*	.05
339	Broderick Thomas	.05
340	*Casey Weldon*	.10
341	Mark Wheeler	.05
342	Vince Workman	.05
343	Willie Anderson	.05
344	Jerome Bettis	.30
345	*Richard Buchanan*	.05
346	Shane Conlan	.05
347	Troy Drayton	.05
348	Henry Ellard	.05
349	Jim Everett	.05
350	Cleveland Gary	.05
351	Sean Gilbert	.05
352	David Lang	.05
353	Todd Lyght	.05
354	*T.J. Rubley*	.10
355	Jackie Slater	.05
356	Russell White	.05
357	Bruce Armstrong	.05
358	Drew Bledsoe	1.00
359	Vincent Brisby	.05
360	Vincent Brown	.05
361	Ben Coates	.10
362	Marv Cook	.05
363	*Ray Crittenden*	.10
364	*Corey Croom*	.05
365	Pat Harlow	.05
366	Dion Lambert	.05
367	Greg McMurtry	.05
368	Leonard Russell	.05
369	Scott Secules	.05
370	Chris Slade	.05
371	Michael Timpson	.05
372	Kevin Turner	.05
373	Ashley Ambrose	.05
374	Dean Biasucci	.05
375	Duane Bickett	.05
376	Quentin Coryatt	.05
377	Rodney Culver	.05
378	*Sean Dawkins*	.25
379	Jeff George	.10
380	Jeff Herrod	.05
381	Jessie Hester	.05
382	Anthony Johnson	.05
383	Reggie Langhorne	.05
384	Roosevelt Potts	.05
385	*William Schultz*	.05
386	Rohn Stark	.05
387	Clarence Verdin	.05
388	Carl Banks	.05
389	Reggie Brooks	.10
390	Earnest Byner	.05
391	Tom Carter	.05
392	Cary Conklin	.05
393	*Pat Ellers*	.05
394	Ricky Ervins	.05
395	Rich Gannon	.05
396	Darrell Green	.05
397	Desmond Howard	.05
398	Chip Lohmiller	.05
399	*Sterling Palmer*	.05
400	Mark Rypien	.05
401	Ricky Sanders	.05
402	*Johnny Thomas*	.05
403	John Copeland	.05
404	Derrick Fenner	.05
405	Alex Gordon	.05
406	Harold Green	.05
407	Lance Gunn	.05
408	David Klingler	.05
409	Ricardo McDonald	.05
410	Tim McGee	.05
411	Reggie Rembert	.05
412	Patrick Robinson	.05
413	Jay Schroeder	.05
414	Erik Wilhelm	.05
415	Alfred Williams	.05
416	Darryl Williams	.05
417	*Sam Adams*	.10
418	*Mario Bates*	.10
419	*James Bostic*	.10
420	*Bucky Brooks*	.10
421	*Jeff Burris*	.10
422	*Shante Carver*	.10
423	*Jeff Cothran*	.05
424	*Lake Dawson*	.10
425	*Trent Dilfer*	2.00
426	*Marshall Faulk*	4.00
427	*Cory Fleming*	.10
428	*William Floyd*	.50
429	*Glenn Foley*	.75
430	*Rob Fredrickson*	.10
431	*Charles Garner*	2.00
432	*Greg Hill*	.50
433	*Charles Johnson*	.50
434	*Calvin Jones*	.10
435	*Jimmy Klingler*	.05
436	*Antonio Langham*	.10
437	*Kevin Lee*	.10
438	*Chuck Levy*	.10
439	*Willie McGinest*	.25
440	*Jamir Miller*	.10
441	*Johnnie Morton*	.30
442	*David Palmer*	.25
443	*Errict Rhett*	.75
444	*Cory Sawyer*	.10
445	*Darnay Scott*	1.00
446	*Heath Shuler*	.25
447	*Lamar Smith*	2.00
448	*Dan Wilkinson*	.10
449	*Bernard Williams*	.10
450	*Bryant Young*	.30

1994 Pacific Crystalline

Crown Collection Crystalline features an action shot of one of the top 20 running backs in the NFL. These cards are made of plastic and have a multi-color pattern on the left half of the card and clear plastic on the right half. The player's name is in the top-left corner, with his position under it and the Pacific Crown Collection logo under it. The player is positioned mostly on the clear side with a small portion of his body located over the pattern. The back features a close-up and stats on the pattern side and the reverse-angle player on the clear.

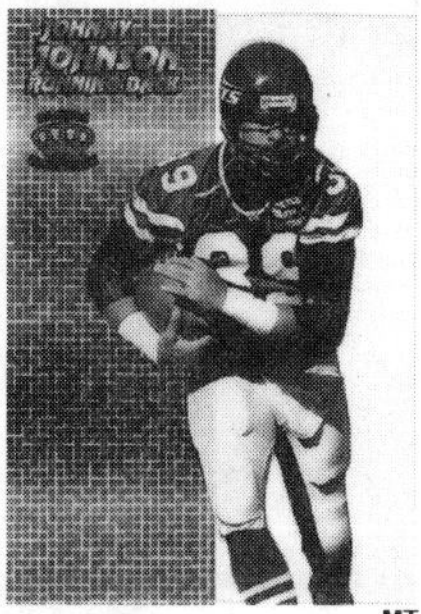

		MT
Complete Set (20):		80.00
Common Player:		2.00
1	Emmitt Smith	35.00
2	Jerome Bettis	7.00
3	Thurman Thomas	10.00
4	Erric Pegram	2.00
5	Barry Sanders	20.00
6	Leonard Russell	2.00
7	Rodney Hampton	6.00
8	Chris Warren	2.00
9	Reggie Brooks	3.00
10	Ron Moore	2.00
11	Gary Brown	2.00
12	Ricky Watters	6.00
13	Johnny Johnson	2.00
14	Rod Bernstine	2.00
15	Marcus Allen	2.00
16	Leroy Thompson	2.00
17	Marion Butts	2.00
18	Herschel Walker	2.00
19	Barry Foster	6.00
20	Roosevelt Potts	2.00

1994 Pacific Gems of the Crown

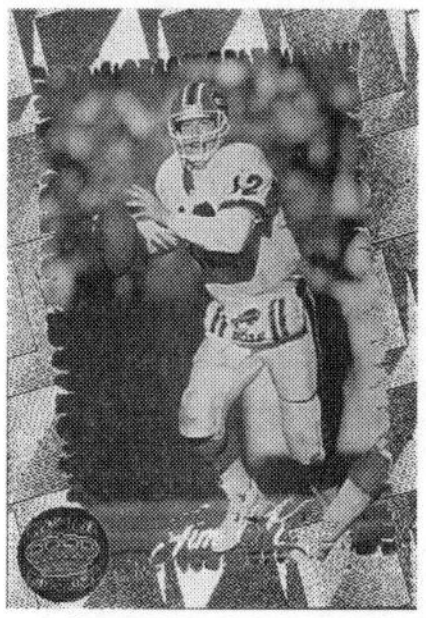

Gems of the Crown present a top offensive player on a card with an etched gold foil border. The Pacific logo appears in the bottom-left corner of this 20-card set, with the player name at the bottom in etched gold foil. The back contains a player close-up and a brief statistics, along with "Gems of the Crown" written across the top-right corner and card numbers in the opposite corner.

		MT
Complete Set (36):		140.00
Common Player:		2.00
Minor Stars:		4.00
1	Troy Aikman	10.00
2	Marcus Allen	4.00
3	Jerome Bettis	6.00
4	Drew Bledsoe	10.00
5	Reggie Brooks	2.00
6	Gary Brown	2.00
7	Tim Brown	4.00
8	Cody Carlson	2.00
9	John Elway	8.00
10	Boomer Esiason	2.00
11	Brett Favre	20.00
12	Rodney Hampton	4.00
13	Alvin Harper	2.00
14	Jeff Hostetler	2.00
15	Jim Kelly	4.00
16	Dan Marino	20.00
17	Eric Martin	2.00
18	O.J. McDuffie	2.00
19	Natrone Means	10.00
20	Rick Mirer	4.00
21	Joe Montana	15.00
22	Herman Moore	6.00
23	Ron Moore	2.00
24	Neil O'Donnell	4.00
25	Erric Pegram	2.00
26	Roosevelt Potts	2.00
27	Jerry Rice	10.00
28	Barry Sanders	12.00
29	Shannon Sharpe	2.00
30	Sterling Sharpe	4.00
31	Emmitt Smith	20.00
32	Thurman Thomas	4.00
33	Herschel Walker	2.00
34	Chris Warren	4.00
35	Ricky Watters	4.00
36	Steve Young	10.00

1994 Pacific Knights of the Gridiron

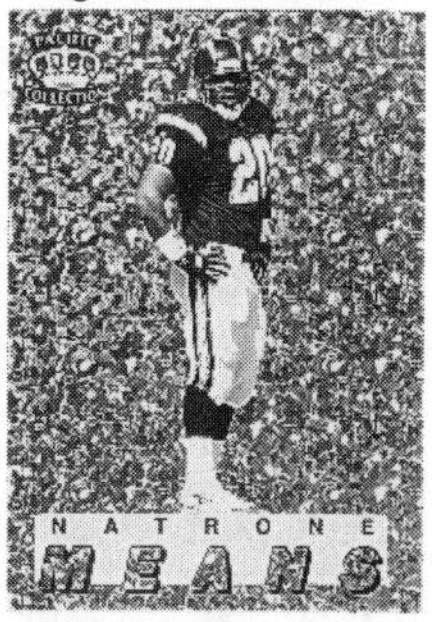

Knights of the Gridiron is a 20-card prism insert that showcases the top rookies and draft picks. Cards show an action-shot of the player with his name at the bottom. His first name is in a color box, depending on his team colors, and his last name is in gold prism and shadowed in a team color. The Pacific logo appears in the top left corner of this shiny gold prism card. The backs show a picture of the player with a large Pacific Crown Collection logo and Knight of the Gridiron, player name and team above the logo.

		MT
Complete Set (20):		130.00
Common Player:		3.00
Minor Stars:		6.00
1	Mario Bates	6.00
2	Jerome Bettis	6.00
3	Drew Bledsoe	16.00
4	Vincent Brisby	3.00
5	Reggie Brooks	3.00
6	Derek Brown	3.00
7	Jeff Burris	3.00
8	Trent Dilfer	6.00
9	Troy Drayton	3.00
10	Marshall Faulk	15.00
11	William Floyd	6.00
12	Rocket Ismail	3.00
13	Terry Kirby	3.00
14	Thomas Lewis	3.00
15	Natrone Means	6.00
16	Rick Mirer	6.00
17	David Palmer	3.00
18	Errict Rhett	6.00
19	Darnay Scott	6.00
20	Heath Shuler	3.00

1994 Pacific Marquee Prisms

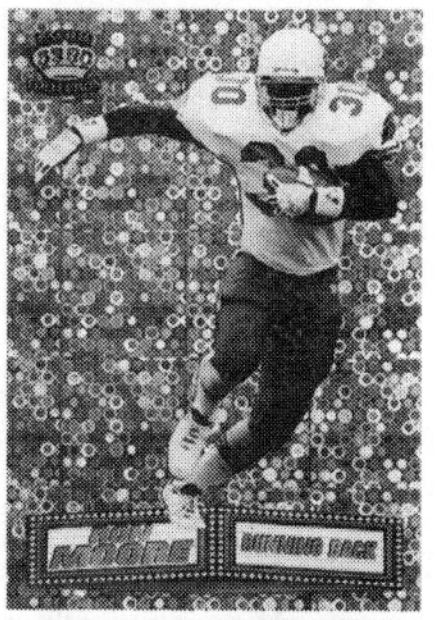

These 36 cards, produced in both silver and gold versions, feature several veteran and younger stars of the NFL. Each card front has a player photo superimposed over either a gold or silver foil background. The Crown Collection logo is in the upper left corner; the player's name and position are at the bottom in a marquee banner. The card back has a player photo on the left and a marquee billboard on the right which says "Now Appearing," followed by the player's name, position and team, plus a card number. A gold or silver card was issued in every pack of 1994 Pacific marquee prism, but gold cards were found at a ratio of only two per every box.

		MT
Complete Set (36):		35.00
Common Player:		.50
Minor Stars:		1.00
Complete Gold Set (36):		250.00
Gold Cards:		4x-8x
1	Troy Aikman	3.00
2	Marcus Allen	1.00
3	Jerome Bettis	1.00
4	Drew Bledsoe	3.00
5	Reggie Brooks	.50
6	Dave Brown	.50
7	Ben Coates	.50
8	Reggie Cobb	.50
9	Curtis Conway	1.00
10	John Elway	2.00
11	Marshall Faulk	3.00
12	Brett Favre	5.00
13	Barry Foster	.50
14	Rodney Hampton	1.00
15	Michael Irvin	1.00
16	Terry Kirby	.50
17	Dan Marino	5.00
18	Natrone Means	2.00

19	Rick Mirer	1.00
20	Joe Montana	3.00
21	Warren Moon	1.00
22	Ron Moore	.50
23	David Palmer	.50
24	Errict Rhett	2.00
25	Jerry Rice	3.00
26	Bucky Richardson	.50
27	Barry Sanders	3.00
28	Shannon Sharpe	.50
29	Sterling Sharpe	1.00
30	Heath Shuler	1.00
31	Emmitt Smith	5.00
32	Irving Spikes	.50
33	Thurman Thomas	1.00
34	Chris Warren	1.00
35	Ricky Watters	1.00
36	Steve Young	2.00

1994 Pacific Prisms

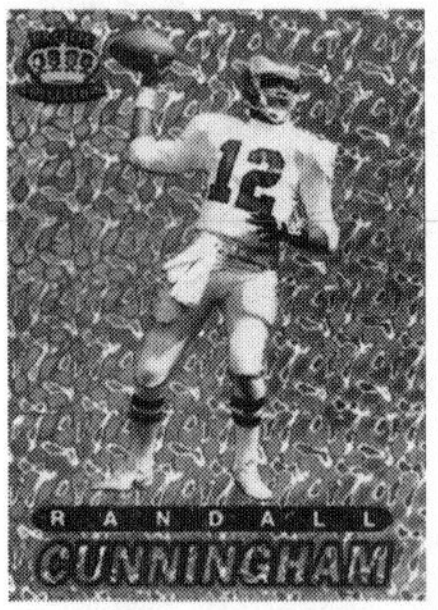

This set offers Pacific's splashy design and technology. The cards have full-color fronts and backs and are printed on a heavier card stock. Production is limited to a maximum of 2,999 individually-numbered 20-box cases. Four or five players from each team are represented in the set, which also includes top draft picks. The cards were done in silver versions (only 16,000 of each card were made) and gold versions (1,138 of each card). The borderless card front has an action photo superimposed on a prism-like background. The card back has the same cutout photo as the front, but the background is blurred. Gold versions are generally worth 4 to 7 times the value of the listed prices.

		MT
Complete Set (126):		160.00
Common Player:		.50
Comp. Gold Set (126):		700.00
Common Gold Player:		2.00
Unlisted Gold Stars:		2x-4x
Comp. Helmet Set (30):		5.00
Pack (1):		2.25
Wax Box (36):		70.00
1	Troy Aikman	10.00
2	Marcus Allen	1.00
3	Morten Andersen	.50
4	Fred Barnett	.50
5	*Mario Bates*	1.00
6	Edgar Bennett	.50
7	Rod Bernstine	.50
8	Jerome Bettis	3.00
9	Steve Beuerlein	.50
10	Brian Blades	.50
11	Drew Bledsoe	10.00
12	Vincent Brisby	1.00
13	Reggie Brooks	.50
14	Derek Brown	.50
15	Gary Brown	.50
16	Tim Brown	1.00
17	Marion Butts	.50
18	Keith Byars	.50
19	Cody Carlson	.50
20	Anthony Carter	.50
21	Tom Carter	.50
22	Gary Clark	.50
23	Ben Coates	1.00
24	Reggie Cobb	.50
25	Curtis Conway	1.50
26	John Copeland	.50
27	Randall Cunningham	.50
28	Willie Davis	.50
29	*Sean Dawkins*	1.50
30	Lawrence Dawsey	.50
31	Richard Dent	.50
32	*Trent Dilfer*	5.00
33	Troy Drayton	.50
34	Vaughn Dunbar	.50
35	Henry Ellard	.50
36	John Elway	5.00
37	Craig Erickson	.50
38	Boomer Esiason	.50
39	*Marshall Faulk*	10.00
40	Brett Favre	16.00
41	*William Floyd*	1.50
42	*Glenn Foley*	1.00
43	Barry Foster	.50
44	Irving Fryar	.50
45	Jeff George	1.00
46	*Scottie Graham*	1.50
47	Rodney Hampton	1.00
48	Jim Harbaugh	.50
49	Alvin Harper	.50
50	Courtney Hawkins	.50
51	Garrison Hearst	3.00
52	Vaughn Hebron	.50
53	*Greg Hill*	1.50
54	Jeff Hostetler	1.00
55	Michael Irvin	1.50
56	Qadry Ismail	.50
57	Rocket Ismail	.50
58	Anthony Johnson	.50
59	*Charles Johnson*	1.50
60	Johnny Johnson	.50
61	Brent Jones	.50
62	Kyle Clifton	.50
63	Jim Kelly	1.50
64	Cortez Kennedy	.50
65	Terry Kirby	1.00
66	David Klingler	.50
67	Erik Kramer	.50
68	Reggie Langhorne	.50
69	*Chuck Levy*	1.00
70	Dan Marino	16.00
71	O.J. McDuffie	1.50
72	Natrone Means	2.00
73	Eric Metcalf	.50
74	Glyn Milburn	.50
75	Anthony Miller	.50
76	Rick Mirer	2.00
77	Johnny Mitchell	.50
78	Scott Mitchell	1.00
79	Joe Montana	10.00
80	Warren Moon	1.00
81	Derrick Moore	.50
82	Herman Moore	4.00
83	Rob Moore	.50
84	Ron Moore	.50
85	*Johnnie Morton*	3.00
86	Neil O'Donnell	.50
87	*David Palmer*	1.00
88	Erric Pegram	.50
89	Carl Pickens	2.00
90	Anthony Pleasant	.50
91	Roosevelt Potts	.50
92	Mike Pritchard	.50
93	Andre Reed	1.00
94	*Errict Rhett*	2.00
95	Jerry Rice	10.00
96	Andre Rison	1.00
97	Greg Robinson	.50
98	T.J. Rubley	.50
99	Leonard Russell	.50
100	Barry Sanders	10.00
101	Deion Sanders	4.00
102	Ricky Sanders	.50
103	Junior Seau	2.00
104	Shannon Sharpe	1.50
105	Sterling Sharpe	1.50
106	*Heath Shuler*	1.00
107	Phil Simms	.50
108	Webster Slaughter	.50
109	Bruce Smith	.50
110	Emmitt Smith	16.00
111	Irv Smith	.50
112	Robert Smith	2.00
113	Vinny Testaverde	1.00
114	Derrick Thomas	1.00
115	Thurman Thomas	2.00
116	Leroy Thompson	.50
117	Lewis Tillman	.50
118	Michael Timpson	.50
119	Herschel Walker	.50
120	Chris Warren	1.50
121	Ricky Watters	2.00
122	Lorenzo White	.50
123	Reggie White	2.00
124	*Dan Wilkinson*	1.50
125	Kevin Williams	1.00
126	Steve Young	5.00

1994 Pacific Prisms Team Helmets

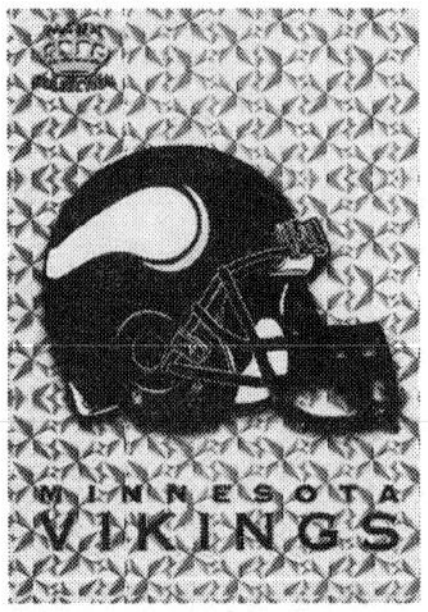

Each of these prism cards features the helmet of an NFL team on the card front, along with a team history and ghosted helmet on the back. The cards, which are numbered on the back (1 of 30, etc.) were random inserts in 1994 Pacific Prisms foil packs. The card front has a borderless prism-like background.

		MT
Complete Set (30):		2.50
Common Player:		.10
1	Arizona Cardinals	.10
2	Atlanta Falcons	.10
3	Buffalo Bills	.10
4	Carolina Panthers	.10
5	Chicago Bears	.10
6	Cincinnati Bengals	.10
7	Cleveland Browns	.10
8	Dallas Cowboys	.10
9	Denver Broncos	.10
10	Detroit Lions	.10
11	Green Bay Packers	.10
12	Houston Oilers	.10
13	Indianapolis Colts	.10
14	Jacksonville Jaguars	.10
15	Kansas City Chiefs	.10
16	Los Angeles Raiders	.10
17	Los Angeles Rams	.10
18	Miami Dolphins	.10
19	Minnesota Vikings	.10
20	New England Patriots	.10
21	New Orleans Saints	.10
22	New York Giants	.10
23	New York Jets	.10
24	Philadelphia Steelers	.10
25	Pittsburgh Steelers	.10
26	San Diego Chargers	.10
27	San Francisco 49ers	.10
28	Seattle Seahawks	.10
29	Tampa Bay Buccaneers	.10
30	Washington Redskins	.10

1994 Pacific Prisms Gold

The 126-card, regular-sized cards are a parallel to the base prism issue. Only 10 percent of the total print run were produced in gold foil.

	MT
Complete Set (126):	900.00
Common Player:	2.50
Veteran Stars:	2.5x-5x
Young Stars/RCs:	1.5x-3x

1994 Pacific Triple Folders

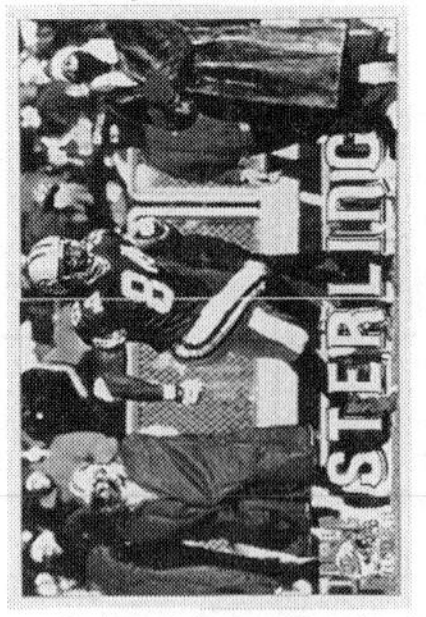

Each card in the 33-card set measures 3-1/2" x 5" when folded, features color photos on all panels. The front panels can be closed and merged into a single action photo. The set, arranged into alphabetical order by teams, was limited to a production run of less than 3,000.

		MT
Complete Set (33):		20.00
Common Player:		.50
1	Ron Moore	.50
2	Erric Pegram	.50
3	Jim Kelly	.75
4	Thurman Thomas	.75
5	Curtis Conway	1.00
6	Vinny Testaverde	.50
7	Troy Aikman	1.75
8	Emmitt Smith	3.00
9	John Elway	1.00
10	Shannon Sharpe	.50
11	Barry Sanders	1.75
12	Brett Favre	3.00
13	Sterling Sharpe	.75
14	Gary Brown	.50
15	Marshall Faulk	1.50
16	Joe Montana	2.00
17	Rocket Ismail	.75
18	Jerome Bettis	1.00
19	Dan Marino	3.00
20	David Palmer	.50
21	Drew Bledsoe	2.00
22	Ben Coates	.75
23	Derrick Ned	.50
24	Rodney Hampton	.75
25	Boomer Esiason	.50
26	Barry Foster	.50
27	Charles Johnson	.50
28	Natrone Means	1.00
29	Steve Young	1.50
30	Rick Mirer	.75
31	Chris Warren	.75
32	Trent Dilfer	1.00
33	Heath Shuler	1.50

1994 Pacific Triple Folders Rookies/Stars

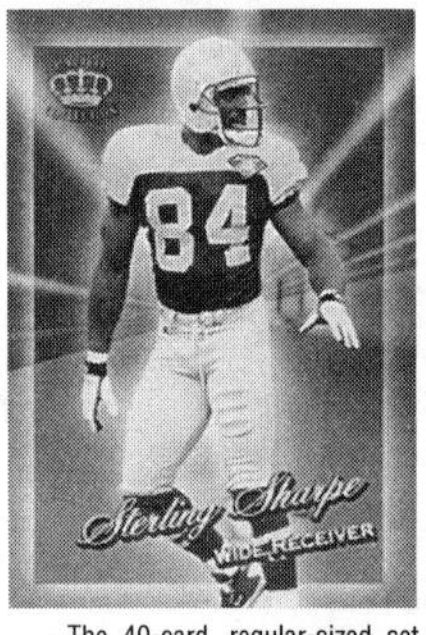

The 40-card, regular-sized set was randomly inserted in Triple Folder packs. The fronts feature color action shots with the player's name and position in gold-foil on the card bottom.

		MT
Complete Set (40):		20.00
Common Player:		.30
1	Ronald Moore	.30
2	Jeff George	.50
3	Jim Kelly	.50
4	Thurman Thomas	.50
5	Curtis Conway	.75
6	Darnay Scott	.60
7	Vinny Testaverde	.30
8	Troy Aikman	1.50
9	Emmitt Smith	3.00
10	John Elway	1.00
11	Shannon Sharpe	.30
12	Barry Sanders	1.50
13	LeShon Johnson	.30
14	Sterling Sharpe	.50
15	Gary Brown	.30
16	Marshall Faulk	1.00
17	Lake Dawson	.30
18	Greg Hill	.60
19	Joe Montana	2.00
20	Tim Brown	.50
21	Jerome Bettis	.60
22	Dan Marino	3.00
23	Terry Allen	.50
24	David Palmer	.30
25	Drew Bledsoe	1.75
26	Ben Coates	.50
27	Michael Haynes	.30
28	Rodney Hampton	.30
29	Thomas Lewis	.30
30	Aaron Glenn	.30
31	Charlie Garner	.30
32	Charles Johnson	.30
33	Byron "Bam" Morris	.50
34	Natrone Means	.75
35	Ricky Watters	.50
36	Steve Young	1.25
37	Rick Mirer	.60
38	Trent Dilfer	1.00
39	Errict Rhett	2.00
40	Heath Shuler	1.50

1995 Pacific

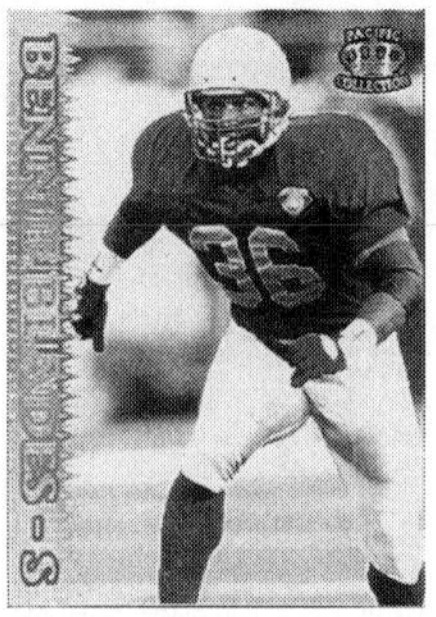

Pacific's 1995 Crown Collection set includes 450 cards, each using double-etched foil technology and etched gold foil. A 40-card subset features the season's top rookie draft picks. Two parallel sets were also created - a hobby only Royal Platinum Pt and a retail only Techn-Chrome Cr (both sets' cards were randomly included nine per every 37 packs). The regular card design has a gold-foiled panel which includes the player's name and position outlined in his team's colors. A full-bleed color photo is on the right, with the Pacific Crown Collection in the upper right. The card back has the player's name at the top, along with a mug shot, position, biographical information and a brief profile. Complete yearly statistics are also included on the back, which incorporates a team logo and the team's colors into the background. Seven insert sets were produced: Gems of the Crown; Gold Die-Cut Crown; Rookies 95; Young Warriors; G-Force; Hometown Heroes; and Cramer's Choice Awards.

		MT
Complete Set (450):		25.00
Common Player:		.05
Minor Stars:		.10
Comp. Platinum Set (450):		150.00
Platinum Cards:		3x-6x
Pack (12):		1.50
Wax Box (36):		50.00
1	Randy Baldwin	.05
2	Tommy Barnhardt	.05
3	Tim McKyer	.05
4	Sam Mills	.05
5	Brian O'Neal	.05
6	Frank Reich	.05
7	Jack Trudeau	.05
8	Vernon Turner	.05
9	*Kerry Collins*	1.00
10	Shawn King	.10
11	Steve Beuerlein	.05
12	Derek Brown	.05
13	Reggie Clark	.10
14	Reggie Cobb	.05
15	Desmond Howard	.05
16	Jeff Lageman	.05
17	Kelvin Pritchett	.05
18	Cedric Tillman	.05
19	*Tony Boselli*	.20
20	*James Stewart*	1.50
21	Eric Davis	.05
22	William Floyd	.30
23	Elvis Grbac	.05
24	Brent Jones	.05
25	Ken Norton Jr.	.05
26	Bart Oates	.05
27	Jerry Rice	.75
28	Deion Sanders	.40
29	John Taylor	.05
30	*Adam Walker*	.10
31	Steve Wallace	.05
32	Ricky Watters	.15
33	Lee Woodall	.05
34	Bryant Young	.05
35	Steve Young	.75
36	*J.J. Stokes*	1.00
37	Troy Aikman	.50
38	Larry Allen	.05
39	Chris Boniol	.05
40	Lincoln Coleman	.05
41	Charles Haley	.05
42	Alvin Harper	.10
43	Chad Hennings	.05
44	Michael Irvin	.20
45	Daryl Johnston	.05
46	Leon Lett	.05
47	Nate Newton	.05
48	Jay Novacek	.05
49	Emmitt Smith	2.00
50	James Washington	.05
51	Kevin Williams	.05
52	*Sherman Williams*	.30
53	Barry Foster	.05
54	Eric Green	.05
55	Kevin Greene	.05
56	Andre Hastings	.05
57	Charles Johnson	.20
58	Greg Lloyd	.05
59	Ernie Mills	.05
60	Byron "Bam" Morris	.10
61	Neil O'Donnell	.10
62	Darren Perry	.05
63	*Yancey Thigpen*	.50
64	Mike Tomczak	.05
65	John L. Williams	.05
66	Rod Woodson	.05
67	*Mark Bruener*	.30
68	*Kordell Stewart*	4.00
69	Jeff Brohm	.10
70	Andre Coleman	.05
71	Rueben Davis	.05
72	Dennis Gibson	.05
73	Darrien Gordon	.05
74	Stan Humphries	.15
75	Shawn Jefferson	.05
76	Tony Martin	.05
77	Natrone Means	.40
78	Shannon Mitchell	.10
79	Leslie O'Neal	.05
80	Alfred Pupunu	.05
81	Stanley Richard	.05
82	Junior Seau	.10
83	Mark Seay	.05
84	Derrick Alexander	.20
85	Carl Banks	.05
86	Issac Booth	.10
87	Rob Burnett	.05
88	Earnest Byner	.05
89	Steve Everitt	.05
90	Leroy Hoard	.05
91	Pepper Johnson	.05
92	Antonio Langham	.05
93	Eric Metcalf	.05
94	Anthony Pleasant	.05
95	Frank Stams	.05
96	Vinny Testaverde	.05
97	Eric Turner	.05
98	Mike Miller	.10
99	Craig Powell	.05
100	Gene Atkins	.05
101	Aubrey Beavers	.05
102	Tim Bowens	.05
103	Keith Byars	.05
104	Bryan Cox	.05
105	Aaron Craver	.05
106	Jeff Cross	.05
107	Irving Fryar	.05
108	Dan Marino	2.00
109	O.J. McDuffie	.05
110	Bernie Parmalee	.20
111	James Saxon	.05
112	Keith Sims	.05
113	Irving Spikes	.05
114	Pete Mitchell	.10
115	Terry Allen	.05
116	Cris Carter	.10
117	Adrian Cooper	.05
118	Bernard Dafney	.05
119	Jack Del Rio	.05
120	Vencie Glenn	.05
121	Qadry Ismail	.05
122	Carlos Jenkins	.05
123	Andrew Jordan	.05
124	Ed McDaniel	.05
125	Warren Moon	.10
126	David Palmer	.05
127	John Randle	.05
128	Jake Reed	.05
129	Derrick Alexander	.15
130	*Chad May*	.30
131	Korey Stringer	.10
132	Bruce Armstrong	.05
133	Drew Bledsoe	1.00
134	Vincent Brisby	.05
135	Troy Brown	.10
136	Vincent Brown	.05
137	Marion Butts	.05
138	Ben Coates	.05
139	Ray Crittenden	.05
140	Maurice Hurst	.05
141	Aaron Jones	.05
142	Willie McGinest	.05
143	Marty Moore	.10
144	Mike Pitts	.05
145	Leroy Thompson	.05
146	Michael Timpson	.05
147	Bennie Blades	.05
148	Jocelyn Borgella	.05
149	Anthony Carter	.05
150	Willie Clay	.05
151	Mel Gray	.05
152	Mike Johnson	.05
153	Dave Kreig	.05
154	Robert Massey	.05
155	Scott Mitchell	.10
156	Herman Moore	.10
157	Johnnie Morton	.05
158	Barry Sanders	1.25
159	Chris Spielman	.05
160	Broderick Thomas	.05
161	Cory Schlesinger	.10
162	Marcus Allen	.10
163	Donnell Bennett	.05
164	J.J. Birden	.05
165	Matt Blundin	.15
166	Steve Bono	.15
167	Dale Carter	.05
168	Lake Dawson	.20
169	Ron Dickerson	.05
170	Lin Elliott	.05
171	Jaime Fields	.05
172	Greg Hill	.20
173	Danan Hughes	.05
174	Neil Smith	.05
175	*Steve Stenstrom*	.20
176	Edgar Bennett	.05
177	Robert Brooks	.05
178	Mark Brunell	.75
179	Doug Evans	.05
180	Brett Favre	2.00
181	Corey Harris	.05
182	LeShon Johnson	.05
183	Sean Jones	.05
184	Lenny McGill	.10
185	Terry Mickens	.05
186	Sterling Sharpe	.10
187	Joe Sims	.05
188	Darrell Thompson	.05
189	Reggie White	.15
190	Craig Newsome	.15
191	Tim Brown	.10
192	Vince Evans	.05
193	Rob Fredrickson	.05
194	*Andrew Glover*	.10
195	Jeff Hostetler	.10
196	Raghib Ismail	.05
197	Jeff Jaeger	.05
198	James Jett	.05
199	Chester McGlockton	.05
200	Don Mosebar	.05
201	Tom Rathman	.05
202	Harvey Williams	.05
203	Steve Wisniewski	.05
204	Alexander Wright	.05
205	*Napoleon Kaufman*	2.00
206	Trace Armstrong	.05
207	Curtis Conway	.10
208	Raymont Harris	.05
209	Erik Kramer	.05
210	Nate Lewis	.05
211	*Shane Matthews*	2.00
212	John Thierry	.05
213	Lewis Tillman	.05
214	Tom Waddle	.05
215	Steve Walsh	.05
216	James Williams	.05
217	Donnell Woolford	.05
218	Chris Zorich	.05
219	*Rashaan Salaam*	.50
220	John Booty	.05
221	Michael Brooks	.05
222	Dave Brown	.05
223	Chris Calloway	.05
224	Gary Downs	.10
225	Kent Graham	.05
226	Keith Hamilton	.05
227	Rodney Hampton	.05
228	Brian Kozlowski	.15
229	Thomas Lewis	.05
230	Dave Meggett	.05
231	Aaron Pierce	.05
232	Mike Sherrard	.05
233	Phillippi Sparks	.05
234	*Tyrone Wheatley*	.40
235	Trev Alberts	.05
236	Aaron Bailey	.05
237	Jason Belser	.05
238	Tony Bennett	.05
239	Kerry Cash	.05
240	Marshall Faulk	1.00
241	Stephen Grant	.10
242	Jeff Herrod	.05
243	Ronald Humphrey	.10
244	Kirk Lowdermilk	.05
245	Don Majkowski	.05
246	Tony McCoy	.05
247	Floyd Turner	.05
248	Lamont Warren	.05
249	Zack Crockett	.10
250	Michael Bankston	.05
251	Larry Centers	.05
252	Gary Clark	.05
253	Ed Cunningham	.05
254	Garrison Hearst	.10
255	Eric Hill	.05
256	Terry Irving	.05
257	Lorenzo Lynch	.05
258	Jamir Miller	.05
259	Ron Moore	.05
260	Terry Samuels	.10
261	Jay Schroeder	.05
262	Eric Swann	.05
263	Aeneas Williams	.05
264	*Frank Sanders*	.75
265	Morten Andersen	.05
266	Mario Bates	.20
267	Derek Brown	.05
268	Darion Conner	.05
269	Quinn Early	.05
270	Jim Everett	.10
271	Michael Haynes	.05
272	Wayne Martin	.05
273	Derrell Mitchell	.10
274	Lorenzo Neal	.05
275	Jimmy Spencer	.05
276	Winfred Tubbs	.05
277	Renaldo Turnbull	.05
278	Jeff Uhlenhake	.05
279	Steve Atwater	.05
280	Keith Burns	.10
281	Butler By'not'e	.15
282	Jeff Campbell	.05
283	Derrick Clark	.10
284	Shane Dronett	.05
285	Jason Elam	.05
286	John Elway	.30
287	Jerry Evans	.10
288	Karl Mecklenburg	.05
289	Glyn Milburn	.05
290	Anthony Miller	.05
291	Tom Rouen	.05
292	Leonard Russell	.05
293	Shannon Sharpe	.05
294	Steve Russ	.10
295	Mel Agee	.05
296	Lester Archambeau	.05
297	Bert Emanuel	.20
298	Jeff George	.10
299	Craig Heyward	.05
300	Bobby Hebert	.05
301	D.J. Johnson	.05
302	Mike Kenn	.05
303	Terance Mathis	.05
304	Clay Matthews	.05
305	Erric Pegram	.05
306	Andre Rison	.10
307	Chuck Smith	.05
308	Jessie Tuggle	.05
309	Lorenzo Styles	.10
310	Cornelius Bennett	.05
311	Bill Brooks	.05
312	Jeff Burris	.05
313	Carwell Gardner	.05
314	Kent Hull	.05
315	Yonel Jourdain	.15
316	Jim Kelly	.10
317	Vince Marrow	.05
318	Pete Metzelaars	.05
319	Andre Reed	.05
320	Kurt Schulz	.05
321	Bruce Smith	.05
322	Darryl Talley	.05
323	Matt Darby	.05
324	Justin Armour	.10
325	*Todd Collins*	.30
326	David Alexander	.05
327	Eric Allen	.05
328	Fred Barnett	.05
329	Randall Cunningham	.05
330	William Fuller	.05
331	Charlie Garner	.05
332	Vaughn Hebron	.05
333	James Joseph	.05
334	Bill Romanowski	.05
335	Ken Rose	.05
336	Jeff Snyder	.05
337	William Thomas	.05
338	Herschel Walker	.05
339	Calvin Williams	.05
340	*Dave Barr*	.25

341 Chidi Ahanotu .05
342 Barney Bussey .05
343 Horace Copeland .05
344 Trent Dilfer .40
345 Craig Erickson .05
346 Paul Gruber .05
347 Courtney Hawkins .05
348 Lonnie Marts .05
349 Martin Mayhew .05
350 Hardy Nickerson .05
351 Errict Rhett .50
352 Lamar Thomas .05
353 Charles Wilson .05
354 Vince Workman .05
355 Derrick Brooks .20
356 *Warren Sapp* .75
357 Sam Adams .05
358 Michael Bates .05
359 Brian Blades .05
360 Carlton Gray .05
361 Bill Hitchcock .05
362 Cortez Kennedy .05
363 Rick Mirer .30
364 Eugene Robinson .05
365 Michael Sinclair .05
366 Steve Smith .05
367 Bob Spitulski .05
368 Rick Tuten .05
369 Chris Warren .10
370 Terrence Warren .10
371 *Christian Fauria* .10
372 *Joey Galloway* 2.00
373 Boomer Esiason .05
374 Aaron Glenn .05
375 Victor Green .10
376 Johnny Johnson .05
377 Mo Lewis .05
378 Ronnie Lott .05
379 Nick Lowery .05
380 Johnny Mitchell .05
381 Rob Moore .05
382 Adrian Murrell .05
383 Anthony Prior .05
384 Brian Washington .05
385 Matt Willig .05
386 *Kyle Brady* .25
387 Willie Anderson .05
388 Johnny Bailey .05
389 Jerome Bettis .25
390 Isaac Bruce .30
391 Shane Conlan .05
392 Troy Drayton .05
393 D'Marco Farr .05
394 Jessie Hester .05
395 Todd Kinchen .05
396 Ron Middleton .05
397 Chris Miller .05
398 Marquez Pope .05
399 Robert Young .05
400 Tony Zendejas .05
401 *Kevin Carter* .20
402 Reggie Brooks .05
403 Tom Carter .05
404 Andre Collins .05
405 Pat Eilers .05
406 Henry Ellard .05
407 Ricky Ervins .05
408 Gus Frerotte .25
409 Ken Harvey .05
410 Jim Lachey .05
411 Brian Mitchell .05
412 Reggie Roby .05
413 Heath Shuler .50
414 Tyronne Stowe .05
415 Tydus Winans .05
416 Cory Raymer .05
417 *Michael Westbrook* 1.00
418 *Jeff Blake* .50
419 Steve Broussard .05
420 Dave Cadigan .05
421 Jeff Cothran .05
422 Derrick Fenner .05
423 James Francis .05
424 Lee Johnson .05
425 Louis Oliver .05
426 Carl Pickens .20
427 Jeff Query .05
428 Corey Sawyer .05
429 Darnay Scott .30
430 Dan Wilkinson .05
431 Alfred Williams .05
432 *Ki-Jana Carter* .50
433 David Dunn .15
434 *John Walsh* .25
435 Gary Brown .05
436 Pat Carter .05
437 Ray Childress .05
438 Ernest Givins .05
439 Haywood Jeffires .05
440 Lamar Lathon .05
441 Bruce Matthews .05
442 Marcus Robertson .05
443 Eddie Robinson .05
444 *Malcolm Seabron* .10
445 Webster Slaughter .05
446 Al Smith .05
447 Billy Joe Tolliver .05
448 Lorenzo White .05
449 *Steve McNair* 3.00
450 *Rodney Thomas* .20

1995 Pacific Blue/Platinum

The two, 450-card card parallel sets were inserted every 37 packs (blue in retail, platinum in hobby).

	MT
Complete Set (45):	225.00
Common Player:	.30
Veteran Stars:	3x-6x
Young Stars:	2x-4x
RCs:	1.5x-3x

1995 Pacific Cramer's Choice

These 1995 Pacific Crown Collection inserts feature six top NFL players in six different categories, as selected by Pacific President and CEO Michael Cramer. The die-cut cards, done in a trophy design, were seeded one per every 720 packs. The front has a marble-like base which includes the Crown logo and designation of the award, plus who won it. The player photo appears in the middle of the metallic silver pyramid design, with another Crown Collection logo at the top of the point. The card back is marble-like, with an extensive quote from Cramer about the player. A small closeup shot is also provided, as is a card number, which uses a "CC" prefix.

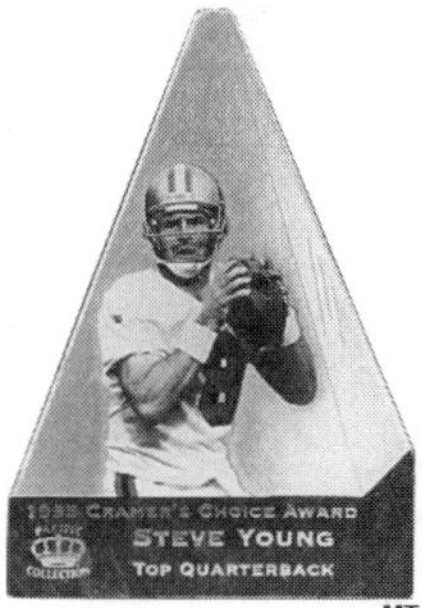

		MT
Complete Set (6):		750.00
Common Player:		50.00
1	Ki-Jana Carter	50.00
2	Emmitt Smith	200.00
3	Marshall Faulk	75.00
4	Jerry Rice	125.00
5	Deion Sanders	75.00
6	Steve Young	125.00

1995 Pacific Gems of the Crown

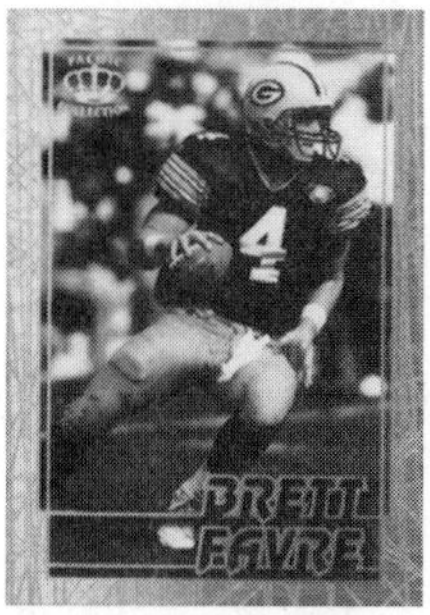

These 36 insert cards feature a color photo on the front, etched by a gold frame. The Pacific Crown Collection logo is in the upper right corner; the player's name is in the bottom right corner, with gold foil outlining the letters. The horizontal back has a closeup shot of the player on the left, with his name, position and team name underneath. On the right is a paragraph summarizing the player's career, plus an insert set logo and a card number (using a GC prefix). Cards were random inserts, two per every 37 packs of 1995 Pacific Crown Collection football.

		MT
Complete Set (36):		180.00
Common Player:		3.00
1	Jim Kelly	5.00
2	Kerry Collins	6.00
3	Darnay Scott	3.00
4	Jeff Blake	6.00
5	Terry Allen	3.00
6	Emmitt Smith	16.00
7	Michael Irvin	5.00
8	Troy Aikman	10.00
9	John Elway	7.00
10	Dave Krieg	3.00
11	Barry Sanders	15.00
12	Brett Favre	16.00
13	Marshall Faulk	8.00
14	Marcus Allen	5.00
15	Tim Brown	3.00
16	Bernie Parmalee	3.00
17	Dan Marino	16.00
18	Cris Carter	3.00
19	Drew Bledsoe	10.00
20	Mario Bates	3.00
21	Rodney Hampton	3.00
22	Ben Coates	3.00
23	Charles Johnson	5.00
24	Byron "Bam" Morris	5.00
25	Stan Humphries	3.00
26	Deion Sanders	6.00
27	Jerry Rice	10.00
28	Ricky Watters	5.00
29	Steve Young	10.00
30	Natrone Means	6.00
31	William Floyd	5.00
32	Chris Warren	5.00
33	Rick Mirer	5.00
34	Jerome Bettis	5.00
35	Errict Rhett	3.00
36	Heath Shuler	5.00

1995 Pacific G-Force

Ten of the NFL's top running backs are featured on these insert cards, randomly included one per every 37 packs of Pacific's 1995 Crown Collection football. The card front has a color photo of the player against a black background which includes several starbursts, plus the number of yards he gained rushing in 1994. "G-Force" is written at the top of the card; the player's name is at the bottom. The card back has a similar design for the background, with a closeup shot of the player in the upper right corner. His name, team name and card number, using a "GF" prefix, are to the left of the photo. A paragraph recapping the player's 1994 accomplishments is featured in the middle of the card.

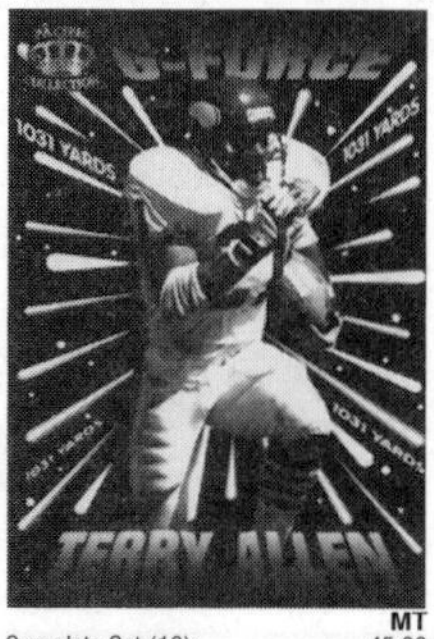

		MT
Complete Set (10):		45.00
Common Player:		2.00
1	Marcus Allen	3.00
2	Terry Allen	2.00
3	Emmitt Smith	12.00
4	Barry Sanders	10.00
5	Marshall Faulk	6.00
6	Rodney Hampton	2.00
7	Natrone Means	3.00
8	Chris Warren	3.00
9	Jerome Bettis	3.00
10	Errict Rhett	2.00

1995 Pacific Gold Crown Die-Cuts

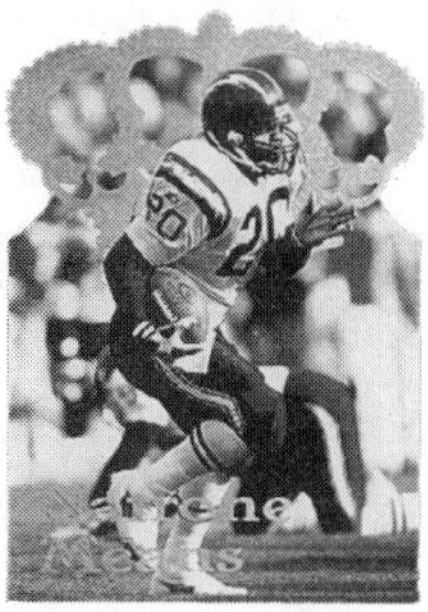

These 36 insert cards could be randomly found two per every 37 packs of 1995 Pacific Crown Collection football. The cards, numbered on the back using a "DC" prefix, feature a full-bleed color action photo on the front, with a die-cut foiled crown at the top. The player's name is at the bottom in foil.

		MT
Complete Set (20):		375.00
Common Player:		7.00
Comp. Flat Gold Set (20):		700.00
Flat Gold Cards:		1x-2x
1	Ki-Jana Carter	7.00
2	Michael Irvin	7.00
3	Emmitt Smith	50.00
4	Troy Aikman	25.00
5	John Elway	15.00
6	Barry Sanders	35.00
7	Marshall Faulk	25.00
8	Dan Marino	50.00
9	Ben Coates	7.00
10	Drew Bledsoe	25.00
11	Byron "Bam" Morris	7.00
12	Jerry Rice	25.00
13	William Floyd	7.00
14	Steve Young	25.00
15	Natrone Means	10.00
16	Deion Sanders	16.00
17	Rick Mirer	7.00
18	Chris Warren	7.00
19	Jerome Bettis	7.00
20	Errict Rhett	7.00

1995 Pacific Hometown Heroes

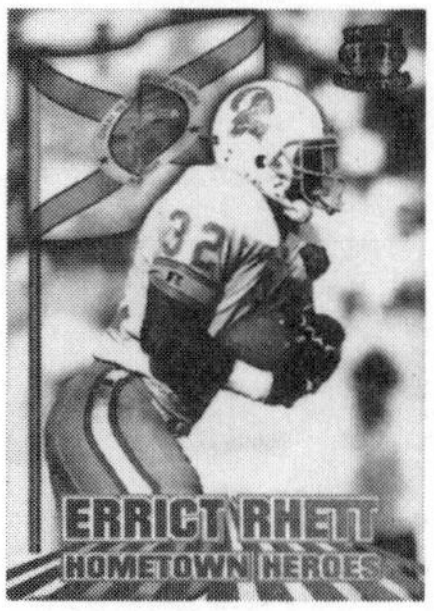

These insert cards feature 10 top NFL stars and pay tribute to the players' hometown. Each card front has a color photo of the player, with his hometown's state flag flying on the left side. His name and "Hometown Hereos" are written in foil at the bottom of the card. The horizontal card back has two photos - one a close-up, the other an action photo of the player framed by the borders of his state. A star is used to pinpoint his city's location on the map. A banner at the top of the card includes the insert set's name, with a recap of where the player started his football career. Cards, randomly included one per every 37 packs of Pacific Crown Collection football, are numbered with an "HH" prefix.

		MT
Complete Set (10):		50.00
Common Player:		3.00
1	Emmitt Smith	12.00
2	Troy Aikman	6.00
3	Barry Sanders	6.00
4	Marshall Faulk	3.00
5	Dan Marino	12.00
6	Drew Bledsoe	6.00
7	Natrone Means	3.00
8	Steve Young	6.00
9	Jerry Rice	6.00
10	Errict Rhett	3.00

1995 Pacific Rookies

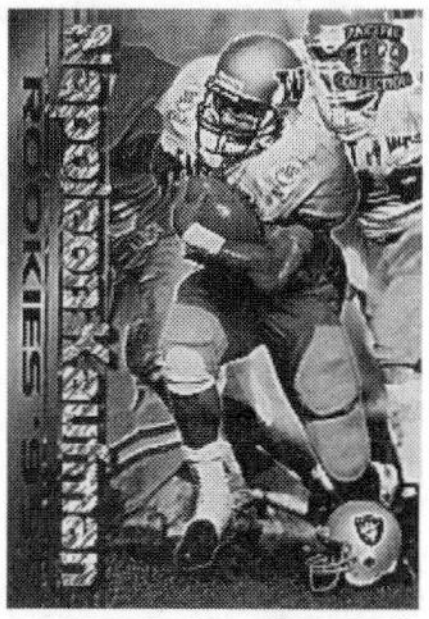

Inserted into 1995 Pacific Crown Collection football packs at a rate of two per every 37 packs, these 20 cards feature top rookies of 1995. The card front has a color photo of the player in his college uniform, with his name in silver foil running down the left side. "Rookies '95" is also written along the side. A football helmet of the team which drafted the player is in the lower right corner. The card back has another photo of the player in the upper left, with his pro team's helmet on the right. The player's name runs across the center of the card, just above a paragraph which summarizes his skills.

		MT
Complete Set (20):		50.00
Common Player:		2.00
1	Dave Barr	2.00
2	Kyle Brady	2.00
3	Mark Bruener	2.00
4	Ki-Jana Carter	2.00
5	Kerry Collins	5.00
6	Todd Collins	2.00
7	Christian Fauria	2.00
8	Joey Galloway	3.00
9	Chris Jones	2.00
10	Napoleon Kaufman	5.00
11	Chad May	2.00
12	Steve McNair	6.00
13	Rashaan Salaam	2.00
14	Warren Sapp	3.00
15	James Stewart	3.00
16	Kordell Stewart	8.00
17	J.J. Stokes	2.00
18	Michael Westbrook	2.00
19	Tyrone Wheatley	2.00
20	Sherman Williams	2.00

1995 Pacific Young Warriors

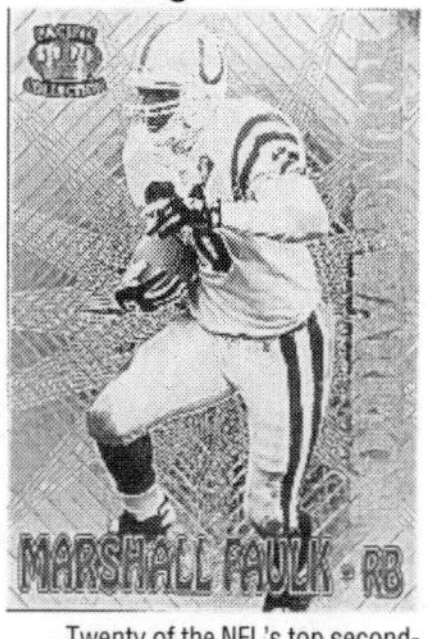

Twenty of the NFL's top second-year stars are featured on these 1995 Pacific Crown Collection inserts. The card front is full gold foil, with "Young Warrior" written down the right side of the card. The Pacific logo is in the upper left corner; the player's name is at the bottom in his team's colors. The back has two pillars, with the insert set name and the player's team name inside at the top. His name is at the very top of the card. Between the two pillars is an image of the player in action. A brief 1994 recap is also given, below the image.

		MT
Complete Set (20):		35.00
Common Player:		2.00
Minor Stars:		3.00
1	Bert Emanuel	3.00
2	Darnay Scott	3.00
3	Dan Wilkinson	2.00
4	Derrick Alexander	2.00
5	Willie McGinest	2.00
6	Marshall Faulk	10.00
7	Lake Dawson	3.00
8	Greg Hill	3.00
9	Tim Bowens	2.00
10	David Palmer	2.00
11	Aaron Glenn	2.00
12	Mario Bates	3.00
13	Charles Johnson	3.00
14	Byron "Bam" Morris	3.00
15	William Floyd	3.00
16	Adam Walker	2.00
17	Bryant Young	3.00
18	Trent Dilfer	3.00
19	Errict Rhett	3.00
20	Heath Shuler	6.00

1995 Pacific Crown Royale

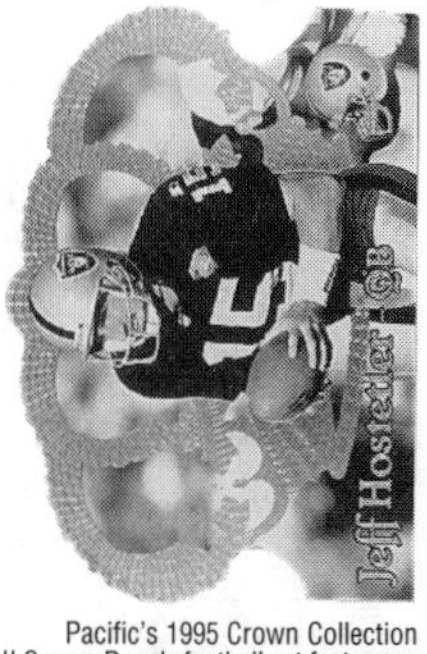

Pacific's 1995 Crown Collection II Crown Royale football set features a hobby first - all cards are die-cut. The horizontal card front has a die-cut crown at the top in gold foil, which is also used for the player's name and position at the bottom. A team helmet also appears at the bottom in the lower right corner. The card back has another color photo of the player, along with a recap of his 1994 season. Hobby and retail versions of Crown Royale were produced. Two distinct parallel sets exist, with distinguishing foils for both hobby and retail versions, and are seeded four per every 25 packs. Three insert sets were created - Pro Bowl Die-Cut, Pride of the NFL and Cramer's Choice Awards.

		MT
Complete Set (144):		150.00
Common Player:		.50
Minor Stars:		1.00
Comp. Copper Set (144):		700.00
Copper Cards:		2x-4x
Comp. Blue Set (144):		1000.
Blue Cards:		3x-6x
Pack (4):		6.50
Wax Box (24):		140.00
1	Lake Dawson	.50
2	Steve Beuerlein	.50
3	Jake Reed	.50
4	Jim Everett	.50
5	Sean Dawkins	.50
6	Jeff Hostetler	.50
7	Marshall Faulk	4.00
8	*Jeff Blake*	3.00
9	Dave Brown	.50
10	Frank Reich	.50
11	Raghib Ismail	.50
12	(Jerry Jones)	4.00
13	Dan Marino	10.00
14	Ricky Watters	1.00
15	Herman Moore	1.50
16	Daryl Johnston	.50
17	Craig Erickson	.50
18	Alexander Wright	.50
19	Reggie White	1.00
20	Andre Rison	.50
21	Fred Barnett	.50
22	*Tyrone Wheatley*	4.00
23	Charles Johnson	1.00
24	*Rashaan Salaam*	1.00
25	Mark Brunell	5.00
26	Derek Loville	.50
27	Garrison Hearst	1.00
28	Ken Norton Jr.	.50
29	*Kerry Collins*	5.00
30	Isaac Bruce	2.00
31	Andre Reed	.50
32	Leon Lett	.50
33	Deion Sanders	4.00
34	Terance Mathis	.50
35	Tim Bowens	.50
36	Shannon Sharpe	.50
37	Quinn Early	.50
38	Jerry Rice	5.00
39	Bruce Smith	.50
40	Drew Bledsoe	5.00
41	Alvin Harper	.50
42	Jim Kelly	1.00
43	*Napoleon Kaufman*	7.00
44	Errict Rhett	1.00
45	Henry Ellard	.50
46	Barry Sanders	7.00
47	Vincent Brisby	.50
48	Chris Zorich	.50
49	Zack Crockett	.50
50	Haywood Jeffires	.50
51	Byron "Bam" Morris	1.00
52	John Kasay	.50
53	Scott Mitchell	.50
54	Boomer Esiason	.50
55	Eric Metcalf	.50
56	Kevin Greene	.50
57	Courtney Hawkins	.50
58	Adrian Murrell	.50
59	Larry Centers	.50
60	Leroy Hoard	.50
61	Lorenzo White	.50
62	Chris Spielman	.50
63	Carl Pickens	1.50
64	Steve Young	5.00
65	Trent Dilfer	1.00
66	Eric Kramer	.50
67	Cortez Kennedy	.50
68	Ray Childress	.50
69	Rick Mirer	1.00
70	Kevin Williams	.50
71	*Joey Galloway*	8.00
72	Dan Wilkinson	.50
73	*Antonio Freeman*	12.00
74	Curtis Conway	1.00
75	Troy Aikman	5.00
76	Natrone Means	1.00
77	Jeff George	1.00
78	*Curtis Martin*	12.00
79	William Floyd	1.00
80	Anthony Miller	.50
81	Greg Hill	1.00
82	Craig Heyward	.50
83	Brian Mitchell	.50
84	Anthony Carter	.50
85	Jerome Bettis	1.00
86	Jim Harbaugh	.50
87	Harvey Williams	.50
88	Tony Martin	.50
89	Rob Moore	.50
90	Neil O'Donnell	.50
91	Cris Carter	.50
92	*Warren Sapp*	3.00
93	Terry Allen	.50
94	Michael Irvin	1.00
95	Heath Shuler	2.00
96	Cornelius Bennett	.50
97	Randy Baldwin	.50
98	Vince Workman	.50
99	Irving Fryar	.50
100	Randall Cunningham	.50
101	*James Stewart*	8.00
102	Stan Humphries	.50
103	Mario Bates	.50
104	Ben Coates	.50
105	Charlie Garner	.50
106	*Todd Collins*	1.00
107	Tim Brown	1.00
108	Edgar Bennett	.50
109	*J.J. Stokes*	3.00
110	Michael Timpson	.50
111	Junior Seau	1.00
112	Bernie Parmalee	1.00
113	Willie McGinest	.50
114	David Dunn	.50
115	*Kyle Brady*	1.50
116	Vinny Testaverde	.50
117	Ernest Givins	.50
118	*Eric Zeier*	2.00
119	Michael Jackson	.50
120	*Chad May*	1.00
121	Dave Krieg	.50
122	Rodney Hampton	.50
123	Darnay Scott	2.00
124	Chris Miller	.50
125	Emmitt Smith	8.00
126	*Steve McNair*	12.00
127	Warren Moon	.50
128	Robert Brooks	1.00
129	Bert Emanuel	1.50
130	John Elway	2.00
131	Chris Warren	1.00
132	Herschel Walker	.50
133	Terry Kirby	.50
134	*Michael Westbrook*	4.00
135	*Kordell Stewart*	10.00
136	*Terrell Davis*	20.00
137	Desmond Howard	.50
138	*Rodney Thomas*	1.00
139	Brett Favre	10.00
140	*Ray Zellars*	1.00
141	Marcus Allen	1.00
142	Gus Frerotte	2.00
143	Steve Bono	1.00
144	Aaron Craver	.50

1995 Pacific Crown Royale Blue Holofoil

The 144-card, regular-size set was inserted into retail packs with the fronts having blue holographic background rather than gold-foil backgrounds.

	MT
Complete Set (144):	850.00
Common Player:	3.00
Veteran Stars:	3.5x-7x
Young Stars:	2.5x-5x
RCs:	2x-4x

1995 Pacific Crown Royale Copper

The 144-card, regular-sized parallel set was randomly inserted in hobby packs and features copper foil instead of gold foil on the die-cut crown.

	MT
Complete Set (144):	700.00
Common Player:	2.00
Veteran Stars:	2.5x-5x
Young Stars:	2x-4x
RCs:	1.5x-3x

1995 Pacific Crown Royale Cramer's Choice Jumbos

These six cards are similar to their 1995 Pacific counterparts, except they are oversized, in a new foil

format. One player is also different; Rashaan Salaam replaces Ki-Jana Carter in the set. The cards are included one per every 16 boxes of Crown Royale football product and represent Mike Cramer's top picks in offensive and defensive categories. Cramer is Pacific's CEO and president. The cards are numbered and have a "CC" prefix.

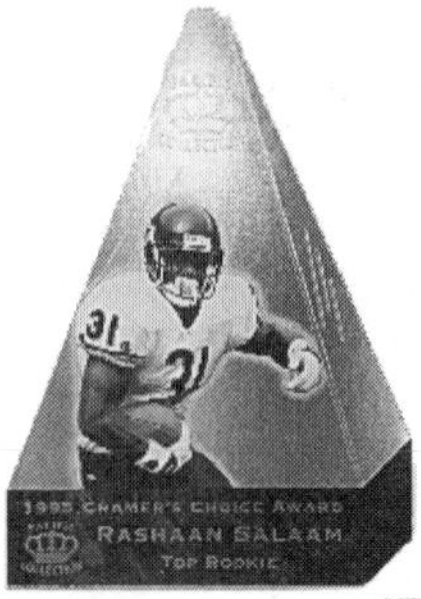

		MT
Complete Set (6):		550.00
Common Player:		50.00
1	Rashaan Salaam	50.00
2	Emmitt Smith	140.00
3	Marshall Faulk	80.00
4	Jerry Rice	90.00
5	Deion Sanders	50.00
6	Steve Young	80.00

1995 Pacific Crown Royale Pride of the NFL

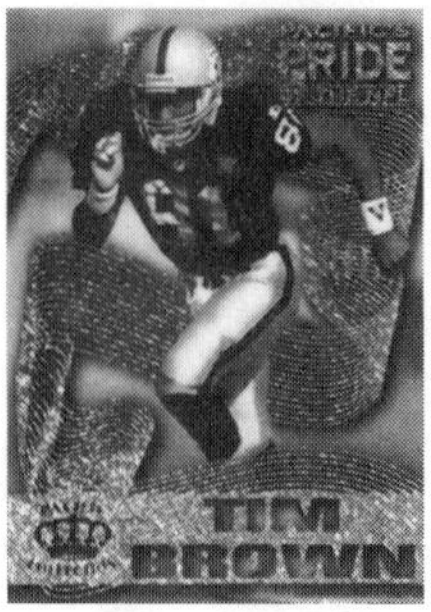

This set represents 36 of the NFL's top players, using a new foil wave design on the card front. The card back is numbered using a "PN" prefix. Cards were random inserts in three of every 25 packs.

		MT
Complete Set (36):		325.00
Common Player:		5.00
1	Jim Kelly	5.00
2	Kerry Collins	18.00
3	Darnay Scott	5.00
4	Jeff Blake	15.00
5	Terry Allen	5.00
6	Emmitt Smith	35.00
7	Michael Irvin	5.00
8	Troy Aikman	20.00
9	John Elway	15.00
10	Napoleon Kaufman	10.00
11	Barry Sanders	20.00
12	Brett Favre	35.00
13	Michael Westbrook	5.00
14	Marcus Allen	5.00
15	Tim Brown	5.00
16	Bernie Parmalee	5.00
17	Dan Marino	35.00
18	Cris Carter	5.00
19	Drew Bledsoe	17.00
20	Mario Bates	5.00
21	Rodney Hampton	5.00
22	Ben Coates	5.00
23	Charles Johnson	5.00
24	Bam Morris	5.00
25	Stan Humphries	5.00
26	Rashaan Salaam	5.00
27	Jerry Rice	17.00
28	Ricky Watters	5.00
29	Steve Young	17.00
30	Natrone Means	5.00
31	William Floyd	5.00
32	Chris Warren	5.00
33	Rick Mirer	5.00
34	Jerome Bettis	8.00
35	Errict Rhett	5.00
36	Heath Shuler	10.00

1995 Pacific Crown Royale Pro Bowl Die Cuts

These 1995 Pacific Crown Royale die-cut cards feature 20 players who participated in the 1995 Pro Bowl game, played in Honolulu, Hawaii. Thus, a palm tree foiled die-cut design is used, and the Pro Bowl logo is displayed on each card. Cards were random inserts, one per every 25 packs. The cards are numbered with the "PB" prefix.

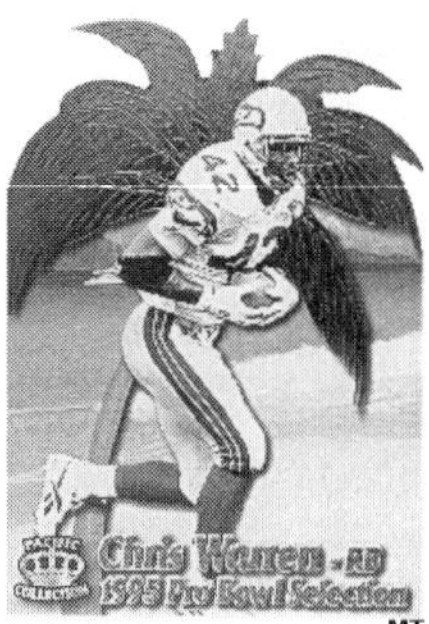

		MT
Complete Set (20):		700.00
Common Player:		15.00
1	Drew Bledsoe	50.00
2	Ben Coates	15.00
3	John Elway	40.00
4	Marshall Faulk	50.00
5	Dan Marino	120.00
6	Natrone Means	20.00
7	Junior Seau	15.00
8	Chris Warren	15.00
9	Rod Woodson	15.00
10	Tim Brown	15.00
11	Troy Aikman	50.00
12	Jerome Bettis	15.00
13	Michael Irvin	15.00
14	Jerry Rice	50.00
15	Barry Sanders	90.00
16	Deion Sanders	40.00
17	Emmitt Smith	120.00
18	Steve Young	40.00
19	Reggie White	15.00
20	Cris Carter	15.00

1995 Pacific Gridiron

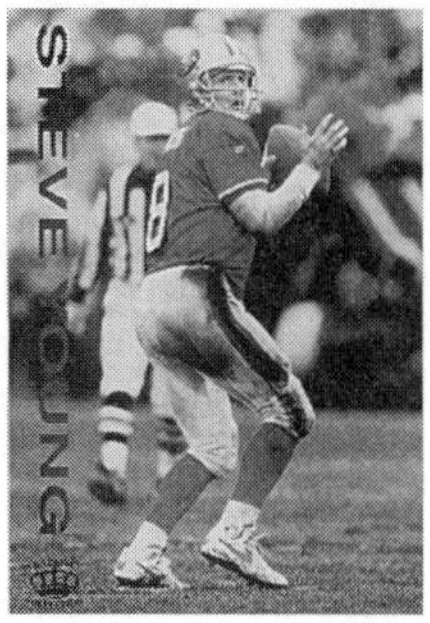

These 3-1/2" x 5" oversized cards capture the NFL's toughest players in their most aggressive and powerful moments on the field. The card front features a full-bleed color photo. The card back details the play on the front in a newspaper-style article and includes a closeup shot of the player. Only 1,500 cases of Pacific's Gridiron were produced. There were 750 hobby cases produced, with each card stamped with blue foil for the player's name on the front. There were also 750 retail cases produced; these cards are stamped with red foil. Each of these sets will also have a "Presidential Series" parallel set, too. The hobby parallel set will be stamped in platinum foil and represent 10 percent of the sets produced. The retail parallel set is stamped in copper foil and represents 10 percent of the sets produced.

		MT
Complete Set (100):		110.00
Common Player:		1.00
Comp. Copper Set (100):		800.00
Common Copper Player:		5.00
Comp. Platinum Set (100):		800.00
Common Platinum Player:		5.00
Copper-Platinum Stars:		3x-6x
Pack (1):		1.50
Wax Box (36):		50.00
1	Natrone Means	3.00
2	Dave Meggett	1.00
3	Curtis Conway	1.00
4	Sam Adams	1.00
5	Quadry Ismail	1.00
6	Steve Young	4.00
7	Errict Rhett	5.00
8	Nate Lewis	1.00
9	Barry Sanders	4.00
10	Sterling Sharpe	1.00
11	Steve Beuerlein	1.00
12	Irving Spikes	1.00
13	Byron "Bam" Morris	1.00
14	Eric Metcalf	1.00
15	Michael Irvin	2.00
16	Dan Marino	8.00
17	Stan Humphries	1.00
18	Leroy Hoard	1.00
19	Marcus Allen	1.00
20	Barry Foster	1.00
21	Rob Moore	1.00
22	Rodney Hampton	1.00
23	Ben Coates	1.00
24	Vernon Turner	1.00
25	Shannon Sharpe	1.00
26	Larry Centers	1.00
27	*Mack Strong*	1.00
28	Reggie White	1.00
29	Harvey Williams	1.00
30	Darnay Scott	2.00
31	Drew Bledsoe	4.00
32	Marshall Faulk	4.00
33	Troy Aikman	4.00
34	Boomer Esiason	1.00
35	Bobby Hebert	1.00
36	Brian Mitchell	1.00
37	Andre Rison	1.00
38	Brett Favre	8.00
39	Don Majkowski	1.00
40	Johnny Johnson	1.00
41	Mark Carrier	1.00
42	James Joseph	1.00
43	Mario Bates	2.00
44	Craig Heyward	1.00
45	Henry Ellard	1.00
46	Thurman Thomas	2.00
47	Jerome Bettis	2.00
48	Dave Brown	1.00
49	Lorenzo White	1.00
50	Joe Montana	5.00
51	Vinny Testaverde	1.00
52	Lake Dawson	2.00
53	Michael Timpson	1.00
54	Ricky Ervins	1.00
55	Cris Carter	1.00
56	Raymont Harris	2.00
57	Andre Coleman	1.00
58	Craig Erickson	1.00
59	Jeff Hostetler	1.00
60	Deion Sanders	2.00
61	Eric Turner	1.00
62	Darryl Johnston	1.00
63	Bernie Parmalee	1.00
64	Ricky Watters	1.00
65	David Palmer	1.00
66	Aaron Glenn	1.00
67	Todd Kinchen	1.00
68	Edgar Bennett	1.00
69	Mel Gray	1.00
70	Randall Cunningham	1.00
71	Michael Haynes	1.00
72	Chris Miller	1.00
73	Glyn Milburn	1.00
74	*Steve McNair*	7.00
75	Lewis Tillman	1.00
76	Chuck Levy	1.00
77	Carl Pickens	1.00
78	Michael Bates	1.00
79	*Jeff Blake*	2.00
80	O.J. McDuffie	1.00
81	Tim Brown	1.00
82	Haywood Jeffires	1.00
83	Jeff Burris	1.00
84	John Elway	4.00
85	Charles Johnson	2.00
86	Emmitt Smith	8.00
87	William Floyd	2.00
88	Herschel Walker	1.00
89	Rick Mirer	3.00
90	Roosevelt Potts	1.00
91	Rod Woodson	1.00
92	Greg Hill	2.00
93	Junior Seau	1.00
94	Dave Krieg	1.00
95	Jim Kelly	1.00
96	Warren Moon	1.00
97	Leroy Thompson	1.00
98	*Ki-Jana Carter*	5.00
99	Herman Moore	2.00
100	Jerry Rice	4.00

1995 Pacific Gridiron Copper/Platinum

The 100-card, regular-size parallel set featured copper/ platinum foil rather than the blue foil. Only 10 percent of the sets produced were copper/platinum.

	MT
Complete Set (100):	800.00
Common Player:	4.00
Veteran Stars:	4x-8x
Young Stars:	3x-6x
RCs:	2x-4x

1995 Pacific Gridiron Gold

The 100-card, regular-sized parallel set features gold foil on the card front instead of red foil. Of the sets produced, only 10 percent were in gold foil.

	MT
Common Player (100):	50.00
Semistars:	100.00
Veteran Stars:	75x-130x
Young Stars/RCs:	50x-90x

1995 Pacific Prisms

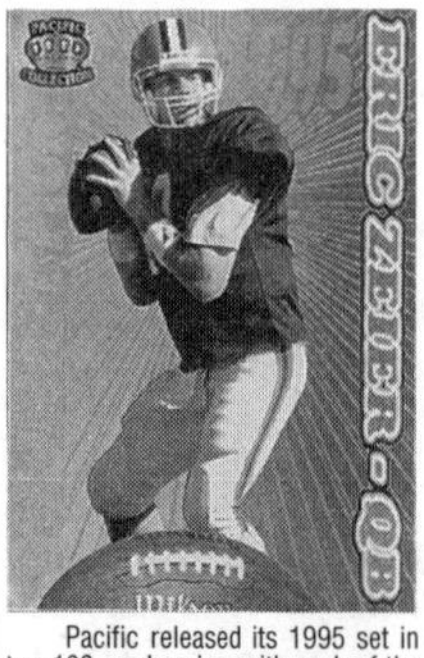

Pacific released its 1995 set in two 108-card series, with each of the 216 cards reprinted in a parallel Gold Prism set (one every 30 Series I packs, two every 37 Series II packs). Each card front has an action photo on the left, along with the player's name in silver foil. A closeup shot appears on the right side of the horizontally-designed card. The back has another action photo of the player against a backdrop with a photo of his team's helmet. A few career accomplishment tidbits are also included on the back. The player's name runs down the right side. Production was limited to 1,500 hobby and 1,500 retail cases for each series. Series I inserts include Red Hot Super Stars, Red Hot Rookies and two Expansion Extra inserts, a Barry Foster card for Carolina and a Steve Beuerlein card for Jacksonville. Series II inserts include Royal Connections, and Kings of the NFL.

		MT
Complete Set (216):		250.00
Complete Series 1 Set (108):		125.00
Complete Series 2 Set (108):		125.00
Common Player:		1.00
Minor Stars:		2.00
Comp. Gold Set (216):		1500.
Comp. Gold Series 1 (108):		750.00
Comp. Gold Series 2 (108):		750.00
Common Gold Player:		3.00
Minor Gold Stars:		5.00
Unlisted Gold Stars:		3x-5x
Comp. Helmet Set (30):		5.00
Comp. SB Logos Set (30):		5.00
Comp. Uniform Set (30):		5.00
Series 1 or 2 Pack (1):		2.00
Series 1 or 2 Wax Box (36):		55.00
1	Chuck Levy	1.00
2	Ron Moore	1.00
3	Jay Schroeder	1.00
4	Bert Emanuel	1.00
5	Terance Mathis	1.00
6	Andre Rison	2.00
7	Bucky Brooks	1.00
8	Jeff Burris	1.00
9	Jim Kelly	2.00
10	Lewis Tillman	1.00
11	Steve Walsh	1.00
12	Chris Zorich	1.00
13	*Jeff Blake*	3.00
14	Steve Broussard	1.00
15	Jeff Cothran	1.00
16	Ernest Byner	1.00
17	Leroy Hoard	1.00
18	Vinny Testaverde	2.00
19	Troy Aikman	7.00
20	Alvin Harper	1.00
21	Leon Lett	1.00
22	Jay Novacek	1.00
23	John Elway	5.00
24	Karl Mecklenburg	1.00
25	Leonard Russell	1.00
26	Mel Gray	1.00
27	Barry Sanders	8.00
28	Dave Krieg	1.00
29	Chris Spielman	1.00
30	Robert Brooks	2.00
31	LeShon Johnson	1.00
32	Sterling Sharpe	2.00
33	Ernest Givins	1.00
34	Billy Joe Tolliver	1.00
35	Lorenzo White	1.00
36	Charles Arbuckle	1.00
37	Sean Dawkins	2.00
38	Marshall Faulk	7.00
39	Marcus Allen	2.00
40	Donnell Bennett	1.00
41	*Matt Blundin*	1.00
42	Greg Hill	2.00
43	Tim Brown	2.00
44	Billy Joe Hobert	2.00
45	Raghib Ismail	1.00
46	James Jett	1.00
47	Tim Bowens	1.00
48	Irving Fryar	1.00
49	O.J. McDuffie	2.00
50	Irving Spikes	1.00
51	Terry Allen	2.00
52	Cris Carter	2.00
53	Amp Lee	1.00
54	Drew Bledsoe	7.00
55	Willie McGinest	1.00
56	Leroy Thompson	1.00
57	Michael Timpson	1.00
58	Michael Haynes	1.00
59	Derrell Mitchell	1.00
60	Dave Brown	1.00
61	Thomas Lewis	1.00
62	Dave Meggett	1.00
63	Boomer Esiason	1.00
64	Aaron Glenn	1.00
65	Ronnie Lott	1.00
66	Randall Cunningham	2.00
67	Charlie Garner	1.00
68	Herschel Walker	1.00
69	Barry Foster	2.00
70	Charles Johnson	2.00
71	*Jim Miller*	2.00
72	Rod Woodson	2.00
73	Andre Coleman	1.00
74	Natrone Means	3.00
75	Shannon Mitchell	1.00
76	Junior Seau	2.00
77	Elvis Grbac	2.00
78	Deion Sanders	3.00
79	*Adam Walker*	1.00
80	Ricky Watters	2.00
81	Michael Bates	1.00
82	Brian Blades	1.00
83	Eugene Robinson	1.00
84	Chris Warren	2.00
85	Jerome Bettis	2.00
86	Troy Drayton	1.00
87	Chris Miller	1.00
88	Trent Dilfer	2.00
89	Hardy Nickerson	1.00
90	Errict Rhett	2.00
91	Henry Ellard	1.00
92	Gus Frerotte	2.00
93	Ricky Irvins	1.00
94	*Dave Barr*	1.00
95	*Kyle Brady*	1.00
96	*Mark Bruener*	2.00
97	*Ki-Jana Carter*	3.00
98	*Kerry Collins*	5.00
99	*Joey Galloway*	8.00
100	*Napoleon Kaufman*	10.00
101	*Steve McNair*	12.00
102	*Craig Newsome*	1.00
103	*Rashaan Salaam*	3.00
104	*Kordell Stewart*	14.00
105	*J.J. Stokes*	3.00
106	*Rodney Thomas*	2.00
107	*Michael Westbrook*	3.00
108	*Tyrone Wheatley*	2.00
109	Larry Centers	1.00
110	Garrison Hearst	2.00
111	Jamir Miller	1.00
112	Jeff George	2.00
113	Craig Heyward	1.00
114	Cornelius Bennett	1.00
115	Andre Reed	1.00
116	Randy Baldwin	1.00
117	Tommy Barnhardt	1.00
118	Sam Mills	1.00
119	Brian O'Neal	1.00
120	Frank Reich	1.00
121	Tony Smith	1.00
122	Lawyer Tillman	1.00
123	Jack Trudeau	1.00
124	Vernon Turner	1.00
125	Curtis Conway	2.00
126	Erik Kramer	1.00
127	Nate Lewis	1.00
128	Carl Pickens	2.00
129	Darnay Scott	2.00
130	Dan Wilkinson	1.00
131	Derrick Alexander	1.00
132	Carl Banks	1.00
133	Michael Irvin	2.00
134	Emmitt Smith	12.00
135	Kevin Williams	1.00
136	Glyn Milburn	1.00
137	Anthony Miller	1.00
138	Shannon Sharpe	1.00
139	Scott Mitchell	1.00
140	Herman Moore	3.00
141	Edgar Bennett	1.00
142	Brett Favre	12.00
143	Reggie White	2.00
144	Gary Brown	1.00
145	Haywood Jeffires	1.00
146	Webster Slaughter	1.00
147	Craig Erickson	1.00
148	Paul Justin	1.00
149	Lamont Warren	1.00
150	Steve Beuerlein	1.00
151	Derek Brown	1.00
152	Mark Brunell	6.00
153	Reggie Cobb	1.00
154	Desmond Howard	1.00
155	Kelvin Pritchett	1.00
156	*James Stewart*	5.00
157	Cedric Tillman	1.00
158	Kimble Anders	1.00
159	Lake Dawson	1.00
160	Keith Byars	1.00
161	Dan Marino	12.00
162	Bernie Parmalee	1.00
163	Qadry Ismail	1.00
164	Warren Moon	2.00
165	Jake Reed	1.00
166	Marion Butts	1.00
167	Ben Coates	1.00
168	Mario Bates	1.00
169	Quinn Early	1.00
170	Jim Everett	1.00
171	Rodney Hampton	1.00
172	Mike Horan	1.00
173	Mike Sherrard	1.00
174	Johnny Johnson	1.00
175	Adrian Murrell	2.00
176	*Andrew Glover*	1.00
177	Jeff Hostetler	1.00
178	Harvey Williams	1.00
179	Fred Barnett	1.00
180	Vaughn Hebron	1.00
181	Jeff Sydner	1.00
182	Kevin Greene	1.00
183	Byron "Bam" Morris	1.00
184	Neil O'Donnell	1.00
185	Stan Humphries	2.00
186	Tony Martin	1.00
187	Mark Seay	1.00
188	William Floyd	2.00
189	Rickey Jackson	1.00
190	Jerry Rice	7.00
191	Steve Young	5.00
192	Cortez Kennedy	1.00
193	Rick Mirer	3.00
194	Jessie Hester	1.00
195	*Curtis Martin*	15.00
196	Horace Copeland	1.00
197	Charles Wilson	1.00
198	Reggie Brooks	1.00
199	Brian Mitchell	1.00
200	Heath Shuler	2.00
201	*Justin Armour*	1.00
202	*Jay Barker*	1.00
203	*Zack Crockett*	1.00
204	*Christian Fauria*	1.00
205	*Antonio Freeman*	8.00
206	*Chad May*	1.00
207	*Frank Sanders*	3.00
208	*Steve Stenstrom*	1.00
209	*Lorenzo Styles*	1.00
210	*Sherman Williams*	1.00
211	*Ray Zellars*	1.00
212	*Eric Zeier*	1.00
213	Joey Galloway	4.00
214	Napoleon Kaufman	1.00
215	Rashaan Salaam	2.00
216	J.J. Stokes	2.00
NNO	Barry Foster (Carolina)	5.00
NNO	Steve Beuerlein (Jacksonville)	5.00

1995 Pacific Prisms Gold

The 216-card, standard-sized parallel set was inserted every 37 packs. The cards feature gold backgrounds instead of silver.

	MT
Complete Set (216):	1600.
Common Player:	3.00
Veteran Stars:	2.5x-5x
Young Stars:	2x-4x
RCs:	1.75x-3.5x

1995 Pacific Prisms Connections

These 1995 Pacific Prism Series II inserts feature 10 top quarterback/receiver combinations; there are 20 cards in the set. Hobby cases feature the receiver halves; retail packs have the 10 quarterback cards. Both appear in one per every 73 of their respective packs. The cards are fitted together to form a particular team's qb/receiver tandem. The quarterback cards, numbered 1-10 using an (A) suffix, have the city name along the top; receiver cards (B) have the team nickname. The players' names run along the bottom of the cards. The foiled background includes team logos, plus half of the Royal Connections logo, which fits with its counterpart to form a circle. The quarterback cards have a throwing quarterback symbol as part of its design; receiver cards have a symbol of a player making a catch. Card backs also have the Royal Connections symbol, a player mug shot and a career summary. In addition to (A) and (B) suffixes, cards are numbered using an "RC" prefix.

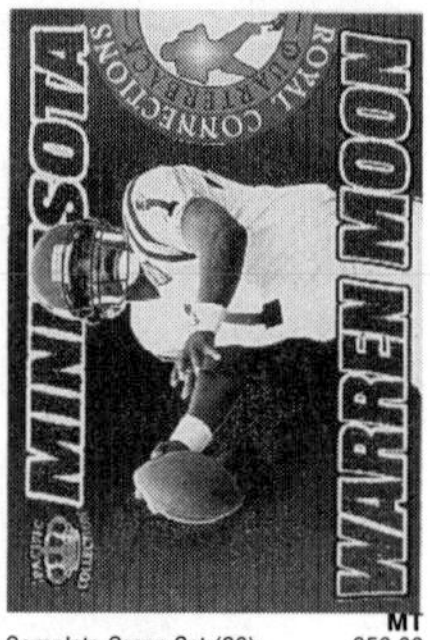

		MT
Complete Green Set (20):		350.00
Common Green Player:		10.00
Complete Blue Set (20):		1000.
Common Blue Player:		20.00
Blue Cards:		2x-4x
1A	Steve Young	40.00
1B	Jerry Rice	40.00
2A	Dan Marino	80.00
2B	Irving Fryar	10.00
3A	Drew Bledsoe	40.00
3B	Ben Coates	10.00
4A	John Elway	25.00
4B	Shannon Sharpe	10.00
5A	Jeff Hostetler	10.00
5B	Tim Brown	10.00
6A	Warren Moon	10.00
6B	Cris Carter	10.00
7A	Neil O'Donnell	10.00
7B	Charles Johnson	10.00
8A	Troy Aikman	40.00
8B	Michael Irvin	10.00
9A	Stan Humphries	10.00
9B	Shawn Jefferson	10.00
10A	Jim Kelly	10.00
10B	Andre Reed	10.00

1995 Pacific Prisms Kings of the NFL

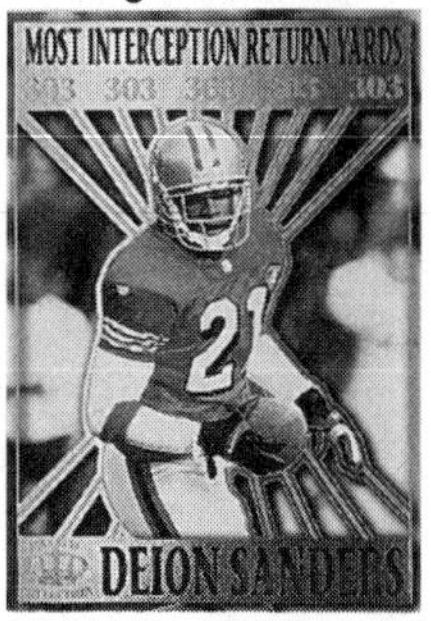

These 10 1995 Pacific Prism Series II football inserts feature statistical leaders from the 1994 season. Cards were inserted one per every 361 packs. The card front has a color action photo of the player, forming the body of a gold foil hourglass which has the category he led the league in listed at the top, along with the statistical number he reached. The bottom of the hourglass has the Pacific Collection Crown icon and the player's name. The card back has a square with a color mug shot inside, with the number he reached adjacent to it, at the top, but below the category heading he led in. His name runs across the middle of the card, followed by a player profile and a few specific examples of when he had productive weeks in his particular category.

		MT
Complete Set (10):		750.00
Common Player:		40.00
1	Emmitt Smith	110.00
2	Steve Young	60.00
3	Jerry Rice	75.00
4	Deion Sanders	40.00
5	Emmitt Smith	110.00
6	Dan Marino	110.00
7	Drew Bledsoe	75.00
8	Barry Sanders	90.00
9	Marshall Faulk	40.00
10	Marshall Faulk, Natrone Means	40.00

A player's name in *italic type* indicates a rookie card.

1995 Pacific Prisms Red Hot Rookies

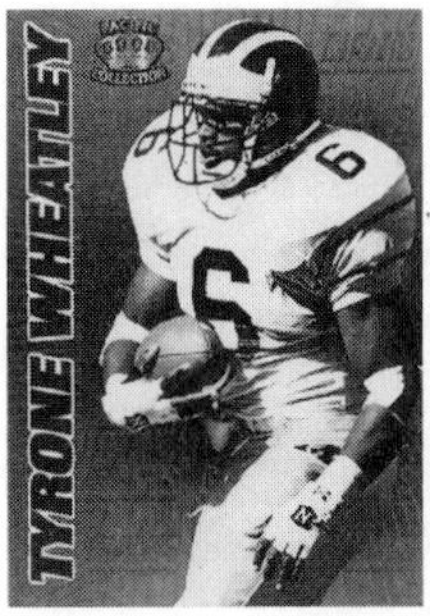

These nine insert cards could be found in 1995 Pacific Prism Series I packs, one per every 73 hobby packs. The cards have a color action photo of the player in his collegiate uniform against a red foil background which has his pro team's nickname printed several times within it. His name runs along the left side of the card. The back, numbered using 1, 2, 3, etc., is horizontal and includes a closeup shot of the player on the left side. A photo of his new pro team appears on the right side. His name, position and pro team are superimposed over the helmet, as is a summary of when the player was selected in the 1995 draft.

		MT
Complete Set (9):		140.00
Common Player:		5.00
Inserted 1:73		
1	Ki-Jana Carter	5.00
2	Joey Galloway	30.00
3	Steve McNair	30.00
4	Tyrone Wheatley	5.00
5	Kerry Collins	15.00
6	Rashaan Salaam	5.00
7	Michael Westbrook	10.00
8	J.J. Stokes	15.00
9	Napoleon Kaufman	30.00

1995 Pacific Prisms Red Hot Stars

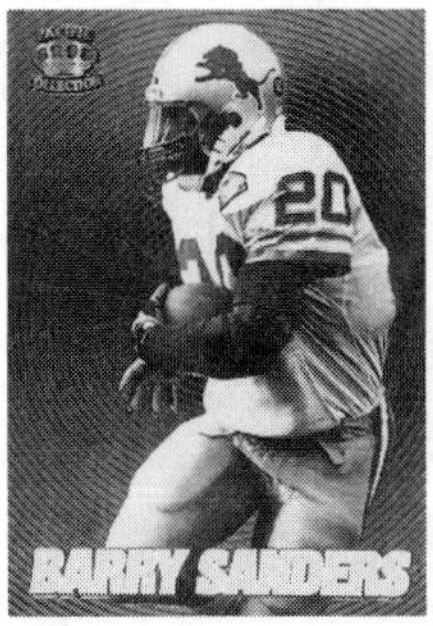

These 1995 Pacific Prism Series I inserts feature nine of the NFL's top stars. The cards were included one per every 73 retail packs. The card front has a color action photo of the player against a red foil spiderweb pattern. The player's name appears at the bottom of the card. The card back, numbered 1, 2, 3, etc., is horizontal and has a closeup shot of the player on the left side. The other side has his name, position, team name and 1994 season recap all superimposed against a football background.

		MT
Complete Set (9):		375.00
Common Player:		30.00
1	Barry Sanders	50.00
2	Steve Young	45.00
3	Emmitt Smith	80.00
4	Drew Bledsoe	45.00
5	Natrone Means	30.00
6	Dan Marino	80.00
7	Marshall Faulk	30.00
8	Jerry Rice	45.00
9	Errict Rhett	30.00

Values quoted in this guide reflect the retail price of a card — the price a collector can expect to pay when buying a card from a dealer. The wholesale price — that which a collector can expect to receive from a dealer when selling cards — will be significantly lower, depending on desirability and condition.

1995 Pacific Prisms Super Bowl Logos

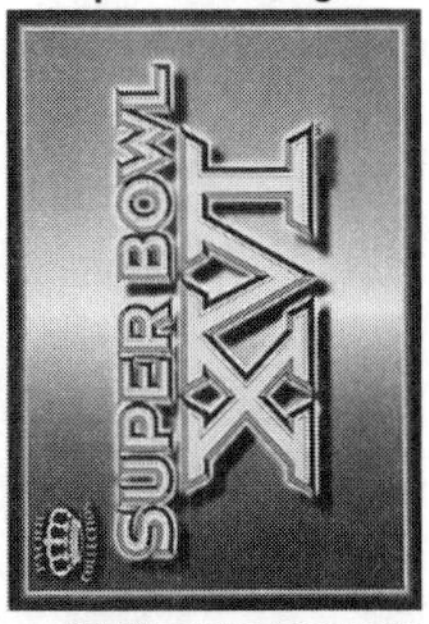

This 30-card insert features the game-specific Super Bowl logo on the front and details of the game on the back. The cards are unnumbered.

		MT
Complete Set (30):		4.00
Common Player:		.15
1	Super Bowl I	.15
2	Super Bowl II	.15
3	Super Bowl III	.15
4	Super Bowl IV	.15
5	Super Bowl V	.15
6	Super Bowl VI	.15
7	Super Bowl VII	.15
8	Super Bowl VIII	.15
9	Super Bowl IX	.15
10	Super Bowl X	.15
11	Super Bowl XI	.15
12	Super Bowl XII	.15
13	Super Bowl XIII	.15
14	Super Bowl XIV	.15
15	Super Bowl XV	.15
16	Super Bowl XVI	.15
17	Super Bowl XVII	.15
18	Super Bowl XVIII	.15
19	Super Bowl XIX	.15
20	Super Bowl XX	.15
21	Super Bowl XXI	.15
22	Super Bowl XXII	.15
23	Super Bowl XXIII	.15
24	Super Bowl XXIV	.15
25	Super Bowl XXV	.15
26	Super Bowl XXVI	.15
27	Super Bowl XXVII	.15
28	Super Bowl XXVIII	.15
29	Super Bowl XXIX	.15
30	Super Bowl XXX	.15

1995 Pacific Prisms Team Helmets

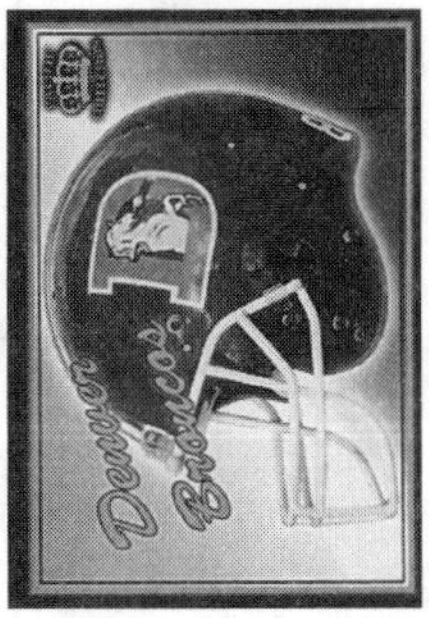

This 30-card insert includes one card for each NFL team. The fronts feature the team helmet and the backs have team history.

		MT
Complete Set (30):		4.00
Common Player:		.15
1	Arizona Cardinals	.15
2	Atlanta Falcons	.15
3	Buffalo Bills	.15
4	Carolina Panthers	.15
5	Chicago Bears	.15
6	Cincinnati Bengals	.15
7	Cleveland Browns	.15
8	Dallas Cowboys	.25
9	Denver Broncos	.15
10	Detroit Lions	.15
11	Green Bay Packers	.25
12	Detroit Lions	.15
13	Indianapolis Colts	.15
14	Jacksonville Jaguars	.15
15	Kansas City Chiefs	.15
16	Los Angeles Raiders	.25
17	Miami Dolphins	.25
18	Minnesota Vikings	.15
19	New England Patriots	.15
20	New Orleans Saints	.15
21	New York Giants	.15
22	New York Jets	.15
23	Philadelphia Eagles	.15
24	Pittsburgh Steelers	.25
25	San Diego Chargers	.15
26	San Francisco 49ers	.25
27	Seattle Seahawks	.15
28	St. Louis Rams	.15
29	Tampa Bay Buccaneers	.15
30	Washington Redskins	.25

1995 Pacific Prisms Team Uniforms

This 30-card insert includes one card per NFL team. The cards feature a horizontal layout with the team uniform on the front and team history on the back.

		MT
Complete Set (30):		4.00
Common Player:		.15
1	Arizona Cardinals	.15
2	Atlanta Falcons	.15
3	Buffalo Bills	.15
4	Carolina Panthers	.15
5	Chicago Bears	.15
6	Cincinnati Bengals	.15
7	Cleveland Browns	.15
8	Dallas Cowboys	.25
9	Denver Broncos	.15
10	Detroit Lions	.15
11	Green Bay Packers	.25
12	Detroit Lions	.15
13	Indianapolis Colts	.15
14	Jacksonville Jaguars	.15
15	Kansas City Chiefs	.15
16	Los Angeles Raiders	.25
17	Miami Dolphins	.25
18	Minnesota Vikings	.15
19	New England Patriots	.15
20	New Orleans Saints	.15
21	New York Giants	.15
22	New York Jets	.15
23	Philadelphia Eagles	.15
24	Pittsburgh Steelers	.25
25	San Diego Chargers	.15
26	San Francisco 49ers	.25
27	Seattle Seahawks	.15
28	St. Louis Rams	.15
29	Tampa Bay Buccaneers	.15
30	Washington Redskins	.25

1995 Pacific Triple Folders

These cards feature two panels on the front which, when closed, form a color action photo of an NFL star player. The format is the same as previous editions, but the 1995 cards have been reduced in size to standard-sized cards. The player's name and the Pacific Crown Collection are on one panel on the front; a team helmet is on the other. When opened up, the inside of the card panels reveal three more photos, with the player's team name in the center. The card back, a green football field, contains a closeup photo of the player, a card number and a brief recap of the 1994 season. Insert sets include: Rookies and Stars (which have different color foil versions for hobby and retail versions, plus another parallel set, with yet another different color foil for each); Team Triple Folders; Crystalline; Big Guns; and Careers.

		MT
Complete Set (48):		35.00
Common Player:		.25
Minor Stars:		.50
Wax Box:		50.00
1	Garrison Hearst	.50
2	*Kerry Collins*	1.50
3	Jeff George	.50
4	Herschel Walker	.25
5	Lake Dawson	.25
6	Cris Carter	.50
7	Byron "Bam" Morris	.25
8	Jim Kelly	.50
9	*Rashaan Salaam*	.50
10	*Eric Zeier*	.50
11	*Curtis Martin*	3.00
12	Jerry Rice	2.00
13	Chris Warren	.50
14	Trent Dilfer	1.00
15	Terry Allen	.50
16	*Jeff Blake*	1.25
17	Drew Bledsoe	2.00
18	Tim Brown	.50
19	*Wayne Chrebet*	3.00
20	Bernie Parmalee	.25
21	Stan Humphries	.25
22	Jerome Bettis	.50
23	*Michael Westbrook*	1.00
24	Charlie Garner	.50
25	Mario Bates	.25
26	Marcus Allen	.50
27	*James Stewart*	2.00
28	Ben Coates	.50
29	*Tyrone Wheatley*	1.50
30	Steve Young	1.50
31	Natrone Means	.50
32	*Terrell Davis*	7.00
33	*Napoleon Kaufman*	2.00
34	Charles Johnson	.50
35	Barry Sanders	4.00
36	John Elway	4.00
37	*Joey Galloway*	2.50
38	Brett Favre	5.00
39	Errict Rhett	.50
40	Gary Brown	.25
41	Reggie White	.50
42	Steve Bono	.50
43	Marshall Faulk	2.00
44	Dan Marino	4.00
45	Emmitt Smith	3.50
46	Troy Aikman	2.00
47	Ricky Watters	.25
48	Michael Irvin	.50
P1	Natrone Means Promo	.50

1995 Pacific Triple Folders Big Guns

Twelve of the NFL's top quarterbacks are featured on these 1995 Pacific Triple Folder inserts, seeded two per every 37 packs. The card front has a color photo of the player against a prism background which has several geometric shapes cut into it. The player's name is in gold foil in the lower left corner; the insert set logo is in the bottom right corner. The horizontal card back has a football as the background, with a mug shot, brief career summary and cannon firing a football superimposed over it. Three opponents' helmets, representing games in which the quarterback had big numbers, are also shown on the back, along with the statistics from those games.

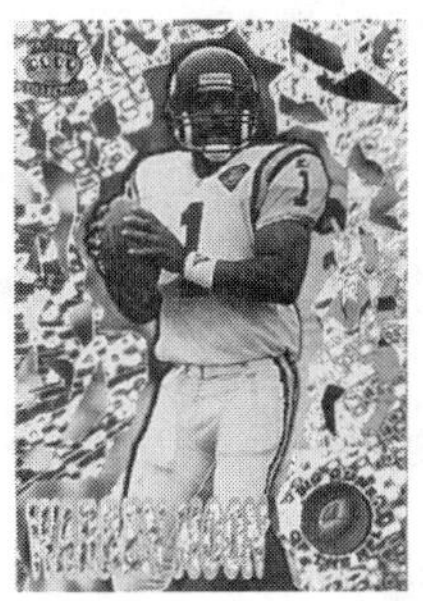

		MT
Complete Set (12):		60.00
Common Player:		2.00
Minor Stars:		4.00
Inserted 2:37		
1	Drew Bledsoe	8.00
2	Dan Marino	12.00
3	Warren Moon	4.00
4	John Elway	12.00
5	Jeff Blake	4.00
6	Brett Favre	15.00
7	Steve Young	7.00
8	Boomer Esiason	4.00
9	Jim Everett	2.00
10	Jim Kelly	4.00
11	Jeff George	4.00
12	Dave Kreig	2.00

1995 Pacific Triple Folders Careers

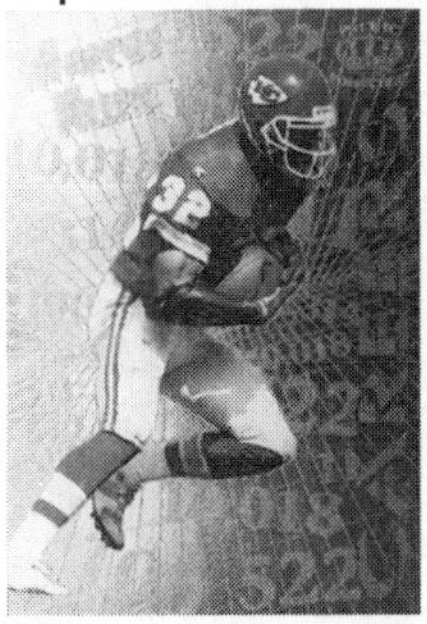

Eight of the NFL's top stars are featured on these 1995 Pacific Triple Folder inserts, seeded one every 181 packs. The metallic card front has a color photo of the player, with his name in the upper left corner, adjacent to the Pacific logo. "Careers" runs down the right side of the card front, which includes several of the player's career numbers scattered throughout the card background. The back, numbered using a "C" prefix, has a closeup shot of the player, plus a recap of some of the key numbers from his career statistics.

		MT
Complete Set (8):		175.00
Common Player:		12.00
Inserted 1:181		
1	Troy Aikman	20.00
2	Marcus Allen	12.00
3	John Elway	35.00
4	Dan Marino	35.00
5	Jerry Rice	20.00
6	Barry Sanders	40.00
7	Emmitt Smith	25.00
8	Steve Young	15.00

1995 Pacific Triple Folders Crystalline

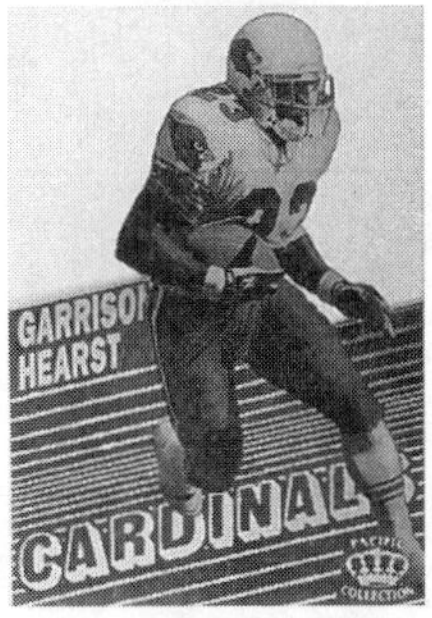

These 1995 Pacific Triple Folder inserts were seeded four per every 37 packs. Each is a plastic card with clear area above the player photo and his team's primary color and gold foil at the bottom for his name, team nickname and Pacific logo. The card back, numbered using a "Cr" prefix, contains the player's name, position, team and biographical information against the shadow of the card front photo. A team helmet, mug shot and brief career summary are also included on the back.

		MT
Complete Set (20):		60.00
Common Player:		1.50
Minor Stars:		3.00
Inserted 4:37		
1	Troy Aikman	5.00
2	Jeff Blake	3.00
3	Drew Bledsoe	4.00
4	Kerry Collins	3.00
5	John Elway	7.50
6	Marshall Faulk	3.00
7	Gus Frerotte	1.50
8	Joey Galloway	3.00
9	Garrison Hearst	1.50
10	Jeff Hostetler	1.50
11	Dan Marino	7.50
12	Natrone Means	3.00
13	Errict Rhett	3.00
14	Rashaan Salaam	1.50
15	Barry Sanders	7.50
16	Deion Sanders	3.00
17	Emmitt Smith	7.50
18	J.J. Stokes	3.00
19	Steve Young	4.00
20	Eric Zeier	1.50

1995 Pacific Triple Folders Rookies and Stars

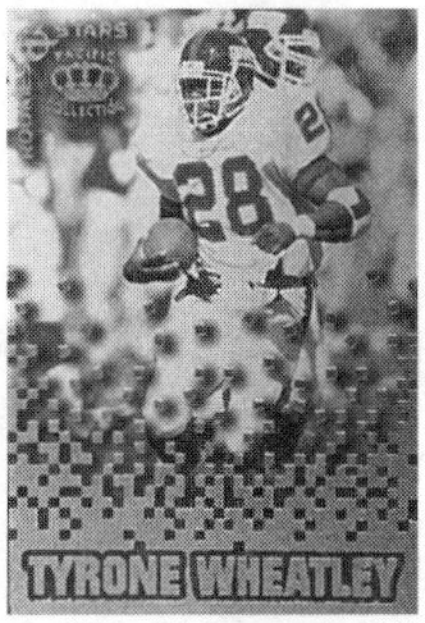

This set features a mix of 36 stars and rookies, featured on different color foiled cards for the retail and hobby versions, plus a third parallel set which uses yet another color for the foil. The hobby and retail inserts were each seeded three per every four of their respective packs, while the parallel cards are seeded three per every 37 packs. The card front features a full-bleed color photo, with foil for the insert set logo and at the bottom for the player's name. The card back, numbered using an "RS" prefix, has a mug shot of the player, plus a brief recap of the player's previous season.

		MT
Complete Gold Set (36):		30.00
Common Gold Player:		.50
Inserted 3:4		
Blue Cards:		1x
Inserted 3:4		
Raspberry Cards:		2x-4x
Inserted 3:37		
Silver Cards:		2x-4x
Inserted 3:37		
1	Garrison Hearst	.50
2	Darrick Holmes	.50
3	Kerry Collins	1.50
4	Rashaan Salaam	.75
5	Jeff Blake	1.00
6	Eric Zeier	1.00
7	Troy Aikman	1.50
8	Eric Bjorson	.50
9	Deion Sanders	1.00
10	Emmitt Smith	2.50
11	Sherman Williams	.50
12	Terrell Davis	7.00
13	John Elway	2.50
14	Barry Sanders	3.00
15	Steve McNair	3.00
16	Marshall Faulk	1.00
17	James Stewart	1.50
18	Steve Bono	.50
19	Tamarick Vanover	.50
20	Dan Marino	2.50
21	Drew Bledsoe	1.50
22	Curtis Martin	3.00
23	Tyrone Wheatley	1.00
24	Tim Brown	.75
25	Napoleon Kaufman	1.75
26	Ricky Watters	.50
27	Natrone Means	.50
28	Jerry Rice	1.50
29	J.J. Stokes	1.00
30	Steve Young	1.25
31	Joey Galloway	2.00
32	Chris Warren	.50
33	Jerome Bettis	.75
34	Errict Rhett	.50
35	Terry Allen	.50
36	Michael Westbrook	1.50

1995 Pacific Triple Folders Teams

These 1995 Pacific Triple Folders feature three players from a team. The two flaps feature one player; the inside features another player, while the back features a third teammate and a card number. The inside of the card uses gold foil stamping for that player's name and the Pacific Crown Collection logo, plus a circle which surrounds the players' team helmet, which is at the bottom of the card. These inserts were randomly included one per every 37 packs.

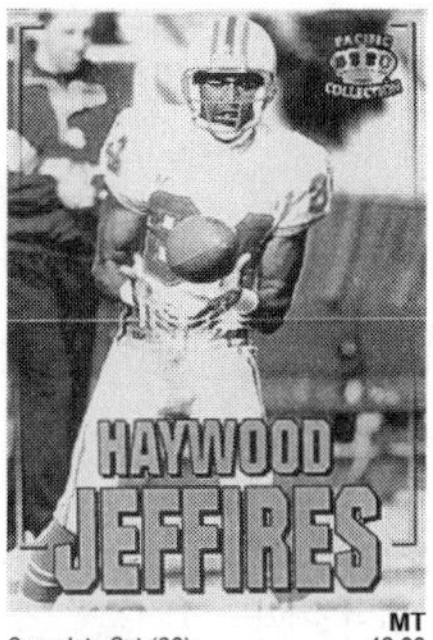

		MT
Complete Set (30):		40.00
Common Player:		.50
Minor Stars:		1.00
Inserted 9:37		
1	Garrison Hearst, Dave Kreig, Rob Moore	1.00
2	Jeff George, Terance Mathis, Eric Metcalf	1.00
3	Darick Holmes, Jim Kelly, Andre Reed	1.00
4	Edgar Bennett, Brett Favre, Reggie White	5.00
5	Haywood Jeffires, Chris Chandler, Steve McNair	2.00
6	Marshall Faulk, Jim Harbaugh, Sean Dawkins	2.00
7	Bob Christian, Tim McKyer, Kerry Collins	2.00
8	Rashaan Salaam, Erik Kramer, Michael Timpson	1.00
9	Carl Pickens, Jeff Blake, Darnay Scott	1.00
10	Leroy Hoard, Andre Rison, Vinny Testaverde	1.00
11	Troy Aikman, Michael Irvin, Emmitt Smith	5.00
12	John Elway, Terrell Davis, Shannon Sharpe	8.00
13	Scott Mitchell, Herman Moore, Barry Sanders	6.00
14	James Stewart, Mark Brunell, Desmond Howard	2.00
15	Marcus Allen, Steve Bono, Greg Hill	1.00
16	Bernie Parmalee, Dan Marino, Irving Fryar	5.00
17	Robert Smith, Warren Moon, Cris Carter	1.50
18	Curtis Martin, Drew Bledsoe, Ben Coates	4.00
19	Mario Bates, Jim Everett, Michael Haynes	.50
20	Rodney Hampton, Dave Brown, Herschel Walker	.50
21	Wayne Chrebet, Kyle Brady, Adrian Murrell	2.50
22	Napoleon Kaufman, Jeff Hostetler, Tim Brown	2.00
23	Ricky Watters, Charlie Garner, Mike Malmua	.75
24	Bam Morris, Mike Tomczak, Charles Johnson	.50
25	Natrone Means, Stan Humphries, Tony Martin	1.00
26	Jerry Rice, Steve Young, J.J. Stokes	3.00
27	Chris Warren, Rick Mirer, Joey Galloway	2.00
28	Jerome Bettis, Kelvin Carter, Isaac Bruce	1.50
29	Errict Rhett, Trent Dilfer, Alvin Harper	1.50
30	Terry Allen, Gus Frerotte, Michael Westbrook	1.00

1996 Pacific Super Bowl Bronze/Gold

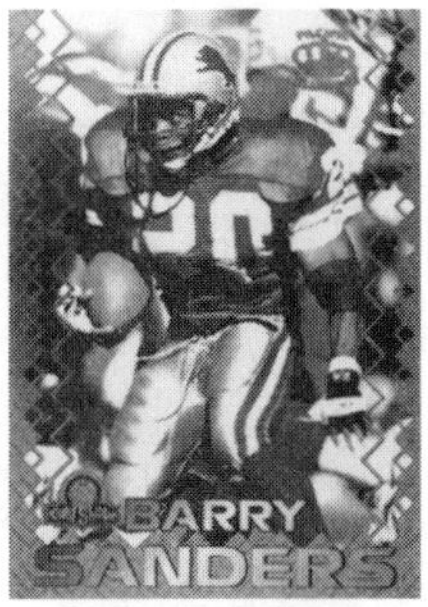

The six-card, standard-size set was produced with both bronze and gold. The bronze set was available to collectors through a special wrapper redemption program at the 1996 Super Bowl Card Show in Phoenix. The gold set was available through a wrapper redemption program with

1995 Triple Folders. The gold cards are parallel to the bronze set, except with a Super Bowl XXX logo on the card fronts.

		MT
Complete Set (6):		14.00
Common Player:		1.00
1	Chris Warren	1.00
2	Kordell Stewart	3.00
3	Curtis Martin	5.00
4	Errict Rhett	2.00
5	Neil O'Donnell	1.00
6	Barry Sanders	4.00

1996 Pacific

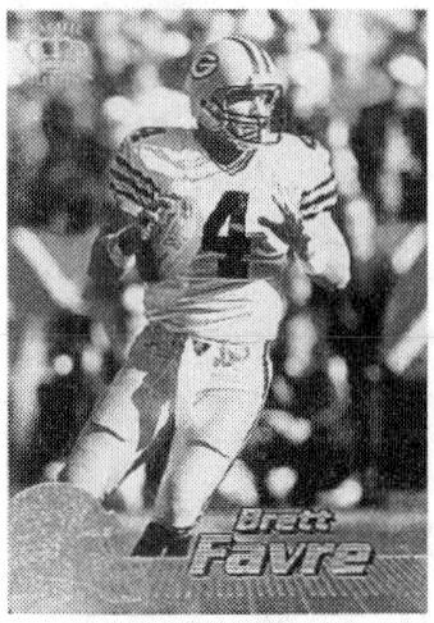

Pacific's 1996 Crown Collection set includes 450 cards (no subsets), each of which has gold-foiled etching along the bottom for the player's name, team helmet and a gridiron. The Pacific logo is also stamped in gold on the front, which features a full-bleed color action photo. The horizontal back has a color closeup shot on one side, with the player's name and position in team colors on the opposite side in the top corner. Underneath is biographical information and a career recap. The card number and a Pacific logo are in the lower right corner. Two parallel versions of the regular set were also made - Scorching Red Foil (nine in every 37 retail packs) and Electric Blue Foil (nine in every 37 hobby packs). There are six insert sets - Card-Supials, Cramer's Choice Awards, Bomb Squad, Gold Crown Die-Cuts, Gems of the Crown and The Zone.

		MT
Complete Set (450):		40.00
Common Player:		.05
Minor Stars:		.10
Comp. Blue or Red (450):		300.00
Blue or Red Cards:		4x-8x
Pack (12):		1.50
Wax Box (36):		48.00
1	Jeff Feagles	.05
2	Rob Moore	.05
3	Clyde Simmons	.05
4	Mike Buck	.05
5	Aeneas Williams	.05
6	*Simeon Rice*	.25
7	Garrison Hearst	.10
8	Eric Swann	.05
9	Dave Krieg	.05
10	*Leeland McElroy*	.75
11	Oscar McBride	.05
12	Frank Sanders	.05
13	Larry Centers	.05
14	Seth Joyner	.05
15	Stevie Anderson	.05
16	Craig Heyward	.05
17	Devin Bush	.05
18	Eric Metcalf	.05
19	Jeff George	.10
20	*Richard Huntley*	4.00
21	*Jamal Anderson*	8.00
22	Bert Emanuel	.05
23	Terance Mathis	.05
24	Roman Fortin	.05
25	Jessie Tuggle	.05
26	Morten Andersen	.05
27	Chris Doleman	.05
28	D.J. Johnson	.05
29	Kevin Ross	.05
30	Michael Jackson	.05
31	Eric Zeier	.05
32	Jonathan Ogden	.05
33	Eric Turner	.05
34	Andre Rison	.05
35	Lorenzo White	.05
36	Earnest Byner	.05
37	Derrick Alexander	.05
38	Brian Kinchen	.05
39	Anthony Pleasant	.05
40	Vinny Testaverde	.05
41	Pepper Johnson	.05
42	Frank Hartley	.05
43	Craig Powell	.05
44	Leroy Hoard	.05
45	Kent Hull	.05
46	Bryce Paup	.05
47	Andre Reed	.05
48	Darick Holmes	.05
49	Russell Copeland	.05
50	Jerry Ostroski	.05
51	Chris Green	.05
52	*Eric Moulds*	2.00
53	Justin Armour	.05
54	Jim Kelly	.10
55	Cornelius Bennett	.05
56	Steve Tasker	.05
57	Thurman Thomas	.10
58	Bruce Smith	.05
59	Todd Collins	.05
60	Shawn King	.05
61	Don Beebe	.05
62	John Kasay	.05
63	Tim McKyer	.05
64	Darion Conner	.05
65	Pete Metzelaars	.05
66	Derrick Moore	.05
67	Blake Brockermeyer	.05
68	*Tim Biakabutuka*	1.00
69	Sam Mills	.05
70	Vince Workman	.05
71	Kerry Collins	.75
72	Carlton Bailey	.05
73	Mark Carrier	.05
74	Donnell Woolford	.05
75	*Walt Harris*	.25
76	John Thierry	.05
77	Al Fontenot	.05
78	Lewis Tillman	.05
79	Curtis Conway	.10
80	Chris Zorich	.05
81	Mark Carrier	.05
82	*Bobby Engram*	.75
83	Alonzo Spellman	.05
84	Rashaan Salaam	.50
85	Michael Timpson	.05
86	Nate Lewis	.05
87	James Williams	.05
88	Jeff Graham	.05
89	Erik Kramer	.05
90	Willie Anderson	.05
91	Tony McGee	.05
92	Marco Battaglia	.05
93	Dan Wilkinson	.05
94	John Walsh	.05
95	Eric Bieniemy	.05
96	Ricardo McDonald	.05
97	Carl Pickens	.10
98	Kevin Sargent	.05
99	David Dunn	.05
100	Jeff Blake	.50
101	Harold Green	.05
102	James Francis	.05
103	John Copeland	.05
104	Darnay Scott	.05
105	Darren Woodson	.05
106	Jay Novacek	.05
107	Charles Haley	.05
108	Mark Tuinei	.05
109	Michael Irvin	.10
110	Troy Aikman	.75
111	Chris Boniol	.05
112	Sherman Williams	.05
113	Deion Sanders	.50
114	Emmitt Smith	2.00
115	Eric Bjornson	.05
116	Nate Newton	.05
117	Larry Allen	.05
118	Kevin Williams	.05
119	Leon Lett	.05
120	John Mobley	.05
121	Anthony Miller	.05
122	Brian Habib	.05
123	Aaron Craver	.05
124	Glyn Milburn	.05
125	Shannon Sharpe	.05
126	Steve Atwater	.05
127	Jason Elam	.05
128	John Elway	.35
129	Reggie Rivers	.05
130	Mike Pritchard	.05
131	Vance Johnson	.05
132	Terrell Davis	1.25
133	Tyrone Braxton	.05
134	Ed McCaffrey	.05
135	Brett Perriman	.05
136	Chris Spielman	.05
137	Luther Elliss	.05
138	Johnnie Morton	.05
139	Zefross Moss	.05
140	Barry Sanders	1.25
141	Lomas Brown	.05
142	Cory Schlesinger	.05
143	Jason Hanson	.05
144	Kevin Glover	.05
145	*Ron Rivers*	.50
146	Aubrey Matthews	.05
147	Reggie Brown	.05
148	Herman Moore	.30
149	Scott Mitchell	.05
150	Brett Favre	2.00
151	Sean Jones	.05
152	Leroy Butler	.05
153	Mark Chmura	.20
154	*Derrick Mayes*	1.00
155	Mark Ingram	.05
156	Antonio Freeman	.05
157	*Chris Darkins*	.25
158	Robert Brooks	.10
159	William Henderson	.05
160	George Koonce	.05
161	Craig Newsome	.05
162	Darius Holland	.05
163	George Teague	.05
164	Edgar Bennett	.05
165	Reggie White	.10
166	Michael Barrow	.05
167	Mel Gray	.05
168	Anthony Dorsett Jr.	.05
169	Roderick Lewis	.05
170	Henry Ford	.05
171	Mark Stepnoski	.05
172	Chris Sanders	.05
173	Anthony Cook	.05
174	Eddie Robinson	.05
175	Steve McNair	.50
176	Haywood Jeffires	.05
177	*Eddie George*	3.50
178	Marion Butts	.05
179	Malcolm Seabron	.05
180	Rodney Thomas	.05
181	Ken Dilger	.05
182	Zack Crockett	.05
183	Tony Bennett	.05
184	Quentin Coryatt	.05
185	Marshall Faulk	.50
186	Sean Dawkins	.05
187	Jim Harbaugh	.05
188	Eugene Daniel	.05
189	Roosevelt Potts	.05
190	Lamont Warren	.05
191	Will Wolford	.05
192	Tony Siragusa	.05
193	Aaron Bailey	.05
194	Trev Alberts	.05
195	*Kevin Hardy*	.10
196	Greg Spann	.05
197	Steve Beuerlein	.05
198	Steve Taneyhill	.05
199	Vaughn Dunbar	.05
200	Mark Brunell	.75
201	Bernard Carter	.05
202	James Stewart	.05
203	Tony Boselli	.05
204	Chris Doering	.05
205	Willie Jackson	.05
206	*Tony Brackens*	.30
207	Ernest Givins	.05
208	Le'Shai Maston	.05
209	Pete Mitchell	.05
210	Desmond Howard	.05
211	Vinnie Clark	.05
212	Jeff Lageman	.05
213	Derrick Walker	.05
214	Dan Saleaumua	.05
215	Derrick Thomas	.05
216	Neil Smith	.05
217	Willie Davis	.05
218	Mark Collins	.05
219	Lake Dawson	.05
220	Greg Hill	.05
221	Anthony Davis	.05
222	Kimble Anders	.05
223	Webster Slaughter	.05
224	Tamarick Vanover	.50
225	Marcus Allen	.10
226	Steve Bono	.10
227	Will Shields	.05
228	*Karim Abdul-Jabbar*	.75
229	Tim Bowens	.05
230	Keith Sims	.05
231	Terry Kirby	.05
232	Gene Atkins	.05
233	Dan Marino	2.00
234	Richmond Webb	.05
235	Gary Clark	.05
236	O.J. McDuffie	.05
237	Marco Coleman	.05
238	Bernie Parmalee	.05
239	Randal Hill	.05
240	Bryan Cox	.05
241	Irving Fryar	.05
242	Derrick Alexander	.05
243	Qadry Ismail	.05
244	Warren Moon	.05
245	Cris Carter	.05
246	Chad May	.05
247	Robert Smith	.05
248	Fuad Reveiz	.05
249	Orlando Thomas	.05
250	Chris Hinton	.05
251	Jack Del Rio	.05
252	Moe Williams	.05
253	Roy Barker	.05
254	Jake Reed	.05
255	Adrian Cooper	.05
256	Curtis Martin	1.50
257	Ben Coates	.05
258	Drew Bledsoe	.75
259	Maurice Hurst	.05
260	Troy Brown	.05
261	Bruce Armstrong	.05
262	Myron Guyton	.05
263	Dave Meggett	.05
264	*Terry Glenn*	1.75
265	Chris Slade	.05
266	Vincent Brisby	.05
267	Willie McGinest	.05
268	Vincent Brown	.05
269	Will Moore	.05
270	Jay Barker	.05
271	Ray Zellars	.05
272	Derek Brown	.05
273	William Roaf	.05
274	Quinn Early	.05
275	Michael Haynes	.05
276	Rufus Porter	.05
277	Renaldo Turnbull	.05
278	Wayne Martin	.05
279	Tyrone Hughes	.05
280	Irv Smith	.05
281	Eric Allen	.05
282	Mark Fields	.05
283	Mario Bates	.05
284	Jim Everett	.05
285	Vince Buck	.05
286	Alex Molden	.05
287	Tyrone Wheatley	.05
288	Chris Calloway	.05
289	Jessie Armstead	.05
290	Arthur Marshall	.05
291	Aaron Pierce	.05
292	Dave Brown	.05
293	Rodney Hampton	.05
294	John Elliott	.05
295	Mike Sherrard	.05
296	Howard Cross	.05
297	Michael Brooks	.05
298	Herschel Walker	.05
299	*Danny Kanell*	.75
300	Keith Elias	.05
301	Bobby Houston	.05
302	Dexter Carter	.05
303	Tony Casillas	.05
304	Kyle Brady	.05
305	Glenn Foley	.05
306	Ron Moore	.05
307	Ryan Yarborough	.05
308	Aaron Glenn	.05
309	Adrian Murrell	.05
310	Boomer Esiason	.05
311	Kyle Clifton	.05
312	Wayne Chrebet	.05
313	Erik Howard	.05
314	*Keyshawn Johnson*	2.50
315	Marvin Washington	.05
316	Johnny Mitchell	.05
317	*Alex Van Dyke*	.50
318	Billy Joe Hobert	.05
319	Andrew Glover	.05
320	Vince Evans	.05
321	Chester McGlockton	.05
322	Pat Swilling	.05
323	Raghib Ismail	.05
324	Eddie Anderson	.05
325	*Rickey Dudley*	.75
326	Steve Wisniewski	.05
327	Harvey Williams	.05
328	Napoleon Kaufman	.05
329	Tim Brown	.10
330	Jeff Hostetler	.05
331	Anthony Smith	.05
332	Terry McDaniel	.05
333	Charlie Garner	.05
334	Ricky Watters	.05
335	Brian Dawkins	.05
336	Randall Cunningham	.05
337	Gary Anderson	.05
338	Calvin Williams	.05
339	Chris T. Jones	.05
340	*Bobby Hoying*	.75
341	William Fuller	.05
342	William Thomas	.05
343	Mike Mamula	.05
344	Fred Barnett	.05
345	Rodney Peete	.05
346	Mark McMillian	.05
347	Bobby Taylor	.05
348	Yancey Thigpen	.35
349	Neil O'Donnell	.05
350	Rod Woodson	.05
351	Kordell Stewart	.75
352	Dermontti Dawson	.05
353	Norm Johnson	.05
354	Ernie Mills	.05
355	Bam Morris	.05
356	Mark Bruener	.05
357	Kevin Greene	.05
358	Greg Lloyd	.05
359	Andre Hastings	.05
360	Erric Pegram	.05
361	Carnell Lake	.05
362	Dwayne Harper	.05
363	Ronnie Harmon	.05
364	Leslie O'Neal	.05
365	John Carney	.05
366	Stan Humphries	.05
367	Brian Roche	.05
368	Terrell Fletcher	.05
369	Shaun Gayle	.05
370	Alfred Pupunu	.05
371	Shawn Jefferson	.05
372	Junior Seau	.05
373	Mark Seay	.05
374	Aaron Hayden	.05
375	Tony Martin	.05
376	Steve Young	.75
377	J.J. Stokes	.50
378	Jerry Rice	.75
379	Derek Loville	.05
380	Lee Woodall	.05
381	*Terrell Owens*	2.50
382	Elvis Grbac	.05
383	Ricky Ervins	.05
384	Eric Davis	.05
385	Dana Stubblefield	.05
386	Gary Plummer	.05
387	Tim McDonald	.05
388	William Floyd	.05
389	Ken Norton Jr.	.05
390	Merton Hanks	.05
391	Bart Oates	.05
392	Brent Jones	.05
393	Steve Broussard	.05
394	Robert Blackmon	.05
395	Rick Tuten	.05
396	Pete Kendall	.05
397	John Friesz	.05
398	Terry Wooden	.05
399	Rick Mirer	.05
400	Chris Warren	.10
401	Joey Galloway	.50
402	Howard Ballard	.05
403	Jason Kyle	.05
404	Kevin Mawae	.05
405	Mack Strong	.05
406	Reggie Brown	.05
407	Cortez Kennedy	.05
408	Sean Gilbert	.05
409	J.T. Thomas	.05
410	Shane Conlan	.05
411	Johnny Bailey	.05
412	Mark Rypien	.05
413	Leonard Russell	.05
414	Troy Drayton	.05
415	Jerome Bettis	.05
416	Jessie Hester	.05
417	Isaac Bruce	.50
418	Roman Phifer	.05
419	Todd Kinchen	.05
420	Alexander Wright	.05
421	Marcus Jones	.05
422	Horace Copeland	.05
423	Eric Curry	.05
424	Courtney Hawkins	.05
425	Alvin Harper	.05
426	Derrick Brooks	.05
427	Errict Rhett	.25
428	Trent Dilfer	.05
429	Hardy Nickerson	.05
430	Brad Culpepper	.05
431	Warren Sapp	.05
432	Reggie Roby	.05
433	Santana Dotson	.05
434	Jerry Ellison	.05
435	Lawrence Dawsey	.05
436	Heath Shuler	.05
437	Stanley Richard	.05
438	Rod Stephens	.05
439	*Stephen Davis*	3.00
440	Terry Allen	.05
441	Michael Westbrook	.40
442	Ken Harvey	.05
443	Coleman Bell	.05
444	Marvcus Patton	.05
445	Gus Frerotte	.05
446	Leslie Shepherd	.05
447	Tom Carter	.05
448	Brian Mitchell	.05
449	Darrell Green	.05
450	Tony Woods	.05

1996 Pacific Blue/Red/Silver

Pacific Crown Collection Football was offered in three different parallel versions - blue, red and silver. Electric Blue versions of the 450-card set were available in hobby packs, with Scorching Red versions in retail, both seeded nine per 37 packs. There was also a Silver version available in special retail packs, with roughly the same production as the Red and Blue set. The only differences in these cards from the base cards is the color of the foil stamping.

	MT
Complete Blue Set (450):	300.00
Blue Cards:	4x-8x
Complete Red Set (450):	300.00
Red Cards:	4x-8x
Complete Silver Set (450):	300.00
Silver Cards:	4x-8x

1996 Pacific Bomb Squad

The NFL's finest quarterback/receiver combinations are spotlighted on these 1996 Pacific inserts. The cards, seeded one per every 73 packs, feature a player on each side against a background of team-colored swirls. The Pacific logo is in the upper left corner; the player's name and position run down the right side of the card. One side has a card number, which uses a "BS" prefix.

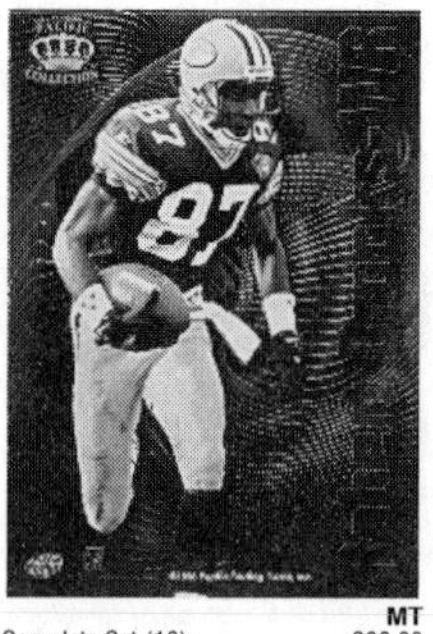

		MT
Complete Set (10):		200.00
Common Player:		10.00
1	Jeff Blake, Carl Pickens	10.00
2	John Elway, Anthony Miller	16.00
3	Scott Mitchell, Herman Moore	10.00
4	Troy Aikman, Jay Novacek	25.00
5	Brett Favre, Robert Brooks	45.00
6	Steve McNair, Chris Sanders	15.00
7	Dan Marino, Irving Fryar	45.00
8	Drew Bledsoe, Terry Glenn	35.00
9	Kordell Stewart,Kordell Stewart	20.00
10	Steve Young, Jerry Rice	25.00

1996 Pacific Card-Supials

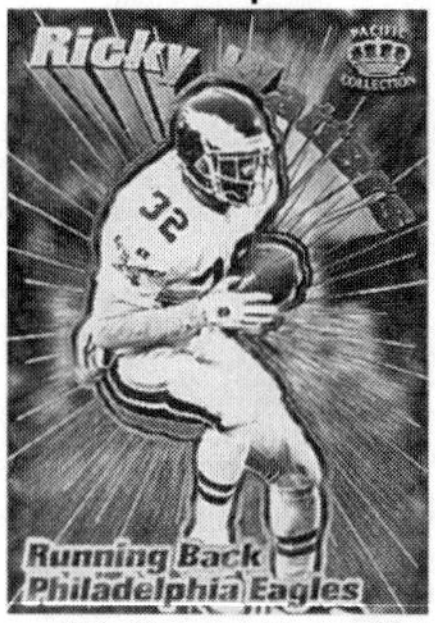

This 36-card Pacific insert set features cards with flashy gold embossing on the front for the Pacific logo, player's name and outline of the letters in the player's position and team name. The back has a little cut in the card, creating a pouch for another mini (1-1/4" x 1-3/4") card of the player - a marsupial. Hence, the name Card-Supials. The card back of the regular card is black-and-white; the mini card, when placed in the pouch, fills in the area with color. The bottom of the card has a brief paragraph about the player, plus a card number (1 of 36, etc.). The mini card's back has the player's name and position along the side. A closeup shot and player profile complete the back. The card is numbered 1a of 36, etc. Cards were seeded one per every 37 packs, but the minis were not always matched up with the larger card.

		MT
Complete Set (72):		500.00
Comp. Large Set (36):		300.00
Comp. Small Set (36):		200.00
Common Large:		4.00
Small Cards: Half Price		
1	Garrison Hearst	4.00
2	Jeff George	4.00
3	Eric Zeier	4.00
4	Jim Kelly	4.00
5	Kerry Collins	8.00
6	Rashaan Salaam	6.00
7	Jeff Blake	6.00
8	Troy Aikman	20.00
9	Emmitt Smith	40.00
10	Terrell Davis	20.00
11	John Elway	10.00
12	Deion Sanders	12.00
13	Barry Sanders	20.00
14	Brett Favre	40.00
15	Steve McNair	10.00
16	Marshall Faulk	6.00
17	Mark Brunell	15.00
18	Tamarick Vanover	6.00
19	Dan Marino	40.00
20	Cris Carter	4.00
21	Keyshawn Johnson	6.00
22	Rodney Hampton	4.00
23	Curtis Martin	25.00
24	Drew Bledsoe	20.00
25	Mario Bates	4.00
26	Napoleon Kaufman	4.00
27	Ricky Watters	4.00
28	Kordell Stewart	20.00
29	Junior Seau	4.00
30	Steve Young	18.00
31	Jerry Rice	20.00
32	Isaac Bruce	8.00
33	Joey Galloway	15.00
34	Chris Warren	4.00
35	Errict Rhett	6.00
36	Michael Westbrook	6.00

1996 Pacific Cramer's Choice Awards

Cramer's Choice Awards return as an insert for Pacific's 1996 football line. The die-cut cards, which showcase some of the NFL's most amazing athletes, have a silver background for the card, which is shaped like a trophy. The cards are the rarest in this product line; they are seeded one per every 721 packs. The back has comments about the player by Michael Cramer, CEO and president of Pacific, who made the selections.

		MT
Complete Set (10):		900.00
Common Player:		40.00
1	Emmitt Smith	100.00
2	John Elway	100.00
3	Barry Sanders	125.00
4	Brett Favre	125.00
5	Reggie White	40.00
6	Dan Marino	100.00
7	Curtis Martin	50.00
8	Keyshawn Johnson	60.00
9	Kordell Stewart	80.00
10	Jerry Rice	80.00

1996 Pacific The Zone

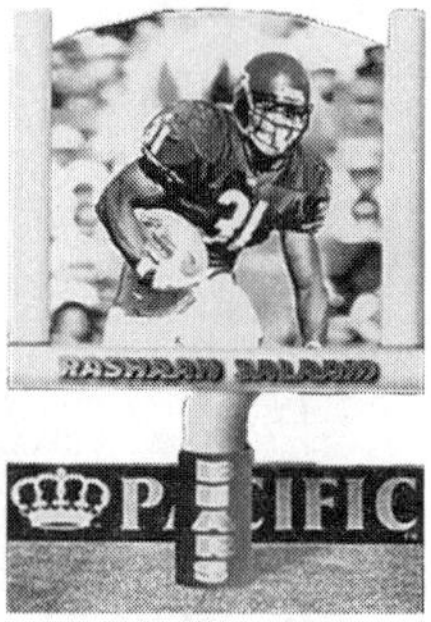

Only the NFL's most productive players who found the end zone on a regular basis in 1995 are featured on these die-cut inserts. The cards were seeded one per every 145 packs. Each card front has a die-cut goal post, with the player photo between the posts. The player's name is in gold foil on the cross bar. His team's name is on the post. Pacific and the logo are in gold foil on the bottom of the card, which has a grassy background. The card back has a closeup shot of the player, his name and a team logo between the posts. His position and city name are on the cross bar. The bottom of the card has a grassy background with a recap of some of the player's accomplishments. The card number is also at the bottom, using a "Z" prefix.

		MT
Complete Set (20):		700.00
Common Player:		10.00
1	Jim Kelly	20.00
2	Rashaan Salaam	10.00
3	Carl Pickens	10.00
4	Jeff Blake	20.00
5	Kerry Collins	20.00
6	Emmitt Smith	70.00
7	Troy Aikman	40.00
8	John Elway	40.00
9	Barry Sanders	50.00
10	Herman Moore	10.00
11	Scott Mitchell	10.00
12	Brett Favre	80.00
13	Robert Brooks	10.00
14	Marshall Faulk	20.00
15	Dan Marino	80.00
16	Drew Bledsoe	40.00
17	Curtis Martin	40.00
18	Steve Young	30.00
19	Jerry Rice	40.00
20	Chris Warren	10.00

1996 Pacific Gold Crown Die-Cuts

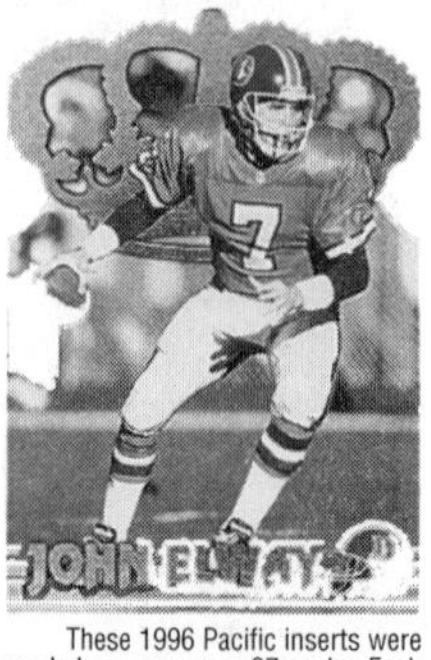

These 1996 Pacific inserts were seeded one per every 37 packs. Each

card features a full-bleed color action photo on the front, with a die-cut gold foiled crown at the top. The player's name is at the bottom in foil, too, next to a team helmet. The card back has the crown image at the top. The player's name runs across the middle, with a closeup shot of the player in a diamond on one side and brief player profile on the other. A card number, using a "GC" prefix, is in the lower left corner.

		MT
Complete Set (20):		350.00
Common Player:		5.00
1	Emmitt Smith	30.00
2	Troy Aikman	20.00
3	Barry Sanders	40.00
4	Kerry Collins	8.00
5	Jeff Blake	5.00
6	John Elway	20.00
7	Terrell Davis	30.00
8	Deion Sanders	15.00
9	Brett Favre	40.00
10	Dan Marino	30.00
11	Eddie George	25.00
12	Curtis Martin	15.00
13	Drew Bledsoe	20.00
14	Keyshawn Johnson	10.00
15	Napoleon Kaufman	10.00
16	Kordell Stewart	20.00
17	Steve Young	15.00
18	Jerry Rice	20.00
19	Joey Galloway	10.00
20	Chris Warren	5.00

1996 Pacific Gems of the Crown

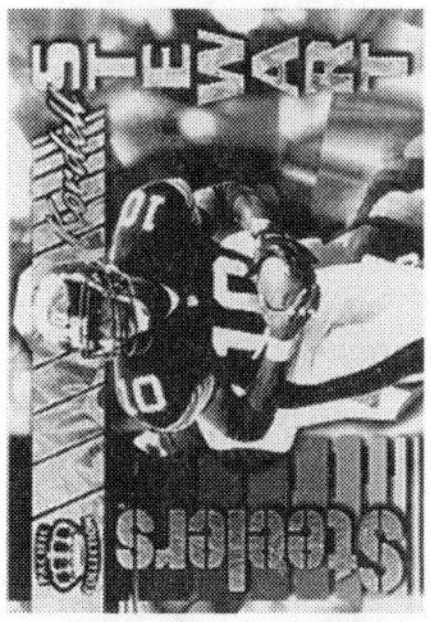

These 1996 Pacific inserts, numbered 19-36, were seeded one per every 37 packs. (Cards 1-18 were inserts in 1996 Dynagon Prism packs.) The horizontal card front has a color photo in the middle, with an outline around it. The team name is stamped in gold along the left side; the player's last name is stamped in gold along the right. A gold-foiled panel along the top has the Pacific logo and the player's first name in the upper right corner.

		MT
Complete Set (18):		130.00
Common Player:		3.00
19	Garrison Hearst	3.00
20	Jeff Blake	8.00
21	Troy Aikman	12.00
22	Deion Sanders	10.00
23	Brett Favre	20.00
24	Robert Smith	3.00
25	Mario Bates	3.00
26	Napoleon Kaufman	3.00
27	Kordell Stewart	12.00
28	Jim Kelly	3.00
29	Jim Harbaugh	3.00
30	Tamarick Vanover	3.00
31	Dan Marino	20.00
32	Warren Moon	3.00
33	Curtis Martin	18.00
34	Rodney Hampton	3.00
35	Ricky Watters	3.00
36	Joey Galloway	10.00

1996 Pacific Power Corps

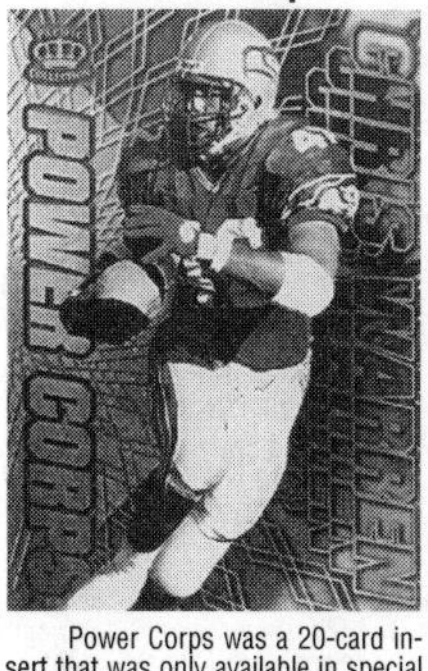

Power Corps was a 20-card insert that was only available in special retail packs on Pacific Crown Collection in 1996. The cards contained the words "Power Corps" running down the left side, with the player's name running down the right side. The cards were numbered PC1-PC20. There were also foil parallel versions of card numbers 1, 11, 14, 17 and 19.

		MT
Complete Set (20):		80.00
Common Player:		2.50
1	Troy Aikman	6.00
2	Jeff Blake	2.50
3	Drew Bledsoe	6.00
4	Kerry Collins	6.00
5	Terrell Davis	8.00
6	John Elway	4.00
7	Marshall Faulk	3.00
8	Brett Favre	12.00
9	Joey Galloway	2.50
10	Garrison Hearst	2.50
11	Dan Marino	12.00
12	Curtis Martin	8.00
13	Steve McNair	6.00
14	Jerry Rice	6.00
15	Rashaan Salaam	4.00
16	Barry Sanders	6.00
17	Emmitt Smith	12.00
18	Kordell Stewart	6.00
19	Chris Warren	2.50
20	Steve Young	4.00

1996 Pacific Crown Royale

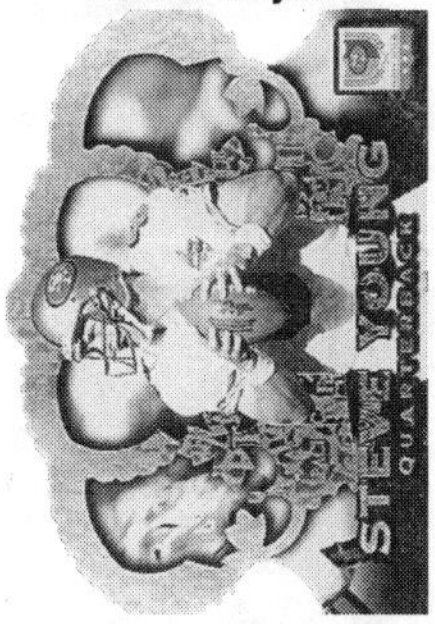

Pacific's 1996 Crown Royale release features 144 regular-size cards that are highlighted by etched, die-cut cards. Each horizontal card is topped with a die-cut gold crown and the front has the player's name, position and team logo. Two parallel versions are available: Royale Blue (hobby) and Royale Silver (retail). Also, five insert sets were inserted: Cramer's Choice Awards, Field Force Etch-Tech, Pro Bowl Die-Cut, Triple Crown Die-Cut and NFL Regime. The 144-card base set was sold in five-card packs and each regular card back was listed by the "CR" prefix.

		MT
Complete Set (144):		150.00
Common Player:		.50
Minor Stars:		1.00
Blue Cards:		2x-4x
Silver Cards:		3x-6x
Pack (5):		6.00
Wax Box (24):		120.00
1	Dan Marino	10.00
2	Frank Sanders	.50
3	*Bobby Engram*	2.00
4	Cornelius Bennett	.50
5	Steve Bono	.50
6	Aaron Hayden	.50
7	Leroy Hoard	.50
8	Brett Perriman	.50
9	Irv Smith	.50
10	Jim Kelly	1.00
11	Rodney Thomas	.50
12	Eric Bieniemy	.50
13	Darnay Scott	1.00
14	Ki-Jana Carter	2.00
15	Kerry Collins	1.50
16	Shannon Sharpe	1.00
17	Michael Westbrook	1.00
18	Steve McNair	6.00
19	*Tony Banks*	5.00
20	Rashaan Salaam	1.00
21	Terrell Fletcher	.50
22	Michael Timpson	.50
23	*Bobby Hoying*	4.00
24	Quinn Early	.50
25	Warren Moon	1.00
26	Tommy Vardell	.50
27	*Marvin Harrison*	12.00
28	Lake Dawson	.50
29	*Karim Abdul-Jabbar*	4.00
30	Chris Warren	2.00
31	Heath Shuler	1.00
32	Bert Emanuel	.50
33	Howard Griffith	.50
34	*Alex Van Dyke*	2.00
35	Isaac Bruce	1.00
36	Mark Brunell	5.00
37	Winslow Oliver	.50
38	O.J. McDuffie	.50
39	*Terrell Owens*	12.00
40	Jerry Rice	5.00
41	Henry Ellard	.50
42	Chris Sanders	.50
43	Craig Heyward	.50
44	*Eddie Kennison*	2.50
45	Terrell Davis	8.00
46	Rodney Hampton	.50
47	Bryan Still	.50
48	Tim Brown	.50
49	*Keyshawn Johnson*	10.00
50	Barry Sanders	12.00
51	Terry Allen	1.00
52	Sean Dawkins	.50
53	Bryce Paup	.50
54	Brett Favre	12.00
55	Deion Sanders	3.00
56	*Kevin Hardy*	2.00
57	Kevin Williams	.50
58	Jeff George	.50
59	*Tim Biakabutuka*	5.00
60	Drew Bledsoe	5.00
61	Michael Jackson	.50
62	James Stewart	.50
63	Mario Bates	.50
64	Daryl Johnston	.50
65	Herman Moore	2.00
66	Ben Coates	.50
67	*Terry Glenn*	7.00
68	Robert Smith	.50
69	Irving Fryar	.50
70	Napoleon Kaufman	.50
71	*Rickey Dudley*	3.00
72	Bernie Parmalee	.50
73	Kyle Brady	.50
74	Neil O'Donnell	.50
75	*Lawrence Phillips*	4.00
76	Hardy Nickerson	.50
77	John Elway	4.00
78	Pete Mitchell	.50
79	Jason Dunn	.50
80	Reggie White	1.00
81	J.J. Stokes	2.00
82	Jake Reed	.50
83	Yancey Thigpen	.50
84	Jonathan Ogden	.50
85	Larry Centers	.50
86	Scott Mitchell	.50
87	Eric Zeier	.50
88	Anthony Miller	.50
89	Brian Blades	.50
90	Cris Carter	.50
91	Kordell Stewart	8.00
92	Charles Way	.50
93	Jeff Hostetler	.50
94	Brad Johnson	5.00
95	Marcus Allen	1.00
96	Errict Rhett	2.00
97	Stan Humphries	.50
98	Michael Haynes	.50
99	Curtis Martin	8.00
100	Troy Aikman	5.00
101	Earnest Byner	.50
102	Vincent Brisby	.50
103	Zack Crockett	.50
104	Haywood Jeffires	.50
105	Joey Galloway	4.00
106	Carl Pickens	1.00
107	*Leeland McElroy*	1.50
108	Adrian Murrell	.50
109	*Joe Horn*	10.00
110	Steve Young	4.00
111	Andre Rison	.50
112	Jim Everett	.50
113	*Jamie Asher*	2.00
114	Steve Walsh	.50
115	Robert Brooks	1.00
116	*Eric Moulds*	8.00
117	Edgar Bennett	.50
118	Greg Lloyd	.50
119	Jerris McPhail	.50
120	Marshall Faulk	3.00
121	Dave Brown	.50
122	Harvey Williams	.50
123	Trent Dilfer	1.00
124	*Eddie George*	15.00
125	Jeff Blake	2.00
126	Mark Chmura	.50
127	Boomer Esiason	.50
128	Jim Harbaugh	.50
129	Bryan Cox	.50
130	Ricky Watters	1.00
131	*Amani Toomer*	2.00
132	Jim Miller	.50
133	Cortez Kennedy	.50
134	Courtney Hawkins	.50
135	Junior Seau	.50
136	Tamarick Vanover	2.00
137	Jerome Bettis	1.00
138	Chris Calloway	.50
139	Rick Mirer	.50
140	Thurman Thomas	1.00
141	Sheddrick Wilson	.50
142	Charlie Garner	.50
143	Erik Kramer	.50
144	Emmitt Smith	10.00

1996 Pacific Crown Royale Blue/Silver

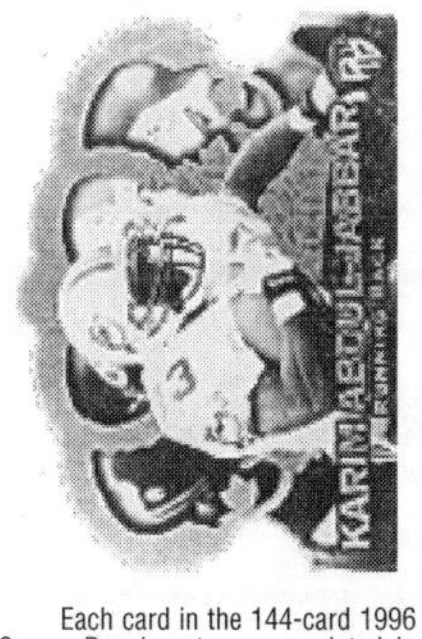

Each card in the 144-card 1996 Crown Royale set were reprinted in two different versions. Hobby packs had Royale Blue parallels, while retail packs had Royale Silver parallels, with both seeded four per 25 packs. These parallel sets are distinguished only by the color of the foil stamping.

	MT
Complete Blue Set (144):	700.00
Blue Cards:	2x-4x
Complete Silver Set (144):	1000.
Silver Cards:	3x-6x

1996 Pacific Crown Royale Cramer's Choice Awards

The large-sized set (5-1/2" x 4") was offered as part of a redemption offer in the Crown Royale set. Redemption cards, inserted every 385 packs, enabled collectors to obtain the 10-card, die-cut set. The cards are cut into the shape of a pyramid and the players honored were chosen by Pacific President and CEO Michael Cramer. The card backs are each listed with the "CC" prefix.

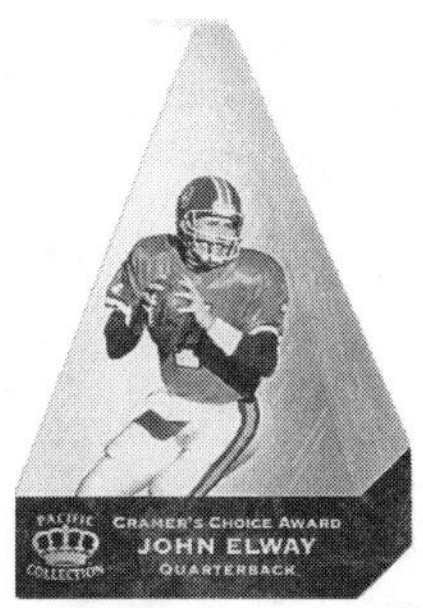

		MT
Complete Set (10):		800.00
Common Player:		50.00
1	John Elway	80.00
2	Brett Favre	125.00
3	Keyshawn Johnson	50.00
4	Dan Marino	125.00
5	Curtis Martin	100.00
6	Jerry Rice	85.00
7	Barry Sanders	100.00
8	Emmitt Smith	125.00
9	Kordell Stewart	75.00
10	Reggie White	50.00

1996 Pacific Crown Royale Triple Crown Die-Cut

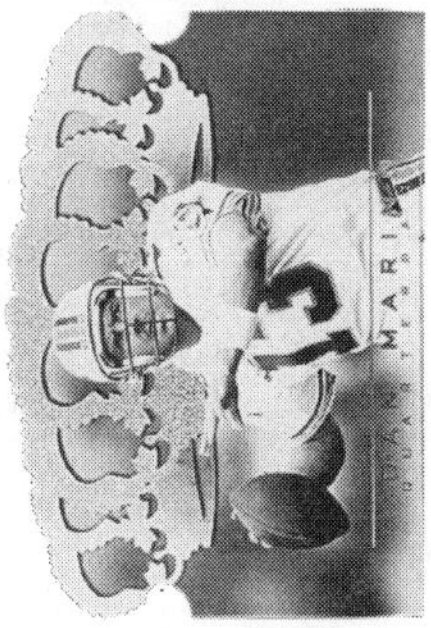

The 10-card, regular-sized, die-cut set honors 10 players who led the league in at least three different categories. Inserted every 73 packs in 1996 Crown Royale, the cards feature a similar die-cut crown design with gold foil as the base cards in Crown Royale. The card backs are labeled with the "TC" prefix and are individually numbered.

		MT
Complete Set (10):		600.00
Common Player:		20.00
1	Troy Aikman	60.00
2	John Elway	40.00
3	Brett Favre	90.00
4	Keyshawn Johnson	20.00
5	Dan Marino	90.00
6	Curtis Martin	80.00
7	Jerry Rice	60.00
8	Barry Sanders	60.00
9	Emmitt Smith	90.00
10	Steve Young	40.00

1996 Pacific Crown Royale Field Force

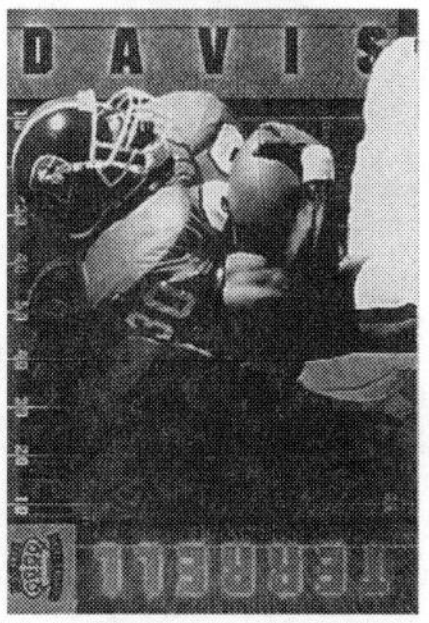

The 20-card, regular-sized set was inserted in 1996 packs of Crown Royale. Inserted every 49 packs, the horizontal cards employ etch-tech design and feature the player's name written on the side margins in foil etching of the player's team colors. The card backs contain a headshot of the player and are numbered with the "FF" prefix.

		MT
Complete Set (20):		900.00
Common Player:		15.00
1	Troy Aikman	60.00
2	Karim Abdul-Jabbar	45.00
3	Jeff Blake	25.00
4	Drew Bledsoe	60.00
5	Lawrence Phillips	35.00
6	Kerry Collins	25.00
7	Terrell Davis	65.00
8	John Elway	40.00
9	Brett Favre	100.00
10	Eddie George	60.00
11	Dan Marino	100.00
12	Curtis Martin	80.00
13	Jerry Rice	65.00
14	Rashaan Salaam	15.00
15	Barry Sanders	60.00
16	Deion Sanders	50.00
17	Emmitt Smith	100.00
18	Kordell Stewart	65.00
19	Chris Warren	15.00
20	Steve Young	50.00

1996 Pacific Crown Royale Pro Bowl Die-Cut

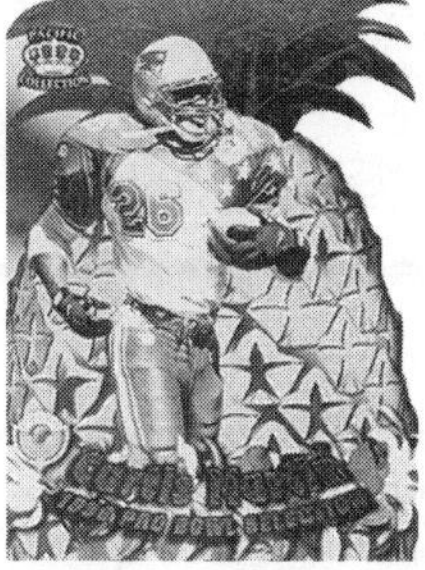

The 20-card, regular-sized, die-cut cards were inserted every 25 packs of Crown Royale. Each player is pictured in his Pro Bowl jersey and is backdropped with a die-cut palm tree and pineapple. The card backs feature an exploding volcano and a headshot of the player and are numbered with the "PB" prefix.

		MT
Complete Set (20):		550.00
Common Player:		10.00
1	Jeff Blake	12.00
2	Mark Chmura	10.00
3	Marshall Faulk	12.00
4	Brett Favre	100.00
5	Charles Haley	10.00
6	Merton Hanks	10.00
7	Greg Lloyd	10.00
8	Dan Marino	100.00
9	Curtis Martin	70.00
10	Anthony Miller	10.00
11	Herman Moore	12.00
12	Bryce Paup	10.00
13	Jerry Rice	50.00
14	Barry Sanders	50.00
15	Junior Seau	10.00
16	Emmitt Smith	100.00
17	Yancey Thigpen	10.00
18	Chris Warren	10.00
19	Ricky Watters	10.00
20	Steve Young	35.00

1996 Pacific Crown Royale NFL Regime

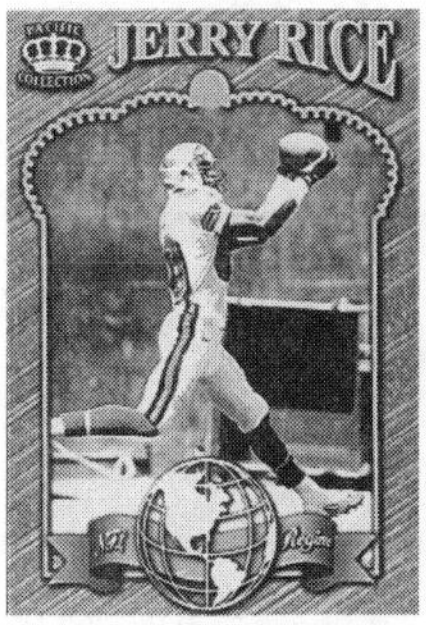

The 110-card, regular-sized set was included in each of the 1996 Crown Royale five-card packs. The card fronts feature a gray border with the player's name on top in red lettering and a white globe centered on a red ribbon which reads "NFL Regime." The card backs contain a headshot of the player and the prefix "NR."

		MT
Complete Set (110):		25.00
Common Player:		.20
Minor Stars:		.40
1	Steve Young	1.00
2	Jamir Miller	.20
3	Tyrone Brown	.20
4	Chris Shelling	.20
5	Warren Moon	.20
6	Shane Bonham	.20
7	Gary Brown	.20
8	Chris Chandler	.20
9	Bradford Banta	.20
10	John Elway	.75
11	Tom McManus	.20
12	Alfred Jackson	.20
13	Jay Barker	.20
14	Kirk Botkin	.20
15	Jim Kelly	.20
16	Lou Benfatti	.20
17	Billy Joe Hobert	.20
18	John Jackson	.20
19	Torin Dorn	.20
20	Drew Bledsoe	1.00
21	Gale Gilbert	.20
22	James Atkins	.20
23	John Lynch	.20
24	James Jenkins	.20
25	Kerry Collins	.50
26	Eric Swann	.20
27	Dan Stryzinski	.20
28	Mike Groh	.20
29	Tim Tindale	.20
30	Kordell Stewart	1.25
31	Frank Garcia	.20
32	Mill Coleman	.20
33	Bracey Walker	.20
34	Ryan McNeil	.20
35	Rodney Hampton	.20
36	John Mobley	.20
37	Derek Russell	.20
38	Jeff George	.20
39	Steve Morrison	.20
40	Rashaan Salaam	.40
41	Ryan Christopherson	.20
42	Darren Anderson	.20
43	Ronnie Williams	.20
44	Scottie Graham	.20
45	Thurman Thomas	.40
46	Corwin Brown	.20
47	Lee DeRamus	.20
48	Ray Agnew	.20
49	Erik Howard	.20
50	Emmitt Smith	2.50
51	Dan Land	.20
52	Vinny Testaverde	.20
53	Myron Bell	.20
54	Keith Lyle	.20
55	Aaron Hayden	.20
56	Jeff Brohm	.20
57	Ronnie Harris	.20
58	Trent Dilfer	.20
59	Browning Nagle	.20
60	Jeff Blake	.75
61	Rich Owens	.20
62	Anthony Edwards	.20
63	Orlando Brown	.20
64	Matthew Campbell	.20
65	Ricky Watters	.40
66	Travis Hannah	.20
67	Melvin Tuten	.20
68	Aaron Taylor	.20
69	Dale Hellestrae	.20
70	Marshall Faulk	1.00
71	Gary Anderson	.20
72	David Williams	.20
73	Jim Harbaugh	.20
74	Ray Hall	.20
75	Dan Marino	2.50
76	Chris Mims	.20
77	Matt Blundin	.20
78	Roy Barker	.20
79	John Burke	.20
80	Troy Aikman	1.25
81	Ed King	.20
82	Stan White	.20
83	Vance Joseph	.20
84	David Klingler	.20
85	Terrell Davis	1.00
86	Bobby Hoying	.20
87	Lethon Flowers	.20
88	Dwayne White	.20
89	Vaughn Parker	.20
90	Jerry Rice	1.25
91	Casey Weldon	.20
92	Rick Mirer	.20
93	Jim Pyne	.20
94	Matt Turk	.20
95	Marcus Allen	.20
96	Rob Moore	.20
97	Ruben Brown	.20
98	Zach Thomas	.20
99	Carwell Gardner	.20
100	Barry Sanders	1.75
101	Ben Coleman	.20
102	Steve Rhem	.20
103	Everett McIver	.20
104	Cole Ford	.20
105	Dave Krieg	.20
106	Anthony Parker	.20
107	Michael Brandon	.20
108	Michael McCrary	.20
109	Chad Fann	.20
110	Brett Favre	2.50

1996 Pacific Dynagon

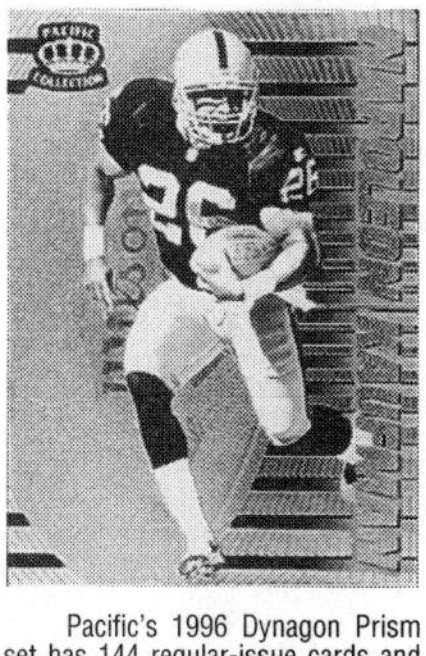

Pacific's 1996 Dynagon Prism set has 144 regular-issue cards and five insert sets. It is sold as a retail and hobby product, with inserts exclusive to both. The regular card front has a gold-foiled football stamped on the left, with a player photo in the middle. The player's name is written along the right side. The card uses the team's primary colors in the design. The horizontal back has a player profile shot on one side, flanked by his name, position and team name, card number and brief career summary. The five insert sets are Dynamic Duos, Gems of the Crown, Kings of the NFL, Tandems and Best Kept Secrets.

		MT
Complete Set (144):		150.00
Common Player:		.75
Minor Stars:		1.50
Comp. Best Kept Secrets (100):		15.00
Common Best Kept Sec.:		.25
Pack (2):		2.00
Wax Box (36):		60.00
1	Larry Centers	.75
2	Garrison Hearst	1.50
3	Dave Krieg	.75
4	Frank Sanders	1.50
5	Jeff George	1.50
6	Craig Heyward	.75
7	Terance Mathis	.75
8	Eric Metcalf	.75
9	Todd Collins	.75
10	Darick Holmes	.75
11	Jim Kelly	1.50
12	*Eric Moulds*	5.00
13	Bryce Paup	.75
14	Thurman Thomas	1.50
15	*Tim Biakabutuka*	2.50
16	Blake Brockermeyer	.75
17	Mark Carrier	.75
18	Kerry Collins	2.00
19	Derrick Moore	.75
20	*Bobby Engram*	2.00
21	Jeff Graham	.75
22	Erik Kramer	.75
23	Rashaan Salaam	1.50
24	Steve Stenstrom	.75
25	Chris Zorich	.75
26	Jeff Blake	2.00
27	David Dunn	.75
28	Carl Pickens	1.50
29	Darnay Scott	.75
30	Earnest Byner	.75
31	Leroy Hoard	.75
32	Keenan McCardell	.75
33	Eric Zeier	.75
34	Troy Aikman	5.00
35	Chris Boniol	.75
36	Michael Irvin	1.50
37	Daryl Johnston	.75
38	Deion Sanders	3.00
39	Emmitt Smith	10.00
40	*Stepfret Williams*	1.50
41	John Elway	5.00
42	Terrell Davis	10.00
43	Anthony Miller	.75
44	Shannon Sharpe	.75
45	Scott Mitchell	.75
46	Herman Moore	1.50
47	Brett Perriman	.75
48	Barry Sanders	10.00
49	Cory Schlesinger	.75
50	Edgar Bennett	.75
51	Robert Brooks	.75
52	Mark Chmura	1.50
53	Brett Favre	10.00
54	Reggie White	1.50
55	*Eddie George*	10.00
56	Steve McNair	4.00
57	Chris Sanders	1.50
58	Rodney Thomas	1.50
59	Ben Bronsen	.75
60	Zack Crockett	.75
61	Marshall Faulk	2.50
62	Jim Harbaugh	.75
63	Mark Brunell	4.00
64	*Kevin Hardy*	1.50
65	Willie Jackson	.75
66	Pete Mitchell	.75
67	James Stewart	.75
68	Marcus Allen	1.50
69	Steve Bono	1.50
70	Lake Dawson	.75
71	Neil Smith	.75
72	Tamarick Vanover	1.50
73	Irving Fryar	.75
74	Terry Kirby	.75
75	Dan Marino	10.00
76	O.J. McDuffie	.75
77	Bernie Parmalee	.75
78	*Stanley Pritchett*	.75
79	Cris Carter	.75
80	Qadry Ismail	.75
81	Chad May	.75
82	Warren Moon	.75
83	Robert Smith	.75
84	Drew Bledsoe	5.00
85	Ben Coates	.75
86	*Terry Glenn*	4.00
87	Curtis Martin	6.00
88	Willie McGinest	.75
89	Mario Bates	.75
90	Jim Everett	.75
91	Wayne Martin	.75
92	Shane Pahukoa	.75
93	Ray Zellars	.75
94	Dave Brown	.75
95	Chris Calloway	.75
96	Rodney Hampton	.75
97	Tyrone Wheatley	.75
98	Wayne Chrebet	.75
99	Glenn Foley	.75
100	*Keyshawn Johnson*	6.00
101	Adrian Murrell	.75
102	*Alex Van Dyke*	1.50
103	Tim Brown	.75
104	Harvey Williams	.75
105	Billy Joe Hobert	.75
106	Raghib Ismail	.75
107	Napoleon Kaufman	1.50
108	Charlie Garner	.75
109	Rodney Peete	.75
110	Ricky Watters	.75
111	Calvin Williams	.75
112	Mark Bruener	.75
113	Kevin Greene	.75
114	Ernie Mills	.75
115	Kordell Stewart	6.00
116	Yancey Thigpen	1.50
117	Dave Barr	.75
118	Jerome Bettis	.75
119	Isaac Bruce	1.50
120	*Lawrence Phillips*	2.00
121	J.T. Thomas	.75
122	Ronnie Harmon	.75
123	Aaron Hayden	1.50
124	Stan Humphries	.75
125	Junior Seau	1.50
126	William Floyd	.75
127	Elvis Grbac	.75
128	Jerry Rice	5.00
129	J.J. Stokes	1.50
130	Steve Young	5.00
131	Joey Galloway	2.00
132	Cortez Kennedy	.75
133	Kevin Mawae	.75
134	Rick Mirer	.75
135	Chris Warren	1.50
136	Trent Dilfer	.75
137	Jerry Ellison	.75
138	Alvin Harper	.75
139	Errict Rhett	1.50
140	Terry Allen	.75
141	Brian Mitchell	.75
142	Gus Frerotte	.75
143	Michael Westbrook	1.50
144	Heath Shuler	1.50

1996 Pacific Dynagon Dynamic Duos

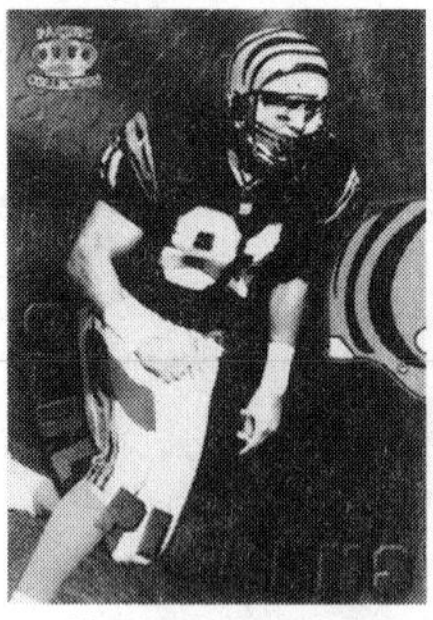

This 24-card 1996 Pacific Dynagon insert set showcases football's best one-two combinations on 12 teams. Cards 1-12 are found in hobby cases, while 13-24 can be found in retail cases; they are seeded in every 37th pack. Each card front has a color action photo against a metallic background which has one half of the team's helmet on it; the two cards can be placed next to each other to complete the helmet and showcase the duo. The back has a closeup shot of the player, with his name, team name and card number (using a "DD" prefix) at the top. His career accomplishments are also summarized.

		MT
Complete Set (24):		275.00
Common Player:		4.00
Minor Stars:		8.00
1	Troy Aikman	20.00
2	Jerry Rice	20.00
3	Brett Favre	40.00
4	Marshall Faulk	8.00
5	Carl Pickens	4.00
6	Terrell Davis	20.00
7	Curtis Martin	20.00
8	Dan Marino	35.00
9	Herman Moore	4.00
10	Kordell Stewart	20.00
11	Emmitt Smith	35.00
12	Trent Dilfer	4.00
13	Deion Sanders	12.00
14	Steve Young	15.00
15	Robert Brooks	4.00
16	Jim Harbaugh	4.00
17	Jeff Blake	8.00
18	John Elway	15.00
19	Drew Bledsoe	20.00
20	Bernie Parmalee	4.00
21	Barry Sanders	25.00
22	Kevin Greene	4.00
23	Sherman Williams	4.00
24	Errict Rhett	8.00

1996 Pacific Dynagon Gems of the Crown

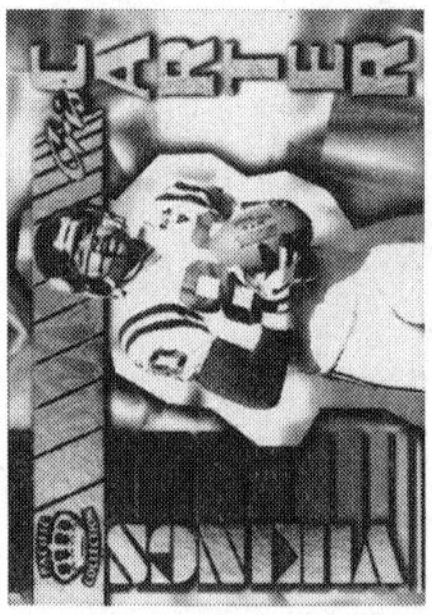

These 36 Pacific insert cards are distributed in two base brands; cards 1-18 are seeded two per every 37 packs of Dynamic Prism, while 19-36 are seeded in Crown Collection Football packs. The horizontal card front has a color action photo in the center. The top has a gold-foiled panel which has the Pacific logo in the upper left corner; the player's last name is in the upper right corner, with his last name stamped in gold down the side. The player's team logo is in gold along the left side, on a panel using team colors. The horizontal back has a color closeup shot on one side, with the player's position and team name below. The opposite side has the player's name in the upper corner, with a brief career summary underneath. The card is numbered using a "GC" prefix.

		MT
Complete Set (18):		80.00
Common Player:		2.00
1	Kerry Collins	5.00
2	Rashaan Salaam	4.00
3	Steve Young	8.00
4	Rodney Thomas	2.00
5	Michael Westbrook	4.00
6	Cris Carter	2.00
7	Jerry Rice	8.00
8	Drew Bledsoe	8.00
9	Steve McNair	6.00
10	Terrell Davis	12.00
11	Barry Sanders	12.00
12	Robert Brooks	2.00
13	Chris Warren	2.00
14	Marshall Faulk	8.00
15	John Elway	5.00
16	Isaac Bruce	4.00
17	Emmitt Smith	15.00
18	Thurman Thomas	2.00

1996 Pacific Dynagon Kings of the NFL

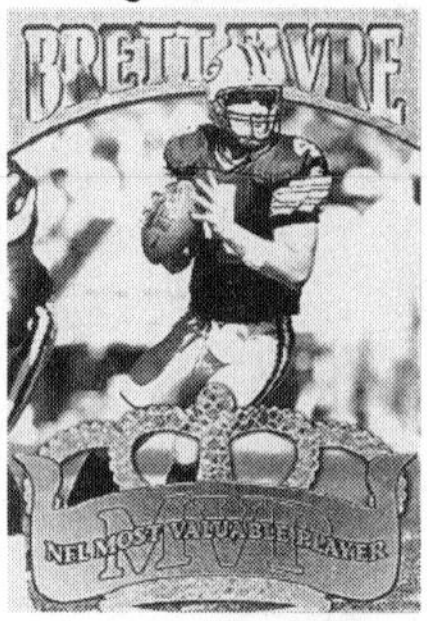

Ten of the NFL's biggest stars are featured on these 1996 Pacific Dynagon inserts. The cards, numbered using a "K" prefix, were seeded one per every 361 packs. The card front is covered with etched foil at the top around the player's name, and at the bottom is a crown with a significant achievement inside it. A color action photo dominates the center of the card. The back has the player's name and team name at the top, with a career summary along the left side. A color action photo is highlighted on the right side. The accomplishment highlighted on the front is indicated at the bottom of the card.

		MT
Complete Set (10):		350.00
Common Player:		15.00
1	Emmitt Smith	40.00
2	Dan Marino	40.00
3	Barry Sanders	50.00
4	Curtis Martin	15.00
5	Brett Favre	50.00
6	Kordell Stewart	15.00
7	Emmitt Smith	40.00
8	Jerry Rice	25.00
9	John Elway	40.00
10	Dan Marino	40.00

1996 Pacific Dynagon Gold Tandems

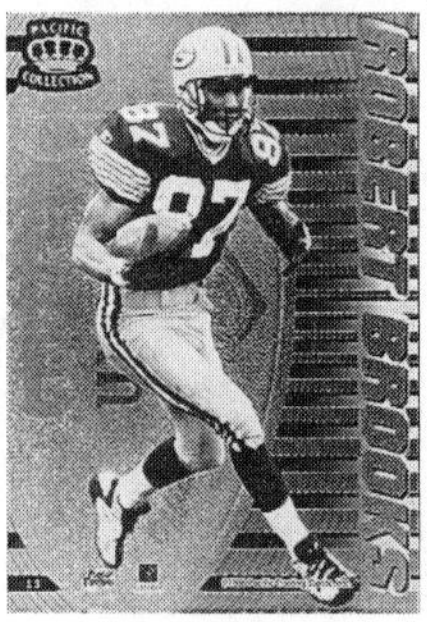

This 72-card parallel set pairs the fronts of two cards from Pacific's main 1996 Dynagon set. The cards were seeded one per every 37 packs.

		MT
Complete Set (72):		1400.
Common Player:		8.00
1	Dan Marino, Troy Aikman	160.00
2	Emmitt Smith, Rashaan Salaam	150.00
3	Jim Kelly, John Elway	50.00
4	Steve Young, Brett Favre	150.00
5	Curtis Martin, Terrell Davis	85.00
6	Kordell Stewart, Napoleon Kaufman	60.00
7	Barry Sanders, Jerry Rice	100.00
8	Joey Galloway, J.J. Stokes	50.00
9	Kerry Collins, Jeff Blake	20.00
10	Deion Sanders, Reggie White	40.00
11	Herman Moore, Mark Chmura	20.00
12	Eric Zeier, Tyrone Wheatley	15.00
13	Errict Rhett, Robert Brooks	25.00
14	Trent Dilfer, Steve McNair	40.00
15	Marshall Faulk, Drew Bledsoe	50.00
16	Tamarick Vanover, Michael Westbrook	25.00
17	Heath Shuler, Jerome Bettis	20.00
18	Isaac Bruce, Tim Brown	25.00
19	Terry Allen, Chris Warren	12.00
20	Brian Mitchell, Alex Van Dyke	12.00
21	Jerry Ellison, Kevin Mawae	8.00
22	Alvin Harper, Stanley Pritchett	8.00
23	Rick Mirer, Elvis Grbac	8.00
24	Cortez Kennedy, Junior Seau	8.00
25	William Floyd, Aaron Hayden	12.00
26	Stan Humphries, Dave Barr	8.00
27	J.T. Thomas, Stepfret Williams	12.00
28	Ronnie Harmon, Yancey Thigpen	12.00
29	Ernie Mills, Calvin Williams	8.00
30	Mark Bruener, Eddie George	50.00
31	Kevin Greene, Eric Moulds	12.00
32	Ricky Watters, Harvey Williams	8.00
33	Rodney Peete, Keyshawn Johnson	35.00
34	Charlie Garner, Adrian Murrell	8.00
35	Raghib Ismail, Wayne Chrebet	8.00
36	Billy Jo Hobert, Glenn Foley	8.00
37	Rodney Hampton, Ben Coates	8.00
38	Chris Calloway, Qadry Ismail	8.00
39	Dave Brown, Warren Moon	8.00
40	Ray Zellars, Robert Smith	8.00
41	Shane Pahukoa, Bernie Parmalee	8.00
42	Wayne Martin, Neil Smith	8.00
43	Jim Everett, Steve Bono	8.00
44	Mario Bates, Terry Kirby	8.00
45	Willie McGinest, Lawrence Phillips	15.00
46	Chad May, Mark Brunell	30.00
47	Cris Carter, O.J. McDuffie	8.00
48	Irving Fryar, Lake Dawson	8.00
49	Marcus Allen, James Stewart	8.00
50	Willie Jackson, Terry Glenn	50.00
51	Pete Mitchell, Kevin Hardy	15.00
52	Jim Harbaugh, Scott Mitchell	8.00
53	Zack Crockett, Rodney Thomas	15.00
54	Ben Bronson, Chris Sanders	8.00
55	Edgar Bennett, Tim Biakabutuka	8.00
56	Brett Perriman, Anthony Miller	8.00
57	Cory Schlesinger, Daryl Johnston	8.00
58	Shannon Sharpe, Michael Irvin	8.00
59	Chris Boniol, Thurman Thomas	8.00
60	Keenan McCardell, Darnay Scott	8.00
61	Leroy Hoard, Chris Zorich	8.00
62	Earnest Byner, Jeff Graham	8.00
63	Carl Pickens, Darick Holmes	8.00
64	David Dunn, Mark Carrier	8.00
65	Steve Stenstrom, Todd Collins	8.00
66	Eric Kramer, Derrick Moore	8.00
67	Larry Centers, Bobby Engram	25.00
68	Garrison Hearst, Jeff George	15.00
69	Dave Krieg, Craig Heyward	8.00
70	Frank Sanders, Terance Mathis	8.00
71	Gus Frerotte, Eric Metcalf	8.00
72	Bryce Paup, Blake Brockermeyer	8.00

1996 Pacific Gridiron

The only oversized football card set on the market returned for a second year in 1996 under the Pacific Pure Gridiron brand. A total of 1,500 cases of the product were produced, meaning the various inserts are rather limited in availability. Each card front uses gold foil stamping for the player's name and Crown Collection logo at the bottom. The photo on the front is a full-bleed color action shot. The back recaps the game from which the photo was taken, and another photo. Five parallel sets were made - Electric Blue (hobby), Scorching Red (retail), Presidential Copper (hobby, four per 37 packs), Presidential Platinum (retail, four per 37) and Presidential Gold (two per 721 packs of both retail and hobby; only 30 of these sets exist). Insert sets include Gold Crown die-cuts, Driving Force, Gridiron Performers and Gridiron Gems.

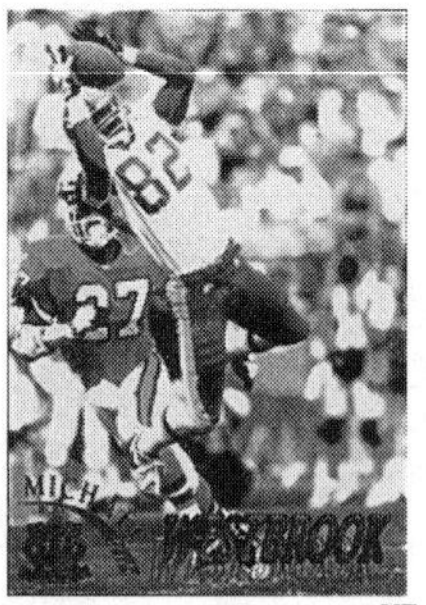

		MT
Complete Set (125):		90.00
Common Player:		.50
Comp. Copper Set (125):		500.00
Common Copper Player:		3.00
Comp. Platinum Set (125):		500.00
Common Platinum Player:		3.00
Copper-Platinum Stars:		3x-6x
Pack (2):		2.00
Wax Box (36):		60.00
1	Larry Centers	.50
2	Garrison Hearst	.50
3	Dave Krieg	.50
4	Frank Sanders	.50
5	*Jamal Anderson*	5.00
6	J.J. Birden	.50
7	Eric Metcalf	.50
8	Jeff George	1.00
9	Cornelius Bennett	.50
10	Todd Collins	.50
11	Darick Holmes	1.00
12	Jim Kelly	1.00
13	Bryce Paup	.50
14	Bob Christian	.50
15	Kerry Collins	4.50
16	Pete Metzelaars	.50
17	Derrick Moore	.50
18	Curtis Conway	.50
19	Jim Flanigan	.50
20	Erik Kramer	.50
21	Rashaan Salaam	2.00
22	Eric Bieniemy	.50
23	Jeff Blake	2.00
24	Tony McGee	.50
25	Darnay Scott	.50
26	Vashone Adams	.50
27	Leroy Hoard	.50
28	Andre Rison	.50
29	Tommy Vardell	.50
30	Troy Aikman	4.00
31	Michael Irvin	1.00
32	Daryl Johnston	.50
33	Deion Sanders	2.00
34	Emmitt Smith	8.00
35	Terrell Davis	5.00
36	John Elway	2.00
37	Ed McCaffrey	.50
38	Anthony Miller	.50
39	Scott Mitchell	.50
40	Brett Perriman	.50
41	Barry Sanders	4.00
42	Chris Spielman	.50
43	Edgar Bennett	.50
44	Robert Brooks	.50
45	Brett Favre	8.00
46	Antonio Freeman	.50
47	Reggie White	.50
48	Haywood Jeffires	.50
49	Steve McNair	3.00
50	Rodney Thomas	1.50
51	Frank Wycheck	.50
52	Ashley Ambrose	.50
53	Mark Brunell	4.00
54	Ken Dilger	.50
55	Marshall Faulk	2.00
56	Jim Harbaugh	.50
57	Tony Boselli	.50
58	Pete Mitchell	.50
59	James Stewart	.50
60	Marcus Allen	.50
61	Steve Bono	.50
62	Lake Dawson	.50
63	Tamarick Vanover	2.00
64	Bryan Cox	.50
65	Dan Marino	8.00
66	O.J. McDuffie	.50
67	Bernie Parmalee	.50
68	Cris Carter	.50
69	Qadry Ismail	.50
70	Warren Moon	.50
71	Robert Smith	.50
72	Drew Bledsoe	4.00
73	Vincent Brisby	.50
74	Ben Coates	.50
75	Curtis Martin	6.00
76	Mario Bates	.50
77	Derek Brown	.50
78	Jim Everett	.50
79	Dave Brown	.50
80	Chris Calloway	.50
81	Rodney Hampton	.50
82	Tyrone Wheatley	.50
83	Kyle Brady	.50
84	Wayne Chrebet	.50
85	Adrian Murrell	.50
86	Tim Brown	.50
87	Rob Carpenter	.50
88	Charlie Garner	.50
89	Daryl Hobbs	.50
90	Napoleon Kaufman	1.50
91	Rodney Peete	.50
92	Ricky Watters	.50
93	Calvin Williams	.50
94	Kevin Greene	.50
95	Greg Lloyd	.50
96	Neil O'Donnell	.50
97	Erric Pegram	.50
98	Kordell Stewart	4.50
99	Yancey Thigpen	2.00
100	Rod Woodson	.50
101	Isaac Bruce	2.00
102	Jerome Bettis	.50
103	J.T. Thomas	.50
104	Ronnie Harmon	.50
105	*Aaron Hayden*	1.50
106	Stan Humphries	.50
107	Alfred Pupunu	.50
108	William Floyd	.50
109	Brent Jones	.50
110	Jerry Rice	4.00
111	J.J. Stokes	2.00
112	John Taylor	.50
113	Steve Young	4.00
114	Harvey Williams	.50
115	John Friesz	.50
116	Joey Galloway	3.00
117	Cortez Kennedy	.50
118	Rick Mirer	.50
119	Chris Warren	1.00
120	Trent Dilfer	.50
121	Alvin Harper	.50
122	Errict Rhett	3.00
123	Terry Allen	.50
124	Gus Frerotte	.50
125	Michael Westbrook	2.50

1996 Pacific Gridiron Copper/Platinum

The 125-card, regular-size parallel set to the Gridiron issue, these sets can be distinguished by the foil on the card fronts. Both Copper and platinum were inserted four times every 37 packs.

	MT
Complete Set (125):	600.00
Common Player:	4.00
Semistars:	7.00
Cop./Plat.:	3x-6x

1996 Pacific Gridiron Gold

The 125-card, regular-sized set paralleled the Gridiron issue. The cards were inserted twice every 721 packs, with just 30 sets produced.

	MT
Common Player (1-125):	50.00
Semistars:	100.00

1996 Pacific Gridiron Driving Force

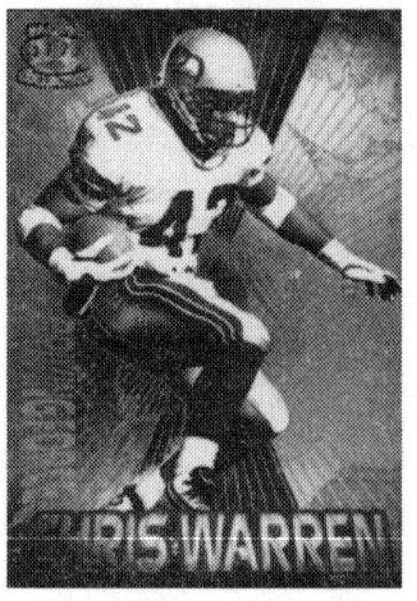

The top 10 running backs in the NFL are highlighted in this 1996 Pacific Pure Gridiron insert set. Cards were seeded one per every 73 packs. The card front has a color action photo, with a team color-coordinated hourglass with gold foil highlights behind the player. Gold foil is also used for the card's background, set name and player's name, which is highlighted in his team's color. The Crown logo is in the upper left corner. The back also uses the player's primary team color for the background, and has a color action photo in the center, with the set name above the photo and the player's name below. A brief recap of the player's 1995 season accomplishments is below the photo. A card number, using a "DF" prefix, is in the lower right corner.

		MT
Complete Set (10):		175.00
Common Player:		10.00
1	Chris Warren	10.00
2	Emmitt Smith	50.00
3	Barry Sanders	25.00
4	Rashaan Salaam	15.00
5	Errict Rhett	25.00
6	Curtis Martin	40.00
7	Garrison Hearst	10.00
8	Marshall Faulk	25.00
9	Terrell Davis	25.00
10	Edgar Bennett	10.00

1996 Pacific Gridiron Gems

These 1996 Pacific Pure Gridiron inserts feature 50 top NFL stars. Cards, numbered on the back using a GG prefix, were randomly inserted three per every four packs. The front has a color action photo in the center, with the Crown logo in the upper left corner. A puzzle-like border is used to frame three sides; a gridiron, with the player's name and brand logo, is stamped along the bottom of the card in green foil. The horizontal back repeats the puzzle pattern and has a color photo on one side and a recap of the player's 1995 achievements on the other.

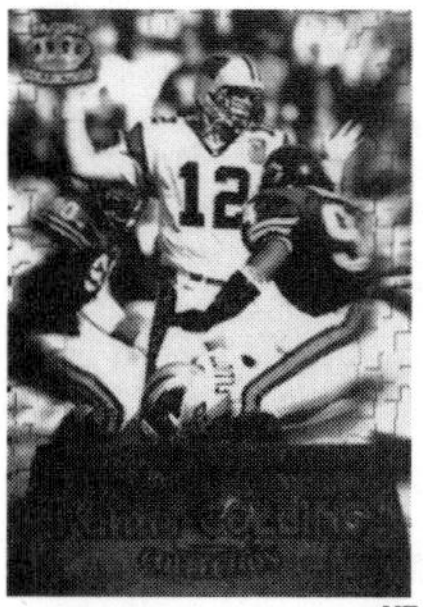

		MT
Complete Set (50):		45.00
Common Player:		.50
1	J.J. Birden	.50
2	Garrison Hearst	.50
3	Bryce Paup	.50
4	Kerry Collins	3.00
5	Alonzo Spellman	.50
6	Chris Zorich	.50
7	Harold Green	.50
8	Lee Johnson	.50
9	Eric Zeier	.50
10	Troy Aikman	3.00
11	Deion Sanders	1.50
12	Emmitt Smith	6.00
13	John Elway	1.50
14	Mike Pritchard	.50
15	Shane Bonham	.50
16	Barry Sanders	3.00
17	Edgar Bennett	.50
18	Brett Favre	6.00
19	Reggie White	.50
20	Eddie Robinson	.50
21	Marshall Faulk	3.00
22	Brian Stablein	.50
23	Don Davey	.50
24	Neil Smith	.50
25	Derrick Thomas	.50
26	Eric Green	.50
27	Jake Reed	.50
28	Troy Brown	.50
29	Will Moore	.50
30	Wesley Walls	.50
31	Herschel Walker	.50
32	Keyshawn Johnson	3.00
33	Billy Joe Hobert	.50
34	Ricky Watters	.50
35	Ernie Mills	.50
36	Kordell Stewart	3.00
37	Terrell Fletcher	.50
38	Junior Seau	.50
39	Elvis Grbac	.50
40	Gary Plummer	.50
41	Jerry Rice	3.00
42	Steve Young	3.00
43	Carlester Crumpler	.50
44	Joey Galloway	3.00
45	Cortez Kennedy	.50
46	Chris Warren	1.00
47	Greg Robinson	.50
48	Errict Rhett	3.00
49	Terry Allen	.50
50	Stanley Richard	.50

1996 Pacific Gridiron Gold Crown Die-Cut

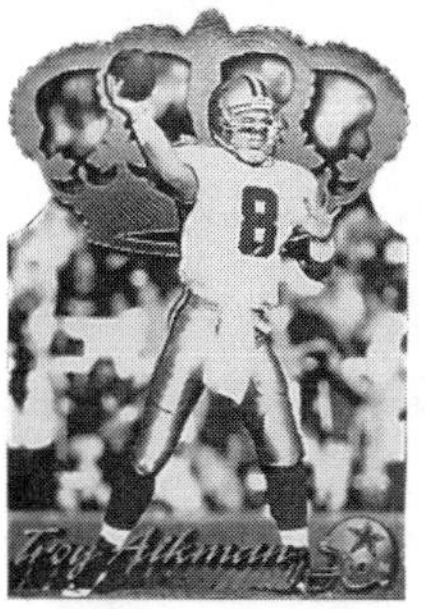

These cards could be obtained by sending in a redemption card bearing the player's name and card number. The cards were seeded one per every 37 packs of 1996 Pacific Pure Gridiron product. The front is a die-cut crown, with gold foil used to complete the crown. Gold foil is also used for the player's name, which is at the bottom adjacent to a team helmet. A full-bleed color action photo is in the center of the card. The back, numbered using a "GC" prefix, has a crown at the top, with a player photo in the center and his name below. Career, 1995 and most prolific games are recapped in brief summaries below.

		MT
Complete Set (20):		400.00
Common Player:		10.00
1	Barry Sanders	30.00
2	Ricky Watters	10.00
3	Troy Aikman	30.00
4	Deion Sanders	20.00
5	Kerry Collins	30.00
6	Dan Marino	50.00
7	Steve Young	30.00
8	Drew Bledsoe	30.00
9	Jerry Rice	30.00
10	Steve McNair	20.00
11	Joey Galloway	25.00
12	John Elway	15.00
13	Terrell Davis	25.00
14	Rashaan Salaam	15.00
15	Kordell Stewart	30.00
16	Emmitt Smith	50.00
17	Curtis Martin	45.00
18	Marshall Faulk	30.00
19	Brett Favre	50.00
20	Chris Warren	10.00

1996 Pacific Gridiron Rock Solid Rookies

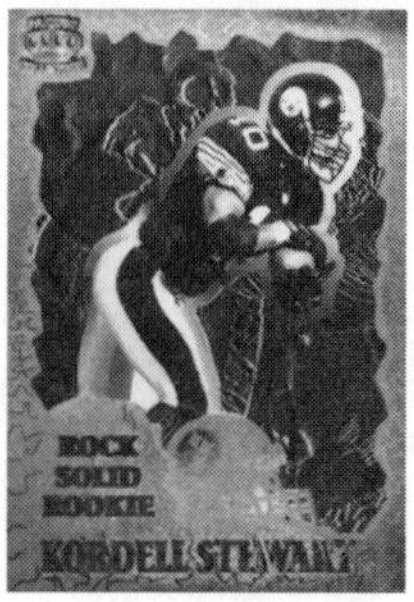

Six of the NFL's top rookies from the 1995 season are featured on these 1996 Pacific Pure Gridiron inserts. The cards, seeded one per every 121 packs, are numbered on the back using an "RP" prefix. The front has a color action photo in the center, with a granite rock background and gold-foil borders. The player's team helmet is at the bottom in gold, too. "Rock Solid Rookie" is written in rock-like letters at the bottom. The Pacific Crown logo is in the upper left corner. The back has the player's name and set name running along opposite sides. A color photo is in a square at the top of the card, while a recap of the player's rookie season is underneath. The background is a gray marble.

		MT
Complete Set (6):		150.00
Common Player:		15.00
1	Joey Galloway	30.00
2	Napoleon Kaufman	15.00
3	Michael Westbrook	20.00
4	Kerry Collins	40.00
5	Aaron Hayden	15.00
6	Kordell Stewart	40.00

1996 Pacific Invincible

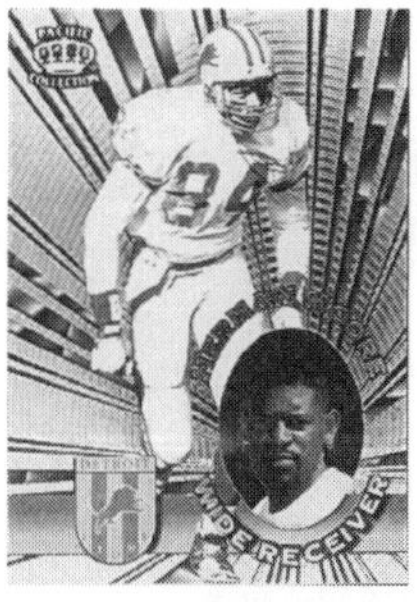

Pacific's 1996 Invincible Football (Prism II) has 150 cards in the set. Each is paralleled in four different versions. The regular card front has a color action photo in the middle, with a gold-foiled sunburst design as a background pattern. The Pacific logo is in the upper left corner; the player's team logo is in a team color-coordinated banner at the bottom. The lower left corner has a small oval with a plastic piece inside featuring the player's mug shot. His name is in gold foil above the photo; his position is below. The back side has a rectangle at the top, with a color photo inside it. The Pacific logo is in the upper left corner. The player's name is below the photo, with a recap of his career comprising most of the back side. The plastic mug shot is reversed on the front and is in the lower left corner. The card number (using an "I" prefix) is at the bottom of the card. The regular cards have four parallel versions. Hobby packs have a bronze parallel (four per 25 packs), while retail packs have a silver parallel (four per 25 packs). Then a platinum (one per 25) and a gold parallel set are found in both hobby and retail packs. There are also four insert sets - Kick-Starters Die-Cuts, Pro Bowl Stars, Smash Mouth, and a 10-card Chris Warren set.

		MT
Complete Set (150):		150.00
Common Player:		1.00
Minor Stars:		2.00
Bronze/Silver Cards:		5x
Platinum Cards:		12x
Comp. C.Warren Set (10):		10.00
Common Warren:		1.00
Pack (3):		3.00
Wax Box (24):		60.00
1	Larry Centers	1.00
2	Garrison Hearst	1.00
3	Seth Joyner	1.00
4	*Simeon Rice*	2.00
5	Eric Swann	1.00
6	Bert Emanuel	1.00
7	Jeff George	1.00
8	Craig Heyward	1.00
9	Terance Mathis	1.00
10	Eric Metcalf	1.00
11	Derrick Alexander	1.00
12	Leroy Hoard	1.00
13	Andre Rison	1.00
14	Tommy Vardell	1.00
15	Eric Zeier	1.00
16	Jim Kelly	2.00
17	*Eric Moulds*	7.00
18	Bryce Paup	1.00
19	Bruce Smith	1.00
20	Thurman Thomas	2.00
21	*Tim Biakabutuka*	4.00
22	Blake Brockermeyer	1.00
23	Kerry Collins	3.00
24	Howard Griffith	1.00
25	Lamar Lathon	1.00
26	Mark Carrier	1.00
27	Curtis Conway	1.00
28	Erik Kramer	1.00
29	Rashaan Salaam	2.00
30	Alonzo Spellman	1.00
31	Jeff Blake BR	4.00
32	Harold Green	1.00
33	Carl Pickens	2.00
34	Darnay Scott	2.00
35	Dan Wilkinson	1.00
36	Troy Aikman	6.00
37	Jay Novacek	1.00
38	Deion Sanders	5.00
39	Emmitt Smith	12.00
40	Kevin Williams	1.00
41	Terrell Davis	12.00
42	John Elway	4.00
43	Anthony Miller	1.00
44	Michael Dean Perry	1.00
45	Shannon Sharpe	1.00
46	Scott Mitchell	1.00
47	Herman Moore	2.00
48	Brett Perriman	1.00
49	Barry Sanders	8.00
50	Chris Spielman	1.00
51	Edgar Bennett	1.00
52	Robert Brooks	1.00
53	Brett Favre	12.00
54	*Derrick Mayes*	3.00
55	Reggie White	2.00
56	*Eddie George*	12.00
57	Haywood Jeffires	1.00
58	Steve McNair	5.00
59	Chris Sanders	2.00
60	Rodney Thomas	2.00
61	Tony Bennett	1.00
62	Quentin Coryatt	1.00
63	Ken Dilger	1.00
64	Marshall Faulk	4.00
65	Jim Harbaugh	1.00
66	Tony Boselli	1.00
67	Mark Brunell	5.00
68	Kevin Hardy	1.00
69	Desmond Howard	1.00
70	James Stewart	1.00
71	Marcus Allen	2.00
72	Steve Bono	1.00
73	Neil Smith	1.00
74	Derrick Thomas	1.00
75	Tamarick Vanover	2.00
76	*Karim Abdul-Jabbar*	3.00
77	Irving Fryar	1.00
78	Eric Green	1.00
79	Dan Marino	12.00
80	Bernie Parmalee	1.00
81	Cris Carter	1.00
82	Warren Moon	1.00
83	Jake Reed	1.00
84	Robert Smith	1.00
85	Moe Williams	1.00
86	Drew Bledsoe	6.00
87	Ben Coates	1.00
88	*Terry Glenn*	6.00
89	Curtis Martin	5.00
90	Dave Meggett	1.00
91	Mario Bates	1.00
92	Jim Everett	1.00
93	Michael Haynes	1.00
94	Torrance Small	1.00
95	Ray Zellars	1.00
96	Kyle Brady	1.00
97	Wayne Chrebet	1.00
98	*Keyshawn Johnson*	8.00
99	Adrian Murrell	1.00
100	*Alex Van Dyke*	2.00
101	Michael Brooks	1.00
102	Dave Brown	1.00
103	Chris Calloway	1.00
104	Rodney Hampton	1.00
105	*Amani Toomer*	2.00
106	Tyrone Wheatley	1.00
107	Tim Brown	1.00
108	*Rickey Dudley*	3.00
109	Billy Joe Hobert	1.00
110	Raghib Ismail	1.00
111	Napoleon Kaufman	1.00
112	Harvey Williams	1.00
113	Charlie Garner	1.00
114	*Bobby Hoying*	2.50
115	Rodney Peete	1.00
116	Ricky Watters	2.00
117	Greg Lloyd	1.00
118	Erric Pegram	1.00
119	Kordell Stewart	7.00
120	Yancey Thigpen	2.00
121	Jon Witman	1.00
122	Aaron Hayden	1.00
123	Stan Humphries	1.00
124	Tony Martin	1.00
125	Leslie O'Neal	1.00
126	Junior Seau	1.00
127	Jerome Bettis	2.00
128	Isaac Bruce	2.00
129	Ernie Conwell	1.00
130	*Lawrence Phillips*	3.00
131	William Floyd	1.00
132	*Terrell Owens*	10.00
133	Jerry Rice	7.00
134	J.J. Stokes	2.00
135	Steve Young	6.00
136	Brian Blades	1.00
137	Christian Fauria	1.00
138	Joey Galloway	6.00
139	Rick Mirer	1.00
140	Chris Warren	2.00
141	Horace Copeland	1.00
142	Trent Dilfer	1.00
143	Alvin Harper	1.00
144	Dave Moore	1.00
145	Errict Rhett	2.00
146	Terry Allen	1.00
147	Gus Frerotte	1.00
148	Brian Mitchell	1.00
149	Heath Shuler	1.00
150	Michael Westbrook	2.00

1996 Pacific Invincible Bronze/Silver/Platinum

Pacific's 150-card Invincible set was paralleled in a total of four different versions. Hobby packs contained Bronze parallels, while retail packs had Silver versions of the base set, with both seeded four per 25 packs. In addition, Invincible Platinums (1:25) and Golds were available in both types of packs at a reduced rate. Each version is distinguished by the color foil used.

	MT
Complete Bronze Set (149):	1000.
Bronze Cards:	3x-6x
Complete Silver Set (149):	1000.
Silver Cards:	3x-6x
Complete Platinum Set (149):	2000.
Platinum Cards:	6x-12x

1996 Pacific Invincible Chris Warren

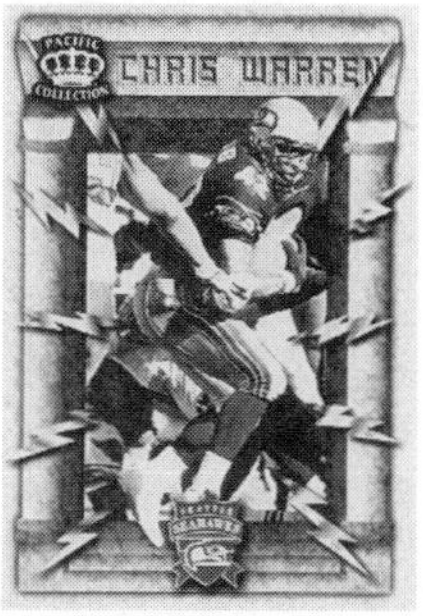

This 10-card set is entirely devoted to Seattle Seahawks running back Chris Warren. Each card features a different action shot of Warren, with cards found every 10 packs.

		MT
Complete Set (10):		10.00
Common Warren:		1.00
1	Chris Warren	1.00
2	Chris Warren	1.00
3	Chris Warren	1.00
4	Chris Warren	1.00
5	Chris Warren	1.00
6	Chris Warren	1.00
7	Chris Warren	1.00
8	Chris Warren	1.00
9	Chris Warren	1.00
10	Chris Warren	1.00

1996 Pacific Invincible Kick-Starters

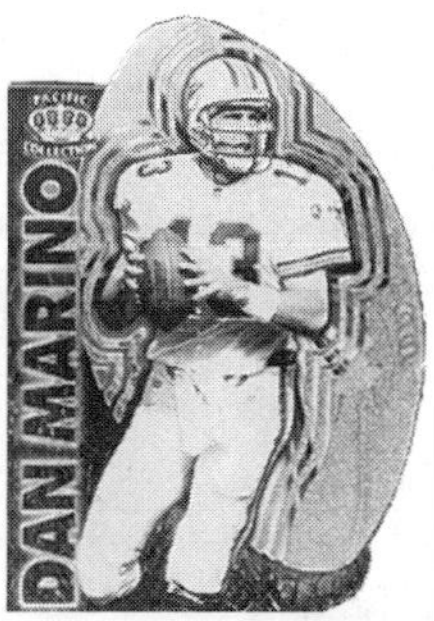

These 1996 Pacific Invincible inserts are the most limited; they are seeded one per every 49 packs. The cards are die-cut into a gold-foiled football with a color action photo on it. The player's name is written along the left side of the card against a grassy background. The Pacific logo is in the upper left corner. The card back has a color action photo on the football part of the card; the right side has the player's name and a recap of a time when the player jump-started his team. The card is numbered using a "KS" prefix.

		MT
Complete Set (20):		500.00
Common Player:		15.00
1	Jeff Blake	18.00
2	Tim Brown	15.00
3	Kerry Collins	20.00
4	John Elway	30.00
5	Marshall Faulk	18.00
6	Brett Favre	75.00
7	Keyshawn Johnson	25.00
8	Dan Marino	75.00
9	Curtis Martin	50.00
10	Steve McNair	25.00
11	Errict Rhett	18.00
12	Jerry Rice	40.00
13	Rashaan Salaam	15.00
14	Barry Sanders	40.00
15	Deion Sanders	30.00
16	Emmitt Smith	75.00
17	Kordell Stewart	40.00
18	Tamarick Vanover	18.00
19	Chris Warren	15.00
20	Ricky Watters	15.00

1996 Pacific Invincible Pro Bowl

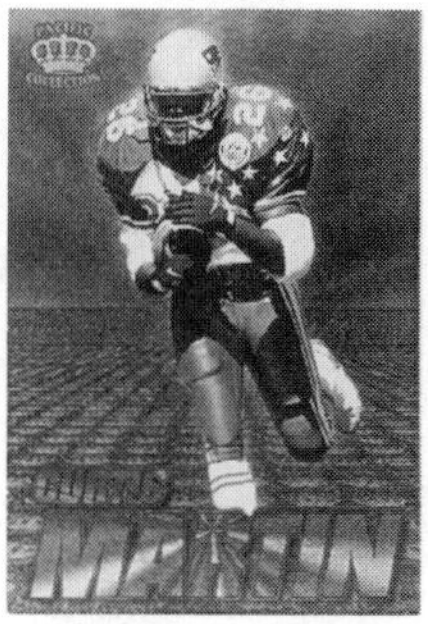

Every 25th pack of 1996 Pacific Invincible has one of these insert cards devoted to participants in the previous Pro Bowl game. Each card front shows the player in his Pro Bowl uniform against a colorful metallic background which incorporates the Pacific logo into the pattern. The player's name is written along the bottom. The horizontal back, numbered using a "PB" prefix, has a close-up shot of the player in his uniform, along with a Pro Bowl logo and a recap of some of his accomplishments as a Pro Bowler.

		MT
Complete Set (20):		175.00
Common Player:		4.00
1	Jeff Blake	6.00
2	Steve Bono	4.00
3	Tim Brown	4.00
4	Cris Carter	4.00
5	Ben Coates	4.00
6	Brett Favre	30.00
7	Jim Harbaugh	4.00
8	Curtis Martin	25.00
9	Warren Moon	4.00
10	Herman Moore	8.00
11	Carl Pickens	4.00
12	Jerry Rice	18.00
13	Barry Sanders	25.00
14	Shannon Sharpe	4.00
15	Emmitt Smith	30.00
16	Yancey Thigpen	7.00
17	Chris Warren	4.00
18	Ricky Watters	4.00
19	Reggie White	4.00
20	Steve Young	14.00

1996 Pacific Invincible Smash-Mouth

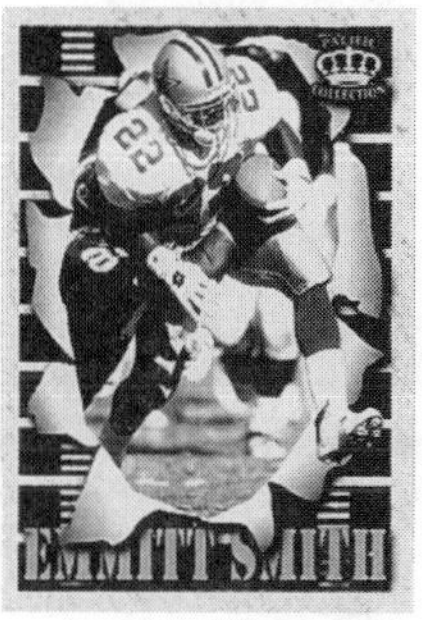

Some of the NFL's most intense players and hardest hitters are featured on these 1996 Pacific Invincible inserts. The cards, numbered on the back using an "SM" prefix, were seeded two per pack. Each card front shows a player busting through a hole against a football field background. The Pacific logo is in the upper right corner; the player's name is along the bottom. The back has a square in the upper right corner which has a mug shot inside. A summary of some of his accomplishments is given below the photo. The player's name, team name and position are written along the left side of the card, below the Pacific logo.

		MT
Complete Set (180):		30.00
Common Player:		.20
Minor Stars:		.40
1	Marcus Dowdell	.20
2	Karl Dunbar	.20
3	Eric England	.20
4	Garrison Hearst	.20
5	Bryan Reeves	.20
6	Simeon Rice	.20
7	Jeff George	.20
8	Bobby Hebert	.20
9	Craig Heyward	.20
10	Dave Richard	.20
11	Elbert Shelley	.20
12	Lonnie Johnson	.20
13	Jim Kelly	.20
14	Corbin Lacina	.20
15	Bryce Paup	.20
16	Sam Rogers	.20
17	Bruce Smith	.20
18	Thurman Thomas	.40
19	Carl Banks	.20
20	Dan Footman	.20
21	Louis Riddick	.20
22	Matt Stover	.20
23	Tommy Barnhardt	.20
24	Kerry Collins	.75
25	Mark Dennis	.20
26	Matt Elliott	.20
27	Eric Guliford	.20
28	Lamar Lathon	.20
29	Joe Cain	.20
30	Marty Carter	.20
31	Robert Green	.20
32	Erik Kramer	.20
33	Todd Perry	.20
34	Rashaan Salaam	.40
35	Alonzo Spellman	.20
36	Jeff Blake	.75
37	Andre Collins	.20
38	Todd Kelly	.20
39	Carl Pickens	.20
40	Kevin Sargent	.20
41	Troy Aikman	1.25
42	Charles Haley	.20
43	Daryl Johnston	.20
44	Nate Newton	.20
45	Deion Sanders	.75
46	Emmitt Smith	3.00
47	Steve Atwater	.20
48	Terrell Davis	1.00
49	John Elway	.75
50	Michael Dean Perry	.20
51	Shannon Sharpe	.20
52	Dave Wyman	.20
53	Bennie Blades	.20
54	Kevin Glover	.20
55	Herman Moore	.50
56	Robert Porcher	.20
57	Barry Sanders	1.25
58	Henry Thomas	.20
59	Edgar Bennett	.20
60	Robert Brooks	.20
61	Brett Favre	3.00
62	Harry Galbreath	.20
63	Sean Jones	.20
64	Reggie White	.40
65	Blaine Bishop	.20
66	Chuck Cecil	.20
67	Cris Dishman	.20
68	Steve McNair	.75
69	Rodney Thomas	.20
70	Jason Belser	.20
71	Ray Buchanan	.20
72	Quentin Coryatt	.20
73	Marshall Faulk	1.00
74	Jim Harbaugh	.20
75	Devon McDonald	.20
76	Tony Boselli	.20
77	Tony Brackens	.20
78	Mark Brunell	.75
79	Don Davey	.20
80	Rich Griffith	.20
81	Kevin Hardy	.20
82	Mickey Washington	.20
83	Louis Aguiar	.20
84	Dan Saleaumua	.20
85	Will Shields	.20
86	Neil Smith	.20
87	Derrick Thomas	.20
88	Tamarick Vanover	.75
89	Gene Atkins	.20
90	Bryan Cox	.20
91	Steve Emtman	.20
92	Chris Gray	.20
93	Dan Marino	3.00
94	Derrick Alexander	.20
95	Cris Carter	.20
96	Jeff Christy	.20
97	Robert Smith	.20
98	Korey Stringer	.20
99	Orlando Thomas	.20
100	Esera Tuaolo	.20
101	Drew Bledsoe	1.00
102	Eddie Cade	.20
103	Mike Jones	.20
104	Curtis Martin	2.00
105	Willie McGinest	.20
106	Chris Slade	.20
107	Eric Allen	.20
108	Mario Bates	.20
109	Jim Dombrowski	.20
110	Wayne Martin	.20
111	William Roaf	.20
112	Irv Smith	.20
113	Michael Brooks	.20
114	Stacey Dillard	.20
115	Rodney Hampton	.20
116	Doug Riesenberg	.20
117	Coleman Rudolph	.20
118	Tyrone Wheatley	.20
119	Kyle Brady	.20
120	Roger Duffy	.20
121	Keyshawn Johnson	1.00
122	Gary Jones	.20
123	Eddie Anderson	.20
124	Rickey Dudley	.40
125	Napoleon Kaufman	.20
126	Greg Skrepenak	.20
127	Pat Swilling	.20
128	Steve Wisniewski	.20
129	William Fuller	.20
130	Kurt Gouvela	.20
131	Andy Harmon	.20
132	Mike Mamula	.20
133	Guy McIntyre	.20
134	Ricky Watters	.20
135	Kevin Greene	.20
136	Bill Johnson	.20
137	Carnell Lake	.20
138	Greg Lloyd	.20
139	Erric Pegram	.20
140	Leon Searcy	.20
141	Shane Conlan	.20
142	Troy Drayton	.20
143	Wayne Gandy	.20
144	Sean Gilbert	.20
145	Carlos Jenkins	.20
146	Lawrence Phillips	.75
147	Aaron Hayden	.20
148	Stan Humphries	.20
149	Leslie O'Neal	.20
150	Bo Orlando	.20
151	Junior Seau	.20
152	Harry Swayne	.20
153	Harris Barton	.20
154	Merton Hanks	.20
155	Rod Milstead	.20

156	Ken Norton Jr.	.20
157	Gary Plummer	.20
158	Jerry Rice	1.50
159	Steve Wallace	.20
160	Steve Young	1.00
161	James Atkins	.20
162	Brian Blades	.20
163	Matt Joyce	.20
164	Cortez Kennedy	.20
165	Kevin Mawae	.20
166	Winston Moss	.20
167	Chris Warren	.40
168	Derrick Brooks	.20
169	Trent Dilfer	.20
170	Santana Dotson	.20
171	Alvin Harper	.20
172	Hardy Nickerson	.20
173	Errict Rhett	.40
174	Warren Sapp	.20
175	Terry Allen	.20
176	John Gesek	.20
177	Ken Harvey	.20
178	Tre Johnson	.20
179	Rod Stephens	.20
180	Michael Westbrook	.40

1996 Pacific Litho-Cel

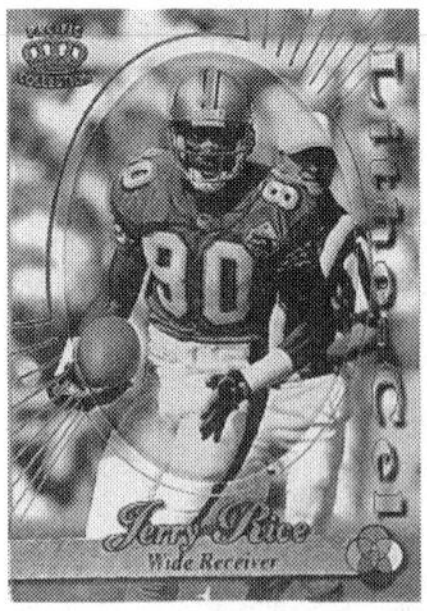

The 100-card, regular-sized set actually is two 100-card sets, with Cel and Litho versions. The Cel cards feature a clear oval center with a blue color image. The Litho cards are the same card fronts, but with a red color, non-clear oval center image. When the Cel card is placed over the Litho card, a 3-D effect makes the center oval image appear in full color. The card backs of the Cel cards are numbered with the "Cel" prefix while the Litho cards feature the same corresponding number with a "Litho" prefix. Litho-Cel came in three-card packs and included Moments In Time, Feature Performers, Game Time, Litho-Proof and Certified Litho-Proof inserts, as well as parallel silver foil (3:25) and Blue-Platinum (retail 3:25) versions. Pacific Litho-Cel was available in three-card packs which contained one Cel card, one Litho card and one Game Time card or other insert card.

		MT
Complete Set (100):		75.00
Common Player:		.25
Minor Stars:		.50
Bronze/Silver:		2x-4x
Wax Box:		70.00
Prices are for both Litho and Cel cards together.		
Pack (3):		3.00
Wax Box (24):		60.00
1	Kent Graham	.25
2	LeShon Johnson	.25
3	*Leeland McElroy*	.75
4	Frank Sanders	.25
5	*Jamal Anderson*	10.00
6	Cornelius Bennett	.25
7	Bobby Hebert	.25
8	Earnest Byner	.25
9	Michael Jackson	.25
10	Vinny Testaverde	.50
11	Jim Kelly	1.00
12	Andre Reed	.50
13	Bruce Smith	.50
14	Thurman Thomas	1.00
15	Kerry Collins	1.00
16	Lamar Lathon	.25
17	Kevin Greene	.25
18	*Bobby Engram*	.75
19	Erik Kramer	.25
20	Rashaan Salaam	.50
21	Jeff Blake	1.00
22	Garrison Hearst	1.00
23	Carl Pickens	.50
24	Darnay Scott	.50
25	Troy Aikman	3.00
26	Eric Bjornson	.25
27	Deion Sanders	1.00
28	Emmitt Smith	5.00
29	Terrell Davis	10.00
30	John Elway	5.00
31	Anthony Miller	.25
32	John Mobley	.25
33	Scott Mitchell	.25
34	Herman Moore	1.00
35	Brett Perriman	.25
36	Barry Sanders	6.00
37	Edgar Bennett	.25
38	Robert Brooks	.25
39	Brett Favre	6.00
40	Reggie White	1.00
41	Chris Chandler	.75
42	*Eddie George*	10.00
43	Steve McNair	3.00
44	Chris Sanders	.25
45	Ken Dilger	.25
46	Marshall Faulk	1.00
47	Jim Harbaugh	.50
48	Mark Brunell	3.00
49	Keenan McCardell	.50
50	James Stewart	.50
51	Marcus Allen	1.00
52	Steve Bono	.50
53	Greg Hill	.50
54	Tamarick Vanover	.50
55	*Karim Abdul-Jabbar*	3.00
56	Dan Marino	5.00
57	*Zach Thomas*	1.50
58	Cris Carter	1.00
59	Warren Moon	.50
60	Robert Smith	1.00
61	Drew Bledsoe	3.00
62	*Terry Glenn*	4.00
63	Curtis Martin	2.00
64	Mario Bates	.25
65	Jim Everett	.50
66	Haywood Jeffires	.25
67	Dave Brown	.25
68	Rodney Hampton	.25
69	*Amani Toomer*	1.00
70	Adrian Murrell	.50
71	Neil O'Donnell	.50
72	*Alex Van Dyke*	.50
73	Tim Brown	.50
74	Jeff Hostetler	.25
75	Napoleon Kaufman	.75
76	Irving Fryar	.25
77	Chris T. Jones	.25
78	Ricky Watters	1.00
79	Jerome Bettis	1.00
80	Kordell Stewart	2.50
81	*Tony Banks*	2.00
82	*Eddie Kennison*	.75
83	*Lawrence Phillips*	2.00
84	Stan Humphries	.25
85	Tony Martin	.25
86	Leonard Russell	.25
87	Junior Seau	.50
88	Jerry Rice	3.00
89	J.J. Stokes	.50
90	Tommy Vardell	.25
91	Steve Young	2.00
92	Joey Galloway	1.00
93	Rick Mirer	.50
94	Chris Warren	.25
95	*Mike Alstott*	3.00
96	Trent Dilfer	.75
97	Nilo Silvan	.25
98	Terry Allen	.50
99	Gus Frerotte	.50
100	Michael Westbrook	.75

1996 Pacific Litho-Cel Bronze/Silver

Each card in the 100-card Litho-Cel set was reprinted in two different foil versions. Silver foil parallels were found in three per 25 hobby packs, while bronze versions were found in three per 25 retail packs. The only difference between these parallels and the regular-issue cards is the color of the foil stamping.

	MT
Complete Bronze Set (100):	700.00
Bronze Cards:	2x-4x
Complete Silver Set (100):	700.00
Silver Cards:	2x-4x

1996 Pacific Litho-Cel Feature Performers

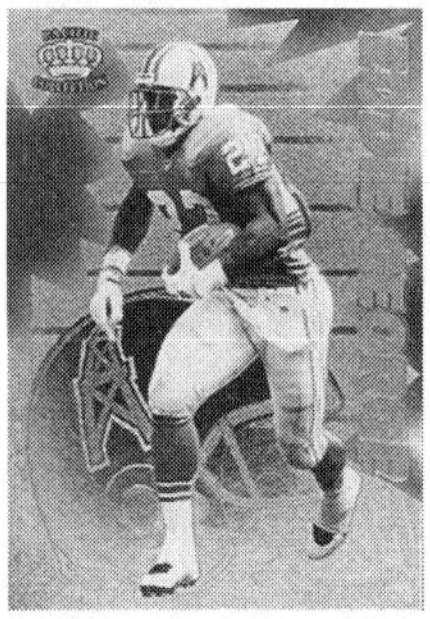

The 20-card, regular-sized inserts were included in every 25 packs of Litho-Cel cards. The card fronts feature the player over gold foil with his respective team helmet outline on the bottom half of the card. The player's name is written in the player's team color down the right side while the backs are numbered with the "FP" prefix.

		MT
Complete Set (20):		300.00
Common Player:		7.00
1	Jim Kelly	7.00
2	Troy Aikman	20.00
3	Deion Sanders	15.00
4	Emmitt Smith	40.00
5	Terrell Davis	30.00
6	John Elway	20.00
7	Herman Moore	10.00
8	Barry Sanders	25.00
9	Robert Brooks	7.00
10	Brett Favre	40.00
11	Eddie George	25.00
12	Jim Harbaugh	7.00
13	Marcus Allen	7.00
14	Karim Abdul-Jabbar	15.00
15	Dan Marino	40.00
16	Joey Galloway	15.00
17	Curtis Martin	30.00
18	Jerome Bettis	10.00
19	Jerry Rice	20.00
20	Steve Young	15.00

1996 Pacific Litho-Cel Litho-Proof

The 36-card, regular-sized set was inserted in every 97 packs of 1996 Litho-Cel cards. The card fronts feature the same color photo and design as the basic Litho-Cel set, without the clear blue cel imaging. Also differentiating between the two sets is a gray seal in the lower left section of the card front which reads, "1996 Pacific Litho Cards - Litho-Proof." The cards are sequentially numbered as "x of 360" and are listed with a "Litho-Proof" prefix. A parallel version, Certified Litho-Proof, features a second seal "Pacific Collection" and is inserted every 481 packs.

		MT
Complete Set (36):		1600.
Common Player:		15.00
Certified Cards:		2x-4x
1	Jim Kelly	15.00
2	Kerry Collins	30.00
3	Rashaan Salaam	30.00
4	Jeff Blake	30.00
5	Carl Pickens	15.00
6	Troy Aikman	80.00
7	Deion Sanders	70.00
8	Emmitt Smith	160.00
9	Terrell Davis	100.00
10	John Elway	70.00
11	Herman Moore	30.00
12	Barry Sanders	120.00
13	Robert Brooks	15.00
14	Brett Favre	160.00
15	Reggie White	15.00
16	Eddie George	90.00
17	Marshall Faulk	50.00
18	Jim Harbaugh	15.00
19	Mark Brunell	70.00
20	Marcus Allen	15.00
21	Steve Bono	15.00
22	Karim Abdul-Jabbar	70.00
23	Dan Marino	160.00
24	Warren Moon	15.00
25	Drew Bledsoe	80.00
26	Curtis Martin	100.00
27	Amani Toomer	15.00
28	Tim Brown	15.00
29	Napoleon Kaufman	15.00
30	Ricky Watters	15.00
31	Jerome Bettis	15.00
32	Kordell Stewart	80.00
33	Jerry Rice	80.00
34	Steve Young	70.00
35	Joey Galloway	70.00
36	Terry Allen	15.00

1996 Pacific Litho-Cel Certified Litho-Proofs

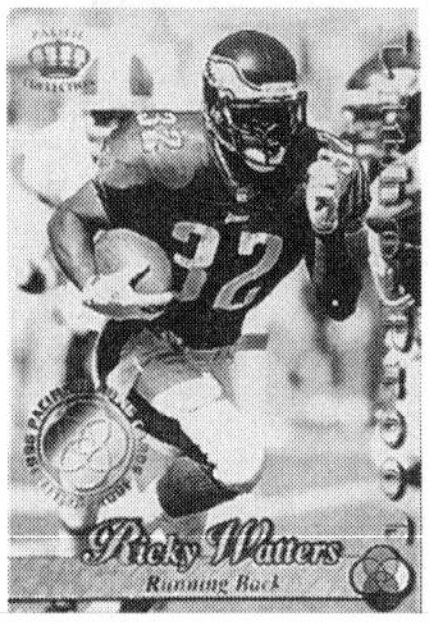

Certified Litho-Proofs are similar to the regular Litho-Proof inserts, but contain a large Pacific Crown Collection logo over top of the Litho-Proof logo in the bottom left corner. Certified Litho-Proofs were inserted at a rate of one per 481 packs.

	MT
Complete Set (36):	6000.
Certified Litho-Proofs:	2x-4x

1996 Pacific Litho-Cel Game Time

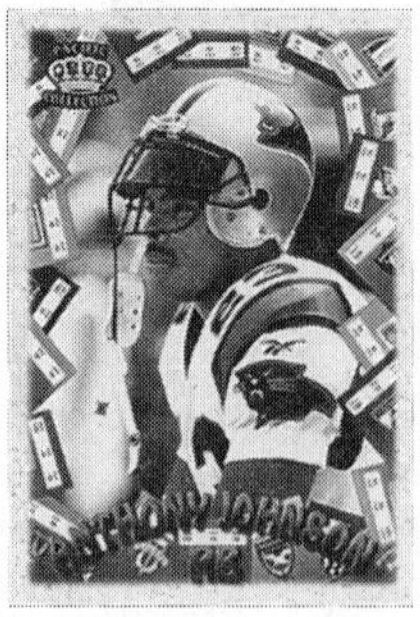

The 96-card, regular-sized set was inserted in each pack of Litho-Cel cards. The card fronts feature the player centered in an array of statistical cut-out boxes and the player's name is written in a curved pattern over the position on the bottom. The card backs feature headshots of the players in the lower lefthand corner, framed in a stop watch. The cards are numbered with the "GT" prefix.

		MT
Complete Set (96):		25.00
Common Player:		.20
Minor Stars:		.40
1	Eddie George	2.00
2	Larry Bowie	.20
3	Jarius Hayes	.20
4	Jamal Anderson	2.00
5	Earnest Hunter	.20
6	Darick Holmes	.20
7	Kerry Collins	.50
8	Raymont Harris	.20
9	Jeff Blake	.50
10	Troy Aikman	1.50
11	Terrell Davis	2.00
12	Kevin Glover	.20
13	Brett Favre	3.00
14	Al Del Greco	.20
15	Marshall Faulk	.75
16	Bryan Barker	.20
17	Rich Gannon	.20
18	Dwight Hollier	.20
19	Dixon Edwards	.20
20	Drew Bledsoe	1.00
21	Paul Green	.20
22	Lawrence Dawsey	.20
23	Ron Carpenter	.20
24	Joe Aska	.20
25	Joe Panos	.20
26	Norm Johnson	.20
27	Tony Banks	.50
28	Darren Bennett	.20
29	Steve Israel	.20
30	Mike Barber	.20
31	Dexter Nottage	.20
32	Kwamie Lassiter	.20
33	Travis Hall	.20
34	Greg Montgomery	.20
35	Jim Kelly	.20
36	Matt Elliott	.20
37	Jack Jackson	.20
38	Ki-Jana Carter	.40
39	Deion Sanders	.50
40	Jason Elam	.20
41	Johnnie Morton	.20
42	Darius Holland	.20
43	Sheddrick Wilson	.20
44	Derrick Frazier	.20
45	Travis Davis	.20
46	Pellom McDaniels	.20
47	Dan Marino	3.00
48	Ben Hanks	.20
49	Tedy Bruschi	.20
50	Tom Hodson	.20
51	Amani Toomer	.50
52	Brian Hansen	.20
53	Paul Butcher	.20
54	Kevin Turner	.20
55	Darren Perry	.20
56	Mike Gruttadauria	.20
57	Charlie Jones	.20
58	Iheanyi Uwaezuoke	.20
59	Glenn Montgomery	.20
60	Mike Alstott	.75
61	Joe Patton	.20
62	Leeland McElroy	.75
63	Robbie Tobeck	.20
64	Vinny Testaverde	.20
65	Chris Spielman	.20
66	Anthony Johnson	.20
67	Todd Sauerbrun	.20
68	Jeff Hill	.20
69	Emmitt Smith	3.00
70	John Elway	1.00
71	Barry Sanders	3.00
72	Brian Williams	.20
73	Chris Gardocki	.20
74	Jimmy Smith	.20
75	Ricky Siglar	.20
76	Tim Ruddy	.20
77	Moe Williams	.20
78	Willie Clay	.20
79	Henry Lusk	.20
80	Brian Williams	.20
81	Ronald Moore	.20
82	Trey Junkin	.20
83	James Willis	.20
84	Joel Steed	.20
85	Jamie Martin	.20
86	Shawn Lee	.20
87	Steve Young	1.00
88	Barrett Robbins	.20
89	Charles Dimry	.20
90	Darryl Pounds	.20
91	Herschel Walker	.20
92	Bill Romanowski	.20
93	David Tate	.20
94	Marrio Grier	.20
95	Rodney Young	.20
96	Lamar Smith	.20

1996 Pacific Litho-Cel Moments in Time

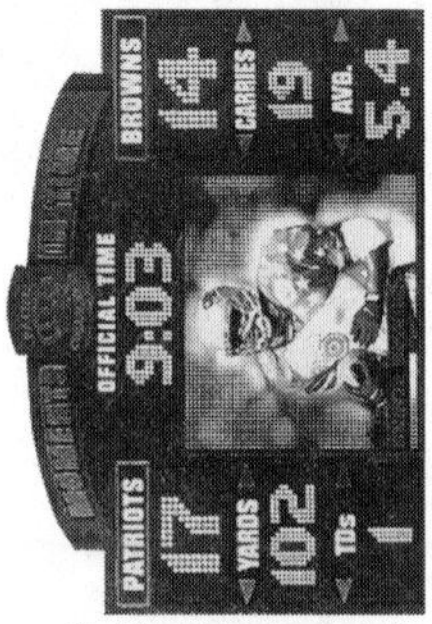

The 20-card, regular-sized, die-cut set was inserted every 49 packs of Litho-Cel cards. The horizontal cards are die-cut in the shape of a scoreboard and feature red-foil printing. The score of a particular game, along with the player's statistics for that game are included on the card front in scoreboard script, while the card back describes the player's performance with a highlight. The cards are numbered with the "MT" prefix.

		MT
Complete Set (20):		500.00
Common Player:		8.00
1	Jim Kelly	8.00
2	Kerry Collins	16.00
3	Rashaan Salaam	8.00
4	Troy Aikman	50.00
5	Deion Sanders	30.00
6	Emmitt Smith	100.00
7	Terrell Davis	50.00
8	John Elway	30.00
9	Barry Sanders	50.00
10	Robert Brooks	8.00
11	Brett Favre	100.00
12	Marshall Faulk	20.00
13	Jim Harbaugh	8.00
14	Steve Bono	8.00
15	Dan Marino	100.00
16	Drew Bledsoe	50.00
17	Curtis Martin	60.00
18	Jerry Rice	50.00
19	Steve Young	40.00
20	Terry Allen	8.00

1997 Pacific

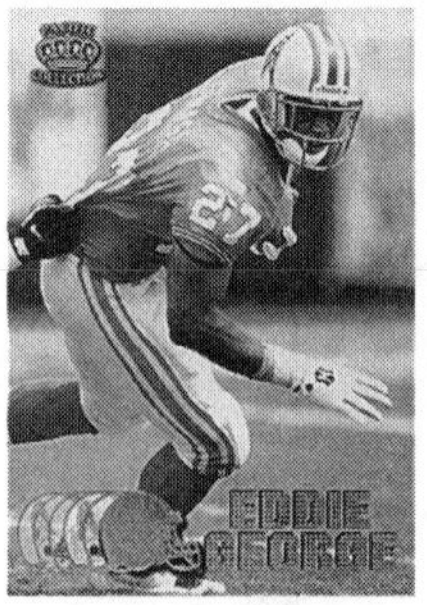

The 450-card set showcases a full-bleed photo on the front, with the Pacific Crown Collection logo in the upper left. The team's helmet is in color in the lower left and reproduced in gold foil towards the bottom center. The player's name is printed in capital gold-foil letters in the lower right of the front. A Copper parallel was inserted 1:1 hobby packs, while a Silver parallel was seeded 1:1 retail packs. A Platinum Blue hobby and retail parallel was included in 1:73 packs. Red-foil parallels were found one per Treat Entertainment U.S. retail pack.

		MT
Complete Set (450):		40.00
Common Player:		.05
Minor Stars:		.10
Copper/Silver Cards:		3x-6x
Blue Cards:		50x-100x
Pack (12):		2.00
Wax Box (36):		60.00
1	Lomas Brown	.05
2	Pat Carter	.05
3	Larry Centers	.05
4	Matt Darby	.05
5	Marcus Dowdell	.05
6	Aaron Graham	.05
7	Kent Graham	.10
8	LeShon Johnson	.05
9	Seth Joyner	.05
10	Leeland McElroy	.10
11	Rob Moore	.05
12	Simeon Rice	.05
13	Eric Swann	.05
14	Aeneas Williams	.05
15	Morten Andersen	.05
16	Jamal Anderson	.20
17	Lester Archambeau	.05
18	Cornelius Bennett	.05
19	J.J. Birden	.05
20	Antone Davis	.05
21	Bert Emanuel	.05
22	Travis Hall	.05
23	Bobby Hebert	.05
24	Craig Heyward	.05
25	Terance Mathis	.05
26	Tim McKyer	.05
27	Eric Metcalf	.05
28	Jessie Tuggle	.05
29	Derrick Alexander	.05
30	Orlando Brown	.05
31	Rob Burnett	.05
32	Earnest Byner	.05
33	Ray Ethridge	.05
34	Steve Everett	.05
35	Carwell Gardner	.05
36	Michael Jackson	.05
37	Jamal Lewis	.05
38	Stevon Moore	.05
39	Bam Morris	.05
40	Jonathan Ogden	.05
41	Vinny Testaverde	.10
42	Todd Collins	.10
43	Russell Copeland	.05
44	Quinn Early	.05
45	John Fina	.05
46	Phil Hansen	.05
47	Eric Moulds	.15
48	Bryce Paup	.05
49	Andre Reed	.05
50	Kurt Schulz	.05
51	Bruce Smith	.05
52	Chris Spielman	.05
53	Steve Tasker	.05
54	Thurman Thomas	.10
55	Carlton Bailey	.05
56	Michael Bates	.05
57	Blake Brockermeyer	.05
58	Mark Carrier	.05
59	Kerry Collins	.25
60	Eric Davis	.05
61	Kevin Greene	.05
62	Raghib Ismail	.05
63	Anthony Johnson	.05
64	Shawn King	.05
65	Greg Kragen	.05
66	Sam Mills	.05
67	Tyrone Poole	.05
68	Wesley Walls	.05
69	Mark Carrier	.05
70	Curtis Conway	.10
71	Bobby Engram	.05
72	Jim Flanigan	.05
73	Al Fontenot	.05
74	Raymont Harris	.05
75	Walt Harris	.05
76	Andy Heck	.05
77	Dave Krieg	.05
78	Rashaan Salaam	.10
79	Vinson Smith	.05
80	Alonzo Spellman	.05
81	Michael Timpson	.05
82	James Williams	.05
83	Ashley Ambrose	.05
84	Eric Bieniemy	.05
85	Jeff Blake	.15
86	Ki-Jana Carter	.10
87	John Copeland	.05
88	David Dunn	.05
89	Jeff Hill	.05
90	Ricardo McDonald	.05
91	Tony McGee	.05
92	Greg Myers	.05
93	Carl Pickens	.10
94	Corey Sawyer	.05
95	Darnay Scott	.05
96	Dan Wilkinson	.05
97	Troy Aikman	1.00
98	Larry Allen	.05
99	Eric Bjornson	.05
100	Ray Donaldson	.05
101	Michael Irvin	.10
102	Daryl Johnson	.05
103	Nate Newton	.05
104	Deion Sanders	.40
105	Jim Schwantz	.05
106	Emmitt Smith	1.75
107	Broderick Thomas	.05
108	Tony Tolbert	.05
109	Erik Williams	.05
110	Sherman Williams	.05
111	Darren Woodson	.05
112	Steve Atwater	.05
113	Aaron Craver	.05
114	Ray Crockett	.05
115	Terrell Davis	1.25
116	Jason Elam	.05
117	John Elway	.60
118	Todd Kinchen	.05
119	Ed McCaffrey	.05
120	Anthony Miller	.05
121	John Mobley	.05
122	Michael Dean Perry	.05
123	Reggie Rivers	.05
124	Shannon Sharpe	.05
125	Alfred Williams	.05
126	Reggie Brown	.05
127	Luther Elliss	.05
128	Kevin Glover	.05
129	Jason Hanson	.05
130	Pepper Johnson	.05
131	Glyn Milburn	.05
132	Scott Mitchell	.05
133	Herman Moore	.15
134	Johnnie Morton	.05
135	Brett Perriman	.05
136	Robert Porcher	.05
137	Ron Rivers	.05
138	Barry Sanders	1.25
139	Henry Thomas	.05
140	Don Beebe	.05
141	Edgar Bennett	.05
142	Robert Brooks	.05
143	LeRoy Butler	.05
144	Mark Chmura	.05
145	Brett Favre	2.00
146	Antonio Freeman	.25
147	Chris Jacke	.05
148	Travis Jervey	.05
149	Sean Jones	.05
150	Dorsey Levens	.10
151	John Michels	.05
152	Craig Newsome	.05
153	Eugene Robinson	.05
154	Reggie White	.10
155	Michael Barrow	.05
156	Blaine Bishop	.05
157	Chris Chandler	.05
158	Anthony Cook	.05
159	Malcolm Floyd	.05
160	Eddie George	1.25
161	Roderick Lewis	.05
162	Steve McNair	.75
163	John Henry Mills	.05
164	Derek Russell	.05
165	Chris Sanders	.05
166	Mark Stepnoski	.05
167	Frank Wycheck	.05
168	Robert Young	.05
169	Trev Alberts	.05
170	Aaron Bailey	.05
171	Tony Bennett	.05
172	Ray Buchanan	.05
173	Quentin Coryatt	.05
174	Eugene Daniel	.05
175	Sean Dawkins	.05
176	Ken Dilger	.05
177	Marshall Faulk	.10
178	Jim Harbaugh	.05
179	Marvin Harrison	.40
180	Paul Justin	.05
181	Lamont Warren	.05
182	Bernard Whittingham	.05
183	Tony Bosselli	.05
184	Tony Brackens	.05
185	Mark Brunell	.75
186	Brian DeMarco	.05
187	Rich Griffith	.05
188	Kevin Hardy	.05
189	Willie Jackson	.05
190	Jeff Lageman	.05
191	Keenan McCardell	.10
192	Natrone Means	.10
193	Pete Mitchell	.05
194	Joel Smeenge	.05
195	Jimmy Smith	.10
196	James Stewart	.05
197	Marcus Allen	.10
198	John Art	.05
199	Kimble Anders	.05
200	Steve Bono	.10
201	Vaughn Booker	.05
202	Dale Carter	.05
203	Mark Collins	.05
204	Greg Hill	.05
205	Joe Horn	.05
206	Dan Saleaumua	.05
207	Will Shields	.05
208	Neil Smith	.05
209	Derrick Thomas	.10
210	Tamarick Vanover	.10
211	Karim Abdul-Jabbar	.25
212	Fred Barnett	.05
213	Tim Bowens	.05
214	Kirby Dar Dar	.05
215	Troy Drayton	.05

216	Craig Erickson	.05
217	Daryl Gardener	.05
218	Randal Hill	.05
219	Dan Marino	1.75
220	O.J. McDuffie	.05
221	Bernie Parmalee	.05
222	Stanley Pritchett	.05
223	Daniel Stubbs	.05
224	Zach Thomas	.20
225	Derrick Alexander	.05
226	Cris Carter	.10
227	Jeff Christy	.05
228	Qadry Ismail	.05
229	Brad Johnson	.05
230	Andrew Jordan	.05
231	Randall McDaniel	.05
232	David Palmer	.05
233	John Randle	.05
234	Jake Reed	.05
235	Scott Sisson	.05
236	Korey Stringer	.05
237	Darryl Talley	.05
238	Orlando Thomas	.05
239	Bruce Armstrong	.05
240	Drew Bledsoe	1.00
241	Willie Clay	.05
242	Ben Coates	.05
243	Frank Collins	.05
244	Terry Glenn	.25
245	Jerome Henderson	.05
246	Shawn Jefferson	.05
247	Dietrich Jells	.05
248	Ty Law	.05
249	Curtis Martin	1.25
250	Willie McGinest	.05
251	David Meggett	.05
252	Lawyer Milloy	.05
253	Chris Slade	.05
254	Je'Rod Cherry	.05
255	Jim Everett	.05
256	Mark Fields	.05
257	Michael Haynes	.05
258	Tyrone Hughes	.05
259	Haywood Jeffires	.05
260	Wayne Martin	.05
261	Mark McMillian	.05
262	Rufus Porter	.05
263	William Roaf	.05
264	Torrance Small	.05
265	Renaldo Turnbull	.05
266	Ray Zellars	.05
267	Jessie Armstead	.05
268	Chad Bratzke	.05
269	Dave Brown	.05
270	Chris Calloway	.05
271	Howard Cross	.05
272	Lawrence Dawsey	.05
273	Rodney Hampton	.05
274	Danny Kanell	.05
275	Arthur Marshall	.05
276	Aaron Pierce	.05
277	Phillippi Sparks	.05
278	Amani Toomer	.05
279	Charles Way	.05
280	Richie Anderson	.05
281	Fred Baxter	.05
282	Wayne Chrebet	.05
283	Kyle Clifton	.05
284	John Elliott	.05
285	Aaron Glenn	.05
286	Jeff Graham	.05
287	Bobby Hamilton	.05
288	Keyshawn Johnson	.40
289	Adrian Murrell	.05
290	Neil O'Donnell	.05
291	Webster Slaughter	.05
292	Alex Van Dyke	.05
293	Marvin Washington	.05
294	Joe Aska	.05
295	Jerry Ball	.05
296	Tim Brown	.10
297	Rickey Dudley	.10
298	Pat Harlow	.05
299	Nolan Harrison	.05
300	Billy Joe Hobert	.05
301	James Jett	.05
302	Napoleon Kaufman	.10
303	Lincoln Kennedy	.05
304	Albert Lewis	.05
305	Chester McGlockton	.05
306	Pat Swilling	.05
307	Steve Wisniewski	.05
308	Darion Conner	.05
309	Ty Detmer	.05
310	Jason Dunn	.05
311	Irving Fryar	.05
312	Jeff Fuller	.05
313	William Fuller	.05
314	Charlie Garner	.05
315	Bobby Hoying	.05
316	Tom Hutton	.05
317	Chris T. Jones	.05
318	Mike Mamula	.05
319	Mark Seay	.05
320	Bobby Taylor	.05
321	Ricky Watters	.10
322	Jahine Arnold	.05
323	Jerome Bettis	.10
324	Chad Brown	.05
325	Mark Bruener	.05
326	Andre Hastings	.05
327	Norm Johnson	.05
328	Levon Kirkland	.05
329	Carnell Lake	.05
330	Greg Lloyd	.05
331	Ernie Mills	.05
332	Orpheus Roye	.05
333	Kordell Stewart	.75
334	Yancey Thigpen	.05
335	Mike Tomczak	.05
336	Rod Woodson	.05
337	Tony Banks	.25
338	Bern Brostek	.05
339	Isaac Bruce	.15
340	Ernie Conwell	.05
341	Keith Crawford	.05
342	Wayne Gandy	.05
343	Harold Green	.05
344	Carlos Jenkins	.05
345	Jimmie Jones	.05
346	Eddie Kennison	.40
347	Todd Lyght	.05
348	Leslie O'Neal	.05
349	Lawrence Phillips	.10
350	Greg Robinson	.05
351	Darren Bennett	.05
352	Lewis Bush	.05
353	Eric Castle	.05
354	Terrell Fletcher	.05
355	Darrien Gordon	.05
356	Kurt Gouveia	.05

357	Aaron Hayden	.05
358	Stan Humphries	.05
359	Tony Martin	.05
360	Vaughn Parker	.05
361	Brian Roche	.05
362	Leonard Russell	.05
363	Junior Seau	.10
364	Roy Barker	.05
365	Harris Barton	.05
366	Dexter Carter	.05
367	Chris Doleman	.05
368	Tyronne Drakeford	.05
369	Elvis Grbac	.05
370	Derek Loville	.05
371	Tim McDonald	.05
372	Ken Norton	.05
373	Terrell Owens	.50
374	Gary Plummer	.05
375	Jerry Rice	1.00
376	Dana Stubblefield	.05
377	Lee Woodall	.05
378	Steve Young	.60
379	Robert Blackmon	.05
380	Brian Blades	.05
381	Carlester Crumpler	.05
382	Christian Fauria	.05
383	John Friesz	.05
384	Joey Galloway	.25
385	Derrick Graham	.05
386	Cortez Kennedy	.05
387	Warren Moon	.10
388	Winston Moss	.05
389	Mike Pritchard	.05
390	Michael Sinclair	.05
391	Lamar Smith	.05
392	Chris Warren	.05
393	Chidi Ahanotu	.05
394	Mike Alstott	.15
395	Reggie Brooks	.05
396	Trent Dilfer	.10
397	Jerry Ellison	.05
398	Paul Gruber	.05
399	Alvin Harper	.05
400	Courtney Hawkins	.05
401	Dave Moore	.05
402	Errict Rhett	.10
403	Warren Sapp	.05
404	Nilo Silvan	.05
405	Regan Upshaw	.05
406	Casey Weldon	.05
407	Terry Allen	.05
408	Jamie Asher	.05
409	Bill Brooks	.05
410	Tom Carter	.05
411	Henry Ellard	.05
412	Gus Frerotte	.05
413	Darrell Green	.05
414	Ken Harvey	.05
415	Tre' Johnson	.05
416	Brian Mitchell	.05
417	Rich Owens	.05
418	Heath Shuler	.10
419	Michael Westbrook	.10
420	*Tony Woods*	.10
421	*Reidel Anthony*	1.50
422	*Darnell Autry*	.50
423	*Tiki Barber*	1.00
424	*Pat Barnes*	.30
425	*Terry Battle*	.10
426	*Will Blackwell*	.30
427	*Peter Boulware*	.10
428	*Rae Carruth*	1.00
429	*Troy Davis*	.50
430	*Jim Druckenmiller*	2.00
431	*Warrick Dunn*	1.25
432	*Marc Edwards*	.10
433	*James Farrior*	.10
434	*Yatil Green*	.50
435	*Byron Hanspard*	.50
436	*Ike Hilliard*	1.50
437	*David LaFleur*	.50
438	*Kevin Lockett*	.25
439	*Sam Madison*	.10
440	*Brian Manning*	.10
441	*Orlando Pace*	.50
442	*Jake Plummer*	2.50
443	*Chad Scott*	.10
444	*Sedrick Shaw*	.30
445	*Antowain Smith*	1.25
446	*Shawn Springs*	.30
447	*Ross Verba*	.20
448	*Bryant Webster*	.10
449	*Renaldo Wynn*	.10
450	*Jimmy Johnson*	.30

1997 Pacific Big Number Die-Cuts

Inserted 1:37 packs, the 20-card die-cut set features the player's last name and jersey number on the front of the card. The backs have the player's name at the top, with the Pacific Crown logo in the upper right. A player photo is in the center, with his highlights located inside a box near the bottom.

		MT
Complete Set (20):		285.00
Common Player:		4.00
Minor Stars:		8.00
Inserted 1:37		
1	Jamal Anderson	15.00
2	Kerry Collins	8.00
3	Troy Aikman	20.00
4	Emmitt Smith	30.00

5	Terrell Davis	35.00
6	John Elway	30.00
7	Barry Sanders	40.00
8	Brett Favre	40.00
9	Eddie George	20.00
10	Mark Brunell	20.00
11	Marcus Allen	8.00
12	Karim Abdul-Jabbar	8.00
13	Dan Marino	30.00
14	Drew Bledsoe	20.00
15	Curtis Martin	15.00
16	Napoleon Kaufman	10.00
17	Jerome Bettis	8.00
18	Eddie Kennison	4.00
19	Jerry Rice	20.00
20	Steve Young	15.00

1997 Pacific Card Supials

Inserted 1:37 packs, the 36-card set features a player photo superimposed on the front, with a gold-foil version of the same photo printed along the right side of the front. The Crown logo is in the upper left, while the player's first name is in the upper right. His last name is printed vertically along the left edge of the front. The backs include a slot where a miniature die-cut card of the player can be inserted. The mini card includes a photo inside a die-cut football, which is sitting on a tee. The team's logo is in the lower right of the mini-card front.

		MT
Complete Set (72):		500.00
Complete Large Set (36):		300.00
Complete Small Set (36):		200.00
Common Large Player:		2.00
Minor Large Stars:		4.00
Small Cards:		.7x
Inserted 1:37		
1	Todd Collins	2.00
2	Kerry Collins	4.00
3	Wesley Walls	2.00
4	Jeff Blake	4.00
5	Troy Aikman	15.00
6	Emmitt Smith	25.00
7	Terrell Davis	25.00
8	John Elway	20.00
9	Herman Moore	4.00
10	Barry Sanders	30.00
11	Brett Favre	30.00
12	Dorsey Levens	4.00
13	Eddie George	15.00
14	Steve McNair	10.00
15	Marshall Faulk	6.00
16	Mark Brunell	15.00
17	Natrone Means	4.00
18	Marcus Allen	4.00
19	Karim Abdul-Jabbar	4.00
20	Dan Marino	25.00
21	Brad Johnson	6.00
22	Drew Bledsoe	15.00
23	Terry Glenn	6.00
24	Curtis Martin	10.00
25	Napoleon Kaufman	8.00
26	Ricky Watters	4.00
27	Jerome Bettis	4.00
28	Kordell Stewart	15.00
29	Tony Banks	4.00
30	Isaac Bruce	4.00
31	Eddie Kennison	4.00
32	Jerry Rice	15.00
33	Steve Young	15.00
34	Joey Galloway	6.00
35	Chris Warren	2.00
36	Gus Frerotte	2.00

1997 Pacific Cramer's Choice Awards

Inserted 1:721 packs, the 10-card set showcases a player photo superimposed over a pyramid die-cut background. "1997 Cramer's Choice Awards" and the Crown logo are printed at the top of the award, while

the gold base of the award includes the Crown logo, player's name and position.

		MT
Complete Set (10):		750.00
Common Player:		25.00
Inserted 1:721		
1	Kevin Greene	25.00
2	Emmitt Smith	125.00
3	Terrell Davis	150.00
4	John Elway	125.00
5	Barry Sanders	150.00
6	Brett Favre	150.00
7	Eddie George	75.00
8	Mark Brunell	75.00
9	Terry Glenn	40.00
10	Jerry Rice	75.00

1997 Pacific Gold Crown Die-Cuts

The 36-card set was inserted 1:37 packs. The top of the cards feature a die-cut gold crown at the top. The player's photo is superimposed over the crown. The bottom of the card front has three gold-foil stripes, with the player's name printed in the center of the middle stripe. A circle at the bottom center features the team logo inside a shield. Eight sun rays are printed diagonally at the bottom of the front.

		MT
Complete Set (36):		575.00
Common Player:		4.00
Minor Stars:		8.00
Inserted 1:37		
1	Larry Centers	4.00
2	Vinny Testaverde	8.00
3	Kerry Collins	8.00
4	Kevin Green	8.00
5	Anthony Johnson	4.00
6	Jeff Blake	8.00
7	Troy Aikman	25.00
8	Emmitt Smith	40.00
9	Terrell Davis	45.00
10	John Elway	40.00
11	Barry Sanders	50.00
12	Brett Favre	50.00
13	Antonio Freeman	12.00
14	Eddie George	25.00
15	Marshall Faulk	8.00
16	Mark Brunell	20.00
17	Jimmy Smith	8.00
18	Marcus Allen	8.00
19	Karim Abdul-Jabbar	8.00
20	Dan Marino	40.00
21	Brad Johnson	12.00
22	Drew Bledsoe	20.00
23	Terry Glenn	12.00
24	Curtis Martin	15.00
25	Adrian Murrell	4.00
26	Tim Brown	4.00
27	Jerome Bettis	12.00
28	Kordell Stewart	20.00
29	Tony Banks	8.00
30	Terrell Owens	25.00
31	Jerry Rice	25.00
32	Steve Young	15.00
33	Chris Warren	4.00
34	Terry Allen	8.00
35	Gus Frerotte	4.00
36	Jim Druckenmiller	8.00

1997 Pacific Mark Brunell

The four-card set was split between Crown Collection and Invincible. Card Nos. 1-2 were seeded 1:72 packs of Crown, while Nos. 3-4 were inserted 1:72 in Invincible packs.

	MT
Complete Set (4):	40.00
Common Player:	10.00

1997 Pacific Team Checklists

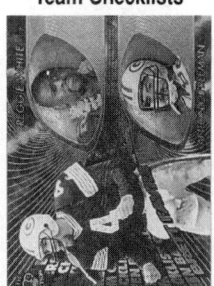

Inserted 1:721 packs, the 20-card die-cut set features the player's last name and jersey number on the front of the card. The backs have the player's name at the top, with the Pacific Crown logo in the upper right. A player photo is in the center, with his highlights located inside a box near the bottom.

The 30-card set is inserted 1:37 packs. The fronts feature an action shot of a player on the left side, with his name printed in gold across his body, while the team's two other stars have each of their head shot printed on football-shaped acetate pieces on the right. Their names appear above the top football and below the bottom football. The team's name and the word "checklist" are repeated many times beginning on the left border and continuing to a thin area on the right side.

		MT
Complete Set (30):		375.00
Common Player:		6.00
Minor Stars:		12.00
Inserted 1:37		
1	Arizona Cardinals	6.00
2	Atlanta Falcons	6.00
3	Baltimore Ravens	6.00
4	Buffalo Bills	12.00
5	Carolina Panthers	12.00
6	Chicago Bears	6.00
7	Cincinnati Bengals	12.00
8	Dallas Cowboys	40.00
9	Denver Broncos	30.00
10	Detroit Lions	50.00
11	Green Bay Packers	50.00
12	Houston Oilers	30.00
13	Indianapolis Colts	6.00
14	Jacksonville Jaguars	20.00
15	Kansas City Chiefs	6.00
16	Miami Dolphins	40.00
17	Minnesota Vikings	6.00
18	New England Patriots	30.00
19	New Orleans Saints	6.00
20	New York Giants	6.00
21	New York Jets	6.00
22	Oakland Raiders	6.00
23	Philadelphia Eagles	6.00
24	Pittsburgh Steelers	15.00
25	St. Louis Rams	12.00
26	San Diego Chargers	6.00
27	San Francisco 49ers	30.00
28	Seattle Seahawks	6.00
29	Tampa Bay Buccaneers	6.00
30	Washington Redskins	6.00

1997 Pacific The Zone

Inserted 1:73 packs, the 20-card set is die-cut in the shape of a goal post. The front has a photo of the player inside the uprights, while his name and position are printed at the base of the goal post.

		MT
Complete Set (20):		475.00
Common Player:		6.00
Minor Stars:		12.00
Inserted 1:73		
1	Kerry Collins	12.00
2	Jeff Blake	12.00
3	Emmitt Smith	40.00
4	Terrell Davis	40.00
5	John Elway	30.00
6	Barry Sanders	50.00
7	Brett Favre	50.00
8	Mark Brunell	25.00
9	Karim Abdul-Jabbar	12.00
10	Dan Marino	40.00
11	Drew Bledsoe	25.00
12	Terry Glenn	12.00
13	Curtis Martin	20.00
14	Napoleon Kaufman	15.00
15	Jerome Bettis	12.00
16	Eddie Kennison	6.00
17	Tony Martin	6.00
18	Jerry Rice	25.00
19	Steve Young	20.00
20	Terry Allen	12.00

1997 Pacific Crown Royale

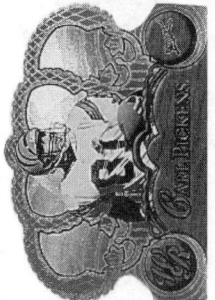

Crown Royale is a 144-card, all die-cut set. The base cards feature a player shot on a crown-shaped die-cut card. The two parallel sets are sil-

ver and holographic gold foil (4:25) and silver and holographic blue foil (1:25). Insert sets include NFL Cel-Fusions, Chalk Talk Laser Cuts, Pro Bowl Die-Cuts, Firestone on Football and Premium-sized Cramer's Choice Awards.

		MT
Complete Set (144):		150.00
Common Player:		.50
Minor Stars:		1.00
Gold/Silver Cards:		2x-4x
Gold/Silver Rookies:		2x
Blue Cards:		6x-12x
Blue Rookies:		3x-6x
Pack (4):		6.00
Wax Box (24):		130.00
1	Larry Centers	.50
2	Kent Graham	1.00
3	LeShon Johnson	.50
4	Leeland McElroy	.50
5	*Jake Plummer*	12.00
6	Jamal Anderson	1.00
7	Chris Chandler	.50
8	*Byron Hanspard*	1.50
9	Michael Haynes	.50
10	Derrick Alexander	.50
11	*Jay Graham*	1.50
12	Michael Jackson	.50
13	Vinny Testaverde	.50
14	Todd Collins	1.00
15	Jay Riemersma	.50
16	*Antowain Smith*	6.00
17	Steve Tasker	.50
18	Thurman Thomas	1.00
19	*Rae Carruth*	4.00
20	Kerry Collins	1.00
21	Anthony Johnson	.50
22	*Fred Lane*	3.00
23	Muhsin Muhammad	.50
24	Wesley Walls	.50
25	*Darnell Autry*	1.00
26	Raymont Harris	1.00
27	Erik Kramer	.50
28	Rick Mirer	.50
29	Rashaan Salaam	1.00
30	Jeff Blake	.50
31	Ki-Jana Carter	.50
32	*Corey Dillon*	10.00
33	Carl Pickens	.50
34	Troy Aikman	6.00
35	Michael Irvin	1.00
36	Daryl Johnston	.50
37	*David LaFleur*	2.00
38	Deion Sanders	3.00
39	Emmitt Smith	10.00
40	Terrell Davis	6.00
41	John Elway	4.00
42	Ed McCaffrey	.50
43	Shannon Sharpe	.50
44	Neil Smith	.50
45	Scott Mitchell	.50
46	Herman Moore	1.00
47	Johnnie Morton	.50
48	Barry Sanders	7.00
49	Robert Brooks	.50
50	Mark Chmura	.50
51	Brett Favre	12.00
52	Antonio Freeman	1.00
53	Dorsey Levens	1.00
54	Reggie White	.50
55	Ken Dilger	.50
56	Marshall Faulk	1.00
57	Jim Harbaugh	.50
58	Marvin Harrison	2.00
59	Mark Brunell	6.00
60	Rob Johnson	.50
61	Keenan McCardell	.50
62	Natrone Means	1.00
63	Jimmy Smith	.50
64	Marcus Allen	1.00
65	*Tony Gonzalez*	6.00
66	Elvis Grbac	.50
67	Greg Hill	.50
68	Tamarick Vanover	.50
69	Karim Abdul-Jabbar	1.50
70	Fred Barnett	.50
71	Dan Marino	10.00
72	O.J. McDuffie	.50
73	Jerris McPhail	.50
74	Cris Carter	.50
75	Randall Cunningham	.50
76	Brad Johnson	1.00
77	Jake Reed	.50
78	Robert Smith	1.00
79	Drew Bledsoe	6.00
80	Ben Coates	.50
81	Terry Glenn	1.50
82	Curtis Martin	6.00
83	*Troy Davis*	1.50
84	Heath Shuler	.50
85	*Danny Wuerffel*	6.00
86	*Tiki Barber*	6.00
87	Dave Brown	.50
88	Rodney Hampton	.50
89	*Ike Hilliard*	1.50
90	Amani Toomer	.50
91	Wayne Chrebet	.50
92	Keyshawn Johnson	2.00
93	Adrian Murrell	1.00
94	Neil O'Donnell	.50
95	Dedric Ward	.50
96	Tim Brown	1.00
97	Jeff George	.50
98	Desmond Howard	.50
99	Napoleon Kaufman	2.00
100	Ty Detmer	.50
101	Irving Fryar	.50
102	Bobby Hoying	.50
103	Ricky Watters	1.00
104	Jerome Bettis	1.00
105	*Will Blackwell*	2.00
106	Charles Johnson	.50
107	*George Jones*	1.00
108	Kordell Stewart	6.00
109	Tony Banks	2.00
110	Isaac Bruce	1.00
111	Eddie Kennison	1.00
112	Lawrence Phillips	1.00
113	Jim Everett	.50
114	Stan Humphries	.50
115	*Freddie Jones*	1.50
116	Tony Martin	.50
117	Junior Seau	.50
118	*Jim Druckenmiller*	8.00
119	Garrison Hearst	.50
120	Brent Jones	.50
121	Terrell Owens	5.00
122	Jerry Rice	6.00

124	Steve Young	4.00
125	Chad Brown	.50
126	Joey Galloway	1.00
127	*Jon Kitna*	12.00
128	Warren Moon	.50
129	Chris Warren	.50
130	Mike Alstott	3.00
131	*Reidel Anthony*	6.00
132	Trent Dilfer	1.00
133	*Warrick Dunn*	6.00
134	Karl Williams	.50
135	Willie Davis	.50
136	Eddie George	8.00
137	*Joey Kent*	1.50
138	Steve McNair	4.00
139	Chris Sanders	.50
140	Terry Allen	.50
141	Jamie Asher	.50
142	Stephen Davis	.50
143	Henry Ellard	.50
144	Gus Frerotte	.50

1997 Pacific Crown Royale Cel-Fusions

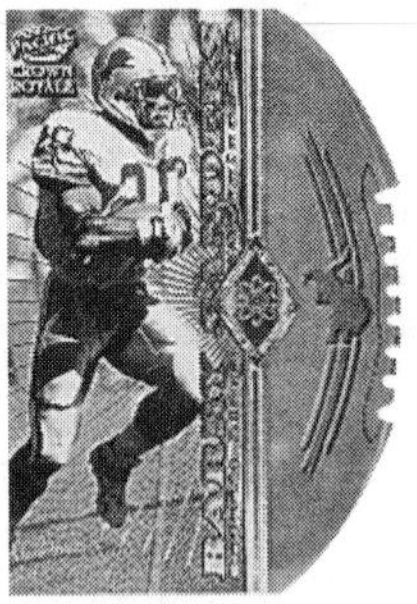

This 20-card insert consists of a die-cut cel football fused to a trading card. The cards were inserted 1:49.

		MT
Complete Set (20):		700.00
Common Player:		12.00
1	Antowain Smith	30.00
2	Troy Aikman	50.00
3	Emmitt Smith	100.00
4	Terrell Davis	50.00
5	John Elway	35.00
6	Barry Sanders	50.00
7	Brett Favre	100.00
8	Mark Brunell	50.00
9	Elvis Grbac	12.00
10	Karim Abdul-Jabbar	20.00
11	Dan Marino	100.00
12	Drew Bledsoe	50.00
13	Curtis Martin	50.00
14	Danny Wuerffel	30.00
15	Tiki Barber	20.00
16	Jeff George	12.00
17	Kordell Stewart	50.00
18	Tony Banks	12.00
19	Jerry Rice	50.00
20	Steve Young	35.00

1997 Pacific Crown Royale Chalk Talk

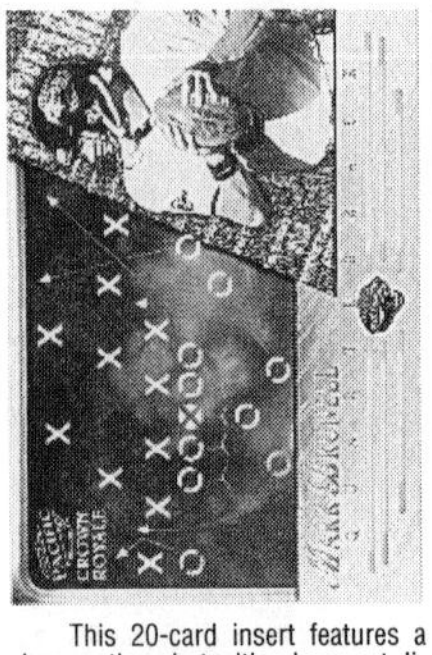

This 20-card insert features a player action shot with a laser cut diagram of one of their signature plays. This set was inserted 1:73.

		MT
Complete Set (20):		900.00
Common Player:		25.00
1	Kerry Collins	30.00
2	Troy Aikman	60.00
3	Emmitt Smith	125.00
4	Terrell Davis	60.00
5	John Elway	40.00
6	Barry Sanders	80.00
7	Brett Favre	150.00
8	Mark Brunell	60.00
9	Marcus Allen	25.00
10	Dan Marino	125.00
11	Drew Bledsoe	60.00
12	Curtis Martin	60.00
13	Troy Davis	25.00
14	Napoleon Kaufman	25.00
15	Jerome Bettis	25.00
16	Jim Druckenmiller	45.00
17	Jerry Rice	60.00
18	Steve Young	40.00
19	Warrick Dunn	70.00
20	Eddie George	85.00

A player's name in *italic type* indicates a rookie card.

1997 Pacific Crown Royale Cramer's Choice Jumbos

Cramer's Choice is a jumbo-sized insert featuring 10 players on cards die-cut to look like trophies. This insert was found one card per box.

		MT
Complete Set (10):		85.00
Common Player:		4.00
1	Deion Sanders	4.00
2	Emmitt Smith	20.00
3	Terrell Davis	10.00
4	John Elway	7.00
5	Barry Sanders	15.00
6	Brett Favre	25.00
7	Mark Brunell	10.00
8	Drew Bledsoe	10.00
9	Jim Druckenmiller	12.00
10	Eddie George	15.00

1997 Pacific Crown Royale Firestone on Football

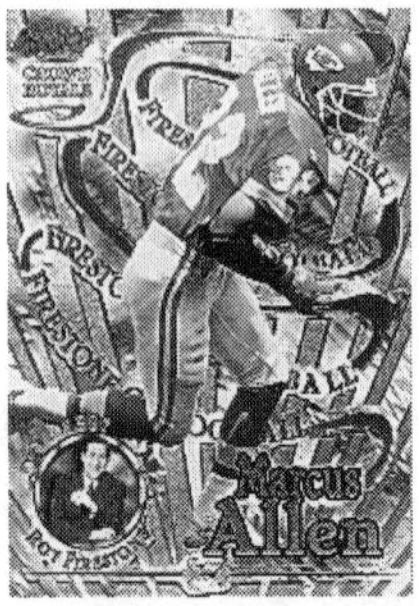

These 20 cards feature players on an etched-foil design. The backs have comments from Roy Firestone. A #21 card was made featuring Firestone with comments from a future Hall of Fame QB on the back. This set was inserted 1:25.

		MT
Complete Set (21):		600.00
Common Player:		7.00
1	Kerry Collins	14.00
2	Troy Aikman	30.00
3	Deion Sanders	18.00
4	Emmitt Smith	60.00
5	Terrell Davis	30.00
6	John Elway	25.00
7	Barry Sanders	40.00
8	Brett Favre	70.00
9	Reggie White	7.00
10	Mark Brunell	30.00
11	Marcus Allen	7.00
12	Dan Marino	60.00
13	Drew Bledsoe	30.00
14	Terry Glenn	14.00
15	Curtis Martin	30.00
16	Jerome Bettis	7.00
17	Jerry Rice	30.00
18	Steve Young	25.00
19	Eddie George	45.00
20	Gus Frerotte	7.00
21	Roy Firestone	7.00

1997 Pacific Crown Royale Pro Bowl Die-Cuts

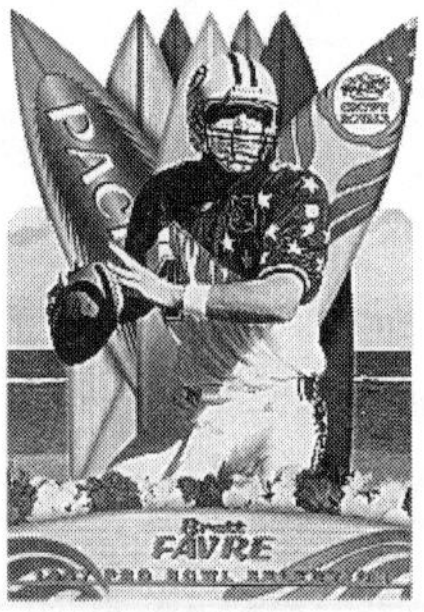

These die-cut cards feature Pro Bowl players against an ocean background. The 20 cards were inserted 1:25.

		MT
Complete Set (20):		500.00
Common Player:		10.00
1	Kerry Collins	20.00
2	Troy Aikman	50.00
3	Deion Sanders	25.00
4	Terrell Davis	50.00
5	John Elway	30.00
6	Shannon Sharpe	10.00
7	Barry Sanders	50.00
8	Brett Favre	100.00
9	Reggie White	10.00
10	Mark Brunell	50.00
11	Derrick Thomas	10.00
12	Drew Bledsoe	50.00
13	Ben Coates	10.00
14	Curtis Martin	50.00
15	Jerome Bettis	10.00
16	Isaac Bruce	10.00
17	Jerry Rice	50.00
18	Steve Young	30.00
19	Terry Allen	10.00
20	Gus Frerotte	10.00

1997 Pacific Dynagon

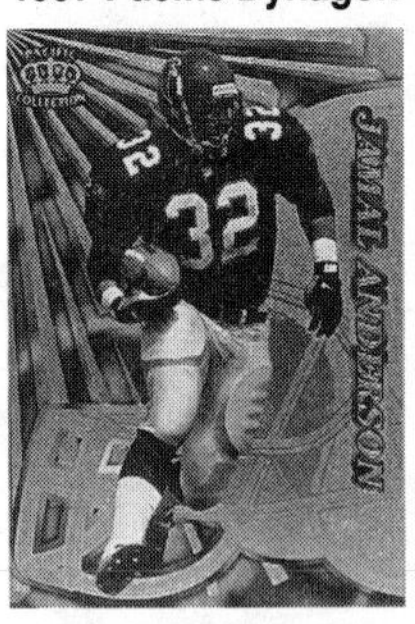

The 1997 Pacific Dynagon prism set consists of 144 regular-sized cards. The card fronts feature a gold-foil helmet background with the player's image outlined on top. The background also has the player's team colors with the player's name printed down the right side. The card backs include a head shot in the upper right-hand corner and a brief career highlight. Included with Dynagon Prism football are Tandems, Careers, Player Of The Week, Royal Connections and Best Kept Secrets insert sets. Each pack of Dynagon Prism contains three cards: one base card, one Best Kept Secrets card and one other insert card. A Silver parallel was available in retail packs (2:37), while a Copper parallel was included in 2:37 hobby packs. Red-foil parallels were found in 4:21 Treat Entertainment U.S. retail packs.

		MT
Complete Set (144):		120.00
Common Player:		.50
Minor Stars:		1.00
Pack (3):		2.50
Wax Box (36):		75.00
1	Larry Centers	.50
2	Kent Graham	.50
3	Leeland McElroy	1.00
4	Frank Sanders	.50
5	Jamal Anderson	1.00
6	Bert Emanuel	.50
7	Bobby Hebert	.50
8	Terance Mathis	.50
9	Eric Metcalf	.50
10	Derrick Alexander	.50
11	Earnest Byner	.50
12	Michael Jackson	.50
13	Vinny Testaverde	.50
14	Quinn Early	.50
15	Jim Kelly	.50
16	Eric Moulds	2.00
17	Andre Reed	.50
18	Bruce Smith	.50
19	Thurman Thomas	1.00
20	Tshimanga Biakabutuka	1.00
21	Mark Carrier	.50
22	Kerry Collins	1.00
23	Kevin Greene	.50
24	Anthony Johnson	.50
25	Wesley Walls	.50
26	Curtis Conway	.50
27	Bobby Engram	1.00
28	Raymont Harris	.50
29	Dave Krieg	.50
30	Rashaan Salaam	1.00
31	Jeff Blake	1.00
32	Ki-Jana Carter	.50
33	Garrison Hearst	.50
34	Carl Pickens	.50
35	Darnay Scott	.50
36	Troy Aikman	5.00
37	Chris Boniol	.50
38	Michael Irvin	1.00
39	Deion Sanders	3.00
40	Emmitt Smith	10.00
41	Herschel Walker	.50
42	Terrell Davis	7.00
43	John Elway	4.00
44	Ed McCaffrey	.50
45	Shannon Sharpe	.50
46	Alfred Williams	.50
47	Scott Mitchell	.50
48	Herman Moore	1.00
49	Brett Perriman	.50
50	Barry Sanders	7.00
51	Edgar Bennett	.50
52	Robert Brooks	.50
53	Mark Chmura	.50
54	Brett Favre	10.00
55	Antonio Freeman	1.50
56	Desmond Howard	.50
57	Reggie White	1.00
58	Chris Chandler	.50
59	Eddie George	7.00
60	James McKeehan	.50
61	Steve McNair	3.50
62	Chris Sanders	.50
63	Sean Dawkins	.50
64	Ken Dilger	.50
65	Marshall Faulk	2.00
66	Jim Harbaugh	.50
67	Marvin Harrison	2.50
68	Tony Boselli	.50
69	Mark Brunell	5.00
70	Keenan McCardell	.50
71	Natrone Means	1.00
72	Jimmy Smith	.50
73	Marcus Allen	1.00
74	Kimble Anders	.50
75	Dale Carter	.50
76	Greg Hill	.50
77	Derrick Thomas	.50
78	Tamarick Vanover	1.00
79	Karim Abdul-Jabbar	1.00
80	Dan Marino	10.00
81	O.J. McDuffie	.50
82	Jerris McPhail	.50
83	Zach Thomas	1.50
84	Cris Carter	.50
85	Brad Johnson	.50
86	Jake Reed	.50
87	Robert Smith	.50
88	Drew Bledsoe	5.00
89	Ben Coates	.50
90	Terry Glenn	1.00
91	Curtis Martin	8.00
92	Willie McGinest	.50
93	Jim Everett	.50
94	Michael Haynes	.50
95	Haywood Jeffires	.50
96	Ray Zellars	.50
97	Dave Brown	.50
98	Rodney Hampton	.50
99	Danny Kanell	.50
100	Thomas Lewis	.50
101	Wayne Chrebet	.50
102	Keyshawn Johnson	2.50
103	Adrian Murrell	.50
104	Neil O'Donnell	.50
105	Tim Brown	.50
106	Rickey Dudley	1.00
107	Jeff Hostetler	.50
108	Napoleon Kaufman	.50
109	Ty Detmer	.50
110	Jason Dunn	.50
111	Irving Fryar	.50
112	Chris T. Jones	.50
113	Ricky Watters	.50
114	Jerome Bettis	1.00
115	Chad Brown	.50
116	Kordell Stewart	4.00
117	Mike Tomczak	.50
118	Rod Woodson	.50
119	Tony Banks	1.50
120	Isaac Bruce	1.50
121	Eddie Kennison	1.00
122	Lawrence Phillips	1.00
123	Terrell Fletcher	.50
124	Stan Humphries	.50
125	Tony Martin	.50
126	Junior Seau	.50
127	Elvis Grbac	.50
128	Terrell Owens	3.00
129	Ted Popson	.50
130	Jerry Rice	5.00
131	Steve Young	4.00
132	John Friesz	.50
133	Joey Galloway	2.00
134	Michael McCrary	.50
135	Lamar Smith	.50
136	Chris Warren	.50
137	Mike Alstott	1.00
138	Trent Dilfer	.50
139	Courtney Hawkins	.50
140	Errict Rhett	1.00
141	Terry Allen	.50
142	Henry Ellard	.50
143	Gus Frerotte	.50
144	Leslie Shepherd	.50

1997 Pacific Dynagon Careers

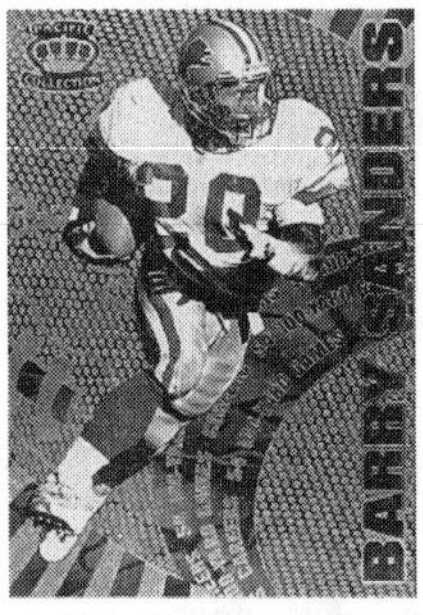

The 10-card, regular-sized cards were inserted every 360 packs in Dynagon Prism. The card fronts feature gold foil in an outline of a football. The player's name is printed down the right side in blue and the player's image is outlined over a crescent-shaped swirl of the player's statistics. The card backs feature a circular photo of the player with several career highlights and are numbered 1-10.

		MT
Complete Set (10):		450.00
Common Player:		30.00
1	Jim Kelly	30.00
2	Emmitt Smith	100.00
3	John Elway	40.00
4	Barry Sanders	90.00
5	Brett Favre	100.00
6	Reggie White	30.00
7	Dan Marino	100.00
8	Drew Bledsoe	50.00
9	Jerry Rice	50.00
10	Steve Young	40.00

1997 Pacific Dynagon Player of the Week

The 20-card, regular-sized set was inserted every 37 packs of Dynagon Prism. The card fronts feature an action shot centered in a diamond. The player's first name is printed on the upper right section of the diamond while the last name appears on the lower left section. The player's team helmet is located in the upper right part of the horizontal card front, centered in a diamond. The card backs feature another shot of the player, again centered in a diamond. The card number corresponds with the week the player excelled during the 1996 season and was voted by visitors to Pacific's website as the Player Of The Week.

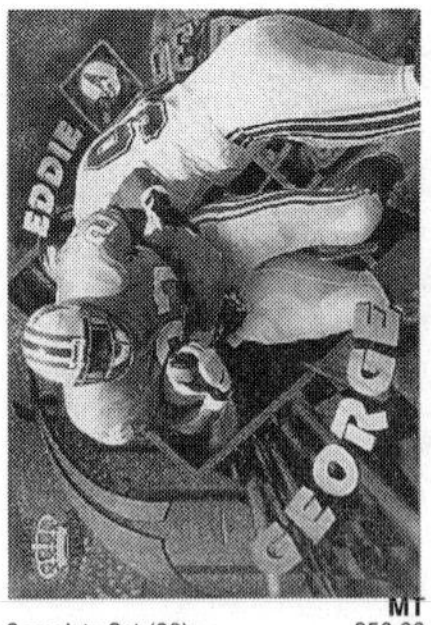

		MT
Complete Set (20):		250.00
Common Player:		5.00
1	Karim Abdul-Jabbar	7.00
2	Eddie George	15.00
3	Curtis Martin	20.00
4	Mark Brunell	15.00
5	John Elway	10.00
6	Drew Bledsoe	15.00
7	Emmitt Smith	30.00
8	Terrell Davis	20.00
9	Troy Aikman	15.00
10	Jerry Rice	15.00
11	Dan Marino	30.00
12	Barry Sanders	25.00
13	Brett Favre	30.00
14	Steve Young	10.00
15	Kerry Collins	5.00
16	Eddie Kennison	5.00
17	Terry Allen	5.00
18	Brett Favre	30.00
19	Desmond Howard	5.00
20	Mark Brunell	15.00

1997 Pacific Dynagon Royal Connections

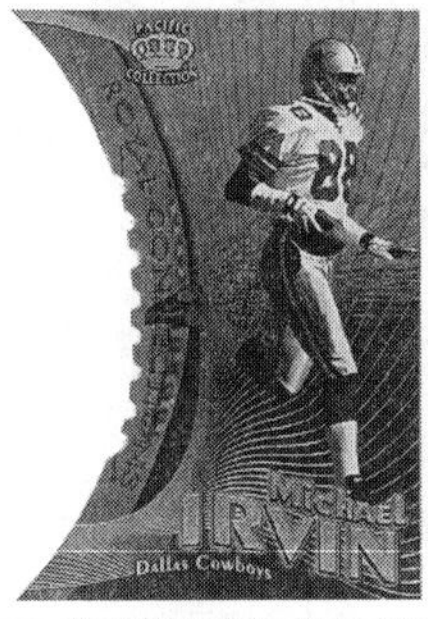

Royal Connections, inserted every 73 packs of 1997 Dynagon Prism, is actually a 30-card, regular-sized, die-cut set that can be fitted with its counterpart to form 15 3-1/2" x 4-1/4" cards. The cards are numbered to 15 with "A" and "B" versions. The A versions feature quarterbacks and the right edge of the card is die-cut in the shape of a football with laces. The "B" versions highlight a wide receiver from a corresponding team and the left side is die-cut to allow the "A" version to fit with it to form a single card.

		MT
Complete Set (30):		425.00
Common Player:		8.00
Minor Stars:		16.00
Inserted 1:73		
1A	Kent Graham	8.00
1B	Larry Centers	8.00
2A	Jim Kelly	16.00
2B	Andre Reed	8.00
3A	Kerry Collins	16.00
3B	Wesley Walls	8.00
4A	Jeff Blake	16.00
4B	Carl Pickens	8.00
5A	Troy Aikman	30.00
5B	Michael Irvin	16.00
6A	John Elway	40.00
6B	Shannon Sharpe	16.00
7A	Brett Favre	60.00
7B	Antonio Freeman	20.00
8A	Mark Brunell	30.00
8B	Keenan McCardell	8.00
9A	Dan Marino	45.00
9B	O.J. McDuffie	8.00
10A	Brad Johnson	16.00
10B	Jake Reed	8.00
11A	Drew Bledsoe	30.00
11B	Terry Glenn	16.00
12A	Ty Detmer	8.00
12B	Irving Fryar	8.00
13A	Kordell Stewart	30.00
13B	Charles Johnson	8.00
14A	Tony Banks	16.00
14B	Isaac Bruce	16.00
15A	Steve Young	25.00
15B	Jerry Rice	30.00

1997 Pacific Dynagon Tandems

Inserted 1:37 packs, the 72 double-fronted cards feature the same 144 players from the base set, with one player on each side. Foiled in emerald, the cards have the numbers printed in the upper right.

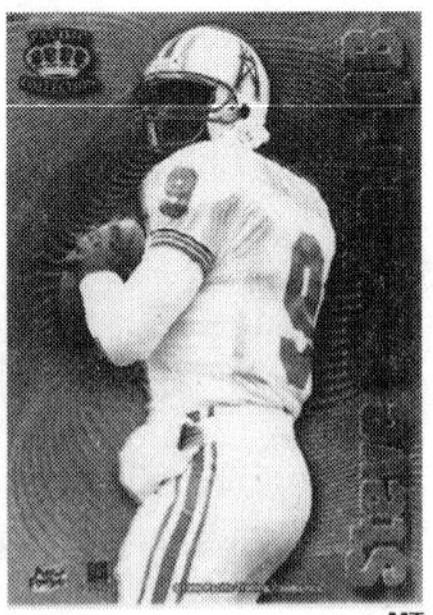

		MT
Complete Set (72):		1300.
Common Player:		10.00
Minor Stars:		20.00
Inserted 1:37		
1	Jerome Bettis, Eddie George	50.00
2	Jamal Anderson, Eric Moulds	50.00
3	Kerry Collins, Kordell Stewart	50.00
4	Jeff Blake, Ty Detmer	20.00
5	Michael Irvin, Tim Brown	20.00
6	Deion Sanders, Ray Zellars	20.00
7	Emmitt Smith, Steve Young	85.00
8	Terrell Davis, Barry Sanders	150.00
9	John Elway, Dan Marino	100.00
10	Robert Brooks, Eddie Kennison	10.00
11	Mark Chmura, Shannon Sharpe	20.00
12	Brett Favre, Mark Brunell	85.00
13	Antonio Freeman, Isaac Bruce	30.00
14	Desmond Howard, Natrone Means	20.00
15	Reggie White, Keyshawn Johnson	20.00
16	Edgar Bennett, Chris Sanders	10.00
17	Terry Glenn, Jerry Rice	60.00
18	Steve McNair, Karim Abdul-Jabbar	30.00
19	Marshall Faulk, Tamarick Vanover	20.00
20	Gus Frerotte, Brad Johnson	20.00
21	Jim Kelly, Tim Biakabutuka	20.00
22	Lawrence Phillips, Ben Coates	20.00
23	Napoleon Kaufman, Terrell Owens	40.00
24	Elvis Grbac, Junior Seau	10.00
25	Drew Bledsoe, Tony Banks	45.00
26	Curtis Martin, Troy Aikman	60.00
27	Curtis Conway, Brett Perriman	10.00
28	Bobby Engram, Larry Centers	10.00
29	Raymont Harris, Eric Metcalf	10.00
30	Dave Krieg, Derrick Alexander	10.00
31	Rashaan Salaam, Leeland McElroy	10.00
32	Ki-Jana Carter, Herman Moore	20.00
33	Garrison Hearst, Earnest Byner	10.00
34	Carl Pickens, Frank Sanders	10.00
35	Darnay Scott, Michael Jackson	10.00
36	Chris Boniol, Kent Graham	10.00
37	Herschel Walker, Thurman Thomas	10.00
38	Ed McCaffrey, Quinn Early	20.00
39	Alfred Williams, Mike Alstott	10.00
40	Scott Mitchell, Mark Carrier	10.00
41	Bert Emanuel, Henry Ellard	10.00
42	Bobby Hebert, Trent Dilfer	20.00
43	Terance Mathis, Andre Reed	10.00
44	Vinny Testaverde, Chris Warren	10.00
45	Bruce Smith, Kevin Greene	10.00
46	Anthony Johnson, Terry Allen	10.00
47	Wesley Walls, Errict Rhett	10.00
48	John Friesz, Jeff Hostetler	10.00
49	Joey Galloway, Leslie Shepherd	20.00
50	Michael McCrary, Chris T. Jones	10.00
51	Lamar Smith, Courtney Hawkins	10.00
52	Rickey Dudley, Jason Dunn	10.00
53	Irving Fryar, Tony Martin	10.00
54	Ted Popson, Ricky Watters	10.00
55	Chad Brown, Zach Thomas	20.00
56	Mike Tomczak, Stan Humphries	10.00

57 Rod Woodson, Willie McGinnest 10.00
58 Terrell Fletcher, Jerris McPhail 10.00
59 O.J. McDuffie, Cris Carter 20.00
60 Jake Reed, Marcus Allen 20.00
61 Robert Smith, Greg Hill 10.00
62 Jim Everett, Dave Brown 10.00
63 Michael Haynes, James McKeehan 10.00
64 Haywood Jeffires, Sean Dawkins 10.00
65 Rodney Hampton, Adrian Murrell 10.00
66 Danny Kanell, Marvin Harrison 20.00
67 Thomas Lewis, Dale Carter 10.00
68 Wayne Chrebet, Ken Dilger 20.00
69 Neil O'Donnell, Chris Chandler 10.00
70 Jim Harbaugh, Jimmy Smith 10.00
71 Derrick Thomas, Tony Boselli 10.00
72 Keenan McCardell, Kimble Anders 10.00

1997 Pacific Invincible

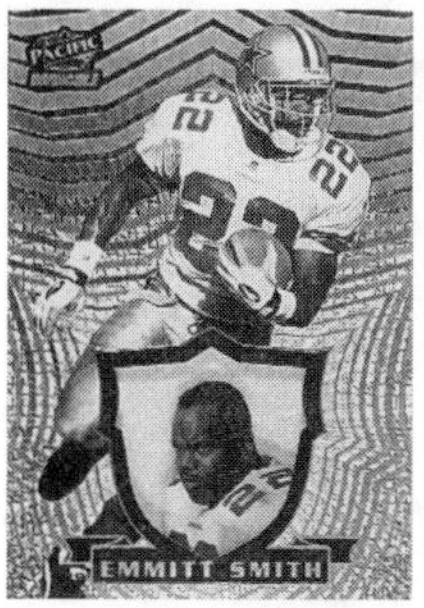

The 150-card set features a player action photo superimposed over a multicolored and gold-foiled background. At the bottom center of the card front is a player head shot printed on acetate. The player's name is printed in gold foil inside a black banner beneath the shield. The Pacific Invincible logo is located in the upper left. The base set is paralleled in Copper foil in hobby packs (2:37), Silver parallel in retail (2:37) and Platinum Blue (1:73). Red-foil parallel was seeded 4:37 in Treat Entertainment U.S. retail packs.

MT
Complete Set (150): 150.00
Common Player: .75
Minor Stars: 1.50
Copper Cards: 4x-8x
Silver Cards: 4x-8x
Blue Cards: 10x-20x
Pack (3): 2.50
Wax Box (36): 80.00
1 Larry Centers .75
2 Kent Graham .75
3 LeShon Johnson .75
4 Leeland McElroy 1.50
5 *Jake Plummer* 7.00
6 Frank Sanders .75
7 Morten Andersen .75
8 Jamal Anderson 1.50
9 Bert Emanuel .75
10 Bobby Hebert .75
11 Roell Preston .75
12 Derrick Alexander .75
13 Michael Jackson .75
14 Bam Morris .75
15 Vinny Testaverde .75
16 Todd Collins 1.50
17 Andre Reed .75
18 *Antowain Smith* 5.00
19 Steve Tasker .75
20 Thurman Thomas 1.50
21 Tim Biakabutuka 1.50
22 *Rae Carruth* 4.00
23 Kerry Collins 2.00
24 Kevin Greene .75
25 Anthony Johnson .75
26 Wesley Walls .75
27 *Darnell Autry* 1.50
28 Curtis Conway .75
29 Raymont Harris .75
30 Rashaan Salaam 1.50
31 Jeff Blake 1.50
32 Ki-Jana Carter 1.50
33 David Dunn .75
34 Carl Pickens .75
35 Darnay Scott .75
36 Troy Aikman 5.00
37 Michael Irvin 1.50
38 Deion Sanders 3.00
39 Emmitt Smith 10.00
40 Herschel Walker .75
41 Kevin Williams .75
42 Steve Atwater .75
43 Terrell Davis 5.00
44 John Elway 4.00
45 Ed McCaffrey .75
46 Shannon Sharpe .75
47 Scott Mitchell .75
48 Herman Moore 1.50
49 Brett Perriman .75
50 Barry Sanders 8.00
51 Edgar Bennett .75
52 Robert Brooks .75
53 Brett Favre 12.00
54 Antonio Freeman 2.00
55 Dorsey Levens .75
56 Reggie White 1.50
57 Eddie George 7.00
58 Steve McNair 4.00
59 Chris Sanders .75
60 Sean Dawkins .75
61 Marshall Faulk 1.50
62 Jim Harbaugh .75
63 Marvin Harrison 2.50
64 Brian Stablein .75
65 Mark Brunell 4.00
66 Keenan McCardell .75
67 Natrone Means 1.50
68 Pete Mitchell .75
69 Jimmy Smith .75
70 Marcus Allen 1.50
71 Kimble Anders .75
72 Greg Hill .75
73 Kevin Lockett .75
74 Derrick Thomas .75
75 Tamarick Vanover .75
76 Karim Abdul-Jabbar 2.00
77 *Yatil Green* 2.00
78 Randal Hill .75
79 Dan Marino 10.00
80 Stanley Pritchett .75
81 Irving Spikes .75
82 Cris Carter .75
83 Brad Johnson .75
84 Robert Smith .75
85 Darryl Talley .75
86 Drew Bledsoe 5.00
87 Ben Coates .75
88 Terry Glenn 2.00
89 Curtis Martin 5.00
90 *Sedrick Shaw* 1.50
91 Mario Bates .75
92 *Troy Davis* 2.00
93 Jim Everett .75
94 Michael Haynes .75
95 *Tiki Barber* 5.00
96 Dave Brown .75
97 Rodney Hampton .75
98 *Ike Hilliard* 4.00
99 Danny Kanell .75
100 Wayne Chrebet .75
101 Keyshawn Johnson 2.50
102 Adrian Murrell .75
103 Neil O'Donnell .75
104 Alex Van Dyke .75
105 Joe Aska .75
106 Tim Brown .75
107 Rickey Dudley .75
108 Napoleon Kaufman 1.50
109 Carl Kidd .75
110 Ty Detmer .75
111 Jason Dunn .75
112 Irving Fryar .75
113 Bobby Hoying .75
114 Ricky Watters 1.50
115 Jerome Bettis 1.50
116 Charles Johnson .75
117 Greg Lloyd .75
118 Kordell Stewart 4.00
119 Rod Woodson .75
120 Tony Banks 2.50
121 Isaac Bruce 1.50
122 Eddie Kennison 1.50
123 Lawrence Phillips 1.50
124 Stan Humphries .75
125 Tony Martin .75
126 *Corey Dillon* 10.00
127 Leonard Russell .75
128 Junior Seau 1.50
129 *Jim Druckenmiller* 6.00
130 Marc Edwards .75
131 Ken Norton Jr. .75
132 Terrell Owens 3.50
133 Jerry Rice 5.00
134 Iheanyi Uwaezuoke .75
135 Steve Young 4.00
136 John Friesz .75
137 Joey Galloway 2.00
138 Warren Moon .75
139 Todd Peterson .75
140 Chris Warren .75
141 Mike Alstott .75
142 *Reidel Anthony* 5.00
143 Trent Dilfer 1.50
144 *Warrick Dunn* 5.00
145 Errict Rhett 1.50
146 Terry Allen .75
147 Henry Ellard .75
148 Gus Frerotte .75
149 Brian Mitchell .75
150 Leslie Shepherd .75

1997 Pacific Invincible Canton, Ohio

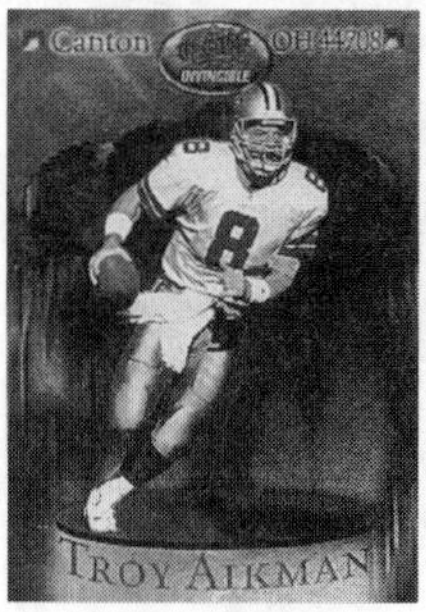

The 10-card Canton, Ohio, chase set was inserted 1:361 packs. The player's photo is superimposed over a crown and multicolored background. The player is standing on an oval, while his name is printed directly beneath it. The chase set's name is printed at the top, with the Invincible logo at the top center.

MT
Complete Set (10): 500.00
Common Player: 30.00
1 Troy Aikman 50.00
2 Emmitt Smith 100.00
3 John Elway 40.00
4 Barry Sanders 90.00
5 Brett Favre 100.00
6 Reggie White 30.00
7 Marcus Allen 30.00
8 Dan Marino 100.00
9 Jerry Rice 50.00
10 Steve Young 40.00

1997 Pacific Invincible Moments in Time

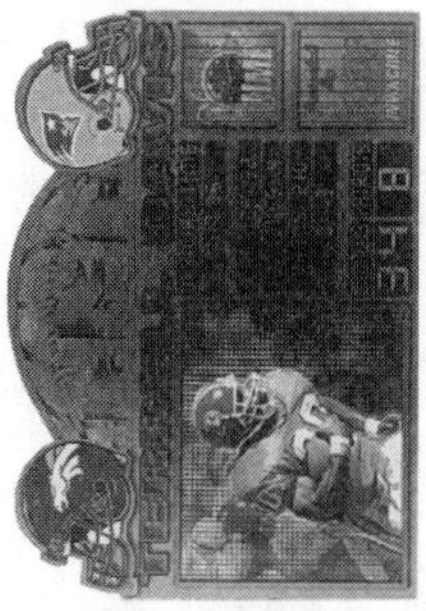

The 20-card Moments in Time was inserted 1:73 packs. The die-cut cards have a scoreboard-like front, with a player photo on the left. His name is printed beneath his team's and opponent's helmets. The date of the game, his yards and stats, along with the score of the game are printed on the front.

MT
Complete Set (20): 800.00
Common Player: 20.00
1 Kerry Collins 30.00
2 Troy Aikman 50.00
3 Emmitt Smith 100.00
4 Terrell Davis 50.00
5 John Elway 35.00
6 Barry Sanders 50.00
7 Brett Favre 100.00
8 Reggie White 20.00
9 Eddie George 50.00
10 Mark Brunell 50.00
11 Marcus Allen 20.00
12 Karim Abdul-Jabbar 30.00
13 Dan Marino 100.00
14 Drew Bledsoe 50.00
15 Terry Glenn 30.00
16 Curtis Martin 50.00
17 Jerome Bettis 20.00
18 Eddie Kennison 20.00
19 Jerry Rice 50.00
20 Steve Young 35.00

1997 Pacific Invincible Pop Cards

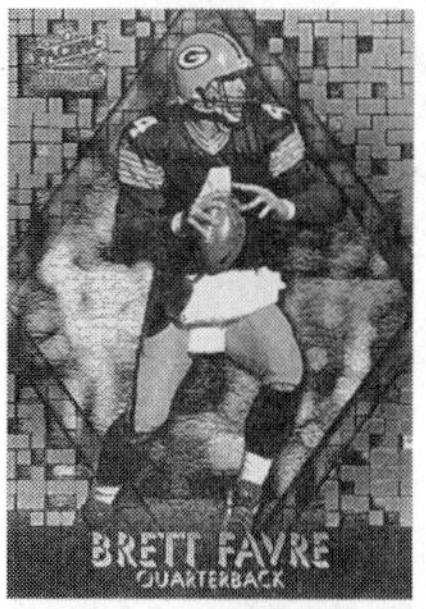

The 10-card set was inserted 2:37 packs. The front of the card included a player photo, which was surrounded by gold-foil squares. The player's name and position are printed at the bottom center. The Pop Card redemption program worked like this: Remove the Pop Card piece from the card back to reveal a player photo and create a new card. If a collector collected all four pieces of a given player's card, the pieces could be sent to Pacific to receive a limited edition gold-foil card of that same player. Details are provided on the backs of each card.

MT
Complete Set (10): 50.00
Common Player: 3.00
1 Kerry Collins 3.00
2 Troy Aikman 6.00
3 Emmitt Smith 12.00
4 John Elway 3.00
5 Barry Sanders 10.00
6 Brett Favre 12.00
7 Mark Brunell 6.00
8 Dan Marino 12.00
9 Drew Bledsoe 6.00
10 Jerry Rice 6.00

1997 Pacific Invincible Smash Mouth

This 220-card bonus set was inserted one or two per pack. The cards feature a player photo on the front inside an oval, surrounded by a metal-diamond-type border. The team's logo is in the lower left, while the player's position is in the lower right. The player's name runs along the bottom of the front. In addition, a Smash Mouth X-tra 59-card set was also inserted one or two cards per pack. The card fronts include a large photo on the left, with the player's name printed in a stencil font vertically along the right border. The backs include a photo in the upper right corner.

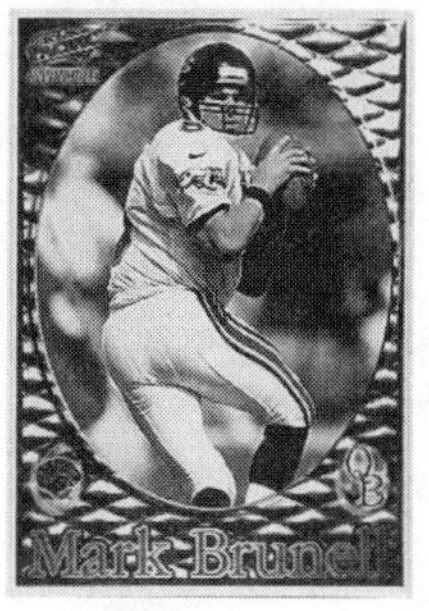

MT
Complete Set (220): 20.00
Common Player: .10
Minor Stars: .20
1 Don Majkowski .10
2 Leo Araguz .10
3 John Carney .10
4 Brett Favre 2.25
5 Cole Ford .10
6 Marty Carter .10
7 John Elway .75
8 Mark Brunell 1.00
9 Rodney Peete .10
10 Jeff Feagles .10
11 Drew Bledsoe 1.00
12 Kerry Collins .75
13 Dan Marino 2.00
14 Torrian Gray .10
15 Reidel Anthony .75
16 Jim Druckenmiller 1.00
17 Jim Everett .10
18 Pat Barnes .20
19 Ike Hilliard .50
20 Barry Sanders 1.25
21 Terry Allen .20
22 Emmitt Smith 2.00
23 Antowain Smith .75
24 Robert Griffith .10
25 Mickey Washington .10
26 Napoleon Kaufman .30
27 Eddie George 1.50
28 Curtis Martin 1.00
29 Anthony Lynn .10
30 Terrell Davis 1.00
31 Steve Broussard .10
32 Ricky Watters .20
33 Karim Abdul-Jabbar .50
34 Thurman Thomas .20
35 Ross Verba .10
36 Jerome Bettis .20
37 Chad Cota .10
38 Antonio Langham .10
39 Brett Maxie .10
40 James Hasty .10
41 Conrad Hamilton .10
42 Chris Warren .10
43 George Jones .10
44 Byron Hanspard .50
45 Henri Crockett .10
46 Brent Alexander .10
47 John Lynch .10
48 Renaldo Wynn .10
49 Jared Tomich .10
50 James Francis .10
51 Brian Williams .10
52 Kevin Mawae .10
53 Marvcus Patton .10
54 Mike Barber .10
55 Robert Jones .10
56 Ernest Dixon .10
57 Mo Lewis .10
58 Peter Boulware .10
59 Wayne Simmons .10
60 Anthony Redmon .10
61 Tim Ruddy .10
62 Victor Green .10
63 Kirk Lowdermilk .10
64 John Jurkovic .10
65 John Jackson .10
66 Kevin Gogan .10
67 Adam Schrieber .10
68 Mike Morris .10
69 Albert Connell .10
70 Tony Mayberry .10
71 Mark Tuinei .10
72 Harry Swayne .10
73 Todd Steussie .10
74 Glenn Parker .10
75 (D'Marco Farr) .10
76 Ed Simmons .10
77 Tarik Glenn .10
78 Rick Hamilton .10
79 Dave Szott .10
80 Jerry Rice 1.00
81 Tim Brown .20
82 Charlie Jones .10
83 Jerry Wunsch .10
84 Lonnie Johnson .10
85 Reggie Johnson .10
86 Willie Davis .10
87 Greg Clark .10
88 Deems May .10
89 J.J. Birden .10
90 Chuck Smith .10
91 Coleman Rudolph .10
92 Leon Johnson .10
93 Trace Armstrong .10
94 John Thierry .10
95 Dean Wells .10
96 Mike Jones .10
97 Mike Lodish .10
98 Tony Siragusa .10
99 Daved Benefield .10
100 Michael Bankston .10
101 Jamal Anderson .20
102 Greg Montgomery .10
103 Mark Maddox .10
104 Matt Elliott .10
105 Joe Cain .10
106 Jeff Blake .20
107 Troy Aikman 1.00
108 Brian Habib .10
109 Pete Chryplewicz .10
110 Earl Dotson .10
111 Joe Bowden .10
112 Marshall Faulk .20
113 Reggie Barlow .10
114 Marcus Allen .20
115 Jeff Buckey .10
116 Mitch Berger .10
117 Corwin Brown .10
118 Troy Davis .50
119 Rodney Hampton .10
120 Tom Knight .10
121 Michael Booker .10
122 Matt Stover .10
123 Mark Pike .10
124 Rohn Stark .10
125 Todd Sauerbrun .10
126 Corey Dillon .50
127 Tyji Armstrong .10
128 Vaughn Hebron .10
129 Antonio London .10
130 Santana Dotson .10
131 Cris Dishman .10
132 Stephen Grant .10
133 Mike Hollis .10
134 Martin Bayless .10
135 Sam Madison .10
136 Esera Tuaolo .10
137 Hason Graham .10
138 Jim Dombrowski .10
139 Bernard Holsey .10
140 Kyle Brady .10
141 David Klingler .10
142 Don Griffin .10
143 Bernard Dafney .10
144 Derrick Harris .10
145 Charles Johnson .10
146 Dedrick Dodge .10
147 Antonio Edwards .10
148 Jorge Diaz .10
149 Marc Logan .10
150 Lou D'Agostino .10
151 Lance Johnstone .10
152 Ray Farmer .10
153 Brenston Buckner .10
154 Tony Banks .50
155 'OMar Ellison .10
156 Derrick Deese .10
157 Howard Ballard .10
158 Ronde Barber .10
159 Gus Frerotte .10
160 Leeland McElroy .10
161 Devin Bush .10
162 Eddie Sutter .10
163 Sam Rogers .10
164 Carl Simpson .10
165 Lee Johnson .10
166 Tony Casillas .10
167 Randy Hilliard .10
168 Ryan McNeil .10
169 William Henderson .10
170 Irv Eatman .10
171 Derwin Gray .10
172 Rob Johnson .10
173 Derrick Walker .10
174 Chris Singleton .10
175 Chris Walsh .10
176 Marty Moore .10
177 Paul Green .10
178 Brian Williams .10
179 Robert Farmer .10
180 Derrick Witherspoon .10
181 Jim Miller .10
182 James Harris .10
183 Shannon Mitchell .10
184 Steve Young .75
185 Ronnie Harris .10
186 Trent Dilfer .25
187 Joe Patton .10
188 Jake Plummer .30
189 Ron George .10
190 Vinny Testaverde .10
191 Ryan Wetnight .10
192 Steve Tovar .10
193 Godfrey Myles .10
194 Rod Smith .10
195 Zefross Moss .10
196 Jerald Sowell .10
197 Jason Layman .10
198 Ray McElroy .10
199 Tom McManus .10
200 Shawn Wooden .10
201 Tony Johnson .10
202 James Farrior .10
203 Marc Woodard .10
204 Chad Scott .10
205 Dwayne White .10
206 Warrick Dunn 2.00
207 Joe Wolf .10
208 Dedric Ward .10
209 Bennie Thompson .10
210 Bracey Walker .10
211 Tracy Scroggins .10
212 Derrick Mason .30
213 Ed King .10
214 Harry Galbreath .10
215 Joel Steed .10
216 Jackie Harris .10
217 Craig Sauer .10
218 Reinard Wilson .10
219 Barron Wortham .10
220 Errict Rhett .10

1997 Pacific Invincible Smash Mouth X-tra

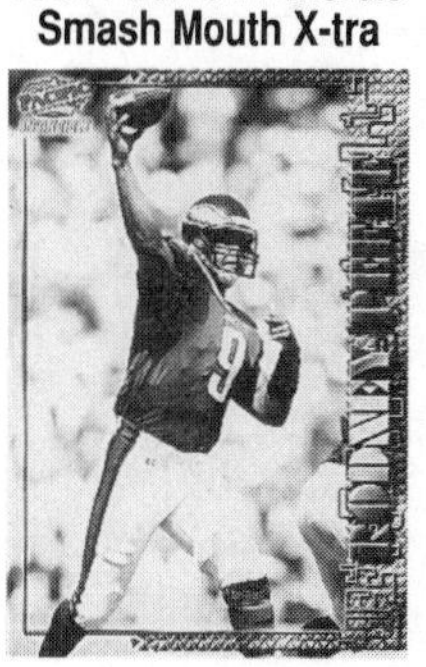

This 59-card set was randomly inserted into packs of Invincible. The card features the player's name running up the right side in team colors, and is numbered in the bottom right corner on the back where the insert name is also indicated.

MT
Complete Set (59): 15.00
Common Player: .10
Minor Stars: .20
1 Steve Young .75
2 Jeff Blake .20
3 Troy Aikman 1.00
4 Brett Favre 2.25
5 Gus Frerotte .10
6 Tony Banks .50
7 John Elway .75
8 Mark Brunell 1.00
9 Rodney Peete .10
10 Trent Dilfer .30
11 Drew Bledsoe 1.00
12 Kerry Collins .75
13 Dan Marino 2.00
14 Vinny Testaverde .10
15 Reidel Anthony .75
16 Jim Druckenmiller 1.00
17 Jim Everett .10
18 Pat Barnes .30
19 Ike Hilliard .50
20 Barry Sanders 1.25
21 Terry Allen .20
22 Emmitt Smith 2.00
23 Antowain Smith .75
24 Jake Plummer .30
25 Vaughn Hebron .10
26 Napoleon Kaufman .25
27 Eddie George 1.50
28 Curtis Martin 1.00
29 Rodney Hampton .10
30 Terrell Davis 1.00
31 Marshall Faulk .20
32 Ricky Watters .20
33 Karim Abdul-Jabbar .50
34 Thurman Thomas .20
35 Troy Davis .50
36 Jerome Bettis .20
37 Warrick Dunn 2.00
38 Leeland McElroy .10
39 William Henderson .10
40 Jamal Anderson .20
41 Errict Rhett .10
42 Chris Warren .10
43 George Jones .10
44 Byron Hanspard .50
45 Jerald Sowell .10
46 Marcus Allen .20
47 Kirk Lowdermilk .10
48 Brian Habib .10
49 Derrick Mason .30
50 Jerry Rice 1.00
51 Albert Connell .10
52 Kyle Brady .10
53 Tim Brown .20
54 Charles Johnson .10
55 Jackie Harris .10
56 Lonnie Johnson .10
57 Deems May .10
58 Peter Boulware .10
59 Wayne Simmons .10

1997 Pacific Philadelphia

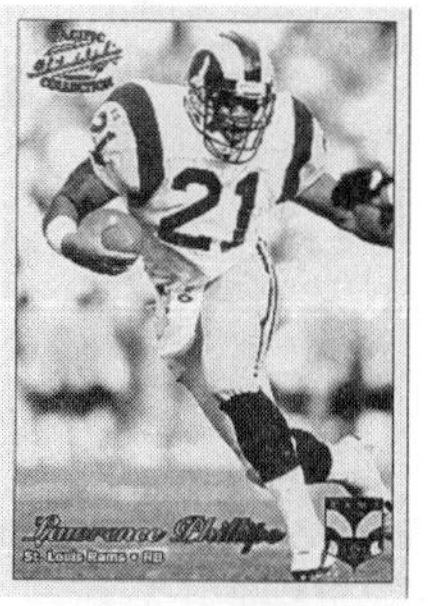

The 330-card set features a white border on the front of the cards, surrounding the player photo. The Philadelphia logo is in the upper left. The bottom left of the photo includes the player's name, team and position. The team's logo is printed in the lower right. The backs included the player's name inside a stripe at the top left, with the card number inside a circle in the upper right. The player's bio, highlights and stats round out the back. Two football player images are printed in the background of the highlights and stats. Red-foil parallels were included one per Treat Entertainment U.S. retail pack.

MT
Complete Set (330): 30.00
Common Player: .05
Minor Stars: .10
Pack (8): 1.50
Wax Box (36): 50.00
1 Kevin Butler .05
2 Larry Centers .05
3 Kent Graham .05
4 Leeland McElroy .10
5 Ronald McKinnon .05
6 Johnny McWilliams .05
7 Brad Ottis .05
8 Frank Sanders .05
9 Rob Selby .05
10 Cedric Smith .05
11 Joe Staysniak .05
12 Cornelius Bennett .05
13 David Brandon .05
14 Tyrone Brown .05
15 John Burrough .05
16 Browning Nagle .05
17 Dan Owens .05
18 Anthony Phillips .05
19 Roell Preston .05

20	Darnell Walker	.05
21	Bob Whitfield	.05
22	Mike Zandofsky	.05
23	Vashone Adams	.05
24	Derrick Alexander	.05
25	Harold Bishop	.05
26	Jeff Blackshear	.05
27	Donny Brady	.05
28	Mike Frederick	.05
29	Tim Goad	.05
30	DeRon Jenkins	.05
31	Ray Lewis	.05
32	Rick Lyle	.05
33	Bam Morris	.05
34	Chris Brantley	.05
35	Jeff Burris	.05
36	Todd Collins	.10
37	Rob Coons	.05
38	Corbin Lacina	.05
39	Emanuel Martin	.05
40	Marlo Perry	.05
41	Sahwn Price	.05
42	Thomas Smith	.05
43	Matt Stevens	.05
44	Thurman Thomas	.15
45	Jay Barker	.05
46	Tshimanga Biakabutuka	.10
47	Kerry Collins	1.50
48	Matt Elliott	.05
49	Howard Griffith	.05
50	Anthony Johnson	.05
51	John Kasay	.05
52	Muhsin Muhammad	.40
53	Winslow Oliver	.05
54	Walter Rasby	.05
55	Gerald Williams	.05
56	Mark Butterfield	.05
57	Bryan Cox	.05
58	Mike Faulkerson	.05
59	Paul Grasmanis	.05
60	Robert Green	.05
61	Jack Jackson	.05
62	Bob Neely	.05
63	Todd Perry	.05
64	Evan Pilgrim	.05
65	Octus Polk	.05
66	Rashaan Salaam	.10
67	Willie Anderson	.05
68	Jeff Blake	.20
69	Scott Brumfield	.05
70	Jeff Cothran	.05
71	Gerald Dixon	.05
72	Garrison Hearst	.05
73	James Hundon	.05
74	Brian Milne	.05
75	Troy Sadowski	.05
76	Tom Tumulty	.05
77	Kimo Von Oelhoffen	.05
78	Troy Aikman	1.50
79	Dale Hellestrae	.05
80	Roger Harper	.05
81	Michael Irvin	.10
82	John Jett	.05
83	Kelvin Martin	.05
84	Deion Sanders	.75
85	Darrin Smith	.05
86	Emmitt Smith	3.00
87	Herschel Walker	.05
88	Charlie Williams	.05
89	Glenn Cadrez	.05
90	Dwayne Carswell	.05
91	Terrell Davis	1.75
92	David Diaz-Infante	.05
93	John Elway	1.00
94	Harold Hasselbach	.05
95	Tory James	.05
96	Bill Musgrave	.05
97	Ralph Tamm	.05
98	Maa Tunavasa	.05
99	Gary Zimmerman	.05
100	Shane Bonham	.05
101	Stephen Boyd	.05
102	Jeff Hartings	.05
103	Hessley Hempstead	.05
104	Scott Kowalkowski	.05
105	Herman Moore	.20
106	Barry Sanders	1.50
107	Tony Semple	.05
108	Ryan Stewart	.05
109	Mike Wells	.05
110	Richard Woodley	.05
111	Brett Favre	3.00
112	Bernardo Harris	.05
113	Keith McKenzie	.05
114	Terry Mickens	.05
115	Doug Pederson	.05
116	Jeff Thomason	.05
117	Adam Timmerman	.05
118	Reggie White	.20
119	Bruce Wilkerson	.05
120	Gabe Wilkens	.05
121	Tyrone Williams	.05
122	Al Del Greco	.05
123	Anthony Dorsett	.05
124	Josh Evans	.05
125	Eddie George	2.00
126	Lemanski Hall	.05
127	Ronnie Harmon	.05
128	Steve McNair	1.00
129	Michael Roan	.05
130	Marcus Robertson	.05
131	Jon Runyan	.05
132	Chris Sanders	.05
133	Kerwin Bell	.05
134	Marshall Faulk	.30
135	Clif Groce	.05
136	Jim Harbaugh	.05
137	Marvin Harrison	1.00
138	Eric Mahlum	.05
139	Tony Mandarich	.05
140	Dedric Mathis	.05
141	Marcus Pollard	.05
142	Scott Slutzker	.05
143	Mark Stock	.05
144	Bucky Brooks	.05
145	Mark Brunell	1.50
146	Kendricke Bullard	.05
147	Randy Jordan	.05
148	Jeff Kopp	.05
149	Le'Shai Maston	.05
150	Keenan McCardell	.05
151	Clyde Simmons	.05
152	Jimmy Smith	.05
153	Rich Tylski	.05
154	Dave Widell	.05
155	Marcus Allen	.10
156	Keith Cash	.05
157	Donnie Edwards	.05
158	Trezelle Jenkins	.05
159	Sean LaChapelle	.05
160	Greg Manusky	.05
161	Steve Matthews	.05
162	Pellom McDaniels	.05
163	Chris Penn	.05
164	Danny Villa	.05
165	Jerome Woods	.05
166	Karim Abdul-Jabbar	1.25
167	John Bock	.05
168	O.J. Brigance	.05
169	Norman Hand	.05
170	Anthony Harris	.05
171	Larry Izzo	.05
172	Charles Jordan	.05
173	Dan Marino	3.00
174	Everett McIver	.05
175	Joe Nedney	.05
176	Robert Wilson	.05
177	David Dixon	.05
178	Charlie Evans	.05
179	Hunter Goodwin	.05
180	Ben Hanks	.05
181	Warren Moon	.10
182	Harold Morrow	.05
183	Fernando Smith	.05
184	Robert Smith	.10
185	Sean Vanhorse	.05
186	Jay Walker	.05
187	DeWayne Washington	.05
188	Moe Williams	.05
189	Mike Bartrum	.05
190	Drew Bledsoe	1.50
191	Troy Brown	.05
192	Chad Eaton	.05
193	Sam Gash	.05
194	Mike Gisler	.05
195	Curtis Martin	1.75
196	Dave Richards	.05
197	Todd Rucci	.05
198	Chris Sullivan	.05
199	Adam Vinatieri	.05
200	Doug Brien	.05
201	Derek Brown	.05
202	Lee DeRamus	.05
203	Jim Everett	.05
204	Mercury Hayes	.05
205	Joe Johnson	.05
206	Henry Lusk	.05
207	Andy McCollum	.05
208	Alex Molden	.05
209	Ray Zellars	.05
210	Marcus Buckley	.05
211	Doug Coleman	.05
212	Percy Ellsworth	.05
213	Rodney Hampton	.05
214	Brian Saxton	.05
215	Jason Sehorn	.05
216	Stan White	.05
217	Corey Widmer	.05
218	Rodney Young	.05
219	Rob Zatechka	.05
220	Henry Bailey	.05
221	Chad Cascadden	.05
222	Wayne Chrebet	.05
223	Tyrone Davis	.05
224	Kwame Ellis	.05
225	Glenn Foley	.05
226	Erik Howard	.05
227	Gary Jones	.05
228	Adrian Murrell	.05
229	Marc Spindler	.05
230	Lonnie Young	.05
231	Eric Zomalt	.05
232	Tim Brown	.10
233	Aundray Bruce	.05
234	Darren Carrington	.05
235	Rick Cunningham	.05
236	Rob Holmberg	.05
237	Jeff Hostetler	.05
238	Lorenzo Lynch	.05
239	Barrett Robbins	.05
240	Dan Turk	.05
241	Harvey Williams	.05
242	Brian Dawkins	.05
243	Ty Detmer	.05
244	Troy Drake	.05
245	Rhett Hall	.05
246	Joe Panos	.05
247	Johnny Thomas	.05
248	Kevin Turner	.05
249	Ricky Watters	.10
250	Derrick Whiterspoon	.05
251	Sylvester Wright	.05
252	Jerome Bettis	.20
253	Carlos Emmons	.05
254	Jason Gildon	.05
255	Jonathan Hayes	.05
256	Kevin Henry	.05
257	Jerry Olsavsky	.05
258	Erric Pegram	.05
259	Brenden Stai	.05
260	Justin Strzelczyk	.05
261	Mike Tomczak	.05
262	Tony Banks	.50
263	Hayward Clay	.05
264	Percell Gaskins	.05
265	Eddie Kennison	.05
266	Aaron Laing	.05
267	Keith Lyle	.05
268	Jamie Martin	.05
269	Lawrence Phillips	.10
270	Zach Wiegert	.05
271	Toby Wright	.05
272	Darren Bennett	.05
273	Tony Berti	.05
274	Freddie Bradley	.05
275	Joe Cocozzo	.05
276	Andre Coleman	.05
277	Marco Coleman	.05
278	Rodney Harrison	.05
279	David Hendrix	.05
280	Leonard Russell	.05
281	Sean Salisbury	.05
282	Dennis Brown	.05
283	Chris Dalman	.05
284	Brent Jones	.05
285	Sean Manuel	.05
286	Marquez Pope	.05
287	Jerry Rice	1.50
288	Kirk Scrafford	.05
289	Iheanyi Uwaezuoke	.05
290	Tommy Vardell	.05
291	Steve Young	1.00
292	James Atkins	.05
293	T.J. Cunningham	.05
294	Stan Gelbaugh	.05
295	James Logan	.05
296	James McKnight	.05
297	Rick Mirer	.10
298	Todd Peterson	.05
299	Fred Thomas	.05
300	Rick Tuten	.05
301	Chris Warren	.05
302	Donnie Abraham	.05
303	Trent Dilfer	.10
304	Kenneth Gant	.05
305	Jeff Gooch	.05
306	Courtney Hawkins	.05
307	Tyoka Jackson	.05
308	Melvin Johnson	.05
309	Lonnie Marts	.05
310	Hardy Nickerson	.05
311	Errict Rhett	.20
312	Terry Allen	.10
313	Flipper Anderson	.05
314	William Bell	.05
315	Scott Blanton	.05
316	Leomont Evans	.05
317	Gus Frerotte	.05
318	Darryl Morrison	.05
319	Matt Turk	.05
320	Jeff Uhlenhake	.05
321	Bryan Walker	.05
322	Mark Brunell (1996 Statistical Leaders)	.75
323	Barry Sanders (1996 Statistical Leaders)	.75
324	Isaac Bruce (1996 Statistical Leaders)	.05
325	Terry Allen (1996 Statistical Leaders)	.05
326	Steve Young (1996 Statistical Leaders)	.50
327	Jerry Rice (1996 Statistical Leaders)	.75
328	Ricky Watters (1996 Statistical Leaders)	.05
329	Kevin Greene (1996 Statistical Leaders)	.05
330	Brett Favre (1996 Statistical Leaders)	1.50

1997 Pacific Philadelphia Gold

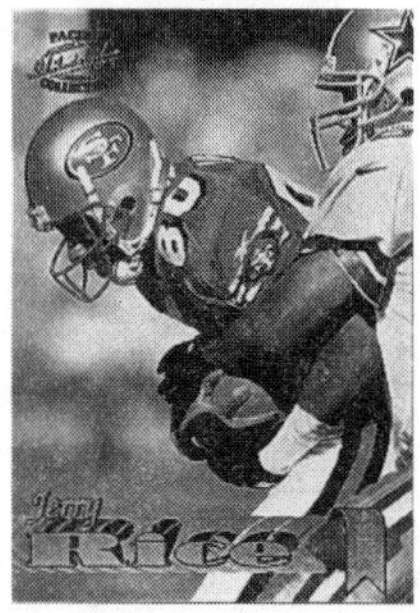

The 200-card set was a bonus in packs of the product. Each pack contained two Philadelphia Gold cards and either one insert card or an additional Philadelphia Gold card per pack. The card fronts showcased a full-bleed photo, with the Philadelphia logo in the upper left. The player's name is printed in gold foil over a gold-foil "spiral background" at the bottom left of the card. The team's logo is printed inside a banner over a football in the lower right. The backs have the player's name, position and highlights along the left, with a photo on the right. The card number is printed inside a circle in the lower right. A Hobby parallel version was printed with copper foil and inserted 2:37 packs. A Retail parallel version was produced with silver foil and inserted 2:37 packs.

		MT
Complete Set (200):		40.00
Common Player:		.15
Minor Stars:		.30
Copper Cards:		2x-4x
Silver Cards:		3x-6x
1	Ryan Christopherson	.15
2	James Dexter	.15
3	Boomer Esiason	.15
4	Jarius Hayes	.15
5	Eric Hill	.15
6	Trey Junkin	.15
7	Kwamie Lassiter	.15
8	Patrick Bates	.15
9	Brad Edwards	.15
10	Roman Fortin	.15
11	Harper LeBel	.15
12	Lorenzo Styles	.15
13	Robbie Tobeck	.15
14	Mike Caldwell	.15
15	Eric Green	.15
16	Brian Kinchen	.15
17	Eric Turner	.15
18	Jerrol Williams	.15
19	Eric Zeier	.15
20	Darick Holmes	.30
21	Ken Irvin	.15
22	Jerry Ostroski	.15
23	Andre Reed	.15
24	Steve Tasker	.15
25	Thurman Thomas	.30
26	Steve Beuerlein	.15
27	Kerry Collins	2.00
28	Eric Davis	.15
29	Norberto Garrido	.15
30	Lamar Lathon	.15
31	Andre Royal	.15
32	Tony Carter	.15
33	Jerry Fontenot	.15
34	Raymont Harris	.30
35	Anthony Marshall	.15
36	Barry Minter	.15
37	Steve Stenstrom	.15
38	Donnell Woolford	.15
39	Ken Blackman	.15
40	Jeff Blake	.50
41	Carl Pickens	.30
42	Artie Smith	.15
43	Ramondo Stallings	.15
44	Melvin Tuten	.15
45	Joe Walter	.15
46	Troy Aikman	2.00
47	Billy Davis	.15
48	Chad Hennings	.15
49	Emmitt Smith	4.00
50	George Teague	.15
51	Kevin Williams	.15
52	Terrell Davis	2.50
53	John Elway	1.25
54	Tom Nalen	.15
55	Bill Romanowski	.15
56	Rod Smith	.15
57	Dan Williams	.15
58	Mike Compton	.15
59	Eric Lynch	.15
60	Aubrey Matthews	.15
61	Pete Metzelaars	.15
62	Herman Moore	.30
63	Barry Sanders	2.00
64	Keith Washington	.15
65	Edgar Bennett	.15
66	Brett Favre	4.00
67	Lamont Hollinquest	.15
68	Keith Jackson	.15
69	Derrick Mayes	.15
60	Andre Rison	.15
71	Eddie George	2.50
72	Mel Gray	.15
73	Darryll Lewis	.15
74	John Henry Mills	.15
75	Rodney Thomas	.15
76	Gary Walker	.15
77	Troy Auzenne	.15
78	Sammie Burroughs	.15
79	Jim Harbaugh	.15
80	Tony McCoy	.15
81	Brian Stablein	.15
82	Kipp Vickers	.15
83	Aaron Beasley	.15
84	Mark Brunell	2.00
85	Don Davey	.15
86	Chris Hudson	.15
87	Greg Huntington	.15
88	Ernie Logan	.15
89	Donnell Bennett	.15
90	Anthony Davis	.15
91	Tim Grunhard	.15
92	Danan Hughes	.15
93	Tony Richardson	.15
94	Tracy Simien	.15
95	Karim Abdul-Jabbar	1.50
96	Dwight Hollier	.15
97	John Kidd	.15
98	Dan Marino	4.00
99	Jerris McPhail	.15
100	Irving Spikes	.15
101	Richmond Webb	.15
102	Jeff Brady	.15
103	Richard Brown	.15
104	Corey Fuller	.15
105	John Gerak	.15
106	Scottie Graham	.15
107	Amp Lee	.15
108	Drew Bledsoe	2.00
109	Tedy Bruschi	.15
110	Todd Collins	.15
111	Bob Kratch	.15
112	Curtis Martin	2.50
113	David Meggett	.15
114	Tom Tupa	.15
115	Eric Allen	.15
116	Mario Bates	.15
117	Clarence Jones	.15
118	Sean Lumpkin	.15
119	Doug Nussmeier	.15
120	Irv Smith	.15
121	Winfred Tubbs	.15
122	Willie Beamon	.15
123	Greg Bishop	.15
124	Dave Brown	.15
125	Gary Downs	.15
126	Thomas Lewis	.15
127	Michael Strahan	.15
128	Tyrone Wheatley	.15
129	Matt Brock	.15
130	Mike Chalenski	.15
131	Roger Duffy	.15
132	John Hudson	.15
133	Frank Reich	.15
134	David Williams	.15
135	Greg Biekert	.15
136	Mike Jones	.15
137	Napoleon Kaufman	.15
138	Carl Kidd	.15
139	Terry McDaniel	.15
140	Mike Morton	.15
141	Orlanda Truitt	.15
142	Gary Anderson	.15
143	Richard Cooper	.15
144	Jimmie Johnson	.15
145	Joe Kelly	.15
146	William Thomas	.15
147	Ricky Watters	.30
148	Ed West	.15
149	Michael Zordich	.15
150	Jerome Bettis	.50
151	Dermontti Dawson	.15
152	Lethon Flowers	.15
153	Charles Johnson	.15
154	Darren Perry	.15
155	Kordell Stewart	2.00
156	Will Wolford	.15
157	Isaac Bruce	.75
158	Kevin Carter	.15
159	Torin Dorn	.15
160	Leo Goeas	.15
161	Gerald McBurrows	.15
162	Chuck Osborne	.15
163	J.T. Thomas	.15
164	Dwayne Gordon	.15
165	Stan Humphries	.15
166	Shawn Lee	.15
167	Chris Mims	.15
168	John Parrella	.15
169	Junior Seau	.15
170	Bryan Still	.15
171	Curtis Buckley	.15
172	William Floyd	.15
173	Merton Hanks	.15
174	Terry Kirby	.15
175	Jerry Rice	2.00
176	J.J. Stokes	.15
177	Jeff Wilkins	.15
178	Bryant Young	.15
179	Sam Adams	.15
180	John Friesz	.15
181	Joey Galloway	.75
182	Pete Kendall	.15
183	Jason Kyle	.15
184	Darryl Williams	.15
185	Ronnie Williams	.15
186	Mike Alstott	.30
187	Trent Dilfer	.30
188	Tyrone Legette	.15
189	Martin Mayhew	.15
190	Jason Odom	.15
191	Warren Sapp	.15
192	Karl Williams	.15
193	Terry Allen	.15
194	Romeo Bandison	.15
195	Alcides Catanho	.15
196	Gus Frerotte	.15
197	William Gaines	.15
198	Ken Harvey	.15
199	Trevor Matich	.15
200	Scott Turner	.15

1997 Pacific Philadelphia Heart of the Game

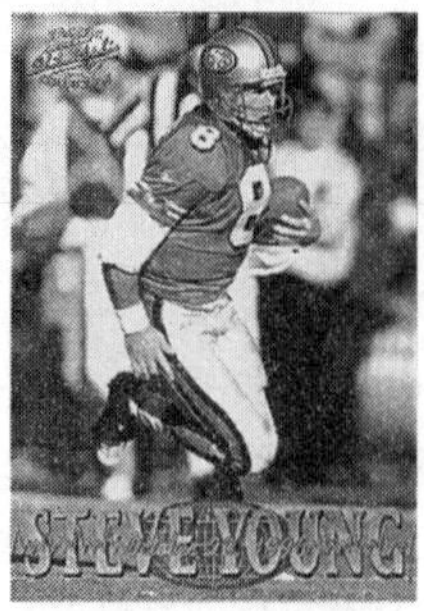

The 20-card set was inserted 1:73 packs. The fronts showcased a full-bleed photo, with the Philadelphia logo in the upper left corner. The player's name is printed in large gold-foil letters at the bottom of the front. In the bottom center of the name is an oval globe. A red heartbeat runs from the lower left to the lower right, with the date of a key game printed in red in the center.

		MT
Complete Set (20):		275.00
Common Player:		6.00
Minor Stars:		12.00
1	Thurman Thomas	6.00
2	Kerry Collins	20.00
3	Troy Aikman	20.00
4	Emmitt Smith	40.00
5	Terrell Davis	20.00
6	John Elway	15.00
7	Barry Sanders	25.00
8	Brett Favre	45.00
9	Antonio Freeman	12.00
10	Marshall Faulk	12.00
11	Mark Brunell	20.00
12	Marcus Allen	6.00
13	Dan Marino	40.00
14	Drew Bledsoe	20.00
15	Curtis Martin	20.00
16	Napoleon Kaufman	6.00
17	Jerome Bettis	12.00
18	Isaac Bruce	12.00
19	Jerry Rice	20.00
20	Steve Young	15.00

1997 Pacific Philadelphia Milestones

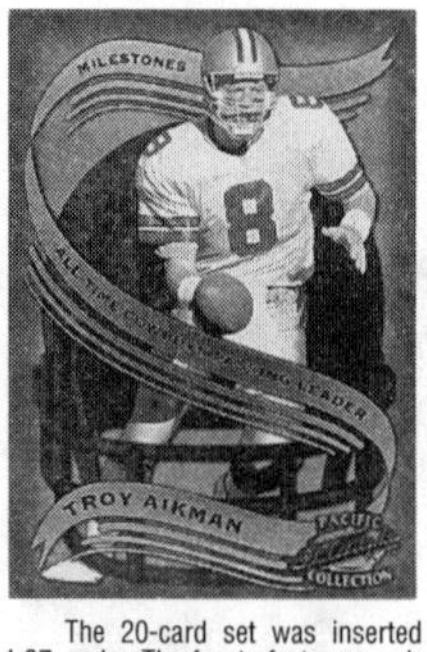

The 20-card set was inserted 1:37 packs. The fronts feature a red-orange border, with a player photo superimposed over a helmet and gold-foil Milestones banner that runs from the upper right to the lower left. The player's milestone is printed in the center of the banner, with his name in the lower left of the banner. The Philadelphia logo is located in the lower right.

		MT
Complete Set (20):		200.00
Common Player:		4.00
Minor Stars:		8.00
1	Simeon Rice	4.00
2	Thurman Thomas	4.00
3	Troy Aikman	15.00
4	Emmitt Smith	30.00
5	Terrell Davis	15.00
6	John Elway	12.00
7	Brett Favre	35.00
8	Desmond Howard	4.00
9	Reggie White	8.00
10	Mark Brunell	15.00
11	Marcus Allen	4.00
12	Karim Abdul-Jabbar	12.00
13	Dan Marino	30.00
14	Drew Bledsoe	15.00
15	Terry Glenn	15.00
16	Curtis Martin	15.00
17	Tony Banks	8.00
18	Jerry Rice	15.00
19	Steve Young	12.00
20	Terry Allen	4.00

1997 Pacific Philadelphia Photoengravings

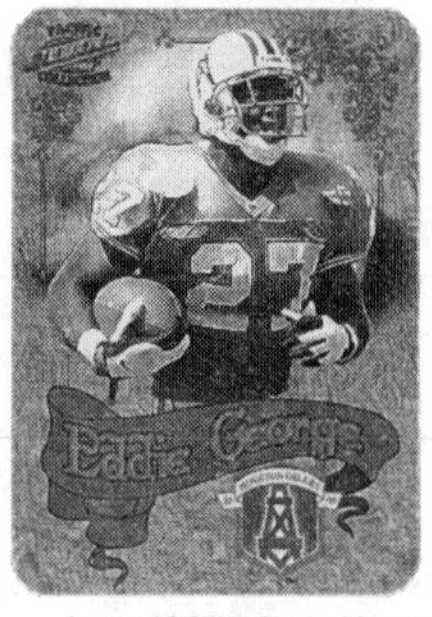

Inserted 2:37 packs, the 36-card set has the look and feel of playing cards. The rounded-bordered cards have a player photo in the center of the card surrounded by a brown border and background. The player's name is printed in black at the bottom center. The Philadelphia logo is located in the upper left of the card front.

		MT
Complete Set (36):		225.00
Common Player:		3.00
Minor Stars:		6.00
1	Thurman Thomas	6.00
2	Kerry Collins	12.00
3	Jeff Blake	6.00
4	Troy Aikman	12.00
5	Deion Sanders	7.00
6	Emmitt Smith	25.00
7	Terrell Davis	15.00
8	John Elway	10.00
9	Herman Moore	6.00
10	Barry Sanders	15.00
11	Brett Favre	30.00
12	Desmond Howard	3.00
13	Dorsey Levens	3.00
14	Eddie George	15.00
15	Marshall Faulk	6.00
16	Jim Harbaugh	3.00
17	Marvin Harrison	6.00
18	Mark Brunell	12.00
19	Keenan McCardell	3.00
20	Karim Abdul-Jabbar	10.00
21	Dan Marino	25.00
22	Brad Johnson	3.00
23	Drew Bledsoe	12.00
24	Terry Glenn	12.00
25	Curtis Martin	12.00
26	Keyshawn Johnson	6.00
27	Tim Brown	3.00
28	Napoleon Kaufman	3.00
29	Ricky Watters	3.00
30	Jerome Bettis	6.00
31	Kordell Stewart	12.00
32	Eddie Kennison	6.00
33	Jerry Rice	12.00
34	Steve Young	10.00
35	Chris Warren	3.00
36	Terry Allen	3.00

1997 Pacific Revolution

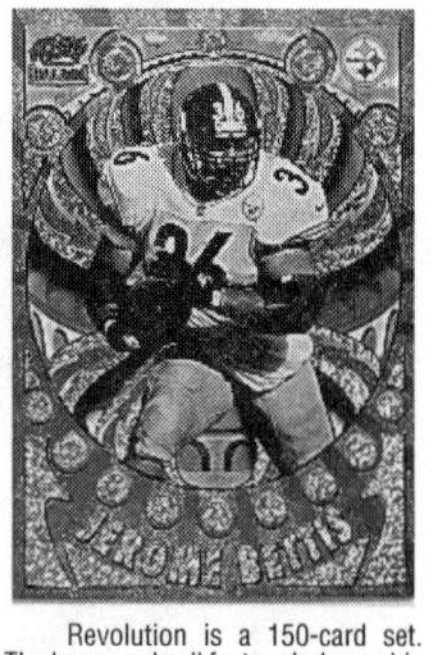

Revolution is a 150-card set. The base cards all feature holographic foil, etching and embossing. Three parallel sets were created: Silver & Holographic Gold (retail, 2:25), Copper & Holographic Silver (hobby, 2:25) and Platinum Blue & Holographic Gold (1:49). The inserts included Proteges, Air Mail Die-Cuts, Silks and Ring Bearer Laser-Cuts.

		MT
Complete Set (150):		75.00
Common Player:		.50
Minor Stars:		1.00
Copper/Red Cards:		4x-8x
Copper/Red Rookies:		2x-4x
Silver Cards:		4x-8x
Silver Rookies:		2x-4x
Blue Cards:		10x-20x
Blue Rookies:		5x-10x
Pack (3):		4.00
Wax Box (24):		80.00
1	Larry Centers	.50
2	Kent Graham	.50
3	Leeland McElroy	.50
4	Rob Moore	.50

5	*Jake Plummer*	10.00
6	Jamal Anderson	1.00
7	Bert Emanuel	.50
8	*Byron Hanspard*	1.50
9	Terance Mathis	.50
10	O.J. Santiago	.50
11	Derrick Alexander	.50
12	Peter Boulware	.50
13	*Jay Graham*	1.00
14	Michael Jackson	.50
15	Vinny Testaverde	.50
16	Todd Collins	1.00
17	Andre Reed	.50
18	Jay Riemersma	.50
19	*Antowain Smith*	3.00
20	Bruce Smith	.50
21	Thurman Thomas	1.00
22	*Rae Carruth*	.75
23	Kerry Collins	1.00
24	Anthony Johnson	.50
25	Muhsin Muhammad	.50
26	Wesley Walls	.50
27	Curtis Conway	1.00
28	Bobby Engram	.50
29	Raymont Harris	.50
30	Rick Mirer	.50
31	Rashaan Salaam	.50
32	Jeff Blake	1.00
33	*Corey Dillon*	10.00
34	Carl Pickens	.50
35	Darnay Scott	.50
36	Troy Aikman	4.00
37	Michael Irvin	1.00
38	Daryl Johnston	.50
39	Deion Sanders	2.00
40	Emmitt Smith	8.00
41	Terrell Davis	4.00
42	John Elway	3.00
43	Ed McCaffrey	.50
44	Shannon Sharpe	.50
45	Neil Smith	.50
46	Scott Mitchell	.50
47	Herman Moore	1.00
48	Johnnie Morton	.50
49	Barry Sanders	7.00
50	Robert Brooks	.50
51	LeRoy Butler	.50
52	Brett Favre	10.00
53	Antonio Freeman	1.00
54	Dorsey Levens	1.00
55	Reggie White	1.00
56	Sean Dawkins	.50
57	Ken Dilger	.50
58	Marshall Faulk	1.00
59	Jim Harbaugh	.50
60	Marvin Harrison	2.00
61	Mark Brunell	4.00
62	Keenan McCardell	.50
63	Natrone Means	1.00
64	Jimmy Smith	.50
65	James Stewart	.50
66	Marcus Allen	1.00
67	*Tony Gonzalez*	5.00
68	Elvis Grbac	.50
69	Greg Hill	.50
70	Andre Rison	.50
71	Karim Abdul-Jabbar	2.00
72	Fred Barnett	.50
73	Dan Marino	8.00
74	O.J. McDuffie	.50
75	Irving Spikes	.50
76	Cris Carter	.50
77	*Matthew Hatchette*	8.00
78	Brad Johnson	1.00
79	Jake Reed	.50
80	Robert Smith	1.00
81	Drew Bledsoe	4.00
82	Ben Coates	.50
83	Terry Glenn	1.50
84	Curtis Martin	4.00
85	Dave Meggett	.50
86	*Troy Davis*	1.50
87	Andre Hastings	.50
88	Heath Shuler	.50
89	Irv Smith	.50
90	*Danny Wuerffel*	4.00
91	Ray Zellars	.50
92	*Tiki Barber*	4.00
93	Dave Brown	.50
94	Chris Calloway	.50
95	Rodney Hampton	.50
96	Amani Toomer	.50
97	Wayne Chrebet	.50
98	Keyshawn Johnson	2.00
99	Adrian Murrell	1.00
100	Neil O'Donnell	.50
101	Dedric Ward	.50
102	Tim Brown	1.00
103	Rickey Dudley	.50
104	Jeff George	.50
105	Desmond Howard	.50
106	Napoleon Kaufman	1.00
107	Ty Detmer	.50
108	Jason Dunn	.50
109	Irving Fryar	.50
110	Rodney Peete	.50
111	Ricky Watters	1.00
112	Jerome Bettis	1.00
113	*Will Blackwell*	1.00
114	Charles Johnson	.50
115	Kordell Stewart	4.00
116	Tony Banks	2.00
117	Isaac Bruce	1.00
118	Ernie Conwell	.50
119	Eddie Kennison	1.00
120	Lawrence Phillips	.50
121	Stan Humphries	.50
122	Tony Martin	.50
123	Eric Metcalf	.50
124	Junior Seau	1.00
125	*Jim Druckenmiller*	3.00
126	Kevin Greene	.50
127	Garrison Hearst	.50
128	Terrell Owens	4.00
129	Jerry Rice	4.00
130	J.J. Stokes	.50
131	Rod Woodson	.50
132	Steve Young	3.00
133	Joey Galloway	1.00
134	Cortez Kennedy	.50
135	*Jon Kitna*	10.00
136	Warren Moon	.50
137	Chris Warren	.50
138	Mike Alstott	2.00
139	*Reidel Anthony*	5.00
140	Trent Dilfer	1.00
141	*Warrick Dunn*	5.00
142	Willie Davis	.50
143	Eddie George	6.00
144	Steve McNair	3.00
145	Chris Sanders	.50
146	Terry Allen	.50
147	Jamie Asher	.50
148	Henry Ellard	.50
149	Gus Frerotte	.50
150	Leslie Shepherd	.50

1997 Pacific Revolution Air Mail

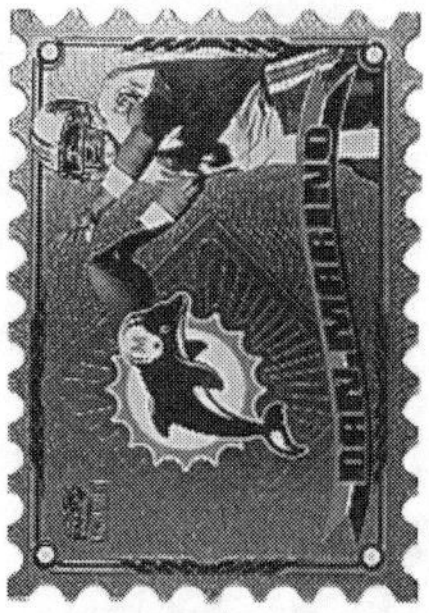

The cards in this 36-card insert are die-cut to look like stamps. They were inserted once in every 25 packs.

		MT
Complete Set (36):		500.00
Common Player:		5.00
Minor Stars:		10.00
1	Vinny Testaverde	5.00
2	Andre Reed	5.00
3	Kerry Collins	10.00
4	Jeff Blake	10.00
5	Troy Aikman	25.00
6	Deion Sanders	15.00
7	Emmitt Smith	50.00
8	Michael Irvin	10.00
9	Terrell Davis	25.00
10	John Elway	18.00
11	Barry Sanders	45.00
12	Brett Favre	60.00
13	Antonio Freeman	10.00
14	Mark Brunell	25.00
15	Marcus Allen	10.00
16	Elvis Grbac	5.00
17	Dan Marino	50.00
18	Brad Johnson	10.00
19	Drew Bledsoe	25.00
20	Terry Glenn	10.00
21	Curtis Martin	25.00
22	Danny Wuerffel	10.00
23	Jeff George	5.00
24	Napoleon Kaufman	10.00
25	Kordell Stewart	25.00
26	Tony Banks	10.00
27	Isaac Bruce	10.00
28	Jim Druckenmiller	30.00
29	Jerry Rice	25.00
30	Steve Young	18.00
31	Warren Moon	5.00
32	Trent Dilfer	10.00
33	Warrick Dunn	40.00
34	Eddie George	40.00
35	Steve McNair	20.00
36	Gus Frerotte	5.00

1997 Pacific Revolution Proteges

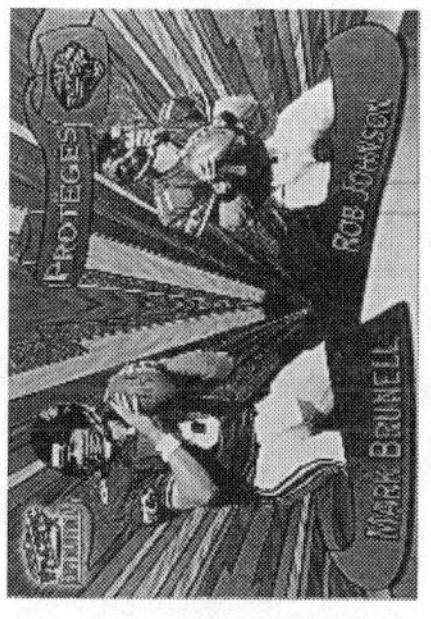

These 20 insert cards feature a proven veteran alongside their young understudy. The foiled cards were inserted 2:25.

		MT
Complete Set (20):		200.00
Common Player:		3.00
1	Kent Graham, Jake Plummer	8.00
2	Jamal Anderson, Byron Hanspard	3.00
3	Thurman Thomas, Antowain Smith	8.00
4	Troy Aikman, Jason Garrett	15.00
5	Emmitt Smith, Sherman Williams	25.00
6	John Elway, Jeff Lewis	12.00
7	Barry Sanders, Ron Rivers	20.00
8	Brett Favre, Doug Pederson	30.00
9	Mark Brunell, Rob Johnson	15.00
10	Marcus Allen, Greg Hill	3.00
11	Dan Marino, Damon Huard	30.00
12	Curtis Martin, Marrio Grier	15.00
13	Heath Shuler, Danny Wuerffel	6.00
14	Rodney Hampton, Tiki Barber	8.00
15	Jerome Bettis, George Jones	3.00
16	Jerry Rice, Terrell Owens	15.00
17	Steve Young, Jim Druckenmiller	12.00
18	Warren Moon, Jon Kitna	3.00
19	Errict Rhett, Warrick Dunn	15.00
20	Terry Allen, Stephen Davis	3.00

1997 Pacific Revolution Ring Bearers

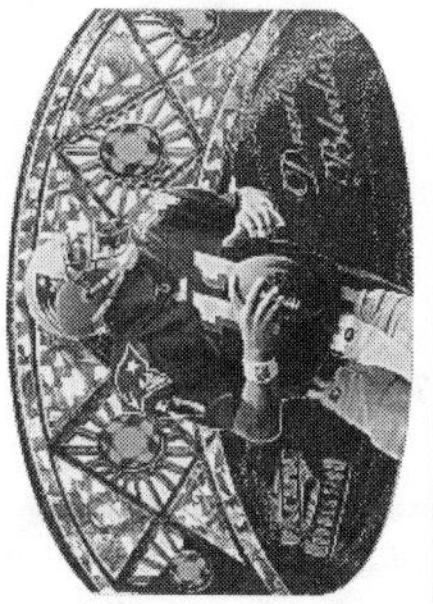

These 10 fully foiled and embossed cards are die-cut and laser-cut to look like a championship ring. The cards feature 10 of the NFL's best and were inserted 1:121.

		MT
Complete Set (12):		500.00
Common Player:		25.00
Inserted 1:121		
1	Emmitt Smith	75.00
2	John Elway	60.00
3	Barry Sanders	100.00
4	Brett Favre	100.00
5	Mark Brunell	50.00
6	Dan Marino	75.00
7	Drew Bledsoe	50.00
8	Steve Young	25.00
9	Warrick Dunn	25.00
10	Eddie George	50.00

1997 Pacific Revolution Silks

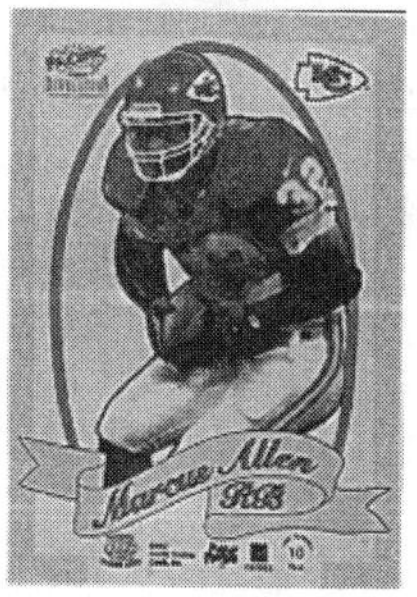

This 18-card, oversized insert features top NFL players on a silk-like material. The cards were inserted 1:49.

		MT
Complete Set (18):		400.00
Common Player:		8.00
1	Kerry Collins	10.00
2	Troy Aikman	25.00
3	Deion Sanders	15.00
4	Emmitt Smith	50.00
5	Terrell Davis	25.00
6	John Elway	18.00
7	Barry Sanders	40.00
8	Brett Favre	60.00
9	Mark Brunell	25.00
10	Marcus Allen	8.00
11	Dan Marino	50.00
12	Drew Bledsoe	25.00
13	Curtis Martin	25.00
14	Jerome Bettis	8.00
15	Jim Druckenmiller	30.00
16	Jerry Rice	25.00
17	Warrick Dunn	40.00
18	Eddie George	40.00

1998 Pacific

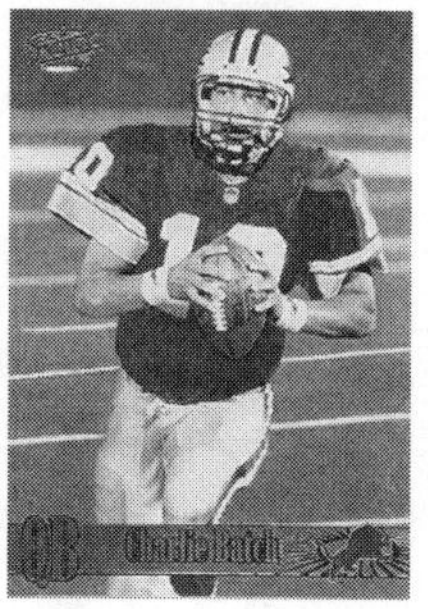

The 450-card silver-foiled main set captures the NFL's pinpoint passes, touchdown runs and goal-line stands with the sharpest action photography. The set is designed with the die-hard football fan in mind, this set delivers outstanding player selection, including the strong crop of rookies from 1998. Each card back includes full year-by-year career stats. A parallel Red version can be found one per special retail pack and the Platinum Blue parallel singles can be found 1:73 packs.

		MT
Complete Set (450):		70.00
Common Player:		.10
Minor Stars:		.20
Common Rookie:		1.00
Platinum Blue Cards:		60x-120x
Platinum Blue Rookies:		10x-20x
Inserted 1:73		
Pack (10):		2.50
Wax Box (36):		80.00
1	Mario Bates	.10
2	Lomas Brown	.10
3	Larry Centers	.10
4	Chris Gedney	.10
5	Terry Irving	.10
6	Tom Knight	.10
7	Eric Metcalf	.10
8	Jamir Miller	.10
9	Rob Moore	.20
10	Joe Nedney	.10
11	Jake Plummer	1.00
12	Simeon Rice	.10
13	Frank Sanders	.10
14	Eric Swann	.10
15	Aeneas Williams	.10
16	Morten Andersen	.10
17	Jamal Anderson	.50
18	Michael Booker	.10
19	Keith Brooking	.10
20	Ray Buchanan	.10
21	Devin Bush	.10
22	Chris Chandler	.20
23	Tony Graziani	.10
24	Harold Green	.10
25	Byron Hanspard	.10
26	Todd Kinchen	.10
27	Tony Martin	.10
28	Terance Mathis	.10
29	Eugene Robinson	.10
30	O.J. Santiago	.10
31	Chuck Smith	.10
32	Jessie Tuggle	.10
33	Bob Whitfield	.10
34	Peter Boulware	.10
35	Jay Graham	.10
36	Eric Green	.10
37	Jim Harbaugh	.20
38	Michael Jackson	.10
39	Jermaine Lewis	.10
40	Ray Lewis	.10
41	Michael McCrary	.10
42	Stevon Moore	.10
43	Jonathan Ogden	.10
44	Errict Rhett	.10
45	Matt Stover	.10
46	Rod Woodson	.10
47	Eric Zeier	.10
48	Ruben Brown	.10
49	Steve Christie	.10
50	Quinn Early	.10
51	John Fina	.10
52	Doug Flutie	.75
53	Phil Hansen	.10
54	Lonnie Johnson	.10
55	Rob Johnson	.20
56	Henry Jones	.10
57	Eric Moulds	.20
58	Andre Reed	.10
59	Antowain Smith	.50
60	Bruce Smith	.10
61	Thurman Thomas	.20
62	Ted Washington	.10
63	Michael Bates	.10
64	Tim Biakabutuka	.10
65	Blake Brockermeyer	.10
66	Mark Carrier	.10
67	Rae Carruth	.10
68	Kerry Collins	.20
69	Doug Evans	.10
70	William Floyd	.10
71	Sean Gilbert	.10
72	Raghib Ismail	.10
73	John Kasay	.10
74	Fred Lane	.20
75	Lamar Lathon	.10
76	Muhsin Muhammad	.10
77	Wesley Walls	.10
78	Edgar Bennett	.10
79	Tom Carter	.10
80	Curtis Conway	.20
81	Bobby Engram	.10
82	*Curtis Enis*	3.00
83	Jim Flanigan	.10
84	Walt Harris	.10
85	Jeff Jaeger	.10
86	Erik Kramer	.10
87	John Mangum	.10
88	Glyn Milburn	.10
89	Barry Minter	.10
90	Chris Penn	.10
91	Todd Sauerbrun	.10
92	James Williams	.10
93	Ashley Ambrose	.10
94	Willie Anderson	.10
95	Eric Bieniemy	.10
96	Jeff Blake	.20
97	Ki-Jana Carter	.10
98	John Copeland	.10
99	Corey Dillon	.75
100	Tony McGee	.10
101	Neil O'Donnell	.20
102	Carl Pickens	.20
103	Kevin Sargent	.10
104	Darnay Scott	.20
105	*Takeo Spikes*	1.00
106	Troy Aikman	1.50
107	Larry Allen	.10
108	Eric Bjornson	.10
109	Billy Davis	.10
110	Jason Garrett	.10
111	Michael Irvin	.20
112	Daryl Johnston	.10
113	David LaFleur	.10
114	Everett McIver	.10
115	Ernie Mills	.10
116	Nate Newton	.10
117	Deion Sanders	.50
118	Emmitt Smith	2.00
119	Kevin Smith	.10
120	Erik Williams	.10
121	Steve Atwater	.10
122	Tyrone Braxton	.10
123	Ray Crockett	.10
124	Terrell Davis	2.00
125	Jason Elam	.10
126	John Elway	1.50
127	Willie Green	.10
128	*Brian Griese*	5.00
129	Tony Jones	.10
130	Ed McCaffrey	.20
131	John Mobley	.10
132	Tom Nalen	.10
133	*Marcus Nash*	2.00
134	Bill Romanowski	.10
135	Shannon Sharpe	.20
136	Neil Smith	.10
137	Rod Smith	.20
138	Keith Traylor	.10
139	Stephen Boyd	.10
140	Mark Carrier	.10
141	*Charlie Batch*	5.00
142	Jason Hanson	.10
143	Scott Mitchell	.20
144	Herman Moore	.50
145	Johnnie Morton	.10
146	Robert Porcher	.10
147	Ron Rivers	.10
148	Barry Sanders	3.00
149	Tracy Scroggins	.10
150	David Sloan	.10
151	Tommy Vardell	.10
152	Kerwin Waldroup	.10
153	Bryant Westbrook	.10
154	Robert Brooks	.10
155	Gilbert Brown	.10
156	LeRoy Butler	.10
157	Mark Chmura	.20
158	Earl Dotson	.10
159	Santana Dotson	.10
160	Brett Favre	3.00
161	Antonio Freeman	.50
162	Raymont Harris	.10
163	William Henderson	.10
164	*Vonnie Holliday*	1.50
165	George Koonce	.10
166	Dorsey Levens	.20
167	Derrick Mayes	.10
168	Craig Newsome	.10
169	Ross Verba	.10
170	Reggie White	.50
171	Elijah Alexander	.10
172	Aaron Bailey	.10
173	Jason Belser	.10
174	Robert Blackmon	.10
175	Zack Crockett	.10
176	Ken Dilger	.10
177	Marshall Faulk	.50
178	Tarik Glenn	.10
179	Marvin Harrison	.20
180	Tony Mandarich	.10
181	*Peyton Manning*	12.00
182	Marcus Pollard	.10
183	Lamont Warren	.10
184	*Tavian Banks*	2.00
185	Reggie Barlow	.10
186	Tony Boselli	.10
187	Tony Brackens	.10
188	Mark Brunell	1.00
189	Kevin Hardy	.10
190	Mike Hollis	.10
191	Jeff Lageman	.10
192	Keenan McCardell	.20
193	Pete Mitchell	.10
194	Bryce Paup	.10
195	Leon Searcy	.10
196	Jimmy Smith	.20
197	James Stewart	.10
198	*Fred Taylor*	5.00
199	Renaldo Wynn	.10
200	Derrick Alexander	.10
201	Kimble Anders	.10
202	Donnell Bennett	.10
203	Dale Carter	.10
204	Anthony Davis	.10
205	Rich Gannon	.10
206	Tony Gonzalez	.20
207	Elvis Grbac	.20
208	James Hasty	.10
209	Leslie O'Neal	.10
210	Andre Rison	.10
211	*Rashaan Shehee*	1.50
212	Will Shields	.10
213	Pete Stoyanovich	.10
214	Derrick Thomas	.20
215	Tamarick Vanover	.10
216	Karim Abdul-Jabbar	.20
217	Trace Armstrong	.10
218	*John Avery*	2.00
219	Tim Bowens	.10
220	Terrell Buckley	.10
221	Troy Drayton	.10
222	Daryl Gardener	.10
223	*Damon Huard*	10.00
224	Charles Jordan	.10
225	Dan Marino	2.00
226	O.J. McDuffie	.10
227	Bernie Parmalee	.10
228	Stanley Pritchett	.10
229	Derrick Rodgers	.10
230	Lamar Thomas	.10
231	Zach Thomas	.20
232	Richmond Webb	.10
233	Derrick Alexander	.10
234	Jerry Ball	.10
235	Cris Carter	.50
236	Randall Cunningham	.50
237	Charles Evans	.10
238	Corey Fuller	.10
239	Andrew Glover	.10
240	Leroy Hoard	.10
241	Brad Johnson	.50
242	Ed McDaniel	.10
243	Randall McDaniel	.10
244	*Randy Moss*	12.00
245	John Randle	.10
246	Jake Reed	.10
247	Dwayne Rudd	.10
248	Robert Smith	.20
249	Bruce Armstrong	.10
250	Drew Bledsoe	1.00
251	Vincent Brisby	.10
252	Tedy Bruschi	.10
253	Ben Coates	.20
254	Derrick Cullors	.10
255	Terry Glenn	.20
256	Shawn Jefferson	.10
257	Ted Johnson	.10
258	Ty Law	.10
259	Willie McGinest	.10
260	Lawyer Milloy	.10
261	Sedrick Shaw	.10
262	Chris Slade	.10
263	Troy Davis	.10
264	Mark Fields	.10
265	Andre Hastings	.10
266	Billy Joe Hobert	.10
267	Qadry Ismail	.10
268	Tony Johnson	.10
269	Sammy Knight	.10
270	Wayne Martin	.10
271	Chris Naeole	.10
272	Keith Poole	.10
273	William Roaf	.10
274	Pio Sagapolutele	.10
275	Danny Wuerffel	.20
276	Ray Zellars	.10
277	Jessie Armstead	.10
278	Tiki Barber	.20
279	Chris Calloway	.10
280	Percy Ellsworth	.10
281	Sam Garnes	.10
282	Kent Graham	.10
283	Ike Hilliard	.10
284	Danny Kanell	.10
285	Corey Miller	.10
286	Phillippi Sparks	.10
287	Michael Strahan	.10
288	Amani Toomer	.10
289	Charles Way	.10
290	Tyrone Wheatley	.10
291	Tito Wooten	.10
292	Kyle Brady	.10
293	Keith Byars	.10
294	Wayne Chrebet	.20
295	John Elliott	.10
296	Glenn Foley	.20
297	Aaron Glenn	.10
298	Keyshawn Johnson	.50
299	Curtis Martin	.50
300	Otis Smith	.10
301	Vinny Testaverde	.20
302	Alex Van Dyke	.10
303	Dedric Ward	.10
304	Greg Biekert	.10
305	Tim Brown	.20
306	Rickey Dudley	.10
307	Jeff George	.20
308	Pat Harlow	.10
309	Desmond Howard	.10
310	James Jett	.10
311	Napoleon Kaufman	.50
312	Lincoln Kennedy	.10
313	Russell Maryland	.10
314	Darrell Russell	.10
315	Eric Turner	.10
316	Steve Wisniewski	.10
317	*Charles Woodson*	3.00
318	James Darling	.10
319	Jason Dunn	.10
320	Irving Fryar	.10
321	Charlie Garner	.20
322	Jeff Graham	.10
323	Bobby Hoying	.20
324	Chad Lewis	.10
325	Rodney Peete	.10
326	Freddie Solomon	.10
327	Duce Staley	.10
328	Bobby Taylor	.10
329	William Thomas	.10
330	Kevin Turner	.10
331	Troy Vincent	.10
332	Jerome Bettis	.50
333	Will Blackwell	.10
334	Mark Bruener	.10
335	Andre Coleman	.10
336	Dermontti Dawson	.10
337	Jason Gildon	.10
338	Courtney Hawkins	.10
339	Charles Johnson	.10
340	Levon Kirkland	.10
341	Carnell Lake	.10
342	Tim Lester	.10
343	Joel Steed	.10
344	Kordell Stewart	1.00
345	Will Wolford	.10
346	Tony Banks	.20
347	Isaac Bruce	.20
348	Ernie Conwell	.10
349	D'Marco Farr	.10
350	Wayne Gandy	.10
351	*Robert Holcombe*	2.00
352	Eddie Kennison	.20
353	Amp Lee	.10
354	Keith Lyle	.10
355	Ryan McNeil	.10
356	Jerald Moore	.20
357	Orlando Pace	.10
358	Roman Phifer	.10
359	David Thompson	.10
360	Darren Bennett	.10
361	John Carney	.10
362	Marco Coleman	.10
363	Terrell Fletcher	.10
364	William Fuller	.10
365	Charlie Jones	.10
366	Freddie Jones	.10
367	*Ryan Leaf*	4.00
368	Natrone Means	.50
369	Junior Seau	.20
370	Terrance Shaw	.10
371	Tremayne Stephens	.10
372	Bryan Still	.10
373	Aaron Taylor	.10
374	Greg Clark	.10
375	Ty Detmer	.10
376	Jim Druckenmiller	.20
377	Marc Edwards	.10
378	Merton Hanks	.10
379	Garrison Hearst	.20
380	Chuck Levy	.10
381	Ken Norton	.10
382	Terrell Owens	.75
383	Marquez Pope	.10
384	Jerry Rice	1.50
385	Irv Smith	.10
386	J.J. Stokes	.20
387	Iheanyi Uwaezuoke	.10
388	Bryant Young	.10
389	Steve Young	.75
390	Sam Adams	.10
391	Chad Brown	.10
392	Christian Fauria	.10
393	Joey Galloway	.50
394	*Ahman Green*	2.50
395	Walter Jones	.10
396	Cortez Kennedy	.10
397	Jon Kitna	.50
398	James McKnight	.10

399	Warren Moon	.20
400	Mike Pritchard	.10
401	Michael Sinclair	.10
402	Shawn Springs	.10
403	Ricky Watters	.20
404	Darryl Williams	.10
405	Mike Alstott	.50
406	Reidel Anthony	.20
407	Derrick Brooks	.10
408	Brad Culpepper	.10
409	Trent Dilfer	.50
410	Warrick Dunn	1.00
411	Bert Emanuel	.10
412	*Jacquez Green*	2.50
413	Paul Gruber	.10
414	Patrick Hape	.10
415	Dave Moore	.10
416	Hardy Nickerson	.10
417	Warren Sapp	.10
418	Robb Thomas	.10
419	Regan Upshaw	.10
420	Karl Williams	.10
421	Blaine Bishop	.10
422	Anthony Cook	.10
423	Willie Davis	.10
424	Al Del Greco	.10
425	*Kevin Dyson*	2.00
426	Henry Ford	.10
427	Eddie George	1.00
428	Jackie Harris	.10
429	Steve McNair	.75
430	Chris Sanders	.10
431	Mark Stepnoski	.10
432	Yancey Thigpen	.20
433	Barron Wortham	.10
434	Frank Wycheck	.10
435	Stephen Alexander	.10
436	Terry Allen	.20
437	Jamie Asher	.10
438	Bob Dahl	.10
439	Stephen Davis	.10
440	Cris Dishman	.10
441	Gus Frerotte	.10
442	Darrell Green	.10
443	Trent Green	.20
444	Ken Harvey	.10
445	*Skip Hicks*	2.00
446	Jeff Hostetler	.10
447	Brian Mitchell	.10
448	Leslie Shepherd	.10
449	Michael Westbrook	.20
450	Dan Wilkinson	.10

1998 Pacific Cramer's Choice Awards

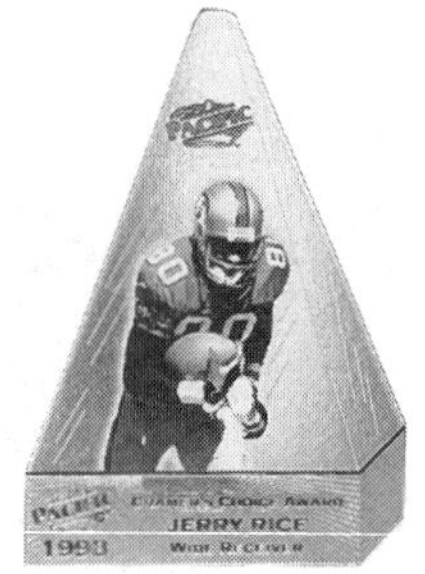

Pacific President/CEO Michael Cramer selected and wrote about the 10 players that are on these die-cut awards. Each card is in the shape of a triangle and were inserted 1:721 packs.

		MT
Complete Set (10):		850.00
Common Player:		50.00
Inserted 1:721		
1	Terrell Davis	125.00
2	John Elway	100.00
3	Barry Sanders	150.00
4	Brett Favre	150.00
5	Peyton Manning	125.00
6	Mark Brunell	70.00
7	Dan Marino	125.00
8	Ryan Leaf	60.00
9	Jerry Rice	85.00
10	Warrick Dunn	50.00

1998 Pacific Dynagon Turf

This sparkling insert features action photography and a mirror-patterned full-foil background. Singles from this 20-card set were inserted 4:37 packs. A parallel Titanium Turf set was added for hobby-only packs. Each single is sequentially numbered to 99.

		MT
Complete Set (20):		100.00
Common Player:		2.00
Inserted 4:37		
Titanium Cards:		7x-14x
Production 99 Sets		
1	Corey Dillon	3.00
2	Troy Aikman	6.00
3	Emmitt Smith	10.00
4	Terrell Davis	10.00
5	John Elway	6.00
6	Barry Sanders	12.00
7	Brett Favre	12.00
8	Peyton Manning	12.00
9	Mark Brunell	5.00
10	Dan Marino	10.00
11	Drew Bledsoe	5.00
12	Curtis Martin	3.00
13	Napoleon Kaufman	2.00
14	Jerome Bettis	2.00
15	Kordell Stewart	5.00
16	Ryan Leaf	6.00
17	Jerry Rice	6.00
18	Steve Young	4.00
19	Warrick Dunn	4.00
20	Eddie George	4.00

1998 Pacific Gold Crown Die-Cuts

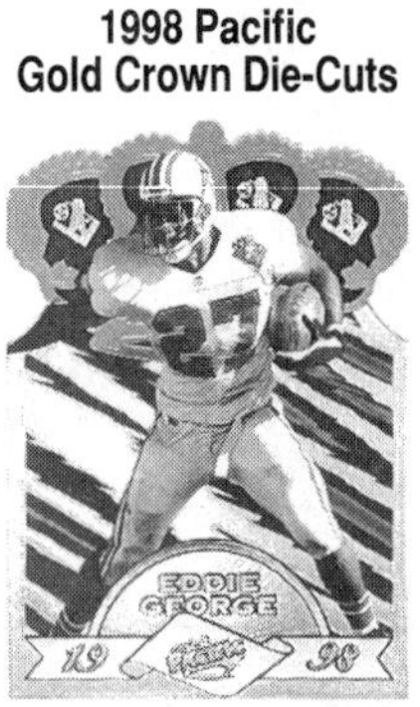

This die-cut dual-foiled insert honors 36 of football's elite players. These singles were created with Pacific's cutting-edge technology and feature super-thick 24-point stock. Singles were inserted 1:37 packs.

		MT
Complete Set (36):		425.00
Common Player:		5.00
Minor Stars:		10.00
Inserted 1:37		
1	Jake Plummer	15.00
2	Antowain Smith	10.00
3	Curtis Enis	12.00
4	Corey Dillon	10.00
5	Troy Aikman	20.00
6	Deion Sanders	10.00
7	Emmitt Smith	30.00
8	Terrell Davis	30.00
9	John Elway	20.00
10	Barry Sanders	40.00
11	Brett Favre	40.00
12	Dorsey Levens	5.00
13	Marshall Faulk	10.00
14	Peyton Manning	40.00
15	Mark Brunell	15.00
16	Fred Taylor	20.00
17	Derrick Thomas	5.00
18	Dan Marino	30.00
19	Brad Johnson	10.00
20	Robert Smith	10.00
21	Drew Bledsoe	15.00
22	Glenn Foley	5.00
23	Curtis Martin	10.00
24	Napoleon Kaufman	10.00
25	Charles Woodson	15.00
26	Jerome Bettis	10.00
27	Kordell Stewart	15.00
28	Ryan Leaf	20.00
29	Garrison Hearst	5.00
30	Jerry Rice	20.00
31	J.J. Stokes	5.00
32	Steve Young	12.00
33	Joey Galloway	10.00
34	Ricky Watters	5.00
35	Warrick Dunn	15.00
36	Eddie George	15.00

1998 Pacific Team Checklists

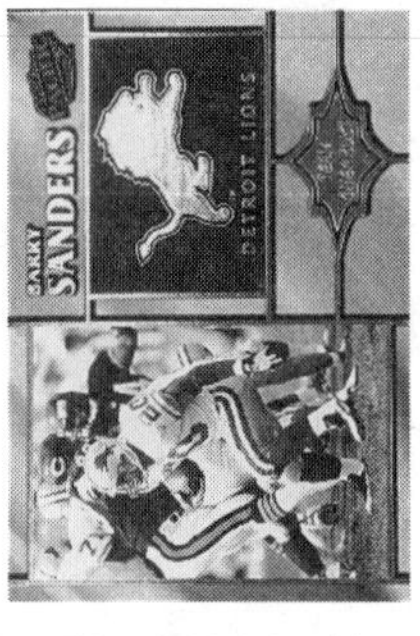

This uniquely-designed insert highlights a team leader side-by-side with the holographic silver-foiled NFL logo of his respective team. On the back you'll find another photo of that player and a complete team checklist. Singles were inserted 2:37 packs.

		MT
Complete Set (30):		150.00
Common Player:		2.00
Minor Stars:		4.00
Inserted 2:37		
1	Jake Plummer	7.00
2	Jamal Anderson	4.00
3	Eric Zeier	2.00
4	Rob Johnson	2.00
5	Fred Lane	2.00
6	Curtis Enis	8.00
7	Corey Dillon	4.00
8	Troy Aikman	10.00
9	John Elway	10.00
10	Barry Sanders	20.00
11	Brett Favre	20.00
12	Peyton Manning	20.00
13	Mark Brunell	8.00
14	Elvis Grbac	2.00
15	Dan Marino	15.00
16	Robert Smith	4.00
17	Drew Bledsoe	8.00
18	Danny Wuerffel	2.00
19	Tiki Barber	2.00
20	Curtis Martin	4.00
21	Napoleon Kaufman	4.00
22	Duce Staley	2.00
23	Kordell Stewart	8.00
24	Tony Banks	4.00
25	Ryan Leaf	10.00
26	Jerry Rice	10.00
27	Warren Moon	4.00
28	Warrick Dunn	7.00
29	Eddie George	7.00
30	Terry Allen	2.00

1998 Pacific Timelines

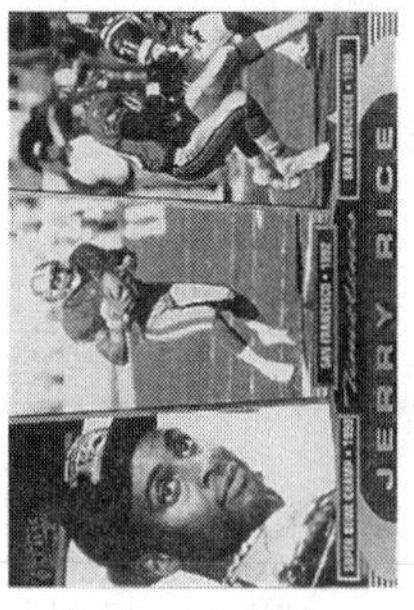

Timelines features 20 superstars, giving a chronological history of each player complete with photos from early in their careers. These singles could be found in hobby-only packs at a ratio of 1:181.

		MT
Complete Set (20):		750.00
Common Player:		10.00
Minor Stars:		20.00
Inserted 1:181 Hobby		
1	Troy Aikman	50.00
2	Deion Sanders	20.00
3	Emmitt Smith	75.00
4	Terrell Davis	75.00
5	John Elway	50.00
6	Barry Sanders	100.00
7	Brett Favre	100.00
8	Peyton Manning	100.00
9	Mark Brunell	35.00
10	Dan Marino	75.00
11	Drew Bledsoe	40.00
12	Curtis Martin	20.00
13	Jerome Bettis	10.00
14	Kordell Stewart	40.00
15	Ryan Leaf	50.00
16	Jerry Rice	50.00
17	Steve Young	30.00
18	Ricky Watters	10.00
19	Warrick Dunn	40.00
20	Eddie George	40.00

1998 Pacific Aurora

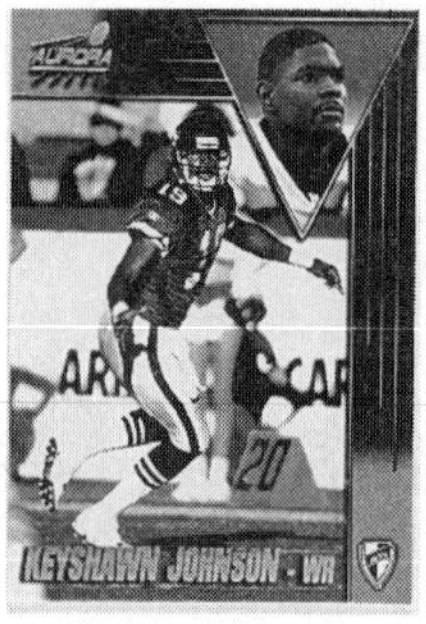

The Aurora main set shines its light on 200 of football's most exciting players, each featured on their own 24-point stock card. Each card back gives you the latest in-depth player information and statistics along with a trivia question.

		MT
Complete Set (200):		75.00
Common Player:		.20
Minor Stars:		.40
Pack (6):		3.00
Wax Box (36):		100.00
1	Rob Moore	.20
2	Jake Plummer	1.50
3	Frank Sanders	.20
4	Eric Swann	.20
5	Jamal Anderson	.75
6	Chris Chandler	.20
7	Byron Hanspard	.20
8	Terance Mathis	.20
9	O.J. Santiago	.20
10	Chuck Smith	.20
11	Jessie Tuggle	.20
12	Jay Graham	.20
13	Jim Harbaugh	.20
14	Michael Jackson	.20
15	*Patrick Johnson*	.40
16	Jermaine Lewis	.20
17	Errict Rhett	.20
18	Rod Woodson	.20
19	Quinn Early	.20
20	Andre Reed	.20
21	Antowain Smith	1.00
22	Bruce Smith	.20
23	Thurman Thomas	.40
24	Ted Washington	.20
25	Michael Bates	.20
26	Rae Carruth	.20
27	Kerry Collins	.40
28	Fred Lane	.40
29	Wesley Walls	.20
30	Edgar Bennett	.20
31	Curtis Conway	.40
32	*Curtis Enis*	4.00
33	Walt Harris	.20
34	Erik Kramer	.20
35	Barry Minter	.20
36	Jeff Blake	.40
37	Corey Dillon	1.25
38	Carl Pickens	.20
39	Darnay Scott	.20
40	Troy Aikman	2.00
41	Michael Irvin	.40
42	Deion Sanders	.75
43	Emmitt Smith	3.00
44	Chris Warren	.20
45	Terrell Davis	3.00
46	John Elway	2.00
47	*Brian Griese*	5.00
48	Ed McCaffrey	.20
49	John Mobley	.20
50	Shannon Sharpe	.40
51	Neil Smith	.20
52	Rod Smith	.20
53	Stephen Boyd	.20
54	Scott Mitchell	.20
55	Herman Moore	.75
56	Johnnie Morton	.20
57	Robert Porcher	.20
58	Barry Sanders	4.00
59	Robert Brooks	.20
60	Mark Chmura	.40
61	Brett Favre	4.00
62	Antonio Freeman	.75
63	*Vonnie Holliday*	1.00
64	Dorsey Levens	.40
65	Ross Verba	.20
66	Reggie White	.40
67	Elijah Alexander	.20
68	Ken Dilger	.20
69	Marshall Faulk	.75
70	Marvin Harrison	.40
71	*Peyton Manning*	15.00
72	Bryan Barker	.20
73	Mark Brunell	1.50
74	Keenan McCardell	.20
75	Jimmy Smith	.20
76	James Stewart	.20
77	Derrick Alexander	.20
78	Kimble Anders	.20
79	Donnell Bennett	.20
80	Elvis Grbac	.20
81	Andre Rison	.20
82	*Rashaan Shehee*	.75
83	Derrick Thomas	.20
84	Karim Abdul-Jabbar	.40
85	Trace Armstrong	.20
86	Charles Jordan	.20
87	Dan Marino	3.00
88	O.J. McDuffie	.20
89	Zach Thomas	.40
90	Cris Carter	.40
91	Charles Evans	.20
92	Andrew Glover	.20
93	Brad Johnson	.40
94	*Randy Moss*	15.00
95	John Randle	.20
96	Jake Reed	.20
97	Robert Smith	.40
98	Bruce Armstrong	.20
99	Drew Bledsoe	1.50
100	Ben Coates	.20
101	*Robert Edwards*	4.00
102	Terry Glenn	.40
103	Willie McGinest	.20
104	Sedrick Shaw	.20
105	*Tony Simmons*	2.00
106	Chris Slade	.20
107	Billy Joe Hobert	.20
108	Qadry Ismail	.20
109	Heath Shuler	.20
110	Lamar Smith	.20
111	Ray Zellars	.20
112	Tiki Barber	.40
113	Chris Calloway	.20
114	Ike Hilliard	.20
115	*Joe Jurevicius*	1.00
116	Danny Kanell	.20
117	Amani Toomer	.20
118	Charles Way	.20
119	Tyrone Wheatley	.20
120	Wayne Chrebet	.20
121	John Elliott	.20
122	Glenn Foley	.20
123	*Scott Frost*	.40
124	Aaron Glenn	.20
125	Keyshawn Johnson	.40
126	Curtis Martin	1.00
127	Vinny Testaverde	.20
128	Tim Brown	.40
129	Rickey Dudley	.20
130	Jeff George	.40
131	James Jett	.20
132	Napoleon Kaufman	.75
133	Darrell Russell	.20
134	*Charles Woodson*	3.00
135	James Darling	.20
136	Koy Detmer	.20
137	Irving Fryar	.20
138	Charlie Garner	.20
139	Bobby Hoying	.20
140	Chad Lewis	.20
141	Duce Staley	.20
142	Kevin Turner	.20
143	Jerome Bettis	.40
144	Will Blackwell	.20
145	Mark Bruener	.20
146	Dermontti Dawson	.20
147	Charles Johnson	.20
148	Levon Kirkland	.20
149	Tim Lester	.20
150	Kordell Stewart	1.50
151	Tony Banks	.75
152	Isaac Bruce	.40
153	*Robert Holcombe*	5.00
154	Eddie Kennison	.40
155	Amp Lee	.20
156	Jerald Moore	.20
157	Charlie Jones	.20
158	Freddie Jones	.20
159	*Ryan Leaf*	4.00
160	Natrone Means	.40
161	Junior Seau	.40
162	Bryan Still	.20
163	Marc Edwards	.20
164	Merton Hanks	.20
165	Garrison Hearst	.40
166	Terrell Owens	.40
167	Jerry Rice	2.00
168	J.J. Stokes	.20
169	Bryant Young	.20
170	Steve Young	1.00
171	Chad Brown	.20
172	Joey Galloway	.75
173	Walter Jones	.20
174	Cortez Kennedy	.20
175	Jon Kitna	.20
176	James McKnight	.20
177	Warren Moon	.40
178	Michael Sinclair	.20
179	Mike Alstott	.40
180	Reidel Anthony	.20
181	Derrick Brooks	.20
182	Trent Dilfer	.40
183	Warrick Dunn	1.50
184	Hardy Nickerson	.20
185	Warren Sapp	.20
186	Willie Davis	.20
187	Eddie George	1.25
188	Steve McNair	.75
189	Jon Runyan	.20
190	Chris Sanders	.20
191	Frank Wycheck	.20
192	Stephen Alexander	.20
193	Terry Allen	.20
194	Stephen Davis	.20
195	Cris Dishman	.20
196	Gus Frerotte	.20
197	Darrell Green	.20
198	*Skip Hicks*	1.50
199	Dana Stubblefield	.20
200	Michael Westbrook	.20

1998 Pacific Aurora Championship Fever

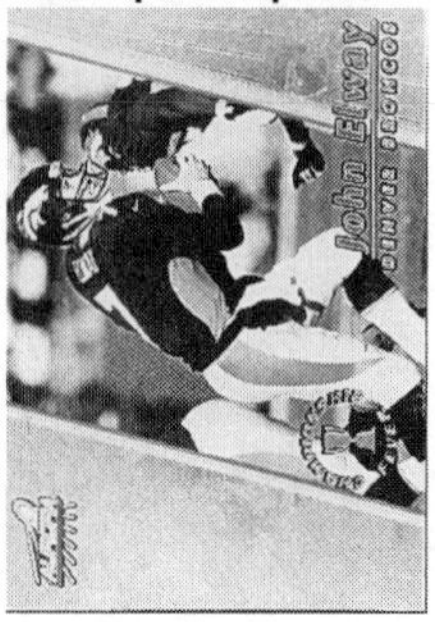

Each of the singles in this 50-card set are printed on gold foil and etched. Singles were inserted one-per-pack. This insert also has three parallel sets. The easiest being the Silvers that are found in retail packs and are sequentially numbered to 250. The Platinum Blues are numbered to 100 and can be found in both hobby and retail packs. The Copper cards are limited to 20 and are found in hobby packs.

		MT
Complete Set (50):		50.00
Common Player:		.30
Minor Stars:		.60
Inserted 1:1		
Silver Cards:		15x-30x
Production 250 Sets		
Platinum Blue Cards:		25x-50x
Production 100 Sets		
Copper Cards:		75x-150x
Production 20 Sets		
1	Jake Plummer	2.00
2	Antowain Smith	1.00
3	Bruce Smith	.30
4	Kerry Collins	.60
5	Kevin Greene	.30
6	Jeff Blake	.30
7	Corey Dillon	1.50
8	Carl Pickens	.30
9	Troy Aikman	3.00
10	Michael Irvin	.60
11	Deion Sanders	.75
12	Emmitt Smith	4.00
13	Terrell Davis	4.00
14	John Elway	3.00
15	Shannon Sharpe	.30
16	Herman Moore	.60
17	Barry Sanders	6.00
18	Brett Favre	6.00
19	Antonio Freeman	.75
20	Dorsey Levens	.60
21	Marshall Faulk	.75
22	Peyton Manning	6.00
23	Mark Brunell	2.00
24	Elvis Grbac	.30
25	Andre Rison	.30
26	Rashaan Shehee	.60
27	Derrick Thomas	.30
28	Dan Marino	4.00
29	Cris Carter	.30
30	Robert Smith	.60
31	Drew Bledsoe	2.00
32	Robert Edwards	3.00
33	Terry Glenn	.60
34	Danny Kanell	.30
35	Keyshawn Johnson	.60
36	Tim Brown	.30
37	Napoleon Kaufman	.75
38	Bobby Hoying	.30
39	Jerome Bettis	.60
40	Kordell Stewart	2.00
41	Ryan Leaf	3.00
42	Jerry Rice	3.00
43	Steve Young	1.50
44	Joey Galloway	.75
45	Mike Alstott	.60
46	Trent Dilfer	.60
47	Warrick Dunn	2.00
48	Eddie George	2.00
49	Steve McNair	.75
50	Gus Frerotte	.30

1998 Pacific Aurora Cubes

The Cubes insert could only be found in hobby boxes and were inserted one per box. Only 20 of the top players from the NFL were included in this insert.

		MT
Complete Set (20):		170.00
Common Player:		4.00
One Per Box		
1	Corey Dillon	6.00
2	Troy Aikman	10.00
3	Emmitt Smith	15.00
4	Terrell Davis	15.00
5	John Elway	10.00
6	Barry Sanders	20.00
7	Brett Favre	20.00
8	Dorsey Levens	4.00
9	Peyton Manning	15.00
10	Mark Brunell	8.00
11	Dan Marino	15.00
12	Drew Bledsoe	8.00
13	Napoleon Kaufman	4.00
14	Jerome Bettis	4.00
15	Kordell Stewart	8.00
16	Ryan Leaf	8.00
17	Jerry Rice	10.00
18	Steve Young	6.00
19	Warrick Dunn	8.00
20	Eddie George	8.00

1998 Pacific Aurora Face Mask Cel-Fusions

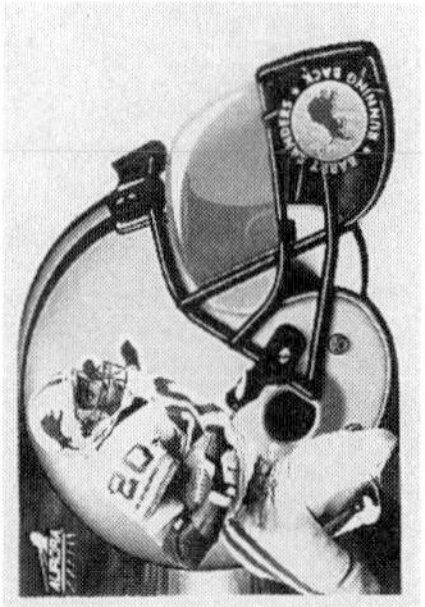

Each player in this 20-card foiled and etched set is profiled against a die-cut helmet that is fused to a cel-portion face mask. Singles were inserted 1:73 packs.

		MT
Complete Set (20):		550.00
Common Player:		10.00
Inserted 1:73		
1	Corey Dillon	15.00
2	Troy Aikman	35.00
3	Emmitt Smith	50.00
4	Terrell Davis	50.00
5	John Elway	35.00
6	Barry Sanders	70.00
7	Brett Favre	70.00
8	Antonio Freeman	10.00
9	Peyton Manning	60.00
10	Mark Brunell	25.00
11	Dan Marino	50.00
12	Drew Bledsoe	25.00
13	Napoleon Kaufman	10.00
14	Jerome Bettis	10.00
15	Kordell Stewart	25.00
16	Ryan Leaf	25.00
17	Jerry Rice	35.00
18	Steve Young	15.00
19	Warrick Dunn	20.00
20	Eddie George	20.00

1998 Pacific Aurora Gridiron Laser-Cuts

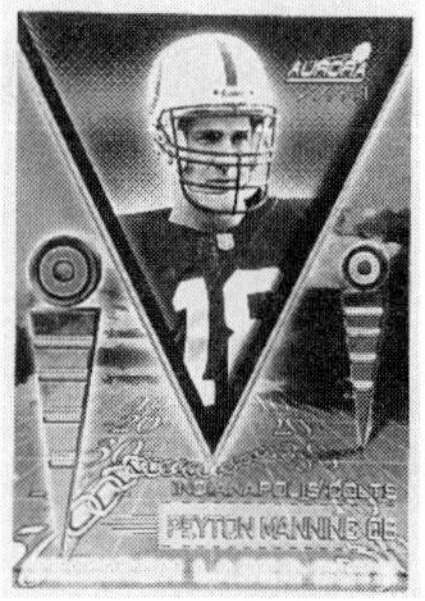

Each single in this 20-card set is laser cut and was inserted 4:37 packs. They could only be found in hobby packs.

		MT
Complete Set (20):		125.00
Common Player:		3.00
Inserted 4:37 Hobby		
1	Jake Plummer	6.00
2	Corey Dillon	5.00
3	Troy Aikman	8.00
4	Emmitt Smith	10.00
5	Terrell Davis	10.00
6	John Elway	8.00
7	Barry Sanders	15.00
8	Brett Favre	15.00
9	Peyton Manning	10.00
10	Mark Brunell	6.00
11	Dan Marino	10.00
12	Drew Bledsoe	6.00
13	Jerome Bettis	3.00
14	Kordell Stewart	6.00
15	Ryan Leaf	7.00
16	Jerry Rice	8.00
17	Steve Young	5.00
18	Warrick Dunn	6.00
19	Eddie George	6.00
20	Steve McNair	4.00

1998 Pacific Aurora NFL Command

This insert salutes 10 NFL stars with this coveted fully-foiled and

etched insert. Singles were inserted 1:361 packs.

		MT
Complete Set (10):		650.00
Common Player:		50.00
Inserted 1:361		
1	Terrell Davis	100.00
2	John Elway	100.00
3	Barry Sanders	125.00
4	Brett Favre	125.00
5	Peyton Manning	100.00
6	Mark Brunell	50.00
7	Dan Marino	100.00
8	Drew Bledsoe	50.00
9	Ryan Leaf	50.00
10	Warrick Dunn	50.00

1998 Pacific Crown Royale

This 144-card base set features football's brightest stars and top rookies on the Crown Royale double-foiled, double-etched, all-die-cut format. The parallel Limited Series cards are printed on 24-point stock and are sequentially numbered to 99.

		MT
Complete Set (144):		125.00
Common Player:		.50
Minor Stars:		1.00
Common Rookie:		1.00
Limited Series Cards:		15x-30x
Limited Series Rookies:		3x-6x
Production 99 Sets		
Pack (6):		5.00
Wax Box (24):		115.00
1	Larry Centers	.50
2	Rob Moore	.50
3	Adrian Murrell	.50
4	Jake Plummer	3.00
5	Jamal Anderson	1.50
6	Chris Chandler	.50
7	*Tim Dwight*	3.00
8	Tony Martin	.50
9	Jay Graham	.50
10	*Patrick Johnson*	2.00
11	Jermaine Lewis	.50
12	Eric Zeier	.50
13	Rob Johnson	1.00
14	Eric Moulds	1.00
15	Antowain Smith	1.50
16	Bruce Smith	.50
17	Steve Beuerlein	.50
18	Anthony Johnson	.50
19	Fred Lane	1.00
20	Muhsin Muhammad	.50
21	Curtis Conway	1.00
22	*Curtis Enis*	6.00
23	Erik Kramer	.50
24	*Tony Parrish*	1.00
25	Corey Dillon	2.00
26	Neil O'Donnell	.50
27	Carl Pickens	1.00
28	*Takeo Spikes*	2.00
29	Troy Aikman	4.00
30	Michael Irvin	1.00
31	Deion Sanders	1.50
32	Emmitt Smith	6.00
33	Chris Warren	.50
34	Terrell Davis	6.00
35	John Elway	4.00
36	*Brian Griese*	12.00
37	Ed McCaffrey	1.00
38	Shannon Sharpe	1.00
39	Rod Smith	1.00
40	*Charlie Batch*	5.00
41	Herman Moore	1.00
42	Johnnie Morton	.50
43	Barry Sanders	8.00
44	Bryant Westbrook	.50
45	Robert Brooks	.50
46	Brett Favre	8.00
47	Antonio Freeman	1.50
48	Raymont Harris	.50
49	*Vonnie Holliday*	3.00
50	Reggie White	1.00
51	Marshall Faulk	1.50
52	*E.G. Green*	3.00
53	Marvin Harrison	1.00
54	*Peyton Manning*	25.00
55	*Jerome Pathon*	3.00
56	*Tavian Banks*	4.00
57	Mark Brunell	3.00
58	Keenan McCardell	.50
59	Jimmy Smith	1.00
60	*Fred Taylor*	10.00
61	Derrick Alexander	.50
62	Tony Gonzalez	.50
63	Elvis Grbac	.50
64	Andre Rison	.50
65	*Rashaan Shehee*	2.00
66	Derrick Thomas	1.00
67	Karim Abdul-Jabbar	1.00
68	*John Avery*	2.00
69	*Oronde Gadsden*	3.00
70	Dan Marino	6.00
71	O.J. McDuffie	.50
72	Cris Carter	1.50
73	Randall Cunningham	1.50
74	Brad Johnson	1.00
75	*Randy Moss*	25.00
76	John Randle	.50
77	Jake Reed	.50
78	Robert Smith	1.00
79	Drew Bledsoe	3.00
80	*Robert Edwards*	7.00
81	Terry Glenn	1.00
82	*Tebucky Jones*	1.00
83	*Tony Simmons*	3.00
84	Mark Fields	.50
85	Andre Hastings	.50
86	Danny Wuerffel	1.00
87	Ray Zellars	.50
88	Tiki Barber	1.00
89	Ike Hilliard	.50
90	*Joe Jurevicius*	2.00
91	Danny Kanell	.50
92	Wayne Chrebet	1.00
93	Glenn Foley	1.00
94	Keyshawn Johnson	1.50
95	Leon Johnson	.50
96	Curtis Martin	1.50
97	Tim Brown	1.00
98	Jeff George	1.00
99	Napoleon Kaufman	1.50
100	*Jon Ritchie*	1.50
101	*Charles Woodson*	7.00
102	Irving Fryar	.50
103	Bobby Hoying	1.00
104	*Allen Rossum*	1.00
105	Duce Staley	.50
106	Jerome Bettis	1.00
107	*Chris Fuamatu-Ma'afala*	3.00
108	Charles Johnson	1.00
109	Levon Kirkland	.50
110	Kordell Stewart	3.00
111	*Hines Ward*	3.00
112	Tony Banks	1.00
113	*Tony Horne*	1.00
114	Eddie Kennison	1.00
115	Amp Lee	.50
116	Freddie Jones	.50
117	*Ryan Leaf*	5.00
118	Natrone Means	1.00
119	*Mikhael Ricks*	3.00
120	Bryan Still	.50
121	Marc Edwards	.50
122	Garrison Hearst	1.50
123	Terrell Owens	1.50
124	Jerry Rice	4.00
125	J.J. Stokes	1.00
126	Steve Young	2.50
127	Joey Galloway	1.50
128	*Ahman Green*	5.00
129	Warren Moon	1.00
130	Ricky Watters	1.00
131	Mike Alstott	1.50
132	Trent Dilfer	1.00
133	Warrick Dunn	3.00
134	*Jacquez Green*	4.00
135	Warren Sapp	.50
136	*Kevin Dyson*	5.00
137	Eddie George	3.00
138	Steve McNair	2.00
139	Yancey Thigpen	1.00
140	*Stephen Alexander*	1.00
141	Terry Allen	1.00
142	Trent Green	1.00
143	*Skip Hicks*	4.00
144	Michael Westbrook	1.00

1998 Pacific Crown Royale Cramer's Choice Awards Jumbos

These singles are identical to the Cramer's Choice awards found in Pacific except for the size. Singles from this set are larger and found on top of boxes at one per. The twist to this insert is the six different parallels with varying foil colors and number of sets produced. The Dark Blues are numbered to 35, Greens are numbered to 30, Reds to 25, Light Blues to 20, Golds to 10 and only one Purple set.

		MT
Complete Set (10):		150.00
Common Player:		10.00
One Per Box		
Dark Blue Cards:		10x-20x
Production 35 Sets		
Green Cards:		10x-20x
Production 30 Sets		
Red Cards:		10x-20x
Production 25 Sets		
Light Blue Cards:		10x-20x
Production 20 Sets		
Gold Cards:		15x-30x
Production 10 Sets		
1	Terrell Davis	15.00
2	John Elway	12.00
3	Barry Sanders	20.00
4	Brett Favre	20.00
5	Peyton Manning	20.00
6	Mark Brunell	10.00
7	Dan Marino	15.00
8	Randy Moss	35.00
9	Jerry Rice	12.00
10	Warrick Dunn	10.00

1998 Pacific Crown Royale Living Legends

The players selected for this insert were based on the dozens of records, awards and championships that each player has earned. Each card in this insert is sequentially numbered to 375.

		MT
Complete Set (10):		300.00
Common Player:		20.00
Production 375 Sets		
1	Troy Aikman	30.00
2	Emmitt Smith	45.00
3	Terrell Davis	45.00
4	John Elway	30.00
5	Barry Sanders	60.00
6	Brett Favre	60.00
7	Mark Brunell	20.00
8	Dan Marino	45.00
9	Drew Bledsoe	25.00
10	Jerry Rice	30.00

1998 Pacific Crown Royale Master Performers

Master Performers includes the top 20 players from the NFL and was inserted 2:25 hobby packs.

		MT
Complete Set (20):		120.00
Common Player:		2.00
Minor Stars:		4.00
Inserted 2:25 Hobby		
1	Corey Dillon	2.00
2	Troy Aikman	7.00
3	Emmitt Smith	10.00
4	Terrell Davis	10.00
5	John Elway	7.00
6	Charlie Batch	8.00
7	Barry Sanders	14.00
8	Brett Favre	14.00
9	Peyton Manning	14.00
10	Mark Brunell	5.00
11	Fred Taylor	6.00
12	Dan Marino	10.00
13	Randy Moss	25.00
14	Drew Bledsoe	5.00
15	Curtis Martin	4.00
16	Kordell Stewart	5.00
17	Ryan Leaf	6.00
18	Jerry Rice	7.00
19	Steve Young	5.00
20	Warrick Dunn	5.00

1998 Pacific Crown Royale Pillars of the Game

These holographic gold foil cards served as the bottom card in every pack and featured a strong mix of NFL mainstays and rising stars. These could only be found in hobby packs.

		MT
Complete Set (25):		45.00
Common Player:		.50
Minor Stars:		1.00
Inserted 1:1 Hobby		
1	Antowain Smith	.50
2	Corey Dillon	1.00
3	Troy Aikman	1.50
4	Emmitt Smith	2.00
5	Terrell Davis	2.00
6	John Elway	1.50
7	Charlie Batch	4.00
8	Barry Sanders	3.00
9	Brett Favre	3.00
10	Antonio Freeman	1.00
11	Peyton Manning	6.00
12	Mark Brunell	1.25
13	Dan Marino	2.00
14	Randy Moss	14.00
15	Drew Bledsoe	1.25
16	Curtis Martin	1.00
17	Napoleon Kaufman	1.00
18	Jerome Bettis	1.00
19	Kordell Stewart	1.25
20	Ryan Leaf	4.00
21	Jerry Rice	1.50
22	Steve Young	1.00
23	Ricky Watters	.50
24	Eddie George	1.25
25	Warrick Dunn	1.25

1998 Pacific Crown Royale Pivotal Players

This 25-card holographic silver foil insert featured some of football's most dynamic superstars along with several top rookies from 1998. Singles were found one-per-pack in hobby packs only.

		MT
Complete Set (25):		30.00
Common Player:		.50
Inserted 1:1 Hobby		
1	Jake Plummer	1.00
2	Antowain Smith	.50
3	Corey Dillon	.75
4	Troy Aikman	1.50
5	Deion Sanders	.50
6	Emmitt Smith	2.00
7	Terrell Davis	2.00
8	John Elway	1.50
9	Charlie Batch	4.00
10	Barry Sanders	3.00
11	Brett Favre	3.00
12	Peyton Manning	6.00
13	Mark Brunell	1.00
14	Fred Taylor	3.00
15	Dan Marino	2.00
16	Randy Moss	14.00
17	Drew Bledsoe	1.25
18	Curtis Martin	.75
19	Napoleon Kaufman	.50
20	Jerome Bettis	.50
21	Kordell Stewart	1.25
22	Ryan Leaf	4.00
23	Jerry Rice	1.50
24	Eddie George	1.25
25	Warrick Dunn	1.00

1998 Pacific Crown Royale Rookie Paydirt

The fully foiled and etched Rookie Paydirt set gave collectors an early look at the top 20 rookies from 1998. Singles were inserted into hobby packs at a ratio of 1:25.

		MT
Complete Set (20):		175.00
Common Player:		3.00
Inserted 1:25 Hobby		
1	Curtis Enis	8.00
2	Marcus Nash	6.00
3	Charlie Batch	15.00
4	Vonnie Holliday	4.00
5	E.G. Green	3.00
6	Peyton Manning	30.00
7	Jerome Pathon	3.00
8	Tavian Banks	6.00
9	Fred Taylor	15.00
10	Rashaan Shehee	3.00
11	John Avery	6.00
12	Randy Moss	60.00
13	Robert Edwards	10.00
14	Charles Woodson	8.00
15	Hines Ward	5.00
16	Ryan Leaf	12.00
17	Mikhael Ricks	4.00
18	Ahman Green	6.00
19	Jacquez Green	8.00
20	Kevin Dyson	8.00

1998 Pacific Omega

Omega football consists of a 250-card base set and five inserts. The base cards have a horizontal layout. The fronts feature three photos separated by a football stitching pattern. The color center photo is duplicated in silver foil on the right. Another color photo is on the left.

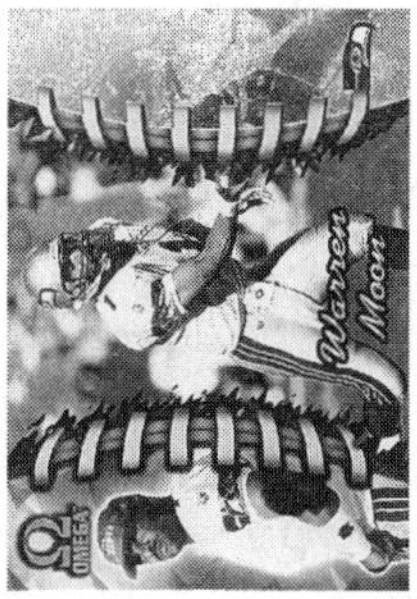

		MT
Complete Set (250):		50.00
Common Player:		.10
Minor Stars:		.20
Pack (8):		2.00
Wax Box (36):		60.00
1	Larry Centers	.10
2	Rob Moore	.10
3	Michael Pittman	.10
4	Jake Plummer	2.00
5	Simeon Rice	.10
6	Frank Sanders	.10
7	Eric Swann	.10
8	Morten Anderson	.10
9	Jamal Anderson	.20
10	Chris Chandler	.10
11	Harold Green	.10
12	Byron Hanspard	.10
13	Terance Mathis	.10
14	O.J. Santiago	.10
15	Peter Boulware	.10
16	Jay Graham	.10
17	Eric Green	.10
18	Michael Jackson	.10
19	Jermaine Lewis	.10
20	Ray Lewis	.10
21	Jonathan Ogden	.10
22	Eric Zeier	.10
23	Steve Christie	.10
24	Todd Collins	.10
25	Quinn Early	.10
26	Eric Moulds	.20
27	Andre Reed	.10
28	Antowain Smith	1.00
29	Bruce Smith	.10
30	Thurman Thomas	.20
31	Ted Washington	.10
32	Michael Bates	.10
33	Tim Biakabutuka	.10
34	Mark Carrier	.10
35	Rae Carruth	.20
36	Kerry Collins	.30
37	Kevin Greene	.10
38	Fred Lane	.20
39	Muhsin Muhammad	.10
40	Wesley Walls	.10
41	Curtis Conway	.20
42	Bobby Engram	.10
43	*Curtis Enis*	3.00
44	Raymont Harris	.10
45	Erik Kramer	.10
46	Chris Penn	.10
47	Ryan Wetnight	.10
48	Jeff Blake	.20
49	Ki-Jana Carter	.10
50	John Copeland	.10
51	Corey Dillon	1.00
52	Tony McGee	.10
53	Carl Pickens	.20
54	Darnay Scott	.10
55	Takeo Spikes	.10
56	Troy Aikman	1.50
57	Eric Bjornson	.10
58	*Greg Ellis*	.20
59	Michael Irwin	.20
60	Daryl Johnston	.10
61	David LaFleur	.10
62	Deion Sanders	.50
63	Emmitt Smith	2.50
64	Jason Garrett	.10
65	Nicky Sualua	.10
66	Steve Atwater	.10
67	Terrell Davis	1.50
68	John Elway	1.50
69	*Brian Griese*	5.00
70	Ed McCaffrey	.10
71	John Mobley	.10
72	*Marcus Nash*	2.00
73	Shannon Sharpe	.20
74	Neil Smith	.10
75	Rod Smith	.20
76	*Charlie Batch*	4.00
77	*Germane Crowell*	3.00
78	Jason Hanson	.10
79	Scott Mitchell	.10
80	Herman Moore	.20
81	Johnnie Morton	.10
82	Barry Sanders	3.00
83	Tommy Vardell	.10
84	Robert Brooks	.10
85	Gilbert Brown	.10
86	Leroy Butler	.10
87	Mark Chmura	.20
88	Brett Favre	3.00
89	Antonio Freeman	.20
90	William Henderson	.10
91	*Vonnie Holliday*	.20
92	Dorsey Levens	.20
93	Reggie White	.20
94	Aaron Bailey	.10
95	Quentin Coryatt	.10
96	Zack Crockett	.10
97	Ken Dilger	.10
98	Marshall Faulk	.20
99	*E.G. Green*	.20
100	Marvin Harrison	.20
101	*Peyton Manning*	12.00
102	Jerome Pathon	.10
103	*Tavian Banks*	3.00
104	Tony Boselli	.10
105	Tony Brackens	.10
106	Mark Brunell	1.25
107	Kevin Hardy	.10
108	Keenan McCardell	.10
109	Pete Mitchell	.10
110	Jimmy Smith	.20
111	James Stewart	.20
112	*Fred Taylor*	6.00
113	Kimble Anders	.10
114	Dale Carter	.10
115	Tony Gonzalez	.10
116	Elvis Grbac	.10
117	Donnell Bennett	.10
118	Andre Rison	.10
119	*Rashaan Shehee*	.50
120	Derrick Thomas	.20
121	Tamarick Vanover	.10
122	Karim Abdul-Jabbar	.30
123	*John Avery*	2.50
124	Troy Drayton	.10
125	John Dutton	.10
126	Craig Erickson	.10
127	Dan Marino	2.50
128	O.J. McDuffie	.10
129	Jerris McPhail	.10
130	Stanley Pritchett	.10
131	Larry Shannon	.10
132	Zach Thomas	.20
133	Cris Carter	.20
134	Randall Cunningham	.20
135	Andrew Glover	.10
136	Brad Johnson	.20
137	Randall McDaniel	.10
138	David Palmer	.10
139	John Randle	.10
140	Jake Reed	.10
141	Robert Smith	.20
142	Drew Bledsoe	1.25
143	Ben Coates	.10
144	*Robert Edwards*	3.00
145	Terry Glenn	.30
146	Shawn Jefferson	.10
147	Willie McGinest	.10
148	Tony Simmons	.10
149	Chris Slade	.10
150	Troy Davis	.10
151	Mark Fields	.10
152	Andre Hastings	.10
153	Billy Joe Hobert	.10
154	William Roaf	.10
155	Heath Shuler	.10
156	Danny Wuerffel	.10
157	Ray Zellars	.10
158	Jessie Armstead	.10
159	Tiki Barber	.20
160	Chris Calloway	.10
161	Mike Cherry	.10
162	Danny Kanell	.10
163	Amani Toomer	.10
164	Charles Way	.10
165	Tyrone Wheatley	.10
166	Kyle Brady	.10
167	Wayne Chrebet	.10
168	Glenn Foley	.20
169	*Scott Frost*	.20
170	Keyshawn Johnson	.20
171	Leon Johnson	.10
172	Alex Van Dyke	.10
173	Dedric Ward	.10
174	Tim Brown	.20
175	Rickey Dudley	.10
176	Jeff George	.20
177	Desmond Howard	.10
178	James Jett	.10
179	Napoleon Kaufman	.50
180	Darrell Russell	.10
181	*Charles Woodson*	3.00
182	Jason Dunn	.10
183	Irving Fryar	.10
184	Charlie Garner	.20
185	Bobby Hoying	.10
186	Chris T. Jones	.10
187	Michael Timpson	.10
188	Kevin Turner	.10
189	Jerome Bettis	.20
190	Will Blackwell	.10
191	Mark Bruener	.10
192	Charles Johnson	.10
193	George Jones	.10
194	Levon Kirkland	.10
195	Kordell Stewart	1.25
196	*Hines Ward*	2.00
197	Tony Banks	.20
198	Isaac Bruce	.20
199	Ernie Conwell	.10
200	*Robert Holcombe*	3.00
201	Eddie Kennison	.20
202	Amp Lee	.10
203	Orlando Pace	.10
204	Charlie Jones	.10
205	Freddie Jones	.10
206	*Ryan Leaf*	3.00
207	Natrone Means	.20
208	Junior Seau	.20
209	Bryan Still	.10
210	Greg Clark	.10
211	Jim Druckenmiller	.20
212	Marc Edwards	.10
213	Garrison Hearst	.20
214	Terrell Owens	.20
215	Jerry Rice	1.50
216	J.J. Stokes	.10
217	Bryant Young	.10
218	Steve Young	1.00
219	Chad Brown	.10
220	Joey Galloway	.30
221	Cortez Kennedy	.10
222	Jon Kitna	.10
223	James McKnight	.10
224	Warren Moon	.20
225	Michael Sinclair	.10
226	Ricky Watters	.20
227	Mike Alstott	.30
228	Reidel Anthony	.20
229	Derrick Brooks	.10
230	Trent Dilfer	.20
231	Warrick Dunn	2.00
232	Dave Moore	.10
233	Hardy Nickerson	.10
234	Warren Sapp	.10
235	Karl Williams	.10
236	Willie Davis	.10
237	*Kevin Dyson*	2.00
238	Eddie George	1.25
239	Derrick Mason	.10
240	Steve McNair	.75
241	Chris Sanders	.10
242	Frank Wycheck	.10
243	Terry Allen	.10
244	Jamie Asher	.10
245	Gus Frerotte	.10
246	Darrell Green	.10
247	*Skip Hicks*	1.50
248	Brian Mitchell	.10
249	Leslie Shepherd	.10
250	Michael Westbrook	.10

1998 Pacific Omega EO Portraits

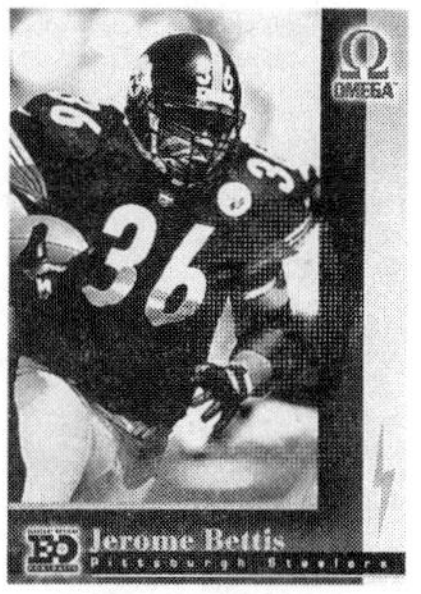

EO Portraits is a 20-card insert seeded 1:73. The cards feature a color player photo with a closeup photo of the player's face laser-cut into the card. A hoobby-only parallel version is numbered to one.

		MT
Complete Set (20):		350.00
Common Player:		10.00
Inserted 1:73		
1	Jake Plummer	25.00
2	Corey Dillon	15.00
3	Troy Aikman	25.00
4	Emmitt Smith	40.00
5	Terrell Davis	25.00
6	John Elway	25.00
7	Barry Sanders	50.00
8	Brett Favre	50.00
9	Dorsey Levens	10.00
10	Peyton Manning	40.00
11	Mark Brunell	20.00
12	Dan Marino	40.00
13	Drew Bledsoe	20.00
14	Jerome Bettis	10.00
15	Kordell Stewart	20.00
16	Ryan Leaf	25.00
17	Jerry Rice	25.00
18	Steve Young	15.00
19	Warrick Dunn	25.00
20	Eddie George	20.00

1998 Pacific Omega Face To Face

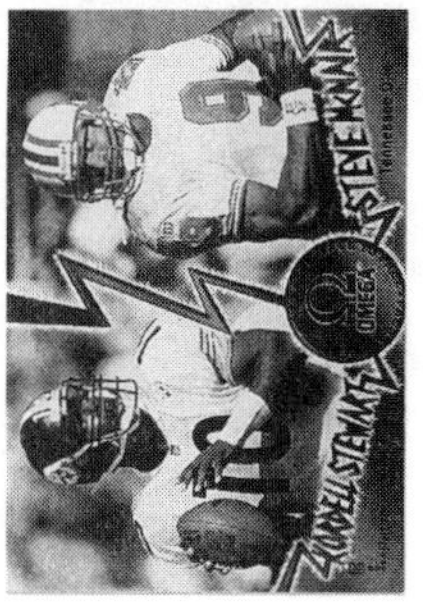

Face To Face is a 10-card insert seeded 1:145. The cards have a horizontal layout and feature two NFL stars on the front.

		MT
Complete Set (10):		300.00
Common Player:		20.00
Inserted 1:145		
1	Peyton Manning, Ryan Leaf	40.00
2	Barry Sanders, Warrick Dunn	50.00
3	Dan Marino, John Elway	40.00
4	Jerry Rice, Antonio Freeman	25.00
5	Jake Plummer, Drew Bledsoe	25.00
6	Corey Dillon, Eddie George	20.00
7	Emmitt Smith, Terrell Davis	40.00
8	Steve Young, Mark Brunell	25.00
9	Kordell Stewart, Steve McNair	25.00
10	Troy Aikman, Brett Favre	50.00

1998 Pacific Omega Online

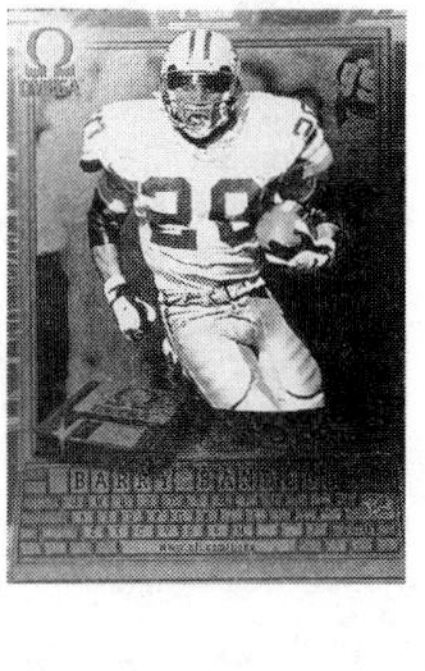

Online is a 36-card insert seeded 4:37. The card is designed to resemble a computer, with the color player photo on the monitor. The player's name, position, team logo and team web page appear on the keyboard at the bottom.

		MT
Complete Set (36):		200.00
Common Player:		2.00
Inserted 4:37		
1	Jake Plummer	10.00
2	Antowain Smith	5.00
3	Curtis Enis	10.00
4	Corey Dillon	6.00
5	Troy Aikman	10.00
6	Emmitt Smith	15.00
7	Terrell Davis	10.00
8	John Elway	10.00
9	Shannon Sharpe	2.00
10	Herman Moore	2.00
11	Barry Sanders	20.00
12	Brett Favre	20.00
13	Antonio Freeman	2.00
14	Dorsey Levens	2.00
15	Peyton Manning	20.00
16	Marshall Faulk	2.00
17	Mark Brunell	8.00
18	Fred Taylor	6.00
19	Dan Marino	15.00
20	Robert Smith	2.00
21	Drew Bledsoe	8.00
22	Tiki Barber	2.00
23	Danny Kanell	2.00
24	Tim Brown	2.00
25	Napoleon Kaufman	5.00
26	Charles Woodson	10.00
27	Jerome Bettis	2.00
28	Kordell Stewart	8.00
29	Ryan Leaf	7.00
30	Jerry Rice	10.00
31	Steve Young	6.00
32	Joey Galloway	2.00
33	Trent Dilfer	2.00
34	Warrick Dunn	10.00
35	Eddie George	8.00
36	Steve McNair	5.00

1998 Pacific Omega Prisms

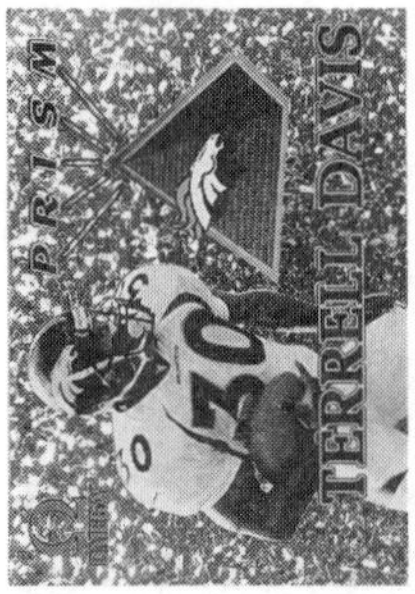

Prism is a 20-card insert seeded one per 37 packs. The cards have a horizontal layout on prismatic foil. A color player photo is on the left with a pyramid and team logo on the right.

		MT
Complete Set (20):		200.00
Common Player:		1.50
Inserted 1:37		
1	Jake Plummer	12.00
2	Corey Dillon	8.00
3	Troy Aikman	12.00
4	Emmitt Smith	20.00
5	Terrell Davis	12.00
6	John Elway	12.00
7	Barry Sanders	25.00
8	Brett Favre	25.00
9	Peyton Manning	25.00
10	Mark Brunell	10.00
11	Dan Marino	20.00
12	Drew Bledsoe	10.00
13	Napoleon Kaufman	6.00
14	Jerome Bettis	1.50
15	Kordell Stewart	10.00
16	Ryan Leaf	10.00
17	Jerry Rice	12.00
18	Steve Young	8.00
19	Warrick Dunn	12.00
20	Eddie George	10.00

1998 Pacific Omega Rising Stars

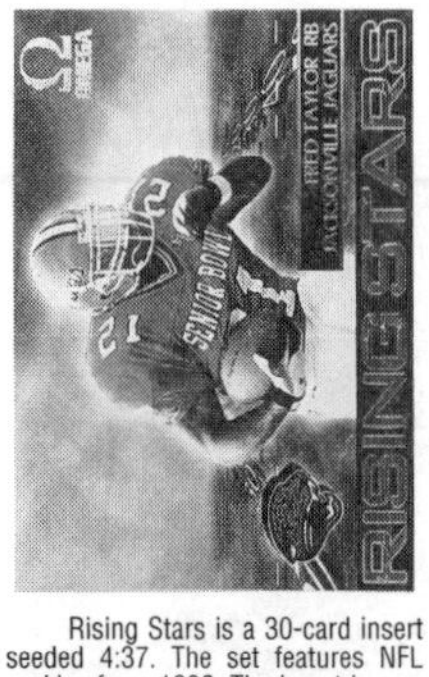

Rising Stars is a 30-card insert seeded 4:37. The set features NFL rookies from 1998. The insert is paralleled five times, each with a different foil color. The blue foil parallel is numbered to 100, red to 75, green to 50, purple to 25 and gold to one.

		MT
Complete Set (30):		90.00
Common Player:		2.00
Inserted 4:37 Hobby		
1	Michael Pittman	2.00
2	Keith Brooking	2.00
3	Duane Starks	2.00
4	Curtis Enis	10.00
5	Marcus Nash	5.00
6	Brian Griese	6.00
7	Terry Fair	2.00
8	Germane Crowell	5.00
9	Charlie Batch	5.00
10	E.G. Green	2.00
11	Peyton Manning	20.00
12	Jerome Pathon	2.00
13	Fred Taylor	8.00
14	Tavian Banks	6.00
15	Rashaan Shehee	4.00
16	John Avery	5.00
17	John Dutton	2.00
18	Robert Edwards	5.00
19	Tony Simmons	4.00
20	Joe Jurevicius	4.00
21	Scott Frost	2.00
22	Charles Woodson	8.00
23	Hines Ward	5.00
24	Robert Holcombe	6.00
25	Az-Zahir Hakim	2.00
26	Ryan Leaf	6.00
27	Ahman Green	6.00
28	Kevin Dyson	5.00
29	Stephen Alexander	2.00
30	Skip Hicks	5.00

1998 Pacific Paramount

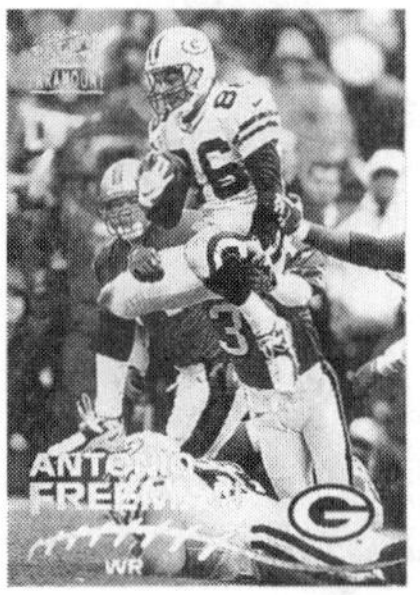

Paramount Football consists of a 250-card base set with three parallels and four inserts. The base cards feature full-bleed photos with the player's name, position and team logo at the bottom. The regular cards have Copper, Silver and Platinum Blue parallels. Inserts include Pro Bowl Die-Cuts, Super Bowl XXXII Highlights, Personal Bests and Kings of the NFL.

		MT
Complete Set (250):		40.00
Common Player:		.10
Minor Stars:		.20
Copper/Silver Cards:		2x-4x
Platinum Blue Cards:		40x-80x
Pack (6):		1.50
Wax Box (36):		50.00
1	Larry Centers	.10
2	Chris Gedney	.10
3	Rob Moore	.10
4	Jake Plummer	1.00
5	Simeon Rice	.10
6	Frank Sanders	.10
7	Mark Smith	.10
8	Eric Swann	.10
9	Jamal Anderson	.20
10	Chris Chandler	.10
11	Bert Emanuel	.10
12	Tony Graziani	.10
13	Byron Hanspard	.20
14	Terance Mathis	.10
15	O.J. Santiago	.10
16	Chuck Smith	.10
17	Derrick Alexander	.10
18	Peter Boulware	.10
19	Jay Graham	.10
20	*Priest Holmes*	7.00
21	Michael Jackson	.10
22	Bam Morris	.10
23	Vinny Testaverde	.20
24	Eric Zeier	.10
25	Todd Collins	.10
26	Quinn Early	.10
27	Bryce Paup	.10
28	Andre Reed	.10
29	Jay Riemersma	.10
30	Antowain Smith	.50
31	Bruce Smith	.10
32	Thurman Thomas	.20
33	Michael Bates	.10
34	Mark Carrier	.10
35	Rae Carruth	.20
36	Kerry Collins	.30
37	Fred Lane	.10
38	Lamar Lathon	.10
39	Muhsin Muhammad	.10
40	Wesley Walls	.10
41	Darnell Autry	.20
42	Curtis Conway	.20
43	Raymont Harris	.20
44	Tyrone Hughes	.10
45	Chris Penn	.10
46	Ricky Proehl	.10
47	Steve Stenstrom	.10
48	Ryan Wetnight	.10
49	Jeff Blake	.20
50	Ki-Jana Carter	.10
51	Corey Dillon	.75
52	David Dunn	.10
53	Boomer Esiason	.10
54	Brian Milne	.10
55	Carl Pickens	.20
56	Darnay Scott	.10
57	Troy Aikman	1.00
58	Eric Bjornson	.10
59	Michael Irvin	.20
60	Daryl Johnston	.10
61	Anthony Miller	.10
62	Deion Sanders	.40
63	Emmitt Smith	1.50
64	Omar Stoutmire	.10
65	Sherman Williams	.10
66	Terrell Davis	1.25
67	John Elway	1.00
68	Darrien Gordon	.10
69	Ed McCaffrey	.10
70	Bill Romanowski	.10
71	Shannon Sharpe	.20
72	Neil Smith	.10
73	Rod Smith	.20
74	Maa Tanuvasa	.10
75	Tommie Boyd	.10
76	Glyn Milburn	.10
77	Scott Mitchell	.10
78	Herman Moore	.20
79	Johnnie Morton	.10
80	Robert Porcher	.10
81	Barry Sanders	1.50
82	Bryant Westbrook	.10
83	Robert Brooks	.10
84	LeRoy Butler	.10
85	Mark Chmura	.20
86	Brett Favre	2.00
87	Antonio Freeman	.20
88	Dorsey Levens	.20
89	Eugene Robinson	.10
90	*Bill Schroeder*	6.00
91	Reggie White	.20
92	Aaron Bailey	.10
93	Quentin Coryatt	.10
94	Zack Crockett	.10
95	Sean Dawkins	.10
96	Ken Dilger	.10
97	Marshall Faulk	.20
98	Jim Harbaugh	.10
99	Marvin Harrison	.20
100	Bryan Barker	.10
101	Tony Boselli	.10
102	Tony Brackens	.10
103	Mark Brunell	1.00
104	Mike Hollis	.10
105	Keenan McCardell	.10
106	Natrone Means	.20
107	Jimmy Smith	.10
108	James Stewart	.10
109	Marcus Allen	.20
110	Kimble Anders	.10
111	Dale Carter	.10
112	Tony Gonzalez	.20
113	Elvis Grbac	.20
114	Greg Hill	.10
115	Andre Rison	.10
116	Will Shields	.10
117	Derrick Thomas	.10
118	Karim Abdul-Jabbar	.30
119	Trace Armstrong	.10
120	*Damon Huard*	10.00
121	Charles Jordan	.10
122	Dan Marino	1.50
123	O.J. McDuffie	.10
124	Irving Spikes	.10
125	Zach Thomas	.10
126	Cris Carter	.10
127	*Charles Woodson*	3.00
128	Brad Johnson	.20
129	Randall McDaniel	.10
130	John Randle	.10
131	Jake Reed	.10
132	Robert Smith	.10
133	Todd Steussie	.10
134	Bruce Armstrong	.10
135	Drew Bledsoe	1.00
136	Ben Coates	.10
137	Derrick Cullors	.10
138	Terry Glenn	.30
139	Shawn Jefferson	.10
140	Curtis Martin	.75
141	Chris Slade	.10
142	Larry Whigham	.10
143	Troy Davis	.20
144	Andre Hastings	.10
145	Randal Hill	.10
146	Sammy Knight	.10
147	William Roaf	.10
148	Heath Shuler	.10
149	Danny Wuerffel	.20
150	Ray Zellars	.10
151	Jessie Armstead	.10
152	Tiki Barber	.40
153	Chris Calloway	.10
154	Danny Kanell	.10
155	David Patten	.10
156	Michael Strahan	.10
157	Charles Way	.10
158	Tyrone Wheatley	.10
159	Kyle Brady	.10
160	Wayne Chrebet	.10
161	Glenn Foley	.10
162	Aaron Glenn	.10
163	Leon Johnson	.10
164	Adrian Murrell	.20
165	Neil O'Donnell	.10
166	Dedric Ward	.10
167	Tim Brown	.20
168	Rickey Dudley	.10
169	Jeff George	.20
170	Desmond Howard	.10
171	James Jett	.10
172	Napoleon Kaufman	.20
173	Chester McGlockton	.10
174	Darrell Russell	.10
175	Ty Detmer	.10
176	Irving Fryar	.10
177	Charlie Garner	.10
178	Bobby Hoying	.10
179	Chad Lewis	.10
180	Duce Staley	.10
181	Kevin Turner	.10
182	Ricky Watters	.20
183	Jerome Bettis	.20
184	Will Blackwell	.10
185	Charles Johnson	.10
186	George Jones	.10
187	Levon Kirkland	.10
188	Carnell Lake	.10
189	Kordell Stewart	1.00
190	Yancey Thigpen	.10
191	Tony Banks	.30
192	Isaac Bruce	.20
193	Ernie Conwell	.10
194	Craig Heyward	.10
195	Eddie Kennison	.20
196	Amp Lee	.10
197	Orlando Pace	.10
198	Torrance Small	.10
199	Gary Brown	.10
200	Kenny Bynum	.10
201	Freddie Jones	.10
202	Tony Martin	.10
203	Eric Metcalf	.10
204	Junior Seau	.20
205	Craig Whelihan	.10
206	William Floyd	.20
207	Merton Hanks	.10
208	Garrison Hearst	.10
209	Brent Jones	.10
210	Terrell Owens	.20
211	Jerry Rice	1.00
212	J.J. Stokes	.10
213	Rod Woodson	.10
214	Steve Young	.50
215	Steve Broussard	.10
216	Joey Galloway	.20
217	Cortez Kennedy	.10
218	Jon Kitna	.10
219	James McKnight	.10
220	Warren Moon	.20
221	Michael Sinclair	.10
222	*Ryan Leaf*	3.00
223	Darryl Williams	.10
224	Mike Alstott	.30
225	Reidel Anthony	.20
226	Derrick Brooks	.10
227	Horace Copeland	.10
228	Trent Dilfer	.20
229	Warrick Dunn	1.00
230	Hardy Nickerson	.10
231	Warren Sapp	.10
232	Karl Williams	.10
233	Blaine Bishop	.10
234	Willie Davis	.10
235	Eddie George	1.25
236	Derrick Mason	.10
237	Bruce Matthews	.10
238	Steve McNair	.75
239	Chris Sanders	.10
240	Rodney Thomas	.10
241	Frank Wycheck	.10
242	Terry Allen	.10
243	Jamie Asher	.10
244	Larry Bowie	.10
245	Albert Connell	.10
246	Stephen Davis	.10
247	Gus Frerotte	.10
248	Ken Harvey	.10
249	Leslie Shepherd	.10
250	Michael Westbrook	.10

1998 Pacific Paramount Copper/Silver

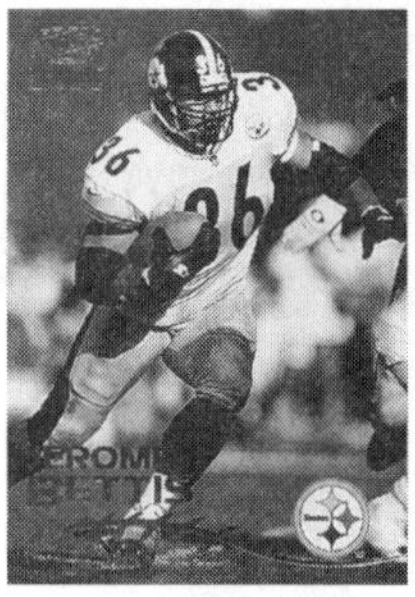

The 250-card base set is paralleled in the Copper hobby-only and Silver retail-only sets (1:1).

	MT
Copper/Silver Cards:	2x-4x

1998 Pacific Paramount Platinum Blue

Platinum Blue is a full parallel of the Paramount base set, seeded one per 73 packs.

	MT
Platinum Blue Cards:	40x-80x

1998 Pacific Paramount Kings of the NFL

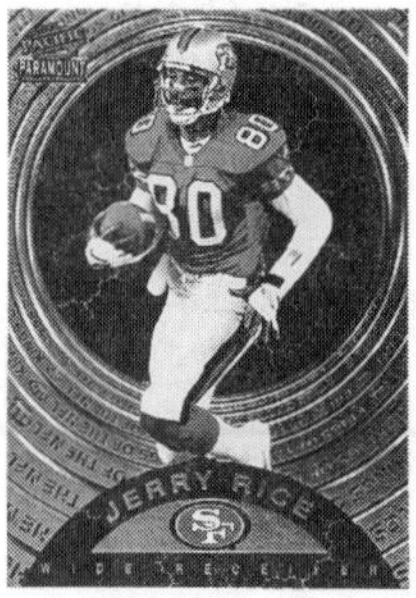

Kings of the NFL is a fully-foiled 20-card insert seeded one per 73 packs. The cards have a color photo with the player's name, position and team logo at the bottom.

		MT
Complete Set (20):		450.00
Common Player:		7.00
1	Antowain Smith	15.00
2	Corey Dillon	20.00
3	Troy Aikman	30.00
4	Emmitt Smith	50.00
5	Terrell Davis	30.00
6	John Elway	30.00
7	Barry Sanders	50.00
8	Brett Favre	60.00
9	Dorsey Levens	7.00
10	Reggie White	7.00
11	Mark Brunell	30.00
12	Dan Marino	50.00
13	Curtis Martin	20.00
14	Drew Bledsoe	30.00
15	Jerome Bettis	7.00
16	Kordell Stewart	30.00
17	Jerry Rice	30.00
18	Steve Young	20.00
19	Warrick Dunn	30.00
20	Eddie George	30.00

1998 Pacific Paramount Personal Bests

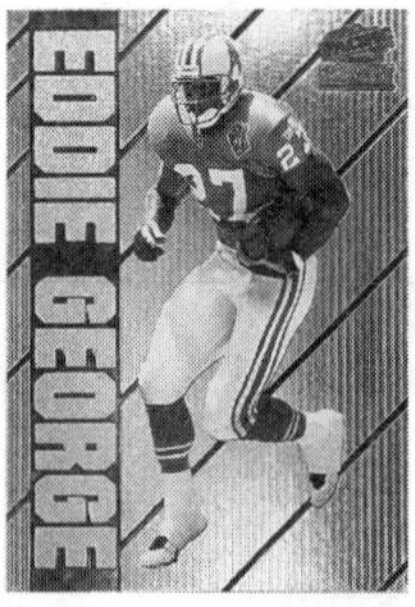

Personal Bests is a 36-card insert seeded 4:37. The cards have a color player photo on holographic silver foil. The player's name is printed vertically on the left.

		MT
Complete Set (36):		100.00
Common Player:		1.50
1	Jake Plummer	8.00
2	Antowain Smith	5.00
3	Kerry Collins	4.00
4	Raymont Harris	1.50
5	Corey Dillon	6.00
6	Troy Aikman	8.00
7	Deion Sanders	4.00
8	Emmitt Smith	10.00
9	Terrell Davis	8.00
10	John Elway	8.00
11	Shannon Sharpe	1.50
12	Herman Moore	1.50
13	Barry Sanders	12.00
14	Brett Favre	16.00
15	Antonio Freeman	1.50
16	Dorsey Levens	1.50
17	Marshall Faulk	1.50
18	Mark Brunell	8.00
19	Dan Marino	10.00
20	Robert Smith	1.50
21	Curtis Martin	6.00
22	Drew Bledsoe	8.00
23	Danny Kanell	1.50
24	Adrian Murrell	1.50
25	Napoleon Kaufman	4.00
26	Jerome Bettis	1.50
27	Kordell Stewart	8.00
28	Terrell Owens	1.50
29	Jerry Rice	8.00
30	Steve Young	5.00
31	Warren Moon	1.50
32	Mike Alstott	4.00
33	Trent Dilfer	1.50
34	Warrick Dunn	8.00
35	Eddie George	8.00
36	Steve McNair	6.00

1998 Pacific Paramount Pro Bowl Die-Cuts

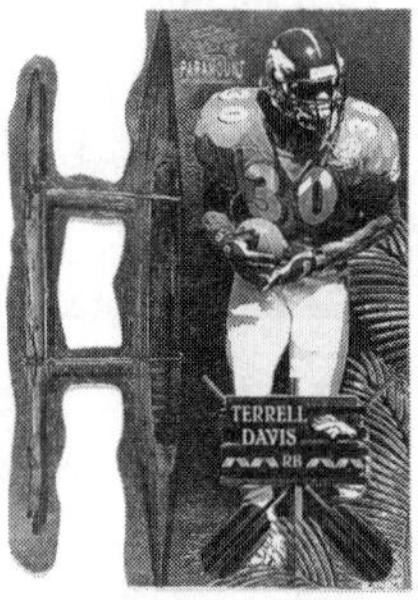

Pro Bowl Die-Cuts is a 20-card insert featuring players in their uniforms from the 1998 Pro Bowl. The background has a Hawaiian theme and the left side of the card features a die-cut outrigger. This set was inserted 1:37.

		MT
Complete Set (20):		200.00
Common Player:		4.00
1	Terrell Davis	20.00
2	John Elway	20.00
3	Shannon Sharpe	4.00
4	Herman Moore	4.00
5	Barry Sanders	30.00
6	Mark Chmura	4.00
7	Brett Favre	40.00
8	Dorsey Levens	4.00
9	Mark Brunell	20.00
10	Andre Rison	4.00
11	Cris Carter	4.00
12	Drew Bledsoe	20.00
13	Ben Coates	4.00
14	Jerome Bettis	4.00
15	Steve Young	10.00
16	Warren Moon	4.00
17	Mike Alstott	10.00
18	Trent Dilfer	4.00
19	Warrick Dunn	20.00
20	Eddie George	20.00

1998 Pacific Paramount Super Bowl XXXII Highlights

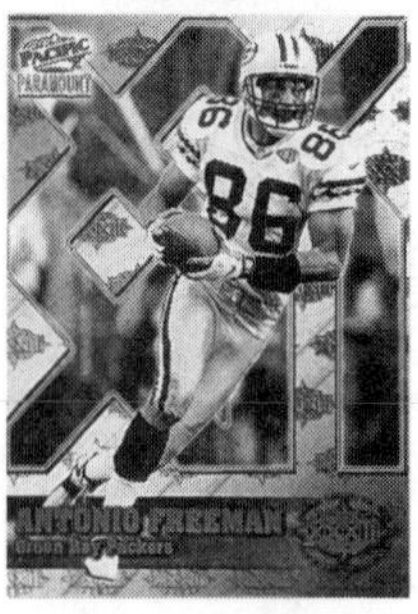

Super Bowl XXXII Highlights is a 10-card insert seeded two per 37 packs. The cards feature photography from the Super Bowl.

		MT
Complete Set (10):		40.00
Common Player:		2.00
1	Terrell Davis	8.00
2	John Elway	8.00
3	John Elway	8.00
4	Brett Favre	12.00
5	Antonio Freeman	4.00
6	Dorsey Levens	4.00
7	Ed McCaffrey	2.00
8	Eugene Robinson	2.00
9	Bill Romanowski	2.00
10	Darren Sharper	2.00

1998 Pacific Revolution

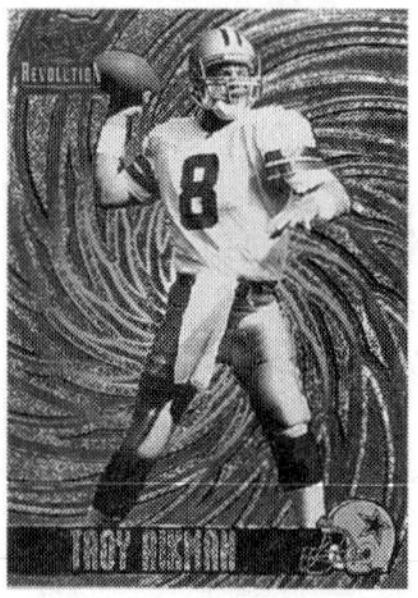

Pacific Revolution Football consists of a 150-card base set with one parallel and five inserts. The base cards feature a color player photo with a swirled foil background. The cards are etched and embossed. The player's name and his team helmet are featured on a black bar on the bottom. The base set is paralleled by Shadow Series. The inserts include Icons, Prime Time Performers, Rookies & Stars, Showstoppers and Touchdown Laser-Cuts.

		MT
Complete Set (150):		125.00
Common Player:		.25
Minor Stars:		.50
Shadow Cards:		10x-20x
Shadow Rookies:		5x-10x
Production 99 Sets		
Pack (3):		4.00
Wax Box (24):		80.00
1	Larry Centers	.25
2	Leeland McElroy	.25
3	Rob Moore	.25
4	Jake Plummer	5.00
5	Frank Sanders	.25
6	Jamal Anderson	.25
7	Chris Chandler	.25
8	Byron Hanspard	.25
9	Jay Graham	.25
10	Michael Jackson	.25
11	Vinny Testaverde	.25
12	Eric Zeier	.25
13	Todd Collins	.25
14	Quinn Early	.25
15	Andre Reed	.25
16	Antowain Smith	2.00
17	Bruce Smith	.25
18	Thurman Thomas	.50
19	Rae Carruth	.50
20	Kerry Collins	.50
21	Wesley Walls	.25
22	Darnell Autry	.50
23	Curtis Conway	.50
24	Bobby Engram	.25
25	*Curtis Enis*	6.00
26	Raymont Harris	.25
27	Jeff Blake	.50
28	Corey Dillon	3.00
29	Carl Pickens	.25
30	Darnay Scott	.25
31	Troy Aikman	5.00
32	Michael Irvin	.50
33	Deion Sanders	2.00
34	Emmitt Smith	8.00
35	Steve Atwater	.25

36 Terrell Davis 5.00
37 John Elway 4.00
38 *Brian Griese* 7.00
39 Ed McCaffrey .25
40 *Marcus Nash* 3.00
41 Shannon Sharpe .25
42 Neil Smith .25
43 Rod Smith .25
44 *Charlie Batch* 7.00
45 *Germane Crowell* 5.00
46 Scott Mitchell .25
47 Herman Moore .50
48 Barry Sanders 7.00
49 Robert Brooks .25
50 Mark Chmura .25
51 Brett Favre 10.00
52 Antonio Freeman .50
53 Dorsey Levens .50
54 Sean Dawkins .25
55 Ken Dilger .25
56 Marshall Faulk .50
57 Marvin Harrison .50
58 *Peyton Manning* 20.00
59 *Tavian Banks* 5.00
60 Tony Brackens .25
61 Mark Brunell 4.00
62 Keenan McCardell .25
63 Natrone Means .50
64 Jimmy Smith .25
65 James Stewart .25
66 *Fred Taylor* 10.00
67 Tony Gonzalez .50
68 Elvis Grbac .25
69 Greg Hill .25
70 Andre Rison .25
71 Derrick Thomas .25
72 Karim Abdul-Jabbar .50
73 *John Avery* 4.00
74 Troy Drayton .25
75 Dan Marino 8.00
76 O.J. McDuffie .25
77 Cris Carter .25
78 Brad Johnson .50
79 John Randle .25
80 Jake Reed .25
81 Robert Smith .50
82 Drew Bledsoe 5.00
83 Ben Coates .25
84 *Robert Edwards* 6.00
85 Terry Glenn .50
86 *Tony Simmons* .25
87 Troy Davis .50
88 Heath Shuler .25
89 Danny Wuerffel .25
90 Ray Zellars .25
91 Tiki Barber 1.00
92 *Joe Jurevicius* 1.50
93 Danny Kanell .25
94 Charles Way .25
95 Tyrone Wheatley .25
96 Wayne Chrebet .25
97 Glenn Foley .50
98 Keyshawn Johnson .50
99 Curtis Martin 3.00
100 Tim Brown .50
101 Rickey Dudley .25
102 Jeff George .50
103 Desmond Howard .25
104 Napoleon Kaufman 1.50
105 *Charles Woodson* 5.00
106 Jason Dunn .25
107 Irving Fryar .25
108 Charlie Garner .25
109 Bobby Hoying .50
110 Jerome Bettis .50
111 Mark Bruener .25
112 Charles Johnson .25
113 Levon Kirkland .25
114 Kordell Stewart 5.00
115 *Hines Ward* 3.00
116 Tony Banks .50
117 Isaac Bruce .50
118 *Robert Holcombe* 5.00
119 Eddie Kennison .50
120 Freddie Jones .25
121 *Ryan Leaf* 5.00
122 Tony Martin .25
123 Junior Seau .50
124 Jim Druckenmiller .50
125 Garrison Hearst .25
126 Terrell Owens .50
127 Jerry Rice 5.00
128 J.J. Stokes .25
129 Steve Young 2.00
130 Joey Galloway .50
131 *Ahman Green* 6.00
132 Cortez Kennedy .25
133 Jon Kitna 3.00
134 James McKnight .25
135 Warren Moon .50
136 Mike Alstott 2.00
137 Reidel Anthony .50
138 Trent Dilfer .50
139 Warrick Dunn 5.00
140 Warren Sapp .25
141 *Kevin Dyson* 4.00
142 Eddie George 5.00
143 Steve McNair 2.00
144 Chris Sanders .25
145 Frank Wycheck .25
146 Stephen Alexander .25
147 Terry Allen .25
148 Gus Frerotte .25
149 *Skip Hicks* 3.00
150 Michael Westbrook .25

1998 Pacific Revolution Icons

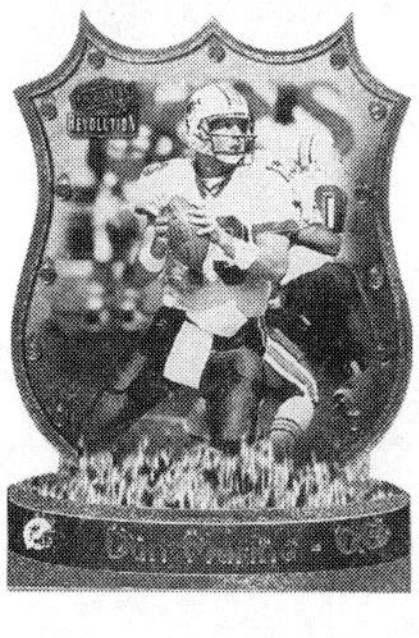

Icons is a 10-card insert seeded one per 121 packs. The cards have a die-cut design resembling the NFL's shield logo.

	MT
Complete Set (10):	500.00
Common Player:	30.00

1 Emmitt Smith 85.00
2 Terrell Davis 50.00
3 John Elway 40.00
4 Barry Sanders 80.00
5 Brett Favre 100.00
6 Mark Brunell 30.00
7 Dan Marino 85.00
8 Jerry Rice 50.00
9 Warrick Dunn 50.00
10 Eddie George 50.00

1998 Pacific Revolution Prime Time Performers

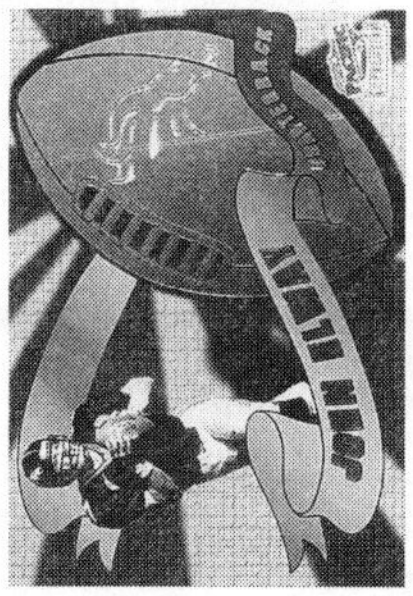

Prime Time Performers is a 20-card insert seeded 1:25. The cards feature a small player photo on the left and a football with the team's logo laser-cut on the right. The cards have a horizontal layout.

	MT
Complete Set (20):	275.00
Common Player:	7.00

1 Jake Plummer 16.00
2 Corey Dillon 12.00
3 Troy Aikman 16.00
4 Deion Sanders 10.00
5 Emmitt Smith 25.00
6 Terrell Davis 16.00
7 John Elway 16.00
8 Barry Sanders 30.00
9 Brett Favre 30.00
10 Peyton Manning 25.00
11 Mark Brunell 16.00
12 Dan Marino 30.00
13 Drew Bledsoe 16.00
14 Jerome Bettis 7.00
15 Kordell Stewart 16.00
16 Jerry Rice 16.00
17 Steve Young 10.00
18 Warrick Dunn 16.00
19 Eddie George 16.00
20 Steve McNair 10.00

1998 Pacific Revolution Rookies and Stars

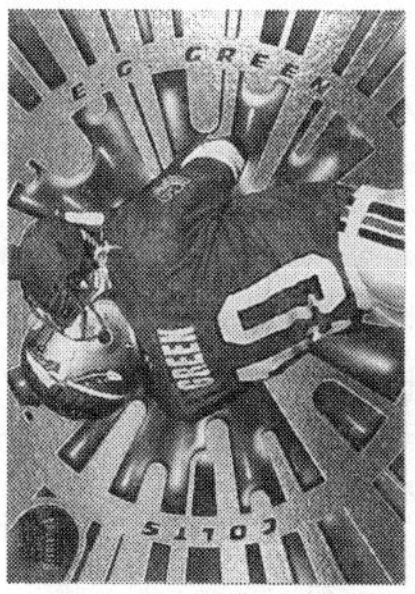

Rookies & Stars is a 30-card hobby-only insert. Seeded 4:25, the set features 20 rookies and 10 established stars. A gold parallel version was also produced. The parallel cards are numbered to 50.

	MT
Complete Set (30):	150.00
Common Player:	1.50
Minor Stars:	3.00
Inserted 4:25 Hobby	
Gold Cards:	8x-16x
Production 50 Sets	

1 Michael Pittman 1.50
2 Curtis Enis 5.00
3 Takeo Spikes 1.50
4 Greg Ellis 3.00
5 Emmitt Smith 10.00
6 Terrell Davis 8.00
7 John Elway 8.00
8 Brian Griese 4.00
9 Marcus Nash 3.00
10 Charlie Batch 6.00
11 Barry Sanders 15.00
12 Brett Favre 15.00
13 Vonnie Holliday 3.00
14 E.G. Green 1.50
15 Peyton Manning 12.00
16 Fred Taylor 6.00
17 John Avery 3.00
18 Dan Marino 10.00
19 Drew Bledsoe 6.00
20 Robert Edwards 6.00
21 Joe Jurevicius 1.50
22 Charles Woodson 6.00
23 Kordell Stewart 6.00
24 Robert Holcombe 4.00
25 Ryan Leaf 6.00
26 Warrick Dunn 6.00
27 Jacquez Green 4.00
28 Kevin Dyson 3.00
29 Eddie George 6.00
30 Stephen Alexander 1.50

1998 Pacific Revolution Shadows

Shadows are a full parallel of the Revolution base set. The parallel cards are numbered to 99.

	MT
Shadow Cards:	10x-20x
Shadow Rookies:	5x-10x

1998 Pacific Revolution Showstoppers

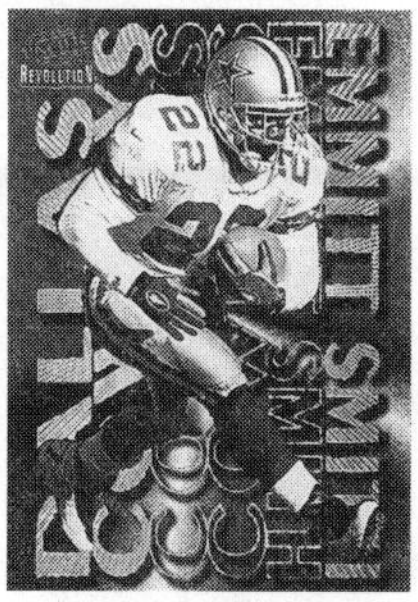

Showstoppers is a 36-card insert seeded two per 25 packs. The background features the player's name and team name printed in holographic silver foil.

	MT
Complete Set (36):	250.00
Common Player:	2.00
Minor Stars:	4.00

1 Jake Plummer 15.00
2 Antowain Smith 7.00
3 Kerry Collins 4.00
4 Corey Dillon 10.00
5 Troy Aikman 15.00
6 Deion Sanders 7.00
7 Emmitt Smith 30.00
8 Terrell Davis 15.00
9 John Elway 12.00
10 Shannon Sharpe 2.00
11 Herman Moore 4.00
12 Barry Sanders 25.00
13 Brett Favre 35.00
14 Antonio Freeman 4.00
15 Dorsey Levens 4.00
16 Peyton Manning 15.00
17 Mark Brunell 12.00
18 Dan Marino 30.00
19 Robert Smith 2.00
20 Drew Bledsoe 15.00
21 Danny Kanell 2.00
22 Curtis Martin 12.00
23 Tim Brown 2.00
24 Napoleon Kaufman 6.00
25 Jerome Bettis 4.00
26 Kordell Stewart 15.00
27 Ryan Leaf 10.00
28 Terrell Owens 2.00
29 Jerry Rice 15.00
30 Steve Young 10.00
31 Ricky Watters 2.00
32 Mike Alstott 6.00
33 Trent Dilfer 2.00
34 Warrick Dunn 15.00
35 Eddie George 15.00
36 Steve McNair 8.00

1998 Pacific Revolution Touchdown

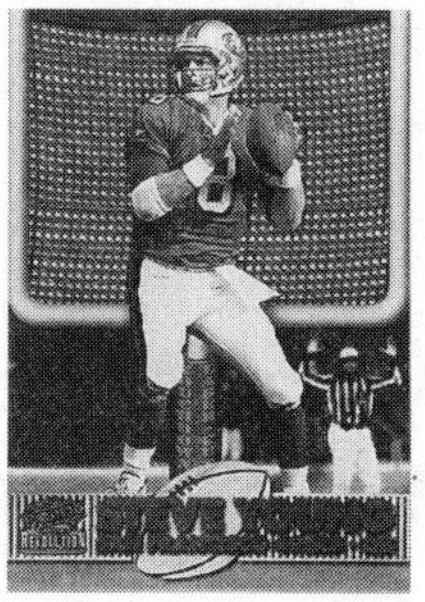

Touchdown Laser-Cuts is a 20-card insert seeded one per 49 packs. The cards have a color player photo in the foreground with a set of goal posts in the background. The netting behind the goal posts is laser-cut.

	MT
Complete Set (20):	250.00
Common Player:	7.00

1 Jake Plummer 15.00
2 Corey Dillon 10.00
3 Troy Aikman 15.00
4 Emmitt Smith 25.00
5 Terrell Davis 15.00
6 John Elway 12.50
7 Barry Sanders 25.00
8 Brett Favre 30.00
9 Dorsey Levens 7.00
10 Peyton Manning 25.00
11 Mark Brunell 12.50
12 Marcus Allen 7.00
13 Dan Marino 25.00
14 Drew Bledsoe 15.00
15 Jerome Bettis 7.00
16 Kordell Stewart 15.00
17 Jerry Rice 15.00
18 Steve Young 10.00
19 Warrick Dunn 15.00
20 Eddie George 15.00

1999 Pacific

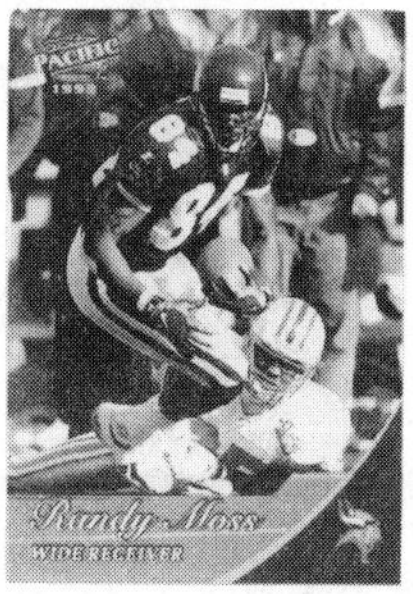

Pacific Football is a 450-card set that includes more than 30 unseeded rookie cards. Copper, Gold, Opening Day and Platinum Blue are the four different parallel sets. Other inserts include: Cramer's Choice, Dynagon Turf, Gold Crown Die Cuts, Pro Bowl Die Cuts, Record Breakers and Team Checklists.

	MT
Complete Set (450):	100.00
Common Player:	.15
Minor Stars:	.30
Common Rookie:	.50
Pack (12):	2.75
Wax Box (24):	60.00

1 Mario Bates .15
2 Larry Centers .15
3 Chris Gedney .15
4 Kwamie Lassiter .15
5 Johnny McWilliams .15
6 Eric Metcalf .15
7 Rob Moore .30
8 Adrian Murrell .15
9 Jake Plummer 1.00
10 Simeon Rice .15
11 Frank Sanders .30
12 Andre Wadsworth .30
13 Aeneas Williams .15
14 Michael Pittman, Ronnie Anderson .15
15 Morten Andersen .15
16 Jamal Anderson .50
17 Lester Archambeau .15
18 Chris Chandler .15
19 Bob Christian .15
20 Steve DeBerg .15
21 Tim Dwight .50
22 Tony Martin .15
23 Terance Mathis .15
24 Eugene Robinson .15
25 O.J. Santiago .15
26 Chuck Smith .15
27 Jessie Tuggle .15
28 Jammi German, Ken Oxendine .15
29 Peter Boulware .15
30 Jay Graham .15
31 Jim Harbaugh .30
32 Priest Holmes .75
33 Michael Jackson .15
34 Jermaine Lewis .15
35 Ray Lewis .15
36 Michael McCrary .15
37 Jonathan Ogden .15
38 Errict Rhett .15
39 James Roe .15
40 Floyd Turner .15
41 Rod Woodson .15
42 Eric Zeier .15
43 Wally Richardson, Patrick Johnson .15
44 Ruben Brown .15
45 Quinn Early .15
46 Doug Flutie .50
47 Sam Gash .15
48 Phil Hansen .15
49 Lonnie Johnson .15
50 Rob Johnson .30
51 Eric Moulds .50
52 Andre Reed .15
53 Jay Riemersma .15
54 Antowain Smith .30
55 Bruce Smith .15
56 Thurman Thomas .30
57 Ted Washington .15
58 Jonathon Linton, Kamil Loud .15
59 Michael Bates .15
60 Steve Beuerlein .15
61 Tshimanga Biakabutuka .15
62 Mark Carrier .15
63 Eric Davis .15
64 William Floyd .15
65 Sean Gilbert .15
66 Kevin Greene .15
67 Raghib Ismail .15
68 Anthony Johnson .15
69 Fred Lane .15
70 Muhsin Muhammad .15
71 Winslow Oliver .15
72 Wesley Walls .15
73 Dameyune Craig, Shane Matthews .15
74 Edgar Bennett .15
75 Curtis Conway .30
76 Bobby Engram .15
77 Curtis Enis .50
78 Ty Hallock .15
79 Walt Harris .15
80 Jeff Jaeger .15
81 Erik Kramer .15
82 Glyn Milburn .15
83 Chris Penn .15
84 Steve Stenstrom .15
85 Ryan Wetnight .15
86 Moses Moreno, James Allen .15
87 Ashley Ambrose .15
88 Brandon Bennett .15
89 Eric Bieniemy .15
90 Jeff Blake .30
91 Corey Dillon .50
92 Paul Justin .15
93 Eric Kresser .15
94 Tremain Mack .15
95 Tony McGee .15
96 Neil O'Donnell .15
97 Carl Pickens .30
98 Darnay Scott .15
99 Takeo Spikes .15
100 Ty Detmer .15
101 Chris Gardocki .15
102 Damon Gibson .15
103 Antonio Langham .15
104 Jerris McPhail .15
105 Irv Smith .15
106 Freddie Solomon .15
107 Scott Milanovich, Fred Brock .15
108 Troy Aikman 1.25
109 Larry Allen .15
110 Eric Bjornson .15
111 Billy Davis .15
112 Michael Irvin .30
113 David LaFleur .15
114 Ernie Mills .15
115 Nate Newton .15
116 Deion Sanders .50
117 Emmitt Smith 1.75
118 Chris Warren .15
119 Bubby Brister .15
120 Terrell Davis 2.00
121 Jason Elam .15
122 John Elway 2.00
123 Willie Green .15
124 Howard Griffith .15
125 Vaughn Hebron .15
126 Ed McCaffrey .30
127 John Mobley .15
128 Bill Romanowski .15
129 Shannon Sharpe .30
130 Neil Smith .15
131 Rod Smith .30
132 Brian Griese, Marcus Nash .50
133 Charlie Batch 1.00
134 Stephen Boyd .15
135 Mark Carrier .15
136 Germane Crowell .30
137 Terry Fair .15
138 Jason Hanson .15
139 Greg Jeffries .15
140 Herman Moore .30
141 Johnnie Morton .15
142 Robert Porcher .15
143 Ron Rivers .15
144 Barry Sanders 2.50
145 Tommy Vardell .15
146 Bryant Westbrook .15
147 Robert Brooks .15
148 LeRoy Butler .15
149 Mark Chmura .15
150 Tyrone Davis .15
151 Brett Favre 2.50
152 Antonio Freeman .50
153 Raymont Harris .15
154 Vonnie Holliday .30
155 Darick Holmes .15
156 Dorsey Levens .30
157 Brian Manning .15
158 Derrick Mayes .15
159 Roell Preston .15
160 Jeff Thomason .15
161 Tyrone Williams .15
162 Corey Bradford, Michael Blair .15
163 Aaron Bailey .15
164 Ken Dilger .15
165 Marshall Faulk .50
166 E.G. Green .30
167 Marvin Harrison .30
168 Craig Heyward .15
169 Peyton Manning 2.50
170 Jerome Pathon .30
171 Marcus Pollard .15
172 Torrance Small .15
173 Mike Vanderjagt .15
174 Lamont Warren .15
175 Tavian Banks .30
176 Reggie Barlow .15
177 Tony Boselli .15
178 Tony Brackens .15
179 Mark Brunell 1.00
180 Kevin Hardy .15
181 Damon Jones .15
182 Jamie Martin .15
183 Keenan McCardell .15
184 Pete Mitchell .15
185 Bryce Paup .15
186 Jimmy Smith .30
187 Fred Taylor 1.50
188 Alvis Whitted, Chris Howard .15
189 Derrick Alexander .15
190 Kimble Anders .15
191 Donnell Bennett .15
192 Dale Carter .15
193 Rich Gannon .15
194 Tony Gonzalez .15
195 Elvis Grbac .15
196 Joe Horn .15
197 Kevin Lockett .15
198 Bam Morris .15
199 Andre Rison .30
200 Derrick Thomas .15
201 Tamarick Vanover .15
202 Gregory Favors, Rashaan Shehee .15
203 Karim Abdul .30
204 Trace Armstrong .15
205 John Avery .30
206 Lorenzo Bromell .15
207 Terrell Buckley .15
208 Oronde Gadsden .30
209 Sam Madison .15
210 Dan Marino 1.75
211 O.J. McDuffie .15
212 Ed Perry .15
213 Jason Taylor .15
214 Lamar Thomas .15
215 Zach Thomas .30
216 Henry Lusk, Nate Jacquet .15
217 Damon Huard, Todd Doxzon .15
218 Gary Anderson .15
219 Cris Carter .50
220 Randall Cunningham .50
221 Andrew Glover .15
222 Matthew Hatchette .15
223 Brad Johnson .50
224 Ed McDaniel .15
225 Randall McDaniel .15
226 Randy Moss 4.00
227 David Palmer .15
228 John Randle .15
229 Jake Reed .15
230 Robert Smith .30
231 Todd Steussie .15
232 Stalin Colinet, Kivuusama Mays .15
233 *Jay Fiedler, Todd Bouman* 8.00
234 Drew Bledsoe 1.00
235 Troy Brown .15
236 Ben Coates .30
237 Derrick Cullors .15
238 Robert Edwards .30
239 Terry Glenn .30
240 Shawn Jefferson .15
241 Ty Law .15
242 Lawyer Milloy .15
243 Lovett Purnell .15
244 Sedrick Shaw .15
245 Tony Simmons .30
246 Chris Slade .15
247 Rod Rutledge, Anthony Ladd .15
248 Chris Floyd, Harold Shaw .15
249 Ink Aleaga .15
250 Cameron Cleeland .30
251 Kerry Collins .30
252 Troy Davis .15
253 Sean Dawkins .15
254 Mark Fields .15
255 Andre Hastings .15
256 Sammy Knight .15
257 Keith Poole .15
258 William Roaf .15
259 Lamar Smith .15
260 Danny Wuerffel .15
261 Josh Wilcox, Brett Bech .15
262 Chris Bordeleau, Wilmont Perry .15
263 Jessie Armstead .15
264 Tiki Barber .15
265 Chad Bratzke .15
266 Gary Brown .15
267 Chris Calloway .15
268 Howard Cross .15
269 Kent Graham .15
270 Ike Hilliard .15
271 Danny Kanell .15
272 Michael Strahan .15
273 Amani Toomer .15
274 Charles Way .15
275 Mike Cherry, Greg Comella .15
276 Kyle Brady .15
277 Keith Byars .15
278 Chad Cascadden .15
279 Wayne Chrebet .30
280 Bryan Cox .15
281 Glenn Foley .30
282 Aaron Glenn .15
283 Keyshawn Johnson .50
284 Leon Johnson .15
285 Mo Lewis .15
286 Curtis Martin .50
287 Otis Smith .15
288 Vinny Testaverde .30
289 Dedric Ward .15
290 Tim Brown .30
291 Rickey Dudley .15
292 Jeff George .30
293 Desmond Howard .15
294 James Jett .15
295 Lance Johnstone .15
296 Randy Jordan .15
297 Napoleon Kaufman .50
298 Lincoln Kennedy .15
299 Terry Mickens .15
300 Darrell Russell .15
301 Harvey Williams .15
302 Jon Ritchie, Charles Woodson .30
303 Rodney Williams, Jermaine Williams .15
304 Koy Detmer .15
305 Hugh Douglas .15
306 Jason Dunn .15
307 Irving Fryar .15
308 Charlie Garner .15
309 Jeff Graham .15
310 Bobby Hoying .15
311 Rodney Peete .15
312 Allen Rossum .15
313 Duce Staley .15
314 William Thomas .15
315 Kevin Turner .15
316 Kaseem Sinceno, Corey Walker .15
317 Jahine Arnold .15
318 Jerome Bettis .30
319 Will Blackwell .15
320 Mark Bruener .15
321 Dermontti Dawson .15
322 Chris Fuamatu-Ma'afala .15
323 Courtney Hawkins .15
324 Richard Huntley .15
325 Charles Johnson .15
326 Levon Kirkland .15
327 Kordell Stewart .75
328 Hines Ward .30
329 DeWayne Washington .15
330 Tony Banks .30
331 Steve Bono .15
332 Isaac Bruce .30
333 June Henley .15
334 Robert Holcombe .30
335 Mike Jones .15
336 Eddie Kennison .15
337 Amp Lee .15
338 Jerald Moore .15
339 Ricky Proehl .15
340 J.T. Thomas .15
341 Derrick Harris, Az-Zahir Hakim .15
342 Roland Williams, Grant Wistrom .15

343 *Kurt Warner,Tony Horne* 45.00
344 Terrell Fletcher .15
345 Greg Jackson .15
346 Charlie Jones .15
347 Freddie Jones .15
348 Ryan Leaf 1.00
349 Natrone Means .30
350 Mikhael Ricks .15
351 Junior Seau .30
352 Bryan Still .15
353 Tremayne Stephens, Ryan Thelwell .15
354 Greg Clark .15
355 Marc Edwards .15
356 Merton Hanks .15
357 Garrison Hearst .30
358 R.W. McQuarters .15
359 Ken Norton Jr. .15
360 Terrell Owens .50
361 Jerry Rice 1.25
362 J.J. Stokes .30
363 Bryant Young .15
364 Steve Young 1.00
365 Chad Brown .15
366 Christian Fauria .15
367 Joey Galloway .50
368 Ahman Green .30
369 Cortez Kennedy .15
370 Jon Kitna .75
371 James McKnight .15
372 Mike Pritchard .15
373 Michael Sinclair .15
374 Shawn Springs .15
375 Ricky Watters .30
376 Darryl Williams .15
377 Robert Wilson, Kerry Joseph .15
378 Mike Alstott .30
379 Reidel Anthony .15
380 Derrick Brooks .15
381 Trent Dilfer .30
382 Warrick Dunn .75
383 Bert Emanuel .15
384 Jacquez Green .30
385 Patrick Hape .15
386 John Lynch .15
387 Dave Moore .15
388 Hardy Nickerson .15
389 Warren Sapp .15
390 Karl Williams .15
391 Blaine Bishop .15
392 Joe Bowden .15
393 Isaac Byrd .15
394 Willie Davis .15
395 Al Del Greco .15
396 Kevin Dyson .30
397 Eddie George .75
398 Jackie Harris .15
399 Dave Krieg .15
400 Steve McNair .50
401 Michael Roan .15
402 Yancey Thigpen .15
403 Frank Wycheck .15
404 Derrick Mason, Steve Matthews .15
405 Stephen Alexander .15
406 Terry Allen .30
407 Jamie Asher .15
408 Stephen Davis .15
409 Darrell Green .15
410 Trent Green .30
411 Skip Hicks .30
412 Brian Mitchell .15
413 Leslie Shepherd .15
414 Michael Westbrook .15
415 Terry Hardy, Rabih Abdullah .15
416 Corey Thomas, Mike Quinn .15
417 Jonathan Quinn, Kelly Holcomb .15
418 Brian Alford, Blake Spence .15
419 Andy Haase, Carlos King .15
420 Karl Hankton, James Thrash .15
421 Fred Beasley, Itula Mili .15
422 *Champ Bailey* 2.50
423 *D'Wayne Bates* 1.00
424 *Michael Bishop* 3.00
425 *David Boston* 3.00
426 *Shawn Bryson* .50
427 *Tim Couch* 6.00
428 *Scott Covington* 1.00
429 *Daunte Culpepper* 7.00
430 *Autry Denson* 1.00
431 *Troy Edwards* 3.00
432 *Kevin Faulk* 3.00
433 *Joe Germaine* 2.00
434 *Torry Holt* 3.00
435 *Brock Huard* 2.00
436 *Sedrick Irvin* 1.50
437 *Edgerrin James* 12.00
438 *Andy Katzenmoyer* 1.00
439 *Shaun King* 4.00
440 *Rob Konrad* .50
441 *Donovan McNabb* 5.00
442 *Cade McNown* 3.00
443 *Billy Miller* 1.00
444 *Dee Miller* 1.00
445 *Sirr Parker* 1.00
446 *Peerless Price* 3.00
447 *Akili Smith* 5.00
448 *Tai Streets* 1.00
449 *Ricky Williams* 6.00
450 *Amos Zereoue* 2.00

1999 Pacific Copper Parallel

This 450-card parallel was a hobby-only release and was sequentially numbered to 99.

MT
Copper Cards: 30x-60x
Copper Rookies: 5x-10x
Production 99 Sets

1999 Pacific Gold Parallel

This 450-card set is a parallel to the base and was hobby only and is sequentially numbered to 199.

MT
Gold Cards: 15x-30x
Gold Rookies: 3x-6x
Production 199 Sets

1999 Pacific Opening Day Parallel

This 450-card set is a parallel to the base and each card is sequentially numbered to 45.

MT
Opening Day Cards: 50x-100x
Opening Day Rookies: 10x-20x
Production 45 Sets

1999 Pacific Platinum Blue Parallel

This is a 450-card set that is a parallel to the base with each single sequentially numbered to 75.

MT
Platinum Blue Cards: 40x-80x
Platinum Blue Rookies: 8x-16x
Production 75 Sets

1999 Pacific Cramer's Choice Awards

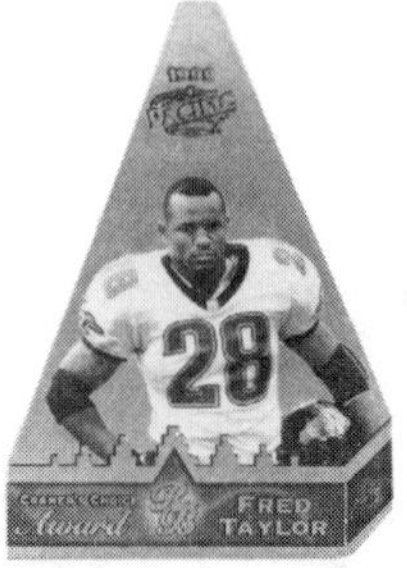

This insert includes the top ten players in the NFL and captures them on a dual-foiled trophy card. Each is die cut in the shape of a pyramid and is sequentially numbered to 299.

MT
Complete Set (10): 950.00
Common Player: 40.00
Production 299 Sets
1 Jamal Anderson 40.00
2 Terrell Davis 125.00
3 John Elway 125.00
4 Barry Sanders 150.00
5 Brett Favre 150.00
6 Peyton Manning 100.00
7 Fred Taylor 85.00
8 Dan Marino 125.00
9 Randall Cunningham 40.00
10 Randy Moss 175.00

1999 Pacific Dynagon Turf

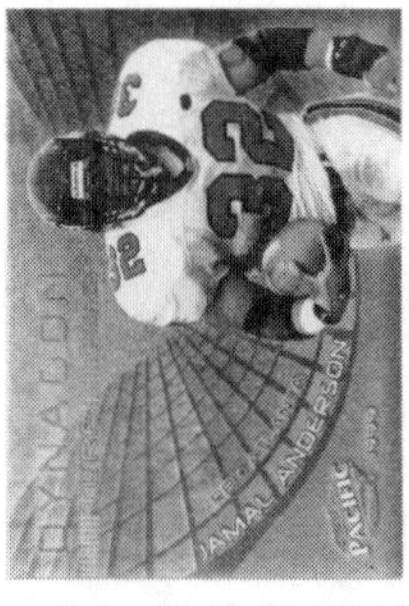

Each card in this 20-card set is printed on a silver-foil card and is horizontal. Singles were inserted 2:25 packs. A parallel Titanium Turf was made and is sequentially numbered to 99.

MT
Complete Set (20): 85.00
Common Player: .75
Minor Stars: 1.50
Inserted 2:25
Titanium Turf Singles: 6x-12x
Production 99 Sets
1 Jake Plummer 6.00
2 Jamal Anderson 1.50
3 Doug Flutie 1.50
4 Emmitt Smith 10.00
5 Terrell Davis 10.00
6 John Elway 10.00
7 Barry Sanders 12.00
8 Brett Favre 12.00
9 Peyton Manning 8.00
10 Mark Brunell 4.00
11 Fred Taylor 6.00
12 Dan Marino 10.00
13 Randall Cunningham 1.50
14 Randy Moss 15.00
15 Drew Bledsoe 4.00
16 Curtis Martin 1.50
17 Jerome Bettis .75
18 Jerry Rice 6.00
19 Jon Kitna 1.50
20 Eddie George 3.00

1999 Pacific Gold Crown Die-Cuts

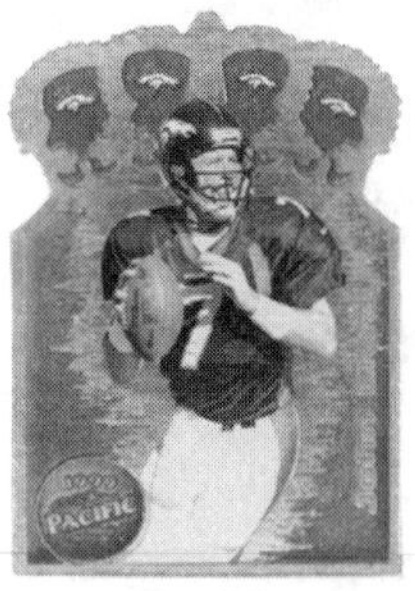

Each card in this 36-card set is printed on dual-foil board and is die cut in the shape of a gold crown. Singles were inserted 1:25 packs.

MT
Complete Set (36): 300.00
Common Player: 3.00
Minor Stars: 6.00
Inserted 1:25
1 Jake Plummer 12.00
2 Jamal Anderson 6.00
3 Priest Holmes 6.00
4 Doug Flutie 6.00
5 Antowain Smith 3.00
6 Corey Dillon 6.00
7 Troy Aikman 15.00
8 Emmitt Smith 20.00
9 Terrell Davis 20.00
10 John Elway 20.00
11 Brian Griese 8.00
12 Charlie Batch 12.00
13 Barry Sanders 30.00
14 Brett Favre 30.00
15 Antonio Freeman 6.00
16 Marshall Faulk 6.00
17 Peyton Manning 20.00
18 Mark Brunell 12.00
19 Fred Taylor 18.00
20 Dan Marino 20.00
21 Randall Cunningham 6.00
22 Randy Moss 35.00
23 Drew Bledsoe 12.00
24 Keyshawn Johnson 6.00
25 Curtis Martin 6.00
26 Napoleon Kaufman 6.00
27 Jerome Bettis 6.00
28 Kordell Stewart 10.00
29 Terrell Owens 8.00
30 Jerry Rice 15.00
31 Steve Young 10.00
32 Joey Galloway 6.00
33 Jon Kitna 6.00
34 Trent Dilfer 3.00
35 Warrick Dunn 8.00
36 Eddie George 8.00

1999 Pacific Pro Bowl Die-Cuts

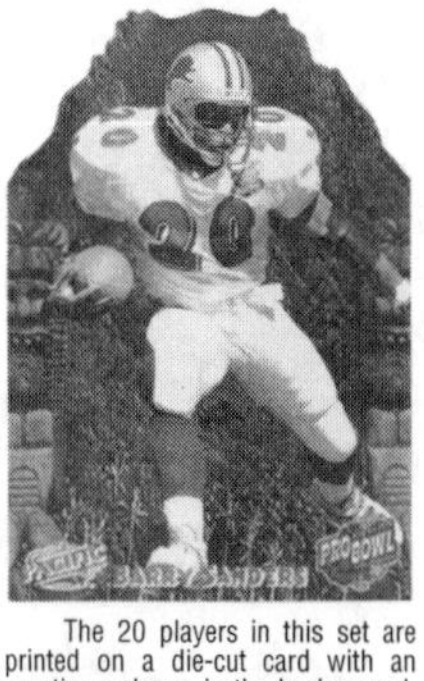

The 20 players in this set are printed on a die-cut card with an erupting volcano in the background. Singles were inserted 1:49 packs.

MT
Complete Set (20): 150.00
Common Player: 4.00
Inserted 1:49
1 Jamal Anderson 6.00
2 Chris Chandler 4.00
3 Doug Flutie 6.00
4 Deion Sanders 6.00
5 Emmitt Smith 20.00
6 Terrell Davis 20.00
7 John Elway 20.00
8 Barry Sanders 30.00
9 Antonio Freeman 6.00
10 Marshall Faulk 6.00
11 Randall Cunningham 6.00
12 Randy Moss 35.00
13 Robert Smith 4.00
14 Ty Law 4.00
15 Keyshawn Johnson 6.00
16 Curtis Martin 6.00
17 Jerry Rice 15.00
18 Steve Young 10.00
19 Mike Alstott 6.00
20 Eddie George 8.00

1999 Pacific Record Breakers

This was a hobby only insert that included record-breaking achievements from 1998. Singles from this 20-card insert were sequentially numbered to 199.

MT
Complete Set (20): 300.00
Common Player: 15.00
Production 199 Sets
1 Jake Plummer 18.00
2 Jamal Anderson 15.00
3 Doug Flutie 18.00
4 Troy Aikman 25.00
5 Emmitt Smith 30.00
6 Terrell Davis 30.00
7 John Elway 30.00
8 Barry Sanders 35.00
9 Brett Favre 40.00
10 Marshall Faulk 18.00
11 Peyton Manning 30.00
12 Mark Brunell 18.00
13 Fred Taylor 20.00
14 Dan Marino 35.00
15 Randall Cunningham 15.00
16 Randy Moss 30.00
17 Drew Bledsoe 18.00
18 Curtis Martin 15.00
19 Jerry Rice 25.00
20 Steve Young 18.00

1999 Pacific Team Checklists

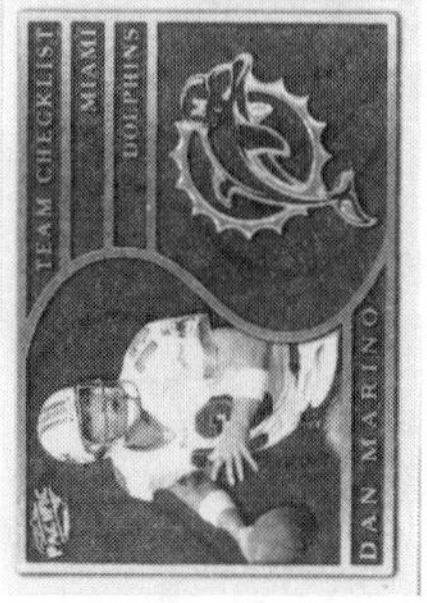

Each card in this 31-card set includes each team with a star player from that team on the fronts of the horizontal card. The backs include the team checklist for each player in the base set. Singles were inserted 2:25 packs.

MT
Complete Set (31): 100.00
Common Player: 1.25
Minor Stars: 2.50
Inserted 2:25
1 Jake Plummer 8.00
2 Jamal Anderson 2.50
3 Priest Holmes 2.50
4 Doug Flutie 2.50
5 Muhsin Muhammad 1.25
6 Curtis Enis 2.50
7 Corey Dillon 2.50
8 Ty Detmer 1.25
9 Emmitt Smith 12.00
10 John Elway 12.00
11 Barry Sanders 16.00
12 Brett Favre 16.00
13 Peyton Manning 10.00
14 Fred Taylor 8.00
15 Andre Rison 1.25
16 Dan Marino 12.00
17 Randy Moss 20.00
18 Drew Bledsoe 6.00
19 Cameron Cleeland 1.25
20 Ike Hilliard 1.25
21 Curtis Martin 2.50
22 Napoleon Kaufman 2.50
23 Duce Staley 1.25
24 Jerome Bettis 2.50
25 Isaac Bruce 2.50
26 Ryan Leaf 4.00
27 Steve Young 4.00
28 Joey Galloway 2.50
29 Warrick Dunn 4.00
30 Eddie George 4.00
31 Michael Westbrook 1.25

1999 Pacific Aurora

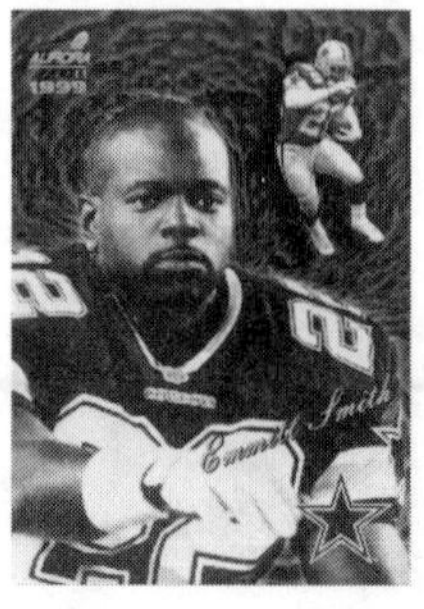

Each card in this 200-card set has a large posed photo and a smaller action photo in a vintage looking sepia color. A total of 150 players were used with 50 star players and rookies duplicated with a pinstripe background and posed photo on front. Inserts include: Premiere Date, Canvas Creations, Championship Fever, Complete Players, Leather Bound and Styrotechs.

MT
Complete Set (200): 65.00
Common Player: .15
Minor Stars: .30
Pack (6): 3.00
Wax Box (24): 65.00
1 *David Boston* 3.00
2 Larry Centers .15
3 Rob Moore .30
4 Adrian Murrell .15
5C Jake Plummer 1.00
5D Jake Plummer 1.00
6C Jamal Anderson .50
6D Jamal Anderson .50
7 Chris Chandler .30
8 Tim Dwight .50
9 Terance Mathis .15
10 O.J. Santiago .15
11C Priest Holmes .50
11D Priest Holmes .50
12 Michael Jackson .15
13 Jermaine Lewis .30
14 Ray Lewis .15
15 Michael McCrary .15
16C Doug Flutie .75
16D Doug Flutie .75
17C Eric Moulds .50
17D Eric Moulds .50
18 *Peerless Price* 2.50
19 Antowain Smith .50
20 Bruce Smith .15
21 Steve Beuerlein .15
22 Tshimanga Biakabutuka .15
23 Kevin Greene .15
24 Muhsin Muhammad .15
25 Wesley Walls .15
26 Curtis Conway .30
27 Bobby Engram .15
28 Curtis Enis .30
29 Erik Kramer .15
30C *Cade McNown* 3.00
30D *Cade McNown* 3.00
31 Jeff Blake .30
32C Corey Dillon .50
32D Corey Dillon .50
33 Carl Pickens .30
34 Darnay Scott .15
35C *Akili Smith* 4.00
35D *Akili Smith* 4.00
36C *Tim Couch* 7.00
36D *Tim Couch* 7.00
37 Ty Detmer .15
38 *Kevin Johnson* 3.00
39 Terry Kirby .15
40C Troy Aikman 1.00
40D Troy Aikman 1.00
41 Michael Irvin .30
42 Raghib Ismail .15
43C Deion Sanders .50
43D Deion Sanders .50
44C Emmitt Smith 1.50
44D Emmitt Smith 1.50
45 Bubby Brister .15
46C Terrell Davis 1.50
46D Terrell Davis 1.50
47 Brian Griese 1.00
48 Ed McCaffrey .30
49C Shannon Sharpe .30
49D Shannon Sharpe .30
50 Rod Smith .30
51C Charlie Batch .75
51D Charlie Batch .75
52 *Sedrick Irvin* 2.00
53C Herman Moore .50
53D Herman Moore .50
54 Johnnie Morton .15
55C Barry Sanders 2.00
55D Barry Sanders 2.00
56 Robert Brooks .15
57C Brett Favre 2.00
57D Brett Favre 2.00
58C Antonio Freeman .50
58D Antonio Freeman .50
59 Dorsey Levens .50
60 Derrick Mayes .30
61 Marvin Harrison .50
62C *Edgerrin James* 12.00
62D *Edgerrin James* 12.00
63C Peyton Manning 1.50
63D Peyton Manning 1.50
64 Jerome Pathon .15
65 Tavian Banks .30
66C Mark Brunell .75
66D Mark Brunell .75
67 Keenan McCardell .15
68 Jimmy Smith .30
69C Fred Taylor 1.00
69D Fred Taylor 1.00
70 Derrick Alexander .15
71 Kimble Anders .15
72 *Michael Cloud* 1.50
73 Elvis Grbac .30
74 Andre Rison .30
75 Karim Abdul .30
76 *James Johnson* 2.00
77C Dan Marino 1.50
77D Dan Marino 1.50
78 O.J. McDuffie .30
79 Lamar Thomas .15
80C Cris Carter .50
80D Cris Carter .50
81 *Daunte Culpepper* 10.00
82C Randall Cunningham .50
82D Randall Cunningham .50
83C Randy Moss 2.50
83D Randy Moss 2.50
84 John Randle .15
85C Robert Smith .50
85D Robert Smith .50
86C Drew Bledsoe .75
86D Drew Bledsoe .75
87 Ben Coates .30
88 *Kevin Faulk* 3.00
89C Terry Glenn .50
89D Terry Glenn .50
90 Ty Law .15
91 Cameron Cleeland .30
92 Andre Hastings .15
93 Billy Joe Hobert .15
94C *Ricky Williams* 7.00
94D *Ricky Williams* 7.00
95 Tiki Barber .15
96 Kent Graham .15
97 Ike Hilliard .15
98 Charles Way .15
99 Wayne Chrebet .50
100C Keyshawn Johnson .50
100D Keyshawn Johnson .50
101C Curtis Martin .50
101D Curtis Martin .50
102C Vinny Testaverde .30
102D Vinny Testaverde .30
103 Dedric Ward .15
104C Tim Brown .30
104D Tim Brown .30
105 Rickey Dudley .15
106 James Jett .15
107 Napoleon Kaufman .50
108 Charles Woodson .50
109 Jeff Graham .15
110 Charles Johnson .15
111C *Donovan McNabb* 6.00
111D *Donovan McNabb* 6.00
112 Duce Staley .30
113C Jerome Bettis .50
113D Jerome Bettis .50
114 *Troy Edwards* 3.00
115 Courtney Hawkins .15
116C Kordell Stewart .50
116D Kordell Stewart .50
117 *Amos Zereoue* 2.50
118 Isaac Bruce .30
119C Marshall Faulk .50
119D Marshall Faulk .50
120 *Joe Germaine* 2.00
121C *Torry Holt* 3.00
121D *Torry Holt* 3.00
122 Amp Lee .15
123 Charlie Jones .15
124 Ryan Leaf .50
125 Natrone Means .30
126 Junior Seau .30
127 Garrison Hearst .50
128C Terrell Owens .50
128D Terrell Owens .50
129C Jerry Rice 1.00
129D Jerry Rice 1.00
130 J.J. Stokes .30
131C Steve Young .75
131D Steve Young .75
132 Chad Brown .15
133C Joey Galloway .50
133D Joey Galloway .50
134 *Brock Huard* 2.00
135C Jon Kitna .50
135D Jon Kitna .50
136C Ricky Watters .30
136D Ricky Watters .30
137C Mike Alstott .50
137D Mike Alstott .50
138 Reidel Anthony .30
139 Trent Dilfer .30
140C Warrick Dunn .50
140D Warrick Dunn .50
141 Jacquez Green .30
142 *Shaun King* 4.00
143C Eddie George .50
143D Eddie George .50
144C Steve McNair .50
144D Steve McNair .50
145 Yancey Thigpen .30
146 Frank Wycheck .15
147 *Champ Bailey* 2.00
148 Skip Hicks .50
149 Brad Johnson .50
150 Michael Westbrook .30

1999 Pacific Aurora Premiere Date Parallel

This 200-card set is a parallel to the base and is sequentially numbered to 77. Singles were only found in hobby product and were inserted 1:25 packs.

MT
Premiere Date Cards: 30x-60x
Premiere Date Rookies: 8x-16x
Production 77 Sets

1999 Pacific Aurora Canvas Creations

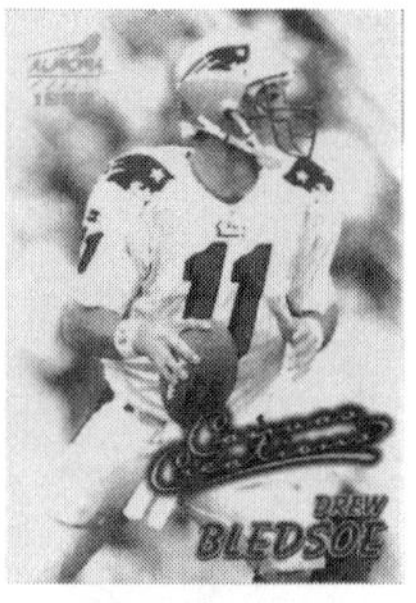

Each player in this 10-card set was printed on real canvas. Singles were inserted 1:193 packs.

MT
Complete Set (10): 275.00
Common Player: 15.00
Inserted 1:193
1 Troy Aikman 30.00
2 Terrell Davis 45.00
3 Barry Sanders 60.00
4 Brett Favre 60.00
5 Peyton Manning 45.00
6 Dan Marino 45.00
7 Randy Moss 60.00
8 Drew Bledsoe 25.00
9 Steve Young 20.00
10 Jon Kitna 15.00

1999 Pacific Aurora Championship Fever

This 20-card set was issued at 4:25 packs. Each card has a parallel Copper issue that was only found in hobby product and are sequentially numbered to 20. A Platinum Blue parallel was also made and are numbered to 100. The retail only Silver parallel are numbered to 250.

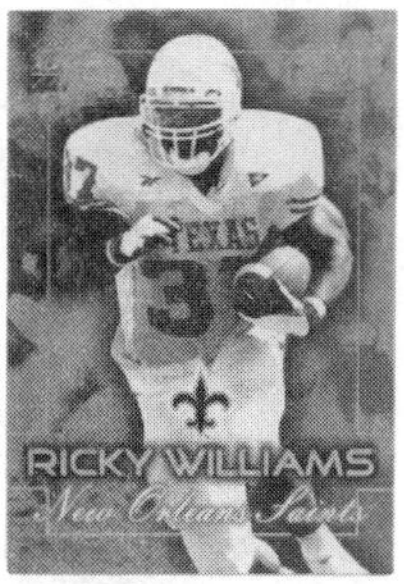

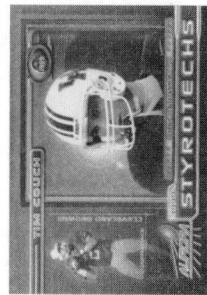

		MT
Complete Set (20):		35.00
Common Player:		1.00
Inserted 4:25		
Copper Cards:		25x-50x
Production 20 Sets		
Platinum Blue Cards:		8x-16x
Production 100 Sets		
1	Jake Plummer	2.50
2	Jamal Anderson	1.00
3	Tim Couch	6.00
4	Troy Aikman	2.50
5	Emmitt Smith	3.50
6	Terrell Davis	3.50
7	Barry Sanders	5.00
8	Brett Favre	5.00
9	Peyton Manning	3.50
10	Fred Taylor	2.50
11	Dan Marino	3.50
12	Randy Moss	5.00
13	Drew Bledsoe	2.00
14	Ricky Williams	6.00
15	Keyshawn Johnson	1.00
16	Terrell Owens	1.00
17	Jerry Rice	2.50
18	Steve Young	1.50
19	Jon Kitna	1.00
20	Eddie George	1.25

1999 Pacific Aurora Complete Players

Ten players were used in this insert with two different cards. One in hobby product and the other in retail. Each product has a 10-card set with each single sequentially numbered to 299. Each card is printed on 10-point double laminated stock with full foil on both sides. A parallel Hologold set was made and inserted into both products and are sequentially numbered to 25.

		MT
Complete Set (10):		125.00
Common Player:		10.00
Production 299 Sets		
Hologold Cards:		4x-8x
Production 25 Sets		
1	Troy Aikman	15.00
2	Terrell Davis	20.00
3	Barry Sanders	30.00
4	Brett Favre	30.00
5	Peyton Manning	20.00
6	Dan Marino	20.00
7	Randy Moss	30.00
8	Drew Bledsoe	10.00
9	Jerry Rice	15.00
10	Steve Young	10.00

1999 Pacific Aurora Leather Bound

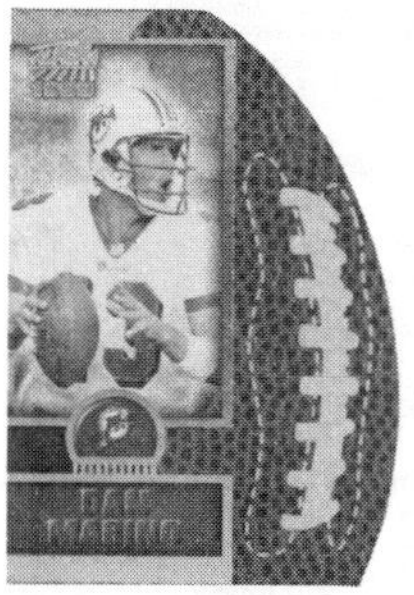

This hobby-only insert features 20 players on a laminated leather football card with white foil embossed laces. They were found 2:25 packs.

		MT
Complete Set (20):		85.00
Common Player:		2.00
Inserted 2:25		
1	Jake Plummer	5.00
2	Jamal Anderson	2.00
3	Tim Couch	12.00
4	Troy Aikman	5.00
5	Emmitt Smith	7.00
6	Terrell Davis	7.00
7	Barry Sanders	10.00
8	Brett Favre	10.00
9	Peyton Manning	7.00
10	Fred Taylor	5.00
11	Dan Marino	7.00
12	Randy Moss	10.00
13	Drew Bledsoe	4.00
14	Ricky Williams	12.00
15	Curtis Martin	2.00
16	Jerome Bettis	2.00
17	Jerry Rice	5.00
18	Steve Young	4.00
19	Jon Kitna	3.00
20	Eddie George	3.00

1999 Pacific Aurora Terrell Owens Autograph

Owens signed a total of 197 cards for Aurora Football. Each card is full foil and hand sequentially numbered.

		MT
Production 197 Sets		
AU1	Terrell Owens Auto	85.00

1999 Pacific Aurora Styrotechs

Each card in this 20-card set is horizontal with two photos of the player. One in color and the other a smaller photo of the player in black and white. Singles are printed on styrene and were inserted 1:25.

		MT
Complete Set (20):		125.00
Common Player:		3.00
Inserted 1:25		
1	Jake Plummer	8.00
2	Jamal Anderson	3.00
3	Tim Couch	16.00
4	Troy Aikman	8.00
5	Emmitt Smith	12.00
6	Terrell Davis	12.00
7	Barry Sanders	16.00
8	Brett Favre	16.00
9	Peyton Manning	12.00
10	Fred Taylor	8.00
11	Dan Marino	12.00
12	Randy Moss	16.00
13	Drew Bledsoe	5.00
14	Ricky Williams	16.00
15	Curtis Martin	3.00
16	Jerry Rice	8.00
17	Steve Young	5.00
18	Joey Galloway	3.00
19	Jon Kitna	4.00
20	Eddie George	4.00

1999 Pacific Crown Royale

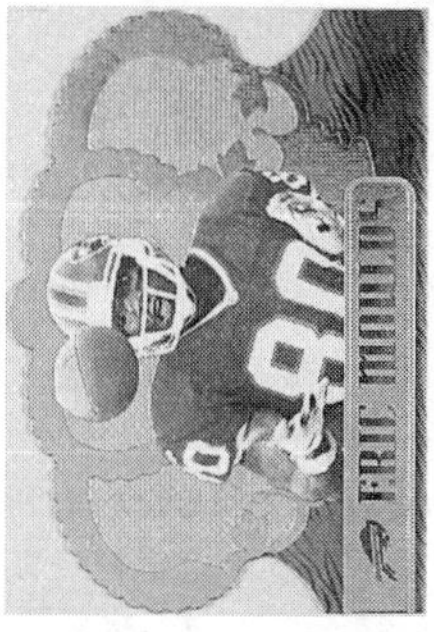

This was a 144-card base set that featured each single die-cut, double-etched and on a double-foiled format. Each veteran card had a gold foil crown while the rookies were printed on a silver foil crown. Parallel sets included Limited Series and Premier Date. Other inserts included: Card Supials, Century 21, Cramer's Choice Jumbos, Franchise Glory, Gold Crown Die Cuts, Rookie Gold and Test of Time. SRP was $5.99 for six-card packs.

		MT
Complete Set (144):		185.00
Common Player:		.30
Minor Stars:		.60
Common Rookie:		2.00
Pack (6):		6.00
Wax Box (24):		120.00
1	*David Boston*	6.00
2	*Chris Greisen*	2.00
3	Rob Moore	.60
4	Jake Plummer	3.00
5	Frank Sanders	.60
6	Jamal Anderson	1.50
7	Chris Chandler	.60
8	Tim Dwight	1.50
9	Byron Hanspard	.60
10	Stoney Case	.30
11	Priest Holmes	1.50
12	Jermaine Lewis	.60
13	*Chris McCalister*	3.00
14	*Brandon Stokley*	2.00
15	Doug Flutie	2.00
16	Eric Moulds	1.50
17	*Peerless Price*	5.00
18	Antowain Smith	1.50
19	Steve Beuerlein	.60
20	Tshimanga Biakabutuka	.60
21	Muhsin Muhammad	1.00
22	Curtis Conway	.60
23	Curtis Enis	1.50
24	Shane Matthews	1.50
25	*Cade McNown*	7.00
26	Marcus Robinson	3.00
27	Jeff Blake	1.00
28	*Scott Covington*	2.00
29	Corey Dillon	1.50
30	*Damon Griffin*	2.00
31	Carl Pickens	1.00
32	*Akili Smith*	12.00
33	*Tim Couch*	20.00
34	*Kevin Johnson*	6.00
35	Terry Kirby	.30
36	Leslie Shepherd	.30
37	Troy Aikman	3.00
38	Raghib Ismail	.30
39	*Wane McGarity*	3.00
40	Deion Sanders	1.50
41	Emmitt Smith	4.00
42	Terrell Davis	4.00
43	Brian Griese	3.00
44	Ed McCaffrey	1.50
45	Shannon Sharpe	.75
46	Rod Smith	1.50
47	Charlie Batch	2.00
48	Germane Crowell	.75
49	*Sedrick Irvin*	4.00
50	Herman Moore	1.50
51	Barry Sanders	6.00
52	Brett Favre	6.00
53	Antonio Freeman	1.50
54	Matt Hasselbeck	1.50
55	Dorsey Levens	1.50
56	*Basil Mitchell*	3.00
57	E.G. Green	.60
58	Marvin Harrison	1.50
59	*Edgerrin James*	30.00
60	Peyton Manning	4.00
61	*Terrence Wilkins*	10.00
62	Mark Brunell	2.00
63	Keenan McCardell	.60
64	Jimmy Smith	1.50
65	Fred Taylor	3.00
66	Derrick Alexander	.30
67	Elvis Grbac	.60
68	Warren Moon	.60
69	*Larry Parker*	2.00
70	Andre Rison	.60
71	*Cecil Collins*	6.00
72	Damon Huard	2.00
73	*James Johnson*	4.00
74	*Rob Konrad*	3.00
75	Dan Marino	4.00
76	O.J. McDuffie	.60
77	Cris Carter	1.50
78	*Daunte Culpepper*	20.00
79	Randall Cunningham	1.50
80	Randy Moss	6.00
81	Robert Smith	1.50
82	*Michael Bishop*	3.00
83	Drew Bledsoe	2.00
84	Ben Coates	.60
85	*Kevin Faulk*	4.00
86	Terry Glenn	1.50
87	Billy Joe Hobert	.30
88	Eddie Kennison	.60
89	Keith Poole	.30
90	*Ricky Williams*	20.00
91	*Sean Bennett*	3.00
92	Kerry Collins	.60
93	Pete Mitchell	.30
94	Amani Toomer	.60
95	Wayne Chrebet	1.50
96	Keyshawn Johnson	1.50
97	Curtis Martin	1.50
98	Tim Brown	1.00
99	*Scott Dreisbach*	2.00
100	Rich Gannon	.60
101	Napoleon Kaufman	1.50
102	Tyrone Wheatley	.60
103	Charles Johnson	.30
104	*Donovan McNabb*	12.00
105	Torrance Small	.30
106	Duce Staley	1.50
107	*Jed Weaver*	2.00
108	Jerome Bettis	1.50
109	*Troy Edwards*	6.00
110	Kordell Stewart	1.50
111	*Amos Zereoue*	4.00
112	Isaac Bruce	1.50
113	Marshall Faulk	1.50
114	*Joe Germaine*	3.00
115	*Torry Holt*	6.00
116	*Kurt Warner*	40.00
117	Jim Harbaugh	.60
118	Erik Kramer	.30
119	Natrone Means	.75
120	Junior Seau	.75
121	*Jeff Garcia*	12.00
122	Terrell Owens	1.50
123	Jerry Rice	3.00
124	J.J. Stokes	.60
125	Steve Young	2.00
126	Sean Dawkins	.30
127	*Brock Huard*	4.00
128	Jon Kitna	2.00
129	Derrick Mayes	.75
130	*Charlie Rogers*	2.00
131	Ricky Watters	1.50
132	Mike Alstott	1.50
133	Trent Dilfer	1.00
134	Warrick Dunn	1.50
135	Eric Zeier	.30
136	*Kevin Daft*	2.00
137	Kevin Dyson	.60
138	Eddie George	1.75
139	Steve McNair	1.75
140	Neil O'Donnell	.60
141	*Champ Bailey*	4.00
142	Albert Connell	.30
143	Stephen Davis	1.50
144	Brad Johnson	1.50

1999 Pacific Crown Royale Limited Series Parallel

This was a 144-card parallel to the base set. Each single was sequentially numbered to 99.

	MT
Limited Ser. Cards:	8x-16x
Limited Ser. Rookies:	2x-4x
Production 99 Sets	

1999 Pacific Crown Royale Premiere Date Parallel

This was a 144-card parallel to the base set. Singles were sequentially numbered to 68 and found 1:25 packs.

	MT
Premiere Date Cards:	10x-20x
Premiere Date Rookies:	3x-6x
Inserted 1:25	
Production 68 Sets	

1999 Pacific Crown Royale Card Supials

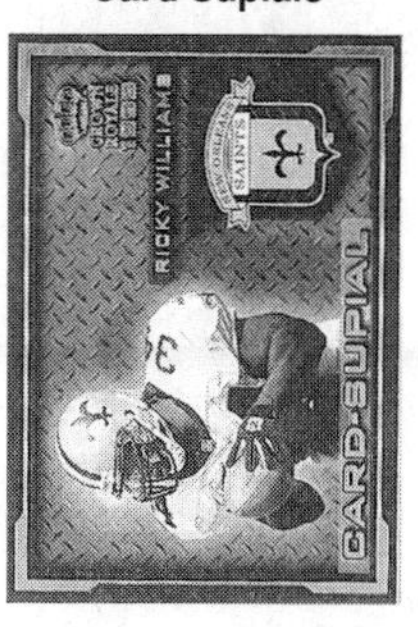

This 20-card insert set included a full-size card with a "Card-Supial" inserted into a special die-cut pouch on the back of the full-size card. The mini (1/4 the full card size) card is inserted into a different player's full-size card. Singles were inserted 2:25 packs.

		MT
Complete Set (20):		100.00
Common Player:		2.00
Small Cards:		.7x
Inserted 2:25		
1	Cade McNown	6.00
2	Tim Couch	10.00
3	Troy Aikman	6.00
4	Emmitt Smith	8.00
5	Barry Sanders	10.00
6	Brett Favre	10.00
7	Edgerrin James	15.00
8	Peyton Manning	8.00
9	Mark Brunell	4.00
10	Fred Taylor	5.00
11	Damon Huard	4.00
12	Dan Marino	8.00
13	Randy Moss	10.00
14	Drew Bledsoe	4.00
15	Ricky Williams	10.00
16	Jerome Bettis	2.00
17	Kurt Warner	15.00
18	Terrell Owens	2.00
19	Jerry Rice	6.00
20	Jon Kitna	3.00

1999 Pacific Crown Royale Century 21

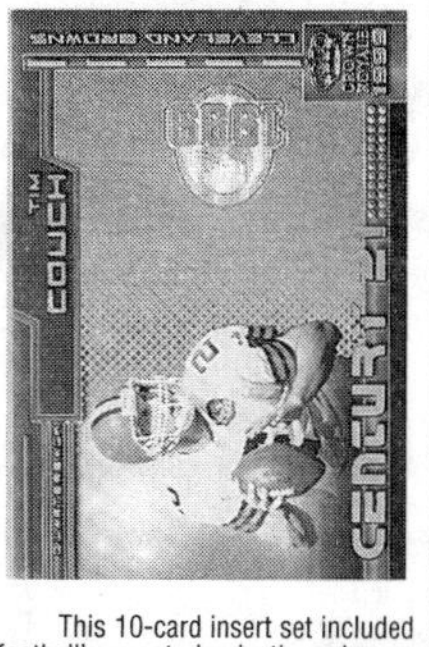

This 10-card insert set included football's most dominating players. Each of the singles were sequentially numbered to 375.

		MT
Complete Set (10):		100.00
Common Player:		7.00
Production 375 Sets		
1	Jake Plummer	10.00
2	Tim Couch	15.00
3	Terrell Davis	15.00
4	Peyton Manning	15.00
5	Mark Brunell	7.00
6	Fred Taylor	10.00
7	Randy Moss	15.00
8	Drew Bledsoe	7.00
9	Ricky Williams	15.00
10	Kurt Warner	30.00

1999 Pacific Crown Royale Cramer's Choice Jumbos

This 10-card insert set included both veterans and a few of the hot rookies from 1999. Singles were inserted one per box. Six different parallel sets were also issued and they include: Dark Blue (#'d to 35), Green (#'d to 30), Red (#'d to 25), Light Blue (#'d to 20), Gold (#'d to 10) and Purple (#'d to 1).

		MT
Complete Set (10):		85.00
Common Player:		5.00
1:Box		
Dark Blue Cards:		6x-12x
Production 35 Sets		
Gold Cards:		15x-30x
Production 10 Sets		
Green Cards:		6x-12x
Production 30 Sets		
Light Blue Cards:		10x-20x
Production 20 Sets		
Purple Cards:		
Production 1 Set		
Red Cards:		10x-20x
Production 25 Sets		
1	Cade McNown	8.00
2	Tim Couch	12.00
3	Emmitt Smith	12.00
4	Edgerrin James	20.00
5	Mark Brunell	8.00
6	Fred Taylor	10.00
7	Randy Moss	15.00
8	Kurt Warner	20.00
9	Jon Kitna	5.00
10	Eddie George	5.00

1999 Pacific Crown Royale Franchise Glory

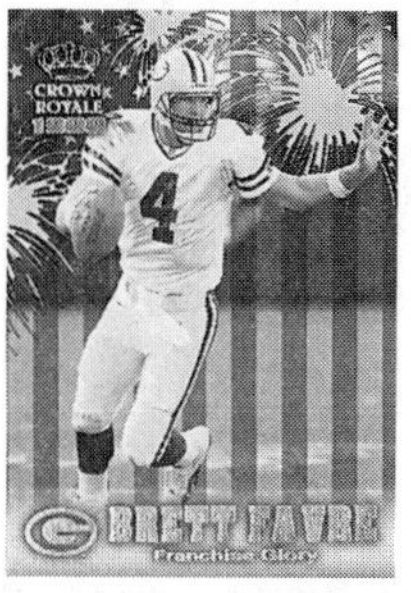

This 25-card insert set included NFL team leaders, veterans and rising stars. Each is printed with the American flag and fireworks in the background. They were found one-per-pack.

		MT
Complete Set (25):		45.00
Common Player:		1.00
Inserted 1:1		
1	Doug Flutie	2.00
2	Corey Dillon	1.00
3	Troy Aikman	3.00
4	Emmitt Smith	4.00
5	Terrell Davis	4.00
6	Herman Moore	1.00
7	Barry Sanders	5.00
8	Brett Favre	5.00
9	Antonio Freeman	1.00
10	Peyton Manning	4.00
11	Mark Brunell	2.00
12	Fred Taylor	3.00
13	Dan Marino	4.00
14	Randy Moss	5.00
15	Drew Bledsoe	2.00
16	Keyshawn Johnson	1.00
17	Jerome Bettis	1.00
18	Marshall Faulk	1.00
19	Kurt Warner	15.00
20	Terrell Owens	1.00
21	Jerry Rice	3.00
22	Steve Young	2.00
23	Warrick Dunn	1.00
24	Eddie George	1.00
25	Brad Johnson	1.00

1999 Pacific Crown Royale Gold Crown Die Cuts

Singles from this six-card insert set were over-sized and sequentially numbered to 976.

		MT
Complete Set (6):		60.00
Common Player:		5.00
Production 976 Sets		
1	Tim Couch	15.00
2	Troy Aikman	10.00
3	Emmitt Smith	10.00
4	Damond Huard	5.00
5	Randy Moss	15.00
6	Kurt Warner	25.00

A card number in parentheses ( ) indicates the set is unnumbered.

1999 Pacific Crown Royale Rookie Gold

This 25-card insert set included the top rookies from 1999. Singles were found one-per-pack. A parallel die-cut version was also made and each of those singles was sequentially numbered to 10.

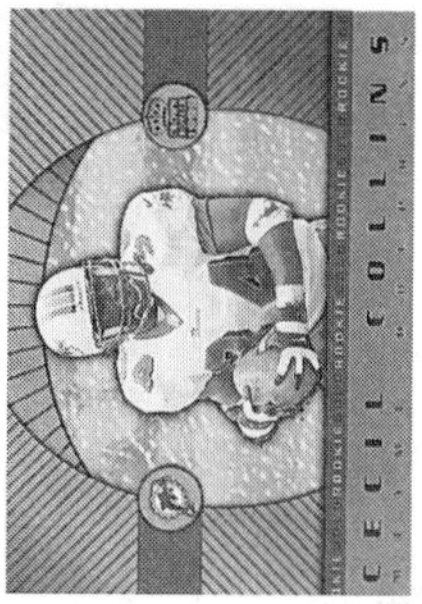

		MT
Complete Set (25):		50.00
Common Player:		1.00
Inserted 1:1		
1	David Boston	3.00
2	Brandon Stokley	1.00
3	Cade McNown	4.00
4	Akili Smith	4.00
5	Tim Couch	6.00
6	Kevin Johnson	3.00
7	Wane McGarity	1.00
8	Edgerrin James	10.00
9	Terrence Wilkins	4.00
10	Cecil Collins	2.00
11	Rob Konrad	1.00
12	James Johnson	1.00
13	Daunte Culpepper	4.00
14	Michael Bishop	1.50
15	Kevin Faulk	1.50
16	Ricky Williams	6.00
17	Scott Dreisbach	1.00
18	Donovan McNabb	4.00
19	Troy Edwards	3.00
20	Amos Zereoue	1.00
21	Joe Germaine	1.00
22	Torry Holt	3.00
23	Brock Huard	1.50
24	Charlie Rogers	1.00
25	Champ Bailey	1.50

1999 Pacific Crown Royale Test of Time

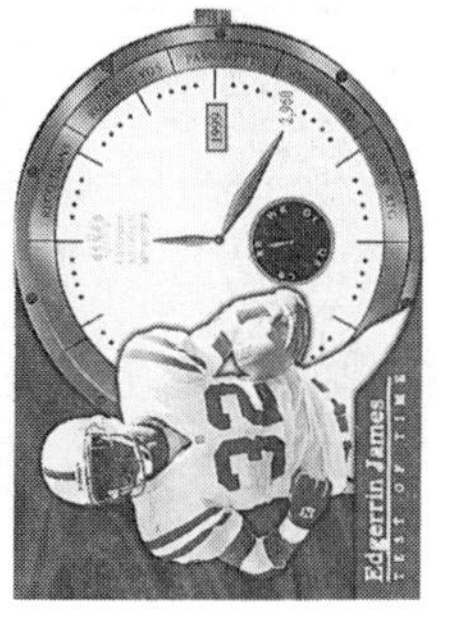

This 10-card insert set included seasoned veterans along with a few rookies. Each player was pictured on a die-cut single with a clock-shaped design. Singles were inserted 1:25 packs.

		MT
Complete Set (10):		65.00
Common Player:		3.00
Inserted 1:25		
1	Tim Couch	12.00
2	Emmitt Smith	10.00
3	Terrell Davis	10.00
4	Barry Sanders	12.00
5	Brett Favre	12.00
6	Antonio Freeman	3.00
7	Edgerrin James	20.00
8	Mark Brunell	5.00
9	Dan Marino	10.00
10	Jerry Rice	8.00

1999 Pacific Omega

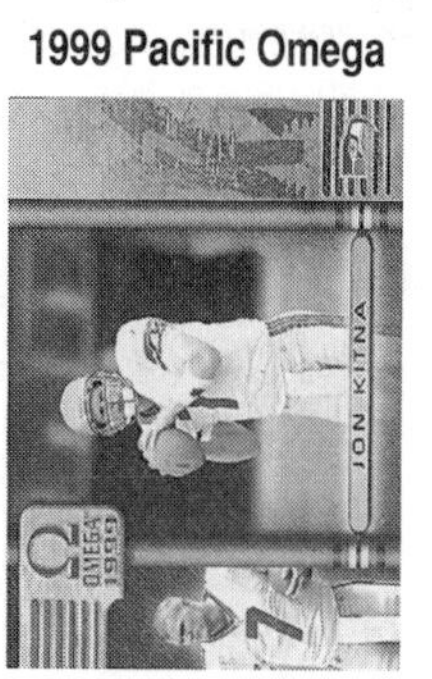

This was a 250-card set that included 48 unseeded rookie cards. Each single was horizontal and used silver foil. Four parallel sets were issued and they include: Copper, Gold, Platinum Blue and Premiere Date. Other inserts include: 5-Star Attack, Draft Class, EO Portraits, Gridiron

Masters and TD 99. SRP was $1.99 for six-card packs.

		MT
Complete Set (250):		60.00
Common Player:		.15
Minor Stars:		.30
Common Rookie:		.50
Pack (6):		2.00
Wax Box (36):		65.00
1	Mario Bates	.15
2	*David Boston*	2.50
3	Rob Moore	.30
4	Adrian Murrell	.15
5	Jake Plummer	1.00
6	Frank Sanders	.15
7	Aeneas Williams	.15
8	*Joel Makovicka,L.J. Shelton*	1.00
9	Jamal Anderson	.50
10	Ray Buchanan	.15
11	Chris Chandler	.30
12	Tim Dwight	.50
13	Byron Hanspard	.15
14	Terance Mathis	.15
15	O.J. Santiago	.15
16	Danny Kanell, Chris Calloway	.15
17	Peter Boulware	.15
18	Priest Holmes	.50
19	Patrick Johnson	.15
20	Jermaine Lewis	.15
21	Ray Lewis	.15
22	Michael McCrary	.15
23	Jonathan Ogden	.15
24	Tony Banks, Scott Mitchell	.15
25	Doug Flutie	.75
26	Rob Johnson	.15
27	Eric Moulds	.50
28	Andre Reed	.15
29	Antowain Smith	.30
30	Bruce Smith	.15
31	Kevin Williams	.15
32	*Shawn Bryson,Peerless Price*	1.75
33	Steve Beuerlein	.15
34	Tshimanga Biakabutuka	.30
35	Rae Carruth	.15
36	*Dameyune Craig*	1.50
37	William Floyd	.15
38	Kevin Greene	.15
39	Muhsin Muhammad	.30
40	Wesley Walls	.15
41	Edgar Bennett	.15
42	*Robert Chancey*	1.00
43	Curtis Conway	.30
44	Bobby Engram	.15
45	Curtis Enis	.50
46	*Cade McNown*	2.50
47	Ryan Wetnight	.15
48	*D'Wayne Bates,Marty Booker*	1.50
49	Jeff Blake	.30
50	*Scott Covington*	1.00
51	Corey Dillon	.50
52	James Hundon	.15
53	Carl Pickens	.30
54	Darnay Scott	.30
55	*Akili Smith*	4.00
56	*Craig Yeast*	1.00
57	*Tim Couch*	8.00
58	Ty Detmer	.15
59	Marc Edwards	.15
60	*Kevin Johnson*	2.50
61	Terry Kirby	.15
62	Sedrick Shaw	.15
63	Leslie Shepherd	.15
64	*Rahim Abdullah,Daylon McCutcheon*	.50
65	Troy Aikman	1.00
66	Michael Irvin	.30
67	David LaFleur	.15
68	*Wane McGarity*	1.00
69	Ernie Mills	.15
70	Deion Sanders	.50
71	Emmitt Smith	1.50
72	Raghib Ismail, James McKnight	.15
73	Bubby Brister	.30
74	*Byron Chamberlain*	1.25
75	Terrell Davis	1.50
76	*Olandis Gary*	4.00
77	Brian Griese	1.00
78	Ed McCaffrey	.50
79	Shannon Sharpe	.30
80	Rod Smith	.30
81	*Travis McGriff,Al Wilson*	1.00
82	Charlie Batch	.75
83	*Chris Claiborne*	1.00
84	Germane Crowell	.30
85	Terry Fair	.15
86	*Sedrick Irvin*	1.50
87	Herman Moore	.50
88	Johnnie Morton	.15
89	Barry Sanders	2.00
90	Mark Chmura	.30
91	Brett Favre	2.00
92	Antonio Freeman	.50
93	Desmond Howard	.15
94	Dorsey Levens	.50
95	Derrick Mayes	.30
96	Bill Schroeder	.30
97	*Aaron Brooks,Dee Miller*	3.00
98	Ken Dilger	.15
99	E.G. Green	.15
100	Marvin Harrison	.50
101	*Edgerrin James*	8.00
102	Peyton Manning	1.50
103	Jerome Pathon	.15
104	Marcus Pollard	.15
105	Derrick Alexander	.15
106	Reggie Barlow	.15
107	Tony Boselli	.15
108	Mark Brunell	.75
109	George Jones	.15
110	Keenan McCardell	.30
111	Jimmy Smith	.30
112	James Stewart	.30
113	Fred Taylor	1.00
114	Kimble Anders	.15
115	*Michael Cloud*	1.00
116	Tony Gonzalez	.30
117	Elvis Grbac	.30
118	Bam Morris	.15
119	Andre Rison	.30
120	Derrick Thomas	.30
121	Karim Abdul	.30
122	Oronde Gadsden	.30
123	*James Johnson*	1.75
124	*Rob Konrad*	1.00
125	Dan Marino	1.50
126	O.J. McDuffie	.30
127	Lamar Thomas	.15
128	Zach Thomas	.30
129	Cris Carter	.50
130	*Daunte Culpepper*	6.00
131	Randall Cunningham	.50
132	Matthew Hatchette	.15
133	Leroy Hoard	.30
134	David Palmer	.15
135	John Randle	.15
136	Randy Moss	2.00
137	Robert Smith	.50
138	Drew Bledsoe	.75
139	Ben Coates	.30
140	*Kevin Faulk*	2.00
141	Terry Glenn	.50
142	Shawn Jefferson	.15
143	Ty Law	.15
144	Tony Simmons	.30
145	*Michael Bishop,Andy Katzenmoyer*	1.75
146	Cameron Cleeland	.30
147	Andre Hastings	.15
148	Billy Joe Hobert	.15
149	Joe Johnson	.15
150	Keith Poole	.15
151	William Roaf	.15
152	Billy Joe Tolliver	.15
153	*Ricky Williams*	8.00
154	Tiki Barber	.30
155	Gary Brown	.15
156	Kent Graham	.15
157	Ike Hilliard	.15
158	David Patten	.15
159	Jason Sehorn	.15
160	Amani Toomer	.15
161	*Joe Montgomery,Luke Petitgout*	1.25
162	Wayne Chrebet	.30
163	Bryan Cox	.15
164	Aaron Glenn	.15
165	Keyshawn Johnson	.50
166	Leon Johnson	.15
167	Curtis Martin	.50
168	Vinny Testaverde	.30
169	Dedric Ward	.15
170	Tim Brown	.30
171	Rickey Dudley	.30
172	James Jett	.15
173	Napoleon Kaufman	.50
174	Jon Ritchie	.15
175	Darrell Russell	.15
176	Charles Woodson	.50
177	Rich Gannon, Heath Shuler	.15
178	Hugh Douglas	.15
179	*Donovan McNabb*	4.00
180	Allen Rossum	.15
181	Duce Staley	.30
182	Kevin Turner	.15
183	Charles Johnson, Doug Pederson	.15
184	*Barry Gardner,Cecil Martin*	.50
185	Jerome Bettis	.50
186	Mark Bruener	.15
187	*Troy Edwards*	2.50
188	Courtney Hawkins	.15
189	Levon Kirkland	.15
190	Kordell Stewart	.50
191	Hines Ward	.30
192	*Malcolm Johnson,Amos Zereoue*	1.75
193	Greg Clark	.15
194	Terrell Fletcher	.15
195	Charlie Jones	.15
196	*Cecil Collins*	4.00
197	Natrone Means	.30
198	Mikhael Ricks	.15
199	Junior Seau	.30
200	Bryan Still	.15
201	Ryan Thelwell	.15
202	Garrison Hearst	.30
203	*Terry Jackson*	.50
204	R.W. McQuarters	.15
205	Terrell Owens	.50
206	Jerry Rice	1.00
207	J.J. Stokes	.30
208	Tommy Vardell	.15
209	Steve Young	.75
210	*Karsten Bailey*	1.00
211	Chad Brown	.15
212	Christian Fauria	.15
213	Joey Galloway	.50
214	Ahman Green	.30
215	*Brock Huard*	1.50
216	Cortez Kennedy	.15
217	Jon Kitna	.75
218	Ricky Watters	.50
219	Isaac Bruce	.50
220	Az-Zahir Hakim	.30
221	June Henley	.15
222	Greg Hill	.15
223	*Torry Holt*	2.50
224	Amp Lee	.15
225	Ricky Proehl	.15
226	Marshall Faulk, Trent Green	.50
227	Mike Alstott	.50
228	Reidel Anthony	.30
229	Trent Dilfer	.30
230	Warrick Dunn	.50
231	Bert Emanuel	.15
232	Jacquez Green	.30
233	Warren Sapp	.15
234	*Shaun King,Anthony McFarland*	3.00
235	*Mike Archie*	.50
236	Kevin Dyson	.30
237	Eddie George	.75
238	Derrick Mason	.15
239	Steve McNair	.75
240	Yancey Thigpen	.30
241	Frank Wycheck	.30
242	*Darran Hall,Jevon Kearse*	2.00
243	Stephen Alexander	.15
244	*Champ Bailey*	1.50
245	Stephen Davis	.50
246	Skip Hicks	.30
247	James Thrash	.15
248	Michael Westbrook	.30
249	Dan Wilkinson	.15
250	Brad Johnson, Larry Centers	.50

1999 Pacific Omega Copper Parallel

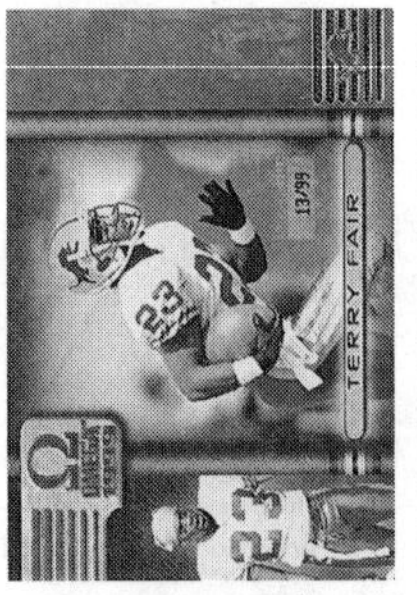

This was a 250-card parallel to the base set. Each of these singles used copper foil rather than silver foil on the base cards. These were only found in hobby packs and each was sequentially numbered to 99.

	MT
Copper Cards:	15x-30x
Copper Rookies:	5x-10x
Production 99 Sets	

1999 Pacific Omega Gold Parallel

This was a 250-card parallel to the base set. Each of these singles used gold foil rather than silver foil on the base cards. These were only found in retail packs and each was sequentially numbered to 299.

	MT
Gold Cards:	8x-16x
Gold Rookies:	2x-4x
Production 299 Sets	

1999 Pacific Omega Platinum Blue Parallel

This was a 250-card parallel to the base set. Each of these singles used blue foil rather than silver foil on the base cards. These were found in both hobby and retail packs and each was sequentially numbered to 75.

	MT
Platinum Blue Cards:	20x-40x
Platinum Blue Rookies:	6x-12x
Production 75 Sets	

1999 Pacific Omega Premiere Date Parallel

This was a 250-card parallel to the base set. Each of these singles used red foil rather than silver foil on the base cards. Each of these singles was sequentially numbered to 60.

	MT
Premiere Date Cards:	20x-40x
Premiere Date Rookies:	6x-12x
Production 60 Sets	

1999 Pacific Omega 5-Star Attack

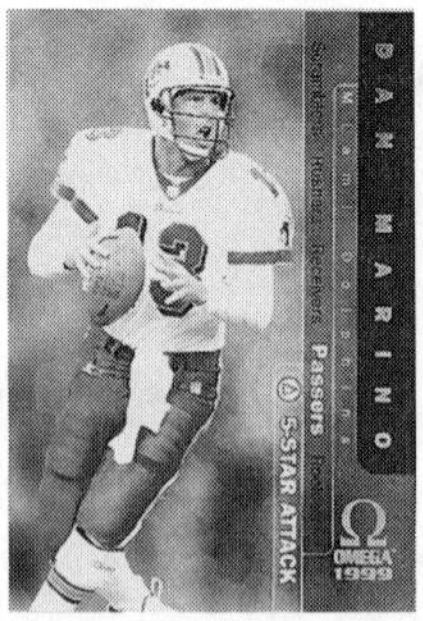

This was a 30-card insert that included the NFL's top stars and premier rookies. Singles were inserted 4:37 packs and could only be found in hobby packs. Five parallel sets were issued and include: Blue (#'d to 100), Red (#'d to 75), Green (#'d to 50), Purple (#'d to 25) and Gold (#'d to 1).

	MT
Complete Set (30):	50.00
Common Player:	.50
Minor Stars:	1.00
Inserted 4:37	
Blue Cards:	5x-10x
Production 100 Sets	
Gold Cards:	
Production 1 Set	
Green Cards:	8x-16x
Production 50 Sets	
Purple Cards:	10x-20x
Production 25 Sets	
Red Cards:	7x-14x
Production 75 Sets	

1	Chris Chandler	.50
2	Tim Couch	6.00
3	Peyton Manning	4.00
4	Dan Marino	4.00
5	Drew Bledsoe	2.00
6	Vinny Testaverde	.50
7	Randall Cunningham	1.00
8	Doug Flutie	1.50
9	Charlie Batch	1.50
10	Mark Brunell	2.00
11	Steve Young	1.75
12	Jon Kitna	1.50
13	Jamal Anderson	1.00
14	Priest Holmes	1.00
15	Emmitt Smith	4.00
16	Fred Taylor	3.00
17	Curtis Martin	1.00
18	Eddie George	1.50
19	Ed McCaffrey	.50
20	Antonio Freeman	1.00
21	Randy Moss	6.00
22	Keyshawn Johnson	1.00
23	Terrell Owens	1.00
24	Joey Galloway	1.00
25	Cade McNown	3.00
26	Akili Smith	3.00
27	Edgerrin James	6.00
28	Daunte Culpepper	3.00
29	Ricky Williams	6.00
30	Donovan McNabb	3.00

1999 Pacific Omega Draft Class

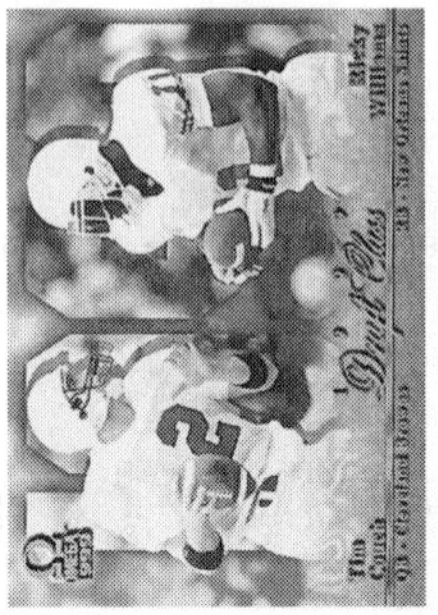

This 10-card insert included two players from the same draft year and pictured them on the front of each card. Singles were inserted 1:145 packs.

		MT
Complete Set (10):		125.00
Common Player:		10.00
Inserted 1:145		
1	1983 (Darrell Green, Dan Marino)	20.00
2	1985 (Jerry Rice, Bruce Smith)	15.00
3	1989 (Troy Aikman, Barry Sanders)	30.00
4	1990 (Shannon Sharpe, Emmitt Smith)	20.00
5	1991 (Brett Favre, Herman Moore)	30.00
6	1993 (Drew Bledsoe, Mark Brunell)	10.00
7	1995 (Terrell Davis, Curtis Martin)	20.00
8	1997 (Warrick Dunn, Jake Plummer)	10.00
9	1998 (Peyton Manning, Randy Moss)	30.00
10	1999 (Tim Couch, Ricky Williams)	25.00

1999 Pacific Omega EO Portraits

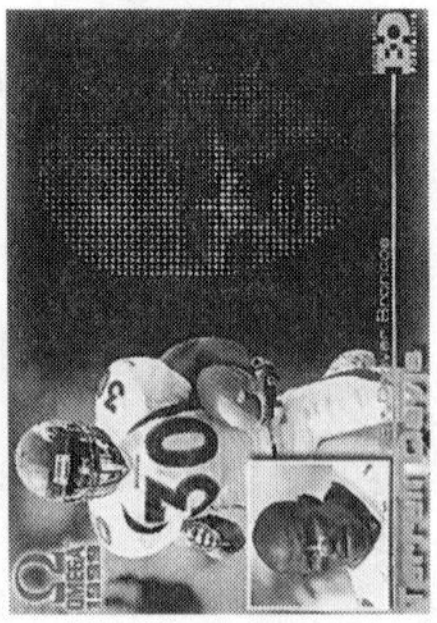

This 20-card insert included mostly veterans and a few rookies. Each single used electro-optical technology and each had the player's portrait laser cut into the card. Singles were inserted 1:73 packs.

		MT
Complete Set (20):		150.00
Common Player:		5.00
Inserted 1:73		
1	Jake Plummer	10.00
2	Jamal Anderson	5.00
3	Akili Smith	10.00
4	Tim Couch	20.00
5	Troy Aikman	10.00
6	Emmitt Smith	15.00
7	Terrell Davis	15.00
8	Barry Sanders	20.00
9	Brett Favre	20.00
10	Peyton Manning	15.00
11	Mark Brunell	8.00
12	Fred Taylor	10.00
13	Dan Marino	15.00
14	Randy Moss	20.00
15	Ricky Williams	20.00
16	Curtis Martin	5.00
17	Jerry Rice	10.00
18	Jon Kitna	8.00
19	Warrick Dunn	5.00
20	Eddie George	8.00

1999 Pacific Omega Gridiron Masters

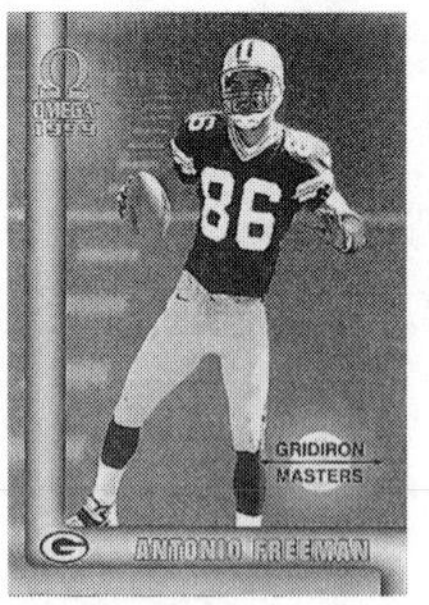

This 36-card insert included both veterans and rookies. Singles were inserted 4:37 packs.

		MT
Complete Set (36):		40.00
Common Player:		.50
Minor Stars:		1.00
Inserted 4:37		
1	David Boston	1.75
2	Jake Plummer	2.50
3	Jamal Anderson	.50
4	Chris Chandler	.50
5	Priest Holmes	1.00
6	Doug Flutie	1.75
7	Akili Smith	2.50
8	Cade McNown	2.50
9	Tim Couch	5.00
10	Deion Sanders	1.00
11	Emmitt Smith	3.50
12	Rod Smith	.50
13	Charlie Batch	1.75
14	Herman Moore	1.00
15	Barry Sanders	5.00
16	Antonio Freeman	1.00
17	Edgerrin James	5.00
18	Mark Brunell	1.75
19	Fred Taylor	2.50
20	Randall Cunningham	1.00
21	Randy Moss	5.00
22	Terry Glenn	1.00
23	Keyshawn Johnson	1.00
24	Curtis Martin	1.00
25	Vinny Testaverde	.50
26	Donovan McNabb	2.50
27	Jerome Bettis	1.00
28	Terrell Owens	1.00
29	Jerry Rice	2.50
30	Steve Young	1.75
31	Joey Galloway	1.00
32	Jon Kitna	1.50
33	Warrick Dunn	1.00
34	Shaun King	1.50
35	Eddie George	1.25
36	Steve McNair	1.25

1999 Pacific Omega TD '99

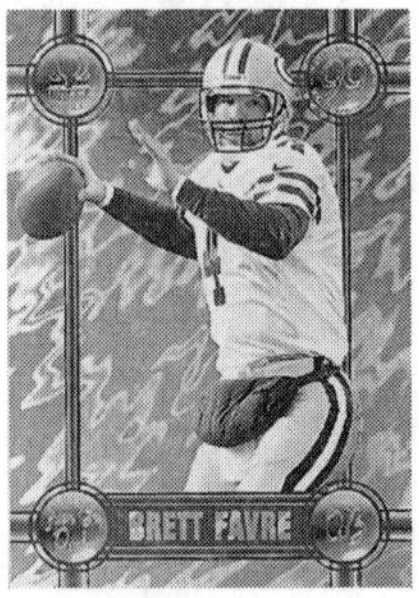

This 20-card insert included the NFL's most renown TD leaders. Each was printed on a prism-style holographic foil board. Singles were inserted 1:37 packs.

		MT
Complete Set (20):		50.00
Common Player:		1.50
Inserted 1:37		
1	Jamal Anderson	1.50
2	Priest Holmes	1.50
3	Doug Flutie	3.00
4	Tim Couch	10.00
5	Troy Aikman	5.00
6	Emmitt Smith	7.00
7	Terrell Davis	7.00
8	Herman Moore	1.50
9	Brett Favre	10.00
10	Antonio Freeman	2.00
11	Mark Brunell	4.00
12	Fred Taylor	5.00
13	Randall Cunningham	2.00
14	Randy Moss	10.00
15	Drew Bledsoe	4.00
16	Terrell Owens	2.00
17	Steve Young	3.00
18	Jon Kitna	3.00
19	Warrick Dunn	3.00
20	Eddie George	3.00

A player's name in *italic type* indicates a rookie card.

1999 Pacific Paramount

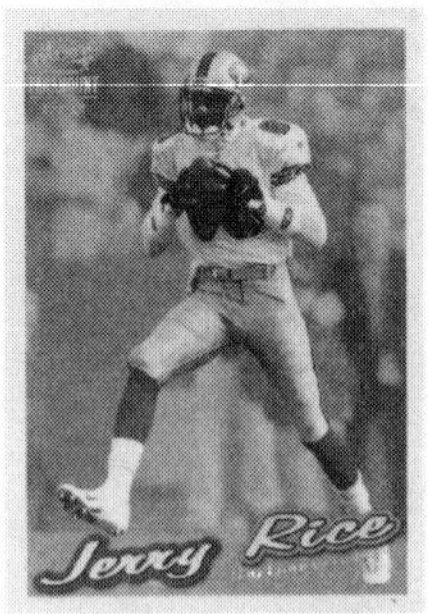

Pacific Paramount Football is a 250-card set that includes all of the top rookies from 1999. The base has six different parallel sets with Copper, Gold, Premiere Date, HoloGold, HoloSilver and Platinum Blue. Other inserts include: Canton Bound, End Zone Net-Fusions, Personal Bests and Team Checklists.

		MT
Complete Set (250):		60.00
Common Player:		.10
Minor Stars:		.20
Common Rookie:		.50
Pack (6):		1.75
Wax Box (36):		50.00
1	*David Boston*	3.00
2	Larry Centers	.10
3	*Joel Makovicka*	1.00
4	Eric Metcalf	.10
5	Rob Moore	.20
6	Adrian Murrell	.20
7	Jake Plummer	1.00
8	Frank Sanders	.20
9	Aeneas Williams	.10
10	Morten Anderson	.10
11	Jamal Anderson	.50
12	Chris Chandler	.20
13	Tim Dwight	.50
14	Terance Mathis	.10
15	*Jeff Paulk*	1.00
16	O.J. Santiago	.10
17	Chuck Smith	.10
18	Peter Boulware	.10
19	Priest Holmes	.50
20	Michael Jackson	.10
21	Jermaine Lewis	.20
22	Ray Lewis	.10
23	Michael McCrary	.10
24	Bennie Thompson	.10
25	Rod Woodson	.10
26	*Shawn Bryson*	.50
27	Doug Flutie	.75
28	Eric Moulds	.50
29	*Peerless Price*	1.50
30	Andre Reed	.10
31	Jay Riemersma	.10
32	Antowain Smith	.50
33	Bruce Smith	.10
34	Michael Bates	.10
35	Steve Beuerlein	.10
36	Tshimanga Biakabutuka	.10
37	Kevin Greene	.10
38	Anthony Johnson	.10
39	Fred Lane	.10
40	Muhsin Muhammad	.10
41	Wesley Walls	.10
42	*D'Wayne Bates*	.75
43	Edgar Bennett	.10
44	*Marty Booker*	.50
45	Curtis Conway	.20
46	Bobby Engram	.10
47	Curtis Enis	.50
48	Erik Kramer	.10
49	*Cade McNown*	2.00
50	Jeff Blake	.20
51	*Scott Covington*	1.00
52	Corey Dillon	.50
53	*Quincy Jackson*	.50
54	Carl Pickens	.20
55	Darnay Scott	.10
56	*Akili Smith*	4.00
57	*Craig Yeast*	.50
58	Jerry Ball	.10
59	*Darrin Chiaverini*	.50
60	*Tim Couch*	10.00
61	Ty Detmer	.10
62	*Kevin Johnson*	1.25
63	Terry Kirby	.10
64	*Daylon McCutcheon*	.50
65	Irv Smith	.10
66	Troy Aikman	1.00
67	*Ebenezer Ekuban*	.50
68	Michael Irvin	.20
69	Daryl Johnston	.10
70	*Wayne McGarity*	.75
71	*Dat Nguyen*	1.00
72	Deion Sanders	.50
73	Emmitt Smith	1.50
74	Bubby Brister	.30
75	Terrell Davis	1.50
76	Jason Elam	.10
77	*Olandis Gary*	4.00
78	Brian Griese	.75
79	Ed McCaffrey	.30
80	*Travis McGriff*	1.00
81	Shannon Sharpe	.20
82	Rod Smith	.20
83	Charlie Batch	.75
84	*Chris Claiborne*	1.00
85	Germane Crowell	.20
86	*Sedrick Irvin*	1.50
87	Herman Moore	.50
88	Johnnie Morton	.10
89	Barry Sanders	2.00
90	Robert Brooks	.10
91	*Aaron Brooks*	3.00
92	Mark Chmura	.20
93	Brett Favre	2.00
94	Antonio Freeman	.50
95	Vonnie Holliday	.20
96	Dorsey Levens	.50

97 *De'Mond Parker* .75
98 Ken Dilger .10
99 Marvin Harrison .30
100 *Edgerrin James* 10.00
101 Peyton Manning 1.50
102 Jerome Pathon .20
103 *Mike Peterson* .50
104 Marcus Pollard .10
105 Tavian Banks .20
106 Reggie Barlow .10
107 Tony Boselli .10
108 Mark Brunell .75
109 Keenan McCardell .10
110 Bryce Paup .10
111 Jimmy Smith .20
112 Fred Taylor 1.00
113 Dave Thomas .10
114 Kimble Anders .10
115 Donnell Bennett .10
116 *Mike Cloud* 1.00
117 Tony Gonzalez .20
118 Elvis Grbac .20
119 *Larry Parker* .50
120 Andre Rison .20
121 *Brian Shay* .50
122 Karim Abdul .30
123 Oronde Gadsden .20
124 *James Johnson* 1.50
125 *Rob Konrad* 1.00
126 Dan Marino 1.50
127 O.J. McDuffie .20
128 Zach Thomas .20
129 Cris Carter .50
130 *Daunte Culpepper* 6.00
131 Randall Cunningham .50
132 Matthew Hatchette .10
133 Leroy Hoard .10
134 Randy Moss 2.00
135 John Randle .10
136 Jake Reed .10
137 Robert Smith .50
138 *Michael Bishop* 2.00
139 Drew Bledsoe .75
140 Ben Coates .20
141 *Kevin Faulk* 2.50
142 Terry Glenn .30
143 Shawn Jefferson .10
144 *Andy Katzenmoyer* 1.00
145 Tony Simmons .20
146 *Cuncho Brown* .50
147 Cameron Cleeland .20
148 Mark Fields .10
149 La'Roi Glover .10
150 Andre Hastings .10
151 Billy Joe Hobert .10
152 William Roaf .10
153 Billy Joe Tolliver .10
154 *Ricky Williams* 10.00
155 Jessie Armstead .10
156 Tiki Barber .20
157 Gary Brown .10
158 Kent Graham .10
159 Ike Hilliard .20
160 *Joe Montgomery* 1.25
161 Amani Toomer .10
162 Charles Way .10
163 Wayne Chrebet .50
164 Bryan Cox .10
165 Aaron Glenn .10
166 Keyshawn Johnson .50
167 Leon Johnson .10
168 Curtis Martin .50
169 Vinny Testaverde .20
170 Dedric Ward .10
171 Tim Brown .20
172 *Dameane Douglas* .75
173 Rickey Dudley .20
174 James Jett .10
175 Napoleon Kaufman .50
176 Darrell Russell .10
177 Harvey Williams .10
178 Charles Woodson .50
179 *Na Brown* .50
180 Hugh Douglas .10
181 *Cecil Martin* .50
182 *Donovan McNabb* 4.00
183 Duce Staley .10
184 Kevin Turner .10
185 Jerome Bettis .50
186 *Troy Edwards* 2.00
187 Jason Gildon .10
188 Courtney Hawkins .10
189 *Malcolm Johnson* .50
190 Kordell Stewart .75
191 *Jerame Tuman* .50
192 *Amos Zereoue* 2.00
193 Isaac Bruce .30
194 Kevin Carter .10
195 *Jeremaine Copeland* .50
196 *Joe Germaine* 1.75
197 Az-Zahir Hakim .20
198 *Torry Holt* 2.50
199 Amp Lee .10
200 Ricky Proehl .10
201 Charlie Jones .10
202 Freddie Jones .10
203 Ryan Leaf .50
204 Natrone Means .30
205 Mikhael Ricks .10
206 Junior Seau .20
207 Bryan Still .10
208 Garrison Hearst .30
209 *Terry Jackson* .50
210 R.W. McQuarters .10
211 Ken Norton Jr. .10
212 Terrell Owens .50
213 Jerry Rice 1.00
214 J.J. Stokes .20
215 *Tai Streets* 1.00
216 Steve Young .75
217 *Karsten Bailey* 1.00
218 Chad Brown .10
219 Joey Galloway .50
220 Ahman Green .20
221 *Brock Huard* 1.50
222 Cortez Kennedy .10
223 Jon Kitna .75
224 Shawn Springs .10
225 Ricky Watters .20
226 Mike Alstott .50
227 Reidel Anthony .20
228 Trent Dilfer .30
229 Warrick Dunn .75
230 Bert Emanuel .10
231 *Martin Gramatica* .50
232 Jacquez Green .20
233 *Shaun King* 3.00
234 *Anthony McFarland* 1.00
235 Warren Sapp .10
236 Willie Davis .10
237 Kevin Dyson .20
238 Eddie George .75
239 *Darran Hall* .50
240 Jackie Harris .10
241 Steve McNair .50
242 Yancey Thigpen .20
243 Frank Wycheck .10
244 Stephen Alexander .10
245 *Champ Bailey* 1.50
246 Stephen Davis .10
247 Darrell Green .10
248 Skip Hicks .50
249 Brian Mitchell .10
250 Michael Westbrook .20

1999 Pacific Paramount Copper Parallel

This is a parallel to the base and could only be found in hobby product at one-per-pack.

	MT
Complete Set (250):	135.00
Copper Cards:	3x
Copper Rookies:	1.5x
Inserted 1:1	

1999 Pacific Paramount HoloGold Parallel

This is a parallel to the base set and was only found in retail product. Each card was sequentially numbered to 199.

	MT
HoloGold Cards:	20x-40x
HoloGold Rookies:	5x-10x
Production 199 Sets	

1999 Pacific Paramount Holographic Silver Parallel

This is a parallel to the base and was inserted into hobby product. Each card was sequentially numbered to 99.

	MT
Silver Cards:	40x-80x
Silver Rookies:	7x-14x
Production 99 Sets	

1999 Pacific Paramount Platinum Blue Parallel

This is a parallel to the base and was inserted in both hobby and retail product. Cards were found 1:73 packs.

	MT
Blue Cards:	40x-80x
Blue Rookies:	7x-14x
Inserted 1:73	

1999 Pacific Paramount Premiere Date Parallel

This is a parallel to the base that was found 1:37 hobby packs and each is sequentially numbered to 62.

	MT
Premiere Date Cards:	50x-100x
Premiere Date Rookies:	9x-18x
Inserted 1:37	

1999 Pacific Paramount Canton Bound

Each card is fully foiled and etched with just ten of the top players heading to Canton. Each card is horizontal and were inserted 1:361 packs. A parallel Proof set was also issued with each card sequentially numbered to 20.

		MT
Complete Set (10):		550.00
Common Player:		40.00
Inserted 1:361		
Proofs:		4x
Production 20 Sets		
1	Troy Aikman	60.00
2	Emmitt Smith	80.00
3	Terrell Davis	80.00
4	Barry Sanders	100.00
5	Brett Favre	100.00
6	Dan Marino	80.00
7	Randy Moss	100.00
8	Drew Bledsoe	50.00
9	Jerry Rice	60.00
10	Steve Young	40.00

1999 Pacific Paramount End Zone Net-Fusions

Each card in this 20-card set has a die-cut design that includes actual netting from behind the goal posts. Singles were inserted 1:73 packs.

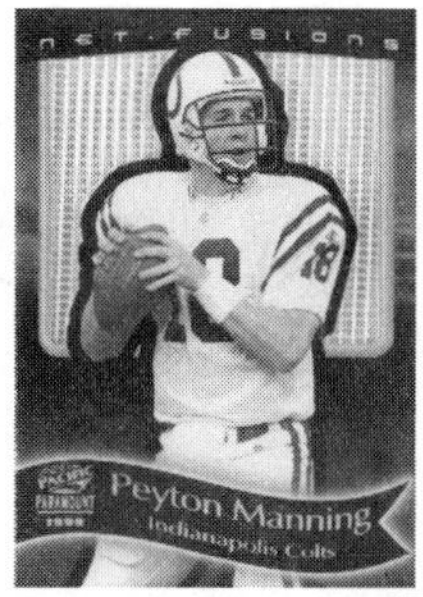
Peyton Manning
Indianapolis Colts

		MT
Complete Set (20):		325.00
Common Player:		10.00
Inserted 1:73		
1	Jake Plummer	20.00
2	Jamal Anderson	10.00
3	Doug Flutie	15.00
4	Tim Couch	40.00
5	Troy Aikman	20.00
6	Emmitt Smith	30.00
7	Terrell Davis	30.00
8	Barry Sanders	40.00
9	Brett Favre	40.00
10	Peyton Manning	30.00
11	Mark Brunell	15.00
12	Fred Taylor	15.00
13	Dan Marino	30.00
14	Randy Moss	40.00
15	Drew Bledsoe	15.00
16	Ricky Williams	40.00
17	Jerry Rice	20.00
18	Steve Young	15.00
19	Jon Kitna	10.00
20	Eddie George	12.00

1999 Pacific Paramount Personal Bests

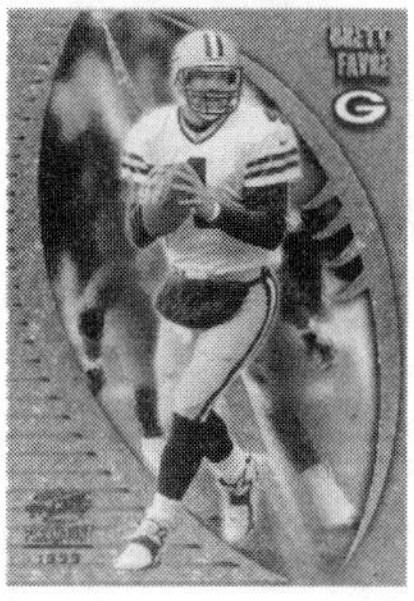

Thirty-six of the NFL's top players are featured on these holographic patterned foil cards. Singles were inserted 1:37 packs.

		MT
Complete Set (36):		225.00
Common Player:		4.00
Inserted 1:37		
1	Jake Plummer	10.00
2	Jamal Anderson	4.00
3	Priest Holmes	6.00
4	Doug Flutie	8.00
5	Antowain Smith	4.00
6	Corey Dillon	4.00
7	Akili Smith	10.00
8	Tim Couch	25.00
9	Troy Aikman	10.00
10	Emmitt Smith	15.00
11	Terrell Davis	15.00
12	Barry Sanders	20.00
13	Brett Favre	20.00
14	Antonio Freeman	4.00
15	Edgerrin James	15.00
16	Peyton Manning	15.00
17	Mark Brunell	8.00
18	Fred Taylor	10.00
19	Dan Marino	15.00
20	Randall Cunningham	4.00
21	Randy Moss	20.00
22	Drew Bledsoe	8.00
23	Kevin Faulk	6.00
24	Ricky Williams	25.00
25	Curtis Martin	4.00
26	Napoleon Kaufman	4.00
27	Donovan McNabb	10.00
28	Jerome Bettis	4.00
29	Kordell Stewart	6.00
30	Terrell Owens	6.00
31	Jerry Rice	10.00
32	Steve Young	8.00
33	Jon Kitna	6.00
34	Warrick Dunn	6.00
35	Eddie George	6.00
36	Steve McNair	4.00

1999 Pacific Paramount Team Checklists

Each card in this 31-card set highlights one player from each team and uses his photo on the front with his name in gold foil. The back has a smaller photo with a checklist of players from that team. Singles were inserted 2:37 packs.

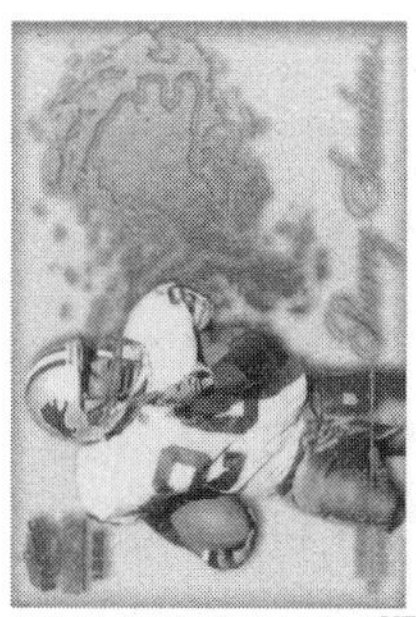

		MT
Complete Set (31):		125.00
Common Player:		1.50
Minor Stars:		3.00
Inserted 2:37		
1	Jake Plummer	6.00
2	Jamal Anderson	3.00
3	Priest Holmes	3.00
4	Doug Flutie	5.00
5	Muhsin Muhammad	1.50
6	Cade McNown	6.00
7	Corey Dillon	3.00
8	Tim Couch	15.00
9	Troy Aikman	6.00
10	Terrell Davis	8.00
11	Barry Sanders	12.00
12	Brett Favre	12.00
13	Peyton Manning	8.00
14	Fred Taylor	6.00
15	Elvis Grbac	1.50
16	Dan Marino	8.00
17	Randy Moss	12.00
18	Drew Bledsoe	5.00
19	Ricky Williams	15.00
20	Ike Hilliard	1.50
21	Curtis Martin	3.00
22	Napoleon Kaufman	3.00
23	Donovan McNabb	6.00
24	Jerome Bettis	3.00
25	Torry Holt	4.00
26	Natrone Means	1.50
27	Jerry Rice	6.00
28	Jon Kitna	4.00
29	Warrick Dunn	4.00
30	Eddie George	4.00
31	Skip Hicks	3.00

1999 Pacific Prisms

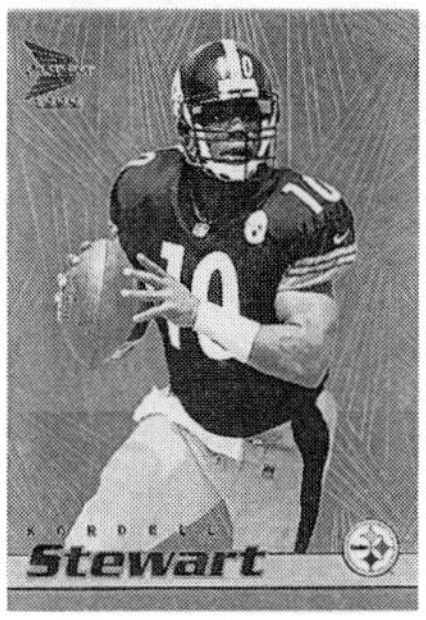
Stewart

This 150-card base set pictured players on a holographic prismatic background. A total of five parallel sets were issued and they include: Holographic Blue, Holographic Gold, Holographic Mirror, Holographic Purple and Premiere Date. Other inserts include: Dial-a-Stats, Ornaments, Prospects and Sunday's Best. SRP was $4.99 for five-card packs.

		MT
Complete Set (150):		90.00
Common Player:		.20
Minor Stars:		.40
Common Rookie:		1.00
Pack (5):		3.50
Wax Box (24):		75.00
1	*David Boston*	3.00
2	Rob Moore	.40
3	Adrian Murrell	.20
4	Jake Plummer	1.50
5	Frank Sanders	.40
6	Jamal Anderson	.75
7	Chris Chandler	.40
8	Tim Dwight	.75
9	Terance Mathis	.20
10	Peter Boulware	.20
11	Priest Holmes	.75
12	Patrick Johnson	.40
13	Jermaine Lewis	.20
14	Doug Flutie	1.25
15	Eric Moulds	.75
16	*Peerless Price*	2.00
17	Antowain Smith	.75
18	Bruce Smith	.20
19	Steve Beuerlein	.40
20	Tim Biakabutuka	.40
21	Muhsin Muhammad	.75
22	Wesley Walls	.20
23	Edgar Bennett	.20
24	Curtis Conway	.40
25	Bobby Engram	.20
26	Curtis Enis	.75
27	*Cade McNown*	3.00
28	Jeff Blake	.40
29	*Scott Covington*	1.00
30	Corey Dillon	.75
31	Carl Pickens	.40
32	*Akili Smith*	6.00
33	*Craig Yeast*	1.00
34	*Tim Couch*	10.00
35	Ty Detmer	.20
36	*Kevin Johnson*	3.00
37	Terry Kirby	.20
38	Leslie Shepherd	.20
39	Troy Aikman	1.50
40	Michael Irvin	.40
41	Deion Sanders	.75
42	Emmitt Smith	2.00
43	Bubby Brister	.40
44	Terrell Davis	2.00
45	Brian Griese	1.50
46	Ed McCaffrey	.75
47	Shannon Sharpe	.40
48	Rod Smith	.75
49	Charlie Batch	1.25
50	Germane Crowell	.75
51	*Sedrick Irvin*	2.00
52	Herman Moore	.75
53	Johnnie Morton	.40
54	Barry Sanders	3.00
55	Mark Chmura	.40
56	Brett Favre	3.00
57	Antonio Freeman	.75
58	Dorsey Levens	.75
59	Ken Dilger	.20
60	Marvin Harrison	.75
61	*Edgerrin James*	15.00
62	Peyton Manning	2.00
63	Jerome Pathon	.20
64	Mark Brunell	1.25
65	Keenan McCardell	.40
66	Jimmy Smith	.75
67	Fred Taylor	1.50
68	Derrick Alexander	.20
69	*Michael Cloud*	1.00
70	Tony Gonzalez	.40
71	Elvis Grbac	.40
72	Andre Rison	.40
73	*Cecil Collins*	3.00
74	Oronde Gadsden	.40
75	*James Johnson*	2.00
76	Dan Marino	2.00
77	O.J. McDuffie	.40
78	Lamar Thomas	.20
79	Cris Carter	.75
80	*Daunte Culpepper*	10.00
81	Randall Cunningham	.75
82	Matthew Hatchette	.40
83	Randy Moss	3.00
84	John Randle	.20
85	Robert Smith	.75
86	Drew Bledsoe	1.25
87	Ben Coates	.40
88	*Kevin Faulk*	2.00
89	Terry Glenn	.75
90	Shawn Jefferson	.20
91	Cameron Cleeland	.40
92	Billy Joe Hobert	.20
93	Keith Poole	.20
94	*Ricky Williams*	10.00
95	Gary Brown	.20
96	Kent Graham	.20
97	Ike Hilliard	.40
98	Amani Toomer	.40
99	Wayne Chrebet	.75
100	Keyshawn Johnson	.75
101	Curtis Martin	.75
102	Vinny Testaverde	.40
103	Tim Brown	.40
104	James Jett	.20
105	Napoleon Kaufman	.75
106	Charles Woodson	.75
107	Koy Detmer	.20
108	*Donovan McNabb*	6.00
109	Duce Staley	.75
110	Kevin Turner	.20
111	Jerome Bettis	.75
112	Mark Bruener	.20
113	*Troy Edwards*	3.00
114	Levon Kirkland	.20
115	Kordell Stewart	.75
116	*Amos Zereoue*	1.50
117	Ryan Leaf	.75
118	Natrone Means	.40
119	Mikhael Ricks	.40
120	Junior Seau	.40
121	Garrison Hearst	.40
122	Terrell Owens	.75
123	Jerry Rice	1.50
124	J.J. Stokes	.40
125	Steve Young	1.25
126	Chad Brown	.20
127	Joey Galloway	.75
128	*Brock Huard*	2.00
129	Jon Kitna	1.00
130	Ricky Watters	.40
131	Isaac Bruce	.75
132	*Joe Germaine*	1.50
133	Marshall Faulk	.75
134	*Torry Holt*	3.00
135	Trent Green	.40
136	Mike Alstott	.75
137	Reidel Anthony	.40
138	Trent Dilfer	.40
139	Warrick Dunn	.75
140	Jacquez Green	.40
141	*Shaun King*	5.00
142	*Darnell McDonald*	1.50
143	Eddie George	1.00
144	Steve McNair	1.00
145	Yancey Thigpen	.40
146	Frank Wycheck	.20
147	*Champ Bailey*	2.00
148	Albert Connell	.40
149	Skip Hicks	.40
150	Michael Westbrook	.40

1999 Pacific Prisms Holographic Blue Parallel

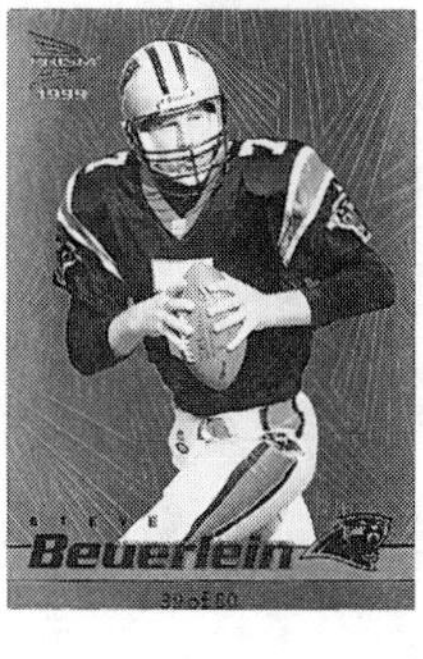
Beuerlein

This was a 150-card parallel to the base set. Each of these singles was printed with blue foil on the background. Singles were found in both hobby and retail packs. Each was sequentially numbered on the front to 80.

	MT
Blue Cards:	12x-24x
Blue Rookies:	4x-8x
Production 80 Sets	

1999 Pacific Prisms Holographic Gold Parallel

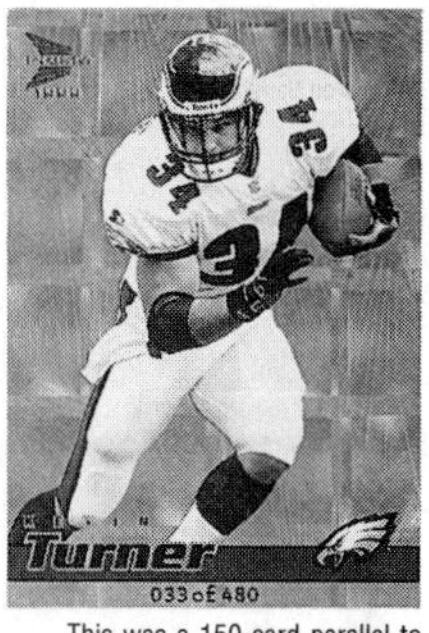
Turner
033 of 480

This was a 150-card parallel to the base set. Each of these singles was printed with gold foil on the background. Singles were found in both hobby and retail packs. Each was sequentially numbered on the front to 480.

	MT
Gold Cards:	3x-6x
Gold Rookies:	2x
Production 480 Sets	

1999 Pacific Prisms Holographic Mirror Parallel

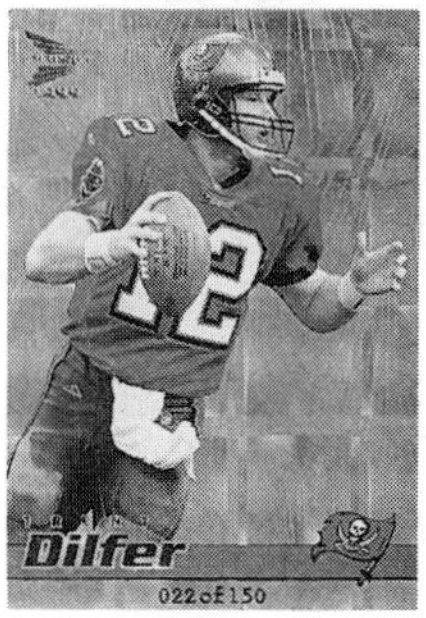
Dilfer
022 of 150

This was a 150-card parallel to the base set. Each of these singles was printed with a mirror foil background. Singles were found in both hobby and retail packs. Each was sequentially numbered on the front to 160.

		MT
Mirror Cards:		10x-20x
Mirror Rookies:		3x-6x
Production 160 Sets		
1	*David Boston*	3.00
2	Rob Moore	.40
3	Adrian Murrell	.20
4	Jake Plummer	1.50
5	Frank Sanders	.40
6	Jamal Anderson	.75
7	Chris Chandler	.40
8	Tim Dwight	.75
9	Terance Mathis	.20
10	Peter Boulware	.20
11	Priest Holmes	.75
12	Patrick Johnson	.40
13	Jermaine Lewis	.20
14	Doug Flutie	1.25
15	Eric Moulds	.75
16	*Peerless Price*	2.00
17	Antowain Smith	.75
18	Bruce Smith	.20
19	Steve Beuerlein	.40
20	Tim Biakabutuka	.40
21	Muhsin Muhammad	.75
22	Wesley Walls	.20
23	Edgar Bennett	.20
24	Curtis Conway	.40
25	Bobby Engram	.20
26	Curtis Enis	.75
27	*Cade McNown*	6.00
28	Jeff Blake	.40
29	*Scott Covington*	1.00
30	Corey Dillon	.75
31	Carl Pickens	.40
32	*Akili Smith*	6.00
33	*Craig Yeast*	1.00
34	*Tim Couch*	10.00
35	Ty Detmer	.20
36	*Kevin Johnson*	3.00
37	Terry Kirby	.20
38	Leslie Shepherd	.20
39	Troy Aikman	1.50
40	Michael Irvin	.40
41	Deion Sanders	.75
42	Emmitt Smith	2.00
43	Bubby Brister	.40
44	Terrell Davis	2.00

45	Brian Griese	1.50
46	Ed McCaffrey	.75
47	Shannon Sharpe	.40
48	Rod Smith	.75
49	Charlie Batch	1.25
50	Germane Crowell	.75
51	*Sedrick Irvin*	2.00
52	Herman Moore	.75
53	Johnnie Morton	.40
54	Barry Sanders	3.00
55	Mark Chmura	.40
56	Brett Favre	3.00
57	Antonio Freeman	.75
58	Dorsey Levens	.75
59	Ken Dilger	.20
60	Marvin Harrison	.75
61	*Edgerrin James*	15.00
62	Peyton Manning	2.00
63	Jerome Pathon	.20
64	Mark Brunell	1.25
65	Keenan McCardell	.40
66	Jimmy Smith	.75
67	Fred Taylor	1.50
68	Derrick Alexander	.20
69	*Michael Cloud*	1.00
70	Tony Gonzalez	.40
71	Elvis Grbac	.40
72	Andre Rison	.40
73	*Cecil Collins*	3.00
74	Oronde Gadsden	.40
75	*James Johnson*	2.00
76	Dan Marino	2.00
77	O.J. McDuffie	.40
78	Lamar Thomas	.20
79	Cris Carter	.75
80	*Daunte Culpepper*	6.00
81	Randall Cunningham	.75
82	Matthew Hatchette	.40
83	Randy Moss	3.00
84	John Randle	.20
85	Robert Smith	.75
86	Drew Bledsoe	1.25
87	Ben Coates	.40
88	*Kevin Faulk*	2.00
89	Terry Glenn	.75
90	Shawn Jefferson	.20
91	Cameron Cleeland	.40
92	Billy Joe Hobert	.20
93	Keith Poole	.20
94	*Ricky Williams*	10.00
95	Gary Brown	.20
96	Kent Graham	.20
97	Ike Hilliard	.40
98	Amani Toomer	.40
99	Wayne Chrebet	.75
100	Keyshawn Johnson	.75
101	Curtis Martin	.75
102	Vinny Testaverde	.40
103	Tim Brown	.40
104	James Jett	.20
105	Napoleon Kaufman	.75
106	Charles Woodson	.75
107	Koy Detmer	.20
108	*Donovan McNabb*	6.00
109	Duce Staley	.75
110	Kevin Turner	.20
111	Jerome Bettis	.75
112	Mark Bruener	.20
113	*Troy Edwards*	3.00
114	Levon Kirkland	.20
115	Kordell Stewart	.75
116	*Amos Zereoue*	1.50
117	Ryan Leaf	.75
118	Natrone Means	.40
119	Mikhael Ricks	.40
120	Junior Seau	.40
121	Garrison Hearst	.40
122	Terrell Owens	.75
123	Jerry Rice	1.50
124	J.J. Stokes	.40
125	Steve Young	1.25
126	Chad Brown	.20
127	Joey Galloway	.75
128	*Brock Huard*	2.00
129	Jon Kitna	1.00
130	Ricky Watters	.40
131	Isaac Bruce	.75
132	*Joe Germaine*	1.50
133	Marshall Faulk	.75
134	*Torry Holt*	3.00
135	Trent Green	.40
136	Mike Alstott	.75
137	Reidel Anthony	.40
138	Trent Dilfer	.40
139	Warrick Dunn	.75
140	Jacquez Green	.40
141	*Shaun King*	5.00
142	*Darnell McDonald*	1.50
143	Eddie George	1.00
144	Steve McNair	1.00
145	Yancey Thigpen	.40
146	Frank Wycheck	.20
147	*Champ Bailey*	2.00
148	Albert Connell	.40
149	Skip Hicks	.40
150	Michael Westbrook	.40

1999 Pacific Prisms Holographic Purple Parallel

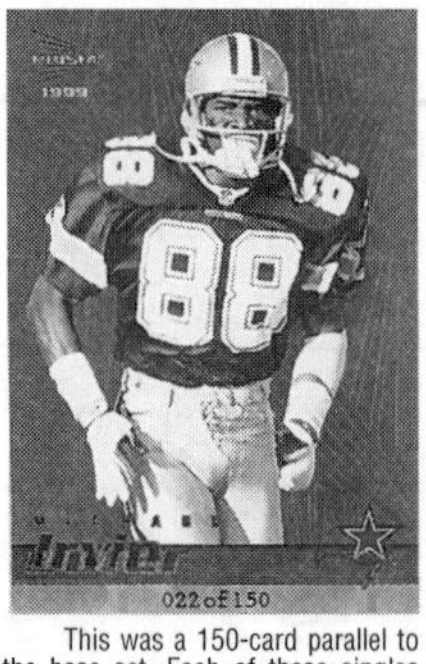

This was a 150-card parallel to the base set. Each of these singles was printed with purple foil on the background. Singles were found only in hobby packs. Each was sequentially numbered on the front to 320.

	MT
Purple Cards:	5x-10x
Purple Rookies:	3x
Production 320 Sets	

1	*David Boston*	3.00
2	Rob Moore	.40
3	Adrian Murrell	.20
4	Jake Plummer	1.50
5	Frank Sanders	.40
6	Jamal Anderson	.75
7	Chris Chandler	.40
8	Tim Dwight	.75
9	Terance Mathis	.20
10	Peter Boulware	.20
11	Priest Holmes	.75
12	Patrick Johnson	.40
13	Jermaine Lewis	.20
14	Doug Flutie	1.25
15	Eric Moulds	.75
16	*Peerless Price*	2.00
17	Antowain Smith	.75
18	Bruce Smith	.20
19	Steve Beuerlein	.40
20	Tim Biakabutuka	.40
21	Muhsin Muhammad	.75
22	Wesley Walls	.20
23	Edgar Bennett	.20
24	Curtis Conway	.40
25	Bobby Engram	.20
26	Curtis Enis	.75
27	*Cade McNown*	6.00
28	Jeff Blake	.40
29	*Scott Covington*	1.00
30	Corey Dillon	.75
31	Carl Pickens	.40
32	*Akili Smith*	6.00
33	*Craig Yeast*	1.00
34	*Tim Couch*	10.00
35	Ty Detmer	.20
36	*Kevin Johnson*	3.00
37	Terry Kirby	.20
38	Leslie Shepherd	.20
39	Troy Aikman	1.50
40	Michael Irvin	.40
41	Deion Sanders	.75
42	Emmitt Smith	2.00
43	Bubby Brister	.40
44	Terrell Davis	2.00
45	Brian Griese	1.50
46	Ed McCaffrey	.75
47	Shannon Sharpe	.40
48	Rod Smith	.75
49	Charlie Batch	1.25
50	Germane Crowell	.75
51	*Sedrick Irvin*	2.00
52	Herman Moore	.75
53	Johnnie Morton	.40
54	Barry Sanders	3.00
55	Mark Chmura	.40
56	Brett Favre	3.00
57	Antonio Freeman	.75
58	Dorsey Levens	.75
59	Ken Dilger	.20
60	Marvin Harrison	.75
61	*Edgerrin James*	15.00
62	Peyton Manning	2.00
63	Jerome Pathon	.20
64	Mark Brunell	1.25
65	Keenan McCardell	.40
66	Jimmy Smith	.75
67	Fred Taylor	1.50
68	Derrick Alexander	.20
69	*Michael Cloud*	1.00
70	Tony Gonzalez	.40
71	Elvis Grbac	.40
72	Andre Rison	.40
73	*Cecil Collins*	3.00
74	Oronde Gadsden	.40
75	*James Johnson*	2.00
76	Dan Marino	2.00
77	O.J. McDuffie	.40
78	Lamar Thomas	.20
79	Cris Carter	.75
80	*Daunte Culpepper*	6.00
81	Randall Cunningham	.75
82	Matthew Hatchette	.40
83	Randy Moss	3.00
84	John Randle	.20
85	Robert Smith	.75
86	Drew Bledsoe	1.25
87	Ben Coates	.40
88	*Kevin Faulk*	2.00
89	Terry Glenn	.75
90	Shawn Jefferson	.20
91	Cameron Cleeland	.40
92	Billy Joe Hobert	.20
93	Keith Poole	.20
94	*Ricky Williams*	10.00
95	Gary Brown	.20
96	Kent Graham	.20
97	Ike Hilliard	.40
98	Amani Toomer	.40
99	Wayne Chrebet	.75
100	Keyshawn Johnson	.75
101	Curtis Martin	.75
102	Vinny Testaverde	.40
103	Tim Brown	.40
104	James Jett	.20
105	Napoleon Kaufman	.75
106	Charles Woodson	.75
107	Koy Detmer	.20
108	*Donovan McNabb*	6.00
109	Duce Staley	.75
110	Kevin Turner	.20
111	Jerome Bettis	.75
112	Mark Bruener	.20
113	*Troy Edwards*	3.00
114	Levon Kirkland	.20
115	Kordell Stewart	.75
116	*Amos Zereoue*	1.50
117	Ryan Leaf	.75
118	Natrone Means	.40
119	Mikhael Ricks	.40
120	Junior Seau	.40
121	Garrison Hearst	.40
122	Terrell Owens	.75
123	Jerry Rice	1.50
124	J.J. Stokes	.40
125	Steve Young	1.25
126	Chad Brown	.20
127	Joey Galloway	.75
128	*Brock Huard*	2.00
129	Jon Kitna	1.00
130	Ricky Watters	.40
131	Isaac Bruce	.75
132	*Joe Germaine*	1.50
133	Marshall Faulk	.75
134	*Torry Holt*	3.00
135	Trent Green	.40
136	Mike Alstott	.75
137	Reidel Anthony	.40
138	Trent Dilfer	.40
139	Warrick Dunn	.75
140	Jacquez Green	.40
141	*Shaun King*	5.00
142	*Darnell McDonald*	1.50
143	Eddie George	1.00
144	Steve McNair	1.00
145	Yancey Thigpen	.40
146	Frank Wycheck	.20
147	*Champ Bailey*	2.00
148	Albert Connell	.40
149	Skip Hicks	.40
150	Michael Westbrook	.40

1999 Pacific Prisms Premiere Date Parallel

This was a 150-card parallel to the base set. Each of these singles was printed with red foil on the background. Singles were found only in hobby packs. Cards were found one-per-box and each was sequentially numbered to 61.

	MT
Premiere Date Cards:	15x-30x
Premiere Date Rookies:	5x-10x
Production 61 Sets	

1999 Pacific Prisms Dial-a-Stats

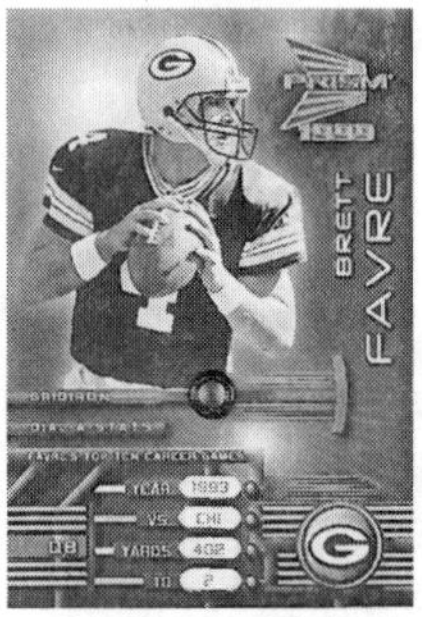

This 10-card insert included a spinning wheel on the card that allowed collectors to dial up a player's top performances. Singles were inserted 1:193 packs.

		MT
Complete Set (10):		185.00
Common Player:		10.00
Inserted 1:193		
1	Tim Couch	40.00
2	Emmitt Smith	30.00
3	Terrell Davis	30.00
4	Barry Sanders	40.00
5	Brett Favre	40.00
6	Mark Brunell	15.00
7	Dan Marino	30.00
8	Ricky Williams	40.00
9	Curtis Martin	10.00
10	Terrell Owens	10.00

1999 Pacific Prisms Ornaments

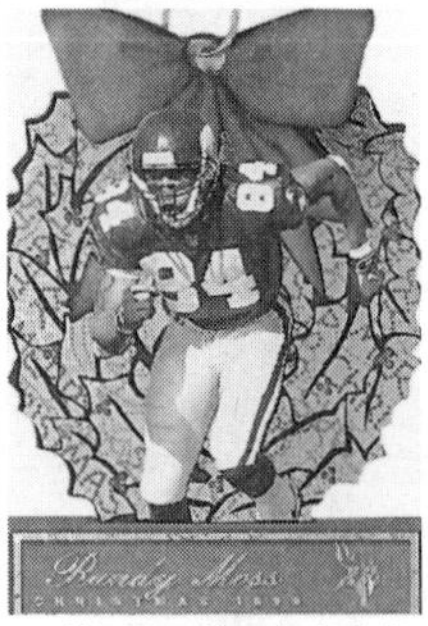

This 20-card insert had a Christmas theme to each single. Five different die cuts could be found in the shapes of Christmas trees, stockings, balls, etc. Each came with a string attached so collectors could hang these on their Christmas trees. Cards were found 1:25 packs.

		MT
Complete Set (20):		150.00
Common Player:		5.00
Inserted 1:25		
1	Jake Plummer	10.00
2	Jamal Anderson	5.00
3	Cade McNown	10.00
4	Tim Couch	15.00
5	Troy Aikman	10.00
6	Deion Sanders	5.00
7	Emmitt Smith	15.00
8	Terrell Davis	15.00
9	Barry Sanders	20.00
10	Brett Favre	20.00
11	Peyton Manning	15.00
12	Mark Brunell	8.00
13	Fred Taylor	10.00
14	Dan Marino	15.00
15	Randy Moss	20.00
16	Drew Bledsoe	8.00
17	Terrell Owens	5.00
18	Jerry Rice	10.00
19	Steve Young	8.00
20	Jon Kitna	5.00

1999 Pacific Prisms Prospects

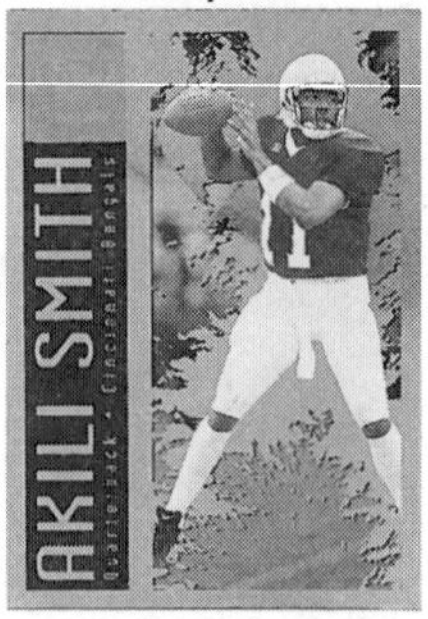

This 10-card insert included rookies from the 1999 NFL Draft. Singles were only found in hobby product and inserted 1:97 packs.

		MT
Complete Set (10):		75.00
Common Player:		5.00
Inserted 1:97		
1	David Boston	5.00
2	Cade McNown	10.00
3	Akili Smith	10.00
4	Tim Couch	15.00
5	Edgerrin James	20.00
6	Cecil Collins	5.00
7	Daunte Culpepper	10.00
8	Ricky Williams	15.00
9	Donovan McNabb	10.00
10	Torry Holt	5.00

1999 Pacific Prisms Sunday's Best

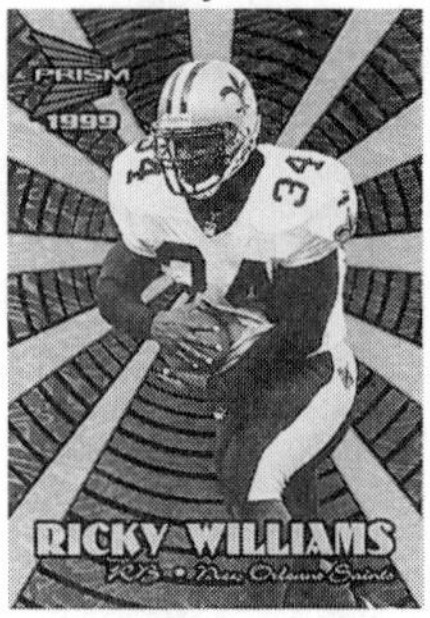

This 20-card insert included a mix of veterans and rookies. Singles were inserted 2:25 packs.

		MT
Complete Set (20):		80.00
Common Player:		2.00
Inserted 2:25		
1	Jake Plummer	5.00
2	Akili Smith	5.00
3	Tim Couch	10.00
4	Emmitt Smith	8.00
5	Terrell Davis	8.00
6	Barry Sanders	10.00
7	Brett Favre	10.00
8	Peyton Manning	10.00
9	Mark Brunell	4.00
10	Fred Taylor	5.00
11	Dan Marino	8.00
12	Randy Moss	10.00
13	Drew Bledsoe	4.00
14	Ricky Williams	10.00
15	Curtis Martin	2.00
16	Terrell Owens	2.00
17	Jerry Rice	5.00
18	Steve Young	3.00
19	Jon Kitna	3.00
20	Eddie George	3.00

1999 Pacific Revolution

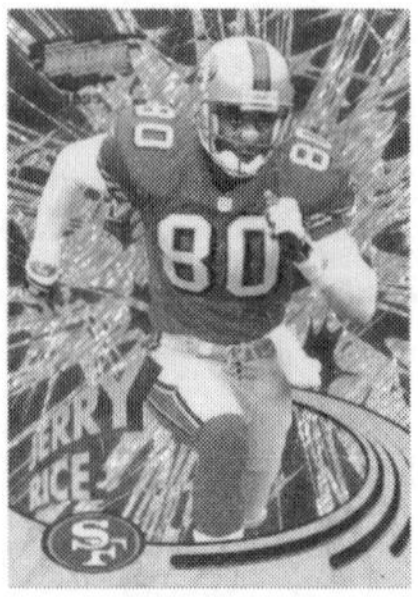

Pacific Revolution is a 175-card set that includes 50 seeded rookies at 1:4 packs. Each card includes dual foiling, etching and embossing. Opening Day, Shadow and Red are three parallel sets. Other inserts include: Chalk Talk, Icons, Showstopper and Thorn in the Side.

		MT
Complete Set (175):		75.00
Common Player:		.25
Minor Stars:		.50
Common Rookie:		1.00
Inserted 1:4		
Pack (3):		4.00
Wax Box (24):		90.00
1	*David Boston*	5.00
2	*Joel Makovicka*	2.00
3	Rob Moore	.50
4	Adrian Murrell	.25
5	Jake Plummer	2.00
6	Frank Sanders	.25
7	Jamal Anderson	1.00
8	Chris Chandler	.50
9	Tim Dwight	.75
10	Terance Mathis	.25
11	*Jeff Paulk*	2.00
12	O.J. Santiago	.25
13	Peter Boulware	.25
14	Priest Holmes	1.00
15	Michael Jackson	.25
16	Jermaine Lewis	.25
17	Doug Flutie	1.50
18	Eric Moulds	1.00
19	*Peerless Price*	4.00
20	Andre Reed	.50
21	Antowain Smith	1.00
22	Bruce Smith	.25
23	Steve Beuerlein	.25
24	Kevin Greene	.25
25	Fred Lane	.25
26	Muhsin Muhammad	.25
27	Wesley Walls	.25
28	*Marty Booker*	1.00
29	Curtis Conway	.50
30	Bobby Engram	.25
31	Curtis Enis	1.00
32	Erik Kramer	.25
33	*Cade McNown*	4.00
34	*Scott Covington*	2.00
35	Corey Dillon	1.25
36	Carl Pickens	.50
37	Darnay Scott	.25
38	*Akili Smith*	7.00
39	*Craig Yeast*	2.00
40	*Darrin Chiaverini*	2.00
41	*Tim Couch*	15.00
42	Ty Detmer	.25
43	*Kevin Johnson*	3.00
44	Terry Kirby	.25
45	*Daylon McCutcheon*	1.00
46	Irv Smith	.25
47	Troy Aikman	2.00
48	Michael Irvin	.75
49	*Wayne McGarity*	2.00
50	*Dat Nguyen*	2.00
51	Deion Sanders	1.00
52	Emmitt Smith	3.00
53	Terrell Davis	3.00
54	John Elway	3.00
55	Brian Griese	1.50
56	Ed McCaffrey	.75
57	*Travis McGriff*	2.00
58	Shannon Sharpe	.50
59	Rod Smith	.50
60	Charlie Batch	1.50
61	*Chris Claiborne*	3.00
62	*Sedrick Irvin*	3.00
63	Herman Moore	1.00
64	Johnnie Morton	.25
65	Barry Sanders	4.00
66	*Aaron Brooks*	6.00
67	Mark Chmura	.50
68	Brett Favre	4.00
69	Antonio Freeman	1.00
70	Dorsey Levens	.75
71	*De'Mond Parker*	1.00
72	Marvin Harrison	.50
73	*Edgerrin James*	15.00
74	Peyton Manning	3.00
75	Jerome Pathon	.25
76	*Mike Peterson*	2.00
77	Reggie Barlow	.25
78	Mark Brunell	1.50
79	Keenan McCardell	.50
80	Jimmy Smith	.75
81	Fred Taylor	2.00
82	*Mike Cloud*	2.00
83	Tony Gonzalez	.50
84	Elvis Grbac	.25
85	*Larry Parker*	1.00
86	Andre Rison	.50
87	*Brian Shay*	1.00
88	Karim Abdul	.75
89	Oronde Gadsden	.50
90	*James Johnson*	3.00
91	*Rob Konrad*	2.00
92	Dan Marino	3.00
93	O.J. McDuffie	.50
94	Cris Carter	1.00
95	*Daunte Culpepper*	12.00
96	Randall Cunningham	1.00
97	*Jim Kleinsasser*	2.00
98	Randy Moss	5.00
99	Jake Reed	.25
100	Robert Smith	.75
101	Drew Bledsoe	1.50
102	Ben Coates	.50
103	*Kevin Faulk*	5.00
104	Terry Glenn	.75
105	Shawn Jefferson	.25
106	*Andy Katzenmoyer*	3.00
107	Cameron Cleeland	.50
108	Andre Hastings	.25
109	Billy Joe Tolliver	.25
110	*Ricky Williams*	15.00
111	Gary Brown	.25
112	Kent Graham	.25
113	Ike Hilliard	.25
114	*Joe Montgomery*	2.00
115	Amani Toomer	.25
116	Wayne Chrebet	.75
117	Keyshawn Johnson	1.00
118	Leon Johnson	.25
119	Curtis Martin	1.00
120	Vinny Testaverde	.50
121	Dedric Ward	.25
122	Tim Brown	.75
123	*Dameane Douglas*	2.00
124	Rickey Dudley	.50
125	James Jett	.25
126	Napoleon Kaufman	1.00
127	Charles Woodson	1.00
128	*Na Brown*	2.00
129	*Cecil Martin*	2.00
130	*Donovan McNabb*	8.00
131	Duce Staley	.25
132	Kevin Turner	.25
133	Jerome Bettis	1.00
134	*Troy Edwards*	4.00
135	Courtney Hawkins	.25
136	*Malcolm Johnson*	2.00
137	Kordell Stewart	1.25
138	*Jerame Tuman*	1.00
139	*Amos Zereoue*	4.00
140	Isaac Bruce	1.00
141	*Joe Germaine*	4.00
142	*Torry Holt*	5.00
143	Amp Lee	.25
144	Ricky Proehl	.25
145	Freddie Jones	.25
146	Ryan Leaf	1.50
147	Natrone Means	1.00
148	Mikhael Ricks	.25
149	Garrison Hearst	.75
150	*Terry Jackson*	2.00
151	Terrell Owens	1.00
152	Jerry Rice	2.00
153	J.J. Stokes	.50
154	Steve Young	1.50
155	*Karsten Bailey*	2.00
156	Joey Galloway	1.00
157	Ahman Green	.50
158	*Brock Huard*	3.00
159	Jon Kitna	1.00
160	Ricky Watters	.75
161	Mike Alstott	1.00
162	Reidel Anthony	.50
163	Trent Dilfer	.75
164	Warrick Dunn	1.25
165	*Shaun King*	6.00
166	*Anthony McFarland*	2.00
167	Kevin Dyson	.50
168	Eddie George	1.25
169	*Darran Hall*	2.00
170	Steve McNair	1.00
171	Frank Wycheck	.25
172	Stephen Alexander	.25
173	*Champ Bailey*	2.50
174	Skip Hicks	.50
175	Michael Westbrook	.25

1999 Pacific Revolution Opening Day Parallel

This is a parallel to the base set and each single is sequentially numbered to 68.

	MT
Opening Day Cards:	20x-40x
Opening Day Rookies:	5x-10x
Production 68 Sets	

1999 Pacific Revolution Red Parallel

This is a parallel to the base set and each single is sequentially numbered to 299.

	MT
Red Cards	3x-6x
Red Rookies:	2x
Production 299 Sets	

1999 Pacific Revolution Shadow Parallel

This is a parallel to the base set and each single is sequentially numbered to 99.

	MT
Shadow Cards:	15x-30x
Shadow Rookies:	4x-8x
Production 99 Sets	

1999 Pacific Revolution Chalk Talk

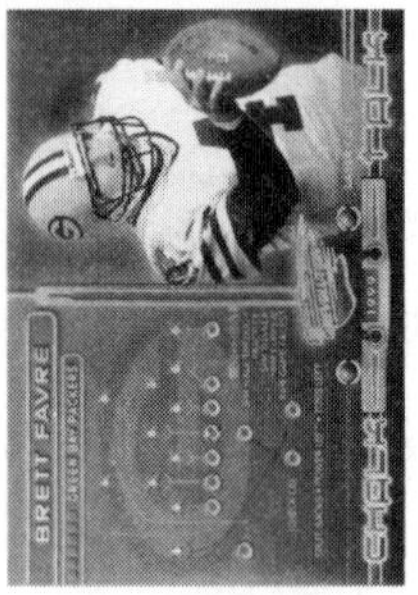

Each card in this 20-card set has the player pictured on a chalk board with a diagram of an offensive play. Singles were inserted 1:49 packs.

		MT
Complete Set (20):		200.00
Common Player:		5.00
Inserted 1:49		
1	Jake Plummer	10.00
2	Jamal Anderson	5.00
3	Doug Flutie	7.00
4	Tim Couch	25.00
5	Troy Aikman	10.00
6	Emmitt Smith	15.00
7	Terrell Davis	15.00
8	John Elway	15.00
9	Barry Sanders	20.00
10	Brett Favre	20.00
11	Peyton Manning	15.00
12	Mark Brunell	8.00
13	Fred Taylor	10.00
14	Dan Marino	15.00
15	Randy Moss	25.00
16	Drew Bledsoe	8.00
17	Ricky Williams	25.00
18	Jerry Rice	10.00
19	Jon Kitna	5.00
20	Eddie George	7.00

1999 Pacific Revolution Icons

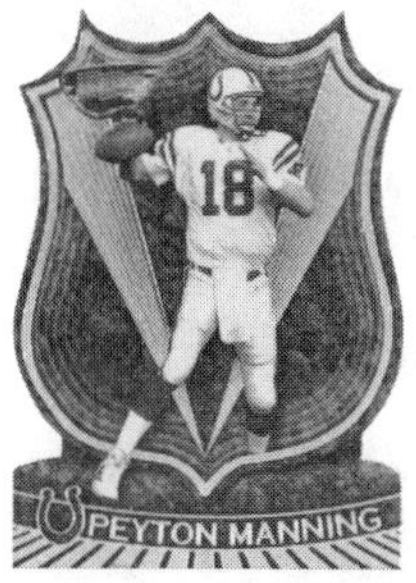

Each card is silver foiled, etched and die-cut. The 10 players in the set were found 1:121 packs.

		MT
Complete Set (10):		275.00
Common Player:		15.00
Inserted 1:121		
1	Emmitt Smith	35.00
2	Terrell Davis	35.00
3	John Elway	35.00
4	Barry Sanders	50.00
5	Brett Favre	50.00
6	Peyton Manning	35.00
7	Dan Marino	35.00
8	Randy Moss	60.00
9	Jerry Rice	25.00
10	Jon Kitna	15.00

1999 Pacific Revolution Showstoppers

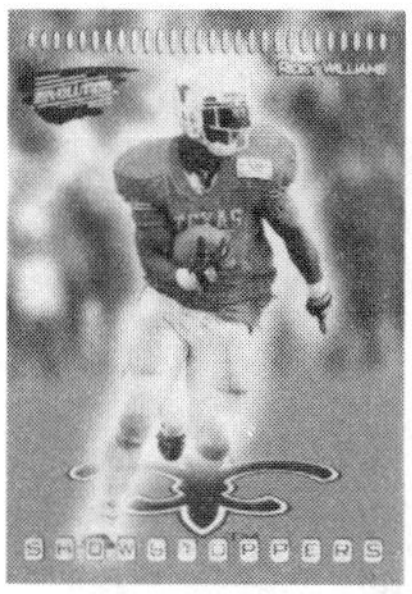

The top 36 players in the NFL are in this insert that is etched and includes silver foil on the fronts. Singles were inserted 2:25 packs.

		MT
Complete Set (36):		160.00
Common Player:		2.50
Minor Stars:		5.00
Inserted 2:25		
1	Jake Plummer	7.50
2	Jamal Anderson	2.50
3	Priest Holmes	5.00
4	Doug Flutie	6.00
5	Antowain Smith	5.00
6	Cade McNown	7.00
7	Tim Couch	20.00
8	Corey Dillon	5.00
9	Akili Smith	7.00
10	Troy Aikman	7.50
11	Emmitt Smith	10.00
12	Terrell Davis	10.00
13	John Elway	10.00
14	Charlie Batch	6.00
15	Barry Sanders	15.00
16	Brett Favre	15.00
17	Antonio Freeman	2.50
18	Edgerrin James	10.00
19	Peyton Manning	10.00
20	Mark Brunell	6.00
21	Fred Taylor	7.50
22	Dan Marino	10.00
23	Randall Cunningham	5.00
24	Randy Moss	15.00
25	Drew Bledsoe	6.00
26	Ricky Williams	20.00
27	Curtis Martin	5.00
28	Napoleon Kaufman	5.00
29	Donovan McNabb	7.00
30	Kordell Stewart	6.00
31	Terrell Owens	5.00
32	Jerry Rice	7.50
33	Steve Young	6.00
34	Jon Kitna	5.00
35	Warrick Dunn	6.00
36	Eddie George	6.00

Values quoted in this guide reflect the retail price of a card — the price a collector can expect to pay when buying a card from a dealer. The wholesale price — that which a collector can expect to receive from a dealer when selling cards — will be significantly lower, depending on desirability and condition.

1999 Pacific Revolution Thorn in the Side

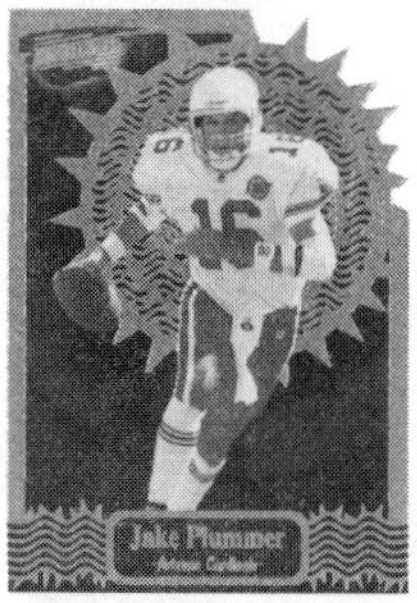

Each card is die cut and on the back includes an analysis of how that player has hurt an opposing team. A total of 20 players were used for this insert and were found 1:25 packs.

		MT
Complete Set (20):		125.00
Common Player:		2.50
Minor Stars:		5.00
Inserted 1:25		
1	Jake Plummer	7.50
2	Jamal Anderson	2.50
3	Doug Flutie	6.00
4	Tim Couch	20.00
5	Troy Aikman	7.50
6	Emmitt Smith	10.00
7	Terrell Davis	10.00
8	John Elway	10.00
9	Barry Sanders	15.00
10	Brett Favre	15.00
11	Peyton Manning	10.00
12	Fred Taylor	7.50
13	Dan Marino	10.00
14	Randy Moss	15.00
15	Drew Bledsoe	6.00
16	Ricky Williams	20.00
17	Curtis Martin	5.00
18	Jerome Bettis	2.50
19	Jerry Rice	7.50
20	Jon Kitna	5.00

2000 Pacific

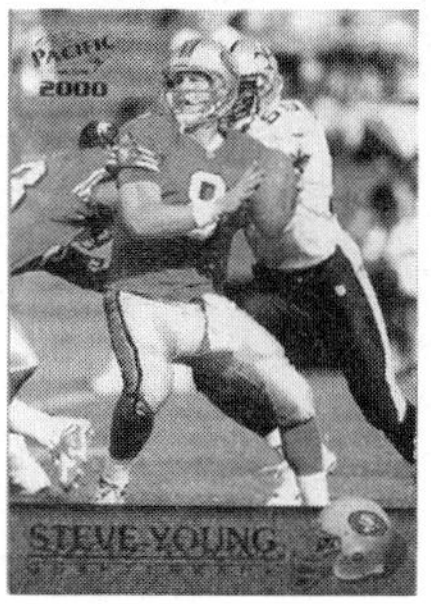

		MT
Complete Set (450):		75.00
Common Player:		.10
Minor Stars:		.20
Common Rookie:		.50
Pack (12):		3.00
Wax Box (36):		85.00
1	Mario Bates	.10
2	David Boston	.50
3	Rob Fredrickson	.10
4	Terry Hardy	.10
5	Rob Moore	.20
6	Adrian Murrell	.20
7	Michael Pittman	.10
8	Jake Plummer	.50
9	Simeon Rice	.10
10	Frank Sanders	.10
11	Aeneas Williams	.10
12	Mac Cody, Andy McCullough	.10
13	*Dennis McKinley*, Joel Makovicka	.50
14	Jamal Anderson	.50
15	Chris Calloway	.10
16	Chris Chandler	.20
17	Bob Christian	.10
18	Tim Dwight	.50
19	Jammi German	.10
20	Ronnie Harris	.10
21	Terance Mathis	.10
22	Ken Oxendine	.10
23	O.J. Santiago	.10
24	Bob Whitfield	.10
25	Eugene Baker, Reggie Kelly	.10
26	Justin Armour	.10
27	Tony Banks	.20
28	Peter Boulware	.10
29	Stoney Case	.10
30	Priest Holmes	.30
31	Qadry Ismail	.10
32	Patrick Johnson	.10
33	Michael McCrary	.10
34	Jonathan Ogden	.10
35	Errict Rhett	.20
36	Duane Starks	.10
37	Doug Flutie	.75
38	Rob Johnson	.20
39	Jonathon Linton	.20
40	Eric Moulds	.50
41	Peerless Price	.30
42	Andre Reed	.20
43	Jay Riemersma	.10
44	Antowain Smith	.30
45	Bruce Smith	.10
46	Thurman Thomas	.20
47	Kevin Williams	.10
48	Bobby Collins, Sheldon Jackson	.10
49	Michael Bates	.10
50	Steve Beuerlein	.20
51	Tshimanga Biakabutuka	.20
52	Antonio Edwards	.10
53	Donald Hayes	.10
54	Patrick Jeffers	.30
55	Anthony Johnson	.10
56	Jeff Lewis	.10
57	Eric Metcalf	.10
58	Muhsin Muhammad	.20
59	Jason Peter	.10
60	Wesley Walls	.20
61	John Allred	.10
62	Marty Booker	.10
63	Curtis Conway	.20
64	Bobby Engram	.10
65	Curtis Enis	.30
66	Shane Matthews	.10
67	Cade McNown	.75
68	Glyn Milburn	.10
69	Jim Miller	.10
70	Marcus Robinson	.50
71	Ryan Wetnight	.10
72	James Allen, Macey Brooks	.10
73	Jeff Blake	.20
74	Corey Dillon	.30
75	Rodney Heath	.10
76	Willie Jackson	.10
77	Tremain Mack	.10
78	Tony McGee	.10
79	Carl Pickens	.20
80	Darnay Scott	.20
81	Akili Smith	.60
82	Takeo Spikes	.10
83	Craig Yeast	.10
84	Michael Basnight, Nick Williams	.10
85	Karim Abdul	.20
86	Darren Chiaverini	.10
87	Tim Couch	1.25
88	Marc Edwards	.10
89	Kevin Johnson	.50
90	Terry Kirby	.10
91	Daylon McCutcheon	.10
92	Jamir Miller	.10
93	Leslie Shepherd	.10
94	Irv Smith	.10
95	Mark Campbell, James Dearth	.10
96	Zola Davis, Damon Dunn	.10
97	Madre Hill, Tarek Selah	.10
98	Troy Aikman	1.25
99	Eric Bjornson	.10
100	Dexter Coakley	.10
101	Greg Ellis	.10
102	Raghib Ismail	.10
103	David LaFleur	.10
104	Ernie Mills	.10
105	Jeff Ogden	.10
106	Ryan Neufeld, Robert Thomas	.10
107	Deion Sanders	.50
108	Emmitt Smith	2.00
109	Chris Warren	.20
110	Mike Lucky, Jason Tucker	.30
111	Byron Chamberlain	.10
112	Terrell Davis	2.00
113	Jason Elam	.10
114	Olandis Gary	.60
115	Brian Griese	.60
116	Ed McCaffrey	.50
117	Trevor Pryce	.10
118	Bill Romanowski	.10
119	Shannon Sharpe	.30
120	Rod Smith	.50
121	Al Wilson	.10
122	Andre Cooper, Chris Watson	.10
123	Charlie Batch	.50
124	Stephen Boyd	.10
125	Chris Claiborne	.10
126	Germane Crowell	.20
127	Terry Fair	.10
128	Gus Frerotte	.10
129	Jason Hanson	.10
130	Greg Hill	.10
131	Herman Moore	.30
132	Johnnie Morton	.10
133	Barry Sanders	2.00
134	David Sloan	.10
135	Brock Olivo, Cory Sauter	.10
136	Corey Bradford	.20
137	Tyrone Davis	.10
138	Brett Favre	2.50
139	Antonio Freeman	.50
140	Vonnie Holliday	.10
141	Dorsey Levens	.50
142	Keith McKenzie	.10
143	Mike McKenzie	.10
144	Bill Schroeder	.10
145	Jeff Thomason	.10
146	Frank Winters	.10
147	Cornelius Bennett	.10
148	Tony Blevins	.10
149	Chad Bratzke	.10
150	Ken Dilger	.10
151	Tarik Glenn	.10
152	E.G. Green	.10
153	Marvin Harrison	.50
154	Edgerrin James	2.50
155	Peyton Manning	2.00
156	Jerome Pathon	.10
157	Marcus Pollard	.10
158	Terrence Wilkins	.10
159	*Issac Jones,Paul Shields*	.50
160	Reggie Barlow	.10
161	Aaron Beasley	.10
162	Tony Boselli	.10
163	Tony Brackens	.10
164	Kyle Brady	.10
165	Mark Brunell	.75
166	Jay Fiedler	.20
167	Kevin Hardy	.10
168	Carnell Lake	.10
169	Keenan McCardell	.20
170	Jonathan Quinn	.10
171	Jimmy Smith	.30
172	James Stewart	.30
173	Fred Taylor	.75
174	*Lenzie Jackson*, Stacey Mack	.50
175	Derrick Alexander	.10
176	Donnell Bennett	.10
177	Donnie Edwards	.10
178	Tony Gonzalez	.30
179	Elvis Grbac	.20
180	James Hasty	.10
181	Joe Horn	.10
182	Lonnie Johnson	.10
183	Kevin Lockett	.10
184	Larry Parker	.10
185	Tony Richardson	.10
186	Rashaan Shehee	.10
187	Tamarick Vanover	.10
188	Trace Armstrong	.10
189	Oronde Gadsden	.10
190	Damon Huard	.20
191	Nate Jacquet	.10
192	J.J. Johnson	.20
193	Rob Konrad	.10
194	Sam Madison	.10
195	Dan Marino	2.00
196	Tony Martin	.10
197	O.J. McDuffie	.20
198	Stanley Pritchett	.10
199	Tim Ruddy	.10
200	Patrick Surtain	.10
201	Zach Thomas	.20
202	Cris Carter	.50
203	Duane Clemons	.10
204	Carlester Crumpler	.10
205	Daunte Culpepper	.75
206	Jeff George	.30
207	Matthew Hatchette	.10
208	Leroy Hoard	.10
209	Randy Moss	2.00
210	John Randle	.10
211	Jake Reed	.10
212	Robert Smith	.50
213	Robert Tate	.10
214	Terry Allen	.20
215	Bruce Armstrong	.10
216	Drew Bledsoe	.75
217	Ben Coates	.20
218	Kevin Faulk	.20
219	Terry Glenn	.30
220	Shawn Jefferson	.10
221	Andy Katzenmoyer	.10
222	Ty Law	.10
223	Willie McGinest	.10
224	Lawyer Milloy	.10
225	Tony Simmons	.10
226	Michael Bishop, Sean Morey	.10
227	Cameron Cleeland	.20
228	Troy Davis	.10
229	*Jake Delhomme*	1.50
230	Andre Hastings	.10
231	Eddie Kennison	.20
232	Wilmont Perry	.10
233	Dino Philyaw	.10
234	Keith Poole	.10
235	William Roaf	.10
236	Billy Joe Tolliver	.10
237	Fred Weary	.10
238	Ricky Williams	1.25
239	*P.J. Franklin,Marvin Powell*	.50
240	Jessie Armstead	.10
241	Tiki Barber	.20
242	Daniel Campbell	.10
243	Kerry Collins	.20
244	Percy Ellsworth	.10
245	Kent Graham	.10
246	Ike Hilliard	.20
247	Cedric Jones	.10
248	Bashir Livingston	.10
249	Pete Mitchell	.10
250	Michael Strahan	.10
251	Amani Toomer	.20
252	Charles Way	.10
253	Andre Weathers	.10
254	Richie Anderson	.10
255	Wayne Chrebet	.50
256	Marcus Coleman	.10
257	Bryan Cox	.10
258	Jason Fabini	.10
259	*Robert Farmer*	.50
260	Keyshawn Johnson	.50
261	Ray Lucas	.30
262	Curtis Martin	.50
263	Kevin Mawae	.10
264	Eric Ogbogu	.10
265	Bernie Parmalee	.10
266	Vinny Testaverde	.30
267	Dedric Ward	.10
268	Eric Barton	.10
269	Tim Brown	.30
270	Tony Bryant	.10
271	Rickey Dudley	.20
272	Rich Gannon	.20
273	Bobby Hoying	.30
274	James Jett	.10
275	Napoleon Kaufman	.30
276	Jon Ritchie	.10
277	Darrell Russell	.10
278	Kenny Shedd	.10
279	Marquis Walker	.10
280	Tyrone Wheatley	.20
281	Charles Woodson	.50
282	Luther Broughton	.10
283	Al Harris	.10
284	Greg Jefferson	.10
285	Dietrich Jells	.10
286	Charles Johnson	.10
287	Chad Lewis	.10
288	Mike Mamula	.10
289	Donovan McNabb	.75
290	Doug Pederson	.10
291	Allen Rossum	.10
292	Torrance Small	.10
293	Duce Staley	.30
294	Jerome Bettis	.50
295	Kris Brown	.10
296	Mark Bruener	.10
297	Troy Edwards	.50
298	Jason Gildon	.10
299	Richard Huntley	.10
300	Bobby Shaw	.10
301	Scott Shields	.10
302	Kordell Stewart	.50
303	Hines Ward	.20
304	Amos Zereoue	.20
305	Matt Cushing, Jerame Tuman	.10
306	Pete Gonzalez,*Anthony Wright*	3.00
307	Isaac Bruce	.50
308	Kevin Carter	.10
309	Marshall Faulk	.50
310	London Fletcher	.10
311	Joe Germaine	.20
312	Az-Zahir Hakim	.20
313	Torry Holt	.50
314	Tony Horne	.20
315	Mike Jones	.10
316	Dexter McCleon	.10
317	Orlando Pace	.10
318	Ricky Proehl	.10
319	Kurt Warner	3.00
320	Roland Williams	.10
321	Grant Winstrom	.10
322	James Hodgins, Justin Watson	.10
323	Jermaine Fazande	.20
324	Jeff Graham	.10
325	Jim Harbaugh	.20
326	Raylee Johnson	.10
327	Charlie Jones	.10
328	Freddie Jones	.10
329	Natrone Means	.20
330	Chris Penn	.10
331	Mikhael Ricks	.10
332	Junior Seau	.20
333	Reginald Davis, Robert Reed	.10
334	Fred Beasley	.10
335	Brenston Buckner	.10
336	Greg Clark	.10
337	Dave Fiore	.10
338	Charlie Garner	.20
339	*Mark Harris*	.50
340	Ramos McDonald	.10
341	Terrell Owens	.50
342	Jerry Rice	1.25
343	Lance Schulters	.10
344	J.J. Stokes	.20
345	Bryant Young	.10
346	Steve Young	.75
347	Jeff Garcia	.50
348	Fabien Bownes	.10
349	Chad Brown	.10
350	Reggie Brown	.10
351	Sean Dawkins	.10
352	Christian Fauria	.10
353	Ahman Green	.20
354	Walter Jones	.10
355	Cortez Kennedy	.10
356	Jon Kitna	.50
357	Derrick Mayes	.20
358	Charlie Rogers	.10
359	Shawn Springs	.10
360	Ricky Watters	.20
361	Donnie Abraham	.10
362	Mike Alstott	.50
363	Reidel Anthony	.20
364	Ronde Barber	.10
365	Derrick Brooks	.10
366	Warrick Dunn	.50
367	Jacquez Green	.20
368	Marcus Jones	.10
369	Shaun King	.75
370	John Lynch	.10
371	Warren Sapp	.10
372	Steve White	.10
373	Martin Gramatica, Kevin McCloud	.10
374	Blaine Bishop	.10
375	Al Del Greco	.10
376	Kevin Dyson	.20
377	Eddie George	.60
378	Jevon Kearse	.60
379	Derrick Mason	.10
380	Bruce Matthews	.10
381	Steve McNair	.60
382	Neil O'Donnell	.20
383	Yancey Thigpen	.20
384	Frank Wycheck	.10
385	Kevin Daft, Larry Brown	.10
386	Stephen Alexander	.10
387	Champ Bailey	.30
388	Larry Centers	.10
389	Marco Coleman	.10
390	Albert Connell	.30
391	Stephen Davis	.50
392	Irving Fryar	.10
393	Skip Hicks	.20
394	Brad Johnson	.50
395	Michael Westbrook	.30
396	Obafemi Ayanbadejo, Lennox Gordon	.10
397	Donald Driver, Ronnie Powell	.10
398	Todd Bouman,*Jeremy Brigham*	.50
399	Brock Huard, Sherdrick Bonner	.30
400	Mike Sellers, Spencer George	.10
401	*Shaun Alexander*	3.00
402	*Lavar Arrington*	3.00
403	*Tom Brady*	1.00
404	*Demario Brown*	.50
405	*Plaxico Burress*	3.00
406	*Trung Canidate*	1.00
407	*Giovanni Carmazzi*	2.50
408	*Kwame Cavil*	1.00
409	*Chrys Chukwuma*	.50
410	*Ron Dayne*	5.00
411	*Reuben Droughns*	1.50
412	*Ron Dugans*	1.00
413	*Deon Dyer*	1.00
414	*Danny Farmer*	1.00
415	*Chafie Fields*	1.00
416	*Trevor Gaylor*	1.00
417	*Sherrod Gideon*	1.00
418	*Joey Goodspeed*	1.00
419	*Joe Hamilton*	1.25
420	*Tony Hartley*	1.00
421	*Todd Husak*	1.00
422	*Trevor Insley*	.50
423	*Thomas Jones*	4.00
424	*Marcus Knight*	.50
425	*Jamal Lewis*	4.00
426	*Anthony Lucas*	1.00
427	*Tee Martin*	2.00
428	*Rondell Mealey*	1.00
429	*Sylvester Morris*	2.00
430	*Chad Morton*	1.00
431	*Dennis Northcutt*	1.50
432	*Chad Pennington*	4.00
433	*Rodnick Phillips*	.50
434	*Mareno Philyaw*	.50
435	*Jerry Porter*	2.00
436	*Travis Prentice*	2.00
437	*Tim Rattay*	1.50
438	*Chris Redman*	2.50
439	*J.R. Redmond*	2.00
440	*Gari Scott*	1.00
441	*Keith Smith*	1.00
442	*Terrelle Smith*	1.00
443	*R. Jay Soward*	2.00
444	*Quinton Spotwood*	1.00
445	*Shyrone Stith*	1.00
446	*Travis Taylor*	2.50
447	*Troy Walters*	1.00
448	*Peter Warrick*	6.00
449	*Dez White*	1.00
450	*Michael Wiley*	1.00

2000 Pacific Copper Parallel

	MT
Copper Cards:	15x-30x
Copper Rookies:	6x-12x
Production 75 Sets	

2000 Pacific Gold Parallel

	MT
Gold Cards:	8x-16x
Gold Rookies:	4x-8x
Production 199 Sets	

2000 Pacific Platinum Blue Draft Picks Parallel

	MT
Complete Set (50):	200.00
Plat. Blue Cards:	2x-4x
Production 399 Sets	

2000 Pacific Premiere Date Parallel

	MT
Premiere Date Cards:	15x-30x
Premiere Date Rookies:	6x-12x
Production 78 Sets	

2000 Pacific Draft Picks 999 Parallel

	MT
Complete Set (50):	125.00
999 Cards:	3x
Production 999 Sets	

2000 Pacific AFC Leaders

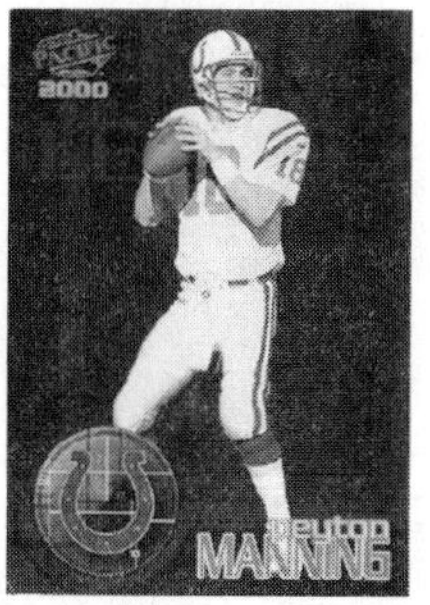

		MT
Complete Set (10):		25.00
Common Player:		1.00
Minor Stars:		2.00
Inserted 1:37		
1	Tim Couch	5.00
2	Olandis Gary	2.50
3	Marvin Harrison	2.00
4	Edgerrin James	6.00
5	Peyton Manning	5.00
6	Mark Brunell	3.00
7	Jimmy Smith	1.00
8	Drew Bledsoe	3.00
9	Keyshawn Johnson	2.00
10	Eddie George	2.50

2000 Pacific Autographs

		MT
Common Player:		7.50
Minor Stars:		15.00
Random Inserts		
51	Tim Biakabutuka	7.50
70	Marcus Robinson	30.00
87	Tim Couch	60.00
229	Jake Delhomme	25.00
307	Isaac Bruce	20.00
319	Kurt Warner	100.00
362	Mike Alstott	20.00
391	Stephen Davis	20.00
401	Shaun Alexander	40.00
403	Tom Brady	15.00
404	Demario Brown	15.00
405	Plaxico Burress	50.00
406	Trung Canidate	15.00
407	Giovanni Carmazzi	25.00
408	Kwame Cavil	7.50
410	Ron Dayne	60.00
411	Reuben Droughns	15.00
412	Ron Dugans	15.00
414	Danny Farmer	15.00
415	Chafie Fields	7.50
417	Sherrod Gideon	7.50
420	Tony Hartley	7.50
421	Todd Husak	7.50
423	Thomas Jones	50.00
424	Marcus Knight	7.50
426	Anthony Lucas	15.00
427	Tee Martin	25.00

428	Rondell Mealey	7.50
429	Sylvester Morris	25.00
431	Dennis Northcutt	25.00
432	Chad Pennington	50.00
434	Mareno Philyaw	7.50
435	Jerry Porter	25.00
436	Travis Prentice	20.00
437	Tim Rattay	20.00
438	Chris Redman	25.00
439	J.R. Redmond	25.00
443	R. Jay Soward	20.00
445	Shyrone Stith	15.00
446	Travis Taylor	25.00
447	Troy Walters	15.00
448	Peter Warrick	75.00
449	Dez White	20.00
450	Michael Wiley	20.00

2000 Pacific Cramer's Choice Awards

		MT
Complete Set (10):		375.00
Common Player:		25.00
Inserted 1:721		
1	Tim Couch	50.00
2	Emmitt Smith	40.00
3	Brett Favre	60.00
4	Edgerrin James	60.00
5	Peyton Manning	50.00
6	Randy Moss	50.00
7	Marshall Faulk	25.00
8	Kurt Warner	85.00
9	Eddie George	25.00
10	Peter Warrick	60.00

2000 Pacific Finest Hour

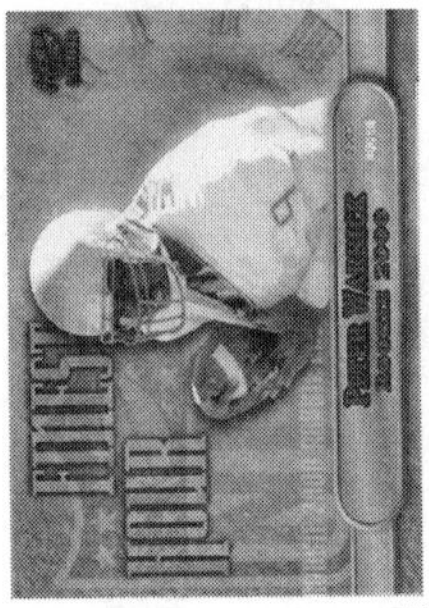

		MT
Complete Set (20):		120.00
Common Player:		3.00
Inserted 1:73		
1	Terrell Davis	8.00
2	Barry Sanders	10.00
3	Brett Favre	12.00
4	Edgerrin James	12.00
5	Drew Bledsoe	5.00
6	Damon Huard	3.00
7	Randy Moss	10.00
8	Kurt Warner	15.00
9	Jerry Rice	6.00
10	Stephen Davis	3.00
11	Shaun Alexander	8.00
12	Peter Warrick	15.00
13	Chris Redman	6.00
14	Chad Pennington	10.00
15	Tom Brady	5.00
16	Plaxico Burress	10.00
17	Todd Husak	3.00
18	Jamal Lewis	10.00
19	Thomas Jones	10.00
20	Ron Dayne	12.00

2000 Pacific Game-Worn Jerseys

		MT
Complete Set (9):		400.00
Common Player:		25.00
Inserted 1:5 Boxes		
1	Kurt Warner	125.00
2	Fred Taylor	60.00
3	Ricky Williams	85.00
4	Ike Hilliard	25.00
5	Tim Brown	25.00
6	Brett Favre	100.00
7	Jon Kitna	25.00
8	Kordell Stewart	45.00
9	Natrone Means	25.00

2000 Pacific Gold Crown Die-Cuts

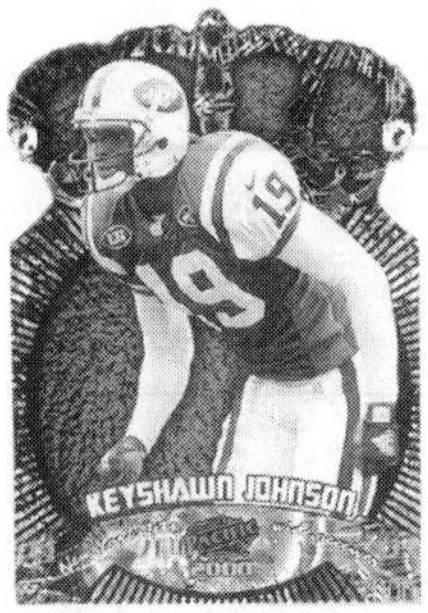

		MT
Complete Set (36):		165.00
Common Player:		2.50
Inserted 1:37		
1	Jake Plummer	2.50
2	Cade McNown	5.00
3	Corey Dillon	2.50
4	Akili Smith	2.50
5	Tim Couch	7.00
6	Kevin Johnson	2.50
7	Olandis Gary	4.00
8	Brian Griese	4.00
9	Marvin Harrison	2.50
10	Edgerrin James	12.00
11	Mark Brunell	4.00
12	Fred Taylor	5.00
13	Damon Huard	2.50
14	Dan Marino	10.00
15	Randy Moss	10.00
16	Drew Bledsoe	4.00
17	Ricky Williams	7.00
18	Keyshawn Johnson	2.50
19	Donovan McNabb	5.00
20	Marshall Faulk	2.50
21	Kurt Warner	15.00
22	Jon Kitna	2.50
23	Jerry Rice	8.00
24	Shaun King	5.00
25	Eddie George	4.00
26	Steve McNair	4.00
27	Stephen Davis	2.50
28	Brad Johnson	2.50
29	Shaun Alexander	10.00
30	Plaxico Burress	12.00
31	Ron Dayne	15.00
32	Joe Hamilton	5.00
33	Thomas Jones	12.00
34	Chad Pennington	12.00
35	Chris Redman	8.00
36	Peter Warrick	20.00

2000 Pacific NFC Leaders

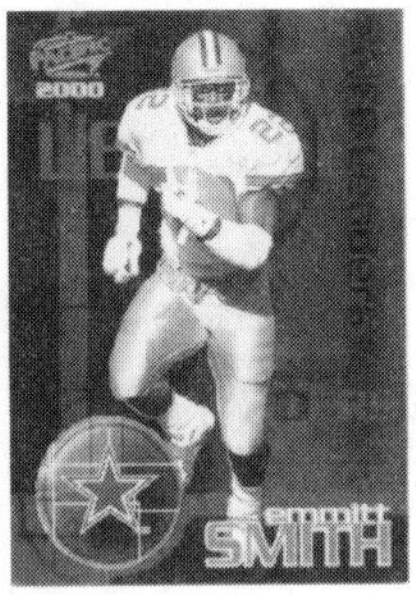

		MT
Complete Set (10):		20.00
Common Player:		1.00
Minor Stars:		2.00
Inserted 1:37		
1	Marcus Robinson	2.00
2	Troy Aikman	4.00
3	Emmitt Smith	5.00
4	Cris Carter	2.00
5	Randy Moss	7.00
6	Isaac Bruce	2.00
7	Marshall Faulk	2.00
8	Kurt Warner	12.00
9	Stephen Davis	1.00
10	Brad Johnson	1.00

2000 Pacific Pro Bowl Die Cuts

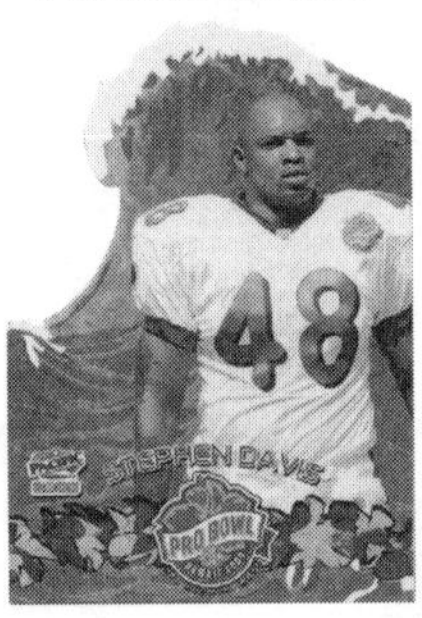

		MT
Complete Set (20):		60.00
Common Player:		1.50
Minor Stars:		3.00
Inserted 1:37		
1	Steve Beuerlein	1.50
2	Corey Dillon	3.00
3	Emmitt Smith	6.00
4	Marvin Harrison	3.00
5	Edgerrin James	10.00
6	Peyton Manning	8.00
7	Mark Brunell	4.00
8	Jimmy Smith	1.50
9	Tony Gonzalez	1.50
10	Cris Carter	3.00
11	Randy Moss	8.00
12	Rich Gannon	1.50
13	Keyshawn Johnson	3.00
14	Terry Glenn	3.00
15	Marshall Faulk	3.00
16	Kurt Warner	15.00
17	Mike Alstott	3.00
18	Eddie George	3.50
19	Stephen Davis	1.50
20	Brad Johnson	1.50

Post-1980 cards in Near Mint condition will generally sell for about 75% of the quoted Mint value. Excellent-condition cards bring no more than 40%.

2000 Pacific Reflections

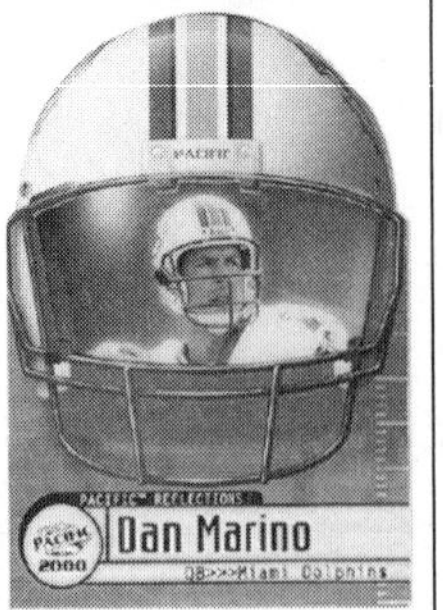

		MT
Complete Set (20):		135.00
Common Player:		5.00
Inserted 1:145		
1	Cade McNown	6.00
2	Tim Couch	10.00
3	Troy Aikman	10.00
4	Emmitt Smith	12.00
5	Terrell Davis	12.00
6	Barry Sanders	12.00
7	Brett Favre	15.00
8	Marvin Harrison	5.00
9	Edgerrin James	15.00
10	Mark Brunell	6.00
11	Fred Taylor	7.00
12	Dan Marino	12.00
13	Randy Moss	12.00
14	Ricky Williams	10.00
15	Marshall Faulk	5.00
16	Kurt Warner	20.00
17	Jon Kitna	5.00
18	Shaun King	6.00
19	Eddie George	5.00
20	Stephen Davis	5.00

2000 Pacific Aurora

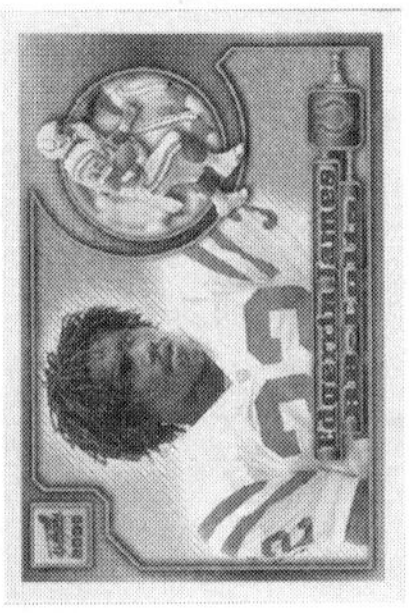

		MT
Complete Set (150):		40.00
Common Player:		.15
Minor Stars:		.30
Common Rookie:		.50
Pack (6):		3.00
Wax Box (36):		75.00
1	David Boston	.50
2	*Thomas Jones*	3.00
3	Rob Moore	.30
4	Jake Plummer	.50
5	Frank Sanders	.15
6	Jamal Anderson	.50
7	Chris Chandler	.30
8	Tim Dwight	.50
9	*Doug Johnson*	1.00
10	Tony Banks	.30
11	Qadry Ismail	.15
12	*Jamal Lewis*	6.00
13	*Chris Redman*	2.00
14	*Travis Taylor*	1.50
15	Doug Flutie	.50
16	Rob Johnson	.30
17	Eric Moulds	.50
18	Peerless Price	.50
19	Antowain Smith	.50
20	Steve Beuerlein	.30
21	Tim Biakabutuka	.15
22	Patrick Jeffers	.50
23	Muhsin Muhammad	.30
24	Curtis Enis	.50
25	Cade McNown	.75
26	Marcus Robinson	.50
27	*Dez White*	1.00
28	Corey Dillon	.50
29	*Ron Dugans*	1.00
30	Darnay Scott	.30
31	Akili Smith	.60
32	*Peter Warrick*	3.50
33	Tim Couch	1.25
34	*JaJuan Dawson*	1.50
35	Kevin Johnson	.50
36	*Dennis Northcutt*	1.25
37	*Travis Prentice*	1.50
38	Troy Aikman	1.00
39	Raghib Ismail	.15
40	Emmitt Smith	1.25
41	Jason Tucker	.30
42	Terrell Davis	1.25
43	Olandis Gary	.60
44	Brian Griese	.60
45	Ed McCaffrey	.30
46	Rod Smith	.30
47	Charlie Batch	.50
48	Germane Crowell	.30
49	*Reuben Droughns*	1.00
50	Herman Moore	.30
51	Barry Sanders	1.75
52	Brett Favre	2.00
53	*Bubba Franks*	1.50
54	Antonio Freeman	.50
55	Dorsey Levens	.50
56	Bill Schroeder	.15
57	Marvin Harrison	.50
58	Edgerrin James	2.00
59	Peyton Manning	1.50
60	Terrence Wilkins	.30
61	Mark Brunell	.75
62	Keenan McCardell	.30
63	Jimmy Smith	.50
64	*R. Jay Soward*	1.25
65	*Shyrone Stith*	1.00
66	Fred Taylor	.75
67	Derrick Alexander	.15
68	Donnell Bennett	.15
69	Tony Gonzalez	.30
70	Elvis Grbac	.30
71	*Sylvester Morris*	2.00
72	Damon Huard	.30
73	J.J. Johnson	.30
74	Dan Marino	1.75
75	Tony Martin	.15
76	O.J. McDuffie	.30
77	*Quinton Spotwood*	.50
78	Cris Carter	.50
79	Daunte Culpepper	.75
80	Randy Moss	1.50
81	Robert Smith	.50
82	*Troy Walters*	.50
83	Drew Bledsoe	.75
84	*Tom Brady*	1.00
85	Kevin Faulk	.50
86	Terry Glenn	.50
87	*J.R. Redmond*	1.50
88	*Marc Bulger*	.75
89	*Sherrod Gideon*	.50
90	Keith Poole	.15
91	Ricky Williams	1.25
92	Kerry Collins	.30
93	*Ron Dayne*	4.00
94	Ike Hilliard	.30
95	Amani Toomer	.30
96	Wayne Chrebet	.30
97	*Laveranues Coles*	1.50
98	Curtis Martin	.50
99	*Chad Pennington*	3.50
100	Vinny Testaverde	.30
101	Tim Brown	.30
102	Rich Gannon	.30
103	Napoleon Kaufman	.50
104	*Jerry Porter*	1.25
105	Tyrone Wheatley	.30
106	Charles Johnson	.15
107	Donovan McNabb	.75
108	*Todd Pinkston*	1.00
109	Duce Staley	.50
110	Jerome Bettis	.50
111	*Plaxico Burress*	2.50
112	Troy Edwards	.50
113	Richard Huntley	.30
114	*Tee Martin*	1.25
115	Kordell Stewart	.50
116	Isaac Bruce	.50
117	*Trung Canidate*	1.00
118	Marshall Faulk	.50
119	Torry Holt	.50
120	Kurt Warner	2.50
121	Jermaine Fazande	.50
122	*Trevor Gaylor*	.50
123	Jim Harbaugh	.15
124	Junior Seau	.30
125	*Giovanni Carmazzi*	1.50
126	Charlie Garner	.30
127	Terrell Owens	.50
128	Jerry Rice	1.00
129	J.J. Stokes	.30
130	Steve Young	.75
131	*Shaun Alexander*	2.50
132	Sean Dawkins	.15
133	Jon Kitna	.50
134	Derrick Mayes	.30
135	Ricky Watters	.30
136	Mike Alstott	.50
137	Warrick Dunn	.50
138	Jacquez Green	.30
139	*Joe Hamilton*	1.25
140	Shaun King	.75
141	Eddie George	.60
142	Jevon Kearse	.50
143	Steve McNair	.50
144	Yancy Thigpen	.15
145	Frank Wycheck	.15
146	Albert Connell	.30
147	Stephen Davis	.50
148	*Todd Husak*	.50
149	Brad Johnson	.50
150	Michael Westbrook	.30

2000 Pacific Aurora Premiere Date Parallel

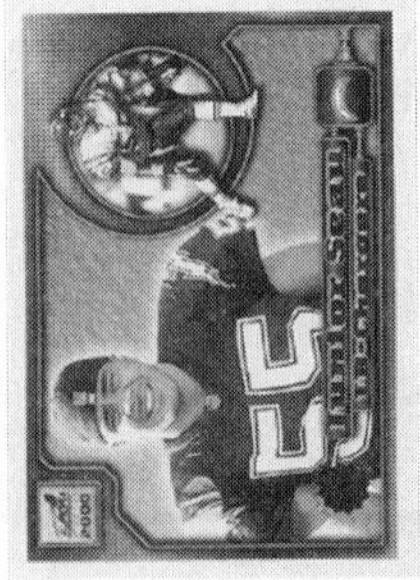

	MT
Prem. Date Cards:	15x-30x
Prem. Date Rookies:	6x-12x
Production 85 Sets	

2000 Pacific Aurora Autographs

		MT
Common Player:		15.00
Randomly Inserted		
2	Thomas Jones 350	30.00
26	Marcus Robinson 350	25.00
27	Dez White 350	15.00
32	Peter Warrick Exch	70.00
34	JaJuan Dawson 350	25.00
43	Olandis Gary 350	20.00
61	Mark Brunell 100	45.00
63	Jimmy Smith 350	20.00
71	Sylvester Morris 350	20.00
77	Quinton Spotwood 350	15.00
88	Marc Bulger 350	15.00
93	Ron Dayne 150	100.00
131	Shaun Alexander 350	30.00
147	Stephen Davis 350	20.00

2000 Pacific Aurora Championship Fever

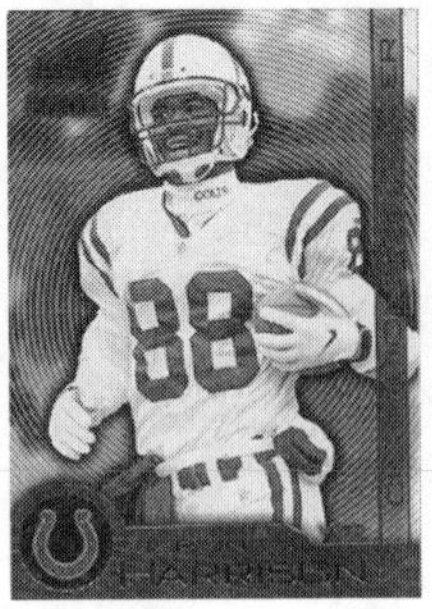

		MT
Complete Set (20):		35.00
Common Player:		1.00
Inserted 4:37		
Copper Cards:		4x-8x
Production 160 Sets		
Platinum Blue Cards:		4x-8x
Production 145 Sets		
1	Thomas Jones	3.00
2	Jamal Lewis	3.00
3	Peter Warrick	5.00
4	Tim Couch	2.00
5	Emmitt Smith	2.50
6	Olandis Gary	1.50
7	Marvin Harrison	1.00
8	Edgerrin James	3.00
9	Mark Brunell	1.50
10	Fred Taylor	1.50
11	Randy Moss	3.00
12	Chad Pennington	4.00
13	Plaxico Burress	4.00
14	Marshall Faulk	1.00
15	Kurt Warner	4.00
16	Shaun Alexander	3.00
17	Jon Kitna	1.00
18	Eddie George	1.50
19	Shaun King	1.50
20	Stephen Davis	1.00

2000 Pacific Aurora Game-Worn Jerseys

		MT
Complete Set (10):		400.00
Common Player:		20.00
Randomly Inserted		
Patch Cards:		
Production 10 Sets		
1	Olandis Gary	30.00
2	Brett Favre	100.00
3	Mark Brunell	45.00
4	Cris Carter	35.00
5	Randy Moss	85.00
6	Ricky Williams	65.00
7	Donovan McNabb	45.00
8	Duce Staley	45.00
9	Junior Seau	20.00
10	Steve McNair	35.00

2000 Pacific Aurora Helmet Styrotechs

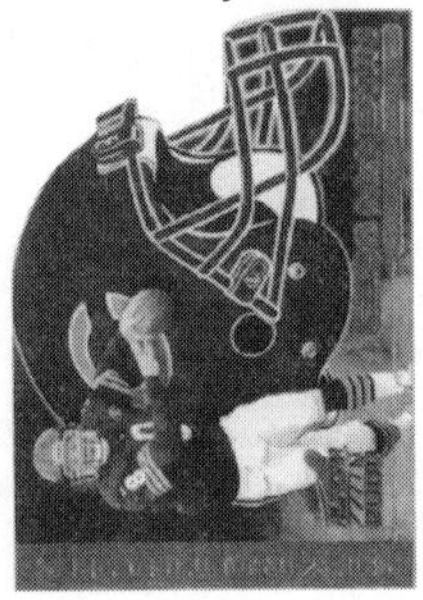

		MT
Complete Set (20):		75.00
Common Player:		3.00
Inserted 1:37		
1	Jake Plummer	3.00
2	Cade McNown	3.50
3	Tim Couch	5.00
4	Troy Aikman	5.00
5	Emmitt Smith	6.00
6	Barry Sanders	8.00
7	Terrell Davis	6.00
8	Brett Favre	10.00
9	Edgerrin James	8.00
10	Peyton Manning	8.00
11	Mark Brunell	4.00
12	Fred Taylor	4.00
13	Drew Bledsoe	4.00
14	Ricky Williams	5.00
15	Randy Moss	10.00
16	Kurt Warner	12.00
17	Jerry Rice	5.00
18	Jon Kitna	3.00
19	Shaun King	3.50
20	Eddie George	3.50

A player's name in *italic type* indicates a rookie card.

2000 Pacific Aurora Rookie Draft Board

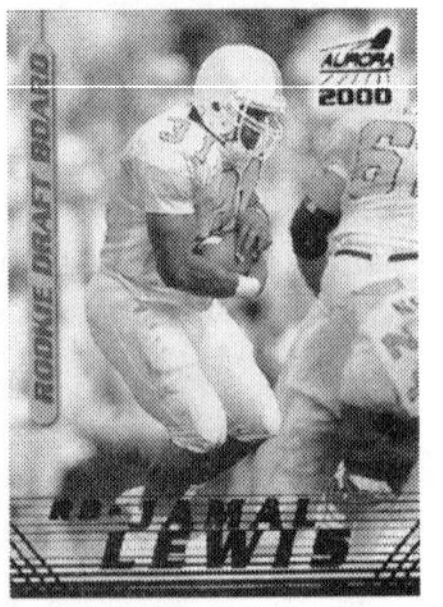

		MT
Complete Set (20):		50.00
Common Player:		1.50
Inserted 2:37		
1	Thomas Jones	5.00
2	Jamal Lewis	5.00
3	Chris Redman	3.00
4	Travis Taylor	3.50
5	Peter Warrick	8.00
6	Dez White	2.00
7	Dennis Northcutt	2.00
8	Travis Prentice	2.50
9	Reuben Droughns	1.50
10	R. Jay Soward	2.00
11	Sylvester Morris	2.50
12	J.R. Redmond	2.50
13	Ron Dayne	8.00
14	Laveranues Coles	1.50
15	Chad Pennington	6.00
16	Plaxico Burress	6.00
17	Tee Martin	2.00
18	Trung Canidate	1.50
19	Giovanni Carmazzi	2.50
20	Shaun Alexander	5.00

2000 Pacific Aurora Team Players

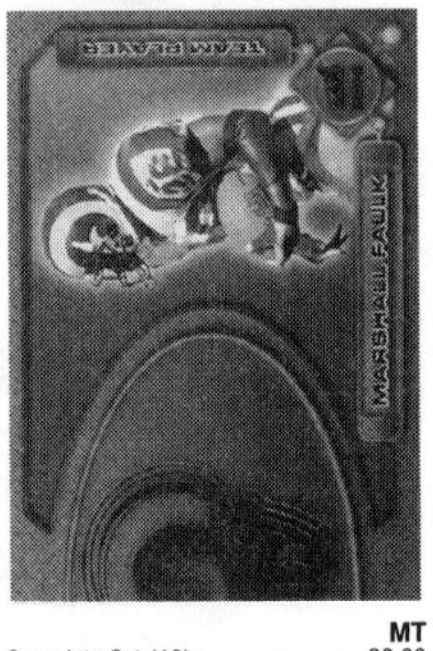

		MT
Complete Set (10):		20.00
Common Player:		1.50
Inserted 1:37		
1	Troy Aikman	3.50
2	Terrell Davis	4.00
3	Antonio Freeman	1.50
4	Peyton Manning	5.00
5	Fred Taylor	2.50
6	Randy Moss	5.00
7	Marshall Faulk	1.50
8	Jerry Rice	3.50
9	Steve McNair	1.50
10	Stephen Davis	1.50

2000 Pacific Crown Royale

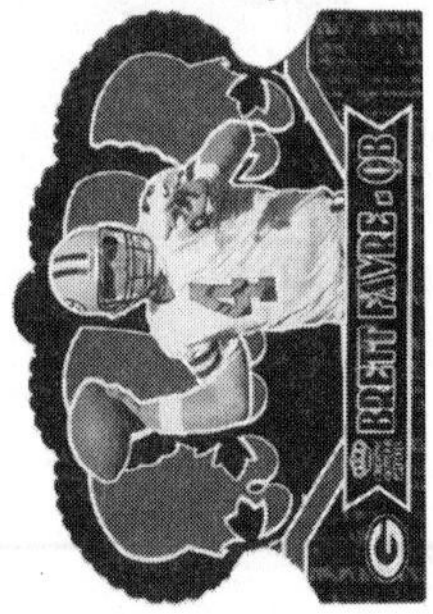

		MT
Complete Set (144):		125.00
Common Player:		.15
Minor Stars:		.30
Common Rookie:		1.00
Pack (6):		6.00
Wax Box (24):		110.00
1	Rob Moore	.30
2	Jake Plummer	1.00
3	Frank Sanders	.30
4	Jamal Anderson	.75
5	Chris Chandler	.30
6	Tim Dwight	.75
7	Tony Banks	.30
8	Priest Holmes	.50
9	Qadry Ismail	.15
10	Doug Flutie	1.00
11	Rob Johnson	.30
12	Eric Moulds	.75
13	Peerless Price	.50

14	Steve Beuerlein	.30
15	Patrick Jeffers	.75
16	Muhsin Muhammad	.30
17	Curtis Enis	.50
18	Cade McNown	1.25
19	Marcus Robinson	.75
20	Corey Dillon	.75
21	Darnay Scott	.30
22	Akili Smith	1.00
23	Karim Abdul	.30
24	Tim Couch	2.00
25	Kevin Johnson	.75
26	Troy Aikman	1.50
27	Joey Galloway	.75
28	Emmitt Smith	2.00
29	Terrell Davis	2.00
30	Olandis Gary	1.00
31	Brian Griese	1.00
32	Ed McCaffrey	.30
33	Charlie Batch	.75
34	Herman Moore	.75
35	Barry Sanders	3.00
36	James Stewart	.50
37	Brett Favre	3.00
38	Antonio Freeman	.75
39	Dorsey Levens	.75
40	Marvin Harrison	.75
41	Edgerrin James	3.00
42	Peyton Manning	2.00
43	Mark Brunell	1.25
44	Keenan McCardell	.30
45	Jimmy Smith	.50
46	Fred Taylor	1.25
47	Derrick Alexander	.15
48	Tony Gonzalez	.30
49	Elvis Grbac	.30
50	Damon Huard	.50
51	J.J. Johnson	.30
52	Dan Marino	2.00
53	O.J. McDuffie	.30
54	Cris Carter	.75
55	Daunte Culpepper	1.25
56	Jeff George	.50
57	Randy Moss	3.00
58	Robert Smith	.75
59	Drew Bledsoe	1.25
60	Terry Glenn	.75
61	Lawyer Milloy	.15
62	Jeff Blake	.30
63	Keith Poole	.15
64	Ricky Williams	2.00
65	Kerry Collins	.30
66	Ike Hilliard	.30
67	Amani Toomer	.30
68	Wayne Chrebet	.50
69	Keyshawn Johnson	.75
70	Ray Lucas	.75
71	Curtis Martin	.75
72	Vinny Testaverde	.50
73	Tim Brown	.50
74	Rich Gannon	.30
75	Napoleon Kaufman	.50
76	Tyrone Wheatley	.30
77	Donovan McNabb	1.25
78	Torrance Small	.15
79	Duce Staley	.75
80	Jerome Bettis	.75
81	Troy Edwards	.75
82	Kordell Stewart	.75
83	Isaac Bruce	.75
84	Marshall Faulk	.75
85	Torry Holt	.75
86	Kurt Warner	4.00
87	Jim Harbaugh	.30
88	Jermaine Fazande	.30
89	Junior Seau	.30
90	Charlie Garner	.30
91	Terrell Owens	.75
92	Jerry Rice	1.50
93	Steve Young	1.00
94	Sean Dawkins	.15
95	Jon Kitna	.50
96	Derrick Mayes	.30
97	Ricky Watters	.50
98	Mike Alstott	.75
99	Warrick Dunn	.75
100	Jacquez Green	.30
101	Shaun King	1.25
102	Kevin Dyson	.30
103	Eddie George	1.00
104	Jevon Kearse	.75
105	Steve McNair	1.00
106	Stephen Davis	.75
107	Brad Johnson	.75
108	Michael Westbrook	.50
109	*Shaun Alexander*	6.00
110	*Tom Brady*	1.50
111	*Marc Bulger*	1.00
112	*Plaxico Burress*	5.00
113	*Giovanni Carmazzi*	3.50
114	*Kwame Cavil*	1.00
115	*Chris Cole*	1.00
116	*Chris Coleman*	1.00
117	*Laveranues Coles*	3.00
118	*Ron Dayne*	10.00
119	*Reuben Droughns*	1.50
120	*Ron Dugans*	1.50
121	*Danny Farmer*	2.00
122	*Chafie Fields*	1.00
123	*Joe Hamilton*	2.00
124	*Todd Husak*	2.00
125	*Darrell Jackson*	3.50
126	*Thomas Jones*	5.00
127	*Jamal Lewis*	12.00
128	*Tee Martin*	3.00
129	*Rondell Mealey*	2.00
130	*Sylvester Morris*	5.00
131	*Chad Morton*	2.00
132	*Dennis Northcutt*	3.00
133	*Chad Pennington*	8.00
134	*Travis Prentice*	4.00
135	*Tim Rattay*	3.00
136	*Chris Redman*	5.00
137	*J.R. Redmond*	3.50
138	*R. Jay Soward*	2.00
139	*Shyrone Stith*	1.50
140	*Travis Taylor*	3.00
141	*Troy Walters*	1.50
142	*Peter Warrick*	8.00
143	*Dez White*	2.00
144	*Michael Wiley*	2.00

2000 Pacific Crown Royale Draft Picks 499 Parallel

		MT
Complete Set (35):		250.00
#'d to 499 Cards:		2.5x
Production 499 Sets		
109	*Shaun Alexander*	7.00
110	*Tom Brady*	2.00
111	*Marc Bulger*	1.00
112	*Plaxico Burress*	10.00
113	*Giovanni Carmazzi*	5.00
114	*Kwame Cavil*	1.00
115	*Chris Cole*	1.00
116	*Chris Coleman*	1.00
117	*Laveranues Coles*	2.00
118	*Ron Dayne*	12.00
119	*Reuben Droughns*	3.00
120	*Ron Dugans*	3.00
121	*Danny Farmer*	2.00
122	*Chafie Fields*	1.00
123	*Joe Hamilton*	2.00
124	*Todd Husak*	2.00
125	*Darrell Jackson*	2.00
126	*Thomas Jones*	7.00
127	*Jamal Lewis*	7.00
128	*Tee Martin*	4.00
129	*Rondell Mealey*	2.00
130	*Sylvester Morris*	4.00
131	*Chad Morton*	2.00
132	*Dennis Northcutt*	3.00
133	*Chad Pennington*	10.00
134	*Travis Prentice*	3.00
135	*Tim Rattay*	3.00
136	*Chris Redman*	5.00
137	*J.R. Redmond*	4.00
138	*R. Jay Soward*	4.00
139	*Shyrone Stith*	2.00
140	*Travis Taylor*	5.00
141	*Troy Walters*	2.00
142	*Peter Warrick*	12.00
143	*Dez White*	3.00
144	*Michael Wiley*	2.00

2000 Pacific Crown Royale Limited Series Parallel

		MT
Limited Cards:		8x-16x
Limited Rookies:		3x-6x
Production 144 Cards		
1	Rob Moore	.30
2	Jake Plummer	1.00
3	Frank Sanders	.30
4	Jamal Anderson	.75
5	Chris Chandler	.30
6	Tim Dwight	.75
7	Tony Banks	.30
8	Priest Holmes	.50
9	Qadry Ismail	.15
10	Doug Flutie	1.00
11	Rob Johnson	.30
12	Eric Moulds	.75
13	Peerless Price	.50
14	Steve Beuerlein	.30
15	Patrick Jeffers	.75
16	Muhsin Muhammad	.30
17	Curtis Enis	.50
18	Cade McNown	1.25
19	Marcus Robinson	.75
20	Corey Dillon	.75
21	Darnay Scott	.30
22	Akili Smith	1.00
23	Karim Abdul	.30
24	Tim Couch	2.00
25	Kevin Johnson	.75
26	Troy Aikman	1.50
27	Joey Galloway	.75
28	Emmitt Smith	2.00
29	Terrell Davis	2.00
30	Olandis Gary	1.00
31	Brian Griese	1.00
32	Ed McCaffrey	.30
33	Charlie Batch	.75
34	Herman Moore	.75
35	Barry Sanders	3.00
36	James Stewart	.50
37	Brett Favre	3.00
38	Antonio Freeman	.75
39	Dorsey Levens	.75
40	Marvin Harrison	.75
41	Edgerrin James	3.00
42	Peyton Manning	2.00
43	Mark Brunell	1.25
44	Keenan McCardell	.30
45	Jimmy Smith	.50
46	Fred Taylor	1.25
47	Derrick Alexander	.15
48	Tony Gonzalez	.30
49	Elvis Grbac	.30
50	Damon Huard	.50
51	J.J. Johnson	.30
52	Dan Marino	2.00
53	O.J. McDuffie	.30
54	Cris Carter	.75
55	Daunte Culpepper	1.25
56	Jeff George	.50
57	Randy Moss	3.00
58	Robert Smith	.75
59	Drew Bledsoe	1.25
60	Terry Glenn	.75
61	Lawyer Milloy	.15
62	Jeff Blake	.30
63	Keith Poole	.15
64	Ricky Williams	2.00
65	Kerry Collins	.30
66	Ike Hilliard	.30
67	Amani Toomer	.30
68	Wayne Chrebet	.50
69	Keyshawn Johnson	.75
70	Ray Lucas	.75
71	Curtis Martin	.75
72	Vinny Testaverde	.50
73	Tim Brown	.50
74	Rich Gannon	.30
75	Napoleon Kaufman	.50
76	Tyrone Wheatley	.30
77	Donovan McNabb	1.25
78	Torrance Small	.15
79	Duce Staley	.75
80	Jerome Bettis	.75
81	Troy Edwards	.75
82	Kordell Stewart	.75
83	Isaac Bruce	.75
84	Marshall Faulk	.75
85	Torry Holt	.75
86	Kurt Warner	4.00
87	Jim Harbaugh	.30
88	Jermaine Fazande	.30
89	Junior Seau	.30
90	Charlie Garner	.30
91	Terrell Owens	.75
92	Jerry Rice	1.50
93	Steve Young	1.00
94	Sean Dawkins	.15
95	Jon Kitna	.50
96	Derrick Mayes	.30
97	Ricky Watters	.50
98	Mike Alstott	.75
99	Warrick Dunn	.75
100	Jacquez Green	.30
101	Shaun King	1.25
102	Kevin Dyson	.30
103	Eddie George	1.00
104	Jevon Kearse	.75
105	Steve McNair	1.00
106	Stephen Davis	.75
107	Brad Johnson	.75
108	Michael Westbrook	.50
109	*Shaun Alexander*	7.00
110	*Tom Brady*	2.00
111	*Marc Bulger*	1.00
112	*Plaxico Burress*	10.00
113	*Giovanni Carmazzi*	5.00
114	*Kwame Cavil*	1.00
115	*Chris Cole*	1.00
116	*Chris Coleman*	1.00
117	*Laveranues Coles*	2.00
118	*Ron Dayne*	12.00
119	*Reuben Droughns*	3.00
120	*Ron Dugans*	3.00
121	*Danny Farmer*	2.00
122	*Chafie Fields*	1.00
123	*Joe Hamilton*	2.00
124	*Todd Husak*	2.00
125	*Darrell Jackson*	2.00
126	*Thomas Jones*	7.00
127	*Jamal Lewis*	7.00
128	*Tee Martin*	4.00
129	*Rondell Mealey*	2.00
130	*Sylvester Morris*	4.00
131	*Chad Morton*	2.00
132	*Dennis Northcutt*	3.00
133	*Chad Pennington*	10.00
134	*Travis Prentice*	3.00
135	*Tim Rattay*	3.00
136	*Chris Redman*	5.00
137	*J.R. Redmond*	4.00
138	*R. Jay Soward*	4.00
139	*Shyrone Stith*	2.00
140	*Travis Taylor*	5.00
141	*Troy Walters*	2.00
142	*Peter Warrick*	12.00
143	*Dez White*	3.00
144	*Michael Wiley*	2.00

2000 Pacific Crown Royale Premiere Date Parallel

		MT
Premiere Cards:		8x-16x
Premiere Rookies:		3x-6x
Production 145 Sets		
1	Rob Moore	.30
2	Jake Plummer	1.00
3	Frank Sanders	.30
4	Jamal Anderson	.75
5	Chris Chandler	.30
6	Tim Dwight	.75
7	Tony Banks	.30
8	Priest Holmes	.50
9	Qadry Ismail	.15
10	Doug Flutie	1.00
11	Rob Johnson	.30
12	Eric Moulds	.75
13	Peerless Price	.50
14	Steve Beuerlein	.30
15	Patrick Jeffers	.75
16	Muhsin Muhammad	.30
17	Curtis Enis	.50
18	Cade McNown	1.25
19	Marcus Robinson	.75
20	Corey Dillon	.75
21	Darnay Scott	.30
22	Akili Smith	1.00
23	Karim Abdul	.30
24	Tim Couch	2.00
25	Kevin Johnson	.75
26	Troy Aikman	1.50
27	Joey Galloway	.75
28	Emmitt Smith	2.00
29	Terrell Davis	2.00
30	Olandis Gary	1.00
31	Brian Griese	1.00
32	Ed McCaffrey	.30
33	Charlie Batch	.75
34	Herman Moore	.75
35	Barry Sanders	3.00
36	James Stewart	.50
37	Brett Favre	3.00
38	Antonio Freeman	.75
39	Dorsey Levens	.75
40	Marvin Harrison	.75
41	Edgerrin James	3.00
42	Peyton Manning	2.00
43	Mark Brunell	1.25
44	Keenan McCardell	.30
45	Jimmy Smith	.30
46	Fred Taylor	1.25
47	Derrick Alexander	.15
48	Tony Gonzalez	.30
49	Elvis Grbac	.30
50	Damon Huard	.50
51	J.J. Johnson	.30
52	Dan Marino	2.00
53	O.J. McDuffie	.30
54	Cris Carter	.75
55	Daunte Culpepper	1.25
56	Jeff George	.50
57	Randy Moss	3.00
58	Robert Smith	.75
59	Drew Bledsoe	1.25
60	Terry Glenn	.75
61	Lawyer Milloy	.15
62	Jeff Blake	.30
63	Keith Poole	.15
64	Ricky Williams	2.00
65	Kerry Collins	.30
66	Ike Hilliard	.30
67	Amani Toomer	.30
68	Wayne Chrebet	.75
69	Keyshawn Johnson	.75
70	Ray Lucas	.75
71	Curtis Martin	.75
72	Vinny Testaverde	.50
73	Tim Brown	.50
74	Rich Gannon	.30
75	Napoleon Kaufman	.50
76	Tyrone Wheatley	.30
77	Donovan McNabb	1.25
78	Torrance Small	.15
79	Duce Staley	.75
80	Jerome Bettis	.75
81	Troy Edwards	.75
82	Kordell Stewart	.75
83	Isaac Bruce	.75
84	Marshall Faulk	.75
85	Torry Holt	.75
86	Kurt Warner	4.00
87	Jim Harbaugh	.30
88	Jermaine Fazande	.30
89	Junior Seau	.30
90	Charlie Garner	.30
91	Terrell Owens	.75
92	Jerry Rice	1.50
93	Steve Young	1.00
94	Sean Dawkins	.15
95	Jon Kitna	.50
96	Derrick Mayes	.30
97	Ricky Watters	.50
98	Mike Alstott	.75
99	Warrick Dunn	.75
100	Jacquez Green	.30
101	Shaun King	1.25
102	Kevin Dyson	.30
103	Eddie George	1.00
104	Jevon Kearse	.75
105	Steve McNair	1.00
106	Stephen Davis	.75
107	Brad Johnson	.75
108	Michael Westbrook	.50
109	*Shaun Alexander*	7.00
110	*Tom Brady*	2.00
111	*Marc Bulger*	1.00
112	*Plaxico Burress*	10.00
113	*Giovanni Carmazzi*	5.00
114	*Kwame Cavil*	1.00
115	*Chris Cole*	1.00
116	*Chris Coleman*	1.00
117	*Laveranues Coles*	2.00
118	*Ron Dayne*	12.00
119	*Reuben Droughns*	3.00
120	*Ron Dugans*	3.00
121	*Danny Farmer*	2.00
122	*Chafie Fields*	1.00
123	*Joe Hamilton*	2.00
124	*Todd Husak*	2.00
125	*Darrell Jackson*	2.00
126	*Thomas Jones*	7.00
127	*Jamal Lewis*	7.00
128	*Tee Martin*	4.00
129	*Rondell Mealey*	2.00
130	*Sylvester Morris*	4.00
131	*Chad Morton*	2.00
132	*Dennis Northcutt*	3.00
133	*Chad Pennington*	10.00
134	*Travis Prentice*	3.00
135	*Tim Rattay*	3.00
136	*Chris Redman*	5.00
137	*J.R. Redmond*	4.00
138	*R. Jay Soward*	4.00
139	*Shyrone Stith*	3.00
140	*Travis Taylor*	5.00
141	*Troy Walters*	2.00
142	*Peter Warrick*	12.00
143	*Dez White*	3.00
144	*Michael Wiley*	2.00

2000 Pacific Crown Royale Autographs

		MT
Common Player:		10.00
Minor Stars:		20.00
Randomly Inserted		
109	Shaun Alexander	30.00
110	Tom Brady	20.00
111	Marc Bulger	10.00
112	Plaxico Burress	60.00
113	Giovanni Carmazzi	30.00
114	Kwame Cavil	10.00
115	Chris Cole	10.00
116	Chris Coleman	10.00
117	Laveranues Coles	20.00
118	Ron Dayne	85.00
119	Reuben Droughns	20.00
120	Ron Dugans	20.00
121	Danny Farmer	20.00
122	Chafie Fields	10.00
123	Joe Hamilton	20.00
124	Todd Husak	10.00
125	Darrell Jackson	10.00
126	Thomas Jones	40.00
127	Jamal Lewis	40.00
128	Tee Martin	25.00
129	Rondell Mealey	10.00
130	Sylvester Morris	25.00
131	Chad Morton	10.00
132	Dennis Northcutt	20.00
133	Chad Pennington	60.00
134	Travis Prentice	25.00
135	Tim Rattay	20.00
136	Chris Redman	30.00
137	J.R. Redmond	25.00
138	R. Jay Soward	25.00
139	Shyrone Stith	10.00
140	Travis Taylor	30.00
141	Troy Walters	10.00
142	Peter Warrick	85.00
143	Dez White	20.00
144	Michael Wiley	20.00

2000 Pacific Crown Royale Cramer's Choice Jumbos

		MT
Complete Set (10):		45.00
Common Player:		2.00
One Per Hobby Box		
Dark Blue Cards:		5x-10x
Production 35 Sets		
Gold Cards:		15x-30x
Production 10 Sets		
Green Cards:		5x-10x
Production 30 Sets		
Light Blue Cards:		7x-14x
Production 20 Sets		
Purple Cards:		
Production 1 Set		
Red Cards:		7x-14x
Production 25 Sets		
1	Tim Couch	5.00
2	Emmitt Smith	6.00
3	Edgerrin James	8.00
4	Damon Huard	2.00
5	Randy Moss	8.00
6	Kurt Warner	10.00
7	Jon Kitna	2.00
8	Eddie George	3.00
9	Chad Pennington	8.00
10	Peter Warrick	10.00

2000 Pacific Crown Royale Fifth Anniversary Jumbos

		MT
Complete Set (6):		35.00
Common Player:		2.50
Inserted 6:10 Boxes		
1	Terrell Davis	7.00
2	Eddie George	4.00
3	Jon Kitna	2.50
4	Randy Moss	10.00
5	Kurt Warner	12.00
6	Peter Warrick	12.00

2000 Pacific Crown Royale First and Ten

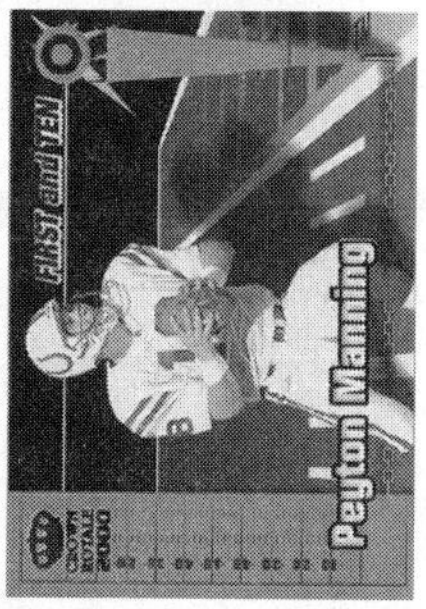

		MT
Complete Set (10):		70.00
Common Player:		7.00
Production 375 Sets		
1	Tim Couch	7.00
2	Troy Aikman	10.00
3	Emmitt Smith	12.00
4	Terrell Davis	12.00
5	Brett Favre	15.00
6	Edgerrin James	15.00
7	Peyton Manning	12.00
8	Randy Moss	12.00
9	Kurt Warner	15.00
10	Jerry Rice	10.00

2000 Pacific Crown Royale Jersey Cards

		MT
Complete Set (9):		325.00
Common Player:		25.00
Randomly Inserted		
1	Eric Moulds	30.00
2	Brett Favre	100.00
3	Antonio Freeman	30.00
4	Ricky Williams	70.00
5	Tiki Barber	25.00
6	Charles Woodson	30.00
7	Isaac Bruce	30.00
8	Kurt Warner	100.00
9	Tim Couch	70.00

2000 Pacific Crown Royale In the Pocket

		MT
Complete Set (20):		75.00
Common Player:		2.00
Mini Cards:		.5x
Inserted 2:25		
1	Tim Couch	4.00
2	Troy Aikman	5.00
3	Emmitt Smith	6.00
4	Charlie Batch	2.00
5	Edgerrin James	8.00
6	Peyton Manning	7.00
7	Mark Brunell	3.00
8	Randy Moss	8.00
9	Drew Bledsoe	3.00
10	Donovan McNabb	3.00
11	Kurt Warner	10.00
12	Jon Kitna	2.00
13	Eddie George	3.00
14	Steve McNair	3.00
15	Brad Johnson	2.00
16	Plaxico Burress	10.00
17	Ron Dayne	12.00
18	Thomas Jones	7.00
19	Chad Pennington	10.00
20	Peter Warrick	12.00

Values quoted in this guide reflect the retail price of a card — the price a collector can expect to pay when buying a card from a dealer. The wholesale price — that which a collector can expect to receive from a dealer when selling cards — will be significantly lower, depending on desirability and condition.

2000 Pacific Crown Royale In Your Face

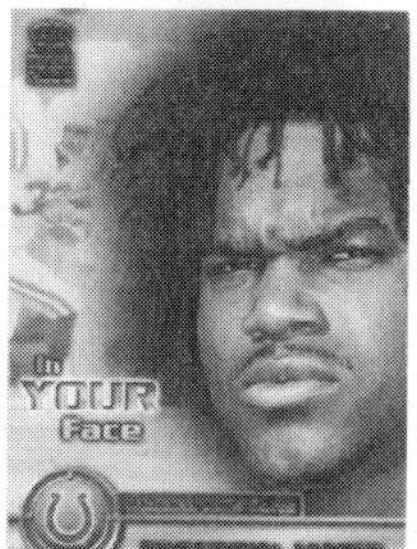

		MT
Complete Set (25):		15.00
Common Player:		.50
Inserted 1:1		
Rainbow Cards:		35x-70x
Production 20 Sets		
1	Jake Plummer	.75
2	Cade McNown	.75
3	Marcus Robinson	.50
4	Corey Dillon	.50
5	Tim Couch	1.25
6	Emmitt Smith	1.50
7	Terrell Davis	1.50
8	Barry Sanders	2.00
9	Marvin Harrison	.50
10	Edgerrin James	2.00
11	Mark Brunell	1.00
12	Fred Taylor	1.00
13	Dan Marino	1.50
14	Randy Moss	2.00
15	Drew Bledsoe	1.00
16	Ricky Williams	1.25
17	Curtis Martin	.50
18	Isaac Bruce	.50
19	Marshall Faulk	.50
20	Kurt Warner	2.50
21	Jerry Rice	1.50
22	Jon Kitna	.50
23	Shaun King	.75
24	Eddie George	.75
25	Stephen Davis	.50

2000 Pacific Crown Royale Productions

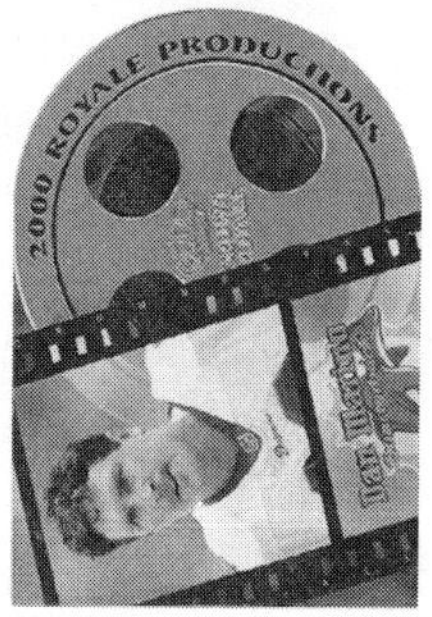

		MT
Complete Set (20):		70.00
Common Player:		2.00
Inserted 1:25		
1	Cade McNown	3.00
2	Tim Couch	5.00
3	Emmitt Smith	6.00
4	Olandis Gary	2.00
5	Barry Sanders	10.00
6	Brett Favre	10.00
7	Edgerrin James	10.00
8	Peyton Manning	8.00
9	Fred Taylor	4.00
10	Damon Huard	2.00
11	Dan Marino	6.00
12	Randy Moss	10.00
13	Drew Bledsoe	4.00
14	Ricky Williams	5.00
15	Marshall Faulk	2.00
16	Kurt Warner	12.00
17	Jerry Rice	6.00
18	Shaun King	3.00
19	Eddie George	3.00
20	Stephen Davis	2.00

2000 Pacific Crown Royale Rookie Royalty

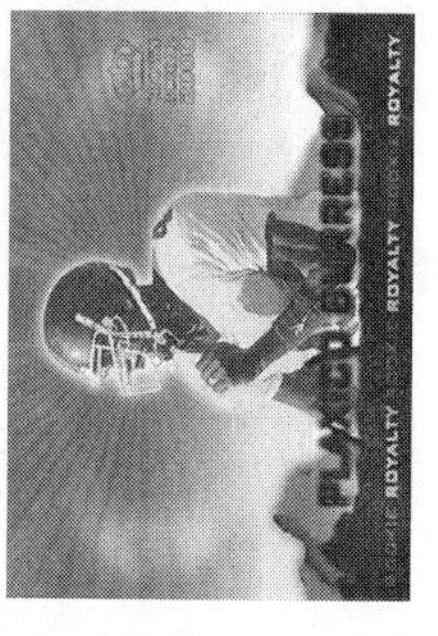

		MT
Complete Set (25):		25.00
Common Player:		.50
Inserted 1:1		
Die-Cut Cards:		30x-60x
Production 10 Sets		
1	Shaun Alexander	2.50
2	Tom Brady	1.00
3	Plaxico Burress	4.00
4	Ron Dayne	5.00
5	Reuben Droughns	1.00
6	Danny Farmer	1.00
7	Chafie Fields	.50
8	Joe Hamilton	1.00
9	Todd Husak	1.00
10	Thomas Jones	3.00
11	Jamal Lewis	3.00
12	Tee Martin	1.50
13	Sylvester Morris	2.00
14	Dennis Northcutt	1.25
15	Chad Pennington	4.00
16	Travis Prentice	1.50
17	Tim Rattay	1.50
18	Chris Redman	1.75
19	J.R. Redmond	1.50
20	R. Jay Soward	1.50
21	Shyrone Stith	.50
22	Travis Taylor	2.00
23	Troy Walters	.50
24	Peter Warrick	5.00
25	Dez White	1.25

2000 Pacific Omega

		MT
Complete Set (250):		450.00
Common Player:		.15
Minor Stars:		.30
Common Rookie:		5.00
Production 500 Sets		
Pack (6):		2.00
Wax Box (36):		50.00
1	David Boston	.50
2	Dave Brown	.15
3	Rob Moore	.30
4	Jake Plummer	.50
5	Simeon Rice	.15
6	Frank Sanders	.30
7	Jamal Anderson	.50
8	Chris Chandler	.30
9	Tim Dwight	.50
10	Terance Mathis	.15
11	Tony Banks	.30
12	Peter Boulware	.15
13	Priest Holmes	.50
14	Qadry Ismail	.15
15	Doug Flutie	.75
16	Rob Johnson	.30
17	Jonathon Linton	.15
18	Eric Moulds	.50
19	Peerless Price	.30
20	Antowain Smith	.30
21	Steve Beuerlein	.30
22	Tshimanga Biakabutuka	.30
23	Patrick Jeffers	.50
24	Muhsin Muhammad	.30
25	Wesley Walls	.15
26	Bobby Engram	.15
27	Curtis Enis	.50
28	Cade McNown	.50
29	Marcus Robinson	.50
30	Willie Anderson	.15
31	Michael Basnight	.15
32	Corey Dillon	.50
33	Akili Smith	.50
34	Tim Couch	1.00
35	Kevin Johnson	.50
36	Wali Rainer	.15
37	Troy Aikman	1.25
38	Dexter Coakley	.15
39	Raghib Ismail	.15
40	Emmitt Smith	1.50
41	Chris Warren	.30
42	Terrell Davis	1.50
43	Olandis Gary	.50
44	Brian Griese	.75
45	Ed McCaffrey	.30
46	Rod Smith	.50
47	Charlie Batch	.50
48	Germane Crowell	.50
49	Herman Moore	.50
50	Johnnie Morton	.30
51	Barry Sanders	1.75
52	Corey Bradford	.30
53	Brett Favre	2.50
54	Antonio Freeman	.50
55	Dorsey Levens	.30
56	Bill Schroeder	.15
57	Ken Dilger	.15
58	Marvin Harrison	.50
59	Edgerrin James	2.00
60	Peyton Manning	1.75
61	Jerome Pathon	.15
62	Terrence Wilkins	.30
63	Mark Brunell	.75
64	Keenan McCardell	.30
65	Jimmy Smith	.50
66	Fred Taylor	.75
67	Derrick Alexander	.15
68	Donnell Bennett	.15
69	Tony Gonzalez	.30
70	Elvis Grbac	.30
71	Tony Richardson	.15
72	Oronde Gadsden	.15
73	Damon Huard	.50
74	J.J. Johnson	.30
75	Dan Marino	1.75
76	Tony Martin	.15
77	O.J. McDuffie	.30
78	Cris Carter	.50
79	Daunte Culpepper	1.00
80	Randy Moss	1.75
81	Robert Smith	.50
82	Drew Bledsoe	.75
83	Kevin Faulk	.30
84	Terry Glenn	.50
85	P.J. Franklin	.15
86	Keith Poole	.15
87	Ricky Williams	1.25
88	Tiki Barber	.50
89	Kerry Collins	.30
90	Ike Hilliard	.30
91	Amani Toomer	.30
92	Wayne Chrebet	.50
93	Ray Lucas	.50
94	Curtis Martin	.50
95	Vinny Testaverde	.30
96	Tim Brown	.50
97	Rich Gannon	.30
98	James Jett	.15
99	Napoleon Kaufman	.50
100	Tyrone Wheatley	.30
101	Charles Woodson	.50
102	Brian Dawkins	.15
103	Charles Johnson	.15
104	Donovan McNabb	.75
105	Torrance Small	.15
106	Duce Staley	.50
107	Jerome Bettis	.50
108	Troy Edwards	.30
109	Richard Huntley	.30
110	Kordell Stewart	.60
111	Hines Ward	.30
112	Isaac Bruce	.50
113	Marshall Faulk	.50
114	Az-Zahir Hakim	.30
115	Torry Holt	.50
116	Tony Horne	.15
117	Kurt Warner	2.50
118	Jermaine Fazande	.30
119	Jeff Graham	.15
120	Jim Harbaugh	.30
121	Mikhael Ricks	.15
122	Junior Seau	.30
123	Jeff Garcia	.50
124	Charlie Garner	.30
125	Terrell Owens	.50
126	Jerry Rice	1.25
127	J.J. Stokes	.30
128	Jon Kitna	.50
129	Derrick Mayes	.30
130	Charlie Rogers	.15
131	Shawn Springs	.15
132	Ricky Watters	.30
133	Mike Alstott	.50
134	Reidel Anthony	.15
135	Warrick Dunn	.50
136	Jacquez Green	.15
137	Shaun King	.75
138	Warren Sapp	.30
139	Kevin Dyson	.30
140	Eddie George	.60
141	Jevon Kearse	.50
142	Steve McNair	.50
143	Yancy Thigpen	.30
144	Frank Wycheck	.15
145	Champ Bailey	.30
146	Larry Centers	.15
147	Albert Connell	.30
148	Stephen Davis	.50
149	Brad Johnson	.30
150	Michael Westbrook	.30
151	*Thomas Jones*	15.00
152	*Jay Tant*	5.00
153	*Doug Johnson*	7.50
154	*Mareno Philyaw*	5.00
155	*Jamal Lewis*	50.00
156	*Chris Redman*	15.00
157	*Travis Taylor*	12.50
158	*Kwame Cavil*	5.00
159	*Corey Moore*	5.00
160	*Deon Grant*	5.00
161	*Frank Murphy*	5.00
162	*Dez White*	5.00
163	*Ron Dugans*	6.00
164	*Tony Hartley*	5.00
165	*Curtis Keaton*	5.00
166	*Peter Warrick*	35.00
167	*Courtney Brown*	7.50
168	*JaJuan Dawson*	7.50
169	*Dennis Northcutt*	7.50
170	*Travis Prentice*	12.50
171	*Aaron Shea*	5.00
172	*Michael Wiley*	6.00
173	*Chris Cole*	5.00
174	*Jarious Jackson*	6.00
175	*Deltha O'Neal*	5.00
176	*Reuben Droughns*	5.00
177	*Bubba Franks*	7.50
178	*Anthony Lucas*	5.00
179	*Rondell Mealey*	6.00
180	*Ibn Green*	5.00
181	*Kevin McDougal*	5.00
182	*R. Jay Soward*	7.50
183	*Shyrone Stith*	6.00
184	*Dante Hall*	5.00
185	*Frank Moreau*	7.50
186	*Sylvester Morris*	17.50
187	*Deon Dyer*	5.00
188	*Ben Kelly*	5.00
189	*Quinton Spotwood*	5.00
190	*Troy Walters*	6.00
191	*Tom Brady*	6.00
192	*J.R. Redmond*	10.00
193	*David Stachelski*	5.00
194	*Marc Bulger*	5.00
195	*Sherrod Gideon*	5.00
196	*Chad Morton*	6.00
197	*Ron Dayne*	40.00
198	*Anthony Becht*	6.00
199	*Laveranues Coles*	7.50
200	*Chad Pennington*	30.00
201	*Sebastian Janikowski*	6.00
202	*Marcus Knight*	5.00
203	*Jerry Porter*	7.50
204	*Todd Pinkston*	7.50
205	*Gari Scott*	5.00
206	*Plaxico Burress*	17.50
207	*Danny Farmer*	6.00
208	*Tee Martin*	6.00
209	*Hank Poteat*	5.00
210	*Trung Canidate*	6.00
211	*Patrick Batteaux*	5.00
212	*Trevor Gaylor*	6.00
213	*Ronney Jenkins*	5.00
214	*Terrence McCaskey*	5.00
215	*JaJuan Seider*	5.00
216	*Giovanni Carmazzi*	7.50
217	*Chafie Fields*	5.00
218	*Jonas Lewis*	5.00
219	*Tim Rattay*	7.50
220	*Shaun Alexander*	25.00
221	*Darrell Jackson*	7.50
222	*James Williams*	5.00
223	*Joe Hamilton*	7.50
224	*Erron Kinney*	5.00
225	*Todd Husak*	6.00
226	Plaxico Burress, Danny Farmer	10.00
227	Ron Dayne, Joe Hamilton	18.00
228	Peter Warrick, Ron Dugans	15.00
229	Thomas Jones, Curtis Keaton	10.00
230	Shaun Alexander, Reuben Droughns	12.00
231	Travis Taylor, Darrell Jackson	8.00
232	Giovanni Carmazzi, Tim Rattay	6.00
233	Trung Canidate, J.R. Redmond	6.00
234	Sylvester Morris, R. Jay Soward	10.00
235	Travis Prentice, Trevor Gaylor	8.00
236	Todd Pinkston, Sherrod Gideon	5.00
237	Frank Murphy, Dez White	5.00
238	Chris Redman, Tom Brady	8.00
239	Jamal Lewis, Tee Martin	20.00
240	Rondell Mealey, Shyrone Stith	5.00
241	Michael Wiley, Chad Morton	6.00
242	Laveranues Coles, Sebastian Janikowski	6.00
243	Troy Walters, Todd Husak	5.00
244	Marc Bulger, Jerry Porter	5.00
245	Mareno Philyaw, Doug Johnson	5.00
246	Dennis Northcutt, Courtney Brown	6.00
247	Jarious Jackson, Chris Cole	5.00
248	JaJuan Dawson, Gari Scott	6.00
249	Quinton Spotwood, Chafie Fields	5.00
250	Chad Pennington, James Williams	15.00

2000 Pacific Omega Copper Parallel

	MT
Copper Cards:	15x-30x
Production 51 Sets	
Inserted 1:73	
No Rookies	

2000 Pacific Omega Gold Parallel

	MT
Gold Cards:	10x-20x
Production 95 Sets	
Inserted 1:37	
No Rookies	

2000 Pacific Omega Platinum Blue Parallel

	MT
Platinum Blue Cards:	15x-30x
Production 51 Sets	
Inserted 1:145	
No Rookies	

2000 Pacific Omega Premiere Date Parallel

	MT
Premiere Date Cards:	10x-20x
Production 92 Sets	
Inserted 1:37	
No Rookies	

2000 Pacific Omega AFC Conference Contenders

		MT
Complete Set (18):		30.00
Common Player:		1.00
Minor Stars:		2.00
Inserted 2:37		
1	Jamal Lewis	10.00
2	Akili Smith	2.00
3	Peter Warrick	7.00
4	Tim Couch	2.50
5	Terrell Davis	5.00
6	Brian Griese	2.00
7	Marvin Harrison	2.00
8	Edgerrin James	6.00
9	Mark Brunell	2.50
10	Fred Taylor	2.50
11	Jimmy Smith	1.00
12	Curtis Martin	2.00
13	Tim Brown	2.00
14	Jerome Bettis	2.00
15	Plaxico Burress	4.00
16	Jon Kitna	1.00
17	Eddie George	2.50
18	Steve McNair	2.00

2000 Pacific Omega Autographs

		MT
Common Player:		20.00
Inserted 1:4 Boxes		
1	Brett Favre	100.00
2	Edgerrin James	85.00
3	Peyton Manning	85.00
4	Mark Brunell	40.00
5	Fred Taylor	40.00
6	Drew Bledsoe	40.00
7	Tyrone Wheatley	20.00
8	Torry Holt	20.00
9	Kurt Warner	100.00
10	Stephen Davis	20.00

2000 Pacific Omega EO Portraits

		MT
Complete Set (20):		75.00
Common Player:		3.00
Inserted 1:73		
1	Jake Plummer	3.00
2	Peter Warrick	10.00
3	Tim Couch	5.00
4	Troy Aikman	6.00
5	Emmitt Smith	8.00
6	Terrell Davis	8.00
7	Brett Favre	12.00
8	Edgerrin James	10.00
9	Peyton Manning	10.00
10	Mark Brunell	4.00
11	Fred Taylor	4.00
12	Randy Moss	10.00
13	Drew Bledsoe	4.00
14	Ricky Williams	5.00
15	Ron Dayne	12.00
16	Chad Pennington	8.00
17	Marshall Faulk	3.00
18	Kurt Warner	10.00
19	Jerry Rice	6.00
20	Eddie George	4.00

2000 Pacific Omega Fourth & Goal

		MT
Complete Set (36):		45.00
Common Player:		.50
Minor Stars:		1.00
Inserted 4:37		
#1-9 Parallel:		3x-6x
Production 100 Sets		
#10-18 Parallel:		5x-10x
Production 50 Sets		
#19-27 Parallel:		12x-24x
Production 25 Sets		
#28-36 Parallel:		20x-40x
Production 10 Sets		
1	Eric Moulds	1.00
2	Marcus Robinson	1.00
3	Antonio Freeman	1.00
4	Marvin Harrison	1.00
5	Jimmy Smith	1.00
6	Cris Carter	1.00
7	Randy Moss	5.00
8	Tim Brown	.50
9	Isaac Bruce	1.00
10	Emmitt Smith	3.50
11	Edgerrin James	5.00
12	Fred Taylor	2.00
13	Robert Smith	1.00
14	Curtis Martin	1.00
15	Marshall Faulk	1.50
16	Warrick Dunn	1.00
17	Eddie George	1.50
18	Stephen Davis	1.00
19	Steve Beuerlein	.50
20	Akili Smith	1.00
21	Tim Couch	2.50
22	Brian Griese	1.50
23	Mark Brunell	2.50
24	Daunte Culpepper	2.50
25	Kurt Warner	5.00
26	Jon Kitna	1.00
27	Shaun King	1.50
28	Thomas Jones	2.50
29	Jamal Lewis	7.00
30	Travis Taylor	1.50
31	Peter Warrick	5.00
32	Ron Dayne	6.00
33	Chad Pennington	4.00
34	Plaxico Burress	3.00
35	Giovanni Carmazzi	1.50
36	Shaun Alexander	2.50

2000 Pacific Omega Game Worn Jerseys

		MT
Complete Set (10):		200.00
Common Player:		15.00
1	Keenan McCardell	15.00
2	Fred Taylor	30.00
3	Dan Marino	75.00
4	Wayne Chrebet	25.00
5	Jerome Bettis	25.00
6	Charles Johnson	15.00
7	Donovan McNabb	35.00
8	Kevin Turner	15.00
9	Brock Huard	20.00
10	Cortez Kennedy	15.00

2000 Pacific Omega Generations

		MT
Complete Set (20):		100.00
Common Player:		5.00
Inserted 1:145		
1	Cade McNown, Dez White	6.00
2	Tim Couch, Dennis Northcutt	10.00
3	Troy Aikman, Chad Pennington	12.00
4	Emmitt Smith, Thomas Jones	15.00
5	Terrell Davis, Jamal Lewis	15.00
6	Brett Favre, Giovanni Carmazzi	15.00
7	Marvin Harrison, Travis Taylor	6.00
8	Edgerrin James, Shaun Alexander	12.00
9	Peyton Manning, Tee Martin	12.00
10	Mark Brunell, R. Jay Soward	6.00
11	Cris Carter, Sylvester Morris	6.00
12	Randy Moss, Peter Warrick	15.00
13	Drew Bledsoe, Tom Brady	6.00
14	Jerome Bettis, Ron Dayne	10.00
15	Marshall Faulk, Trung Canidate	5.00
16	Kurt Warner, Chris Redman	15.00
17	Jerry Rice, Plaxico Burress	10.00
18	Warrick Dunn, J.R. Redmond	6.00
19	Eddie George, Reuben Droughns	6.00
20	Stephen Davis, Travis Prentice	6.00

2000 Pacific Omega NFC Conference Contenders

		MT
Complete Set (18):		25.00
Common Player:		1.00
Minor Stars:		2.00
Inserted 2:37		
1	Thomas Jones	3.00
2	Cade McNown	2.00
3	Ron Dayne	6.00
4	Donovan McNabb	2.50
5	Emmitt Smith	5.00
6	Jake Plummer	2.00
7	Randy Moss	5.00
8	Marshall Faulk	2.00
9	Kurt Warner	6.00
10	Ricky Williams	3.00
11	Marcus Robinson	2.00
12	Warrick Dunn	2.00
13	Jerry Rice	4.00
14	Jamal Anderson	2.00
15	Cris Carter	2.00
16	Brad Johnson	1.00
17	Stephen Davis	2.00
18	Shaun King	2.50

2000 Pacific Omega Stellar Performers

		MT
Complete Set (20):		50.00
Common Player:		2.50
Inserted 1:37		
1	Tim Couch	3.50
2	Troy Aikman	5.00
3	Emmitt Smith	7.00
4	Brian Griese	3.00
5	Brett Favre	10.00
6	Edgerrin James	8.00
7	Peyton Manning	8.00
8	Mark Brunell	3.50
9	Fred Taylor	3.50
10	Randy Moss	8.00
11	Drew Bledsoe	3.50
12	Isaac Bruce	2.50
13	Marshall Faulk	2.50
14	Kurt Warner	10.00
15	Jerry Rice	5.00
16	Jon Kitna	2.50
17	Shaun King	3.00
18	Eddie George	3.00
19	Steve McNair	2.50
20	Stephen Davis	2.50

2000 Pacific Paramount

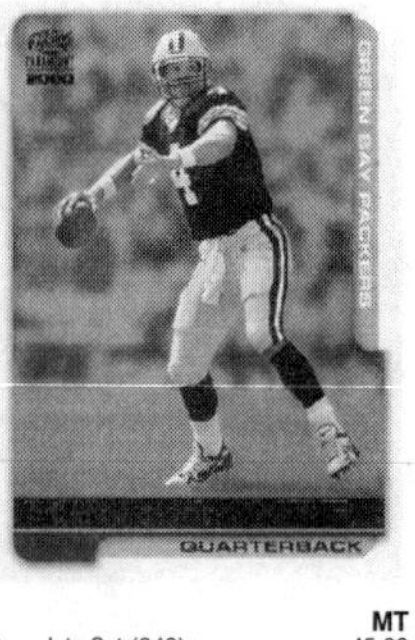

		MT
Complete Set (249):		45.00
Common Player:		.10
Minor Stars:		.20
Common Rookie:		.50
Pack (6):		2.00
Wax Box (36):		60.00
Card #242 Never Released		
1	David Boston	.30
2	*Thomas Jones*	2.00
3	Rob Moore	.20
4	Jake Plummer	.50
5	Simeon Rice	.10
6	Frank Sanders	.20
7	*Raynoch Thompson*	.50
8	Jamal Anderson	.40
9	Chris Chandler	.20
10	Bob Christian	.10
11	Tim Dwight	.30
12	Byron Hanspard	.10
13	Terance Mathis	.10
14	*Mareno Philyaw*	.50
15	Tony Banks	.20
16	Priest Holmes	.30
17	Qadry Ismail	.10
18	Patrick Johnson	.10
19	*Jamal Lewis*	2.00
20	*Chris Redman*	1.25
21	Shannon Sharpe	.20
22	*Travis Taylor*	1.50
23	*Erik Flowers*	.75
24	Doug Flutie	.50
25	Rob Johnson	.20
26	Jonathon Linton	.10
27	*Corey Moore*	.50
28	Eric Moulds	.40
29	Peerless Price	.30
30	Jay Riemersma	.10
31	Antowain Smith	.30
32	*Rashard Anderson*	.75
33	Steve Beuerlein	.20
34	Tshimanga Biakabutuka	.20
35	Donald Hayes	.10
36	Patrick Jeffers	.30
37	Jeff Lewis	.20
38	Muhsin Muhammad	.30
39	Wesley Walls	.10
40	Bobby Engram	.10
41	Curtis Enis	.30
42	Cade McNown	.75
43	Jim Miller	.10
44	Marcus Robinson	.40
45	*Brian Urlacher*	1.00
46	*Dez White*	1.00
47	Michael Basnight	.10
48	Corey Dillon	.30
49	*Ron Dugans*	.75
50	Willie Jackson	.10
51	Darnay Scott	.20
52	Akili Smith	.50
53	*Peter Warrick*	4.00
54	*Courtney Brown*	1.50
55	Darrin Chiaverini	.20
56	Tim Couch	1.00
57	Kevin Johnson	.40
58	Terry Kirby	.10
59	*Dennis Northcutt*	1.00
60	*Travis Prentice*	1.00
61	Leslie Shepherd	.10
62	Troy Aikman	1.00
63	Joey Galloway	.30
64	Raghib Ismail	.10
65	David LaFleur	.10
66	Emmitt Smith	1.25
67	Jason Tucker	.20
68	Chris Warren	.10
69	*Michael Wiley*	1.00
70	Desmond Clark	.10
71	*Chris Cole*	.50
72	Terrell Davis	1.25
73	Olandis Gary	.50
74	Brian Griese	.50
75	*Jarious Jackson*	.75
76	Ed McCaffrey	.30
77	*Delthea O'Neal*	.50
78	Rod Smith	.30
79	Charlie Batch	.40
80	Germane Crowell	.30
81	*Reuben Droughns*	1.00
82	Terry Fair	.10
83	Herman Moore	.30
84	Johnnie Morton	.20
85	Barry Sanders	1.50
86	James Stewart	.20
87	Corey Bradford	.20
88	Tyrone Davis	.10
89	Brett Favre	1.50
90	*Bubba Franks*	1.25
91	Antonio Freeman	.30
92	Matt Hasselbeck	.20
93	Dorsey Levens	.30
94	*Anthony Lucas*	.75
95	Bill Schroeder	.20
96	Ken Dilger	.10
97	E.G. Green	.10
98	Marvin Harrison	.40
99	Edgerrin James	1.50
100	Peyton Manning	1.25
101	Jerome Pathon	.10
102	*Marcus Washington*	.50
103	Terrence Wilkins	.30
104	Kyle Brady	.10
105	Mark Brunell	.60
106	Kevin Hardy	.10
107	Keenan McCardell	.20
108	Jimmy Smith	.30
109	*R. Jay Soward*	1.25
110	*Shyrone Stith*	.50
111	Fred Taylor	.60
112	Alvis Whitted	.10
113	Derrick Alexander	.10
114	Kimble Anders	.10
115	Donnell Bennett	.10
116	Tony Gonzalez	.20
117	Elvis Grbac	.20
118	Kevin Lockett	.10
119	*Sylvester Morris*	1.25
120	Tony Richardson	.10
121	*Deon Dyer*	.50
122	Oronde Gadsden	.20
123	Damon Huard	.30
124	J.J. Johnson	.20
125	Dan Marino	1.25
126	Tony Martin	.10
127	O.J. McDuffie	.20
128	Zach Thomas	.20
129	Cris Carter	.30
130	Daunte Culpepper	.75
131	Leroy Hoard	.10
132	*Chris Hovan*	.50
133	Randy Moss	1.50
134	John Randle	.20
135	Robert Smith	.30
136	*Troy Walters*	.75
137	Drew Bledsoe	.60
138	*Tom Brady*	.75
139	Troy Brown	.10
140	Kevin Faulk	.20
141	Terry Glenn	.30
142	*J.R. Redmond*	1.25
143	Tony Simmons	.20
144	*David Stachelski*	.75
145	Jeff Blake	.20
146	*Marc Bulger*	.75
147	Cameron Cleeland	.20
148	*Sherrod Gideon*	.50
149	*Darren Howard*	.50
150	*Chad Morton*	.50
151	Keith Poole	.10
152	Ricky Williams	1.00
153	Tiki Barber	.20
154	Kerry Collins	.20
155	*Ron Dayne*	4.00
156	Ike Hilliard	.20
157	Joe Jurevicius	.10
158	Pete Mitchell	.10
159	Joe Montgomery	.10
160	Amani Toomer	.20
161	*John Abraham*	.50
162	*Anthony Becht*	.75
163	Wayne Chrebet	.30
164	*Laveranues Coles*	.75
165	Ray Lucas	.30
166	Curtis Martin	.30
167	*Chad Pennington*	3.00
168	Vinny Testaverde	.30
169	Dedric Ward	.20
170	Tim Brown	.30
171	Rich Gannon	.20
172	Bobby Hoying	.20
173	James Jett	.10
174	Napoleon Kaufman	.30
175	*Jerry Porter*	1.00
176	Tyrone Wheatley	.20
177	Charles Woodson	.30
178	Dameane Douglas	.10
179	Charles Johnson	.20
180	Donovan McNabb	.75
181	*Todd Pinkston*	.75
182	*Gari Scott*	.50
183	Torrance Small	.10
184	Duce Staley	.30
185	Jerome Bettis	.30

186	*Plaxico Burress*	2.00
187	Troy Edwards	.30
188	*Danny Farmer*	.75
189	Richard Huntley	.20
190	*Tee Martin*	1.25
191	Kordell Stewart	.40
192	Hines Ward	.20
193	Isaac Bruce	.30
194	*Trung Canidate*	.75
195	Marshall Faulk	.40
196	Az-Zahir Hakim	.20
197	Torry Holt	.40
198	Tony Horne	.10
199	Ricky Proehl	.10
200	Kurt Warner	1.75
201	Jermaine Fazande	.20
202	*Trevor Gaylor*	.75
203	Jeff Graham	.10
204	Jim Harbaugh	.20
205	Freddie Jones	.20
206	Mikhael Ricks	.10
207	Junior Seau	.20
208	Fred Beasley	.10
209	*Giovanni Carmazzi*	1.50
210	Jeff Garcia	.30
211	Charlie Garner	.20
212	Terrell Owens	.40
213	*Tim Rattay*	1.25
214	Jerry Rice	1.00
215	J.J. Stokes	.20
216	Steve Young	.60
217	*Shaun Alexander*	2.00
218	Sean Dawkins	.10
219	*Darrell Jackson*	.75
220	Jon Kitna	.40
221	Derrick Mayes	.20
222	Charlie Rogers	.10
223	Shawn Springs	.10
224	Ricky Watters	.30
225	Mike Alstott	.40
226	Reidel Anthony	.20
227	Warrick Dunn	.40
228	Jacquez Green	.20
229	*Joe Hamilton*	1.00
230	Keyshawn Johnson	.40
231	Shaun King	.75
232	Warren Sapp	.20
233	*Keith Bulluck*	.50
234	Kevin Dyson	.20
235	Eddie George	.50
236	Jevon Kearse	.50
237	*Erron Kinney*	.50
238	Steve McNair	.50
239	Neil O'Donnell	.20
240	Yancy Thigpen	.20
241	Frank Wycheck	.10
243	Champ Bailey	.20
244	Larry Centers	.10
245	Albert Connell	.20
246	Stephen Davis	.30
247	*Todd Husak*	.75
248	Brad Johnson	.30
249	*Chris Samuels*	.75
250	Michael Westbrook	.20

2000 Pacific Paramount Draft Picks 325 Parallel

	MT
Draft Pick Cards:	5x-10x
Production 325 Sets	

2000 Pacific Paramount HoloGold Parallel

	MT
HoloGold Cards:	10x-20x
HoloGold Rookies:	6x-12x
Production 199 Sets	
Retail Only	

2000 Pacific Paramount HoloSilver Parallel

	MT
HoloSilver Cards:	15x-30x
HoloSilver Rookies:	8x-16x
Production 99 Sets	
Hobby Only	

2000 Pacific Paramount Platinum Blue Parallel

	MT
Platinum Blue Cards:	15x-30x
Platinum Blue Rookies:	8x-16x
Production 67 Sets	

2000 Pacific Paramount Premiere Date Parallel

	MT
Premiere Date Cards:	15x-30x
Premiere Date Rookies:	8x-16x
Production 79 Sets	
Hobby Only	

Post-1980 cards in Near Mint condition will generally sell for about 75% of the quoted Mint value. Excellent-condition cards bring no more than 40%.

2000 Pacific Paramount Draft Report

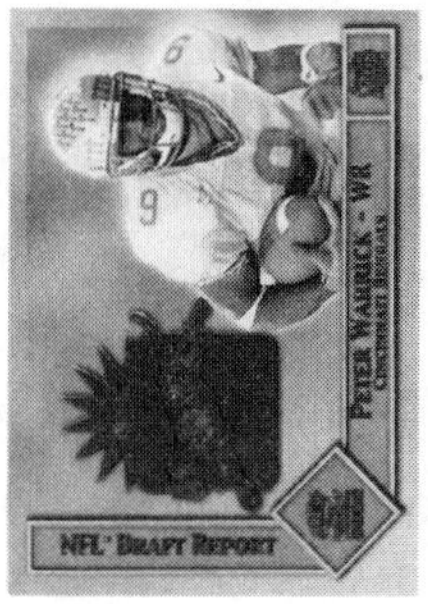

		MT
Complete Set (31):		65.00
Common Player:		1.00
Minor Stars:		2.00
Inserted 2:37		
1	Thomas Jones	4.00
2	Mareno Philyaw	1.00
3	Jamal Lewis	4.00
4	Erik Flowers	1.00
5	Rashard Anderson	1.00
6	Dez White	2.00
7	Peter Warrick	8.00
8	Dennis Northcutt	2.00
9	Michael Wiley	2.00
10	Delthea O'Neal	1.00
11	Reuben Droughns	2.00
12	Anthony Lucas	1.00
13	Marcus Washington	1.00
14	R. Jay Soward	2.50
15	Sylvester Morris	2.50
16	Deon Dyer	1.00
17	Troy Walters	2.00
18	J.R. Redmond	3.00
19	Marc Bulger	1.00
20	Ron Dayne	8.00
21	Chad Pennington	6.00
22	Jerry Porter	2.00
23	Todd Pinkston	1.00
24	Plaxico Burress	6.00
25	Trung Canidate	2.00
26	Trevor Gaylor	1.00
27	Giovanni Carmazzi	3.50
28	Shaun Alexander	4.00
29	Joe Hamilton	2.00
30	Erron Kinney	1.00
31	Todd Husak	1.50

2000 Pacific Paramount End Zone Net-Fusions

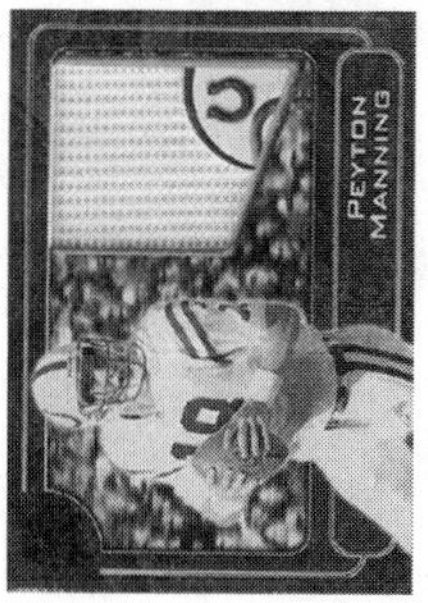

		MT
Complete Set (20):		140.00
Common Player:		3.00
Inserted 1:73		
1	Jake Plummer	3.00
2	Cade McNown	6.00
3	Tim Couch	8.00
4	Troy Aikman	8.00
5	Emmitt Smith	10.00
6	Terrell Davis	10.00
7	Brett Favre	15.00
8	Edgerrin James	15.00
9	Peyton Manning	15.00
10	Mark Brunell	6.00
11	Fred Taylor	6.00
12	Drew Bledsoe	6.00
13	Ricky Williams	8.00
14	Randy Moss	15.00
15	Marshall Faulk	3.00
16	Kurt Warner	15.00
17	Jerry Rice	8.00
18	Jon Kitna	3.00
19	Eddie George	4.00
20	Stephen Davis	3.00

2000 Pacific Paramount Game Used Footballs

		MT
Complete Set (10):		350.00
Common Player:		25.00
Randomly Inserted		
1	Troy Aikman	40.00
2	Emmitt Smith	50.00
3	Olandis Gary	25.00
4	Brett Favre	60.00
5	Edgerrin James	60.00
6	Peyton Manning	60.00
7	Randy Moss	60.00
8	Drew Bledsoe	35.00
9	Kurt Warner	60.00
10	Jerry Rice	40.00

2000 Pacific Paramount Sculptures

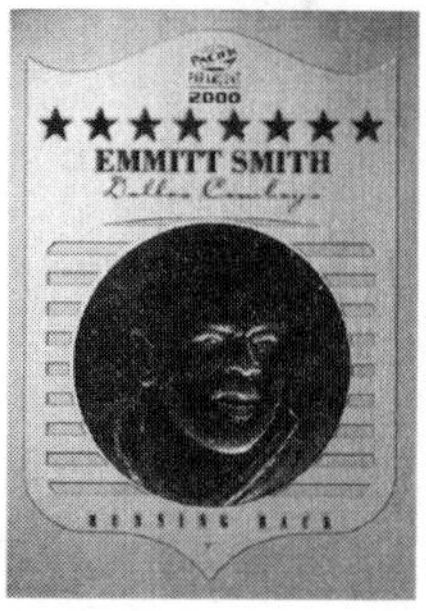

		MT
Complete Set (10):		140.00
Common Player:		10.00
Inserted 1:361		
Proof Cards:		4x-8x
Production 20 Sets		
Canvas Proof Cards:		
Production 1 Set		
1	Peter Warrick	40.00
2	Tim Couch	20.00
3	Emmitt Smith	25.00
4	Edgerrin James	30.00
5	Mark Brunell	15.00
6	Fred Taylor	15.00
7	Randy Moss	30.00
8	Kurt Warner	35.00
9	Eddie George	12.00
10	Stephen Davis	10.00

2000 Pacific Paramount Zoned In

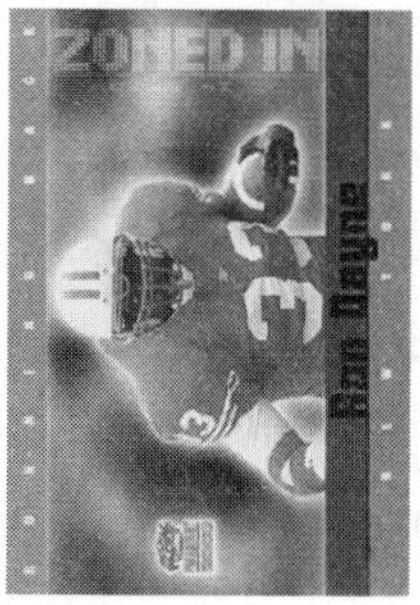

		MT
Complete Set (36):		160.00
Common Player:		2.50
Inserted 1:37		
1	Thomas Jones	8.00
2	Jake Plummer	2.50
3	Jamal Lewis	8.00
4	Cade McNown	4.00
5	Marcus Robinson	2.50
6	Peter Warrick	12.00
7	Tim Couch	5.00
8	Troy Aikman	6.00
9	Emmitt Smith	7.00
10	Barry Sanders	8.00
11	Terrell Davis	7.00
12	Brian Griese	4.00
13	Brett Favre	10.00
14	Marvin Harrison	2.50
15	Edgerrin James	10.00
16	Peyton Manning	10.00
17	Mark Brunell	4.00
18	Fred Taylor	4.00
19	Drew Bledsoe	4.00
20	Ricky Williams	6.00
21	Ron Dayne	12.00
22	Chad Pennington	10.00
23	Randy Moss	10.00
24	Donovan McNabb	4.00
25	Plaxico Burress	10.00
26	Isaac Bruce	2.50
27	Marshall Faulk	2.50
28	Kurt Warner	12.00
29	Jerry Rice	7.00
30	Shaun Alexander	7.00
31	Jon Kitna	2.50
32	Shaun King	4.00
33	Eddie George	4.00
34	Steve McNair	2.50
35	Stephen Davis	2.50
36	Brad Johnson	2.50

2000 Pacific Prism

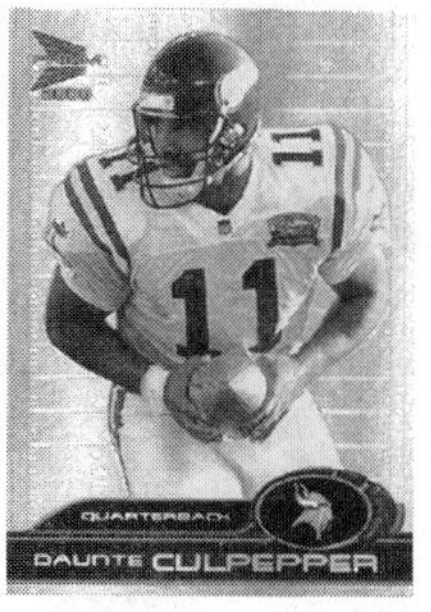

		MT
Complete Set (200):		600.00
Common Player:		.15
Minor Stars:		.30
Common Rookie:		4.00
Production 1,000 Sets		
Pack (5):		5.00
Wax Box (24):		75.00
1	David Boston	.50
2	Jake Plummer	.50
3	Jamal Anderson	.50
4	Chris Chandler	.30
5	Tim Dwight	.50
6	Terance Mathis	.15
7	Tony Banks	.30
8	Priest Holmes	.50
9	Doug Flutie	.75
10	Rob Johnson	.30
11	Eric Moulds	.50
12	Antowain Smith	.30
13	Steve Beuerlein	.30
14	Tim Biakabutuka	.30
15	Muhsin Muhammad	.30
16	Bobby Engram	.15
17	Curtis Enis	.30
18	Cade McNown	.75
19	Marcus Robinson	.50
20	Corey Dillon	.50
21	Akili Smith	.50
22	Tim Couch	1.25
23	Kevin Johnson	.50
24	Troy Aikman	1.50
25	Joey Galloway	.50
26	Raghib Ismail	.15
27	Emmitt Smith	1.75
28	Terrell Davis	1.75
29	Olandis Gary	.50
30	Brian Griese	.75
31	Charlie Batch	.50
32	Herman Moore	.30
33	Johnnie Morton	.15
34	Brett Favre	2.50
35	Antonio Freeman	.50
36	Dorsey Levens	.50
37	Marvin Harrison	.50
38	Edgerrin James	2.50
39	Peyton Manning	2.00
40	Mark Brunell	1.00
41	Keenan McCardell	.30
42	Jimmy Smith	.50
43	Fred Taylor	1.00
44	Donnell Bennett	.15
45	Tony Gonzalez	.30
46	Elvis Grbac	.30
47	Damon Huard	.50
48	J.J. Johnson	.15
49	Cris Carter	.50
50	Daunte Culpepper	1.25
51	Randy Moss	2.00
52	Robert Smith	.50
53	Drew Bledsoe	1.00
54	Kevin Faulk	.30
55	Terry Glenn	.50
56	Jeff Blake	.30
57	Ricky Williams	1.50
58	Kerry Collins	.30
59	Ike Hilliard	.30
60	Amani Toomer	.30
61	Wayne Chrebet	.50
62	Curtis Martin	.50
63	Vinny Testaverde	.50
64	Tim Brown	.50
65	Rich Gannon	.30
66	Napoleon Kaufman	.50
67	Tyrone Wheatley	.30
68	Donovan McNabb	1.00
69	Duce Staley	.50
70	Jerome Bettis	.50
71	Troy Edwards	.50
72	Kordell Stewart	.60
73	Isaac Bruce	.50
74	Torry Holt	.50
75	Marshall Faulk	.50
76	Kurt Warner	2.50
77	Jermaine Fazande	.30
78	Jim Harbaugh	.30
79	Ryan Leaf	.30
80	Junior Seau	.30
81	Jeff Garcia	.50
82	J.J. Stokes	.30
83	Terrell Owens	.50
84	Jerry Rice	1.50
85	Jon Kitna	.50
86	Derrick Mayes	.30
87	Ricky Watters	.30
88	Mike Alstott	.50
89	Warrick Dunn	.50
90	Jacquez Green	.15
91	Shaun King	1.00
92	Eddie George	.75
93	Jevon Kearse	.50
94	Steve McNair	.60
95	Carl Pickens	.30
96	Stephen Davis	.50
97	Jeff George	.50
98	Brad Johnson	.50
99	Deion Sanders	.50
100	Michael Westbrook	.30
101	*Jabari Issa*	4.00
102	*Thomas Jones*	15.00
103	*Sekou Sanyika*	4.00
104	*Jay Tant*	4.00
105	*Raynoch Thompson*	4.00
106	*Doug Johnson*	6.00
107	*Mark Simoneau*	4.00
108	*Jamal Lewis*	50.00
109	*Chris Redman*	15.00
110	*Travis Taylor*	10.00
111	*Kwame Cavil*	4.00
112	*Corey Moore*	4.00
113	*Rashard Anderson*	6.00
114	*Lester Towns*	4.00
115	*Paul Edinger*	4.00
116	*Brian Urlacher*	25.00
117	*Dez White*	6.00
118	*Ron Dugans*	6.00
119	*Danny Farmer*	6.00
120	*Curtis Keaton*	6.00
121	*Peter Warrick*	35.00
122	*Courtney Brown*	8.00
123	*Lamar Chapman*	4.00
124	*JaJuan Dawson*	8.00
125	*Dennis Northcutt*	8.00
126	*Travis Prentice*	12.50
127	*Aaron Shea*	4.00
128	*Spergon Wynn*	6.00
129	*Dwayne Goodrich*	4.00
130	*Orantes Grant*	4.00
131	*Kareem Larrimore*	4.00
132	*Michael Wiley*	6.00
133	*Mike Anderson*	45.00
134	*Chris Cole*	4.00
135	*Jarious Jackson*	8.00
136	*Jerry Johnson*	4.00
137	*Kenoy Kennedy*	4.00
138	*Deltha O'Neal*	6.00
139	*Reuben Droughns*	6.00
140	*Barret Green*	4.00
141	*Bubba Franks*	8.00
142	*Kevin McDougal*	4.00
143	*Marcus Washington*	4.00
144	*T.J. Slaughter*	4.00
145	*R. Jay Soward*	8.00
146	*Shyrone Stith*	6.00
147	*William Bartee*	4.00
148	*Dante Hall*	4.00
149	*Frank Moreau*	8.00
150	*Sylvester Morris*	20.00
151	*Deon Dyer*	4.00
152	*Ben Kelly*	4.00
153	*Tyrone Carter*	4.00
154	*Doug Chapman*	4.00
155	*Troy Walters*	6.00
156	*Tom Brady*	6.00
157	*Patrick Pass*	6.00
158	*J.R. Redmond*	10.00
159	*Marc Bulger*	4.00
160	*Darren Howard*	4.00
161	*Chad Morton*	8.00
162	*Mareno Philyaw*	4.00
163	*Terrelle Smith*	4.00
164	*Ralph Brown*	4.00
165	*Ron Dayne*	40.00
166	*Brandon Short*	4.00
167	*John Abraham*	4.00
168	*Anthony Becht*	8.00
169	*Laveranues Coles*	8.00
170	*Shaun Ellis*	4.00
171	*Chad Pennington*	30.00
172	*Sebastian Janikowski*	6.00
173	*Jerry Porter*	8.00
174	*Todd Pinkston*	8.00
175	*Gari Scott*	4.00
176	*Corey Simon*	8.00
177	*Plaxico Burress*	20.00
178	*Tee Martin*	8.00
179	*Hank Poteat*	4.00
180	*Rogers Beckett*	4.00
181	*Trevor Gaylor*	6.00
182	*Ronney Jenkins*	6.00
183	*Giovanni Carmazzi*	8.00
184	*Chafie Fields*	6.00
185	*Ahmed Plummer*	6.00
186	*Tim Rattay*	8.00
187	*Jeff Ulenhake*	4.00
188	*Shaun Alexander*	25.00
189	*Darrell Jackson*	8.00
190	*Rodnick Phillips*	4.00
191	*James Williams*	4.00
192	*Trung Canidate*	6.00
193	*Joe Hamilton*	8.00
194	*Demario Brown*	4.00
195	*Keith Bulluck*	4.00
196	*Chris Coleman*	4.00
197	*Erron Kinney*	4.00
198	*Billy Volek*	4.00
199	*Todd Husak*	6.00
200	*Chris Samuels*	6.00

2000 Pacific Prism Graded Series

	MT
7.5	.5x Reg. Set
8.0	.75x Reg Set
8.5	1x Reg Set
9	1.5x Reg Set

Common Player:

101	Jabari Issa 8.0 (133)
102	Thomas Jones 8.0 (91)
102	Thomas Jones 8.5 (42)
103	Sekou Sanyika 8.0 (129)
103	Sekou Sanyika 8.5 (4)
104	Jay Tant 8.0 (2)
104	Jay Tant 8.5 (105)
104	Jay Tant 9.0 (26)
105	Raynoch Thompson 8.0 (128)
105	Raynoch Thompson 8.5 (5)
106	Doug Johnson 8.0 (133)
107	Mark Simoneau 8.0 (127)
107	Mark Simoneau 8.5 (6)
108	Jamal Lewis 8.0 (133)
109	Chris Redman 8.0 (68)
109	Chris Redman 8.5 (63)
109	Chris Redman 9.0 (2)
110	Travis Taylor 7.5 (1)
110	Travis Taylor 8.0 (132)
111	Kwame Cavil 8.0 (133)
112	Corey Moore 8.0 (125)
112	Corey Moore 8.5 (8)
113	Rashard Anderson 8.0 (128)
113	Rashard Anderson 8.5 (5)
114	Lester Towns 8.0 (126)
114	Lester Towns 8.5 (7)
115	Paul Edinger 8.0 (99)
115	Paul Edinger 8.5 (33)
115	Paul Edinger 9.0 (1)
116	Brian Urlacher 8.0 (132)
116	Brian Urlacher 8.5 (1)
117	Dez White 8.0 (133)
118	Ron Dugans 8.0 (133)
119	Danny Farmer 8.0 (96)
119	Danny Farmer 8.5 (37)
121	Peter Warrick 8.0 (131)
121	Peter Warrick 8.5 (2)
122	Courtney Brown 8.0 (64)
122	Courtney Brown 8.5 (68)
122	Courtney Brown 9.0 (1)
123	Lamar Chapman 8.0 (132)
123	Lamar Chapman 8.5 (1)
124	JaJuan Dawson 8.0 (116)
124	JaJuan Dawson 8.5 (16)
124	JaJuan Dawson 9.0 (1)
125	Dennis Northcutt 8.0 (130)
125	Dennis Northcutt 8.5 (3)
126	Travis Prentice 8.0 (133)
127	Aaron Shea 8.0 (133)
128	Spergon Wynn 8.0 (132)
128	Spergon Wynn 8.5 (1)
129	Dwayne Goodrich 8.0 (133)
130	Orantes Grant 8.0 (129)
130	Orantes Grant 8.5 (4)
131	Kareem Larrimore 8.0 (116)
131	Kareem Larrimore 8.5 (17)
132	Michael Wiley 8.0 (128)
132	Michael Wiley 8.5 (5)
133	Mike Anderson 8.0 (132)
133	Mike Anderson 8.5 (1)
134	Chris Cole 8.0 (132)
134	Chris Cole 8.5 (1)
135	Jarious Jackson 8.0 (132)
135	Jarious Jackson 8.5 (1)
136	Jerry Johnson 8.0 (124)
136	Jerry Johnson 8.5 (9)
137	Kenoy Kennedy 8.0 (72)
137	Kenoy Kennedy 8.5 (59)
137	Kenoy Kennedy 9.0 (2)
138	Deltha O'Neal 8.0 (131)
138	Deltha O'Neal 8.5 (2)
139	Reuben Droughns 8.0 (3)
139	Reuben Droughns 8.5 (129)
139	Reuben Droughns 9.0 (1)
140	Barrett Green 8.0 (121)
140	Barrett Green 8.5 (12)
141	Bubba Franks 8.5 (103)
141	Bubba Franks 9.0 (30)
142	Kevin McDougal 8.0 (123)
142	Kevin McDougal 8.5 (10)
144	T.J. Slaughter 8.0 (133)
145	R. Jay Soward 8.5 (27)
145	R. Jay Soward 9.0 (106)
146	Shyrone Stith 8.0 (18)
146	Shyrone Stith 8.5 (109)
146	Shyrone Stith 9.0 (6)
147	William Bartee 8.0 (133)
148	Dante Hall 8.0 (121)
148	Dante Hall 8.5 (12)
149	Frank Moreau 8.0 (133)
150	Sylvester Morris 8.0 (90)
150	Sylvester Morris 8.5 (43)
151	Deon Dyer 8.0 (131)
151	Deon Dyer 8.5 (2)
155	Troy Walters 8.5 (21)
155	Troy Walters 9.0 (102)
155	Troy Walters 9.5 (10)
157	Patrick Pass 8.0 (133)
158	J.R. Redmond 8.0 (133)
159	Marc Bulger 8.0 (2)
159	Marc Bulger 8.5 (60)
159	Marc Bulger 9.0 (70)
159	Marc Bulger 9.5 (1)
161	Chad Morton 8.0 (130)
161	Chad Morton 8.5 (3)
162	Mareno Philyaw 8.0 (16)
162	Mareno Philyaw 8.5 (115)
162	Mareno Philyaw 9.0 (2)
164	Ralph Brown 8.0 (126)
164	Ralph Brown 8.5 (7)
165	Ron Dayne 8.0 (42)
165	Ron Dayne 8.5 (83)
165	Ron Dayne 9.0 (8)
166	Brandon Short 8.0 (122)
166	Brandon Short 8.5 (11)
167	John Abraham 8.0 (4)
167	John Abraham 8.5 (26)
167	John Abraham 9.0 (95)
167	John Abraham 9.5 (8)
168	Anthony Becht 8.0 (133)
169	Laveranues Coles 8.0 (133)
170	Shaun Ellis 8.0 (132)
170	Shaun Ellis 8.5 (1)
171	Chad Pennington 8.0 (133)
172	Sebastian Janikowski 8.0 (123)
172	Sebastian Janikowski 8.5 (10)
173	Jerry Porter 8.0 (133)
174	Todd Pinkston 8.0 (129)
174	Todd Pinkston 8.5 (4)
175	Gari Scott 8.0 (133)
176	Corey Simon 8.0 (130)
176	Corey Simon 8.5 (3)
177	Plaxico Burress 8.0 (132)
177	Plaxico Burress 8.5 (1)
178	Tee Martin 8.0 (133)
179	Hank Poteat 8.0 (133)
180	Rogers Beckett 8.0 (133)
181	Trevor Gaylor 8.0 (133)
182	Ronney Jenkins 8.0 (133)
183	Giovanni Carmazzi 8.0 (110)
183	Giovanni Carmazzi 8.5 (23)
184	Chafie Fields 8.0 (130)
184	Chafie Fields 8.5 (3)
185	Ahmed Plummer 8.0 (133)
186	Tim Rattay 8.0 (129)
186	Tim Rattay 8.5 (4)
187	Jeff Ulbrich 8.0 (85)
187	Jeff Ulbrich 8.5 (48)
188	Shaun Alexander 7.5 (1)

188	Shaun Alexander 8.0 (130)	
188	Shaun Alexander 8.5 (2)	
189	Darrell Jackson 8.0 (22)	
189	Darrell Jackson 8.5 (84)	
189	Darrell Jackson 9.0 (27)	
190	Rodnick Phillips 8.0 (133)	
191	James Williams 8.0 (133)	
192	Trung Canidate 8.0 (133)	
193	Joe Hamilton 8.0 (132)	
193	Joe Hamilton 8.5 (1)	
194	Demario Brown 8.0 (133)	
195	Keith Bulluck 8.0 (133)	
196	Chris Coleman 8.0 (132)	
196	Chris Coleman 8.5 (1)	
197	Erron Kinney 8.5 (133)	
198	Billy Volek 8.0 (77)	
198	Billy Volek 8.5 (55)	
198	Billy Volek 9.0 (1)	
199	Todd Husak 8.0 (133)	
200	Chris Samuels 8.0 (131)	
200	Chris Samuels 8.5 (2)	

2000 Pacific Prism Holographic Blue Parallel

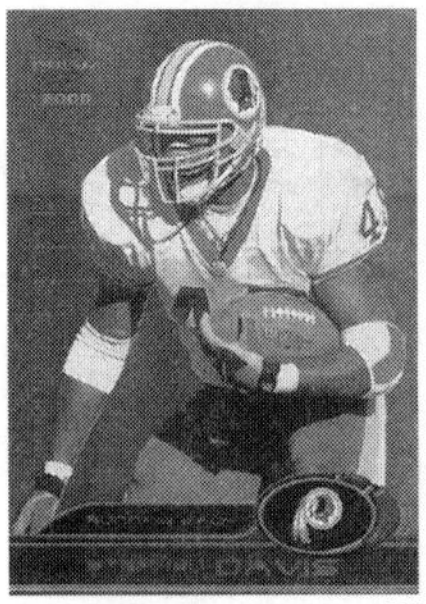

	MT
Blue Cards:	7x-14x
Production 100 Sets	

2000 Pacific Prism Holographic Gold Parallel

	MT
Gold Cards:	12x-24x
Production 50 Sets	

2000 Pacific Prism Holographic Mirror Parallel

	MT
Mirror Cards:	9x-18x
Production 75 Sets	

2000 Pacific Prism Premiere Date Parallel

	MT
Premiere Date Cards:	5x-10x
Production 138 Sets	

2000 Pacific Prism Fortified with Stars

		MT
Complete Set (10):		85.00
Common Player:		8.00
Inserted 1:97		
1	Apple Jakes (Jake Plummer)	8.00
2	BledsOe's (Drew Bledsoe)	10.00
3	Cap'n Couch (Tim Couch)	12.00
4	Frosted PlaxicO's (Plaxico Burress)	20.00
5	Frosted Favre's (Brett Favre)	30.00
6	Alpha-Bettis (Jerome Bettis)	8.00
7	Peerless Price Krispies (Peerless Price)	8.00
8	Special K itna (Jon Kitna)	8.00
9	Jerry Rice Chex (Jerry Rice)	20.00
10	Tyrone Wheatley's (Tyrone Wheatley)	8.00

2000 Pacific Prism Game Worn Jerseys

		MT
Complete Set (10):		175.00
Common Player:		15.00
Randomly Inserted		
1	Mark Brunell	20.00
2	Wayne Chrebet	15.00
3	Randall Cunningham	15.00
4	Drew Bledsoe	20.00
5	Kordell Stewart	20.00
6	Dan Marino	60.00
7	Steve Young	30.00
8	Jerry Rice	35.00
9	Fred Taylor	25.00
10	Jon Kitna	15.00

2000 Pacific Prism MVP Candidates

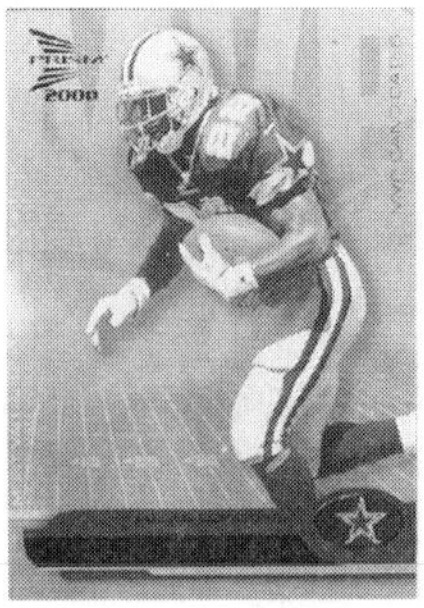

		MT
Complete Set (10):		40.00
Common Player:		2.00
Inserted 1:25		
1	Peter Warrick	8.00
2	Emmitt Smith	6.00
3	Brett Favre	10.00
4	Edgerrin James	8.00
5	Peyton Manning	8.00
6	Randy Moss	8.00
7	Ricky Williams	5.00
8	Marshall Faulk	2.00
9	Kurt Warner	10.00
10	Eddie George	3.00

2000 Pacific Prism Rookie Dial-A-Stats

		MT
Complete Set (10):		120.00
Common Player:		6.00
Inserted 1:193		
1	Thomas Jones	12.00
2	Jamal Lewis	40.00
3	Peter Warrick	30.00
4	Plaxico Burress	15.00
5	Ron Dayne	35.00
6	Chad Pennington	25.00
7	Shaun Alexander	20.00
8	Chris Redman	12.00
9	R. Jay Soward	6.00
10	Laveranues Coles	6.00

2000 Pacific Prism ROY Candidates

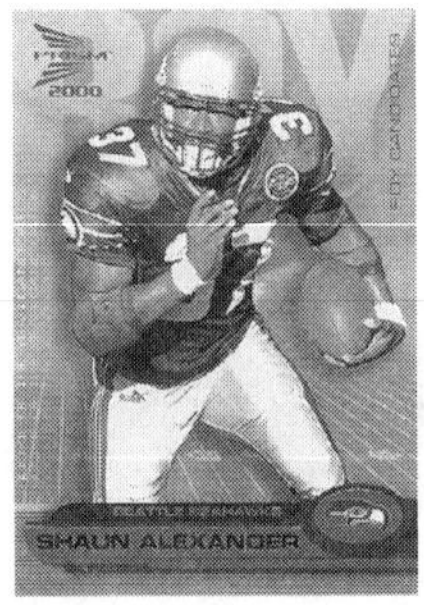

		MT
Complete Set (10):		30.00
Common Player:		1.50
Inserted 1:25		
1	Thomas Jones	3.00
2	Jamal Lewis	10.00
3	Travis Taylor	2.00
4	Peter Warrick	7.00
5	Sylvester Morris	3.50
6	Doug Chapman	1.50
7	Ron Dayne	8.00
8	Chad Pennington	6.00
9	Plaxico Burress	3.50
10	Shaun Alexander	5.00

2000 Pacific Prism Sno-Globe Die Cuts

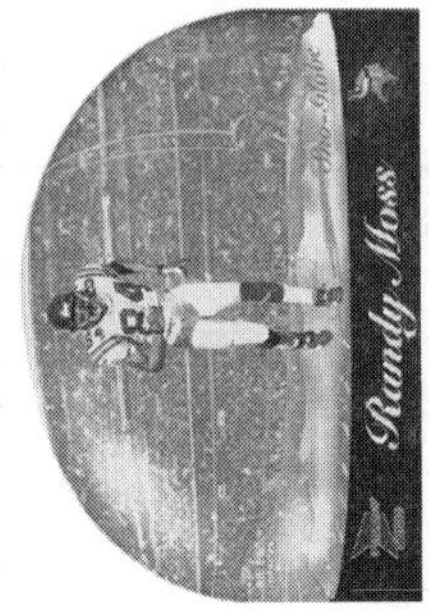

		MT
Complete Set (20):		100.00
Common Player:		4.00
Inserted 1:25		
1	Jamal Anderson	4.00
2	Cade McNown	5.00
3	Tim Couch	6.00
4	Troy Aikman	10.00
5	Emmitt Smith	12.00
6	Terrell Davis	12.00
7	Brian Griese	5.00
8	Brett Favre	18.00
9	Peyton Manning	15.00
10	Edgerrin James	15.00
11	Mark Brunell	5.00
12	Damon Huard	4.00
13	Randy Moss	15.00
14	Drew Bledsoe	5.00
15	Jon Kitna	5.00
16	Marshall Faulk	4.00
17	Kurt Warner	18.00
18	Eddie George	5.00
19	Steve McNair	4.00
20	Stephen Davis	4.00

2000 Pacific Private Stock

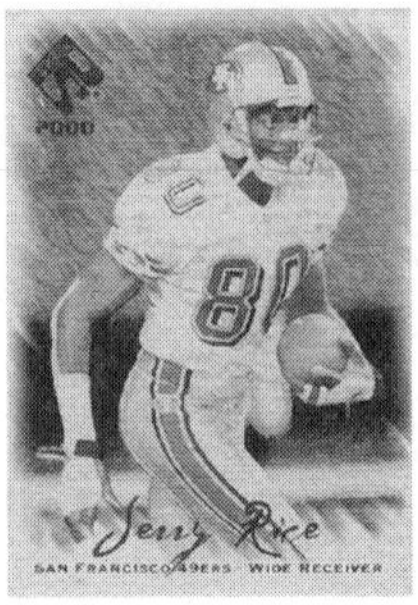

		MT
Complete Set (150):		1000.
Common Player:		.20
Minor Stars:		.40
Common Rookie:		15.00
Production 278 Sets		
Pack (7):		6.00
Wax Box (22):		90.00
1	Rob Moore	.40
2	Jake Plummer	.75
3	Frank Sanders	.40
4	Jamal Anderson	.75
5	Chris Chandler	.40
6	Tim Dwight	.75
7	Tony Banks	.40
8	Priest Holmes	.75
9	Doug Flutie	1.00
10	Rob Johnson	.40
11	Eric Moulds	.75
12	Antowain Smith	.40
13	Steve Beuerlein	.40
14	Tshimanga Biakabutuka	.40
15	Patrick Jeffers	.75
16	Muhsin Muhammad	.40
17	Curtis Enis	.40
18	Cade McNown	1.00
19	Marcus Robinson	.75
20	Corey Dillon	.75
21	Akili Smith	.75
22	Tim Couch	1.25
23	Kevin Johnson	.40
24	Troy Aikman	1.75
25	Raghib Ismail	.20
26	Emmitt Smith	2.25
27	Terrell Davis	2.25
28	Olandis Gary	.75
29	Brian Griese	1.00
30	Ed McCaffrey	.75
31	Charlie Batch	.75
32	Germane Crowell	.75
33	Herman Moore	.75
34	Barry Sanders	2.50
35	Brett Favre	3.00
36	Antonio Freeman	.75
37	Dorsey Levens	.75
38	Marvin Harrison	.75
39	Edgerrin James	3.00
40	Peyton Manning	2.50
41	Terrence Wilkins	.75
42	Mark Brunell	1.25
43	Keenan McCardell	.40
44	Jimmy Smith	.75
45	Fred Taylor	1.25
46	Derrick Alexander	.20
47	Donnell Bennett	.20
48	Tony Gonzalez	.40
49	Elvis Grbac	.40
50	Damon Huard	.75
51	J.J. Johnson	.20
52	Dan Marino	2.50
53	O.J. McDuffie	.20
54	Cris Carter	.75
55	Daunte Culpepper	1.50
56	Randy Moss	2.50
57	Robert Smith	.75
58	Drew Bledsoe	1.25
59	Kevin Faulk	.40
60	Terry Glenn	.75
61	Keith Poole	.20
62	Ricky Williams	2.00
63	Kerry Collins	.40
64	Ike Hilliard	.20
65	Amani Toomer	.20
66	Wayne Chrebet	.75
67	Ray Lucas	.75
68	Curtis Martin	.75
69	Tim Brown	.75
70	Rich Gannon	.40
71	Napoleon Kaufman	.75
72	Donovan McNabb	1.25
73	Duce Staley	.75
74	Jerome Bettis	.75
75	Troy Edwards	.75
76	Kordell Stewart	.75
77	Isaac Bruce	.75
78	Marshall Faulk	.75
79	Torry Holt	.75
80	Kurt Warner	3.00
81	Jermaine Fazande	.20
82	Jim Harbaugh	.20
83	Junior Seau	.40
84	Charlie Garner	.40
85	Terrell Owens	.75
86	Jerry Rice	1.75
87	Jon Kitna	.75
88	Derrick Mayes	.40
89	Ricky Watters	.40
90	Mike Alstott	.75
91	Warrick Dunn	.75
92	Jacquez Green	.20
93	Shaun King	1.25
94	Eddie George	1.00
95	Jevon Kearse	.75
96	Steve McNair	.75
97	Yancey Thigpen	.20
98	Stephen Davis	.75
99	Brad Johnson	.75
100	Michael Westbrook	.40
101	*Thomas Jones*	45.00
102	*Doug Johnson*	20.00
103	*Mareno Philyaw*	15.00
104	*Jamal Lewis*	150.00
105	*Chris Redman*	45.00
106	*Travis Taylor*	30.00
107	*Frank Murphy*	15.00
108	*Dez White*	20.00
109	*Ron Dugans*	20.00
110	*Curtis Keaton*	20.00
111	*Peter Warrick*	100.00
112	*Courtney Brown*	25.00
113	*JaJuan Dawson*	25.00
114	*Dennis Northcutt*	25.00
115	*Travis Prentice*	40.00
116	*Michael Wiley*	20.00
117	*Chris Cole*	15.00
118	*Jarious Jackson*	20.00
119	*Reuben Droughns*	20.00
120	*Bubba Franks*	25.00
121	*Anthony Lucas*	15.00
122	*Rondell Mealey*	20.00
123	*R. Jay Soward*	25.00
124	*Shyrone Stith*	20.00
125	*Sylvester Morris*	50.00
126	*Quinton Spotwood*	20.00
127	*Troy Walters*	20.00
128	*Tom Brady*	20.00
129	*J.R. Redmond*	30.00
130	*Marc Bulger*	15.00
131	*Sherrod Gideon*	20.00
132	*Ron Dayne*	125.00
133	*Anthony Becht*	20.00
134	*Laveranues Coles*	25.00
135	*Chad Pennington*	85.00
136	*Sebastian Janikowski*	20.00
137	*Jerry Porter*	25.00
138	*Todd Pinkston*	25.00
139	*Gari Scott*	15.00
140	*Plaxico Burress*	50.00
141	*Danny Farmer*	20.00
142	*Tee Martin*	20.00
143	*Trung Canidate*	20.00
144	*Trevor Gaylor*	20.00
145	*Giovanni Carmazzi*	25.00
146	*Tim Rattay*	25.00
147	*Shaun Alexander*	75.00
148	*Darrell Jackson*	30.00
149	*Joe Hamilton*	25.00
150	*Todd Husak*	20.00

2000 Pacific Private Stock Retail Version Parallel

	MT
Complete Set (150):	500.00
Retail Cards:	1x
Retail Rookies:	.1x
Production 650 Sets	

2000 Pacific Private Stock Gold Parallel

	MT
Gold Cards:	5x-10x
Gold Rookies:	.2x
Production 181 Sets	

2000 Pacific Private Stock Premiere Date Parallel

	MT
Premiere Date Cards:	7x-14x
Premiere Date Rookies:	.1x
Production 95 Sets	

2000 Pacific Private Stock Silver Parallel

	MT
Silver Cards:	3x-6x
Silver Rookies:	.1x
Production 330 Sets	

2000 Pacific Private Stock Artist's Canvas

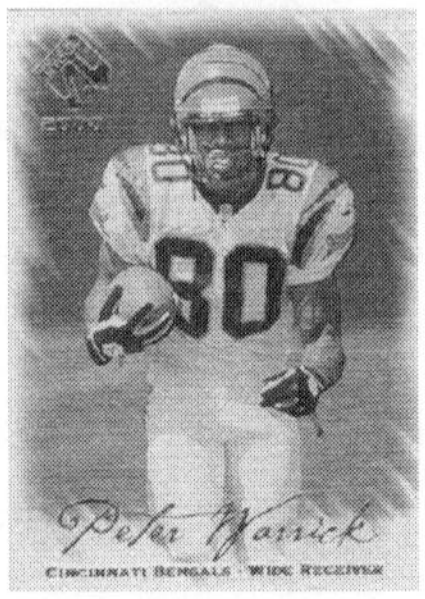

		MT
Complete Set (20):		180.00
Common Player:		7.00
Inserted 1:45		
1	Jamal Lewis	25.00
2	Peter Warrick	15.00
3	Tim Couch	12.00
4	Emmitt Smith	20.00
5	Olandis Gary	7.00
6	Marvin Harrison	7.00
7	Edgerrin James	25.00
8	Mark Brunell	12.00
9	Fred Taylor	12.00
10	Randy Moss	25.00
11	Ron Dayne	20.00
12	Chad Pennington	12.00
13	Jerome Bettis	7.00
14	Plaxico Burress	10.00
15	Marshall Faulk	7.00
16	Kurt Warner	30.00
17	Jon Kitna	7.00
18	Eddie George	10.00
19	Shaun King	10.00
20	Stephen Davis	7.00

2000 Pacific Private Stock Extreme Action

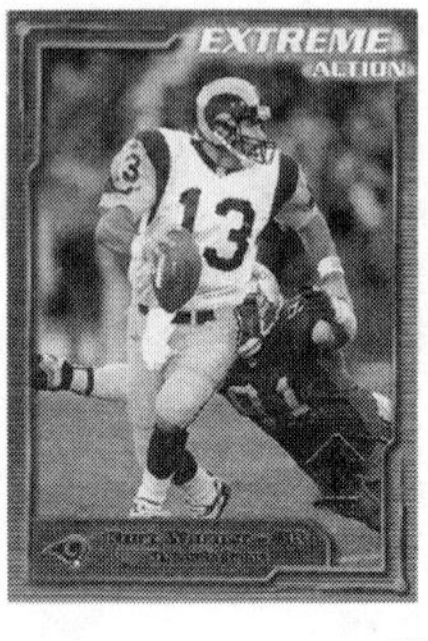

		MT
Complete Set (20):		60.00
Common Player:		2.50
Inserted 2:23		
1	Jake Plummer	2.50
2	Tim Couch	4.00
3	Emmitt Smith	8.00
4	Olandis Gary	2.50
5	Marvin Harrison	2.50
6	Edgerrin James	10.00
7	Mark Brunell	4.00
8	Fred Taylor	4.00
9	Randy Moss	10.00
10	Drew Bledsoe	4.00
11	Ricky Williams	5.00
12	Ron Dayne	12.00
13	Donovan McNabb	4.00
14	Isaac Bruce	2.50
15	Marshall Faulk	2.50
16	Kurt Warner	12.00
17	Jon Kitna	2.50
18	Shaun King	3.00
19	Steve McNair	2.50
20	Stephen Davis	2.50

2000 Pacific Private Stock Private Signings

		MT
Complete Set (36):		
Common Player:		10.00
1	Thomas Jones	10.00
2	Jamal Lewis	30.00
3	Chris Redman	25.00
4	Travis Taylor	20.00
5	Dez White	15.00
6	Peter Warrick	25.00
7	Courtney Brown	25.00
8	JaJuan Dawson	10.00
9	Dennis Northcutt	10.00
10	Travis Prentice	10.00
11	Michael Wiley	10.00
12	Chris Cole	10.00
13	Reuben Droughns	10.00
14	Anthony Lucas	10.00
15	Rondell Mealey	10.00
16	R. Jay Soward	10.00
17	Shyrone Stith	10.00
18	Sylvester Morris	20.00
19	Quinton Spotwood	10.00
20	Troy Walters	10.00
21	J.R. Redmond	20.00
22	Marc Bulger	10.00
23	Ron Dayne	25.00
24	Laveranues Coles	10.00
25	Chad Pennington	30.00
26	Jerry Porter	15.00
27	Todd Pinkston	15.00
28	Plaxico Burress	40.00
29	Danny Farmer	15.00
30	Tee Martin	15.00
31	Chafie Fields	10.00
32	Tim Rattay	10.00
33	Shaun Alexander	50.00
34	Darrell Jackson	10.00
35	Joe Hamilton	15.00
36	Todd Husak	15.00

Post-1980 cards in Near Mint condition will generally sell for about 75% of the quoted Mint value. Excellent-condition cards bring no more than 40%.

2000 Pacific Private Stock PS 2000 Action

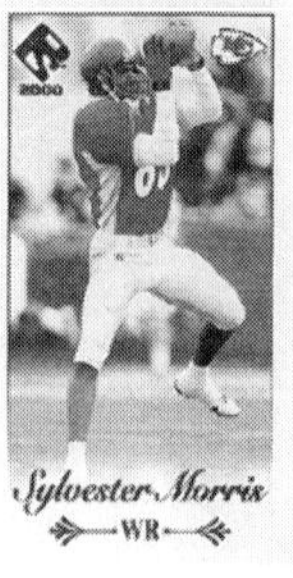

		MT
Complete Set (60):		25.00
Common Player:		.30
Minor Stars:		.60
Inserted 2:1		
1	Thomas Jones	.75
2	Jake Plummer	.60
3	Jamal Lewis	2.00
4	Chris Redman	.75
5	Travis Taylor	.60
6	Doug Flutie	.60
7	Cade McNown	.60
8	Marcus Robinson	.60
9	Dez White	.30
10	Akili Smith	.60
11	Peter Warrick	1.25
12	Tim Couch	.75
13	Dennis Northcutt	.60
14	Travis Prentice	.60
15	Troy Aikman	1.00
16	Emmitt Smith	1.25
17	Terrell Davis	1.25
18	Olandis Gary	.60
19	Brian Griese	.60
20	Reuben Droughns	.30
21	Barry Sanders	1.50
22	Brett Favre	1.75
23	Antonio Freeman	.30
24	Marvin Harrison	.60
25	Edgerrin James	1.50
26	Peyton Manning	1.50
27	Mark Brunell	.60
28	R. Jay Soward	.30
29	Fred Taylor	.75
30	Sylvester Morris	.75
31	Dan Marino	1.50
32	Cris Carter	.60
33	Randy Moss	1.50
34	Drew Bledsoe	.75
35	J.R. Redmond	.60
36	Ricky Williams	.75
37	Ron Dayne	1.50
38	Laveranues Coles	.60
39	Curtis Martin	.60
40	Chad Pennington	1.00
41	Napoleon Kaufman	.30
42	Donovan McNabb	.60
43	Jerome Bettis	.30
44	Plaxico Burress	.75
45	Tee Martin	.60
46	Isaac Bruce	.60
47	Marshall Faulk	.60
48	Kurt Warner	1.75
49	Giovanni Carmazzi	.60
50	Terrell Owens	.60
51	Jerry Rice	1.00
52	Shaun Alexander	1.00
53	Jon Kitna	.60
54	Warrick Dunn	.60
55	Joe Hamilton	.60
56	Shaun King	.60
57	Eddie George	.60
58	Steve McNair	.60
59	Stephen Davis	.60
60	Brad Johnson	.30

2000 Pacific Private Stock PS 2000 New Wave

		MT
Complete Set (25):		85.00
Common Player:		2.00
Minor Stars:		4.00
Production 202 Sets		
1	Jake Plummer	4.00
2	Eric Moulds	2.00
3	Cade McNown	4.00
4	Marcus Robinson	4.00
5	Akili Smith	4.00
6	Tim Couch	6.00
7	Kevin Johnson	2.00
8	Olandis Gary	4.00
9	Brian Griese	5.00
10	Marvin Harrison	4.00
11	Edgerrin James	15.00
12	Peyton Manning	15.00
13	Fred Taylor	6.00
14	Tony Gonzalez	2.00
15	Damon Huard	4.00
16	Randy Moss	15.00
17	Ricky Williams	8.00
18	Donovan McNabb	6.00
19	Duce Staley	4.00
20	Kurt Warner	16.00
21	Terrell Owens	4.00
22	Jon Kitna	4.00
23	Shaun King	10.00
24	Steve McNair	4.00
25	Stephen Davis	4.00

2000 Pacific Private Stock PS 2000 Rookies

		MT
Complete Set (25):		150.00
Common Player:		4.00
Production 106 Sets		
1	Thomas Jones	10.00

2	Jamal Lewis	30.00
3	Chris Redman	10.00
4	Travis Taylor	6.00
5	Dez White	4.00
6	Ron Dugans	4.00
7	Peter Warrick	20.00
8	Dennis Northcutt	5.00
9	Travis Prentice	8.00
10	Reuben Droughns	4.00
11	R. Jay Soward	4.00
12	Sylvester Morris	12.00
13	Troy Walters	4.00
14	J.R. Redmond	6.00
15	Ron Dayne	25.00
16	Laveranues Coles	5.00
17	Chad Pennington	18.00
18	Jerry Porter	4.00
19	Todd Pinkston	4.00
20	Plaxico Burress	12.00
21	Tee Martin	5.00
22	Giovanni Carmazzi	5.00
23	Shaun Alexander	15.00
24	Joe Hamilton	5.00
25	Todd Husak	4.00

2000 Pacific Private Stock PS 2000 Stars

		MT
	Complete Set (25):	65.00
	Common Player:	2.00
	Minor Stars:	4.00
	Production 298 Sets	
1	Jamal Anderson	4.00
2	Doug Flutie	5.00
3	Troy Aikman	8.00
4	Emmitt Smith	10.00
5	Terrell Davis	10.00
6	Herman Moore	2.00
7	Barry Sanders	10.00
8	Brett Favre	15.00
9	Antonio Freeman	4.00
10	Dorsey Levens	4.00
11	Mark Brunell	6.00
12	Dan Marino	12.00
13	Cris Carter	4.00
14	Robert Smith	4.00
15	Drew Bledsoe	6.00
16	Curtis Martin	4.00
17	Tim Brown	4.00
18	Napoleon Kaufman	4.00
19	Jerome Bettis	4.00
20	Isaac Bruce	4.00
21	Marshall Faulk	4.00
22	Jerry Rice	8.00
23	Warrick Dunn	4.00
24	Eddie George	5.00
25	Brad Johnson	2.00

2000 Pacific Private Stock Reserve

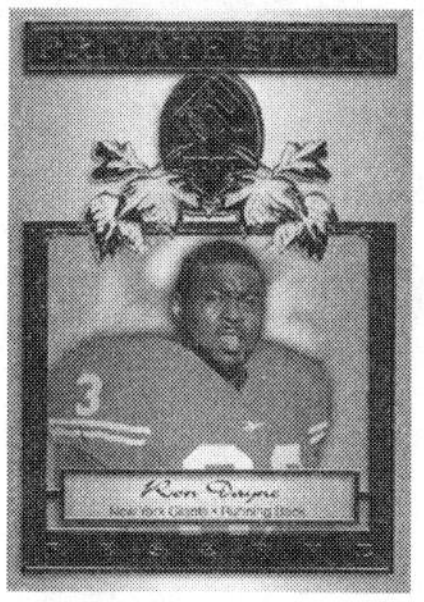

		MT
	Complete Set (20):	125.00
	Common Player:	4.00
	Inserted 1:23	
1	Cade McNown	4.00
2	Peter Warrick	12.00
3	Tim Couch	6.00
4	Troy Aikman	8.00
5	Emmitt Smith	10.00
6	Terrell Davis	10.00
7	Barry Sanders	12.00
8	Brett Favre	15.00
9	Edgerrin James	12.00
10	Peyton Manning	12.00
11	Mark Brunell	6.00
12	Fred Taylor	6.00
13	Randy Moss	12.00
14	Ron Dayne	15.00
15	Chad Pennington	10.00
16	Marshall Faulk	4.00
17	Kurt Warner	15.00
18	Jerry Rice	8.00
19	Shaun Alexander	8.00
20	Eddie George	5.00

2000 Pacific Revolution

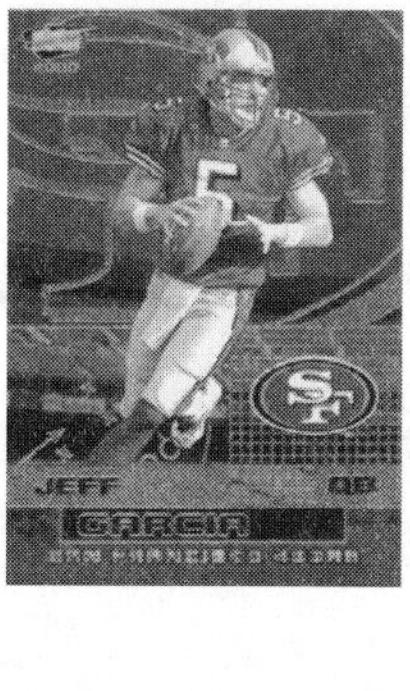

		MT
	Complete Set (150):	375.00
	Common Player:	.20
	Minor Stars:	.40
	Common Rookie:	5.00
	Production 300 Sets	
	Pack (3plus Graded):	25.00
	Wax Box (6):	125.00
1	David Boston	1.00
2	Jake Plummer	1.00
3	Frank Sanders	.40
4	Jamal Anderson	1.00
5	Chris Chandler	.40
6	Tim Dwight	.75
7	Terance Mathis	.20
8	Tony Banks	.40
9	Qadry Ismail	.20
10	Shannon Sharpe	.40
11	Rob Johnson	.75
12	Eric Moulds	1.00
13	Peerless Price	.75
14	Antowain Smith	.40
15	Steve Beuerlein	.40
16	Tshimanga Biakabutuka	.40
17	Muhsin Muhammad	.40
18	Curtis Enis	.40
19	Cade McNown	1.00
20	Marcus Robinson	1.00
21	Corey Dillon	1.00
22	Akili Smith	1.00
23	Tim Couch	2.00
24	Kevin Johnson	.75
25	Troy Aikman	2.50
26	Raghib Ismail	.20
27	Emmitt Smith	3.00
28	Terrell Davis	3.00
29	Brian Griese	1.25
30	Ed McCaffrey	.75
31	Charlie Batch	1.00
32	Herman Moore	.75
33	James Stewart	.40
34	Brett Favre	4.00
35	Antonio Freeman	.75
36	Dorsey Levens	.75
37	Marvin Harrison	1.00
38	Edgerrin James	3.50
39	Peyton Manning	3.00
40	Terrence Wilkins	.40
41	Mark Brunell	1.50
42	Keenan McCardell	.40
43	Jimmy Smith	.75
44	Fred Taylor	1.50
45	Derrick Alexander	.20
46	Tony Gonzalez	.50
47	Elvis Grbac	.50
48	Damon Huard	.75
49	J.J. Johnson	.40
50	O.J. McDuffie	.40
51	Cris Carter	1.00
52	Daunte Culpepper	2.00
53	Randy Moss	3.00
54	Robert Smith	1.00
55	Drew Bledsoe	1.50
56	Terry Glenn	1.00
57	Jeff Blake	.75
58	Ricky Williams	2.50
59	Tiki Barber	.75
60	Kerry Collins	.50
61	Ike Hilliard	.40
62	Amani Toomer	.40
63	Wayne Chrebet	.75
64	Curtis Martin	1.00
65	Vinny Testaverde	.75
66	Dedric Ward	.40
67	Tim Brown	.75
68	Napoleon Kaufman	.50
69	Tyrone Wheatley	.50
70	Charles Johnson	.40
71	Donovan McNabb	1.50
72	Duce Staley	1.00
73	Jerome Bettis	1.00
74	Troy Edwards	.50
75	Kordell Stewart	.75
76	Isaac Bruce	1.00
77	Marshall Faulk	1.25
78	Az-Zahir Hakim	.50
79	Torry Holt	.75
80	Kurt Warner	4.00
81	Curtis Conway	.40
82	Jermaine Fazande	.50
83	Ryan Leaf	.50
84	Junior Seau	.40
85	Jeff Garcia	1.00
86	Charlie Garner	.50
87	Terrell Owens	1.00
88	Jerry Rice	2.50
89	Jon Kitna	.75
90	Derrick Mayes	.40
91	Ricky Watters	.75
92	Mike Alstott	1.00
93	Warrick Dunn	1.00
94	Keyshawn Johnson	1.00
95	Shaun King	1.00
96	Eddie George	1.25
97	Jevon Kearse	1.00
98	Steve McNair	1.00
99	Stephen Davis	1.00
100	Brad Johnson	.75
101	*Thomas Jones*	20.00
102	*Doug Johnson*	10.00
103	*Jamal Lewis*	70.00
104	*Chris Redman*	25.00
105	*Travis Taylor*	15.00
106	*Avion Black*	5.00
107	*Kwame Cavil*	5.00
108	*Sammy Morris*	15.00
109	*Dez White*	10.00
110	*Ron Dugans*	10.00
111	*Danny Farmer*	10.00
112	*Curtis Keaton*	5.00
113	*Peter Warrick*	40.00
114	*Dennis Northcutt*	15.00
115	*Travis Prentice*	20.00
116	*Kevin Thompson*	5.00
117	*Spergon Wynn*	8.00
118	*Michael Wiley*	10.00
119	*Mike Anderson*	60.00
120	*Chris Cole*	5.00
121	*Jarious Jackson*	8.00
122	*Charles Lee*	5.00
123	*Anthony Lucas*	5.00
124	*R. Jay Soward*	10.00
125	*Shyrone Stith*	8.00
126	*Sylvester Morris*	25.00
127	*Doug Chapman*	25.00
128	*Tom Brady*	10.00
129	*Shockmain Davis*	8.00
130	*J.R. Redmond*	15.00
131	*Ron Dayne*	35.00
132	*Ron Dixon*	12.00
133	*Laveranues Coles*	20.00
134	*Windrell Hayes*	5.00
135	*Chad Pennington*	35.00
136	*Jerry Porter*	10.00
137	*Todd Pinkston*	10.00
138	*Plaxico Burress*	25.00
139	*Trung Canidate*	10.00
140	*Trevor Gaylor*	8.00
141	*Giovanni Carmazzi*	12.00
142	*Tim Rattay*	12.00
143	*Shaun Alexander*	30.00
144	*Darrell Jackson*	15.00
145	*James Williams*	5.00
146	*Joe Hamilton*	10.00
147	*Aaron Stecker*	8.00
148	*Billy Volek*	8.00
149	*Bashir Yamini*	5.00
150	*Todd Husak*	10.00

2000 Pacific Revolution Premiere Date Parallel

	MT
Premiere Date Cards:	7x-14x
Inserted 1:7	
Production 85 Sets	

2000 Pacific Revolution Red Parallel

	MT
Red Cards:	6x-12x
Production 99 Sets	

2000 Pacific Revolution Silver Parallel

	MT
Silver Cards:	7x-14x
Production 80 Sets	

2000 Pacific Revolution First Look

		MT
	Complete Set (36):	75.00
	Common Player:	1.00
	Minor Stars:	2.00
	Inserted 4:25	
1	Thomas Jones	3.00
2	Doug Johnson	1.00
3	Jamal Lewis	10.00
4	Chris Redman	4.00
5	Travis Taylor	2.50
6	Sammy Morris	2.50
7	Dez White	1.00
8	Ron Dugans	1.00
9	Curtis Keaton	1.00
10	Peter Warrick	7.00
11	Courtney Brown	2.00
12	Dennis Northcutt	2.00
13	Travis Prentice	3.00
14	Mike Anderson	10.00
15	Bubba Franks	2.00
16	R. Jay Soward	2.00
17	Frank Moreau	2.00
18	Sylvester Morris	4.00
19	Deon Dyer	1.00
20	Doug Chapman	3.00
21	Tom Brady	2.00
22	Aaron Brooks	2.00
23	Ron Dayne	6.00
24	Laveranues Coles	2.50
25	Chad Pennington	6.00
26	Jerry Porter	2.00
27	Todd Pinkston	2.00
28	Plaxico Burress	4.00
29	Tee Martin	2.50
30	Trung Canidate	2.00
31	JaJuan Seider	1.00
32	Giovanni Carmazzi	2.50
33	Paul Smith	1.00
34	Darrell Jackson	2.50
35	Shaun Alexander	5.00
36	Joe Hamilton	2.50

2000 Pacific Revolution Game Worn Jerseys

		MT
	Common Player:	15.00
1	Rod Woodson 1145	15.00
2	Jamir Miller 1295	15.00
3	Olandis Gary 75	35.00
4	Brett Favre 15	175.00
5	Mark Brunell 735	30.00
6	Keenan McCardell 679	15.00
7	Fred Taylor 380	35.00
8	Dan Marino 777	50.00
9	Cris Carter 235	35.00
10	Randy Moss 85	85.00
11	Drew Bledsoe 645	30.00
12	Ricky Williams 35	100.00
13	Koy Detmer 726	15.00
14	Torrance Small 481	15.00
15	Duce Staley 35	75.00
16	Jerome Bettis 65	30.00
17	Junior Seau 60	25.00
18	Jerry Rice 828	50.00
19	Brock Huard	20.00
20	Steve McNair 52	50.00

Post-1980 cards in Near Mint condition will generally sell for about 75% of the quoted Mint value. Excellent-condition cards bring no more than 40%.

2000 Pacific Revolution Making The Grade Black

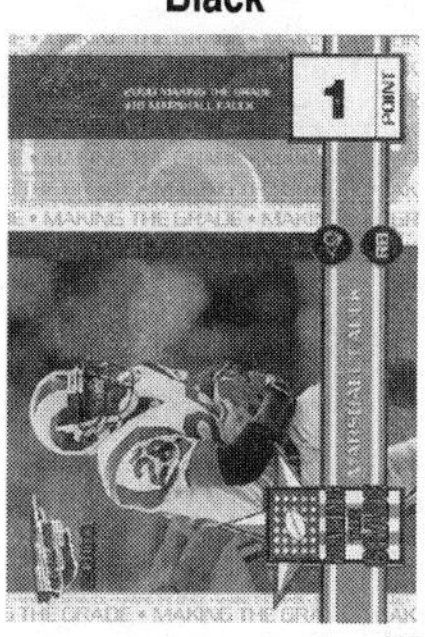

		MT
	Complete Set (20):	40.00
	Common Player:	1.00
	Inserted 4:13	
	Red Cards:	3x
	Inserted 1:49	
	Gold Cards:	5x
	Inserted 1:97	
1	Peter Warrick	4.00
2	Tim Couch	2.00
3	Troy Aikman	3.00
4	Emmitt Smith	4.00
5	Terrell Davis	3.50
6	Brian Griese	1.50
7	Brett Favre	6.00
8	Peyton Manning	5.00
9	Edgerrin James	5.00
10	Mark Brunell	2.00
11	Fred Taylor	2.00
12	Randy Moss	5.00
13	Ricky Williams	2.50
14	Ron Dayne	4.00
15	Chad Pennington	4.00
16	Marshall Faulk	1.50
17	Kurt Warner	6.00
18	Jerry Rice	3.00
19	Eddie George	1.50
20	Steve McNair	1.00

2000 Pacific Revolution Ornaments

		MT
	Complete Set (20):	125.00
	Common Player:	4.00
	Inserted 1:25	
1	Thomas Jones	6.00
2	Jake Plummer	4.00
3	Jamal Anderson	4.00
4	Jamal Lewis	20.00
5	Cade McNown	4.00
6	Corey Dillon	4.00
7	Peter Warrick	12.00
8	Troy Aikman	10.00
9	Emmitt Smith	12.00
10	Mike Anderson	20.00
11	Marvin Harrison	4.00
12	Edgerrin James	15.00
13	Peyton Manning	15.00
14	Mark Brunell	8.00
15	Daunte Culpepper	8.00
16	Ron Dayne	10.00
17	Plaxico Burress	8.00
18	Marshall Faulk	6.00
19	Kurt Warner	15.00
20	Jerry Rice	10.00

2000 Pacific Revolution Shields

		MT
	Complete Set (20):	150.00
	Common Player:	5.00
	Inserted 1:97	
1	Peter Warrick	18.00
2	Tim Couch	10.00
3	Troy Aikman	12.00
4	Emmitt Smith	15.00
5	Terrell Davis	15.00
6	Brett Favre	20.00
7	Edgerrin James	18.00
8	Peyton Manning	18.00
9	Mark Brunell	8.00
10	Daunte Culpepper	10.00
11	Randy Moss	18.00
12	Drew Bledsoe	8.00
13	Ricky Williams	10.00
14	Chad Pennington	15.00
15	Marshall Faulk	7.00
16	Kurt Warner	20.00
17	Eddie George	7.00
18	Steve McNair	5.00
19	Stephen Davis	5.00
20	Brad Johnson	5.00

2000 Pacific Vanguard

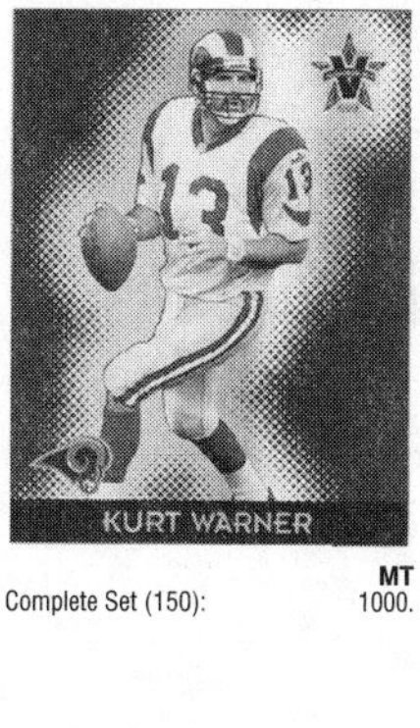

		MT
	Complete Set (150):	1000.
	Common Player:	.25
	Minor Stars:	.50
	Common Rookie:	20.00
	Production 762 Sets	
	Pack (4):	4.00
	Wax Box (24):	80.00
1	Tony Banks	.50
2	Priest Holmes	.50
3	Qadry Ismail	.25
4	Doug Flutie	1.00
5	Rob Johnson	.50
6	Eric Moulds	.75
7	Peerless Price	.75
8	Antowain Smith	.75
9	Corey Dillon	.75
10	Darnay Scott	.50
11	Akili Smith	1.00
12	Tim Couch	2.00
13	Kevin Johnson	.75
14	Terry Kirby	.25
15	Terrell Davis	2.25
16	Olandis Gary	1.00
17	Brian Griese	1.00
18	Ed McCaffrey	.50
19	Rod Smith	.75
20	Marvin Harrison	.75
21	Edgerrin James	3.00
22	Peyton Manning	2.50
23	Terrence Wilkins	.75
24	Mark Brunell	1.25
25	Keenan McCardell	.50
26	Jimmy Smith	.75
27	Fred Taylor	1.50
28	Derrick Alexander	.25
29	Donnell Bennett	.25
30	Tony Gonzalez	.50
31	Elvis Grbac	.50
32	Damon Huard	.50
33	J.J. Johnson	.50
34	Dan Marino	2.50
35	Tony Martin	.25
36	O.J. McDuffie	.25
37	Drew Bledsoe	1.25
38	Kevin Faulk	.50
39	Terry Glenn	.75
40	Wayne Chrebet	.50
41	Ray Lucas	.75
42	Curtis Martin	.75
43	Vinny Testaverde	.75
44	Tim Brown	.50
45	Rich Gannon	.50
46	Napoleon Kaufman	.75
47	Tyrone Wheatley	.50
48	Jerome Bettis	.75
49	Troy Edwards	.75
50	Richard Huntley	.50
51	Kordell Stewart	.75
52	Jermaine Fazande	.50
53	Jim Harbaugh	.50
54	Mikhael Ricks	.25
55	Junior Seau	.50
56	Brock Huard	.50
57	Jon Kitna	.75
58	Derrick Mayes	.50
59	Ricky Watters	.50
60	Eddie George	1.00
61	Jevon Kearse	1.00
62	Steve McNair	1.00
63	Yancy Thigpen	.25
64	David Boston	.75
65	Rob Moore	.50
66	Jake Plummer	.75
67	Frank Sanders	.25
68	Jamal Anderson	.75
69	Chris Chandler	.50
70	Tim Dwight	.75
71	Terance Mathis	.25
72	Steve Beuerlein	.50
73	Tshimanga Biakabutuka	.50
74	Patrick Jeffers	.75
75	Muhsin Muhammad	.50
76	Bobby Engram	.25
77	Curtis Enis	.75
78	Cade McNown	1.25
79	Marcus Robinson	.75
80	Troy Aikman	1.75
81	Raghib Ismail	.25
82	Emmitt Smith	2.25
83	Jason Tucker	.25
84	Chris Warren	.25
85	Charlie Batch	.75
86	Germane Crowell	.75
87	Herman Moore	.50
88	Johnnie Morton	.25
89	Barry Sanders	2.50
90	Brett Favre	3.00
91	Antonio Freeman	.75
92	Dorsey Levens	.75
93	Bill Schroeder	.25
94	Cris Carter	.75
95	Daunte Culpepper	1.25
96	Randy Moss	3.00
97	Robert Smith	.75
98	Cameron Cleeland	.50
99	Keith Poole	.25
100	Ricky Williams	2.00
101	Tiki Barber	.75
102	Kerry Collins	.50
103	Ike Hilliard	.50
104	Amani Toomer	.50
105	Charles Johnson	.25
106	Donovan McNabb	1.25
107	Torrance Small	.25
108	Duce Staley	.75
109	Isaac Bruce	.75
110	Marshall Faulk	.75
111	Torry Holt	.75
112	Kurt Warner	3.50
113	Charlie Garner	.50
114	Terrell Owens	.75
115	Jerry Rice	1.75
116	J.J. Stokes	.50
117	Steve Young	1.25
118	Mike Alstott	.75
119	Reidel Anthony	.50
120	Warrick Dunn	.75
121	Jacquez Green	.50
122	Shaun King	1.25
123	Stephen Davis	.75
124	Brad Johnson	.50
125	Michael Westbrook	.50
126	*Thomas Jones*	50.00
127	*Jamal Lewis*	120.00
128	*Chris Redman*	50.00
129	*Travis Taylor*	30.00
130	*Dez White*	25.00
131	*Ron Dugans*	25.00
132	*Peter Warrick*	85.00
133	*Dennis Northcutt*	25.00
134	*Travis Prentice*	35.00
135	*Reuben Droughns*	20.00
136	*R. Jay Soward*	30.00
137	*Sylvester Morris*	50.00
138	*Troy Walters*	20.00
139	*Tom Brady*	20.00
140	*J.R. Redmond*	30.00
141	*Marc Bulger*	20.00
142	*Ron Dayne*	85.00
143	*Laveranues Coles*	30.00
144	*Chad Pennington*	70.00
145	*Jerry Porter*	25.00
146	*Plaxico Burress*	50.00
147	*Trung Canidate*	25.00
148	*Giovanni Carmazzi*	35.00
149	*Shaun Alexander*	60.00
150	*Todd Husak*	20.00

2000 Pacific Vanguard Premiere Date Parallel

	MT
Premiere Date Cards:	7x-14x
Production 138 Sets	

2000 Pacific Vanguard Purple Parallel

	MT
Purple Cards:	7x-14x

2000 Pacific Vanguard Cosmic Force

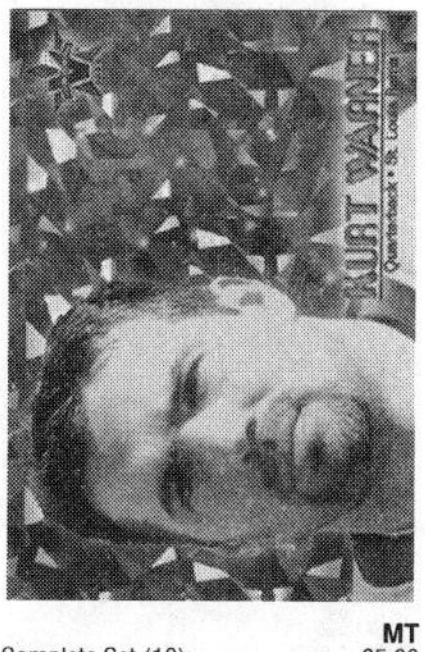

		MT
	Complete Set (10):	65.00
	Common Player:	5.00
	Inserted 1:73	
1	Tim Couch	5.00
2	Troy Aikman	6.00
3	Emmitt Smith	7.00
4	Terrell Davis	7.00
5	Barry Sanders	8.00
6	Brett Favre	10.00
7	Edgerrin James	10.00
8	Peyton Manning	10.00
9	Randy Moss	10.00
10	Kurt Warner	12.00

2000 Pacific Vanguard Game-Worn Jerseys

		MT
	Complete Set (14):	425.00
	Common Player:	20.00
	Randomly Inserted	
1	Cris Carter	35.00
2	Randall Cunningham	25.00
3	Randy Moss	85.00
4	Ricky Williams	65.00
5	Wayne Chrebet	30.00
6	Koy Detmer	20.00
7	Donovan McNabb	45.00
8	Torrance Small	20.00
9	Duce Staley	40.00
10	Jerome Bettis	30.00
11	Kordell Stewart	35.00
12	Jerry Rice	65.00
13	Steve Young	50.00
14	Steve McNair	35.00

2000 Pacific Vanguard Game-Worn Jerseys Duals

		MT
	Complete Set (6):	475.00
	Common Player:	45.00
	Production 200 Sets	
1	Cris Carter, Randy Moss	150.00
2	Ricky Williams, Jerome Bettis	100.00
3	Duce Staley, Donovan McNabb	85.00
4	Jerome Bettis, Kordell Stewart	45.00
5	Jerry Rice, Randy Moss	175.00
6	Steve Young, Steve McNair	60.00

2000 Pacific Vanguard Game-Worn Jerseys Dual Patches

		MT
	Inserted 1:5,000	
1	Olandis Gary, Ricky Williams 12	175.00
2	Mark Brunell, Steve Young 15	250.00
3	Cris Carter, Randy Moss 25	250.00
4	Jerome Bettis, Kordell Stewart 35	125.00
5	Jerry Rice, Randy Moss 19	350.00

6	Steve McNair, Donovan McNabb 25	175.00

2000 Pacific Vanguard Gridiron Architects

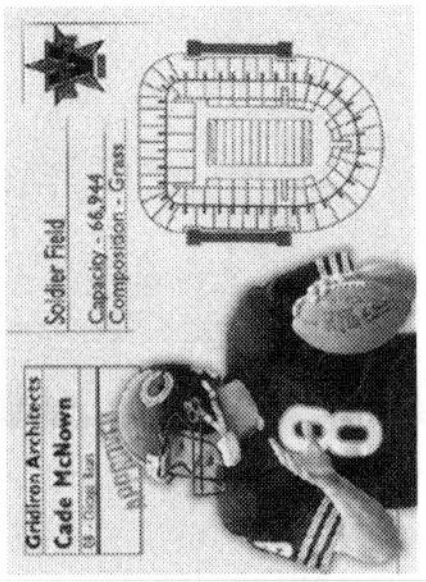

		MT
Complete Set (20):		65.00
Common Player:		2.00
Inserted 1:25		
1	Jake Plummer	2.00
2	Cade McNown	3.00
3	Tim Couch	4.50
4	Troy Aikman	4.50
5	Emmitt Smith	6.00
6	Terrell Davis	6.00
7	Brett Favre	8.00
8	Edgerrin James	8.00
9	Peyton Manning	8.00
10	Fred Taylor	3.50
11	Dan Marino	8.00
12	Randy Moss	8.00
13	Drew Bledsoe	3.50
14	Curtis Martin	2.00
15	Terrell Owens	2.00
16	Marshall Faulk	2.00
17	Kurt Warner	10.00
18	Shaun King	3.00
19	Eddie George	2.50
20	Stephen Davis	2.00

2000 Pacific Vanguard High Voltage

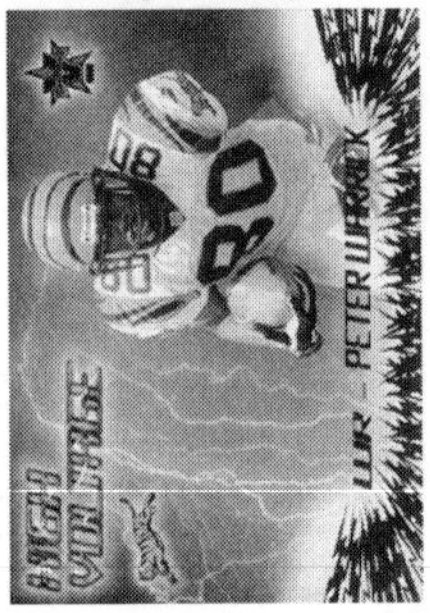

		MT
Complete Set (36):		18.00
Common Player:		.50
Inserted 1:1		
Gold Cards:		7x-14x
Production 199 Sets		
Green Cards:		10x-20x
Production 99 Sets		
Red Cards:		4x-8x
Production 299 Sets		
1	Thomas Jones	1.50
2	Jamal Lewis	1.50
3	Eric Moulds	.50
4	Marcus Robinson	.50
5	Corey Dillon	.50
6	Peter Warrick	2.50
7	Tim Couch	1.00
8	Kevin Johnson	.50
9	Emmitt Smith	1.25
10	Olandis Gary	.75
11	Brian Griese	.75
12	Charlie Batch	.50
13	Antonio Freeman	.50
14	Marvin Harrison	.50
15	Edgerrin James	1.50
16	Mark Brunell	.75
17	Fred Taylor	.75
18	Damon Huard	.50
19	Cris Carter	.50
20	Daunte Culpepper	.75
21	Randy Moss	1.50
22	Ron Dayne	2.50
23	Curtis Martin	.50
24	Chad Pennington	2.00
25	Jerome Bettis	.50
26	Plaxico Burress	2.00
27	Isaac Bruce	.50
28	Marshall Faulk	.50
29	Kurt Warner	1.75
30	Giovanni Carmazzi	1.00
31	Shaun Alexander	1.50
32	Jon Kitna	.50
33	Eddie George	.50
34	Warrick Dunn	.50
35	Shaun King	.75
36	Stephen Davis	.50

Post-1980 cards in Near Mint condition will generally sell for about 75% of the quoted Mint value. Excellent-condition cards bring no more than 40%.

2000 Pacific Vanguard Press Hobby

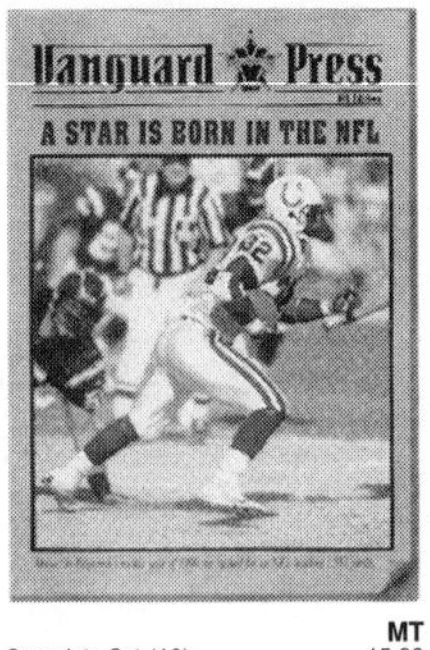

		MT
Complete Set (10):		15.00
Common Player:		1.00
Inserted 2:25 Hobby		
1	Peter Warrick	4.00
2	Tim Couch	1.50
3	Terrell Davis	2.00
4	Edgerrin James	3.00
5	Peyton Manning	3.00
6	Fred Taylor	1.25
7	Drew Bledsoe	1.25
8	Chad Pennington	3.00
9	Jon Kitna	1.00
10	Eddie George	1.00

2000 Pacific Vanguard Press Retail

		MT
Complete Set (10):		15.00
Common Player:		1.00
Inserted 2:25 Retail		
1	Thomas Jones	2.00
2	Cade McNown	1.25
3	Troy Aikman	1.75
4	Emmitt Smith	2.00
5	Brett Favre	3.00
6	Randy Moss	3.00
7	Ron Dayne	4.00
8	Marshall Faulk	1.00
9	Kurt Warner	4.00
10	Stephen Davis	1.00

2001 Pacific

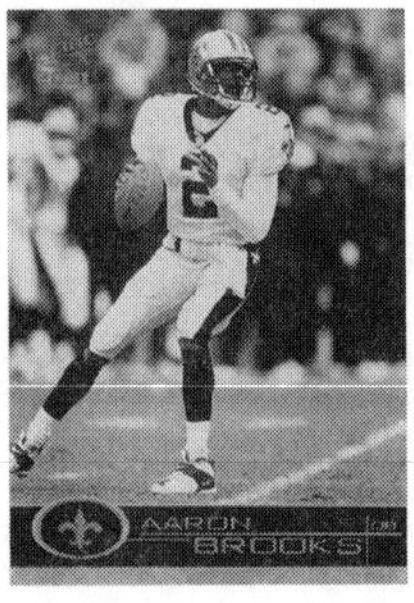

		MT
Complete Set (530):		550.00
Common Player:		.15
Minor Stars:		.30
Common Rookie:		2.00
Rookie QB Numbered to 1,000		
Rookie RB Numbered to 1,500		
Rookie WR Numbered to 1,750		
Rookie Other Numbered to 2,500		
Pack (10):		3.00
Wax Box (36):		90.00
1	David Boston	.50
2	Mac Cody	.15
3	Chris Gedney	.15
4	Chris Griesen	.15
5	Terry Hardy	.15
6	Mar Tay Jenkins	.15
7	Thomas Jones	.50
8	Joel Makovicka	.15
9	Tywan Mitchell	.15
10	Rob Moore	.15
11	Michael Pittman	.15
12	Jake Plummer	.50
13	Frank Sanders	.15
14	Aeneas Williams	.15
15	Jamal Anderson	.50
16	Eugene Baker	.15
17	Chris Chandler	.30
18	Tim Dwight	.30
19	Brian Finneran	.15
20	Jammi German	.15
21	Shawn Jefferson	.15
22	Doug Johnson	.30
23	Danny Kanell	.15
24	Reggie Kelly	.15
25	Terance Mathis	.15
26	Derek Rackley	.15
27	Ron Rivers	.15
28	Maurice Smith	.15
29	Sam Adams	.15
30	Obafemi Ayanbadejo	.15
31	Tony Banks	.30
32	Trent Dilfer	.30
33	Sam Gash	.15
34	Priest Holmes	.30
35	Qadry Ismail	.15
36	Pat Johnson	.15
37	Jamal Lewis	1.50
38	Jermaine Lewis	.15
39	Ray Lewis	.15
40	Chris Redman	.75
41	Shannon Sharpe	.30
42	Brandon Stokley	.15
43	Travis Taylor	.50
44	Shawn Bryson	.15
45	Kwame Cavil	.15
46	Sam Cowart	.15
47	Doug Flutie	.75
48	Rob Johnson	.30
49	Jonathon Linton	.15
50	Jeremy McDaniel	.15
51	Sammy Morris	.50
52	Eric Moulds	.50
53	Peerless Price	.30
54	Jay Riemersma	.15
55	Antowain Smith	.30
56	Chris Watson	.15
57	Marcelius Wiley	.15
58	Michael Bates	.15
59	Steve Beuerlein	.30
60	Tshimanga Biakabutuka	.30
61	Isaac Byrd	.15
62	Dameyune Craig	.30
63	William Floyd	.15
64	Karl Hankton	.15
65	Donald Hayes	.15
66	Chris Hetherington	.15
67	Brad Hoover	.50
68	Patrick Jeffers	.30
69	Muhsin Muhammad	.30
70	Iheanyi Uwaezuoke	.15
71	Wesley Walls	.15
72	James Allen	.30
73	Marlon Barnes	.15
74	D'Wayne Bates	.15
75	Marty Booker	.15
76	Macey Brooks	.15
77	Bobby Engram	.15
78	Curtis Enis	.30
79	Mark Hartsell	.15
80	Eddie Kennison	.15
81	Shane Matthews	.15
82	Cade McNown	.50
83	Jim Miller	.15
84	Marcus Robinson	.50
85	Brian Urlacher	1.00
86	Dez White	.15
87	Brandon Bennett	.15
88	Steve Bush	.15
89	Corey Dillon	.50
90	Ron Dugans	.15
91	Danny Farmer	.15
92	Damon Griffin	.15
93	Clif Groce	.15
94	Curtis Keaton	.15
95	Scott Mitchell	.15
96	Darnay Scott	.15
97	Akili Smith	.50
98	Peter Warrick	1.00
99	Nick Williams	.15
100	Craig Yeast	.15
101	Bobby Brown	.15
102	Darrin Chiaverini	.15
103	Tim Couch	.75
104	JaJuan Dawson	.15
105	Marc Edwards	.15
106	Kevin Johnson	.30
107	Dennis Northcutt	.30
108	David Patten	.15
109	Doug Pederson	.15
110	Travis Prentice	.50
111	Errict Rhett	.15
112	Aaron Shea	.15
113	Kevin Thompson	.15
114	Jamel White	.15
115	Spergon Wynn	.15
116	Troy Aikman	1.00
117	Chris Brazzell	.15
118	Randall Cunningham	.30
119	Jackie Harris	.15
120	Damon Hodge	.15
121	Raghib Ismail	.15
122	David LaFleur	.15
123	Wane McGarity	.15
124	James McKnight	.15
125	Emmitt Smith	1.25
126	Clint Stoerner	.50
127	Jason Tucker	.15
128	Michael Wiley	.30
129	Anthony Wright	.15
130	Mike Anderson	1.25
131	Dwayne Carswell	.15
132	Byron Chamberlain	.15
133	Desmond Clark	.15
134	Chris Cole	.15
135	KaRon Coleman	.15
136	Terrell Davis	1.25
137	Gus Frerotte	.15
138	Olandis Gary	.50
139	Brian Griese	.50
140	Howard Griffith	.15
141	Jarious Jackson	.15
142	Ed McCaffrey	.30
143	Scottie Montgomery	.15
144	Rod Smith	.30
145	Charlie Batch	.30
146	Stoney Case	.15
147	Germane Crowell	.30
148	Larry Foster	.15
149	Desmond Howard	.15
150	Sedrick Irvin	.15
151	Herman Moore	.30
152	Johnnie Morton	.15
153	Robert Porcher	.15
154	Cory Sauter	.15
155	Cory Schlesinger	.15
156	David Sloan	.15
157	Brian Stablein	.15
158	James Stewart	.30
159	Corey Bradford	.15
160	Tyrone Davis	.15
161	Donald Driver	.15
162	Brett Favre	2.00
163	Bubba Franks	.30
164	Antonio Freeman	.30
165	Herbert Goodman	.15
166	Ahman Green	.30
167	Matt Hasselbeck	.50
168	William Henderson	.15
169	Charles Lee	.15
170	Dorsey Levens	.30
171	Bill Schroeder	.30
172	Darren Sharper	.15
173	Matt Snider	.15
174	Danny Wuerffel	.15
175	Ken Dilger	.15
176	Jim Finn	.15
177	Lennox Gordon	.15
178	E.G. Green	.15
179	Marvin Harrison	.50
180	Kelly Holcomb	.15
181	Trevor Insley	.15
182	Edgerrin James	1.50
183	Peyton Manning	1.50
184	Kevin McDougal	.15
185	Jerome Pathon	.15
186	Marcus Pollard	.15
187	Justin Snow	.15
188	Terrence Wilkins	.15
189	Reggie Barlow	.15
190	Kyle Brady	.15
191	Mark Brunell	.75
192	Kevin Hardy	.15
193	Anthony Johnson	.15
194	Stacey Mack	.15
195	Jamie Martin	.15
196	Keenan McCardell	.30
197	Daimon Shelton	.15
198	Jimmy Smith	.50
199	R. Jay Soward	.30
200	Shyrone Stith	.30
201	Fred Taylor	.60
202	Alvis Whitted	.15
203	Jermaine Williams	.15
204	Derrick Alexander	.15
205	Kimble Anders	.15
206	Donnell Bennett	.15
207	Mike Cloud	.15
208	Todd Collins	.15
209	Tony Gonzalez	.30
210	Elvis Grbac	.30
211	Dante Hall	.15
212	Kevin Lockett	.15
213	Warren Moon	.30
214	Frank Moreau	.30
215	Sylvester Morris	.50
216	Larry Parker	.15
217	Tony Richardson	.15
218	Trace Armstrong	.15
219	Autry Denson	.15
220	Bert Emanuel	.15
221	Jay Fiedler	.30
222	Oronde Gadsden	.15
223	Damon Huard	.30
224	J.J. Johnson	.15
225	Rob Konrad	.15
226	Tony Martin	.15
227	O.J. McDuffie	.30
228	Mike Quinn	.15
229	Lamar Smith	.50
230	Jason Taylor	.15
231	Thurman Thomas	.30
232	Zach Thomas	.30
233	Todd Bouman	.15
234	Bubby Brister	.30
235	Cris Carter	.50
236	Daunte Culpepper	1.00
237	John Davis	.15
238	Robert Griffith	.15
239	Matthew Hatchette	.15
240	Jim Kleinsasser	.15
241	Randy Moss	1.50
242	John Randle	.30
243	Robert Smith	.30
244	Chris Walsh	.15
245	Troy Walters	.15
246	Moe Williams	.15
247	Michael Bishop	.50
248	Drew Bledsoe	.75
249	Troy Brown	.15
250	Tedy Bruschi	.15
251	Tony Carter	.15
252	Shockmain Davis	.15
253	Kevin Faulk	.30
254	Terry Glenn	.50
255	Ty Law	.15
256	Lawyer Milloy	.15
257	J.R. Redmond	.30
258	Harold Shaw	.30
259	Tony Simmons	.30
260	Jermaine Wiggins	.30
261	Jeff Blake	.15
262	Aaron Brooks	.50
263	Cameron Cleeland	.30
264	Andrew Glover	.15
265	La'Roi Glover	.15
266	Joe Horn	.30
267	Kevin Houser	.50
268	Willie Jackson	.15
269	Jerald Moore	.15
270	Chad Morton	.30
271	Keith Poole	.15
272	Terrelle Smith	.30
273	Ricky Williams	.75
274	Robert Wilson	.15
275	Jessie Armstead	.15
276	Tiki Barber	.50
277	Mike Cherry	.15
278	Kerry Collins	.30
279	Greg Comella	.15
280	Thabiti Davis	.15
281	Ron Dayne	1.00
282	Ron Dixon	.30
283	Ike Hilliard	.30
284	Joe Jurevicius	.30
285	Jason Sehorn	.15
286	Michael Strahan	.15
287	Amani Toomer	.30
288	Craig Walendy	.15
289	Damon Washington	.15
290	Richie Anderson	.15
291	Anthony Becht	.15
292	Wayne Chrebet	.30
293	Laveranues Coles	.50
294	Bryan Cox	.15
295	Marvin Jones	.15
296	Mo Lewis	.15
297	Ray Lucas	.50
298	Curtis Martin	.50
299	Bernie Parmalee	.15
300	Chad Pennington	1.00
301	Jerald Sowell	.15
302	Dwight Stone	.15
303	Vinny Testaverde	.30
304	Dedric Ward	.30
305	Tim Brown	.30
306	Zack Crockett	.15
307	Scott Dreisbach	.15
308	Rickey Dudley	.15
309	David Dunn	.15
310	Mondriel Fulcher	.15
311	Rich Gannon	.30
312	James Jett	.15
313	Randy Jordan	.15
314	Napoleon Kaufman	.30
315	Rodney Peete	.15
316	Jerry Porter	.30
317	Andre Rison	.30
318	Tyrone Wheatley	.30
319	Charles Woodson	.30
320	Darnell Autry	.15
321	Na Brown	.15
322	Hugh Douglas	.15
323	Charles Johnson	.15
324	Chad Lewis	.15
325	Cecil Martin	.15
326	Donovan McNabb	.75
327	Brian Mitchell	.15
328	Todd Pinkston	.30
329	Ron Powlus	.30
330	Stanley Pritchett	.15
331	Torrance Small	.15
332	Duce Staley	.50
333	Troy Vincent	.15
334	Chris Warren	.30
335	Jerome Bettis	.50
336	Plaxico Burress	.50
337	Troy Edwards	.30
338	Chris Fuamatu-Ma'afala	.15
339	Cory Geason	.15
340	Kent Graham	.15
341	Courtney Hawkins	.15
342	Richard Huntley	.15
343	Tee Martin	.30
344	Bobby Shaw	.30
345	Kordell Stewart	.50
346	Hines Ward	.30
347	Destry Wright	.15
348	Amos Zereoue	.15
349	Isaac Bruce	.50
350	Trung Canidate	.50
351	Marshall Faulk	.60
352	London Fletcher	.15
353	Joe Germaine	.30
354	Trent Green	.50
355	Az-Zahir Hakim	.30
356	James Hodgins	.15
357	Robert Holcombe	.15
358	Torry Holt	.30
359	Tony Horne	.15
360	Ricky Proehl	.15
361	Chris Thomas	.15
362	Kurt Warner	1.75
363	Justin Watson	.15
364	Kenny Bynum	.15
365	Robert Chancey	.15
366	Curtis Conway	.15
367	Jermaine Fazande	.30
368	Terrell Fletcher	.15
369	Trevor Gaylor	.15
370	Jeff Graham	.15
371	Jim Harbaugh	.30
372	Rodney Harrison	.15
373	Ronney Jenkins	.15
374	Freddie Jones	.15
375	Reggie Jones	.30
376	Ryan Leaf	.30
377	Junior Seau	.30
378	Fred Beasley	.15
379	Greg Clark	.15
380	Jeff Garcia	.50
381	Charlie Garner	.30
382	Terry Jackson	.15
383	Brian Jennings	.15
384	Travis Jervey	.15
385	Jonas Lewis	.15
386	Terrell Owens	.50
387	Jerry Rice	1.00
388	Paul Smith	.15
389	J.J. Stokes	.30
390	Tai Streets	.30
391	Justin Swift	.15
392	Shaun Alexander	.50
393	Karsten Bailey	.15
394	Chad Brown	.15
395	Sean Dawkins	.15
396	Christian Fauria	.15
397	Brock Huard	.30
398	Darrell Jackson	.30
399	Jon Kitna	.30
400	Derrick Mayes	.30
401	Itula Mili	.15
402	Charlie Rogers	.15
403	Mack Strong	.15
404	Ricky Watters	.30
405	James Williams	.15
406	Rabih Abdullah	.15
407	Mike Alstott	.50
408	Reidel Anthony	.15
409	Derrick Brooks	.15
410	Warrick Dunn	.50
411	Jacquez Green	.30
412	Joe Hamilton	.30
413	Keyshawn Johnson	.50
414	Shaun King	.50
415	*Charles Kirby*	1.00
416	Warren Sapp	.30
417	Aaron Stecker	.15
418	Todd Yoder	.15
419	Eric Zeier	.15
420	Chris Coleman	.15
421	Kevin Dyson	.30
422	Eddie George	.60
423	Jevon Kearse	.50
424	Erron Kinney	.15
425	Mike Leach	.15
426	Derrick Mason	.30
427	Steve McNair	.50
428	Lorenzo Neal	.15
429	Carl Pickens	.30
430	Chris Sanders	.15
431	Yancey Thigpen	.15
432	Rodney Thomas	.15
433	Frank Wycheck	.15
434	Stephen Alexander	.15
435	Champ Bailey	.30
436	Larry Centers	.15
437	Albert Connell	.15
438	Stephen Davis	.50
439	Zeron Flemister	.15
440	Irving Fryar	.15
441	Jeff George	.30
442	Skip Hicks	.30
443	Todd Husak	.30
444	Brad Johnson	.30
445	Adrian Murrell	.15
446	Deion Sanders	.50
447	Mike Sellers	.15
448	Derrius Thompson	.15
449	James Thrash	.30
450	Michael Westbrook	.30
451	*Alex Bannister AUTO*	10.00
452	*Kevan Barlow AUTO*	10.00
453	*Drew Brees AUTO*	75.00
454	*Travis Henry AUTO*	20.00
455	*Chad Johnson AUTO*	15.00
456	*Mike McMahon AUTO*	15.00
457	*Bobby Newcombe AUTO*	15.00
458	*Sage Rosenfels AUTO*	20.00
459	*LaDainian Tomlinson AUTO*	60.00
460	*Chris Weinke AUTO*	35.00
461	*Tay Cody*	4.00
462	*Adam Archuleta*	4.00
463	*Will Allen*	4.00
464	*Moran Norris*	4.00
465	*Tommy Polley*	4.00
466	*Ennis Davis*	4.00
467	*Jamar Fletcher*	5.00
468	*Derrick Gibson*	4.00
469	*Sedrick Hodge*	4.00
470	*Willie Howard*	4.00
471	*Steve Hutchinson*	4.00
472	*Michael Stone*	2.00
473	*Vinny Sutherland*	6.00
474	*Joe Tafoya*	2.00
475	*Maurice Williams*	4.00
476	*Pork Chop Womack*	4.00
477	*Chad Ward*	4.00
478	*Scotty Anderson*	4.00
479	*Gary Baxter*	4.00
480	*Marques Tuiasosopo*	15.00
481	*Tim Hasselbeck*	8.00
482	*Clevan Thomas*	4.00
483	*Marcus Stroud*	4.00
484	*John Schlecht*	2.00
485	*Brandon Spoon*	4.00
486	*Alex Lincoln*	4.00
487	*Anthony Thomas*	30.00
488	*Freddie Mitchell*	10.00
489	*Brian Allen*	4.00
490	*Zeke Moreno*	4.00
491	*Tony Driver*	4.00
492	*Kynan Forney*	2.00
493	*Reggie Wayne*	12.00
494	*Larry Casher*	4.00
495	*Fred Wakefield*	4.00
496	*Jeff Backus*	4.00
497	*Jarrod Cooper*	2.00
498	*Heath Evans*	4.00
499	*James Jackson*	8.00
500	*Jabari Holloway*	4.00
501	*Quincy Morgan*	10.00
502	*Josh Booty*	8.00
503	*Ja'Mar Toombs*	4.00
504	*Jason McKinley*	6.00
505	*Reggie White*	5.00
506	*Todd Heap*	5.00
507	*Rudi Johnson*	6.00
508	*Marvin "Snoop" Minnis*	5.00
509	*David Terrell*	20.00
510	*Torrance Marshall*	4.00
511	*Michael Bennett*	25.00
512	*Chris Chambers*	15.00
513	*Ben Leard*	6.00
514	*Ron Gardner*	12.00
515	*Michael Vick*	75.00
516	*Josh Heupel 1000 RED*	20.00
517	*Jesse Palmer 1000 RED*	12.00
518	*Quincy Carter 1000 RED*	12.00
519	*A.J. Freely 1000 RED*	8.00
520	*David Rivers 1000 RED*	8.00
521	*Deuce McAllister 1500 RED*	25.00
522	*LaMont Jordan 1500 RED*	15.00
523	*David Allen 1500 RED*	10.00
524	*Correll Buckhelter 1500 RED*	10.00
525	*Travis Minor 1500 RED*	10.00
526	*Koren Robinson 1750 RED*	20.00
527	*Santana Moss 1750 RED*	20.00
528	*Robert Ferguson 1750 RED*	15.00
529	*T.J. Houshmandzadeh 1750 RED*	10.00
530	*Cedrick Wilson 1750 RED*	10.00

2001 Pacific All-Rookie Team

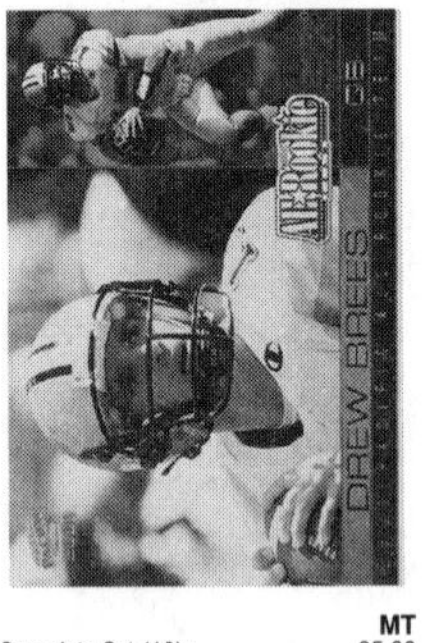

		MT
Complete Set (10):		35.00
Common Player:		4.00
Inserted 1:37		
1	Kevan Barlow	5.00
2	Travis Henry	5.00
3	Chad Johnson	4.00
4	LaDainian Tomlinson	10.00
5	Chris Weinke	6.00
6	Drew Brees	12.00
7	Anthony Thomas	5.00
8	Freddie Mitchell	5.00
9	Reggie Wayne	5.00
10	Marques Tuiasosopo	6.00

2001 Pacific Cramer's Choice Awards

		MT
Complete Set (10):		200.00
Common Player:		12.00
Production 99 Sets		
1	Trent Dilfer	12.00
2	Jamal Lewis	45.00
3	Emmitt Smith	40.00
4	Brett Favre	60.00
5	Edgerrin James	40.00

6	Peyton Manning	40.00
7	Randy Moss	40.00
8	Marshall Faulk	25.00
9	Kurt Warner	50.00
10	Eddie George	20.00

2001 Pacific Game-Worn Jerseys

		MT
Common Player:		20.00
Production 99 Sets		
1	Thomas Jones	25.00
2	Jake Plummer	25.00
3	Rod Woodson	20.00
4	Rob Johnson	20.00
5	Corey Dillon	25.00
6	Akili Smith	25.00
7	Peter Warrick	40.00
8	Mark Brunell	40.00
9	Keenan McCardell 20	35.00
10	Fred Taylor	30.00
11	Dan Marino	120.00
12	Trent Green	25.00
13	Kurt Warner	80.00
14	Jerry Rice 20	100.00
15	Brock Huard 20	40.00

2001 Pacific Game-Used Footballs

		MT
Common Player:		40.00
Production 99 Sets		
1	Jamal Lewis	70.00
2	Peter Warrick	50.00
3	Mike Anderson	70.00
4	Edgerrin James	70.00
5	Daunte Culpepper	70.00
6	Randy Moss	70.00
7	Ron Dayne	50.00
8	Marshall Faulk	60.00
9	Kurt Warner	80.00
10	Eddie George	40.00

2001 Pacific Gold Crown Die-Cuts

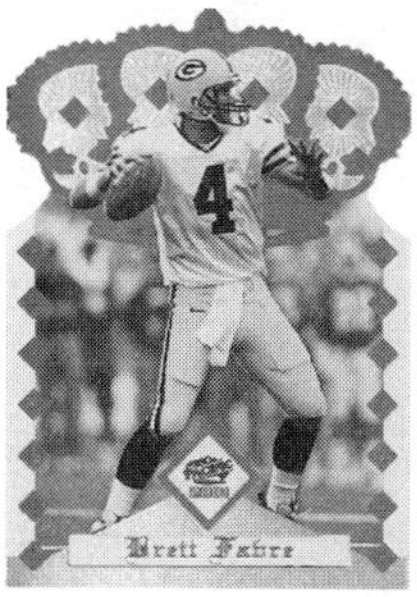
Brett Favre

		MT
Complete Set (30):		125.00
Common Player:		2.00
Minor Stars:		4.00
Inserted 1:73		
1	Jamal Lewis	12.00
2	Corey Dillon	4.00
3	Peter Warrick	7.00
4	Troy Aikman	8.00
5	Emmitt Smith	10.00
6	Mike Anderson	12.00
7	Terrell Davis	10.00
8	Brian Griese	5.00
9	Brett Favre	20.00
10	Marvin Harrison	4.00
11	Edgerrin James	12.00
12	Peyton Manning	12.00
13	Mark Brunell	5.00
14	Fred Taylor	5.00
15	Cris Carter	4.00
16	Daunte Culpepper	8.00
17	Randy Moss	12.00
18	Drew Bledsoe	5.00
19	Ricky Williams	6.00
20	Kerry Collins	2.00
21	Ron Dayne	7.00
22	Curtis Martin	4.00
23	Donovan McNabb	6.00
24	Jerome Bettis	4.00
25	Isaac Bruce	4.00
26	Marshall Faulk	5.00
27	Kurt Warner	15.00
28	Jeff Garcia	4.00
29	Jerry Rice	8.00
30	Steve McNair	4.00

2001 Pacific Impact Zone

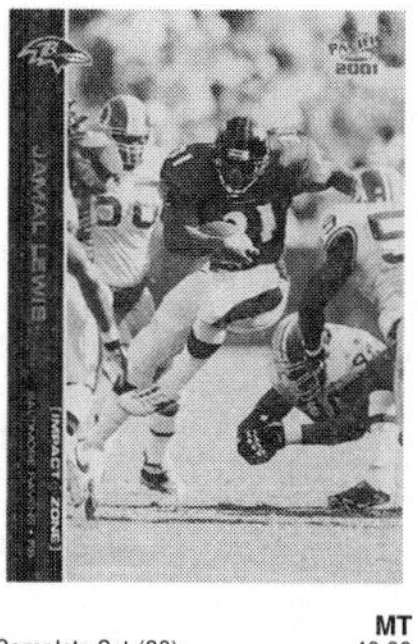
JAMAL LEWIS

		MT
Complete Set (20):		40.00
Common Player:		1.00
Minor Stars:		2.00
Inserted 1:37		
1	Jamal Lewis	6.00
2	Corey Dillon	2.00
3	Peter Warrick	4.00
4	Emmitt Smith	5.00
5	Mike Anderson	5.00
6	Brian Griese	2.00
7	Edgerrin James	6.00
8	Mark Brunell	2.50
9	Fred Taylor	2.50
10	Randy Moss	7.00
11	Ricky Williams	2.50
12	Ron Dayne	3.00
13	Curtis Martin	2.00
14	Rich Gannon	1.00
15	Donovan McNabb	3.00
16	Marshall Faulk	2.50
17	Jerry Rice	5.00
18	Mike Alstott	2.00
19	Warrick Dunn	2.00
20	Eddie George	2.50

2001 Pacific Pro Bowl Die-Cuts

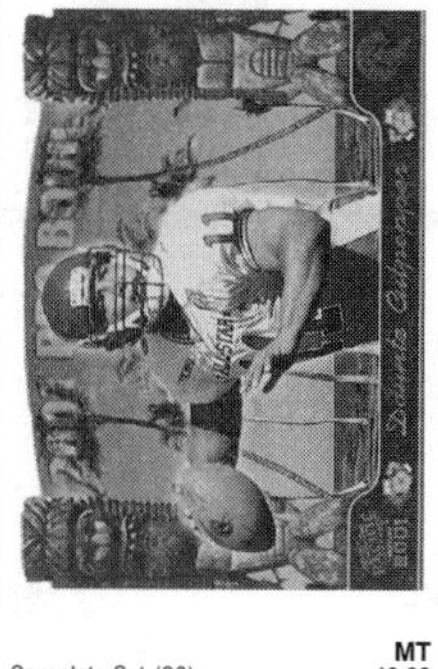
Daunte Culpepper

		MT
Complete Set (20):		40.00
Common Player:		1.50
Minor Stars:		3.00
Inserted 1:37		
1	Eric Moulds	3.00
2	Corey Dillon	3.00
3	Marvin Harrison	3.00
4	Edgerrin James	7.00
5	Peyton Manning	7.00
6	Jimmy Smith	1.50
7	Tony Gonzalez	1.50
8	Elvis Grbac	1.50
9	Cris Carter	3.00
10	Daunte Culpepper	5.00
11	Joe Horn	1.50
12	Rich Gannon	1.50
13	Donovan McNabb	4.00
14	Torry Holt	3.00
15	Jeff Garcia	3.00
16	Terrell Owens	3.00
17	Warrick Dunn	3.00
18	Eddie George	4.00
19	Derrick Mason	1.50
20	Stephen Davis	3.00

2001 Pacific War Room

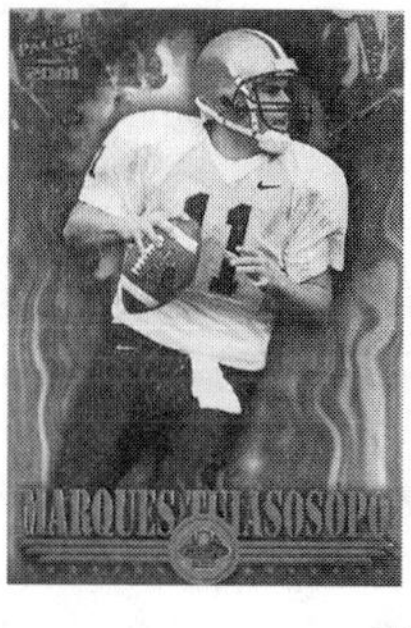
MARQUES TUIASOSOPO

		MT
Complete Set (20):		50.00
Common Player:		2.50
Inserted 1:73		
1	Alex Bannister	2.50
2	Kevan Barlow	5.00
3	Travis Henry	5.00
4	Chad Johnson	3.00
5	Mike McMahon	3.00
6	Sage Rosenfels	3.00
7	LaDainian Tomlinson	10.00
8	Chris Weinke	6.00
9	Drew Brees	12.00
10	Anthony Thomas	5.00
11	Freddie Mitchell	4.00
12	Reggie Wayne	4.00
13	Marques Tuiasosopo	5.00
14	Quincy Morgan	4.00
15	Josh Booty	2.50
16	Tim Hasselbeck	4.00
17	James Jackson	2.50
18	Rudi Johnson	2.50
19	Marvin Minnis	2.50
20	Bobby Newcombe	3.00

Post-1980 cards in Near Mint condition will generally sell for about 75% of the quoted Mint value. Excellent-condition cards bring no more than 40%.

2001 Pacific Canvas Impressions

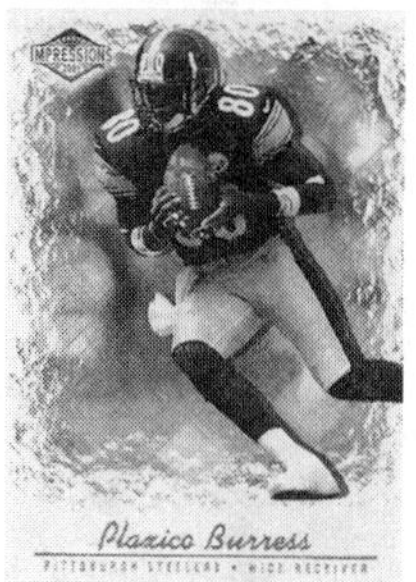
Plaxico Burress
PITTSBURGH STEELERS • WIDE RECEIVER

		MT
Complete Set (144):		75.00
Common Player:		.30
Minor Stars:		.60
Common Rookie:		5.00
Inserted 1:17		
Production 117 Sets		
Pack (3):		6.00
Wax Box (16):		80.00
1	David Boston	1.00
2	Thomas Jones	.60
3	Rob Moore	.30
4	Michael Pittman	.60
5	Jake Plummer	1.00
6	Jamal Anderson	1.00
7	Chris Chandler	.60
8	Shawn Jefferson	.30
9	Terance Mathis	.30
10	Elvis Grbac	.75
11	Qadry Ismail	.60
12	Jamal Lewis	2.75
13	Ray Lewis	.75
14	Shannon Sharpe	.60
15	Shawn Bryson	.30
16	Rob Johnson	.75
17	Sammy Morris	.60
18	Eric Moulds	1.00
19	Peerless Price	1.00
20	Tim Biakabutuka	.60
21	Richard Huntley	.30
22	Patrick Jeffers	.75
23	Jeff Lewis	.30
24	Muhsin Muhammad	.75
25	James Allen	.75
26	Marcus Robinson	1.00
27	Brian Urlacher	2.50
28	Corey Dillon	1.25
29	Jon Kitna	.75
30	Akili Smith	.75
31	Peter Warrick	1.25
32	Tim Couch	1.50
33	Kevin Johnson	.75
34	Dennis Northcutt	.60
35	Travis Prentice	.75
36	Joey Galloway	1.00
37	Raghib Ismail	.60
38	Emmitt Smith	3.00
39	Mike Anderson	2.25
40	Terrell Davis	2.75
41	Brian Griese	1.25
42	Ed McCaffrey	1.00
43	Rod Smith	1.00
44	Charlie Batch	1.00
45	Germane Crowell	.75
46	Herman Moore	.60
47	Johnnie Morton	.30
48	James Stewart	.60
49	Brett Favre	5.00
50	Antonio Freeman	1.25
51	Ahman Green	1.25
52	Dorsey Levens	.60
53	Bill Schroeder	.60
54	Marvin Harrison	1.25
55	Edgerrin James	3.50
56	Peyton Manning	4.00
57	Jerome Pathon	.30
58	Terrence Wilkins	.60
59	Mark Brunell	1.25
60	Keenan McCardell	.60
61	Jimmy Smith	1.00
62	Fred Taylor	1.25
63	Derrick Alexander	.60
64	Tony Gonzalez	.75
65	Trent Green	.75
66	Priest Holmes	1.00
67	Jay Fiedler	1.00
68	Oronde Gadsden	.60
69	O.J. McDuffie	.60
70	Cade McNown	.75
71	Lamar Smith	1.00
72	Zach Thomas	.75
73	Cris Carter	1.25
74	Daunte Culpepper	2.50
75	Randy Moss	4.00
76	Moe Williams	.30
77	Drew Bledsoe	1.50
78	Kevin Faulk	.60
79	Charles Johnson	.30
80	J.R. Redmond	.60
81	Jeff Blake	.75
82	Aaron Brooks	1.25
83	Albert Connell	.60
84	Joe Horn	1.00
85	Ricky Williams	2.00
86	Tiki Barber	.75
87	Kerry Collins	1.00
88	Ron Dayne	2.50
89	Ike Hilliard	.60
90	Amani Toomer	.60
91	Richie Anderson	.30
92	Wayne Chrebet	1.00
93	Laveranues Coles	1.00
94	Curtis Martin	1.25
95	Chad Pennington	2.00
96	Vinny Testaverde	1.00
97	Tim Brown	1.25
98	Rich Gannon	1.00
99	Charlie Garner	.75
100	Jerry Rice	2.75
101	Tyrone Wheatley	.60
102	Charles Woodson	.75
103	Darnell Autry	.30
104	Donovan McNabb	2.00
105	Duce Staley	1.25
106	James Thrash	.60
107	Jerome Bettis	1.25
108	Plaxico Burress	1.25
109	Bobby Shaw	.60
110	Kordell Stewart	1.25
111	Hines Ward	.75
112	Isaac Bruce	1.25
113	Marshall Faulk	1.50
114	Az-Zahir Hakim	1.00
115	Torry Holt	1.25
116	Kurt Warner	5.00
117	Curtis Conway	.60
118	Tim Dwight	.75
119	Doug Flutie	1.25
120	Jeff Graham	.30
121	Jeff Garcia	1.25
122	Garrison Hearst	1.25
123	Terrell Owens	1.25
124	J.J. Stokes	1.00
125	Tai Streets	1.00
126	Shaun Alexander	1.50
127	Matt Hasselbeck	1.00
128	Darrell Jackson	1.00
129	Ricky Watters	1.25
130	Mike Alstott	1.25
131	Warrick Dunn	1.25
132	Jacquez Green	.75
133	Brad Johnson	1.00
134	Keyshawn Johnson	1.25
135	Warren Sapp	.75
136	Kevin Dyson	.60
137	Eddie George	1.50
138	Jevon Kearse	1.00
139	Derrick Mason	1.00
140	Steve McNair	1.25
141	Champ Bailey	1.00
142	Stephen Davis	1.25
143	Jeff George	1.00
144	Michael Westbrook	1.00
145	*Bobby Newcombe*	10.00
146	*Corey Brown*	10.00
147	*Quentin McCord*	5.00
148	*Vinny Sutherland*	12.00
149	*Michael Vick*	70.00
150	*Chris Barnes*	12.00
151	*Tim Hasselbeck*	10.00
152	*Todd Heap*	12.00
153	*Nate Clements*	10.00
154	*Reggie Germany*	10.00
155	*Travis Henry*	25.00
156	*Dee Brown*	5.00
157	*Dan Morgan*	12.00
158	*Steve Smith*	10.00
159	*Chris Weinke*	30.00
160	*David Terrell*	40.00
161	*Anthony Thomas*	60.00
162	*T.J. Houshmandzadeh*	10.00
163	*Chad Johnson*	12.00
164	*Rudi Johnson*	12.00
165	*James Jackson*	15.00
166	*Andre King*	8.00
167	*Quincy Morgan*	15.00
168	*Quincy Carter*	30.00
169	*Kevin Kasper*	12.00
170	*Scotty Anderson*	10.00
171	*Mike McMahon*	25.00
172	*Robert Ferguson*	12.00
173	*Jamal Reynolds*	10.00
174	*Reggie Wayne*	20.00
175	*Marcus Stroud*	10.00
176	*Derrick Blaylock*	10.00
177	*Ryan Helming*	10.00
178	*Marvin "Snoop" Minnis*	20.00
179	*Chris Chambers*	30.00
180	*Josh Heupel*	15.00
181	*Travis Minor*	12.00
182	*Michael Bennett*	35.00
183	*Deuce McAllister*	25.00
184	*Onomo Ojo*	5.00
185	*Will Allen*	10.00
186	*Jonathan Carter*	10.00
187	*Jesse Palmer*	12.00
188	*Corey Alston*	5.00
189	*LaMont Jordan*	15.00
190	*Santana Moss*	25.00
191	*Derek Combs*	10.00
192	*Derrick Gibson*	10.00
193	*Ken-Yon Rambo*	10.00
194	*Marques Tuiasosopo*	25.00
195	*Correll Buckhelter*	20.00
196	*Freddie Mitchell*	20.00
197	*Chris Taylor*	10.00
198	*Adam Archuleta*	12.00
199	*Damione Lewis*	10.00
200	*Francis St.Paul*	10.00
201	*Milton Wynn*	10.00
202	*Drew Brees*	50.00
203	*LaDainian Tomlinson*	60.00
204	*Kevan Barlow*	20.00
205	*Andre Carter*	12.00
206	*Cedrick Wilson*	8.00
207	*Alex Bannister*	12.00
208	*Josh Booty*	12.00
209	*Heath Evans*	8.00
210	*Ken Lucas*	8.00
211	*Koren Robinson*	25.00
212	*Dan Alexander*	12.00
213	*Eddie Berlin*	10.00
214	*Rod Gardner*	25.00
215	*Darnerian McCants*	8.00
216	*Sage Rosenfels*	15.00

2001 Pacific Canvas Impressions Classic Images

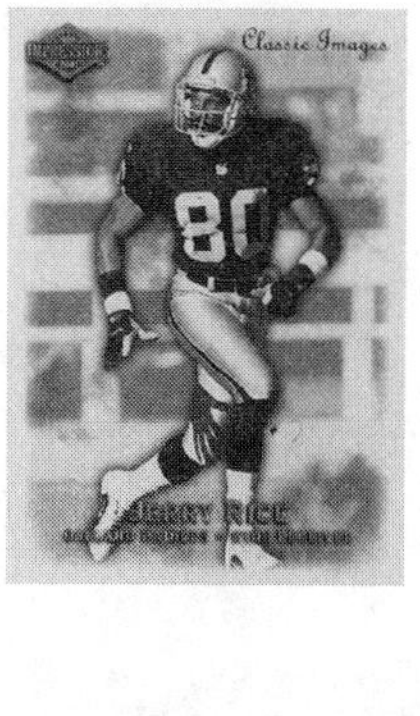
Classic Images
JERRY RICE

		MT
Complete Set (10):		60.00
Common Player:		6.00
Inserted 1:65		
1	Emmitt Smith	8.00
2	Terrell Davis	7.00
3	Brett Favre	15.00
4	Edgerrin James	10.00
5	Peyton Manning	10.00
6	Daunte Culpepper	7.00
7	Randy Moss	10.00
8	Jerry Rice	8.00
9	Donovan McNabb	6.00
10	Kurt Warner	15.00

2001 Pacific Canvas Impressions First Impressions

		MT
Complete Set (20):		85.00
Common Player:		3.00
Inserted 1:33		
1	Michael Vick	15.00
2	Travis Henry	5.00
3	Chris Weinke	6.00
4	David Terrell	7.00
5	Anthony Thomas	10.00
6	Chad Johnson	3.00
7	Quincy Carter	6.00
8	Reggie Wayne	4.00
9	Chris Chambers	6.00
10	Michael Bennett	8.00
11	Deuce McAllister	5.00
12	Jesse Palmer	3.00
13	LaMont Jordan	3.00
14	Santana Moss	5.00
15	Marques Tuiasosopo	5.00
16	Freddie Mitchell	5.00
17	Drew Brees	12.00
18	LaDainian Tomlinson	12.00
19	Rod Gardner	5.00
20	Sage Rosenfels	3.00

2001 Pacific Canvas Impressions Future Foundations

		MT
Common Player:		25.00
Inserted 1:257		
Production 50 Sets		
1	Michael Vick	70.00
2	Chris Weinke	35.00
3	David Terrell	40.00
4	Michael Bennett	40.00
5	Deuce McAllister	30.00
6	Santana Moss	25.00
7	Freddie Mitchell	25.00
8	Drew Brees	50.00
9	LaDainian Tomlinson	60.00
10	Koren Robinson	25.00

2001 Pacific Canvas Impressions Lasting Impressions

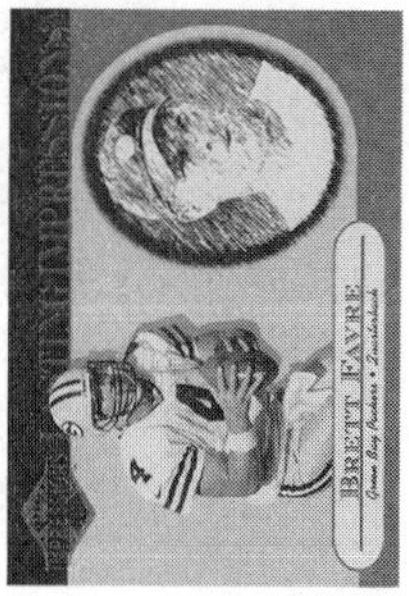
BRETT FAVRE

		MT
Complete Set (20):		60.00
Common Player:		1.50
Inserted 1:17		
1	Jamal Lewis	3.50
2	Peter Warrick	1.50
3	Emmitt Smith	5.00
4	Mike Anderson	3.00
5	Terrell Davis	4.00
6	Brian Griese	2.00
7	Brett Favre	8.00
8	Edgerrin James	6.00
9	Peyton Manning	6.00
10	Mark Brunell	2.00
11	Daunte Culpepper	4.00
12	Randy Moss	6.00
13	Drew Bledsoe	2.00
14	Ricky Williams	3.00
15	Ron Dayne	3.00
16	Jerry Rice	4.00
17	Donovan McNabb	3.00
18	Marshall Faulk	2.00
19	Kurt Warner	8.00
20	Eddie George	2.00

Values quoted in this guide reflect the retail price of a card — the price a collector can expect to pay when buying a card from a dealer. The wholesale price — that which a collector can expect to receive from a dealer when selling cards — will be significantly lower, depending on desirability and condition.

2001 Pacific Canvas Impressions Renderings

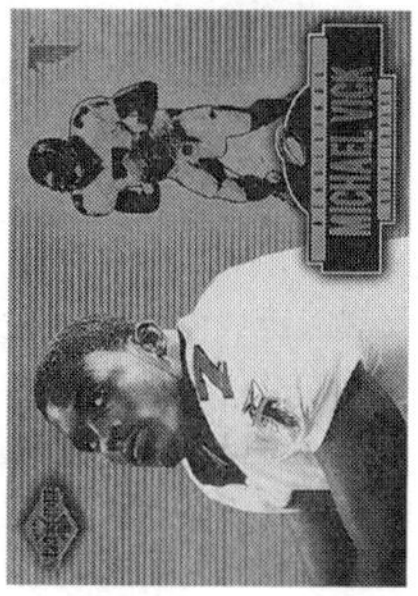
MICHAEL VICK

		MT
Complete Set (20):		35.00
Common Player:		1.00
Inserted 2:17		
1	Michael Vick	6.00
2	Travis Henry	2.00
3	Chris Weinke	3.00
4	David Terrell	3.50
5	Anthony Thomas	4.50
6	Chad Johnson	1.00
7	James Jackson	1.25
8	Quincy Carter	2.75
9	Reggie Wayne	1.50
10	Chris Chambers	2.50
11	Michael Bennett	3.00
12	Deuce McAllister	2.00
13	LaMont Jordan	1.00
14	Santana Moss	2.00
15	Marques Tuiasosopo	2.00
16	Freddie Mitchell	2.00
17	Drew Brees	5.00
18	LaDainian Tomlinson	6.00
19	Kevan Barlow	1.50
20	Rod Gardner	2.00

2001 Pacific Canvas Impressions Triple Threads

		MT
Common Player:		12.00
Inserted 3:17		
1	David Boston, Thomas Jones, Jake Plummer	20.00
2	Joel Makovicka, Dennis McKinley, Stephen Davis	12.00
3	Jamal Anderson, Mike Alstott, Stephen Davis	25.00
4	Qadry Ismail, Pat Johnson, Brandon Stokley	12.00
5	Tim Biakabutuka, Brad Hoover, Muhsin Muhammad	12.00
6	Chris Weinke, Marques Tuiasosopo, Drew Brees	60.00
7	Richard Huntley, Dan Kreider, Amos Zereoue	15.00
8	Shane Matthews, Cade McNown, Jim Miller	18.00
9	Bobby Engram, Marcus Robinson, Dez White	20.00
10	Ron Dugans, Danny Farmer, Craig Yeast	12.00
11	Steve Bush, Tony McGee, Brad St. Louis	12.00
12	Corey Dillon, Ricky Watters, Eddie George	25.00
13	JaJuan Dawson, Travis Prentice, Errict Rhett	12.00
14	Tim Couch, Troy Aikman, Kurt Warner	60.00
15	Desmond Clark, KaRon Coleman, Howard Griffith	12.00
16	Gus Frerotte, Ed McCaffrey, Rod Smith	20.00
17	Brian Griese, Brett Favre, Drew Bledsoe	60.00
18	Terrell Davis, Curtis Martin, LaDainian Tomlinson	60.00
19	Charlie Batch, Johnnie Morton, James Stewart	18.00
20	Herbert Goodman, Ahman Green, Dorsey Levens	18.00
21	Marvin Harrison, Edgerrin James, Peyton Manning	65.00
22	Ken Dilger, Lennox Gordon, Terrence Wilkins	12.00
23	Mark Brunell, Jimmy Smith, Fred Taylor	20.00
24	Jay Fiedler, Oronde Gadsden, Lamar Smith	20.00
25	Cris Carter, Daunte Culpepper, Randy Moss	60.00
26	Shockmain Davis, Kevin Faulk, Terry Glenn	15.00
27	Jeff Blake, Aaron Brooks, Joe Horn	20.00
28	Tiki Barber, Kerry Collins, Ron Dayne	25.00
29	Wayne Chrebet, Dwight Stone, Vinny Testaverde	15.00
30	Tim Brown, Rich Gannon, Tyrone Wheatley	25.00
31	Plaxico Burress, Troy Edwards, Courtney Hawkins	25.00
32	Giovanni Carmazzi, Rick Mirer, Tim Rattay	18.00

33 Shaun Alexander, Darrell Jackson, James Williams 20.00
34 Reggie Brown, Charlie Rogers, Mack Strong 12.00
35 Reidel Anthony, Jacquez Green, Keyshawn Johnson 18.00

2001 Pacific Dynagon DMX

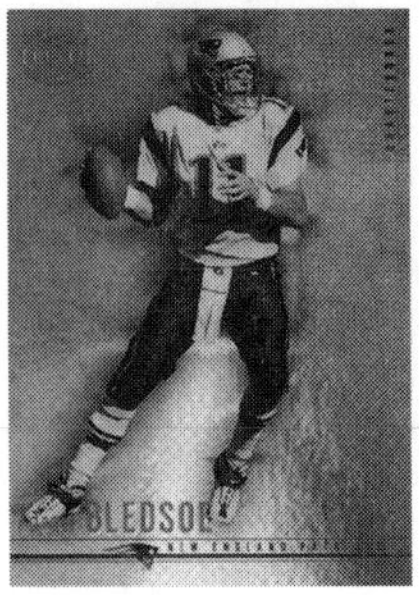

MT
Complete Set (147): 1000.
Common Player: .25
Minor Stars: .50
Cards #132, 136, 148 never released
Pack (5) 7.00
Wax Box (22): 120.00
1 David Boston 1.00
2 Thomas Jones 1.00
3 Jake Plummer 1.00
4 Jamal Anderson 1.00
5 Tim Dwight 1.00
6 Elvis Grbac 1.00
7 Jamal Lewis 3.00
8 Ray Lewis .50
9 Shannon Sharpe .50
10 Rob Johnson .50
11 Eric Moulds 1.00
12 Peerless Price .75
13 Tim Biakabutuka .50
14 Patrick Jeffers .75
15 Muhsin Muhammad .75
16 James Allen .50
17 Cade McNown 1.00
18 Marcus Robinson 1.00
19 Brian Urlacher 2.00
20 Corey Dillon 1.00
21 Akili Smith 1.00
22 Peter Warrick 2.00
23 Tim Couch 1.50
24 Kevin Johnson 1.00
25 Randall Cunningham 1.00
26 Emmitt Smith 2.50
27 Mike Anderson 3.00
28 Terrell Davis 2.50
29 Brian Griese 1.25
30 Ed McCaffrey 1.00
31 Rod Smith 1.00
32 Charlie Batch 1.00
33 Johnnie Morton .50
34 James Stewart .75
35 Brett Favre 4.00
36 Antonio Freeman 1.00
37 Ahman Green 1.00
38 Marvin Harrison 1.00
39 Edgerrin James 3.00
40 Peyton Manning 3.00
41 Mark Brunell 1.25
42 Keenan McCardell .50
43 Jimmy Smith 1.00
44 Fred Taylor 1.25
45 Derrick Alexander .50
46 Tony Gonzalez .50
47 Sylvester Morris 1.00
48 Jay Fiedler 1.00
49 Oronde Gadsden .25
50 Lamar Smith 1.00
51 Cris Carter 1.00
52 Daunte Culpepper 2.00
53 Randy Moss 3.00
54 Drew Bledsoe 1.25
55 Terry Glenn 1.00
56 J.R. Redmond 1.00
57 Aaron Brooks 1.00
58 Joe Horn 1.00
59 Ricky Williams 1.50
60 Tiki Barber 1.00
61 Kerry Collins 1.00
62 Ron Dayne 2.00
63 Amani Toomer .25
64 Wayne Chrebet .75
65 Curtis Martin 1.00
66 Vinny Testaverde .75
67 Tim Brown 1.00
68 Rich Gannon 1.00
69 Tyrone Wheatley 1.00
70 Charles Johnson .50
71 Donovan McNabb 1.50
72 Duce Staley 1.00
73 Jerome Bettis 1.00
74 Plaxico Burress 1.00
75 Kordell Stewart 1.00
76 Isaac Bruce 1.00
77 Marshall Faulk 1.25
78 Torry Holt 1.00
79 Kurt Warner 3.50
80 Curtis Conway .50
81 Doug Flutie 1.25
82 Jeff Garcia 1.00
83 Charlie Garner .75
84 Terrell Owens 1.00
85 Jerry Rice 2.50
86 Shaun Alexander 1.00
87 Matt Hasselbeck 1.00
88 Darrell Jackson 1.00
89 Mike Alstott 1.00
90 Warrick Dunn 1.00
91 Brad Johnson 1.00
92 Keyshawn Johnson 1.00
93 Shaun King 1.00
94 Eddie George 1.25
95 Jevon Kearse 1.00
96 Derrick Mason 1.00
97 Steve McNair 1.00
98 Stephen Davis 1.00
99 Jeff George 1.00
100 Deion Sanders 1.00
101 *Michael Bennett 199* 60.00
102 *Drew Brees 199* 100.00
103 *Chris Chambers 199* 60.00
104 *LaMont Jordan 199* 30.00
105 *Deuce McAllister 199* 50.00
106 *Koren Robinson 199* 50.00
107 *David Terrell 199* 75.00
108 *LaDainian Tomlinson 199* 120.00
109 *Marques Tuiasosopo 199* 45.00
110 *Michael Vick 199* 150.00
111 *Chris Weinke 199* 60.00
112 *Kevan Barlow 499* 20.00
113 *Josh Booty 499* 15.00
114 *Rod Gardner 499* 30.00
115 *Todd Heap 499* 15.00
116 *Travis Henry 499* 30.00
117 *James Jackson 499* 20.00
118 *Chad Johnson 499* 20.00
119 *Rudi Johnson 499* 20.00
120 *Ben Leard 499* 12.00
121 *Quincy Morgan 499* 20.00
122 *Marvin "Snoop" Minnis 499* 25.00
123 *Freddie Mitchell 499* 25.00
124 *Sage Rosenfels 499* 20.00
125 *Anthony Thomas 499* 75.00
126 *Reggie Wayne 499* 30.00
127 *Dan Alexander 699* 12.00
128 *Will Allen 699* 10.00
129 *Scotty Anderson 699* 10.00
130 *Adam Archuleta 699* 12.00
131 *Alex Bannister 699* 12.00
133 *Tay Cody 699* 8.00
134 *Tony Dixon 699* 8.00
135 *Heath Evans 699* 8.00
137 *Derrick Gibson 699* 8.00
138 *Edgerton Hartwell 699* 8.00
139 *Tim Hasselbeck 699* 12.00
140 *Jabari Holloway 699* 10.00
141 *Torrance Marshall 699* 10.00
142 *Jason McKinley 699* 10.00
143 *Mike McMahon 699* 15.00
144 *Bobby Newcombe 699* 12.00
145 *Moran Norris 699* 8.00
146 *Tommy Polley 699* 8.00
147 *Vinny Sutherland 699* 12.00
149 *Reggie White 699* 12.00
150 *Cedrick Wilson 699* 10.00

2001 Pacific Dynagon DMX Retail

MT
Complete Set (150): 150.00
Common Rookie: 1.00
Inserted 1:4
101 Michael Bennett 7.00
102 Drew Brees 12.00
103 Chris Chambers 2.00
104 LaMont Jordan 2.00
105 Deuce McAllister 5.00
106 Koren Robinson 4.00
107 David Terrell 6.00
108 LaDainian Tomlinson 8.00
109 Marques Tuiasosopo 3.00
110 Michael Vick 18.00
111 Chris Weinke 5.00
112 Kevan Barlow 2.00
113 Josh Booty 2.00
114 Rod Gardner 4.00
115 Todd Heap 1.50
116 Travis Henry 3.00
117 James Jackson 2.00
118 Chad Johnson 2.00
119 Rudi Johnson 1.50
120 Ben Leard 1.00
121 Quincy Morgan 2.50
122 Marvin "Snoop" Minnis 2.50
123 Freddie Mitchell 2.50
124 Sage Rosenfels 2.00
125 Anthony Thomas 15.00
126 Reggie Wayne 3.00
127 Dan Alexander 2.00
128 Will Allen 1.00
129 Scotty Anderson 1.00
130 Adam Archuleta 1.50
131 Alex Bannister 2.00
132 Gary Baxter 1.00
133 Tay Cody 1.00
134 Tony Dixon 1.00
135 Heath Evans 1.00
136 Jamar Fletcher 1.50
137 Derrick Gibson 1.00
138 Edgerton Hartwell 1.00
139 Tim Hasselbeck 1.00
140 Jabari Holloway 1.50
141 Torrance Marshall 1.50
142 Jason McKinley 1.00
143 Mike McMahon 2.00
144 Bobby Newcombe 1.50
145 Moran Norris 1.00
146 Tommy Polley 1.00
147 Vinny Sutherland 1.50
148 Ja'Mar Toombs 1.00
149 Reggie White 1.50
150 Cedrick Wilson 1.00

2001 Pacific Dynagon DMX Big Numbers

MT
Complete Set (20): 50.00
Common Player: 3.00
Production 799 Sets
1 Cade McNown 3.00
2 Peter Warrick 6.00
3 Tim Couch 5.00
4 Mike Anderson 10.00
5 Brian Griese 5.00
6 Cris Carter 3.00
7 Mark Brunell 5.00
8 Drew Bledsoe 5.00
9 Ricky Williams 6.00
10 Ron Dayne 6.00
11 Curtis Martin 3.00
12 Rich Gannon 3.00
13 Jerome Bettis 3.00
14 Torry Holt 3.00
15 Jeff Garcia 3.00
16 Jerry Rice 8.00
17 Warrick Dunn 3.00
18 Eddie George 3.50
19 Steve McNair 3.00
20 Stephen Davis 3.00

2001 Pacific Dynagon DMX Canton Bound

MT
Complete Set (10): 225.00
Common Player: 15.00
Production 99 Sets
1 Emmitt Smith 35.00
2 Brett Favre 50.00
3 Edgerrin James 40.00
4 Peyton Manning 40.00
5 Dan Marino 40.00
6 Cris Carter 15.00
7 Randy Moss 40.00
8 Marshall Faulk 20.00
9 Kurt Warner 40.00
10 Jerry Rice 30.00

2001 Pacific Dynagon DMX Dynamic Duos

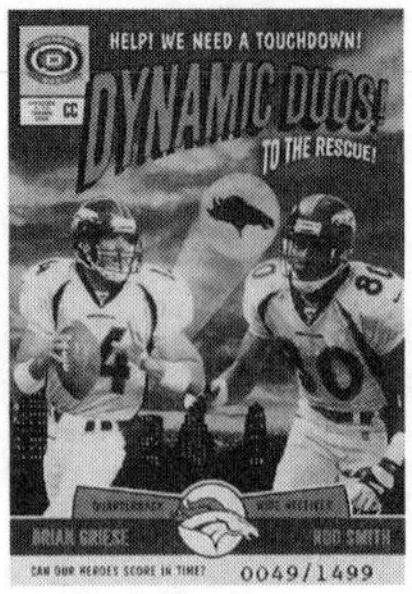

MT
Complete Set (20): 45.00
Common Player: 2.00
Production 1,499 Sets
1 Jake Plummer, David Boston 2.00
2 Jamal Lewis, Priest Holmes 6.00
3 Rob Johnson, Eric Moulds 2.00
4 Cade McNown, Marcus Robinson 2.00
5 Corey Dillon, Peter Warrick 4.00
6 Tim Couch, Kevin Johnson 3.00
7 Mike Anderson, Terrell Davis 6.00
8 Brian Griese, Rod Smith 3.00
9 Brett Favre, Antonio Freeman 10.00
10 Peyton Manning, Marvin Harrison 8.00
11 Mark Brunell, Fred Taylor 3.00
12 Daunte Culpepper, Randy Moss 8.00
13 Drew Bledsoe, Terry Glenn 3.00
14 Tiki Barber, Ron Dayne 4.00
15 Rich Gannon, Tim Brown 2.00
16 Donovan McNabb, Duce Staley 3.00
17 Kurt Warner, Torry Holt 8.00
18 Jeff Garcia, Terrell Owens 2.00
19 Mike Alstott, Warrick Dunn 2.00
20 Steve McNair, Derrick Mason 2.00

2001 Pacific Dynagon DMX Freshman Phenoms

MT
Complete Set (10): 130.00
Common Player: 7.00
Production 599 Sets
1 Michael Bennett 18.00
2 Drew Brees 30.00
3 Josh Heupel 12.00
4 Deuce McAllister 15.00
5 Santana Moss 15.00
6 Ken-Yon Rambo 7.00
7 Koren Robinson 12.00
8 David Terrell 18.00
9 LaDainian Tomlinson 25.00
10 Michael Vick 50.00

2001 Pacific Dynagon DMX Game-Used Footballs

MT
Common Player: 15.00
Inserted 1:82
Production 214 Sets
1 Jamal Lewis 40.00
2 Peter Warrick 25.00
3 Tim Couch 20.00
4 Emmitt Smith 40.00
5 Mike Anderson 30.00
6 Terrell Davis 30.00
7 Brett Favre 50.00
8 Edgerrin James 40.00
9 Peyton Manning 40.00
10 Mark Brunell 20.00
11 Fred Taylor 15.00
12 Daunte Culpepper 30.00
13 Randy Moss 40.00
14 Drew Bledsoe 20.00
15 Ricky Williams 25.00
16 Donovan McNabb 25.00
17 Marshall Faulk 20.00
18 Kurt Warner 40.00
19 Jerry Rice 35.00
20 Eddie George 20.00

2001 Pacific Dynagon DMX Logo Optics

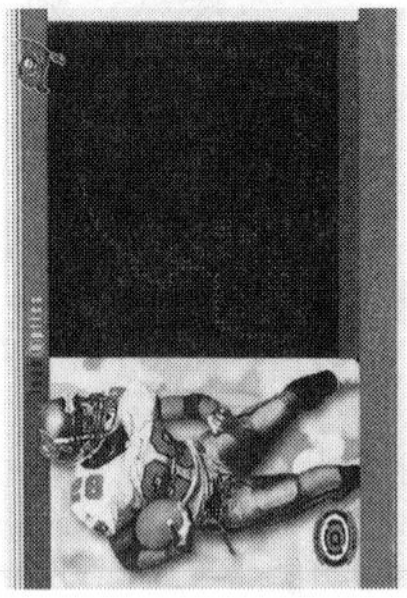

MT
Complete Set (20): 40.00
Common Player: 1.50
Production 499 Sets
1 Jamal Lewis 6.00
2 Eric Moulds 2.00
3 Corey Dillon 2.00
4 Emmitt Smith 6.00
5 Terrell Davis 5.00
6 Brian Griese 2.50
7 Edgerrin James 7.00
8 Fred Taylor 2.50
9 Lamar Smith 1.50
10 Daunte Culpepper 5.00
11 Ricky Williams 4.00
12 Curtis Martin 2.00
13 Tyrone Wheatley 1.50
14 Donovan McNabb 4.00
15 Jerome Bettis 2.00
16 Marshall Faulk 2.00
17 Jeff Garcia 2.00
18 Warrick Dunn 2.00
19 Eddie George 2.00
20 Stephen Davis 2.00

2001 Pacific Dynagon DMX Premiere Players

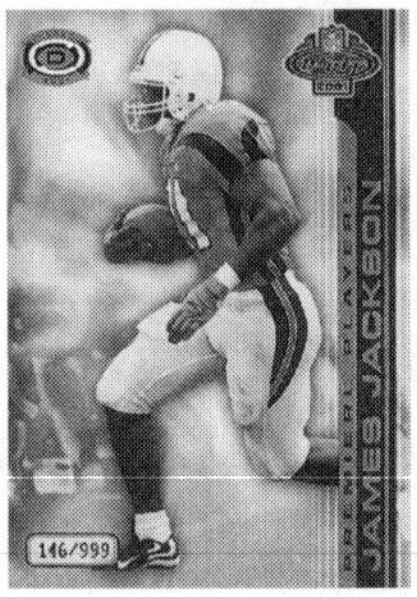

MT
Complete Set (20): 100.00
Common Player: 2.00
Production 999 Sets
1 David Allen 2.00
2 Kevan Barlow 3.00
3 Michael Bennett 10.00
4 Drew Brees 15.00
5 Chris Chambers 3.00
6 Josh Heupel 7.00
7 James Jackson 3.00
8 LaMont Jordan 3.00
9 Deuce McAllister 8.00
10 Freddie Mitchell 4.00
11 Santana Moss 8.00
12 Ken-Yon Rambo 2.00
13 Koren Robinson 7.00
14 David Terrell 10.00
15 Anthony Thomas 7.00
16 LaDainian Tomlinson 12.00
17 Marques Tuiasosopo 5.00
18 Michael Vick 25.00
19 Reggie Wayne 6.00
20 Chris Weinke 7.00

2001 Pacific Dynagon DMX Top of the Class

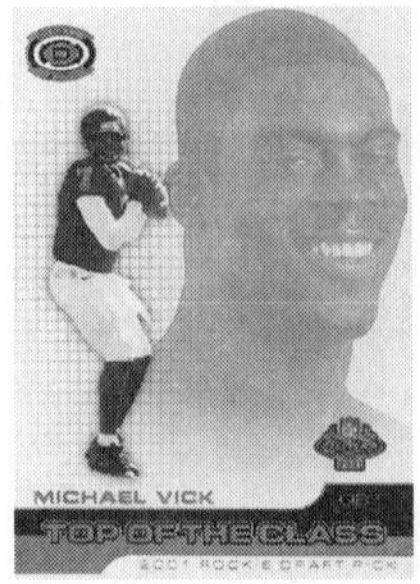

MT
Complete Set (25): 40.00
Common Player: 1.00
Inserted 1:1
1 Kevan Barlow 1.50
2 Michael Bennett 4.00
3 Drew Brees 7.00
4 Chris Chambers 1.50
5 Rod Gardner 2.50
6 Travis Henry 2.00
7 Josh Heupel 3.00
8 James Jackson 1.00
9 Chad Johnson 1.00
10 LaMont Jordan 1.00
11 Deuce McAllister 3.00
12 Mike McMahon 1.00
13 Marvin "Snoop" Minnis 1.50
14 Travis Minor 1.50
15 Freddie Mitchell 2.00
16 Santana Moss 3.00
17 Ken-Yon Rambo 1.00
18 Koren Robinson 2.50
19 David Terrell 4.00
20 Anthony Thomas 2.50
21 LaDainian Tomlinson 5.00
22 Marques Tuiasosopo 2.00
23 Michael Vick 10.00
24 Reggie Wayne 2.50
25 Chris Weinke 3.00

2001 Pacific Invincible

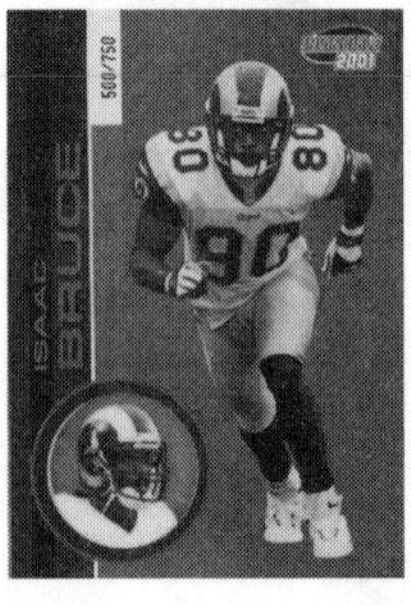

MT
Complete Set (300): 850.00
Common Player: .75
Minor Stars: 1.50
Common Rookie: 7.00
Production 299 Sets
Common RK Jersey: 40.00
Production 250 Sets
Pack (3): 6.00
Wax Box (20): 85.00
1 David Boston 2.50
2 Mar Tay Jenkins .75
3 Thomas Jones .75
4 Rob Moore .75
5 Michael Pittman .75
6 Jake Plummer 2.50
7 Frank Sanders .75
8 Jamal Anderson 2.50
9 Chris Chandler .75
10 Jammi German .75
11 Shawn Jefferson .75
12 Doug Johnson .75
13 Terance Mathis .75
14 Elvis Grbac .75
15 Qadry Ismail .75
16 Jamal Lewis 6.00
17 Jermaine Lewis .75
18 Ray Lewis .75
19 Chris Redman 2.50
20 Shannon Sharpe .75
21 Travis Taylor .75
22 Shawn Bryson .75
23 Rob Johnson .75
24 Jeremy McDaniel .75
25 Sammy Morris .75
26 Eric Moulds .75
27 Peerless Price .75
28 Antowain Smith .75
29 Michael Bates .75
30 Tim Biakabutuka .75
31 Isaac Byrd .75
32 Brad Hoover 2.50
33 Patrick Jeffers .75
34 Jeff Lewis .75
35 Muhsin Muhammad .75
36 Wesley Walls .75
37 James Allen .75
38 Marty Booker .75
39 Macey Brooks .75
40 Bobby Engram .75
41 Cade McNown 2.50
42 Marcus Robinson 2.50
43 Brian Urlacher 5.00
44 Dez White .75
45 Brandon Bennett .75
46 Corey Dillon 2.50
47 Danny Farmer .75
48 Jon Kitna 2.50
49 Darnay Scott .75
50 Akili Smith 2.50
51 Peter Warrick 5.00
52 Craig Yeast .75
53 Tim Couch 3.00
54 JaJuan Dawson .75
55 Curtis Enis .75
56 Kevin Johnson 2.50
57 Dennis Northcutt .75
58 Travis Prentice .75
59 Errict Rhett .75
60 Tony Banks .75
61 Randall Cunningham 1.30
62 Raghib Ismail .75
63 Wane McGarity .75
64 Carl Pickens .75
65 Emmitt Smith 7.00
66 Jason Tucker .75
67 Michael Wiley .75
68 Mike Anderson 6.00
69 Terrell Davis 6.00
70 Gus Frerotte .75
71 Olandis Gary .75
72 Brian Griese 3.00
73 Eddie Kennison .75
74 Ed McCaffrey 2.50
75 Rod Smith .75
76 Charlie Batch 2.50
77 Germane Crowell .75
78 Larry Foster .75
79 Desmond Howard .75
80 Herman Moore .75
81 Johnnie Morton .75
82 Robert Porcher .75
83 James Stewart .75
84 Donald Driver .75
85 Brett Favre 10.00
86 Bubba Franks .75
87 Antonio Freeman 2.50
88 Ahman Green .75
89 William Henderson .75
90 Dorsey Levens .75
91 Bill Schroeder .75
92 Ken Dilger .75
93 E.G. Green .75
94 Marvin Harrison 2.50
95 Edgerrin James 7.00
96 Peyton Manning 8.00
97 Jerome Pathon .75
98 Marcus Pollard .75
99 Terrence Wilkins .75
100 Kyle Brady .75
101 Mark Brunell 3.00
102 Stacey Mack .75
103 Keenan McCardell .75
104 Jimmy Smith .75
105 R. Jay Soward .75
106 Shyrone Stith .75
107 Fred Taylor 3.00
108 Derrick Alexander .75
109 Kimble Anders .75
110 Todd Collins .75
111 Tony Gonzalez .75
112 Trent Green .75
113 Priest Holmes .75
114 Frank Moreau .75
115 Sylvester Morris .75
116 Tony Richardson .75
117 Jay Fiedler 2.50
118 Oronde Gadsden .75
119 J.J. Johnson .75
120 Ray Lucas .75
121 Tony Martin .75
122 O.J. McDuffie .75
123 James McKnight .75
124 Lamar Smith .75
125 Jason Taylor .75
126 Zach Thomas .75
127 Cris Carter 2.50
128 Daunte Culpepper 5.00
129 Randy Moss 8.00
130 Chris Walsh .75
131 Troy Walters .75
132 Moe Williams .75
133 Drew Bledsoe 3.00
134 Troy Brown .75
135 Kevin Faulk .75
136 Terry Glenn .75
137 Ty Law .75
138 Lawyer Milloy .75
139 David Patten .75
140 J.R. Redmond .75
141 Tony Simmons .75
142 Jeff Blake .75
143 Aaron Brooks 2.50
144 Albert Connell .75
145 Joe Horn .75
146 Willie Jackson .75
147 Chad Morton .75
148 Keith Poole .75
149 Ricky Williams 4.00
150 Robert Wilson .75
151 Jessie Armstead .75
152 Tiki Barber .75
153 Kerry Collins .75
154 Ron Dayne 5.00
155 Ron Dixon .75
156 Ike Hilliard .75
157 Jason Sehorn .75
158 Michael Strahan .75
159 Amani Toomer .75
160 Richie Anderson .75
161 Wayne Chrebet .75
162 Laveranues Coles 2.50
163 Matthew Hatchette .75
164 Marvin Jones .75
165 Curtis Martin 2.50
166 Chad Pennington 5.00
167 Vinny Testaverde .75
168 Dedric Ward .75
169 Tim Brown 2.50
170 Zack Crockett .75
171 Rich Gannon .75
172 James Jett .75
173 Randy Jordan .75
174 Andre Rison .75
175 Tyrone Wheatley .75
176 Charles Woodson .75
177 Darnell Autry .75
178 Charles Johnson .75
179 Chad Lewis .75
180 Donovan McNabb 4.00
181 Todd Pinkston .75
182 Stanley Pritchett .75
183 Torrance Small .75
184 Duce Staley 2.50
185 Jerome Bettis 2.50
186 Plaxico Burress 2.50
187 Troy Edwards .75
188 Courtney Hawkins .75
189 Richard Huntley .75
190 Bobby Shaw .75
191 Kordell Stewart 2.50
192 Hines Ward .75
193 Isaac Bruce 2.50
194 Trung Canidate .75
195 Marshall Faulk 3.00
196 Az-Zahir Hakim .75
197 Torry Holt 2.50
198 Tony Horne .75
199 Ricky Proehl .75
200 Kurt Warner 8.00
201 Aeneas Williams .75
202 Curtis Conway .75
203 Tim Dwight 2.50
204 Jermaine Fazande .75
205 Terrell Fletcher .75
206 Doug Flutie 3.00
207 Jeff Graham .75
208 Freddie Jones .75
209 Reggie Jones .75
210 Junior Seau .75
211 Fred Beasley .75
212 Jeff Garcia 2.50
213 Charlie Garner .75
214 Terrell Owens 2.50
215 Jerry Rice 6.00
216 Paul Smith .75
217 J.J. Stokes .75
218 Tai Streets .75
219 Shaun Alexander 3.00
220 Karsten Bailey .75
221 Matt Hasselbeck .75
222 Brock Huard .75
223 Darrell Jackson 2.50

224	Shawn Springs	.75
225	Ricky Watters	.75
226	James Williams	.75
227	Mike Alstott	2.50
228	Reidel Anthony	.75
229	Warrick Dunn	2.50
230	Jacquez Green	.75
231	Keyshawn Johnson	2.50
232	Brad Johnson	2.50
233	Shaun King	2.50
234	Warren Sapp	.75
235	Kevin Dyson	.75
236	Eddie George	3.00
237	Jevon Kearse	2.50
238	Derrick Mason	.75
239	Steve McNair	2.50
240	Chris Sanders	.75
241	Rodney Thomas	.75
242	Frank Wycheck	.75
243	Stephen Alexander	.75
244	Larry Centers	.75
245	Stephen Davis	2.50
246	Irving Fryar	.75
247	Jeff George	.75
248	Kevin Lockett	.75
249	James Thrash	.75
250	Michael Westbrook	.75
251	*Bobby Newcombe*	10.00
252	*Alge Crumpler*	10.00
253	*Vinny Sutherland*	10.00
254	*Michael Vick*	125.00
255	*Travis Henry*	20.00
256	*Dan Morgan*	15.00
257	*Chris Weinke*	60.00
258	*David Terrell*	50.00
259	*Anthony Thomas*	100.00
260	*T.J. Houshmandzadeh*	7.00
261	*Chad Johnson*	12.00
262	*Rudi Johnson*	12.00
263	*James Jackson*	12.00
264	*Quincy Morgan*	15.00
265	*Scotty Anderson*	7.00
266	*Mike McMahon*	10.00
267	*Robert Ferguson*	15.00
268	*Reggie Wayne*	15.00
269	*Marvin "Snoop" Minnis*	15.00
270	*Chris Chambers*	12.00
271	*Josh Heupel*	15.00
272	*Travis Minor*	15.00
273	*Michael Bennett*	30.00
274	*Ben Leard*	7.00
275	*Deuce McAllister*	20.00
276	*Moran Norris*	7.00
277	*Jesse Palmer*	12.00
278	*LaMont Jordan*	12.00
279	*Santana Moss*	25.00
280	*Ken-Yon Rambo*	10.00
281	*Marques Tuiasosopo*	40.00
282	*Correl Buckhalter*	15.00
283	*A.J. Feely*	7.00
284	*Freddie Mitchell*	40.00
285	*Joey Getherall*	12.00
286	*Chris Taylor*	10.00
287	*Adam Archuleta*	10.00
288	*David Rivers*	7.00
289	*Drew Brees*	100.00
290	*LaDainian Tomlinson*	100.00
291	*Kevan Barlow*	12.00
292	*Cedrick Wilson*	10.00
293	*Alex Bannister*	12.00
294	*Josh Booty*	10.00
295	*Heath Evans*	7.00
296	*Koren Robinson*	30.00
297	*Dan Alexander*	12.00
298	*Rod Gardner*	30.00
299	*Sage Rosenfels*	12.00
300	*David Allen*	10.00

2001 Pacific Invincible Afterburners

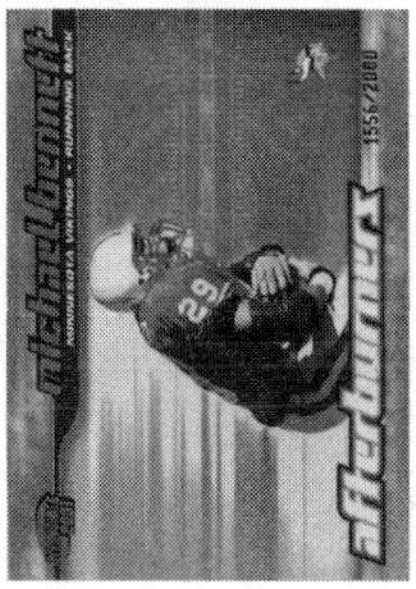

		MT
Complete Set (20):		45.00
Common Player:		1.00
Production 2,000 Sets		
1	Jamal Lewis	6.00
2	Eric Moulds	1.00
3	David Terrell	6.00
4	Corey Dillon	2.00
5	Peter Warrick	4.00
6	Marvin Harrison	2.00
7	Edgerrin James	7.00
8	Jimmy Smith	1.00
9	Fred Taylor	3.00
10	Sylvester Morris	1.00
11	Chris Chambers	2.00
12	Michael Bennett	7.00
13	Randy Moss	8.00
14	Santana Moss	5.00
15	Tim Brown	2.00
16	Isaac Bruce	2.00
17	Marshall Faulk	3.00
18	Torry Holt	2.00
19	LaDainian Tomlinson	10.00
20	Warrick Dunn	2.00

Post-1980 cards in Near Mint condition will generally sell for about 75% of the quoted Mint value. Excellent-condition cards bring no more than 40%.

2001 Pacific Invincible Fast Forward

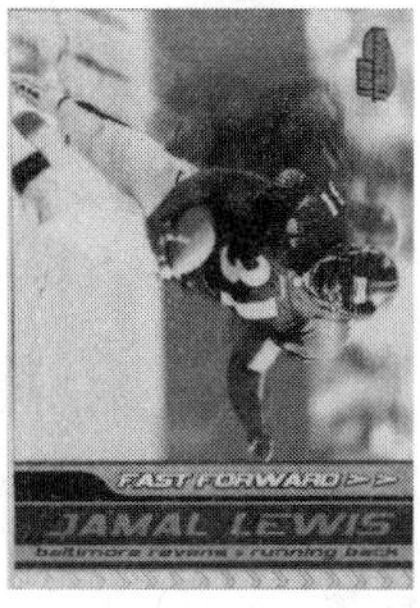

		MT
Complete Set (20):		85.00
Common Player:		2.00
Production 1,000 Sets		
1	Jamal Lewis	8.00
2	Eric Moulds	2.00
3	Emmitt Smith	12.00
4	Mike Anderson	10.00
5	Marvin Harrison	4.00
6	Jimmy Smith	2.00
7	Cris Carter	4.00
8	Daunte Culpepper	8.00
9	Randy Moss	15.00
10	Ricky Williams	6.00
11	Ron Dayne	2.00
12	Curtis Martin	4.00
13	Rich Gannon	2.00
14	Jerome Bettis	4.00
15	Isaac Bruce	4.00
16	Marshall Faulk	5.00
17	Torry Holt	4.00
18	Kurt Warner	15.00
19	Jeff Garcia	4.00
20	Jerry Rice	10.00

2001 Pacific Invincible Heat-Seekers

		MT
Complete Set (20):		100.00
Common Player:		2.50
Production 750 Sets		
1	Jake Plummer	5.00
2	Michael Vick	25.00
3	Rob Johnson	2.50
4	Cade McNown	5.00
5	Akili Smith	5.00
6	Tim Couch	7.00
7	Brian Griese	6.00
8	Charlie Batch	5.00
9	Brett Favre	25.00
10	Peyton Manning	20.00
11	Mark Brunell	6.00
12	Daunte Culpepper	10.00
13	Drew Bledsoe	6.00
14	Aaron Brooks	6.00
15	Rich Gannon	2.50
16	Marques Tuiasosopo	5.00
17	Kurt Warner	20.00
18	Jeff Garcia	5.00
19	Steve McNair	5.00
20	Jeff George	2.50

2001 Pacific Invincible Main Set Jersey Variations-Blue

		MT
Complete Set (50):		
Common Player:		10.00
1	David Boston	15.00
4	Rob Moore	10.00
8	Jamal Anderson	10.00
9	Chris Chandler	10.00
23	Rob Johnson	10.00
26	Eric Moulds	10.00
30	Tim Biakabutuka	10.00
37	James Allen	10.00
40	Bobby Engram	10.00
53	Tim Couch	20.00
56	Kevin Johnson	10.00
65	Emmitt Smith	30.00
68	Mike Anderson	10.00
69	Terrell Davis	20.00
72	Brian Griese	15.00
76	Charlie Batch	10.00
83	James Stewart	10.00
85	Brett Favre	40.00
101	Mark Brunell	20.00
103	Keenan McCardell	10.00
104	Jimmy Smith	10.00
108	Derrick Alexander	10.00
115	Sylvester Morris	10.00
117	Jay Fiedler	10.00
127	Cris Carter	10.00
128	Daunte Culpepper	20.00
129	Randy Moss	20.00
142	Jeff Blake	10.00
145	Joe Horn	10.00
149	Ricky Williams	15.00
152	Tiki Barber	10.00
153	Kerry Collins	10.00
159	Amani Toomer	10.00
165	Curtis Martin	15.00
166	Chad Pennington	15.00
167	Vinny Testaverde	10.00
169	Tim Brown	15.00
171	Rich Gannon	10.00
175	Tyrone Wheatley	10.00
196	Az-Zahir Hakim	10.00
200	Kurt Warner	30.00
206	Doug Flutie	10.00
210	Junior Seau	15.00
215	Jerry Rice	20.00
219	Shaun Alexander	15.00
223	Darrell Jackson	10.00
225	Ricky Watters	10.00
235	Kevin Dyson	10.00
236	Eddie George	15.00
239	Steve McNair	15.00

2001 Pacific Invincible Main Set Jersey Variations-Red

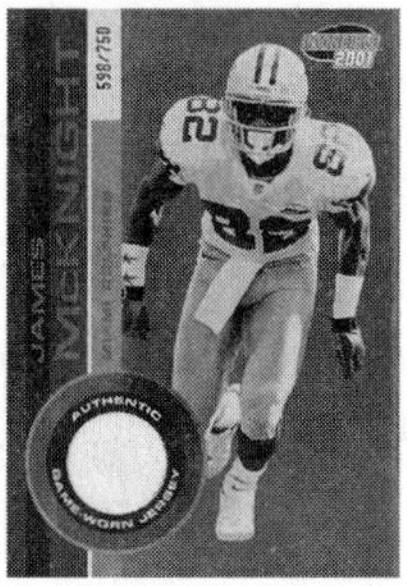

		MT
Complete Set (50):		
Common Player:		5.00
2	Mar Tay Jenkins	5.00
5	Michael Pittman	5.00
10	Jammi German	5.00
11	Shawn Jefferson	5.00
14	Elvis Grbac	5.00
22	Shawn Bryson	5.00
27	Peerless Price	5.00
31	Isaac Byrd	5.00
33	Patrick Jeffers	5.00
35	Muhsin Muhammad	5.00
39	Macey Brooks	5.00
42	Marcus Robinson	10.00
49	Darnay Scott	5.00
50	Akili Smith	10.00
52	Craig Yeast	5.00
55	Curtis Enis	5.00
57	Dennis Northcutt	5.00
62	Raghib Ismail	5.00
67	Michael Wiley	5.00
73	Eddie Kennison	5.00
74	Ed McCaffrey	5.00
75	Rod Smith	5.00
77	Germane Crowell	5.00
80	Herman Moore	5.00
87	Antonio Freeman	5.00
91	Bill Schroeder	5.00
100	Kyle Brady	5.00
105	R. Jay Soward	5.00
106	Shyrone Stith	5.00
109	Kimble Anders	5.00
118	Oronde Gadsden	5.00
122	O.J. McDuffie	5.00
126	James McKnight	5.00
147	Chad Morton	5.00
155	Ron Dixon	5.00
160	Richie Anderson	5.00
161	Wayne Chrebet	5.00
163	Matthew Hatchette	5.00
174	Andre Rison	5.00
176	Charles Woodson	10.00
194	Trung Canidate	5.00
199	Ricky Proehl	5.00
202	Curtis Conway	5.00
203	Tim Dwight	5.00
204	Jermaine Fazande	5.00
217	J.J. Stokes	10.00
218	Tai Streets	5.00
220	Karsten Bailey	5.00
238	Derrick Mason	5.00
248	Kevin Lockett	5.00

2001 Pacific Invincible New Sensations

		MT
Complete Set (30):		60.00
Common Player:		1.25
Production 1,250 Sets		
1	Vinny Sutherland	1.00
2	Michael Vick	15.00
3	Travis Henry	2.50
4	Chris Weinke	4.00
5	David Terrell	6.00
6	Anthony Thomas	4.00
7	Chad Johnson	1.50
8	James Jackson	1.50
9	Quincy Morgan	2.00
10	Mike McMahon	1.50
11	Reggie Wayne	2.50
12	Marvin "Snoop" Minnis	2.00
13	Chris Chambers	1.50
14	Josh Heupel	4.00
15	Travis Minor	2.00
16	Michael Bennett	7.00
17	Deuce McAllister	5.00
18	LaMont Jordan	1.50
19	Santana Moss	4.00
20	Ken-Yon Rambo	1.25
21	Marques Tuiasosopo	2.50
22	Correl Buckhalter	2.00
23	Freddie Mitchell	3.00
24	Drew Brees	8.00
25	LaDainian Tomlinson	8.00
26	Kevan Barlow	2.00
27	Josh Booty	1.25
28	Koren Robinson	4.00
29	Rod Gardner	4.00
30	Sage Rosenfels	1.50

2001 Pacific Invincible Rookie Die-Cuts

		MT
Complete Set (10):		175.00
Common Player:		15.00
Production 100 Sets		
1	Michael Vick	70.00
2	Chris Weinke	20.00
3	David Terrell	30.00
4	Michael Bennett	30.00
5	Deuce McAllister	25.00
6	Freddie Mitchell	15.00
7	Drew Brees	40.00
8	LaDainian Tomlinson	40.00
9	Koren Robinson	15.00
10	Rod Gardner	15.00

2001 Pacific Invincible School Colors

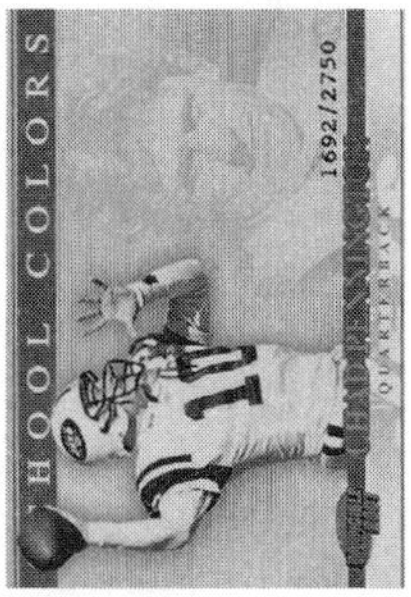

		MT
Complete Set (60):		125.00
Common Player:		1.00
Minor Stars:		2.00
Production 2,750 Sets		
1	Doug Flutie	3.00
2	Tim Hasselbeck	2.00
3	Darrell Jackson	2.00
4	Jesse Palmer	1.00
5	Emmitt Smith	7.00
6	Fred Taylor	2.00
7	Warrick Dunn	2.00
8	Marvin "Snoop" Minnis	2.00
9	Travis Minor	2.00
10	Peter Warrick	4.00
11	Chris Weinke	5.00
12	Terrell Davis	6.00
13	Olandis Gary	6.00
14	Randy Moss	8.00
15	Chad Pennington	4.00
16	James Jackson	2.00
17	Edgerrin James	7.00
18	Santana Moss	5.00
19	Reggie Wayne	3.00
20	Brian Griese	3.00
21	David Terrell	6.00
22	Anthony Thomas	4.00
23	Tyrone Wheatley	1.00
24	Ahman Green	1.00
25	Dan Alexander	2.00
26	Correl Buckhalter	2.00
27	Bobby Newcombe	1.00
28	Torry Holt	2.00
29	Koren Robinson	4.00
30	Jerome Bettis	2.00
31	Tim Brown	2.00
32	Joey Getherall	1.00
33	Jabari Holloway	1.00
34	David Boston	2.00
35	Cris Carter	2.00
36	Eddie George	3.00
37	Ken-Yon Rambo	1.00
38	Kevan Barlow	2.00
39	Curtis Martin	2.00
40	Mike Alstott	2.00
41	Drew Brees	8.00
42	Vinny Sutherland	1.00
43	Marvin Harrison	2.00
44	Kevin Johnson	2.00
45	Donovan McNabb	4.00
46	Travis Henry	3.00
47	Jamal Lewis	5.00
48	Peyton Manning	8.00
49	Troy Aikman	5.00
50	Cade McNown	2.00
51	Freddie Mitchell	4.00
52	Keyshawn Johnson	2.00
53	Junior Seau	1.00
54	Rob Johnson	1.00
55	Mark Brunell	3.00
56	Corey Dillon	2.00
57	Marques Tuiasosopo	3.00
58	Ron Dayne	4.00
59	Michael Bennett	6.00
60	Chris Chambers	2.00

2001 Pacific Invincible Widescreen

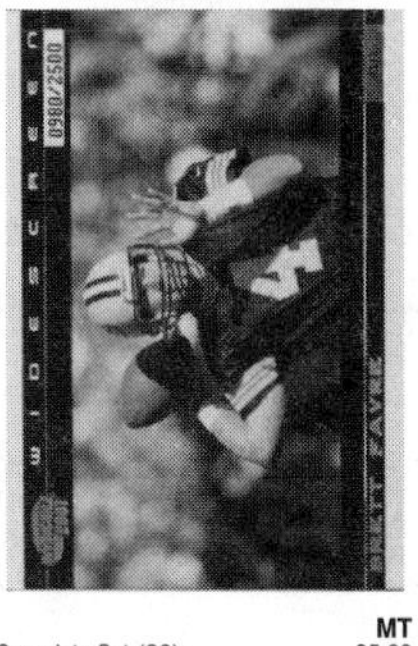

		MT
Complete Set (20):		35.00
Common Player:		1.00
Production 2,500 Sets		
1	Corey Dillon	2.00
2	Peter Warrick	4.00
3	Tim Couch	3.00
4	Kevin Johnson	2.00
5	Brian Griese	3.00
6	Brett Favre	10.00
7	Peyton Manning	8.00
8	Fred Taylor	3.00
9	Sylvester Morris	1.00
10	Drew Bledsoe	3.00
11	Tyrone Wheatley	1.00
12	Donovan McNabb	4.00
13	Jerome Bettis	2.00
14	Plaxico Burress	2.00
15	Jeff Garcia	2.00
16	Terrell Owens	2.00
17	Shaun Alexander	3.00
18	Eddie George	3.00
19	Derrick Mason	1.00
20	Steve McNair	2.00

2001 Pacific Invincible XXXVI

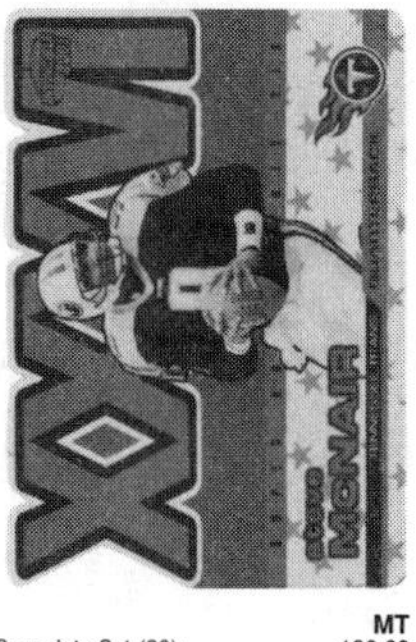

		MT
Complete Set (20):		120.00
Common Player:		2.50
Production 499 Sets		
1	Jamal Lewis	10.00
2	Rob Johnson	2.50
3	Mike Anderson	12.00
4	Terrell Davis	12.00
5	Brett Favre	25.00
6	Marvin Harrison	5.00
7	Edgerrin James	15.00
8	Mark Brunell	6.00
9	Cris Carter	5.00
10	Daunte Culpepper	10.00
11	Ricky Williams	8.00
12	Ron Dayne	8.00
13	Curtis Martin	5.00
14	Rich Gannon	2.50
15	Donovan McNabb	8.00
16	Marshall Faulk	6.00
17	Kurt Warner	20.00
18	Warrick Dunn	5.00
19	Eddie George	6.00
20	Steve McNair	5.00

2001 Pacific Prism Atomic

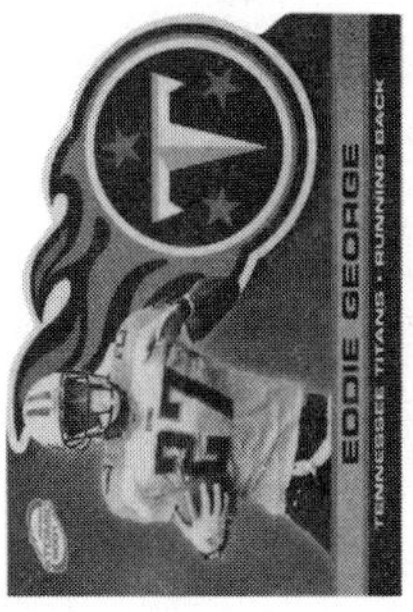

		MT
Complete Set (198):		250.00
Common Player:		.25
1	David Boston	.60
2	Thomas Jones	.25
3	Rob Moore	.25
4	Michael Pittman	.25
5	Jake Plummer	.25
6	Jamal Anderson	.25
7	Chris Chandler	.25
8	Shawn Jefferson	.25
9	Terance Mathis	.25
10	Elvis Grbac	.25
11	Qadry Ismail	.25
12	Jamal Lewis	1.50
13	Ray Lewis	.25
14	Shannon Sharpe	.25
15	Shawn Bryson	.25
16	Rob Johnson	.25
17	Sammy Morris	.25
18	Eric Moulds	.25
19	Peerless Price	.25
20	Tim Biakabutuka	.25
21	Richard Huntley	.25
22	Patrick Jeffers	.25
23	Jeff Lewis	.25
24	Muhsin Muhammad	.25
25	James Allen	.25
26	Cade McNown	.25
27	Marcus Robinson	.25
28	Brian Urlacher	1.50
29	Corey Dillon	.60
30	Jon Kitna	.25
31	Akili Smith	.60
32	Peter Warrick	.60
33	Tim Couch	1.00
34	Kevin Johnson	.25
35	Dennis Northcutt	.25
36	Travis Prentice	.25
37	Tony Banks	.25
38	Joey Galloway	.25
39	Raghib Ismail	.25
40	Emmitt Smith	2.00
41	Anthony Wright	.25
42	Mike Anderson	1.00
43	Terrell Davis	1.00
44	Olandis Gary	.25
45	Brian Griese	.75
46	Ed McCaffrey	.25
47	Rod Smith	.25
48	Charlie Batch	.25
49	Germane Crowell	.25
50	Herman Moore	.25
51	Johnnie Morton	.25
52	James Stewart	.25
53	Brett Favre	4.00
54	Antonio Freeman	.25
55	Ahman Green	.75
56	Dorsey Levens	.25
57	Bill Schroeder	.25
58	Marvin Harrison	.60
59	Edgerrin James	3.00
60	Peyton Manning	3.00
61	Jerome Pathon	.25
62	Terrence Wilkins	.25
63	Mark Brunell	.75
64	Keenan McCardell	.25
65	Jimmy Smith	.25
66	Fred Taylor	.60
67	Derrick Alexander	.25
68	Tony Gonzalez	.25
69	Trent Green	.50
70	Priest Holmes	.50
71	Sylvester Morris	.25
72	Jay Fiedler	.25
73	Oronde Gadsden	.25
74	O.J. McDuffie	.25
75	Lamar Smith	.25
76	Zach Thomas	.50
77	Daunte Culpepper	2.00
78	Cris Carter	.25
79	Randy Moss	3.00
80	Chris Walsh	.25
81	Moe Williams	.25
82	Drew Bledsoe	1.00
83	Kevin Faulk	.25
84	Terry Glenn	.50
85	Charles Johnson	.25
86	J.R. Redmond	.25
87	Jeff Blake	.25
88	Aaron Brooks	1.00
89	Albert Connell	.25
90	Joe Horn	.25
91	Ricky Williams	1.00
92	Tiki Barber	.25
93	Kerry Collins	.25
94	Ron Dayne	.75
95	Ike Hilliard	.25
96	Amani Toomer	.25
97	Richie Anderson	.25
98	Wayne Chrebet	.25
99	Curtis Martin	.50
100	Chad Pennington	.25
101	Vinny Testaverde	.25
102	Tim Brown	.50
103	Rich Gannon	.25
104	Charlie Garner	.25
105	Jerry Rice	2.00
106	Tyrone Wheatley	.25
107	Charles Woodson	.75
108	Darnell Autry	.25
109	Donovan McNabb	1.00
110	Duce Staley	.25
111	James Thrash	.25
112	Jerome Bettis	.60
113	Plaxico Burress	1.00
114	Bobby Shaw	.25
115	Kordell Stewart	.75
116	Hines Ward	.25
117	Isaac Bruce	.75
118	Marshall Faulk	2.00
119	Az-Zahir Hakim	.25
120	Torry Holt	.25
121	Kurt Warner	3.00
122	Curtis Conway	.25
123	Tim Dwight	.25
124	Doug Flutie	.75
125	Dave Dickerson	.25
126	Jeff Garcia	.50
127	Terrell Owens	.75
128	J.J. Stokes	.25
129	Tai Streets	.25
130	Shaun Alexander	.50
131	Matt Hasselbeck	.25
132	Darrell Jackson	.25
133	Ricky Watters	.25
134	Mike Alstott	.50
135	Warrick Dunn	.50
136	Jacquez Green	.25
137	Brad Johnson	.25
138	Keyshawn Johnson	.50
139	Warren Sapp	.25
140	Kevin Dyson	.25
141	Eddie George	1.00
142	Jevon Kearse	.25
143	Derrick Mason	.25
144	Steve McNair	1.00
145	Champ Bailey	.75
146	Stephen Davis	.50
147	Jeff George	.25
148	Michael Westbrook	.25
149	*Quentin McCord*	3.00
150	*Vinny Sutherland*	3.00
151	*Michael Vick*	30.00
152	*Chris Barnes*	3.00
153	*Reggie Germany*	3.00
154	*Travis Henry*	5.00
155	*Dee Brown*	3.00
156	*Dan Morgan*	5.00
157	*Steve Smith*	.25
158	*Chris Weinke*	15.00
159	*David Terrell*	15.00
160	*Anthony Thomas*	30.00
161	*Chad Johnson*	5.00
162	*Rudi Johnson*	5.00
163	*James Jackson*	3.00
164	*Andre King*	3.00
165	*Quincy Morgan*	5.00
166	*Quincy Carter*	10.00
167	*Kevin Kasper*	5.00
168	*Scotty Anderson*	5.00
169	*Mike McMahon*	15.00
170	*Robert Ferguson*	5.00
171	*Reggie Wayne*	10.00
172	*Derrick Blaylock*	5.00
173	*Marvin "Snoop" Minnis*	10.00
174	*Chris Chambers*	25.00
175	*Josh Heupel*	10.00
176	*Travis Minor*	10.00
177	*Michael Bennett*	25.00
178	*Deuce McAllister*	25.00
179	*Jonathan Carter*	5.00
180	*Jesse Palmer*	5.00
181	*LaMont Jordan*	5.00
182	*Santana Moss*	10.00
183	*Ken-Yon Rambo*	3.00
184	*Marques Tuiasosopo*	10.00
185	*Correl Buckhalter*	5.00
186	*Freddie Mitchell*	10.00
187	*Milton Wynn*	3.00
188	*Drew Brees*	25.00
189	*LaDainian Tomlinson*	25.00
190	*Kevan Barlow*	5.00
191	*Cedrick Wilson*	3.00
192	*Alex Bannister*	3.00
193	*Josh Booty*	3.00
194	*Koren Robinson*	5.00
195	*Eddie Berlin*	3.00
196	*Rod Gardner*	10.00
197	*Darnerian McCants*	5.00
198	*Sage Rosenfels*	5.00

2001 Pacific Prism Atomic Atomic Energy

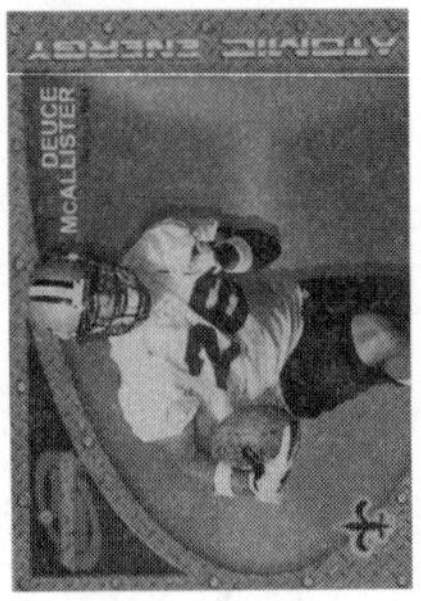

		MT
Complete Set (20):		50.00
Common Player:		1.00
1	Michael Vick	8.00
2	Travis Henry	2.00
3	Chris Weinke	4.00
4	David Terrell	4.00
5	Anthony Thomas	8.00
6	Quincy Carter	2.00
7	Reggie Wayne	2.00
8	Josh Heupel	2.00
9	Michael Bennett	4.00
10	Deuce McAllister	4.00
11	Jesse Palmer	2.00
12	LaMont Jordan	1.00
13	Santana Moss	3.00
14	Marques Tuiasosopo	3.00
15	Freddie Mitchell	3.00
16	Drew Brees	4.00
17	LaDainian Tomlinson	4.00
18	Koren Robinson	2.00
19	Rod Gardner	2.00
20	Sage Rosenfels	1.00

2001 Pacific Prism Atomic Core Players

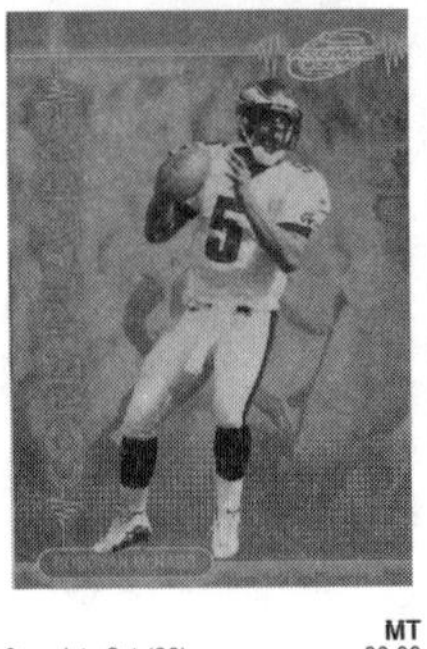

		MT
Complete Set (20):		30.00
Common Player:		1.00
1	Jamal Lewis	2.00
2	Peter Warrick	1.00
3	Tim Couch	2.00
4	Emmitt Smith	3.00
5	Mike Anderson	2.00
6	Terrell Davis	1.00
7	Brett Favre	5.00
8	Edgerrin James	3.00
9	Peyton Manning	3.00
10	Fred Taylor	1.00
11	Randy Moss	4.00
12	Ricky Williams	1.00
13	Ron Dayne	1.00
14	Jerry Rice	3.00
15	Donovan McNabb	2.00
16	Marshall Faulk	2.00
17	Kurt Warner	4.00
18	Jeff Garcia	1.00
19	Eddie George	2.00
20	Steve McNair	1.00

A player's name in *italic type* indicates a rookie card.

2001 Pacific Prism Atomic Game-Worn Jerseys

		MT
Complete Set (150):		
Common Player:		10.00
1	Mac Cody	10.00
2	MarTay Jenkins	10.00
3	Thomas Jones	10.00
4	Rob Moore	10.00
5	Chris Chandler	10.00
6	Bob Christian	10.00
7	Jamal Lewis	15.00
8	Larry Centers	10.00
9	Rob Johnson	10.00
10	Peerless Price	10.00
11	Brad Hoover	10.00
12	Muhsin Muhammad	10.00
13	Chris Weinke	30.00
14	James Allen	10.00
15	Macey Brooks	10.00
16	Bobby Engram	10.00
17	Anthony Thomas	40.00
18	Brian Urlacher	30.00
19	Corey Dillon	10.00
20	Bobby Brown	10.00
21	Tim Couch	15.00
22	Curtis Enis	10.00
23	Emmitt Smith	50.00
24	Anthony Wright	10.00
25	Mike Anderson	25.00
26	Eddie Kennison	10.00
27	James Stewart	10.00
28	Brett Favre	50.00
29	Bubba Franks	10.00
30	William Henderson	10.00
31	Marvin Harrison	15.00
32	Edgerrin James	30.00
33	Peyton Manning	30.00
34	Mark Brunell	10.00
35	Keenan McCardell	10.00
36	Jimmy Smith	10.00
37	R. Jay Soward	10.00
38	Fred Taylor	15.00
39	Sylvester Morris	10.00
40	Autrey Denson	10.00
41	Jay Fiedler	10.00
42	J.J. Johnson	10.00
43	Zach Thomas	10.00
44	Cris Carter	10.00
45	Daunte Culpepper	25.00
46	Randy Moss	50.00
47	Drew Bledsoe	15.00
48	Aaron Brooks	15.00
49	Joe Horn	10.00
50	Terrelle Smith	10.00
51	Tiki Barber	10.00
52	Kerry Collins	10.00
53	Greg Comella	10.00
54	Ron Dixon	10.00
55	Ike Hilliard	10.00
56	Joe Jurevicius	10.00
57	Richie Anderson	10.00
58	Laveranues Coles	10.00
59	Matthew Hatchette	10.00
60	Curtis Martin	10.00
61	Dwight Stone	10.00
62	Vinny Testaverde	10.00
63	David Dunn	10.00
64	Napoleon Kaufman	10.00
65	Jerry Porter	30.00
66	Jerry Rice	10.00
67	Andre Rison	10.00
68	Marques Tuiasosopo	25.00
69	Tyrone Wheatley	10.00
70	Charles Woodson	10.00
71	Donovan McNabb	25.00
72	Freddie Mitchell	25.00
73	Duce Staley	10.00
74	Ernie Conwell	10.00
75	Marshall Faulk	25.00
76	Az-Zahir Hakim	10.00
77	Torry Holt	10.00
78	Ricky Proehl	10.00
79	Drew Brees	30.00
80	Curtis Conway	10.00
81	Freddie Jones	10.00
82	Junior Seau	10.00
83	LaDainian Tomlinson	30.00
84	Jeff Garcia	10.00
85	Terrell Owens	15.00
86	J.J. Stokes	10.00
87	Tai Streets	10.00
88	Karsten Bailey	10.00
89	Brock Huard	10.00
90	James Williams	10.00
91	Reidel Anthony	10.00
92	Jacquez Green	10.00
93	Joe Hamilton	10.00
94	Keyshawn Johnson	15.00
95	Warren Sapp	10.00
96	Kevin Dyson	10.00
97	Jevon Kearse	10.00
98	Derrick Mason	10.00
99	Stephen Alexander	10.00
100	Kevin Lockett	10.00
101	Michael Pittman	10.00
102	Jake Plummer	10.00
103	Jamal Anderson	10.00
104	Qadry Ismail	10.00
105	Pat Johnson	10.00
106	Chris Redman	10.00
107	Brandon Stokley	10.00
108	Travis Taylor	10.00
109	Tim Biakabutuka	10.00
110	Richard Huntley	10.00
111	Marcus Robinson	10.00
112	Ron Dugans	10.00
113	Scott Mitchell	10.00
114	Darnay Scott	10.00
115	Akili Smith	10.00
116	Craig Yeast	10.00
117	JaJuan Dawson	10.00
118	Travis Prentice	10.00
119	Errict Rhett	10.00
120	Spergon Wynn	10.00
121	Brian Griese	15.00
122	Germane Crowell	10.00
123	Herman Moore	10.00
124	Antonio Freeman	10.00
125	Tom Brady	50.00
126	Shockmain Davis	10.00
127	Kevin Faulk	10.00
128	Curtis Jackson	10.00
129	Jeff Blake	10.00
130	Amani Toomer	10.00
131	Wayne Chrebet	10.00
132	Chad Pennington	15.00
133	Tim Brown	15.00
134	Rich Gannon	10.00
135	Darnell Autry	10.00
136	Brian Mitchell	10.00
137	Plaxico Burress	15.00
138	Troy Edwards	10.00
139	Courtney Hawkins	10.00
140	Dan Kreider	10.00
141	Bobby Shaw	10.00
142	Hines Ward	10.00
143	Amos Zereoue	10.00
144	Giovanni Carmazzi	10.00
145	Greg Clark	10.00
146	Rick Mirer	10.00
147	Tim Rattay	10.00
148	Darrell Jackson	10.00
149	Ricky Watters	15.00
150	Chris Sanders	10.00

Post-1980 cards in Near Mint condition will generally sell for about 75% of the quoted Mint value. Excellent-condition cards bring no more than 40%.

2001 Pacific Prism Atomic Rookie Reaction

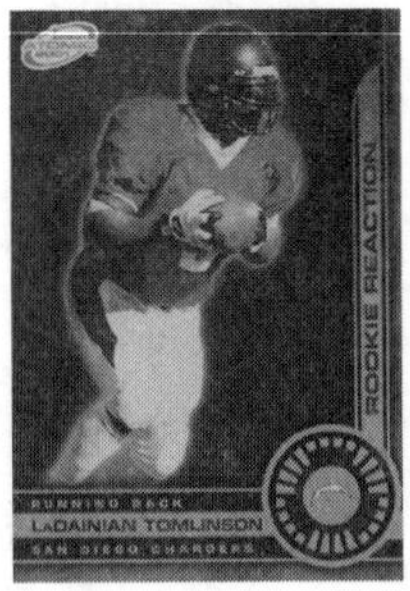

		MT
Complete Set (20):		55.00
Common Player:		1.00
1	Michael Vick	8.00
2	Travis Henry	2.00
3	Chris Weinke	4.00
4	David Terrell	6.00
5	Anthony Thomas	8.00
6	James Jackson	2.00
7	Quincy Carter	4.00
8	Reggie Wayne	2.00
9	Josh Heupel	1.00
10	Michael Bennett	4.00
11	Deuce McAllister	4.00
12	LaMont Jordan	1.00
13	Santana Moss	3.00
14	Marques Tuiasosopo	3.00
15	Freddie Mitchell	4.00
16	Drew Brees	6.00
17	LaDainian Tomlinson	6.00
18	Kevan Barlow	2.00
19	Koren Robinson	2.00
20	Rod Gardner	3.00

2001 Pacific Prism Atomic Strategic Arms

		MT
Complete Set (10):		175.00
Common Player:		10.00
1	Michael Vick	40.00
2	Tim Couch	10.00
3	Brian Griese	10.00
4	Brett Favre	50.00
5	Peyton Manning	40.00
6	Mark Brunell	10.00
7	Daunte Culpepper	15.00
8	Drew Bledsoe	15.00
9	Donovan McNabb	15.00
10	Kurt Warner	40.00

2001 Pacific Prism Atomic Statosphere

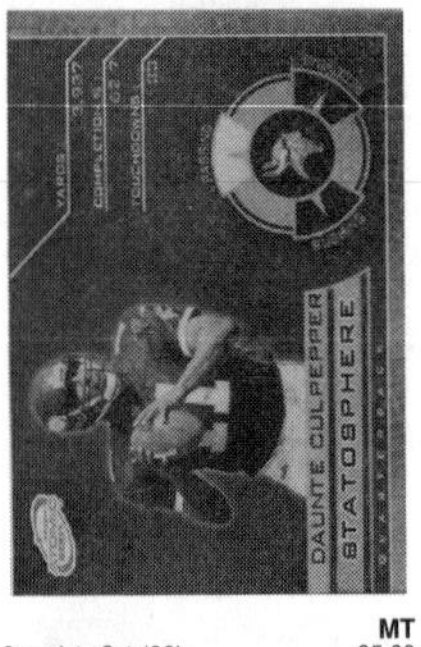

		MT
Complete Set (20):		35.00
Common Player:		1.00
1	Chris Weinke	3.00
2	Tim Couch	1.00
3	Brian Griese	1.00
4	Peyton Manning	4.00
5	Mark Brunell	1.00
6	Daunte Culpepper	2.50
7	Drew Bledsoe	1.50
8	Kurt Warner	4.00
9	Jeff Garcia	1.00
10	Steve McNair	1.00
11	Jamal Lewis	2.50
12	Peter Warrick	1.00
13	Emmitt Smith	3.00
14	Terrell Davis	1.00
15	Edgerrin James	3.00
16	Fred Taylor	1.00
17	Randy Moss	4.00
18	Ricky Williams	1.00
19	Jerry Rice	3.00
20	Marshall Faulk	2.00

Values quoted in this guide reflect the retail price of a card — the price a collector can expect to pay when buying a card from a dealer. The wholesale price — that which a collector can expect to receive from a dealer when selling cards — will be significantly lower, depending on desirability and condition.

2001 Pacific Prism Atomic Team Nucleus

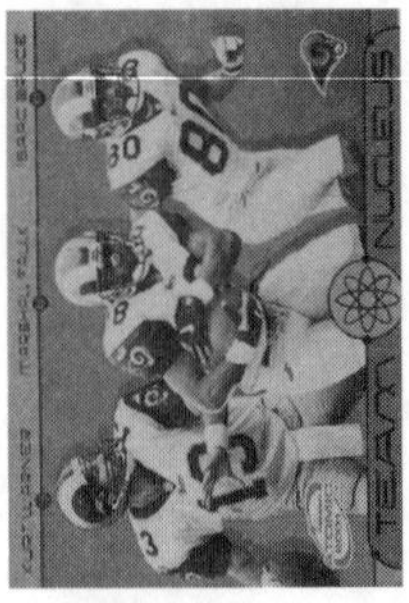

		MT
Complete Set (10):		30.00
Common Player:		2.00
1	Brian Urlacher, Anthony Thomas, David Terrell	5.00
2	Chad Johnson, Corey Dillon, Peter Warrick	2.00
3	Brian Griese, Terrell Davis, Mike Anderson	2.00
4	Reggie Wayne, Edgerrin James, Marvin Harrison	4.00
5	Mark Brunell, Fred Taylor, Jimmy Smith	2.00
6	Daunte Culpepper, Michael Bennett, Randy Moss	6.00
7	Chad Pennington, LaMont Jordan, Santana Moss	3.00
8	Kurt Warner, Marshall Faulk, Isaac Bruce	5.00
9	Doug Flutie, Drew Brees, LaDainian Tomlinson	6.00
10	Steve McNair, Eddie George, Derrick Mason	2.00

2001 Pacific Private Stock

		MT
Complete Set (175):		1000.
Common Player:		.25
Minor Stars:		.50
Common Rookie:		7.00
Production 200 Sets		
Pack (7):		15.00
Wax Box (10):		110.00
1	David Boston	1.00
2	Thomas Jones	.50
3	Jake Plummer	1.00
4	Jamal Anderson	1.00
5	Chris Chandler	.50
6	Eric Zeier	.25
7	Elvis Grbac	.75
8	Jamal Lewis	2.50
9	Shannon Sharpe	.50
10	Rob Johnson	.75
11	Eric Moulds	1.00
12	Peerless Price	.75
13	Tim Biakabutuka	.50
14	Jeff Lewis	.50
15	Muhsin Muhammad	.75
16	James Allen	.75
17	Cade McNown	1.00
18	Marcus Robinson	1.00
19	Brian Urlacher	2.00
20	Corey Dillon	1.00
21	Jon Kitna	.75
22	Akili Smith	1.00
23	Peter Warrick	2.00
24	Tim Couch	1.25
25	Kevin Johnson	.75
26	Travis Prentice	.75
27	Raghib Ismail	.50
28	Emmitt Smith	2.50
29	Mike Anderson	2.50
30	Terrell Davis	2.00
31	Brian Griese	1.25
32	Ed McCaffrey	1.00
33	Charlie Batch	1.00
34	Germane Crowell	.75
35	James Stewart	.75
36	Brett Favre	4.00
37	Antonio Freeman	.75
38	Ahman Green	.75
39	Marvin Harrison	1.00
40	Edgerrin James	2.75
41	Peyton Manning	3.00
42	Mark Brunell	1.25
43	Jimmy Smith	.75
44	Fred Taylor	1.25
45	Derrick Alexander	.50
46	Tony Gonzalez	.75
47	Trent Green	.75
48	Priest Holmes	.50
49	Jay Fiedler	1.00
50	Oronde Gadsden	.50
51	Lamar Smith	.75
52	Cris Carter	1.00
53	Daunte Culpepper	2.00
54	Randy Moss	3.00
55	Drew Bledsoe	1.25
56	Kevin Faulk	.50
57	Terry Glenn	.75
58	Jeff Blake	.50
59	Aaron Brooks	1.00
60	Joe Horn	.75
61	Ricky Williams	1.50
62	Tiki Barber	1.00
63	Kerry Collins	.75
64	Ron Dayne	1.75
65	Amani Toomer	.50
66	Wayne Chrebet	.50
67	Curtis Martin	1.00
68	Vinny Testaverde	.75
69	Tim Brown	.75
70	Rich Gannon	.50
71	Charlie Garner	.50
72	Jerry Rice	2.00
73	Tyrone Wheatley	.50
74	Donovan McNabb	1.50
75	Duce Staley	1.00
76	Jerome Bettis	1.00
77	Kordell Stewart	1.00
78	Hines Ward	.50
79	Isaac Bruce	1.00
80	Marshall Faulk	1.25
81	Torry Holt	1.00
82	Kurt Warner	3.00
83	Curtis Conway	.50
84	Doug Flutie	1.25
85	Jeff Garcia	1.00
86	Terrell Owens	1.00
87	Shaun Alexander	1.25
88	Matt Hasselbeck	1.00
89	Darrell Jackson	.50
90	Ricky Watters	.75
91	Mike Alstott	1.00
92	Warrick Dunn	1.00
93	Keyshawn Johnson	1.00
94	Brad Johnson	.75
95	Eddie George	1.25
96	Derrick Mason	.75
97	Steve McNair	1.00
98	Stephen Davis	1.00
99	Jeff George	.75
100	Michael Westbrook	.75
101	*Bobby Newcombe*	12.00
102	*Corey Brown*	10.00
103	*Alge Crumpler*	12.00
104	*Vinny Sutherland*	12.00
105	*Michael Vick*	100.00
106	*Chris Barnes*	12.00
107	*Todd Heap*	12.00
108	*Nate Clements*	10.00
109	*Tim Hasselbeck*	12.00
110	*Travis Henry*	40.00
111	*Dee Brown*	10.00
112	*Dan Morgan*	12.00
113	*Steve Smith*	10.00
114	*Chris Weinke*	40.00
115	*John Capel*	12.00
116	*David Terrell*	50.00
117	*Anthony Thomas*	80.00
118	*T.J. Houshmandzadeh*	10.00
119	*Chad Johnson*	20.00
120	*Rudi Johnson*	20.00
121	*James Jackson*	25.00
122	*Quincy Morgan*	25.00
123	*Quincy Carter*	40.00
124	*Kevin Kasper*	12.00
125	*Scotty Anderson*	7.00
126	*Mike McMahon*	15.00
127	*Robert Ferguson*	20.00
128	*David Martin*	7.00
129	*Jamal Reynolds*	12.00
130	*Reggie Wayne*	30.00
131	*Richmond Flowers*	10.00
132	*Marcus Stroud*	10.00
133	*Derrick Blaylock*	7.00
134	*Marvin "Snoop" Minnis*	25.00
135	*Chris Chambers*	40.00
136	*Jamar Fletcher*	12.00
137	*Josh Heupel*	35.00
138	*Travis Minor*	20.00
139	*Michael Bennett*	40.00
140	*Deuce McAllister*	40.00
141	*Moran Norris*	7.00
142	*Onomo Ojo*	10.00
143	*Will Allen*	10.00
144	*Jonathan Carter*	7.00
145	*Jesse Palmer*	15.00
146	*LaMont Jordan*	20.00
147	*Santana Moss*	35.00
148	*Derek Combs*	10.00
149	*Derrick Gibson*	7.00
150	*Javon Green*	7.00
151	*Ken-Yon Rambo*	15.00
152	*Marques Tuiasosopo*	35.00
153	*Correll Buckhalter*	20.00
154	*Freddie Mitchell*	35.00
155	*Joey Getherall*	7.00
156	*Chris Taylor*	7.00
157	*Adam Archuleta*	15.00
158	*David Rivers*	10.00
159	*Francis St. Paul*	7.00
160	*Drew Brees*	80.00
161	*LaDainian Tomlinson*	80.00
162	*David Allen*	12.00
163	*Kevan Barlow*	25.00
164	*Andre Carter*	10.00
165	*Cedrick Wilson*	12.00
166	*Alex Bannister*	15.00
167	*Josh Booty*	12.00
168	*Heath Evans*	7.00
169	*Koren Robinson*	35.00
170	*Margin Hooks*	7.00
171	*Dan Alexander*	15.00
172	*Eddie Berlin*	7.00
173	*Rod Gardner*	35.00
174	*Darnerian McCants*	10.00
175	*Sage Rosenfels*	20.00

2001 Pacific Private Stock Artist's Reserve

		MT
Common Player:		20.00
Production 99 Sets		
1	Michael Vick	75.00
2	Chris Weinke	30.00
3	David Terrell	25.00
4	Quincy Carter	20.00
5	Michael Bennett	40.00
6	Deuce McAllister	25.00
7	Marques Tuiasosopo	20.00
8	Drew Brees	50.00
9	LaDainian Tomlinson	50.00
10	Koren Robinson	20.00

2001 Pacific Private Stock Game-Worn Jersey

		MT
Complete Set (150):		
Common Player:		5.00
1	Thomas Jones	5.00
2	Rob Moore	5.00
3	Jake Plummer	5.00
4	Frank Sanders	5.00
5	Chris Chandler	5.00
6	Doug Johnson	5.00
7	Terance Mathis	5.00
8	Randall Cunningham	5.00
9	Elvis Grbac	5.00
10	Jamal Lewis	15.00
11	Ray Lewis	10.00
12	Shawn Bryson	5.00
13	Kwame Cavil	5.00
14	Jonathon Linton	5.00
15	Jeremy McDaniel	5.00
16	Eric Moulds	5.00
17	Thurman Thomas	10.00
18	Michael Bates	5.00
19	Dameyune Craig	5.00
20	William Floyd	5.00
21	Patrick Jeffers	5.00
22	Wesley Walls	5.00
23	Chris Weinke (college)	18.00
24	Marlon Barnes	5.00
25	D'Wayne Bates	5.00
26	Marty Booker	5.00
27	Cade McNown	10.00
28	Anthony Thomas (college)	25.00
29	Brian Urlacher	15.00
30	Brandon Bennett	5.00
31	Curtis Keaton	5.00
32	Jon Kitna	5.00
33	Peter Warrick	10.00
34	Darrin Chiaverini	5.00
35	Tim Couch	10.00
36	Rickey Dudley	5.00
37	Curtis Enis	5.00
38	Kevin Johnson	5.00
39	Dennis Northcutt	5.00
40	Troy Aikman	15.00
41	Wane McGarity	5.00
42	Carl Pickens	5.00
43	Emmitt Smith	20.00
44	Michael Wiley	5.00
45	Anthony Wright	5.00
46	Mike Anderson	5.00
47	Steve Beuerlein	5.00
48	Terrell Davis	10.00
49	Olandis Gary	5.00
50	Brian Griese	10.00
51	Eddie Kennison	5.00
52	Deltha O'Neal	5.00
53	Keith Poole	5.00
54	Bill Romanowski	5.00
55	Charlie Batch	5.00
56	Desmond Howard	5.00
57	Sedrick Irvin	5.00
58	Tyrone Davis	5.00
59	Donald Driver	5.00
60	Brett Favre	30.00
61	Ahman Green	10.00
62	Charles Lee	5.00
63	Bill Schroeder	5.00
64	E.G. Green	5.00
65	Edgerrin James	20.00
66	Peyton Manning	25.00
67	Jerome Pathon	5.00
68	Marcus Pollard	5.00
69	Kyle Brady	5.00
70	Mark Brunell	10.00
71	Jamie Martin	5.00
72	Keenan McCardell	5.00
73	Shyrone Stith	5.00
74	Fred Taylor	10.00
75	Alvis Whitted	5.00
76	Derrick Alexander	5.00
77	Kimble Anders	5.00
78	Mike Cloud	5.00
79	Trent Green	5.00
80	Tony Horne	5.00
81	Warren Moon	10.00
82	Rob Konrad	5.00
83	Ray Lucas	5.00
84	Tony Martin	5.00
85	O.J. McDuffie	5.00
86	James McKnight	5.00
87	Leslie Shepherd	5.00
88	Dedric Ward	5.00
89	Cris Carter	10.00
90	Daunte Culpepper	15.00
91	Randy Moss	25.00
92	Jake Reed	5.00
93	Robert Smith	5.00
94	Moe Williams	5.00
95	Michael Bishop	5.00
96	Drew Bledsoe	10.00
97	Troy Brown	5.00
98	Bert Emanuel	5.00
99	David Patten	5.00
100	J.R. Redmond	10.00
101	Albert Connell	5.00
102	Willie Jackson	5.00
103	Chad Morton	5.00
104	Ricky Williams	10.00
105	Ron Dayne	10.00
106	Ron Dixon	5.00
107	Joe Jurevicius	5.00
108	Richie Anderson	5.00
109	Matthew Hatchette	5.00
110	Chad Pennington	10.00
111	Reggie Barlow	5.00
112	Napoleon Kaufman	5.00
113	Jerry Rice	20.00
114	Andre Rison	5.00
115	Marques Tuiasosopo (college)	15.00
116	Charles Woodson	10.00
117	Donovan McNabb	10.00
118	Freddie Mitchell (college)	10.00
119	Trung Canidate	5.00
120	Marshall Faulk	15.00
121	Kurt Warner	25.00
122	Drew Brees (college)	25.00
123	Tim Dwight	5.00
124	Jermaine Fazande	5.00
125	Doug Flutie	15.00
126	LaDainian Tomlinson (college)	25.00
127	Jeff Garcia	10.00
128	Tai Streets	5.00
129	Shaun Alexander	10.00
130	Matt Hasselbeck	5.00
131	Warrick Dunn	5.00
132	Shaun King	5.00
133	Ryan Leaf	5.00
134	Eddie George	10.00
135	Jevon Kearse	5.00
136	Steve McNair	10.00
137	Chris Sanders	5.00
138	Donnell Bennett	5.00
139	Kevin Lockett	5.00
140	David Boston	10.00
141	Thomas Jones	5.00
142	Jake Plummer	5.00
143	Corey Dillon	10.00
144	Akili Smith	10.00
145	Peter Warrick	10.00

146 Isaac Bruce 10.00
147 Marshall Faulk 15.00
148 Az-Zahir Hakim 5.00
149 Torry Holt 5.00
150 Kurt Warner 25.00

2001 Pacific Private Stock Game Worn Gear

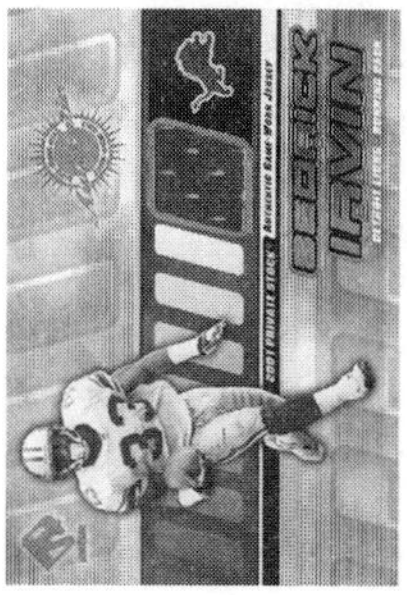

		MT
Common Player:		7.00
Inserted 1:1		
1	Thomas Jones 600	10.00
2	Rob Moore 500	10.00
3	Jake Plummer 1148	10.00
4	Frank Sanders 250	10.00
5	Chris Chandler 600	10.00
6	Doug Johnson 2000	7.00
7	Terance Mathis 750	7.00
8	Randall Cunningham 1000	7.00
9	Elvis Grbac 1250	10.00
10	Jamal Lewis 500	30.00
11	Ray Lewis 1250	7.00
12	Shawn Bryson 500	7.00
13	Kwame Cavil 2000	7.00
14	Jonathon Linton 2000	7.00
15	Jeremy McDaniel 1500	7.00
16	Eric Moulds 1250	10.00
17	Thurman Thomas 1224	12.00
18	Michael Bates 200	10.00
19	Dameyune Craig 2000	7.00
20	William Floyd 2000	7.00
21	Patrick Jeffers 500	12.00
22	Wesley Walls 500	7.00
23	Chris Weinke 1000	30.00
24	Marlon Barnes 2000	7.00
25	D'Wayne Bates 2000	7.00
26	Marty Booker 2000	7.00
27	Cade McNown 1000	15.00
28	Anthony Thomas 1000	20.00
29	Brian Urlacher 625	25.00
30	Brandon Bennett 2000	7.00
31	Curtis Keaton 500	10.00
32	Jon Kitna 2000	12.00
33	Peter Warrick 400	20.00
34	Darrin Chiaverini 2000	7.00
35	Tim Couch 500	20.00
36	Rickey Dudley 2000	7.00
37	Curtis Enis 750	7.00
38	Kevin Johnson 1250	10.00
39	Dennis Northcutt 750	12.00
40	Troy Aikman 1250	30.00
41	Wane McGarity 500	7.00
42	Carl Pickens 1000	7.00
43	Emmitt Smith 400	45.00
44	Michael Wiley 1250	7.00
45	Anthony Wright 750	12.00
46	Mike Anderson 400	30.00
47	Steve Beuerlein 750	10.00
48	Terrell Davis 400	30.00
49	Olandis Gary 1250	12.00
50	Brian Griese 400	25.00
51	Eddie Kennison 750	10.00
52	Deltha O'Neal 2000	7.00
53	Bill Romanowski 2000	7.00
54	Charlie Batch 1250	10.00
55	Desmond Howard 500	12.00
56	Sedrick Irvin 2000	7.00
57	Tyrone Davis 500	7.00
58	Donald Driver 2000	7.00
59	Brett Favre 723	45.00
60	Ahman Green 400	12.00
61	Charles Lee 2000	7.00
62	Bill Schroeder 500	10.00
63	E.G. Green 1500	7.00
64	Edgerrin James 500	40.00
65	Peyton Manning 500	50.00
66	Jerome Pathon 1500	7.00
67	Marcus Pollard 2000	7.00
68	Kyle Brady 1250	7.00
69	Mark Brunell 500	25.00
70	Jamie Martin 2000	7.00
71	Keenan McCardell 750	10.00
72	Shyrone Stith 1250	7.00
73	Fred Taylor 1500	20.00
74	Alvis Whitted 2000	7.00
75	Derrick Alexander 1000	7.00
76	Kimble Anders 1250	7.00
77	Mike Cloud 2000	7.00
78	Trent Green 1398	10.00
79	Tony Horne 1500	7.00
80	Warren Moon 2000	15.00
81	Rob Konrad 2000	7.00
82	Ray Lucas 2000	7.00
83	Tony Martin 500	10.00
84	O.J. McDuffie 750	10.00
85	James McKnight 500	10.00
86	Leslie Shepherd 2000	7.00
87	Dedric Ward 2000	7.00
88	Cris Carter 1000	15.00
89	Daunte Culpepper 400	30.00
90	Randy Moss 400	45.00
91	Jake Reed 2000	7.00
92	Robert Smith 1500	7.00
93	Moe Williams 500	10.00
94	Michael Bishop 2000	10.00
95	Drew Bledsoe 500	20.00
96	Troy Brown 2000	7.00
97	Bert Emanuel 500	10.00
98	David Patten 2000	7.00
99	J.R. Redmond 2000	7.00
100	Albert Connell 2000	7.00
101	Willie Jackson 250	15.00
102	Chad Morton 250	12.00
103	Keith Poole 2000	7.00
104	Ricky Williams 731	20.00
105	Ron Dayne 625	15.00
106	Ron Dixon 750	10.00
107	Joe Jurevicius 1000	7.00
108	Richie Anderson 750	7.00
109	Matthew Hatchette 750	10.00
110	Chad Pennington 625	20.00
111	Reggie Barlow 1500	7.00
112	Napoleon Kaufman 1000	7.00
113	Jerry Rice 750	30.00
114	Andre Rison 750	10.00
115	Marques Tuiasosopo 1000	15.00
116	Charles Woodson 750	10.00
117	Donovan McNabb 500	25.00
118	Freddie Mitchell 1000	20.00
119	Trung Canidate 750	10.00
120	Marshall Faulk 400	20.00
121	Kurt Warner 200	40.00
122	Drew Brees 1000	45.00
123	Tim Dwight 500	12.00
124	Jermaine Fazande 1250	7.00
125	Doug Flutie 1250	15.00
126	LaDainian Tomlinson 1000	45.00
127	Jeff Garcia 1400	15.00
128	Tai Streets 750	12.00
129	Shaun Alexander 500	20.00
130	Matt Hasselbeck 750	12.00
131	Warrick Dunn 1500	12.00
132	Shaun King 2000	10.00
133	Ryan Leaf 2000	7.00
134	Eddie George 400	25.00
135	Jevon Kearse 750	15.00
136	Steve McNair 900	12.00
137	Chris Sanders 750	7.00
138	Donnell Bennett 2000	7.00
139	Kevin Lockett 750	7.00
140	David Boston 200	25.00
141	Thomas Jones 200	25.00
142	Jake Plummer 200	15.00
143	Corey Dillon 200	25.00
144	Akili Smith 200	20.00
145	Peter Warrick 200	25.00
146	Isaac Bruce 200	25.00
147	Marshall Faulk 200	30.00
148	Az-Zahir Hakim 200	15.00
149	Torry Holt 200	20.00
150	Kurt Warner 200	50.00

2001 Pacific Private Stock Game Worn Gear Patch

		MT
Common Player:		12.00
1	Thomas Jones 100	20.00
2	Rob Moore 200	15.00
3	Jake Plummer 225	20.00
4	Frank Sanders 250	15.00
5	Chris Chandler 150	20.00
6	Doug Johnson 300	15.00
7	Terance Mathis 250	12.00
8	Randall Cunningham 200	18.00
9	Elvis Grbac 300	20.00
10	Jamal Lewis 100	70.00
11	Ray Lewis 300	20.00
12	Shawn Bryson 300	15.00
13	Kwame Cavil 300	12.00
14	Jonathon Linton 300	12.00
15	Jeremy McDaniel 300	12.00
16	Eric Moulds 250	20.00
17	Thurman Thomas 250	25.00
18	Michael Bates 300	12.00
19	Dameyune Craig 300	12.00
20	William Floyd 300	12.00
21	Patrick Jeffers 250	15.00
22	Wesley Walls 250	12.00
24	Marlon Barnes 300	12.00
25	D'Wayne Bates 300	12.00
26	Marty Booker 300	12.00
27	Cade McNown 200	20.00
29	Brian Urlacher 100	50.00
30	Brandon Bennett 300	12.00
31	Curtis Keaton 50	20.00
32	Jon Kitna 300	20.00
33	Peter Warrick 25	60.00
34	Darrin Chiaverini 300	12.00
35	Tim Couch 100	35.00
36	Rickey Dudley 300	12.00
37	Curtis Enis 250	12.00
38	Kevin Johnson 250	15.00
39	Dennis Northcutt 300	12.00
40	Troy Aikman 225	50.00
41	Wane McGarity 250	12.00
42	Carl Pickens 200	12.00
43	Emmitt Smith 100	70.00
44	Michael Wiley 300	12.00
45	Anthony Wright 150	30.00
46	Mike Anderson 100	50.00
47	Steve Beuerlein 200	15.00
48	Terrell Davis 100	50.00
49	Olandis Gary 225	15.00
50	Brian Griese 100	40.00
51	Eddie Kennison 250	12.00
52	Deltha O'Neal 300	12.00
53	Bill Romanowski 300	12.00
54	Charlie Batch 250	20.00
55	Desmond Howard 250	12.00
56	Sedrick Irvin 300	12.00
57	Tyrone Davis 250	12.00
58	Donald Driver 300	12.00
59	Brett Favre 125	85.00
60	Ahman Green 75	25.00
61	Charles Lee 300	12.00
62	Bill Schroeder 300	12.00
63	E.G. Green 250	12.00
64	Edgerrin James 100	60.00
65	Peyton Manning 100	75.00
66	Jerome Pathon 300	12.00
67	Marcus Pollard 300	12.00
68	Kyle Brady 300	12.00
69	Mark Brunell 100	40.00
70	Jamie Martin 300	12.00
71	Keenan McCardell 100	20.00
72	Shyrone Stith 300	12.00
73	Fred Taylor 250	30.00
74	Alvis Whitted 300	12.00
75	Derrick Alexander 300	12.00
76	Kimble Anders 300	12.00
77	Mike Cloud 300	12.00
78	Trent Green 250	25.00
79	Tony Horne 250	15.00
80	Warren Moon 300	25.00
81	Rob Konrad 300	12.00
82	Ray Lucas 300	12.00
83	Tony Martin 250	12.00
84	O.J. McDuffie 250	15.00
85	James McKnight 250	12.00
86	Leslie Shepherd 300	12.00
87	Dedric Ward 300	12.00
88	Cris Carter 225	25.00
89	Daunte Culpepper 25	100.00
90	Randy Moss 25	150.00
91	Jake Reed 300	12.00
92	Robert Smith 275	12.00
93	Moe Williams 250	12.00
94	Michael Bishop 300	18.00
95	Drew Bledsoe 100	40.00
96	Troy Brown 300	12.00
97	Bert Emanuel 250	12.00
98	David Patten 300	12.00
99	J.R. Redmond 300	12.00
100	Albert Connell 300	12.00
101	Willie Jackson 250	12.00
102	Chad Morton 300	12.00
103	Keith Poole 300	12.00
104	Ricky Williams 100	45.00
105	Ron Dayne 100	45.00
106	Ron Dixon 250	20.00
107	Joe Jurevicius 200	12.00
108	Richie Anderson 250	12.00
109	Matthew Hatchette 250	12.00
110	Chad Pennington 100	45.00
111	Reggie Barlow 250	12.00
112	Napoleon Kaufman 200	20.00
113	Jerry Rice 100	80.00
114	Andre Rison 250	15.00
116	Charles Woodson 250	20.00
117	Donovan McNabb 100	40.00
119	Trung Canidate 250	12.00
120	Marshall Faulk 25	85.00
121	Kurt Warner 25	125.00
123	Tim Dwight 250	25.00
124	Jermaine Fazande 300	12.00
125	Doug Flutie 250	35.00
127	Jeff Garcia 250	30.00
128	Tai Streets 250	15.00
129	Shaun Alexander 100	30.00
130	Matt Hasselbeck 200	25.00
131	Warrick Dunn 250	25.00
132	Shaun King 300	18.00
133	Ryan Leaf 300	12.00
134	Eddie George 100	40.00
135	Jevon Kearse 150	30.00
136	Steve McNair 225	25.00
137	Chris Sanders 150	15.00
138	Donnell Bennett 300	12.00
139	Kevin Lockett 250	12.00

2001 Pacific Private Stock Moments In Time

		MT
Complete Set (15):		130.00
Common Player:		8.00
Production 499 Sets		
1	Michael Vick	45.00
2	Travis Henry	10.00
3	Chris Weinke	15.00
4	David Terrell	12.00
5	Anthony Thomas	10.00
6	Quincy Carter	12.00
7	Michael Bennett	20.00
8	Deuce McAllister	12.00
9	Santana Moss	10.00
10	Marques Tuiasosopo	8.00
11	Freddie Mitchell	10.00
12	Drew Brees	30.00
13	LaDainian Tomlinson	30.00
14	Koren Robinson	10.00
15	Rod Gardner	10.00

2001 Pacific Private Stock PS-2001

		MT
Common Player:		.20
1	David Boston	.50
2	Thomas Jones	.20
3	Jake Plummer	.20
4	Jamal Anderson	.20
5	Terance Mathis	.20
6	Elvis Grbac	.20
7	Jamal Lewis	1.00
8	Chris Redman	.20
9	Shannon Sharpe	.40
10	Travis Taylor	.20
11	Rob Johnson	.40
12	Eric Moulds	.20
13	Peerless Price	.40
14	Tim Biakabutuka	.20
15	Patrick Jeffers	.20
16	Muhsin Muhammad	.20
17	James Allen	.20
18	Cade McNown	.40
19	Marcus Robinson	.20
20	Brian Urlacher	1.50
21	Corey Dillon	.40
22	Peter Warrick	.40
23	Tim Couch	1.00
24	Kevin Johnson	.20
25	Dennis Northcutt	.20
26	Travis Prentice	.20
27	Raghib Ismail	.20
28	Emmitt Smith	2.00
29	Mike Anderson	.50
30	Terrell Davis	.50
31	Brian Griese	.50
32	Ed McCaffrey	.20
33	Charlie Batch	.20
34	Johnnie Morton	.20
35	James Stewart	.20
36	Brett Favre	3.00
37	Antonio Freeman	.20
38	Ahman Green	.75
39	Marvin Harrison	.50
40	Jerome Pathon	.20
41	Terrence Wilkins	.20
42	Mark Brunell	.50
43	Keenan McCardell	.20
44	Jimmy Smith	.20
45	Fred Taylor	.50
46	Derrick Alexander	.20
47	Tony Gonzalez	.20
48	Trent Green	.20
49	Sylvester Morris	.20
50	Jay Fiedler	.20
51	Oronde Gadsden	.20
52	Lamar Smith	.20
53	Cris Carter	.50
54	Doug Chapman	.20
55	Daunte Culpepper	2.00
56	Drew Bledsoe	1.00
57	Kevin Faulk	.20
58	Terry Glenn	.20
59	J.R. Redmond	.50
60	Jeff Blake	.20
61	Aaron Brooks	1.00
62	Joe Horn	.20
63	Ricky Williams	1.00
64	Tiki Barber	.20
65	Kerry Collins	.20
66	Ron Dayne	1.00
67	Amani Toomer	.20
68	Curtis Martin	.50
69	Chad Pennington	1.00
70	Vinny Testaverde	.20
71	Tim Brown	.50
72	Rich Gannon	.20
73	Jerry Rice	1.00
74	Tyrone Wheatley	.20
75	Donovan McNabb	.50
76	Duce Staley	.20
77	Jerome Bettis	.50
78	Kordell Stewart	.50
79	Isaac Bruce	.50
80	Marshall Faulk	1.00
81	Az-Zahir Hakim	.20
82	Torry Holt	.50
83	Tim Dwight	.20
84	Doug Flutie	1.00
85	Jeff Garcia	.50
86	Terrell Owens	.50
87	Shaun Alexander	1.00
88	Matt Hasselbeck	.20
89	Darrell Jackson	.20
90	Ricky Watters	.40
91	Mike Alstott	.40
92	Warrick Dunn	.40
93	Brad Johnson	.20
94	Keyshawn Johnson	.40
95	Eddie George	1.00
96	Derrick Mason	.20
97	Steve McNair	.50
98	Stephen Davis	.50
99	Jeff George	.20
100	Michael Westbrook	.20
101	Bobby Newcombe	1.00
102	Alge Crumpler	1.00
103	Vinny Sutherland	1.00
104	Todd Heap	1.00
105	Tim Hasselbeck	1.00
106	Travis Henry	1.00
107	Dee Brown	1.00
108	Dan Morgan	1.00
109	Steve Smith	1.00
110	Chris Weinke	2.00
111	Anthony Thomas	2.50
112	T.J. Houshmandzadeh	1.00
113	Chad Johnson	1.00
114	Rudi Johnson	1.00
115	James Jackson	1.00
116	Quincy Morgan	1.50
117	Quincy Carter	1.50
118	Kevin Kasper	1.00
119	Scotty Anderson	1.00
120	Mike McMahon	2.00
121	Robert Ferguson	1.00
122	Reggie Wayne	1.00
123	Derrick Blaylock	1.00
124	Marvin "Snoop" Minnis	1.50
125	Chris Chambers	2.00
126	Jamar Fletcher	1.00
127	Josh Heupel	1.50
128	Travis Minor	1.00
129	Michael Bennett	2.50
130	Deuce McAllister	2.50
131	Moran Norris	1.00
132	Will Allen	1.00
133	Jonathan Carter	1.00
134	Jesse Palmer	1.00
135	LaMont Jordan	1.00
136	Ken-Yon Rambo	1.00
137	Marques Tuiasosopo	2.00
138	Correll Buckhelter	1.00
139	Freddie Mitchell	2.00
140	Chris Taylor	1.00
141	Adam Archuleta	1.00
142	Francis St. Paul	1.00
143	Kevan Barlow	1.00
144	Cedrick Wilson	1.00
145	Alex Bannister	1.00
146	Josh Booty	1.00
147	Heath Evans	1.00
148	Dan Alexander	1.00
149	Eddie Berlin	1.00
150	Rod Gardner	1.50
151	Darnerian McCants	1.00
152	Sage Rosenfels	1.00

2001 Pacific Private Stock PS-2001 Blue Back

		MT
Complete Set (10):		
Common Player:		
Not priced due to limited production		
153	Michael Vick	
154	David Terrell	
155	Edgerrin James	
156	Peyton Manning	
157	Randy Moss	
158	Santana Moss	
159	Kurt Warner	
160	Drew Brees	
161	LaDainian Tomlinson	
162	Koren Robinson	

2001 Pacific Private Stock Reserve

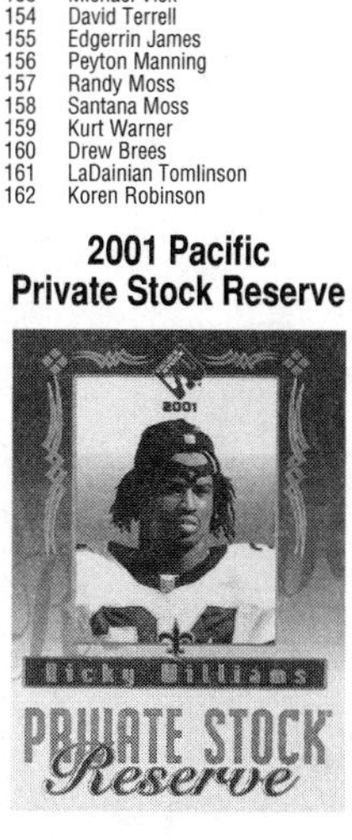

		MT
Complete Set (20):		85.00
Common Player:		3.00
Inserted 1:21		
1	Jamal Lewis	7.00
2	Peter Warrick	5.00
3	Emmitt Smith	8.00
4	Mike Anderson	7.00
5	Terrell Davis	7.00
6	Brian Griese	4.00
7	Brett Favre	12.00
8	Edgerrin James	8.00
9	Peyton Manning	10.00
10	Mark Brunell	4.00
11	Daunte Culpepper	6.00
12	Randy Moss	10.00
13	Drew Bledsoe	4.00
14	Ricky Williams	5.00
15	Ron Dayne	5.00
16	Donovan McNabb	4.00
17	Marshall Faulk	4.00
18	Kurt Warner	10.00
19	Eddie George	4.00
20	Steve McNair	3.00

2001 Pacific Titanium Hobby

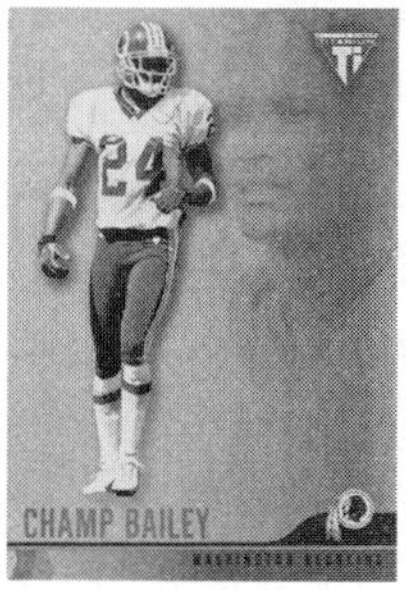

		MT
Complete Set (208):		
Commons		.25
Rookie commons $10.00		
1	David Boston	1.00
2	Thomas Jones	.25
3	Rob Moore	.25
4	Michael Pittman	.25
5	Jake Plummer	.25
6	Jamal Anderson	.50
7	Chris Chandler	.25
8	Shawn Jefferson	.25
9	Terance Mathis	.25
10	Terry Allen	.25
11	Jason Brookins	1.50
12	Elvis Grbac	.25
13	Qadry Ismail	.25
14	Jamal Lewis	2.00
15	Ray Lewis	.50
16	Shannon Sharpe	.50
17	Shawn Bryson	.25
18	Rob Johnson	.25
19	Sammy Morris	.40
20	Eric Moulds	.25
21	Peerless Price	.25
22	Tim Biakabutuka	.25
23	Patrick Jeffers	.25
24	Muhsin Muhammad	.25
25	James Allen	.25
26	Shane Mathews	.25
27	Marcus Robinson	.50
28	Brian Urlacher	2.50
29	Corey Dillon	.50
30	Jon Kitna	.25
31	Akili Smith	.50
32	Peter Warrick	.50
33	Tim Couch	1.25
34	Kevin Johnson	.25
35	Dennis Northcutt	.25
36	Joey Galloway	.25
37	Raghib Ismail	.25
38	Emmitt Smith	2.50
39	Mike Anderson	1.50
40	Terrell Davis	1.50
41	Brian Griese	1.25
42	Ed McCaffrey	.25
43	Rod Smith	.25
44	Charlie Batch	.25
45	Germane Crowell	.25
46	Herman Moore	.25
47	Johnnie Morton	.25
48	James Stewart	.25
49	Brett Favre	4.00
50	Antonio Freeman	.25
51	Ahman Green	.60
52	Bill Schroeder	.25
53	Marvin Harrison	.60
54	Edgerrin James	2.50
55	Peyton Manning	3.00
56	Jerome Pathon	.25
57	Terrence Wilkins	.25
58	Mark Brunell	1.00
59	Keenan McCardell	.25
60	Jimmy Smith	.25
61	Fred Taylor	1.00
62	Derrick Alexander	.25
63	Tony Gonzalez	.25
64	Trent Green	.25
65	Priest Holmes	.60
66	Jay Fiedler	.25
67	Oronde Gadsden	.25
68	James McKnight	.25
69	Lamar Smith	.25
70	Zach Thomas	.60
71	Cris Carter	.60
72	Daunte Culpepper	2.00
73	Randy Moss	3.00
74	Drew Bledsoe	1.00
75	Troy Brown	.25
76	Charles Johnson	.25
77	J.R. Redmond	1.00
78	Antowain Smith	.25
79	Jeff Blake	.25
80	Aaron Brooks	1.00
81	Albert Connell	.25
82	Joe Horn	.25
83	Ricky Williams	1.50
84	Tiki Barber	.25
85	Kerry Collins	.25
86	Ron Dayne	.60
87	Ike Hilliard	.25
88	Amani Toomer	.25
89	Richie Anderson	.25
90	Wayne Chrebet	.25
91	Laveranues Coles	.25
92	Curtis Martin	.60
93	Chad Pennington	.75
94	Vinny Testaverde	.25
95	Tim Brown	.60
96	Rich Gannon	.25
97	Charlie Garner	.25
98	Jerry Rice	2.50
99	Tyrone Wheatley	.25
100	Charles Woodson	.75
101	Donovan McNabb	2.00
102	Todd Pinkston	.25
103	Duce Staley	.25
104	James Thrash	.25
105	Jerome Bettis	.60
106	Plaxico Burress	1.00
107	Tommy Maddox	.25
108	Bobby Shaw	.25
109	Kordell Stewart	.60
110	Hines Ward	.25
111	Isaac Bruce	.60
112	Marshall Faulk	1.50
113	Az-Zahir Hakim	.25
114	Torry Holt	.25
115	Kurt Warner	3.00
116	Curtis Conway	.25
117	Tim Dwight	.25
118	Doug Flutie	1.00
119	Jeff Graham	.25
120	Jeff Garcia	.60
121	Garrison Hearst	.25
122	Terrell Owens	.60
123	J.J. Stokes	.25
124	Tai Streets	.25
125	Shaun Alexander	1.50
126	Matt Hasselbeck	.25
127	Darrell Jackson	.25
128	Ricky Watters	.60
129	Mike Alstott	.60
130	Warrick Dunn	.60
131	Jacquez Green	.25
132	Brad Johnson	.25
133	Keyshawn Johnson	.60
134	Warren Sapp	.50
135	Kevin Dyson	.25
136	Eddie George	1.25
137	Mike Green	.25
138	Jevon Kearse	.25
139	Derrick Mason	.25
140	Steve McNair	.60
141	Champ Bailey	.50
142	Stephen Davis	.75
143	Jeff George	.25
144	Michael Westbrook	.25
145	*Bill Gramatica*	10.00
146	*Arnold Jackson*	10.00
147	*Bobby Newcombe*	10.00
148	*Marcel Shipp*	10.00
149	*Quentin McCord*	10.00
150	*Michael Vick*	175.00
151	*Chris Barnes*	10.00
152	*Todd Heap*	10.00
153	*Reggie Germany*	10.00
154	*Travis Henry*	40.00
155	*Chris Taylor*	10.00
156	*Dee Brown*	10.00
157	*Dan Morgan*	10.00
158	*Steve Smith*	10.00
159	*Chris Weinke*	75.00
160	*David Terrell*	75.00
161	*Anthony Thomas*	175.00
162	*T.J. Houshmandzadeh*	10.00
163	*Chad Johnson*	10.00
164	*Rudi Johnson*	10.00
165	*James Jackson*	40.00
166	*Andre King*	10.00
167	*Quincy Morgan*	40.00
168	*Quincy Carter*	75.00
169	*Ken-Yon Rambo*	10.00
170	*Kevin Kasper*	10.00
171	*Scotty Anderson*	15.00
172	*Mike McMahon*	75.00
173	*Robert Ferguson*	15.00
174	*David Martin*	15.00
175	*Reggie Wayne*	50.00
176	*Richmond Flowers*	10.00
177	*Derrick Blaylock*	10.00
178	*Marvin "Snoop" Minnis*	40.00
179	*Chris Chambers*	75.00
180	*Josh Heupel*	40.00
181	*Travis Minor*	15.00
182	*Michael Bennett*	75.00
183	*Cedric James*	10.00
184	*Deuce McAllister*	75.00
185	*Onomo Ojo*	10.00
186	*Jonathan Carter*	10.00
187	*Jesse Palmer*	25.00
188	*LaMont Jordan*	15.00
189	*Derek Combs*	10.00
190	*Marques Tuiasosopo*	75.00
191	*Correll Buckhalter*	40.00
192	*Freddie Mitchell*	40.00
193	*Adam Archuleta*	10.00
194	*Francis St. Paul*	10.00
195	*Drew Brees*	125.00
196	*LaDainian Tomlinson*	125.00
197	*Kevan Barlow*	40.00
198	*Vinny Sutherland*	10.00
199	*Cedrick Wilson*	10.00
200	*Alex Bannister*	10.00
201	*Koren Robinson*	20.00
202	*Milton Wynn*	10.00
203	*Dan Alexander*	10.00
204	*Eddie Berlin*	10.00
205	*Justin McCareins*	10.00
206	*Rod Gardner*	40.00
207	*Darnerian McCants*	10.00
208	*Sage Rosenfels*	25.00

2001 Pacific Titanium Hobby Double-Sided Jerseys

		MT
Complete Set (125):		
Common Player:		10.00
1	Bobby Newcombe, Arnold Jackson	10.00
2	Marcel Shipp, Bill Gramatica	10.00
3	LaMont Jordan, Rod Gardner	20.00

4 Quentin McCord, Vinny Sutherland 10.00
5 Michael Vick, Quincy Carter 50.00
6 Chris Barnes, Todd Heap 10.00
7 Reggie Germany, Travis Henry 15.00
8 Dee Brown, Steve Smith 10.00
9 Chris Weinke, Josh Heupel 40.00
10 Dan Morgan, Adam Archuleta 10.00
11 David Terrell, Anthony Thomas 50.00
12 T.J. Houshmandzadeh, Chad Johnson 10.00
13 Rudi Johnson, James Jackson 20.00
14 Andre King, Quincy Morgan 15.00
15 Kevin Kasper, Richmond Flowers 10.00
16 Scotty Anderson, Mike McMahon 20.00
17 Robert Ferguson, David Martin 20.00
18 Reggie Wayne, Freddie Mitchell 25.00
19 Derrick Blaylock, Marvin "Snoop" Minnis 20.00
20 Chris Chambers, Travis Minor 40.00
21 Michael Bennett, Cedric James 40.00
22 Deuce McAllister, Onomo Ojo 40.00
23 Jonathan Carter, Jesse Palmer 15.00
24 Derek Combs, Ken-Yon Rambo 10.00
25 Marques Tuiasosopo, Sage Rosenfels 25.00
26 Correll Buckhalter, Dan Alexander 10.00
27 Chris Taylor, Darnerian McCants 10.00
28 Francis St. Paul, Milton Wynn 10.00
29 Drew Brees, LaDainian Tomlinson 50.00
30 Kevan Barlow, Cedrick Wilson 10.00
31 Alex Bannister, Koren Robinson 10.00
32 Eddie Berlin, Justin McCareins 10.00
33 Na Brown, Chad Lewis 10.00
34 Terry Hardy, David Sloan 10.00
35 Tywan Mitchell, Dennis McKinley 10.00
36 Bryan Gilmore, Jermaine Lewis 10.00
37 David Boston, Jimmy Smith 20.00
38 MarTay Jenkins, R. Jay Soward 10.00
39 Thomas Jones, Fred Taylor 20.00
40 Frank Sanders, Terrell Owens 15.00
41 Chris Gedney, Frank Wycheck 10.00
42 Chris Griesen, Neil O'Donnell 10.00
43 Jammi German, Shawn Jefferson 10.00
44 Reggie Kelly, Maurice Smith 10.00
45 Tony Martin, Derrick Alexander 10.00
46 Jamal Anderson, Curtis Martin 15.00
47 Jamal Lewis, Mike Anderson 25.00
48 Shannon Sharpe, Tony Gonzalez 15.00
49 Ray Lewis, Bryan Cox 15.00
50 Elvis Grbac, Kerry Collins 10.00
51 Obafemi Ayanbadejo, Chris Fuamatu-Ma'afala 10.00
52 Antowain Smith, Sammy Morris 10.00
53 Thurman Thomas, J.J. Johnson 15.00
54 Donald Hayes, Chris Hetherington 10.00
55 Isaac Byrd, Reggie White 10.00
56 Brad Hoover, Steve Beuerlein 10.00
57 Tim Biakabutuka, William Floyd 10.00
58 Shane Matthews, Jim Miller 10.00
59 Marcus Robinson, Johnnie Morton 10.00
60 Dez White, Sylvester Morris 10.00
61 Brian Urlacher, Zach Thomas 50.00
62 Clif Groce, Nick Williams 10.00
63 Corey Dillon, Peter Warrick 15.00
64 Damon Griffin, Tremain Mack 10.00
65 Danny Farmer, Craig Yeast 10.00
66 Marco Battaglia, Takeo Spikes 10.00
67 Damay Scott, Bill Schroeder 10.00
68 Kevin Thompson, Jamel White 10.00
69 Tim Couch, Jake Plummer 20.00
70 Kevin Johnson, Antonio Freeman 10.00
71 Dennis Northcutt, Keenan McCardell 10.00
72 Aaron Shea, Marc Edwards 10.00
73 Raghib Ismail, Jason Tucker 10.00
74 Troy Hambrick, Darren Woodson 10.00
75 Jeff Garcia, Warren Moon 20.00
76 Wane McGarity, James McKnight 10.00
77 Emmitt Smith, Eddie George 50.00
78 Dwayne Carswell, Byron Chamberlain 10.00
79 Terrell Davis, Brian Griese 25.00
80 Rod Smith, Oronde Gadsden 10.00
81 Ed McCaffrey, Torry Holt 10.00
82 Germane Crowell, Herman Moore 10.00
83 Larry Foster, Allen Rossum 10.00
84 James Stewart, Robert Smith 10.00
85 Charlie Batch, Steve McNair 15.00
86 Herbert Goodman, De'Mond Parker 10.00
87 Dorsey Levens, Lamar Smith 10.00
88 Brett Favre, Kurt Warner 75.00
89 E.G. Green, Jerome Pathon 10.00
90 Edgerrin James, Peyton Manning 50.00
91 Marvin Harrison, Amani Toomer 15.00
92 Anthony Johnson, Stacey Mack 10.00
93 Mark Brunell, Chris Chandler 20.00
94 Sean Dawkins, Derrick Mayes 10.00
95 Priest Holmes, Charlie Garner 15.00
96 Kimble Anders, Mike Alstott 10.00
97 Leslie Shepherd, Bert Emanuel 10.00
98 O.J. McDuffie, J.J. Stokes 10.00
99 Chris Walsh, Troy Walters 10.00
100 Daunte Culpepper, Randy Moss 50.00
101 Cris Carter, Wayne Chrebet 10.00
102 Charles Johnson, Torrance Small 10.00
103 Drew Bledsoe, Rich Gannon 15.00
104 Damon Huard, Brock Huard 10.00
105 Jeff Blake, Chad Morton 10.00
106 Willie Jackson, Kevin Dyson 10.00
107 Ron Dayne, Tiki Barber 15.00
108 Jason Sehorn, Charles Woodson 15.00
109 Ron Dixon, Az-Zahir Hakim 10.00
110 Chad Pennington, Vinny Testaverde 15.00
111 Tim Brown, Jerry Rice 50.00
112 Andre Rison, Tai Streets 10.00
113 Tyrone Wheatley, Shaun Alexander 20.00
114 Donovan McNabb, Duce Staley 20.00
115 Jerome Bettis, Kordell Stewart 25.00
116 Orlando Pace, Justin Watson 10.00
117 Curtis Conway, Doug Flutie 20.00
118 Fred Beasley, Paul Smith 10.00
119 Christian Fauria, Itula Mili 10.00
120 Darrell Jackson, Ricky Watters 10.00
121 Trent Dilfer, Tony Banks 10.00
122 Rabih Abdullah, Aaron Stecker 10.00
123 Dave Moore, Erron Kinney 10.00
124 Yancey Thigpen, Rodney Thomas 10.00
125 Deion Sanders, Champ Bailey 20.00

2001 Pacific Titanium Hobby Fantasy Football

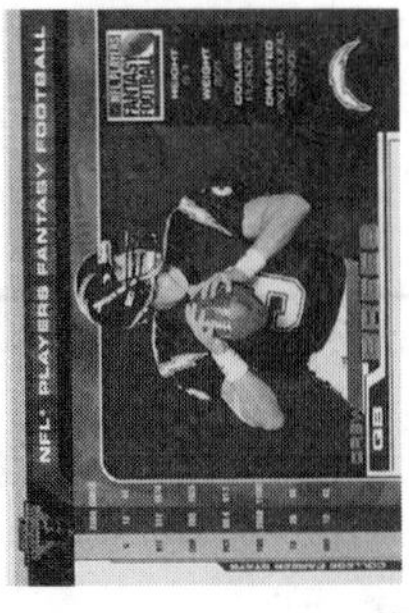

		MT
Complete Set (25):		80.00
Common Player:		2.00
1	Michael Vick	8.00
2	Travis Henry	3.00
3	Chris Weinke	6.00
4	David Terrell	6.00
5	Anthony Thomas	8.00
6	Chad Johnson	2.00
7	James Jackson	3.00
8	Quincy Morgan	3.00
9	Quincy Carter	3.00
10	Kevin Kasper	2.00
11	Reggie Wayne	4.00
12	Marvin "Snoop" Minnis	3.00
13	Chris Chambers	6.00
14	Travis Minor	3.00
15	Michael Bennett	6.00
16	Deuce McAllister	6.00
17	Santana Moss	4.00
18	Marques Tuiasosopo	5.00
19	Correll Buckhalter	2.00
20	Freddie Mitchell	5.00
21	Drew Brees	6.00
22	LaDainian Tomlinson	6.00
23	Kevan Barlow	3.00
24	Koren Robinson	3.00
25	Rod Gardner	5.00

2001 Pacific Titanium Hobby Monday Knights

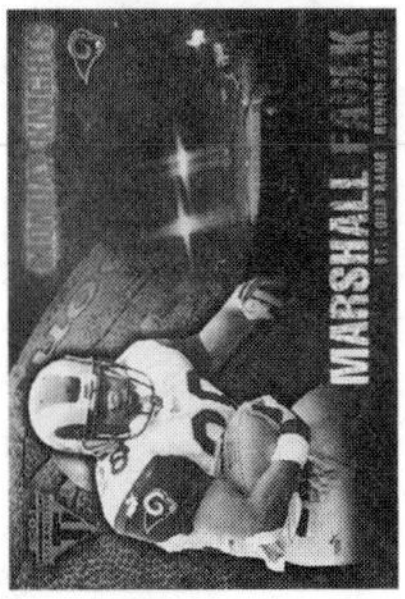

		MT
Complete Set (25):		50.00
Common Player:		1.00
1	Emmitt Smith	5.00
2	Mike Anderson	3.00
3	Terrell Davis	3.00
4	Brian Griese	2.00
5	Rod Smith	1.00
6	Brett Favre	8.00
7	Antonio Freeman	1.00
8	Ahman Green	1.50
9	Edgerrin James	5.00
10	Peyton Manning	6.00
11	Mark Brunell	2.00
12	Jimmy Smith	1.00
13	Fred Taylor	1.00
14	Cris Carter	1.00
15	Daunte Culpepper	4.00
16	Randy Moss	6.00
17	Rich Gannon	1.00
18	Jerry Rice	5.00
19	Donovan McNabb	4.00
20	Duce Staley	2.00
21	Isaac Bruce	1.50
22	Marshall Faulk	3.00
23	Kurt Warner	6.00
24	Eddie George	2.50
25	Steve McNair	1.50

2001 Pacific Titanium Hobby Titanium Team

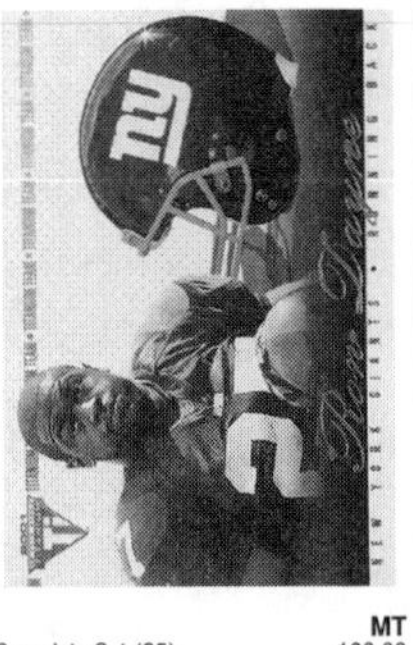

		MT
Complete Set (25):		100.00
Common Player:		2.00
1	Corey Dillon	2.00
2	Peter Warrick	2.00
3	Tim Couch	5.00
4	Emmitt Smith	10.00
5	Mike Anderson	6.00
6	Olandis Gary	2.00
7	Brian Griese	5.00
8	Brett Favre	15.00
9	Edgerrin James	10.00
10	Peyton Manning	12.00
11	Mark Brunell	5.00
12	Fred Taylor	5.00
13	Daunte Culpepper	8.00
14	Randy Moss	12.00
15	Drew Bledsoe	5.00
16	Aaron Brooks	5.00
17	Ricky Williams	5.00
18	Ron Dayne	4.00
19	Jerry Rice	10.00
20	Donovan McNabb	8.00
21	Marshall Faulk	8.00
22	Kurt Warner	12.00
23	Jeff Garcia	2.00
24	Eddie George	5.00
25	Steve McNair	2.00

2001 Pacific Titanium Retail

	MT
Complete Set (216):	
Common Player:	
#'s 1-144 .5X of hobby	
#'s 145-216 .1X of hobby	

2001 Pacific Vanguard

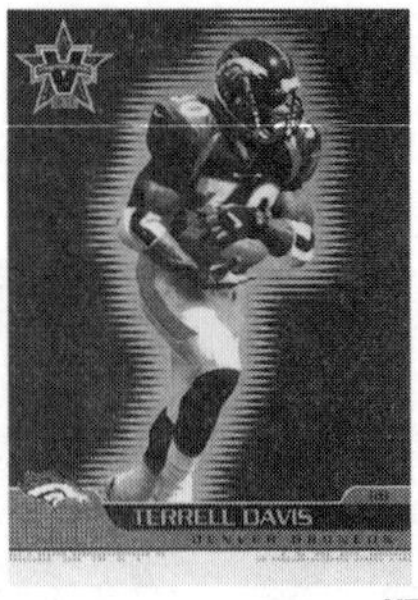

		MT
Complete Set (150):		500.00
Common Player:		.25
Minor Stars:		.50
Common Rookie:		5.00
Production 450 Sets		
Pack (4):		4.00
Wax Box (24):		65.00
1	David Boston	.75
2	Thomas Jones	.75
3	Jake Plummer	.75
4	Jamal Anderson	.75
5	Chris Chandler	.50
6	Elvis Grbac	.75
7	Jamal Lewis	2.00
8	Shannon Sharpe	.50
9	Rob Johnson	.50
10	Eric Moulds	.75
11	Peerless Price	.50
12	Tim Biakabutuka	.50
13	Muhsin Muhammad	.75
14	James Allen	.75
15	Cade McNown	.75
16	Marcus Robinson	.75
17	Corey Dillon	.75
18	Akili Smith	.75
19	Peter Warrick	.75
20	Tim Couch	1.00
21	Kevin Johnson	.75
22	Travis Prentice	.50
23	Raghib Ismail	.50
24	Emmitt Smith	2.00
25	Mike Anderson	2.00
26	Terrell Davis	1.75
27	Brian Griese	1.00
28	Ed McCaffrey	.75
29	Rod Smith	.75
30	Charlie Batch	.75
31	Johnnie Morton	.50
32	James Stewart	.75
33	Brett Favre	3.00
34	Antonio Freeman	.75
35	Ahman Green	.75
36	Bill Schroeder	.50
37	Marvin Harrison	.75
38	Edgerrin James	2.00
39	Peyton Manning	2.50
40	Terrence Wilkins	.50
41	Mark Brunell	1.00
42	Keenan McCardell	.50
43	Jimmy Smith	.75
44	Fred Taylor	1.00
45	Derrick Alexander	.50
46	Tony Gonzalez	.50
47	Sylvester Morris	.75
48	Jay Fiedler	.75
49	Oronde Gadsden	.50
50	Lamar Smith	.50
51	Cris Carter	.75
52	Daunte Culpepper	1.50
53	Randy Moss	2.50
54	Drew Bledsoe	1.00
55	Terry Glenn	.75
56	J.R. Redmond	.75
57	Jeff Blake	.50
58	Joe Horn	.50
59	Ricky Williams	1.25
60	Tiki Barber	.75
61	Kerry Collins	.50
62	Ron Dayne	1.25
63	Amani Toomer	.50
64	Wayne Chrebet	.50
65	Curtis Martin	.75
66	Vinny Testaverde	.50
67	Tim Brown	.50
68	Rich Gannon	.50
69	Tyrone Wheatley	.50
70	Charles Johnson	.25
71	Donovan McNabb	1.25
72	Duce Staley	.75
73	Jerome Bettis	.75
74	Kordell Stewart	.50
75	Hines Ward	.50
76	Isaac Bruce	.75
77	Marshall Faulk	1.00
78	Torry Holt	.75
79	Kurt Warner	2.50
80	Curtis Conway	.50
81	Tim Dwight	.50
82	Doug Flutie	1.00
83	Junior Seau	.50
84	Jeff Garcia	.75
85	Terrell Owens	.75
86	Jerry Rice	2.00
87	Shaun Alexander	1.00
88	Matt Hasselbeck	.75
89	Darrell Jackson	.50
90	Mike Alstott	.75
91	Warrick Dunn	.75
92	Keyshawn Johnson	.75
93	Brad Johnson	.50
94	Kevin Dyson	.25
95	Eddie George	1.00
96	Derrick Mason	.75
97	Steve McNair	.75
98	Stephen Davis	.75
99	Jeff George	.50
100	Michael Westbrook	.50
101	*Bobby Newcombe*	10.00
102	*Alge Crumpler*	10.00
103	*Vinny Sutherland*	10.00
104	*Michael Vick*	60.00
105	*Todd Heap*	10.00
106	*Nate Clements*	5.00
107	*Travis Henry*	25.00
108	*Dan Morgan*	10.00
109	*Chris Weinke*	30.00
110	*David Terrell*	25.00
111	*Anthony Thomas*	50.00
112	*T.J. Houshmandzadeh*	5.00
113	*Chad Johnson*	12.00
114	*Rudi Johnson*	12.00
115	*James Jackson*	15.00
116	*Quincy Morgan*	15.00
117	*Quincy Carter*	25.00
118	*Scotty Anderson*	5.00
119	*Mike McMahon*	10.00
120	*Robert Ferguson*	10.00
121	*Reggie Wayne*	15.00
122	*Marvin "Snoop" Minnis*	15.00
123	*Chris Chambers*	15.00
124	*Jamar Fletcher*	8.00
125	*Josh Heupel*	18.00
126	*Travis Minor*	10.00
127	*Michael Bennett*	30.00
128	*Deuce McAllister*	25.00
129	*Will Allen*	5.00
130	*Jesse Palmer*	10.00
131	*LaMont Jordan*	12.00
132	*Santana Moss*	18.00
133	*Ken-Yon Rambo*	10.00
134	*Marques Tuiasosopo*	25.00
135	*Correl Buckhalter*	15.00
136	*A.J. Feeley*	5.00
137	*Freddie Mitchell*	20.00
138	*Chris Taylor*	5.00
139	*Adam Archuleta*	10.00
140	*Drew Brees*	50.00
141	*LaDainian Tomlinson*	50.00
142	*Kevan Barlow*	15.00
143	*Cedrick Wilson*	8.00
144	*Alex Bannister*	8.00
145	*Josh Booty*	8.00
146	*Heath Evans*	5.00
147	*Koren Robinson*	20.00
148	*Dan Alexander*	8.00
149	*Rod Gardner*	25.00
150	*Sage Rosenfels*	10.00

2001 Pacific Vanguard Bombs Away

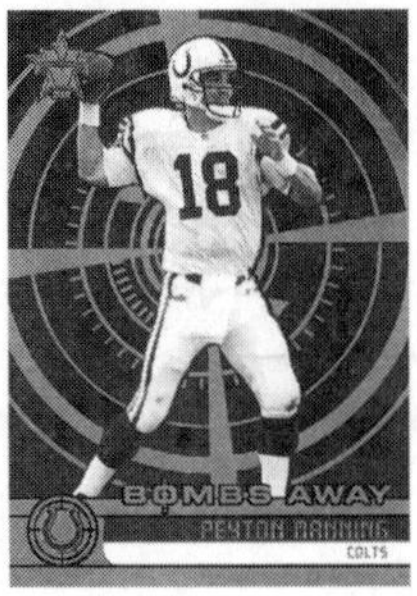

		MT
Complete Set (30):		140.00
Common Player:		3.00
1	Michael Vick	12.00
2	Chris Weinke	10.00
3	Tim Couch	5.00
4	Brian Griese	5.00
5	Brett Favre	15.00
6	Peyton Manning	12.00
7	Mark Brunell	5.00
8	Daunte Culpepper	8.00
9	Drew Bledsoe	5.00
10	Rich Gannon	3.00
11	Donovan McNabb	8.00
12	Kurt Warner	12.00
13	Drew Brees	10.00
14	Jeff Garcia	5.00
15	Steve McNair	5.00
16	Eric Moulds	3.00
17	David Terrell	10.00
18	Peter Warrick	5.00
19	Marvin Harrison	5.00
20	Jimmy Smith	3.00
21	Cris Carter	3.00
22	Santana Moss	5.00
23	Tim Brown	5.00
24	Freddie Mitchell	8.00
25	Isaac Bruce	5.00
26	Torry Holt	3.00
27	Terrell Owens	5.00
28	Jerry Rice	10.00
29	Koren Robinson	5.00
30	Rod Gardner	8.00

2001 Pacific Vanguard Double Sided Jerseys

		MT
Common Player:		12.00
Inserted 2:25		
1	Jake Plummer, David Boston	20.00
2	Rob Moore, Frank Sanders	12.00
3	Thomas Jones, Michael Pittman	12.00
4	Chris Gedney, Ernie Conwell	12.00
5	Chris Griesen, Neil O'Donnell	12.00
6	Chris Chandler, Terance Mathis	12.00
7	Tim Biakabutuka, Steve Beuerlein	15.00
8	Brad Hoover, Moe Williams	12.00
9	Chris Weinke, Freddie Mitchell	45.00
10	Patrick Jeffers, Tim Dwight	20.00
11	Reggie White, Jevon Kearse	20.00
12	Wesley Walls, Frank Wycheck	15.00
13	Bobby Engram, Dez White	12.00
14	Cade McNown, James Allen	20.00
15	Shane Matthews, Jim Miller	15.00
16	Brian Urlacher, Zach Thomas	60.00
17	Anthony Thomas, LaDainian Tomlinson	60.00
18	Corey Dillon, Peter Warrick	25.00
19	Ron Dugans, Danny Farmer	15.00
20	Randall Cunningham, Anthony Wright	12.00
21	Troy Aikman, Emmitt Smith	60.00
22	Wane McGarity, James McKnight	15.00
23	Jason Tucker, Ricky Proehl	12.00
24	Carl Pickens, Kevin Dyson	15.00
25	Brian Griese, Olandis Gary	30.00
26	Dwayne Carswell, Byron Chamberlain	12.00
27	Mike Anderson, Terrell Davis	40.00
28	Gus Frerotte, Matt Hasselbeck	18.00
29	Herman Moore, Johnnie Morton	15.00
30	James Stewart, Larry Foster	15.00
31	Desmond Howard, Tony Martin	12.00
32	Ahman Green, Herbert Goodman	20.00
33	Brett Favre, Antonio Freeman	50.00
34	Dorsey Levens, De'Mond Parker	15.00
35	Tyrone Davis, Bubba Franks	15.00
36	William Henderson, Greg Comella	12.00
37	Autry Denson, J.J. Johnson	12.00
38	Chris Walsh, Troy Walters	12.00
39	Cris Carter, Robert Smith	25.00
40	Daunte Culpepper, Randy Moss	70.00
41	Damon Huard, Bert Emanuel	15.00
42	Jeff Blake, Willie Jackson	15.00
43	Kerry Collins, Joe Jurevicius	15.00
44	Tiki Barber, Ron Dayne	25.00
45	Jason Sehorn, Aeneas Williams	15.00
46	Amani Toomer, Chris Sanders	15.00
47	Tyrone Wheatley, Napoleon Kaufman	15.00
48	Marques Tuiasosopo, Drew Brees	45.00
49	Kurt Warner, Marshall Faulk	50.00
50	Eddie George, Steve McNair	25.00

2001 Pacific Vanguard In Focus

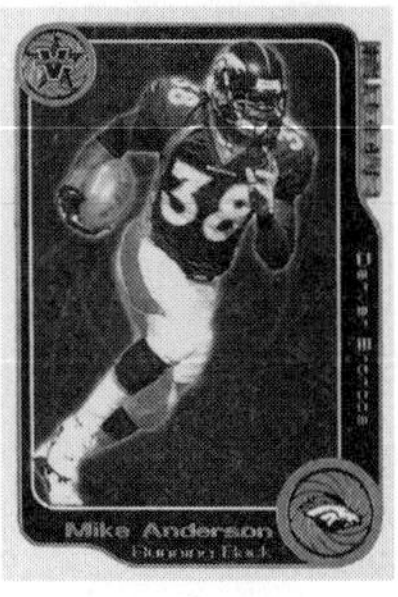

		MT
Common Player:		15.00
Production 99 Sets		
1	Jamal Lewis	25.00
2	Emmitt Smith	30.00
3	Mike Anderson	30.00
4	Terrell Davis	25.00
5	Brett Favre	45.00
6	Edgerrin James	30.00
7	Peyton Manning	35.00
8	Mark Brunell	15.00
9	Daunte Culpepper	25.00
10	Randy Moss	35.00
11	Ricky Williams	20.00
12	Donovan McNabb	20.00
13	Marshall Faulk	15.00
14	Kurt Warner	35.00
15	Jerry Rice	25.00

2001 Pacific Vanguard Prime Prospects

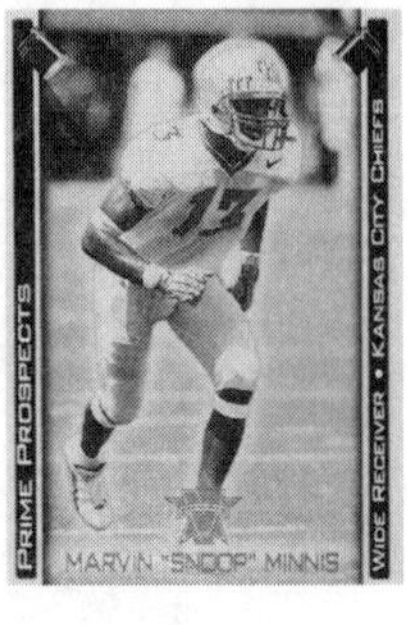

	MT
Complete Set (36):	45.00
Common Player:	.75
Inserted 1:1	
1 Michael Vick	10.00
2 Travis Henry	2.50
3 Dan Morgan	.75
4 Chris Weinke	4.00
5 David Terrell	2.50
6 Anthony Thomas	2.00
7 Chad Johnson	1.00
8 James Jackson	1.25
9 Quincy Morgan	1.50
10 Quincy Carter	2.50
11 Mike McMahon	1.25
12 Robert Ferguson	.75
13 Reggie Wayne	.75
14 Marvin "Snoop" Minnis	1.50
15 Chris Chambers	1.50
16 Josh Heupel	1.75
17 Travis Minor	.75
18 Michael Bennett	5.00
19 Deuce McAllister	2.50
20 Jesse Palmer	.75
21 LaMont Jordan	1.25
22 Santana Moss	1.75
23 Ken-Yon Rambo	.75
24 Marques Tuiasosopo	2.00
25 Correl Buckhalter	1.50
26 Freddie Mitchell	1.75
27 Adam Archuleta	1.00
28 Drew Brees	4.50
29 LaDainian Tomlinson	6.00
30 Kevan Barlow	1.50
31 Cedrick Wilson	.75
32 Alex Bannister	.75
33 Koren Robinson	2.00
34 Dan Alexander	1.00
35 Rod Gardner	2.50
36 Sage Rosenfels	1.00

2001 Pacific Vanguard V-Team

	MT
Complete Set (25):	85.00
Common Player:	2.50
Production 1,499 Sets	
1 Jamal Lewis	6.00
2 Corey Dillon	2.50
3 Peter Warrick	4.00
4 Tim Couch	4.00
5 Emmitt Smith	8.00
6 Mike Anderson	7.00
7 Terrell Davis	7.00
8 Brian Griese	3.50
9 Marvin Harrison	2.50
10 Edgerrin James	8.00
11 Peyton Manning	10.00
12 Mark Brunell	3.50
13 Fred Taylor	3.00
14 Cris Carter	2.50
15 Randy Moss	10.00
16 Drew Bledsoe	3.50
17 Ricky Williams	5.00
18 Ron Dayne	5.00
19 Donovan McNabb	5.00
20 Marshall Faulk	4.00
21 Kurt Warner	10.00
22 Jeff Garcia	2.50
23 Jerry Rice	7.00
24 Eddie George	4.00
25 Steve McNair	2.50

2001 Pacific Vanguard V-Team Rookies

	MT
Complete Set (30):	100.00
Common Player:	2.00
Production 999 Sets	
1 Michael Vick	18.00
2 Travis Henry	6.00
3 Chris Weinke	10.00
4 David Terrell	7.00
5 Anthony Thomas	5.00
6 Chad Johnson	3.00
7 James Jackson	4.00
8 Quincy Morgan	5.00
9 Quincy Carter	6.00
10 Mike McMahon	3.00
11 Robert Ferguson	2.00
12 Reggie Wayne	4.00
13 Marvin "Snoop" Minnis	4.00
14 Chris Chambers	4.00
15 Josh Heupel	5.00
16 Travis Minor	2.50
17 Michael Bennett	12.00
18 Deuce McAllister	6.00
19 Jesse Palmer	2.00
20 LaMont Jordan	3.00
21 Santana Moss	5.00
22 Marques Tuiasosopo	5.00
23 Correl Buckhalter	4.00
24 A.J. Feeley	2.00
25 Freddie Mitchell	5.00
26 Drew Brees	10.00
27 LaDainian Tomlinson	12.00
28 Koren Robinson	5.00
29 Rod Gardner	6.00
30 Sage Rosenfels	3.00

1961 Packers Lake to Lake

The 36-card, 2-1/2" x 3-1/4" set was issued by Lake to Lake out of Sheboygan, Wis. The card fronts feature a player shot with the card number and the player's number, height, weight and college attended. The card backs give offers for premium upgrades, such as a football or a ceramic figurine. Cards 1-8 and 17-24 are much more difficult to obtain.

Complete Set (36):	625.00
Common Player (1-8/17-24):	25.00
Common Player (9-16/25-32):	2.50
Common Player (33-36):	5.00
Common SP:	25.00
1 Jerry Kramer (SP)	45.00
2 Norm Masters (SP)	25.00
3 Willie Davis (SP)	50.00
4 Bill Quinlan (SP)	25.00
5 Jim Temp (SP)	25.00
6 Emlen Tunnell (SP)	45.00
7 Gary Knafelc (SP)	25.00
8 Hank Jordan (SP)	45.00
9 Bill Forester	15.00
10 Paul Hornung	15.00
11 Jesse Whittenton	2.50
12 Andy Cverko	2.50
13 Jim Taylor	10.00
14 Hank Gremminger	2.50
15 Tom Moore	3.00
16 John Symank	2.50
17 Max McGee (SP)	40.00
18 Bart Starr (SP)	85.00
19 Ray Nitschke (SP)	65.00
20 Dave Hanner (SP)	30.00
21 Tom Bettis (SP)	25.00
22 Fuzzy Thurston (SP)	30.00
23 Lew Carpenter (SP)	25.00
24 Boyd Dowler (SP)	30.00
25 Ken Iman	2.50
26 Bob Skoronski	2.50
27 Forrest Gregg	7.50
28 Jim Ringo	7.50
29 Ron Kramer	3.00
30 Herb Adderley	12.00
31 Dan Currie	2.50
32 John Roach	2.50
33 Dale Hackbart	5.00
34 Larry Hickman	5.00
35 Nelson Toburen	5.00
36 Willie Wood	12.00

1966 Packers Mobil Posters

The eight-poster, 11" x 14" set features color action art with blank backs. The posters were available with envelopes which gave the art's title and number.

	NM
Complete Set (8):	80.00
Common Player:	10.00
1 The Pass (Bart Star back to pass)	25.00
2 The Block (Jerry Kramer blocking for Elijah Pitts)	12.00
3 The Punt (Don Chandler punting)	10.00
4 The Sweep (Jim Taylor following blocking)	15.00
5 The Catch (Boyd Dowler)	12.00
6 The Tackle	10.00
7 The Touchdown (Tom Moore scoring)	12.00
8 The Extra Point (Don Chandler with Bart Starr holding)	12.00

1969 Packers Drenks Potato Chip Pins

The 20-pin, 1-1/8" in diameter set were issued by Drenks Potato Chips. The pins have a black and white headshot with green and white backgrounds. "Green Bay Packers" appears on the top edge while the bottom edge has the player's name and position.

	NM
Complete Set (20):	80.00
Common Player:	2.00
1 Herb Adderley	8.00
2 Lionel Aldridge	2.00
3 Donny Anderson	3.00
4 Ken Bowman	2.00
5 Carroll Dale	2.00
6 Willie Davis	8.00
7 Boyd Dowler	3.00
8 Marv Fleming	2.00
9 Gale Gillingham	2.00
10 Jim Grabowski	3.00
11 Forrest Gregg	6.00
12 Don Horn	2.00
13 Bob Jeter	2.00
14 Hank Jordan	8.00
15 Ray Nitschke	10.00
16 Elijah Pitts	3.00
17 Dave Robinson	3.00
18 Bart Starr	16.00
19 Travis Williams	3.00
20 Willie Wood	8.00

1969 Packers Tasco Prints

The seven-piece, 11" x 16" print set features artwork of the player with his name and position, with the backs blank.

	NM
Complete Set (7):	50.00
Common Player:	10.00
1 Donny Anderson	10.00
2 Boyd Dowler	10.00
3 Jim Grabowski	10.00
4 Hank Jordan	15.00
5 Ray Nitschke	25.00
6 Bart Starr	30.00
7 Willie Wood	15.00

1972 Packers Team Issue

The 45-card, 8" x 10" set was printed on glossy paper and featured posed player shots. The card front bottoms have the player's name and position while the backs are blank.

	NM
Complete Set (45):	50.00
Common Player:	2.00
1 Ken Bowman	2.00
2 John Brockington	4.00
3 Bob Brown (DT)	2.00
4 Willie Buchanon	3.00
5 Fred Carr	2.00
6 Jim Carter	2.00
7 Carroll Dale	3.00
8 Carroll Dale (Action pose)	2.00
9 Dan Devine (CO/GM)	3.00
10 Ken Ellis	2.00
11 Len Garrett	2.00
12 Gale Gillingham	2.00
13 Leland Glass	2.00
14 Charlie Hall	2.00
15 Jim Hill	2.00
16 Dick Himes	2.00
17 Bob Hudson (Head shot)	2.00
18 Bob Hudson (Kneeling pose)	2.00
19 Kevin Hunt	2.00
20 Scott Hunter	3.00
21 Dave Kopay	2.00
22 Bob Kroll	2.00
23 Pete Lammons	2.00
24 MacArthur Lane	4.00
25 Bill Lueck	2.00
26 Al Matthews	2.00
27 Mike McCoy	2.00
28 Rich McGeorge	2.00
29 Charlie Napper	2.00
30 Ray Nitschke	10.00
31 Charles Pittman	3.00
32 Malcolm Snider (action pose, Falcons Uniform)	2.00
33 Malcolm Snider (Kneeling pose)	2.00
34 Jon Staggers	2.00
35 Bart Starr	12.00
36 Jerry Tagge	3.00
37 Isaac Thomas (Action pose)	2.00
38 Isaac Thomas (Kneeling pose)	2.00
39 Vern Vanoy	2.00
40 Ron Widby (Action pose, Cowboys uniform)	2.00
41 Ron Widby (Kneeling pose)	2.00
42 Clarence Williams	2.00
43 Perry Williams	2.00
44 Keith Wortman	2.00
45 Coaching Staff (Bart Starr, Hank Kuhlmann, Dave Hanner, Burt Gustafson, John Polonchek, Don Doll, Red Cochran, Dan Devine, Rollie Dotsch)	12.00

1974 Packers Team Issue

The 14-card, 6" x 9" set featured the players in posed shots with facsimile autographs and blank backs.

	NM
Complete Set (14):	25.00
Common Player:	3.00
1 John Brockington	5.00
2 Willie Buchanon	4.00
3 Fred Carr	4.00
4 Jim Carter	4.00
5 Jack Concannon	4.00
6 Bill Curry	5.00
7 John Hadl	5.00
8 Bill Lueck	4.00
9 Chester Marcol	4.00
10 Rich McGeorge	4.00
11 Alden Roche	3.00
12 Barry Smith	3.00
13 Barty Smith	3.00
14 Clarence Williams	3.00

1983 Packers Police

The 19-card, 2-5/8" x 4-1/8" set featured action shots on white card stock with three different card backs: First Wisconsin Bank, Waukesha Police and without First Wisconsin Bank, with the latter one being the most rare set. "Packer Tips" are given on the back.

	MT
Complete Set (19):	20.00
Common Player:	1.00
10 Jan Stenerud	2.00
12 Lynn Dickey	1.50
14 Johnnie Gray	1.00
29 Mike McCoy	1.25
40 Eddie Lee Ivery	1.50
52 George Cumby	1.00
53 Mike Douglass	1.25
54 Larry McCarren	1.00
59 John Anderson	1.25
63 Terry Jones	1.00
64 Sid Kitson	1.00
68 Greg Koch	1.00
80 James Lofton	4.00
82 Paul Coffman	1.50
83 John Jefferson	2.00
85 Phillip Epps	1.50
87 Ezra Johnson	1.00
90 Bart Starr (CO)	4.00

1984 Packers Police

83 • John Jefferson
6-1 Wide Receiver
204 lbs. Arizona State

The 25-card, 2-5/8" x 4" set was sponsored by First Wisconsin Bank, local law enforcement and the Packers. The card backs contain "Packer Tips."

	MT
Complete Set (25):	10.00
Common Player:	.40
1 John Jefferson	.60
2 Forrest Gregg (CO)	2.00
3 John Anderson	.50
4 Eddie Garcia	.40
5 Tim Lewis	.40
6 Jessie Clark	.40
7 Karl Swanke	.40
8 Lynn Dickey	1.00
9 Eddie Lee Ivery	.60
10 Dick Modzelewski (CO) (Defensive Coord.)	.40
11 Mark Murphy	.40
12 Dave Drechsler	.40
13 Mike Douglass	.40
14 James Lofton	2.50
15 Bucky Scribner	.40
16 Randy Scott	.40
17 Mark Lee	.50
18 Gerry Ellis	.40
19 Terry Jones	.40
20 Bob Schnelker (CO) (Offensive Coord.)	.40
21 George Cumby	.40
22 George Cumby	.40
23 Larry McCarren	.40
24 Sid Kitson	.40
25 Paul Coffman	.50

1985 Packers Police

80 • James Lofton
6-3 Wide Receiver
197 lbs. Stanford

The 25-card, 2-3/4" x 4" set, as with the previous year's, was issued by First Wisconsin Bank, local law enforcement and Green Bay and contains "Packer Tips" on the card backs.

	MT
Complete Set (25):	8.00
Common Player:	.40
1 Forrest Gregg (CO)	1.75
2 Paul Coffman	.60
3 Terry Jones	.40
4 Ron Hallstrom	.40
5 Eddie Lee Ivery	.60
6 John Anderson	.40
7 Tim Lewis	.40
8 Bob Schnelker (CO) (Offensive Coord.)	.40
9 Al Del Greco	.40
10 Mark Murphy	.40
11 Tim Huffman	.40
12 Del Rodgers	.40
13 Mark Lee	.40
14 Tom Flynn	.40
15 Dick Modzelewski (CO) (Defensive Corrd.)	.40
16 Randy Scott	.40
17 Bucky Scribner	.40
18 George Cumby	.40
19 James Lofton	2.50
20 Mike Douglass	.50
21 Alphonso Carreker	.40
22 Greg Koch	.40
23 Gerry Ellis	.40
24 Ezra Johnson	.40
25 Lynn Dickey	.75

1986 Packers Police

The 25-card, 2-3/4" x 4" set was sponsored by local law enforcement, First Wisconsin Bank and the Packers. The card backs feature player bios and stats, as well as a safety tip.

	MT
Complete Set (25):	8.00
Common Player:	.35
10 Al Del Greco	.35
12 Lynn Dickey	.60
16 Randy Wright	.60
26 Tim Lewis	.35
31 Gerry Ellis	.35
33 Jessie Clark	.35
37 Mark Murphy	.50
40 Eddie Lee Ivery	.50
41 Tom Flynn	.35
42 Gary Ellerson	.35
55 Randy Scott	.35
58 Mark Cannon	.35
63 John Anderson	.35
65 Ron Hallstrom	.35
67 Karl Swanke	.35
76 Alphonso Carreker	.35
80 James Lofton	1.50
82 Paul Coffman	.50
85 Phillip Epps	.50
90 Ezra Johnson	.50
91 Brian Noble	.50
93 Robert Brown	.35
94 Charles Martin	.35
99 John Dorsey	.35
Forrest Gregg (CO)	1.25

1987 Packers Police

Measuring 2-3/4" x 4", the 22-card set showcased "1987 Packers" at the top, with a photo in the center and the Packers' helmet, player's jersey number and name under the photo. The card backs, printed in green on white paper stock, has the player's name and jersey number at the top, his bio and highlights follow. A safety tip is also included on the back. The cards were sponsored by local law enforcement agencies, the Packers, Employers Health Insurance Co. and Arson Task Force. Approximately 35,000 sets were handed out. Card Nos. 5, 6 and 20 were never distributed as they featured players who were waived or traded before the set was released.

	MT
Complete Set (22):	8.00
Common Player:	.35
1 Forrest Gregg (CO)	1.00
2 George Greene	.35
3 Ron Hallstrom	.35
4 Ezra Johnson	.35
7 Robert Brown	.35
8 Tom Neville	.35
9 Rich Moran	.35
10 Ken Ruettgers	.50
11 Alan Veingrad	.35
12 Mark Lee	.35
13 John Dorsey	.35
14 Paul Ott Carruth	.35
15 Randy Wright	.50
16 Phillip Epps	.50
17 Al Del Greco	.35
18 Tim Harris	1.00
19 Kenneth Davis	1.00
21 John Anderson	.50
22 Mark Murphy	.35
23 Ken Stills	.35
24 Brian Noble	.50
25 Mark Cannon	.35

1988 Packers Police

Measuring 2-3/4" x 4", the 25-card set was anchored by a large photo to on the front, with the player's name, number, height, weight and position listed at the bottom. The Packers' helmet appears in the lower right. The card backs included a Packers' helmet at the top, with a "Packers Tips" boxed in section underneath. The set was sponsored by Copps, Brown County Arson Task Force, local law enforcement agencies and the Packers.

	MT
Complete Set (25):	10.00
Common Player:	.40
1 John Anderson	.50
2 Jerry Boyarsky	.40
3 Don Bracken	.40
4 Dave Brown	.40
5 Mark Cannon	.40
6 Alphonso Carreker	.40
7 Paul Ott Carruth	.40
8 Kenneth Davis	.75
9 John Dorsey	.40
10 Brent Fullwood	.40
11 Tiger Greene	.40
12 Ron Hallstrom	.40
13 Tim Harris	.75
14 Johnny Holland	.50
15 Lindy Infante (CO)	.75
16 Mark Lee	.50
17 Don Majkowski	.75
18 Rich Moran	.40
19 Mark Murphy	.50
20 Ken Ruettgers	.50
21 Walter Stanley	.60
22 Keith Uecker	.40
23 Ed West	.40
24 Randy Wright	.40
25 Max Zendejas	.40

1989 Packers Police

Measuring 2-3/4" x 4", the 15-card set showcases a photo on the card front, with the player's name, jersey number, position and year in the league listed below. The Packers' helmet is at the bottom center. The backs have a Packers Tip boxed in the center, with the Packers' logo at the top. The card number is listed at the bottom center of the text box. The front photo is bordered in yellow, with the card printed on white stock.

	MT
Complete Set (15):	5.00
Common Player:	.35
1 Lindy Infante (CO)	.50
2 Don Majkowski	.60
3 Brent Fullwood	.35
4 Mark Lee	.50
5 Dave Brown	.50
6 Mark Murphy	.50
7 Johnny Holland	.50
8 John Anderson	.50
9 Ken Ruettgers	.50
10 Sterling Sharpe	2.00
11 Ed West	.35
12 Walter Stanley	.50
13 Brian Noble	.50
14 Shawn Patterson	.35

1990 Packers Police

Measuring 2-3/4" x 4", the 20-card set is anchored by a large photo on the front. "Packers '90" is printed at the top, with the player's name, number, position and year in the league listed under the photo. The Packers' helmet is located in the lower left.

	MT
Complete Set (20):	5.00
Common Player:	.25
1 Lindy Infante (CO)	.35
2 Keith Woodside	.25
3 Chris Jacke	.25
4 Chuck Cecil	.35
5 Tony Mandarich	.25
6 Brent Fullwood	.25
7 Robert Brown	.25
8 Scott Stephen	.25
9 Anthony Dilweg	.25
10 Mark Murphy	.25
11 Johnny Holland	.35
12 Sterling Sharpe	1.00
13 Tim Harris	.35
14 Ed West	.25
15 Jeff Query	.25
16 Mark Lee	.25
17 Rich Moran	.25
18 Perry Kemp	.25
19 Brian Noble	.35
20 Don Majkowski	.50

1990 Packers 25th Anniversary

Pacific Trading Cards produced this 45-card standard sized set, while Champion Cards released it. The card fronts feature a 25th Anniversary pennant in the upper left, either a color or sepia-toned photo and the player's name and position. The Packers' helmet is pictured in the lower right corner. The backs feature the player's name, position and number at the top. His bio and career highlights are also listed. The card's number is printed in the lower right.

	MT
Complete Set (45):	10.00
Common Player:	.25
1 Introduction Card	.50
2 Bart Starr	2.00
3 Herb Adderley	.75
4 Bob Skoronski	.25
5 Tom Brown	.35
6 Lee Roy Caffey	.25
7 Ray Nitschke	1.00
8 Carroll Dale	.35
9 Jim Taylor	1.25
10 Ken Bowman	.25
11 Gale Gillingham	.35
12 Jim Grabowski	.50
13 Dave Robinson	.50
14 Donny Anderson	.50
15 Willie Wood	.75
16 Zeke Bratkowski	.50
17 Doug Hart	.25
18 Jerry Kramer	.75
19 Marv Fleming	.35
20 Lionel Aldridge	.35
21 Red Mack (UER) (Text reads returned to football before the following season should be retired)	.25
22 Ron Kostelnik	.25
23 Boyd Dowler	.50
24 Vince Lombardi (CO)	1.25
25 Forrest Gregg	.75
26 Max McGee (Superstar)	.35
27 Fuzzy Thurston	.50
28 Bob Brown (DT)	.35
29 Willie Davis	.75
30 Elijah Pitts	.50
31 Hank Jordan	.75
32 Bart Starr	2.00
33 Super Bowl I (Jim Taylor)	.75
34 1996 Packers	.50
35 Max McGee	.50
36 Jim Weatherwax	.25
37 Bob Long	.25
38 Don Chandler	.35
39 Bill Anderson	.25
40 Tommy Crutcher	.25
41 Dave Hathcock	.25
42 Steve Wright	.25
43 Phil Vandersea	.25
44 Bill Curry	.50
45 Bob Jeter	.35

1991 Packers Police

The green-bordered, 20-card set features a yellow banner in the up-

per left corner of the card front which includes "1991 Packers." The photo is surrounded by a green and yellow border. The player's name and position are printed in the upper right, while his year in the league and his college are printed inside a yellow band at the bottom of the card. The Packers' logo is printed in the lower right of the photo. Numbered "of 20," the card backs feature "1991 Packer Tips." The sponsors' logos appear at the bottom of the standard-sized card backs. Each card back is vertical, except for the Lambeau Field card which is horizontal.

		MT
Complete Set (20):		5.00
Common Player:		.30
1	Lambeau Field	.30
2	Sterling Sharpe	1.00
3	James Campen	.30
4	Chuck Cecil	.40
5	Lindy Infante (CO)	.40
6	Keith Woodside	.30
7	Perry Kemp	.30
8	Johnny Holland	.40
9	Don Majkowski	.40
10	Tony Bennett	.50
11	Leroy Butler	.40
12	Tony Mandarich	.30
13	Darrell Thompson	.40
14	Matt Brock	.30
15	Charles Wilson	.50
16	Brian Noble	.40
17	Ed West	.30
18	Chris Jacke	.30
19	Blair Kiel	.40
20	Mark Murphy	.30

1991 Packers Super Bowl II

The 25th anniversary of the Packers' Super Bowl II victory is honored on this standard-sized 50-card set. The card fronts include a photo which is surrounded by a dark green border. The player's name, Packers' logo and Super Bowl II are located inside a yellow band at the bottom of the card. The card backs feature the player's name, bio and highlights, along with his stats. A photo credit and "Copyright Champion Cards" appear at the bottom left. The card number is printed at the bottom center inside a football.

		MT
Complete Set (50):		10.00
Common Player:		.25
1	Intro Card Super Bowl Trophy	.50
2	Steve Wright	.25
3	Jim Flanigan	.25
4	Tom Brown	.35
5	Tommy Joe Crutcher	.35
6	Doug Hart	.35
7	Bob Hyland	.25
8	John Rowser	.25
9	Bob Skoronski	.25
10	Jim Weatherwax	.25
11	Ben Wilson	.25
12	Don Horn	.35
13	Allen Brown	.25
14	Dick Capp	.25
15	Super Bowl II Action (Donny Anderson)	.50
16	Ice Bowl: The Play (Bart Starr)	1.00
17	Chuck Mercein	.35
18	Herb Adderley	.75
19	Ken Bowman	.25
20	Lee Roy Caffey	.35
21	Carroll Dale	.35
22	Marv Fleming	.35
23	Jim Grabowski	.50
24	Bob Jeter	.35
25	Jerry Kramer	.75
26	Max McGee	.50
27	Elijah Pitts	.50
28	Bart Starr	1.50
29	Fuzzy Thurston	.50
30	Willie Wood	.75
31	Lionel Aldridge	.35
32	Donny Anderson	.50
33	Zeke Bratkowski	.50
34	Bob Brown (DT)	.35
35	Don Chandler	.35
36	Willie Davis	.75
37	Boyd Dowler	.50
38	Gale Gillingham	.35
39	Hank Jordan	.75
40	Ron Kostelnik	.25
41	Vince Lombardi (CO)	1.25
42	Bob Long	.25
43	Ray Nitschke	1.00
44	Dave Robinson	.50
45	Bart Starr (MVP)	1.25
46	Travis Williams	.35
47	1967 Packers Team	.50
48	Ice Bowl Game Summary	.25
49	Ice Bowl	.25
50	NNO Packer Pro Shop	.25

1992 Packers Hall of Fame

This 110-card set, available only at the Packer Hall of Fame Gift Shop, honors 106 members of the Packer Hall of Fame. The card fronts are anchored by a photo inside an oval. The Packers Hall of Fame logo appears in the upper left, with an old Packers' logo in the upper right. The player's name, position and jersey number are included inside a gold rectangle at the bottom of the card, which is bordered in green. Card backs have the player's name in green inside a gold banner at the top. His bio and highlights appear at the center of the horizontal card back. The card number is printed at the bottom center inside a helmet. Card No. 1 does not exist, but two No. 45 cards were printed.

		MT
Complete Set (110):		20.00
Common Player:		.10
2	Red Dunn	.20
3	Mike Michalske	.50
4	Cal Hubbard	.50
5	Johnny (Blood) McNally	.50
6	Verne Lewellen	.10
7	Cub Buck	.10
8	Whitey Woodin	.10
9	Jug Earp	.10
10	Charlie Mathys	.10
11	Andrew Turnbull (PRES)	.10
12	Curly Lambeau (Founder/Coach)	.50
13	George Calhoun (PUB)	.10
14	Boob Darling	.10
15	Eddie Jankowski	.10
16	Swede Johnston	.10
17	George Svendsen	.10
18	Bob Monnett	.10
19	Joe Laws	.10
20	Tiny Engebretsen	.10
21	Milt Gantenbein	.10
22	Hank Bruder	.10
23	Clarke Hinkle	.50
24	Lon Evans	.10
25	Buckets Goldenberg	.10
26	Nate Barrager	.10
27	Arnie Herber	.30
28	Lee Joannes (PRES)	.10
29	Jerry Clifford (VP)	.10
30	Pete Tinsley	.10
31	Buford Ray	.10
32	Andy Uram	.10
33	Larry Craig	.10
34	Charlie Brock	.10
35	Ted Fritsch	.20
36	Lou Brock	.10
37	Carl Mulleneaux	.10
38	Harry Jacunski	.10
39	Cecil Isbell	.30
40	Bud Svendsen	.10
41	Russ Letlow	.10
42	Don Hutson	.75
43	Irv Comp	.10
44	John Martinkovic	.10
45A	Bobby Dillon	.20
45B	Lavern Dilweg (UER) (Back is that of card 45 card, Bobby Dillon)	.50
46	Wilner Burke (Band Director)	.10
47	Dick Wildung	.10
48	Billy Howton	.30
49	Tobin Rote	.30
50	Jim Ringo	.50
51	Deral Teteak	.10
52	Bob Forte	.10
53	Tony Canadeo	.50
54	Al Carmichael	.10
55	Bob Mann	.10
56	Jack Vainisi (Scout)	.10
57	Ken Bowman	.10
58	Bob Skoronski	.10
59	Dave Hanner	.20
60	Bill Forester	.20
61	Fred Cone	.10
62	Lionel Aldridge	.20
63	Carroll Dale	.20
64	Howard Ferguson	.10
65	Gary Knafelc	.10
66	Ron Kramer	.20
67	Forrest Gregg	.50
68	Phil Bengtson (CO)	.10
69	Dan Currie	.10
70	Al Schneider (Contributor)	.10
71	Bob Jeter	.20
72	Jesse Whittenton	.20
73	Hank Gremminger	.10
74	Ron Kostelnik	.10
75	Gale Gillingham	.20
76	Lee Roy Caffey	.20
77	Hank Jordan	.50
78	Boyd Dowler	.30
79	Fred Carr	.20
80	Bud Jorgensen (TR)	.10
81	Eugene Brusky (Team Physician)	.10
82	Fred Trowbridge (Executive Committee)	.10
83	Jan Stenerud	.50
84	Jerry Atkinson (Contributor)	.10
85	Larry McCarren	.10
86	Fred Leicht (Executive Committee)	.10
87	Max McGee	.30
88	Zeke Bratkowski	.30
89	Dave Robinson	.30
90	Herb Adderley	.50
91	Dominic Olejniczak (President)	.20
92	Jerry Kramer	.50
93	Super Bowl I	.20
94	Don Chandler	.10
95	John Brockington	.30
96	Lynn Dickey	.20
97	Bart Starr	1.00
98	Willie Wood	.50
99	Packer Hall of Fame	.20
100	Donny Anderson	.20
101	Chester Marcol	.20
102	Fuzzy Thurston	.20
103	Paul Hornung	.75
104	Jim Taylor	.75
105	Vince Lombardi (CO)	.75
106	Willie Davis	.50
107	Ray Nitschke	.50
108	Elijah Pitts	.20
109	NNO Honor Roll (Checklist Card)	.20
110	NNO Packer Hall of Fame (Catalog Order Form)	.20

1992 Packers Police

This unnumbered 20-card set is anchored by a color photo on the front. The backs of the cards have text printed in green on a white background. The logos of the various sponsors also appear. This set has one of the first cards to feature Brett Favre as a Packer.

		MT
Complete Set (20):		10.00
Common Player:		.25
1	Tony Bennett	.50
2	Matt Brock	.25
3	Leroy Butler	.25
4	Vinnie Clark	.35
5	Brett Favre	6.00
6	Jackie Harris	.50
7	Johnny Holland	.25
8	Mike Holmgren (CO)	1.50
9	Chris Jacke	.25
10	Sherman Lewis (CO)	.25
11	Don Majkowski	.35
12	Tony Mandrich	.25
13	Paul McJulien	.25
14	Brian Noble	.35
15	Bryce Paup	2.00
16	Ray Rhodes (CO)	1.00
17	Tootie Robbins	.25
18	Sterling Sharpe	.75
19	Darrell Thompson	.25
20	Ron Wolf (GM)	.35

1993 Packers Archives Postcards

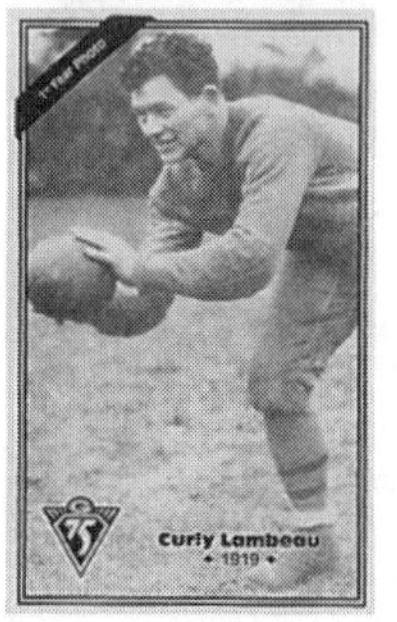

Measuring 3-1/2" x 5-1/2", this 40-postcard set features Packer players from the team's 75-year history. A photo dominates the card fronts, which are bordered in white. Card fronts also include the Packers' 75th anniversary logo and the player's name and year the photo was taken. The horizontal card backs are divided in half, with the player's name, bio and highlights printed on the left side. The right side of the card back includes the Champion Cards' logo printed over the Vince Lombardi Trophy. The card number is printed inside a football at the bottom center.

		MT
Complete Set (40):		10.00
Common Player:		.50
1	The First Team 1919	.75
2	The 1920s	.50
3	The 1930s	.50
4	The 1940s	.50
5	The 1950s	.50
6	The 1960s	.50
7	The 1970s	.50
8	The 1980s	.50
9	The 1990s	.50
10	Curly Lambeau (1919)	.75
11	Jim Ringo (1953)	.75
12	Ice Bowl 1967	.75
13	Jerry Kramer (1958)	.75
14	Ray Nitschke (1958)	1.00
15	Fuzzy Thurston (1959)	.75
16	James Lofton (1978-86)	.75
17	Super Bowl I Action	.75
18	Don Hutson (1935-45)	1.00
19	Tony Canadeo (1941-43, 46-52)	.75
20	Bobby Dillon (1952-59)	.50
21	The Quarterback	.75
22	Willie Wood (1960-71)	.75
23	Dave Beverly (1975-80)	.50
24	James Lofton (1978)	.75
25	Tim Harris (1986-90)	.75
26	1929 Championship Team	.50
27	1930 Championship Team	.50
28	1931 Championship Team	.50
29	1936 Championship Team	.50
30	1939 Championship Team	.50
31	1944 Championship Team	.50
32	1961 Championship Team	.75
33	1962 Championship Team	.75
34	1965 Championship Team	.75
35	1966 Championship Team	.75
36	1967 Championship Team	.75
37	Old City Stadium	.50
38	New City Stadium	.50
39	Lambeau Field-1992	.50
40	NNO Title Card (3-3/4" x 5-3/4")	.75

1993 Packers Police

The 20-card set is bordered in white on the front, with a color photo anchoring it. The Packers' 75th anniversary logo appears inside the photo in the upper left. "Celebrating 75 seasons of Pro Football 1919-1993" is printed under the photo. The vertical card backs have the Packers' helmet in the upper left, with the player's name, position, year in the league and college listed to the right. Elementary students' saftey tips are printed in the center of the card. The card number "of 20" is located under the tip. Various sponsor logos appear at the bottom of the card backs.

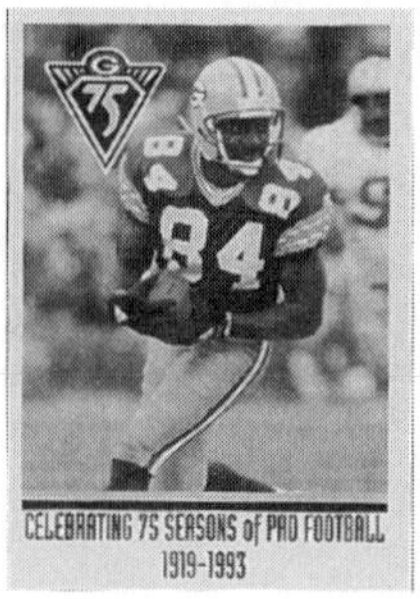

		MT
Complete Set (20):		8.00
Common Player:		.25
1	Ron Wolf (GM)	.25
2	Wayne Simmons	.35
3	James Campen	.25
4	Matt Brock	.25
5	Mike Holmgren (CO)	1.00
6	Brian Noble	.35
7	Ken O'Brien	.35
8	George Teague	.35
9	Brett Favre	4.00
10	LeRoy Butler	.35
11	Harry Galbreath	.25
12	Chris Jacke	.35
13	Sterling Sharpe	.75
14	Terrell Buckley	.35
15	Ken Ruettgers	.35
16	Johnny Holland	.35
17	Edgar Bennett	1.50
18	Jackie Harris	.50
19	Tony Bennett	.50
20	Reggie White	1.50

1994 Packers Police

The 20-card set includes a color photo on the front, with "1994 Green Bay Packers" printed at the top. The player's name and jersey number are printed inside a green band under the photo. Numbered "of 20," the card backs include the Packers' logo in the upper left, with the player's number, name, position, year in the league and college listed to the right. A student tip is printed in the center of the card back. Logos from the various sponsors are printed at the bottom.

		MT
Complete Set (20):		8.00
Common Player:		.30
1	Sherman Lewis	.30
2	Sterling Sharpe	.75
3	Ken Ruettgers	.40
4	Reggie White	1.00
5	Edgar Bennett	1.00
6	Fritz Shurmur (CO)	.40
7	Brett Favre	3.00
8	John Jurkovic	.50
9	Robert Brooks	2.00
10	Reggie Cobb	.30
11	Bryce Paup	.75
12	Harry Galbreath	.30
13	Mike Holmgren (CO)	.50
14	Ed West	.30
15	Sean Jones	.50
16	Ron Wolf (GM)	.30
17	Chris Jacke	.40
18	Wayne Simmons	.40
19	LeRoy Butler	.30
20	George Teague	.40

1995 Packers Safety Fritsch

Produced by Larry Fritsch Cards, the 20-card set showcases a color photo on the front, with "Packers" printed vertically along the left side inside a ghosted area. A 1995 diamond logo is located at the upper left. The player's name and number are printed inside a yellow stripe at the bottom. The cards are bordered in green on the front. Card backs feature the player's name, number, position, year in the league and college at the top, with a student tip printed below it. The card number "of 20" is printed in the lower center, above the various sponsors' names.

		MT
Complete Set (20):		8.00
Common Player:		.30
1	Mike Holmgren (CO)	.40
2	Ron Wolf (VP/GM)	.30
3	Brett Favre	3.00
4	Ty Detmer	1.00
5	Chris Jacke	.50
6	Craig Hentrich	.30
7	Craig Newsome	.30
8	George Teague	.50
9	Edgar Bennett	1.00
10	LeRoy Butler	.30
11	George Koonce	.30
12	John Jurkovic	.50
13	Aaron Taylor	.30
14	Ken Ruettgers	.30
15	Robert Brooks	1.50
16	Mark Chmura	1.50
17	Reggie White	1.00
18	Doug Evans	.30
19	Sean Jones	.50
20	Wayne Simmons	.50

1996 Packers Police

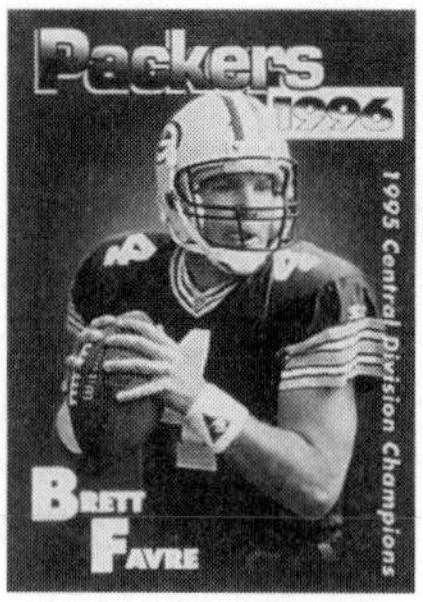

The 20-card standard-sized set features a photo of the player placed over a two-toned green background. "Packers 1996" is featured at the top, while "1995 Central Division Champions" is printed in yellow along the right side of the card. The player's name is printed in yellow in the lower left. The card backs, numbered "of 20," has the player's name position, jersey number and university at the top. A student tip is located in the center, with the card number underneath it. The various sponsors are listed at the bottom.

		MT
Complete Set (20):		8.00
Common Player:		.30
1	Edgar Bennett	.30
2	Robert Brooks	.50
3	Gilbert Brown	.75
4	LeRoy Butler	.30
5	Mark Chmura	.50
6	Santana Dotson	.30
7	Doug Evans	.30
8	Brett Favre	3.00
9	Antonio Freeman	.75
10	Craig Hendricks	.30
11	Chris Jacke	.30
12	Wayne Simmons	.30
13	George Koonce	.30
14	Craig Newsome	.30
15	Ron Wolf	.50
16	Ken Ruettgers	.20
17	Keith Jackson	.30
18	Aaron Taylor	.30
19	Reggie White	1.00
20	Mike Holmgren	.50

1997 Packers Playoff

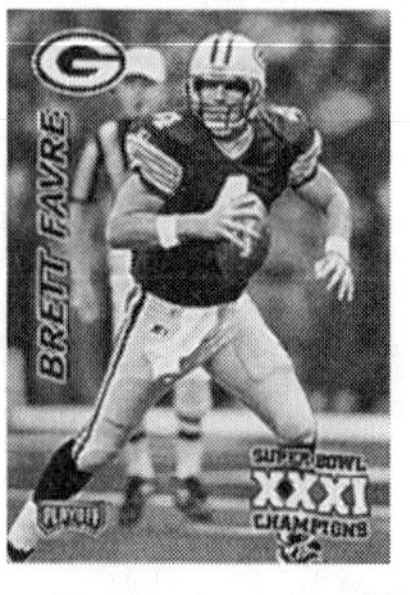

This 50-card set commemorates the Packers' Super Bowl XXXI victory. The card fronts contain a color action shot and the Super Bowl logo. The backs have player information and the final score of the Super Bowl with the Superdome as the background.

		MT
Complete Set (50):		30.00
Common Player:		.40
1	Super Bowl XXXI Champions (Scoreboard Photo)	.50
2	Brett Favre MVP	3.00
3	Minister of Defense (Reggie White)	1.50
4	Desmond Howard MVP	.50
5	NFC Championship Trophy Presentation	.40
6	Mike Holmgren CO	.50
7	Brett Favre	5.00
8	Chris Jacke	.40
9	Craig Hentrich	.40
10	Craig Newsome	.50
11	Dorsey Levens	2.00
12	Doug Evans	.40
13	Edgar Bennett	.50
14	Leroy Butler	.50
15	Eugene Robinson	.40
16	Brian Williams	.50
17	Frank Winters	.40
18	Ron Cox	.40
19	Wayne Simmons	.40
20	Adam Timmerman	.40
21	Bruce Wilkerson	.40
22	Santana Dotson	.50
23	Earl Dotson	.40
24	Aaron Taylor	.40
25	Desmond Howard	.50
26	Don Beebe	.50
27	Andre Rison	.50
28	Antonio Freeman	2.00
29	Terry Mickens	.40
30	Keith Jackson	.50
31	Mark Chmura	1.00
32	Reggie White	1.50
33	Gilbert Brown	.50
34	Sean Jones	.50
35	Robert Brooks, George Koonce	.75
36	Derrick Mayes, Gary Brown	.50
37	Jim McMahon	.50
38	William Henderson	.40
39	Travis Jervey, Roderick Mullen	.50
40	Tyrone Williams	.40
41	John Michels	.50
42	Mike Prior	.40
43	Calvin Jones, Jeff Thomason	.40
44	Brett Favre	3.00
45	Jeff Dellenbach	.40
46	Bernardo Harris	.40
47	Darius Holland	.40
48	Lamont Hollinquest	.40
49	Lindsay Knapp	.40
50	Gabe Wilkins	.40

1997 Packers Police

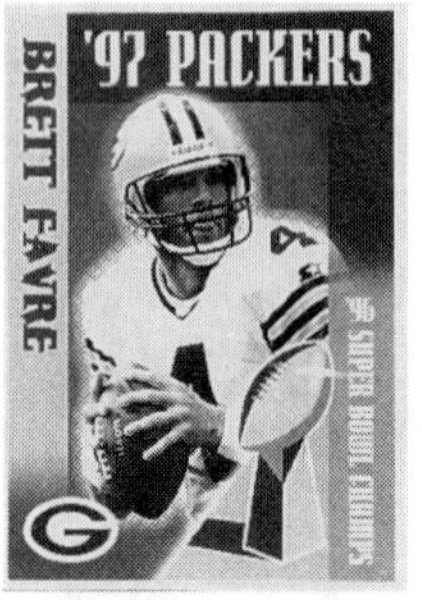

This 20-card Packers set boasts the Vince Lombardi Trophy in the lower right and the words "96 Super Bowl Champs" down the right side. Fronts capture a color photo of the player cut out over a purple background, with the player's name down the left side in a vertical gold strip. Card backs are numbered "of 20" and have the player's name, number, position, college and various sponsors. Included in the background is a photo of the Packers' three Super Bowl trophies.

		MT
Complete Set (20):		8.00
Common Player:		.30
1	Super Bowl XXXI Trophy	.50
2	Mike Holmgren	.50
3	Ron Wolf	.50
4	Brett Favre	3.00
5	Reggie White	1.00
6	LeRoy Butler	.30
7	Frank Winters	.30
8	Aaron Taylor	.30
9	Robert Brooks	.50
10	Gilbert Brown	.75
11	Mark Chmura	.50
12	Earl Dotson	.30
13	Santana Dotson	.30
14	Doug Evans	.30
15	Antonio Freeman	.75
16	William Henderson	.30
17	Craig Hentrich	.30
18	Dorsey Levens	1.00
19	Craig Newsome	.30
20	Edgar Bennett	.30

1988 Panini Stickers

These stickers, which each measure 2-1/8" x 2-3/4", were made to be stored in a special collector's album which was produced. John Elway is featured on the cover of the album, which has the stickers arranged on pages according to the way they are numbered. The sticker number appears on both sides of the sticker. The front of the sticker has a close-up shot of the player, between two team color-coded bars. His team's name is above the photo; his name is below the photo. The stickers were sold in packs which also included one of three types of foil stickers - team name stickers, team helmet stickers, and team uniform stickers. Each team name sticker was produced with a player sticker, listed in parenthesis. Backs for the team name stickers had a referee signal, while helmet foils had a stadium shot and uniform foils had a mascot cartoon on the back.

		MT
Complete Set (447):		35.00
Common Player:		.05
1	Super Bowl XXII Program Cover	.15
2	Bills Helmet	.05
3	Bills Action	.05
4	Cornelius Bennett	.50
5	Chris Burkett	.05
6	Derrick Burroughs	.05
7	Shane Conlan	.25
8	Ronnie Harmon	.25
9	Jim Kelly	.80
10	Buffalo Bills	.05
11	Mark Kelso	.05
12	Nate Odomes	.05
13	Andre Reed	.25

14 Fred Smerlas .05
15 Bruce Smith .25
16 Uniform .05
17 Bengals Helmet .05
18 Bengals Action .05
19 Jim Breech .05
20 James Brooks .10
21 Eddie Brown .10
22 Cris Collinsworth .10
23 Boomer Esiason .20
24 Rodney Holman .10
25 Bengals .05
26 Larry Kinnebrew .05
27 Tim Krumrie .05
28 Anthony Munoz .15
29 Reggie Williams .10
30 Carl Zander .05
31 Uniform .05
32 Browns Helmet .05
33 Browns Action .15
34 Earnest Byner .10
35 Hanford Dixon .05
36 Bob Golic .10
37 Mike Johnson .05
38 Bernie Kosar .30
39 Kevin Mack .10
40 Browns .05
41 Clay Matthews .15
42 Gerald McNeil .05
43 Frank Minnifield .05
44 Ozzie Newsome .15
45 Cody Risien .05
46 Uniform .05
47 Broncos Helmet .05
48 Broncos Action .05
49 Keith Bishop .05
50 Tony Dorsett .35
51 John Elway 1.25
52 Simon Fletcher .25
53 Mark Jackson .10
54 Vance Johnson .10
55 Broncos .05
56 Rulon Jones .05
57 Rick Karlis .05
58 Karl Mecklenburg .10
59 Ricky Nattiel .10
60 Sammy Winder .05
61 Uniform .05
62 Oilers Helmet .05
63 Oilers Action .25
64 Keith Bostic .05
65 Steve Brown .05
66 Ray Childress .15
67 Jeff Donaldson .05
68 John Grimsley .05
69 Robert Lyles .05
70 Oilers .05
71 Drew Hill .10
72 Warren Moon .85
73 Mike Munchak .15
74 Mike Rozier .10
75 Johnny Meads .05
76 Uniform .05
77 Colts Helmet .05
78 Colts Action .15
79 Albert Bentley .10
80 Dean Biasucci .05
81 Duane Bickett .15
82 Bill Brooks .15
83 Johnny Cooks .05
84 Eric Dickerson .40
85 Colts .05
86 Ray Donaldson .05
87 Chris Hinton .10
88 Cliff Odom .05
89 Barry Krauss .10
90 Jack Trudeau .15
91 Uniform .05
92 Chiefs Helmet .05
93 Chiefs Action .05
94 Carlos Carson .05
95 Deron Cherry .10
96 Dino Hackett .05
97 Bill Kenney .05
98 Albert Lewis .10
99 Nick Lowery .10
100 Chiefs .05
101 Bill Maas .05
102 Christian Okoye .15
103 Stephone Paige .10
104 Paul Palmer .05
105 Kevin Ross .05
106 Uniform .05
107 Raiders Helmet .05
108 Raiders Action .25
109 Marcus Allen .35
110 Todd Christensen .15
111 Mike Haynes .15
112 Bo Jackson .60
113 James Lofton .20
114 Howie Long .15
115 Raiders .05
116 Rod Martin .05
117 Vann McElroy .05
118 Bill Pickel .05
119 Don Mosebar .05
120 Stacey Toran .05
121 Uniform .05
122 Dolphins Helmet .05
123 Dolphins Action .05
124 John Bosa .05
125 Mark Clayton .15
126 Mark Duper .10
127 Lorenzo Hampton .05
128 William Judson .05
129 Dan Marino 2.50
130 Dolphins .05
131 John Offerdahl .10
132 Reggie Roby .05
133 Jackie Shipp .05
134 Dwight Stephenson .10
135 Troy Stradford .10
136 Uniform .05
137 Patriots Helmet .05
138 Patriots Action .05
139 Bruce Armstrong .05
140 Raymond Clayborn .05
141 Reggie Dupard .05
142 Steve Grogan .10
143 Craig James .25
144 Ronnie Lippett .05
145 Patriots .05
146 Fred Marion .05
147 Stanley Morgan .15
148 Mosi Tatupu .05
149 Andre Tippett .10
150 Garin Veris .05
151 Uniform .05
152 Jets Helmet .05
153 Jets Action .05
154 Bob Crable .05
155 Mark Gastineau .10
156 Pat Leahy .05
157 Johnny Hector .10
158 Marty Lyons .10
159 Freeman McNeil .15
160 Jets .05
161 Ken O'Brien .10
162 Mickey Shuler .10
163 Al Toon .10
164 Roger Vick .05
165 Wesley Walker .10
166 Uniform .05
167 Steelers Helmet .05
168 Steelers Action .05
169 Walter Abercrombie .05
170 Gary Anderson .05
171 Todd Blackledge .05
172 Thomas Everett .15
173 Delton Hall .05
174 Bryan Hinkle .05
175 Steelers .05
176 Earnest Jackson .10
177 Louis Lipps .10
178 David Little .05
179 Mike Merriweather .10
180 Mike Webster .15
181 Uniform .05
182 Chargers Helmet .05
183 Chargers Action .05
184 Gary Anderson .15
185 Chip Banks .10
186 Martin Bayless .05
187 Chuck Ehin .05
188 Venice Glenn .05
189 Lionel James .05
190 Chargers .05
191 Mark Malone .05
192 Ralf Mojsiejenko .05
193 Billy Ray Smith .10
194 Lee Williams .15
195 Kellen Winslow .15
196 Uniform .05
197 Seahawks Helmet .05
198 Seahawks Action .10
199 Eugene Robinson .05
200 Jeff Bryant .05
201 Ray Butler .05
202 Jacob Green .10
203 Norm Johnson .10
204 Dave Krieg .10
205 Seahawks .05
206 Steve Largent .75
207 Joe Nash .05
208 Curt Warner .10
209 Bobby Joe Edmonds .10
210 Daryl Turner .05
211 Uniform .05
212 AFC Logo .05
213 Bernie Kosar .35
214 Curt Warner .10
215 Jerry Rice, Steve Largent 1.25
216 Mark Bavaro, Anthony Munoz .15
217 Gary Zimmerman, Bill Fralic .10
218 Dwight Stephenson, Mike Munchak .10
219 Joe Montana 3.00
220 Charles White, Eric Dickerson .40
221 Morten Andersen, Vai Sikahema .10
222 Bruce Smith, Reggie White .30
223 Michael Carter, Steve McMichael .10
224 Jim Arnold .05
225 Carl Banks, Andre Tippett .10
226 Barry Wilburn, Mike Singletary .10
227 Hanford Dixon, Frank Minnifield .05
228 Ronnie Lott, Joey Browner .15
229 NFC Logo .05
230 Gary Clark .15
231 Richard Dent .15
232 Falcons Helmet .05
233 Falcons Action .05
234 Rick Bryan .10
235 Bobby Butler .05
236 Tony Casillas .15
237 Floyd Dixon .05
238 Rick Donnelly .05
239 Bill Fralic .10
240 Falcons .05
241 Mike Gann .05
242 Chris Miller .40
243 Robert Moore .05
244 John Rade .05
245 Gerald Riggs .10
246 Uniform .05
247 Bears Helmet .05
248 Bears Action .15
249 Neal Anderson .30
250 Jim Covert .10
251 Richard Dent .15
252 Dave Duerson .05
253 Dennis Gentry .05
254 Jay Hilgenberg .10
255 Bears .05
256 Jim McMahon .20
257 Steve McMichael .10
258 Matt Suhey .05
259 Mike Singletary .20
260 Otis Wilson .10
261 Uniform .05
262 Cowboys Helmet .05
263 Cowboys Action .15
264 Bill Bates .10
265 Doug Crosbie .05
266 Ron Francis .05
267 Jim Jeffcoat .15
268 Ed "Too Tall" Jones .20
269 Eugene Lockhart .05
270 Cowboys .05
271 Danny Noonan .05
272 Steve Pelleur .10
273 Herschel Walker .20
274 Everson Walls .10
275 Randy White .05
276 Uniform .05
277 Lions Helmet .05
278 Lions Action .05
279 Jim Arnold .10
280 Jerry Ball .05
281 Michael Cofer .05
282 Keith Ferguson .05
283 Dennis Gibson .05
284 James Griffin .05
285 Lions .05
286 James Jones .10
287 Chuck Long .10
288 Pete Mandley .05
289 Eddie Murray .05
290 Garry James .05
291 Uniform .05
292 Packers Helmet .05
293 Packers Action .05
294 John Anderson .05
295 Dave Brown .10
296 Alphonso Carreker .05
297 Kenneth Davis .20
298 Phillip Epps .05
299 Brent Fullwood .05
300 Packers .05
301 Tim Harris .15
302 Johnny Holland .10
303 Mark Murphy .05
304 Brian Noble .05
305 Walter Stanley .10
306 Uniform .05
307 Rams Helmet .05
308 Rams Action .05
309 Jim Collins .05
310 Henry Ellard .15
311 Jim Everett .30
312 Jerry Gray .05
313 LeRoy Irvin .05
314 Mike Lansford .05
315 Los Angeles Rams .05
316 Mel Owens .05
317 Jackie Slater .10
318 Doug Smith .05
319 Charles White .10
320 Mike Wilcher .05
321 Uniform .05
322 Vikings Helmet .05
323 Vikings Action .05
324 Joey Browner .10
325 Anthony Carter .15
326 Chris Doleman .15
327 D.J. Dozier .10
328 Steve Jordan .10
329 Tommy Kramer .10
330 Vikings .05
331 Darrin Nelson .10
332 Jesse Solomon .10
333 Scott Studwell .10
334 Wade Wilson .35
335 Gary Zimmerman .05
336 Uniform .05
337 Saints Helmet .05
338 Saints Action .15
339 Morten Andersen .10
340 Bruce Clark .05
341 Brad Edelman .05
342 Bobby Hebert .15
343 Dalton Hilliard .10
344 Rickey Jackson .15
345 Saints .05
346 Vaughan Johnson .10
347 Rueben Mayes .10
348 Sam Mills .10
349 Lionel Manuel .35
350 Dave Waymer .05
351 Uniform .05
352 Giants Helmet .05
353 Giants Action .05
354 Carl Banks .15
355 Mark Bavaro .15
356 Jim Burt .05
357 Harry Carson .10
358 Terry Kinard .05
359 Lionel Manuel .05
360 Giants .05
361 Leonard Marshall .10
362 George Martin .05
363 Joe Morris .10
364 Phil Simms .50
365 George Adams .05
366 Uniform .05
367 Eagles Helmet .05
368 Eagles Action .25
369 Jerome Brown .30
370 Keith Byars .15
371 Randall Cunningham .40
372 Terry Hoage .15
373 Seth Joyner .20
374 Mike Quick .05
375 Eagles .05
376 Clyde Simmons .20
377 Anthony Toney .05
378 Andre Waters .05
379 Reggie White .35
380 Roynell Young .05
381 Uniform .05
382 Cardinals Helmet .05
383 Cardinals Action .05
384 Robert Awalt .05
385 Roy Green .15
386 Neil Lomax .10
387 Stump Mitchell .10
388 Niko Noga .06
389 Freddie Joe Nunn .05
390 Cardinals .05
391 Luis Sharpe .10
392 Vai Sikahema .10
393 J.T. Smith .10
394 Leonard Smith .05
395 Lonnie Young .05
396 Uniform .05
397 49ers Helmet .05
398 49ers Action 1.50
399 Dwaine Board .05
400 Michael Carter .10
401 Roger Craig .25
402 Jeff Fuller .05
403 Don Griffin .05
404 Ronnie Lott .20
405 49ers .05
406 Joe Montana 3.00
407 Tom Rathman .25
408 Jerry Rice 1.50
409 Keena Turner .05
410 Michael Walter .05
411 Uniform .05
412 Bucs Helmet .05
413 Bucs Action .10
414 Mark Carrier .25
415 Gerald Carter .05
416 Ron Holmes .10
417 Rod Jones .05
418 Calvin Magee .05
419 Ervin Randle .05
420 Buccaneers .05
421 Donald Igwebuike .05
422 Vinny Testaverde .25
423 Jackie Walker .05
424 Chris Washington .05
425 James Wilder .10
426 Uniform .05
427 Redskins Helmet .05
428 Redskins Action .10
429 Gary Clark .15
430 Monte Coleman .05
431 Darrell Green .10
432 Charles Mann .10
433 Kelvin Bryant .10
434 Art Monk .25
435 Redskins .05
436 Ricky Sanders .15
437 Jay Schroeder .15
438 Alvin Walton .05
439 Barry Wilburn .10
440 Doug Williams .10
441 Uniform .05
442 Super Bowl Action .05
443 Super Bowl Action .05
444 Doug Williams (Super Bowl MVP) .15
445 Super Bowl Action .05
446 Super Bowl Action .05
447 Super Bowl Action .05
---- Panini Album (John Elway on cover) 2.00

1989 Panini Stickers

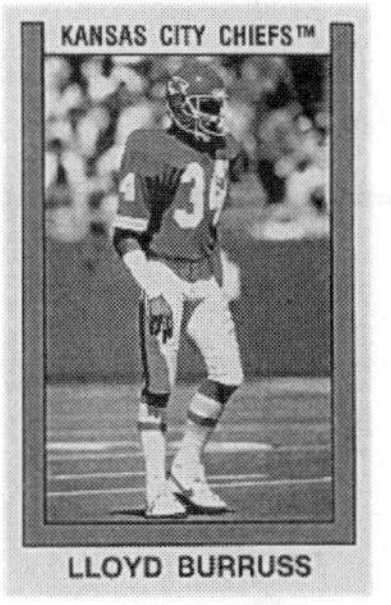

These 1989 stickers from Panini are slightly larger than those issued in 1988, measuring 1-15/16" x 3."

MT
Complete Set (416): 30.00
Common Player: .05
1 SB XXIII Program .10
2 SB XXIII Program .05
3 Floyd Dixon .05
4 Tony Casillas .10
5 Bill Fralic .10
6 Aundray Bruce .05
7 Scott Case .05
8 Rick Donnelly .05
9 Atlanta logo .05
10 Helmet .05
11 Marcus Cotton .05
12 Chris Miller .25
13 Robert Moore .05
14 Bobby Butler .05
15 Rick Bryan .05
16 John Settle .10
17 Jim McMahon .15
18 Neal Anderson .15
19 Dave Duerson .05
20 Steve McMichael .05
21 Jay Hilgenberg .05
22 Dennis McKinnon .05
23 Chicago logo .05
24 Helmet .05
25 Richard Dent .15
26 Dennis Gentry .05
27 Mike Singletary .15
28 Vestee Jackson .05
29 Mike Tomczak .15
30 Dan Hampton .15
31 Michael Irvin 1.75
32 Eugene Lockhart .10
33 Herschel Walker .30
34 Kelvin Martin .15
35 Jim Jeffcoat .10
36 Everson Walls .10
37 Dallas logo .05
38 Helmet .05
39 Danny Noonan .05
40 Ray Alexander .05
41 Garry Cobb .05
42 Ed "Too Tall" Jones .15
43 Kevin Brooks .05
44 Bill Bates .10
45 Detroit logo .05
46 Chuck Long .10
47 Jim Arnold .05
48 Michael Cofer .05
49 Eddie Murray .05
50 Keith Ferguson .05
51 Pete Mandley .05
52 Helmet .05
53 Jerry Ball .05
54 Bennie Blades .15
55 Dennis Gibson .05
56 Chris Spielman .15
57 Eric Williams .05
58 Lomas Brown .10
59 Johnny Holland .10
60 Tim Harris .15
61 Mark Murphy .05
62 Walter Stanley .10
63 Brent Fullwood .05
64 Ken Ruettgers .10
65 Green Bay logo .05
66 Helmet .05
67 John Anderson .05
68 Brian Noble .05
69 Sterling Sharpe 1.50
70 Keith Woodside .10
71 Mark Lee .05
72 Don Majkowski .15
73 Aaron Cox .10
74 LeRoy Irvin .05
75 Jim Everett .15
76 Mike Lansford .05
77 Mike Wilcher .05
78 Henry Ellard .10
79 Rams helmet .05
80 Jerry Gray .05
81 Doug Smith .05
82 Tom Newberry .10
83 Jackie Slater .10
84 Greg Bell .10
85 Kevin Greene .10
86 Chris Doleman .10
87 Steve Jordan .10
88 Jesse Solomon .05
89 Randall McDaniel .05
90 Hassan Jones .10
91 Joey Browner .10
92 Vikings logo .05
93 Helmet .05
94 Anthony Carter .10
95 Gary Zimmerman .05
96 Wade Wilson .15
97 Scott Studwell .10
98 Keith Millard .10
99 Carl Lee .10
100 Morten Andersen .10
101 Bobby Hebert .15
102 Rueben Mayes .10
103 Sam Mills .10
104 Vaughan Johnson .10
105 Pat Swilling .15
106 Saints logo .05
107 Helmet .05
108 Brad Edelman .05
109 Craig Heyward .15
110 Eric Martin .10
111 Dalton Hilliard .10
112 Lonzell Hill .05
113 Rickey Jackson .10
114 Erik Howard .05
115 Phil Simms .35
116 Leonard Marshall .10
117 Joe Morris .10
118 Bart Oates .10
119 Mark Bavaro .10
120 Giants logo .05
121 Helmet .05
122 Terry Kinard .05
123 Carl Banks .10
124 Lionel Manuel .05
125 Stephen Baker .15
126 Pepper Johnson .10
127 Jim Burt .05
128 Cris Carter .35
129 Mike Quick .10
130 Terry Hoage .05
131 Keith Jackson .80
132 Clyde Simmons .15
133 Eric Allen .05
134 Eagles logo .05
135 Helmet .05
136 Randall Cunningham .40
137 Mike Pitts .05
138 Keith Byars .10
139 Seth Joyner .15
140 Jerome Brown .15
141 Reggie White .30
142 Jay Novacek .30
143 Neil Lomax .10
144 Ken Harvey .10
145 Freddie Joe Nunn .05
146 Robert Awalt .05
147 Niko Noga .05
148 Phoenix logo .05
149 Helmet .05
150 Tim McDonald .25
151 Roy Green .10
152 Stump Mitchell .10
153 J.T. Smith .10
154 Luis Sharpe .05
155 Vai Sikhema .10
156 Jeff Fuller .05
157 Joe Montana 3.00
158 Harris Barton .05
159 Michael Carter .10
160 Jeff Fuller .05
161 Jerry Rice 2.00
162 49ers logo .05
163 Helmet .05
164 Tom Rathman .15
165 Roger Craig .20
166 Ronnie Lott .30
167 Charles Haley .15
168 John Taylor .50
169 Michael Walter .05
170 Ron Hall .05
171 Ervin Randle .05
172 James Wilder .10
173 Ron Holmes .05
174 Mark Carrier .15
175 William Howard .05
176 Tampa Bay logo .05
177 Helmet .05
178 Lars Tate .05
179 Vinny Testaverde .20
180 Paul Gruber .05
181 Bruce Hill .10
182 Reuben Davis .05
183 Ricky Reynolds .05
184 Ricky Sanders .15
185 Gary Clark .15
186 Mark May .05
187 Darrell Green .10
188 Jim Lachey .10
189 Doug Williams .10
190 Helmet .05
191 Redskins logo .05
192 Kelvin Bryant .05
193 Charles Mann .05
194 Alvin Walton .05
195 Art Monk .20
196 Barry Wilburn .05
197 Mark Rypien .25
198 NFC logo .05
199 Scott Case .05
200 Herschel Walker .30
201 Herschel Walker, Roger Craig .25
202 Henry Ellard, Jerry Rice .65
203 Bruce Matthews, Tom Newberry .05
204 Gary Zimmerman, Anthony Munoz .10
205 Boomer Esiason .15
206 Jay Hilgenberg .10
207 Keith Jackson .25
208 Reggie White, Bruce Smith .25
209 Keith Millard, Tim Krumrie .10
210 Carl Lee, Frank Minnifield .05
211 Joey Browner, Deron Cherry .10
212 Shane Conlan .10
213 Mike Singletary .15
214 Cornelius Bennett .15
215 AFC logo .05
216 Boomer Esiason .25
217 Erik McMillan .10
218 Jim Kelly .60
219 Cornelius Bennett .15
220 Fred Smerlas .10
221 Shane Conlan .10
222 Scott Norwood .05
223 Mark Kelso .05
224 Bills logo .05
225 Helmet .05
226 Thurman Thomas 1.50
227 Pete Metzelaars .05
228 Bruce Smith .25
229 Art Still .10
230 Kent Hull .10
231 Andre Reed .25
232 Tim Krumrie .05
233 Boomer Esiason .25
234 Ickey Woods .10
235 Eric Thomas .10
236 Rodney Holman .10
237 Jim Skow .05
238 Bengals helmet .05
239 James Brooks .10
240 David Fulcher .10
241 Carl Zander .05
242 Eddie Brown .10
243 Max Montoya .05
244 Anthony Munoz .15
245 Felix Wright .05
246 Clay Matthews .15
247 Hanford Dixon .05
248 Ozzie Newsome .15
249 Bernie Kosar .25
250 Kevin Mack .10
251 Bengals Helmet .05
252 Brian Brennan .05
253 Reggie Langhorne .05
254 Cody Risien .05
255 Webster Slaughter .15
256 Mike Johnson .05
257 Frank Minnifield .05
258 Mike Horan .05
259 Dennis Smith .10
260 Ricky Nattiel .05
261 Karl Mecklenburg .10
262 Keith Bishop .05
263 John Elway 1.50
264 Broncos helmet .05
265 Broncos logo .05
266 Simon Fletcher .15
267 Vance Johnson .10
268 Tony Dorsett .35
269 Greg Kragen .10
270 Mike Harden .05
271 Mark Jackson .05
272 Warren Moon .75
273 Mike Rozier .10
274 Houston logo .05
275 Allen Pinkett .10
276 Tony Zendejas .05
277 Alonzo Highsmith .10
278 Johnny Meads .05
279 Helmet .05
280 Mike Munchak .10
281 John Grimsley .05
282 Ernest Givins .15
283 Drew Hill .10
284 Bruce Matthews .10
285 Ray Childress .10
286 Colts logo .05
287 Chris Hinton .10
288 Clarence Verdin .10
289 Jon Hand .15
290 Chris Chandler .15
291 Eugene Daniel .05
292 Dean Biasucci .05
293 Helmet .05
294 Duane Bickett .10
295 Rohn Stark .05
296 Albert Bentley .10
297 Bill Brooks .10
298 O'Brien Alston .05
299 Ray Donaldson .05
300 Carlos Carson .05
301 Lloyd Burruss .05
302 Steve DeBerg .15
303 Irv Eatman .05
304 Dino Hackett .05
305 Albert Lewis .10
306 Chiefs helmet .05
307 Chiefs logo .05
308 Deron Cherry .10
309 Paul Palmer .05
310 Neil Smith .40
311 Christian Okoye .10
312 Stephone Paige .10
313 Bill Maas .05
314 Marcus Allen .40
315 Vann McElroy .05
316 Mervyn Fernandez .10
317 Bill Pickel .05
318 Greg Townsend .10
319 Tim Brown 1.25
320 Raiders logo .05
321 Helmet .05
322 James Lofton .15
323 Willie Gault .10
324 Jay Schroeder .10
325 Matt Millen .05
326 Howie Long .10
327 Bo Jackson .50
328 Lorenzo Hampton .05
329 Jarvis Williams .05
330 Jim C. Jensen .05
331 Dan Marino 2.50
332 John Offerdahl .10
333 Brian Sochia .05
334 Miami logo .05
335 Helmet .05
336 Ferrell Edmunds .05
337 Mark Brown .05
338 Mark Duper .10
339 Troy Stradford .05
340 T.J. Turner .05
341 Mark Clayton .15
342 Patriots logo .05
343 Johnny Rembert .05
344 Garin Veris .05
345 Stanley Morgan .10
346 John Stephens .15
347 Fred Marion .05
348 Irving Fryar .15
349 Helmet .05
350 Andre Tippett .10
351 Roland James .05
352 Brent Williams .05
353 Raymond Clayborn .05
354 Tony Eason .10
355 Bruce Armstrong .05
356 Jets logo .05
357 Marty Lyons .10

358	Bobby Humphrey	.05
359	Pat Leahy	.05
360	Mickey Shuler	.10
361	James Hasty	.05
362	Ken O'Brien	.10
363	Helmet	.05
364	Alex Gordon	.05
365	Al Toon	.10
366	Erik McMillan	.10
367	Johnny Hector	.10
368	Wesley Walker	.10
369	Freeman McNeil	.10
370	Steelers logo	.05
371	Gary Anderson	.05
372	Rodney Carter	.05
373	Merril Hoge	.10
374	David Little	.05
375	Bubby Brister	.15
376	Thomas Everett	.10
377	Helmet	.05
378	Rod Woodson	.40
379	Bryan Hinkle	.05
380	Tunch Ilkin	.05
381	Aaron Jones	.05
382	Louis Lipps	.10
383	Warren Williams	.05
384	Anthony Miller	.75
385	Gary Anderson	.15
386	Lee Williams	.10
387	Lionel James	.10
388	Gary Plummer	.05
389	Gill Byrd	.10
390	Chargers helmet	.05
391	Ralf Mojsiejenko	.05
392	Rod Bernstine	.25
393	Keith Browner	.05
394	Billy Ray Smith	.10
395	Leslie O'Neal	.15
396	Jamie Holland	.05
397	Tony Woods	.10
398	Bruce Scholtz	.05
399	Joe Nash	.05
400	Curt Warner	.10
401	John L. Williams	.10
402	Bryan Millard	.05
403	Seahawks logo	.05
404	Helmet	.05
405	Steve Largent	.30
406	Norm Johnson	.10
407	Jacob Green	.10
408	Dave Krieg	.10
409	Paul Moyer	.05
410	Brian Blades	.50
411	SB XXIII	.05
412	Jerry Rice	1.50
413	SB XXIII	.10
414	SB XXIII	.10
415	SB XXIII	.10
416	SB XXIII	.10
----	Panini Album (Joe Montana on conver)	4.00

1990 Panini Stickers

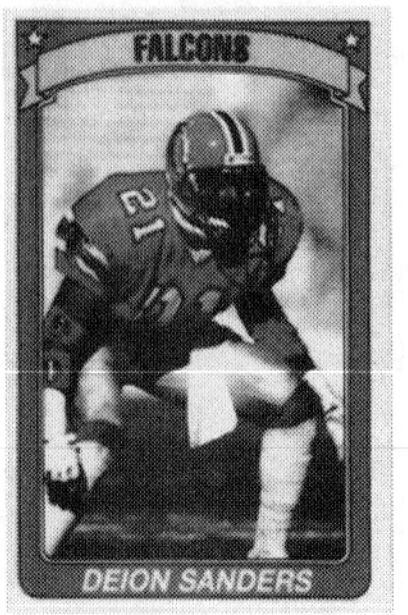

These stickers were intended to be stored in an album titled "The Hitters." Ronnie Lott, Mike Singletary and Lawrence Taylor are featured on the album cover. The stickers measure 1-7/8" x 2-15/16" and have a color action photo on the front, using a design distinctly different from those used the two years before.

		MT
	Complete Set (396):	20.00
	Common Player:	.05
1	Super Bowl XXIV Program Cover (top)	.15
2	Super Bowl XXIV Program Cover (bottom)	.10
3	Bills Crest	.05
4	Thurman Thomas	.50
5	Nate Odomes	.05
6	Jim Kelly	.45
7	Cornelius Bennett	.20
8	Scott Norwood	.05
9	Mark Kelso	.05
10	Kent Hull	.05
11	Jim Ritcher	.05
12	Darryl Talley	.10
13	Bruce Smith	.15
14	Shane Conlan	.10
15	Andre Reed	.15
16	Jason Buck	.05
17	David Fulcher	.10
18	Jim Skow	.05
19	Anthony Munoz	.15
20	Eric Thomas	.05
21	Eric Ball	.05
22	Tim Krumrie	.05
23	James Brooks	.10
24	Bengals Crest	.05
25	Rodney Holman	.05
26	Boomer Esiason	.25
27	Eddie Brown	.10
28	Tim McGee	.10
29	Browns Crest	.05
30	Mike Johnson	.05
31	David Grayson	.05
32	Thane Gash	.05
33	Robert Banks	.05
34	Eric Metcalf	.20
35	Kevin Mack	.10
36	Reggie Langhorne	.05
37	Webster Slaughter	.10
38	Felix Wright	.05
39	Bernie Kosar	.25
40	Frank Minnifield	.05
41	Clay Matthews	.15
42	Vance Johnson	.10
43	Ron Holmes	.05
44	Melvin Bratton	.10
45	Greg Kragen	.05
46	Karl Mecklenburg	.10
47	Dennis Smith	.10
48	Bobby Humphrey	.10
49	Simon Fletcher	.10
50	Broncos Crest	.05
51	Michael Brooks	.05
52	Steve Atwater	.10
53	John Elway	.80
54	David Treadwell	.05
55	Oilers Crest	.05
56	Bubba McDowell	.05
57	Ray Childress	.10
58	Bruce Matthews	.05
59	Allen Pinkett	.10
60	Warren Moon	.55
61	John Grimsley	.05
62	Alonzo Highsmith	.10
63	Mike Munchak	.10
64	Ernest Givins	.10
65	Johnny Meads	.05
66	Drew Hill	.10
67	William Fuller	.05
68	Duane Bickett	.10
69	Jack Trudeau	.10
70	Jon Hand	.10
71	Chris Hinton	.10
72	Bill Brooks	.10
73	Donnell Thompson	.05
74	Jeff Herrod	.10
75	Andre Rison	.25
76	Colts Crest	.05
77	Chris Chandler	.10
78	Ray Donaldson	.05
79	Albert Bentley	.10
80	Keith Taylor	.05
81	Chiefs Crest	.05
82	Leonard Griffin	.05
83	Dino Hackett	.05
84	Christian Okoye	.10
85	Chris Martin	.10
86	John Alt	.05
87	Kevin Ross	.10
88	Steve DeBerg	.10
89	Albert Lewis	.10
90	Stephone Paige	.10
91	Derrick Thomas	.40
92	Neil Smith	.15
93	Pete Mandley	.10
94	Howie Long	.10
95	Greg Townsend	.05
96	Mervyn Fernandez	.10
97	Scott Davis	.05
98	Steve Beuerlein	.40
99	Mike Dyal	.05
100	Willie Gault	.10
101	Eddie Anderson	.05
102	Raiders Crest	.05
103	Trey McDaniel	.05
104	Bo Jackson	.30
105	Steve Wisniewski	.05
106	Steve Smith	.10
107	Dolphins Crest	.05
108	Mark Clayton	.15
109	Louis Oliver	.10
110	Jarvis Williams	.05
111	Ferrell Edmunds	.05
112	Jeff Cross	.05
113	John Offerdahl	.10
114	Brian Sochia	.05
115	Dan Marino	2.00
116	Jim C. Jensen	.05
117	Sammie Smith	.05
118	Reggie Roby	.05
119	Roy Foster	.05
120	Bruce Armstrong	.05
121	Steve Grogan	.10
122	Hart Lee Dykes	.05
123	Andre Tippett	.10
124	Johnny Rembert	.05
125	Ed Reynolds	.05
126	Cedric Jones	.05
127	Vincent Brown	.05
128	Patriots Crest	.05
129	Brent Williams	.05
130	John Stephens	.10
131	Eric Sievers	.05
132	Maurice Hurst	.05
133	Jets Crest	.05
134	Johnny Hector	.05
135	Eric McMillan	.05
136	Jeff Lageman	.05
137	Al Toon	.10
138	James Hasty	.05
139	Kyle Clifton	.05
140	Ken O'Brien	.10
141	Jim Sweeney	.10
142	JoJo Townsell	.10
143	Dennis Byrd	.20
144	Mickey Shuler	.10
145	Alex Gordon	.05
146	Keith Willis	.05
147	Louis Lipps	.10
148	David Little	.05
149	Greg Lloyd	.10
150	Carnell Lake	.10
151	Tim Worley	.10
152	Dwayne Woodruff	.05
153	Gerald Williams	.05
154	Steelers Crest	.05
155	Merril Hoge	.10
156	Bubby Brister	.10
157	Tunch Ilkin	.05
158	Rod Woodson	.15
159	Charger Crest	.05
160	Leslie O'Neal	.10
161	Billy Ray Smith	.05
162	Marion Butts	.15
163	Lee Williams	.10
164	Gill Byrd	.10
165	Jim McMahon	.15
166	Courtney Hall	.05
167	Burt Grossman	.15
168	Gary Plummer	.05
169	Anthony Miller	.40
170	Billy Joe Tolliver	.15
171	Venice Glenn	.05
172	Andy Heck	.05
173	Brian Blades	.15
174	Bryan Millard	.05
175	Tony Woods	.05
176	Rufus Porter	.05
177	Dave Wyman	.05
178	John L. Williams	.10
179	Jacob Green	.05
180	Seahawks Crest	.05
181	Eugene Robinson	.05
182	Jeff Bryant	.05
183	Dave Krieg	.10
184	Joe Nash	.05
185	Christian Okoye	.05
186	Felix Wright	.05
187	Rod Woodson	.10
188	Barry Sanders, Christian Okoye	.75
189	Jerry Rice, Sterling Sharpe	1.00
190	Bruce Matthews	.05
191	Jay Hilgenberg	.05
192	Tom Newbury	.05
193	Anthony Munoz	.10
194	Jim Lachey	.05
195	Keith Jackson	.15
196	Joe Montana	1.50
197	David Fulcher, Ronnie Lott	.10
198	Albert Lewis, Eric Allen	.05
199	Reggie White	.20
200	Keith Millard	.05
201	Chris Doleman	.05
202	Mike Singletary	.15
203	Tim Harris	.05
204	Lawrence Taylor	.20
205	Rich Camarillo	.05
206	Sterling Sharpe	.25
207	Chris Doleman	.05
208	Barry Sanders	.55
209	Falcons Crest	.05
210	Michael Haynes	.30
211	Scott Case	.05
212	Marcus Cotton	.05
213	Chris Miller	.15
214	Keith Jones	.05
215	Tim Green	.05
216	Deion Sanders	.50
217	Shawn Collins	.10
218	John Settle	.05
219	Bill Fralic	.05
220	Aundray Bruce	.05
221	Jessie Tuggle	.05
222	James Thornton	.05
223	Dennis Gentry	.05
224	Richard Dent	.15
225	Jay Hilgenberg	.05
226	Steve McMichael	.05
227	Brad Muster	.10
228	Donnell Woodford	.05
229	Mike Singletary	.15
230	Bears Crest	.05
231	Mark Bortz	.05
232	Kevin Butler	.05
233	Neal Anderson	.10
234	Trace Armstrong	.05
235	Cowboys Crest	.05
236	Mark Tuinei	.10
237	Tony Tolbert	.05
238	Eugene Lockhart	.10
239	Daryl Johnston	.05
240	Troy Aikman	3.00
241	Jim Jeffcoat	.10
242	James Dixon	.05
243	Jesse Solomon	.05
244	Ken Norton	.25
245	Kelvin Martin	.05
246	Danny Noonan	.05
247	Michael Irvin	.50
248	Eric Williams	.05
249	Richard Johnson	.05
250	Michael Cofer	.05
251	Chris Spielman	.10
252	Rodney Peete	.20
253	Bennie Blades	.10
254	Jerry Ball	.05
255	Eddie Murray	.08
256	Lions Crest	.05
257	Barry Sanders	1.75
258	Jerry Holmes	.05
259	Dennis Gibson	.05
260	Lomas Brown	.05
261	Packers Crest	.05
262	Dave Brown	.05
263	Mark Murphy	.05
264	Perry Kemp	.05
265	Don Majkowski	.10
266	Chris Jacke	.05
267	Keith Woodside	.10
268	Tony Mandarich	.10
269	Robert Brown	.05
270	Sterling Sharpe	.75
271	Tim Harris	.10
272	Brent Fullwood	.05
273	Brian Noble	.05
274	Alvin Wright	.05
275	Flipper Anderson	.10
276	Jackie Slater	.10
277	Kevin Greene	.10
278	Pete Holohan	.05
279	Tom Newberry	.05
280	Jerry Gray	.05
281	Henry Ellard	.10
282	Rams Crest	.05
283	LeRoy Irvin	.05
284	Jim Everett	.15
285	Greg Bell	.10
286	Doug Smith	.05
287	Vikings Crest	.05
288	Joey Browner	.10
289	Wade Wilson	.15
290	Chris Doleman	.10
291	Al Noga	.05
292	Herschel Walker	.20
293	Henry Thomas	.05
294	Steve Jordan	.10
295	Anthony Carter	.10
296	Keith Millard	.10
297	Carl Lee	.05
298	Randall McDaniel	.05
299	Gary Zimmerman	.05
300	Morten Andersen	.05
301	Rickey Jackson	.10
302	Sam Mills	.05
303	Hoby Brenner	.05
304	Dalton Hilliard	.05
305	Robert Massey	.05
306	John Fourcade	.10
307	Lonzell Hill	.05
308	Saints Crest	.05
309	Jim Dombrowski	.05
310	Pat Swilling	.15
311	Vaughan Johnson	.05
312	Eric Martin	.10
313	Giants Crest	.05
314	Ottis Anderson	.10
315	Myron Guyton	.05
316	Terry Kinard	.05
317	Mark Bavaro	.10
318	Phil Simms	.25
319	Lawrence Taylor	.30
320	Odessa Turner	.05
321	Erik Howard	.05
322	Mark Collins	.05
323	Dave Meggett	.15
324	Leonard Marshall	.05
325	Carl Banks	.10
326	Anthony Toney	.05
327	Seth Joyner	.15
328	Cris Carter	.20
329	Eric Allen	.05
330	Keith Jackson	.20
331	Clyde Simmons	.10
332	Byron Evans	.05
333	Keith Byars	.10
334	Eagles Crest	.05
335	Reggie White	.25
336	Izel Jenkins	.05
337	Jerome Brown	.15
338	David Alexander	.05
339	Cardinals Crest	.05
340	Rich Camarillo	.05
341	Ken Harvey	.05
342	Luis Sharpe	.05
343	Timm Rosenbach	.10
344	Tim McDonald	.15
345	Vai Sikahema	.05
346	Freddie Joe Nunn	.05
347	Ernie Jones	.05
348	J.T. Smith	.10
349	Eric Hill	.05
350	Roy Green	.10
351	Anthony Bell	.05
352	Kevin Fagan	.05
353	Roger Craig	.15
354	Ronnie Lott	.20
355	Mike Cofer	.05
356	John Taylor	.20
357	Joe Montana	3.00
358	Charles Haley	.10
359	Guy McIntyre	.05
360	49ers Crest	.05
361	Pierce Holt	.15
362	Tom Rathman	.15
363	Jerry Rice	1.50
364	Michael Carter	.10
365	Buccaneers Crest	.05
366	Lars Tate	.05
367	Paul Gruber	.10
368	Winston Moss	.05
369	Reuben Davis	.05
370	Mark Robinson	.05
371	Bruce Hill	.05
372	Kevin Murphy	.05
373	Ricky Reynolds	.05
374	Harry Hamilton	.05
375	Vinny Testaverde	.15
376	Mark Carrier	.15
377	Ervin Randle	.05
378	Ricky Sanders	.10
379	Charles Mann	.10
380	Jim Lachey	.10
381	Wilber Marshall	.10
382	A.J. Johnson	.05
383	Darrell Green	.10
384	Mark Rypien	.15
385	Gerald Riggs	.10
386	Redskins Crest	.05
387	Alvin Walton	.05
388	Art Monk	.15
389	Gary Clark	.15
390	Earnest Byner	.10
391	SB XXIV Action (Jerry Rice)	.75
392	SB XXIV Action (49er Offensive Line)	.15
393	SB XXIV Action (Tom Rathman)	.25
394	SB XXIV Action (Chet Brooks)	.10
395	SB XXIV Action (John Elway)	1.00
396	SB XXIV Action (Joe Montana)	3.00
----	Panini Album	2.00

1995 Panthers SkyBox

The Panthers' inaugural season is commemorated on this 21-card set. The card fronts feature a full-bleed photo, with the player's name and position listed on a team-colored band near the bottom. The Panther logo is featured next to the name. The backs include a photo on the right, with the player's name, bio and highlights inside a box on the left. The card number is printed inside a circle in the upper right. Stats are located in the lower right.

		MT
	Complete Set (21):	15.00
	Common Player:	.75
1	John Kasay	.75
2	Kerry Collins	4.00
3	Frank Reich	1.25
4	Rod Smith	.75
5	Tim McKyer	.75
6	Randy Baldwin	.75
7	Bubba McDowell	.75
8	Tyrone Poole	1.00
9	Sam Mills	1.00
10	Carlton Bailey	.75
11	Darion Conner	.75
12	Lamar Lathon	.75
13	Blake Brockermeyer	1.00
14	Mike Fox	.75
15	Don Beebe	1.00
16	Mark Carrier	1.00
17	Pete Metzelaars	.75
18	Shawn King	.75
19	Howard Griffith	.75
20	Bob Christian	1.00
NNO	Cover Card (checklist back)	.75

1996 Panthers Fleer/SkyBox Impact Promo Sheet

This six-card promo sheet was distributed by Fleer/SkyBox at the NFL Experience Card Show in Charlotte in 1996. It features six players from the Carolina Panthers.

		MT
	Complete Sheet (1):	5.00
	Common Sheet:	5.00
1	Promo Sheet (Tim Biakabutuka, Lamar Lathon, Muhsin Muhammad, Kerry Collins, Tyrone Poole, Mark Carrier WR)	5.00

1974 Parker Brothers Pro Draft

These 50 cards were included inside a Parker Brothers board game called Pro Draft. The cards, featuring only offensive players, were produced by Topps and use the identical design as the 1974 Topps set. However, some differences can be noted on certain cards. Some of the game cards have 1972 statistics on the card backs, and others have different player poses on the front (#s 23, 49, 116, 124, 126 and 127). Players with an * have 1972 statistics. Card numbers in this set are identical to the card numbers the players have in the regular 1974 Topps set.

		NM
	Complete Set (50):	75.00
	Common Player:	1.25
4	Ken Bowman	1.25
6	Jerry Smith	3.00
7	Ed Podolak	2.50
9	Pat Matson	1.25
11	Frank Pitts	2.00
15	Winston Hill	1.25
18	Rich Coady	2.00
19	Ken Willard	3.75
21	Ben Hawkins	2.00
23	Norm Snead (vertical pose)	10.00
24	Jim Yarborough	2.00
28	Bob Hayes	5.00
32	Dan Dierdorf	8.00
35	Essex Johnson	2.00
39	Mike Siani	1.25
42	Del Williams	1.25
43	Don McCauley	2.00
44	Randy Jackson	2.00
46	Gene Washington	3.50
49	Bob Windsor (vertical pose)	6.00
50	John Hadl	4.00
52	Steve Owens	4.00
54	Rayfield Wright	2.00
57	Milt Sunde	2.00
58	Bill Kilmer	5.50
61	Rufus Mayes	2.00
63	Gene Washington	2.50
65	Eugene Upshaw	4.50
75	Fred Willis	2.00
77	Tom Neville	1.25
78	Ted Kwalick	3.00
80	John Niland	2.00
81	Ted Fritsch Jr.	1.25
83	Jack Snow	3.00
87	Mike Phipps	3.00
90	MacArthur Lane	3.00
95	Calvin Hill	3.50
98	Len Rohde	1.25
101	Gary Garrison	2.50
103	Len St. Jean	1.25
107	Jim Mitchell	2.00
109	Harry Schuh	1.25
110	Greg Pruitt	5.00
111	Ed Flanagan	1.25
113	Chuck Foreman	6.00
116	Charlie Johnson (vertical pose)	8.00
119	Roy Jefferson	4.00
124	Forrest Blue (not All-Pro on card)	6.00
126	Tom Mack (not All-Pro on card)	8.00
127	Bob Tucker (not All-Pro on card)	6.00

1989 Parker Brothers Talking Football

Licensed by the NFL Players Association, the 34-card set features a "Superstar Lineup Talking Football" logo in the upper left. Up to three player photos can appear on the front of the card. The NFLPA logo also appears on the front of the card. The backs of the cards, which are unnumbered, include the name of player (s), bio and highlights. The bottom right of the card back carries a Parker Brothers copyright.

		MT
	Complete Set (34):	90.00
	Common Player:	2.00
1	AFC Team Roster	2.00
2	Marcus Allen	5.00
3	Cornelius Bennett, John Offerdahl	3.00
4	Keith Bishop, Mike Munchak	2.00
5	Keith Bostic, Deron Cherry, Hanford Dixon	2.00
6	Carlos Carson, Stanley Morgan	2.00
7	Todd Christensen, Mickey Shuler	2.50
8	Eric Dickerson	4.00
9	Ray Donaldson, Irving Fryar	2.00
10	Jacob Green, Bruce Smith	2.00
11	Mark Haynes, Frank Minnifield, Dennis Smith	2.00
12	Chris Hinton, Anthony Munoz	2.50
13	Steve Largent, Al Toon	5.00
14	Howie Long, Bill Maas	3.00
15	Nick Lowery, Reggie Roby	2.00
16	Dan Marino	25.00
17	Karl Mecklenburg, Andre Tippett	2.50
18	NFC Team Roster	2.00
19	Morten Andersen, Jim Arnold	2.00
20	Carl Banks, Mike Singletary	3.00
21	Mark Bavaro, Doug Cosbie	2.50
22	Joey Browner, Darrell Green, Leonard Smith	2.00
23	Anthony Carter, Jerry Rice	12.00
24	Gary Clark, Mike Quick	4.00
25	Richard Dent, Chris Doleman	3.00
26	Brad Edelman, Bill Fralic	2.00
27	Carl Ekern, Rickey Jackson	2.00
28	Jerry Gray, LeRoy Irvin, Ronnie Lott	2.50
29	Mel Gray, Jay Hilgenberg	3.00
30	Dexter Manley, Reggie White	2.50
31	Rueben Mayes	2.00
32	Joe Montana	20.00
33	Jackie Slater, Gary Zimmerman	2.00
34	Herschel Walker	3.00

1988 Patriots Holsum

Available only in specially marked packages of Holsum Bread, the 12 standard-sized cards feature the Holsum logo in the upper left, with "1988 Annual Collectors' Edition" printed in the upper right. The player photo dominates the front, while the player's name and team are located inside a box beneath the photo. The card backs include the player's facsimile autograph, jersey number, bio and card number "of 12" printed at the top. The remainder of the card back is filled with stats and various logos.

		MT
	Complete Set (12):	40.00
	Common Player:	4.00
1	Andre Tippett	4.00
2	Stanley Morgan	6.00
3	Steve Grogan	6.00
4	Ronnie Lippett	4.00
5	Kenneth Sims	4.00
6	Pete Brock	4.00
7	Sean Farrell	4.00
8	Garin Veris	4.00
9	Mosi Tatupu	4.00
10	Raymond Clayborn	5.00
11	Tony Franklin	4.00
12	Reggie Dupard	4.00

1988 Walter Payton Commemorative

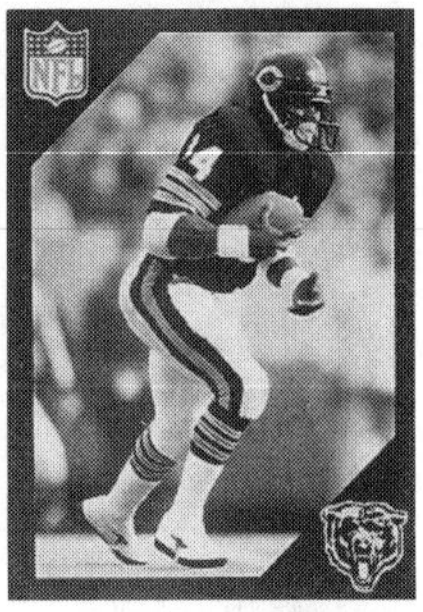

Chicagoland Processing Corp. produced 16,726 of these sets to commemorate the total rushing yards Hall of Fame running back Walter Payton gained during his career with the Chicago Bears. The 132-card set chronicles his illustrious career; each card recaptures a significant moment. The standard-size cards were packaged in a blue plastic box and were issued in conjunction with a soft-cover book titled "Sweetness." Each card front has a dark blue border around an action photo. The Bears' logo and NFL logo are also on the front. The cards are numbered on the back and have a title and text which ties to the photo on the front. The cards are listed by the title used on the back.

		MT
	Complete Set (132):	50.00
	Common Player:	.50
1	Leading Scorer in NCAA History	2.00
2	1975 Game-by-Game	.50
3	Vs. New York Jets	.50
4	Vs. Miami Dolphins	.50
5	Vs. Baltimore/Indianapolis Colts	.50
6	Vs. Buffalo Bills	.50
7	Vs. New England Patriots	.50
8	Vs. Houston Oilers	.50
9	Vs. Pittsburgh Steelers	.50
10	Vs. Cincinnati Bengals	.50
11	Vs. Cleveland Browns	.50
12	Vs. Kansas City Chiefs	.50
13	Vs. Oakland/Los Angeles Raiders	.50
14	Vs. San Diego Chargers	.50
15	Vs. Denver Broncos	.50
16	Vs. Seattle Seahawks	.50

17 Vs. Washington Redskins .50
18 Vs. New York Giants .50
19 Vs. Dallas Cowboys .50
20 Vs. St. Louis Cardinals .50
21 Vs. Philadelphia Eagles .50
22 Vs. New Orleans Saints .50
23 Vs. Atlanta Falcons .50
24 Vs. Los Angeles Rams .50
25 Vs. San Francisco 49ers .50
26 Vs. Detroit Lions .50
27 Vs. Minnesota Vikings .50
28 Vs. Tampa Bay Buccaneers .50
29 Vs. Green Bay Packers .50
30 1976 Game-by-Game .50
31 Appears in Nine Pro Bowls .50
32 Post-Season Stats .50
33 Owns 23 Bear Records .50
34 Season-by-Season Statistics .50
35 1977 Game-by-Game .50
36 Most Yards Gained, Rushing .50
37 Most Combined Yards, Career .50
38 Most Rushing Touchdowns .50
39 Most Games, 100 Yards Rushing, Career .50
40 Consecutive Combined 2000-Yard Seasons .50
41 Most Yards Gained, Rushing, Game .50
42 Most Rushing Attempts, Career .50
43 Most Combined Attempts, Career .50
44 Most Seasons, 1000 Yards Rushing .50
45 1978 Game-by-Game .50
46 Top 10 Average Per Carry Days 1 .50
47 Top 10 Average Per Carry Days 2 .50
48 Top 10 Average Per Carry Days 3 .50
49 Top 10 Average Per Carry Days 4 .50
50 Top 10 Average Per Carry Days 5 .50
51 Top 10 Average Per Carry Days 6 .50
52 Top 10 Average Per Carry Days 7 .50
53 Top 10 Average Per Carry Days 8 .50
54 Top 10 Average Per Carry Days 9 .50
55 Top 10 Average Per Carry Days 10 .50
56 1979 Game-by-Game .50
57 In Training Didn't Play Until 11th Grad .50
58 In Training Running the Hill .50
59 In Training Jumping Rope .50
60 In Training .50
61 Personal Life Interests Include... .50
62 Personal Life Corporate Spokesman .50
63 Personal Life Family Man .50
64 Personal Life Realtives in NFL .50
65 "Sweetness" autobiography written, 1978 .50
66 National Committee, Child Abuse Preven. .50
67 Chicago 1986 Sports Father of the Year .50
68 Active in Many Charities .50
69 Personal Life Parade Grand Marshall .50
70 1980 Game-by-Game .50
71 1976 TSN MFC Player of the Year .50
72 1976 Chicago Red Cloud Athlete of the Y .50
73 1977 UPI Atlete of the Year .50
74 1977 PFWA NFL MVP .50
75 1977 UPI and TSN NFC Player of the Year .50
76 1977 All Pro Pick AP, UPI, and NEA .50
77 1977 PFWA,NEA,Mut.Radio, AP,FB Dig., POT .50
78 TSN NFC All-Star 1976-79 .50
79 TSN NFL All-Star 1980,1984, and 1985 .50
80 1981 Game-by-Game .50
81 As Quarterback .50
82 Kickoff Return .50
83 Complete Player .50
84 Toouchdown .50
85 1982 Game-by-Game .50
86 Most Consecutive Games, Career .50
87 Five Longest Runs .50
88 Pass Receiving .50
89 Ditka on Payton .50
90 1983 Game-by-Game .50
91 Breaks Career Rushing Record .50
92 Breaks Career Rushing .50
93 Breaks Career Rushing .50
94 Breaks Career Rushing .50
95 1984 Game-by-Game .50
96 Bears Win 1985 NFC Champ. over Rams .50
97 Super Bowl XX .50
98 Super Bowl XX .50
99 Super Bowl XX .50
100 Super Bowl XX .50
101 1985 Game-by-Game .50
102 Sweetness .50
103 Sweetness Choice to Pro Bowl Squad 1977 .50
104 Sweetness .50
105 Sweetness 1979 Pro Bowl Starter,AP NFC .50
106 Sweetness .50
107 Sweetness .50
108 Sweetness .50
109 Sweetness .50
110 1986 Game-by-Game .50
111 Final Season Goodbye to Green Bay .50
112 Final Season .50
113 Last Regular Season Home Game .50
114 Last Reg.Season Home Game,Number Retire .50
115 Last Home Game,Presented with Portrait .50
116 Last Regular Season Home Game .50
117 Soldier Field,Known As Payton's Place .50
118 Last Regular Season Home Game .50
119 Last Regular Season Game vs. Raiders .50
120 Last Regular Season Game .50
121 Last Reg. Season Game, Catches 2 Passes .50
122 Last Regular Season Game .50
123 Last Regular Season Game .50
124 Plays 190th Game, Bears All-Time Record .50
125 Last Regular Season Game .50
126 Ends Career with 21,803 Combined Yards .50
127 Finishes w/4542 Career Receiving Yards .50
128 16,726 Career Rushing Yards .50
129 1987 Game-by-Game .50
130 The End of an Era .50
131 Thanks for the Memories .50
132 Last Few Moments 2.00

1976 Pepsi Discs

This set was regionally produced in the Cincinnati area; hence the majority of the discs feature members of the Cincinnati Bengals (#s 21-40). The remaining discs feature top NFL stars. The cards are valued with the tab intact; this is how they are commonly found. The tab was used to hang the disc from a bottle included in six packs of Pepsi products. Each disc is 3-1/2" in diameter and features a player photo, biographical information and 1975 statistics on the front. Discs 1, 5, 7, 8 and 14 are reportedly scarcer than the others because they were short-printed. A free, personalized T-shirt was also offered to those who sent in 200 capliners which read "Pepsi Players." The shirt would picture either Ken Anderson or Archie Griffin, with the collector's first name. It would say "To my buddy xxxx, Best Wishes, Ken Anderson."

		NM
Complete Set (40):		90.00
Common Player:		.50
1	Steve Bartkowski	22.00
2	Lydell Mitchell	1.50
3	Wally Chambers	.50
4	Doug Buffone	.50
5	Jerry Sherk	22.00
6	Drew Pearson	1.00
7	Otis Armstrong	22.00
8	Charlie Sanders	20.00
9	John Brockington	.75
10	Curley Culp	.75
11	Jan Stenerud	1.50
12	Lawrence McCutcheon	.75
13	Chuck Foreman	1.00
14	Bob Pollard	20.00
15	Ed Marinaro	12.00
16	Jack Lambert	5.00
17	Terry Metcalf	.75
18	Mel Gray	.75
19	Russ Washington	.50
20	Charley Taylor	2.50
21	Ken Anderson	2.50
22	Bob Brown	.50
23	Ron Carpenter	.50
24	Tom Casanova	1.25
25	Boobie Clark	1.00
26	Isaac Curtis	1.00
27	Lenvil Elliott	.50
28	Stan Fritts	.50
29	Vernon Holland	.50
30	Bob Johnson	1.00
31	Ken Johnson	.50
32	Bill Kollar	.50
33	Jim LeClair	.75
34	Chip Myers	.75
35	Lemar Parrish	.75
36	Rob Pritchard	.50
37	Bob Trumpy	1.50
38	Sherman White	.50
39	Archie Griffin	1.50
40	John Shinners	.50

1964 Philadelphia

This was Philly's first of four straight 198-card sets, and Philly covered the NFL players while Topps, possibly unable to reach an agreement with the NFL, showcased only American Football League players. For the first time, a card with a team play and a black-and-white photo of the coach was included in a football card set. As would be the case throughout the Philly run, cards are numbered alphabetically by player's last name and by city name. Two checklists appear at the end of each of the four Philly sets. Rookies in this set include John Mackey, Tom Matte, Jack Pardee, Mick Tingelhoff, Irv Cross, and Hall of Famers Herb Adderly, Willie Davis and Merlin Olsen. Making their debut on cards on coaches' issues were Don Shula, Vince Lombardi and Allie Sherman. Second-year cards in the set include Bob Lilly and Jim Marshall. This set held the final regular-issue cards of Gino Marchetti, Night Train Lane, Joe Schmidt, Jerry Kramer, Frank Gifford, Y.A. Tittle, and Bob St. Clair. One error does exist in the set -- card #169 does not picture Garland Boyette as advertised, it's unclear who the player actually is. \

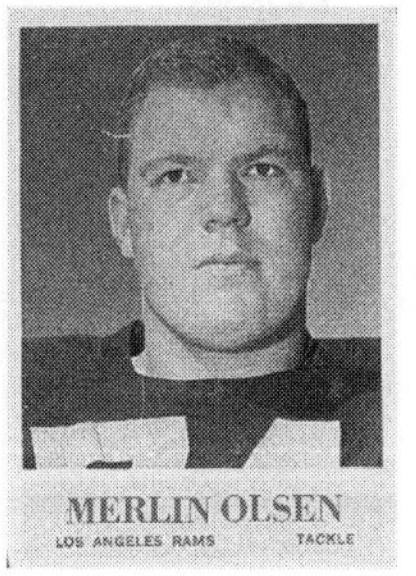

		NM
Complete Set (198):		875.00
Common Player:		1.75
Wax Pack (5):		190.00
1	Raymond Berry	20.00
2	Tom Gilburg	1.75
3	*John Mackey*	25.00
4	Gino Marchetti	4.00
5	Jim Martin	1.75
6	*Tom Matte*	6.00
7	Jimmy Orr	1.75
8	Jim Parker	3.00
9	Bill Pellington	1.75
10	Alex Sandusky	1.75
11	Dick Szymanski	1.75
12	Johnny Unitas	40.00
13	Baltimore Colts Team	1.75
14	Don Shula	25.00
15	Doug Atkins	2.50
16	Ron Bull	1.75
17	Mike Ditka	32.00
18	Joe Fortunato	1.75
19	Willie Galimore	1.75
20	Joe Marconi	1.75
21	*Bennie McRae*	2.00
22	Johnny Morris	1.75
23	*Richie Petitbon*	2.50
24	Mike Pyle	1.75
25	*Roosevelt Taylor*	4.00
26	Bill Wade	1.75
27	Chicago Bears Team	1.75
28	George Halas	10.00
29	Johnny Brewer	1.75
30	Jim Brown	65.00
31	*Gary Collins*	6.00
32	Vince Costello	1.75
33	Galen Fiss	1.75
34	Bill Glass	1.75
35	*Ernie Green*	4.00
36	Rich Kreitling	1.75
37	John Morrow	1.75
38	Frank Ryan	3.00
39	*Charlie Scales*	3.00
40	*Dick Schafrath*	2.00
41	Cleveland Browns Team	1.75
42	Cleveland Browns Play of the Year (Blanton Collier)	1.75
43	Don Bishop	1.75
44	*Frank Clarke*	3.00
45	Mike Connelly	1.75
46	Lee Folkins	1.75
47	*Cornell Green*	5.00
48	Bob Lilly	40.00
49	Amos Marsh	1.75
50	Tommy McDonald	1.75
51	Don Meredith	35.00
52	*Pettis Norman*	2.00
53	Don Perkins	2.00
54	Guy Resse	1.75
55	Dallas Cowboys Team	1.75
56	Tom Landry	12.00
57	Terry Barr	1.75
58	Roger Brown	1.75
59	Gail Cogdill	1.75
60	John Gordy	1.75
61	Dick Lane	4.00
62	Yale Lary	4.00
63	Dan Lewis	1.75
64	Darris McCord	1.75
65	Earl Morrall	5.00
66	Joe Schmidt	4.00
67	*Pat Studstill*	4.00
68	*Wayne Walker*	4.00
69	Detroit Lions Team	1.75
70	Detroit Lions Player of the Year (George Wilson)	1.75
71	*Herb Adderley*	30.00
72	*Willie Davis*	30.00
73	Forrest Gregg	4.00
74	Paul Hornung	25.00
75	Henry Jordan	1.75
76	Jerry Kramer	5.00
77	Tom Moore	1.75
78	Jim Ringo	4.00
79	Bart Starr	40.00
80	Jim Taylor	15.00
81	*Jess Whittenton*	2.50
82	Willie Wood	8.00
83	Green Bay Packers Team	1.75
84	Vince Lombardi	24.00
85	Jon Arnett	1.75
86	*Pervis Atkins*	2.00
87	Dick Bass	1.75
88	Carroll Dale	1.75
89	Roman Gabriel	6.00
90	Ed Meador	1.75
91	*Merlin Olsen*	50.00
92	*Jack Pardee*	7.00
93	Jim Phillips	1.75
94	Carver Shannon	1.75
95	Frank Varrichione	1.75
96	Danny Villanueva	1.75
97	Los Angeles Rams team	1.75
98	Los Angeles Rams Play of the Year (Harland Svare)	1.75
99	*Grady Alderman*	2.00
100	Larry Bowie	1.75
101	*Bill Brown*	5.00
102	*Paul Flatley*	2.00
103	Rip Hawkins	1.75
104	Jim Marshall	8.00
105	Tommy Mason	1.75
106	Jim Prestel	1.75
107	Jerry Reichow	1.75
108	Ed Sharockman	1.75
109	Fran Tarkenton	30.00
110	*Mick Tingelhoff*	8.00
111	Minnesota Vikings Team	1.75
112	Norm Van Brocklin	4.00
113	Erich Barnes	1.75
114	Roosevelt Brown	3.00
115	Don Chandler	1.75
116	Darrell Dess	1.75
117	Frank Gifford	45.00
118	Dick James	1.75
119	Jim Katcavage	1.75
120	John Lovetere	1.75
121	*Dick Lynch*	2.00
122	Jim Patton	1.75
123	Del Shofner	1.75
124	Y.A. Tittle	20.00
125	New York Giants Team	1.75
126	Player of the year (Allie Sherman)	1.75
127	Sam Baker	1.75
128	Maxie Baughan	1.75
129	Timmy Brown	1.75
130	Mike Clark	1.75
131	*Irv Cross*	6.00
132	Ted Dean	1.75
133	Ron Goodwin	1.75
134	King Hill	1.75
135	Clarence Peaks	1.75
136	Pete Retzlaff	1.75
137	Jim Schrader	1.75
138	Norm Snead	3.00
139	Philadelphia Eagles Team	1.75
140	Philadelphia Eagles Play of the Year (Joe Kuharich)	1.75
141	*Gary Ballman*	3.00
142	Charley Bradshaw	1.75
143	Ed Brown	1.75
144	John Henry Johnson	5.00
145	Joe Krupa	1.75
146	Bill Mack	1.75
147	Lou Michaels	1.75
148	Buzz Nutter	1.75
149	Myron Pottios	1.75
150	John Reger	1.75
151	Mike Sandusky	1.75
152	Clendon Thomas	1.75
153	Pittsburgh Steelers Team	1.75
154	Pittsburgh Steelers Play of the Year (Buddy Parker)	1.75
155	*Kermit Alexander*	3.00
156	Bernie Casey	1.75
157	Dan Colchico	1.75
158	Clyde Conner	1.75
159	Tommy Davis	1.75
160	Matt Hazeltine	1.75
161	*Jim Johnson*	15.00
162	*Don Lisbon*	2.00
163	Lamar McHan	1.75
164	Bob St. Clair	4.00
165	J.D. Smith	1.75
166	Abe Woodson	1.75
167	San Francisco 49ers Team	1.75
168	San Francisco 49ers Play of the Year (Red Hickey)	1.75
169	Garland Boyette	1.75
170	Bobby Joe Conrad	1.75
171	*Bob DeMarco*	3.00
172	*Ken Gray*	3.00
173	Jimmy Hill	1.75
174	Charlie Johnson	3.00
175	Ernie McMillan	1.75
176	Dale Meinert	1.75
177	Luke Owens	1.75
178	Sonny Randle	1.75
179	Joe Robb	1.75
180	Bill Stacy	1.75
181	St. Louis Cardinals Team	1.75
182	St. Louis Cardinals Play of the Year (Wally Lem)	1.75
183	Bill Barnes	1.75
184	Don Bosseler	1.75
185	Sam Huff	6.00
186	Sonny Jurgensen	18.00
187	Ed Khayat	1.75
188	Riley Mattson	1.75
189	Bobby Mitchell	6.00
190	John Nisby	1.75
191	Vince Promuto	1.75
192	Joe Rutgens	1.75
193	Lonnie Sanders	1.75
194	Jim Steffen	1.75
195	Washington Redskins Team	1.75
196	Washington Redskins Play of the Year (Bill McPeak)	1.75
197	Checklist 1	1.75
198	Checklist 2	1.75

1965 Philadelphia

This Philly set was the second one of NFLers issued in its four-year run during the mid-60s. The standard-size 198-card set lists players alphabetically by last name, and alphabetically by city name. Card fronts show the player name in a black box below the photo, with the NFL logo to the right. Card backs had a rub-off game below the statistics. Play of the year cards displayed a diagrammed play the team had used; accompanying it on the front of the card is a small black-and-white picture of the coach. Team cards were once again issued, as were set checklists. One error in the set has Merlin Olsen spelled "Olson" on the checklist card. Rookies in this set include Hall of Famers Paul Warfield and Charley Taylor; all-time interception leader Paul Krause; future NFL head coach Floyd Peters; Carl Eller; Fred Cox; Jack Concannon; Jim Bakken and Pat Fischer. Second-year cards in the set depict Hall of Famers Herb Adderly, Willie Davis, Ray Nitschke (his first Philly card), Vince Lombardi, Deacon Jones, and Merlin Olsen. Others include Mick Tinglehoff, Allie Sherman and Irv Cross. The final regular-issue cards of these players are also in the set: Hall of Famers Yale Lary, Norm Van Brocklin (on a play of the year card), John Henry Johnson, and Sam Huff. This set also had the last regular-issue card of Roosevelt Grier.

		NM
Complete Set (198):		775.00
Common Player:		1.50
Wax Pack (5):		190.00
1	Baltimore Colts Team	11.00
2	Raymond Berry	6.00
3	Bob Boyd	1.50
4	Wendell Harris	1.50
5	Jerry Logan	1.50
6	Tony Lorick	1.50
7	Lou Michaels	1.50
8	Lenny Moore	6.00
9	Jimmy Orr	1.50
10	Jim Parker	3.00
11	Dick Szymanski	1.50
12	Johnny Unitas	35.00
13	*Bob Vogel*	1.50
14	Don Shula	14.00
15	Chicago Bears Team	1.50
16	Jon Arnett	1.50
17	Doug Atkins	3.00
18	*Rudy Bukich*	3.00
19	Mike Ditka	25.00
20	Dick Evey	1.50
21	Joe Fortunato	1.50
22	*Bobby Joe Green*	1.50
23	Johnny Morris	1.50
24	Mike Pyle	1.50
25	Roosevelt Taylor	1.50
26	Bill Wade	1.50
27	Bob Wetoska	1.50
28	George Halas	6.00
29	Cleveland Browns Team	1.50
30	Walter Beach	1.50
31	Jim Brown	60.00
32	Gary Collins	1.50
33	Bill Glass	1.50
34	Ernie Green	1.50
35	*Jim Houston*	3.00
36	Dick Modzelewski	1.50
37	Bernie Parrish	1.50
38	Walter Roberts	1.50
39	Frank Ryan	1.50
40	Dick Schafrath	1.50
41	*Paul Warfield*	75.00
42	Cleveland Browns Play of the Year (Blanton Collier)	1.50
43	Dallas Cowboys Team	1.50
44	Frank Clarke	1.50
45	Mike Connelly	1.50
46	Buddy Dial	1.50
47	Bob Lilly	20.00
48	*Tony Liscio*	1.75
49	Tommy McDonald	1.50
50	Don Meredith	25.00
51	Pettis Norman	1.50
52	Don Perkins	2.00
53	*Mel Renfro*	30.00
54	Jim Ridlon	1.50
55	Jerry Tubbs	1.50
56	Tom Landry	7.00
57	Detroit Lions Team	1.50
58	Terry Barr	1.50
59	Roger Brown	1.50
60	Gail Cogdill	1.50
61	Jim Gibbons	1.50
62	John Gordy	1.50
63	Yale Lary	3.00
64	*Dick LeBeau*	4.00
65	Earl Morrall	4.00
66	Nick Pietrosante	1.50
67	Pat Studstill	1.50
68	Wayne Walker	1.50
69	Tom Watkins	1.50
70	Detroit Lions Play of the Year (George Wilson)	1.50
71	Green Bay Packers Team	1.50
72	Herb Adderley	8.00
73	Willie Davis	8.00
74	Boyd Dowler	1.50
75	Forrest Gregg	4.00
76	Paul Hornung	25.00
77	Henry Jordan	1.50
78	Tom Moore	1.50
79	Ray Nitschke	15.00
80	*Elijah Pitts*	5.00
81	Bart Starr	25.00
82	Jim Taylor	14.00
83	Willie Wood	8.00
84	Vince Lombardi	12.00
85	Los Angeles Rams Team	1.50
86	Dick Bass	1.50
87	Roman Gabriel	5.00
88	Roosevelt Grier	3.00
89	Deacon Jones	8.00
90	*Lamar Lundy*	3.00
91	Marlin McKeever	1.50
92	Ed Meador	1.50
93	*Bill Munson*	3.00
94	Merlin Olsen	17.00
95	Bobby Smith	1.50
96	Frank Varrichione	1.50
97	Ben Wilson	1.50
98	Los Angeles Rams Play of the Year (Harland Svare)	1.50
99	Minnesota Vikings Team	1.50
100	Grady Alderman	1.50
101	*Hal Bedsole*	1.50
102	Bill Brown	1.50
103	Bill Butler	1.50
104	*Fred Cox*	4.00
105	*Carl Eller*	26.00
106	Paul Flatley	1.50
107	Jim Marshall	6.00
108	Tommy Mason	1.50
109	George Rose	1.50
110	Fran Tarkenton	30.00
111	Mick Tingelhoff	2.00
112	Norm Van Brocklin	3.00
113	New York Giants Team	1.50
114	Erich Barnes	1.50
115	Roosevelt Brown	4.00
116	Clarence Childs	1.50
117	Jerry Hillebrand	1.50
118	Greg Larson	1.50
119	Dick Lynch	1.50
120	*Joe Morrison*	4.00
121	Lou Slaby	1.50
122	*Aaron Thomas*	2.50
123	Steve Thurlow	1.50
124	Ernie Wheelwright	1.50
125	*Gary Wood*	1.50
126	New York Giants Play of the Year (Allie Sherman)	1.50
127	Philadelphia Eagles Team	1.50
128	Sam Baker	1.50
129	Maxie Baughan	1.50
130	Timmy Brown	1.50
131	*Jack Concannon*	1.50
132	Irv Cross	2.50
133	Earl Gros	1.50
134	Dave Lloyd	1.50
135	Floyd Peters	4.00
136	Nate Ramsey	1.50
137	Pete Retzlaff	1.50
138	Jim Ringo	4.00
139	Norm Snead	2.00
140	Philadelphia Eagles Play of the Year (Joe Kuharich)	1.50
141	Pittsburgh Steelers Team	1.50
142	John Baker	1.50
143	Gary Ballman	1.50
144	Charley Bradshaw	1.50
145	Ed Brown	1.50
146	Dick Haley	1.50
147	John Henry Johnson	4.50
148	Brady Keys	1.50
149	Ray Lemek	1.50
150	Ben McGee	1.50
151	Clarence Peaks	1.50
152	Myron Pottios	1.50
153	Clendon Thomas	1.50
154	Pittsburgh Steelers Play of the Year (Buddy Parker)	1.50
155	St. Louis Cardinals Team	1.50
156	*Jim Bakken*	4.50
157	Joe Childress	1.50
158	Bobby Joe Conrad	1.50
159	Bob DeMarco	1.50
160	*Pat Fischer*	4.50
161	Irv Goode	1.50
162	Ken Gray	1.50
163	Charlie Johnson	1.50
164	Bill Koman	1.50
165	Dale Meinert	1.50
166	*Jerry Stovall*	2.50
167	Abe Woodson	1.50
168	St. Louis Cardinals Play of the Year (Wally Lemon)	1.50
169	San Francisco 49ers Team	1.50
170	Kermit Alexander	1.50
171	John Brodie	12.00
172	Bernie Casey	1.50
173	John David Crow	1.50
174	Tommy Davis	1.50
175	Matt Hazeltine	1.50
176	Jim Johnson	1.50
177	Charlie Krueger	1.50
178	Roland Lakes	1.50
179	*George Mira*	5.00
180	*Dave Parks*	4.00
181	John Thomas	1.50
182	Jack Christiansen	2.00
183	Washington Redskins Team	1.50
184	Pervis Atkins	1.50
185	Preston Carpenter	1.50
186	Angelo Coia	1.50
187	Sam Huff	6.00
188	Sonny Jurgensen	15.00
189	*Paul Krause*	16.00
190	Jim Martin	1.50
191	Bobby Mitchell	6.00
192	John Nisby	1.50
193	John Paluck	1.50
194	Vince Promuto	1.50
195	*Charley Taylor*	60.00
196	Bill McPeak	1.50
197	Checklist 1	20.00
198	Checklist 2	35.00

1966 Philadelphia

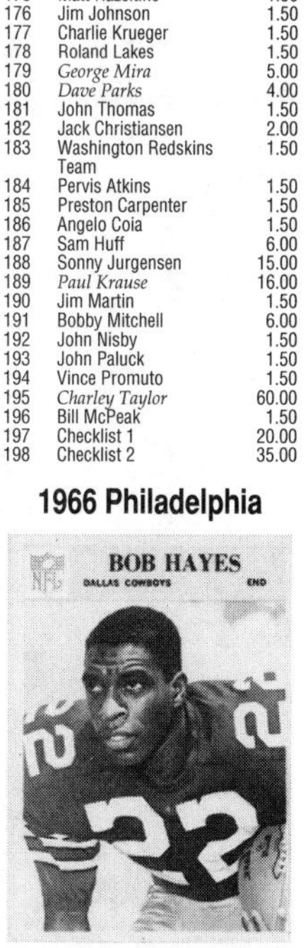

This 198-card set of NFL players is best known for the inclusion of rookie cards of Gale Sayers and Dick Butkus (the other significant rookie card is that of Bob Hayes). This was the final year regular-issue cards were produced of players including Hall of Famers Lenny Moore, Jim Parker, Jim Brown, Roosevelt Brown, and Jim Ringo. The 198-card set lists players in alphabetical order according to city. The play card for each team features a color action photo on the front, with a description of the play on the back.

		NM
	Complete Set (198):	875.00
	Common Player:	1.50
	Wax Pack (5):	215.00
1	Falcons Logo	8.00
2	Larry Benz	1.50
3	Dennis Claridge	1.50
4	Perry Lee Dunn	1.50
5	Dan Grimm	1.50
6	Alex Hawkins	1.50
7	Ralph Heck	1.50
8	Frank Lasky	1.50
9	Guy Reese	1.50
10	Bob Richards	1.50
11	Ron Smith	1.50
12	Ernie Wheelwright	1.50
13	Atlanta Falcons Roster	1.50
14	Baltimore Colts Team Card	1.50
15	Raymond Berry	7.00
16	Bob Boyd	1.50
17	Jerry Logan	1.50
18	John Mackey	6.00
19	Tom Matte	1.50
20	Lou Michaels	1.50
21	Lenny Moore	6.00
22	Jimmy Orr	1.50
23	Jim Parker	1.50
24	Johnny Unitas	30.00
25	Bob Vogel	1.50
26	Baltimore Colts Play Card	1.50
27	Chicago Bears Team Card	1.50
28	Doug Atkins	1.50
29	Rudy Bukich	1.50
30	Ron Bull	1.50
31	*Dick Butkus*	185.00
32	Mike Ditka	25.00
33	Joe Fortunato	1.50
34	Bobby Joe Green	1.50
35	Roger LeClerc	1.50
36	Johnny Morris	1.50
37	Mike Pyle	1.50
38	*Gale Sayers*	210.00
39	Gale Sayers (Bears)	25.00
40	Cleveland Browns Team Card	1.50
41	Jim Brown	55.00
42	Gary Collins	1.50
43	Ross Fichtner	1.50
44	Ernie Green	1.50
45	*Gene Hickerson*	2.00
46	Jim Houston	1.50
47	John Morrow	1.50
48	Walter Roberts	1.50
49	Frank Ryan	1.50
50	Dick Schafrath	1.50
51	*Paul Wiggin*	2.00
52	Cleveland Browns Play Card	1.50
53	Dallas Cowboys Team Card	1.50
54	*George Andrie*	2.00
55	Frank Ryan	1.50
56	Mike Connelly	1.50
57	Cornell Green	1.50
58	*Bob Hayes*	25.00
59	*Chuck Howley*	10.00
60	Bob Lilly	15.00
61	Don Meredith	25.00
62	Don Perkins	1.50
63	Mel Renfro	8.00
64	Danny Villanueva	1.50
65	Dallas Cowboys Play Card	1.50
66	Detroit Lions Team Card	1.50
67	Roger Brown	1.50
68	John Gordy	1.50
69	Alex Karras	10.00
70	Dick LeBeau	1.50
71	Amos Marsh	1.50
72	Milt Plum	1.50
73	Bobby Smith	1.50
74	Wayne Rasmussen	1.50
75	Pat Studstill	1.50
76	Wayne Walker	1.50
77	Tom Watkins	1.50
78	Detroit Lions Play Card	1.50
79	Green Bay Packers Team Card	1.50
80	Herb Adderley	5.00
81	*Lee Roy Caffey*	2.00
82	Don Chandler	1.50
83	Willie Davis	5.00
84	Boyd Dowler	1.50
85	Forrest Gregg	4.00
86	Tom Moore	1.50
87	Ray Nitschke	10.00
88	Bart Starr	25.00
89	Jim Taylor	13.00
90	Willie Wood	4.50
91	Green Bay Packers Play Card	1.50
92	Los Angeles Rams Team Card	1.50
93	Willie Brown	1.50
94	Dick Bass, Roman Gabriel	2.50
95	Bruce Gossett	2.50
96	Deacon Jones	6.00
97	Tommy McDonald	1.50
98	Marlin McKeever	1.50
99	Aaron Martin	1.50
100	Ed Meador	1.50
101	Bill Munson	2.00
102	Merlin Olsen	9.00
103	Jim Stiger	1.50
104	Los Angeles Rams Play Card	1.50
105	Minnesota Vikings Team Card	1.50
106	Grady Alderman	1.50
107	Bill Brown	1.50
108	Fred Cox	1.50
109	Paul Flatley	1.50
110	Rip Hawkins	1.50
111	Tommy Mason	1.50
112	Ed Sharockman	1.50
113	Gordon Smith	1.50
114	Fran Tarkenton	20.00
115	Mick Tinglehoff	2.00
116	*Bobby Walden*	2.00
117	Minnesota Vikings Play Card	1.50
118	New York Giants Team Card	1.50
119	Roosevelt Brown	4.00
120	*Henry Carr*	2.00
121	Clarence Childs	1.50
122	*Tucker Frederickson*	2.00
123	Jerry Hillebrand	1.50
124	Greg Larson	1.50
125	*Spider Lockhart*	3.00
126	Dick Lynch	1.50
127	Earl Morrall, Bob Scholtz	1.50
128	Joe Morrison	1.50
129	Steve Thurlow	1.50
130	New York Giants Play Card	1.50
131	Philadelphia Ealges Team Card	1.50
132	Sam Baker	1.50
133	Maxie Baughan	1.50
134	*Bob Brown*	6.00
135	Timmy Brown	1.50
136	Irv Cross	2.00
137	Earl Gros	1.50
138	Ray Poage	1.50
139	Nate Ramsey	1.50
140	Pete Retzlaff	1.50
141	Jim Ringo	3.50
142	Norm Snead	2.00
143	Philadelphia Eagles Play Card	1.50
144	Pittsburgh Steelers Team Card	1.50
145	Gary Ballman	1.50
146	Charley Bradshaw	1.50
147	Jim Butler	1.50
148	Mike Clark	1.50
149	*Dick Hoak*	2.00
150	*Roy Jefferson*	2.00
151	Frank Lambert	1.50
152	Mike Lind	1.50
153	*Bill Nelsen*	4.00
154	Clarence Peaks	1.50
155	Clendon Thomas	1.50
156	Pittsburgh Steelers Play Card	1.50
157	St. Louis Cardinals Team Card	1.50
158	Jim Bakken	1.50
159	Bobby Joe Conrad	1.50
160	*Willis Crenshaw*	2.00
161	Bob DeMarco	1.50
162	Pat Fischer	2.00
163	Charlie Johnson	2.00
164	Dale Meinert	1.50
165	Sonny Randle	1.50
166	*Sam Silas*	2.00
167	Bill Triplett	1.50
168	Larry Wilson	4.00
169	St. Louis Cardinals Play Card	1.50
170	San Francisco 49ers Team Card	1.50
171	Kermit Alexander	1.50
172	Bruce Bosley	1.50
173	John Brodie	9.00
174	Bernie Casey	1.50
175	John David Crow	1.50
176	Tommy Davis	1.50
177	Jim Johnson	1.50
178	Gary Lewis	1.50
179	Dave Parks	1.50
180	Walter Rock	1.50
181	*Ken Willard*	4.00
182	San Francisco 49ers Play Card	1.50
183	Washington Redskins Team Card	1.50
184	Rickie Harris	1.50
185	Sonny Jurgensen	9.00
186	Paul Krause	5.00
187	Bobby Mitchell	5.00
188	Vince Promuto	1.50
189	*Pat Richter*	3.00
190	Joe Rutgens	1.50
191	John Sample	1.50
192	Lonnie Sanders	1.50
193	Jim Steffen	1.50
194	Charley Taylor	18.00
195	Washington Redskins Play Card	1.50
196	Referee signals	5.00
197	Checklist 1	15.00
198	Checklist 2	40.00

1967 Philadelphia

This was the last time until 1989 that Topps would face a direct challenge in the football card market, as the Philadelphia Chewing Gum Corp. ceased production of football cards after this issue. (The company returned with sets of NFL Hall of Famers in 1988 and 1989). The 198-card set has yellow borders on the front, and backs were printed on white or brown card stock. As usual, teams were grouped alphabetically by city name, players were grouped alphabetically by last name. Team logo cards rounded out the grouping of each team. There is an error in the set: on card #14, Raymond Berry, the picture actually shows Bob Boyd. Also, the roster for the New Orleans Saints team card (#121) was included on the back of the logo card (#132); the set includes team picture cards and team logo cards for all other teams except the expansion Saints (The front of the card reads, "On the back of this card are names of New Orleans players and the teams from which they were picked" while the back simply has a capsule on the Saints' New Orleans impact). Another error, on card #26 reads "Bukich" on the front and "Buckich" on the back. Rookies in this set include Tommy Nobis, Leroy Kelly, Lee Roy Jordan, and Chris Hanburger. Second-year cards include Dick Butkus, Gale Sayers, Bob Brown, Roy Jefferson, Jim Bakken and Ken Willard. This was the last year for regular-issue cards of Hall of Famers Forrest Gregg and Paul Hornung. The first members of the New Orleans Saints made their debut in the '67 Philly set.

		NM
	Complete Set (198):	650.00
	Common Player:	1.50
	Wax Pack (5):	180.00
1	Falcons Team	5.00
2	*Junior Coffey*	1.50
3	Alex Hawkins	1.50
4	*Randy Johnson*	3.00
5	Lou Kirouac	1.50
6	Billy Martin	1.50
7	*Tommy Nobis*	16.00
8	*Jerry Richardson*	6.00
9	Marion Rushing	1.50
10	Ron Smith	1.50
11	Ernie Wheelwright	1.50
12	Atlanta Falcons Insignia	1.50
13	Baltimore Colts Team	1.50
14	Raymond Berry	5.00
15	Bob Boyd	1.50
16	Ordell Braase	1.50
17	Alvin Haymond	1.50
18	Tony Lorick	1.50
19	Lenny Lyles	1.50
20	John Mackey	5.00
21	Tom Matte	1.50
22	Lou Michaels	1.50
23	Johnny Unitas	30.00
24	Baltimore Colts Insignia	1.50
25	Chicago Bears Team	1.50
26	Rudy Bukich	1.50
27	Ron Bull	1.50
28	Dick Butkus	60.00
29	Mike Ditka	25.00
30	*Dick Gordon*	1.50
31	Roger LeClerc	1.50
32	Bennie McRae	1.50
33	Richie Petibon	2.50
34	Mike Pyle	1.50
35	Gale Sayers	75.00
36	Chicago Bears Insignia	1.50
37	Cleveland Browns Team	1.50
38	Johnny Brewer	1.50
39	Gary Collins	1.50
40	Ross Fichtner	1.50
41	Ernie Green	1.50
42	Gene Hickerson	1.50
43	*Leroy Kelly*	30.00
44	Frank Ryan	1.50
45	Dick Schafrath	1.50
46	Paul Warfield	20.00
47	John Wooten	1.50
48	Cleveland Browns Insignia	1.50
49	Dallas Cowboys Team	1.50
50	George Andrie	1.50
51	Cornell Green	1.50
52	Bob Hayes	10.00
53	Chuck Howley	1.50
54	*Lee Roy Jordan*	22.00
55	Bob Lilly	12.00
56	*Dave Manders*	2.00
57	Don Meredith	20.00
58	*Dan Reeves*	33.00
59	Mel Renfro	2.50
60	Dallas Cowboys Insignia	1.50
61	Detroit Lions Team	1.50
62	Roger Brown	1.50
63	Gail Cogdill	1.50
64	John Gordy	1.50
65	Ron Kramer	1.50
66	Dick LeBeau	1.50
67	*Mike Lucci*	6.00
68	Amos Marsh	1.50
69	Tom Nowatzke	1.50
70	Pat Studstill	1.50
71	Karl Sweetan	1.50
72	Detroit Lions Insignia	1.50
73	Green Bay Packers Team	1.50
74	Herb Adderley	4.50
75	Lee Roy Caffey	1.50
76	Willie Davis	4.50
77	Forrest Gregg	4.00
78	Henry Jordan	1.50
79	Ray Nitschke	6.00
80	*Dave Robinson*	5.00
81	Bob Skoronski	1.50
82	Bart Starr	20.00
83	Willie Wood	5.00
84	Green Bay Packers Insignia	1.50
85	Los Angeles Rams Team	1.50
86	Dick Bass	1.50
87	Maxie Baughan	1.50
88	Roman Gabriel	4.00
89	Bruce Gossett	1.50
90	Deacon Jones	5.00
91	Tommy McDonald	1.50
92	Marlin McKeever	1.50
93	Tom Moore	1.50
94	Merlin Olsen	7.00
95	Clancy Williams	1.50
96	Los Angeles Rams Insignia	1.50
97	Minnesota Vikings Team	1.50
98	Grady Alderman	1.50
99	Bill Brown	1.50
100	Fred Cox	1.50
101	Paul Flatley	1.50
102	Dale Hackbart	1.50
103	Jim Marshall	3.00
104	Tommy Mason	1.50
105	Milt Sunde	1.50
106	Fran Tarkenton	20.00
107	Mick Tingelhoff	2.00
108	Minnesota Vikings Insignia	1.50
109	New York Giants Team	1.50
110	Henry Carr	1.50
111	Clarence Childs	1.50
112	Allen Jacobs	1.50
113	*Homer Jones*	2.00
114	Tom Kennedy	1.50
115	Spider Lockhart	1.50
116	Joe Morrison	1.50
117	Francis Peay	1.50
118	Jeff Smith	1.50
119	Aaron Thomas	1.50
120	New York Giants Team	1.50
121	New Orleans Saints Team	2.00
122	Charley Bradshaw	1.50
123	Paul Hornung	18.00
124	Elbert Kimbrough	1.50
125	Earl Leggett	1.50
126	Obert Logan	1.50
127	Riley Mattson	1.50
128	John Morrow	1.50
129	Bob Scholtz	1.50
130	*Dave Whitsell*	2.00
131	Gary Wood	1.50
132	New Orleans Saints Insignia	1.50
133	Philadelphia Eagles Team	1.50
134	Sam Baker	1.50
135	Bob Brown	2.00
136	Jim Brown	1.50
137	Earl Gros	1.50
138	Dave Lloyd	1.50
139	Floyd Peters	1.50
140	Pete Retzlaff	1.50
141	Joe Scarpati	1.50
142	Norm Snead	2.00
143	Jim Skaggs	1.50
144	Philadelphia Eagles Insignia	1.50
145	Pittsburgh Steelers Team	1.50
146	Bill Asbury	1.50
147	John Baker	1.50
148	Gary Ballman	1.50
149	Mike Clark	1.50
150	Riley Gunnels	1.50
151	John Hilton	1.50
152	Roy Jefferson	1.50
153	Brady Keys	1.50
154	Ben McGee	1.50
155	Bill Nelsen	2.00
156	Pittsburgh Steelers Insignia	1.50
157	St. Louis Cardinals Team	1.50
158	Jim Bakken	1.50
159	Bobby Joe Conrad	1.50
160	Ken Gray	1.50
161	Charlie Johnson	2.00
162	Joe Robb	1.50
163	*Johnny Roland*	4.00
164	Roy Shivers	1.50
165	*Jackie Smith*	15.00
166	Jerry Stovall	1.50
167	Larry Wilson	4.00
168	St. Louis Cardinals Insignia	1.50
169	San Francisco 49ers Team	1.50
170	Kermit Alexander	1.50
171	Bruce Bosley	1.50
172	John Brodie	7.50
173	Bernie Casey	1.50
174	Tommy Davis	1.50
175	Howard Mudd	1.50
176	Dave Parks	1.50
177	John Thomas	1.50
178	*Dave Wilcox*	5.00
179	Ken Willard	1.50
180	San Francisco 49ers Insignia	1.50
181	Washington Redskins Team	1.50
182	*Charlie Gogolak*	2.00
183	*Chris Hanburger*	8.00
184	*Len Hauss*	3.00
185	Sonny Jurgensen	8.00
186	Bobby Mitchell	5.00
187	Bris Owens	1.50
188	Jim Shorter	1.50
189	*Jerry Smith*	2.00
190	Charley Taylor	7.50
191	A.D. Whitfield	1.50
192	Washington Redskins Insignia	1.50
193	Cleveland Browns	5.00
194	New York Giants Play Card (Joe Morrison)	1.50
195	Atlanta Falcons Play Card (Ernie Wheelwright)	1.50
196	Referee Signals	2.00
197	Checklist 1	18.00
198	Checklist 2	35.00

1991 Pinnacle Promo Panels

The 18-card, 5" x 7" panel set each features four preview cards from Pinnacle's 1991 football debut and were issued at the Super Bowl XXVI Card Show. The four-card panels have the same design as the regular-issue set.

		MT
	Complete Set (18):	100.00
	Common Player:	3.00
1	John Alt, Eric Green, Don Mosebar, Greg Townsend	3.00
2	Bruce Armstrong, Joe Montana, Jim Lachey, Bruce Matthews	8.00
3	Don Beebe, Irving Fryar, Ricky Proehl, Vinny Testaverde	4.00
4	Duane Bickett, Tony Bennett, John Friesz, Rob Burnett	3.00
5	Mark Bortz, Warren Moon, Jim Breech, Eric Metcalf	4.00
6	Roger Craig, Issiac Holt, Kevin Mack, Shane Conlan	4.00
7	Wendell Davis, Gaston Green, Tony Mandarich, Merril Hoge	3.00
8	Dermontti Dawson, Jerry Gray, Nick Lowery, Scott Case	3.00
9	Chris Doleman, Troy Aikman, Sterling Sharpe, Sean Landeta	8.00
10	Darryl Henley, Karl Mecklenberg, Sam Mills, Rod Woodson	4.00
11	Mark Higgs, Jay Schroeder, Mark Carrier, Jim Everett	4.00
12	Jay Hilgenberg, Dan Marino, Anthony Carter, Howie Long	15.00
13	Louis Lipps, John Offerdahl, Herschel Walker, Jeff George	4.00
14	Greg McMurtry, Henry Ellard, Brian Mitchell, Mark Clayton	4.00
15	Nate Odomes, Allen Pinkett, Don Majkowski, Dave Meggett	3.00
16	Andre Rison, Jeff Hostetler, Hugh Millen, Jack Del Rio	4.00
17	Emmitt Smith, Dennis Smith, Bill Brooks, Bobby Hebert	18.00
18	Reyna Thompson, Louis Oliver, Steve Broussard, Andre Reed	4.00

1991 Pinnacle

Score's first effort at a premium edition is its 415-card 1991 Pinnacle set. Each card front features an action shot and a mug shot against a black background with white borders. The back has an action photo superimposed against a black background, plus statistics, a profile and a biography. An anti-counterfeit band appears on the back of each card. Subsets include Head-to-Head, Technicians, Game Winners, Idols and Sidelines. There are also 58 rookies featured in the set; their cards have green backgrounds on the front, and a mug shot on the back. A standard-size Emmitt Smith promotional card was also created. It is identical in design to its regular set's counterpart, except the text on the back of the promo card mentions Smith's holdout before the season. Twelve four-card panels (5" x 7" each) were also made and use the same design as the regular 1991 cards. Each card in the panel has the same number as its counterpart in the regular set, but the panel is unnumbered.

		MT
	Complete Set (415):	35.00
	Common Player:	.10
	Minor Stars:	.20
	Foil Pack (12):	2.00
	Foil Wax Box (36):	40.00
1	Warren Moon	.30
2	Morten Andersen	.10
3	Rohn Stark	.10
4	Mark Bortz	.10
5	*Mark Higgs*	.10
6	Troy Aikman	4.00
7	John Elway	1.50
8	Neal Anderson	.10
9	Chris Doleman	.10
10	Jay Schroeder	.10
11	Sterling Sharpe	.40
12	Steve DeBerg	.10
13	Ronnie Lott	.10
14	Sea Landeta	.10
15	Jim Everett	.10
16	Jim Breech	.10
17	Barry Foster	.10
18	Mike Merriweather	.10
19	Eric Metcalf	.40
20	Mark Carrier	.10
21	James Brooks	.10
22	Nate Odomes	.10
23	Rodney Hampton	.50
24	Chris Miller	.10
25	Roger Craig	.10
26	Louis Oliver	.10
27	Allen Pinkett	.10
28	Bubby Brister	.10
29	Reyna Thompson	.10
30	Issiac Holt	.10
31	Steve Broussard	.10
32	Christian Okoye	.10
33	Dave Meggett	.10
34	Andre Reed	.20
35	Shane Conlan	.10
36	Eric Ball	.10
37	Johnny Bailey	.10
38	Don Majkowski	.10
39	Gerald Williams	.10
40	Kevin Mack	.10
41	Jeff Herrod	.10
42	Emmitt Smith	6.00
43	Wendell Davis	.10
44	Lorenzo White	.10
45	Andre Rison	.20
46	Jerry Gray	.10
47	Dennis Smith	.10
48	Gaston Green	.10
49	Dermontti Dawson	.10
50	Jeff Hostetler	.30
51	Nick Lowery	.10
52	Merril Hoge	.10
53	Bobby Hebert	.10
54	Scott Case	.10
55	Jack Del Rio	.10
56	Cornelius Bennett	.10
57	Tony Mandarich	.10
58	Bill Brooks	.10
59	Jessie Tuggle	.10
60	*Hugh Millen*	.10
61	Tony Bennett	.10
62	*Chris Dishman*	.10
63	*Darryl Henley*	.10
64	Duane Bickett	.10
65	Jay Hilgenberg	.10
66	Joe Montana	3.50
67	Bill Fralic	.10
68	Sam Mills	.10
69	Bruce Armstrong	.10
70	Dan Marino	5.00
71	Jim Lachey	.10
72	Rod Woodson	.10
73	Simon Fletcher	.10
74	Bruce Matthews	.10
75	Howie Long	.10
76	John Friesz	.10
77	Karl Mecklenburg	.10
78	John L. Williams	.10
79	*Rob Burnett*	.10
80	Anthony Carter	.10
81	Henry Ellard	.10
82	Don Beebe	.10
83	Louis Lipps	.10
84	Greg McMurty	.10
85	Will Wolford	.10
86	Eric Green	.20
87	Irving Fryar	.10
88	John Offerdahl	.10
89	John Alt	.10
90	Tom Tupa	.10
91	Don Mosebar	.10
92	Jeff George	1.00
93	Vinny Testaverde	.20
94	Greg Townsend	.10
95	Derrick Fenner	.10
96	Brian Mitchell	.20
97	Herschel Walker	.10
98	Ricky Proehl	.10
99	Mark Clayton	.10
100	Derrick Thomas	.20
101	Jim Harbaugh	.50
102	Barry Word	.10
103	Jerry Rice	4.00
104	Keith Byars	.10
105	Marion Butts	.10
106	Rich Moran	.10
107	Thurman Thomas	.75
108	Stephone Paige	.10
109	David Johnson	.10
110	William Perry	.10
111	Haywood Jeffires	.10
112	Rodney Peete	.10
113	Andy Heck	.10
114	Kevin Ross	.10
115	Michael Carter	.10
116	Tim McKyer	.10
117	Kenneth Davis	.10
118	Richmond Webb	.10
119	Rich Camarillo	.10
120	James Francis	.10
121	Craig Heyward	.10
122	Hardy Nickerson	.10
123	Michael Brooks	.10
124	Fred Barnett	.30
125	Cris Carter	.40
126	Brian Jordan	.10
127	Pat Leahy	.10
128	Kevin Greene	.10
129	Trace Armstrong	.10
130	Eugene Lockhart	.10
131	Albert Lewis	.10
132	Ernie Jones	.10
133	Eric Martin	.10
134	Anthony Thompson	.10
135	Tim Krumrie	.10
136	James Lofton	.10
137	John Taylor	.10
138	Jeff Cross	.10
139	Tommy Kane	.10
140	Robb Thomas	.10
141	Gary Anderson	.10
142	Mark Murphy	.10
143	Rickey Jackson	.10
144	Ken O'Brien	.10
145	Ernest Givins	.10
146	Jessie Hester	.10
147	Deion Sanders	1.75
148	*Keith Henderson*	.10
149	Chris Singleton	.10
150	Rod Bernstine	.10
151	Quinn Early	.10
152	Boomer Esiason	.10
153	Mike Gann	.10
154	Dino Hackett	.10
155	Perry Kemp	.10
156	Mark Ingram	.10
157	Daryl Johnston	.75
158	Eugene Daniel	.10
159	Dalton Hilliard	.10
160	Rufus Porter	.10
161	Tunch Ilkin	.10
162	James Hasty	.10
163	Keith McKeller	.10
164	Heath Sherman	.10
165	Vai Sikahema	.10
166	Pat Terrell	.10
167	Anthony Munoz	.10
168	*Brad Edwards*	.10
169	Tom Rathman	.10
170	Steve McMichael	.10
171	Vaughan Johnson	.10
172	*Nate Lewis*	.10
173	Mark Rypien	.10
174	Rob Moore	.10
175	Tim Green	.10
176	Tony Casillas	.10
177	Jon Hand	.10
178	Todd McNair	.10
179	*Toi Cook*	.10
180	Eddie Brown	.10
181	Mark Jackson	.10
182	Pete Stoyanovich	.10
183	*Bryce Paup*	2.00
184	Anthony Miller	.20
185	Dan Saleaumua	.10
186	Guy McIntyre	.10
187	Broderick Thomas	.10
188	Frank Warren	.10
189	Drew Hill	.10
190	Reggie White	.40
191	Chris Hinton	.10
192	David Little	.10
193	David Fulcher	.10
194	Clarence Verdin	.10
195	Junior Seau	1.00
196	Blair Thomas	.10
197	Stan Brock	.10
198	Gary Clark	.10
199	Michael Irvin	.75
200	Ronnie Harmon	.10
201	Steve Young	3.00
202	Brian Noble	.10
203	Dan Stryzinski	.10
204	Darryl Talley	.10
205	David Alexander	.10
206	Pat Swilling	.10
207	Gary Plummer	.10
208	Robert Delpino	.10

209	Norm Johnson	.10
210	Mike Singletary	.10
211	Anthony Johnson	.10
212	Eric Allen	.10
213	Gill Fenerty	.10
214	Neil Smith	.10
215	Joe Phillips	.10
216	Ottis Anderson	.10
217	LeRoy Butler	.10
218	Ray Childress	.10
219	Rodney Holman	.10
220	Kevin Fagan	.10
221	Bruce Smith	.10
222	Brad Muster	.10
223	Mike Horan	.10
224	Steve Atwater	.10
225	Rich Gannon	.10
226	Anthony Pleasant	.10
227	Steve Jordan	.10
228	Lomas Broan	.10
229	Jackie Slater	.10
230	Brad Baxter	.10
231	Joe Morris	.10
232	Marcus Allen	.20
233	Chris Warren	1.00
234	Johnny Johnson	.10
235	Phil Simms	.10
236	Dave Krieg	.10
237	Jim McMahon	.10
238	Richard Dent	.10
239	*John Washington*	.10
240	Sammie Smith	.10
241	Brian Brennan	.10
242	Cortez Kennedy	.20
243	Tim McDonald	.10
244	Charles Haley	.10
245	Joey Browner	.10
246	Eddie Murray	.10
247	Bob Golic	.10
248	Myron Guyton	.10
249	Dennis Byrd	.10
250	Barry Sanders	4.00
251	Clay Matthews	.10
252	Pepper Johnson	.10
253	*Eric Swann*	1.00
254	Lamar Lathon	.10
255	Andre Tippett	.10
256	Tom Newberry	.10
257	Kyle Clifton	.10
258	Leslie O'Neal	.10
259	Bubba McDowell	.10
260	Scott Davis	.10
261	Wilber Marshall	.10
262	Marv Cook	.10
263	Jeff Lageman	.10
264	Mike Young	.10
265	Gary Zimmerman	.10
266	Mike Munchak	.10
267	David Treadwell	.10
268	Steve Wisniewski	.10
269	Mark Duper	.10
270	Chris Spielman	.10
271	Brett Perriman	.50
272	Lionel Washington	.10
273	Lawrence Taylor	.20
274	Mark Collins	.10
275	Mark Carrier	.10
276	Paul Gruber	.10
277	Earnest Byner	.10
278	Andre Collins	.10
279	Reggie Cobb	.10
280	Art Monk	.20
281	*Henry Jones*	.20
282	*Mike Pritchard*	.75
283	*Moe Gardner*	.20
284	*Chris Zorich*	.50
285	*Keith Traylor*	.20
286	*Mike Dumas*	.20
287	*Ed King*	.20
288	*Russell Maryland*	.20
289	*Alfred Williams*	.20
290	*Derek Russell*	.20
291	*Vinnie Clark*	.20
292	*Mike Croel*	.20
293	*Todd Marinovich*	.20
294	*Phil Hansen*	.20
295	*Aaron Craver*	.20
296	*Nick Bell*	.20
297	*Kenny Walker*	.20
298	*Roman Phifer*	.20
299	*Kanavis McGhee*	.20
300	*Ricky Ervins*	.20
301	*Jim Price*	.20
302	*John Johnson*	.20
303	George Thornton	.10
304	Huey Richardson	.10
305	*Harry Colon*	.20
306	*Antone Davis*	.20
307	*Todd Lyght*	.30
308	*Bryan Cox*	1.00
309	*Brad Goebel*	.20
310	*Eric Moten*	.20
311	*John Kasay*	.30
312	*Esera Tuaolo*	.20
313	*Bobby Wilson*	.20
314	*Mo Lewis*	.20
315	*Harvey Williams*	1.00
316	Mike Stonebreaker	.10
317	*Charles McRae*	.20
318	*John Flannery*	.20
319	*Ted Washington*	.20
320	*Stanley Richard*	.20
321	*Browning Nagle*	.50
322	*Ed McCaffery*	3.50
323	*Jeff Graham*	2.00
324	Stan Thomas	.10
325	*Lawrence Dawsey*	.20
326	*Eric Bieniemy*	.30
327	*Tim Barnett*	.20
328	*Erric Pegram*	1.50
329	Lamar Rogers	.10
330	*Ernie Mills*	.20
331	*Pat Harlow*	.20
332	*Greg Lewis*	.20
333	*Jarrod Bunch*	.20
334	*Dan McGwire*	.20
335	*Randal Hill*	.50
336	*Leonard Russell*	.50
337	Carnell Lake	.10
338	Brian Blades	.10
339	Darrell Green	.10
340	Bobby Humphrey	.10
341	Mervyn Fernandez	.10
342	Ricky Sanders	.10
343	Keith Jackson	.20
344	Carl Banks	.10
345	Gill Byrd	.10
346	Al Toon	.10
347	Stephen Baker	.10
348	Randall Cunningham	.10
349	Flipper Anderson	.10
350	Jay Novacek	.10
351	Young/Smith (HH)	.40
352	Sanders/Browner (HH)	.75
353	Montana/Carrier (HH)	.50
354	Thomas/Taylor (HH)	.20
355	Rice/Green (HH)	.50
356	Warren Moon (TECH)	.20
357	Anthony Munoz (TECH)	.10
358	Barry Sanders (TECH)	1.50
359	Jerry Rice (TECH)	1.00
360	Joey Browner (TECH)	.10
361	Morten Andersen (TECH)	.10
362	Sean Landeta (TECH)	.10
363	Thurman Thomas (GW)	.20
364	Emmitt Smith (GW)	3.00
365	Gaston Green (GW)	.10
366	Barry Sanders (GW)	2.00
367	Christian Okoye (GW)	.10
368	Earnest Byner (GW)	.10
369	Neal Anderson (GW)	.10
370	Herschel Walker (GW)	.10
371	Rodney Hampton (GW)	.20
372	Darryl Talley (IDOL)	.10
373	Mark Carrier (IDOL)	.10
374	Jim Breech (IDOL)	.10
375	Rodney Hampton (IDOL)	.20
376	Kevin Mack (IDOL)	.10
377	Steve Jordan (IDOL)	.10
378	Boomer Esiason (IDOL)	.10
379	Steve DeBerg (IDOL)	.10
380	Al Toon (IDOL)	.10
381	Ronnie Lott (IDOL)	.10
382	Henry Ellard (IDOL)	.10
383	Troy Aikman (IDOL)	1.25
384	Thurman Thomas	.50
385	Dan Marino (IDOL)	1.75
386	Howie Long (IDOL)	.10
387	Immaculate Reception (Franco Harris)	.10
388	Esera Tuaolo	.10
389	Super Bowl XXVI (Super Bowl Records)	.10
390	Charles Mann	.10
391	Kenny Walker	.10
392	Reggie Roby	.10
393	*Bruce Pickens*	.20
394	Ray Childress (SL)	.10
395	Karl Mecklenburg (SL)	.10
396	Dean Biasucci (SL)	.10
397	John Alt (SL)	.10
398	Marcus Allen (SL)	.10
399	John Offerdahl (SL)	.10
400	Richard Tardits (SL)	.10
401	Al Toon (SL)	.10
402	Joey Browner (SL)	.10
403	Spencer Tillman (SL)	.10
404	Jay Novacek (SL)	.10
405	Stephen Braggs (SL)	.10
406	Mike Tice (SL)	.10
407	Kevin Greene (SL)	.10
408	Reggie White (SL)	.20
409	Brian Noble (SL)	.10
410	Bart Oates (SL)	.10
411	Art Monk (SL)	.10
412	Ron Wolfley (SL)	.10
413	Louis Lipps (SL)	.10
414	*Dante Jones* (SL)	.20
415	Kenneth Davis (SL)	.10

1992 Pinnacle Samples

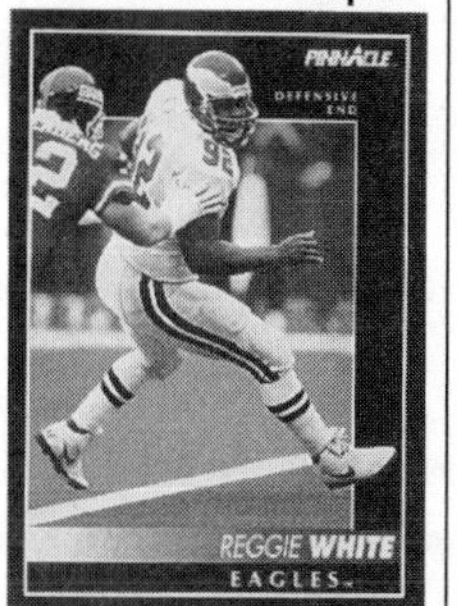

The six-card, standard-size set features six cards from the 1992 Pinnacle football set with the same design, as well as the same card numbers on the backs as their regular-issue counterparts.

		MT
Complete Set (6):		5.00
Common Player:		1.00
1	Reggie White	2.00
5	Pepper Johnson	1.00
19	Chris Spielman	1.00
59	Mike Croel	1.00
100	Bobby Hebert	1.00
102	Rodney Hampton	1.50

1992 Pinnacle

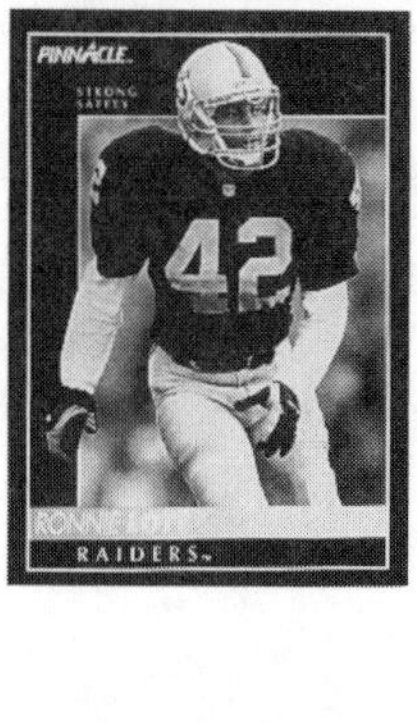

Score decreased its second Pinnacle set to 360 cards. The fronts have action shots with a white frame and black border. Parts of the photos extend over the background, giving them a cut-out look. The player's name is at the bottom of the card in a team color-coded bar. The horizontal backs have black backgrounds with white borders and a purple band that contains the player's name. Also included on the backs are a profile, biography, statistics and a mug shot. Subsets include Rookies, Sidelines, Game Winners, Hall of Famers and Idols. Insert sets include Team Pinnacle cards (13) and Team 2000 (30 cards). A six-card promotional set was also produced to preview the regular set. The cards have a similar design to the regular set, but each card back is marked as a "SAMPLE."

		MT
Complete Set (360):		20.00
Common Player:		.05
Minor Stars:		.10
Pack (16):		.75
Wax Box (36):		25.00
1	Reggie White	.10
2	Eric Green	.05
3	Craig Heyward	.05
4	Phil Simms	.05
5	Pepper Johnson	.05
6	Sean Landeta	.05
7	Dino Hackett	.05
8	Andre Ware	.05
9	Ricky Nattiel	.05
10	Jim Price	.05
11	Jim Ritcher	.05
12	Kelly Stouffer	.05
13	Ray Crockett	.05
14	Steve Tasker	.05
15	Barry Sanders	3.50
16	Pat Swilling	.05
17	Moe Gardner	.05
18	Steve Young	2.50
19	Chris Spielman	.05
20	Richard Dent	.05
21	Anthony Munoz	.05
22	Thurman Thomas	.50
23	Ricky Sanders	.05
24	Steve Atwater	.05
25	Tony Tolbert	.05
26	Haywood Jeffires	.05
27	Duane Bickett	.05
28	Tim McDonald	.05
29	Cris Carter	.10
30	Derrick Thomas	.10
31	Hugh Millen	.05
32	Bart Oates	.05
33	Darryl Talley	.05
34	Marion Butts	.05
35	Pete Stoyanovich	.05
36	Ronnie Lott	.10
37	Simon Fletcher	.05
38	Morten Andersen	.05
39	Clyde Simmons	.05
40	Mark Rypien	.05
41	Henry Ellard	.05
42	Michael Irvin	.50
43	Louis Lipps	.05
44	John L. Williams	.05
45	Broderick Thomas	.05
46	Don Majkowski	.05
47	William Perry	.05
48	David Fulcher	.05
49	Tony Bennett	.05
50	Clay Matthews	.05
51	Warren Moon	.10
52	Bruce Armstrong	.05
53	Bill Brooks	.05
54	Greg Townsend	.05
55	Steve Broussard	.05
56	Mel Gray	.05
57	Kevin Mack	.05
58	Emmitt Smith	5.00
59	Mike Croel	.05
60	Brian Mitchell	.05
61	Bennie Blades	.05
62	Carnell Lake	.05
63	Cornelius Bennett	.05
64	Darrell Thompson	.05
65	Jessie Hester	.05
66	Marv Cook	.05
67	Tim Brown	.10
68	Mark Duper	.05
69	Robert Delpino	.05
70	Eric Martin	.05
71	Wendell Davis	.05
72	Vaughan Johnson	.05
73	Brian Blades	.05
74	Ed King	.05
75	Gaston Green	.05
76	Christian Okoye	.05
77	Rohn Stark	.05
78	Kevin Greene	.05
79	Jay Novacek	.10
80	Chip Lohmiller	.05
81	Cris Dishman	.05
82	Ethan Horton	.05
83	Pat Harlow	.05
84	Mark Ingram	.05
85	Mark Carrier	.05
86	Sam Mills	.05
87	Mark Higgs	.05
88	Keith Jackson	.10
89	Gary Anderson	.05
90	Ken Harvey	.05
91	Anthony Carter	.05
92	Randall McDaniel	.05
93	Johnny Johnson	.10
94	Shane Conlan	.05
95	Sterling Sharpe	.10
96	Guy McIntyre	.05
97	Albert Lewis	.05
98	Chris Doleman	.05
99	Andre Rison	.10
100	Bobby Hebert	.05
101	Dan Owens	.05
102	Rodney Hampton	.10
103	Ernie Jones	.05
104	Reggie Cobb	.05
105	Wilber Marshall	.05
106	Mike Munchak	.05
107	Cortez Kennedy	.05
108	Todd Lyght	.05
109	Burt Grossman	.05
110	Ferrell Edmunds	.05
111	Jim Everett	.05
112	Hardy Nickerson	.05
113	Andre Tippett	.05
114	Ronnie Harmon	.05
115	Andre Waters	.05
116	Ernest Givins	.05
117	Eric Hill	.05
118	Erric Pegram	.10
119	Jarrod Bunch	.05
120	Marcus Allen	.10
121	Barry Foster	.05
122	Kent Hull	.05
123	Neal Anderson	.05
124	Stephen Braggs	.05
125	Nick Lowery	.05
126	Jeff Hostetler	.10
127	Michael Carter	.05
128	Don Warren	.05
129	Brad Baxter	.05
130	John Taylor	.05
131	Harold Green	.05
132	Mike Merriweather	.05
133	Gary Clark	.05
134	Vince Buck	.05
135	Dan Saleaumua	.05
136	Gary Zimmerman	.05
137	Richmond Webb	.05
138	Art Monk	.10
139	Mervyn Fernandez	.05
140	Mark Jackson	.05
141	Freddie Joe Nunn	.05
142	Jeff Lageman	.05
143	Kenny Walker	.05
144	Mark Carrier	.05
145	Jon Vaughn	.05
146	Greg Davis	.05
147	Bubby Brister	.05
148	Mo Lewis	.05
149	Howie Long	.05
150	Rod Bernstine	.05
151	Nick Bell	.05
152	Terry Allen	.50
153	William Fuller	.05
154	Dexter Carter	.05
155	Gene Atkins	.05
156	Don Beebe	.05
157	Mark Collins	.05
158	Jerry Ball	.05
159	Fred Barnett	.05
160	Rodney Holman	.05
161	Stephen Baker	.05
162	Jeff Graham	.10
163	Leonard Russell	.10
164	Jeff Gossett	.05
165	Vinny Testaverde	.05
166	Maurice Hurst	.05
167	Louis Oliver	.05
168	Jim Morrissey	.05
169	Greg Kragen	.05
170	Andre Collins	.05
171	Dave Meggett	.05
172	Keith Henderson	.05
173	Vince Newsome	.05
174	Chris Hinton	.05
175	James Hasty, Steve Sewell	.05
176	John Offerdahl	.05
177	Lomas Brown	.05
178	Neil O'Donnell	.10
179	Leonard Marshall	.05
180	Bubba McDowell	.05
181	Herman Moore	2.00
182	Rob Moore	.05
183	Earnest Byner	.05
184	Keith McCants	.05
185	Floyd Turner	.05
186	Steve Jordan	.05
187	Nate Odomes	.05
188	Jeff Herrod	.05
189	Jim Harbaugh	.10
190	Jessie Tuggle	.05
191	Al Smith	.05
192	Lawrence Dawsey	.05
193	*Steve Bono*	1.00
194	Greg Lloyd	.10
195	Steve Wisniewski	.05
196	Larry Kelm	.05
197	Tommy Kane	.05
198	*Mark Schlereth*	.05
199	Ray Childress	.05
200	Vincent Brown	.05
201	Rodney Peete	.10
202	Dennis Smith	.05
203	Bruce Matthews	.05
204	Rickey Jackson	.05
205	Eric Allen	.05
206	Rich Camarillo	.05
207	Jim Lachey	.05
208	Kevin Ross	.05
209	Irving Fryar	.05
210	Mark Clayton	.05
211	Keith Byars	.05
212	John Elway	.75
213	Harris Barton	.05
214	Aeneas Williams	.05
215	Rich Gannon	.05
216	Toi Cook	.05
217	Rod Woodson	.10
218	Gary Anderson	.05
219	Reggie Roby	.05
220	Karl Mecklenburg	.05
221	Rufus Porter	.05
222	Jon Hand	.05
223	Tim Barnett	.05
224	Eric Swann	.10
225	Eugene Robinson	.05
226	Mike Young	.05
227	Frank Warren	.05
228	Mike Kenn	.05
229	Tim Green	.05
230	Barry Word	.05
231	Mike Pritchard	.05
232	John Kasay	.05
233	Derek Russell	.05
234	Jim Breech	.05
235	Pierce Holt	.05
236	Tim Krumrie	.05
237	William Roberts	.05
238	Erik Kramer	.10
239	Brett Perriman	.10
240	Reyna Thompson	.05
241	Chris Miller	.05
242	Drew Hill	.05
243	Curtis Duncan	.05
244	Seth Joyner	.05
245	Ken Norton	.05
246	Calvin Williams	.05
247	James Joseph	.05
248	*Bennie Thompson*	.05
249	Tunch Ilkin	.05
250	Brad Edward	.05
251	Jeff Jaeger	.05
252	Gill Byrd	.05
253	Jeff Feagles	.05
254	*Jamie Dukes*	.05
255	Greg McMurtry	.05
256	Anthony Johnson	.05
257	Lamar Lathon	.05
258	John Roper	.05
259	Lorenzo White	.05
260	Brian Noble	.05
261	Chris Singleton	.05
262	Todd Marinovich	.05
263	Jay Hilgenberg	.05
264	Kyle Clifton	.05
265	Tony Casillas	.05
266	James Francis	.05
267	Eddie Anderson	.05
268	Tim Harris	.05
269	James Lofton	.05
270	Jay Schroeder	.05
271	Ed West	.05
272	Don Mosebar	.05
273	Jackie Slater	.05
274	*Fred McAfee*	.05
276	Charles Mann	.05
277	Ron Hall	.05
278	Darrell Green	.05
279	Jeff Cross	.05
280	Jeff Wright	.05
281	Issiac Holt	.05
282	Dermontti Dawson	.05
283	Michael Haynes	.05
284	Tony Mandarich	.05
285	Leroy Hoard	.05
286	Darryl Henley	.05
287	Tim McGee	.05
288	Willie Gault	.05
289	Dalton Hilliard	.05
290	Tim McKyer	.05
291	Tom Waddle	.05
292	Eric Thomas	.05
293	Herschel Walker	.05
294	Donnell Woolford	.05
295	James Brooks	.05
296	Brad Muster	.05
297	Brent Jones	.05
298	Erik Howard	.05
299	Alvin Harper	.10
300	Joey Browner	.05
301	Jack Del Rio	.05
302	Cleveland Gary	.05
303	Brett Favre	5.00
304	Freeman McNeil	.05
305	Willie Green	.05
306	Percy Snow	.05
307	Neil Smith	.05
308	Eric Bieniemy	.05
309	Keith Traylor	.05
310	Ernie Mills	.05
311	Will Wolford	.05
312	Robert Young	.05
313	Anthony Smith	.05
314	*Robert Porcher*	.50
315	*Leon Searcy*	.05
316	*Amp Lee*	.20
317	*Siran Stacy*	.05
318	*Patrick Rowe*	.05
319	*Chris Mims*	.05
320	*Matt Elliott*	.05
321	*Ricardo McDonald*	.05
322	*Keith Hamilton*	.05
323	*Edgar Bennett*	1.00
324	*Chris Hakel*	.05
325	*Dexter McNabb*	.05
326	*Roderick Milstead*	.05
327	*Joe Bowden*	.05
328	*Brian Bollinger*	.05
329	*Darryl Williams*	.05
330	*Tommy Vardell*	.15
331	Glenn Parker	.05
332	Herschel Walker	.05
333	Mike Cofer	.05
334	Mark Rypien	.05
335	Andre Rison	.10
336	Henry Ellard	.05
337	Rob Moore	.05
338	Fred Barnett	.05
339	Mark Clayton	.05
340	Eric Martin	.05
341	Irving Fryar	.05
342	Tim Brown	.10
343	Sterling Sharpe	.10
344	Gary Clark	.05
345	John Mackey	.05
346	Lem Barney	.05
347	John Riggins	.05
348	Marion Butts	.05
349	Jeff Lageman	.05
350	Eric Green	.05
351	Reggie White	.10
352	Marv Cook	.05
353	John Elway, Roger Staubach	.50
354	Steve Tasker	.05
355	Nick Lowery	.05
356	Mark Clayton	.05
357	Warren Moon	.10
358	Eric Metcalf	.05
359	Charles Haley	.05
360	*Terrell Buckley*	.05

1992 Pinnacle Team Pinnacle

Each of these 13 insert cards features two players on it, one on each side. Score randomly included the cards in 1992 Score Pinnacle packs at a rate of one per every 36 packs. The cards have a gold foil stripe at the bottom with the player's name and position. A black stripe beneath this gold stripe has a card number (1 of 13, etc.), but this number only appears on one side of the card. An offensive player is featured on one side, while a standout defensive counterpart is on the other. The cards feature the artwork of Christopher Greco.

		MT
Complete Set (13):		80.00
Common Player:		5.00
Minor Stars:		10.00
1	Mark Rypien, Ronnie Lott	5.00
2	Barry Sanders, Derrick Thomas	20.00
3	Thurman Thomas, Pat Swilling	10.00
4	Eric Green, Steve Atwater	5.00
5	Haywood Jeffires, Darrell Green	5.00
6	Michael Irvin, Eric Allen	10.00
7	Bruce Matthews, Jerry Ball	5.00
8	Steve Wisniewski, Pepper Johnson	5.00
9	William Roberts, Karl Mecklenburg	5.00
10	Jim Lachey, William Fuller	5.00
11	Anthony Munoz, Reggie White	10.00
12	Mel Gray, Steve Tasker	5.00
13	Jeff Jaeger, Jeff Gossett	5.00

1992 Pinnacle Team 2000

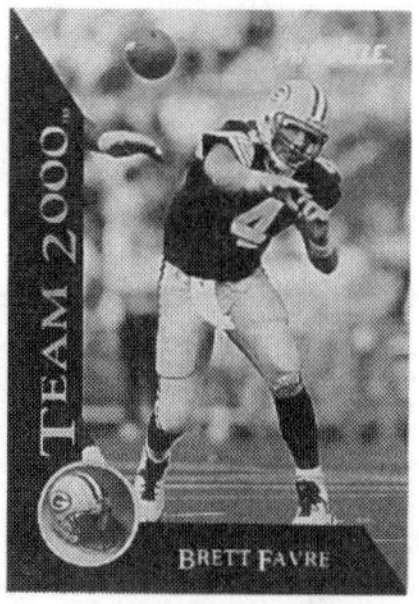

The NFL's projected stars of the year 2000 are featured on these inserts, available randomly two per 27-card jumbo pack of 1992 Score Pinnacle football. The card is framed on the left and bottom by a black border. "Team 2000" is written in gold foil along the left side of the card; the player's name is in gold foil at the bottom. A team helmet logo intersects the two borders. The card back has a career summary and player photo against a black background. The horizontally-designed back also has a card number (1 of 30, etc.).

		MT
Complete Set (30):		15.00
Common Player:		.25
Minor Stars:		.50
1	Todd Marinovich	.25
2	Rodney Hampton	.50
3	Mike Croel	.25
4	Leonard Russell	.50
5	Herman Moore	.75
6	Rob Moore	.50
7	Jon Vaughn	.25
8	Lamar Lathon	.25
9	Ed King	.25
10	Moe Gardner	.25
11	Barry Foster	.25
12	Eric Green	.25
13	Kenny Walker	.25
14	Tim Barnett	.25
15	Derrick Thomas	.50
16	Steve Atwater	.25
17	Nick Bell	.25
18	John Friesz	.50
19	Emmitt Smith	3.00
20	Eric Swann	.25
21	Barry Sanders	4.00
22	Mark Carrier	.25
23	Brett Favre	4.00
24	James Francis	.25
25	Lawrence Dawsey	.25
26	Keith McCants	.25
27	Broderick Thomas	.25
28	Mike Pritchard	.25
29	Bruce Pickens	.25
30	Todd Lyght	.25

1993 Pinnacle Samples

The six-card, standard size set gave collectors a preview of the 1993 base set by issuing the first six cards of the regular-issue set. The cards were distributed in 7-1/2" x 7" panels with two rows of three cards.

		MT
Complete Set (6):		8.00
Common Player:		1.00
1	Brett Favre	6.00
2	Tommy Vardell	1.00
3	Jarrod Bunch	1.00
4	Mike Croel	1.00
5	Morten Andersen	1.00
6	Barry Foster	1.00

1993 Pinnacle

Score's 1993 Pinnacle set has 360 cards and includes two subsets - Hall of Famers and Hometown Heroes. The cards have black backgrounds, with the player's team name at the top and his name at the bottom of the card. Backs have a mug shot, one-year and career statistics, a profile and biographical information. Insert sets include Men of Autumn (55 cards), Rookies (25), Super Bowl XXVII (10), Team 2001 (30) and Team Pinnacle (13 cards). Six sample cards on a 7-1/2" x 7" panel was also produced as previews of the regular set. The cards are similar in design to the regular set, including numbers, but the sample cards are labeled as such

on the backs under the anti-counterfeit band.

		MT
Complete Set (360):		25.00
Common Player:		.10
Minor Stars:		.20
Autograph F. Harris:		25.00
Wax Box:		60.00
1	Brett Favre	4.00
2	Tommy Vardell	.10
3	Jarrod Bunch	.10
4	Mike Croel	.10
5	Morten Andersen	.10
6	Barry Foster	.30
7	Chris Spielman	.10
8	Jim Jeffcoat	.10
9	Ken Ruettgers	.10
10	Cris Dishman	.10
11	Ricky Watters	.30
12	Alfred Williams	.10
13	Mark Kelso	.10
14	Moe Gardner	.10
15	Terry Allen	.10
16	Willie Gault	.10
17	Bubba McDowell	.10
18	Brian Mitchell	.10
19	Karl Mecklenburg	.10
20	Jim Everett	.20
21	Bobby Humphrey	.10
22	Tim Krumrie	.10
23	Ken Norton	.10
24	Wendell Davis	.10
25	Brad Baxter	.10
26	Mel Gray	.10
27	Jon Vaughn	.10
28	James Hasty	.10
29	Chris Warren	.50
30	Tim Harris	.10
31	Eric Metcalf	.10
32	Rob Moore	.10
33	Charles Haley	.10
34	Leonard Marshall	.10
35	Jeff Graham	.10
36	Eugene Robinson	.10
37	Darryl Talley	.10
38	Brent Jones	.10
39	Reggie Roby	.10
40	Bruce Armstrong	.10
41	Audray McMillian	.10
42	Bern Brostek	.10
43	Tony Bennett	.10
44	Albert Lewis	.10
45	Derrick Thomas	.25
46	Cris Carter	.20
47	Richmond Webb	.10
48	Sean Landeta	.10
49	Cleveland Gary	.10
50	Mark Carrier	.10
51	Lawrence Dawsey	.10
52	Lamar Lathon	.10
53	Nick Bell	.10
54	Curtis Duncan	.10
55	Irving Fryar	.10
56	Seth Joyner	.10
57	Jay Novacek	.10
58	John L. Williams	.10
59	Amp Lee	.10
60	Marion Butts	.10
61	Clyde Simmons	.10
62	Rich Gannon	.10
63	Anthony Johnson	.10
64	Dave Meggett	.10
65	James Francis	.10
66	Trace Armstrong	.10
67	Mo Lewis	.10
68	Cornelius Bennett	.10
69	Mark Duper	.10
70	Frank Reich	.10
71	Eric Green	.10
72	Bruce Matthews	.10
73	Steve Broussard	.10
74	Anthony Carter	.10
75	Sterling Sharpe	.30
76	Mike Kenn	.10
77	Andre Rison	.30
78	Todd Marinovich	.10
79	Vincent Brown	.10
80	Harold Green	.10
81	Art Monk	.10
82	Reggie Cobb	.10
83	Johnny Johnson	.10
84	Tommy Kane	.10
85	Rohn Stark	.10
86	Steve Tasker	.10
87	Ronnie Harmon	.10
88	Pepper Johnson	.10
89	Hardy Nickerson	.10
90	Alvin Harper	.20
91	Louis Oliver	.10
92	Rod Woodson	.25
93	Sam Mills	.10
94	Randall McDaniel	.10
95	Johnny Holland	.10
96	Jackie Slater	.10
97	Don Mosebar	.10
98	Andre Ware	.10
99	Kelvin Martin	.10
100	Emmitt Smith	4.00
101	Michael Brooks	.10
102	Dan Saleaumua	.10
103	John Elway	1.00
104	Henry Jones	.10
105	William Perry	.10
106	James Lofton	.10
107	Carnell Lake	.10
108	Chip Lohmiller	.10
109	Andre Tippett	.10
110	Barry Word	.10
111	Haywood Jeffires	.10
112	Kenny Walker	.10
113	John Randle	.10
114	Donnell Woolford	.10
115	Johnny Bailey	.10
116	Marcus Allen	.25
117	Mark Jackson	.10
118	Ray Agnew	.10
119	Gill Byrd	.10
120	Kyle Clifton	.10
121	Marv Cook	.10
122	Jerry Ball	.10
123	Steve Jordan	.10
124	Shannon Sharpe	.25
125	Brian Blades	.10
126	Rodney Hampton	.30
127	Bobby Hebert	.10
128	Jessie Tuggle	.10
129	Tom Newberry	.10
130	Keith McCants	.10
131	Richard Dent	.10
132	Herman Moore	1.00
133	Michael Irvin	.50
134	Ernest Givins	.10
135	Mark Rypien	.10
136	Leonard Russell	.10
137	Reggie White	.25
138	Thurman Thomas	.50
139	Nick Lowery	.10
140	Al Smith	.10
141	Jackie Harris	.10
142	Duane Bickett	.10
143	Lawyer Tillman	.10
144	Steve Wisniewski	.10
145	Derrick Fenner	.10
146	Harris Barton	.10
147	Rich Camarillo	.10
148	John Offerdahl	.10
149	Mike Johnson	.10
150	Ricky Reynolds	.10
151	Fred Barnett	.10
152	Nate Newton	.10
153	Chris Doleman	.10
154	Todd Scott	.10
155	Tim McKyer	.10
156	Ken Harvey	.10
157	Jeff Feagles	.10
158	Vince Workman	.10
159	Bart Oates	.10
160	Chris Miller	.10
161	Pete Stoyanovich	.10
162	Steve Wallace	.10
163	Dermontti Dawson	.10
164	Kenneth Davis	.10
165	Mike Munchak	.10
166	George Jamison	.10
167	Christian Okoye	.10
168	Chris Hinton	.10
169	Vaughan Johnson	.10
170	Gaston Green	.10
171	Kevin Greene	.10
172	Rob Burnett	.10
173	Norm Johnson	.10
174	Eric Hill	.10
175	Lomas Brown	.10
176	Chip Banks	.10
177	Greg Townsend	.10
178	David Fulcher	.10
179	Gary Anderson	.10
180	Brian Washington	.10
181	Brett Perriman	.10
182	Chris Chandler	.10
183	Phil Hansen	.10
184	Mark Clayton	.10
185	Frank Warren	.10
186	Tim Brown	.30
187	Mark Stepnoski	.10
188	Bryan Cox	.10
189	Gary Zimmerman	.10
190	Neil O'Donnell	.30
191	Anthony Smith	.10
192	Craig Heyward	.10
193	Keith Byars	.10
194	Sean Salisbury	.10
195	Todd Lyght	.10
196	Jessie Hester	.10
197	Rufus Porter	.10
198	Steve Christie	.10
199	Nate Lewis	.10
200	Barry Sanders	3.00
201	Michael Haynes	.10
202	John Taylor	.10
203	John Friesz	.10
204	William Fuller	.10
205	Dennis Smith	.10
206	Adrian Cooper	.10
207	Henry Thomas	.10
208	Gerald Williams	.10
209	Chris Burkett	.10
210	Broderick Thomas	.10
211	Marvin Washington	.10
212	Bennie Blades	.10
213	Tony Casillas	.10
214	Bubby Brister	.10
215	Don Griffin	.10
216	Jeff Cross	.10
217	Derrick Walker	.10
218	Lorenzo White	.10
219	Ricky Sanders	.10
220	Rickey Jackson	.10
221	Simon Fletcher	.10
222	Troy Vincent	.10
223	Gary Clark	.10
224	Stanley Richard	.10
225	Dave Krieg	.10
226	Warren Moon	.25
227	Reggie Langhorne	.10
228	Kent Hull	.10
229	Ferrell Edmunds	.10
230	Cortez Kennedy	.20
231	Hugh Millen	.10
232	Eugene Chung	.10
233	Rodney Peete	.10
234	Tom Waddle	.10
235	David Klingler	.10
236	Mark Carrier	.10
237	Jay Schroeder	.10
238	James Jones	.10
239	Phil Simms	.10
240	Steve Atwater	.10
241	Jeff Herrod	.10
242	Dale Carter	.10
243	*Glenn Cadrez*	.10
244	Wayne Martin	.10
245	Willie Davis	.10
246	Lawrence Taylor	.20
247	Stan Humphries	.50
248	Byron Evans	.10
249	Wilber Marshall	.10
250	*Michael Bankston*	.10
251	Steve McMichael	.10
252	Brad Edwards	.10
253	Will Wolford	.10
254	Paul Gruber	.10
255	Steve Young	2.00
256	Chuck Cecil	.10
257	Pierce Holt	.25
258	Anthony Miller	.20
259	Carl Banks	.10
260	Brad Muster	.10
261	Clay Matthews	.10
262	Rod Bernstine	.10
263	Tim Barnett	.10
264	Greg Lloyd	.10
265	Sean Jones	.10
266	J.J. Birden	.10
267	Tim McDonald	.10
268	Charles Mann	.10
269	Bruce Smith	.10
270	Sean Gilbert	.10
271	Ricardo McDonald	.10
272	Jeff Hostetler	.20
273	Russell Maryland	.10
274	*Dave Brown*	1.00
275	Ronnie Lott	.10
276	Jim Kelly	.25
277	Joe Montana	3.00
278	Eric Allen	.10
279	Browning Nagle	.10
280	Neal Anderson	.10
281	Troy Aikman	2.00
282	Ed McCaffrey	.10
283	Robert Jones	.10
284	Dalton Hilliard	.10
285	Johnny Mitchell	.10
286	Jay Hilgenberg	.10
287	Eric Martin	.10
288	Steve Emtman	.10
289	Vaughn Dunbar	.10
290	Mark Wheeler	.10
291	Leslie O'Neal	.10
292	Jerry Rice	2.00
293	Neil Smith	.10
294	Kerry Cash	.10
295	Dan McGwire	.10
296	Carl Pickens	1.00
297	Terrell Buckley	.10
298	Randall Cunningham	.25
299	Santana Dotson	.10
300	Keith Jackson	.10
301	Jim Lachey	.10
302	Dan Marino	3.50
303	Lee Williams	.10
304	Burt Grossman	.10
305	Kevin Mack	.10
306	Pat Swilling	.10
307	*Arthur Marshall*	.20
308	Jim Harbaugh	.10
309	Kurt Barber	.10
310	Harvey Williams	.10
311	Ricky Ervins	.10
312	Willie Anderson	.10
313	Bernie Kosar	.20
314	Boomer Esiason	.20
315	Deion Sanders	1.00
316	Ray Childress	.10
317	Howie Long	.10
318	Henry Ellard	.10
319	Marco Coleman	.10
320	Chris Mims	.10
321	Quentin Coryatt	.10
322	Jason Hanson	.10
323	Ricky Proehl	.10
324	Randal Hill	.10
325	Vinny Testaverde	.20
326	Jeff George	.20
327	Junior Seau	.40
328	Earnest Byner	.10
329	Andre Reed	.20
330	Phillippi Sparks	.10
331	Kevin Ross	.10
332	Clarence Verdin	.10
333	Darryl Henley	.10
334	Dana Hall	.10
335	Greg McMurtry	.10
336	Ron Hall	.10
337	Darrell Green	.10
338	Carlton Bailey	.10
339	Irv Eatman	.10
340	Greg Kragen	.10
341	Wade Wilson	.10
342	Klaus Wilmsmeyer	.10
343	Derek Brown	.10
344	Erik Williams	.10
345	Jim McMahon	.10
346	Mike Sherrard	.10
347	Mark Bavaro	.10
348	Anthony Munoz	.10
349	Eric Dickerson	.10
350	Steve Beuerlein	.10
351	Tim McGee	.10
352	Terry McDaniel	.10
353	Dan Fouts (Hall of Fame)	.20
354	Chuck Noll (Hall of Fame)	.10
355	Bill Walsh (Hall of Fame)	.10
356	Larry Little (Hall of Fame)	.10
357	Todd Marinovich (Hometown Hero)	.10
358	Jeff George (Hometown Hero)	.20
359	Bernie Kosar (Hometown Hero)	.10
360	Rob Moore (Hometown Hero)	.10

1993 Pinnacle Men of Autumn

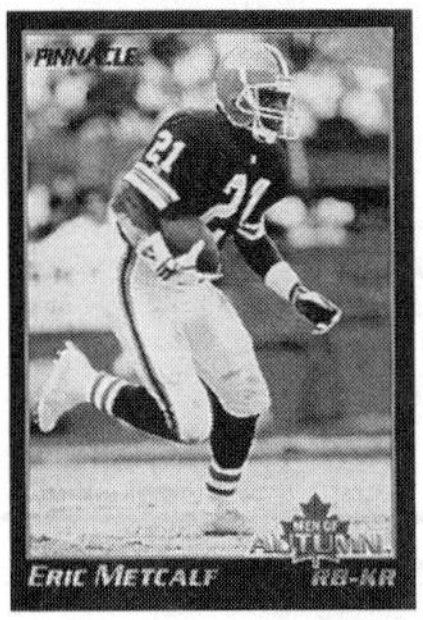

These 55 cards were randomly inserted into 1993 Score football 16-card foil packs. The cards feature a glossy black laminate with a color action photo with a red frame. The set's logo is at the bottom, along with the player's name and position, which are in gold foil. Each back is horizontal and numbered and has a closeup shot of the player, plus a brief career summary.

		MT
Complete Set (55):		15.00
Common Player:		.25
Minor Stars:		.50
1	Andre Rison	.50
2	Thurman Thomas	.50
3	Wendell Davis	.25
4	Harold Green	.25
5	Eric Metcalf	.25
6	Michael Irvin	.50
7	John Elway	1.50
8	Barry Sanders	3.00
9	Sterling Sharpe	.50
10	Warren Moon	.50
11	Rohn Stark	.25
12	Derrick Thomas	.50
13	Terry McDaniel	.25
14	Cleveland Gary	.25
15	Dan Marino	3.00
16	Terry Allen	.25
17	Marv Cook	.25
18	Bobby Hebert	.25
19	Rodney Hampton	.50
20	Brad Baxter	.25
21	Reggie White	.50
22	Ricky Proehl	.25
23	Barry Foster	.50
24	Junior Seau	.50
25	Steve Young	2.00
26	Cortez Kennedy	.25
27	Reggie Cobb	.25
28	Mark Rypien	.25
29	Deion Sanders	1.00
30	Bruce Smith	.25
31	Richard Dent	.25
32	Alfred Williams	.25
33	Clay Matthews	.25
34	Emmitt Smith	4.00
35	Simon Fletcher	.25
36	Chris Spielman	.25
37	Brett Favre	4.00
38	Bruce Matthews	.25
39	Jeff Herrod	.25
40	Nick Lowery	.25
41	Steve Wisniewski	.25
42	Jim Everett	.25
43	Keith Jackson	.25
44	Chris Doleman	.25
45	Irving Fryar	.25
46	Rickey Jackson	.25
47	Pepper Johnson	.25
48	Randall Cunningham	.50
49	Rich Camarillo	.25
50	Rod Woodson	.50
51	Ronnie Harmon	.25
52	Ricky Watters	.50
53	Chris Warren	.50
54	Lawrence Dawsey	.25
55	Wilber Marshall	.25

1993 Pinnacle Rookies

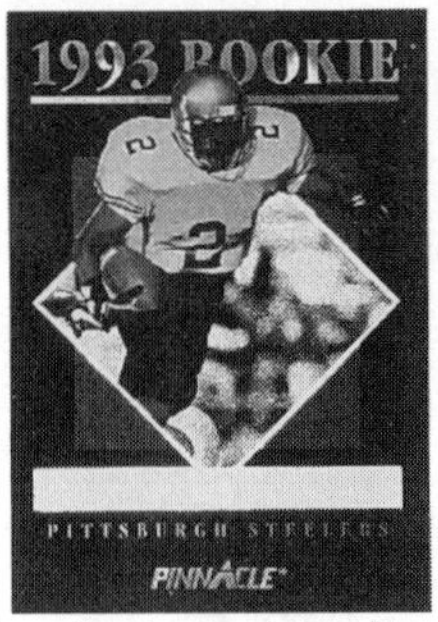

These inserts cards have a black front with a color action photo emerging from a diamond-shaped metallic design in the middle. The set's name and Pinnacle logo are foil stamped in copper on the card, too. A metallic bar in team colors contains the player's name and team. The back is black and has a copper panel which includes career information. The player's name is in copper at the top of the card, which is also numbered 1 of 25, etc. Cards were reportedly randomly inserted one per every 36 1993 Pinnacle foil packs and feature several of the NFL's top rookies in 1993.

		MT
Complete Set (25):		400.00
Common Player:		7.00
1	Drew Bledsoe	175.00
2	Garrison Hearst	30.00
3	John Copeland	7.00
4	Eric Curry	7.00
5	Curtis Conway	25.00
6	Lincoln Kennedy	7.00
7	Jerome Bettis	50.00
8	Dan Williams	7.00
9	Patrick Bates	7.00
10	Brad Hopkins	7.00
11	Wayne Simmons	7.00
12	Rick Mirer	10.00
13	Tom Carter	7.00
14	Irv Smith	7.00
15	Marvin Jones	7.00
16	Deon Figures	7.00
17	Leonard Renfro	7.00
18	O.J. McDuffie	20.00
19	Dana Stubblefield	14.00
20	Carlton Gray	7.00
21	Demetrius DuBose	7.00
22	Troy Drayton	7.00
23	Natrone Means	30.00
24	Reggie Brooks	7.00
25	Glyn Milburn	14.00

1993 Pinnacle Super Bowl XXVII

The 1993 Super Bowl Champion Dallas Cowboys are featured on this 10-card insert set. Cards were randomly inserted in foil packs, one per hobby box of 1993 Pinnacle. Horizontal fronts feature a borderless color photo, plus a blue stripe that has the set name in blue foil. The backs are horizontal, too, and has the player's name, game highlights, Buffalo Bills and Cowboys helmets and the Super Bowl logo. Each card is numbered 1 of 10, etc.

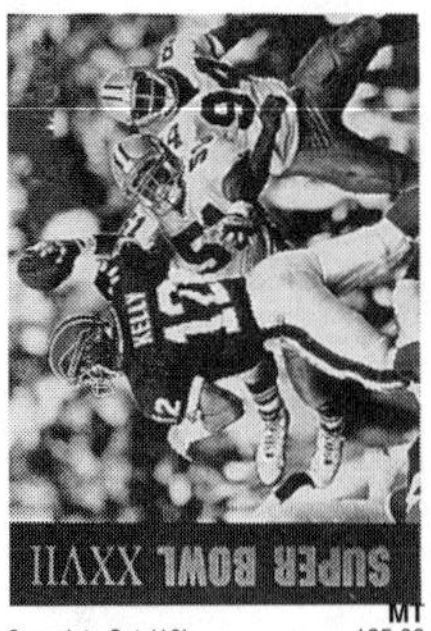

		MT
Complete Set (10):		125.00
Common Player:		10.00
1	Rose Bowl	10.00
2	Dominant "D"	10.00
3	Emmitt Smith	50.00
4	Ken Norton Jr.	10.00
5	Michael Irvin	20.00
6	Jay Novacek	10.00
7	Charles Haley	10.00
8	Leon Lett	10.00
9	Alvin Harper	10.00
10	Sweet Victory	10.00

1993 Pinnacle Team Pinnacle

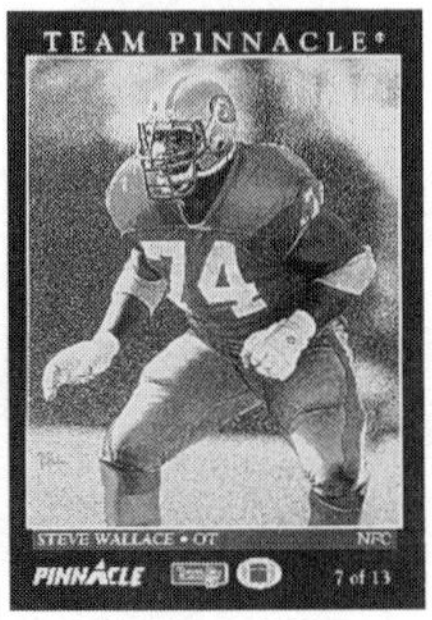

Each of these cards features two player paintings on it - one per side. An AFC player is featured with his NFC counterpart at that position. The paintings are framed by a thin white border and a larger black one. The player's name, position and conference are given in a stripe at the bottom. Both sides are numbered 1 of 13, etc. Cards were random inserts in 1993 Pinnacle foil packs, at least one per every 90 packs.

		MT
Complete Set (13):		250.00
Common Player:		10.00
1	Troy Aikman, Joe Montana	120.00
2	Thurman Thomas, Emmitt Smith	75.00
3	Rodney Hampton, Barry Foster	10.00
4	Sterling Sharpe, Anthony Miller	15.00
5	Haywood Jeffires, Michael Irvin	15.00
6	Jay Novacek, Keith Jackson	10.00
7	Richmond Webb, Steve Wallace	10.00
8	Reggie White, Leslie O'Neal	10.00
9	Cortez Kennedy, Sean Gilbert	10.00
10	Derrick Thomas, Wilber Marshall	10.00
11	Sam Mills, Junior Seau	15.00
12	Rod Woodson, Deion Sanders	20.00
13	Steve Atwater, Tim McDonald	10.00

1993 Pinnacle Team 2001

Promising young NFL players who might become stars by the year 2001 are featured in this 30-card insert set. A wide black stripe along the left and bottom of the card front borders a color action photo of the player. The set's and player's name are stamped in gold foil at the bottom, too, near a team logo. The back is done in a horizontal format and has a player mug shot and a black panel with a 1992 recap, team name and position, plus the player's name in gold foil. Cards, numbered 1 of 27, etc., were randomly inserted in 1993 Pinnacle 27-card super packs, one per pack.

		MT
Complete Set (30):		15.00
Common Player:		.50
Minor Stars:		1.00
1	Junior Seau	1.00
2	Cortez Kennedy	.50
3	Carl Pickens	3.00
4	David Klingler	.50
5	Santana Dotson	.50
6	Sean Gilbert	.50
7	Brett Favre	8.00
8	Steve Emtman	.50
9	Rodney Hampton	1.00
10	Browning Nagle	.50
11	Amp Lee	.50
12	Vaughn Dunbar	.50
13	Quentin Coryatt	.50
14	Marco Coleman	.50
15	Johnny Mitchell	.50
16	Arthur Marshall	.50
17	Dale Carter	.50
18	Henry Jones	.50
19	Terrell Buckley	.50
20	Tommy Vardell	.50
21	Tommy Maddox	.50
22	Barry Foster	1.00
23	Herman Moore	3.00
24	Ricky Watters	1.00
25	Mike Croel	.50
26	Russell Maryland	.50
27	Terry Allen	.50
28	Jon Vaughn	.50
29	Todd Marinovich	.50
30	Jeff Graham	.50

1994 Pinnacle Samples

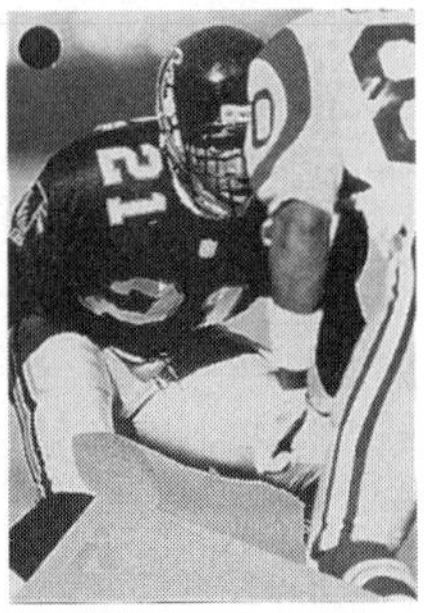

The 10-card, regular-size set was issued as a preview for the 1994 regular-issue set. The cards have the same design as the cards in the base set, complete with same card-back numbers, but with a hole punched in a corner.

		MT
Complete Set (10):		10.00
Common Player:		.75
1	Deion Sanders (last line of text reads "es for a 17.7-yard...")	1.50
3	Trophy Collection (Barry Sanders) (name in brown ink on back)	2.50
24	Sean Gilbert (last line on text reads "mage to earn...")	.75
30	Alvin Harper (last line of text reads "tions and scored...")	.75
32	Derrick Thomas (last line of text reads "bles last season")	.75
85	James Jett (hometown/drafted line 1-3/16" long instead of 1-5/16")	.75
214	Chuck Levy (card number in white letters)	.75
DP8	William Floyd (last line of text reads "over would-be tacklers.")	1.25
NNO	Ad Card	.75
NNO	Pick Pinnacle Redemp. Card. (no player name on front)	.75

1994 Pinnacle

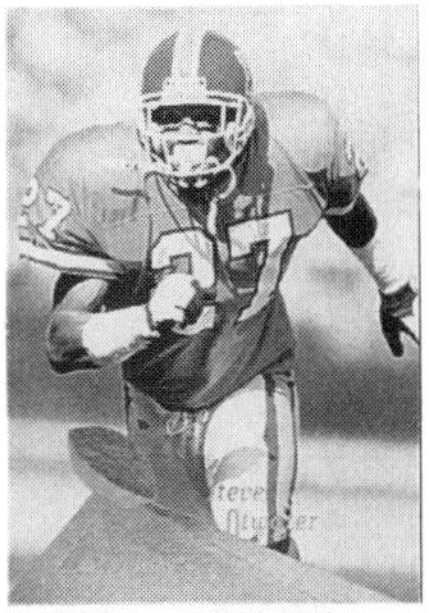

Pinnacle football 1994 contained full-bleed action shots with a gold foil football appearing on top of a large, textured, gold foil pyramid. Each player's name also appears in gold foil. The backs contain a close-up of the player and statistics on a football background. There were six insert sets in Pinnacle football: Trophy Collection, Team Pinnacle, Pick Pinnacle, Draft Pinnacle, Pinnacle Passer and Performers. Trophy is a 270-card parallel set that utilizes the Dufex printing process on regular-issue cards. Cards from the set are inserted at a rate of one-per-four packs. These cards feature the same shot as in the regular set, but have a Dufex background (shiny with silver highlights). Card backs are the same, except for a Trophy Collection logo in

the bottom-right corner. Three insert sets were also made: Draft Picks, Performers and Team Pinnacle.

	MT
Complete Set (270):	25.00
Common Player:	.10
Minor Stars:	.20
Comp. Trophy Coll. (270):	500.00
Common Trophy:	2.00
Trophy Minor Stars:	4.00
Unlisted Trophy Stars:	10x-20x
Hobby Pack (14):	4.00
Hobby Wax Box (24):	80.00
Retail Pack (14):	3.00
Retail Wax Box (36):	70.00

1	Deion Sanders	.75
2	Eric Metcalf	.10
3	Barry Sanders	2.50
4	Ernest Givins	.10
5	Phil Simms	.10
6	Rod Woodson	.20
7	Michael Irvin	.20
8	Cortez Kennedy	.20
9	Eric Martin	.10
10	Jeff Hostetler	.20
11	Sterling Sharpe	.30
12	John Elway	1.00
13	Neal Anderson	.10
14	Terry Kirby	.20
15	Jim Everett	.10
16	Lawrence Dawsey	.10
17	Kelvin Martin	.10
18	Tim McGee	.10
19	Cris Carter	.20
20	Ronnie Harmon	.10
21	Jim Kelly	.30
22	Steve Young	1.50
23	Johnny Johnson	.10
24	Sean Gilbert	.10
25	Brian Mitchell	.10
26	Carl Pickens	.10
27	Tim Brown	.20
28	Reggie Langhorne	.10
29	Webster Slaughter	.10
30	Alvin Harper	.20
31	Andre Rison	.20
32	Derrick Thomas	.20
33	Irving Fryar	.10
34	Vinny Testaverde	.10
35	Steve Beuerlein	.10
36	Brett Favre	3.00
37	Barry Foster	.20
38	Vaughan Johnson	.10
39	Carlton Bailey	.10
40	Steve Emtman	.10
41	Anthony Miller	.10
42	Jeff Cross	.10
43	Trace Armstrong	.10
44	Derek Russell	.10
45	Vincent Brisby	.30
46	Mark Jackson	.10
47	Eugene Robinson	.10
48	John Friesz	.10
49	Scott Mitchell	.20
50	Steve Atwater	.10
51	Ken Norton	.10
52	Vincent Brown	.10
53	Morten Andersen	.10
54	Gary Anderson	.10
55	Eric Curry	.10
56	Henry Jones	.10
57	Willie Anderson	.10
58	Pat Swilling	.10
59	Erric Pegram	.10
60	Bruce Matthews	.10
61	Willie Davis	.10
62	O.J. McDuffie	.20
63	Qadry Ismail	.20
64	Anthony Smith	.10
65	Eric Allen	.10
66	Marion Butts	.10
67	Chris Miller	.10
68	Terrell Buckley	.10
69	Thurman Thomas	.30
70	Roosevelt Potts	.10
71	Tony McGee	.10
72	Jason Hanson	.10
73	Victor Bailey	.10
74	Albert Lewis	.10
75	Nate Odomes	.10
76	Ben Coates	.20
77	Warren Moon	.20
78	Derek Brown	.10
79	David Klingler	.10
80	Cleveland Gary	.10
81	Emmitt Smith	3.00
82	Jay Novacek	.10
83	Dana Stubblefield	.20
84	Michael Brooks	.10
85	James Jett	.10
86	J.J. Birden	.10
87	William Fuller	.10
88	Glyn Milburn	.10
89	Tim Worley	.10
90	Brett Perriman	.10
91	Randall Cunningham	.20
92	Drew Bledsoe	2.00
93	Jerome Bettis	1.00
94	Boomer Esiason	.10
95	Garrison Hearst	.20
96	Bruce Smith	.10
97	Jackie Harris	.10
98	Jeff George	.20
99	Tom Waddle	.10
100	John Copeland	.10
101	Bobby Hebert	.10
102	Joe Montana	2.00
103	Herman Moore	.75
104	Rick Mirer	.20
105	Ricky Watters	.20
106	Neil O'Donnell	.20
107	Herschel Walker	.10
108	Rob Moore	.10
109	Reggie Brooks	.10
110	Tommy Vardell	.10
111	Eric Green	.10
112	Stan Humphries	.20
113	Greg Robinson	.10
114	Eric Swann	.10
115	Courtney Hawkins	.10
116	Andre Reed	.10
117	Steve McMichael	.10
118	Gary Brown	.10
119	Terry Allen	.10
120	Dan Marino	3.00
121	Gary Clark	.10
122	Chris Warren	.20
123	Pierce Holt	.10
124	Anthony Carter	.10
125	Quentin Coryatt	.10
126	Harold Green	.10
127	Leonard Russell	.10
128	Tim McDonald	.10
129	Chris Spielman	.10
130	Cody Carlson	.10
131	Ron Moore	.10
132	Renaldo Turnbull	.10
133	Ronnie Lott	.10
134	Natrone Means	.75
135	Keith Byars	.10
136	Henry Ellard	.10
137	Steve Jordan	.10
138	Calvin Williams	.10
139	Brian Blades	.10
140	Michael Jackson	.10
141	Charles Haley	.10
142	Curtis Conway	.10
143	Nick Lowery	.10
144	Bill Brooks	.10
145	Michael Haynes	.10
146	Willie Green	.10
147	Duane Bickett	.10
148	Shannon Sharpe	.20
149	Ricky Proehl	.10
150	Troy Aikman	1.50
151	Mike Sherrard	.10
152	Reggie Cobb	.10
153	Norm Johnson	.10
154	Neil Smith	.10
155	James Francis	.10
156	Greg McMurtry	.10
157	Greg Townsend	.10
158	Mel Gray	.10
159	Rocket Ismail	.10
160	Leslie O'Neal	.10
161	Johnny Mitchell	.10
162	Brent Jones	.10
163	Chris Doleman	.10
164	Seth Joyner	.10
165	Marco Coleman	.10
166	Mark Higgs	.10
167	John L. Williams	.10
168	Darrell Green	.10
169	Mark Carrier	.10
170	Reggie White	.20
171	Darryl Talley	.10
172	Russell Maryland	.10
173	Mark Collins	.10
174	Chris Jacke	.10
175	Richard Dent	.10
176	John Taylor	.10
177	Rodney Hampton	.20
178	Dwight Stone	.10
179	Cornelius Bennett	.10
180	Cris Dishman	.10
181	Jerry Rice	1.50
182	Rod Bernstine	.10
183	Keith Hamilton	.10
184	Keith Jackson	.10
185	Craig Erickson	.10
186	Marcus Allen	.20
187	Marcus Robertson	.10
188	Junior Seau	.20
189	*LeShon Johnson*	.40
190	*Perry Klein*	.30
191	*Bryant Young*	.50
192	*Byron Morris*	.50
193	*Jeff Cothran*	.20
194	*Lamar Smith*	3.00
195	*Calvin Jones*	.40
196	*James Bostic*	.20
197	*Dan Wilkinson*	.40
198	*Marshall Faulk*	5.00
199	*Heath Shuler*	.50
200	*Willie McGinest*	.40
201	*Trev Alberts*	.30
202	*Trent Dilfer*	3.00
203	*Sam Adams*	.30
204	*Charles Johnson*	1.00
205	*Johnnie Morton*	.75
206	*Thomas Lewis*	.20
207	*Greg Hill*	.50
208	*William Floyd*	1.00
209	*Derrick Alexander*	.50
210	*Darnay Scott*	1.50
211	*Lake Dawson*	.30
212	*Errict Rhett*	1.00
213	*Kevin Lee*	.30
214	*Chuck Levy*	.30
215	*David Palmer*	.50
216	*Ryan Yarborough*	.30
217	*Charlie Garner*	3.00
218	*Mario Bates*	.30
219	*Jamir Miller*	.20
220	*Bucky Brooks*	.30
221	*Donnell Bennett*	.30
222	Kevin Greene	.10
223	LeRoy Butler	.10
224	Anthony Pleasant	.10
225	Steve Christie	.10
226	Bill Romanowski	.10
227	Darren Carrington	.10
228	Chester McGlockton	.10
229	Jack Del Rio	.10
230	Kevin Smith	.10
231	Chris Zorich	.10
232	Donnell Woolford	.10
233	Tony Casillas	.10
234	Terry McDaniel	.10
235	Ray Childress	.10
237	Clyde Simmons	.10
238	Dante Jones	.10
239	Karl Mecklenburg	.10
240	Daryl Johnston	.10
241	Hardy Nickerson	.10
242	Jeff Lageman	.10
243	Lewis Tillman	.10
244	Jim McMahon	.10
245	Mike Pritchard	.10
246	Harvey Williams	.10
247	Sean Jones	.10
248	Stevon Moore	.10
249	Pete Metzelaars	.10
250	Mike Johnson	.10
251	Chris Slade	.20
252	Jessie Hester	.10
253	Louis Oliver	.10
254	Ken Harvey	.10
255	Bryan Cox	.10
256	Erik Kramer	.10
257	Andy Harmon	.10
258	Rickey Jackson	.10
259	Mark Carrier	.10
260	Greg Lloyd	.10
261	Robert Brooks	.10
262	Dave Brown	.20
263	Dennis Smith	.10
264	Michael Dean Perry	.10
265	Dan Saleaumua	.10
266	Mo Lewis	.10
267	Checklist	.10
268	Checklist	.10
269	Checklist	.10
270	Checklist	.10
271SP	Jerry Rice TD King	7.00
NNO	Drew Bledsoe Pin. Pass.	70.00

1994 Pinnacle Trophy Collection

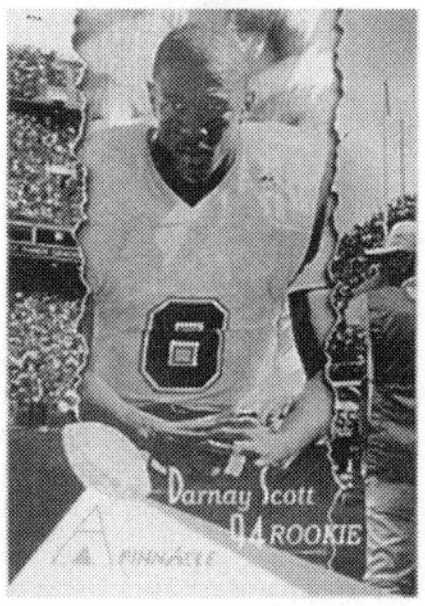

The 270-card, regular-size set was a parallel Dufex version of the base card set, inserted every four packs.

	MT
Complete Set (270):	600.00
Common Player:	1.50
Veteran Stars:	8x-16x
Young Stars:	7x-14x
RCs:	5x-10x

1994 Pinnacle Draft Pinnacle

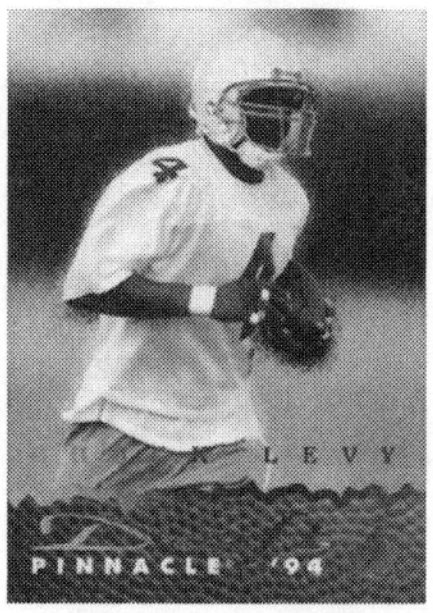

Draft Pinnacle displays the NFL's top 10 picks in their NFL uniforms. The bottom of the card shows a football texture background with "Draft" printed in gold, along with the Pinnacle logo, while "Pinnacle '94" is printed in white. The rest of the front pictures the draft pick. The back is made of half football texture with a brief biography and the other half contains a picture of the player. Cards are numbered DP 1 through DP 10.

	MT
Complete Set (10):	40.00
Common Player:	.50
Minor Stars:	1.00
Dufex Cards:	1x

1	Dan Wilkinson	1.00
2	Marshall Faulk	15.00
3	Heath Shuler	1.00
4	Trent Dilfer	15.00
5	Charles Johnson	1.00
6	Johnnie Morton	5.00
7	Darnay Scott	7.00
8	William Floyd	1.00
9	Errict Rhett	7.00
10	Chuck Levy	.50

1994 Pinnacle Performers

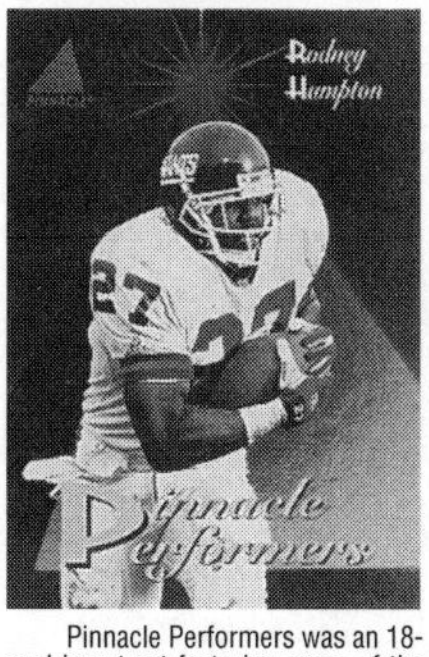

Pinnacle Performers was an 18-card insert set featuring some of the top talent in the NFL. These were inserted exclusively into jumbo packs at a rate of one every four packs.

	MT
Complete Set (18):	55.00
Common Player:	.50
Minor Stars:	1.00
Inserted 1:4 Jumbo	

1	Troy Aikman	5.00
2	Emmitt Smith	8.00
3	Sterling Sharpe	1.00
4	Barry Sanders	10.00
5	Jerry Rice	5.00
6	Steve Young	4.00
7	John Elway	8.00
8	Michael Irvin	1.00
9	Jerome Bettis	1.00
10	Tim Brown	1.00
11	Joe Montana	6.00
12	Reggie Brooks	.50
13	Brett Favre	10.00
14	Drew Bledsoe	5.00
15	Ricky Watters	1.00
16	Garrison Hearst	1.00
17	Rodney Hampton	.50
18	Dan Marino	8.00

1994 Pinnacle Team Pinnacle

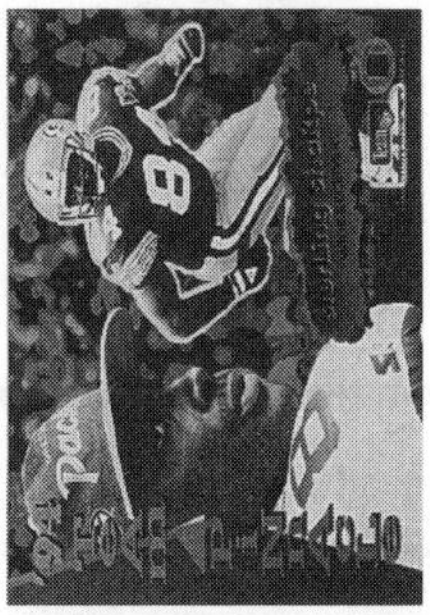

Team Pinnacle is a double-fronted, 10-card insert set that was found one in every 90 packs. Cards feature two top performers at a variety of different positions.

	MT
Complete Set (10):	275.00
Common Player:	10.00

1	Troy Aikman, Joe Montana	90.00
2	Brett Favre, Rick Mirer	60.00
3	Thurman Thomas, Emmitt Smith	60.00
4	Barry Sanders, Barry Foster	40.00
5	Jerome Bettis, Natrone Means	20.00
6	Tim Brown, Sterling Sharpe	10.00
7	Anthony Miller, Jerry Rice	40.00
8	Michael Irvin, James Jett	10.00
9	Reggie White, Bruce Smith	10.00
10	Cortez Kennedy, Sean Gilbert	10.00

1994 Pinnacle Canton Bound

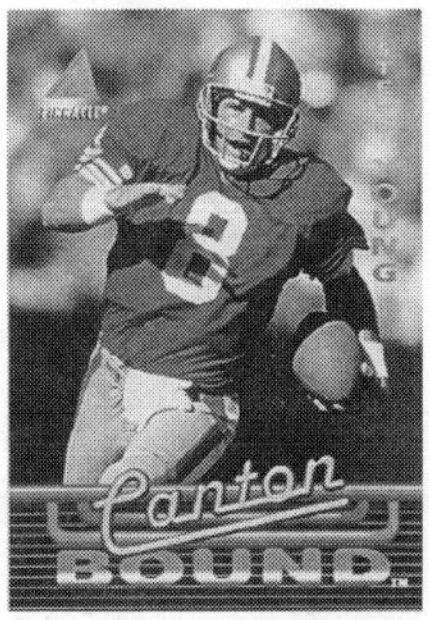

The Canton Bound NFL boxed set was released by Pinnacle containing 25 cards. It featured the game's most accomplished veterans and the brightest young stars. Pinnacle produced 100,000 numbered sets, each came with a factory seal and serial number. The cards showcase a full-bleed design with the player's name and Pinnacle logo in gold-foil. At the bottom of the card is the "Canton Bound" neon logo. The back of the card includes two photos, the player's bio, highlights, 1993 and career stats.

	MT
Complete Set (25):	10.00
Common Player:	.25

1	Troy Aikman	1.50
2	Emmitt Smith	3.00
3	Barry Sanders	1.50
4	Jerry Rice	1.50
5	Sterling Sharpe	.35
6	Ronnie Lott	.35
7	John Elway	1.00
8	Joe Montana	1.50
9	Reggie White	.35
10	Thurman Thomas	.50
11	Bruce Smith	.35
12	Cortez Kennedy	.35
13	Dan Marino	3.00
14	James Lofton	.35
15	Art Monk	.35
16	Warren Moon	.35
17	Barry Foster	.25
18	Steve Young	1.00
19	Phil Simms	.35
20	Richard Dent	.25
21	Marcus Allen	.35
22	Junior Seau	.50
23	Michael Irvin	.50
24	Deion Sanders	.75
25	Jerome Bettis	.50
26	Ronnie Lott Sample	1.50

1994 Pinnacle/Sportflics Super Bowl

This seven-card set was distributed at the 1994 Super Bowl Show in Atlanta, and was available by exchanging three Pinnacle Brands wrappers for one card. These Magic Motion cards were produced in the following quantities: Gary Brown and Emmitt Smith (3,000); Sterling Sharpe and Jerome Bettis/Reggie Brooks and Drew Bledsoe/Rick Mirer (2,000); and Jerry Rice and Deion Sanders (1,000).

	MT
Complete Set (7):	250.00
Common Player:	15.00

1	Gary Brown	15.00
2	Emmitt Smith	60.00
3	Sterling Sharpe	25.00
4	Jerome Bettis, Reggie Brooks	30.00
5	Drew Bledsoe, Rick Mirer	40.00
6	Jerry Rice	50.00
7	Deion Sanders	50.00

1995 Pinnacle Promos

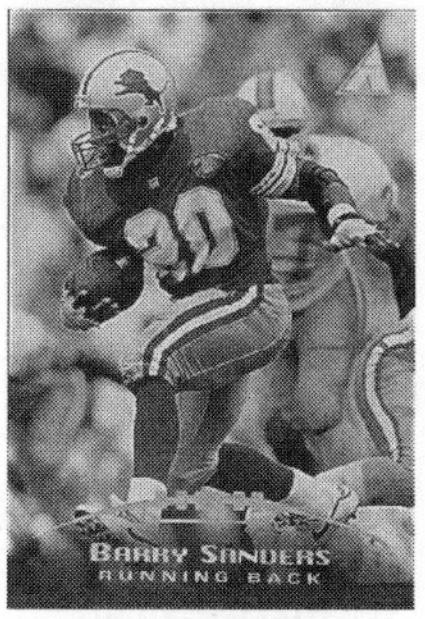

This four-card set was used to promote the 1995 Pinnacle set. It included two regular-issue cards, one Showcase insert and a header card.

	MT
Complete Set (4):	7.00
Common Player:	.50

1	Showcase Card (Dan Marino)	4.00
39	Barry Sanders	2.00
62	Steve Young	1.25
NNO	Ad Card	.50

1995 Pinnacle

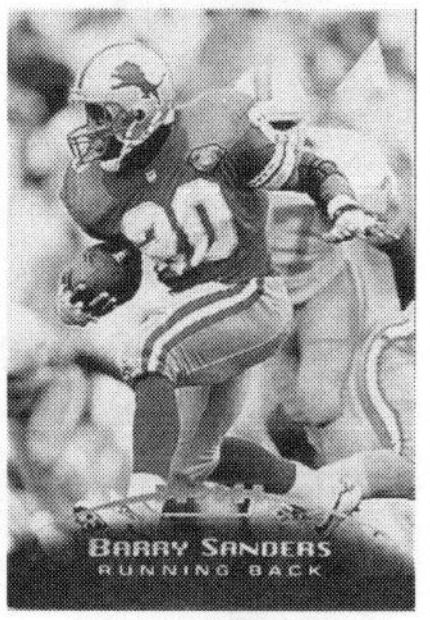

Pinnacle's 1995 football set has 250 cards plus two Dufex parallel sets. Each regular card front has a full-bleed color action photo on the front, with a Pinnacle logo in an upper corner. The player's name and position are stamped in gold foil at the bottom of the card, along with the seams of a football. The card back has a color photo, player profile, biographical information and 1994 and career statistics. There are four subsets within the main set - Draft Picks, Pinnacle Passers, Checklists and a "Judge" card, which pays tribute to Steve Young for passing the bar exam. Parallel sets are Trophy Collection, which reprints all 250 cards on a dufex design, and Artist's Proofs, which parallels the Trophy Collection, but has an Artist's Proof stamp on each card. Five insert sets were made: Showcase, Black 'n Blue, Team Pinnacle, Clear Shots and Gamebreakers.

	MT
Complete Set (250):	30.00
Common Player:	.10
Minor Stars:	.20
Comp. Trophy Coll. Set (250):	550.00
Trophy Collection Cards:	6x-12x
Comp. Art. Proof Set (250):	2500.
Artist Proof Cards:	30x-60x
Card #193 Montana AP was never made.	
Hobby Pack (12):	2.50
Hobby Wax Box (24):	60.00
Retail Pack (12):	2.00
Retail Wax Box (24):	60.00

1	Reggie White	.20
2	Troy Aikman	1.00
3	Willie Davis	.10
4	Jerry Rice	1.00
5	Bruce Smith	.10
6	Keith Byars	.10
7	Chris Warren	.20
8	Erik Kramer	.10
9	Leon Lett	.10
10	Greg Lloyd	.10
11	Jackie Harris	.10
12	Irving Fryar	.10
13	Rodney Hampton	.10
14	Michael Irvin	.30
15	Michael Haynes	.10
16	Irving Spikes	.10
17	Calvin Williams	.10
18	Ken Norton Jr.	.10
19	Herman Moore	.20
20	Lewis Tillman	.10
21	Cortez Kennedy	.10
22	Dan Marino	2.50
23	Erric Pegram	.10
24	Tim Brown	.20
25	*Jeff Blake*	.50
26	Brett Favre	2.50
27	Garrison Hearst	.20
28	Ronnie Harmon	.10
29	Qadry Ismail	.10
30	Ben Coates	.10
31	Deion Sanders	.60
32	John Elway	.50
33	Natrone Means	.60
34	Derrick Alexander	.30
35	Craig Heyward	.10
36	Jake Reed	.10
37	Steve Walsh	.10
38	John Randle	.10
39	Barry Sanders	2.00
40	Tydus Winans	.10
41	Thomas Lewis	.10
42	Jim Kelly	.30
43	Gus Frerotte	.40
44	Cris Carter	.20
45	Kevin Williams	.10
46	Dave Meggett	.10
47	Pat Swilling	.10
48	Neil O'Donnell	.20
49	Terance Mathis	.10
50	Desmond Howard	.10
51	Bryant Young	.10
52	Stan Humphries	.20
53	Alvin Harper	.10
54	Henry Ellard	.10
55	Jessie Hester	.10
56	Lorenzo White	.10
57	John Friesz	.10
58	Anthony Smith	.10
59	Bert Emanuel	.40
60	Gary Clark	.10
61	Bill Brooks	.10
62	Steve Young	1.00
63	Jerome Bettis	.30
64	John Taylor	.10
65	Ricky Proehl	.10
66	Junior Seau	.20
67	Bubby Brister	.10
68	Neil Smith	.10
69	Dan McGwire	.10
70	Brett Perriman	.10
71	Chris Spielman	.10
72	Jeff George	.20
73	Emmitt Smith	2.50
74	Chris Penn	.10
75	Derrick Fenner	.10
76	Reggie Brooks	.10
77	Chris Chandler	.10
78	Rod Woodson	.10
79	Isaac Bruce	.30
80	Reggie Cobb	.10
81	Bryce Paup	.10
82	Warren Moon	.20
83	Bryan Reeves	.10
84	Lake Dawson	.30
85	Larry Centers	.10
86	Marshall Faulk	1.00
87	Jim Harbaugh	.10
88	Ray Childress	.10
89	Eric Metcalf	.10
90	Ernie Mills	.10
91	Lamar Lathon	.10
92	Errict Rhett	.20
93	David Klingler	.10
94	Vincent Brown	.10
95	Andre Rison	.10
96	Brian Mitchell	.10
97	Mark Rypien	.10
98	Eugene Robinson	.10
99	Eric Green	.10
100	Rocket Ismail	.10
101	Flipper Anderson	.10
102	Randall Cunningham	.10
103	Ricky Watters	.20
104	Amp Lee	.10
105	Ernest Givins	.10
106	Daryl Johnston	.10
107	Dave Krieg	.10
108	Dana Stubblefield	.10
109	Torrance Small	.10
110	*Yancey Thigpen*	.50
111	Chester McGlockton	.10
112	Craig Erickson	.10
113	Herschel Walker	.10
114	Mike Sherrard	.10
115	Tony McGee	.10
116	Adrian Murrell	.10
117	Frank Reich	.10
118	Hardy Nickerson	.10
119	Andre Reed	.10
120	Leonard Russell	.10
121	Eric Allen	.10
122	Jeff Hostetler	.10
123	Barry Foster	.10
124	Anthony Miller	.10
125	Shawn Jefferson	.10
126	Richie Anderson	.10
127	Steve Bono	.20
128	Seth Joyner	.10
129	Darnay Scott	.60
130	Johnny Mitchell	.10
131	Eric Swann	.10
132	Drew Bledsoe	1.50
133	Marcus Allen	.20
134	Carl Pickens	.20
135	Michael Brooks	.10
136	John L. Williams	.10
137	Steve Beuerlein	.10
138	Robert Smith	.10
139	O.J. McDuffie	.10
140	Haywood Jeffires	.10
141	Aeneas Williams	.10

142	Rick Mirer	.40
143	William Floyd	.50
144	Fred Barnett	.10
145	Leroy Hoard	.10
146	Terry Kirby	.10
147	Boomer Esiason	.10
148	Ken Harvey	.10
149	Cleveland Gary	.10
150	Brian Blades	.10
151	Eric Turner	.10
152	Vinny Testaverde	.10
153	Ron Moore	.10
154	Curtis Conway	.10
155	Johnnie Morton	.10
156	Kenneth Davis	.10
157	Scott Mitchell	.10
158	Sean Gilbert	.10
159	Shannon Sharpe	.10
160	Mark Seay	.10
161	Cornelius Bennett	.10
162	Heath Shuler	.75
163	Bam Morris	.50
164	Robert Brooks	.10
165	Glyn Milburn	.10
166	Gary Brown	.10
167	Jim Everett	.10
168	Steve Atwater	.10
169	Darren Woodson	.10
170	Mark Ingram	.10
171	Donnell Woolford	.10
172	Trent Dilfer	.50
173	Charlie Garner	.10
174	Charles Johnson	.40
175	Mike Pritchard	.10
176	Derek Brown	.10
177	Chris Miller	.10
178	Charles Haley	.10
179	J.J. Birden	.10
180	Jeff Graham	.10
181	Bernie Parmalee	.30
182	Mark Brunell	1.00
183	Greg Hill	.40
184	Michael Timpson	.10
185	Terry Allen	.10
186	Ricky Ervins	.10
187	Dave Brown	.10
188	Dan Wilkinson	.10
189	Jay Novacek	.10
190	Harvey Williams	.10
191	Mario Bates	.30
192	Steve Young	.50
193	Joe Montana	2.00
194	Steve Young	.50
195	Troy Aikman	.40
196	Drew Bledsoe	.75
197	Dan Marino	1.00
198	John Elway	.20
199	Brett Favre	.75
200	Heath Shuler	.40
201	Warren Moon	.20
202	Jim Kelly	.20
203	Jeff Hostetler	.20
204	Rick Mirer	.20
205	Dave Brown	.10
206	Randall Cunningham	.10
207	Neil O'Donnell	.10
208	Jim Everett	.10
209	*Ki-Jana Carter*	.30
210	*Steve McNair*	4.00
211	*Michael Westbrook*	1.50
212	*Kerry Collins*	2.00
213	*Joey Galloway*	3.00
214	*Kyle Brady*	.20
215	*J.J. Stokes*	1.50
216	*Tyrone Wheatley*	.50
217	*Rashaan Salaam*	.30
218	*Napoleon Kaufman*	1.50
219	*Frank Sanders*	.30
220	*Stoney Case*	.20
221	*Todd Collins*	.30
222	*Warren Sapp*	.75
223	*Sherman Williams*	.20
224	*Rob Johnson*	1.50
225	*Mark Bruener*	.20
226	*Derrick Brooks*	.20
227	*Chad May*	.20
228	*James Stewart*	.20
229	*Ray Zellars*	.20
230	*Dave Barr*	.20
231	*Kordell Stewart*	3.00
232	*Jimmy Oliver*	.20
233	*Tony Boselli*	.30
234	*James Stewart*	1.75
235	*Derrick Alexander*	.20
236	*Lovell Pinkney*	.20
237	*John Walsh*	.20
238	*Tyrone Davis*	.20
239	*Joe Aska*	.20
240	*Korey Stringer*	.20
241	*Hugh Douglas*	.20
242	*Christian Fauria*	.20
243	*Terrell Fletcher*	.20
244	Dan Marino CL	.40
245	Drew Bledsoe CL	.40
246	John Elway CL	.20
247	Emmitt Smith CL	.40
248	Steve Young CL	.25
249	Barry Sanders CL	.50
250	Jerry Rice CL	.25

1995 Pinnacle Artist's Proof

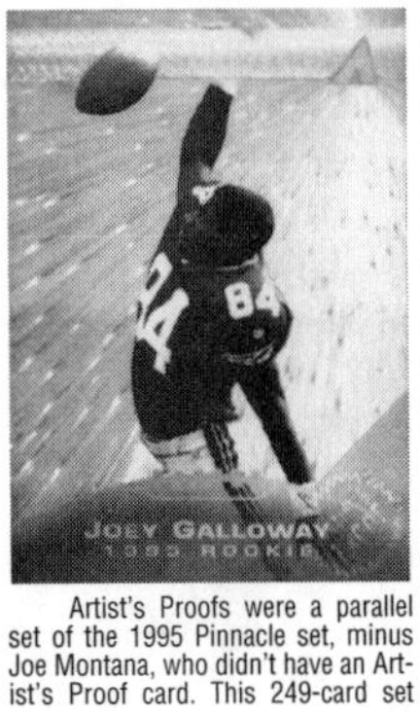

Artist's Proofs were a parallel set of the 1995 Pinnacle set, minus Joe Montana, who didn't have an Artist's Proof card. This 249-card set features the same all-foil dufex printing as the Trophy Collection parallel, but is identified by a round seal that includes the Artist's Proof logo. This parallel set was seeded every 48 packs.

	MT
Complete Set (249):	2600.
Common Player:	7.00
Semistars	10.00
193 Montana AP Not Issued	
AP Veteran Stars:	35x-65x
AP Young Stars:	25x-45x
AP RCs:	15x-30x

1995 Pinnacle Trophy Collection

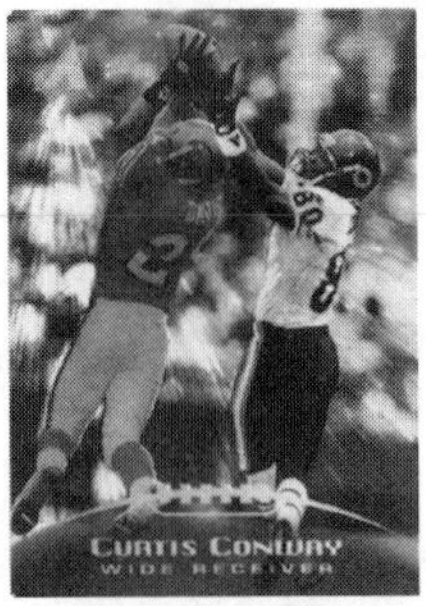

This 250-card parallel set was included in every four packs of Pinnacle Football and is printed in all-foil dufex. The cards have the same photo on the front as regular-issue cards, but have the words Trophy Collection written in large letters on the back.

	MT
Complete Set (250):	600.00
Common Player:	1.25
Veteran Stars:	6x-12x
Young Stars:	4x-8x
RCs:	2.5x-5x

1995 Pinnacle Black 'N Blue

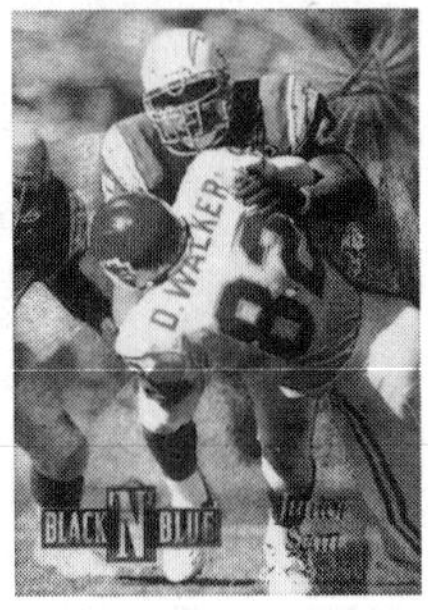

These 1995 Pinnacle football cards picture some of the NFL's toughest players. The cards, featuring a micro-etched foil design for the front, were seeded one per every 18 jumbo packs.

		MT
Complete Set (30):		250.00
Common Player:		7.00
1	Junior Seau	7.00
2	Bam Morris	7.00
3	Craig Heyward	7.00
4	Drew Bledsoe	25.00
5	Barry Sanders	25.00
6	Jerome Bettis	7.00
7	William Floyd	7.00
8	Greg Lloyd	7.00
9	John Elway	15.00
10	Jerry Rice	25.00
11	Kevin Greene	7.00
12	Errict Rhett	7.00
13	Steve Young	25.00
14	Bruce Smith	7.00
15	Steve Atwater	7.00
16	Natrone Means	7.00
17	Ben Coates	7.00
18	Reggie White	7.00
19	Ken Harvey	7.00
20	Dan Marino	50.00
21	Marshall Faulk	7.00
22	Seth Joyner	7.00
23	Rod Woodson	7.00
24	Hardy Nickerson	7.00
25	Brett Favre	50.00
26	Bryan Cox	7.00
27	Rodney Hampton	7.00
28	Jeff Hostetler	7.00
29	Brent Jones	7.00
30	Emmitt Smith	50.00

1995 Pinnacle Clear Shots

These 1995 Pinnacle football inserts are one of the most exclusive ones in the base brand; they are seeded one per every 60 packs. The cards display 10 of the league's best veterans on a clear plastic card stock overprinted with rainbow holographic foil. The process is called Spectroview.

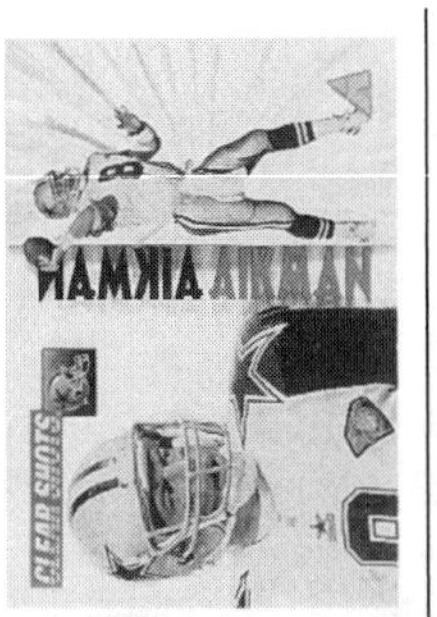

		MT
Complete Set (10):		125.00
Common Player:		5.00
1	Jerry Rice	15.00
2	Dan Marino	30.00
3	Steve Young	15.00
4	Drew Bledsoe	15.00
5	Emmitt Smith	30.00
6	Barry Sanders	18.00
7	Marshall Faulk	5.00
8	Troy Aikman	15.00
9	Ki-Jana Carter	5.00
10	Steve McNair	15.00

1995 Pinnacle Gamebreakers

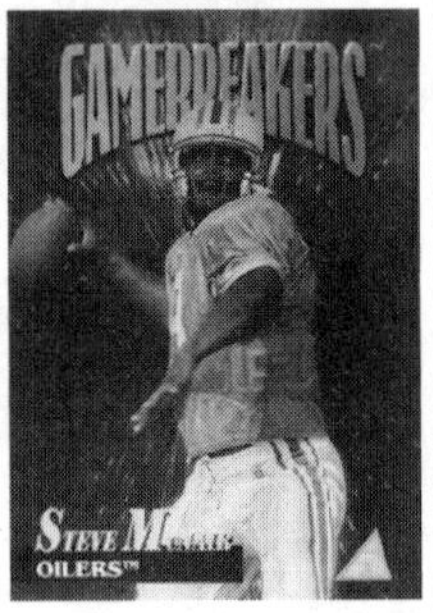

These 15 insert cards were exclusive to 1995 Pinnacle hobby packs, one per every 24 hobby packs. The card front has a metallic shine to it, with the insert set name featured at the top of the card. The player's name and team name are in the lower left corner, opposite the Pinnacle base brand logo.

		MT
Complete Set (15):		150.00
Common Player:		4.00
1	Marshall Faulk	4.00
2	Emmitt Smith	20.00
3	Steve Young	10.00
4	Ki-Jana Carter	4.00
5	Drew Bledsoe	10.00
6	Troy Aikman	10.00
7	Rashaan Salaam	4.00
8	Tyrone Wheatley	4.00
9	Dan Marino	20.00
10	Natrone Means	4.00
11	Barry Sanders	12.00
12	Jerry Rice	10.00
13	Bam Morris	4.00
14	Steve McNair	10.00
15	Kerry Collins	6.00

1995 Pinnacle Showcase

This 1995 Pinnacle insert set features 21 top NFL stars, using black-and-white portraits for the card fronts. The front design also uses silver foil stamping for the player's name and brand name. A silver bar outlines the letters in the word "Showcase." The card back, numbered 1 of 21, etc., has another black-and-white photo, but this one is an action shot, unlike the front one, which shows the player without his helmet on. The insert set icon and a facsimile autograph are also included on the card back. Cards were seeded one per every 18 packs.

		MT
Complete Set (21):		80.00
Common Player:		3.00
1	Drew Bledsoe	7.00
2	Joey Galloway	7.00
3	Steve Young	7.00
4	Joe Aska	3.00
5	Barry Sanders	7.00
6	Troy Aikman	7.00
7	Dan Marino	14.00
8	Randall Cunningham	3.00
9	John Elway	5.00
10	Brett Favre	14.00
11	Jim Kelly	3.00
12	Warren Moon	3.00
13	Dave Brown	3.00
14	Jeff Hostetler	3.00
15	Rick Mirer	4.00
16	Ki-Jana Carter	3.00
17	Kerry Collins	5.00
18	J.J. Stokes	3.00
19	Kordell Stewart	10.00
20	Michael Westbrook	3.00
21	Todd Collins	3.00

1995 Pinnacle Team Pinnacle

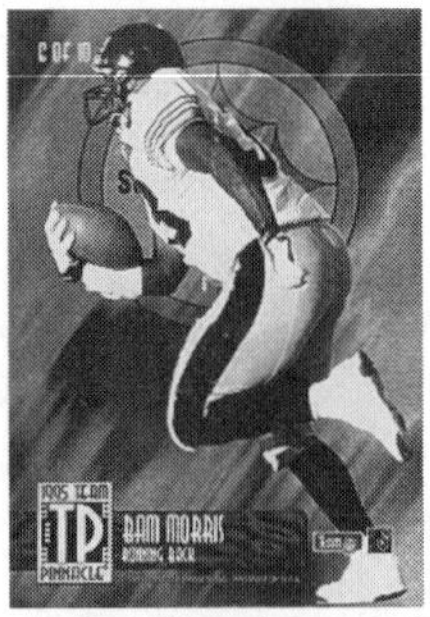

These cards are the rarest of all 1995 Pinnacle football inserts, seeded one per every 90 packs. The 10 cards feature some of the hottest AFC and NFC players at their positions, back-to-back. The set has 20 variations, because each card exists with just one side printed with Pinnacle's exclusive textured-foil process. The player is pictured against a background which shows his team's logo.

		MT
Complete Set (10):		275.00
Common Player:		14.00
1	Steve Young, Drew Bledsoe	30.00
2	Emmitt Smith, Marshall Faulk	40.00
3	Barry Sanders, Natrone Means	30.00
4	Troy Aikman, Dan Marino	50.00
5	Jerry Rice, Tim Brown	30.00
6	Errict Rhett, Bam Morris	14.00
7	Brett Favre, John Elway	50.00
8	Ki-Jana Carter, Rashaan Salaam	14.00
9	Steve McNair, Kerry Collins	25.00
10	Michael Westbrook, Joey Galloway	14.00

1995 Pinnacle Super Bowl Card Show

The four-card, standard-size set was available at the 1995 NFL Experience in exchange for five Pinnacle-brand wrappers. Gold Zone (2,000) and Platinum (1,000) cards were also randomly issued.

		MT
Complete Set (4):		25.00
Common Player:		3.50
1	Jeff Blake	6.00
2	Drew Bledsoe	12.00
3	Marshall Faulk	8.00
4	Natrone Means	3.50

1995 Pinnacle Club Collection Promos

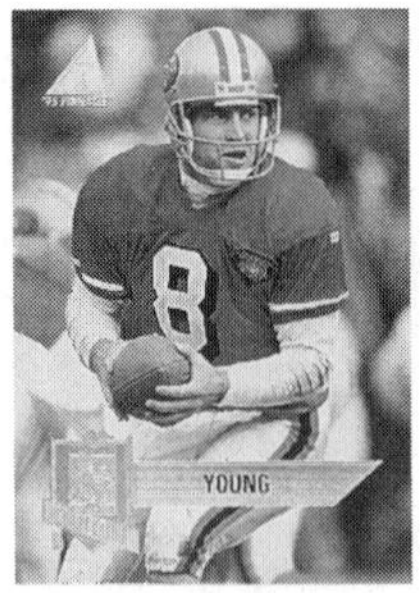

The four-card, standard-size set, issued in a cello pack, previewed the 1995 Pinnacle Club Collection series. The set contained two base cards, one Arms Race card and an advertisement card. The card backs are identified with a "Promo" stamp.

		MT
Complete Set (4):		8.00
Common Player:		.50
1	Steve Young	2.00
11	Dan Marino	4.00
AR11	Arm's Race (Drew Bledsoe)	2.00
NNO	Pinnacle Ad Card	.50

1995 Pinnacle Club Collection

This set, in conjunction with Pinnacle's sponsorship of the NFL Quarterback Club, features 20 members of the NFL's Quarterback Club. Each player in the 261-card set has at least four cards - a regular one and three subset cards. The subset cards are: Xs and Os, which feature the players with an Xs and Os graphic design of their favorite plays; Rookie Replay, which shows the players from their rookie season; and Defining Moment, which highlights top performances for each player. A pin redemption card was also produced; it was seeded one per every 24 packs and entitles the finder to one of 20 Quarterback Club pins if the card is mailed in. There were three insert sets made: Arms Race and Aerial Assault, both of which are dedicated to the quarterbacks, and Spotlight, which focuses on non-quarterbacks. An interactive game that goes along with the Arms Race insert was also designed; as each featured quarterback accumulates statistics, collectors earned chances at winning prizes.

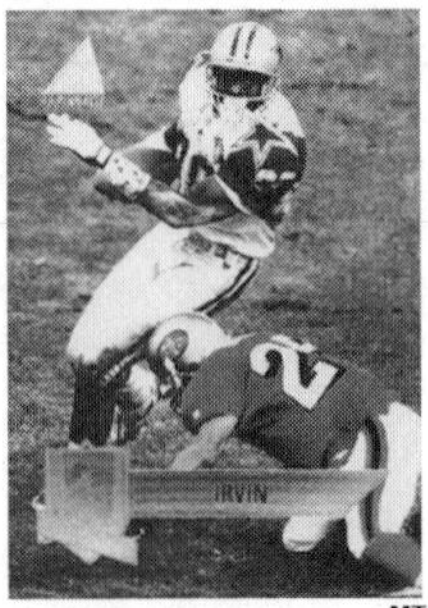

		MT
Complete Set (261):		25.00
Common Player:		.05
Minor Stars:		.10
Each player has nine cards.		
Pack (12):		1.50
Wax Box (24):		25.00
1	Steve Young (R)	.50
2	Steve Young	.50
3	Steve Young	.50
4	Steve Young	.50
5	Steve Young	.50
6	Steve Young	.50
7	Steve Young (XO)	.50
8	Steve Young (RR)	.50
9	Steve Young (DM)	.50
10	Dan Marino (R)	1.00
11	Dan Marino	1.00
12	Dan Marino	1.00
13	Dan Marino	1.00
14	Dan Marino	1.00
15	Dan Marino	1.00
16	Dan Marino (XO)	1.00
17	Dan Marino (RR)	1.00
18	Dan Marino (DM)	1.00
19	Troy Aikman (R)	.40
20	Troy Aikman	.40
21	Troy Aikman	.40
22	Troy Aikman	.40
23	Troy Aikman	.40
24	Troy Aikman	.40
25	Troy Aikman (XO)	.40
26	Troy Aikman (RR)	.40
27	Troy Aikman (DM)	.40
28	Drew Bledsoe (R)	.50
29	Drew Bledsoe	.50
30	Drew Bledsoe	.50
31	Drew Bledsoe	.50
32	Drew Bledsoe	.50
33	Drew Bledsoe	.50
34	Drew Bledsoe (XO)	.50
35	Drew Bledsoe (RR)	.50
36	Drew Bledsoe (DM)	.50
37	Bubby Brister (R)	.05
38	Bubby Brister	.05
39	Bubby Brister	.05
40	Bubby Brister	.05
41	Bubby Brister	.05
42	Bubby Brister	.05
43	Bubby Brister (XO)	.05
44	Bubby Brister (RR)	.05
45	Bubby Brister (DM)	.05
46	Dave Brown (R)	.05
47	Dave Brown	.05
48	Dave Brown	.05
49	Dave Brown	.05
50	Dave Brown	.05
51	Dave Brown	.05
52	Dave Brown (XO)	.05
53	Dave Brown (RR)	.05
54	Dave Brown (DM)	.05
55	Randall Cunningham (R)	.10
56	Randall Cunningham	.10
57	Randall Cunningham	.10
58	Randall Cunningham	.10
59	Randall Cunningham	.10
60	Randall Cunningham	.10
61	Randall Cunningham (XO)	.10
62	Randall Cunningham (RR)	.10
63	Randall Cunningham (DM)	.10
64	John Elway (R)	.30
65	John Elway	.30
66	John Elway	.30
67	John Elway	.30
68	John Elway	.30
69	John Elway	.30
70	John Elway (XO)	.30
71	John Elway (RR)	.30
72	John Elway (DM)	.30
73	Boomer Esiason (R)	.05
74	Boomer Esiason	.05
75	Boomer Esiason	.05
76	Boomer Esiason	.05
77	Boomer Esiason	.05
78	Boomer Esiason	.05
79	Boomer Esiason (XO)	.05
80	Boomer Esiason (RR)	.05
81	Boomer Esiason (DM)	.05
82	Jim Everett (R)	.05
83	Jim Everett	.05
84	Jim Everett	.05
85	Jim Everett	.05
86	Jim Everett	.05
87	Jim Everett	.05
88	Jim Everett (XO)	.05
89	Jim Everett (RR)	.05
90	Jim Everett (DM)	.05
91	Brett Favre (R)	.50
92	Brett Favre	.50
93	Brett Favre	.50
94	Brett Favre	.50
95	Brett Favre	.50
96	Brett Favre	.50
97	Brett Favre (XO)	.50
98	Brett Favre (RR)	.50
99	Brett Favre (DM)	.50
100	Jim Harbaugh (R)	.05
101	Jim Harbaugh	.05
102	Jim Harbaugh	.05
103	Jim Harbaugh	.05
104	Jim Harbaugh	.05
105	Jim Harbaugh	.05
106	Jim Harbaugh (XO)	.05
107	Jim Harbaugh (RR)	.05
108	Jim Harbaugh (DM)	.05
109	Jeff Hostetler (R)	.05
110	Jeff Hostetler	.05
111	Jeff Hostetler	.05
112	Jeff Hostetler	.05
113	Jeff Hostetler	.05
114	Jeff Hostetler	.05
115	Jeff Hostetler (XO)	.05
116	Jeff Hostetler (RR)	.05
117	Jeff Hostetler (DM)	.05
118	Michael Irvin (R)	.25
119	Michael Irvin	.25
120	Michael Irvin	.25
121	Michael Irvin	.25
122	Michael Irvin	.25
123	Michael Irvin	.25
124	Michael Irvin (XO)	.25
125	Michael Irvin (RR)	.25
126	Michael Irvin (DM)	.25
127	Jim Kelly (R)	.20
128	Jim Kelly	.20
129	Jim Kelly	.20
130	Jim Kelly	.20
131	Jim Kelly	.20
132	Jim Kelly	.20
133	Jim Kelly (XO)	.20
134	Jim Kelly (RR)	.20
135	Jim Kelly (DM)	.20
136	David Klingler (R)	.05
137	David Klingler	.05
138	David Klingler	.05
139	David Klingler	.05
140	David Klingler	.05
141	David Klingler	.05
142	David Klingler (XO)	.05
143	David Klingler (RR)	.05
144	David Klingler (DM)	.05
145	Bernie Kosar (R)	.05
146	Bernie Kosar	.05
147	Bernie Kosar	.05
148	Bernie Kosar	.05
149	Bernie Kosar	.05
150	Bernie Kosar	.05
151	Bernie Kosar (XO)	.05
152	Bernie Kosar (RR)	.05
153	Bernie Kosar (DM)	.05
154	Chris Miller (R)	.05
155	Chris Miller	.05
156	Chris Miller	.05
157	Chris Miller	.05
158	Chris Miller	.05
159	Chris Miller	.05
160	Chris Miller (XO)	.05
161	Chris Miller (RR)	.05
162	Chris Miller (DM)	.05
163	Rick Mirer (R)	.25
164	Rick Mirer	.25
165	Rick Mirer	.25
166	Rick Mirer	.25
167	Rick Mirer	.25
168	Rick Mirer	.25
169	Rick Mirer (XO)	.25
170	Rick Mirer (RR)	.25
171	Rick Mirer (DM)	.25
172	Warren Moon (R)	.10
173	Warren Moon	.10
174	Warren Moon	.10
175	Warren Moon	.10
176	Warren Moon	.10
177	Warren Moon	.10
178	Warren Moon (XO)	.10
179	Warren Moon (RR)	.10
180	Warren Moon (DM)	.10
181	Neil O'Donnell (R)	.05
182	Neil O'Donnell	.05
183	Neil O'Donnell	.05
184	Neil O'Donnell	.05
185	Neil O'Donnell	.05
186	Neil O'Donnell	.05
187	Neil O'Donnell (XO)	.05
188	Neil O'Donnell (RR)	.05
189	Neil O'Donnell (DM)	.05
190	Jerry Rice (R)	.50
191	Jerry Rice	.50
192	Jerry Rice	.50
193	Jerry Rice	.50
194	Jerry Rice	.50
195	Jerry Rice	.50
196	Jerry Rice (XO)	.50
197	Jerry Rice (RR)	.50
198	Jerry Rice (DM)	.50
199	Mark Rypien (R)	.05
200	Mark Rypien	.05
201	Mark Rypien	.05
202	Mark Rypien	.05
203	Mark Rypien	.05
204	Mark Rypien	.05
205	Mark Rypien (XO)	.05
206	Mark Rypien (RR)	.05
207	Mark Rypien (DM)	.05
208	Barry Sanders (R)	.50
209	Barry Sanders	.50
210	Barry Sanders	.50
211	Barry Sanders	.50
212	Barry Sanders	.50
213	Barry Sanders	.50
214	Barry Sanders (XO)	.50
215	Barry Sanders (RR)	.50
216	Barry Sanders (DM)	.50
217	Junior Seau (R)	.10
218	Junior Seau	.10
219	Junior Seau	.10
220	Junior Seau	.10
221	Junior Seau	.10
222	Junior Seau	.10
223	Junior Seau (XO)	.10
224	Junior Seau (RR)	.10
225	Junior Seau (DM)	.10
226	Emmitt Smith (R)	1.00
227	Emmitt Smith	1.00
228	Emmitt Smith	1.00

229	Emmitt Smith	1.00
230	Emmitt Smith	1.00
231	Emmitt Smith	1.00
232	Emmitt Smith (XO)	1.00
233	Emmitt Smith (RR)	1.00
234	Emmitt Smith (DM)	1.00
235	Phil Simms (R)	.05
236	Phil Simms	.05
237	Phil Simms	.05
238	Phil Simms	.05
239	Phil Simms	.05
240	Phil Simms	.05
241	Phil Simms (XO)	.05
242	Phil Simms (RR)	.05
243	Phil Simms (DM)	.05
244	Heath Shuler (R)	.30
245	Heath Shuler	.30
246	Heath Shuler	.30
247	Heath Shuler	.30
248	Heath Shuler	.30
249	Heath Shuler	.30
250	Heath Shuler (XO)	.30
251	Heath Shuler (RR)	.30
252	Heath Shuler (DM)	.30
253	Frank Reich (R)	.05
254	Frank Reich	.05
255	Frank Reich	.05
256	Frank Reich	.05
257	Frank Reich	.05
258	Frank Reich (XO)	.05
259	Frank Reich (RR)	.05
260	Frank Reich (DM)	.05
261	Frank Reich	.05

1995 Pinnacle Club Collection Aerial Assault

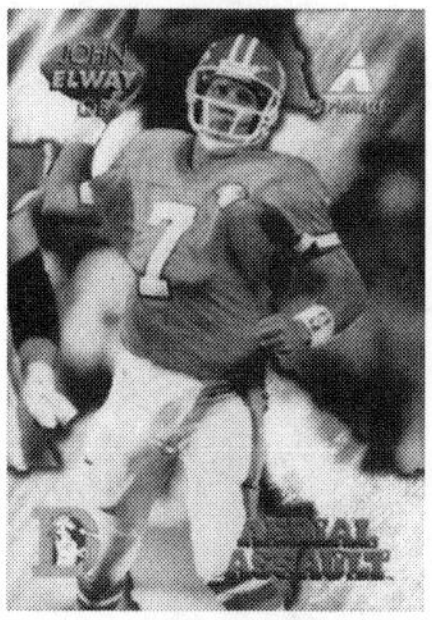

These 18 cards have all-foil printing on one side, and Pinnacle's exclusive Dufex textured-foil printing on the other. Both sides say "Aerial Assault," but only the all-foil side has a card number, which uses an "AA" prefix. This side also has a brief recap of the player's accomplishments. Cards were random inserts, one per every 36 packs of 1995 Pinnacle Club Collection football.

		MT
Complete Set (18):		125.00
Common Player:		3.00
1	Troy Aikman	20.00
2	Dave Brown	3.00
3	Drew Bledsoe	20.00
4	Randall Cunningham	3.00
5	Jim Everett	3.00
6	Jeff Hostetler	3.00
7	David Klingler	3.00
8	Dan Marino	45.00
9	Rick Mirer	3.00
10	Neil O'Donnell	3.00
11	Brett Favre	20.00
12	Boomer Esiason	3.00
13	Jim Harbaugh	3.00
14	John Elway	10.00
15	Steve Young	20.00
16	Warren Moon	3.00
17	Jim Kelly	3.00
18	Heath Shuler	15.00

1995 Pinnacle Club Collection Arms Race

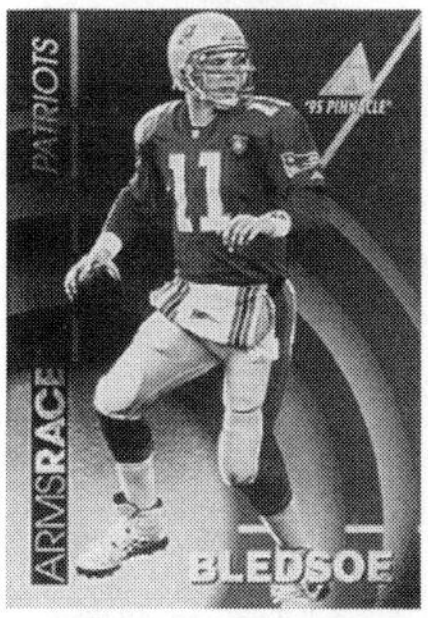

These cards, featuring double-sided Gold Rush technology that puts all-foil printing on both sides of the card, were from an interactive game-card insert set comprised of 18 members of the Quarterback Club. As each quarterback gained points for TD passes, victories and in six statistical categories, the card holder would move closer toward winning prizes. Collectors who had the card of the highest point total finisher at the end of the season had chances at the prizes. Cards were seeded one per every 18 packs. The front of the card had a gold-foiled scope as a background, with the color action photo in the foreground. Arms Race and the player's team name are along the left side of the card. The player's last name is in the lower left corner. The card back, numbered 1 of 18, etc., has a closeup shot of the player on the top half, with a scope as a background. The bottom half has contest rules for the game sweepstakes, plus the set logo.

		MT
Complete Set (18):		60.00
Common Player:		3.00
1	Steve Young	10.00
2	Troy Aikman	10.00
3	John Elway	7.00
4	Dan Marino	18.00
5	Brett Favre	10.00
6	Heath Shuler	8.00
7	Jim Kelly	5.00
8	Randall Cunningham	3.00
9	Dave Brown	3.00
10	Jim Everett	3.00
11	Drew Bledsoe	10.00
12	Rick Mirer	3.00
13	Jeff Hostetler	3.00
14	Neil O'Donnell	3.00
15	Warren Moon	5.00
16	Boomer Esiason	3.00
17	Chris Miller	3.00
18	David Klingler	3.00

1995 Pinnacle Club Collection Spotlight

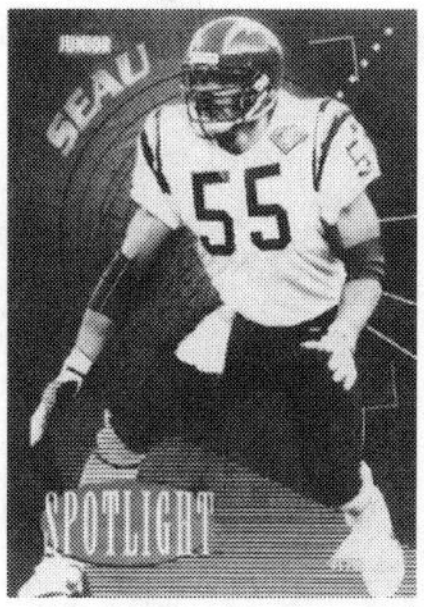

These five cards pay a special tribute to superstars who are not quarterbacks. The cards use a micro-etching process that puts fine textured lines into a holographic foil, creating a flashy effect for the front. Cards were random inserts, one per every 90 packs of 1995 Pinnacle Club Collection.

		MT
Complete Set (5):		60.00
Common Player:		5.00
1	Emmitt Smith	35.00
2	Barry Sanders	20.00
3	Jerry Rice	20.00
4	Michael Irvin	5.00
5	Junior Seau	5.00

1995 Pinnacle Dial Corporation

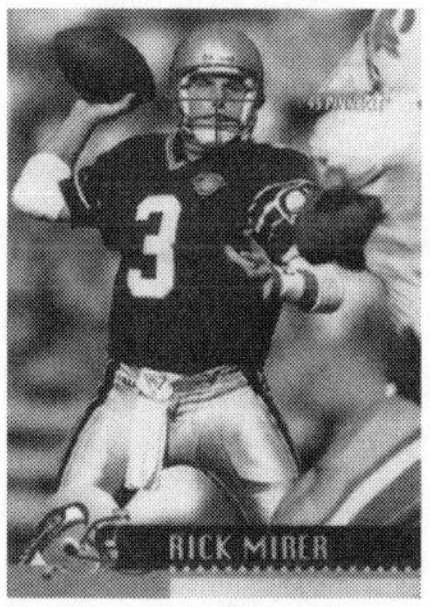

The 30-card, regular-sized cards were issued as part of a promotion sponsored by Dial soap and Purex laundry products. UPC labels from these products could be sent in, with $2.50, for the set. As part of the promotion, 90-card sheets were awarded with Bruce Smith signatures. The cards are numbered with the "DC" prefix.

		MT
Complete Set (30):		15.00
Common Player:		.30
1	Troy Aikman	1.50
2	Frank Reich	.30
3	Drew Bledsoe	1.50
4	Bubby Brister	.30
5	Dave Brown	.30
6	Randall Cunningham	.30
7	John Elway	1.00
8	Boomer Esiason	.30
9	Jim Everett	.30
10	Bruce Smith	.30
11	Brett Favre	3.00
12	Jim Harbaugh	.40
13	Jeff Hostetler	.30
14	Michael Irvin	.60
15	Jim Kelly	.40
16	David Klingler	.30
17	Bernie Kosar	.30
18	Dan Marino	3.00
19	Chris Miller	.30
20	Rick Mirer	.60
21	Warren Moon	.40
22	Neil O'Donnell	.40
23	Jerry Rice	1.50
24	Mark Rypien	.30
25	Barry Sanders	1.50
26	Junior Seau	.60
27	Heath Shuler	.40
28	Phil Simms	.30
29	Emmitt Smith	3.00
30	Steve Young	1.00
P1	Uncut Sheet Prize	45.00

1996 Pinnacle Super Bowl Card Show

The 15-card, standard-size set features color action shots over a metallic Dufex background. The card fronts feature a Super Bowl XXX Card Show logo while the horizontal backs have a player shot with a highlight. Pinnacle distributed the set in three-card packs in exchange for two Pinnacle wrappers.

		MT
Complete Set (15):		15.00
Common Player:		.40
1	Steve Young	1.25
2	Dan Marino	3.00
3	Troy Aikman	1.50
4	Drew Bledsoe	1.50
5	John Elway	3.00
6	Brett Favre	3.00
7	Jim Harbaugh	.40
8	Jeff Hostetler	.40
9	Michael Irvin	.75
10	Jim Kelly	.75
11	Warren Moon	.75
12	Jerry Rice	1.50
13	Barry Sanders	3.00
14	Junior Seau	.75
15	Emmitt Smith	2.50

1996 Pinnacle

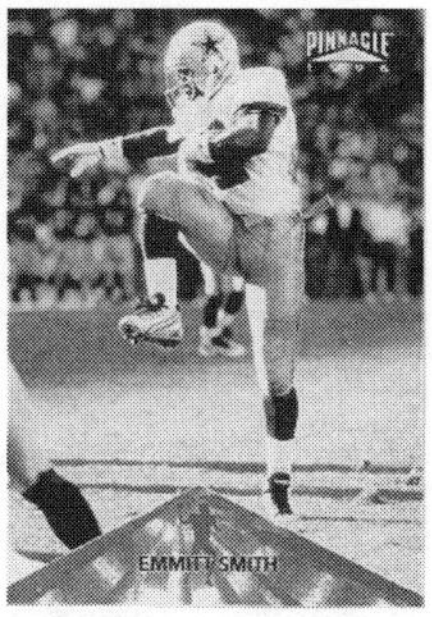

Pinnacle's 1996 football set includes 200 cards in the regular set, including 30 Rookies, six Bid For Six subset cards, five checklists and a Brett Favre Cheesehead card. The set is paralleled twice in normal packs - Trophy Collection (one in five packs, these cards use all-foil Dufex) and Artist's Proof (one in 47 packs, these have a holographic gold foil stamp). These parallel cards are labeled accordingly on them. Each regular card has a full-bleed color action photo on the front, with a Pinnacle logo in an upper corner. The player's name is in a gold-foiled triangle at the bottom. The card back has logo in an upper corner, with the card number in white in a black square. The upper half of the card has a photo; the lower half has a brief profile, stats, biographical information, the player's name and team logo, and his position. Insert sets include Black 'N Blue, Double Disguise, On the Line, Team Pinnacle and 321 Die-Cut Jersey cards. Pinnacle also offers hobby-exclusive packs called premium stock, which contain 25 cards and carry a suggested retail price of $6.99. In these packs each common card in the set is printed on a super-premium, 24-point card stock featuring silver foil stamping. Premium stock packs also have five inserts - Trophy Collection, Artist's Proofs, Team Pinnacle, Double Disguise and an exclusive rainbow holographic foil version of 321.

		MT
Complete Set (200):		25.00
Common Player:		.10
Minor Stars:		.20
Comp. Trophy Coll. (200):		500.00
Trophy Coll. Cards:		10x-20x
Comp. Artist's Proof (200):		1500.
Artist's Proof Cards:		25x-50x
Comp. Premium Stock (200):		50.00
Premium Cards:		2x
Hobby Pack (10):		2.25
Hobby Wax Box (24):		55.00
Prem. Stock Pack (25):		8.00
Prem. Stock Wax Box (8):		55.00
1	Emmitt Smith	2.50
2	Robert Brooks	.20
3	Joey Galloway	.75
4	Dan Marino	2.50
5	Frank Sanders	.20
6	Cris Carter	.10
7	Jeff Blake	.75
8	Steve McNair	.75
9	Tamarick Vanover	.75
10	Andre Reed	.10
11	Junior Seau	.10
12	Alvin Harper	.10
13	Trent Dilfer	.10
14	Kordell Stewart	1.00
15	Kyle Brady	.10
16	Charles Haley	.10
17	Greg Lloyd	.10
18	Mario Bates	.10
19	Shannon Sharpe	.10
20	Scott Mitchell	.10
21	Craig Heyward	.10
22	Marcus Allen	.10
23	Curtis Martin	1.75
24	Drew Bledsoe	1.00
25	Jerry Rice	1.00
26	Charlie Garner	.10
27	Michael Irvin	.10
28	Curtis Conway	.10
29	Terrell Davis	1.25
30	Jeff Hostetler	.10
31	Neil O'Donnell	.10
32	Errict Rhett	.50
33	Stan Humphries	.10
34	Jeff Graham	.10
35	Floyd Turner	.10
36	Vincent Brisby	.10
37	Steve Young	1.00
38	Carl Pickens	.10
39	Terance Mathis	.10
40	Brett Favre	2.50
41	Ki-Jana Carter	.40
42	Jim Everett	.10
43	Marshall Faulk	.75
44	William Floyd	.10
45	Deion Sanders	.50
46	Garrison Hearst	.10
47	Chris Sanders	.10
48	Isaac Bruce	.75
49	Natrone Means	.10
50	Troy Aikman	1.25
51	Ben Coates	.10
52	Tony Martin	.10
53	Rod Woodson	.10
54	Edgar Bennett	.10
55	Eric Zeier	.10
56	Steve Bono	.10
57	Tim Brown	.10
58	Kevin Williams	.10
59	Erik Kramer	.10
60	Jim Kelly	.10
61	Larry Centers	.10
62	Terrell Fletcher	.10
63	Michael Westbrook	.20
64	Kerry Collins	.50
65	Jay Novacek	.10
66	J.J. Stokes	.20
67	John Elway	.50
68	Jim Harbaugh	.10
69	Aeneas Williams	.10
70	Tyrone Wheatley	.10
71	Chris Warren	.20
72	Rodney Thomas	.10
73	Jeff George	.10
74	Rick Mirer	.10
75	Yancey Thigpen	.50
76	Herman Moore	.50
77	Gus Frerotte	.10
78	Anthony Miller	.10
79	Ricky Watters	.10
80	Sherman Williams	.10
81	Hardy Nickerson	.10
82	Henry Ellard	.10
83	Aaron Craver	.10
84	Rodney Peete	.10
85	Eric Metcalf	.10
86	Brian Blades	.10
87	Rob Moore	.10
88	Kimble Anders	.10
89	Harvey Williams	.10
90	Thurman Thomas	.20
91	Dave Brown	.10
92	Terry Allen	.10
93	Ken Norton	.10
94	Reggie White	.20
95	Mark Chmura	.20
96	Bert Emanuel	.10
97	Brett Perriman	.10
98	Antonio Freeman	.10
99	Brian Mitchell	.10
100	Orlando Thomas	.10
101	Aaron Hayden	.10
102	Quinn Early	.10
103	Lovell Pinkney	.10
104	Napoleon Kaufman	.20
105	Daryl Johnston	.10
106	Steve Tasker	.10
107	Brent Jones	.10
108	Mark Brunell	.75
109	Leslie O'Neal	.10
110	Irving Fryar	.10
111	Jim Miller	.10
112	Sean Dawkins	.10
113	Boomer Esiason	.10
114	Heath Shuler	.10
115	Bruce Smith	.10
116	Russell Maryland	.10
117	Jake Reed	.10
118	O.J. McDuffie	.10
119	Erik Williams	.10
120	Willie McGinest	.10
121	Terry Kirby	.10
122	Fred Barnett	.10
123	Andre Hastings	.10
124	Dale Hellestrae	.10
125	Darren Woodson	.10
126	Steve Atwater	.10
127	Quentin Coryatt	.10
128	Derrick Thomas	.10
129	Nate Newton	.10
130	Kevin Greene	.10
131	Barry Sanders	1.25
132	Warren Moon	.10
133	Rashaan Salaam	.50
134	Rodney Hampton	.10
135	James Stewart	.10
136	Erric Pegram	.10
137	Bryan Cox	.10
138	Adrian Murrell	.10
139	Robert Smith	.10
140	Bernie Parmalee	.10
141	Bryce Paup	.10
142	Darick Holmes	.10
143	Hugh Douglas	.10
144	Ken Dilger	.10
145	Derek Loville	.10
146	Horace Copeland	.10
147	Wayne Chrebet	.10
148	Andre Coleman	.10
149	Greg Hill	.10
150	Eric Swann	.10
151	Tyrone Hughes	.10
152	Ernie Mills	.10
153	*Terry Glenn*	2.00
154	*Cedric Jones*	.10
155	*Leeland McElroy*	.30
156	*Bobby Engram*	.50
157	*Willie Anderson*	.10
158	*Mike Alstott*	1.75
159	*Alex Van Dyke*	.20
160	*Jeff Lewis*	.50
161	*Keyshawn Johnson*	3.00
162	*Regan Upshaw*	.10
163	*Eric Moulds*	2.50
164	*Tim Biakabutuka*	1.00
165	*Kevin Hardy*	.20
166	*Marvin Harrison*	3.00
167	*Karim Abdul-Jabbar*	1.00
168	*Tony Brackens*	.30
169	*Stepfret Williams*	.10
170	*Eddie George*	4.00
171	*Lawrence Phillips*	.75
172	*Danny Kanell*	.50
173	*Derrick Mayes*	1.00
174	*Daryl Gardener*	.10
175	*Jonathan Ogden*	.10
176	*Alex Molden*	.10
177	*Chris Darkins*	.20
178	*Stephen Davis*	4.00
179	*Rickey Dudley*	.30
180	*Eddie Kennison*	.50
181	*Simeon Rice*	.40
182	*Bobby Hoying*	.75
183	Troy Aikman	.50
184	Emmitt Smith	1.00
185	Michael Irvin	.10
186	Deion Sanders	.25
187	Daryl Johnston	.10
188	Jay Novacek	.10
189	Steve Young	.40
190	Jerry Rice	.50
191	J.J. Stokes	.10
192	Ken Norton	.10
193	William Floyd	.10
194	Brent Jones	.10
195	(Dan Marino CL)	.40
196	(Brett Favre CL)	.30
197	(Emmitt Smith CL)	.40
198	(Barry Sanders CL)	.30
199	Checklist (Emmitt Smith, Dan Marino, Brett Favre, Barry Sanders CL)	.30
200	Brett Favre Cheese	2.50

1996 Pinnacle Trophy Collection

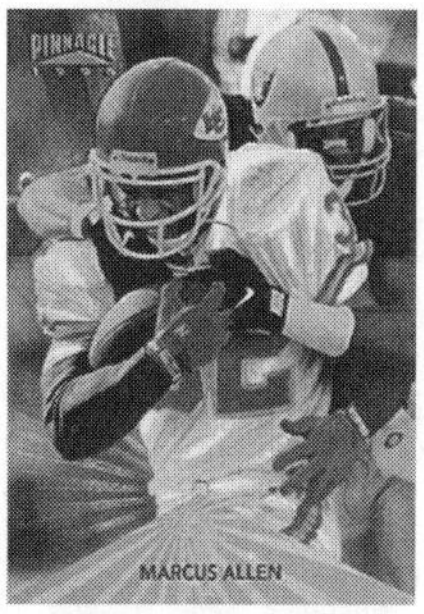

Trophy Collection features all 200 cards from 1996 Pinnacle, reprinted in Dufex foil fronts and a stamp on the back that reads "Trophy Collection." Regular packs had Trophy Collection cards every five packs, while Premium Stock packs contained them every two packs. There is no difference between regular and Premium Stock cards in Trophy Collection.

	MT
Complete Trophy Set (200):	500.00
Trophy Cards:	10x-20x

1996 Pinnacle Foils

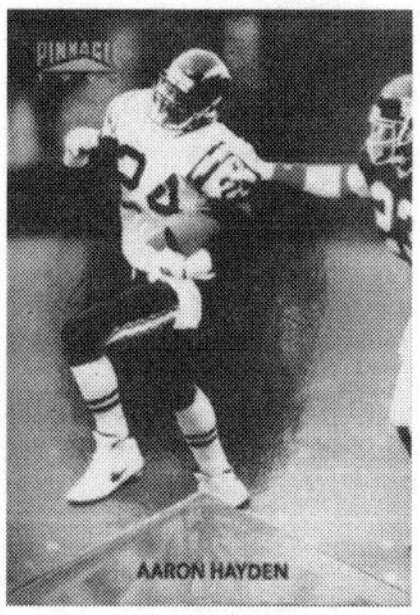

Pinnacle Foils were available only in All-Foil packs, which were available in retail locations. These Foils were the "regular-issue" cards of All-Foil packs that also included Black and Blue inserts.

	MT
Complete Set (200):	35.00
Foil Cards:	1.5x

1996 Pinnacle Artist's Proofs

This 200-card parallel set features each card in 1996 Pinnacle Football, but includes a holographic Artist's Proof logo on the front, as well as a logo on the back. Artist's Proofs were included in every 48 hobby and retail packs. Regular Artist's Proofs contained gold foil at the bottom of the card in contrast to Premium Stock Artist's Proofs that included silver foil and are included in a separate entry.

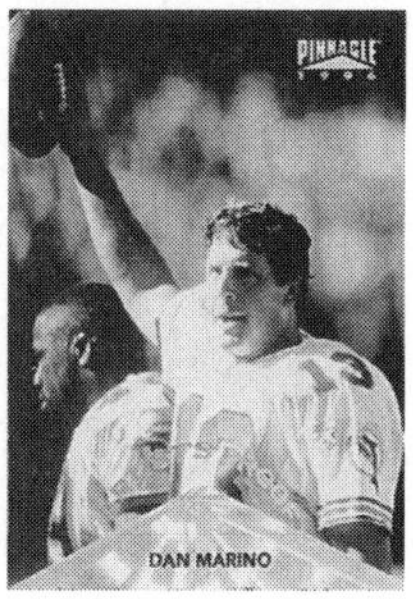

	MT
Complete Set (200):	1500.
Artist's Proof Cards:	25x-50x

1996 Pinnacle Premium Stock

Pinnacle Premium Stock was issued as a hobby exclusive product that was offered in addition to regular Pinnacle Football. The base cards were different in that they had silver foil at the bottom instead of gold foil. Packs of Premium Stock contained 25 cards, and included Artist's Proofs, Trophy Collection, Team Pinnacle, Die-Cut Jerseys and Double Disguise inserts. Only the Artist's Proofs and Die-Cut Jerseys are different than regular-issue inserts.

	MT
Complete Set (200):	50.00
Premium Stock Cards:	2x

1996 Pinnacle Premium Stock Artist's Proofs

Each card in the 200-card Premium Stock set was featured in the parallel Artist's Proof insert. This means that the Premium Stock Artist's Proofs feature silver foil on the fronts instead of gold foil on the regular-issue Artist's Proofs. Premium Stock Artist's Proofs were inserted every 12 packs.

	MT
Complete Set (200):	1500.
PS Artist's Proofs:	25x-50x

1996 Pinnacle Die-Cut Jerseys

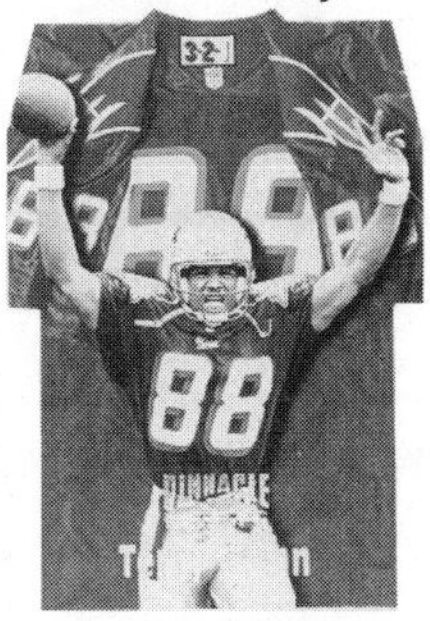

The best and youngest players in the NFL - those with three or less years of experience - are featured on these die-cut Pinnacle insert cards. The cards are hobby-exclusive; they were seeded one per every 23 hobby packs. The card front has a color action shot against a die-cut version of his jersey. "3-2-1" is included as a tag in the jersey's collar. The Pinnacle logo and player's name are stamped in gold foil along the bottom of the card. The back of the card uses the back of the player's jersey as a background. A second photo appears, along with a team logo, a brief summary of one of his accomplishments, and a card number (1 of 20, etc.).

		MT
Complete Set (20):		160.00
Common Player:		4.00
Comp. Holofoil (20):		320.00
Holofoil Cards		2x
1	Errict Rhett	6.00
2	Marshall Faulk	8.00
3	Isaac Bruce	8.00
4	William Floyd	4.00
5	Heath Shuler	4.00

6	Kerry Collins	8.00
7	Kordell Stewart	14.00
8	Rashaan Salaam	6.00
9	Terrell Davis	18.00
10	Rodney Thomas	4.00
11	Curtis Martin	20.00
12	Steve McNair	10.00
13	J.J. Stokes	8.00
14	Joey Galloway	10.00
15	Michael Westbrook	6.00
16	Keyshawn Johnson	10.00
17	Lawrence Phillips	8.00
18	Terry Glenn	18.00
19	Tim Biakabutuka	8.00
20	Eddie George	20.00

1996 Pinnacle Premium Stock Die-Cut Jerseys

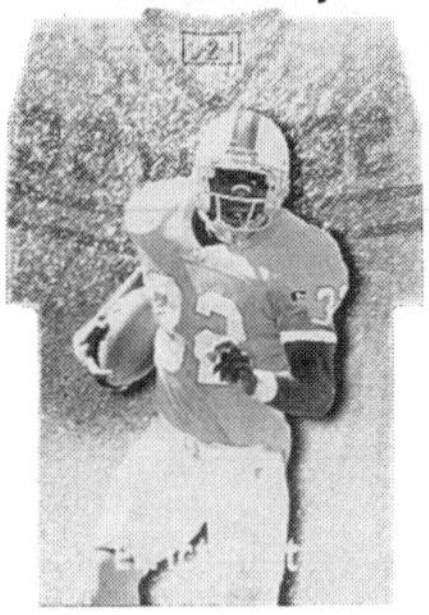

Premium Stock packs included a unique version of the Die-cut Jerseys that featured the fronts in prismatic foil. These versions of Die-Cut Jerseys were inserted every six packs and only included in Premium Stock.

	MT
Complete Set (20):	320.00
PS Die-Cut Jerseys:	2x

1996 Pinnacle Double Disguise

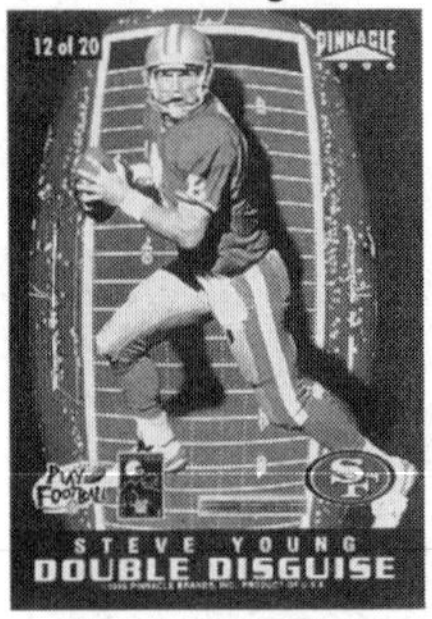

These 1996 Pinnacle inserts showcase five players in 20 different combinations. The cards are printed on plastic and are covered with an opaque plastic protector which is meant to be peeled off. Each side features combinations of Emmitt Smith, Dan Marino, Brett Favre, Kerry Collins and Steve Young matched up. The card's background shows the length of a football field as seen through a fisheye lens. The front side uses gold-foil stamping for the Pinnacle logo, player's name and set name. These are not in foil on the opposite side, which has a card number (1 of 20, etc.). The cards were seeded one per every 18 packs.

		MT
Complete Set (20):		150.00
Common Player:		4.00
1	Emmitt Smith, Emmitt Smith	15.00
2	Emmitt Smith, Dan Marino	15.00
3	Emmitt Smith, Brett Favre	12.00
4	Emmitt Smith, Steve Young	10.00
5	Dan Marino, Dan Marino	12.00
6	Dan Marino, Emmitt Smith	15.00
7	Dan Marino, Kerry Collins	10.00
8	Dan Marino, Steve Young	10.00
9	Kerry Collins, Kerry Collins	4.00
10	Kerry Collins, Dan Marino	10.00
11	Kerry Collins, Brett Favre	10.00
12	Kerry Collins, Steve Young	4.00
13	Brett Favre, Brett Favre	10.00
14	Brett Favre, Kerry Collins	10.00
15	Brett Favre, Dan Marino	10.00
16	Brett Favre, Emmitt Smith	12.00
17	Steve Young, Steve Young	4.00
18	Steve Young, Brett Favre	8.00
19	Steve Young, Emmitt Smith	10.00
20	Steve Young, Kerry Collins	4.00

1996 Pinnacle Black 'N Blue

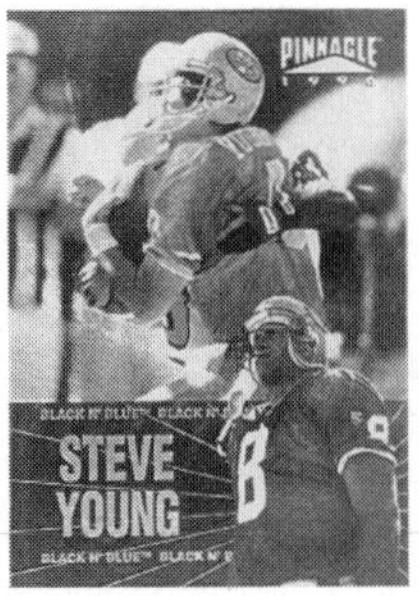

Twenty-five of the NFL's most rugged players show the hard-nosed, aggressive play which has earned them a spot in this set. The cards were seeded one per every 33 magazine packs. Each card front has two photos on it.

		MT
Complete Set (25):		275.00
Common Player:		5.00
1	Steve Young	15.00
2	Troy Aikman	20.00
3	Dan Marino	40.00
4	Michael Irvin	5.00
5	Jerry Rice	20.00
6	Emmitt Smith	40.00
7	Brett Favre	40.00
8	Drew Bledsoe	20.00
9	John Elway	15.00
10	Barry Sanders	25.00
11	Cris Carter	5.00
12	Jeff Blake	5.00
13	Chris Warren	5.00
14	Kerry Collins	8.00
15	Natrone Means	5.00
16	Herman Moore	5.00
17	Steve McNair	10.00
18	Ricky Watters	5.00
19	Tamarick Vanover	10.00
20	Deion Sanders	15.00
21	Terrell Davis	20.00
22	Rodney Thomas	5.00
23	Rashaan Salaam	8.00
24	Darick Holmes	5.00
25	Eric Zeier	5.00

1996 Pinnacle Team Pinnacle

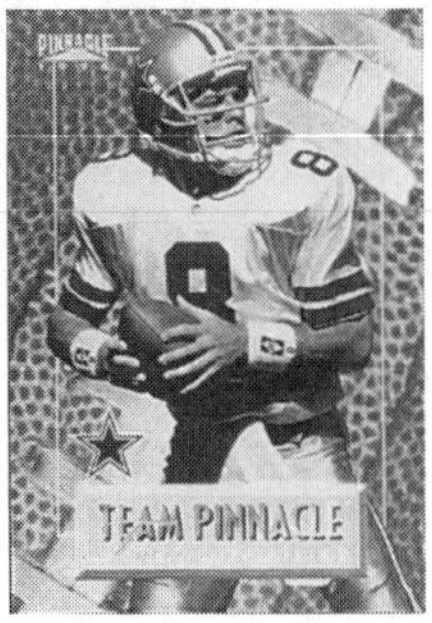

These 1996 Pinnacle inserts feature the best AFC player at each position on a card that is complemented by the top NFC position player on the flip side. The cards were seeded one per every 90 packs for both hobby and retail packs. The design shows a pinstripe-framed color action photo against a football background. The player's name, position and Team Pinnacle are written in a rectangle at the bottom. The card is numbered 1 of 20, etc.

		MT
Complete Set (10):		150.00
Common Player:		8.00
Inserted 1:90		
1	Troy Aikman, Drew Bledsoe	15.00
2	Steve Young, Jeff Blake	12.00
3	Brett Favre, John Elway	40.00
4	Kerry Collins, Dan Marino	30.00
5	Emmitt Smith, Curtis Martin	30.00
6	Barry Sanders, Chris Warren	35.00
7	Errict Rhett, Marshall Faulk	8.00
8	Jerry Rice, Carl Pickens	15.00
9	Michael Irvin, Joey Galloway	8.00
10	Isaac Bruce, Kordell Stewart	12.00

1996 Pinnacle On the Line

The NFL's top pass catchers are featured on these 1996 Pinnacle inserts. The cards, seeded one per every 23 retail packs, use Dufex for the design. The card front has a full-bleed color action photo on it, with the player's name at the bottom near a grid which says "On the Line." The Pinnacle logo is in an upper corner.

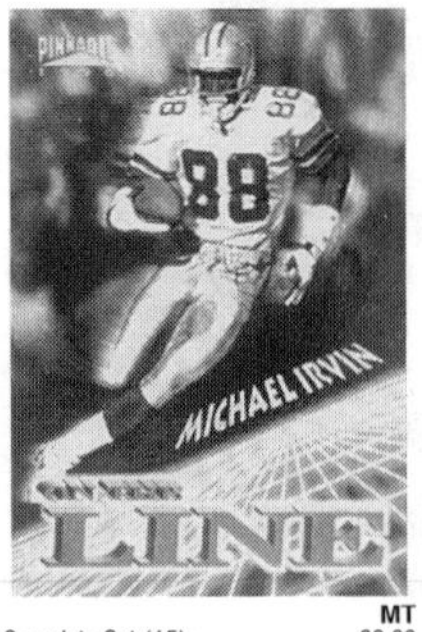

		MT
Complete Set (15):		80.00
Common Player:		3.00
1	Michael Irvin	3.00
2	Robert Brooks	3.00
3	Herman Moore	6.00
4	Cris Carter	3.00
5	Chris Sanders	3.00
6	Jerry Rice	20.00
7	Michael Westbrook	3.00
8	Carl Pickens	3.00
9	Bobby Engram	6.00
10	Alex Van Dyke	3.00
11	Keyshawn Johnson	12.00
12	Terry Glenn	18.00
13	Eric Moulds	8.00
14	Marvin Harrison	13.00
15	Eddie Kennison	6.00

1996 Laser View

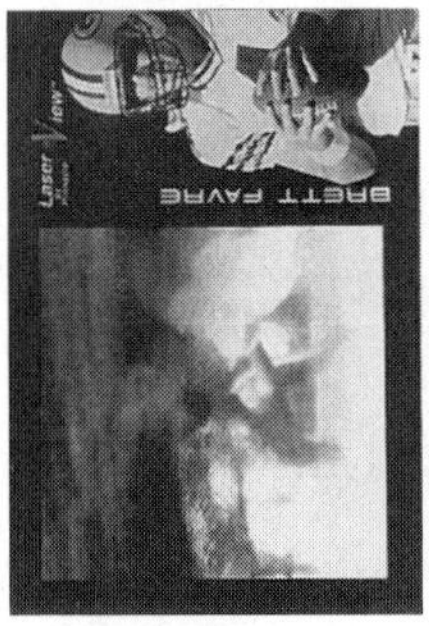

Each of these 1996 Pinnacle Laserview cards features nearly four seconds of taped replay action from NFL Films in the form of a hologram. Each regular card has the hologram on one side, with a small action photo, the player's name and the Laser-View logo on the opposite. The background of the horizontal card front is black. The card back has a ghosted image for the background, with a small action photo, biographical information, a card number, team logo and brief writeup toward the top of the card. Two team-colored stripes separate this information from the player's name, position and 1995 and career statistics at the bottom. Laserview Gold parallel gold-foiled cards were seeded every 12th pack. Other inserts include Eye on the Prize and Inscriptions. Every box also comes with a Pinnacle authenticator lens that allows collectors to prove the authenticity of the printing. A small box on the back of each card has a multi-colored pattern of lines that can only be read by the lens; the message "PBI 96" appears when this is done. If the lens is turned another way, a rainbow pattern appears. Pinnacle claims no counterfeit techniques would be able to duplicate this printing because the pattern of lines is so thin.

		MT
Complete Set (40):		50.00
Common Player:		.50
Minor Stars:		1.00
Gold Cards:		2x-3x
Pack (1):		4.00
Wax Box (24):		75.00
1	Jim Kelly	1.00
2	Troy Aikman	5.00
3	Michael Irvin	1.00
4	Emmitt Smith	10.00
5	John Elway	4.00
6	Barry Sanders	5.00
7	Brett Favre	10.00
8	Jim Harbaugh	.50
9	Dan Marino	10.00
10	Warren Moon	.50
11	Drew Bledsoe	5.00
12	Jim Everett	.50
13	Jeff Hostetler	.50
14	Neil O'Donnell	.50
15	Junior Seau	.50
16	Jerry Rice	5.00
17	Steve Young	4.00
18	Rick Mirer	1.00
19	Boomer Esiason	.50
20	Bernie Kosar	.50
21	Heath Shuler	1.00
22	Dave Brown	.50
23	Jeff Blake	1.00
24	Kerry Collins	1.50
25	Kordell Stewart	5.00
26	Scott Mitchell	.50
27	Kerry Collins PE	3.00
28	Troy Aikman PE	3.00
29	Kordell Stewart PE	3.00
30	Michael Irvin PE	.50
31	Emmitt Smith PE	5.00
32	John Elway PE	1.00
33	Barry Sanders PE	3.00
34	Brett Favre PE	5.00
35	Dan Marino PE	5.00
36	Drew Bledsoe PE	3.00
37	Neil O'Donnell PE	.50
38	Jerry Rice PE	3.00
39	Steve Young PE	2.00
40	Jeff Blake PE	2.00

1996 Laser View Golds

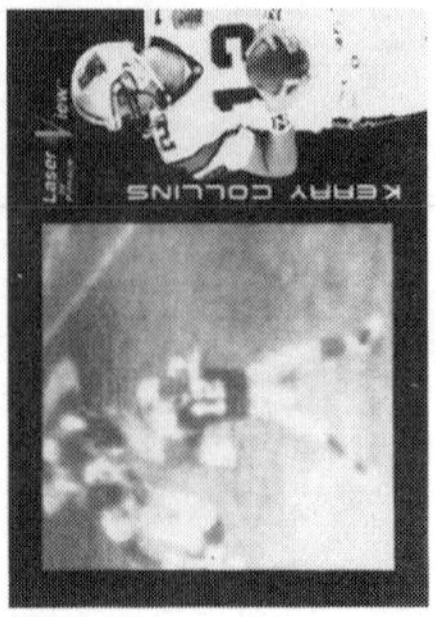

This 40-card parallel set used all 40 cards in the regular-issue Laser-View set in a gold version. Gold parallels were found every 12 packs.

	MT
Complete Set (40):	150.00
Golds:	2x-3x

1996 Laser View Eye on the Prize

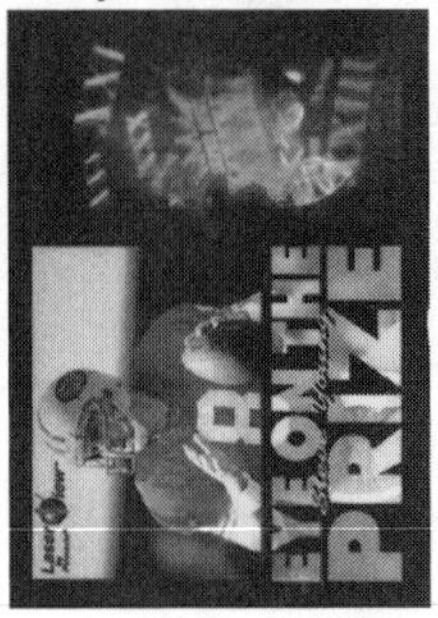

This 1996 Pinnacle Laserview insert spotlights 12 of the NFL's elite superstars as they compete for the coveted Lombardi Trophy as winners of the Super Bowl. The cards put a different holographic angle on the play-ers by picturing the player with a holographic background. The cards were seeded one per every 24 packs.

		MT
Complete Set (12):		100.00
Common Player:		3.00
1	Troy Aikman	10.00
2	Emmitt Smith	20.00
3	Michael Irvin	3.00
4	Steve Young	8.00
5	Jerry Rice	10.00
6	Dan Marino	20.00
7	John Elway	8.00
8	Junior Seau	3.00
9	Neil O'Donnell	3.00
10	Jeff Hostetler	3.00
11	Jim Kelly	3.00
12	Kordell Stewart	10.00

1996 Laser View Inscriptions

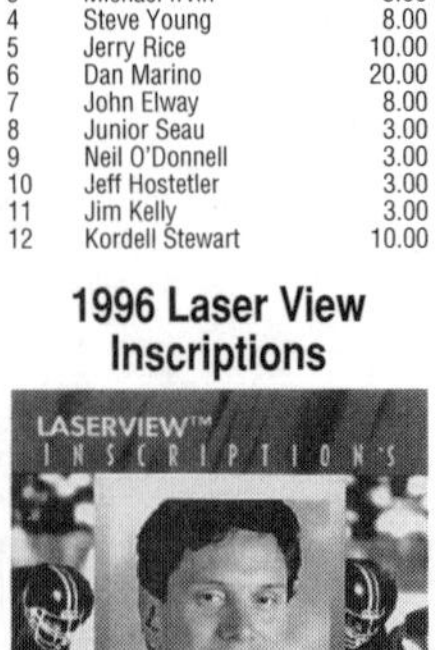

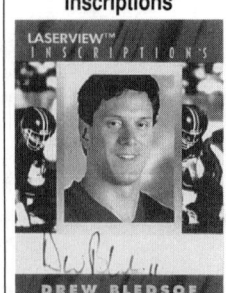

This 1996 Pinnacle Laserview insert set features 25 of the top members of the NFL Quarterback Club who each signed a serial-numbered card. The cards, seeded one per every 24 packs, are printed on clear plastic stock which gives collectors a backwards-forwards look at the signature. The front has a color panel at the top which includes the brand and set names, with a color mug shot underneath framed in yellow. The closeup shot is flanked by a black-and-white action scene. The player's signature is below his photo, followed by another colored band at the bottom which has the player's name and team name inside. The back, which shows reverse images of the front, includes the serial number in a white rectangle at the top.

	MT
Complete Set (25):	1450.
Jeff Blake 3125	40.00
Drew Bledsoe 2775	100.00
Dave Brown 3100	20.00
Mark Brunell 3200	90.00
Kerry Collins 3000	50.00
John Elway 3100	100.00
Boomer Esiason 1500	160.00
Jim Everett 3100	20.00
Brett Favre 4850	125.00
Jeff George 2900	30.00
Jim Harbaugh 3500	25.00
Jeff Hostetler 3750	20.00
Michael Irvin 3050	25.00
Jim Kelly 3100	40.00
Bernie Kosar 3200	20.00
Erik Kramer 3150	20.00
Rick Mirer 3150	30.00
Scott Mitchell 4900	20.00
Warren Moon 2800	25.00
Neil O'Donnell 1600	50.00
Jerry Rice 900	350.00
Barry Sanders 2900	150.00
Junior Seau 3000	25.00
Heath Shuler 3100	25.00
Steve Young 1950	110.00

1996 Pinnacle Mint Cards

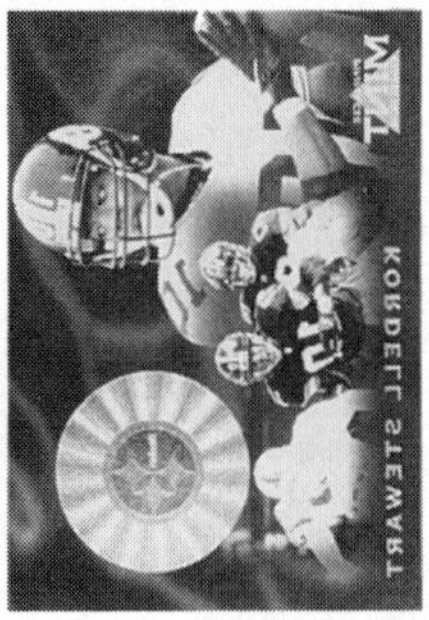

The 30-card, regular-sized set comes in three-card packs and contains two coin cards and one regular-issue card. The die-cut coin cards feature a closeup player shot and an action shot on the front with the same action shot in black and white on the back. The cards have a circular cutout in the upper right quadrant where the included brass, nickel- silver or gold coins fit. The regular-issue cards feature a foil team emblem (where the hole is on the coin cards) in brass (common), silver (1:20) or gold (1:48). Each of the 30 players represented in the set are members of the Quarterback Club.

		MT
Complete Die-Cut (30):		18.00
Common Player:		.20
Minor Stars:		.40
Bronze Cards:		2x
Silver Cards:		4x-8x
Gold Cards:		10x-20x
Wax Box:		30.00
1	Troy Aikman	1.50
2	John Elway	.75
3	Jim Kelly	.40
4	Dan Marino	3.00
5	Warren Moon	.20
6	Steve Young	1.50
7	Jerry Rice	1.50
8	Boomer Esiason	.20
9	Jim Everett	.20
10	Brett Favre	3.00
11	Jim Harbaugh	.40
12	Jeff Hostetler	.20
13	Neil O'Donnell	.20
14	Drew Bledsoe	1.50
15	Rick Mirer	.20
16	Emmitt Smith	3.00
17	Barry Sanders	1.50
18	Junior Seau	.20
19	Dave Brown	.20
20	Heath Shuler	.20
21	Jeff Blake	.40
22	Kerry Collins	.75
23	Scott Mitchell	.20
24	Kordell Stewart	1.50
25	Jeff George	.20
26	Mark Brunell	1.00
27	Erik Kramer	.20
28	Bernie Kosar	.20
29	Frank Reich	.20
30	Randall Cunningham	.20

1996 Pinnacle Mint Coins

The 30-piece set was included twice in every three-pack of Pinnacle Mint Collection football. Two variations of the common brass coin were available: nickel-silver (1:20) and 24 kt. gold (1:48). Solid silver coins were also inserted every 2,300 packs and one redemption card was available for an all-gold coin with the odds being one in 47,200. The coin face has the image of the player's face with his name, team and uniform number. The coin backs feature the Quarterback Club logo, as each of the 30 players represented in the set are members.

		MT
Complete Brass (30):		50.00
Common Brass Coin:		.75
Minor Brass Stars:		1.50
Nickel Coins:		2x-4x
Gold Plated Coins:		4x-8x
1	Troy Aikman	4.00
2	John Elway	3.00
3	Jim Kelly	1.50
4	Dan Marino	8.00
5	Warren Moon	.75
6	Steve Young	3.00
7	Jerry Rice	4.00
8	Boomer Esiason	.75
9	Jim Everett	.75
10	Brett Favre	8.00
11	Jim Harbaugh	.75
12	Jeff Hostetler	.75
13	Neil O'Donnell	.75
14	Drew Bledsoe	4.00
15	Rick Mirer	.75
16	Emmitt Smith	8.00
17	Barry Sanders	4.00
18	Junior Seau	1.50
19	Dave Brown	.75
20	Heath Shuler	.75
21	Jeff Blake	1.50
22	Kerry Collins	1.50
23	Scott Mitchell	.75
24	Kordell Stewart	4.00
25	Jeff George	.75
26	Mark Brunell	3.00
27	Erik Kramer	.75
28	Bernie Kosar	.75
29	Frank Reich	.75
30	Randall Cunningham	.75

1996 Pinnacle Bimbo Bread

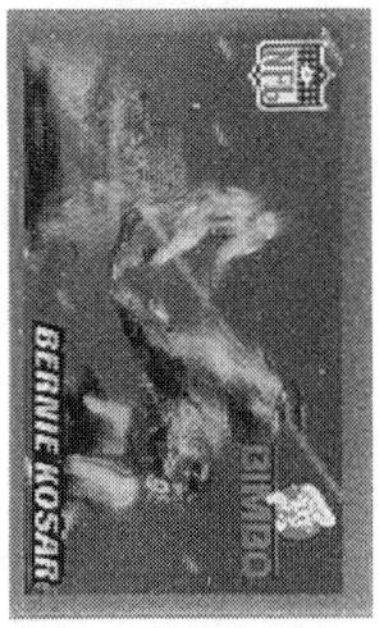

These magic motion cards were distributed in Mexico through Bimbo Bakery products. The 30 cards measure 1-1/2" x 2-1/2" and feature a magic motion photo and the Bimbo logo on the front. The backs have another player photo and biographical information.

		MT
Complete Set (30):		300.00
Common Player:		4.00
1	Troy Aikman	30.00
2	Michael Irvin	8.00
3	Emmitt Smith	60.00
4	Jim Kelly	8.00
5	John Elway	25.00
6	Barry Sanders	35.00
7	Brett Favre	70.00
8	Jim Harbaugh	4.00
9	Dan Marino	60.00
10	Warren Moon	4.00
11	Drew Bledsoe	30.00
12	Jim Everett	4.00
13	Jeff Hostetler	4.00
14	Neil O'Donnell	4.00
15	Junior Seau	6.00
16	Jerry Rice	30.00
17	Steve Young	20.00
18	Rick Mirer	4.00
19	Jeff Blake	8.00
20	David Klingler	4.00
21	Boomer Esiason	4.00
22	Heath Shuler	4.00
23	Dave Brown	4.00
24	Bernie Kosar	4.00
25	Kordell Stewart	30.00
26	Mark Brunell	30.00
27	Kerry Collins	25.00
28	Scott Mitchell	4.00
29	Erik Kramer	4.00
30	Jeff George	6.00

Values quoted in this guide reflect the retail price of a card — the price a collector can expect to pay when buying a card from a dealer. The wholesale price — that which a collector can expect to receive from a dealer when selling cards — will be significantly lower, depending on desirability and condition.

1997 Pinnacle

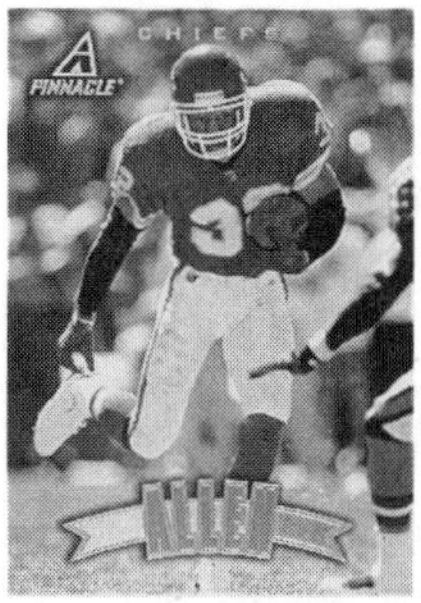

Pinnacle Football has a 200-card base set. Both sides feature a player action photo. Pinnacle Football also has two partial base set parallels (Artist's Proof and Trophy Collection) and three inserts. Trophy Collection utilizes Dufex technology. Artist's Proof parallels Trophy Collection by adding the Artist's Proof stamp. The parallel sets are re-numbered. The inserts include Epix (24 cards, 1:19), Scoring Core (24 cards, 1:89) and Team Pinnacle (10 cards, 1:240).

		MT
Complete Set (200):		25.00
Common Player:		.10
Minor Stars:		.20
Trophy Cards:		5x-10x
Trophy Rookies:		3x-6x
Inserted 1:9		
Artist Proof Cards:		15x-30x
Artist Proof Rookies:		8x-16x
Inserted 1:39		
Pack (10):		3.00
Wax Box (18):		48.00
1	Brett Favre	2.50
2	Dan Marino	2.00
3	Emmitt Smith	2.00
4	Steve Young	.75
5	Drew Bledsoe	1.00
6	Eddie George	1.50
7	Barry Sanders	1.25
8	Jerry Rice	1.00
9	John Elway	.75
10	Troy Aikman	1.00
11	Kerry Collins	.25
12	Rick Mirer	.10
13	Jim Harbaugh	.10
14	Elvis Grbac	.10
15	Gus Frerotte	.10
16	Neil O'Donnell	.10
17	Jeff George	.10
18	Kordell Stewart	1.00
19	Junior Seau	.20
20	Vinny Testaverde	.10
21	Terry Glenn	.30
22	Anthony Johnson	.10
23	Boomer Esiason	.10
24	Terrell Owens	.50
25	Natrone Means	.20
26	Marcus Allen	.20
27	James Jett	.10
28	Chris T. Jones	.10
29	Stan Humphries	.10
30	Keith Byars	.10
31	John Friesz	.10
32	Mike Alstott	.20
33	Eddie Kennison	.40
34	Eric Moulds	.10
35	Frank Sanders	.10
36	Daryl Johnston	.10
37	Cris Carter	.10
38	Errict Rhett	.20
39	Ben Coates	.10
40	Shannon Sharpe	.10
41	Jamal Anderson	.20
42	Tim Biakabutuka	.10
43	Jeff Blake	.20
44	Michael Irvin	.20
45	Terrell Davis	1.00
46	Bam Morris	.10
47	Rashaan Salaam	.10
48	Adrian Murrell	.20
49	Ty Detmer	.10
50	Terry Allen	.10
51	Mark Brunell	1.00
52	O.J. McDuffie	.10
53	Willie McGinest	.10
54	Chris Warren	.10
55	Trent Dilfer	.20
56	Jerome Bettis	.20
57	Tamarick Vanover	.10
58	Ki-Jana Carter	.10
59	Ray Zellars	.10
60	J.J. Stokes	.10
61	Cornelius Bennett	.10
62	Scott Mitchell	.10
63	Tyrone Wheatley	.10
64	Steve McNair	.75
65	Tony Banks	.40
66	James Stewart	.10
67	Robert Smith	.10
68	Thurman Thomas	.20
69	Mark Chmura	.10
70	Napoleon Kaufman	.20
71	Ken Norton	.10
72	Herschel Walker	.10
73	Joey Galloway	.20
74	Neil Smith	.10
75	Simeon Rice	.10
76	Michael Jackson	.10
77	Muhsin Muhammad	.10
78	Kevin Hardy	.10
79	Irving Fryar	.10
80	Eric Swann	.10
81	Yancey Thigpen	.10
82	Jim Everett	.10
83	Karim Abdul-Jabbar	.30
84	Garrison Hearst	.10
85	Lawrence Phillips	.20
86	Bryan Cox	.10
87	Larry Centers	.10
88	Wesley Walls	.10
89	Curtis Conway	.10
90	Darnay Scott	.10
91	Anthony Miller	.10
92	Edgar Bennett	.10
93	Willie Green	.10
94	Kent Graham	.10
95	Dave Brown	.10
96	Wayne Chrebet	.10
97	Ricky Watters	.20
98	Tony Martin	.10
99	Warren Moon	.10
100	Curtis Martin	1.00
101	Dorsey Levens	.30
102	Jim Pyne	.10
103	Antonio Freeman	.30
104	Leeland McElroy	.10
105	Isaac Bruce	.20
106	Chris Sanders	.10
107	Tim Brown	.10
108	Greg Lloyd	.10
109	Terrell Buckley	.10
110	Deion Sanders	.40
111	Carl Pickens	.10
112	Bobby Engram	.10
113	Andre Reed	.10
114	Terance Mathis	.10
115	Herman Moore	.20
116	Robert Brooks	.10
117	Ken Dilger	.10
118	Keenan McCardell	.10
119	Andre Hastings	.10
120	Willie Davis	.10
121	Bruce Smith	.10
122	Rob Moore	.10
123	Johnnie Morton	.10
124	Sean Dawkins	.10
125	Mario Bates	.10
126	Henry Ellard	.10
127	Derrick Alexander	.10
128	Kevin Green	.10
129	Derrick Thomas	.10
130	Rod Woodson	.10
131	Rodney Hampton	.10
132	Marshall Faulk	.20
133	Michael Westbrook	.10
134	Erik Kramer	.10
135	Todd Collins	.10
136	Bill Romanowski	.10
137	Jake Reed	.10
138	Heath Shuler	.10
139	Keyshawn Johnson	.40
140	Marvin Harrison	.40
141	Andre Rison	.10
142	Zach Thomas	.20
143	Eric Metcalf	.10
144	Amani Toomer	.10
145	Desmond Howard	.10
146	Jimmy Smith	.10
147	Brad Johnson	.10
148	Troy Vincent	.10
149	Bryce Paup	.10
150	Reggie White	.20
151	*Jake Plummer*	2.50
152	*Darnell Autry*	.25
153	*Tiki Barber*	.75
154	*Pat Barnes*	.30
155	*Orlando Pace*	.20
156	*Peter Boulware*	.10
157	*Shawn Springs*	.20
158	*Troy Davis*	.30
159	*Ike Hilliard*	.75
160	*Jim Druckenmiller*	1.50
161	*Warrick Dunn*	1.25
162	*James Farrior*	.10
163	*Tony Gonzalez*	.75
164	*Darrell Russell*	.10
165	*Byron Hanspard*	.50
166	*Corey Dillon*	2.00
167	*Kenny Holmes*	.10
168	*Walter Jones*	.10
169	*Danny Wuerffel*	.75
170	*Tom Knight*	.10
171	*David LaFleur*	.40
172	*Kevin Lockett*	.10
173	*Will Blackwell*	.20
174	*Reidel Anthony*	1.00
175	*Dwayne Rudd*	.10
176	*Yatil Green*	.30
177	*Antowain Smith*	1.25
178	*Rae Carruth*	.75
179	*Bryant Westbrook*	.10
180	*Reinard Wilson*	.10
181	*Joey Kent*	.30
182	*Renaldo Wynn*	.10
183	Brett Favre	1.25
184	Emmitt Smith	1.00
185	Dan Marino	1.00
186	Troy Aikman	.50
187	Jerry Rice	.50
188	Drew Bledsoe	.50
189	Eddie George	.75
190	Terry Glenn	.10
191	John Elway	.30
192	Steve Young	.30
193	Mark Brunell	.50
194	Barry Sanders	.50
195	Kerry Collins	.30
196	Curtis Martin	.50
197	Terrell Davis	.50
198	Checklist	.10
199	Checklist	.10
200	Checklist	.10

1997 Pinnacle Trophy Collection

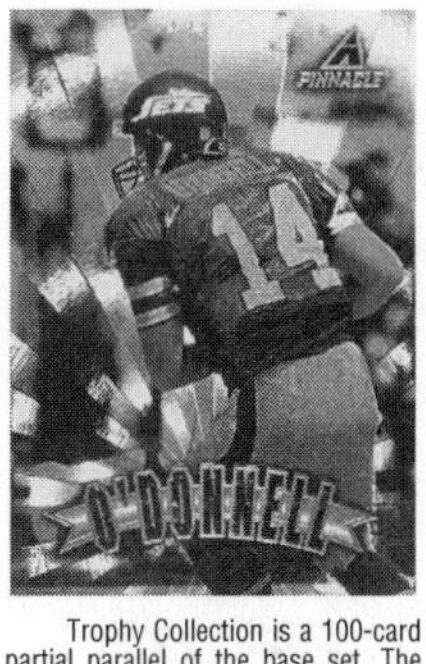

Trophy Collection is a 100-card partial parallel of the base set. The cards were re-numbered and feature Dufex technology. They were inserted one per nine packs.

		MT
Complete Set (100):		250.00
Common Player:		1.00
Minor Stars:		2.00
P1	Brett Favre	25.00
P2	Dan Marino	20.00
P3	Emmitt Smith	20.00
P4	Steve Young	8.00
P5	Drew Bledsoe	12.00
P6	Eddie George	16.00
P7	Barry Sanders	12.00
P8	Jerry Rice	12.00
P9	John Elway	10.00
P10	Troy Aikman	12.00
P11	Kerry Collins	3.00
P12	Rick Mirer	1.00
P13	Jim Harbaugh	1.00
P14	Elvis Grbac	1.00
P15	Gus Frerotte	1.00
P16	Neil O'Donnell	1.00
P17	Jeff George	1.00
P18	Kordell Stewart	12.00
P19	Junior Seau	1.00
P20	Vinny Testaverde	1.00
P21	Terry Glenn	10.00
P22	Natrone Means	2.00
P23	Marcus Allen	2.00
P24	Stan Humphries	1.00
P25	John Friesz	1.00
P26	Cris Carter	1.00
P27	Shannon Sharpe	1.00
P28	Tim Biakabutuka	1.00
P29	Jeff Blake	2.00
P30	Michael Irvin	2.00
P31	Terrell Davis	12.00
P32	Rashaan Salaam	1.00
P33	Adrian Murrell	2.00
P34	Ty Detmer	1.00
P35	Mark Brunell	12.00
P36	Chris Warren	1.00
P37	Trent Dilfer	2.00
P38	Jerome Bettis	2.00
P39	Scott Mitchell	1.00
P40	Steve McNair	10.00
P41	Tony Banks	3.00
P42	Joey Galloway	2.00
P43	Karim Abdul-Jabbar	8.00
P44	Lawrence Phillips	2.00
P45	Dave Brown	1.00
P46	Warren Moon	1.00
P47	Curtis Martin	12.00
P48	Dorsey Levens	2.00
P49	Deion Sanders	5.00
P50	Herman Moore	2.00
P51	Bruce Smith	1.00
P52	Keyshawn Johnson	2.00
P53	Reggie White	2.00
P54	Jake Plummer	10.00
P55	Darnell Autry	4.00
P56	Tiki Barber	8.00
P57	Pat Barnes	4.00
P58	Orlando Pace	2.00
P59	Peter Boulware	1.00
P60	Shawn Springs	2.00
P61	Troy Davis	3.00
P62	Ike Hilliard	6.00
P63	Jim Druckenmiller	12.00
P64	Warrick Dunn	20.00
P65	James Farrior	1.00
P66	Tony Gonzalez	5.00
P67	Darrell Russell	1.00
P68	Byron Hanspard	3.00
P69	Corey Dillon	12.00
P70	Kenny Holmes	1.00
P71	Walter Jones	1.00
P72	Danny Wuerffel	10.00
P73	Tom Knight	1.00
P74	David LaFleur	5.00
P75	Kevin Lockett	1.00
P76	Will Blackwell	2.00
P77	Reidel Anthony	8.00
P78	Dwayne Rudd	1.00
P79	Yatil Green	6.00
P80	Antowain Smith	12.00
P81	Rae Carruth	6.00
P82	Bryant Westbrook	2.00
P83	Reinard Wilson	1.00
P84	Joey Kent	2.00
P85	Renaldo Wynn	1.00
P86	Brett Favre	12.00
P87	Emmitt Smith	10.00
P88	Dan Marino	10.00
P89	Troy Aikman	6.00
P90	Jerry Rice	6.00
P91	Drew Bledsoe	6.00
P92	Eddie George	8.00
P93	Terry Glenn	4.00
P94	John Elway	4.00
P95	Steve Young	4.00
P96	Mark Brunell	6.00
P97	Barry Sanders	6.00
P98	Kerry Collins	2.00
P99	Curtis Martin	6.00
P100	Terrell Davis	6.00

1997 Pinnacle Artist's Proof

Artist's Proof is a 100-card partial parallel of Pinnacle Football. The cards feature Dufex technology and the Artist's Proof stamp. The cards are re-numbered from one to 100.

		MT
Complete Set (100):		850.00
Common Player:		3.00
Minor Stars:		6.00
P1	Brett Favre	75.00
P2	Dan Marino	60.00
P3	Emmitt Smith	60.00
P4	Steve Young	20.00
P5	Drew Bledsoe	40.00
P6	Eddie George	50.00
P7	Barry Sanders	40.00
P8	Jerry Rice	40.00
P9	John Elway	30.00
P10	Troy Aikman	40.00
P11	Kerry Collins	8.00
P12	Rick Mirer	3.00
P13	Jim Harbaugh	3.00
P14	Elvis Grbac	3.00
P15	Gus Frerotte	3.00
P16	Neil O'Donnell	3.00
P17	Jeff George	3.00
P18	Kordell Stewart	40.00
P19	Junior Seau	3.00
P20	Vinny Testaverde	3.00
P21	Terry Glenn	30.00
P22	Natrone Means	6.00
P23	Marcus Allen	6.00
P24	Stan Humphries	3.00
P25	John Friesz	3.00
P26	Cris Carter	3.00
P27	Shannon Sharpe	3.00
P28	Tim Biakabutuka	3.00
P29	Jeff Blake	6.00
P30	Michael Irvin	6.00
P31	Terrell Davis	40.00
P32	Rashaan Salaam	3.00
P33	Adrian Murrell	6.00
P34	Ty Detmer	3.00
P35	Mark Brunell	40.00
P36	Chris Warren	3.00
P37	Trent Dilfer	6.00
P38	Jerome Bettis	6.00
P39	Scott Mitchell	3.00
P40	Steve McNair	30.00
P41	Tony Banks	8.00
P42	Joey Galloway	6.00
P43	Karim Abdul-Jabbar	20.00
P44	Lawrence Phillips	6.00
P45	Dave Brown	3.00
P46	Warren Moon	3.00
P47	Curtis Martin	40.00
P48	Dorsey Levens	6.00
P49	Deion Sanders	20.00
P50	Herman Moore	6.00
P51	Bruce Smith	3.00
P52	Keyshawn Johnson	6.00
P53	Reggie White	6.00
P54	Jake Plummer	25.00
P55	Darnell Autry	12.00
P56	Tiki Barber	20.00
P57	Pat Barnes	10.00
P58	Orlando Pace	6.00
P59	Peter Boulware	3.00
P60	Shawn Springs	6.00
P61	Troy Davis	8.00
P62	Ike Hilliard	15.00
P63	Jim Druckenmiller	30.00
P64	Warrick Dunn	50.00
P65	James Farrior	3.00
P66	Tony Gonzalez	12.00
P67	Darrell Russell	3.00
P68	Byron Hanspard	8.00
P69	Corey Dillon	30.00
P70	Kenny Holmes	3.00
P71	Walter Jones	3.00
P72	Danny Wuerffel	25.00
P73	Tom Knight	3.00
P74	David LaFleur	12.00
P75	Kevin Lockett	3.00
P76	Will Blackwell	6.00
P77	Reidel Anthony	20.00
P78	Dwayne Rudd	3.00
P79	Yatil Green	15.00
P80	Antowain Smith	25.00
P81	Rae Carruth	15.00
P82	Bryant Westbrook	6.00
P83	Reinard Wilson	3.00
P84	Joey Kent	6.00
P85	Renaldo Wynn	3.00
P86	Brett Favre	40.00
P87	Emmitt Smith	30.00
P88	Dan Marino	30.00
P89	Troy Aikman	20.00
P90	Jerry Rice	20.00
P91	Drew Bledsoe	20.00
P92	Eddie George	25.00
P93	Terry Glenn	15.00
P94	John Elway	15.00
P95	Steve Young	15.00
P96	Mark Brunell	20.00
P97	Barry Sanders	20.00
P98	Kerry Collins	8.00
P99	Curtis Martin	20.00
P100	Terrell Davis	20.00

1997 Pinnacle Epix

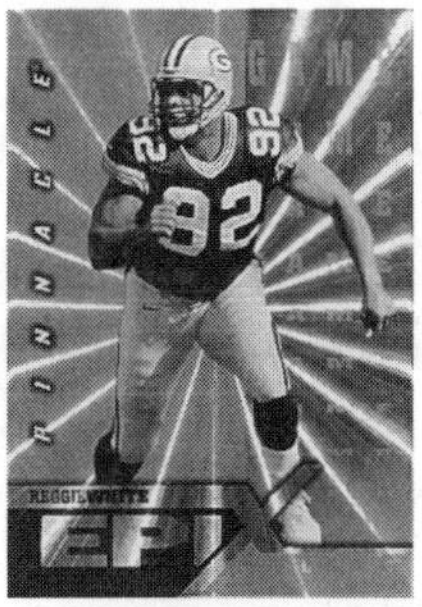

Epix is a 24-card insert which features holographic effects. The set consists of Game, Moment and Season cards which highlight each player's top performances. Orange, Purple and Emerald versions of each card were produced. The overall insertion rate for Epix was 1:19.

		MT
Complete Set (24):		400.00
Common Game (E1-E8):		4.00
Common Moment (E9-E16):		12.00
Common Season (E17-E24):		8.00
Purple Cards:		2x
Emerald Cards:		3x
1	Emmitt Smith	25.00
2	Troy Aikman	15.00
3	Terrell Davis	15.00
4	Drew Bledsoe	15.00
5	Jeff George	4.00
6	Kerry Collins	10.00
7	Antonio Freeman	4.00
8	Herman Moore	4.00
9	Barry Sanders	50.00
10	Brett Favre	80.00
11	Michael Irvin	12.00
12	Steve Young	30.00
13	Mark Brunell	40.00
14	Jerome Bettis	12.00
15	Deion Sanders	25.00
16	Jeff Blake	12.00
17	Dan Marino	50.00
18	Eddie George	35.00
19	Jerry Rice	25.00
20	John Elway	20.00
21	Curtis Martin	20.00
22	Kordell Stewart	25.00
23	Junior Seau	8.00
24	Reggie White	8.00

1997 Pinnacle Scoring Core

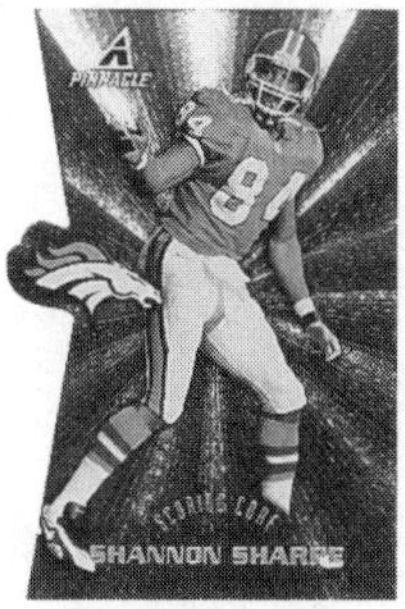

Scoring Core is a 24-card insert seeded 1:89 packs. Each card is specially die-cut and features foil-etching.

		MT
Complete Set (24):		375.00
Common Player:		4.00
Minor Stars:		8.00
1	Emmitt Smith	50.00
2	Troy Aikman	30.00
3	Michael Irvin	8.00
4	Robert Brooks	4.00
5	Brett Favre	60.00
6	Antonio Freeman	8.00
7	Curtis Martin	30.00
8	Drew Bledsoe	30.00
9	Terry Glenn	8.00
10	Tim Biakabutuka	4.00
11	Kerry Collins	8.00
12	Muhsin Muhammad	4.00
13	Karim Abdul-Jabbar	15.00
14	Dan Marino	50.00
15	O.J. McDuffie	4.00
16	Terrell Davis	30.00
17	John Elway	20.00
18	Shannon Sharpe	4.00
19	Garrison Hearst	4.00
20	Steve Young	20.00
21	Jerry Rice	30.00
22	Natrone Means	8.00
23	Mark Brunell	30.00
24	Keenan McCardell	4.00

1997 Pinnacle Team Pinnacle

Team Pinnacle is a 10-card insert consisting of double-sided foil cards. The cards feature two players from the same position, one from each conference. Team Pinnacle cards were inserted 1:240.

		MT
Complete Set (10):		400.00
Common Player:		25.00
1	Dan Marino, Troy Aikman	80.00
2	Drew Bledsoe, Brett Favre	100.00
3	Mark Brunell, Kerry Collins	50.00
4	John Elway, Steve Young	40.00
5	Terrell Davis, Emmitt Smith	80.00
6	Curtis Martin, Barry Sanders	50.00
7	Eddie George, Tim Biakabutuka	60.00
8	Karim Abdul-Jabbar, Lawrence Phillips	25.00
9	Terry Glenn, Jerry Rice	50.00
10	Joey Galloway, Michael Irvin	25.00

1997 Pinnacle Inscriptions

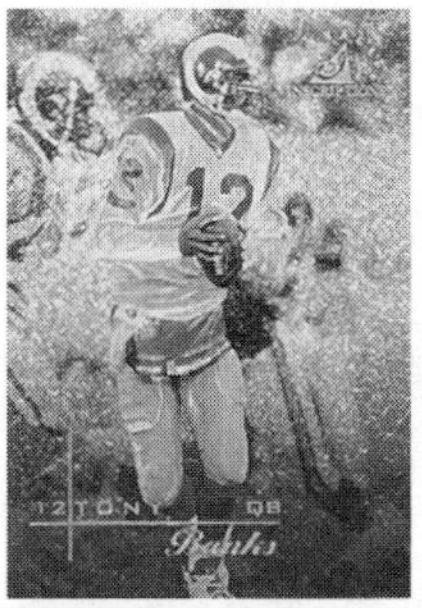

Inscriptions consists of a 50-card base set, two parallel sets and two inserts. The base set features a color player photo with a black and white background. The parallel sets are Challenge Collection (1:7) and Artist's Proof (1:35). Artist's Proof features Dufex technology and the Artist's Proof seal. The inserts are Autographs (30 cards, 1:23) and V2 (18 cards, 1:11). Each pack contained three cards and was packaged in a collectable box.

		MT
Complete Set (50):		75.00
Common Player:		.50
Minor Stars:		1.00
Artist Proof Cards:		8x-16x
Chall. Collection Cards:		2x-4x
Pack (3):		7.00
Wax Box (24):		150.00
1	Mark Brunell	4.00
2	Steve Young	3.00
3	Rick Mirer	.50
4	Brett Favre	10.00
5	Tony Banks	1.00
6	Elvis Grbac	.50
7	John Elway	3.00
8	Troy Aikman	4.00
9	Neil O'Donnell	.50
10	Kordell Stewart	4.00
11	Drew Bledsoe	4.00
12	Kerry Collins	1.00
13	Dan Marino	8.00
14	Jeff George	1.00
15	Scott Mitchell	.50
16	Jim Harbaugh	.50
17	Dave Brown	.50
18	Jeff Blake	1.00
19	Trent Dilfer	1.00
20	Barry Sanders	5.00
21	Jerry Rice	4.00
22	Emmitt Smith	8.00
23	Vinny Testaverde	.50
24	Warren Moon	.50
25	Junior Seau	.50
26	Gus Frerotte	.50
27	Heath Shuler	.50
28	Erik Kramer	.50
29	Boomer Esiason	.50
30	Jim Kelly	1.00
31	Mark Brunell	2.00
32	Steve Young	1.50
33	Brett Favre	5.00
34	Tony Banks	1.00
35	John Elway	1.50
36	Troy Aikman	2.00
37	Kordell Stewart	2.00
38	Drew Bledsoe	2.00
39	Kerry Collins	1.00
40	Dan Marino	4.00
41	Jim Harbaugh	.50
42	Jeff Blake	.50
43	Barry Sanders	2.50
44	Jerry Rice	2.00
45	Emmitt Smith	4.00
46	Rick Mirer	.50
47	Jeff George	.50
48	Neil O'Donnell	.50
49	Elvis Grbac	.50
50	Scott Mitchell	.50

1997 Pinnacle Inscriptions Autographs

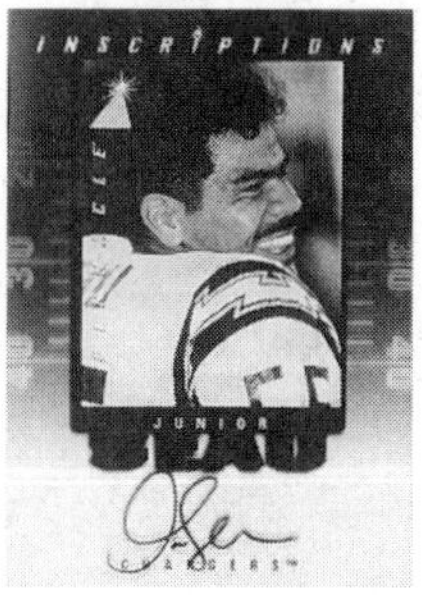

Autographs is a 30-card insert which was seeded one per 23 packs. The cards are plastic, signed by the player and hand-numbered. Each player signed a different number of cards.

	MT
Common Player:	25.00
Minor Stars:	50.00
Tony Banks 1925	50.00
Jeff Blake 1470	50.00
Drew Bledsoe 1970	150.00
Dave Brown 1970	25.00
Mark Brunell 2000	150.00
Kerry Collins 1300	100.00
Trent Dilfer 1950	50.00
John Elway 1975	150.00
Jim Everett 2000	25.00
Brett Favre 215	700.00
Gus Frerotte 1975	25.00
Jeff George 1935	25.00
Elvis Grbac 1985	25.00
Jim Harbaugh 1975	25.00
Jeff Hostetler 2000	25.00
Jim Kelly 1925	50.00
Bernie Kosar 1975	25.00
Eric Kramer 2000	25.00
Dan Marino 440	500.00
Rick Mirer 2000	25.00
Scott Mitchell 1995	25.00
Warren Moon 1975	25.00
Neil O'Donnell 1990	25.00
Jerry Rice 950	300.00
Junior Seau 1900	25.00
Heath Shuler 1965	25.00
Emmitt Smith 220	600.00
Kordell Stewart 1495	150.00
Vinny Testaverde 1975	25.00
Steve Young 1900	125.00

Post-1980 cards in Near Mint condition will generally sell for about 75% of the quoted Mint value. Excellent-condition cards bring no more than 40%.

1997 Pinnacle Inscriptions V2

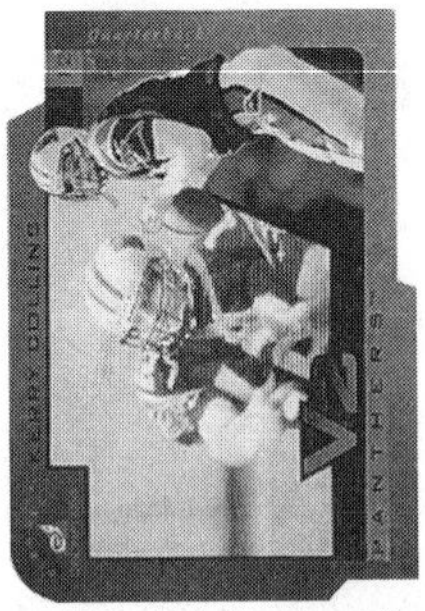

V2 is a 18-card insert consisting of plastic motion cards. Inserted 1:11, the cards came with a clear-coat protector.

		MT
	Complete Set (18):	200.00
	Common Player:	4.00
	Minor Stars:	8.00
1	Mark Brunell	15.00
2	Steve Young	10.00
3	Brett Favre	35.00
4	Tony Banks	8.00
5	John Elway	10.00
6	Troy Aikman	15.00
7	Kordell Stewart	15.00
8	Drew Bledsoe	15.00
9	Kerry Collins	8.00
10	Dan Marino	30.00
11	Barry Sanders	20.00
12	Jerry Rice	15.00
13	Emmitt Smith	30.00
14	Neil O'Donnell	4.00
15	Scott Mitchell	4.00
16	Jim Harbaugh	4.00
17	Jeff Blake	8.00
18	Trent Dilfer	8.00

1997 Pinnacle Inside

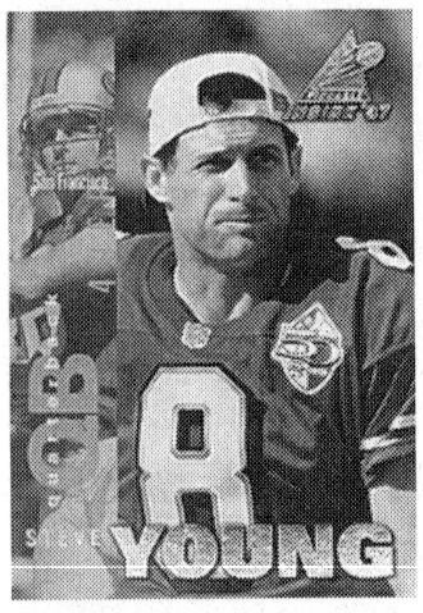

Pinnacle Inside featured a 150-card base set and 28 collectible cans. The base cards include three different player shots. Silver Lining (1:7) and Gridiron Gold (1:63) were the parallel sets. The inserts are Fourth & Goal and Autographed Cards.

		MT
	Complete Set (150):	40.00
	Common Player:	.20
	Minor Stars:	.40
	Silver Cards:	6x-12x
	Silver Rookies:	3x-6x
	Inserted 1:7	
	Gridiron Gold Cards:	20x-40x
	Gridiron Gold Rookies:	10x-20x
	Inserted 1:63	
	Wax Box (48):	120.00
1	Troy Aikman	1.50
2	Dan Marino	3.00
3	Barry Sanders	3.00
4	Drew Bledsoe	1.50
5	Kerry Collins	.50
6	Emmitt Smith	3.00
7	Brett Favre	3.00
8	John Elway	1.00
9	Jerry Rice	1.50
10	Mark Brunell	1.50
11	Elvis Grbac	.20
12	Junior Seau	.20
13	Eddie George	1.75
14	Steve Young	1.00
15	Terrell Davis	1.50
16	Thurman Thomas	.40
17	Deion Sanders	.75
18	Terrell Owens	.75
19	Neil O'Donnell	.20
20	Carl Pickens	.20
21	Marcus Allen	.40
22	Ricky Watters	.40
23	Vinny Testaverde	.20
24	Kordell Stewart	1.25
25	Tony Banks	.75
26	Terry Glenn	.50
27	Todd Collins	.20
28	Robert Brooks	.40
29	Heath Shuler	.20
30	Shannon Sharpe	.20
31	Michael Westbrook	.20
32	Reggie White	.40
33	Brad Johnson	.20
34	Tamarick Vanover	.20
35	Larry Centers	.20
36	Terance Mathis	.20
37	Hardy Nickerson	.20
38	Jamal Anderson	.40
39	Kevin Hardy	.20
40	Stan Humphries	.20
41	Chris Warren	.20
42	Tim Brown	.20
43	Joey Galloway	.60
44	Boomer Esiason	.20
45	Jake Reed	.20
46	Kent Graham	.20
47	Marshall Faulk	.40
48	Sean Dawkins	.20
49	Dave Brown	.20
50	Willie Green	.20
51	Andre Hastings	.20
52	Erik Kramer	.20
53	Michael Irvin	.40
54	Gus Frerotte	.20
55	Winslow Oliver	.20
56	Jimmy Smith	.20
57	Derrick Alexander	.20
58	Adrian Murrell	.20
59	Ki-Jana Carter	.20
60	Garrison Hearst	.20
61	Chris Sanders	.20
62	Johnnie Morton	.20
63	Lawrence Phillips	.40
64	Bobby Engram	.20
65	Tim Biakabutuka	.40
66	Anthony Johnson	.20
67	Keyshawn Johnson	.60
68	Jeff George	.20
69	Errict Rhett	.20
70	Cris Carter	.20
71	Chris T. Jones	.20
72	Eric Moulds	.20
73	Rick Mirer	.20
74	Keenan McCardell	.20
75	Simeon Rice	.20
76	Eddie Kennison	.75
77	Herman Moore	.40
78	Jim Harbaugh	.20
79	Robert Smith	.20
80	Bruce Smith	.20
81	John Friesz	.20
82	Irving Fryar	.20
83	Edgar Bennett	.20
84	Ty Detmer	.20
85	Curtis Conway	.20
86	Napoleon Kaufman	.20
87	Tony Martin	.20
88	Amani Toomer	.20
89	Willie McGinest	.20
90	Daryl Johnston	.20
91	Stanley Pritchett	.20
92	Chris Chandler	.20
93	Natrone Means	.20
94	Kimble Anders	.20
95	Steve McNair	1.00
96	Curtis Martin	1.50
97	O.J. McDuffie	.20
98	Ben Coates	.20
99	Jerome Bettis	.40
100	Andre Reed	.20
101	Jeff Blake	.40
102	Wesley Walls	.20
103	Warren Moon	.20
104	Isaac Bruce	.40
105	Terry Allen	.20
106	Rodney Hampton	.20
107	Karim Abdul-Jabbar	.50
108	Marvin Harrison	.75
109	Dorsey Levens	.20
110	Rashaan Salaam	.40
111	Scott Mitchell	.20
112	Darnay Scott	.20
113	Aeneas Williams	.20
114	Trent Dilfer	.20
115	Antonio Freeman	.40
116	Jim Everett	.20
117	Muhsin Muhammad	.20
118	Rickey Dudley	.20
119	Mike Alstott	.20
120	*Jim Druckenmiller*	2.50
121	*Tiki Barber*	1.50
122	*Ike Hilliard*	1.25
123	*Orlando Pace*	.50
124	*Jake Plummer*	2.00
125	*Yatil Green*	.75
126	*Byron Hanspard*	.75
127	*James Farrior*	.20
128	*Corey Dillon*	2.50
129	*Pat Barnes*	.50
130	*Kenny Holmes*	.20
131	*Rae Carruth*	1.25
132	*Danny Wuerffel*	1.50
133	*Darnell Autry*	.75
134	*Reidel Anthony*	2.00
135	*Darrell Russell*	.20
136	*Will Blackwell*	.50
137	*Peter Boulware*	.20
138	*Shawn Springs*	.50
139	*Joey Kent*	.75
140	*Troy Davis*	.75
141	*Antowain Smith*	1.50
142	*Walter Jones*	.20
143	*Tony Gonzalez*	.75
144	*David LaFleur*	.75
145	*Warrick Dunn*	1.25
146	*Bryant Westbrook*	.20
147	*Dwayne Rudd*	.20
148	*Tom Knight*	.20
149	*Kevin Lockett*	.20
150	Checklist	.20

1997 Pinnacle Inside Cans

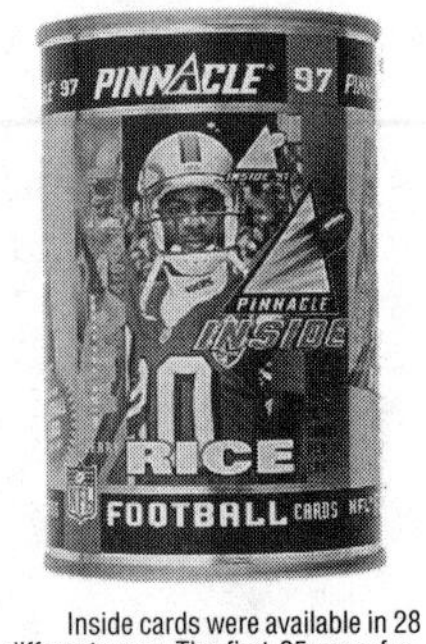

Inside cards were available in 28 different cans. The first 25 cans featured a single player with the image of their Inside card on the outside of the can. Three special cans - Brett Favre MVP, Dan Marino passing record and Ice Bowl commemorative - were also issued. A Gold Can parallel set was also created. Gold Cans were found once per 47 cans.

		MT
	Complete Set (28):	30.00
	Common Can:	.50
	Common Sealed Can:	3.00
	Sealed Cans:	1x-2x
	Gold Cans:	4x-8x
	Gold Sealed Cans:	8x-16x
1	Brett Favre	3.00
2	Dan Marino	2.50
3	Emmitt Smith	2.50
4	Troy Aikman	1.50
5	Barry Sanders	1.50
6	Kerry Collins	1.00
7	Mark Brunell	1.50
8	John Elway	1.00
9	Steve Young	1.00
10	Jerry Rice	1.50
11	Terrell Davis	1.50
12	Curtis Martin	1.50
13	Terry Glenn	1.00
14	Eddie George	2.00
15	Jeff Blake	.50
16	Kordell Stewart	1.50
17	Rick Mirer	.50
18	Karim Abdul-Jabbar	1.00
19	Jeff George	.50
20	Keyshawn Johnson	.50
21	Jim Harbaugh	.50
22	Drew Bledsoe	1.50
23	Deion Sanders	1.00
24	Tony Banks	1.00
25	Jerome Bettis	.50
26	Brett Favre (MVP)	3.00
27	Dan Marino (Passing)	2.50
28	Ice Bowl	2.50

1997 Pinnacle Inside Fourth & Goal

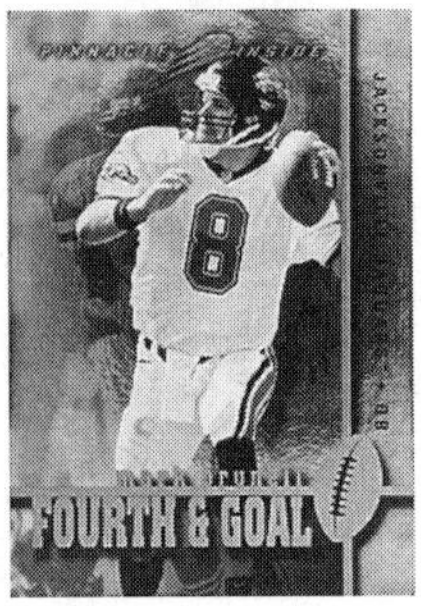

This 20-card insert features clutch players on a foil card. These cards were inserted 1:23.

		MT
	Complete Set (20):	500.00
	Common Player:	10.00
1	Brett Favre	60.00
2	Drew Bledsoe	30.00
3	Troy Aikman	30.00
4	Mark Brunell	30.00
5	Steve Young	25.00
6	Vinny Testaverde	10.00
7	Dan Marino	50.00
8	Kerry Collins	15.00
9	John Elway	25.00
10	Emmitt Smith	50.00
11	Barry Sanders	30.00
12	Eddie George	40.00
13	Terrell Davis	30.00
14	Curtis Martin	30.00
15	Terry Glenn	15.00
16	Jerry Rice	30.00
17	Herman Moore	10.00
18	Jeff Blake	10.00
19	Warrick Dunn	35.00
20	Antowain Smith	20.00

1997 Pinnacle Mint Cards

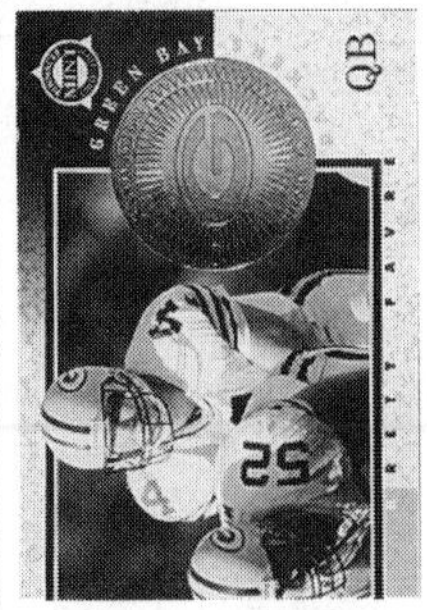

This 30-card base set features a player photo and a foil stamped bronze medallion on the front. A die-cut parallel was created to hold the set's coins. The other parallels are Silver Team Pinnacle (silver foil printing, 1:15) and Gold Team Pinnacle (gold Dufex etched foil, 1:47). Inserts include Commemorative Collection, a six-card set capturing the top moments of 1996 with silver foil and inserted 1:31. Pinnacle Mint also includes Solid Gold Redemption Cards. The solid gold cards are a parallel of the regular set. One redemption card per player was issued and they were inserted 1:47,000.

		MT
	Complete Die-Cut (30):	20.00
	Common Player:	.20
	Minor Stars:	.40
	Bronze Cards:	1x-2x
	Silver Cards:	6x-12x
	Gold Cards:	12x-24x
	Wax Box:	60.00
1	Brett Favre	2.50
2	Drew Bledsoe	1.25
3	Mark Brunell	1.25
4	Kerry Collins	.50
5	Troy Aikman	1.25
6	Steve Young	1.00
7	Dan Marino	2.00
8	Barry Sanders	1.25
9	John Elway	1.00
10	Emmitt Smith	2.00
11	Rick Mirer	.20
12	Kordell Stewart	1.25
13	Tony Banks	.75
14	Jeff George	.20
15	Jerry Rice	1.25
16	Jeff Blake	.40
17	Jim Harbaugh	.20
18	Heath Shuler	.20
19	Scott Mitchell	.20
20	Neil O'Donnell	.20
21	Brett Favre (Minted Highlights)	1.25
22	Drew Bledsoe (Minted Highlights)	.75
23	Mark Brunell (Minted Highlights)	.75
24	Kerry Collins (Minted Highlights)	.40
25	Troy Aikman (Minted Highlights)	.50
26	Dan Marino (Minted Highlights)	1.00
27	Barry Sanders (Minted Highlights)	.75
28	Emmitt Smith (Minted Highlights)	1.00
29	Tony Banks (Minted Highlights)	.20
30	John Elway (Minted Highlights)	.50

1997 Pinnacle Mint Coins

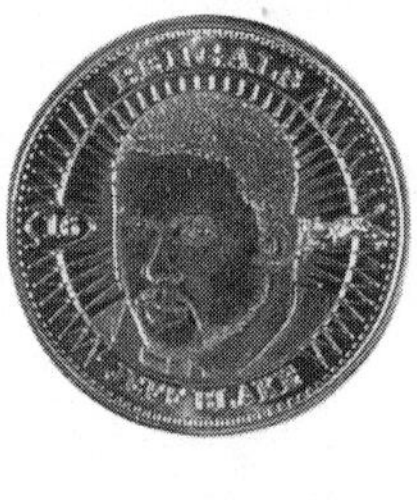

The 30-base coins feature each players face and match up with one of the base cards. Six parallels of the base coins were made. Nickel-Silver (1:20), Gold Plated (1:47), Brass Proof (numbered to 500), Silver Proof (numbered to 250), Gold Proof (numbered to 100) and Solid Silver (1:288) versions were all added to Pinnacle Mint. The only insert is Commemorative Collection.

		MT
	Complete Brass (30):	60.00
	Common Brass Coin:	.75
	Minor Brass Stars:	1.50
	Nickel Coins:	2.5x-5x
	Gold Plated Coins:	6x-12x
1	Brett Favre	8.00
2	Drew Bledsoe	4.00
3	Mark Brunell	4.00
4	Kerry Collins	2.00
5	Troy Aikman	4.00
6	Steve Young	3.00
7	Dan Marino	6.00
8	Barry Sanders	4.00
9	John Elway	3.00
10	Emmitt Smith	6.00
11	Rick Mirer	.75
12	Kordell Stewart	4.00
13	Tony Banks	1.50
14	Jeff George	.75
15	Jerry Rice	4.00
16	Jeff Blake	1.50
17	Jim Harbaugh	.75
18	Heath Shuler	.75
19	Scott Mitchell	.75
20	Neil O'Donnell	.75
21	Brett Favre (Minted Highlights)	4.00
22	Drew Bledsoe (Minted Highlights)	2.50
23	Mark Brunell (Minted Highlights)	2.50
24	Kerry Collins (Minted Highlights)	1.50
25	Troy Aikman (Minted Highlights)	1.75
26	Dan Marino (Minted Highlights)	3.00
27	Barry Sanders (Minted Highlights)	2.50
28	Emmitt Smith (Minted Highlights)	3.00
29	Tony Banks (Minted Highlights)	.75
30	John Elway (Minted Highlights)	1.75

A player's name in *italic* type indicates a rookie card.

1997 Pinnacle Mint Commemorative Cards

This six-card insert highlights six top moments of 1996. The cards feature silver foil and were inserted 1:31.

		MT
	Complete Set (6):	60.00
	Common Player:	8.00
1	Barry Sanders	25.00
2	Brett Favre	18.00
3	Mark Brunell	8.00
4	Emmitt Smith	16.00
5	Dan Marino	16.00
6	Jerry Rice	8.00

1997 Pinnacle Mint Commemorative Coins

These six coins are double-sized brass and match up with the Commemorative Collection cards. They also highlight top events of 1996 and were inserted 1:31.

		MT
	Complete Set (6):	120.00
	Common Player:	16.00
1	Barry Sanders	25.00
2	Brett Favre	35.00
3	Mark Brunell	16.00
4	Emmitt Smith	35.00
5	Dan Marino	35.00
6	Jerry Rice	16.00

1997 Pinnacle Totally Certified Platinum Red

Platinum Red is considered the "base set" for Totally Certified. Each card in the 150-card set is sequentially-numbered to 4,999. The cards feature a micro-etched holographic mylar finish. Platinum Blue (one per pack) and Platinum Gold (1:79) parallels were also included in this series.

		MT
	Complete Set (150):	250.00
	Common Player:	.75
	Minor Stars:	1.50
	Common Rookie:	1.00
	Reds Sequentially #'d to 4,999	
	Pack (3):	7.00
	Wax Box (18):	100.00
1	Emmitt Smith	12.00
2	Dan Marino	12.00
3	Brett Favre	15.00
4	Steve Young	7.00
5	Kerry Collins	7.00
6	Troy Aikman	10.00
7	Drew Bledsoe	10.00
8	Eddie George	7.00
9	Jerry Rice	10.00
10	John Elway	12.00
11	Barry Sanders	15.00
12	Mark Brunell	8.00
13	Elvis Grbac	1.50
14	Tony Banks	1.50
15	Vinny Testaverde	1.50
16	Rick Mirer	.75
17	Carl Pickens	1.50
18	Deion Sanders	3.00
19	Terry Glenn	3.00
20	Heath Shuler	.75
21	Dave Brown	.75
22	Keyshawn Johnson	3.00
23	Jeff George	3.00
24	Ricky Watters	1.50
25	Kordell Stewart	5.00
26	Junior Seau	1.50
27	Terrell Owens	3.00
28	Warren Moon	1.50
29	Isaac Bruce	3.00
30	Steve McNair	5.00
31	Gus Frerotte	.75
32	Trent Dilfer	1.50
33	Shannon Sharpe	1.50
34	Scott Mitchell	.75
35	Antonio Freeman	3.00
36	Jim Harbaugh	1.50
37	Natrone Means	1.50
38	Marcus Allen	3.00
39	Karim Abdul-Jabbar	1.50
40	Tim Biakabutuka	1.50
41	Jeff Blake	3.00
42	Michael Irvin	3.00
43	Herschel Walker	.75
44	Curtis Martin	4.00
45	Eddie Kennison	1.50
46	Napoleon Kaufman	3.00
47	Larry Centers	.75
48	Jamal Anderson	3.00
49	Derrick Alexander	.75
50	Bruce Smith	1.50
51	Wesley Walls	.75
52	Rod Smith	1.50
53	Keenan McCardell	1.50
54	Robert Brooks	1.50
55	Willie Green	.75
56	Jake Reed	.75
57	Joey Galloway	3.00
58	Eric Metcalf	.75
59	Chris Sanders	.75
60	Jeff Hostetler	.75
61	Kevin Greene	.75
62	Frank Sanders	1.50
63	Dorsey Levens	3.00
64	Sean Dawkins	.75
65	Cris Carter	3.00
66	Andre Hastings	.75
67	Amani Toomer	1.50
68	Adrian Murrell	1.50
69	Ty Detmer	1.50
70	Yancey Thigpen	1.50
71	Jim Everett	1.50
72	Todd Collins	.75
73	Curtis Conway	1.50
74	Herman Moore	3.00
75	Neil O'Donnell	1.50
76	Rod Woodson	1.50
77	Tony Martin	.75
78	Kent Graham	.75
79	Andre Reed	1.50
80	Reggie White	3.00
81	Thurman Thomas	3.00
82	Garrison Hearst	1.50
83	Chris Warren	1.50
84	Wayne Chrebet	3.00
85	Chris T. Jones	.75
86	Anthony Miller	.75
87	Chris Chandler	1.50
88	Terrell Davis	12.00
89	Mike Alstott	3.00
90	Terry Allen	1.50
91	Jerome Bettis	3.00
92	Stan Humphries	.75
93	Andre Rison	1.50
94	Marshall Faulk	4.00
95	Erik Kramer	.75
96	O.J. McDuffie	1.50
97	Robert Smith	3.00
98	Keith Byars	.75
99	Rodney Hampton	.75
100	Desmond Howard	.75
101	Lawrence Phillips	1.50
102	Michael Westbrook	1.50
103	Johnnie Morton	1.50
104	Ben Coates	1.50
105	J.J. Stokes	1.50
106	Terance Mathis	1.50
107	Errict Rhett	1.50
108	Tim Brown	3.00
109	Marvin Harrison	3.00
110	Muhsin Muhammad	1.50
111	Bam Morris	.75
112	Mario Bates	.75
113	Jimmy Smith	3.00
114	Irving Fryar	1.50
115	Tamarick Vanover	.75
116	Brad Johnson	3.00
117	Rashaan Salaam	.75
118	Ki-Jana Carter	.75
119	Tyrone Wheatley	1.50
120	John Friesz	1.50
121	*Orlando Pace*	2.00
122	*Jim Druckenmiller*	4.00
123	*Byron Hanspard*	4.00
124	*David LaFleur*	2.00
125	*Reidel Anthony*	6.00
126	*Antowain Smith*	7.00
127	*Bryant Westbrook*	2.00
128	*Fred Lane*	4.00
129	*Tiki Barber*	12.00
130	*Shawn Springs*	2.00
131	*Ike Hilliard*	6.00
132	*James Farrior*	1.00
133	*Darrell Russell*	2.00
134	*Walter Jones*	1.00
135	*Tom Knight*	1.00
136	*Yatil Green*	2.00
137	*Joey Kent*	2.00
138	*Kevin Lockett*	1.00
139	*Troy Davis*	2.00
140	*Darnell Autry*	4.00
141	*Pat Barnes*	4.00
142	*Rae Carruth*	2.00
143	*Will Blackwell*	2.00
144	*Warrick Dunn*	10.00
145	*Corey Dillon*	25.00
146	*Dwayne Rudd*	2.00
147	*Reinard Wilson*	1.00
148	*Peter Boulware*	2.00
149	*Tony Gonzalez*	10.00
150	*Danny Wuerffel*	4.00

1997 Pinnacle Totally Certified Platinum Blue

Platinum Blue cards are sequentially-numbered to 2,499. They feature a micro-etched holographic mylar finish and were seeded one per pack.

	MT
Complete Set (150):	500.00
Platinum Blue Cards:	2x
Production 2,499 Sets	
Inserted 1:1	

1997 Pinnacle Totally Certified Platinum Gold

Platinum Gold cards feature a micro-etched holographic mylar finish. Each card is sequentially-numbered to 30 and they were inserted 1:79.

	MT
Platinum Gold Cards:	25x
Platinum Gold Rookies:	7x-14x
Production 30 Sets	
Inserted 1:79	

1997 Pinnacle X-Press

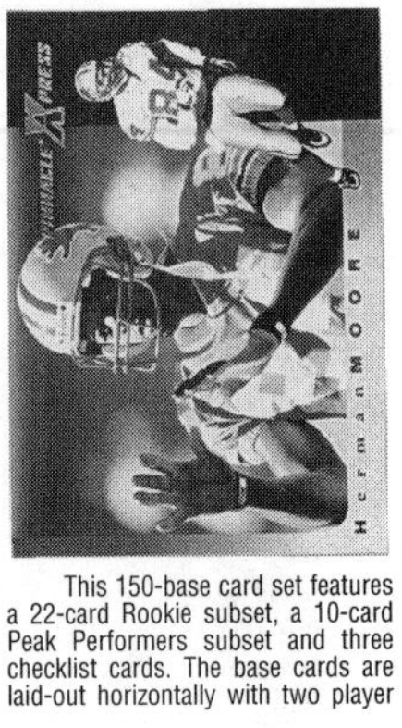

This 150-base card set features a 22-card Rookie subset, a 10-card Peak Performers subset and three checklist cards. The base cards are laid-out horizontally with two player

photos on the front. The inserts included the Pursuit of Paydirt interactive game, Metal Works, Bombs Away and Divide & Conquer. Autumn Warriors is a base set parallel. The silver foil cards were inserted 1:7.

		MT
Complete Set (150):		25.00
Common Player:		.05
Minor Stars:		.10
Aut. Warrior Cards:		6x-12x
Aut. Warrior Rookies:		3x-6x
Hobby Pack (8):		2.00
Hobby Wax Box (24):		42.00
Retail Pack (8):		2.00
Retail Wax Box (36):		65.00
Metal Works Wax Box:		15.00
1	Drew Bledsoe	1.00
2	Steve Young	.75
3	Brett Favre	2.25
4	John Elway	.75
5	Dan Marino	2.00
6	Jerry Rice	1.00
7	Tony Banks	.40
8	Kerry Collins	.25
9	Mark Brunell	1.00
10	Troy Aikman	1.00
11	Barry Sanders	1.25
12	Elvis Grbac	.05
13	Eddie George	1.50
14	Terry Glenn	.25
15	Kordell Stewart	1.00
16	Junior Seau	.10
17	Herman Moore	.10
18	Gus Frerotte	.05
19	Warren Moon	.05
20	Emmitt Smith	2.00
21	Chris Chandler	.05
22	Rashaan Salaam	.05
23	Sean Dawkins	.05
24	Tyrone Wheatley	.05
25	Lawrence Phillips	.05
26	Ty Detmer	.05
27	Vinny Testaverde	.05
28	Dorsey Levens	.10
29	Ricky Watters	.10
30	Natrone Means	.10
31	Curtis Conway	.05
32	Larry Centers	.05
33	Johnnie Morton	.05
34	Desmond Howard	.05
35	Marcus Allen	.10
36	Cris Carter	.05
37	James Stewart	.05
38	Frank Sanders	.05
39	Bruce Smith	.05
40	Carl Pickens	.05
41	Neil O'Donnell	.05
42	Trent Dilfer	.10
43	Rodney Peete	.05
44	Terance Mathis	.05
45	Muhsin Muhammad	.05
46	Jake Reed	.05
47	Jim Harbaugh	.05
48	Todd Collins	.05
49	Ki-Jana Carter	.05
50	Scott Mitchell	.05
51	Kevin Hardy	.05
52	Stanley Pritchett	.05
53	Dave Brown	.05
54	Jeff George	.05
55	Stan Humphries	.05
56	Isaac Bruce	.10
57	Eric Moulds	.05
58	Robert Brooks	.05
59	Steve McNair	.75
60	Adrian Murrell	.10
61	Mike Alstott	.10
62	Michael Jackson	.05
63	Tamarick Vanover	.05
64	Edgar Bennett	.05
65	Andre Hastings	.05
66	Robert Smith	.05
67	Thurman Thomas	.10
68	Tim Biakabutuka	.05
69	Rick Mirer	.05
70	Deion Sanders	.50
71	Curtis Martin	1.00
72	Garrison Hearst	.05
73	Kent Graham	.05
74	Anthony Johnson	.05
75	Antonio Freeman	.10
76	Marshall Faulk	.10
77	O.J. McDuffie	.05
78	Heath Shuler	.05
79	Napoleon Kaufman	.10
80	Aeneas Williams	.05
81	Hardy Nickerson	.05
82	Keenan McCardell	.05
83	Erik Kramer	.05
84	Ben Coates	.05
85	Shannon Sharpe	.05
86	Tony Martin	.05
87	Chris Sanders	.05
88	Jamal Anderson	.05
89	Karim Abdul-Jabbar	.50
90	Keyshawn Johnson	.40
91	Terrell Owens	.50
92	Michael Irvin	.10
93	John Friesz	.05
94	Chris Warren	.05
95	Errict Rhett	.05
96	Terry Allen	.10
97	Michael Westbrook	.05
98	Simeon Rice	.05
99	Willie Green	.05
100	Jerome Bettis	.10
101	Reggie White	.10
102	Bert Emanuel	.05
103	Zach Thomas	.10
104	Tim Brown	.05
105	Darnay Scott	.05
106	Terrell Davis	1.00
107	Andre Reed	.05
108	Amani Toomer	.05
109	Irving Fryar	.05
110	Joey Galloway	.10
111	Marvin Harrison	.40
112	Derrick Alexander	.05
113	Jeff Blake	.20
114	Brad Johnson	.10
115	Eddie Kennison	.40
116	*Rae Carruth*	.75
117	*Tony Gonzalez*	.50
118	*Joey Kent*	.10
119	*Peter Boulware*	.10
120	*Orlando Pace*	.20
121	*David LaFleur*	.50
122	*Darnell Autry*	.50
123	*Tiki Barber*	1.00
124	*Troy Davis*	.50
125	*Jim Druckenmiller*	1.50
126	*Corey Dillon*	2.00
127	*Ike Hilliard*	.75
128	*Reidel Anthony*	1.00
129	*Byron Hanspard*	.50
130	*Antowain Smith*	1.00
131	*Jake Plummer*	1.25
132	*Warrick Dunn*	1.00
133	*Bryant Westbrook*	.10
134	*Darrell Russell*	.10
135	*Yatil Green*	.50
136	*Shawn Springs*	.10
137	*Danny Wuerffel*	.75
138	*Brett Favre* (Peak Performer)	1.00
139	Emmitt Smith (Peak Performer)	1.00
140	Barry Sanders (Peak Performer)	.50
141	Troy Aikman (Peak Performer)	.50
142	Drew Bledsoe (Peak Performer)	.50
143	Jerry Rice (Peak Performer)	.50
144	Dan Marino (Peak Performer)	1.00
145	John Elway (Peak Performer)	.30
146	Kerry Collins (Peak Performer)	.30
147	Mark Brunell (Peak Performer)	.30
148	Checklist (Brett Favre)	.50
149	Checklist (Dan Marino)	.50
150	Checklist (Troy Aikman)	.25

1997 Pinnacle X-Press Bombs Away

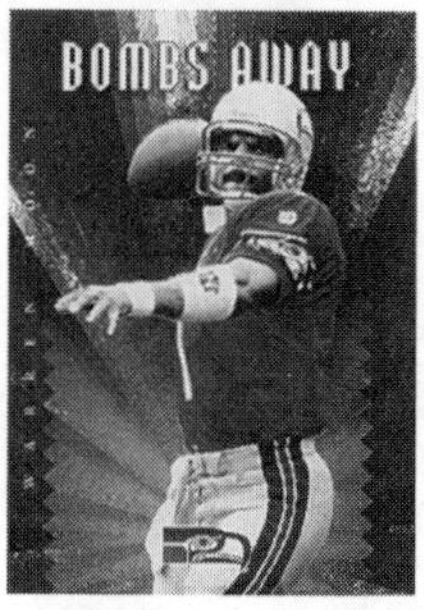

This 18-card insert features top quarterbacks on a full foil, micro-etched card. Bombs Away was inserted 1:19.

		MT
Complete Set (18):		100.00
Common Player:		2.00
Minor Stars:		4.00
1	Brett Favre	20.00
2	Dan Marino	18.00
3	Troy Aikman	10.00
4	Drew Bledsoe	10.00
5	Kerry Collins	5.00
6	Mark Brunell	10.00
7	John Elway	8.00
8	Steve Young	8.00
9	Jeff Blake	4.00
10	Kordell Stewart	10.00
11	Jeff George	2.00
12	Rick Mirer	2.00
13	Neil O'Donnell	2.00
14	Scott Mitchell	2.00
15	Jim Harbaugh	2.00
16	Warren Moon	2.00
17	Trent Dilfer	4.00
18	Jim Druckenmiller	8.00

1997 Pinnacle X-Press Divide & Conquer

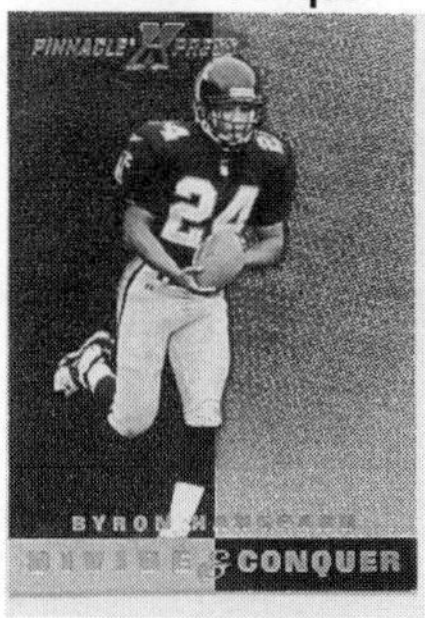

Divide & Conquer is a 20-card insert on full foil, micro-etched card stock. The cards feature a player action shot and heliogram print technology. They are numbered to 500.

		MT
Complete Set (20):		750.00
Common Player:		7.00
1	Tim Biakabutuka	7.00
2	Karim Abdul-Jabbar	30.00
3	Jerome Bettis	14.00
4	Eddie George	80.00
5	Terrell Davis	60.00
6	Barry Sanders	60.00
7	Emmitt Smith	100.00
8	Brett Favre	120.00
9	Dan Marino	100.00
10	Troy Aikman	60.00
11	Jerry Rice	60.00
12	Drew Bledsoe	60.00
13	Kerry Collins	15.00
14	Mark Brunell	60.00
15	John Elway	45.00
16	Steve Young	45.00
17	Warrick Dunn	90.00
18	Byron Hanspard	25.00
19	Troy Davis	40.00
20	Jeff Blake	14.00

1997 Pinnacle X-Press Pursuit of Paydirt-Quarterbacks

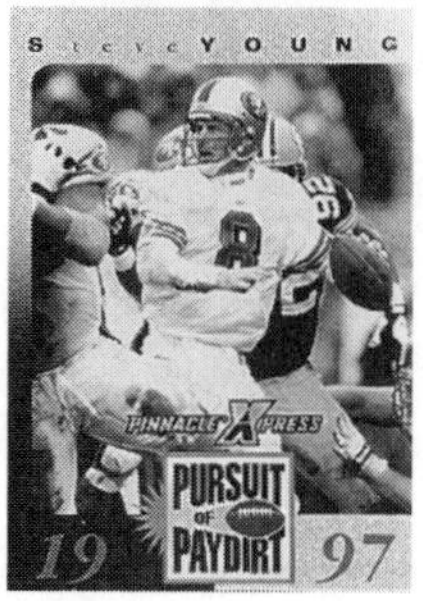

The Pursuit of Paydirt insert was an interactive game which ran during the 1997 season. This 30-card insert (found 1:2) featured quarterbacks and gave collectors the chance to win if they found the QB who led the league in touchdowns during the season.

		MT
Complete Set (30):		25.00
Common Player:		.25
Minor Stars:		.50
1	Drew Bledsoe	2.00
2	Steve Young	1.50
3	Brett Favre	4.50
4	John Elway	1.50
5	Dan Marino	4.00
6	Tony Banks	1.00
7	Kerry Collins	.75
8	Mark Brunell	2.00
9	Troy Aikman	2.00
10	Elvis Grbac	.25
11	Kordell Stewart	2.00
12	Gus Frerotte	.25
13	Warren Moon	.25
14	Chris Chandler	.25
15	Rick Mirer	.25
16	Vinny Testaverde	.25
17	Neil O'Donnell	.25
18	Trent Dilfer	.50
19	Rodney Peete	.25
20	Jim Harbaugh	.25
21	Todd Collins	.25
22	Scott Mitchell	.25
23	Dave Brown	.25
24	Jeff George	.25
25	Stan Humphries	.25
26	Steve McNair	1.50
27	Heath Shuler	.25
28	Jeff Blake	.50
29	Brad Johnson	.25
30	Jim Druckenmiller	2.00

1997 Pinnacle X-Press Pursuit of Paydirt-Running Backs

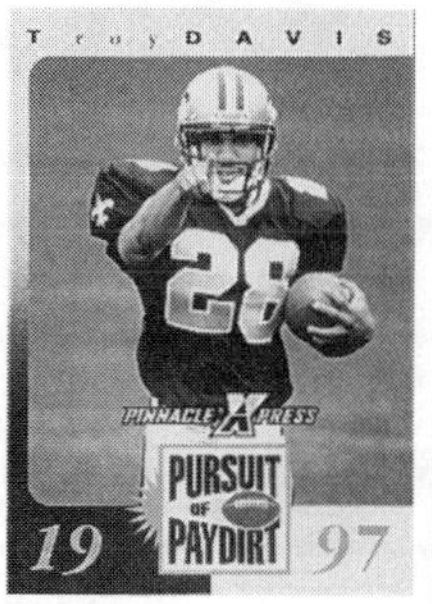

This 30-card insert featured running backs and gave collectors the chance to win prizes if they could match the leading TD scorer with the number of TDs he made. This insert was found 1:2.

		MT
Complete Set (30):		25.00
Common Player:		.25
Minor Stars:		.50
1	Errict Rhett	.25
2	Terry Allen	.50
3	Jerome Bettis	.50
4	Terrell Davis	2.00
5	Tiki Barber	1.50
6	Troy Davis	1.25
7	Byron Hanspard	1.25
8	Greg Hill	.25
9	Barry Sanders	2.00
10	Eddie George	3.00
11	Emmitt Smith	4.00
12	Rashaan Salaam	.25
13	Tyrone Wheatley	.25
14	Lawrence Phillips	.25
15	Ricky Watters	.50
16	Natrone Means	.50
17	Marcus Allen	.50
18	James Stewart	.25
19	Ki-Jana Carter	.25
20	Dorsey Levens	.50
21	Robert Smith	.25
22	Thurman Thomas	.50
23	Tim Biakabutuka	.25
24	Curtis Martin	2.00
25	Garrison Hearst	.25
26	Marshall Faulk	.50
27	Napoleon Kaufman	1.00
28	Jamal Anderson	.25
29	Karim Abdul-Jabbar	1.50
30	Chris Warren	.25

1997 Pinnacle Rembrandt

This nine-card set was inserted one per box of Rembrandt's Ultra-PRO plastic sheets. The cards feature an action shot and a bronze-colored foil section. Silver and gold foil parallel sets were also created. Collectors who assembled an entire bronze, silver or gold set could redeem them for prizes from Rembrandt.

		MT
Complete Set (9):		20.00
Common Player:		1.50
*Gold Cards:		6x-12x
*Silver Cards:		3x-6x
1	Brett Favre	5.00
2	Troy Aikman	2.00
3	John Elway	1.50
4	Dan Marino	4.00
5	Drew Bledsoe	2.00
6	Emmitt Smith	4.00
7	Jerry Rice	2.00
8	Barry Sanders	2.50
9	Mark Brunell	2.00

1992 Playoff Promos

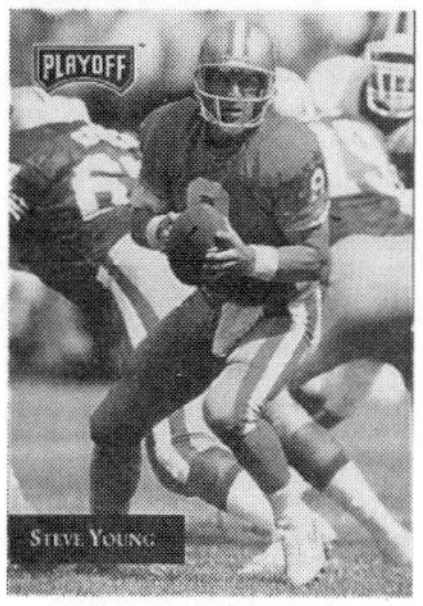

This seven-card promotional set gave collectors a glimpse of what Playoff's 1992 set would look like. These cards were printed on 22-point stock. The player's names were printed in silver inside a black box at the bottom of the card. The card backs, numbered "of 6 promo," feature a full-bleed photo, with the player's name located along the left margin of the card. A write-up about the player was included in the lower left of the card back.

		MT
Complete Set (7):		15.00
Common Player:		1.00
1	Calvin Williams	1.25
2	John Elway	4.00
3	Dalton Hilliard	1.00
4	Steve Young	4.00
5	Emmitt Smith	8.00
6	Mike Golic	1.00
NNO	Header/Intro Card	1.00

1992 Playoff

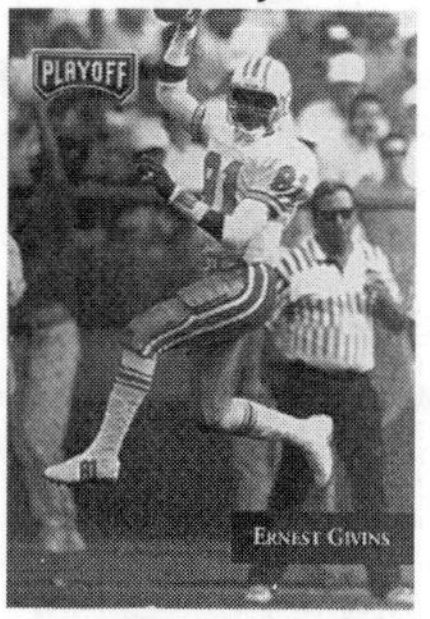

This 150-card set features standard-size cards printed on stock which is thicker than usual. The card front has a full-bleed color photo, plus the player's name in a black bar at the bottom. Most of the backgrounds are black-and-white and, using a metallic-like process, give the cards depth. The card back has a close-up shot of the player, plus his team's name in a team color-coded bar. Information contained in a black box details the player's performance from a key game during the previous season. There were also seven promotional cards made as previews of the regular 1992 set.

		MT
Complete Set (150):		45.00
Common Player:		.25
Minor Stars:		.50
Pack (8):		1.50
Wax Box (36):		40.00
1	Emmitt Smith	10.00
2	Steve Young	5.00
3	Jack Del Rio	.25
4	Bobby Hebert	.25
5	Shannon Sharpe	.25
6	Gary Clark	.25
7	Christian Okoye	.25
8	Ernest Givins	.25
9	Mike Horan	.25
10	Dennis Gentry	.25
11	Michael Irvin	1.00
12	Eric Floyd	.25
13	Brent Jones	.25
14	Anthony Carter	.25
15	Tony Martin	.75
16	Greg Lewis ("Returning" should be "returned" on back)	.25
17	Todd McNair	.25
18	Earnest Byner	.25
19	Steve Beuerlein	.25
20	Roger Craig	.25
21	Mark Higgs	.25
22	Guy McIntyre	.25
23	Don Warren	.25
24	Alvin Harper	.50
25	Mark Jackson	.25
26	Chris Doleman	.25
27	Jesse Sapolu	.25
28	Tony Talbert	.25
29	Wendell Davis	.25
30	Dan Saleaumua	.25
31	Jeff Bostic	.25
32	Jay Novacek	.25
33	Cris Carter	.50
34	Tony Paige	.25
35	Greg Kragen	.25
36	Jeff Dellenbach	.25
37	Keith DeLong	.25
38	Todd Scott	.25
39	Jeff Feagles	.25
40	Mike Saxon	.25
41	Martin Mayhew	.25
42	*Steve Bono*	1.00
43	*Willie Davis*	.50
44	Mark Stepnoski	.25
45	Harry Newsome	.25
46	Thane Gash	.25
47	Gaston Green	.25
48	James Washington	.25
49	Kenny Walker	.25
50	*Jeff Davidson*	.25
51	Shane Conlan	.25
52	Richard Dent	.25
53	Haywood Jeffires	.25
54	Harry Galbreath	.25
55	Terry Allen	1.00
56	Tommy Barnhardt	.25
57	Mike Golic	.25
58	Dalton Hilliard	.25
59	Danny Copeland	.25
60	*Jerry Fontenot*	.25
61	Kelvin Martin	.25
62	Mark Kelso	.25
63	Wymon Henderson	.25
64	Mark Rypien	.25
65	Bobby Humphrey	.25
66	Rich Gannon (Tarkington misspelled, Minneapolis instead of Minnesota on back)	.25
67	Darren Lewis	.25
68	Barry Foster	.25
69	Ken Norton	.25
70	James Lofton	.25
71	Trace Armstrong	.25
72	Vestee Jackson	.25
73	Clyde Simmons	.25
74	Brad Muster	.25
75	Cornelius Bennett	.25
76	Mike Merriweather	.25
77	John Elway	2.00
78	Herschel Walker	.25
79	Hassan Jones (Minneapolis instead of Minnesota on back)	.25
80	Jim Harbaugh	.50
81	Issiac Holt	.25
82	David Alexander	.25
83	Brian Mitchell	.25
84	Mark Tuinei	.25
85	Tom Rathman	.25
86	Reggie White	.50
87	William Perry	.25
88	Jeff Wright	.25
89	Keith Kartz	.25
90	Andre Waters	.25
91	Darryl Talley	.25
92	Morten Andersen	.25
93	Tom Waddle	.25
94	Felix Wright (Minneapolis instead of Minnesota on back)	.25
95	Keith Jackson	.25
96	Art Monk	.50
97	Seth Joyner	.25
98	Steve McMichael	.25
99	Thurman Thomas	1.00
100	Warren Moon	.75
101	Tony Casillas	.25
102	Vance Johnson	.25
103	*Doug Dawson*	.25
104	Bill Maas	.25
105	Mark Clayton	.25
106	Hoby Brenner	.25
107	Gary Anderson	.25
108	Marc Logan	.25
109	Ricky Sanders	.25
110	Vai Sikahema	.25
111	Neil Smith	.25
112	Cody Carlson	.25
113	Jimmie Jones	.25
114	Pat Swilling	.25
115	Neil O'Donnell	1.00
116	Chip Lohmiller	.25
117	Mike Croel	.25
118	Pete Metzelaars	.25
119	Ray Childress	.25
120	Fred Banks	.25
121	Derek Kennard	.25
122	Daryl Johnston	.25
123	Lorenzo White (Minneapolis instead of Minnesota on back)	.25
124	Hardy Nickerson	.25
125	Derrick Thomas	.50
126	Steve Walsh	.25
127	Doug Widell	.25
128	Calvin Williams	.25
129	Tim Harris	.25
130	Rod Woodson	.50
131	Craig Heyward	.25
132	Barry Word	.25
133	Mark Duper	.25
134	Tim Johnson	.25
135	John Gesek	.25
136	Steve Jackson	.25
137	Dave Krieg	.25
138	Barry Sanders	7.00
139	Michael Haynes	.25
140	Eric Metcalf	.25
141	Stan Humphries	1.00
142	Sterling Sharpe	.50
143	Todd Marinovich	.25
144	Rodney Hampton	1.00
145	Rodney Peete	.50
146	*Darryl Williams*	.25
147	*Darren Perry*	.25
148	*Terrell Buckley*	.25
149	*Amp Lee*	.75
150	Ricky Watters	1.50

1993 Playoff Promos

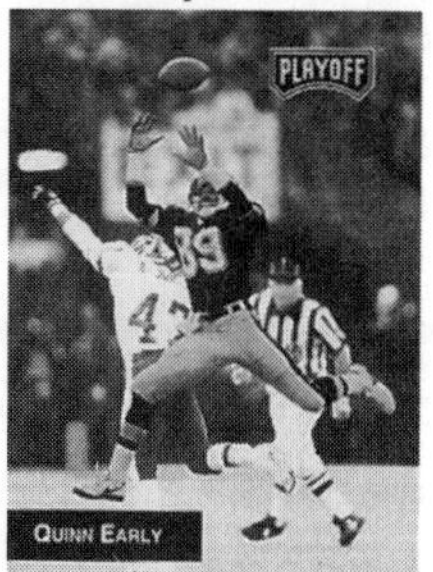

This six-card promotional set gave collectors a glimpse of what the 1993 Playoff set would look like. The card fronts feature the Playoff logo at the top and the player's name, printed in silver inside a black box, near the bottom of the card. The card backs have a full-bleed photo, with the player's name inside a box on the upper left corner. A write-up about the player is included in the lower right. The cards, printed on 22-point stock, are numbered "of 6 promo."

		MT
Complete Set (6):		12.00
Common Player:		1.00
1	Emmitt Smith	6.00
2	Barry Foster	1.00
3	Quinn Early	1.00
4	Tim Brown	1.50
5	Steve Young	3.00
6	Sterling Sharpe	1.50

1993 Playoff

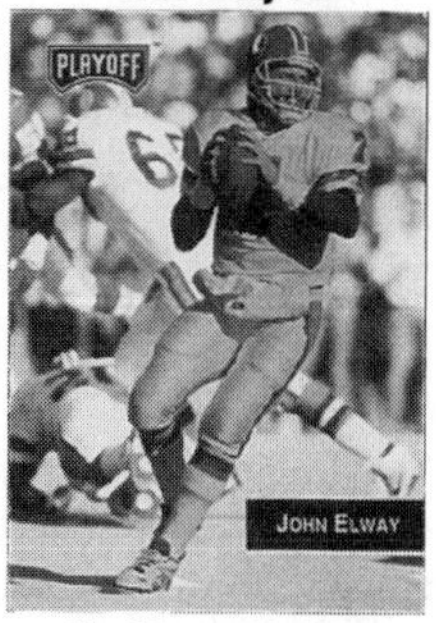

Playoff increased its 1993 set to 315 cards. Subsets within the regular set include "The Backs" (#s 277-282, featuring top running backs), "Connections" (#s 283-292, featuring top quarterback/wide receiver combinations), and "Rookies" (#s 293-315). Redemption cards were randomly inserted in packs for "Headliner" (six cards) and "Rookie Roundup" (10 cards) sets. Other insert sets included Checklists (eight cards), Playoff Club (seven cards), and Brett Favre and Ricky Watters (five cards each). Six promotional cards, which have the same design as the regular cards, were also made.

		MT
Complete Set (315):		60.00
Common Player:		.15
Minor Stars:		.25
Comp. Promo Set (6):		10.00
Hobby Pack (8):		1.75
Hobby Wax Box (24):		30.00
Retail Pack (8):		1.50
Retail Wax Box (24):		25.00
1	Troy Aikman	3.00
2	Jerry Rice	3.00
3	Keith Jackson	.15
4	Sean Gilbert	.15
5	Jim Kelly	.25
6	Junior Seau	.25
7	Deion Sanders	2.00
8	Joe Montana	4.00
9	Terrell Buckley	.15
10	Emmitt Smith	5.00
11	Pete Stoyanovich	.15
12	Randall Cunningham	.25
13	Boomer Esiason	.25
14	Mike Saxon	.15
15	Chuck Cecil	.15
16	Vinny Testaverde	.25

17	Jeff Hostetler	.25
18	Mark Clayton	.15
19	Nick Bell	.15
20	Frank Reich	.15
21	Henry Ellard	.15
22	Andre Reed	.25
23	Mark Ingram	.15
24	Mike Brim	.15
25	Bernie Kosar	.25
26	Jeff George	.25
27	Tommy Maddox	.15
28	*Kent Graham*	.75
29	David Klingler	.15
30	Robert Delpino	.15
31	Kevin Fagan	.15
32	Mark Bavaro	.15
33	Harold Green	.15
34	Shawn McCarthy	.15
35	Ricky Proehl	.15
36	Eugene Robinson	.15
37	Phil Simms	.15
38	David Lang	.15
39	Santana Dotson	.15
40	Brett Perriman	.15
41	Jim Harbaugh	.15
42	Keith Byars	.15
43	Quentin Coryatt	.15
44	Louis Oliver	.15
45	Howie Long	.15
46	Mike Sherrard	.15
47	Earnest Byner	.15
48	Neil Smith	.15
49	Audray McMillan	.15
50	Vaughn Dunbar	.15
51	Ronnie Lott	.15
52	Clyde Simmons	.15
53	Kevin Scott	.15
54	Bubby Brister	.15
55	Randal Hill	.15
56	Pat Swilling	.15
57	Steve Beuerlein	.15
58	Gary Clark	.15
59	Brian Noble	.15
60	Leslie O'Neal	.15
61	Vincent Brown	.15
62	Edgar Bennett	.25
63	Anthony Carter	.15
64	Glenn Cadez	.15
65	Dalton Hilliard	.15
66	James Lofton	.15
67	Walter Stanley	.15
68	Tim Harris	.15
69	Carl Banks	.15
70	Andre Ware	.15
71	Karl Mecklenburg	.15
72	Russell Maryland	.15
73	LeRoy Thompson	.15
74	Tommy Kane	.15
75	Dan Marino	5.00
76	Darrell Fullington	.15
77	Jessie Tuggle	.15
78	Bruce Smith	.15
79	Neal Anderson	.15
80	Kevin Mack	.15
81	Shane Dronett	.15
82	Nick Lowery	.15
83	Sheldon White	.15
84	Willie (Flipper) Anderson	.15
85	Jeff Herrod	.15
86	Dwight Stone	.15
87	Dave Krieg	.15
88	Bryan Cox	.15
89	Greg McMurty	.15
90	Rickey Jackson	.15
91	Ernie Mills	.15
92	Browning Nagle	.15
93	John Taylor	.15
94	Eric Dickerson	.15
95	Johnny Holland	.15
96	Anthony Miller	.15
97	Fred Barnett	.15
98	Ricky Ervins	.15
99	Leonard Russell	.15
100	Lawrence Taylor	.25
101	Tony Casillas	.15
102	John Elway	1.50
103	Bennie Blades	.15
104	Harry Sydney	.15
105	Bubba McDowell	.15
106	Todd McNair	.15
107	Steve Smith	.15
108	Jim Everett	.25
109	Bobby Humphrey	.15
110	Rich Gannon	.15
111	Marv Cook	.15
112	Wayne Martin	.15
113	Sean Landeta	.15
114	Brad Baxter	.15
115	Reggie White	.25
116	Johnny Johnson	.15
117	Jeff Graham	.15
118	*Darren Carrington*	.25
119	Ricky Watters	.25
120	Art Monk	.25
121	Cornelius Bennett	.15
122	Wade Wilson	.15
123	Daniel Stubbs	.15
124	Brad Muster	.15
125	Mike Tomczak	.15
126	Jay Novacek	.15
127	Shannon Sharpe	.25
128	Rodney Peete	.15
129	Daryl Johnston	.15
130	Warren Moon	.25
131	Willie Gault	.15
132	Tony Martin	.15
133	Terry Allen	.15
134	Hugh Millen	.15
135	Rob Moore	.15
136	*Andy Harmon*	.15
137	Kelvin Martin	.15
138	Rod Woodson	.25
139	Nate Lewis	.15
140	Darryl Talley	.15
141	Guy McIntyre	.15
142	John L. Williams	.15
143	Brad Edwards	.15
144	Trace Armstrong	.15
145	Kenneth Davis	.15
146	Clay Matthews	.15
147	Gaston Green	.15
148	Chris Spielman	.15
149	Cody Carlson	.15
150	Derrick Thomas	.25
151	Terry McDaniel	.15
152	Kevin Greene	.15
153	Roger Craig	.15
154	Craig Heyward	.15
155	Rodney Hampton	.25
156	Heath Sherman	.15
157	Mark Stepnoski	.15
158	Chris Chandler	.15
159	Rob Berstine	.15
160	Pierce Holt	.15
161	Wilber Marshall	.15
162	Reggie Cobb	.15
163	Tom Rathman	.15
164	Michael Haynes	.15
165	Nate Odomes	.15
166	Tom Waddle	.15
167	Eric Ball	.15
168	Brett Favre	5.00
169	Michael Jackson	.15
170	Lorenzo White	.15
171	Cleveland Gary	.15
172	Jay Schroeder	.15
173	Tony Paige	.15
174	Jack Del Rio	.15
175	Jon Vaughn	.15
176	Morten Andersen	.15
177	Chris Burkett	.15
178	Vai Sikahema	.15
179	Ronnie Harmon	.15
180	Amp Lee	.15
181	Chip Lohmiller	.15
182	Steve Broussard	.15
183	Don Beebe	.15
184	Tommy Vardell	.15
185	Keith Jennings	.15
186	Simon Fletcher	.15
187	Mel Gray	.15
188	Vince Workman	.15
189	Haywood Jeffires	.15
190	Barry Word	.15
191	Ethan Horton	.15
192	Mark Higgs	.15
193	Irving Fryar	.15
194	Charles Haley	.15
195	Steve Bono	1.00
196	Mike Golic	.15
197	Gary Anderson	.15
198	Sterling Sharpe	.25
199	Andre Tippett	.15
200	Thurman Thomas	1.00
201	Chris Miller	.15
202	Henry Jones	.15
203	Mo Lewis	.15
204	Marion Butts	.15
205	Mike Johnson	.15
206	Alvin Harper	.25
207	Ray Childress	.15
208	Anthony Newman	.15
209	Tony Bennett	.15
210	*Antony Newman*	.15
211	Christian Okoye	.15
212	Marcus Allen	.25
213	Jackie Harris	.15
214	Mark Duper	.15
215	Cris Carter	.25
216	John Stephens	.15
217	Barry Sanders	3.50
218	Herman Moore	2.00
219	Marvin Washington	.15
220	Calvin Williams	.15
221	John Randle	.15
222	Marco Coleman	.15
223	Eric Martin	.15
224	David Meggett	.15
225	Brian Washington	.15
226	Barry Foster	.25
227	Michael Zordich	.15
228	Stan Humphries	.25
229	Mike Cofer	.15
230	Chris Warren	1.00
231	Keith McCants	.15
232	Mark Rypien	.15
233	James Francis	.15
234	Andre Rison	.25
235	William Perry	.15
236	Chip Banks	.15
237	Willie Davis	.15
238	Chris Doleman	.15
239	Tim Brown	.25
240	Darren Perry	.15
241	Johnny Bailey	.15
242	Ernest Givins	.15
243	John Carney	.15
244	Cortez Kennedy	.25
245	Lawrence Dawsey	.15
246	Martin Mayhew	.15
247	Shane Conlan	.15
248	J.J. Birden	.15
249	Quinn Early	.15
250	Michael Irvin	.25
251	Neil O'Donnell	.25
252	Stan Gelbaugh	.15
253	Drew Hill	.15
254	Wendell Davis	.15
255	Tim Johnson	.15
256	Seth Joyner	.15
257	Derrick Fenner	.15
258	Steve Young	3.00
259	Jackie Slater	.15
260	Eric Metcalf	.15
261	Rufus Porter	.15
262	Ken Norton	.15
263	Tim McDonald	.15
264	Mark Jackson	.15
265	Hardy Nickerson	.15
266	Anthony Munoz	.15
267	Mark Carrier	.15
268	Mike Pritchard	.15
269	Steve Emtman	.15
270	Ricky Sanders	.15
271	Robert Massey	.15
272	Pete Metzelaars	.15
273	Reggie Langhorne	.15
274	Tim McGee	.15
275	*Reggie Rivers*	.15
276	Jimmie Jones	.15
277	Lorenzo White	.15
278	Emmitt Smith	3.00
279	Thurman Thomas	.25
280	Barry Sanders	2.00
281	Rodney Hampton	.25
282	Barry Foster	.25
283	Troy Aikman	1.50
284	Michael Irvin	.25
285	Brett Favre	2.00
286	Sterling Sharpe	.25
287	Steve Young	2.00
288	Jerry Rice	2.00
289	Stan Humphries	.25
290	Anthony Miller	.25
291	Dan Marino	3.00
292	Keith Jackson	.15
293	*Patrick Bates*	.25
294	*Jerome Bettis*	3.00
295	*Drew Bledsoe*	8.00
296	*Tom Carter*	.25
297	*Curtis Conway*	2.00
298	*John Copeland*	.25
299	*Eric Curry*	.25
300	*Reggie Brooks*	.25
301	*Steve Everitt*	.25
302	*Deon Figures*	.25
303	*Garrison Hearst*	3.00
304	*Qadry Ismail*	1.00
305	*Marvin Jones*	.25
306	*Lincoln Kennedy*	.25
307	*O.J. McDuffie*	3.00
308	*Rick Mirer*	.50
309	*Wayne Simmons*	.25
310	*Irv Smith*	.25
311	*Robert Smith*	3.00
312	*Dana Stubblefield*	1.50
313	*George Teague*	.25
314	*Dan Williams*	.25
315	*Kevin Williams*	.50

1993 Playoff Checklists

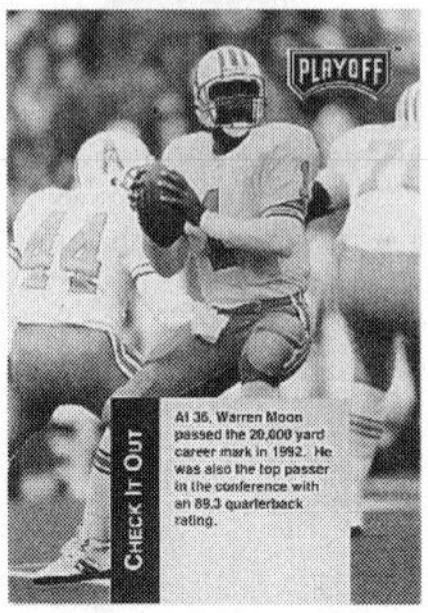

Randomly seeded in packs, this eight-card set showcases an action shot of a player. A silver box, featuring highlights about the player, is included at the bottom of the card. The box is bordered on the left side by a black box which has "Check It Out" inside it. The card back features a portion of the checklist printed inside a white area in the center of the card. The top of the card has a red stripe, while the bottom of the card has a black stripe.

		MT
Complete Set (8):		7.00
Common Player:		.75
1A	Warren Moon (UER) (Kosar misspelled Kozar)	1.00
1B	Warren Moon (COR)	1.00
2	Barry Sanders	1.00
3	Deion Sanders	1.00
4	Ron Woodson	1.00
5	Junior Seau	1.00
6	Mark Rypien	.75
7	Derrick Thomas	1.00
8	Dallas Players (Daryl Johnston, Alvin Harper, Michael Irvin) (UER) (Stan Humphries listed as 299; should be 289)	.75

1993 Playoff Club

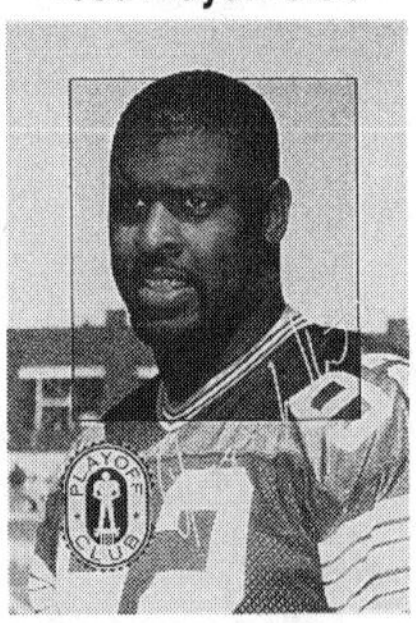

These insert cards feature a gold Playoff Club logo on the card front which distinguishes it as an insert card from the regular Playoff cards. A color player closeup shot, surrounded by a black-and-white background, is also included on the card front. The player has also signed his signature in gold ink. The back, numbered using a "PC" prefix, gives a summary of the player's career against a grey Playoff Club logo which is ghosted in the background. These were inserted into retail and hobby boxes.

		MT
Complete Set (7):		25.00
Common Player:		2.00
1	Joe Montana	15.00
2	Art Monk	2.00
3	Lawrence Taylor	4.00
4	Ronnie Lott	2.00
5	Reggie White	4.00
6	Anthony Munoz	2.00
7	Jackie Slater	2.00

1993 Playoff Brett Favre

Green Bay Packer quarterback Brett Favre is featured in this five-card insert set. The fronts have a metallic shine to them and feature a full-bleed color photo. A black box at the bottom contains Favre's name. The card back has a ghosted image of Favre throwing a pass, plus season highlights against a green background. Cards, numbered 1 of 5, etc., were randomly inserted in hobby display boxes.

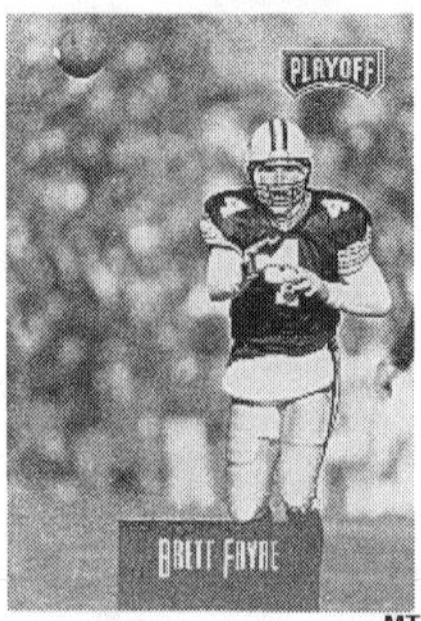

		MT
Complete Set (5):		100.00
Common Favre:		20.00
1	The Early Years (Brett Favre)	20.00
2	The College Years (Brett Favre)	20.00
3	Turning Pro (Brett Favre)	20.00
4	Green Bay Star (Brett Favre)	20.00
5	1992: The Storybook Season (Brett Favre)	20.00

1993 Playoff Headliners Redemption

Randomly seeded in retail foil packs, the redemption card could be redeemed for this six-card set. Overall, 48,475 redemption cards were inserted into packs. The card front features a gray background with silver type. A color photo of the player is featured, with the player's name located inside a black box at the top of the card front. The Headliners' logo is printed to the right of the player's name. The card backs showcase the player's name and highlights printed inside a black box at the top, with the card number in the upper right. A headshot of the player is located in the center of the card back. The cards are numbered with an "H" prefix.

		MT
Complete Set (6):		25.00
Common Player:		1.00
1	Brett Favre	14.00
2	Sterling Sharpe	2.00
3	Emmitt Smith	14.00
4	Jerry Rice	7.00
5	Thurman Thomas	2.00
6	David Klingler	1.00
NNO	Headliner Redemption	1.00

1993 Playoff Promo Inserts

Each 1993 Playoff special retail pack included one promo insert (or Playoff Ricky Watters card). The full-bleed photo on the card front includes the Playoff logo at the top and the player's name in silver inside a black rectangle, located at the bottom left. The player is highlighted in color, with the background in black-and-white. Showcased on the card back are highlights from the player's career. With the card number in the upper right (labeled "Promo X of 6"), the player's name appears in white inside a black band in the upper left corner.

		MT
Complete Set (6):		10.00
Common Player:		1.50
1	Michael Irvin	1.50
2	Barry Foster	1.50
3	Quinn Early	1.50
4	Tim Brown	1.50
5	Reggie White	2.00
6	Sterling Sharpe	2.00

1993 Playoff Rookie Roundup Redemption

A 10-card set would be given to collectors in exchange for a 1993 Playoff Rookie Roundup Redemption card, which was found in hobby foil packs. The mail-in offer expired on July 3, 1994. Silver type over a gray background served as the backdrop to the color photo of the player. The Rookie Roundup and the Playoff logos also appear on the card front. The player's name is printed in the lower right corner. The card back has a color photo of the player in the center, over a white background with gray team logos in the background. A black box at the bottom of the card back houses the player's name and 1993 highlights. Overall, 15,683 exchange cards were printed. Cards are prefixed with "R."

		MT
Complete Set (10):		40.00
Common Player:		2.00
1	Jerome Bettis	10.00
2	Drew Bledsoe	15.00
3	Reggie Brooks	3.00
4	Derek Brown (RB)	3.00
5	Garrison Hearst	6.00
6	Terry Kirby	3.00
7	Glyn Milburn	3.00
8	Rick Mirer	6.00
9	Roosevelt Potts	2.00
10	Dana Stubblefield	3.00
NNO	Rookie Roundup Redemption Card	.50

1993 Playoff Ricky Watters

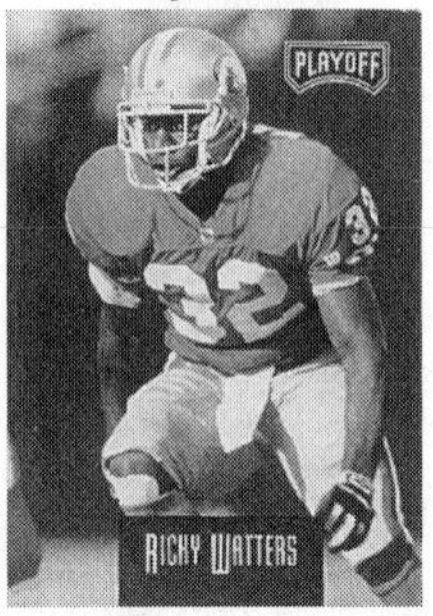

This five-card set features San Francisco 49er running back Ricky Watters. The front has a full-bleed color photo against a metallic background. Watters' name is at the bottom of the card in a black box. The Playoff logo is also on the front. The back has a ghosted image of Watters running the ball, plus career highlights against a tan background. Cards, which are numbered 1 of 5, etc., were randomly inserted in retail display boxes.

		MT
Complete Set (5):		20.00
Common Watters:		4.00
1	The Early Years (Ricky Watters)	4.00
2	Irish Eyes Were Smiling (Ricky Watters)	4.00
3	The Bay Watters (Ricky Watters)	4.00
4	A Second-Year Rookie (Ricky Watters)	4.00
5	Rookie of the Year (Ricky Watters)	4.00

1993 Playoff Contenders Promos

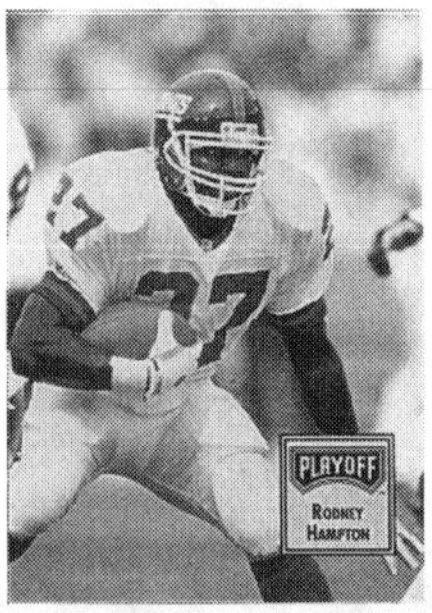

This six-card promotional set gave collectors a glimpse of what the 1993 Contenders set would look like. The borderless fronts showcase the Playoff logo and player's name inside of a silver box at the bottom of the card. A color photo of the player is located on the left of the horizontal card back. The right side is a team-colored area which includes the player's team helmet, his name and his season highlight. In the upper right is the card number, which is indicated with a Roman numeral.

		MT
Complete Set (6):		12.00
Common Player:		.75
1	Drew Bledsoe	3.00
2	Neil Smith	.75
3	Rick Mirer	1.00
4	Rodney Hampton	.75
5	Barry Sanders	2.50
6	Emmitt Smith	4.00

1993 Playoff Contenders

This 150-card Playoff Contenders set uses a unique ink-on-foil printing process called Tekchrome. The cards are printed on a heavy card stock, making them among the thickest and sturdiest in the hobby. Cards include photos and game information from the 1993 season; the set is primarily composed of players from teams that were most likely to make the NFL playoffs, plus 49 top rookies and free agents from the season. The set also includes two insert sets - "Rookie Contenders" (10 of the top first-year players) and a five-card set tracing the collegiate and professional career of Seattle Seahawk rookie quarterback Rick Mirer. The regular cards have the player's name and Playoff logo in a silver box on the card front.

		MT
Complete Set (150):		35.00
Common Player:		.15
Minor Stars:		.25
Pack (7):		2.00
Wax Box (24):		40.00
1	Brett Favre	4.00
2	Thurman Thomas	.25
3	Barry Word	.15
4	Herman Moore	1.00
5	Reggie Langhorne	.15
6	Wilber Marshall	.15
7	Ricky Watters	.25
8	Marcus Allen	.25
9	Jeff Hostetler	.25
10	Steve Young	2.00
11	Bobby Hebert	.15
12	David Klingler	.15
13	Craig Heyward	.15
14	Andre Reed	.25
15	Tommy Vardell	.15
16	Anthony Carter	.15
17	Mel Gray	.15
18	Dan Marino	4.00
19	Haywood Jeffires	.15
20	Joe Montana	3.00
21	Tim Brown	.25
22	Jim McMahon	.15
23	Scott Mitchell	.25
24	Rickey Jackson	.15
25	Troy Aikman	2.00
26	Rodney Hampton	.25
27	Fred Barnett	.15
28	Gary Clark	.15
29	Barry Foster	.25
30	Brian Blades	.15
31	Tim McDonald	.15
32	Kelvin Martin	.15
33	Henry Jones	.15
34	Erric Pegram	.15
35	Don Beebe	.15
36	Eric Metcalf	.15
37	Charles Haley	.15
38	Robert Delpino	.15
39	Leonard Russell	.15
40	Jackie Harris	.15
41	Ernest Givins	.15
42	Willie Davis	.15
43	Alexander Wright	.15
44	Keith Byars	.15
45	David Meggett	.15
46	Johnny Johnson	.15
47	Mark Bavaro	.15
48	Seth Joyner	.15
49	Junior Seau	.25
50	Emmitt Smith	4.00
51	Shannon Sharpe	.25
52	Rodney Peete	.15
53	Andre Rison	.25
54	Cornelius Bennett	.15
55	Mark Carrier	.15
56	Mark Clayton	.15
57	Warren Moon	.25
58	J.J. Birden	.15
59	Howie Long	.15
60	Irving Fryar	.15
61	Mark Jackson	.15
62	Eric Martin	.15
63	Herschel Walker	.15
64	Cortez Kennedy	.25
65	Steve Beuerlein	.15
66	Jim Kelly	.25
67	Bernie Kosar	.25
68	Pat Swilling	.15
69	Michael Irvin	.25
70	Harvey Williams	.15
71	Steve Smith	.15
72	Wade Wilson	.15
73	Phil Simms	.15
74	Vinny Testaverde	.25
75	Barry Sanders	2.50
76	Ken Norton	.15
77	Rod Woodson	.25
78	Webster Slaughter	.15
79	Derrick Thomas	.25
80	Mike Sherrard	.15
81	Calvin Williams	.15
82	Jay Novacek	.15
83	Michael Brooks	.15
84	Randall Cunningham	.25
85	Chris Warren	.50
86	Johnny Mitchell	.15
87	Jim Harbaugh	.15
88	Rod Bernstine	.15
89	John Elway	1.00
90	Jerry Rice	2.00
91	Brent Jones	.15
92	Cris Carter	.25
93	Alvin Harper	.25
94	*Horace Copeland*	.50
95	Raghib Ismail	.25
96	*Darrin Smith*	.25
97	*Reggie Brooks*	.25
98	*Demetrius DuBose*	.25
99	*Eric Curry*	.25
100	*Rick Mirer*	.75
101	*Carlton Gray*	.15
102	*Dana Stubblefield*	1.00
103	*Todd Kelly*	.15
104	*Natrone Means*	2.00
105	*Darrien Gordon*	.50
106	*Deon Figures*	.30
107	*Garrison Hearst*	3.00
108	*Ron Moore*	.50
109	*Leonard Renfro*	.15
110	*Lester Holmes*	.15
111	*Vaughn Hebron*	.25
112	*Marvin Jones*	.25
113	*Irv Smith*	.25
114	*Willie Roaf*	.25
115	*Derek Brown*	.25
116	*Vincent Brisby*	1.00
117	*Drew Bledsoe*	7.00
118	*Gino Torretta*	.25
119	*Robert Smith*	3.00
120	*Qadry Ismail*	1.00
121	*O.J. McDuffie*	1.75
122	*Terry Kirby*	.75
123	*Troy Drayton*	1.00

124	*Jerome Bettis*	3.00
125	*Patrick Bates*	.25
126	*Rossevelt Potts*	.25
127	*Tom Carter*	.40
128	*Patrick Robinson*	.25
129	*Brad Hopkins*	.15
130	*George Teague*	.40
131	Wayne Simmons	.15
132	*Mark Brunell*	7.00
133	*Ryan McNeil*	.15
134	*Dan Williams*	.15
135	*Glyn Milburn*	.50
136	*Kevin Williams*	1.50
137	*Derrick Lassic*	.25
138	Steve Everitt	.25
139	*Lance Gunn*	.25
140	*John Copeland*	.25
141	*Curtis Conway*	2.00
142	*Thomas Smith*	.25
143	*Russell Copeland*	1.00
144	*Lincoln Kennedy*	.25
145	Boomer Esiason	.15
146	Neil Smith	.15
147	Jack Del Rio	.15
148	Morten Andersen	.15
149	Sterling Sharpe (CL)	.15
150	Reggie White	.25

1993 Playoff Contenders Rick Mirer

These five cards, devoted to Seattle Seahawks first-round draft pick Rick Mirer, were randomly inserted in 1993 Playoff Contenders packs. The fronts have a borderless color action shot with a metallic shine. Mirer's name is at the bottom in a black box. Mirer's photo from the front of card 3 is used as a ghosted image for all five card backs. Career highlights and a card number, 1 of 5, etc., are also given on the backs.

		MT
Complete Set (5):		40.00
Common Mirer:		8.00
1	This Kid Can Play (Rick Mirer)	8.00
2	Notre Dame All-American (Rick Mirer)	8.00
3	First-Round Draft Pick (Rick Mirer)	8.00
4	Seattle in the Hunt (Rick Mirer)	8.00
5	A Tough Guy (Rick Mirer)	8.00

1993 Playoff Contenders Rookie Contenders

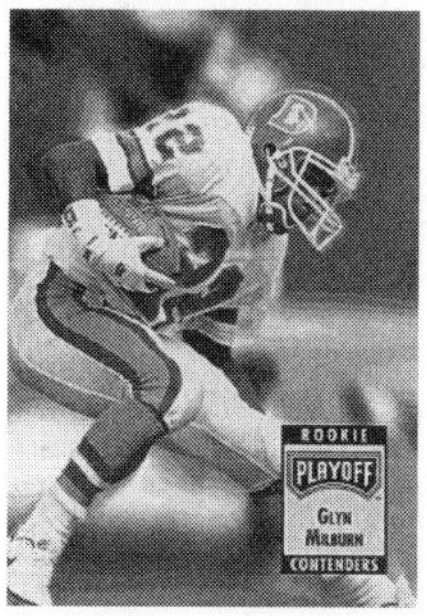

These 10 inserts cards, randomly included in 1993 Playoff Contenders packs, feature 10 of the top rookies in 1993. Each card front has a borderless color action photo, with a metallic shine and blurred background. The player's name and set logo appear in the lower left corner in a gold box. Each card is white and has the player's name at the top; the set name is given in white in two black bands, one on top and the other on the bottom. The backs are numbered and include a summary of the player's collegiate accomplishments.

		MT
Complete Set (10):		120.00
Common Player:		5.00
1	Jerome Bettis	20.00
2	Drew Bledsoe	45.00
3	Reggie Brooks	5.00
4	Derek Brown	5.00
5	Garrison Hearst	20.00
6	Vaughn Hebron	5.00
7	Qadry Ismail	10.00
8	Derrick Lassic	5.00
9	Glyn Milburn	5.00
10	Dana Stubblefield	7.00

1994 Playoff Prototypes

This six-card set gave collectors a glimpse of what the 1994 Playoff set would look like. A full-bleed color photo dominates the front, with the Playoff logo near the bottom, located inside an oval that also housed the player's name. The card back also had a full-bleed shot of the player, with his name in a black box next to his helmet. Below the name on the unnumbered card back is the player's career highlights.

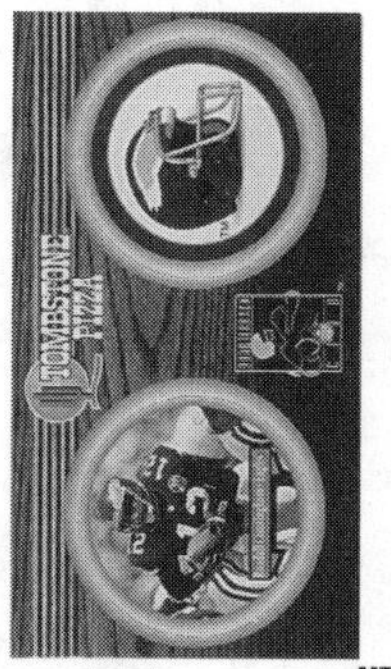

		MT
Complete Set (6):		8.00
Common Player:		1.00
1	Marcus Allen	1.00
2	Rick Mirer	1.25
3	Barry Sanders	2.00
4	Junior Seau	1.25
5	Sterling Sharpe	1.00
6	Emmitt Smith	3.00

1994 Playoff

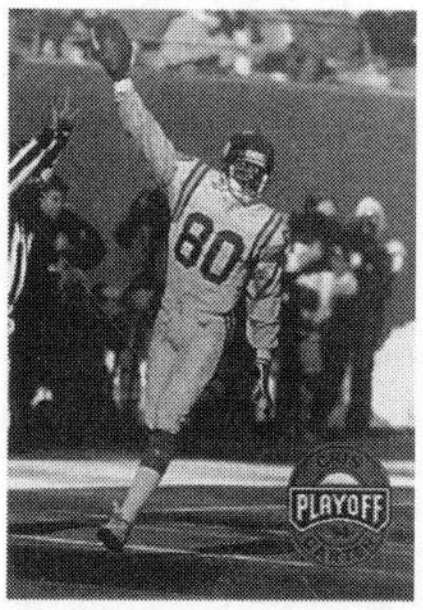

These Playoff cards use the company's Tekchrome II ink-on-foil process for the full-color card fronts. The photo is full-bleed and has the set's logo in the upper right corner. The card back has another photo of the player, along with his name and team helmet. A brief player profile is also included. Subsets within the main set include Sack Pack, Ground Attack, Summerall's Best and Rookies. Insert sets include the Silver Playoff Club, which features Gale Sayers (some of them are autographed); the Jerome Bettis Collection; the Jerry Rice Collection; the Playoff Club; the Barry Sanders Collection; and the Headliners. Six prototype cards were also produced, previewing the regular cards.

		MT
Complete Set (336):		45.00
Common Player:		.15
Pack (8):		2.25
Wax Box (24):		40.00
1	Joe Montana	2.00
2	Derrick Thomas	.35
3	Dan Marino	4.00
4	Cris Carter	.25
5	Boomer Esiason	.30
6	Bruce Smith	.25
7	Andre Rison	.40
8	Curtis Conway	.40
9	Michael Irvin	.50
10	Shannon Sharpe	.35
11	Pat Swilling	.25
12	John Parrella	.15
13	Mel Gray	.15
14	Ray Childress	.15
15	Willie Davis	.15
16	Raghib Ismail	.45
17	Jim Everett	.20
18	Mark Higgs	.15
19	Trace Armstrong	.15
20	Jim Kelly	.60
21	Rob Burnett	.15
22	Jay Novacek	.35
23	Robert Delpino	.15
24	Brett Perriman	.15
25	Troy Aikman	2.00
26	Reggie White	.30
27	Lorenzo White	.15
28	Bubba McDowell	.15
29	Steve Emtman	.15
30	Brett Favre	4.00
31	Derek Russell	.15
32	Jeff Hostetler	.20
33	Henry Ellard	.15
34	Jack Del Rio	.15
35	Mike Saxon	.15
36	Rickey Jackson	.15
37	Phil Simms	.25
38	Quinn Early	.15
39	Russell Copeland	.15
40	Carl Pickens	.25
41	Lance Gunn	.15
42	Bernie Kosar	.15
43	John Elway	1.00
44	George Teague	.30
45	Nick Lowery	.25
46	Haywood Jeffires	.25
47	Will Shields	.15
48	Daryl Johnson	.20
49	Pete Metzelaars	.15
50	Warren Moon	.25
51	Cornelius Bennett	.20
52	Vinny Testaverde	.20
53	*John Mangun*	.15
54	Tommy Vardell	.25
55	*Lincoln Coleman*	.60
56	Karl Mecklenburg	.15
57	Jackie Harris	.20
58	Curtis Duncan	.15
59	Quentin Coryatt	.25
60	Tim Brown	.35
61	Irving Fryar	.30
62	Sean Gilbert	.25
63	Qadry Ismail	.25
64	Irv Smith	.25
65	Mark Jackson	.15
66	Ronnie Lott	.20
67	Henry Jones	.15
68	Horace Copeland	.25
69	John Copeland	.15
70	Mark Carrier	.15
71	Michael Jackson	.25
72	Jason Elam	.20
73	Rod Bernstine	.20
74	Wayne Simmons	.25
75	Cody Carlson	.15
76	Alexander Wright	.15
77	Shane Conlan	.15
78	Keith Jackson	.25
79	Sean Salisbury	.15
80	Vaughan Johnson	.15
81	Rob Moore	.15
82	Andre Reed	.30
83	David Klingler	.35
84	Jim Harbaugh	.15
85	*John Jett*	.30
86	Sterling Sharpe	.25
87	Webster Slaughter	.20
88	J.J. Birden	.15
89	O.J. McDuffie	.60
90	Andre Tippett	.15
91	Don Beebe	.15
92	Mark Stepnoski	.15
93	Neil Smith	.20
94	Terry Kirby	.85
95	Wade Wilson	.15
96	Darryl Talley	.15
97	Anthony Smith	.15
98	Willie Roaf	.25
99	Mo Lewis	.15
100	James Washington	.15
101	Nate Odomes	.15
102	Chris Gedney	.15
103	Joe Walter	.15
104	Alvin Harper	.20
105	Simon Fletcher	.25
106	Rodney Peete	.15
107	Terrell Buckley	.15
108	Jeff George	.30
109	James Jett	.50
110	Tony Casillas	.15
111	Marco Coleman	.15
112	Anthony Carter	.15
113	Lincoln Kennedy	.20
114	Chris Calloway	.15
115	Randall Cunningham	.20
116	Steve Beuerlein	.25
117	Neil O'Donnell	.30
118	Stan Humphries	.15
119	John Taylor	.20
120	Cortez Kennedy	.20
121	Santana Dotson	.15
122	Thomas Smith	.15
123	Kevin Williams	.30
124	Andre Ware	.15
125	Ethan Horton	.15
126	Mike Sherrard	.15
127	Fred Barnett	.15
128	Rickey Proehl	.15
129	Kevin Greene	.15
130	John Carney	.15
131	Tim McDonald	.25
132	Rick Mirer	1.00
133	Blair Thomas	.15
134	Hardy Nickerson	.15
135	Heath Sherman	.15
136	Andre Hastings	.15
137	Randal Hill	.15
138	Mike Cofer	.15
139	Brian Blades	.15
140	Earnest Byner	.15
141	Bill Bates	.15
142	Junior Seau	.20
143	Johnny Bailey	.15
144	Dwight Stone	.15
145	Todd Kelly	.15
146	Tyrone Montgomery	.15
147	Herschel Walker	.15
148	Gary Clark	.15
149	Eric Green	.20
150	Steve Young	2.00
151	Anthony Miller	.25
152	Dana Stubblefield	.50
153	*Dean Wells*	.15
154	Vincent Brisby	.60
155	Chris Chandler	.15
156	Clyde Simmons	.15
157	Rod Woodson	.20
158	Nate Lewis	.15
159	Martin Harrison	.15
160	Kelvin Martin	.15
161	Craig Erickson	.25
162	Johnny Mitchell	.20
163	Calvin Williams	.20
164	Deon Figures	.30
165	Tom Rathman	.15
166	Rick Hamilton	.15
167	John L. Williams	.15
168	Demetrius Dubose	.15
169	Michael Brooks	.15
170	Marion Butts	.30
171	Brent Jones	.20
172	Bobby Hebert	.20
173	Brad Edwards	.15
174	Dave Wyman	.15
175	Herman Moore	1.00
176	Leroy Butler	.20
177	Reggie Langhorne	.15
178	Dave Krieg	.15
179	Patrick Bates	.15
180	Erik Kramer	.15
181	Troy Drayton	.30
182	David Meggett	.15
183	Eric Allen	.30
184	Mark Bavaro	.15
185	Leslie O'Neal	.25
186	Jerry Rice	2.00
187	Desmond Howard	.25
188	Deion Sanders	1.00
189	Bill Maas	.15
190	Frank Wycheck	.15
191	Ernest Givins	.25
192	Terry McDaniel	.15
193	Bryan Cox	.20
194	Guy McIntyre	.15
195	Pierce Holt	.15
196	Fred Stokes	.15
197	Mike Pritchard	.25
198	Terry Obee	.15
199	Mark Collins	.15
200	Drew Bledsoe	3.00
201	Barry Wood	.15
202	Derrick Lassic	.35
203	Chris Spielman	.15
204	*John Jurkovic*	.25
205	Ken Norton Jr.	.15
206	Dale Carter	.20
207	Chris Doleman	.25
208	Keith Hamilton	.15
209	Andy Harmon	.15
210	John Friesz	.15
211	Steve Bono	.20
212	Mark Rypien	.15
213	Ricky Sanders	.15
214	Michael Haynes	.35
215	Todd McNair	.15
216	Leon Lett	.15
217	Scott Mitchell	.50
218	*Mike Morris*	.15
219	Darrin Smith	.15
220	Jim McMahon	.15
221	Garrison Hearst	1.50
222	Leroy Thompson	.15
223	Darren Carrington	.15
224	Pete Stoyanovich	.15
225	Chris Miller	.20
226	Bruce Smith	.30
227	Simon Fletcher	.30
228	Reggie White	.20
229	Neil Smith	.20
230	Chris Doleman	.20
231	Keith Hamilton	.15
232	Dana Stubblefield	.20
233	Erric Pegram	.40
234	Thurman Thomas	.50
235	Lewis Tillman	.15
236	Harold Green	.15
237	Eric Metcalf	.20
238	Emmitt Smith	4.00
239	Glyn Milburn	.20
240	Barry Sanders	3.00
241	Edgar Bennett	.20
242	Gary Brown	.20
243	Rossevelt Potts	.15
244	Marcus Allen	.25
245	Greg Robinson	.15
246	Jerome Bettis	.75
247	Keith Byars	.15
248	Robert Smith	.50
249	Leonard Russell	.20
250	Derek Brown	.55
251	Rodney Hampton	.55
252	Johnny Johnson	.15
253	Vaughn Hebron	.15
254	Ron Moore	.40
255	Barry Foster	.50
256	Natrone Means	.75
257	Ricky Watters	.30
258	Chris Warren	.15
259	Vince Workman	.15
260	Reggie Brooks	.30
261	Carolina Panthers	.20
262	Jacksonville Jaguars	.20
263	Troy Aikman	1.75
264	Barry Sanders	1.50
265	Emmitt Smith	2.00
266	Michael Irvin	.40
267	Jerry Rice	1.00
268	Shannon Sharpe	.25
269	Bob Kratch	.15
270	Howard Ballard	.15
271	Erik Williams	.15
272	Guy McIntyre	.15
273	Kelvin Williams	.25
274	Mel Gray	.15
275	Eddie Murray	.15
276	Mark Stepnoski	.15
277	Tommy Barnhardt	.15
278	Derrick Thomas	.30
279	Ken Norton Jr.	.20
280	Chris Spielman	.15
281	Deion Sanders	.75
282	Mark Collins	.15
283	Bruce Smith	.20
284	Reggie White	.20
285	Sean Gilbert	.25
286	Cortez Kennedy	.20
287	Steve Atwater	.15
288	Tim McDonald	.15
289	Jerome Bettis	.75
290	Dana Stubblefield	.20
291	*Bert Emanuel*	1.00
292	*Jeff Burris*	.30
293	*Bucky Brooks*	.65
294	*Dan Wilkinson*	.85
295	*Darnay Scott*	2.00
296	*Derrick Alexander*	.75
297	*Antonio Langham*	.50
298	*Shante Carver*	.40
299	*Shelby Hill*	.25
300	*Larry Allen*	.30
301	*Johnnie Morton*	.75
302	*Van Malone*	.25
303	*Aaron Taylor*	.35
304	*Marshall Faulk*	8.00
305	Eric Mahlum	.25
306	*Trev Alberts*	.90
307	*Greg Hill*	.50
308	*Donnell Bennett*	.30
309	*Rob Fredrickson*	.25
310	*James Folston*	.25
311	*Isaac Bruce*	5.00
312	*Tim Ruddy*	.25
313	*Aubrey Beavers*	.25
314	*David Palmer*	.50
315	*DeWayne Washington*	.45
316	*Willie McGinest*	.50
317	*Mario Bates*	.30
318	*Kevin Lee*	.50
319	*Jason Sehorn*	.15
320	*Thomas Randolph*	.35
321	*Ryan Yarborough*	.40
322	*Bernard Williams*	.25
323	*Chuck Levy*	.75
324	*Jamir Miller*	.50
325	*Charles Johnson*	1.00
326	*Bryant Young*	.35
327	*William Floyd*	.50
328	*Kevin Mitchell*	.25
329	*Sam Adams*	.50
330	*Kevin Mawae*	.15
331	*Errict Rhett*	1.00
332	*Trent Dilfer*	1.00
333	*Heath Shuler*	.50
334	*Aaron Glenn*	.40
335	*Todd Steussie*	.30
336	*Toby Wright*	.15

1994 Playoff Jerome Bettis

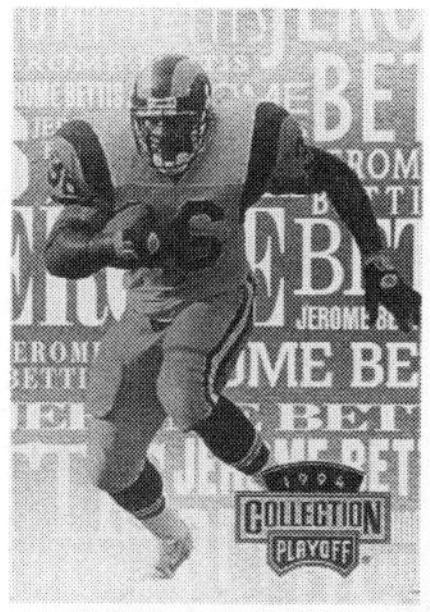

1993 NFL Rookie of the Year Jerome Bettis is featured in this five-card insert set. Cards devoted to the Los Angeles Rams running back were random inserts in 1994 Playoff hobby packs. Each card front has a color action photo against a silver foil background which has Bettis' name written on it in several different typefaces. The "1994 Playoff Collection" logo is also on the front, in the lower right corner. The yellow backs have biographical information about Bettis, and the card title, plus a card number.

		MT
Complete Set (5):		50.00
Common Bettis:		10.00
1	Jerome Bettis	10.00
2	Jerome Bettis	10.00
3	Jerome Bettis	10.00
4	Jerome Bettis	10.00
5	Jerome Bettis	10.00

1994 Playoff Checklists

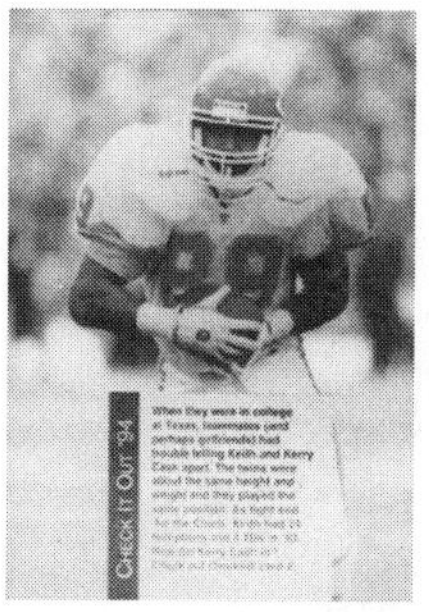

Full-bleed metallic color photos dominate the front, with the featured player's highlights printed inside a silver box at the bottom center. The card backs, numbered "of 10," highlight a portion of the set's checklists. The cards were randomly seeded.

		MT
Complete Set (10):		5.00
Common Player:		.50
1	Keith Cash	.50
2	Kerry Cash	.50
3	Qadry Ismail	.75
4	Rocket Ismail	.75
5	Bruce Matthews	.50
6	Clay Matthews	.50
7	Shannon Sharpe	1.00
8	Sterling Sharpe	1.00
9	John Taylor	.50
10	Keith Taylor	.50

1994 Playoff Club

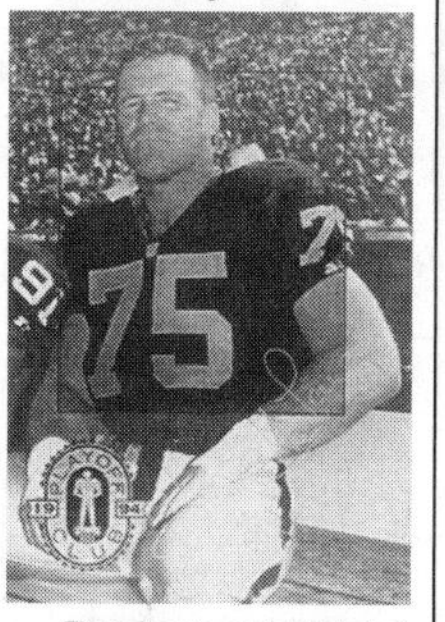

These inserts, randomly included in 1994 Playoff packs, feature six future Hall of Famers. Each card has a borderless front with a metallic action photo. The set logo appears at the bottom of the card, along with a facsimile autograph. The card back is white and has the player's name and a career summary. Backs are numbered with a "PC" prefix.

		MT
Complete Set (6):		35.00
Commom Player:		2.75
8	Jerry Rice	20.00
9	Marcus Allen	5.00
10	Howie Long	5.00
11	Clay Matthews	2.75
12	Richard Dent	2.75
13	Morten Andersen	2.75

1994 Playoff Headliners Redemption

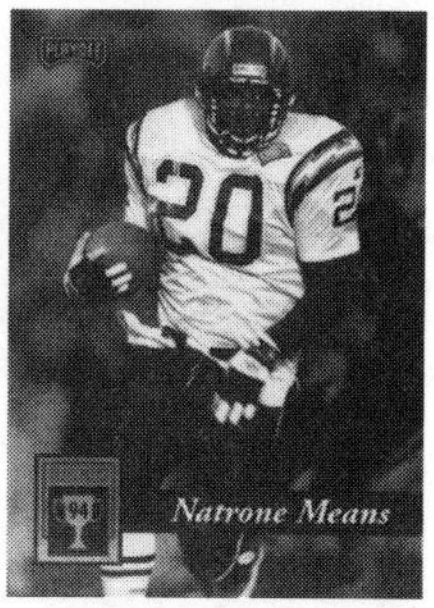

In exchange for a redemption card, a collector would receive this six-card set. Card fronts have a prism effect, with the player's name and Headliners' logo printed at the bottom. Showcased on the horizontal card back is a headshot of the player, his name and an explanation of his 1994 milestone.

		MT
Complete Set (6):		18.00
Common Player:		2.00
1	Tim Brown	3.00
2	Bernie Parmalee	2.00
3	Sterling Sharpe	3.00
4	Natrone Means	4.00
5	Alvin Harper	2.00
6	Deion Sanders	6.00
NNO	Headliners Redemption	.50

1994 Playoff Jerry Rice

San Francisco 49er wide receiver Jerry Rice is featured in this five-card insert set. Cards were randomly included in 1994 Playoff retail display packs. The card front has a color action photo against a foil background, plus a "1994 Playoff Collection" logo. The card back has another photo and career summary, plus a card number.

		MT
Complete Set (5):		120.00
Common Rice:		25.00
1	Born to Run (Jerry Rice)	25.00
2	All American (Jerry Rice)	25.00
3	The 49ers Start the Dynasty (Jerry Rice)	25.00
4	The Offensive Player of the Year (Again, Jerry Rice)	25.00
5	Breaking Jim Brown's Record (Jerry Rice)	25.00

1994 Playoff Rookie Roundup Redemption

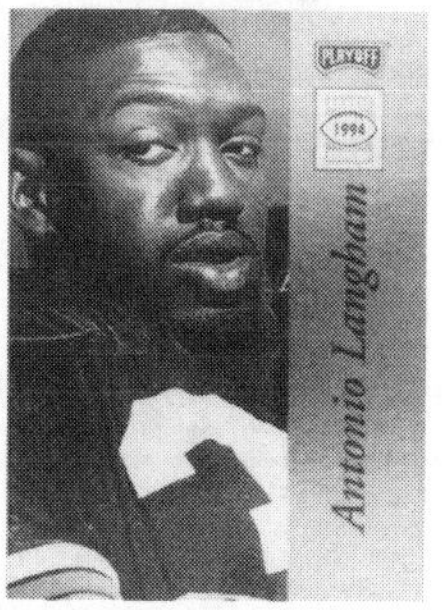

A mail-in offer allowed collectors to exchange the redemption card for this nine-card set. The exchange card was randomly seeded in packs. Card fronts have a photo of the player, with a team-colored border on either side of the card. Located on the horizontal backs are a full-bleed photo, with his name and biographical information printed inside boxes. This offer expired Dec. 31, 1995.

		MT
Complete Set (9):		30.00
Common Player:		3.00
1	Heath Shuler	6.00
2	David Palmer	3.00
3	Dan Wilkinson	3.00
4	Marshall Faulk	10.00
5	Charlie Garner	4.00
6	Errict Rhett	8.00
7	Trent Dilfer	5.00
8	Antonio Langham	3.00
9	Gus Frerotte	6.00
NNO	Redemption Card	.50

1994 Playoff Barry Sanders

Detroit Lions running back Barry Sanders is highlighted in this five-card insert set. Cards were randomly included in Playoff's Four Star Edition of the set. These sets were distributed to selected hobby stores, Wal-Mart, Books-A-Million, Walden Books and other retail stores.

		MT
Complete Set (5):		120.00
Common Sanders:		25.00
1	Barry Sanders	25.00
2	Barry Sanders	25.00
3	Barry Sanders	25.00
4	Barry Sanders	25.00
5	Barry Sanders	25.00

1994 Playoff Super Bowl Redemption

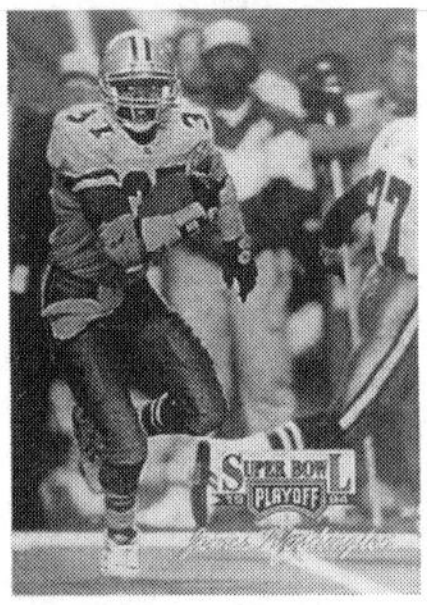

This six-card set, which featured Dallas players, was traded to collectors in exchange for a redemption card through a mail-in offer. The redemption card was randomly seeded in packs. A Super Bowl Playoff logo, along with the player's name, are printed at the top of the full-bleed card fronts. The horizontal card backs have the Super Bowl Playoff logo, Cowboys and Bills helmets and the player's Super Bowl accomplishments.

		MT
Complete Set (6):		30.00
Common Player:		2.50
1	Troy Aikman	10.00
2	Emmitt Smith	20.00
3	Leon Lett	2.50
4	Michael Irvin	3.00
5	James Washington	2.50
6	Darrin Smith	2.50
NNO	Super Bowl Redemption	1.00

1994 Playoff Julie Bell Art Redemption

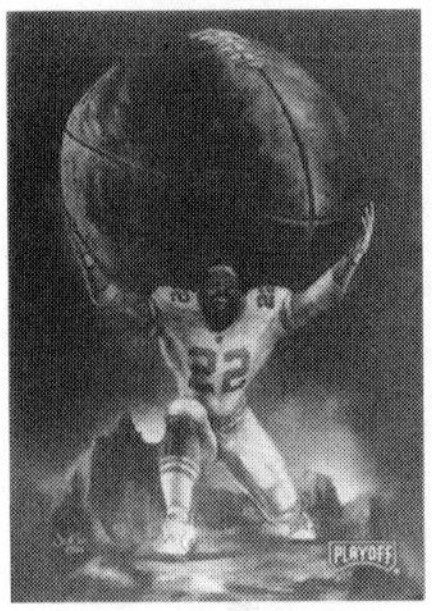

Fantasy artist Julie Bell used her talents to create this six-card set,featuring players in superhuman poses. The fronts are borderless, with a Playoff logo. The backs have a repeat of a portion of the artwork, along with a quote from Bell. "Julie Bell's Fantasy Football" is printed at the top. The set was available as a mail-in offer with a redemption found randomly inserted in packs.

		MT
Complete Set (6):		20.00
Common Player:		2.00
1	Emmitt Smith	10.00
2	Marcus Allen	2.00
3	Junior Seau	3.00
4	Barry Sanders	5.00
5	Rick Mirer	2.00
6	Sterling Sharpe	2.00

1994 Playoff Super Bowl Promos

To commemorate Super Bowl XXVIII, Playoff produced this six-card set. The full-bleed fronts have the player's name and the Playoff logo printed in an oval at the bottom of the card. The white card backs, numbered "of 6 promo," showcase the Super Bowl XXVIII logo in the center.

		MT
Complete Set (6):		16.00
Common Player:		1.50
1	Jerry Rice	6.00
2	Daryl Johnston	1.50
3	Herschel Walker	1.50
4	Reggie White	2.50
5	Scott Mitchell	2.00
6	Thurman Thomas	2.50

1994 Playoff Contenders Promos

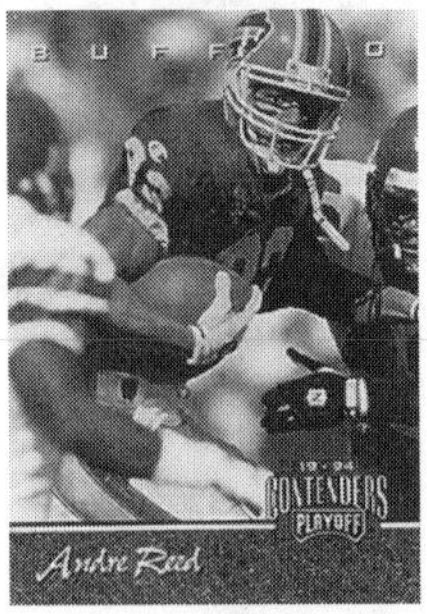

This seven-card set gave collectors a glimpse of what the 1994 Playoff Contenders set would look like. The city name of the player's team was printed at the top of the card fronts, with the player's name in silver foil on a green border at the bottom. The Playoff Contenders' logo is also included at the bottom. The unnumbered card backs have a headshot of the player, with his highlights printed below. The NFL's 75th anniversary logo is located above the write-up.

		MT
Complete Set (7):		10.00
Common Player:		1.00
1	Qadry Ismail	2.50
2	Daryl Johnston	1.50
3	John Jurkovic	1.00
4	Eric Metcalf	2.00
5	Andre Reed	1.50
6	Calvin Williams	1.00
7	Title Card	1.00

1994 Playoff Contenders

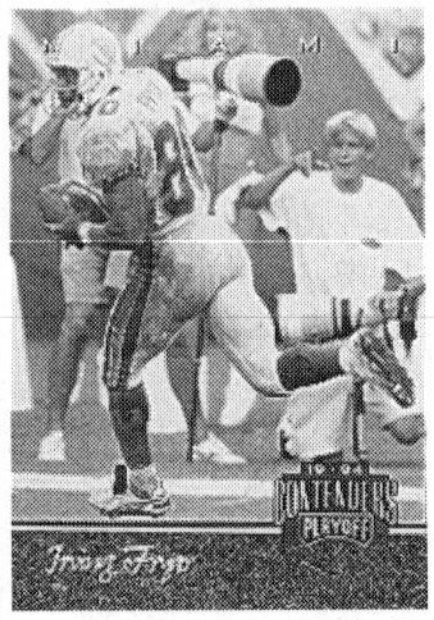

This 120-card set uses Playoff's patented, ink-on-foil Tekchrome printing process. Fronts capture the player in an intense game action photo. A grass strip at the bottom contains the player's name; his team's name is at the top of the card. A set logo appears in the lower right corner. The card back has a close-up shot of the player, which takes up two-thirds of the card. A blue strip at the bottom of the card contains some biographical information. The entire background is grey marble. A 27-card Draft Pick subset is contained within the main set. There were also four insert sets produced - 75th Anniversary Throwbacks, Rookie Contenders, Sophomore Contenders and Back-To-Backs.

		MT
Complete Set (120):		40.00
Common Player:		.15
Minor Stars:		.30
Pack (7):		8.00
Wax Box (24):		160.00
1	Drew Bledsoe	3.00
2	Barry Sanders	3.00
3	Jerry Rice	3.00
4	Rod Woodson	.30
5	Irving Fryar	.15
6	Charles Haley	.15
7	Chris Warren	.30
8	Craig Erickson	.15
9	Eric Metcalf	.15
10	Marcus Allen	.30
11	Chris Miller, Charles Johnson	.15
12	Andre Rison	.30
13	Art Monk	.30
14	Calvin Williams	.15
15	Shannon Sharpe, Bryant Young	.15
16	Rodney Hampton	.30
17	Marion Butts	.15
18	John Jurkovic	.50
19	Jim Kelly	.30
20	Emmitt Smith	5.00
21	Jeff Hostetler	.30
22	Barry Foster	.30
23	Boomer Esiason	.30
24	Jim Harbaugh	.15
25	Joe Montana	3.00
26	Jeff George	.50
27	Warren Moon	.30
28	Steve Young	3.00
29	Randall Cunningham	.30
30	Shawn Jefferson	.15
31	Cortez Kennedy	.30
32	Reggie Brooks	.15
33	Alvin Harper	.30
34	Brent Jones	.15
35	O.J. McDuffie	.40
36	Jerome Bettis	1.00
37	Daryl Johnston	.15
38	Herman Moore	1.00
39	Dave Meggett	.15
40	Reggie White	.30
41	Junior Seau	.50
42	Dan Marino	5.00
43	Scott Mitchell	.15
44	John Elway	4.00
45	Troy Aikman	3.00
46	Terry Allen	.15
47	David Klingler	.15
48	Stan Humphries	.40
49	Rick Mirer	.30
50	Neil O'Donnell	.30
51	Keith Jackson	.15
52	Ricky Watters	.30
53	Dave Brown	.30
54	Neil Smith	.15
55	Johnny Mitchell	.15
56	Jackie Harris	.15
57	Terry Kirby	.15
58	Willie Davis	.15
59	Rob Moore	.15
60	Nate Newton	.15
61	Deion Sanders	2.00
62	John Taylor	.15
63	Sterling Sharpe	.30
64	Natrone Means	1.00
65	Steve Beuerlein	.15
66	Erik Kramer	.15
67	Qadry Ismail	.15
68	Johnny Johnson	.15
69	Herschel Walker	.15
70	Mark Stepnoski	.15
71	Brett Favre	5.00
72	Dana Stubblefield	.15
73	Bruce Smith	.15
74	Leroy Hoard	.15
75	Steve Walsh	.15
76	Jay Novacek	.15
77	Derrick Thomas	.30
78	Keith Byars	.15
79	Ben Coates	.40
80	Lorenzo Neal	.15
81	Ronnie Lott	.15
82	Tim Brown	.30
83	Michael Irvin	.50
84	Ron Moore	.15
85	Andre Reed	.30
86	James Jett	.15
87	Curtis Conway	.15
88	*Bernie Parmalee*	.30
89	Keith Cash	.15
90	Russell Copeland	.15
91	Kevin Williams	.50
92	Gary Brown	.15
93	Thurman Thomas	.50
94	*Jamir Miller*	.30
95	*Bert Emanuel*	2.00
96	*Buck Brooks*	.50
97	*Jeff Burris*	.50
98	*Antonio Langham*	.50
99	*Derrick Alexander*	.50
100	*Dan Wilkinson*	.50
101	*Shante Carver*	.40
102	*Johnnie Morton*	.75
103	*LeShon Johnson*	.50
104	*Marshall Faulk*	5.00
105	*Greg Hill*	.50
106	*Lake Dawson*	.30
107	*Irving Spikes*	.50
108	*David Palmer*	.50
109	*Willie McGinest*	.50
110	*Joe Johnson*	.30
111	*Aaron Glenn*	.30
112	*Charlie Garner*	3.00
113	*Charles Johnson*	.50
114	*Byron Bam Morris*	.50
115	*Bryant Young*	.75
116	*William Floyd*	.50
117	*Trent Dilfer*	3.00
118	*Errict Rhett*	1.00
119	*Heath Shuler*	.50
120	*Gus Frerotte*	1.00

1994 Playoff Contenders Back-to-Back

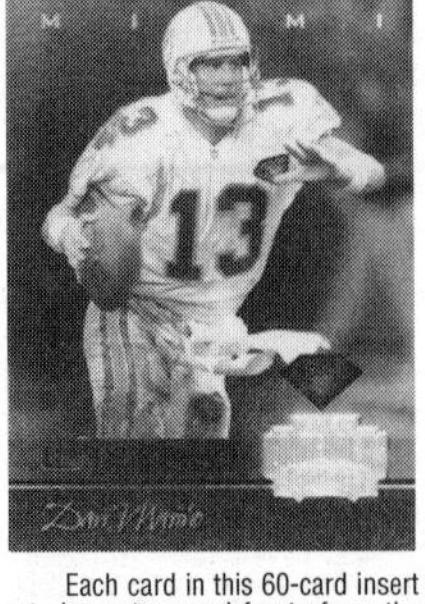

Each card in this 60-card insert set shows two card fronts from the 120 regular cards. The card fronts are matched up so that two key players from the same position appear on the card. Team names and Playoff Contenders logos are foil stamped on the cards, and the photos are embossed, meaning they are raised up off the card.

		MT
Complete Set (60):		1250.
Common Player:		12.50
Minor Stars:		25.00
Inserted 1:24		
1	Joe Montana, Dan Marino	150.00
2	Drew Bledsoe, John Elway	100.00
3	Jerry Rice, Sterling Sharpe	75.00
4	Barry Sanders, Emmitt Smith	150.00
5	Troy Aikman, Steve Young	75.00
6	Erik Kramer, Steve Walsh	12.50
7	Nate Newton, Bruce Smith	12.50
8	Johnny Mitchell, Aaron Glenn	12.50
9	Neil O'Donnell, Charles Johnson	12.50
10	Herman Moore, Calvin Williams	25.00
11	Alvin Harper, Michael Irvin	25.00
12	Jim Harbaugh, Curtis Conway	25.00
13	Brett Favre, LeShon Johnson	125.00
14	Marshall Faulk, Eric Metcalf	35.00
15	Qadry Ismail, David Palmer	12.50
16	Deion Sanders, Andre Rison	35.00
17	Jackie Harris, Errict Rhett	12.50
18	Keith Jackson, Keith Byars	12.50
19	Dave Meggett, Jeff Burris	12.50
20	Dana Stubblefield, William Floyd	12.50
21	Randall Cunningham, Reggie White	25.00
22	Shannon Sharpe, Keith Cash	25.00
23	Marcus Allen, Greg Hill	25.00
24	Irving Fryar, Russell Copeland	12.50
25	Johnny Johnson, Willie McGinest	12.50
26	John Taylor, Brent Jones	12.50
27	Terry Kirby, Bernie Parmalee	12.50
28	Ricky Watters, Ronnie Lott	25.00
29	Scott Mitchell, Johnnie Morton	12.50
30	O.J. McDuffie, Irving Spikes	12.50
31	Shawn Jefferson, Andre Reed	12.50
32	Rodney Hampton, Lorenzo Neal	12.50
33	Chris Miller, Joe Johnson	12.50
34	Charles Haley, Thurman Thomas	25.00
35	Herschel Walker, Charlie Garner	12.50
36	Natrone Means, Stan Humphries	25.00
37	Willie Davis, Lake Dawson	12.50
38	Dave Brown, Gary Brown	12.50
39	Jerome Bettis, Terry Allen	35.00
40	Cortez Kennedy, Junior Seau	12.50
41	David Klingler, Derrick Alexander	12.50
42	Chris Warren, Bucky Brooks	12.50
43	Mark Stepnoski, Kevin Williams	12.50
44	Steve Beuerlein, Ron Moore	12.50
45	Rob Moore, James Jett	12.50
46	Neil Smith, Derrick Thomas	12.50
47	Rick Mirer, Bryant Young	12.50
48	Daryl Johnston, Jay Novacek	12.50
49	Reggie Brooks, Gus Frerotte	12.50
50	Barry Foster, Byron "Bam" Morris	12.50
51	Art Monk, Heath Shuler	12.50
52	Craig Erickson, Trent Dilfer	25.00
53	Jeff George, Bert Emanuel	12.50
54	Rod Woodson, Antonio Langham	12.50
55	Marion Butts, Ben Coates	12.50
56	John Jurkovic, Dan Wilkinson	12.50
57	Jim Kelly, Shante Carver	25.00
58	Jeff Hostetler, Tim Brown	12.50
59	Boomer Esiason, Jamir Miller	12.50
60	Warren Moon, Terry Allen	25.00

1994 Playoff Contenders Rookie Contenders

Six first-year standouts are showcased in this 1994 Playoff Contenders insert set, which combines three different foil effects. Each card has a split background, with the left side having a glittery silver foil and the right side having a purple foil. The player's name is written in silver foil within the purple foil. Above his name is a Rookie Contender logo stamped in foil. Below his name is a Playoff logo. These cards are inserted one per 48 packs.

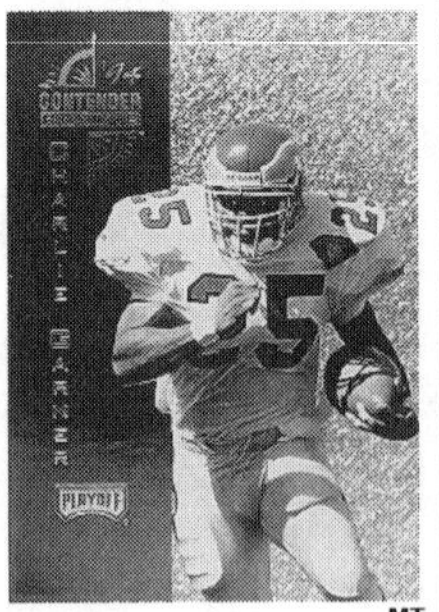

		MT
Complete Set (6):		125.00
Common Player:		10.00
Minor Stars:		15.00
1	Marshall Faulk	45.00
2	Charles Garner	15.00
3	Trent Dilfer	15.00
4	Heath Shuler	10.00
5	Dan Wilkinson	10.00
6	David Palmer	10.00

1994 Playoff Contenders Sophomore Contenders

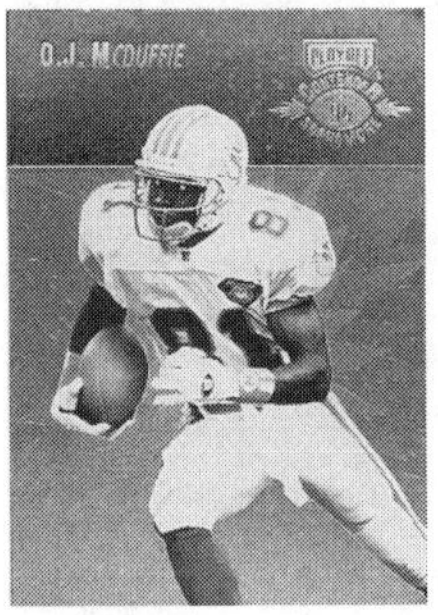

Six of the top second-year NFL players are featured on these insert cards, available at a rate of one per 48 packs. These cards feature a foil-etched burst-pattern design. The top one third of the card has a purple prism design. It has the player's name on the left and a Sophomore Contenders logo on the right, both in silver foil. The bottom two-thirds has the player on a silver burst-patterned background.

		MT
Complete Set (6):		100.00
Common Player:		5.00
1	Drew Bledsoe	50.00
2	Jerome Bettis	10.00
3	Natrone Means	12.00
4	Rick Mirer	7.00
5	Reggie Brooks	5.00
6	O.J. McDuffie	5.00

1994 Playoff Contenders Throwbacks

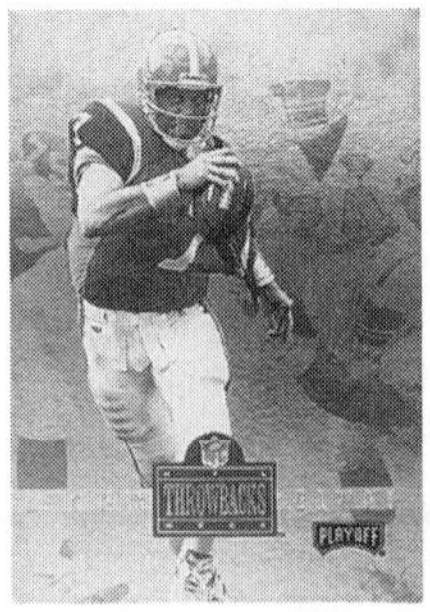

This 30-card insert set shows at least one star from each NFL team in his "Throwback" uniform. The front shows the player in a foil-enhanced background. A strip across the bottom contains the player's name in silver foil, with an NFL Throwback Week logo centered on this strip. These cards were randomly included in Playoff Contender packs at a ratio of one per 12 packs.

		MT
Complete Set (30):		200.00
Common Player:		5.00
1	Larry Centers	5.00
2	Andre Rison	5.00
3	Jim Kelly	8.00
4	Curtis Conway	5.00
5	David Klingler	5.00
6	Vinny Testaverde	5.00
7	Troy Aikman	15.00
8	Emmitt Smith	30.00
9	John Elway	12.00
10	Barry Sanders	20.00
11	Sterling Sharpe	8.00
12	Gary Brown	5.00
13	Jim Harbaugh	5.00
14	Joe Montana	15.00
15	Tim Brown	8.00
16	Chris Miller	5.00
17	Dan Marino	30.00
18	Terry Allen	5.00
19	Marion Butts	5.00
20	Jim Everett	5.00
21	Dave Brown	5.00
22	Johnny Johnson	5.00
23	Randall Cunningham	5.00
24	Barry Foster	5.00
25	Stan Humphries	8.00
26	Jerry Rice	15.00
27	Steve Young	12.00
28	Chris Warren	8.00
29	Errict Rhett	5.00
30	John Freisz	5.00

1995 Playoff Absolute-Prime

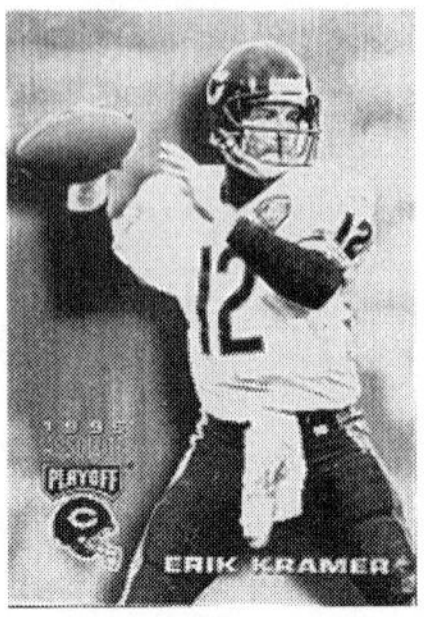

Playoff's 1995 200-card football set was released in two different designs - a hobby version (Absolute) and a totally different retail version (Prime). The hobby-only Absolute features a Pigskins Preview insert set devoted to six NFC players, a Quad Series parallel set (four players per card), and Die-Cut Helmets. Common to both Absolute and Prime packs are Unsung Heroes and First Draft Picks for the two new expansion teams - Jacksonville and Carolina. Playoff Prime has the remaining six Pigskin Preview cards, which are devoted to AFC players. Draft Picks cards are a subset of the regular set.

		MT
Complete Absolute Set (200):		35.00
Common Absolute Player:		.15
Minor Absolute Stars:		.30
Complete Prime Set (200):		17.00
Prime Cards:		.5x
Absolute Pack (8):		2.50
Absolute Box (24):		45.00
Prime Pack (8):		1.50
Prime Wax Box (24):		26.00
1	John Elway	.50
2	Reggie White	.30
3	Errict Rhett	.30
4	Deion Sanders	.75
5	Raghib Ismail	.15
6	Jerome Bettis	.30
7	Randall Cunningham	.15
8	Mario Bates	.50
9	Dave Brown	.15
10	Stan Humphries	.30
11	Drew Bledsoe	1.50
12	Neil O'Donnell	.30
13	Dan Marino	3.00
14	Larry Centers	.15
15	Craig Heyward	.15
16	Bruce Smith	.15
17	Erik Kramer	.15
18	*Jeff Blake*	.50
19	Vinny Testaverde	.15
20	Barry Sanders	2.00
21	Boomer Esiason	.15
22	Emmitt Smith	3.00
23	Warren Moon	.30
24	Junior Seau	.30
25	Heath Shuler	1.25
26	Jackie Harris	.15
27	Terance Mathis	.15
28	Raymont Harris	.15
29	Jim Kelly	.30
30	Dan Wilkinson	.15
31	Herman Moore	.50
32	Shannon Sharpe	.15
33	Antonio Langham	.15
34	Charles Haley	.15
35	Brett Favre	3.00
36	Marshall Faulk	.30
37	Neil Smith	.15
38	Harvey Williams	.15
39	Johnny Bailey	.15
40	O.J. McDuffie	.15
41	David Palmer	.15
42	Willie McGinest	.15
43	Quinn Early	.15
44	Johnny Johnson	.15
45	Derek Brown	.15
46	Charlie Garner	.15
47	Bam Morris	.30
48	Natrone Means	.30
49	Ken Norton	.15
50	Troy Aikman	1.25
51	Reggie Brooks	.15
52	Trent Dilfer	.50
53	Cortez Kennedy	.15
54	Chuck Levy	.15
55	Jeff George	.30
56	Steve Young	1.25
57	Lewis Tillman	.15
58	Carl Pickens	.30

59	Brett Perriman	.15
60	Jay Novacek	.15
61	Greg Hill	.30
62	James Jett	.15
63	Terry Kirby	.15
64	Qadry Ismail	.15
65	Ben Coates	.15
66	Kevin Greene	.15
67	Bryant Young	.15
68	Brian Mitchell	.15
69	Steve Walsh	.15
70	Darnay Scott	.75
71	Daryl Johnston	.15
72	Glyn Milburn	.15
73	Tim Brown	.30
74	Isaac Bruce	.50
75	Bernie Parmalee	.30
76	Terry Allen	.15
77	Jim Everett	.15
78	Thomas Lewis	.15
79	Vaughn Hebron	.15
80	Rod Woodson	.15
81	Rick Mirer	.40
82	Dana Stubblefield	.15
83	Bert Emanuel	.50
84	Andre Reed	.15
85	Jeff Graham	.15
86	Johnnie Morton	.15
87	LeShon Johnson	.15
88	Michael Irvin	.40
89	Derrick Alexander	.15
90	Lake Dawson	.50
91	Cody Carlson	.15
92	Chris Warren	.30
93	William Floyd	.50
94	Charles Johnson	.30
95	Roosevelt Potts	.15
96	Cris Carter	.30
97	Aaron Glenn	.15
98	Curtis Conway	.30
99	Kevin Williams	.15
100	Jerry Rice	1.25
101	Frank Reich	.15
102	Harold Green	.15
103	Russell Copeland	.15
104	Rob Moore	.15
105	Edgar Bennett	.15
106	Darren Carrington	.15
107	Tommy Maddox	.15
108	Dave Meggett	.15
109	Fred Barnett	.15
110	Mark Seay	.15
111	Gus Frerotte	.50
112	Brent Jones	.15
113	Chris Miller	.15
114	Cedric Tillman	.15
115	Mark Ingram	.15
116	Eric Turner	.15
117	Mark Carrier	.15
118	Garrison Hearst	.30
119	Craig Erickson	.15
120	Derek Russell	.15
121	Mike Sherrard	.15
122	Horace Copeland	.15
123	Jack Trudeau	.15
124	Leroy Hoard	.15
125	Gary Brown	.15
126	Mel Gray	.15
127	Steve Beuerlein	.15
128	Marcus Allen	.30
129	Irving Fryar	.15
130	Marion Butts	.15
131	Ricky Watters	.30
132	Tony Martin	.15
133	Lawrence Dawsey	.15
134	Ronnie Harmon	.15
135	Herschel Walker	.15
136	Michael Haynes	.15
137	Eric Green	.15
138	Steve Bono	.40
139	Jamir Miller	.15
140	Rod Smith	.15
141	Andre Rison	.30
142	Eric Metcalf	.15
143	Michael Timpson	.15
144	Cornelius Bennett	.15
145	Sean Dawkins	.30
146	Scott Mitchell	.15
147	Ray Childress	.15
148	Jim Harbaugh	.30
149	Reggie Cobb	.15
150	Willie Roaf	.15
151	Stevie Anderson	.15
152	Barry Foster	.15
153	Joe Montana	2.00
154	David Klingler	.15
155	Chris Chandler	.15
156	Carnell Lake	.15
157	Calvin Williams	.15
158	Kenneth Davis	.15
159	Tydus Winans	.15
160	Sam Adams	.15
161	Ron Moore	.15
162	Vincent Brisby	.15
163	Alvin Harper	.15
164	Jake Reed	.15
165	Jeff Hostetler	.15
166	Mark Brunell	1.50
167	Leonard Russell	.15
168	Greg Truitt	.15
169	Pete Metzelaars	.15
170	Dave Krieg	.15
171	Lorenzo White	.15
172	Robert Brooks	.30
173	Willie Davis	.15
174	Irving Spikes	.15
175	Rodney Hampton	.15
176	Erric Pegram	.15
177	Brian Blades	.15
178	Shawn Jefferson	.15
179	Tyrone Poole	.15
180	*Rob Johnson*	4.00
181	*Ki-Jana Carter*	1.00
182	*Steve McNair*	5.00
183	*Michael Westbrook*	1.00
184	*Kerry Collins*	2.00
185	*Kevin Carter*	.30
186	*Tony Boselli*	.30
187	*Joey Galloway*	4.00
188	*Kyle Brady*	.50
189	*J.J. Stokes*	1.00
190	*Warren Sapp*	.75
191	*Tyrone Wheatley*	.75
192	*Napoleon Kaufman*	4.00
193	*James Stewart*	2.00
194	*Rashaan Salaam*	1.00
195	*Ray Zellars*	.75
196	*Todd Collins*	.75
197	*Sherman Williams*	.50
198	*Frank Sanders*	1.00
199	*Terrell Fletcher*	.50
200	*Chad May*	.50
DP1	Tony Boselli Draft	3.00
DP2	Kerry Collins Draft	10.00

1995 Playoff Unsung Heroes

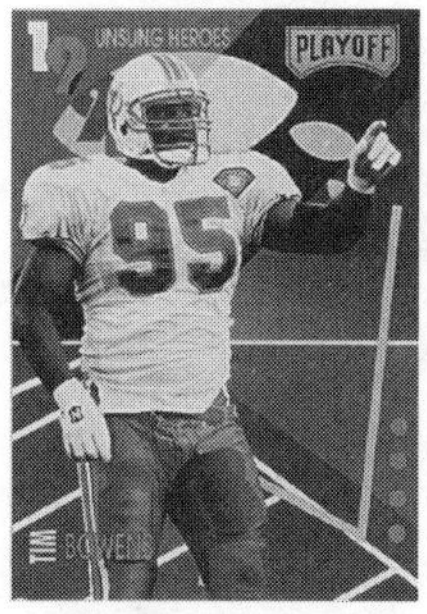

These 28 cards were inserted in both 1995 Playoff Absolute and Prime packs, one per 13 packs. The card front has a color photo of the player against a football field pattern. "Unsung Heroes" and the Playoff logo are stamped in gold in the upper corners. The player's name is in the lower left corner. The card back has goal posts which have a brief recap of the player's 1994 season between them.

		MT
Complete Set (28):		25.00
Common Player:		.75
Minor Stars:		1.50
1	Garth Jax	.75
2	Craig Heyward	.75
3	Steve Tasker	.75
4	Raymont Harris	.75
5	Jeff Blake	2.00
6	Bob Dahl	.75
7	Jason Garrett	.75
8	Gary Zimmerman	.75
9	Tom Beer	.75
10	John Jurkovic	.75
11	Spencer Tillman	.75
12	Devon McDonald	.75
13	John Alt	.75
14	Steve Wisniewski	.75
15	Tim Bowens	.75
16	Amp Lee	.75
17	Todd Rucci	.75
18	Tyrone Hughes	.75
19	Michael Strahan	.75
20	Brad Baxter	.75
21	Mark Bavaro	.75
22	Yancy Thigpen	1.50
23	Courtney Hall	.75
24	Eric Davis	.75
25	Rufus Porter	.75
26	Jackie Slater	.75
27	Courtney Hawkins	.75
28	Gus Frerotte	1.50

1995 Playoff Absolute Die Cut Helmets

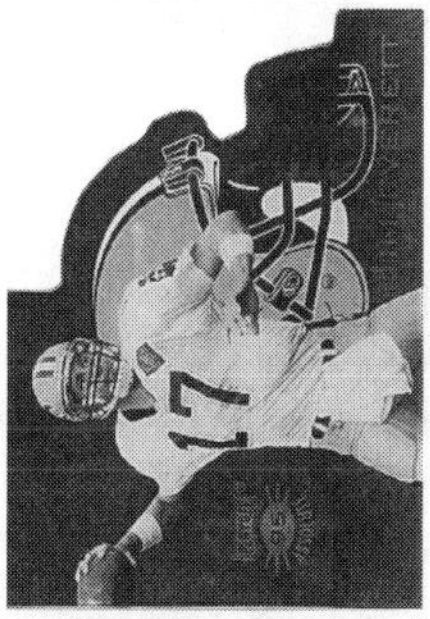

These die-cut cards feature all 30 teams with a star player from each club on a clear plastic card. The front has a color photo of the player against a background of his team's helmet. His name appears in the lower right corner. The back of the card, numbered using an "HDC" prefix, has a white outline of the helmet and photo depicted on the front. These inserts were randomly included in hobby-only 1995 Playoff Absolute Packs, one per 25.

		MT
Complete Set (30):		600.00
Common Player:		6.00
Minor Stars:		12.00
1	Garrison Hearst	12.00
2	Jim Kelly	12.00
3	Jeff Blake	12.00
4	Emmitt Smith	70.00
5	John Elway	30.00
6	Brett Favre	70.00
7	Marshall Faulk	25.00
8	Marcus Allen	12.00
9	Jerome Bettis	12.00
10	Dan Marino	70.00
11	Cris Carter	12.00
12	Drew Bledsoe	45.00
13	Jim Everett	6.00
14	Rodney Hampton	6.00
15	Natrone Means	12.00
16	Steve Young	30.00
17	Rick Mirer	12.00
18	Errict Rhett	30.00
19	Heath Shuler	25.00
20	Lewis Tillman	6.00
21	Barry Sanders	45.00
22	Leroy Hoard	6.00
23	Rod Woodson	12.00
24	Gary Brown	6.00
25	Terance Mathis	6.00
26	Frank Reich	6.00
27	Steve Beuerlein	6.00
28	Raghib Ismail	6.00
29	Johnny Johnson	6.00
30	Charlie Garner	6.00

1995 Playoff Absolute Pigskin Previews

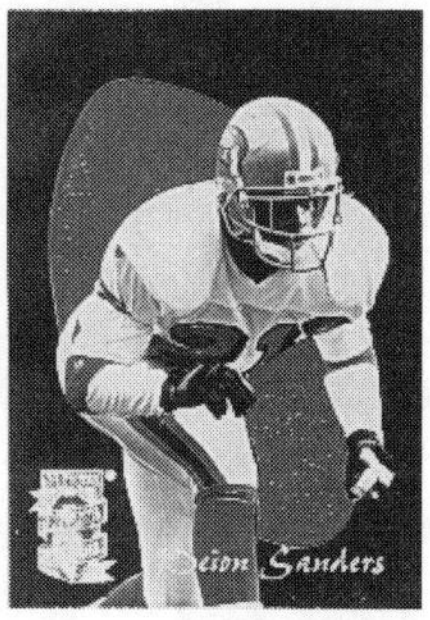

These hobby-only 1995 Playoff Absolute inserts feature six NFC stars. Cards were randomly included one per 145 packs. The front has a color photo superimposed over a leather football. Gold foil stamping is used at the bottom for the player's name and insert set logo. The card back has a color photo of the player against his team's city skyline. A brief recap of the player's 1994 accomplishments is given at the top of the card; his 1994 and career stats are listed in a panel at the bottom.

		MT
Complete Set (6):		400.00
Common Player:		20.00
1	Emmitt Smith	150.00
2	Steve Young	80.00
3	Barry Sanders	80.00
4	Deion Sanders	65.00
5	Cris Carter	20.00
6	Errict Rhett	20.00

1995 Playoff Absolute Quad Series

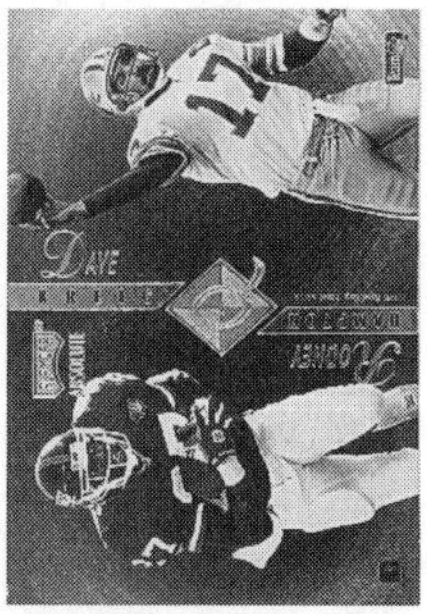

These 50 cards are a creative variation as a parallel set to Playoff's 1995 Absolute set. Each card features four players on it, two per side. Their names and the set and insert set logos are stamped in gold foil down the middle of the card. The backgrounds for each player are a pattern of metallic swirls. One side has a card number, using a "Q" prefix.

		MT
Complete Set (50):		1600.
Common Player:		10.00
Minor Stars:		16.00
1	Joe Montana, Steve Young, Dan Marino, John Elway	225.00
2	Troy Aikman, Drew Bledsoe, Brett Favre, Rick Mirer	225.00
3	Trent Dilfer, Heath Shuler, Mark Brunell, Jeff Blake	60.00
4	Randall Cunningham, Warren Moon, Jim Kelly, Boomer Esiason	16.00
5	Dave Brown, Jeff George, Stan Humphries, Jim Everett	16.00
6	Barry Sanders, Emmitt Smith, Marshall Faulk, Errict Rhett	175.00
7	Marcus Allen, Ricky Watters, William Floyd, Natrone Means	25.00
8	Garrison Hearst, Jerome Bettis, Lewis Tillman, Gary Brown	25.00
9	Michael Irvin, Jerry Rice, Tim Brown, Cris Carter	90.00
10	Pete Metzelaars, Bam Morris, Ben Coates, Andre Rison	16.00
11	Reggie White, Bruce Smith, Junior Seau, Deion Sanders	35.00
12	Rob Moore, Larry Centers, Jamir Miller, Chuck Levy	10.00
13	Craig Haywood, Terance Mathis, Bert Emanuel, Eric Metcalf	10.00
14	Kenneth Davis, Andre Reed, Russell Copeland, Cornelius Bennett	10.00
15	Frank Reich, Jack Trudeau, Mark Carrier, Tyrone Poole	10.00
16	Jeff Graham, Curtis Conway, Erik Kramer, Steve Walsh	16.00
17	Carl Pickens, Darnay Scott, Harold Green, David Klinger	16.00
18	Vinny Testaverde, Derrick Alexander, Leroy Hoard, Lorenzo White	10.00
19	Charles Haley, Kevin Williams, Daryl Johnston, Jay Novacek	10.00
20	Glyn Milburn, Leonard Russell, Derek Russell, Shannon Sharpe	10.00
21	Scott Mitchell, Brett Perriman, Herman Moore, Johnnie Morton	16.00
22	Edgar Bennett, LeShon Johnson, Robert Brooks, Mark Ingram	10.00
23	Cody Carlson, Mel Gray, Chris Chandler, Ray Childress	10.00
24	Jim Harbaugh, Craig Erickson, Roosevelt Potts, Sean Dawkins	10.00
25	Steve Beuerlein, Rob Johnson, Cedric Tillman, Reggie Cobb	10.00
26	Greg Hill, Willie Davis, Lake Dawson, Steve Bono	16.00
27	Jeff Hostetler, Harvey Williams, James Jett, Raghib Ismail	10.00
28	Bernie Parmalee, Irving Spikes, Terry Kirby, Irving Fryar	10.00
29	Terry Allen, David Palmer, Qadry Ismail, Jake Reed	10.00
30	Marion Butts, Vincent Brisby, Dave Meggett, Willie McGinest	10.00
31	Willie Roaf, Mario Bates, Quinn Early, Michael Haynes	10.00
32	Herschel Walker, Mike Sherrard, Derek Brown, Thomas Lewis	10.00
33	Stevie Anderson, Aaron Glenn, Johnny Johnson, Ron Moore	10.00
34	Calvin Williams, Fred Barnett, Vaughn Hebron, Charlie Garner	10.00
35	Neil O'Donnell, Charles Johnson, Rod Woodson, Erric Pegram	16.00
36	Ronnie Harmon, Shawn Jefferson, Tony Martin, Mark Seay	10.00
37	Brent Jones, Dana Stubblefield, Bryant Young, Ken Norton	10.00
38	Chris Warren, Cortez Kennedy, Sam Adams, Brian Blades	10.00
39	Tommy Maddox, Chris Miller, Johnny Bailey, Isaac Bruce	50.00
40	Lawrence Dawsey, Alvin Harper, Jackie Harris, Horace Copeland	10.00
41	Gus Frerotte, Brian Mitchell, Reggie Brooks, Tydus Winans	25.00
42	Steve McNair, Kerry Collins, Todd Collins, Chad May	100.00
43	Ki-Jana Carter, Tyrone Wheatley, Napoleon Kaufman, Rashaan Salaam	40.00
44	Terrell Fletcher, Sherman Williams, Ray Zellars, James Stewart	16.00
45	Michael Westbrook, Joseph Galloway, J.J. Stokes, Frank Sanders	40.00
46	Kevin Carter, Tony Boselli, Warren Sapp, Kyle Brady	16.00
47	Greg Truitt, Dan Wilkinson, Eric Turner, Antonio Langham	10.00
48	Carnell Lake, Neil Smith, Rod Smith, Kevin Greene	10.00
49	O.J. McDuffie, Darren Carrington, Michael Timpson, Raymont Harris	10.00
50	Rodney Hampton, Dave Krieg, Barry Foster, Kevin Greene	10.00

1995 Playoff Prime Fantasy Team

These inserts, available in 1995 Playoff Prime retail packs, were seeded at a ratio of one per 25 packs. Each clear plastic card features a star player against an exciting multi-color holographic foil background. If the card is moved to change the angle of the light, the phrase "Playoff Fantasy Team" flashes in three different dimensions.

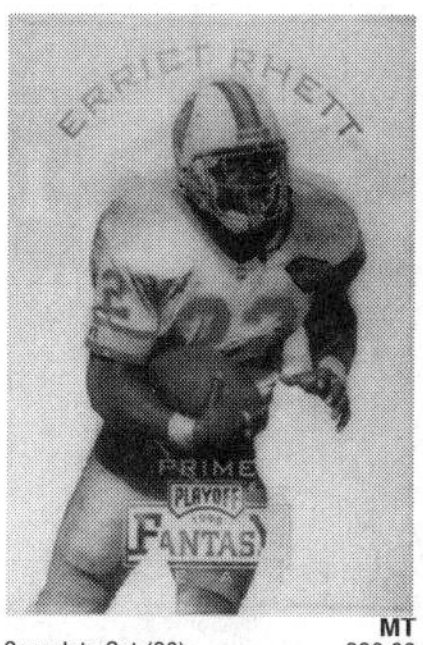

		MT
Complete Set (20):		220.00
Common Player:		3.00
Minor Stars:		6.00
1	Jerome Bettis	6.00
2	Shannon Sharpe	3.00
3	Fuad Reveiz	3.00
4	John Carney	3.00
5	Steve Young	20.00
6	Brett Favre	40.00
7	Tim Brown	6.00
8	Ben Coates	3.00
9	Marshall Faulk	15.00
10	Stan Humphries	3.00
11	Dan Marino	40.00
12	Jerry Rice	25.00
13	Errict Rhett	12.00
14	Chris Warren	6.00
15	Barry Sanders	25.00
16	Cris Carter	6.00
17	Michael Irvin	6.00
18	Emmitt Smith	40.00
19	Terance Mathis	3.00
20	Herman Moore	6.00

1995 Playoff Prime Minis

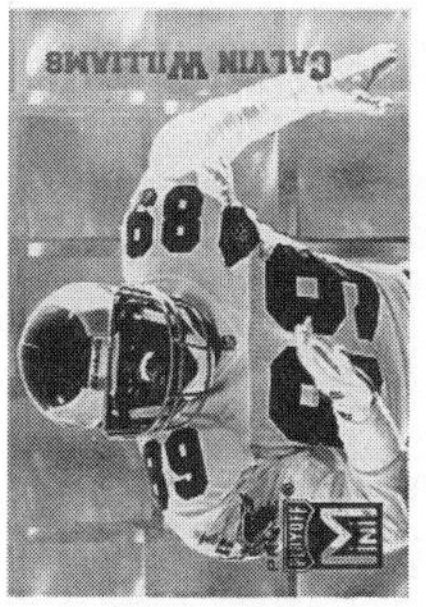

These 1995 Playoff Prime Mini insert cards were seeded one per every seven retail packs. The cards are a miniature version of the 200-card base set; each measures 2-1/4" x 3-1/8" and isolates the corresponding base set player photo against a holographic foil background. Blue foil is used for the player's name along the right side of the card, and the set icon, printed in the lower left corner. The card back has a closeup shot of the player toward the top, along with the card number. Below the photo is a brief player profile.

		MT
Complete Set (200):		700.00
Common Player:		2.00
Minor Stars:		4.00
1	John Elway	14.00
2	Reggie White	4.00
3	Errict Rhett	20.00
4	Deion Sanders	18.00
5	Raghib Ismail	2.00
6	Jerome Bettis	6.00
7	Randall Cunningham	4.00
8	Mario Bates	8.00
9	Dave Brown	2.00
10	Stan Humphries	4.00
11	Drew Bledsoe	30.00
12	Neil O'Donnell	4.00
13	Dan Marino	50.00
14	Larry Centers	2.00
15	Craig Heyward	2.00
16	Bruce Smith	2.00
17	Erik Kramer	4.00
18	Jeff Blake	20.00
19	Vinny Testaverde	4.00
20	Barry Sanders	40.00
21	Boomer Esiason	2.00
22	Emmitt Smith	50.00
23	Warren Moon	4.00
24	Junior Seau	4.00
25	Heath Shuler	15.00
26	Jackie Harris	2.00
27	Terance Mathis	2.00
28	Raymont Harris	4.00
29	Jim Kelly	6.00
30	Dan Wilkinson	2.00
31	Herman Moore	12.00
32	Shannon Sharpe	4.00
33	Antonio Langham	2.00
34	Charles Haley	2.00
35	Brett Favre	50.00
36	Marshall Faulk	30.00
37	Neil Smith	2.00
38	Harvey Williams	2.00
39	Johnny Bailey	2.00
40	O.J. McDuffie	2.00
41	David Palmer	2.00
42	Willie McGinest	2.00
43	Quinn Early	2.00
44	Johnny Johnson	2.00
45	Derek Brown	2.00
46	Charlie Garner	2.00
47	Bam Morris	10.00
48	Natrone Means	10.00
49	Ken Norton	2.00
50	Troy Aikman	30.00
51	Reggie Brooks	2.00
52	Trent Dilfer	14.00
53	Cortez Kennedy	2.00
54	Chuck Levy	2.00
55	Jeff George	6.00
56	Steve Young	30.00
57	Lewis Tillman	2.00
58	Carl Pickens	6.00
59	Brett Perriman	4.00
60	Jay Novacek	2.00
61	Greg Hill	8.00
62	James Jett	2.00
63	Terry Kirby	2.00
64	Qadry Ismail	2.00
65	Ben Coates	2.00
66	Kevin Greene	2.00
67	Bryant Young	2.00
68	Brian Mitchell	2.00
69	Steve Walsh	2.00
70	Darnay Scott	14.00
71	Daryl Johnston	2.00
72	Glyn Milburn	2.00
73	Tim Brown	4.00
74	Isaac Bruce	25.00
75	Bernie Parmalee	2.00
76	Terry Allen	2.00
77	Jim Everett	2.00
78	Thomas Lewis	2.00
79	Vaughn Hebron	2.00
80	Rod Woodson	4.00
81	Rick Mirer	10.00
82	Dana Stubblefield	4.00
83	Bert Emanuel	4.00
84	Andre Reed	4.00
85	Jeff Graham	2.00
86	Johnnie Morton	2.00
87	LeShon Johnson	2.00
88	Michael Irvin	12.00
89	Derrick Alexander	2.00
90	Lake Dawson	8.00
91	Cody Carlson	2.00
92	Chris Warren	6.00
93	William Floyd	12.00
94	Charles Johnson	6.00
95	Roosevelt Potts	2.00
96	Cris Carter	4.00
97	Aaron Glenn	2.00
98	Curtis Conway	4.00
99	Kevin Williams	4.00
100	Jerry Rice	30.00
101	Frank Reich	2.00
102	Harold Green	2.00
103	Russell Copeland	2.00
104	Rob Moore	2.00
105	Edgar Bennett	2.00
106	Darren Carrington	2.00
107	Tommy Maddox	2.00
108	Dave Meggett	2.00
109	Fred Barnett	2.00
110	Mark Seay	2.00
111	Gus Frerotte	12.00
112	Brent Jones	2.00
113	Chris Miller	2.00
114	Cedric Tillman	2.00
115	Mark Ingram	2.00
116	Eric Turner	2.00
117	Mark Carrier	2.00
118	Garrison Hearst	6.00
119	Craig Erickson	2.00
120	Derek Russell	2.00
121	Mike Sherrard	2.00
122	Horace Copeland	2.00
123	Jack Trudeau	2.00
124	Leroy Hoard	2.00
125	Gary Brown	2.00
126	Mel Gray	2.00
127	Steve Beuerlein	2.00
128	Marcus Allen	6.00
129	Irving Fryar	2.00
130	Marion Butts	2.00
131	Ricky Watters	6.00
132	Tony Martin	2.00
133	Lawrence Dawsey	2.00
134	Ronnie Harmon	2.00
135	Herschel Walker	2.00
136	Michael Haynes	2.00
137	Eric Green	2.00
138	Steve Bono	6.00
139	Jamir Miller	2.00
140	Rod Smith	2.00
141	Andre Rison	4.00
142	Eric Metcalf	2.00
143	Michael Timpson	2.00
144	Cornelius Bennett	2.00
145	Sean Dawkins	4.00
146	Scott Mitchell	4.00
147	Ray Childress	2.00
148	Jim Harbaugh	4.00
149	Reggie Cobb	2.00
150	Willie Roaf	2.00
151	Stevie Anderson	2.00
152	Barry Foster	2.00
153	Joe Montana	30.00
154	David Klingler	2.00
155	Chris Chandler	2.00
156	Carnell Lake	2.00
157	Calvin Williams	2.00
158	Kenneth Davis	2.00
159	Tydus Winans	2.00
160	Sam Adams	2.00
161	Ron Moore	2.00
162	Vincent Brisby	2.00
163	Alvin Harper	4.00
164	Jake Reed	2.00
165	Jeff Hostetler	4.00
166	Mark Brunell	20.00
167	Leonard Russell	2.00
168	Greg Truitt	2.00
169	Pete Metzelaars	2.00
170	Dave Krieg	2.00
171	Lorenzo White	2.00
172	Robert Brooks	4.00
173	Willie Davis	2.00
174	Irving Spikes	2.00
175	Rodney Hampton	2.00
176	Eric Pegram	2.00
177	Brian Blades	2.00
178	Shawn Jefferson	2.00
179	Tyrone Poole	2.00
180	Rob Johnson	6.00
181	Ki-Jana Carter	4.00
182	Steve McNair	25.00
183	Michael Westbrook	4.00
184	Kerry Collins	30.00
185	Kevin Carter	6.00
186	Tony Boselli	6.00

187 Joseph Galloway 25.00
188 Kyle Brady 6.00
189 J.J. Stokes 10.00
190 Warren Sapp 6.00
191 Tyrone Wheatley 7.00
192 Napoleon Kaufman 12.00
193 James Stewart 6.00
194 Rashaan Salaam 10.00
195 Ray Zellars 6.00
196 Todd Collins 6.00
197 Sherman Williams 6.00
198 Frank Sanders 10.00
199 Terrell Fletcher 6.00
200 Chad May 6.00

1995 Playoff Prime Pigskin Previews

These retail-only 1995 Playoff Prime inserts feature six AFC stars. Cards were randomly included one per 145 packs. The front has a color photo superimposed over a leather football. Gold foil stamping is used for the player's name and insert set logo. The card back has a color photo of the player against his team's city skyline. A brief recap of the player's 1994 accomplishments is given at the top of the card; his 1994 and career stats are listed in a panel at the bottom.

MT
Complete Set (6): 350.00
Common Player: 20.00
7 Dan Marino 125.00
8 Marshall Faulk 40.00
9 Natrone Means 30.00
10 Tim Brown 20.00
11 Drew Bledsoe 70.00
12 Marcus Allen 20.00

1995 Playoff Night of the Stars

Playoff produced this six-card set to hand out to those attending the 1995 National Sports Collectors Convention Trade Show in St. Louis. The set was also available at the Playoff booth during the National by exchanging 10 wrappers for one of the six cards. The borderless fronts featured the "Night of the Stars," the player's name, Playoff logo and team helmet at the bottom. The backs include the player's name and an endorsement for the 1995 National.

MT
Complete Set (6): 20.00
Common Player: 2.00
1 Jerome Bettis 4.00
2 Ben Coates 2.00
3 Deion Sanders 5.00
4 Ki-Jana Carter 2.00
5 Steve McNair 8.00
6 Errict Rhett 2.00

1995 Playoff Super Bowl Card Show

To commemorate the Super Bowl XXIX Card Show, Playoff produced this eight-card set. Overall, 3,000 of each card was issued. A color photo of the player is printed over a red, silver and gold-foil background. In the upper left is the player's name in silver foil. The card backs have the player's name, highlights and the Super Bowl XXIX logo. The card number is printed in the upper right of the card back, which sports a black background.

MT
Complete Set (8): 25.00
Common Player: 2.00
1 Marshall Faulk 8.00
2 Heath Shuler 3.00
3 David Palmer 2.00
4 Errict Rhett 3.00
5 Charlie Garner 3.00
6 Irving Spikes 2.00
7 Shante Carver 2.00
8 Greg Hill 3.00

1995 Playoff Contenders

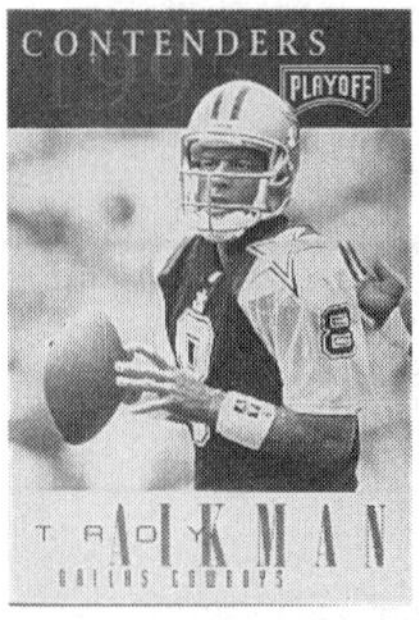

As with previous editions, Playoff's 1995 Contenders set emphasizes players whose teams are in contention for post-season play. The 150-card set includes a 30-card Rookies subset and three insert sets. The regular card uses a metallic process which gives the card a depth to it. The band at the top and the player's name use a team-related color, as does the back, which includes a closeup shot of the player and a brief recap of a game in which he had a key role. Insert sets include Hog Heaven Pigskins, Rookie Kickoff and Back-to-Backs, a 75-card parallel set which includes two players per card.

MT
Complete Set (150): 35.00
Common Player: .20
Minor Stars: .40
Pack (6): 3.50
Wax Box (24): 80.00
1 Steve Young 1.50
2 *Jeff Blake* 1.00
3 Rick Mirer .40
4 Brett Favre 4.00
5 Heath Shuler 1.00
6 Steve Bono .40
7 John Elway 1.50
8 Troy Aikman 2.00
9 Rodney Peete .20
10 Gus Frerotte .50
11 Drew Bledsoe 1.50
12 Jim Kelly .40
13 Dan Marino 4.00
14 Errict Rhett 1.00
15 Jeff Hostetler .20
16 Erik Kramer .20
17 Jim Everett .20
18 Elvis Grbac .20
19 Scott Mitchell .20
20 Barry Sanders 1.50
21 Deion Sanders 1.00
22 Emmitt Smith 4.00
23 Garrison Hearst .40
24 Mario Bates .40
25 Mark Brunell 1.00
26 Robert Smith .20
27 Rodney Hampton .20
28 Marshall Faulk .40
29 Greg Hill .40
30 Bernie Parmalee .20
31 Natrone Means .40
32 Marcus Allen .40
33 Bam Morris .40
34 Edgar Bennett .20
35 Vincent Brisby .20
36 Jerome Bettis .40
37 Craig Heyward .20
38 Anthony Miller .20
39 Curtis Conway .20
40 William Floyd .40
41 Chris Warren .40
42 Terry Kirby .20
43 Herschel Walker .20
44 Eric Metcalf .20
45 Darnay Scott .40
46 Jackie Harris .20
47 Dana Stubblefield .20
48 Daryl Johnston .20
49 Dave Meggett .20
50 Ricky Watters .40
51 Ken Norton .20
52 Boomer Esiason .20
53 Lake Dawson .40
54 Eric Green .20
55 Junior Seau .40
56 *Yancey Thigpen* 1.00
57 James Jett .20
58 Leonard Russell .20
59 Brent Jones .20
60 Trent Dilfer .40
61 Terance Mathis .20
62 Jeff George .20
63 Alvin Harper .20
64 Terry Allen .20
65 Stan Humphries .20
66 Robert Green .20
67 Bryce Paup .40
68 *Tamarick Vanover* .75
69 Desmond Howard .20
70 Derek Loville .20
71 Dave Brown .20
72 Carl Pickens .40
73 Gary Clark .20
74 Gary Brown .20
75 Brett Perriman .20
76 Charlie Garner .20
77 Ben Coates .20
78 Bruce Smith .20
79 Erric Pegram .20
80 Jerry Rice 1.50
81 Tim Brown .20
82 John Taylor .20
83 Will Moore .20
84 Jay Novacek .20
85 Kevin Williams .20
86 Raghib Ismail .20
87 Robert Brooks .40
88 Michael Irvin .40
89 Mark Chmura .75
90 Shannon Sharpe .20
91 Henry Ellard .20
92 Reggie White .40
93 Isaac Bruce .50
94 Charles Haley .20
95 Jake Reed .20
96 Pete Metzelaars .20
97 Dave Krieg .20
98 Tony Martin .20
99 Charles Jordan .20
100 Bert Emanuel .50
101 Andre Rison .20
102 Jeff Graham .20
103 O.J. McDuffie .20
104 Randall Cunningham .20
105 Harvey Williams .20
106 Cris Carter .20
107 Irving Fryar .20
108 Jim Harbaugh .20
109 Bernie Kosar .20
110 Charles Johnson .40
111 Warren Moon .40
112 Neil O'Donnell .40
113 Fred Barnett .20
114 Herman Moore .75
115 Chris Miller .20
116 Vinny Testaverde .20
117 Craig Erickson .20
118 Qadry Ismail .20
119 Willie Davis .20
120 Michael Jackson .20
121 *Stoney Case* .40
122 *Frank Sanders* .50
123 *Todd Collins* .40
124 *Kerry Collins* 2.00
125 *Sherman Williams* .40
126 *Terrell Davis* 8.00
127 *Luther Elliss* .40
128 *Steve McNair* 4.00
129 *Chris Sanders* 1.00
130 *Ki-Jana Carter* 1.00
131 *Rodney Thomas* .50
132 *Tony Boselli* .40
133 *Rob Johnson* 3.00
134 *James Stewart* 1.50
135 *Chad May* .40
136 *Eric Bjornson* .40
137 *Tyrone Wheatley* .50
138 *Kyle Brady* .40
139 *Curtis Martin* 4.00
140 *Eric Zeier* .50
141 *Ray Zellars* .40
142 *Napoleon Kaufman* 3.00
143 *Mike Mamula* .40
144 *Mark Bruener* .50
145 *Kordell Stewart* 5.00
146 *J.J. Stokes* 1.00
147 *Joey Galloway* 2.50
148 *Warren Sapp* .75
149 *Michael Westbrook* 1.00
150 *Rashaan Salaam* 1.00

1995 Playoff Contenders Back-to-Back

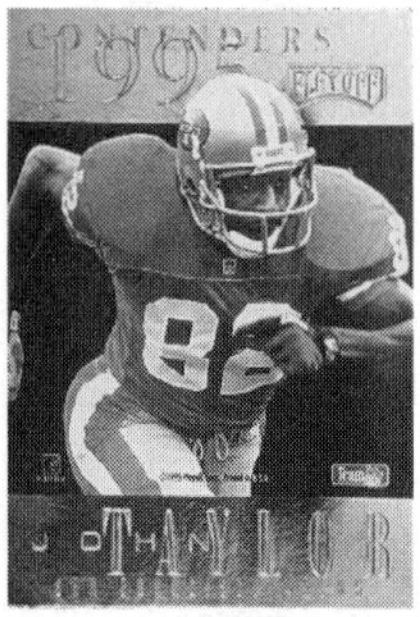

This 1995 Playoff Contenders insert set is a 75-card parallel set which features two players per card, one on each side. The cards use foil stamping for the player's name and set logo, which appear at the bottom and top, respectively. The cards have a glossier finish than their regular counterparts. These inserts are seeded one per 19 packs.

MT
Complete Set (75): 1000.
Common Player: 5.00
Minor Stars: 10.00
Inserted 1:19
1 Troy Aikman, Dan Marino 50.00
2 Emmitt Smith, Marshall Faulk 40.00
3 Brett Favre, John Elway 60.00
4 Steve Young, Drew Bledsoe 25.00
5 Barry Sanders, Errict Rhett 50.00
6 Deion Sanders, Jerry Rice 25.00
7 Jeff Blake, Rick Mirer 5.00
8 Michael Irvin, Tim Brown 10.00
9 Chris Warren, Ricky Watters 10.00
10 Herman Moore, Vincent Brisby 10.00
11 James Jett, Eric Metcalf 5.00
12 Henry Ellard, Terance Mathis 5.00
13 Curtis Conway, Isaac Bruce 10.00
14 Steve Bono, Jeff Hostetler 5.00
15 Greg Hill, Harvey Williams 5.00
16 Garrison Hearst, Jerome Bettis 10.00
17 Jay Novacek, Brent Jones 5.00
18 Reggie White, Bruce Smith 10.00
19 Eric Green, Shannon Sharpe 10.00
20 Gus Frerotte, Jeff George 10.00
21 Erik Kramer, Brian Mitchell 5.00
22 Warren Moon, Jim Kelly 10.00
23 Mark Chmura, Ben Coates 5.00
24 Trent Dilfer, Heath Shuler 10.00
25 Craig Heyward, Edgar Bennett 5.00
26 Jim Everett, Dave Brown 5.00
27 Bert Emanuel, Andre Rison 5.00
28 Robert Brooks, Alvin Harper 5.00
29 Desmond Howard, Tony Martin 5.00
30 Rodney Peete, Fred Barnett 5.00
31 Natrone Means, William Floyd 10.00
32 Brett Perriman, Raghib Ismail 5.00
33 Cris Carter, Irving Fryar 10.00
34 Tamarick Vanover, Darnay Scott 5.00
35 Charles Haley, Dana Stubblefield 5.00
36 Bryce Paup, Ken Norton 5.00
37 Marcus Allen, Herschel Walker 10.00
38 Leonard Russell, Terry Allen 5.00
39 Junior Seau, Derrick Loville 5.00
40 Lake Dawson, Charles Johnson 5.00
41 Kevin Williams, Charles Jordan 5.00
42 Jeff Graham, Carl Pickens 5.00
43 Anthony Miller, O.J. McDuffie 5.00
44 Elvis Grbac, Jim Harbaugh 5.00
45 Dave Meggett, Terry Kirby 5.00
46 Dave Krieg, Stan Humphries 5.00
47 Mark Brunell, Boomer Esiason 20.00
48 Craig Erickson, Vinny Testaverde 5.00
49 Randall Cunningham, Bernie Kosar 10.00
50 Erric Pegram, Charlie Garner 5.00
51 Will Moore, Gary Clark 5.00
52 Qadry Ismail, Willie Davis 5.00
53 Neil O'Donnell, Chris Miller 5.00
54 Mario Bates, Robert Smith 5.00
55 Rodney Hampton, Bernie Parmalee 5.00
56 Bam Morris, Daryl Johnston 5.00
57 Jackie Harris, Jake Reed 5.00
58 John Taylor, Pete Metzelaars 5.00
59 Yancey Thigpen, Michael Jackson 5.00
60 Gary Brown, Robert Green 5.00
61 Rashaan Salaam, Napoleon Kaufman 15.00
62 Mark Bruener, Kyle Brady 5.00
63 Ki-Jana Carter, Rodney Thomas 5.00
64 Chad May, Steve McNair 15.00
65 Frank Sanders, J.J. Stokes 10.00
66 Mike Mamula, Warren Sapp 5.00
67 Stoney Case, Kordell Stewart 30.00
68 Terrell Davis, Curtis Martin 50.00
69 Sherman Williams, Chris Sanders 5.00
70 James Stewart, Eric Bjornson 5.00
71 Tyrone Wheatley, Ray Zellars 5.00
72 Tony Boselli, Luther Elliss 5.00
73 Rob Johnson, Todd Collins 15.00
74 Kerry Collins, Eric Zeier 10.00
75 Joey Galloway, Michael Westbrook 15.00

1995 Playoff Contenders Hog Heaven

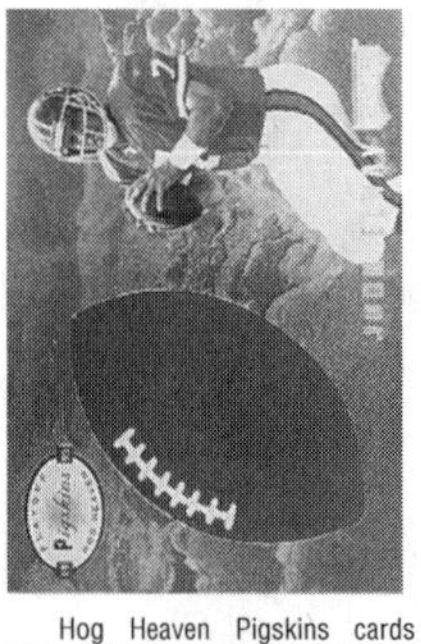

Hog Heaven Pigskins cards were randomly inserted one per 48 packs of 1995 Playoff Contenders football packs. The thick cards, which showcase 30 players, feature a photo among cloud formations, next to a leather football. The set logo is in the upper left corner; the player's name is in gold foil in the lower right hand corner of the horizontally-designed card. The card back is all leather and features a caricature of the player, plus his name, position and team name. The card number uses an "HH" prefix.

MT
Complete Set (30): 425.00
Common Player: 5.00
Minor Stars: 10.00
Inserted 1:48
1 Troy Aikman 30.00
2 Marcus Allen 10.00
3 Jeff Blake 10.00
4 Drew Bledsoe 30.00
5 Steve Bono 5.00
6 Isaac Bruce 10.00
7 Trent Dilfer 10.00
8 John Elway 45.00
9 Marshall Faulk 15.00
10 Brett Favre 60.00
11 Gus Frerotte 5.00
12 Irving Fryar 5.00
13 Jeff George 10.00
14 Rodney Hampton 5.00
15 Garrison Hearst 10.00
16 Michael Irvin 10.00
17 Erik Kramer 5.00
18 Dan Marino 45.00
19 Natrone Means 10.00
20 Errict Rhett 5.00
21 Jerry Rice 30.00
22 Barry Sanders 60.00
23 Deion Sanders 15.00
24 Shannon Sharpe 5.00
25 Emmitt Smith 45.00
26 Robert Smith 10.00
27 Chris Warren 5.00
28 Reggie White 10.00
29 Harvey Williams 5.00
30 Steve Young 25.00

1995 Playoff Contenders Rookie Kick Off

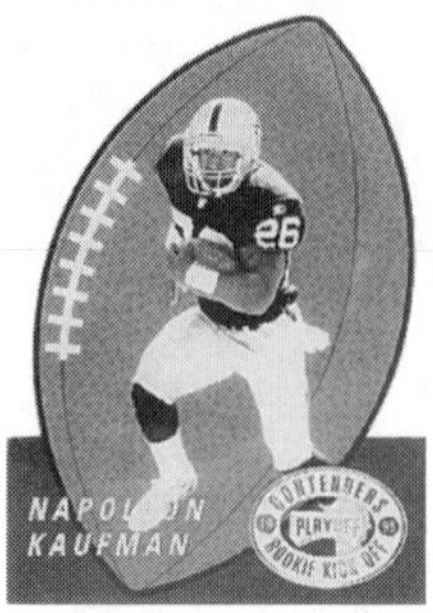

These 1995 Playoff Absolute inserts were seeded one per 24 packs. Thirty rookies appear on a plastic die-cut card shaped like a football waiting to be kicked off. The player's name and set logo are in gold foil at the bottom. The card back is blank.

MT
Complete Set (30): 400.00
Common Player: 3.00
1 Eric Bjornson 7.00
2 Tony Boselli 7.00
3 Kyle Brady 7.00
4 Mark Bruener 6.00
5 Ki-Jana Carter 6.00
6 Stoney Case 6.00
7 Kerry Collins 12.00
8 Todd Collins 6.00
9 Terrell Davis 75.00
10 Luther Elliss 7.00
11 Joey Galloway 15.00
12 Rob Johnson 7.00
13 Napoleon Kaufman 25.00
14 Mike Mamula 7.00
15 Curtis Martin 50.00
16 Chad May 7.00
17 Steve McNair 35.00
18 Rashaan Salaam 10.00
19 Chris Sanders 10.00
20 Frank Sanders 10.00
21 Warren Sapp 7.00
22 James Stewart 7.00
23 Kordell Stewart 50.00
24 J.J. Stokes 10.00
25 Rodney Thomas 3.00
26 Michael Westbrook 10.00
27 Tyrone Wheatley 7.00
28 Sherman Williams 7.00
29 Eric Zeier 7.00
30 Ray Zellars 7.00

1996 Playoff National Promos

Handed out at the 1996 National Sports Collectors Convention in Anaheim, this seven-card set was available through a wrapper redemption program at the show. Three wrappers from a Playoff product could be exchanged for one card. A foil box of wrappers was good for the complete set. The card fronts featured a photo of the player over a background of a California scene. The "17th National Sports Collectors Convention" is printed along one side of the acetate card. The card backs are the reverse of the fronts, with the player's bio written in the shadow of the player. The cards are numbered "x/7." Kordell Stewart's card was only available through the foil box complete set redemption offer.

MT
Complete Set (7): 35.00
Common Player: 3.00
1 Kordell Stewart 8.00
2 Curtis Martin 10.00
3 Tyrone Wheatley 3.00
4 Joey Galloway 5.00
5 Steve McNair 6.00
6 Kerry Collins 8.00
7 Napoleon Kaufman 4.00

1996 Playoff Super Bowl Card Show

As a redemption offer at the Super Bowl XXX Card Show, Playoff issued this six-card set. Player photos are showcased over Arizona desert scenery. The player's name is printed along one side of the card, with the Playoff logo in one of the lower corners. The Super Bowl Card Show logo is located in one of the upper corners. The card back features the Super Bowl Card Show logo at the top, with the player's highlights printed in a box at the bottom. The cards are numbered "X/6." A collector could exchange a Playoff wrapper for a different card each day of the show, which was held in Tempe, Ariz. A collector could receive the entire set in exchange for 10 wrappers. The cards have a 1995 copyright date on the card back.

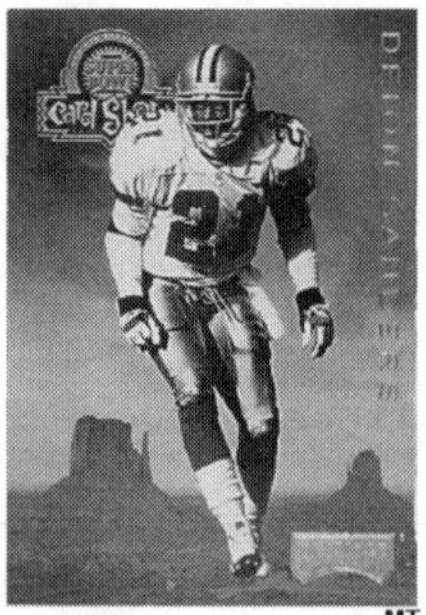

MT
Complete Set (6): 17.00
Common Player: 2.00
1 Deion Sanders 4.00
2 Rashaan Salaam 3.00
3 Garrison Hearst 2.00
4 Robert Brooks 2.00
5 Barry Sanders 5.00
6 Errict Rhett 3.00

1996 Playoff Absolute Promos

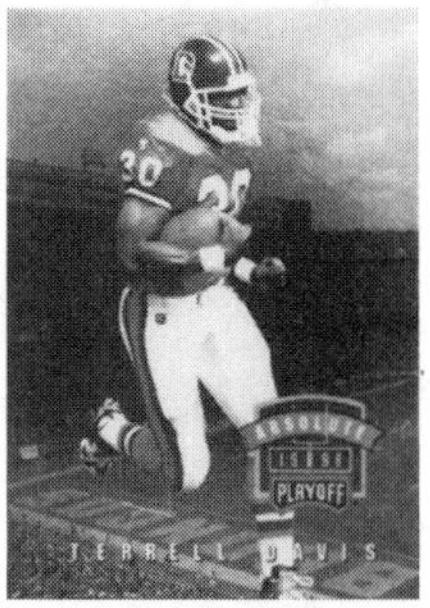

This six-card promo set gave collectors and dealers a sneak peak at the designs for 1996 Playoff Absolute. The same six players are featured in Prime Promos, but the photos and logos are different.

MT
Complete Set (6): 20.00
Common Player: 1.50
Terrell Davis 7.00
Tamarick Vanover 3.00
Rashaan Salaam 3.00
J.J. Stokes 3.00
Antonio Freeman 3.00
Zack Crockett 1.50

1996 Playoff Absolute

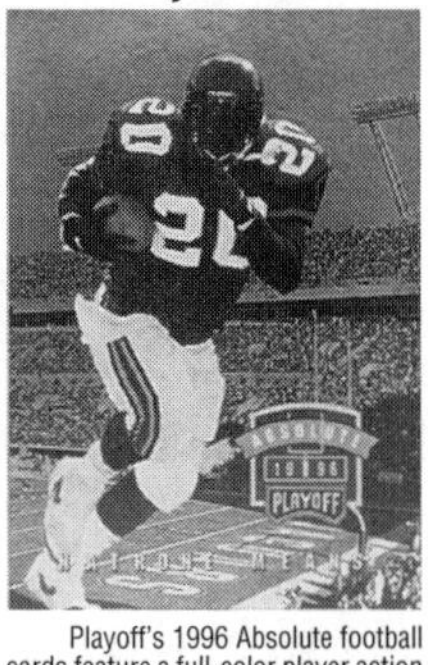

Playoff's 1996 Absolute football cards feature a full-color player action photo on the front, set against a colorful snapshot of the player's stadium with a game in progress. Each card back has a head-and-shoulder shot of the player, complete career and 1995 NFL statistics and an intriguing or unusual fact about the player. A 20-card subset of the top 1996 draft choices is included within the main set. Four insert sets were also produced: Metal X (also in Prime), Xtreme Team, Quad Series and Unsung Heroes (also in Prime). In an innovative pack-within-a-pack concept, three types of color-coded packs are available within 1996 Playoff Absolute boxes. Each box of 1996 Playoff Absolute contains 24 Red packs, each containing five cards, and either a White or Blue inner pack. Each Red pack contains five base cards from the #1-100 low level series, plus one White or Blue inner pack, and a potential random insert card. Each White inner pack contains one base card from the #101-150 mid

level series, or a random insert card. Each box includes approximately 18 White inner packs. Each Blue inner pack has one base card from the #150-200 high level series, or a random insert card. Each box includes approximately six Blue inner packs.

MT
Complete Set (200): 150.00
Complete Red Set (100): 15.00
Complete White Set (50): 45.00
Complete Blue Set (50): 90.00
Common Red (1-100): .10
Common White (101-150): .40
Common Blue (151-200): 1.00
Pack (6): 3.50
Wax Box (24): 65.00
1 Jim Kelly .20
2 Michael Irvin .20
3 Jim Harbaugh .10
4 Warren Moon .20
5 Rick Mirer .10
6 Drew Bledsoe 1.25
7 Steve Young 1.50
8 Junior Seau .20
9 Sherman Williams .10
10 Jay Novacek .10
11 Bill Brooks .10
12 Steve Bono .20
13 Leroy Hoard .10
14 Willie Jackson .10
15 Irving Fryer .10
16 Tony McGee .10
17 Neil O'Donnell .20
18 Fred Barnett .10
19 Erric Pegram .10
20 Derrick Moore .10
21 Johnnie Morton .10
22 James Jett .10
23 Tim Brown .20
24 Kevin Miniefield .10
25 Jim McMahon .10
26 Brian Blades .10
27 Henry Ellard .10
28 Calvin Williams .10
29 Chris Chandler .10
30 Rod Woodson .10
31 Ronnie Harmon .10
32 Brent Jones .10
33 Qadry Ismail .10
34 Steve Tasker .10
35 Eric Green .10
36 Brian Mitchell .10
37 Herschel Walker .10
38 Sean Dawkins .10
39 Bryce Paup .10
40 Dorsey Levens .25
41 Andre Rison .10
42 Lamont Warren .10
43 Earnest Byner .10
44 *Bobby Engram* 1.00
45 *Simeon Rice* .25
46 Michael Jackson .10
47 *Marvin Harrison* 3.00
48 Thurman Thomas .20
49 Charles Haley .10
50 Rob Moore .10
51 Bryan Cox .10
52 Horace Copeland .10
53 Rodney Peete .10
54 Jeff Graham .10
55 Charles Johnson .10
56 Natrone Means .20
57 Terrell Fletcher .10
58 Eric Bieniemy .10
59 *Karim Abdul-Jabbar* 1.00
60 Quinn Early .10
61 Mark Bruener .10
62 Shawn Jefferson .10
63 Vinny Testaverde .10
64 *Derrick Mayes* 1.25
65 Mario Bates .10
66 J.J. Birden .10
67 *Eddie Kennison* .75
68 Steve Walsh .10
69 Mark Chmura .30
70 Mike Sherrard .10
71 Boomer Esiason .10
72 *Alex Van Dyke* .75
73 Jake Reed .10
74 Jackie Harris .10
75 Mark Rypien .10
76 Chris Calloway .10
77 *Amani Toomer* .50
78 Terrell Davis 8.00
79 Raghib Ismail .10
80 Derek Loville .10
81 Ben Coates .10
82 Kyle Brady .10
83 Willie Green .10
84 Randall Cunningham .10
85 Amp Lee .10
86 Bert Emanual .10
87 *Jason Dunn* .25
88 Michael Haynes .10
89 Robert Green .10
90 Willie Davis .10
91 O.J. McDuffie .10
92 Harold Green .10
93 Ken Dilger .10
94 Brett Perriman .10
95 Eric Zeier .10
96 Jerome Bettis .10
97 *Rickey Dudley* .75
98 Darnay Scott .10
99 Mark Brunell 1.00
100 Christian Fauria .10
101 Jeff Blake .75
102 Troy Aikman 5.00
103 John Elway 3.00
104 Barry Sanders 7.00
105 Curtis Conway .75
106 Wayne Chrebet .40
107 Lake Dawson .40
108 Jerry Rice 5.00
109 Kevin Williams .40
110 Zack Crockett .40
111 Vincent Brisby .40
112 Rodney Thomas .75
113 Rodney Hampton .40
114 Adrian Murrell .40
115 Bruce Smith .40
116 Napoleon Kaufman .75
117 Bam Morris .40
118 Anthony Miller .40
119 *Aaron Hayden* 1.00
120 Joey Galloway 4.00
121 Trent Dilfer .75
122 Stoney Case .40
123 Tamarick Vanover .75
124 Eric Metcalf .40
125 Marcus Allen .40
126 James Stewart .40
127 Charlie Garner .40
128 Yancey Thigpen 1.25
129 William Floyd .40
130 Terry Allen .40
131 Robert Smith .40
132 Todd Kinchen .40
133 Gus Frerotte .40
134 Frank Sanders .75
135 Scott Mitchell .40
136 Greg Hill .40
137 Edgar Bennett .40
138 Alvin Harper .40
139 Reggie White .40
140 Craig Heyward .40
141 Todd Collins .40
142 Ernie Mills .40
143 *Keyshawn Johnson* 6.00
144 Mark Carrier .40
145 Robert Brooks .40
146 Bernie Parmalee .40
147 Carl Pickens .75
148 *Kevin Hardy* .75
149 *Jonathan Ogden* .75
150 *Lawrence Phillips* 2.50
151 Emmitt Smith 25.00
152 Brett Favre 25.00
153 Dan Marino 25.00
154 Jim Everett 1.00
155 Dave Brown 1.00
156 Jeff Hostetler 1.00
157 Heath Shuler 1.00
158 Daryl Johnston 1.00
159 Terance Mathis 1.00
160 Curtis Martin 16.00
161 Ray Zellars 1.00
162 Ricky Watters 1.00
163 Chris Warren 1.00
164 Larry Centers 1.00
165 Steve McNair 10.00
166 Terry Kirby 1.00
167 Rob Johnson 1.00
168 Dave Meggett 1.00
169 Antonio Freeman 1.00
170 Marshall Faulk 5.00
171 Andre Hastings 1.00
172 Stan Humphries 1.00
173 Errict Rhett 1.00
174 Michael Westbrook 1.50
175 Deion Sanders 7.00
176 Jeff George 2.00
177 Cris Carter 1.50
178 Chris Sanders 1.50
179 Ki-Jana Carter 1.50
180 Kordell Stewart 12.00
181 Isaac Bruce 2.00
182 *Terry Glenn* 6.00
183 Garrison Hearst 1.00
184 Erik Kramer 1.00
185 *Leeland McElroy* 2.00
186 Rashaan Salaam 2.00
187 Kimble Anders 1.00
188 Chad May 1.00
189 Tony Martin 1.00
190 J.J. Stokes 7.00
191 Darick Holmes 1.00
192 *Eric Moulds* 10.00
193 Shannon Sharpe 1.00
194 *Tim Biakabutuka* 5.00
195 *Eddie George* 15.00
196 *Mike Alstott* 7.00
197 Kerry Collins 3.00
198 Harvey Williams 1.00
199 Herman Moore 2.00
200 Tyrone Wheatley 1.00

1996 Playoff Absolute/ Prime Metal XL

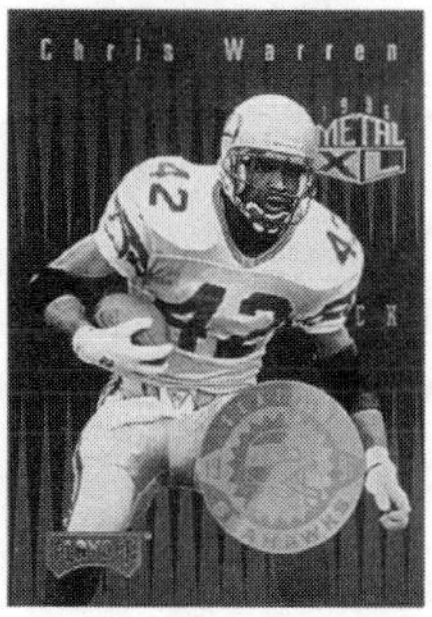

These cards were available in both 1996 Playoff Absolute (#s 1-18) and 1996 Playoff Prime (#s 19-36). The cards introduce the first-ever concept of a collector coin and card in one. A metal coin commemorating each player's team is imbedded in each card. Cards were available only in Blue inner packs, one in 96 packs.

MT
Complete Set (36): 800.00
Comp. Absolute Set (18): 500.00
Comp. Prime Set (18): 300.00
Common Player: 10.00
1 Troy Aikman 40.00
2 Emmitt Smith 80.00
3 Barry Sanders 40.00
4 Brett Favre 80.00
5 Dan Marino 80.00
6 Jerry Rice 40.00
7 Marshall Faulk 25.00
8 Curtis Martin 60.00
9 Rashaan Salaam 20.00
10 Harvey Williams 10.00
11 Ricky Watters 10.00
12 Yancey Thigpen 10.00
13 Chris Warren 10.00
14 Errict Rhett 20.00
15 Terry Allen 10.00
16 Robert Brooks 10.00
17 Anthony Miller 10.00
18 Erik Kramer 10.00
19 Michael Irvin 10.00
20 John Elway 35.00
21 Jim Harbaugh 10.00
22 Steve Young 35.00
23 Deion Sanders 35.00
24 Terrell Davis 50.00
25 Reggie White 10.00
26 Herman Moore 20.00
27 Rodney Hampton 10.00
28 Cris Carter 10.00
29 Isaac Bruce 25.00
30 Kordell Stewart 40.00
31 Brett Perriman 10.00
32 Joey Galloway 35.00
33 Drew Bledsoe 40.00
34 J.J. Stokes 15.00
35 Napoleon Kaufman 10.00
36 Tim Brown 10.00

1996 Playoff Absolute Quad Series

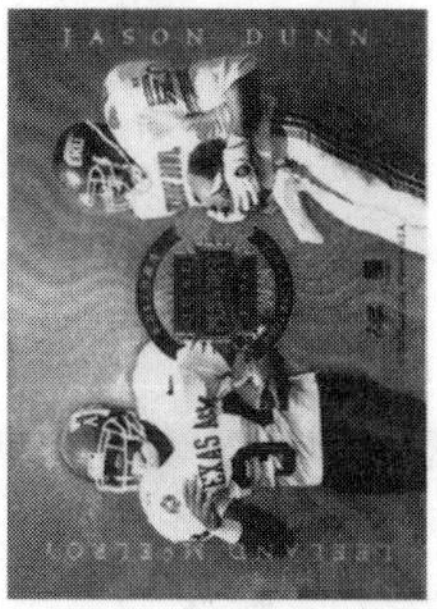

These 35 insert cards were available only in Playoff's 1996 Absolute Red packs, one in 24. Each card features four players on it. There were also five rookies-only Quad cards produced. The background is foiled, with a silver-stamped insert set logo with the player's team name around it. The player's names are stamped in copper foil on each side of the card. Copper is also used for a card number, which appears on one side only.

MT
Complete Set (35): 700.00
Common Player: 7.50
Minor Stars: 15.00
1 Stoney Case, Garrison Hearst, Rob Moore, Frank Sanders 7.50
2 J.J. Birden, Bert Emanuel, Jeff George, Craig Heyward 7.50
3 Todd Collins, Bill Brooks, Jim Kelly, Bryce Paup 7.50
4 Mark Carrier, Kerry Collins, Willie Green, Derrick Moore 50.00
5 Curtis Conway, Robert Green, Erik Kramer, Kevin Miniefield 7.50
6 Eric Bieniemy, Jeff Blake, Harold Green, Tony McGee 7.50
7 Earnest Byner, Michael Jackson, Andre Rison, Eric Zeier 7.50
8 Michael Irvin, Jay Novacek, Deion Sanders, Kevin Williams 30.00
9 Terrell Davis, John Elway, Anthony Miller, Shannon Sharpe 40.00
10 Scott Mitchell, Herman Moore, Johnnie Morton, Brett Perriman 15.00
11 Edgar Bennett, Mark Chmura, Antonio Freeman, Reggie White 15.00
12 Chris Chandler, Steve McNair, Chris Sanders, Rodney Thomas 30.00
13 Zack Crockett, Sean Dawkins, Ken Dilger, Jim Harbaugh 7.50
14 Mark Brunell, Willie Jackson, Rob Johnson, James Stewart 25.00
15 Marcus Allen, Kimble Anders, Lake Dawson, Tamarick Vanover 15.00
16 Eric Green, Terry Kirby, O.J. McDuffie, Bernie Parmalee 7.50
17 Cris Carter, Warren Moon, Robert Smith, Chad May 15.00
18 Drew Bledsoe, Vincent Brisby, Ben Coates, Dave Meggett 40.00
19 Mario Bates, Jim Everett, Michael Haynes, Ray Zellars 7.50
20 Dave Brown, Chris Calloway, Rodney Hampton, Tyrone Wheatley 15.00
21 Kyle Brady, Wayne Chrebet, Adrian Murrell, Neil O'Donnell 7.50
22 Tim Brown, Jeff Hostetler, Raghib Ismail, Napoleon Kaufman 15.00
23 Charlie Garner, Rodney Peete, Ricky Watters, Calvin Williams 7.50
24 Andre Hastings, Ernie Mills, Kordell Stewart, Rod Woodson 45.00
25 Terrell Fletcher, Ronnie Harmon, Aaron Hayden, Junior Seau 15.00
26 William Floyd, Derek Loville, J.J. Stokes, Steve Young 40.00
27 Brian Blades, Christian Fauria, Joey Galloway, Rick Mirer 35.00
28 Mark Rypien, Isaac Bruce, Todd Kinchen, Steve Walsh 20.00
29 Horace Copeland, Trent Dilfer, Alvin Harper, Jackie Harris 15.00
30 Henry Ellard, Gus Frerotte, Heath Shuler, Michael Westbrook 15.00
31 Keyshawn Johnson, Kevin Hardy, Simeon Rice, Jonathan Ogden 70.00
32 Lawrence Phillips, Tim Biakabutuka, Terry Glenn, Rickey Dudley 60.00
33 Eddie George, Marvin Harrison, Eric Moulds, Eddie Kennison 60.00
34 Derrick Mayes, Karim Abdul-Jabbar, Alex Van Dyke, Bobby Engram 50.00
35 Leeland McElroy, Jason Dunn, Mike Alstott, Amani Toomer 30.00

1996 Playoff Absolute/Prime Unsung Heroes

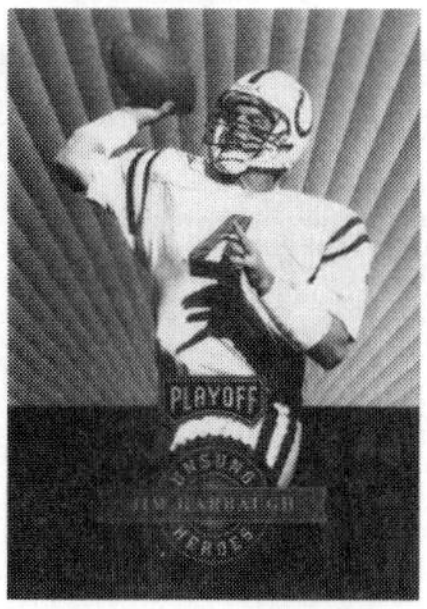

These cards were available in 1996 Playoff Absolute (#s 1- 15, NFC players) and 1996 Playoff Prime (#s 16-30, AFC players). The cards, which utilize a brand-new Tekchrome design, honor players long on desire and grit, but short on headlines. The players were chosen by fans in nationwide voting and were honored at the 23rd Annual NFLPA Banquet in March 1996 to benefit the Washington D.C. chapter of the Special Olympics. The cards were only available in Red packs, one in 24 packs. Fronts have a color action photo, with the brand/insert set logos and player's name toward the bottom.

MT
Complete Set (30): 30.00
Complete Absolute Set (15): 13.00
Complete Prime Set (15): 17.00
Common Player: .50
Minor Stars: 1.00
Inserted 1:24
1 Bill Bates .50
2 Jeff Brady .50
3 Ray Brown .50
4 Isaac Bruce 2.00
5 Larry Centers 1.00
6 Mark Chmura 1.00
7 Keith Elias .50
8 Robert Green .50
9 Andy Harmon .50
10 Rodney Holman .50
11 Derek Loville 1.00
12 J.J. McCleskey .50
13 Sam Mills .50
14 Hardy Nickerson 1.00
15 Jessie Tuggle .50
16 Eric Bieniemy .50
17 Blaine Bishop .50
18 Mark Brunell 5.00
19 Wayne Chrebet 1.50
20 Vince Evans .50
21 Sam Gash .50
22 Tim Grunhard .50
23 Jim Harbaugh 1.00
24 Dwayne Harper .50
25 Bernie Parmalee .50
26 Reggie Rivers .50
27 Eugene Robinson .50
28 Kordell Stewart 6.00
29 Steve Tasker .50
30 Bennie Thompson .50

1996 Playoff Absolute Xtreme Team

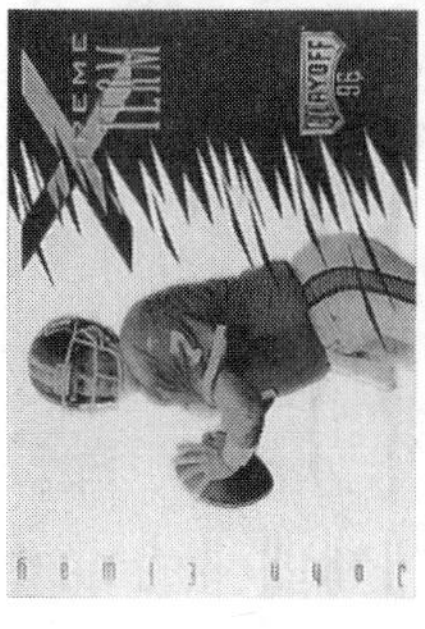

Thirty of the game's most coveted players appear to jump out at you on these 1996 Playoff Absolute cards. Each card is clear plastic, foil-enhanced, and available only in White inner packs (one in 24 packs). Fronts have a color action photo on one side against a clear background that has the player's name (along the left side) and a team logo showing through. The player's name is stamped in gold foil along the left side. The right side has a color panel with a gold-foil stamped brand logo. Gold foil is also used for part of the X in the insert set logo. The card back (numbered XT01, etc.) has a reverse angle of the photo from the front, plus a brief recap of the player's accomplishments.

MT
Complete Set (30): 300.00
Common Player: 5.00
Minor Stars: 10.00
1 Troy Aikman 20.00
2 Emmitt Smith 40.00
3 Jerry Rice 20.00
4 Dan Marino 40.00
5 Brett Favre 40.00
6 Barry Sanders 25.00
7 Michael Irvin 10.00
8 John Elway 15.00
9 Joey Galloway 15.00
10 Steve Young 15.00
11 Deion Sanders 15.00
12 Terrell Davis 25.00
13 Herman Moore 10.00
14 Reggie White 5.00
15 Cris Carter 5.00
16 Rodney Hampton 5.00
17 Isaac Bruce 10.00
18 Brett Perriman 5.00
19 Curtis Conway 5.00
20 Scott Mitchell 5.00
21 Rashaan Salaam 10.00
22 Robert Brooks 5.00
23 Marshall Faulk 12.00
24 Curtis Martin 30.00
25 Harvey Williams 5.00
26 Yancey Thigpen 5.00
27 Chris Warren 10.00
28 Errict Rhett 10.00
29 Terry Allen 5.00
30 Carl Pickens 10.00

1996 Playoff Prime Promos

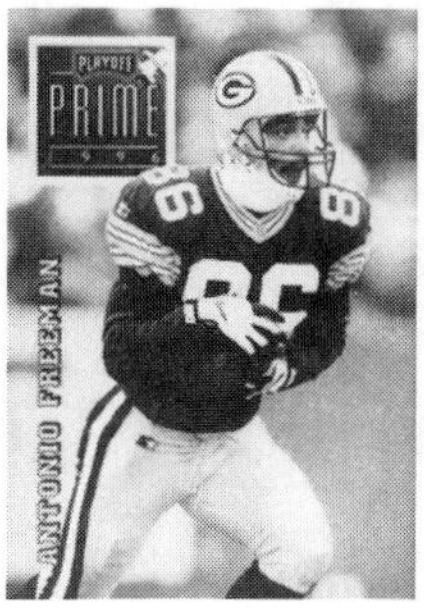

This six-card promo set gave collectors and dealers a sneak peak at the designs for 1996 Playoff Prime. The same six players were featured in 1996 Absolute Promos, but the photos and logos are different.

MT
Complete Set (6): 20.00
Common Player: 1.50
Terrell Davis 7.00
Tamarick Vanover 3.00
Rashaan Salaam 3.00
J.J. Stokes 3.00
Antonio Freeman 3.00
Zack Crockett 1.50

1996 Playoff Prime

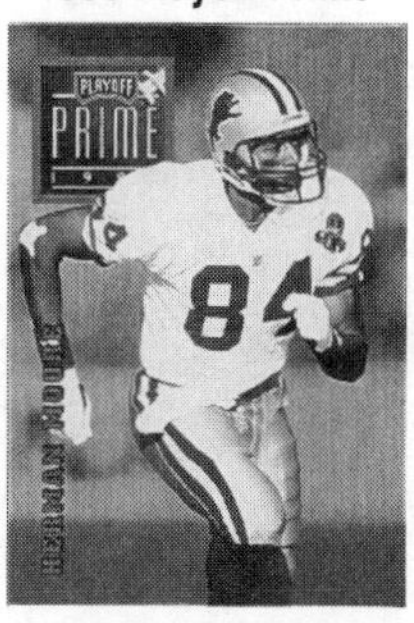

Playoff's 1996 Prime set is its 200-card retail version. The checklist order and card design are different than Prime's Absolute hobby version. Four insert sets are available; Prime Boss Hog is exclusive to Prime retail packs, while Metal XL and Unsung Heroes are in hobby and retail packs, with the retail versions picking up the numbering where the hobby versions ended. 1996 Playoff Prime also continues the pack-within-a-pack concept explained in the 1996 Playoff Absolute set introduction in this book.

MT
Complete Set (200): 200.00
Comp. Bronze Set (100): 10.00
Comp. Silver Set (50): 60.00
Comp. Gold Set (50): 130.00
Common Bronze: .10
Common Silver: .40
Common Gold: 1.00
Pack (6): 2.50
Wax Box (24): 55.00
1 Brett Favre 4.00
2 Jerry Rice 1.50
3 Troy Aikman 1.50
4 Bruce Smith .10
5 Marshall Faulk 1.25
6 Erik Kramer .10
7 Carl Pickens .20
8 Anthony Miller .10
9 Cris Carter .10
10 Todd Kinchen .10
11 Stoney Case .10
12 Chris Calloway .10
13 Andre Rison .10
14 Bill Brooks .10
15 Shawn Jefferson .10
16 Eric Zeier .10
17 Yancey Thigpen .30
18 Edgar Bennett .10
19 Garrison Hearst .20
20 Daryl Johnston .10
21 Tyrone Wheatley .10
22 Darick Holmes .10
23 Dave Brown .10
24 *Leeland McElroy* .30
25 Craig Heyward .10
26 *Kevin Hardy* .30
27 Scott Mitchell .10
28 Willie Green .10
29 Vincent Brisby .10
30 Mike Tomczak .10
31 Luther Ellis .10
32 Mike Pritchard .10
33 Robert Green .10
34 Jeff Graham .10
35 Tamarick Vanover .30
36 William Floyd .10
37 Alvin Harper .10
38 Stan Humphries .10
39 Herman Moore .40
40 Tony Martin .10
41 Jonathan Ogden .10
42 Randall Cunningham .10
43 Chris Warren .20
44 Bobby Hobert .10
45 Jerome Bettis .10
46 Joey Galloway 1.25
47 Ernie Mills .10
48 Steve McNair 1.00
49 *Karim Abdul-Jabbar* 1.00
50 Chad May .10
51 Jim Everett .10
52 Robert Smith .10
53 Tony Boselli .10
54 William Henderson .10
55 *Terry Glenn* 2.50
56 Neil O'Donnell .10
57 Chris Chandler .10
58 Michael Jackson .10
59 *Jason Dunn* .30
60 James Stewart .10
61 Greg Hill .10
62 Mark Carrier .10
63 Bernie Parmalee .10
64 Chris Sanders .30
65 Jeff Hostetler .10
66 *Eric Moulds* 4.00
67 James Jett .10
68 Henry Ellard .10
69 Mario Bates .10
70 Natrone Means .20
71 *Bobby Engram* 1.25
72 Christian Fauria .10
73 Gus Frerotte .10
74 Aaron Hayden .30
75 Reggie White .20
76 Dave Meggett .10
77 Harvey Williams .10
78 Terance Mathis .10
79 Bam Morris .10
80 Trent Dilfer .10
81 Irving Fryar .10
82 Quinn Early .10
83 Lake Dawson .10
84 Todd Collins .10
85 Eric Metcalf .10
86 *Tim Biakabutuka* 1.25
87 Rob Johnson .10
88 Charlie Garner .10
89 Mike Mamula .10
90 Steve Walsh .10
91 Charles Haley .10
92 *Mike Alstott* 2.00
93 Wayne Chrebet .10
94 Vinny Testaverde .10
95 Fred Barnett .10
96 Boomer Esiason .10
97 Zack Crockett .10
98 Kevin Williams .10
99 Eric Bieniemy .10
100 Bryan Cox .10
101 Larry Centers .40
102 Jeff George .75
103 Bryce Paup .40
104 Kerry Collins 1.00
105 Derrick Moore .40
106 Adrian Murrell .40
107 Harold Green .40
108 Ki-Jana Carter .75
109 Sherman Williams .40
110 Deion Sanders 2.50
111 Emmitt Smith 12.00
112 Shannon Sharpe .40
113 Johnnie Morton .40
114 *Eddie Kennison* 1.50
115 *Marvin Harrison* 8.00
116 *Amani Toomer* 1.00
117 *Rickey Dudley* 1.00
118 *Alex Van Dyke* 1.00
119 Dorsey Levens 2.00
120 Antonio Freeman .40
121 Willie Davis .40
122 Lamont Warren .40
123 Sean Dawkins .40
124 Willie Jackson .40
125 Kimble Anders .40
126 Dan Marino 12.00
127 Terry Kirby .40
128 Amp Lee .40
129 Jake Reed .40
130 Curtis Martin 8.00
131 Ray Zellars .40

132	Herschel Walker	.40
133	Mike Sherrard	.40
134	Kyle Brady	.40
135	Raghib Ismail	.40
136	Ricky Watters	.40
137	Kordell Stewart	5.00
138	Andre Hastings	.40
139	Ronnie Harmon	.40
140	Terrell Fletcher	.40
141	J.J. Stokes	3.00
142	Brent Jones	.40
143	Tony McGee	.40
144	Brian Blades	.40
145	Isaac Bruce	.75
146	Erric Rhett	.75
147	Warren Sapp	.40
148	Horace Copeland	.40
149	Heath Shuler	.75
150	Michael Westbrook	.75
151	Frank Sanders	1.00
152	Rob Moore	1.00
153	Bert Emanuel	1.00
154	J.J. Birden	1.00
155	Thurman Thomas	2.00
156	Jim Kelly	2.00
157	Curtis Conway	2.00
158	Darnay Scott	2.00
159	Jeff Blake	2.00
160	Jay Novacek	1.00
161	Michael Irvin	2.00
162	John Elway	15.00
163	Terrell Davis	20.00
164	Barry Sanders	15.00
165	Brett Perriman	1.00
166	*Keyshawn Johnson*	10.00
167	*Eddie George*	14.00
168	*Derrick Mayes*	3.50
169	*Simeon Rice*	2.00
170	*Lawrence Phillips*	5.00
171	Robert Brooks	2.00
172	Mark Chmura	1.50
173	Rodney Thomas	1.00
174	Jim Harbaugh	1.00
175	Ken Dilger	1.00
176	Mark Brunell	10.00
177	Steve Bono	2.00
178	Marcus Allen	2.00
179	O.J. McDuffie	1.00
180	Eric Green	1.00
181	Warren Moon	2.00
182	Drew Bledsoe	12.00
183	Ben Coates	1.00
184	Michael Haynes	1.00
185	Rodney Hampton	1.00
186	Rashaan Salaam	2.00
187	Napoleon Kaufman	1.00
188	Tim Brown	1.00
189	Rodney Peete	1.00
190	Calvin Williams	1.00
191	Erric Pegram	1.00
192	Mark Bruener	1.00
193	Junior Seau	2.00
194	Steve Young	10.00
195	Derek Loville	1.00
196	Rick Mirer	2.00
197	Mark Rypien	1.00
198	Jackie Harris	1.00
199	Tracy Allen	1.00
200	Brian Mitchell	1.00

1996 Playoff Prime Boss Hogs

These cards were exclusive inserts in 1996 Playoff Prime retail packs.

		MT
Complete Set (18):		675.00
Common Player:		15.00
1	Curtis Martin	75.00
2	Chris Warren	15.00
3	Emmitt Smith	100.00
4	Barry Sanders	60.00
5	Rashaan Salaam	30.00
6	Marshall Faulk	40.00
7	Errict Rhett	35.00
8	Thurman Thomas	30.00
9	Kerry Collins	30.00
10	Dan Marino	100.00
11	Jerry Rice	60.00
12	Troy Aikman	60.00
13	Jeff George	15.00
14	Brett Favre	100.00
15	Robert Brooks	15.00
16	John Elway	25.00
17	Deion Sanders	30.00
18	Kordell Stewart	50.00

1996 Playoff Prime X's and O's

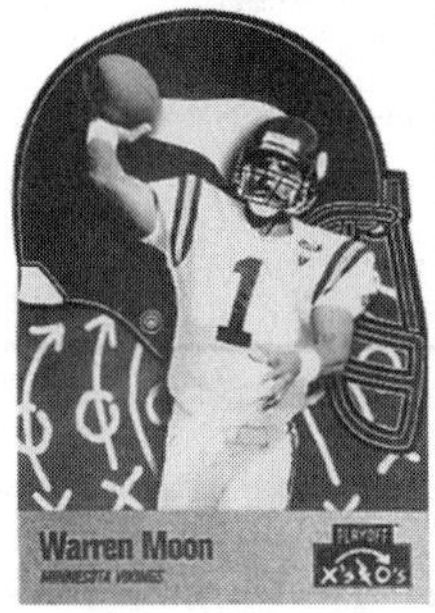

X's & O's is a 200-card parallel set of Prime, and was inserted one per 7.2 packs. It is considered a parallel set since it has an identical checklist to the base set, but X's & O's were printed on a die-cut plastic surface, with the player's team helmet in the background. There is a holographic strip on the bottom that includes the player's name, position and an X's & O's logo.

		MT
Complete Set (200):		850.00
Common Player:		2.00
Minor Stars:		4.00
1	Brett Favre	50.00
2	Jerry Rice	30.00
3	Troy Aikman	25.00
4	Bruce Smith	2.00
5	Marshall Faulk	25.00
6	Erik Kramer	2.00
7	Carl Pickens	4.00
8	Anthony Miller	2.00
9	Cris Carter	4.00
10	Todd Kinchen	2.00
11	Stoney Case	2.00
12	Chris Calloway	2.00
13	Andre Rison	2.00
14	Bill Brooks	2.00
15	Shawn Jefferson	2.00
16	Eric Zeier	2.00
17	Yancey Thigpen	15.00
18	Edgar Bennett	2.00
19	Garrison Hearst	4.00
20	Daryl Johnston	2.00
21	Tyrone Wheatley	2.00
22	Darick Holmes	4.00
23	Dave Brown	2.00
24	Leeland McElroy	10.00
25	Craig Heyward	2.00
26	Kevin Hardy	4.00
27	Scott Mitchell	2.00
28	Willie Green	2.00
29	Vincent Brisby	2.00
30	Mike Tomczak	2.00
31	Luther Ellis	2.00
32	Mike Pritchard	2.00
33	Robert Green	2.00
34	Jeff Graham	2.00
35	Tamarick Vanover	15.00
36	William Floyd	4.00
37	Alvin Harper	2.00
38	Stan Humphries	2.00
39	Herman Moore	15.00
40	Tony Martin	2.00
41	Jonathan Ogden	2.00
42	Randall Cunningham	2.00
43	Chris Warren	4.00
44	Bobby Hobert	2.00
45	Jerome Bettis	4.00
46	Joey Galloway	20.00
47	Ernie Mills	2.00
48	Steve McNair	20.00
49	Karim Abdul-Jabbar	25.00
50	Chad May	2.00
51	Jim Everett	2.00
52	Robert Smith	4.00
53	Tony Boselli	2.00
54	William Henderson	2.00
55	Terry Glenn	30.00
56	Neil O'Donnell	4.00
57	Chris Chandler	2.00
58	Michael Jackson	2.00
59	Jason Dunn	4.00
60	James Stewart	2.00
61	Greg Hill	2.00
62	Mark Carrier	2.00
63	Bernie Parmalee	2.00
64	Chris Sanders	2.00
65	Jeff Hostetler	2.00
66	Eric Moulds	12.00
67	James Jett	2.00
68	Henry Ellard	2.00
69	Mario Bates	2.00
70	Natrone Means	4.00
71	Bobby Engram	12.00
72	Christian Fauria	2.00
73	Gus Frerotte	2.00
74	Aaron Hayden	4.00
75	Reggie White	4.00
76	Dave Meggett	2.00
77	Harvey Williams	2.00
78	Terance Mathis	2.00
79	Bam Morris	2.00
80	Trent Dilfer	2.00
81	Irving Fryar	2.00
82	Quinn Early	2.00
83	Lake Dawson	2.00
84	Todd Collins	2.00
85	Eric Metcalf	2.00
86	Tim Biakabutuka	20.00
87	Rob Johnson	6.00
88	Charlie Garner	2.00
89	Mike Mamula	2.00
90	Steve Walsh	2.00
91	Charles Haley	2.00
92	Mike Alstott	20.00
93	Wayne Chrebet	2.00
94	Vinny Testaverde	2.00
95	Fred Barnett	2.00
96	Boomer Esiason	2.00
97	Zack Crockett	2.00
98	Kevin Williams	2.00
99	Eric Bieniemy	2.00
100	Bryan Cox	2.00
101	Larry Centers	2.00
102	Jeff George	6.00
103	Bryce Paup	2.00
104	Kerry Collins	6.00
105	Derrick Moore	2.00
106	Adrian Murrell	2.00
107	Harold Green	2.00
108	Ki-Jana Carter	6.00
109	Sherman Williams	2.00
110	Deion Sanders	15.00
111	Emmitt Smith	50.00
112	Shannon Sharpe	2.00
113	Johnnie Morton	2.00
114	Eddie Kennison	15.00
115	Marvin Harrison	20.00
116	Amani Toomer	6.00
117	Rickey Dudley	10.00
118	Alex Van Dyke	8.00
119	Dorsey Levens	6.00
120	Antonio Freeman	2.00
121	Willie Davis	2.00
122	Lamont Warren	2.00
123	Sean Dawkins	2.00
124	Willie Jackson	2.00
125	Kimble Anders	2.00
126	Dan Marino	50.00
127	Terry Kirby	2.00
128	Amp Lee	2.00
129	Jake Reed	2.00
130	Curtis Martin	40.00
131	Ray Zellars	2.00
132	Herschel Walker	2.00
133	Mike Sherrard	2.00
134	Kyle Brady	2.00
135	Raghib Ismail	2.00
136	Ricky Watters	4.00
137	Kordell Stewart	25.00
138	Andre Hastings	2.00
139	Ronnie Harmon	2.00
140	Terrell Fletcher	2.00
141	J.J. Stokes	15.00
142	Brent Jones	2.00
143	Tony McGee	2.00
144	Brian Blades	2.00
145	Isaac Bruce	15.00
146	Errict Rhett	15.00
147	Warren Sapp	2.00
148	Horace Copeland	2.00
149	Heath Shuler	4.00
150	Michael Westbrook	15.00
151	Frank Sanders	2.00
152	Rob Moore	2.00
153	Bert Emanuel	2.00
154	J.J. Birden	2.00
155	Thurman Thomas	4.00
156	Jim Kelly	4.00
157	Curtis Conway	4.00
158	Darnay Scott	4.00
159	Jeff Blake	15.00
160	Jay Novacek	2.00
161	Michael Irvin	6.00
162	John Elway	35.00
163	Terrell Davis	60.00
164	Barry Sanders	50.00
165	Brett Perriman	2.00
166	Keyshawn Johnson	20.00
167	Eddie George	40.00
168	Derrick Mayes	10.00
169	Simeon Rice	4.00
170	Lawrence Phillips	6.00
171	Robert Brooks	4.00
172	Mark Chmura	4.00
173	Rodney Thomas	4.00
174	Jim Harbaugh	4.00
175	Ken Dilger	2.00
176	Mark Brunell	25.00
177	Steve Bono	4.00
178	Marcus Allen	4.00
179	O.J. McDuffie	2.00
180	Eric Green	2.00
181	Warren Moon	2.00
182	Drew Bledsoe	30.00
183	Ben Coates	2.00
184	Michael Haynes	2.00
185	Rodney Hampton	2.00
186	Rashaan Salaam	10.00
187	Napoleon Kaufman	6.00
188	Tim Brown	2.00
189	Rodney Peete	2.00
190	Calvin Williams	2.00
191	Erric Pegram	2.00
192	Mark Bruener	2.00
193	Junior Seau	4.00
194	Steve Young	25.00
195	Derek Loville	2.00
196	Rick Mirer	4.00
197	Mark Rypien	2.00
198	Jackie Harris	2.00
199	Terry Allen	2.00
200	Brian Mitchell	2.00

1996 Playoff Prime Surprise

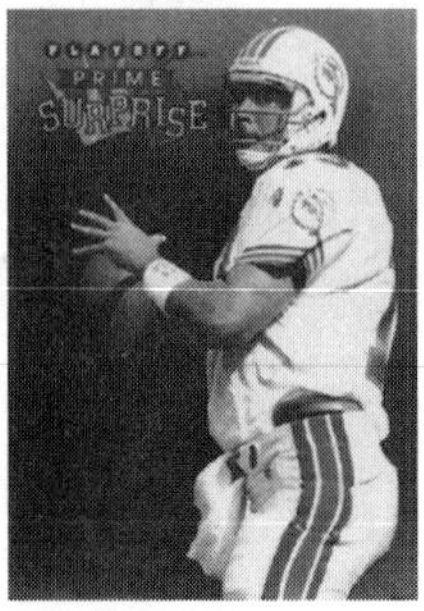

This 14-card set was inserted in Prime at a rate of one in 288 packs.

		MT
Complete Set (14):		375.00
Common Player:		10.00
Minor Stars:		20.00
Inserted 1:288		
1	Dan Marino	50.00
2	Brett Favre	60.00
3	Emmitt Smith	50.00
4	Kordell Stewart	30.00
5	Jerry Rice	30.00
6	Troy Aikman	30.00
7	Barry Sanders	60.00
8	Curtis Martin	25.00
9	Marshall Faulk	20.00
10	Joey Galloway	20.00
11	Robert Brooks	10.00
12	Deion Sanders	25.00
13	Reggie White	10.00
14	Marcus Allen	10.00

1996 Playoff Prime Playoff Honors

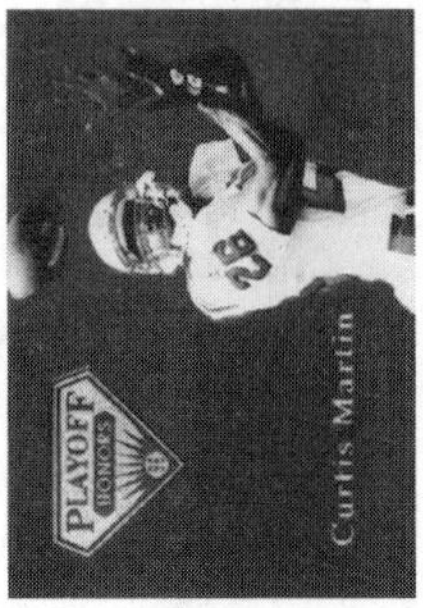

This 1996 Playoff Prime set features three of the NFL's brightest stars - Brett Favre, Emmitt Smith and Curtis Martin. The leather cards are seeded one per 7,200 packs.

		MT
Complete Set (3):		500.00
Common Player:		100.00
Inserted 1:7,200		
1	Emmitt Smith	175.00
2	Curtis Martin	100.00
3	Brett Favre	250.00

1996 Playoff Unsung Heroes Banquet

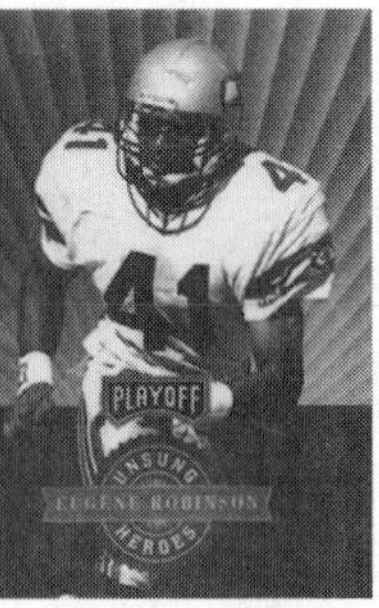

To honor the NFL's Unsung Heroes, Playoff produced this 30-card set which was handed out at the March 8, 1996 NFL Players Award Banquet in Washington, D.C. The card fronts have a color photo of the player over a purple striped background. At the bottom of the front, are "1996," and the Playoff and Unsung Heroes' logos. The card backs have a color photo of the player, his name and why he was named an Unsung Hero. The date of the banquet is also featured at the top of the horizontal card backs.

		MT
Complete Set (30):		20.00
Common Player:		.50
Minor Stars:		1.00
1	Bill Bates	.50
2	Jeff Brady	.50
3	Ray Brown	.50
4	Isaac Bruce	2.00
5	Larry Centers	1.00
6	Mark Chmura	1.00
7	Keith Elias	.50
8	Robert Green	.50
9	Andy Harmon	.50
10	Rodney Holman	.50
11	Derek Loville	1.00
12	J.J. McCleskey	.50
13	Sam Mills	.50
14	Hardy Nickerson	1.00
15	Jessie Tuggle	.50
16	Eric Bieniemy	.50
17	Blaine Bishop	.50
18	Mark Brunell	6.00
19	Wayne Chrebet	2.00
20	Vince Evans	.50
21	Sam Gash	.50
22	Tim Grunhard	.50
23	Jim Harbaugh	1.00
24	Dwayne Harper	.50
25	Bernie Parmalee	.50
26	Reggie Rivers	.50
27	Eugene Robinson	.50
28	Kordell Stewart	5.00
29	Steve Tasker	.50
30	Bennie Thompson	.50

1996 Playoff Contenders Leather

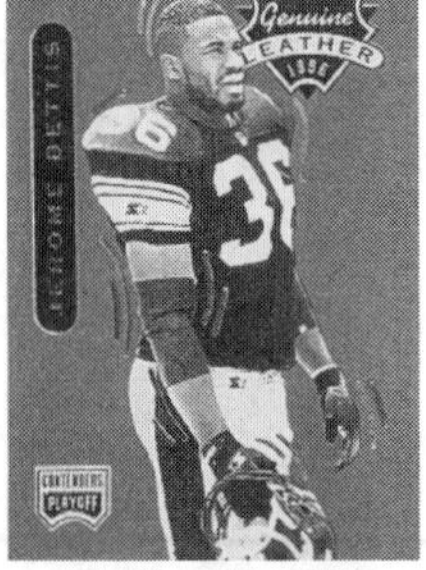

This 100-card base set lives up to its name, with a leather card front. The player's name, which can be printed in green, purple or red, is printed inside a black oval along the left side of the card. The Playoff Contenders' and Genuine Leather logos appear on the front. If the player's name is printed in green foil, it is a "Scarce" card, which was most frequently inserted. Purple foil is a "Rare" card, seeded one per 11 packs. Red foil is "Ultra Rare," and seeded one per 22 packs. The card backs include a full-bleed photo of the player. The card number is printed in the upper right.

		MT
Complete Set (100):		1200.
Common Player:		.75
Pack (3):		6.00
Wax Box (12):		60.00
1	Brett Favre R	100.00
2	Steve Young P	20.00
3	Herman Moore P	5.00
4	Jim Harbaugh P	3.00
5	Curtis Martin R	60.00
6	Junior Seau	.75
7	John Elway R	45.00
8	Troy Aikman R	50.00
9	Terry Allen	.75
10	Kordell Stewart R	50.00
11	Drew Bledsoe R	50.00
12	Jim Kelly R	10.00
13	Dan Marino R	100.00
14	Andre Rison	.75
15	Jeff Hostetler	.75
16	Scott Mitchell	.75
17	Carl Pickens	.75
18	Larry Centers R	5.00
19	Craig Heyward	.75
20	Barry Sanders R	60.00
21	Deion Sanders P	15.00
22	Emmitt Smith R	100.00
23	Rashaan Salaam P	9.00
24	Mario Bates	.75
25	Lawrence Phillips R	10.00
26	Napoleon Kaufman P	7.00
27	Rodney Hampton	.75
28	Marshall Faulk R	20.00
29	Trent Dilfer	.75
30	Leeland McElroy	3.00
31	Marcus Allen	2.00
32	Ricky Watters R	10.00
33	Karim Abdul-Jabbar R	40.00
34	Herschel Walker	.75
35	Thurman Thomas	2.00
36	Jerome Bettis	2.00
37	Gus Frerotte P	3.00
38	Neil O'Donnell P	3.00
39	Rick Mirer	.75
40	Mike Alstott P	15.00
41	Vinny Testaverde P	3.00
42	Derek Loville	.75
43	Ben Coates	.75
44	Steve McNair	6.00
45	Bobby Engram	2.00
46	Yancey Thigpen	.75
47	Lake Dawson	.75
48	Terrell Davis	10.00
49	Kerry Collins P	6.00
50	Eric Metcalf	.75
51	Stanley Pritchett P	3.00
52	Robert Brooks	.75
53	Isaac Bruce R	10.00
54	Tim Brown	.75
55	Edgar Bennett	.75
56	Warren Moon	.75
57	Jerry Rice R	50.00
58	Michael Westbrook	2.00
59	Keyshawn Johnson R	30.00
60	Steve Bono	.75
61	Derrick Mayes	2.00
62	Erik Kramer	.75
63	Rodney Peete	.75
64	Eddie Kennison P	6.00
65	Derrick Thomas	.75
66	Joey Galloway P	15.00
67	Amani Toomer	2.00
68	Reggie White P	7.00
69	Heath Shuler R	7.00
70	Dave Brown R	7.00
71	Tony Banks	6.00
72	Chris Warren R	7.00
73	J.J. Stokes R	8.00
74	Rickey Dudley	3.00
75	Stan Humphries	.75
76	Jason Dunn	.75
77	Tyrone Wheatley P	3.00
78	Jim Everett R	7.00
79	Cris Carter P	3.00
80	Alex Van Dyke	2.00
81	O.J. McDuffie	.75
82	Mark Chmura	.75
83	Terry Glenn	10.00
84	Boomer Esiason	.75
85	Bruce Smith	.75
86	Curtis Conway P	3.00
87	Ki-Jana Carter	2.00
88	Tamarick Vanover	2.00
89	Michael Jackson	.75
90	Mark Brunell P	20.00
91	Tim Biakabutuka P	12.00
92	Anthony Miller P	3.00
93	Marvin Harrison P	15.00
94	Jeff George R	7.00
95	Jeff Blake P	6.00
96	Eddie George R	50.00
97	Eric Moulds	2.00
98	Mike Tomczak P	3.00
99	Chris Sanders P	3.00
100	Chris Chandler	.75

1996 Playoff Contenders Pennants

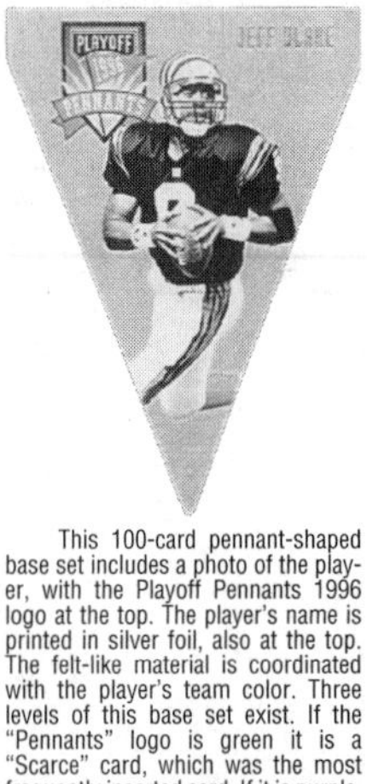

This 100-card pennant-shaped base set includes a photo of the player, with the Playoff Pennants 1996 logo at the top. The player's name is printed in silver foil, also at the top. The felt-like material is coordinated with the player's team color. Three levels of this base set exist. If the "Pennants" logo is green it is a "Scarce" card, which was the most frequently inserted card. If it is purple, it is "Rare" and inserted one per eight packs. If it is red, it is "Ultra Rare" and inserted one per 16 packs. Card backs also have the felt-like surface, with the player's name in a colored bar in the middle.

		MT
Complete Set (100):		800.00
Common Player:		1.00
1	Brett Favre R	90.00
2	Steve Young R	40.00
3	Herman Moore R	10.00
4	Jim Harbaugh R	6.00
5	Curtis Martin R	40.00
6	Junior Seau	1.00
7	John Elway R	35.00
8	Troy Aikman P	20.00
9	Terry Allen	1.00
10	Kordell Stewart R	40.00
11	Drew Bledsoe	10.00
12	Jim Kelly P	6.00
13	Dan Marino P	40.00
14	Andre Rison	1.00
15	Jeff Hostetler	1.00
16	Scott Mitchell	1.00
17	Carl Pickens R	6.00
18	Larry Centers P	3.00
19	Craig Heyward	1.00
20	Barry Sanders P	20.00
21	Deion Sanders R	20.00
22	Emmitt Smith R	90.00
23	Rashaan Salaam R	10.00
24	Mario Bates	1.00
25	Lawrence Phillips	5.00
26	Napoleon Kaufman	1.00
27	Rodney Hampton	1.00
28	Marshall Faulk P	10.00
29	Trent Dilfer	1.00
30	Leeland McElroy P	5.00
31	Marcus Allen P	6.00
32	Ricky Watters	2.00
33	Karim Abdul-Jabbar	4.00
34	Herschel Walker P	3.00
35	Thurman Thomas R	10.00
36	Jerome Bettis P	6.00
37	Gus Frerotte	1.00
38	Neil O'Donnell	1.00
39	Rick Mirer	1.00
40	Mike Alstott R	20.00
41	Vinny Testaverde R	6.00
42	Derek Loville	1.00
43	Ben Coates	1.00
44	Steve McNair R	25.00
45	Bobby Engram P	6.00
46	Yancey Thigpen	1.00
47	Lake Dawson	1.00
48	Terrell Davis P	40.00
49	Kerry Collins R	10.00
50	Eric Metcalf	1.00
51	Stanley Pritchett R	6.00
52	Robert Brooks R	6.00
53	Isaac Bruce	3.00
54	Tim Brown	1.00
55	Edgar Bennett P	3.00
56	Warren Moon	1.00
57	Jerry Rice R	40.00
58	Michael Westbrook	2.00
59	Keyshawn Johnson	5.00
60	Steve Bono R	6.00
61	Derrick Mayes P	6.00
62	Erik Kramer P	3.00
63	Rodney Peete	1.00
64	Eddie Kennison	6.00
65	Derrick Thomas	1.00
66	Joey Galloway R	15.00
67	Amani Toomer P	6.00
68	Reggie White	2.00
69	Heath Shuler	1.00
70	Dave Brown	1.00
71	Tony Banks P	8.00
72	Chris Warren	1.00
73	J.J. Stokes	2.00
74	Rickey Dudley P	7.00
75	Stan Humphries	1.00
76	Jason Dunn P	3.00
77	Tyrone Wheatley	1.00
78	Jim Everett	1.00
79	Cris Carter P	3.00
80	Alex Van Dyke P	6.00
81	O.J. McDuffie	1.00
82	Mark Chmura P	3.00
83	Terry Glenn P	20.00
84	Boomer Esiason R	6.00
85	Bruce Smith	1.00
86	Curtis Conway	1.00
87	Ki-Jana Carter	2.00
88	Tamarick Vanover	2.00
89	Michael Jackson	1.00
90	Mark Brunell	10.00
91	Tim Biakabutuka R	25.00
92	Anthony Miller	1.00
93	Marvin Harrison R	20.00
94	Jeff George P	3.00
95	Jeff Blake R	10.00
96	Eddie George	12.00
97	Eric Moulds P	10.00
98	Mike Tomczak	1.00
99	Chris Sanders	1.00
100	Chris Chandler	1.00

1996 Playoff Contenders Open Field

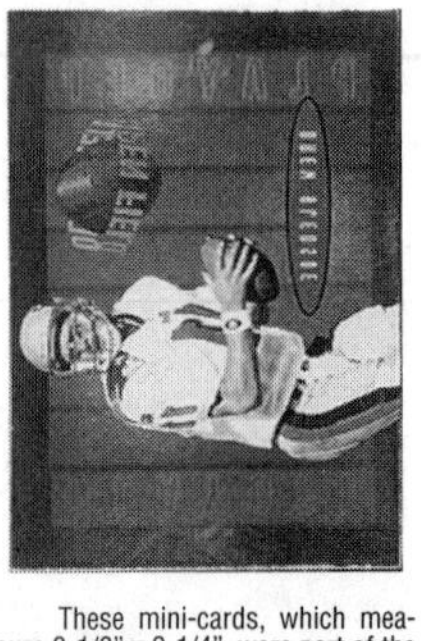

These mini-cards, which measure 3-1/8" x 2-1/4", were part of the Contenders base set. A color photo of

the player is showcased, with a holographic background of a football field. The Open Field logo also is included in the hologram. Three levels of this base set exist. The "Scarce" cards, which have the player's name in a green oval, are the most frequently inserted. The "Rare" cards have the oval in purple and were inserted one per five packs. The "Ultra Rare" cards have the oval in red and are seeded one per nine packs. Card backs have a photo on the left, with a "Playoff The Wall Fact" on the right.

		MT
Complete Set (100):		400.00
Common Player:		.75
1	Brett Favre P	20.00
2	Steve Young R	15.00
3	Herman Moore P	4.00
4	Jim Harbaugh	.75
5	Curtis Martin P	15.00
6	Junior Seau P	2.00
7	John Elway P	10.00
8	Troy Aikman R	18.00
9	Terry Allen	.75
10	Kordell Stewart P	12.00
11	Drew Bledsoe	6.00
12	Jim Kelly	2.00
13	Dan Marino R	35.00
14	Andre Rison P	2.00
15	Jeff Hostetler	.75
16	Scott Mitchell R	3.00
17	Carl Pickens	.75
18	Larry Centers	.75
19	Craig Heyward R	3.00
20	Barry Sanders R	20.00
21	Deion Sanders P	8.00
22	Emmitt Smith P	20.00
23	Rashaan Salaam R	6.00
24	Mario Bates P	2.00
25	Lawrence Phillips P	3.00
26	Napoleon Kaufman	.75
27	Rodney Hampton	.75
28	Marshall Faulk R	10.00
29	Trent Dilfer	.75
30	Leeland McElroy R	6.00
31	Marcus Allen	2.00
32	Ricky Watters P	4.00
33	Karim Abdul-Jabbar P	15.00
34	Herschel Walker R	3.00
35	Thurman Thomas	2.00
36	Jerome Bettis	2.00
37	Gus Frerotte R	3.00
38	Neil O'Donnell	.75
39	Rick Mirer	.75
40	Mike Alstott	3.00
41	Vinny Testaverde	.75
42	Derek Loville	.75
43	Ben Coates	.75
44	Steve McNair	3.00
45	Bobby Engram R	6.00
46	Yancey Thigpen	.75
47	Lake Dawson P	2.00
48	Terrell Davis	8.00
49	Kerry Collins P	4.00
50	Eric Metcalf	.75
51	Stanley Pritchett	.75
52	Robert Brooks P	2.00
53	Isaac Bruce P	3.00
54	Tim Brown P	2.00
55	Edgar Bennett	.75
56	Warren Moon P	2.00
57	Jerry Rice P	15.00
58	Michael Westbrook	2.00
59	Keyshawn Johnson P	8.00
60	Steve Bono	.75
61	Derrick Mayes R	6.00
62	Erik Kramer	.75
63	Rodney Peete	.75
64	Eddie Kennison	4.00
65	Derrick Thomas	.75
66	Joey Galloway R	10.00
67	Amani Toomer R	6.00
68	Reggie White R	6.00
69	Heath Shuler P	2.00
70	Dave Brown	.75
71	Tony Banks R	6.00
72	Chris Warren	.75
73	J.J. Stokes	2.00
74	Rickey Dudley R	6.00
75	Stan Humphries	.75
76	Jason Dunn R	3.00
77	Tyrone Wheatley	.75
78	Jim Everett	.75
79	Cris Carter	.75
80	Alex Van Dyke R	6.00
81	O.J. McDuffie P	2.00
82	Mark Chmura	.75
83	Terry Glenn R	25.00
84	Boomer Esiason	.75
85	Bruce Smith	.75
86	Curtis Conway	.75
87	Ki-Jana Carter R	6.00
88	Tamarick Vanover P	4.00
89	Michael Jackson R	3.00
90	Mark Brunell	6.00
91	Tim Biakabutuka	4.00
92	Anthony Miller	.75
93	Marvin Harrison	4.00
94	Jeff George	.75
95	Jeff Blake	4.00
96	Eddie George P	20.00
97	Eric Moulds R	12.00
98	Mike Tomczak R	3.00
99	Chris Sanders	.75
100	Chris Chandler	.75

1996 Playoff Contenders Leather Accents

The difference between Genuine Leather and Genuine Leather Accents parallel set is Accents has the Genuine Leather and Playoff Contenders' logo and name oval in teal foil. Different scarcities also exist with the green, purple and red foils on the player's names. The card backs have a full-bleed photo, with the card number in the upper right. "Accent" is printed in teal foil in the lower center on the card back. One card was seeded per 216 packs.

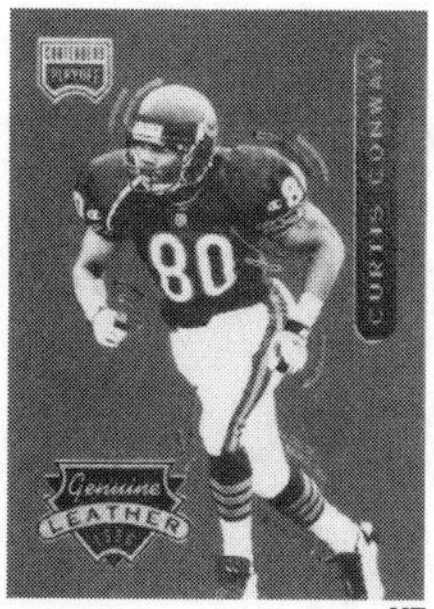

		MT
Common Player:		10.00
Minor Stars:		20.00
1	Brett Favre	125.00
2	Steve Young	50.00
3	Herman Moore	20.00
4	Jim Harbaugh	10.00
5	Curtis Martin	40.00
6	Junior Seau	20.00
7	John Elway	100.00
8	Troy Aikman	60.00
9	Terry Allen	10.00
10	Kordell Stewart	50.00
11	Drew Bledsoe	60.00
12	Jim Kelly	20.00
13	Dan Marino	100.00
14	Andre Rison	10.00
15	Jeff Hostetler	10.00
16	Scott Mitchell	10.00
17	Carl Pickens	20.00
18	Larry Centers	10.00
19	Craig Heyward	10.00
20	Barry Sanders	125.00
21	Deion Sanders	40.00
22	Emmitt Smith	100.00
23	Rashaan Salaam	20.00
24	Mario Bates	10.00
25	Lawrence Phillips	20.00
26	Napoleon Kaufman	20.00
27	Rodney Hampton	10.00
28	Marshall Faulk	30.00
29	Trent Dilfer	20.00
30	Leeland McElroy	10.00
31	Marcus Allen	20.00
32	Ricky Watters	20.00
33	Karim Abdul-Jabbar	20.00
34	Herschel Walker	10.00
35	Thurman Thomas	20.00
36	Jerome Bettis	20.00
37	Gus Frerotte	10.00
38	Neil O'Donnell	10.00
39	Rick Mirer	10.00
40	Mike Alstott	25.00
41	Vinny Testaverde	20.00
42	Derek Loville	10.00
43	Ben Coates	20.00
44	Steve McNair	40.00
45	Bobby Engram	10.00
46	Yancey Thigpen	10.00
47	Lake Dawson	10.00
48	Terrell Davis	100.00
49	Kerry Collins	20.00
50	Eric Metcalf	10.00
51	Stanley Pritchett	10.00
52	Robert Brooks	10.00
53	Isaac Bruce	25.00
54	Tim Brown	20.00
55	Edgar Bennett	10.00
56	Warren Moon	20.00
57	Jerry Rice	60.00
58	Michael Westbrook	20.00
59	Keyshawn Johnson	40.00
60	Steve Bono	10.00
61	Derrick Mayes	20.00
62	Erik Kramer	10.00
63	Rodney Peete	10.00
64	Eddie Kennison	10.00
65	Derrick Thomas	20.00
66	Joey Galloway	30.00
67	Amani Toomer	10.00
68	Reggie White	20.00
69	Heath Shuler	10.00
70	Dave Brown	10.00
71	Tony Banks	20.00
72	Chris Warren	10.00
73	J.J. Stokes	20.00
74	Rickey Dudley	10.00
75	Stan Humphries	10.00
76	Jason Dunn	10.00
77	Tyrone Wheatley	20.00
78	Jim Everett	10.00
79	Cris Carter	20.00
80	Alex Van Dyke	10.00
81	O.J. McDuffie	10.00
82	Mark Chmura	10.00
83	Terry Glenn	25.00
84	Boomer Esiason	10.00
85	Bruce Smith	10.00
86	Curtis Conway	10.00
87	Ki-Jana Carter	10.00
88	Tamarick Vanover	10.00
89	Michael Jackson	10.00
90	Mark Brunell	60.00
91	Tim Biakabutuka	20.00
92	Anthony Miller	10.00
93	Marvin Harrison	40.00
94	Jeff George	20.00
95	Jeff Blake	10.00
96	Eddie George	50.00
97	Eric Moulds	20.00
98	Mike Tomczak	10.00
99	Chris Sanders	10.00
100	Chris Chandler	10.00

1996 Playoff Contenders Ground Hogs

This insert set, which was seeded one per 44 packs, featured a leather front. A rainbow foil "swoosh" follows behind the player. The Ground Hogs logo appears in one of the lower corners. The player's name is in gold foil at the top of the card. The card back has the Playoff Contenders' logo in the upper left and the card number, prefixed by "GH," in the upper right. A color photo of the player is featured on the back, with the running back in focus and the background blurry.

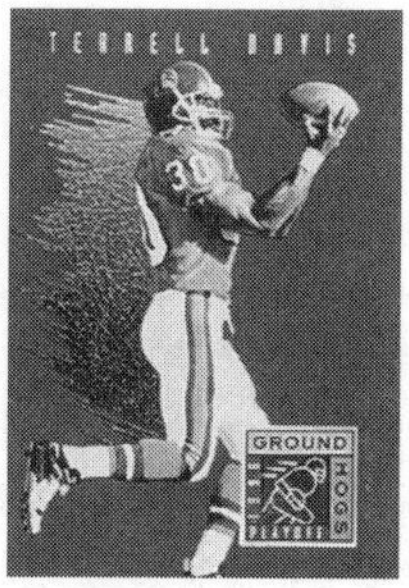

		MT
Complete Set (8):		160.00
Common Player:		15.00
1	Emmitt Smith	30.00
2	Barry Sanders	40.00
3	Marshall Faulk	20.00
4	Curtis Martin	20.00
5	Chris Warren	15.00
6	Ricky Watters	15.00
7	Thurman Thomas	15.00
8	Terrell Davis	30.00

1996 Playoff Contenders Pennant Flyers

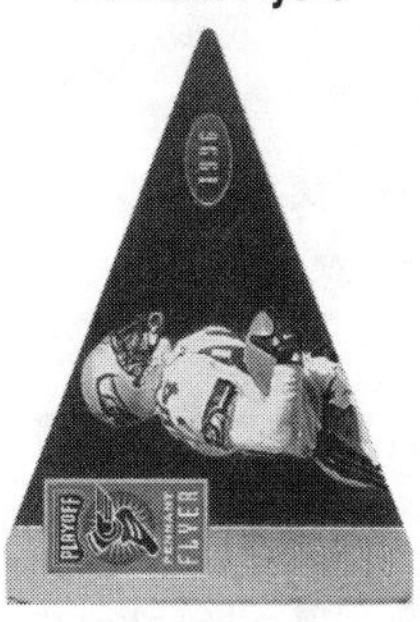

This pennant-shaped insert set includes a felt-like surface on the right, with the player's last name embossed on the left in a gold-foil bar along the left border. The Playoff Pennant Flyer logo is pictured on the front, with "1996" embossed in a gold-foil oval. The player's team's main color is used for the felt on the front and back. The card backs include the player's full name embossed in the gold-foil band, team logo inside a circle and a gold-foil embossed Playoff Contenders' logo. These were seeded one per 48 packs. The card numbers are prefixed with "PF."

		MT
Complete Set (8):		125.00
Common Player:		10.00
1	Jerry Rice	45.00
2	Joey Galloway	15.00
3	Isaac Bruce	15.00
4	Herman Moore	15.00
5	Carl Pickens	10.00
6	Yancey Thigpen	10.00
7	Deion Sanders	20.00
8	Robert Brooks	10.00

1996 Playoff Contenders Air Command

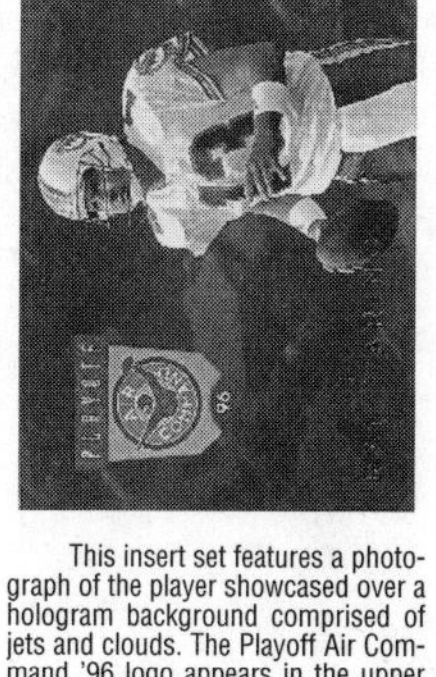

This insert set features a photograph of the player showcased over a hologram background comprised of jets and clouds. The Playoff Air Command '96 logo appears in the upper left. The player's name is printed in gold foil in the lower left. The card back has a silver and blue etched-foil background and a color photo of the player. The Playoff Contenders logo is in the upper left, with the card number, prefixed by "AC," in the upper right. Each card measures 3-1/8" x 2-1/4". The cards were inserted one per 96 packs.

		MT
Complete Set (8):		125.00
Common Player:		10.00
1	Dan Marino	25.00
2	Brett Favre	35.00
3	Troy Aikman	20.00
4	Mike Tomczak	10.00
5	John Elway	25.00
6	Jeff George	15.00
7	Chris Chandler	10.00
8	Steve Bono	10.00

1996 Playoff Contenders Honors

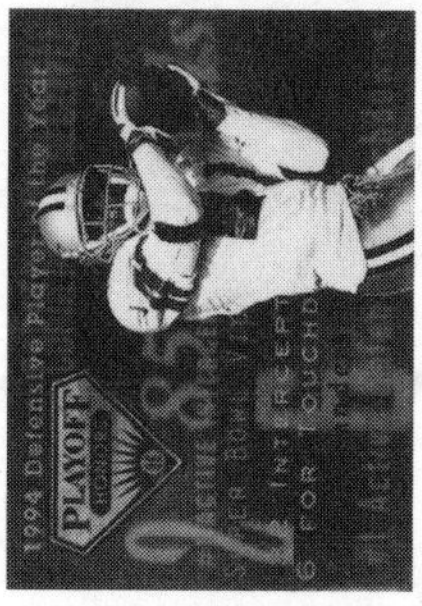

A continuation from Prime, this insert set had a new design that featured the Playoff Honors' logo and player's name in teal foil on the front of the card. The holographic background includes the various achievements of the player. The card back has a full-bleed photo of the player. The card numbers, prefixed by a "PH," are in the upper right. One card was seeded per 7,200 packs.

		MT
Complete Set (3):		500.00
Common Player:		50.00
4	Dan Marino	200.00
5	Deion Sanders	50.00
6	Marcus Allen	50.00

1996 Playoff Illusions

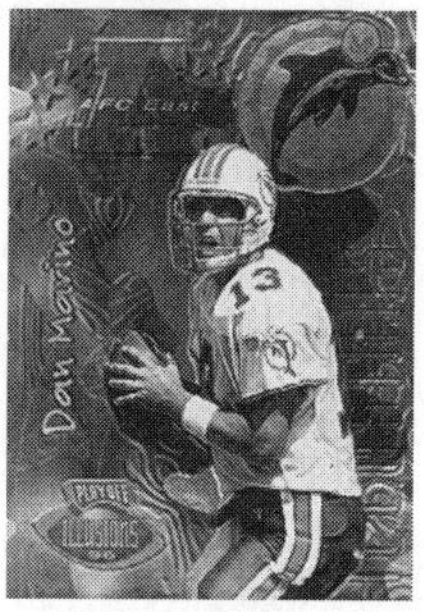

The 120-card set's base cards are printed in different color schemes and graphics. The set features six different designs, each representing the six NFL divisions, as well as two levels of insertions. Cards #s 1-63 appeared approximately 3.5 cards per pack, while card #s 64-120 were found approximately one card per pack.

		MT
Complete Set (120):		125.00
Common Player (1-63):		.25
Common Player (64-120):		.50
Pack (5):		2.50
Wax Box (24):		55.00
1	Troy Aikman	2.00
2	Larry Centers	.25
3	Terance Mathis	.25
4	Calvin Williams	.25
5	Jim Kelly	.25
6	*Tim Biakabutuka*	1.50
7	Rashaan Salaam	.75
8	Ki-Jana Carter	.50
9	Anthony Miller	.25
10	Deion Sanders	1.25
11	Scott Mitchell	.25
12	Robert Brooks	.25
13	Willie Davis	.25
14	Zack Crockett	.25
15	James Stewart	.25
16	Tamarick Vanover	.75
17	Stanley Pritchett	.25
18	Warren Moon	.25
19	Shawn Jefferson	.25
20	Shannon Sharpe	.25
21	Jim Everett	.25
22	Dave Brown	.25
23	Adrian Murrell	.25
24	*Rickey Dudley*	.75
25	Chris T. Jones	.25
26	Andre Hastings	.25
27	Stan Humphries	.25
28	Steve Young	1.50
29	Joey Galloway	1.50
30	Jim Harbaugh	.25
31	*Eddie Kennison*	1.00
32	*Mike Alstott*	2.50
33	Michael Westbrook	.50
34	*Leeland McElroy*	.75
35	Erik Kramer	.25
36	Mark Chmura	.25
37	Cris Carter	.25
38	Ben Coates	.25
39	Wayne Chrebet	.25
40	Jerome Bettis	.50
41	Tim Brown	.25
42	Jason Dunn	.25
43	William Henderson	.25
44	Rick Mirer	.25
45	J.J. Stokes	.50
46	Rodney Peete	.25
47	Neil O'Donnell	.25
48	Tyrone Wheatley	.25
49	*Terry Glenn*	2.50
50	Junior Seau	.25
51	Jake Reed	.25
52	O.J. McDuffie	.25
53	Steve Bono	.25
54	Steve McNair	2.00
55	Antonio Freeman	.50
56	Johnnie Morton	.25
57	Eric Metcalf	.25
58	Andre Reed	.25
59	*Bobby Engram*	1.00
60	Gus Frerotte	.25
61	Jeff Blake	.75
62	Erric Pegram	.25
63	Jeff Hostetler	.25
64	Edgar Bennett	.50
65	*Eddie George*	10.00
66	*Marvin Harrison*	7.00
67	LeShon Johnson	.50
68	*Jamal Anderson*	10.00
69	Thurman Thomas	1.00
70	Barry Sanders	5.00
71	*Muhsin Muhammad*	4.00
72	Robert Green	.50
73	Garrison Hearst	.50
74	John Elway	4.00
75	Herman Moore	1.00
76	Chris Chandler	.50
77	Marshall Faulk	1.50
78	Mark Brunell	4.00
79	*Tony Banks*	3.00
80	Terrell Davis	8.00
81	Marcus Allen	1.00
82	Dan Marino	10.00
83	Robert Smith	.50
84	Curtis Martin	7.00
85	*Amani Toomer*	1.00
86	Napoleon Kaufman	.50
87	Ricky Watters	.50
88	Kordell Stewart	5.00
89	*Keyshawn Johnson*	6.00
90	Emmitt Smith	10.00
91	Chris Warren	.50
92	Isaac Bruce	1.50
93	Terry Allen	.50
94	Trent Dilfer	.50
95	Vinny Testaverde	.50
96	Bruce Smith	.50
97	Kerry Collins	2.00
98	Curtis Conway	.50
99	*Karim Abdul-Jabbar*	2.00
100	Brett Favre	10.00
101	Carl Pickens	.50
102	Brett Perriman	.50
103	Keith Jackson	.50
104	Drew Bledsoe	5.00
105	Rodney Hampton	.50
106	Ray Zellars	.50
107	Jeff Graham	.50
108	Irving Fryar	.50
109	*Lawrence Phillips*	2.00
110	Jerry Rice	5.00
111	Mike Tomczak	.50
112	Tony Martin	.50
113	Brian Blades	.50
114	Bill Brooks	.50
115	Rob Moore	.50
116	Quinn Early	.50
117	Darnay Scott	.50
118	Ken Dilger	.50
119	Derek Loville	.50
120	Reggie White	1.00

1996 Playoff Illusions Spectralusion Elite

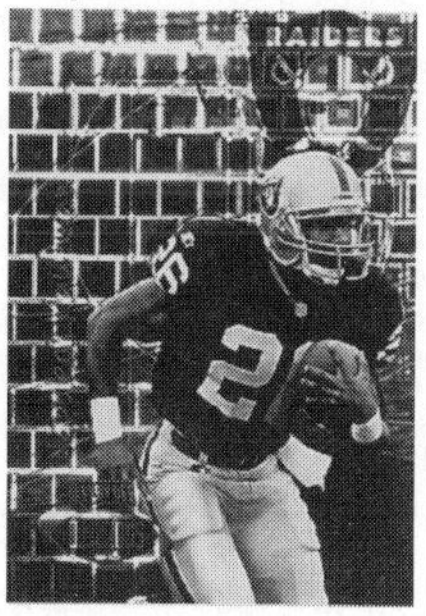

This 120-card parallel set utilizes Illusion printing technology and silver holographic foil background. It is one of four different parallel sets associated with the Illusion product, and is the easiest to get with a one per five packs insertion rate.

		MT
Complete Set (120):		300.00
Common Player:		1.00
Spectralusion Dominion:		10x-20x
Complete XXXI Set (120):		600.00
XXXI Cards:		2x
XXXI Spectralusion Dominion:		6x-12x
1	Troy Aikman	10.00
2	Larry Centers	1.00
3	Terance Mathis	1.00
4	Calvin Williams	1.00
5	Jim Kelly	2.00
6	Tim Biakabutuka	4.00
7	Rashaan Salaam	2.00
8	Ki-Jana Carter	2.00
9	Anthony Miller	1.00
10	Deion Sanders	7.00
11	Scott Mitchell	1.00
12	Robert Brooks	1.00
13	Willie Davis	1.00
14	Zack Crockett	1.00
15	James Stewart	1.00
16	Tamarick Vanover	5.00
17	Stanley Pritchett	1.00
18	Warren Moon	1.00
19	Shawn Jefferson	1.00
20	Shannon Sharpe	1.00
21	Jim Everett	1.00
22	Dave Brown	1.00
23	Adrian Murrell	1.00
24	Rickey Dudley	4.00
25	Chris T. Jones	1.00
26	Andre Hastings	1.00
27	Stan Humphries	1.00
28	Steve Young	8.00
29	Joey Galloway	7.00
30	Jim Harbaugh	1.00
31	Eddie Kennison	6.00
32	Mike Alstott	8.00
33	Michael Westbrook	2.00
34	Leeland McElroy	2.00
35	Erik Kramer	1.00
36	Mark Chmura	1.00
37	Cris Carter	1.00
38	Ben Coates	1.00
39	Wayne Chrebet	1.00
40	Jerome Bettis	2.00
41	Tim Brown	1.00
42	Jason Dunn	1.00
43	William Henderson	1.00
44	Rick Mirer	1.00
45	J.J. Stokes	2.00
46	Rodney Peete	1.00
47	Neil O'Donnell	1.00
48	Tyrone Wheatley	1.00
49	Terry Glenn	12.00
50	Junior Seau	1.00
51	Jake Reed	1.00
52	O.J. McDuffie	1.00
53	Steve Bono	1.00
54	Steve McNair	5.00
55	Antonio Freeman	1.00
56	Johnnie Morton	1.00
57	Eric Metcalf	1.00
58	Andre Reed	1.00
59	Bobby Engram	4.00
60	Gus Frerotte	1.00
61	Jeff Blake	4.00
62	Erric Pegram	1.00
63	Jeff Hostetler	1.00
64	Edgar Bennett	1.00
65	Eddie George	12.00
66	Marvin Harrison	8.00
67	LeShon Johnson	1.00
68	Jamal Anderson	20.00
69	Thurman Thomas	2.00
70	Barry Sanders	12.00
71	Muhsin Muhammad	2.00
72	Robert Green	1.00
73	Garrison Hearst	1.00
74	John Elway	7.00
75	Herman Moore	3.00
76	Chris Chandler	1.00
77	Marshall Faulk	4.00
78	Mark Brunell	6.00
79	Tony Banks	5.00
80	Terrell Davis	20.00
81	Marcus Allen	2.00
82	Dan Marino	20.00
83	Robert Smith	1.00
84	Curtis Martin	12.00
85	Amani Toomer	2.00
86	Napoleon Kaufman	8.00
87	Ricky Watters	2.00
88	Kordell Stewart	10.00
89	Keyshawn Johnson	8.00
90	Emmitt Smith	20.00
91	Chris Warren	1.00
92	Isaac Bruce	5.00
93	Terry Allen	1.00
94	Trent Dilfer	1.00
95	Vinny Testaverde	1.00
96	Bruce Smith	1.00
97	Kerry Collins	3.00
98	Curtis Conway	1.00
99	Karim Abdul-Jabbar	10.00
100	Brett Favre	20.00
101	Carl Pickens	1.00
102	Brett Perriman	1.00
103	Keith Jackson	1.00
104	Drew Bledsoe	10.00
105	Rodney Hampton	1.00
106	Ray Zellars	1.00
107	Jeff Graham	1.00
108	Irving Fryar	1.00
109	Lawrence Phillips	2.00
110	Jerry Rice	10.00
111	Mike Tomczak	1.00
112	Tony Martin	1.00
113	Brian Blades	1.00
114	Bill Brooks	1.00
115	Rob Moore	1.00
116	Quinn Early	1.00
117	Darnay Scott	1.00
118	Ken Dilger	1.00
119	Derek Loville	1.00
120	Reggie White	2.00

1996 Playoff Illusions Spectralusion Dominion

Spectralusion Dominion was a 120-card parallel set that utilized Illusion printing technology and a gold holographic foil background. These parallel cards were inserted every 192 packs.

	MT
Spec. Dominion Cards:	10x-20x

1996 Playoff Illusions XXXI

XXXI reprints all 120 cards in the base set in a die-cut, parallel that features the Roman numerals XXXI across the top of the card. This parallel set is inserted at a rate of one per 12 packs. These cards are also featured in a more difficult gold holographic parallel called Spectralusion Dominion.

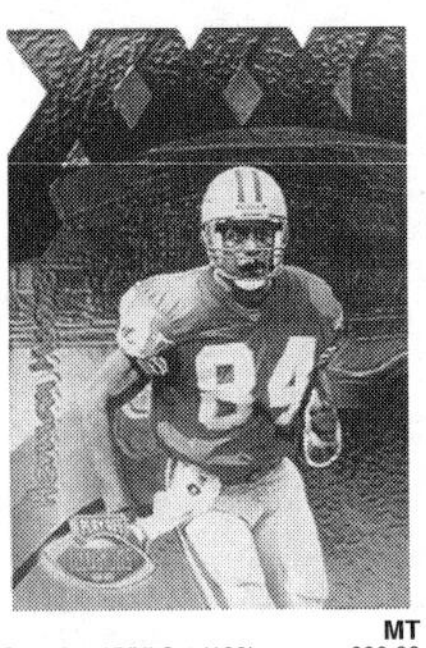

	MT
Complete XXXI Set (120):	600.00
XXXI Cards:	2x

1996 Playoff Illusions XXXI Spectralusion Dominion

XXXI Spectralusion Dominion reprints the die-cut XXXI cards and adds a gold holographic background. These parallel cards are found in every 96 packs.

	MT
XXXI Spec. Dominion:	6x-12x

1996 Playoff Illusions Optical Illusions

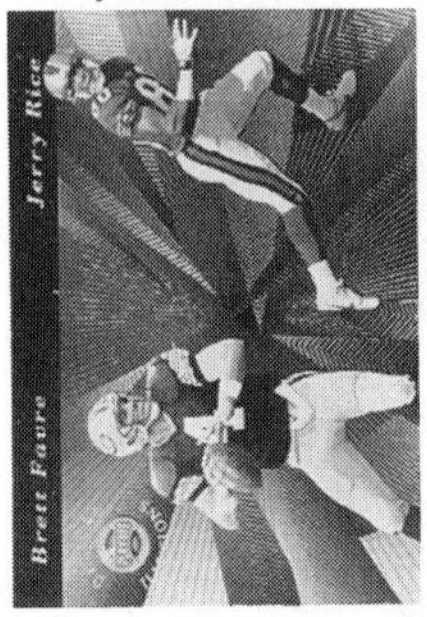

This 18-card chase set, found one per 96 packs, featured Troy Aikman handing off to Barry Sanders and Brett Favre passing to Jerry Rice.

		MT
Complete Set (18):		800.00
Common Player:		15.00
1	Brett Favre, Jerry Rice	150.00
2	Troy Aikman, Barry Sanders	120.00
3	Dan Marino, Emmitt Smith	175.00
4	Warren Moon, Carl Pickens	15.00
5	John Elway, Herman Moore	60.00
6	Steve Young, Anthony Miller	60.00
7	Jim Harbaugh, Terrell Davis	60.00
8	Kordell Stewart, Kordell Stewart	70.00
9	Deion Sanders, Deion Sanders	50.00
10	Kerry Collins, Curtis Martin	90.00
11	Scott Mitchell, Robert Brooks	15.00
12	Jeff Blake, Tony Martin	25.00
13	Mark Brunell, Marshall Faulk	50.00
14	Drew Bledsoe, Jerome Bettis	70.00
15	Gus Frerotte, Karim Abdul-Jabbar	40.00
16	Steve Bono, Ricky Watters	15.00
17	Chris Chandler, Terry Allen	15.00
18	Tony Banks, Keyshawn Johnson	40.00

1996 Playoff Trophy Contenders

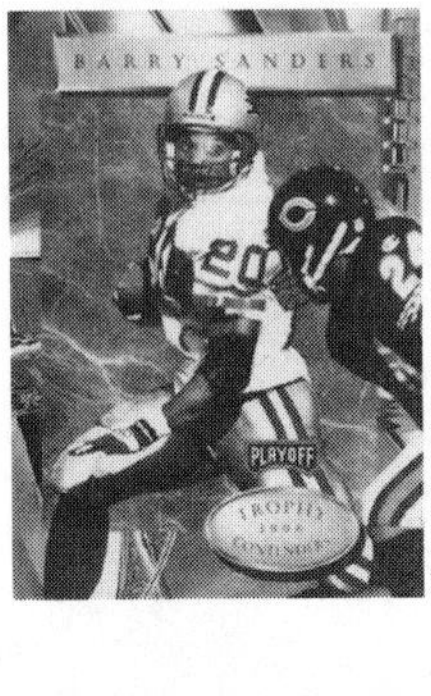

Playoff Trophy Contenders' regular 1996 football set puts a cap on the 1995 NFL season by highlighting members of the two teams in the Super Bowl - the Pittsburgh Steelers and Dallas Cowboys. Each regular card front has the player's name in a bar at the top. An action photo is in the center of the card; the Playoff and insert set logos are toward the bottom. The back has a color photo of the player, with the player's name and team at the top. A brief player profile and 1995 statistics are also included. The Steelers and Cowboys are featured in a 60-card mini parallel set called Back-to-Back. The first 11 cards in the set have an opposing player from each team on different card sides. Rookie Stallions and Playoff Zone cards are also included as inserts in packs, as are special cards redeemable for Wilson commemorative Super Bowl XXX footballs.

		MT
Complete Set (120):		26.00
Common Player:		.10
Minor Stars:		.20
Pack (6):		3.00
Wax Box (24):		55.00
1	Brett Favre	3.00
2	Troy Aikman	1.50
3	Dan Marino	3.00
4	Emmitt Smith	3.00
5	Marshall Faulk	1.50
6	Jeff Blake	1.00
7	John Elway	1.00
8	Steve Young	1.50
9	Curtis Martin	4.00
10	Kordell Stewart	2.50
11	Drew Bledsoe	1.50
12	Jim Kelly	.20
13	Steve Bono	.20
14	Neil O'Donnell	.20
15	Jeff Hostetler	.10
16	Jim Harbaugh	.10
17	Jim Everett	.10
18	Erric Pegram	.10
19	Tyrone Wheatley	.20
20	Barry Sanders	1.50
21	Deion Sanders	1.00
22	Harvey Williams	.10
23	Garrison Hearst	.20
24	*Aaron Hayden*	1.00
25	Dorsey Levens	.30
26	Napoleon Kaufman	.50
27	Rodney Hampton	.10
28	Scott Mitchell	.10
29	Greg Hill	.10
30	Charlie Garner	.10
31	Rashaan Salaam	1.00
32	Errict Rhett	1.00
33	Bam Morris	.20
34	Edgar Bennett	.10
35	Jeff George	.10
36	Rodney Peete	.10
37	Stan Humphries	.10
38	Kimble Anders	.10
39	Natrone Means	.25
40	Sherman Williams	.10
41	Eric Metcalf	.10
42	Chris Warren	.10
43	Marcus Allen	.10
44	Bill Brooks	.10
45	Wayne Chrebet	.10
46	Irving Fryar	.10
47	Tony Martin	.10
48	Daryl Johnston	.10
49	O.J. McDuffie	.10
50	Frank Sanders	.50
51	Ken Norton	.10
52	Jake Reed	.10
53	Bert Emanuel	.10
54	Floyd Turner	.10
55	Junior Seau	.10
56	Ernie Mills	.10
57	Mark Pike	.10
58	Warren Moon	.10
59	Mike Mamula	.10
60	Kerry Collins	.50
61	Nate Newton	.10
62	Terry Allen	.10
63	Bernie Parmalee	.10
64	James Stewart	.10
65	Isaac Bruce	1.00
66	Lake Dawson	.10
67	Terance Mathis	.10
68	Chris Sanders	.50
69	Anthony Miller	.10
70	Jay Novacek	.10
71	Sean Dawkins	.10
72	J.J. Birden	.10
73	Calvin Williams	.10
74	Rick Mirer	.10
75	Steve McNair	1.50
76	Lamont Warren	.10
77	Rod Woodson	.10
78	Larry Brown	.10
79	Zack Crockett	.10
80	Jerry Rice	1.50
81	Tim Brown	.10
82	Yancey Thigpen	.75
83	J.J. Stokes	1.00
84	Herman Moore	.50
85	Kevin Williams	.10
86	Gus Frerotte	.10
87	Robert Brooks	.10
88	Michael Irvin	.50
89	Steve Tasker	.10
90	Joey Galloway	1.50
91	Kevin Greene	.10
92	Reggie White	.10
93	Cris Carter	.10
94	Charles Haley	.10
95	Bryce Paup	.10
96	Heath Shuler	.10
97	Eric Zeier	.20
98	Antonio Freeman	.10
99	Erik Kramer	.10
100	Derek Loville	.10
101	Rodney Thomas	.50
102	Terrell Davis	2.00
103	Ricky Watters	.10
104	Craig Heyward	.10
105	Terry Kirby	.10
106	Bruce Smith	.10
107	Curtis Conway	.10
108	Charles Johnson	.10
109	Brett Perriman	.10
110	Carl Pickens	.20
111	Michael Westbrook	1.00
112	Brent Jones	.10
113	Ken Dilger	.10
114	Fred Barnett	.10
115	Mark Bruener	.10
116	Tamarick Vanover	.20
117	Quinn Early	.10
118	Mark Chmura	.10
119	Andre Hastings	.10
120	Craig Newsome	.10

1996 Playoff Trophy Contenders Mini Back-to-Backs

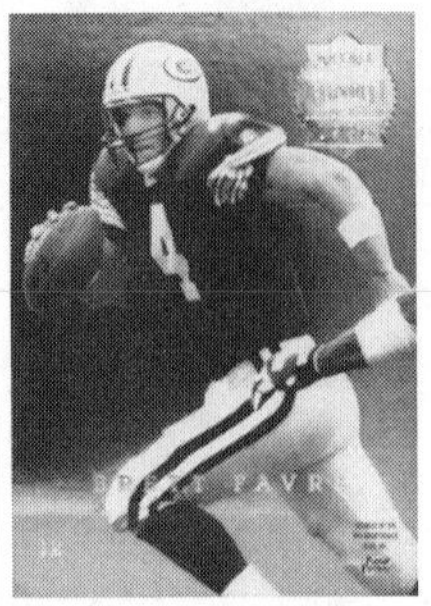

Eleven members from the Super Bowl participants, the Dallas Cowboys and Pittsburgh Steelers, are highlighted on the first 11 cards in this 1996 Playoff Trophy Contenders insert set. The mini cards form a 60-card parallel set to the main set, putting those 120 cards in a back-to-back format. These cards are seeded one per 17 packs.

		MT
Complete Set (60):		900.00
Common Player:		10.00
Minor Stars:		20.00
1	Troy Aikman, Neil O'Donnell	50.00
2	Sherman Williams, Kordell Stewart	45.00
3	Deion Sanders, Andre Hastings	35.00
4	Emmitt Smith, Bam Morris	90.00
5	Daryl Johnston, Eric Pegram	10.00
6	Nate Newton, Kevin Greene	10.00
7	Larry Brown, Charles Johnson	10.00
8	Jay Novacek, Mark Bruener	10.00
9	Kevin Williams, Yancey Thigpen	25.00
10	Michael Irvin, Ernie Mills	25.00
11	Charles Haley, Rod Woodson	10.00
12	Brett Favre, Steve Young	90.00
13	Edgar Bennett, Derek Loville	10.00
14	Reggie White, Ken Norton	10.00
15	Robert Brooks, Jerry Rice	60.00
16	Dorsey Levens, J.J. Stokes	20.00
17	Mark Chmura, Brent Jones	10.00
18	Craig Newsome, Antonio Freeman	20.00
19	Dan Marino, Jim Kelly	90.00
20	Bernie Parmalee, Bruce Smith	10.00
21	Irving Fryar, Bill Brooks	10.00
22	O.J. McDuffie, Steve Tasker	10.00
23	Terry Kirby, Bryce Paup	10.00
24	Jim Harbaugh, Steve Bono	20.00
25	Marshall Faulk, Greg Hill	20.00
26	Lamont Warren, Marcus Allen	10.00
27	Floyd Turner, Kimble Anders	10.00
28	Sean Dawkins, Lake Dawson	10.00
29	Zack Crockett, Tamarick Vanover	20.00
30	Scott Mitchell, Rodney Peete	10.00
31	Barry Sanders, Ricky Watters	60.00
32	Brett Perriman, Calvin Williams	10.00
33	Herman Moore, Fred Barnett	25.00
34	Stan Humphries, Jeff George	20.00
35	Natrone Means, Craig Heyward	20.00
36	Aaron Hayden, Terance Mathis	10.00
37	Junior Seau, Bert Emanuel	10.00
38	Tony Martin, J.J. Birden	10.00
39	Jeff Blake, Carl Pickens	20.00
40	Erik Kramer, Curtis Conway	20.00
41	Garrison Hearst, Frank Sanders	25.00
42	John Elway, Anthony Miller	30.00
43	Steve McNair, Chris Sanders	45.00
44	Warren Moon, Cris Carter	20.00
45	Drew Bledsoe, Curtis Martin	90.00
46	Jim Everett, Quinn Early	10.00
47	Rodney Hampton, Tyrone Wheatley	10.00
48	Jeff Hostetler, Tim Brown	10.00
49	Rick Mirer, Joey Galloway	25.00
50	Gus Frerotte, Michael Westbrook	20.00
51	Heath Shuler, Terry Allen	20.00
52	Charlie Garner, Mike Mamula	10.00
53	Harvey Williams, Napoleon Kaufman	25.00
54	Errict Rhett, Rashaan Salaam	20.00
55	Mark Pike, Kerry Collins	25.00
56	Ken Dilger, Eric Zeier	25.00
57	Chris Warren, Terrell Davis	50.00
58	Isaac Bruce, Jake Reed	25.00
59	Eric Metcalf, Wayne Chrebet	10.00
60	James Stewart, Rodney Thomas	25.00

1996 Playoff Trophy Contenders Playoff Zone

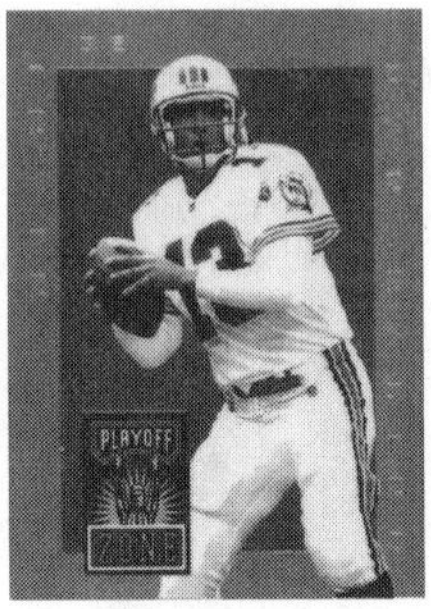

This 36-card insert set captures some of the top NFL players on gold and silver foil backgrounds. The player's name is written in the foil along the right side, while his team's name and position are in the upper left corner. The Playoff Zone logo, showing a referee signaling a touchdown, is in the lower left corner. Cards were seeded one per 24 packs of 1996 Playoff Trophy Contenders.

		MT
Complete Set (36):		350.00
Common Player:		5.00
Minor Stars:		10.00
1	Troy Aikman	30.00
2	Jeff Blake	10.00
3	John Elway	15.00
4	Brett Favre	50.00
5	Jeff George	5.00
6	Jim Harbaugh	5.00
7	Erik Kramer	5.00
8	Dan Marino	50.00
9	Scott Mitchell	5.00
10	Warren Moon	5.00
11	Neil O'Donnell	10.00
12	Steve Young	30.00
13	Marcus Allen	5.00
14	Terry Allen	5.00
15	Edgar Bennett	5.00
16	Marshall Faulk	30.00
17	Rodney Hampton	5.00
18	Craig Heyward	5.00
19	Errict Rhett	10.00
20	Barry Sanders	30.00
21	Emmitt Smith	50.00
22	Chris Warren	10.00
23	Ricky Watters	5.00
24	Harvey Williams	5.00
25	Robert Brooks	10.00
26	Isaac Bruce	10.00
27	Cris Carter	5.00
28	Curtis Conway	5.00
29	Michael Irvin	10.00
30	Anthony Miller	5.00
31	Herman Moore	10.00
32	Brett Perriman	5.00
33	Carl Pickens	10.00
34	Jerry Rice	30.00
35	Deion Sanders	20.00
36	Yancey Thigpen	10.00

1996 Playoff Trophy Contenders Rookie Stallions

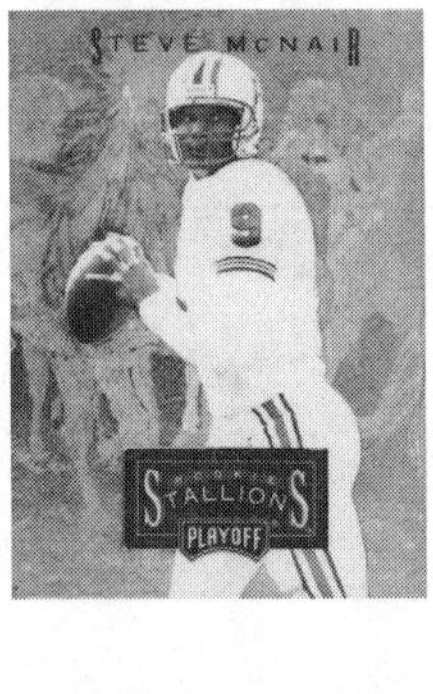

The top 20 rookies from the 1995 season are featured on these 1996 Playoff Trophy Contenders insert cards. Cards, seeded one per 24 packs, are gold-foil etched, with "Stallions" etched into the background.

		MT
Complete Set (20):		300.00
Common Player:		5.00
Minor Stars:		10.00
1	Mark Bruener	5.00
2	Wayne Chrebet	10.00
3	Kerry Collins	15.00
4	Zack Crockett	5.00
5	Terrell Davis	30.00
6	Antonio Freeman	5.00
7	Joey Galloway	20.00
8	Napoleon Kaufman	10.00
9	Curtis Martin	40.00
10	Steve McNair	25.00
11	Rashaan Salaam	20.00
12	Chris Sanders	10.00
13	Frank Sanders	10.00
14	Kordell Stewart	30.00
15	J.J. Stokes	20.00
16	Rodney Thomas	10.00
17	Tamarick Vanover	20.00
18	Michael Westbrook	20.00
19	Tyrone Wheatley	10.00
20	Eric Zeier	10.00

1997 Playoff Absolute

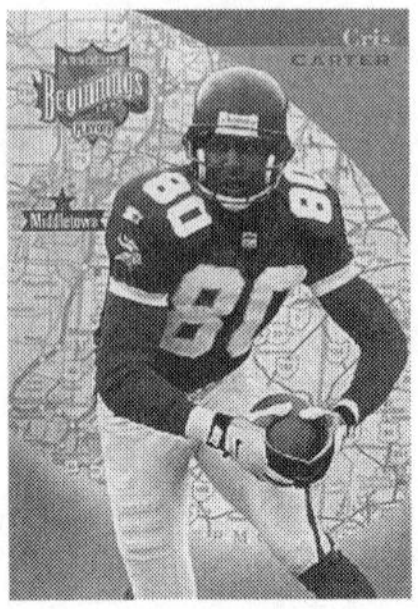

The 200-card set showcases an action shot of the player with a map of his hometown serving as the background on the card front. Named "Absolute Beginnings," the backs include the player's bio at the top left and the card number in the upper right inside a shape of an NFL shield. A headshot of the player is featured in the left center, while his name, number, position and team, along with interesting facts regarding the player's hometown and his pre-collegiate years are included to the right of the photo. His 1996 and total stats are printed along the bottom. The base set has three levels of color coded insertion ratios: Green (card #s 1-100, 3.5 per pack), Blue (#s 101-150, 1 per pack) and Red (#s 151-200, 1 per every 2 packs). The backs for each colored card are identical. The cards are standard size.

		MT
Complete Set (200):		170.00
Comp. Green Set (100):		20.00
Comp. Blue Set (50):		40.00
Comp. Red Set (50):		110.00
Common Green (1-100):		.10
Minor Green Stars:		.20
Common Blue (101-150):		.40
Minor Blue Stars:		.75
Common Red (151-200):		1.00
Minor Red Stars:		2.00
Pack (6):		4.00
Wax Box (24):		85.00
1	Marcus Allen	.20
2	Eric Bieniemy	.10
3	Jason Dunn	.10
4	Jim Harbaugh	.20
5	Michael Westbrook	.20
6	*Tiki Barber*	2.00
7	Frank Reich	.10
8	Irving Fryar	.10
9	Courtney Hawkins	.10
10	Eric Zeier	.10
11	Kent Graham	.10
12	Trent Dilfer	.20
13	Neil O'Donnell	.10
14	*Reidel Anthony*	2.00
15	Jeff Hostetler	.10
16	Lawrence Phillips	.20
17	Dave Brown	.10
18	Mike Tomczak	.10
19	Jake Reed	.10
20	Anthony Miller	.10
21	Eric Metcalf	.10
22	*Sedrick Shaw*	.50
23	Anthony Johnson	.10
24	Mario Bates	.10
25	Dorsey Levens	.30
26	Stan Humphries	.10
27	Ben Coates	.10
28	Tyrone Wheatley	.10
29	Adrian Murrell	.10
30	William Henderson	.10
31	*Warrick Dunn*	1.50
32	LeShon Johnson	.10
33	James Stewart	.10
34	Edgar Bennett	.10
35	Raymont Harris	.10
36	Leroy Butler	.10
37	Darren Woodson	.10
38	*Darnell Autry*	.40
39	Johnnie Morton	.10
40	William Floyd	.10
41	Terrell Fletcher	.10
42	Leonard Russell	.10
43	Henry Ellard	.10
44	Terrell Owens	.75
45	John Friesz	.10
46	*Antowain Smith*	2.00
47	Charles Johnson	.10
48	Rickey Dudley	.10
49	Lake Dawson	.10
50	Bert Emanuel	.10
51	Zach Thomas	.30
52	Ernest Byner	.10
53	*Yatil Green*	.75
54	Chris Spielman	.10
55	Muhsin Muhammad	.30
56	Bobby Engram	.20
57	Eric Bjornson	.10
58	Willie Green	.10
59	Derrick Mayes	.10
60	Chris Sanders	.10
61	Jimmy Smith	.10
62	*Tony Gonzalez*	.75
63	Rich Gannon	.10
64	Stanley Pritchett	.10
65	Brad Johnson	.10
66	Rodney Peete	.10
67	Sam Gash	.10
68	Chris Calloway	.10
69	Chris T. Jones	.10
70	*Will Blackwell*	.50
71	Mark Bruener	.10
72	Terry Kirby	.10
73	Brian Blades	.10
74	Craig Heyward	.10
75	Jamie Asher	.10
76	Terance Mathis	.10
77	*Troy Davis*	.50
78	Bruce Smith	.10
79	Simeon Rice	.10
80	Fred Barnett	.10
81	Tim Brown	.20
82	James Jett	.10
83	Mark Carrier	.10
84	Shawn Jefferson	.10
85	Ken Dilger	.10
86	*Rae Carruth*	1.00
87	Keenan McCardell	.10
88	Michael Irvin	.20
89	Mark Chmura	.20
90	Derrick Alexander	.10
91	Andre Reed	.10
92	Ed McCaffrey	.10
93	Erik Kramer	.10
94	Albert Connell	.10
95	Frank Wycheck	.10
96	Zach Crockett	.10
97	Jim Everett	.10
98	Michael Haynes	.10
99	Jeff Graham	.10
100	Brent Jones	.10
101	Troy Aikman	3.50
102	*Byron Hanspard*	.50
103	Robert Brooks	.50
104	Karim Abdul-Jabbar	2.50
105	Drew Bledsoe	3.50
106	Napoleon Kaufman	.40
107	Steve Young	2.50
108	Leeland McElroy	.40
109	Jamal Anderson	1.50
110	*David LaFleur*	1.75
111	Vinny Testaverde	.40
112	Eric Moulds	.75
113	Tim Biakabutuka	.75
114	Rick Mirer	.75
115	Jeff Blake	.75
116	Jim Schwantz	.40
117	Herman Moore	1.00
118	*Ike Hilliard*	4.00
119	Reggie White	.75
120	Steve McNair	2.00
121	Marshall Faulk	1.25
122	Natrone Means	.75
123	Greg Hill	.40
124	O.J. McDuffie	.40
125	Robert Smith	.40
126	*Bryant Westbrook*	1.25
127	Ray Zellars	.40
128	Rodney Hampton	.40
129	Wayne Chrebet	.40
130	Desmond Howard	.75
131	Ty Detmer	.75
132	Erric Pegram	.40
133	Yancey Thigpen	.40
134	*Danny Wuerffel*	4.00
135	Charlie Jones	.40
136	Chris Warren	.75
137	Isaac Bruce	1.25
138	Errict Rhett	1.00
139	Gus Frerotte	.40
140	Frank Sanders	.40
141	Todd Collins	.40
142	*Jake Plummer*	10.00
143	Darnay Scott	.75
144	Rashaan Salaam	.75
145	Terrell Davis	4.00
146	Scott Mitchell	.40
147	Junior Seau	.75
148	Warren Moon	.40
149	Wesley Walls	.40
150	Daryl Johnston	.40
151	Brett Favre	14.00
152	Emmitt Smith	12.00
153	Dan Marino	12.00
154	Larry Centers	1.00
155	Michael Jackson	1.00
156	Kerry Collins	2.00
157	Curtis Conway	2.00
158	Peter Boulware	1.00
159	Carl Pickens	2.00
160	Shannon Sharpe	2.00
161	Brett Perriman	1.00
162	Eddie George	8.00
163	Mark Brunell	6.00
164	Tamarick Vanover	2.00
165	Cris Carter	1.00
166	*Corey Dillion*	10.00
167	Curtis Martin	7.00
168	Amani Toomer	1.00
169	Jeff George	1.00
170	Kordell Stewart	6.00
171	Garrison Hearst	1.00
172	Tony Banks	3.00
173	Mike Alstott	2.00
174	*Jim Druckenmiller*	10.00
175	Chris Chandler	1.00
176	Bam Morris	1.00
177	Billy Joe Hobert	1.00
178	Ernie Mills	1.00
179	Ki-Jana Carter	1.00
180	Deion Sanders	4.00
181	Ricky Watters	2.00
182	*Shawn Springs*	3.00
183	Barry Sanders	10.00
184	Antonio Freeman	3.00
185	Marvin Harrison	3.00
186	Elvis Grbac	1.00
187	Terry Glenn	5.00
188	Willie Roaf	1.00

189	Keyshawn Johnson	3.00
190	*Orlando Pace*	3.00
191	Jerome Bettis	2.00
192	Tony Martin	1.00
193	Jerry Rice	6.00
194	Joey Galloway	2.00
195	Terry Allen	2.00
196	Eddie Kennison	3.00
197	Thurman Thomas	2.00
198	Darrell Russell	1.00
199	Rob Moore	1.00
200	John Elway	5.00

1997 Playoff Absolute Autographed Pennants

Measuring 3-1/2" x 5", one of the eight signed pennants were randomly inserted in boxes of Playoff Absolute. The cards are numbered with an "A" prefix.

		MT
Complete Set (8):		600.00
Common Player:		40.00
1	Kordell Stewart	125.00
2	Eddie George	175.00
3	Karim Abdul-Jabbar	75.00
4	Mike Alstott	40.00
5	Terry Glenn	80.00
6	Napoleon Kaufman	40.00
7	Terry Allen	40.00
8	Tim Brown	40.00

1997 Playoff Absolute Chip Shots

Inserted one per pack, the Chip Shots resembled poker chips. The chips, which measure approximately 1-1/2" in diameter, were available in assorted colors. The plastic tokens were a 200-player parallel of the base set.

		MT
Complete Set (200):		220.00
Common Player:		.40
Minor Stars:		.75
1	Marcus Allen	.75
2	Eric Bieniemy	.40
3	Jason Dunn	.40
4	Jim Harbaugh	.40
5	Michael Westbrook	.40
6	Tiki Barber	4.00
7	Frank Reich	.40
8	Irving Fryar	.40
9	Courtney Hawkins	.40
10	Eric Zeier	.40
11	Kent Graham	.40
12	Trent Dilfer	.75
13	Neil O'Donnell	.40
14	Reidel Anthony	4.00
15	Jeff Hostetler	.40
16	Lawrence Phillips	.75
17	Dave Brown	.40
18	Mike Tomczak	.40
19	Jake Reed	.40
20	Anthony Miller	.40
21	Eric Metcalf	.40
22	Sedrick Shaw	1.00
23	Anthony Johnson	.40
24	Mario Bates	.40
25	Dorsey Levens	1.00
26	Stan Humphries	.40
27	Ben Coates	.40
28	Tyrone Wheatley	.40
29	Adrian Murrell	.40
30	William Henderson	.40
31	Warrick Dunn	10.00
32	LeShon Johnson	.40
33	James Stewart	.40
34	Edgar Bennett	.40
35	Raymont Harris	.40
36	Leroy Butler	.40
37	Darren Woodson	.40
38	Darnell Autry	2.00
39	Johnnie Morton	.40
40	William Floyd	.40
41	Terrell Fletcher	.40
42	Leonard Russell	.40
43	Henry Ellard	.40
44	Terrell Owens	4.00
45	John Friesz	.40
46	Antowain Smith	5.00
47	Charles Johnson	.40
48	Rickey Dudley	.40
49	Lake Dawson	.40
50	Bert Emanuel	.40
51	Zach Thomas	1.00
52	Ernest Byner	.40
53	Yatil Green	3.00
54	Chris Spielman	.40
55	Muhsin Muhammad	.75
56	Bobby Engram	.75
57	Eric Bjornson	.40
58	Willie Green	.40
59	Derrick Mayes	.40
60	Chris Sanders	.40
61	Jimmy Smith	.40
62	Tony Gonzalez	1.00
63	Rich Gannon	.40
64	Stanley Pritchett	.40
65	Brad Johnson	.75
66	Rodney Peete	.40
67	Sam Gash	.40
68	Chris Calloway	.40
69	Chris T. Jones	.40
70	Will Blackwell	.75
71	Mark Bruener	.40
72	Terry Kirby	.40
73	Brian Blades	.40
74	Craig Heyward	.40
75	Jamie Asher	.40
76	Terance Mathis	.40
77	Troy Davis	3.00
78	Bruce Smith	.40
79	Simeon Rice	.40
80	Fred Barnett	.40
81	Tim Brown	.40
82	James Jett	.40
83	Mark Carrier	.40
84	Shawn Jefferson	.40
85	Ken Dilger	.40
86	Rae Carruth	2.00
87	Keenan McCardell	.75
88	Michael Irvin	.75
89	Mark Chmura	.40
90	Derrick Alexander	.40
91	Andre Reed	.40
92	Ed McCaffrey	.40
93	Erik Kramer	.40
94	Albert Connell	.40
95	Frank Wycheck	.40
96	Zach Crockett	.40
97	Jim Everett	.40
98	Michael Haynes	.40
99	Jeff Graham	.40
100	Brent Jones	.40
101	Troy Aikman	7.00
102	Byron Hanspard	2.00
103	Robert Brooks	.75
104	Karim Abdul-Jabbar	4.00
105	Drew Bledsoe	7.00
106	Napoleon Kaufman	.75
107	Steve Young	4.00
108	Leeland McElroy	.40
109	Jamal Anderson	1.00
110	David LaFleur	1.50
111	Vinny Testaverde	.40
112	Eric Moulds	.75
113	Tim Biakabutuka	.75
114	Rick Mirer	.40
115	Jeff Blake	1.00
116	Jim Schwantz	.40
117	Herman Moore	1.00
118	Ike Hilliard	4.00
119	Reggie White	.75
120	Steve McNair	4.00
121	Marshall Faulk	1.00
122	Natrone Means	.75
123	Greg Hill	.40
124	O.J. McDuffie	.40
125	Robert Smith	.40
126	Bryant Westbrook	1.00
127	Ray Zellars	.40
128	Rodney Hampton	.40
129	Wayne Chrebet	.40
130	Desmond Howard	.40
131	Ty Detmer	.40
132	Erric Pegram	.40
133	Yancey Thigpen	.40
134	Danny Wuerffel	4.00
135	Charlie Jones	.40
136	Chris Warren	.40
137	Isaac Bruce	1.00
138	Errict Rhett	.75
139	Gus Frerotte	.40
140	Frank Sanders	.40
141	Todd Collins	.75
142	Jake Plummer	6.00
143	Darnay Scott	.40
144	Rashaan Salaam	.75
145	Terrell Davis	8.00
146	Scott Mitchell	.40
147	Junior Seau	.75
148	Warren Moon	.40
149	Wesley Walls	.40
150	Daryl Johnston	.40
151	Brett Favre	14.00
152	Emmitt Smith	12.00
153	Dan Marino	12.00
154	Larry Centers	.40
155	Michael Jackson	.40
156	Kerry Collins	1.00
157	Curtis Conway	.75
158	Peter Boulware	.75
159	Carl Pickens	.40
160	Shannon Sharpe	.40
161	Brett Perriman	.40
162	Eddie George	10.00
163	Mark Brunell	7.00
164	Tamarick Vanover	.75
165	Cris Carter	.40
166	Corey Dillion	6.00
167	Curtis Martin	8.00
168	Amani Toomer	.40
169	Jeff George	.40
170	Kordell Stewart	7.00
171	Garrison Hearst	.40
172	Tony Banks	3.00
173	Mike Alstott	3.00
174	Jim Druckenmiller	7.00
175	Chris Chandler	.40
176	Bam Morris	.40
177	Billy Joe Hobert	.40
178	Ernie Mills	.40
179	Ki-Jana Carter	.40
180	Deion Sanders	3.00
181	Ricky Watters	.75
182	Shawn Springs	1.00
183	Barry Sanders	10.00
184	Antonio Freeman	1.00
185	Marvin Harrison	3.00
186	Elvis Grbac	.40
187	Terry Glenn	6.00
188	Willie Roaf	.40
189	Keyshawn Johnson	3.00
190	Orlando Pace	2.00
191	Jerome Bettis	.75
192	Tony Martin	.40
193	Jerry Rice	7.00
194	Joey Galloway	1.00
195	Terry Allen	.40
196	Eddie Kennison	3.00
197	Thurman Thomas	.75
198	Darrell Russell	.75
199	Rob Moore	.40
200	John Elway	4.00

1997 Playoff Absolute Leather Quads

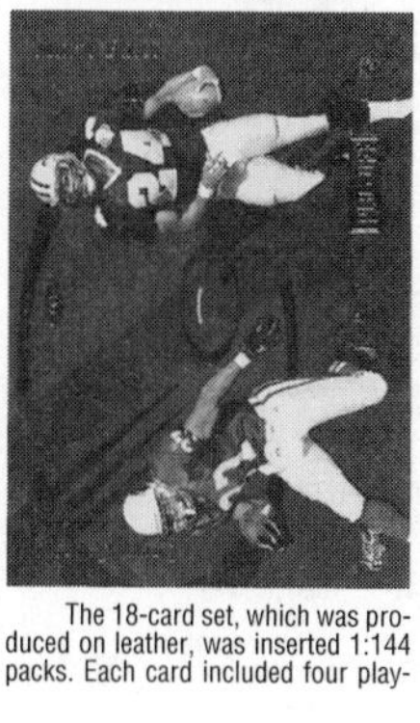

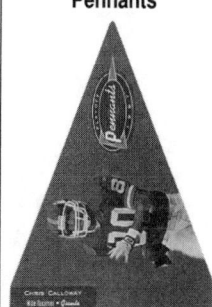

The 18-card set, which was produced on leather, was inserted 1:144 packs. Each card included four players, with two appearing on each side. The player photos are superimposed over the leather background. The players' names are printed vertically in green along the left and right borders. "Leather Quad" is printed in white over a black stripe which runs diagonally between the two players' photos. The Playoff logo and "1997" are printed in green at the bottom center on both sides of the cards. The card numbers appear in the top center inside a green oval on both sides of the cards with a "LQ" prefix.

		MT
Complete Set (18):		1200.
Common Player:		20.00
Minor Stars:		40.00
1	Brett Favre, Jerry Rice, Dan Marino, Emmitt Smith	300.00
2	Barry Sanders, Terrell Davis, Eddie George, Curtis Martin	180.00
3	Kordell Stewart, Herman Moore, Elvis Grbac, Chris Warren	75.00
4	Troy Aikman, Leeland McElroy, Cris Carter, Zach Thomas	75.00
5	Drew Bledsoe, Jamal Anderson, Michael Jackson, Jim Harbaugh	75.00
6	John Elway, Reggie White, Warren Moon, Terrell Owens	60.00
7	Kerry Collins, Rashaan Salaam, Shannon Sharpe, Ricky Watters	75.00
8	Mark Brunell, Eric Moulds, Mario Bates, Larry Centers	75.00
9	Karim Abdul-Jabbar, Robert Brooks, Jerome Bettis, Carl Pickens	60.00
10	Steve Young, Tim Biakabutuka, Jeff George, Tony Martin	50.00
11	Terry Glenn, Jeff Blake, Mike Alstott, Curtis Conway	50.00
12	Joey Galloway, Antonio Freeman, Anthony Johnson, Rick Mirer	40.00
13	Steve McNair, Marshall Faulk, Jimmy Smith, Isaac Bruce	50.00
14	Deion Sanders, Tony Banks, Vinny Testaverde, Rodney Hampton	40.00
15	Marvin Harrison, Lawrence Phillips, Thurman Thomas, Chris Chandler	20.00
16	Keyshawn Johnson, Napoleon Kaufman, Gus Frerotte, Greg Hill	20.00
17	Eddie Kennison, Terry Allen, Scott Mitchell, Errict Rhett	20.00
18	Warrick Dunn, Orlando Pace, Jim Druckenmiller, Darrell Russell	80.00

1997 Playoff Absolute Pennants

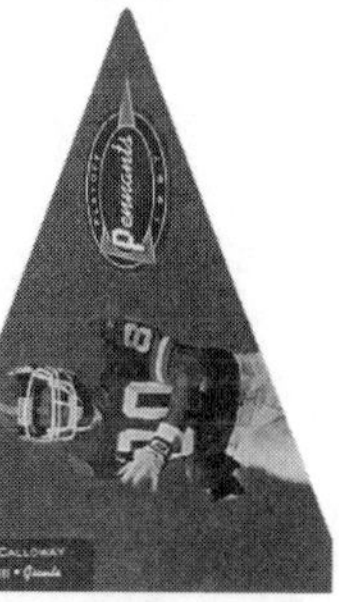

Inserted one per box, the pennants measure 3-1/2" x 5". Each of the 192 pennants in the set have a felt-like feel to them. The pennant fronts have the player's name printed inside a rectangle in the upper left, while a cutout color action photo of the player is included in the center of the pennant. The Playoff Pennants 1997 logo is on the right of the front. The vertical backs have the player's name, appropriate logos and pennant number in a stripe at the top. The player's headshot is included inside a circle in the center of the back, which also has a felt-like feel to it. The Playoff Pennants' logo is on the bottom of the back.

		MT
Common Player:		5.00
Minor Stars:		10.00
1	Marcus Allen	10.00
2	Eric Bieniemy	5.00
3	Jason Dunn	5.00
4	Jim Harbaugh (QBC)	5.00
5	Michael Westbrook	5.00
6	Tiki Barber	10.00
7	Frank Reich (QBC)	5.00
8	Irving Fryar	5.00
9	Courtney Hawkins	5.00
10	Eric Zeier	5.00
11	Kent Graham	5.00
12	Trent Dilfer (QBC)	10.00
13	Neil O'Donnell (QBC)	5.00
14	Reidel Anthony	30.00
15	Jeff Hostetler (QBC)	5.00
16	Lawrence Phillips	10.00
17	Dave Brown (QBC)	5.00
18	Mike Tomczak	5.00
19	Jake Reed	5.00
20	Anthony Miller	5.00
21	Eric Metcalf	5.00
22	Sedrick Shaw	20.00
23	Anthony Johnson	5.00
24	Mario Bates	5.00
25	Dorsey Levens	10.00
26	Stan Humphries	5.00
27	Ben Coates	5.00
28	Tyrone Wheatley	5.00
29	Adrian Murrell	5.00
30	William Henderson	5.00
31	Warrick Dunn	65.00
32	LeShon Johnson	5.00
33	James Stewart	5.00
34	Edgar Bennett	5.00
35	Raymont Harris	5.00
36	Leroy Butler	5.00
37	Darren Woodson	5.00
38	Darnell Autry	20.00
39	Johnnie Morton	5.00
40	William Floyd	10.00
41	Terrell Fletcher	5.00
42	Leonard Russell	5.00
43	Henry Ellard	5.00
44	Terrell Owens	40.00
45	John Friesz	5.00
46	Antowain Smith	25.00
47	Charles Johnson	5.00
48	Rickey Dudley	5.00
49	Lake Dawson	5.00
50	Bert Emanuel	5.00
51	Zach Thomas	15.00
52	Earnest Byner	5.00
53	Yatil Green	25.00
54	Chris Spielman	5.00
55	Muhsin Muhammad	5.00
56	Bobby Engram	5.00
57	Eric Bjornson	5.00
58	Willie Green	5.00
59	Derrick Mayes	5.00
60	Chris Sanders	5.00
61	Jimmy Smith	5.00
62	Tony Gonzalez	20.00
63	Rich Gannon	5.00
64	Stanley Pritchett	5.00
65	Brad Johnson	10.00
66	Rodney Peete (QBC)	5.00
67	Sam Gash	5.00
68	Chris Galloway	5.00
69	Chris T. Jones	5.00
70	Will Blackwell	10.00
71	Mark Bruener	5.00
72	Terry Kirby	5.00
73	Brian Blades	5.00
74	Craig Heyward	5.00
75	Jamie Asher	5.00
76	Terance Mathis	5.00
77	Troy Davis	10.00
78	Bruce Smith	5.00
79	Simeon Rice	5.00
80	Fred Barnett	5.00
81	Jerry Rice	75.00
82	James Jett	5.00
83	Mark Carrier	5.00
84	Shawn Jefferson	5.00
85	Ken Dilger	5.00
86	Rae Carruth	25.00
87	Keenan McCardell	10.00
88	Michael Irvin (QBC)	10.00
89	Mark Chmura	10.00
90	Derrick Alexander	5.00
91	Andre Reed	5.00
92	Ed McCaffrey	5.00
93	Erik Kramer (QBC)	5.00
94	Albert Connell	5.00
95	Frank Wycheck	5.00
96	Zach Crockett	5.00
97	Jim Everett (QBC)	5.00
98	Michael Haynes	5.00
99	Jeff Graham	5.00
100	Brent Jones	5.00
101	Troy Aikman (QBC)	75.00
102	Byron Hanspard	25.00
103	Robert Brooks	10.00
104	Joey Galloway	15.00
105	Drew Bledsoe (QBC)	75.00
106	Eddie Kennison	10.00
107	Steve Young (QBC)	50.00
108	Leeland McElroy	10.00
109	Jamal Anderson	15.00
110	David LaFleur	20.00
111	Vinny Testaverde	5.00
112	Eric Moulds	5.00
113	Tim Biakabutuka	10.00
114	Rick Mirer (QBC)	5.00
115	Jeff Blake (QBC)	15.00
116	Jim Schwantz	5.00
117	Herman Moore	15.00
118	Ike Hilliard	25.00
119	Reggie White	10.00
120	Steve McNair (QBC)	65.00
121	Marshall Faulk	10.00
122	Natrone Means	10.00
123	Greg Hill	5.00
124	O.J. McDuffie	5.00
125	Robert Smith	5.00
126	Bryant Westbrook	10.00
127	Ray Zellars	5.00
128	Rodney Hampton	5.00
129	Wayne Chrebet	5.00
130	Desmond Howard	5.00
131	Ty Detmer	5.00
132	Erric Pegram	5.00
133	Yancey Thigpen	5.00
134	Danny Wuerffel	25.00
135	Charlie Jones	5.00
136	Chris Warren	5.00
137	Isaac Bruce	15.00
138	Errict Rhett	10.00
139	Gus Frerotte (QBC)	5.00
140	Frank Sanders	5.00
141	Todd Collins	10.00
142	Jake Plummer	30.00
143	Darnay Scott	5.00
144	Rashaan Salaam	10.00
145	Terrell Davis	75.00
146	Scott Mitchell (QBC)	5.00
147	Junior Seau (QBC)	10.00
148	Warren Moon (QBC)	5.00
149	Wesley Walls	5.00
150	Daryl Johnston	5.00
151	Brett Favre (QBC)	130.00
152	Emmitt Smith (QBC)	100.00
153	Dan Marino (QBC)	100.00
154	Larry Centers	5.00
155	Michael Jackson	5.00
156	Kerry Collins (QBC)	10.00
157	Curtis Conway	10.00
158	Peter Boulware	5.00
159	Carl Pickens	10.00
160	Shannon Sharpe	5.00
161	Brett Perriman	5.00
162	Thurman Thomas	10.00
163	Mark Brunell (QBC)	75.00
164	Tamarick Vanover	10.00
165	Cris Carter	10.00
166	Corey Dillon	40.00
167	Curtis Martin	60.00
168	Amani Toomer	5.00
169	Jeff George (QBC)	5.00
170	Darrell Russell	5.00
171	Garrison Hearst	5.00
172	Tony Banks (QBC)	10.00
173	Rob Moore	5.00
174	Jim Druckenmiller	45.00
175	Chris Chandler	5.00
176	Bam Morris	5.00
177	Billy Joe Hobert	5.00
178	Ernie Mills	5.00
179	Ki-Jana Carter	10.00
180	Deion Sanders	35.00
181	Ricky Watters	10.00
182	Shawn Springs	20.00
183	Barry Sanders (QBC)	85.00
184	Antonio Freeman	15.00
185	Marvin Harrison	35.00
186	Elvis Grbac (QBC)	5.00
187	John Elway (QBC)	50.00
188	Willie Roaf	5.00
189	Keyshawn Johnson	35.00
190	Orlando Pace	15.00
191	Jerome Bettis	10.00
192	Tony Martin	5.00

1997 Playoff Absolute Playoff Honors

This three-card set, which was inserted 1:7,200 packs, was a continuation from the 1996 Playoff Prime and Contenders sets. The felt-like cards feature a player photo superimposed over a checkered background on the front. The Playoff Honors' logo appears in one of the upper corners of the card, with the player's name printed in a lower corner. The cards carry a prefix of "PF."

		MT
Complete Set (3):		350.00
Common Player:		50.00
7	Jerry Rice	125.00
8	Reggie White	50.00
9	John Elway	200.00

1997 Playoff Absolute Reflex

The 200-card set is a parallel of the base set printed on mirror board. The card fronts have "Reflex" printed at the top, with the player's photo superimposed over a silver mirror background. "Playoff '97" is printed vertically along the left border, while his name is printed vertically along the right border. The cards were inserted 1:288 packs.

		MT
Common Player:		30.00
Minor Stars:		60.00
1	Brett Favre	750.00
2	Dorsey Levens	60.00
3	Antonio Freeman	60.00
4	Robert Brooks	30.00
5	Mark Chmura	60.00
6	Reggie White	60.00
7	Drew Bledsoe	350.00
8	Curtis Martin	275.00
9	Ben Coates	30.00
10	Terry Glenn	100.00
11	Kerry Collins	75.00
12	Tim Biakabutuka	30.00
13	Anthony Johnson	30.00
14	Wesley Walls	30.00
15	Muhsin Muhammad	30.00
16	Mark Brunell	350.00
17	Natrone Means	60.00
18	Jimmy Smith	30.00
19	John Elway	400.00
20	Terrell Davis	400.00
21	Anthony Miller	30.00
22	Shannon Sharpe	30.00
23	Steve Young	300.00
24	Garrison Hearst	30.00
25	Jerry Rice	350.00
26	Troy Aikman	350.00
27	Deion Sanders	200.00
28	Emmitt Smith	600.00
29	Michael Irvin	60.00
30	Kordell Stewart	350.00
31	Jerome Bettis	60.00
32	Charles Johnson	30.00
33	Ty Detmer	30.00
34	Ricky Watters	60.00
35	Irving Fryar	30.00
36	Todd Collins	30.00
37	Thurman Thomas	60.00
38	Bruce Smith	30.00
39	Eric Moulds	30.00
40	Brad Johnson	60.00
41	Robert Smith	60.00
42	Cris Carter	60.00
43	Elvis Grbac	30.00
44	Greg Hill	30.00
45	Marcus Allen	60.00
46	Gus Frerotte	30.00
47	Terry Allen	30.00
48	Michael Westbrook	30.00
49	Jim Harbaugh	60.00
50	Marshall Faulk	60.00
51	Marvin Harrison	100.00
52	Jeff Blake	60.00
53	Ki-Jana Carter	30.00
54	Carl Pickens	30.00
55	Junior Seau	60.00
56	Tony Martin	30.00
57	Dan Marino	600.00
58	Karim Abdul-Jabbar	100.00
59	Stanley Pritchett	30.00
60	Zach Thomas	30.00
61	Steve McNair	250.00
62	Eddie George	350.00
63	Chris Sanders	30.00
64	Rick Mirer	30.00
65	Rashaan Salaam	60.00
66	Curtis Conway	30.00
67	Bobby Engram	30.00
68	Kent Graham	30.00
69	Leeland McElroy	30.00
70	Larry Centers	30.00
71	Frank Sanders	30.00
72	Jeff George	60.00
73	Napoleon Kaufman	200.00
74	Desmond Howard	30.00
75	Tim Brown	60.00
76	John Friesz	30.00
77	Chris Warren	30.00
78	Joey Galloway	100.00
79	Tony Banks	100.00
80	Lawrence Phillips	60.00
81	Isaac Bruce	100.00
82	Eddie Kennison	100.00
83	Errict Rhett	60.00
84	Mike Alstott	125.00
85	Rodney Hampton	30.00
86	Amani Toomer	30.00
87	Scott Mitchell	30.00
88	Barry Sanders	525.00
89	Herman Moore	60.00
90	Vinny Testaverde	30.00
91	Bam Morris	30.00
92	Michael Jackson	30.00
93	Chris Chandler	30.00
94	Eric Metcalf	30.00
95	Jamal Anderson	60.00
96	Jim Everett	30.00
97	Mario Bates	30.00
98	Wayne Chrebet	30.00
99	Adrian Murrell	60.00
100	Keyshawn Johnson	60.00
101	William Henderson	30.00
102	Edgar Bennett	30.00
103	LeRoy Butler	30.00
104	Derrick Mayes	30.00
105	Sedrick Shaw	60.00
106	Sam Gash	30.00
107	Shawn Jefferson	30.00
108	Mark Carrier	30.00
109	Rae Carruth	100.00
110	Ernie Mills	30.00
111	James Stewart	30.00
112	Keenan McCardell	30.00
113	Willie Green	30.00
114	Ed McCaffrey	30.00
115	William Floyd	30.00
116	Terrell Owens	100.00
117	Terry Kirby	30.00
118	Brent Jones	30.00
119	Jim Schwantz	30.00
120	Jim Druckenmiller	150.00
121	Darren Woodson	30.00
122	Eric Bjornson	30.00
123	David LaFleur	60.00
124	Daryl Johnston	30.00
125	Mike Tomczak	30.00
126	Will Blackwell	30.00
127	Mark Bruener	30.00
128	Erric Pegram	30.00
129	Yancey Thigpen	30.00
130	Jason Dunn	30.00
131	Chris T. Jones	30.00
132	Rodney Peete	30.00
133	Antowain Smith	150.00
134	Chris Spielman	30.00
135	Andre Reed	30.00
136	Billy Joe Hobert	30.00
137	Jake Reed	30.00
138	Tamarick Vanover	30.00
139	Lake Dawson	30.00
140	Tony Gonzalez	60.00
141	Rich Gannon	30.00
142	Henry Ellard	30.00
143	Jamie Asher	30.00
144	Albert Connell	30.00
145	Ken Dilger	30.00
146	Zack Crockett	30.00
147	Eric Bieniemy	30.00
148	Darnay Scott	30.00
149	Corey Dillon	175.00
150	Stan Humphries	30.00
151	Terrell Fletcher	30.00
152	Leonard Russell	30.00
153	Charlie Jones	30.00
154	Yatil Green	100.00
155	Fred Barnett	30.00
156	O.J. McDuffie	30.00
157	Frank Wycheck	30.00
158	Raymont Harris	30.00
159	Darnell Autry	60.00
160	Erik Kramer	30.00
161	LeShon Johnson	30.00
162	Simeon Rice	30.00
163	Jake Plummer	200.00
164	Rob Moore	30.00
165	Jeff Hostetler	30.00
166	Rickey Dudley	30.00
167	James Jett	30.00
168	Darrell Russell	30.00
169	Brian Blades	30.00
170	Warren Moon	60.00
171	Shawn Springs	30.00
172	Craig Heyward	30.00
173	Orlando Pace	60.00
174	Courtney Hawkins	30.00
175	Trent Dilfer	60.00
176	Reidel Anthony	100.00
177	Warrick Dunn	200.00
178	Tiki Barber	100.00
179	Dave Brown	30.00
180	Tyrone Wheatley	30.00
181	Chris Calloway	30.00
182	Ike Hilliard	100.00
183	Frank Reich	30.00
184	Johnnie Morton	30.00
185	Bryant Westbrook	30.00
186	Brett Perriman	30.00
187	Eric Zeier	30.00
188	Earnest Byner	30.00
189	Derrick Alexander	30.00
190	Peter Boulware	30.00
191	Bert Emanuel	30.00
192	Terance Mathis	30.00
193	Byron Hanspard	75.00
194	Troy Davis	75.00
195	Michael Haynes	30.00
196	Ray Zellars	30.00
197	Danny Wuerffel	75.00
198	Willie Roaf	30.00
199	Neil O'Donnell	30.00
200	Jeff Graham	30.00

1997 Playoff Absolute Unsung Heroes

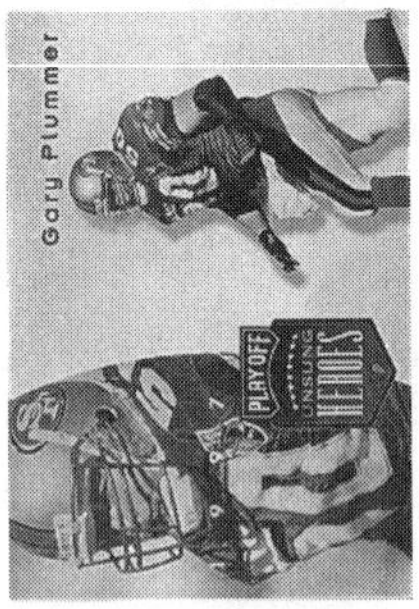

The 30-card set honors the players selected as the 1996 Playoff/Players Inc. Unsung Heroes, which were voted on by the fans and players. In its third year, the set includes a color photo of the player superimposed over a silver background on the right side of the front. His name is printed in the upper right. A black-and-white close-up photo, which is an enlarged version of the color photo, is printed on the left side of the card, with "1997" printed over the top of it. The Unsung Heroes logo is printed at the bottom. The backs are numbered inside a red box in the upper left. The player's name, bio and write-up are printed on the left side over a green background. Along the right side of the back is a color headshot of the player. The cards were inserted 1:12 packs.

		MT
Complete Set (30):		25.00
Common Player:		.50
Minor Stars:		1.00
Inserted 1:12		
1	Larry Centers	1.25
2	Jessie Tuggle	.50
3	Stevon Moore	.50
4	Mark Pike	.50
5	Anthony Johnson	.50
6	Anthony Carter	.50
7	Eric Bieniemy	.50
8	Jim Schwantz	.50
9	Tyrone Braxton	.50
10	Bennie Blades	.50
11	Don Beebe	.50
12	Barron Wortham	.50
13	Jason Belser	.50
14	Mickey Washington	.50
15	Dave Szott	.50
16	Zach Thomas	2.50
17	Chris Walsh	.50
18	Sam Gash	.50
19	Willie Roaf	1.00
20	Charles Way	.50
21	Wayne Chrebet	2.00
22	Russell Maryland	.50
23	Michael Zordich	.50
24	Tim Lester	.50
25	Harold Green	.50
26	Rodney Harrison	.50
27	Gary Plummer	.50
28	Winston Moss	.50
29	Robb Thomas	.50
30	Darrick Brownlow	.50

1997 Playoff Contenders

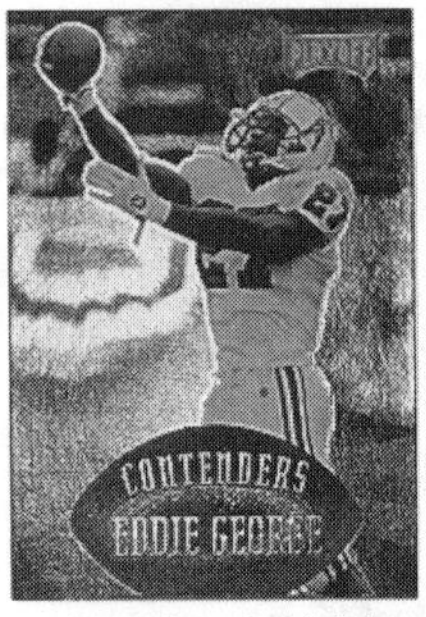

Playoff Contenders includes a 150-card base set. Printed on 30 pt. stock, these cards feature player shots on each side, with foil etching and holographic technology. The player's name is added in silver on each side. A Blue Level parallel version was included in 1:4 packs, while a Red Level version was sequentially numbered to 25. Inserts include Playoff Clash, Leather Die-Cut Helmets, Playoff Plaques, Playoff Pennants and Playoff Rookie Wave Pennants.

		MT
Complete Set (150):		140.00
Common Player:		.50
Minor Stars:		1.00
Blue Cards:		2x-4x
Blue Rookies:		2x
Inserted 1:4		
Red Cards:		40x-80x
Red Rookies:		20x-40x
Production 25 Sets		
Pack (4):		7.50
Wax Box (12):		80.00
1	Kent Graham	.50
2	Leeland McElroy	.50
3	Rob Moore	.50
4	Frank Sanders	.50
5	*Jake Plummer*	10.00
6	Chris Chandler	.50
7	Bert Emanuel	.50
8	O.J. Santiago	.50
9	*Byron Hanspard*	3.00
10	Vinny Testaverde	.50
11	Michael Jackson	.50
12	Ernest Byner	.50
13	Jermaine Lewis	.50
14	Derrick Alexander	.50
15	*Jay Graham*	1.00
16	Todd Collins	1.00
17	Thurman Thomas	1.00
18	Bruce Smith	.50
19	Andre Reed	.50
20	Quinn Early	.50
21	*Antowain Smith*	6.00
22	Kerry Collins	1.50
23	Tim Biakabutuka	.50
24	Anthony Johnson	.50
25	Wesley Johnson	.50
26	*Fred Lane*	3.00
27	*Rae Carruth*	4.00
28	Raymont Harris	.50
29	Rick Mirer	.50
30	*Darnell Autry*	3.00
31	Jeff Blake	1.00
32	Ki-Jana Carter	1.00
33	Carl Pickens	.50
34	Darnay Scott	.50
35	*Corey Dillon*	12.00
36	Troy Aikman	6.00
37	Emmitt Smith	10.00
38	Michael Irvin	1.00
39	Deion Sanders	3.00
40	Anthony Miller	.50
41	Eric Bjornson	.50
42	*David LaFleur*	3.00
43	John Elway	4.00
44	Terrell Davis	6.00
45	Shannon Sharpe	.50
46	Ed McCaffrey	.50
47	Rod Smith	.50
48	Scott Mitchell	.50
49	Barry Sanders	7.00
50	Herman Moore	2.00
51	Brett Favre	12.00
52	Dorsey Levens	1.00
53	William Henderson	.50
54	Derrick Mayes	.50
55	Antonio Freeman	1.00
56	Robert Brooks	.50
57	Mark Chmura	.50
58	Reggie White	1.00
59	Darren Sharper	.50
60	Jim Harbaugh	.50
61	Marshall Faulk	1.00
62	Marvin Harrison	2.00
63	Mark Brunell	6.00
64	Natrone Means	1.00
65	Jimmy Smith	.50
66	Keenan McCardell	.50
67	Elvis Grbac	.50
68	Greg Hill	.50
69	Marcus Allen	1.00
70	Andre Rison	.50
71	Kimble Anders	.50
72	*Tony Gonzalez*	6.00
73	*Pat Barnes*	2.00
74	Dan Marino	10.00
75	Karim Abdul-Jabbar	3.00
76	Zach Thomas	1.00
77	O.J. McDuffie	.50
78	*Brian Manning*	1.00
79	Brad Johnson	1.00
80	Cris Carter	1.00
81	Jake Reed	.50
82	Robert Smith	1.00
83	Drew Bledsoe	6.00
84	Curtis Martin	6.00
85	Ben Coates	.50
86	Terry Glenn	3.00
87	Shawn Jefferson	.50
88	Heath Shuler	.50
89	Mario Bates	.50
90	Andre Hastings	.50
91	*Troy Davis*	3.00
92	*Danny Wuerffel*	4.00
93	Dave Brown	.50
94	Chris Calloway	.50
95	*Tiki Barber*	6.00
96	Mike Cherry	.50
97	Neil O'Donnell	.50
98	Keyshawn Johnson	2.00
99	Adrian Murrell	1.00
100	Wayne Chrebet	.50
101	Dedric Ward	.50
102	Leon Johnson	.50
103	Jeff George	1.00
104	Napoleon Kaufman	2.00
105	Tim Brown	1.00
106	James Jett	.50
107	Ty Detmer	.50
108	Ricky Watters	1.00
109	Irving Fryar	.50
110	Michael Timpson	.50
111	Chad Lewis	.50
112	Kordell Stewart	6.00
113	Jerome Bettis	1.00
114	Charles Johnson	.50
115	*George Jones*	1.00
116	*Will Blackwell*	1.00
117	Stan Humphries	.50
118	Junior Seau	1.00
119	*Freddie Jones*	1.00
120	Steve Young	4.00
121	Jerry Rice	6.00
122	Garrison Hearst	.50
123	William Floyd	.50
124	Terrell Owens	3.00
125	J.J. Stokes	.50
126	Marc Edwards	.50
127	*Jim Druckenmiller*	8.00
128	Warren Moon	.50
129	Chris Warren	.50
130	Joey Galloway	1.00
131	*Shawn Springs*	1.00
132	Tony Banks	3.00
133	Lawrence Phillips	1.00
134	Isaac Bruce	1.00
135	Eddie Kennison	2.00
136	*Orlando Pace*	1.00
137	Trent Dilfer	1.00
138	Mike Alstott	3.00
139	Horace Copeland	.50
140	Jackie Harris	.50
141	*Warrick Dunn*	4.00
142	*Reidel Anthony*	6.00
143	Steve McNair	5.00
144	Eddie George	8.00
145	Chris Sanders	.50
146	Gus Frerotte	.50
147	Terry Allen	.50
148	Henry Ellard	.50
149	Leslie Shepherd	.50
150	Michael Westbrook	.50

1997 Playoff Contenders Clash

Clash is a 12-card insert highlighting some of the NFL's top matchups. The cards feature two players with their team helmets die-cut in the background. Silver Level cards were inserted 1:48 and Blue Level cards were found 1:192.

		MT
Complete Set (12):		500.00
Common Player:		20.00
Blue Cards:		3x
1	Brett Favre, Troy Aikman	100.00
2	Barry Sanders, Brad Johnson	75.00
3	Curtis Martin, Warrick Dunn	50.00
4	Steve Young, John Elway	40.00
5	Jerry Rice, Marcus Allen	50.00
6	Dan Marino, Drew Bledsoe	85.00
7	Terrell Davis, Napoleon Kaufman	50.00
8	Eddie George, Emmitt Smith	85.00
9	Mark Brunell, Tim Brown	40.00
10	Kerry Collins, Reggie White	25.00
11	Deion Sanders, Carl Pickens	20.00
12	Mike Alstott, Keyshawn Johnson	20.00

1997 Playoff Contenders Leather Helmets

This 18-card insert features a die-cut leather helmet. The Silver Level was found 1:24, Blue Level 1:216 and the Red Parallel was numbered to 25.

		MT
Complete Set (18):		425.00
Common Player:		6.00
Minor Stars:		12.00
Inserted 1:24		
Blue Cards:		2x-4x
Inserted 1:216		
Red Cards:		5x-10x
Production 25 Sets		
1	Dan Marino	40.00
2	Troy Aikman	25.00
3	Brett Favre	50.00
4	Barry Sanders	50.00
5	Drew Bledsoe	25.00
6	Deion Sanders	12.00
7	Curtis Martin	15.00
8	Warrick Dunn	20.00
9	Napoleon Kaufman	12.00
10	Eddie George	20.00
11	Antowain Smith	12.00
12	Emmitt Smith	40.00
13	John Elway	30.00
14	Steve Young	15.00
15	Mark Brunell	25.00
16	Terrell Davis	40.00
17	Terry Glenn	6.00
18	Terrell Owens	12.00

1997 Playoff Contenders Pennants

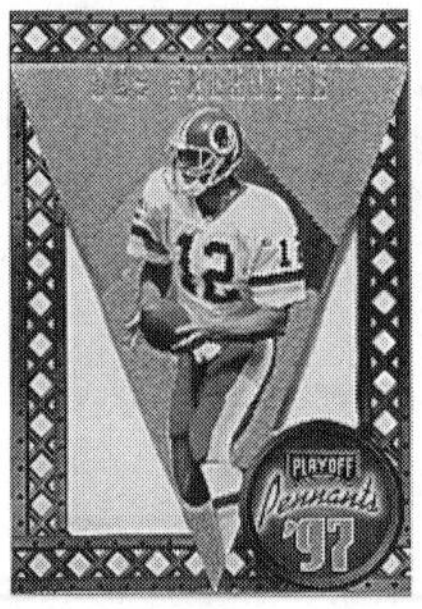

Pennants features player shots on a fuzzy pennant. The 36 cards came in Silver Level (1:12) and Blue Parallel (1:72) versions.

		MT
Complete Set (36):		600.00
Common Player:		4.00
Minor Stars:		8.00
Blue Cards:		4x
1	Dan Marino	40.00
2	Kordell Stewart	25.00
3	Drew Bledsoe	25.00
4	Kerry Collins	10.00
5	John Elway	20.00
6	Trent Dilfer	8.00
7	Jerry Rice	25.00
8	Emmitt Smith	40.00
9	Jeff George	4.00
10	Eddie George	30.00
11	Terrell Davis	25.00
12	Mike Alstott	10.00
13	Jim Druckenmiller	20.00
14	Antowain Smith	15.00
15	Marcus Allen	8.00
16	Jerome Bettis	8.00
17	Terrell Owens	8.00
18	Gus Frerotte	4.00
19	Troy Aikman	25.00
20	Andre Rison	4.00
21	Mark Brunell	25.00
22	Antonio Freeman	8.00
23	Brett Favre	50.00
24	Steve McNair	20.00
25	Barry Sanders	40.00
26	Steve Young	20.00
27	Curtis Martin	25.00
28	Napoleon Kaufman	8.00
29	Deion Sanders	12.00
30	Terry Glenn	18.00
31	Warrick Dunn	25.00
32	Danny Wuerffel	10.00
33	Elvis Grbac	4.00
34	Cris Carter	4.00
35	Joey Galloway	8.00
36	Corey Dillon	20.00

1997 Playoff Contenders Plaques

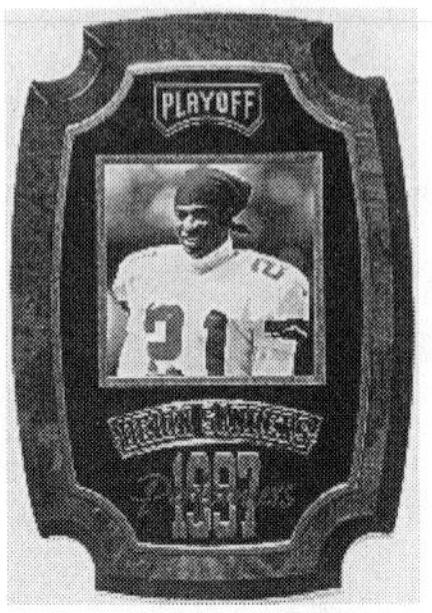

These 45 die-cut cards feature a player shot on a card designed to resemble a plaque. Plaques were made in Silver Level (1:12) and Blue Parallel (1:36) versions.

		MT
Complete Set (45):		600.00
Common Player:		4.00
Minor Stars:		8.00
Blue Cards:		3x
1	Jim Druckenmiller	20.00
2	Danny Wuerffel	10.00
3	Antowain Smith	15.00
4	Warrick Dunn	30.00
5	Terrell Owens	8.00
6	Elvis Grbac	4.00
7	Andre Rison	4.00
8	Tim Brown	4.00
9	Trent Dilfer	8.00
10	Brad Johnson	4.00
11	Deion Sanders	12.00
12	Dan Marino	50.00
13	Kerry Collins	10.00
14	Steve McNair	20.00
15	Eddie George	30.00
16	Ricky Watters	8.00
17	Jerome Bettis	8.00
18	Robert Brooks	4.00
19	Keyshawn Johnson	8.00
20	Antonio Freeman	8.00
21	Eddie Kennison	8.00
22	Mike Alstott	10.00
23	Brett Favre	60.00
24	Troy Aikman	25.00
25	Emmitt Smith	50.00
26	Terrell Davis	25.00
27	John Elway	20.00
28	Barry Sanders	35.00
29	Steve Young	20.00
30	Curtis Martin	25.00
31	Cris Carter	4.00
32	Drew Bledsoe	25.00
33	Mark Brunell	25.00
34	Kordell Stewart	25.00
35	Tony Banks	10.00
36	Napoleon Kaufman	8.00
37	Marcus Allen	8.00
38	Terry Glenn	10.00
39	Herman Moore	8.00
40	Michael Irvin	8.00
41	Joey Galloway	8.00
42	Karim Abdul-Jabbar	10.00
43	Reggie White	8.00
44	Jerry Rice	25.00
45	Gus Frerotte	4.00

1997 Playoff Contenders Rookie Wave

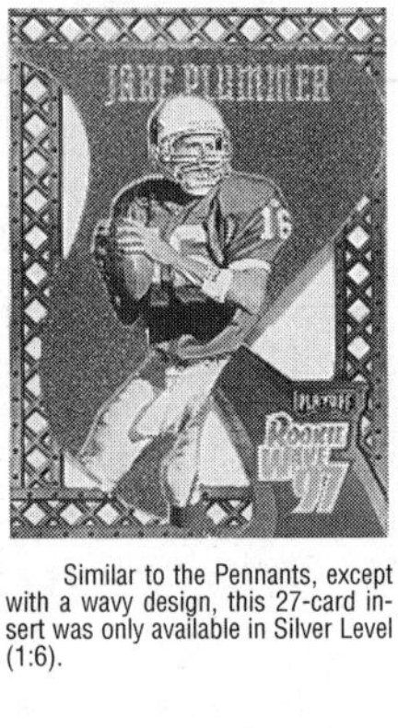

Similar to the Pennants, except with a wavy design, this 27-card insert was only available in Silver Level (1:6).

		MT
Complete Set (27):		150.00
Common Player:		1.50
Minor Stars:		3.00
1	Jim Druckenmiller	10.00
2	Antowain Smith	12.00
3	Will Blackwell	3.00
4	Tiki Barber	3.00
5	Rae Carruth	6.00
6	Jay Graham	3.00
7	Darnell Autry	4.00
8	David LaFleur	4.00
9	Tony Gonzalez	4.00
10	Chad Lewis	1.50
11	Freddie Jones	3.00
12	Shawn Springs	3.00
13	Danny Wuerffel	5.00
14	Warrick Dunn	15.00
15	Troy Davis	5.00
16	Reidel Anthony	8.00
17	Jake Plummer	25.00
18	Byron Hanspard	5.00
19	Fred Lane	4.00
20	Corey Dillon	12.00
21	Darren Sharper	3.00
22	Pat Barnes	5.00
23	Mike Cherry	1.50
24	Leon Johnson	1.50
25	George Jones	3.00
26	Marc Edwards	1.50
27	Orlando Pace	3.00

1997 Playoff Zone

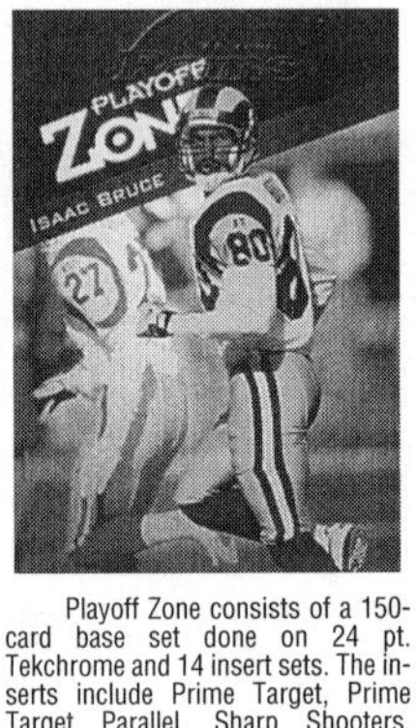

Playoff Zone consists of a 150-card base set done on 24 pt. Tekchrome and 14 insert sets. The inserts include Prime Target, Prime Target Parallel, Sharp Shooters, Sharp Shooters Parallel, Rookies, Close-Ups, Frenzy and Treasures as well as a "1 of 5" parallel set of each insert. The parallels are limited to five each and are sequentially numbered.

		MT
Complete Set (150):		40.00
Common Player:		.10
Minor Stars:		.20
Pack (10):		2.00
Wax Box (36):		60.00
1	Brett Favre	3.00
2	Dorsey Levens	.20
3	William Henderson	.10
4	Derrick Mayes	.10
5	Antonio Freeman	.20
6	Robert Brooks	.10
7	Mark Chmura	.10
8	Reggie White	.20
9	Randall Cunningham	.10
10	Brad Johnson	.20
11	Robert Smith	.10
12	Cris Carter	.10
13	Jake Reed	.10
14	Trent Dilfer	.20
15	Errict Rhett	.10
16	Mike Alstott	.20
17	Scott Mitchell	.10
18	Barry Sanders	2.00
19	Herman Moore	.20
20	Erik Kramer	.10
21	Rick Mirer	.10
22	Rashaan Salaam	.10
23	Troy Aikman	1.50
24	Deion Sanders	.75
25	Emmitt Smith	2.50
26	Daryl Johnston	.10
27	Anthony Miller	.10
28	Eric Bjornson	.10
29	Michael Irvin	.20
30	Chris Jones	.10
31	Ty Detmer	.10
32	Ricky Watters	.20
33	Irving Fryar	.10
34	Rodney Peete	.10
35	Jeff Hostetler	.10
36	Terry Allen	.20
37	Michael Westbrook	.10
38	Gus Frerotte	.10
39	Frank Sanders	.10
40	Larry Centers	.10
41	Kent Graham	.10
42	Dave Brown	.10
43	Rodney Hampton	.10
44	Tyrone Wheatley	.10
45	Chris Calloway	.10
46	Ernie Mills	.10
47	Tim Biakabutuka	.10
48	Anthony Johnson	.10
49	Wesley Walls	.10
50	Muhsin Muhammad	.10
51	Kerry Collins	.30
52	Terrell Owens	1.00
53	Garrison Hearst	.10
54	Jerry Rice	1.50
55	Steve Young	1.00
56	Lawrence Phillips	.10
57	Isaac Bruce	.20
58	Eddie Kennison	.50
59	Tony Banks	.75
60	Heath Shuler	.10
61	Andre Hastings	.10
62	Mario Bates	.10
63	Chris Chandler	.10
64	Jamal Anderson	.10
65	Bert Emanuel	.10
66	Drew Bledsoe	1.50
67	Curtis Martin	1.50
68	Ben Coates	.10
69	Terry Glenn	.40
70	Dan Marino	2.50
71	Karim Abdul-Jabbar	.40
72	Fred Barnett	.10
73	O.J. McDuffie	.10
74	Jim Harbaugh	.10
75	Marshall Faulk	.20
76	Zack Crockett	.10
77	Ken Dilger	.10
78	Marvin Harrison	.50
79	Keyshawn Johnson	.50
80	Neil O'Donnell	.10
81	Adrian Murrell	.20
82	Wayne Chrebet	.10
83	Todd Collins	.10
84	Thurman Thomas	.20
85	Bruce Smith	.10
86	Eric Moulds	.10
87	Rob Johnson	.10
88	Mark Brunell	1.50
89	Natrone Means	.20
90	Jimmy Smith	.10
91	Keenan McCardell	.10
92	Kordell Stewart	1.50
93	Jerome Bettis	.20
94	Charles Johnson	.10
95	Courtney Hawkins	.10
96	Greg Lloyd	.10
97	Ki-Jana Carter	.10
98	Carl Pickens	.10
99	Jeff Blake	.20
100	Steve McNair	1.00
101	Chris Sanders	.10
102	Eddie George	2.00
103	Vinny Testaverde	.10
104	Michael Jackson	.10
105	Derrick Alexander	.10
106	Willie Green	.10
107	Shannon Sharpe	.10
108	Rod Smith	.10
109	Terrell Davis	1.50
110	John Elway	1.00
111	Elvis Grbac	.10
112	Greg Hill	.10
113	Marcus Allen	.20
114	Derrick Thomas	.10
115	Brett Perriman	.10
116	Andre Rison	.10
117	Rickey Dudley	.10
118	Tim Brown	.10
119	Desmond Howard	.10
120	Napoleon Kaufman	.30
121	Jeff George	.10
122	Warren Moon	.10
123	John Friesz	.10
124	Chris Warren	.10
125	Joey Galloway	.20
126	Stan Humphries	.10
127	Tony Martin	.10
128	Eric Metcalf	.10
129	Jim Everett	.10
130	*Warrick Dunn*	1.50
131	*Reidel Anthony*	2.50
132	*Derrick Mason*	1.00
133	*Joey Kent*	.20
134	*Will Blackwell*	.20
135	*Jim Druckenmiller*	3.00
136	*Byron Hanspard*	.50
137	*John Allred*	.10
138	*David LaFleur*	1.00
139	*Danny Wuerffel*	2.00
140	*Tiki Barber*	2.00
141	*Ike Hilliard*	1.50
142	*Troy Davis*	.30
143	*Sedrick Shaw*	.10
144	*Tony Gonzalez*	1.00
145	*Jake Plummer*	4.00
146	*Antowain Smith*	2.00
147	*Rae Carruth*	1.75
148	*Darnell Autry*	1.00
149	*Corey Dillon*	4.00
150	*Orlando Pace*	.20

1997 Playoff Zone Close-Up

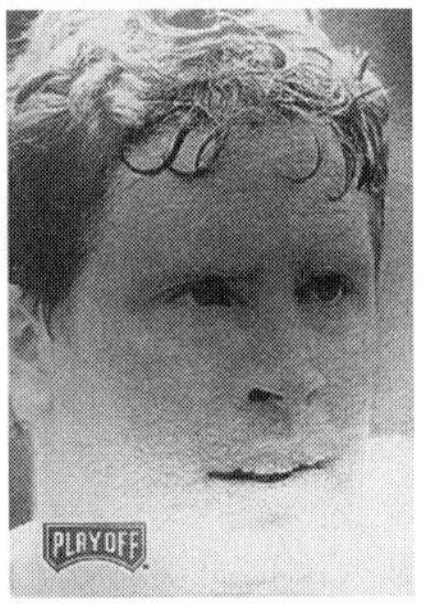

This 32-card insert features helmetless close-ups of top NFL players. The cards were inserted 1:6.

		MT
Complete Set (32):		100.00
Common Player:		.75
Minor Stars:		1.50
1	Brett Favre	12.00
2	Mark Brunell	5.00
3	Dan Marino	10.00
4	Kerry Collins	2.00
5	Troy Aikman	5.00
6	Drew Bledsoe	5.00
7	John Elway	4.00
8	Kordell Stewart	5.00
9	Steve Young	4.00
10	Steve McNair	4.00
11	Tony Banks	3.00
12	Emmitt Smith	10.00
13	Barry Sanders	8.00
14	Jerry Rice	5.00
15	Deion Sanders	3.00
16	Terrell Davis	5.00
17	Curtis Martin	5.00
18	Karim Abdul-Jabbar	3.00
19	Terry Glenn	2.00
20	Eddie George	8.00
21	Keyshawn Johnson	1.50
22	Marvin Harrison	2.00
23	Muhsin Muhammad	.75

24	Joey Galloway	1.50
25	Terrell Owens	3.00
26	Antonio Freeman	1.50
27	Ricky Watters	1.50
28	Jeff Blake	1.50
29	Reggie White	1.50
30	Michael Irvin	1.50
31	Eddie Kennison	2.00
32	Robert Brooks	.75

1997 Playoff Zone Frenzy

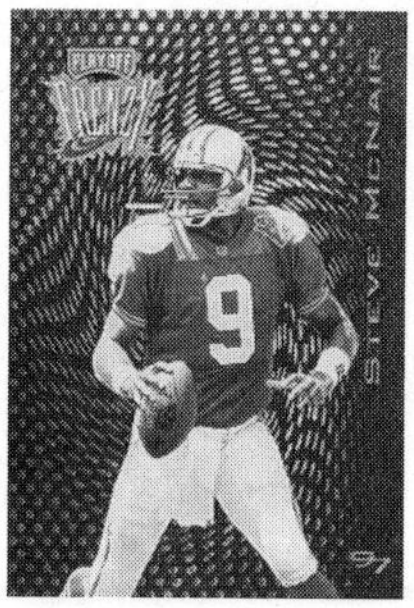

This 26-card insert set was done on etched foil cards and inserted 1:12.

		MT
Complete Set (26):		175.00
Common Player:		1.00
Minor Stars:		2.00
1	Brett Favre	25.00
2	Dan Marino	20.00
3	Troy Aikman	10.00
4	Drew Bledsoe	10.00
5	John Elway	10.00
6	Kordell Stewart	10.00
7	Steve Young	6.00
8	Steve McNair	6.00
9	Tony Banks	4.00
10	Emmitt Smith	20.00
11	Barry Sanders	15.00
12	Deion Sanders	4.00
13	Terrell Davis	10.00
14	Curtis Martin	8.00
15	Karim Abdul-Jabbar	4.00
16	Terry Glenn	2.00
17	Eddie George	10.00
18	Keyshawn Johnson	2.00
19	Marvin Harrison	2.00
20	Joey Galloway	2.00
21	Antonio Freeman	2.00
22	Jeff Blake	2.00
23	Michael Irvin	2.00
24	Eddie Kennison	2.00
25	Reggie White	2.00
26	Robert Brooks	1.00

1997 Playoff Zone Prime Target

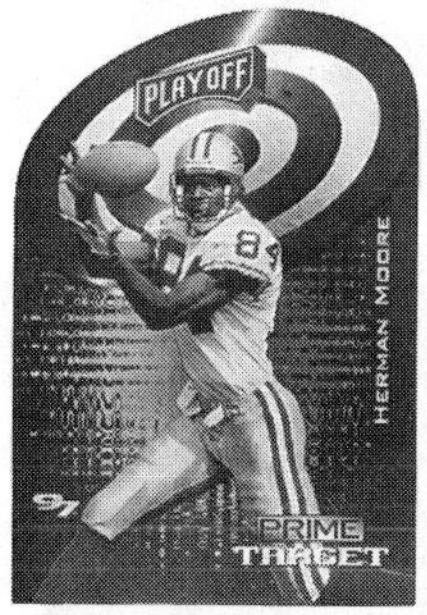

This 20-card insert features the NFL's top pass catchers backed by a blue and silver die-cut target design. This set had an insert rate of 1:24.

		MT
Complete Set (20):		170.00
Common Player:		4.00
Minor Stars:		8.00
Red Cards:		3x
1	Emmitt Smith	25.00
2	Barry Sanders	20.00
3	Jerry Rice	15.00
4	Terrell Davis	15.00
5	Curtis Martin	15.00
6	Karim Abdul-Jabbar	10.00
7	Terry Glenn	12.00
8	Eddie George	20.00
9	Keyshawn Johnson	8.00
10	Joey Galloway	8.00
11	Antonio Freeman	8.00
12	Herman Moore	8.00
13	Tim Brown	4.00
14	Michael Irvin	8.00
15	Isaac Bruce	8.00
16	Eddie Kennison	8.00
17	Shannon Sharpe	4.00
18	Cris Carter	4.00
19	Napoleon Kaufman	8.00
20	Carl Pickens	4.00

Post-1980 cards in Near Mint condition will generally sell for about 75% of the quoted Mint value. Excellent-condition cards bring no more than 40%.

1997 Playoff Zone Rookies

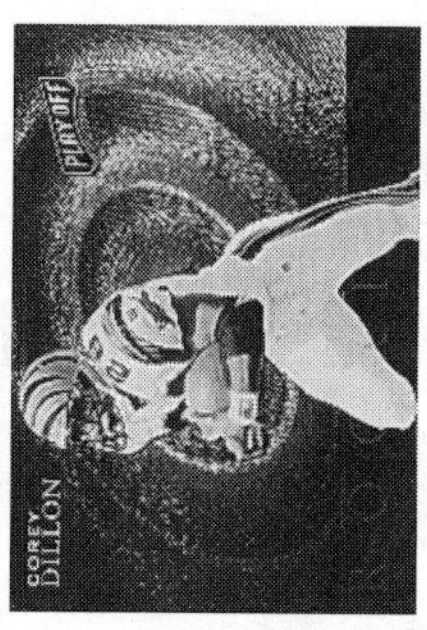

This insert features 24 rookies on etched foil cards. The cards were inserted 1:8.

		MT
Complete Set (24):		100.00
Common Player:		1.00
Minor Stars:		2.00
1	Jake Plummer	20.00
2	George Jones	1.00
3	Pat Barnes	4.00
4	Brian Manning	1.00
5	O.J. Santiago	1.00
6	Byron Hanspard	4.00
7	Antowain Smith	8.00
8	Rae Carruth	6.00
9	Darnell Autry	4.00
10	Corey Dillon	10.00
11	David LaFleur	4.00
12	Tony Gonzalez	4.00
13	Sedrick Shaw	4.00
14	Danny Wuerffel	6.00
15	Troy Davis	6.00
16	Ike Hilliard	6.00
17	Tiki Barber	6.00
18	Will Blackwell	1.00
19	Jim Druckenmiller	8.00
20	Orlando Pace	2.00
21	Warrick Dunn	12.00
22	Reidel Anthony	7.00
23	Derrick Mason	2.50
24	Joey Kent	2.00

1997 Playoff Zone Sharpshooters

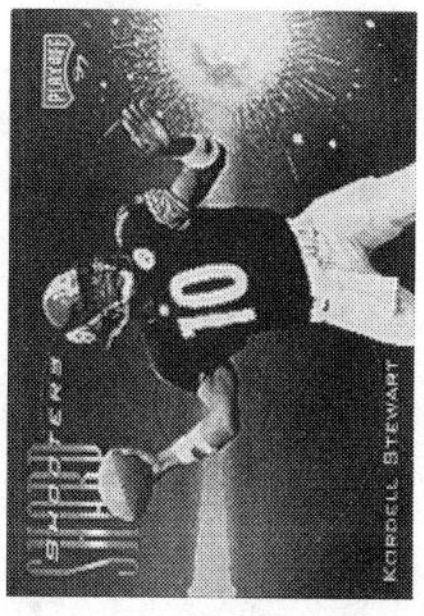

The top NFL QBs are highlighted in this 18-card set with flaming graphics in the background. The cards were inserted 1:72.

		MT
Complete Set (18):		160.00
Common Player:		3.00
Minor Stars:		6.00
Red Cards:		2x
1	Brett Favre	35.00
2	Dan Marino	30.00
3	John Elway	12.00
4	Troy Aikman	15.00
5	Drew Bledsoe	15.00
6	Todd Collins	3.00
7	Brad Johnson	6.00
8	Stan Humphries	3.00
9	John Friesz	3.00
10	Tony Banks	8.00
11	Ty Detmer	3.00
12	Steve McNair	12.00
13	Rob Johnson	3.00
14	Kordell Stewart	15.00
15	Danny Wuerffel	12.00
16	Jim Druckenmiller	12.00
17	Jake Plummer	10.00
18	Kerry Collins	6.00

1997 Playoff Zone Treasures

This 12-card insert features the top collectible NFL players. The cards were inserted 1:196.

		MT
Complete Set (12):		700.00
Common Players:		25.00
1	Brett Favre	120.00
2	Dan Marino	100.00
3	Troy Aikman	50.00
4	Drew Bledsoe	50.00
5	Emmitt Smith	100.00
6	Barry Sanders	75.00
7	Warrick Dunn	60.00
8	Deion Sanders	25.00
9	Terrell Davis	50.00
10	Curtis Martin	40.00
11	Tiki Barber	25.00
12	Eddie George	50.00

1997 Playoff 1st & 10

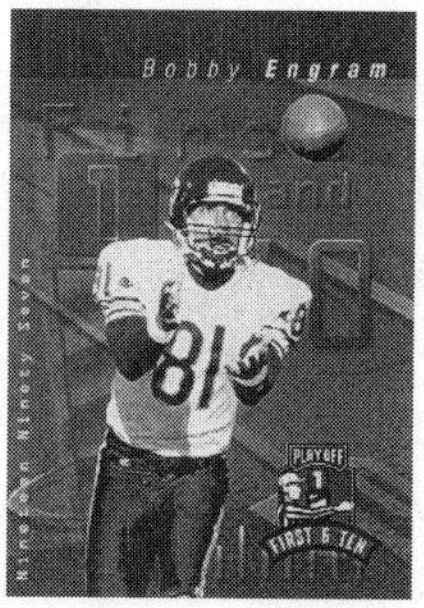

The 250-card set features a color photo of a player superimposed over a purple "1st and 10" background on the front. The player's name is printed in light purple in the upper center and right, while "Nineteen Ninety Seven" appears vertically along the lower left border. The "1st and 10" logo appears in the lower right. The backs have the card number in the upper right, while the player's number, position, name, highlights, bio and stats all are printed along the left side over a purple "1st and 10" background. The player's head shot is printed on the right. In addition, a Kickoff parallel 250-card set was inserted 1:9 packs. The card fronts are identical to the base cards except they are printed on translucent lucite and a gold-foil Kickoff logo is stamped in the upper left. The only printing on the backs are the Players Inc., Play Football and the Playoff 1997 copyright tag line.

		MT
Complete Set (250):		30.00
Common Player:		.10
Minor Stars:		.20
Kickoff Cards:		10x-20x
Kickoff Rookies:		5x-10x
Inserted 1:9		
Pack (10):		55.00
Wax Box (36):		
1	Marcus Allen	.20
2	Eric Bieniemy	.10
3	Jason Dunn	.10
4	Jim Harbaugh	.10
5	Michael Westbrook	.10
6	*Tiki Barber*	1.00
7	Frank Reich	.10
8	Irving Fryar	.10
9	Courtney Hawkins	.10
10	Eric Zeier	.10
11	Kent Graham	.10
12	Trent Dilfer	.10
13	Neil O'Donnell	.10
14	*Reidel Anthony*	1.00
15	Jeff Hostetler	.10
16	Lawrence Phillips	.20
17	Dave Brown	.10
18	Mike Tomczak	.10
19	Jake Reed	.10
20	Anthony Miller	.10
21	Eric Metcalf	.10
22	*Sedrick Shaw*	.50
23	Anthony Johnson	.10
24	Mario Bates	.10
25	Dorsey Levens	.25
26	Stan Humphries	.10
27	Ben Coates	.10
28	Tyrone Wheatley	.10
29	Adrian Murrell	.10
30	William Henderson	.10
31	*Warrick Dunn*	1.50
32	LeShon Johnson	.10
33	James Stewart	.10
34	Edgar Bennett	.10
35	Raymont Harris	.10
36	Leroy Butler	.10
37	Darren Woodson	.10
38	*Darnell Autry*	.75
39	Johnnie Morton	.10
40	William Floyd	.10
41	Terrell Fletcher	.10
42	Leonard Russell	.10
43	Henry Ellard	.10
44	Terrell Owens	.50
45	John Friesz	.10
46	*Antowain Smith*	1.25
47	Charles Johnson	.10
48	Rickey Dudley	.10
49	Lake Dawson	.10
50	Bert Emanuel	.10
51	Zach Thomas	.25
52	Earnest Byner	.10
53	*Yatil Green*	.75
54	Chris Spielman	.10
55	Muhsin Muhammad	.10
56	Bobby Engram	.10
57	Eric Bjornson	.10
58	Willie Green	.10
59	Derrick Mayes	.10
60	Chris Sanders	.10
61	Jimmy Smith	.10
62	*Tony Gonzalez*	.50
63	Rich Gannon	.10
64	Stanley Pritchett	.10
65	Brad Johnson	.10
66	Rodney Peete	.10
67	Sam Gash	.10
68	Chris Calloway	.10
69	Chris T. Jones	.10
70	*Will Blackwell*	.20
71	Mark Bruener	.10
72	Terry Kirby	.10
73	Brian Blades	.10
74	Craig Heyward	.10
75	Jamie Asher	.10
76	Terance Mathis	.10
77	*Troy Davis*	.30
78	Bruce Smith	.10
79	Simeon Rice	.10
80	Fred Barnett	.10
81	Tim Brown	.10
82	James Jett	.10
83	Mark Carrier	.10
84	Shawn Jefferson	.10
85	Ken Dilger	.10
86	*Rae Carruth*	.75
87	Keenan McCardell	.10
88	Michael Irvin	.20
89	Mark Chmura	.10
90	Derrick Alexander	.10
91	Andre Reed	.10
92	Ed McCaffrey	.10
93	Erik Kramer	.10
94	Albert Connell	.10
95	Frank Wycheck	.10
96	Zack Crockett	.10
97	Jim Everett	.10
98	Michael Haynes	.10
99	Jeff Graham	.10
100	Brent Jones	.10
101	Troy Aikman	1.00
102	*Byron Hanspard*	.75
103	Robert Brooks	.10
104	Karim Abdul-Jabbar	.75
105	Drew Bledsoe	1.00
106	Napoleon Kaufman	.50
107	Steve Young	.50
108	Leeland McElroy	.20
109	Jamal Anderson	.20
110	*David LaFleur*	.50
111	Vinny Testaverde	.10
112	Eric Moulds	.20
113	Tim Biakabutuka	.20
114	Rick Mirer	.10
115	Jeff Blake	.20
116	Jim Schwantz	.50
117	Herman Moore	.20
118	*Ike Hilliard*	1.00
119	Reggie White	.20
120	Steve McNair	.50
121	Marshall Faulk	.20
122	Natrone Means	.20
123	Greg Hill	.10
124	O.J. McDuffie	.10
125	Robert Smith	.10
126	*Bryant Westbrook*	.20
127	Ray Zellars	.10
128	Rodney Hampton	.10
129	Wayne Chrebet	.10
130	Desmond Howard	.10
131	Ty Detmer	.10
132	Erric Pegram	.10
133	Yancey Thigpen	.10
134	*Danny Wuerffel*	.75
135	Charlie Jones	.10
136	Chris Warren	.10
137	Isaac Bruce	.25
138	Errict Rhett	.20
139	Gus Frerotte	.10
140	Frank Sanders	.10
141	Todd Collins	.10
142	*Jake Plummer*	3.00
143	Darnay Scott	.10
144	Rashaan Salaam	.20
145	Terrell Davis	1.50
146	Scott Mitchell	.10
147	Junior Seau	.20
148	Warren Moon	.10
149	Wesley Walls	.10
150	Daryl Johnston	.10
151	Brett Favre	2.25
152	Emmitt Smith	2.00
153	Dan Marino	2.00
154	Larry Centers	.10
155	Michael Jackson	.10
156	Kerry Collins	.30
157	Curtis Conway	.20
158	*Peter Boulware*	.20
159	Carl Pickens	.10
160	Shannon Sharpe	.10
161	Brett Perriman	.10
162	Eddie George	1.50
163	Mark Brunell	1.00
164	Tamarick Vanover	.20
165	Cris Carter	.10
166	*Corey Dillon*	2.50
167	Curtis Martin	1.25
168	Amani Toomer	.10
169	Jeff George	.10
170	Kordell Stewart	.75
171	Garrison Hearst	.10
172	Tony Banks	.50
173	Mike Alstott	.20
174	*Jim Druckenmiller*	.75
175	Chris Chandler	.10
176	Bam Morris	.10
177	Billy Joe Hobert	.10
178	Ernie Mills	.10
179	Ki-Jana Carter	.10
180	Deion Sanders	.50
181	Ricky Watters	.20
182	*Shawn Springs*	.30
183	Barry Sanders	1.25
184	Antonio Freeman	.30
185	Marvin Harrison	.50
186	Elvis Grbac	.10
187	Terry Glenn	1.00
188	Willie Roaf	.10
189	Keyshawn Johnson	.50
190	*Orlando Pace*	.30
191	Jerome Bettis	.20
192	Tony Martin	.10
193	Jerry Rice	1.00
194	Joey Galloway	.30
195	Terry Allen	.10
196	Eddie Kennison	.50
197	Thurman Thomas	.20
198	*Darrell Russell*	.20
199	Rob Moore	.10
200	John Elway	.50
201	Quinn Early	.10
202	Kevin Greene	.10
203	Robert Green	.10
204	Tony Carter	.10
205	Michael Timpson	.10
206	Kevin Smith	.10
207	Herschel Walker	.10
208	Steve Atwater	.10
209	Tyrone Braxton	.10
210	Willie Davis	.10
211	Lamont Warren	.10
212	Sean Dawkins	.10
213	Dale Carter	.10
214	Kimble Anders	.10
215	Derrick Thomas	.10
216	Chris Penn	.10
217	Irving Spikes	.10
218	Amp Lee	.10
219	Qadry Ismail	.10
220	Dave Meggett	.10
221	Tyrone Hughes	.10
222	Haywood Jeffires	.10
223	Torrance Small	.10
224	Danny Kanell	.10
225	Thomas Lewis	.10
226	Kyle Brady	.10
227	Harvey Williams	.10
228	Bobby Hoying	.10
229	Charlie Garner	.10
230	Andre Hastings	.10
231	Heath Shuler	.10
232	J.J. Stokes	.10
233	Ken Norton	.10
234	Steve Walsh	.10
235	Harold Green	.10
236	Reggie Brooks	.10
237	Robb Thomas	.10
238	Brian Mitchell	.10
239	Bill Brooks	.10
240	Leslie Shepherd	.10
241	Jay Graham	.10
242	*Kevin Lockett*	.20
243	*Derrick Mason*	1.00
244	*Marc Edwards*	.20
245	*Joey Kent*	.40
246	*Pat Barnes*	.50
247	Sherman Williams	.10
248	Ray Brown	.10
249	Stephen Davis	.10
250	Lamar Smith	.10

1997 Playoff 1st & 10 Chip Shots

Similar to a poker chip, the 250 plastic Chip Shot tokens were inserted one per pack. The fronts have the player's name at the top, while his photo is in the center. The Playoff logo and team name are printed at the bottom, with the token number appearing on the left and right sides of the front. The backs have "Chip Shot" printed at the top, with the Playoff logo in the center. "'97" is printed on the left and right of the token. "NFL" appears at the bottom.

		MT
Complete Set (250):		200.00
Common Player:		.25
Minor Stars:		.50
1	Marcus Allen	.50
2	Eric Bieniemy	.25
3	Jason Dunn	.25
4	Jim Harbaugh	.25
5	Michael Westbrook	.25
6	Tiki Barber	3.00
7	Frank Reich	.25
8	Irving Fryar	.25
9	Courtney Hawkins	.25
10	Eric Zeier	.25
11	Kent Graham	.25
12	Trent Dilfer	.25
13	Neil O'Donnell	.25
14	Reidel Anthony	3.00
15	Jeff Hostetler	.25
16	Lawrence Phillips	.50
17	Dave Brown	.25
18	Mike Tomczak	.25
19	Jake Reed	.25
20	Anthony Miller	.25
21	Eric Metcalf	.25
22	Sedrick Shaw	.75
23	Anthony Johnson	.25
24	Mario Bates	.25
25	Dorsey Levens	.25
26	Stan Humphries	.25
27	Ben Coates	.25
28	Tyrone Wheatley	.25
29	Adrian Murrell	.25
30	William Henderson	.25
31	Warrick Dunn	8.00
32	LeShon Johnson	.25
33	James Stewart	.25
34	Edgar Bennett	.25
35	Raymont Harris	.25
36	Leroy Butler	.25
37	Darren Woodson	.25
38	Darnell Autry	1.50
39	Johnnie Morton	.25
40	William Floyd	.25
41	Terrell Fletcher	.25
42	Leonard Russell	.25
43	Henry Ellard	.25
44	Terrell Owens	3.00
45	John Friesz	.25
46	Antowain Smith	4.00
47	Charles Johnson	.25
48	Rickey Dudley	.25
49	Lake Dawson	.25
50	Bert Emanuel	.25
51	Zach Thomas	.75
52	Earnest Byner	.25
53	Yatil Green	1.00
54	Chris Spielman	.25
55	Muhsin Muhammad	.25
56	Bobby Engram	.25
57	Eric Bjornson	.25
58	Willie Green	.25
59	Derrick Mayes	.25
60	Chris Sanders	.25
61	Jimmy Smith	.25
62	Tony Gonzalez	.75
63	Rich Gannon	.25
64	Stanley Pritchett	.25
65	Brad Johnson	.25
66	Rodney Peete	.25
67	Sam Gash	.25
68	Chris Calloway	.25
69	Chris T. Jones	.25
70	Will Blackwell	.50
71	Mark Bruener	.25
72	Terry Kirby	.25
73	Brian Blades	.25
74	Craig Heyward	.25
75	Jamie Asher	.25
76	Terance Mathis	.25
77	Troy Davis	1.00
78	Bruce Smith	.25
79	Simeon Rice	.25
80	Fred Barnett	.25
81	Tim Brown	.25
82	James Jett	.25
83	Mark Carrier	.25
84	Shawn Jefferson	.25
85	Ken Dilger	.25
86	Rae Carruth	2.50
87	Keenan McCardell	.25
88	Michael Irvin	.50
89	Mark Chmura	.25
90	Derrick Alexander	.25
91	Andre Reed	.25
92	Ed McCaffrey	.25
93	Erik Kramer	.25
94	Albert Connell	.25
95	Frank Wycheck	.25
96	Zack Crockett	.25
97	Jim Everett	.25
98	Michael Haynes	.25
99	Jeff Graham	.25
100	Brent Jones	.25
101	Troy Aikman	5.00
102	Byron Hanspard	2.00
103	Robert Brooks	.25
104	Karim Abdul-Jabbar	1.00
105	Drew Bledsoe	5.00
106	Napoleon Kaufman	.25
107	Steve Young	3.00
108	Leeland McElroy	.25
109	Jamal Anderson	.50
110	David LaFleur	.75
111	Vinny Testaverde	.25
112	Eric Moulds	.50
113	Tim Biakabutuka	.50
114	Rick Mirer	.25
115	Jeff Blake	.50
116	Jim Schwantz	.25
117	Herman Moore	.50
118	Ike Hilliard	3.00
119	Reggie White	.50
120	Steve McNair	4.00
121	Marshall Faulk	.50
122	Natrone Means	.50
123	Greg Hill	.25
124	O.J. McDuffie	.25
125	Robert Smith	.25
126	Bryant Westbrook	.50
127	Ray Zellars	.25
128	Rodney Hampton	.25
129	Wayne Chrebet	.25
130	Desmond Howard	.25
131	Ty Detmer	.25
132	Erric Pegram	.25
133	Yancey Thigpen	.25
134	Danny Wuerffel	3.00
135	Charlie Jones	.25
136	Chris Warren	.25
137	Isaac Bruce	.75
138	Errict Rhett	.50
139	Gus Frerotte	.25
140	Frank Sanders	.25
141	Todd Collins	.25
142	Jake Plummer	4.00
143	Darnay Scott	.25
144	Rashaan Salaam	.50
145	Terrell Davis	6.00
146	Scott Mitchell	.25
147	Junior Seau	.50
148	Warren Moon	.25
149	Wesley Walls	.25
150	Daryl Johnston	.25
151	Brett Favre	10.00
152	Emmitt Smith	8.00
153	Dan Marino	8.00
154	Larry Centers	.25
155	Michael Jackson	.25
156	Kerry Collins	1.00
157	Curtis Conway	.50
158	Peter Boulware	.50
159	Carl Pickens	.25
160	Shannon Sharpe	.25
161	Brett Perriman	.25
162	Eddie George	6.00
163	Mark Brunell	5.00
164	Tamarick Vanover	.50
165	Cris Carter	.25
166	Corey Dillon	5.00
167	Curtis Martin	6.00
168	Amani Toomer	.25
169	Jeff George	.25
170	Kordell Stewart	5.00
171	Garrison Hearst	.25
172	Tony Banks	2.00
173	Mike Alstott	2.00
174	Jim Druckenmiller	5.00
175	Chris Chandler	.25
176	Bam Morris	.25
177	Billy Joe Hobert	.25
178	Ernie Mills	.25
179	Ki-Jana Carter	.25
180	Deion Sanders	2.50
181	Ricky Watters	.50
182	Shawn Springs	.50
183	Barry Sanders	8.00
184	Antonio Freeman	1.50
185	Marvin Harrison	2.50
186	Elvis Grbac	.25
187	Terry Glenn	1.00
188	Willie Roaf	.25
189	Keyshawn Johnson	2.50
190	Orlando Pace	.50
191	Jerome Bettis	.50
192	Tony Martin	.25
193	Jerry Rice	5.00
194	Joey Galloway	1.00
195	Terry Allen	.25
196	Eddie Kennison	2.50
197	Thurman Thomas	.50
198	Darrell Russell	.50
199	Rob Moore	.25
200	John Elway	3.00
201	Quinn Early	.25
202	Kevin Greene	.25
203	Robert Green	.25
204	Tony Carter	.25
205	Michael Timpson	.25
206	Kevin Smith	.25
207	Herschel Walker	.25
208	Steve Atwater	.25
209	Tyrone Braxton	.25
210	Willie Davis	.25
211	Lamont Warren	.25
212	Sean Dawkins	.25
213	Dale Carter	.25
214	Kimble Anders	.25
215	Derrick Thomas	.25
216	Chris Penn	.25
217	Irving Spikes	.25
218	Amp Lee	.25
219	Qadry Ismail	.25
220	Dave Meggett	.25
221	Tyrone Hughes	.25
222	Haywood Jeffires	.25
223	Torrance Small	.25
224	Danny Kanell	.25
225	Thomas Lewis	.25
226	Kyle Brady	.25
227	Harvey Williams	.25
228	Bobby Hoying	.25
229	Charlie Garner	.25
230	Andre Hastings	.25

231	Heath Shuler	.25
232	J.J. Stokes	.25
233	Ken Norton	.25
234	Steve Walsh	.25
235	Harold Green	.25
236	Reggie Brooks	.25
237	Robb Thomas	.25
238	Brian Mitchell	.25
239	Bill Brooks	.25
240	Leslie Shepherd	.25
241	Jay Graham	.25
242	Kevin Lockett	.50
243	Derrick Mason	.75
244	Marc Edwards	.50
245	Joey Kent	.75
246	Pat Barnes	.75
247	Sherman Williams	.25
248	Ray Brown	.25
249	Stephen Davis	.25
250	Lamar Smith	.25

1997 Playoff 1st & 10 Extra Point Autograph

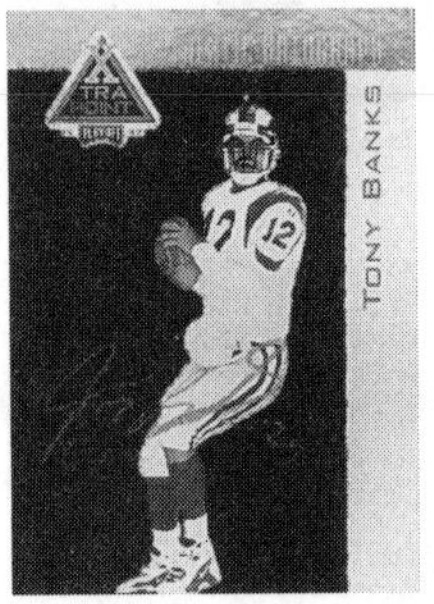

Inserted 1:444 packs, the autographed cards are signed by either Tony Banks or Terrell Davis. The cards have a gold-foil stripe at the top front with "Authentic Autograph" embossed on it. The Extra Point logo appears in the upper left. Black felt surrounds the photo of the respective player. The autograph is signed on the felt and into the photo. The player's name is listed inside a white stripe on the right border of the front. The backs, which are numbered with an "XPA" prefix, have a photo bordered in black. The number appears in an oval in the upper right.

		MT
Complete Set (2):		200.00
Common Player:		50.00
1	Tony Banks	50.00
2	Terrell Davis	150.00

1997 Playoff 1st & 10 Hot Pursuit

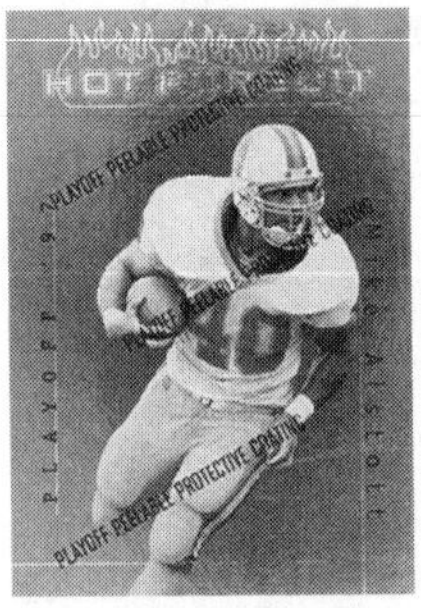

Inserted 1:180 packs, the 100-card set has the player photo superimposed on an orange background on the front. The Hot Pursuit logo is in the top center, while "Playoff '97" is printed vertically along the left border and the player's name is printed vertically along the right border. The card fronts did include a Playoff peelable protective coating. The backs featured a full-bleed photo of the player, with the card number in the upper right.

		MT
Compete Set (100):		1250.
Common Player:		5.00
Minor Stars:		10.00
1	Brett Favre	100.00
2	Dorsey Levens	20.00
3	Antonio Freeman	20.00
4	Robert Brooks	5.00
5	Mark Chmura	5.00
6	Reggie White	10.00
7	Drew Bledsoe	50.00
8	Curtis Martin	25.00
9	Ben Coates	10.00
10	Terry Glenn	20.00
11	Kerry Collins	10.00
12	Tim Biakabutuka	10.00
13	Anthony Johnson	5.00
14	Wesley Walls	10.00
15	Muhsin Muhammad	10.00
16	Mark Brunell	50.00
17	Natrone Means	10.00
18	Jimmy Smith	20.00
19	John Elway	100.00
20	Terrell Davis	100.00
21	Anthony Miller	5.00
22	Shannon Sharpe	10.00
23	Steve Young	30.00
24	Garrison Hearst	20.00
25	Jerry Rice	50.00
26	Troy Aikman	50.00
27	Deion Sanders	20.00
28	Emmitt Smith	80.00
29	Michael Irvin	20.00
30	Kordell Stewart	25.00
31	Jerome Bettis	20.00
32	Charles Johnson	5.00
33	Ty Detmer	5.00
34	Ricky Watters	10.00
35	Irving Fryar	5.00
36	Todd Collins	5.00
37	Thurman Thomas	10.00
38	Bruce Smith	10.00
39	Eric Moulds	20.00
40	Brad Johnson	20.00
41	Robert Smith	20.00
42	Cris Carter	20.00
43	Elvis Grbac	10.00
44	Greg Hill	10.00
45	Marcus Allen	20.00
46	Gus Frerotte	5.00
47	Terry Allen	10.00
48	Michael Westbrook	20.00
49	Jim Harbaugh	10.00
50	Marshall Faulk	25.00
51	Marvin Harrison	25.00
52	Jeff Blake	10.00
53	Ki-Jana Carter	10.00
54	Carl Pickens	10.00
55	Junior Seau	10.00
56	Tony Martin	10.00
57	Dan Marino	100.00
58	Karim Abdul-Jabbar	10.00
59	Stanley Pritchett	5.00
60	Zach Thomas	10.00
61	Steve McNair	25.00
62	Eddie George	50.00
63	Chris Sanders	5.00
64	Rick Mirer	5.00
65	Rashaan Salaam	5.00
66	Curtis Conway	10.00
67	Bobby Engram	5.00
68	Kent Graham	5.00
69	Leeland McElroy	5.00
70	Larry Centers	5.00
71	Frank Sanders	10.00
72	Jeff George	10.00
73	Napoleon Kaufman	10.00
74	Desmond Howard	5.00
75	Tim Brown	20.00
76	John Friesz	10.00
77	Chris Warren	10.00
78	Joey Galloway	60.00
79	Tony Banks	20.00
80	Lawrence Phillips	10.00
81	Isaac Bruce	25.00
82	Eddie Kennison	10.00
83	Errict Rhett	10.00
84	Mike Alstott	25.00
85	Rodney Hampton	5.00
86	Amani Toomer	10.00
87	Scott Mitchell	5.00
88	Barry Sanders	100.00
89	Herman Moore	20.00
90	Vinny Testaverde	20.00
91	Bam Morris	5.00
92	Michael Jackson	5.00
93	Chris Chandler	5.00
94	Eric Metcalf	5.00
95	Jamal Anderson	20.00
96	Jim Everett	5.00
97	Mario Bates	5.00
98	Wayne Chrebet	10.00
99	Adrian Murrell	5.00
100	Keyshawn Johnson	20.00

1997 Playoff 1st & 10 Xtra Point

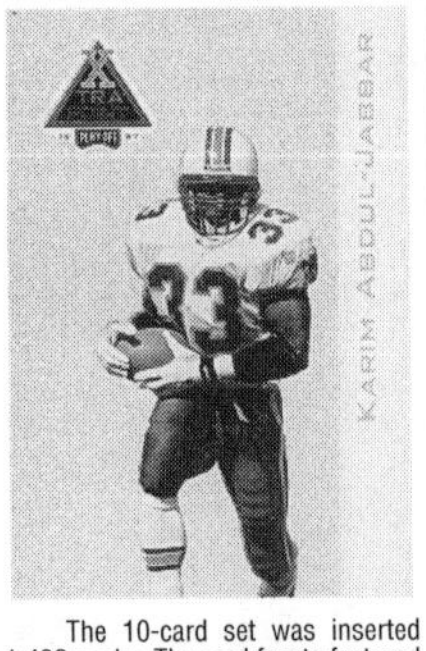

The 10-card set was inserted 1:432 packs. The card fronts featured the Extra Point logo in the upper left, and a player photo in the center. Both were surrounded by felt. The player's name is printed inside a white stripe along the right border. The card backs, which featured a prefix of "XP," have the player photo surrounded by felt. The card's number is printed inside an oval in the upper right.

		MT
Complete Set (10):		275.00
Common Player:		10.00
Inserted 1:432		
Autographs 1:4,454		
1	Kordell Stewart	20.00
2	Dan Marino	45.00
3	Brett Favre	60.00
4	Emmitt Smith	45.00
5	John Elway	45.00
6	Eddie George	30.00
7	Karim Abdul-Jabbar	10.00
8	Terry Glenn	12.00
9	Curtis Martin	15.00
10	Joey Galloway	15.00
A1	Tony Banks Auto	40.00
A2	Terrell Davis Auto	160.00

1997 Playoff Sports Cards Picks

Playoff produced this six-card set which was distributed to collectors who purchased a subscription to Sports Cards magazine at the 1997 National.

		MT
Complete Set (6):		8.00
Common Player:		1.00
1	Brett Favre	3.00
2	Barry Sanders	2.00
3	Terrell Davis	1.50
4	Jerry Rice	1.50
5	Deion Sanders	1.00
6	Kordell Stewart	1.50

1997 Playoff Super Bowl Card Show

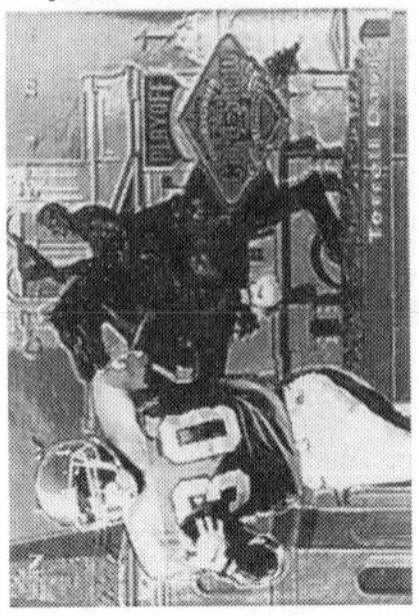

This set was available through wrapper redemption at the 1997 Super Bowl Card Show. Each card was available in exchange for three Playoff wrappers opened at the Playoff booth. The only exception is the Terrell Davis card, which could only be obtained by redeeming an entire box of wrappers for a complete seven-card set. The cards are not numbered.

		MT
Complete Set (7):		20.00
Common Player:		2.00
1	Terry Allen	2.00
2	Jerome Bettis	3.00
3	Terrell Davis	5.00
4	Marshall Faulk	3.00
5	Eddie George	8.00
6	Deion Sanders	3.50
7	Reggie White	3.00

1998 Playoff Absolute Hobby

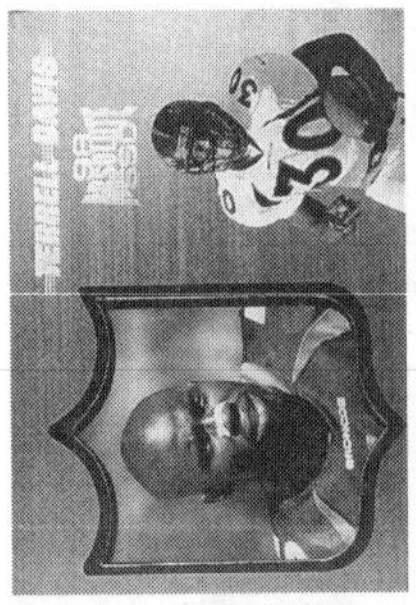

Absolute SSD was made for the hobby-only and contained 200 cards on super-thick 24-point stock. The horizontal cards featured brushed silver foil with a celluloid player image laminated between the front and back. Playoff also produced a retail version, called Absolute, which included all 200 cards, but on a thinner stock with a different twist to some of the inserts. The set was paralleled twice, in a Silver foil version and a Gold foil version numbered to 25 sets. Inserts include: Checklists, Draft Picks, Honors, Marino Milestones, Platinum Quads, Shields, Red Zone and Statistically Speaking.

		MT
Complete Set (200):		225.00
Common Player:		.50
Minor Stars:		1.00
Silver Cards:		3x
Silver Rookies:		2x
Inserted 1:3		
Gold Cards:		50x-100x
Gold Rookies:		7x-14x
Production 25 Sets		
Pack (5):		8.00
Wax Box (16):		110.00
1	John Elway	6.00
2	*Marcus Nash*	8.00
3	*Brian Griese*	12.00
4	Terrell Davis	8.00
5	Rod Smith	1.00
6	Shannon Sharpe	1.00
7	Ed McCaffrey	.50
8	Brett Favre	12.00
9	Dorsey Levens	1.00
10	Derrick Mayes	.50
11	Antonio Freeman	1.00
12	Robert Brooks	.50
13	Mark Chmura	1.00
14	Reggie White	1.00
15	Kordell Stewart	5.00
16	*Hines Ward*	8.00
17	Jerome Bettis	1.00
18	Charles Johnson	.50
19	Courtney Hawkins	.50
20	Will Blackwell	.50
21	Mark Bruener	.50
22	Steve Young	4.00
23	Jim Druckenmiller	1.00
24	Garrison Hearst	1.00
25	*R.W. McQuarters*	2.00
26	Marc Edwards	.50
27	Irv Smith	.50
28	Jerry Rice	6.00
29	Terrell Owens	1.00
30	J.J. Stokes	1.00
31	Elvis Grbac	1.00
32	*Rashaan Shehee*	2.00
33	Donnell Bennett	.50
34	Kimble Anders	.50
35	Ted Popson	.50
36	Derrick Alexander	.50
37	Tony Gonzalez	1.00
38	Andre Rison	1.00
39	Brad Johnson	1.00
40	*Randy Moss*	25.00
41	Robert Smith	1.00
42	Leroy Hoard	.50
43	Cris Carter	1.00
44	Jake Reed	.50
45	Drew Bledsoe	6.00
46	*Tony Simmons*	1.00
47	*Chris Floyd*	1.00
48	*Robert Edwards*	12.00
49	Shawn Jefferson	.50
50	Ben Coates	.50
51	Terry Glenn	1.00
52	Trent Dilfer	1.00
53	*Jacquez Green*	6.00
54	Warrick Dunn	6.00
55	Mike Alstott	1.00
56	Reidel Anthony	1.00
57	Bert Emanuel	.50
58	Warren Sapp	.50
59	*Charlie Batch*	10.00
60	*Germane Crowell*	8.00
61	Scott Mitchell	.50
62	Barry Sanders	12.00
63	Tommy Vardell	.50
64	Herman Moore	1.00
65	Johnnie Morton	.50
66	Mark Brunell	5.00
67	*Jonathan Quinn*	1.00
68	*Fred Taylor*	15.00
69	James Stewart	.50
70	Jimmy Smith	1.00
71	Damon Jones	.50
72	Keenan McCardell	.50
73	Dan Marino	10.00
74	*Larry Shannon*	1.00
75	*John Avery*	8.00
76	Troy Drayton	.50
77	Stanley Pritchett	.50
78	Karim Abdul-Jabbar	1.00
79	O.J. McDuffie	1.00
80	Yatil Green	1.00
81	Danny Kanell	.50
82	Tiki Barber	1.00
83	Tyrone Wheatley	.50
84	Charles Way	.50
85	Gary Brown	.50
86	*Brian Alford*	1.00
87	*Joe Jurevicius*	2.00
88	Ike Hilliard	1.00
89	Troy Aikman	6.00
90	Deion Sanders	3.00
91	Emmitt Smith	10.00
92	Chris Warren	1.00
93	Daryl Johnston	.50
94	Michael Irvin	1.00
95	David LaFleur	.50
96	*Kevin Dyson*	7.00
97	Steve McNair	5.00
98	Eddie George	5.00
99	Yancey Thigpen	.50
100	Frank Wycheck	.50
101	Glenn Foley	1.00
102	Vinny Testaverde	1.00
103	Keyshawn Johnson	1.00
104	Curtis Martin	3.00
105	Keith Byars	.50
106	*Scott Frost*	1.00
107	Wayne Chrebet	.50
108	Warren Moon	1.00
109	*Ahman Green*	10.00
110	Steve Broussard	.50
111	Ricky Watters	1.00
112	Joey Galloway	1.00
113	Mike Pritchard	.50
114	Brian Blades	.50
115	Gus Frerotte	.50
116	*Skip Hicks*	6.00
117	Terry Allen	.50
118	Michael Westbrook	1.00
119	Jamie Asher	.50
120	Leslie Shepherd	.50
121	Jeff Blake	1.00
122	Corey Dillon	4.00
123	Carl Pickens	1.00
124	Tony McGee	.50
125	Darnay Scott	.50
126	Kerry Collins	1.00
127	Fred Lane	1.00
128	William Floyd	.50
129	Rae Carruth	.50
130	Wesley Walls	.50
131	Muhsin Muhammad	.50
132	Jake Plummer	6.00
133	Adrian Murrell	1.00
134	*Michael Pittman*	1.00
135	Larry Centers	.50
136	Frank Sanders	.50
137	Rob Moore	.50
138	*Andre Wadsworth*	3.00
139	Mario Bates	.50
140	Chris Chandler	.50
141	Byron Hanspard	1.00
142	Jamal Anderson	1.00
143	Terance Mathis	.50
144	O.J. Santiago	.50
145	Tony Martin	.50
146	*Jammi German*	1.00
147	Jim Harbaugh	.50
148	Errict Rhett	.50
149	Michael Jackson	.50
150	*Patrick Johnson*	1.00
151	Eric Green	.50
152	Doug Flutie	4.00
153	Rob Johnson	1.00
154	Antowain Smith	3.00
155	Bruce Smith	.50
156	Eric Moulds	.50
157	Andre Reed	.50
158	Erik Kramer	.50
159	Darnell Autry	.50
160	Edgar Bennett	.50
161	*Curtis Enis*	8.00
162	Curtis Conway	1.00
163	*E.G. Green*	1.00
164	*Jerome Pathon*	2.00
165	*Peyton Manning*	25.00
166	Marshall Faulk	1.00
167	Zack Crockett	.50
168	Ken Dilger	.50
169	Marvin Harrison	1.00
170	Danny Wuerffel	.50
171	Lamar Smith	.50
172	Ray Zellars	.50
173	Qadry Ismail	.50
174	Sean Dawkins	.50
175	Andre Hastings	.50
176	Jeff George	1.00
177	*Charles Woodson*	10.00
178	Napoleon Kaufman	3.00
179	*Jon Ritchie*	1.00
180	Desmond Howard	.50
181	Tim Brown	.50
182	James Jett	.50
183	Rickey Dudley	.50
184	Bobby Hoying	.50
185	Rodney Peete	.50
186	Charlie Garner	.50
187	Irving Fryar	.50
188	Chris T. Jones	.50
189	Jason Dunn	.50
190	Tony Banks	1.00
191	*Robert Holcombe*	12.00
192	Craig Heyward	.50
193	Isaac Bruce	1.00
194	*Az-Zahir Hakim*	1.00
195	Eddie Kennison	1.00
196	*Mikhael Ricks*	1.00
197	*Ryan Leaf*	10.00
198	Natrone Means	1.00
199	Junior Seau	1.00
200	Freddie Jones	.50

1998 Playoff Absolute Hobby Silver/Gold

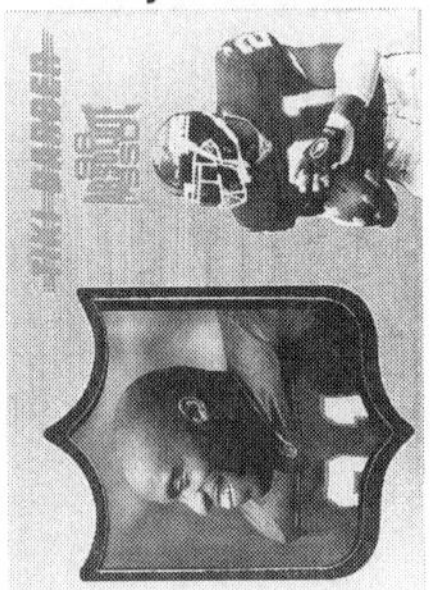

Two parallel versions of the 200-card Absolute SSD set exist. Silver foil versions were printed on a silver foil versus the team colored foil used on base cards. These were inserted one per three packs. Gold versions were printed on gold foil and sequentially numbered to 25 on the back.

	MT
Silver Cards:	3x
Silver Rookies:	2x
Gold Cards:	50x-100x
Gold Rookies:	7x-14x

1998 Playoff Absolute Hobby Checklist

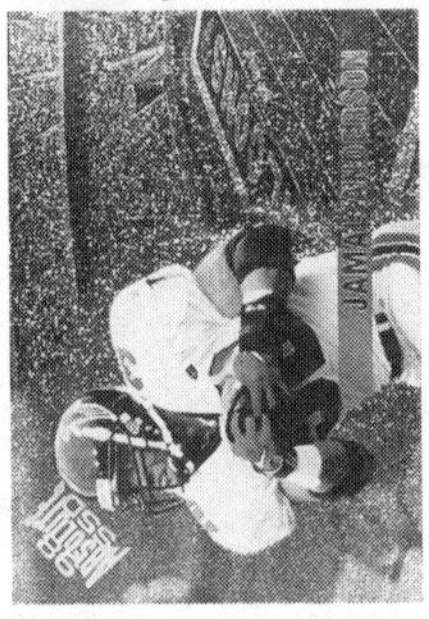

This 30-card insert featured a horizontal shot of a key player from one of the NFL teams, with that team's home stadium in the background. On the back, each player card from that team is listed. Checklists were inserted one per 19 packs.

		MT
Complete Set (30):		300.00
Common Player:		5.00
Inserted 1:19		
1	Jake Plummer	15.00
2	Jamal Anderson	5.00
3	Jim Harbaugh	5.00
4	Rob Johnson	5.00
5	Fred Lane	5.00
6	Curtis Enis	15.00
7	Corey Dillon	12.00
8	Troy Aikman	20.00
9	Terrell Davis	20.00
10	Barry Sanders	30.00
11	Brett Favre	30.00
12	Peyton Manning	30.00
13	Mark Brunell	12.00
14	Elvis Grbac	5.00
15	Dan Marino	25.00
16	Cris Carter	5.00
17	Drew Bledsoe	15.00
18	Ray Zellars	5.00
19	Charles Way	5.00
20	Curtis Martin	8.00
21	Napoleon Kaufman	8.00
22	Irving Fryar	5.00
23	Kordell Stewart	15.00
24	Tony Banks	5.00
25	Ryan Leaf	15.00
26	Jerry Rice	20.00
27	Warren Moon	5.00
28	Warrick Dunn	15.00
29	Eddie George	15.00
30	Terry Allen	5.00

1998 Playoff Absolute Hobby Draft Picks

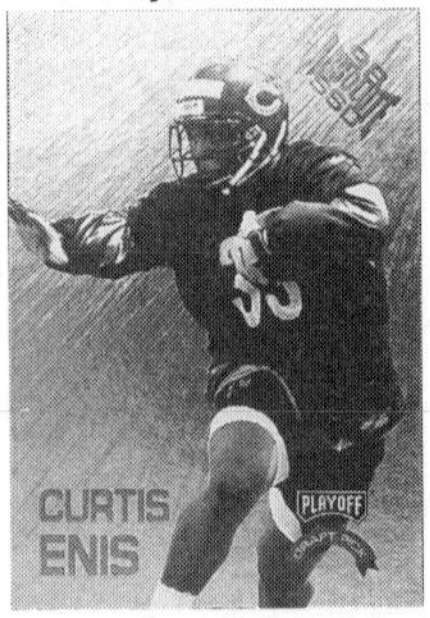

This 36-card insert set featured top players from the 1998 NFL Draft over a foil background. These were inserted one per 10 packs. In addition, Bronze versions of each card were available only through special three-card packs that contained only these Bronze versions. Those packs were inserted one per four boxes.

		MT
Complete Set (36):		300.00
Common Player:		4.00
Minor Stars:		6.00
Inserted 1:10		
1	Peyton Manning	30.00
2	Ryan Leaf	15.00
3	Andre Wadsworth	6.00
4	Charles Woodson	15.00
5	Curtis Enis	12.00
6	Fred Taylor	20.00
7	Kevin Dyson	10.00
8	Robert Edwards	10.00
9	Randy Moss	40.00
10	R.W. McQuarters	4.00
11	John Avery	10.00
12	Marcus Nash	10.00
13	Jerome Pathon	4.00
14	Jacquez Green	12.00
15	Robert Holcombe	10.00
16	Patrick Johnson	4.00
17	Germane Crowell	8.00
18	Tony Simmons	4.00
19	Joe Jurevicius	6.00
20	Mikhael Ricks	4.00
21	Charlie Batch	20.00
22	Jon Ritchie	4.00
23	Scott Frost	4.00
24	Skip Hicks	6.00
25	Brian Alford	4.00
26	E.G. Green	4.00
27	Jammi German	4.00
28	Ahman Green	12.00
29	Chris Floyd	4.00
30	Larry Shannon	4.00
31	Jonathan Quinn	4.00
32	Rashaan Shehee	6.00
33	Brian Griese	12.00
34	Hines Ward	8.00
35	Michael Pittman	4.00
36	Az-Zahir Hakim	4.00

1998 Playoff Absolute Hobby Marino Milestones

Playoff continued its 15-card Marino Milestones insert, with cards 6-10 inserted one per 397 packs of Absolute. Cards 1-5 were found in Prestige SSD and 11-15 were inserted into Momentum SSD. All versions were signed and featured a different record of Dan Marino's.

		MT
Complete Set (5):		600.00
Common Player:		125.00
Inserted 1:397		
6	Dan Marino (7,452)	125.00
7	Dan Marino (56/9)	125.00
8	Dan Marino (5,084)	125.00
9	Dan Marino (9)	125.00
10	Dan Marino (96.0)	125.00

1998 Playoff Absolute Hobby Platinum Quads

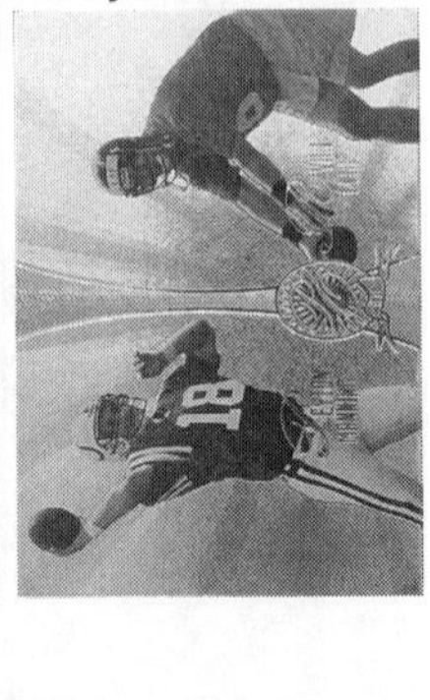

Platinum Quads was an 18-card insert that captured four players on a single card, with two per side. Cards were printed horizontally with the player's image appearing over foil with a "sunburst" etch. These were inserted one per 73 packs of Absolute SSD.

		MT
Complete Set (18):		1100.
Common Player:		30.00
Inserted 1:73		
1	Brett Favre, John Elway, Barry Sanders, Warrick Dunn	150.00
2	Dan Marino, Terrell Davis, Napoleon Kaufman, Jerome Bettis	125.00
3	Jerry Rice, Brad Johnson, Marshall Faulk, Jimmy Smith	80.00
4	Troy Aikman, Herman Moore, Mark Chmura, Gus Frerotte	80.00
5	Steve Young, Mike Alstott, Tiki Barber, Keyshawn Johnson	50.00
6	Kordell Stewart, Robert Brooks, Karim Abdul-Jabbar, Shannon Sharpe	60.00
7	Mark Brunell, Dorsey Levens, Carl Pickens, Rob Moore	60.00
8	Drew Bledsoe, Joey Galloway, Tim Brown, Fred Lane	60.00
9	Eddie George, Rob Johnson, Irving Fryar, Andre Rison	50.00
10	Jake Plummer, Antonio Freeman, Steve McNair, Warren Moon	50.00
11	Emmitt Smith, Cris Carter, Junior Seau, Danny Kanell	125.00
12	Corey Dillon, Jake Reed, Curtis Martin, Bobby Hoying	50.00
13	Deion Sanders, Jim Druckenmiller, Reidel Anthony, Terry Allen	30.00
14	Antowain Smith, Wesley Walls, Isaac Bruce, Terry Glenn	30.00
15	Charlie Batch, Scott Frost, Jonathan Quinn, Brian Griese	50.00
16	Kevin Dyson, Randy Moss, Marcus Nash, Jerome Pathon	125.00
17	Curtis Enis, Fred Taylor, Robert Edwards, John Avery	65.00
18	Peyton Manning, Ryan Leaf, Andre Wadsworth, Charles Woodson	100.00

1998 Playoff Absolute Hobby Playoff Honors

This three-card insert continued Playoff's Honors insert through all of its products, and was numbered PH13-PH15. These die-cut cards showed the player's image over a large black Playoff logo with white letters. Honors were inserted one per 3,970 packs of Absolute SSD.

		MT
Complete Set (3):		400.00
Common Player:		75.00
Inserted 1:3,970		
13	John Elway	250.00
14	Jerome Bettis	75.00
15	Steve Young	100.00

1998 Playoff Absolute Hobby Red Zone

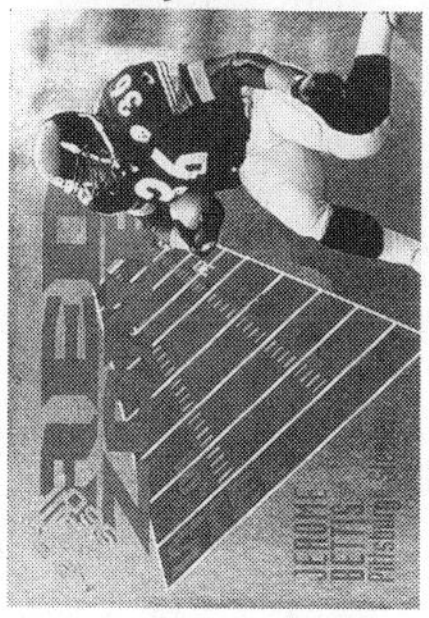

Red Zone featured 26 different players on a horizontal card with a mock-football field across the background. The insert name was printed in large letters in red foil, with his photo off to the right side. These were inserted one per 19 packs.

		MT
Complete Set (26):		250.00
Common Player:		4.00
Inserted 1:19		
1	Terrell Davis	20.00
2	Jerome Bettis	4.00
3	Mike Alstott	4.00
4	Brett Favre	35.00
5	Mark Brunell	15.00
6	Jeff George	4.00
7	John Elway	20.00
8	Troy Aikman	20.00
9	Steve Young	15.00
10	Kordell Stewart	15.00
11	Drew Bledsoe	20.00
12	James Jett	4.00
13	Dan Marino	25.00
14	Brad Johnson	4.00
15	Jake Plummer	15.00
16	Karim Abdul-Jabbar	4.00
17	Eddie George	15.00
18	Warrick Dunn	15.00
19	Cris Carter	4.00
20	Barry Sanders	35.00
21	Corey Dillon	10.00
22	Steve McNair	10.00
23	Herman Moore	4.00
24	Antonio Freeman	4.00
25	Dorsey Levens	4.00
26	James Stewart	4.00

1998 Playoff Absolute Hobby Shields

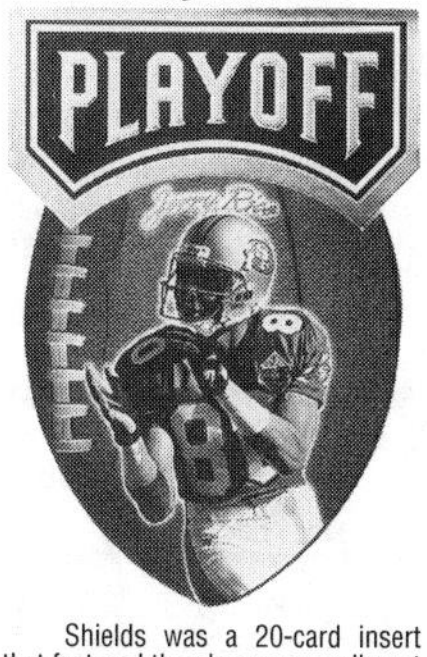

Shields was a 20-card insert that featured the player over a die-cut football with the Playoff logo cut across the top. These were inserted one per 37 packs.

		MT
Complete Set (20):		350.00
Common Player:		10.00
Inserted 1:37		
1	Terrell Davis	25.00
2	Corey Dillon	15.00
3	Dorsey Levens	10.00
4	Brett Favre	50.00
5	Warrick Dunn	20.00
6	Jerome Bettis	10.00
7	John Elway	25.00
8	Troy Aikman	25.00
9	Mark Brunell	20.00
10	Kordell Stewart	20.00
11	Eddie George	20.00
12	Jerry Rice	25.00
13	Dan Marino	40.00
14	Emmitt Smith	40.00
15	Napoleon Kaufman	10.00
16	Ryan Leaf	20.00
17	Curtis Martin	15.00
18	Peyton Manning	40.00
19	Cris Carter	10.00
20	Barry Sanders	50.00

1998 Playoff Absolute Hobby Statistically Speaking

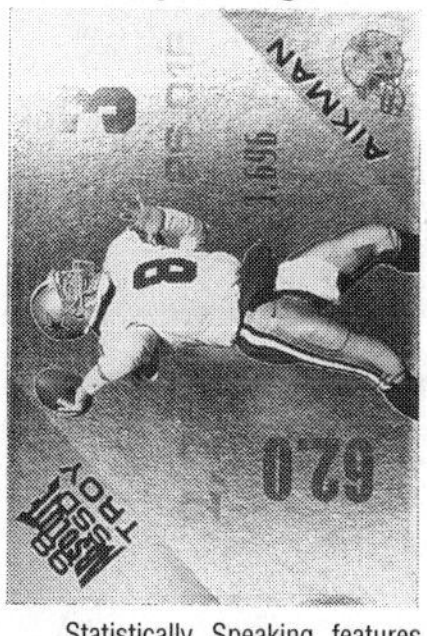

Statistically Speaking features 18 cards, with the player shown over a brushed foil background that highlights individual numbers of the featured player. These were inserted one per 55 packs.

		MT
Complete Set (18):		350.00
Common Player:		7.00
Inserted 1:55		
1	Jerry Rice	25.00
2	Barry Sanders	50.00
3	Deion Sanders	12.00
4	Brett Favre	50.00
5	Curtis Martin	12.00
6	Warrick Dunn	20.00
7	John Elway	25.00
8	Steve Young	15.00
9	Cris Carter	7.00
10	Kordell Stewart	20.00
11	Terrell Davis	25.00
12	Irving Fryar	7.00
13	Dan Marino	40.00
14	Tim Brown	7.00
15	Jerome Bettis	7.00
16	Troy Aikman	25.00
17	Napoleon Kaufman	15.00
18	Emmitt Smith	40.00

A card number in parentheses ( ) indicates the set is unnumbered.

1998 Playoff Contenders Leather

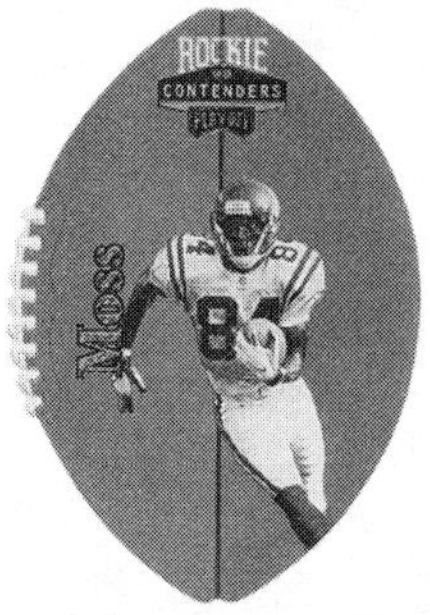

Leather cards are one of three base sets found in Contenders. Each Leather card is printed on actual leather with three different foil stamps and are found one-per-pack. The 100-card set included 70 veterans and 30 rookies from 1998. The parallel Red set has the players last name in red foil. Singles from this insert were found 1:9 hobby packs.

		MT
Complete Set (100):		225.00
Common Player:		.50
Minor Stars:		1.00
Common Rookie:		1.00
Inserted 1:1		
Red Cards:		3x
Red Rookies:		2x
Inserted 1:9		
Pack (5):		10.00
Wax Box (16):		130.00
1	Adrian Murrell	.50
2	Michael Pittman	2.00
3	Jake Plummer	5.00
4	Andre Wadsworth	3.00
5	Jamal Anderson	2.00
6	Chris Chandler	1.00
7	Tim Dwight	4.00
8	Patrick Johnson	3.00
9	Jermaine Lewis	.50
10	Doug Flutie	3.00
11	Antowain Smith	2.00
12	Muhsin Muhammad	.50
13	Bobby Engram	.50
14	Curtis Enis	5.00
15	Alonzo Mayes	1.00
16	Corey Dillon	3.00
17	Carl Pickens	1.00
18	Troy Aikman	5.00
19	Michael Irvin	2.00
20	Deion Sanders	2.00
21	Emmitt Smith	7.00
22	Terrell Davis	8.00
23	John Elway	8.00
24	Brian Griese	8.00
25	Rod Smith	1.00
26	Charlie Batch	8.00
27	Germane Crowell	4.00
28	Terry Fair	3.00
29	Herman Moore	1.00
30	Barry Sanders	10.00
31	Brett Favre	10.00
32	Antonio Freeman	1.50
33	Vonnie Holliday	3.00
34	Reggie White	1.50
35	Marshall Faulk	1.50
36	Marvin Harrison	1.00
37	Peyton Manning	20.00
38	Jerome Pathon	3.00
39	Tavian Banks	3.00
40	Mark Brunell	4.00
41	Keenan McCardell	1.00
42	Fred Taylor	12.00
43	Elvis Grbac	.50
44	Andre Rison	1.00
45	Rashaan Shehee	2.00
46	Karim Abdul-Jabbar	1.00
47	John Avery	4.00
48	Dan Marino	8.00
49	O.J. McDuffie	1.00
50	Cris Carter	1.50
51	Brad Johnson	1.50
52	Randy Moss	20.00
53	Robert Smith	1.50
54	Drew Bledsoe	4.00
55	Ben Coates	1.00
56	Robert Edwards	7.00
57	Chris Floyd	2.00
58	Terry Glenn	1.50
59	Cameron Cleeland	4.00
60	Kerry Collins	.50
61	Danny Kanell	.50
62	Charles Way	.50
63	Glenn Foley	1.00
64	Keyshawn Johnson	1.50
65	Curtis Martin	1.50
66	Tim Brown	1.00
67	Jeff George	1.00
68	Napoleon Kaufman	1.50
69	Charles Woodson	5.00
70	Irving Fryar	.50
71	Bobby Hoying	1.00
72	Jerome Bettis	1.00
73	Kordell Stewart	4.00
74	Hines Ward	3.00
75	Ryan Leaf	5.00
76	Natrone Means	1.00
77	Mikhael Ricks	3.00
78	Junior Seau	1.00
79	Garrison Hearst	1.00
80	Terrell Owens	1.50
81	Jerry Rice	5.00
82	Steve Young	3.00
83	Joey Galloway	1.50
84	Ahman Green	3.00
85	Warren Moon	1.00
86	Ricky Watters	1.00
87	Tony Banks	1.00
88	Isaac Bruce	1.00
89	Robert Holcombe	3.00
90	Mike Alstott	1.50
91	Trent Dilfer	.50
92	Warrick Dunn	4.00
93	Jacquez Green	4.00
94	Kevin Dyson	4.00
95	Eddie George	4.00
96	Steve McNair	2.00
97	Yancey Thigpen	.50
98	Terry Allen	1.00
99	Skip Hicks	4.00
100	Michael Westbrook	.50

1998 Playoff Contenders Leather Gold

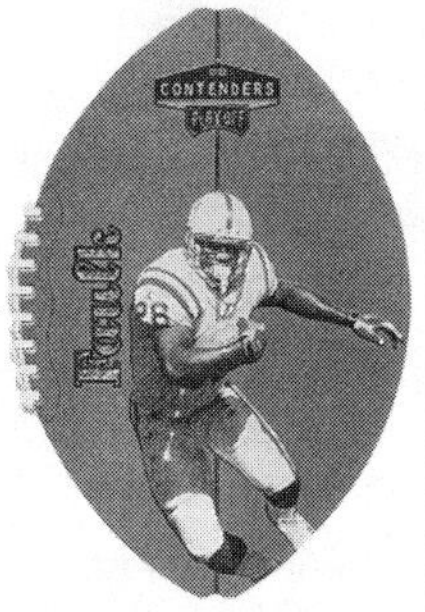

This insert parallel's the Leather set but each single is sequentially numbered to a player's featured stat. The cards look identical to the base Leather card except for the player's last name is in gold foil and the numbering is stamped on the back.

		MT
Common Player:		10.00
Minor Stars:		20.00
1	Adrian Murrell/27	30.00
2	Michael Pittman/32	30.00
3	Jake Plummer/53	100.00
4	Andre Wadsworth/29	50.00
5	Jamal Anderson/29	75.00
6	Chris Chandler/94	20.00
7	Tim Dwight/39	75.00
8	Patrick Johnson/55	20.00
9	Jermaine Lewis/42	20.00
10	Doug Flutie/48	75.00
11	Antowain Smith/28	75.00
12	Muhsin Muhammad/52	20.00
13	Bobby Engram/78	10.00
14	Curtis Enis/36	75.00
15	Alonzo Mayes/92	10.00
16	Corey Dillon/27	100.00
17	Carl Pickens/52	25.00
18	Troy Aikman/62	100.00
19	Michael Irvin/61	30.00
20	Deion Sanders/36	50.00
21	Emmitt Smith/40	200.00
22	Terrell Davis/35	275.00
23	John Elway/27	250.00
24	Brian Griese/33	125.00
25	Rod Smith/70	20.00
26	Charlie Batch/23	150.00
27	Germane Crowell/53	35.00
28	Terry Fair/42	30.00
29	Herman Moore/52	30.00
30	Barry Sanders/33	300.00
31	Brett Favre/35	300.00
32	Antonio Freeman/58	50.00
33	Vonnie Holliday/64	30.00
34	Reggie White/36	75.00
35	Marshall Faulk/47	50.00
36	Marvin Harrison/73	20.00
37	Peyton Manning/36	250.00
38	Jerome Pathon/69	20.00
39	Tavian Banks/33	45.00
40	Mark Brunell/52	85.00
41	Keenan McCardell/85	10.00
42	Fred Taylor/31	225.00
43	Elvis Grbac/29	35.00
44	Andre Rison/72	10.00
45	Rashaan Shehee/72	20.00
46	Karim Abdul-Jabbar/44	60.00
47	John Avery/26	60.00
48	Dan Marino/16	500.00
49	O.J. McDuffie/35	30.00
50	Cris Carter/89	20.00
51	Brad Johnson/37	50.00
52	Randy Moss/25	650.00
53	Robert Smith/90	20.00
54	Drew Bledsoe/28	175.00
55	Ben Coates/42	30.00
56	Robert Edwards/27	100.00
57	Chris Floyd/63	10.00
58	Terry Glenn/50	40.00
59	Cameron Cleeland/50	30.00
60	Kerry Collins/39	30.00
61	Danny Kanell/53	20.00
62	Charles Way/76	10.00
63	Glenn Foley/56	20.00
64	Keyshawn Johnson/70	25.00
65	Curtis Martin/41	40.00
66	Tim Brown/60	30.00
67	Jeff George/29	40.00
68	Napoleon Kaufman/40	50.00
69	Charles Woodson/27	120.00
70	Irving Fryar/75	10.00
71	Bobby Hoying/53	20.00
72	Jerome Bettis/31	65.00
73	Kordell Stewart/22	150.00
74	Hines Ward/55	30.00
75	Ryan Leaf/33	125.00
76	Natrone Means/78	20.00
77	Mikhael Ricks/47	25.00
78	Junior Seau/33	40.00
79	Garrison Hearst/74	25.00
80	Terrell Owens/60	35.00
81	Jerry Rice/16	325.00
82	Steve Young/19	175.00
83	Joey Galloway/72	25.00
84	Ahman Green/42	40.00
85	Warren Moon/25	85.00
86	Ricky Watters/56	25.00
87	Tony Banks/51	20.00
88	Isaac Bruce/56	30.00
89	Robert Holcombe/35	45.00
90	Mike Alstott/88	25.00
91	Trent Dilfer/38	45.00
92	Warrick Dunn/39	75.00
93	Jacquez Green/61	30.00
94	Kevin Dyson/60	30.00
95	Eddie George/30	150.00
96	Steve McNair/52	45.00
97	Yancey Thigpen/79	10.00
98	Terry Allen/58	30.00
99	Skip Hicks/48	45.00
100	Michael Westbrook/45	20.00

1998 Playoff Contenders Pennant

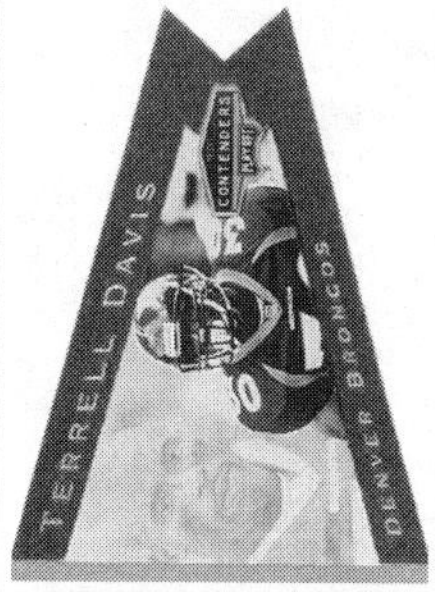

Pennant singles are printed on conventional stock with felt-like flocking and foil stamping. The 100-card set includes 70 veterans and 30 rookies from 1998. Pennant cards are found one-per-pack. Each player in the set has six different cards with each having a different color felt. The parallel Red singles are the same as the base except for the foil on the card is red. Singles are found 1:9 packs. The parallel Gold cards are in gold foil and are sequentially numbered to 98.

		MT
Complete Set (100):		225.00
Common Player:		.50
Minor Stars:		1.00
Common Rookie:		1.00
Each Card Issued In Six Colors		
Inserted 1:1		
Red Cards:		3x
Red Rookies:		2x
Inserted 1:9		
Gold Cards:		6x-12x
Gold Rookies:		4x-8x
Production 98 Sets		
1	Jake Plummer	5.00
2	Frank Sanders	.50
3	Jamal Anderson	2.00
4	Tim Dwight	6.00
5	Jammi German	2.00
6	Tony Martin	1.00
7	Jim Harbaugh	1.00
8	Rod Woodson	.50
9	Rob Johnson	1.00
10	Eric Moulds	1.50
11	Antowain Smith	1.50
12	Steve Beuerlein	.50
13	Fred Lane	1.00
14	Curtis Enis	5.00
15	Corey Dillon	3.00
16	Neil O'Donnell	.50
17	Carl Pickens	1.00
18	Darnay Scott	.50
19	Takeo Spikes	2.00
20	Troy Aikman	5.00
21	Michael Irvin	1.00
22	Deion Sanders	1.50
23	Emmitt Smith	7.00
24	Chris Warren	.50
25	Terrell Davis	8.00
26	John Elway	6.00
27	Brian Griese	6.00
28	Ed McCaffrey	1.50
29	Marcus Nash	3.00
30	Shannon Sharpe	1.00
31	Rod Smith	1.00
32	Charlie Batch	10.00
33	Germane Crowell	3.00
34	Herman Moore	1.00
35	Barry Sanders	10.00
36	Mark Chmura	1.00
37	Brett Favre	10.00
38	Antonio Freeman	1.50
39	Reggie White	1.00
40	Marshall Faulk	1.50
41	E.G. Green	2.50
42	Peyton Manning	15.00
43	Jerome Pathon	2.00
44	Mark Brunell	4.00
45	Jonathan Quinn	2.00
46	Fred Taylor	12.00
47	Tony Gonzalez	.50
48	Andre Rison	1.00
49	Karim Abdul-Jabbar	1.00
50	John Avery	3.00
51	Dan Marino	7.00
52	Cris Carter	1.50
53	Randall Cunningham	1.50
54	Brad Johnson	1.50
55	Randy Moss	30.00
56	Robert Smith	1.00
57	Drew Bledsoe	4.00
58	Robert Edwards	5.00
59	Terry Glenn	1.50
60	Tony Simmons	2.50
61	Tiki Barber	1.00
62	Joe Jurevicius	2.00
63	Danny Kanell	.50
64	Keyshawn Johnson	1.50
65	Curtis Martin	1.50
66	Vinny Testaverde	1.00
67	Tim Brown	1.00
68	Jeff George	1.00
69	Napoleon Kaufman	1.50
70	Jon Ritchie	2.00
71	Charles Woodson	5.00
72	Irving Fryar	.50
73	Duce Staley	1.00
74	Jerome Bettis	1.50
75	Chris Fuamatu-Ma'afala	2.00
76	Kordell Stewart	4.00
77	Hines Ward	2.50
78	Ryan Leaf	8.00
79	Natrone Means	1.50
80	Mikhael Ricks	2.00
81	Garrison Hearst	1.50
82	R.W. McQuarters	2.00
83	Jerry Rice	5.00
84	J.J. Stokes	1.00
85	Steve Young	3.00
86	Joey Galloway	1.50
87	Ahman Green	3.00
88	Warren Moon	1.00
89	Ricky Watters	1.00
90	Isaac Bruce	1.00
91	Robert Holcombe	2.50
92	Mike Alstott	1.50
93	Trent Dilfer	1.00
94	Warrick Dunn	3.00
95	Jacquez Green	3.00
96	Kevin Dyson	3.00
97	Eddie George	4.00
98	Steve McNair	2.00
99	Terry Allen	1.00
100	Skip Hicks	3.00

1998 Playoff Contenders Ticket

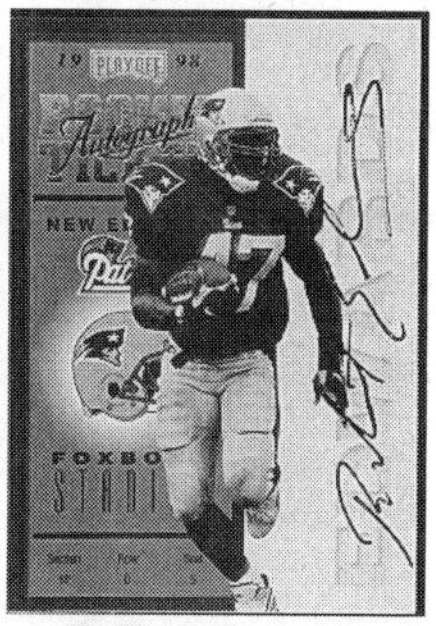

The 99-card Ticket set is made up 80 veterans and 19 rookies and was inserted one-per-pack. Each Ticket card was printed on conventional stock with foil stamping and has a ticket design to it. All of the rookie cards in the set are autographed. The quantities vary from player to player depending on how many they signed. A parallel Red and Gold insert was also produced. Red's were found 1:9 hobby packs and the Gold's were sequentially numbered to 25. The name on the fronts will either be in red or gold depending on which single you have.

		MT
Complete Set (99):		2500.
Common Player:		.50
Minor Stars:		1.00
Common Rookie Autograph:		25.00
Inserted 1:1		
Red Cards:		3x
Red Rookies: .		2x
Inserted 1:9		
Gold Cards:		35x-70x
Gold Rookies:		2x
Production 25 Sets		
1	Rob Moore	1.00
2	Jake Plummer	4.00
3	Jamal Anderson	1.50
4	Terance Mathis	.50
5	Priest Holmes	6.00
6	Michael Jackson	.50
7	Eric Zeier	.50
8	Andre Reed	.50
9	Antowain Smith	1.50
10	Bruce Smith	.50
11	Thurman Thomas	1.00
12	Raghib Ismail	.50
13	Wesley Walls	.50
14	Curtis Conway	1.00
15	Jeff Blake	1.00
16	Corey Dillon	2.00
17	Carl Pickens	1.00
18	Troy Aikman	5.00
19	Michael Irvin	1.00
20	Ernie Mills	.50
21	Deion Sanders	1.50
22	Emmitt Smith	7.00
23	Terrell Davis	8.00
24	John Elway	6.00
25	Neil Smith	.50
26	Rod Smith	1.00
27	Herman Moore	1.00
28	Johnnie Morton	.50
29	Barry Sanders	10.00
30	Robert Brooks	.50
31	Brett Favre	10.00
32	Antonio Freeman	1.50
33	Dorsey Levens	1.50
34	Reggie White	1.50
35	Marshall Faulk	1.50
36	Mark Brunell	4.00
37	Jimmy Smith	1.00
38	James Stewart	.50
39	Donnell Bennett	.50
40	Andre Rison	1.00
41	Derrick Thomas	1.00
42	Karim Abdul-Jabbar	1.00
43	Dan Marino	7.00
44	Cris Carter	1.50
45	Brad Johnson	1.00
46	Robert Smith	1.00
47	Drew Bledsoe	4.00
48	Terry Glenn	1.50
49	Lamar Smith	.50
50	Ike Hilliard	.50
51	Danny Kanell	.50
52	Wayne Chrebet	1.50
53	Keyshawn Johnson	1.50
54	Curtis Martin	1.50
55	Tim Brown	1.00
56	Rickey Dudley	.50
57	Jeff George	1.00
58	Napoleon Kaufman	1.50
59	Irving Fryar	.50
60	Jerome Bettis	1.50

61	Charles Johnson	.50
62	Kordell Stewart	4.00
63	Natrone Means	1.00
64	Bryan Still	.50
65	Garrison Hearst	1.50
66	Jerry Rice	5.00
67	Steve Young	3.00
68	Joey Galloway	1.50
69	Warren Moon	1.00
70	Ricky Watters	1.00
71	Isaac Bruce	1.00
72	Mike Alstott	1.50
73	Reidel Anthony	1.00
74	Trent Dilfer	1.00
75	Warrick Dunn	3.00
76	Warren Sapp	.50
77	Eddie George	4.00
78	Steve McNair	2.00
79	Terry Allen	1.00
80	Gus Frerotte	.50
81	Andre Wadsworth AUTO	25.00
82	Tim Dwight AUTO	50.00
83	Curtis Enis AUTO/400	50.00
85	Charlie Batch AUTO	60.00
86	Germane Crowell AUTO	75.00
87	Peyton Manning AUTO/200	1200.
88	Jerome Pathon AUTO	30.00
89	Fred Taylor AUTO	200.00
90	Tavian Banks AUTO	30.00
92	Randy Moss AUTO/300	700.00
93	Robert Edwards AUTO	75.00
94	Hines Ward AUTO	30.00
95	Ryan Leaf AUTO/200	100.00
96	Mikhael Ricks AUTO	25.00
97	Ahman Green AUTO	150.00
98	Jacquez Green AUTO	50.00
99	Kevin Dyson AUTO	50.00
100	Skip Hicks AUTO	30.00
103	Chris Fuamatu-Ma'afala AUTO	25.00

1998 Playoff Contenders Checklist

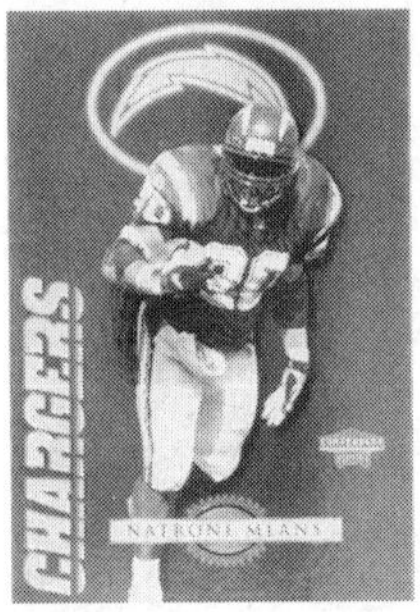

Each card in this 30-card set displays the top star from each club on the front and a checklist of each player from that team featured in our three base sets on the back. Each card measures 3" x 5" and was found one-per-box.

		MT
Complete Set (30):		150.00
Common Player:		2.50
Minor Stars:		5.00
Inserted 1:Box		
1	Jake Plummer	8.00
2	Jamal Anderson	5.00
3	Jermaine Lewis	2.50
4	Antowain Smith	5.00
5	Muhsin Muhammad	2.50
6	Curtis Enis	5.00
7	Corey Dillon	6.00
8	Deion Sanders	5.00
9	Terrell Davis	18.00
10	Barry Sanders	20.00
11	Brett Favre	20.00
12	Peyton Manning	15.00
13	Mark Brunell	8.00
14	Andre Rison	2.50
15	Dan Marino	15.00
16	Randy Moss	30.00
17	Drew Bledsoe	8.00
18	Kerry Collins	5.00
19	Danny Kanell	2.50
20	Curtis Martin	5.00
21	Tim Brown	2.50
22	Irving Fryar	2.50
23	Kordell Stewart	8.00
24	Natrone Means	5.00
25	Steve Young	6.00
26	Isaac Bruce	5.00
27	Warren Moon	5.00
28	Warrick Dunn	8.00
29	Eddie George	8.00
30	Terry Allen	5.00

1998 Playoff Contenders Honors

This is an insert that began with 1996 Playoff Prime and has continued throughout Playoff products over the past three years. Cards 19-21 can be found in this insert and are found 1:3,241 hobby packs.

		MT
Complete Set (3):		300.00
Common Player:		75.00
Inserted 1:3,241 Hobby		
19	Dan Marino	150.00
20	Jerry Rice	100.00
21	Mark Brunell	75.00

A card number in parentheses ( ) indicates the set is unnumbered.

1998 Playoff Contenders MVP Contenders

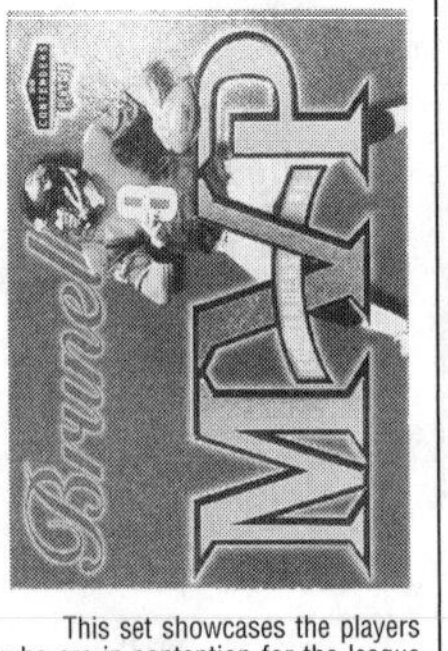

This set showcases the players who are in contention for the league MVP. Each card is printed on holographic stock with an MVP graphic stamped in gold foil. Singles were inserted 1:19 hobby packs.

		MT
Complete Set (36):		160.00
Common Player:		4.00
Inserted 1:19		
1	Terrell Davis	18.00
2	Jerry Rice	10.00
3	Jerome Bettis	4.00
4	Brett Favre	20.00
5	Natrone Means	4.00
6	Steve Young	6.00
7	John Elway	12.00
8	Troy Aikman	10.00
9	Steve McNair	4.00
10	Kordell Stewart	8.00
11	Drew Bledsoe	8.00
12	Tim Brown	4.00
13	Dan Marino	15.00
14	Mark Brunell	8.00
15	Marshall Faulk	4.00
16	Jake Plummer	8.00
17	Corey Dillon	6.00
18	Carl Pickens	4.00
19	Keyshawn Johnson	4.00
20	Barry Sanders	20.00
21	Deion Sanders	4.00
22	Emmitt Smith	15.00
23	Antowain Smith	4.00
24	Curtis Martin	4.00
25	Cris Carter	4.00
26	Napoleon Kaufman	4.00
27	Eddie George	8.00
28	Warrick Dunn	8.00
29	Antonio Freeman	4.00
30	Joey Galloway	4.00
31	Herman Moore	4.00
32	Jamal Anderson	6.00
33	Terry Glenn	4.00
34	Garrison Hearst	4.00
35	Robert Smith	4.00
36	Mike Alstott	4.00

1998 Playoff Contenders Rookie of the Year

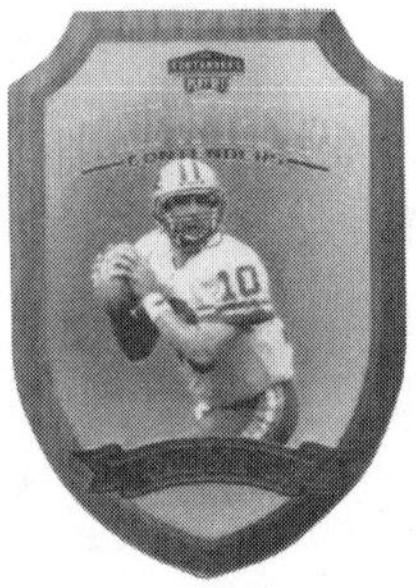

Playoff included the top 12 rookies from '98 who were battling for the rookie of the year award. Each card is printed on a wood-grain finish with two types of foil stamping. Singles were inserted 1:55 hobby packs.

		MT
Complete Set (12):		160.00
Common Player:		7.00
Inserted 1:55		
1	Tim Dwight	10.00
2	Curtis Enis	10.00
3	Charlie Batch	20.00
4	Peyton Manning	30.00
5	Fred Taylor	25.00
6	John Avery	7.00
7	Randy Moss	60.00
8	Robert Edwards	10.00
9	Charles Woodson	10.00
10	Ryan Leaf	12.00
11	Jacquez Green	7.00
12	Kevin Dyson	7.00

1998 Playoff Contenders Rookie Stallions

Only the top NFL draftees were featured in this 18-card set. Each card was printed on all micro-etched foil stock with silver foil stamping. Singles were inserted 1:19 hobby packs.

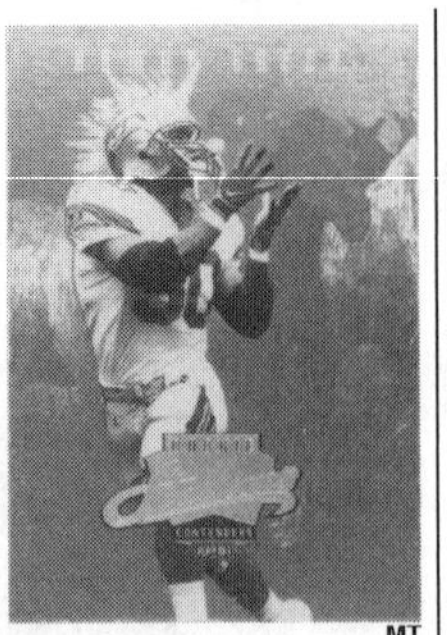

		MT
Complete Set (18):		100.00
Common Player:		2.50
Minor Stars:		5.00
Inserted 1:19		
1	Tim Dwight	6.00
2	Curtis Enis	6.00
3	Brian Griese	8.00
4	Charlie Batch	12.00
5	Germane Crowell	5.00
6	Peyton Manning	20.00
7	Tavian Banks	5.00
8	Fred Taylor	18.00
9	Rashaan Shehee	2.50
10	John Avery	5.00
11	Randy Moss	40.00
12	Robert Edwards	6.00
13	Charles Woodson	7.00
14	Ryan Leaf	10.00
15	Ahman Green	5.00
16	Jacquez Green	5.00
17	Kevin Dyson	5.00
18	Skip Hicks	5.00

1998 Playoff Contenders Super Bowl Leather

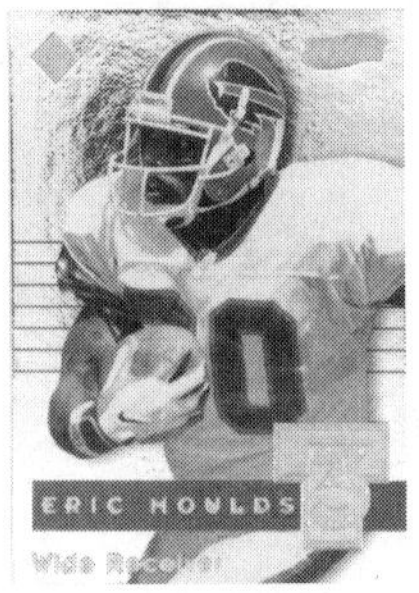

Each card in this set highlights a piece of an actual game-used football from Super Bowl XXXII. Each card back features a replica of the letter from the NFL verifying the authenticity of the ball. Cards are printed on conventional stock with foil stamping and were inserted 1:2,401 hobby packs.

		MT
Complete Set (6):		1000.
Common Player:		75.00
Inserted 1:2,401		
1	Brett Favre	350.00
2	John Elway	275.00
3	Robert Brooks	75.00
4	Rod Smith	100.00
5	Antonio Freeman	125.00
6	Terrell Davis	300.00

1998 Playoff Contenders Touchdown Tandems

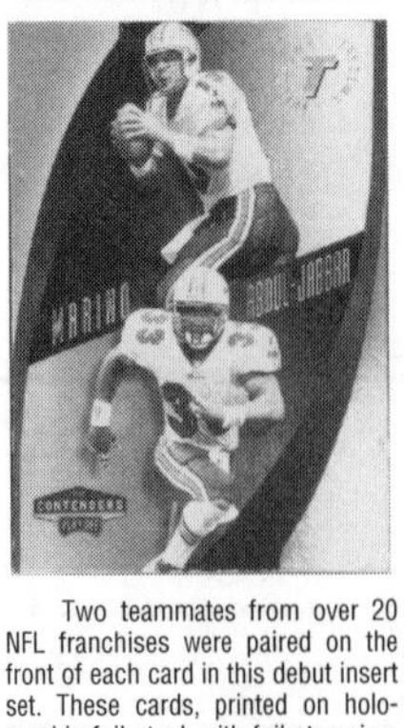

Two teammates from over 20 NFL franchises were paired on the front of each card in this debut insert set. These cards, printed on holographic foil stock with foil stamping, show the players known for carrying the scoring load for their respective clubs. Singles were found 1:19 hobby packs.

		MT
Complete Set (24):		150.00
Common Player:		4.00
Inserted 1:19		
1	Brett Favre, Antonio Freeman	20.00
2	Dan Marino, Karim Abdul-Jabbar	15.00
3	Emmitt Smith, Troy Aikman	15.00
4	Barry Sanders, Herman Moore	20.00
5	Eddie George, Steve McNair	8.00
6	Robert Edwards, Drew Bledsoe	8.00
7	Terrell Davis, Rod Smith	15.00
8	Mark Brunell, Fred Taylor	12.00
9	Jerry Rice, Steve Young	10.00
10	Jerome Bettis, Kordell Stewart	8.00
11	Curtis Martin, Keyshawn Johnson	4.00
12	Mike Alstott, Warrick Dunn	6.00
13	Isaac Bruce, Tony Banks	4.00
14	Adrian Murrell, Jake Plummer	8.00
15	Tim Brown, Napoleon Kaufman	4.00
16	Cris Carter, Randy Moss	30.00
17	Joey Galloway, Ricky Watters	4.00
18	Peyton Manning, Marshall Faulk	15.00
19	Ryan Leaf, Natrone Means	8.00
20	Carl Pickens, Corey Dillon	4.00
21	Doug Flutie, Antowain Smith	6.00
22	Randall Cunningham, Robert Smith	4.00
23	Chris Chandler, Jamal Anderson	5.00
24	John Elway, Ed McCaffrey	12.00

1998 Playoff Momentum Hobby

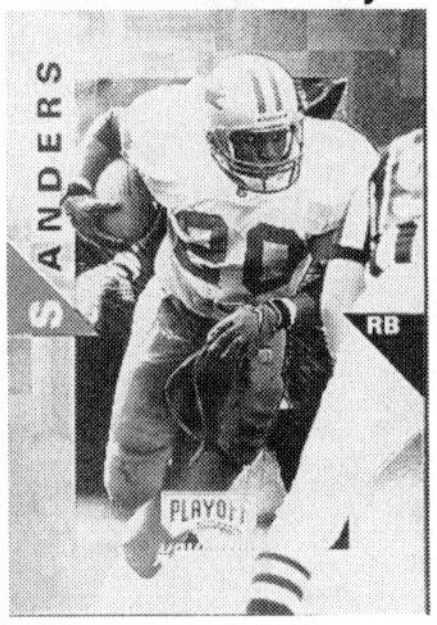

Each card in this 250-card set was printed on premium doublesided metalized mylar with double micro-etching on both sides. The shortprinted Rookie subset included 48 rising NFL stars and were inserted 1:6 packs. Each card also has a Red and Gold parallel version. The Reds were inserted 1:4 hobby packs while the Golds were sequentially numbered to 25.

		MT
Complete Set (250):		425.00
Common Player:		.30
Minor Stars:		.60
Common Rookie:		4.00
Inserted 1:6		
Red Cards:		2x-4x
Red Rookies:		1.2x
Inserted 1:4		
Gold Cards:		50x-100x
Gold Rookies:		3x-6x
Production 25 Sets		
Hobby Pack (5):		8.00
Hobby Wax Box (16):		120.00
1	Jake Plummer	5.00
2	Eric Metcalf	.30
3	Adrian Murrell	.30
4	Larry Centers	.30
5	Frank Sanders	.30
6	Rob Moore	.60
7	*Andre Wadsworth*	8.00
8	Chris Chandler	.60
9	Jamal Anderson	1.00
10	Tony Martin	.30
11	Terrance Mathis	.30
12	*Tim Dwight*	15.00
13	*Jammi German*	8.00
14	O.J. Santiago	.30
15	Jim Harbaugh	.60
16	Eric Zeier	.30
17	*Duane Starks*	8.00
18	Rod Woodson	.30
19	Errict Rhett	.30
20	Jay Graham	.30
21	Ray Lewis	.30
22	Michael Jackson	.30
23	Jermaine Lewis	.30
24	*Patrick Johnson*	4.00
25	Eric Green	.30
26	Doug Flutie	3.00
27	Rob Johnson	.60
28	Antowain Smith	2.00
29	Thurman Thomas	.60
30	*Jonathon Linton*	5.00
31	Bruce Smith	.30
32	Eric Moulds	.60
33	Kevin Williams	.30
34	Andre Reed	.30
35	Steve Beurlein	.30
36	Kerry Collins	.60
37	Anthony Johnson	.30
38	Fred Lane	.60
39	William Floyd	.30
40	Raghib Ismail	.30
41	Wesley Walls	.30
42	Muhsin Muhammad	.30
43	Rae Carruth	.30
44	Kevin Greene	.30
45	Greg Lloyd	.30
46	*Moses Moreno*	8.00
47	Erik Kramer	.30
48	Edgar Bennett	.30
49	*Curtis Enis*	5.00
50	Curtis Conway	.60
51	Bobby Engram	.30
52	*Alonzo Mayes*	4.00
53	Jeff Blake	.60
54	Neil O'Donnell	.30
55	Corey Dillon	3.00
56	*Takeo Spikes*	4.00
57	Carl Pickens	.60
58	Tony McGee	.30
59	Darnay Scott	.30
60	Troy Aikman	4.00
61	Deion Sanders	1.00
62	Emmitt Smith	8.00
63	Darren Woodson	.30
64	Chris Warren	.30
65	Daryl Johnston	.30
66	Ernie Mills	.30
67	Billy Davis	.30
68	Michael Irvin	.60
69	David LaFleur	.30
70	John Elway	8.00
71	*Brian Griese*	25.00
72	Steve Atwater	.30
73	Terrell Davis	8.00
74	Rod Smith	.60
75	*Marcus Nash*	25.00
76	Shannon Sharpe	.60
77	Ed McCaffrey	.60
78	Neil Smith	.30
79	*Charlie Batch*	10.00
80	*Germane Crowell*	15.00
81	Scott Mitchell	.60
82	Barry Sanders	10.00
83	*Terry Fair*	8.00
84	Herman Moore	1.00
85	Johnnie Morton	.30
86	Brett Favre	10.00
87	Rick Mirer	.30
88	Dorsey Levens	.60
89	William Henderson	.30
90	Derrick Mayes	.30
91	Antonio Freeman	1.00
92	Robert Brooks	.30
93	Mark Chmura	.30
94	*Vonnie Holliday*	8.00
95	Reggie White	1.00
96	*E.G. Green*	8.00
97	*Jerome Pathon*	8.00
98	*Peyton Manning*	40.00
99	Marshall Faulk	1.00
100	Zack Crockett	.30
101	Ken Dilger	.30
102	Marvin Harrison	.60
103	Mark Brunell	3.00
104	*Jonathan Quinn*	8.00
105	*Tavian Banks*	20.00
106	*Fred Taylor*	15.00
107	James Stewart	.30
108	Jimmy Smith	.60
109	Keenan McCardell	.30
110	Elvis Grbac	.30
111	Rich Gannon	.30
112	*Rashaan Shehee*	8.00
113	Donnell Bennett	.30
114	Kimble Anders	.30
115	Derrick Thomas	.30
116	Kevin Lockett	.30
117	Derrick Alexander	.30
118	Tony Gonzalez	.60
119	Andre Rison	.30
120	Craig Erickson	.30
121	Dan Marino	8.00
122	*John Avery*	25.00
123	Karim Abdul-Jabbar	.60
124	Zach Thomas	.60
125	O.J. McDuffie	.30
126	Troy Drayton	.30
127	Randall Cunningham	1.00
128	Brad Johnson	.60
129	Robert Smith	.60
130	Cris Carter	1.00
131	*Randy Moss*	40.00
132	Jake Reed	.30
133	John Randle	.30
134	Drew Bledsoe	3.00
135	*Tony Simmons*	15.00
136	Sedrick Shaw	.30
137	*Chris Floyd*	4.00
138	*Robert Edwards*	25.00
139	*Rod Rutledge*	4.00
140	Shawn Jefferson	.30
141	Ben Coates	.60
142	Terry Glenn	.60
143	Heath Shuler	.30
144	Danny Wuerffel	.30
145	Troy Davis	.30
146	Qadry Ismail	.30
147	Ray Zellars	.30
148	Lamar Smith	.30
149	*Cameron Cleeland*	12.00
150	Sean Dawkins	.30
151	Andre Hastings	.30
152	Danny Kanell	.30
153	Tiki Barber	.60
154	Tyrone Wheatley	.30
155	Charles Way	.30
156	Gary Brown	.30
157	*Shaun Williams*	4.00
158	Chris Calloway	.30
159	Amani Toomer	.30
160	*Brian Alford*	4.00
161	*Joe Jurevicius*	8.00
162	Ike Hilliard	.30
163	Michael Strahan	.30
164	Glenn Foley	.60
165	Vinny Testaverde	.60
166	Keyshawn Johnson	.60
167	Curtis Martin	1.00
168	Leon Johnson	.30
169	Keith Byars	.30
170	Wayne Chrebet	.60
171	Kyle Brady	.30
172	Dedric Ward	.30
173	Jeff George	.60
174	*Charles Woodson*	15.00
175	Napoleon Kaufman	1.00
176	*Jon Ritchie*	4.00
177	Tim Brown	.60
178	James Jett	.30
179	Rickey Dudley	.30
180	Bobby Hoying	.30
181	Duce Staley	3.00
182	Charlie Garner	.30
183	Irvin Fryar	.30
184	Jeff Graham	.30
185	Jason Dunn	.30
186	Kordell Stewart	3.00
187	Jerome Bettis	1.00
188	Andre Coleman	.30
189	*Chris Fuamatu-Ma'afala*	10.00
190	Charles Johnson	.30
191	*Hines Ward*	20.00
192	Mark Bruener	.30
193	Courtney Hawkins	.30
194	Will Blackwell	.30
195	Levon Kirkland	.30
196	*Mikhael Ricks*	15.00
197	*Ryan Leaf*	15.00
198	Natrone Means	.60
199	Junior Seau	.60
200	Bryan Still	.30
201	Freddie Jones	.30
202	Steve Young	2.00
203	Jim Druckenmiller	1.00
204	Garrison Hearst	.60
205	*R.W. McQuarters*	8.00
206	Merton Hanks	.30
207	Marc Edwards	.30
208	Jerry Rice	4.00
209	Terrell Owens	1.50
210	J.J. Stokes	.30
211	Tony Banks	.60
212	*Robert Holcombe*	20.00
213	Greg Hill	.30
214	Amp Lee	.30
215	Jerald Moore	.30
216	Isaac Bruce	.60
217	*Az-Zahir Hakim*	8.00
218	Eddie Kennison	.30
219	*Grant Wistrom*	4.00
220	Warren Moon	.60
221	*Ahman Green*	15.00
222	Steve Broussard	.30
223	Ricky Watters	.60
224	James McKnight	.30
225	Joey Galloway	1.00
226	Mike Pritchard	.30
227	Trent Dilfer	.60
228	Warrick Dunn	3.00
229	Mike Alstott	1.00
230	John Lynch	.30
231	*Jacquez Green*	8.00
232	Reidel Anthony	.60
233	Bert Emanuel	.30
234	Warren Sapp	.30
235	Steve McNair	1.50
236	Eddie George	3.00
237	Chris Sanders	.30
238	Yancey Thigpen	.30
239	Willie Davis	.30
240	*Kevin Dyson*	10.00
241	Frank Wycheck	.30
242	Trent Green	.60
243	Gus Frerotte	.30
244	*Skip Hicks*	25.00
245	Terry Allen	.30
246	Stephen Davis	.30
247	*Stephen Alexander*	4.00
248	Michael Westbrook	.60
249	Dana Stubblefield	.30
250	Dan Wilkinson	.30

1998 Playoff Momentum Hobby Class Reunion Quads

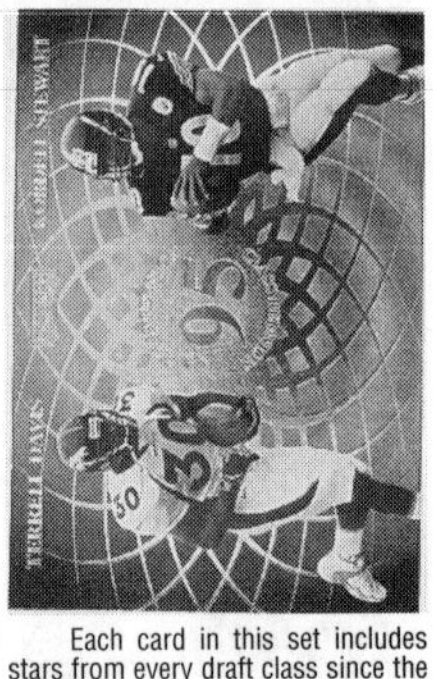

Each card in this set includes stars from every draft class since the famous one in 1983. Four players drafted in the same year appear on each card (two on the front, two on the back). Cards are printed on doublesided mirror foil stock with micro-etching on each side as well as gold foil stamping. Singles were inserted 1:81 hobby packs.

		MT
Complete Set (16):		700.00
Common Player:		20.00
Inserted 1:81		
1	1983 (Dan Marino, John Elway, Bruce Matthews, Darrell Green)	75.00
2	1984 (Steve Young, Irving Fryar, Reggie White, Jeff Hostetler)	35.00
3	1985 (Jerry Rice, Bruce Smith, Andre Reed, Doug Flutie)	50.00
4	1986 (Keith Byars, Leslie O'Neal, Seth Joyner, Ray Brown)	20.00
5	1987 (Cris Carter, Vinny Testaverde, Jim Harbaugh, Rod Woodson)	20.00
6	1988 (Tim Brown, Chris Chandler, Michael Irvin, Neil Smith)	20.00
7	1989 (Troy Aikman, Barry Sanders, Deion Sanders, Andre Rison)	100.00

8	1990 (Emmitt Smith, Jeff George, Neil O'Donnell, Shannon Sharpe)	75.00
9	1991 (Brett Favre, Herman Moore, Yancey Thigpen, Ricky Watters)	100.00
10	1992 (Mark Chmura, Brad Johnson, Carl Pickens, Robert Brooks)	20.00
11	1993 (Drew Bledsoe, Jerome Bettis, Mark Brunell, Garrison Hearst)	40.00
12	1994 (Trent Dilfer, Dorsey Levens, Marshall Faulk, Isaac Bruce)	25.00
13	1995 (Terrell Davis, Kordell Stewart, Napoleon Kaufman, Curtis Martin)	75.00
14	1996 (Eddie George, Keyshawn Johnson, Karim Abdul-Jabbar, Terry Glenn)	40.00
15	1997 (Warrick Dunn, Corey Dillon, Jake Plummer, Antowain Smith)	40.00
16	1998 (Peyton Manning, Ryan Leaf, Curtis Enis, Randy Moss)	125.00

1998 Playoff Momentum Hobby EndZone Xpress

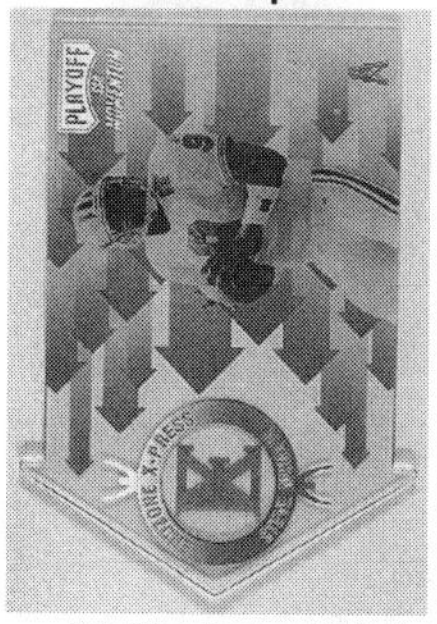

This 29-card set spotlights the NFL's best who have a knack for getting into the end zone. Each card is printed on die-cut clear plastic with holographic foil stamping. Singles were found 1:9 hobby packs.

		MT
Complete Set (29):		250.00
Common Player:		2.00
Minor Stars:		4.00
Inserted 1:9		
1	Jake Plummer	10.00
2	Herman Moore	2.00
3	Terrell Davis	18.00
4	Antowain Smith	5.00
5	Curtis Enis	10.00
6	Corey Dillon	7.00
7	Troy Aikman	12.00
8	John Elway	12.00
9	Barry Sanders	25.00
10	Brett Favre	25.00
11	Peyton Manning	25.00
12	Mark Brunell	10.00
13	Andre Rison	2.00
14	Dan Marino	18.00
15	Randy Moss	35.00
16	Drew Bledsoe	10.00
17	Jerome Bettis	4.00
18	Tim Brown	2.00
19	Antonio Freeman	4.00
20	Napoleon Kaufman	4.00
21	Emmitt Smith	18.00
22	Kordell Stewart	10.00
23	Curtis Martin	6.00
24	Ryan Leaf	12.00
25	Jerry Rice	12.00
26	Joey Galloway	4.00
27	Warrick Dunn	10.00
28	Eddie George	10.00
29	Steve McNair	7.00

1998 Playoff Momentum Hobby Headliners

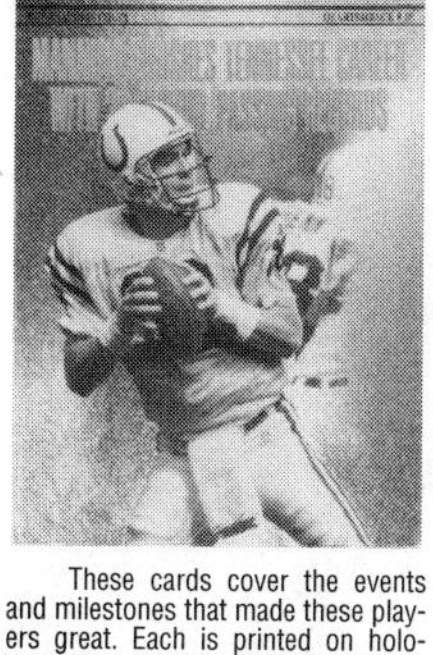

These cards cover the events and milestones that made these players great. Each is printed on holographic stock with foil stamping. Singles were inserted 1:49 hobby packs.

		MT
Complete Set (23):		650.00
Common Player:		15.00
Inserted 1:49		
1	Brett Favre	80.00
2	Jerry Rice	40.00
3	Barry Sanders	80.00
4	Troy Aikman	40.00
5	Warrick Dunn	30.00
6	Dan Marino	60.00
7	John Elway	40.00
8	Drew Bledsoe	30.00
9	Kordell Stewart	30.00
10	Mark Brunell	30.00
11	Eddie George	30.00
12	Terrell Davis	60.00
13	Emmitt Smith	60.00
14	Steve McNair	20.00
15	Mike Alstott	15.00
16	Peyton Manning	80.00
17	Antonio Freeman	15.00
18	Curtis Martin	20.00
19	Terry Glenn	15.00
20	Brad Johnson	15.00
21	Karim Abdul-Jabbar	15.00
22	Ryan Leaf	40.00
23	Jerome Bettis	15.00

1998 Playoff Momentum Hobby Playoff Honors

This insert has appeared in most Playoff products since it debuted in 1996 Prime. These singles (#16-18) were inserted 1:3,841 hobby packs.

		MT
Complete Set (3):		400.00
Common Player:		100.00
Inserted 1:3,841		
PH16	Brett Favre	225.00
PH17	Kordell Stewart	100.00
PH18	Troy Aikman	125.00

1998 Playoff Momentum Hobby Marino Milestones

The final five cards (#11-15) of this chase set were inserted into Momentum packs at a ratio of 1:385. All cards are printed on premium card stock with film laminates and foil stamping designed to showcase the soon to be "Hall of Fame" autograph of Dan found on each.

	MT
Complete Set (11-15):	600.00
Common Player:	125.00
Inserted 1:385	

1998 Playoff Momentum Hobby NFL Rivals

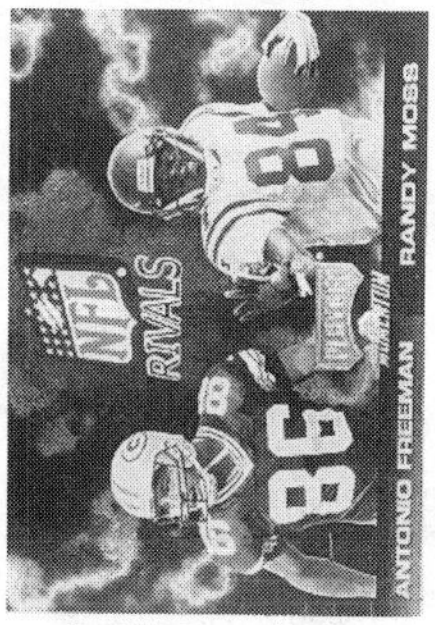

Top NFL stars and rookie rivals were paired together on the front of these tough inserts. Each card in this 22-card set is printed on premium mirror foil board stock with gold foil stamping. Each was inserted 1:49 packs.

		MT
Complete Set (22):		650.00
Common Player:		15.00
Inserted 1:49		
1	Mark Brunell, John Elway	40.00
2	Jerome Bettis, Eddie George	30.00
3	Barry Sanders, Emmitt Smith	80.00
4	Dan Marino, Drew Bledsoe	60.00
5	Troy Aikman, Jake Plummer	40.00
6	Terrell Davis, Napoleon Kaufman	60.00
7	Cris Carter, Herman Moore	15.00
8	Warrick Dunn, Dorsey Levens	30.00
9	Kordell Stewart, Steve McNair	30.00
10	Curtis Martin, Antowain Smith	20.00
11	Jerry Rice, Michael Irvin	40.00
12	Steve Young, Brett Favre	80.00
13	Corey Dillon, Fred Taylor	50.00
14	Tim Brown, Andre Rison	15.00
15	Mike Alstott, Robert Smith	15.00
16	Brad Johnson, Scott Mitchell	15.00
17	Robert Edwards, John Avery	25.00
18	Deion Sanders, Rob Moore	15.00
19	Antonio Freeman, Randy Moss	100.00
20	Peyton Manning, Ryan Leaf	80.00
21	Curtis Enis, Jacquez Green	30.00
22	Keyshawn Johnson, Terry Glenn	15.00

1998 Playoff Momentum Hobby Rookie Double Feature

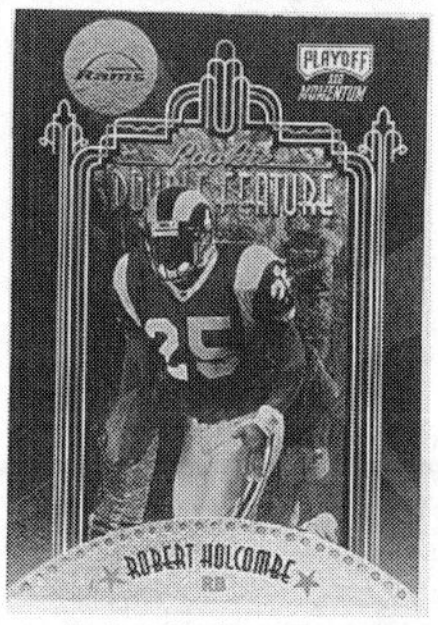

Each card in this set was printed on doublesided foil board with three patterned micro-etches on each side. Two rookies with similar styles of play are matched in this 20-card chase set. One on the front and one on the back. Singles were inserted 1:17 hobby packs.

		MT
Complete Set (20):		200.00
Common Player:		4.00
Inserted 1:17		
1	Peyton Manning, Brian Griese	30.00
2	Ryan Leaf, Charlie Batch	25.00
3	Charles Woodson, Terry Fair	12.00
4	Curtis Enis, Tavian Banks	12.00
5	Fred Taylor, John Avery	20.00
6	Kevin Dyson, E.G. Green	10.00
7	Robert Edwards, Chris Fuamatu-Ma'afala	12.00
8	Randy Moss, Tim Dwight	40.00
9	Marcus Nash, Joe Jurevicius	10.00
10	Jerome Pathon, Az-Zahir Hakim	6.00
11	Jacquez Green, Tony Simmons	10.00
12	Robert Holcombe, Jon Ritchie	8.00
13	Cameron Cleeland, Alonzo Mayes	6.00
14	Patrick Johnson, Mikhael Ricks	4.00
15	Germane Crowell, Hines Ward	10.00
16	Skip Hicks, Chris Floyd	8.00
17	Brian Alford, Jammi German	4.00
18	Ahman Green, Rashaan Shehee	8.00
19	Jonathan Quinn, Moses Moreno	4.00
20	R.W. McQuarters, Duane Starks	4.00
		4.00

1998 Playoff Momentum Hobby Team Threads

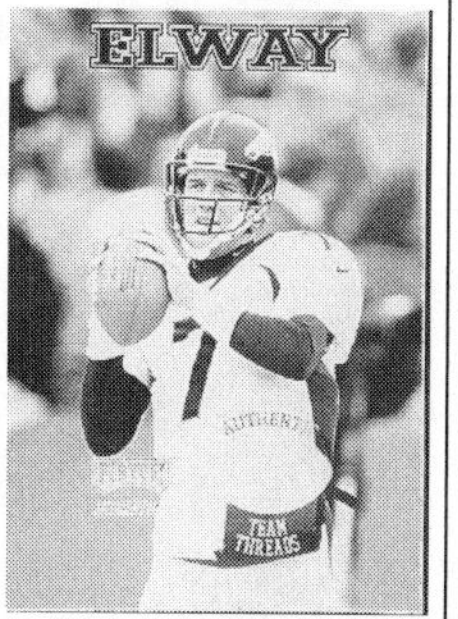

Each card in this 20-card set showcased authentic team jerseys that the pros use. All the Home jerseys were in color while the parallel Away jerseys were in white. Home jerseys could be found 1:33 hobby packs while the Away singles were tougher at 1:65.

		MT
Complete Set (20):		350.00
Common Player:		7.00
Inserted 1:33		
Away Cards:		2x
Inserted 1:65		
1	Jerry Rice	20.00
2	Terrell Davis	30.00
3	Warrick Dunn	15.00
4	Brett Favre	40.00
5	Napoleon Kaufman	10.00
6	Corey Dillon	10.00
7	John Elway	20.00
8	Troy Aikman	20.00
9	Mark Brunell	15.00
10	Kordell Stewart	15.00
11	Drew Bledsoe	15.00
12	Curtis Martin	10.00
13	Dan Marino	30.00
14	Jerome Bettis	7.00
15	Eddie George	15.00
16	Ryan Leaf	20.00
17	Jake Plummer	15.00
18	Peyton Manning	40.00
19	Steve Young	12.00
20	Barry Sanders	40.00

1998 Playoff Momentum Retail

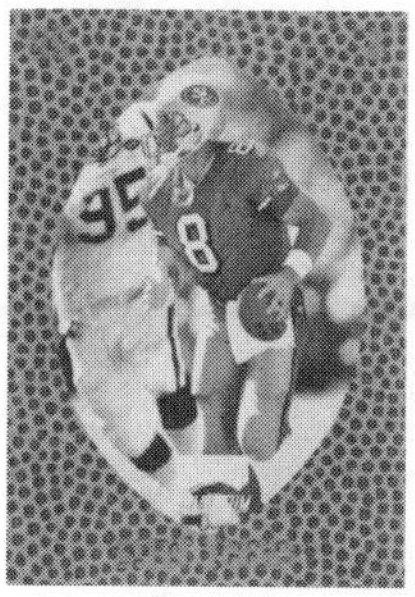

Each of the base cards in this set have a pigskin embossed style to them. Rookie cards are seeded at 1:3 retail packs. Each card has a parallel Red version with singles found 1:4 retail packs.

		MT
Complete Set (250):		150.00
Common Player:		.15
Minor Stars:		.30
Common Rookie:		1.00
Inserted 1:3		
Red Cards:		3x
Red Rookies:		1.5x
Inserted 1:4		
Wax Box:		60.00
1	Karim Abdul	.50
2	Troy Aikman	1.50
3	Derrick Alexander	.15
4	*Stephen Alexander*	3.00
5	*Brian Alford*	2.00
6	Terry Allen	.30
7	Mike Alstott	.50
8	Kimble Anders	.15
9	Jamal Anderson	.75
10	Reidel Anthony	.30
11	Steve Atwater	.15
12	*John Avery*	4.00
13	*Tavian Banks*	3.50
14	Tony Banks	.30
15	Tiki Barber	.15
16	*Charlie Batch*	10.00
17	Donnell Bennett	.15
18	Edgar Bennett	.15
19	Jerome Bettis	.50
20	Steve Beuerlein	.15
21	Will Blackwell	.15
22	Jeff Blake	.30
23	Drew Bledsoe	1.25
24	Kyle Brady	.15
25	Robert Brooks	.30
26	Steve Broussard	.15
27	Gary Brown	.15
28	Tim Brown	.30
29	Isaac Bruce	.30
30	Mark Bruener	.15
31	Mark Brunell	1.25
32	Keith Byars	.15
33	Chris Calloway	.15
34	Rae Carruth	.15
35	Cris Carter	.50
36	Larry Centers	.15
37	Chris Chandler	.50
38	Mark Chmura	.30
39	Wayne Chrebet	.50
40	*Cameron Cleeland*	3.00
41	Ben Coates	.30
42	Kerry Collins	.30
43	Andre Coleman	.15
44	Curtis Conway	.30
45	Zack Crockett	.15
46	*Germane Crowell*	5.00
47	Randall Cunningham	1.00
48	Billy Davis	.15
49	Stephen Davis	.15
50	Terrell Davis	2.50
51	Troy Davis	.15
52	Willie Davis	.15
53	Sean Dawkins	.15
54	Trent Dilfer	.30
55	Ken Dilger	.15
56	Corey Dillon	1.00
57	Troy Drayton	.15
58	Jim Druckenmiller	.30
59	Rickey Dudley	.15
60	Jason Dunn	.15
61	Warrick Dunn	1.25
62	*Tim Dwight*	4.00
63	*Kevin Dyson*	4.00
64	Marc Edwards	.15
65	*Robert Edwards*	7.00
66	John Elway	2.50
67	Bert Emanuel	.15
68	Bobby Engram	.15
69	*Curtis Enis*	6.00
70	Craig Erickson	.15
71	*Terry Fair*	3.00
72	Marshall Faulk	.75
73	Brett Favre	3.00
74	*Chris Floyd*	1.00
75	William Floyd	.15
76	Doug Flutie	1.00
77	Glenn Foley	.30
78	Antonio Freeman	.50
79	Gus Frerotte	.30
80	Irving Fryar	.15
81	*Chris Fuamatu-Ma'afala*	2.00
82	Joey Galloway	.50
83	Rich Gannon	.15
84	Charlie Garner	.15
85	Eddie George	1.25
86	Jeff George	.30
87	*Jammi German*	3.00
88	Terry Glenn	.50
89	Tony Gonzalez	.30
90	Jay Graham	.15
91	Jeff Graham	.15
92	Elvis Grbac	.30
93	*Ahman Green*	3.00
94	*E.G. Green*	3.00
95	Eric Green	.15
96	*Jacquez Green*	4.00
97	Trent Green	.50
98	Kevin Greene	.15
99	*Brian Griese*	10.00
100	*Az-Zahir Hakim*	3.00
101	Merton Hanks	.15
102	Jim Harbaugh	.30
103	Marvin Harrison	.30
104	Andre Hastings	.15
105	Courtney Hawkins	.15
106	Garrison Hearst	.50
107	William Henderson	.15
108	*Skip Hicks*	5.00
109	Greg Hill	.15
110	Ike Hilliard	.15
111	*Robert Holcombe*	3.00
112	*Vonnie Holliday*	3.00
113	Bobby Hoying	.30
114	Michael Irvin	.30
115	Qadry Ismail	.15
116	Raghib Ismail	.15
117	Michael Jackson	.15
118	Shawn Jefferson	.15
119	James Jett	.15
120	Anthony Johnson	.15
121	Brad Johnson	.50
122	Charles Johnson	.15
123	Keyshawn Johnson	.50
124	Leon Johnson	.15
125	*Patrick Johnson*	3.00
126	Rob Johnson	.50
127	Daryl Johnston	.15
128	Freddie Jones	.15
129	*Joe Jurevicius*	3.00
130	Danny Kanell	.15
131	Napoleon Kaufman	.50
132	Eddie Kennison	.30
133	Levon Kirkland	.15
134	Erik Kramer	.15
135	David LaFleur	.15
136	Fred Lane	.30
137	*Ryan Leaf*	6.00
138	Amp Lee	.15
139	Dorsey Levens	.50
140	Jermaine Lewis	.30
141	Ray Lewis	.15
142	*Jonathon Linton*	3.00
143	Greg Lloyd	.15
144	Kevin Lockett	.15
145	John Lynch	.15
146	*Peyton Manning*	25.00
147	Dan Marino	2.00
148	Curtis Martin	.50
149	Tony Martin	.30
150	Terance Mathis	.15
151	*Alonzo Mayes*	1.00
152	Derrick Mayes	.15
153	Ed McCaffrey	.30
154	Keenan McCardell	.30
155	O.J. McDuffie	.30
156	Tony McGee	.15
157	James McKnight	.15
158	Steve McNair	.75
159	*R.W. McQuarters*	2.00
160	Natrone Means	.50
161	Eric Metcalf	.15
162	Ernie Mills	.15
163	Rick Mirer	.15
164	Scott Mitchell	.30
165	Warren Moon	.30
166	Herman Moore	.50
167	Jerald Moore	.15
168	Rob Moore	.30
169	*Moses Moreno*	2.00
170	Johnnie Morton	.15
171	*Randy Moss*	25.00
172	Eric Moulds	.75
173	Muhsin Muhammad	.15
174	Adrian Murrell	.30
175	*Marcus Nash*	4.00
176	Neil O'Donnell	.15
177	Terrell Owens	.75
178	*Jerome Pathon*	3.00
179	Carl Pickens	.50
180	Jake Plummer	1.25
181	Mike Pritchard	.15
182	*Jonathan Quinn*	3.00
183	John Randle	.15
184	Andre Reed	.30
185	Jake Reed	.30
186	Errict Rhett	.15
187	Jerry Rice	1.50
188	*Mikhael Ricks*	3.00
189	Andre Rison	.30
190	*John Ritchie*	2.00
191	*Rod Rutledge*	1.00
192	Barry Sanders	3.00
193	Chris Sanders	.15
194	Deion Sanders	.50
195	Frank Sanders	.15
196	O.J. Santiago	.30
197	Warren Sapp	.15
198	Darnay Scott	.15
199	Junior Seau	.30
200	Shannon Sharpe	.30
201	Sedrick Shaw	.15
202	*Rashaan Shehee*	2.00
203	Heath Shuler	.15
204	*Tony Simmons*	4.00
205	Antowain Smith	.50
206	Bruce Smith	.15
207	Emmitt Smith	2.00
208	Jimmy Smith	.50
209	Lamar Smith	.15
210	Neil Smith	.15
211	Robert Smith	.30
212	Rod Smith	.30
213	*Takeo Spikes*	2.00
214	Duce Staley	1.00
215	*Duane Starks*	2.00
216	James Stewart	.15
217	Kordell Stewart	1.25
218	Bryan Still	.15
219	J.J. Stokes	.30
220	Michael Strahan	.15
221	Dana Stubblefield	.15
222	*Fred Taylor*	15.00
223	Vinny Testaverde	.30
224	Yancey Thigpen	.15
225	Derrick Thomas	.15
226	Thurman Thomas	.30
227	Zach Thomas	.30
228	Amani Toomer	.15
229	*Andre Wadsworth*	4.00
230	Wesley Walls	.15
231	Dedric Ward	.15
232	*Hines Ward*	3.00
233	Chris Warren	.30
234	Ricky Watters	.50
235	Charles Way	.15
236	Michael Westbrook	.15
237	Tyrone Wheatley	.15
238	Reggie White	.50
239	Dan Wilkinson	.15
240	Kevin Williams	.15
241	*Shaun Williams*	1.00
242	*Grant Wistrom*	2.00
243	*Charles Woodson*	7.00
244	Darren Woodson	.15
245	Rod Woodson	.15
246	Danny Wuerffel	.15
247	Frank Wycheck	.15
248	Steve Young	1.00
249	Eric Zeier	.15
250	Ray Zellars	.15

1998 Playoff Momentum Retail Class Reunion Tandems

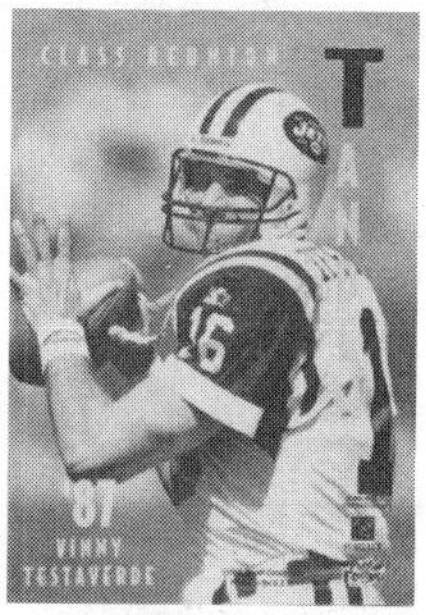

The idea behind this insert was to pick two of the top players drafted from a specific season and picture one on the front and the other on the back. The set starts with the year 1983 and ends with 1998. Singles were inserted 1:121 retail packs.

		MT
Complete Set (16):		500.00
Common Player:		12.00
Minor Stars:		24.00
Inserted 1:121		
1	Dan Marino, John Elway	70.00
2	Steve Young, Reggie White	30.00
3	Jerry Rice, Bruce Smith	40.00
4	Keith Byars, Leslie O'Neal	12.00
5	Cris Carter, Vinny Testaverde	24.00
6	Tim Brown, Michael Irvin	24.00
7	Troy Aikman, Barry Sanders	80.00
8	Emmitt Smith, Jeff George	60.00
9	Brett Favre, Herman Moore	80.00
10	Brad Johnson, Carl Pickens	24.00
11	Drew Bledsoe, Mark Brunell	40.00
12	Dorsey Levens, Isaac Bruce	24.00
13	Terrell Davis, Kordell Stewart	70.00
14	Eddie George, Keyshawn Johnson	35.00
15	Warrick Dunn, Jake Plummer	35.00
16	Peyton Manning, Ryan Leaf	50.00

1998 Playoff Momentum Retail EndZone X-press

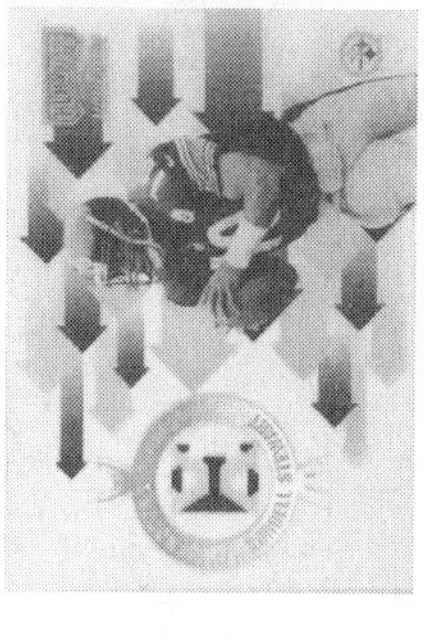

Each card in this set is similar to the hobby version except these singles aren't die cut. They are printed on plastic with gold foil and were inserted 1:13 retail packs.

		MT
Complete Set (29):		100.00
Common Player:		1.00
Minor Stars:		2.00
Inserted 1:13		
1	Jake Plummer	5.00
2	Herman Moore	2.00
3	Terrell Davis	8.00
4	Antowain Smith	2.00
5	Curtis Enis	3.00
6	Corey Dillon	3.00
7	Troy Aikman	6.00
8	John Elway	6.00
9	Barry Sanders	10.00
10	Brett Favre	10.00
11	Peyton Manning	10.00
12	Mark Brunell	6.00
13	Andre Rison	1.00
14	Dan Marino	8.00
15	Randy Moss	20.00
16	Drew Bledsoe	6.00
17	Jerome Bettis	2.00
18	Tim Brown	1.00
19	Antonio Freeman	2.00
20	Napoleon Kaufman	2.00
21	Emmitt Smith	8.00
22	Kordell Stewart	6.00
23	Curtis Martin	4.00
24	Ryan Leaf	5.00
25	Jerry Rice	6.00
26	Joey Galloway	2.00
27	Warrick Dunn	5.00
28	Eddie George	5.00
29	Steve McNair	3.00

1998 Playoff Momentum Retail Headliners

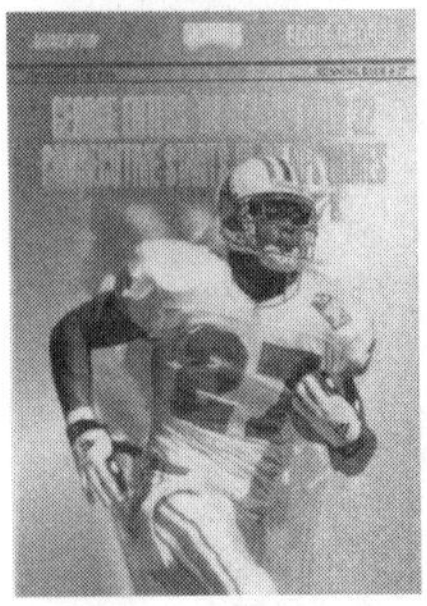

These red foil front cards highlight a record that the player had set in the past. Singles were found 1:73 retail packs.

		MT
Complete Set (23):		275.00
Common Player:		7.00
Inserted 1:73		
1	Brett Favre	40.00
2	Jerry Rice	20.00
3	Barry Sanders	40.00
4	Troy Aikman	20.00
5	Warrick Dunn	15.00
6	Dan Marino	30.00
7	John Elway	25.00
8	Drew Bledsoe	15.00
9	Kordell Stewart	15.00
10	Mark Brunell	15.00
11	Eddie George	15.00
12	Terrell Davis	35.00
13	Emmitt Smith	30.00
14	Steve McNair	10.00
15	Mike Alstott	7.00
16	Peyton Manning	30.00
17	Antonio Freeman	10.00
18	Curtis Martin	10.00
19	Terry Glenn	7.00
20	Brad Johnson	7.00
21	Karim Abdul	7.00
22	Ryan Leaf	15.00
23	Jerome Bettis	7.00

1998 Playoff Momentum Retail NFL Rivals

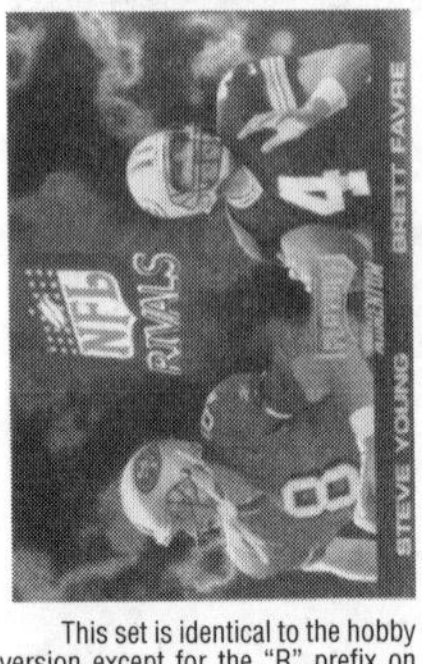

This set is identical to the hobby version except for the "R" prefix on these retail singles. Each card pictures two players who compete at the same position. Singles are found 1:73 retail packs.

		MT
Complete Set (22):		280.00
Common Player:		10.00
Inserted 1:73		
1	Mark Brunell, John Elway	20.00
2	Jerome Bettis, Eddie George	15.00
3	Barry Sanders, Emmitt Smith	40.00
4	Dan Marino, Drew Bledsoe	30.00
5	Troy Aikman, Jake Plummer	20.00
6	Terrell Davis, Napoleon Kaufman	30.00
7	Cris Carter, Herman Moore	10.00
8	Warrick Dunn, Dorsey Levens	15.00
9	Kordell Stewart, Steve McNair	15.00
10	Curtis Martin, Antowain Smith	10.00
11	Jerry Rice, Michael Irvin	20.00
12	Steve Young, Brett Favre	40.00
13	Corey Dillon, Fred Taylor	20.00
14	Tim Brown, Andre Rison	10.00
15	Mike Alstott, Robert Smith	10.00
16	Brad Johnson, Scott Mitchell	10.00
17	Robert Edwards, John Avery	15.00
18	Deion Sanders, Rob Moore	10.00
19	Antonio Freeman, Randy Moss	50.00
20	Peyton Manning, Ryan Leaf	35.00
21	Curtis Enis, Jacquez Green	15.00
22	Keyshawn Johnson, Terry Glenn	10.00

1998 Playoff Momentum Retail Rookie Double Feature

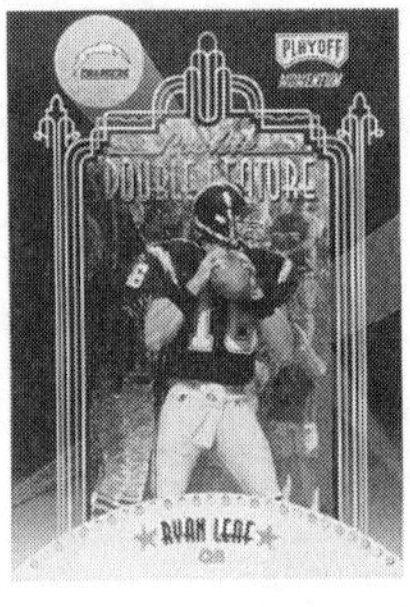

The hobby version of this set features two players on one card, where this set has the players on their own card. Each card also has the "R" prefix before the card number and were found 1:25 retail packs.

		MT
Complete Set (40):		220.00
Common Player:		2.00
Minor Stars:		4.00
Inserted 1:25		
1	Peyton Manning	30.00
2	Ryan Leaf	10.00
3	Charles Woodson	10.00
4	Curtis Enis	8.00
5	Fred Taylor	15.00
6	Kevin Dyson	6.00
7	Robert Edwards	8.00
8	Randy Moss	60.00
9	Marcus Nash	6.00
10	Jerome Pathon	4.00
11	Jacquez Green	6.00
12	Robert Holcombe	5.00
13	Cameron Cleeland	5.00
14	Patrick Johnson	4.00
15	Germane Crowell	6.00
16	Skip Hicks	6.00
17	Brian Alford	2.00
18	Ahman Green	5.00
19	Jonathan Quinn	4.00
20	R.W. McQuarters	4.00
21	Brian Griese	10.00
22	Charlie Batch	18.00
23	Terry Fair	4.00
24	Tavian Banks	5.00
25	John Avery	6.00
26	E.G. Green	4.00
27	Chris Fuamatu-Ma'afala	4.00
28	Tim Dwight	6.00
29	Joe Jurevicius	4.00
30	Az-Zahir Hakim	4.00
31	Tony Simmons	5.00
32	Jon Ritchie	4.00
33	Alonzo Mayes	2.00
34	Mikhael Ricks	4.00
35	Hines Ward	4.00
36	Chris Floyd	2.00
37	Jammi German	4.00
38	Rashaan Shehee	4.00
39	Moses Moreno	2.00
40	Duane Starks	4.00

1998 Playoff Momentum Retail Team Jerseys

Team Jersey cards feature a photo of the player on the front and a piece of an authentic jersey on the back. It isn't an actual game worn but a jersey that the pros use. The Home versions carry a colored swatch and were inserted 1:49 retail packs. The parallel Away versions feature the white jerseys and were inserted 1:97 packs.

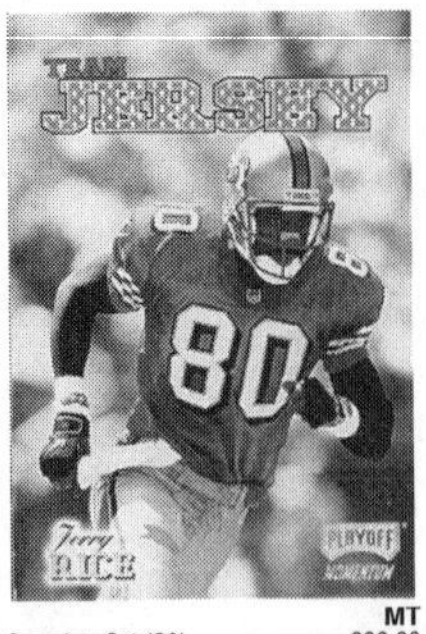

		MT
Complete Set (20):		600.00
Common Player:		15.00
Inserted 1:49		
Away Cards:		1.5x
Inserted 1:97		
1	Jerry Rice	30.00
2	Terrell Davis	50.00
3	Warrick Dunn	25.00
4	Brett Favre	60.00
5	Napoleon Kaufman	15.00
6	Corey Dillon	15.00
7	John Elway	30.00
8	Troy Aikman	30.00
9	Mark Brunell	25.00
10	Kordell Stewart	25.00
11	Drew Bledsoe	25.00
12	Curtis Martin	15.00
13	Dan Marino	50.00
14	Jerome Bettis	15.00
15	Eddie George	25.00
16	Ryan Leaf	25.00
17	Jake Plummer	30.00
18	Peyton Manning	50.00
19	Steve Young	20.00
20	Barry Sanders	60.00

1998 Playoff Prestige

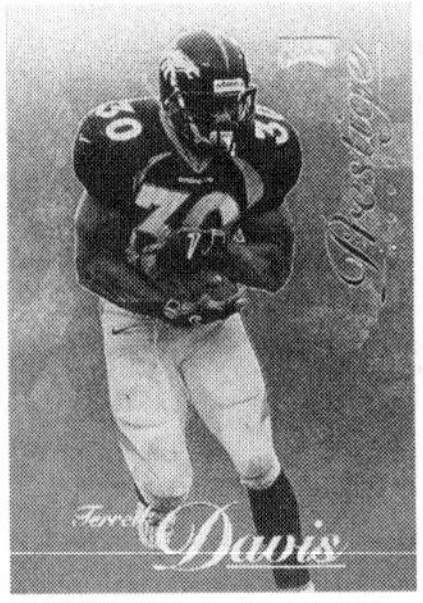

Prestige was a 200-card set that arrived with two different looks - one in hobby and one in retail. Prestige SSD cards are printed on 30-point etched silver foil stock. Retail versions are printed on thinner stock, with a foil strip across the bottom. While hobby cards are paralleled in red and gold versions, retail cards are paralleled in red and green foil versus the silver foil used on base cards. Inserts include: Alma Mater (both retail and hobby), Award Winning Performers (both), Best of the NFL (both), Checklists (both), Draft Picks (both), Honors (hobby), Inside the Numbers (both) and Marino Milestones (hobby).

		MT
Complete Set (200):		170.00
Common Player:		.30
Minor Stars:		.60
Common Rookie (165-200):		1.50
Red Cards:		2x-4x
Red Rookies:		2x
Gold Cards:		40x-80x
Gold Rookies:		12x-25x
Hobby Pack (5):		7.50
Hobby Wax Box (16):		105.00
Retail Pack (7):		2.50
Retail Wax Box (24):		60.00
1	John Elway	6.00
2	Steve Atwater	.30
3	Terrell Davis	6.00
4	Bill Romanowski	.30
5	Rod Smith	.30
6	Shannon Sharpe	.60
7	Ed McCaffrey	.30
8	Neil Smith	.30
9	Brett Favre	8.00
10	Dorsey Levens	.60
11	LeRoy Butler	.30
12	Antonio Freeman	.60
13	Robert Brooks	.30
14	Mark Chmura	.60
15	Gilbert Brown	.30
16	Kordell Stewart	3.00
17	Jerome Bettis	.60
18	Carnell Lake	.30
19	Dermontti Dawson	.30
20	Charles Johnson	.30
21	Greg Lloyd	.30
22	Levon Kirkland	.30
23	Steve Young	3.00
24	Jim Druckenmiller	.60
25	Garrison Hearst	.30
26	Merton Hanks	.30
27	Ken Norton	.30
28	Jerry Rice	5.00
29	Terrell Owens	.60
30	J.J. Stokes	.30
31	Trent Dilfer	.60
32	Warrick Dunn	4.00
33	Mike Alstott	.75
34	Reidel Anthony	.60
35	Warren Sapp	.30
36	Elvis Grbac	.30
37	Kimble Anders	.30
38	Ted Popson	.30
39	Derrick Thomas	.30
40	Tony Gonzalez	.60
41	Andre Rison	.30
42	Derrick Alexander	.30
43	Brad Johnson	.60
44	Robert Smith	.30
45	Randall McDaniel	.30
46	Cris Carter	.30
47	Jake Reed	.30
48	John Randle	.30
49	Drew Bledsoe	4.00
50	Willie Clay	.30
51	Chris Slade	.30
52	Willie McGinest	.30
53	Shawn Jefferson	.30
54	Ben Coates	.30
55	Terry Glenn	.60
56	Jason Hanson	.30
57	Scott Mitchell	.30
58	Barry Sanders	8.00
59	Herman Moore	.60
60	Johnnie Morton	.30
61	Mark Brunell	4.00
62	James Stewart	.30
63	Tony Boselli	.30
64	Jimmy Smith	.30
65	Keenan McCardell	.30
66	Dan Marino	8.00
67	Troy Drayton	.30
68	Bernie Parmalee	.30
69	Karim Abdul-Jabbar	.75
70	Zach Thomas	.30
71	O.J. McDuffie	.30
72	Tim Bowens	.30
73	Danny Kanell	.30
74	Tiki Barber	.60
75	Tyrone Wheatley	.30
76	Charles Way	.30
77	Jason Sehorn	.30
78	Ike Hilliard	.60
79	Michael Strahan	.30
80	Troy Aikman	4.00
81	Deion Sanders	2.00
82	Emmitt Smith	7.00
83	Darren Woodson	.30
84	Daryl Johnston	.30
85	Michael Irvin	.60
86	David LaFleur	.60
87	Glenn Foley	.30
88	Neil O'Donnell	.30
89	Keyshawn Johnson	.60
90	Aaron Glenn	.30
91	Wayne Chrebet	.30
92	Curtis Martin	2.00
93	Steve McNair	2.00
94	Eddie George	3.00
95	Bruce Matthews	.30
96	Frank Wycheck	.30
97	Yancey Thigpen	.30
98	Gus Frerotte	.30
99	Terry Allen	.30
100	Michael Westbrook	.30
101	Jamie Asher	.30
102	Marshall Faulk	.60
103	Zack Crockett	.30
104	Ken Dilger	.30
105	Marvin Harrison	.60
106	Chris Chandler	.30
107	Byron Hanspard	.60
108	Jamal Anderson	.60
109	Terance Mathis	.30
110	Peter Boulware	.30
111	Michael Jackson	.30
112	Jim Harbaugh	.60
113	Errict Rhett	.30
114	Antowain Smith	3.00
115	Thurman Thomas	.60
116	Bruce Smith	.30
117	Doug Flutie	3.00
118	Rob Johnson	.60
119	Kerry Collins	.75
120	Fred Lane	.30
121	Wesley Walls	.30
122	William Floyd	.30
123	Kevin Greene	.30
124	Erik Kramer	.30
125	Darnell Autry	.60
126	Curtis Conway	.30
127	Edgar Bennett	.30
128	Jeff Blake	.60
129	Corey Dillon	3.00
130	Carl Pickens	.30
131	Darnay Scott	.30
132	Jake Plummer	4.00
133	Larry Centers	.30
134	Frank Sanders	.30
135	Rob Moore	.30
136	Adrian Murrell	.60
137	Troy Davis	.60
138	Ray Zellars	.30
139	Willie Roaf	.30
140	Andre Hastings	.30
141	Jeff George	.60
142	Napoleon Kaufman	.75
143	Desmond Howard	.30
144	Tim Brown	.30
145	James Jett	.30
146	Rickey Dudley	.30
147	Bobby Hoying	.60
148	Duce Staley	2.00
149	Charlie Garner	.30
150	Irving Fryar	.30
151	Chris T. Jones	.30
152	Tony Banks	.60
153	Craig Heyward	.30
154	Isaac Bruce	.60
155	Eddie Kennison	.60
156	Junior Seau	.30
157	Tony Martin	.30
158	Freddie Jones	.30
159	Natrone Means	.60
160	Warren Moon	.60
161	Steve Broussard	.30
162	Joey Galloway	.60
163	Brian Blades	.30
164	Ricky Watters	.60
165	*Peyton Manning*	25.00
166	*Ryan Leaf*	8.00
167	*Andre Wadsworth*	3.00
168	*Charles Woodson*	8.00
169	*Curtis Enis*	7.00
170	*Fred Taylor*	15.00
171	*Kevin Dyson*	5.00
172	*Robert Edwards*	8.00
173	*Randy Moss*	25.00
174	*R.W. McQuarters*	1.50
175	*John Avery*	5.00
176	*Marcus Nash*	5.00
177	*Jerome Pathon*	3.00
178	*Jacquez Green*	6.00
179	*Robert Holcombe*	6.00
180	*Patrick Johnson*	1.50
181	*Germane Crowell*	7.00
182	*Tony Simmons*	3.00
183	*Joe Jurevicius*	3.00
184	*Mikhael Ricks*	1.50
185	*Charlie Batch*	10.00
186	*Jon Ritchie*	1.50
187	*Scott Frost*	1.50
188	*Skip Hicks*	5.00
189	*Brian Alford*	1.50
190	*E.G. Green*	3.00
191	*Jammi German*	1.50
192	*Ahman Green*	7.00
193	*Chris Floyd*	1.50
194	*Larry Shannon*	1.50
195	*Jonathan Quinn*	2.00
196	*Rashaan Shehee*	3.00
197	*Brian Griese*	10.00
198	*Hines Ward*	5.00
199	*Michael Pittman*	1.50
200	*Az-Zahir Hakim*	5.00

1998 Playoff Prestige Red Hobby

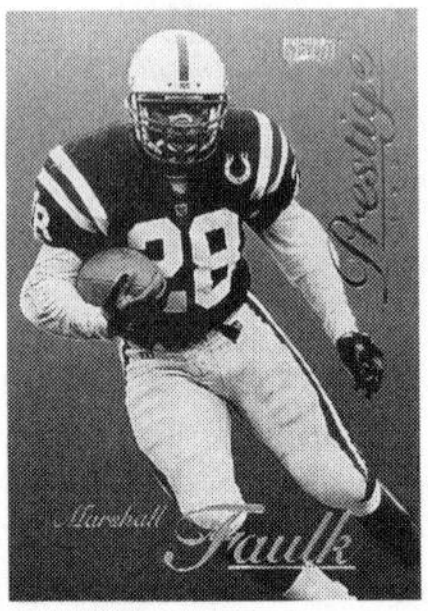

All 200 cards in Prestige SSD were paralleled in this red foil version. Red parallels were seeded one per three packs.

	MT
Red Cards:	3x
Red Rookies:	2x

1998 Playoff Prestige Gold

All 200 cards in Prestige were available in a gold foil parallel version. These were sequentially numbered to 25 on the card back.

	MT
Gold Cards:	50x-100x
Gold Rookies:	12x-25x

1998 Playoff Prestige Alma Maters

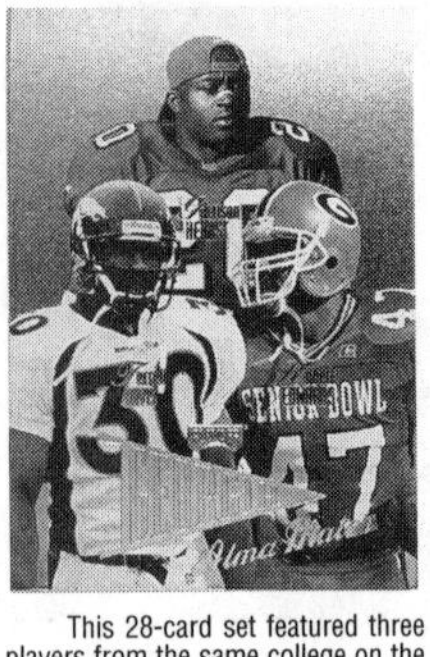

This 28-card set featured three players from the same college on the silver foilboard. The back showed the same three players are gave a "Did you Know?" statistic about each. Silver versions were seeded one per 17 hobby packs, while Blue versions were seeded one per 25 retail packs.

		MT
Complete Set (28):		375.00
Common Player:		6.00
1	Favre, Jackson, P. Carter	45.00
2	Irvin, Maryland, Testaverde	6.00
3	Dunn, Wadsworth, Boulware	20.00
4	D. Sanders, Bennett, B. Johnson	12.00
5	E. Smith, F. Taylor, Anthony	30.00
6	A. Smith, Anders, Lathon	12.00
7	Barry Sanders, R.J. McQuarters, Thurman Thomas	40.00
8	Leaf, Bledsoe, Hansen	25.00
9	Brunell, Moon, Shehee	20.00
10	Kaufman, Dillon, Pathon	15.00
11	Manning, Pickens, R. White	40.00
12	K. Stewart, Carruth, Westbrook	20.00
13	Enis, Collins, McDuffie	20.00
14	George, Hoying, Dudley	20.00
15	C. Carter, Glenn, Galloway	6.00
16	Grbac, Harbaugh, Woodson	15.00
17	Elway, McCaffrey, Milburn	20.00
18	T. Davis, Hearst, Edwards	25.00
19	Walker, Hastings, Ward	6.00
20	Marino, C. Martin, Heyward	40.00
21	Aikman, Stokes, Hicks	25.00
22	Seau, K. Johnson, Morton	6.00
23	Bettis, T. Brown, Watters	6.00
24	Faulk, Scott, Hakim	6.00
25	B. Smith, Druckenmiller, Freeman	6.00
26	Plummer, Woodson, Bates	20.00
27	H. Moore, Barber, Way	6.00
28	Avery, Walls, Bowens	6.00

1998 Playoff Prestige Award Winning Performers

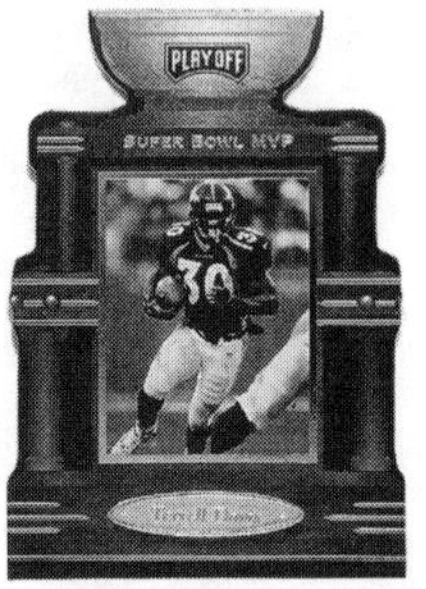

This 22-card insert showcased top players on a large trophy, with the record they achieved and the Playoff logo near the top of the trophy. Hobby versions of this inserted were printed on silver foil, die-cut around the trophy and inserted one per 65 packs, while retail versions were printed on blue foil, not die-cut and inserted one per 97 packs.

		MT
Complete Set (22):		750.00
Common Player:		15.00
1	Terrell Davis	60.00
2	Troy Aikman	50.00
3	Brett Favre	90.00
4	Barry Sanders	90.00
5	Warrick Dunn	45.00
6	John Elway	50.00
7	Jerome Bettis	15.00
8	Jake Plummer	45.00
9	Corey Dillon	25.00
10	Jerry Rice	50.00
11	Steve Young	30.00
12	Mark Brunell	35.00
13	Drew Bledsoe	45.00
14	Dan Marino	75.00
15	Kordell Stewart	45.00
16	Emmitt Smith	75.00
17	Deion Sanders	20.00
18	Mike Alstott	15.00
19	Herman Moore	15.00
20	Cris Carter	15.00
21	Eddie George	35.00
22	Dorsey Levens	15.00

1998 Playoff Prestige Best of the NFL

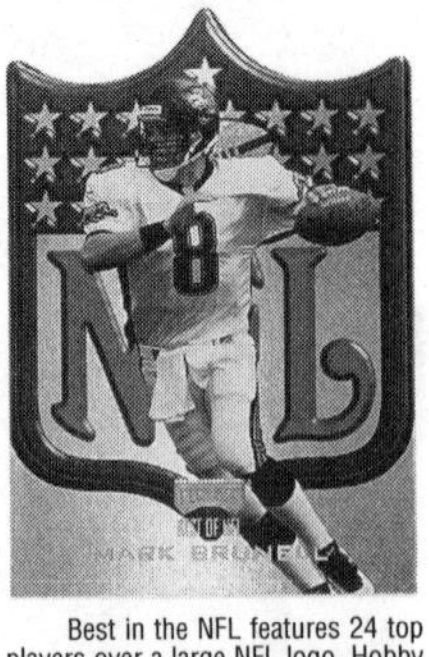

Best in the NFL features 24 top players over a large NFL logo. Hobby versions of this insert were die-cut around the top of the NFL shield and inserted one per 33 hobby packs, while retail versions were not die-cut and inserted one per 49 retail packs.

		MT
Complete Set (24):		400.00
Common Player:		6.00
1	Terrell Davis	25.00
2	Troy Aikman	25.00
3	Brett Favre	50.00
4	Barry Sanders	40.00
5	Warrick Dunn	20.00

6	John Elway	25.00
7	Jerome Bettis	6.00
8	Jake Plummer	20.00
9	Corey Dillon	15.00
10	Jerry Rice	25.00
11	Steve Young	15.00
12	Mark Brunell	20.00
13	Drew Bledsoe	25.00
14	Dan Marino	40.00
15	Kordell Stewart	25.00
16	Emmitt Smith	40.00
17	Deion Sanders	15.00
18	Mike Alstott	6.00
19	Herman Moore	6.00
20	Cris Carter	6.00
21	Eddie George	25.00
22	Dorsey Levens	6.00
23	Peyton Manning	35.00
24	Ryan Leaf	25.00

1998 Playoff Prestige Checklist

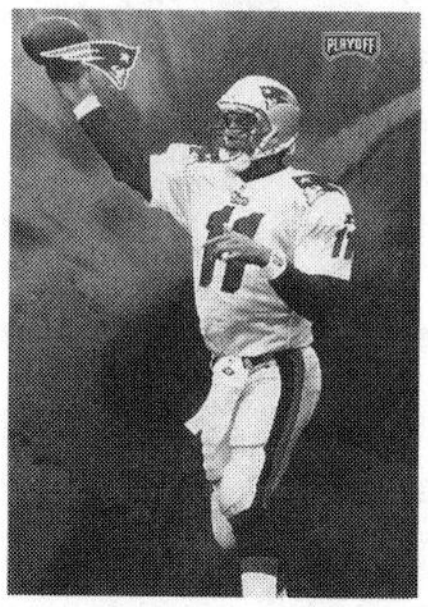

This 30-card insert arrived in both retail and hobby packs, and contained a star player from each NFL team on the front and shots of each player on that team's cards on the back. Silver hobby versions were seeded one per 17 hobby packs, while gold retail versions were seeded one per 17 retail packs.

		MT
Complete Set (30):		350.00
Common Player:		4.00
1	Jake Plummer	20.00
2	Byron Hanspard	4.00
3	Michael Jackson	4.00
4	Antowain Smith	10.00
5	Wesley Walls	4.00
6	Erik Kramer	4.00
7	Corey Dillon	15.00
8	Troy Aikman	25.00
9	John Elway	20.00
10	Barry Sanders	35.00
11	Brett Favre	40.00
12	Peyton Manning	35.00
13	Mark Brunell	20.00
14	Andre Rison	4.00
15	Dan Marino	35.00
16	Cris Carter	4.00
17	Drew Bledsoe	25.00
18	Troy Davis	4.00
19	Danny Kanell	4.00
20	Glenn Foley	4.00
21	Napoleon Kaufman	6.00
22	Bobby Hoying	4.00
23	Kordell Stewart	25.00
24	Isaac Bruce	6.00
25	Ryan Leaf	25.00
26	Jerry Rice	25.00
27	Joey Galloway	6.00
28	Warrick Dunn	20.00
29	Eddie George	25.00
30	Gus Frerotte	4.00

1998 Playoff Prestige Draft Picks

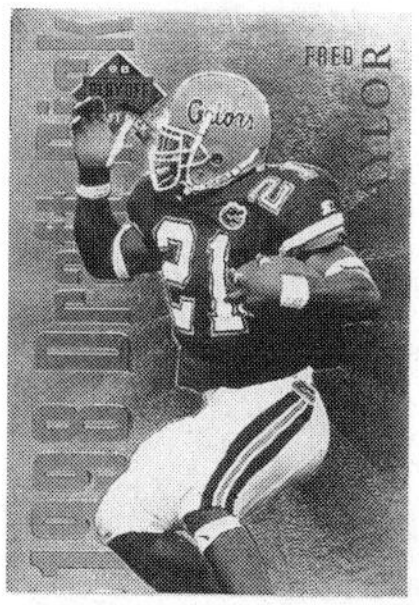

This 30-card insert featured the top draft picks from 1998. Silver versions were seeded one per nine hobby packs, while Silver Jumbos were inserted one per hobby box. Bronze standard sized cards were seeded one per nine retail packs, while Bronze Jumbos were inserted one per retail box. Green standard sized cards and Green Jumbos were also available, but only in special retail boxes, and both seeded one per box.

		MT
Complete Set (33):		250.00
Common Player:		3.00
Jumbos:		1x
1	Peyton Manning	30.00
2	Ryan Leaf	15.00
3	Andre Wadsworth	6.00
4	Charles Woodson	12.00
5	Curtis Enis	12.00
6	Fred Taylor	15.00
7	Kevin Dyson	10.00
8	Robert Edwards	12.00
9	Randy Moss	40.00
10	R.W. McQuarters	3.00
11	John Avery	10.00
12	Marcus Nash	10.00
13	Jerome Pathon	3.00
14	Jacquez Green	10.00
15	Robert Holcombe	10.00
16	Patrick Johnson	3.00
17	Germane Crowell	3.00
18	Tony Simmons	6.00
19	Joe Jurevicius	6.00
20	Mikhael Ricks	3.00
21	Charlie Batch	12.00
22	Jon Ritchie	3.00
23	Scott Frost	3.00
24	Skip Hicks	10.00
25	Brian Alford	3.00
26	E.G. Green	3.00
27	Jammi German	3.00
28	Ahman Green	12.00
29	Chris Floyd	3.00
30	Larry Shannon	3.00
31	Jonathan Quinn	3.00
32	Rashaan Shehee	6.00
33	Brian Griese	12.00

1998 Playoff Prestige Playoff Honors

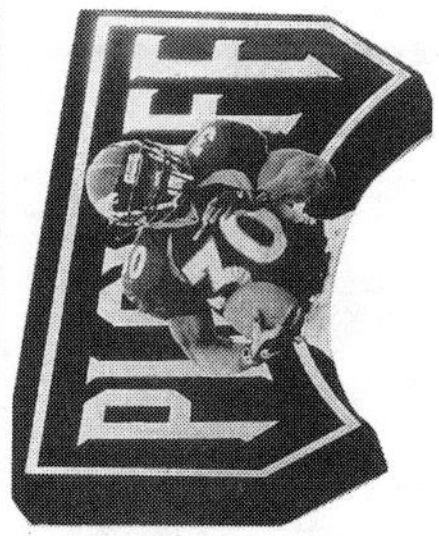

This three-card insert was found only in hobby packs of Pretige. The cards were unnumbered and are listed alphabetically. The were inserted one per 3,200 packs.

		MT
Complete Set (3):		400.00
Common Player:		75.00
PH10	Terrell Davis	150.00
PH11	Barry Sanders	200.00
PH12	Warrick Dunn	75.00

1998 Playoff Prestige Inside the Numbers

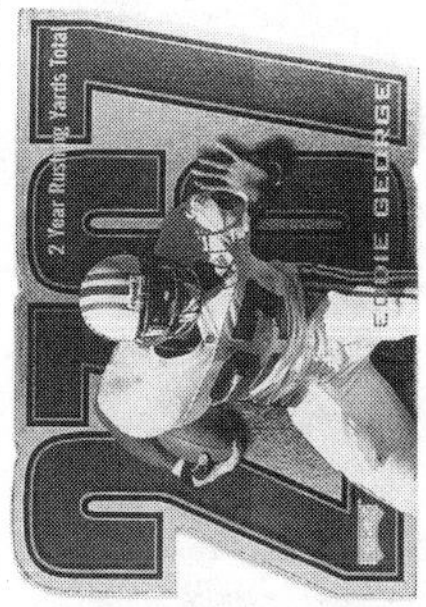

This 18-card insert set featured a player over some statistic that he has achieved. Hobby versions were die-cut and inserted one per 49 hobby packs, while retail not die-cut and inserted one per 72 retail packs.

		MT
Complete Set (18):		450.00
Common Player:		10.00
1	Barry Sanders	75.00
2	Terrell Davis	45.00
3	Jerry Rice	30.00
4	Kordell Stewart	30.00
5	Dan Marino	60.00
6	Warrick Dunn	30.00
7	Corey Dillon	20.00
8	Drew Bledsoe	30.00
9	Herman Moore	10.00
10	Troy Aikman	30.00
11	Brett Favre	75.00
12	Mark Brunell	25.00
13	Tim Brown	10.00
14	Jerome Bettis	10.00
15	Eddie George	30.00
16	Dorsey Levens	10.00
17	Napoleon Kaufman	10.00
18	John Elway	40.00

1998 Playoff Prestige Marino Milestones

The first five Marino Milestones cards were inserted into Prestige SSD at a rate of one per 321 packs. Each card highlighted a different record held by Marino, and no unautographed versions were available. Cards 6-10 were inserted into Absolute SSD and 11-15 were in Momentum SSD.

		MT
Complete Set (5):		600.00
Common Player:		125.00
1	55.416 (Dan Marino)	125.00
2	13/4 (Dan Marino)	125.00
3	6 (Dan Marino)	125.00
4	48 (Dan Marino)	125.00
5	2.03 (Dan Marino)	125.00

1998 Playoff Prestige Retail

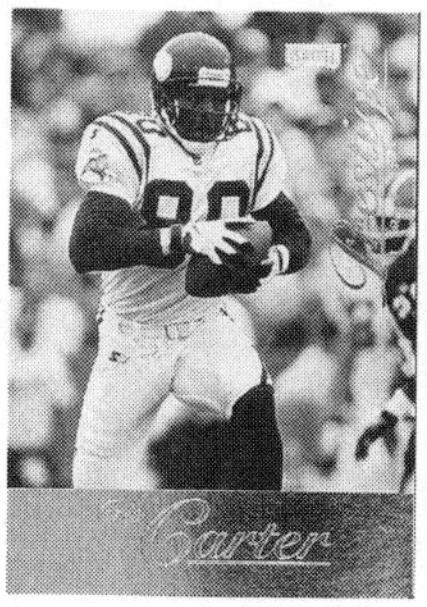

Prestige Retail contained the same 200-card checklist that the hobby version had, but was printed on a thinner card stock and featured silver strip across the bottom with the player's name embossed in it. This set was paralleled in both a red (retail) and green (specail retail jumbos) foil set.

	MT
Complete Set (200):	75.00
Common Player:	.20
Minor Stars:	.40
Red Stars:	3x
Red Rookies:	2x
Inserted 1:3	
Green Stars:	3x
Green Rookies:	2x
Inserted 1:1 Special Retail Pack	
Wax Box:	55.00

1998 Playoff Prestige Red/Green Retail

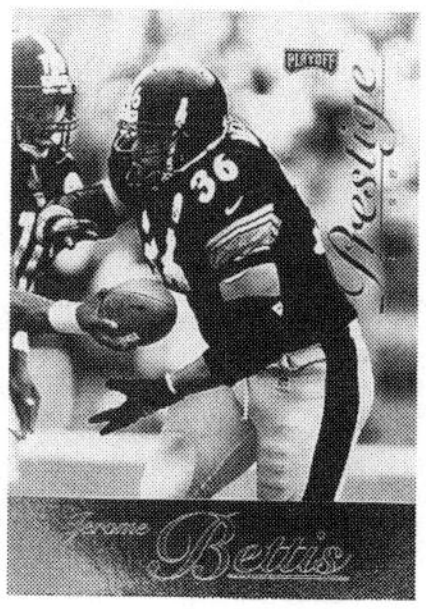

Each card in the Prestige retail set was paralleled in both red and green foil versions. The 200-card set contained either red foil (retail) or green foil (special retail) across the bottom instead of the silver used on base cards. Red foil versions were seeded one per three packs, while green foil versions were seeded one per Jumbo retail pack.

	MT
Red/Green Cards:	1.5x
Red/Green Rookies:	1x

1998 Playoff Super Bowl Show

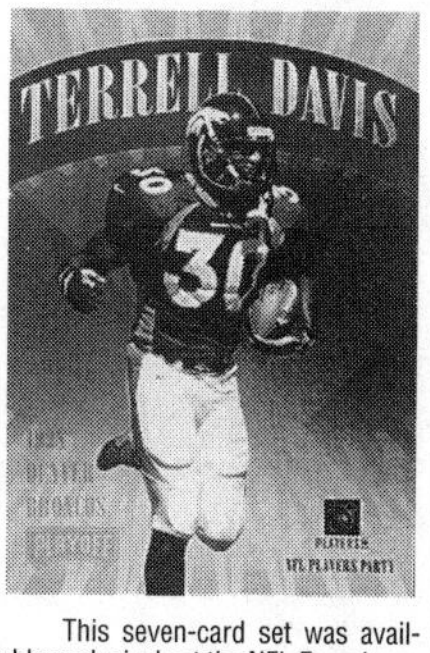

This seven-card set was available exclusively at the NFL Experience Show in conjunction with Super Bowl XXXII. The cards are horizontal with the player's image superimposed over Qualcomm Stadium and the player's last name running up the right side. The backs capture a superimposed shot of the player over San Diego scenery with the card number in the upper right.

		MT
Complete Set (7):		18.00
Common Player:		1.00
1	Trent Dilfer	2.00
2	Tony Martin	1.00
3	Terrell Davis	7.00
4	Antonio Freeman	2.00
5	Herschel Walker	1.00
6	Kordell Stewart	5.00
7	Drew Bledsoe	4.00

1999 Playoff Absolute EXP

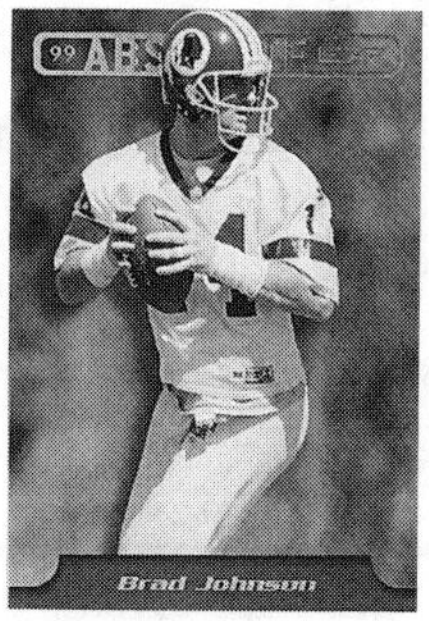

This was a 200-card set that included 40 unseeded rookie cards. Each single was printed on 20-point stock with foil stamping. Inserts included: Tools of the Trade (parallel), Absolute Heroes, Absolute Rookies, Extreme Team, Terrell Davis Salute, Rookie Reflex, Barry Sanders Commemorative and Team Jersey Tandems. SRP was $2.99 for eight-card packs.

		MT
Complete Set (200):		70.00
Common Player:		.15
Minor Stars:		.30
Common Rookie:		.50
SSD Pack (4):		6.00
SSD Wax Box (18):		100.00
EXP Pack (8):		3.00
EXP Wax Box (24):		65.00
1	*Tim Couch*	5.00
2	*Donovan McNabb*	4.00
3	*Akili Smith*	3.00
4	*Edgerrin James*	10.00
5	*Ricky Williams*	6.00
6	*Torry Holt*	3.00
7	*Champ Bailey*	1.50
8	*David Boston*	3.00
9	*Chris Claiborne*	1.00
10	*Chris McAlister*	1.00
11	*Daunte Culpepper*	6.00
12	*Cade McNown*	3.00
13	*Troy Edwards*	3.00
14	*Kevin Johnson*	3.00
15	*James Johnson*	2.50
16	*Rob Konrad*	1.00
17	*Jim Kleinsasser*	1.00
18	*Kevin Faulk*	2.00
19	*Joe Montgomery*	1.50
20	*Shaun King*	3.00
21	*Peerless Price*	2.50
22	*Mike Cloud*	1.00
23	*Jermaine Fazande*	1.00
24	*D'Wayne Bates*	1.00
25	*Brock Huard*	1.50
26	*Marty Booker*	1.50
27	*Karsten Bailey*	1.00
28	*Shawn Bryson*	.50
29	*Jeff Paulk*	1.00
30	*Sedrick Irvin*	1.75
31	*Craig Yeast*	1.00
32	*Joe Germaine*	1.50
33	*Dameane Douglas*	.50
34	*Brandon Stokley*	.50
35	*Larry Parker*	.50
36	*Wane McGarity*	1.00
37	*Na Brown*	.50
38	*Cecil Collins*	1.00
39	*Darrin Chiaverini*	.50
40	*Madre Hill*	.50
41	Adrian Murrell	.30
42	Jake Plummer	1.50
43	Frank Sanders	.30
44	Rob Moore	.30
45	Andre Wadsworth	.30
46	Simeon Rice	.15
47	Eric Swann	.15
48	Terance Mathis	.15
49	Tim Dwight	.50
50	Jamal Anderson	.50
51	Chris Chandler	.30
52	Chris Calloway	.15
53	O.J. Santiago	.15
54	Jermaine Lewis	.30
55	Priest Holmes	.50
56	Scott Mitchell	.50
57	Tony Banks	.30
58	Rod Woodson	.15
59	Andre Reed	.15
60	Thurman Thomas	.30
61	Bruce Smith	.15
62	Rob Johnson	.30
63	Eric Moulds	.50
64	Doug Flutie	1.00
65	Antowain Smith	.50
66	Tim Biakabutuka	.30
67	Muhsin Muhammad	.30
68	Steve Beuerlein	.30
69	Bobby Engram	.15
70	Curtis Conway	.30
71	Curtis Enis	.50
72	Edgar Bennett	.15
73	Jeff Blake	.30
74	Darnay Scott	.30
75	Carl Pickens	.30
76	Corey Dillon	.50
77	Ty Detmer	.15
78	Leslie Shepherd	.15
79	Sedrick Shaw	.15
80	Raghib Ismail	.15
81	Emmitt Smith	2.00
82	Michael Irvin	.30
83	Troy Aikman	1.50
84	Deion Sanders	.50
85	Darren Woodson	.15
86	Chris Warren	.15
87	John Elway	2.00
88	Brian Griese	1.25
89	Shannon Sharpe	.30
90	Terrell Davis	2.00
91	Bubby Brister	.30
92	Ed McCaffrey	.30
93	Rod Smith	.30
94	Germane Crowell	.30
95	Johnnie Morton	.15
96	Barry Sanders	3.00
97	Herman Moore	.50
98	Charlie Batch	1.00
99	Mark Chmura	.30
100	Derrick Mayes	.30
101	Dorsey Levens	.50
102	Brett Favre	3.00
103	Antonio Freeman	.50
104	Robert Brooks	.15
105	Desmond Howard	.15
106	Jerome Pathon	.15
107	Marvin Harrison	.50
108	Peyton Manning	2.00
109	E.G. Green	.15
110	Tavian Banks	.30
111	Keenan McCardell	.30
112	Jimmy Smith	.50
113	Mark Brunell	1.25
114	Fred Taylor	1.50
115	Bam Morris	.15
116	Andre Rison	.30
117	Elvis Grbac	.30
118	Warren Moon	.30
119	Tony Gonzalez	.30
120	Derrick Alexander	.15
121	Rashaan Shehee	.15
122	Zach Thomas	.30
123	Oronde Gadsden	.30
124	Dan Marino	2.00
125	Karim Abdul	.30
126	O.J. McDuffie	.30
127	Jake Reed	.30
128	John Randle	.15
129	Randy Moss	3.00
130	Cris Carter	.50
131	Randall Cunningham	.50
132	Robert Smith	.50
133	Terry Glenn	.50
134	Ben Coates	.30
135	Drew Bledsoe	1.25
136	Ty Law	.15
137	Tony Simmons	.30
138	Eddie Kennison	.15
139	Cam Cleeland	.30
140	Ike Hilliard	.15
141	Joe Jurevicius	.15
142	Gary Brown	.15
143	Kerry Collins	.30
144	Tiki Barber	.30
145	Jason Sehorn	.15
146	Dedric Ward	.15
147	Vinny Testaverde	.30
148	Wayne Chrebet	.50
149	Curtis Martin	.50
150	Keyshawn Johnson	.50
151	James Jett	.15
152	Napoleon Kaufman	.50
153	Tim Brown	.30
154	Charles Woodson	.50
155	Rickey Dudley	.30
156	Charles Johnson	.15
157	Duce Staley	.30
158	Chris Fuamatu-Ma'afala	.15
159	Jerome Bettis	.50
160	Kordell Stewart	.75
161	Levon Kirkland	.15
162	Hines Ward	.30
163	Mikhael Ricks	.15
164	Natrone Means	.30
165	Ryan Leaf	.50
166	Jim Harbaugh	.30
167	Junior Seau	.30
168	Steve Young	1.00
169	J.J. Stokes	.30
170	Terrell Owens	.50
171	Jerry Rice	1.50
172	Garrison Hearst	.50
173	Ricky Watters	.30
174	Jon Kitna	.75
175	Joey Galloway	.50
176	Ahman Green	.30
177	Isaac Bruce	.50
178	Marshall Faulk	.50
179	Trent Green	.50
180	Amp Lee	.15
181	Greg Hill	.15
182	Warren Sapp	.15
183	Hardy Nickerson	.15
184	Trent Dilfer	.30
185	Reidel Anthony	.30
186	Jacquez Green	.30
187	Warrick Dunn	.50
188	Mike Alstott	.50
189	Kevin Dyson	.30
190	Eddie George	.75
191	Yancey Thigpen	.30
192	Steve McNair	.75
193	Willie Davis	.15
194	Frank Wycheck	.15
195	Darrell Green	.15
196	Stephen Alexander	.15
197	Albert Connell	.15
198	Michael Westbrook	.30
199	Brad Johnson	.50
200	Skip Hicks	.30

1999 Playoff Absolute EXP Tools of the Trade Parallel

This was a 200-card parallel to the base set. Each single was printed on foil board with holographic foil stamping. Defensive players were sequentially numbered to 1,000, wide receivers to 750, running backs to 500 and quarterbacks to 250.

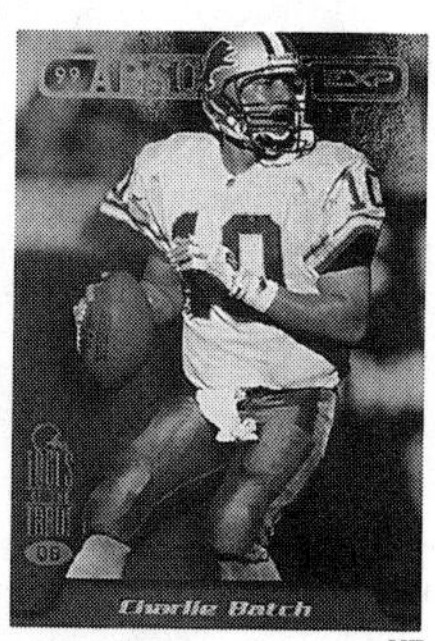

	MT
Defensive Cards:	3x-6x
Defensive Rookies:	2x
Production 1,000 Sets	
Receiver Cards:	3x-6x
Receiver Rookies:	3x
Production 750 Sets	
Running Back Cards:	5x-10x
Running Back Rookies:	4x
Production 500 Sets	
Quarterback Cards:	7x-14x
Quarterback Rookies:	6x
Production 250 Sets	

1999 Playoff Absolute EXP Absolute Heroes

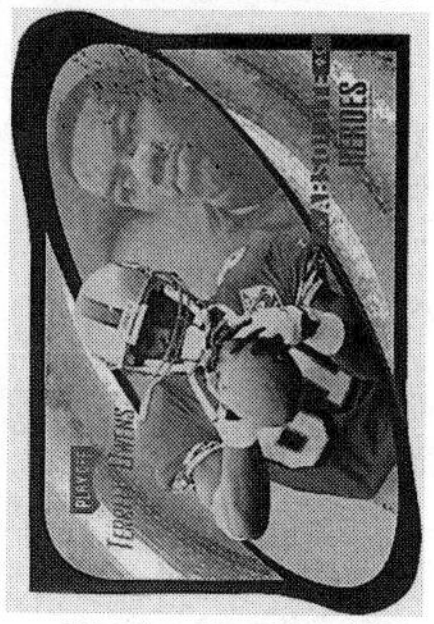

This 24-card insert included superstars and highlighted them on mirror board with red foil stamping and silver borders. Singles were inserted 1:25 packs.

		MT
Complete Set (24):		65.00
Common Player:		2.00
Inserted 1:25		
1	Terrell Owens	2.00
2	Troy Aikman	5.00
3	Cris Carter	2.00
4	Brett Favre	10.00
5	Jamal Anderson	2.00
6	Doug Flutie	3.00
7	John Elway	7.00
8	Steve Young	3.00
9	Jerome Bettis	2.00
10	Emmitt Smith	7.00
11	Drew Bledsoe	4.00
12	Fred Taylor	5.00
13	Dan Marino	7.00
14	Antonio Freeman	2.00
15	Mark Brunell	4.00
16	Jake Plummer	5.00
17	Warrick Dunn	2.00
18	Peyton Manning	7.00
19	Randy Moss	10.00
20	Barry Sanders	10.00
21	Keyshawn Johnson	2.00
22	Eddie George	2.00
23	Terrell Davis	7.00
24	Jerry Rice	5.00

1999 Playoff Absolute EXP Absolute Rookies

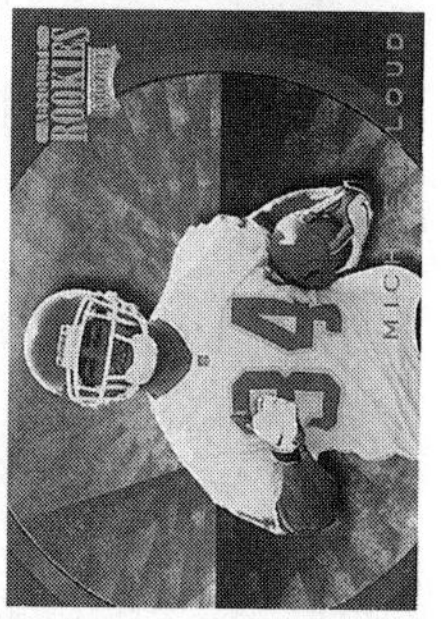

This 36-card insert included the hottest rookies from the '99 NFL Draft and pictured them on holographic board with bronze foil stamping. Each single had green borders. Cards were found 1:13 packs.

		MT
Complete Set (36):		60.00
Common Player:		.75
Inserted 1:13		
1	Champ Bailey	1.50
2	Karsten Bailey	.75
3	D'Wayne Bates	.75

4	Marty Booker	.75
5	David Boston	3.00
6	Shawn Bryson	.75
7	Chris Claiborne	.75
8	Mike Cloud	.75
9	Cecil Collins	5.00
10	Tim Couch	10.00
11	Daunte Culpepper	5.00
12	Demeane Douglas	.75
13	Troy Edwards	3.00
14	Kevin Faulk	2.00
15	Jermaine Fazande	.75
16	Joe Germaine	1.50
17	Torry Holt	3.00
18	Brock Huard	1.50
19	Edgerrin James	10.00
20	James Johnson	2.00
21	Kevin Johnson	3.00
22	Shaun King	3.00
23	Jim Kleinsasser	.75
24	Rob Konrad	.75
25	Chris McAlister	.75
26	Travis McGriff	.75
27	Donovan McNabb	5.00
28	Cade McNown	5.00
29	Joe Montgomery	1.50
30	Larry Parker	.75
31	Jeff Paulk	.75
32	Peerless Price	2.00
33	Akili Smith	5.00
34	Brandon Stokley	.75
35	Ricky Williams	10.00
36	Craig Yeast	.75

1999 Playoff Absolute EXP Extreme Team

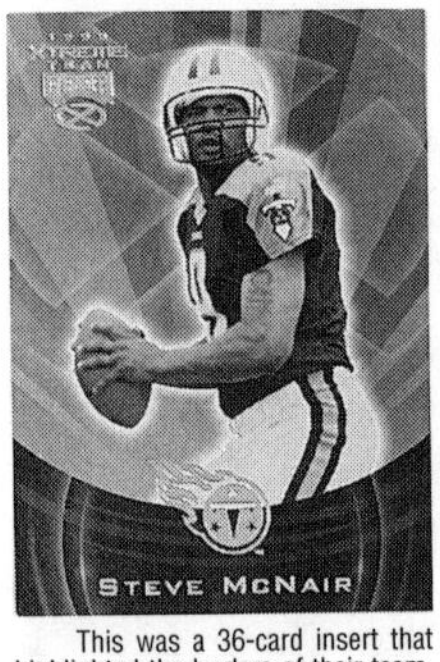

This was a 36-card insert that highlighted the leaders of their team. Each was featured with holographic foil with foil stamping. Singles were inserted 1:25 packs.

		MT
Complete Set (36):		150.00
Common Player:		2.50
Inserted 1:25		
1	Steve Young	4.00
2	Fred Taylor	6.00
3	Kordell Stewart	3.00
4	Emmitt Smith	8.00
5	Barry Sanders	12.00
6	Jerry Rice	6.00
7	Jake Plummer	6.00
8	Eric Moulds	2.50
9	Randy Moss	12.00
10	Steve McNair	3.00
11	Curtis Martin	2.50
12	Dan Marino	8.00
13	Peyton Manning	8.00
14	Jon Kitna	3.00
15	Napoleon Kaufman	2.50
16	Eddie George	3.00
17	Brett Favre	12.00
18	Marshall Faulk	2.50
19	John Elway	8.00
20	Corey Dillon	2.50
21	Terrell Davis	8.00
22	Randall Cunningham	3.00
23	Mark Brunell	5.00
24	Tim Brown	2.50
25	Drew Bledsoe	5.00
26	Jerome Bettis	2.50
27	Charlie Batch	3.50
28	Jamal Anderson	2.50
29	Mike Alstott	2.50
30	Troy Aikman	6.00
31	Dorsey Levens	3.00
32	Joey Galloway	2.50
33	Skip Hicks	2.50
34	Terrell Owens	2.50
35	Keyshawn Johnson	2.50
36	Doug Flutie	4.00

1999 Playoff Absolute EXP Terrell Davis Salute

This was a 5-card set that highlighted Davis' 1998 season. Singles were inserted 1:289 packs. The first 150 of each single was autographed and sequentially numbered.

		MT
Complete Set (5):		60.00
Common Player:		12.00
Inserted 1:289		
Autographed Cards:		8x
Production 150 Sets		
1	Terrell Davis	12.00
2	Terrell Davis	12.00
3	Terrell Davis	12.00
4	Terrell Davis	12.00
5	Terrell Davis	12.00

1999 Playoff Absolute EXP Rookie Reflex

This was an 18-card set that highlighted the top rookies from 1999. Each single was printed on holographic foil board with micro-etching. Singles were found 1:49 packs.

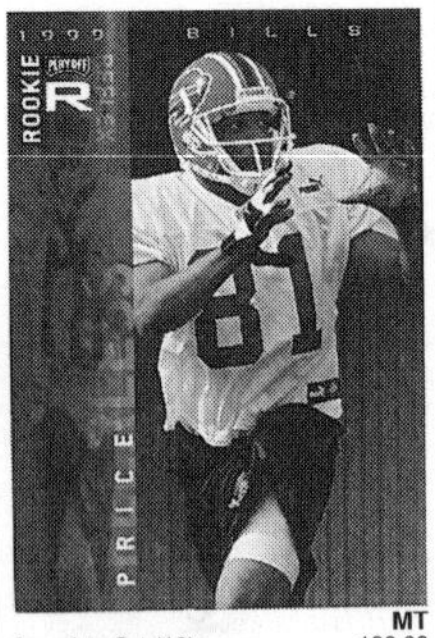

		MT
Complete Set (18):		120.00
Common Player:		3.00
Inserted 1:49		
1	Peerless Price	6.00
2	Daunte Culpepper	12.00
3	Joe Montgomery	4.00
4	David Boston	8.00
5	Shaun King	8.00
6	Champ Bailey	4.00
7	Rob Konrad	3.00
8	Torry Holt	8.00
9	Kevin Faulk	6.00
10	Ricky Williams	25.00
11	James Johnson	6.00
12	Edgerrin James	25.00
13	Kevin Johnson	8.00
14	Akili Smith	12.00
15	Troy Edwards	8.00
16	Donovan McNabb	12.00
17	Cade McNown	12.00
18	Tim Couch	25.00

1999 Playoff Absolute EXP Barry Sanders Commemorative

This was a 5-card insert that commemorated the career of Barry Sanders. Singles were found 1:289 packs.

		MT
Complete Set (5):		75.00
Common Player:		15.00
Inserted 1:289		
2	Barry Sanders	15.00
3	Barry Sanders	15.00
4	Barry Sanders	15.00
5	Barry Sanders	15.00
6	Barry Sanders	15.00

1999 Playoff Absolute EXP Team Jersey Tandems

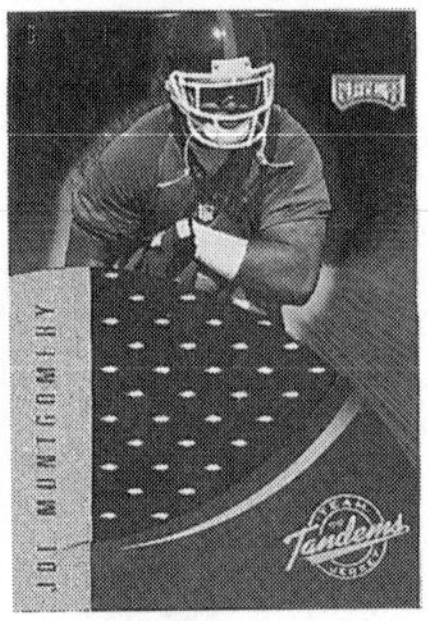

This was a 31-card insert that pictured a tandem with a swatch of a home and away authentic team jersey. One player was pictured on each side and singles were inserted 1:97 packs.

		MT
Complete Set (31):		1300.
Common Player:		25.00
Inserted 1:97		
1	Jake Plummer, David Boston	50.00
2	Troy Aikman, Emmitt Smith	85.00
3	Skip Hicks, Brad Johnson	35.00
4	Joe Montgomery, Ike Hilliard	25.00
5	Charles Johnson, Donovan McNabb	50.00
6	Randy Moss, Cris Carter	100.00
7	Warrick Dunn, Mike Alstott	25.00
8	Barry Sanders, Charlie Batch	100.00
9	Antonio Freeman, Brett Favre	100.00
10	Curtis Enis, Cade McNown	50.00
11	Tim Biakabutuka, Muhsin Muhammad	25.00
12	Eddie Kennison, Ricky Williams	100.00
13	Steve Young, Jerry Rice	50.00
14	Marshall Faulk, Torry Holt	40.00
15	Jamal Anderson, Chris Chandler	25.00
16	Dan Marino, O.J. McDuffie	85.00
17	Drew Bledsoe, Terry Glenn	50.00
18	Eric Moulds, Doug Flutie	50.00
19	Peyton Manning, Edgerrin James	100.00
20	Keyshawn Johnson, Wayne Chrebet	35.00
21	Kordell Stewart, Jerome Bettis	35.00
22	Mark Brunell, Fred Taylor	50.00
23	Tim Couch, Kevin Johnson	100.00
24	Carl Pickens, Akili Smith	50.00
25	Jermaine Lewis, Tony Banks	25.00
26	Eddie George, Steve McNair	40.00
27	Napoleon Kaufman, Tim Brown	25.00
28	John Elway, Terrell Davis	85.00
29	Jon Kitna, Joey Galloway	35.00
30	Andre Rison, Elvis Grbac	25.00
31	Natrone Means, Mikhael Ricks	25.00

1999 Playoff Absolute SSD

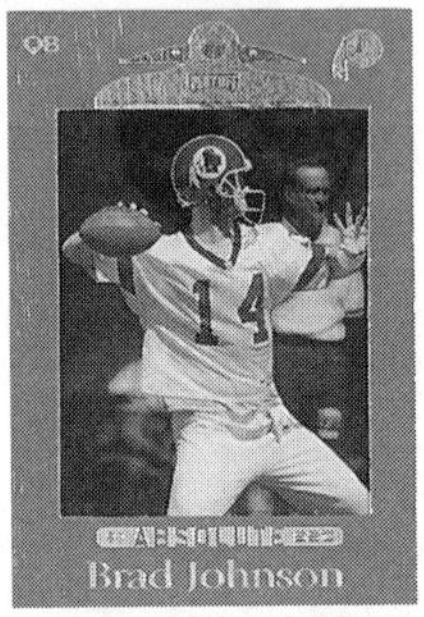

This was a 200-card set that included 50 short printed singles. The 31 Checklist cards were found 1:9 packs and the 19 Canton Absolute cards were found 1:17. Each of the regular 150 base cards were found in five different colors. Blue, Green, Purple and Red were all found at equal ratios. The Orange singles were in shorter quanities and valued higher. Each base card featured the player in a cell window with foil stamping and wood grain embossing. Parallel sets included: Coaches Collection Gold and Coaches Collection Silver. Partial parallel sets included: Honor Red, Honor Gold and Honor Silver. Other insert sets included: Boss Hogs Autographs, Force, Heroes, Rookie Roundup, Rookies and Team Jersey Quads.

		MT
Complete Set (200):		250.00
Common Player:		.30
Minor Stars:		.60
Common Canton:		4.00
Inserted 1:17		
Common CL:		2.50
Inserted 1:9		
Common Rookie:		1.00
Blue,Green,Purple,Red:		1x
Orange Cards:		5x-10x
Orange Canton:		3x
Orange CL:		3x
Orange Rookies:		3x
Wax Box:		60.00
1	Rob Moore	.60
2	Frank Sanders	.30
3	Jake Plummer	2.50
4	Adrian Murrell	.30
5	Chris Chandler	.60
6	Jamal Anderson	1.00
7	Tim Dwight	1.00
8	Terance Mathis	.30
9	Priest Holmes	1.00
10	Jermaine Lewis	.30
11	Antowain Smith	.60
12	Doug Flutie	2.00
13	Eric Moulds	1.00
14	Muhsin Muhammad	.60
15	Tim Biakabutuka	.60
16	Curtis Enis	1.00
17	Curtis Conway	.60
18	Bobby Engram	.30
19	Corey Dillon	1.00
20	Carl Pickens	.60
21	Darnay Scott	.60
22	Sedrick Shaw	.30
23	Leslie Shepherd	.30
24	Ty Detmer	.30
25	Deion Sanders	1.00
26	Troy Aikman	3.00
27	Michael Irvin	.60
28	Emmitt Smith	4.50
29	Raghib Ismail	.30
30	Rod Smith	.60
31	Ed McCaffrey	.60
32	Bubby Brister	.60
33	Terrell Davis	4.50
34	Shannon Sharpe	.60
35	Brian Griese	3.00
36	John Elway	4.50
37	Charlie Batch	2.00
38	Herman Moore	1.00
39	Barry Sanders	6.00
40	Johnnie Morton	.30
41	Antonio Freeman	1.00
42	Brett Favre	6.00
43	Dorsey Levens	1.00
44	Derrick Mayes	.60
45	Mark Chmura	.60
46	Peyton Manning	4.50
47	Marvin Harrison	1.00
48	Jerome Pathon	.30
49	Fred Taylor	3.00
50	Mark Brunell	2.50
51	Jimmy Smith	1.00
52	Keenan McCardell	.60
53	Elvis Grbac	.60
54	Andre Rison	.60
55	Bam Morris	.30
56	O.J. McDuffie	.60
57	Karim Abdul	.60
58	Dan Marino	4.50
59	Oronde Gadsden	.60
60	Robert Smith	1.00
61	Randall Cunningham	1.00
62	Cris Carter	1.00
63	Randy Moss	6.00
64	Drew Bledsoe	2.50
65	Ben Coates	.60
66	Terry Glenn	1.00
67	Cameron Cleeland	.60
68	Eddie Kennison	.30
69	Kerry Collins	.60
70	Gary Brown	.30
71	Joe Jurevicius	.30
72	Ike Hilliard	.60
73	Keyshawn Johnson	1.00
74	Curtis Martin	1.00
75	Wayne Chrebet	1.00
76	Tim Brown	.60
77	Napoleon Kaufman	1.00
78	James Jett	.30
79	Duce Staley	1.00
80	Charles Johnson	.30
81	Kordell Stewart	1.00
82	Jerome Bettis	1.00
83	Chris Fuamatu-Ma'afala	.30
84	Jim Harbaugh	.60
85	Ryan Leaf	1.00
86	Natrone Means	.60
87	Mikhael Ricks	.30
88	Garrison Hearst	.75
89	Jerry Rice	3.00
90	Terrell Owens	1.00
91	J.J. Stokes	.60
92	Steve Young	2.00
93	Joey Galloway	1.00
94	Jon Kitna	1.00
95	Ricky Watters	.60
96	Trent Green	.60
97	Marshall Faulk	1.00
98	Isaac Bruce	1.00
99	Mike Alstott	1.00
100	Warrick Dunn	1.00
101	Jacquez Green	.60
102	Reidel Anthony	.60
103	Trent Dilfer	.60
104	Steve McNair	1.25
105	Yancey Thigpen	.60
106	Eddie George	1.25
107	Kevin Dyson	.60
108	Skip Hicks	.60
109	Brad Johnson	1.00
110	Michael Westbrook	.60
111	Thurman Thomas CA	4.00
112	Andre Reed CA	4.00
113	Emmitt Smith CA	12.00
114	Troy Aikman CA	10.00
115	Deion Sanders CA	4.00
116	John Elway CA	12.00
117	Terrell Davis CA	12.00
118	Barry Sanders CA	15.00
119	Brett Favre CA	15.00
120	Warren Moon CA	4.00
121	Dan Marino CA	12.00
122	Cris Carter CA	6.00
123	Vinny Testaverde CA	4.00
124	Tim Brown CA	4.00
125	Jerome Bettis CA	4.00
126	Junior Seau CA	4.00
127	Jerry Rice CA	10.00
128	Steve Young CA	8.00
129	Eddie George CA	6.00
130	Dan Marino CL	8.00
131	Vinny Testaverde CL	2.50
132	Drew Bledsoe CL	6.00
133	Peyton Manning CL	8.00
134	Doug Flutie CL	6.00
135	Akili Smith CL	5.00
136	Tim Couch CL	8.00
137	Kordell Stewart CL	5.00
138	Fred Taylor CL	6.00
139	Steve McNair CL	5.00
140	Priest Holmes CL	2.50
141	Terrell Davis CL	8.00
142	Jon Kitna CL	5.00
143	Tim Brown CL	2.50
144	Natrone Means CL	2.50
145	Andre Rison CL	2.50
146	Troy Aikman CL	7.00
147	Kerry Collins CL	2.50
148	Jake Plummer CL	6.00
149	Brad Johnson CL	5.00
150	Donovan McNabb CL	5.00
151	Barry Sanders CL	10.00
152	Brett Favre CL	10.00
153	Cade McNown CL	5.00
154	Mike Alstott CL	2.50
155	Randy Moss CL	10.00
156	Ricky Williams CL	8.00
157	Muhsin Muhammad CL	2.50
158	Marshall Faulk CL	5.00
159	Jamal Anderson CL	2.50
160	Jerry Rice CL	6.00
161	*Tim Couch*	12.00
162	*Donovan McNabb*	7.00
163	*Akili Smith*	7.00
164	*Edgerrin James*	15.00
165	*Ricky Williams*	10.00
166	*Torry Holt*	5.00
167	*Champ Bailey*	3.00
168	*David Boston*	5.00
169	*Chris Claiborne*	2.00
170	*Chris McAlister*	2.00
171	*Daunte Culpepper*	12.00
172	*Cade McNown*	5.00
173	*Troy Edwards*	5.00
174	*Kevin Johnson*	5.00
175	*James Johnson*	3.00
176	*Rob Konrad*	1.00
177	*Jim Kleinsasser*	2.00
178	*Kevin Faulk*	3.00
179	*Joe Montgomery*	2.00
180	*Shaun King*	7.00
181	*Peerless Price*	4.00
182	*Mike Cloud*	1.00
183	*Jermaine Fazande*	2.00
184	*D'Wayne Bates*	1.00
185	*Brock Huard*	3.00
186	*Marty Booker*	1.00
187	*Karsten Bailey*	1.00
188	*Shawn Bryson*	1.00
189	*Jeff Paulk*	1.00
190	*Sedrick Irvin*	3.00
191	*Craig Yeast*	1.00
192	*Joe Germaine*	2.00
193	*Demeane Douglas*	1.00
194	*Brandon Stokley*	1.00
195	*Larry Parker*	1.00
196	*Wane McGarity*	1.00
197	*Na Brown*	1.00
198	*Cecil Collins*	4.00
199	*Darrin Chiaverini*	2.00
200	*Madre Hill*	1.00

1999 Playoff Absolute SSD Coaches Collection Gold

This was a 200-card parallel to the base set. Each single was sequentially numbered to 25.

	MT
Gold Cards:	25x-50x
Gold Canton:	8x-16x
Gold CL:	5x-10x
Gold Rookies:	8x-16x
Production 25 Sets	

1999 Playoff Absolute SSD Coaches Collection Silver

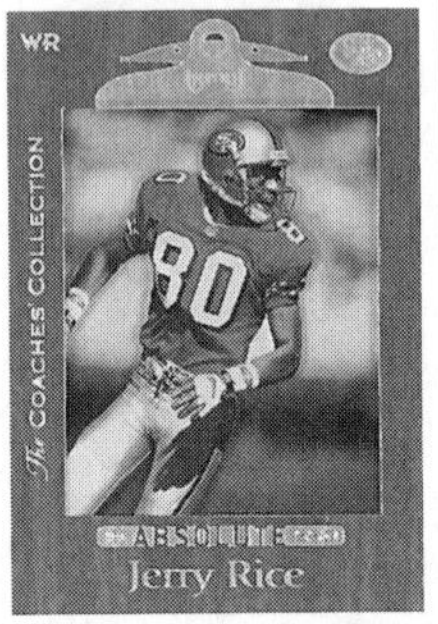

This was a 200-card parallel to the base set. Each of these singles was sequentially numbered to 500.

	MT
Silver Cards:	2x-4x
Silver Canton:	2x
Silver CL:	2x
Silver Rookies:	2x
Production 500 Sets	

1999 Playoff Absolute SSD Honors Red

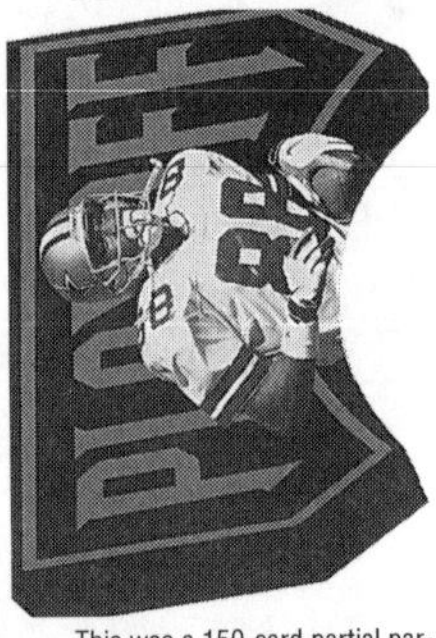

This was a 150-card partial parallel to the base set. Each single had the Playoff logo in the background. Each card was sequentially numbered to 200.

	MT
Red Cards:	5x-10x
Red Rookies:	3x
Production 200 Sets	
Gold Cards:	25x-50x
Gold Rookies:	8x-16x
Production 25 Sets	
Silver Cards:	8x-16x
Silver Rookies:	3x-6x
Production 100 Sets	

1999 Playoff Absolute SSD Boss Hogs Autographs

This 10-card insert set included autographs of the top playmakers and each signed on real football leather. Each single was sequentially numbered to 400.

		MT
Complete Set (10):		550.00
Common Player:		25.00
Production 400 Sets		
1	Ricky Williams	125.00
2	Terrell Davis	75.00
3	Mike Alstott	25.00
4	Jake Plummer	50.00
5	Vinny Testaverde	25.00
6	Cris Carter	25.00
7	Peyton Manning	125.00
8	Natrone Means	25.00
9	Eddie George	35.00
10	Barry Sanders	150.00

1999 Playoff Absolute SSD Force

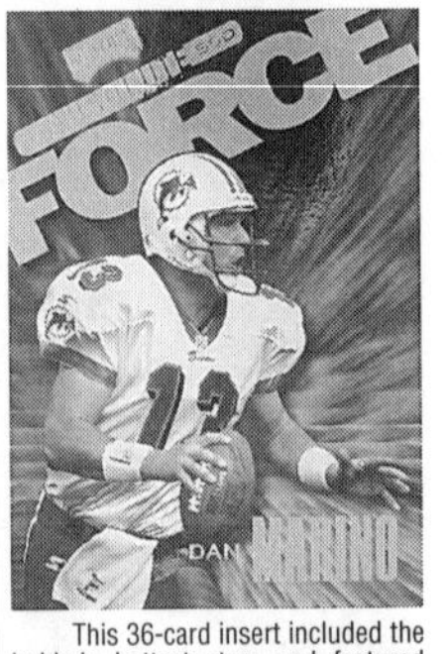

This 36-card insert included the hobby's hottest stars and featured them on a mirror board with gold foil stamping. Singles were found 1:19 packs.

		MT
Complete Set (36):		150.00
Common Player:		4.00
Inserted 1:19		
1	Steve Young	6.00
2	Fred Taylor	8.00
3	Kordell Stewart	4.00
4	Emmitt Smith	10.00
5	Barry Sanders	15.00
6	Jerry Rice	8.00
7	Jake Plummer	7.00
8	Eric Moulds	4.00
9	Randy Moss	15.00
10	Steve McNair	4.00
11	Curtis Martin	4.00
12	Dan Marino	10.00
13	Peyton Manning	10.00
14	Jon Kitna	4.00
15	Napoleon Kaufman	4.00
16	Keyshawn Johnson	4.00
17	Eddie George	5.00
18	Antonio Freeman	4.00
19	Doug Flutie	6.00
20	Brett Favre	15.00
21	Marshall Faulk	4.00
22	John Elway	10.00
23	Warrick Dunn	4.00
24	Corey Dillon	4.00
25	Terrell Davis	10.00
26	Randall Cunningham	4.00
27	Cris Carter	4.00
28	Mark Brunell	6.00
29	Tim Brown	4.00
30	Drew Bledsoe	6.00
31	Jerome Bettis	4.00
32	Charlie Batch	5.00
33	Jamal Anderson	4.00
34	Mike Alstott	4.00
35	Troy Aikman	8.00
36	Terrell Owens	4.00

1999 Playoff Absolute SSD Heroes

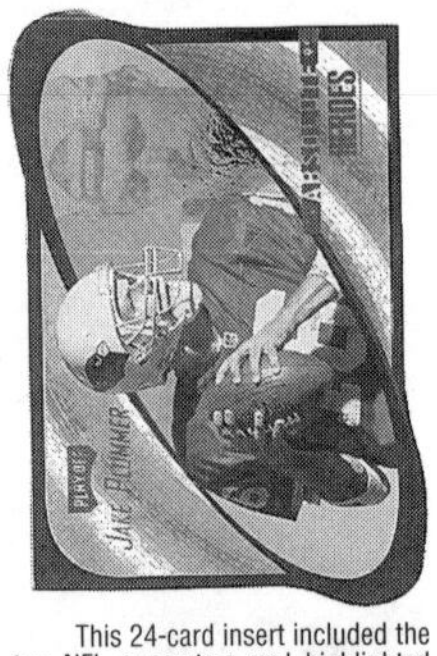

This 24-card insert included the top NFL superstars and highlighted them on a die-cut mirror board with red foil stamping and micro-etching. Singles were found 1:19 packs. A parallel Red (#'d to 100) and Jumbo (one per hobby box) version was also issued.

		MT
Complete Set (24):		125.00
Common Player:		3.00
Inserted 1:19		
Jumbo Cards:		1x
1:Box		
Red Cards: 4x-8x		
Production 100 Sets		
1	Terrell Owens	3.00
2	Troy Aikman	6.00
3	Cris Carter	3.00
4	Brett Favre	12.00
5	Jamal Anderson	3.00
6	Doug Flutie	4.00
7	John Elway	8.00
8	Steve Young	4.00
9	Jerome Bettis	3.00
10	Emmitt Smith	8.00
11	Drew Bledsoe	5.00
12	Fred Taylor	6.00
13	Dan Marino	8.00
14	Antonio Freeman	3.00
15	Mark Brunell	5.00
16	Jake Plummer	5.00
17	Warrick Dunn	3.00
18	Peyton Manning	8.00
19	Randy Moss	12.00
20	Barry Sanders	12.00
21	Keyshawn Johnson	3.00
22	Eddie George	4.00
23	Terrell Davis	8.00
24	Jerry Rice	6.00

1999 Playoff Absolute SSD Rookie Roundup

This 18-card insert included both first and second round picks from the 1999 NFL Draft. First round pick cards were inserted 1:46 packs and second round picks were inserted 1:69. Each single was printed on mirror board with foil stamping.

		MT
Complete Set (18):		125.00
Common Player:		5.00
1st Rounders Inserted 1:46		
2nd Rounders Inserted 1:69		
1	Peerless Price	8.00
2	Daunte Culpepper	12.00
3	Joe Montgomery	5.00
4	David Boston	8.00
5	Shaun King	15.00
6	Champ Bailey	5.00
7	Rob Konrad	5.00
8	Torry Holt	8.00
9	Kevin Faulk	7.00
10	Ricky Williams	20.00
11	James Johnson	5.00
12	Edgerrin James	30.00
13	Kevin Johnson	10.00
14	Akili Smith	12.00
15	Troy Edwards	8.00
16	Donovan McNabb	12.00
17	Cade McNown	12.00
18	Tim Couch	20.00

1999 Playoff Absolute SSD Rookies

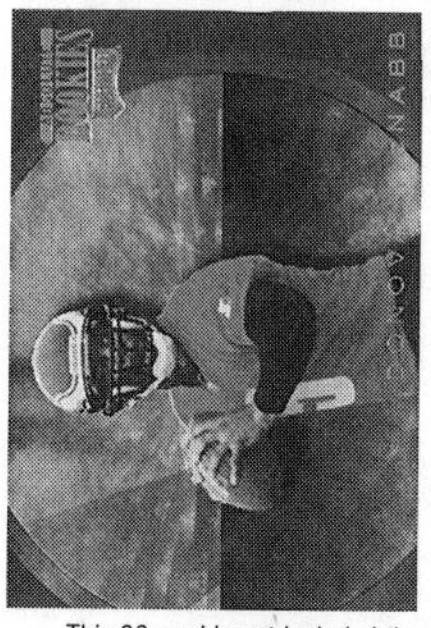

This 36-card insert included the hottest rookies from the '99 NFL Draft. Each was printed on holographic foil board with blue foil stamping. Singles were inserted 1:10 packs. A parallel Red version was also made and each of those singles were sequentially numbered to 100.

		MT
Complete Set (36):		75.00
Common Player:		1.00
Minor Stars:		2.00
Inserted 1:10		
Red Cards:		5x-10x
Production 100 Sets		
1	Champ Bailey	2.50
2	Karsten Bailey	1.00
3	D'Wayne Bates	1.00
4	Marty Booker	1.00
5	David Boston	4.00
6	Shawn Bryson	1.00
7	Chris Claiborne	2.00
8	Mike Cloud	2.00
9	Cecil Collins	4.00
10	Tim Couch	10.00
11	Daunte Culpepper	6.00
12	Demeane Douglas	1.00
13	Troy Edwards	4.00
14	Kevin Faulk	3.00
15	Jermaine Fazande	2.00
16	Joe Germaine	2.00
17	Torry Holt	4.00
18	Brock Huard	2.50
19	Edgerrin James	15.00
20	James Johnson	2.50
21	Kevin Johnson	4.00
22	Shaun King	6.00
23	Jim Kleinsasser	2.00
24	Rob Konrad	2.00
25	Chris McAlister	2.00
26	Travis McGriff	1.00
27	Donovan McNabb	6.00
28	Cade McNown	6.00
29	Joe Montgomery	2.00
30	Larry Parker	1.00
31	Jeff Paulk	1.00
32	Peerless Price	3.00
33	Akili Smith	6.00
34	Brandon Stokley	1.00
35	Ricky Williams	10.00
36	Craig Yeast	1.00

Post-1980 cards in Near Mint condition will generally sell for about 75% of the quoted Mint value. Excellent-condition cards bring no more than 40%.

1999 Playoff Absolute SSD Team Jersey Quads

This 31-card insert showcased an authentic team jersey and four superstars from each NFL team. Each was printed on a foil board with micro etching. Singles were inserted 1:73 packs.

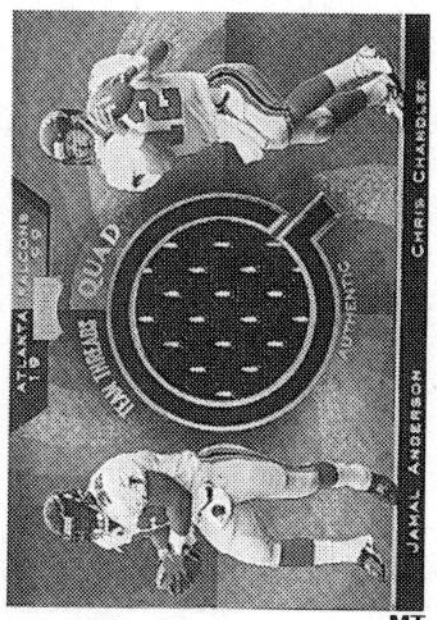

		MT
Complete Set (31):		1600.
Common Player:		20.00
Minor Stars:		40.00
Inserted 1:73		
1	David Boston, Adrian Murrell, Jake Plummer, Frank Sanders	60.00
2	Troy Aikman, Michael Irvin, Deion Sanders, Emmitt Smith	85.00
3	Champ Bailey, Skip Hicks, Brad Johnson, Michael Westbrook	40.00
4	Gary Brown, Kerry Collins, Ike Hilliard, Joe Montgomery	20.00
5	Na Brown, Charles Johnson, Donovan McNabb, Duce Staley	60.00
6	Cris Carter, Randall Cunningham, Randy Moss, Robert Smith	100.00
7	Mike Alstott, Reidel Anthony, Trent Dilfer, Warrick Dunn	40.00
8	Charlie Batch, Herman Moore, Johnnie Morton, Barry Sanders	100.00
9	Mark Chmura, Brett Favre, Antonio Freeman, Dorsey Levens	100.00
10	Curtis Conway, Bobby Engram, Curtis Enis, Cade McNown	60.00
11	Steve Beuerlein, Tim Biakabutuka, Muhsin Muhammad, Wesley Walls	20.00
12	Cam Cleeland, Eddie Kennison, Willie Roaf, Ricky Williams	75.00
13	Garrison Hearst, Terrell Owens, Jerry Rice, Steve Young	85.00
14	Isaac Bruce, Marshall Faulk, Trent Green, Torry Holt	40.00
15	Jamal Anderson, Chris Chandler, Tim Dwight, Terrance Mathis	20.00
16	Karim Abdul, Cecil Collins, Dan Marino, O.J. McDuffie	100.00
17	Drew Bledsoe, Ben Coates, Kevin Faulk, Terry Glenn	60.00
18	Doug Flutie, Eric Moulds, Peerless Price, Antowain Smith	60.00
19	Marvin Harrison, Edgerrin James, Peyton Manning, Jerome Pathon	125.00
20	Wayne Chrebet, Keyshawn Johnson, Curtis Martin, Vinny Testaverde	40.00
21	Jerome Bettis, Troy Edwards, Kordell Stewart, Hines Ward	50.00
22	Mark Brunell, Keenan McCardell, Jimmy Smith, Fred Taylor	60.00
23	Tim Couch, Kevin Johnson, Sedrick Shaw, Leslie Shepherd	85.00
24	Corey Dillon, Carl Pickens, Darnay Scott, Akili Smith	50.00
25	Tony Banks, Priest Holmes, Jermaine Lewis, Chris McAllister	20.00
26	Kevin Dyson, Eddie George, Steve McNair, Yancey Thigpen	40.00
27	Tim Brown, James Jett, Napoleon Kaufman, Charles Woodson	40.00
28	Terrell Davis, John Elway, Ed McCaffrey, Rod Smith	100.00
29	Joey Galloway, Ahman Green, Jon Kitna, Ricky Watters	40.00
30	Mike Cloud, Elvis Grbac, Bam Morris, Andre Rison	20.00
31	Ryan Leaf, Natrone Means, Mikhael Ricks, Junior Seau	20.00

1999 Playoff Contenders SSD

This was a 200-card base set that had 44 Rookie Tickets and 15 short-printed Playoff Tickets (1:7). Each card was printed on 30-point embossed holographic foil stock with foil stamping. Each of the Rookie Tickets were autographed by that player. Parallel sets included: Finesse Gold, Power Blue and Speed Red. Other inserts included: Game Day Souvenirs, MVP Contenders, Quads, Round Numbers Autographs, ROY Contenders, ROY Contenders Autographs, Touchdown Tandems and Triple Threat. SRP was $7.99 for four-card packs.

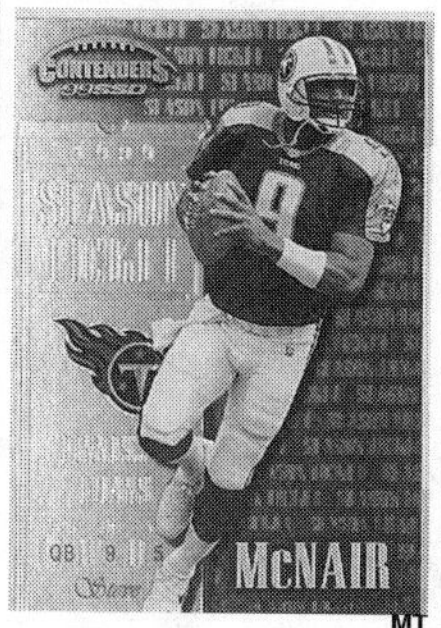

		MT
Complete Set (200):		2500.
Common Player:		.30
Minor Stars:		.60
Common Rookie Auto:		12.00
Common PT:		2.00
Inserted 1:7		
Pack (4):		20.00
Wax Box (14):		260.00
1	Randy Moss	8.00
2	Randall Cunningham	1.00
3	Cris Carter	1.00
4	Robert Smith	1.00
5	Jake Reed	.60
6	Albert Connell	.60
7	Jeff George	1.00
8	Brett Favre	8.00
9	Antonio Freeman	1.00
10	Dorsey Levens	1.00
11	Mark Chmura	.60
12	Mike Alstott	1.00
13	Warrick Dunn	1.00
14	Trent Dilfer	.60
15	Jacquez Green	.60
16	Reidel Anthony	.60
17	Warren Sapp	.60
18	Amani Toomer	.30
19	Curtis Enis	1.00
20	Curtis Conway	.60
21	Bobby Engram	.30
22	Barry Sanders	8.00
23	Charlie Batch	2.50
24	Herman Moore	1.00
25	Johnnie Morton	.30
26	Greg Hill	.30
27	Germane Crowell	.60
28	Kerry Collins	.60
29	Ike Hilliard	.30
30	Joe Jurevicius	.30
31	Stephen Davis	1.00
32	Brad Johnson	1.00
33	Skip Hicks	.60
34	Michael Westbrook	.60
35	Jake Plummer	3.00
36	Adrian Murrell	.30
37	Frank Sanders	.60
38	Rob Moore	.60
39	Gary Brown	.30
40	Duce Staley	1.00
41	Charles Johnson	.30
42	Emmitt Smith	6.00
43	Troy Aikman	4.00
44	Michael Irvin	.60
45	Deion Sanders	1.00
46	Raghib Ismail	.30
47	Jerry Rice	4.00
48	Terrell Owens	1.00
49	Steve Young	2.50
50	Garrison Hearst	.60
51	J.J. Stokes	.60
52	Lawrence Phillips	.60
53	Jamal Anderson	1.00
54	Chris Chandler	.60
55	Terance Mathis	.30
56	Tim Dwight	1.00
57	Charlie Garner	.60
58	Chris Calloway	.30
59	Eddie Kennison	.30
60	Billy Joe Hobert	.30
61	Tim Biakabutuka	.60
62	Muhsin Muhammad	.60
63	*Olandis Gary 1825*	45.00
64	Wesley Walls	.60
65	Isaac Bruce	1.00
66	Marshall Faulk	1.00
67	Kordell Stewart	1.00
68	Jerome Bettis	1.00
69	Hines Ward	.60
70	Corey Dillon	1.00
71	Carl Pickens	.60
72	Darnay Scott	.60
73	Steve McNair	1.75
74	Eddie George	1.75
75	Yancey Thigpen	.60
76	Kevin Dyson	.60
77	Fred Taylor	4.00
78	Mark Brunell	3.00
79	Jimmy Smith	1.00
80	Keenan McCardell	.60
81	James Stewart	.60
82	Jermaine Lewis	.30
83	Priest Holmes	1.00
84	Stoney Case	.30
85	Errict Rhett	.60
86	Bill Schroeder	.60
87	Terry Kirby	.30
88	Leslie Shepherd	.30
89	*Terrence Wilkins 825*	75.00
90	Dan Marino	6.00
91	O.J. McDuffie	.60
92	Karim Abdul	.60
93	Zach Thomas	.60
94	Terry Allen	.60
95	Tony Martin	.30
96	Drew Bledsoe	3.00
97	Terry Glenn	1.00
98	Ben Coates	.60
99	Tony Simmons	.60
100	Curtis Martin	1.00
101	Keyshawn Johnson	1.00
102	Vinny Testaverde	.60
103	Wayne Chrebet	1.00
104	Peyton Manning	6.00
105	Marvin Harrison	1.00
106	E.G. Green	.30
107	Doug Flutie	2.50
108	Thurman Thomas	.60
109	Andre Reed	.60
110	Eric Moulds	1.00
111	Antowain Smith	1.00
112	Bruce Smith	.60
113	Terrell Davis	6.00
114	John Elway	6.00
115	Ed McCaffrey	.75
116	Rod Smith	.75
117	Shannon Sharpe	.60
118	*Jeff Garcia 325*	450.00
119	Brian Griese	3.00
120	*Justin Watson 325*	150.00
121	Bubby Brister	.60
122	Ryan Leaf	1.00
123	Natrone Means	.75
124	Mikhael Ricks	.30
125	Junior Seau	.60
126	Jim Harbaugh	.60
127	Andre Rison	.60
128	Elvis Grbac	.60
129	Bam Morris	.60
130	Rashaan Shehee	.30
131	Warren Moon	.60
132	Tony Gonzalez	.60
133	Derrick Alexander	.30
134	Jon Kitna	1.50
135	Ricky Watters	.60
136	Joey Galloway	1.00
137	Ahman Green	.60
138	Derrick Mayes	.60
139	Tyrone Wheatley	.60
140	Napoleon Kaufman	1.00
141	Tim Brown	.60
142	Charles Woodson	1.00
143	Rich Gannon	.60
144	Rickey Dudley	.60
145	Az-Zahir Hakim	.60
146	*Kurt Warner 1825*	400.00
147	*Sean Bennett*	15.00
148	*Brandon Stokley*	12.00
149	*Amos Zereoue 1325*	30.00
150	*Brock Huard 1325*	40.00
151	*Tim Couch 1025*	150.00
152	*Ricky Williams 725*	225.00
153	*Donovan McNabb 525*	375.00
154	*Edgerrin James 525*	650.00
155	*Torry Holt 1025*	120.00
156	*Daunte Culpepper 1025*	325.00
157	*Akili Smith 1025*	85.00
158	*Champ Bailey 1725*	30.00
159	*Chris Claiborne*	12.00
160	*Chris McAlister*	12.00
161	*Troy Edwards 1225*	30.00
162	*Jevon Kearse 325*	130.00
163	*Darnell McDonald*	12.00
164	*David Boston 1025*	50.00
165	*Peerless Price 1325*	30.00
166	*Cecil Collins*	15.00
167	*Rob Konrad*	15.00
168	*Cade McNown 1025*	40.00
169	*Shawn Bryson*	12.00
170	*Kevin Faulk 1325*	40.00
171	*Corby Jones*	12.00
172	*James Johnson 1325*	25.00
173	*Autry Denson*	20.00
174	*Sedrick Irvin*	20.00
175	*Michael Bishop 1825*	45.00
176	*Joe Germaine 825*	30.00
177	*De'Mond Parker*	20.00
178	*Shaun King 1825*	25.00
179	*D'Wayne Bates*	12.00
180	*Tai Streets 1825*	40.00
181	*Na Brown*	12.00
182	*Desmond Clark*	12.00
183	*Jim Kleinsasser*	15.00
184	*Kevin Johnson 1325*	35.00
185	*Joe Montgomery*	20.00
186	John Elway PT	8.00
187	Dan Marino PT	8.00
188	Jerry Rice PT	6.00
189	Barry Sanders PT	12.00
190	Steve Young PT	4.00
191	Doug Flutie PT	4.00
192	Troy Aikman PT	6.00
193	Drew Bledsoe PT	5.00
194	Brett Favre PT	12.00
195	Randall Cunningham PT	2.00
196	Terrell Davis PT	8.00
197	Kordell Stewart PT	2.00
198	Keyshawn Johnson PT	2.00
199	Jake Plummer PT	5.00
200	Peyton Manning PT	8.00

1999 Playoff Contenders SSD Finesse Gold Parallel

This was a 200-card parallel insert that showcased each single with a gold background. Singles were sequentially numbered to 25.

	MT
Gold Cards:	20x-40x
Gold Rookies:	3x
Gold PT Cards:	10x-20x
Production 25 Sets	

1999 Playoff Contenders SSD Power Blue Parallel

This was a 200-card parallel insert that had each single printed with a blue background. Each card was sequentially numbered to 50.

	MT
Blue Cards:	10x-20x
Blue Rookies:	1.5x
Blue PT Cards:	5x-10x
Production 50 Sets	

A card number in parentheses ( ) indicates the set is unnumbered.

1999 Playoff Contenders SSD Speed Red Parallel

This was a 200-card parallel insert to the base set. Each of these singles were printed with a red background and were sequentially numbered to 100.

	MT
Red Cards:	5x-10x
Red Rookies:	1.2x
Red PT Cards:	3x-6x
Production 100 Sets	

1999 Playoff Contenders SSD Game Day Souvenirs

This 15-card insert included swatches of game-dated, game-used footballs from the 1998-99 season. Singles were found 1:308 packs.

		MT
Complete Set (15):		1250.
Common Player:		50.00
Inserted 1:308		
1	Terrell Owens	50.00
2	Jerry Rice	100.00
3	Steve Young	75.00
4	Akili Smith	50.00
5	Tim Couch	125.00
6	Mark Brunell	75.00
7	Eddie George	60.00
8	Dorsey Levens	50.00
9	Brett Favre	150.00
10	Antonio Freeman	50.00
11	Ricky Williams	125.00
12	Steve McNair	60.00
13	Kurt Warner	250.00
14	John Elway	125.00
15	Terrell Davis	125.00

1999 Playoff Contenders SSD MVP Contenders

This 20-card insert included candidates for the NFL's MVP award. Each single was printed with actual leather in the background. Singles were inserted 1:43 packs.

		MT
Complete Set (20):		160.00
Common Player:		5.00
Inserted 1:43		
1	Jamal Anderson	5.00
2	Eddie George	7.00
3	Emmitt Smith	20.00
4	Jerry Rice	15.00
5	Barry Sanders	30.00
6	Keyshawn Johnson	5.00
7	Brett Favre	30.00
8	Randy Moss	30.00
9	Mark Brunell	10.00
10	Fred Taylor	15.00
11	Dan Marino	20.00
12	Peyton Manning	20.00
13	Drew Bledsoe	10.00
14	Antonio Freeman	5.00
15	Steve Young	10.00
16	Terrell Davis	20.00
17	Terrell Owens	5.00
18	Troy Aikman	15.00
19	Steve McNair	7.00
20	Jake Plummer	10.00

1999 Playoff Contenders SSD Quads

This 12-card insert featured two powerful, potential playoff opponents on each side of the card. Each card was printed on holographic board with micro-etching. Singles were found 1:57 packs.

		MT
Complete Set (12):		225.00
Common Player:		10.00
Inserted 1:57		
1	Jake Plummer, David Boston, Emmitt Smith, Troy Aikman	25.00
2	Jerry Rice, Steve Young, Jamal Anderson, Chris Chandler	20.00
3	Randy Moss, Cris Carter, Brett Favre, Antonio Freeman	35.00
4	Warrick Dunn, Mike Alstott, Stephen Davis, Brad Johnson	10.00
5	Cade McNown, Curtis Enis, Barry Sanders, Charlie Batch	30.00
6	Ricky Williams, Eddie Kennison, Marshall Faulk, Torry Holt	25.00
7	Kordell Stewart, Jerome Bettis, Eddie George, Steve McNair	15.00
8	Doug Flutie, Eric Moulds, Drew Bledsoe, Terry Glenn	15.00
9	Dan Marino, Cecil Collins, Keyshawn Johnson, Curtis Martin	25.00
10	Terrell Davis, Brian Griese, Mark Brunell, Fred Taylor	20.00
11	Jon Kitna, Joey Galloway, Napoleon Kaufman, Tim Brown	10.00
12	Peyton Manning, Edgerrin James, Tim Couch, Kevin Johnson	70.00

1999 Playoff Contenders SSD Round Numbers Autographs

This 10-card insert included autographs from one of ten pairs of rookies drafted from the same round. Both the player's image and autograph appeared on the front of the cards. Singles were inserted 1:109 packs.

		MT
Complete Set (10):		650.00
Common Player:		30.00
Inserted 1:109		
1	Kevin Johnson, Peerless Price	50.00
2	Ricky Williams, Edgerrin James	275.00
3	Donovan McNabb, Akili Smith	75.00
4	Sean Bennett, Brandon Stokley	30.00
5	Tim Couch, Cade McNown	150.00
6	David Boston, Troy Edwards	50.00
7	Daunte Culpepper, Torry Holt	75.00
8	Kevin Faulk, James Johnson	40.00
9	Joe Montgomery, Rob Konrad	30.00
10	Cecil Collins, De'Mond Parker	40.00

1999 Playoff Contenders SSD ROY Contenders

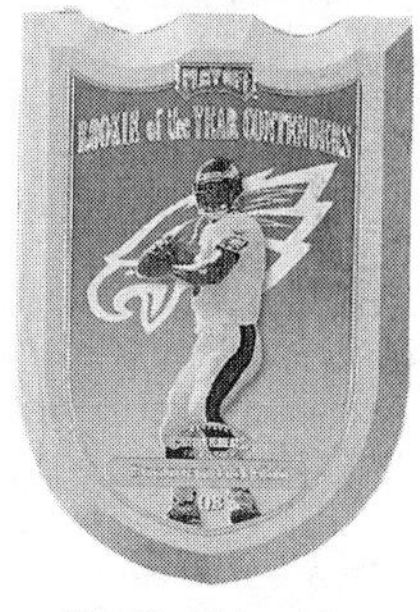

This 12-card insert included rookies who would challenge for the Rookie of the Year Award. Each single was printed on actual wood and inserted 1:29 packs. A parallel autographed version was also issued with each of those singles sequentially numbered to 100.

		MT
Complete Set (12):		100.00
Common Player:		5.00
Inserted 1:29		
1	Tim Couch	20.00
2	Donovan McNabb	12.00
3	Akili Smith	10.00
4	Daunte Culpepper	12.00
5	Cade McNown	12.00
6	Edgerrin James	25.00
7	Ricky Williams	20.00
8	Cecil Collins	5.00
9	Torry Holt	8.00
10	David Boston	8.00
11	Troy Edwards	8.00
12	Champ Bailey	5.00

1999 Playoff Contenders SSD ROY Contenders Autographs

This was a 12-card parallel to the ROY Contenders insert. Each of these singles were printed on actual wood and sequentially numbered to 100.

		MT
Complete Set (12):		1000.
Common Player:		25.00
Production 100 Sets		
1	Tim Couch	180.00
2	Donovan McNabb	100.00
3	Akili Smith	80.00
4	Daunte Culpepper	100.00
5	Cade McNown	100.00
6	Edgerrin James	250.00
7	Ricky Williams	180.00
8	Cecil Collins	25.00
9	Torry Holt	60.00
10	David Boston	50.00
11	Troy Edwards	50.00
12	Champ Bailey	25.00

1999 Playoff Contenders SSD Touchdown Tandems

This was a 24-card insert that matched up two touchdown-scoring teammates and each was printed on dual-sided holographic foil board. Singles were inserted 1:15 packs. A parallel die-cut version was also issued with each of those singles se-

quentially numbered to the player's 1998 TD total.

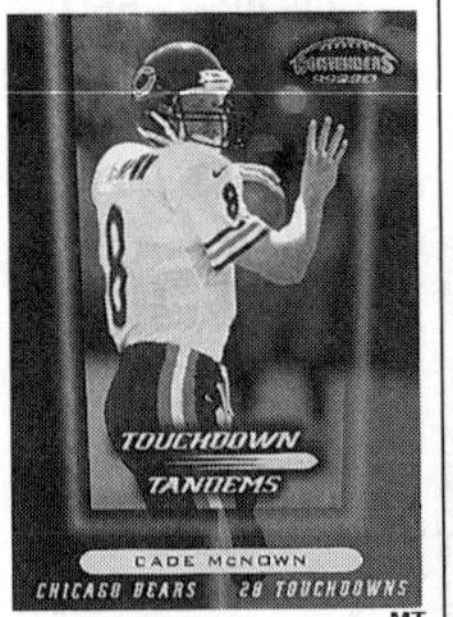

		MT
Complete Set (24):		100.00
Common Player:		2.00
Minor Stars:		4.00
Inserted 1:15		
1	Keyshawn Johnson, Curtis Martin	2.00
2	Dan Marino, Tony Martin	10.00
3	Drew Bledsoe, Terry Glenn	5.00
4	Peyton Manning, Marvin Harrison	10.00
5	Doug Flutie, Thurman Thomas	4.00
6	Steve McNair, Eddie George	4.00
7	Kordell Stewart, Jerome Bettis	4.00
8	Akili Smith, Carl Pickens	5.00
9	Mark Brunell, Jimmy Smith	5.00
10	Jon Kitna, Joey Galloway	4.00
11	John Elway, Terrell Davis	10.00
12	Napoleon Kaufman, Tim Brown	2.00
13	Troy Aikman, Emmitt Smith	10.00
14	Jake Plummer, Rob Moore	5.00
15	Donovan McNabb, Charles Johnson	6.00
16	Brad Johnson, Michael Westbrook	2.00
17	Brett Favre, Antonio Freeman	12.00
18	Randall Cunningham, Randy Moss	12.00
19	Mike Alstott, Warrick Dunn	2.00
20	Cade McNown, Curtis Enis	6.00
21	Barry Sanders, Herman Moore	12.00
22	Steve Young, Jerry Rice	8.00
23	Chris Chandler, Jamal Anderson	2.00
24	Marshall Faulk, Isaac Bruce	4.00

1999 Playoff Contenders SSD Touchdown Tandems Die Cuts

This was a 24-card parallel to the Touchdown Tandem insert. Each of these singles were die-cut and sequentially numbered to the player's 1998 TD total.

		MT
Common Player:		15.00
1	Keyshawn Johnson, Curtis Martin 20	45.00
2	Dan Marino, Tony Martin 29	120.00
3	Drew Bledsoe, Terry Glenn 23	50.00
4	Peyton Manning, Marvin Harrison 33	120.00
5	Doug Flutie, Thurman Thomas 24	50.00
6	Steve McNair, Eddie George 25	45.00
7	Kordell Stewart, Jerome Bettis 16	45.00
8	Akili Smith, Carl Pickens 41	25.00
9	Mark Brunell, Jimmy Smith 28	50.00
10	Jon Kitna, Joey Galloway 18	35.00
11	John Elway, Terrell Davis 46	70.00
12	Napoleon Kaufman, Tim Brown 11	35.00
13	Troy Aikman, Emmitt Smith 29	85.00
14	Jake Plummer, Rob Moore 26	50.00
15	Donovan McNabb, Charles Johnson 37	40.00
16	Brad Johnson, Michael Westbrook 13	40.00
17	Brett Favre, Antonio Freeman 46	60.00
18	Randall Cunningham, Randy Moss 52	50.00
19	Mike Alstott, Warrick Dunn 11	45.00
20	Cade McNown, Curtis Enis 28	70.00
21	Barry Sanders, Herman Moore 9	225.00
22	Steve Young, Jerry Rice 51	35.00
23	Chris Chandler, Jamal Anderson 43	15.00
24	Marshall Faulk, Isaac Bruce 11	50.00

1999 Playoff Contenders SSD Triple Threat

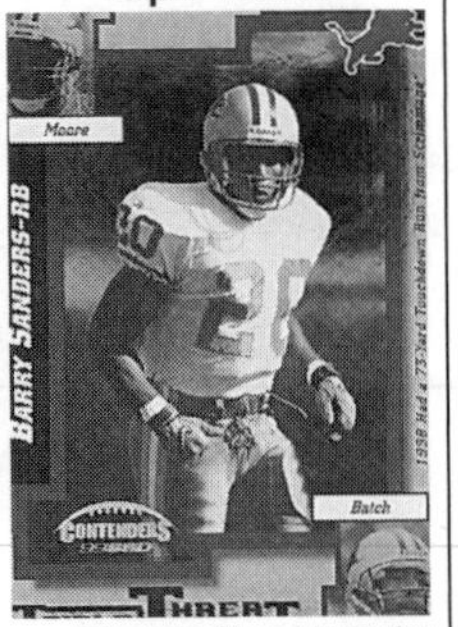

This was a 20-card insert that pictured three teammates on a mirror board with foil stamping. Singles were inserted 1:15 packs. A Triple Threat parallel was issued with one of the teammates on the front of each card for a total of 60 cards. Each was sequentially numbered to a player-specific stat.

		MT
Complete Set (20):		70.00
Common Player:		2.50
Inserted 1:15		
1	Jake Plummer, David Boston, Frank Sanders	5.00
2	Deion Sanders, Troy Aikman, Emmitt Smith	7.00
3	Terrell Owens, Jerry Rice, Steve Young	5.00
4	Dan Marino, O.J. McDuffie, Cecil Collins	7.00
5	Keyshawn Johnson, Wayne Chrebet, Curtis Martin	2.50
6	Jamal Anderson, Chris Chandler, Terance Mathis	2.50
7	Brian Griese, Terrell Davis, Shannon Sharpe	7.00
8	Fred Taylor, Mark Brunell, Keenan McCardell	5.00
9	Randy Moss, Cris Carter, Randall Cunningham	10.00
10	Antonio Freeman, Brett Favre, Dorsey Levens	10.00
11	Brad Johnson, Skip Hicks, Champ Bailey	2.50
12	Barry Sanders, Herman Moore, Charlie Batch	10.00
13	Eddie George, Steve McNair, Yancey Thigpen	4.00
14	Kordell Stewart, Jerome Bettis, Troy Edwards	3.00
15	Antowain Smith, Eric Moulds, Doug Flutie	3.00
16	Terry Glenn, Kevin Faulk, Drew Bledsoe	4.00
17	Mike Alstott, Warrick Dunn, Shaun King	6.00
18	Peyton Manning, Marvin Harrison, Edgerrin James	15.00
19	Corey Dillon, Akili Smith, Carl Pickens	3.00
20	Isaac Bruce, Torry Holt, Marshall Faulk	4.00

1999 Playoff Contenders SSD Triple Threat Parallel

This was a 60-card parallel to the Triple Threat insert. Each single featured one of the teammates on the front. Each was sequentially numbered to the player-specific stat.

		MT
Common Player:		8.00
1	Jake Plummer 17	85.00
2	Deion Sanders 16	45.00
3	Terrell Owens 14	45.00
4	Dan Marino 23	200.00
5	Keyshawn Johnson 10	60.00
6	Jamal Anderson 14	50.00
7	Brian Griese 33	60.00
8	Fred Taylor 14	125.00
9	Randy Moss 17	275.00
10	Antonio Freeman 14	50.00
11	Brad Johnson 48	15.00
12	Barry Sanders 73	80.00
13	Eddie George 37	45.00
14	Kordell Stewart 11	60.00
15	Antowain Smith 8	45.00
16	Terry Glenn 86	12.00
17	Mike Alstott 8	85.00
18	Peyton Manning 26	225.00
19	Corey Dillon 66	15.00
20	Isaac Bruce 80	12.00
21	David Boston 13	100.00
22	Troy Aikman 12	150.00
23	Jerry Rice 75	45.00
24	O.J. McDuffie 90	8.00
25	Wayne Chrebet 63	15.00
26	Chris Chandler 25	30.00
27	Terrell Davis 21	100.00
28	Mark Brunell 20	85.00
29	Cris Carter 12	70.00
30	Brett Favre 31	150.00
31	Skip Hicks 8	50.00
32	Herman Moore 82	8.00
33	Steve McNair 15	75.00
34	Jerome Bettis 4	100.00
35	Eric Moulds 84	12.00
36	Kevin Faulk 12	75.00
37	Warrick Dunn 50	30.00
38	Marvin Harrison 61	20.00
39	Akili Smith 32	75.00
40	Torry Holt 11	120.00
41	Frank Sanders 89	8.00
42	Emmitt Smith 13	175.00
43	Steve Young 36	75.00
44	Cecil Collins 28	50.00
45	Curtis Martin 60	15.00
46	Terance Mathis 11	30.00
47	Shannon Sharpe 10	45.00
48	Keenan McCardell 67	8.00
49	Randall Cunningham 34	40.00
50	Dorsey Levens 50	25.00
51	Champ Bailey 22	50.00
52	Charlie Batch 98	25.00
53	Yancey Thigpen 13	30.00
54	Troy Edwards 27	70.00
55	Doug Flutie 20	85.00
56	Drew Bledsoe 20	85.00
57	Shaun King 36	100.00
58	Edgerrin James 17	500.00
59	Carl Pickens 67	8.00
60	Marshall Faulk 78	15.00

1999 Playoff Momentum SSD

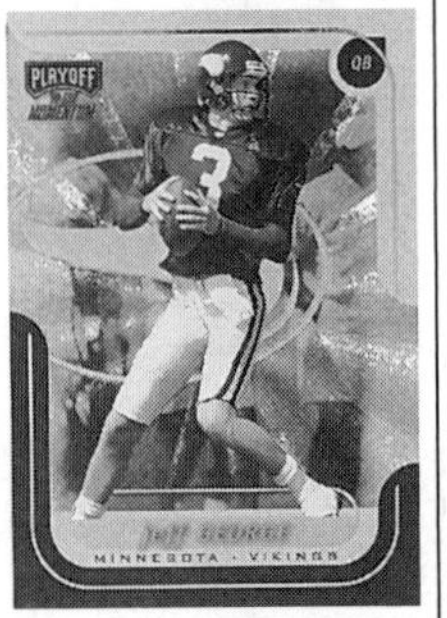

This was a 200-card base set that was divided into three tiers. Cards #1-100 were printed on foil board with micro- etching and inserted 4:1 packs. Cards #101-150 were printed on clear plastic with dual-sided holographic foil stamping and inserted 1:1. Rookie cards #151-200 were printed on clear plastic with clear holographic foil and micro-etching and inserted 1:5 packs. Parallel sets included O's and X's. Other inserts included: Chart Toppers, Terrell Davis Salute, Gridiron Force, Hog Heaven, Rookie Quads, Rookie Recall, Barry Sanders Commemorate, Star Gazing and Team Thread Checklists. SRP was $4.99 for five-card packs.

		MT
Complete Set (200):		375.00
Common Player:		.15
Minor Stars:		.30
Common Player (101-150):		.25
Minor Stars (101-150):		.50
Inserted 1:1		
Common Rookie:		2.50
Inserted 1:5		
Pack (5):		6.00
Wax Box (18):		95.00
1	Rob Moore	.30
2	Adrian Murrell	.15
3	Frank Sanders	.30
4	Andre Wadsworth	.15
5	Tim Dwight	.75
6	Terance Mathis	.15
7	Priest Holmes	.75
8	Jermaine Lewis	.15
9	Scott Mitchell	.15
10	Patrick Johnson	.30
11	Tony Banks	.30
12	Thurman Thomas	.30
13	Andre Reed	.30
14	Bruce Smith	.15
15	Tim Biakabutuka	.30
16	Muhsin Muhammad	.50
17	Wesley Walls	.30
18	Rae Carruth	.15
19	Curtis Conway	.30
20	Bobby Engram	.15
21	Jeff Blake	.30
22	Darnay Scott	.30
23	Ty Detmer	.15
24	Leslie Shepherd	.15
25	Sedrick Shaw	.15
26	Michael Irvin	.30
27	Raghib Ismail	.15
28	Ed McCaffrey	.50
29	Marcus Nash	.30
30	Shannon Sharpe	.30
31	Neil Smith	.15
32	Rod Smith	.50
33	Bubby Brister	.30
34	Germane Crowell	.30
35	Johnnie Morton	.15
36	Bill Schroeder	.15
37	Mark Chmura	.30
38	Marvin Harrison	.75
39	E.G. Green	.15
40	Jerome Pathon	.15
41	Keenan McCardell	.30
42	Jimmy Smith	.75
43	Kyle Brady	.15
44	Tavian Banks	.30
45	Warren Moon	.30
46	Derrick Alexander	.15
47	Elvis Grbac	.30
48	Andre Rison	.30
49	Bam Morris	.30
50	Rashaan Shehee	.30
51	Karim Abdul	.30
52	John Avery	.30
53	Tony Martin	.15
54	O.J. McDuffie	.30
55	Oronde Gadsden	.30
56	Robert Smith	.75
57	Jeff George	.75
58	Jake Reed	.30
59	Leroy Hoard	.30
60	Terry Allen	.30
61	Terry Glenn	.75
62	Ben Coates	.30
63	Tony Simmons	.30
64	Cameron Cleeland	.30
65	Eddie Kennison	.15
66	Billy Joe Hobert	.15
67	Amani Toomer	.30
68	Kerry Collins	.30
69	Ike Hilliard	.30
70	Gary Brown	.15
71	Joe Jurevicius	.15
72	Wayne Chrebet	.75
73	Vinny Testaverde	.30
74	Charles Woodson	.50
75	James Jett	.15
76	Charles Johnson	.15
77	Duce Staley	.50
78	Hines Ward	.30
79	Jim Harbaugh	.30
80	Ryan Leaf	.75
81	Junior Seau	.30
82	Mikhael Ricks	.15
83	Garrison Hearst	.50
84	J.J. Stokes	.30
85	Lawrence Phillips	.30
86	Derrick Mayes	.30
87	Mike Pritchard	.15
88	Ahman Green	.30
89	Ricky Watters	.50
90	Robert Holcombe	.30
91	Isaac Bruce	.75
92	Trent Dilfer	.50
93	Reidel Anthony	.30
94	Jacquez Green	.30
95	Warren Sapp	.30
96	Kevin Dyson	.30
97	Yancey Thigpen	.30
98	Stephen Davis	.75
99	Irving Fryar	.15
100	Michael Westbrook	.50
101	Jake Plummer	2.00
102	Jamal Anderson	1.00
103	Chris Chandler	.50
104	Doug Flutie	1.50
105	Eric Moulds	1.00
106	Antowain Smith	.50
107	Jonathon Linton	.50
108	Curtis Enis	1.00
109	Corey Dillon	1.00
110	Carl Pickens	.50
111	Emmitt Smith	3.00
112	Troy Aikman	2.00
113	Deion Sanders	1.00
114	John Elway	3.00
115	Terrell Davis	3.00
116	Brian Griese	2.00
117	Barry Sanders	4.00
118	Charlie Batch	1.50
119	Herman Moore	1.00
120	Brett Favre	4.00
121	Antonio Freeman	1.00
122	Dorsey Levens	1.00
123	Peyton Manning	3.00
124	Fred Taylor	2.00
125	Mark Brunell	1.50
126	Dan Marino	3.00
127	Randy Moss	4.00
128	Cris Carter	1.00
129	Randall Cunningham	1.00
130	Drew Bledsoe	1.50
131	Keyshawn Johnson	1.00
132	Curtis Martin	1.00
133	Tim Brown	.75
134	Napoleon Kaufman	1.00
135	Kordell Stewart	1.00
136	Jerome Bettis	1.00
137	Natrone Means	.75
138	Jerry Rice	2.00
139	Steve Young	1.50
140	Terrell Owens	1.00
141	Joey Galloway	1.00
142	Jon Kitna	1.00
143	Marshall Faulk	1.00
144	*Kurt Warner*	50.00
145	Warrick Dunn	1.00
146	Mike Alstott	1.00
147	Eddie George	1.25
148	Steve McNair	1.25
149	Brad Johnson	1.00
150	Skip Hicks	.25
151	*Tim Couch*	30.00
152	*Donovan McNabb*	20.00
153	*Akili Smith*	20.00
154	*Edgerrin James*	40.00
155	*Ricky Williams*	30.00
156	*Torry Holt*	12.00
157	*Champ Bailey*	8.00
158	*David Boston*	12.00
159	*Chris Claiborne*	5.00
160	*Chris McAlister*	5.00
161	*Daunte Culpepper*	20.00
162	*Cade McNown*	12.00
163	*Troy Edwards*	12.00
164	*Jevon Kearse*	10.00
165	*Kevin Johnson*	12.00
166	*James Johnson*	8.00
167	*Reginald Kelly*	2.50
168	*Rob Konrad*	4.00
169	*Jim Kleinsasser*	4.00
170	*Kevin Faulk*	8.00
171	*Joe Montgomery*	5.00
172	*Shaun King*	20.00
173	*Peerless Price*	8.00
174	*Michael Cloud*	5.00
175	*Jermaine Fazande*	5.00
176	*D'Wayne Bates*	2.50
177	*Brock Huard*	8.00
178	*Marty Booker*	2.50
179	*Karsten Bailey*	2.50
180	*Shawn Bryson*	2.50
181	*Jeff Paulk*	2.50
182	*Travis McGriff*	2.50
183	*Amos Zereoue*	4.00
184	*Craig Yeast*	2.50
185	*Joe Germaine*	5.00
186	*Dameane Douglas*	2.50
187	*Sedrick Irvin*	8.00
188	*Brandon Stokley*	2.50
189	*Larry Parker*	2.50
190	*Sean Bennett*	2.50
191	*Wane McGarity*	2.50
192	*Olandis Gary*	25.00
193	*Na Brown*	2.50
194	*Aaron Brooks*	15.00
195	*Cecil Collins*	12.00
196	*Darrin Chiaverini*	4.00
197	*Kevin Daft*	2.50
198	*Darnell McDonald*	4.00
199	*Joel Makovicka*	4.00
200	*Michael Bishop*	7.00

1999 Playoff Momentum SSD O's Parallel

This was a 200-card parallel to the base set. Each single was printed on holographic foil board with foil stamping. Cards were sequentially numbered to 25.

	MT
O's Cards:	50x-100x
O's Cards (101-150):	35x-70x
O's Rookies (144,151-200):	3x-6x
Production 25 Sets	

1999 Playoff Momentum SSD X's Parallel

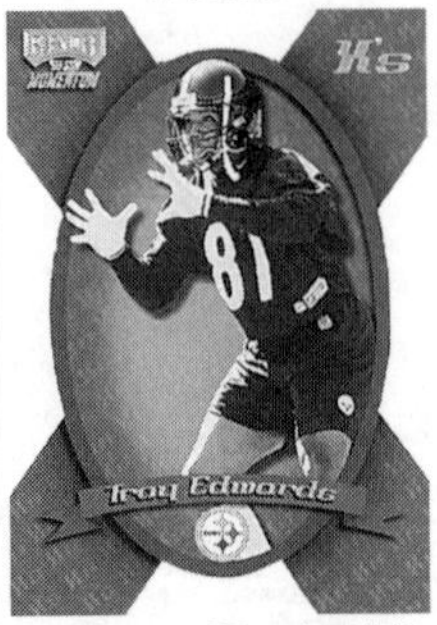

This was a 200-card parallel to the base set. Each was die cut in the shape of the letter "X" and was printed on holographic foil board with foil stamping. They were sequentially numbered to 300.

	MT
X's Cards:	6x-12x
X's Cards (101-150):	5x-10x
X's Rookies (144,151-200):	1.5x
Production 300 Sets	

1999 Playoff Momentum SSD Chart Toppers

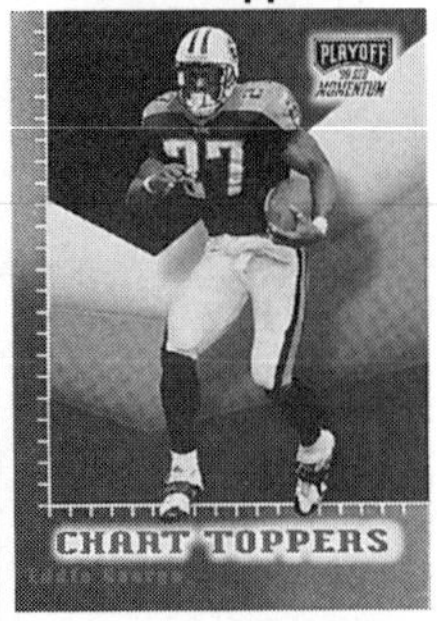

This 24-card insert included some of the top veteran and rookies in the NFL. Each was printed on holographic foil board with holographic foil stamping. Singles were found 1:33 packs.

		MT
Complete Set (24):		150.00
Common Player:		3.00
Inserted 1:33		
1	Donovan McNabb	8.00
2	Randy Moss	15.00
3	Cade McNown	8.00
4	Brett Favre	15.00
5	Edgerrin James	20.00
6	Dan Marino	12.00
7	Jamal Anderson	3.00
8	Barry Sanders	15.00
9	Kordell Stewart	3.00
10	John Elway	12.00
11	Eddie George	4.00
12	Terrell Davis	12.00
13	Ricky Williams	12.00
14	Peyton Manning	12.00
15	Tim Couch	12.00
16	Emmitt Smith	12.00
17	Doug Flutie	6.00
18	Troy Aikman	10.00
19	Steve Young	6.00
20	Jerry Rice	10.00
21	Mark Brunell	6.00
22	Fred Taylor	10.00
23	Jake Plummer	10.00
24	Drew Bledsoe	6.00

1999 Playoff Momentum SSD Terrell Davis Salute

This was a 5-card insert that covered Davis' career. Singles were numbered 11-15 and they were found 1:255 packs. The first 150 of each card were autographed and sequentially numbered.

		MT
Complete Set (5):		60.00
Common Player:		12.00
Inserted 1:255		
Common Autograph:		75.00
Production 150 Sets		
11	Terrell Davis	12.00
12	Terrell Davis	12.00
13	Terrell Davis	12.00
14	Terrell Davis	12.00
15	Terrell Davis	12.00

1999 Playoff Momentum SSD Gridiron Force

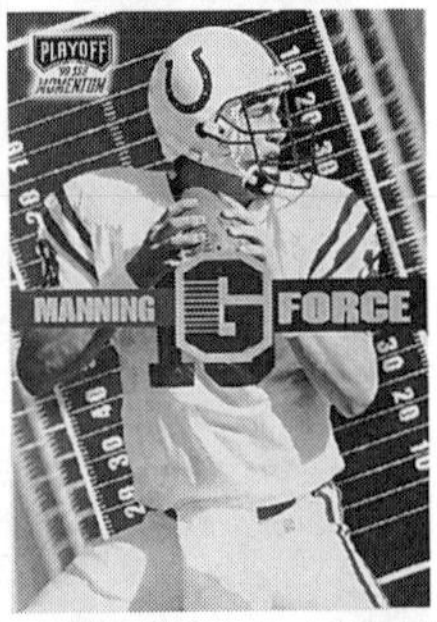

This 24-card insert included some of the top players in the NFL. Each was printed on holographic foil board with gold foil stamping. Singles were inserted 1:17 packs.

		MT
Complete Set (24):		85.00
Common Player:		2.00
Inserted 1:17		
1	Cris Carter	2.00
2	Brett Favre	12.00
3	Jamal Anderson	2.00
4	Dan Marino	10.00
5	Deion Sanders	2.00
6	Barry Sanders	12.00
7	Jerome Bettis	2.00
8	John Elway	10.00
9	Eddie George	3.00
10	Peyton Manning	10.00
11	Warrick Dunn	2.00
12	Troy Aikman	6.00
13	Keyshawn Johnson	2.00
14	Jerry Rice	6.00
15	Terrell Owens	2.00
16	Randy Moss	12.00
17	Fred Taylor	6.00
18	Mark Brunell	4.00
19	Steve Young	4.00
20	Drew Bledsoe	4.00
21	Kordell Stewart	2.00
22	Emmitt Smith	10.00
23	Terrell Davis	10.00
24	Jake Plummer	6.00

1999 Playoff Momentum SSD Hog Heaven

This 12-card insert pictured the players on a die-cut card with real football leather and foil stamping. Singles were inserted 1:81 packs.

		MT
Complete Set (12):		200.00
Common Player:		15.00
Inserted 1:81		
1	Ricky Williams	30.00
2	Terrell Davis	20.00
3	Emmitt Smith	20.00
4	Brett Favre	30.00
5	Fred Taylor	15.00
6	Tim Couch	30.00
7	John Elway	20.00
8	Dan Marino	20.00
9	Randy Moss	30.00
10	Barry Sanders	30.00
11	Jerry Rice	20.00
12	Jake Plummer	15.00

1999 Playoff Momentum SSD Rookie Quads

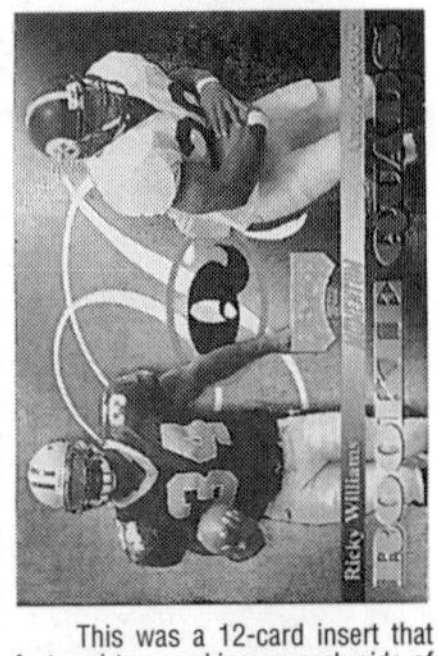

This was a 12-card insert that featured two rookies on each side of the card on a mirror board with micro-etching. Singles were inserted

1:97 packs. A parallel Gold version was also issued and each of those singles included holographic gold foil stamping and were sequentially numbered to 50.

	MT
Complete Set (12):	230.00
Common Player:	10.00
Inserted 1:97	
Gold Cards:	2x
Production 50 Sets	

1	Tim Couch, Aaron Brooks, Shaun King, Michael Bishop	40.00
2	Edgerrin James, Michael Cloud, Jeff Paulk, Joel Makovicka	50.00
3	Torry Holt, Reginald Kelly, Marty Booker, Dameane Douglas	20.00
4	Champ Bailey, Chris Claiborne, Chris McAlister, Anthony McFarland	10.00
5	David Boston, Jim Kleinsasser, Karsten Bailey, Brandon Stokley	15.00
6	Ricky Williams, Amos Zereoue, Cecil Collins, Olandis Gary	50.00
7	Donovan McNabb, Brock Huard, Daunte Culpepper, Scott Covington	30.00
8	James Johnson, Jermaine Fazande, Sedrick Irvin, Sean Bennett	15.00
9	Troy Edwards, Peerless Price, Travis McGriff, Larry Parker	25.00
10	Rob Konrad, Kevin Faulk, Joe Montgomery, Shawn Bryson	10.00
11	Cade McNown, Joe Germaine, Akili Smith, Chris Griesen	30.00
12	Kevin Johnson, D'Wayne Bates, Craig Yeast, Wane McGarity	20.00

1999 Playoff Momentum SSD Rookie Recall

This was a 30-card insert that featured photos of NFL stars on the front with their rookie photos on the back. Singles were found 1:49 packs.

	MT
Complete Set (30):	185.00
Common Player:	5.00
Inserted 1:49	

1	Jerome Bettis	5.00
2	Tim Brown	5.00
3	Cris Carter	5.00
4	Marshall Faulk	5.00
5	Doug Flutie	8.00
6	Randall Cunningham	5.00
7	Brett Favre	20.00
8	Dan Marino	15.00
9	Barry Sanders	20.00
10	John Elway	15.00
11	Emmitt Smith	15.00
12	Troy Aikman	12.00
13	Jerry Rice	12.00
14	Steve Young	8.00
15	Randy Moss	20.00
16	Peyton Manning	15.00
17	Fred Taylor	10.00
18	Jake Plummer	10.00
19	Drew Bledsoe	8.00
20	Mark Brunell	8.00
21	Charlie Batch	7.00
22	Antonio Freeman	5.00
23	Curtis Martin	5.00
24	Eddie George	5.00
25	Kordell Stewart	5.00
26	Jamal Anderson	5.00
27	Curtis Enis	5.00
28	Terrell Davis	15.00
29	Eric Moulds	5.00
30	Terrell Owens	5.00

1999 Playoff Momentum SSD Barry Sanders Commemorate

This was a five-card insert that covered the career of Barry Sanders. Singles were numbered 7 to 11 and found 1:275 packs.

	MT
Complete Set (5):	100.00
Common Player:	20.00
Inserted 1:275	

1	Barry Sanders	20.00
2	Barry Sanders	20.00
3	Barry Sanders	20.00
4	Barry Sanders	20.00
5	Barry Sanders	20.00

1999 Playoff Momentum SSD Star Gazing

This was a 45-card insert that was divided into three levels. The Red singles were the first eight cards in the set, each was autographed and found 1:185 packs. The next 22 cards were Blue and they were inserted 1:17 packs. The last 15 cards were Green and they were issued at 1:65 packs. Each single had a parallel Gold version and each of those singles were sequentially numbered to 50.

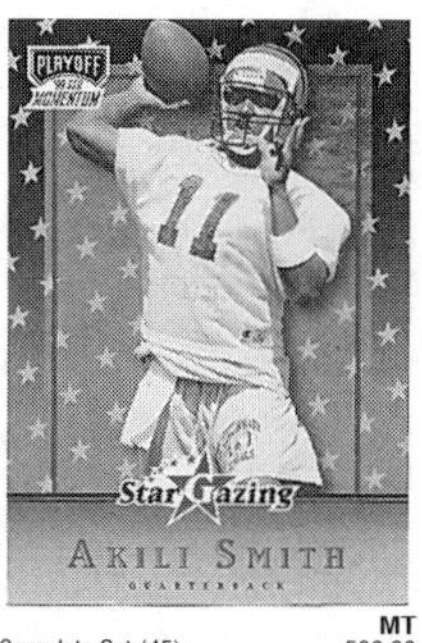

	MT
Complete Set (45):	500.00
Common Red Auto. (1-8):	25.00
Inserted 1:185	
Common Blue (9-30):	1.50
Inserted 1:17	
Common Green (31-45):	5.00
Inserted 1:65	

1	Terrell Davis (red)	75.00
2	Dan Marino (red)	100.00
3	Joey Galloway (red)	25.00
4	Steve McNair (red)	25.00
5	Doug Flutie (red)	35.00
6	Kordell Stewart (red)	25.00
7	Fred Taylor (red)	45.00
8	Jamal Anderson (red)	25.00
9	Karim Abdul (blue)	1.50
10	Mike Alstott (blue)	3.00
11	Jerome Bettis (blue)	1.50
12	Carl Pickens (blue)	1.50
13	Cris Carter (blue)	3.00
14	Randall Cunningham (blue)	3.00
15	Corey Dillon (blue)	3.00
16	Tim Dwight (blue)	1.50
17	Cade McNown (blue)	5.00
18	Marshall Faulk (blue)	3.00
19	Napoleon Kaufman (blue)	1.50
20	Antonio Freeman (blue)	1.50
21	Edgerrin James (blue)	15.00
22	Terrell Owens (blue)	3.00
23	Garrison Hearst (blue)	1.50
24	Keyshawn Johnson (blue)	3.00
25	Akili Smith (blue)	5.00
26	Curtis Martin (blue)	3.00
27	Dorsey Levens (blue)	1.50
28	Deion Sanders (blue)	3.00
29	Herman Moore (blue)	1.50
30	Eric Moulds (blue)	1.50
31	Randy Moss (green)	15.00
32	Eddie George (green)	5.00
33	Barry Sanders (green)	15.00
34	John Elway (green)	12.00
35	Peyton Manning (green)	12.00
36	Emmitt Smith (green)	12.00
37	Troy Aikman (green)	10.00
38	Jerry Rice (green)	10.00
39	Mark Brunell (green)	6.00
40	Steve Young (green)	6.00
41	Tim Couch (green)	15.00
42	Ricky Williams (green)	15.00
43	Donovan McNabb (green)	10.00
44	Drew Bledsoe (green)	6.00
45	Brett Favre (green)	15.00

1999 Playoff Momentum SSD Team Threads

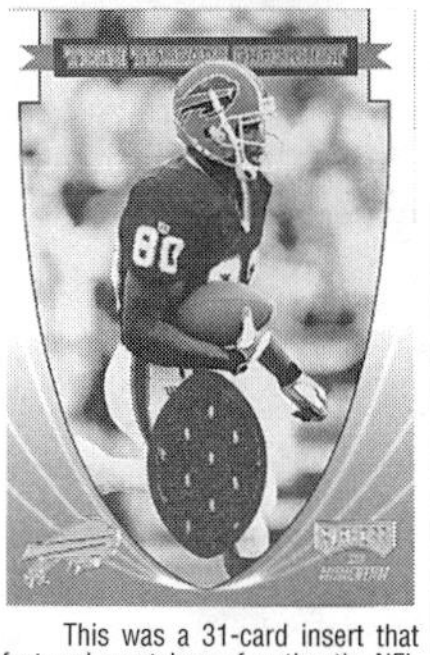

This was a 31-card insert that featured swatches of authentic NFL team jerseys on the front and back of each card. Singles were inserted 1:17 packs.

	MT
Complete Set (31):	425.00
Common Player:	5.00
Minor Stars:	10.00
Inserted 1:17	

1	Dan Marino	30.00
2	Drew Bledsoe	15.00
3	Keyshawn Johnson	10.00
4	Eric Moulds	10.00
5	Peyton Manning	30.00
6	Natrone Means	5.00
7	Jon Kitna	10.00
8	Bam Morris	5.00
9	Tim Brown	5.00
10	Terrell Davis	30.00
11	Kordell Stewart	10.00
12	Fred Taylor	20.00
13	Tim Couch	30.00
14	Eddie George	12.00
15	Priest Holmes	10.00
16	Akili Smith	15.00
17	Emmitt Smith	30.00
18	Skip Hicks	5.00
19	Jake Plummer	15.00
20	Donovan McNabb	20.00
21	Ike Hilliard	5.00
22	Barry Sanders	40.00
23	Cade McNown	20.00
24	Randy Moss	40.00
25	Brett Favre	40.00
26	Mike Alstott	5.00
27	Marshall Faulk	15.00
28	Ricky Williams	30.00
29	Jamal Anderson	5.00
30	Jerry Rice	20.00
31	Tim Biakabutuka	5.00

1999 Playoff Prestige EXP

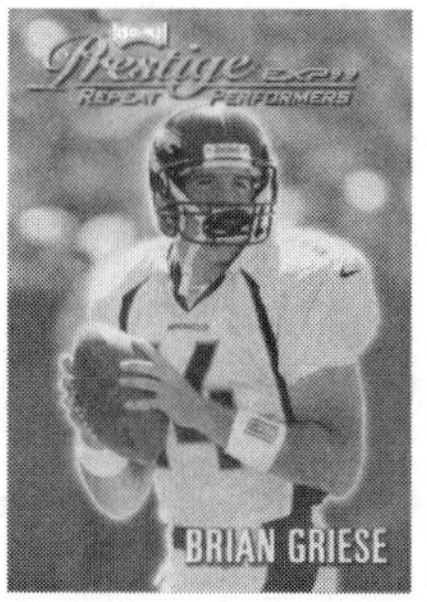

This 200-card set was a retail only release that included 40 unseeded rookie cards. It had two parallel sets with Reflections Gold and Reflections Silver. Other inserts include: Alma Maters, Checklists, Crowd Pleasers, Terrell Davis Salute, Draft Picks, Performers and Stars of the NFL.

	MT
Complete Set (200):	70.00
Common Player:	.20
Minor Stars:	.40
Common Rookie:	.50
SSD Pack (5):	7.00
SSD Wax Box (16):	100.00
EXP Pack (8):	3.50
EXP Wax Box (24):	75.00

1	*Anthony McFarland*	1.00
2	*Al Wilson*	1.00
3	*Jevon Kearse*	3.00
4	*Aaron Brooks*	4.00
5	*Travis McGriff*	1.00
6	*Jeff Paulk*	1.00
7	*Shawn Bryson*	.50
8	*Karsten Bailey*	1.00
9	*Mike Cloud*	1.00
10	*James Johnson*	2.00
11	*Tai Streets*	1.00
12	*Jermaine Fazande*	1.00
13	*Ebenezer Ekuban*	.50
14	*Joe Montgomery*	1.50
15	*Craig Yeast*	1.00
16	*Joe Germaine*	2.00
17	*Andy Katzenmoyer*	1.50
18	*Kevin Faulk*	3.00
19	*Chris McAlister*	1.00
20	*Sedrick Irvin*	2.00
21	*Brock Huard*	2.00
22	*Cade McNown*	3.00
23	*Shaun King*	4.00
24	*Amos Zereoue*	2.50
25	*Dameane Douglas*	1.00
26	*D'Wayne Bates*	1.00
27	*Kevin Johnson*	3.00
28	*Rob Konrad*	1.50
29	*Troy Edwards*	3.00
30	*Peerless Price*	2.50
31	*Daunte Culpepper*	5.00
32	*Akili Smith*	4.00
33	*David Boston*	3.00
34	*Chris Claiborne*	1.50
35	*Torry Holt*	3.00
36	*Champ Bailey*	2.00
37	*Edgerrin James*	10.00
38	*Donovan McNabb*	5.00
39	*Ricky Williams*	8.00
40	*Tim Couch*	8.00
41	Charles Woodson (Repeat Performers)	.20
42	Skip Hicks (Repeat Performers)	.20
43	Brian Griese (Repeat Performers)	.75
44	Tim Dwight (Repeat Performers)	.20
45	Ryan Leaf (Repeat Performers)	.50
46	Curtis Enis (Repeat Performers)	.20
47	Charlie Batch (Repeat Performers)	.75
48	Fred Taylor (Repeat Performers)	1.00
49	Peyton Manning (Repeat Performers)	1.50
50	Randy Moss (Repeat Performers)	2.00
51	Jim Harbaugh (Trading Places)	.20
52	Warren Moon (Trading Places)	.75
53	Jeff George (Trading Places)	.20
54	Rich Gannon (Trading Places)	.20
55	Scott Mitchell (Trading Places)	.20
56	Kerry Collins (Trading Places)	.20
57	Brad Johnson (Trading Places)	.75
58	Charles Johnson (Trading Places)	.20
59	Chris Calloway (Trading Places)	.20
60	Tyrone Wheatley (Trading Places)	.20
61	Michael Westbrook	.40
62	Skip Hicks	.75
63	Terry Allen	.20
64	Albert Connell	.20
65	Kevin Dyson	.40
66	Frank Wycheck	.20
67	Yancey Thigpen	.40
68	Steve McNair	.75
69	Eddie George	1.00
70	Eric Zeier	.20
71	Jacquez Green	.40
72	Reidel Anthony	.40
73	Warren Sapp	.20
74	Mike Alstott	.75
75	Warrick Dunn	1.00
76	Trent Dilfer	.40
77	Ahman Green	.40
78	Joey Galloway	.75
79	Ricky Watters	.40
80	Jon Kitna	1.00
81	Amp Lee	.20
82	Isaac Bruce	.40
83	Robert Holcombe	.20
84	Greg Hill	.20
85	Marshall Faulk	.75
86	Trent Green	.75
87	J.J. Stokes	.40
88	Terrell Owens	.75
89	Jerry Rice	2.00
90	Garrison Hearst	.75
91	Steve Young	1.25
92	Junior Seau	.40
93	Mikhael Ricks	.20
94	Natrone Means	.40
95	Ryan Leaf	.75
96	Courtney Hawkins	.20
97	Chris Fuamatu-Ma'afala	.20
98	Jerome Bettis	.75
99	Kordell Stewart	.75
100	Bobby Hoying	.40
101	Charlie Garner	.40
102	Duce Staley	.40
103	Charles Woodson	.75
104	James Jett	.20
105	Rickey Dudley	.20
106	Tim Brown	.50
107	Napoleon Kaufman	.75
108	Wayne Chrebet	.50
109	Keyshawn Johnson	.75
110	Vinny Testaverde	.40
111	Curtis Martin	.75
112	Joe Jurevicius	.20
113	Tiki Barber	.20
114	Ike Hilliard	.20
115	Kent Graham	.20
116	Gary Brown	.20
117	Lamar Smith	.20
118	Eddie Kennison	.20
119	Cameron Cleeland	.20
120	Tony Simmons	.20
121	Ben Coates	.40
122	Darick Holmes	.20
123	Terry Glenn	.75
124	Drew Bledsoe	1.50
125	Leroy Hoard	.20
126	Jake Reed	.20
127	Randy Moss	4.00
128	Cris Carter	.75
129	Robert Smith	.75
130	Randall Cunningham	.75
131	Lamar Thomas	.20
132	John Avery	.40
133	O.J. McDuffie	.40
134	Dan Marino	3.00
135	Karim Abdul	.40
136	Rashaan Shehee	.20
137	Derrick Alexander	.20
138	Bam Morris	.20
139	Andre Rison	.40
140	Elvis Grbac	.40
141	Tavian Banks	.20
142	Keenan McCardell	.20
143	Jimmy Smith	.40
144	Fred Taylor	2.00
145	Mark Brunell	1.50
146	Jerome Pathon	.20
147	Marvin Harrison	.40
148	Peyton Manning	3.00
149	Robert Brooks	.20
150	Mark Chmura	.40
151	Antonio Freeman	.75
152	Dorsey Levens	.75
153	Brett Favre	4.00
154	Johnnie Morton	.20
155	Germane Crowell	.40
156	Barry Sanders	4.00
157	Herman Moore	.75
158	Charlie Batch	1.25
159	Marcus Nash	.20
160	Shannon Sharpe	.40
161	Rod Smith	.40
162	Ed McCaffrey	.40
163	Terrell Davis	3.00
164	John Elway	3.00
165	Ernie Mills	.20
166	Michael Irvin	.40
167	Deion Sanders	.75
168	Emmitt Smith	3.00
169	Troy Aikman	2.00
170	Chris Spielman	.20
171	Terry Kirby	.20
172	Ty Detmer	.20
173	Leslie Shepherd	.20
174	Darnay Scott	.20
175	Jeff Blake	.40
176	Carl Pickens	.40
177	Corey Dillon	.75
178	Bobby Engram	.20
179	Curtis Conway	.40
180	Curtis Enis	.75
181	Muhsin Muhammad	.20
182	Steve Beuerlein	.20
183	Tim Biakabutuka	.20
184	Bruce Smith	.20
185	Andre Reed	.20
186	Thurman Thomas	.40
187	Eric Moulds	.75
188	Antowain Smith	.75
189	Doug Flutie	1.25
190	Jermaine Lewis	.20
191	Priest Holmes	.75
192	O.J. Santiago	.20
193	Tim Dwight	.75
194	Terrance Mathis	.20
195	Chris Chandler	.40
196	Jamal Anderson	.75
197	Rob Moore	.40
198	Frank Sanders	.20
199	Adrian Murrell	.20
200	Jake Plummer	1.50

1999 Playoff Prestige EXP Reflections Gold Parallel

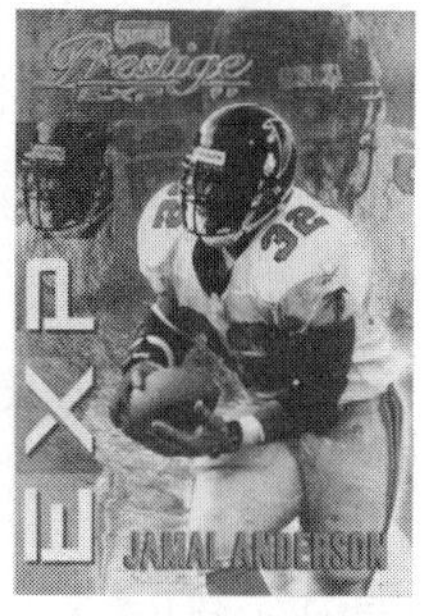

This is a parallel to the base set and each single is the same as the base card except for these singles are printed on a gold foil card and are sequentially numbered to 1,000.

	MT
Complete Set (200):	280.00
Gold Cards:	3x-6x
Gold Rookies:	3x
Production 1,000 Sets	

1999 Playoff Prestige EXP Reflections Silver Parallel

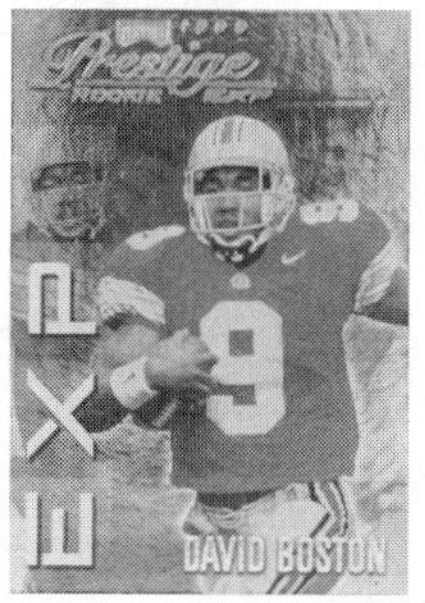

This is a parallel to the base set and is identical to the base card except each single is printed on a silver foil card and is sequentially numbered to 3,250.

	MT
Complete Set (200):	140.00
Silver Cards:	2x
Silver Rookies:	1.5x
Production 3,250 Sets	

1999 Playoff Prestige EXP Alma Maters

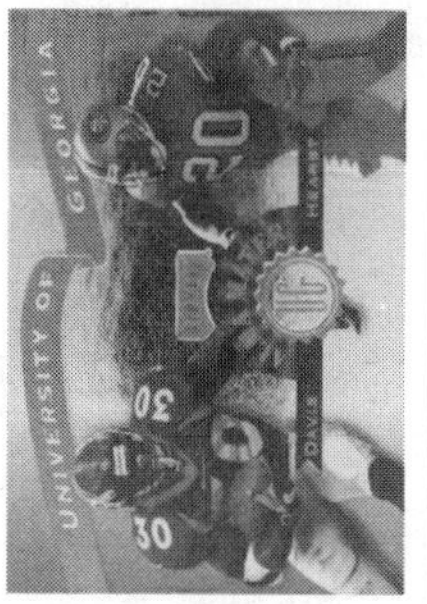

Each card in this 30-card set pictures two players that went to the same college. Singles were inserted 1:25 packs.

	MT
Complete Set (30):	100.00
Common Player:	2.00
Minor Stars:	4.00
Inserted 1:25	

1	Priest Holmes, Ricky Williams	12.00
2	Tim Couch, Dermonti Dawson	12.00
3	Terrell Davis, Garrison Hearst	8.00
4	Troy Brown, Randy Moss	10.00
5	Barry Sanders, Thurman Thomas	10.00
6	Emmitt Smith, Fred Taylor	8.00
7	Doug Flutie, Bill Romanowski	5.00
8	Brett Favre, Michael Jackson	10.00
9	Charlie Batch, Ron Rice	5.00
10	Mark Brunell, Chris Chandler	5.00
11	Warrick Dunn, Deion Sanders	4.00
12	Cris Carter, Eddie George	4.00
13	Drew Bledsoe, Ryan Leaf	5.00
14	Corey Dillon, Napoleon Kaufman	2.00
15	Jerome Bettis, Tim Brown	2.00
16	Marshall Faulk, Darnay Scott	2.00
17	Tiki Barber, Herman Moore	2.00
18	Jamal Anderson, Chris Fuamatu-Ma'afala	2.00
19	Troy Aikman, Cade McNown	7.00
20	Brian Griese, Charles Woodson	6.00
21	Charles Johnson, Kordell Stewart	4.00
22	Kevin Faulk, Eddie Kennison	4.00
23	Donovan McNabb, Rob Moore	5.00
24	Steve McNair, John Thierry	4.00
25	Michael Irvin, Vinny Testaverde	2.00
26	Randall Cunningham, Keenan McCardell	4.00
27	Keyshawn Johnson, Junior Seau	2.00
28	Karim Abdul, Skip Hicks	2.00
29	Curtis Enis, O.J. McDuffie	2.00
30	Joey Galloway, Robert Smith	2.00

1999 Playoff Prestige EXP Checklists

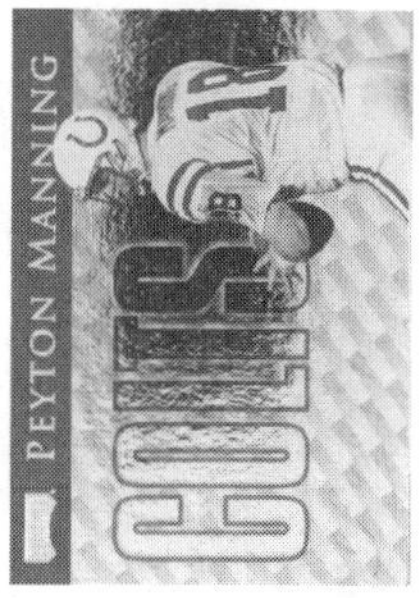

This 31-card set includes a card for each NFL team and highlights one player on the front of these silver foil singles. The backs include photos of each player on that team in the base set and includes their card number. Singles were inserted 1:25 packs.

	MT
Complete Set (31):	85.00
Common Player:	1.50
Minor Stars:	3.00
Inserted 1:25	

1	Jake Plummer	6.00
2	Chris Chandler	1.50
3	Priest Holmes	3.00
4	Doug Flutie	4.00
5	Wesley Walls	1.50
6	Curtis Enis	3.00
7	Corey Dillon	3.00
8	Kevin Johnson	3.00
9	Troy Aikman	6.00
10	Terrell Davis	8.00
11	Barry Sanders	12.00
12	Antonio Freeman	3.00
13	Peyton Manning	8.00
14	Fred Taylor	6.00
15	Andre Rison	1.50
16	Dan Marino	8.00
17	Randy Moss	12.00
18	Kevin Faulk	4.00
19	Ricky Williams	12.00
20	Joe Montgomery	3.00
21	Vinny Testaverde	1.50
22	Tim Brown	3.00
23	Duce Staley	1.50
24	Jerome Bettis	3.00
25	Natrone Means	3.00
26	Terrell Owens	3.00
27	Joey Galloway	3.00
28	Isaac Bruce	3.00
29	Mike Alstott	3.00
30	Eddie George	4.00
31	Skip Hicks	3.00

1999 Playoff Prestige EXP Crowd Pleasers

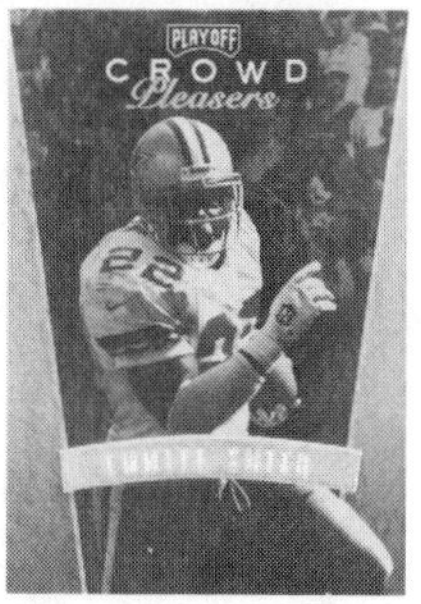

Each card in this 30-card set highlights the hottest players who fill

the stadiums. Singles were inserted 1:49 packs.

		MT
Complete Set (30):		200.00
Common Player:		2.50
Minor Stars:		5.00
Inserted 1:49		
1	Terrell Davis	15.00
2	Fred Taylor	10.00
3	Corey Dillon	5.00
4	Eddie George	6.00
5	Napoleon Kaufman	5.00
6	Jamal Anderson	5.00
7	Tim Couch	20.00
8	Emmitt Smith	15.00
9	Deion Sanders	5.00
10	Garrison Hearst	2.50
11	Peyton Manning	15.00
12	Ricky Williams	20.00
13	Barry Sanders	20.00
14	Jerry Rice	10.00
15	Jake Plummer	8.00
16	Tim Brown	2.50
17	Terrell Owens	5.00
18	Dan Marino	15.00
19	Chris Chandler	2.50
20	Drew Bledsoe	7.00
21	Charlie Batch	6.00
22	Mark Brunell	7.00
23	Troy Aikman	10.00
24	John Elway	15.00
25	Jon Kitna	5.00
26	Jerome Bettis	5.00
27	Brett Favre	20.00
28	Steve Young	6.00
29	Randy Moss	20.00
30	Antonio Freeman	5.00

1999 Playoff Prestige EXP Terrell Davis Salute

This 5-card set highlights 15 milestones in Davis' career. Each single is sequentially numbered to 750 and the first 150 of each single were autographed.

		MT
Complete Set (5):		60.00
Common Player:		12.00
Production 750 Sets		
Common Autographs:		85.00
First 150-cards were signed		
1	Terrell Davis	12.00
2	Terrell Davis	12.00
3	Terrell Davis	12.00
4	Terrell Davis	12.00
5	Terrell Davis	12.00

1999 Playoff Prestige EXP Draft Picks

This insert includes the top 30 players drafted in 1999. It pictures each player in their college uniform on a silver foil card. Singles were inserted 1:13 packs.

		MT
Complete Set (30):		60.00
Common Player:		1.00
Minor Stars:		2.00
Inserted 1:13		
1	Tim Couch	12.00
2	Ricky Williams	12.00
3	Donovan McNabb	5.00
4	Edgerrin James	7.00
5	Champ Bailey	2.50
6	Torry Holt	4.00
7	Chris Claiborne	2.00
8	David Boston	4.00
9	Akili Smith	5.00
10	Daunte Culpepper	5.00
11	Peerless Price	3.00
12	Troy Edwards	4.00
13	Rob Konrad	1.00
14	Kevin Johnson	4.00
15	D'Wayne Bates	2.00
16	Cecil Collins	5.00
17	Amos Zereoue	3.00
18	Shaun King	3.00
19	Cade McNown	5.00
20	Brock Huard	2.50
21	Sedrick Irvin	2.50
22	Chris McAlister	1.00
23	Kevin Faulk	3.00
24	Jevon Kearse	2.50
25	Joe Germaine	2.50
26	Andy Katzenmoyer	2.00
27	Joe Montgomery	2.00
28	Al Wilson	1.00
29	Jermaine Fazande	1.00
30	Ebenezer Ekuban	1.00

1999 Playoff Prestige EXP Performers

This 24-card insert includes the top performers from 1998. Singles were inserted 1:97 packs.

		MT
Complete Set (24):		200.00

Common Player: 3.00
Minor Stars: 6.00
Inserted 1:97

		MT
1	Marshall Faulk	6.00
2	Jake Plummer	15.00
3	Antonio Freeman	6.00
4	Brett Favre	30.00
5	Troy Aikman	15.00
6	Randy Moss	30.00
7	John Elway	20.00
8	Mark Brunell	10.00
9	Jamal Anderson	6.00
10	Doug Flutie	8.00
11	Drew Bledsoe	12.00
12	Barry Sanders	30.00
13	Dan Marino	20.00
14	Randall Cunningham	6.00
15	Steve Young	8.00
16	Carl Pickens	3.00
17	Peyton Manning	20.00
18	Herman Moore	6.00
19	Eddie George	7.00
20	Fred Taylor	15.00
21	Garrison Hearst	6.00
22	Emmitt Smith	20.00
23	Jerry Rice	15.00
24	Terrell Davis	20.00

1999 Playoff Prestige EXP Barry Sanders Commemorative

This was a special insert found 1:289 packs that was commemorating Sanders run for the record.

		MT
Inserted 1:289		
RR1	Barry Sanders	20.00

1999 Playoff Prestige EXP Stars of the NFL

Each card in this 20-card set is printed on clear plastic and is die cut. Singles were inserted 1:73 packs.

		MT
Complete Set (20):		160.00
Common Player:		5.00
Inserted 1:73		
1	Jerry Rice	12.00
2	Steve Young	8.00
3	Drew Bledsoe	10.00
4	Jamal Anderson	5.00
5	Eddie George	6.00
6	Keyshawn Johnson	5.00
7	Kordell Stewart	6.00
8	Barry Sanders	25.00
9	Tim Brown	5.00
10	Mark Brunell	8.00
11	Fred Taylor	12.00
12	Randy Moss	25.00
13	Peyton Manning	18.00
14	Emmitt Smith	18.00
15	Deion Sanders	5.00
16	Troy Aikman	12.00
17	Brett Favre	25.00
18	Dan Marino	18.00
19	Terrell Davis	18.00
20	John Elway	18.00

1999 Playoff Prestige SSD

Prestige SSD was a 200-card set that was a hobby-only product. It had 50 short prints with 40 rookies and 10 Repeat Performers that were inserted 1:2 packs. It has a parallel Spectrum insert in five different colors that include Blue, Gold, Green, Purple and Red. Other inserts include: Alma Maters, Checklists, Checklists Autographs, Draft Picks, For the Record, Gridiron Heritage, Inside the Numbers and Barry Sanders Run for the Record.

		MT
Complete Set (200):		175.00
Common Player:		.50
Minor Stars:		.50
Common RP (151-160):		1.00
Common Rookie:		2.00
Inserted 1:2		
Wax Box:		100.00
1	Jake Plummer	2.50
2	Adrian Murrell	.25
3	Frank Sanders	.50
4	Rob Moore	.25
5	Jamal Anderson	1.00
6	Chris Chandler	.50
7	Terrance Mathis	.25
8	Tim Dwight	1.00
9	O.J. Santiago	.25
10	Priest Holmes	1.50
11	Jermaine Lewis	.50
12	Doug Flutie	1.50
13	Antowain Smith	1.00
14	Eric Moulds	1.00
15	Thurman Thomas	.50
16	Andre Reed	.25
17	Bruce Smith	.25

18	Tim Biakabutuka	.50
19	Steve Beuerlein	.25
20	Muhsin Muhammed	.25
21	Curtis Enis	1.00
22	Curtis Conway	.50
23	Bobby Engram	.25
24	Corey Dillon	1.00
25	Carl Pickens	.50
26	Jeff Blake	.50
27	Darnay Scott	.25
28	Leslie Shepherd	.25
29	Ty Detmer	.25
30	Terry Kirby	.25
31	Chris Spielman	.25
32	Troy Aikman	2.50
33	Emmitt Smith	4.00
34	Deion Sanders	1.00
35	Michael Irvin	.50
36	Ernie Mills	.25
37	John Elway	4.00
38	Terrell Davis	4.00
39	Ed McCaffrey	.50
40	Rod Smith	.50
41	Shannon Sharpe	.50
42	Marcus Nash	.25
43	Charlie Batch	2.00
44	Herman Moore	1.00
45	Barry Sanders	5.00
46	Germane Crowell	.50
47	Johnnie Morton	.25
48	Brett Favre	5.00
49	Dorsey Levens	1.00
50	Antonio Freeman	1.00
51	Mark Chmura	.50
52	Robert Brooks	.50
53	Peyton Manning	4.00
54	Marvin Harrison	.50
55	Jerome Pathon	.25
56	Mark Brunell	2.00
57	Fred Taylor	2.50
58	Jimmy Smith	.50
59	Keenan McCardell	.25
60	Tavian Banks	.50
61	Elvis Grbac	.25
62	Andre Rison	.50
63	Bam Morris	.25
64	Derrick Alexander	.25
65	Rashaan Shehee	.25
66	Karim Abdul	.75
67	Dan Marino	4.00
68	O.J. McDuffie	.50
69	John Avery	.50
70	Lamar Thomas	.25
71	Randall Cunningham	1.00
72	Robert Smith	.75
73	Cris Carter	1.00
74	Randy Moss	6.00
75	Jake Reed	.25
76	Leroy Hoard	.25
77	Drew Bledsoe	2.00
78	Terry Glenn	.75
79	Darick Holmes	.25
80	Ben Coates	.50
81	Tony Simmons	.50
82	Cam Cleeland	.50
83	Eddie Kennison	.25
84	Lamar Smith	.25
85	Gary Brown	.25
86	Kent Graham	.25
87	Ike Hilliard	.50
88	Tiki Barber	.50
89	Joe Jurevicius	.50
90	Curtis Martin	1.00
91	Vinny Testaverde	1.00
92	Keyshawn Johnson	1.00
93	Wayne Chrebet	1.00
94	Napoleon Kaufman	1.00
95	Tim Brown	.50
96	Rickey Dudley	.25
97	James Jett	.25
98	Charles Woodson	1.00
99	Duce Staley	.25
100	Charlie Garner	.25
101	Bobby Hoying	.25
102	Kordell Stewart	1.50
103	Jerome Bettis	1.00
104	Chris Fuamatu-Ma'afala	.25
105	Courtney Hawkins	.25
106	Ryan Leaf	1.50
107	Natrone Means	.75
108	Mikhael Ricks	.50
109	Junior Seau	.50
110	Steve Young	2.00
111	Garrison Hearst	1.00
112	Jerry Rice	2.50
113	Terrell Owens	1.00
114	J.J. Stokes	.50
115	Trent Green	1.00
116	Marshall Faulk	1.00
117	Greg Hill	.25
118	Robert Holcombe	.50
119	Isaac Bruce	.75
120	Amp Lee	.25
121	Jon Kitna	1.50
122	Ricky Watters	.50
123	Joey Galloway	.50
124	Ahman Green	.50
125	Trent Dilfer	.75
126	Warrick Dunn	1.50
127	Mike Alstott	1.00
128	Warren Sapp	.25
129	Reidel Anthony	.50
130	Jacquez Green	.50
131	Eric Zeier	.25
132	Eddie George	1.50
133	Steve McNair	.50
134	Yancey Thigpen	.50
135	Frank Wycheck	.25
136	Kevin Dyson	.50
137	Albert Connell	.25
138	Terry Allen	.50
139	Skip Hicks	.50
140	Michael Westbrook	.50
141	Tyrone Wheatley (Trading Places)	.25
142	Chris Calloway (Trading Places)	.25
	Charles Johnson (Trading Places)	.25
144	Brad Johnson (Trading Places)	.50
145	Kerry Collins (Trading Places)	.50
146	Scott Mitchell (Trading Places)	.25
147	Rich Gannon (Trading Places)	.25
148	Jeff George (Trading Places)	.25

149	Warren Moon (Trading Places)	.25
150	Jim Harbaugh (Trading Places)	.25
151	Randy Moss (Repeat Performers)	10.00
152	Peyton Manning (Repeat Performers)	8.00
153	Fred Taylor (Repeat Performers)	6.00
154	Charlie Batch (Repeat Performers)	3.00
155	Curtis Enis (Repeat Performers)	1.00
156	Ryan Leaf (Repeat Performers)	2.00
157	Tim Dwight (Repeat Performers)	2.00
158	Brian Griese (Repeat Performers)	3.00
159	Skip Hicks (Repeat Performers)	1.00
160	Charles Woodson (Repeat Performers)	2.00
161	Tim Couch	15.00
162	Ricky Williams	15.00
163	Donovan McNabb	12.00
164	Edgerrin James	25.00
165	Champ Bailey	6.00
166	Torry Holt	10.00
167	Chris Claiborne	4.00
168	David Boston	10.00
169	Akili Smith	10.00
170	Peerless Price	8.00
171	Troy Edwards	10.00
172	Rob Konrad	3.00
173	Kevin Johnson	10.00
174	D'Wayne Bates	3.00
175	Daunte Culpepper	20.00
176	Dameane Douglas	2.00
177	Amos Zereoue	6.00
178	Shaun King	12.00
179	Cade McNown	8.00
180	Brock Huard	5.00
181	Sedrick Irvin	5.00
182	Chris McAlister	4.00
183	Kevin Faulk	6.00
184	Andy Katzenmoyer	4.00
185	Joe Germaine	5.00
186	Craig Yeast	2.00
187	Joe Montgomery	3.00
188	Ebenezer Ekuban	3.00
189	Jermaine Fazande	2.00
190	Tai Streets	2.00
191	James Johnson	6.00
192	Mike Cloud	3.00
193	Karsten Bailey	2.00
194	Shawn Bryson	2.00
195	Jeff Paulk	2.00
196	Travis McGriff	3.00
197	Aaron Brooks	10.00
198	Jevon Kearse	7.00
199	Al Wilson	3.00
200	Anthony McFarland	2.00

1999 Playoff Prestige SSD Spectrum Blue Parallel

This is a 200-card parallel to the base and is the same except for the background color is in blue and the foil on the fronts are also in blue. Each card is sequentially numbered on the back to 500. There is also a Gold, Green, Purple and Red version that are also numbered to 500 and are only different by the colors on the fronts of the cards.

		MT
Complete Set (200):		600.00
Spectrum Blue Cards:		4x
Spectrum Blue Rookies:		1x
Production 500 Sets		

Prices and production are the same for Gold, Green, Purple and Red.

1999 Playoff Prestige SSD Alma Maters

Each of these horizontal cards picture two players that went to the same college and put them on a foil card. Singles were inserted 1:17 packs. A parallel Jumbo version was also produced and inserted as a box topper.

		MT
Complete Set (30):		185.00
Common Player:		4.00
Inserted 1:17		
Jumbos:		1x
One Per Box		
1	Priest Holmes, Ricky Williams	30.00
2	Tim Couch, Dermontti Dawson	30.00
3	Terrell Davis, Garrison Hearst	15.00
4	Troy Brown, Randy Moss	25.00
5	Barry Sanders, Thurman Thomas	25.00
6	Emmitt Smith, Fred Taylor	15.00
7	Doug Flutie, Bill Romanowski	8.00
8	Brett Favre, Michael Jackson	25.00
9	Charlie Batch, Ron Rice	4.00
10	Mark Brunell, Chris Chandler	8.00
11	Warrick Dunn, Deion Sanders	7.00
12	Cris Carter, Eddie George	7.00
13	Drew Bledsoe, Ryan Leaf	8.00
14	Corey Dillon, Napoleon Kaufman	4.00
15	Jerome Bettis, Tim Brown	4.00
16	Marshall Faulk, Darnay Scott	4.00
17	Tiki Barber, Herman Moore	4.00
18	Jamal Anderson, Chris Fuamatu-Ma'afala	4.00
19	Troy Aikman, Cade McNown	12.00
20	Brian Griese, Charles Woodson	8.00
21	Charles Johnson, Kordell Stewart	4.00
22	Kevin Faulk, Eddie Kennison	7.00
23	Donovan McNabb, Rob Moore	8.00
24	Steve McNair, John Thierry	6.00
25	Michael Irvin, Vinny Testaverde	4.00
26	Randall Cunningham, Keenan McCardell	4.00
27	Keyshawn Johnson, Junior Seau	6.00
28	Karim Abdul, Skip Hicks	4.00
29	Curtis Enis, O.J. McDuffie	4.00
30	Joey Galloway, Robert Smith	4.00

1999 Playoff Prestige SSD Checklist

Each NFL team has a card in this 31-card insert with a player from each team on the fronts of the foil singles. The backs have a small picture from each player on that team with their card number next to it. Singles were found 1:17 packs.

		MT
Complete Set (31):		200.00
Common Player:		2.50
Minor Stars:		5.00
Inserted 1:17		
1	Jake Plummer	12.00
2	Chris Chandler	2.50
3	Priest Holmes	6.00
4	Doug Flutie	8.00
5	Wesley Walls	2.50
6	Curtis Enis	5.00
7	Corey Dillon	5.00
8	Kevin Johnson	6.00
9	Troy Aikman	12.00
10	Terrell Davis	18.00
11	Barry Sanders	25.00
12	Antonio Freeman	5.00
13	Peyton Manning	18.00
14	Fred Taylor	12.00
15	Andre Rison	2.50
16	Dan Marino	18.00
17	Randy Moss	25.00
18	Kevin Faulk	8.00
19	Ricky Williams	25.00
20	Joe Montgomery	5.00
21	Vinny Testaverde	2.50
22	Tim Brown	5.00
23	Duce Staley	2.50
24	Jerome Bettis	5.00
25	Natrone Means	2.50
26	Terrell Owens	5.00
27	Joey Galloway	5.00
28	Isaac Bruce	5.00
29	Mike Alstott	5.00
30	Eddie George	6.00
31	Skip Hicks	5.00

1999 Playoff Prestige SSD Checklist Autographs

These cards are identical to the Checklist insert except for that each of these singles are autographed on the fronts. Each is sequentially numbered to 250.

		MT
Complete Set (31):		2000.
Common Player:		20.00
Minor Stars:		40.00
Production 250 Sets		
1	Jake Plummer	85.00
2	Chris Chandler	20.00
3	Priest Holmes	40.00
4	Doug Flutie	60.00
5	Wesley Walls	40.00
6	Curtis Enis	40.00
7	Corey Dillon	40.00
8	Kevin Johnson	40.00
9	Troy Aikman	120.00
10	Terrell Davis	150.00
11	Barry Sanders	250.00
12	Antonio Freeman	40.00
13	Peyton Manning	150.00
14	Fred Taylor	100.00
15	Andre Rison	20.00
16	Dan Marino	200.00
17	Randy Moss	250.00
18	Kevin Faulk	60.00
19	Ricky Williams	250.00
20	Joe Montgomery	40.00
21	Vinny Testaverde	40.00
22	Tim Brown	40.00
23	Duce Staley	40.00
24	Jerome Bettis	40.00
25	Natrone Means	20.00
26	Terrell Owens	50.00
27	Joey Galloway	50.00
28	Isaac Bruce	40.00
29	Mike Alstott	40.00
30	Eddie George	50.00
31	Skip Hicks	40.00

Top of column right:

28	Isaac Bruce	5.00
29	Mike Alstott	5.00
30	Eddie George	6.00
31	Skip Hicks	5.00

1999 Playoff Prestige SSD Draft Picks

This insert includes the top 30 players drafted in 1999. It pictures each player in their college uniform on a silver foil card. Singles were inserted 1:13 packs.

Each card in this 30-card set is printed on a silver-foiled card with a blue foil background. Singles were inserted 1:9 packs.

		MT
Complete Set (30):		135.00
Common Player:		2.00
Minor Stars:		4.00
Inserted 1:9		
1	Tim Couch	30.00
2	Ricky Williams	30.00
3	Donovan McNabb	10.00
4	Edgerrin James	15.00
5	Champ Bailey	5.00
6	Torry Holt	8.00
7	Chris Claiborne	4.00
8	David Boston	8.00
9	Akili Smith	10.00
10	Daunte Culpepper	10.00
11	Peerless Price	6.00
12	Troy Edwards	6.00
13	Rob Konrad	4.00
14	Kevin Johnson	8.00
15	D'Wayne Bates	4.00
16	Cecil Collins	8.00
17	Amos Zereoue	6.00
18	Shaun King	10.00
19	Cade McNown	10.00
20	Brock Huard	5.00
21	Sedrick Irvin	4.00
22	Chris McAlister	2.00
23	Kevin Faulk	8.00
24	Jevon Kearse	5.00
25	Joe Germaine	5.00
26	Andy Katzenmoyer	4.00
27	Joe Montgomery	4.00
28	Al Wilson	2.00

29	Jermaine Fazande	2.00
30	Ebenezer Ekuban	2.00

1999 Playoff Prestige SSD For the Record

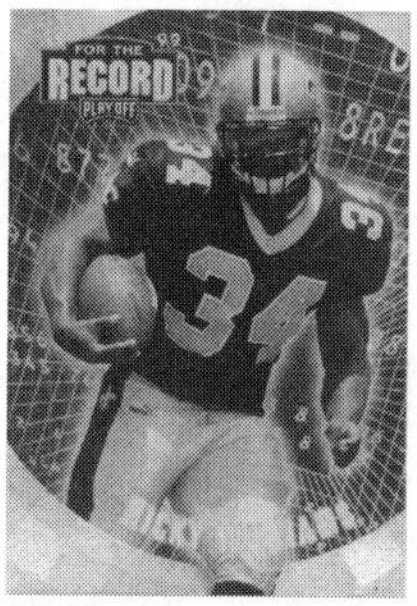

Each card in this set has a player that broke a record in 1998 or projections for a player in 1999. They were printed on a holographic foil board with the name in gold foil. Singles were found 1:161 packs.

		MT
Complete Set (30):		750.00
Common Player:		15.00
Inserted 1:161		
1	Mark Brunell	30.00
2	Jerry Rice	40.00
3	Peyton Manning	50.00
4	Barry Sanders	70.00
5	Deion Sanders	15.00
6	Eddie George	20.00
7	Corey Dillon	15.00
8	Jerome Bettis	15.00
9	Curtis Martin	15.00
10	Ricky Williams	70.00
11	Jake Plummer	40.00
12	Emmitt Smith	50.00
13	Dan Marino	50.00
14	Terrell Davis	50.00
15	Fred Taylor	40.00
16	Warrick Dunn	20.00
17	Steve McNair	15.00
18	Cris Carter	15.00
19	Mike Alstott	15.00
20	Steve Young	25.00
21	Charlie Batch	25.00
22	Tim Couch	70.00
23	Jamal Anderson	15.00
24	Randy Moss	70.00
25	Brett Favre	70.00
26	Drew Bledsoe	30.00
27	Troy Aikman	40.00
28	John Elway	50.00
29	Kordell Stewart	20.00
30	Keyshawn Johnson	15.00

1999 Playoff Prestige SSD Gridiron Heritage

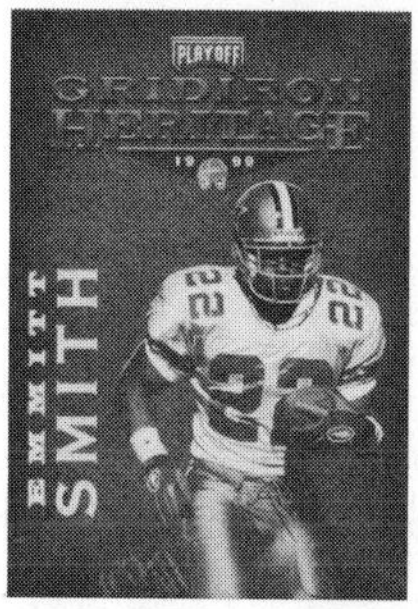

Each card in this 24-card set tracks the players career from high school to the NFL. Each is printed on actual leather and were inserted 1:33 packs.

		MT
Complete Set (24):		375.00
Common Player:		10.00
Inserted 1:33		
1	Randy Moss	40.00
2	Terrell Davis	30.00
3	Brett Favre	40.00
4	Barry Sanders	30.00
5	Peyton Manning	30.00
6	John Elway	30.00
7	Fred Taylor	20.00
8	Cris Carter	10.00
9	Jamal Anderson	10.00
10	Jake Plummer	20.00
11	Steve Young	15.00
12	Mark Brunell	15.00
13	Dan Marino	30.00
14	Emmitt Smith	30.00
15	Deion Sanders	10.00
16	Troy Aikman	20.00
17	Drew Bledsoe	15.00
18	Jerry Rice	20.00
19	Ricky Williams	40.00
20	Tim Couch	40.00
21	Jerome Bettis	10.00
22	Eddie George	12.00
23	Marshall Faulk	10.00
24	Terrell Owens	12.00

A card number in parentheses ( ) indicates the set is unnumbered.

1999 Playoff Prestige SSD Inside the Numbers

Each card in this 20-card set is printed on clear plastic and each is sequentially numbered to a different number. Overall odds for these cards were 1:49 packs.

		MT
Complete Set (20):		300.00
Common Player:		10.00
Inserted 1:49		
1	Tim Brown 1012	10.00
2	Charlie Batch 2178	10.00
3	Deion Sanders 226	15.00
4	Eddie George 1294	15.00
5	Keyshawn Johnson 1131	10.00
6	Jamal Anderson 1846	10.00
7	Steve Young 4170	12.00
8	Tim Couch 4275	30.00
9	Ricky Williams 6279	25.00
10	Jerry Rice 1157	25.00
11	Randy Moss 1313	50.00
12	Edgerrin James 1416	30.00
13	Peyton Manning 3739	20.00
14	John Elway 2803	25.00
15	Terrell Davis 2008	25.00
16	Fred Taylor 1213	20.00
17	Brett Favre 4212	25.00
18	Jake Plummer 3737	12.00
19	Mark Brunell 2601	12.00
20	Barry Sanders 1491	50.00

1999 Playoff Prestige SSD Barry Sanders

This is a 10-card st that celebrates Sanders ten years of pursuit for the rushing record. Singles were found 1:161 packs.

	MT
Complete Set (10):	750.00
Common Player:	75.00
Inserted 1:161	

2000 Playoff Absolute

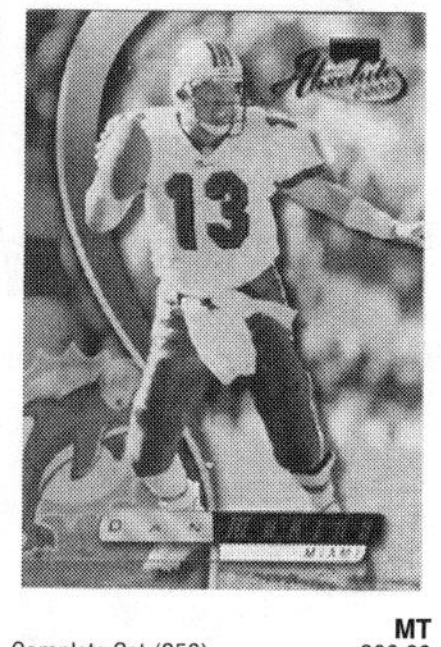

		MT
Complete Set (250):		200.00
Common Player:		.15
Minor Stars:		.30
Common Rookies:		1.50
Production 3,000 Sets		
Pack (6):		4.00
Wax Box (20):		60.00
1	Frank Sanders	.30
2	Rob Moore	.30
3	Jake Plummer	.50
4	David Boston	.50
5	Chris Chandler	.30
6	Tim Dwight	.50
7	Terance Mathis	.15
8	Jamal Anderson	.30
9	Priest Holmes	.50
10	Tony Banks	.30
11	Jermaine Lewis	.15
12	Qadry Ismail	.15
13	Brandon Stokley	.30
14	Shannon Sharpe	.30
15	Trent Dilfer	.30
16	Eric Moulds	.50
17	Doug Flutie	.75
18	Antowain Smith	.30
19	Jonathon Linton	.30
20	Peerless Price	.30
21	Rob Johnson	.30
22	Muhsin Muhammad	.30
23	Wesley Walls	.30
24	Tim Biakabutuka	.30
25	Steve Beuerlein	.30
26	Patrick Jeffers	.50
27	Natrone Means	.30
28	Curtis Enis	.30
29	Bobby Engram	.15
30	Marcus Robinson	.50
31	Marty Booker	.30
32	Cade McNown	.50
33	Darnay Scott	.30
34	Carl Pickens	.30
35	Corey Dillon	.30
36	Akili Smith	.50
37	Michael Basnight	.15
38	Karim Abdul	.30
39	Tim Couch	1.25
40	Kevin Johnson	.50
41	Darrin Chiaverini	.15
42	Errict Rhett	.30
43	Emmitt Smith	1.75
44	Michael Irvin	.30
45	Raghib Ismail	.15
46	Troy Aikman	1.50
47	Jason Tucker	.30
48	Randall Cunningham	.30
49	Joey Galloway	.50
50	Ed McCaffrey	.30
51	Rod Smith	.30
52	Brian Griese	.75
53	John Elway	2.00
54	Terrell Davis	1.75
55	Olandis Gary	.50
56	Johnnie Morton	.30
57	Charlie Batch	.50
58	Barry Sanders	2.00
59	Germane Crowell	.50
60	Herman Moore	.50
61	James Stewart	.30
62	Corey Bradford	.15
63	Dorsey Levens	.50
64	Antonio Freeman	.50
65	Brett Favre	2.50
66	Bill Schroeder	.15
67	Marvin Harrison	.50
68	Peyton Manning	1.75
69	Terrence Wilkins	.30
70	Edgerrin James	2.00
71	Keenan McCardell	.30
72	Mark Brunell	1.00
73	Fred Taylor	1.00
74	Jimmy Smith	.50
75	Elvis Grbac	.30
76	Tony Gonzalez	.30
77	Donnell Bennett	.15
78	Warren Moon	.30
79	Kimble Anders	.15
80	Dan Marino	2.00
81	O.J. McDuffie	.30
82	Tony Martin	.15
83	James Johnson	.30
84	Thurman Thomas	.30
85	Randy Moss	2.00
86	Cris Carter	.50
87	Robert Smith	.50
88	Daunte Culpepper	1.25
89	Terry Glenn	.50
90	Drew Bledsoe	1.00
91	Kevin Faulk	.30
92	Ricky Williams	1.50
93	Jeff Blake	.30
94	Jake Reed	.30
95	Amani Toomer	.30
96	Kerry Collins	.30
97	Tiki Barber	.30
98	Ike Hilliard	.30
99	Curtis Martin	.50
100	Vinny Testaverde	.30
101	Wayne Chrebet	.50
102	Ray Lucas	.30
103	Tyrone Wheatley	.30
104	Napoleon Kaufman	.30
105	Tim Brown	.50
106	Rich Gannon	.30
107	Duce Staley	.50
108	Donovan McNabb	1.00
109	Kordell Stewart	.50
110	Jerome Bettis	.50
111	Troy Edwards	.30
112	Junior Seau	.30
113	Jim Harbaugh	.30
114	Ryan Leaf	.50
115	Jermaine Fazande	.30
116	Curtis Conway	.30
117	Terrell Owens	.50
118	Charlie Garner	.30
119	Jerry Rice	1.50
120	Steve Young	1.00
121	Jeff Garcia	.50
122	Derrick Mayes	.50
123	Ricky Watters	.50
124	Jon Kitna	.50
125	Sean Dawkins	.15
126	Az-Zahir Hakim	.30
127	Isaac Bruce	.50
128	Marshall Faulk	.60
129	Trent Green	.50
130	Kurt Warner	2.50
131	Torry Holt	.50
132	Jacquez Green	.30
133	Warren Sapp	.30
134	Mike Alstott	.50
135	Warrick Dunn	.50
136	Shaun King	1.00
137	Keyshawn Johnson	.50
138	Eddie George	.60
139	Yancey Thigpen	.30
140	Steve McNair	.50
141	Kevin Dyson	.30
142	Frank Wycheck	.15
143	Jevon Kearse	.50
144	Stephen Davis	.50
145	Brad Johnson	.50
146	Michael Westbrook	.30
147	Albert Connell	.30
148	Bruce Smith	.30
149	Jeff George	.30
150	Deion Sanders	.50
151	Peter Warrick	12.00
152	Courtney Brown	4.00
153	Plaxico Burress	7.00
154	Corey Simon	4.00
155	Thomas Jones	6.00
156	Travis Taylor	5.00
157	Shaun Alexander	8.00
158	Chris Redman	6.00
159	Chad Pennington	10.00
160	Jamal Lewis	15.00
161	Brian Urlacher	7.00
162	Bubba Franks	4.00
163	Dez White	2.00
164	Ahmed Plummer	1.50
165	Ron Dayne	12.00
166	Shaun Ellis	1.50
167	Sylvester Morris	6.00
168	Deltha O'Neal	1.50
169	R. Jay Soward	2.50
170	Sherrod Gideon	1.50
171	John Abraham	1.50
172	Travis Prentice	5.00
173	Darrell Jackson	4.00
174	Giovanni Carmazzi	4.00
175	Anthony Lucas	1.50
176	Danny Farmer	2.50
177	Dennis Northcutt	3.00
178	Troy Walters	2.00
179	Laveranues Coles	4.00
180	Kwame Cavil	1.50
181	Tee Martin	4.00
182	J.R. Redmond	3.00
183	Tim Rattay	4.00
184	Jerry Porter	2.50
185	Sebastian Janikowski	2.50
186	Michael Wiley	2.50
187	Reuben Droughns	2.00
188	Trung Canidate	2.00
189	Shyrone Stith	2.00
190	Ian Gold	1.50
191	Hank Poteat	1.50
192	Darren Howard	1.50
193	Rob Morris	1.50
194	Marc Bulger	1.50
195	Tom Brady	8.00
196	Doug Johnson	3.00
197	Todd Husak	2.00
198	Gari Scott	1.50
199	Erron Kinney	1.50
200	Nate Webster	1.50
201	Anthony Becht	1.50
202	Sammy Morris	3.00
203	Rondell Mealey	2.00
204	Doug Chapman	1.50
205	Rogers Beckett	1.50
206	Ron Dugans	2.50
207	Deon Dyer	1.50
208	Marcus Knight	1.50
209	Thomas Hamner	1.50
210	Joe Hamilton	3.00
211	Todd Pinkston	3.00
212	Chris Cole	1.50
213	Ron Dixon	3.00
214	JaJuan Dawson	3.00
215	Terrelle Smith	1.50
216	Curtis Keaton	2.00
217	Keith Bulluck	1.50
218	John Engelberger	1.50
219	Raynoch Thompson	1.50
220	Cornelius Griffin	1.50
221	William Bartee	1.50
222	Fred Robbins	1.50
223	Dwayne Goodrich	1.50
224	Deon Grant	1.50
225	Jacoby Shepherd	1.50
226	Ben Kelly	1.50
227	Corey Moore	1.50
228	Aaron Shea	1.50
229	Trevor Gaylor	2.50
230	Frank Moreau	2.50
231	Avion Black	1.50
232	Paul Smith	1.50
233	Dante Hall	1.50
234	Muneer Moore	1.50
235	James Whalen	1.50
236	Chad Morton	2.50
237	Frank Murphy	1.50
238	Mareno Philyaw	1.50
239	James Williams	1.50
240	Mike Anderson	15.00
241	Jarious Jackson	2.50
242	Demario Brown	1.50
243	Chris Coleman	1.50
244	Rashard Anderson	1.50
245	John Jones	1.50
246	Erik Flowers	1.50
247	JaJuan Seider	1.50
248	Leon Murray	1.50
249	Bashir Yamini	1.50
250	Na'il Diggs	1.50

2000 Playoff Absolute Coaches Honors Parallel

	MT
Complete Set (250):	1000.
Coaches Honors Cards:	5x-10x
Coaches Honors Rookies:	2x
Production 300 Sets	

2000 Playoff Absolute Players Honors Parallel

	MT
Player Honors Cards:	30x-60x
Player Honors Rookies:	6x-12x
Production 10 Sets	

2000 Playoff Absolute Boss Hoggs

		MT
Complete Set (20):		600.00
Common Player:		12.00
Minor Stars:		20.00
Inserted 1:298		
Production 200 Sets		
1	Eric Moulds	20.00
2	Cade McNown	20.00
3	Tim Couch	35.00
4	Terrell Davis	45.00
5	Barry Sanders	75.00
6	Peyton Manning	75.00
7	Edgerrin James	65.00
8	Marvin Harrison	24.00
9	Mark Brunell	30.00
10	Fred Taylor	30.00
11	Dan Marino	85.00
12	Cris Carter	24.00
13	Drew Bledsoe	30.00
14	Ricky Williams	40.00
15	Curtis Martin	24.00
16	Kurt Warner	85.00
17	Isaac Bruce	24.00
18	Eddie George	30.00
19	Steve McNair	24.00
20	Brad Johnson	12.00

2000 Playoff Absolute Canton Absolutes

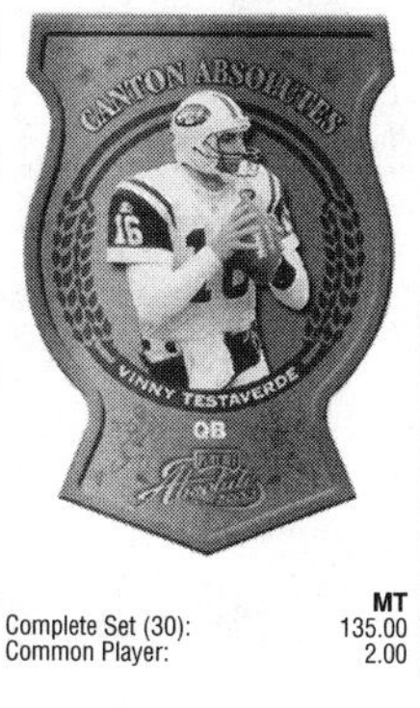

	MT
Complete Set (30):	135.00
Common Player:	2.00
Minor Stars:	4.00
Inserted 1:39	

1	Tim Couch	6.00
2	Emmitt Smith	10.00
3	Troy Aikman	8.00
4	John Elway	12.00
5	Terrell Davis	10.00
6	Barry Sanders	12.00
7	Brett Favre	15.00
8	Peyton Manning	12.00
9	Edgerrin James	12.00
10	Mark Brunell	6.00
11	Dan Marino	12.00
12	Randy Moss	12.00
13	Drew Bledsoe	6.00
14	Jerry Rice	8.00
15	Steve Young	5.00
16	Kurt Warner	15.00
17	Eddie George	5.00
18	Deion Sanders	4.00
19	Antonio Freeman	4.00
20	Warren Moon	2.00
21	Cris Carter	4.00
22	Randall Cunningham	4.00
23	Curtis Martin	4.00
24	Tim Brown	4.00
25	Marshall Faulk	5.00
26	Michael Irvin	4.00
27	Thurman Thomas	4.00
28	Vinny Testaverde	2.00
29	Ricky Watters	2.00
30	Jeff George	2.00

2000 Playoff Absolute Extreme Team

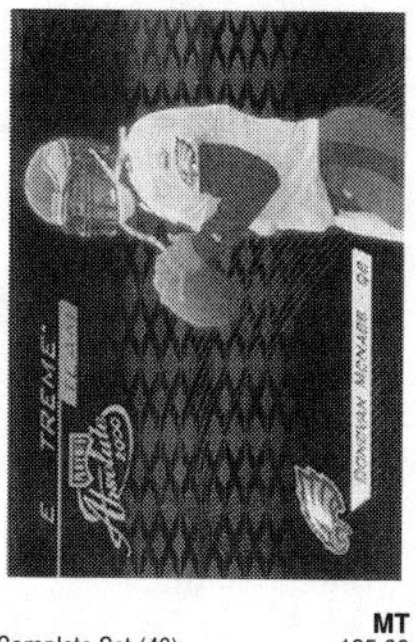

		MT
Complete Set (40):		125.00
Common Player:		1.50
Minor Stars:		3.00
Inserted 1:18		
1	Jake Plummer	3.00
2	Tim Couch	5.00
3	Terrell Davis	8.00
4	Brett Favre	12.00
5	Peyton Manning	10.00
6	Edgerrin James	10.00
7	Mark Brunell	5.00
8	Fred Taylor	5.00
9	Randy Moss	12.00
10	Drew Bledsoe	5.00
11	Ricky Williams	6.00
12	Kurt Warner	12.00
13	Eddie George	3.50
14	Cade McNown	3.00
15	Kevin Johnson	3.00
16	Joey Galloway	3.00
17	Olandis Gary	3.00
18	Dorsey Levens	3.00
19	Marvin Harrison	3.00
20	Daunte Culpepper	5.00
21	Duce Staley	3.00
22	Donovan McNabb	4.00
23	Marshall Faulk	3.50
24	Shaun King	3.00
25	Keyshawn Johnson	3.00
26	Steve McNair	3.00
27	Stephen Davis	3.00
28	Brad Johnson	1.50
29	Akili Smith	3.00
30	Brian Griese	3.00
31	Emmitt Smith	8.00
32	Isaac Bruce	3.00
33	Peter Warrick	10.00
34	Jamal Lewis	15.00
35	Thomas Jones	5.00
36	Plaxico Burress	6.00
37	Travis Taylor	4.00
38	Ron Dayne	10.00
39	Chad Pennington	10.00
40	Shaun Alexander	8.00

2000 Playoff Absolute Ground Hoggs

		MT
Common Player:		25.00
Inserted 1:188		
Production 135 Sets		
Autographs:		3x
#1,9,17,22 & 28 signed their first 25 cards.		
1	Jake Plummer	25.00
2	Muhsin Muhammad 75	25.00
3	Emmitt Smith	85.00
4	Ricky Watters	25.00
5	Terrell Davis	75.00
6	Brett Favre	100.00
7	Dorsey Levens	25.00
8	Antonio Freeman	25.00
9	Edgerrin James	85.00
10	Marvin Harrison	25.00
11	Mark Brunell	50.00
12	Fred Taylor	50.00
13	Jimmy Smith	25.00
14	James Johnson	25.00
15	Dan Marino	125.00
16	Jon Kitna	25.00
17	Ricky Williams	60.00
18	Curtis Martin	35.00
19	Wayne Chrebet	25.00
20	Steve Young	60.00
21	Junior Seau	25.00
22	Kurt Warner	125.00
23	Marshall Faulk	45.00
24	Eddie George	45.00
25	Steve McNair	25.00
26	Joey Galloway	25.00
27	Jerry Rice	85.00
28	Jevon Kearse	30.00
29	Stephen Davis	25.00
30	Albert Connell	25.00

2000 Playoff Absolute Hogg Heaven Points

		MT
Common Player:		10.00
500 points redeemable for autographed fb		
1	Cade McNown	10.00
2	Jim Harbaugh	10.00
3	Brad Johnson	10.00
4	Steve Young	20.00
5	Jake Plummer	15.00
6	Chris Chandler	10.00
7	Tony Banks	10.00
8	Bubby Brister	10.00
9	Kordell Stewart	15.00
10	Warren Moon	15.00
11	Donovan McNabb	20.00
12	Jim Kelly	15.00
13	Peyton Manning	35.00
14	Hogg Heaven	10.00

2000 Playoff Absolute Leather

		MT
Common Player 350:		12.00
Common Player 175:		15.00
Laces Numbered to 20:		3x
Laces Numbered to 10:		4x
TA8	Troy Aikman 175	50.00
MA40	Mike Alstott 350	15.00
RA85	Reidel Anthony 175	15.00
MB35	Michael Basnight 175	15.00
JB36	Jerome Bettis 350	15.00
SB7	Steve Beuerlein 350	12.00
TB21	Tim Biakabutuka 350	12.00
JB18	Jeff Blake 175	15.00
DB11	Drew Bledsoe 350	30.00
DB89	David Boston 350	15.00
TB81	Tim Brown 350	15.00
IB80	Isaac Bruce 350	20.00
MB8A	Mark Brunell 350	30.00
MB8B	Mark Brunell 175	50.00
CC80	Cris Carter 175	20.00
DC84	Darren Chiaverini 175	15.00
WC80	Wayne Chrebet 175	20.00
BC85	Ben Coates 175	15.00
AC83	Albert Connell 175	15.00
CC80	Curtis Conway 175	15.00
TC2	Tim Couch 350	30.00
RC7	Randall Cunningham 175	15.00
SD48	Stephen Davis 175	20.00
TD30	Terrell Davis 175	60.00
TD7	Trent Dilfer 175	15.00
CD28	Corey Dillon 350	20.00
RD83	Rickey Dudley 175	15.00
WD28	Warrick Dunn 350	15.00
TD83	Tim Dwight 350	15.00
KD87	Kevin Dyson 175	15.00
TE81	Troy Edwards 350	15.00
JE7	John Elway 175	100.00
BE81	Bobby Engram 175	15.00
CE44	Curtis Enis 350	12.00
MF28A	Marshall Faulk 175	30.00
MF28B	Marshall Faulk 175	30.00
BF4A	Brett Favre 350	60.00
BF4B	Brett Favre 175	85.00
AF86A	Antonio Freeman 350	15.00
AF86B	Antonio Freeman 175	20.00
OG86	Oronde Gadsden 175	15.00
RG12	Rich Gannon 175	15.00
JG5	Jeff Garcia 350	25.00
CG25	Charlie Garner 350	12.00
EG27A	Eddie George 350	25.00
EG27B	Eddie George 175	40.00
JG87	Jami Germaine 175	15.00
TG88	Terry Glenn 175	20.00
JH4	Jim Harbaugh 175	15.00
MH88	Marvin Harrison 175	25.00
PH33	Priest Holmes 175	20.00
TH88	Torry Holt 175	20.00
DH11	Damon Huard 175	20.00
QI87	Qadry Ismail 175	15.00
RI81	Raghib Ismail 175	15.00
EJ32	Edgerrin James 175	65.00
BJ14	Brad Johnson 175	20.00
JJ32	James Johnson 350	12.00
KJ85	Kevin Johnson 350	15.00
KJ19	Keyshawn Johnson 175	20.00
RJ11	Rob Johnson 175	20.00
NK26	Napoleon Kaufman 175	20.00
JK90A	Jevon Kearse 350	15.00
JK90B	Jevon Kearse 175	20.00
LK99	LaVonne Kirkland 175	15.00
DL25A	Dorsey Levens 350	15.00
DL25B	Dorsey Levens 175	20.00
JL84	Jermaine Lewis 175	15.00
SM29	Sam Madison 175	15.00
PM18	Peyton Manning 350	60.00
DM13	Dan Marino 350	75.00
CM28	Curtis Martin 175	20.00
TM80	Tony Martin 175	15.00
TM81	Terance Mathis 175	15.00
BM74	Bruce Matthews 175	15.00
DM87	Derrick Mayes 175	15.00
EM87	Ed McCaffrey 175	20.00
KM87	Keenan McCardell 350	15.00
OM81	O.J. McDuffie 175	15.00
DM5	Donovan McNabb 350	25.00
SM9A	Steve McNair 350	20.00
SM9B	Steve McNair 175	25.00
NM20	Natrone Means 175	15.00
HM84	Herman Moore 175	20.00
RM85	Rob Moore 350	12.00
JM87	Johnnie Morton 175	15.00
RM84	Randy Moss 175	85.00
EM80	Eric Moulds 350	15.00
MM87	Muhsin Muhammad 350	12.00
NO14	Neil O'Donnell 175	15.00
TO81A	Terrell Owens 175	25.00
TO81B	Terrell Owens 175	25.00
CP81	Carl Pickens 175	15.00
JP16	Jake Plummer 350	20.00
PP81	Peerless Price 175	20.00
ER23	Errict Rhett 175	15.00
JR80A	Jerry Rice 350	40.00
JR80B	Jerry Rice 175	65.00

BS20 Barry Sanders 350 60.00
DS21 Deion Sanders 175 20.00
FS81 Frank Sanders 350 15.00
WS99 Warren Sapp 350 15.00
DS86 Darnay Scott 175 15.00
JS55 Junior Seau 175 20.00
AS11 Akili Smith 350 20.00
AS23 Antowain Smith 350 15.00
BS78 Bruce Smith 350 15.00
ES22 Emmitt Smith 175 70.00
JS82 Jimmy Smith 350 15.00
RS26 Robert Smith 175 20.00
RS80 Rod Smith 175 20.00
DS22 Duce Staley 350 15.00
JS33 James Stewart 350 15.00
KS10 Kordell Stewart 350 20.00
JS83 J.J. Stokes 175 20.00
FT28A Fred Taylor 350 25.00
FT28B Fred Taylor 175 40.00
VT16 Vinny Testaverde 175 20.00
YT82 Yancey Thigpen 175 20.00
TT34 Thurman Thomas 350 15.00
ZT54 Zach Thomas 175 20.00
HW86 Hines Ward 175 20.00
KW13A Kurt Warner 350 70.00
KW13B Kurt Warner 175 85.00
MW82 Michael Westbrook 175 20.00
TW47 Tyrone Wheatley 175 20.00
RW92 Reggie White 350 15.00
RW34 Ricky Williams 350 45.00
FW89 Frank Wycheck 175 15.00
SY8 Steve Young 350 30.00

2000 Playoff Absolute Rookie Reflex

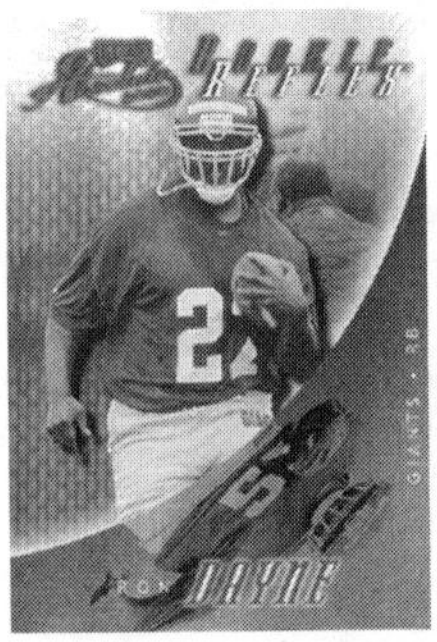

MT
Complete Set (30): 50.00
Common Player: 1.25
Minor Stars: 2.50
Inserted 1:10
Gold Cards: 3x-6x
Production 100 Sets
1 Peter Warrick 8.00
2 Jamal Lewis 12.00
3 Thomas Jones 5.00
4 Plaxico Burress 5.00
5 Travis Taylor 3.00
6 Ron Dayne 8.00
7 Bubba Franks 2.50
8 Chad Pennington 7.00
9 Shaun Alexander 6.00
10 Sylvester Morris 5.00
11 R. Jay Soward 2.50
12 Trung Canidate 1.25
13 Dennis Northcutt 2.50
14 Todd Pinkston 2.50
15 Jerry Porter 1.25
16 Travis Prentice 3.50
17 Giovanni Carmazzi 2.50
18 Ron Dugans 1.25
19 Erron Kinney 1.25
20 Dez White 1.25
21 Chris Cole 1.25
22 Doug Chapman 1.25
23 Chris Redman 4.00
24 J.R. Redmond 3.00
25 Laveranues Coles 3.00
26 JaJuan Dawson 2.50
27 Darrell Jackson 3.00
28 Reuben Droughns 1.25
29 Curtis Keaton 1.25
30 Gari Scott 1.25

2000 Playoff Absolute Tag Team Quads

MT
Complete Set (31): 300.00
Common Player: 10.00
Inserted 1:79
1 Jake Plummer, David Boston, Thomas Jones, Frank Sanders 12.00
2 Jamal Anderson, Tim Dwight, Chris Chandler, Terance Mathis 10.00
3 Tony Banks, Travis Taylor, Shannon Sharpe, Jamal Lewis 30.00
4 Rob Johnson, Eric Moulds, Antowain Smith, Peerless Price 10.00
5 Steve Beuerlein, Tim Biakabutuka, Patrick Jeffers, Muhsin Muhammad 10.00
6 Curtis Enis, Cade McNown, Marcus Robinson, Dez White 12.00
7 Corey Dillon, Akili Smith, Peter Warrick, Ron Dugans 25.00
8 Tim Couch, Errict Rhett, Kevin Johnson, Courtney Brown 15.00
9 Raghib Ismail, Emmitt Smith, Troy Aikman, Joey Galloway 25.00
10 Terrell Davis, Ed McCaffrey, Olandis Gary, Brian Griese 20.00
11 James Stewart, Charlie Batch, Herman Moore, Germane Crowell 10.00
12 Brett Favre, Bubba Franks, Dorsey Levens, Antonio Freeman 25.00
13 Peyton Manning, Marvin Harrison, Edgerrin James, Terrence Wilkins 30.00
14 Keenan McCardell, Mark Brunell, Jimmy Smith, Fred Taylor 15.00
15 Elvis Grbac, Sylvester Morris, Tony Gonzalez, Derrick Alexander 12.00
16 James Johnson, O.J. McDuffie, Tony Martin, Damon Huard 10.00
17 Randy Moss, Robert Smith, Cris Carter, Daunte Culpepper 30.00
18 Drew Bledsoe, Kevin Faulk, J.R. Redmond, Terry Glenn 15.00
19 Sherrod Gideon, Ricky Williams, Jeff Blake, Jake Reed 12.00
20 Kerry Collins, Amani Toomer, Ron Dayne, Ike Hilliard 20.00
21 Curtis Martin, Wayne Chrebet, Chad Pennington, Vinny Testaverde 15.00
22 Tim Brown, Napoleon Kaufman, Rich Gannon, Tyrone Wheatley 10.00
23 Donovan McNabb, Corey Simon, Todd Pinkston, Duce Staley 12.00
24 Plaxico Burress, Troy Edwards, Kordell Stewart, Jerome Bettis 12.00
25 Jim Harbaugh, Junior Seau, Curtis Conway, Jermaine Fazande 10.00
26 Charlie Garner, Jerry Rice, Terrell Owens, Steve Young 15.00
27 Derrick Mayes, Shaun Alexander, Ricky Watters, Jon Kitna 12.00
28 Kurt Warner, Torry Holt, Isaac Bruce, Marshall Faulk 30.00
29 Warrick Dunn, Keyshawn Johnson, Shaun King, Mike Alstott 12.00
30 Kevin Dyson, Eddie George, Steve McNair, Jevon Kearse 12.00
31 Albert Connell, Brad Johnson, Michael Westbrook, Stephen Davis 10.00

2000 Playoff Absolute Tools of the Trade

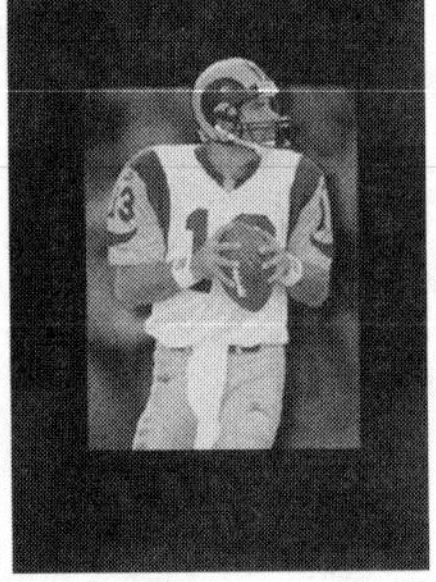

MT
Complete Set (60): 200.00
Common Player (#1-20): 2.00
Production 2,000 Sets
Die-Cut Cards (#1-20): 6x-12x
Production 25 Sets
Common Player (#21-40): 2.50
Production 1,500 Sets
Die-Cut Cards (#21-40): 4x-8x
Production 50 Sets
Common Player (#41-60): 3.00
Production 1,000 Sets
Die-Cut Cards (#41-60): 3x
Production 100 Sets
1 Jake Plummer 2.50
2 Tim Couch 4.00
3 Troy Aikman 7.00
4 John Elway 10.00
5 Charlie Batch 2.00
6 Brett Favre 12.00
7 Peyton Manning 10.00
8 Mark Brunell 4.00
9 Dan Marino 10.00
10 Drew Bledsoe 4.00
11 Steve Young 4.00
12 Kurt Warner 12.00
13 Cade McNown 2.50
14 Daunte Culpepper 4.00
15 Donovan McNabb 3.00
16 Jon Kitna 2.00
17 Steve McNair 2.00
18 Brad Johnson 2.00
19 Akili Smith 2.00
20 Chad Pennington 8.00
21 Emmitt Smith 10.00
22 Terrell Davis 10.00
23 Barry Sanders 12.00
24 Edgerrin James 10.00
25 Fred Taylor 4.00
26 Ricky Williams 6.00
27 Eddie George 4.00
28 Jamal Anderson 2.50
29 Corey Dillon 2.50
30 Dorsey Levens 2.50
31 Robert Smith 2.50
32 Curtis Martin 2.50
33 Jerome Bettis 2.50
34 Marshall Faulk 3.00
35 Stephen Davis 2.50
36 Jamal Lewis 25.00
37 Thomas Jones 6.00
38 Ron Dayne 15.00
39 Shaun Alexander 10.00
40 Trung Canidate 2.50
41 Randy Moss 15.00
42 Jerry Rice 10.00
43 Eric Moulds 4.00
44 Kevin Johnson 3.00
45 Joey Galloway 4.00
46 Antonio Freeman 4.00
47 Marvin Harrison 4.00
48 Cris Carter 4.00
49 Tim Brown 3.00
50 Terrell Owens 4.00
51 Keyshawn Johnson 4.00
52 Muhsin Muhammad 3.00
53 Patrick Jeffers 4.00
54 Marcus Robinson 4.00
55 Jimmy Smith 4.00
56 Amani Toomer 3.00
57 Isaac Bruce 4.00
58 Peter Warrick 15.00
59 Plaxico Burress 10.00
60 Travis Taylor 6.00

2000 Playoff Contenders

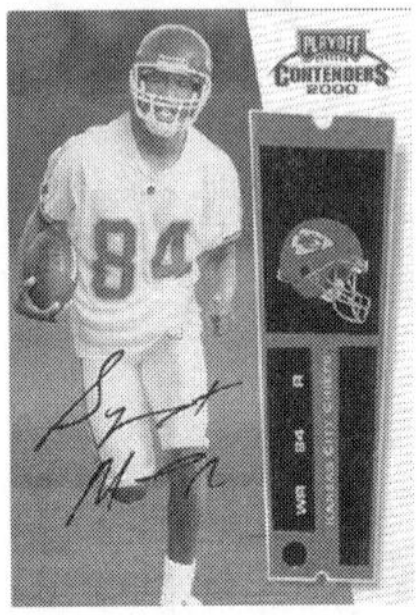

MT
Complete Set (200): 2250.
Common Player: .25
Minor Stars: .50
Common Rookie: 8.00
Common Europe Ticket: 5.00
Common Playoff Ticket: 20.00
Pack (5): 12.00
Wax Box (12): 120.00
1 David Boston .75
2 Jake Plummer .75
3 Chris Chandler .50
4 Jamal Anderson .75
5 Tim Dwight .75
6 Qadry Ismail .25
7 Tony Banks .50
8 Lamar Smith .50
9 Doug Flutie 1.00
10 Eric Moulds .75
11 Peerless Price .75
12 Rob Johnson .50
13 Muhsin Muhammad .50
14 Reggie White .50
15 Steve Beuerlein .50
16 Cade McNown .75
17 Derrick Alexander .25
18 Marcus Robinson .75
19 Akili Smith .75
20 Corey Dillon .75
21 Kevin Johnson .75
22 Tim Couch 1.50
23 Emmitt Smith 2.00
24 Joey Galloway .75
25 Raghib Ismail .25
26 Troy Aikman 1.50
27 Brian Griese 1.00
28 Ed McCaffrey .50
29 John Elway 2.00
30 Olandis Gary .75
31 Rod Smith .75
32 Terrell Davis 2.00
33 Charlie Batch .75
34 Germane Crowell .75
35 James Stewart .50
36 Barry Sanders 2.00
37 Antonio Freeman .75
38 Brett Favre 3.00
39 Dorsey Levens .75
40 Edgerrin James 2.50
41 Marvin Harrison .75
42 Peyton Manning 2.50
43 Fred Taylor 1.25
44 Jimmy Smith .75
45 Mark Brunell 1.25
46 Elvis Grbac .50
47 Tony Gonzalez .50
48 Dan Marino 2.00
49 Joe Horn .50
50 Jay Fiedler .50
51 Thurman Thomas .50
52 Cris Carter .75
53 Daunte Culpepper 1.50
54 Randy Moss 2.50
55 Robert Smith .75
56 Drew Bledsoe 1.25
57 Terry Glenn .75
58 Ricky Williams 1.75
59 Amani Toomer .50
60 Kerry Collins .50
61 Curtis Martin .75
62 Vinny Testaverde .50
63 Wayne Chrebet .75
64 Rich Gannon .50
65 Tim Brown .75
66 Tyrone Wheatley .50
67 Donovan McNabb 1.25
68 Duce Staley .75
69 Jerome Bettis .75
70 Jermaine Fazande .50
71 Junior Seau .50
72 Donald Hayes .50
73 Charlie Garner .50
74 Jeff Garcia .75
75 Jerry Rice 1.50
76 Steve Young 1.25
77 Terrell Owens .75
78 Tiki Barber .50
79 Tim Biakabutuka .50
80 Ricky Watters .50
81 Isaac Bruce .75
82 Kurt Warner 3.00
83 Marshall Faulk 1.00
84 Torry Holt .75
85 Keyshawn Johnson .75
86 Mike Alstott .75
87 Shaun King .75
88 Warren Sapp .50
89 Warrick Dunn .75
90 Eddie George 1.00
91 Jevon Kearse .75
92 Steve McNair .75
93 Carl Pickens .50
94 Albert Connell .50
95 Brad Johnson .50
96 Bruce Smith .50
97 Deion Sanders .75
98 Jeff George .50
99 Michael Westbrook .50
100 Stephen Davis .75
101 *Courtney Brown SP* 135.00
102 *Corey Simon* 20.00
103 *Brian Urlacher* 75.00
104 *Deon Grant* 8.00
105 *Peter Warrick* 75.00
106 *Jamal Lewis* 100.00
107 *Thomas Jones* 45.00
108 *Plaxico Burress* 45.00
109 *Travis Taylor* 30.00
110 *Ron Dayne* 75.00
111 *Bubba Franks* 35.00
112 *Chad Pennington* 100.00
113 *Shaun Alexander* 85.00
114 *Sylvester Morris* 45.00
115 *Mike Anderson* 50.00
116 *R. Jay Soward* 20.00
117 *Trung Canidate* 15.00
118 *Dennis Northcutt* 20.00
119 *Todd Pinkston* 20.00
120 *Jerry Porter* 20.00
121 *Travis Prentice* 30.00
122 *Giovanni Carmazzi* 25.00
123 *Ron Dugans* 15.00
124 *Dez White* 15.00
125 *Chris Cole* 12.00
126 *Ron Dixon* 20.00
127 *Chris Redman* 50.00
128 *J.R. Redmond* 25.00
129 *Laveranues Coles* 25.00
130 *JaJuan Dawson* 20.00
131 *Darrell Jackson* 25.00
132 *Reuben Droughns* 15.00
133 *Doug Chapman* 20.00
134 *Curtis Keaton* 12.00
135 *Gari Scott* 12.00
136 *Danny Farmer* 15.00
137 *Trevor Gaylor* 12.00
138 *Avion Black* 8.00
139 *Michael Wiley* 15.00
140 *Sammy Morris* 25.00
141 *Tee Martin* 25.00
142 *Troy Walters* 15.00
143 *Marc Bulger* 15.00
144 *Tom Brady* 60.00
145 *Todd Husak* 20.00
146 *Tim Rattay* 25.00
147 *Jarious Jackson* 35.00
148 *Joe Hamilton* 20.00
149 *Shyrone Stith* 12.00
150 *Kwame Cavil* 10.00
151 *Antonio Banks* 5.00
152 *Jonathan Brown* 5.00
153 *Ontiwaun Carter* 5.00
154 *Jeremaine Copeland* 5.00
155 *Ralph Dawkins* 5.00
156 *Marques Douglas* 5.00
157 *Kevin Drake* 5.00
158 *Damon Dunn* 5.00
159 *Todd Floyd* 5.00
160 *Tony Graziani* 8.00
161 *Derrick Ham* 5.00
162 *Duane Hawthorne* 5.00
163 *Alonzo Johnson* 5.00
164 *Mark Kacmarynski* 5.00
165 *Eric Kresser* 5.00
166 *Jim Kubiak* 5.00
167 *Blaine McElmurry* 5.00
168 *Scott Milanovich* 8.00
169 *Norman Miller* 5.00
170 *Sean Morey* 5.00
171 *Jeff Ogden* 8.00
172 *Pepe Pearson* 8.00
173 *Ron Powlus* 25.00
174 *Jason Shelley* 5.00
175 *Ben Snell* 5.00
176 *Aaron Stecker* 8.00
177 *L.C. Stevens* 5.00
178 *Mike Sutton* 5.00
179 *Damian Vaughn* 5.00
180 *Ted White* 5.00
181 *Marcus Crandell* 5.00
182 *Darryl Daniel* 5.00
183 *Jessie Haynes* 5.00
184 *Matt Lytle* 5.00
185 *Deon Mitchell* 5.00
186 *Kendrick Nord* 5.00
187 *Ronnie Powell* 5.00
188 *Selucio Sanford* 5.00
189 *Corey Thomas* 5.00
190 *Vershan Jackson* 5.00
191 Jake Plummer PT 20.00
192 Jim Kelly PT 30.00
193 Bernie Kosar PT 30.00
194 Marvin Harrison PT 25.00
195 Fred Taylor PT 30.00
196 Kerry Collins PT 25.00
197 Kurt Warner PT 85.00
198 Jevon Kearse PT 25.00
199 Brad Johnson PT 20.00
200 Jeff George PT 20.00

Post-1980 cards in Near Mint condition will generally sell for about 75% of the quoted Mint value. Excellent-condition cards bring no more than 40%.

2000 Playoff Contenders Championship Ticket Parallel

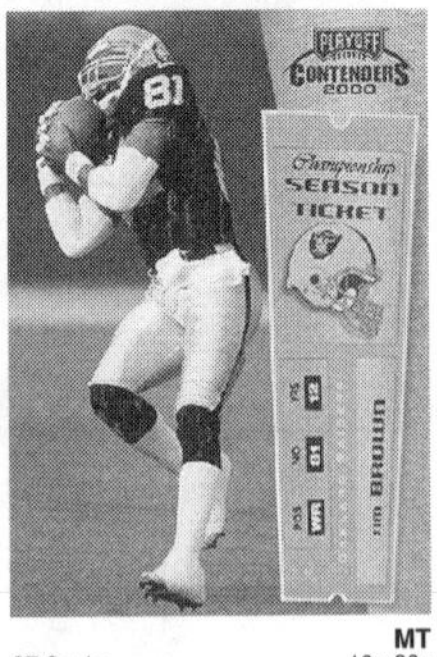

MT
CT Cards: 10x-20x
CT European Ticket: 2x
CT Playoff Ticket: 1.5x
Production 100 Sets
1 David Boston .75
2 Jake Plummer .75
3 Chris Chandler .50
4 Jamal Anderson .75
5 Tim Dwight .75
6 Qadry Ismail .25
7 Tony Banks .50
8 Lamar Smith .50
9 Doug Flutie 1.00
10 Eric Moulds .75
11 Peerless Price .75
12 Rob Johnson .50
13 Muhsin Muhammad .50
14 Reggie White .50
15 Steve Beuerlein .50
16 Cade McNown .75
17 Derrick Alexander .25
18 Marcus Robinson .75
19 Akili Smith .75
20 Corey Dillon .75
21 Kevin Johnson .75
22 Tim Couch 1.50
23 Emmitt Smith 2.00
24 Joey Galloway .75
25 Raghib Ismail .25
26 Troy Aikman 1.50
27 Brian Griese 1.00
28 Ed McCaffrey .50
29 John Elway 2.00
30 Olandis Gary .75
31 Rod Smith .75
32 Terrell Davis 2.00
33 Charlie Batch .75
34 Germane Crowell .75
35 James Stewart .50
36 Barry Sanders 2.00
37 Antonio Freeman .75
38 Brett Favre 3.00
39 Dorsey Levens .75
40 Edgerrin James 2.50
41 Marvin Harrison .75
42 Peyton Manning 2.50
43 Fred Taylor 1.25
44 Jimmy Smith .75
45 Mark Brunell 1.25
46 Elvis Grbac .50
47 Tony Gonzalez .50
48 Dan Marino 2.00
49 Joe Horn .50
50 Jay Fiedler .50
51 Thurman Thomas .50
52 Cris Carter .75
53 Daunte Culpepper 1.50
54 Randy Moss 2.50
55 Robert Smith .75
56 Drew Bledsoe 1.25
57 Terry Glenn .75
58 Ricky Williams 1.75
59 Amani Toomer .50
60 Kerry Collins .50
61 Curtis Martin .75
62 Vinny Testaverde .50
63 Wayne Chrebet .75
64 Rich Gannon .50
65 Tim Brown .75
66 Tyrone Wheatley .50
67 Donovan McNabb 1.25
68 Duce Staley .75
69 Jerome Bettis .75
70 Jermaine Fazande .50
71 Junior Seau .50
72 Donald Hayes .50
73 Charlie Garner .50
74 Jeff Garcia .75
75 Jerry Rice 1.50
76 Steve Young 1.25
77 Terrell Owens .75
78 Tiki Barber .50
79 Tim Biakabutuka .50
80 Ricky Watters .50
81 Isaac Bruce .75
82 Kurt Warner 3.00
83 Marshall Faulk 1.00
84 Torry Holt .75
85 Keyshawn Johnson .75
86 Mike Alstott .75
87 Shaun King .75
88 Warren Sapp .50
89 Warrick Dunn .75
90 Eddie George 1.00
91 Jevon Kearse .75
92 Steve McNair .75
93 Carl Pickens .50
94 Albert Connell .50
95 Brad Johnson .50
96 Bruce Smith .50
97 Deion Sanders .75
98 Jeff George .50
99 Michael Westbrook .50
100 Stephen Davis .75
101 Courtney Brown
102 Corey Simon 25.00
103 Brian Urlacher 100.00
104 Deon Grant 10.00
105 Peter Warrick 175.00
106 Jamal Lewis 250.00
107 Thomas Jones 60.00
108 Plaxico Burress 60.00
109 Travis Taylor 40.00
110 Ron Dayne 135.00
111 Bubba Franks 45.00
112 Chad Pennington 135.00
113 Shaun Alexander 100.00
114 Sylvester Morris 60.00
115 Mike Anderson 175.00
116 R. Jay Soward 25.00
117 Trung Canidate 20.00
118 Dennis Northcutt 25.00
119 Todd Pinkston 25.00
120 Jerry Porter 25.00
121 Travis Prentice 40.00
122 Giovanni Carmazzi 35.00
123 Ron Dugans 20.00
124 Dez White 20.00
125 Chris Cole 15.00
126 Ron Dixon 25.00
127 Chris Redman 85.00
128 J.R. Redmond 35.00
129 Laveranues Coles 35.00
130 JaJuan Dawson 25.00
131 Darrell Jackson 35.00
132 Reuben Droughns 20.00
133 Doug Chapman 25.00
134 Curtis Keaton 15.00
135 Gari Scott 15.00
136 Danny Farmer 20.00
137 Trevor Gaylor 15.00
138 Avion Black 10.00
139 Michael Wiley 20.00
140 Sammy Morris 35.00
141 Tee Martin 35.00
142 Troy Walters 20.00
143 Marc Bulger 20.00
144 Tom Brady 20.00
145 Todd Husak 25.00
146 Tim Rattay 35.00
147 Jarious Jackson 45.00
148 Joe Hamilton 25.00
149 Shyrone Stith 15.00
150 Kwame Cavil 12.00
151 Antonio Banks 7.00
152 Jonathan Brown 7.00
153 Ontiwaun Carter 7.00
154 Jeremaine Copeland 7.00
155 Ralph Dawkins 7.00
156 Marques Douglas 7.00
157 Kevin Drake 7.00
158 Damon Dunn 7.00
159 Todd Floyd 7.00
160 Tony Graziani 10.00
161 Derrick Ham 7.00
162 Duane Hawthorne 7.00
163 Alonzo Johnson 7.00
164 Mark Kacmarynski 7.00
165 Eric Kresser 7.00
166 Jim Kubiak 7.00
167 Blaine McElmurry 7.00
168 Scott Milanovich 10.00
169 Norman Miller 7.00
170 Sean Morey 7.00
171 Jeff Ogden 10.00
172 Pepe Pearson 10.00
173 Ron Powlus 35.00
174 Jason Shelley 7.00
175 Ben Snell 7.00
176 Aaron Stecker 10.00
177 L.C. Stevens 7.00
178 Mike Sutton 7.00
179 Damian Vaughn 7.00
180 Ted White 7.00
181 Marcus Crandell 7.00
182 Darryl Daniel 7.00
183 Jessie Haynes 7.00
184 Matt Lytle 7.00
185 Deon Mitchell 7.00
186 Kendrick Nord 7.00
187 Ronnie Powell 7.00
188 Selucio Sanford 7.00
189 Corey Thomas 7.00
190 Vershan Jackson 7.00
191 Jake Plummer PT 25.00
192 Jim Kelly PT 40.00
193 Bernie Kosar PT 40.00
194 Marvin Harrison PT 35.00
195 Fred Taylor PT 40.00
196 Kerry Collins PT 35.00
197 Kurt Warner PT 120.00
198 Jevon Kearse PT 35.00
199 Brad Johnson PT 25.00
200 Jeff George PT 25.00

2000 Playoff Contenders Championship Fabrics

MT
Complete Set (45): 1250.
Common Player: 15.00
Single Jerseys #'d to 300
Single Pants #'d to 300
Single Jerseys/Pants #'d to 100
Double Jerseys #'d to 25
Double Pants #'d to 25
Double Jerseys/Pants #'d to 25
1 Az-Zahir Hakim P 20.00
2 Grant Wistrom P 15.00
3 Isaac Bruce P 25.00
4 Kevin Carter P 15.00
5 Kurt Warner P 45.00
6 Marshall Faulk P 25.00
7 Tony Horne P 15.00
8 Robert Holcombe P 15.00
9 Todd Collins P 15.00
10 Torry Holt P 25.00
11 Az-Zahir Hakim J 20.00
12 Grant Wistrom J 15.00
13 Isaac Bruce J 25.00
14 Kevin Carter J 15.00
15 Kurt Warner J 45.00
16 Marshall Faulk J 25.00
17 Tony Horne J 15.00
18 Robert Holcombe J 15.00
19 Todd Collins J 15.00
20 Torry Holt J 25.00
21 Az-Zahir Hakim PJ 40.00
22 Grant Wistrom PJ 30.00
23 Isaac Bruce PJ 85.00
24 Kevin Carter PJ 30.00
25 Kurt Warner PJ 100.00
26 Marshall Faulk PJ 85.00
27 Tony Horne PJ 30.00
28 Robert Holcombe PJ 30.00
29 Todd Collins PJ 30.00
30 Torry Holt PJ 40.00
31 Kurt Warner, Torry Holt 150.00
32 Marshall Faulk, Isaac Bruce P 75.00

33 Tony Horne, Az-Zahir Hakim P 40.00
34 Grant Wistrom, Robert Holcombe P 30.00
35 Todd Collins, Kevin Carter P 30.00
36 Kurt Warner, Marshall Faulk J 150.00
37 Isaac Bruce, Torry Holt J 70.00
38 Kevin Carter, Az-Zahir Hakim J 40.00
39 Grant Wistrom, Robert Holcombe J 30.00
40 Todd Collins, Tony Horne J 40.00
41 Isaac Bruce, Kurt Warner PJ 150.00
42 Torry Holt, Marshall Faulk PJ 75.00
43 Az-Zahir Hakim, Robert Holcombe PJ 40.00
44 Kevin Carter, Tony Horne PJ 40.00
45 Grant Wistrom, Todd Collins PJ 40.00

2000 Playoff Contenders Hawaii Five-O

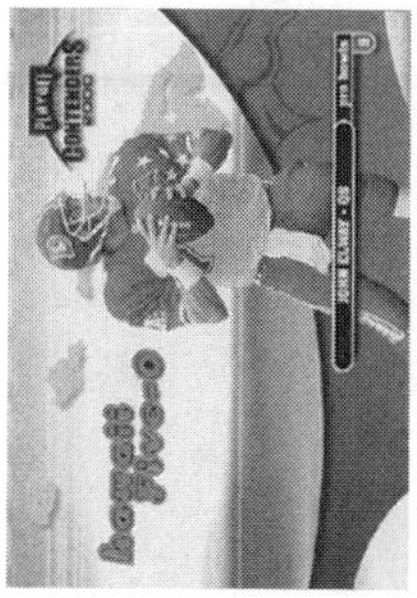

MT
Complete Set (50): 85.00
Common Player: 1.00
Minor Stars: 2.00
Inserted 1:11
1 Steve Beuerlein 1.00
2 Muhsin Muhammad 2.00
3 Jim Kelly 3.00
4 Doug Flutie 3.00
5 Reggie White 2.00
6 Corey Dillon 2.00
7 Emmitt Smith 6.00
8 Troy Aikman 5.00
9 Randall Cunningham 2.00
10 John Elway 7.00
11 Terrell Davis 6.00
12 Barry Sanders 7.00
13 Herman Moore 1.00
14 Brett Favre 10.00
15 Dorsey Levens 1.00
16 Antonio Freeman 1.00
17 Peyton Manning 8.00
18 Edgerrin James 8.00
19 Marvin Harrison 2.00
20 Mark Brunell 3.50
21 Jimmy Smith 1.00
22 Warren Moon 2.00
23 Dan Marino 7.00
24 Randy Moss 8.00
25 Cris Carter 2.00
26 Robert Smith 2.00
27 Drew Bledsoe 3.50
28 Tony Gonzalez 1.00
29 Rich Gannon 1.00
30 Curtis Martin 2.00
31 Vinny Testaverde 1.00
32 Frank Wycheck 1.00
33 Jerome Bettis 2.00
34 Junior Seau 1.00
35 Jerry Rice 5.00
36 Steve Young 3.50
37 Ricky Watters 1.00
38 Kurt Warner 10.00
39 Marshall Faulk 2.50
40 Isaac Bruce 2.00
41 Keyshawn Johnson 2.00
42 Mike Alstott 2.00
43 Warren Sapp 1.00
44 Eddie George 2.50
45 Jevon Kearse 2.00
46 Carl Pickens 1.00
47 Terry Glenn 1.00
48 Brad Johnson 1.00
49 Bruce Smith 1.00
50 Deion Sanders 2.00

2000 Playoff Contenders MVP Contenders

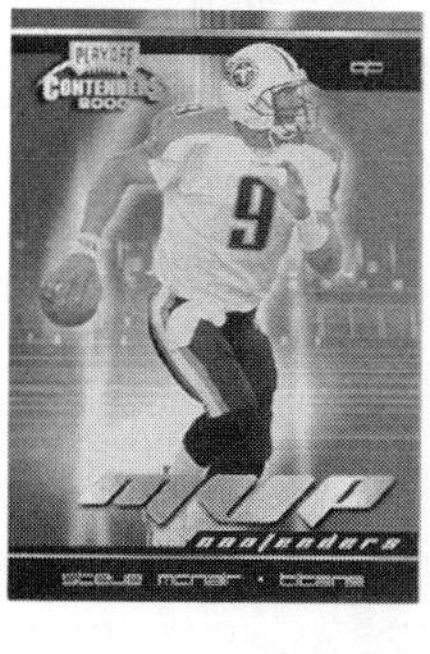

MT
Complete Set (30): 100.00
Common Player: 2.00
Minor Stars: 4.00
Inserted 1:35
1 Cade McNown 4.00
2 Tim Couch 7.00
3 Troy Aikman 10.00
4 Terrell Davis 12.00
5 Drew Bledsoe 7.00
6 Ricky Williams 8.00
7 Jerry Rice 10.00
8 Jamal Anderson 4.00
9 Dorsey Levens 4.00
10 Cris Carter 4.00
11 Emmitt Smith 12.00
12 Brett Favre 15.00
13 Peyton Manning 12.00
14 Edgerrin James 12.00
15 Fred Taylor 6.00
16 Randy Moss 12.00
17 Curtis Martin 4.00
18 Marshall Faulk 5.00
19 Steve McNair 4.00
20 Stephen Davis 4.00
21 Mark Brunell 7.00
22 Daunte Culpepper 7.00
23 Kurt Warner 15.00
24 Eddie George 5.00
25 Marvin Harrison 4.00
26 Isaac Bruce 4.00
27 Shaun King 5.00
28 Keyshawn Johnson 4.00
29 Brad Johnson 4.00
30 Jimmy Smith 4.00

2000 Playoff Contenders Quads

MT
Complete Set (15): 100.00
Common Player: 6.00
Inserted 1:59
1 Plaxico Burress, Jerome Bettis, Travis Prentice, Tim Couch 15.00
2 Troy Aikman, Emmitt Smith, Brad Johnson, Stephen Davis 12.00
3 Curtis Martin, Chad Pennington, Edgerrin James, Peyton Manning 18.00
4 Shaun King, Keyshawn Johnson, Daunte Culpepper, Randy Moss 15.00
5 Fred Taylor, Eddie George, Mark Brunell, Steve McNair 10.00
6 Ricky Watters, Jerry Porter, Tim Brown, Shaun Alexander 10.00
7 Antonio Freeman, Brett Favre, Marcus Robinson, Cade McNown 12.00
8 Donovan McNabb, Duce Staley, Kerry Collins, Ron Dayne 12.00
9 Jamal Lewis, Akili Smith, Peter Warrick, Travis Taylor 18.00
10 Jeff Blake, Ricky Williams, Thomas Jones, Jake Plummer 10.00
11 Jerry Rice, Terrell Owens, Marshall Faulk, Kurt Warner 15.00
12 Drew Bledsoe, Peerless Price, Terry Glenn, Eric Moulds 6.00
13 Terrell Davis, Brian Griese, Sylvester Morris, Elvis Grbac 12.00
14 Steve Beuerlein, Muhsin Muhammad, Jamal Anderson, Chris Chandler 6.00
15 Ryan Leaf, Jermaine Fazande, Jay Fiedler, Damon Huard 6.00

2000 Playoff Contenders Ultimate Quads

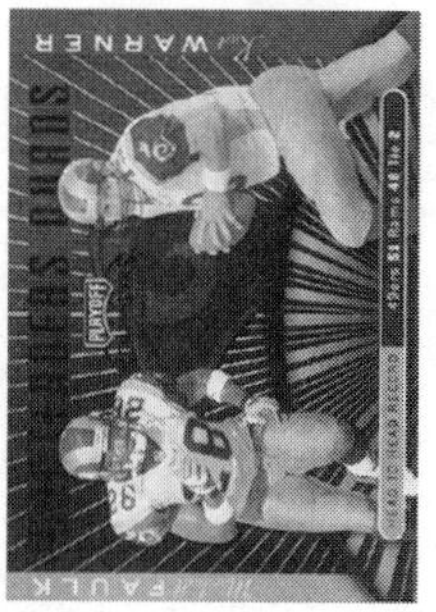

MT
Complete Set (15): 400.00
Common Player: 25.00
#'d to Stat
1 Plaxico Burress, Jerome Bettis, Travis Prentice, Tim Couch 94 30.00
2 Troy Aikman, Emmitt Smith, Brad Johnson, Stephen Davis 80 35.00
3 Curtis Martin, Chad Pennington, Edgerrin James, Peyton Manning 60 60.00
4 Shaun King, Keyshawn Johnson, Daunte Culpepper, Randy Moss 44 75.00
5 Fred Taylor, Eddie George, Mark Brunell, Steve McNair 10 75.00
6 Ricky Watters, Jerry Porter, Tim Brown, Shaun Alexander 44 40.00
7 Antonio Freeman, Brett Favre, Marcus Robinson, Cade McNown 159 30.00
8 Donovan McNabb, Duce Staley, Kerry Collins, Ron Dayne 131 30.00
9 Jamal Lewis, Akili Smith, Peter Warrick, Travis Taylor 8 150.00
10 Jeff Blake, Ricky Williams, Thomas Jones, Jake Plummer 22 45.00
11 Jerry Rice, Terrell Owens, Marshall Faulk, Kurt Warner 101 50.00
12 Drew Bledsoe, Peerless Price, Terry Glenn, Eric Moulds 80 25.00
13 Terrell Davis, Brian Griese, Sylvester Morris, Elvis Grbac 80 45.00
14 Steve Beuerlein, Muhsin Muhammad, Jamal Anderson, Chris Chandler 10 50.00
15 Ryan Leaf, Jermaine Fazande, Jay Fiedler, Damon Huard 21 25.00

2000 Playoff Contenders Round Numbers Autographs

MT
Complete Set (15): 400.00
Common Player: 20.00
Inserted 1:173
1 Jamal Lewis, Travis Taylor 100.00
2 Thomas Jones, Shaun Alexander 50.00
3 Plaxico Burress, Chad Pennington 60.00
4 Sylvester Morris, R. Jay Soward 40.00
5 Todd Pinkston, Jerry Porter 20.00
6 J.R. Redmond, Doug Chapman 20.00
7 Giovanni Carmazzi, Chris Redman 35.00
8 Travis Prentice, JaJuan Dawson 25.00
9 Ron Dugans, Laveranues Coles 20.00
10 Corey Simon, Brian Urlacher 50.00
11 Marc Bulger, Tom Brady 20.00
12 Tim Rattay, Joe Hamilton 25.00
13 Trevor Gaylor, Avion Black 20.00
14 Chris Cole, Ron Dixon 20.00
15 Curtis Keaton, Gari Scott 20.00

2000 Playoff Contenders Round Numbers Autographs Gold

MT
Common Player: 30.00
Randomly Inserted
1 Jamal Lewis, Travis Taylor 10 250.00
2 Thomas Jones, Shaun Alexander 10 100.00
3 Plaxico Burress, Chad Pennington 10 125.00
4 Sylvester Morris, R. Jay Soward 10 85.00
5 Todd Pinkston, Jerry Porter 20 50.00
6 J.R. Redmond, Doug Chapman 30 40.00
7 Giovanni Carmazzi, Chris Redman 30 75.00
8 Travis Prentice, JaJuan Dawson 30 50.00
9 Ron Dugans, Laveranues Coles 30 50.00
10 Corey Simon, Brian Urlacher 10 100.00
11 Marc Bulger, Tom Brady 60 30.00
12 Tim Rattay, Joe Hamilton 70 40.00
13 Trevor Gaylor, Avion Black 40 30.00
14 Chris Cole, Ron Dixon 30 35.00
15 Curtis Keaton, Gari Scott 40 30.00

Values quoted in this guide reflect the retail price of a card — the price a collector can expect to pay when buying a card from a dealer. The wholesale price — that which a collector can expect to receive from a dealer when selling cards — will be significantly lower, depending on desirability and condition.

2000 Playoff Contenders ROY Contenders

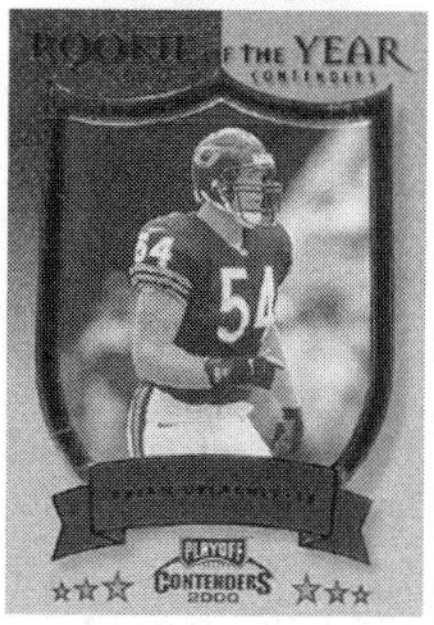

MT
Complete Set (20): 50.00
Common Player: 2.50
Inserted 1:23
1 Thomas Jones 4.00
2 Jamal Lewis 12.00
3 Travis Taylor 3.00
4 Brian Urlacher 6.00
5 Peter Warrick 10.00
6 Travis Prentice 3.00
7 Courtney Brown 2.50
8 Bubba Franks 2.50
9 R. Jay Soward 2.50
10 Sylvester Morris 5.00
11 J.R. Redmond 3.00
12 Ron Dayne 10.00
13 Chad Pennington 7.50
14 Laveranues Coles 3.00
15 Jerry Porter 2.50
16 Todd Pinkston 2.50
17 Corey Simon 2.50
18 Plaxico Burress 5.00
19 Shaun Alexander 6.00
20 Darrell Jackson 3.00

2000 Playoff Contenders ROY Contenders Autographs

MT
Complete Set (20): 750.00
Common Player: 25.00
Production 100 Sets
1 Thomas Jones 40.00
2 Jamal Lewis 125.00
3 Travis Taylor 30.00
4 Brian Urlacher 70.00
5 Peter Warrick 100.00
6 Travis Prentice 30.00
7 Courtney Brown 25.00
8 Bubba Franks 25.00
9 R. Jay Soward 25.00
10 Sylvester Morris 50.00
11 J.R. Redmond 30.00
12 Ron Dayne 100.00
13 Chad Pennington 75.00
14 Laveranues Coles 30.00
15 Jerry Porter 25.00
16 Todd Pinkston 25.00
17 Corey Simon 25.00
18 Plaxico Burress 50.00
19 Shaun Alexander 60.00
20 Darrell Jackson 30.00

2000 Playoff Contenders Touchdown Tandems

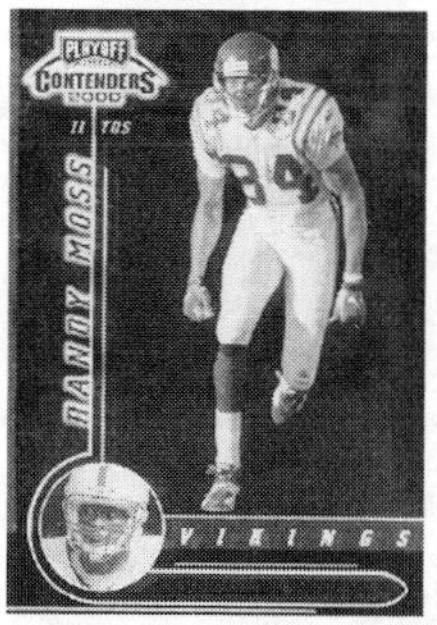

MT
Complete Set (30): 65.00
Common Player: 1.25
Minor Stars: 2.50
Inserted 1:11
1 Randy Moss, Marvin Harrison 6.00
2 Kurt Warner, Peyton Manning 7.00
3 Marshall Faulk, Edgerrin James 6.00
4 Eddie George, Fred Taylor 2.50
5 Emmitt Smith, Stephen Davis 5.00
6 Isaac Bruce, Jerry Rice 4.00
7 Antonio Freeman, Cris Carter 1.25
8 Drew Bledsoe, Mark Brunell 2.50
9 Jake Plummer, Steve McNair 1.25
10 Curtis Martin, Duce Staley 1.25
11 Keyshawn Johnson, Marcus Robinson 1.25
12 Dan Marino, Steve Young 6.00
13 Brett Favre, Troy Aikman 8.00
14 Tim Brown, Eric Moulds 1.25
15 Jerome Bettis, Mike Alstott 1.25
16 Dorsey Levens, James Stewart 1.25
17 Olandis Gary, Ricky Watters 1.25
18 Brian Griese, Charlie Batch 2.50
19 Terrell Owens, Torry Holt 1.25
20 Jimmy Smith, Joey Galloway 1.25
21 Kevin Johnson, Michael Westbrook 1.25
22 Corey Dillon, Ricky Williams 3.50
23 Donovan McNabb, Akili Smith 2.50
24 Tim Couch, Cade McNown 3.00
25 Shaun King, Jon Kitna 2.50
26 Peter Warrick, Plaxico Burress 7.00
27 Jamal Lewis, Shaun Alexander 10.00
28 Ron Dayne, Thomas Jones 7.00
29 Sylvester Morris, Travis Taylor 4.00
30 Chad Pennington, Chris Redman 6.00

2000 Playoff Contenders Touchdown Tandems Total

MT
Common Player: 30.00
Randomly Inserted
1 Randy Moss, Marvin Harrison 23 85.00
2 Kurt Warner, Peyton Manning 67 60.00
3 Marshall Faulk, Edgerrin James 20 75.00
4 Eddie George, Fred Taylor 15 35.00
5 Emmitt Smith, Stephen Davis 28 70.00
6 Isaac Bruce, Jerry Rice 17 85.00
7 Antonio Freeman, Cris Carter 19 30.00
8 Drew Bledsoe, Mark Brunell 33 35.00
9 Jake Plummer, Steve McNair 21 30.00
10 Curtis Martin, Duce Staley 9 45.00
11 Keyshawn Johnson, Marcus Robinson 17 35.00
12 Dan Marino, Steve Young 15 150.00
13 Brett Favre, Troy Aikman 39 70.00
14 Tim Brown, Eric Moulds 13 30.00
15 Jerome Bettis, Mike Alstott 14 30.00
16 Dorsey Levens, James Stewart 22 30.00
17 Olandis Gary, Ricky Watters 12 35.00
18 Brian Griese, Charlie Batch 27 30.00
19 Terrell Owens, Torry Holt 10 45.00
20 Jimmy Smith, Joey Galloway 7 40.00
21 Kevin Johnson, Michael Westbrook 17 30.00
22 Corey Dillon, Ricky Williams 7 60.00
23 Donovan McNabb, Akili Smith 10 40.00
24 Tim Couch, Cade McNown 23 40.00
25 Shaun King, Jon Kitna 30 35.00
26 Peter Warrick, Plaxico Burress 20 50.00
27 Jamal Lewis, Shaun Alexander 26 100.00
28 Ron Dayne, Thomas Jones 35 45.00
29 Sylvester Morris, Travis Taylor 19 35.00
30 Chad Pennington, Chris Redman 67 35.00

2000 Playoff Momentum

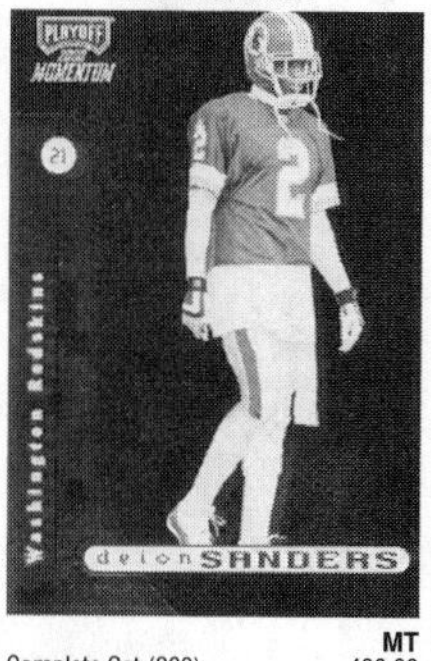

MT
Complete Set (200): 400.00
Common Player: .20
Minor Stars: .40
Common Rookie: 4.00
Production 750 Sets
Pack (6): 5.00
Wax Box (16): 65.00
1 David Boston .50
2 Jake Plummer .50
3 Chris Chandler .20
4 Jamal Anderson .50
5 Tim Dwight .40
6 Qadry Ismail .20
7 Peerless Price .40
8 Antowain Smith .40
9 Eric Moulds .50
10 Rob Johnson .40
11 Natrone Means .40
12 Muhsin Muhammad .40
13 Steve Beuerlein .40
14 Patrick Jeffers .50
15 Curtis Enis .40
16 Cade McNown .50
17 Marcus Robinson .50
18 Corey Dillon .50
19 Akili Smith .50
20 Carl Pickens .40
21 Tim Couch 1.00
22 Kevin Johnson .40
23 Troy Aikman 1.25
24 Emmitt Smith 1.50
25 Joey Galloway .50
26 Raghib Ismail .20
27 Olandis Gary .50
28 John Elway 1.50
29 Brian Griese .60
30 Ed McCaffrey .40
31 Terrell Davis 1.50
32 Charlie Batch .50
33 James Stewart .40
34 Germane Crowell .40
35 Barry Sanders 1.50
36 Herman Moore .40
37 Antonio Freeman .50
38 Dorsey Levens .50
39 Brett Favre 2.50
40 Edgerrin James 2.00
41 Marvin Harrison .50
42 Peyton Manning 2.00
43 Fred Taylor .75
44 Keenan McCardell .40
45 Mark Brunell .75
46 Jimmy Smith .40
47 Elvis Grbac .40
48 Tony Gonzalez .40
49 James Johnson .40
50 Dan Marino 1.50
51 Thurman Thomas .40
52 Cris Carter .50
53 Robert Smith .40
54 Randy Moss 2.00
55 Daunte Culpepper 1.00
56 Terry Glenn .40
57 Kevin Faulk .40
58 Drew Bledsoe .75
59 Ricky Williams 1.25
60 Amani Toomer .40
61 Kerry Collins .40
62 Vinny Testaverde .40
63 Curtis Martin .50
64 Rich Gannon .40
65 Tyrone Wheatley .40
66 Napoleon Kaufman .40
67 Tim Brown .50
68 Duce Staley .50
69 Donovan McNabb .75
70 Kordell Stewart .50
71 Troy Edwards .40
72 Jerome Bettis .50
73 Jim Harbaugh .40
74 Jermaine Fazande .40
75 Steve Young .75
76 Charlie Garner .40
77 Terrell Owens .50
78 Jerry Rice 1.25
79 Jeff Garcia .50
80 Ricky Watters .40
81 Jon Kitna .40
82 Marshall Faulk .60
83 Isaac Bruce .50
84 Torry Holt .40
85 Kurt Warner 2.50
86 Keyshawn Johnson .50
87 Warrick Dunn .50
88 Mike Alstott .50
89 Warren Sapp .40
90 Shaun King .50
91 Eddie George .60
92 Steve McNair .50
93 Jevon Kearse .50
94 Bruce Smith .20
95 Deion Sanders .50
96 Albert Connell .40
97 Michael Westbrook .40
98 Brad Johnson .50
99 Jeff George .40
100 Stephen Davis .50
101 *Peter Warrick* 25.00
102 *Jamal Lewis* 50.00
103 *Thomas Jones* 12.00
104 *Plaxico Burress* 15.00
105 *Travis Taylor* 10.00
106 *Ron Dayne* 25.00
107 *Bubba Franks* 8.00
108 *Sebastian Janikowski* 8.00
109 *Chad Pennington* 25.00
110 *Shaun Alexander* 20.00
111 *Sylvester Morris* 15.00
112 *Anthony Becht* 6.00
113 *R. Jay Soward* 8.00
114 *Trung Canidate* 8.00
115 *Dennis Northcutt* 10.00
116 *Todd Pinkston* 8.00
117 *Jerry Porter* 8.00
118 *Travis Prentice* 12.00
119 *Giovanni Carmazzi* 10.00
120 *Ron Dugans* 8.00
121 *Erron Kinney* 4.00
122 *Dez White* 6.00
123 *Chris Cole* 4.00
124 *Ron Dixon* 10.00
125 *Chris Redman* 15.00
126 *J.R. Redmond* 10.00
127 *Laveranues Coles* 12.00
128 *JaJuan Dawson* 8.00
129 *Darrell Jackson* 12.00
130 *Reuben Droughns* 4.00
131 *Doug Chapman* 12.00
132 *Terrelle Smith* 4.00
133 *Curtis Keaton* 4.00
134 *Gari Scott* 4.00
135 *Courtney Brown* 10.00
136 *Corey Simon* 8.00
137 *Brian Urlacher* 20.00

138	*Shaun Ellis*	4.00
139	*John Abraham*	4.00
140	*Delthea O'Neal*	4.00
141	*Rashard Anderson*	4.00
142	*Ahmed Plummer*	4.00
143	*Chris Hovan*	4.00
144	*Erik Flowers*	4.00
145	*Rob Morris*	4.00
146	*Keith Bullock*	4.00
147	*Darren Howard*	4.00
148	*John Engelberger*	4.00
149	*Ian Gold*	4.00
150	*Raynoch Thompson*	4.00
151	*Cornelius Griffin*	4.00
152	*Rogers Beckett*	4.00
153	*Dwayne Goodrich*	4.00
154	*Barrett Green*	4.00
155	*Kevin Thompson*	4.00
156	*Ben Kelly*	4.00
157	*Danny Farmer*	6.00
158	*Aaron Shea*	4.00
159	*Trevor Gaylor*	6.00
160	*Mike Brown*	4.00
161	*Frank Moreau*	8.00
162	*Deon Dyer*	4.00
163	*Avion Black*	4.00
164	*Spergon Wynn*	8.00
165	*Billy Volek*	6.00
166	*Michael Wiley*	8.00
167	*Dante Hall*	4.00
168	*Ronney Jenkins*	4.00
169	*Sammy Morris*	10.00
170	*Kevin McDougal*	4.00
171	*Tee Martin*	8.00
172	*Troy Walters*	6.00
173	*Chad Morton*	8.00
174	*Jamel White*	4.00
175	*Shockmain Davis*	6.00
176	*Mario Edwards*	4.00
177	*Brandon Short*	4.00
178	*James Williams*	4.00
179	*Mike Anderson*	45.00
180	*Tom Brady*	15.00
181	*Na'il Diggs*	4.00
182	*Todd Husak*	8.00
183	*JaJuan Seider*	4.00
184	*Tim Rattay*	10.00
185	*Jarious Jackson*	8.00
186	*Joe Hamilton*	10.00
187	*Shyrone Stith*	6.00
188	*Mondriel Fulcher*	4.00
189	*Bashir Yamini*	4.00
190	*Herbert Goodman*	6.00
191	*Mike Green*	4.00
192	*Demario Brown*	4.00
193	*Charles Lee*	4.00
194	*Doug Johnson*	8.00
195	*Windrell Hayes*	4.00
196	*Julian Peterson*	4.00
197	*Kwame Cavil*	4.00
198	*Hank Poteat*	4.00
199	*Clint Stoerner*	12.00
200	*Mark Simoneau*	4.00

2000 Playoff Momentum Game Day Souvenirs Jerseys

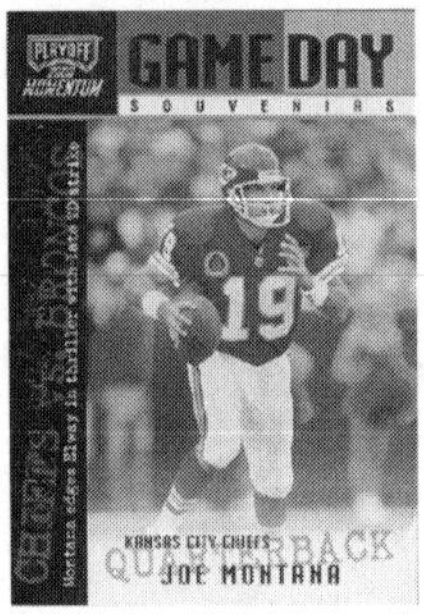

		MT
Complete Set (45):		
Common Player:		50.00
1	Joe Montana	125.00
2	Dan Marino	100.00
3	Joe Montana	125.00
4	John Elway	100.00
5	Terry Bradshaw	100.00
6	Roger Staubach	100.00
7	Bob Griese	75.00
8	Fran Tarkenton	75.00
9	Phil Simms	75.00
10	Lawrence Taylor	75.00
11	Ronnie Lott	75.00
12	Boomer Esiason	75.00
13	Joe Namath	125.00
14	Don Maynard	50.00
15	Howie Long	75.00
16	Marcus Allen	75.00
17	Jim Kelly	50.00
18	Thurman Thomas	50.00
19	Fred Taylor	50.00
20	Mark Brunell	50.00
21	Randy Moss	75.00
22	Antonio Freeman	50.00
23	Ricky Williams	50.00
24	Tim Couch	50.00
25	Kurt Warner	100.00
26	Eddie George	50.00
27	Troy Aikman	75.00
28	Steve Young	75.00
29	Dorsey Levens	50.00
30	Barry Sanders	75.00
31	Joe Montana, Dan Marino	300.00
32	Joe Montana, John Elway	300.00
33	Terry Bradshaw, Roger Staubach	200.00
34	Bob Griese, Fran Tarkenton	150.00
35	Phil Simms, Lawrence Taylor	150.00
36	Ronnie Lott, Boomer Esiason	100.00
37	Joe Namath, Don Maynard	175.00
38	Howie Long, Marcus Allen	100.00
39	Jim Kelly, Thurman Thomas	100.00
40	Fred Taylor, Mark Brunell	100.00
41	Randy Moss, Antonio Freeman	100.00
42	Ricky Williams, Tim Couch	100.00
43	Kurt Warner, Eddie George	150.00
44	Troy Aikman, Steve Young	150.00
45	Dorsey Levens, Barry Sanders	150.00

2000 Playoff Momentum Generations

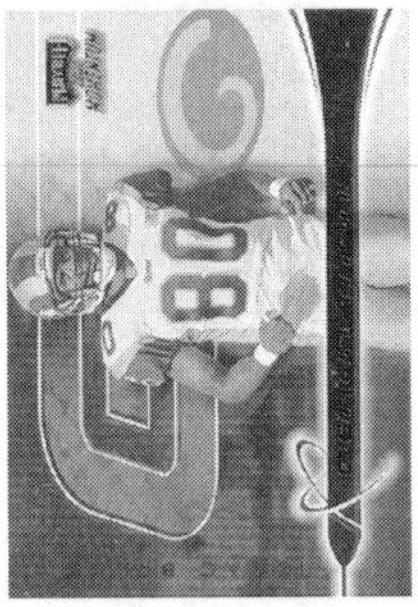

		MT
Complete Set (50):		60.00
Common Player:		.75
1	Jake Plummer	.75
2	Tim Couch	1.00
3	Emmitt Smith	2.00
4	Troy Aikman	2.00
5	John Elway	4.00
6	Terrell Davis	2.00
7	Barry Sanders	3.00
8	Brett Favre	4.00
9	Peyton Manning	3.00
10	Edgerrin James	3.00
11	Mark Brunell	2.00
12	Fred Taylor	1.00
13	Dan Marino	3.00
14	Randy Moss	3.00
15	Drew Bledsoe	2.00
16	Ricky Williams	2.00
17	Jerry Rice	4.00
18	Steve Young	2.00
19	Kurt Warner	4.00
20	Eddie George	2.00
21	Eric Moulds	1.00
22	Cade McNown	.75
23	Corey Dillon	1.00
24	Kevin Johnson	.75
25	Joey Galloway	.75
26	Dorsey Levens	.75
27	Antonio Freeman	.75
28	Marvin Harrison	2.00
29	Daunte Culpepper	3.00
30	Cris Carter	1.00
31	Curtis Martin	1.00
32	Tim Brown	1.00
33	Donovan McNabb	2.00
34	Terrell Owens	1.00
35	Peter Warrick	1.00
36	Jamal Lewis	3.00
37	Thomas Jones	2.00
38	Plaxico Burress	3.00
39	Travis Taylor	.75
40	Ron Dayne	2.00
41	Chad Pennington	3.00
42	Shaun Alexander	3.00
43	Marshall Faulk	2.00
44	Keyshawn Johnson	.75
45	Steve McNair	1.00
46	Stephen Davis	.75
47	Brad Johnson	.75
48	Akili Smith	.75
49	Brian Griese	1.00
50	Isaac Bruce	.75

2000 Playoff Momentum Rookie Quads

		MT
Complete Set (12):		
Common Player:		5.00
1	Peter Warrick, Avion Black, Ron Dugans, Charles Lee	8.00
2	Plaxico Burress, Trevor Gaylor, JaJuan Dawson, Dez White	10.00
3	Travis Taylor, Danny Farmer, Jerry Porter, Laveranues Coles	5.00
4	Gari Scott, Sylvester Morris, Todd Pinkston, Ron Dixon	5.00
5	Darrell Jackson, R. Jay Soward, Dennis Northcutt, Chris Cole	5.00
6	Jamal Lewis, Ronney Jenkins, Doug Chapman, Reuben Droughns	10.00
7	Thomas Jones, Chad Morton, J.R. Redmond, Curtis Keaton	5.00
8	Ron Dayne, Sammy Morris, Travis Prentice, Frank Moreau	10.00
9	Shaun Alexander, Dante Hall, Trung Canidate, Michael Wiley	10.00
10	Chad Pennington, Todd Husak, Tee Martin, Billy Volek	12.00
11	Giovanni Carmazzi, Tim Rattay, Chris Redman, Tom Brady	30.00
12	Courtney Brown, Shaun Ellis, Corey Simon, Brian Urlacher	25.00

2000 Playoff Momentum Rookie Tandems

		MT
Complete Set (24):		75.00
Common Player:		2.00
1	Peter Warrick, Avion Black	5.00
2	Ron Dugans, Charles Lee	2.00
3	Plaxico Burress, Trevor Gaylor	5.00
4	Dez White, JaJuan Dawson	2.00
5	Travis Taylor, Danny Farmer	2.00
6	Jerry Porter, Laveranues Coles	4.00
7	Sylvester Morris, Gari Scott	2.00
8	Todd Pinkston, Ron Dixon	2.00
9	R. Jay Soward, Darrell Jackson	2.00
10	Dennis Northcutt, Chris Cole	2.00
11	Jamal Lewis, Ronney Jenkins	10.00
12	Reuben Droughns, Doug Chapman	2.00
13	Thomas Jones, Chad Morton	5.00
14	J.R. Redmond, Curtis Keaton	2.00
15	Ron Dayne, Sammy Morris	5.00
16	Travis Prentice, Frank Moreau	2.00
17	Shaun Alexander, Dante Hall	10.00
18	Trung Canidate, Michael Wiley	2.00
19	Chad Pennington, Todd Husak	5.00
20	Tee Martin, Billy Volek	3.00
21	Giovanni Carmazzi, Tim Rattay	2.00
22	Chris Redman, Tom Brady	25.00
23	Courtney Brown, Shaun Ellis	2.00
24	Corey Simon, Brian Urlacher	20.00

2000 Playoff Momentum Signing Bonus Quads

		MT
Complete Set (3):		
Common Player:		
1	Peter Warrick, R. Jay Soward, Sylvester Morris, Plaxico Burress	150.00
2	Jamal Lewis, Dez White, Shaun Alexander, Travis Taylor	100.00
3	Thomas Jones, Chris Redman, Chad Pennington, Ron Dayne	100.00

2000 Playoff Momentum Signing Bonus Tandems

		MT
Complete Set (6):		
Common Player:		
1	Peter Warrick, R. Jay Soward	100.00
2	Plaxico Burress, Sylvester Morris	125.00
3	Jamal Lewis, Dez White	100.00
4	Travis Taylor, Shaun Alexander	125.00
5	Thomas Jones, Chris Redman	50.00
6	Ron Dayne, Chad Pennington	100.00

2000 Playoff Prestige

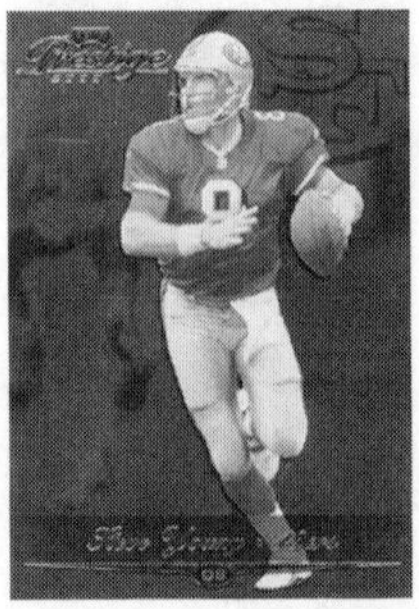

		MT
Complete Set (300):		450.00
Common Player:		.15
Minor Stars:		.30
Common Performer:		1.00
Production 2,500 Sets		
Common Rookie:		2.50
Production 2,500 Sets		
Pack (6):		6.00
Wax Box (16):		75.00
1	Frank Sanders	.30
2	Rob Moore	.30
3	Michael Pittman	.50
4	Jake Plummer	.50
5	David Boston	.50
6	Chris Chandler	.30
7	Tim Dwight	.50
8	Shawn Jefferson	.15
9	Terance Mathis	.15
10	Jamal Anderson	.50
11	Byron Hanspard	.15
12	Ken Oxendine	.15
13	Priest Holmes	.50
14	Tony Banks	.30
15	Shannon Sharpe	.30
16	Rod Woodson	.15
17	Jermaine Lewis	.15
18	Qadry Ismail	.15
19	Eric Moulds	.50
20	Doug Flutie	.50
21	Jay Riemersma	.15
22	Antowain Smith	.30
23	Jonathon Linton	.30
24	Peerless Price	.30
25	Rob Johnson	.30
26	Muhsin Muhammad	.30
27	Wesley Walls	.15
28	Tim Biakabutuka	.30
29	Steve Beuerlein	.30
30	Patrick Jeffers	.50
31	Natrone Means	.30
32	Curtis Enis	.50
33	Bobby Engram	.15
34	Marcus Robinson	.50
35	Marty Booker	.15
36	Cade McNown	.75
37	Darnay Scott	.30
38	Carl Pickens	.30
39	Corey Dillon	.50
40	Akili Smith	.60
41	Michael Basnight	.15
42	Kareem Abdul Jabbar	.30
43	Tim Couch	1.25
44	Kevin Johnson	.50
45	Darrin Chiaverini	.15
46	Errict Rhett	.15
47	Emmitt Smith	1.50
48	Deion Sanders	.50
49	Michael Irvin	.30
50	Raghib Ismail	.15
51	Troy Aikman	1.00
52	Jason Tucker	.15
53	Joey Galloway	.50
54	David LaFleur	.15
55	Wane McGarity	.15
56	Ed McCaffrey	.50
57	Rod Smith	.30
58	Brian Griese	.60
59	John Elway	1.50
60	Gus Frerotte	.15
61	Neil Smith	.15
62	Terrell Davis	1.50
63	Olandis Gary	.60
64	Johnnie Morton	.15
65	Charlie Batch	.50
66	Barry Sanders	1.50
67	James Stewart	.50
68	Germane Crowell	.50
69	Sedrick Irvin	.15
70	Herman Moore	.30
71	Corey Bradford	.50
72	Dorsey Levens	.50
73	Antonio Freeman	.50
74	Brett Favre	2.00
75	De'Mond Parker	.15
76	Bill Schroeder	.15
77	Donald Driver	.15
78	E.G. Green	.15
79	Marvin Harrison	.50
80	Peyton Manning	1.75
81	Terrence Wilkins	.50
82	Edgerrin James	1.75
83	Keenan McCardell	.30
84	Mark Brunell	.75
85	Fred Taylor	.75
86	Jimmy Smith	.50
87	Derrick Alexander	.15
88	Andre Rison	.30
89	Elvis Grbac	.30
90	Tony Gonzalez	.30
91	Donnell Bennett	.15
92	Warren Moon	.30
93	Kimble Anders	.15
94	Tony Richardson	.15
95	Jay Fiedler	.30
96	Zach Thomas	.30
97	Oronde Gadsden	.15
98	Dan Marino	1.50
99	O.J. McDuffie	.30
100	Tony Martin	.15
101	James Johnson	.15
102	Rob Konrad	.15
103	Damon Huard	.50
104	Thurman Thomas	.30
105	Randy Moss	2.00
106	Cris Carter	.50
107	Robert Smith	.50
108	Randall Cunningham	.50
109	John Randle	.15
110	Leroy Hoard	.15
111	Daunte Culpepper	.75
112	Matthew Hatchette	.15
113	Troy Brown	.15
114	Tony Simmons	.30
115	Terry Glenn	.50
116	Ben Coates	.30
117	Drew Bledsoe	.75
118	Terry Allen	.15
119	Kevin Faulk	.15
120	Ricky Williams	1.25
121	*Jake Delhomme*	1.50
122	Jake Reed	.30
123	Jeff Blake	.30
124	Amani Toomer	.15
125	Kerry Collins	.30
126	Tiki Barber	.30
127	Ike Hilliard	.15
128	Joe Montgomery	.15
129	Sean Bennett	.15
130	Curtis Martin	.50
131	Vinny Testaverde	.50
132	Wayne Chrebet	.30
133	Ray Lucas	.30
134	Tyrone Wheatley	.30
135	Napoleon Kaufman	.30
136	Tim Brown	.30
137	Rickey Dudley	.15
138	James Jett	.15
139	Rich Gannon	.30
140	Charles Woodson	.50
141	Duce Staley	.50
142	Donovan McNabb	.75
143	Na Brown	.15
144	Kordell Stewart	.50
145	Jerome Bettis	.50
146	Hines Ward	.30
147	Troy Edwards	.50
148	Curtis Conway	.30
149	Junior Seau	.30
150	Jim Harbaugh	.30
151	Jermaine Fazande	.30
152	Terrell Owens	.50
153	J.J. Stokes	.30
154	Charlie Garner	.50
155	Jerry Rice	1.00
156	Garrison Hearst	.50
157	Steve Young	.75
158	Jeff Garcia	.50
159	Derrick Mayes	.30
160	Ahman Green	.30
161	Ricky Watters	.30
162	Jon Kitna	.50
163	Karsten Bailey	.15
164	Sean Dawkins	.15
165	Az-Zahir Hakim	.30
166	Isaac Bruce	.50
167	Marshall Faulk	.50
168	Trent Green	.50
169	Kurt Warner	2.00
170	Torry Holt	.50
171	Robert Holcombe	.15
172	Kevin Carter	.15
173	Keyshawn Johnson	.50
174	Jacquez Green	.30
175	Reidel Anthony	.30
176	Warren Sapp	.30
177	Mike Alstott	.50
178	Warrick Dunn	.50
179	Trent Dilfer	.30
180	Shaun King	.75
181	Neil O'Donnell	.15
182	Eddie George	.60
183	Yancey Thigpen	.15
184	Steve McNair	.60
185	Kevin Dyson	.30
186	Frank Wycheck	.15
187	Jevon Kearse	.60
188	Adrian Murrell	.15
189	Jeff George	.50
190	Stephen Davis	.50
191	Stephen Alexander	.15
192	Darrell Green	.15
193	Skip Hicks	.15
194	Brad Johnson	.50
195	Michael Westbrook	.30
196	Albert Connell	.30
197	Irving Fryar	.15
198	Bruce Smith	.15
199	Champ Bailey	.30
200	Larry Centers	.15
201	Jake Plummer	1.00
202	Doug Flutie	1.50
203	Eric Moulds	1.00
204	Muhsin Muhammad	1.00
205	Marcus Robinson	1.50
206	Cade McNown	2.00
207	Corey Dillon	1.00
208	Tim Couch	3.00
209	Kevin Johnson	1.00
210	Emmitt Smith	3.00
211	Troy Aikman	2.50
212	Brian Griese	1.50
213	Olandis Gary	1.50
214	Germane Crowell	1.00
215	Brett Favre	6.00
216	Charlie Batch	1.00
217	Antonio Freeman	1.00
218	Dorsey Levens	1.00
219	Peyton Manning	4.00
220	Edgerrin James	5.00
221	Marvin Harrison	1.00
222	Fred Taylor	2.00
223	Mark Brunell	2.00
224	Jimmy Smith	1.00
225	Dan Marino	4.00
226	Randy Moss	4.00
227	Cris Carter	1.00
228	Robert Smith	1.00
229	Drew Bledsoe	2.00
230	Terry Glenn	1.00
231	Ricky Williams	3.00
232	Amani Toomer	1.00
233	Keyshawn Johnson	1.00
234	Curtis Martin	1.00
235	Ray Lucas	1.00
236	Tim Brown	1.00
237	Duce Staley	1.00
238	Donovan McNabb	2.00
239	Jerry Rice	2.50
240	Jon Kitna	1.00
241	Isaac Bruce	1.00
242	Kurt Warner	6.00
243	Torry Holt	1.00
244	Mike Alstott	1.00
245	Marshall Faulk	1.00
246	Shaun King	2.00
247	Eddie George	1.50
248	Steve McNair	1.00
249	Stephen Davis	1.00
250	Brad Johnson	1.00
251	*Rondell Mealey*	3.00
252	*Peter Warrick*	20.00
253	*Courtney Brown*	5.00
254	*Plaxico Burress*	12.00
255	*Corey Simon*	4.00
256	*Thomas Jones*	10.00
257	*Travis Taylor*	6.00
258	*Shaun Alexander*	12.00
259	*Chris Redman*	10.00
260	*Chad Pennington*	15.00
261	*Jamal Lewis*	30.00
262	*Bubba Franks*	5.00
263	*Dez White*	4.00
264	*Ron Dayne*	20.00
265	*Sylvester Morris*	12.00
266	*R. Jay Soward*	4.00
267	*Sherrod Gideon*	3.00
268	*Travis Prentice*	7.50
269	*Darrell Jackson*	7.00
270	*Giovanni Carmazzi*	5.00
271	*Anthony Lucas*	3.00
272	*Danny Farmer*	4.00
273	*Dennis Northcutt*	5.00
274	*Troy Walters*	3.00
275	*Laveranues Coles*	7.00
276	*Tee Martin*	4.00
277	*J.R. Redmond*	6.00
278	*Jerry Porter*	4.00
279	*Sebastian Janikowski*	4.00
280	*Michael Wiley*	4.00
281	*Reuben Droughns*	3.00
282	*Trung Canidate*	4.00
283	*Shyrone Stith*	3.00
284	*Trevor Gaylor*	3.00
285	*Marc Bulger*	2.50
286	*Tom Brady*	8.00
287	*Todd Husak*	3.00
288	*Jarious Jackson*	3.00
289	*Terrelle Smith*	2.50
290	*Chad Morton*	5.00
291	*Chris Cole*	3.00
292	*Kwame Cavil*	2.50
293	*JuJuan Dawson*	4.00
294	*Curtis Keaton*	3.00
295	*Tim Rattay*	5.00
296	*Joe Hamilton*	4.00
297	*Gari Scott*	3.00
298	*Mike Anderson*	30.00
299	*Ron Dugans*	4.00
300	*Todd Pinkston*	4.00

2000 Playoff Prestige Spectrum Green Parallel

	MT
Green Cards:	40x-80x
Green Performers:	15x-30x
Green Rookies:	2x-4x
Production 25 Sets	

2000 Playoff Prestige Spectrum Red Parallel

	MT
Red Cards:	15x-30x
Red Performers:	6x-12x
Red Rookies:	1.5x
Production 100 Sets	

2000 Playoff Prestige Alma Mater Materials

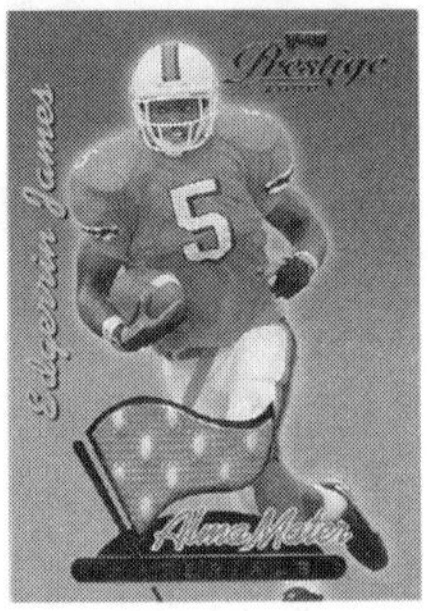

		MT
Complete Set (10):		475.00
Common Player:		25.00
Inserted 1:335		
Patch Cards:		2x
Inserted 1:2,005		
AM1	John Elway	125.00
AM2	Drew Bledsoe	60.00
AM3	Ricky Williams	85.00
AM4	Edgerrin James	150.00
AM5	Fred Taylor	70.00
AM6	J.J. Stokes	25.00
AM7	Eddie George	50.00
AM8	Frank Wycheck	25.00
AM9	Tim Biakabutuka	25.00
AM10	Ryan Leaf	25.00

2000 Playoff Prestige Award Winning Materials

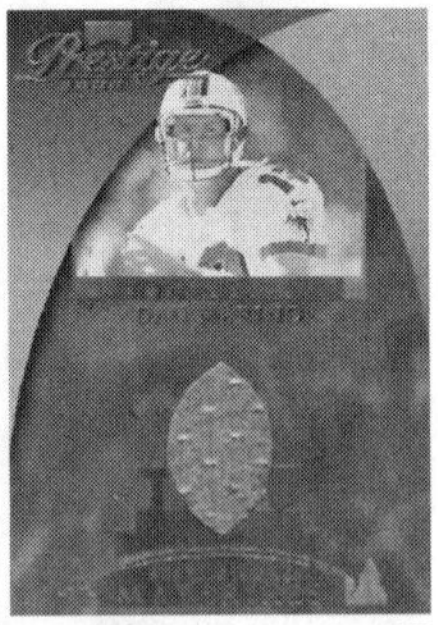

		MT
Common Player:		45.00
Inserted 1:429		
Single Jerseys #'d to 75		
Triple Jerseys #'d to 25		
AW1	Brett Favre	150.00
AW2	Barry Sanders	150.00
AW3	Thurman Thomas	45.00
AW4	Brett Favre, Barry Sanders, Thurman Thomas	275.00
AW5	Dan Marino	150.00
AW6	Steve Young	65.00
AW7	Kurt Warner	150.00
AW8	Dan Marino, Steve Young, Kurt Warner	325.00
AW9	John Elway	150.00
AW10	Terrell Davis	85.00
AW11	Phil Simms	45.00
AW12	John Elway, Terrell Davis, Phil Simms	250.00
AW13	Troy Aikman	85.00
AW14	Emmitt Smith	100.00
AW15	Jerry Rice	85.00
AW16	Troy Aikman, Emmitt Smith, Jerry Rice	250.00
AW17	Randy Moss	150.00

AW18	Eddie George	50.00
AW19	Jerome Bettis	45.00
AW20	Randy Moss, Eddie George, Jerome Bettis	200.00
AW21	Edgerrin James	150.00
AW22	Curtis Martin	45.00
AW23	Marshall Faulk	50.00
AW24	Edgerrin James, Curtis Martin, Marshall Faulk	200.00

2000 Playoff Prestige Award Winning Performers

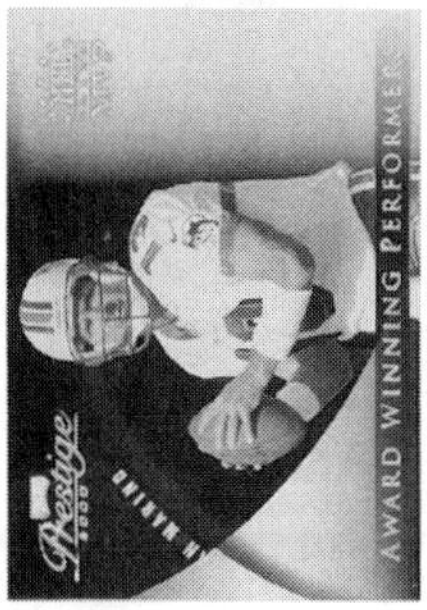

		MT
Complete Set (24):		65.00
Common Player:		1.00
Minor Stars:		2.00
Inserted 1:31		
AW1	Brett Favre	6.00
AW2	Barry Sanders	6.00
AW3	Thurman Thomas	1.00
AW4	Brett Favre, Barry Sanders, Thurman Thomas	5.00
AW5	Dan Marino	5.00
AW6	Steve Young	2.50
AW7	Kurt Warner	6.00
AW8	Dan Marino, Steve Young, Kurt Warner	5.00
AW9	John Elway	5.00
AW10	Terrell Davis	4.00
AW11	Phil Simms	1.00
AW12	John Elway, Terrell Davis, Phil Simms	5.00
AW13	Troy Aikman	4.00
AW14	Emmitt Smith	4.00
AW15	Jerry Rice	4.00
AW16	Troy Aikman, Emmitt Smith, Jerry Rice	4.00
AW17	Randy Moss	6.00
AW18	Eddie George	2.00
AW19	Jerome Bettis	1.00
AW20	Randy Moss, Eddie George, Jerome Bettis	4.00
AW21	Edgerrin James	5.00
AW22	Curtis Martin	1.00
AW23	Marshall Faulk	2.00
AW24	Edgerrin James, Curtis Martin, Marshall Faulk	3.00

2000 Playoff Prestige Award Winning Signatures

		MT
Common Player:		45.00
Inserted 1:330		
Single Autos #'d to 100		
Triple Autos #'d to 25		
AW1	Brett Favre	175.00
AW2	Barry Sanders	150.00
AW3	Thurman Thomas	45.00
AW4	Brett Favre, Barry Sanders, Thurman Thomas	350.00
AW5	Dan Marino	150.00
AW6	Steve Young	65.00
AW7	Kurt Warner	175.00
AW8	Dan Marino, Steve Young, Kurt Warner	425.00
AW9	John Elway	150.00
AW10	Terrell Davis	85.00
AW11	Phil Simms	45.00
AW12	John Elway, Terrell Davis, Phil Simms	350.00
AW13	Troy Aikman	100.00
AW14	Emmitt Smith	125.00
AW15	Jerry Rice	100.00
AW16	Troy Aikman, Emmitt Smith, Jerry Rice	425.00
AW17	Randy Moss	150.00
AW18	Eddie George	50.00
AW19	Jerome Bettis	45.00
AW20	Randy Moss, Eddie George, Jerome Bettis	300.00
AW21	Edgerrin James	150.00
AW22	Curtis Martin	45.00
AW23	Marshall Faulk	50.00
AW24	Edgerrin James, Curtis Martin, Marshall Faulk	275.00

Values quoted in this guide reflect the retail price of a card — the price a collector can expect to pay when buying a card from a dealer. The wholesale price — that which a collector can expect to receive from a dealer when selling cards — will be significantly lower, depending on desirability and condition.

2000 Playoff Prestige Draft Picks

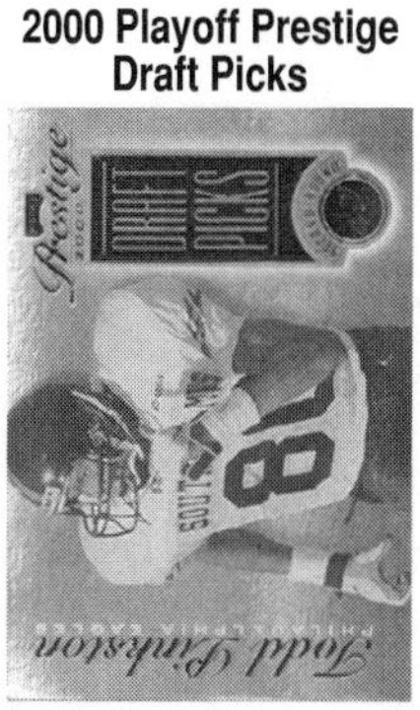

		MT
Complete Set (30):		60.00
Common Player:		1.00
Minor Stars:		2.00
Inserted 1:8		
DP1	Joe Hamilton	2.00
DP2	Peter Warrick	10.00
DP3	Courtney Brown	3.00
DP4	Plaxico Burress	6.00
DP5	Thomas Jones	5.00
DP6	Travis Taylor	3.50
DP7	Shaun Alexander	5.00
DP8	Chris Redman	3.00
DP9	Chad Pennington	6.00
DP10	Jamal Lewis	5.00
DP11	Bubba Franks	2.00
DP12	Dez White	2.00
DP13	Ron Dayne	10.00
DP14	Sylvester Morris	3.00
DP15	R. Jay Soward	2.50
DP16	Travis Prentice	3.00
DP17	Darrell Jackson	2.50
DP18	Giovanni Carmazzi	3.00
DP19	Danny Farmer	1.00
DP20	Dennis Northcutt	2.50
DP21	Laveranues Coles	2.00
DP22	J.R. Redmond	2.50
DP23	Jerry Porter	2.00
DP24	Reuben Droughns	2.00
DP25	Trung Canidate	2.00
DP26	Trevor Gaylor	2.00
DP27	Chris Cole	1.00
DP28	Tim Rattay	2.50
DP29	Ron Dugans	2.00
DP30	Todd Pinkston	2.00

2000 Playoff Prestige Human Highlight Film

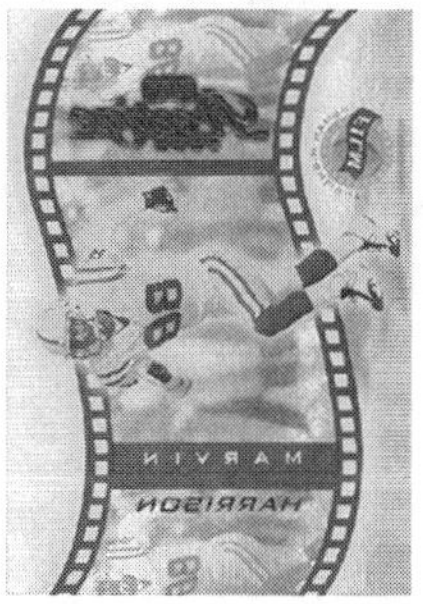

		MT
Complete Set (70):		125.00
Common Player:		1.25
Minor Stars:		2.50
Inserted 1:15		
Gold Cards:		4x-8x
Production 50 Sets		
HH1	Randy Moss	10.00
HH2	Brett Favre	10.00
HH3	Dan Marino	8.00
HH4	Barry Sanders	8.00
HH5	John Elway	8.00
HH6	Peyton Manning	10.00
HH7	Terrell Davis	7.00
HH8	Emmitt Smith	7.00
HH9	Troy Aikman	6.00
HH10	Jerry Rice	6.00
HH11	Fred Taylor	4.00
HH12	Jake Plummer	2.50
HH13	Charlie Batch	2.50
HH14	Drew Bledsoe	3.50
HH15	Mark Brunell	3.50
HH16	Steve Young	3.50
HH17	Eddie George	3.00
HH18	Mike Alstott	2.50
HH19	Jamal Anderson	2.50
HH20	Jerome Bettis	2.50
HH21	Tim Brown	1.25
HH22	Cris Carter	2.50
HH23	Stephen Davis	2.50
HH24	Corey Dillon	2.50
HH25	Warrick Dunn	2.50
HH26	Curtis Enis	1.25
HH27	Marshall Faulk	2.50
HH28	Doug Flutie	3.00
HH29	Antonio Freeman	2.50
HH30	Joey Galloway	2.50
HH31	Terry Glenn	2.50
HH32	Marvin Harrison	2.50
HH33	Brad Johnson	2.50
HH34	Keyshawn Johnson	2.50
HH35	Jon Kitna	2.50
HH36	Dorsey Levens	2.50
HH37	Curtis Martin	2.50
HH38	Steve McNair	2.50
HH39	Eric Moulds	2.50
HH40	Terrell Owens	2.50
HH41	Deion Sanders	2.50
HH42	Antowain Smith	1.25
HH43	Robert Smith	2.50
HH44	Duce Staley	2.50
HH45	Kordell Stewart	2.50
HH46	Isaac Bruce	2.50
HH47	Germane Crowell	2.50
HH48	Michael Irvin	2.50
HH49	Ed McCaffrey	2.50
HH50	Muhsin Muhammad	2.50
HH51	Jimmy Smith	2.50
HH52	James Stewart	2.50
HH53	Amani Toomer	1.25
HH54	Ricky Watters	2.50
HH55	Michael Westbrook	2.50
HH56	Brian Griese	3.00
HH57	Marcus Robinson	2.50
HH58	Kurt Warner	10.00
HH59	Edgerrin James	10.00
HH60	Tim Couch	5.00
HH61	Ricky Williams	5.00
HH62	Donovan McNabb	3.00
HH63	Cade McNown	3.00
HH64	Daunte Culpepper	3.50
HH65	Akili Smith	3.00
HH66	Torry Holt	2.50
HH67	Peerless Price	2.50
HH68	Kevin Johnson	2.50
HH69	Shaun King	3.00
HH70	Olandis Gary	3.00

2000 Playoff Prestige Inside the Numbers

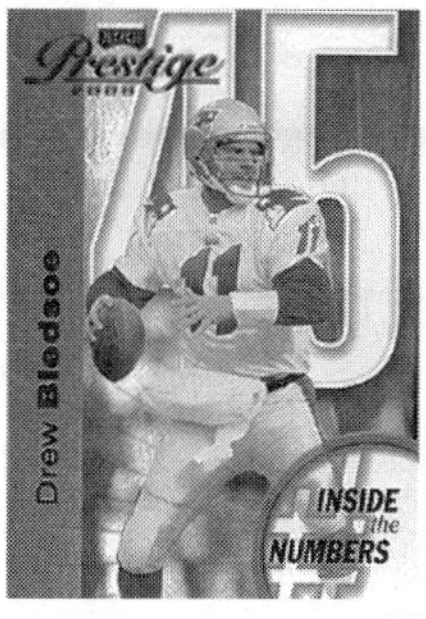

		MT
Complete Set (100):		275.00
Common Player:		1.50
Minor Stars:		3.00
Inserted 1:15		
IN1	Ricky Williams	6.00
IN2	Edgerrin James	12.00
IN3	Brett Favre	12.00
IN4	Donovan McNabb	5.00
IN5	James Stewart	1.50
IN6	Corey Dillon	3.00
IN7	Tim Couch	6.00
IN8	Doug Flutie	4.00
IN9	Jake Plummer	3.00
IN10	Akili Smith	4.00
IN11	Jerry Rice	8.00
IN12	Brian Griese	4.00
IN13	Peyton Manning	12.00
IN14	Fred Taylor	5.00
IN15	Brad Johnson	3.00
IN16	Courtney Brown	5.00
IN17	Randy Moss	12.00
IN18	Deion Sanders	3.00
IN19	Bruce Smith	1.50
IN20	Natrone Means	1.50
IN21	Dez White	4.00
IN22	Robert Smith	3.00
IN23	Jon Kitna	3.00
IN24	Duce Staley	3.00
IN25	Emmitt Smith	10.00
IN26	Dennis Northcutt	4.00
IN27	Antowain Smith	1.50
IN28	Mike Alstott	3.00
IN29	Ike Hilliard	1.50
IN30	Ed McCaffrey	3.00
IN31	Cade McNown	4.00
IN32	Jamal Lewis	10.00
IN33	Ron Dayne	15.00
IN34	Isaac Bruce	3.00
IN35	Tim Brown	1.50
IN36	Steve Beuerlein	1.50
IN37	Olandis Gary	3.00
IN38	Shyrone Stith	3.00
IN39	Jerome Bettis	3.00
IN40	Todd Pinkston	3.00
IN41	Kurt Warner	12.00
IN42	Peter Warrick	15.00
IN43	Steve Young	5.00
IN44	Corey Simon	3.00
IN45	Drew Bledsoe	5.00
IN46	Ron Dugans	4.00
IN47	Germane Crowell	3.00
IN48	Dan Marino	10.00
IN49	Eric Moulds	3.00
IN50	Peerless Price	3.00
IN51	Travis Taylor	6.00
IN52	Torry Holt	3.00
IN53	Charlie Batch	3.00
IN54	Shaun Alexander	10.00
IN55	John Elway	10.00
IN56	Amani Toomer	1.50
IN57	Thomas Jones	10.00
IN58	David Boston	3.00
IN59	Terrell Davis	10.00
IN60	Marvin Harrison	3.00
IN61	Priest Holmes	3.00
IN62	Troy Aikman	8.00
IN63	Chris Redman	6.00
IN64	Eddie George	4.00
IN65	Plaxico Burress	12.00
IN66	Kevin Johnson	3.00
IN67	Chad Pennington	12.00
IN68	Marshall Faulk	3.00
IN69	Sylvester Morris	6.00
IN70	Jimmy Smith	3.00
IN71	Dorsey Levens	3.00
IN72	Joey Galloway	3.00
IN73	Daunte Culpepper	4.50
IN74	Curtis Martin	3.00
IN75	Shaun King	4.00
IN76	Stephen Davis	3.00
IN77	Danny Farmer	3.00
IN78	Travis Prentice	6.00
IN79	Terrell Owens	3.00
IN80	Jamal Anderson	3.00
IN81	Antonio Freeman	3.00
IN82	Mark Brunell	5.00
IN83	Steve McNair	3.00
IN84	Marcus Robinson	3.00
IN85	Keenan McCardell	1.50
IN86	Jevon Kearse	3.00
IN87	Thurman Thomas	1.50
IN88	Patrick Jeffers	3.00
IN89	Keyshawn Johnson	3.00
IN90	Terry Glenn	3.00
IN91	Jerry Porter	4.00
IN92	J.R. Redmond	5.00
IN93	Yancey Thigpen	1.50
IN94	Troy Edwards	3.00
IN95	Cris Carter	3.00
IN96	Muhsin Muhammad	1.50
IN97	Ricky Watters	3.00
IN98	R. Jay Soward	4.00
IN99	Barry Sanders	10.00
IN100	James Johnson	1.50

2000 Playoff Prestige League Leader Quads

		MT
Complete Set (12):		125.00
Common Player:		10.00
Inserted 1:159		
1	Peyton Manning, Rich Gannon, Ray Lucas, Mark Brunell	30.00
2	Elvis Grbac, Tony Banks, Steve McNair, Jon Kitna	10.00
3	Kurt Warner, Steve Beuerlein, Jeff George, Brad Johnson	30.00
4	Charlie Batch, Gus Frerotte, Chris Chandler, Troy Aikman	12.00
5	Edgerrin James, Curtis Martin, Eddie George, Ricky Watters	25.00
6	Corey Dillon, Olandis Gary, Jerome Bettis, Tyrone Wheatley	10.00
7	Stephen Davis, Emmitt Smith, Marshall Faulk, Duce Staley	20.00
8	Charlie Garner, Dorsey Levens, Robert Smith, Mike Alstott	10.00
9	Marvin Harrison, Jimmy Smith, Tim Brown, Kevin Johnson	12.00
10	Terry Glenn, Raghib Ismail, Tony Martin, Darnay Scott	10.00
11	Randy Moss, Marcus Robinson, Germane Crowell, Muhsin Muhammad	25.00
12	Amani Toomer, Cris Carter, Michael Westbrook, Isaac Bruce	12.00

2000 Playoff Prestige Team Checklist

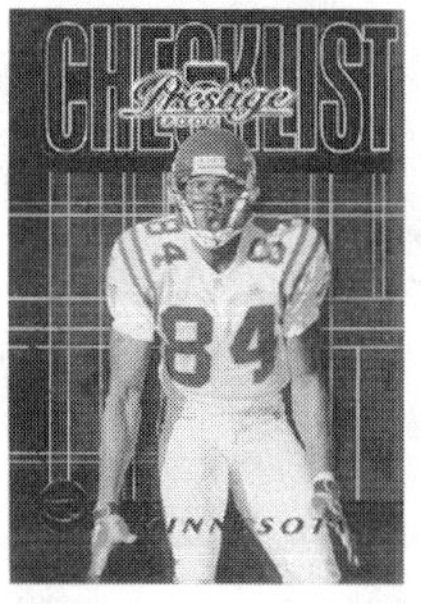

		MT
Complete Set (93):		300.00
Common Player (1-31):		1.00
Inserted 1:15		
Common Player (32-62):		1.50
Inserted 1:31		
Common Player (63-93):		10.00
Inserted 1:63		
CL1	Jake Plummer	1.00
CL2	Jamal Anderson	1.00
CL3	Jamal Lewis	3.50
CL4	Rob Johnson	1.00
CL5	Muhsin Muhammad	1.00
CL6	Marcus Robinson	1.00
CL7	Peter Warrick	5.00
CL8	Tim Couch	2.50
CL9	Emmitt Smith	3.50
CL10	Terrell Davis	3.50
CL11	Charlie Batch	1.00
CL12	Brett Favre	5.00
CL13	Peyton Manning	5.00
CL14	Mark Brunell	2.00
CL15	Elvis Grbac	1.00
CL16	Dan Marino	3.50
CL17	Randy Moss	5.00
CL18	Drew Bledsoe	2.00
CL19	Jeff Blake	1.00
CL20	Kerry Collins	1.00
CL21	Chad Pennington	4.00
CL22	Tim Brown	1.00
CL23	Duce Staley	1.00
CL24	Jerome Bettis	1.00
CL25	Jim Harbaugh	1.00
CL26	Jerry Rice	3.00
CL27	Jon Kitna	1.00
CL28	Kurt Warner	5.00
CL29	Keyshawn Johnson	1.00
CL30	Eddie George	1.50
CL31	Stephen Davis	1.00
CL32	Thomas Jones	5.00
CL33	Chris Chandler	1.50
CL34	Tony Banks	1.50
CL35	Eric Moulds	1.50
CL36	Tim Biakabutuka	1.50
CL37	Curtis Enis	1.50
CL38	Corey Dillon	1.50
CL39	Courtney Brown	3.00
CL40	Troy Aikman	4.00
CL41	Brian Griese	2.00
CL42	Herman Moore	1.50
CL43	Antonio Freeman	1.50
CL44	Edgerrin James	6.00
CL45	Fred Taylor	3.00
CL46	Derrick Alexander	1.50
CL47	James Johnson	1.50
CL48	Cris Carter	1.50
CL49	Terry Glenn	1.50
CL50	Sherrod Gideon	1.50
CL51	Ron Dayne	8.00
CL52	Curtis Martin	1.50
CL53	Rich Gannon	1.50
CL54	Todd Pinkston	2.00
CL55	Kordell Stewart	1.50
CL56	Junior Seau	1.50
CL57	Steve Young	3.00
CL58	Shaun Alexander	5.00
CL59	Marshall Faulk	1.50
CL60	Shaun King	2.50
CL61	Jevon Kearse	1.50
CL62	Brad Johnson	1.50
CL63	Frank Sanders	10.00
CL64	Tim Dwight	15.00
CL65	Qadry Ismail	10.00
CL66	Antowain Smith	10.00
CL67	Patrick Jeffers	15.00
CL68	Cade McNown	30.00
CL69	Akili Smith	25.00
CL70	Kevin Johnson	15.00
CL71	Joey Galloway	15.00
CL72	Olandis Gary	20.00
CL73	Germane Crowell	15.00
CL74	Dorsey Levens	15.00
CL75	Marvin Harrison	20.00
CL76	Jimmy Smith	15.00
CL78	Tony Martin	10.00
CL79	Daunte Culpepper	40.00
CL80	Kevin Faulk	10.00
CL81	Ricky Williams	50.00
CL82	Amani Toomer	10.00
CL83	Ray Lucas	15.00
CL84	Tyrone Wheatley	10.00
CL85	Donovan McNabb	30.00
CL86	Troy Edwards	20.00
CL87	Jermaine Fazande	15.00
CL88	Charlie Garner	15.00
CL89	Derrick Mayes	10.00
CL90	Isaac Bruce	20.00
CL91	Mike Alstott	20.00
CL92	Steve McNair	25.00
CL93	Albert Connell	10.00

2000 Playoff Prestige Xtra Points

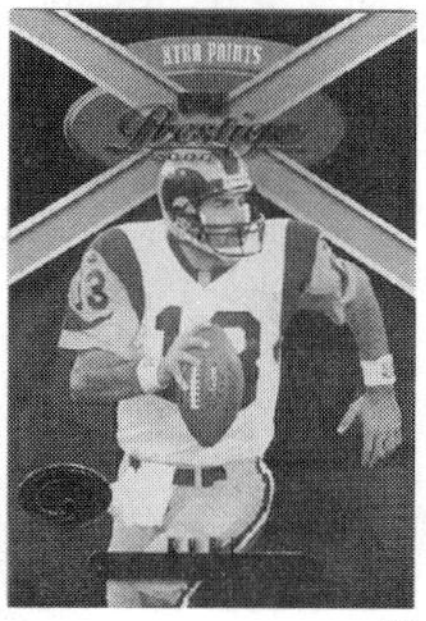

		MT
Complete Set (40):		125.00
Common Player:		2.00
Minor Stars:		4.00
Inserted 1:47		
XP1	Randy Moss	12.00
XP2	Brett Favre	12.00
XP3	Dan Marino	10.00
XP4	Peyton Manning	12.00
XP5	Emmitt Smith	10.00
XP6	Troy Aikman	8.00
XP7	Jerry Rice	8.00
XP8	Fred Taylor	5.00
XP9	Jake Plummer	4.00
XP10	Drew Bledsoe	5.00
XP11	Mark Brunell	5.00
XP12	Eddie George	4.00
XP13	Cris Carter	4.00
XP14	Stephen Davis	4.00
XP15	Corey Dillon	4.00
XP16	Marshall Faulk	4.00
XP17	Doug Flutie	4.00
XP18	Antonio Freeman	4.00
XP19	Terry Glenn	4.00
XP20	Marvin Harrison	4.00
XP21	Brad Johnson	4.00
XP22	Keyshawn Johnson	4.00
XP23	Jon Kitna	4.00
XP24	Dorsey Levens	4.00
XP25	Curtis Martin	4.00
XP26	Steve McNair	4.00
XP27	Isaac Bruce	4.00
XP28	Germane Crowell	4.00
XP29	Muhsin Muhammad	2.00
XP30	Jimmy Smith	4.00
XP31	Brian Griese	4.00
XP32	Marcus Robinson	4.00
XP33	Kurt Warner	12.00
XP34	Edgerrin James	12.00
XP35	Tim Couch	7.00
XP36	Ricky Williams	7.00
XP37	Torry Holt	4.00
XP38	Kevin Johnson	4.00
XP39	Shaun King	4.00
XP40	Olandis Gary	4.00

Post-1980 cards in Near Mint condition will generally sell for about 75% of the quoted Mint value. Excellent-condition cards bring no more than 40%.

2001 Playoff Absolute Memorabilia

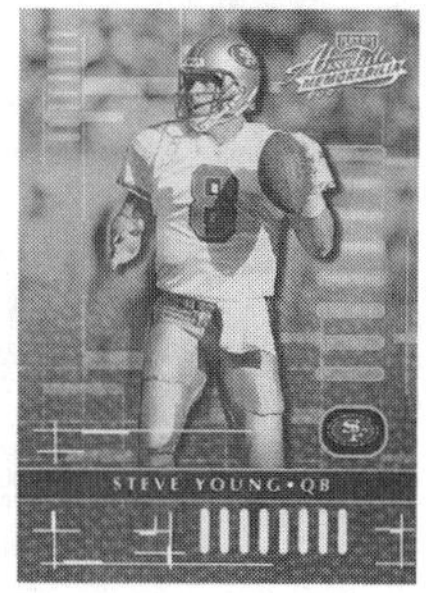

		MT
Complete Set (185):		850.00
Common Player:		.25
Minor Stars:		.50
Common Rookie:		2.00
Rookie Production 1,750 Sets		
Common RPM (151-185):		10.00
Production 850 Sets		
Pack (6):		10.00
Wax Box (18):		150.00
1	David Boston	1.00
2	Jake Plummer	1.00
3	Thomas Jones	.25
4	Jamal Anderson	1.00
5	Chris Redman	.25
6	Jamal Lewis	2.50
7	Qadry Ismail	.25
8	Ray Lewis	.25
9	Shannon Sharpe	.25
10	Travis Taylor	.25
11	Trent Dilfer	.25
12	Elvis Grbac	.25
13	Eric Moulds	.25
14	Rob Johnson	.25
15	Muhsin Muhammad	.25
16	Brian Urlacher	2.00
17	Cade McNown	1.00
18	Marcus Robinson	1.00
19	Akili Smith	1.00
20	Corey Dillon	1.00
21	Peter Warrick	2.00
22	Courtney Brown	.25
23	Tim Couch	1.25
24	Emmitt Smith	3.00
25	Troy Aikman	2.00
26	Brian Griese	1.25
27	Ed McCaffrey	1.00
28	John Elway	3.00
29	Mike Anderson	3.00
30	Rod Smith	.25
31	Terrell Davis	2.50
32	Barry Sanders	2.50
33	James Stewart	.25
34	Ahman Green	.25
35	Antonio Freeman	1.00
36	Brett Favre	4.00
37	Edgerrin James	2.50
38	Marvin Harrison	1.00
39	Peyton Manning	3.00
40	Fred Taylor	1.25
41	Jimmy Smith	.25
42	Keenan McCardell	.25
43	Mark Brunell	1.25
44	Sylvester Morris	.25
45	Tony Gonzalez	.25
46	Dan Marino	3.00
47	Jay Fiedler	1.00
48	Lamar Smith	.25
49	Cris Carter	1.00
50	Daunte Culpepper	2.00
51	Randy Moss	3.00
52	Drew Bledsoe	1.25
53	Terry Glenn	.25
54	Aaron Brooks	1.00
55	Joe Horn	.25
56	Ricky Williams	1.50
57	Amani Toomer	.25
58	Ike Hilliard	.25
59	Kerry Collins	.25
60	Ron Dayne	2.00
61	Tiki Barber	.25
62	Chad Pennington	2.00
63	Curtis Martin	1.00
64	Laveranues Coles	1.00
65	Vinny Testaverde	.25
66	Wayne Chrebet	.25
67	Charles Woodson	.25
68	Rich Gannon	.25
69	Tim Brown	1.00
70	Tyrone Wheatley	.25
71	Corey Simon	.25
72	Donovan McNabb	1.50
73	Duce Staley	1.00
74	Jerome Bettis	1.00
75	Plaxico Burress	1.00
76	Doug Flutie	1.25
77	Junior Seau	.25
78	Charlie Garner	.25
79	Jeff Garcia	1.00
80	Jerry Rice	2.00
81	Steve Young	1.25
82	Terrell Owens	1.00
83	Darrell Jackson	1.00
84	Ricky Watters	.25
85	Shaun Alexander	1.25
86	Isaac Bruce	1.00
87	Kurt Warner	3.00
88	Marshall Faulk	1.25
89	Torry Holt	1.00
90	Brad Johnson	1.00
91	Keyshawn Johnson	1.00
92	Mike Alstott	1.00
93	Shaun King	1.00
94	Warren Sapp	.25
95	Warrick Dunn	1.00
96	Eddie George	1.25
97	Jevon Kearse	1.00
98	Steve McNair	1.00
99	Jeff George	.25
100	Stephen Davis	1.00
101	*Jason McKinley*	2.00
102	*Bobby Newcombe*	5.00
103	*Cedrick Wilson*	5.00
104	*Ken-Yon Rambo*	5.00

105	Kevin Kasper	5.00
106	Jamal Reynolds	5.00
107	Scotty Anderson	4.00
108	T.J. Houshmandzadeh	4.00
109	Chris Taylor	4.00
110	Vinny Sutherland	4.00
111	Jabari Holloway	4.00
112	Shad Meier	4.00
113	Correl Buckhalter	6.00
114	Dan Alexander	4.00
115	David Allen	5.00
116	LaMont Jordan	6.00
117	Nate Clements	4.00
118	Reggie White	5.00
119	Javon Green	4.00
120	Shaun Rogers	2.00
121	Heath Evans	4.00
122	Moran Norris	2.00
123	Ben Leard	4.00
124	David Rivers	4.00
125	A.J. Feely	4.00
126	Boo Williams	2.00
127	Ronney Daniels	4.00
128	Alge Crumpler	5.00
129	Todd Heap	5.00
130	Tim Hasselbeck	5.00
131	Josh Booty	5.00
132	Jamie Winborn	4.00
133	Brian Allen	2.00
134	Sedrick Hodge	2.00
135	Tommy Polley	4.00
136	Torrance Marshall	4.00
137	Damione Lewis	4.00
138	Marcus Stroud	4.00
139	Aaron Schobel	2.00
140	DeLawrence Grant	2.00
141	Fred Smoot	5.00
142	Jamar Fletcher	5.00
143	Ken Lucas	4.00
144	Will Allen	4.00
145	Adam Archuleta	5.00
146	Derrick Gibson	2.00
147	Jarrod Cooper	2.00
148	Eddie Berlin	4.00
149	Steve Smith	4.00
150	Willie Middlebrooks	4.00
151	Michael Vick	100.00
152	Drew Brees	75.00
153	Chris Weinke	50.00
154	Marques Tuiasosopo	35.00
155	Mike McMahon	20.00
156	Deuce McAllister	60.00
157	Leonard Davis	10.00
158	LaDainian Tomlinson	75.00
159	Anthony Thomas	75.00
160	Travis Henry	30.00
161	James Jackson	20.00
162	Michael Bennett	50.00
163	Kevan Barlow	25.00
164	Travis Minor	25.00
165	David Terrell	60.00
166	Santana Moss	50.00
167	Rod Gardner	40.00
168	Quincy Morgan	25.00
169	Freddie Mitchell	40.00
170	Reggie Wayne	35.00
171	Koren Robinson	40.00
172	Chad Johnson	20.00
173	Chris Chambers	20.00
174	Josh Heupel	25.00
175	Andre Carter	15.00
176	Justin Smith	15.00
177	Richard Seymour	10.00
178	Dan Morgan	20.00
179	Gerard Warren	20.00
180	Robert Ferguson	25.00
181	Sage Rosenfels	20.00
182	Rudi Johnson	15.00
183	Marvin "Snoop" Minnis	25.00
184	Jesse Palmer	15.00
185	Quincy Carter	30.00

2001 Playoff Absolute Memorabilia Autograph Mini Helmet

		MT
Common Helmet:		25.00
Inserted 1:Box		
1	Alex Bannister 250	35.00
2	Barry Sanders 20	200.00
3	Cade McNown 1024	30.00
4	Chuck Foreman 600	35.00
5	Jake Plummer 1003	35.00
6	Jake Plummer CHR 19	125.00
7	Jevon Kearse 40	60.00
8	John Elway 40	200.00
9	Kurt Warner 119	130.00
10	Peyton Manning 287	125.00
11	Rich Gannon 1033	35.00
12	Trent Dilfer SB 100	60.00
13	Donovan McNabb 58	90.00
14	Dan Marino 80	180.00
15	Jim Kelly 20	170.00
16	Jim Kelly, Rob Johnson 18	185.00
17	Kerry Collins 18	85.00
18	Steve Young 20	200.00
19	Steve Young, Jeff Garcia 18	200.00
20	Troy Aikman 86	120.00
21	Troy Aikman CHR 34	175.00
22	Charlie Joiner 511	25.00
23	Charlie Taylor 485	25.00
24	Cliff Branch 554	35.00
25	Cliff Branch CHR 6	150.00
26	Jeff Garcia 1000	40.00
27	John Hannah 500	25.00
28	Kevin Greene 474	25.00
29	Kevin Greene CHR 24	85.00
30	Randall Cunningham 70	40.00
31	Ricky Williams 1046	50.00
32	Rob Johnson 501	35.00
33	Willie Brown 1005	25.00
34	Bob Lilly 600	40.00
35	Drew Pearson 600	35.00
36	Mike McMahon 289	35.00
37	Mike McMahon CHR 9	100.00
38	Drew Brees 273	120.00
39	Drew Brees CHR 24	225.00
40	Gerard Warren 250	30.00
41	James Jackson 238	35.00
42	James Jackson CHR 12	100.00
43	Ken-Yon Rambo 226	30.00
44	Ken-Yon Rambo CHR 24	85.00
45	LaDainian Tomlinson 226	120.00
46	LaDainian Tomlinson CHR 24	230.00
47	LaMont Jordan 237	35.00
48	Michael Bennett 251	100.00
49	Quincy Carter 236	75.00
50	Quincy Carter CHR 12	175.00
51	Quincy Morgan 238	45.00
52	Quincy Morgan CHR 12	120.00
53	Reggie Wayne 232	60.00
54	Reggie Wayne CHR 18	125.00
55	Sage Rosenfels 250	40.00
56	Santana Moss 238	65.00
57	Travis Minor 250	45.00
58	Rod Gardner 226	60.00
59	Chad Johnson 249	40.00
60	Chris Chambers 242	45.00
61	Chris Chambers CHR 12	180.00
62	Chris Weinke 226	75.00
63	Chris Weinke CHR 24	150.00
64	Deuce McAllister 224	80.00
65	Deuce McAllister CHR 24	150.00
66	Jesse Palmer 250	40.00
67	Justin Smith 239	35.00
68	Justin Smith CHR 11	100.00
69	Kevan Barlow 226	50.00
70	Kevan Barlow CHR 24	110.00
71	Robert Ferguson 226	50.00
72	Robert Ferguson CHR 24	110.00
73	Rudi Johnson 238	45.00
74	Rudi Johnson CHR 11	100.00
75	Anthony Thomas 238	60.00
76	Anthony Thomas CHR 12	125.00
77	Freddie Mitchell 217	50.00
78	Freddie Mitchell CHR 22	110.00
79	Koren Robinson 227	60.00
80	Koren Robinson CHR 23	120.00
81	Marvin "Snoop" Minnis 225	40.00
82	Marvin "Snoop" Minnis CHR 24	85.00
83	Michael Vick 226	150.00
84	Michael Vick CHR 24	300.00
85	Richard Seymour 228	25.00
86	Richard Seymour CHR 22	50.00
87	Todd Heap 225	35.00
88	Todd Heap CHR 22	70.00
89	Travis Henry 225	45.00
90	Travis Henry CHR 24	90.00
91	Will Allen 252	25.00
92	Harvey Martin 250	40.00

2001 Playoff Absolute Memorabilia Ground Hoggs

		MT
Common Player:		15.00
Production 125 Sets		
GH1	Amani Toomer	15.00
GH2	Antonio Freeman	20.00
GH3	Brett Favre	100.00
GH4	Bruce Mathews	15.00
GH5	Chad Pennington	40.00
GH6	Champ Bailey	20.00
GH7	Charles Woodson	20.00
GH8	Charlie Batch	15.00
GH9	Chris Samuels	15.00
GH10	Cris Carter	30.00
GH11	Curtis Martin	25.00
GH12	Dan Marino	125.00
GH13	Darrell Green	15.00
GH14	Darren Woodson	15.00
GH15	Daunte Culpepper	45.00
GH16	Deion Sanders	35.00
GH17	Derrick Mason	15.00
GH18	Eddie George	30.00
GH19	Edgerrin James	60.00
GH20	Emmitt Smith	70.00
GH21	Frank Wycheck	15.00
GH22	Fred Taylor	30.00
GH23	Ike Hilliard	15.00
GH24	Isaac Bruce	25.00
GH25	Jeff George	20.00
GH26	Jerry Rice	45.00
GH27	Jessie Armstead	15.00
GH28	Jevon Kearse	20.00
GH29	Jimmy Smith	15.00
GH30	Keyshawn Johnson	25.00
GH31	Lamar Smith	15.00
GH32	Laveranues Coles	15.00
GH33	Mark Brunell	30.00
GH34	Marshall Faulk	30.00
GH35	Marvin Harrison	25.00
GH36	Peerless Price	15.00
GH37	Peyton Manning	70.00
GH38	Raghib Ismail	15.00
GH39	Robert Smith	15.00
GH40	Ron Dayne	35.00
GH41	Stephen Davis	25.00
GH42	Terrell Owens	25.00
GH43	Terry Glenn	15.00
GH44	Tyrone Wheatley	15.00
GH45	Vinny Testaverde	15.00
GH46	Warren Moon	20.00
GH47	Warren Sapp	15.00
GH48	Wayne Chrebet	15.00
GH49	Willie McGinest	15.00
GH50	Zach Thomas	20.00

Values quoted in this guide reflect the retail price of a card — the price a collector can expect to pay when buying a card from a dealer. The wholesale price — that which a collector can expect to receive from a dealer when selling cards — will be significantly lower, depending on desirability and condition.

2001 Playoff Absolute Memorabilia Leather & Laces

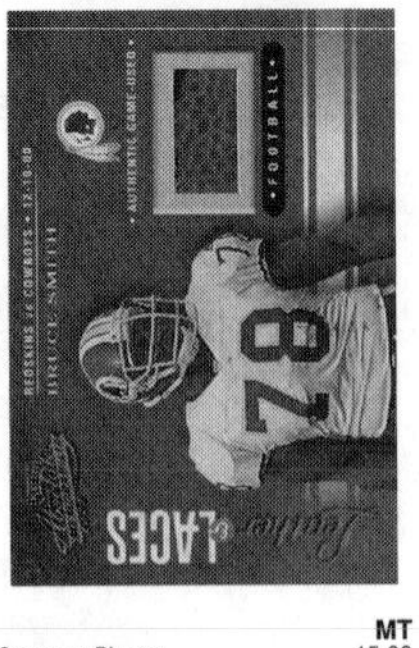

		MT
Common Player:		15.00
#1-16 Production 825 Sets		
#17-34 Production 550 Sets		
#35-50 Production 275 Sets		
Combos:		3x
#1-16 Production 75 Sets		
#17-34 Production 50 Sets		
#35-50 Production 25 Sets		
LL1	David Boston	15.00
LL2	Thomas Jones	10.00
LL3	Akili Smith	15.00
LL4	Cris Carter	25.00
LL5	Tiki Barber	15.00
LL6	Jevon Kearse	15.00
LL7	Jamal Anderson	20.00
LL8	Corey Simon	10.00
LL9	Deion Sanders	25.00
LL10	Stephen Davis	15.00
LL11	Peter Warrick	20.00
LL12	Kerry Collins	15.00
LL13	Bruce Smith	15.00
LL14	Jake Plummer	15.00
LL15	Darren Woodson	10.00
LL16	Steve McNair	20.00
LL17	Brian Urlacher	30.00
LL18	Cade McNown	20.00
LL19	Marcus Robinson	20.00
LL20	Corey Dillon	25.00
LL21	Emmitt Smith	45.00
LL22	Brett Favre	60.00
LL23	Peyton Manning	50.00
LL24	Fred Taylor	20.00
LL25	Mark Brunell	20.00
LL26	Dan Marino	50.00
LL27	Daunte Culpepper	30.00
LL28	Randy Moss	40.00
LL29	Drew Bledsoe	25.00
LL30	Ron Dayne	20.00
LL31	Donovan McNabb	25.00
LL32	Jerome Bettis	20.00
LL33	Jerry Rice	35.00
LL34	Eddie George	25.00
LL35	Isaac Bruce	30.00
LL36	Ray Lewis	20.00
LL37	Tim Couch	40.00
LL38	Eric Moulds	20.00
LL39	Doug Flutie	30.00
LL40	Edgerrin James	50.00
LL41	Curtis Martin	20.00
LL42	Wayne Chrebet	20.00
LL43	Jamal Lewis	40.00
LL44	Kurt Warner	60.00
LL45	Barry Sanders	60.00
LL46	Marvin Harrison	25.00
LL47	Ricky Williams	25.00
LL48	Jimmy Smith	15.00
LL49	Tim Brown	25.00
LL50	Troy Aikman	50.00

2001 Playoff Absolute Memorabilia Tools of the Trade

		MT
Common Player:		15.00
Glove Production 50 Sets		
Pants Production 100 Sets		
Facemask Production 125 Sets		
Jersey Production 300 Sets		
TT1	Antonio Freeman	20.00
TT2	Barry Sanders	50.00
TT3	Brett Favre	60.00
TT4	Brian Griese	25.00
TT5	Donovan McNabb	30.00
TT6	Daunte Culpepper	40.00
TT7	Drew Bledsoe	30.00
TT8	Emmitt Smith	50.00
TT9	Jamal Lewis	35.00
TT10	Jimmy Smith	15.00
TT11	Edgerrin James	45.00
TT12	Mike Anderson	30.00
TT13	Peyton Manning	60.00
TT14	Randy Moss	60.00
TT15	Rich Gannon	30.00
TT16	Ricky Williams	30.00
TT17	Steve McNair	25.00
TT18	Terrell Owens	25.00
TT19	Ricky Watters	15.00
TT20	Warren Sapp	25.00
TT21	Champ Bailey	40.00
TT22	Courtney Brown	25.00
TT23	Deion Sanders	30.00
TT24	Derrick Mason	25.00
TT25	Eddie George	30.00
TT26	Jevon Kearse	40.00
TT27	Keyshawn Johnson	35.00
TT28	Ron Dayne	40.00
TT29	Terry Glenn	30.00
TT30	Wayne Chrebet	25.00
TT31	Curtis Martin	30.00
TT32	Corey Dillon	30.00
TT33	Cris Carter	35.00
TT34	Junior Seau	30.00
TT35	Jerome Bettis	30.00
TT36	Warrick Dunn	30.00
TT37	Eric Moulds	30.00
TT38	Stephen Davis	25.00
TT39	Steve Young	45.00
TT40	Troy Aikman	60.00
TT41	Dan Marino	100.00
TT42	Isaac Bruce	25.00
TT43	Jerry Rice	50.00
TT44	John Elway	100.00
TT45	Kurt Warner	60.00
TT46	Mark Brunell	30.00
TT47	Marshall Faulk	30.00
TT48	Terrell Davis	50.00
TT49	Tim Couch	30.00
TT50	Torry Holt	20.00

2001 Playoff Contenders

		MT
Complete Set (100):		25.00
Common Player:		.30
Minor Stars:		.50
Common Rookie (101-200):		10.00
Pack (5):		6.00
Box (16):		85.00
1	David Boston	.60
2	Jake Plummer	.50
3	Jamal Anderson	.50
4	Chris Chandler	.30
5	Elvis Grbac	.50
6	Brandon Stokley	.30
7	Travis Taylor	.50
8	Ray Lewis	.50
9	Rob Johnson	.50
10	Eric Moulds	.50
11	Tim Biakabutuka	.30
12	Muhsin Muhammad	.30
13	James Allen	.30
14	Brian Urlacher	1.25
15	Peter Warrick	.60
16	Corey Dillon	.60
17	Tim Couch	.75
18	Kevin Johnson	.50
19	Rickey Dudley	.30
20	Emmitt Smith	2.00
21	Joey Galloway	.50
22	Brian Griese	1.00
23	Terrell Davis	1.50
24	Mike Anderson	1.00
25	Ed McCaffrey	.50
26	Rod Smith	.50
27	Charlie Batch	.50
28	James Stewart	.50
29	Germane Crowell	.30
30	Johnnie Morton	.30
31	Brett Favre	3.00
32	Ahman Green	.60
33	Antonio Freeman	.50
34	Peyton Manning	2.00
35	Edgerrin James	2.00
36	Marvin Harrison	.75
37	Jerome Pathon	.30
38	Mark Brunell	1.00
39	Fred Taylor	.75
40	Keenan McCardell	.30
41	Jimmy Smith	.50
42	Trent Green	.50
43	Priest Holmes	.50
44	Tony Gonzalez	.50
45	Derrick Alexander	.50
46	Jay Fiedler	.50
47	Lamar Smith	.50
48	Zach Thomas	.30
49	Oronde Gadsden	.30
50	Daunte Culpepper	1.50
51	Randy Moss	2.00
52	Cris Carter	.50
53	Drew Bledsoe	1.00
54	J.R. Redmond	.30
55	Troy Brown	.30
56	Aaron Brooks	1.00
57	Ricky Williams	1.25
58	Joe Horn	.30
59	Kerry Collins	.60
60	Tiki Barber	.50
61	Ron Dayne	.50
62	Ike Hilliard	.30
63	Vinny Testaverde	.50
64	Curtis Martin	.60
65	Wayne Chrebet	.50
66	Laveranues Coles	.50
67	Rich Gannon	.60
68	Tyrone Wheatley	.50
69	Tim Brown	.75
70	Jerry Rice	2.00
71	Donovan McNabb	1.50
72	Duce Staley	.50
73	Todd Pinkston	.30
74	Kordell Stewart	.75
75	Jerome Bettis	.60
76	Plaxico Burress	.75
77	Doug Flutie	1.00
78	Junior Seau	.50
79	Jeff Garcia	1.00
80	Garrison Hearst	.50
81	Terrell Owens	.75
82	Matt Hasselbeck	.60
83	Ricky Watters	.50
84	Shaun Alexander	1.25
85	Darrell Jackson	.50
86	Kurt Warner	2.50
87	Marshall Faulk	1.00
88	Isaac Bruce	.75
89	Torry Holt	.75
90	Brad Johnson	.60
91	Keyshawn Johnson	.75
92	Warrick Dunn	.50
93	Warren Sapp	.50
94	Steve McNair	.60
95	Eddie George	1.00
96	Derrick Mason	.50
97	Jevon Kearse	.50
98	Stephen Davis	.60
99	Bruce Smith	.30
100	Michael Westbrook	.50
101	Adam Archuleta	40.00
102	Alex Bannister	15.00
103	Alge Crumpler	10.00
104	Andre Carter	20.00
105	Anthony Thomas	100.00
106	Ben Leard	10.00
107	Bobby Newcombe	15.00
108	Brian Allen	10.00
109	Carlos Polk	10.00
110	Casey Hampton	25.00
111	Cedric Scott	10.00
112	Cedrick Wilson	12.00
113	Chad Johnson	15.00
114	Chris Chambers	75.00
115	Chris Weinke	50.00
116	Correll Buckhalter	30.00
117	Damione Lewis	25.00
118	Dan Morgan	30.00
119	Daniel Guy	12.00
120	David Allen	15.00
121	David Terrell	60.00
122	Ken Lucas	10.00
123	Deuce McAllister	90.00
124	Drew Brees	125.00
125	Eddie Berlin	25.00
126	Eddie "Boo" Williams	20.00
127	Ennis Davis	10.00
128	Freddie Mitchell	40.00
129	Gary Baxter	10.00
130	Gerard Warren	15.00
131	Hakim Akbar	10.00
132	Heath Evans	10.00
133	Jabari Holloway	12.00
134	Jamal Reynolds	15.00
135	James Jackson	30.00
136	Jamie Winborn	10.00
137	Javon Green	12.00
138	Jesse Palmer	25.00
139	Dominic Rhodes	75.00
140	Josh Heupel	25.00
141	Justin Smith	15.00
142	Karon Riley	10.00
143	Keith Adams	25.00
144	Kendrell Bell	60.00
145	Kenny Smith	10.00
146	Kenyatta Walker	20.00
147	Ken-Yon Rambo	15.00
148	Kevan Barlow	30.00
149	Koren Robinson	40.00
150	LaDainian Tomlinson	100.00
151	LaMont Jordan	40.00
152	Leonard Davis	25.00
153	Marcus Stroud	10.00
154	Marques Tuiasosopo	40.00
155	Marvin "Snoop" Minnis	30.00
156	Michael Bennett	80.00
157	Michael Vick	175.00
158	Mike McMahon	40.00
159	Moran Norris	10.00
160	Morlon Greenwood	10.00
161	Nate Clements	20.00
162	Quincy Carter	125.00
163	Quincy Morgan	20.00
164	Jamar Fletcher	25.00
165	Reggie Germany	25.00
166	Reggie Wayne	40.00
167	Reggie White	12.00
168	Richard Seymour	25.00
169	Robert Carswell	20.00
170	Robert Ferguson	20.00
171	Rod Gardner	40.00
172	Ronney Daniels	15.00
173	Rudi Johnson	15.00
174	Sage Rosenfels	25.00
175	Santana Moss	40.00
176	Shaun Rogers	10.00
177	T.J. Houshmandzadeh	10.00
178	Tim Hasselbeck	15.00
179	Todd Heap	12.00
180	Tony Stewart	12.00
181	Torrance Marshall	10.00
182	Travis Henry	30.00
183	Travis Minor	25.00
184	Vinny Sutherland	15.00
185	Will Allen	15.00
186	Willie Howard	10.00
187	Willie Middlebrooks	20.00
188	Derrick Blaylock	12.00
189	A.J. Feeley	20.00
190	Steve Smith	15.00
191	Onome Ojo	10.00
192	Dee Brown	12.00
193	Kevin Kasper	20.00
194	Dave Dickenson	20.00
195	Chris Barnes	12.00
196	Scotty Anderson	15.00
197	Chris Taylor	12.00
198	Cedric James	12.00
199	Justin McCareins	12.00
200	Tommy Polley	25.00

2001 Playoff Contenders MVP Contenders

		MT
Complete Set (20):		50.00
Common Player:		1.00
Inserted 1:16		
1	Brett Favre	8.00
2	Brian Griese	2.50
3	Corey Dillon	2.00
4	Cris Carter	2.00
5	Daunte Culpepper	4.00
6	Drew Bledsoe	2.50
7	Eddie George	2.50
8	Edgerrin James	5.00
9	Emmitt Smith	5.00
10	Isaac Bruce	2.00
11	Aaron Brooks	2.50
12	Jerry Rice	5.00
13	Kurt Warner	6.00
14	Mark Brunell	2.00
15	Marshall Faulk	2.50
16	Peyton Manning	6.00
17	Randy Moss	6.00
18	Ray Lewis	2.00
19	Ricky Williams	3.00
20	Stephen Davis	2.00

2001 Playoff Contenders ROY Contenders

		MT
Complete Set (20):		60.00
Common Player:		2.00
Inserted 1:32		
1	Anthony Thomas	10.00
2	Chad Johnson	2.00
3	Chris Chambers	5.00
4	Chris Weinke	4.00
5	David Terrell	6.00
6	Deuce McAllister	4.00
7	Drew Brees	8.00
8	Freddie Mitchell	4.00
9	James Jackson	2.50
10	Kevan Barlow	3.00
11	Koren Robinson	4.00
12	LaDainian Tomlinson	8.00
13	Marvin "Snoop" Minnis	3.00
14	Michael Bennett	5.00
15	Michael Vick	10.00
16	Quincy Carter	5.00
17	Quincy Morgan	2.50
18	Reggie Wayne	4.00
19	Travis Henry	3.00
20	Travis Minor	2.50

2001 Playoff Contenders ROY Contenders Autographs

		MT
Common Player:		40.00
Production 50 Sets		
1	Anthony Thomas	150.00
2	Chad Johnson	40.00
3	Chris Chambers	75.00
4	Chris Weinke	60.00
5	David Terrell	75.00
6	Deuce McAllister	60.00
7	Drew Brees	125.00
8	Freddie Mitchell	50.00
9	James Jackson	40.00
10	Kevan Barlow	40.00
11	Koren Robinson	50.00
12	LaDainian Tomlinson	100.00
13	Marvin "Snoop" Minnis	40.00
14	Michael Bennett	75.00
15	Michael Vick	150.00
16	Quincy Carter	60.00
17	Quincy Morgan	40.00
18	Reggie Wayne	40.00
19	Travis Henry	40.00
20	Travis Minor	40.00

2001 Playoff Contenders Round Numbers Autographs

		MT
Common Player:		25.00
1	Michael Vick, LaDainian Tomlinson	200.00
2	Deuce McAllister, Michael Bennett	60.00
3	David Terrell, Koren Robinson	60.00
4	Nate Clements, Will Allen	25.00
5	Todd Heap, Reggie Wayne	40.00
6	Richard Seymour, Justin Smith	25.00
7	Drew Brees, Quincy Carter	125.00
8	Anthony Thomas, Travis Henry	125.00
9	Chad Johnson, Quincy Morgan	25.00
10	Robert Ferguson, Chris Chambers	40.00
11	Shaun Rogers, Kendrell Bell	50.00
12	Kevan Barlow, Travis Minor	30.00
13	James Jackson, Marvin "Snoop" Minnis	30.00
14	Rudi Johnson, Correll Buckhalter	25.00
15	Chris Weinke, Jesse Palmer	40.00

2001 Playoff Contenders Round Numbers Gold

"Many cards too rare to price."

		MT
Complete Set (15):		
Common Player:		
1	Michael Vick/10, LaDainian Tomlinson/10	
2	Deuce McAllister/10, Michael Bennett/10	
3	David Terrell/10, Koren Robinson/10	
4	Nate Clements/10, Will Allen/10	
5	Todd Heap/10, Reggie Wayne/10	
6	Richard Seymour/10, Justin Smith/10	
7	Drew Brees/20, Quincy Carter/20	250.00
8	Anthony Thomas/20, Travis Henry/10	
9	Chad Johnson/20, Quincy Morgan/20	75.00
10	Robert Ferguson/20, Chris Chambers/20	250.00
11	Shaun Rogers/20, Kendrell Bell/20	75.00
12	Kevan Barlow/30, Travis Minor/30	40.00
13	James Jackson/30, Marvin "Snoop" Minnis/30	40.00
14	Rudi Johnson/40, Correll Buckhalter/40	40.00
15	Chris Weinke/40, Jesse Palmer/40	100.00

2001 Playoff Honors

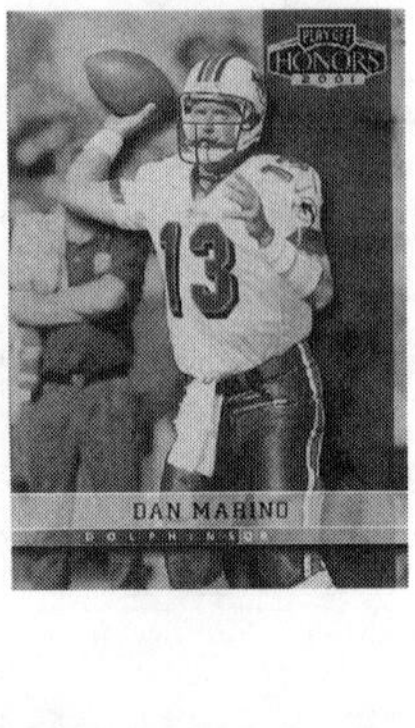

		MT
Complete Set (235):		1000.
Common Player:		.25
Minor Stars:		.50
Common Rookie (#101-200):		5.00
Production 250 Sets		
Common Rookie (#201-235):		10.00
Production 725 Sets		
Cards #209, #211 & #221 Released		Never
Pack (6):		11.00
Wax Box (16):		145.00
1	Rob Johnson	.50
2	Eric Moulds	.75
3	Marvin Harrison	.75
4	Edgerrin James	2.00
5	Peyton Manning	2.50
6	Jay Fiedler	.75
7	Lamar Smith	.50
8	Zach Thomas	.50
9	Dan Marino	3.00
10	Drew Bledsoe	1.00
11	Terry Glenn	.50
12	Wayne Chrebet	.75
13	Curtis Martin	.75
14	Chad Pennington	1.25
15	Vinny Testaverde	.50
16	Corey Dillon	.75
17	Jon Kitna	.75
18	Akili Smith	.75
19	Peter Warrick	1.00
20	Kevin Johnson	.75
21	Tim Couch	1.00
22	Eddie George	1.00
23	Steve McNair	.75
24	Jevon Kearse	.75
25	Jerome Bettis	.75
26	Kordell Stewart	.75
27	Plaxico Burress	.75
28	Mark Brunell	1.00
29	Keenan McCardell	.50
30	Jimmy Smith	.75
31	Fred Taylor	1.00
32	Elvis Grbac	.50
33	Jamal Lewis	2.00
34	Ray Lewis	.75
35	Mike Anderson	2.00
36	Terrell Davis	1.50
37	John Elway	3.00
38	Brian Griese	1.00
39	Ed McCaffrey	.75
40	Tony Gonzalez	.75
41	Trent Green	.75
42	Sylvester Morris	.50
43	Tim Brown	.75
44	Rich Gannon	.50
45	Charlie Garner	.50
46	Tyrone Wheatley	.50
47	Charles Woodson	.75
48	Tim Dwight	.50
49	Doug Flutie	1.00
50	Junior Seau	.50
51	Shaun Alexander	1.00
52	Matt Hasselbeck	.75
53	Ricky Watters	.50
54	Tony Banks	.50
55	Joey Galloway	.75
56	Emmitt Smith	2.00
57	Troy Aikman	1.50
58	Kerry Collins	.50
59	Ron Dayne	1.25
60	Donovan McNabb	1.25
61	Duce Staley	.75
62	David Boston	.75
63	Thomas Jones	.50
64	Jake Plummer	.75
65	Stephen Davis	.75
66	Jeff George	.50
67	Michael Westbrook	.50
68	Deion Sanders	.75
69	James Allen	.50
70	Cade McNown	.75
71	Marcus Robinson	.75
72	Brian Urlacher	1.50
73	Germane Crowell	.75
74	Charlie Batch	.75
75	James Stewart	.50
76	Brett Favre	3.50
77	Antonio Freeman	.75
78	Ahman Green	.75
79	Cris Carter	.75
80	Daunte Culpepper	1.50
81	Randy Moss	2.50
82	Mike Alstott	.75
83	Warrick Dunn	.75
84	Brad Johnson	.50
85	Keyshawn Johnson	.75
86	Warren Sapp	.50
87	Jamal Anderson	.75
88	Chris Chandler	.50
89	Isaac Bruce	.75
90	Marshall Faulk	1.00
91	Torry Holt	.75
92	Kurt Warner	3.00
93	Aaron Brooks	1.00
94	Albert Connell	.25
95	Ricky Williams	1.25
96	Jeff Garcia	.75
97	Terrell Owens	.75
98	Steve Young	1.00
99	Jerry Rice	1.75
100	Jeff Lewis	.25
101	*Rashard Casey*	10.00
102	*A.J. Feeley*	10.00
103	*Josh Booty*	10.00
104	*LaMont Jordan*	10.00
105	*Ben Leard*	10.00
106	*David Rivers*	10.00
107	*Tim Hasselbeck*	10.00
108	*Jason McKinley*	10.00
109	*Correl Buckhalter*	20.00
110	*Dan Alexander*	10.00
111	*Derrick Blaylock*	10.00
112	*Chris Barnes*	12.00
113	*Dadrian Brown*	10.00
114	*Derek Combs*	10.00
115	*David Allen*	10.00
116	*DeAngelo Evans*	10.00
117	*Reggie White*	10.00
118	*Heath Evans*	10.00
119	*George Layne*	10.00
120	*Moran Norris*	5.00
121	*Bhawoh Jue*	5.00
122	*Dustin McClintock*	10.00
123	*Ja'Mar Toombs*	10.00
124	*Steve Smith*	10.00
125	*Milton Wynn*	10.00
126	*Justin McCareins*	10.00
127	*Jarrod Cooper*	10.00
128	*Vinny Sutherland*	12.00
129	*Alex Bannister*	12.00
130	*Scotty Anderson*	10.00
131	*Onomo Ojo*	10.00
132	*Darnerian McCants*	10.00
133	*Eddie Berlin*	10.00
134	*Jonathan Carter*	10.00
135	*Bobby Newcombe*	10.00
136	*Cedrick Wilson*	10.00
137	*Kevin Kasper*	15.00
138	*Francis St. Paul*	10.00
139	*David Martin*	10.00
140	*T.J. Houshmandzadeh*	10.00
141	*John Capel*	10.00
142	*Reggie Germany*	10.00
143	*Chris Taylor*	10.00
144	*Ken-Yon Rambo*	10.00
145	*Richmond Flowers*	10.00
146	*Quentin McCord*	10.00
147	*Andre King*	10.00
148	*Eddie "Boo" Williams*	5.00
149	*Daniel Guy*	5.00
150	*Javon Green*	10.00
151	*Ronney Daniels*	10.00
152	*Alge Crumpler*	15.00
153	*Tony Driver*	10.00
154	*Shad Meier*	10.00
155	*Jabari Holloway*	10.00
156	*Ryan Pickett*	10.00
157	*Billy Baber*	10.00
158	*Tony Stewart*	10.00
159	*Arther Love*	10.00
160	*Orlando Huff*	10.00
161	*Nate Clements*	10.00
162	*Will Allen*	10.00
163	*Willie Middlebrooks*	10.00
164	*Jamar Fletcher*	10.00
165	*Ken Lucas*	10.00
166	*Fred Smoot*	10.00
167	*Michael Stone*	5.00
168	*Tony Dixon*	5.00
169	*Andre Dyson*	5.00
170	*Gary Baxter*	10.00
171	*Adam Archuleta*	15.00
172	*Derrick Gibson*	5.00
173	*Edgerton Hartwell*	10.00
174	*Jamal Reynolds*	10.00
175	*Richard Seymour*	10.00
176	*Aaron Schobel*	10.00
177	*Paul Toviessi*	5.00
178	*DeLawrence Grant*	5.00
179	*Karon Riley*	5.00
180	*Cedric Scott*	10.00
181	*Damione Lewis*	10.00
182	*Marcus Stroud*	10.00
183	*Casey Hampton*	10.00
184	*Willie Howard*	10.00
185	*Shaun Rogers*	5.00
186	*Kenny Smith*	5.00
187	*Marcus Bell*	5.00
188	*Mario Fatafehi*	10.00
189	*Kendrell Bell*	30.00
190	*Tommy Polley*	10.00
191	*Jamie Winborn*	10.00
192	*Sedrick Hodge*	10.00
193	*Torrance Marshall*	10.00
194	*Eric Westmoreland*	10.00
195	*Brian Allen*	5.00
196	*Morlon Greenwood*	10.00
197	*Brandon Spoon*	10.00
198	*Carlos Polk*	10.00
199	*Alex Lincoln*	10.00
200	*Keith Adams*	10.00
201	*Kevan Barlow*	20.00
202	*Michael Bennett*	35.00
203	*Drew Brees*	60.00
204	*Quincy Carter*	30.00
205	*Andre Carter*	10.00
206	*Chris Chambers*	25.00
207	*Robert Ferguson*	10.00
208	*Rod Gardner*	30.00
210	*Travis Henry*	25.00
212	*Chad Johnson*	15.00
213	*Rudi Johnson*	15.00
214	*Sage Rosenfels*	15.00
215	*Deuce McAllister*	30.00
216	*Mike McMahon*	15.00
217	*Marvin "Snoop" Minnis*	20.00
218	*Travis Minor*	15.00
219	*Freddie Mitchell*	25.00
220	*Quincy Morgan*	20.00
222	*Santana Moss*	25.00
223	*Jesse Palmer*	15.00
224	*Koren Robinson*	25.00
225	*Josh Heupel*	15.00
226	*Justin Smith*	10.00
227	*David Terrell*	35.00
228	*Anthony Thomas*	60.00
229	*LaDainian Tomlinson*	60.00
230	*Marques Tuiasosopo*	25.00
231	*Michael Vick*	70.00
232	*Gerard Warren*	15.00
233	*Reggie Wayne*	20.00
234	*Chris Weinke*	30.00
235	*Leonard Davis*	10.00

2001 Playoff Honors Alma Mater Materials

		MT
Complete Set (15):		
Common Player:		15.00
1	Shaun Alexander	20.00
2	Drew Bledsoe	20.00
3	Earl Campbell	25.00
4	Larry Csonka	15.00
5	Terrell Davis	20.00
6	Tony Dorsett	25.00
7	John Elway	75.00
8	Eddie George	20.00
9	Edgerrin James	40.00
10	Keyshawn Johnson	20.00
11	Jevon Kearse	15.00
12	Fred Taylor	15.00
13	Ricky Williams	20.00
14	Olandis Gary	15.00
15	E.G. Green	15.00

Post-1980 cards in Near Mint condition will generally sell for about 75% of the quoted Mint value. Excellent-condition cards bring no more than 40%.

2001 Playoff Honors Game Day Jerseys

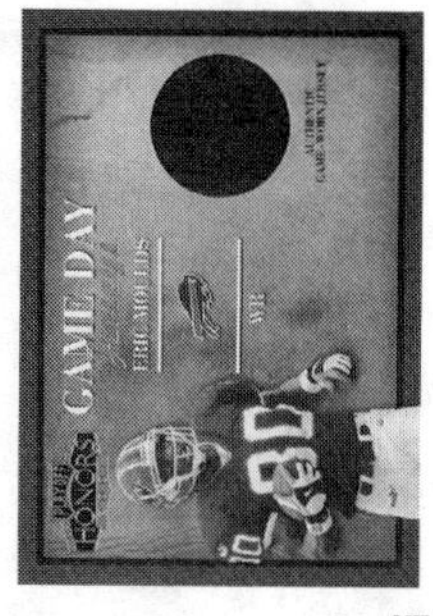

		MT
Complete Set (50):		
Common Player:		5.00
1	Troy Aikman	25.00
2	Mike Anderson	10.00
3	Jerome Bettis	10.00
4	Drew Bledsoe	10.00
5	Aaron Brooks	10.00
6	Isaac Bruce	5.00
7	Tim Brown	10.00
8	Mark Brunell	10.00
9	Cris Carter	5.00
10	Kerry Collins	5.00
11	Tim Couch	10.00
12	Daunte Culpepper	15.00
13	Stephen Davis	10.00
14	Terrell Davis	15.00
15	Ron Dayne	15.00
16	Corey Dillon	10.00
17	Warrick Dunn	5.00
18	John Elway	30.00
19	Marshall Faulk	15.00
20	Brett Favre	40.00
21	Eddie George	10.00
22	Brian Griese	10.00
23	Marvin Harrison	5.00
24	Torry Holt	5.00
25	Edgerrin James	25.00
26	Keyshawn Johnson	5.00
27	Jevon Kearse	5.00
28	Jamal Lewis	25.00
29	Peyton Manning	15.00
30	Dan Marino	30.00
31	Curtis Martin	10.00
32	Donovan McNabb	10.00
33	Steve McNair	10.00
34	Joe Montana	30.00
35	Randy Moss	10.00
36	Eric Moulds	5.00
37	Jake Plummer	5.00
38	Jerry Rice	25.00
39	Barry Sanders	25.00
40	Deion Sanders	20.00
41	Warren Sapp	5.00
42	Junior Seau	5.00
43	Emmitt Smith	30.00
44	Fred Taylor	10.00
45	Zach Thomas	10.00
46	Brian Urlacher	40.00
47	Kurt Warner	30.00
48	Peter Warrick	10.00
49	Ricky Williams	10.00
50	Steve Young	30.00

2001 Playoff Honors Rookie Tandem/ Quad Materials

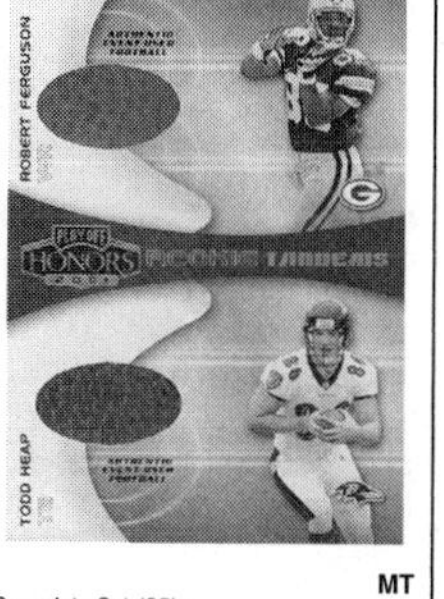

		MT
Complete Set (25):		
Common Player:		10.00
1	Michael Vick, Quincy Carter	20.00
2	Chris Weinke, Mike McMahon	20.00
3	Drew Brees, LaDainian Tomlinson	30.00
4	Anthony Thomas, David Terrell	40.00
5	Sage Rosenfels, Rod Gardner	10.00
6	Rudi Johnson, Chad Johnson	10.00
7	Josh Heupel, Travis Minor	10.00
8	James Jackson, Quincy Morgan	10.00
9	Koren Robinson, Reggie Wayne	10.00
10	Freddie Mitchell, Santana Moss	20.00
11	Michael Bennett, Deuce McAllister	25.00
12	Travis Henry, Kevan Barlow	15.00
13	Chris Chambers, Marvin "Snoop" Minnis	15.00
14	Robert Ferguson, Todd Heap	10.00
15	Marques Tuiasosopo, Jesse Palmer	20.00
16	Justin Smith, Gerard Warren	10.00
17	Andre Carter, Dan Morgan	10.00
18	Michael Vick, Quincy Carter, Chris Weinke, Mike McMahon	75.00
19	Drew Brees, LaDainian Tomlinson, Anthony Thomas, David Terrell	125.00
20	Sage Rosenfels, Rod Gardner, Rudi Johnson, Chad Johnson	20.00
21	Josh Heupel, Travis Minor, James Jackson, Quincy Morgan	30.00
22	Koren Robinson, Reggie Wayne, Freddie Mitchell, Santana Moss	30.00
23	Michael Bennett, Deuce McAllister, Travis Henry, Kevan Barlow	50.00
24	Chris Chambers, Marvin "Snoop" Minnis, Robert Ferguson, Todd Heap	50.00
25	Marques Tuiasosopo, Jesse Palmer, Justin Smith, Gerard Warren	25.00

1985 Police Raiders/Rams

Broken down into two 15-card subsets for each team, the cards are not numbered, except with the player's uniform numerals. It was sponsored by KIIS Radio, the Rams and Raiders and the Los Angeles County Sheriff's Department. Card fronts include a photo of the player, with his name underneath, along with his team's helmet and sponsor logo. Card backs have the player's name, uniform number, position, bio and a safety message printed in black. The cards measure 2-13/16 x 4-1/8".

		MT
Complete Set (30):		20.00
Common Raiders (1-15):		.75
Common Rams (16-30):		.50
1	Marcus Allen	4.00
2	Lyle Alzado	1.50
3	Todd Christensen	1.00
4	Dave Dalby	.75
5	Mike Davis	.75
6	Ray Guy	1.00
7	Frank Hawkins	.75
8	Lester Hayes	1.00
9	Mike Haynes	1.00
10	Howie Long	2.00
11	Rod Martin	.75
12	Mickey Marvin	.75
13	Jim Plunkett	1.25
14	Brad Van Pelt	.75
15	Dokie Williams	.75
16	Bill Bain	.50
17	Mike Barber	.50
18	Dieter Brock	.75
19	Nolan Cromwell	.75
20	Eric Dickerson	3.00
21	Reggie Doss	.50
22	Carl Ekern	.50
23	Kent Hill	.50
24	LeRoy Irvin	.75
25	Johnnie Johnson	.50
26	Jeff Kemp	.50
27	Mike Lansford	.50
28	Mel Owens	.50
29	Barry Redden	.50
30	Mike Wilcher	.50

1986 Police Bears/Patriots

Featuring the two teams from Super Bowl XX, this 17-card set measures 2-5/8" x 4-1/4". The card fronts boast a photo of the player, with his name, uniform number and position at the bottom. The card backs have "Super Bowl Superstars 1986 presents" at the top, with a safety tip listed at the bottom of the card. The card number is located in the lower right. Chicago players are on card #s 2-9, while New England players are highlighted on #s 10-17.

		MT
Complete Set (17):		15.00
Common Player:		.50
1	Title Card (Checklist on back of card)	.75
2	Richard Dent	2.00
3	Walter Payton	6.00
4	William Perry	1.00
5	Jim McMahon	1.50
6	Dave Duerson	.75
7	Gary Fencik	.75
8	Otis Wilson	.75
9	Willie Gault	1.00
10	Craig James	1.00
11	Fred Marion	.50
12	Ronnie Lippett	.50
13	Stanley Morgan	1.00
14	John Hannah	1.00
15	Andre Tippett	1.00
16	Tony Franklin	.50
17	Tony Eason	1.00

1976 Popsicle Teams

Each NFL team is represented in this 28-card set, which features a color action shot on the front of each card, plus the corresponding team's helmet. The back provides a historical overview of the team. The cards, which are unnumbered, are listed below alphabetically. Each one is 3-3/8" x 2-1/8" and resembles a thin plastic credit card with rounded corners. A title card, which says "Pro Quarterback, Pro Football's Leading Magazine," was also produced.

		NM
Complete Set (30):		40.00
Common Player:		2.50
(1)	Atlanta Falcons	2.50
(2)	Baltimore Colts	2.50
(3)	Buffalo Bills	2.50
(4)	Chicago Bears	2.50
(5)	Cincinnati Bengals	2.50
(6)	Cleveland Browns	2.50
(7)	Dallas Cowboys	4.00
(8)	Denver Broncos	2.50
(9)	Detriot Lions	2.50
(10)	Green Bay Packers	2.50
(11)	Houston Oilers	2.50
(12)	Kansas City Chiefs	2.50
(13)	Los Angeles Rams	2.50
(14)	Miami Dolphins	4.00
(15)	Minnesota Vikings	2.50
(16)	New England Patriots	2.50
(17)	New Orleans Saints	2.50
(18A)	New York Giants (Giants on helmet)	3.50
(18B)	New York Giants (New York on helmet)	4.50
(19)	New York Jets	2.50
(20)	Oakland Raiders	4.00
(21)	Philadelphia Eagles	2.50
(22)	Pittsburgh Steelers	4.00
(23)	St. Louis Cardinals	2.50
(24)	San Diego Chargers	2.50
(25)	San Francisco 49ers	3.00
(26)	Seattle Seahawks	2.50
(27)	Tampa Bay Buccaneers	2.50
(28)	Washington Redskins	3.50
----	Title Card, Pro Quarterback	30.00

1962 Post Cereal

Post Cereal's only U.S. football issue, the 1962 set is complete at 200 cards. The blank-backed cards were printed on the back panels of various Post cereals and measure the standard 2-1/2" x 3-1/2" when properly cut. Like the Post Cereal baseball issues from the same period, the cards must be very carefully cut from the boxes to be considered in top condition. Players who were pictured on boxes of the less-popular cereals are scarcer and more valuable, explaining the higher prices on about two dozen of the cards listed below.

		NM
Complete Set (200):		2500.
Common Player:		3.50
1	Dan Currie	3.50
2	Boyd Dowler	3.50
3	Bill Forester	3.50
4	Forrest Gregg	4.00
5	Dave Hanner	3.50
6	Paul Hornung	14.00
7	Henry Jordan	3.50
8	Jerry Kramer	12.00
9	Max McGee	3.50
10	Tom Moore	100.00
11	Jim Ringo	6.00
12	Bart Starr	20.00
13	Jim Taylor	12.00
14	Fred Thurston	3.50
15	Kess Whittenton	3.50
16	Erich Barnes	3.50
17	Roosevelt Grier	5.00
18	Bob Gaiters	3.50
19	Roosevelt Brown	5.00
20	Sam Huff	8.00
21	Jim Katcavage	3.50
22	Cliff Livingston	3.50
23	Dick Lynch	3.50
24	Joe Morrison	20.00
25	Dick Nolan	18.00
26	Andy Robustelli	5.00
27	Kyle Rote	7.00
28	Del Shofner	25.00
29	Y.A. Tittle	60.00
30	Alex Webster	3.50
31	Bill Barnes	3.50
32	Maxie Baughan	3.50
33	Chuck Bednarik	8.00
34	Tom Brookshier	6.00
35	Jimmy Carr	3.50
36	Ted Dean	3.50
37	Sonny Jurgensen	12.00
38	Tommy McDonald	3.50
39	Clarence Peaks	3.50
40	Pete Retzlaff	3.50
41	Jesse Richardson	30.00
42	Leo Sugar	3.50
43	Bobby Walston	40.00
44	Chuck Weber	3.50
45	Ed Khayat	3.50
46	Howard Cassady	3.50
47	Gail Cogdill	3.50
48	Jim Gibbons	3.50
49	Bill Glass	3.50
50	Alex Karras	3.50
51	Dick Lane	3.50
52	Yale Lary	3.50
53	Dan Lewis	3.50
54	Darris McCord	50.00
55	Jim Martin	3.50
56	Earl Morrall	3.50
57	Jim Ninowski	3.50
58	Nick Pietrosante	3.50
59	Joe Schmidt	50.00
60	Harley Sewell	3.50
61	Jim Brown	60.00
62	Galen Fiss	40.00
63	Bob Gain	3.50
64	Jim Houston	3.50
65	Mike McCormack	3.50
66	Gene Hickerson	3.50
67	Bob Mitchell	3.50
68	John Morrow	3.50
69	Bernie Parrish	3.50
70	Milt Plum	3.50
71	Ray Renfro	3.50
72	Dick Schafrath	3.50
73	Jim Ray Smith	3.50
74	Sam Baker	220.00
75	Paul Wiggin	3.50
76	Raymond Berry	3.50
77	Bob Boyd	3.50
78	Ordell Braase	3.50
79	Art Donovan	3.50
80	Dee Mackey	3.50
81	Gino Marchetti	3.50
82	Lenny Moore	3.50
83	Jim Mutscheller	3.50
84	Steve Myhra	3.50
85	Jimmy Orr	3.50
86	Jim Parker	3.50
87	Bill Pellington	3.50
88	Alex Sandusky	3.50
89	Dick Szymanski	3.50
90	Johnny Unitas	25.00
91	Bruce Bosley	3.50
92	John Brodie	12.00
93	Dave Baker	125.00
94	Tommy Davis	3.50
95	Bob Harrison	3.50
96	Matt Hazeltine	3.50
97	Jim Johnson	50.00
98	Bill Kilmer	8.00
99	Jerry Mertens	3.50
100	Frank Morze	3.50
101	R.C. Owens	3.50
102	J.D. Smith	3.50
103	Bob St. Clair	60.00
104	Monty Stickles	3.50
105	Abe Woodson	3.50
106	Doug Atkins	3.50
107	Ed Brown	3.50
108	J.C. Caroline	3.50
109	Rick Casares	3.50
110	Angelo Coia	175.00
111	Mike Ditka	20.00
112	Joe Fortunato	3.50
113	Willie Galimore	3.50
114	Bill George	5.50
115	Stan Jones	3.50
116	Johnny Morris	5.50
117	Larry Morris	40.00
118	Rich Pettibon	3.50
119	Bill Wade	4.00
120	Maury Youmans	3.50
121	Preston Carpenter	3.50
122	Buddy Dial	3.50
123	Bobby Joe Green	3.50
124	Mike Henry	3.50
125	John Henry Johnson	5.50
126	Bobby Layne	15.00
127	Gene Lipscomb	5.50
128	Lou Michaels	3.50
129	John Nisby	3.50
130	John Reger	3.50
131	Mike Sandusky	3.50
132	George Tarasovic	3.50
133	Tom Tracy	40.00
134	Glynn Gregory	3.50
135	Frank Clarke	40.00
136	Mike Connelly	40.00
137	L.G. Dupre	3.50
138	Bob Fry	3.50
139	Allen Green	60.00
140	Bill Howton	3.50
141	Bob Lilly	12.00
142	Don Meredith	16.00
143	Dick Moegle	3.50
144	Don Perkins	5.50
145	Jerry Tubbs	60.00
146	J.W. Lockett	3.50
147	Ed Cook	3.50
148	John David Crow	5.50
149	Sam Etcheverry	5.50
150	Frank Fuller	3.50
151	Prentice Gault	3.50
152	Jimmy Hill	3.50
153	Bill Koman	40.00
154	Larry Wilson	5.50
155	Dale Meinert	3.50
156	Ed Henke	3.50
157	Sonny Randle	3.50
158	Ralph Guglielmi	40.00
159	Joe Childress	3.50
160	Jon Arnett	5.50
161	Dick Bass	3.50
162	Zeke Bratkowski	5.50
163	Carroll Dale	3.50
164	Art Hunter	3.50
165	John Lovetere	3.50
166	Lamar Lundy	3.50
167	Ollie Matson	8.00
168	Ed Meador	3.50
169	Jack Pardee	60.00
170	Jim Phillips	3.50
171	Les Richter	3.50
172	Frank Ryan	3.50
173	Frank Varrichione	3.50
174	Grady Alderman	3.50
175	Rip Hawkins	3.50
176	Don Joyce	60.00
177	Bill Lapham	3.50
178	Tommy Mason	3.50
179	Hugh McElhenny	3.50
180	Dave Middleton	3.50
181	Dick Pesonen	3.50
182	Karl Rubke	3.50
183	George Shaw	3.50
184	Fran Tarkenton	35.00
185	Mel Triplett	3.50
186	Frank Youso	40.00
187	Bill Bishop	3.50
188	Bill Anderson	40.00
189	Don Bosseler	3.50
190	Fred Hageman	3.50
191	Sam Horner	3.50
192	Jim Kerr	3.50
193	Joe Krakoski	150.00
194	Fred Dugan	3.50
195	John Paluck	3.50
196	Vince Promuto	3.50
197	Joe Rutgens	3.50
198	Norm Snead	5.50
199	Andy Stynchula	3.50
200	Bob Toneff	3.50

1962 Post Booklets

Measuring 5" x 3", each of the four booklets included 15 pages. The booklet covers include a drawing of the player, with his name, position and team, along with the title. The book covers are numbered in the upper right with a prefix of "book."

		NM
Complete Set (4):		65.00
Common Player:		10.00
1	Football Formations To Watch (Jon Arnett) (Important Rules of the Game)	10.00

2	Fundamentals of Football (Paul Hornung)	25.00
3	How To Play On Offense (Sonny Jurgensen) (How To Call Signals And Key Plays)	20.00
4	How To Play Defense (Sam Huff)	15.00

1977 Pottsville Maroons

This 1977 17-card set commemorates the 1925 NFL champion team with photos of the players on the front. The player's name, number and team are printed at the bottom of the card front. The back include the player's name, number, bio, position and career highlights. At the bottom of the card back is the 1977 copyright line, which attributes the set to the estate of Joseph C. Zacko Sr. and executor Russel F. Zacko.

		NM
Complete Set (17):		25.00
Common Player:		1.50
1	Team History	1.50
2	The Symbolic Shoe	1.50
3	Jack Ernst	1.50
4	Tony Latone	1.50
5	Duke Osborn	1.50
6	Frank Bucher	1.50
7	Frankie Racis	1.50
8	Russ Hathaway	1.50
9	W.H. Flanagan	1.50
10	Charlie Berry	3.00
11	Russ Stein, Herb Stein	1.50
12	Howard Lebengood	1.50
13	Denny Hughes	1.50
14	Barney Wentz	1.50
15	Eddie Doyle (UER) (Bio says American troops landed in Africa 1943; should be 1942)	1.50
16	Walter French	1.50
17	Dick Rauch	3.00

1994 Predators Arena Team Issue

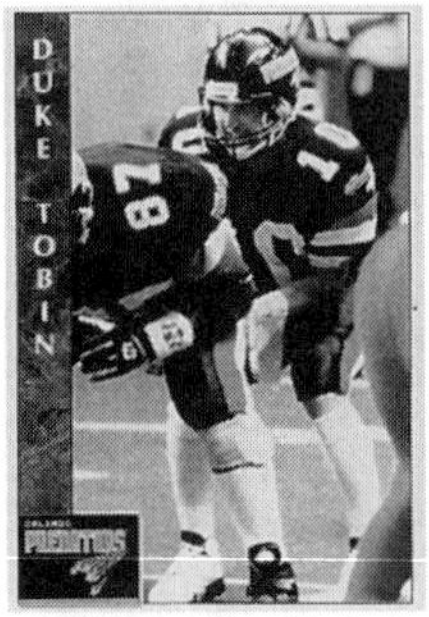

This set was issued by the Orlando Predators of the Arena Football League and sold through their concession stands and gift shop. The cards are unnumbered.

		MT
Complete Set (27):		7.00
Common Player:		.25
1	Ben Bennett	.25
2	Henry Brown	.25
3	Webbie Burnett	.25
4	Jorge Cimadevilla	.25
5	Bernard Clark	.25
6	Wayne Dickson	.25
7	Eric Drakes	.25
8	Chris Ford	.25
9	Victor Hall	.25
10	Paul McGowan	.25
11	Perry Moss CO	.25
12	Jerry Odom	.25
13	Billy Owens	.25
14	Marshall Roberts	.25
15	Durwood Roquemore	.25
16	Rusty Russell DL	.25
17	Tony Scott	.25
18	Ricky Shaw	.25
19	Alex Shell	.25
20	Bill Stewart	.25
21	Duke Tobin	.25
22	Barry Wagner	.25
23	Jackie Walker	.25
24	Herkie Walls	.25
25	Isaac Williams	.25
26	Coaches	.25
27	The Klaw (mascot)	.25

1994 Press Pass SB Photo Board

Measuring 10" x 14", these Photo Boards showcased color photos of both Buffalo and Dallas players on the front, along with the Super Bowl logo in gold foil. Each of the boards are individually numbered of 50,000. The product was sold at the Super Bowl Card Show in Atlanta. The backs include photos and statistic leaders in both conferences.

		MT
Complete Set (1):		10.00
Common Panel:		10.00
1	SB XXVIII Photo Board (John Elway, Rick Mirer, Reggie Langhorne, Neil Smith, Nate Odomes, Thurman Thomas, Steve Young, Jerome Bettis, Sterling Sharpe, Reggie White, Deion Sanders, Emmitt Smith)	10.00

1996 Press Pass

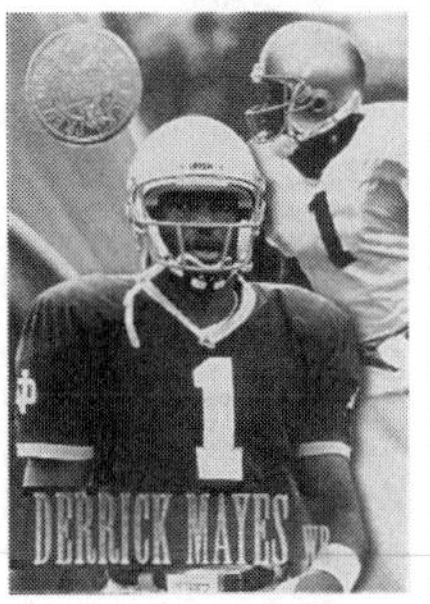

Top rookies slated to make NFL debuts in 1996 are featured in this 55-card 1996 Press Pass Football Draft Picks set, the company's first devoted to football. Each card front has a pair of color action photos on it, along with gold foil stamping which is used for the player's name at the bottom and the brand logo in the upper left corner. The back has the player's name, college and card number at the top, with a box below with information about his college career. In the center is a circle with statistics around the diameter and a color photo in the center. Another box below the photo has biographical information in it. Three parallel sets were also created. First, autographed versions of all 55 cards are available at a rate of one per every 72 packs. Next, Emerald Proofs were limited to only 380 of each card, with an insertion rate of one per every 36 packs. Last, each pack includes a Holofoil version of the set, which features a holographic finish on the front. Insert sets include Crystal Ball, and four different denominations of Prime Time Phone cards of nine different players.

		MT
Complete Set (55):		25.00
Common Player:		.25
Comp. Holofoil Set (55):		50.00
Holofoil Cards: 1x-2x		
Comp. Emerald Proof (55):		500.00
Emerald Proof Cards: 10x-20x		
1	Keyshawn Johnson	3.00
2	Jonathan Ogden	.25
3	Duane Clemons	.25
4	Kevin Hardy	.25
5	Eddie George	5.00
6	Karim Abdul-Jabbar	1.50
7	Terry Glenn	1.50
8	Leeland McElroy	1.00
9	Simeon Rice	.25
10	Roman Oben	.25
11	Daryl Gardener	.25
12	Marcus Coleman	.25
13	Christian Peter	.25
14	Tim Biakabutuka	1.00
15	Eric Moulds	.75
16	Chris Darkins	.50
17	Andre Johnson	.25
18	Lawyer Milloy	.25
19	Jon Runyan	.25
20	Mike Alstott	.50
21	Jeff Hartings	.25
22	Amani Toomer	.75
23	Danny Kanell	.75
24	Marco Battaglia	.50
25	Stephen Davis	.75
26	Johnny McWilliams	.50
27	Israel Ifeanyi	.25
28	Scott Slutzker	.50
29	Bryant Mix	.25
30	Brian Roche	.25
31	Stanley Pritchett	.25
32	Jerome Woods	.25
33	Tommie Frazier	.25
34	Stepfret Williams	.25
35	Ray Mickens	.25
36	Alex Van Dyke	.50
37	Bobby Hoying	.50
38	Tony Brackens	.25
39	Dietrich Jells	.25
40	Jason Odom	.25
41	Randall Godfrey	.25
42	Willie Anderson	.25
43	Tony Banks	.25
44	Michael Cheever	.25
45	Jerod Cherry	.25
46	Chris Doering	.25
47	Steve Taneyhill	.25
48	Kyle Wachholz	.25
49	Dusty Zeigler	.25
50	Derrick Mayes	.50
51	Orpheus Roye	.25
52	Sedric Clark	.25
53	Richard Huntley	.25
54	Donnie Edwards	.25
55	Zach Thomas	.25

1996 Press Pass Holofoil

The 55-card, standard-size set was issued as a parallel to the base Press Pass set. The cards were inserted in each pack and featured holofoil stock.

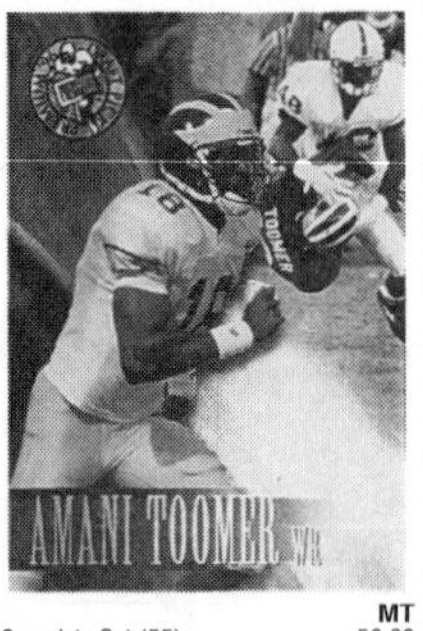

	MT
Complete Set (55):	50.00
Common Player:	.30
Stars:	2x

1996 Press Pass Holofoil Emerald Proofs

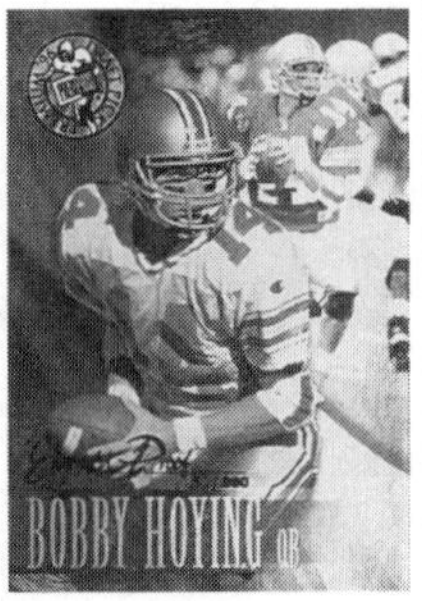

The 55-card, standard-size set was a parallel issue to the base set. Inserted every 36 packs, the cards feature holofoil stock with "Emerald Proof" printed on each card front. Production of each card was limited to just 280.

	MT
Complete Set (55):	375.00
Common Player:	1.00
Stars:	8x-16x

1996 Press Pass Autographs

The 12-card, standard-size set, inserted every 72 packs, is similar to the base cards, except with the player's autograph on the card front. The card backs inform the collector that he/she has received a "limited edition" signed card.

		MT
Complete Set (12):		200.00
Common Player:		10.00
1	Karim Abdul-Jabbar	35.00
2	Tony Banks	18.00
3	Tim Biakabutuka	30.00
4	Duane Clemons	10.00
5	Stephen Davis	30.00
6	Chris Doering	10.00
7	Bobby Hoying	25.00
8	Keyshawn Johnson	45.00
9	Danny Kanell	15.00
10	Leeland McElroy	20.00
11	Jonathan Ogden	10.00
12	Steve Taneyhill	10.00

1996 Press Pass Crystal Ball

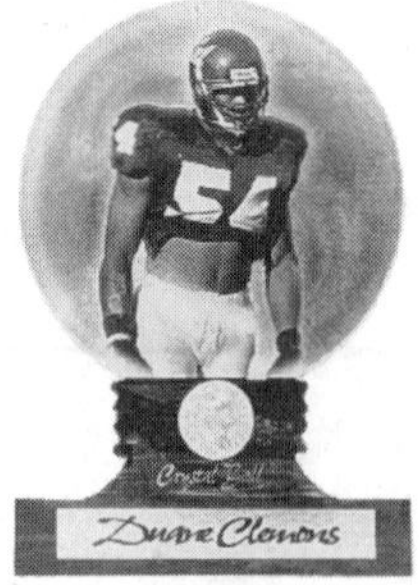

These 1996 Press Pass inserts were seeded one per 18 packs. The die-cut cards, numbered using a "CB" prefix, have a crystal ball on the front with a player photo inside. His name is written along the base of the crystal ball. The back has the player's name inside the ball with an analysis of the player's talents. The card number is in a circle in the lower left corner.

		MT
Complete Set (12):		120.00
Common Player:		5.00
1	Lawyer Milloy	5.00
2	Terry Glenn	15.00
3	Duane Clemons	5.00
4	Kevin Hardy	5.00
5	Eddie George	25.00
6	Jonathan Ogden	5.00
7	Karim Abdul-Jabbar	15.00
8	Tim Biakabutuka	12.00
9	Eric Moulds	8.00
10	Danny Kanell	6.00
11	Israel Ifeanyi	5.00
12	Keyshawn Johnson	40.00

1996 Press Pass Prime Time Phone Cards

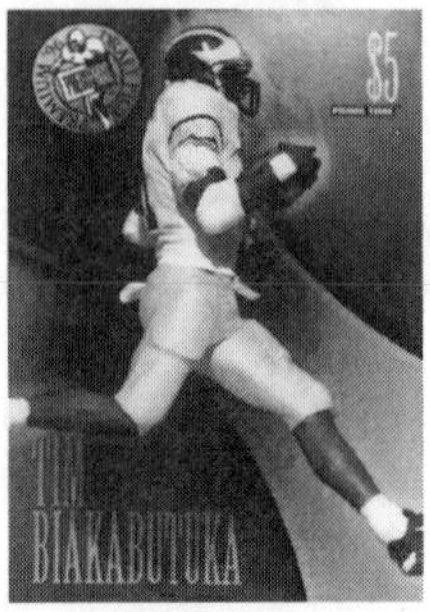

Four different denominations - $5, $10, $20 and $1,996 - are used for these Prime Time Phone cards, found one every 36 packs of 1996 Press Pass Football Draft Picks product. Nine players are featured on the cards, which have a color action photo on the front, plus the denomination. The back, numbered using a "PT" prefix, has instructions on how to use the card.

		MT
Complete Set (9):		120.00
Common Player:		10.00
Ten Dollar Cards:		2x-4x
Twenty Dollar Cards:		3x-6x
1	Keyshawn Johnson	30.00
2	Jonathan Ogden	10.00
3	Tommie Frazier	12.00
4	Eddie George	20.00
5	Karim Abdul-Jabbar	15.00
6	Terry Glenn	15.00
7	Leeland McElroy	12.00
8	Tim Biakabutuka	18.00
9	Kevin Hardy	10.00

1996 Press Pass Paydirt

The 75-card, standard-size set was issued in five-card packs. The set is the retail version and includes inserts such as: Paydirt Holofoil, Paydirt Red Foil, Paydirt Autographs and Paydirt Eddie George.

		MT
Complete Set (75):		30.00
Common Player:		.10
1	Keyshawn Johnson	4.00
2	Jonathan Ogden	.25
3	Duane Clemons	.40
4	Kevin Hardy	.50
5	Eddie George	3.50
6	Karim Abdul-Jabbar	2.00
7	Terry Glenn	3.00
8	Leeland McElroy	2.00
9	Simeon Rice	.40
10	Roman Oben	.10
11	Daryl Gardener	.40
12	Marcus Coleman	.10
13	Christian Peter	.10
14	Tim Biakabutuka	3.00
15	Eric Moulds	1.25
16	Chris Darkins	1.00
17	Andre Johnson	.10
18	Lawyer Milloy	.25
19	Jon Runyan	.10
20	Mike Alstott	1.50
21	Jeff Hartings	.10
22	Amani Toomer	1.25
23	Danny Kanell	1.25
24	Marco Battaglia	.60
25	Stephen Davis	1.00
26	Johnny McWilliams	.40
27	Israel Ifeanyi	.10
28	Scott Slutzker	.10
29	Bryant Mix	.10
30	Brian Roche	.10
31	Stanley Pritchett	.40
32	Jerome Woods	.10
33	Tommie Frazier	1.50
34	Stepfret Williams	.75
35	Ray Mickens	.10
36	Alex Van Dyke	1.00
37	Bobby Hoying	1.25
38	Tony Brackens	.10
39	Dietrich Jells	.10
40	Jason Odom	.10
41	Randall Godfrey	.10
42	Willie Anderson	.25
43	Tony Banks	.75
44	Michael Cheever	.10
45	Je'Rod Cherry	.25
46	Chris Doering	.25
47	Steve Taneyhill	.40
48	Kyle Wachholz	.40
49	Dusty Zeigler	.10
50	Derrick Mayes	1.25
51	Orpheus Roye	.10
52	Sedric Clark	.10
53	Richard Huntley	.10
54	Donnie Edwards	.25
55	Zach Thomas	.10
56	Alex Molden	.30
57	Jimmy Herndon	.10
58	Mike Alstott	1.50
59	Scott Greene	.40
60	Danny Kanell	1.25
61	Jonathan Ogden	.25
62	Simeon Rice	.40
63	Kevin Hardy	.50
64	Jon Runyan	.10
65	Stephen Davis	1.00
66	Tim Biakabutuka	3.00
67	Terry Glenn	3.00
68	Leeland McElroy	2.00
69	Eric Moulds	1.25
70	Karim Abdul-Jabbar	2.00
71	Lawyer Milloy	.25
72	Derrick Mayes	1.25
73	Tommie Frazier	1.50
74	Bobby Hoying	1.25
75	Kyle Wachholz (CL)	.10

1996 Press Pass Paydirt Holofoil

The 75-card, standard-size set, a parallel to the base set with holofoil paper, was inserted every four packs.

	MT
Complete Set (75):	125.00
Common Player:	.40
Stars:	2x-4x

1996 Press Pass Paydirt Red Foil

The 75-card, regular-size set was inserted in each pack of Paydirt and was also known as Torquers. The foil wrappers incorrectly describe the parallel set as having "blue foil."

	MT
Complete Set (75):	60.00
Common Player:	.20
Stars:	1x-2x

1996 Press Pass Paydirt Autographs

The 16-card, standard-size set was inserted every 72 packs of Paydirt. The card fronts contain the player's autograph while the backs inform the collectors of his/her pull. The cards are unnumbered.

		MT
Complete Set (16):		250.00
Common Player:		10.00
1	Karim Abdul-Jabbar	35.00
2	Tony Banks	30.00
3	Tim Biakabutuka	20.00
4	Duane Clemons	10.00
5	Stephen Davis	30.00
6	Chris Doering	10.00
7	Bobby Hoying	25.00
8	Keyshawn Johnson	30.00
9	Danny Kanell	15.00
10	Derrick Mayes	15.00
11	Leeland McElroy	20.00
12	Lawyer Milloy	10.00
13	Eric Moulds	15.00
14	Jonathan Ogden	10.00
15	Steve Taneyhill	10.00
16	Alex Van Dyke	15.00

1996 Press Pass Paydirt Eddie George

The four-card, standard-size set features the 1995 Heisman Trophy winner. The cards were inserted into packs at a progressive rate. Card No. 1 was every 36 packs; card No. 2 was every 72; card No. 3 every 216, and card No. 4 every 864 packs. The cards are numbered with the "EG" prefix.

		MT
Complete Set (4):		150.00
Common Player:		7.00
1	Eddie George	7.00
2	Eddie George	14.00
3	Eddie George	40.00
4	Eddie George	125.00

1996 Press Pass Paydirt Game Breakers

The 12-card, standard-size set was inserted every 18 packs and features players who excelled in college. The cards are numbered with the "GB" prefix.

		MT
Complete Set (12):		70.00
Common Player:		4.00
1	Lawyer Milloy	4.00
2	Terry Glenn	15.00
3	Duane Clemons	4.00
4	Kevin Hardy	6.00
5	Eddie George	18.00
6	Jonathan Ogden	4.00
7	Karim Abdul-Jabbar	12.00
8	Tim Biakabutuka	10.00
9	Eric Moulds	8.00
10	Danny Kanell	6.00
11	Leeland McElroy	8.00
12	Keyshawn Johnson	10.00

1997 Press Pass

The 55-card set features full-bleed fronts, with the player's name, position and Press Pass logo at the bottom in gold foil. The backs have a player photo on the left over a "groovy" multicolored background. The player's name, bio, highlights and stats are printed on the right side. Red Zone is a red-foil parallel which was inserted 1:1 hobby packs. Torquers, which is a blue-foil parallel, was inserted 1:1 mass market packs. In addition, a 50-card all-foil die-cut "set within a set" was inserted 1:1 pack.

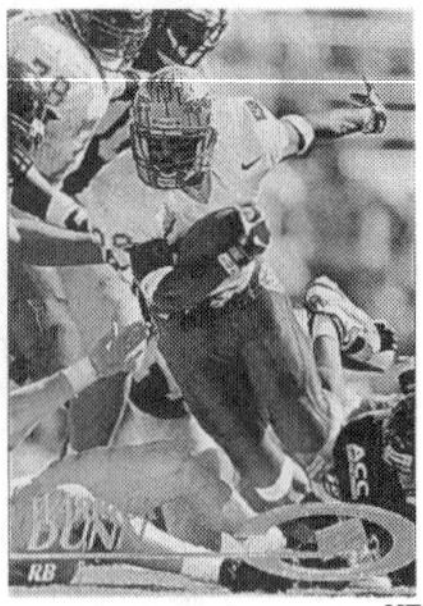

		MT
Complete Set (50):		15.00
Common Player:		.10
Minor Stars:		.20
Combine Cards:		2x
Red Zone Cards:		2x
1	Orlando Pace	1.00
2	Warrick Dunn	2.00
3	Danny Wuerffel	2.00
4	Darnell Autry	.75
5	Troy Davis	1.25
6	Jake Plummer	.75
7	Corey Dillon	.50
8	Reidel Anthony	1.25
9	Byron Hanspard	.75
10	Tiki Barber	.75
11	Ike Hilliard	1.25
12	Rae Carruth	1.00
13	Yatil Green	1.25
14	Peter Boulware	.10
15	Jim Druckenmiller	1.50
16	Pat Barnes	.20
17	Trevor Pryce	.10
18	Kevin Lockett	.10
19	Koy Detmer	.20
20	Bryant Westbrook	.40
21	Darrell Russell	.20
22	Tony Gonzalez	.30
23	Shawn Springs	.50
24	Chris Canty	.10
25	David LaFleur	.50
26	Dwayne Rudd	.10
27	Bob Sapp	.10
28	Mike Vrabel	.10
29	Antowain Smith	.50
30	Keith Poole	.10
31	Sedrick Shaw	.10
32	Tremain Mack	.10
33	Matt Russell	.10
34	Reinard Wilson	.10
35	Marc Edwards	.10
36	Greg Jones	.10
37	Michael Booker	.10
38	James Farrior	.10
39	Danny Wuerffel	.75
40	Troy Davis	.50
41	Corey Dillon	.10
42	Jake Plummer	.30
43	Peter Boulware, Reinard Wilson	.10
44	Eddie Robinson	.20
45	Bobby Bowden	.75
46	Steve Spurrier	1.00
47	Gary Barnett	.10
49	Checklist (Tom Osborne)	.50
50	Checklist (Jarrett Irons)	.10

1997 Press Pass Combine

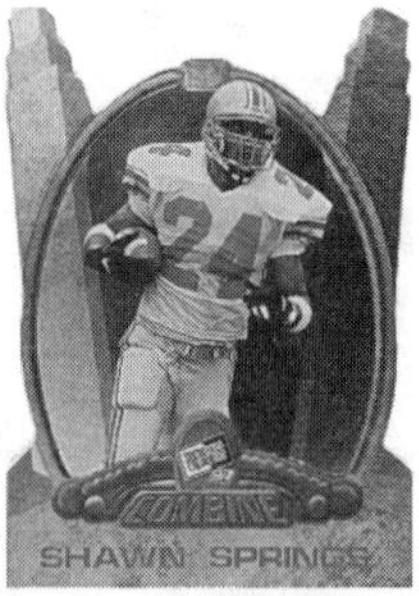

Combine was a 50-card parallel set to the Press Pass Draft Picks set that was included one per pack. These die-cut cards were printed on silver foil and include towers up both sides. The word "Combine" and the player's name is printed in red letters across the bottom.

	MT
Combine Cards:	2x

1997 Press Pass Red Zone

Red Zone was another parallel set to the 50-card Press Pass Draft Picks. These parallels were identical to base cards except they were printed with red foil on the front instead of the gold foil used on base cards. Red Zone parallels were inserted one per pack.

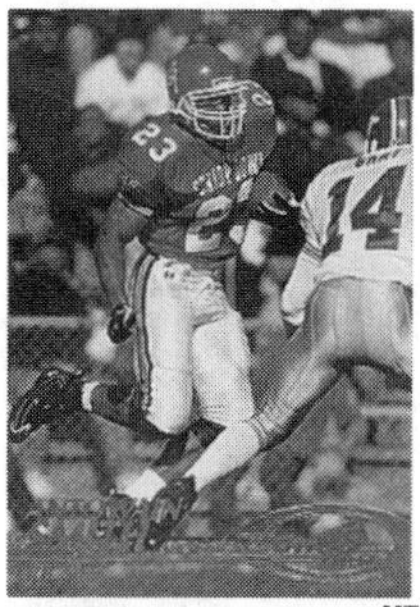

	MT
Red Zone Cards:	2x

1997 Press Pass Big 12

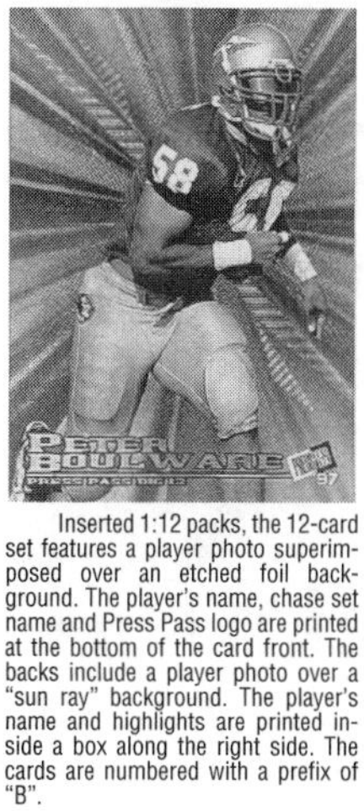

Inserted 1:12 packs, the 12-card set features a player photo superimposed over an etched foil background. The player's name, chase set name and Press Pass logo are printed at the bottom of the card front. The backs include a player photo over a "sun ray" background. The player's name and highlights are printed inside a box along the right side. The cards are numbered with a prefix of "B".

		MT
Complete Set (12):		45.00
Common Player:		2.00
1	Orlando Pace	5.00
2	Peter Boulware	2.00
3	Shawn Springs	4.00
4	Warrick Dunn	12.00
5	Dwayne Rudd	2.00
6	Rae Carruth	6.00
7	Bryant Westbrook	4.00
8	Darrell Russell	2.00
9	Yatil Green	6.00
10	David LaFleur	4.00
11	Jim Druckenmiller	8.00
12	Reidel Anthony	6.00

1997 Press Pass Can't Miss

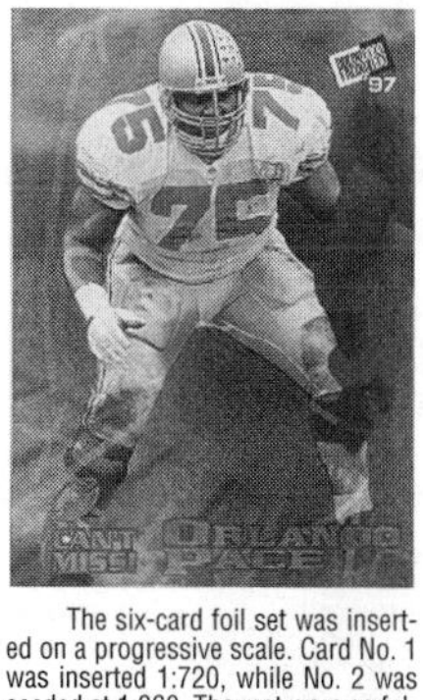

The six-card foil set was inserted on a progressive scale. Card No. 1 was inserted 1:720, while No. 2 was seeded at 1:360. The rest were as follows: No. 3 1:180, No. 4 1:90, No. 5 1:45 and No. 6 1:36. The player's photo is superimposed over a foil background. A football field and X's and O's also appear on the front. The Can't Miss logo and the player's name are printed at the bottom. The backs have a photo of each of the six players. The numbers have a prefix of "CM".

		MT
Complete Set (6):		225.00
Common Player:		10.00
1	Warrick Dunn	100.00
2	Jim Druckenmiller	60.00
3	Yatil Green	45.00
4	Orlando Pace	30.00
5	Rae Carruth	20.00
6	Peter Boulware	10.00

1997 Press Pass Head-Butt

Inserted 1:18 packs, the nine-card set features the player's photo superimposed over the player's college helmet. The Head Butt logo is in gold foil at the bottom, while the player's name is printed inside a gold-foil stripe at the bottom center. The backs have the player's photo printed over his college helmet. The bottom of the card back has the player's name and his highlights. The card numbers carry a prefix of "HB". A die-cut parallel version is randomly seeded 1:36 packs.

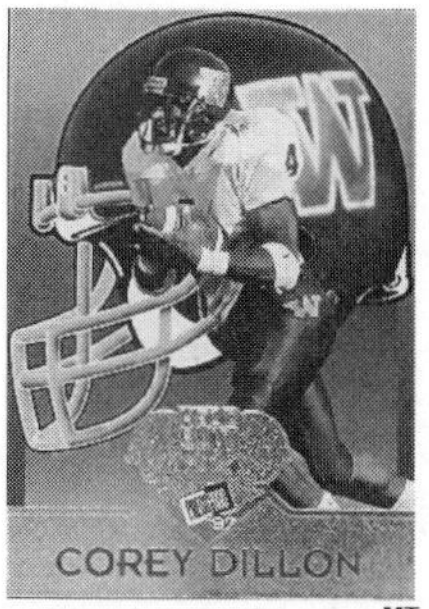

		MT
Complete Set (9):		60.00
Common Player:		3.00
Die Cuts:		2x
1	Warrick Dunn	16.00
2	Orlando Pace	8.00
3	Troy Davis	10.00
4	Reidel Anthony	10.00
5	Rae Carruth	10.00
6	Yatil Green	10.00
7	Corey Dillon	3.00
8	Danny Wuerffel	12.00
9	Darnell Autry	8.00

1997 Press Pass Marquee Matchups

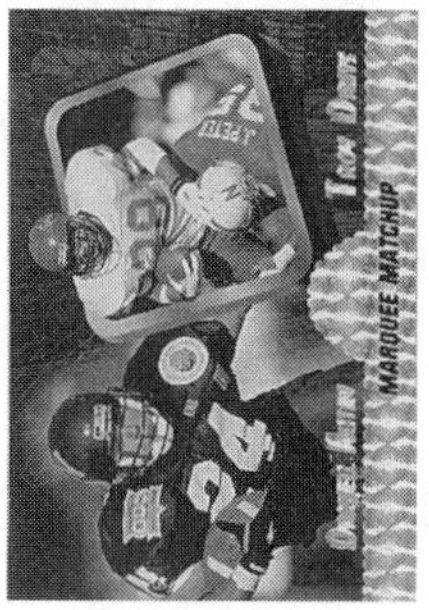

Inserted 1:18 packs, the nine-card set features two players on the front, with their names printed at the bottom in prism foil. "Marquee Matchup" is printed in black inside a prism stripe at the bottom of the front. The backs have two player photos, their names and highlights. The card numbers are prefixed by "MM".

		MT
Complete Set (9):		40.00
Common Player:		2.00
1	Jim Druckenmiller, Danny Wuerffel	12.00
2	Warrick Dunn, Corey Dillon	10.00
3	Darnell Autry, Troy Davis	8.00
4	Byron Hanspard, Tiki Barber	6.00
5	Reidel Anthony, Bryant Westbrook	5.00
6	Orlando Pace, Peter Boulware	4.00
7	Rae Carruth, Ike Hilliard	5.00
8	Yatil Green, Shawn Springs	5.00
9	David LaFleur, Tony Gonzalez	2.00

1998 Press Pass

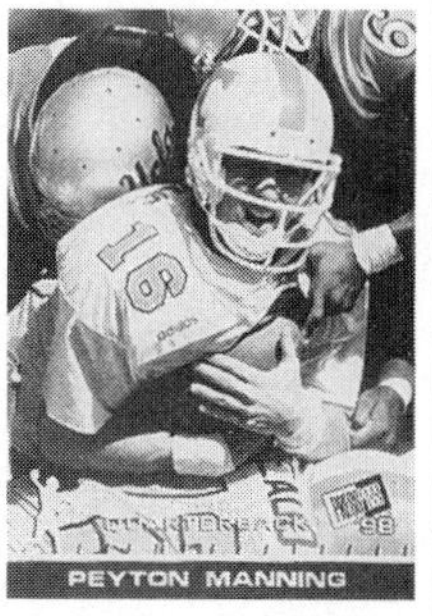

Press Pass Draft Picks Football contained 50 cards in 1998, with 45 players eligible for the 1998 NFL Draft, four coaches and a checklist card featuring Peyton Manning. Cards featured a black strip across the bottom identifying the player, with his position and several logo above over the bottom of the player photograph. The set was paralleled in Paydirt (hobby), Pickoffs (retail), Reflectors and Reflector Solos sets. Inserts include: Fields of Fury, Head Butt, Jerseys, Kick-off, Triple Threat and Trophy Case.

		MT
Complete Set (50):		18.00
Common Player:		.10
Minor Stars:		.20
Paydirt Cards:		2x
Pickoff Cards:		2x
Reflectors:		25x-50x
Wax Box:		60.00
1	Peyton Manning	3.50
2	Ryan Leaf	2.50
3	Charles Woodson	1.50
4	Andre Wadsworth	.75
5	Randy Moss	5.00
6	Curtis Enis	1.50
7	T. Thomas	.10
8	Flozell Adams	.10
9	Jason Peter	.10
10	Brian Simmons	.10
11	Takeo Spikes	.10
12	Michael Myers	.10
13	Kevin Dyson	.75
14	Grant Wistrom	.10
15	Fred Taylor	2.00
16	Germane Crowell	.75
17	Sam Cowart	.10
18	Anthony Simmons	.10
19	Robert Edwards	1.50
20	Shaun Williams	.10
21	Phil Savoy	.10
22	Leonard Little	.10
23	Saladin McCullough	.10
24	Duane Starks	.10
25	John Avery	.75
26	Vonnie Holliday	.50
27	Tim Dwight	.50
28	Donovin Darius	.10
29	Alonzo Mayes	.30
30	Jerome Pathon	.30
31	Brian Kelly	.10
32	Hines Ward	.50
33	Jacquez Green	.75
34	Marcus Nash	.75
35	Ahman Green	.75
36	Joe Jurevicius	.50
37	Tavian Banks	1.00
38	Donald Hayes	.30
39	Robert Holcombe	.75
40	Eric Green	.50
41	John Dutton	.30
42	Skip Hicks	.75
43	Patrick Johnson	.10
44	Keith Brooking	.10
45	Alan Faneca	.10
46	Steve Spurrier	1.00
47	Mike Price	.10
48	Bobby Bowden	.75
49	Tom Osborne	1.00
50	Manning - Checklist	1.50

1998 Press Pass Paydirt

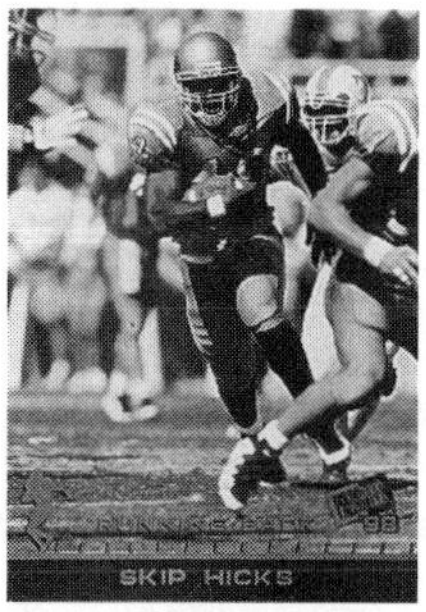

Paydirt included all 50 cards, but were distinguised by red foil stamping versus the gold used on base cards. These were found in hobby packs only and inserted one per pack.

	MT
Paydirt Cards:	2x

1998 Press Pass Pickoff

Pickoff included parallel versions of all 50 cards, but were distinguished by silver foil stamping on the front versus the gold foil used on base cards. These were retail exclusive and inserted one per pack.

	MT
Pickoff Cards:	2x

1998 Press Pass Reflectors

This 50-card parallel set was seeded one per 180 packs and arrived with a protective covering over the card. This covering could be peeled back to reveal a holofoil finish. Reflectors were numbered with a "R" prefix. In addition, Solos versions of Reflectors were also available, with only one existing set. These were distinguised by a "Solos 1 of 1" stamp on the card back.

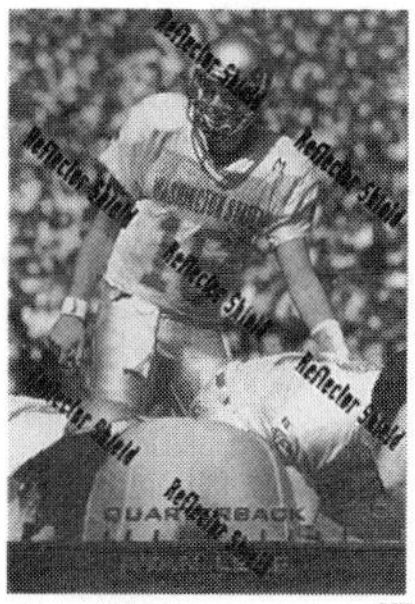

	MT
Reflector Cards:	25x-50x

1998 Press Pass Autographs

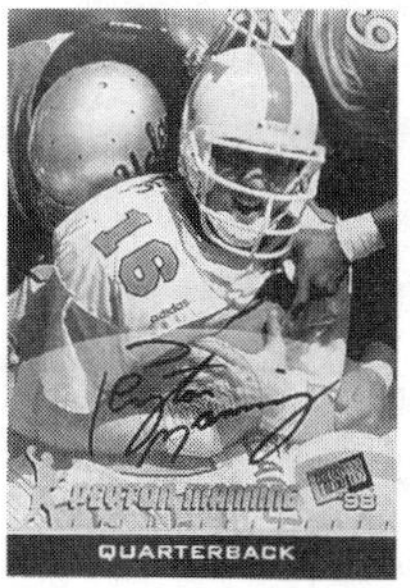

Autographed versions of Press Pass cards were seeded one per 18 hobby packs and one per 36 retail packs. They were similar to base cards, except for a faded area across the bottom of the photograph that included the player's signature. Backs were green, with the word "Autograph" in large white letters and a paragraph that congratulated the collector and certified the card. Autographs were unnumbered and are listed in alphabetical order.

		MT
Complete Set (38):		300.00
Common Player:		8.00
Minor Stars:		12.00
1	John Avery	12.00
2	Tavian Banks	20.00
3	Bobby Bowden	20.00
4	Germane Crowell	20.00
5	Donovin Darius	8.00
6	Tim Dwight	15.00
7	Kevin Dyson	20.00
8	Robert Edwards	30.00
9	Curtis Enis	30.00
10	Alan Faneca	8.00
11	Ahman Green	20.00
12	Jacquez Green	25.00
13	Donald Hayes	12.00
14	Skip Hicks	15.00
15	Robert Holcombe	12.00
16	Vonnie Holliday	15.00
17	Patrick Johnson	8.00
18	Joe Jurevicius	15.00
19	Brian Kelly	8.00
20	Ryan Leaf	50.00
21	Peyton Manning	100.00
22	Alonzo Mayes	12.00
23	Randy Moss	125.00
24	Michael Myers	8.00
25	Marcus Nash	15.00
26	Tom Osborne	25.00
27	Jason Peter	8.00
28	Mike Price	8.00
29	Phil Savoy	12.00
30	Anthony Simmons	8.00
31	Brian Simmons	8.00
32	Takeo Spikes	12.00
33	Steve Spurrier	25.00
34	Fred Taylor	40.00
35	Andre Wadsworth	15.00
36	Hines Ward	15.00
37	Shaun Williams	8.00
38	Grant Wistrom	8.00

1998 Press Pass Fields of Fury

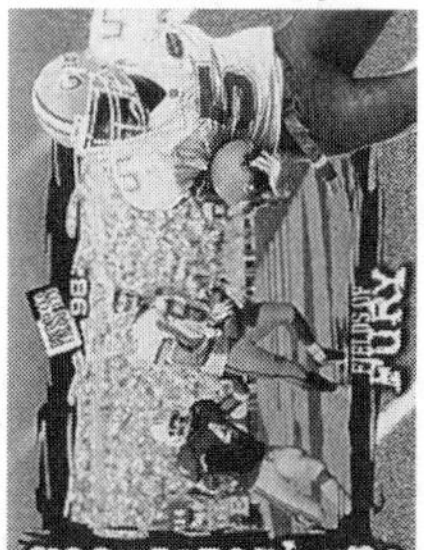

This horizontal, nine-card set featured the player off to the right side, with a game highlight of him roughly bordered in black across the majority of the card. Fields of Fury were numbered with a "FF" prefix and inserted one per 36 packs.

		MT
Complete Set (9):		90.00
Common Player:		7.00
1	Peyton Manning	30.00
2	Marcus Nash	10.00
3	Ryan Leaf	12.00
4	Randy Moss	40.00
5	Robert Edwards	8.00
6	Curtis Enis	10.00
7	Kevin Dyson	10.00
8	Fred Taylor	12.00
9	Jacquez Green	7.00

1998 Press Pass Head Butt

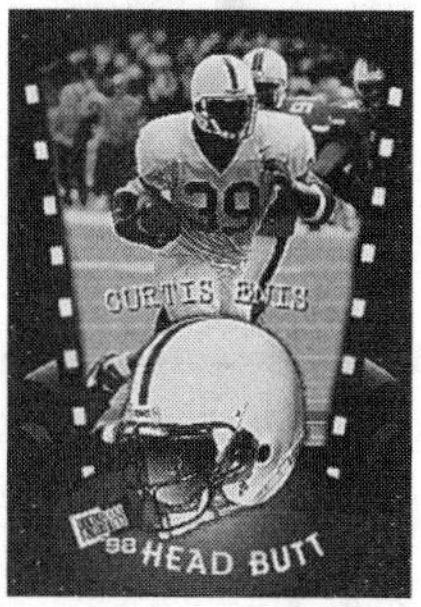

Head Butt was a nine-card insert that included a film-like shot of the player over a black background, with his embossed college team helmet at the bottom center. These were numbered with a "HB" prefix and inserted one per 18 packs. Die-cut versions were seeded one per 36 packs.

		MT
Complete Set (9):		50.00
Common Player:		3.00
Die-Cut Cards:		2x
1	Peyton Manning	18.00
2	Charles Woodson	8.00
3	Ryan Leaf	7.00
4	Curtis Enis	8.00
5	Jacquez Green	3.00
6	Ahman Green	3.00
7	Randy Moss	20.00
8	Tavian Banks	6.00
9	Robert Edwards	7.00

1998 Press Pass Jerseys

Jerseys was a four-card insert that featured a swatch of the player's game-used college jersey embedded in the front. These were sequentially numbered to 425 sets, numbered with a "JC" prefix and inserted one per 720 packs.

		MT
Complete Set (4):		500.00
Common Player:		70.00
PM	Peyton Manning	200.00
RL	Ryan Leaf	125.00
KD	Kevin Dyson	70.00
TB	Tavian Banks	70.00

1998 Press Pass Kick-Off

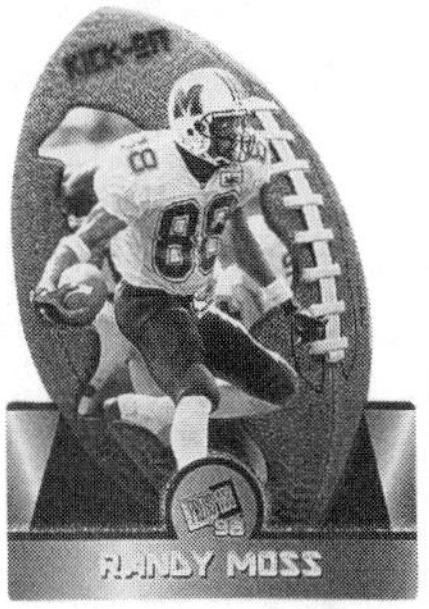

Kick-Off included 36 of the players from the base set on a die-cut, football-shaped card. The player's image and the football were both embossed. These were numbered with a "KO" prefix and inserted one per pack in both hobby and retail.

		MT
Complete Set (36):		30.00
Common Player:		.20
Minor Stars:		.40
1	Peyton Manning	6.00
2	Ryan Leaf	3.00
3	Charles Woodson	3.00
4	Andre Wadsworth	1.50
5	Randy Moss	8.00
6	Curtis Enis	3.00
7	Donald Hayes	.20
8	Flozell Adams	.20
9	Jason Peter	.20
10	Brian Simmons	.20
11	Takeo Spikes	.20
12	Germane Crowell	.20
13	Donovin Darius	.20
14	Grant Wistrom	.20
15	Alonzo Mayes	.20
16	Kevin Dyson	1.50
17	John Avery	1.50
18	Anthony Simmons	.20
19	Robert Edwards	1.50
20	Shaun Williams	.20
21	Leonard Little	.20
22	Skip Hicks	1.50
23	Phil Savoy	.20
24	Tavian Banks	2.00
25	Robert Holcombe	1.00
26	Eric Green	1.00
27	Tim Dwight	.20
28	Saladin McCullough	.20
29	Fred Taylor	1.50
30	Jerome Pathon	.20
31	Brian Kelly	.20
32	Hines Ward	1.00
33	Jacquez Green	1.00
34	Marcus Nash	1.50
35	Ahman Green	1.50
36	Joe Jurevicius	.20

1998 Press Pass Triple Threat

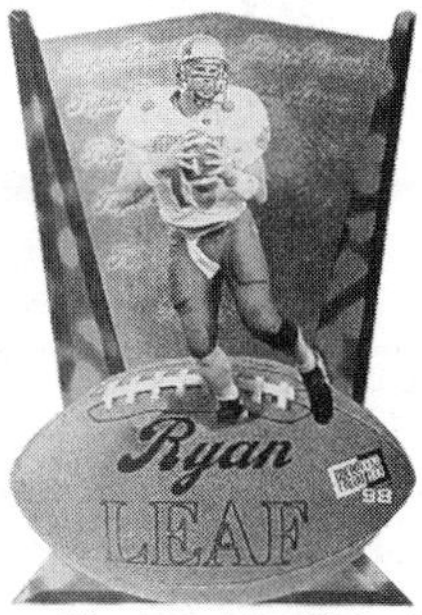

This nine-card insert featured three different players, with each having three different fit-together cards to form a three-card panel. They were numbered with a "TT" prefix and inserted one per 12 packs.

		MT
Complete Set (9):		40.00
Common Player:		3.00
1	Peyton Manning	8.00
2	Peyton Manning	8.00
3	Peyton Manning	8.00
4	Ryan Leaf	6.00
5	Ryan Leaf	6.00
6	Ryan Leaf	6.00
7	Charles Woodson	3.00
8	Charles Woodson	3.00
9	Charles Woodson	3.00

1998 Press Pass Trophy Case

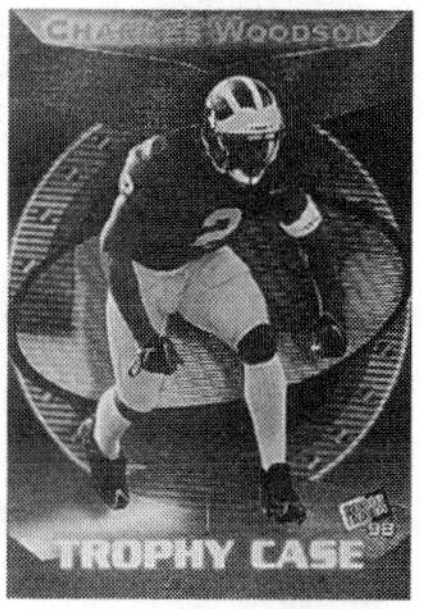

This 12-card insert was printed on silver foilboard, with the player's name across the top and the insert name across the bottom. Trophy Case cards are numbered with a "TC" prefix and inserted one per nine packs.

		MT
Complete Set (12):		40.00
Common Player:		2.00
1	Peyton Manning	12.00
2	Ryan Leaf	6.00
3	Charles Woodson	6.00
4	Randy Moss	16.00
5	Curtis Enis	6.00
6	Grant Wistrom	2.00
7	Kevin Dyson	4.00
8	Fred Taylor	6.00
9	Tavian Banks	4.00
10	Ahman Green	2.00
11	Skip Hicks	4.00
12	Andre Wadsworth	4.00

A card number in parentheses ( ) indicates the set is unnumbered.

1999 Press Pass

This 45-card set includes all of the top draft picks from 1999. Each is pictured in his college uniform and each name is in gold foil. Three parallel sets were made with Paydirt, Torquers and Reflectors. Other inserts include: Autographs, Big Numbers, Game Jerseys, Goldenarm, Hardware and X's and O's.

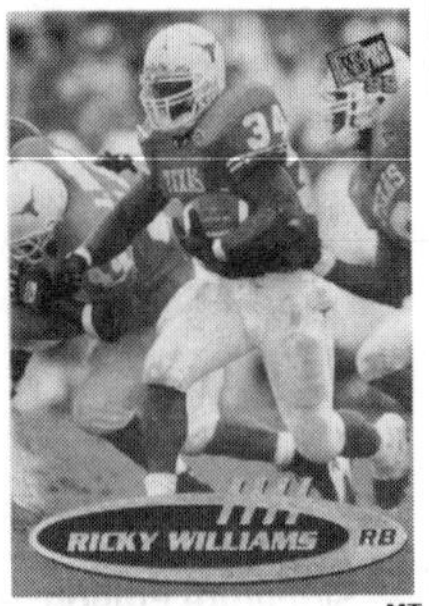

	MT
Complete Set (45):	20.00
Common Player:	.10
Minor Stars:	.20
Paydirt Cards:	1.5x
Inserted 1:1 Hobby	
Torquer Cards:	1.5x
Inserted 1:1 Mass	
Reflector Cards:	12x-24x
Inserted 1:180	
Pack (4):	2.50
Wax Box (32):	65.00
1 Ricky Williams	3.00
2 Tim Couch	3.00
3 Champ Bailey	.50
4 Chris Claiborne	.20
5 Donovan McNabb	2.00
6 Edgerrin James	5.00
7 Akili Smith	2.00
8 John Tait	.10
9 Jevon Kearse	1.00
10 Torry Holt	1.25
11 Troy Edwards	1.25
12 Chris McAlister	.20
13 Daunte Culpepper	2.00
14 Andy Katzenmoyer	.20
15 David Boston	1.25
16 Ebenezer Ekuban	.10
17 Peerless Price	.75
18 Shaun King	2.00
19 Joe Germaine	.30
20 Brock Huard	.50
21 Michael Bishop	.50
22 Amos Zereoue	.30
23 Sedrick Irvin	.50
24 Autry Denson	.20
25 Kevin Faulk	.50
26 James Johnson	.50
27 D'Wayne Bates	.20
28 Kevin Johnson	1.25
29 Tai Streets	.30
30 Craig Yeast	.20
31 Dre Bly	.10
32 Anthony Poindexter	.10
33 Jared DeVries	.10
34 Rob Konrad	.20
35 Dat Nguyen	.10
36 Cade McNown	2.00
37 Scott Covington	.20
38 Jon Jansen	.10
39 Rufus French	.10
40 Mike Rucker	.10
41 Aaron Gibson	.10
42 Kris Farris	.10
43 Anthony McFarland	.10
44 Matt Stinchcomb	.10
45 Checklist (Dee Miller)	.10

1999 Press Pass Autographs

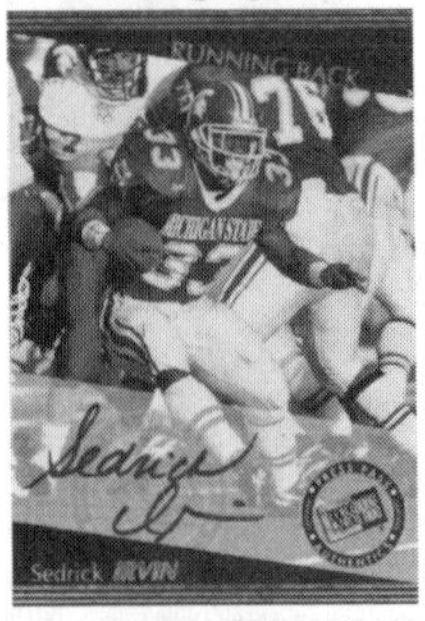

Each autographed card in this set has the same photo as his base card but the name is in smaller type and the autograph is above it. Singles were inserted 1:16 packs.

	MT
Complete Set (50):	750.00
Common Player:	6.00
Minor Stars:	12.00
Inserted 1:16 Hobby	
Inserted 1:36 Retail	
Champ Bailey	15.00
D'Wayne Bates	12.00
Michael Bishop	15.00
Dre Bly	6.00
David Boston	25.00
Chris Claiborne	12.00
Mike Cloud	12.00
Tim Couch	75.00
Scott Covington	12.00
Daunte Culpepper	35.00
Autry Denson	12.00
Jared DeVries	6.00
Antwan Edwards	12.00
Troy Edwards	25.00
Ebenezer Ekuban	6.00
Kris Farris	6.00
Kevin Faulk	15.00
Rufus French	6.00
Joe Germaine	12.00
Aaron Gibson	6.00
Torry Holt	25.00
Brock Huard	15.00
Sedrick Irvin	15.00
Edgerrin James	100.00
Jon Jansen	6.00
James Johnson	15.00
Kevin Johnson	25.00
Andy Katzenmoyer	12.00
Jevon Kearse	20.00
Shaun King	35.00
Rob Konrad	12.00
Chris McAlister	12.00
Darnell McDonald	12.00
Anthony McFarland	6.00
Donovan McNabb	35.00
Cade McNown	35.00
Dee Miller	6.00
Dat Nguyen	6.00
Mike Peterson	6.00
Anthony Poindexter	6.00
Peerless Price	20.00
Mike Rucker	6.00
Akili Smith	35.00
Matt Stinchcomb	6.00
Tai Streets	12.00
John Tait	6.00
Jerame Tuman	6.00
Ricky Williams	75.00
Craig Yeast	6.00
Amos Zereoue	12.00

1999 Press Pass Big Numbers

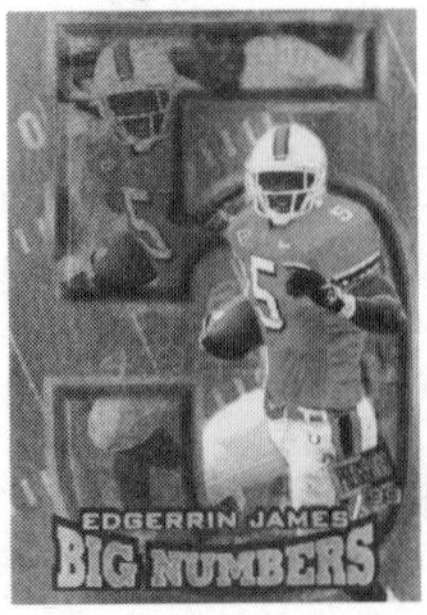

Each card in this 9-card set is printed on foil board with a photo of the player and the number that he was drafted in the background. Singles were inserted 1:16 packs. A parallel Die Cut version was also made with each single the same except for die cut. Those were found 1:32 packs.

	MT
Complete Set (9):	30.00
Common Player:	2.50
Inserted 1:16	
Die-Cut Cards:	2x
Inserted 1:32	
1 Tim Couch	7.00
2 Ricky Williams	7.00
3 Donovan McNabb	5.00
4 Edgerrin James	10.00
5 Peerless Price	3.00
6 Amos Zereoue	2.50
7 Daunte Culpepper	5.00
8 Tai Streets	2.50
9 Akili Smith	5.00

1999 Press Pass Goldenarm

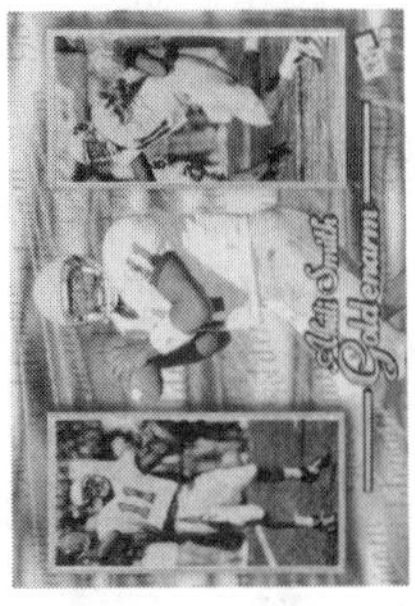

Each card in this 9-card set is horizontal and includes the top quarterbacks drafted in 1999. They were printed on foil board and were inserted 1:10 packs.

	MT
Complete Set (9):	25.00
Common Player:	1.50
Inserted 1:10	
1 Tim Couch	7.00
2 Donovan McNabb	4.00
3 Akili Smith	4.00
4 Daunte Culpepper	4.00
5 Cade McNown	4.00
6 Brock Huard	1.50
7 Joe Germaine	1.50
8 Shaun King	4.00
9 Michael Bishop	2.00

1999 Press Pass Hardware

Only the top rookies were included in this 12-card insert that was inserted 1:8 packs.

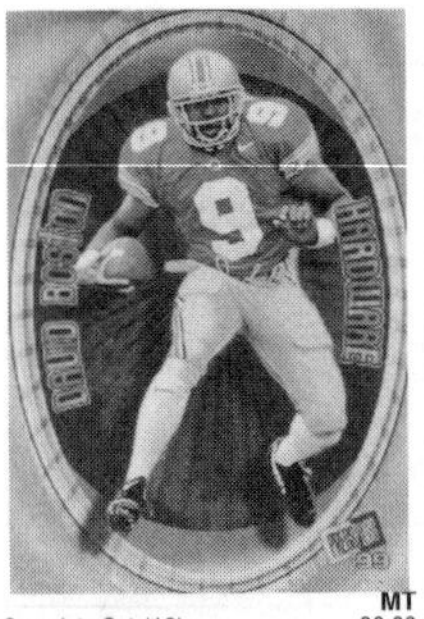

	MT
Complete Set (12):	30.00
Common Player:	1.50
Inserted 1:8	
1 Cade McNown	3.50
2 Ricky Williams	7.00
3 Torry Holt	2.00
4 Tim Couch	7.00
5 David Boston	2.00
6 Troy Edwards	2.00
7 Michael Bishop	1.50
8 Mike Cloud	1.50
9 Champ Bailey	1.50
10 Kevin Faulk	1.50
11 Autry Denson	1.50
12 Donovan McNabb	3.50

1999 Press Pass Jersey Cards

Each single in this 6-card set features a piece of game-used jersey on the card. Singles were found 1:640 packs.

	MT
Complete Set (6):	425.00
Common Player:	40.00
Inserted 1:640 Hobby	
Inserted 1:720 Mass	
TC Tim Couch (redemption)	175.00
DC Daunte Culpepper	80.00
TH Torry Holt	60.00
AS Akili Smith	80.00
CM Cade McNown	80.00
PP Peerless Price	40.00

1999 Press Pass "X's and O's"

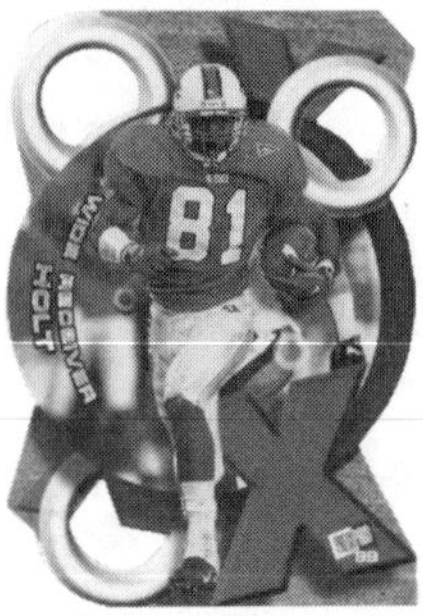

The top 36 players from the base set were included in this insert that was found one-per-pack. Each is die cut and embossed on extra thick stock.

	MT
Complete Set (36):	20.00
Common Player:	.25
Minor Stars:	.50
Inserted 1:1	
1 Ricky Williams	4.00
2 Tim Couch	4.00
3 Champ Bailey	.75
4 Donovan McNabb	2.00
5 Edgerrin James	6.00
6 Akili Smith	2.00
7 Torry Holt	1.25
8 Troy Edwards	1.25
9 Daunte Culpepper	2.00
10 Andy Katzenmoyer	.50
11 David Boston	1.25
12 Peerless Price	.75
13 Shaun King	2.00
14 Joe Germaine	.50
15 Brock Huard	.75
16 Michael Bishop	.75
17 Amos Zereoue	.50
18 Sedrick Irvin	.75
19 Autry Denson	.50
20 Kevin Faulk	.75
21 James Johnson	.75
22 D'Wayne Bates	.50
23 Kevin Johnson	1.25
24 Tai Streets	.50
25 Cade McNown	2.00
26 Scott Covington	.50
27 Chris Claiborne	.50
28 Jevon Kearse	1.00
29 Rob Konrad	.25
30 Dat Nguyen	.25
31 Chris McAlister	.50
32 Craig Yeast	.25
33 Anthony Poindexter	.25
34 Dre Bly	.25
35 Mike Rucker	.25
36 Checklist (Tim Couch)	2.00

A player's name in *italic type* indicates a rookie card.

2000 Press Pass

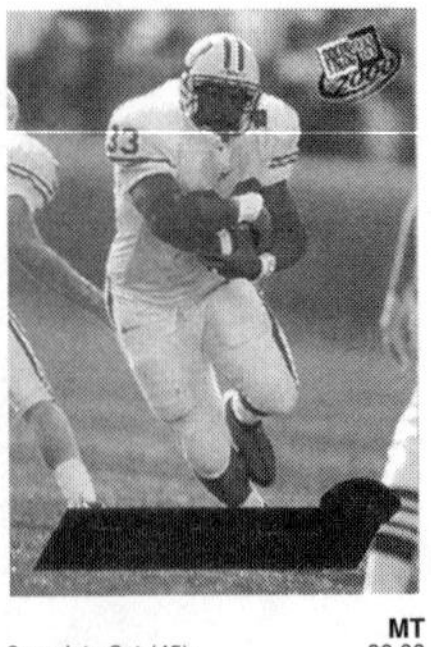

	MT
Complete Set (45):	20.00
Common Player:	.20
Minor Stars:	.40
Pack (5):	3.50
Wax Box (24):	60.00
1 Peter Warrick	3.00
2 Travis Claridge	.20
3 Courtney Brown	.75
4 Plaxico Burress	2.00
5 Chad Pennington	2.00
6 Thomas Jones	2.00
7 Ron Dayne	2.50
8 Brian Urlacher	.75
9 Corey Simon	.40
10 Chris Samuels	.40
11 Stockar McDougle	.20
12 Deon Grant	.40
13 Cosey Coleman	.20
14 Sylvester Morris	1.00
15 Shyrone Stith	.40
16 Shaun Alexander	1.50
17 Dez White	.60
18 John Engelberger	.40
19 Tim Rattay	.60
20 Todd Pinkston	.60
21 John Abraham	.40
22 R. Jay Soward	1.00
23 Shaun Ellis	.40
24 Keith Bullock	.40
25 Jerry Porter	1.00
26 Darren Howard	.40
27 Joe Hamilton	.60
28 Delthea O'Neal	.40
29 Chris Redman	1.25
30 Deon Dyer	.40
31 Jamal Lewis	2.00
32 Chris Hovan	.40
33 Raynoch Thompson	.40
34 Travis Taylor	1.25
35 Sebastian Janikowski	.40
36 Travis Prentice	1.00
37 Tom Brady	.50
38 Tee Martin	1.00
39 JR Redmond	1.00
40 Dennis Northcutt	.75
41 Laveranues Coles	.60
42 Danny Farmer	.60
43 Darrell Jackson	.50
44 Chris McIntosh	.20
45 Checklist (Peter Warrick CL)	1.25

2000 Press Pass Gold Parallel

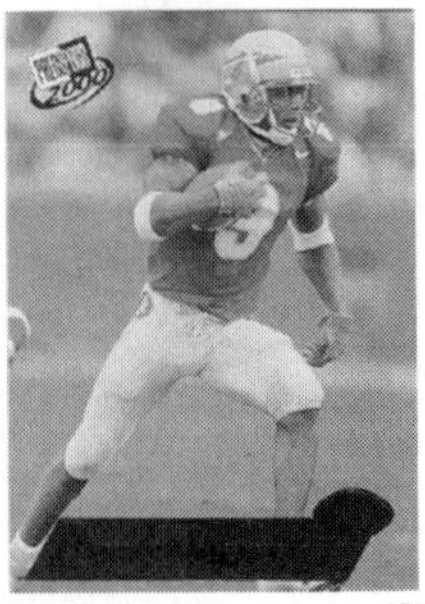

	MT
Complete Set (45):	24.00
Gold Cards:	1.2x
Inserted 1:1 Hobby	

2000 Press Pass Reflectors Parallel

	MT
Complete Set (45):	240.00
Reflector Cards:	5x-10x
Inserted 1:72	
Production 500 Sets	

2000 Press Pass Torquers Parallel

	MT
Complete Set (45):	36.00
Torquers Cards:	1.5x
Inserted 1:1 Retail	

Post-1980 cards in Near Mint condition will generally sell for about 75% of the quoted Mint value. Excellent-condition cards bring no more than 40%.

2000 Press Pass Autographs

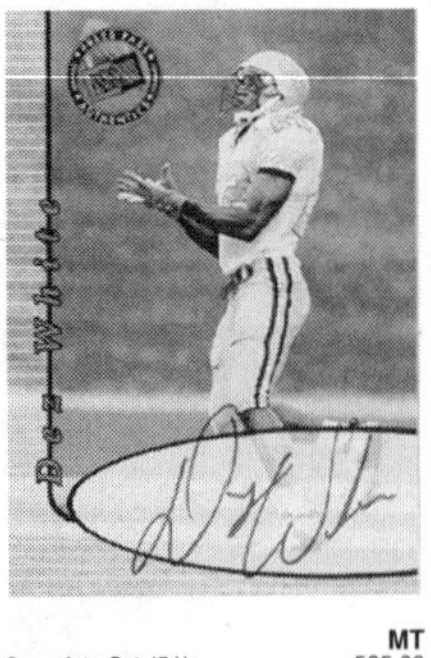

	MT
Complete Set (51):	525.00
Common Player:	5.00
Minor Stars:	10.00
Inserted 1:8	
Holofoil Cards:	2x
Production 100 Sets	
John Abraham	10.00
Shaun Alexander	30.00
Tom Brady	10.00
Courtney Brown	15.00
Keith Bulluck	10.00
Plaxico Burress	40.00
Giovanni Carmazzi	25.00
Kwame Cavil	10.00
Travis Claridge	5.00
Cosey Coleman	5.00
Laveranues Coles	12.00
Ron Dayne	50.00
Na'il Diggs	10.00
Ron Dugans	10.00
Deon Dyer	10.00
Shaun Ellis	10.00
John Engelberger	10.00
Danny Farmer	12.00
Deon Grant	10.00
Joe Hamilton	12.00
Chris Hovan	10.00
Darren Howard	10.00
Darrell Jackson	10.00
Sebastian Janikowski	10.00
Thomas Jones	40.00
Jamal Lewis	40.00
Tee Martin	20.00
Stockar McDougle	5.00
Chris McIntosh	5.00
Corey Moore	10.00
Rob Morris	10.00
Sylvester Morris	20.00
Dennis Northcutt	15.00
Delthea O'Neal	10.00
Chad Pennington	40.00
Todd Pinkston	12.00
Jerry Porter	20.00
Travis Prentice	20.00
Tim Rattay	12.00
Chris Redman	25.00
J.R. Redmond	20.00
Chris Samuels	10.00
Corey Simon	10.00
Marvel Smith	5.00
Shyrone Stith	10.00
Travis Taylor	25.00
Raynoch Thompson	10.00
Brian Urlacher	15.00
Todd Wade	5.00
Peter Warrick	60.00
Dez White	12.00

2000 Press Pass Autographs Holofoils Parallel

	MT
Holofoil Cards:	2x
Production 100 Sets	

2000 Press Pass Big Numbers

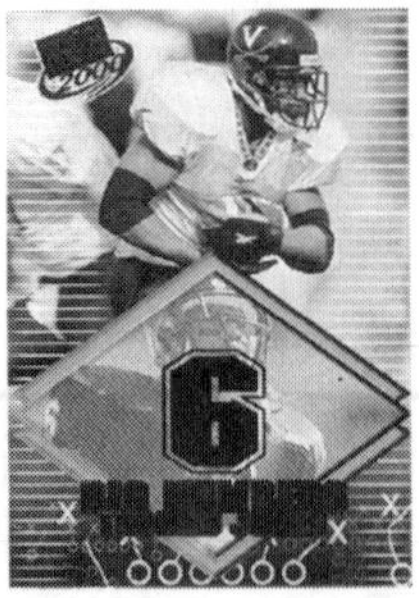

	MT
Complete Set (8):	15.00
Common Player:	2.00
Inserted 1:12	
Die-Cut Cards:	2x
Inserted 1:24	
BN1 Peter Warrick	5.00
BN2 Ron Dayne	4.00
BN3 Courtney Brown	2.00
BN4 Plaxico Burress	3.00
BN5 Shaun Alexander	3.00
BN6 Thomas Jones	3.00
BN7 Chad Pennington	3.00
BN8 Chris Redman	2.00

2000 Press Pass Big Numbers Die Cuts Parallel

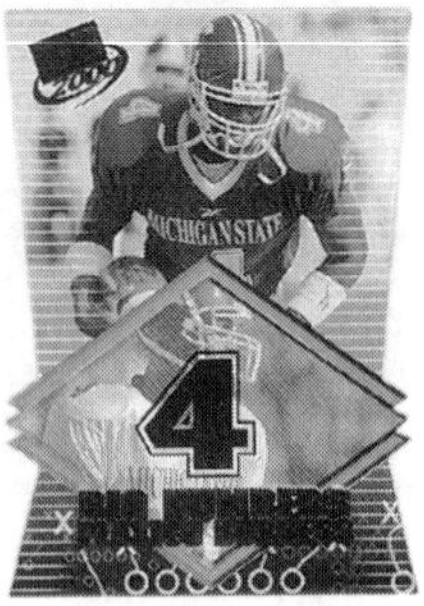

	MT
Die-Cut Cards:	2x
Inserted 1:24	

2000 Press Pass Breakout

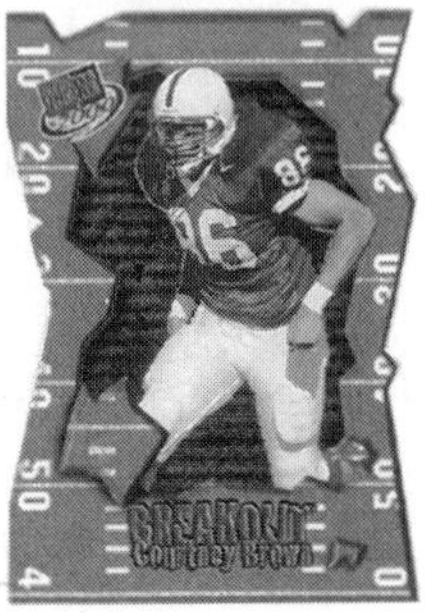

	MT
Complete Set (35):	20.00
Common Player:	.25
Minor Stars:	.50
Inserted 1:1	
BO1 Peter Warrick	3.00
BO2 Sebastian Janikowski	.50
BO3 Courtney Brown	.75
BO4 Plaxico Burress	2.00
BO5 Chad Pennington	2.00
BO6 Thomas Jones	2.00
BO7 Ron Dayne	2.50
BO8 Brian Urlacher	.75
BO9 Deon Dyer	.50
BO10 Chris Samuels	.50
BO11 Stockar McDougle	.25
BO12 Deon Grant	.50
BO13 Cosey Coleman	.25
BO14 Shyrone Stith	.50
BO15 Tim Rattay	.75
BO16 Shaun Alexander	1.50
BO17 Dez White	.75
BO18 John Engelberger	.50
BO19 Laveranues Coles	.75
BO20 J.R. Redmond	1.00
BO21 R. Jay Soward	1.00
BO22 Chris McIntosh	.25
BO23 Shaun Ellis	.50
BO24 Keith Bullock	.50
BO25 Jerry Porter	1.00
BO26 Darren Howard	.50
BO27 Tee Martin	1.00
BO28 Delthea O'Neal	.50
BO29 Chris Redman	1.25
BO30 Danny Farmer	.75
BO31 Jamal Lewis	2.00
BO32 Chris Hovan	.50
BO33 Corey Simon	.50
BO34 Travis Taylor	1.25
BO35 Checklist (Ron Dayne CL)	1.00

2000 Press Pass Game Jerseys

	MT
Complete Set (6):	400.00
Common Player:	30.00
Inserted 1:380 Hobby	
Inserted 1:720 Retail	
Production 475 Sets	
JC1 Ron Dayne	100.00
JC2 Thomas Jones	85.00
JC3 Chad Pennington	85.00
JC4 Chris Redman	50.00
JC5 Corey Simon	30.00
JC6 Peter Warrick	125.00

2000 Press Pass Gridiron

	MT
Complete Set (3):	10.00
Common Player:	3.00
Inserted 1:1 Special Retail Box	
1 Peter Warrick	5.00
2 Chad Pennington	3.00
3 Ron Dayne	4.00

A card number in parentheses ( ) indicates the set is unnumbered.

2000 Press Pass Paydirt

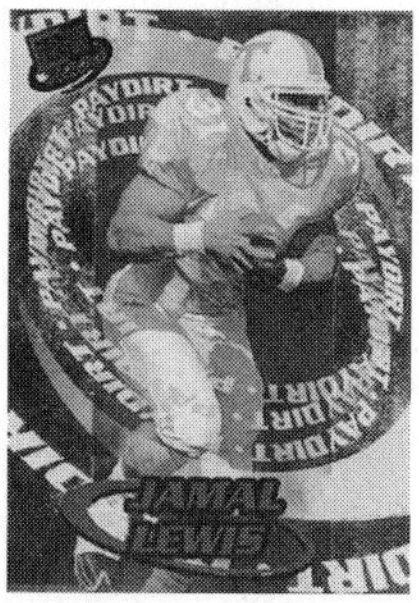

	MT
Complete Set (12):	25.00
Common Player:	.75
Minor Stars:	1.50
Inserted 1:16	
PD1 Peter Warrick	6.00
PD2 Plaxico Burress	4.00
PD3 Chad Pennington	4.00
PD4 Thomas Jones	4.00
PD5 Ron Dayne	5.00
PD6 Shyrone Stith	.75
PD7 Shaun Alexander	3.00
PD8 Chris Redman	3.00
PD9 Dez White	1.50
PD10 Jamal Lewis	4.00
PD11 J.R. Redmond	2.00
PD12 Travis Taylor	2.00

2000 Press Pass Power Picks

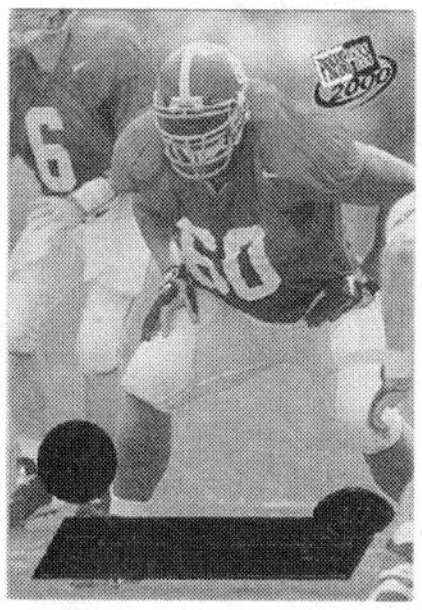

	MT
Complete Set (10):	12.00
Common Player:	.50
Minor Stars:	1.00
Inserted 1:12	
PP1 Peter Warrick	4.00
PP2 Courtney Brown	1.50
PP3 Plaxico Burress	2.00
PP4 Chad Pennington	2.00
PP5 Thomas Jones	2.00
PP6 Ron Dayne	3.00
PP7 Corey Simon	1.00
PP8 Shaun Alexander	1.50
PP9 Brian Urlacher	1.00
PP10 Chris Samuels	.50

2000 Press Pass Showbound

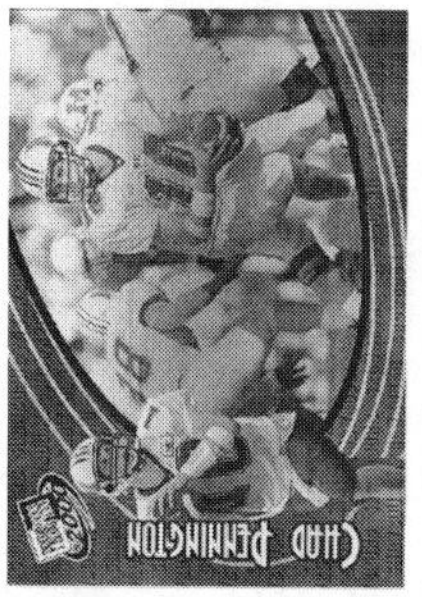

	MT
Complete Set (8):	10.00
Common Player:	.50
Inserted 1:8	
SB1 Peter Warrick	3.00
SB2 Dez White	.75
SB3 Courtney Brown	1.50
SB4 Plaxico Burress	1.50
SB5 Chad Pennington	1.50
SB6 Thomas Jones	1.50
SB7 Ron Dayne	2.00
SB8 Shaun Alexander	1.00

Post-1980 cards in Near Mint condition will generally sell for about 75% of the quoted Mint value. Excellent-condition cards bring no more than 40%.

2001 Press Pass

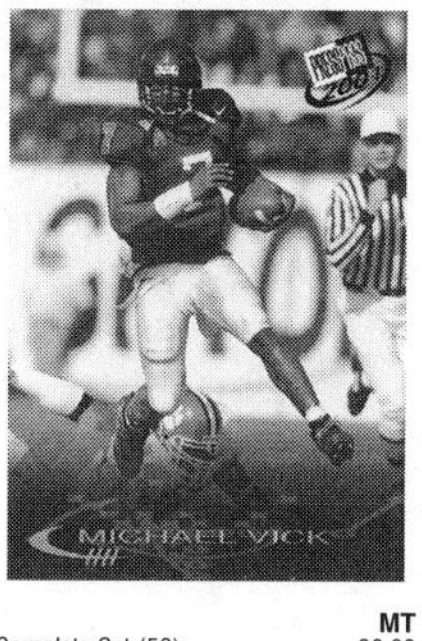

	MT
Complete Set (50):	30.00
Common Player:	.20
Minor Stars:	.40
Common Power Pick (46-50):	3.00
Inserted 1:16	
Pack (5):	3.50
Wax Box (24):	65.00
1 (Michael Vick)	2.50
2 Drew Brees	4.00
3 Michael Vick	5.00
4 Chris Weinke	2.00
5 Marques Tuiasosopo	1.25
6 Josh Booty	1.25
7 Josh Heupel	1.50
8 Sage Rosenfels	.50
9 Mike McMahon	.50
10 Deuce McAllister	2.00
11 LaDainian Tomlinson	2.50
12 LaMont Jordan	1.25
13 James Jackson	.75
14 Travis Henry	1.25
15 Anthony Thomas	1.00
16 Travis Minor	.75
17 Michael Bennett	2.00
18 Kevan Barlow	.75
19 Rudi Johnson	1.00
20 Santana Moss	2.00
21 Quincy Morgan	1.25
22 Rod Gardner	2.00
23 David Terrell	2.00
24 Chris Chambers	1.00
25 Reggie Wayne	2.00
26 Ken-Yon Rambo	.60
27 Chad Johnson	.60
28 Marvin "Snoop" Minnis	.60
29 Freddie Mitchell	.75
30 Koren Robinson	2.00
31 Bobby Newcombe	.60
32 Robert Ferguson	.75
33 Todd Heap	.20
34 Steve Hutchinson	.20
35 Leonard Davis	.20
36 Kenyatta Walker	.20
37 Justin Smith	.20
38 Jamal Reynolds	.20
39 Richard Seymour	.20
40 Shaun Rogers	.20
41 Gerard Warren	.20
42 Jamar Fletcher	.40
43 Gary Baxter	.20
44 Nate Clements	.20
45 Derrick Gibson	.40
46 Drew Brees PP	5.00
47 Michael Vick PP	6.00
48 Deuce McAllister PP	3.00
49 LaDainian Tomlinson PP	4.00
50 David Terrell PP	3.00

2001 Press Pass Autograph Cards

	MT
Common Player:	5.00
Inserted 1:8	
1 Michael Vick	100.00
2 Drew Brees	60.00
3 Marques Tuiasosopo	25.00
4 Chris Weinke	20.00
5 Sage Rosenfels	5.00
6 Jesse Palmer	5.00
7 Mike McMahon	5.00
8 Josh Booty	5.00
9 LaDainian Tomlinson	45.00
10 Deuce McAllister	35.00
11 Michael Bennett	30.00
12 Anthony Thomas	20.00
13 LaMont Jordan	20.00
14 Travis Henry	15.00
15 James Jackson	10.00
16 Rudi Johnson	12.00
17 David Terrell	35.00
18 Koren Robinson	35.00
19 Rod Gardner	35.00
20 Santana Moss	35.00
21 Reggie Wayne	25.00
22 Quincy Morgan	15.00
23 Chad Johnson	8.00
24 Robert Ferguson	10.00
25 Chris Chambers	12.00
26 Marvin "Snoop" Minnis	5.00
27 Bobby Newcombe	5.00
28 Ken-Yon Rambo	5.00
29 Todd Heap	5.00
30 Jabari Holloway	5.00
31 Nate Clements	5.00
32 Jamar Fletcher	5.00
33 Kenyatta Walker	5.00
34 Jeff Bakus	5.00
35 Steve Hutchinson	5.00
36 Chad Ward	5.00
37 Jamal Reynolds	5.00
38 Justin Smith	5.00
39 Gerard Warren	5.00
40 Casey Hampton	5.00
41 Ennis Davis	5.00
42 Moran Norris	5.00
43 Tommy Polley	5.00
44 Quinton Caver	5.00
45 Torrance Marshall	5.00
46 Brian Allen	5.00
47 Dominic Raiola	5.00

2001 Press Pass Big Numbers

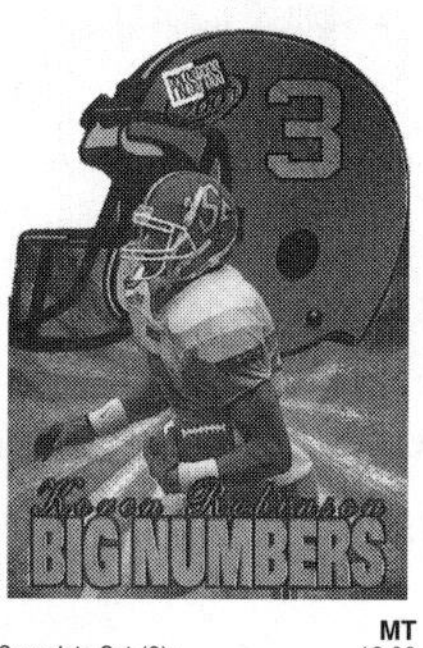

	MT
Complete Set (9):	12.00
Common Player:	1.25
Inserted 1:12	
Die-Cut Cards:	1.5x
Inserted 1:24	
BN1 Drew Brees	3.00
BN2 Michael Vick	4.00
BN3 Deuce McAllister	1.50
BN4 LaDainian Tomlinson	2.00
BN5 Santana Moss	1.50
BN6 David Terrell	1.50
BN7 Freddie Mitchell	1.25
BN8 Koren Robinson	1.50
BN9 Chad Johnson	1.25

2001 Press Pass Breakout

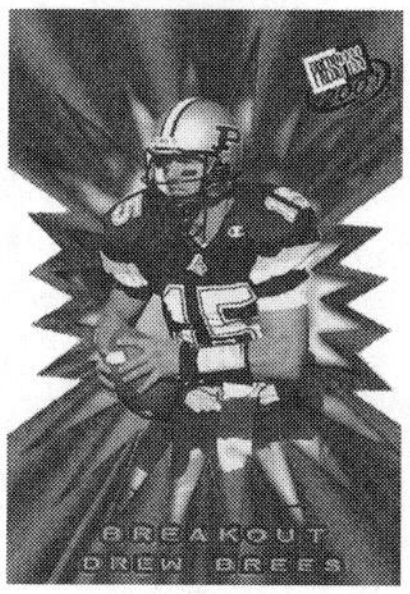

	MT
Complete Set (36):	25.00
Common Player:	.25
Minor Stars:	.50
Inserted 1:1	
B1 Drew Brees	3.00
B2 Michael Vick	4.00
B3 Chris Weinke	1.50
B4 Marques Tuiasosopo	1.00
B5 Josh Heupel	1.00
B6 Sage Rosenfels	.50
B7 Mike McMahon	.50
B8 Deuce McAllister	1.50
B9 LaDainian Tomlinson	2.00
B10 LaMont Jordan	1.00
B11 James Jackson	.50
B12 Travis Henry	.75
B13 Anthony Thomas	.75
B14 Michael Bennett	1.25
B15 Kevan Barlow	.50
B16 Rudi Johnson	.75
B17 Travis Minor	.50
B18 Ken-Yon Rambo	.50
B19 Santana Moss	1.50
B20 Quincy Morgan	1.00
B21 Rod Gardner	1.50
B22 David Terrell	1.50
B23 Chris Chambers	.75
B24 Reggie Wayne	1.50
B25 Chad Johnson	.50
B26 Marvin "Snoop" Minnis	.50
B27 Freddie Mitchell	.75
B28 Koren Robinson	1.50
B29 Todd Heap	.25
B30 Leonard Davis	.25
B31 Kenyatta Walker	.25
B32 Jamal Reynolds	.25
B33 Richard Seymour	.25
B34 Justin Smith	.25
B35 Jamar Fletcher	.50
B36 David Terrell	1.50

A player's name in *italic* type indicates a rookie card.

2001 Press Pass Jersey Cards

	MT
Common Player:	30.00
Inserted 1:320	
JC/MB Michael Bennett	35.00
JC/DB Drew Brees	75.00
JC/JS Justin Smith	30.00
JC/LT LaDainian Tomlinson	50.00
JC/MV Michael Vick	125.00
JC/CW Chris Weinke	40.00

A card number in parentheses ( ) indicates the set is unnumbered.

2001 Press Pass Paydirt

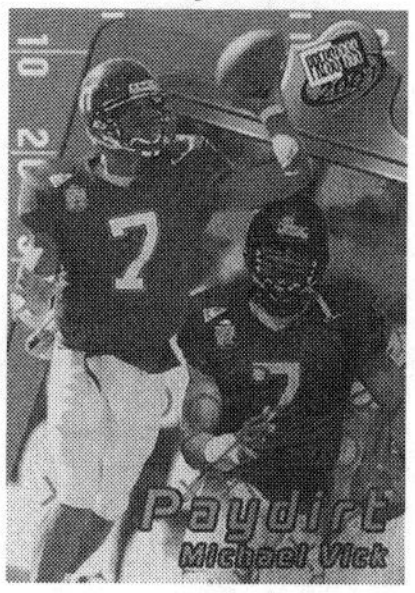

	MT
Complete Set (6):	15.00
Common Player:	1.50
Inserted 1:24	
PD1 Drew Brees	4.00
PD2 Michael Vick	5.00
PD3 Deuce McAllister	2.00
PD4 LaDainian Tomlinson	3.00
PD5 Santana Moss	1.50
PD6 David Terrell	1.50

2001 Press Pass Power Pick Autographs

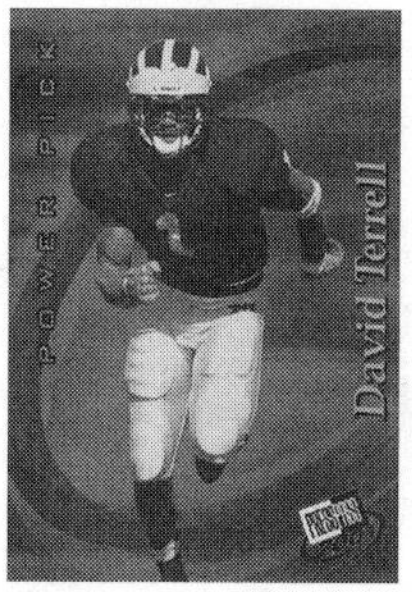

	MT
Common Player:	35.00
Inserted 1:320	
Production 250 Sets	
1 Michael Vick	125.00
2 LaDainian Tomlinson	50.00
3 David Terrell	45.00
4 Koren Robinson	45.00
5 Santana Moss	45.00
6 Deuce McAllister	45.00
7 Michael Bennett	35.00
8 Drew Brees	75.00
9 Chris Weinke	40.00

2001 Press Pass Showbound

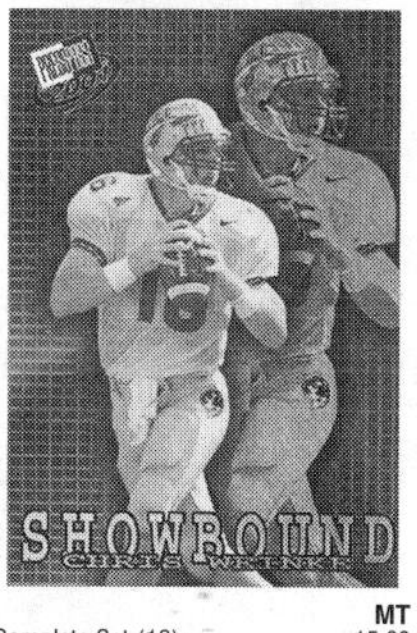

	MT
Complete Set (12):	15.00
Common Player:	.75
Inserted 1:12	
SB1 Drew Brees	3.00
SB2 Michael Vick	4.00
SB3 Chris Weinke	1.50
SB4 Koren Robinson	1.50
SB5 Deuce McAllister	1.50
SB6 Michael Bennett	1.25
SB7 LaDainian Tomlinson	2.00
SB8 Santana Moss	1.50
SB9 Rod Gardner	1.50
SB10 David Terrell	1.50
SB11 Chris Chambers	.75
SB12 Chad Johnson	.75

Values quoted in this guide reflect the retail price of a card — the price a collector can expect to pay when buying a card from a dealer. The wholesale price — that which a collector can expect to receive from a dealer when selling cards — will be significantly lower, depending on desirability and condition.

2001 Press Pass Signature Edition

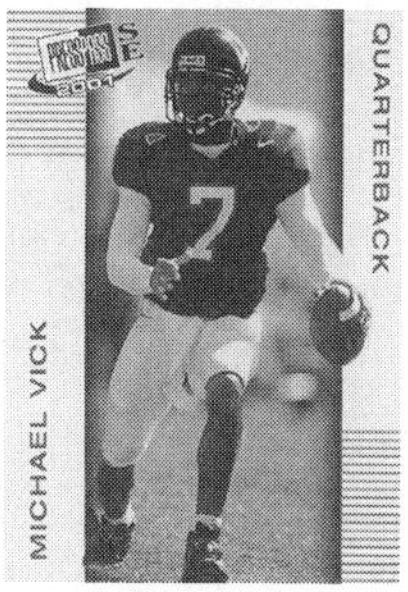

	MT
Complete Set (45):	45.00
Common Player:	.30
Minor Stars:	.60
Pack (4):	11.00
Wax Box (12):	100.00
1 Michael Vick	6.00
2 Drew Brees	4.50
3 Quincy Carter	1.75
4 Marques Tuiasosopo	1.50
5 Chris Weinke	2.50
6 Sage Rosenfels	1.00
7 Jesse Palmer	.75
8 Mike McMahon	.75
9 Josh Booty	.75
10 Josh Heupel	2.50
11 LaDainian Tomlinson	3.50
12 Deuce McAllister	2.50
13 Michael Bennett	3.00
14 Anthony Thomas	2.00
15 LaMont Jordan	1.25
16 Travis Henry	1.50
17 James Jackson	1.25
18 Kevan Barlow	1.00
19 Travis Minor	1.25
20 Rudi Johnson	1.00
21 David Terrell	3.00
22 Koren Robinson	2.50
23 Rod Gardner	2.50
24 Santana Moss	3.00
25 Freddie Mitchell	1.50
26 Reggie Wayne	1.75
27 Quincy Morgan	1.00
28 Chris Chambers	1.25
29 Robert Ferguson	1.25
30 Chad Johnson	1.25
31 Marvin "Snoop" Minnis	1.25
32 Todd Heap	.75
33 Steve Hutchinson	.60
34 Leonard Davis	.30
35 Kenyatta Walker	.30
36 Justin Smith	.75
37 Andre Carter	.75
38 Jamal Reynolds	.75
39 Gerard Warren	.75
40 Richard Seymour	.30
41 Damione Lewis	.75
42 Jamar Fletcher	.75
43 Nate Clements	.60
44 Derrick Gibson	.30
45 David Terrell CL	1.50

2001 Press Pass Signature Edition Autographs

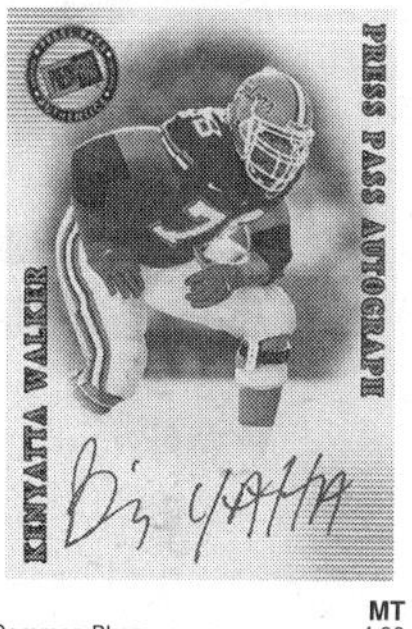

	MT
Common Player:	4.00
Minor Stars:	8.00
Inserted 1:1	
1 Anthony Thomas	15.00
2 Ben Leard	8.00
3 Bobby Newcombe	8.00
4 Brian Allen	4.00
5 Chad Johnson	10.00
6 Chad Ward	4.00
7 Chris Chambers	10.00
8 Chris Weinke	20.00
9 Dan Alexander	8.00
10 David Terrell	25.00
11 Deuce McAllister	20.00
12 Dominic Raiola	4.00
13 Drew Brees	30.00
14 Ennis Davis	4.00
15 Freddie Mitchell	12.00
16 Gerard Warren	8.00
17 Jabari Holloway	4.00
18 Jamal Reynolds	8.00
19 James Jackson	10.00
20 Jamie Winborn	4.00
21 Jeff Backus	4.00
22 Jesse Palmer	8.00
23 Josh Booty	8.00
24 Josh Heupel	20.00
25 Justin Smith	8.00
26 Kenyatta Walker	4.00
27 Ken-Yon Rambo	8.00
28 Kevan Barlow	10.00
29 Koren Robinson	15.00
30 LaDainian Tomlinson	30.00
31 LaMont Jordan	12.00
32 Marques Tuiasosopo	12.00
33 Maurice Williams	4.00
34 Michael Bennett	25.00
36 Mike McMahon	8.00
37 Moran Norris	4.00
38 Quincy Morgan	10.00
39 Reggie Wayne	12.00
40 Richard Seymour	4.00
41 Robert Ferguson	10.00
42 Rod Gardner	15.00
43 Rudi Johnson	10.00
44 Sage Rosenfels	10.00
45 Santana Moss	25.00
46 Marvin "Snoop" Minnis	12.00
47 Steve Hutchinson	4.00
48 Todd Heap	8.00
49 Tommy Polley	4.00
50 Travis Henry	12.00
51 Travis Minor	10.00
52 Willie Howard	4.00

2001 Press Pass Signature Edition Autographs Silver

	MT
Silver Cards:	1.5x
Production 250 Sets	
Blue Cards:	3x
Production 25 Sets	
Michael Vick	100.00

2001 Press Pass Signature Edition Class of 2001

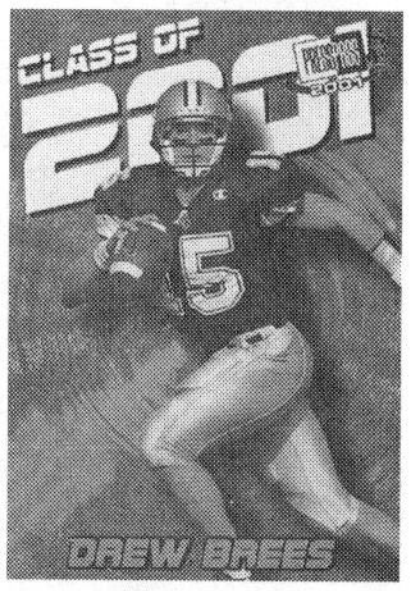

	MT
Complete Set (9):	25.00
Common Player:	2.00
Inserted 1:6	
CL1 Michael Vick	8.00
CL2 LaDainian Tomlinson	5.00
CL3 David Terrell	4.00
CL4 Koren Robinson	3.00
CL5 Santana Moss	4.00
CL6 Deuce McAllister	3.50
CL7 Freddie Mitchell	2.00
CL8 Drew Brees	6.00
CL9 Chris Weinke	3.00

2001 Press Pass Signature Edition Game Jersey

	MT
Complete Set (6):	400.00
Common Player:	25.00
Inserted 1:96	
Production 250 Sets	
J/MB Michael Bennett	60.00
J/DB Drew Brees	85.00
J/JS Justin Smith	25.00
J/LT LaDainian Tomlinson	75.00
J/MV Michael Vick	125.00
J/CW Chris Weinke	40.00
Michael Vick, Drew Brees	125.00

2001 Press Pass Signature Edition Game Jersey Autograph

	MT
Production 25 Sets	
AJC/MB Michael Bennett	150.00
AJC/DB Drew Brees	200.00
AJC/LT LaDainian Tomlinson	175.00
AJC/MV Michael Vick 15	350.00
AJC/CW Chris Weinke	125.00

2001 Press Pass Signature Edition Game Jersey Uniform

	MT
Production 25 Sets	
JN/MB Michael Bennett	150.00
JN/DB Drew Brees	200.00
JN/JS Justin Smith	50.00
JN/LT LaDainian Tomlinson	175.00
JN/MV Michael Vick	250.00
JN/CW Chris Weinke	125.00

2001 Press Pass Signature Edition Jersey Patch Swatch

	MT
Complete Set (6):	
Common Player:	
JP/MB Michael Bennett	150.00
JP/DB Drew Brees	200.00
JP/JS Justin Smith	50.00
JP/LT LaDainian Tomlinson	175.00
JP/MV Michael Vick	250.00
JP/CW Chris Weinke	125.00

2001 Press Pass Signature Edition Old School

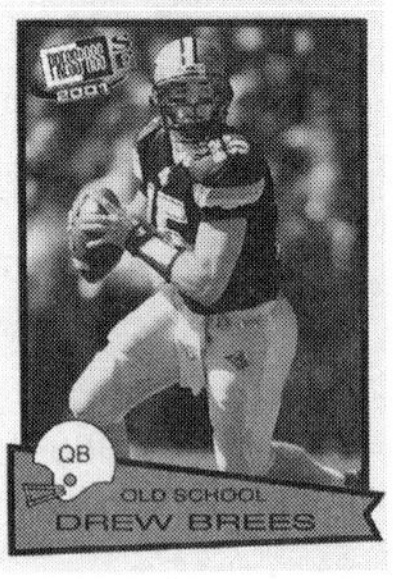

		MT
Complete Set (27):		45.00
Common Player:		.50
Minor Stars:		1.00
Inserted 1:2		
OS1	Michael Vick	8.00
OS2	Drew Brees	6.00
OS3	Chris Weinke	3.00
OS4	LaDainian Tomlinson	5.00
OS5	Deuce McAllister	3.00
OS6	Michael Bennett	4.00
OS7	Anthony Thomas	2.50
OS8	LaMont Jordan	1.50
OS9	Travis Henry	2.00
OS10	James Jackson	1.25
OS11	Kevan Barlow	1.00
OS12	David Terrell	4.00
OS13	Koren Robinson	2.50
OS14	Rod Gardner	2.50
OS15	Santana Moss	4.00
OS16	Freddie Mitchell	1.75
OS17	Reggie Wayne	2.00
OS18	Quincy Morgan	1.25
OS19	Chad Johnson	1.25
OS20	Chris Chambers	1.25
OS21	Todd Heap	1.00
OS22	Justin Smith	1.00
OS23	Andre Carter	1.00
OS24	Leonard Davis	.50
OS25	Kenyatta Walker	.50
OS26	Richard Seymour	.50
OS27	Michael Vick CL	4.00

2001 Press Pass Signature Edition Rookievision

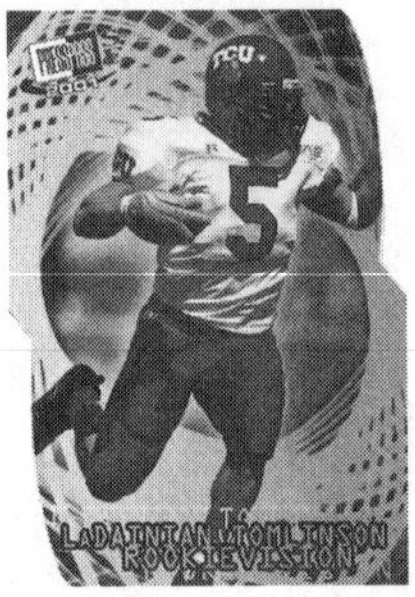

		MT
Complete Set (12):		30.00
Common Player:		1.00
Inserted 1:3		
RV1	Michael Vick	8.00
RV2	LaDainian Tomlinson	5.00
RV3	David Terrell	4.00
RV4	Koren Robinson	2.50
RV5	Rod Gardner	2.50
RV6	Deuce McAllister	3.50
RV7	Santana Moss	4.00
RV8	Michael Bennett	4.00
RV9	Freddie Mitchell	2.00
RV10	Todd Heap	1.00
RV11	Drew Brees	6.00
RV12	Chad Johnson	1.75

2001 Press Pass Signature Edition Up Close

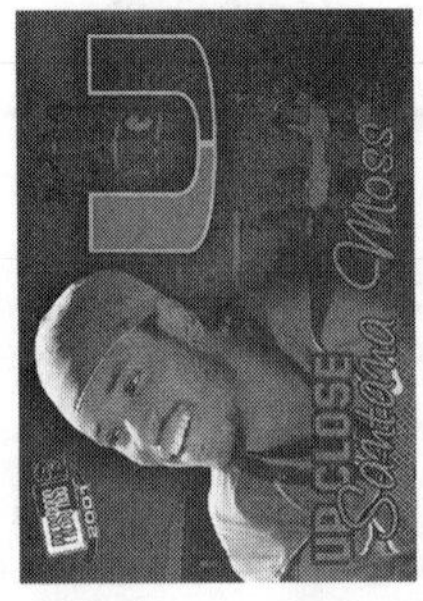

		MT
Complete Set (6):		20.00
Common Player:		2.50
Inserted 1:9		
UC1	Michael Vick	8.00
UC2	Drew Brees	6.00
UC3	LaDainian Tomlinson	5.00
UC4	David Terrell	4.00
UC5	Deuce McAllister	2.50
UC6	Santana Moss	4.00

1993-94 Pro Athletes Outreach

Measuring 7-1/8" x 4-1/8", the 12-card set was made up of triple-fold cards, which showcased a player photo on the right panel. Beneath the photo is the PAO logo, player's name and position. The player's career highlights and his Christian philosophy also are featured on the unnumbered card.

		MT
Complete Set (12):		6.00
Common Player:		.50
1	Mark Boyer	.50
2	Gill Byrd	.50
3	Darren Carrington	.50
4	Paul Coffman	.50
5	Burnell Dent	.50
6	Johnny Holland	.50
7	Jeff Kemp	1.00
8	Steve Largent	3.00
9	John Offerdahl	.50
10	Stephone Paige	.50
11	Doug Smith	.50
12	Rob Taylor	.50

1990 Pro Line Samples

These Pro Line samples can be identified from the regular set's card by several factors, including having the word SAMPLE written on the card back next to a player head shot. The card fronts have photos which are entirely different, or cropped differently, than their regular counterparts. The front also has a silver border; the regular cards are full-bleed. Some backs also have different photos than those used in the regular set and quotes. Card numbers are from 1-37, using all the odd numbers except 15.

		MT
Complete Set (18):		120.00
Common Player:		7.00
1	Charles Mann	7.00
3	Troy Aikman	25.00
5	Boomer Esiason	10.00
7	Warren Moon	12.00
9	Bill Fralic	7.00
11	Lawrence Taylor	10.00
13	George Seifert	7.00
17	Dan Marino	20.00
19	Jim Everett	10.00
21	John Elway	12.00
23	Jeff George	10.00
25	Lindy Infante	7.00
27	Dan Reeves	7.00
29	Steve Largent	12.00
31	Roger Craig	10.00
33	Marty Schottenheimer	7.00
35	Mike Ditka	8.00
37	Sam Wyche	7.00

1991 Pro Line Portraits

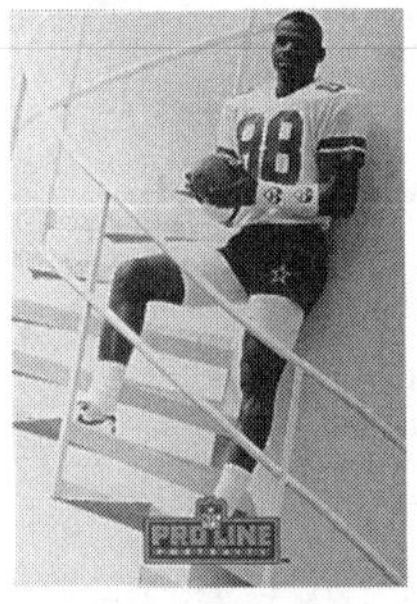

This set of high-end cards issued by NFL Properties shows a number of past and present NFL players in posed shots, wearing team apparel without football equipment. These cards were issued in August 1991 in 12-card wax packs. Some 250,000 autographed, embossed and unnumbered were randomly packed. Cards are not licensed by the NFL Players Association, so non-association members such as Eric Dickerson, Michael Dean Perry, Jim Kelly, Bernie Kosar, Webster Slaughter and Cornelius Bennett appear here while they don't appear in any other 1991 sets. A subset, Spirit Collectibles, shows seven player wives. Two other cards, Pro Line Portraits Collectible #1 (Ahmad Rashad and family) and #2 (Payne Stewart), were limited to 10,000 randomly issued cards. Each card in the regular set was also autographed.

		MT
Complete Set (300):		4.50
Common Player:		.03
Pack (12):		.40
Wax Box (36):		12.00
1	Jim Kelly	.20
2	Carl Banks	.03
3	Neal Anderson	.03
4	James Brooks	.03
5	Reggie Langhorne	.03
6	Robert Awalt	.03
7	Greg Kragen	.03
8	Steve Young	.50
9	*Nick Bell*	.10
10	Ray Childress	.03
11	Albert Bentley	.03
12	Albert Lewis	.03
13	Howie Long	.03
14	Willie Anderson	.03
15	Mark Clayton	.03
16	*Jarrod Bunch*	.10
17	Bruce Armstrong	.03
18	*Vinnie Clark*	.10
19	Rob Moore	.10
20	Eric Allen	.03
21	Timm Rosenbach	.03
22	Gary Anderson	.03
23	Martin Bayless	.03
24	Kevin Fagan	.03
25	Brian Blades	.03
26	Gary Anderson	.03
27	Earnest Bymer	.03
28	O.J. Simpson	1.00
29	Dan Henning	.03
30	Sean Landeta	.03
31	James Lofton	.03
32	Mike Singletary	.03
33	David Fulcher	.03
34	Mark Murphy	.03
35	Issiac Holt	.03
36	Dennis Smith	.03
37	Lomas Brown	.03
38	Ernest Givins	.03
39	Duane Bickett	.03
40	Barry Word	.03
41	Tony Mandarich	.03
42	Cleveland Gary	.03
43	Ferrell Edmunds	.03
44	*Randal Hill*	.25
45	Irving Fryar	.03
46	*Henry Jones*	.10
47	Blair Thomas	.03
48	Andre Waters	.03
49	J.T. Smith	.03
50	Thomas Everett	.03
51	Marion Butts	.03
52	Tom Rathman	.03
53	Vann McElroy	.03
54	Mark Carrier (T.B.)	.03
55	Jim Lachey	.03
56	Joe Theismann	.03
57	Jerry Glanville	.03
58	Doug Riesenberg	.03
59	Cornelius Bennett	.03
60	Mark Carrier (Chi.)	.03
61	Rodney Holman	.03
62	Leroy Hoard	.03
63	Michael Irvin	.65
64	Bobby Humphrey	.03
65	Mel Gray	.03
66	Brian Noble	.03
67	Al Smith	.03
68	Eric Dickerson	.10
69	Steve DeBerg	.03
70	Jay Schroeder	.03
71	Irv Pankey	.03
72	Reggie Roby	.03
73	Wade Wilson	.03
74	Reggie Rembert	.03
75	*Russell Maryland*	.40
76	Al Toon	.03
77	Randall Cunningham	.10
78	Lonnie Young	.03
79	Carnell Lake	.03
80	Brut Grossman	.03
81	Jim Mora	.03
82	Dave Krieg	.03
83	Bruce Hill	.03
84	Ricky Sanders	.03
85	Roger Staubach	.10
86	Richard Williamson	.03
87	Everson Walls	.03
88	Shane Conlan	.03
89	Mike Ditka	.10
90	Mark Bortz	.03
91	Tim McGee	.03
92	Michael Dean Perry	.10
93	Danny Noonan	.03
94	Mark Jackson	.03
95	Chris Miller	.03
96	*Ed McCaffrey*	.50
97	Lorenzo White	.10
98	Ray Donaldson	.03
99	Nick Lowery	.03
100	Steve Smith	.03
101	Jackie Slater	.03
102	Louis Oliver	.03
103	*Kanavis McGhee*	.10
104	Ray Agnew	.03
105	Sam Mills	.03
106	Bill Pickel	.03
107	Keith Byars	.03
108	Ricky Proehl	.10
109	Merril Hoge	.03
110	Rod Berstine	.03
111	Andy Heck	.03
112	Broderick Thomas	.03
113	Andre Reed	.03
114	Paul Warfield	.03
115	Bill Belichick	.03
116	Ottis Anderson	.03
117	Andre Reed	.10
118	Andre Rison	.20
119	Dexter Carter	.03
120	Anthony Munoz	.03
121	Bernie Kosar	.03
122	Alonzo Highsmith	.03
123	David Treadwell	.03
124	Rodney Peete	.03
125	Haywood Jeffires	.15
126	Clarence Verdin	.03
127	Christian Okoye	.03
128	Greg Townsend	.03
129	Tom Newberry	.03
130	Keith Sims	.03
131	Myron Guyton	.03
132	Andre Tippett	.03
133	Steve Walsh	.03
134	Erik McMillan	.03
135	Jim McMahon	.03
136	Derek Hill	.03
137	David Johnson	.03
138	Leslie O'Neal	.03
139	Pierce Holt	.03
140	Cortez Kennedy	.20
141	Danny Peebles	.03
142	Alvin Walton	.03
143	Drew Pearson	.03
144	Dick MacPherson	.03
145	Erik Howard	.03
146	Steve Tasker	.03
147	Bill Fralic	.03
148	Don Warren	.03
149	Eric Thomas	.03
150	Jack Pardee	.03
151	Gary Zimmerman	.03
152	Leonard Marshall	.03
153	Chris Spielman	.03
154	Sam Wyche	.03
155	Rohn Stark	.03
156	Stephone Paige	.03
157	Lionel Washington	.03
158	Henry Ellard	.03
159	Dan Marino	.75
160	Lindy Infante	.03
161	*Dan McGwire*	.10
162	Ken O'Brien	.03
163	Tim McDonald	.03
164	Louis Lipps	.03
165	Billy Joe Tolliver	.03
166	Harris Barton	.03
167	Tony Woods	.03
168	Matt Millen	.03
169	Gale Sayers	.03
170	Ron Meyer	.03
171	William Roberts	.03
172	Thurman Thomas	.25
173	Steve McMichael	.03
174	Ickey Woods	.03
175	Eugene Lockhart	.03
176	George Seifert	.03
177	Keith Jones	.03
178	Jack Trudeau	.03
179	Kevin Porter	.03
180	Ronnie Lott	.10
181	Marty Schottenhelmer	.03
182	Morten Andersen	.03
183	Anthony Thompson	.03
184	Tim Worley	.03
185	Billy Ray Smith	.03
186	David Whitmore	.03
187	Jacob Green	.03
188	*Browning Nagle*	.15
189	Franco Harris	.10
190	Art Shell	.03
191	Bart Oates	.03
192	William Perry	.03
193	Chuck Noll	.03
194	Troy Aikman	1.00
195	Jeff George	.15
196	Derrick Thomas	.15
197	Roger Craig	.03
198	John Fourcade	.03
199	Rod Woodson	.03
200	Anthony Miller	.03
201	Jerry Rice	.75
202	Eugene Robinson	.03
203	Charles Mann	.03
204	Mel Blount	.03
205	Don Shula	.03
206	John Elliott	.03
207	Jay Hilgenberg	.03
208	Deron Cherry	.03
209	Dan Reeves	.03
210	*Roman Phifer*	.10
211	David Little	.03
212	Lee Williams	.03
213	John Taylor	.10
214	Monte Coleman	.03
215	Walter Payton	.10
216	John Robinson	.03
217	Pepper Johnson	.03
218	Tom Thayer	.03
219	Dan Saleumua	.03
220	Ernest Spears	.03
221	Bubby Brister	.03
222	Junior Seau	.20
223	Brent Jones	.03
224	Rufus Porter	.03
225	Jack Kemp	.10
226	Wayne Fontes	.03
227	Phil Simms	.10
228	Shaun Gayle	.03
229	Bill Maas	.03
230	Renaldo Turnbull	.03
231	Bryan Hinkle	.03
232	Gary Plummer	.03
233	Jerry Burns	.03
234	Lawrence Taylor	.10
235	Joe Gibbs	.03
236	Neil Smith	.03
237	Rich Kotite	.03
238	Jim Covert	.03
239	Tim Grunhard	.03
240	Joe Bugel	.03
241	Dave Wyman	.03
242	Maruy Buford	.03
243	Kevin Ross	.03
244	Jimmy Johnson	.03
245	Jim Morrissey	.03
246	Jeff Hostetler	.20
247	Andre Ware	.10
248	Steve Largent	.10
249	Chuck Knox	.03
250	Boomer Esiason	.10
251	Kevin Butler	.03
252	Bruce Smith	.03
253	Webster Slaughter	.03
254	Mike Sherrard	.03
255	Steve Broussard	.03
256	Warren Moon	.15
257	John Elway	.25
258	Bob Golic	.03
259	Jim Everett	.03
260	Bruce Coslet	.03
261	James Francis	.03
262	Eric Dorsey	.03
263	Marcus Dupree	.03
264	Hart Lee Dykes	.03
265	Vinny Testaverde	.03
266	Chip Lohmiller	.03
267	John Riggins	.03
268	Mike Schad	.03
269	Kevin Greene	.03
270	Dean Biasucci	.03
271	*Mike Pritchard*	.40
272	*Ted Washington*	.10
273	*Alfred Williams*	.15
274	*Chris Zorich*	.15
275	Reggie Barrett	.03
276	Chris Hinton	.03
277	Tracy Johnson	.10
278	Jim Harbaugh	.03
279	John Roper	.03
280	Mike Dumas	.03
281	*Herman Moore*	3.50
282	*Eric Turner*	.15
283	Steve Atwater	.03
284	Michael Cofer (Det.)	.03
285	Darion Conner	.03
286	Darryl Talley	.03
287	Donnell Woolford	.03
288	Keith McCants	.03
289	Ray Handley	.03
290	Ahmad Rashad	.03
291	*Eric Swann*	.15
292	Dalton Hilltiard	.03
293	Rickey Jackson	.03
294	Vaughan Johnson	.03
295	Eric Martin	.03
296	Pat Swilling	.03
297	Anthony Carter	.03
298	Guy McIntyre	.03
299	Bennie Blades	.03
300	Paul Farren	.03

1991 Pro Line Portraits Autographs

Each card in the regular set was also autographed. The card is the same as the regular one, except it is not numbered. These cards command premium prices and were random inserts in packs, about one every three boxes.

		MT
Complete Set (301):		5250.
Common Player:		6.00
Minor Stars:		12.00
1A	Jim Kelly (Autopenned)	20.00
1B	Jim Kelly (Real Signature)	250.00
2	Carl Banks	6.00
3	Neal Anderson	6.00
4	James Brooks	6.00
5	Reggie Langhorne	60.00
6	Robert Awalt	6.00
7	Greg Kragen	6.00
8	Steve Young	125.00
9	Nick Bell	6.00
10	Ray Childress	12.00
11	Albert Bentley	6.00
12	Albert Lewis (Most signatures are cut off)	60.00
13	Howie Long	35.00
14	Flipper Anderson	12.00
15	Mark Clayton	12.00
16	Jarrod Bunch	6.00
17	Bruce Armstrong	6.00
18	Vinnie Clark	6.00
19	Rob Moore	20.00
20	Eric Allen	6.00
21	Timm Rosenbach	6.00
22	Gary Anderson (K)	6.00
23	Martin Bayless	6.00
24	Kevin Fagan	6.00
25	Brian Blades	12.00
26	Gary Anderson (RB)	6.00
27	Earnest Byner	6.00
28	O.J. Simpson (RET)	300.00
29	Dan Henning (CO)	6.00
30	Sean Landeta	6.00
31	James Lofton	25.00
32	Mike Singletary	40.00
33	David Fulcher	6.00
34	Mark Murphy	6.00
35	Issiac Holt	6.00
36	Dennis Smith	6.00
37	Lomas Brown	6.00
38	Ernest Givins	12.00
39	Duane Bickett	6.00
40	Barry Word	6.00
41	Tony Mandarich	12.00
42	Cleveland Gary	12.00
43	Ferrell Edmunds	6.00
44	Randal Hill	12.00
45	Irving Fryar	12.00
46	Henry Jones	6.00
47	Blair Thomas	6.00
48	Andre Waters	6.00
49	J.T. Smith	6.00
50	Thomas Everett	6.00
51	Marion Butts	6.00
52	Tom Rathman	12.00
53	Vann McElroy	6.00
54	Mark Carrier (WR)	6.00
55	Jim Lachey	6.00
56	Joe Theismann (RET)	30.00
57	Jerry Glanville (CO)	12.00
58	Doug Riesenberg	6.00
59	Cornelius Bennett	12.00
60	Mark Carrier (DB)	100.00
61	Rodney Holman	225.00
62	Leroy Hoard	12.00
63	Michael Irvin	35.00
64	Bobby Humphrey	6.00
65	Mel Gray	12.00
66	Brian Noble	6.00
67	Al Smith	6.00
68	Eric Dickerson	30.00
69	Steve DeBerg	12.00
70	Jay Schroeder	12.00
71	Irv Pankey	6.00
72	Reggie Roby	12.00
73	Wade Wilson	12.00
74	Johnny Rembert	6.00
75	Russell Maryland	12.00
76	Al Toon	12.00
77	Randall Cunningham	30.00
78	Lonnie Young	6.00
79	Carnell Lake	12.00
80	Brut Grossman	6.00
81	Jim Mora (CO)	6.00
82	Dave Krieg	12.00
83	Bruce Hill	6.00
84	Ricky Sanders	12.00
85	Roger Staubach (RET)	150.00
86	Richard Williamson (CO)	6.00
87	Everson Walls	12.00
88	Shane Conlan	6.00
89	Mike Ditka (CO)	40.00
90	Mark Bortz	6.00
91	Tim McGee	6.00
92	Michael Dean Perry	12.00
93	Danny Noonan	6.00
94	Mark Jackson	12.00
95	Chris Miller	12.00
96	Ed McCaffrey	25.00
97	Lorenzo White	12.00
98	Ray Donaldson	6.00
99	Nick Lowery (May be autopenned)	6.00
100	Steve Smith	6.00
101	Jackie Slater	12.00
102	Louis Oliver	6.00
103	Kanavis McGhee	6.00
104	Ray Agnew	6.00
105	Sam Mills	12.00
106	Bill Pickel	12.00
107	Keith Byars	12.00
108	Ricky Proehl	12.00
109	Merril Hoge	6.00
110	Rod Berstine	6.00
111	Andy Heck	6.00
112	Broderick Thomas	6.00
113	Andre Collins	6.00
114	Paul Warfield (RET)	25.00
115	Bill Belichick (CO)	12.00
116	Ottis Anderson	12.00
117	Andre Reed	25.00
118A	Andre Rison (Ball-point pen)	15.00
118B	Andre Rison (Signed in Sharpie)	30.00
119	Dexter Carter	12.00
120	Anthony Munoz	12.00
121	Bernie Kosar	15.00
122	Alonzo Highsmith	60.00
123	David Treadwell	6.00
124	Rodney Peete	12.00
125	Haywood Jeffires	12.00
126	Clarence Verdin	6.00
127	Christian Okoye	12.00
128	Greg Townsend	125.00
129	Tom Newberry	6.00
130	Keith Sims	6.00
131	Myron Guyton	6.00
132	Andre Tippett	6.00
133	Steve Walsh	12.00
134	Erik McMillan	6.00
135	Jim McMahon	280.00
136	Derek Hill	6.00
137	D.J. Johnson	6.00
138	Leslie O'Neal	12.00
139	Pierce Holt	6.00
140	Cortez Kennedy	12.00
141	Danny Peebles	6.00
142	Alvin Walton	6.00
143	Drew Pearson (RET)	12.00
144	Dick MacPherson (CO)	6.00
145	Erik Howard	6.00
146	Steve Tasker	6.00
147	Bill Fralic	6.00
148	Don Warren	6.00
149	Eric Thomas	6.00
150	Jack Pardee (CO)	6.00
151	Gary Zimmerman	6.00
152	Leonard Marshall (Frequently miscut)	12.00
153	Chris Spielman	12.00
154	Sam Wyche (CO)	6.00
155	Rohn Stark	6.00
156	Stephone Paige	6.00
157	Lionel Washington (Most signatures are cut off)	120.00
158	Henry Ellard	12.00
159	Dan Marino	200.00
160	Lindy Infante (CO)	6.00
161	Dan McGwire	6.00
162	Ken O'Brien	12.00
163	Tim McDonald	6.00
164	Louis Lipps	6.00
165	Billy Joe Tolliver	12.00
166	Harris Barton	6.00
167	Tony Woods	6.00
168	Matt Millen	12.00
169	Gale Sayers (RET)	35.00
170	Ron Meyer (CO)	12.00
171	William Roberts	6.00
172	Thurman Thomas	30.00
173	Steve McMichael	6.00
174	Ickey Woods	6.00
175	Eugene Lockhart	6.00
176	George Seifert (CO)	12.00
177	Keith Jones	6.00
178	Jack Trudeau	6.00
179	Kevin Porter	6.00
180	Ronnie Lott	15.00
181	Marty Schottenheimer (CO)	12.00
182	Morten Andersen	12.00
183	Anthony Thompson	6.00
184	Tim Worley	6.00
185	Billy Ray Smith	6.00
186	David Whitmore	6.00
187	Jacob Green	6.00
188	Browning Nagle	6.00
189	Franco Harris (RET) (Most signatures are cut off)	45.00
190	Art Shell (CO)	15.00
191	Bart Oates	6.00
192	William Perry	12.00
193	Chuck Noll (CO)	30.00
194	Troy Aikman	100.00
195	Jeff George	25.00
196	Derrick Thomas	40.00
197	Roger Craig	12.00
198	John Fourcade	6.00
199	Rod Woodson	12.00
200	Anthony Miller	12.00
201	Jerry Rice	150.00
202	Eugene Robinson	6.00
203	Charles Mann	6.00
204	Mel Blount (RET)	12.00
205	Don Shula (CO)	45.00
206	John Elliott	6.00
207	Jay Hilgenberg	6.00
208	Deron Cherry	6.00
209	Dan Reeves (CO)	12.00
210	Roman Phifer	6.00
211	David Little	6.00
212	Lee Williams	6.00
213	John Taylor	12.00
214	Monte Coleman	6.00
215	Walter Payton (RET)	150.00
216	John Robinson (CO)	6.00
217	Pepper Johnson	6.00
218	Tom Thayer	6.00
219	Dan Saleumua	6.00
220	Ernest Spears	6.00
221	Bubby Brister (Signed Bubby 6)	12.00
222	Junior Seau	20.00
223	Brent Jones	12.00
224	Rufus Porter	6.00
225	Jack Kemp (RET) (Autopenned)	30.00
226	Wayne Fontes (CO)	6.00
227	Phil Simms	30.00
228	Shaun Gayle	6.00
229	Bill Maas	6.00
230	Renaldo Turnbull	6.00
231	Bryan Hinkle	6.00
232	Gary Plummer	6.00
233	Jerry Burns (CO)	6.00
234	Lawrence Taylor	40.00
235	Joe Gibbs (CO)	20.00
236	Neil Smith (Most signatures are cut off)	60.00
237	Rich Kotite (CO)	6.00
238	Jim Covert	6.00
239	Tim Grunhard (Two different signatures known for this card)	6.00

240	Joe Bugel (CO)	6.00
241	Dave Wyman	6.00
242	Maruy Buford	6.00
243	Kevin Ross	6.00
244	Jimmy Johnson (CO)	40.00
245	Jim Morrissey	6.00
246	Jeff Hostetler	12.00
247	Andre Ware	12.00
248	Steve Largent (RET)	40.00
249	Chuck Knox (CO)	12.00
250	Boomer Esiason	12.00
251	Kevin Butler	6.00
252	Bruce Smith	12.00
253	Webster Slaughter	6.00
254	Mike Sherrard	6.00
255	Steve Broussard	6.00
256	Warren Moon	35.00
257	John Elway	100.00
258	Bob Golic	6.00
259	Jim Everett	12.00
260	Bruce Coslet (CO)	6.00
261	James Francis	280.00
262	Eric Dorsey	6.00
263	Marcus Dupree	6.00
264	Hart Lee Dykes	6.00
265	Vinny Testaverde	15.00
266	Chip Lohmiller	6.00
267	John Riggins (RET)	50.00
268	Mike Schad	6.00
269	Kevin Greene	12.00
270	Dean Biasucci	6.00
271	Mike Pritchard	6.00
272	Ted Washington	6.00
273	Alfred Williams	6.00
274	Chris Zorich	6.00
275	Reggie Barrett	6.00
276	Chris Hinton	6.00
277	Tracy Johnson	6.00
278	Jim Harbaugh	12.00
279	John Roper	6.00
280	Mike Dumas	6.00
281	Herman Moore	60.00
282	Eric Turner	6.00
283	Steve Atwater	6.00
284	Michael Cofer	6.00
285	Darion Conner	6.00
286	Darryl Talley	6.00
287	Donnell Woolford	6.00
288	Keith McCants	6.00
289	Ray Handley (CO)	6.00
290	Ahmad Rashad (RET)	175.00
291	Eric Swann	12.00
292	Dalton Hilliard (Signatures usually miscut)	25.00
293	Rickey Jackson	6.00
294	Vaughan Johnson	6.00
295	Eric Martin	6.00
296	Pat Swilling	12.00
297	Anthony Carter (Signatures usually miscut)	25.00
298	Guy McIntyre	75.00
299	Bennie Blades	6.00
300	Paul Farren	6.00
PLC2	Payne Stewart (Golfer)	85.00
NNO	Santa Claus Sendaway (Signed)	30.00
	Santa Claus Sendaway (Signed and numbered)	60.00

1991 Pro Line Portraits Collectibles

These two cards were randomly inserted in 1991 Pro Line foil packs and feature NBC sports commentator Ahmad Rashad and pro golfer Payne Stewart. The Stewart card shows him kissing a trophy and offers a tip on the back on how to approach the game. The card, like the Rashad card, has a number on the back, along with the words "Pro Line Portraits Collectible." The Rashad card pictures him and his family on the front, including his wife, TV actress, Phylicia. The back, in a horizontal format, has a quote from Rashad about the importance of family life.

		MT
Complete Set (2):		20.00
Common Player:		10.00
1	Rashad Family (Ahmad Rashad)	10.00
2	Golfer (Payne Stewart)	10.00

1991 Pro Line Portraits Wives

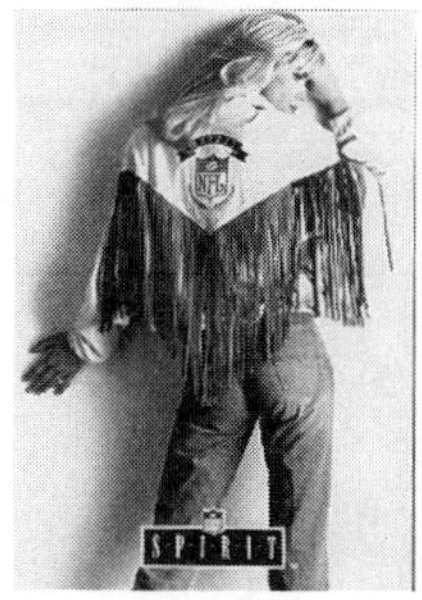

Wives of some of the most popular NFL players are featured in this seven-card "Spirit" set. The cards are numbered on the back and were included in the 1991 Pro Line Portraits set.

		MT
Common Wife:		.05
1	Jennifer Montana	.25
2	Babette Kosar	.05
3	Janet Elway	.05
4	Michelle Oates	.05
5	Toni Lipps	.05
6	Stacey O'Brien	.05
7	Phylicia Rashad	.20

1991 Pro Line Portraits Wives Autographs

The seven-card, standard-size set featured wives of top NFL players and was inserted in packs of 1991 NFL Pro Line. The Rashad signed card was limited to 15, thus giving it its high value. The cards are identical to the seven wives featured in the base set, except with signatures.

		MT
Complete Set (7):		550.00
Common Player:		15.00
1	Jennifer Montana	75.00
2	Babette Kosar	15.00
3	Janet Elway	15.00
4	Michelle Oates	15.00
5	Toni Lipps	15.00
6	Stacey O'Brien	15.00
7	Phylicia Rashad	450.00

1991 Pro Line Punt, Pass and Kick

Eleven NFL quarterbacks are featured in this 12-card set issued to promote nationwide Punt, Pass and Kick competitions. Each card front has a full bleed posed shot of the player, along with Pro Line Portraits and Punt, Pass and Kick logos. The card back is numbered and includes a player head shot and a quote from him about being a successful NFL quarterback. A checklist card was also produced.

		MT
Complete Set (11):		75.00
Common Player:		5.00
1	Troy Aikman	20.00
2	Bubby Brister	5.00
3	Randall Cunningham	8.00
4	John Elway	8.00
5	Boomer Esiason	7.00
6	Jim Everett	5.00
7	Jim Kelly	10.00
8	Bernie Kosar	7.00
9	Dan Marino	15.00
10	Warren Moon	10.00
11	Phil Simms	7.00

1991 Pro Line Profiles Anthony Munoz

Cincinnati Bengals lineman Anthony Munoz is profiled in this set of cards, which was included inside Super Bowl XXVI programs. The cards chronicle Munoz's career and are listed below according to the topic presented on the card back. Each back is also numbered. A full-color photo appears on the card front, along with the Pro Line Profiles logo. The back has a smaller photo and provides information and quotes from Munoz about his life, community service projects, his family and his NFL career.

		MT
Complete Set (9):		4.00
Common Player:		.50
1	1991 NFL Man of Year	.50
2	Little League player	.50
3	1980 Rose Bowl	.50
4	Community Service	.50
5	Portrait	.50
6	1981 AFC Championship Game	.50
7	1992 Pro Bowl	.50
8	Super Bowl XVI and XXIII	.50
9	Physical Fitness Video	.50

1992 Pro Line Draft Day

The two-card, regular-size set features top pick Steve Emtman on one card with NFL coaches on the other. The card back features Emtman on No. 1 with a quote, an ESPN announcer Chris Berman on No. 2, also with a quote.

		MT
Complete Set (2):		4.00
Common Player:		2.00
1	Steve Emtman	2.00
2	Coaches Photo	2.00

1992 Pro Line Mobil

This 72-card set was available in nine-card packs in an eight-week promotion in Southern California. It could be obtained by purchasing eight or more gallons of Mobil Super Unleaded Plus. The first nine cards are from 1991 Portraits, while the final 63 cards are from 1992 Portraits, both of which are produced by NFL Properties. The first pack included a checklist card, a title card and a card for each of the seven players featured, with the dates that their nine-card packs would be available. Card number nine of Eric Dickerson in a Raiders' uniform is an exclusive to the set. Only one player is featured per pack, with cards numbered "X of 9."

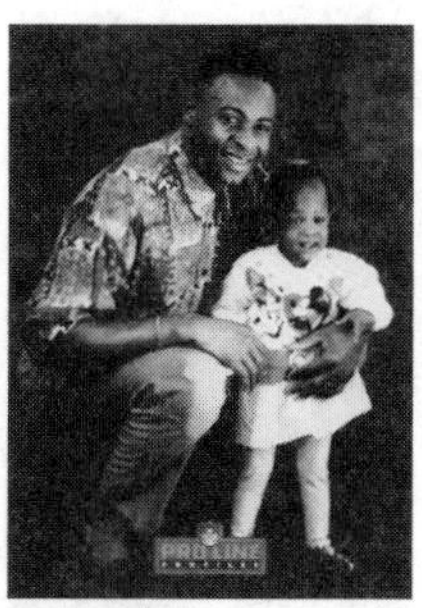

		MT
Complete Set (72):		8.00
Common Player:		.10
1	Title Card (October 3-9)	.10
2	Checklist	.10
3	Ronnie Lott	.15
4	Junior Seau	.40
5	Jim Everett	.10
6	Howie Long	.15
7	Jerry Rice	1.00
8	Art Shell (CO)	.15
9	Eric Dickerson	.25
10	Ronnie Lott (October 10-16) (Making Hit)	.15
11	Ronnie Lott (Little Leaguer)	.15
12	Ronnie Lott (Playing for USC)	.15
13	Ronnie Lott (Exultation)	.15
14	Ronnie Lott (Portrait)	.15
15	Ronnie Lott (Behind Bar)	.15
16	Ronnie Lott (With Family)	.15
17	Ronnie Lott (Catching Ball)	.15
18	Ronnie Lott (Tuxedo)	.15
19	Junior Seau (October 17-23) (With Ball)	.25
20	Junior Seau (Young Junior)	.25
21	Junior Seau (Pointing)	.25
22	Junior Seau (Over Fallen Opponent)	.25
23	Junior Seau (Portrait)	.25
24	Junior Seau (With Wife)	.25
25	Junior Seau (Running in Surf)	.25
26	Junior Seau (Weightlifting)	.25
27	Junior Seau (Seaweed Boa)	.25
28	Jim Everett (October 24-30) (Looking for Receiver)	.10
29	Jim Everett (Young Jim)	.10
30	Jim Everett (Playing for Purdue)	.10
31	Jim Everett (With Parents, Sister)	.10
32	Jim Everett (Portrait)	.10
33	Jim Everett (Eluding Rush)	.10
34	Jim Everett (Fishing)	.10
35	Jim Everett (Handing Off)	.10
36	Jim Everett (Studio Photo)	.10
37	Howie Long (October 31-November 6) (Hand Up to Block Pass)	.15
38	Howie Long (High School Footballer)	.15
39	Howie Long (Closing in for Sack)	.15
40	Howie Long (With Family)	.15
41	Howie Long (Portrait)	.15
42	Howie Long (Fundraising for Kids)	.15
43	Howie Long (Hitting the Heavy Bag)	.15
44	Howie Long (Taking Swipe at Ball)	.15
45	Howie Long (Studio Photo)	.15
46	Jerry Rice (November 7-13) (With Trophy)	.50
47	Jerry Rice (Avoiding Block)	.50
48	Jerry Rice (Eluding Steeler)	.50
49	Jerry Rice (With Family)	.50
50	Jerry Rice (Portrait)	.50
51	Jerry Rice (With Toddler)	.50
52	Jerry Rice (Playing Tennis)	.50
53	Jerry Rice (Scoring TD)	.50
54	Jerry Rice (Studio Photo)	.50
55	Art Shell (CO) (November 14-20) (In Front of his Team)	.15
56	Art Shell (CO) (At Maryland State)	.15
57	Art Shell (CO) (Blocking Viking)	.15
58	Art Shell (CO) (Playing Basketball)	.15
59	Art Shell (CO) (Portrait)	.15
60	Art Shell (CO) (Talking to Player)	.15
61	Art Shell (CO) (In Front of TV)	.15
62	Art Shell (CO) (Blocking for Raiders)	.15
63	Art Shell (CO) (With Teddy Bear)	.15
64	Eric Dickerson (November 21-30) (Studio Suit Up)	.15
65	Eric Dickerson (Running for SMU)	.15
66	Eric Dickerson (With Mom)	.15
67	Eric Dickerson (49ers in Pursuit)	.15
68	Eric Dickerson (Portrait)	.15
69	Eric Dickerson (Running for Colts)	.15
70	Eric Dickerson (On Training Ramp)	.15
71	Eric Dickerson (Running Against Rams)	.15
72	Eric Dickerson (Posed With Football)	.15

1992 Pro Line Prototypes

The 13-card, regular-size set was distributed by Pro Line to sample its upcoming releases. Featured in the sample set are Profiles, Spirit and Portraits. The Profiles backs have "Prototype" printed while Portraits backs have "Sample."

		MT
Complete Set (13):		8.00
Common Player:		.50
12	Kathie Lee Gifford	1.00
28	Thurman Thomas (Bills' uniform, action shot)	.75
29	Thurman Thomas (With his mother)	.75
30	Thurman Thomas (OSU Cowboy uniform, action shot)	.75
31	Thurman Thomas (With family)	.75
32	Thurman Thomas (Color portrait)	.75
33	Thurman Thomas (Action shot, Suepr Bowl XXV)	.75
34	Thurman Thomas (Fishing)	.75
35	Thurman Thomas (Stretching on track)	.75
36	Thurman Thomas (Close-up photo)	.75
379	Jessie Tuggle	.50
386	Neil O'Donnell	.50
NNO	Advertisement Card	.50

1992 Pro Line Portraits

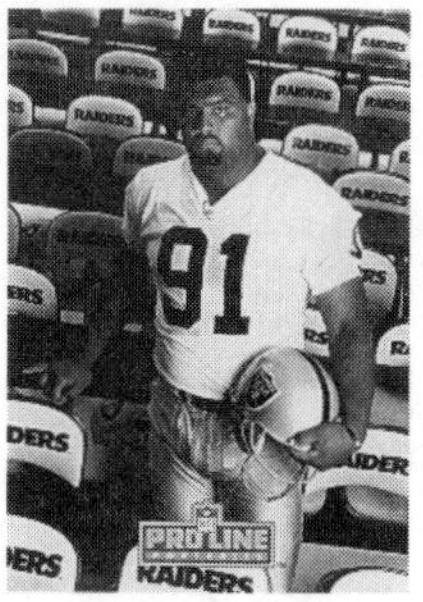

This 1992 Pro Line Portraits set continues numbering where the 1991 set ended, starting at #301. The front has a full-bleed color non-action photo; the back has a mug shot and player information. CO means coach; RET means retired. There were also cards autographed by the players. These command premium prices. They are identical to those in the regular set, except they are unnumbered. Cards 349, 370, 417, 428, 451 and 462 were never signed, however.

		MT
Complete Set (167):		7.00
Common Player:		.04
Pack (12):		.40
Wax Box (36):		12.00
301	*Steve Emtman*	.15
302	Al Edwards	.04
303	Wendell Davis	.05
304	Lewis Billups	.04
305	Brian Brennan	.04
306	John Gesek	.04
307	*Terrell Buckley*	.25
308	*Johnny Mitchell*	.60
309	LeRoy Butler	.04
310	William Fuller	.04
311	Bill Brooks	.06
312	Dino Hackett	.04
313	Willie Gault	.06
314	Aaron Cox	.04
315	Jeff Cross	.04
316	Emmitt Smith	2.00
317	Marv Cook	.06
318	Gill Fenerty	.06
319	*Jeff Carlson*	.20
320	Brad Baxter	.06
321	Fred Barnett	.10
322	Kurt Barber	.10
323	Eric Green	.06
324	Greg Clark	.10
325	Keith DeLong	.04
326	Patrick Hunter	.04
327	*Troy Vincent*	.10
328	Gary Clark	.08
329	Joe Montana	1.75
330	Michael Haynes	.25
331	*Edgar Bennett*	.50
332	Darren Lewis	.15
333	Derrick Fenner	.06
334	Rob Burnett	.04
335	Alvin Harper	.40
336	Vance Johnson	.06
337	William White	.04
338	Sterling Sharpe	.50
339	Sean Jones	.04
340	Jeff Herrod	.04
341	Chris Martin	.04
342	Ethan Horton	.04
343	Robert Delpino	.06
344	Mark Higgs	.15
345	Chris Doleman	.06
346	Tom Hodson	.06
347	Craig Heyward	.06
348	Cary Conklin	.08
349	James Hasty	.04
350	Antone Davis	.04
351	Ernie Jones	.04
352	Greg Lloyd	.04
353	John Friesz	.06
354	Charles Haley	.06
355	*Tracy Scroggins*	.20
356	Paul Gruber	.06
357	Ricky Ervins	.10
358	Brad Muster	.06
359	Deion Sanders	.20
360	*Mitch Frerotte*	.10
361	Stan Thomas	.04
362	Harold Green	.08
363	Eric Metcalf	.06
364	Ken Norton Jr.	.06
365	Dave Widell, Doug Widell	.04
366	Mike Tomczak	.06
367	Bubba McDowell	.04
368	Jessie Hester	.04
369	Ervin Randle	.04
370	Tony Smith	.04
371	Pat Terrell	.04
372	Jim C. Jensen	.04
373	Mike Merriweather	.06
374	Chris Singleton	.04
375	Floyd Turner	.04
376	Jim Sweeney	.04
377	Keith Jackson	.15
378	Walter Reeves	.04
379	Neil O'Donnell	.50
380	Nate Lewis	.12
381	Keith Henderson	.04
382	Kelly Stouffer	.04
383	Ricky Reynolds	.04
384	Joe Jacoby	.04
385	(Fred Biletnikoff) (RET)	.10
386	Jessie Tuggle	.04
387	Tom Waddle	.12
388	Dave Shula (CO)	.10
389	*Van Waiters*	.10
390	Jay Novacek	.12
391	Michael Young	.04
392	Mike Holmgren	.08
393	Doug Smith	.04
394	Mike Prior	.04
395	Harvey Williams	.10
396	Aaron Wallace	.04
397	Tony Zendejas	.04
398	Sammie Smith	.06
399	Henry Thomas	.04
400	Jon Vaughn	.12
401	Brian Washington	.04
402	*Leon Searcy*	.10
403	Lance Smith	.04
404	Warren Williams	.04
405	(Bobby Ross) (CO)	.10
406	Harry Sydney	.04
407	John L. Williams	.06
408	Ken Willis	.04
409	Brian Mitchell	.06
410	(Dick Butkus) (RET)	.10
411	(Chuck Knox) (CO)	.04
412	*Robert Porcher*	.25
413	Calvin Williams	.10
414	(Bill Cowher) (CO)	.10
415	Eric Moore	.04
416	*Derek Brown*	.20
417	(Dennis Greene) (CO)	.10
418	Tom Flores (CO)	.04
419	*Dale Carter*	.30
420	(Tony Dorsett) (RET)	.10
421	*Marco Coleman*	.40
422	(Sam Wyche) (CO)	.04
423	Ray Crockett	.04
424	Dan Fouts (RET)	.10
425	Hugh Millen	.15
426	*Quentin Coryatt*	.40
427	Brian Jordan	.06
428	(Frank Gifford) (RET)	.10
429	*Toby Caston*	.10
430	(Ted Marchibroda) (CO)	.04
431	Cris Carter	.06
432	Tim Krumrie	.04
433	(Otto Graham) (CO)	.10
434	*Vaughn Dunbar*	.25
435	*John Fina*	.10
436	(Sonny Jurgensen) (RET)	.10
437	*Robert Jones*	.15
438	Steve DeOssie	.04
439	(Eddie LeBaron) (RET)	.04
440	*Chester McGlockton*	.15
441	(Ken Stabler) (RET)	.10
442	(Joe DeLamielleure) (RET)	.04
443	(Charley Taylor) (RET)	.10
444	*Greg Skrepenak*	.10
445	(Y.A. Tittle) (RET)	.10
446	*Chuck Smith*	.10
447	(Kellen Winslow) (RET)	.10
448	*Kevin Smith*	.30
449	*Phillippi Sparks*	.12
450	*Alonzo Spellman*	.20
451	Mark Rypien	.10
452	*Darryl Williams*	.15
453	*Tommy Vardell*	.20
454	*Tommy Maddox*	.30
455	*Steve Israel*	.12
456	*Marquez Pope*	.12
457	*Eugene Chung*	.10
458	(Lynn Swann) (RET)	.10
459	*Sean Gilbert*	.40
460	*Chris Mims*	.30
461	(Al Davis)	.04
462	Richard Todd	.04
463	Mike Fox	.04
464	*David Klingler*	.40
465	*Darren Woodson*	.12
466	*Jason Hanson*	.12
467	(Lem Barney) (RET)	.10
1NNO	Santa Sendaway	5.00
2NNO	Mrs. Claus Sendaway	7.00
1NNO	Santa Sendaway	5.00
2NNO	Mrs. Claus Sendaway	7.00

1992 Pro Line Portraits Checklists

These checklist cards were randomly included in 1992 Pro Line Portraits foil packs. The cards use letters instead of card numbers. The card fronts form a 3x3 puzzle which shows the Pro Line Collection emblem on a screened background with NFL logos. The backs include checklists for the 1991-92 Portraits series, 1992 Profiles series and collectible series.

		MT
Complete Set (9):		1.00
Common Checklists:		.15
A	Introduction Card	.15
B	Checklist 1-75	.15
C	Checklist 76-150	.15
D	Checklist 151-225	.15
E	Checklist 226-300	.15
F	Checklist 301-375	.15
G	Checklist 376-450	.15
H	Checklist 451-467 and inserts	.15
I	Checklist Profiles	.15

1992 Pro Line Portraits Autographs

This 1992 Pro Line Portraits set was autographed by the players. These command premium prices. They are identical to those in the regular set, except they are unnumbered. Cards 349, 370, 417, 428, 451 and 462 were never signed, however.

		MT
Complete Set (161):		1200.
Common Player:		4.00
Minor Stars:		8.00
301	Steve Emtman	4.00
302	Al Edwards	4.00
303	Wendell Davis	4.00
304	Lewis Billups	8.00
305	Brian Brennan	4.00
306	John Gesek	4.00
307	Terrell Buckley	8.00
308	Johnny Mitchell	4.00
309	LeRoy Butler	4.00
310	William Fuller	4.00
311	Bill Brooks	4.00
312	Dino Hackett	4.00
313	Willie Gault	4.00
314	Aaron Cox	4.00
315	Jeff Cross	4.00
316	Emmitt Smith	85.00
317	Marv Cook	4.00
318	Gill Fenerty	4.00
319	Jeff Carlson	4.00
320	Brad Baxter	4.00
321	Fred Barnett	8.00
322	Kurt Barber	4.00
323	Eric Green	4.00
324	Greg Clark	4.00
325	Keith DeLong	4.00
326	Patrick Hunter	4.00
327	Troy Vincent	8.00
328	Gary Clark	8.00
329	Joe Montana	120.00
330	Michael Haynes	8.00
331	Edgar Bennett	8.00
332	Darren Lewis	4.00
333	Derrick Fenner	4.00
334	Rob Burnett	4.00
335	Alvin Harper	8.00
336	Vance Johnson	4.00
337	William White	4.00
338	Sterling Sharpe	20.00
339	Sean Jones	4.00
340	Jeff Herrod	4.00
341	Chris Martin	4.00
342	Ethan Horton	4.00
343	Robert Delpino	4.00
344	Mark Higgs	4.00
345	Chris Doleman	4.00
346	Tom Hodson	4.00
347	Craig Heyward	4.00
348	Cary Conklin	4.00
349	James Hasty	4.00
350	Antone Davis	4.00
351	Ernie Jones	4.00
352	Greg Lloyd	8.00
353	John Friesz	8.00
354	Charles Haley	8.00
355	Tracy Scroggins	4.00
356	Paul Gruber	4.00
357	Ricky Ervins	4.00
358	Brad Muster	4.00
359	Deion Sanders (Deion also signed and numbered 200 cards from his personal stock; these are worth double)	40.00
360	Mitch Frerotte	4.00
361	Stan Thomas	4.00
362	Harold Green	4.00
363	Eric Metcalf	8.00
364	Ken Norton Jr.	8.00
365	Dave Widell, Doug Widell	8.00
366	Mike Tomczak	8.00
367	Bubba McDowell	4.00
368	Jessie Hester (Signed in ballpoint pen)	4.00
369	Ervin Randle	4.00
370	Tony Smith	4.00
371	Pat Terrell	4.00
372	Jim C. Jensen	4.00
373	Mike Merriweather	4.00
374	Chris Singleton	4.00
375	Floyd Turner	4.00
376	Jim Sweeney	4.00
377	Keith Jackson	8.00
378	Walter Reeves	4.00
379	Neil O'Donnell	8.00
380	Nate Lewis	4.00
381	Keith Henderson	4.00
382	Kelly Stouffer	4.00
383	Ricky Reynolds	4.00
384	Joe Jacoby	4.00
385	(Fred Biletnikoff) (RET)	180.00
386	Jessie Tuggle	4.00
387	Tom Waddle	4.00

388 Dave Shula (CO) 4.00
389 Van Waiters 4.00
390 Jay Novacek 8.00
391 Michael Young 4.00
392 Mike Holmgren (CO) 25.00
393 Doug Smith 4.00
394 Mike Prior 4.00
395 Harvey Williams 8.00
396 Aaron Wallace 4.00
397 Tony Zendejas 4.00
398 Sammie Smith 4.00
399 Henry Thomas 4.00
400 Jon Vaughn 4.00
401 Brian Washington 4.00
402 Leon Searcy 4.00
403 Lance Smith 4.00
404 Warren Williams 4.00
405 (Bobby Ross) (CO) 4.00
406 Harry Sydney 4.00
407 John L. Williams 4.00
408 Ken Willis 4.00
409 Brian Mitchell 4.00
410 (Dick Butkus) (RET) 25.00
411 (Chuck Knox) (CO) 4.00
412 Robert Porcher 4.00
413 Calvin Williams 4.00
414 (Bill Cowher) (CO) 15.00
415 Eric Moore 4.00
416 Derek Brown (TE) 4.00
417 (Dennis Greene) (CO) 8.00
418 Tom Flores (CO) 4.00
419 Dale Carter 4.00
420 (Tony Dorsett) (RET) 25.00
421 Marco Coleman 4.00
422 (Sam Wyche) (CO) 4.00
423 Ray Crockett 4.00
424 Dan Fouts (RET) 15.00
425 Hugh Millen 4.00
426 Quentin Coryatt 8.00
427 Brian Jordan 8.00
428 (Frank Gifford) (RET) 12.00
429 Toby Caston 4.00
430 (Ted Marchibroda) (CO) 4.00
431 Cris Carter 35.00
432 Tim Krumrie 4.00
433 (Otto Graham) (CO) 25.00
434 Vaughn Dunbar 4.00
435 John Fina 4.00
436 (Sonny Jurgensen) (RET) 20.00
437 Robert Jones 4.00
438 Steve DeOssie 4.00
439 (Eddie LeBaron) (RET) 8.00
440 Chester McGlockton 8.00
441 (Ken Stabler) (RET) 25.00
442 (Joe DeLamielleure) (RET) 4.00
443 (Charley Taylor) (RET) 8.00
444 Greg Skrepenak 4.00
445 (Y.A. Tittle) (RET) 25.00
446 Chuck Smith 4.00
447 (Kellen Winslow) (RET) 8.00
448 Kevin Smith 4.00
449 Phillippi Sparks 4.00
450 Alonzo Spellman 4.00
451 Mark Rypien 4.00
452 Darryl Williams 4.00
453 Tommy Vardell 4.00
454 Tommy Maddox 4.00
455 Steve Israel 4.00
456 Marquez Pope 4.00
457 Eugene Chung 4.00
458 (Lynn Swann) (RET) 75.00
459 Sean Gilbert 8.00
460 Chris Mims 4.00
461 (Al Davis) (OWN) 325.00
462 Richard Todd 4.00
463 Mike Fox 4.00
464 David Klingler 8.00
465 Darren Woodson 8.00
466 Jason Hanson 4.00
467 (Lem Barney) (RET) 8.00
NNO Santa Claus 8.00
NNO Mrs. Santa Claus 8.00

1NNO Santa Sendaway 5.00
2NNO Mrs. Claus Sendaway 7.00

1992 Pro Line Portraits Collectibles

These cards continue numbering where two prior special insert cards left off the preceding year. Each card front has a full-color photo and the set logo; the back has the card number with a "PLC" suffix and a quote on a silver background. Cards were random inserts in 1992 Pro Line foil packs.

		MT
Complete Set (6):		12.00
Common Player:		2.00
3	Coaches Photo (Chris Berman)	2.00
4	Joe Gibbs CO (Racing)	2.00
5	Gifford Family (Frank, Kathie Lee, Cody)	2.00
6	Dale Jarrett (NASCAR driver)	4.00
7	Paul Tagliabue COM (Autographed)	2.00
8	Don Shula, Dave Shula (CO)	3.00

1992 Pro Line Portraits Collectibles Autographs

Randomly seeded in 1992 Pro Line foil packs, the cards are anchored by a borderless photo on the front, with the Pro Line logo at the bottom. The card backs, which are unnumbered, have a quote from the featured person in a silver-colored area. His autograph is signed over his photo on the bottom of the card back.

		MT
Complete Set (4):		160.00
Common Player:		5.00
3	Coaches Photo (Chris Berman)	25.00
6	Dale Jarrett (NASCAR driver)	40.00
7	Paul Tagliabue (COM) (Autopenned)	5.00
8	Don Shula CO, Dave Shula CO	100.00

1992 Pro Line Portraits QB Gold

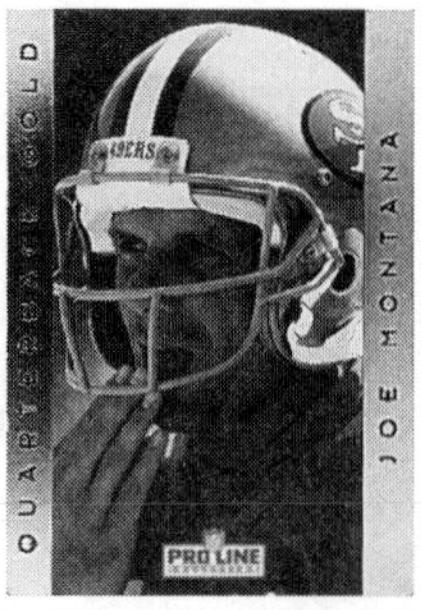

These 18 insert cards, randomly included in 1992 Pro Line foil packs, feature some of the top quarterbacks in the NFL. Each card front has a color action photo on it, with gold foil stripes on the left and right borders. The player's name and "Quarterback Gold" are printed in black in the foil stripes. The backs also have gold stripes for borders; they are at the top and bottom. Statistics are given against a white background. The cards are also numbered on the back. Pro Line stated it put an average of three of these insert cards in each box it made. The company also sent a complete set to dealers who ordered a hobby case of the cards.

		MT
Complete Set (18):		10.00
Common Player:		.25
Minor Stars:		.50
1	Troy Aikman	1.50
2	Bubby Brister	.25
3	Randall Cunningham	.50
4	John Elway	1.00
5	Boomer Esiason	.25
6	Jim Everett	.25
7	Jeff George	.50
8	Jim Harbaugh	.25
9	Jeff Hostetler	.25
10	Jim Kelly	.50
11	Bernie Kosar	.25
12	Dan Marino	3.00
13	Chris Miller (Birthdate incorrectly listed as 8-91-65)	.25
14	Joe Montana	1.50
15	Warren Moon	.50
16	Mark Rypien	.25
17	Phil Simms	.25
18	Steve Young	1.50

1992 Pro Line Portraits Rookie Gold

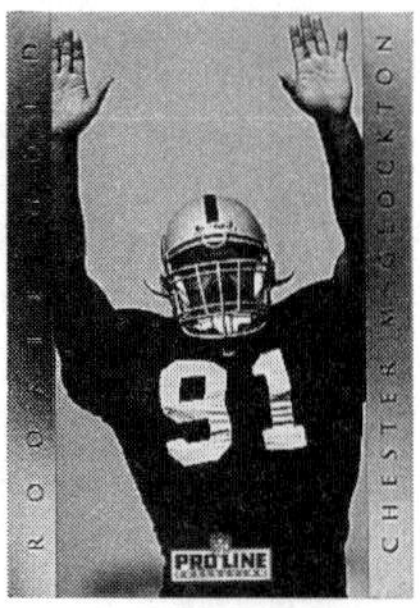

These insert cards, randomly included one per every 1992 Pro Line jumbo pack, feature some of the top rookies in the NFL. Each card front shows a color action photo, with gold foil stripes creating borders on the right and left sides. The player's name and "Rookie Gold" are printed in black in the stripes. The backs have white backgrounds with collegiate statistics in black, plus a card number. Gold foil stripes appear at the top and bottom of the card, too. A complete set of the cards was sent to every dealer for each hobby case they ordered.

		MT
Complete Set (28):		12.00
Common Player:		.30
1	Tony Smith	.50
2	John Fina	.30
3	Alonzo Spellman	.50
4	David Klinger	1.75
5	Tommy Vardell	.60
6	Kevin Smith	.60
7	Tommy Maddox	1.25
8	Robert Porcher	.50
9	Terrell Buckley	.60
10	Eddie Robinson	.30
11	Steve Emtman	.30
12	Quentin Coryatt	.75
13	Dale Carter	.50
14	Chester McGlockton	.30
15	Sean Gilbert	.75
16	Troy Vincent	.50
17	Robert Harris	.30
18	Eugene Chung	.30
19	Vaughn Dunbar	.60
20	Derek Brown	.50
21	Johnny Mitchell	1.50
22	Siran Stacy	.50
23	Tony Sacca	.50
24	Leon Searcy	.30
25	Chris Mims	.60
26	Dana Hall	.50
27	Courtney Hawkins	.75
28	Shane Collins	.30

1992 Pro Line Portraits Team NFL

Celebrities and entertainers from outside the sporting world are featured on these five insert cards. Each card front shows the entertainer/celebrity wearing his favorite team's apparel. The backs, done in a horizontal format, have a silver panel which contains a quote from the person. The back is numbered with a "TNC" prefix and has team color-coded stripes at the top.

		MT
Complete Set (5):		10.00
Common Player:		1.50
1	Muhammad Ali	5.00
2	Milton Berle	2.50
3	Don Mattingly	3.00
4	Martin Mull	1.50
5	Isiah Thomas	2.50

1992 Pro Line Portraits Team NFL Autographs

This five-card set features stars from other sports and celebrities, with each personality pictured on the card front in their favorite team's attire. This unnumbered set marks the debut of Pro Line's Team Collectible cards, and includes a very limited number of signed Muhammad Ali cards, with his birth name Cassius Clay.

		MT
Complete Set (5):		200.00
Common Player:		20.00
1A	Muhammad Ali	150.00
1B	Muhammad Ali	475.00
2	Milton Berle	30.00
3	Don Mattingly	50.00
4	Martin Mull	20.00
5	Isiah Thomas	25.00

1992 Pro Line Portraits Wives

These insert cards, included in 1992 Pro Line Portraits packs, continue with numbers from where a similar set ended in 1991. The cards feature full-bleed photos of wives whose husbands are star coaches or players in the NFL. The card back has a profile shot of the wife, plus a quote from her. A card number is also included on the back. Each of the wives, except Kathie Lee Gifford, autographed her cards, too. They are identical to the regular cards, except they are unnumbered with a "SC" prefix and command premium prices.

		MT
Complete Set (16):		1.00
Common Wives:		.10
8	Ortancis Carter	.10
9	Faith Cherry	.10
10	Kaye Cowher	.10
11	Dainnese Gault	.10
12	Kathie Lee Gifford	.20
13	Carole Hinton	.10
14	Diane Long	.10
15	Karen Lott	.10
16	Felicia Moon	.10
17	Cindy Noble	.10
18	Line Seifert	.10
19	Mitzi Testaverde	.10
20	Robin Swilling	.10
21	Lesley Visser (ANN)	.20
22	Toni Doleman	.10
23	Diana Ditka (with Mike Ditka)	.20

1992 Pro Line Portraits Wives Autographs

These insert cards, included in 1992 Pro Line Portraits packs, continue with numbers from where a similar set endedin 1991. Each of the wives, except Kathie Lee Lee Gifford, autographed her cards. They are identical to the regular cards, except they are unnumbered and command premium prices.

		MT
Complete Set (16):		90.00
Common Wives:		6.00
8	Ortancis Carter	6.00
9	Faith Cherry	6.00
10	Kaye Cowher	6.00
11	Dainnese Gault	6.00
12	Kathie Lee Gifford	6.00
13	Carole Hinton	6.00
14	Diane Long	6.00
15	Karen Lott	6.00
16	Felicia Moon	6.00
17	Cindy Noble	6.00
18	Line Seifert	6.00
19	Mitzi Testaverde	6.00
20	Robin Swilling	6.00
21	Lesley Visser (ANN)	20.00
22	Toni Doleman	6.00
23	Diana Ditka (with Mike Ditka)	6.00

1992 Pro Line Profiles

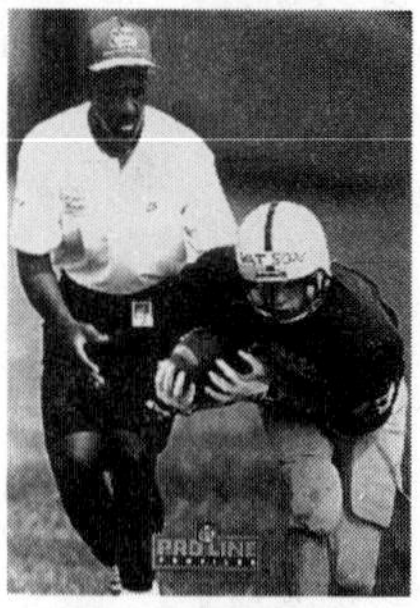

This set features nine-card sets for 55 pro football players. Each card set traces the player's progress from his collegiate days to his professional career and life off the field. The card front has a full-bleed color action shot; the back has an action shot and a quote from the player. A 10-card Art Monk set was also offered by a mail-in exchange.

		MT
Complete Set (504):		12.00
Common Player:		.04
Pack (12):		.35
Wax Box (36):		10.00
NNO	Art Monk (Collection Bonus Set title card)	1.00
1	Ronnie Lott (Tackling opponent (1-9))	.06
2	Ronnie Lott (As youth, in baseball uniform)	.06
3	Ronnie Lott (Playing for USC)	.06
4	Ronnie Lott (Arms raised in triumph)	.06
5	Ronnie Lott (Portrait by Chris Hopkins)	.06
6	Ronnie Lott (At the Sports City Cafe)	.06
7	Ronnie Lott (With family)	.06
8	Ronnie Lott (Catching)	.06
9	Ronnie Lott (In tuxedo)	.06
10	Rodney Peete (Right arm raised (10-18))	.10
11	Rodney Peete (As youth, in football uniform)	.10
12	Rodney Peete (Playing baseball)	.10
13	Rodney Peete (In sweats with ball)	.10
14	Rodney Peete (Portrait by Merv Corning)	.10
15	Rodney Peete (Looking for receiver)	.10
16	Rodney Peete (Playing pool)	.10
17	Rodney Peete (Passing)	.10
18	Rodney Peete (Injured)	.10
19	Carl Banks (In action on field (19-27))	.04
20	Carl Banks (Playing basketball at Beecher High School)	.04
21	Carl Banks (In Michigan State uniform)	.04
22	Carl Banks (With family)	.04
23	Carl Banks (Portrait by Merv Corning)	.04
24	Carl Banks (Talking, wearing suit)	.04
25	Carl Banks (Tackling opponent)	.04
26	Carl Banks (On the air)	.04
27	Carl Banks (Close-up)	.04
28	Thurman Thomas (Running with ball, blue jersey (28-36))	.40
29	Thurman Thomas (With mother, Terlisha Cockrell)	.25
30	Thurman Thomas (At Oklahoma State)	.25
31	Thurman Thomas (With family)	.25
32	Thurman Thomas (Portrait by Gary Kelley)	.25
33	Thurman Thomas (Running with ball, white jersey)	.25
34	Thurman Thomas (Fishing)	.25
35	Thurman Thomas (Stretching)	.25
36	Thurman Thomas (Close-up)	.25
37	Roger Staubach (With Heisman Trophy (37-45))	.15
38	Roger Staubach (At Naval Academy)	.15
39	Roger Staubach (In Navy dress whites)	.15
40	Roger Staubach (Front view, running with ball)	.15
41	Roger Staubach (Portrait by John Collier)	.15
42	Roger Staubach (Passing, side view)	.15
43	Roger Staubach (With family)	.15
44	Roger Staubach (With young person at Daytop, substance abuse recovery facility)	.15
45	Roger Staubach (Calling the play)	.15
46	Jerry Rice (With MVP trophy (46-54))	.50
47	Jerry Rice (At Mississippi Valley State)	.50
48	Jerry Rice (Running with ball)	.50
49	Jerry Rice (With family)	.50
50	Jerry Rice (Portrait by Gary Kelley)	.50
51	Jerry Rice (With March of Dimes Ambassador, Ashley Johnson)	.50
52	Jerry Rice (Playing tennis)	.50
53	Jerry Rice (Arms raised in triumph)	.50
54	Jerry Rice (Close-up)	.50
55	Vinny Testaverde (Posed with Heisman (55-63))	.04
56	Vinny Testaverde (At Fork Union Military Academy)	.04
57	Vinny Testaverde (Playing for the University of Miami)	.04
58	Vinny Testaverde (Passing)	.04
59	Vinny Testaverde (Portrait by Merv Corning)	.04
60	Vinny Testaverde (Running with ball)	.04
61	Vinny Testaverde (With family)	.04
62	Vinny Testaverde (View from hips up, fist raised in triumph)	.04
63	Vinny Testaverde (With Vince Hanley)	.04
64	Anthony Carter (Manuevering around opponent, with ball 64-72))	.06
65	Anthony Carter (In high school football game, black-and-white)	.06
66	Anthony Carter (At Michigan, running with ball)	.06
67	Anthony Carter (Fishing)	.06
68	Anthony Carter (Portrait by John Collier)	.06
69	Anthony Carter (Running, looking over shoulder)	.06
70	Anthony Carter (With family)	.06
71	Anthony Carter (Catching pass)	.06
72	Anthony Carter (Close-up)	.06
73	Sterling Sharpe (Catching (73-81))	.35
74	Sterling Sharpe (Passing, in high school)	.35
75	Sterling Sharpe (Walking on field at South Carolina)	.35
76	Sterling Sharpe (With books on SC campus)	.35
77	Sterling Sharpe (Portrait by Chris Hopkins)	.35
78	Sterling Sharpe (Running with ball against Rams)	.35
79	Sterling Sharpe (At the piano)	.35
80	Sterling Sharpe (Running with ball against Lions)	.35
81	Sterling Sharpe (In brick arch with football)	.35
82	Anthony Munoz (With NFL Man of the Year award (82-90))	.04
83	Anthony Munoz (As youth, batting)	.04
84	Anthony Munoz (Playing for USC)	.04
85	Anthony Munoz (With child at Children's Hospital)	.04
86	Anthony Munoz (Portrait by Merv Corning)	.04
87	Anthony Munoz (Blocking opponent)	.04
88	Anthony Munoz (Holding baby, with fellow players and children)	.04
89	Anthony Munoz (In action for Bengals)	.04
90	Anthony Munoz (Close-up)	.04
91	Bubby Brister (Passing, white jersey (91-99))	.04
92	Bubby Brister (NLU uniform)	.04
93	Bubby Brister (Baseball unform)	.04
94	Bubby Brister (With kids at Ronald McDonald House)	.04
95	Bubby Brister (Portrait by Greg Spalenka)	.04
96	Bubby Brister (Wearing western attire)	.04
97	Bubby Brister (Running with ball, white jersey)	.04
98	Bubby Brister (Passing, black jersey)	.04
99	Bubby Brister (Close-up)	.04
100	Bernie Kosar (Passing, white jersey (100-108))	.10
101	Bernie Kosar (In high school)	.10
102	Bernie Kosar (Playing for Miami)	.10
103	Bernie Kosar (Being tackled)	.10
104	Bernie Kosar (Portrait by Greg Spalenka)	.10
105	Bernie Kosar (With family)	.10
106	Bernie Kosar (Playing golf)	.10
107	Bernie Kosar (Looking for receiver)	.10
108	Bernie Kosar (Close-up)	.10
109	Art Shell (On sidelines (109-117))	.06
110	Art Shell (At Maryland State)	.06
111	Art Shell (Playing for Raiders)	.06
112	Art Shell (Playing basketball with sons)	.06
113	Art Shell (Portrait by Chris Hopkins)	.06
114	Art Shell (Talking to player on sidelines)	.06
115	Art Shell (In front of big screen TV)	.06
116	Art Shell (In line of scrimmage)	.06
117	Art Shell (With teddy bear)	.06
118	Don Shula (With players)	.06
119	Don Shula (At John Carroll University)	.06
120	Don Shula (Coaching Baltimore Colts)	.06
121	Don Shula (With son, Mike)	.06
122	Don Shula (Portrait by Merv Corning)	.06
123	Don Shula (With daughters)	.06
124	Don Shula (With Dan Marino)	.06
125	Don Shula (With doctor at the Don Shula Foundation)	.06
126	Don Shula (With Super Bowl trophies)	.06
127	Joe Gibbs (Writing out play)	.06
128	Joe Gibbs (Playing for San Diego State)	.06
129	Joe Gibbs (Coaching on sidelines)	.06
130	Joe Gibbs (With sons)	.06
131	Joe Gibbs (Portrait by John Collier)	.06
132	Joe Gibbs (Reading in office)	.06
133	Joe Gibbs (With Youth For Tomorrow group)	.06
134	Joe Gibbs (In front of race car)	.06
135	Joe Gibbs (In front of Church)	.06
136	Junior Seau (Holding ball (136-144))	.15
137	Junior Seau (As youth, in football uniform)	.15
138	Junior Seau (At USC)	.15
139	Junior Seau (Finger pointing up)	.15
140	Junior Seau (Portrait by Merv Corning)	.15
141	Junior Seau (With wife, Gina)	.15
142	Junior Seau (Running on beach)	.15
143	Junior Seau (Lifting weights)	.15
144	Junior Seau (In swim trunks with seaweed)	.15
145	Al Toon (Running with ball, white jersey 145-153))	.06
146	Al Toon (During Pee-Wee football days)	.06
147	Al Toon (On the field at Wisconsin)	.06
148	Al Toon (With family)	.06
149	Al Toon (Portrait by Gary Kelley)	.06
150	Al Toon (Catching)	.06
151	Al Toon (Working out)	.06
152	Al Toon (Running with ball, green jersey)	.06
153	Al Toon (Close-up)	.06
154	Jack Kemp (In office (154-162))	.10
155	Jack Kemp (Portrait from Occidental College)	.10
156	Jack Kemp (Playing for Chargers)	.10
157	Jack Kemp (With family)	.10
158	Jack Kemp (Portrait by Merv Corning)	.10
159	Jack Kemp (Playing for Buffalo)	.10
160	Jack Kemp (Passing)	.10
161	Jack Kemp (With son, Jeff)	.10
162	Jack Kemp (In Washington)	.10
163	Jim Harbaugh (Passing, blue jersey (163-171))	.10
164	Jim Harbaugh (Playing in high school)	.10
165	Jim Harbaugh (Playing for Michigan)	.10
166	Jim Harbaugh (Passing, white jersey)	.10
167	Jim Harbaugh (Portrait by Gary Kelley)	.10
168	Jim Harbaugh (With children in children's home)	.10
169	Jim Harbaugh (Working out)	.10
170	Jim Harbaugh (Calling play)	.10
171	Jim Harbaugh (Close-up)	.10
172	Dan McGwire (From waist up (172-180))	.15
173	Dan McGwire (At Purdue)	.15
174	Dan McGwire (At San Diego)	.15
175	Dan McGwire (From waist down)	.15
176	Dan McGwire (Portrait by Chris Hopkins)	.15

177 Dan McGwire (Passing, blue jersey) .15
178 Dan McGwire (Passing, white jersey) .15
179 Dan McGwire (Working out) .15
180 Dan McGwire (With wife, Dana) .15
181 Troy Aikman (Passing, wearing blue jersey (181-189)) .75
182 Troy Aikman (As youth) .75
183 Troy Aikman (Passing, at UCLA) .75
184 Troy Aikman (Preparing to pass, with Cowboys) .75
185 Troy Aikman (Portrait by Greg Spalenka) .75
186 Troy Aikman (Golfing) .75
187 Troy Aikman (Looking for opening, front view) .75
188 Troy Aikman (In sweats, passing) .75
189 Troy Aikman (In cowboy hat) .75
190 Keith Byars (With little brother (190-198)) .06
191 Keith Byars (Childhood picture) .06
192 Keith Byars (High School football photo) .06
193 Keith Byars (Ohio State photo, red jersey) .06
194 Keith Byars (Portrait by Chris Hopkins) .06
195 Keith Byars (Working out) .06
196 Keith Byars (Running, green jersey) .06
197 Keith Byars (Running, white jersey) .06
198 Keith Byars (Close-up) .06
199 Timm Rosenbach (Running with ball, red jersey 199-207)) .04
200 Timm Rosenbach (In high school football uniform) .04
201 Timm Rosenbach (At Washington State) .04
202 Timm Rosenbach (With wife, Kerry) .04
203 Timm Rosenbach (Portrait by John Collier) .04
204 Timm Rosenbach (Passing, white jersey) .04
205 Timm Rosenbach (Roping a calf) .04
206 Timm Rosenbach (Working out) .04
207 Timm Rosenbach (Seated on hay, in western attire) .04
208 Gary Clark (In the end zone (208-216)) .12
209 Gary Clark (Playing for James Madison University) .12
210 Gary Clark (Catching ball in end zone) .12
211 Gary Clark (With daughter) .12
212 Gary Clark (Portrait by John Collier) .12
213 Gary Clark (Running, slouched position) .12
214 Gary Clark (Playing basketball) .12
215 Gary Clark (Lifted by teammates) .12
216 Gary Clark (Close-up) .12
217 Chris Doleman (Playing for Vikings, white jersey 217-225)) .04
218 Chris Doleman (In Pittsburgh uniform) .04
219 Chris Doleman (With wife, Toni, and dog) .04
220 Chris Doleman (Playing for Vikings, blue jersey) .04
221 Chris Doleman (Portrait by John Collier) .04
222 Chris Doleman (Working out) .04
223 Chris Doleman (Leaping over opponent) .04
224 Chris Doleman (Playing golf) .04
225 Chris Doleman (Close-up) .04
226 John Elway (Passing, orange jersey (226-234)) .25
227 John Elway (Playing for Stanford) .25
228 John Elway (Passing, white jersey) .25
229 John Elway (With family) .25
230 John Elway (Portrait by Greg Spalenka) .25
231 John Elway (Working out) .25
232 John Elway (Sitting on car) .25
233 John Elway (Running with ball) .25
234 John Elway (Close-up) .25
235 Boomer Esiason (Calling play (235-243)) .15
236 Boomer Esiason (In high school) .15
237 Boomer Esiason (In Terps uniform) .15
238 Boomer Esiason (Passing) .15
239 Boomer Esiason (Portrait by Greg Spalenka) .15
240 Boomer Esiason (With dogs) .15
241 Boomer Esiason (With Kinny McQuade) .15
242 Boomer Esiason (Looking for pass receiver) .15
243 Boomer Esiason (Close-up) .15
244 Jim Everett (Passing, white jersey (244-252)) .10
245 Jim Everett (In high school uniform) .10
246 Jim Everett (Playing for Purdue) .10
247 Jim Everett (With family) .10
248 Jim Everett (Portrait by Greg Spalenka) .10
249 Jim Everett (Running with ball, blue jersey) .10
250 Jim Everett (Fishing) .10
251 Jim Everett (Handing off ball) .10
252 Jim Everett (Close-up) .10
253 Eric Green (Running with ball (253-261)) .04
254 Eric Green (With coach Sam Rutigliano) .04
255 Eric Green (Being blocked by opponent) .04
256 Eric Green (Playing basketball) .04
257 Eric Green (Portrait by Merv Corning) .04
258 Eric Green (In locker room) .04
259 Eric Green (Blocking opponent) .04
260 Eric Green (Catching) .04
261 Eric Green (Close-up) .04
262 Jerry Glanville (On motorcycle (262-270)) .04
263 Jerry Glanville (With Lions coaching staff) .04
264 Jerry Glanville (Coaching, clapping) .04
265 Jerry Glanville (With family) .04
266 Jerry Glanville (Portrait by Gary Kelley) .04
267 Jerry Glanville (Coaching, with players) .04
268 Jerry Glanville (In race car) .04
269 Jerry Glanville (With country music stars) .04
270 Jerry Glanville (In black western attire) .04
271 Jeff Hostetler (Passing, blue jersey (271-279)) .12
272 Jeff Hostetler (Playing for West Virginia) .12
273 Jeff Hostetler (Lifting weights) .12
274 Jeff Hostetler (With family) .12
275 Jeff Hostetler (Portrait by John Collier) .12
276 Jeff Hostetler (Passing, white jersey) .12
277 Jeff Hostetler (At Ronald McDonald house) .12
278 Jeff Hostetler (With father-in-law) .12
279 Jeff Hostetler (Close-up) .12
280 Haywood Jeffires (Catching, Houston uniform (280-288)) .15
281 Haywood Jeffires (Playing for North Carolina) .15
282 Haywood Jeffires (With wife, Robin) .15
283 Haywood Jeffires (Pushing past opponent) .15
284 Haywood Jeffires (Portrait by John Collier) .15
285 Haywood Jeffires (With car) .15
286 Haywood Jeffires (With Boy and Girls Club members) .15
287 Haywood Jeffires (Being tackled) .15
288 Haywood Jeffires (Close-up) .15
289 Michael Irvin (Running with ball (289-297)) .40
290 Michael Irvin (Playing basketball) .40
291 Michael Irvin (In Miami uniform) .40
292 Michael Irvin (With wife, Sandy) .40
293 Michael Irvin (Portrait by Gary Kelley) .40
294 Michael Irvin (Catching) .40
295 Michael Irvin (With student, Nyna Sherte) .40
296 Michael Irvin (Playing in Pro Bowl) .40
297 Michael Irvin (Close-up) .40
298 Steve Largent (Catching, blue jersey (298-306)) .10
299 Steve Largent (Playing for Tulsa) .10
300 Steve Largent (With family) .10
301 Steve Largent (At school for disabled children) .10
302 Steve Largent (Portrait by Chris Hopkins) .10
303 Steve Largent (Catching, white jersey) .10
304 Steve Largent (In dress attire) .10
305 Steve Largent (Running, white jersey) .10
306 Steve Largent (Close-up) .10
307 Ken O'Brien (Passing, side view (307-315)) .04
308 Ken O'Brien (With University of California-Davis) .04
309 Ken O'Brien (With family) .04
310 Ken O'Brien (Passing, front view) .04
311 Ken O'Brien (Portrait by Chris Hopkins) .04
312 Ken O'Brien (Shaking hands with Tony Eason) .04
313 Ken O'Brien (Playing golf) .04
314 Ken O'Brien (Handing off the ball) .04
315 Ken O'Brien (Close-up) .04
316 Christian Okoye (Running with ball, red jersey 316-324)) .06
317 Christian Okoye (Close-up at Asuza Pacific Univ.) .06
318 Christian Okoye (Cooking) .06
319 Christian Okoye (Running with ball, white jersey) .06
320 Christian Okoye (Portrait by Chris Hopkins) .06
321 Christian Okoye (In Nigerian attire) .06
322 Christian Okoye (With daughter, Christiana) .06
323 Christian Okoye (Withstanding an opponent) .06
324 Christian Okoye (In casual attire) .06
325 Michael Dean Perry (Blocking opponent, white jersey 325-333)) .12
326 Michael Dean Perry (Playing for Clemson) .12
327 Michael Dean Perry (Blocking opponent, brown jersey) .12
328 Michael Dean Perry (With family) .12
329 Michael Dean Perry (Portrait by Merv Corning) .12
330 Michael Dean Perry (At Children's Hospital) .12
331 Michael Dean Perry (Playing basketball) .12
332 Michael Dean Perry (Blocking opponent, horizontal shot) .12
333 Michael Dean Perry (With AFC Player of the Year trophy) .12
334 Chris Miller (Passing, black jersey (334-342)) .10
335 Chris Miller (As youth, fishing) .10
336 Chris Miller (Playing for Oregon) .10
337 Chris Miller (In baseball uniform) .10
338 Chris Miller (Portrait by Greg Spalenka) .10
339 Chris Miller (Running with ball) .10
340 Chris Miller (With wife, Jennifer) .10
341 Chris Miller (In the Pro Bowl) .10
342 Chris Miller (Close-up) .10
343 Phil Simms (Passing, blue jersey (343-351)) .10
344 Phil Simms (Calling the play) .10
345 Phil Simms (With family) .10
346 Phil Simms (Playing pool) .10
347 Phil Simms (Portrait by Greg Spalenka) .10
348 Phil Simms (Running with ball) .10
349 Phil Simms (With young man from the Eastern Christian School for handicapped children) .10
350 Phil Simms (Passing, white jersey) .10
351 Phil Simms (Close-up) .10
352 Bruce Smith (Tackling opponent, white jersey 352-360)) .06
353 Bruce Smith (At Virginia Tech) .06
354 Bruce Smith (Close-up in game) .06
355 Bruce Smith (With wife, Carmen) .06
356 Bruce Smith (Portrait by John Collier) .06
357 Bruce Smith (In Pro Bowl) .06
358 Bruce Smith (Working out) .06
359 Bruce Smith (Blocking, blue jersey) .06
360 Bruce Smith (Close-up) .06
361 Derrick Thomas (Running, red jersey (361-369)) .15
362 Derrick Thomas (At the University of Alabama) .15
363 Derrick Thomas (With his father's Air Force momentos) .15
364 Derrick Thomas (Seated on helmet) .15
365 Derrick Thomas (Portrait by Merv Corning) .15
366 Derrick Thomas (With motivational program participants) .15
367 Derrick Thomas (Posed with Limo) .15
368 Derrick Thomas (In Pro Bowl) .15
369 Derrick Thomas (Close-up) .15
370 Pat Swilling (Relaxed against tree (370-378)) .06
371 Pat Swilling (At Georgia Tech) .06
372 Pat Swilling (With family) .06
373 Pat Swilling (Running on field) .06
374 Pat Swilling (Portrait by John Collier) .06
375 Pat Swilling (Working out) .06
376 Pat Swilling (Tackling opponent on icy field) .06
377 Pat Swilling (With underprivileged children) .06
378 Pat Swilling (Relaxed at home) .06
379 Eric Dickerson (Close-up in Rams football gear 379-387)) .10
380 Eric Dickerson (Playing for SMU) .10
381 Eric Dickerson (With great aunt Viola) .10
382 Eric Dickerson (Running with ball, Rams uniform) .10
383 Eric Dickerson (Portrait by Merv Corning) .10
384 Eric Dickerson (Running with ball, Colts uniform) .10
385 Eric Dickerson (Working out) .10
386 Eric Dickerson (Leaping over other players, Colts uniform) .10
387 Eric Dickerson (Close-up) .10
388 Howie Long (Being blocked by opponent (388-396)) .06
389 Howie Long (At Villanova) .06
390 Howie Long (Rushing quarterback) .06
391 Howie Long (With family) .06
392 Howie Long (Portrait by Chris Hopkins) .06
393 Howie Long (On sidelines) .06
394 Howie Long (Boxing) .06
395 Howie Long (Blocking pass) .06
396 Howie Long (Close-up) .06
397 Mike Singletary (Crouched, ready for play) .06
398 Mike Singletary (At Baylor) .06
399 Mike Singletary (With children) .06
400 Mike Singletary (In the gym) .06
401 Mike Singletary (Portrait by Gary Kelley) .06
402 Mike Singletary (Rushing, white jersey) .06
403 Mike Singletary (With Man of the Year Award) .06
404 Mike Singletary (Tackling, blue jersey) .06
405 Mike Singletary (In sweatshirt) .06
406 John Taylor (Celebrating on the field (406-414)) .10
407 John Taylor (In high school) .10
408 John Taylor (Playing for Delaware State) .10
409 John Taylor (Posed with bowling ball and pins) .10
410 John Taylor (Portrait by John Collier) .10
411 John Taylor (With family) .10
412 John Taylor (With kids from Northern Light School) .10
413 John Taylor (Catching) .10
414 John Taylor (Close-up) .10
415 Andre Tippett (Blocking opponent, arms outspread) .04
416 Andre Tippett (At Iowa State (416-423)) .04
417 Andre Tippett (With daughter, Janea Lynn) .04
418 Andre Tippett (In Okinawa with karate masters) .04
419 Andre Tippett (Portrait by Gary Kelley) .04
420 Andre Tippett (Running on the field) .04
421 Andre Tippett (Performing karate move) .04
422 Andre Tippett (In action, from knees up) .04
423 Andre Tippett (Close-up) .04
424 Jim Kelly (Passing, white jersey (424-432)) .25
425 Jim Kelly (With Punt, Pass, and Kick trophy) .25
426 Jim Kelly (Passing for Miami) .25
427 Jim Kelly (With family) .25
428 Jim Kelly (Portrait by Greg Spalenka) .25
429 Jim Kelly (With sports jersey collection) .25
430 Jim Kelly (With young cancer patients) .25
431 Jim Kelly (Calling play) .25
432 Jim Kelly (Close-up) .25
433 Mark Rypien (Passing, horizontal shot (433-441)) .10
434 Mark Rypien (In high school football uniform) .10
435 Mark Rypien (At Washington State) .10
436 Mark Rypien (Playing golf) .10
437 Mark Rypien (Portrait by Merv Corning) .10
438 Mark Rypien (With family) .10
439 Mark Rypien (Passing, vertical shot) .10
440 Mark Rypien (With young cystic fibrosis patients) .10
441 Mark Rypien (Close-up) .10
442 Warren Moon (Passing, white jersey (442-450)) .20
443 Warren Moon (As youth, in football uniform) .20
444 Warren Moon (Playing for Washington) .20
445 Warren Moon (With Edmonton Eskimos) .20
446 Warren Moon (Portrait by Greg Spalenka) .20
447 Warren Moon (With family) .20
448 Warren Moon (Calling the play) .20
449 Warren Moon (In his office) .20
450 Warren Moon (Posed with football and helmet) .20
451 Deion Sanders (In position for a play (451-459)) .15
452 Deion Sanders (As youth, in football uniform) .15
453 Deion Sanders (With Florida State) .15
454 Deion Sanders (Playing baseball) .15
455 Deion Sanders (Portrait by Gary Kelley) .15
456 Deion Sanders (Running with ball) .15
457 Deion Sanders (With family) .15
458 Deion Sanders (Walking on field) .15
459 Deion Sanders (Close-up) .15
460 Lawrence Taylor (Facing opponent, blue jersey (460-468)) .10
461 Lawrence Taylor (At North Carolina State) .10
462 Lawrence Taylor (Side view, white jersey) .10
463 Lawrence Taylor (Playing golf on football field) .10
464 Lawrence Taylor (Portrait by Chris Hopkins) .10
465 Lawrence Taylor (In Honolulu) .10
466 Lawrence Taylor (In front of his restaurant) .10
467 Lawrence Taylor (Steping over Jets player) .10
468 Lawrence Taylor (Close-up) .10
469 Randall Cunningham (Looking for receiver) .15
470 Randall Cunningham (In Pop Warner team uniform) .15
471 Randall Cunningham (Playing for UNLV) .15
472 Randall Cunningham (Running with ball) .15
473 Randall Cunningham (Portrait by Greg Spalenka) .15
474 Randall Cunningham (Playing golf) .15
475 Randall Cunningham (Passing) .15
476 Randall Cunningham (Working out) .15
477 Randall Cunningham (In dress attire) .15
478 Earnest Byner (Redskins uniform, running, side view 478-486)) .06
479 Earnest Byner (At East Carolina, black and white) .06
480 Earnest Byner (Browns, brown jersey) .06
481 Earnest Byner (With family) .06
482 Earnest Byner (Portrait by Chris Hopkins) .06
483 Earnest Byner (Browns, white jersey) .06
484 Earnest Byner (Fishing) .06
485 Earnest Byner (Redskins, uniform, running, front view) .06
486 Earnest Byner (In workout attire) .06
487 Mike Ditka (On sideline, in shirt and tie 487-495)) .10
488 Mike Ditka (Playing for Bears) .10
489 Mike Ditka (With family) .10
490 Mike Ditka (Playing for Cowboys) .10
491 Mike Ditka (Portrait by Garry Kelley) .10
492 Mike Ditka (With antique car) .10
493 Mike Ditka (Playing golf) .10
494 Mike Ditka (Eating) .10
495 Mike Ditka (Close-up) .10
496 Art Monk (Catching, close-up (496-504)) .75
497 Art Monk (Running hurdles in high school) .75
498 Art Monk (Running with ball, front view) .75
499 Art Monk (With family) .75
500 Art Monk (Portrait by Gary Kelley) .75
501 Art Monk (With youth at his football camp) .75
502 Art Monk (Running with ball, side view) .75
503 Art Monk (Working out) .75
504 Art Monk (Ready to catch ball, hands extended) .75

1992 Pro Line Profiles Autographs

Profiles Autographs run parallel to the Profiles set and were inserted in Pro Line foil packs at a rate of one per box. The cards were signed in black Sharpies, embossed with an NFL seal and are missing the card number to distinguish them from regular cards. Cards signed by Jack Kemp, Chris Miller and Mark Rypien do not exist, as well as cards 46-49, 56, 58, 356, 376, 383, 457-459 and 504. Art Monk's autographed cards were the first ones sent to wrapper redemption offers and do not have the card numbers removed and are not considered part of the set. Prices below are for the entire set of that player.

	MT
Complete Set (457):	3200.
Troy Aikman (181-189):	45.00
Carl Banks (19-27):	4.00
Bubby Brister (91-99):	4.00
Keith Byars (190-198):	4.00
Earnest Byner (478-486):	4.00
Anthony Carter (64-72):	4.00
Gary Clark (208-216):	4.00
Randall Cunningham (469-477):	20.00
Eric Dickerson (379-387):	10.00
Mike Ditka (487-495):	20.00
Chris Doleman (217-225):	4.00
John Elway (226-234):	45.00
Boomer Esiason (235-243):	8.00
Jim Everett (244-252):	25.00
Joe Gibbs (127-135):	8.00
Jerry Glanville (262-270):	4.00
Eric Green (253-261):	4.00
Jim Harbaugh (163-171):	4.00
Jeff Hostetler (271-279):	4.00
Michael Irvin (289-297):	20.00
Haywood Jeffires (280-288):	4.00
Jim Kelly (424-432):	20.00
Jack Kemp (154-162):	25.00
Bernie Kosar (100-108):	4.00
Steve Largent (298-306):	25.00
Howie Long (388-396):	20.00
Ronnie Lott (1-9):	8.00
Dan McGwire (172-180):	4.00
Art Monk (496-504):	35.00
Warren Moon (442-450):	10.00
Anthony Munoz (82-90):	8.00
Ken O'Brien (307-315):	4.00
Christian Okoye (316-324):	4.00
Rodney Peete (10-18):	4.00
Michael D. Perry (325-333):	4.00
Jerry Rice (46-54):	50.00
Timm Rosenbach (199-207):	4.00
Deion Sanders (451-459):	30.00
Junior Seau (136-144):	8.00
Sterling Sharpe (73-81):	10.00
Art Shell (109-117):	8.00
Don Shula (118-126):	20.00
Phil Simms (343-351):	15.00
Mike Singletary (397-405):	15.00
Bruce Smith (352-360):	8.00
Roger Staubach (37-45):	25.00
Pat Swilling (370-378):	4.00
John Taylor (406-414):	4.00
Lionel Taylor (460-468):	10.00
Vinny Testaverde (55-63):	8.00
Derrick Thomas (361-369):	35.00
Thurman Thomas (28-36):	12.00
Andre Tippett (415-423):	4.00
Al Toon (145-153):	4.00

1992-93 Pro Line SB Program

Numbered "of 9," the nine-card set chronicles the career of Steve Young from BYU to the L.A. Express to Tampa Bay and San Francisco. Showcased on the front are borderless photos, with his name in a strip at the top and the Pro Line logo at the bottom. The card back includes a photo, along with highpoints of his life and football career. A promo card was included with copies of the 1993 Super Bowl program.

		MT
Complete Set (9):		8.00
Common Player:		1.00
1	Steve Young (Just after release of ball)	1.00
2	Steve Young (Posed beside statue of Brigham Young)	1.00
3	Steve Young (in BYU uniform)	1.00
4	Steve Young (in Los Angeles Express uniform USFL)	1.00
5	Steve Young (Portrait)	1.00
6	Steve Young (in Tampa Bay Buccaneers uniform)	1.00
7	Steve Young (Posed with children for the Children's Miracle Network)	1.00
8	Steve Young (in San Francisco 49ers uniform)	1.00
9	Steve Young (Close-up shot, posed in law library)	1.00

1993 Pro Line Live Draft Day NYC

This 10-card set included cards which featured the four possible top

draft picks of the 1993 draft with different teams. The set was housed in a cellophane pack and given to attendees at the NFL Draft in New York. The fronts include a photo, with a colored stripe down the right side which includes the player's name and possible team, along with the NFL Draft logo. The Classic Pro Line Live logo is in the lower left. The card backs have a photo at the top, with a write-up, stats and the card number printed below. To add to the confusion, each card was No. 1. Classic produced 1,000 sets.

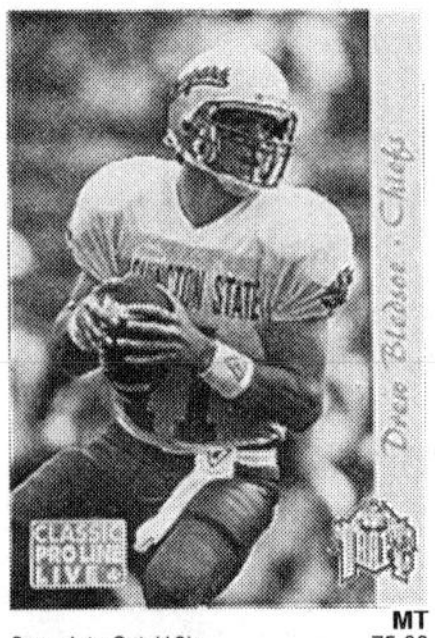

		MT
Complete Set (10):		75.00
Common Player:		2.50
1A	Drew Bledsoe	20.00
1B	Drew Bledsoe	20.00
1C	Drew Bledsoe	20.00
1D	Eric Curry	2.50
1E	Eric Curry	2.50
1F	Marvin Jones	2.50
1G	Marvin Jones	2.50
1H	Rick Mirer	7.00
1I	Rick Mirer	7.00
1J	Rick Mirer	7.00

1993 Pro Line Live Draft Day QVC

Resembling the Draft Day New York City set on the front, the backs of the 10-card set included the Classic Pro Line Live logo, draft date and set number "of 9,300" printed over a continuous background of "Draft Day 1993." The cards also featured different versions with the players on different teams. The set was produced for sale on the QVC television network.

		MT
Complete Set (10):		20.00
Common Player:		1.00
1A	Drew Bledsoe	4.00
1B	Drew Bledsoe	4.00
1C	Drew Bledsoe	4.00
1D	Eric Curry	1.00
1E	Eric Curry	1.00
1F	Marvin Jones	1.00
1G	Marvin Jones	1.00
1H	Rick Mirer	2.00
1I	Rick Mirer	2.00
1J	Rick Mirer	2.00

1993 Pro Line Previews

Randomly seeded in 1993 Classic Football Draft Picks foil packs, the five-card set focused on the previous five No. 1 NFL Draft picks. According to Classic, 12,000 of each card was produced. Versions of Pro Line Live, Portraits and Profiles are on the card fronts, while the backs for each card are identical, listing the season and the player's name. The cards carry a "PL" prefix.

		MT
Complete Set (5):		45.00
Common Player:		4.00
1	Troy Aikman (Live)	20.00
2	Jeff George (Profile)	6.00
3	Russell Maryland (Live)	4.00
4	Steve Emtman	4.00
5	Drew Bledsoe (Portrait)	20.00

1993 Pro Line Live

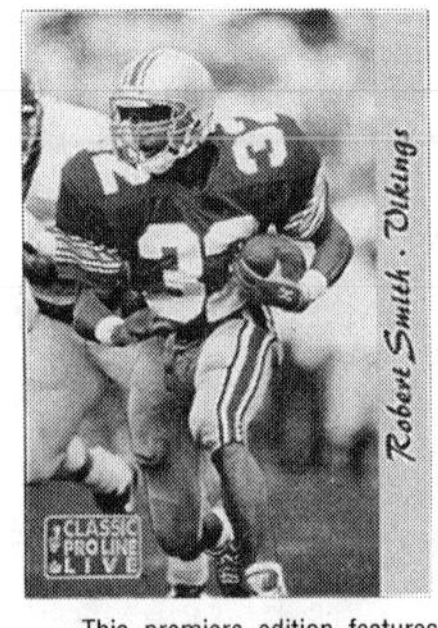

This premiere edition features 285 Classic Pro Line Live cards, 48 Portraits cards and 13 nine-card Profiles sets. The card front has a full-bleed color action photo with the team and player's name on the right in its corresponding color. The back has an action photo and player information. Randomly inserted autographed cards were also issued, two per case. Players (35) signed between 900-1,050 cards; the autograph and the limited-edition card number appear on the card front. The card front is basically the same design as those in the regular set. The card back indicates the card is a limited-edition autographed card. The players who signed cards are #s 7, 16, 23, 34, 46, 51, 67, 70, 76, 79, 87, 88, 91, 96, 99, 107, 108, 109, 119, 120, 121, 124, 129, 131, 146, 151, 158, 160, 188, 199, 201, 217, 227, 231, and 242. These command premium prices.

		MT
Complete Set (285):		15.00
Common Player:		.05
Minor Stars:		.10
Pack (12):		.50
Wax Box (36):		15.00
1	Michael Haynes	.10
2	Chris Hinton	.05
3	Pierce Holt	.05
4	Chris Miller	.10
5	Mike Pritchard	.05
6	Andre Rison	.20
7	Deion Sanders	.50
8	Jessie Tuggle	.05
9	*Lincoln Kennedy*	.10
10	*Roger Harper*	.10
11	Cornelius Bennett	.05
12	Henry Jones	.05
13	Jim Kelly	.20
14	Bill Brooks	.05
15	Nate Odomes	.05
16	Andre Reed	.10
17	Frank Reich	.05
18	Bruce Smith	.05
19	Steve Tasker	.05
20	Thurman Thomas	.20
21	*Thomas Smith*	.10
22	*John Parrella*	.10
23	Neal Anderson	.05
24	Mark Carrier	.05
25	Jim Harbaugh	.10
26	Darren Lewis	.05
27	Steve McMichael	.05
28	Alonzo Spellman	.05
29	Tom Waddle	.05
30	*Curtis Conway*	.50
31	Carl Simpson	.05
32	David Fulcher	.05
33	Harold Green	.05
34	David Klingler	.10
35	Tim Krumrie	.05
36	Carl Pickens	.50
37	Alfred Williams	.05
38	Darryl William	.05
39	*John Copeland*	.10
40	*Tony McGee*	.10
41	Bernie Kosar	.05
42	Kevin Mack	.05
43	Clay Mathews	.05
44	Eric Metcalf	.05
45	Michael Dean Perry	.05
46	Vinny Testaverde	.20
47	Jerry Ball	.05
48	Tommy Vardell	.05
49	*Steve Everitt*	.10
50	*Dan Footman*	.10
51	Troy Aikman	.75
52	Daryl Johnston	.05
53	Tony Casillas	.05
54	Charles Haley	.05
55	Alvin Harper	.10
56	Michael Irvin	.20
57	Robert Jones	.05
58	Russell Maryland	.10
59	Nate Newton	.05
60	Ken Norton	.05
61	Jay Novacek	.05
62	Emmitt Smith	1.50
63	Kevin Smith	.05
64	*Kevin Williams*	.20
65	*Darrin Smith*	.10
66	Steve Atwater	.05
67	Rod Bernstine	.05
68	Mike Croel	.05
69	John Elway	1.00
70	Tommy Maddox	.10
71	Karl Mecklenburg	.05
72	Shannon Sharpe	.20
73	Dennis Smith	.05
74	*Dan Williams*	.10
75	*Glyn Milburn*	.20
76	Pat Swilling	.05
77	Bernie Blades	.05
78	Herman Moore	.50
79	Rodney Peete	.05
80	Brett Perriman	.05
81	Barry Sanders	2.00
82	Chris Spielman	.05
83	Andre Ware	.05
84	*Ryan McNeil*	.10
85	*Antonio London*	.10
86	Tony Bennett	.05
87	Terrell Buckley	.10
88	Brett Favre	2.00
89	Brian Noble	.05
90	Ken O'Brien	.05
91	Sterling Sharpe	.20
92	Reggie White	.20
93	John Stephens	.05
94	*Wayne Simmons*	.10
95	*George Teague*	.10
96	Ray Childress	.05
97	Curtis Duncan	.05
98	Ernest Givins	.05
99	Haywood Jeffires	.10
100	Bubba McDowell	.05
101	Warren Moon	.20
102	Al Smith	.05
103	Lorenzo White	.05
104	*Brad Hopkins*	.10
105	*Michael Barrow*	.10
106	Duane Bickett	.05
107	Quentin Coryatt	.10
108	Steve Emtman	.10
109	Jeff George	.20
110	Anthony Johnson	.05
111	Reggie Langhorne	.05
112	Jack Trudeau	.05
113	Clarence Verdin	.05
114	Sean Dawkins	.05
115	*Roosevelt Potts*	.10
116	Dale Carter	.05
117	Dave Krieg	.05
118	Nick Lowery	.05
119	Christian Okoye	.05
120	Neil Smith	.05
121	Derrick Thomas	.20
122	Harvey Williams	.05
123	Barry Word	.05
124	Joe Montana	1.00
125	Marcus Allen	.20
126	James Lofton	.05
127	Nick Bell	.05
128	Tim Brown	.20
129	Eric Dickerson	.10
130	Jeff Hostetler	.10
131	Howie Long	.05
132	Todd Marinovich	.05
133	Greg Townsend	.05
134	*Patrick Bates*	.10
135	Billy Joe Hobart	.05
136	Willie Anderson	.05
137	Shane Conlan	.05
138	Henry Ellard	.05
139	Jim Everett	.10
140	Cleveland Gary	.05
141	Sean Gilbert	.05
142	Todd Lyght	.05
143	*Jerome Bettis*	1.50
144	*Troy Drayton*	.20
145	Louis Oliver	.05
146	Marco Coleman	.05
147	Bryan Cox	.05
148	Mark Duper	.05
149	Irving Fryar	.05
150	Mark Higgs	.05
151	Keith Jackson	.10
152	Dan Marino	1.50
153	Troy Vincent	.05
154	Richmond Webb	.05
155	*O.J. McDuffie*	.75
156	*Terry Kirby*	.20
157	Terry Allen	.20
158	Anthony Carter	.05
159	Cris Carter	.50
160	Chris Doleman	.05
161	Randall McDaniel	.05
162	Audray McMillian	.05
163	Henry Thomas	.05
164	Gary Zimmerman	.05
165	*Robert Smith*	1.00
166	*Qadry Ismail*	.20
167	Vincent Brown	.05
168	Marv Cook	.05
169	Greg McMurtry	.05
170	Jon Vaughn	.05
171	Leonard Russell	.10
172	Andre Tippett	.05
173	Scott Zolak	.05
174	*Drew Bledsoe*	3.00
175	*Chris Slade*	.10
176	Morten Andersen	.05
177	Vaughn Dunbar	.05
178	Rickey Jackson	.05
179	Vaughan Johnson	.05
180	Eric Martin	.05
181	Sam Mills	.05
182	Brad Muster	.05
183	*Willie Roaf*	.10
184	*Irv Smith*	.20
185	*Reggie Freeman*	.10
186	Michael Brooks	.05
187	*Dave Brown*	.20
188	Rodney Hampton	.20
189	Pepper Johnson	.05
190	Ed McCaffrey	.30
191	David Meggett	.05
192	Bart Oates	.05
193	Phil Simms	.10
194	Lawrence Taylor	.20
195	Michael Strahan	.05
196	Brad Baxter	.05
197	Johnny Johnson	.10
198	Boomer Esiason	.10
199	Ronnie Lott	.10
200	Johnny Mitchell	.10
201	Rob Moore	.20
202	Browning Nagle	.05
203	Blair Thomas	.05
204	*Marvin Jones*	.10
205	*Coleman Rudolph*	.10
206	Eric Allen	.05
207	Fred Barnett	.10
208	Tim Harris	.05
209	Randall Cunningham	.20
210	Seth Joyner	.05
211	Clyde Simmons	.05
212	Herschel Walker	.10
213	Calvin Williams	.05
214	*Lester Holmes*	.10
215	*Leonard Renfro*	.10
216	Chris Chandler	.20
217	Gary Clark	.05
218	Ken Harvey	.05
219	Randal Hill	.05
220	Steve Beuerlein	.10
221	Ricky Proehl	.05
222	Timm Rosenbach	.05
223	*Garrison Hearst*	1.00
224	*Ernest Dye*	.10
225	Bubby Brister	.05
226	Dermontti Dawson	.05
227	Barry Foster	.05
228	Kevin Greene	.05
229	Merril Hoge	.05
230	Greg Lloyd	.05
231	Neil O'Donnell	.20
232	Rod Woodson	.10
233	*Deon Figures*	.10
234	*Chad Brown*	.20
235	Marion Butts	.05
236	Gill Byrd	.05
237	Ronnie Harmon	.05
238	Stan Humphries	.10
239	Anthony Miller	.05
240	Leslie O'Neil	.05
241	Stanley Richard	.05
242	Junior Seau	.20
243	*Darrien Gordon*	.20
244	*Natrone Means*	1.00
245	Dana Hall	.05
246	Brent Jones	.10
247	Tim McDonald	.05
248	Steve Bono	.20
249	Jerry Rice	1.00
250	John Taylor	.10
251	Ricky Watters	.20
252	Steve Young	.75
253	*Dana Stubblefield*	.20
254	*Todd Kelly*	.10
255	Brian Blades	.05
256	Ferrell Edmunds	.05
257	Stan Gelbaugh	.05
258	Cortez Kennedy	.10
259	Dan McGwire	.10
260	Chris Warren	.10
261	John L. Williams	.05
262	David Wyman	.05
263	*Rick Mirer*	.25
264	*Carlton Gray*	.10
265	Marty Carter	.05
266	Reggie Cobb	.05
267	Lawrence Dawsey	.05
268	Santana Dotson	.05
269	Craig Erickson	.10
270	Paul Gruber	.05
271	Keith McCants	.05
272	Broderick Thomas	.05
273	*Eric Curry*	.10
274	*Demetrius Duboise*	.10
275	Earnest Byner	.05
276	Ricky Ervins	.05
277	Brad Edwards	.05
278	Jim Lachey	.05
279	Charles Mann	.05
280	Carl Banks	.05
281	Art Monk	.10
282	Mark Rypien	.10
284	*Tom Carter*	.10
285	*Reggie Brooks*	.20

1993 Pro Line Live Autographs

Randomly seeded two per 10-box case, the card fronts carry the same design as the regular cards, with the autograph signed over the photo. The backs congratulate the winner of the autograph. The Classic, NFL and NFLPA logos appear at the bottom. The cards are unnumbered, but are listed below respective of the player's regular card.

		MT
Complete Set (38):		1200.
Common Player:		10.00
Minor Stars:		20.00
7	Deion Sanders (900)	75.00
16	Andre Reed (1050)	20.00
23	Neal Anderson (1050)	10.00
34	David Klingler (1200)	10.00
46	Vinny Testaverde (900)	30.00
51	Troy Aikman (700)	80.00
67	Rod Bernstine (1000)	10.00
70	Tommy Maddox (1050)	10.00
76	Pat Swilling (950)	10.00
79	Rodney Peete (1000)	10.00
87	Terrell Buckley (1050)	20.00
88	Brett Favre (650)	200.00
91	Sterling Sharpe (1050)	20.00
96	Ray Childress (950)	10.00
99	Haywood Jeffires (950)	10.00
107	Quentin Coryatt (900)	10.00
108	Steve Emtman (800)	10.00
109	Jeff George (1050)	20.00
119	Christian Okoye (900)	10.00
120	Neil Smith (1050)	20.00
121	Derrick Thomas (550)	35.00
124	Joe Montana (600)	200.00
129	Eric Dickerson (900)	20.00
131	Howie Long (950)	20.00
146	Marco Coleman (1000)	10.00
151	Keith Jackson (650)	10.00
158	Anthony Carter (950)	10.00
160	Chris Doleman (1000)	10.00
188	Rodney Hampton (650)	20.00
199	Ronnie Lott (1050)	20.00
201	Rob Moore (950)	30.00
212	Herschel Walker (400)	20.00
217	Gary Clark (1050)	10.00
227	Barry Foster (750)	10.00
231	Neil O'Donnell (1050)	20.00
242	Junior Seau (900)	20.00
275	Earnest Byner (750)	10.00
281	Art Monk (750)	20.00

1993 Pro Line Live Future Stars

The 28-card set was seeded one per Pro Line Live jumbo pack. The fronts are anchored with a photo, with a colored stripe running along the right side of the card. The player's name and team appears in the stripe. The Pro Line Live logo is located in the lower left. The backs have the photo at the top, with his name and position in the upper left. His highlights and stats are printed in a colored rectangle at the bottom of the card. The card fronts also boast a gold-foil stamp of "1 of 22,000" printed to the inside of the stripe on the right side. The cards are numbered with "FS."

		MT
Complete Set (28):		15.00
Common Player:		.25
Minor Stars:		.50
1	Patrick Bates	.25
2	Jerome Bettis	2.00
3	Drew Bledsoe	4.50
4	Tom Carter	.25
5	Curtis Conway	.75
6	Steve Everitt	.25
7	Deon Figures	.25
8	Darrien Gordon	.25
9	Lester Holmes	.25
10	Brad Hopkins	.25
11	Marvin Jones	.50
12	Lincoln Kennedy	.25
13	O.J. McDuffie	1.00
14	Rick Mirer	.50
15	Willie Roaf	.50
16	Will Shields	.25
17	Wayne Simmons	.25
18	Robert Smith	2.00
19	Thomas Smith	.25
20	Michael Strahan	.50
21	Dana Stubblefield	.50
22	Dan Williams	.25
23	Kevin Williams (WR)	.50
24	Garrison Hearst	2.00
25	John Copeland	.25
26	Ryan McNeil	.25
27	Eric Curry	.25
28	Roosevelt Potts	.25

1993 Pro Line Live Illustrated

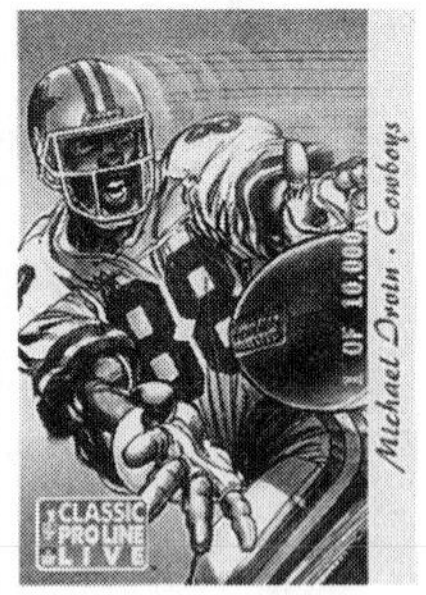

Artwork was the main feature of this six-card set, created by artist Neal Adams. The fronts showcase artwork on the left, with the player's name and team in a colored stripe on the right side. The Pro Line logo is in the lower left. "One of 10,000" is printed along the inside of the stripe on the right side. The backs carry the same design as the base cards, but are numbered with a prefix of "SP." The cards were seeded three per case. Classic produced 10,000 of each card.

		MT
Complete Set (6):		20.00
Common Player:		2.00
1	Troy Aikman	4.50
2	Jerry Rice	6.00
3	Michael Irvin	2.00
4	Thurman Thomas	2.00
5	Lawrence Taylor	2.00
6	Deion Sanders	3.00

1993 Pro Line Live LPs

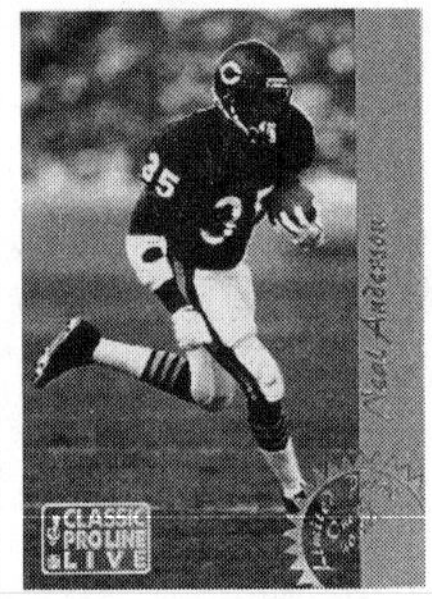

Randomly seeded in packs, the 20-card set included a large photo on the front, with the player's name in a colored stripe on the right side. The Pro Line logo is in the lower left corner, while a "one of 40,000" gold-foil seal is on the right corner. The backs, prefixed with an "LP," have the player's name in the upper left of the photo. The player's write-up is included beneath the photo, with the card number in the lower right.

		MT
Complete Set (20):		30.00
Common Player:		.75
Minor Stars:		1.50
1	Chris Webber (Dunking football)	2.00
2	Shaquille O'Neal (Wearing street clothes)	5.00
3	Jamal Mashburn (Wearing ProLine apparel)	1.50
4	Marcus Allen	1.50
5	Neal Anderson	.75
6	Reggie Cobb	.75
7	Rod Bernstine	.75
8	Barry Word	.75
9	Troy Aikman	3.00
10	Brett Favre	6.00
11	Ricky Watters	1.50
12	Terry Allen	1.50
13	Rodney Hampton	.75
14	Garrison Hearst	1.50
15	Jerome Bettis	1.50
16	Barry Foster	.75
17	Harold Green	.75
18	Tommy Vardell	.75
19	Lorenzo White	.75
20	Marion Butts	.75

1993 Pro Line Live Tonx

Randomly seeded in packs, the six-milk cap set previewed the NFL Tonx set. The milk cap, which measures 1-5/8 inches in diameter, could be removed from the standard size card. The front of the disc features a full-bleed photo, while the back has the team's helmet, player name and Tonx logo. The card front announces that Tonx is coming in the fall, while the card back explains the Tonx set. Each card is unnumbered.

		MT
Complete Set (6):		6.00
Common Player:		.50
1	Troy Aikman	2.00
2	Michael Irvin	.50
3	Jerry Rice	1.50
4	Deion Sanders	1.00
5	Lawrence Taylor	.50
6	Thurman Thomas	.50

1993 Pro Line Portraits

These cards continue where the numbers from the 1992 Pro Line Portraits left off, at #468. The players are featured in non-game photos on the front, with a small mug shot on the card back. A quote from the player also appears on the back.

		MT
Complete Set (44):		7.50
Common Player:		.05
468	*Willie Roaf*	.15
469	Terry Allen	.15
470	Jerry Ball	.05
471	Patrick Bates	.15
472	Ray Bentley	.05
473	*Jerome Bettis*	.50
474	Steve Beuerlein	.10
475	*Drew Bledsoe*	3.00
476	*Dave Brown*	.10
477	Gill Byrd	.05
478	Tony Casillas	.05
479	Chuck Cecil	.05
480	Reggie Cobb	.05
481	Pat Harlow	.05
482	*John Copeland*	.25
483	Bryan Cox	.05
484	*Eric Curry*	.25
485	Jeff Lageman	.05
486	Brett Favre	.75
487	Barry Foster	.25
488	Gaston Green	.05
489	Rodney Hampton	.25
490	Tim Harris	.05
491	*Garrison Hearst*	1.00
492	Tony Smith	.05
493	*Marvin Jones*	.20
494	*Lincoln Kennedy*	.25
495	Wilber Marshall	.05
496	Terry McDaniel	.05
497	*Rick Mirer*	.50
498	Art Monk	.08
499	Mike Munchak	.05
500	Frank Reich	.05
501	Barry Sanders	1.00
502	Shannon Sharpe	.05
503	*Gino Torretta*	.25
504	Ricky Watters	.40
505	Richmond Webb	.05
506	Reggie White	.25
507	Bert Jones	.05
508	Billy Kilmer	.05
509	John Mackey	.05
510	Archie Manning	.05
511	Harvey Martin	.05

1993 Pro Line Portraits Autographs

The 26-card set includes a full-bleed photo on the front, with the Pro Line logo in the bottom center. The card front is autographed. The back has the player's name in the upper left, team in the upper right and a quote in the center of the card. His photo is at the bottom center.

		MT
Complete Set (26):		750.00
Common Player:		20.00
468	Willie Roaf	20.00
471	Patrick Bates	20.00
473	Jerome Bettis	45.00
474	Steve Beuerlein	20.00
478	Tony Casillas	20.00
479	Chuck Cecil	20.00
480	Reggie Cobb	20.00
481	Pat Harlow	20.00
482	John Copeland	20.00
484	Eric Curry	20.00
485	Jeff Lageman	20.00
486	Brett Favre	250.00
488	Gaston Green	20.00
489	Rodney Hampton	25.00
492	Tony Smith	20.00
493	Marvin Jones	20.00
494	Lincoln Kennedy	20.00
496	Terry McDaniel	20.00
499	Mike Munchak	20.00
500	Frank Reich	25.00
502	Shannon Sharpe	35.00
503	Gino Torretta	20.00
507	Bert Jones (TB)	20.00
508	Billy Kilmer (TB)	30.00
510	Archie Manning (TB)	30.00
511	Harvey Martin (TB)	20.00

1993 Pro Line Portraits Wives

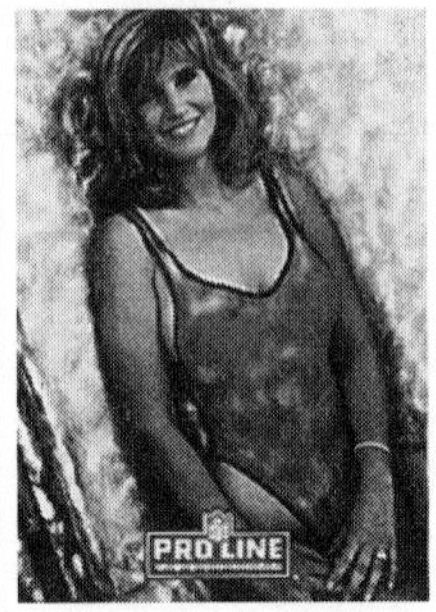

This four-card set features wives of NFL players and was inserted into packs of 1993 Pro Line. The cards are numbered SC25-SC28 in a continuation from 1992 Pro Line Wives, however card number SC24 was never produced.

		MT
Complete Set (4):		.50
Common Player:		.15
25	Annette Rypien	.15
26	Ann Stark	.15
27	Cindy Walker	.15
28	Cindy Reed	.15

1993 Pro Line Portraits Wives Autographs

The set features the same design as the Portraits Wives set, except these are autographed. Three of the four wives featured in the basic set signed cards, with the exception of Cindy Walker.

		MT
Complete Set (3):		75.00
Common Player:		25.00
25	Annette Rypien	25.00
26	Ann Stark	25.00
28	Cindy Reed	25.00

1994 Pro Line Live Draft Day Prototypes

The 1994 Draft was previewed by this 13-card set. The fronts are anchored with a borderless photo, with the NFL Draft logo in the upper right and the player's name and possible team at the bottom. The backs showcase a cutout of a portion of a photo, with the rest of the photo grayed out. The cards are numbered by a prefix of "FD" in the upper right. The backs state, "1994 NFL Draft Day prototype set April 24, 1994, limited edition 1 of 19,940."

		MT
Complete Set (13):		25.00
Common Player:		1.00
1	Dan Wilkinson	1.00
2	Dan Wilkinson	1.00
3	Marshall Faulk	5.00
4	Marshall Faulk	5.00
5	Marshall Faulk	5.00
6	1989 First Pick (Troy Aikman)	3.00
7	Trent Dilfer	2.00
8	Trent Dilfer	2.00
9	Heath Shuler	3.00
10	Heath Shuler	3.00
11	Aaron Glenn	1.00
12	Aaron Glenn	1.00
13	Dan Wilkinson	1.00

1994 Pro Line Live Previews

This five-card set boasts a full-bleed photo on the front, with the Classic Pro Line Preview logo in the upper left and player's name and team at the bottom. The backs, numbered in the lower left with a prefix of "PL," have the player's name and position in the upper left and his highlights and bio in a stripe along the left side of the card. An action shot and his stats are printed over his photo. The back also has a tagline which says the card is one of 12,000.

		MT
Complete Set (5):		45.00
Common Player:		7.00
1	Troy Aikman	12.00
2	Jerry Rice	12.00
3	Steve Young	10.00
4	Rick Mirer	7.00
5	Drew Bledsoe	12.00

1994 Pro Line Live

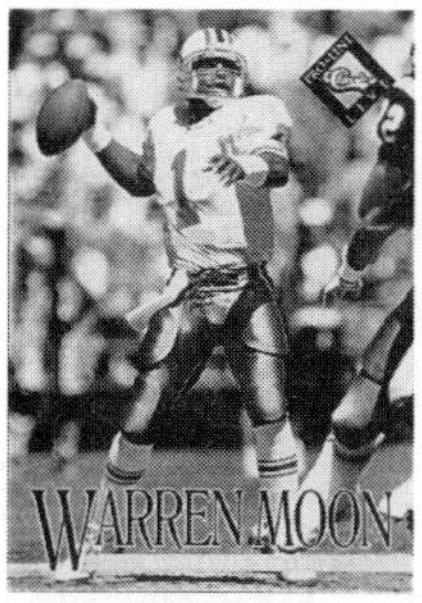

Classic Games Inc. produced the 405-card 1994 Pro Line Live set. The set includes 327 NFL veterans and 62 rookies. Each card front has a borderless color action photo on the front, along with the player's name and team and set logo. The back has another color photo of the player, with statistics, biographical information and a brief career summary. More than 150 players also autographed their cards; these cards, issued one per box, command premium values. Two subsets were also made, featuring the league's two new expansion teams (the Jacksonville Jaguars and Carolina Panthers), and the player illustrations of comic book artist Neal Adams (#s 401-405). There were also three insert sets produced. Emmitt Smith is honored with 15,000 sequentially-numbered inserts, while another set honors 45 players who were MVP candidates. Collectors who obtained one of the 2,083 cards of the 1994 NFL MVP could redeem it for a limited, uncut sheet of the 45 cards. The other insert series previews the company's 1994 Basketball Draft Pick series.

		MT
Complete Set (405):		20.00
Common Player:		.05
Minor Stars:		.10
Pack (10):		1.50
Wax Box (36):		40.00
1	Emmitt Smith	1.50
2	Andre Rison	.10
3	Deion Sanders	.50
4	Jeff George	.10
5	Cornelius Bennett	.05
6	Jim Kelly	.25
7	Andre Reed	.10
8	Bruce Smith	.05
9	Thurman Thomas	.25
10	Mark Carrier	.05
11	Curtis Conway	.25
12	Donnell Woolford	.05
13	Chris Zorich	.05
14	Erik Kramer	.10
15	John Copeland	.05
16	Harold Green	.05
17	David Klingler	.10
18	Tony McGee	.05
19	Carl Pickens	.25
20	Michael Jackson	.10
21	Eric Metcalf	.10
22	Michael Dean Perry	.05
23	Vinny Testaverde	.25
24	Eric Turner	.05
25	Tommy Vardell	.05
26	Troy Aikman	1.00
27	Charles Haley	.05
28	Michael Irvin	.25
29	Pierce Holt	.05
30	Russell Maryland	.05
31	Erik Williams	.05
32	Thomas Everett	.05
33	Steve Atwater	.10
34	John Elway	1.50
35	Glyn Milburn	.10
36	Shannon Sharpe	.25
37	Anthony Miller	.05
38	Barry Sanders	2.00
39	Chris Spielman	.05
40	Pat Swilling	.05
41	Brett Perriman	.05
42	Herman Moore	.30
43	Scott Mitchell	.10
44	Edgar Bennett	.05
45	Terrell Buckley	.10
46	LeRoy Butler	.05
47	Brett Favre	2.00
48	Jackie Harris	.05
49	Sterling Sharpe	.25
50	Reggie White	.25
51	Gary Brown	.10
52	Cody Carlson	.05
53	Ray Childress	.05
54	Ernest Givins	.05
55	Bruce Matthews	.05
56	Quentin Coryatt	.05
57	Steve Emtman	.05
58	Roosevelt Potts	.05
59	Tony Bennett	.05
60	Marcus Allen	.25
61	Joe Montana	1.00
62	Neil Smith	.05
63	Derrick Thomas	.10
64	Dale Carter	.05
65	Tim Brown	.25
66	Jeff Hostetler	.05
67	Terry McDaniel	.05
68	Chester McGlockton	.05
69	Anthony Smith	.05
70	Albert Lewis	.05
71	Jerome Bettis	.50
72	Shane Conlan	.05
73	Troy Drayton	.10
74	Sean Gilbert	.05
75	Chris Miller	.05
76	Bryan Cox	.05
77	Irving Fryar	.05
78	Keith Jackson	.05
79	Terry Kirby	.10
80	Dan Marino	1.50
81	O.J. McDuffie	.25
82	Terry Allen	.25
83	Cris Carter	.50
84	Chris Doleman	.05
85	Randall McDaniel	.05
86	John Randle	.10
87	Robert Smith	.50
88	Jason Belser	.05
89	Jack Del Rio	.05
90	Vincent Brown	.05
91	Ben Coates	.10
92	Chris Slade	.05
93	Derek Brown	.05
94	Morten Andersen	.05
95	Willie Roaf	.05
96	Irv Smith	.05
97	Tyrone Hughes	.05
98	Michael Haynes	.05
99	Jim Everett	.05
100	Michael Brooks	.05
101	Leroy Thompson	.05
102	Rodney Hampton	.10
103	David Meggett	.05
104	Phil Simms	.10
105	Boomer Esiason	.10
106	Johnny Johnson	.05
107	Gary Anderson	.05
108	Mo Lewis	.05
109	Ronnie Lott	.10
110	Johnny Mitchell	.05
111	Howard Cross	.05
112	Victor Bailey	.05
113	Fred Barnett	.05
114	Randall Cunningham	.25
115	Calvin Williams	.05
116	Steve Beuerlein	.05
117	Gary Clark	.05
118	Ron Moore	.05
119	Ricky Proehl	.05
120	Eric Swann	.05
121	Barry Foster	.05
122	Kevin Greene	.05
123	Greg Lloyd	.05
124	Neil O'Donnell	.10
125	Rod Woodson	.05
126	Ronnie Harmon	.05
127	Mark Higgs	.05
128	Stan Humphries	.10
129	Leslie O'Neal	.05
130	Chris Mims	.05
131	Stanley Richard	.05
132	Junior Seau	.10
133	Brent Jones	.05
134	Tim McDonald	.05
135	Jerry Rice	1.00
136	Dana Stubblefield	.10
137	Ricky Watters	.25
138	Steve Young	.75
139	Cortez Kennedy	.05
140	Rick Mirer	.10
141	Eugene Robinson	.05
142	Chris Warren	.10
143	Nate Odomes	.05
144	Howard Ballard	.05
145	Willie Anderson	.05
146	Chris Jacke	.05
147	Santana Dotson	.05
148	Craig Erickson	.05
149	Hardy Nickerson	.05
150	Lawrence Dawsey	.05
151	Terry Wooden	.05
152	Ethan Horton	.05
153	John Kasay	.05
154	Desmond Howard	.05
155	Ken Harvey	.05
156	William Fuller	.05
157	Clyde Simmons	.05
158	Randal Hill	.05
159	Garrison Hearst	.50
160	Mike Pritchard	.05
161	Jessie Tuggle	.05
162	Erric Pegram	.05
163	Kevin Ross	.05
164	Bill Brooks	.05
165	Darryl Talley	.05
166	Steve Tasker	.05
167	Pete Stoyanovich	.05
168	Dante Jones	.05
169	Vencie Glenn	.05
170	Tom Waddle	.05
171	Harlon Barnett	.05
172	Trace Armstrong	.05
173	Tim Worley	.05
174	Alfred Williams	.05
175	Louis Oliver	.05
176	Darryl Williams	.05
177	Clay Matthews	.05
178	Kyle Clifton	.05
179	Alvin Harper	.05
180	Jay Novacek	.05
181	Ken Norton	.05
182	Kevin Williams	.10
183	Daryl Johnson	.05
184	Rod Bernstine	.10
185	Karl Mecklenburg	.05
186	Dennis Smith	.05
187	Robert Delpino	.05
188	Bennie Blades	.05
189	Jason Hanson	.05
190	Derrick Moore	.05
191	Mark Clayton	.05
192	Webster Slaughter	.05
193	Haywood Jeffires	.05
194	Bubba McDowell	.05
195	Warren Moon	.25
196	Al Smith	.05
197	Bill Romanowski	.05
198	John Carney	.05
199	Kerry Cash	.05
200	Darren Carrington	.05
201	Jeff Lageman	.05
202	Tracy Simien	.05
203	Willie Davis	.05
204	Dan Saleaumua	.05
205	Raghib Ismail	.05
206	James Jett	.10
207	Todd Lyght	.05
208	Roman Phifer	.05
209	Jimmie Jones	.10
210	Jeff Cross	.05
211	Eric Davis	.05
212	Keith Byars	.05
213	Richmond Webb	.05
214	Anthony Carter	.05
215	Henry Thomas	.05
216	Andre Tippett	.05
217	Rickey Jackson	.05
218	Vaughan Johnson	.05
219	Eric Martin	.05
220	Sam Mills	.05
221	Renaldo Turnbull	.05
222	Mark Collins	.05
223	Mike Johnson	.05
224	Rob Moore	.25
225	Seth Joyner	.05
226	Herschel Walker	.10
227	Eric Green	.05
228	Marion Butts	.05
229	John Friesz	.10
230	John Taylor	.05
231	Dexter Carter	.05
232	Brian Blades	.05
233	Reggie Cobb	.05
234	Paul Gruber	.05
235	Ricky Reynolds	.05
236	Vince Workman	.05
237	Darrell Green	.05
238	Jim Lachey	.05
239	James Hasty	.05
240	Howie Long	.10
241	Aeneas Williams	.05
242	Mike Kenn	.05
243	Henry Jones	.05
244	Kenneth Davis	.05
245	Tim Krumrie	.05
246	Derrick Fenner	.05
247	Mark Carrier	.05
248	Robert Porcher	.05
249	Darren Woodson	.05
250	Kevin Smith	.05
251	Mark Stepnoski	.05
252	Simon Fletcher	.05
253	Derek Russell	.05
254	Mike Croel	.05
255	Johnny Holland	.05
256	Bryce Paup	.05
257	Cris Dishman	.05
258	Sean Jones	.05
259	Marcus Robertson	.05
260	Steve Jackson	.05
261	Jeff Herrod	.05
262	John Alt	.05
263	Nick Lowery	.05
264	Greg Robinson	.05
265	Alexander Wright	.05
266	Steve Wisniewski	.05
267	Henry Ellard	.05
268	Tracy Scroggins	.05
269	Jackie Slater	.05
270	Troy Vincent	.05
271	Qadry Ismail	.10
272	Steve Jordan	.05
273	Leonard Russell	.05
274	Maurice Hurst	.05
275	*Scottie Graham*	.10
276	Carlton Bailey	.05
277	John Elliott	.05
278	Corey Miller	.05
279	Brad Baxter	.05
280	Brian Washington	.05
281	Tim Harris	.05
282	Byron Evans	.05
283	Dermontti Dawson	.05
284	Carnell Lake	.05
285	Jeff Graham	.05
286	Merton Hanks	.05
287	Harris Barton	.05
288	Guy McIntyre	.05
289	Kelvin Martin	.05
290	John Williams	.05
291	Courtney Hawkins	.05
292	Vaughn Hebron	.05
293	Brian Mitchell	.05
294	Andre Collins	.05
295	Art Monk	.10
296	Mark Rypien	.05
297	Ricky Sanders	.05
298	Eric Hill	.05
299	Larry Centers	.05
300	Norm Johnson	.05
301	Pete Metzelaars	.05
302	Ricardo McDonald	.05
303	Stevon Moore	.05
304	Mike Sherrard	.05
305	Andy Harmon	.05
306	Anthony Johnson	.05
307	J.J. Birden	.05
308	Neal Anderson	.05
309	Lewis Tillman	.05
310	Richard Dent	.10
311	Nate Newton	.05
312	*Sean Dawkins*	.25
313	Lawrence Taylor	.25
314	Wilber Marshall	.05
315	Tim Carter	.05
316	Reggie Brooks	.10
317	Eric Curry	.05
318	Horace Copeland	.05
319	Natrone Means	.50
320	Eric Allen	.05
321	Marvin Jones	.05
322	Keith Hamilton	.05
323	Vincent Brisby	.10
324	Drew Bledsoe	1.00
325	Tom Rathman	.05
326	Ed McCaffrey	.30
327	Steve Israel	.05
328	*Dan Wilkinson*	.25
329	*Marshall Faulk*	4.00
330	*Heath Shuler*	.50
331	*Willie McGinest*	.25
332	*Trev Alberts*	.25
333	*Trent Dilfer*	2.50
334	*Bryant Young*	.50
335	*Sam Adams*	.25
336	*Antonio Langham*	.25
337	*Jamir Miller*	.25
338	*John Thierry*	.25
339	*Aaron Glenn*	.25
340	*Joe Johnson*	.10
341	*Bernard Williams*	.10
342	*Wayne Gandy*	.10
343	*Aaron Taylor*	.10
344	*Charles Johnson*	.25
345	*DeWayne Washington*	.10
346	*Todd Steussie*	.25
347	*Tim Bowens*	.10
348	*Johnnie Morton*	.40
349	*Rob Fredrickson*	.10
350	*Shante Carver*	.10
351	*Thomas Lewis*	.10
352	*Greg Hill*	.50
353	*Henry Ford*	.10
354	*Jeff Burris*	.10
355	*William Floyd*	.50
356	*Derrick Alexander*	.25
357	*Darnay Scott*	.75
358	*Isaac Bruce*	4.00
359	*Errict Rhett*	.50
360	*Kevin Lee*	.10
361	*Chuck Levy*	.25
362	*David Palmer*	.50
363	*Ryan Yarborough*	.10
364	*Charlie Garner*	2.50
365	*Isaac Davis*	.10
366	*Mario Bates*	.25
367	*Bert Emanuel*	.75
368	*Thomas Randolph*	.10
369	*Bucky Brooks*	.10
370	*Allen Aldridge*	.10
371	*Charlie Ward*	.50
372	*Audrey Beavers*	.10
373	*Donnell Bennett*	.50
374	*Jason Sehorn*	.25
375	*Lonnie Johnson*	.25
376	*Tyronne Drakeford*	.10
377	*Andre Coleman*	.10
378	*Lamar Smith*	2.50
379	*Calvin Jones*	.10
380	*LeShon Johnson*	.10
381	*Byron Morris*	.50
382	*Lake Dawson*	.25
383	*Corey Sawyer*	.10
384	*Willie Jackson*	.10
385	*Perry Klein*	.10
386	*Ronnie Woolfork*	.10
387	*Doug Nussmeier*	.10
388	*Rob Waldrop*	.10
389	*Glenn Foley*	.50
390	Aikman, Irvin	.50
391	Young, Rice	.50
392	Favre, Sharpe	1.00
393	Kelly, Reed	.10
394	Elway, Sharpe	.75
395	Carolina Panthers	.05
396	Jacksonville Jaguars	.05
397	Checklist #1	.05
398	Checklist #2	.05
399	Checklist #3	.05
400	Checklist #4	.05
401	Sterling Sharpe	.10
402	Derrick Thomas	.05
403	Joe Montana	.50
404	Emmitt Smith	.75
405	Barry Sanders	1.00

1994 Pro Line Live Autographs

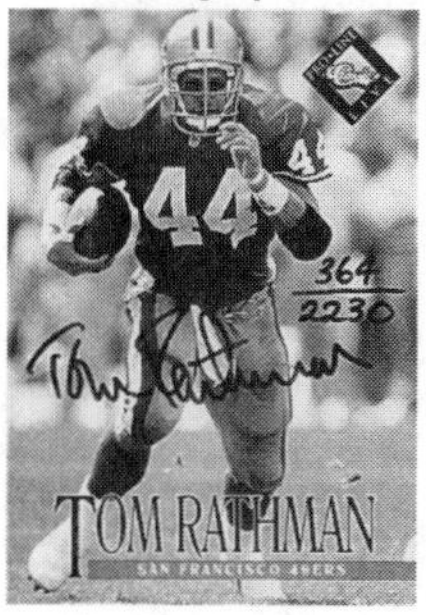

This 132-card autographed set showcases the same design as the base cards, except they are signed and numbered on the front. The card backs congratulate the collector on receiving an autographed card. The Pro Line Live logo is in the center of the unnumbered card back. The cards are numbered below according to the player's base card number.

		MT
Complete Set (132):		2750.
Common Player:		10.00
Minor Stars:		20.00
Inserted 1:36		
1	Emmitt Smith (925)	125.00
4	Jeff George (2140)	20.00
12	Donnell Woolford (1000)	10.00
14	Eric Kramer (1020)	10.00
17	David Klingler (2140)	10.00
20	Michael Jackson (1490)	10.00
24	Eric Turner (1030)	10.00
25	Tommy Vardell (1000)	10.00
26	Troy Aikman (340)	125.00
28	Michael Irvin (450)	25.00
29	Pierce Holt (2020)	10.00
30	Russell Maryland (1945)	10.00
33	Steve Atwater (1040)	10.00
34	John Elway (1000)	100.00
35	Glyn Milburn (440)	20.00
36	Shannon Sharpe (1020)	20.00
37	Anthony Miller (2070)	10.00
47	Brett Favre (1130)	100.00
49	Sterling Sharpe (450)	35.00
51	Gary Brown (950)	20.00
53	Ray Childress (2240)	10.00
56	Quentin Coryatt (970)	10.00
57	Steve Emtman (1900)	10.00
61	Joe Montana (920)	150.00
62	Neil Smith (1000)	20.00
63	Derrick Thomas (1087)	50.00
64	Dale Carter (1031)	10.00
65	Tim Brown (1920)	20.00
66	Jeff Hostetler (955)	10.00
67	Terry McDaniel (1980)	10.00
72	Shane Conlan (1110)	10.00
73	Troy Drayton (450)	20.00
77	Irving Fryar (1040)	10.00
78	Keith Jackson (1020)	10.00
93	Derek Brown (RB/449)	10.00
96	Irv Smith (470)	20.00
97	Tyrone Hughes (470)	10.00
99	Jim Everett (1265)	10.00
102	Rodney Hampton (1090)	20.00
105	Boomer Esiason (920)	20.00
109	Ronnie Lott (910)	20.00
112	Victor Bailey (450)	20.00
116	Steve Beuerlein (970)	20.00
119	Ricky Proehl (1020)	10.00
121	Barry Foster (1080)	10.00
127	Mark Higgs (980)	10.00
129	Leslie O'Neal (2050)	10.00
133	Brent Jones (1880)	10.00
134	Tim McDonald (2040)	10.00
138	Steve Young (925)	75.00
149	Hardy Nickerson (1175)	10.00
159	Garrison Hearst (1435)	25.00
162	Erric Pegram (1020)	10.00
164	Bill Brooks (1030)	10.00
177	Clay Matthews (2000)	10.00
184	Rod Bernstine (1010)	10.00
187	Robert Delpino (1030)	10.00
208	Roman Phifer (2140)	10.00
212	Keith Byars (1020)	10.00
213	Richmond Webb (1020)	10.00
214	Anthony Carter (1020)	10.00
216	Andre Tippett (1090)	10.00
220	Sam Mills (1115)	10.00
221	Renaldo Turnbull (945)	10.00
224	Rob Moore (1025)	20.00
228	Marion Butts (2040)	10.00
229	John Friesz (2150)	20.00
230	John Taylor (1030)	10.00
238	Jim Lachey (1850)	10.00
244	Kenneth Davis (1170)	10.00
266	Steve Wisniewski (2150)	10.00
269	Jackie Slater (1110)	10.00
271	Qadry Ismail (450)	20.00
277	John Elliott (2150)	10.00
279	Brad Baxter (1070)	10.00
284	Carnell Lake (1985)	10.00
287	Harris Barton (2120)	10.00
294	Andre Collins (1100)	10.00
315	Tom Carter (460)	10.00
316	Reggie Brooks (460)	20.00
318	Horace Copeland (450)	10.00
319	Natrone Means (445)	40.00
320	Eric Allen (1980)	10.00
324	Drew Bledsoe (1150)	65.00
325	Tom Rathman (2230)	10.00
326	Ed McCaffrey (2030)	25.00
327	Steve Israel (2020)	10.00
328	Dan Wilkinson (1960)	10.00
329	Marshall Faulk (2230)	50.00
330	Heath Shuler (2020)	20.00
331	Willie McGinest (3520)	10.00
333	Trent Dilfer (2680)	20.00
336	Antonio Langham (1240)	10.00
338	John Thierry (1150)	10.00
339	Aaron Glenn (1140)	10.00
342	Wayne Gandy (1040)	10.00
343	Aaron Taylor (950)	10.00
344	Charles Johnson	10.00
345	DeWayne Washington (1040)	10.00
348	Johnnie Morton (2945)	10.00
349	Rob Fredrickson (1160)	10.00
350	Shante Carver (1160)	10.00
351	Thomas Lewis (1140)	10.00
352	Greg Hill (1145)	20.00
353	Henry Ford (1110)	10.00
354	Jeff Burris (1140)	10.00
355	William Floyd (950)	20.00
356	Derrick Alexander (WR/950)	20.00
357	Darnay Scott (1400)	20.00
359	Errict Rhett (1120)	20.00
360	Kevin Lee (1190)	10.00
361	Chuck Levy (950)	10.00
362	David Palmer (950)	20.00
364	Charlie Garner (1130)	20.00
365	Isaac Davis (1150)	10.00
366	Mario Bates (1145)	10.00
368	Thomas Randolph (1100)	10.00
369	Bucky Brooks (1090)	10.00
372	Aubrey Beavers (1150)	10.00
373	Donnell Bennett (1130)	20.00
374	Jason Sehorn (950)	20.00
377	Andre Coleman (1000)	10.00
378	Lamar Smith (1130)	10.00
379	Calvin Jones (960)	10.00
381	Byron "Bam" Morris (1130)	20.00
382	Lake Dawson (1100)	10.00
384	Willie Jackson (1140)	10.00
385	Perry Klein (1000)	10.00
386	Ronnie Woolfork (360)	20.00
387	Doug Nussmeier (1150)	10.00
389	Glenn Foley (890)	20.00
390	Troy Aikman, Michael Irvin (Combo/345)	225.00
391	Steve Young, Jerry Rice (Combo/450)	275.00

1994 Pro Line Live MVP Sweepstakes

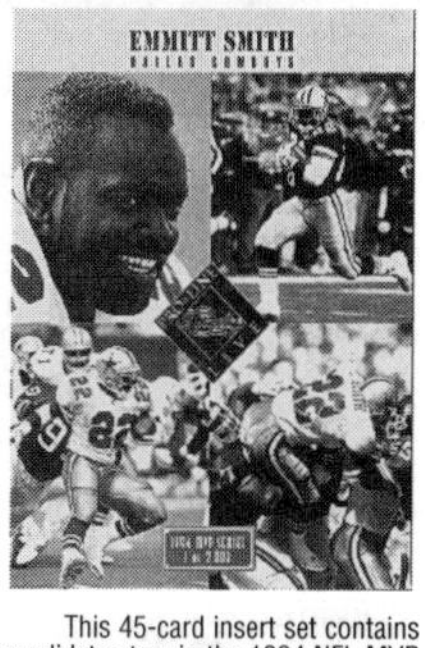

This 45-card insert set contains candidates to win the 1994 NFL MVP Award. Collectors who obtain one of the 2,083 cards of the eventual 1994 NFL MVP could redeem the card for a limited-edition uncut sheet of the 45 cards. Each card front has four player photos on it. Card backs are numbered with an "MVP" prefix.

		MT
Complete Set (45):		200.00
Common Player:		2.50
Minor Stars:		5.00
Inserted 1:72		
1	Jeff George	5.00
2	Andre Rison	5.00
3	Jim Kelly	5.00
4	Thurman Thomas	5.00
5	Troy Aikman	15.00
6	Emmitt Smith	20.00
7	Michael Irvin	5.00
8	John Elway	20.00
9	Brett Favre	30.00
10	Sterling Sharpe	5.00
11	Barry Sanders	30.00
12	Scott Mitchell	2.50
13	Gary Brown	2.50
14	Warren Moon	5.00
15	Marcus Allen	5.00
16	Joe Montana	20.00
17	Tim Brown	5.00
18	Jeff Hostetler	2.50
19	Dan Marino	20.00
20	Terry Kirby	2.50
21	Terry Allen	5.00
22	Drew Bledsoe	15.00
23	Chris Miller	2.50
24	Jerome Bettis	5.00
25	Derek Brown	2.50
26	Rodney Hampton	2.50
27	Phil Simms	2.50
28	Randall Cunningham	5.00
29	Barry Foster	2.50
30	Neil O'Donnell	2.50
31	Boomer Esiason	2.50
32	Johnny Johnson	2.50
33	Garrison Hearst	7.00
34	Ron Moore	2.50
35	Natrone Means	7.00
36	Steve Young	10.00
37	Ricky Watters	5.00
38	Jerry Rice	15.00
39	Rick Mirer	5.00
40	Chris Warren	2.50

41	Reggie Brooks	2.50
42	Marshall Faulk	7.00
43	Heath Shuler	5.00
44	Trent Dilfer	10.00
45	Field Card	2.50

1994 Pro Line Live Spotlight

The chromium cards have the player's name and the Spotlight logo inside a border on the left side of the card. The Classic Pro Line logo is in the upper left. The cards were seeded one per 16-card pack. The card backs, numbered in the lower left with a prefix of "PB," have the player's name, position, team and bio inside a stripe on the left side. A photo is anchored on the right side of the card, with his stats printed toward the bottom.

		MT
Complete Set (25):		25.00
Common Player:		.25
Minor Stars:		.50
1	Trent Dilfer	1.00
2	Heath Shuler	.50
3	Marshall Faulk	2.00
4	Troy Aikman	1.50
5	Emmitt Smith	2.00
6	Thurman Thomas	.50
7	Andre Rison	.50
8	Jerry Rice	1.50
9	Sterling Sharpe	.50
10	Brett Favre	3.00
11	Steve Young	1.00
12	Drew Bledsoe	1.50
13	Rick Mirer	.50
14	Barry Sanders	3.00
15	Joe Montana	2.00
16	Jerome Bettis	.50
17	Ricky Watters	.50
18	Rodney Hampton	.25
19	Tim Brown	.50
20	Reggie Brooks	.25
21	Natrone Means	.50
22	Marcus Allen	.50
23	Gary Brown	.25
24	Barry Foster	.25
25	Dan Marino	2.00

1995 Pro Line Previews

These five cards preview the design of Classic's micro-lined insert cards from its 1995 NFL Pro Line set. The Game Breakers, seeded one per box of 1995 Classic NFL Rookies product, feature players who have the ability to change the course of a game at any moment. The insert set logo is in the lower left corner; the Classic Pro Line brand logo is in the upper left corner. The player's name and position are in a black band at the bottom. The card back is numbered using a "GP" prefix.

		MT
Complete Set (5):		35.00
Common Player:		5.00
1	Dan Marino	15.00
2	Natrone Means	5.00
3	Joe Montana	8.00
4	Barry Sanders	8.00
5	Deion Sanders	7.00

1995 Pro Line Previews Phone Cards $2

These four cards were random inserts in 1995 Classic Basketball Rookies packs, one per two boxes of the product. The cards preview 1995 Classic Pro Line Series II $2 phone cards.

		MT
Complete Set (4):		45.00
Common Player:		8.00
1	Troy Aikman	12.00
2	Drew Bledsoe	18.00
3	Ki-Jana Carter	8.00
4	Marshall Faulk	18.00

1995 Pro Line Previews Phone Cards $5

These four cards were random inserts in 1995 Classic Basketball Rookies packs, seeded one per case of the product. The cards preview the 1995 Classic NFL Pro Line Series II $5 phone cards.

		MT
Complete Set (4):		90.00
Common Player:		16.00
1	Troy Aikman	20.00
2	Drew Bledsoe	35.00
3	Ki-Jana Carter	16.00
4	Marshall Faulk	35.00

1995 Pro Line

Only in Classic's 1995 NFL Pro Line will collectors find cards autographed by some of the NFL's marquee players, including Steve Young, Emmitt Smith and Drew Bledsoe. The complete Pro Line series has 400 cards from all 30 NFL teams, including the expansion Jacksonville Jaguars and Carolina Panthers. Forty rookies, including the first 32 selected in the draft, are also included in the set. Each card, which has 29 percent thicker stock than before, has a full-bleed color action photo on the front. The player's name is in the lower left corner; the player's team is in a bar along the bottom, with his position above the bar. The Pro Line logo is in the upper left corner. The card back has a color photo on one side, with a recap of the previous season, biographical information and stats on the other. The card number is in the upper left corner in a box. As a bonus, more than 100 top NFL players personally signed a maximum of 2,500 cards each. One autographed card was guaranteed to be in every box. Pro Line also continued its Hot Boxes program. Each pack in a Hot Box contains 40 percent inserts. Hot Boxes were randomly inserted one in every 10 cases. Exclusive to Hot Boxes are 10 Team Record Breaker acetate cards sequentially numbered to 350. Other insert sets include Pro Line Impact, MVP Interactive cards, Game Breaker cards, Pro Line Silver cards and Basketball Rookies Preview cards. A parallel insert set of the regular cards printed on silver foil board was also produced; these cards were included one per pack.

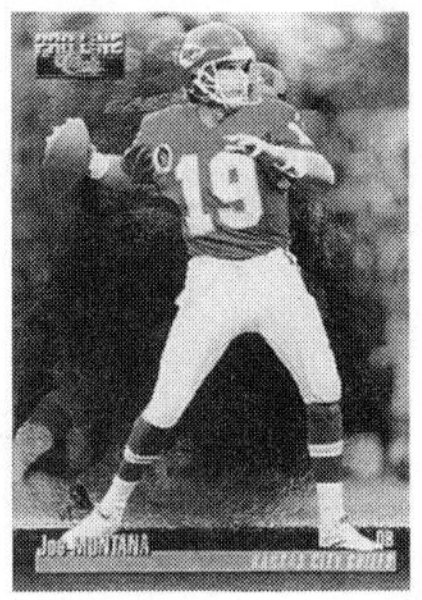

		MT
Complete Set (400):		20.00
Common Player:		.05
Minor Stars:		.10
Comp. Silver Set (400):		80.00
Silver Cards: 2x-4x		
Comp. Print. Proof (400):		700.00
Print. Proof Cards: 15x-30x		
Comp. PP Silver Set (400):		1400.
PP Silver Cards: 2x PP		
Series 1 Pack (10):		1.50
Series 1 Wax Box (36):		45.00
Series 2 Pack (6):		3.50
Series 2 Wax Box (18)		55.00
1	Garrison Hearst	.10
2	Anthony Miller	.05
3	Brett Favre	1.50
4	Jessie Hester	.05
5	Mike Fox	.05
6	*Jeff Blake*	1.00
7	J.J. Birden	.05
8	Greg Jackson	.05
9	Leon Lett	.05
10	Bruce Matthews	.05
11	Andre Reed	.05
12	Joe Montana	1.00
13	Craig Heyward	.05
14	Henry Ellard	.05
15	Chris Spielman	.05
16	Tony Woods	.05
17	Carl Banks	.05
18	*Eric Zeier*	.75
19	Michael Brooks	.05
20	Kevin Ross	.05
21	Qadry Ismail	.05
22	Mel Gray	.05
23	Ty Law	.15
24	Mark Collins	.05
25	Neil O'Donnell	.10
26	Ellis Johnson	.15
27	Rick Mirer	.40
28	Fred Barnett	.05
29	*Mike Mamula*	.10
30	Jim Jeffcoat	.05
31	Reggie Cobb	.05
32	Mark Carrier	.05
33	Darnay Scott	.40
34	Michael Jackson	.05
35	Terrell Buckley	.05
36	Nolan Harrison	.05
37	Thurman Thomas	.20
38	Anthony Smith	.05
39	Phillippi Sparks	.05
40	Cornelius Bennett	.05
41	Robert Young	.05
42	Pierce Holt	.05
43	Greg Lloyd	.05
44	*Chad May*	.10
45	Darrien Gordon	.05
46	Bryan Cox	.05
47	Junior Seau	.10
48	Al Smith	.05
49	Chris Slade	.05
50	Hardy Nickerson	.05
51	Brad Baxter	.05
52	Darryl Lewis	.05
53	Bryant Young	.05
54	Chris Warren	.05
55	Darion Conner	.05
56	Thomas Everett	.05
57	Charles Haley	.05
58	Chris Mims	.05
59	Sean Jones	.05
60	*Tamarick Vanover*	1.00
61	Daryl Johnston	.05
62	*Rashaan Salaam*	1.00
63	James Hasty	.05
64	Dante Jones	.05
65	Darren Perry	.05
66	Troy Drayton	.05
67	Mark Fields	.10
68	Brian Williams	.10
69	Steve Bono	.15
70	Eric Allen	.05
71	Chris Zorich	.05
72	Dave Brown	.05
73	Ken Norton	.05
74	Wayne Martin	.05
75	Mo Lewis	.05
76	Johnny Mitchell	.05
77	Todd Lyght	.05
78	Erric Pegram	.05
79	Kevin Greene	.05
80	Randal Hill	.05
81	Brett Perriman	.05
82	Mike Sherrard	.05
83	Curtis Conway	.05
84	Mark Tuinei	.05
85	Mark Seay	.05
86	Randy Baldwin	.05
87	Ricky Ervins	.05
88	Chester McGlockton	.05
89	*Tyrone Wheatley*	.50
90	Michael Barrow	.05
91	Kenneth Davis	.05
92	*Napoleon Kaufman*	2.00
93	Webster Slaughter	.05
94	Darren Woodson	.05
95	Pete Stoyanovich	.05
96	Jimmie Jones	.05
97	Craig Erickson	.05
98	*Michael Westbrook*	1.00
99	*Steve McNair*	2.50
100	Errict Rhett	.50
101	Devin Bush	.15
102	Dewayne Washington	.05
103	Bart Oates	.05
104	Aaron Pierce	.05
105	*Warren Sapp*	.50
106	Eric Green	.05
107	Glyn Milburn	.05
108	Johnny Johnson	.05
109	Marshall Faulk	.75
110	William Thomas	.05
111	George Koonce	.05
112	Dana Stubblefield	.05
113	Steve Tovar	.05
114	Steve Israel	.05
115	Brent Williams	.05
116	Shane Conlan	.05
117	Winston Moss	.05
118	Nate Newton	.05
119	Michael Irvin	.20
120	Jeff Lageman	.05
121	*Ki-Jana Carter*	2.00
122	Dan Marino	1.50
123	Tony Casillas	.05
124	*Kevin Carter*	.20
125	Warren Moon	.10
126	Byron Morris	.40
127	Ben Coates	.10
128	Michael Bankston	.05
129	Anthony Parker	.05
130	LeRoy Butler	.05
131	Tony Bennett	.05
132	Alvin Harper	.05
133	Tim Brown	.10
134	Tom Carter	.05
135	Lorenzo White	.05
136	Shane Dronett	.05
137	John Elliott	.05
138	Korey Stringer	.05
139	Jerry Rice	.50
140	*Sherman Williams*	.10
141	Kevin Turner	.05
142	Randall Cunningham	.10
143	Vinny Testaverde	.05
144	Tim Bowens	.05
145	Russell Maryland	.05
146	Chris Miller	.05
147	Vince Buck	.05
148	Willie Clay	.05
149	Jeff Graham	.05
150	Shannon Sharpe	.10
151	Carnell Lake	.05
152	*Mark Bruener*	.30
153	James Washington	.05
154	Pepper Johnson	.05
155	Bert Emanuel	.20
156	Mark Stepnoski	.05
157	Robert Jones	.05
158	Cris Dishman	.05
159	Henry Jones	.05
160	Henry Thomas	.05
161	John L. Williams	.05
162	Joe Cain	.05
163	Mike Johnson	.05
164	Merton Hanks	.05
165	Deion Sanders	.35
166	William Floyd	.25
167	Leroy Thompson	.05
168	Ray Childress	.05
169	Donnell Woolford	.05
170	Tony Siragusa	.05
171	Chad Brown	.05
172	Stanley Richard	.05
173	*Rob Johnson*	2.00
174	Derrick Brooks	.10
175	Drew Bledsoe	.75
176	Maurice Hurst	.05
177	Ricky Watters	.10
178	Myron Guyton	.05
179	Ricky Proehl	.05
180	Haywood Jeffires	.05
181	Michael Strahan	.05
182	Charles Wilson	.05
183	Mark Carrier	.05
184	*James Stewart*	1.25
185	Andy Harmon	.05
186	Ronnie Lott	.05
187	Clay Matthews	.05
188	John Carney	.05
189	Andre Rison	.10
190	Aeneas Williams	.05
191	Alexander Wright	.05
192	Desmond Howard	.05
193	Herman Moore	.10
194	Alfred Williams	.05
195	Tyrone Poole	.10
196	Darren Mickell	.05
197	Steve Young	.50
198	Roman Phifer	.05
199	Darrell Green	.05
200	Terry Wooden	.05
201	Chris Calloway	.05
202	Lewis Tillman	.05
203	Cris Carter	.10
204	Jim Everett	.05
205	Adrian Murrell	.05
206	Barry Sanders	1.25
207	Mario Bates	.25
208	Shawn Lee	.05
209	Charles Mincy	.05
210	*Kerry Collins*	2.00
211	Steve Walsh	.05
212	Chris Chandler	.05
213	Bennie Blades	.05
214	Kevin Williams	.05
215	Jim Kelly	.10
216	Marion Butts	.05
217	Jay Novacek	.05
218	Shawn Jefferson	.05
219	O.J. McDuffie	.05
220	Ray Seals	.05
221	Arthur Marshall	.05
222	Karl Mecklenburg	.05
223	Terance Mathis	.05
224	David Klinger	.05
225	Rod Woodson	.05
226	Quentin Coryatt	.05
227	Leroy Hoard	.05
228	Brian Blades	.05
229	Rob Moore	.05
230	Boomer Esiason	.05
231	Dave Krieg	.05
232	Sterling Sharpe	.10
233	Marcus Allen	.10
234	John Randle	.05
235	Craig Powell	.05
236	John Elway	.25
237	Mark Ingram	.05
238	Cortez Kennedy	.05
239	Brent Jones	.05
240	Ken Harvey	.05
241	Keenan McCardell	.05
242	Dan Wilkinson	.05
243	Don Beebe	.05
244	Jack Del Rio	.05
245	Byron Evans	.05
246	Ron Moore	.05
247	Edgar Bennett	.05
248	William Fuller	.05
249	James Williams	.05
250	Neil Smith	.05
251	Sam Mills	.05
252	Willie McGinest	.05
253	Howard Cross	.05
254	Troy Aikman	.60
255	Herschel Walker	.05
256	Dale Carter	.05
257	Sean Dawkins	.15
258	Greg Hill	.25
259	Stan Humphries	.10
260	Erik Kramer	.05
261	Leslie O'Neal	.05
262	Trezelle Jenkins	.10
263	Antonio Langham	.05
264	Bryce Paup	.05
265	Jake Reed	.05
266	Richmond Webb	.05
267	Eric Davis	.05
268	Mark McMillian	.05
269	*John Walsh*	.25
270	Irving Fryar	.05
271	Raghib Ismail	.05
272	Phil Hansen	.05
273	*J.J. Stokes*	1.00
274	*Craig Newsome*	.10
275	Leonard Russell	.05
276	Derrick Deese	.05
277	Broderick Thomas	.05
278	Bobby Houston	.05
279	Lamar Lathon	.05
280	Eugene Robinson	.05
281	Dan Saleaumua	.05
282	*Kyle Brady*	.10
283	John Taylor	.05
284	*Tony Boselli*	.10
285	Seth Joyner	.05
286	Steve Beuerlein	.05
287	Sam Adams	.05
288	Frank Reich	.05
289	Patrick Hunter	.05
290	Sean Gilbert	.05
291	Dermontti Dawson	.05
292	Shaun Gayle	.05
293	Vincent Brown	.05
294	Terry Kirby	.05
295	Courtney Hawkins	.05
296	Carl Pickens	.05
297	Luther Elliss	.10
298	Steve Atwater	.05
299	James Francis	.05
300	Rob Burnett	.05
301	Keith Hamilton	.05
302	Rob Fredrickson	.05
303	Jerome Bettis	.30
304	Emmitt Smith	1.50
305	Clyde Simmons	.05
306	Reggie White	.10
307	Rodney Hampton	.05
308	Steve Emtman	.05
309	*Hugh Douglas*	.10
310	Bernie Parmalee	.20
311	Trent Dilfer	.40
312	Willie Anderson	.05
313	Heath Shuler	.75
314	Rod Smith	.05
315	*Ray Zellars*	.10
316	Robert Brooks	.05
317	Lee Woodall	.05
318	Robert Porcher	.05
319	*Todd Collins*	.10
320	Willie Roaf	.05
321	Erik Williams	.05
322	Steve Wisniewski	.05
323	Derrick Alexander	.20
324	Frank Warren	.05
325	Kelvin Pritchett	.05
326	Dennis Gibson	.05
327	Jason Belser	.05
328	Vincent Brisby	.05
329	Calvin Williams	.05
330	Derek Brown	.05
331	Blake Brockermeyer	.05
332	Jeff Herrod	.05
333	Darryl Williams	.05
334	Aaron Glenn	.05
335	Eric Metcalf	.05
336	Billy Milner	.05
337	Terry McDaniel	.05
338	Trace Armstrong	.05
339	*Yancey Thigpen*	1.00
340	Jackie Harris	.05
341	Jeff George	.10
342	Darryl Talley	.05
343	Marcus Robertson	.05
344	Robert Massey	.05
345	Jessie Tuggle	.05
346	Scott Mitchell	.05
347	Harvey Williams	.05
348	*Jack Jackson*	.10
349	Brian Mitchell	.05
350	Lawrence Dawsey	.05
351	Erik Howard	.05
352	Quinn Early	.05
353	Terry Allen	.05
354	Simon Fletcher	.05
355	Eric Turner	.05
356	Natrone Means	.40
357	*Frank Sanders*	.20
358	Michael Timpson	.05
359	Michael Haynes	.05
360	Ruben Brown	.05
361	Troy Vincent	.05
362	Floyd Turner	.05
363	Larry Centers	.05
364	Eric Swann	.05
365	Albert Lewis	.05
366	Barry Foster	.05
367	Michael Dean Perry	.05
368	Jumpy Geathers	.05
369	*Kordell Stewart*	4.00
370	Chuck Smith	.05
371	Lake Dawson	.20
372	Terry Hoage	.05
373	Jeff Cross	.05
374	Tony McGee	.05
375	Eric Curry	.05
376	Harold Green	.05
377	Eric Hill	.05
378	Ray Buchanan	.05
379	Willie Davis	.05
380	*Chris Jones*	.20
381	Martin Mayhew	.05
382	Anthony Pleasant	.05
383	*Joey Galloway*	2.00
384	Anthony Morgan	.05
385	Harlon Barnett	.05
386	Bruce Smith	.05
387	Jeff Hostetler	.05
388	Randall McDaniel	.05
389	David Meggett	.05
390	Bill Romanowski	.05
391	Gary Brown	.05
392	Charles Johnson	.20
393	Chris Doleman	.05
394	Tony Martin	.05
395	Raymont Harris	.15
396	John Copeland	.05
397	Checklist #1 (Emmitt Smith)	.40
398	Checklist #2 (Steve Young)	.25
399	Checklist #3 (Marshall Faulk)	.40
400	Checklist #4 (Ki-Jana Carter)	.40

1995 Pro Line Printer's Proofs

Packaged two per hobby box, this set is a parallel to the base set. "Printer's Proof" is printed near the bottom of the card front. Overall, 400 of each card were printed.

	MT
Complete Set (400):	700.00
Common Player:	1.25
Veteran Stars:	10x-20x
Young Stars:	10x-18x
RCs:	5x-10x

1995 Pro Line Printer's Proof Silver

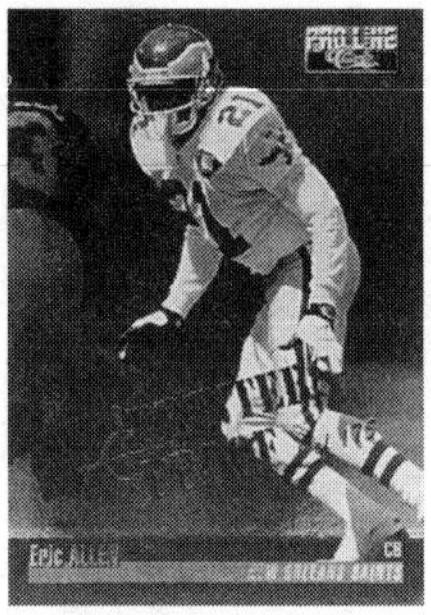

Randomly seeded one per hobby box, this set is a parallel to the 400-card base set. "Printer's Proof" is printed on the front over silver foil. Overall, 175 of each card were produced.

	MT
Complete Set (400):	1300.
Common Player:	2.50
Semistars	4.00
Veteran Stars:	25x-50x
Young Stars:	20x-35x
RCs:	15x-30x

1995 Pro Line Silver

Randomly seeded one per hobby and retail pack, this is a 400-card parallel to the base set. A silver-foil background is the distinguishing feature of this set.

	MT
Complete Set (400):	80.00
Common Player:	.20
Veteran Stars:	2x-4x
Young Stars:	1.5x-3x
RCs:	2x

1995 Pro Line Autographs

Randomly seeded one per box, the 128-card set was signed by NFL players, who signed less than 2,500 cards each. The card fronts have the identical design to the base cards, while the backs offer congratulations to the card holder for picking up an autographed card.

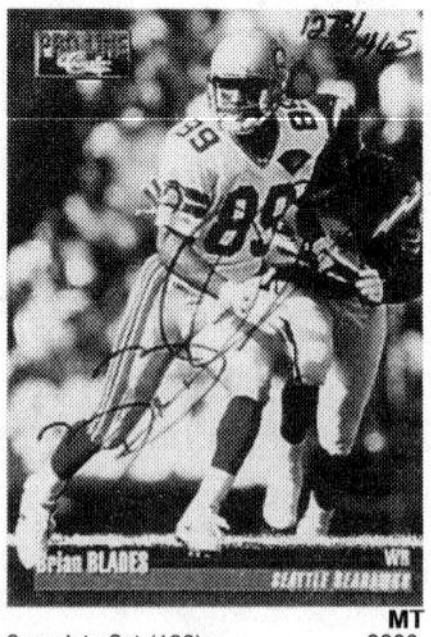

		MT
Complete Set (128):		2200.
Common Player:		10.00
1	Garrison Hearst (1460)	25.00
2	Anthony Miller (2385)	12.00
5	Mike Fox (1445)	10.00
6	Jeff Blake (1200)	40.00
7	J.J. Birden (775)	12.00
9	Leon Lett (1550)	12.00
11	Andre Reed (1440)	12.00
13A	Craig Heyward (1200)	12.00
13B	Craig Heyward (265AP)	12.00
14	Henry Ellard (1440)	12.00
18	Eric Zeier (500)	30.00
21	Qadry Ismail (1170)	12.00
23	Ty Law (1460)	10.00
24	Mark Collins (1430)	10.00
29	Mike Mamula (1250)	10.00
34	Michael Jackson (1200)	12.00
40A	Cornelius Bennett (1200)	12.00
40B	Cornelius Bennett (255AP)	12.00
42	Pierce Holt (1440)	10.00
44A	Chad May (1180)	12.00
44B	Chad May (2410AP)	12.00
45	Darrien Gordon (2400)	10.00
48	Al Smith (1360)	10.00
49A	Chris Slade (1100)	10.00
49B	Chris Slade (2417AP)	10.00
57	Charles Haley (1420)	12.00
59	Sean Jones (2385)	12.00
60	Tamarick Vanover (1155)	30.00
62	Rashaan Salaam (1320)	30.00
66	Troy Drayton (1375)	10.00
68A	Brian Williams (1175)	10.00
68B	Brian Williams (2670AP)	10.00
68C	Brian Williams (865AP)	10.00
70A	Eric Allen (1225)	10.00
70B	Eric Allen (2398AP)	10.00
70C	Eric Allen (745AP)	10.00
81A	Brett Perriman (1380)	12.00
81B	Brett Perriman (935)	12.00
82	Mike Sherrard (1450)	12.00
83	Curtis Conway (1200)	15.00
86A	Randy Baldwin (1435)	10.00
86B	Randy Baldwin (2405AP)	10.00
86C	Randy Baldwin (760AP)	10.00
88	Chester McGlockton (1280)	12.00
97A	Craig Erickson (630)	12.00
97B	Craig Erickson (890AP)	12.00
99	Steve McNair (3490)	40.00
100	Errict Rhett (1400)	45.00
106	Eric Green (1460)	12.00
109	Marshall Faulk (1030)	75.00
114A	Steve Israel (1200)	10.00
114B	Steve Israel (2413AP)	10.00
114C	Steve Israel (750AP)	10.00
119	Michael Irvin (1490)	15.00
126	Byron "Bam" Morris (1430)	12.00
127	Ben Coates (1175)	15.00
131	Tony Bennett (1475)	12.00
133	Tim Brown (2410)	15.00
137	John Elliott (2380)	10.00
140	Sherman Williams (1460)	12.00
142	Randall Cunningham (470)	30.00
143	Vinny Testaverde (1020)	12.00
145	Russell Maryland (1250)	12.00
149	Jeff Graham (1465)	12.00
155	Bert Emanuel (1445)	15.00
156	Mark Stepnoski (1500)	10.00
160	Henry Thomas (1420)	10.00
168A	Ray Childress (1200)	10.00
168B	Ray Childress (235AP)	10.00
173A	Rob Johnson (2815)	15.00
173B	Rob Johnson (500)	15.00
174	Derrick Brooks (1470)	12.00
175	Drew Bledsoe (515)	125.00
179	Ricky Proehl (1475)	10.00
180	Haywood Jeffires (1470)	12.00
185	Andy Harmon (1200)	10.00
186	Ronnie Lott (1900)	15.00
187	Clay Matthews (2385)	12.00
193	Herman Moore (2070)	20.00
197	Steve Young (500)	100.00
198	Roman Phifer (2395)	10.00
202	Lewis Tillman (1170)	12.00
207	Mario Bates (1480)	15.00
210	Kerry Collins (3300)	45.00
211A	Steve Walsh (1185)	12.00
211B	Steve Walsh (1015AP)	12.00
215	Jim Kelly (470)	40.00
217	Jay Novacek (1195)	12.00
218A	Shawn Jefferson (1200)	12.00
218B	Shawn Jefferson (240AP)	12.00
221A	Arthur Marshall (1165)	10.00
221B	Arthur Marshall (2400AP)	10.00
221C	Arthur Marshall (870AP)	10.00
226	Quentin Coryatt (1400)	12.00

228 Brian Blades (1465) 12.00
230 Boomer Esiason (1700) 12.00
231 Dave Krieg (1470) 12.00
234A John Randle (1170) 12.00
234B John Randle (2400AP) 12.00
234C John Randle (757AP) 12.00
238 Cortez Kennedy (1380) 12.00
241A Keenan McCardell (1235) 12.00
241B Keenan McCardell (2403AP) 12.00
243A Don Beebe (1200) 12.00
243B Don Beebe (275AP) 12.00
244A Jack Del Rio (1480) 10.00
244B Jack Del Rio (930AP) 10.00
247 Edgar Bennett (1475) 12.00
250 Neil Smith (1465) 12.00
251 Sam Mills (1470) 12.00
252A Willie McGinest (1160) 12.00
252B Willie McGinest (2407AP) 12.00
252C Willie McGinest (754AP) 12.00
254 Troy Aikman (500) 125.00
256 Dale Carter (1400) 12.00
258 Greg Hill (1455) 12.00
262 Trezelle Jenkins (1470) 10.00
263A Antonio Langham (1200) 10.00
263B Antonio Langham (1200) 10.00
265 Jake Reed (1470) 12.00
268A Mark McMillian (1175) 10.00
268B Mark McMillian (2400AP) 10.00
268C Mark McMillian (1175) 10.00
269 John Walsh (3340) 12.00
270 Irving Fryar (1500) 12.00
273 J.J. Stokes (1435) 35.00
276A Derrick Deese (1200) 10.00
276B Derrick Deese (2375AP) 10.00
276C Derrick Deese (735AP) 10.00
285 Seth Joyner (1480) 10.00
286 Steve Beuerlein (1465) 12.00
289 Patrick Hunter (2375) 10.00
292A Shaun Gayle 10.00
292B Shaun Gayle (265AP) 10.00
294 Terry Kirby (1450) 12.00
295 Courtney Hawkins (1445) 10.00
297 Luther Elliss (1470) 12.00
304 Emmitt Smith (500) 200.00
305 Clyde Simmons (735) 12.00
307 Rodney Hampton (1120) 15.00
308 Steve Emtman (2365) 10.00
311A Trent Dilfer (2010) 15.00
311B Trent Dilfer (306AP) 15.00
312 Flipper Anderson (1140) 12.00
313A Heath Shuler (2000) 25.00
313B Heath Shuler (366AP) 35.00
320A Willie Roaf (1200) 12.00
320B Willie Roaf (245AP) 12.00
329 Calvin Williams (1200) 12.00
331A Blake Brockermeyer (1445) 12.00
331B Blake Brockermeyer (2315AP) 12.00
337 Terry McDaniel (2340) 10.00
341 Jeff George (1295) 15.00
345A Jessie Tuggle (1200) 10.00
345B Jessie Tuggle (195AP) 10.00
348 Jack Jackson (1475) 12.00
352 Quinn Early (1200) 12.00
356 Natrone Means (1058) 15.00
359 Michael Haynes (1180) 12.00
361 Troy Vincent (1490) 10.00
366 Barry Foster (1455) 12.00
367A Michael Dean Perry (1200) 12.00
367B Michael Dean Perry (295AP) 12.00
374 Tony McGee (1385) 12.00
379 Willie Davis (1500) 12.00
383 Joey Galloway (1445) 45.00
390 Bill Romanowski (1450) 10.00

1995 Pro Line Bonus Card Jumbos

This complete set of 14 over-sized cards was issued in four series. Cards 1-3 were inserted in 1995 Classic NFL Rookies cases (one per hobby case); cards 4-8 were inserted in 1995 Classic Pro Line cases (one per case); cards 9-11 were inserted in 1995 Classic NFL Pro Line Series II cases (one per case); cards 13-15 were inserted in 1996 Classic NFL Experience (one per case). Cards are sequentially numbered up to 2,500 and measure 4-3/4" x 2-1/2". There was no #12 card made.

		MT
Complete Set (14):		175.00
Comp. Series 1 (3):		30.00
Comp. Series 2 (5):		70.00
Comp. Series 3 (3):		30.00
Comp. Series 4 (3):		45.00
Common Player:		6.00
1	Ki-Jana Carter	6.00
2	Steve McNair	12.00
3	Kerry Collins	15.00
4	Deion Sanders	10.00
5	Steve Young	15.00
6	Emmitt Smith	30.00
7	Natrone Means	6.00
8	Drew Bledsoe	14.00
9	Troy Aikman	14.00
10	Marshall Faulk	6.00
11	J.J. Stokes	6.00
13	Emmitt Smith	30.00
14	Rashaan Salaam	6.00

1995 Pro Line Field Generals

These 10 insert cards were randomly included one per every 60 packs of 1995 Classic NFL Pro Line Series II product. The acetate cards, featuring some of the NFL's leaders on the field, are sequentially numbered to 1,700. Card backs are numbered using a "G" prefix.

		MT
Complete Set (10):		300.00
Common Player:		15.00
1	Marshall Faulk	15.00
2	Emmitt Smith	50.00
3	Steve Young	20.00
4	Ki-Jana Carter	15.00
5	Rashaan Salaam	15.00
6	Dan Marino	50.00
7	J.J. Stokes	15.00
8	Drew Bledsoe	30.00
9	Brett Favre	50.00
10	Barry Sanders	30.00

1995 Pro Line Game of the Week

The 60-card interactive game set showcased two teams in a key game from the 1995 season. "H" or "V" prefixes are listed on the back and stand for home or visitor. A set of 30 NFL Pro Line silver-foil winning cards with the final score printed on the card was given to the first 1,000 collectors who redeemed 21-30 different game cards. In addition, 2,500 collectors who redeemed 10-20 winning game cards received a set of 30 Pro Line winning cards with the score stamped on them. Those who redeemed 30 winning cards were entered into a drawing for a Steve Young or Jerry Rice game-used jersey.

		MT
Complete Set (60):		25.00
Common Player:		.40
1	Barry Sanders, Reggie White	1.50
2	Jeff Hostetler, John Elway	.75
3	Michael Westbrook, Ricky Watters	.75
4	Jim Kelly, Mo Lewis	.60
5	Marshall Faulk, Jerome Bettis	1.00
6	Natrone Means, Bam Morris	.60
7	Seth Joyner, Michael Irvin	.60
8	Errict Rhett, Heath Shuler	1.00
9	Junior Seau, Randall Cunningham	.60
10	Drew Bledsoe, Steve Young	1.00
11	Dave Krieg, Kerry Collins	1.50
12	Steve Beuerlein, Alvin Harper	.40
13	Ben Coates, Troy Vincent	.60
14	Jerry Rice, Michael Irvin	1.50
15	Rodney Hampton, Cortez Kennedy	.60
16	Ray Childress, Leroy Hoard	.40
17	Thurman Thomas, Irving Fryar	.60
18	Andre Rison, Ki-Jana Carter	.75
19	Dan Marino, Boomer Esiason	2.00
20	Brett Favre, Warren Moon	2.00
21	Anthony Miller, Tim Brown	.40
22	Chris Warren, Steve Bono	.60
23	Shannon Sharpe, Neil Smith	.40
24	John Randle, Dana Stubblefield	.40
25	Jim Everett, Terance Mathis	.40
26	Troy Aikman, Mike Mamula	1.50
27	Trent Dilfer, Cris Carter	.60
28	Steve Walsh, Scott Mitchell	.40
29	Greg Lloyd, Vinny Testaverde	.60
30	Jeff George, Garrison Hearst	.60

1995 Pro Line Game Breakers

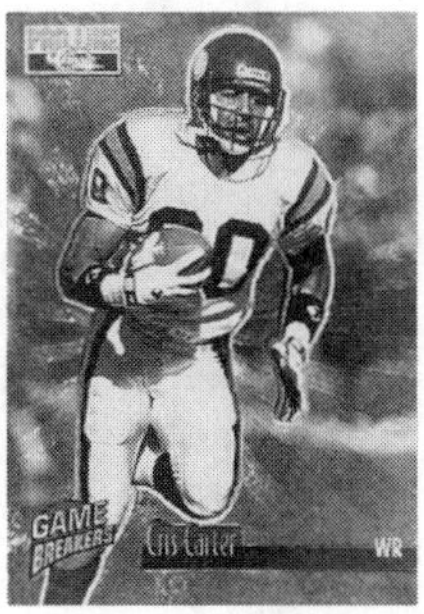

These 1995 Classic NFL Pro Line insert cards use an attention-grabbing micro-lined foil-board for the cards. The cards, featuring players who can break a game open at any moment, were randomly seeded one per box of the football product. Cards are numbered using a "GB" prefix. Printer's Proof cards were also made for these inserts.

		MT
Complete Set (30):		130.00
Common Player:		2.00
Minor Stars:		4.00
Comp. Prin. Proof Set (30):		800.00
Printer's Proofs:		4x-8x
1	Troy Aikman	10.00
2	Drew Bledsoe	10.00
3	Tim Brown	4.00
4	Cris Carter	4.00
5	Ki-Jana Carter	7.00
6	Kerry Collins	10.00
7	John Elway	8.00
8	Marshall Faulk	4.00
9	Brett Favre	20.00
10	Garrison Hearst	4.00
11	Michael Irvin	6.00
12	Jim Kelly	4.00
13	Dan Marino	20.00
14	Natrone Means	6.00
15	Eric Metcalf	2.00
16	J.J. Stokes	6.00
17	Carl Pickens	2.00
18	Jerry Rice	10.00
19	Andre Rison	4.00
20	Barry Sanders	10.00
21	Deion Sanders	6.00
22	Junior Seau	4.00
23	Emmitt Smith	20.00
24	Thurman Thomas	4.00
25	Ricky Watters	4.00
26	Reggie White	4.00
27	Rod Woodson	2.00
28	Steve Young	10.00
29	Rashaan Salaam	6.00
30	Michael Westbrook	5.00

1995 Pro Line Grand Gainers

The 30-card retail-only set has an action photo, with white mesh in the background on the top half of the card front, while the bottom half included the photo background. The player's name and position are printed in a box in the lower right, with the Grand Gainers' logo in the lower left. The backs include an action photo of the player, his name, position and write-up on the left. The player's yardage is printed inside a stripe on the right side of the card back, which are numbered with a "G" prefix.

		MT
Complete Set (30):		25.00
Common Player:		.40
1	Barry Sanders	2.00
2	Emmitt Smith	4.00
3	Natrone Means	.60
4	Marshall Faulk	1.00
5	Errict Rhett	1.00
6	Jerry Rice	2.00
7	Tim Brown	.60
8	Cris Carter	.60
9	Irving Fryar	.40
10	Ben Coates	.40
11	Fred Barnett	.40
12	Andre Rison	.40
13	Drew Bledsoe	2.00
14	Dan Marino	4.00
15	Warren Moon	.60
16	Steve Young	1.50
17	Brett Favre	4.00
18	John Elway	1.50
19	Randall Cunningham	.40
20	Stan Humphries	.60
21	Jim Kelly	.60
22	Ki-Jana Carter	1.00
23	Rodney Hampton	.60
24	Tyrone Wheatley	.60
25	J.J. Stokes	1.00
26	Michael Irvin	.40
27	Herman Moore	.75
28	Kerry Collins	2.50
29	Steve McNair	2.00
30	Rob Johnson	.60

1995 Pro Line Images Previews

This five-card preview of the 1995 Images series was inserted one per 18 packs of Series Two.

		MT
Complete Set (5):		25.00
Common Player:		3.00
1	Emmitt Smith	10.00
2	Steve Young	4.00
3	Drew Bledsoe	5.00
4	Kerry Collins	7.00
5	Marshall Faulk	3.00

1995 Pro Line Impact

These 30 exclusive cards of Impact NFL superstars are each sequentially numbered to only 4,500. The horizontal cards were seeded at a rate of one per every box of 1995 Classic Pro Line football product. A rarer version, Pro Line Golden Impact was also created. These cards, each sequentially numbered to 1,750, were seeded one per 90 packs.

		MT
Complete Set (30):		140.00
Common Player:		2.00
Minor Stars:		4.00
Comp. Golden Set (30):		375.00
Gold Cards:		2x-4x
1	Jim Kelly	4.00
2	Thurman Thomas	4.00
3	Troy Aikman	10.00
4	Michael Irvin	6.00
5	Emmitt Smith	18.00
6	John Elway	8.00
7	Barry Sanders	10.00
8	Brett Favre	18.00
9	Reggie White	4.00
10	Marshall Faulk	4.00
11	Ki-Jana Carter	4.00
12	Tim Brown	4.00
13	Jeff Hostetler	2.00
14	Dan Marino	18.00
15	Drew Bledsoe	15.00
16	Ben Coates	2.00
17	Rodney Hampton	2.00
18	Randall Cunningham	4.00
19	Ricky Watters	4.00
20	Bam Morris	6.00
21	Natrone Means	6.00
22	Junior Seau	4.00
23	Jerry Rice	10.00
24	Steve Young	10.00
25	William Floyd	6.00
26	Rick Mirer	6.00
27	Chris Warren	2.00
28	Jerome Bettis	6.00
29	Alvin Harper	4.00
30	Heath Shuler	6.00

1995 Pro Line MVP Redemption

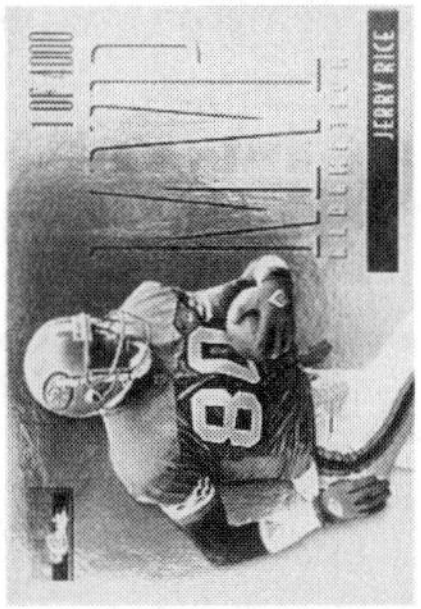

These 1995 Classic NFL Pro Line inserts feature foil-board cards of the top 34 candidates for the Associated Press' 1995 Offensive MVP Award, plus one field card. Cards which depicted the MVP winner were winners and were redeemable for one of the following prizes: winner cards stamped 1 of 4,000 were redeemable for a prepaid $50 phone card of the player; winner cards hand-numbered to 200 were redeemable for a $100 phone card of the player; the winner card hand-numbered "1/200" was redeemable for the $100 phone card and a complete 1995 Pro Line autographed set of more than 100 cards. The MVP Interactive cards were seeded an average of one per two boxes.

		MT
Complete Set (35):		200.00
Common Player:		3.00
1	Garrison Hearst	4.00
2	Terance Mathis	3.00
3	Jim Kelly	4.00
4	Thurman Thomas	4.00
5	Kerry Collins	10.00
6	Rashaan Salaam	5.00
7	Ki-Jana Carter	4.00
8	Andre Rison	3.00
9	Troy Aikman	12.00
10	Michael Irvin	3.00
11	Emmitt Smith	25.00
12	John Elway	10.00
13	Barry Sanders	15.00
14	Brett Favre	30.00
15	Marshall Faulk	3.00
16	Marcus Allen	3.00
17	Jeff Hostetler	3.00
18	Dan Marino	25.00
19	Cris Carter	3.00
20	Warren Moon	4.00
21	Drew Bledsoe	15.00
22	Ben Coates	3.00
23	Rodney Hampton	3.00
24	Boomer Esiason	3.00
25	Ricky Watters	4.00
26	Barry Foster	3.00
27	Natrone Means	4.00
28	Rick Mirer	4.00
29	Chris Warren	3.00
30	Jerry Rice	15.00
31	Steve Young	10.00
32	Jerome Bettis	5.00
33	Errict Rhett	6.00
34	Heath Shuler	5.00
35	Field Card	4.00

1995 Pro Line National Attention

Randomly seeded in Pro Line National boxes sold by dealers who had a booth at the National Convention in St. Louis, Mo., the 10-card set is numbered with a prefix of "NA".

		MT
Complete Set (10):		60.00
Common Player:		4.00
1	Jerome Bettis	6.00
2	Sean Gilbert	4.00
3	Chris Miller	4.00
4	Troy Aikman	15.00
5	Kevin Carter	4.00
6	Marshall Faulk	8.00
7	Drew Bledsoe	15.00
8	Shane Conlan	4.00
9	Emmitt Smith	25.00
10	Steve Young	10.00

1995 Pro Line Phone Cards $1

Phone cards were randomly inserted into 1995 Classic NFL Series II packs at a ratio of one per pack, and at least three $2 cards and a $5 card per box. Printer's Proof versions were also made of these $1 cards. They are stamped with a printer's proof logo and are numbered 1 of 699. The proof cards were seeded at a ratio of one per 44 packs.

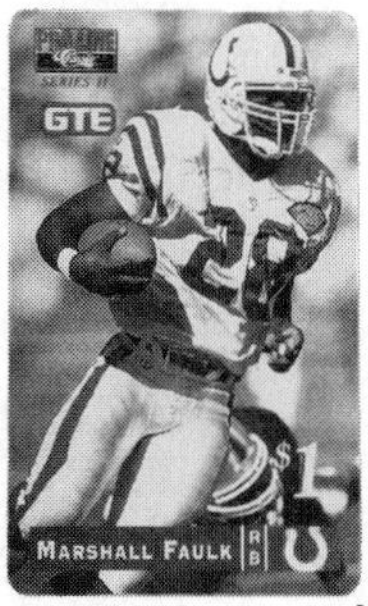

		MT
Complete Set (30):		40.00
Common Player:		1.50
Comp. Art. Proofs Set (30):		75.00
Artist Proofs Cards:		2x-4x
1	Kerry Collins	3.00
2	Barry Foster	1.50
3	Jeff Blake	2.00
4	Troy Aikman	2.00
5	Reggie White	1.50
6	Marshall Faulk	3.00
7	Steve Bono	1.50
8	Drew Bledsoe	3.00
9	Byron Morris	1.50
10	Rodney Hampton	1.50
11	Trent Dilfer	2.00
12	Errict Rhett	3.00
13	Heath Shuler	2.00
14	Mike Mamula	1.50
15	Ricky Watters	1.50
16	Stan Humphries	1.50
17	Natrone Means	2.00
18	William Floyd	2.00
19	Joey Galloway	2.00
20	Ki-Jana Carter	2.00
21	Andre Rison	1.50
22	Steve McNair	2.00
23	Napoleon Kaufman	1.50
24	Kyle Brady	1.50
25	Desmond Howard	1.50
26	Ben Coates	1.50
27	Eric Metcalf	1.50
28	Steve Beurlein	1.50
29	Deion Sanders	2.00
30	J.J. Stokes	2.00

1995 Pro Line Phone Cards $2

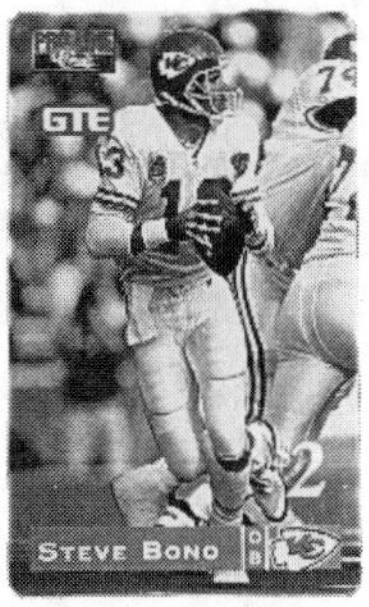

Phone cards were randomly inserted into 1995 Classic NFL Pro Line Series II packs at a ratio of one per pack, and at least three $2 cards and one $5 card in every box. Printer's proof versions were also made of these $2 cards. They are stamped with a printer's proof logo and are numbered 1 of 494. The proof cards are seeded at a ratio of one per 75 packs.

		MT
Complete Set (25):		90.00
Common Player:		2.50
Comp. Art. Proofs Set (25):		175.00
Artist Proofs Cards:		2x-4x
1	Troy Aikman	6.00
2	Marshall Faulk	4.00
3	Drew Bledsoe	3.00
4	Byron Morris	2.50
5	Rodney Hampton	2.50
6	Errict Rhett	3.00
7	Heath Shuler	3.00
8	Mike Mamula	2.50
9	Ricky Watters	2.50
10	Stan Humphries	2.50
11	Natrone Means	3.00
12	William Floyd	2.00
13	Kerry Collins	3.00
14	Barry Foster	2.50
15	Ki-Jana Carter	3.00
16	Andre Rison	2.50
17	Steve McNair	3.00
18	Kyle Brady	2.50
19	Deion Sanders	5.00
20	J.J. Stokes	5.00
21	Jeff Blake	5.00
22	Eric Metcalf	2.50
23	Steve Beuerlein	2.50
24	Eric Green	2.50
25	Steve Bono	2.50

1995 Pro Line Phone Cards $5

Phone cards were randomly inserted into 1995 Classic NFL Pro Line Series II packs at a ratio of one per pack, and at least three $2 cards and a $5 card in every box. Printer's proof versions were also made of these $5 cards. They are stamped with a printer's proof logo and are numbered 1 of 297. The proof cards were seeded at a ratio of one per 210 packs.

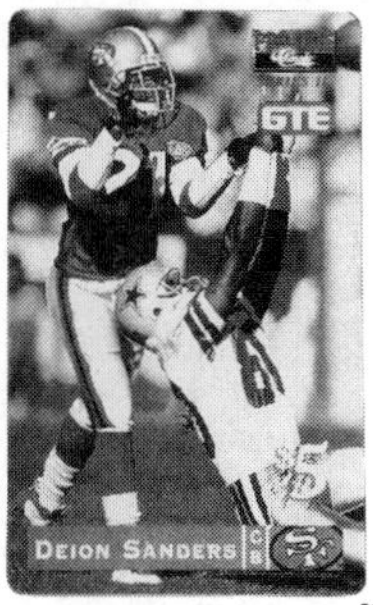

		MT
Complete Set (15):		100.00
Common Player:		7.00
1	Marshall Faulk	18.00
2	Troy Aikman	12.00
3	Drew Bledsoe	17.00
4	Deion Sanders	10.00
5	Kerry Collins	14.00
6	Steve McNair	12.00
7	Kyle Brady	7.00
8	J.J. Stokes	10.00
9	Ki-Jana Carter	12.00
10	Emmitt Smith	20.00
11	William Floyd	10.00
12	Ricky Watters	7.00
13	Reggie White	7.00
14	Warren Sapp	7.00
15	Steve Young	12.00

1995 Pro Line Phone Cards $20

Phone cards were randomly inserted into 1995 Classic NFL Pro Line Series II packs at a ratio of one per pack, and at least three $2 cards and a $5 card in every box. The higher denominations were seeded at scarcer rates.

		MT
Complete Set (5):		125.00
Common Player:		30.00
1	Steve Young	30.00
2	Drew Bledsoe	30.00
3	Marshall Faulk	40.00
4	Ki-Jana Carter	30.00
5	Kerry Collins	30.00

1995 Pro Line Phone Cards $100

One phone card is seeded in each pack of 1995 Classic Pro Line Series II packs; at least three $2 cards and a $5 card are in every box. These $100 phone cards, featuring four NFL stars and a promising rookie, were fairly scarce.

		MT
Complete Set (5):		600.00
Common Player:		100.00
1	Emmitt Smith	200.00
2	Steve Young	150.00
3	Drew Bledsoe	100.00
4	Ki-Jana Carter	100.00
5	Troy Aikman	150.00

1995 Pro Line Phone Cards $1,000

Phone cards were randomly inserted into 1995 Classic NFL Pro Line Series II packs, one per every pack, and at least three $2 cards and one $5 card in every box. The higher the denomination, the more exclusive the number made.

		MT
Complete Set (4):		5000.
Common Player:		900.00
1	Steve Young	1250.
2	Drew Bledsoe	900.00
3	Ki-Jana Carter	900.00
4	Troy Aikman	1400.

1995 Pro Line Phone Cards $1,500

Dallas Cowboys' star running back Emmitt Smith is featured on this 1995 Classic NFL Pro Line Series II phone card insert. This card is the scarcest of the phone card inserts.

		MT
Complete Set (1):		2000.
Common Player:		2000.
1	Emmitt Smith	2000.

1995 Pro Line Pogs

The 30-card retail-only set included an action photo on the front, with two Pogs punched out on the card. The backs have the player's name and stats. The cards carry a "C" prefix.

		MT
Complete Set (30):		8.00
Common Player:		.25

1	Steve Walsh, Rashaan Salaam	.35
2	Kerry Collins, Barry Foster	.75
3	Jim Kelly, Thurman Thomas	.35
4	Terance Mathis, Jeff George	.25
5	Garrison Hearst, Seth Joyner	.25
6	Barry Sanders, Herman Moore	.75
7	John Elway, Shannon Sharpe	.50
8	Troy Aikman, Emmitt Smith	1.50
9	Leroy Hoard, Andre Rison	.25
10	Jeff Blake, Ki-Jana Carter	.50
11	Marcus Allen, Steve Bono	.35
12	Tony Boselli, Steve Beuerlein	.25
13	Marshall Faulk, Quentin Coryatt	.35
14	Steve McNair, Gary Brown	.35
15	Brett Favre, Reggie White	1.50
16	Jim Everett, Michael Bates	.35
17	Drew Bledsoe, Ben Coates	.75
18	Warren Moon, Cris Carter	.35
19	Dan Marino, Irving Fryar	1.50
20	Jeff Hostetler, Tim Brown	.35
21	Kevin Greene, Bam Morris	.35
22	Derek Brown, Rodney Hampton	.25
23	Boomer Esiason, Mo Lewis	.25
24	Randall Cunningham, Ricky Watters	.25
25	Natrone Means, Junior Seau	.25
26	Heath Shuler, Michael Westbrook	.35
27	Trent Dilfer, Errict Rhett	.35
28	Jerome Bettis, Ki-Jana Carter	.35
29	Steve Young, Jerry Rice	1.00
30	Rick Mirer, Chris Warren	.35

1995 Pro Line Precision Cuts

These 20 die-cut cards feature NFL superstars on silver foil board. The cards were exclusive inserts in 1995 Classic Pro Line Series II cases, one per 45 packs. The cards are sequentially numbered up to 1,250.

		MT
Complete Set (20):		375.00
Common Player:		7.00
1	Jim Kelly	9.00
2	John Elway	14.00
3	Kerry Collins	25.00
4	Ki-Jana Carter	7.00
5	Andre Rison	7.00
6	Troy Aikman	25.00
7	Emmitt Smith	50.00
8	Barry Sanders	40.00
9	Warren Moon	9.00
10	Jeff Hostetler	7.00
11	Dan Marino	50.00
12	Drew Bledsoe	35.00
13	Rodney Hampton	7.00
14	Ricky Watters	9.00
15	Byron Morris	7.00
16	Natrone Means	7.00
17	Steve Young	25.00
18	Jerry Rice	25.00
19	J.J. Stokes	18.00
20	Errict Rhett	7.00

1995 Pro Line Pro Bowl

The 30-card set was seeded one per box in $1.99 retail packs. The ticket-shaped die-cut fronts have an action photo of the player on a silver-foil background. Every card showcases the number "250392" on the top and bottom. The card backs, numbered with a "PB" prefix, have another action shot, with the player's name, position and write-up included.

		MT
Complete Set (30):		50.00
Common Player:		1.00
1	Seth Joyner	1.00
2	Andre Reed	1.00
3	Bruce Smith	1.50
4	Michael Irvin	1.50
5	Troy Aikman	3.00
6	Emmitt Smith	6.00
7	Charles Haley	1.00
8	Shannon Sharpe	1.00
9	John Elway	2.00
10	Barry Sanders	3.00
11	Reggie White	1.25
12	Marshall Faulk	2.00
13	Tim Brown	1.25
14	Chester McGlockton	1.00
15	Dan Marino	6.00
16	Cris Carter	1.25
17	Warren Moon	1.25
18	Ben Coates	1.25
19	Drew Bledsoe	2.50
20	Rod Woodson	1.25
21	Natrone Means	1.25
22	Leslie O'Neal	1.25
23	Junior Seau	1.25
24	Jerry Rice	3.00
25	Chris Warren	1.25
26	Brent Jones	1.00
27	Steve Young	2.50
28	Dana Stubblefield	1.00
29	Deion Sanders	2.00
30	Jerome Bettis	1.25

1995 Pro Line Record Breakers

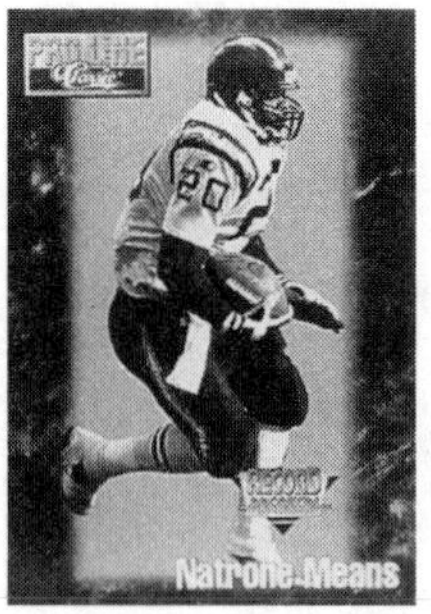

These Record Breaker acetate cards were exclusive inserts in 1995 Classic NFL Pro Line Hot Boxes. Each pack in a Hot Box contains 40 percent inserts. Hot Boxes were randomly inserted one per 10 cases of 1995 Classic NFL Pro Line cases. Cards 1-5 were hobby inserts; 6-10 were retail inserts. They carried a "RB" prefix. Cards were sequentially numbered up to 350.

		MT
Complete Set (10):		500.00
Common Player:		20.00
1	Drew Bledsoe	75.00
2	Cris Carter	20.00
3	Jerry Rice	75.00
4	Steve Young	75.00
5	Marshall Faulk	40.00
6	Emmitt Smith	125.00
7	Barry Sanders	75.00
8	Natrone Means	20.00
9	Ben Coates	20.00
10	Bruce Smith	20.00

1995 Pro Line Series II

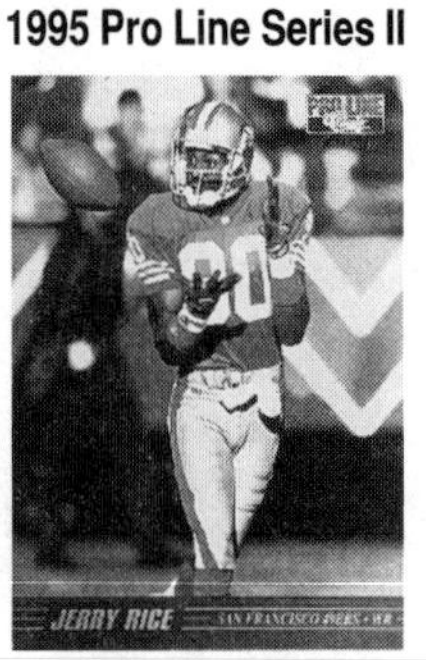

Classic's 1995 NFL Pro Line Series II contains 75 cards, including the NFL's top stars, most promising rookies and traded veterans in their new uniforms. The basic format for the cards is similar to the Series I cards, but the cards can be distinguished because they say Series II on the front. Exclusive to hobby cases is a 75-card parallel set of Printer's Proofs cards, which feature holographic foil-stamped logos. These cards are seeded one per 18 packs in hobby cases. Phone cards have a dominant presence in Series II, with denominations of $1, $2, $5, $20, $100 and $1,000. One phone card appears in each pack and at least three $2 cards and one $5 phone card are in a box. Printer's Proof versions of the $1 (one per 44 packs), $2 (one per 75) and $5 (one per 210) also exist. The $1 phone cards are stamped with the printer's proof logo and are numbered 1 of 699. The $2 cards are also stamped with the logo and are numbered 1 of 494, while the $5 cards are stamped and numbered 1 of 297. Other inserts include Precision Cut, NFL Images Preview cards, Field Generals, and a continuation of Classic's oversized bonus cards program. These micro-lined cards are numbered 9-11 in the bonus series and are sequentially numbered to 1,250. One oversized bonus card is packed in every case of 1995 Pro Line Series II product.

		MT
Complete Set (75):		15.00
Common Player:		.05
Minor Stars:		.10
Comp. Prin. Proof Set (75):		250.00
Printers Proof Cards:		8x-16x
1	Jim Kelly	.10
2	Steve Walsh	.05
3	Jeff Blake	1.00
4	Vinny Testaverde	.05
5	Jeff Hostetler	.05
6	Dan Marino	1.50
7	Cris Carter	.10
8	Drew Bledsoe	1.00
9	Jim Everett	.05
10	Neil O'Donnell	.05
11	Rodney Hampton	.05
12	Troy Aikman	.75
13	John Elway	.50
14	Barry Sanders	1.25
15	Reggie White	.10
16	Marshall Faulk	.50
17	Marcus Allen	.10
18	James Stewart	.10
19	Randall Cunningham	.10
20	Natrone Means	.50
21	Rick Mirer	.40
22	Jerry Rice	.75
23	Errict Rhett	.50
24	Heath Shuler	.50
25	Jerome Bettis	.25
26	Garrison Hearst	.10
27	Jeff George	.10
28	Andre Reed	.05
29	Warren Moon	.10
30	Ben Coates	.05
31	Mario Bates	.20
32	Byron Morris	.40
33	Dave Brown	.05
34	Emmitt Smith	1.50
35	Anthony Miller	.05
36	Herman Moore	.10
37	Brett Favre	1.50
38	Steve Bono	.20
39	Stan Humphries	.05
40	Steve Young	.75
41	Trent Dilfer	.30
42	Chris Miller	.05
43	Herschel Walker	.05
44	Michael Irvin	.20
45	Junior Seau	.10
46	Deion Sanders	.40
47	William Floyd	.30
48	Ki-Jana Carter	.75
49	Kerry Collins	1.00
50	Steve McNair	1.00
51	Tony Boselli	.10
52	Kyle Brady	.10
53	Mike Mamula	.05
54	Warren Sapp	.10
55	J.J. Stokes	.75
56	Joey Galloway	1.00
57	Hugh Douglas	.05
58	Michael Westbrook	.50
59	Napoleon Kaufman	.50
60	Rashaan Salaam	1.00
61	Tyrone Wheatley	.50
62	*Terrell Fletcher*	.50
63	Eric Metcalf	.05
64	Kevin Carter	.05
65	Andre Rison	.05
66	Eric Green	.05
67	Dave Meggett	.05
68	Ricky Watters	.10
69	Steve Beuerlein	.05
70	Craig Erickson	.05
71	Michael Dean Perry	.05
72	Alvin Harper	.05
73	Rob Moore	.05
74	Frank Reich	.05
75	Checklist	.05

1995 Pro Line Series II Printer's Proofs

The 75-card set is a parallel to the Series II cards. Seeded one per 18 packs, the cards have a printer's proof logo on the front.

	MT
Complete Set (75):	300.00
Common Player:	1.50
PP Veteran Stars:	10x-18x
PP Young Stars:	7.5x-15x
PP RCs:	5x-10x

1996 Pro Line

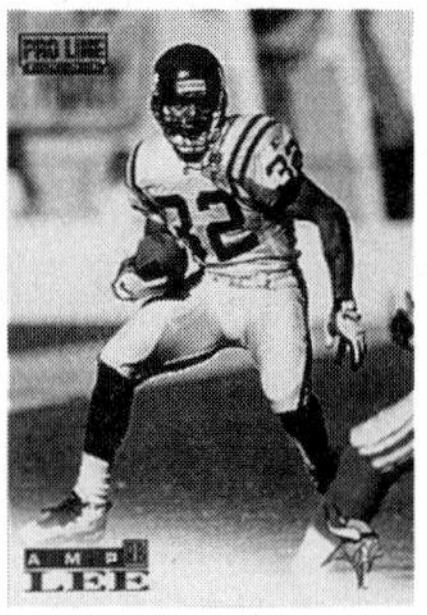

Pro Line's 1996 football offers one autographed card in every box and cards of newly-signed free agents and rookies. Each regular card front has a full-bleed color action photo on it, with the Pro Line logo at the top. The player's name and position are in the lower left corner, opposite his team's logo. The card back has a color photo on the right, flanked by a recap of some of the player's accomplishments. The player's name, position and card number are at the top; a team logo, biographical information and statistics are along the bottom. The autographed cards of players are available in blue and gold foil-stamped versions, with gold ones limited to a maximum of 250 cards. One autographed card is seeded in every 25th pack. Five cards are jointly autographed by a quarterback/wide receiver combination. Other inserts include Cels, Cover Story, Rivalries and Touchdown Performers.

		MT
Complete Set (350):		25.00
Common Player:		.05
Minor Stars:		.10
Complete PP Set (350):		500.00
Printer's Proof Cards:		10x-20x
Pack (10):		1.75
Wax Box (36):		50.00
1	Troy Aikman	1.00
2	Steve Young	1.00
3	John Elway	.50
4	Jim Kelly	.10
5	Dan Marino	2.00
6	Brett Favre	2.00
7	Kerry Collins	1.25
8	Jeff Blake	.50
9	Stan Humphries	.05
10	Steve Bono	.05
11	Jeff George	.10
12	Mark Brunell	.75
13	Scott Mitchell	.05
14	Steve McNair	1.00
15	Jeff Hostetler	.05
16	Jim Everett	.05
17	Rick Mirer	.05
18	Boomer Esiason	.05
19	Neil O'Donnell	.05
20	Dave Brown	.05
21	Erik Kramer	.05
22	Trent Dilfer	.05
23	Jim Harbaugh	.05
24	Vinny Testaverde	.05
25	Thurman Thomas	.10
26	Rodney Peete	.05
27	Gus Frerotte	.05
28	Warren Moon	.05
29	Eric Zeier	.05
30	Randall Cunningham	.05
31	Heath Shuler	.40
32	John Friesz	.05
33	Tommy Maddox	.05
34	Glenn Foley	.05
35	Drew Bledsoe	.75
36	Kordell Stewart	1.25
37	Natrone Means	.15
38	Errict Rhett	.30
39	Rashaan Salaam	.30
40	Emmitt Smith	2.00
41	Larry Centers	.05
42	Terrell Davis	1.00
43	Marshall Faulk	.50
44	Rodney Hampton	.05
45	Byron Morris	.05
46	Chris Warren	.15
47	Curtis Martin	2.00
48	Ricky Watters	.05
49	Marcus Allen	.05
50	Barry Sanders	1.25
51	Edgar Bennett	.05
52	Adrian Murrell	.05
53	James Stewart	.05
54	Leroy Hoard	.05
55	Jerome Bettis	.05
56	Craig Heyward	.05
57	Harvey Williams	.05
58	Bernie Parmalee	.05
59	Garrison Hearst	.05
60	Terry Allen	.05
61	Charlie Garner	.05
62	Dorsey Levens	.10
63	Derek Loville	.05
64	Greg Hill	.05
65	Derrick Moore	.05
66	Rodney Thomas	.40
67	Daryl Johnston	.05
68	Mario Bates	.05
69	*Aaron Hayden*	.10
70	Napoleon Kaufman	.05
71	Terry Kirby	.05
72	Glyn Milburn	.05
73	Robert Smith	.05
74	Ki-Jana Carter	.40
75	Tyrone Wheatley	.05
76	Erric Pegram	.05
77	Brian Mitchell	.05
78	Vaughn Dunbar	.05
79	Dave Meggett	.05
80	Scottie Graham	.05
81	Darick Holmes	.05
82	Marion Butts	.05
83	Harold Green	.05
84	Zack Crockett	.05
85	Amp Lee	.05
86	Lamont Warren	.05
87	Mark Chmura	.25
88	Irving Fryar	.05
89	Tim Brown	.05
90	Michael Irvin	.05
91	Tony Martin	.05
92	Alvin Harper	.05
93	Darnay Scott	.05
94	Eric Metcalf	.05
95	Michael Timpson	.05
96	Sean Dawkins	.05
97	Qadry Ismail	.05
98	Yancey Thigpen	.50
99	Joey Galloway	1.00
100	Herman Moore	.25
101	J.J. Stokes	.10
102	Wayne Chrebet	.05
103	Ernest Givins	.05
104	Michael Jackson	.05
105	Henry Ellard	.05
106	Thomas Lewis	.05
107	Anthony Miller	.05
108	Terance Mathis	.05
109	Horace Copeland	.05
110	Raghib Ismail	.05
111	Quinn Early	.05
112	Haywood Jeffires	.05
113	Mark Carrier	.05
114	Brent Jones	.05
115	Ben Coates	.05
116	Ken Dilger	.05
117	Irv Smith	.05
118	Jay Novacek	.05
119	Tony McGee	.05
120	Troy Drayton	.05
121	Johnny Mitchell	.05
122	Rob Moore	.05
123	Kevin Williams	.05
124	O.J. McDuffie	.05
125	Carl Pickens	.10
126	Curtis Conway	.05
127	Ed McCaffery	.05
128	Arthur Marshall	.05
129	Ernie Mills	.05
130	Cris Carter	.05
131	Isaac Bruce	.50
132	Brian Blades	.05
133	Michael Westbrook	.10
134	Andre Reed	.05
135	Andre Rison	.05
136	Brett Perriman	.05
137	Willie Jackson	.05
138	Ryan Yarborough	.05
139	Chris T. Jones	.05
140	Jerry Rice	1.00
141	Lake Dawson	.05
142	Robert Brooks	.05
143	Vincent Brisby	.05
144	Desmond Howard	.05
145	Johnnie Morton	.05
146	Steve Tasker	.05
147	Ty Detmer	.05
148	Todd Kinchen	.05
149	Mike Sherrard	.05
150	Eric Green	.05
151	Mark Bruener	.05
152	Kyle Brady	.05
153	Frank Sanders	.05
154	Willie Green	.05
155	Jeff Graham	.05
156	Bert Emanuel	.05
157	Courtney Hawkins	.05
158	Mark Seay	.05
159	Chris Calloway	.05
160	John Taylor	.05
161	Fred Barnett	.05
162	Tamarick Vanover	.60
163	Keenan McCardell	.05
164	Bill Brooks	.05
165	Alexander Wright	.05
166	Jake Reed	.05
167	Floyd Turner	.05
168	Mike Pritchard	.05
169	Lawrence Dawsey	.05
170	Shawn Jefferson	.05
171	Michael Haynes	.05
172	Shannon Sharpe	.05
173	Jackie Harris	.05
174	Daryl Hobbs	.05
175	Chris Sanders	.25
176	Willie Davis	.05
177	Marco Coleman	.05
178	Pat Swilling	.05
179	Alonzo Spellman	.05
180	Simon Fletcher	.05
181	Sean Gilbert	.05
182	Tracy Scroggins	.05
183	Hugh Douglas	.05
184	Eric Swann	.05
185	Russell Maryland	.05
186	Warren Sapp	.05
187	Jim Flanigan	.05
188	Cortez Kennedy	.05
189	Andy Harmon	.05
190	Dan Saleaumua	.05
191	Kelvin Pritchett	.05
192	John Randle	.05
193	Dan Wilkinson	.05
194	Chester McGlockton	.05
195	Leon Lett	.05
196	Neil Smith	.05
197	Mike Mamula	.05
198	Mike Jones	.05
199	Reggie White	.05
200	Anthony Pleasant	.05
201	Phil Hansen	.05
202	Ray Seals	.05
203	Tony Bennett	.05
204	Leslie O'Neal	.05
205	Jeff Cross	.05
206	Anthony Cook	.05
207	Clyde Simmons	.05
208	Renaldo Turnbull	.05
209	Charles Haley	.05
210	John Copeland	.05
211	John Thierry	.05
212	Michael Strahan	.05
213	Jeff Lageman	.05
214	William Fuller	.05
215	Rickey Jackson	.05
216	Wayne Martin	.05
217	Steve Emtman	.05
218	Shawn Lee	.05
219	Chris Zorich	.05
220	Henry Thomas	.05
221	Dana Stubblefield	.05
222	D'Marco Farr	.05
223	Pierce Holt	.05
224	Sean Jones	.05
225	Robert Porcher	.05
226	Kevin Carter	.05
227	Chris Doleman	.05
228	Tony Tolbert	.05
229	Bruce Smith	.05
230	Marvin Washington	.05
231	Blaine Bishop	.05
232	Bryant Young	.05
233	Rob Burnett	.05
234	*Lawrence Phillips*	.50
235	Trev Alberts	.05
236	Eric Curry	.05
237	Anthony Smith	.05
238	Sam Mills	.05
239	Seth Joyner	.05
240	Quentin Coryatt	.05
241	Levon Kirkland	.05
242	Cornelius Bennett	.05
243	Chris Spielman	.05
244	Mo Lewis	.05
245	Lee Woodall	.05
246	Derrick Thomas	.05
247	Willie McGinest	.05
248	Terry Wooden	.05
249	Greg Lloyd	.05
250	Jack Del Rio	.05
251	Hardy Nickerson	.05
252	Michael Barrow	.05
253	Lamar Lathon	.05
254	Bryan Cox	.05
255	Randy Kirk	.05
256	Jessie Tuggle	.05
257	Roman Phifer	.05
258	Ken Harvey	.05
259	Junior Seau	.05
260	Pepper Johnson	.05
261	Chris Slade	.05
262	Gary Plummer	.05
263	Wayne Simmons	.05
264	Bryce Paup	.05
265	William Thomas	.05
266	Kevin Greene	.05
267	*Bobby Engram*	1.00
268	Ken Norton	.05
269	Eric Hill	.05
270	Darion Conner	.05
271	Tyrone Poole	.05
272	Cris Dishman	.05
273	Marcus Jones	.05
274	Rod Woodson	.05
275	Mark McMillan	.05
276	Dale Carter	.05
277	Darrell Green	.05
278	Donnell Woolford	.05
279	Troy Vincent	.05
280	Larry Brown	.05
281	Aeneas Williams	.05
282	Eric Allen	.05
283	Ray Buchanan	.05
284	Ty Law	.05
285	Eric Davis	.05
286	Todd Lyght	.05
287	Terry McDaniel	.05
288	Darryl Lewis	.05
289	Deion Sanders	.50
290	Phillippi Sparks	.05
291	Bobby Taylor	.05
292	Mark Collins	.05
293	Steve Atwater	.05
294	Stanley Richard	.05
295	Stevon Moore	.05
296	Bennie Blades	.05
297	Tim McDonald	.05
298	Shaun Gayle	.05
299	Darren Woodson	.05
300	Mark Carrier	.05
301	Carnell Lake	.05
302	James Washington	.05
303	LeRoy Butler	.05
304	Henry Jones	.05
305	Darryl Williams	.05
306	Darren Perry	.05
307	Merton Hanks	.05
308	Orlando Thomas	.05
309	Eric Turner	.05
310	Nate Newton	.05
311	Steve Wisniewski	.05
312	Derrick Deese	.05
313	Larry Allen	.05
314	Aaron Taylor	.05
315	Blake Brockermeyer	.05
316	William Roaf	.05
317	John Elliott	.05
318	*Keyshawn Johnson*	2.00
319	*Karim Abdul-Jabbar*	1.00
320	*Kevin Hardy*	.30
321	Duane Clemons	.05
322	Jevon Langford	.05
323	*Mike Alstott*	1.50
324	Scott Greene	.05
325	*Derrick Mayes*	.75
326	Chris Doering	.05
327	*Amani Toomer*	.10
328	*Eric Moulds*	1.50
329	Alex Molden	.05
330	Lawyer Milloy	.05
331	Daryl Gardener	.05
332	Randall Godfrey	.05
333	Willie Anderson	.05
334	*Tony Banks*	.50
335	*Jeff Lewis*	.50
336	Roman Oben	.05
337	Andre Johnson	.05
338	Brian Roche	.05
339	Johnny McWilliams	.05
340	*Alex Van Dyke*	.10
341	Ray Mickens	.05
342	*Marvin Harrison*	2.00
343	*Terry Glenn*	1.75
344	*Tim Biakabutuka*	1.00
345	*Simeon Rice*	.30
346	Cedric Jones	.05
347	*Eddie George*	3.50
348	Checklist 1	.05
349	Checklist 2	.30
350	Checklist 3	.30

1996 Pro Line National

This 350-card parallel set was inserted 1:1 in 1996 Pro Line National packs. The card fronts feature the 1996 National logo printed in silver foil. Each card is numbered one of 499.

	MT
Complete Set (350):	400.00
Common Player:	.50
National Stars:	4x-8x
National RCs:	2x-4x

1996 Pro Line Printer's Proof

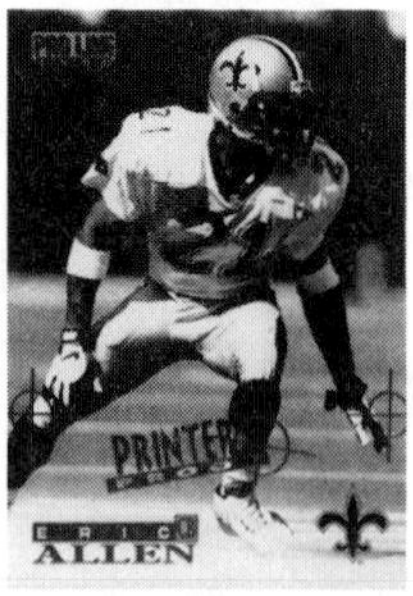

Inserted at a rate of one per 10 packs, this 350-card set parallels the regular-issue set. Printer's Proof cards are distinguished by a large red foil "Printer's Proof" stamp.

	MT
Complete Set (350):	500.00
Printer's Proof Cards:	10x-20x

1996 Pro Line Autographs

This 73-card insert features authentic player autographs printed in gold foil. The cards were inserted 1:170 in hobby and retail packs and 1:200 in jumbo packs. The cards in this insert are not numbered. Blue foil versions were inserted 1:25 hobby and retail and 1:90 jumbo.

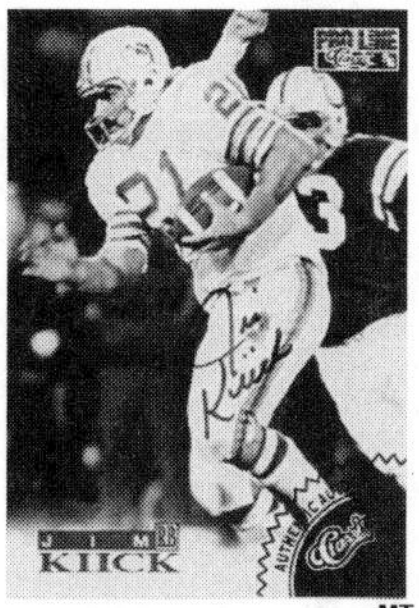

		MT
Complete Set (73):		2700.
Common Gold Foil:		20.00
Comp. Blue Set (68):		650.00
Common Blue Foil:		10.00
Blue Cards:		.5x
1	Troy Aikman, Emmitt Smith (Gold only)	500.00
2	Eric Allen	20.00
3	Mike Alstott	40.00
4	Tony Banks	40.00
5	Blaine Bishop	20.00
6	Drew Bledsoe	150.00
7	Tim Brown	25.00
8	Marion Butts	20.00
9	Sedric Clark	20.00
10	Duane Clemons	20.00
11	Marco Coleman	20.00
12	Eric Davis	20.00
13	Derrick Deese	20.00
14	Jack Del Rio	20.00
15	Ty Detmer	30.00
16	Chris Doering	20.00
17	Jumbo Elliott	20.00
18	Marshall Faulk	60.00
19	Glenn Foley	20.00
20	John Friesz	20.00
21	Daryl Gardener	20.00
22	Randall Godfrey	20.00
23	Scott Greene	20.00
24	Rhett Hall	20.00
25	Merton Hanks	20.00
26	Kevin Hardy	20.00
27	Richard Huntley	20.00
28	Michael Jackson	20.00
29	Ron Jaworski	25.00
30	Andre Johnson	20.00
31	Keyshawn Johnson	100.00
32	Keyshawn Johnson, Neil O'Donnell (Gold only)	175.00
33	Mike Jones	20.00
34	Jim Kick	20.00
35	Jeff Lewis	25.00
36	Tommy Maddox	20.00
37	Arthur Marshall	20.00
38	Russell Maryland	20.00
39	Derrick Mayes	40.00
40	Ed McCaffrey	20.00
41	Keenan McCardell	25.00
42	Terry McDaniel	20.00
43	Tim McDonald	20.00
44	Willie McGinest	20.00
45	Mark McMillian	20.00
46	Johnny McWilliams	20.00
47	Ray Mickens	20.00
48	Anthony Miller	20.00
49	Rick Mirer	20.00
50	Alex Molden	20.00
51	Johnnie Morton	25.00
52	Eric Moulds	30.00
53	Roman Oben	20.00
54	Neil O'Donnell (Gold only)	60.00
55	Leslie O'Neal	20.00
56	Roman Phifer	20.00
57	Gary Plummer	20.00
58	Jim Plunkett	20.00
59	Stanley Pritchett	20.00
60	John Randle	20.00
61	Brian Roche	20.00
62	Orpheus Roye	20.00
63	Mark Seay	20.00
64	Mike Sherrard	20.00
65	Chris Slade	20.00
66	Scott Slutzker	20.00
67	Emmitt Smith (Gold only)	350.00
68	Steve Taneyhill	20.00
69	Robb Thomas	20.00
70	William Thomas	20.00
71	Alex Van Dyke	20.00
72	Randy White	30.00
73	Steve Young (Gold only)	150.00

1996 Pro Line Cels

Each of thse 1996 Pinnacle inserts features a top NFL veteran or rookie on an acetate card and contains two foil stamps on it. The cards were seeded exclusively in hobby packs, one per 75 packs. They are numbered with a "C" prefix.

		MT
Complete Set (20):		350.00
Common Player:		6.00
1	Bryce Paup	6.00
2	Kerry Collins	30.00
3	Troy Aikman	35.00
4	Deion Sanders	20.00
5	Emmitt Smith	50.00
6	Steve McNair	20.00
7	Drew Bledsoe	30.00
8	Kordell Stewart	30.00
9	Ricky Watters	6.00
10	Jerry Rice	35.00
11	Steve Young	25.00
12	Errict Rhett	15.00
13	Brett Favre	50.00
14	Jeff Blake	20.00
15	Joey Galloway	25.00
16	Herman Moore	6.00
17	Curtis Martin	30.00
18	Keyshawn Johnson	20.00
19	Eddie George	25.00
20	Simeon Rice	6.00

1996 Pro Line Rivalries

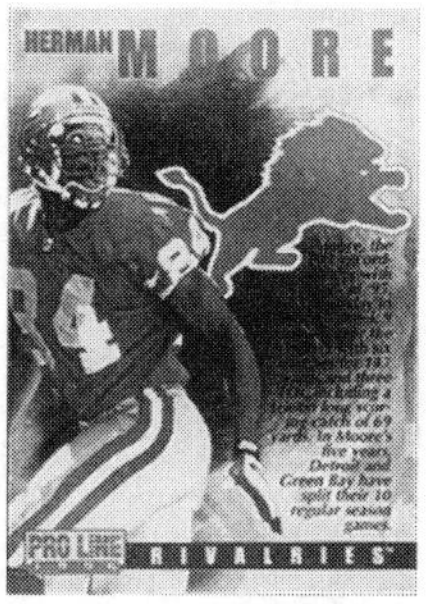

This 30-card 1996 Pro Line insert set provides an in-depth look at some of the NFL's most heated battles. Each card side features an action shot of one of two players along with a decorative foil stamp, used for the player's name. His team logo and highlights from the two team's rivalries are also on each side. The metallic background shows a ghosted image of the player's opponent. A card number, using an "R" prefix, is on one side only. Cards were seeded one per every 10 packs.

		MT
Complete Set (20):		200.00
Common Player:		3.00
1	Drew Bledsoe, Jim Kelly	12.00
2	Dan Marino, Greg Lloyd	20.00
3	Kordell Stewart, Mark Brunell	12.00
4	Tamarick Vanover, Napoleon Kaufman	12.00
5	John Elway, Jeff Blake	8.00
6	Emmitt Smith, Ricky Watters	20.00
7	Troy Aikman, Steve Young	12.00
8	Deion Sanders, Gus Frerotte	8.00
9	Brett Favre, Errict Rhett	20.00
10	Rashaan Salaam, Warren Moon	10.00
11	Kerry Collins, Ken Norton Jr.	12.00
12	Jeff George, Isaac Bruce	8.00
13	Rod Woodson, Rodney Thomas	3.00
14	Herman Moore, Reggie White	3.00
15	Marshall Faulk, Curtis Martin	16.00
16	Keyshawn Johnson, Marvin Harrison	20.00
17	Kevin Hardy, Alex Molden	3.00
18	Terry Glenn, Simeon Rice	12.00
19	Eddie George, Tim Biakabutuka	16.00
20	Karim Abdul-Jabbar, Cedric Jones	8.00

1996 Pro Line Cover Story

This 20-card set was inserted one per 30 periodical packs. The cards feature a newspaper design and carry a "CS" prefix on the card number. The insert is made up of a mix of top 1995 players as well as some of the top rookies from 1996.

		MT
Complete Set (20):		125.00
Common Player:		2.00
1	Bryce Paup	2.00
2	Kerry Collins	12.00
3	Rashaan Salaam	5.00
4	Troy Aikman	12.00
5	Emmitt Smith	25.00
6	Herman Moore	4.00
7	Curtis Martin	18.00
8	Kordell Stewart	12.00
9	Ricky Watters	2.00
10	Carl Pickens	2.00
11	Joey Galloway	8.00
12	Errict Rhett	5.00
13	Deion Sanders	7.00
14	Reggie White	4.00
15	Hugh Douglas	2.00
16	Tamarick Vanover	7.00
17	Derrick Mayes	2.00
18	Marvin Harrison	7.00
19	Tim Biakabutuka	6.00
20	Terry Glenn	12.00

Values quoted in this guide reflect the retail price of a card — the price a collector can expect to pay when buying a card from a dealer. The wholesale price — that which a collector can expect to receive from a dealer when selling cards — will be significantly lower, depending on desirability and condition.

1996 Pro Line Touchdown Performers

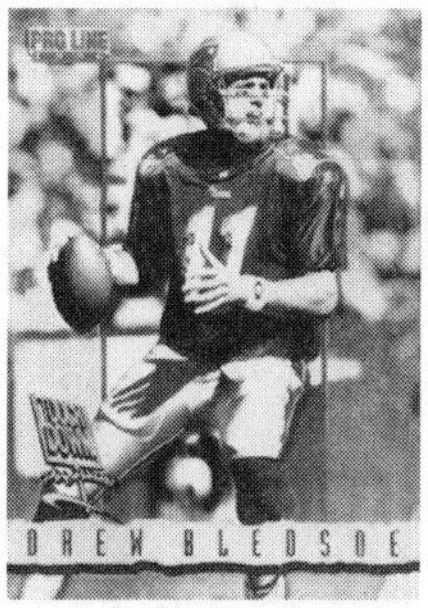

Touchdown Performers is a 20-card insert that was found every 75 retail packs. The cards are numbered TD1-TD20.

		MT
Complete Set (20):		250.00
Common Player:		5.00
1	Kerry Collins	20.00
2	Troy Aikman	20.00
3	Deion Sanders	12.00
4	Emmitt Smith	40.00
5	Mark Brunell	15.00
6	Steve McNair	15.00
7	Marshall Faulk	15.00
8	Dan Marino	40.00
9	Cris Carter	5.00
10	Drew Bledsoe	18.00
11	Yancey Thigpen	5.00
12	Jerry Rice	20.00
13	J.J. Stokes	14.00
14	Terrell Davis	25.00
15	Carl Pickens	5.00
16	Joey Galloway	16.00
17	Kordell Stewart	20.00
18	Isaac Bruce	14.00
19	Keyshawn Johnson	20.00
20	Amani Toomer	5.00

1996 Pro Line II Intense

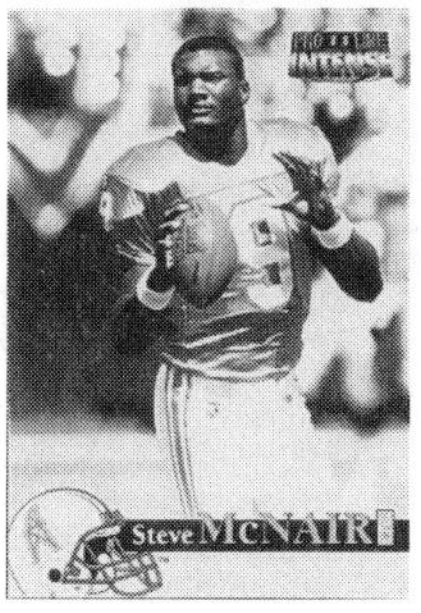

Pro Line II Intense features 100 cards, a parallel set and four insert sets. Each regular card has a full-bleed color photo on the front, with the Intense logo at the top. The player's name and position are in a bar along the bottom, flanked by a team helmet in the lower left corner. The back has a card number and the player's name at the top, with a photo on one side and statistics on the other. A box with biographical information is in the lower left corner. There were also parallel Double Intensity cards made; they were seeded one per five packs and are stamped in bronze on the front. Three other insert sets were also made - Determined and $3 and $5 Sprint Foncards. There's an average of $11 in phone time in every box.

		MT
Complete Set (100):		20.00
Common Player:		.05
Minor Stars:		.10
Double Intensity:		4x-8x
Pack (5):		1.25
Wax Box (36):		35.00
1	Kerry Collins	1.25
2	Jeff George	.05
3	Mark Brunell	1.00
4	Steve McNair	.75
5	Rick Mirer	.05
6	Dave Brown	.05
7	Rashaan Salaam	.50
8	Marshall Faulk	.50
9	Erric Pegram	.05
10	Cris Carter	.05
11	Eric Allen	.05
12	Jim Kelly	.05
13	Jeff Blake	.50
14	Stan Humphries	.05
15	Scott Mitchell	.05
16	Jeff Hostetler	.05
17	Rodney Peete	.05
18	Warren Moon	.05
19	Errict Rhett	.40
20	Terrell Davis	2.00
21	J.J. Stokes	.10
22	Marco Coleman	.05
23	Heath Shuler	.05
24	Duane Clemons	.05
25	*Amani Toomer*	.10
26	Leslie O'Neal	.05
27	Tamarick Vanover	.50
28	Steve Bono	.05
29	Jim Everett	.05
30	Erik Kramer	.05
31	Trent Dilfer	.10
32	Jim Harbaugh	.05
33	Vinny Testaverde	.05
34	Rodney Hampton	.05
35	Chris Warren	.10
36	Curtis Martin	2.00
37	*Eddie Kennison*	.50
38	Herman Moore	.40
39	Terance Mathis	.05
40	Carl Pickens	.05
41	Isaac Bruce	.50
42	Reggie White	.10
43	Junior Seau	.05
44	Bryce Paup	.05
45	Deion Sanders	.50
46	Thurman Thomas	.10
47	Gus Frerotte	.05
48	Jerome Bettis	.10
49	Michael Irvin	.10
50	Wayne Chrebet	.05
51	*Bobby Engram*	.75
52	Marcus Jones	.05
53	Daryl Gardener	.05
54	*Alex Van Dyke*	.10
55	Cedric Jones	.05
56	Regan Upshaw	.05
57	*Jason Dunn*	.30
58	Mark Chmura	.25
59	Ray Lewis	.25
60	*Rickey Dudley*	.20
61	*Leeland McElroy*	.20
62	Derrick Thomas	.05
63	*Bobby Hoying*	.75
64	Robert Brooks	.05
65	Tim Brown	.05
66	Michael Westbrook	.40
67	Jim Miller	.05
68	Aaron Hayden	.05
69	Marcus Allen	.05
70	Troy Aikman	1.00
71	Steve Young	.75
72	Neil O'Donnell	.05
73	Drew Bledsoe	.75
74	Emmitt Smith	2.00
75	Ki-Jana Carter	.30
76	Irving Fryar	.05
77	Joey Galloway	.75
78	Russell Maryland	.05
79	Kordell Stewart	1.00
80	Barry Sanders	1.25
81	Bryan Cox	.05
82	*Keyshawn Johnson*	1.50
83	*Karim Abdul-Jabbar*	1.75
84	*Kevin Hardy*	.30
85	Rodney Thomas	.05
86	John Elway	.50
87	Dan Marino	2.00
88	Brett Favre	2.00
89	John Mobley	.05
90	Jonathan Ogden	.05
91	*Eddie George*	2.50
92	*Simeon Rice*	.25
93	*Tim Biakabutuka*	1.00
94	*Terry Glenn*	1.75
95	*Marvin Harrison*	1.00
96	*Lawrence Phillips*	.50
97	Natrone Means	.10
98	Jerry Rice	.75
99	Ricky Watters	.10
100	Checklist	.05

1996 Pro Line II Intense Double Intensity

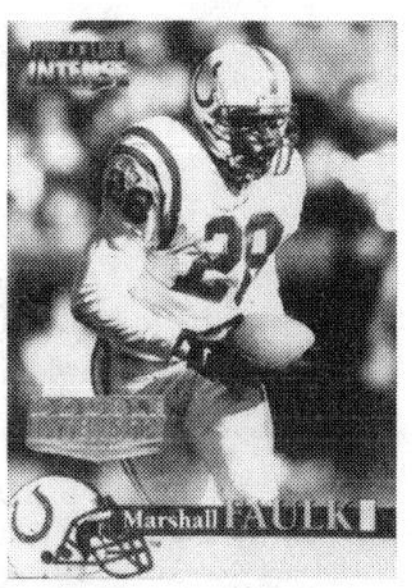

Pro Line II Intense Double Intensity was a 100-card parallel set that included the words "Double Intensity" on the front in foil. These parallel cards were inserted at a rate of one per five packs.

	MT
Complete Set (100):	160.00
Double Intensity Cards:	4x-8x

1996 Pro Line II Intense Determined

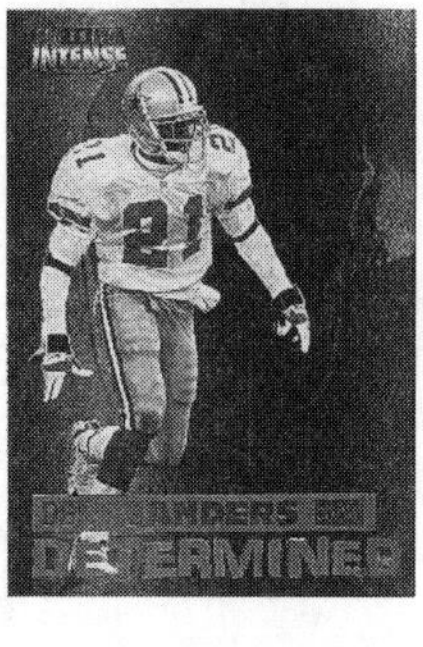

These 1996 Pro Line II inserts offer an in-depth view of the look and determination of 20 of the NFL's fiercest competitors. Each card front has an action photo of the player against a metallic ghosted close-up image of him as the background. The Pro Line II logo is at the top of the card; the player's name and position are in a bar at the bottom, above the word "Determined." The card back, numbered 1 of 20, etc., has a full-bleed color action photo on it, with an oval toward the bottom which recaps some of the player's achievements.

		MT
Complete Set (20):		250.00
Common Player:		4.00
1	Kerry Collins	15.00
2	Troy Aikman	15.00
3	Herman Moore	6.00
4	Mark Brunell	15.00
5	Dan Marino	30.00
6	Kordell Stewart	15.00
7	Junior Seau	4.00
8	Steve Young	12.00
9	John Elway	12.00
10	Emmitt Smith	30.00
11	Steve McNair	10.00
12	Drew Bledsoe	15.00
13	Joey Galloway	12.00
14	Deion Sanders	10.00
15	Kevin Hardy	4.00
16	Keyshawn Johnson	12.00
17	Marvin Harrison	10.00
18	Tim Biakabutuka	4.00
19	Eddie George	25.00
20	Terry Glenn	20.00

1996 Pro Line II Intense $3 Phone Cards

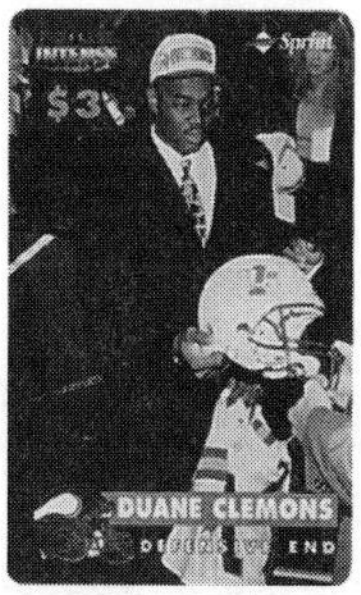

Fifty top players are featured in this 1996 Pro Line II insert set, which is licensed by the NFL and sponsored by Sprint. The cards, randomly inserted one per 18 packs, contain $3 worth of prepaid Sprint long-distance calling. The card front has the brand and Sprint logos at the top; the player's name, position and a team helmet are at the bottom. The card back explains how to use the card and when it expires.

		MT
Complete Set (50):		250.00
Common Player:		3.00
1	Jim Kelly	3.00
2	Kerry Collins	8.00
3	Jeff George	3.00
4	Troy Aikman	8.00
5	John Elway	5.00
6	Herman Moore	4.00
7	Barry Sanders	8.00
8	Brett Favre	12.00
9	Jim Harbaugh	3.00
10	Steve Bono	3.00
11	Dan Marino	16.00
12	Drew Bledsoe	6.00
13	Jim Everett	3.00
14	Neil O'Donnell	3.00
15	Ricky Watters	3.00
16	Junior Seau	3.00
17	Jerry Rice	8.00
18	Errict Rhett	3.00
19	Joey Galloway	6.00
20	Steve Young	6.00
21	Kordell Stewart	8.00
22	Rodney Hampton	3.00
23	Curtis Martin	12.00
24	Mark Brunell	6.00
25	Steve McNair	5.00
26	Deion Sanders	5.00
27	Carl Pickens	3.00
28	Michael Irvin	3.00
29	Tamarick Vanover	3.00
30	Emmitt Smith	15.00
31	Chris Warren	3.00
32	Stan Humphries	3.00
33	J.J. Stokes	5.00
34	Tim Biakabutuka	5.00
35	Keyshawn Johnson	10.00
36	Simeon Rice	3.00
37	Jonathan Ogden	3.00
38	Rashaan Salaam	4.00
39	Bobby Engram	4.00
40	John Mobley	3.00
41	Derrick Mayes	3.00
42	Eddie George	8.00
43	Marvin Harrison	7.00
44	Kevin Hardy	3.00
45	Karim Abdul-Jabbar	8.00
46	Duane Clemons	3.00
47	Terry Glenn	8.00
48	Cedric Jones	3.00
49	Rickey Dudley	3.00
50	Lawrence Phillips	8.00

A player's name in *italic type* indicates a rookie card.

1996 Pro Line II Intense $5 Phone Cards

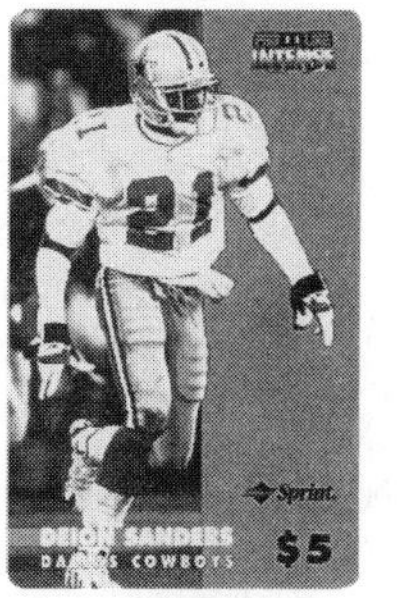

Twenty top players are featured in this 1996 Pro Line II insert set, which is licensed by the NFL and sponsored by Sprint. The cards, randomly inserted one per 35 packs, contain $5 worth of prepaid Sprint long-distance calling. The card front has the brand logo at the top; the Sprint logo, denomination and player's name and team are at the bottom. The card back explains how to use the card and when it expires.

		MT
Complete Set (20):		150.00
Common Player:		6.00
1	Kerry Collins	10.00
2	Troy Aikman	10.00
3	Herman Moore	6.00
4	Mark Brunell	10.00
5	Dan Marino	20.00
6	Kordell Stewart	10.00
7	Junior Seau	6.00
8	Steve Young	8.00
9	John Elway	6.00
10	Emmitt Smith	20.00
11	Steve McNair	6.00
12	Drew Bledsoe	8.00
13	Joey Galloway	8.00
14	Deion Sanders	8.00
15	Kevin Hardy	6.00
16	Keyshawn Johnson	12.00
17	Marvin Harrison	10.00
18	Tim Biakabutuka	9.00
19	Eddie George	10.00
20	Terry Glenn	12.00

1996 Pro Line Memorabilia

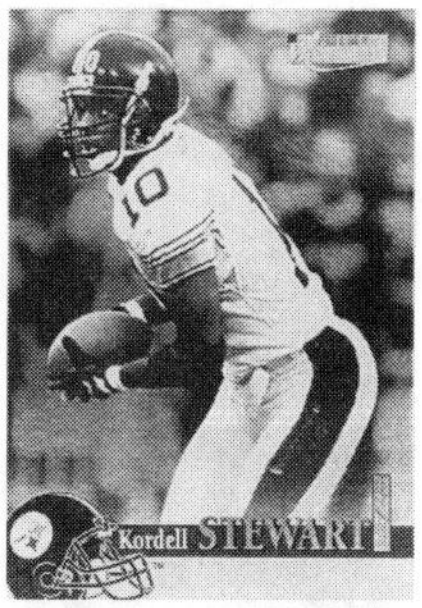

Pro Line Memorabilia was the third installment of Pro Line Football in 1996. The same 100 players from Intense were used, but with different designs. Memorabilia included one autographed memorabilia redemption card, two autographed cards, with one of a 1996 NFL first-round pick, as well as two inserts - Down the Stretch and Producers.

		MT
Complete Set (100):		25.00
Common Player:		.10
Minor Stars:		.20
Pack (5):		1.25
Box (24):		100.00
1	Kerry Collins	1.50
2	Jeff George	.10
3	Mark Brunell	1.50
4	Steve McNair	1.00
5	Rick Mirer	.20
6	Dave Brown	.10
7	Rashaan Salaam	.30
8	Marshall Faulk	.30
9	Erric Pegram	.10
10	Cris Carter	.10
11	Eric Allen	.10
12	Jim Kelly	.20
13	Jeff Blake	.30
14	Stan Humphries	.10
15	Scott Mitchell	.10
16	Jeff Hostetler	.10
17	Rodney Peete	.10
18	Warren Moon	.20
19	Errict Rhett	.30
20	Terrell Davis	1.75
21	J.J. Stokes	.20
22	Marco Coleman	.10
23	Heath Shuler	.20
24	Duane Clemons	.10
25	Amani Toomer	.20
26	Leslie O'Neal	.10
27	Tamarick Vanover	.20
28	Steve Bono	.10
29	Jim Everett	.10
30	Erik Kramer	.10
31	Trent Dilfer	.20

32	Jim Harbaugh	.10
33	Vinny Testaverde	.10
34	Rodney Hampton	.10
35	Chris Warren	.10
36	Curtis Martin	1.75
37	Eddie Kennison	1.50
38	Herman Moore	.30
39	Terance Mathis	.10
40	Carl Pickens	.20
41	Isaac Bruce	.30
42	Reggie White	.20
43	Junior Seau	.20
44	Bryce Paup	.10
45	Deion Sanders	.75
46	Thurman Thomas	.20
47	Gus Frerotte	.10
48	Tony Mandarich	.10
49	Michael Irvin	.20
50	Wayne Chrebet	.10
51	Bobby Engram	1.00
52	Marcus Jones	.10
53	Daryl Gardener	.10
54	Alex Van Dyke	.20
55	Andre Rison	.10
56	Regan Upshaw	.10
57	Jason Dunn	.10
58	Mark Chmura	.20
59	Ray Lewis	.25
60	Rickey Dudley	.30
61	Leeland McElroy	.20
62	Derrick Thomas	.10
63	Bobby Hoying	.20
64	Robert Brooks	.20
65	Tim Brown	.20
66	Michael Westbrook	.20
67	Jim Miller	.10
68	Aaron Hayden	.10
69	Marcus Allen	.20
70	Troy Aikman	1.50
71	Steve Young	1.00
72	Neil O'Donnell	.10
73	Drew Bledsoe	1.50
74	Emmitt Smith	3.00
75	Ki-Jana Carter	.20
76	Irving Fryar	.10
77	Joey Galloway	.50
78	Russell Maryland	.10
79	Kordell Stewart	1.50
80	Barry Sanders	1.50
81	Bryan Cox	.10
82	Keyshawn Johnson	1.50
83	Karim Abdul-Jabbar	2.00
84	Kevin Hardy	.20
85	Rodney Thomas	.10
86	John Elway	1.00
87	Dan Marino	3.00
88	Brett Favre	3.00
89	Eric Metcalf	.10
90	Jonathan Ogden	.20
91	Eddie George	3.00
92	Simeon Rice	.20
93	Tim Biakabutuka	.30
94	Terry Glenn	2.50
95	Marvin Harrison	1.50
96	Lawrence Phillips	.30
97	Natrone Means	.20
98	Jerry Rice	1.50
99	Ricky Watters	.20
100	Checklist (Emmitt Smith)	.50

1996 Pro Line Memorabilia Stretch Drive

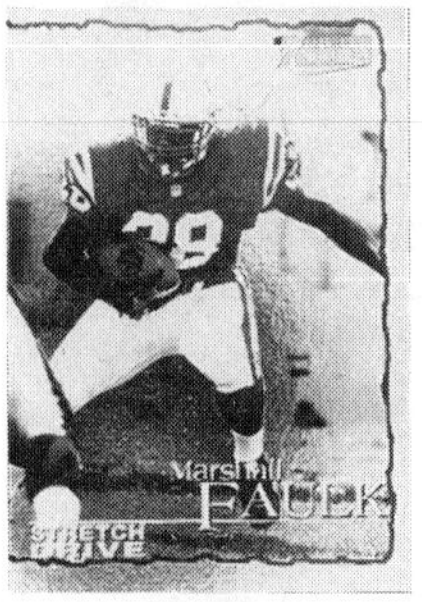

Stretch Drive featured 30 top players on a foil background, with cards numbered DS1-DS30. Regular versions were inserted every three packs, while Signature Series versions, which had facsimile signatures, were inserted every 25 packs.

		MT
Complete Set (30):		150.00
Common Player:		2.50
Minor Stars:		5.00
1	Jim Kelly	5.00
2	Kerry Collins	10.00
3	Rashaan Salaam	5.00
4	Jeff Blake	5.00
5	Deion Sanders	6.00
6	Troy Aikman	10.00
7	Emmitt Smith	18.00
8	John Elway	8.00
9	Terrell Davis	12.00
10	Barry Sanders	10.00
11	Herman Moore	5.00
12	Brett Favre	18.00
13	Steve McNair	8.00
14	Eddie George	12.00
15	Marshall Faulk	5.00
16	Marvin Harrison	6.00
17	Dan Marino	18.00
18	Curtis Martin	12.00
19	Drew Bledsoe	10.00
20	Terry Glenn	10.00
21	Neil O'Donnell	2.50
22	Keyshawn Johnson	6.00
23	Ricky Watters	5.00
24	Kordell Stewart	10.00
25	J.J. Stokes	2.50
26	Steve Young	8.00
27	Joey Galloway	6.00
28	Lawrence Phillips	5.00
29	Isaac Bruce	5.00
30	Errict Rhett	5.00

1996 Pro Line Memorabilia Producers

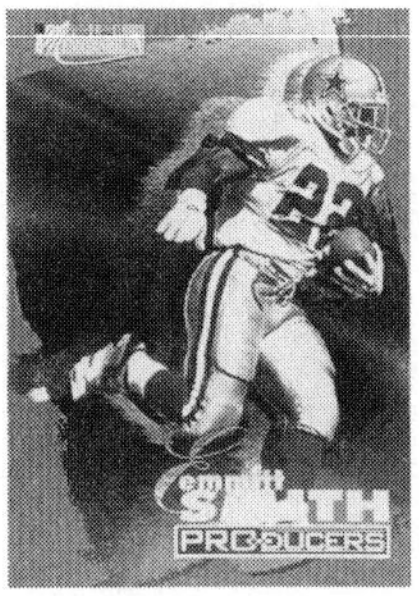

Producers was a 10-card insert found in every six packs of Memorabilia. Cards in this insert were numbered P1-P10. There are also Signature Series Producers, which have facsimile signatures, inserted every 100 packs.

		MT
Complete Set (10):		50.00
Common Player:		1.00
Minor Stars:		2.00
Silver Signatures:		2x-4x
1	Keyshawn Johnson	3.00
2	Barry Sanders	5.00
3	Eddie George	8.00
4	Emmitt Smith	10.00
5	Jerry Rice	5.00
6	Brett Favre	10.00
7	Marshall Faulk	1.00
8	Dan Marino	10.00
9	Deion Sanders	4.00
10	Ricky Watters	1.00

1996 Pro Line Memorabilia Rookie Autographs

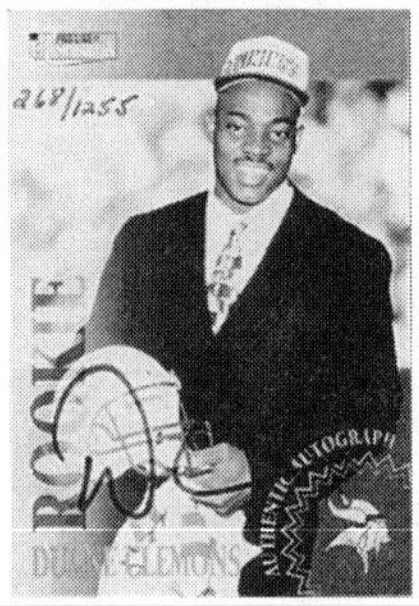

This 15-card insert features autographs of NFL rookies from 1996 and was inserted 1:12. Each card is limited to a different production number and sequentially numbered. The cards are not numbered within the insert set.

		MT
Complete Set (15):		900.00
Common Player:		15.00
1	Tim Biakabutuka/210	75.00
2	Tim Biakabutuka/600, Eddie George	200.00
3	Duane Clemons/1255	15.00
4	Daryl Gardener/1390	15.00
5	Eddie George/395	175.00
6	Terry Glenn/600, Keyshawn Johnson	175.00
7	Kevin Hardy/940	20.00
8	Jeff Hartings/1370	15.00
9	Andre Johnson/1370	15.00
10	Keyshawn Johnson/195	125.00
11	Pete Kendall/1495	15.00
12	Alex Molden/1320	15.00
13	Eric Moulds/1010	30.00
14	Jamain Stephens/795	15.00
15	Jerome Woods/1375	15.00

1996 Pro Line DC III

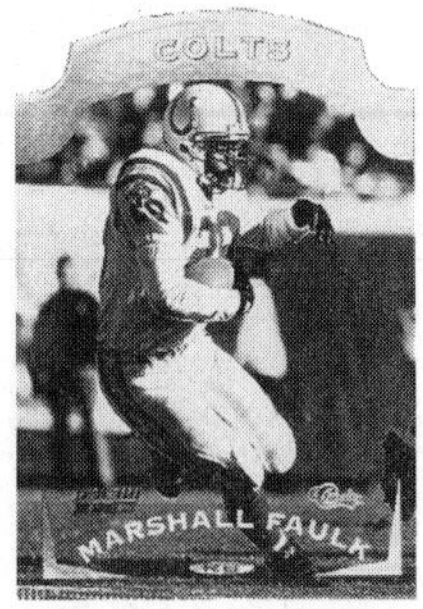

Pro Line III DC, by Classic, follows the hobby trend with all 100 cards printed on a die-cut design. Every card is printed on 24-point stock, die-cut around the top. The back has final statistics from the 1995 season, plus career totals, biographical information, a color action photo, and trivial notes about the player. There were also insert sets created for the set: Road to the Super Bowl and All-Pro/All-Pro Rookies.

		MT
Complete Set (100):		50.00
Common Player:		.20
Minor Stars:		.40
Pack (5):		4.50
Wax Box (24):		80.00
1	Emmitt Smith	6.00
2	Larry Centers	.20
3	Jeff George	.40
4	Jim Kelly	.40
5	Kerry Collins	4.00
6	Erik Kramer	.20
7	Jeff Blake	2.00
8	Andre Rison	.20
9	John Elway	1.50
10	Herman Moore	.75
11	Robert Brooks	.50
12	Steve McNair	3.00
13	Jim Harbaugh	.20
14	Mark Brunell	1.00
15	Steve Bono	.40
16	Dan Marino	6.00
17	Warren Moon	.40
18	Drew Bledsoe	3.00
19	Jim Everett	.20
20	Rodney Hampton	.20
21	Kyle Brady	.20
22	Jeff Hostetler	.20
23	Neil O'Donnell	.40
24	Ricky Watters	.20
25	Isaac Bruce	1.50
26	Steve Young	3.00
27	Stan Humphries	.20
28	Joey Galloway	3.00
29	Errict Rhett	2.00
30	Terry Allen	.20
31	Eric Swann	.20
32	Craig Heyward	.20
33	Bryce Paup	.20
34	Sam Mills	.20
35	Jim Flanigan	.20
36	Carl Pickens	.40
37	Pepper Johnson	.20
38	Troy Aikman	3.00
39	Terrell Davis	3.00
40	Scott Mitchell	.20
41	Brett Favre	6.00
42	Chris Sanders	1.00
43	Marshall Faulk	3.00
44	James Stewart	.20
45	Marcus Allen	.20
46	Bernie Parmalee	.20
47	Cris Carter	.20
48	Ben Coates	.20
49	Quinn Early	.20
50	Tyrone Wheatley	.40
51	Adrian Murrell	.20
52	Tim Brown	.20
53	Yancey Thigpen	1.50
54	Andy Harmon	.20
55	Jerome Bettis	.20
56	Jerry Rice	3.00
57	Natrone Means	.50
58	Chris Warren	.40
59	Warren Sapp	.20
60	Michael Westbrook	2.00
61	Aeneas Williams	.20
62	Eric Metcalf	.20
63	Bruce Smith	.20
64	Rashaan Salaam	2.00
65	Michael Irvin	.75
66	Anthony Miller	.20
67	Barry Sanders	3.00
68	Reggie White	.40
69	Rodney Thomas	1.50
70	Zack Crockett	.20
71	Neil Smith	.20
72	Bryan Cox	.20
73	Curtis Martin	5.00
74	Eric Allen	.20
75	Hugh Douglas	.20
76	Napoleon Kaufman	.75
77	Greg Lloyd	.20
78	Charlie Garner	.20
79	Lee Woodall	.20
80	Tony Martin	.20
81	Cortez Kennedy	.20
82	Gus Frerotte	.40
83	Darick Holmes	.50
84	Jay Novacek	.20
85	Brett Perriman	.20
86	Mark Chmura	.40
87	Chester McGlockton	.20
88	Dave Brown	.20
89	William Thomas	.20
90	Ken Norton	.20
91	Junior Seau	.40
92	Deion Sanders	2.00
93	J.J. Stokes	2.00
94	Kordell Stewart	3.00
95	Tamarick Vanover	2.00
96	Ken Harvey	.20
97	John Randle	.20
98	Lamont Warren	.20
99	Dorsey Levens	.40
100	Frank Sanders	1.00

1996 Pro Line DC III All-Pros

These cards, printed on 24-point fabric stock, were inserted one per 100 packs of 1996 Pro Line III DC product. The card back is numbered using an "AP" prefix.

		MT
Complete Set (20):		650.00
Common Player:		8.00
1	Bryce Paup	8.00
2	Kerry Collins	50.00
3	Rashaan Salaam	30.00
4	Emmitt Smith	80.00
5	Terrell Davis	60.00
6	Herman Moore	8.00
7	Barry Sanders	50.00
8	Brett Favre	80.00
9	Marshall Faulk	30.00
10	Dan Marino	80.00
11	Cris Carter	8.00
12	Curtis Martin	70.00
13	Hugh Douglas	8.00
14	Kordell Stewart	45.00
15	Jerry Rice	45.00
16	J.J. Stokes	30.00
17	Joey Galloway	40.00
18	Isaac Bruce	25.00
19	Steve McNair	40.00
20	Tim Brown	8.00

1996 Pro Line DC III Road to the Super Bowl

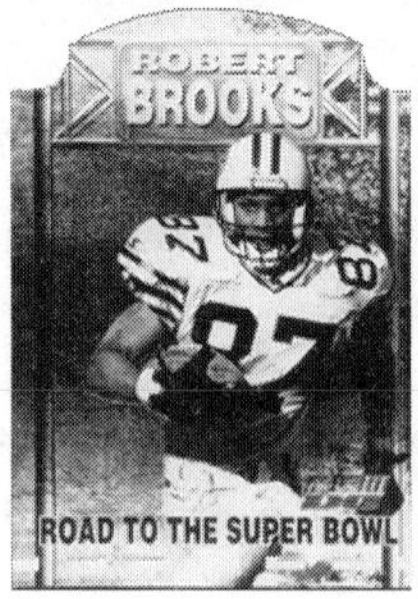

The key members and moments in the 1995 season are captured in this 30-card Road to the Super Bowl set. The cards, which were inserted one per 15 packs of 1996 Pro Line III DC product, have the player's name at the top, with "Road to the Super Bowl" written along the bottom. The back has statistics or a brief box score of the game being recalled, plus a photo of the player inside a circle. A map of Phoenix is used as a background motif on both sides of the card. The card number is listed as 1 of 30, etc..

		MT
Complete Set (30):		300.00
Common Player:		4.00
Minor Stars:		8.00
1	Larry Centers	4.00
2	Eric Metcalf	4.00
3	Jim Kelly	8.00
4	Bryce Paup	4.00
5	Kerry Collins	20.00
6	Carl Pickens	8.00
7	Emmitt Smith	45.00
8	Michael Irvin	8.00
9	Troy Aikman	25.00
10	Terrell Davis	25.00
11	Barry Sanders	25.00
12	Herman Moore	8.00
13	Brett Favre	45.00
14	Robert Brooks	8.00
15	Jim Harbaugh	4.00
16	Tony Bennett	4.00
17	Steve Bono	8.00
18	Dan Marino	45.00
19	Cris Carter	4.00
20	Curtis Martin	30.00
21	Tim Brown	4.00
22	Ricky Watters	4.00
23	Yancey Thigpen	15.00
24	Neil O'Donnell	4.00
25	Kordell Stewart	25.00
26	Isaac Bruce	15.00
27	Tony Martin	4.00
28	Steve Young	25.00
29	Jerry Rice	25.00
30	Chris Warren	8.00

1997 Pro Line

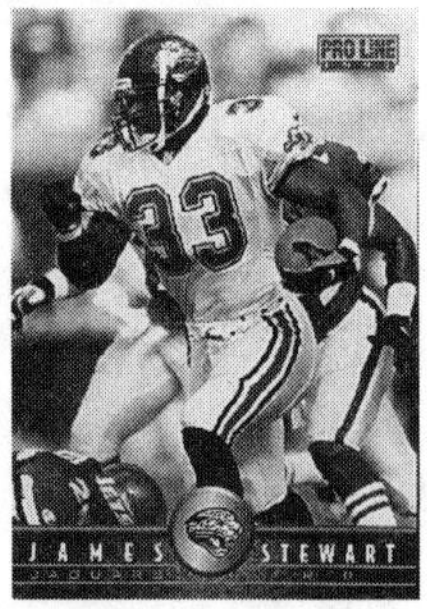

The 300-card set featured a full-bleed photo with a stripe at the bottom that included the player's name, team and position. The team's logo is included inside a circle at the bottom center. The Pro Line logo is in the upper left.

		MT
Complete Set (300):		30.00
Common Player:		.05
Minor Stars:		.10
Pack (8):		2.50
Wax Box (28):		60.00
1	Larry Centers	.05
2	Kent Graham	.05
3	LeShon Johnson	.05
4	Leeland McElroy	.10
5	Rob Moore	.05
6	Simeon Rice	.05
7	Frank Sanders	.05
8	Eric Swann	.05
9	Aeneas Williams	.05
10	Jamal Anderson	.15
11	Cornelius Bennett	.05
12	Ray Buchanan	.05
13	Bert Emanuel	.05
14	Terance Mathis	.05
15	Eric Metcalf	.05
16	Jessie Tuggle	.05
17	Derrick Alexander	.05
18	Earnest Byner	.05
19	Michael Jackson	.05
20	Antonio Langham	.05
21	Ray Lewis	.05
22	Bam Morris	.05
23	Jonathan Ogden	.05
24	Vinny Testaverde	.05
25	Eric Moulds	.10
26	Todd Collins	.05
27	Quinn Early	.05
28	Phil Hansen	.05
29	Darick Holmes	.10
30	Bryce Paup	.05
31	Andre Reed	.05
32	Bruce Smith	.05
33	Chris Spielman	.05
34	Matt Stevens	.05
35	Steve Tasker	.05
36	Thurman Thomas	.10
37	Mark Carrier	.05
38	Kerry Collins	.25
39	Tim Biakabutuka	.25
40	Eric Davis	.05
41	Kevin Greene	.05
42	Anthony Johnson	.05
43	Lamar Lathon	.05
44	Sam Mills	.05
45	Wesley Walls	.05
46	Muhsin Muhammad	.10
47	Mark Carrier	.05
48	Curtis Conway	.10
49	Bryan Cox	.05
50	Bobby Engram	.05
51	Raymont Harris	.05
52	Walt Harris	.05
53	Rick Mirer	.05
54	Rashaan Salaam	.10
55	Alonzo Spellman	.05
56	Ashley Ambrose	.05
57	Jeff Blake	.15
58	Ki-Jana Carter	.10
59	John Copeland	.05
60	James Francis	.05
61	Tony McGee	.05
62	Carl Pickens	.10
63	Darnay Scott	.05
64	Steve Tovar	.05
65	Dan Wilkinson	.05
66	Troy Aikman	1.00
67	Eric Bjornson	.05
68	Michael Irvin	.10
69	Daryl Johnston	.05
70	Nate Newton	.05
71	Deion Sanders	.40
72	Emmitt Smith	2.00
73	Kevin Smith	.05
74	Kevin Williams	.05
75	Darren Woodson	.05
76	Mark Tuinei	.05
77	Steve Atwater	.05
78	Terrell Davis	1.25
79	John Elway	.75
80	Ed McCaffrey	.05
81	Anthony Miller	.05
82	John Mobley	.05
83	Michael Dean Perry	.05
84	Shannon Sharpe	.05
85	Alfred Williams	.05
86	Reggie Brown	.05
87	Luther Elliss	.05
88	Scott Mitchell	.05
89	Herman Moore	.15
90	Johnnie Morton	.05
91	Brett Perriman	.05
92	Robert Porcher	.05
93	Barry Sanders	1.25
94	Henry Thomas	.05
95	Edgar Bennett	.05
96	Robert Brooks	.10
97	Gilbert Brown	.05
98	LeRoy Butler	.05
99	Mark Chmura	.05
100	Brett Favre	2.25
101	Santana Dotson	.05
102	Antonio Freeman	.20
103	Dorsey Levens	.20
104	Wayne Simmons	.05
105	Reggie White	.10
106	Willie Davis	.05
107	Eddie George	1.50
108	Darryll Lewis	.05
109	Steve McNair	.30
110	Marcus Robertson	.05
111	Chris Sanders	.05
112	Al Smith	.05
113	Tony Bennett	.05
114	Quentin Coryatt	.05
115	Ken Dilger	.05
116	Sean Dawkins	.05
117	Marshall Faulk	.20
118	Jim Harbaugh	.05
119	Marvin Harrison	.30
120	Jeff Herrod	.05
121	Tony Boselli	.05
122	Tony Brackens	.05
123	Mark Brunell	1.00
124	Kevin Hardy	.05
125	Jeff Lageman	.05
126	Keenan McCardell	.05
127	Natrone Means	.10
128	Eddie Robinson	.05
129	Jimmy Smith	.05
130	James Stewart	.05
131	Marcus Allen	.10
132	Dale Carter	.05
133	Mark Collins	.05
134	Lake Dawson	.05
135	Greg Hill	.05
136	Sean LaChapelle	.05
137	Chris Penn	.05
138	Derrick Thomas	.05
139	Tamarick Vanover	.10
140	Elvis Grbac	.05
141	Karim Abdul-Jabbar	.30
142	Fred Barnett	.05
143	Terrell Buckley	.05
144	Daryl Gardener	.05
145	Randal Hill	.05
146	Dan Marino	2.00
147	O.J. McDuffie	.05
148	Jerris McPhail	.05
149	Zach Thomas	.20
150	Cris Carter	.05
151	Dixon Edwards	.05
152	Leroy Hoard	.05
153	Qadry Ismail	.05
154	Brad Johnson	.05
155	John Randle	.05
156	Jake Reed	.05
157	Robert Smith	.05
158	Orlando Thomas	.05
159	DeWayne Washington	.05
160	Drew Bledsoe	1.00
161	Tedy Bruschi	.05
162	Willie Clay	.05
163	Ben Coates	.05
164	Terry Glenn	.25
165	Shawn Jefferson	.05
166	Ty Law	.05
167	Curtis Martin	1.25
168	Willie McGinest	.05
169	Chris Slade	.05
170	Eric Allen	.05
171	Mario Bates	.05
172	Jim Everett	.05
173	Michael Haynes	.05
174	Wayne Martin	.05
175	Torrance Small	.05
176	Dave Brown	.05
177	Chris Calloway	.05
178	Rodney Hampton	.05
179	Danny Kanell	.05
180	Thomas Lewis	.05
181	Jason Sehorn	.05
182	Amani Toomer	.05
183	Charles Way	.05
184	Tyrone Wheatley	.05
185	Wayne Chrebet	.05
186	Hugh Douglas	.05
187	Aaron Glenn	.05
188	Jeff Graham	.05
189	Keyshawn Johnson	.30
190	Mo Lewis	.05
191	Adrian Murrell	.05
192	Neil O'Donnell	.05
193	Tim Brown	.05
194	Rickey Dudley	.10
195	Jeff George	.10
196	Napoleon Kaufman	.05
197	Russell Maryland	.05
198	Terry McDaniel	.05
199	Chester McGlockton	.05
201	Pat Swilling	.05
200	Desmond Howard	.05
202	Ty Detmer	.05
203	Jason Dunn	.05
204	Ray Farmer	.05
205	Irving Fryar	.05
206	Chris T. Jones	.05
207	Bobby Taylor	.05
208	William Thomas	.05
209	Hollis Thomas	.05
210	Kevin Turner	.05
211	Ricky Watters	.10
212	Jerome Bettis	.10
213	Andre Hastings	.05
214	Charles Johnson	.05
215	Levon Kirkland	.05
216	Carnell Lake	.05
217	Greg Lloyd	.05
218	Darren Perry	.05
219	Kordell Stewart	.75
220	Rod Woodson	.05
221	Andre Coleman	.05
222	Marco Coleman	.05
223	Leonard Russell	.05
224	Stan Humphries	.05
225	Shawn Lee	.05
226	Tony Martin	.05
227	Chris Mims	.05
228	Junior Seau	.10
229	Chris Doleman	.05
230	William Floyd	.05
231	Merton Hanks	.05
232	Brent Jones	.05
233	Terry Kirby	.05
234	Ken Norton	.05
235	Terrell Owens	.75
236	Jerry Rice	1.00
237	Bryant Young	.05
238	Steve Young	.75
239	Garrison Hearst	.05
240	Brian Blades	.05
241	Chad Brown	.05
242	John Friesz	.05
243	Joey Galloway	.30
244	Cortez Kennedy	.05
245	Chris Warren	.05
246	Darryl Williams	.05
247	Tony Banks	.30
248	Isaac Bruce	.15
249	Kevin Carter	.05
250	Eddie Kennison	.10
251	Todd Lyght	.05
252	Leslie O'Neal	.05
253	Anthony Parker	.05
254	Roman Phifer	.05
255	Lawrence Phillips	.10
256	Mike Alstott	.15
257	Derrick Brooks	.05
258	Trent Dilfer	.10
259	Jackie Harris	.05
260	Hardy Nickerson	.05
261	Errict Rhett	.10
262	Warren Sapp	.05
263	Terry Allen	.05
264	Jamie Asher	.05
265	Henry Ellard	.05
266	Gus Frerotte	.05
267	Sean Gilbert	.05
268	Darrell Green	.05
269	Ken Harvey	.05
270	Brian Mitchell	.05
271	Michael Westbrook	.05
272	*Koy Detmer*	.30
273	*Yatil Green*	.40
274	*Troy Davis*	.30
275	*Darrell Russell*	.05
276	*Warrick Dunn*	1.00
277	*David LaFleur*	.30
278	*Tony Gonzalez*	.30
279	*Jake Plummer*	2.50
280	*Antowain Smith*	1.25
281	*Peter Boulware*	.05
282	*Shawn Springs*	.25
283	*Bryant Westbrook*	.10
284	*Rae Carruth*	.30
285	*Corey Dillon*	2.00
286	*Byron Hanspard*	.30
287	*Greg Jones*	.05
288	*Trevor Pryce*	.05
289	*Michael Booker*	.05
290	*Orlando Pace*	.40
291	*James Farrior*	.05
292	*Walter Jones*	.05
293	*Reinard Wilson*	.05
294	*Ike Hilliard*	1.00

295	*Kenard Lang*	.05
296	*Reidel Anthony*	1.00
297	(Brett Favre CL)	.75
298	(Kerry Collins CL)	.30
299	(Drew Bledsoe CL)	.30
300	(Terrell Davis CL)	.50

1997 Pro Line Board Members

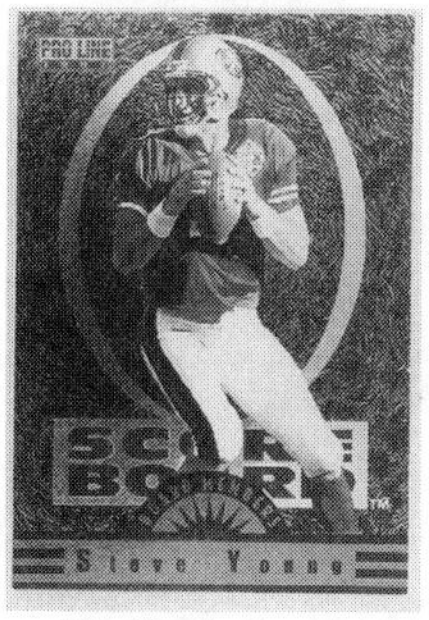

This 15-card set was inserted 1:112 packs. It includes an inside look at the NFL Players that Score Board has signed to exclusive spokesman contracts. The cards are numbered with a "B" prefix.

		MT
Complete Set (15):		275.00
Common Player:		7.00
1	Troy Aikman	25.00
2	Kerry Collins	14.00
3	Terrell Davis	25.00
4	Brett Favre	50.00
5	Gus Frerotte	7.00
6	Emmitt Smith	40.00
7	Kordell Stewart	25.00
8	Steve Young	20.00
9	Eddie George	30.00
10	Terry Glenn	14.00
11	Troy Davis	7.00
12	Darrell Russell	7.00
13	Peter Boulware	7.00
14	Warrick Dunn	30.00
15	Rae Carruth	15.00

1997 Pro Line Brett Favre

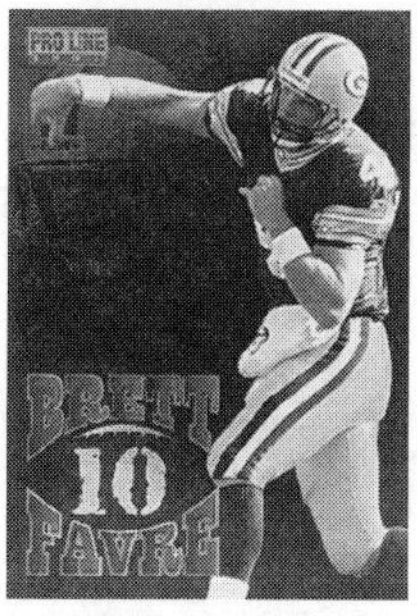

This 10-card set, which was inserted 1:28 packs, is an interactive insert series that focuses on Brett Favre. All 10 cards could be redeemed for autographed memorabilia. All sets redeemed won either an autographed jersey or a Super Bowl XXXI autographed plaque.

		MT
Complete Set (10):		150.00
Common Player:		10.00
1	Brett Favre	10.00
2	Brett Favre	10.00
3	Brett Favre	10.00
4	Brett Favre	10.00
5	Brett Favre	10.00
6	Brett Favre	10.00
7	Brett Favre	10.00
8	Brett Favre	10.00
9	Brett Favre	10.00
10	Brett Favre	75.00

1997 Pro Line Rivalries

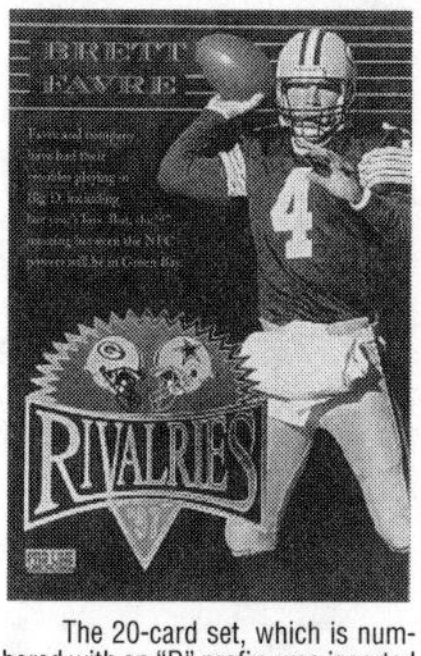

The 20-card set, which is numbered with an "R" prefix, was inserted 1:35 packs. The double-front cards provide insight into the top games of the 1997 campaign.

		MT
Complete Set (20):		275.00
Common Player:		4.00
1	John Elway, Derrick Thomas	15.00
2	Jeff Blake, Vinny Testaverde	4.00
3	Emmitt Smith, Ricky Watters	35.00
4	Jim Harbaugh, Thurman Thomas	4.00
5	Barry Sanders, Reggie White	20.00
6	Desmond Howard, Junior Seau	4.00
7	Dan Marino, Hugh Douglas	35.00
8	Jerome Bettis, Carl Pickens	4.00
9	Mark Brunell, Kordell Stewart	25.00
10	Karim Abdul-Jabbar, Bruce Smith	10.00
11	Rashaan Salaam, Brad Johnson	4.00
12	Steve Young, Kerry Collins	20.00
13	Brett Favre, Troy Aikman	40.00
14	Drew Bledsoe, Marshall Faulk	20.00
15	Steve McNair, Ki-Jana Carter	15.00
16	Jerry Rice, Terrell Davis	25.00
17	Deion Sanders, Dave Brown	15.00
18	Darrell Russell, Orlando Pace	4.00
19	Warrick Dunn, Bryant Westbrook	20.00
20	Yatil Green, Reidel Anthony	6.00

1997 Pro Line Gems

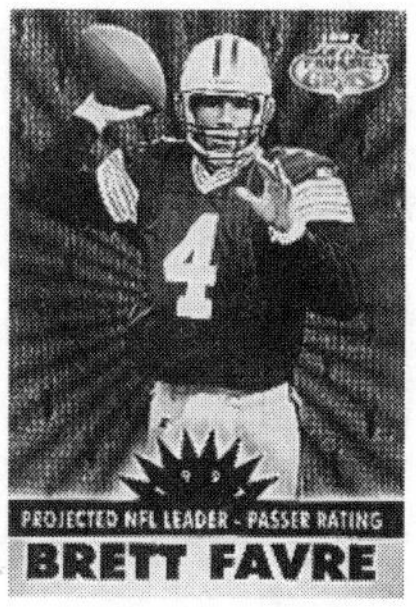

The 100-card base set consists of three subsets. Veterans is a 60-card set on blue foil-stamped cards, Rookies features 30 black foil-stamped cards and Leaders is a 10-card set with black and blue foil-stamping. The insert sets include Gems of the NFL, Championship Ring and Through the Years.

		MT
Complete Set (100):		35.00
Common Player:		.10
Minor Stars:		.20
Pack (4):		4.00
Wax Box (24):		80.00
1	Brett Favre	3.50
2	Robert Brooks	.10
3	Reggie White	.20
4	Drew Bledsoe	1.50
5	Curtis Martin	1.50
6	Terry Glenn	.30
7	Kerry Collins	.30
8	Kevin Greene	.10
9	Troy Aikman	1.50
10	Emmitt Smith	3.00
11	Deion Sanders	.75
12	John Elway	1.00
13	Terrell Davis	1.50
14	Kordell Stewart	1.50
15	Jerome Bettis	.20
16	Steve Young	1.00
17	Jerry Rice	1.50
18	Bruce Smith	.10
19	Thurman Thomas	.20
20	Jim Harbaugh	.10
21	Marshall Faulk	.20
22	Marvin Harrison	.50
23	Ricky Watters	.20
24	Seth Joyner	.10
25	Mark Brunell	1.50
26	Natrone Means	.20
27	Dan Marino	3.00
28	Zach Thomas	.50
29	Karim Abdul-Jabbar	.50
30	Isaac Bruce	.20
31	Eddie Kennison	.30
32	Tony Banks	.50
33	Tony Martin	.10
34	Junior Seau	.20
35	Barry Sanders	1.50
36	Herman Moore	.20
37	Leeland McElroy	.10
38	Jamal Anderson	.20
39	Rick Mirer	.10
40	Rashaan Salaam	.10
41	Vinny Testaverde	.10
42	Elvis Grbac	.10
43	Cris Carter	.10
44	Brad Johnson	.20
45	Keyshawn Johnson	.50
46	Adrian Murrell	.10
47	Joey Galloway	.30
48	Trent Dilfer	.20
49	Gus Frerotte	.10
50	Terry Allen	.10
51	Tim Brown	.10
52	Desmond Howard	.10
53	Jeff George	.10
54	Heath Shuler	.10
55	Steve McNair	1.25
56	Eddie George	2.00
57	Jeff Blake	.20
58	Carl Pickens	.10
59	Dave Brown	.10
60	Brett Favre	1.50
61	Antowain Smith	1.50
62	Emmitt Smith	1.25
63	Terry Glenn	.50
64	Herman Moore	.10
65	Barry Sanders	.50
66	Derrick Thomas	.10
67	Brett Favre	1.50
68	Warrick Dunn	2.50
69	Emmitt Smith	1.25
70	Brett Favre	1.50
71	Orlando Pace	.10
72	Darrell Russell	.10
73	Shawn Springs	.10
74	Warrick Dunn	3.00
75	Tiki Barber	.30
76	Tom Knight	.10
77	Peter Boulware	.10
78	David LaFleur	.50
79	Tony Gonzalez	.50
80	Yatil Green	.30
81	Ike Hilliard	.30
82	James Farrior	.10
83	Jim Druckenmiller	2.00
84	Jon Harris	.10
85	Walter Jones	.10
86	Reidel Anthony	1.25
87	Jake Plummer	1.50
88	Reinard Wilson	.10
89	Kevin Lockett	.10
90	Rae Carruth	1.00
91	Byron Hanspard	.50
92	Renaldo Wynn	.10
93	Troy Davis	.75
94	Duce Staley	.75
95	Kenard Lang	.10
96	Freddie Jones	.75
97	Corey Dillon	2.00
98	Antowain Smith	1.50
99	Dwayne Rudd	.10
100	Warrick Dunn	.75

1997 Pro Line Gems Gems of the NFL

This 15-card insert features either a sapphire or emerald gemstone on a 23-karat gold card. These cards were seeded one per box (24 packs per box). The cards are numbered with a "G" prefix.

		MT
Complete Set (15):		400.00
Common Player:		5.00
1	Kerry Collins	10.00
2	Troy Aikman	25.00
3	Emmitt Smith	45.00
4	Terrell Davis	25.00
5	Barry Sanders	60.00
6	Brett Favre	50.00
7	Eddie George	35.00
8	Mark Brunell	25.00
9	Dan Marino	45.00
10	Curtis Martin	25.00
11	Terry Glenn	10.00
12	Jerome Bettis	5.00
13	Steve Young	15.00
14	Jerry Rice	25.00
15	Warrick Dunn	40.00

1997 Pro Line Gems Championship Ring

This card featured Brett Favre and his Super Bowl XXXI championship ring. The card contains a real diamond and was inserted one per case (10 boxes per case, 24 packs per box).

		MT
Complete Set (1):		100.00
Common Player:		100.00
CR1	Brett Favre	100.00

1997 Pro Line Gems Through the Years

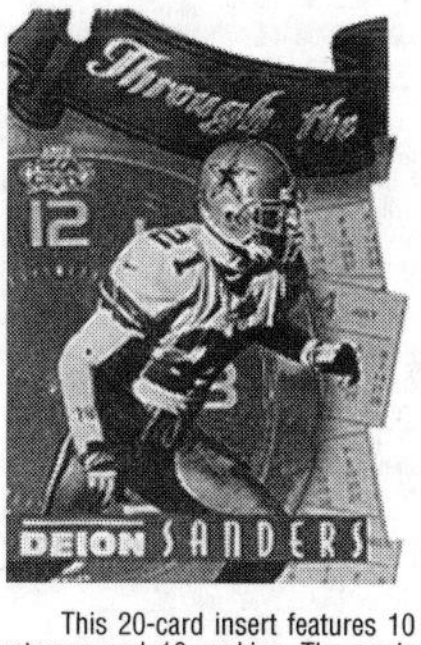

This 20-card insert features 10 veterans and 10 rookies. The cards are die-cut to fit one of the rookies' cards with one of the veterans'. The cards were inserted 1:12. The cards are numbered with a "TY" prefix.

		MT
Complete Set (20):		150.00
Common Player:		2.50
Minor Stars:		5.00
1	Emmitt Smith	20.00
2	Brett Favre	25.00
3	Deion Sanders	8.00
4	Dan Marino	20.00
5	Barry Sanders	15.00
6	Herman Moore	5.00
7	Curtis Martin	10.00
8	Jerome Bettis	5.00
9	Mark Brunell	10.00
10	Jerry Rice	10.00
11	Warrick Dunn	15.00
12	Jim Druckenmiller	10.00
13	Shawn Springs	2.50
14	Tony Banks	5.00
15	Byron Hanspard	5.00
16	Ike Hilliard	5.00
17	Antowain Smith	10.00
18	Eddie George	15.00
19	Jake Plummer	15.00
20	Terry Glenn	5.00

1997 Pro Line DC III

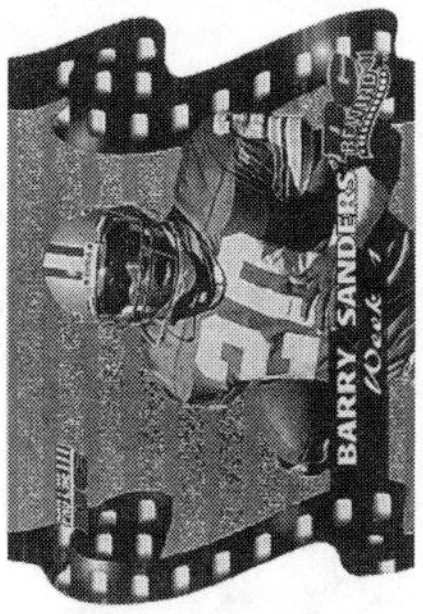

The 100-card, regular-sized, die-cut set includes two subsets: Rewind and DC Top Ten. The first 67 cards in the set are die-cut in a circular pattern with a rectangular base. Cards 68-89 are die-cut with wave outlines on the sides (Rewind) while cards 90-100 are horizontal with the top die-cut in the shape of a football. All cards have gold foil.

		MT
Complete Set (100):		50.00
Common Player:		.20
Minor Stars:		.40
Pack (4):		4.00
Wax Box (24):		90.00
1	Emmitt Smith	5.00
2	Rod Woodson	.20
3	Eddie George	3.50
4	Ty Detmer	.20
5	Zach Thomas	1.00
6	Kevin Greene	.20
7	Michael Jackson	.20
8	Isaac Bruce	1.00
9	Joey Galloway	1.50
10	Bryant Young	.20
11	Terrell Davis	3.00
12	Mark Brunell	2.00
13	Marvin Harrison	1.50
14	Jake Reed	.20
15	Terry Allen	.20
16	Kordell Stewart	2.00
17	Reggie White	.40
18	Michael Irvin	.40
19	Tony Martin	.20
20	Barry Sanders	2.50
21	Tony Boselli	.20
22	Carl Pickens	.20
23	Simeon Rice	.20
24	Adrian Murrell	.20
25	Lamar Lathon	.20
26	Thurman Thomas	.40
27	Tim Brown	.20
28	Karim Abdul-Jabbar	.75
29	Brad Johnson	.20
30	Keenan McCardell	.20
31	Keyshawn Johnson	1.50
32	Ricky Watters	.40
33	Michael McCrary	.20
34	Brett Favre	5.00
35	Steve McNair	2.00
36	Herman Moore	.40
37	Tony Banks	1.00
38	Deion Sanders	1.75
39	Kerry Collins	.75
40	Shannon Sharpe	.20
41	Drew Bledsoe	2.50
42	Jim Everett	.20
43	Jamal Anderson	.40
44	Irving Fryar	.20
45	Terry Glenn	.75
46	Jerry Rice	2.50
47	Curtis Martin	3.50
48	Curtis Conway	.20
49	Jerome Bettis	.40
50	Vinny Testaverde	.20
51	Mike Alstott	.75
52	Anthony Johnson	.20
53	Dan Marino	5.00
54	Junior Seau	.20
55	Steve Young	1.75
56	Troy Aikman	2.50
57	Jimmy Smith	.20
58	Cris Carter	.20
59	Gus Frerotte	.20
60	Marcus Allen	.40
61	Rodney Hampton	.20
62	Bruce Smith	.20
63	Leroy Butler	.20
64	Jeff Blake	.75
65	Antonio Freeman	.20
66	John Elway	1.75
67	Checklist	.20
68	Barry Sanders	1.50
69	Troy Aikman	1.00
70	Jerome Bettis	.20
71	Mark Brunell	1.00
72	Junior Seau	.20
73	John Elway	.75
74	Chad Brown	.20
75	Irving Fryar	.20
76	Drew Bledsoe	1.00
77	Jerry Rice	1.00
78	Larry Centers	.20
79	Terrell Davis	1.50
80	Carl Pickens	.20
81	Emmitt Smith	2.00
82	Kerry Collins	1.00
83	Eddie Kennison	.20
84	Kordell Stewart	1.00
85	Natrone Means	.20
86	Curtis Martin	1.50
87	Dorsey Levens	.20
88	Desmond Howard	.20
89	Checklist (Brett Favre MVP)	2.00
90	Brett Favre	2.00
91	Terrell Davis	1.50
92	Kevin Greene	.20
93	Terry Allen	.20
94	Barry Sanders	1.50
95	John Elway	.75
96	Ricky Watters	.20
97	Reggie White	.20
98	Jerome Bettis	.20
99	Jerry Rice	1.00
100	Checklist (Brett Favre CL)	2.00

1997 Pro Line DC III Perennial/Future All-Pros

The 20-card, regular-sized, die-cut set was inserted every 24 packs of Pro Line III DC football. The cards feature the same die-cut design as the Rewind subset in the base set, except the cards in Perennial/Future All-Pros are vertical, making the wave cut design on the card's top and bottom. The cards feature bronze foil on the top and bottom and the backs are numbered as "x of 20." The backs have a color action shot imaged over a white background with a black-and-white closeup behind a brief statistical analysis. The cards are numbered with an "AP" prefix.

		MT
Complete Set (20):		475.00
Common Player:		7.00
1	Emmitt Smith	60.00
2	Brett Favre	60.00
3	Jerry Rice	30.00
4	Steve Young	25.00
5	Barry Sanders	30.00
6	Reggie White	15.00
7	Ricky Watters	7.00
8	Lawrence Phillips	7.00
9	Kerry Collins	14.00
10	Mark Brunell	30.00
11	John Elway	25.00
12	Dan Marino	60.00
13	Drew Bledsoe	30.00
14	Curtis Martin	45.00
15	Terrell Davis	35.00
16	Karim Abdul-Jabbar	14.00
17	Marvin Harrison	15.00
18	Keyshawn Johnson	15.00
19	Terry Glenn	14.00
20	Eddie George	30.00

1997 Pro Line DC III Road to the Super Bowl

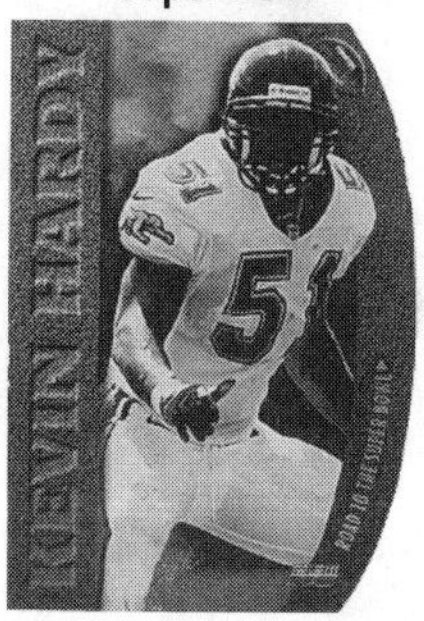

The 30-card, regular-sized, die-cut set was inserted every 12 packs of Pro Line III DC. The cards feature the same die-cut design as the DC Top Ten subset in the base set. The cards are numbered with a "SB" prefix.

		MT
Complete Set (30):		400.00
Common Player:		5.00
1	Ricky Watters	10.00
2	Ty Detmer	5.00
3	Emmitt Smith	50.00
4	Troy Aikman	25.00
5	Kerry Collins	10.00
6	Kevin Greene	5.00
7	Steve Young	20.00
8	Jerry Rice	25.00
9	Brett Favre	50.00
10	Reggie White	10.00
11	Cris Carter	5.00
12	Brad Johnson	5.00
13	Drew Bledsoe	25.00
14	Curtis Martin	35.00
15	Bruce Smith	5.00
16	Thurman Thomas	5.00
17	Jim Harbaugh	5.00
18	Marshall Faulk	15.00
19	Mark Brunell	25.00
20	Natrone Means	5.00
21	John Elway	20.00
22	Terrell Davis	30.00
23	Kordell Stewart	25.00
24	Jerome Bettis	10.00
25	Eddie George	30.00
26	Dan Marino	50.00
27	Terry Glenn	10.00
28	Antonio Freeman	10.00
29	Anthony Johnson	5.00
30	Kevin Hardy	5.00

1998 Pro Line DC III

Pro Line DC III was a 100-card, all die-cut set that included 20 DC Rewind subset cards and 10 Rookie Uprising subset cards. The primary base cards feature the player in an oval shot with gold foil extended and squared off on all four corners, with the Pro Line DC logo in the upper right corner. Inserts in the product included: Clear Cuts, X-Tra Effort, Decade Draft, SB Team Totals and Choice Cuts. Each card and insert was also included in a Perfect Cut 1 of 1 set that was encapsulated in a PSA container and graded Mint. This included 170 total cards and these were available through redemptions.

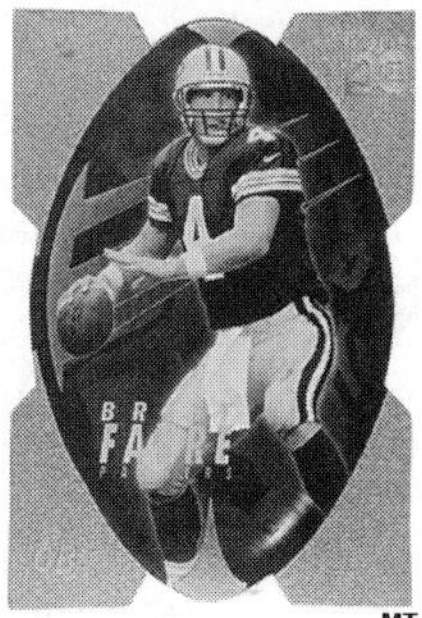

		MT
Complete Set (100):		50.00
Common Player:		.30
Minor Stars:		.60
Pack (4):		6.00
Wax Box (24):		90.00
1	Drew Bledsoe	2.00
2	Emmitt Smith	3.00
3	Dana Stubblefield	.30
4	Brett Favre	4.00
5	Derrick Alexander	.30
6	Bert Emanuel	.30
7	Joey Galloway	.60
8	Terrell Davis	2.00
9	Mark Brunell	2.00
10	Marshall Faulk	.60
11	Jake Reed	.30
12	Terry Allen	.30
13	Kordell Stewart	2.00
14	Reggie White	.60
15	Michael Irvin	.60
16	Tony Martin	.30
17	Barry Sanders	3.00
18	Carl Pickens	.30
19	Bobby Hoying	.30
20	Adrian Murrell	.60
21	Jeff George	.60
22	Tim Brown	.30
23	Karim Abdul-Jabbar	.60
24	Robert Smith	.30
25	Eddie George	2.50
26	Corey Dillon	1.50
27	Keyshawn Johnson	.60
28	Ricky Watters	.60
29	Robert Brooks	.30
30	Antonio Freeman	.60
31	Danny Kanell	.30
32	Steve McNair	1.50
33	Antowain Smith	1.50
34	Warrick Dunn	3.00
35	Napoleon Kaufman	.60
36	Trent Dilfer	.60
37	Herman Moore	.60
38	Brad Johnson	.30
39	Deion Sanders	1.00
40	Kerry Collins	1.25
41	Shannon Sharpe	.30
42	Irving Fryar	.30
43	Dorsey Levens	.60
44	Jerry Rice	2.00
45	Curtis Martin	2.00
46	Jerome Bettis	.60
47	Raymont Harris	.30
48	Vinny Testaverde	.30
49	Dan Marino	3.00
50	Junior Seau	.30
51	Steve Young	1.50
52	Troy Aikman	2.00
53	Jimmy Smith	.30
54	Ben Coates	.30
55	Gus Frerotte	.30
56	Marcus Allen	.60
57	Bruce Smith	.30
58	Jeff Blake	.60
59	John Elway	1.50
60	Rod Smith	.30
61	Andre Rison	.30
62	Isaac Bruce	.60
63	Cris Carter	.30
64	Danny Wuerffel	1.00
65	Rob Moore	.30
66	Garrison Hearst	.30
67	Warren Moon	.30
68	Checklist (Jerome Bettis)	.30
69	Marcus Allen (DC Rewind)	.30
70	James Stewart (DC Rewind)	.30
71	Karim Abdul-Jabbar (DC Rewind)	.30
72	Joey Galloway (DC Rewind)	.30
73	Corey Dillon (DC Rewind)	1.50
74	Andre Rison (DC Rewind)	.30
75	Napoleon Kaufman (DC Rewind)	.30
76	Dorsey Levens (DC Rewind)	.30
77	Irving Fryar (DC Rewind)	.30
78	Eric Metcalf (DC Rewind)	.30
79	Darrien Gordon (DC Rewind)	.30
80	Neil O'Donnell (DC Rewind)	.30
81	Rod Woodson (DC Rewind)	.30
82	Rob Johnson (DC Rewind)	.30
83	Michael Westbrook (DC Rewind)	.30
84	Jake Plummer (DC Rewind)	1.50

85	Bobby Hoying (DC Rewind)	.30
86	Adrian Murrell (DC Rewind)	.30
87	Jim Druckenmiller (DC Rewind)	1.50
88	Warren Moon (DC Rewind)	.30
89	Checklist (Dorsey Levens) (DC Rewind)	.30
90	Tony Gonzalez (Rookie Uprising)	.30
91	Jim Druckenmiller (Rookie Uprising)	1.50
92	Corey Dillon (Rookie Uprising)	1.50
93	Darrell Russell (Rookie Uprising)	.30
94	Byron Hanspard (Rookie Uprising)	1.00
95	Rae Carruth (Rookie Uprising)	1.00
96	Peter Boulware (Rookie Uprising)	.30
97	Troy Davis (Rookie Uprising)	1.00
98	Reidel Anthony (Rookie Uprising)	1.25
99	Tiki Barber (Rookie Uprising)	1.25
100	Checklist (Jake Plummer) (Rookie Uprising)	.30

1998 Pro Line DC III Choice Cuts

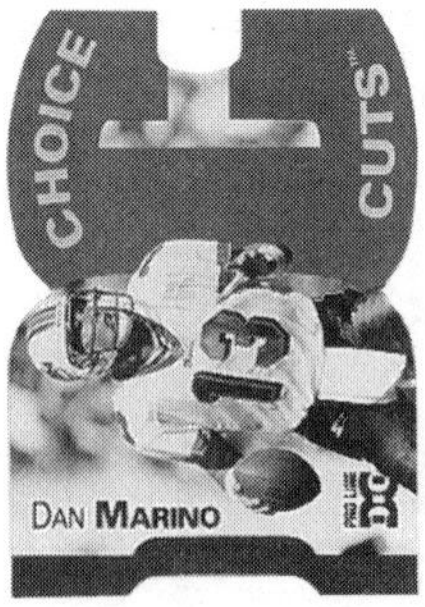

Choice Cuts were randomly inserted into packs of Pro Line DC III. The cards are horizontal and die-cut in design, with the player featured on the left side, and a large blue "C" die-cut out of the right side. The insert name is included in the blue "C" with "Choice" on the top and "Cuts" across the bottom. Choice Cuts are numbered on the back with a "CHC" prefix, with 10 cards in the set.

		MT
Complete Set (10):		75.00
Common Player:		3.00
1	Deion Sanders	6.00
2	Jerome Bettis	3.00
3	Troy Aikman	12.00
4	Jerry Rice	12.00
5	Mark Brunell	12.00
6	Curtis Martin	10.00
7	Cris Carter	3.00
8	Steve Young	8.00
9	Reggie White	3.00
10	Dan Marino	20.00

1998 Pro Line DC III Clear Cuts

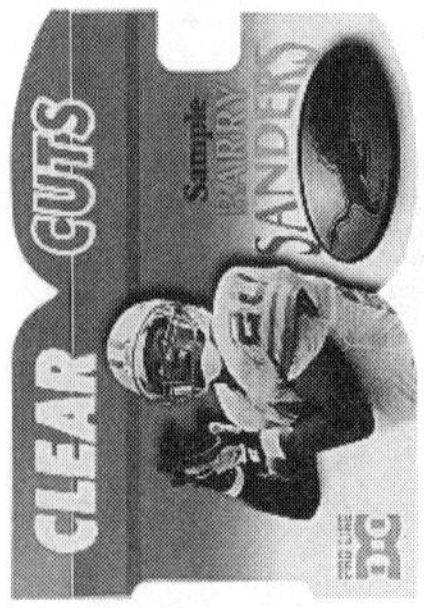

This 10-card set was printed on horizontal plastic that was die-cut. Clear Cuts were hobby exclusive, inserted one per 95 packs and sequentially numbered to 500. Cards featured the insert name printed across the top, with a gold foil finish. A color shot of the player was centered on the card, with his name and team logo off to the right. Clear Cuts inserts were numbered on the back with a "CLC" prefix.

		MT
Complete Set (10):		475.00
Common Player:		20.00
1	John Elway	40.00
2	Drew Bledsoe	50.00
3	Terrell Davis	50.00
4	Brett Favre	100.00
5	Cris Carter	20.00
6	Eddie George	75.00
7	Kordell Stewart	50.00
8	Warrick Dunn	75.00
9	Tim Brown	20.00
10	Barry Sanders	85.00

1998 Pro Line DC III Decade Draft

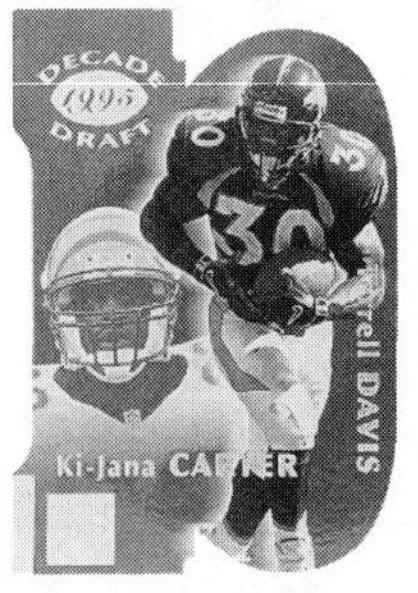

Decade Draft was a 10-card insert that was inserted at a rate of one per 24 packs in Pro Line DC III. The cards are die-cut in the shape of a "D" with foil etched around the edge. An action shot of the player is shown on the right side of the card with a closer shot on the left. Decade Draft inserts are numbered with a "DD" prefix on the back.

		MT
Complete Set (10):		120.00
Common Player:		2.50
1	T. Aikman, B. Sanders	25.00
2	J. George, E. Smith	20.00
3	R. Maryland, B. Favre	30.00
4	S. Emtman, C. Pickens	2.50
5	D. Bledsoe, D. Bledsoe	12.00
6	D. Wilkinson, M. Faulk	5.00
7	K. Carter, T. Davis	20.00
8	K. Johnson, E. George	15.00
9	O. Pace, W. Dunn	15.00
10	1998 Top Draft Pick	8.00

1998 Pro Line DC III Team Totals

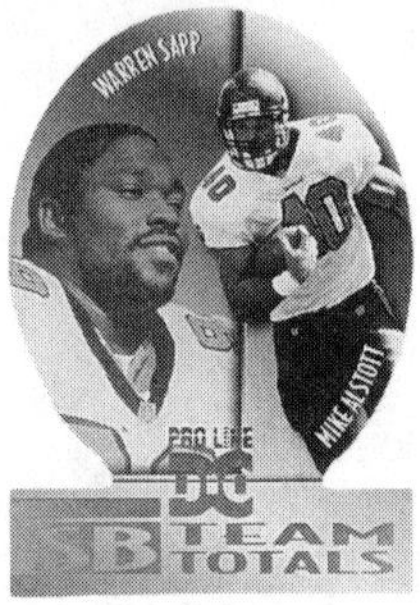

Team Totals was a 30-card insert that was found in packs of Pro Line DC III at a rate of one per eight packs. The cards were die-cut in the shape of a crystal ball, with the insert name across the bottom in gold foil and two shots of the player in the ball part - an action shot on the right and a close-up on the left. Team Totals inserts are numbered on the back with a "TT" prefix.

		MT
Complete Set (30):		100.00
Common Player:		2.00
Minor Stars:		4.00
1	Ben Coates, Willie McGinest	2.00
2	Michael Irvin, Deion Sanders	6.00
3	Carl Pickens, Dan Wilkinson	2.00
4	LeRoy Butler, Antonio Freeman	6.00
5	Adrian Murrell, Hugh Douglas	3.00
6	Raymont Harris, Bryan Cox	2.00
7	Ricky Watters, William Thomas	4.00
8	Neil Smith, Shannon Sharpe	3.00
9	Dana Stubblefield, Garrison Hearst	3.00
10	Keenan McCardell, Jeff Lageman	2.00
11	Rae Carruth, Lamar Lathon	4.00
12	Yancey Thigpen, Greg Lloyd	2.00
13	Chris Calloway, Michael Strahan	2.00
14	Troy Davis, Wayne Martin	3.00
15	Warren Moon, Cortez Kennedy	3.00
16	Rob Moore, Simeon Rice	2.00
17	O.J. McDuffie, Zach Thomas	3.00
18	John Randle, Robert Smith	3.00
19	Derrick Thomas, Elvis Grbac	3.00
20	Antowain Smith, Bruce Smith	10.00
21	Jeff George, Darrell Russell	2.00
22	Steve McNair, Darryll Lewis	10.00
23	Isaac Bruce, Leslie O'Neal	4.00
24	Junior Seau, Tony Martin	3.00
25	Warren Sapp, Mike Alstott	4.00
26	Jessie Tuggle, Jamal Anderson	2.00
27	Michael Jackson, Peter Boulware	2.00
28	Quentin Coryatt, Marvin Harrison	4.00
29	Bryant Westbrook, Scott Mitchell	2.00
30	Michael Westbrook, Darrell Green	3.00

1998 Pro Line DC III X-Tra Effort

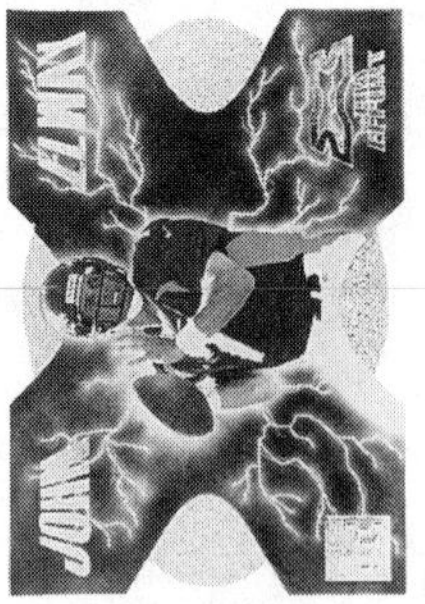

X-Tra Effort inserts are die-cut in the shape of an "X" on a horizontal format. Card fronts have the player's first name in the top left corner, his last name in the top right corner, a Pro Line DC logo in the bottom left and the insert name in the bottom right corner. The player is centered in the card with lightning bolts coming out on all sides. In addition, the front bears gold foil on all sides of the "X" as if a gold oval was set in back of the card to form a second layer. X-Tra Effort was a 20-card insert that was found one per 24 hobby packs and sequentially numbered to 1,000 sets. Cards carried an "XE" prefix on the back card number.

		MT
Complete Set (20):		325.00
Common Player:		5.00
1	Reggie White	8.00
2	Emmitt Smith	40.00
3	Junior Seau	5.00
4	Brett Favre	50.00
5	Warrick Dunn	30.00
6	Keyshawn Johnson	8.00
7	Dan Marino	40.00
8	Thurman Thomas	5.00
9	Steve Young	15.00
10	Curtis Martin	20.00
11	Karim Abdul-Jabbar	10.00
12	John Elway	20.00
13	Marcus Allen	8.00
14	Napoleon Kaufman	8.00
15	Irving Fryar	5.00
16	Mark Brunell	20.00
17	Andre Rison	5.00
18	Herman Moore	8.00
19	Jerry Rice	20.00
20	Kordell Stewart	20.00

1988 Pro Set Test Designs

Philadelphia Eagles quarterback Randall Cunningham is featured on these five prototype cards, used to preview Pro Set's 1989 debut set. The card numbers are the same on each card, but five different designs were used for the fronts. These are indicated with the corresponding card. Each card back is designed horizontally, with a mug shot, statistics, player profile and biographical information provided.

		MT
Complete Set (5):		160.00
Common Player:		40.00
315A	Randall Cunningham (No team or name listed on card front; borderless; logo is vertical)	40.00
315B	Randall Cunningham (No team or name listed on card front; border is silver; logo is vertical)	40.00
315C	Randall Cunningham (Name and team are listed on card front; borderless; logo is horizontal)	40.00
315D	Randall Cunningham (Team and name listed on card front; border is black; logo is horizontal)	40.00
315E	Randall Cunningham (Team and name listed on card front; border is gray; logo is horizontal)	40.00

1988 Pro Set Test

These promotional cards, used to preview Pro Set's debut set in 1989, can be distinguished from regular cards in several manners. First, each of the card backs is designed in a vertical fashion; the regular cards use a horizontal format. Also, the card number includes a # symbol before it. Plus, all the photos used for the fronts, except for the Jerry Rice photo, are different than those used on the regular cards.

		MT
Complete Set (8):		200.00
Common Player:		10.00
1	Dan Marino	80.00
2	Jerry Rice	65.00
3	Eric Dickerson	25.00
4	Reggie White	25.00
5	Mike Singletary	15.00
6	Frank Minnifield	10.00
7	Phil Simms	25.00
8	Jim Kelly	45.00

1989 Pro Set Promos

These five cards preview Pro Set's 1989 card design. The Santa Claus card was given to dealers, NFL representatives and members of the hobby press in December 1989. The Super Bowl card was given to those who attended the card show at Super Bowl XXIV in New Orleans in January 1990. The three player cards were samples which were mistakenly handed out at card shows in San Francisco and Chicago. The Bush and Lofton cards were intended to be included in Pro Set's Series II cards, but were bumped for Eric Dickerson and Greg Townsend. Sanders was given #446.

		MT
Complete Set (5):		125.00
Common Player:		10.00
445	Thomas Sanders	20.00
455	Blair Bush	20.00
463	James Lofton	25.00
1989	Santa Claus	50.00

1989 Pro Set

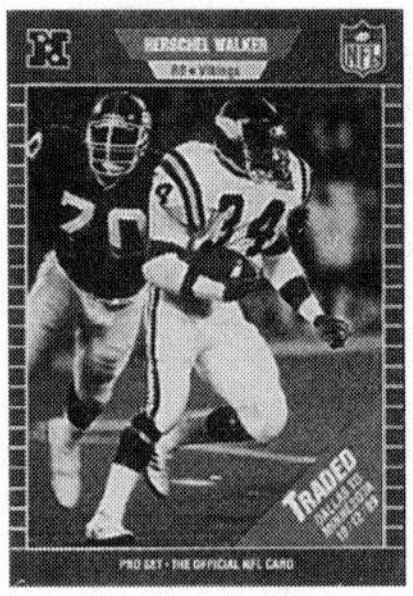

Pro Set's premier football issue was released in two series in the summer and fall of 1989. Printed on heavy white cardboard stock, the standard-size cards come in a variety of colors and feature full-color action shots on the front, full-color head shots on the back, and biographical notes and statistics on the back. The 615-card set (541 player/coach cards, 23 Super Bowl cards, 30 announcer cards, 20 Final Update cards, one commissioner card) was not released in factory-issued sets. Pro Set is the only one of the three 1989 football card sets featuring coaches cards. Pro Set released its first series in late July 1989, and its second series in September 1989. The third series, labeled "Final Update" on the boxes only, contained 20 additional cards of traded players, rookies and players not previously included in the set. Along with the re-released Art Shell card, these blue-bordered cards were included with Series I and II cards. Art Shell cards were printed on separate sheets and were inserted into late Series II and all Final Update print runs; the card was usually found on top of the pack.

		MT
Complete Set (561):		30.00
Complete Series 1 (440):		8.00
Complete Series 2 (100):		20.00
Complete Series 3 (21):		2.00
Common Player:		.03
Minor Stars:		.10
Series 1 Pack (14):		.45
Series 1 Box (36):		8.50
Series 2 or 3 Pack (14):		1.00
Series 2 or 3 Wax Box (36):		24.00
1	Stacey Bailey	.03
2	*Aundray Bruce*	.03
3	Rick Bryan	.03
4	Bobby Butler	.03
5	*Scott Case*	.10
6	Tony Casillas	.03
7	Floyd Dixon	.03
8	Rick Donnelly	.03
9	Bill Fralic	.03
10	Mike Gann	.03
11	Mike Kenn	.03
12	*Chris Miller*	.25
13	John Rade	.03
14	Gerald Riggs	.03
15	*John Settle*	.10
16	Marion Campbell	.03
17	Cornelius Bennett	.10
18	Derrick Burroughs	.03
19	Shane Conlan	.03
20	Ronnie Harmon	.03
21	*Kent Hull*	.10
22	Jim Kelly	.50
23	Mark Kelso	.03
24	Pete Metzelaars	.03
25	Scott Norwood	.03
26	Andre Reed	.10
27	Fred Smerlas	.03
28	Bruce Smith	.10
29	Leonard Smith	.03
30	Art Still	.03
31	Darryl Talley	.03
32	*Thurman Thomas*	1.50
33	Will Wolford	.03
34	Marv Levy (C)	.03
35	Neal Anderson	.03
36	Kevin Butler	.03
37	Jim Covert	.03
38	Richard Dent	.10
39	Dave Duerson	.03
40	Dennis Gentry	.03
41	Dan Hampton	.03
42	Jay Hilgenberg	.03
43	Dennis McKinnon	.03
44	Jim McMahon	.10
45	Steve McMichael	.03
46	*Brad Muster*	.10
47	William Perry ERR	3.00
48	Ron Rivera	.03
49	*Vestee Jackson*	.03
50	Mike Singletary	.10
51	Mike Tomczak	.03
52	*Keith Van Horne*	.03
53	Mike Ditka (C HOF stripe)	.10
54	Lewis Billups	.03
55	James Brooks	.03
56	Eddie Brown	.03
57	*Jason Buck*	.03
58	Boomer Esiason	.10
59	David Fulcher	.03
60	*Rodney Holman*	.10
61	Reggie Williams	.03
62	*Joe Kelly*	.03
63	Tim Krumrie	.03
64	Tim McGee	.03
65	Max Montoya	.03
66	Anthony Munoz	.10
67	Jim Skow	.03
68	*Eric Thomas*	.03
69	Leon White	.03
70	Ickey Woods	.03
71	Carl Zander	.03
72	Sam Wyche (C)	.03
73	Brian Brennan	.03
74	Earnest Byner	.03
75	Hanford Dixon	.03
76	Mike Pagel	.03
77	Bernie Kosar	.10
78	*Reggie Langhorne*	.10
79	Kevin Mack	.03
80	Clay Matthews	.03
81	Gerald McNeil	.03
82	Frank Minnifield	.03
83	Cody Risien	.03
84	Webster Slaughter	.10
85	Felix Wright	.03
86	Bud Carson (C)	.03
87	Bill Bates	.03
88	Kevin Brooks	.03
89	*Michael Irvin*	1.50
90	Jim Jeffcoat	.03
91	Too Tall Jones	.03
92	Eugene Lockhart	.03
93	*Nate Newton*	.20
94	Danny Noonan	.03
95	Steve Pelluer	.03
96	Herschel Walker	.10
97	Everson Walls	.03
98	Jimmy Johnson (C)	.10
99	Keith Bishop	.03
100	John Elway DRAFT	4.00
100a	John Elway TRADE	2.00
101	*Simon Fletcher*	.10
102	Mike Harden	.03
103	Mike Horan	.03
104	Mark Jackson	.03
105	Vance Johnson	.03
106	Rulon Jones	.03
107	Clarence Kay	.03
108	Karl Mecklenburg	.03
109	Ricky Nattiel	.03
110	*Steve Sewell*	.10
111	Dennis Smith	.03
112	Gerald Willhite	.03
113	Sammy Winder	.03
114	Dan Reeves	.10
115	Jim Arnold	.03
116	*Jerry Ball*	.10
117	*Bennie Blades*	.10
118	Lomas Brown	.03
119	Michael Cofer	.03
120	Garry James	.03
121	James Jones	.03
122	Chuck Long	.03
123	Pete Mandley	.03
124	Eddie Murray	.03
125	*Chris Speilman*	.10
126	Dennis Gibson	.03
127	Wayne Fontes (C)	.03
128	John Anderson	.03
129	Brent Fullwood	.03
130	Mark Cannon	.03
131	Tim Harris	.03
132	Mark Lee	.03
133	*Don Majkowski*	.10
134	Mark Murphy	.03
135	Brian Noble	.03
136	*Ken Ruettgers*	.03
137	Johnny Holland	.03
138	Randy Wright	.03
139	Lindy Infante (C)	.03
140	Steve Brown	.03
141	Ray Childress	.03
142	Jeff Donaldson	.03
143	Ernest Givins	.10
144	John Grimsley	.03
145	Alonzo Highsmith	.03
146	Drew Hill	.03
147	Robert Lyles	.03
148	*Bruce Matthews*	.10
149	Warren Moon	.25
150	Mike Munchak	.03
151	*Allen Pinkett*	.10
152	Mike Rozier	.03
153	Tony Zendejas	.03
154	Jerry Glanville (C)	.10
155	Albert Bentley	.03
156	Dean Biasucci	.03
157	Duane Bickett	.03
158	Bill Brooks	.03
159	*Chris Chandler*	2.00
160	Pat Beach	.03
161	Ray Donaldson	.03
162	Jon Hand	.03
163	Chris Hinton	.03
164	Rohn Stark	.03
165	Fredd Young	.03
166	Ron Meyer (C)	.03
167	Lloyd Burruss	.03
168	Carlos Carson	.03
169	Deron Cherry	.03
170	Irv Eatman	.03
171	Dino Hackett	.03
172	Steve DeBerg	.03
173	Albert Lewis	.03
174	Nick Lowery	.03
175	Bill Maas	.03
176	Christian Okoye	.10
177	Stephone Paige	.03
178	Mark Addickes	.03
179	*Kevin Ross*	.10
180	*Neil Smith*	.50
181	Marty Schottenheimer (C)	.03
182	Marcus Allen	.25
183	*Tim Brown*	1.50
184	Willie Gault	.03
185	Bo Jackson	.25
186	Howie Long	.10
187	Vann McElroy	.03
188	Matt Millen	.10
189	*Don Mosebar*	.03
190	Bill Pickel	.03
191	Jerry Robinson	.03
192	Jay Schroeder	.03
193	Stacey Toran	.10
193a	Stacey Toran (1961-1989)	.50
194	Mike Shanahan (C)	.10
195	Greg Bell	.03
196	Ron Brown	.03
197	*Aaron Cox*	.03
198	Henry Ellard	.03
199	Jim Everett	.10
200	Jerry Gray	.03
201	Kevin Greene	.10
202	Pete Holohan	.03
203	LeRoy Irvin	.03
204	Mike Lansford	.03
205	*Tom Newberry*	.10
206	Mel Owens	.03
207	Jackie Slater	.03
208	Doug Smith	.03
209	Mike Wilcher	.03
210	John Robinson (C)	.03
211	John Bosa	.03
212	Mark Brown	.03
213	Mark Clayton	.03
214	*Ferrell Edmunds* (corrected)	.10
214a	*Ferrell Edmonds* (error)	.50
215	Roy Foster	.03
216	Lorenzo Hampton	.03
217	Jim Jensen	.03
218	William Judson	.03
219	*Eric Kumerow*	.03
220	Dan Marino	2.00
221	John Offerdahl	.03
222	Fuad Reveiz	.03
223	Reggie Roby	.03
224	Brian Sochia	.03
225	Don Shula (C)	.20
226	Alfred Anderson	.03
227	Joey Browner	.03
228	Anthony Carter	.03
229	Chris Doleman	.03
230	*Hassan Jones*	.03
231	Steve Jordan	.03
232	Tommy Kramer	.03
233	*Carl Lee*	.03
234	*Kirk Lowdermilk*	.10
235	*Randall McDaniel*	.10
236	Doug Martin	.03
237	Keith Millard	.03
238	Darrin Nelson	.03
239	Jesse Solomon	.03
240	Scott Studwell	.03
241	Wade Wilson	.03
242	Gary Zimmerman	.03
243	Jerry Burns (C)	.03
244	*Bruce Armstrong*	.10
245	Raymond Clayburn	.03
246	Reggie Dupard	.03
247	Tony Eason	.03
248	Sean Farrell	.03
249	Doug Flutie	.75
250	*Brent Williams*	.03
251	Roland James	.03
252	Ronnie Lippett	.03
253	Fred Marion	.03
254	Lawrence McGrew	.03
255	Stanley Morgan	.03
256	*Johnny Rembert*	.03
257	*John Stephens*	.10
258	Andre Tippett	.03
259	Garin Veris	.03
260	Ray Berry (C HOF stripe)	.10
261	Morten Andersen	.10
262	Hoby Brenner	.03
263	Stan Brock	.03
264	Brad Edelmann	.03
265	James Geathers	.03
266	Bobby Hebert ("touchdown passers")	.50
266a	Bobby Hebert ("touchdown passes")	.10
267	*Craig Heyward*	.10
268	Lonzell Hill	.03
269	Dalton Hilliard	.03
270	Rickey Jackson	.03
271	Steve Korte	.03
272	Eric Martin	.03
273	Reuben Mayes	.03
274	Sam Mills	.03
275	*Brett Perriman*	.25
276	Pat Swilling	.10
277	John Tice	.03
278	Jim Mora (C)	.03
279	Eric Moore	.03
280	Carl Banks	.03
281	Mark Bavaro	.03
282	Maurice Carthon	.03
283	*Mark Collins*	.10
284	Erik Howard	.03
285	Terry Kinard	.03
286	Sean Landeta	.03
287	Lionel Manuel	.03
288	Leonard Marshall	.03
289	Joe Morris	.03
290	Bart Oates	.03
291	Phil Simms	.10
292	Lawrence Taylor	.20

293	Bill Parcells (C)	.10
294	Dave Cadigan	.03
295	*Kyle Clifton*	.10
296	Alex Gordon	.03
297	*James Hasty*	.10
298	Johnny Hector	.03
299	Bobby Humphery	.03
300	Pat Leahy	.03
301	Marty Lyons	.03
302	*Reggie McElroy*	.10
303	*Erik McMillan*	.10
304	Freeman McNeil	.03
305	Ken O'Brien	.03
306	Pat Ryan	.03
307	Mickey Shuler	.03
308	Al Toon	.03
309	JoJo Townsell	.03
310	Roger Vick	.03
311	Joe Walton (C)	.03
312	Jerome Brown	.03
313	Keith Byars	.03
314	*Cris Carter*	2.50
315	Randall Cunningham	.40
316	Terry Hoage	.03
317	Wes Hopkins	.03
318	*Keith Jackson*	.20
319	Mike Quick	.03
320	Mike Reichenbach	.03
321	Dave Rimington	.03
322	John Teltschik	.03
323	Anthony Toney	.03
324	Andre Waters	.03
325	Reggie White	.25
326	Luis Zendejas	.03
327	Buddy Ryan (C)	.03
328	Robert Awalt	.03
329	*Tim McDonald*	.10
330	Roy Green	.03
331	Neil Lomax	.03
332	Cedric Mack	.03
333	Stump Mitchell	.03
334	Niko Noga	.03
335	*Jay Novacek*	.25
336	Freddie Joe Nunn	.03
337	Luis Sharpe	.03
338	Vai Sikahema	.03
339	J.T. Smith	.03
340	Ron Wolfley	.03
341	Gene Stallings (C)	.03
342	Gary Anderson (Pit.)	.03
343	*Bubby Brister*	.75
344	*Dermontti Dawson*	.10
345	*Thomas Everett*	.10
346	Delton Hall	.03
347	*Bryan Hinkle*	.10
348	*Merril Hoge*	.10
349	Tunch Ilken	.03
350	*Aaron Jones*	.10
351	Louis Lipps	.03
352	David Little	.03
353	*Hardy Nickerson*	.20
354	*Rod Woodson*	.75
355	Chuck Noll ("One of the only three") (C)	.15
355a	Chuck Noll ("One of only two") (C)	.15
356	Gary Anderson (S.D.)	.03
357	*Rod Berstine*	.10
358	Gill Byrd	.03
359	Vencie Glenn	.03
360	Dennis McKnight	.03
361	Lionel James	.03
362	Mark Malone	.03
363	*Anthony Miller 14.8*	.40
363a	*Anthony Miller 3*	.40
364	Ralf Mojsiejenko	.03
365	Leslie O'Neal	.03
366	Jamie Holland	.03
367	Lee Williams	.03
368	Dan Henning	.03
369	*Harris Barton*	.10
370	Michael Carter	.03
371	*Mike Cofer* (S.F.)	.10
372	Roger Craig	.03
373	Riki Ellison	.03
374	Jim Fahnhorst	.03
375	John Frank	.03
376	Jeff Fuller	.03
377	Don Griffin	.03
378	Charles Haley	.10
379	Ronnie Lott	.10
380	Tim McKyer	.03
381	Joe Montana	1.50
382	Tom Rathman	.03
383	Jerry Rice	1.50
384	*John Taylor*	.25
385	Keena Turner	.03
386	Michael Walter	.03
387	Bubba Paris	.03
388	Steve Young	1.00
389	*George Siefert* (C)	.10
390	*Brian Blades*	.20
391	Brian Bosworth (Seahawks)	.10
391a	Brian Bosworth (Seattle)	.10
392	Jeff Bryant	.03
393	Jacob Green	.03
394	Norm Johnson	.03
395	Dave Krieg	.03
396	Steve Largent	.15
397	Bryan Millard	.03
398	Paul Moyer	.03
399	Joe Nash	.03
400	Rufus Porter	.03
401	*Eugene Robinson*	.20
402	Bruce Scholtz	.03
403	*Kelly Stouffer*	.10
404	Curt Warner 1455 (yards 1,455)	1.00
404a	Curt Warner (yards 6,074)	.15
405	John L. Williams	.03
406	*Tony Woods*	.10
407	David Wyman	.03
408	Chuck Knox (C)	.03
409	*Mark Carrier*	.50
410	Randy Grimes	.03
411	*Paul Gruber*	.10
412	Harry Hamilton	.03
413	Ron Holmes	.03
414	Donald Igwebuike	.03
415	Dan Turk	.03
416	Ricky Reynolds	.03
417	Bruce Hill	.03
418	Lars Tate	.03
419	Vinny Testaverde	.30
420	James Wilder	.03
421	Ray Perkins (C)	.03
422	Jeff Bostic	.03
423	Kelvin Bryant	.03
424	Gary Clark	.10
425	Monte Coleman	.03
426	Darrell Green	.03
427	Joe Jacoby	.03
428	Jim Lachey	.03
429	Charles Mann	.03
430	Dexter Manley	.03
431	Darryl Grant	.03
432	*Mark May*	.10
433	Art Monk	.15
434	*Mark Rypien*	.20
435	Ricky Sanders	.03
436	*Alvin Walton*	.10
437	Don Warren	.03
438	Jamie Morris	.03
439	Doug Williams	.03
440	Joe Gibbs (C)	.10
441	Marcus Cotton	.03
442	Joel Williams	.03
443	Joe Devlin	.03
444	Robb Riddick	.03
445	William Perry	.03
446	*Thomas Sanders*	.03
447	Brian Blades	.03
448	Cris Collinsworth	.10
449	Stanford Jennings	.03
450	Barry Krauss	.03
451	Ozzie Newsome	.10
452	Mike Oliphant	.03
453	Tony Dorsett	.15
454	Bruce McNorton	.03
455	Eric Dickerson	.20
456	Keith Bostic	.03
457	Sam Clancy	.03
458	Jack Del Rio	.03
459	Mike Webster	.03
460	Bob Golic	.03
461	Otis Wilson	.03
462	Mike Haynes	.03
463	Greg Townsend	.03
464	Mark Duper	.03
465	E.J. Junior	.03
466	Troy Stradford	.03
467	Mike Merriweather	.03
468	Irving Fryar	.10
469	*Vaughan Johnson*	.03
470	Pepper Johnson	.03
471	Gary Reasons	.03
472	*Perry Williams*	.10
473	Wesley Walker	.03
474	Anthony Bell	.03
475	Earl Ferrell	.03
476	Craig Wolfley	.03
477	Billy Ray Smith	.03
478	Jim McMahon	.10
478a	Jim McMahon (traded)	.40
479	Eric Wright	.03
480	Earnest Byner	.10
480a	Earnest Byner (traded)	.30
481	Russ Grimm	.03
482	Wilber Marshall	.03
483	Gerald Riggs	.03
484	*Brian Davis*	.10
485	*Shawn Collins*	.10
486	*Deion Sanders*	2.00
487	*Trace Armstrong*	.10
488	*Donnell Woolford*	.20
489	*Eric Metcalf*	.25
490	*Troy Aikman*	3.00
491	*Steve Walsh*	.20
492	*Steve Atwater*	.30
493	*Bobby Humphrey*	.10
494	*Barry Sanders*	15.00
495	*Tony Mandarich*	.20
496	*David Williams*	.10
497	*Andre Rison*	1.00
498	*Derrick Thomas*	1.00
499	*Cleveland Gary*	.20
500	*Bill Hawkins*	.10
501	*Louis Oliver*	.10
502	*Sammie Smith*	.10
503	*Hart Lee Dykes*	.10
504	*Wayne Martin*	.10
505	*Brian Williams*	.10
506	*Jeff Lageman*	.10
507	*Eric Hill*	.10
508	*Joe Wolf*	.10
509	*Timm Rosenbach*	.10
510	*Tom Ricketts*	.10
511	*Tim Worley*	.10
512	*Burt Grossman*	.10
513	*Keith DeLong*	.10
514	*Andy Heck*	.10
515	*Broderick Thomas*	.10
516	*Don Beebe*	.25
517	*James Thornton*	.10
518	*Eric Kattus*	.10
519	*Bruce Kozerski*	.10
520	*Brian Washington*	.10
521	*Rodney Peete*	.25
522	*Erik Affholter*	.10
523	*Anthony Dilweg*	.10
524	*O'Brien Alston*	.10
525	*Mike Elkins*	.10
526	*Jonathan Hayes*	.10
527	*Terry McDaniel*	.10
528	*Frank Stams*	.10
529	*Darryl Ingram*	.10
530	*Henry Thomas*	.10
531	*Eric Coleman*	.10
532	*Sheldon White*	.10
533	*Eric Allen*	.20
534	Robert Drummond	.03
535	Gizmo Williams ("Scouting Photo")	10.00
535a	Gizmo Williams (no "Scouting Photo")	.25
535b	Gizmo Williams (no "Scouting Photo," "Canadian Football" on back)	.15
536	*Billy Joe Tolliver*	.20
537	*Danny Stubbs*	.10
538	*Wesley Walls*	.40
539	James Jefferson (no stripe)	.30
539a	James Jefferson (Pro Set Prospect stripe)	.10
540	Tracy Rocker	.03
541	Art Shell (C)	.10
542	*Lemuel Stinson*	.15
543	*Tyrone Braxton*	.10
543a	*Tyrone Braxton* (back photo actually Ken Bell)	.10
544	*David Treadwell*	.10
545	*Willie Anderson*	.20
546	*Dave Meggett*	.25
547	*Lewis Tillman*	.20
548	*Carnell Lake*	.20
549	*Marion Butts*	.20
550	*Sterling Sharpe*	1.00
551	Ezra Johnson	.03
552	*Clarence Verdin*	.10
553	Mervyn Fernandez	.03
554	Ottis Anderson	.10
555	Gary Hogeboom	.03
556	Paul Palmer	.03
557	Jesse Solomon	.03
558	Chip Banks	.03
559	Steve Pelluer	.03
560	Darrin Nelson	.03
561	Herschel Walker	.10
CC1	Pete Rozelle	.50

1989 Pro Set Announcer Inserts

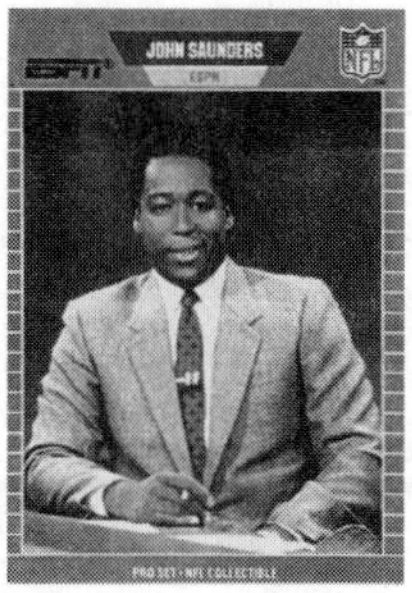

This set of 30 cards was issued in Pro Set's Series II wax packs, one per pack. Like the Super Bowl inserts, the glossy cards are standard size. They feature color photos (bordered in bright orange) of the announcer on the front and back - if the announcer is a former player, a shot of him in action is shown. If the announcer made it to the Hall of Fame as a player (Terry Bradshaw, O.J. Simpson), a yellow stripe bearing a "Hall of Fame" label is in the lower left corner of his action picture. Pro Set had announced the names of the players of its first 20 cards in its premier issue of Pro Set Gazette. Since the initial announcement, Pro Set acquired the rights to NBC announcers and added them shortly before the presses began to roll. Verne Lundquist was apparently substituted for Dan Jiggetts just before the print run began.

		MT
Complete Set (30):		5.00
Common Player:		.08
1	Dan Dierdorf	.25
2	Frank Gifford	.75
3	Al Michaels	.15
4	Pete Axthelm	.08
5	Chris Berman	.25
6	Tom Jackson	.15
7	Mike Patrick	.08
8	John Saunders	.08
9	Joe Theismann	.30
10	Steve Sabol	.08
11	Jack Buck	.08
12	Terry Bradshaw	.50
13	James Brown	.08
14	Dan Fouts	.30
15	Dick Butkus	.50
16	Irv Cross	.08
17	Brent Musberger	.15
18	Ken Stabler	.25
19	Dick Stockton	.08
20	Hank Stram	.08
21	Verne Lundquist	.08
22	Will McDonough	.08
23	Bob Costas	.25
24	Dick Enberg	.15
25	Joe Namath	.65
26	Bob Trumpy	.08
27	Merlin Olsen	.25
28	Ahmad Rashad	.30
29	O.J. Simpson	2.00
30	Bill Walsh	.30

1989 Pro Set Super Bowl Inserts

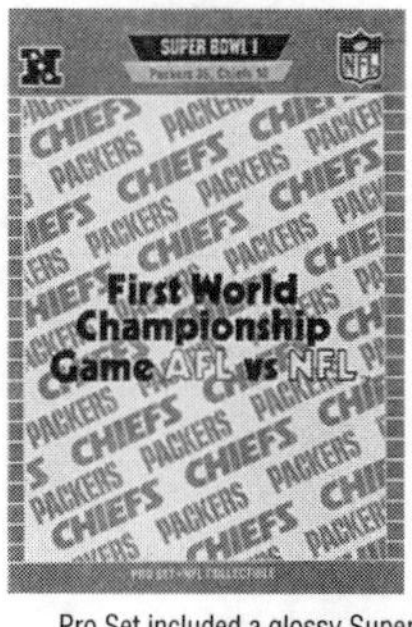

Pro Set included a glossy Super Bowl card (1 through 23) in each wax pack of its 1989 Series I cards. The standard-size cards show the official logo of each Super Bowl surrounded by a bright orange border on the front of the card, with the stylized names of the two participating teams in the background. Card backs include a recap of the game and a line score.

		MT
Complete Set (23):		5.00
Common Player:		.25
1	Super Bowl I	.25
2	Super Bowl II	.25
3	Super Bowl IV	.25
4	Super Bowl IV	.25
5	Super Bowl V	.25
6	Super Bowe VI	.25
7	Super Bowl VII	.25
8	Super Bowl VIII	.25
9	Super Bowl IX	.25
10	Super Bowl X	.25
11	Super Bowl XI	.25
12	Super Bowl XII	.25
13	Super Bowl XIII	.25
14	Super Bowl XIV	.25
15	Super Bowl XV	.25
16	Super Bowl XVI	.25
17	Super Bowl XVII	.25
18	Super Bowl XVIII	.25
19	Super Bowl XIX	.25
20	Super Bowl XX	.25
21	Super Bowl XXI	.25
22	Super Bowl XXII	.25
23	Super Bowl XXIII	.25

1989 Pro Set GTE SB Album

This 40-card set was made available to those who attended the Super Bowl XXIV game in New Orleans in 1990. Players from the participants in the game, the San Francisco 49ers and Denver Broncos, are represented in the set. The card numbers are identical to those in the regular set, but these cards can be distinguished from the regulars by the NFC or AFC Champs designation on the card front, along with the Super Bowl logo. GTE issued the cards in conjunction with Pro Set, and created a card album to hold the set.

		MT
Complete Set (40):		30.00
Common Player:		.40
99	Keith Bishop	.40
100	John Elway	6.00
101	Simon Fletcher	.60
103	Mike Horan	.40
104	Mark Jackson	.70
105	Vance Johnson	.60
107	Clarence Kay	.40
108	Karl Mecklenburg	.60
109	Ricky Nattiel	.60
110	Steve Sewell	.50
111	Dennis Smith	.50
113	Sammy Winder	.50
114	Dan Reeves CO	.60
369	Harris Barton	.40
370	Michael Carter	.60
371	Mike Cofer	.40
372	Roger Craig	1.75
374	Jim Fahnhorst	.40
377	Don Griffin	.50
378	Charles Haley	.60
379	Ronnie Lott	2.50
380	Tim McKyer	.50
381	Joe Montana	11.00
382	Tom Rathman	.75
383	Jerry Rice	8.00
384	John Taylor	2.00
385	Keena Turner	.50
386	Michael Walter	.40
387	Bubba Paris	.60
388	Steve Young	4.00
389	George Seifert CO	.50
479	Eric Wright	.60
492	Steve Atwater	1.00
493	Bobby Humphrey	.75
537	Danny Stubbs	.40
543	Tyrone Braxton	.50
544	David Treadwell	.40
----	AFC Logo XXIV Collectible	.60
----	NFC logo XXIV Collectible	.60
----	Superdome XXIV Collectible	.60

1990 Pro Set Draft Day

Each of these cards, numbered 669, was issued by Pro Set on the day of the 1990 NFL draft to present various scenarios for the draft. The card fronts preview Pro Set's 1990 main set design; each back uses a horizontal format and includes a mug shot, biographical information and a player profile.

		MT
Complete Set (3):		25.00
Common Player:		3.00
669A	Jeff George	12.00
669B	Jeff George	12.00
669D	Keith McCants	3.00

1990 Pro Set

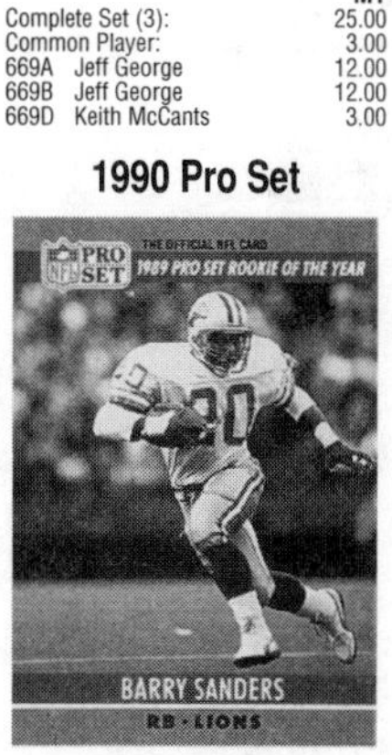

Pro Set's Series I was issued in late May of 1990. The sophomore set for the Dallas-based company was its first using its own printing press, and that allowed Pro Set to create die-cut borderless cards. Again, several insert cards were included throughout Series I: Paul Tagliabue was randomly included in early Series I wax packs; golfer Payne Stewart was added to the rotation; and Jeff George completed the rotating triumverate in late Series I printings. Because of a squabble over what card companies he wanted to appear with, Eric Dickerson was not to appear in any 1990 card sets. Pro Set already had a card of him created, however, and was forced to pull them by hand from Series I. Some, however, did get through to the hobby. Issued in November 1990, the second series of Pro Set was, unlike the year before, not included in Series I wax boxes. In addition, space was saved in the middle of the set for the mail-in Final Update offer. Five cards were inserted on a rotating basis in every 50th pack: Paul Tagliabue (carried over from Series I), Payne Stewart (same), Santa Claus, Joe Robbie, and Marvel Comics Super Pro. The Final Update was available in late January through a mail-in offer. It included 28 cards, plus three other special cards: card 799, which featured Ronnie Lott in his role as a spokesman for the NFL's "Stay in School" program; the Series I Andre Rison card with a traded stripe; and cards 800, Emmitt Smith and Mark Carrier, the 1990 NFL Pro Set Rookies of the Year in the 1991 Pro Set design. One correction was made very early in the print run. The text on the back of card 772, Dexter Manley, originally read, "Reinstated by Paul Tagliabue 11 weeks into the 1990 season after suspension for violating the league's substance-abuse policy." According to reports, Manley's agent objected to the wording, and it was changed to "After missing the first 10 weeks of the 1990 season, Dexter returned to the NFL." Very few of the original cards were issued.

		MT
Complete Set (801):		15.00
Complete Series 1 (377):		6.00
Complete Series 2 (392):		6.00
Complete Series 3 (32):		3.00
Common Player:		.03
Series 1 Pack (14+1):		.35
Series 1 Wax Box (36):		8.00
Series 2 Pack (14+1):		.50
Series 2 Wax Box (36):		11.00
1	Barry Sanders (ROY)	.75
2	Joe Montana (SPL, back reads "Kelly-3,521 yards")	.50
2a	Joe Montana (SPL, back corrected to "Kelly: 3,130 yards")	.75
3	Lindy Infante (SPL)	.03
4	Warren Moon (SPL)	.10
5	Keith Millard (SPL)	.03
6	Derrick Thomas (SPL)	.10
7	Ottis Anderson (SPL)	.03
8	Joe Montana (LL)	.50
9	Christian Okoye (SPL)	.03
10	Thurman Thomas	.25
11	Mike Cofer (SPL)	.03
12	Dalton Hilliard (SPL)	.03
13	Sterling Sharpe (LL)	.20
14	Rich Camarillo (LL)	.03
15	Walter Stanley (SPL, #8 on back)	.10
15a	Walter Stanley (SPL, #86 on back)	.10
16	Rod Woodson (LL)	.03
17	Felix Wright (LL)	.03
18	Chris Doleman (SPL, error back)	.10
18a	Chris Doleman (SPL, back corrected to 104.5 sacks for Taylor; "Townsent" corrected to "Townsend")	.10
19	Andre Ware (SPL)	.10
19a	Andre Ware (SPL, drafted stripe added)	.10
20	Mohammed Elewonibi (SPL)	.05
20a	Mohammed Elewonibi (SPL, drafted stripe added)	.05
21	Percy Snow (SPL)	.05
21a	Percy Snow (SPL, drafted stripe added)	.05
22	Anthony Thompson (SPL)	.10
22a	Anthony Thompson (SPL, drafted stripe added)	.10
23	Buck Buchanan (HOF)	.03
24	Bob Griese (HOF)	.03
25	Franco Harris (HOF)	.05
25a	Franco Harris (HOF, corrected birthdate: 3/7/50)	.05
26	Ted Hendricks (HOF)	.03
27	Jack Lambert (HOF)	.08
27a	Jack Lambert (HOF, corrected birthdate 7/8/52)	.08
28	Tom Landry (HOF)	.06
29	Bob St. Clair (HOF)	.03
30	Aundray Bruce	.06
31	Tony Casillas	.03
32	Shawn Collins	.03
33	Marcus Cotton	.03
34	Bill Fralic	.03
35	Chris Miller	.06
36	Deion Sanders	.30
37	John Settle	.03
38	Jerry Glanville	.03
39	Cornelius Bennett	.03
40	Jim Kelly	.35
41	Mark Kelso	.03
42	Scott Norwood	.03
43	*Nate Odomes*	.30
44	Scott Radecic	.03
45	Jim Ritcher	.03
46	Leonard Smith	.03
47	Darryl Talley	.03
48	Marv Levy (C)	.03
49	Neal Anderson	.03
50	Kevin Butler	.03
51	Jim Covert	.03
52	Richard Dent	.03
53	Jay Hilgenberg	.03
54	Steve McMichael	.03
55	Ron Morris	.03
56	John Roper	.03
57	Mike Singletary	.03
59	Mike Ditka (C)	.03
60	Lewis Billups	.03
61	Eddie Brown	.03
62	Jason Buck	.03
63	Rickey Dixon (no bio notes under photo)	.10
63a	Rickey Dixon (with bio notes)	.10
64	Tim McGee	.03
65	Eric Thomas	.03
66	Ickey Woods	.03
67	Carl Zander	.03
68	Sam Wyche (C, no bio notes under photo)	.05
68a	Sam Wyche (C, corrected)	.05
69	Paul Farren	.03
70	Thane Gash	.03
71	David Grayson	.03
72	Bernie Kosar	.03
73	Reggie Langhorne	.03
74	Eric Metcalf	.03
75	Ozzie Newsome	.10
75a	Ozzie Newsome (corrected hometown: Muscle Shoals, AL)	.10
75	Cody Risien (SP)	.10
76	Felix Wright	.03
77	Bud Carson (C)	.03
78	Troy Aikman	1.00
79	Michael Irvin	.30
80	Jim Jeffcoat	.03
81	Crawford Ker	.03
82	Eugene Lockhart	.03
83	*Kelvin Martin*	.25
84	*Ken Norton Jr.*	.50
85	Jimmy Johnson (C)	.03
86	Steve Atwater	.03
87	Tyrone Braxton	.03
88	John Elway	.40
89	Simon Fletcher	.03
90	Ron Holmes	.03
91	Bobby Humphrey	.03
92	Vance Johnson	.03
93	Ricky Nattiel	.03
94	Dan Reeves	.03
95	Jim Arnold	.03
96	Jerry Ball	.03
97	Bennie Blades	.03
98	Lomas Brown	.03
99	Michael Cofer	.03
100	Richard Johnson	.03
101	Eddie Murray	.03
102	Barry Sanders	1.25
103	Chris Spielman	.03
104	*William White*	.08
105	*Eric Williams*	.08
106	Wayne Fontes (C)	.03
107	Brent Fullwood	.03
108	*Ron Hallstrom*	.08
109	Tim Harris	.03
110	Johnny Holland (no name, number on back)	1.00
110a	Johnny Holland (corrected)	.15
111	Perry Kemp (Ken Stills photo on back)	.10
111a	Perry Kemp (corrected)	.10
112	Don Majkowski	.03
113	Mark Murphy	.03
114	Sterling Sharpe	.20
114a	Sterling Sharpe (corrected birthplace: Chicago, IL)	.20
115	Ed West	.03
116	Lindy Infante (C)	.03
117	Steve Brown	.03
118	Ray Childress	.03
119	Ernest Givins	.03
120	John Grimsley	.03
121	Alonzo Highsmith	.03
122	Drew Hill	.03
123	Bubba McDowell	.03
124	Dean Steinkuhler	.03
125	Lorenzo White	.10
126	Tony Zendejas	.03
127	Jack Pardee (C)	.03
128	Albert Bentley	.03
129	Dean Biasucci	.03
130	Duane Bickett	.03
131	Bill Brooks	.03
132	John Hand	.03
133	Mike Prior	.03
134	Andre Rison (no stripe)	.25
134a	Andre Rison (with stripe)	.50
135	Rohn Stark	.03
136	Donnell Thompson	.03
137	Clarence Verdin	.03
138	Fredd Young	.03
139	Ron Meyer (C)	.03
140	*John Alt*	.08
141	Steve DeBerg	.03
142	Irv Eatman	.03
143	Dino Hackett	.03
144	Nick Lowery	.03
145	Bill Maas	.03
146	Stephone Paige	.03
147	Neil Smith	.25
148	Marty Schottenheimer (C)	.03
149	Steve Beuerlein	.25
150	Tim Brown	.35
151	Mike Dyal	.03
152	Mervyn Fernandez	.10
152a	Mervyn Fernandez (status corrected to "Drafted 10th round '83")	.10
153	Willie Gault	.03
154	Bob Golic	.03
155	Bo Jackson	.40
156	Don Mosebar	.03
157	Steve Smith	.03
158	Greg Townsend	.03

159 *Bruce Wilkerson* .08
160 Steve Wisniewski .03
161 Art Shell (C) .10
161a Art Shell (C, birthdate corrected to 11/26/46) .10
162 Willie Anderson .10
163 Greg Bell .03
164 Henry Ellard .03
165 Jim Everett .03
166 Jerry Gray .03
167 Kevin Greene .03
168 Pete Holohan .03
169 *Larry Kelm* .08
170 Tom Newberry .03
171 Vince Newsome .03
172 Irv Pankey .03
173 Jackie Slater .03
174 *Fred Strickland* .08
175 Mike Wilcher .03
176 John Robinson (C) .03
177 Mark Clayton .03
178 Roy Foster .03
179 *Harry Galbreath* .08
180 Jim Jensen .03
181 Dan Marino .75
182 Louis Oliver .03
183 Sammie Smith .03
184 Brian Sochia .03
185 Don Shula (C) .03
186 Joey Browner .03
187 Anthony Carter .03
188 Chris Doleman .03
189 Steve Jordan .03
190 Carl Lee .03
191 Randall McDaniel .03
192 Mike Merriweather .03
193 Keith Millard .03
194 Al Noga .03
195 Scott Studwell .03
196 Henry Thomas .03
197 Herschel Walker .03
198 Wade Wilson .03
199 Gary Zimmerman .03
200 Jerry Burns (C) .03
201 *Vincent Brown* .15
202 Hart Lee Dykes .03
203 Sean Farrell .03
204 Fred Marion (49er with belt) .05
204a Fred Marion (corrected) .05
205 Stanley Morgan .03
206 Eric Sievers .03
207 John Stephens .03
208 Andre Tippett .03
209 Rod Rust (C) .03
210 Morten Andersen (name in white on back) .10
210a Morten Andersen (corrected) .10
211 Brad Edelman .03
212 John Fourcade .03
213 Dalton Hilliard .03
214 Rickey Jackson .03
215 Vaughan Johnson .03
216 Eric Martin (name in white on back) .05
216a Eric Martin (corrected) .05
217 Sam Mills .03
218 Pat Swilling .03
219 *Frank Warren* .08
220 Jim Wilks .03
221 Jim Mora (C, name in white on back) .03
221a Jim Mora (C, corrected) .03
222 Raul Allegre .03
223 Carl Banks .03
224 John Elliot .03
225 Erik Howard .03
226 Pepper Johnson .03
227 Leonard Marshall .03
228 David Meggett .10
229 Bart Oates .03
230 Phil Simms .10
231 Lawrence Taylor .10
232 Bill Parcells (C) .03
233 Troy Benson .03
234 Kyle Clifton .03
235 Johnny Hector .03
236 Jeff Lageman .03
237 Pat Leahy .03
238 Freeman McNeil .03
239 Ken O'Brien .03
240 Al Toon .03
241 JoJo Townsell .03
242 Bruce Coslet (C) .03
243 Eric Allen .03
244 Jerome Brown .03
245 Keith Byars .03
246 Cris Carter .35
247 Randall Cunningham .15
248 Keith Jackson .25
249 Mike Quick .03
250 Clyde Simmons .03
251 Andre Waters .03
252 Reggie White .15
253 Buddy Ryan (C) .03
254 Rich Camarillo .03
255 Earl Ferrell .03
256 Roy Green .03
257 *Ken Harvey* .08
258 *Ernie Jones* .10
259 Tim McDonald .03
260 Timm Rosenbach .03
261 Luis Sharpe .03
262 Vai Sikahema .03
263 J.T. Smith .03
264 Ron Wolfley .03
265 Joe Bugel (C) .03
266 Gary Anderson .03
267 Bubby Brister .10
268 Merril Hoge .03
269 Carnell Lake .03
270 Louis Lipps .03
271 David Little .03
272 Greg Lloyd .03
273 Keith Willie .03
274 Tim Worley .03
275 Chuck Noll (C) .03
276 Marion Butts .06
277 Gill Byrd .03
278 Vencie Glenn .03
279 Burt Grossman .03
280 Gary Plummer .03
281 Billy Ray Smith .03
282 Billy Joe Tolliver .03
283 Dan Henning (C) .03
284 Harris Barton .03
285 Michael Carter .03
286 Mike Cofer .03
287 Roger Craig .03
288 Don Griffin .03
289 Charles Haley .05
289a Charles Haley (stats corrected to 5 total fumble recoveries) .05
290 *Pierce Holt* .10
291 Ronnie Lott .10
292 Guy McIntyre .03
293 Joe Montana 1.00
294 Tom Rathman .03
295 Jerry Rice .75
296 *Jesse Sapolu* .05
297 John Taylor .20
298 Michael Walter .03
299 George Seifert (C) .03
300 Jeff Bryant .03
301 Jacob Green .03
302 Norm Johnson .03
303 Bryan Millard .03
304 Joe Nash .03
305 Eugene Robinson .03
306 John L. Williams .03
307 Dave Wyman .03
308 Chuck Knox (C) .03
309 Mark Carrier .03
310 Paul Gruber .03
311 Harry Hamilton .03
312 Bruce Hill .03
313 Donald Igwebuike .03
314 Kevin Murphy .03
315 Ervin Randle .03
316 Mark Robinson .03
317 Lars Tate .03
318 Vinny Testaverde .08
319 Ray Perkins (C, no name, number on back) .05
319a Ray Perkins (C, corrected) .05
320 Earnest Byner .03
321 Gary Clark .15
322 Darryl Grant .03
323 Darrell Green .03
324 Jim Lachey .03
325 Charles Mann .03
326 Wilber Marshall .03
327 Ralf Mojsiejenko .03
328 Art Monk .03
329 Gerald Riggs .03
330 Mark Rypien .10
331 Ricky Sanders .03
332 Alvin Walton .03
333 Joe Gibbs (C) .03
334 Aloha Stadium - PB .03
335 Brian Blades (PB) .03
336 James Brooks (PB) .03
337 Shane Conlan (PB) .03
338 Eric Dickerson 4.00
339 Ray Donaldson (PB) .03
340 Ferrell Edmunds .03
341 Boomer Esiason (PB) .06
342 David Fulcher (PB) .03
343 Chris Hinton (PB, no traded stripe) .05
343a Chris Hinton (PB, traded) .05
344 Rodney Holman (PB) .06
345 Kent Hull (PB) .03
346 Tunch Ilkin (PB) .03
347 Mike Johnson (PB) .03
348 Greg Kragen (PB) .03
349 Dave Krieg (PB) .03
350 Albert Lewis (PB) .03
351 Howie Long (PB) .03
352 Bruce Matthews .03
353 Clay Matthews (PB) .03
354 Erik McMillan (PB) .03
355 Karl Mecklenberg (PB) .03
356 Anthony Miller (PB) .25
357 Frank Minnifield (PB) .03
358 Max Montoya (PB) .03
359 Warren Moon (PB) .08
360 Mike Munchak (PB) .03
361 Anthony Munoz (PB) .03
362 John Offerdahl (PB) .03
363 Christian Okoye (PB) .03
364 Leslie O'Neal (PB) .06
365 Rufus Porter (PB) .03
366 Andre Reed (PB) .06
367 Johnny Rembert (PB) .03
368 Reggie Roby (PB) .03
369 Kevin Ross (PB) .03
370 Webster Slaughter (PB) .03
371 Bruce Smith (PB) .06
372 Dennis Smith .03
373 Derrick Thomas (PB) .06
374 Thurman Thomas .25
375 David Treadwell (PB) .03
376 Lee Williams (PB) .03
377 Rod Woodson (PB) .03
378 Bud Carson (PB) .03
379 Eric Allen (PB) .03
380 Neal Anderson (PB) .03
381 Jerry Ball (PB) .03
382 Joey Browner (PB) .03
383 Rich Camarillo (PB) .03
384 Mark Carrier (PB) .03
385 Roger Craig (PB) .03
386 Randall Cunningham (PB) .10
387 Chris Doleman (PB) .03
388 Henry Ellard (PB) .03
389 Bill Fralic (PB) .03
390 Brent Fullwood (PB) .03
391 Jerry Gray (PB) .03
392 Kevin Greene (PB) .03
393 Tim Harris (PB) .03
394 Jay Hilgenberg (PB) .03
395 Dalton Hilliard (PB) .03
396 Keith Jackson (PB) .08
397 Vaughan Johnson (PB) .03
398 Steve Jordan (PB) .03
399 Carl Lee (PB) .03
400 Ronnie Lott (PB) .06
401 Don Majkowski (PB) .03
402 Charles Mann (PB) .03
403 Randall McDaniel (PB) .03
404 Tim McDonald (PB) .03
405 Guy McIntyre (PB) .03
406 Dave Meggett (PB) .03
407 Keith Millard (PB) .03
408 Joe Montana (PB) .50
409 Eddie Murray .03
410 Tom Newberry (PB) .03
411 Jerry Rice (PB) .40
412 Mark Rypien (PB) .03
413 Barry Sanders (PB) .75
414 Luis Sharpe (PB) .03
415 Sterling Sharpe (PB) .20
416 Mike Singletary (PB) .03
417 Jackie Slater (PB) .03
418 Doug Smith (PB) .03
419 Chris Spielman (PB) .03
420 Pat Swilling (PB) .03
421 John Taylor (PB) .10
422 Lawrence Taylor (PB) .10
423 Reggie White (PB) .08
424 Ron Wolfley (PB) .03
425 Gary Zimmerman (PB) .03
426 John Robinson (PB) .03
427 Scott Case .03
428 Mike Kenn .03
429 Mike Gann .03
430 *Tim Green* .08
431 *Michael Haynes* .30
432 *Jessie Tuggle* .20
433 John Rade .03
434 Andre Rison .25
435 Don Beebe .03
436 Ray Bentley .03
437 Shane Conlan .03
438 Kent Hull .03
439 Pete Metzelaars .03
440 Andre Reed .15
441 Frank Reich .15
442 Leon Seals .08
443 Bruce Smith .03
444 Thurman Thomas .40
445 Will Wolford .03
446 Trace Armstrong .03
447 *Mark Bortz* .10
448 *Tom Thayer* .10
449 Dan Hampton (DE back) .05
449a Dan Hampton (DT back) .05
451 Dennis Gentry .03
452 Jim Harbaugh .10
453 Vestee Jackson .03
454 Brad Muster .03
455 William Perry .03
456 Ron Rivera .03
457 James Thornton .03
458 Mike Tomczak .03
459 Donnell Woolford .03
460 Eric Ball .03
461 James Brooks .03
462 David Fulcher .03
463 Boomer Esiason .10
464 Rodney Holman .03
465 Bruce Kozerski .03
466 Tim Krumrie .03
467 Anthony Munoz .03
468 Brian Blados .03
469 Mike Baab .03
470 Brian Brennan .03
471 Raymond Clayborn .03
472 Mike Johnson .03
473 Kevin Mack .03
474 Clay Matthews .03
475 Frank Minnifield .03
476 Gregg Rakoczy .03
477 Webster Slaughter .03
478 James Dixon .03
479 Robert Awalt .03
480 Dennis McKinnon .03
481 Danny Noonan .03
482 Jesse Soloman .03
483 Danny Stubbs .03
484 Steve Walsh .03
485 *Michael Brooks* .25
486 Mark Jackson .03
487 Greg Kragen .03
488 *Ken Lanier* .08
489 Karl Mecklenburg .03
490 Steve Sewell .03
491 Dennis Smith .03
492 David Treadwell .03
493 *Michael Young* .08
494 *Robert Clark* .10
495 Dennis Gibson .03
496 *Kevin Glover* (C-G back) .15
496a *Kevin Glover* (G back) .10
497 Mel Gray .03
498 Rodney Peete .10
499 Dave Brown .03
500 Jerry Holmes .03
501 Chris Jacke .03
502 Alan Veingrad .03
503 Mark Lee .03
504 Tony Mandarich .03
505 Brian Noble .03
506 Jeff Query .03
507 Ken Ruettgers .03
508 Patrick Allen .03
509 Curtis Duncan .03
510 William Fuller .03
511 *Haywood Jeffires* .50
512 Sean Jones .03
513 Terry Kinard .03
514 Bruce Matthews .03
515 Gerald McNeil .03
516 *Greg Montgomery* .08
517 Warren Moon .20
518 Mike Munchak .03
519 Allen Pinkett .03
520 Pat Beach .03
521 Eugene Daniel .03
522 Kevin Call .03
523 Ray Donaldson .03
524 *Jeff Herrod* .08
525 Keith Taylor .03
526 Jack Trudeau .03
527 Deron Cherry .03
528 Jeff Donaldson .03
529 Albert Lewis .03
530 Pete Mandley .03
531 *Chris Martin* .08
532 Christian Okoye .03
533 Steve Pelluer .08
534 Kevin Ross .03
535 Dan Saleaumua .03
536 Derrick Thomas .25
537 Mike Webster .03
538 Marcus Allen .03
539 Greg Bell .03
540 Thomas Benson .03
541 Ron Brown .03
542 Scott Davis .03
543 Riki Ellison .03
544 Jamie Holland .03
545 Howie Long .03
546 Terry McDaniel .03
547 Max Montoya .03
548 Jay Schroeder .03
549 Lionel Washington .03
550 Robert Delpino .03
551 Bobby Humphery .03
552 Mike Lansford .03
553 *Michael Stewart* .08
554 Doug Smith .03
555 Curt Warner .03
556 Alvin Wright .03
557 Jeff Cross .03
558 *Jeff Dellenbach* .08
559 Mark Duper .03
560 Ferrell Edmunds .03
561 Tim McKyer .03
562 John Offerdahl .03
563 Reggie Roby .03
564 Pete Stovanovich .03
565 Alfred Anderson .03
566 Ray Berry .03
567 Rick Fenney .03
568 *Rich Gannon* 2.00
569 Tim Irwin .03
570 Hassan Jones .03
571 Cris Carter .30
572 Kirk Lowdermilk .03
573 *Reggie Rutland* .08
574 Ken Stills .03
575 Bruce Armstrong .03
576 Irving Fryar .03
577 Roland James .03
578 Robert Perryman .03
579 Cedric Jones .03
580 Steve Grogan .03
581 Johnny Rembert .03
582 Ed Reynolds .03
583 Brent Williams .03
584 Marc Wilson .03
585 Hoby Brenner .03
586 Stan Brock .03
587 *Jim Dombrowski* .08
588 *Joel Hilgenberg* .10
589 Robert Massey .03
590 Floyd Turner .10
591 Ottis Anderson .03
592 Mark Bavaro .03
593 Maurice Carthon .03
594 *Eric Dorsey* .10
595 Myron Guyton .03
596 *Jeff Hostetler* .75
597 Sean Landeta .03
598 Lionel Manuel .03
599 *Odessa Turner* .10
600 Perry Williams .03
601 James Hasty .03
602 Erik McMillan .03
603 Alex Gordon .03
604 Ron Stallworth .03
605 *Byron Evans* .10
606 *Ron Heller* .10
607 Wes Hopkins (black, red fumble/interceptions head) .10
607a Wes Hopkins (red fumble/interceptions head) .10
608 Mickey Shuler .03
609 Seth Joyner .03
610 Jim McMahon .03
611 Mike Pitts .03
612 Izel Jenkins .03
613 Anthony Bell .03
614 David Galloway .03
615 Eric Hill .03
616 Cedric Mack .03
617 Freddie Joe Nunn .03
618 Tootie Robbins .03
619 *Tom Tupa* .10
620 Joe Wolf .03
621 Dermontti Dawson .03
622 Thomas Everett .03
623 Tunch Ilken .03
624 Hardy Nickerson .03
625 *Gerald Williams* .08
626 Rod Woodson (black, red fumbles/interceptions head) .25
626a Rod Woodson (red fumbles/interceptions head) .25
627 Rod Bernstine (error TE) .25
627a Rod Bernstine (corrected RB) .15
628 Courtney Hall .03
629 Ronnie Harmon .03
630 Anthony Miller (WR back) .25
630a Anthony Miller (WR-KR back) .20
630b Anthony Miller (WR-KR back, front) .20
631 Joe Phillips .03
632 Leslie O'Neal (LB-DE front) .20
632a Leslie O'Neal (LB front) .15
633 David Richards (G-T back) .05
633a David Richards (G back) .05
634 Mark Vlasic .08
635 Lee Williams .03
636 Chet Brooks .03
637 Keena Turner .03
638 Kevin Fagan .03
639 *Brent Jones* .70
640 Matt Millen .03
641 Bubba Paris .03
642 *Bill Romanowski* .10
643 Fred Smerlas .03
644 Dave Waymer .03
645 Steve Young .40
646 Brian Blades .10
647 Andy Heck .03
648 Dave Krieg .03
649 Rufus Porter .03
650 Kelly Stouffer .03
651 Tony Woods .03
652 Gary Anderson .03
653 Reuben Davis .03
654 Randy Grimes .03
655 Ron Hall .03
656 Eugene Marve .03
657 Curt Jarvis (no "Official NFL card") .05
657a Curt Jarvis ("Official NFL card" added) .05
658 Ricky Reynolds .03
659 Broderick Thomas .03
660 Jeff Bostic .03
661 *Todd Bowles* .10
662 Ravin Caldwell .03
663 Russ Grimm .03
664 Joe Jacoby .03
665 Mark May .03
666 Walter Stanley .03
667 Don Warren .03
668 *Stan Humphries* .75
669 *Jeff George* (Illinois) 1.00
670 *Blair Thomas* (R1) .10
671 *Cortez Kennedy* .25
672 *Keith McCants* (R1) .08
673 *Junior Seau* 1.00
674 *Mark Carrier* .25
675 *Andre Ware* (R1) .10
676 *Chris Singleton* (R1) .10
677 *Richmond Webb* (R1) .15
678 *Ray Agnew* (R1) .08
679 *Anthony Smith* .30
680 *James Francis* (R1) .10
681 Percy Snow (R1) .03
682 *Renaldo Turnbull* .35
683 *Lamar Lathon* (R1) .10
684 *James Williams* (R1) .10
685 *Emmitt Smith* 3.00
686 *Tony Bennett* .25
687 *Darrell Thompson* .20
688 Steve Broussard (R1) .08
689 *Eric Green* .25
690 *Ben Smith* (R1) .08
691 *Bern Brostek* (R1) .08
692 *Rodney Hampton* 1.25
693 *Dexter Carter* (R1) .10
694 *Rob Moore* 1.50
695 *Alexander Wright* (R2) .20
696 *Darion Conner* (R2) .10
697 Reggie Rembert (R2) .03
698 *Terry Wooden* (R2, back number 51) .05
698a *Terry Wooden* (R2, back number 90) .05
699 *Reggie Cobb* .60
700 Anthony Thompson (R2) .03
701 Fred Washington (R2) .05
701a Fred Washington (Final Update memorial) .05
702 *Ron Cox* (R2) .10
703 *Robert Blackmon* (R2) .10
704 *Dan Owens* (R2) .10
705 *Anthony Johnson* (R2) .15
706 *Aaron Wallace* (R2) .15
707 *Harold Green* .35
708 *Keith Sims* (R2) .10
709 *Tim Grunhard* (R2) .10
710 Jeff Alm (R2) .03
711 *Carwell Gardner* .10
712 *Ken Davidson* (R2) .10
713 *Vince Buck* (R2) .10
714 *Leroy Hoard* (R2) .50
715 *Andre Collins* (R2) .08
716 *Dennis Brown* (R2) .08
717 *Leroy Butler* .20
718 *Pat Terrell* (R2, back number 41) .20
718a *Pat Terrell* (R2, back number 37) .10
719 Mike Bellamy (R2) .03
720 *Mike Fox* (R2) .08
721 *Alton Montgomery* (R2) .08
722 *Eric Davis* (R2) .08
723 *Oliver Barnett* (PR, DT front) .30
723a *Oliver Barnett* (PR, NT front) .10
724 *Houston Hoover* (PR) .08
725 *Howard Ballard* (PR) .08
726 *Keith McKeller* (PR) .08
727 *Wendell Davis* .10
728 *Peter Tom Willis* (PR) .10
729 Bernard Clark (PR) .03
730 *Doug Widell* (PR) .10
731 Eric Andolsek (PR) .03
732 *Jeff Campbell* (PR) .08
733 *Marc Spindler* (PR) .08
734 Keith Woodside (PR) .03
735 *Willis Peguese* (PR) .08
736 Frank Stams (PR) .03
737 Jeff Uhlenhake (PR) .03
738 Todd Kalis (PR) .03
739 Tom Hodson (PR) .03
740 Greg McMurtry (PR) .03
741 Mike Buck (PR) .03
742 Kevin Haverdink (PR) .03
743 *Johnny Bailey* (PR, back number 46) .50
743a *Johnny Bailey* (PR, back number 22) .25
744 *Eric Moore* (PR, no prospect stripe) .10
744a *Eric Moore* (PR, stripe added) .10
745 *Tony Stargell* (PR) .08
746 *Fred Barnett* .60
747 Walter Reeves (PR) .03
748 Derek Hill (PR) .03
749 *Quinn Early* (PR) .35
750 *Ronald Lewis* (PR) .05
751 *Ken Clark* (PR) .05
752 Garry Lewis (PR) .03
753 James Lofton .03
754 Jim Morrissey .03
755 Jim Shofner .03
756 *Jimmie Jones* .10
757 Jay Novacek .40
758 *Jessie Hester* .20
759 *Barry Word* .30
760 *Eddie Anderson* .08
761 Cleveland Gary .08
762 Marcus Dupree .03
763 *David Griggs* .08
764 Rueben Mayes .03
765 Stephen Baker .08
766 Reyna Thompson .03
767 Everson Walls .03
768 *Brad Baxter* .25
769 Steve Walsh .03
770 *Heath Sherman* .20
771 *Johnny Johnson* .10
772 Dexter Manley .03
773 *Rickey Proehl* .50
774 Frank Cornish .03
775 *Tommy Kane* .10
776 *Derrick Fenner* .10
777 *Steve Christie* .10
778 *Wayne Haddix* .08
779 Richard Williamson .03
780 *Brian Mitchell* .50
781 American Bowl London .03
782 American Bowl Berlin .03
783 American Bowl Tokyo .03
784 American Bowl Montreal .03
785 Paul Tagliabue (NR, "peered through the Berlin Wall") .05
785a Paul Tagliabue (NR, "posed at the Berlin Wall") .05
786 Al Davis (NR) .10
787 Jerry Glanville (NR) .03
788 WLF (NR) .03
789 Overseas (NR) .03
790 Mike Mularkey (PC) .03
791 Gary Reasons (PC) .03
792 Maurice Hurst, Drew Hill (PC) .03
793 Ronnie Lott (PC) .03
794 Barry Sanders, Felix Wright (PC) .75
795 George Seifert (PC) .03
796 Doug Smith (PC) .03
797 Doug Widell (PC) .03
798 Cris Carter, Todd Bowles (PC) .03
799 Ronnie Lott (Stay in School) .03
800 Mark Carrier, Emmitt Smith (ROY) 1.00
SC3 Joe Robbie Stadium 1.00
CC2 Paul Tagliabue 1.00
NNO Lombardi Trophy (2-9,999) 50.00
SC2 Santa Claus 1.00
SC Super Pro 1.00
NNO Super Bowl XXIVB logo .30
SP1 Payne Stewart 1.00

1990 Pro Set Super Bowl MVPs

These 1990 Pro Set Series II inserts feature the 24 players who were named MVP of a Super Bowl. Each card front has a portrait of the player done by artist Merv Corning. Two silver panels are also on the front, one on top, the other at the bottom. The player's name is in the bottom panel, which is bordered by two stripes featuring the player's team colors. The horizontal card back has a color action photo and summary of the player's Super Bowl achievement. The cards are numbered on the back in a chronological manner, beginning with Super Bowl I.

MT
Complete Set (24): 4.00
Common Player: .10
1 Super Bowl I (Bart Starr) .30
2 Super Bowl II (Bart Starr) .30
3 Super Bowl III (Joe Namath) .50
4 Super Bowl IV (Len Dawson) .20
5 Super Bowl V (Chuck Howley) .10
6 Super Bowl VI (Roger Staubach) .50
7 Super Bowl VII (Jake Scott) .10
8 Super Bowl VIII (Larry Csonka) .30
9 Super Bowl IX (Franco Harris) .30
10 Super Bowl X (Lynn Swann) .20
11 Super Bowl XI (Fred Biletnikoff) .20
12 Super Bowl XII (Harvey Martin) .10
13 Super Bowl XIII (Terry Bradshaw) .40
14 Super Bowl XIV (Terry Bradshaw) .40
15 Super Bowl XV (Jim Plunkett) .20
16 Super Bowl XVI (Joe Montana) .50
17 Super Bowl XVII (John Riggins) .20
18 Super Bowl XVIII (Marcus Allen) .20
19 Super Bowl XIX (Joe Montana) .50
20 Super Bowl XX (Richard Dent) .10
21 Super Bowl XXI (Phil Simms) .20
22 Super Bowl XXII (Doug Williams) .10
23 Super Bowl XXIII (Jerry Rice) .30
24 Super Bowl XXIV (Joe Montana) .50

1990 Pro Set Theme Art

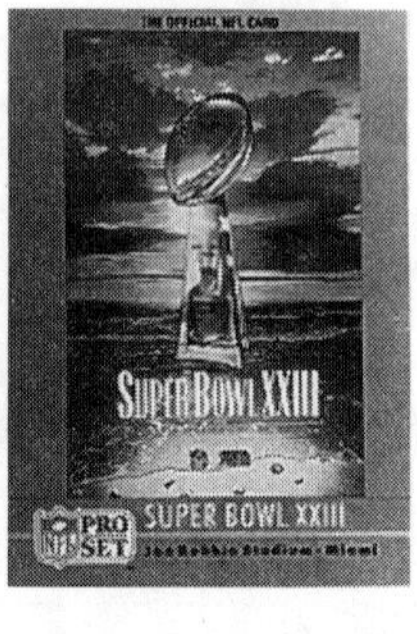

The 25-card set spotlights Super Bowl theme art on the front, which resembles the cover art of Super Bowl programs. The Pro Set logo is in the lower left, with the Super Bowl listed in the lower right, with the site and city name listed beneath. Card backs include a photo of the winning team's championship ring. The Super Bowl number and date, along with the score, are listed at the top, with background text also included. The cards were seeded one per 1990 Pro Set Series I pack.

		MT
Complete Set (24):		3.00
Common Player:		.15
1	Super Bowl I	.15
2	Super Bowl II	.15
3	Super Bowl III	.15
4	Super Bowl IV	.15
5	Super Bowl V	.15
6	Super Bowl VI	.15
7	Super Bowl VII	.15
8	Super Bowl VIII	.15
9	Super Bowl IX	.15
10	Super Bowl X	.15
11	Super Bowl XI	.15
12	Super Bowl XII	.15
13	Super Bowl XIII UER (Colgate University 7, sould be Colgate 13)	.15
14	Super Bowl XIV	.15
15	Super Bowl XV	.15
16	Super Bowl XVI	.15
17	Super Bowl XVII	.15
18	Super Bowl XVIII	.15
19	Super Bowl XIX	.15
20	Super Bowl XX	.15
21	Super Bowl XXI	.15
22A	Super Bowl XXII ERR (Jan. 31, 1989 on back)	.50
22B	Super Bowl XXII COR (Jan. 31, 1988 on back)	.15
23	Super Bowl XXIII	.15
24	Super Bowl XXIV Theme Art	.15

1990 Pro Set Collect-A-Books

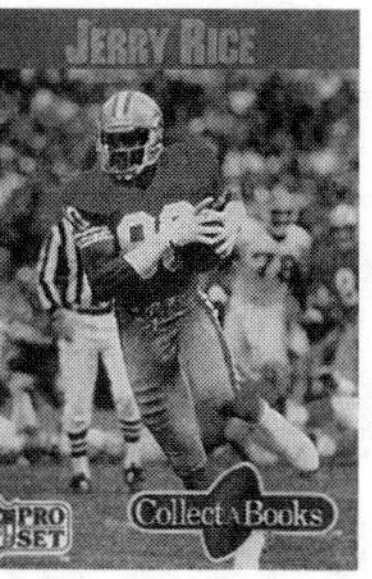

These 2-1/2" x 3-1/2" 8-page booklets were issued in three series of 12. Each series came in its own box, and included one player who was a rookie. The front of the booklet has an action photo of the player, along with his name, and set logos. Page two has a color mug shot of the player; pages 3-4 provide a career summary in text form. Pages 6-7 are a double-page action photo of the player; page 8 has statistics and trademark information. Two players who have booklets - Eric Dickerson and Michael Dean Perry - were not included in Pro Set's regular 1990 card set.

		MT
Complete Set (36):		7.50
Common Player:		.15
1	Jim Kelly	.50
2	Andre Ware	.20
3	Phil Simms	.25
4	Bubby Brister	.20
5	Bernie Kosar	.25
6	Eric Dickerson	.25
7	Barry Sanders	.75
8	Jerry Rice	1.00
9	Keith Millard	.15
10	Erik McMillan	.15
11	Ickey Woods	.15
12	Mike Singletary	.25
13	Randall Cunningham	.30
14	Boomer Esiason	.25
15	John Elway	.25
16	Wade Wilson	.20
17	Troy Aikman	1.50
18	Dan Marino	1.50
19	Lawrence Taylor	.35
20	Roger Craig	.25
21	Merril Hoge	.15
22	Christian Okoye	.15
23	Blair Thomas	.15
24	William Perry	.20
25	Bill Fralic	.15
26	Warren Moon	.30
27	Jim Everett	.20
28	Jeff George	.50
29	Shane Conlan	.15
30	Carl Banks	.15
31	Charles Mann	.15
32	Anthony Munoz	.25
33	Dan Hampton	.25
34	Michael Dean Perry	.15
35	Joey Browner	.15
36	Ken O'Brien	.20

A player's name in *italic type* indicates a rookie card.

1990 Pro Set Pro Bowl 106

Participants in the annual Pro Bowl game are honored in this 106-card set produced by Pro Set. The set includes a white binder which features the Pro Bowl game logo on the front cover. The cards, except for four, are identical to their corresponding numbered counterparts in the regular set; there is no indication they were in the Pro Bowl set. However, four players who are featured in the Final Update set have "1990 Final Update" on the front (#s 754, 766, 771 and 778). This is not written on the fronts of the regular update cards.

		MT
Complete Set (106):		10.00
Common Player:		.03
39	Cornelius Bennett	.10
40	Jim Kelly	.25
49	Neal Anderson	.05
52	Richard Dent	.05
53	Jay Hilgenberg	.03
57	Mike Singletary	.08
86	Steve Atwater	.05
91	Bobby Humphrey	.03
96	Jerry Ball	.03
98	Lomas Brown	.03
102	Barry Sanders	1.00
114	Sterling Sharpe	.75
118	Ray Childress	.05
119	Ernest Givins	.05
122	Drew Hill	.05
135	Rohn Stark	.03
137	Clarence Verdin	.03
144	Nick Lowery	.03
155	Bo Jackson	.40
156	Don Mosebar	.03
158	Greg Townsend	.05
160	Steve Wisniewski	.03
173	Jackie Slater	.05
186	Joey Browner	.05
188	Chris Doleman	.05
189	Steve Jordan	.03
190	Carl Lee	.03
191	Randall McDaniel	.05
210	Morten Andersen	.05
215	Vaughan Johnson	.03
218	Pat Swilling	.05
226	Pepper Johnson	.03
229	Bart Oates	.03
231	Lawrence Taylor	.15
244	Jerome Brown	.03
247	Randall Cunningham	.15
248	Keith Jackson	.15
252	Reggie White	.25
271	David Little	.03
276	Marion Butts	.10
289	Charles Haley	.05
291	Ronnie Lott	.10
292	Guy McIntyre	.03
293	Joe Montana	1.00
295	Jerry Rice	.75
320	Earnest Byner	.03
321	Gary Clark	.05
323	Darrell Green	.05
324	Jim Lachey	.03
334	Pro Bowl Aloha Stadium	.03
434	Andre Rison	.25
438	Kent Hull	.03
440	Andre Reed	.15
443	Bruce Smith	.10
444	Thurman Thomas	.25
447	Mark Bortz	.03
462	David Fulcher	.03
464	Rodney Holman	.03
467	Anthony Munoz	.10
491	Dennis Smith	.03
497	Mel Gray	.03
514	Bruce Matthews	.03
517	Warren Moon	.25
529	Albert Lewis	.05
534	Kevin Ross	.03
536	Derrick Thomas	.20
557	Jeff Cross	.03
560	Ferrell Edmunds	.03
562	John Offerdahl	.05
575	Bruce Armstrong	.03
597	Sean Landeta	.03
626	Rod Woodson	.20
630	Anthony Miller	.10
632	Leslie O'Neal	.05
677	Richmond Webb	.05
754	Steve Tasker	8.00
766	Reyna Thompson	8.00
771	Johnny Johnson	12.00
778	Wayne Haddix	8.00
800	Mark Carrier	.10
SB1	Super Bowl I	.15
SB2	Super Bowl II	.15
SB3	Super Bowl III	.15
SB4	Super Bowl IV	.15
SB5	Super Bowl V	.15
SB6	Super Bowl VI	.15
SB7	Super Bowl VII	.15
SB8	Super Bowl VIII	.15
SB9	Super Bowl IX	.15
SB10	Super Bowl X	.15
SB11	Super Bowl XI	.15
SB12	Super Bowl XII	.15
SB13	Super Bowl XIII	.15
SB14	Super Bowl XIV	.15
SB15	Super Bowl XV	.15
SB16	Super Bowl XVI	.15
SB17	Super Bowl XVII	.15
SB18	Super Bowl XVIII	.15
SB19	Super Bowl XIX	.15
SB20	Super Bowl XX	.15
SB21	Super Bowl XXI	.15
SB22	Super Bowl XXII	.15
SB23	SUper Bowl XXIII	.15
SB24	Super Bowl XXIV	.15

1990 Pro Set Super Bowl 160

This set was issued in its own commemorative box and traces the history of the Super Bowl in four categories - Super Bowl Tickets, Super Bowl Supermen, Super Bowl Super Moments, and puzzle cards, which make up art for Super Bowl XXV. Cards were also sold in packs of eight and were originally given away at Texas Stadium during the Dallas Cowboys Pro Set Sports Collectors Show.

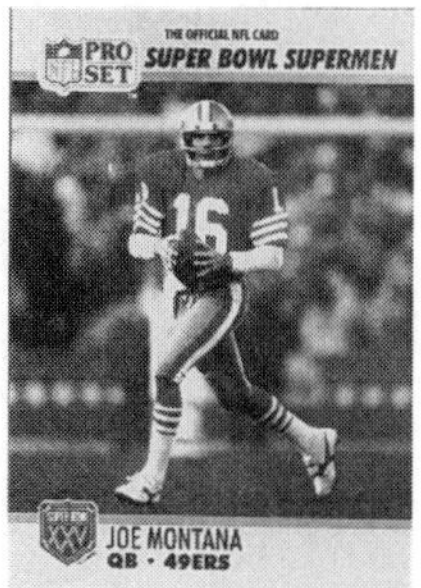

		MT
Complete Set (160):		5.00
Common Player:		.05
Common Puzzle:		.03
1	SB 1 Ticket	.10
2	SB II Ticket	.05
3	SB III Ticket	.05
4	SB IV Ticket	.05
5	SB V Ticket	.05
6	SB VI Ticket	.05
7	SB VII Ticket	.05
8	SB VIII Ticket	.05
9	SB IV Ticket	.05
10	SB X Ticket	.05
11	SB XI Ticket	.05
12	SB XII Ticket	.05
13	SB XIII Ticket	.05
14	SB XIV Ticket	.05
15	SB XV Ticket	.05
16	SB XVI Ticket	.05
17	SB XVII Ticket	.05
18	SB XVIII Ticket	.05
19	SB XIX Ticket	.05
20	SB XX Ticket	.05
21	SB XXI Ticket	.05
22	SB XXII Ticket	.05
23	SB XXIII Ticket	.05
24	SB XXIV Ticket	.05
25	Tom Flores (CO)	.05
26	Joe Gibbs (CO)	.05
27	Tom Landry (CO)	.15
28	Vince Lombardi (CO)	.15
29	Chuck Noll (CO)	.10
30	Don Shula (CO)	.15
31	Bill Walsh (CO)	.15
32	Terry Bradshaw	.25
33	Joe Montana	.50
34	Joe Namath	.35
35	Jim Plunkett	.10
36	Bart Starr	.20
37	Roger Staubach	.35
38	Marcus Allen	.20
39	Roger Craig	.10
40	Larry Csonka	.10
41	Franco Harris	.10
42	John Riggins	.10
43	Timmy Smith	.05
44	Matt Snell	.05
45	Fred Biletnikoff	.10
46	Cliff Branch	.05
47	Max McGee	.10
48	Jerry Rice	.50
49	Ricky Sanders	.05
50	George Sauer	.05
51	John Stallworth	.10
52	Lynn Swann	.15
53	Dave Casper	.05
54	Marv Fleming	.05
55	Dan Ross	.05
56	Forrest Gregg	.10
57	Winston Hill	.05
58	Joe Jacoby	.05
59	Anthony Munoz	.10
60	Art Shell	.10
61	Rayfield Wright	.05
62	Ron Yary	.05
63	Randy Cross	.05
64	Jerry Kramer	.10
65	Bob Kuechenberg	.05
66	Larry Little	.05
67	Gerry Mullins	.05
68	John Niland	.05
69	Gene Upshaw	.10
70	Dave Dalby	.05
71	Jim Langer	.05
72	Dwight Stephenson	.05
73	Mike Webster	.10
74	Ross Browner	.05
75	Willie Davis	.10
76	Richard Dent	.10
77	L.C. Greenwood	.10
78	Ed "Too Tall" Jones	.10
79	Harvey Martin	.05
80	Dwight White	.05
81	Buck Buchanan	.10
82	Curley Culp	.05
83	Manny Fernandez	.05
84	Joe Greene	.15
85	Bob Lilly	.15
86	Alan Page	.15
87	Randy White	.10
88	Nick Buoniconti	.10
89	Lee Roy Jordan	.10
90	Jack Lambert	.15
91	Willie Lanier	.10
92	Ray Nitschke	.15
93	Mike Singletary	.15
94	Carl Banks	.05
95	Charles Haley	.05
96	Jack Ham	.10
97	Ted Hendricks	.10
98	Chuck Howley	.05
99	Rod Martin	.05
100	Herb Adderley	.10
101	Mel Blount	.10
102	Willie Brown	.10
103	Lester Hayes	.05
104	Mike Haynes	.05
105	Ronnie Lott	.15
106	Mel Renfro	.05
107	Eric Wright	.05
108	Dick Anderson	.05
109	David Fulcher	.05
110	Cliff Harris	.05
111	Johnny Robinson	.05
112	Jake Scott	.05
113	Donnie Shell	.05
114	Mike Wagner	.05
115	Willie Wood	.10
116	Ray Guy	.10
117	Lee Johnson	.05
118	Larry Seiple	.05
119	Jerrel Wilson	.05
120	Kevin Butler	.05
121	Don Chandler	.05
122	Jan Stenerud	.10
123	Jim Turner	.05
124	Ray Wersching	.05
125	Larry Anderson	.05
126	Stanford Jennings	.05
127	Mike Nelms	.05
128	John Taylor	.10
129	Fulton Walker	.05
130	E.J. Holub	.05
131	George Siefert CO	.05
132	Jim Taylor	.10
133	Joe Theismann	.15
134	Johnny Unitas	.25
135	Reggie Williams	.05
136	Two Networks (Paul Christman, Frank Gifford)	.05
137	First Fly-Over (Military jets)	.05
138	Weeb Ewbank (Super Bowl Super Moment)	.05
139	Otis Taylor (Super Bowl Super Moment)	.05
140	Jim O'Brien (Super Bowl Super Moment)	.05
141	Garo Yepremian (Super Bowl Super Moment)	.05
142	(Pete Rozelle, Art Rooney)	.05
143	Percy Howard (Super Bowl Super Moment)	.05
144	Jackie Smith (Super Bowl Super Moment)	.05
145	Record Crowd (Super Bowl Super Moment)	.05
146	Yellow Ribbon UER (Fourth line says more than year, should say more than a year)	.05
147	(Dan Bunz, Charles Alexander) (Super Bowl Super Moment)	.05
148	Smurfs (Redskins) (Super Bowl Super Moment)	.05
149	(William "The Fridge" Perry) (Scores, Super Bowl Super Moment)	.05
150	Phil McConkey (Super Bowl Super Moment)	.05
151	Doug Williams (Super Bowl Super Moment)	.05
152	Top row left	.03
153	Top row middle XXV Theme Art Puzzle	.03
154	Top row left XXV Theme Art Puzzle	.03
155	Center row left XXV Theme Art Puzzle	.03
156	Center row right XXV Theme Art Puzzle	.03
157	Center row right XXV Theme Art Puzzle	.03
158	Bottom row left VVX Theme Art Puzzle	.03
159	Bottom row right XXV Theme Art Puzzle	.03
160	Bottom row right XXV Theme Art Puzzle	.03
	Special Offer Card	.10

1990 Pro Set Super Bowl Binder

This 56-card set, with Buick as its sponsor, was given to those who attended Super Bowl XXV between the New York Giants and Buffalo Bills. Included within the set are a cover card for Buick, a commemorative card for the 2-millionth Super Bowl fan, cards for the NFC and AFC Championship trophies, and a Ronnie Lott Stay in School card from Pro Set's Final Update set. Players from the two participating Super Bowl teams are featured in the set, along with 27 cards featuring fans' choices for the Silver Anniversary Super Bowl Team. Super Bowl participants' cards have the same photos as their counterparts in the regular set, but have NFC or AFC Champions designated on the front. A binder with pages that hold four cards per page was also issued to store the cards in.

		MT
Complete Set (56):		25.00
Common Player:		.25
1	Vince Lombardi	.35
2	Joe Montana	4.00
3	Larry Csonka	.50
4	Franco Harris	.50
5	Jerry Rice	3.00
6	Lynn Swann	.50
7	Forrest Gregg	.35
8	Art Shell	.35
9	Jerry Kramer	.25
10	Gene Upshaw	.35
11	Mike Webster	.35
12	Dave Casper	.25
13	Jan Stenerud	.35
14	John Taylor	.35
15	L.C. Greenwood	.25
16	Ed "Too Tall" Jones	.35
17	Joe Greene	.50
18	Randy White	.50
19	Jack Lambert	.50
20	Mike Singletary	.35
21	Jack Ham	.35
22	Ted Hendricks	.35
23	Mel Blount	.35
24	Ronnie Lott	.50
25	Donnie Shell	.25
26	Willie Wood	.35
27	Ray Guy	.35
SC1	2,000,000th Fan	.50
SC2	Buick Checklist Card	.50
SC3	Lamar Hunt Trophy	.50
SC4	George Halas Trophy	.50
799	Ronnie Lott Education	.35
39	Cornelius Bennett	.50
40	Jim Kelly	1.50
47	Darryl Talley	.25
48	Marv Levy (CO)	.25
437	Shane Conlan	.25
438	Kent Hull	.25
440	Andre Reed	1.00
443	Bruce Smith	1.00
444	Thurman Thomas	2.50
725	Howard Ballard	.25
753	James Lofton	.50
754	Steve Tasker	.25
223	Carl Banks	.25
226	Pepper Johnson	.25
228	Dave Meggett	.25
230	Phil Simms	.50
231	Lawrence Taylor	.75
232	Bill Parcells (CO)	.35
591	Ottis Anderson	.50
592	Mark Bavaro	.25
596	Jeff Hostetler	.35
692	Rodney Hampton	1.00
765	Stephen Baker	.25
766	Reyna Thompson	.25

1991 Pro Set Draft Day

These cards, issued in conjunction with the 1991 NFL draft, create different scenarios regarding the first selection in the draft. Each card is numbered 694 and features the player in his collegiate uniform. The card back is in a horizontal format and has another player photo on it, plus biographical information and statistics.

		MT
Complete Set (8):		250.00
Common Player:		20.00
694A	Nick Bell	25.00
694B	Mike Croel	25.00
694C	Raghib (Rocket) Ismail (Cowboys)	65.00
694D	Raghib (Rocket) Ismail (Falcons)	50.00
694E	Raghib (Rocket) Ismail (Patriots)	50.00
694F	Todd Lyght	20.00
694G	Russell Maryland	25.00
694H	Dan McGwire	30.00

1991 Pro Set Promos

These six promotional cards were distributed in various manners. Each is unnumbered. The Kids on the Block card was given away during the Super Bowl XXV Football Clinic, which featured NFL stars talking about drug education. The card was sponsored by Pro Set, Sports Illustrated for Kids and The Learning Channel, which broadcast the clinic. The Super Bowl XXV Card Show II card is similiar to the Card Show I issued in 1989, except the front gives the date of the second card show, which occurred Jan. 24-27, 1991. The cards for William Roberts and Michael Dean Perry (there were two versions for the Perry card) were intended to be in the previously issued Pro Bowl set, but were withdrawn. The Emmitt Smith card was a mail-in offer through the Pro Set Gazette, a quarterly publication designed to provide an overview of the hobby to young collectors.

		MT
Complete Set (6):		150.00
Common Player:		2.00
NNO	NLF Kids on the Block (Tele-clinic)	2.00
NNO	Super Bowl XXV (Card Show II)	5.00
NNO	Michael Dean Perry Pro Bowl (unnumbered, with Pro Set logo)	75.00
NNO	Michael Dean Perry Pro Bowl (unnumbered, without Pro Set logo)	50.00
NNO	William Roberts Pro Bowl (unnumbered)	50.00
NNO	Emmitt Smith Gazette (Pro Set Gazette)	4.00
----	Pro Bowl Special (Michael Dean Perry)	50.00
----	Pro Bowl Special (Michael Dean Perry) (with Pro Set logo)	75.00
----	Pro Bowl Special (William Roberts)	50.00
----	Gazette (Emmitt Smith) (Given away with pro Set Gazette mail-ou t)	3.00

1991 Pro Set

Released in late April, Pro Set's third annual football set was again divided into two series. Subsets added this year to Series I include Heisman Heroes, Super Bowl XXV Replay, NFL Officials, and Think About It messages. World League of American Football cards made their debut in Series I as well. Again, randomly-packed insert cards were included in Series I: Super Bowl XXV logo, Walter Payton and Team 34, a mini Pro Set Gazette, Red Grange, Russell Maryland 31 Draft Pick (only in Series I), and 1,000 autographed Lawrence Taylor cards. (Key: L - leader, M - milestone, HOF - Hall of Fame, AW - college award winner, HH - Heisman hero, SBR - Super Bowl XXV replay, R - 1990 replay, NR - newsreel, O - official, M - NFL message, NFC - all-NFC team, C - coach).

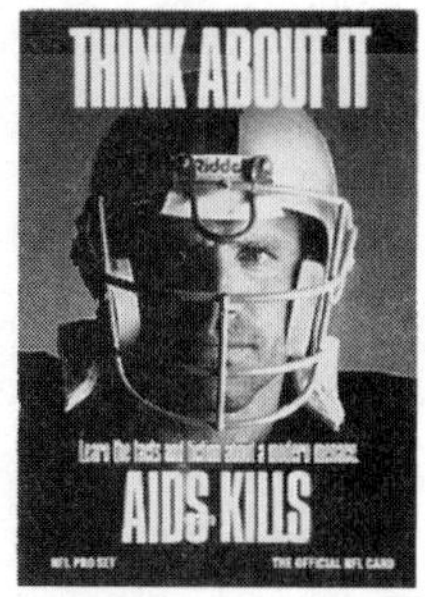

		MT
Complete Set (850):		18.00
Complete Series 1 (405):		7.00
Complete Series 2 (407):		7.00
Complete Final (38):		4.00
Common Player:		.03
Series 1 Pack (14):		.20
Series 1 Wax Box (36):		5.00
Series 2 Pack (14):		.30
Series 2 Wax Box (36):		10.00
1	Emmitt Smith (LL)	1.00
2	Mark Carrier (LL)	.25
3	Joe Montana (LL)	.50
4	Art Shell (LL)	.03
5	Mike Singletary (LL)	.03
6	Bruce Smith (LL)	.04
7	Barry Word (LL)	.03
8	Jim Kelly (LL, with NFLPA logo)	.25
8a	Jim Kelly (LL, without NFLPA logo)	.20
8b	Jim Kelly (LL, without NFLPA logo, with registered symbol)	6.00
9	Warren Moon (LL)	.08
10	Barry Sanders (LL)	.50
11	Jerry Rice (LL)	.40
12	Jay Novacek (LL)	.05
13	Thurman Thomas (LL)	.20
14	Nick Lowery (LL)	.03
15	Mike Horan (LL)	.03
16	Clarence Verdin (LL)	.03
17	Kevin Clark (LL)	.03
18	Mark Carrier (LL)	.03
19	Derrick Thomas (LL, error: Bills helmet on front)	15.00
19a	Derrick Thomas (LL, corrected: Chiefs helmet on front)	.25
20	Ottis Anderson (M)	.03
21	Roger Craig (M)	.03
22	Art Monk (M)	.05
23	Chuck Noll (M)	.03
24	Randall Cunningham (M)	.08
25	Dan Marino (M)	.40
26	Charles Haley (M)	.03
27	Earl Campbell (HOF)	.10
28	John Hannah (HOF)	.03
29	Stan Jones (HOF)	.03
30	Tex Schramm (HOF)	.03
31	Jan Stenerud (HOF)	.03
32	*Russell Maryland* (AW)	.40
33	*Chris Zorich* (AW)	.15
34	*Darryl Lewis* (AW)	.03
35	*Alfred Williams* (AW)	.08
36	*Raghib Ismail* (AW)	1.00
37	*Ty Detmer* (HH)	1.00
38	Andre Ware (HH)	.05
39	Barry Sanders (HH)	.50
40	Tim Brown (HH)	.05
41	Vinny Testaverde (HH)	.03
42	Bo Jackson (HH)	.15
43	Mike Rozier (HH)	.03
44	Herschel Walker (HH)	.03
45	Marcus Allen (HH)	.04
46	James Lofton (SBR, with NFLPA logo)	.05
46a	James Lofton (SBR, NFLPA logo removed)	.08
47	Bruce Smith (SBR, "Official NFL Card" in white)	.15
47a	Bruce Smith (SBR, "Official NFL Card" in black)	.10
48	Myron Guyton (SBR)	.03
49	Stephen Baker (SBR)	.03
50	Mark Ingram (SBR)	.03
51	O.J. Anderson (SBR)	.03
52	Thurman Thomas	.20
53	Matt Bahr (SBR)	.03
54	Scott Norwood (SBR)	.03
55	Stephen Baker	.03
56	Carl Banks	.03
57	Mark Collins	.03
58	Steve DeOssie	.03
59	Eric Dorsey	.03
60	John Elliott	.03
61	Myron Guyton	.03
62	Rodney Hampton	.50
63	Jeff Hostetler	.15
64	Erik Howard	.03
65	Mark Ingram	.03
66	*Greg Jackson*	.08
67	Leonard Marshall	.03
68	David Meggett	.03
69	Eric Moore	.03
70	Bart Oates	.03
71	Gary Reasons	.03
72	Bill Parcells (C)	.03
73	Howard Ballard	.03
74	Cornelius Bennett (with NFLPA logo)	.25
74a	Cornelius Bennett (NFLPA logo removed)	.10
75	Shane Conlan	.03
76	Kent Hull	.03
77	Kirby Jackson	.03
78	Jim Kelly (w/o logo)	.35
79	Mark Kelso	.03
80	Nate Odomes	.03
81	Andre Reed	.08

82	Jim Ritcher	.03
83	Bruce Smith	.03
84	Darryl Talley	.03
85	Steve Tasker	.03
86	Thurman Thomas	.35
87	James Williams	.03
88	Will Wolford	.03
89	Jeff Wright	.03
90	Marv Levy (C)	.03
91	Steve Broussard	.03
92	Darion Conner (error: "Drafted 1st Round '99")	6.00
92a	Darion Conner (corrected: "Drafted 2nd Round '90")	.15
93	Bill Fralic	.03
94	Tim Green	.03
95	Michael Haynes	.03
96	Chris Hinton	.03
97	Chris Miller	.03
98	Deion Sanders	.20
99	Jerry Glanville (C)	.03
100	Kevin Butler	.03
101	Mark Carrier (Chi.)	.03
102	Jim Covert	.03
103	Richard Dent	.03
104	Jim Harbaugh	.08
105	Brad Muster	.03
106	Lemuel Stinson	.03
107	Keith Van Horne	.03
108	Mike Ditka (C)	.05
109	Lewis Billups	.03
110	James Brooks	.03
111	Boomer Esiason	.10
112	James Francis	.03
113	David Fulcher	.03
114	Rodney Holman	.03
115	Tim McGee	.03
116	Anthony Munoz	.03
117	Sam Wyche (C)	.03
118	Paul Farren	.03
119	Thane Gash	.03
120	Mike Johnson	.03
121	Bernie Kosar (with NFLPA logo)	.05
121a	Bernie Kosar (NFLPA logo removed)	.10
122	Clay Matthews	.03
123	Eric Metcalf	.03
124	Frank Minnifield	.03
125	Webster Slaughter (with NFLPA logo)	.05
125a	Webster Slaughter (NFLPA logo removed)	.05
126	Bill Belichick (C)	.03
127	Tommie Agee	.03
128	Troy Aikman	1.00
129	Jack Del Rio	.03
130	*John Gesek*	.06
131	Issiac Holt	.03
132	Michael Irvin	.55
133	Ken Norton	.03
134	Daniel Stubbs	.03
135	Jimmy Johnson (C)	.05
136	Steve Atwater (AW)	.03
137	Michael Brooks	.03
138	John Elway	.35
139	Wymon Henderson	.03
140	Bobby Humphrey	.03
141	Mark Jackson	.03
142	Karl Mecklenburg	.03
143	Doug Widell	.03
144	Dan Reeves (C)	.03
145	Eric Andolsek	.03
146	Jerry Ball	.03
147	Bennie Blades	.03
148	Lomas Brown	.03
149	Robert Clark	.03
150	Michael Cofer	.03
151	Dan Owens	.03
152	Rodney Peete	.03
153	Wayne Fontes (C)	.03
154	Tim Harris	.03
155	Johnny Holland	.03
156	Don Majkowski	.03
157	Tony Mandarich	.03
158	Mark Murphy	.03
159	Brian Noble	.03
160	Jeff Query	.03
161	Sterling Sharpe	.20
162	Lindy Infante (C)	.03
163	Ray Childress	.03
164	Ernest Givins	.03
165	Richard Johnson	.03
166	Bruce Matthews	.03
167	Warren Moon	.15
168	Mike Munchak	.03
169	Al Smith	.03
170	Lorenzo White	.08
171	Jack Pardee (C)	.03
172	Albert Bentley	.03
173	Duane Bickett	.03
174	Bill Brooks	.03
175	Eric Dickerson (with NFLPA logo, error text: 667)	.50
175a	Eric Dickerson (NFLPA logo removed, error text: 667)	1.25
175b	Eric Dickerson (NFLPA logo removed, corrected text: 677))	.25
176	Ray Donaldson	.03
177	Jeff George	.20
178	Jeff Herrod	.03
179	Clarence Verdin	.03
180	Ron Meyer (C)	.03
181	John Alt	.03
182	Steve DeBerg	.03
183	Albert Lewis	.03
184	Nick Lowery	.03
185	Christian Okoye	.03
186	Stephone Paige	.03
187	Kevin Porter	.03
188	Derrick Thomas	.15
189	Marty Schottenheimer (C)	.03
190	Willie Gault	.03
191	Howie Long	.03
192	Terry McDaniel	.03
193	Jay Schroeder	.03
194	Steve Smith	.03
195	Greg Townsend	.03
196	Lionel Washington	.03
197	Steve Wisniewski	.03
198	Art Shell (C)	.03
199	Henry Ellard	.03
200	Jim Everett	.03
201	Jerry Gray	.03
202	Kevin Greene	.03
203	Buford McGee	.03
204	Tom Newberry	.03
205	Frank Stams, David Wyman	.03
206	Alvin Wright	.03
207	John Robinson (C)	.03
208	Jeff Gross	.03
209	Mark Duper	.03
210	Dan Marino	.75
211	Tim McKyer	.05
211a	Tim McKyer (traded stripe added)	.05
212	John Offerdahl	.03
213	Sammie Smith	.03
214	Richmond Webb	.03
215	Jarvis Williams	.03
216	Don Shula (C)	.03
217	Darrell Fullington (missing registered symbol by NFLPA logo)	.05
217a	Darrell Fullington (corrected)	.05
218	Tim Irwin	.03
219	Mike Merriweather	.03
220	Keith Millard	.03
221	Al Noga	.03
222	Henry Thomas	.03
223	Wade Wilson	.03
224	Gary Zimmerman	.03
225	Jerry Burns (C)	.03
226	Bruce Armstrong	.03
227	Marv Cook	.03
228	Hart Lee Dykes	.03
229	Tom Hodson	.03
230	Ronnie Lippett	.03
231	Ed Reynolds	.03
232	Chris Singleton	.03
233	John Stephens	.03
234	Dick MacPherson (C)	.03
235	Stan Brock	.03
236	Craig Heyward	.03
237	Vaughan Johnson	.03
238	Robert Massey	.03
239	Brett Maxie	.03
240	Rueben Mayes	.03
241	Pat Swilling	.03
242	Renaldo Turnbull	.03
243	Jim Mora (C)	.03
244	Kyle Clifton	.03
245	Jeff Criswell	.03
246	James Hasty	.03
247	Erik McMillan	.03
248	*Scott Mersereau*	.05
249	Ken O'Brien	.03
250	Blair Thomas (with NFLPA logo)	.30
250a	Blair Thomas (NFLPA logo removed)	.10
251	Al Toon	.03
252	Bruce Coslet (C)	.03
253	Eric Allen (AW, FC)	.03
254	Fred Barnett	.10
255	Keith Byars	.03
256	Randall Cunningham	.10
257	Seth Joyner	.03
258	Clyde Simmons	.03
259	Jessie Small	.03
260	Andre Waters	.03
261	Rich Kotite (C)	.03
262	Roy Green	.03
263	Ernie Jones	.03
264	Tim McDonald	.03
265	Timm Rosenbach	.03
266	Rod Saddler	.03
267	Luis Sharpe	.03
268	Anthony Thompson	.03
269	*Marcus Turner*	.08
270	Joe Bugel (C)	.03
271	Gary Anderson (Pit.)	.03
272	Dermontti Dawson	.03
273	Eric Green	.10
274	Merril Hoge	.03
275	Tunch Ilkin	.03
276	David Johnson	.03
277	Louis Lipps	.03
278	Rod Woodson	.05
279	Chuck Noll (C)	.03
280	Martin Bayless	.03
281	Marion Butts	.05
282	Gill Byrd	.03
283	Burt Grossman	.03
284	Courtney Hall	.03
285	Anthony Miller	.03
286	Leslie O'Neal	.03
287	Billy Joe Tolliver	.03
288	Dan Henning (C)	.03
289	Dexter Carter	.03
290	Michael Carter	.03
291	Kevin Fagan	.03
292	Pierce Holt	.03
293	Guy McIntyre	.03
294	Tom Rathman	.03
295	John Taylor	.08
296	Steve Young	.50
297	George Seifert (C)	.03
298	Brian Blades	.03
299	Jeff Bryant	.03
300	Norm Johnson	.03
301	Tommy Kane	.03
302	Cortez Kennedy	.20
303	Bryan Millard	.03
304	John L. Williams	.03
306	Chuck Knox (C, with NFLPA logo)	.10
306a	Chuck Knox (NFLPA logo removed)	.40
307	Gary Anderson (T.B.)	.03
308	Reggie Cobb	.10
309	Randy Grimes	.03
310	Harry Hamilton	.03
311	Bruce Hill	.03
312	Eugene Marve	.03
313	Ervin Randle	.03
314	Vinny Testaverde	.08
315	Richard Williamson (C)	.03
316	Ernest Byner	.03
317	Gary Clark	.08
318	Andre Collins (with NFLPA logo)	.05
318a	Andre Collins (NFLPA logo removed)	.05
319	Darryl Grant	.03
320	Chip Lohmiller	.03
321	Martin Mayhew	.03
322	Mark Rypien	.08
323	Alvin Walton	.03
324	Joe Gibbs	.03
325	Jerry Glanville (R)	.03
326	Nate Odomes (with NFLPA logo)	.05
326a	Nate Odomes (NFLPA logo removed)	.05
327	Boomer Esiason	.03
328	Steve Tasker (with NFLPA logo)	.05
328a	Steve Tasker (NFLPA logo removed)	.05
329	Jerry Rice	.25
330	Jeff Rutledge	.03
331	KC defense (R)	.03
332	Rams (R)	.03
333	John Taylor (R)	.03
334	Randall Cunningham (with NFLPA logo)	.10
334a	Randall Cunningham (NFLPA logo removed)	.10
335	Bo Jackson	.10
336	Lawrence Taylor	.08
337	Warren Moon	.10
338	Alan Grant	.03
339	Steve DeBerg	.03
340	Playoff (Mark Clayton) (TM on Chief #27's shoulder)	.05
340a	Playoff (Mark Clayton) (TM away from Chief #27)	.05
341	Playoff (Jim Kelly) (with NFLPA logo)	.05
341a	Playoff (Jim Kelly) (NFLPA logo removed)	.05
342	NFC Championship (Matt Bahr) (R)	.03
343	*Robert Tisch*	.08
344	Sam Jankovich	.03
345	John Elway	.08
346	Bo Jackson	.08
347	Paul Tagliabue	.03
348	Ronnie Lott	.05
349	Super Bowl XXV Teleclinic	.03
350	Whitney Houston	.08
351	U.S. Troops	.03
352	Art McNally (O)	.03
353	Dick Jorgensen (O)	.03
354	Jerry Seeman (O)	.03
355	Jim Tunney (O)	.03
356	Gerry Austin (O)	.03
357	Gene Barth (O)	.03
358	Red Cashion (O)	.03
359	Tom Dooley (O)	.03
360	Johnny Grier (O)	.03
361	Pat Haggerty (O)	.03
362	Dale Hamer (O)	.03
363	Dick Hantak (O)	.03
364	Jerry Markbreit (O)	.03
365	Gordon McCarter (O)	.03
366	Bob McElwee (O)	.03
367	Howard Roe (O)	.03
368	Tom White (O)	.03
369	Norm Schachter (O)	.03
370	Warren Moon (small type)	.12
370a	Warren Moon (large type)	.10
371	Boomer Esiason (small type)	.05
371a	Boomer Esiason (large type)	.05
372	Troy Aikman (small type)	.50
372a	Troy Aikman (large type)	.50
373	Carl Banks (small type)	.05
373a	Carl Banks (large type)	.05
374	Jim Everett (small type)	.05
374a	Jim Everett (large type)	.05
375	Anthony Munoz (small type, error back: "dificul", "latrapar", error front: "Quadante," "Antony")	.05
375a	Anthony Munoz (small type, corrected back: "dicifil", "atrapar", error front: "Quadante," "Antony")	.05
375b	Anthony Munoz (large type, error front: "Quadante," "Antony")	.05
375c	Anthony Munoz (large type, corrected front: "Quedate," "Anthony")	.05
376	Ray Childress (small type)	.05
376a	Ray Childress (large type)	.05
377	Charles Mann (small type)	.05
377a	Charles Mann (large type)	.05
378	Jackie Slater (small type)	.05
378a	Jackie Slater (large type)	.05
379	Jerry Rice (NFC)	.25
380	Andre Rison (NFC)	.10
381	Jim Lachey (NFC)	.03
382	Jackie Slater (NFC)	.03
383	Randall McDaniel (NFC)	.03
384	Mark Bortz (NFC)	.03
385	Jay Hilgenberg (NFC)	.03
386	Keith Jackson (NFC)	.05
387	Joe Montana (NFC)	.50
388	Barry Sanders (NFC)	.50
389	Neal Anderson (NFC)	.05
390	Reggie White (NFC)	.05
391	Chris Doleman (NFC)	.03
392	Jerome Brown (NFC)	.03
393	Charles Haley (NFC)	.03
394	Lawrence Taylor (NFC)	.05
395	Pepper Johnson (NFC)	.03
396	Mike Singletary (NFC)	.05
397	Darrell Green (NFC)	.03
398	Carl Lee (NFC)	.03
399	Joey Browner (NFC)	.03
400	Ronnie Lott (NFC)	.05
401	Sean Landeta (NFC)	.03
402	Morten Andersen (NFC)	.03
403	Mel Gray (NFC)	.03
404	Reyna Thompson (NFC)	.03
405	Jimmy Johnson (NFC)	.03
406	Andre Reed	.05
407	Anthony Miller	.03
408	Anthony Munoz	.03
409	Bruce Armstrong	.03
410	Bruce Matthews	.03
411	Mike Munchak	.03
412	Kent Hull	.03
413	Rodney Holman	.03
414	Warren Moon	.10
415	Thurman Thomas	.15
416	Marion Butts	.05
417	Bruce Smith	.03
418	Greg Townsend	.03
419	Ray Childress	.03
420	Derrick Thomas	.08
421	Leslie O'Neal	.03
422	John Offerdahl	.03
423	Shane Conlan	.03
424	Rod Woodson	.04
425	Albert Lewis	.03
426	Steve Atwater	.03
427	David Fulcher	.03
428	Rohn Stark	.03
429	Nick Lowery	.03
430	Clarence Verdin	.03
431	Steve Tasker	.03
432	Art Shell	.03
433	Scott Case	.03
434	Tory Epps	.03
435	Mike Gann	.03
436	Brian Jordan	.03
437	Mike Kenn	.03
438	John Rade	.03
439	Andre Rison	.30
440	Mike Rozier	.03
441	Jessie Tuggle	.03
442	Don Beebe	.03
443	*John Davis*	.08
444	James Lofton	.03
445	Keith McKeller	.03
446	Frank Reich	.03
447	Scott Norwood	.03
448	Frank Reich	.03
449	Leon Seals	.03
450	Leonard Smith	.03
451	Neal Anderson	.03
452	Trace Armstrong	.03
453	Mark Bortz	.03
454	Wendell Davis	.05
455	Shaun Gayle	.03
456	Jay Hilgenberg	.03
457	Steve McMichael	.03
458	Mike Singletary	.05
459	Donnell Woolford	.03
460	Jim Breech	.03
461	Eddie Brown	.03
462	Barney Bussey	.03
463	Bruce Kozerski	.03
464	Tim Krumrie	.03
465	Bruce Reimers	.03
466	*Kevin Walker*	.08
467	Ickey Woods	.03
468	Carl Zander	.03
469	Mike Baab	.03
470	Brian Brennan	.03
471	*Rob Burnett*	.08
472	Raymond Clayborn	.03
473	Reggie Langhorne	.03
474	Kevin Mack	.03
475	Anthony Pleasant	.03
476	Joe Morris	.03
477	Dan Fike	.03
478	Ray Horton	.03
479	Jim Jeffcoat	.03
480	Jimmie Jones	.03
481	Kelvin Martin	.03
482	Nate Newton	.03
483	Danny Noonan	.03
484	Jay Novacek	.10
485	Emmitt Smith	2.00
486	*James Washington*	.08
487	Simon Fletcher	.03
488	Ron Holmes	.03
489	Mike Horan	.03
490	Vance Johnson	.03
491	Keith Kartz	.03
492	Greg Kragen	.03
493	Ken Lanier	.03
494	Warren Powers	.03
495	Dennis Smith	.03
496	Jeff Campbell	.03
497	Ken Dallafior	.03
498	Dennis Gibson	.03
499	Kevin Glover	.03
500	Mel Gray	.03
501	Eddie Murray	.03
502	Barry Sanders	1.25
503	Chris Spielman	.03
504	William White	.03
505	*Matt Brock*	.08
506	Robert Brown	.03
507	LeRoy Butler	.03
508	James Campen	.03
509	Jerry Holmes	.03
510	Perry Kemp	.03
511	Ken Ruettgers	.03
512	Scott Stephen	.03
513	Ed West	.03
514	*Cris Dishman*	.08
515	Curtis Duncan	.03
516	Drew Hill	.03
517	Haywood Jeffires	.10
518	Sean Jones	.03
519	Lamar Lathon	.03
520	Don Maggs	.03
521	Bubba McDowell	.03
522	Johnny Meads	.03
523	Chip Banks (error no text)	.03
523a	Chip Banks (corrected)	.03
524	Pat Beach	.03
525	Sam Clancy	.03
526	Eugene Daniel	.03
527	Jon Hand	.03
528	Jessie Hester	.03
529	Mike Prior (error no textual information)	.08
529a	Mike Prior (corrected)	.03
530	Keith Taylor	.03
531	Donnell Thompson	.03
532	Dino Hackett	.03
533	David Lutz	.03
534	Chris Martin	.03
535	Kevin Ross	.03
536	Dan Saleaumua	.03
537	Neil Smith	.05
538	Percy Snow	.03
539	Robb Thomas	.03
540	Barry Word	.08
541	Marcus Allen	.05
542	Eddie Anderson	.03
543	Scott Davis	.03
544	Mervyn Fernandez	.03
545	Ethan Horton	.03
546	Ronnie Lott	.08
547	Don Mosebar	.03
548	Jerry Robinson	.03
549	Aaron Wallace	.03
550	Flipper Anderson	.05
551	Cleveland Gary	.03
552	Damone Johnson	.03
553	Duval Love	.03
554	Irv Pankey	.03
555	Mike Piel	.03
556	Jackie Slater	.03
557	Michael Stewart	.03
558	Pat Terrell	.03
559	J.B. Brown	.03
560	Mark Clayton	.03
561	Ferrell Edmunds	.03
562	Harry Galbreath	.03
563	David Griggs	.03
564	Jim C. Jensen	.03
565	Louis Oliver	.03
566	Tony paige	.05
567	Keith Sims	.03
568	Joey Browner	.03
569	Anthony Carter	.05
570	Chris Doleman	.03
571	Rich Gannon	.05
572	Hassan Jones	.03
573	Steve Jordan	.03
574	Carl Lee	.03
575	Randall McDaniel	.03
576	Herschel Walker	.05
577	Ray Agnew	.03
578	Vincent Brown	.03
579	Irving Fryar	.05
580	Tim Goad	.03
581	Maurice Hurst	.03
582	Fred Marion	.03
583	Johnny Rembert	.03
584	Andre Tippett	.03
585	Brent Williams	.03
586	Morten Andersen	.03
587	*Toi Cook*	.08
588	Jim Dombrowski	.03
589	Dalton Hilliard	.05
590	Rickey Jackson	.03
591	Eric Martin	.03
592	Sam Mills	.03
593	Bobby Hebert	.03
594	Steve Walsh	.03
595	Ottis Anderson	.03
596	Pepper Johnson	.03
597	*Bob Kratch*	.05
598	Sean Landeta	.03
599	Doug Riesenberg	.03
600	William Roberts	.03
601	Phil Simms	.05
602	Lawrence Taylor	.08
603	Everson Walls	.03
604	Brad Baxter	.05
605	Dennis Byrd	.03
606	Jeff Lageman	.03
607	Pat Leahy	.03
608	Rob Moore	.08
609	Joe Mott	.03
610	Tony Stargell	.03
611	Brian Washington	.03
612	*Marvin Washington*	.15
613	David Alexander	.03
614	Jerome Brown	.03
615	Byron Evans	.03
616	Ron Heller	.03
617	Wes Hopkins	.03
618	Keith Jackson	.10
619	Heath Sherman	.03
620	Reggie White	.10
621	Calvin Williams	.10
622	Ken Harvey	.03
623	Eric Hill	.03
624	Johnny Johnson	.20
625	Freddie Joe Nunn	.03
626	Ricky Proehl	.08
627	Tootie Robbins	.03
628	Jay Taylor	.03
629	Tom Tupa	.03
630	*Jim Wahler*	.08
631	Bubby Brister	.03
632	Thomas Everett	.03
633	Bryan Hinkle	.03
634	Carnell Lake	.03
635	David Little	.03
636	Hardy Nickerson	.03
637	Gerald Williams	.03
638	Keith Willis	.03
639	Tim Worley	.03
640	Rod Bernstine	.03
641	Frank Cornish	.03
642	Gary Plummer	.03
643	*Henry Rolling*	.08
644	Sam Seale	.03
645	Junior Seau	.20
646	Billy Ray Smith	.03
647	Broderick Thompson	.03
648	*Derrick Walker*	.08
649	Todd Bowles	.03
650	Don Griffin	.03
651	Charles Haley	.03
652	Brent Jones	.03
653	Joe Montana	1.00
654	Jerry Rice	.75
655	Bill Romanowski	.03
656	Michael Walter	.03
657	Dave Waymer	.03
658	Jeff Chadwick	.03
659	Derrick Fenner	.03
660	Nesby Glasgow	.03
661	Jacob Green	.03
662	*Dwayne Harper*	.08
663	Andy Heck	.03
664	Dave Krieg	.03
665	Rufus Porter	.03
666	Eugene Robinson	.03
667	Mark Carrier	.03
668	Steve Christie	.03
669	Reuben Davis	.03
670	Paul Gruber	.03
671	Wayne Haddix	.03
672	Ron Hall	.03
673	Keith McCants	.05
674	Ricky Reynolds	.03
675	Mark Robinson	.03
676	Jeff Bostic	.03
677	Darrell Green	.05
678	Markus Koch	.03
679	Jim Lachey	.03
680	Charles Mann	.03
681	Wilber Marshall	.03
682	Art Monk	.05
683	Gerald Riggs	.03
684	Ricky Sanders	.03
685	Ray Handley replaces Bill Parcels	.03
686	NFL Announces Expansion	.03
687	Miami Gets Super Bowl XXIX	.03
688	George Young named NFL Executive of yea	.03
689	Five-millionith fan visits Pro FB HOF	.03
690	Sports Illustrated poll pro football #1	.03
691	American Bowl London	.03
692	American Bowl Berlin	.03
693	American Bowl Tokyo	.03
694	Joe Ferguson (LEG)	.03
695	Carl Hairston (LEG)	.03
696	Dan Hampton (LEG)	.03
697	Mike Haynes (LEG)	.03
698	Marty Lyons (LEG)	.03
699	Ozzie Newsome (LEG)	.08
700	Scott Studwell (LEG)	.03
701	Mike Webster (LEG)	.04
702	Dwayne Woodruff (LEG)	.03
703	Larry Kennan (CO)	.03
704	*Stan Gelbaugh*	.08
705	John Brantley	.03
706	Danny Lockett	.03
707	*Anthony Parker*	.08
708	Dan Crossman	.03
709	Eric Wilkerson	.03
710	*Judd Garrett*	.08
711	Tony Baker	.03
712	1st Place BW (Randall Cunningham)	.06
713	2nd Place BW (Mark Ingram)	.03
714	3rd Place BW (Pete Holohan, Barney Bussey, Carl Carter)	.03
715	1st Place Color Action (Sterling Sharpe)	.08
716	2nd Place Color Action (Jim Harbaugh)	.04
717	3rd Place Color Action (Anthony Miller, David Fulcher)	.03
718	1st Place Color Feature (Bill Parcels, Lawrence Taylor) (CO)	.03
719	Patriotic Crowd (2nd Place Color Feature)	.03
720	3rd Place Color Feature (Alfredo Roberts)	.03
721	Read And Study (Ray Bentley)	.03
722	Never Give Up (Earnest Byner)	.03
723	Steroids Destroy (Bill Fralic)	.03
724	Don't Polute (Joe Jacoby)	.03
725	AIDS Kills (Howie Long)	.03
726	School's The Ticket (Dan Montana)	.40
727	Leer Y Estudiar (Ron Rivera)	.03
728	Be The Best (Mike Singletary)	.05
729	Chill (Cornelius Bennett)	.03
730	Russell Maryland	.20
731	*Eric Turner*	.20
732	*Bruce Pickens*	.08
733	*Mike Croel*	.15
734	*Todd Lyght*	.15
735	*Eric Swann*	.10
736	*Charles McRae*	.10
737	*Antone Davis*	.10
738	*Stanley Richard*	.30
739	*Herman Moore*	2.50
740	*Pat Harlow*	.08
741	*Alvin Harper*	.30
742	*Mike Pritchard*	.50
743	*Leonard Russell*	.15
744	*Huey Richardson*	.04
745	*Dan McGwire*	.10
746	*Bobby Wilson*	.08
747	*Alfred Williams*	.10
748	*Vinnie Clark*	.08
749	*Kelvin Pritchett*	.10
750	*Harvey Williams*	1.00
751	*Stan Thomas*	.05
752	*Randal Hill*	.35
753	*Todd Marinovich*	.08
754	*Ted Washington*	.08
755	*Henry Jones*	.20
756	*Jarrod Bunch*	.10
757	*Mike Dumas*	.05
758	*Ed King*	.08
759	*Reggie Johnson*	.08
760	*Roman Phifer*	.10
761	*Mike Jones*	.10
762	*Brett Favre*	5.00
763	*Browning Nagle*	.20
764	*Esera Tuaolo*	.05
765	George Thornton	.03
766	*Dixon Edwards*	.05
767	Darryll Lewis	.03
768	*Eric Bieniemy*	.05
769	*Shane Curry*	.05
770	*Jerome Henderson*	.06
771	*Wesley Carroll*	.10
772	*Nick Bell*	.15
773	John Flannery	.03
774	*Ricky Watters*	1.50
775	*Jeff Graham*	.75
776	*Eric Moten*	.08
777	*Jesse Campbell*	.08
778	*Chris Zorich*	.10
779	Joe Valerio	.03
780	*Doug Thomas*	.08
781	Lamar Rogers	.04
782	*John Johnson*	.08
783	*Phil Hansen*	.08
784	*Kanavis McGhee*	.05
785	*Calvin Stephens*	.05
786	*James Jones*	.10
787	Reggie Barrett	.03
788	*Aeneas Williams*	.10
789	*Aaron Craver*	.10
790	*Keith Traylor*	.08
791	*Godfrey Myles*	.08
792	*Mo Lewis*	.08
793	James Richard	.03
794	*Carlos Jenkins*	.20
795	*Lawrence Dawsey*	.25
796	*Don Davey*	.04
797	*Jake Reed*	1.00
798	Dave McCloughan	.03
799	*Eric Williams*	.15
800	*Steve Jackson*	.10
801	Bob Dahl	.03

802	*Ernie Mills*	.10
803	David Daniels	.03
804	Rob Selby	.03
805	*Ricky Ervins*	.20
806	*Tim Barnett*	.20
807	*Chris Gardocki*	.04
808	*Kevin Donnalley*	.04
809	*Robert Wilson*	.04
810	*Chuck Webb*	.04
811	*Darryl Wren*	.08
812	*Ed McCaffrey*	3.00
813	Shula's 300th Victory	.05
814	Raiders-49ers Sell Out Coliseum	.03
815	NFL International	.03
816	*Moe Gardner*	.08
817	*Tim McKyer*	.05
818	*Tom Waddle*	.50
819	*Michael Jackson*	.75
820	Tony Casillas	.03
821	Gaston Green	.03
822	*Kenny Walker*	.08
823	*Willie Green*	.30
824	*Erik Kramer*	1.00
825	*William Fuller*	.05
826	*Allen Pinkett*	.04
827	*Rick Venturi*	.04
828	*Bill Maas*	.04
829	*Jeff Jaeger*	.04
830	Robert Delpino	.04
831	*Mark Higgs*	.50
832	Reggie Roby	.03
833	*Terry Allen*	1.50
834	Cris Carter	.25
835	John Randle	.40
836	*Hugh Millen*	.25
837	*Jon Vaughn*	.25
838	Gill Fenerty	.03
839	Floyd Turner	.03
840	Irv Eatman	.03
841	Lonnie Young	.03
842	Jim McMahon	.05
843	Randal Hill	.05
844	Barry Foster	.45
845	*Neil O'Donnell*	1.50
846	John Friesz	.10
847	Broderick Thomas	.03
848	Brian Mitchell	.10
849	*Mike Utley*	.15
850	Mike Croel	.08

1991 Pro Set WLAF Helmets

Each of these 10 cards features a helmet for a team in the World League of American Football in its initial season. The cards, random inserts in 1991 Pro Set Series I packs, are numbered on the back and include information about the team depicted on the front, plus a schedule.

		MT
Complete Set (10):		3.00
Common Helmet:		.30
1	Barcelona Dragons	.30
2	Birmingham Fire	.30
3	Frankfurt Galaxy	.30
4	London Monarchs	.30
5	Montreal Machine	.30
6	NY-NJ Knights	.30
7	Orlando Thunder	.30
8	Raleigh-Durham Skyhawks	.30
9	Sacramento Surge	.30
10	San Antonio Riders	.30

1991 Pro Set WLAF Inserts

These cards, featuring players from each of the 10 teams in the World League of American Football during its initial season in 1991, were random inserts in 1991 Pro Set Series I packs. Each team is represented by its quarterback and head coach, at least. The card front has the set's logo in an upper corner and indicates it is an official World League card. The back also has the set logo, plus a player profile and head shot. Card numbering includes "World League Collectible" above the number.

		MT
Complete Set (32):		6.00
Common Player:		.10
1	Mike Lynn	.35
2	Larry Kennan	.10
3	Jack Bicknell	.10
4	Scott Erney	.20
5	A.J. Green	.25
6	Chan Gailey	.10
7	Paul McGowan	.15
8	Brent Pease	.20
9	Jack Elway	.30
10	Mike Perez	.30
11	Mike Tetter	.10
12	Larry Kennan	.10
13	Corris Ervin	.10
14	John Witkowski	.25
15	Jacques Dussault	.10
16	Ray Savage	.10
17	Kevin Sweeney	.50
18	Mouse Davis	.50
19	Todd Hammel	.20
20	Anthony Parker	.30
21	Don Matthews	.15
22	Kerwin Bell	.30
23	Wayne Davis	.10
24	Roman Gabriel	.60
25	John Carter	.20
26	Mark Maye	.20
27	Kay Stephenson	.20
28	Ben Bennett	.50
29	Shawn Knight	.20
30	Mike Riley	.10
31	Jason Garrett	.15
32	Greg Gilbert	.20

A card number in parentheses ( ) indicates the set is unnumbered.

1991 Pro Set Cinderella Story

This nine-card perforated sheet was available inside The Official NFL Pro Set Card Book. The card fronts are similar to the design Pro Set used for its 1991 set, except there are four cards which have black-and-white photos instead of color ones. Each card back is numbered indicating it is in the Cinderella Story set, which profiles players who have achieved success in the NFL despite formidable roadblocks in their paths. If a card is perforated from the sheet, it measures the standard 2-1/2" x 3-1/2".

		MT
Complete Set (9):		8.00
Common Player:		.60
1	Rocky Bleier	1.00
2	Tom Dempsey	.60
3	Dan Hampton	.75
4	Charlie Hennigan	.60
5	Dante Lavelli	.75
6	Jim Plunkett	.75
7	1968 New York Jets (Joe Namath Handing Off)	1.50
8	1981 San Francisco 49ers (Joe Montana Passing)	3.00
9	1979 Tampa Bay Bucs (Ricky Bell Running)	.60

1991 Pro Set National Banquet

Each of these cards can be identified by the National Sports Collectors Convention logo on the front. The cards, which feature full-bleed color photos, were given away during the convention, held in Anaheim, Calif. Each card back is numbered and includes a player profile, biographical information and a mug shot.

		MT
Complete Set (5):		5.00
Common Player:		.50
1	Ronnie Lott	1.50
2	Roy Firestone (Television celebrity)	1.25
3	Roger Craig	1.25
4	ProFiles Television Show (Craig James, Tim Brant)	1.00
5	Title Card	.50

1991 Pro Set Platinum

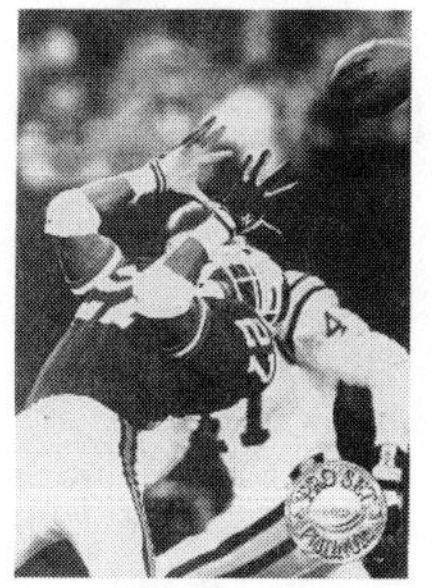

Pro Set issued this 315-card set in two series - 150 and 165 cards each. The glossy cards have full-bleed color action photos on the front, along with the Pro Set Platinum logo. The card backs use a horizontal format and include another action photo, plus the player's name, team and position. A "Platinum Performer" feature is also included, highlighting an outstanding performance by the player. Each series is numbered alphabetically by team, beginning with Atlanta. Subsets include "Special Teams" (#s 128-135), "Platinum Performance" (#s 136-150) and "Platinum Prospects" (#s 286-315). Random insert cards include "Special Collectibles" (numbered PC1-PC10) and redemption cards for a limited-edition Platinum card of Paul Brown or Emmitt Smith.

		MT
Complete Set (315):		12.00
Complete Series 1 (150):		5.00
Complete Series 2 (165):		7.00
Common Player:		.05
Pack (16):		.20
Wax Box (36):		6.00
1	Chris Miller	.05
2	Andre Rison	.25
3	Tim Green	.05
4	Jessie Tuggle	.05
5	Thurman Thomas	.40
6	Darryl Talley	.05
7	Kent Hull	.05
8	Bruce Smith	.05
9	Shane Conlan	.05
10	Jim Harbaugh	.08
11	Neal Anderson	.08
12	Mark Bortz	.05
13	Richard Dent	.05
14	Steve McMichael	.05
15	James Brooks	.05
16	Boomer Esiason	.08
17	Tim Krumrie	.05
18	James Francis	.05
19	Lewis Billups	.05
20	Eric Metcalf	.05
21	Kevin Mack	.05
22	Clay Matthews	.05
23	Mike Johnson	.05
24	Troy Aikman	1.00
25	Emmitt Smith	2.00
26	Daniel Stubbs	.05
27	Ken Norton	.05
28	John Elway	.40
29	Bobby Humphrey	.05
30	Simon Fletcher	.05
31	Karl Mecklenburg	.05
32	Rodney Peete	.05
33	Barry Sanders	1.00
34	Michael Cofer	.05
35	Jerry Ball	.05
36	Sterling Sharpe	.20
37	Tony Mandarich	.05
38	Brian Noble	.05
39	Tim Harris	.05
40	Warren Moon	.15
41	Ernest Givins	.05
42	Mike Munchak	.05
43	Sean Jones	.05
44	Ray Childress	.05
45	Jeff George	.30
46	Albert Bentley	.05
47	Duane Bickett	.05
48	Steve DeBerg	.05
49	Christian Okoye	.05
50	Neil Smith	.05
51	Derrick Thomas	.25
52	Willie Gault	.05
53	Don Mosebar	.05
54	Howie Long	.05
55	Greg Townsend	.05
56	Terry McDaniel	.05
57	Jackie Slater	.05
58	Jim Everett	.05
59	Cleveland Gary	.05
60	Mike Piel	.05
61	Jerry Gray	.05
62	Dan Marino	.75
63	Sammie Smith	.05
64	Richmond Webb	.05
65	Louis Oliver	.05
66	Ferrell Edmunds	.05
67	Jeff Cross	.05
68	Wade Wilson	.05
69	Chris Doleman	.05
70	Joey Browner	.05
71	Keith Millard	.05
72	John Stephens	.05
73	Andre Tippett	.05
74	Brent Williams	.05
75	Craig Heyward	.05
76	Eric Martin	.05
77	Pat Swilling	.05
78	Sam Mills	.05
79	Jeff Hostetler	.25
80	Ottis Anderson	.05
81	Lawrence Taylor	.10
82	Pepper Johnson	.05
83	Blair Thomas	.05
84	Al Toon	.05
85	Ken O'Brien	.05
86	Erik McMillan	.05
87	Dennis Byrd	.05
88	Randall Cunningham	.10
89	Fred Barnett	.15
90	Seth Joyner	.05
91	Reggie White	.15
92	Timm Rosenbach	.05
93	Johnny Johnson	.25
94	Tim McDonald	.05
95	Freddie Joe Nunn	.05
96	Bubby Brister	.08
97	Gary Anderson	.05
98	Merril Hoge	.05
99	Keith Willis	.05
100	Rod Woodson	.08
101	Billy Joe Tolliver	.05
102	Marion Butts	.08
103	Rod Benstine	.05
104	Lee Williams	.05
105	Burt Grossman	.05
106	Tom Rathman	.05
107	John Taylor	.10
108	Michael Carter	.05
109	Guy McIntyre	.05
110	Pierce Holt	.05
111	John L. Williams	.05
112	Dave Krieg	.05
113	Bryan Millard	.05
114	Cortez Kennedy	.30
115	Derrick Fenner	.05
116	Vinny Testaverde	.08
117	Reggie Cobb	.25
118	Gary Anderson	.05
119	Bruce Hill	.05
120	Wayne Haddix	.05
121	Broderick Thomas	.05
122	Keith McCants	.05
123	Andre Collins	.05
124	Earnest Byner	.05
125	Jim Lachey	.05
126	Mark Rypien	.10
127	Charles Mann	.05
128	Nick Lowery	.05
129	Chip Lohmiller	.05
130	Mike Horan	.05
131	Rohn Stark	.05
132	Sean Landeta	.05
133	Clarence Verdin	.05
134	Johnny Bailey	.05
135	Herschel Walker	.05
136	Bo Jackson	.40
137	Dexter Carter	.05
138	Warren Moon	.10
139	Joe Montana	1.00
140	Jerry Rice	.75
141	Deion Sanders	.30
142	Ronnie Lippett	.05
143	Terance Mathis	.05
144	Gaston Green	.05
145	Dean Biasucci	.05
146	Charles Haley	.05
147	Derrick Thomas	.25
148	Lawrence Taylor	.10
149	Art Shell	.05
150	Bill Parcells	.05
151	Steve Broussard	.05
152	Darion Conner	.05
153	Bill Fralic	.05
154	Mike Gann	.05
155	Tim McKyer	.05
156	Don Beebe	.05
157	Cornelius Bennett	.05
158	Andre Reed	.10
159	Leonard Smith	.05
160	Will Wolford	.05
161	Mark Carrier	.05
162	Wendell Davis	.10
163	Jay Hilgenberg	.05
164	Brad Muster	.05
165	Mike Singletary	.05
166	Eddie Brown	.05
167	David Fulcher	.05
168	Rodney Holman	.05
169	Anthony Munoz	.05
170	Craig Taylor	.05
171	Mike Baab	.05
172	David Grayson	.05
173	Reggie Langhorne	.05
174	Joe Morris	.05
175	Kevin Gogan	.10
176	Jack Del Rio	.05
177	Issiac Holt	.05
178	Michael Irvin	.60
179	Jay Novacek	.15
180	Steve Atwater	.05
181	Mark Jackson	.05
182	Ricky Nattiel	.05
183	Warren Powers	.05
184	Dennis Smith	.05
185	Bennie Blades	.05
186	Lomas Brown	.05
187	Robert Clark	.05
188	Mel Gray	.05
189	Chris Spielman	.05
190	Johnny Holland	.05
191	Don Majkowski	.05
192	*Bryce Paup*	.50
193	Darrell Thompson	.15
194	Ed West	.05
195	Cris Dishman	.15
196	Drew Hill	.05
197	Bruce Matthews	.05
198	Bubba McDowell	.05
199	Allen Pinkett	.05
200	Bill Brooks	.05
201	Jeff Herrod	.05
202	Anthony Johnson	.10
203	Mike Prior	.05
204	John Alt	.05
205	Stephone Paige	.05
206	Kevin Ross	.05
207	Dan Saleaumua	.05
208	Barry Word	.10
209	Marcus Allen	.05
210	Roger Craig	.05
211	Ronnie Lott	.10
212	Winston Moss	.05
213	Jay Schroeder	.05
214	Robert Delpino	.05
215	Henry Ellard	.05
216	Kevin Greene	.05
217	Tom Newberry	.05
218	Michael Stewart	.05
219	Mark Duper	.05
220	*Mark Higgs*	.30
221	John Offerdahl	.05
222	Keith Sims	.05
223	Anthony Carter	.05
224	Cris Carter	.05
225	Steve Jordan	.05
226	Randall McDaniel	.05
227	Al Noga	.05
228	Ray Agnew	.05
229	Bruce Armstrong	.05
230	Bruce Armstrong	.05
231	Greg McMurtry	.05
232	Chris Singleton	.05
233	Morten Andersen	.05
234	Vince Buck	.05
235	Gill Fenerty	.05
236	Rickey Jackson	.05
237	Vaughan Johnson	.05
238	Carl Banks	.05
239	Mark Collins	.05
240	Rodney Hampton	.50
241	David Meggett	.05
242	Bart Oates	.05
243	Kyle Clifton	.05
244	Jeff Lageman	.05
245	Freeman McNeil	.05
246	Rob Moore	.20
247	Eric Allen	.05
248	Keith Byars	.05
249	Keith Jackson	.10
250	Jim McMahon	.05
251	Andre Waters	.05
252	Ken Harvey	.05
253	Ernie Jones	.05
254	Luis Sharpe	.05
255	Anthony Thompson	.05
256	Tom Tupa	.05
257	Eric Green	.10
258	Barry Foster	.50
259	Bryan Hinkle	.05
260	Tunch Ilkin	.05
261	Louis Lipps	.05
262	Gill Byrd	.05
263	John Friesz	.10
264	Anthony Miller	.05
265	Junior Seau	.25
266	Ronnie Harmon	.05
267	Harris Barton	.05
268	Todd Bowles	.05
269	Don Griffin	.05
270	Bill Romanowski	.05
271	Steve Young	.50
272	Brian Blades	.05
273	Jacob Green	.05
274	Rufus Porter	.05
275	Eugene Robinson	.05
276	Mark Carrier	.05
277	Reuben Davis	.05
278	Paul Gruber	.05
279	Gary Clark	.10
280	Darrell Green	.05
281	Wilber Marshall	.05
282	Matt Millen	.05
283	Alvin Walton	.05
284	Joe Gibbs	.05
285	Don Shula	.05
286	*Larry Brown*	.15
287	*Mike Croel*	.30
288	*Antone Davis*	.10
289	*Ricky Ervins*	.25
290	*Brett Favre*	1.75
291	*Pat Harlow*	.10
292	*Michael Jackson*	.60
293	*Henry Jones*	.25
294	*Aaron Craver*	.10
295	*Nick Bell*	.25
296	*Todd Lyght*	.15
297	*Todd Marinovich*	.10
298	*Russell Maryland*	.35
299	*Kanavis McGhee*	.10
300	*Dan McGwire*	.15
301	Charles McRae	.10
302	Eric Moten	.10
303	Jerome Henderson	.10
304	*Browning Nagle*	.25
305	*Mike Pritchard*	.35
306	*Stanley Richard*	.30
307	*Randal Hill*	.25
308	*Leonard Russell*	1.00
309	*Eric Swann*	.15
310	*Phil Hansen*	.15
311	*Moe Gardner*	.15
312	*Jon Vaughn*	.15
313	*Aeneas Williams*	.10
314	*Alfred Williams*	.15
315	*Harvey Williams*	.35

1991 Pro Set Platinum PC

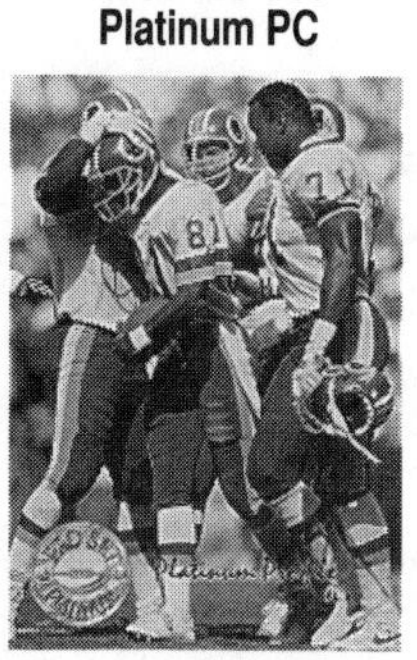

These 10 insert cards were randomly included in Series II Platinum packs. Each is numbered on the card back using a "PC" prefix. The card front has a full-bleed color action photo, plus the set logo. The back has another photo and player summary, all designed in a horizontal format. The cards were divided into three subsets - Platinum Profile, Platinum Photo and Platinum Game Breaker.

		MT
Complete Set (10):		10.00
Common Player:		.50
1	Bobby Hebert	.50
2	Art Monk	.50
3	Kenny Walker	.50
4	Low Fives	.50
5	Kevin Mack	.50
6	Neal Anderson	.50
7	Gaston Green	.50
8	Barry Sanders	3.00
9	Emmitt Smith	5.00
10	Thurman Thomas	1.50

1991 Pro Set Spanish

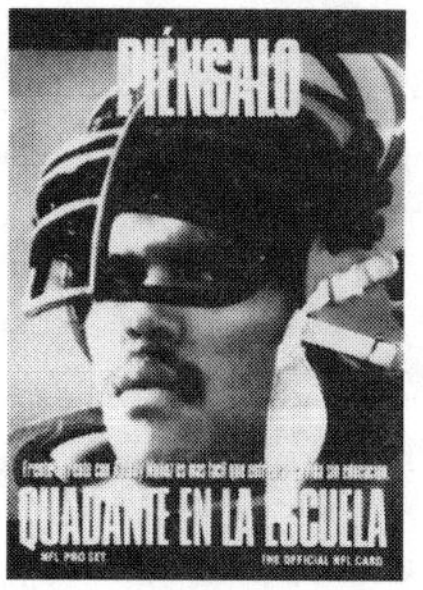

These cards have the same photos on them as their regular 1991 Pro Set counterparts, but the card numbers have been changed. Also, the big difference is that all text and information on the card is in Spanish. Five insert cards (ES1-ES5) were also randomly included in packs.

		MT
Complete Set (300):		10.00
Common Player:		.03
1	Steve Broussard	.03
2	Darion Conner	.03
3	Tory Epps	.03
4	Bill Fralic	.03
5	Mike Gann	.03
6	Chris Miller	.15
7	Andre Rison	.20
8	Deion Sanders	.25
9	Jessie Tuggle	.03
10	Cornelius Bennett	.10
11	Shane Conlan	.05
12	Kent Hull	.03
13	Kirby Jackson	.03
14	James Lofton	.15
15	Andre Reed	.15
16	Bruce Smith	.15
17	Darryl Talley	.05
18	Thurman Thomas	.50
19	Neal Anderson	.15
20	Trace Armstrong	.03
21	Mark Carrier	.07
22	Wendell Davis	.03
23	Richard Dent	.15
24	Jim Harbaugh	.10
25	Ron Rivera	.03
26	Mike Singletary	.15
27	Lemuel Stinson	.03
28	James Brooks	.03
29	Eddie Brown	.03
30	Boomer Esiason	.15
31	James Francis	.03
32	David Fulcher	.03
33	Rodney Holman	.03
34	Anthony Munoz	.10
35	Bruce Reimers	.03
36	Ickey Woods	.05
37	Mike Baab	.03
38	Brian Brennan	.03
39	Raymond Clayborn	.03
40	Mike Johnson	.03
41	Clay Matthews	.03
42	Eric Metcalf	.07
43	Frank Minnifield	.03
44	Joe Morris	.05
45	Anthony Pleasant	.03
46	Troy Aikman	1.00
47	Jack Del Rio	.03
48	Issiac Holt	.03
49	Michael Irvin	.50
50	Jimmie Jones	.03
51	Nate Newton	.03
52	Danny Noonan	.03
53	Jay Novacek	.07
54	Emmitt Smith	2.00
55	Steve Atwater	.05
56	Michael Brooks	.03
57	John Elway	.25
58	Mike Horan	.03
59	Mark Jackson	.03
60	Karl Mecklenburg	.03
61	Warren Powers	.03
62	Dennis Smith	.03
63	Doug Widell	.03
64	Jerry Ball	.05
65	Bennie Blades	.05
66	Robert Clark	.03
67	Ken Dallafior	.03
68	Mel Gray	.07
69	Eddie Murray	.05
70	Rodney Peete	.05
71	Barry Sanders	.75
72	Chris Spielman	.07
73	Robert Brown	.03
74	LeRoy Butler	.07
75	Perry Kemp	.03
76	Don Majkowski	.05
77	Tony Mandarich	.03
78	Mark Murphy	.03
79	Brian Noble	.03
80	Sterling Sharpe	.50
81	Ed West	.03
82	Ray Childress	.03
83	Cris Dishman	.03
84	Ernest Givins	.07
85	Drew Hill	.05
86	Haywood Jeffires	.07
87	Lamar Lathon	.03
88	Bruce Matthews	.07
89	Bubba McDowell	.03
90	Warren Moon	.25
91	Chip Banks	.03
92	Albert Bentley	.05
93	Duane Bickett	.03
94	Bill Brooks	.03
95	Sam Clancy	.03
96	Ray Donaldson	.03
97	Jeff George	.25
98	Mike Prior	.03
99	Clarence Verdin	.03
100	Steve DeBerg	.05
101	Albert Lewis	.03
102	Christian Okoye	.05
103	Kevin Ross	.03
104	Stephone Paige	.03
105	Kevin Porter	.03
106	Percy Snow	.03
107	Derrick Thomas	.20
108	Barry Word	.05
109	Marcus Allen	.20
110	Mervyn Fernandez	.03
111	Howie Long	.07
112	Ronnie Lott	.15
113	Terry McDaniel	.03
114	Max Montoya	.03
115	Don Mosebar	.03
116	Jay Schroeder	.10
117	Greg Townsend	.03
118	Flipper Anderson	.07
119	Henry Ellard	.07
120	Jim Everett	.10
121	Kevin Greene	.07
122	Damone Johnson	.03
123	Buford McGee	.03
124	Tom Newberry	.05
125	Michael Stewart	.03
126	Alvin Wright	.03
127	Mark Clayton	.05
128	Jeff Cross	.03
129	Mark Duper	.05
130	Ferrell Edmunds	.03
131	Dan Marino	.75
132	Tim McKyer	.03
133	John Offerdahl	.05
134	Louis Oliver	.03
135	Sammie Smith	.03
136	Joey Browner	.05
137	Anthony Carter	.10
138	Chris Doleman	.05
139	Hassan Jones	.03
140	Steve Jordan	.05
141	Carl Lee	.03
142	Al Noga	.03
143	Henry Thomas	.03
144	Herschel Walker	.15
145	Ray Agnew	.03
146	Bruce Armstrong	.03
147	Marv Cook	.05
148	Irving Fryar	.07
149	Tommy Hodson	.07
150	Fred Marion	.03
151	Johnny Rembert	.03
152	Chris Singleton	.03
153	Andre Tippett	.07
154	Morten Andersen	.10
155	Toi Cook	.03
156	Craig Heyward	.05
157	Dalton Hilliard	.03
158	Rickey Jackson	.07
159	Vaughan Johnson	.07
160	Rueben Mayes	.03
161	Pat Swilling	.07
162	Bobby Hebert	.07
163	Ottis Anderson	.10
164	Carl Banks	.05
165	Rodney Hampton	.25
166	Jeff Hostetler	.15
167	Mark Ingram	.05
168	Leonard Marshall	.03
169	David Meggett	.05
170	Lawrence Taylor	.25
171	Everson Walls	.03
172	Brad Baxter	.03
173	Jeff Lageman	.03
174	Pat Leahy	.03
175	Erik McMillan	.03
176	Scott Mersereau	.03
177	Rob Moore	.10

178	Ken O'Brien	.07
179	Blair Thomas	.10
180	Al Toon	.07
181	Eric Allen	.03
182	Jerome Brown	.03
183	Keith Byars	.05
184	Randall Cunningham	.15
185	Byron Evans	.03
186	Keith Jackson	.05
187	Heath Sherman	.03
188	Clyde Simmons	.03
189	Reggie White	.20
190	Rich Camarillo	.03
191	Johnny Johnson	.15
192	Ernie Jones	.03
193	Tim McDonald	.03
194	Freddie Joe Nunn	.03
195	Luis Sharpe	.03
196	Jay Taylor	.03
197	Anthony Thompson	.03
198	Tom Tupa	.03
199	Gary Anderson	.05
200	Bubby Brister	.10
201	Eric Green	.07
202	Bryan Hinkle	.03
203	Merril Hoge	.03
204	Carnell Lake	.03
205	Louis Lipps	.03
206	Keith Willis	.03
207	Rod Woodson	.10
208	Rod Bernstine	.05
209	Marion Butts	.07
210	Anthony Miller	.10
211	Leslie O'Neal	.03
212	Henry Rolling	.03
213	Junior Seau	.15
214	Billy Ray Smith	.03
215	Broderick Thompson	.03
216	Derrick Walker	.05
217	Dexter Carter	.03
218	Don Griffin	.03
219	Charles Haley	.05
220	Pierce Holt	.03
221	Joe Montana	1.00
222	Jerry Rice	.75
223	John Taylor	.10
224	Michael Walter	.03
225	Steve Young	.25
226	Brian Blades	.05
227	Jeff Bryant	.03
228	Jacob Green	.03
229	Tommy Kane	.03
230	Dave Krieg	.07
231	Bryan Millard	.03
232	Rufus Porter	.03
233	Eugene Robinson	.03
234	John L. Williams	.03
235	Gary Anderson	.03
236	Mark Carrier	.05
237	Reggie Cobb	.05
238	Rueben Davis	.03
239	Paul Gruber	.03
240	Harry Hamilton	.03
241	Keith McCants	.03
242	Ricky Reynolds	.03
243	Vinny Testaverde	.10
244	Earnest Byner	.05
245	Gary Clark	.10
246	Andre Collins	.03
247	Darrell Green	.07
248	Jim Lachey	.03
249	Charles Mann	.03
250	Wilber Marshall	.05
251	Art Monk	.10
252	Mark Rypien	.10
253	Russell Maryland	.15
254	Mike Croel	.03
255	Stanley Richard	.03
256	Leonard Russell	.03
257	Dan McGwire	.10
258	Todd Marinovich	.05
259	Eric Swann	.03
260	Mike Pritchard	.03
261	Alfred Williams	.03
262	Brett Favre	1.25
263	Browning Nagle	.07
264	Darryll Lewis	.03
265	Nick Bell	.03
266	Jeff Graham	.03
267	Eric Moten	.03
268	Roman Phifer	.03
269	Eric Bieniemy	.03
270	Phil Hansen	.03
271	Reggie Barrett	.03
272	Aeneas Williams	.07
273	Aaron Craver	.03
274	Lawrence Dawsey	.03
275	Ricky Ervins	.03
276	Jake Reed	.10
277	Eric Williams	.10
278	Tim Barnett	.10
279	Keith Traylor	.03
280	Jerry Rice	.25
281	Jim Lachey	.03
282	Barry Sanders	.50
283	Neal Anderson	.07
284	Reggie White	.15
285	Lawrence Taylor	.15
286	Mike Singletary	.10
287	Joey Browner	.05
288	Morten Andersen	.05
289	Andre Reed	.10
290	Anthony Munoz	.07
291	Warren Moon	.20
292	Thurman Thomas	.25
293	Ray Childress	.05
294	Derrick Thomas	.15
295	Rod Woodson	.10
296	Steve Atwater	.05
297	David Fulcher	.03
298	Anthony Munoz	.10
299	Ron Rivera	.03
300	Cornelius Bennett	.10
E1	Tom Flores	2.00
E2	Anthony Munoz	2.00
E3	Tony Casillas	2.00
E4	Super Bowl XXVI	2.00
E5	Felicidades	2.00

1991 Pro Set UK Sheets

Measuring 5-1/8" x 11-3/4", the five six-card strips were used as a promotion in a Middlesex, England, newspaper called Today. Released one strip per week in Sunday papers during Fall 1991, the unperforated strips were numbered 1-5. Each player card is numbered identically to his 1991 regular-issue cards.

		MT
Complete Set (5):		25.00
Common Player:		2.00
1	Quarterbacks (200 Jim Everett, 167 Warren Moon, 111 Boomer Esiason, 128 Troy Aikman, 726 Dan Marino, 138 John Elway)	10.00
2	Running Backs (576 Herschel Walker, 213 Sammie Smith, 722 Earnest Byner, 123 Eric Metcalf, 485 Emmitt Smith)	10.00
3	Receivers (209 Mark Duper, 654 Jerry Rice, 251 Al Toon, 161 Sterling Sharpe, 618 Keith Jackson, 115 Tim McGee)	6.00
4	Kickers (460 Jim Breech, 447 Scott Norwood, 489 Mike Horan, 300 Norm Johnson, 184 Nick Lowery, 401 Sean Landeta)	2.00
5	Defensive (728 Mike Singletary, 56 Carl Banks, 98 Deion Sanders, 191 Howie Long, 131 Issiac Holt, 241 Pat Swilling)	3.00

1991 Pro Set WLAF

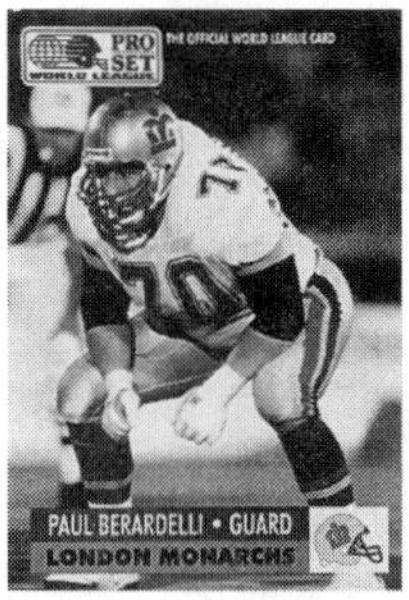

These cards feature players from the World League of American Football. This logo and a notation that the card is an "Official World League Card" are on the front, which has a full-bleed color action photo. The back has a card number, player profile, biographical information and a mug shot. Each back is designed in a horizontal format.

		MT
Complete Set (150):		5.00
Common Player:		.05
1	World League Logo	.15
2	Mike Lynn	.15
3	First Weekend	.15
4	World Bowl Trophy	.30
5	Jon Horton	.05
6	Stan Gelbaugh	.50
7	Dan Crossman	.05
8	Marlon Brown	.10
9	Judd Garrett	.25
10	Barcelona Dragons	.05
11	Birmingham Fire	.05
12	Frankfurt Galaxy	.05
13	London Monarchs	.05
14	Montreal Machine	.05
15	NY-NJ Knights	.05
16	Orlando Thunder	.05
17	Raleigh-Durham Skyhawks	.05
18	Sacramento Surge	.05
19	San Antonio Riders	.05
20	Eric Wilkerson	.05
21	Stan Gelbaugh	.35
22	Judd Garrett	.15
23	Tony Baker	.05
24	Byron Williams	.05
25	Chris Mohr	.10
26	Errol Tucker	.05
27	Carl Painter	.05
28	Anthony Parker	.10
29	Danny Lockett	.10
30	Scott Adams	.05
31	Jim Bell	.05
32	Lydell Carr	.15
33	Bruce Clark	.15
34	Demetrius Davis	.10
35	Scott Erney	.10
36	Ron Goetz	.05
37	Xisco Marcos	.05
38	Paul Palmer	.15
39	Tony Rice	.40
40	Bobby Sign	.05
41	Gene Taylor	.05
42	Barry Voorhees	.05
43	Jack Bicknell	.10
44	Kenny Bell	.05
45	Willie Bouyer	.05
46	John Brantley	.10
47	Elroy Harris	.05
48	James Henry	.05
49	John Holland	.10
50	Arhur Hunter	.05
51	Eric Jones	.05
52	Kirk Maggio	.05
53	Paul McGowan	.05
54	John Miller	.10
55	Maurice Oliver	.05
56	Darrel Phillips	.05
57	Chan Gailey	.05
58	Tony Baker	.10
59	Tim Broady	.05
60	Garry Frank	.05
61	Jason Johnson	.05
62	Stefan Maslo	.05
63	Mark Mraz	.05
64	Yepi Pau'u	.05
65	Mike Perez	.25
66	Mike Teeter	.05
67	Chris Williams	.05
68	Jack Elway	.20
69	Theo Adams	.05
70	Jeff Alexander	.05
71	Phillip Alexander	.05
72	Paul Berardelli	.10
73	Dana Brinson	.05
74	Marlon Brown	.05
75	Dedrick Dodge	.05
76	Victor Ebubedike	.05
77	Corris Ervin	.10
78	Steve Gabbard	.05
79	Judd Garrett	.15
80	Stan Gelbaugh	.75
81	Roy Hart	.05
82	Jon Horton	.05
83	Danny Lockett	.15
84	Doug Marrone	.05
85	Ken Sale	.05
86	Larry Kennan	.05
87	Mike Cadore	.05
88	K.D. Dunn	.05
89	Ricky Johnson	.05
90	Chris Mohr	.05
91	Bjorn Nittmo	.10
92	Michael Proctor	.05
93	Richard Shelton	.15
94	Tracy Simien	.30
95	Jacques Dussault	.05
96	Cornell Burbage	.10
97	Joe Campbell	.05
98	Monty Gilbreath	.05
99	Jeff Graham	.25
100	Kip Lewis	.05
101	Bob Lilljedahl	.05
102	Falanda Newton	.10
103	Anthony Parker	.10
104	Caesar Rentie	.05
105	Ron Sancho	.10
106	Craig Schlicting	.10
107	Lonnie Turner	.05
108	Eric Wilkerson	.10
109	Tony Woods	.10
110	Darrell "Mouse" Davis	.15
111	Kerwin Bell	.30
112	Wayne Davis	.05
113	John Guerrero	.05
114	Myron Jones	.05
115	Eric Mitchel	.20
116	Billy Owens	.05
117	Carl Painter	.10
118	Rob Sterling	.05
119	Errol Tucker	.05
120	Byron Williams	.05
121	Mike Withycombe	.05
122	Don Matthews	.05
123	Jon Carter	.05
124	Marvin Hargrove	.10
125	Clarkston Hines	.05
126	Ray Jackson	.05
127	Bobby McAllister	.25
128	Darryl McGill	.05
129	Pat McGuirk	.10
130	Shawn Woodson	.10
131	Roman Gabriel	.25
132	Greg Coauette	.05
133	Mike Eklins	.15
134	Victor Floyd	.05
135	Shawn Knight	.10
136	Pete Najarian	.05
137	Carl Parker	.10
138	Richard Stephens	.05
139	Curtis Wilson	.05
140	Kay Stephenson	.10
141	Ricky Blake	.25
142	Donnie Gardner	.05
143	Jason Garrett	.25
144	Mike Johnson	.05
145	Undra Johnson	.10
146	John Layfield	.05
147	Mark Ledbetter	.05
148	Gary Richard	.05
149	Tim Walton	.05
150	Mike Riley	.05

1991 Pro Set WLAF World Bowl Combo 43

This set combines Pro Set's helmet and 32-card insert sets into one issue. Fans who attended the World Bowl Game in Wembley Stadium in London, England, received the set. The cards have been renumbered from the original sets, and the helmet cards can be identified by the chronological text which is on the back instead of a team schedule.

		MT
Complete Set (43):		15.00
Common Player:		.25
1	PRES (Mike Lynn)	.75
2	League Opener London 24, Frankfurt 11	.50
3	Jack Bicknell	.50
4	Scott Erney	.40
5	Anthony Greene	.50
6	Chan Gailey	.50
7	Paul McGowan	.25
8	Brent Pease	.50
9	Jack Elway	.80
10	Mike Perez	.75
11	Mike Teeter	.25
12	Larry Kennan	.25
13	Corris Ervin	.25
14	John Witkowski	.50
15	Jacques Dussault	.25
16	Ray Savage	.35
17	Kevin Sweeney	.65
18	Mouse Davis	.65
19	Todd Hammel	.50
20	Anthony Parker	.50
21	Don Matthews	.25
22	Kerwin Bell	.75
23	Wayne Davis	.25
24	Roman Gabriel	.75
25	Jon Carter	.50
26	Bobby McAllister	1.00
27	Kay Stephenson	.25
28	Mike Elkins	1.00
29	Shawn Knight	.50
30	Mike Riley	.25
31	Jason Garrett	.75
32	Greg Gilbert	.50
33	World Bowl Trophy	4.00
34	Barcelona Dragons Helmet	.60
35	Birmingham Fire Helmet	.60
36	Frankfurt Galaxy Helmet	.60
37	London Monarchs Helmet	.60
38	Montreal Machine Helmet	.60
39	NY-NJ Knights Helmet	.60
40	Orlando Thunder Helmet	.60
41	Ral.-Durham Skyhawks Helmet	.60
42	Sacramento Surge Helmet	.60
43	San Antonio Riders Helmet	.60

1991 Pro Set Super Bowl XXVI AMEX Binder

American Express sponsored this 49-card set which was sold to commemorate Super Bowl XXVI in Minneapolis. The cards were included in an album, which holds four cards per page. Representatives from the Super Bowl teams - the Buffalo Bills and Washington Redskins - are included in the set. The cards have the same photos and numbers as their regular set counterparts, except these are marked with an AFC or NFC Champs logo on the front.

		MT
Complete Set (49):		25.00
Common Player:		.40
1	The NFL Experience	1.00
2	Super Bowl XXVI	.50
3	AFC Standings	.50
4	NFC Standings	.50
5	The Metrodome	.50
73	Howard Ballard	.40
74	Cornelius Bennett	.75
75	Shane Conlan	.50
76	Kent Hull	.50
77	Kirby Jackson	.40
79	Mark Kelso	.40
80	Nate Odomes	.40
81	Andre Reed	.90
82	Jim Ritcher	.40
83	Bruce Smith	.75
84	Darryl Talley	.50
86	Thurman Thomas	3.00
88	Will Wolford	.40
89	Jeff Wright	.40
90	Marv Levy	.40
300	Cornelius Bennett	.50
316	Earnest Byner	.60
317	Gary Clark	.90
318	Andre Collins	.50
320	Chip Lohmiller	.40
321	Martin Mayhew	.40
322	Mark Rypien	.75
323	Alvin Walton	.40
324	Joe Gibbs	.50
370	Warren Moon	.75
444	James Lofton	.75
445	Keith McKeller	.50
449	Leon Seals	.40
450	Leonard Smith	.40
676	Jeff Bostic	.40
677	Darrell Green	.75
678	Markus Koch	.40
679	Jim Lachey	.50
680	Charles Mann	.50
681	Wilber Marshall	.50
682	Art Monk	.75
683	Gerald Riggs	.50
684	Ricky Sanders	.75
725	Howie Long	.75
726	Dan Marino	2.00
746	Bobby Wilson	.50
805	Ricky Ervins	.75
848	Brian Mitchell	.75
(1)	Jim Kelly	20.00
(1)	Jim Kelly	20.00

1992 Pro Set

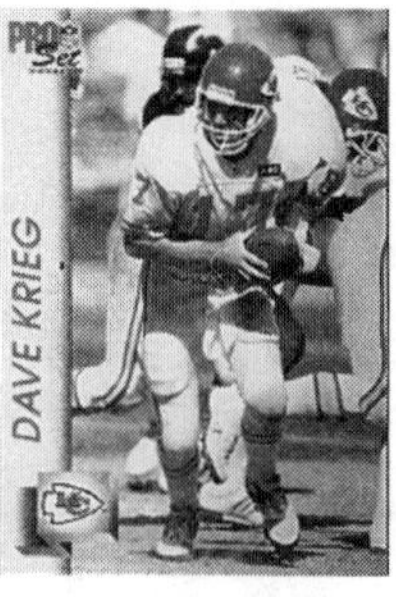

Pro Set issued its 700-card 1992 set in two series - 400 and 300 cards. The fronts have full-bleed color action photos and the player's name and NFL/Pro Set logos at the bottom. The backs, using a horizontal format, offer statistics, a biography, career highlights and a close-up shot of the player. Subsets include Statistical Leaders, Milestones, Draft Day, Innovators, 1991 Replays, Super Bowl XXVI Replays, Pro Set Newsreel, Magic Numbers, Play Smart, NFC Spirit of the Game, AFC Pro Bowl Stars, NFC Pro Bowl Stars, and six miscellaneous cards. Insert cards include an Emmitt Smith hologram set of four cards (ES1-ES4), Hall of Fame 2000 (10 cards), Team MVPs (30 gold-foil stamped cards), a Santa Claus card, Ground Force, Hall of Fame Inductees and a Pro Set Emmitt Smith Power Preview special offer card.

		MT
Complete Set (700):		20.00
Complete Series 1 (400):		10.00
Complete Series 2 (300):		10.00
Common Player:		.05
Minor Stars:		.10
Series 1 Pack (14):		.25
Series 1 Wax Box (36):		8.00
Series 2 Pack (14):		.40
Series 2 Wax Box (36):		12.00
1	Mike Croel (LL)	.05
2	Thurman Thomas (LL)	.10
3	Wayne Fontes (CO) (LL)	.05
4	Anthony Munoz (LL)	.05
5	Steve Young (LL)	.25
6	Warren Moon (LL)	.10
7	Emmitt Smith (LL)	.50
8	Haywood Jeffires (LL)	.05
9	Marv Cook (LL)	.05
10	Michael Irvin (LL)	.10
11	Thurman Thomas (LL)	.10
12	Chip Lohmiller (LL)	.05
13	Barry Sanders (LL)	.75
14	Reggie Roby (LL)	.05
15	Mel Gray (LL)	.05
16	Ronnie Lott (LL)	.05
17	Pat Swilling (LL)	.05
18	Reggie White (LL)	.10
19	Haywood Jeffires (ML)	.05
20	Pat Leahy (ML)	.05
21	James Lofton (ML)	.05
22	Art Monk (ML)	.10
23	Don Shula (ML)	.05
24	Nick Lowery (ML)	.05
25	John Elway (ML)	.50
26	Chicago Bears (ML)	.05
27	Marcus Allen (ML)	.10
28	*Terrell Buckley*	.20
29	*Amp Lee*	.10
30	*Chris Mims*	.10
31	*Leon Searcy*	.10
32	*Jimmy Smith*	2.00
33	*Siran Stacy*	.10
34	Pete Gogolak	.05
35	Cheerleaders	.05
36	Houston Astrodome	.05
37	Christian Okoye (Week 1)	.05
38	Don Beebe (Week 2)	.05
39	Wendell Davis (Week 3)	.05
40	Don Shula (CO, Week 4)	.05
41	Ronnie Lott (Week 5)	.05
42	Art Monk (Week 6)	.10
43	Thurman Thomas (Week 7)	.10
44	John Stephens (Week 8)	.05
45	Herschel Walker (Week 9)	.05
46	Chris Burkett (Week 10)	.05
47	Line Play (Week 11)	.05
48	Andre Rison (Week 12)	.10
49	Steve Beuerlein, Michael Irvin (Week 13)	.10
50	Irving Fryar (Week 14)	.05
51	Bill's Defense (Week 15)	.05
52	Kelvin Martin (Week 16)	.05
53	Bruce Coslet (CO, Week 17)	.05
54	Fred Jones (AFC Wild Card)	.05
55	Oilers' Run-and-Shoot (AFC Wild Card)	.05
56	Bill Bates (NFC Wild Card)	.05
57	Michael Haynes (NFC Wild Card)	.05
58	Bronco Interception (AFC Divisional Playoff)	.05
59	Thurman Thomas (AFC Divisional Playoff)	.10
60	Erik Kramer (NFC Divisional Playoff)	.05
61	Darrell Green (NFC Divisional Playoff)	.05
62	Carlton Bailey (AFC Championship)	.05
63	Mark Rypien (NFC Championship)	.05
64	TD Reversed, FG Blocked	.05
65	Brad Edwards (Picks Off First of Two)	.05
66	Rypien to Byner, Rypien to Byner	.05
67	Riggs Puts Redskins Up	.05
68	Gouvela Interceptions Buries Bills	.05
69	Thurman Thomas	.20
70	Clark Catches Rypien's Second TD	.05
71	Bills Convert Late Break	.05
72	Redskins Run Out the Clock	.05
73	Jeff Bostic	.05
74	Earnest Byner	.05
75	Gary Clark	.05
76	Andre Collins	.05
77	Darrell Green	.05
78	Joe Jacoby	.05
79	Jim Lachey	.05
80	Chip Lohmiller	.05
81	Charles Mann	.05
82	Martin Mayhew	.05
83	Matt Millen	.05
84	Brian Mitchell	.05
85	Art Monk	.10
86	Gerald Riggs	.05
87	Mark Rypien	.05
88	Fred Stokes	.05
89	Bobby Wilson	.05
90	Joe Gibbs	.05
91	Howard Ballard	.05
92	Cornelius Bennett	.10
93	Kenneth Davis	.05
94	Al Edwards	.05
95	Kent Hull	.05
96	Kirby Jackson	.05
97	Mark Kelso	.05
98	James Lofton	.10
99	Keith McKeller	.05
100	Nate Odomes	.05
101	Jim Ritcher	.05
102	Leon Seals	.05
103	Steve Tasker	.05
104	Darryl Talley	.05
105	Thurman Thomas	.20
106	Will Wolford	.05
107	Jeff Wright	.05
108	Marv Levy	.05
109	Darion Conner	.05
110	Bill Fralic	.05
111	Moe Gardner	.05
112	Michael Haynes	.05
113	Chris Miller	.05
114	Eric Pegram	.05
115	Bruce Pickens	.05
116	Andre Rison	.20
117	Jerry Glanville	.05
118	Neal Anderson	.05
119	Trace Armstrong	.05
120	Wendell Davis	.05
121	Richard Dent	.10
122	Jay Hilgenberg	.05
123	Lemuel Stinson	.05
124	Stan Thomas	.05
125	Tom Waddle	.05
126	Mike Ditka	.10
127	James Brooks	.05
128	Eddie Brown	.05
129	David Fulcher	.05
130	Harold Green	.05
131	Tim Krumrie	.05
132	Anthony Munoz	.05
133	Craig Taylor	.05
134	Eric Thomas	.05
135	David Shula	.05
136	Mike Baab	.05
137	Brian Brennan	.05
138	Michael Jackson	.10
139	James Jones	.05
140	Ed King	.05
141	Clay Matthews	.05
142	Eric Metcalf	.05
143	Joe Morris	.05
144	Bill Belichick	.05
145	Steve Beuerlein	.05
146	Larry Brown	.05
147	Ray Horton	.05
148	Ken Norton	.05
150	Emmitt Smith	1.50
151	Mark Stepnoski	.05
152	Alexander Wright	.05
153	Jimmy Johnson	.10
154	Mike Croel	.05
155	John Elway	.75
156	Gaston Green	.05
157	Wymon Henderson	.05
158	Karl Mecklenburg	.05
159	Warren Powers	.05
160	Steve Sewell	.05
161	Doug Widell	.05
162	Dan Reeves	.05
163	Eric Andolsek	.05
164	Jerry Ball	.05
165	Bennie Blades	.05
166	Ray Crockett	.05
167	Willie Green	.05
168	Erik Kramer	.05
169	Barry Sanders	2.00
170	Chris Spielman	.05
171	Wayne Fontes	.05
172	Vinnie Clark	.05
173	Tony Mandarich	.05
174	Brian Noble	.05
175	Bryce Paup	.05
176	Sterling Sharpe	.20
177	Darrell Thompson	.05
178	Esera Tuaolo	.05
179	Ed West	.05
180	Mike Holmgren	.20
181	Ray Childress	.05
182	Cris Dishman	.05
183	Curtis Duncan	.05
184	William Fuller	.05
185	Lamar Lathon	.05
186	Warren Moon	.20
187	*Bo Orlando*	.10
188	Lorenzo White	.05
189	Jack Pardee	.05
190	Chip Banks	.05
191	Dean Biasucci	.05
192	Bill Brooks	.05
193	Ray Donaldson	.05
194	Jeff Herrod	.05
195	Mike Prior	.05
196	Mark Vander Poel	.05
197	Clarence Verdin	.05
198	Ted Marchibroda	.05
199	John Alt	.05
200	Deron Cherry	.05
201	Steve DeBerg	.05
202	Nick Lowery	.05
203	Neil Smith	.05
204	Derrick Thomas	.20
205	Joe Valerio	.05
206	Barry Word	.05
207	Marty Schottenheimer	.05
208	Marcus Allen	.20
209	Nick Bell	.05
210	Tim Brown	.20
211	Howie Long	.10
212	Ronnie Lott	.10
213	Todd Marinovich	.05
214	Greg Townsend	.05
215	Steve Wright	.05
216	Art Shell	.05
217	Flipper Anderson	.05
218	Robert Delpino	.05
219	Henry Ellard	.05
220	Kevin Greene	.05
221	Todd Lyght	.05
222	Tom Newberry	.05
223	Roman Phifer	.05
224	Michael Stewart	.05
225	Chuck Knox	.05
226	Aaron Craver	.05
227	Jeff Cross	.05
228	Mark Duper	.05
229	Ferrell Edmunds	.05
230	Jim C. Jensen	.05
231	Louis Oliver	.05
232	Reggie Roby	.05
233	Sammie Smith	.05
234	Don Shula	.10
235	Joey Browner	.05

236	Anthony Carter	.05
237	Chris Doleman	.05
238	Steve Jordan	.05
239	Kirk Lowdermilk	.05
240	Henry Thomas	.05
241	Herschel Walker	.10
242	Felix Wright	.05
243	Dennis Green	.10
244	Ray Agnew	.05
245	Marv Cook	.05
246	Irving Fryar	.10
247	Pat Harlow	.05
248	Hugh Millen	.05
249	Leonard Russell	.10
250	Andre Tippett	.05
251	Jon Vaughn	.05
252	Dick MacPherson	.05
253	Morten Andersen	.10
254	Bobby Hebert	.05
255	Joel Hilgenberg	.05
256	Vaughan Johnson	.05
257	Sam Mills	.05
258	Pat Swilling	.05
259	Floyd Turner	.05
260	Steve Walsh	.05
261	Jim Mora	.05
262	Stephen Baker	.05
263	Mark Collins	.05
264	Rodney Hampton	.10
265	Jeff Hostetler	.10
266	Erik Howard	.05
267	Sean Landeta	.05
268	Gary Reasons	.05
269	Everson Walls	.05
270	Ray Handley	.05
271	*Louis Aguiar*	.10
272	Brad Baxter	.05
273	Chris Burkett	.05
274	Irv Eatman	.05
275	Jeff Lageman	.05
276	Freeman McNeil	.05
277	Rob Moore	.20
278	Lonnie Young	.05
279	Bruce Coslet	.05
280	Jerome Brown	.05
281	Keith Byars	.05
282	Bruce Collie	.05
283	Keith Jackson	.10
284	James Joseph	.05
285	Seth Joyner	.05
286	Andre Waters	.05
287	Reggie White	.20
288	Rich Kotite	.05
289	Rich Camarillo	.05
290	Garth Jax	.05
291	Ernie Jones	.05
292	Tim McDonald	.05
293	Rod Saddler	.05
294	Anthony Thompson	.05
295	Tim Tupa	.05
296	Ron Wolfley	.05
297	Joe Bugel	.05
298	Gary Anderson	.05
299	Jeff Graham	.10
300	Eric Green	.05
301	Bryan Hinkle	.05
302	Tunch Ilkin	.05
303	Louis Lipps	.05
304	Neil O'Donnell	.10
305	Rod Woodson	.05
306	Bill Cowher	.05
307	Eric Bieniemy	.05
308	Marion Butts	.05
309	John Friesz	.10
310	Courtney Hall	.05
311	Ronnie Harmon	.05
312	Henry Rolling	.05
313	Billy Ray Smith	.05
314	George Thornton	.05
315	Bobby Ross	.05
316	Todd Bowles	.05
317	Michael Carter	.05
318	Don Griffin	.05
319	Charles Haley	.10
320	Brent Jones	.05
321	John Taylor	.10
322	Ted Washington	.05
323	Steve Young	.50
324	George Seifert	.10
325	Brian Blades	.05
326	Jacob Green	.05
327	Patrick Hunter	.05
328	Tommy Kane	.05
329	Cortez Kennedy	.10
330	Dave Krieg	.05
331	Rufus Porter	.05
332	John L. Williams	.05
333	Tom Flores	.05
334	Gary Anderson	.05
335	Mark Carrier	.05
336	Reuben Davis	.05
337	Lawrence Dawsey	.05
338	Keith McCants	.05
339	Vinny Testaverde	.20
340	Broderick Thomas	.05
341	Robert Wilson	.05
342	Sam Wyche	.05
343	1991 Teacher of the Year	.05
344	Owners Reject Instant Replay	.05
345	NFL Experience Unveiled	.05
346	Noll Retires Tosses Coin	.05
347	Isaac Curtis, Tim McGee	.05
348	Drew Pearson, Michael Irvin	.10
349	Billy Sims, Barry Sanders	.50
350	Kenny Stabler, Todd Marinovich	.05
351	Craig James, Leonard Russell	.05
352	Bob Golic (Graffiti It's a Sign of Ignorance)	.05
353	Pat Harlow (Vote, Let Your Choice Be Heard)	.05
354	Esera Tuaolo (Stand Tall, Be Proud of Your Heritage)	.05
355	Mark Schlereth (Save the Environment Be a Team Player)	.05
356	Trace Armstrong (Drug Abuse Stay in Control)	.05
357	Eric Bieniemy (Save a Life Buckle Up)	.05
358	Bill Romanowski (Education Stay in School)	.05
359	Irv Eatman (Exercise Be Active)	.05
360	Jonathan Hayes (Diabetes Be Your Best)	.05
361	Atlanta Falcons	.05
362	Chicago Bears	.05
363	Dallas Cowboys	.05
364	Detroit Lions	.05
365	Green Bay Packers	.05
366	Los Angeles Rams	.05
367	Minnesota Vikings	.05
368	New Orleans Saints	.05
369	New York Giants	.05
370	Philadelphia Eagles	.05
371	Phoenix Cardinals	.05
372	San Francisco 49ers	.05
373	Tampa Bay Buccaneers	.05
374	Washington Redskins	.05
375	Steve Atwater	.05
376	Cornelius Bennett	.05
377	Tim Brown	.10
378	Marion Butts	.05
379	Ray Childress	.05
380	Mark Clayton	.05
381	Marv Cook	.05
382	Cris Dishman	.05
383	William Fuller	.05
384	Gaston Green	.05
385	Jeff Jaeger	.05
386	Haywood Jeffires	.05
387	James Lofton	.05
388	Ronnie Lott	.05
389	Karl Mecklenburg	.05
390	Warren Moon	.10
391	Anthony Munoz	.05
392	Dennis Smith	.05
393	Neil Smith	.05
394	Darryl Talley	.05
395	Derrick Thomas	.10
396	Thurman Thomas	.20
397	Greg Townsend	.05
398	Richmond Webb	.05
399	Rod Woodson	.05
400	Dan Reeves	.05
401	Troy Aikman (PB)	.30
402	PB (Eric Allen)	.05
403	PB (Bennie Blades)	.05
404	PB (Lomas Brown)	.05
405	PB (Mark Carrier)	.05
406	PB (Gary Clark)	.05
407	PB (Mel Gray)	.05
408	PB (Darrell Green)	.05
409	PB (Michael Irvin)	.10
410	PB (Vaughan Johnson)	.05
411	PB (Seth Joyner)	.05
412	PB (Jim Lachey)	.05
413	PB (Chip Lohmiller)	.05
414	PB (Charles Mann)	.05
415	PB (Chris Miller)	.05
416	PB (Sam Mills)	.05
417	PB (Bart Oates)	.05
418	PB (Jerry Rice)	.30
419	PB (Andre Rison)	.10
420	PB (Mark Rypien)	.05
421	PB (Barry Sanders)	.75
422	PB (Deion Sanders)	.10
423	PB (Mark Schlereth)	.05
424	PB (Mike Singletary)	.05
425	(Emmitt Smith PB)	.50
426	PB (Pat Swilling)	.05
427	PB (Reggie White)	.10
428	Rick Bryan	.05
429	Tim Green	.05
430	Drew Hill	.05
431	Norm Johnson	.05
432	Keith Jones	.05
433	Mike Pritchard	.10
434	Deion Sanders	.50
435	*Tony Smith*	.10
436	Jessie Tuggle	.05
437	Steve Christie	.05
438	Shane Conlan	.05
439	*Matt Darby*	.10
440	*John Fina*	.05
441	Henry Jones	.05
442	Jim Kelly	.20
443	Pete Metzelaars	.05
444	Andre Reed	.10
445	Bruce Smith	.05
446	*Troy Auzenne*	.10
447	Mark Carrier	.05
448	*Will Furrer*	.10
449	Jim Harbaugh	.10
450	Brad Muster	.05
451	Darren Lewis	.05
452	Mike Singletary	.10
453	*Alonzo Spellman*	.20
454	Chris Zorich	.05
455	Jim Breech	.05
456	Boomer Esiason	.10
457	James Francis	.05
458	Derrick Fenner	.05
459	*David Klingler*	.20
460	Tim McGee	.05
461	*Carl Pickens*	1.00
462	Alfred Williams	.05
463	*Darryl Williams*	.10
464	Mark Bavaro	.05
465	Jay Hilgenberg	.05
466	Leroy Hoard	.10
467	Bernie Kosar	.10
468	Michael Dean Perry	.10
469	*Todd Philcox*	.10
470	*Patrick Rowe*	.10
471	*Tommy Vardell*	.20
472	Everson Walls	.05
473	Troy Aikman	.75
474	*Kenneth Gant*	.10
475	Charles Haley	.05
476	Michael Irvin	.20
477	*Robert Jones*	.10
478	Russell Maryland	.10
479	Jay Novacek	.10
480	*Kevin Smith*	.10
481	Tony Tolbert	.05
482	Steve Atwater	.05
483	*Shane Dronett*	.10
484	Simon Fletcher	.05
485	Greg Lewis	.05
486	*Tommy Maddox*	.20
487	Shannon Sharpe	.20
488	Dennis Smith	.05
489	Sammie Smith	.05
490	Kenny Walker	.05
491	Lomas Brown	.05
492	Mike Farr	.05
493	Mel Gray	.05
494	*Jason Hanson*	.10
495	Herman Moore	.75
496	Rodney Peete	.05
497	*Robert Porcher*	.10
498	Kelvin Pritchett	.05
499	Andre Ware	.05
500	*Sanjay Beach*	.10
501	*Edgar Bennett*	.20
502	Lewis Billups	.05
503	Terrell Buckley	.20
504	Ty Detmer	.10
505	Brett Favre	2.50
506	Johnny Holland	.05
507	*Dexter McNabb*	.10
508	Vince Workman	.05
509	Cody Carlson	.05
510	Ernest Givins	.05
511	Jerry Gray	.05
512	Haywood Jeffires	.10
513	Bruce Matthews	.05
514	Bubba McDowell	.05
515	*Bucky Richardson*	.10
516	Webster Slaughter	.05
517	Al Smith	.05
518	Mel Agee	.10
519	*Ashley Ambrose*	.10
520	Kevin Call	.05
521	Ken Clark	.05
522	*Quentin Coryatt*	.20
523	*Steve Emtman*	.10
524	Jeff George	.20
525	Jessie Hester	.05
526	Anthony Johnson	.05
527	Tim Barnett	.05
528	Martin Bayless	.05
529	J.J. Birden	.05
530	*Dale Carter*	.20
531	Dave Krieg	.05
532	Albert Lewis	.05
533	Nick Lowery	.05
534	Christian Okoye	.05
535	Harvey Williams	.10
536	Aundray Bruce	.05
537	Eric Dickerson	.10
538	Willie Gault	.05
539	Ethan Horton	.05
540	Jeff Jaeger	.05
541	Napoleon McCallum	.05
542	*Chester McGlockton*	.10
543	Steve Smith	.05
544	Steve Wisniewski	.05
545	Marc Boutte	.05
546	Pat Carter	.05
547	Jim Everett	.05
548	Cleveland Gary	.05
549	*Sean Gilbert*	.20
550	Steve Israel	.05
551	*Todd Kinchen*	.20
552	Jackie Slater	.05
553	Tony Zendejas	.05
554	Robert Clark	.05
555	Mark Clayton	.05
556	*Marco Coleman*	.10
557	Bryan Cox	.05
558	(Keith Jackson) (Card says drafted in '88, but acquired as free agent in '92)	.05
559	Dan Marino	1.25
560	John Offerdahl	.05
561	*Troy Vincent*	.20
562	Richmond Webb	.05
563	Terry Allen	.20
564	Cris Carter	.50
565	Roger Craig	.10
566	Rich Gannon	.10
567	Hassan Jones	.05
568	Randall McDaniel	.05
569	Al Noga	.05
570	Todd Scott	.05
571	*Van Waiters*	.10
572	Bruce Armstrong	.05
573	*Gene Chilton*	.10
574	*Eugene Chung*	.10
575	*Todd Collins*	.10
576	Hart Lee Dykes	.05
577	*David Howard*	.10
578	Eugene Lockhart	.05
579	Greg McMurtry	.05
580	*Rodney Smith*	.05
581	Gene Atkins	.05
582	Vince Buck	.05
583	Wesley Carroll	.05
584	Jim Dombrowski	.05
585	*Vaughn Dunbar*	.10
586	Craig Heyward	.05
587	Dalton Hilliard	.05
588	Wayne Martin	.05
589	Renaldo Turnbull	.05
590	Carl Banks	.05
591	*Derek Brown*	.10
592	Jarrod Bunch	.05
593	Mark Ingram	.05
594	Ed McCaffrey	.30
595	Phil Simms	.10
596	*Phillippi Sparks*	.10
597	Lawrence Taylor	.20
598	Lewis Tillman	.05
599	Kyle Clifton	.05
600	Mo Lewis	.05
601	Terance Mathis	.05
602	Scott Mersereau	.05
603	*Johnny Mitchell*	.20
604	Browning Nagle	.10
605	Ken O'Brien	.05
606	Al Toon	.05
607	Marvin Washington	.05
608	Eric Allen	.05
609	Fred Barnett	.05
610	John Booty	.05
611	Randall Cunningham	.20
612	Rich Miano	.05
613	Clyde Simmons	.05
614	Siran Stacy	.05
615	Herschel Walker	.10
616	Calvin Williams	.05
617	Chris Chandler	.20
618	Randal Hill	.10
619	Johnny Johnson	.10
620	Lorenzo Lynch	.05
621	Robert Massey	.05
622	Ricky Proehl	.05
623	Timm Rosenbach	.05
624	*Tony Sacca*	.10
625	(Aeneas Williams) (name misspelled Aaneas)	.10
626	Bubby Brister	.05
627	Barry Foster	.05
628	Merril Hoge	.05
629	David Johnson	.05
630	David Little	.05
631	Greg Lloyd	.05
632	Ernie Mills	.05
633	*Leon Searcy*	.10
634	Dwight Stone	.05
635	*Sam Anno*	.10
636	Burt Grossman	.05
637	Stan Humphries	.10
638	Nate Lewis	.05
639	Anthony Miller	.05
640	Chris Mims	.05
641	*Marquez Pope*	.20
642	Stanley Richard	.05
643	Junior Seau	.20
644	*Brian Bollinger*	.05
645	*Steve Bono*	.30
646	Dexter Carter	.10
647	*Dana Hall*	.05
648	Amp Lee	.10
649	Joe Montana	1.25
650	Tom Rathman	.05
651	Jerry Rice	.75
652	Ricky Watters	.20
653	Robert Blackmon	.05
654	John Kasay	.05
655	*Ronnie Lee*	.10
656	Dan McGwire	.10
657	*Ray Roberts*	.10
658	Kelly Stouffer	.05
659	Chris Warren	.20
660	Tony Woods	.05
661	David Wyman	.05
662	*Reggie Cobb*	.10
663A	(Steve DeBerg) (incorrect career yardage 1,455; found in foil packs)	.05
663B	(Steve DeBerg) (correct career yardage 31,455; found in jumbo packs)	.05
664	*Santana Dotson*	.20
665	Craig Erickson	.10
666	Paul Gruber	.05
667	Ron Hall	.05
668	*Courtney Hawkins*	.10
669	Charles McRae	.05
670	Ricky Reynolds	.05
671	Monte Coleman	.05
672	Brad Edwards	.05
673	(James Geathers) (card says played in New Orleans '89; should say Washington)	.05
674	Kelly Goodburn	.05
675	Kurt Gouveia	.05
676	*Chris Hakel*	.10
677	Wilber Marshall	.05
678	Ricky Sanders	.05
679	Mark Schlereth	.05
680	Spirit of the Game (Rich Stadium)	.05
681	Spirit of the Game (Boomer Esiason) (with tiger cub)	.05
682	Spirit of the Game (The Dog Pound)	.05
683	Spirit of the Game (Bronco Statue)	.05
684	Spirit of the Game ("Luv Ya Blue")	.05
685	Spirit of the Game (Hoosier Dome)	.05
686	Spirit of the Game (Mack Lee Hill, Tracy Simien) (Mack Lee Hill Award)	.05
687	Spirit of the Game (The Team of the Decades)	.05
688	Spirit of the Game (Dolphins' helmet)	.05
689	Spirit of the Game (Francis J. Kilroy) (VP)	.05
690	Spirit of the Game (Team mascot)	.05
691	Spirit of the Game (Steelers' helmet)	.05
692	Spirit of the Game (Charger in parachute)	.05
693	Spirit of the Game (Kingdome)	.05
694	Play Smart (Stephen Baker)	.05
695	Hank Williams Jr.	.20
696	NEW (Brian Baldinger, Gary Baldinger, Rich Baldinger) (3 Brothers in NFL)	.05
697	NEW (Japan Bowl August 2, 1992)	.05
698	NEW (Georgia Dome)	.05
699	NEW (Theme Art Super Bowl XXVII)	.05
700	Super Bowl XXVI MVP (Mark Rypien)	.10
AU150	Emmitt Smith AUTO (Certified Autograph)	200.00
AU168	Erik Kramer AUTO (Certified Autograph)	40.00
NNO	Power Preview (Emmitt Smith)	1.00
NNO	Santa Claus (Spirit of the Game)	.50

1992 Pro Set Emmitt Smith Holograms

Dallas Cowboys' star running back Emmitt Smith is featured on these four insert holograms offered randomly in 1992 Pro Set foil packs. Each card front represents a different part of Smith's career. The red, white and blue backs have player profile information, 1991 and projected stats and a career summary. Cards are numbered ES1-ES4, with those numbered ES1 being the easiest to find, while the ES4 cards were the most difficult to find.

		MT
Complete Set (4):		60.00
Common Smith:		7.00
1	Stats 1990-1999	7.00
2	Drafted by Cowboys	10.00
3	Rookie of the Year	20.00
4	NFL Rushing Leader	30.00

1992 Pro Set Gold MVPs

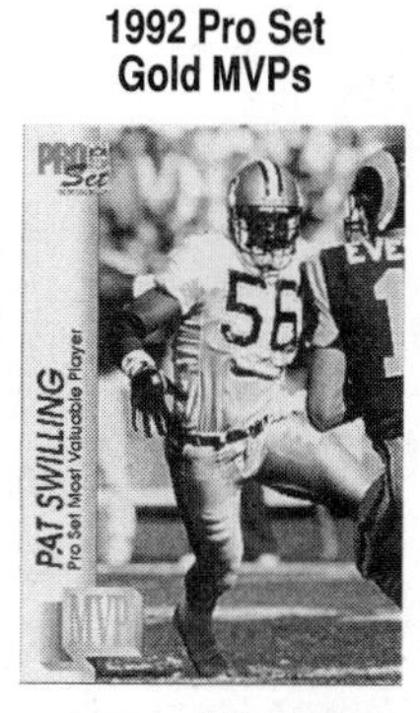

A most valuable player from each of the 28 NFL teams has been selected for this insert set. Two coaches were also selected. Cards 1-15, Series I jumbo pack inserts, have full-bleed action photos, plus a diamond-shaped "92 MVP" emblem on the front. The player's name is stamped in gold foil near the Pro Set/NFL logo. The horizontal card backs have statistics, a career summary and close-up shot. Series II pack inserts, cards 16-30, have a two-toned stripe on the left, plus a gray box in the lower left corner which has "MVP" stamped in gold foil. The backs are screened and have career information and a close-up shot of the player. All cards are numbered with an "MVP" prefix; AFC players are cards 1-14; NFC cards are 16-29. Coaches' cards are Don Shula (15) and Jimmy Johnson (30).

		MT
Complete Set (30):		15.00
Common Player:		.10
Minor Stars:		.20
1	Thurman Thomas	.40
2	Anthony Munoz	.10
3	Clay Matthews	.10
4	John Elway	2.00
5	Warren Moon	.40
6	Bill Brooks	.10
7	Derrick Thomas	.20
8	Todd Marinovich	.10
9	Mark Higgs	.10
10	Leonard Russell	.20
11	Rob Moore	.40
12	Rod Woodson	.20
13	Marion Butts	.10
14	Brian Blades	.10
15	Don Shula	.20
16	Deion Sanders	1.00
17	Neal Anderson	.10
18	Emmitt Smith	3.00
19	Barry Sanders	4.00
20	Brett Favre	5.00
21	Kevin Greene	.10
22	Terry Allen	.40
23	Pat Swilling	.10
24	Rodney Hampton	.20
25	Randall Cunningham	.50
26	Randall Hill	.10
27	Jerry Rice	1.50
28	Vinny Testaverde	.40
29	Mark Rypien	.20
30	Jimmy Johnson	.20

1992 Pro Set Ground Force

These cards are identical to their counterparts in the regular 1992 Pro Set issue, except they are stamped with a "Ground Force" logo in gold foil on the front. They share the same number as their counterparts in the regular issue's Ground Force subset. The gold-foiled inserts were included in foil packs of numbered hobby cases only.

		MT
Complete Set (6):		50.00
Common Player:		3.00
86	Gerald Riggs	3.00
105	Thurman Thomas	8.00
118	Neal Anderson	3.00
150	Emmitt Smith	35.00
206	Barry Word	3.00
249	Leonard Russell	3.00

1992 Pro Set HOF Inductees

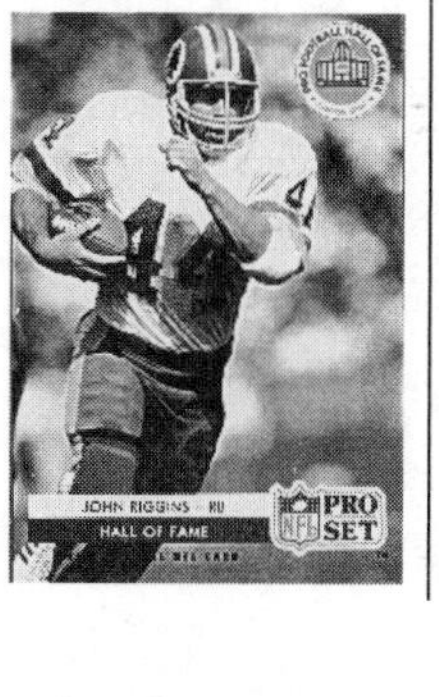

These cards, numbered with an "SC" prefix, are a "Special Collectibles" subset that features the 1992 Pro Football Hall of Fame Inductees. The cards, random inserts in 1992 Pro Set packs, have the Hall of Fame's logo on the front, along with the Pro Set logo, and show an action photo of the player. The card back has a career summary and a portrait shot.

		MT
Complete Set (4):		1.50
Common Player:		.40
1	Lem Barney	.40
2	Al Davis	.40
3	John Mackey	.40
4	John Riggins	.50

1992 Pro Set HOF 2000

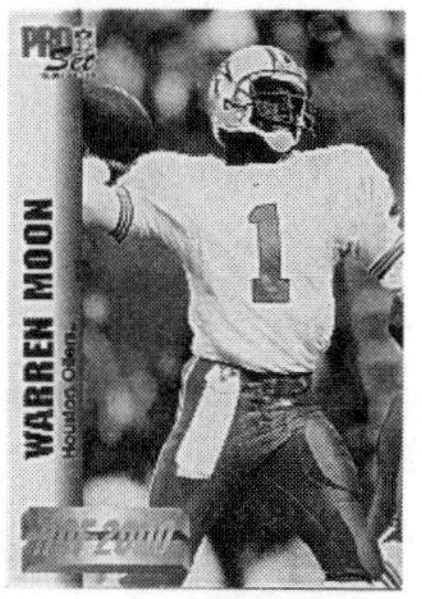

Randomly inserted in Series II foil packs, the 10-card set honors players which Pro Set said would be inducted into the Hall of Fame shortly after the year 2000. The card fronts are identical to the base cards, with the player's name in a white stripe along the left and his team name listed beneath it. The HOF-2000 logo appears on a 3-D band in the lower left. Card backs have HOF-2000 listed at the top, with the player's name, position and team printed below it. Inside a 3-D text box is a write-up on the player's career. The cards are numbered inside a small rectangle in the lower right.

		MT
Complete Set (10):		20.00
Common Player:		1.50
Minor Stars:		3.00
1	Marcus Allen	3.00
2	Richard Dent	1.50
3	Eric Dickerson	3.00
4	Ronnie Lott	1.50
5	Art Monk	1.50
6	Joe Montana	8.00
7	Warren Moon	3.00
8	Anthony Munoz	1.50
9	Mike Singletary	3.00
10	Lawrence Taylor	3.00

1992 Pro Set Club

This nine-card set was used as a football practice educational tool. The full-bleed card fronts include photos which deal with various football skills. The bottom of each card includes the card's caption inside a purple stripe. The Pro Set Club logo is located on the left side of the stripe. The card backs include details on the skill highlighted on the front. The text is printed inside a yellow box. Card numbers are printed inside an oval in the lower right.

		MT
Complete Set (9):		5.00
Common Player:		.75
1	Quarterback Throwing Pass	.75
2	Coach Reviewing Play Strategy	.75
3	Team Stretching	.75
4	Offensive Play	.75
5	Kickoff	.75
6	Player's Stance	.75
7	Football Is a Spectator Sport	.75
8	Defensive Practice	.75
9	Play in Motion	.75

1992 Pro Set Emmitt Smith Promo Sheet

Measuring 7" x 13" and numbered to 2,000, this five-card sheet was used to promote the signing of Emmitt Smith as the Pro Set spokesman. Showcased on the sheet are his 1990, 1991, 1991 Platinum, 1991 Platinum Game Breaker and 1992 cards with a checklist back.

		MT
Complete Set (1):		10.00
Common Sheet:		10.00
NNO	Emmitt Smith Sheet (five cards featured numberd of 2000)	10.00

1992 Pro Set Power

This 330-card UV-coated set features action photos on the fronts with a semi-ghosted background. The player's name is in red letters at the

bottom. The backs are in a horizontal format and feature the team and player name printed in the team's colors. A player profile is also included. A 10-card insert set, "Power Combos," was also made and features pairs of teammates. The cards were random inserts in foil packs.

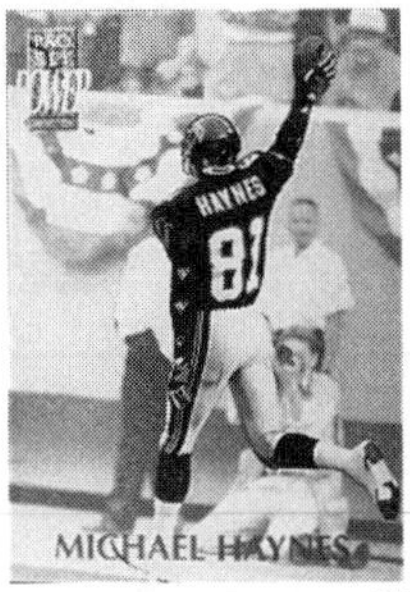

		MT
Complete Set (330):		15.00
Common Player:		.05
Wax Box:		15.00
1	Warren Moon	.30
2	Mike Horan	.05
3	Bobby Hebert	.05
4	Jim Harbaugh	.05
5	Sean Landeta	.05
6	Bubby Brister	.05
7	John Elway	.50
8	Troy Aikman	1.00
9	Rodney Peete	.05
10	Dan McGwire	.05
11	Mark Rypien	.10
12	Randall Cunningham	.20
13	Dan Marino	1.50
14	Vinny Testaverde	.05
15	Jeff Hostetler	.35
16	Joe Montana	1.00
17	Dave Krieg	.05
18	Jeff Jaeger	.05
19	Bernie Kosar	.05
20	Barry Sanders	1.00
21	Deion Sanders	.40
22	Emmitt Smith	2.00
23	Mel Gray	.05
24	Stanley Richard	.05
25	Brad Muster	.05
26	Rod Woodson	.10
27	Rodney Hampton	.50
28	Darrell Green	.05
29	Barry Foster	.50
30	Dave Meggett	.05
31	Lonnie Young	.05
32	Marcus Allen	.05
33	Merril Hoge	.05
34	Thurman Thomas	.25
35	Neal Anderson	.10
36	Bennie Blades	.05
37	Pat Terrell	.05
38	Nick Bell	.20
39	Johnny Johnson	.20
40	Bill Bates	.05
41	Keith Byars	.05
42	Ronnie Lott	.05
43	Elvis Patterson	.05
44	Lorenzo White	.05
45	Tony Stargell	.05
46	Tim McDonald	.05
47	Kirby Jackson	.05
48	Lionel Washington	.05
49	Dennis Smith	.05
50	Mike Singletary	.05
51	Mike Croel	.05
52	Pepper Johnson	.05
53	Vaughn Johnson	.05
54	Chris Spielman	.05
55	Junior Seau	.10
56	Lawrence Taylor	.15
57	Clay Matthews	.05
58	Derrick Thomas	.20
59	Seth Joyner	.05
60	Stan Thomas	.05
61	Nate Newton	.05
62	Matt Brock	.05
63	*Gene Chilton*	.15
64	Randall McDaniel	.05
65	Max Montoya	.05
66	Joe Jacoby	.05
67	Russell Maryland	.25
68	Ed King	.05
69	*Mark Schlereth*	.15
70	Charles McRae	.05
71	Charles Mann	.05
72	William Perry	.05
73	Simon Fletcher	.05
74	Paul Gruber	.05
75	Howie Long	.05
76	Steve McMichael	.05
77	Karl Mecklenberg	.05
78	Anthony Munoz	.05
79	Ray Childress	.05
80	Jerry Rice	1.00
81	Art Monk	.10
82	John Taylor	.10
83	Andre Reed	.25
84	Haywood Jeffires	.25
85	Mark Duper	.05
86	Fred Barnett	.25
87	Tom Waddle	.15
88	Michael Irvin	.25
89	Brian Blades	.05
90	Neil Smith	.05
91	Kevin Greene	.05
92	Reggie White	.30
93	Jerry Ball	.05
94	Charles Haley	.05
95	Richard Dent	.05
96	Clyde Simmons	.05
97	Cornelius Bennett	.05
98	Eric Swann	.05
99	Doug Smith	.05
100	Jim Kelly	.40
101	Michael Jackson	.30
102	Steve Christie	.05
103	Timm Rosenbach	.05
104	Brett Favre	1.25
105	Jeff Feagles	.05
106	Kevin Butler	.10
107	Boomer Esiason	.25
108	Steve Young	1.00
109	Norm Jackson	.05
110	Jay Schroeder	.05
111	Jeff George	.40
112	Chris Miller	.05
113	*Steve Bono*	1.00
114	Neil O'Donnell	.50
115	*David Klingler*	.35
116	Rich Gannon	.10
117	Chris Chandler	.05
118	Stan Gelbaugh	.05
119	Scott Mitchell	.50
120	Mark Carrier	.05
121	Terry Allen	.55
122	Tim McKyer	.05
123	Barry Wood	.20
124	Freeman McNeil	.05
125	Louis Oliver	.05
126	Jarvis Williams	.05
127	Steve Atwater	.05
128	Cris Dishman	.05
129	Eric Dickerson	.05
130	Brad Baxter	.05
131	Frank Minnifield	.05
132	Ricky Watters	.50
133	David Fulcher	.05
134	Herschel Walker	.05
135	Christian Okoye	.05
136	Jerome Henderson	.05
137	Nate Odomes	.05
138	Todd Scott	.05
139	Robert Delpino	.05
140	Gary Anderson	.05
141	Todd Lyght	.05
142	Chris Warren	.30
143	*Mike Brim*	.15
144	Tom Rathman	.05
145	*Dexter McNabb*	.10
146	Vince Workman	.05
147	Anthony Jackson	.05
148	Brian Washington	.05
149	David Tate	.05
150	Johnny Holland	.05
151	Monte Coleman	.05
152	Keith McCants	.05
153	*Eugene Seale*	.10
154	Al Smith	.05
155	Andre Collins	.05
156	Pat Swilling	.05
157	Rickey Jackson	.05
158	Wilbur Marshall	.05
159	Kyle Clifton	.05
160	Fred Stokes	.05
161	Lance Smith	.05
162	Guy McIntyre	.05
163	Bill Maas	.05
164	Gerald Perry	.05
165	Bart Oates	.05
166	Tony Jones	.05
167	Moe Gardner	.05
168	Joe Wolf	.05
169	Tim Krumrie	.05
170	Leonard Marshall	.05
171	Kevin Call	.05
172	Keith Kartz	.05
173	Ron Heller	.05
174	Steve Wallace	.05
175	Tony Casillas	.05
176	Tim Irwin	.05
177	Pat Harlow	.05
178	Bruce Smith	.05
179	Jim Lachey	.05
180	Andre Rison	.50
181	Michael Haynes	.60
182	Rod Bernstine	.05
183	Mark Clayton	.05
184	Jay Novacek	.25
185	Rob Moore	.05
186	Willie Green	.20
187	Ricky Proehl	.05
188	Al Toon	.05
189	Webster Slaughter	.05
190	Tony Bennett	.05
191	Jeff Cross	.05
192	Michael Dean Perry	.05
193	Greg Townsend	.05
194	Alfred Williams	.05
195	William Fuller	.05
196	Cortez Kennedy	.05
197	Henry Thomas	.05
198	Esera Tuaolo	.05
199	Tim Green	.05
200	Keith Jackson	.15
201	Don Majkowski	.05
202	Steve Beuerlein	.40
203	Hugh Millen	.05
204	Browning Nagel	.15
205	Chip Lohmiller	.05
206	Phil Simms	.15
207	Jim Everett	.05
208	Erik Kramer	.05
209	Todd Marinovich	.05
210	Henry Jones	.15
211	Dwight Stone	.05
212	Andre Waters	.05
213	Darryl Henley	.05
214	Mark Higgs	.15
215	Dalton Hilliard	.05
216	Earnest Byner	.05
217	Eric Metcalf	.05
218	Gill Byrd	.05
219	*Robert Williams*	.10
220	Kenneth Davis	.05
221	Larry Brown	.05
222	Mark Collins	.05
223	Vinnie Clark	.05
224	Patrick Hunter	.05
225	Gaston Green	.05
226	Everson Walls	.05
227	Harold Green	.05
228	Albert Lewis	.05
229	Don Griffin	.05
230	Lorenzo Lynch	.05
231	Brian Mitchell	.05
232	Thomas Everett	.05
233	Leonard Russell	.50
234	Eric Bieniemy	.05
235	John L. Williams	.05
236	Leroy Hoard	.05
237	Darren Lewis	.05
238	Reggie Cobb	.15
239	Steve Broussard	.05
240	Marion Butts	.05
241	Mike Pritchard	.25
242	Dexter Carter	.05
243	Aeneas Williams	.05
244	Bruce Pickens	.05
245	Harvey Williams	.15
246	Bobby Humphrey	.05
247	Duane Bickett	.05
248	James Francis	.05
249	Broderick Thomas	.05
250	Chip Banks	.05
251	Bryan Cox	.05
252	Sam Mills	.05
253	Ken Norton	.05
254	Jeff Harrod	.05
255	John Roper	.05
256	Darryl Talley	.05
257	Andre Tippett	.05
258	Jeff Lageman	.05
259	Chris Doleman	.05
260	Shane Conlan	.05
261	Jessie Tuggle	.05
262	Eric Hill	.05
263	Bruce Armstrong	.05
264	Bill Fralic	.05
265	Alvin Harper	.60
266	Bill Brooks	.05
267	Henry Ellard	.05
268	Cris Carter	.05
269	Irving Fryar	.05
270	Lawrence Dawsey	.05
271	James Lofton	.05
272	Ernest Givins	.05
273	Terance Mathis	.05
274	Randal Hill	.15
275	Eddie Brown	.05
276	Tim Brown	.50
277	Anthony Carter	.05
278	Wendell Davis	.05
279	Mark Ingram	.05
280	Anthony Miller	.05
281	Clarence Verdin	.05
282	Willie Anderson	.05
283	Ricky Sanders	.05
284	Steve Jordan	.05
285	Gary Clark	.05
286	Sterling Sharpe	.20
287	Herman Moore	.65
288	Stephen Baker	.05
289	Marv Cook	.05
290	Ernie Jones	.05
291	Eric Green	.05
292	Mervyn Fernandez	.05
293	Greg McMurty	.05
294	Quinn Early	.05
295	Tim Harris	.05
296	*Will Furrer*	.25
297	*Jason Hanson*	.15
298	*Chris Hakel*	.15
299	Ty Detmer	.20
300	David Klingler	.30
301	*Amp Lee*	.30
302	*Troy Vincent*	.30
303	*Kevin Smith*	.30
304	*Terrell Buckley*	.20
305	*Dana Hall*	.25
306	*Tony Smith*	.20
307	*Steve Israel*	.25
308	*Vaughn Dunbar*	.20
309	*Ashley Ambrose*	.10
310	*Edgar Bennett*	.50
311	*Dale Carter*	.40
312	*Rodney Culver*	.25
313	*Matt Darby*	.15
314	*Tommy Vardell*	.30
315	*Quentin Coryatt*	.40
316	*Robert Jones*	.25
317	*Joe Bowden*	.10
318	*Eugene Chung*	.10
319	*Troy Auzenne*	.10
320	*Santana Dotson*	.25
321	*Greg Skrepenak*	.10
322	*Steve Emtman*	.20
323	*Carl Pickens*	2.00
324	*Johnny Mitchell*	.75
325	*Patrick Rowe*	.25
326	*Alonzo Spellman*	.35
327	*Robert Porcher*	.30
328	*Chris Mims*	.30
329	*Marc Boutte*	.10
330	*Shane Dronett*	.35

1992 Pro Set Power Power Combos

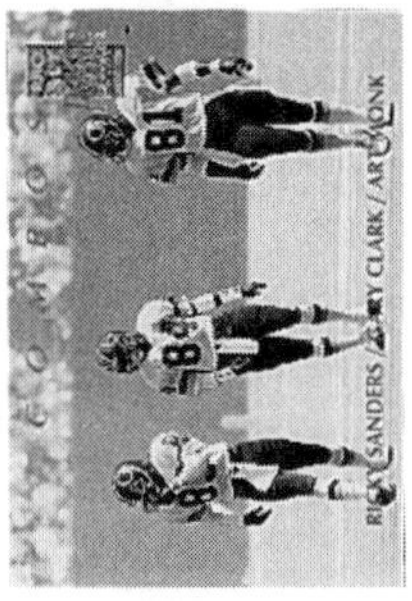

These cards feature top offensive and defensive combinations from the same team. The front of each card has a color photo of the two players together, with a ghosted background. "Combos" and "Power" are written at the top of the card in holographic letters. The cards are numbered on the back and have a purple background which contains player biographical information and a summary of their roles with their team. This information is framed by a marble-like border all the way around the card. The cards were randomly included in Pro Set Power foil packs.

		MT
Complete Set (10):		45.00
Common Player:		3.00
1	Steve Emtman, Quentin Coryatt	5.00
2	Barry Word, Christian Okoye	3.00
3	Sam Mills, Vaughan Johnson	3.00
4	Broderick Thomas, Keith McCants	3.00
5	Michael Irvin, Emmitt Smith	30.00
6	Jerry Ball, Chris Spielman	3.00
7	Rickey Sanders, Gary Clark, Art Monk	4.00
8	Dave Johnson, Rod Woodson	4.50
9	Bill Fralic, Chris Hinton	3.00
10	Irving Fryar, Marv Cook	3.00

1992-93 Pro Set Super Bowl XXVII

Inserted into Super Bowl XXVII GTE seat cushions at the Super Bowl and available by mail - with either a Bills or Cowboys mini-binder - for $22, the 38-card set was packaged in two cello packs. Reports have said 7,000 sets were issued for the mail-in offer. The cards are identical to the regular-issue cards, with the exception of the Super Bowl XXVII logo and AFC or NFC Champions listed under the player's name on the card fronts. Card backs are numbered "XXVII," except Marco Coleman who was named Pro Set Rookie of the Year. There are NFC and AFC logo cards and a Newsreel card included in the set.

		MT
Complete Set (38):		10.00
Common Player:		.20
1	AFC Logo	.20
2	Cornelius Bennett	.30
3	Steve Christie	.20
4	Shane Conlan	.20
5	Matt Darby	.20
6	Kenneth Davis	.20
7	John Fina	.20
8	Henry Jones	.30
9	Jim Kelly	.50
10	Marv Levy (CO)	.20
11	James Lofton	.30
12	Pete Metzelaars	.20
13	Nate Odomes	.20
14	Andre Reed	.40
15	Bruce Smith	.40
16	Darryl Talley	.20
17	Steve Tasker	.30
18	Thurman Thomas	.75
19	NFC Logo	.20
20	Troy Aikman	2.00
21	Steve Beuerlein	.30
22	(Tony Casillas)	.20
23	Kenneth Gant	.30
24	Charles Haley	.30
25	Alvin Harper	.30
26	Michael Irvin	.75
27	Jimmy Johnson (CO)	.30
28	Robert Jones	.20
29	Russell Maryland	.30
30	Nate Newton	.30
31	Ken Norton	.30
32	Jay Novacek	.40
33	Emmitt Smith	4.00
34	Kevin Smith	.30
35	Mark Stepnoski	.20
36	Tony Tolbert	.20
37	Newsreel Art, Super Bowl XXVII	.20
38	Marco Coleman (PS-ROY)	.30

1992-93 Pro Set Power Emmitt Smith

Produced as a premium for Pro Set Series II, the 10-card set honors Emmitt Smith's career. The set was offered through a chase card which was randomly seeded in Series II foil packs. The set was available through the mail in exchange for 10 1992 Pro Set first or second series wrappers and 10 1992 Pro Set Power wrappers, in addition to $7.50 for shipping. Those collectors who paid $20 more would receive one of 7,500 Smith-autographed cards. The card fronts have a borderless photo, with Pro Set Power printed in one of the upper corners. A blue stripe at the bottom includes Smith's name and card caption. The backs, numbered "of 10," include a "Report Card" and highlights.

		MT
Complete Set (10):		20.00
Common Player:		2.50
1	Title Card (Emmitt Smith)	2.50
2	Drafted by the (Emmitt Smith)	2.50
3	Emmitt Scores Four Touchdowns (Emmitt Smith)	2.50
4	Pro Set Offensive Rookie of the Year (Emmitt Smith)	2.50
5	Cowboys Beat Undefeated Redskins (Emmitt Smith)	2.50
6	Cowboys Beat Chicago In Playoffs (Emmitt Smith)	2.50
7	Back-to-Back Rushing Titles (Emmitt Smith)	2.50
8	Emmitt's Three Pro Bowls (Emmitt Smith)	2.50
9	Emmitt's Super Day (Emmitt Smith)	2.50
10	Running Back of the 90's (Emmitt Smith)	2.50

1993 Pro Set Promos

Measuring 8" x 13-1/2", the 10-card unperforated sheets featuring six different cards were given to dealers, card show attendees and promoters. In addition, single cards were also handed out. The sheet included a bottom row of five Emmitt Smith cards. The card fronts have a full-bleed photo, with the player's name, team logo and 1993 Pro Set logo printed inside "a ripped away" area. Card backs feature a player photo at the top, with the player's name, position and team in the "ripped away" area along the left border. The player's bio, highlights and stats are printed underneath the photo.

		MT
Complete Set (6):		8.00
Common Player:		.75
1	Jerome Bettis	2.00
2	Reggie Brooks	1.00
3	Cortez Kennedy	1.00
4	Junior Seau	1.00
5	Emmitt Smith	4.00
6	Wade Wilson	.75

1993 Pro Set

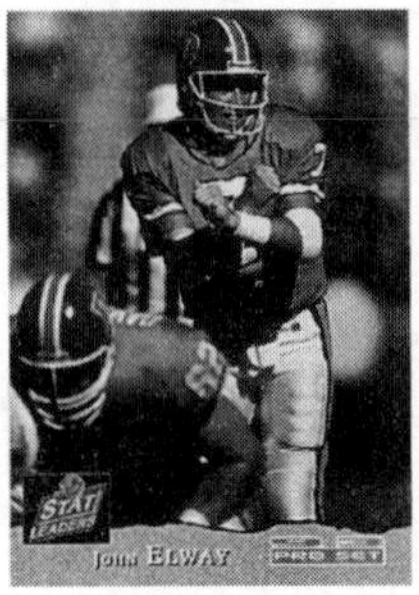

Pro Set's 1993 set consists of one series of 449 cards featuring full-bleed photos on the fronts and backs. The player's name and team logo appear at the bottom of the card over a gray slate panel that stretches along the left side of the back of the card. The backs include statistics for the past three years and lifetime totals, plus biographical information. Insert sets include prism cards for "All Rookie Forecast" (27 cards) and "Rookie Running Backs" (14); "College Connections" (10 cards, each featuring a pair of players from the same college) and "Rookie Quarterbacks" (6 cards).

		MT
Complete Set (449):		15.00
Common Player:		.05
Minor Stars:		.10
Pack (15):		.60
Wax Box (36):		15.00
1	Marco Coleman (LL)	.05
2	Steve Young (LL)	.25
3	Mike Holmgren (LL)	.10
4	John Elway (LL)	.40
5	Steve Young (LL)	.25
6	Dan Marino (LL)	.75
7	Emmitt Smith (LL)	.75
8	Sterling Sharpe (LL)	.10
9	Jay Novacek (LL)	.05
10	Sterling Sharpe (LL)	.10
11	Thurman Thomas (LL)	.10
12	Pete Stoyanovich (LL)	.05
13	Greg Montgomery (LL)	.05
14	Johnny Bailey (LL)	.05
15	Jon Vaughn (LL)	.05
16	Jones/McMillan, Jones/McMillan (LL)	.05
17	Clyde Simmons (LL)	.05
18	Cortez Kennedy (LL)	.05
19	AFC Wildcard	.05
20	AFC Wildcard	.05
21	NFC Wildcard	.05
22	NFC Wildcard	.05
23	AFC Divisional	.05
24	AFC Divisional	.75
25	NFC Divisional	.50
26	NFC Divisional (Watters)	.10
27	AFC Championship	.05
28	NFC Championship	.05
29	SB 28 Theme Art	.05
30	Troy Aikman	.75
31	Thomas Everett	.05
32	Charles Haley	.05
33	Alvin Harper	.10
34	Michael Irvin	.20
35	Robert Jones	.05
36	Russell Maryland	.05
37	Ken Norton	.05
38	Jay Novacek	.05
39	Emmitt Smith	1.75
40	*Darrin Smith*	.20
41	Mark Stepnoski	.05
42	*Kevin Williams*	.20
43	Daryl Johnston	.05
44	*Derrick Lassic*	.10
45	Don Beebe	.05
46	Cornelius Bennett	.05
47	Bill Brooks	.05
48	Kenneth Davis	.05
49	Jim Kelly	.20
50	Andre Reed	.10
51	Bruce Smith	.05
52	*Thomas Smith*	.10
53	Darryl Talley	.05
54	Thurman Thomas	.10
55	*Reggie Copeland*	.20
56	Scott Christie	.05
57	Pete Metzelaars	.05
58	Frank Reich	.05
59	Henry Jones	.05
60	Vinny Clark	.05
61	Eric Dickerson	.05
62	Jumpy Geathers	.05
63	*Roger Harper*	.10
64	Michael Haynes	.05
65	Bobby Hebert	.05
66	*Lincoln Kennedy*	.10
67	Chris Miller	.10
68	Andre Rison	.10
69	Deion Sanders	.50
70	Jessie Tuggle	.05
71	*Ron George*	.10
72	Eric Pegram	.05
73	Melvin Jenkins	.05
74	Pierce Holt	.05
75	Neal Anderson	.05
76	Mark Carrier	.05
77	*Curtis Conway*	.75
78	Richard Dent	.05
79	Jim Harbaugh	.10
80	Craig Heyward	.05
81	Darren Lewis	.05
82	Alonzo Spellman	.05
83	Tom Waddle	.05
84	Wendall Davis	.05
85	Chris Zorich	.05
86	*Carl Simpson*	.10
87	*Chris Gedney*	.20
88	Trace Armstrong	.05
89	Peter Tom Willis	.05
90	*John Copeland*	.10
91	Derrick Fenner	.05
92	James Francis	.05
93	Harold Green	.05
94	David Klingler	.10
95	Tim Krumrie	.05
96	*Tony McGee*	.10
97	Carl Pickens	.75
98	Alfred Williams	.05
99	Doug Pelrey	.10
100	*Lance Gunn*	.10
101	Jay Schroeder	.05
102	*Steve Tovar*	.10
103	Jeff Query	.05
104	*Ty Parten*	.10
105	Jerry Ball	.05
106	Mark Carrier	.05
107	Rob Burnett	.05
108	Michael Jackson	.10
109	Mike Johnson	.05
110	Bernie Kosar	.10
111	Clay Matthews	.05
112	Eric Metcalf	.05
113	Michael Dean Perry	.05
114	Vinny Testaverde	.20
115	Eric Turner	.05
116	Tommy Vardell	.05
117	Leroy Hoard	.05
118	*Steve Everitt*	.10
119	Everson Walls	.05
120	Steve Atwater	.05
121	Rod Bernstine	.05
122	Mike Croel	.05
123	John Elway	1.00
124	Simon Fletcher	.05
125	*Glyn Milburn*	.20
126	*Reggie Rivers*	.10
127	Shannon Sharpe	.20
128	Dennis Smith	.05
129	*Dan Williams*	.10
130	*Rondell Jones*	.10
131	*Jason Elam*	.20
132	*Arthur Marshall*	.10
133	Gary Zimmerman	.05
134	Karl Mecklenberg	.05
135	Bennie Blades	.05
136	Lomas Brown	.05
137	Bill Fralic	.05
138	Mel Gray	.05
139	Willie Green	.05
140	*Ryan McNeil*	.10
141	Rodney Peete	.05
142	Barry Sanders	2.00
143	Chris Spielman	.05
144	Pat Swilling	.05
145	Andre Ware	.05
146	Herman Moore	.50
147	Tim McKyer	.05
148	Brett Perriman	.05
149	*Antonio London*	.10
150	Edgar Bennett	.10
151	Terrell Buckley	.05
152	Brett Favre	2.00
153	Jackie Harris	.05
154	Johnny Holland	.05
155	Sterling Sharpe	.10
156	*Tim Hauck*	.10
157	*George Teague*	.25
158	Reggie White	.20
159	Mark Clayton	.05
160	Ty Detmer	.10
161	*Wayne Simmons*	.10
162	*Mark Brunell*	3.00
163	Tony Bennett	.05
164	Brian Noble	.05
165	Cody Carlson	.05
166	Ray Childress	.05
167	Cris Dishman	.05
168	Curtis Duncan	.05
169	*Brad Hopkins*	.10
170	Haywood Jeffires	.05
171	Wilber Marshall	.05
172	*Michael Barrow*	.10
173	Bubba McDowell	.05
174	Warren Moon	.20
175	Webster Slaughter	.05
176	*Travis Hannah*	.10
177	Lorenzo White	.05
178	Ernest Givins	.05
179	Keith McCants	.05
180	Kerry Cash	.05
181	Quentin Coryatt	.05
182	Kirk Lowdermilk	.05
183	Rodney Cullver	.05
184	Rohn Stark	.05
185	Steve Emtman	.05
186	Jeff George	.20
187	Jeff Herrod	.05
188	Reggie Langhorne	.05
189	*Roosevelt Potts*	.10
190	Jack Trudeau	.05
191	Will Wolford	.05
192	Jessie Hester	.05
193	Anthony Johnson	.10
194	*Ray Buchanan*	.10
195	Dale Carter	.05
196	Willie Davis	.05
197	John Alt	.05
198	Joe Montana	1.00
199	*Will Shields*	.10
200	Neil Smith	.05
201	Derrick Thomas	.10
202	Harvey Williams	.05
203	Marcus Allen	.20
204	J.J. Birden	.05
205	Tim Barnett	.05
206	Albert Lewis	.05
207	Nick Lowery	.05
208	Dave Krieg	.05

209	Keith Cash	.05
210	*Patrick Bates*	.10
211	Nick Bell	.05
212	Tim Brown	.20
213	Willie Gault	.05
214	Ethan Horton	.05
215	Jeff Hostetler	.10
216	Howie Long	.05
217	Greg Townsend	.05
218	Rocket Ismail	.10
219	Alexander Wright	.05
220	*Greg Robinson*	.10
221	*Billy Joe Hobert*	.20
222	Steve Wisenienski	.05
223	Steve Smith	.05
224	Vince Evans	.05
225	Willie Anderson	.05
226	*Jerome Bettis*	1.50
227	*Troy Drayton*	.25
228	Henry Ellard	.05
229	Jim Everett	.10
230	Tony Zendejas	.05
231	Todd Lyght	.05
232	Todd Kinchen	.10
233	Jackie Slater	.05
234	Fred Stokes	.05
235	*Russell White*	.10
236	Cleveland Gary	.05
237	*Sean Lachapelle*	.20
238	Steve Israel	.05
239	Shane Conlan	.05
240	Keith Byars	.05
241	Marco Coleman	.05
242	Bryan Cox	.05
243	Irving Fryar	.05
244	Richmond Webb	.05
245	Mark Higgs	.05
246	*Terry Kirby*	.30
247	Mark Ingram	.05
248	John Offerdahl	.05
249	Keith Jackson	.05
250	Dan Marino	2.00
251	*O.J. McDuffie*	.75
252	Louis Oliver	.05
253	Pete Stoyanovich	.05
254	Troy Vincent	.10
255	Anthony Carter	.05
256	Cris Carter	.20
257	Roger Craig	.05
258	Jack Del Rio	.05
259	Chris Doleman	.05
260	Barry Word	.05
261	*Qadry Ismail*	.25
262	Jim McMahon	.05
263	*Robert Smith*	1.25
264	Fred Strickland	.05
265	Randall McDaniel	.05
266	Carl Lee	.05
267	*Orlanda Truitt*	.10
268	Terry Allen	.10
269	Audray McMillan	.05
270	*Drew Bledsoe*	3.00
271	Eugene Chug	.05
272	Marv Cook	.05
273	Pat Harlow	.05
274	Greg McMurty	.05
275	Leonard Russell	.05
276	*Chris Slade*	.10
277	Andre Tippett	.05
278	*Vincent Brisby*	.25
279	Ben Coates	.30
280	*Sam Gash*	.10
281	Bruce Armstrong	.05
282	Rod Smith	.20
283	Michael Timpson	.05
284	*Scott Sisson*	.10
285	Morten Anderson	.05
286	*Reggie Freeman*	.10
287	Dalton Hilliard	.05
288	Rickey Jackson	.05
289	Vaughan Johnson	.05
290	Eric Martin	.05
291	Sam Mills	.05
292	Brad Muster	.05
293	*Willie Roaf*	.20
294	*Irv Smith*	.20
295	Wade Wilson	.05
296	*Derek Brown*	.10
297	Quinn Early	.05
298	Steve Walsh	.05
299	Renaldo Turnbull	.05
300	*Jessie Armstead*	.10
301	Carlton Bailey	.05
302	Michael Brooks	.05
303	Rodney Hampton	.05
304	Ed McCaffrey	.10
305	Dave Meggett	.05
306	Bart Oates	.05
307	Mike Sherrard	.05
308	Phil Simms	.10
309	Lawrence Taylor	.10
310	Mark Jackson	.05
311	Jarrod Bunch	.05
312	Howard Cross	.05
313	Michael Strahan	.05
314	Marcus Buckley	.05
315	Brad Baxter	.05
316	*Adrian Murrell*	1.00
317	Boomer Esiason	.10
318	Johnny Johnson	.05
319	*Marvin Jones*	.20
320	Jeff Lageman	.05
321	Ronnie Lott	.10
322	Leonard Marshall	.05
323	Johnny Mitchell	.05
324	Rob Moore	.10
325	Browning Nagle	.05
326	Blair Thomas	.05
327	Brian Washington	.05
328	Terrance Mathis	.10
329	Kyle Clifton	.05
330	Eric Allen	.05
331	*Victor Bailey*	.10
332	Fred Barnett	.05
333	Mark Bavaro	.05
334	Randall Cunningham	.10
335	Ken O'Brien	.05
336	Seth Joyner	.05
337	*Leonard Renfro*	.10
338	Heath Sherman	.05
339	Clyde Simmons	.05
340	Herschel Walker	.10
341	Calvin Williams	.05
342	Bubby Brister	.05
343	*Vaughn Hebron*	.10
344	Keith Millard	.05
345	Johnny Bailey	.05
346	Steve Beuerlein	.10
347	Chuck Cecil	.05
348	*Larry Centers*	.20
349	Chris Chandler	.10
350	*Ernest Dye*	.10
351	*Garrison Hearst*	1.00
352	Randal Hill	.05
353	John Booty	.05
354	Gary Clark	.05
355	*Ron Moore*	.10
356	Ricky Proehl	.05
357	Eric Swann	.05
358	Ken Harvey	.05
359	*Ben Coleman*	.10
360	*Deon Figures*	.20
361	Barry Foster	.05
362	Jeff Graham	.05
363	Eric Green	.05
364	Kevin Greene	.05
365	*Andre Hastings*	.10
366	Greg Lloyd	.05
367	Neil O'Donnell	.10
368	Dwight Stone	.05
369	Mike Tomczak	.05
370	Rod Woodson	.10
371	*Chad Brown*	.20
372	Ernie Mills	.05
373	Darren Perry	.05
374	Leon Searcy	.05
375	Marion Butts	.05
376	John Carney	.10
377	Ronnie Harmon	.05
378	Stan Humphries	.10
379	Nate Lewis	.05
380	*Natrone Means*	1.00
381	Anthony Miller	.05
382	Chris Mims	.05
383	Leslie O'Neal	.05
384	*Joe Coccozzo*	.10
385	Junior Seau	.10
386	Jerrol Williams	.05
387	John Friesz	.05
388	*Darrien Gordon*	.10
389	Derrick Walker	.05
390	Dana Hall	.05
391	Brent Jones	.05
392	*Todd Kelly*	.10
393	Amp Lee	.10
394	Tim McDonald	.05
395	Jerry Rice	1.00
396	*Dana Stubblefield*	.40
397	John Taylor	.05
398	Ricky Watters	.20
399	Steve Young	.75
400	Steve Bono	.30
401	*Adrian Hardy*	.10
402	Tom Rathman	.05
403	*Elvis Grbac*	1.50
404	Bill Romanowski	.05
405	Brian Blades	.05
406	Ferrell Edmunds	.05
407	*Carlton Gray*	.10
408	Cortez Kennedy	.05
409	Kelvin Martin	.05
410	Dan McGwire	.05
411	*Rick Mirer*	.30
412	Rufus Porter	.05
413	Chris Warren	.20
414	Jon Vaughn	.05
415	John L. Williams	.05
416	Eugene Robinson	.05
417	*Michael McCrary*	.10
418	*Michael Bates*	.20
419	Stan Gelbaugh	.05
420	Reggie Cobb	.05
421	*Eric Curry*	.10
422	Lawrence Dawsey	.05
423	Santana Dotson	.05
424	Craig Erickson	.10
425	Ron Hall	.05
426	Courtney Hawkins	.05
427	Broderick Thomas	.05
428	Vince Workman	.05
429	*Demetrius DuBose*	.10
430	*Lamar Thomas*	.10
431	*John Lynch*	.20
432	Hardy Nickerson	.05
433	*Horace Copeland*	.20
434	Steve DeBerg	.05
435	Joe Jacoby	.05
436	*Tom Carter*	.10
437	Andre Collins	.05
438	Darrell Green	.05
439	Desmond Howard	.10
440	Chip Lohmiller	.05
441	Charles Mann	.05
442	Tim McGee	.05
443	Art Monk	.10
444	Mark Rypien	.05
445	Ricky Sanders	.05
446	Brian Mitchell	.05
447	*Reggie Brooks*	.10
448	Carl Banks	.05
449	Cary Conklin	.05

1993 Pro Set All-Rookies

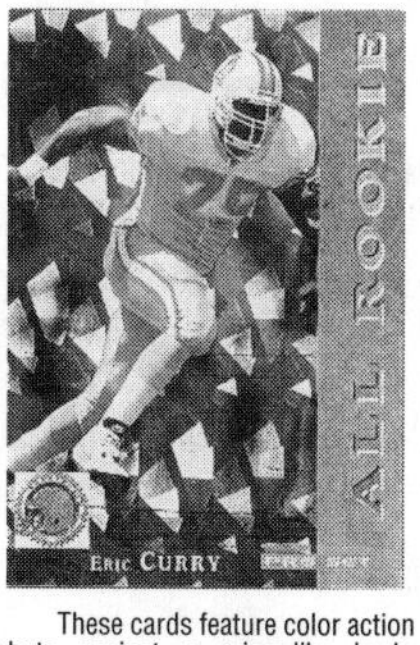

These cards feature color action shots against a prism-like background. Twenty-seven of the NFL's top rookie prospects are featured on these cards, which were random inserts in 1993 Pro Set foil packs. The player's name is at the bottom of the card, while the set's name is in a brown stripe along the right side. The numbered card back is green and has a football field ghosted over it. A player biography and team logo are also included. The player's name and card number are inside a gray stripe running along the left side of the card.

		MT
Complete Set (27):		10.00
Common Player:		.20
Minor Stars:		.40
1	Rick Mirer	.40
2	Garrison Hearst	1.75
3	Jerome Bettis	1.75
4	Vincent Brisby	.20
5	O.J. McDuffie	.75
6	Curtis Conway	.75
7	Raghib Ismail	.20
8	Steve Everitt	.20
9	Ernest Dye	.20
10	Todd Rucci	.20
11	Willie Roaf	.40
12	Lincoln Kennedy	.20
13	Irv Smith	.20
14	Jason Elam	.20
15	Derrick Alexander	.20
16	John Copeland	.20
17	Eric Curry	.20
18	Dana Stubblefield	.40
19	Leonard Renfro	.20
20	Marvin Jones	.20
21	Demetrius DuBose	.20
22	Chris Slade	.20
23	Darrin Smith	.20
24	Deon Figures	.20
25	Darrien Gordon	.20
26	Patrick Bates	.20
27	George Teague	.20

1993 Pro Set College Connections

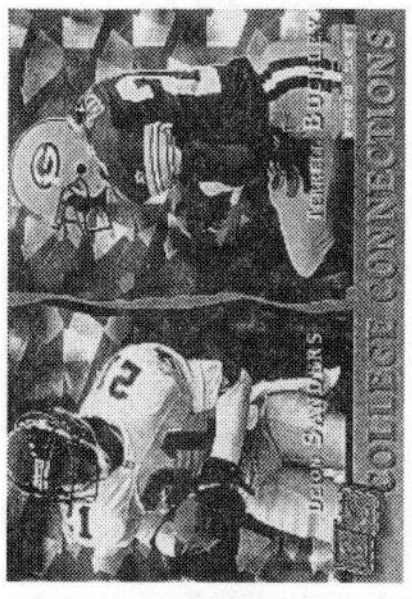

College teammates who've become stars in the NFL are featured on these insert cards, randomly included in 1993 jumbo packs. Each card front is horizontal and features two small color action photos of the teammates against a silver prism-like background. A gray stripe at the bottom has the set's name. Each back has two panels which compare the players and give biographical information about them. The cards are numbered with a "CC" prefix.

		MT
Complete Set (10):		35.00
Common Player:		1.00
Minor Stars:		2.00
1	Barry Sanders, Thurman Thomas	6.00
2	Jerome Bettis, Reggie Brooks	2.00
3	Neal Anderson, Emmitt Smith	5.00
4	Raghib Ismail, Tim Brown	1.00
5	Rodney Hampton, Garrison Hearst	2.00
6	Derrick Thomas, Cornelius Bennett	1.00
7	Steve Young, Jim McMahon	3.00
8	Rick Mirer, Joe Montana	5.00
9	Terrell Buckley, Deion Sanders	3.00
10	Drew Bledsoe, Mark Rypien	5.00

1993 Pro Set Rookie Quarterbacks

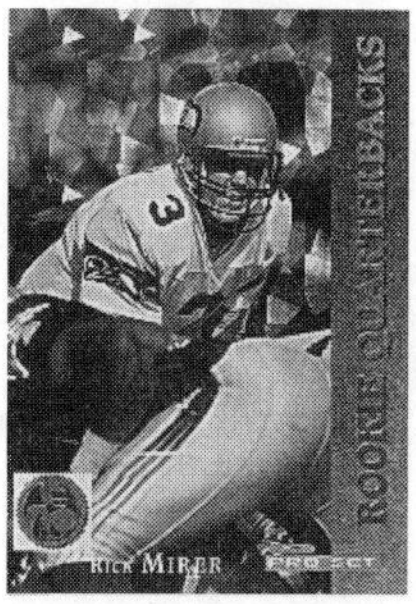

These cards, randomly inserted in 1993 Pro Set jumbo packs, have color action shots on them against a prism-like background. The set name is in a gray stripe along the right side; the player's name is at the bottom of the card. The pink backs have a team logo and career highlights and are numbered with a "RQ" prefix. The player's name is in a purple stripe which runs along the left side of the card.

		MT
Complete Set (6):		10.00
Common Player:		.20
1	Drew Bledsoe	3.00
2	Rick Mirer	.40
3	Mark Brunell	3.00
4	Billy Joe Hobert	.20
5	Trent Green	4.00
6	Elvis Grbac	1.50

1993 Pro Set Rookie Running Backs

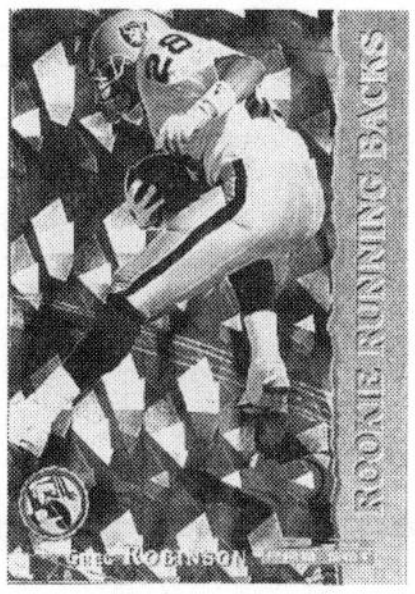

Fourteen promising rookie running backs are featured on these cards, which were random inserts in 1993 Pro Set foil packs. Each card front has a color action shot against a prism background. The player's name is at the bottom of the card; the set name runs along the right side in a brown stripe. The backs, numbered with a "RRB" prefix, are gray and have a light brown stripe along the left side containing the player's name. His career highlights, team, position and biography are also given.

		MT
Complete Set (14):		10.00
Common Player:		.20
Minor Stars:		.40
1	Derrick Lassic	.20
2	Reggie Brooks	.20
3	Garrison Hearst	1.75
4	Ron Moore	.20
5	Robert Smith	1.75
6	Jerome Bettis	1.75
7	Russell White	.20
8	Derek Brown	.20
9	Roosevelt Potts	.20
10	Terry Kirby	.40
11	Glyn Milburn	.40
12	Greg Robinson	.20
13	Natrone Means	1.50
14	Vaughn Hebron	.20

1993 Pro Set Power Prototypes

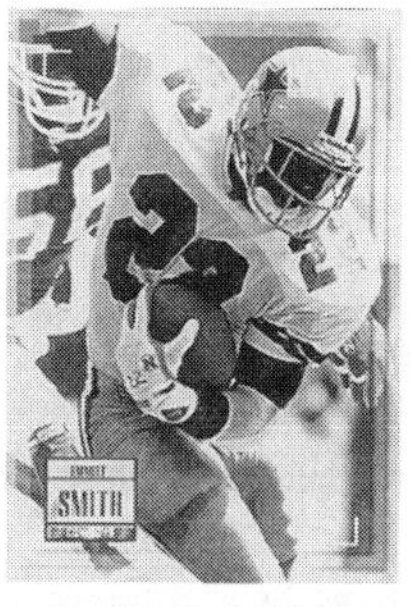

The 10-card set previewed the 1993 Pro Set Power series. The card fronts have the Pro Set Power logo in one of the upper corners, with the player's name and team listed in a red, white and blue box at the bottom of the full-bleed cards. The backs include a horizontal photo, along with a rating system and career highlights. The cards are numbered in the upper left. "Prototype" is printed at the bottom center.

		MT
Complete Set (10):		10.00
Common Player:		.50
20	Barry Sanders	2.00
22	Emmitt Smith	4.00
26	Rod Woodson	.50
32	Ricky Watters	.75
37	Larry Centers	.50
71	Santana Dotson	.50
80	Jerry Rice	2.00
138	Reggie Rivers	.50
193	Trace Armstrong	.50
NNO	Title/Ad Card	.50

1993 Pro Set Power

Pro Set Power's 1993 set has 200 cards. The fronts are similar to the 1992 look; the player is featured in a color action shot against a ghosted background. The player's name and team are at the bottom left; the foil-stamped Pro Set Power logo is in the upper right. The card back has a summary of the player's 1992 season, including statistics and a rating guide. His name appears at the top between team color-coded bars. Below that is an action photo. Insert sets include All-Power Defense (25 cards), Power Moves (30), Draft Picks (30), and Power Combos (10).

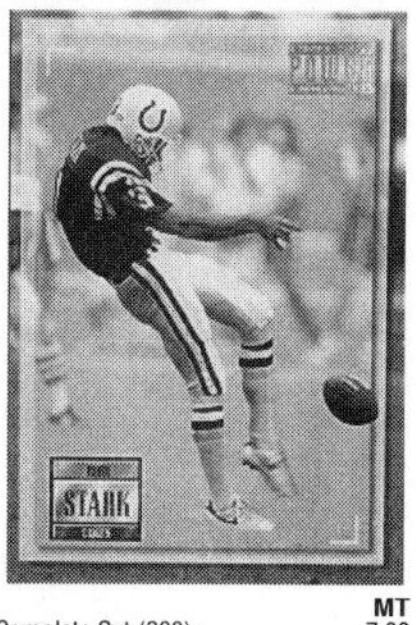

		MT
Complete Set (200):		7.00
Common Player:		.05
Minor Stars:		.10
Comp. Gold Set (200):		16.00
Gold Cards:		1x-2x
Wax Box:		15.00
1	Warren Moon	.20
2	Steve Christie	.05
3	Jim Breech	.05
4	Brett Favre	1.00
5	Sean Landeta	.05
6	Jim Arnold	.05
7	John Elway	.50
8	Troy Aikman	1.00
9	Rodney Peete	.10
10	Pete Stoyanovich	.05
11	Mark Rypien	.05
12	Jim Kelly	.20
13	Dan Marino	1.25
14	Neil O'Donnell	.10
15	David Klingler	.10
16	Rich Gannon	.05
17	Dave Krieg	.05
18	Jeff Jaeger	.05
19	Bernie Kosar	.05
20	Barry Sanders	1.00
21	Deion Sanders	.40
22	Emmitt Smith	1.25
23	Barry Word	.05
24	Stanley Richard	.05
25	Louis Oliver	.05
26	Rod Woodson	.10
27	Rodney Hampton	.20
28	Cris Dishman	.05
29	Barry Foster	.10
30	Dave Meggett	.05
31	Kevin Ross	.05
32	Ricky Watters	.20
33	Darren Lewis	.05
34	Thurman Thomas	.20
35	Rodney Culver	.05
36	Bennie Blades	.05
37	*Larry Centers*	.20
38	Todd Scott	.05
39	Darren Perry	.05
40	Robert Massey	.05
41	Keith Byars	.05
42	Chris Warren	.10
43	Cleveland Gary	.05
44	Lorenzo White	.05
45	Tony Stargell	.05
46	Bennie Thompson	.05
47	A.J. Johnson	.05
48	Daryl Johnston	.05
49	Dennis Smith	.05
50	Johnny Holland	.05
51	Ken Norton Jr.	.05
52	Pepper Johnson	.05
53	Vaughn Johnson	.05
54	Chris Spielman	.05
55	Junior Seau	.20
56	Chris Doleman	.05
57	Rickey Jackson	.05
58	Derrick Thomas	.10
59	Seth Joyner	.05
60	Stan Thomas	.05
61	Nate Newton	.05
62	Matt Brock	.05
63	Mike Munchak	.05
64	Randall McDaniel	.05
65	Ron Hallstrom	.05
66	Andy Heck	.05
67	Russell Maryland	.05
68	Bruce Wilkerson	.05
69	Mark Schlereth	.05
70	John Fina	.05
71	Santana Dotson	.05
72	Don Mosebar	.05
73	Simon Fletcher	.05
74	Paul Gruber	.05
75	Howard Ballard	.05
76	John Alt	.05
77	Carlton Hasselrig	.05
78	Bruce Smith	.05
79	Ray Childress	.05
80	Jerry Rice	.75
81	Art Monk	.10
82	John Taylor	.05
83	Andre Reed	.10
84	Sterling Sharpe	.10
85	Sam Graddy	.05
86	Fred Barnett	.05
87	Ricky Proehl	.05
88	Michael Irvin	.25
89	Webster Slaughter	.05
90	Tony Bennett	.05
91	Leslie O'Neal	.05
92	Michael Dean Perry	.05
93	Greg Townsend	.05
94	Anthony Smith	.05
95	Richard Dent	.05
96	Clyde Simmons	.05
97	Cornelius Bennett	.05
98	Eric Swann	.05
99	Cortez Kennedy	.05
100	Emmitt Smith	.75
101	Michael Jackson	.05
102	Lin Elliott	.05
103	Rohn Stark	.05
104	Jim Harbaugh	.05
105	Greg Davis	.05
106	Mike Cofer	.05
107	Morten Andersen	.05
108	Steve Young	.75
109	Norm Johnson	.05
110	Dan McGwire	.05
111	Jim Everett	.05
112	Randall Cunningham	.10
113	Steve Bono	.20
114	Cody Carlson	.05
115	Jeff Hostetler	.10
116	Rich Camarillo	.05
117	Chris Chandler	.05
118	Stan Gelbaugh	.05
119	Tony Sacca	.05
120	Henry Jones	.05
121	Terry Allen	.05
122	Amp Lee	.05
123	Mel Gray	.05
124	Jon Vaughn	.05
125	Bubba McDowell	.05
126	Audray McMilliam	.05
127	Terrell Buckley	.05
128	Dana Hall	.05
129	Eric Dickerson	.05
130	Martin Bayless	.05
131	Steve Israel	.05
132	Vaughn Dunbar	.05
133	Ronnie Harmon	.05
134	Dale Carter	.05
135	Neal Anderson	.05
136	Merton Hanks	.05
137	James Washington	.05
138	*Reggie Rivers*	.05
139	Bruce Pickens	.05
140	Gary Anderson	.05
141	Eugene Robinson	.05
142	*Charles Mincy*	.10
143	Matt Darby	.05
144	Tom Rathman	.05
145	Mike Prior	.05
146	Sean Lumpkin	.05
147	Greg Jackson	.05
148	Wes Hopkins	.05
149	David Tate	.05
150	James Francis	.05
151	Brian Cox	.05
152	Keith McCants	.05
153	Mark Stepnoski	.05
154	Al Smith	.05
155	Robert Jones	.05
156	Lawrence Taylor	.10
157	Clay Matthews	.05
158	Wilber Marshall	.05
159	Mike Johnson	.05
160	Adam Schreiber	.05
161	Tim Grunhard	.05
162	Mark Bortz	.05
163	Gene Chilton	.05
164	Jamie Dukes	.05
165	Bart Oates	.05
166	Kevin Gogan	.05
167	Kent Hull	.05
168	Ed King	.05
169	Eugene Chung	.05
170	Troy Auzenne	.05
171	Charles Mann	.05
172	William Perry	.05
173	Mike Lodish	.05
174	Bruce Matthews	.05
175	Tony Casillas	.05
176	Steve Wisenewski	.05
177	Karl Mecklenberg	.05
178	Richmond Webb	.05
179	Erik Williams	.05
180	Andre Rison	.10
181	Michael Haynes	.05
182	Don Beebe	.05
183	Anthony Miller	.05
184	Jay Novacek	.05
185	Rob Moore	.05
186	Willie Green	.05
187	Tom Waddle	.05
188	Keith Jackson	.05
189	Steve Tasker	.05
190	Marco Coleman	.05
191	Jeff Wright	.05
192	Burt Grossman	.05
193	Trace Armstong	.05
194	Charles Haley	.05
195	Greg Lloyd	.05
196	Marc Boutte	.05
197	Rufus Porter	.05
198	Dennis Gibson	.05
199	Shane Dronett	.05
200	Joe Montana	1.00
H1	Emmitt Smith HOLO	25.00
H2	Emmitt Smith HOLO	25.00

1993 Pro Set Power Gold

Inserted one per pack, this set was a parallel to the Power base cards. The Power logo is printed in gold foil, which is very similar to the silver foil. If the card is held at the correct angle, the gold foil can be differentiated.

	MT
Complete Set (200):	20.00
Common Player:	.10
Gold Cards:	1x-2x

1993 Pro Set Power All-Power Defense

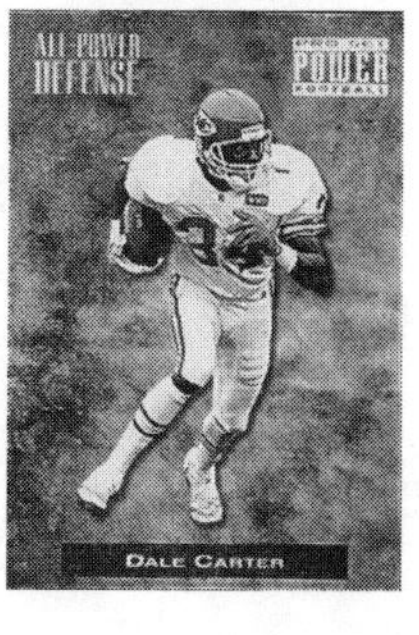

Twenty-five top NFL defensive players are featured on these cards, which were randomly inserted at a rate of two per jumbo pack. Each card front has a borderless color photo against a brown background. A black rectangle at the bottom includes the player's name in yellow letters. The back is also in brown, and includes the player's name, team, position and biography in a yellow box in the upper left corner. A career summary is also given in red lettering. Cards are numbered with an "APD" prefix. Scarcer gold-foil versions were also made for each card.

		MT
Complete Set (25):		5.00
Common Player:		.20
Minor Stars:		.40
Comp. Gold Set (25):		10.00
Gold Cards:		1x-2x
1	Clyde Simmons	.20
2	Anthony Smith	.20
3	Ray Childress	.20
4	Michael Dean Perry	.40
5	Bruce Smith	.40
6	Cortez Kennedy	.40
7	Charles Haley	.20
8	Marco Coleman	.20
9	Alonzo Spellman	.20
10	Junior Seau	.75
11	Ken Norton	.20
12	Derrick Thomas	.40
13	Wilber Marshall	.20
14	Chris Doleman	.20
15	Seth Joyner	.20
16	Al Smith	.20
17	Deion Sanders	.75
18	Rod Woodson	.40
19	Audray McMillian	.20
20	Dale Carter	.20
21	Terrell Buckley	.20
22	Bennie Thompson	.20
23	Chris Spielman	.20
24	Lawrence Taylor	.40
25	Tony Bennett	.20

1993 Pro Set Power Combos

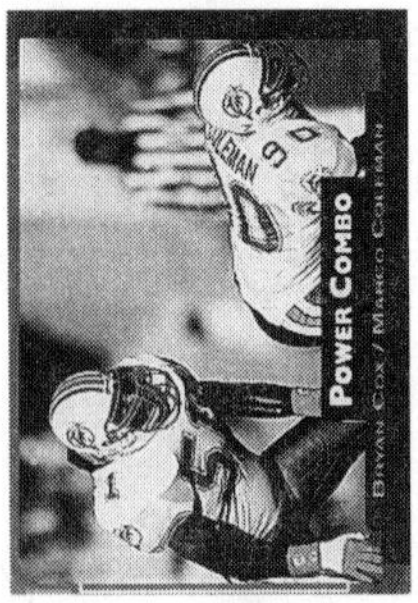

Two players are featured on the front of each card in this Pro Set Power insert set. Cards were random inserts in foil packs. Each card front has a black, blue and purple border, along with the players' names in red in a black bar at the bottom. The card back has a purple rectangle at the top, which has the players' team name in it in yellow lettering. Their names, positions, uniform numbers, career summaries and highlights are featured on the back against a green background with borders in the same color as those on the front. Gold versions and prism versions, were also made for each card.

		MT
Complete Set (10):		6.00
Common Player:		.50
Minor Stars:		1.00
Comp. Gold Set (10):		12.00
Gold Cards:		1x-2x
Comp. Prism Set (10):		18.00
Prism Cards:		1x-3x
1	Emmitt Smith, Barry Sanders	3.00
2	Terrell Buckley, Sterling Sharpe	1.00
3	Junior Seau, Gary Plummer	1.00
4	Deion Sanders, Tim McKyer	1.00
5	Bruce Smith, Darryl Talley	.50
6	Warren Moon, Webster Slaughter	.50
7	Chris Doleman, Henry Thomas	.50
8	Karl Mecklenberg, Michael Brooks	.50
9	Ken Norton, Robert Jones	.50
10	Bryan Cox, Marco Coleman	.50

1993 Pro Set Power Draft Picks

These cards feature color action photos on the front against a black-and-white background. The cards, random inserts in 1993 Pro Set Power packs, feature top rookies in the NFL for the 1993 season; the player's name is in red at the bottom. The card back also has the player's name in red at the top, and is in a horizontal format. The player's name and player biography are also included. Cards are numbered with a "PDP" prefix. Gold foil versions were also made for each card.

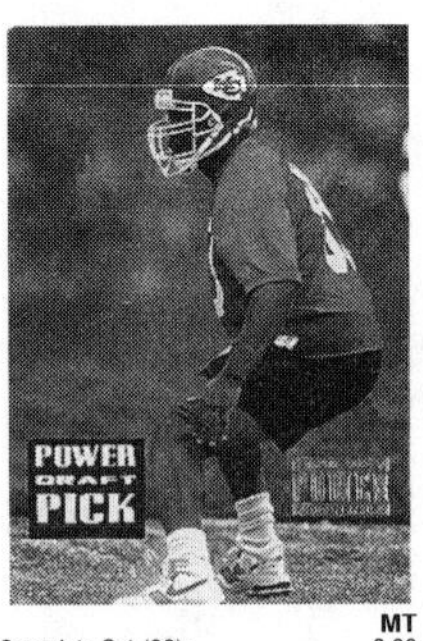

		MT
Complete Set (30):		8.00
Common Player:		.10
Minor Stars:		.20
Comp. Gold Set (30):		16.00
Gold Cards:		1x-2x
1	Lincoln Kennedy	.10
2	Thomas Smith	.10
3	Robert Smith	1.00
4	John Copeland	.20
5	Dan Footman	.10
6	Darrin Smith	.20
7	Qadry Ismail	.50
8	Ryan McNeil	.10
9	George Teague	.20
10	Brad Hopkins	.10
11	Ernest Dye	.10
12	Jaime Fields	.10
13	Patrick Bates	.10
14	Jerome Bettis	1.00
15	O.J. McDuffie	.75
16	Gino Torretta	.10
17	Drew Bledsoe	2.50
18	Irv Smith	.10
19	Marcus Buckley	.10
20	Coleman Rudolph	.10
21	Leonard Renfro	.10
22	Garrison Hearst	1.00
23	Deon Figures	.20
24	Natrone Means	1.00
25	Todd Kelly	.10
26	Carlton Gray	.10
27	Eric Curry	.10
28	Tom Carter	.20
29	AFC Stars	.10
30	NFC Stars	.10

1993 Pro Set Power Moves

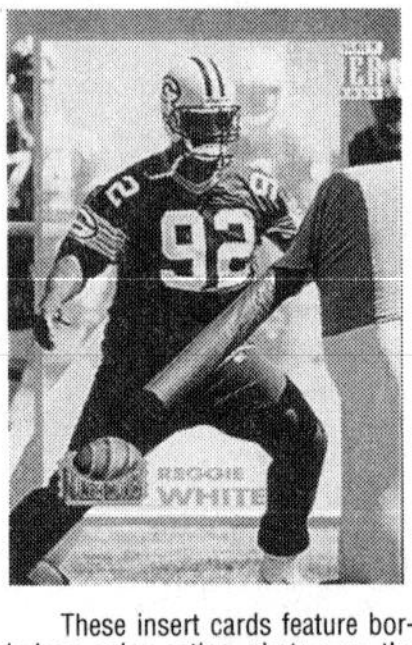

These insert cards feature borderless color action photos on the front, with a ghosted version of the same photo on the back. The front has a red frame for a border, with the player's name in red at the bottom. The back has the set name in white in a black stripe along the left side, with the player's name and his team name in black in a gray plaque at the top. Cards are numbered with a "PM" prefix. Card numbers 1-30 were randomly inserted in 1993 Pro Set Power packs; cards 31-40 were random inserts in 1993 Pro Set Power jumbo packs. Scarcer gold-foil versions were also made for each card.

		MT
Complete Set (40):		5.00
Common Player:		.10
Minor Stars:		.20
Comp. Gold Set (40):		10.00
Gold Cards:		1x-2x
1	Bobby Hebert	.20
2	Billy Brooks	.10
3	Vinny Testaverde	.20
4	Hugh Millen	.10
5	Rod Berstine	.10
6	Robert Delpino	.10
7	Pat Swilling	.10
8	Reggie White	.30
9	Aaron Cox	.10
10	Joe Montana	2.00
11	Gaston Green	.10
12	Jeff Hostetler	.20
13	Shane Conlan	.10
14	Irv Eatman	.10
15	Mark Ingram	.10
16	Irving Fryar	.10
17	Don Majkowski	.10
18	(Will Wolford)	.10
19	Boomer Esiason	.20
20	Ronnie Lott	.10
21	Johnny Johnson	.10
22	Steve Beuerlein	.10
23	Chuck Cecil	.10
24	Gary Clark	.10
25	Kevin Greene	.10
26	Jerrol Williams	.10
27	Tim McDonald	.10
28	Ferrell Edmunds	.10
29	Kelvin Martin	.10
30	Hardy Nickerson	.10
31	Jerry Ball	.10
32	Jim McMahon	.10
33	Marcus Allen	.30
34	John Stephens	.10
35	John Booty	.10
36	Wade Wilson	.10
37	Mark Bavaro	.10
38	Bill Fralic	.10
39	Mark Clayton	.10
40	Mike Sherrard	.10

1993 Pro Set Power Update Power Moves

These insert cards feature color action photos on the front, with a purple border framed with blue and red lines. The player's name is at the bottom in yellow letters. The card backs, numbered with a "PMVD" prefix, have a biography and season highlights, plus a date when he was traded. Helmets for his old and new team appear at the top, too. The background has shades of purple and white. These inserts shared packs with 1993 Pro Set Power Update Power Prospects cards.

		MT
Complete Set (50):		4.00
Common Player:		.10
Minor Stars:		.20
Comp. Gold Set (50):		8.00
Gold Cards:		1x-2x
1	Bobby Hebert	.20
2	Bill Brooks	.10
3	Vinny Testaverde	.20
4	Hugh Millen	.10
5	Rod Bernstine	.10
6	Robert Delpino	.10
7	Pat Swilling	.10
8	Reggie White	.30
9	Aaron Cox	.10
10	Joe Montana	2.00
11	Vinnie Clark (Name misspelled Vinny on card)	.10
12	Jeff Hostetler	.20
13	Shane Conlan	.10
14	Irv Eatman	.10
15	Mark Ingram	.10
16	Irving Fryar	.10
17	Don Majkowski	.10
18	Will Wolford	.10
19	Boomer Esiason	.20
20	Ronnie Lott	.10
21	Johnny Johnson	.10
22	Steve Beuerlein	.10
23	Chuck Cecil	.10
24	Gary Clark	.10
25	Kevin Greene	.10
26	Jerrol Williams	.10
27	Tim McDonald	.10
28	Ferrell Edmunds	.10
29	Kelvin Martin	.10
30	Hardy Nickerson	.10
31	Jumpy Geathers	.10
32	Craig Heyward	.10
33	Tim McKyer	.10
34	Mark Carrier	.10
35	Gary Zimmerman	.10
36	Jay Schroeder	.10
37	Keith Millard	.10
38	Vince Workman	.10
39	Kirk Lowdermilk	.10
40	Fred Stokes	.10
41	Ernie Jones	.10
42	Keith Byars	.10
43	Carlton Bailey	.10
44	Michael Brooks	.10
45	Tim McGee	.10
46	Leonard Marshall	.10
47	Bubby Brister	.10
48	Mike Tomczak	.10
49	Mark Jackson	.10
50	Wade Wilson	.10

1993 Pro Set Power Update Power Prospects

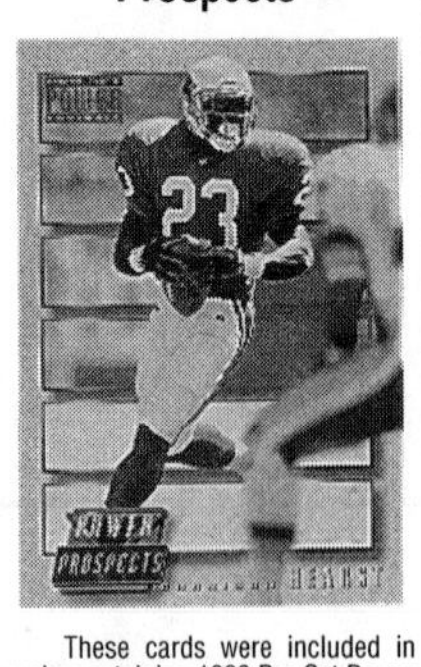

These cards were included in packs containing 1993 Pro Set Power Update Power Moves cards. Each card has a color action photo framed by gray borders. A horizontally-patterned background is also used on the front. The player's name is in yellow at the bottom on the front, while it and his team helmet appear at the top in a panel on the back. The back is gray and contains a career summary and a number, which uses a "PP" prefix. Gold versions were also made for each card.

		MT
Complete Set (60):		10.00
Common Player:		.10
Minor Stars:		.20
Comp. Gold Set (60):		20.00
Gold Cards:		1x-2x
1	*Drew Bledsoe*	2.50
2	*Rick Mirer*	.25
3	*Trent Green*	10.00
4	*Mark Brunell*	3.00
5	*Billy Joe Hobert*	.20
6	*Ron Moore*	.40
7	*Elvis Grbac*	.50
8	*Garrison Hearst*	1.00
9	*Jerome Bettis*	1.00
10	*Reggie Brooks*	.25
11	*Robert Smith*	1.00
12	*Vaughn Hebron*	.10
13	*Derek Brown*	.25
14	*Roosevelt Potts*	.20
15	*Terry Kirby*	.30
16	*Glyn Milburn*	.30
17	*Greg Robinson*	.10
18	*Natrone Means*	1.00
19	*Curtis Conway*	.50
20	*James Jett*	.75
21	*O.J. McDuffie*	.50
22	Raghib Ismail	.20
23	*Qadry Ismail*	.40
24	*Kevin Williams*	.60
25	*Victor Bailey*	.20
26	*Vincent Brisby*	.60
27	*Irv Smith*	.10
28	*Troy Drayton*	.40
29	Wayne Simmons	.10
30	*Marvin Jones*	.10
31	*Demetrius DuBase*	.10
32	*Chad Brown*	.40
33	*Michael Barrow*	.10
34	*Darrin Smith*	.20
35	*Deon Figures*	.20
36	*Darrien Gordon*	.20
37	Patrick Bates	.10
38	*George Teague*	.20
39	*Lance Gunn*	.10
40	*Tom Carter*	.20
41	*Carlton Gray*	.20
42	*John Copeland*	.20
43	*Eric Curry*	.25
44	*Dana Stubblefield*	.40
45	*Leonard Renfro*	.10
46	*Dan Williams*	.10
47	*Todd Kelly*	.10
48	*Chris Slade*	.40
49	*Carl Simpson*	.10
50	*Coleman Rudolph*	.10
51	*Michael Strahan*	.10
52	*Dan Footman*	.10
53	*Steve Everitt*	.10
54	*Will Shields*	.10
55	*Ben Coleman*	.10
56	*William Roaf*	.10
57	*Lincoln Kennedy*	.10
58	*Brad Hopkins*	.10
59	*Ernest Dye*	.10
60	*Jason Elam*	.10

1993 Pro Set Power Update Prospects Gold

Featuring a gold-foil stamp on the card fronts, this 60-card set is a parallel to the Power Update base set.

	MT
Complete Set (60):	25.00
Common Player:	.10
Gold Cards:	1x-2x

1993 Pro Set Power Update Combos

These inserts were randomly included in 1993 Pro Set Power Update packs. Each card front features two players on it, in a horizontal format. Their names are at the bottom in red letters. The backs are horizontal too, and include the players' names at the top, along with career highlights for them against a turf-like background. Cards are numbered with a "PC" prefix. Gold versions and prism versions.

		MT
Complete Set (10):		10.00
Common Player:		.50
Minor Stars:		1.00
Comp. Gold Set (10):		20.00
Gold Cards:		1x-2x
Comp. Prism Set (10):		30.00
Prism Cards:		1x-3x
1	Andre Rison, Michael Haynes, Mike Pritchard, Drew Hill	.50
2	Steve Young, Jerry Rice	3.00
3	Jim Kelly, Frank Reich	1.00
4	Alvin Harper, Michael Irvin	1.50
5	Rod Woodson, Deon Figures	.50
6	Bruce Smith, Cornelius Bennett	.50
7	Bryan Cox, Marco Coleman	.50
8	Troy Aikman, Emmitt Smith	4.00
9	Tim Brown, Raghib Ismail	1.00
10	Art Monk, Desmond Howard, Ricky Sanders	.50

1993 Pro Set Power Update Impact Rookies

These cards feature top rookies entering the 1993 season. Each card front has an action photo framed by a gold border. The player's name is in yellow at the bottom. The back is gray and includes the player's team name and helmet at the top, along with the college he attended, position and collegiate highlights underneath. Cards were numbered with an "IR" prefix.

		MT
Complete Set (15):		10.00
Common Player:		.25
Minor Stars:		.50
1	Rick Mirer	2.00
2	Drew Bledsoe	3.00
3	Jerome Bettis	1.00
4	Derek Brown	.50
5	Roosevelt Potts	.25
6	Glyn Milburn	.50
7	Adrian Murrell	.50
8	Victor Bailey	.25
9	Vincent Brisby	.50
10	O.J. McDuffie	1.00
11	James Jett	.50
12	Eric Curry	.25
13	Dana Stubblefield	.50
14	William Roaf	.25
15	Patrick Bates	.25

1994 Pro Set National Promos

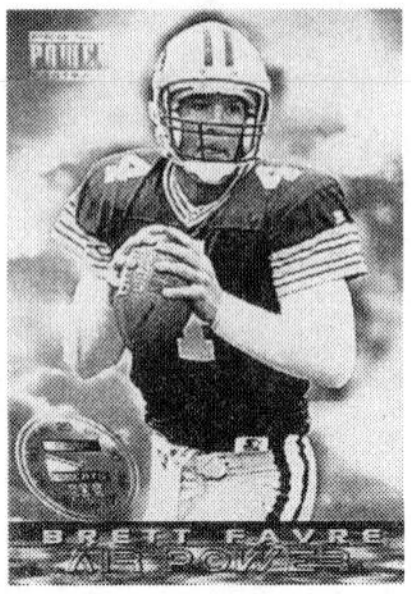

Six of eight cards were handed out at the Pro Set booth at the 1994 National Sports Collectors Convention. The cards, numbered by a letter, were promos from either Pro Set football, Power football or Power racing. A title card, which was unnumbered, featured the National logo and was individually numbered "of 10,000." The Garrison Hearst and Richmond Webb cards were inserts in "Tuff Stuff" magazine. The card backs have "proto" printed inside a strip at the bottom.

		MT
Complete Set (8):		14.00
Common Player:		1.00
1	Fire Power (Jerome Bettis)	2.00
2	Drew Bledsoe	3.00
3	Green Bay Packers, Air Power (Brett Favre, Sterling Sharpe)	5.00
4	Ronald Moore	1.00
5	Power Line (Willie Roaf)	1.00
6	Garrison Hearst	1.50
7	Richmond Webb	1.00
NNO	Title Card (1994 National)	1.00

Q

1991 Quarterback Legends

This 50-card set, produced by NFL Quarterback Legends, comes in a special commemorative box. Each card front has a full-bleed color action photo, with the set logo and name given at the bottom of the card in a checkerboard pattern. The card back has the sponsors' logos, a card number, a color photo, statistics and a career summary. The design is horizontal. Cards were released at the Quarterback Legends Show in Nashville, Tenn., in January 1992.

		MT
Complete Set (50):		20.00
Common Player:		.25
1	Ken Anderson	.75
2	Steve Bartkowski	.35
3	George Blanda	1.50
4	Terry Bradshaw	2.00
5	Zeke Bratkowski	.25
6	John Brodie	.50
7	Charley Conerly	.50
8	Len Dawson	.50
9	Lynn Dickey	.25
10	Joe Ferguson	.25
11	Vince Ferragamo	.25
12	Tom Flores	.35
13	Dan Fouts	1.00
14	Roman Gabriel	.35
15	Otto Graham	.75
16	Bob Griese	1.25
17	Steve Grogan	.35
18	John Hadl	.35
19	James Harris	.25
20	Jim Hart	.25
21	Ron Jaworski	.25
22	Charlie Johnson	.25
23	Bert Jones	.35
24	Sonny Jurgensen	.75
25	Joe Kapp	.25
26	Billy Kilmer	.50
27	Daryle Lamonica	.35
28	Greg Landry	.25
29	Neil Lomax	.25
30	Archie Manning	.40
31	Earl Morrall	.35
32	Craig Morton	.35
33	Gifford Nielsen	.25
34	Dan Pastorini	.25
35	Jim Plunkett	.35
36	Norm Snead	.25
37	Ken Stabler	.75
38	Bart Starr	1.50
39	Roger Staubach	3.00
40	Joe Theismann	.75
41	Y.A. Tittle	.75
42	Johnny Unitas	1.50
43	Bill Wade	.25
44	Danny White	.35
45	Doug Williams	.25
46	Jim Zorn	.35
47	Legendary Feats (Otto Graham)	1.00
48	Legendary Feats (Johnny Unitas)	1.00
49	Legendary Feats (Bart Starr)	1.00
50	Legendary Feats (Terry Bradshaw)	1.75

1992 Quarterback Greats GE

Members of the Quarterback Club are represented in this 12-card set sponsored by General Electric. The QB Club, GE and NFL Team Players logos all appear on the card back, which is numbered. The card front has a color action photo against a red background. The player's name is at the top of the card in white letters. Quarterback Greats is also written on the card front. The back has a career summary and player statistics. Cards were available through a mail-in offer utilizing proofs of purchase seals. An unnumbered checklist card was also produced for the set.

		MT
Complete Set (12):		10.00
Common Player:		.50
1	Troy Aikman	5.00
2	Bubby Brister	.75
3	Randall Cunningham	1.00
4	John Elway	2.00
5	Boomer Esiason	.75
6	Jim Everett	.75
7	Jim Kelly	1.50
8	Bernie Kosar	.50
9	Dan Marino	4.00
10	Warren Moon	1.00
11	Phil Simms	.50
NNO	Title Card (Checklist)	.25

1993 Quarterback Legends

These cards feature color photos of some of the NFL's best quarterbacks, against a sepia-toned background. The set name runs vertically along the left side of the card, written in bronze letters. The card back is numbered and includes a career summary and closeup shot of the player.

		MT
Complete Set (50):		15.00
Common Player:		.20
1	Checklist Card	.25
2	Ken Anderson	.50
3	Steve Bartkowski	.25
4	George Blanda	1.00
5	Terry Bradshaw	1.50
6	Zeke Bratkowski	.20
7	John Brodie	.50
8	Charley Conerly	.50
9	Len Dawson	.50
10	Lynn Dickey	.20
11	Joe Ferguson	.20
12	Vince Ferragamo	.20
13	Tom Flores	.25
14	Dan Fouts	.75
15	Roman Gabriel	.25
16	Otto Graham	.75
17	Bob Griese	1.00
18	Steve Grogan	.25
19	John Hadl	.25
20	James Harris	.20
21	Jim Hart	.20
22	Ron Jaworski	.20
23	Charlie Johnson	.20
24	Bert Jones	.25
25	Sonny Jurgensen	.50
26	Joe Kapp	.20
27	Billy Kilmer	.25
28	Daryle Lamonica	.20
29	Greg Landry	.20
30	Neil Lomax	.20
31	Archie Manning	.50
32	Earl Morrall	.25
33	Craig Morton	.25
34	Gifford Nielsen	.20
35	Dan Pastorini	.20
36	Jim Plunkett	.25
37	Norm Snead	.20
38	Ken Stabler	.75
39	Bart Starr	1.00
40	Roger Staubach	2.00
41	Joe Theismann	.75
42	Y.A. Tittle	.75
43	Johnny Unitas	1.00
44	Bill Wade	.20
45	Danny White	.25
46	Doug Williams	.20
47	Jim Zorn	.20
48	Miracle Streak (George Blanda)	.75
49	Perfect Season (Bob Griese, Earl Morrall)	.50
50	Record Setting Super Bowl XXII (Doug Williams)	.25

R

1935 R311-2 Premium Photos

Measuring 6" x 8", these 17 photos feature both collegiate and professional players. The black-and-white photos have blank backs. The photos could be ordered from National Chicle in exchange for 20 wrappers given to the retailer. The photos are listed in alphabetical order by the player's name or team.

		NM
Complete Set (17):		3000.
Common Player:		175.00
1	Joe Bach	175.00
2	Eddie Casey	175.00
3	George Christensen	175.00
4	Red Grange	525.00
5	TD Next Stop (Stan Kostka)	175.00
6	Fordham Back (Joe Maniaci) (26 with ball, shown trying to gain around left end)	175.00
7	Harry Newman	175.00
8	Walter Switzer (Cornell quarterback)	175.00
9	Chicago Bears, 1934 Western Champs	300.00
10	New York Giants, 1934 World's Champs	350.00
11	Notre Dame's Quick Kick Against Army, 1934	220.00
12	Pittsburgh in Rough Going Against the Navy 1945	175.00
13	Pittsburgh Pirates, 1935 Football Club	250.00
14	Touchdown: Morton of Yale	175.00
15	A Tight Spot	175.00
16	Cotton Goes Places	175.00
17	Boston Redskins, The Greatest Tackle Picture Ever Photographed (Ace Gutowky, Steve Hokuf)	220.00

1985 Raiders Shell Oil Posters

Measuring 11-5/8" x 18", the five posters were available at participating Southern California Shell gas stations during the 1985 season. Color artwork of Raider players in action are included on the poster fronts. The backs are blank, except for the Pro Bowl poster which has the Raiders and Shell logos and the release schedule of the posters.

		MT
Complete Set (5):		25.00
Common Player:		5.00
1	Pro Bowl (No release date)	6.00
2	Defensive Front (September)	6.00
3	Deep Secondary (October)	5.00
4	Big Offensive Line (November)	5.00
5	Scores (December)	5.00

1985 Raiders Smokey

Measuring 2-5/8" x 4-1/8", the four-card set is anchored by a photo on the front, with the player's name, position and team at the bottom. The Raiders' logo and Kodak logo are printed on the lower left and right, respectively. The card backs have the player's name and his highlights on the left. A fire safety tip and cartoon are included on the right. The cards are numbered on the backs. The sponsors and Kodak logos are printed at the bottom of the card fronts.

		MT
Complete Set (4):		3.00
Common Player:		.35
1	Marcus Allen	1.50
2	Tom Flores (CO)	.50
3	Howie Long	1.25
4	Rod Martin	.35

1987 Raiders Smokey Color-Grams

This 14-page booklet includes 13 player drawings and one of Smokey and Huddles. Featured on a page are a 5-5/8" x 3-11/16" postcard and a perforated card which measures 2-1/2" x 3-11/16". Each booklet measures 8-1/8" x 3-11/16". The postcard fronts have "Arsonbusters" printed at the top, with a Smokey the Bear and two Raiders logos printed at the bottom. The cards, which are unnumbered, are listed by page number.

		MT
Complete Set (14):		25.00
Common Player:		1.25
1	Smokey and Huddles	1.25
2	Matt Millen	1.50
3	Rod Martin	1.50
4	Sean Jones	2.50
5	Dokie Williams	1.25
6	Don Mosebar	1.50
7	Todd Christensen	2.50
8	Bill Pickel	1.25
9	Marcus Allen	8.00
10	Charley Hannah	1.25
11	Howie Long	3.00
12	Vann McElroy	1.50
13	Reggie McKenzie	1.25
14	Mike Haynes	2.00

1988 Raiders Police

Measuring 2-3/4" x 4-1/8", the 12-card set is anchored by a large photo on the front, with "Los Angeles Raiders," Texaco logo and Raiders' logo printed at the top. The player's number, name and position are listed beneath the photo. The card backs, which are numbered, have the player's name, number, position, bio, safety tip and L.A.P.D. shield.

		MT
Complete Set (12):		8.00
Common Player:		.40
1	Vann McElroy	.40
2	Bill Pickel	.40
3	Marcus Allen	2.00
4	Rod Martin	.50
5	Lionel Washington	.50
6	Don Mosebar	.50
7	Reggie McKenzie	.40
8	Todd Christensen	.75
9	Bo Jackson	2.50
10	James Lofton	1.25
11	Howie Long	1.00
12	Mike Shanahan (CO)	.75

1988 Raiders Smokey

Measuring 3" x 5", the 14-card set showcases "Arsonbusters" at the top of the photo. The player's name and position are printed at the bottom of the photo. The Smokey the Bear and Raiders' logos are printed at the bottom of the black-bordered card fronts. The unnumbered card backs have the player's name, position, bio and safety tip cartoon.

		MT
Complete Set (14):		10.00
Common Player:		.75
1	Marcus Allen	4.00
2	Todd Christensen	1.00
3	Bo Jackson	4.00
4	James Lofton	2.00
5	Howie Long	1.50
6	Rod Martin	1.00
7	Vann McElroy	.75
8	Don Mosebar	1.00
9	Bill Pickel	.75
10	Jerry Robinson	.75
11	Mike Shanahan (CO)	1.50
12	Smokey Bear	.75
13	Stacey Toran	.75
14	Greg Townsend	1.00

1989 Raiders Swanson

The three cards were printed on a perforated strip, which also included two Swanson Hungry-Man dinner coupons. The cards measure 2-1/2" x 3-3/4". The card fronts have a black-and-white player photo inside an oval, with "Hungry Man" printed in a stripe in the upper left corner. The player's name is printed at the bottom. The card backs, which are unnumbered, showcase the player's name, bio and highlights. The Swanson Hungry-Man logo is printed at the top of the horizontal card backs.

		MT
Complete Set (3):		8.00
Common Player:		2.50
1	Marcus Allen	5.00
2	Howie Long	3.00
3	Jim Plunkett	2.50

1990 Raiders Smokey

The 16-card set is anchored on the front with a large photo. "Los Angeles Raiders" is printed above the photo, while the player's name and number are printed beneath the photo. The Smokey the Bear logo is in the lower left. The card fronts are bordered in black. The unnumbered card backs have the player's name, position, bio, Raiders' logos and safety tip cartoon.

		MT
Complete Set (16):		10.00
Common Player:		.75
1	Eddie Anderson	1.00
2	Tom Benson	.75
3	Mervyn Fernandez	1.25
4	Bob Golic	1.00
5	Jeff Gossett	.75
6	Rory Graves	.75
7	Jeff Jaeger	.75
8	Howie Long	2.00
9	Don Mosebar	1.00
10	Jay Schroeder	1.25
11	Art Shell (CO)	2.00
12	Greg Townsend	1.25
13	Lionel Washington	1.00
14	Steve Wisniewski	1.25
15	Commitment to Excellence (Helmet and Super Bowl trophies)	.75
16	Denise Franzen (Cheerleader)	.75

A player's name in *italic* type indicates a rookie card.

1990-91 Raiders Main Street Dairy

The six half-pint milk cartons have the Raiders logo, player head shot, his name, position, team and safety tip printed on a panel. The cartons measure 4-1/2" x 6" when they are collapsed. Released in the Los Angeles metro area, the cartons were produced in three colors -- brown (chocolate lowfat), red (vitamin D) and blue (two percent lowfat).

		MT
Complete Set (6):		15.00
Common Player:		2.50
1	Bob Golic (Blue)	3.50
2	Terry McDaniel (Brown)	2.50
3	Don Mosebar (Red)	2.50
4	Jay Schroeder (Blue)	3.50
5	Art Shell (CO) (Red)	5.00
6	Steve Wisniewski (Brown)	2.50

1991 Raiders Police

The 12-card set showcases a color action photo on the front, with the player's name printed in a gray stripe above the photo. The Raiders and sponsor logos are printed at the bottom of the card front. The card backs are numbered, have the player's name, position, bio and safety tip. The sponsors are listed at the bottom, while the card number is printed inside a football in the upper right.

		MT
Complete Set (12):		15.00
Common Player:		1.00
1	Art Shell (CO)	3.00
2	Marcus Allen	3.00
3	Mervyn Fernandez	1.50
4	Willie Gault	1.50
5	Howie Long	2.00
6	Don Mosebar	1.25
7	Winston Moss	1.00
8	Jay Schroeder	1.50
9	Steve Wisniewski	1.25
10	Ethan Horton	1.00
11	Lionel Washington	1.25
12	Greg Townsend	1.50

1991 Raiders Adohr Farms Dairy

These 10 half-pint milk cartons have the Raiders' logo, player head-shot, safety tip, player's name, position and team printed on one of the panels. The cartons measure 4-1/2" x 6" when collapsed. The cartons were printed in two colors -- blue (two percent lowfat) and red (vitamin D). The Greg Townsend carton was the only one to be released in both colors. The cartons are unnumbered.

		MT
Complete Set (10):		25.00
Common Player:		2.50
1	Jeff Gossett (Red)	2.50
2	Ethan Horton (Blue)	2.50
3	Jeff Jaeger (Red)	2.50
4	Ronnie Lott (Blue)	5.00
5	Terry McDaniel (Red)	2.50
6	Don Mosebar (Red)	2.50
7	Jay Schroeder (Red)	3.50
8	Art Shell (CO) (Red)	5.00
9	Greg Townsend (Red or blue)	3.50
10	Steve Wisniewski (Red)	2.50

1993-94 Raiders Adohr Farms Dairy

The six half-pint milk cartons have the Raiders' logo, player head-shot, safety tip, player's name and position printed on one of the panels. The cartons measure 4-1/2" x 6" when collapsed. According to reports, 2 million cartons were sold through Los Angeles area schools and hospitals during a two-week period. The cartons are unnumbered.

		MT
Complete Set (6):		15.00
Common Player:		2.50
1	Jeff Gossett	2.50
2	Ethan Horton	2.50
3	Terry McDaniel	2.50
4	Don Mosebar	2.50
5	Art Shell (CO)	5.00
6	Steve Wisniewski	2.50

1994-95 Raiders Adohr Farms Dairy

The four half-pint milk cartons showcase the Raiders' logo, player headshot, safety tip, player's name and position on one of the carton's panels. The cartons measure 4-1/2" x 6" when collapsed. Five million sets were distributed during a three-week period to hospitals, schools, airlines and the general public. The cartons are not numbered.

		MT
Complete Set (4):		15.00
Common Player:		3.50
1	Jeff Jaeger	3.50
2	Terry McDaniel	3.50
3	Art Shell (CO)	6.00
4	Steve Wisniewski	3.50

1950 Rams Admiral

Measuring 3-1/2" x 5-1/2", the 35-card set features a posed black-and-white photo on the front of the card, with "Your Admiral dealer presents..." and the player's name printed in a black area at the top. Beneath the photo are the card number and player bio. The backs have a Rams schedule on one half, while the other half is blank. Card Nos. 26-35 are blank-backed and are a bit smaller than the other cards in the set.

		NM
Complete Set (35):		110.00
Common Player:		20.00
1	Joe Stydahar (CO)	30.00
2	Hampton Pool (CO)	20.00
3	Fred Naumetz	20.00
4	Jack Finlay	20.00
5	Gil Bouley	20.00
6	Bob Reinhard	20.00
7	Bob Boyd	25.00
8	Bob Waterfield	100.00
9	Mel Hein (CO)	40.00
10	Howard Hickey (CO)	25.00
11	Ralph Pasquariello	20.00
12	Jack Zilly	20.00
13	Tom Kalmanir	20.00
14	Norm Van Brocklin	125.00
15	Woodley Lewis	25.00
16	Glenn Davis	50.00
17	Dick Hoerner	20.00
18	Bob Kelley (ANN)	20.00
19	Paul (Tank) Younger	30.00
20	George Sims	20.00
21	Dick Huffman	20.00
22	Tom Fears	50.00
23	Vitamin Smith	25.00
24	Elroy Hirsch	75.00
25	Don Paul	25.00
26	Bill Lange	20.00
27	Paul Barry	20.00
28	Deacon Dan Towler	30.00
29	Vic Vasicek	20.00
30	Bill Smyth	20.00
31	Larry Brink	20.00
32	Jerry Williams	20.00
33	Stan West	20.00
34	Art Statuto	20.00
35	Ed Champagne	20.00

1953 Rams Black Border

Measuring 4-1/4" x 6-3/8", the 36-card set is anchored by a large photo and bordered in black. A facsimile autograph is printed near the bottom of the photo. The unnumbered card backs have the player's name, bio and highlights. The set was available from the Rams. Some cards from the 1953-55 and 1957 Rams Black Border sets are very similar, with the excepton of different information on the card backs.

		NM
Complete Set (36):		175.00
Common Player:		3.00
1	Ben Agajanian	3.00
2	Bob Boyd (Born in Riverside)	3.00
3	Larry Brink	3.00
4	Rudy Bukich	5.00
5	Tom Dahms (4 text lines)	3.00
6	Dick Daugherty (Regular Ram ...)	3.00
7	Jack Dwyer (Played 1951 ...)	3.00
8	Tom Fears (1952 stats)	10.00
9	Bob Fry (Was sprinter)	3.00
10	Frank Fuller (Attended ...)	3.00
11	Norbert Hecker	3.00
12	Elroy Hirsch (1952 stats)	12.00
13	John Hock (Just completed ...)	3.00
14	Bob Kelley (ANN) (Signature in upper left of photo)	3.00
15	Dick Lane	12.00
16	Woodley Lewis (Ram utility ...)	4.00
17	Tom McCormick (Set three ...)	3.00
18	Lewis Bud McFadin (Came to Rams ...)	3.00
19	Leon McLaughlin (Played every ...)	3.00
20	Brad Myers	3.00
21	Don Paul (A five year ...)	4.00
22	Hampton Pool (CO) (Hampton Pool ...)	3.00
23	Duane Putnam (As rookie ...)	4.00
24	Volney Quinlan (Nickname ...)	4.00
25	Herb Rich	3.00
26	Andy Robustelli (Rams' regular ...)	10.00
27	Vitamin Smith	4.00
28	Harland Svare (Attended ...)	3.00
29	Len Teeuws	3.00
30	Harry Thompson (Used at ...)	3.00
31	Charley Toogood (Been defensive ...)	3.00
32	Deacon Dan Towler (National football)	7.00
33	Norm Van Brocklin (1952 stats)	20.00
34	Stan West (Rams' regular)	3.00
35	Paul (Tank) Younger (1952 stats)	6.00
36	Coaches (John Sauer, William Battles, Howard (Red) Hickey)	4.00

1954 Rams Black Border

Measuring 4-1/4" x 6-3/8", the front is anchored by a large black-and-white photo, bordered in black. A facsimile autograph also appears near the bottom of the photo. The unnumbered backs have the player's name, bio and career highlights. The 36-card set was available from the Rams.

		NM
Complete Set (36):		175.00
Common Player:		3.00
1	Bob Boyd (One of fastest ...)	3.00
2	Bob Carey	3.00
3	Bobby Cross	3.00
4	Tom Dahms (5 text lines)	3.00
5	Don Doll	3.00
6	Jack Dwyer (Regular defensive ...)	3.00
7	Tom Fears (1953 stats)	20.00
8	Bob Griffin (All American ...)	3.00
9	Art Hauser (Was fastest ...)	3.00
10	Hall Haynes	3.00
11	Elroy Hirsch (1953 stats)	12.00
12	Ed Hughes	3.00
13	Bob Kelley (ANN) (Signature across photo)	3.00
14	Woodley Lewis (Established ...)	4.00
15	Gene Lipscomb	10.00
16	Tom McCormick (Rams' regular)	3.00
17	Bud McFadin (Although ...)	3.00
18	Leon McLaughlin (Started every ...)	3.00
19	Paul Miller (Lettered at ...)	3.00
20	Don Paul (One of two ...)	4.00
21	Hampton Pool (CO) (Since taking ...)	3.00
22	Duane Putnam (Offensive guard)	4.00
23	Volney Quinlan (Had best ...)	4.00
24	Les Richter (Rated one ...)	7.00
25	Andy Robustelli (L.A.'s regular ...)	10.00
26	Willard Sherman (Played at ...)	4.00
27	Harland Svare (An outside ...)	3.00
28	Harry Thompson (Played offensive ...)	3.00
29	Charley Toogood	3.00
30	Deacon Dan Towler (Since becoming ...)	7.00
31	Norm Van Brocklin (1953 stats)	20.00
32	Bill Wade (Selected as)	8.00
33	Duane Wardlow	3.00
34	Stan West (Virtually ...)	3.00
35	Paul (Tank) Younger (1953 stats)	7.00
36	Coaches (Bill Battles, Howard Hickey, John Sauer, Dick Voris, Buck Weaver, Hampton Pool)	4.00

1955 Rams Black Border

Measuring 4-1/4" x 6-3/8", the 37-card set is anchored by a large black-and-white photo on the front and bordered in black. A facsimile autograph appears near the bottom of the photo. The backs include the player's name, bio and career highlights. The cards are unnumbered and were available as a set from the Rams.

		NM
Complete Set (37):		175.00
Common Player:		3.00
1	Jack Bighead	3.00
2	Bob Boyd	3.00
3	Don Burroughs	3.00
4	Jim Cason	3.00
5	Bobby Cross	3.00
6	Jack Ellena	3.00
7	Tom Fears	10.00
8	Sid Fournet	3.00
9	Frank Fuller	4.00
10	Sid Gillman (and staff)	7.00
11	Bob Griffin	3.00
12	Art Hauser	3.00
13	Hall Haynes	3.00
14	Elroy Hirsch	12.00
15	John Hock	3.00
16	Glenn Holtzman	3.00
17	Ed Hughes	3.00
18	Woodley Lewis	4.00
19	Gene Lipscomb	10.00
20	Tom McCormick	3.00
21	Bud McFadin	3.00
22	Leon McLaughlin	3.00
23	Paul Miller	3.00
24	Larry Morris	3.00
25	Don Paul	4.00
26	Duane Putnam	4.00
27	Volney Quinlan	4.00
28	Les Richter	7.00
29	Andy Robustelli	10.00
30	Willard Sherman	4.00
31	Corky Taylor	3.00
32	Charley Toogood	3.00
33	Deacon Dan Towler	7.00
34	Norm Van Brocklin	20.00
35	Bill Wade	8.00
36	Ron Waller	3.00
37	Paul (Tank) Younger	7.00

A card number in parentheses ( ) indicates the set is unnumbered.

1956 Rams White Border

Measuring 4-1/4" x 6-3/8", the 37-card set is anchored by a black-and-white photo on the front and bordered in white. A facsimile autograph appears near the bottom of the photo. The unnumbered card backs have the player's name, bio and career highlights. The set was available from the Rams.

		NM
Complete Set (37):		175.00
Common Player:		3.00
1	Bob Boyd	3.00
2	Rudy Bukich	5.00
3	Don Burroughs	3.00
4	Jim Cason	3.00
5	Leon Clarke	4.00
6	Dick Daugherty	3.00
7	Jack Ellena	3.00
8	Tom Fears	10.00
9	Sid Fournet	3.00
10	Bob Fry	3.00
11	Sid Gillman, Joseph Madro, Jack Faulkner, Joe Thomas, Lowell Storm (Coaches)	7.00
12	Bob Griffin	3.00
13	Art Hauser	3.00
14	Elroy Hirsch	12.00
15	John Hock	3.00
16	Bobby Holladay	3.00
17	Glenn Holtzman	3.00
18	Bob Kelley (ANN)	3.00
19	Joe Marconi	4.00
20	Bud McFadin	3.00
21	Paul Miller	3.00
22	Ron Miller	3.00
23	Larry Morris	3.00
24	John Morrow	3.00
25	Brad Myers	3.00
26	Hugh Pitts	3.00
27	Duane Putnam	3.00
28	Les Richter	7.00
29	Willard Sherman	4.00
30	Charley Toogood	3.00
31	Norm Van Brocklin	20.00
32	Bill Wade	7.00
33	Ron Waller	4.00
34	Duane Wardlow	3.00
35	Jesse Whittenton	4.00
36	Tom Wilson	4.00
37	Paul (Tank) Younger	7.00

1957 Rams Black Border

Measuring 4-1/4" x 6-3/8", the 38-card set is anchored by a large photo on the front bordered in black. A facsimile autograph appears near the bottom of the photo. The card backs include the player's name, bio and career highlights. The cards are unnumbered and were sold as a set by the Rams.

		NM
Complete Set (38):		175.00
Common Player:		3.00
1	Jon Arnett	8.00
2	Bob Boyd (Frequently called ...)	4.00
3	Alex Bravo	3.00
4	Bill Brundige (ANN)	3.00
5	Don Burroughs	3.00
6	Jerry Castete	3.00
7	Leon Clarke	4.00
8	Paige Cothren	3.00
9	Dick Daugherty (Has the ...)	3.00
10	Bob Dougherty	3.00
11	Bob Fry (One of the ...)	3.00
12	Frank Fuller (One of the ...)	3.00
13	Coaches (Sid Gillman, Joseph Madro, George Allen, Jack Faulkner, Lowell Storm)	10.00
14	Bob Griffin (After four ...)	3.00
15	Art Hauser (One of the ...)	3.00
16	Elroy Hirsch (A legendary ...)	12.00
17	John Hock (Teamed with ...)	3.00
18	Glenn Holtzman	3.00
19	John Houser	3.00
20	Bob Kelley (ANN) (Signature near right border of photo)	3.00
21	Lamar Lundy	8.00
22	Joe Marconi	3.00
23	Paul Miller (From a ...)	3.00
24	Larry Morris	3.00
25	Ken Panfil	3.00
26	Jack Pardee	12.00
27	Duane Putnam (Named to a ...)	4.00
28	Les Richter (One of the ...)	7.00
29	Willard Sherman (One of the ...)	4.00
30	Del Shofner	8.00
31	Bill Ray Smith	6.00
32	George Strugar	3.00
33	Norm Van Brocklin (When Van Brocklin ...)	25.00
34	Bill Wade (In the first ...)	7.00
35	Ron Waller	3.00
36	Jesse Whittenton	4.00
37	Tom Wilson	4.00
38	Paul (Tank) Younger (One of a ...)	7.00

1959 Rams Bell Brand

The 40-card set is anchored by a color photo on the front, with the player's name, position and team at the bottom. The numbered card backs have the player's name, position, bio

and career highlights, along with an advertisement for Bell Snacks on the left side. The right side has an ad for fans to buy L.A. Rams' Signature Merchandise. The card number is located in the upper left corner. The cards were included in specially marked bags of Bell's potato chips and corn chips.

		NM
	Complete Set (40):	1500.
	Common Player:	30.00
1	Bill Wade	45.00
2	Buddy Humphrey	30.00
3	Frank Ryan	50.00
4	Ed Meador	40.00
5	Tom Wilson	30.00
6	Don Burroughs	30.00
7	Jon Arnett	45.00
8	Del Shofner	45.00
9	Jack Pardee	50.00
10	Ollie Matson	75.00
11	Joe Marconi	30.00
12	Jim Jones	30.00
13	Jack Morris	30.00
14	Willard Sherman	40.00
15	Clendon Thomas	40.00
16	Les Richter	40.00
17	John Morrow	30.00
18	Lou Michaels	40.00
19	Bob Reifsnyder	30.00
20	John Guzik	30.00
21	Duane Putnam	30.00
22	John Houser	30.00
23	Buck Lansford	30.00
24	Gene Selawski	30.00
25	John Baker	30.00
26	Bob Fry	30.00
27	John Lovetere	30.00
28	George Strugar	30.00
29	Roy Wilkins	30.00
30	Charley Bradshaw	30.00
31	Gene Brito	40.00
32	Jim Phillips	40.00
33	Leon Clarke	40.00
34	Lamar Lundy	45.00
35	Sam Williams	30.00
36	Sid Gillman (CO)	60.00
37	Jack Faulkner (CO)	30.00
38	Joseph Madro (CO)	30.00
39	Don Paul (CO)	30.00
40	Lou Rymkus (CO)	40.00

1960 Rams Bell Brand

The 39-card standard sized set features the identical design on the front and back as the 1959 set, except the fronts of the 1960 set has yellow borders (the 1959 set had white borders). Card Nos. 1-18, with the exception of No. 2, are duplicate photos from the 1959 set. These cards were also inserted into specially marked bags of Bell's Snacks. Card No. 2 of Gene Selawski was pulled from the set early in the season because he was waived from the team. However, the card was available from the company.

		NM
	Complete Set (39):	2000.
	Common Player (1-18):	25.00
	Common Player (19-39):	50.00
1	Joe Marconi	25.00
2	Gene Selawski (SP)	1200.
3	Frank Ryan	40.00
4	Ed Meador	30.00
5	Tom Wilson	25.00
6	Gene Brito	30.00
7	Jon Arnett	35.00
8	Buck Lansford	25.00
9	Jack Pardee	45.00
10	Ollie Matson	65.00
11	John Lovetere	25.00
12	Bill Jolko	25.00
13	Jim Phillips	30.00
14	Lamar Lundy	35.00
15	Del Shofner	40.00
16	Les Richter	30.00
17	Bill Wade	35.00
18	Lou Michaels	30.00
19	Dick Bass	60.00
20	Charley Britt	50.00
21	Willard Sherman	60.00
22	George Strugar	50.00
23	Bob Long	50.00
24	Danny Villanueva	60.00
25	Jim Boeke	50.00
26	Clendon Thomas	50.00
27	Art Hunter	50.00
28	Carl Karilivacz	50.00
29	John Baker	50.00
30	Charley Bradshaw	50.00
31	John Guzik	50.00
32	Buddy Humphrey	50.00
33	Carroll Dale	60.00
34	Don Ellensick	50.00
35	Ray Hord	50.00
36	Charles Janerette	50.00
37	John Kenerson	50.00
38	Jerry Stalcup	50.00
39	Bob Waterfield (CO)	125.00

1973 Rams Team Issue

Measuring 7" x 8-3/4", the six sheets are anchored on the front by color photos. Bordered in white, the fronts have the player's name and team listed beneath the photo. The blank-backed cards are unnumbered.

		NM
	Complete Set (6):	32.00
	Common Player:	2.50
1	Jim Bertelsen	2.50
2	John Hadl	7.00
3	Harold Jackson	5.00
4	Merlin Olsen	10.00
5	Isiah Robertson	3.50
6	Jack Snow	3.50

1980 Rams Police

Measuring 2-5/8" x 4-1/8", the 14-card set is anchored by a large photo. The player's name, number, position and team are printed beneath the photo. The Rams' and Kiwanis' logos appear in the lower left and right, respectively, on the card fronts. The backs have Rams' tips inside a box, with the sponsors listed at the bottom. The cards are unnumbered. The cards were handed out by police officers for 14 weeks.

		NM
	Complete Set (14):	20.00
	Common Player:	1.00
11	Pat Haden	3.50
15	Vince Ferragamo	2.50
21	Nolan Cromwell	2.50
26	Wendell Tyler	2.50
32	Cullen Bryant	1.25
53	Jim Youngblood	1.25
59	Bob Brudzinski	1.00
61	Rich Saul	1.00
77	Doug France	1.00
82	Willie Miller	1.00
85	Jack Youngblood	4.00
88	Preston Dennard	1.00
90	Larry Brooks	1.00
xx0	Ray Malavasi (CO)	1.00

1985 Rams Smokey

Measuring 4" x 6", the 24-card set showcases the player's last name at the top of the card, with a photo of the player standing with Smokey the Bear printed in the center of the card front. The Rams' logo, helmet and Smokey the Bear logo are printed beneath the photo on the front. The backs include the card number, player name, position and bio, along with a safety tip cartoon.

		MT
	Complete Set (24):	15.00
	Common Player:	.50
1	George Andrews	.50
2	Bill Bain	.50
3	Russ Bolinger	.50
4	Jim Collins	.50
5	Nolan Cromwell	1.00
6	Reggie Doss	.50
7	Carl Ekern	.50
8	Vince Ferragamo	1.00
9	Gary Green	.50
10	Mike Guman	.50
11	David Hill	.50
12	LeRoy Irvin (SP)	4.00
13	Mark Jerue	.50
14	Johnnie Johnson	.75
15	Jeff Kemp	1.00
16	Mel Owens	.50
17	Irv Pankey	.50
18	Doug Smith	.75
19	Ivory Sully	.50
20	Jack Youngblood	1.50
21	Mike McDonald	.50
22	Norwood Vann	.50
23	Smokey Bear (Unnumbered)	.50
24	Smokey Bear (Reggie Doss, Gary Green, Johnnie Johnson, Carl Ekern) (Unnumbered)	.75

1987 Rams Jello/General Foods

Jello and Bird's Eye sponsored this 10-card set, which features a large photo, with the Rams' helmet in the upper left and the NFL shield in the upper right. The Jello and Bird's Eye logos are in the lower left and right, respectively, with the player's name and position printed in the bottom center of the card front. The card backs have the player's name and number at the top, with his bio inside an oval in the center. His career highlights are listed at the bottom of the card, along with the Jello and Bird's Eye logos. The cards are unnumbered.

		MT
	Complete Set (10):	5.00
	Common Player:	.35
1	Ron Brown	.50
2	Nolan Cromwell	.60
3	Eric Dickerson	2.00
4	Carl Ekern	.35
5	Jim Everett	2.00
6	Dennis Harrah	.35
7	LeRoy Irvin	.50
8	Mike Lansford	.35
9	Jackie Slater	.60
10	Doug Smith	.50

1987 Rams Oscar Mayer

This 19-card set celebrated the Rams Special Teams Player of the Week. The player's photo appears inside a ripped-out hole in the center of the card. The Rams' helmet and Oscar Mayer logo are on the lower left and right, respectively. The player's name and position are listed beneath the photo. The fronts have a baby blue background. The unnumbered card backs have the player's name, bio Rams' helmet and Oscar Mayer logo.

		MT
	Complete Set (19):	14.00
	Common Player:	.75
1	Sam Anno	.75
2	Ron Brown	1.00
3	Nolan Cromwell	1.25
4	Henry Ellard	1.50
5	Jerry Gray	1.00
6	Kevin Greene	3.00
7	Mike Guman	.75
8	Dale Hatcher	.75
9	Clifford Hicks	.75
10	Mark Jerue	.75
11	Johnnie Johnson	1.00
12	Larry Kelm	.75
13	Mike Lansford	.75
14	Vince Newsome	.75
15	Michael Stewart	.75
16	Mickey Sutton	.75
17	Tim Tyrrell	.75
18	Norwood Vann	.75
19	Charles White	1.25

1989 Rams Police

Released as a 16-card perforated sheet, the cards have a photo of the player, with his name and position, along with the Rams' helmet and Frito-Lay logos beneath the helmet. The card backs, numbered "of 16," have the Rams' helmet and Frito-Lay logo in the upper corners, followed by the player's name, position and quote. McGruff the Crime Dog's safety tip is also included on the back. The 7-11 and police badge logos are in the lower corners, with the card number centered at the bottom.

		MT
	Complete Set (16):	10.00
	Common Player:	1.00
1	John Robinson	2.00
2	Jim Everett	2.50
3	Doug Smith	1.25
4	Duval Love	1.00
5	Henry Ellard	2.00
6	Mel Owens	1.00
7	Jerry Gray	1.25
8	Kevin Greene	2.00
9	Vince Newsome	1.00
10	Irv Pankey	1.00
11	Tom Newberry	1.25
12	Pete Holohan	1.00
13	Mike Lansford	1.00
14	Greg Bell	1.25
15	Jackie Slater	1.25
16	Dale Hatcher	1.00

1990 Rams Smokey

Full-bleed photos are on the fronts of this 12-card set, while the backs have a black-and-white photo of the player and his bio. The cards are unnumbered and sponsored by local fire departments. The cards measure 3-3/4" x 5-3/4".

		MT
	Complete Set (12):	8.00
	Common Player:	.75
1	Aaron Cox	.75
2	Henry Ellard	1.25
3	Jim Everett	1.50
4	Jerry Gray	1.00
5	Kevin Greene	1.50
6	Pete Holohan	.75
7	Mike Lansford	.75
8	Vince Newsome	.75
9	Doug Reed	.75
10	Jackie Slater	1.00
11	Fred Strickland	.75
12	Mike Wilcher	.75

1992 Rams Carl's Jr.

The 21-card set is anchored on the front with a photo, with the Rams' helmet in the lower left, player's name, position and number in the lower center and "Drug abuse is life abuse" in the bottom right. The card backs include a photo of the player in the upper left, with his name, position, number and bio printed beneath it. A safety message is printed to the right of the photo, with the card number printed inside a black box in the upper right. The player's stats and highlights are listed on the right side, along with Carl's Jr.'s logo and the other sponsors' logos. Reportedly, 80,000 sets were distributed.

		MT
	Complete Set (21):	10.00
	Common Player:	.60
1	Carl Karcher (Founder)	.60
2	Happy Star (Carl's Jr. symbol)	.75
3	Tony Zendejas	.60
4	Henry Ellard	1.25
5	Jackie Slater	.75
6	Bern Brostek	.60
7	Cleveland Gary	.75
8	Larry Kelm	.60
9	Roman Phifer	.75
10	Jim Everett	1.25
11	Anthony Newman	.60
12	Steve Israel	.60
13	Marc Boutte	.75
14	Darryl Henley	.60
15	Michael Stewart	.60
16	Flipper Anderson	1.25
17	Kevin Greene	1.25
18	Sean Gilbert	1.25
NNOO	Skippy (Be Drug Free)	.75
NNOO	Spike (Be Drug Free)	.75
NNOO	Wise Owl Mike (Be Drug Free)	.75

1994 Rams L.A. Times

Measuring 5-1/2" x 8-1/2", the 32-sheet set was printed by the Los Angeles Times on semi-gloss stock. Showcased on the fronts is a large color photo, with the player's last name printed along the right side. The "Collector Series" logo is located in the upper left, while the L.A. Rams' logo and helmet are printed inside a yellow stripe at the bottom of the card front. The sheets are numbered "of 32" on the fronts. The backs have the player's name in a stripe at the top, with his jersey number, position, bio, headshot, career highlights and 1994 Rams' schedule following underneath. The sheets were included in weekend editions of the L.A. Times.

		MT
	Complete Set (32):	10.00
	Common Player:	.40
1	Toby Wright	.40
2	Tim Lester	.40
3	Shane Conlan	.50
4	Troy Drayton	.50
5	Fred Stokes	.40
6	Jerome Bettis	1.25
7	Jimmie Jones	.40
8	Henry Rolling	.40
9	Anthony Newman	.40
10	Flipper Anderson	.75
11	Steve Israel	.40
12	Johnny Bailey	.40
13	Jackie Slater	.50
14	Chris Chandler	.50
15	Sean Landeta	.40
16	Bern Brostek	.40
17	Roman Phifer	.40
18	Robert Young	.50
19	Leo Goeas	.40
20	Chris Miller	.75
21	Darryl Ashmore	.40
22	Joe Kelly	.40
23	Wayne Gandy	.50
24	Tony Zendejas	.40
25	Tom Newberry	.40
26	David Lang	.40
27	Sean Gilbert	.50
28	Chris Martin	.40
29	Thomas Homco	.40
30	Chuck Knox (CO)	.50
31	Todd Lyght	.50
32	Jerome Bettis, Sean Gilbert	.75

1995 Rams Upper Deck McDonald's

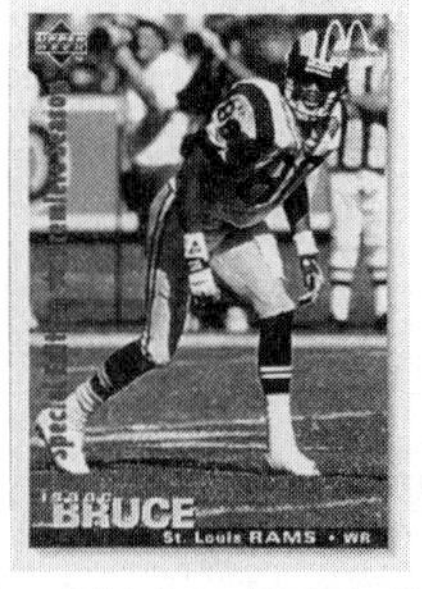

Sold in five-card packs for 79 cents at St. Louis area McDonald's restaurants, the 26-card set featured the Upper Deck logo in the upper left and McDonald's logo in top right. The player's name is in the lower left, with the team name and his position at the bottom right. Printed along the left side of the photo is "Special Edition" and "Premiere Season." The backs, prefixed with "McD," have the player's name, team, position and bio at the top above the photo, while the player's stats are printed beneath the photo. Proceeds from the sales of this set went to the Ronald McDonald Children's Charities.

		MT
	Complete Set (26):	8.00
	Common Player:	.25
1	Johnny Bailey	.25
2	Jerome Bettis	.50
3	Isaac Bruce	2.00
4	Kevin Carter	.50
5	Shane Conlan	.25
6	Troy Drayton	.35
7	Wayne Gandy	.35
8	Sean Gilbert	.35
9	Jessie Hester	.25
10	Bern Brostek	.25
11	Jimmie Jones	.25
12	Todd Kinchen	.35
13	Sean Landeta	.25
14	Thomas Homco	.25
15	Todd Lyght	.25
16	Keith Lyle	.25
17	Chris Miller	.35
18	Toby Wright	.25
19	Anthony Parker	.25
20	Roman Phifer	.25
21	Leonard Russell	.25
22	Jackie Slater	.35
23	Fred Stokes	.25
24	Alexander Wright	.25
25	Robert Young	.35
NNO	Checklist Card	.35

1996 Ravens Score Board/Exxon

Score Board produced this set which was distributed at Baltimore-area Exxon stations. The nine-card set was sold in four-card packs (three players and a checklist) and carried a "BR" prefix.

		MT
	Complete Set (9):	2.50
	Common Player:	.25
1	Vinny Testaverde	.40
2	Eric Zeier	.40
3	Earnest Byner	.25
4	Derrick Alexander	.75
5	Michael Jackson	.40
6	Jonathan Ogden	.25
7	Ray Lewis	.25
8	Eric Turner	.25
9	Ravens Checklist	.25

1939 Redskins Matchbooks

Measuring 1-1/2" x 4-1/2" when folded out, the 20 matchbooks have a black-and-white headshot of the player at the top, with his facsimile autograph, position, college and bio listed underneath. The back side says, "This is one of 20 autographed pictures of the Washington Redskins. Compliments of The Ross Jewelry Co." The inside of the matchbook has the official 1939 Redskins schedule. The matchbooks are unnumbered.

		NM
	Complete Set (20):	525.00
	Common Matchbook:	10.00
1	Jim Barber (SP)	125.00
2	Sammy Baugh	65.00
3	Hal Bradley	10.00
4	Vic Carroll	10.00
5	Bud Erickson	10.00
6	Andy Farkas	12.00
7	Frank Filchock	12.00
8	Ray Flaherty (CO)	18.00
9	Don Irwin	10.00
10	Ed Justice	10.00
11	Jim Karcher	10.00
12	Max Krause	10.00
13	Charley Malone	10.00
14	Bob Masterson	10.00
15	Wayne Millner	20.00
16	Mickey Parks	10.00
17	Ernie Pinckert	12.00
18	Steve Slivinski (SP)	125.00
19	Clem Stralka	10.00
20	Jay Turner	10.00

1940 Redskins Matchbooks

This 20-matchbook set is very similar in design to the 1939 set. The 1940 set has a headshot of the player, a facsimile autograph, his position, college and bio showcased on the front. The backside of the matchbook states, "This is one of 20 autographed pictures of the Washington Redskins. Compliments of Ross Jewelry Co." The inside of the matchbooks have the official 1940 Redskins' schedule. Prices listed here are for matchbooks missing the matches, but with the strikers intact.

		NM
	Complete Set (20):	225.00
	Common Player:	10.00
1	Jim Barber	10.00
2	Sammy Baugh	45.00
3	Vic Carroll	10.00
4	Glen Edwards	25.00
5	Andy Farkas	12.00
6	Dick Farman	10.00
7	Bob Hoffman	10.00
8	Don Irwin	10.00
9	Charley Malone	10.00
10	Bob Masterson	10.00
11	Wayne Millner	20.00
12	Mickey Parks	10.00
13	Ernie Pinckert	12.00
14	Bo Russell	10.00
15	Clyde Shugart	10.00
16	Steve Slivinski	10.00
17	Clem Stralka	10.00
18	Dick Todd	12.00
19	Bill Young	10.00
20	Roy Zimmerman	10.00

1941 Redskins Matchbooks

Measuring 1-1/2" x 4-1/2" when folded out, the 20 matchbooks have a headshot of the player at the top of the front, with his facsimile autograph, position, college and bio listed beneath. The backside of the cover states, "This is one of 20 autographed pictures of the Washington Redskins. Compliments of Home Laundry." The phone number Atlantic 2400 is also included. The inside features the 1941 official Redskins' schedule.

		NM
	Complete Set (20):	195.00
	Common Player:	8.00
1	Ki Aldrich	10.00
2	Jim Barber	8.00
3	Sammy Baugh	40.00
4	Vic Carroll	8.00
5	Fred Davis	8.00
6	Andy Farkas	10.00
7	Dick Farman	8.00
8	Frank Filchock	10.00
9	Ray Flaherty (CO)	12.00
10	Bob Masterson	8.00
11	Bob McChesney	8.00
12	Wayne Millner	15.00
13	Wilbur Moore	10.00
14	Bob Seymour	8.00
15	Clyde Shugart	8.00
16	Clem Stralka	8.00
17	Robert Titchenal	8.00
18	Dick Todd	10.00
19	Bill Young	8.00
20	Roy Zimmerman	8.00

1942 Redskins Matchbooks

Measuring 1-1/2" x 4-1/2" when folded out, the 20 matchbooks follow the same design as the previous sets. A player headshot is showcased on the front, with his facsimile signature, position, college and bio printed beneath. The back of the cover states, "This is one of 20 autographed pictures of the Washington Redskins. Compliments of Home Laundry Atlantic 2400." The inside of the covers have the official 1942 Redskins' schedule, plus an ad for Home Laundry.

		NM
	Complete Set (20):	195.00
	Common Player:	8.00
1	Ki Aldrich	10.00
2	Sammy Baugh	45.00
3	Joe Beinor	8.00
4	Vic Carroll	8.00
5	Ed Cifers	8.00
6	Fred Davis	8.00
7	Glen Edwards	16.00
8	Andy Farkas	10.00
9	Dick Farman	8.00
10	Ray Flaherty (CO)	12.00
11	Al Krueger	8.00
12	Bob Masterson	8.00
13	Bob McChesney	8.00
14	Wilbur Moore	10.00
15	Bob Seymour	8.00
16	Clyde Shugart	8.00
17	Clem Stralka	8.00
18	Dick Todd	10.00
19	Willie Wilkin	8.00
20	Bill Young	8.00

1951-52 Redskins Matchbooks

Measuring 1-1/2" x 4-1/2" when folded out, the 20 matchbooks have the player headshot on the front, followed by a facsimile signature, position, college and bio. The backs state, "This is one of 20 autographed pictures of the Washington Redskins. Compliments of Jack Blank, President, Arcade Pontiac Co. ADams 8500." The outside of the matchbooks have the Redskins' logo on black and gold. An advertisement for Arcade Pontiac is printed on the back, also in color. The matchbooks are unnumbered.

		NM
	Complete Set (25):	225.00
	Common Player:	8.00
1	John Badaczewski	8.00
2A	Head Coach (Herman Ball) (CO)	8.00
2B	Assistant Coach (Herman Ball) (CO)	8.00
3	Sammy Baugh	40.00
4	Ed Berrang (1951)	10.00
5	Dan Brown (1951)	10.00
6	Al DeMao	8.00
7	Harry Dowda (1952)	10.00
8	Chuck Drazenovich	8.00
9	Bill Dudley (1951)	15.00
10	Harry Gilmer	12.00
11	Robert Goode (1951)	10.00
12	Leon Heath (1952)	10.00
13	Charlie Justice (1952)	15.00
14	Lou Karras	8.00
15	Eddie LeBaron (1952)	12.00
16	Paul Lipscomb	8.00
17	Laurie Niemi	8.00
18	John Papit (1952)	10.00
19	James Peebles (1951)	10.00
20	Ed Quirk	8.00
21	Jim Ricca (1952)	10.00
22	James Staton (1951)	10.00
23	Hugh Taylor	10.00
24	Joe Tereshinski	8.00
25	Dick Todd (CO) (1952)	10.00

1958-59 Redskins Matchbooks

Measuring 1-1/2" x 4-1/2" when folded out, the 20 matchbooks went with a totally different design than in years past. This set features a cutout of a player headshot printed below the Redskins' logo and "Famous Redskins." The years he played with the Redskins are listed to the left of the headshot. The back of the cover has an ad for First Federal Savings. The inside includes the player's name and bio, along with an ad for First Federal Savings. The matchbooks, which are unnumbered, are printed on gray cardboard.

		NM
	Complete Set (20):	195.00
	Common Player:	8.00
1	Steve Bagarus (58)	8.00
2	Cliff Battles (58)	15.00
3	Sammy Baugh (58)	40.00
4	Gene Brito (58)	10.00
5	Jim Castiglia (58)	8.00
6	Al DeMao (58)	8.00
7	Chuck Drazenovich (59)	10.00
8	Bill Dudley (59)	18.00
9	Al Fiorentino (59)	8.00
10	Don Irwin (59)	8.00
11	Eddie LeBaron (58)	10.00
12	Wayne Millner (58)	12.00
13	Wilbur Moore (58)	10.00
14	Jim Schrader (59)	8.00
15	Riley Smith (59)	8.00
16	Mike Sommer (59)	8.00
17	Joe Tereshinski (58)	8.00
18	Dick Todd (59)	10.00
19	Willie Wilkin (59)	8.00
20	Casimir Witucki	8.00

1960-61 Redskins Matchbooks

Measuring 1-1/2" x 4-1/2" when folded out, the 20 matchbooks are

very similar in design to the 1958-59 set except this 1960-61 set is printed on off-white cardboard. The front has a headshot of the player, along with the Redskins' logo and "Famous Redskins." The player's bio is printed on the back, along with "This is one of twenty famous Redskins presented for you by your 1st Federal Savings and Loan Association of Washington, Bethesda Branch." The matchbooks are not numbered.

		NM
Complete Set (20):		175.00
Common Player:		8.00
1	Bill Anderson (61)	10.00
2	Don Bosseler (60)	10.00
3	Glen Edwards (60)	15.00
4	Ralph Guglielmi (61)	10.00
5	Bill Hartman (60)	8.00
6	Norbert Hecker (61)	8.00
7	Dick James (61)	10.00
8	Charlie Justice (60)	15.00
9	Ray Krause (61)	8.00
10	Ray Lemek (61)	8.00
11	Tommy Mont (60)	8.00
12	John Olszewski (61)	10.00
13	John Paluck (61)	8.00
14	Jim Peebles (60)	8.00
15	Bo Russell (60)	8.00
16	Jim Schrader (61)	8.00
17	Louis Stephens (61)	8.00
18	Ed Sutton (60)	8.00
19	Bob Toneff (60)	10.00
20	Lavern Torgeson (60)	10.00

1960 Redskins Jay Publishing

Measuring 5" x 7", the 12-card set is anchored by a black-and-white posed photo on the front. The cards are unnumbered and blank-backed. Originally, the cards were sold for 25 cents in 12-photo packs.

		NM
Complete Set (12):		50.00
Common Player:		5.00
1	Sam Baker	6.00
2	Don Bosseler	6.00
3	Gene Brito	5.00
4	Johnny Carson	5.00
5	Chuck Drazenovich	5.00
6	Ralph Guglielmi	6.00
7	Dick James	5.00
8	Eddie LeBaron	7.50
9	Jim Podoley	5.00
10	Jim Schrader	5.00
11	Ed Sutton	5.00
12	Albert Zagers	5.00

1969 Redskins High's Dairy

Measuring 8" x 10", the eight-card set includes Alex Fournier artwork on the front. The player's facsimile signature is printed near the bottom of the artwork. On the left side of the unnumbered card backs is the player's name, bio and stats, while on the right side is data on Fournier. The portraits were available two ways - they could be purchased at High's Dairy Stores or consumers could purchase two half gallons of milk and recieve a free portrait.

		NM
Complete Set (8):		100.00
Common Player:		6.00
1	Chris Hanburger	10.00
2	Len Hauss	8.00
3	Sam Huff	15.00
4	Sonny Jurgensen	25.00
5	Carl Kammerer	6.00
6	Brig Owens	6.00
7	Pat Richter	8.00
8	Charley Taylor	20.00

1972 Redskins Caricature

Dick Shuman and Compu-Set, Inc. produced this 15-card set. The 8" x 10" cards feature a caricature of a Washington Redskin player. The cards are unnumbered and blank-backed.

		NM
Complete Set (16):		130.00
Common Player:		8.00
1	Mike Bass	10.00
2	Verlon Biggs	8.00
3	Mike Bragg	8.00
4	Speedy Duncan	10.00
5	Pat Fischer	10.00
6	Chris Hanburger	10.00
7	Curt Knight	8.00
8	Ron McDole	8.00
9	Brig Owens	8.00
10	Jack Pardee	10.00
11	Richie Petibon	10.00
12	Myron Pottios	8.00
13	Manny Sistrunk	8.00
14	Diron Talbert	8.00
15	Ted Vactor	8.00
16	Cover Card (Jack Pardee, Mike Bass, Manny Sistrunk, Chris Hanburger)	10.00

1981 Redskins Frito-Lay Schedules

Measuring 3-1/2" x 7-1/2", the 30 schedules are anchored by a color photo on the inside. Included on the collectibles are the 1981 Redskins' schedule, player photo and his name and bio, along with sponsor logos. The schedules are unnumbered.

		MT
Complete Set (30):		30.00
Common Player:		.50
1	Coy Bacon	.75
2	Perry Brooks	.50
3	Dave Butz	.75
4	Rickey Claitt	.50
5	Monte Coleman	.75
6	Mike Connell	.50
7	Brad Dusek	.75
8	Ike Forte	.50
9	Clarence Harmon	.50
10	Terry Hermeling	.50
11	Wilbur Jackson	.50
12	Mike Kruczek	.50
13	Bob Kuziel	.50
14	Joe Lavender	.75
15	Karl Lorch	.50
16	LeCharls McDaniel	.50
17	Rich Milot	.50
18	Art Monk	3.00
19	Mark Moseley	1.00
20	Mark Murphy	.75
21	Mike Nelms	.50
22	Neal Olkewicz	.50
23	Lemar Parrish	.75
24	Tony Peters	.50
25	Ron Saul	.50
26	George Starke	.50
27	Joe Theismann	2.00
28	Ricky Thompson	.50
29	Don Warren	.75
30	Jeris White	.50

1982 Redskins Frito-Lay Schedules

Measuring 3-1/2" x 7-1/2", the 15 schedule set boasts a color photo of the player on the inside, with "Redskins' '82 Schedule" printed on another panel. The player's name and bio are also included on the schedules.

		MT
Complete Set (15):		15.00
Common Player:		.50
1	Dave Butz	.75
2	Monte Coleman	.75
3	Brad Dusek	.50
4	Joe Lavender	.75
5	Art Monk	2.00
6	Mark Moseley	1.00
7	Mark Murphy	.75
8	Mike Nelms	.50
9	Neal Olkewicz	.50
10	Tony Peters	.50
11	John Riggins	3.00
12	George Starke	.50
13	Joe Theismann	2.00
14	Don Warren	.75
15	Joe Washington	1.00

1982 Redskins Police

Measuring 2-5/8" x 4-1/8", the 15-card set includes a photo of the player on the front, with the Redskins' helmet on the lower left. On the bottom right are the player's number, name, position and team. The backs have a boxed-in "Redskins/PACT Tips." The Frito-Lay and PACT logos appear at the bottom corners. The cards are numbered.

		MT
Complete Set (15):		10.00
Common Player:		.50
1	Dave Butz	.75
2	Art Monk	2.50
3	Mark Murphy	.50
4	Monte Coleman	.75
5	Mark Moseley	.75
6	George Starke	.50
7	Perry Brooks	.50
8	Joe Washington	.75
9	Don Warren	.75
10	Joe Lavender	.50
11	Joe Theismann	2.00
12	Tony Peters	.50
13	Neal Olkewicz	.50
14	Mike Nelms	.50
15	John Riggins	2.00

1983 Redskins Frito-Lay Schedules

Measuring 2-1/2" x 3-1/2", the 15-schedule set showcases an action photo, along with the player's name and bio. The schedules are unnumbered.

		MT
Complete Set (15):		15.00
Common Player:		.50
1	Charlie Brown	.75
2	Dave Butz	.75
3	The Hogs	.75
4	Dexter Manley	.75
5	Rich Milot	.50
6	Art Monk	1.50
7	Mark Moseley	.75
8	Mark Murphy	.50
9	Mike Nelms	.50
10	Neal Olkewicz	.50
11	Tony Peters	.50
12	John Riggins	2.00
13	Joe Theismann	2.00
14	Joe Washington	.75
15	Jeris White	.50

1983 Redskins Police

Measuring 2-5/8" x 4-1/8", the 16-card set was handed out one per week by police officers. The card fronts are anchored by a large photo, with the player's number, position, name and bio beneath it. The Redskins' helmet is in the lower left corner, with "Washington Redskins, Super Bowl XVII Champions" printed at the bottom right. The backs, numbered "of 16," have a boxed-in "Redskins PACT Tips" and the player's bio and highlights. The Frito-Lay and PACT logos are printed in the lower left and right corners, respectively. Jeris White's card is tough to locate, as his card was never handed out because he held out during the season.

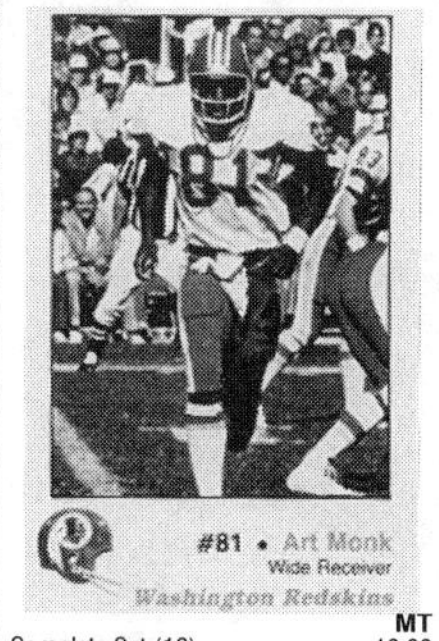

		MT
Complete Set (16):		10.00
Common Player:		.50
1	Joe Washington	1.00
2	The Hogs (Offensive Line)	.75
3	Mark Moseley	1.00
4	Monte Coleman	.50
5	Mike Nelms	.50
6	Neal Olkewicz	.50
7	Joe Theismann	3.00
8	Charlie Brown	.75
9	Dave Butz	.75
10	Jeris White (SP)	1.50
11	Mark Murphy	.50
12	Dexter Manley	.75
13	Art Monk	3.00
14	Rich Milot	.50
15	Vernon Dean	.50
16	John Riggins	2.00

1984 Redskins Frito-Lay Schedules

Measuring 3-1/2" x 7-1/2", the 15 schedules boast a color photo of the player, along with his name and bio. The schedules are unnumbered.

		MT
Complete Set (15):		15.00
Common Player:		.50
1	Charlie Brown	.75
2	Dave Butz	.75
3	Ken Coffey	.50
4	Clint Didier	.50
5	Darryl Grant	.50
6	Darrell Green	1.00
7	Jeff Hayes	.50
8	The Hogs	.75
9	Rich Milot	.50
10	Art Monk	1.50
11	Mark Murphy	.50
12	John Riggins	1.50
13	Joe Theismann	1.50
14	Don Warren	.75
15	Joe Washington	.75

1984 Redskins Police

Measuring 2-5/8" x 4-1/8", the 16-card set showcases a color photo on the front, with the player's name, number and position printed beneath the photo. The player's facsimile signature and "NFC Champion Redskins" is printed in the lower right. The Redskins' helmet is located in the lower left. The card backs, numbered "of 16," have the "Redskins/PACT Tip" at the top, while the player's name, bio and highlights are printed below. The Frito-Lay and PACT logos are printed in the lower left and right, respectively.

		MT
Complete Set (16):		8.00
Common Player:		.35
1	John Riggins	1.25
2	Darryl Grant	.35
3	Art Monk	1.50
4	Neal Olkewicz	.35
5	The Hogs	.50
6	Jeff Hayes	.35
7	Joe Theismann	1.25
8	Clint Didier	.35
9	Mark Murphy	.35
10	Don Warren	.50
11	Darrell Green	1.00
12	Dave Butz	.50
13	Ken Coffey	.35
14	Rich Milot	.35
15	Charlie Brown	.50
16	Joe Washington	.50

1985 Redskins Frito-Lay Schedules

Measuring 3-1/2" x 7-1/2", the 16 schedules showcase a photo of a legendary Washington Redskins' player. The schedules are unnumbered.

		MT
Complete Set (16):		15.00
Common Player:		.50
1	Cliff Battles	.75
2	Sammy Baugh	1.50
3	Larry Brown	.75
4	Bill Dudley	.75
5	Turk Edwards	.75
6	Pat Fischer	.50
7	Chris Hanburger	.50
8	Len Hauss	.50
9	Ken Houston	.75
10	Sam Huff	1.00
11	Sonny Jurgenson	1.00
12	Billy Kilmer	.50
13	Wayne Millner	.50
14	Bobby Mitchell	.75
15	Brig Owens	.50
16	Charley Taylor	1.00

1985 Redskins Police

Measuring 2-5/8" x 4-1/8", the 16-card set has the Washington Redskins' logo at the top of the card front, with the player photo in the center. Beneath the photo are the player's number, position and name. The backs, numbered "of 16," have "Redskins/PACT Tips" at the top. Printed in the center of the back are the player's name, number, position, bio and career highlights. The Frito-Lay and PACT logos are located in the lower left and right, respectively.

		MT
Complete Set (16):		5.00
Common Player:		.35
1	Darrell Green	.75
2	Clint Didier	.35
3	Neal Olkewicz	.35
4	Darryl Grant	.35
5	Joe Jacoby	.50
6	Vernon Dean	.35
7	Joe Theismann	1.00
8	Mel Kaufman	.35
9	Calvin Muhammad	.35
10	Dexter Manley	.50
11	John Riggins	1.00
12	Mark May	.50
13	Dave Butz	.35
14	Art Monk	1.25
15	Russ Grimm	.50
16	Charles Mann	.50

1986 Redskins Frito-Lay Schedules

These 16 schedules feature the Redskins' 50th Anniversary logo on the front and Frito-Lay's logos on the back. When opened, the left panel contains the preseason and postseason schedules, the center panel has a player photo and the right panel features the regular season schedule. The other panel has basic player information. The schedules are unnumbered.

		MT
Complete Set (16):		20.00
Common Player:		1.00
1	Cliff Battles	1.50
2	Sammy Baugh	2.00
3	Larry Brown	1.00
4	Bill Dudley	1.50
5	Turk Edwards	1.00
6	Pat Fischer	1.00
7	Chris Hanburger	1.00
8	Len Hauss	1.00
9	Sam Huff	2.00
10	Ken Houston	1.50
11	Sonny Jurgensen	2.00
12	Billy Kilmer	1.50
13	Wayne Millner	1.50
14	Bobby Mitchell	2.00
15	Brig Owens	1.00
16	Charley Taylor	2.00

1986 Redskins Police

Measuring 2-5/8" x 4-1/8", the 16-card set has a Washington Redskins' pennant in the upper left corner of the front. Inside the pennant is a facsimile signature of the player. His number, name and position is printed to the right of the pennant. The photo fills up the bottom portion of the card front. The backs, numbered "of 16," have the player's name inside a pennant at the top, with his number, position, bio and career highlights printed beneath it. Quick quiz and crime prevention tips are also included on the back. The Frito-Lay, PACT and WMAL radio logos are printed at the bottom.

		MT
Complete Set (16):		5.00
Common Player:		.35
1	Darrell Green	.75
2	Joe Jacoby	.50
3	Charles Mann	.50
4	Jay Schroeder	.50
5	Raphel Cherry	.35
6	Russ Grimm	.50
7	Mel Kaufman	.35
8	Gary Clark	1.25
9	Vernon Dean	.35
10	Mark May	.50
11	Dave Butz	.50
12	Jeff Bostic	.50
13	Dean Hamel	.35
14	Dexter Manley	.50
15	George Rogers	.50
16	Art Monk	1.00

1987 Redskins Frito-Lay Schedules

Measuring 3-1/2" x 7-1/2", the 16 schedule set includes an action photo of the player. The schedules are unnumbered.

		MT
Complete Set (16):		15.00
Common Player:		.50
1	Jeff Bostic	.75
2	Kelvin Bryant	.75
3	Dave Butz	.75
4	Gary Clark	1.00
5	Steve Cox	.50
6	Clint Didier	.50
7	Darryl Grant	.50
8	Darrell Green	.75
9	Joe Jacoby	.75
10	Dexter Manley	.75
11	Charles Mann	.75
12	Mark May	.75
13	Art Monk	1.00
14	Jay Schroeder	.75
15	Alvin Walton	.50
16	Don Warren	.75

1987 Redskins Police

Measuring 2-5/8" x 4-1/8", the 16-card set has the Washington Redskins' logo at the top, with the player photo anchoring the middle. The player's name is printed at the bottom of the card front. The backs, numbered "Week X of 16," have the player's number inside a football in the upper left. The player's name, position, bio and career highlights are also listed on the back. "Did you know?" and a tip from McGruff the Crime Dog round out the back, along with Frito-Lay and PACT logos at the bottom right.

		MT
Complete Set (16):		5.00
Common Player:		.30
1	Joe Jacoby	.40
2	Gary Clark	.75
3	Dexter Manley	.40
4	Darrell Green	.40
5	Alvin Walton	.30
6	Clint Didier	.30
7	Art Monk	1.00
8	Darryl Grant	.30
9	Kelvin Bryant	.40
10	Jay Schroeder	.40
11	Don Warren	.40
12	Steve Cox	.30
13	Mark May	.40
14	Jeff Bostic	.40
15	Charles Mann	.40
16	Dave Butz	.40

1988 Redskins Frito-Lay Schedules

Measuring 3-1/2" x 7-1/2", the 16 schedules boast an action photo of a player, with his name and bio. A photo of the Super Bowl trophy is showcased on these schedules, which are unnumbered.

		MT
Complete Set (16):		15.00
Common Player:		.50
1	Jeff Bostic	.75
2	Dave Butz	.75
3	Gary Clark	1.00
4	Brian Davis	.50
5	Joe Jacoby	.75
6	Markus Koch	.50
7	Charles Mann	.75
8	Wilbur Marshall	.75
9	Mark May	.75
10	Raleigh McKenzie	.50
11	Art Monk	1.00
12	Ricky Sanders	.75
13	Alvin Walton	.50
14	Don Warren	.75
15	Barry Wilburn	.50
16	Doug Williams	1.00

1988 Redskins Police

Measuring 2-5/8" x 4-1/8", the 16-card set has the Washington Redskins' logo (with the Vince Lombardi Super Bowl Trophy printed where the "i" in Redskins would appear) located in the upper left. The player's number and name are printed in the upper right. A color photo covers the remaining portion of the card front. The backs, numbered with a "Week X," have the player's name and number at the top, followed by his bio, career highlights and a safety tip. The logos printed at the bottom from left to right are Mobil, PACT and Jello.

		MT
Complete Set (16):		5.00
Common Player:		.30
1	Jeff Bostic	.40
2	Dave Butz	.40
3	Gary Clark	.75
4	Brian Davis	.30
5	Joe Jacoby	.40
6	Markus Koch	.30
7	Charles Mann	.40
8	Wilber Marshall	.40
9	Mark May	.40
10	Raleigh McKenzie	.30
11	Art Monk	1.00
12	Ricky Sanders	.75
13	Alvin Walton	.30
14	Don Warren	.40
15	Barry Wilburn	.30
16	Doug Williams	.75

1989 Redskins Mobil Schedules

Measuring 3-1/2" x 7-1/2", the 16 schedules showcase a color player photo, along with the 1989 schedule. These schedules are unnumbered.

		MT
Complete Set (16):		10.00
Common Player:		.40
1	Ravin Caldwell	.40
2	Gary Clark	1.00
3	Monte Coleman	.60
4	Brian Davis	.40
5	Joe Jacoby	.60
6	Jim Lachey	.60
7	Chip Lohmiller	.60
8	Charles Mann	.60
9	Wilbur Marshall	.60
10	Mark May	.60
11	Raleigh McKenzie	.40
12	Art Monk	1.00
13	Mark Rypien	.60
14	Ricky Sanders	.60
15	Don Warren	.60
16	Doug Williams	.75

1989 Redskins Police

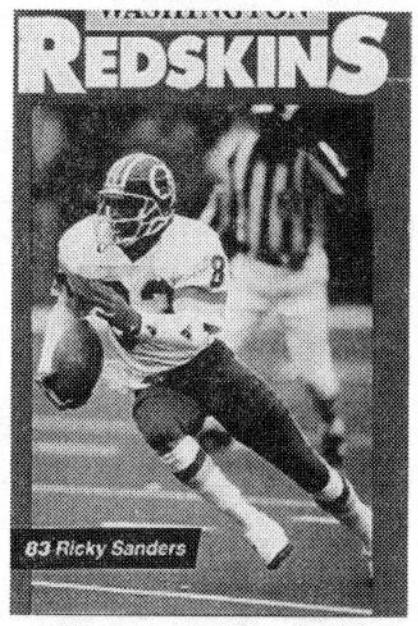

Measuring 2-5/8" x 4-1/8", the 16-card set has "Washington" in a stripe at the top of the card front, with "Redskins" printed beneath it. The player photo has the player's name and number inside a stripe near the bottom. The unnumbered card backs have the player's number and name at the top, along with his bio, career highlights, safety tip and "Did you know?" The Mobil, PACT and Fox-TV 5 logos are printed at the bottom of the card backs.

		MT
Complete Set (16):		5.00
Common Player:		.30
11	Mark Rypien	.60
17	Doug Williams	.60
21	Earnest Byner	.40
22	Jamie Morris	.30
28	Darrell Green	.40
34	Brian Davis	.30
37	Gerald Riggs	.40
50	Ravin Caldwell	.30
52	Neal Olkewicz	.30
58	Wilber Marshall	.40
73	Mark May	.40
74	Markus Koch	.30
81	Art Monk	1.00
83	Ricky Sanders	.60
84	Gary Clark	.75
85	Don Warren	.40

1990 Redskins Mobil Schedules

Measuring 3-1/2" x 7-1/2", the 16 pocket schedules boast a color action photo of the player. The schedules are unnumbered.

		MT
Complete Set (16):		10.00
Common Player:		.40
1	Jeff Bostic	.60
2	Earnest Byner	.60
3	Gary Clark	.75
4	Darryl Grant	.40
5	Darrell Green	.60
6	Jim Lachey	.60
7	Chip Lohmiller	.60
8	Charles Mann	.60
9	Wilbur Marshall	.60
10	Ralf Mojsiejenko	.40
11	Art Monk	1.00
12	Gerald Riggs	.60
13	Mark Rypien	.60
14	Ricky Sanders	.60
15	Alvin Walton	.40
16	Don Warren	.60

1990 Redskins Police

Measuring 3-1/2" x 7-1/2", the 16-card set includes a Washington Redskins' logo at the top, with the player's name and number at the bottom of the card front. The unnumbered card backs have the player's name, number, bio, career highlights, safety tip and "Did you know?" Printed at the bottom of the card backs are the Mobil, PACT and Fox-TV 5 logos.

		MT
Complete Set (16):		5.00
Common Player:		.25
1	Todd Bowles	.25
2	Earnest Byner	.35
3	Ravin Caldwell	.25
4	Gary Clark	.60
5	Darrell Green	.35
6	Jimmie Johnson	.25
7	Jim Lachey	.35
8	Chip Lohmiller	.35
9	Charles Mann	.35
10	Greg Manusky	.25
11	Wilber Marshall	.35
12	Art Monk	.75
13	Gerald Riggs	.35
14	Mark Rypien	.35
15	Alvin Walton	.25
16	Don Warren	.35

1991 Redskins Mobil Schedules

Measuring 2-1/2" x 3-1/2", the 16 pocket schedules boast a photo of

the player on the front. The player's name and bio also are printed on the unnumbered schedule.

		MT
	Complete Set (16):	10.00
	Common Player:	.40
1	Earnest Byner	.60
2	Gary Clark	.75
3	Andre Collins	.60
4	Kurt Gouveia	.40
5	Darrell Green	.60
6	Jimmie Johnson	.40
7	Markus Koch	.40
8	Jim Lachey	.60
9	Chip Lohmiller	.40
10	Charles Mann	.60
11	Martin Mayhew	.40
12	Art Monk	1.00
13	Mark Rypien	.60
14	Mark Schlereth	.40
15	Ed Simmons	.40
16	Eric Williams	.40

1991 Redskins Police

Measuring 2-5/8" x 4-1/8", the 16-card set has "Washington" printed inside a gold stripe at the top, while "Redskins" is printed vertically along the left side. The player photo is to the right of "Redskins." The player's number is printed inside a circle at the bottom, with his name inside a black stripe at the bottom. The backs have the player's name, number, bio, career highlights, safety tip and "Did you know?" The logos printed on the bottom, from left to right, are Mobil, PACT and Fox-TV 5. The cards are unnumbered.

		MT
	Complete Set (16):	5.00
	Common Player:	.25
1	John Brandes	.25
2	Earnest Byner	.35
3	Gary Clark	.60
4	Andre Collins	.35
5	Darrell Green	.35
6	Joey Howard	.25
7	Tim Johnson	.25
8	Jim Lachey	.35
9	Chip Lohmiller	.25
10	Charles Mann	.35
11	Art Monk	.75
12	Mark Rypien	.35
13	Mark Schlereth	.25
14	Fred Stokes	.25
15	Don Warren	.35
16	Eric Williams	.25

1992 Redskins Mobil Schedules

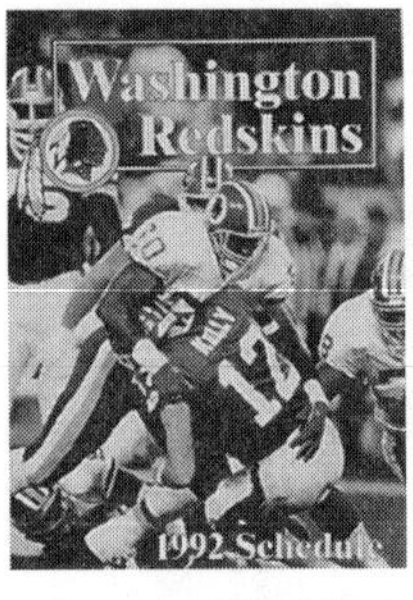

Measuring 2-1/2" x 3-1/2", the 16 pocket schedules have a color action photo of the player, along with his name and bio. The schedules are unnumbered.

		MT
	Complete Set (16):	10.00
	Common Player:	.40
1	Gary Clark	.75
2	Brad Edwards	.60
3	Ricky Ervins	.75
4	Jumpy Geathers	.40
5	Darrell Green	.60
6	Joe Jacoby	.60
7	Tim Johnson	.40
8	Charles Mann	.60
9	Wilber Marshall	.60
10	Ron Middleton	.40
11	Brian Mitchell	.75
12	Art Monk	1.00
13	Jim Lachey	.60
14	Chip Lohmiller	.40
15	Mark Rypien	.60
16	Fred Stokes	.40

1992 Redskins Police

Measuring 2-1/2" x 4-1/8", the 16-card set has "Washington Redskins" printed in the upper right, with the Vince Lombardi Trophy in the upper left of the photo. The player's number is printed inside a circle on the lower left of the photo, while the player's name is printed inside the border at the bottom of the card front. The card backs, which are unnumbered, have the player's number, name, bio, career highlights and tip. The sponsor logos, from left to right, are Mobil, PACT and Fox-TV 5.

		MT
	Complete Set (16):	5.00
	Common Player:	.30
1	Jeff Bostic	.40
2	Earnest Byner	.40
3	Gary Clark	.60
4	Monte Coleman	.40
5	Andre Collins	.40
6	Danny Copeland	.30
7	Kurt Gouveia	.30
8	Darrell Green	.40
9	Jim Lachey	.40
10	Charles Mann	.40
11	Wilber Marshall	.40
12	Raleigh McKenzie	.30
13	Art Monk	1.00
14	Mark Rypien	.40
15	Mark Schlereth	.30
16	Eric Williams	.30

1993 Redskins Mobil Schedules

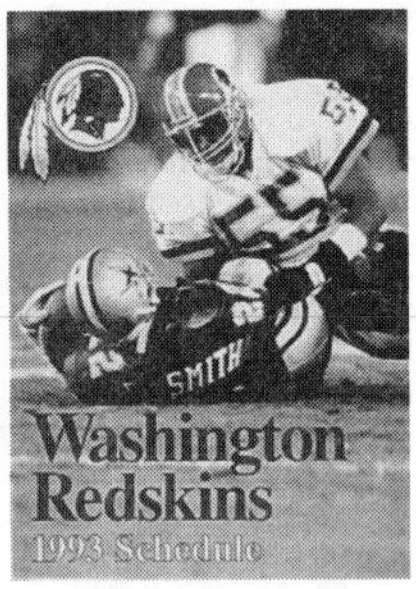

Measuring 2-1/2" x 3-1/2", the 16 pocket schedules have an action photo on the front, along with the player's name and bio. The schedules are unnumbered.

		MT
	Complete Set (16):	10.00
	Common Player:	.40
1	Todd Bowles	.40
2	Earnest Byner	.60
3	Monte Coleman	.60
4	Andre Collins	.60
5	Shane Collins	.40
6	Danny Copeland	.40
7	Kurt Gouveia	.40
8	Darrell Green	.60
9	A.J. Johnson	.40
10	Jim Lachey	.40
11	Ron Middleton	.40
12	Brian Mitchell	.75
13	Mark Rypien	.60
14	Ricky Sanders	.60
15	Mark Schlereth	.40
16	Ed Simmons	.40

1993 Redskins Police

Measuring 2-3/4" x 4-1/8", the 16-card set has "Washington Redskins" printed at the top, with a photo in the middle. The Redskins' helmet is in the lower left, with the player's name and number printed beneath the photo to the right of the helmet. The unnumbered card backs have the player's name, number, bio, career highlights and safety tip. The sponsor logos printed at the bottom, from left to right, are Mobil, PACT and Cellular One.

		MT
	Complete Set (16):	5.00
	Common Player:	.30
1	Ray Brown	.30
2	Andre Collins	.40
3	Brad Edwards	.30
4	Matt Elliott	.30
5	Ricky Ervins	.40
6	Darrell Green	.40
7	Desmond Howard	.60
8	Joe Jacoby	.40
9	Tim Johnson	.30
10	Jim Lachey	.40
11	Chip Lohmiller	.30
12	Charles Mann	.40
13	Raleigh McKenzie	.30
14	Brian Mitchell	.50
15	Terry Orr	.30
16	Mark Rypien	.40

1994 Redskins Mobil Schedules

Measuring 2-1/2" x 3-1/2", the 16 pocket schedules showcase an action photo of the player, along with his name and bio. The schedules are unnumbered.

		MT
	Complete Set (16):	10.00
	Common Player:	.40
1	Reggie Brooks	.60
2	Ray Brown	.40
3	Tom Carter	.60
4	Shane Collins	.40
5	Darrell Green	.60
6	Ken Harvey	.60
7	Lamont Hollinquest	.40
8	Desmond Howard	.60
9	Tim Johnson	.40
10	Jim Lachey	.60
11	Chip Lohmiller	.40
12	Chip Lohmiller	.60
13	Sterling Palmer	.40
14	Heath Shuler	1.50
15	Bobby Wilson	.40
16	Frank Wycheck	.40

1995 Redskins Program Sheets

Measuring 8" x 10", the eight sheets were inserted into Redskins' GameDay programs during the regular season. The sheets showcase stadium photographs taken during championship games. The sheets are unnumbered.

		MT
	Complete Set (8):	20.00
	Common Player:	3.00
1	9/3/95 vs. Cardinals. Redskins vs. Bears, 1937, 1943. (Wrigley Field)	3.00
2	9/10/95 vs. Raiders. Redskins vs. Bears, 1940, 1942. (Griffith Stadium)	3.00
3	10/1/95 vs. Cowboys. Redskins vs. Rams, 1945. (Cleveland Stadium)	3.00
4	10/22/95 vs. Lions. Redskins vs. Dolphins, S.B. VII. (L.A. Coliseum)	3.00
5	10/29/95 vs. Giants. Redskins vs. Dolphins, S.B. XVII. (Rose Bowl)	3.00
6	11/19/95 vs. Seahawks. Redskins vs. Raiders, S.B. XVIII. (Tampa Stadium)	3.00
7	11/26/95 vs. Eagles. Skins vs. Broncos, S.B. XXII. (Jack Murphy Stadium)	3.00
8	12/24/95 vs. Panthers. Redskins vs. Bills, S.B. XXVI. (H.H.H. Metrodome)	3.00

1996 Redskins Score Board/Exxon

This nine-card set was produced by Score Board and distributed by Washington D.C. area Exxon stations. The cards were sold in four-card packs, which contained three player cards and one checklist. They have a "WR" prefix.

		MT
	Complete Set (9):	3.00
	Common Player:	.25
1	Gus Frerotte	.75
2	Terry Allen	.50
3	Henry Ellard	.50
4	Michael Westbrook	1.00
5	Brian Mitchell	.25
6	Sean Gilbert	.25
7	Ken Harvey	.25
8	Darrell Green	.50
9	Redskins Checklist	.25

1993 Rice Council

Athletes from football, baseball, swimming, bobsledding and tennis are honored in this 10-card set produced by the USA Rice Council in Houston, Texas. Troy Aikman and Warren Moon are the two football players featured in the set. Showcased on the fronts are a color photo, player's name and USA Rice Council logo. The fronts are bordered in red or blue. The backs, which are numbered in the upper right corner, have the player's name, team and position, along with his bio. A recipe also is included on the back.

		MT
	Complete Set (10):	10.00
	Common Player:	.25
1	Steve Sax	.50
2	Troy Aikman	4.00
3	Roger Clemens	1.50
4	Zina Garrison	.75
5	Warren Moon	1.50
6	Summer Sanders	.75
7	Steve Sax	.50
8	Brian Shimer	.25
9	Food Guide Pyramid	.25
10	Ten Tips to Healthy Eating for Kids	.25

S

1976 Saga Discs

Cards from this set parallel the 1976 Crane Disk singles. Instead of having the Crane logo on the back they have the Saga logo. Cards from this set are much tougher to find than the Crane singles.

		NM
	Complete Set (30):	750.00
	Common Player:	9.00
1	Ken Anderson	9.00
2	Otis Armstrong	9.00
3	Steve Barkowski	9.00
4	Terry Bradshaw	9.00
5	John Brockington	9.00
6	Doug Buffone	9.00
7	Wally Chambers	9.00
8	Isaac Curtis	9.00
9	Chuck Foreman	9.00
10	Roman Gabriel	9.00
11	Mel Gray	9.00
12	Joe Greene	9.00
13	James Harris	9.00
14	Jim Hart	9.00
15	Billy Kilmer	9.00
16	Greg Landry	9.00
17	Ed Marinaro	9.00
18	Lawrence McCutcheon	9.00
19	Terry Metcalf	9.00
20	Lydell Mitchell	9.00
21	Jim Otis	9.00
22	Alan Page	9.00
23	Walter Payton	9.00
24	Greg Pruitt	9.00
25	Charlie Sanders	9.00
26	Ron Shanklin	9.00
27	Roger Staubach	9.00
28	Jan Stenerud	9.00
29	Charley Taylor	9.00
30	Roger Wehrli	9.00

1999 Sage

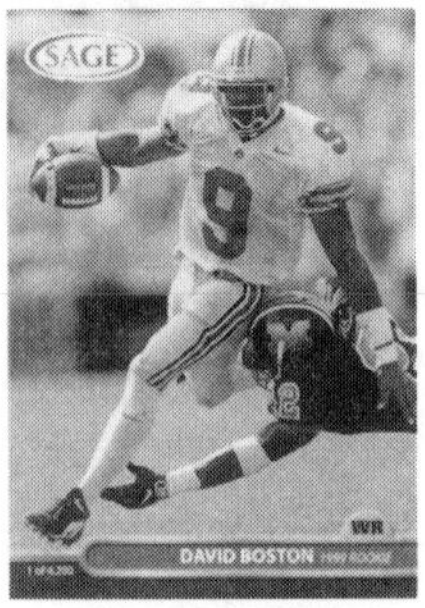

This was the premiere issue of Sage Football. It released a 50-card prospect set that included all of the top picks from 1999 except for Ricky Williams. Only 4,200 of each player was produced. Inserts included five different levels of autographs with Red, Bronze, Silver, Gold and Platinum.

		MT
	Complete Set (50):	35.00
	Common Player:	.25
	Minor Stars:	.50
	Pack (3):	10.00
	Wax Box (12):	100.00
1	Rahim Abdullah	.25
2	Jerry Azumah	.25
3	Champ Bailey	1.00
4	D'Wayne Bates	.50
5	Michael Bishop	1.00
6	David Boston	1.50
7	Fernando Bryant	.25
8	Tony Bryant	.25
9	Chris Claiborne	.50
10	Mike Cloud	.50
11	Cecil Collins	1.25
12	Tim Couch	5.00
13	Daunte Culpepper	2.50
14	Jared DeVries	.25
15	Adrian Dingle	.25
16	Antwan Edwards	.50
17	Troy Edwards	1.50
18	Kevin Faulk	1.00
19	Rufus French	.25
20	Martin Gramatica	.50
21	Torry Holt	1.50
22	Sedrick Irvin	.75
23	Edgerrin James	8.00
24	Jon Jansen	.25
25	Andy Katzenmoyer	.50
26	Jevon Kearse	1.50
27	Patrick Kerney	.25
28	Lamar King	.25
29	Shaun King	2.50
30	Jim Kleinsasser	.50
31	Rob Konrad	.50
32	Brian Kuklick	.25
33	Chris McAlister	.50
34	Darrell McDonald	.50
35	Reggie McGrew	.25
36	Donovan McNabb	2.50
37	Cade McNown	2.50
38	Dat Nguyen	.50
39	Solomon Page	.25
40	Mike Peterson	.25
41	Anthony Poindexter	.25
42	Peerless Price	1.00
43	Michael Rucker	.25
44	L.J. Shelton	.25
45	Akili Smith	2.50
46	John Tait	.25
47	Fred Vinson	.25
48	Al Wilson	.25
49	Antoine Winfield	.25
50	Damien Woody	.25

1999 Sage Autographs

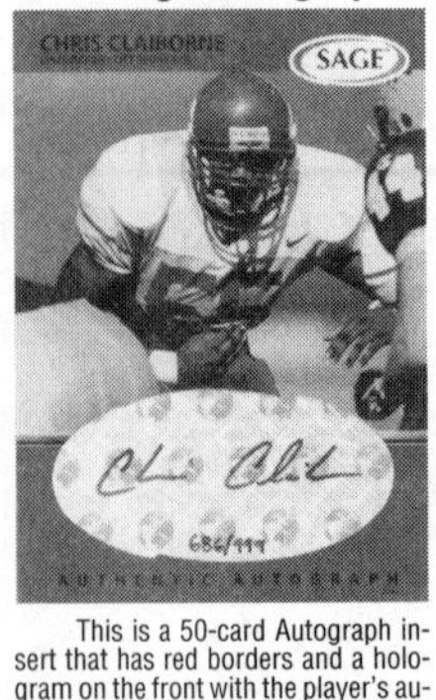

This is a 50-card Autograph insert that has red borders and a hologram on the front with the player's autograph and sequentially numbered. Most players signed a total of 999 except for ten players.

		MT
	Complete Set (50):	550.00
	Common Player:	4.00
	Minor Stars:	8.00
1	Rahim Abdullah 999	4.00
2	Jerry Azumah 999	4.00
3	Champ Bailey 999	12.00
4	D'Wayne Bates 999	8.00
5	Michael Bishop 999	12.00
6	David Boston 869	20.00
7	Fernando Bryant 999	4.00
8	Tony Bryant 999	4.00
9	Chris Claiborne 999	8.00
10	Mike Cloud 434	15.00
11	Cecil Collins 999	15.00
12	Tim Couch 999	60.00
13	Daunte Culpepper 419	40.00
14	Jared DeVries 887	4.00
15	Adrian Dingle 999	4.00
16	Antwan Edwards 999	8.00
17	Troy Edwards 999	20.00
18	Kevin Faulk 999	12.00
19	Rufus French 999	4.00
20	Martin Gramatica 999	8.00
21	Torry Holt 999	20.00
22	Sedrick Irvin 999	12.00
23	Edgerrin James 859	75.00
24	Jon Jansen 999	4.00
25	Andy Katzenmoyer 209	35.00
26	Jevon Kearse 999	15.00
27	Patrick Kerney 879	4.00
28	Lamar King 999	4.00
29	Shaun King 999	30.00
30	Jim Kleinsasser 999	8.00
31	Rob Konrad 999	8.00
32	Brian Kuklick 999	4.00
33	Chris McAlister 999	8.00
34	Darrell McDonald 999	15.00
35	Reggie McGrew 999	4.00
36	Donovan McNabb 999	30.00
37	Cade McNown 209	75.00
38	Dat Nguyen 999	8.00
39	Solomon Page 999	4.00
40	Mike Peterson 999	4.00
41	Anthony Poindexter 999	4.00
42	Peerless Price 232	30.00
43	Michael Rucker 999	4.00
44	L.J. Shelton 999	4.00
45	Akili Smith 419	40.00
46	John Tait 999	4.00
47	Fred Vinson 999	4.00
48	Al Wilson 999	4.00
49	Antoine Winfield 999	4.00
50	Damien Woody 999	4.00

1999 Sage Autographs Bronze

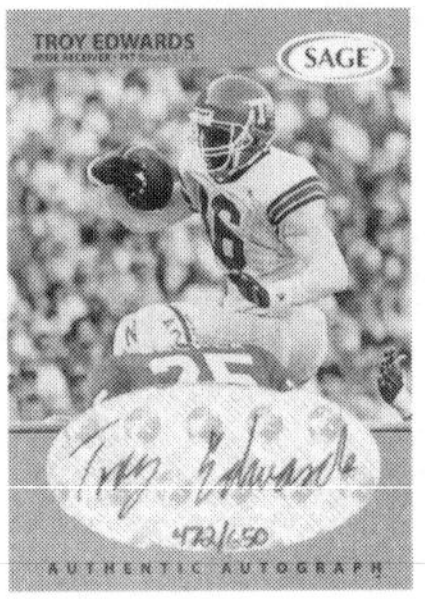

This insert is the same as the Red Autographs except for the borders are Bronze and the players only signed a total of 650. A few of the players signed less.

		MT
	Complete Set (50):	725.00
	Common Player:	6.00
	Minor Stars:	12.00
1	Rahim Abdullah 650	12.00
2	Jerry Azumah 650	12.00
3	Champ Bailey 650	15.00
4	D'Wayne Bates 650	12.00
5	Michael Bishop 650	15.00
6	David Boston 565	30.00
7	Fernando Bryant 650	6.00
8	Tony Bryant 650	6.00
9	Chris Claiborne 650	12.00
10	Mike Cloud 280	20.00
11	Cecil Collins 650	18.00
12	Tim Couch 650	75.00
13	Daunte Culpepper 285	45.00
14	Jared DeVries 575	6.00
15	Adrian Dingle 650	6.00
16	Antwan Edwards 650	12.00
17	Troy Edwards 650	20.00
18	Kevin Faulk 650	15.00
19	Rufus French 650	6.00
20	Martin Gramatica 650	12.00
21	Torry Holt 650	20.00
22	Sedrick Irvin 650	15.00
23	Edgerrin James 570	100.00
24	Jon Jansen 650	6.00
25	Andy Katzenmoyer 140	45.00
26	Jevon Kearse 650	20.00
27	Patrick Kerney 585	12.00
28	Lamar King 650	6.00
29	Shaun King 650	30.00
30	Jim Kleinsasser 650	12.00
31	Rob Konrad 650	12.00
32	Brian Kuklick 650	6.00
33	Chris McAlister 650	12.00
34	Darrell McDonald 650	15.00
35	Reggie McGrew 650	6.00
36	Donovan McNabb 650	30.00
37	Cade McNown 140	85.00
38	Dat Nguyen 650	6.00
39	Solomon Page 650	6.00
40	Mike Peterson 650	6.00
41	Anthony Poindexter 650	6.00
42	Peerless Price 150	35.00
43	Michael Rucker 650	6.00
44	L.J. Shelton 650	6.00
45	Akili Smith 285	45.00
46	John Tait 650	6.00
47	Fred Vinson 650	6.00
48	Al Wilson 650	6.00
49	Antoine Winfield 650	6.00
50	Damien Woody 650	6.00

1999 Sage Autographs Gold

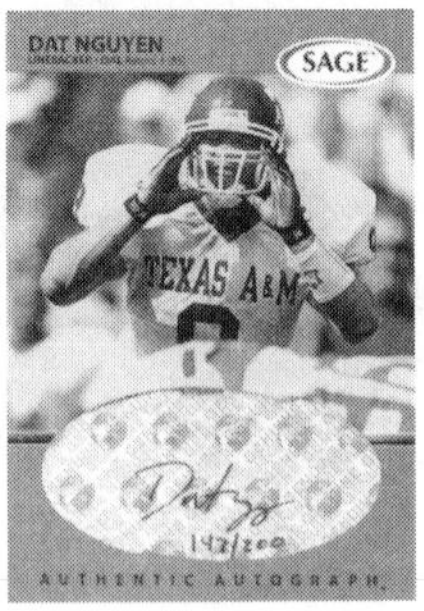

This insert is the same as the Red set except for the borders are in gold and most players in the set signed only 200.

		MT
	Common Player:	12.00
	Minor Stars:	20.00
1	Rahim Abdullah 200	12.00
2	Jerry Azumah 200	12.00
3	Champ Bailey 200	25.00
4	D'Wayne Bates 200	20.00
5	Michael Bishop 200	25.00
6	David Boston 174	45.00
7	Fernando Bryant 200	12.00
8	Tony Bryant 200	12.00
9	Chris Claiborne 200	20.00
10	Mike Cloud 88	35.00
11	Cecil Collins 200	30.00
12	Tim Couch 200	125.00
13	Daunte Culpepper 90	75.00
14	Jared DeVries 185	20.00
15	Adrian Dingle 200	12.00
16	Antwan Edwards 200	20.00
17	Troy Edwards 200	35.00
18	Kevin Faulk 200	25.00
19	Rufus French 200	12.00
20	Martin Gramatica 200	20.00
21	Torry Holt 200	35.00
22	Sedrick Irvin 200	25.00
23	Edgerrin James 175	150.00
24	Jon Jansen 200	12.00
25	Andy Katzenmoyer 45	75.00
26	Jevon Kearse 200	30.00
27	Patrick Kerney 175	12.00
28	Lamar King 200	12.00
29	Shaun King 200	50.00
30	Jim Kleinsasser 200	20.00
31	Rob Konrad 200	20.00
32	Brian Kuklick 200	12.00
33	Chris McAlister 200	20.00
34	Darrell McDonald 200	25.00
35	Reggie McGrew 200	12.00
36	Donovan McNabb 200	50.00
37	Cade McNown 45	150.00
38	Dat Nguyen 200	12.00
39	Solomon Page 200	12.00
40	Mike Peterson 200	12.00
41	Anthony Poindexter 200	12.00
42	Peerless Price 46	60.00
43	Michael Rucker 200	12.00
44	L.J. Shelton 200	12.00
45	Akili Smith 90	75.00
46	John Tait 200	12.00
47	Fred Vinson 200	12.00
48	Al Wilson 200	12.00
49	Antoine Winfield 200	12.00
50	Damien Woody 200	12.00

1999 Sage Autographs Platinum

This insert is the same as the Red Autographs except most of the players only signed 50 cards and the borders are in platinum.

		MT
	Common Player:	15.00
	Minor Stars:	30.00
1	Rahim Abdullah 50	15.00
2	Jerry Azumah 50	15.00
3	Champ Bailey 50	35.00
4	D'Wayne Bates 50	30.00
5	Michael Bishop 50	35.00
6	David Boston 43	60.00
7	Fernando Bryant 50	15.00
8	Tony Bryant 50	15.00
9	Chris Claiborne 50	30.00
10	Mike Cloud 22	45.00
11	Cecil Collins 50	40.00
12	Tim Couch 50	175.00
13	Daunte Culpepper 25	130.00
14	Jared DeVries 47	15.00
15	Adrian Dingle 50	15.00
16	Antwan Edwards 50	40.00
17	Troy Edwards 50	55.00
18	Kevin Faulk 50	60.00
19	Rufus French 50	15.00
20	Martin Gramatica 50	15.00
21	Torry Holt 50	60.00
22	Sedrick Irvin 50	40.00
23	Edgerrin James 45	150.00
24	Jon Jansen 50	15.00
25	Andy Katzenmoyer 15	100.00
26	Jevon Kearse 50	45.00
27	Patrick Kerney 45	15.00
28	Lamar King 50	15.00
29	Shaun King 50	45.00
30	Jim Kleinsasser 50	15.00
31	Rob Konrad 50	40.00
32	Brian Kuklick 50	40.00
33	Chris McAlister 50	40.00
34	Darrell McDonald 50	40.00
35	Reggie McGrew 50	40.00
36	Donovan McNabb 50	80.00
37	Cade McNown 15	150.00
38	Dat Nguyen 50	40.00

39	Solomon Page 50	15.00
40	Mike Peterson 50	15.00
41	Anthony Poindexter 50	15.00
42	Peerless Price 13	100.00
43	Michael Rucker 50	15.00
44	L.J. Shelton 50	15.00
45	Akili Smith 25	120.00
46	John Tait 50	15.00
47	Fred Vinson 50	15.00
48	Al Wilson 50	15.00
49	Antoine Winfield 50	15.00
50	Damien Woody 50	15.00

1999 Sage Autographs Silver

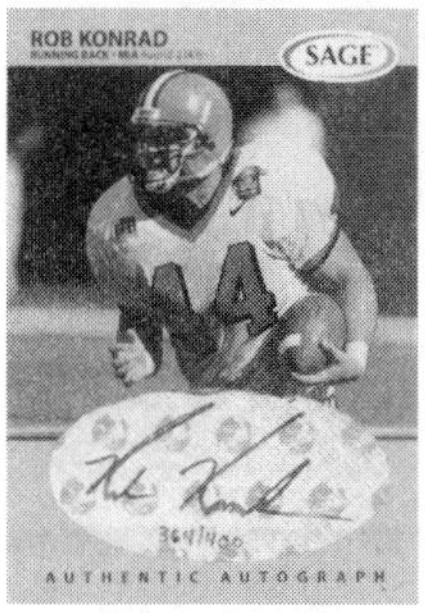

This insert is the same as the Red Autographs except most of the players signed a total of 400 cards and the borders are in silver.

		MT
Common Player:		10.00
Minor Stars:		15.00
1	Rahim Abdullah 400	15.00
2	Jerry Azumah 400	15.00
3	Champ Bailey 400	20.00
4	D'Wayne Bates 400	15.00
5	Michael Bishop 400	30.00
6	David Boston 348	45.00
7	Fernando Bryant 400	15.00
8	Tony Bryant 400	10.00
9	Chris Claiborne 400	20.00
10	Mike Cloud 175	30.00
11	Cecil Collins 400	30.00
12	Tim Couch 400	100.00
13	Daunte Culpepper 180	75.00
14	Jared DeVries 355	10.00
15	Adrian Dingle 400	10.00
16	Antwan Edwards 400	15.00
17	Troy Edwards 400	30.00
18	Kevin Faulk 400	35.00
19	Rufus French 400	10.00
20	Martin Gramatica 400	10.00
21	Torry Holt 400	35.00
22	Sedrick Irvin 400	20.00
23	Edgerrin James 350	75.00
24	Jon Jansen 400	10.00
25	Andy Katzenmoyer 90	55.00
26	Jevon Kearse 400	25.00
27	Patrick Kerney 365	10.00
28	Lamar King 400	10.00
29	Shaun King 400	20.00
30	Jim Kleinsasser 400	10.00
31	Rob Konrad 400	15.00
32	Brian Kuklick 400	15.00
33	Chris McAlister 400	15.00
34	Darnell McDonald 400	20.00
35	Reggie McGrew 400	15.00
36	Donovan McNabb 400	50.00
37	Cade McNown 90	80.00
38	Dat Nguyen 400	15.00
39	Solomon Page 400	10.00
40	Mike Peterson 400	10.00
41	Anthony Poindexter 400	10.00
42	Peerless Price 93	50.00
43	Michael Rucker 400	10.00
44	L.J. Shelton 400	10.00
45	Akili Smith 180	65.00
46	John Tait 400	10.00
47	Fred Vinson 400	10.00
48	Al Wilson 400	10.00
49	Antoine Winfield 400	10.00
50	Damien Woody 400	10.00

2000 Sage Autographed

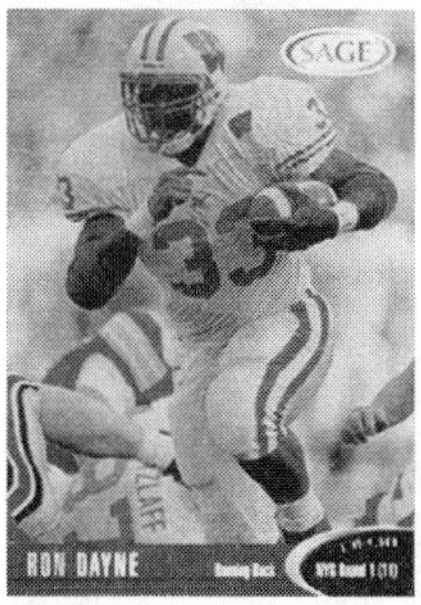

		MT
Complete Set (50):		30.00
Common Player:		.25
Minor Stars:		.50
Pack (3):		10.00
Wax Box (12):		110.00
1	John Abraham	.25
2	Shaun Alexander	2.00
3	LaVar Arrington	2.00
4	Courtney Brown	1.25
5	Keith Bulluck	.25
6	Plaxico Burress	3.50
7	Giovanni Carmazzi	1.75
8	Kwame Cavil	.50
9	Cosey Coleman	.25
10	Laveranues Coles	1.00
11	Tim Couch	2.00
12	Ron Dayne	5.00
13	Reuben Droughns	1.00
14	Shaun Ellis	.25
15	John Engelberger	.25
16	Danny Farmer	.75
17	Dwayne Goodrich	.25
18	Deon Grant	.25
19	Chris Hovan	.25
20	Darren Howard	.25
21	Todd Husak	.75
22	Thomas Jones	2.75
23	Curtis Keaton	.75
24	Jamal Lewis	2.50
25	Anthony Lucas	.50
26	Tee Martin	1.25
27	Stockar McDougle	.25
28	Corey Moore	.25
29	Rob Morris	.25
30	Sammy Morris	.25
31	Sylvester Morris	1.25
32	Chad Pennington	3.50
33	Todd Pinkston	.75
34	Ahmed Plummer	.75
35	Jerry Porter	1.25
36	Travis Prentice	1.25
37	Tim Rattay	1.25
38	Chris Redman	1.50
39	J.R. Redmond	1.50
40	Chris Samuels	.75
41	Brandon Short	.25
42	Corey Simon	.50
43	R. Jay Soward	1.25
44	Shyrone Stith	.25
45	Raynoch Thompson	.25
46	Brian Urlacher	1.00
47	Todd Wade	.25
48	Troy Walters	.50
49	Dez White	1.00
50	Michael Wiley	.75
51	Ron Dayne AUTO SP	150.00

2000 Sage Autographed Red Autographs

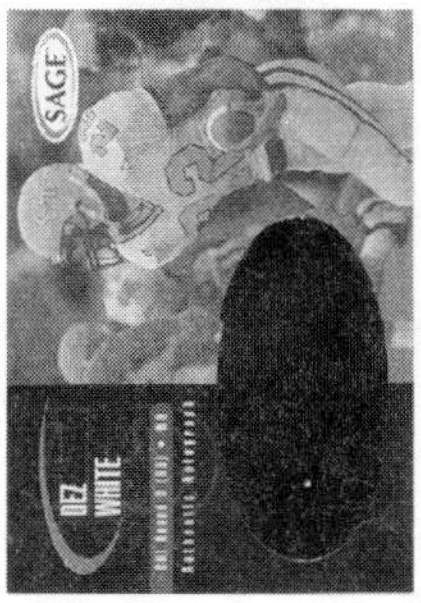

		MT
Complete Set (47):		600.00
Common Player:		4.00
Minor Stars:		8.00
Inserted 1:2		
Production 999 Sets		
1	John Abraham 999	4.00
2	Shaun Alexander 999	20.00
3	LaVar Arrington 514	30.00
4	Courtney Brown 514	20.00
6	Plaxico Burress 999	35.00
7	Giovanni Carmazzi 999	18.00
8	Kwame Cavil 999	8.00
9	Cosey Coleman 999	4.00
10	Laveranues Coles 999	10.00
11	Tim Couch 339	80.00
12	Ron Dayne 309	85.00
13	Reuben Droughns 999	10.00
14	Shaun Ellis 999	4.00
15	John Engelberger 999	4.00
16	Danny Farmer 999	10.00
17	Dwayne Goodrich 999	4.00
18	Deon Grant 999	4.00
19	Chris Hovan 999	4.00
20	Darren Howard 999	4.00
21	Todd Husak 999	8.00
22	Thomas Jones 999	30.00
23	Curtis Keaton 999	8.00
24	Jamal Lewis 999	25.00
25	Anthony Lucas 999	4.00
26	Tee Martin 999	15.00
28	Corey Moore 999	4.00
29	Rob Morris 999	4.00
30	Sammy Morris 999	4.00
31	Sylvester Morris 999	15.00
32	Chad Pennington 689	50.00
33	Todd Pinkston 999	8.00
34	Ahmed Plummer 999	8.00
35	Jerry Porter 999	12.00
36	Travis Prentice 999	15.00
37	Tim Rattay 999	12.00
38	Chris Redman 999	15.00
39	J.R. Redmond 999	15.00
40	Chris Samuels 999	10.00
41	Brandon Short 999	4.00
43	R. Jay Soward 999	12.00
44	Shyrone Stith 999	4.00
45	Raynoch Thompson 999	4.00
46	Brian Urlacher 999	10.00
47	Todd Wade 999	4.00
48	Troy Walters 999	4.00
49	Dez White 999	10.00
50	Michael Wiley 999	8.00

Post-1980 cards in Near Mint condition will generally sell for about 75% of the quoted Mint value. Excellent-condition cards bring no more than 40%.

2000 Sage Autographed Bronze Autographs

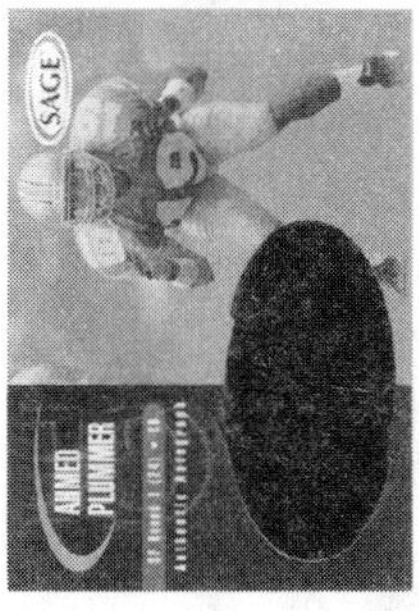

		MT
Complete Set (48):		700.00
Common Player:		5.00
Minor Stars:		10.00
Inserted 1:4		
Production 650 Sets		
1	John Abraham 650	5.00
2	Shaun Alexander 650	30.00
3	LaVar Arrington 340	40.00
4	Courtney Brown 340	30.00
6	Plaxico Burress 650	45.00
7	Giovanni Carmazzi 650	25.00
8	Kwame Cavil 650	10.00
9	Cosey Coleman 650	5.00
10	Laveranues Coles 650	15.00
11	Tim Couch 230	100.00
12	Ron Dayne 215	100.00
13	Reuben Droughns 650	15.00
14	Shaun Ellis 650	5.00
15	John Engelberger 650	5.00
16	Danny Farmer 650	12.00
17	Dwayne Goodrich 650	5.00
18	Deon Grant 650	5.00
19	Chris Hovan 650	5.00
20	Darren Howard 650	5.00
21	Todd Husak 650	10.00
22	Thomas Jones 650	35.00
23	Curtis Keaton 650	10.00
24	Jamal Lewis 650	30.00
25	Anthony Lucas 650	10.00
26	Tee Martin 650	15.00
27	Stockar McDougle 650	5.00
28	Corey Moore 650	5.00
29	Rob Morris 650	5.00
30	Sammy Morris 650	5.00
31	Sylvester Morris 650	20.00
32	Chad Pennington 455	60.00
33	Todd Pinkston 650	10.00
34	Ahmed Plummer 650	10.00
35	Jerry Porter 650	15.00
36	Travis Prentice 650	15.00
37	Tim Rattay 650	15.00
38	Chris Redman 650	20.00
39	J.R. Redmond 650	20.00
40	Chris Samuels 650	10.00
41	Brandon Short 650	5.00
43	R. Jay Soward 650	18.00
44	Shyrone Stith 650	5.00
45	Raynoch Thompson 650	5.00
46	Brian Urlacher 650	15.00
47	Todd Wade 650	5.00
48	Troy Walters 650	10.00
49	Dez White 650	12.00
50	Michael Wiley 650	10.00

2000 Sage Autographed Gold Autographs

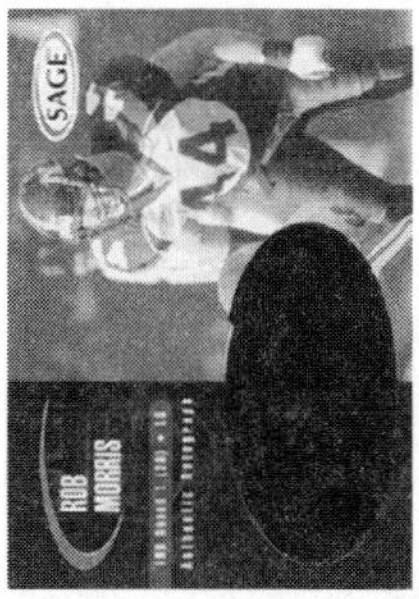

		MT
Complete Set (48):		1200.
Common Player:		8.00
Minor Stars:		16.00
Inserted 1:12		
Production 200 Sets		
1	John Abraham 200	8.00
2	Shaun Alexander 200	50.00
3	LaVar Arrington 105	60.00
4	Courtney Brown 105	50.00
6	Plaxico Burress 200	70.00
7	Giovanni Carmazzi 200	40.00
8	Kwame Cavil 200	16.00
9	Cosey Coleman 200	8.00
10	Laveranues Coles 200	20.00
11	Tim Couch 70	140.00
12	Ron Dayne 70	160.00
13	Reuben Droughns 200	20.00
14	Shaun Ellis 200	8.00
15	John Engelberger 200	8.00
16	Danny Farmer 200	18.00
17	Dwayne Goodrich 200	8.00
18	Deon Grant 200	8.00
19	Chris Hovan 200	8.00
20	Darren Howard 200	8.00
21	Todd Husak 200	16.00
22	Thomas Jones 200	60.00
23	Curtis Keaton 200	16.00
24	Jamal Lewis 200	50.00
25	Anthony Lucas 200	16.00
26	Tee Martin 200	25.00
27	Stockar McDougle 200	8.00
28	Corey Moore 200	8.00
29	Rob Morris 200	8.00
30	Sammy Morris 200	8.00
31	Sylvester Morris 200	30.00
32	Chad Pennington 140	85.00
33	Todd Pinkston 200	16.00
34	Ahmed Plummer 200	16.00
35	Jerry Porter 200	25.00
36	Travis Prentice 200	30.00
37	Tim Rattay 200	30.00
38	Chris Redman 200	30.00
39	J.R. Redmond 200	30.00
40	Chris Samuels 200	16.00
41	Brandon Short 200	8.00
43	R. Jay Soward 200	30.00
44	Shyrone Stith 200	8.00
45	Raynoch Thompson 200	8.00
46	Brian Urlacher 200	20.00
47	Todd Wade 200	8.00
48	Troy Walters 200	16.00
49	Dez White 200	20.00
50	Michael Wiley 200	16.00

2000 Sage Autographed Platinum Autographs

		MT
Common Player:		10.00
Minor Stars:		20.00
Inserted 1:46		
Production 50 Sets		
1	John Abraham 50	10.00
2	Shaun Alexander 50	65.00
3	LaVar Arrington 30	80.00
4	Courtney Brown 30	75.00
6	Plaxico Burress 50	100.00
7	Giovanni Carmazzi 50	50.00
8	Kwame Cavil 50	20.00
9	Cosey Coleman 50	10.00
10	Laveranues Coles 50	30.00
11	Tim Couch 20	170.00
12	Ron Dayne 20	200.00
13	Reuben Droughns 50	30.00
14	Shaun Ellis 50	10.00
15	John Engelberger 50	10.00
16	Danny Farmer 50	25.00
17	Dwayne Goodrich 50	10.00
18	Deon Grant 50	10.00
19	Chris Hovan 50	10.00
20	Darren Howard 50	10.00
21	Todd Husak 50	20.00
22	Thomas Jones 50	85.00
23	Curtis Keaton 50	20.00
24	Jamal Lewis 50	75.00
25	Anthony Lucas 50	20.00
26	Tee Martin 50	40.00
28	Corey Moore 50	10.00
29	Rob Morris 50	10.00
30	Sammy Morris 50	10.00
31	Sylvester Morris 50	40.00
32	Chad Pennington 35	150.00
33	Todd Pinkston 50	20.00
34	Ahmed Plummer 50	25.00
35	Jerry Porter 50	40.00
36	Travis Prentice 50	45.00
37	Tim Rattay 50	45.00
38	Chris Redman 50	50.00
39	J.R. Redmond 50	50.00
40	Chris Samuels 50	25.00
41	Brandon Short 50	10.00
43	R. Jay Soward 50	40.00
44	Shyrone Stith 50	10.00
45	Raynoch Thompson 50	10.00
46	Brian Urlacher 50	30.00
47	Todd Wade 50	10.00
48	Troy Walters 50	20.00
49	Dez White 50	30.00
50	Michael Wiley 50	25.00

2000 Sage Autographed Silver Autographs

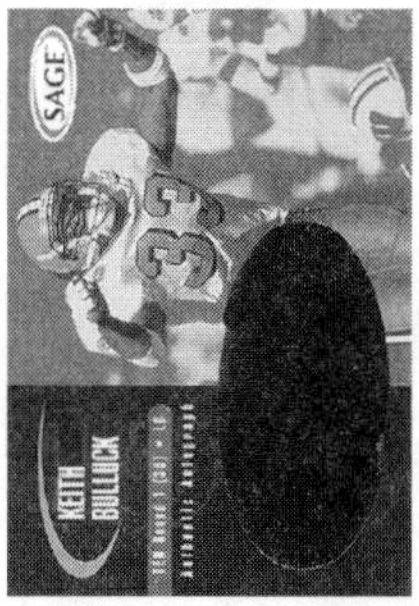

		MT
Complete Set (49):		900.00
Common Player:		6.00
Minor Stars:		12.00
Inserted 1:6		
Production 400 Sets		
1	John Abraham 400	6.00
2	Shaun Alexander 400	40.00
3	LaVar Arrington 210	50.00
4	Courtney Brown 210	40.00
6	Plaxico Burress 400	55.00
7	Giovanni Carmazzi 400	30.00
8	Kwame Cavil 400	12.00
9	Cosey Coleman 400	6.00
10	Laveranues Coles 400	15.00
11	Tim Couch 140	120.00
12	Ron Dayne 135	130.00
13	Reuben Droughns 400	15.00
14	Shaun Ellis 400	6.00
15	John Engelberger 400	6.00
16	Danny Farmer 400	12.00
17	Dwayne Goodrich 400	6.00
18	Deon Grant 400	6.00
19	Chris Hovan 400	6.00
20	Darren Howard 400	6.00
21	Todd Husak 400	12.00
22	Thomas Jones 400	40.00
23	Curtis Keaton 400	12.00
24	Jamal Lewis 400	40.00
25	Anthony Lucas 400	12.00
26	Tee Martin 400	20.00
27	Stockar McDougle 400	6.00
28	Corey Moore 400	6.00
29	Rob Morris 400	6.00
30	Sammy Morris 400	6.00
31	Sylvester Morris 400	20.00
32	Chad Pennington 280	75.00
33	Todd Pinkston 400	12.00
34	Ahmed Plummer 400	12.00
35	Jerry Porter 400	20.00
36	Travis Prentice 400	20.00
37	Tim Rattay 400	20.00
38	Chris Redman 400	25.00
39	J.R. Redmond 400	25.00
40	Chris Samuels 400	12.00
41	Brandon Short 400	6.00
42	Corey Simon 400	12.00
43	R. Jay Soward 400	20.00
44	Shyrone Stith 400	6.00
45	Raynoch Thompson 400	6.00
46	Brian Urlacher 400	15.00
47	Todd Wade 400	6.00
48	Troy Walters 400	12.00
49	Dez White 400	15.00
50	Michael Wiley 400	15.00

2000 Sage Hit

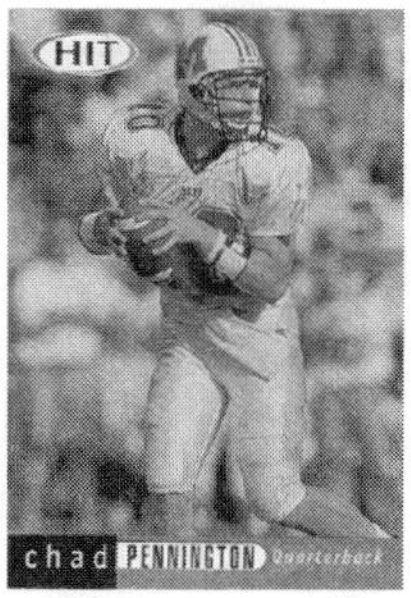

		MT
Complete Set (50):		25.00
Common Player:		.25
Minor Stars:		.50
Pack (5):		3.50
Wax Box (24):		60.00
1	Jerry Porter	1.25
2	Tim Couch	2.00
3	Chris Samuels	.50
4	Plaxico Burress	2.50
5	Michael Wiley	.75
6	Thomas Jones	2.50
7	Chris Redman	1.50
8	Anthony Lucas	.75
9	Kwame Cavil	.50
10	Chad Pennington	2.50
11	LaVar Arrington	2.00
12	Giovanni Carmazzi	1.50
13	Tim Rattay	1.00
14	Laveranues Coles	.75
15	Mario Edwards	.25
16	John Engelberger	.25
17	Tee Martin	1.25
18	R. Jay Soward	1.25
19	Ahmed Plummer	.50
20	Na'il Diggs	.50
21	J.R. Redmond	1.25
22	Dez White	.75
23	Reuben Droughns	.75
24	Sylvester Morris	1.25
25	Cosey Coleman	.25
26	Corey Moore	.50
27	Curtis Keaton	.50
28	Danny Farmer	.75
29	Travis Claridge	.25
30	Troy Walters	.50
31	Jamal Lewis	2.50
32	Shaun King	1.25
33	Ron Dayne	3.00
34	Keith Bulluck	.50
35	Corey Simon	.50
36	Deon Dyer	.50
37	Shaun Alexander	2.00
38	Shyrone Stith	.50
39	Shaun Ellis	.50
40	Todd Pinkston	.75
41	Travis Prentice	1.25
42	Chris Hovan	.50
43	Brandon Short	.50
44	Brian Urlacher	1.00
45	Rob Morris	.50
46	Raynoch Thompson	.50
47	Deon Grant	.50
48	Stockar McDougle	.25
49	Darren Howard	.50
50	Courtney Brown	1.25

2000 Sage Hit NGR Parallel

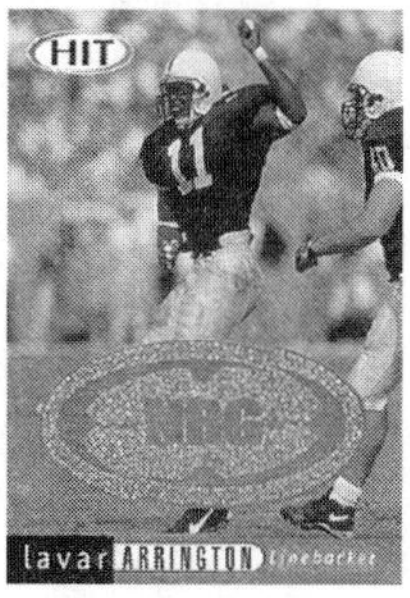

		MT
Complete Set (50):		40.00
NGR Cards:		1.5x
Inserted 1:1.5		

2000 Sage Hit Autographs Emerald

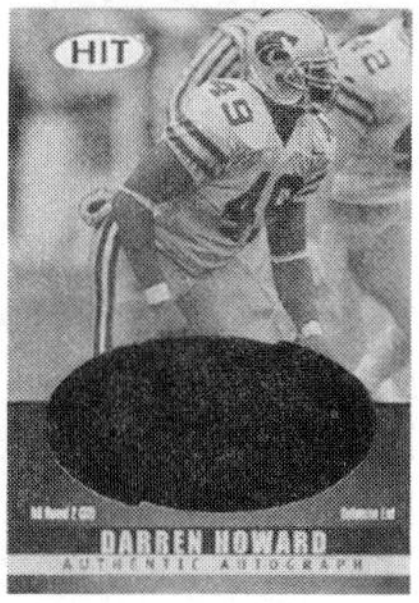

		MT
Complete Set (49):		650.00
Common Player:		5.00
Minor Stars:		10.00
Inserted 1:12		
Emerald Die Cuts:		2x
Inserted 1:40		
Diamond Cards:		1.5x
Inserted 1:20		
Diamond Die Cuts:		3x
Inserted 1:100		
1	Jerry Porter	20.00
2	Tim Couch	50.00
3	Chris Samuels	10.00
4	Plaxico Burress	40.00
5	Michael Wiley	10.00
6	Thomas Jones	30.00
7	Chris Redman	20.00
8	Anthony Lucas	10.00
9	Kwame Cavil	10.00
10	Chad Pennington	65.00
11	LaVar Arrington	50.00
12	Giovanni Carmazzi	25.00
13	Tim Rattay	10.00
14	Laveranues Coles	10.00
15	Mario Edwards	5.00
16	John Engelberger	5.00
17	Tee Martin	20.00
18	R. Jay Soward	15.00
19	Ahmed Plummer	10.00
20	Na'il Diggs	10.00
21	J.R. Redmond	15.00
22	Dez White	10.00
23	Reuben Droughns	10.00
24	Sylvester Morris	15.00
25	Cosey Coleman	10.00
26	Corey Moore	10.00
27	Curtis Keaton	10.00
28	Danny Farmer	10.00
29	Travis Claridge	5.00
30	Troy Walters	10.00
31	Jamal Lewis	35.00
32	Shaun King	30.00
33	Ron Dayne	85.00
35	Corey Simon	10.00
36	Deon Dyer	10.00
37	Shaun Alexander	30.00
38	Shyrone Stith	10.00
39	Shaun Ellis	10.00
40	Todd Pinkston	10.00
41	Travis Prentice	10.00
42	Chris Hovan	10.00
43	Brandon Short	10.00
44	Brian Urlacher	12.00
45	Rob Morris	10.00
46	Raynoch Thompson	10.00
47	Deon Grant	10.00
48	Stockar McDougle	10.00
49	Darren Howard	10.00
50	Courtney Brown	40.00

A card number in parentheses ( ) indicates the set is unnumbered.

2000 Sage Hit Autographs Emerald Die Cut Parallel

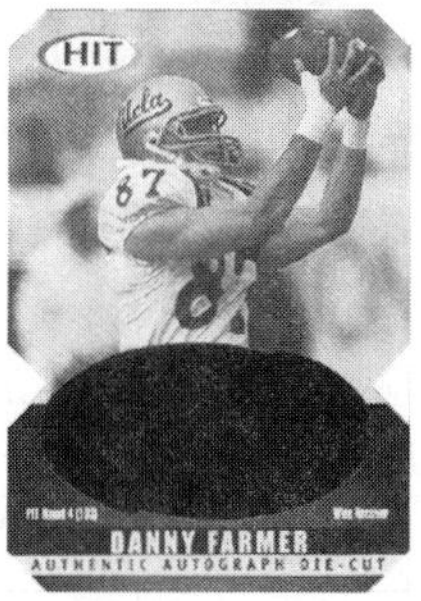

		MT
Emerald Die Cuts:		2x
Inserted 1:40		

A player's name in *italic type* indicates a rookie card.

2000 Sage Hit Autographs Diamond Parallel

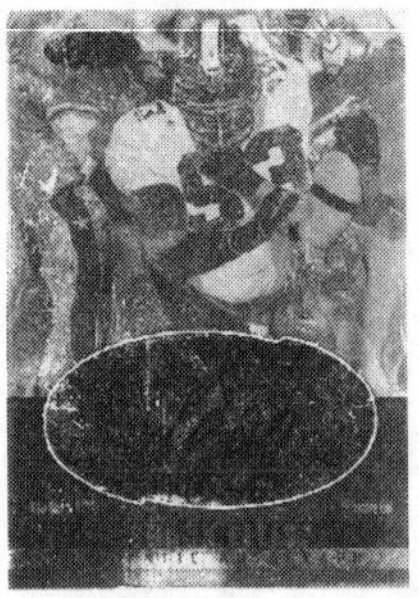

		MT
Diamond Cards:		1.5x
Inserted 1:20		

2000 Sage Hit Autographs Diamond Die Cut Parallel

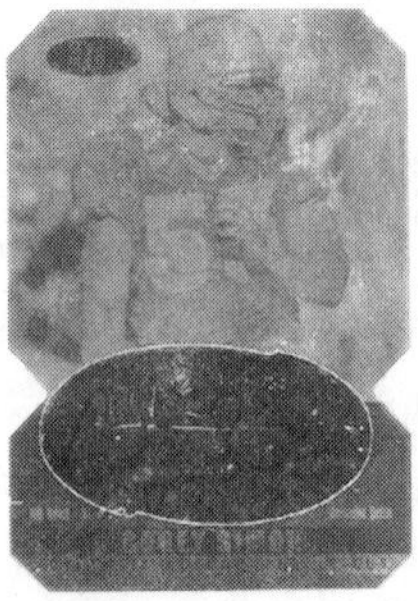

		MT
Diamond Die Cuts:		3x
Inserted 1:100		

2000 Sage Hit Prospectors Emerald

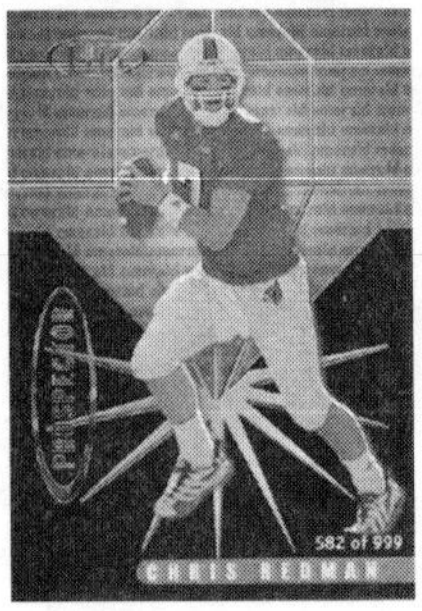

		MT
Complete Set (20):		65.00
Common Player:		3.00
Production 999 Sets		
Inserted 1:24		
Emerald Die Cuts: 2x		
Production 300 Sets		
Inserted 1:80		
Diamond Cards: 1.5x		
Production 600 Sets		
Inserted 1:40		
Diamond Die Cuts: 2x-4x		
Production 100 Sets		
Inserted 1:240		
P1	Shaun Alexander	7.00
P2	LaVar Arrington	6.00
P3	Courtney Brown	4.00
P4	Plaxico Burress	8.00
P5	Giovanni Carmazzi	5.00
P6	Tim Couch	6.00
P7	Ron Dayne	10.00
P8	Thomas Jones	8.00
P9	Shaun King	4.00
P10	Jamal Lewis	8.00
P11	Tee Martin	4.00
P12	Sylvester Morris	4.00
P13	Chad Pennington	8.00
P14	Jerry Porter	4.00
P15	Travis Prentice	4.00
P16	Tim Rattay	3.00
P17	Chris Redman	4.00
P18	R. Jay Soward	3.00
P19	Dez White	3.00
P20	Michael Wiley	3.00

2000 Sage Hit Prospectors Emerald Die Cut Parallel

		MT
Emerald Die Cuts:		2x
Production 300 Sets		
Inserted 1:80		

2000 Sage Hit Prospectors Diamond Parallel

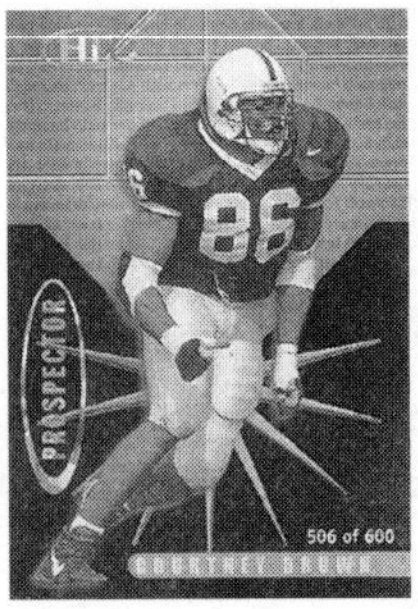

		MT
Diamond Cards:		1.5x
Production 600 Sets		
Inserted 1:40		

2000 Sage Hit Prospectors Diamond Die Cut Parallel

		MT
Diamond Die Cuts:		2x-4x
Production 100 Sets		
Inserted 1:240		

2001 Sage HIT

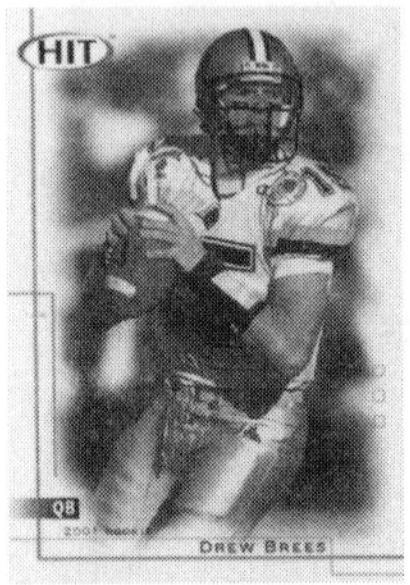

		MT
Complete Set (50):		25.00
Common Player:		.25
Minor Stars:		.50
Pack (5):		3.50
Wax Box (24):		75.00
1	David Terrell	3.00
2	Jamar Fletcher	.50
3	Koren Robinson	2.50
4	Ken-Yon Rambo	.75
5	LaDainian Tomlinson	4.00
6	Santana Moss	3.00
7	Michael Vick	6.00
8	Steve Hutchinson	.50
9	Robert Ferguson	1.00
10	Torrance Marshall	.50
11	Scotty Anderson	.50
12	Derrick Gibson	.50
13	Marcus Stroud	.50
14	Josh Heupel	2.00
15	Drew Brees	4.00
16	Gerard Warren	1.00
17	Quincy Carter	1.50
18	Gary Baxter	.50
19	Alex Bannister	1.25
20	Travis Henry	1.75
21	Andre Dyson	.25
22	Deuce McAllister	3.00
23	Rod Gardner	2.00
24	Jamie Winborn	.50
25	Will Allen	.50
26	Kenyatta Walker	.25
27	Tim Hasselbeck	.75
28	Alge Crumpler	.75
29	Michael Bennett	3.00
30	LaMont Jordan	1.25
31	Jeff Backus	.50
32	Rudi Johnson	1.25
33	Willie Howard	.50
34	Josh Booty	.75
35	Todd Heap	.75
36	Correll Buckhalter	1.00
37	Jesse Palmer	.75
38	Carlos Polk	.50
39	Richard Seymour	.50
40	Adam Archuleta	.75
41	James Jackson	1.00
42	Willie Middlebrooks	.50
43	Ja'Mar Toombs	.50
44	Chris Chambers	1.50
45	Reggie Germany	.50
46	Casey Hampton	.50
47	Reggie Wayne	1.50
48	Jamal Reynolds	.50
49	Justin Smith	.75
50	Quincy Morgan	1.00

Post-1980 cards in Near Mint condition will generally sell for about 75% of the quoted Mint value. Excellent-condition cards bring no more than 40%.

2001 Sage HIT A-Game

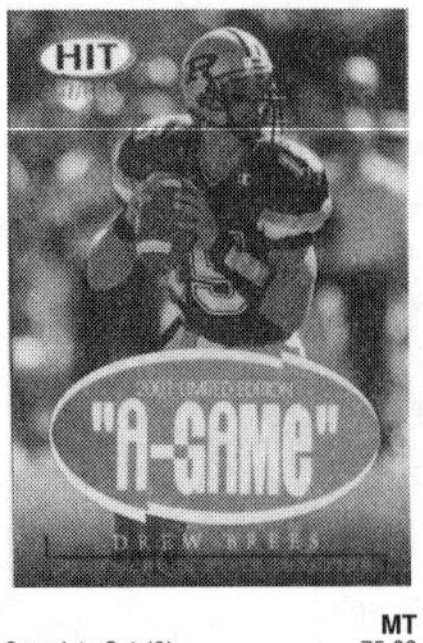

		MT
Complete Set (9):		75.00
Common Player:		10.00
Inserted 1:42		
Production 600 Sets		
1	Drew Brees	12.00
2	Drew Brees	12.00
3	Drew Brees	12.00
4	David Terrell	10.00
5	David Terrell	10.00
6	David Terrell	10.00
7	Michael Vick	15.00
8	Michael Vick	15.00
9	Michael Vick	15.00

2001 Sage HIT Autographs

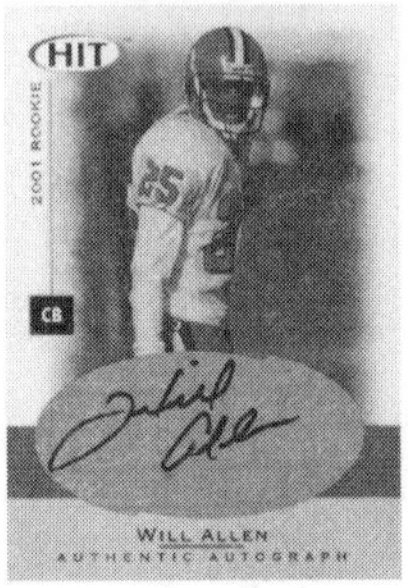

		MT
Common Player:		7.00
Inserted 1:9		
Die-Cut Cards:		2x
Inserted 1:26		
Production 250 Sets		
Foilboard Cards:		2x
Inserted 1:13		
Foilboard Die-Cut Cards:		3x
Inserted 1:64		
Production 100 Sets		
Overall inserted 1:4		
1	David Terrell	25.00
2	Jamar Fletcher	
3	Koren Robinson	20.00
4	Ken-Yon Rambo	7.00
5	LaDainian Tomlinson	40.00
6	Santana Moss	30.00
7	Michael Vick	75.00
8	Steve Hutchinson	7.00
9	Robert Ferguson	12.00
10	Torrance Marshall	10.00
11	Scotty Anderson	7.00
12	Derrick Gibson	
13	Marcus Stroud	7.00
14	Josh Heupel	30.00
15	Drew Brees	50.00
16	Gerard Warren	
17	Quincy Carter	15.00
18	Gary Baxter	7.00
19	Alex Bannister	12.00
20	Travis Henry	20.00
21	Andre Dyson	7.00
22	Deuce McAllister	25.00
23	Rod Gardner	20.00
24	Jamie Winborn	7.00
25	Will Allen	10.00
26	Kenyatta Walker	7.00
27	Tim Hasselbeck	12.00
28	Alge Crumpler	7.00
29	Michael Bennett	25.00
30	LaMont Jordan	12.00
31	Jeff Backus	7.00
32	Rudi Johnson	12.00
33	Willie Howard	7.00
34	Josh Booty	10.00
35	Todd Heap	10.00
36	Correll Buckhalter	10.00
37	Jesse Palmer	12.00
38	Carlos Polk	7.00
39	Richard Seymour	7.00
40	Adam Archuleta	10.00
41	James Jackson	
42	Willie Middlebrooks	7.00
43	Ja'Mar Toombs	
44	Chris Chambers	12.00
45	Reggie Germany	7.00
46	Casey Hampton	
47	Reggie Wayne	15.00
48	Jamal Reynolds	10.00
49	Justin Smith	10.00
50	Quincy Morgan	10.00

2001 Sage HIT Jerseys

		MT
Complete Set (9):		500.00
Common Player:		60.00
Inserted 1:205		
Production 175 Sets		
1	Michael Vick	150.00
2	Michael Vick	150.00
3	Michael Vick	150.00
4	Drew Brees	85.00
5	Drew Brees	85.00
6	Drew Brees	85.00
7	David Terrell	60.00
8	David Terrell	60.00
9	David Terrell	60.00

2001 Sage HIT Prospector Emerald

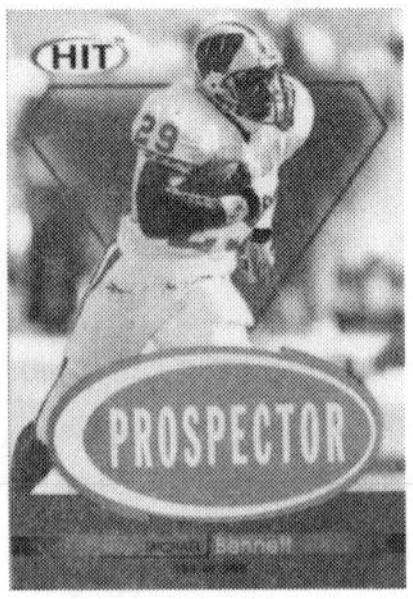

		MT
Complete Set (15):		85.00
Common Player:		3.00
Inserted 1:19		
Production 999 Sets		
Emerald Die-Cut Cards:		2x
Inserted 1:63		
Production 299 Sets		
Diamond Cards:		1.5x
Inserted 1:32		
Production 599 Sets		
Diamond Die-Cut Cards:		4x
Inserted 1:190		
Production 99 Sets		
1	Michael Bennett	8.00
2	Drew Brees	15.00
3	Quincy Carter	4.00
4	Chris Chambers	4.00
5	Rod Gardner	7.00
6	Josh Heupel	7.00
7	LaMont Jordan	4.00
8	Deuce McAllister	10.00
9	Quincy Morgan	3.00
10	Santana Moss	10.00
11	Koren Robinson	8.00
12	David Terrell	10.00
13	LaDainian Tomlinson	12.00
14	Michael Vick	20.00
15	Reggie Wayne	4.00

2001 Sage HIT Rarefied

		MT
Complete Set (50):		75.00
Common Player:		.75
Minor Stars:		1.50
Inserted 1:3		
Production 2,001 Sets		
Silver Cards:		2x
Inserted 1:6		
Production 999 Sets		
Gold Cards:		3x
Inserted 1:11		
Production 500 Sets		
R1	Will Allen	.75
R2	Adam Archuleta	1.50
R3	Jeff Backus	.75
R4	Alex Bannister	2.00
R5	Gary Baxter	.75
R6	Michael Bennett	5.00
R7	Josh Booty	1.50
R8	Drew Brees	10.00
R9	Correl Buckhalter	2.00
R10	Quincy Carter	2.50
R11	Chris Chambers	2.00
R12	Alge Crumpler	.75
R13	Andre Dyson	.75
R14	Robert Ferguson	2.50
R15	Jamar Fletcher	1.50
R16	Rod Gardner	4.00
R17	Reggie Germany	.75
R18	Derrick Gibson	.75
R19	Casey Hampton	.75
R20	Tim Hasselbeck	1.50
R21	Todd Heap	.75
R22	Travis Henry	3.00
R23	Josh Heupel	4.50
R24	Willie Howard	.75
R25	Steve Hutchinson	.75
R26	James Jackson	2.00
R27	Rudi Johnson	2.00
R28	LaMont Jordan	2.00
R29	Torrance Marshall	.75
R30	Deuce McAllister	5.00
R31	Willie Middlebrooks	.75
R32	Quincy Morgan	2.00
R33	Santana Moss	5.00
R34	Jesse Palmer	.75
R35	Carlos Polk	.75
R36	Ken-Yon Rambo	1.50
R37	Jamal Reynolds	.75
R38	Koren Robinson	5.00
R39	Richard Seymour	.75
R40	Justin Smith	1.50
R41	Fred Smoot	.75
R42	Marcus Stroud	.75
R43	David Terrell	6.00
R44	LaDainian Tomlinson	8.00
R45	Ja'Mar Toombs	.75
R46	Michael Vick	12.00
R47	Kenyatta Walker	.75
R48	Gerard Warren	1.50
R49	Reggie Wayne	3.00
R50	Jamie Winborn	.75

A card number in parentheses ( ) indicates the set is unnumbered.

2001 Sage Autographed

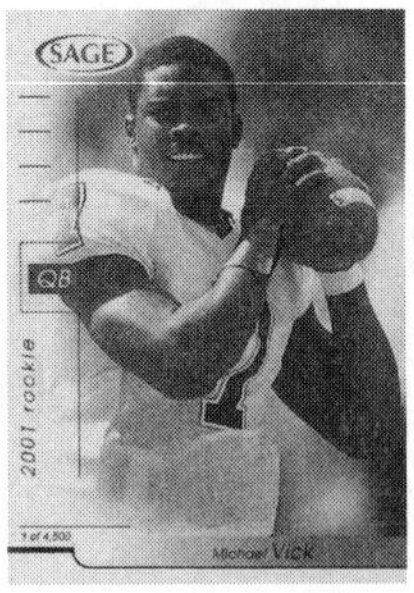

		MT
Complete Set (50):		25.00
Common Player:		.25
Minor Stars:		.50
Production 4,500 Sets		
Pack (3):		12.00
Wax Box (12):		100.00
A1	Will Allen	.25
A2	Adam Archuleta	.75
A3	Jeff Backus	.50
A4	Alex Bannister	.75
A5	Gary Baxter	.25
A6	Michael Bennett	3.00
A7	Josh Booty	.50
A8	Drew Brees	4.00
A9	Correl Buckhalter	.75
A10	Quincy Carter	1.50
A11	Chris Chambers	1.00
A12	Alge Crumpler	.50
A13	Andre Dyson	.25
A14	Robert Ferguson	1.50
A15	Jamar Fletcher	.75
A16	Rod Gardner	2.00
A17	Reggie Germany	1.25
A18	Derrick Gibson	.50
A19	Casey Hampton	.25
A20	Tim Hasselbeck	.75
A21	Todd Heap	.50
A22	Travis Henry	1.50
A23	Josh Heupel	2.50
A24	Willie Howard	.25
A25	Steve Hutchinson	.50
A26	James Jackson	1.25
A27	Rudi Johnson	1.00
A28	LaMont Jordan	1.00
A29	Torrance Marshall	.50
A30	Deuce McAllister	2.50
A31	Willie Middlebrooks	.25
A32	Quincy Morgan	1.00
A33	Santana Moss	2.50
A34	Jesse Palmer	.75
A35	Carlos Polk	.25
A36	Ken-Yon Rambo	.50
A37	Jamal Reynolds	.50
A38	Koren Robinson	2.00
A39	Richard Seymour	.25
A40	Justin Smith	.75
A41	Fred Smoot	.50
A42	Marcus Stroud	.50
A43	David Terrell	2.75
A44	LaDainian Tomlinson	3.50
A45	Ja'Mar Toombs	.25
A46	Michael Vick	6.00
A47	Kenyatta Walker	.50
A48	Gerard Warren	1.00
A49	Reggie Wayne	1.75
A50	Jamie Winborn	.50

2001 Sage Autographed Bronze

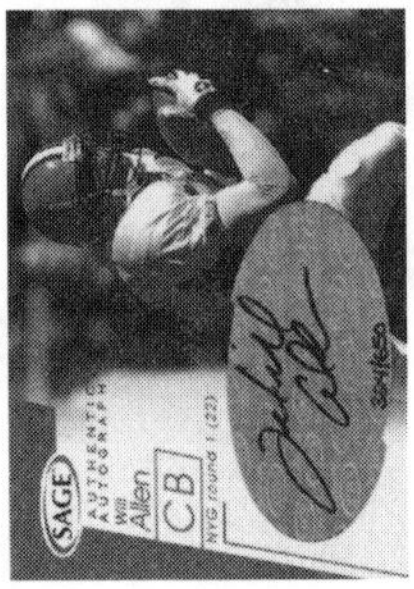

		MT
Common Player:		6.00
Inserted 1:4		
Production 650 Sets		
A1	Will Allen 650	6.00
A2	Adam Archuleta 650	6.00
A3	Jeff Backus 600	6.00
A4	Alex Bannister 650	8.00
A5	Gary Baxter 650	6.00
A6	Michael Bennett 650	30.00
A7	Josh Booty 600	6.00
A8	Drew Brees 500	50.00
A9	Correl Buckhalter 650	12.00
A10	Quincy Carter 650	15.00
A11	Chris Chambers 650	10.00
A12	Alge Crumpler 650	6.00
A13	Andre Dyson 650	6.00
A14	Robert Ferguson 650	12.00
A16	Rod Gardner 650	18.00
A17	Reggie Germany 650	12.00
A18	Derrick Gibson 650	6.00
A19	Casey Hampton 650	6.00
A20	Tim Hasselbeck 600	7.00
A21	Todd Heap 650	6.00
A22	Travis Henry 600	18.00
A23	Josh Heupel 650	25.00
A24	Willie Howard 600	6.00
A25	Steve Hutchinson 650	6.00
A26	James Jackson 650	10.00
A27	Rudi Johnson 650	8.00
A28	LaMont Jordan 650	10.00
A29	Torrance Marshall 650	6.00
A30	Deuce McAllister 500	30.00
A31	Willie Middlebrooks 650	6.00
A32	Quincy Morgan 650	10.00
A33	Santana Moss 650	30.00
A34	Jesse Palmer 650	7.00
A35	Carlos Polk 650	6.00
A36	Ken-Yon Rambo 500	6.00
A37	Jamal Reynolds 650	6.00
A38	Koren Robinson 650	18.00
A39	Richard Seymour 650	6.00
A40	Justin Smith 650	8.00
A41	Fred Smoot 650	6.00
A42	Marcus Stroud 600	6.00
A43	David Terrell 425	25.00
A44	LaDainian Tomlinson 650	35.00
A45	Ja'Mar Toombs 650	6.00
A46	Michael Vick 325	85.00
A47	Kenyatta Walker 650	6.00
A49	Reggie Wayne 650	15.00
A50	Jamie Winborn 650	6.00

2001 Sage Autographed Gold

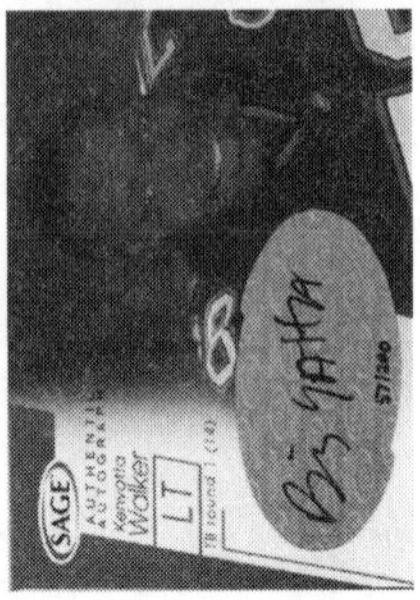

		MT
Common Player:		10.00
Inserted 1:12		
Production 200 Sets		
A1	Will Allen 200	10.00
A2	Adam Archuleta 200	12.00
A3	Jeff Backus 200	10.00
A4	Alex Bannister 200	15.00
A5	Gary Baxter 200	10.00
A6	Michael Bennett 200	50.00
A7	Josh Booty 200	10.00
A8	Drew Brees 150	85.00
A9	Correl Buckhalter 200	20.00
A10	Quincy Carter 200	25.00
A11	Chris Chambers 200	18.00
A12	Alge Crumpler 200	10.00
A13	Andre Dyson 200	10.00
A14	Robert Ferguson 200	20.00
A16	Rod Gardner 200	30.00
A17	Reggie Germany 200	25.00
A18	Derrick Gibson 200	10.00
A19	Casey Hampton 200	10.00
A20	Tim Hasselbeck 200	12.00
A21	Todd Heap 200	10.00
A22	Travis Henry 200	30.00
A23	Josh Heupel 200	40.00
A24	Willie Howard 200	10.00
A25	Steve Hutchinson 200	10.00
A26	James Jackson 200	16.00
A27	Rudi Johnson 200	15.00
A28	LaMont Jordan 200	16.00
A29	Torrance Marshall 200	10.00
A30	Deuce McAllister 150	50.00
A31	Willie Middlebrooks 200	10.00
A32	Quincy Morgan 200	15.00
A33	Santana Moss 200	45.00
A34	Jesse Palmer 200	12.00
A35	Carlos Polk 200	10.00
A36	Ken-Yon Rambo 150	10.00
A37	Jamal Reynolds 200	10.00
A38	Koren Robinson 200	30.00
A39	Richard Seymour 200	10.00
A40	Justin Smith 200	12.00
A41	Fred Smoot 200	10.00
A42	Marcus Stroud 200	10.00
A43	David Terrell 130	40.00
A44	LaDainian Tomlinson 200	60.00
A45	Ja'Mar Toombs 200	10.00
A46	Michael Vick 100	150.00
A47	Kenyatta Walker 200	10.00
A49	Reggie Wayne 200	25.00
A50	Jamie Winborn 200	10.00

2001 Sage Autographed Platinum

		MT
Common Player:		20.00
Inserted 1:46		
Production 50 Sets		
A1	Will Allen 50	20.00
A2	Adam Archuleta 50	20.00
A3	Jeff Backus 50	20.00
A4	Alex Bannister 50	25.00
A5	Gary Baxter 50	20.00
A6	Michael Bennett 50	100.00
A7	Josh Booty 50	20.00
A8	Drew Brees 40	150.00
A9	Correl Buckhalter 50	35.00
A10	Quincy Carter 50	45.00
A11	Chris Chambers 50	30.00
A12	Alge Crumpler 50	20.00
A13	Andre Dyson 50	20.00
A14	Robert Ferguson 50	40.00
A16	Rod Gardner 50	60.00
A17	Reggie Germany 50	45.00
A18	Derrick Gibson 50	20.00
A19	Casey Hampton 50	20.00
A20	Tim Hasselbeck 50	25.00
A21	Todd Heap 50	20.00
A22	Travis Henry 50	60.00
A23	Josh Heupel 50	75.00
A24	Willie Howard 50	20.00
A25	Steve Hutchinson 50	20.00
A26	James Jackson 50	30.00

A27	Rudi Johnson 50	25.00
A28	LaMont Jordan 50	35.00
A29	Torrance Marshall 50	20.00
A30	Deuce McAllister 40	100.00
A31	Willie Middlebrooks 50	20.00
A32	Quincy Morgan 50	35.00
A33	Santana Moss 50	90.00
A34	Jesse Palmer 50	25.00
A35	Carlos Polk 50	20.00
A36	Ken-Yon Rambo 40	20.00
A37	Jamal Reynolds 50	20.00
A38	Koren Robinson 50	60.00
A39	Richard Seymour 50	20.00
A40	Justin Smith 50	25.00
A41	Fred Smoot 50	20.00
A42	Marcus Stroud 50	20.00
A43	David Terrell 35	80.00
A44	LaDainian Tomlinson 50	125.00
A45	Ja'Mar Toombs 50	20.00
A46	Michael Vick 25	275.00
A47	Kenyatta Walker 50	20.00
A49	Reggie Wayne 50	50.00
A50	Jamie Winborn 50	20.00

2001 Sage Autographed Red

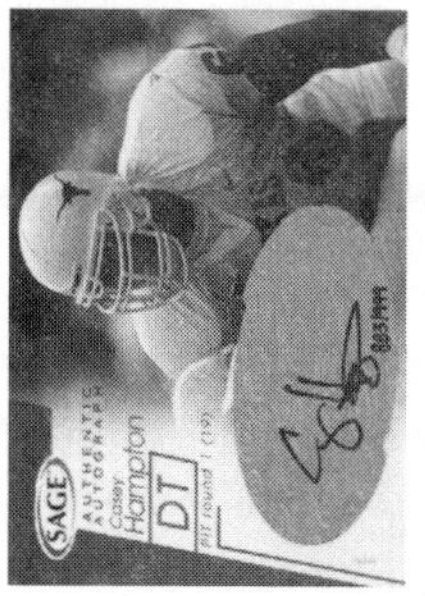

		MT
Common Player:		5.00
Inserted 1:2		
Production 999 Sets		
A1	Will Allen 999	5.00
A2	Adam Archuleta 999	5.00
A3	Jeff Backus 900	6.00
A4	Alex Bannister 999	7.00
A5	Gary Baxter 999	5.00
A6	Michael Bennett 999	25.00
A7	Josh Booty 900	6.00
A8	Drew Brees 749	40.00
A9	Correl Buckhalter 999	10.00
A10	Quincy Carter 999	12.00
A11	Chris Chambers 999	8.00
A12	Alge Crumpler 999	5.00
A13	Andre Dyson 999	5.00
A14	Robert Ferguson 999	10.00
A16	Rod Gardner 999	15.00
A17	Reggie Germany 999	10.00
A18	Derrick Gibson 999	5.00
A19	Casey Hampton 999	5.00
A20	Tim Hasselbeck 900	6.00
A21	Todd Heap 999	6.00
A22	Travis Henry 800	15.00
A23	Josh Heupel 999	18.00
A24	Willie Howard 900	5.00
A25	Steve Hutchinson 999	5.00
A26	James Jackson 999	8.00
A27	Rudi Johnson 999	7.00
A28	LaMont Jordan 999	8.00
A29	Torrance Marshall 999	5.00
A30	Deuce McAllister 749	30.00
A31	Willie Middlebrooks 999	5.00
A32	Quincy Morgan 999	8.00
A33	Santana Moss 999	25.00
A34	Jesse Palmer 999	6.00
A35	Carlos Polk 999	5.00
A36	Ken-Yon Rambo 749	5.00
A37	Jamal Reynolds 999	5.00
A38	Koren Robinson 999	15.00
A39	Richard Seymour 999	5.00
A40	Justin Smith 999	7.00
A41	Fred Smoot 999	5.00
A42	Marcus Stroud 900	5.00
A43	David Terrell 649	25.00
A44	LaDainian Tomlinson 999	30.00
A45	Ja'Mar Toombs 999	5.00
A46	Michael Vick 499	75.00
A47	Kenyatta Walker 999	5.00
A49	Reggie Wayne 999	12.00
A50	Jamie Winborn 999	5.00

2001 Sage Autographed Silver

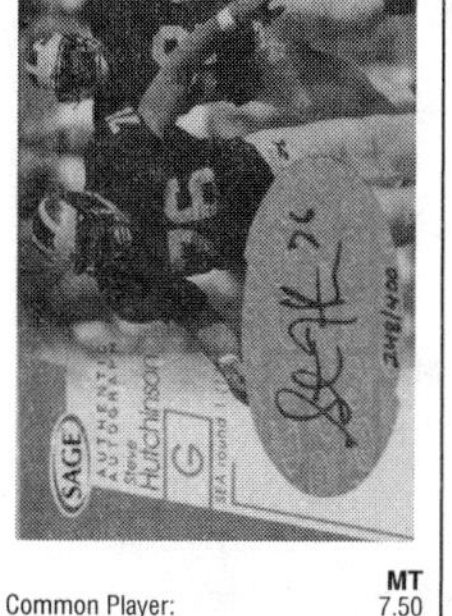

		MT
Common Player:		7.50
Inserted 1:6		
Production 400 Sets		
A1	Will Allen 400	7.50
A2	Adam Archuleta 400	7.50
A3	Jeff Backus 400	7.50
A4	Alex Bannister 400	10.00
A5	Gary Baxter 400	7.50
A6	Michael Bennett 400	40.00
A7	Josh Booty 400	7.50
A8	Drew Brees 300	60.00
A9	Correl Buckhalter 400	15.00
A10	Quincy Carter 400	18.00
A11	Chris Chambers 400	12.00
A12	Alge Crumpler 400	7.50
A13	Andre Dyson 400	7.50
A14	Robert Ferguson 400	15.00
A16	Rod Gardner 400	25.00
A17	Reggie Germany 400	18.00
A18	Derrick Gibson 400	7.50
A19	Casey Hampton 400	7.50
A20	Tim Hasselbeck 400	10.00
A21	Todd Heap 400	7.50
A22	Travis Henry 400	25.00
A23	Josh Heupel 400	30.00
A24	Willie Howard 400	7.50
A25	Steve Hutchinson 400	7.50
A26	James Jackson 400	12.00
A27	Rudi Johnson 400	10.00
A28	LaMont Jordan 400	12.00
A29	Torrance Marshall 400	7.50
A30	Deuce McAllister 300	40.00
A31	Willie Middlebrooks 400	7.50
A32	Quincy Morgan 400	12.00
A33	Santana Moss 400	35.00
A34	Jesse Palmer 400	10.00
A35	Carlos Polk 400	7.50
A36	Ken-Yon Rambo 300	7.50
A37	Jamal Reynolds 400	7.50
A38	Koren Robinson 400	25.00
A39	Richard Seymour 400	7.50
A40	Justin Smith 400	10.00
A41	Fred Smoot 400	7.50
A42	Marcus Stroud 400	7.50
A43	David Terrell 260	30.00
A44	LaDainian Tomlinson 400	45.00
A45	Ja'Mar Toombs 400	7.50
A46	Michael Vick 200	100.00
A47	Kenyatta Walker 400	7.50
A49	Reggie Wayne 400	18.00
A50	Jamie Winborn 400	7.50

2001 Sage Autographed Jerseys

		MT
Complete Set (3):		200.00
Common Player:		45.00
Inserted 1:205		
Production 175 Sets		
J1	Michael Vick	125.00
J2	Drew Brees	75.00
J3	David Terrell	45.00

2001 Sage Autographed Michael Vick Specials

		MT
Complete Set (2):		
Common Player:		
MV1	Vick Authentic Jersey	50.00
MV2	Vick Authentic Autograph	50.00

1968-69 Saints 8x10

Measuring 8" x 10", the 35 black-and-white photo cards feature members of the 1968-69 Saints teams. The backs are unnumbered and blank.

		NM
Complete Set (35):		120.00
Common Player:		3.00
1	Dan Abramowicz	6.00
2	Doug Atkins	7.50
3	Tom Barrington	4.00
4	Jim Boeke	3.00
5	Johnny Brewer	4.00
6	Bo Burris	3.00
7	Bill Cody	3.00
8	Ted Davis	3.00
9	John Douglas	3.00
10	Charles Durkee	3.00
11	John Gilliam	4.00
12	Jim Hester	3.00
13	Gene Howard	3.00
14	Les Kelley	3.00
15	Jake Kupp	4.00
16	Earl Leggett	3.00
17	Archie Manning	20.00
18	Don McCall	3.00
19	Tom McNeill	3.00
20	Richard Neal	3.00
21	Dave Parks	4.00
22	Dave Parks (with small inset photo)	4.00
23	Ray Poage	3.00
24	David Rowe	3.00
25	Roy Schmidt	3.00
26	Randy Schultz	3.00
27	Brian Schweda	3.00
28	Monty Stickles	3.00
29	Steve Stonebreaker	4.00
30	Jerry Sturm	3.00
31	Mike Tilleman	3.00
32	Joe Wendryhoski	3.00
33	Ernie Wheelwright	3.00
34	Fred Whittingham	3.00
35	Del Williams	3.00

1974 Saints Circle Inset

Measuring 8" x 10", the 22 photos showcase a black-and-white action photo on the front, with a player headshot picture inside a circle inset. Printed at the bottom of the card are the player's name, position and team name. The backs are unnumbered and blank.

		NM
Complete Set (22):		120.00
Common Player:		5.00
1	John Beasley	5.00
2	Tom Blanchard	6.00
3	Larry Cipa	5.00
4	Don Coleman	5.00
5	Wayne Colman	5.00
6	Jack DeGrenier	5.00
7	Rick Kingrea	5.00
8	Phil LaPorta	5.00
9	Odell Lawson	5.00
10	Archie Manning	20.00
11	Alvin Maxson	6.00
12	Bill McClard	5.00
13	Bill McNeill	5.00
14	Jim Merlo	6.00
15	Rick Middleton	5.00
16	Derland Moore	5.00
17	Jerry Moore	5.00
18	Joel Parker	5.00
19	Jess Phillips	5.00
20	Terry Schmidt	5.00
21	Paul Seal	5.00
22	Dave Thompson	5.00

1979 Saints Coke

The 45 cards are anchored by a black-and-white player headshot, with the Coca-Cola logo in an oval in the upper right. The Saints logo is in the lower left and the player's name is printed in the lower right. The fronts of the cards are bordered in red. The card backs have the card number inside a helmet in the upper left, while the player's name is to the right of the helmet. His position is printed inside a banner. Beneath the banner is the player's bio. The Coca-Cola logo is located at the bottom center.

		NM
Complete Set (45):		60.00
Common Player:		1.00
1	Archie Manning	8.00
2	Ed Burns	1.00
3	Bobby Scott	1.50
4	Russell Erxleben	1.50
5	Eric Felton	1.00
6	David Gray	1.00
7	Ricky Ray	1.00
8	Clarence Chapman	1.00
9	Kim Jones	1.00
10	Mike Strachan	1.00
11	Tony Galbreath	2.00
12	Tom Myers	1.50
13	Chuck Muncie	3.00
14	Jack Holmes	1.00
15	Don Schwartz	1.00
16	Ralph McGill	1.00
17	Ken Bordelon	1.00
18	Jim Kovach	1.00
19	Pat Hughes	1.00
20	Reggie Mathis	1.00
21	Jim Merlo	1.00
22	Joe Federspiel	1.00
23	Don Reese	1.00
24	Roger Finnie	1.00
25	John Hill	1.00
26	Barry Bennett	1.00
27	Dave Lafary	1.00
28	Robert Woods	1.00
29	Conrad Dobler	1.50
30	John Watson	1.00
31	Fred Sturt	1.00
32	J.T. Taylor	1.00
33	Mike Fultz	1.00
34	Joe Campbell	1.00
35	Derland Moore	1.00
36	Elex Price	1.00
37	Elois Grooms	1.00
38	Emanuel Zanders	1.00
39	Ike Harris	1.00
40	Tinker Owens	1.50
41	Rich Mauti	1.00
42	Henry Childs	1.50
43	Larry Hardy	1.00
44	Brooks Williams	1.00
45	Wes Chandler	3.50

1992 Saints McDag

Showcased on the front of the 32-card set is "Saints '92" inside a brown border on the left side. The photo is located on the right, with the Saints' logo in the lower left of the photo. The player's name is printed in a gold stripe at the bottom of the front. The backs, which are unnumbered, have the player's name, position, bio, number, career highlights and safety tips. The Behavioral Health and Saints logos are printed on the lower left and right, respectively. The cards were produced by McDag Productions.

		MT
Complete Set (32):		12.00
Common Player:		.25
1	Morten Andersen	.50
2	Gene Atkins	.25
3	Toi Cook	.25
4	Tommy Barnhardt	.25
5	Hoby Brenner	.40
6	Stan Brock	.40
7	Vince Buck	.40
8	Wesley Carroll	.40
9	Jim Dombrowski	.25
10	Vaughn Dunbar	.50
11	Quinn Early	.75
12	Bobby Hebert	.50
13	Craig Heyward	.60
14	Joel Hilgenberg	.25
15	Dalton Hilliard	.40
16	Rickey Jackson	.40
17	Vaughan Johnson	.25
18	Reginald Jones	.25
19	Eric Martin	.40
20	Wayne Martin	.40
21	Brett Maxie	.25
22	Fred McAfee	.40
23	Sam Mills	.40
24	Jim Mora (CO)	.40
25	Pat Swilling	.50
26	John Tice	.25
27	Renaldo Turnbull	.40
28	Floyd Turner	.40
29	Steve Walsh	.25
30	Frank Warren	.25
31	Jim Wilks	.25
32	Saints Cheerleaders	.40

1962 Salada Coins

These coins, featuring 154 pro football players, are color- color-coded according to the team the player plays for; each team has a specific rim color. The fronts feature a color head-and-shoulders shot of the player without his helmet on. The backs are numbered and contain advertising for Salada Tea and Junket brand desserts. Brief biographical information, including the collegiate school the player attended, is also given. Each coin measures 1-1/2" diameter. The set can sometimes be found as a complete set in its own custom box. Double- and triple-printed coins are indicated by (DP) and (TP) and are easier to find than the others.

		NM
Complete Set (154):		3000.
Common Player DP:		7.50
Common Player SP:		25.00
1	Johnny Unitas	175.00
2	Lenny Moore	85.00
3	Jim Parker	50.00
4	Gino Marchetti	60.00
5	Dick Szymanski	25.00
6	Alex Sandusky	25.00
7	Raymond Berry	90.00
8	Jimmy Orr	30.00
9	Ordell Braase	25.00
10	Bill Pellington	25.00
11	Bob Boyd	25.00
12	Paul Hornung (DP)	25.00
13	Jim Taylor (DP)	20.00
14	Henry Jordan (DP)	8.00
15	Dan Currie (DP)	8.00
16	Bill Forester (DP)	8.00
17	Dave Hanner (DP)	8.00
18	Bart Starr (DP)	30.00
19	Max McGee (DP)	7.50
20	Jerry Kramer (DP)	9.00
21	Forrest Gregg (DP)	15.00
22	Jim Ringo (DP)	15.00
23	Billy Kilmer	55.00
24	Charlie Krueger	25.00
25	Bob St. Clair	50.00
26	Abe Woodson	25.00
27	Jimmy Johnson	65.00
28	Matt Hazeltine	25.00
29	Bruce Bosley	25.00
30	Dan Conners	25.00
31	John Brodie	80.00
32	J.D. Smith	25.00
33	Monty Stickles	25.00
34	Johnny Morris (DP)	9.00
35	Stan Jones (DP)	15.00
36	J.C. Caroline (DP)	8.00
37	Richie Petitbon (DP)	9.00
38	Joe Fortunato (DP)	9.00
39	Larry Morris (DP)	6.00
40	Doug Atkins (DP)	12.00
41	Billy Wade (DP)	7.50
42	Rick Casares (DP)	9.00
43	Willie Galimore (DP)	9.00
44	Angelo Coia (DP)	8.00
45	Ollie Matson	65.00
46	Carroll Dale	30.00
47	Ed Meador	30.00
48	Jon Arnett	35.00
49	Joe Marconi	25.00
50	John LoVetere	25.00
51	Red Phillips	25.00
52	Zeke Bratkowski	35.00
53	Dick Bass	30.00
54	Les Richter	30.00
55	Art Hunter (DP)	8.00
56	Jim Brown (TP)	65.00
57	Mike McCormack (DP)	12.00
58	Bob Gain (DP)	8.00
59	Paul Wiggin (DP)	7.50
60	Jim Houston (DP)	7.50
61	Ray Renfro (DP)	7.50
62	Galen Fiss (DP)	8.00
63	J.R. Smith (DP)	8.00
64	John Morrow (DP)	8.00
65	Gene Hickerson (DP)	8.00
66	Jim Ninowski (DP)	7.50
67	Tom Tracy	30.00
68	Buddy Dial	30.00
69	Mike Sandusky	30.00
70	Lou Michaels	30.00
71	Preston Carpenter	25.00
72	John Reger	25.00
73	John Henry Johnson	65.00
74	Gene Lipscomb	40.00
75	Mike Henry	30.00
76	George Tarasovic	25.00
77	Bobby Layne	70.00
78	Harley Sewell (DP)	8.00
79	Darris McCord (DP)	8.00
80	Yale Lary (DP)	12.00
81	Jim Gibbons (DP)	8.00
82	Gail Codgill (DP)	8.00
83	Nick Pietrosante (DP)	9.00
84	Alex Karras (DP)	15.00
85	Dick Lane (DP)	12.00
86	Joe Schmidt (DP)	15.00
87	John Gordy (DP)	8.00
88	Milt Plum (DP)	7.50
89	Andy Stynchula	25.00
90	Bob Toneff	25.00
91	Bill Anderson	30.00
92	Sam Horner	25.00
93	Norm Snead	30.00
94	Bobby Mitchell	65.00
95	Billy Barnes	25.00
96	Rod Breedlove	25.00
97	Fred Hageman	25.00
98	Vince Promuto	25.00
99	Joe Rutgens	25.00
100	Maxie Baughan (DP)	9.00
101	Pete Retzlaff (DP)	7.50
102	Tom Brookshier (DP)	9.00
103	Sonny Jurgensen (DP)	25.00
104	Ed Khayat (DP)	6.00
105	Chuck Bednarik (DP)	15.00
106	Tommy McDonald (DP)	9.00
107	Bobby Walston (DP)	8.00
108	Ted Dean (DP)	8.00
109	Clarence Peaks (DP)	8.00
110	Jimmy Carr (DP)	8.00
111	Sam Huff (DP)	15.00
112	Erich Barnes (DP)	7.50
113	Del Shofner (DP)	9.00
114	Bob Gaiters (DP)	8.00
115	Alex Webster (DP)	9.00
116	Dick Modzelewski (DP)	7.50
117	Jim Katcavage (DP)	7.50
118	Roosevelt Brown (DP)	15.00
119	Y.A. Tittle (DP)	25.00
120	Andy Robustelli (DP)	12.00
121	Dick Lynch (DP)	7.50
122	Don Webb (DP)	8.00
123	Larry Eisenhauer (DP)	8.00
124	Babe Parilli (DP)	7.50
125	Charles Long (DP)	8.00
126	Billy Lott (DP)	8.00
127	Harry Jacobs (DP)	8.00
128	Bob Dee (DP)	8.00
129	Ron Burton (DP)	7.50
130	Jim Colclough (TP)	3.00
131	Gino Cappelletti (DP)	9.00
132	Tommy Addison (DP)	8.00
133	Larry Grantham (DP)	7.50
134	Dick Christy (DP)	8.00
135	Bill Mathis (DP)	7.50
136	Butch Songin (DP)	8.00
137	Dainard Paulson (DP)	8.00
138	Roger Ellis (DP)	8.00
139	Mike Hudock (DP)	8.00
140	Don Maynard (DP)	20.00
141	Al Dorow (DP)	7.50
142	Jack Klotz (DP)	8.00
143	Lee Riley (DP)	8.00
144	Bill Atkins (DP)	8.00
145	Art Baker (DP)	8.00
146	Stew Barber (DP)	8.00
147	Glen Bass (DP)	8.00
148	Al Bemiller (DP)	8.00
149	Richie Lucas (DP)	7.50
150	Archie Matsos (DP)	8.00
151	Warren Rabb (DP)	8.00
152	Ken Rice (DP)	8.00
153	Billy Shaw (DP)	7.50
154	Laverne Torczon (DP)	8.00

1959 San Giorgio Flipbooks

Measuring 5-3/4" x 3-9/16", the 17 flipbooks showcase movement of a player on 14 different photos. When the photos are separated and sorted, the photos go into motion when they are flipped. Players from the Washington Redskins, Philadelphia Eagles and Pittsburgh Steelers are pictured in the set. Many collectors prefer the flipbooks to be intact and uncut.

		NM
Complete Set (17):		2500.
Common Player:		150.00
1	Sam Baker	175.00
2	Bill Barnes	150.00
3	Chuck Bednarik	300.00
4	Don Bosseler	150.00
5	Darrell Brewster	150.00
6	Jack Butler	150.00
7	Proverb Jacobs	150.00
8	Eddie LeBaron	200.00
9	Tommy McDonald	175.00
10	Ed Meadows	150.00
11	Gern Nagler	150.00
12	Clarence Peaks	150.00
13	Pete Retzlaff	175.00
14	Mike Sommer	175.00
15	Tom Tracy	175.00
16	Bobby Walston	150.00
17	Chuck Weber	150.00

1989 Score Promos

These cards were used to promote Score's debut football set. They are basically identical to the 1989 regular issue, but these six promo cards can be distinguished from the regular set by the use of a registered symbol on them instead of a trademark symbol. Also, the stats on these promo cards are carried out to only one decimal place on the card back; the regular cards carry out the stats to two places. These cards were sent to dealers along with order forms for the 1989 set.

		MT
Complete Set (6):		75.00
Common Player:		5.00
1	Joe Montana	35.00
2	Bo Jackson	15.00
3	Boomer Esiason	12.00
4	Roger Craig	8.00
5	Too Tall Jones (Registered seven sacks, regular card issue has registered 7.0 sacks)	5.00
6	Phil Simms (Moorehead State, should say Morehead State; photo cropping has Score logo blocking part of the ball)	8.00

1989 Score

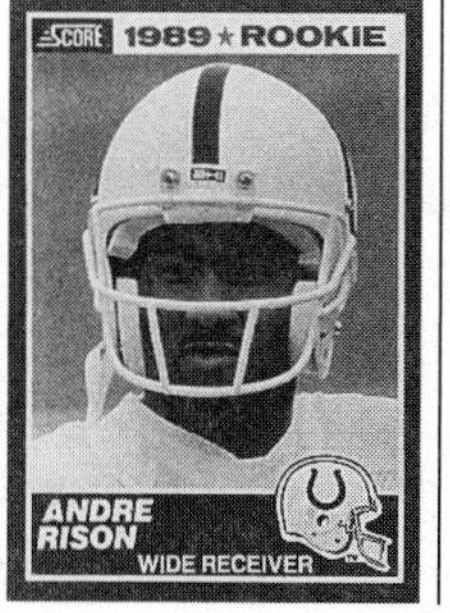

Score's premier set of football cards, a 330-card edition, was released in August 1989. An additional 110 cards were released as a boxed updated set to hobby shops in January 1990 and were numbered 331-440 with an "S" following the number. Score expanded its print run and corrected several errors in the regular set: #101, Keith Jackson (wrong uniform number on back); #122, Ricky Sanders (wrong uniform number on back); #126, Ron Hall (wrong photos on front and back); #188 Mark Carrier (wrong photo -- original back showed Bruce Hill); #218, Willie Gault (photo showed Greg Townsend); #293, Keith Jackson's All Pro card (wrong uniform number on back); #305, Tim Brown (photo showed James Lofton); and #316, Eric Thomas (wrong uniform number on back). The corrected cards were issued in both wax boxes and in factory sets, a Score spokesman said. The corrected cards are scarcer than the error cards. Score was the first set to include the same year's first-round draft picks. Rookies in this set include Barry Sanders, Deion Sanders, Troy Aikman, Louis Oliver, Dave Meggett, Erik McMillan and Don Majkowski.

		MT
Complete Set (330):		130.00
Comp. Factory Set (330):		150.00
Common Player:		.10
Minor Stars:		.20
Pack (15):		20.00
Wax Box (36):		545.00
1	Joe Montana	3.00
2	Bo Jackson	1.00
3	Boomer Esiason	.20
4	Roger Craig	.10
5	Ed Jones	.10
6	Phil Simms	.20
7	Dan Hampton	.10
8	*John Settle*	.10
9	Bernie Kosar	.20
10	Al Toon	.10
11	*Bubby Brister*	3.00
12	Mark Clayton	.10
13	Dan Marino	4.00
14	Joe Morris	.10
15	Warren Moon	1.00
16	Chuck Long	.10
17	Mark Jackson	.10
18	*Michael Irvin*	5.00
19	Bruce Smith	.10
20	Anthony Carter	.10
21	Charles Haley	.20
22	Dave Duerson	.10
23	Troy Stradford	.10
24	Freeman McNeil	.10
25	Jerry Gray	.10
26	Bill Maas	.10
27	*Chris Chandler*	6.00
28	*Tom Newberry*	.10
29	Albert Lewis	.10
30	Jay Schroeder	.10
31	Dalton Hilliard	.10
32	Tony Eason	.10
33	Rick Donnelly	.10
34	Herschel Walker	.20
35	Wesley Walker	.10
36	Chris Doleman	.20
37	Pat Swilling	.20
38	Joey Browner	.10
39	Shane Conlan	.10
40	Mike Tomczak	.10
41	Webster Slaughter	.10
42	Ray Donaldson	.10
43	Christian Okoye	.10
44	Jon Bosa	.10
45	*Aaron Cox*	.10
46	Bobby Hebert	.10
47	Carl Banks	.10
48	Jeff Fuller	.10
49	Gerald Willhite	.10
50	Mike Singletary	.10
51	Stanley Morgan	.10
52	Mark Bavaro	.10
53	Mickey Shuler	.10
54	Keith Millard	.10
55	Andre Tippett	.10
56	Vance Johnson	.10
57	*Bennie Blades*	.20
58	Tim Harris	.10
59	Hanford Dixon	.10
60	*Chris Miller*	1.50
61	Cornelius Bennett	.75
62	Neal Anderson	.10
63	Ickey Woods	.10
64	Gary Anderson	.10
65	*Vaughan Johnson*	.20
66	Ronnie Lippett	.10
67	Mike Quick	.10
68	Roy Green	.10
69	Tim Krumrie	.10
70	Mark Malone	.10
71	James Jones	.10
72	*Cris Carter*	20.00
73	Ricky Nattiel	.10
74	Jim Arnold	.10
75	Randall Cunningham	1.00
76	John L. Williams	.10
77	*Paul Gruber*	.10
78	*Rod Woodson*	4.00
79	Ray Childress	.10
80	Doug Williams	.10
81	Deron Cherry	.10
82	John Offerdahl	.10
83	Louis Lipps	.10
84	Neil Lomax	.10
85	Wade Wilson	.10
86	*Tim Brown*	12.00
87	Chris Hinton	.10
88	Stump Mitchell	.10
89	Tunch Ilkin	.10
90	Steve Pelluer	.10
91	Brian Noble	.10
92	Reggie White	1.00
93	*Aundray Bruce*	.10
94	Garry James	.10
95	Drew Hill	.10
96	Anthony Munoz	.10
97	James Wilder	.10
98	Dexter Manley	.10
99	Lee Williams	.10

100	Dave Krieg	.10
101	*Keith Jackson* ERR (incorrect number 84)	1.00
101a	*Keith Jackson* COR (correct number 88)	1.00
102	Luis Sharpe	.10
103	Kevin Greene	.20
104	Duane Bickett	.10
105	*Mark Rypien*	.75
106	Curt Warner	.10
107	Jacob Green	.10
108	Gary Clark	.20
109	*Bruce Matthews*	1.00
110	Bill Fralic	.10
111	Bill Bates	.10
112	Jeff Bryant	.10
113	Charles Mann	.10
114	Richard Dent	.10
115	Bruce Hill	.10
116	*Mark May*	.10
117	*Mark Collins*	.10
118	Ron Holmes	.10
119	*Scott Case*	.20
120	Tom Rathman	.10
121	Dennis McKinnon	.10
122	Ricky Sanders ERR (incorrect number 46)	.25
122a	Ricky Sanders COR (correct number 83)	.50
123	Michael Carter	.10
124	Ozzie Newsome	.10
125	Irving Fryar	.10
126	*Ron Hall* ERR (wrong photo)	.25
126a	*Ron Hall* COR (corrected photo)	.50
127	Clay Matthews	.10
128	Leonard Marshall	.10
129	Kevin Mack	.10
130	Art Monk	.20
131	Garin Veris	.10
132	Steve Jordan	.10
133	Frank Minnifield	.10
134	Eddie Brown	.10
135	Stacey Bailey	.10
136	Rickey Jackson	.10
137	Henry Ellard	.10
138	Jim Burt	.10
139	Jerome Brown	.10
140	*Rodney Holman*	.20
141	Sammy Winder	.10
142	Marcus Cotton	.10
143	Jim Jeffcoat	.10
144	Reuben Mayes	.10
145	Jim McMahon	.10
146	Reggie Williams	.10
147	John Anderson	.10
148	*Harris Barton*	.20
149	Philip Epps	.10
150	Jay Hilgenberg	.10
151	Earl Ferrell	.10
152	Andre Reed	.50
153	Dennis Gentry	.10
154	Max Montoya	.10
155	Darrin Nelson	.10
156	Jeff Chadwick	.10
157	James Brooks	.10
158	Keith Bishop	.10
159	Robert Awalt	.10
160	Marty Lyons	.10
161	Johnny Hector	.10
162	Tony Casillas	.10
163	*Kyle Clifton*	.20
164	Cody Risien	.10
165	Jamie Holland	.10
166	*Merril Hoge*	.10
167	*Chris Spielman*	1.50
168	Carlos Carson	.10
169	*Jerry Ball*	.20
170	*Don Majkowski*	.20
171	Everson Walls	.10
172	Mike Rozier	.10
173	Matt Millen	.10
174	Karl Mecklenberg	.10
175	Paul Palmer	.10
176	*Brian Blades*	1.00
177	Brent Fullwood	.10
178	*Anthony Miller*	1.00
179	Brian Sochia	.10
180	*Stephen Baker*	.20
181	Jesse Solomon	.10
182	John Grimsley	.10
183	Timmy Newsome	.10
184	*Steve Sewell*	.10
185	Dean Biasucci	.10
186	Alonzo Highsmith	.10
187	Randy Grimes	.10
188	*Mark Carrier* ERR (back shows Bruce Hill)	1.50
188a	Mark Carrier COR (corrected)	1.50
189	Vann McElroy	.10
190	Greg Bell	.10
191	*Quinn Early*	2.00
192	Lawrence Taylor	.50
193	Albert Bentley	.10
194	Ernest Givins	.20
195	Jackie Slater	.10
196	Jim Sweeney	.10
197	Freddie Joe Nunn	.10
198	Keith Byars	.10
199	*Hardy Nickerson*	1.50
200	*Steve Beuerlein*	5.00
201	*Bruce Armstrong*	.20
202	Lionel Manuel	.10
203	J.T. Smith	.10
204	*Mark Ingram*	1.00
205	Fred Smerlas	.10
206	*Bryan Hinkle*	.10
207	Steve McMichael	.10
208	Nick Lowery	.10
209	Jack Trudeau	.10
210	Lorenzo Hampton	.10
211	*Thurman Thomas*	5.00
212	Steve Young	2.00
213	James Lofton	.10
214	Jim Covert	.10
215	Ronnie Lott	.20
216	Stephone Paige	.10
217	Mark Duper	.10
218	Willie Gault ERR (shows Greg Townsend)	.25
218a	Willie Gault COR (corrected)	.50
219	*Ken Ruettgers*	.10
220	*Kevin Ross*	.10
221	Jerry Rice	3.00
222	Billy Ray Smith	.10
223	Jim Kelly	1.00
224	Vinny Testaverde	.40
225	Steve Largent	.75
226	*Warren Williams*	.10
227	Morten Andersen	.10
228	Bill Brooks	.10
229	*Reggie Langhorne*	.20
230	Pepper Johnson	.10
231	Pat Leahy	.10
232	Fred Marion	.10
233	Gary Zimmerman	.10
234	Marcus Allen	.50
235	*Gaston Green*	.20
236	*John Stephens*	.20
237	Terry Kinard	.10
238	*John Taylor*	1.50
239	Brian Bosworth	.10
240	Anthony Toney	.10
241	Ken O'Brien	.10
242	Howie Long	.10
243	Doug Flutie	2.00
244	Jim Everett	.30
245	*Broderick Thomas*	.20
246	*Deion Sanders*	12.00
247	*Donnell Woolford*	1.00
248	*Wayne Martin*	.75
249	*David Williams*	.10
250	Bill Hawkins	.10
251	*Eric Hill*	.10
252	*Burt Grossman*	.20
253	Tracy Rocker	.10
254	*Steve Wisniewski*	.20
255	*Jessie Small*	.10
256	David Braxton	.10
257	*Barry Sanders*	80.00
258	*Derrick Thomas*	5.00
259	*Eric Metcalf*	2.00
260	*Keith DeLong*	.20
261	Hart Lee Dykes	.10
262	*Sammie Smith*	.20
263	*Steve Atwater*	1.00
264	*Eric Ball*	.20
265	*Don Beebe*	1.00
266	Brian Williams	.10
267	*Jeff Lageman*	.30
268	*Tim Worley*	.20
269	Tony Mandarich	.10
270	*Troy Aikman*	40.00
271	*Andy Heck*	.20
272	*Andre Rison*	5.00
273	AFC Championship Game	.20
274	NFC Championship (Joe Montana)	1.00
275	Joe Montana, Jerry Rice	2.00
276	Rodney Carter	.10
277	Mark Jackson, Vance Johnson, Ricky Nattiel	.10
278	John Williams, Curt Warner	.10
279	Joe Montana, Jerry Rice	2.00
280	Roy Green, Neil Lomax	.10
281	Randall Cunningham, Keith Jackson	.20
282	Chris Doleman, Keith Millard	.10
283	Mark Duper, Mark Clayton	.10
284	Allen, Jackson	.50
285	Frank Minnifield (AP)	.10
286	Bruce Matthews (AP)	.10
287	Joey Browner (AP)	.10
288	Jay Hilgenberg (AP)	.10
289	*Carl Lee* (AP)	.10
290	Scott Norwood (AP)	.10
291	John Taylor (AP)	.50
292	Jerry Rice (AP)	1.00
293	Keith Jackson ERR (AP, incorrect number)	.50
293a	Keith Jackson COR (AP, corrected)	.50
294	Gary Zimmerman (AP)	.10
295	Lawrence Taylor (AP)	.20
296	Reggie White (AP)	.20
297	Roger Craig (AP)	.10
298	Boomer Esiason (AP)	.10
299	Cornelius Bennett (AP)	.10
300	Mike Horan (AP)	.10
301	Deron Cherry (AP)	.10
302	Tom Newberry (AP)	.10
303	Mike Singletary (AP)	.10
304	Shane Conlan (AP)	.10
305	Tim Brown ERR (AP, shows James Lofton)	2.00
305a	Tim Brown COR (AP, corrected)	2.00
306	Henry Ellard (AP)	.10
307	Bruce Smith (AP)	.10
308	Tim Krumrie (AP)	.10
309	Anthony Munoz (AP)	.10
310	Darrell Green (SB)	.10
311	Anthony Miller (SB)	.50
312	Wesley Walker (SB)	.10
313	Ron Brown (SB)	.10
314	Bo Jackson (SB)	.40
315	Philip Epps (SB)	.10
316	*Eric Thomas* ERR (SB, wrong number)	.25
316a	*Eric Thomas* COR (SB, corrected)	.50
317	Herschel Walker (SB)	.20
318	Jacob Green (PD)	.10
319	Andre Tippett	.10
320	Freddie Joe Nunn (PD)	.10
321	Reggie White (PD)	.20
322	Lawrence Taylor (PD)	.20
323	Greg Townsend (PD)	.10
324	Tim Harris (PD)	.10
325	Bruce Smith (PD)	.10
326	Tony Dorsett (RB)	.30
327	Steve Largent (RB)	.50
328	Tim Brown (RB)	2.00
329	Joe Montana (RB)	1.50
330	Tom Landry (Tribute)	1.00

1989 Score Supplemental

These 110 cards continue with numbers where the 1989 Score regular set left off at - 330. The cards are numbered using an "S" prefix, however. The design is similar to the regular issue's, but the supplemental cards have purple borders. The cards were distributed as a complete, boxed set only.

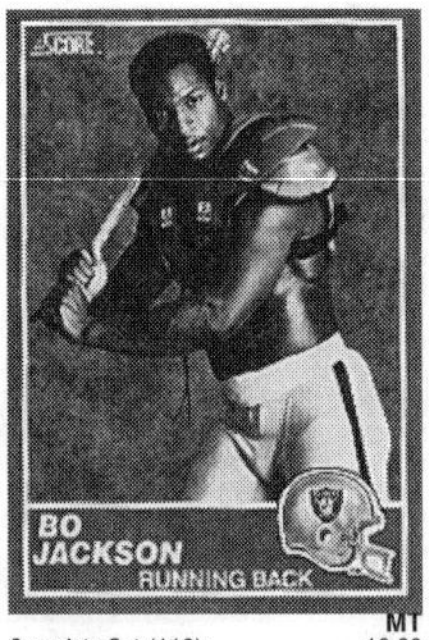

		MT
	Complete Set (110):	10.00
	Common Player:	.05
	Minor Stars:	.10
331	Herschel Walker	.10
332	*Allen Pinkett*	.05
333	*Sterling Sharpe*	4.00
334	*Alvin Walton*	.05
335	*Frank Reich*	.50
336	*Jim Thornton*	.05
337	David Fulcher	.05
338	Raul Allegre	.05
339	John Elway	3.00
340	Michael Cofer	.05
341	Jim Skow	.05
342	Steve DeBerg	.05
343	Mervyn Fernandez	.05
344	Mike Lansford	.05
345	Reggie Roby	.05
346	Raymond Clayborn	.05
347	Lonzell Hill	.05
348	Ottis Anderson	.05
349	*Erik McMillan*	.05
350	*Al Harris*	.05
351	*Jack Del Rio*	1.00
352	Gary Anderson	.10
353	Jim McMahon	.10
354	Keena Turner	.05
355	*Tony Woods*	.05
356	Donald Igwebuike	.05
357	Gerald Riggs	.05
358	Eddie Murray	.05
359	Dino Hackett	.05
360	*Brad Muster*	.05
361	Paul Palmer	.05
362	Jerry Robinson	.05
363	*Simon Fletcher*	.50
364	Tommy Kramer	.05
365	Jim C. Jensen	.05
366	*Lorenzo White*	.50
367	Fredd Young	.05
368	Ron Jaworski	.05
369	Mel Owens	.05
370	Dave Waymer	.05
371	Sean Landeta	.05
372	Sam Mills	.05
373	Todd Blackledge	.05
374	JoJo Townsell	.05
375	Ron Wolfley	.05
376	Ralf Mojsiejenko	.05
377	Eric Wright	.05
378	Newsby Glasgow	.05
379	Darryl Talley	.05
380	*Eric Allen*	.40
381	Dennis Smith	.05
382	John Tice	.05
383	Jesse Solomon	.05
384	Bo Jackson	1.50
385	Mike Merriweather	.05
386	Maurice Carthon	.05
387	Dave Grayson	.05
388	Wilber Marshall	.05
389	David Wyman	.05
390	*Thomas Everett*	.05
391	Alex Gordon	.05
392	D.J. Dozier	.05
393	*Scott Radecic*	.05
394	Eric Thomas	.05
395	Mike Gann	.05
396	William Perry	.05
397	Carl Hariston	.05
398	Billy Ard	.05
399	Donnell Thompson	.05
400	Mike Webster	.05
401	Scott Davis	.05
402	Sean Farrell	.05
403	*Mike Golic*	.05
404	Mike Kenn	.05
405	*Keith Van Horne*	.05
406	Bob Golic	.05
407	*Neil Smith*	2.50
408	*Dermontti Dawson*	.05
409	Leslie O'Neal	.10
410	Matt Bahr	.05
411	*Guy McIntyre*	.10
412	Bryan Millard	.05
414	*Rob Taylor*	.05
415	Tony Zendejas	.05
416	Vai Sikahema	.05
417	Gary Reasons	.05
418	*Shawn Collins*	.05
419	*Mark Green*	.05
420	*Courtney Hall*	.05
421	*Bobby Humphrey*	.05
422	*Myron Guyton*	.05
423	Darryl Ingram	.05
424	*Chris Jacke*	.10
425	Keith Jones	.05
426	*Robert Massey*	.05
427	*Bubba McDowell*	.05
428	*Dave Meggett*	1.00
429	*Louis Oliver*	.05
430	Danny Peebles	.05
431	*Rodney Peete*	1.00
432	*Jeff Query*	.10
433	*Timm Rosenbach*	.05
434	*Frank Stams*	.05
435	*Lawyer Tillman*	.05
436	*Billy Joe Tolliver*	.10
437	*Floyd Turner*	.30
438	*Steve Walsh*	.75
439	*Joe Wolf*	.05
440	*Trace Armstrong*	.05

A player's name in *italic type* indicates a rookie card.

1989 Score Franco Harris

This card, which has two versions, was given to those who received Franco Harris' autograph at the Super Bowl show in New Orleans. The unnumbered standard-size cards have identical fronts and are similar in design to Score's 1989 regular set. The difference on the card backs is in the text which describes Harris' status as a potential Hall of Famer. Earlier versions say Harris was a "sure-shot" to be elected to the Hall of Fame. He was elected during the show, so the text was changed to say "Hall of Famer." The "sure-shot" cards are scarcer.

		MT
	Complete Set (2):	135.00
	Common Player:	65.00
1A	Franco Harris (Sure-shot)	80.00
1B	Franco Harris (Hall of Famer)	65.00

1990 Score Promos

These cards were sent to dealers along with order forms for Score's 1990 regular set. The design is similar to the regular issue, except the photos are cropped tighter. They also use a registered symbol on them, not the trademark symbol which is used on the regular cards.

		MT
	Complete Set (3):	18.00
	Common Player:	2.50
20	Barry Sanders	14.00
184	Robert Delpino	2.50
256	Cornelius Bennett	5.00

1990 Score

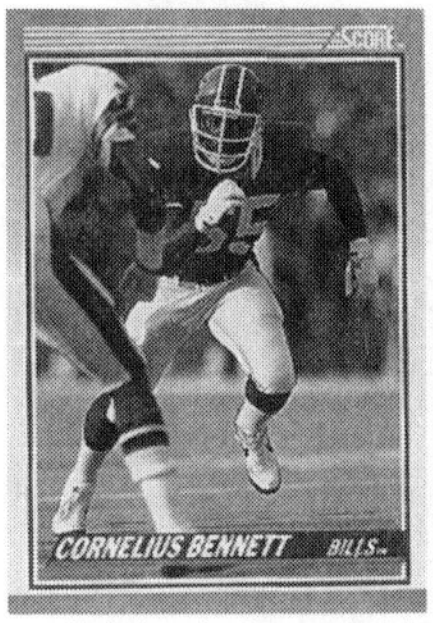

Variations in the set include #134, Kevin Butler (uncorrected photo on back shows him wearing a helmet; corrected photo shows him without helmet), #136, Vai Sikahema (uncorrected photo on back shows him wearing a helmet; corrected photo to shows him without a helmet), #147, Joey Browner (uncorrected back shows him looking into the sun; corrected back show more of a profile); #208, Ralf Mojsiejenko (uncorrected stats read "Chargers"; corrected stats read "Redskins."); and #600, Buck Buchanan (uncorrected back says he was the first player selected in the '83 AFL draft; it was corrected to read the '63 draft). Note: Rookie cards in the first series contained no information on which NFL team the player was drafted by; thus they are considered first cards, not rookie cards. (Key: HG - Hot Gun; GF - Ground Force; DP - draft pick)

		MT
	Complete Set (660):	8.00
	Complete Series 1 (1-330):	4.00
	Complete Series 2 (331-660):	4.00
	Common Player:	.04
	Series 1 Pack (16):	.50
	Series 1 Wax Box (36):	9.00
	Series 2 Pack (6):	.30
	Series 2 Wax Box (36):	5.00
1	Joe Montana	1.00
2	Christian Okoye	.04
3	Mike Singletary	.04
4	Jim Everett	.05
5	Phil Simms	.10
6	Brent Fullwood	.04
7	Bill Fralic	.04
8	Leslie O'Neal	.04
9	John Taylor	.20
10	Bo Jackson	.40
11	John Stephens	.05
12	Art Monk	.05
13	Dan Marino	1.50
14	John Settle	.04
15	Don Majkowski	.04
16	Bruce Smith	.04
17	Brad Muster	.04
18	Jason Buck	.04
19	James Brooks	.04
20	Barry Sanders	1.25
21	Troy Aikman	1.00
22	Allen Pinkett	.04
23	Duane Bickett	.04
24	Kevin Ross	.04
25	John Elway	.40
26	Jeff Query	.04
27	Eddie Murray	.04
28	Richard Dent	.04
29	Lorenzo White	.15
30	Eric Metcalf	.10
31	*Jeff Dellenbach*	.10
32	Leon White	.04
33	Jim Jeffcoat	.04
34	Herschel Walker	.04
35	Mike Johnson	.04
36	Joe Phillips	.04
37	Willie Gault	.04
38	Keith Millard	.04
39	Fred Marion	.04
40	Boomer Esiason	.20
41	Dermontti Dawson	.04
42	Dino Hackett	.04
43	Reggie Roby	.04
44	Roger Vick	.04
45	Bobby Hebert	.15
46	Don Beebe	.15
47	Neal Anderson	.10
48	Johnny Holland	.04
49	Bobby Humphrey	.04
50	Lawrence Taylor	.10
51	Billy Ray Smith	.04
52	Robert Perryman	.04
53	Gary Anderson	.04
54	Raul Allegre	.04
55	Pat Swilling	.04
56	Chris Doleman	.04
57	Andre Reed	.20
58	Seth Joyner	.04
59	Bart Oates	.04
60	Bernie Kosar	.04
61	Dave Krieg	.04
62	Lars Tate	.04
63	Scott Norwood	.04
64	Kyle Clifton	.04
65	Alan Veingrad	.04
66	Gerald Riggs	.04
67	Tim Worley	.04
68	Rodney Holman	.04
69	Tony Zendejas	.04
70	Chris Miller	.10
71	Wilber Marshall	.04
72	*Skip McClendon*	.10
73	Jim Covert	.04
74	Sam Mills	.04
75	Chris Hinton	.04
76	Irv Eatman	.04
77	Bubba Paris	.04
78	John Elliott	.04
79	Thomas Everett	.04
80	Steve Smith	.04
81	Jackie Slater	.04
82	*Kelvin Martin*	.25
83	JoJo Townsell	.04
84	Jim Jensen	.04
85	Bobby Humphrey	.04
86	Mike Dyal	.04
87	Andre Rison	.25
88	Brian Sochia	.04
89	Greg Bell	.04
90	Dalton Hilliard	.04
91	Carl Banks	.04
92	Dennis Smith	.04
93	Bruce Matthews	.04
94	Charles Haley	.04
95	Deion Sanders	.35
96	Stephone Paige	.04
97	Marion Butts	.10
98	Howie Long	.04
99	Donald Igwebuike	.04
100	Roger Craig	.04
101	Charles Mann	.04
102	Fredd Young	.04
103	Chris Jacke	.04
104	Scott Case	.04
105	Warren Moon	.25
106	Clyde Simmons	.04
107	Steve Atwater	.04
108	Morten Andersen	.04
109	Eugene Marve	.04
110	Thurman Thomas	.40
111	Carnell Lake	.04
112	Jim Kelly	.30
113	Stanford Jennings	.04
114	Jacob Green	.04
115	Karl Mecklenberg	.04
116	Ray Childress	.04
117	Erik McMillan	.04
118	Harry Newsome	.04
119	James Dixon	.04
120	Hassan Jones	.04
121	Eric Allen	.04
122	Felix Wright	.04
123	Merril Hoge	.04
124	Eric Ball	.04
125	Willie Anderson	.10
126	James Jefferson	.04
127	Tim McDonald	.04
128	Larry Kinnebrew	.04
129	Mark Collins	.04
130	Ickey Woods	.04
131	Jeff Donaldson	.04
132	Rich Camarillo	.04
133	Melvin Bratton	.04
134	Kevin Butler (helmet)	.05
134a	Kevin Butler (without helmet)	.05
135	Albert Bentley	.04
136	Vai Sikahema (helmet on back)	.08
136a	Vai Sikahema (without helmet)	.08
137	*Todd McNair*	.10
138	Alonzo Highsmith	.04
139	Brian Blades	.10
140	Jeff Lageman	.04
141	Eric Thomas	.04
142	Derek Hill	.04
143	Rick Fenney	.04
144	Herman Heard	.04
145	Steve Young	1.00
146	Kent Hull	.04
147	Joey Browner	.04
148	Frank Minnifield	.04
149	Robert Massey	.04
150	Dave Meggett	.10
151	Bubba McDowell	.04
152	*Rickey Dixon*	.10
153	Ray Donaldson	.04
154	Alvin Walton	.04
155	Mike Cofer	.04
156	Darryl Talley	.04
157	A.J. Johnson	.04
158	Jerry Gray	.04
159	Keith Byars	.04
160	Andy Heck	.04
161	Mike Munchak	.04
162	Dennis Gentry	.04
163	Timm Rosenbach	.04
164	Randall McDaniel	.04
165	Pat Leahy	.04
166	Bubby Brister	.10
167	Aundray Bruce	.04
168	Bill Brooks	.04
169	*Eddie Anderson*	.10
170	Ronnie Lott	.10
171	Jay Hilgenberg	.04
172	Joe Nash	.04
173	Simon Fletcher	.04
174	Shane Conlan	.04
175	Sean Landeta	.04
176	*John Alt*	.10
177	Clay Matthews	.04
178	Anthony Munoz	.04
179	Pete Holohan	.04
180	Robert Awalt	.04
181	Rohn Stark	.04
182	Vance Johnson	.04
184	Robert Delpino	.04
185	Drew Hill	.04
186	Reggie Langhorne	.04
187	Lonzell Hill	.04
188	Tom Rathman	.04
189	*Greg Montgomery*	.10
190	Leonard Smith	.04
191	Chris Spielman	.04
192	Tom Newberry	.04
193	Chris Carter	.35
194	Kevin Porter	.04
195	Donnell Thompson	.04
196	Vaughan Johnson	.04
197	Steve McMichael	.04
198	Jim Sweeney	.04
199	Rich Karlis	.04
200	Jerry Rice	1.00
201	Dan Hampton	.04
202	Jim Lachey	.04
203	Reggie White	.15
204	Jerry Ball	.04
205	Russ Grimm	.04
206	*Tim Green*	.08
207	Shawn Collins	.04
208	Ralf Mojsiejenko (Chargers on back)	.05
208a	Ralf Mojsiejenko (Redskins on back)	.05
209	Trace Armstrong	.04
210	Keith Jackson	.25
211	Jamie Holland	.04
212	Mark Clayton	.04
213	Jeff Cross	.04
214	Bob Gagliano	.04
215	Louis Oliver	.04
216	Jim Arnold	.04
217	*Robert Clark*	.08
218	Gill Byrd	.04
219	Rodney Peete	.08
220	Anthony Miller	.30
221	Steve Grogan	.04
222	Vince Newsome	.04
223	Tom Benson	.04
224	Kevin Murphy	.04
225	Henry Ellard	.04
226	Richard Johnson	.04
227	Jim Skow	.04
228	Keith Jones	.04
229	Dave Brown	.04
230	Marcus Allen	.04
231	Steve Walsh	.04
232	Jim Harbaugh	.10
233	Mel Gray	.04
234	David Treadwell	.04
235	John Offerdahl	.04
236	Gary Reasons	.04
237	Tim Krumrie	.04
238	Dave Duerson	.04
239	Gary Clark	.10
240	Mark Jackson	.04
241	Mark Murphy	.04
242	Jerry Holmes	.04
243	Tim McGee	.04
244	Mike Tomczak	.04
245	Sterling Sharpe	.10
246	Bennie Blades	.04
247	*Ken Harvey*	.10
248	Ron Heller	.04
249	Louis Lipps	.04
250	Wade Wilson	.04
251	Freddie Joe Nunn	.04
252	Jerome Brown	.04
253	Myron Guyton	.04
254	*Nate Odomes*	.25
255	Rod Woodson	.25
256	Cornelius Bennett	.04
257	Keith Woodside	.04
258	Jeff Uhlenhake	.04
259	Harry Hamilton	.04
260	Mark Bavaro	.04
261	Vinny Testaverde	.10
262	Steve DeBerg	.04
263	Steve Wisniewski	.04
264	Pete Mandley	.04
265	Tim Harris	.04
266	Jack Trudeau	.04
267	Mark Kelso	.04
268	Brian Noble	.04
269	*Jessie Tuggle*	.20
270	Ken O'Brien	.04
271	David Little	.04
272	Pete Stoyanovich	.04
273	*Odessa Turner*	.10
274	Anthony Toney	.04
275	Tunch Ilkin	.04
276	Carl Lee	.04
277	Hart Lee Dykes	.04
278	Al Noga	.04
279	Greg Lloyd	.04
280	Billy Joe Tolliver	.04
281	Kirk Lowdermilk	.04
282	Earl Ferrell	.04
283	Eric Sievers	.04
284	Steve Jordan	.04
285	Burt Grossman	.04
286	Johnny Rembert	.04
287	*Jeff Jaeger*	.10
288	James Hasty	.04
289	Tony Mandarich	.10
290	*Chris Singleton* (DP)	.10
291	Lynn James (DP, FC)	.10
292	*Andre Ware* (DP)	.20
293	*Ray Agnew* (DP)	.10
294	*Joel Smeenge* (DP)	.10
295	*Marc Spindler* (DP)	.10
296	*Renaldo Turnbull* (DP)	.40
297	Reggie Rembert (DP)	.04
298	Jeff Alm (DP)	.04
299	*Cortez Kennedy* (DP)	.30
300	*Blair Thomas* (DP)	.10
301	*Pat Terrell* (DP)	.10
302	*Junior Seau* (DP)	1.00
303	Mohammed Elewonibi (DP)	.04
304	*Tony Bennett* (DP)	.35
305	*Percy Snow* (DP)	.08

306	*Richmond Webb* (DP)	.15
307	*Rodney Hampton* (DP)	1.00
308	*Barry Foster* (DP)	.10
309	*John Friesz* (DP)	.25
310	*Ben Smith* (DP)	.08
311	Joe Montana (HG)	.50
312	Jim Everett (HG)	.04
313	Mark Rypien (HG)	.08
314	Phil Simms (HG)	.08
315	Don Majkowski (HG)	.04
316	Boomer Esiason (HG)	.10
317	Warren Moon (HG)	.10
318	Jim Kelly (HG)	.10
319	Bernie Kosar (HG)	.04
320	Dan Marino (HG)	.40
321	Christian Okoye (GF)	.04
322	Thurman Thomas (GF)	.20
323	James Brooks (GF)	.04
324	Bobby Humphrey (GF)	.04
325	Barry Sanders (GF)	.75
326	Neal Anderson (GF)	.04
327	Dalton Hilliard (GF)	.04
328	Greg Bell (GF)	.04
329	Roger Craig (GF)	.04
330	Bo Jackson (GF)	.20
331	Don Warren	.04
332	Rufus Porter	.04
333	Sammie Smith	.04
334	Lewis Tillman	.20
335	Michael Walter	.04
336	Marc Logan	.04
337	*Ron Hallstrom*	.08
338	Stanley Morgan	.04
339	Mark Robinson	.04
340	Frank Reich	.20
341	Chip Lohmiller	.10
342	Steve Beuerlein	.25
343	John L. Williams	.04
344	Irving Fryar	.04
345	Anthony Carter	.04
346	Al Toon	.04
347	J.T. Smith	.04
348	*Pierce Holt*	.10
349	Ferrell Edmunds	.04
350	Mark Rypien	.15
351	Paul Gruber	.04
352	Ernest Givins	.04
353	Ervin Randle	.04
354	Guy McIntyre	.04
355	Webster Slaughter	.04
356	Reuben Davis	.04
357	Rickey Jackson	.04
358	Earnest Byner	.04
359	Eddie Brown	.04
360	Troy Stradford	.04
361	Pepper Johnson	.04
362	Ravin Caldwell	.04
363	*Chris Mohr*	.08
364	Jeff Bryant	.04
365	Bruce Collie	.04
366	Courtney Hall	.04
367	Jerry Olsavsky	.04
368	David Galloway	.04
369	Wes Hopkins	.04
370	Johnny Hector	.04
371	Clarence Verdin	.04
372	Nick Lowery	.04
373	Tim Brown	.45
374	Kevin Greene	.04
375	Leonard Marshall	.04
376	Roland James	.04
377	Scott Studwell	.04
378	Jarvis Williams	.04
379	Mike Saxon	.04
380	Kevin Mack	.04
381	Joe Kelly	.04
382	*Tom Thayer*	.10
383	Roy Green	.04
384	*Michael Brooks*	.20
385	Michael Cofer	.04
386	Ken Ruettgers	.04
387	Dean Steinkuhler	.04
388	Maurice Carthon	.04
389	Ricky Sanders	.04
390	*Winton Moss*	.10
391	Tony Woods	.04
392	Keith DeLong	.04
393	David Wyman	.04
394	Vencie Glenn	.04
395	Harris Barton	.04
396	Bryan Hinkle	.04
397	Derek Kennard	.04
398	*Heath Sherman*	.20
399	Troy Benson	.04
400	Gary Zimmerman	.04
401	Mark Duper	.04
402	Eugene Lockhart	.04
403	Tim Manoa	.04
404	Reggie Williams	.04
405	*Mark Bortz*	.10
406	Mike Kenn	.04
407	John Grimsley	.04
408	*Bill Romanowski*	.10
409	Perry Kemp	.04
410	Norm Johnson	.04
411	Broderick Thomas	.04
412	Joe Wolf	.04
413	Andre Waters	.04
414	Jason Staurovsky	.04
415	Eric Martin	.04
416	Joe Prokop	.04
417	Steve Sewell	.04
418	Cedric Jones	.04
419	Alphonso Carreker	.04
420	Keith Willis	.04
421	Bobby Butler	.04
422	John Roper	.04
423	Tim Spencer	.04
424	*Jesse Sapolu*	.08
425	Ron Wolfley	.04
426	Doug Smith	.04
427	William Howard	.04
428	Keith Van Horne	.04
429	Tony Jordan	.04
430	Mervyn Fernandez	.04
431	*Shaun Gayle*	.10
432	Ricky Nattiel	.04
433	Albert Lewis	.04
434	*Fred Banks*	.10
435	Henry Thomas	.04
436	Chet Brooks	.04
437	Mark Ingram	.04
438	Jeff Gossett	.04
439	Mike Wilcher	.04
440	Deron Cherry	.04
441	Mike Rozier	.04
442	Jon Hand	.04
443	Ozzie Newsome	.10
444	Sammy Martin	.04
445	Luis Sharpe	.04
446	Lee Williams	.04
447	*Chris Martin*	.10
448	Kevin Fagan	.04
449	Gene Lang	.04
450	Greg Townsend	.04
451	Robert Lyles	.04
452	Eric Hill	.04
453	John Teltschik	.04
454	Vestee Jackson	.04
455	Bruce Reimers	.04
456	*Butch Rolle*	.10
457	Lawyer Tillman	.04
458	Andre Tippett	.04
459	James Thornton	.04
460	Randy Grimes	.04
461	Larry Roberts	.04
462	Ron Holmes	.04
463	Mike Wise	.04
464	*Danny Copeland*	.10
465	*Bruce Wilkerson*	.10
466	Mike Quick	.04
467	Mickey Shuler	.04
468	Mike Prior	.04
469	Ron Rivera	.04
470	Dean Biasucci	.04
471	Perry Williams	.04
472	Darren Comeaux	.04
473	Freeman McNeil	.04
474	Tyrone Braxton	.04
475	Jay Schroeder	.04
476	Naz Worthen	.04
477	Lionel Washington	.04
478	Carl Zander	.04
479	Al Baker	.04
480	Mike Merriweather	.04
481	Mike Gann	.04
482	Brent Williams	.04
483	Eugene Robinson	.04
484	Ray Horton	.04
485	Bruce Armstrong	.04
486	John Fourcade	.04
487	Lewis Billups	.04
489	Ken Sims	.04
490	Chris Chandler	.04
491	Mark Lee	.04
492	Johnny Meads	.04
493	Tim Irwin	.04
494	E.J. Junior	.04
495	Hardy Nickerson	.04
496	Rob McGovern	.04
497	*Fred Strickland*	.10
498	*Reggie Rutland*	.10
499	Mel Owens	.04
500	Derrick Thomas	.25
501	Jerrol Williams	.04
502	*Maurice Hurst*	.10
503	*Larry Kelm*	.10
504	Herman Fontenot	.04
505	Pat Beach	.04
506	*Haywood Jeffires*	.85
507	Neil Smith	.25
508	Cleveland Gary	.10
509	William Perry	.04
510	Michael Carter	.04
511	Walker Lee Ashley	.04
512	Bob Golic	.04
513	*Danny Villa*	.08
514	Matt Millen	.04
515	Don Griffin	.04
516	Jonathan Hayes	.04
517	*Gerald Williams*	.08
518	Scott Fulhage	.04
519	Irv Pankey	.04
520	*Randy Dixon*	.08
521	Terry McDaniel	.04
522	Dan Saleaumua	.04
523	Darrin Nelson	.04
524	Leonard Griffin	.04
525	Michael Ball	.04
526	*Ernie Jones*	.25
527	Tony Eason	.04
528	Ed Reynolds	.04
529	Gary Hogeboom	.04
530	Don Mosebar	.04
531	Ottis Anderson	.04
532	Bucky Scribner	.04
533	Aaron Cox	.04
534	Sean Jones	.04
535	Doug Flutie	.75
536	Leo Lewis	.04
537	Art Still	.04
538	Matt Bahr	.04
539	Keena Turner	.04
540	Sammy Winder	.04
541	Mike Webster	.04
542	*Doug Riesenberg*	.10
543	Dan Fike	.04
544	Clarence Kay	.04
545	Jim Burt	.04
546	Mike Horan	.04
547	Al Harris	.04
548	Maury Buford	.04
549	Jerry Robinson	.04
550	Tracy Rocker	.04
551	Karl Mecklenburg (CC)	.04
552	Lawrence Taylor (CC)	.08
553	Derrick Thomas (CC)	.20
554	Mike Singletary (CC)	.04
555	Tim Harris (CC)	.04
556	Jerry Rice (RM)	.40
557	Art Monk (RM)	.04
558	Mark Carrier (RM)	.04
559	Andre Reed (RM)	.08
560	Sterling Sharpe (RM)	.30
561	Herschel Walker (GF)	.04
562	Ottis Anderson (GF)	.04
563	Randall Cunningham (HG)	.08
564	John Elway (HG)	.20
565	David Fulcher (AP)	.04
566	Ronnie Lott (AP)	.04
567	Jerry Gray (AP)	.04
568	Albert Lewis (AP)	.04
569	Karl Mecklenburg (AP)	.04
570	Mike Singletary (AP)	.04
571	Lawrence Taylor (AP)	.08
572	Tim Harris (AP)	.04
573	Keith Millard (AP)	.04
574	Reggie White (AP)	.04
575	Chris Doleman (AP)	.04
576	Dave Meggett (AP)	.04
577	Rod Woodson (AP)	.04
578	Sean Landeta (AP)	.04
579	Eddie Murray (AP)	.04
580	Barry Sanders (AP)	.75
581	Christian Okoye (AP)	.04
582	Joe Montana (AP)	.50
583	Jay Hilgenberg (AP)	.04
584	Bruce Matthews (AP)	.04
585	Tom Newberry (AP)	.04
586	Gary Zimmerman (AP)	.04
587	Anthony Munoz (AP)	.04
588	Keith Jackson (AP)	.08
589	Sterling Sharpe (AP)	.30
590	Jerry Rice (AP)	.40
591	Bo Jackson (RB)	.15
592	Steve Largent (RB)	.10
593	Flipper Anderson (RB)	.04
594	Joe Montana (RB)	.50
595	Franco Harris (HOF)	.08
596	Bob St. Clair (HOF)	.04
597	Tom Landry (HOF)	.08
598	Jack Lambert (HOF)	.04
599	Ted Hendricks (HOF)	.04
600	Buck Buchanan (HOF, "drafted '83")	.05
600a	Buck Buchanan (HOF, "drafted '63")	.05
601	Bob Griese (HOF)	.04
602	Super Bowl	.04
603	Vince Lombardi	.04
604	Mark Carrier	.04
605	Randall Cunningham	.10
606	Percy Snow (C90)	.04
607	Andre Ware (C90)	.10
608	Blair Thomas (C90)	.04
609	Eric Green (C90)	.10
610	Reggie Rembert (C90)	.04
611	Richmond Webb (C90)	.10
612	Bern Brostek (C90)	.04
613	James Williams (C90)	.04
614	Mark Carrier (C90)	.04
615	Renaldo Turnbull (C90)	.20
616	Cortez Kennedy (C90)	.40
617	Keith McCants (C90)	.04
618	*Anthony Thompson* (DP)	.10
619	*LeRoy Butler* (DP)	.20
620	*Aaron Wallace* (DP)	.10
621	*Alexander Wright* (DP)	.15
622	*Keith McCants* (DP)	.10
623	*Jimmie Jones* (DP)	.10
624	*Anthony Johnson* (DP)	.20
625	Fred Washington (DP)	.04
626	Mike Bellamy (DP)	.04
627	*Mark Carrier* (DP)	.20
628	*Harold Green* (DP)	.25
629	*Eric Green* (DP)	.40
630	*Andre Collins* (DP)	.10
631	*Lamar Lathon* (DP)	.10
632	*Terry Wooden* (DP)	.10
633	Jesse Anderson (DP)	.04
634	*Jeff George* (DP)	1.25
635	*Carwell Gardner* (DP)	.10
636	*Darrell Thompson*	.25
637	Vince Buck (DP)	.10
638	Mike Jones (DP)	.04
639	*Charles Arbuckle* (DP)	.10
640	*Dennis Brown* (DP)	.10
641	*James Williams* (DP)	.10
642	*Bern Brostek* (DP)	.10
643	*Darion Conner* (DP)	.08
644	*Mike Fox* (DP)	.08
645	*Cary Conklin* (DP)	.40
646	*Tim Grunhard* (DP)	.08
647	*Ron Cox* (DP)	.08
648	*Keith Sims* (DP)	.08
649	*Alton Montgomery* (DP)	.10
650	*Greg McMurtry* (DP)	.10
651	*Scott Mitchell* (DP)	.75
652	Tim Ryan (DP)	.04
653	Jeff Mills (DP)	.04
654	*Ricky Proehl* (DP)	.50
655	*Steve Broussard* (DP)	.08
656	*Peter Tom Willis* (DP)	.15
657	*Dexter Carter* (DP)	.15
658	Tony Casillas	.04
659	Joe Morris	.04
660	Greg Kragen	.04

1990 Score Hot Card

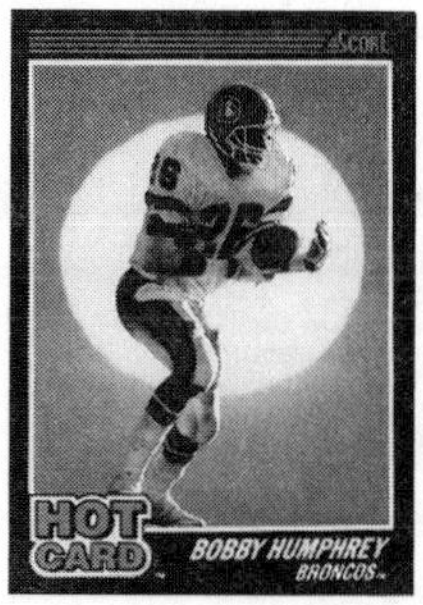

Score test-marketed a 100-card football blister pack subset in August 1990, available only at select retail accounts. Blister packs featuring 100 assorted cards from Series I and Series II. As an incentive to buy the blister packs, one "Hot Card" was included in each blister pack.

		MT
Complete Set (10):		30.00
Common Player:		1.75
1	Joe Montana	6.00
2	Bo Jackson	2.50
3	Barry Sanders	6.00
4	Jerry Rice	6.00
5	Eric Metcalf	1.75
6	Don Majkowski	1.75
7	Christian Okoye	1.75
8	Bobby Humphrey	1.75
9	Dan Marino	12.00
10	Sterling Sharpe	3.00

1990 Score Update

These cards were sold in sets only to hobby stores and included traded players as well as rookies in team uniforms.

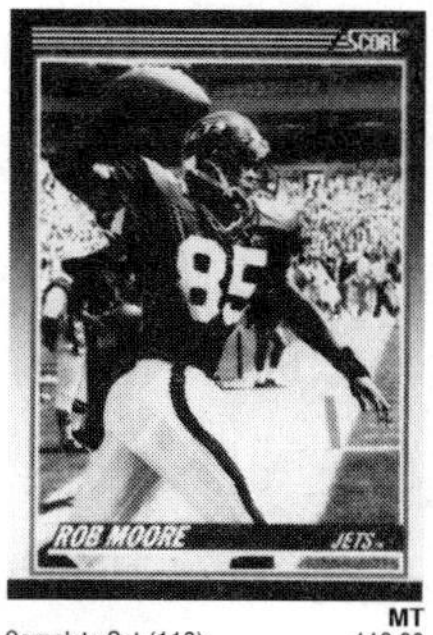

		MT
Complete Set (110):		110.00
Common Player:		.10
Minor Stars:		.20
1	Marcus Dupree	.10
2	Jerry Kauric	.10
3	Everson Walls	.10
4	Elliott Smith	.10
5	*Donald Evans*	.10
6	Jerry Holmes	.10
7	*Dan Stryzinski*	.10
8	Gerald McNeil	.10
9	*Rick Tuten*	.10
10	Mickey Shuler	.10
11	Jay Novacek	1.00
12	*Eric Williams*	.20
13	Stanley Morgan	.10
14	*Wayne Haddix*	.20
15	Gary Anderson	.20
16	*Stan Humphries*	1.00
17	Raymond Clayborn	.10
18	*Mark Boyer*	.10
19	Dave Waymer	.10
20	Andre Rison	.50
21	Daniel Stubbs	.10
22	Mike Rozier	.10
23	Damian Johnson	.10
24	Don Smith	.10
25	Max Montoya	.10
26	Terry Kinard	.10
27	Herb Welch	.10
28	Cliff Odom	.10
29	John Kidd	.10
30	*Barry Word*	.20
31	Rich Karlis	.10
32	Mike Baab	.10
33	Ronnie Harmon	.10
34	Jeff Donaldson	.10
35	Riki Ellison	.10
36	Steve Walsh	.20
37	*Bill Lewis*	.10
38	Tim McKyer	.10
39	James Wilder	.10
40	Tony Paige	.10
41	*Derrick Fenner*	.20
42	Thane Gash	.10
43	Dave Duerson	.10
44	Clarence Weathers	.10
45	Matt Bahr	.10
46	Alonzo Highsmith	.10
47	Joe Kelly	.10
48	Chris Hinton	.10
49	Bobby Humphery	.10
50	Greg Bell	.10
51	Fred Smerlas	.10
52	Dennis McKinnon	.10
53	Jim Skow	.10
54	Renaldo Turnbull	.20
55	Bern Brostek	.10
56	*Charles Wilson*	.10
57	Keith McCants	.10
58	Alexander Wright	.20
59	*Ian Beckles*	.10
60	*Eric Davis*	.20
61	Chris Singleton	.10
62	*Rob Moore*	10.00
63	Darion Conner	.10
64	Tim Gunhard	.10
65	Junior Seau	4.00
66	Tony Stargell	.10
67	Anthony Thompson	.20
68	Cortez Kennedy	.50
69	Darrell Thompson	.10
70	*Calvin Williams*	.20
71	Rodney Hampton	1.50
72	Terry Wooden	.10
73	Leo Goeas	.10
74	Ken Willis	.10
75	Ricky Proehl	.75
76	*Steve Christie*	.50
77	Andre Ware	.20
78	Jeff George	3.00
79	Walter Wilson	.10
80	*Johnny Bailey*	.20
81	*Harold Green*	.20
82	Mark Carrier	.50
83	Frank Cornish	.10
84	James Williams	.10
85	*James Francis*	.20
86	Percy Snow	.10
87	Anthony Johnson	1.00
88	Tim Ryan	.10
89	*Dan Owens*	.20
90	Aaron Wallace	.10
91	Steve Broussard	.20
92	Eric Green	.50
93	Blair Thomas	.20
94	*Robert Blackmon*	.20
95	*Alan Grant*	.10
96	Andre Collins	.10
97	Dexter Carter	.20
98	*Reggie Cobb*	.20
99	Dennis Brown	.10
100	*Kenny Davidson*	.10
101	*Emmitt Smith*	100.00
102	Jeff Alm	.10
103	Alton Montgomery	.10
104	Tony Bennett	.20
105	*Johnny Johnson*	.50
106	*Leroy Hoard*	1.50
107	Ray Agnew	.10
108	Richmond Webb	.20
109	Keith Sims	.10
110	Barry Foster	.20

1990 Score 100 Hottest

These cards featuring 100 top NFL players, have the same photos on them as the regular issue 1990 Score cards, but they are numbered differently. Publications International published a magazine to accompany the set; the magazine offered additional information about the players.

		MT
Complete Set (100):		15.00
Common Player:		.10
1	Bo Jackson	.25
2	Joe Montana	2.00
3	Deion Sanders	.50
4	Dan Marino	1.25
5	Barry Sanders	1.00
6	Neal Anderson	.15
7	Phil Simms	.20
8	Bobby Humphrey	.10
9	Roger Craig	.20
10	John Elway	.60
11	James Brooks	.15
12	Ken O'Brien	.10
13	Thurman Thomas	.50
14	Troy Aikman	2.00
15	Karl Mecklenburg	.10
16	Dave Krieg	.10
17	Chris Spielman	.10
18	Tim Harris	.15
19	Tim Worley	.10
20	Clay Matthews	.15
21	Lars Tate	.10
22	Hart Lee Dykes	.10
23	Cornelius Bennett	.15
24	Anthony Miller	.15
25	Lawrence Taylor	.30
26	Jay Hilgenberg	.10
27	Tom Rathman	.15
28	Brian Blades	.25
29	David Fulcher	.10
30	Cris Carter	.40
31	Marcus Allen	.30
32	Eric Metcalf	.15
33	Bruce Smith	.15
34	Jim Kelly	.60
35	Wade Wilson	.15
36	Rich Camarillo	.10
37	Boomer Esiason	.20
38	John Offerdahl	.10
39	Vance Johnson	.10
40	Ronnie Lott	.20
41	Kevin Ross	.15
42	Greg Bell	.10
43	Erik McMillan	.10
44	Mike Singletary	.20
45	Roger Vick	.10
46	Keith Jackson	.30
47	Henry Ellard	.15
48	Gary Anderson	.15
49	Art Monk	.30
50	Jim Everett	.15
51	Anthony Munoz	.15
52	Ray Childress	.15
53	Howie Long	.20
54	Chris Hinton	.10
55	John Stephens	.20
56	Reggie White	.25
57	Rodney Peete	.15
58	Don Majkowski	.10
59	Michael Cofer	.10
60	Bubby Brister	.10
61	Jerry Gray	.10
62	Rodney Holman	.10
63	Vinny Testaverde	.20
64	Sterling Sharpe	.65
65	Keith Millard	.10
66	Jim Lachey	.10
67	Dave Meggett	.15
68	Brent Fullwood	.10
69	Bobby Hebert	.15
70	Joey Browner	.10
71	Flipper Anderson	.15
72	Tim McGee	.10
73	Eric Allen	.10
74	Charles Haley	.25
75	Christian Okoye	.15
76	Herschel Walker	.20
77	Kelvin Martin	.15
78	Bill Fralic	.10
79	Leslie O'Neal	.15
80	Bernie Kosar	.20
81	Eric Sievers	.10
82	Timm Rosenbach	.10
83	Steve DeBerg	.15
84	Duane Bickett	.10
85	Chris Doleman	.15
86	Carl Banks	.15
87	Vaughan Johnson	.10
88	Dennis Smith	.10
89	Billy Joe Tolliver	.15
90	Dalton Hilliard	.10
91	John Taylor	.20
92	Mark Rypien	.20
93	Chris Miller	.30
94	Mark Clayton	.15
95	Andre Reed	.25
96	Warren Moon	.50
97	Bruce Matthews	.10
98	Rod Woodson	.25
99	Pat Swilling	.10
100	Jerry Rice	1.25

1990 Score Young Superstars

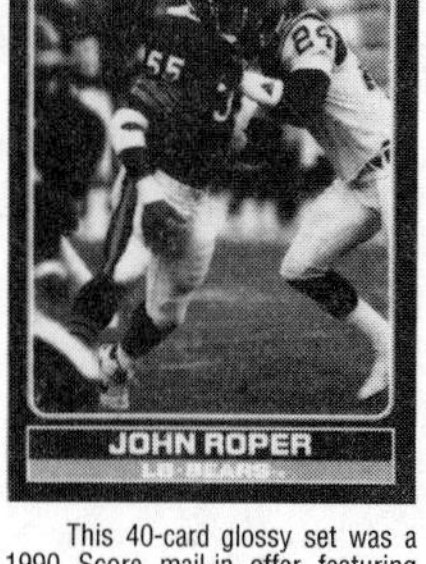

This 40-card glossy set was a 1990 Score mail-in offer featuring some of the top young players in the NFL. Each card front has an action photo framed by black borders. Each back has a full color close-up photo, plus statistics, a card number, team logo and career summary.

		MT
Complete Set (40):		8.00
Common Player:		.10
1	Barry Sanders	1.50
2	Bobby Humphrey	.40
3	Ickey Woods	.20
4	Shawn Collins	.10
5	Dave Meggett	.25
6	Keith Jackson	.25
7	Sterling Sharpe	.25
8	Troy Aikman	.75
9	Tim McDonald	.10
10	Tim Brown	.25
11	Trace Armstrong	.10
12	Eric Metcalf (Led Bears in rushing, should be Browns)	.20
13	Derrick Thomas	.35
14	Eric Hill	.10
15	Deion Sanders	.50
16	Steve Atwater	.15
17	Carnell Lake	.10
18	Andre Reed	.30
19	Chris Spielman	.15
20	Eric Allen	.10
21	Erik McMillan	.15
22	Louis Oliver	.10
23	Robert Massey	.10
24	John Roper	.10
25	Burt Grossman	.15
26	Chris Jacke	.10
27	Steve Wisniewski	.10
28	Alonzo Highsmith	.15
29	Mark Carrier	.20
30	Bruce Armstrong	.10
31	Jerome Brown	.10
32	Cornelius Bennett	.20
33	Flipper Anderson	.15
34	Brian Blades	.25
35	Anthony Miller	.20
36	Thurman Thomas	.90
37	Chris Miller	.35
38	Aundray Bruce	.15
39	Robert Clark	.15
40	Robert Delpino	.15

1990 Score Final Five

These five cards were inserted in 1990 Score Football factory sets and feature the last five picks in the 1990 NFL Draft. The "Final Five" logo is on each card front, along with a color photo of the player selected. The back has his name, position and summary of his collegiate accomplishments. Cards are numbered with a "B" prefix.

		MT
Complete Set (5):		.50
Common Player:		.05
1	Judd Garrett	.05
2	Matt Stover	.15
3	Ken McMichael	.05
4	Demetrius Davis	.05
5	Elliott Searcy	.05

1990 Score Franco Harris

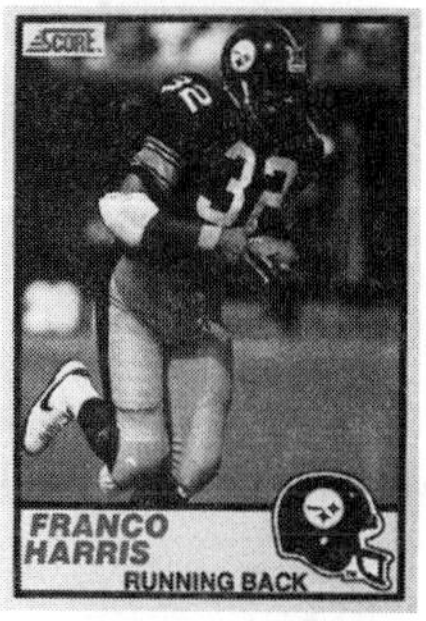

This card was given away to collectors who acquired Franco Harris' autograph at the Super Bowl Card Show in Tampa. The card is unnumbered and features a Leroy Nieman painting of Harris on the front with a picture of him celebrating a Super Bowl win on the back. Production of this card was estimated between 1,500 and 5,000.

		MT
Complete Set (1):		100.00
Common Player:		100.00
1	Franco Harris	100.00

1991 Score Promos

These six cards were designed to preview Score's 1991 regular set. The card numbers, which are on the card back, are identical to those in the regular set, except for Lawrence Taylor, who is #529 in the regular set. The prototype cards can be distinguished from the regular cards by several differences, including: the statistics on the back are in blue-green, not green; the promo cards omit the tiny trademark symbol next to the Team NFL logo; and cards 1, 5 and 7 are cropped slightly different.

		MT
Complete Set (6):		10.00
Common Player:		1.00
1	Joe Montana	5.00
4	Lawrence Taylor	1.25

5	Derrick Thomas	1.50
6	Mike Singletary	1.00
7	Boomer Esiason	1.25
12	Randall Cunningham	1.50

1991 Score

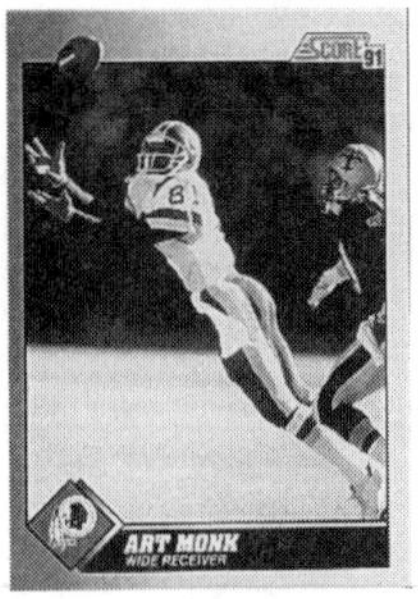

Score's 1991 first series was released in May 1991. The size increased by 15 cards over the previous year's Series I. Carried over from Score baseball was the "Dream Team" subset - this time featuring card-size profile shots with a smaller action insert. Artist Chris Greco worked on the MVP and Top Leader cards. Because Draft Pick cards carry no NFL team designation, they technically are not considered true rookie cards. (Key: DP - Draft Pick, 90 - 90-Plus Club, TL - Top Leader, DT - Dream Team)

		MT
Complete Set (686):		9.00
Factory Set (690):		9.00
Complete Series 1 (345):		4.50
Complete Series 2 (341):		4.50
Common Player:		.04
Pack (16):		.20
Wax Box (36):		5.00
1	Joe Montana	1.00
2	Eric Allen	.04
3	Rohn Stark	.04
4	Frank Reich	.04
5	Derrick Thomas	.25
6	Mike Singletary	.04
7	Boomer Esiason	.10
8	Matt Millen	.04
9	Chris Spielman	.04
10	Gerald McNeil	.04
11	Nick Lowery	.04
12	Randall Cunningham	.10
13	Marion Butts	.04
14	Tim Brown	.25
15	Emmitt Smith	1.75
16	Rich Camarillo	.04
17	Mike Merriweather	.04
18	Derrick Fenner	.10
19	Clay Matthews	.04
20	Barry Sanders	1.75
21	James Brooks	.04
22	Alton Montgomery	.04
23	Steve Atwater	.04
24	Ron Morris	.04
25	Brad Muster	.04
26	Andre Rison	.25
27	Brian Brennan	.04
28	Leonard Smith	.04
29	Kevin Butler	.04
30	Tim Harris	.04
31	Jay Novacek	.15
32	Eddie Murray	.04
33	Keith Woodside	.04
34	*Ray Crockett*	.10
35	Eugene Lockhart	.04
36	Bill Romanowski	.04
37	Eddie Brown	.04
38	Eugene Daniel	.04
39	Scott Fulhage	.04
40	Harold Green	.10
41	Mark Jackson	.04
42	Sterling Sharpe	.10
43	Mel Gray	.04
44	Jerry Holmes	.04
45	Allen Pinkett	.04
46	Warren Powers	.04
47	Rodney Peete	.04
48	Lorenzo White	.10
49	Dan Owens	.10
50	James Francis	.04
51	Ken Norton	.04
52	Ed West	.04
53	Andre Reed	.10
54	John Grimsley	.04
55	Michael Cofer	.04
56	Chris Doleman	.04
57	Pat Swilling	.04
58	Jessie Tuggle	.04
59	Mike Johnson	.04
60	Steve Walsh	.04
61	Sam Mills	.04
62	Don Mosebar	.04
63	Jay Hilgenberg	.04
64	Cleveland Gary	.04
65	Andre Tippett	.04
66	Tom Newberry	.04
67	Maurice Hurst	.04
68	Louis Oliver	.04
69	Fred Marion	.04
70	Christian Okoye	.04
71	Marv Cook	.04
72	Darryl Talley	.04
73	Rick Fenney	.04
74	Kelvin Martin	.04
75	Howie Long	.04
76	Steve Wisniewski	.04
77	Karl Mecklenburg	.04
78	Dan Saleaumua	.04
79	Ray Childress	.04
80	Henry Ellard	.04
81	Ernest Givins	.04
82	Ferrell Edmunds	.04
83	Steve Jordan	.04
84	Tony Mandarich	.04
85	Eric Martin	.04
86	Rich Gannon	.10
87	Irving Fryar	.04
88	Tom Rathman	.04
89	Dan Hampton	.04
90	Barry Word	.10
91	Kevin Greene	.04
92	Sean Landeta	.04
93	Trace Armstrong	.04
94	Dennis Byrd	.04
95	Timm Rosenbach	.04
96	Anthony Toney	.04
97	Tim Krumrie	.04
98	Jerry Ball	.04
99	Tim Green	.04
100	Bo Jackson	.35
101	Myron Guyton	.04
102	Mike Mularkey	.04
103	Jerry Gray	.04
104	Scott Stephen	.04
106	Lomas Brown	.04
107	David Little	.04
108	Brad Baxter	.10
109	Freddie Joe Nunn	.04
110	Dave Meggett	.04
111	Mark Rypien	.10
112	Warren Williams	.04
113	Ron Rivera	.04
114	Terance Mathis	.10
115	Anthony Munoz	.04
116	Jeff Bryant	.04
117	Issaic Holt	.04
118	Steve Sewell	.04
119	Tim Newton	.04
120	Emile Harry	.04
121	Gary Anderson (Pitt.)	.04
122	Mark Lee	.04
123	Alfred Anderson	.04
124	Tony Blaylock	.04
125	Ernest Byner	.04
126	Bill Maas	.04
127	Keith Taylor	.04
128	Cliff Odom	.04
129	Bob Golic	.04
130	Bart Oates	.04
131	Jim Arnold	.04
132	Jerr Herrod	.04
133	Bruce Armstrong	.04
134	Craig Heyward	.06
135	Joey Browner	.04
136	Darren Comeaux	.04
137	Pat Beach	.04
138	Dalton Hilliard	.06
139	David Treadwell	.04
140	Gary Anderson (T.B.)	.04
141	Eugene Robinson	.04
142	Scott Case	.04
143	Paul Farren	.04
144	Gill Fenerty	.04
145	Tim Irwin	.04
146	Norm Johnson	.04
147	Willie Gault	.06
148	Clarence Verdin	.04
149	Jeff Uhlenhake	.04
150	Erik McMillan	.04
151	Kevin Ross	.04
152	Pepper Johnson	.04
153	Bryan Hinkle	.04
154	Gary Clark	.08
155	Robert Delpino	.04
156	Doug Smith	.04
157	Chris Martin	.04
158	Ray Berry	.04
159	Steve Christie	.04
160	Don Smith	.04
161	Greg McMurtry	.04
162	Jack Del Rio	.04
163	Floyd Dixon	.04
164	Buford McGee	.04
165	Brett Maxie	.04
166	Morten Andersen	.06
167	Kent Hull	.04
168	Skip McClendon	.04
169	Keith Sims	.04
170	Leonard Marshall	.04
171	Tony Woods	.04
172	Byron Evans	.04
173	*Rob Burnett*	.15
174	Tory Epps	.04
175	*Toi Cook*	.10
176	John Elliott	.04
177	Tommie Agee	.04
178	Keith Van Horne	.04
179	Dennis Smith	.04
180	James Lofton	.04
181	Art Monk	.04
182	Anthony Carter	.04
183	Louis Lipps	.04
184	Bruce Hill	.04
185	Mike Young	.04
186	Eric Green	.10
187	*Barney Bussey*	.10
188	Curtis Duncan	.04
189	Robert Awalt	.04
190	Johnny Johnson	.20
191	Jeff Cross	.04
192	Keith McKeller	.04
193	Robert Brown	.04
194	Vincent Brown	.04
195	Calvin Williams	.20
196	Sean Jones	.04
197	Willie Drewrey	.04
198	Bubba McDowell	.04
199	Al Noga	.04
200	Ronnie Lott	.10
201	Warren Moon	.20
202	Chris Hinton	.04
203	Jim Sweeney	.04
204	Wayne Haddix	.04
205	*Tim Jorden*	.10
206	Marvin Allen	.04
207	*Jim Morrissey*	.10
208	Ben Smith	.04
209	William White	.04
210	Jim Jensen	.04
211	Doug Reed	.04
212	Ethan Horton	.04
213	Chris Jacke	.04
214	Johnny Hector	.04
215	Drew Hill	.04
216	Roy Green	.04
217	Dean Steinhuhler	.04
218	Cedric Mack	.04
219	Chris Miller	.04
220	Keith Byars	.04
221	Lewis Billups	.04
222	Roger Craig	.04
223	Shaun Gayle	.04
224	Mike Rozier	.04
225	Troy Aikman	1.00
226	Bobby Humphrey	.04
227	Eugene Marve	.04
228	Michael Carter	.04
229	Richard Johnson	.04
230	Billy Joe Tolliver	.08
231	Mark Murphy	.04
232	John L. Williams	.04
233	Ronnie Harmon	.08
234	Thurman Thomas	.40
235	Martin Mayhew	.04
236	Richmond Webb	.04
237	Gerald Riggs	.04
238	Mike Prior	.04
239	Mike Gann	.04
240	Alvin Walton	.04
241	Tim McGee	.04
242	Bruce Matthews	.04
243	Johnny Holland	.04
244	Martin Bayless	.04
245	Eric Metcalf	.04
246	John Alt	.04
247	Max Montoya	.04
248	Rod Bernstine	.04
249	Paul Gruber	.04
250	Charles Haley	.04
251	Scott Norwood	.04
252	Michael Haddix	.04
253	Ricky Sanders	.06
254	Ervin Randle	.04
255	Duane Bickett	.04
256	Mike Munchak	.04
257	Keith Jones	.04
258	Riki Ellison	.04
259	Vince Newsome	.04
260	Lee Williams	.04
261	Steve Smith	.04
262	Sam Clancy	.04
263	Pierce Holt	.04
264	Jim Harbaugh	.08
265	Dino Hackett	.04
266	Andy Heck	.04
267	Leo Goeas	.04
268	Russ Grimm	.04
269	Gill Byrd	.04
270	Neal Anderson	.08
271	Jackie Slater	.04
272	Joe Nash	.04
273	Todd Bowles	.04
274	D.J. Dozier	.04
275	Kevin Fagan	.04
276	Don Warren	.04
277	Jim Jeffcoat	.04
278	Bruce Smith	.08
279	Cortez Kennedy	.25
280	Thane Gash	.04
281	Perry Kemp	.04
282	John Taylor	.10
283	Stephone Paige	.04
284	Paul Skansi	.04
285	Shawn Collins	.04
286	Mervyn Fernandez	.04
287	Daniel Stubbs	.04
288	Chip Lohmiller	.04
289	Brian Blades	.04
290	Mark Carrier	.04
291	Carl Zander	.04
292	David Wyman	.04
293	Jeff Bostic	.04
294	Irv Pankey	.04
295	Keith Millard	.04
296	Jamie Mueller	.04
297	Bill Fralic	.04
298	Wendell Davis	.08
299	Ken Clarke	.04
300	Wymon Henderson	.04
301	Jeff Campbell	.04
302	*Cody Carlson*	.35
303	*Matt Brock*	.10
304	Maurice Carthon	.04
305	*Scott Mersereau*	.10
306	Steve Wright	.04
307	J.B. Brown	.04
308	Ricky Reynolds	.04
309	Darryl Pollard	.04
310	Donald Evans	.04
311	*Nick Bell* (DP)	.20
312	*Pat Harlow* (DP)	.10
313	*Dan McGwire* (DP)	.10
314	Mike Dumas (DP)	.04
315	*Mike Croel* (DP)	.20
316	Chris Smith (DP)	.04
317	*Kenny Walker* (DP)	.10
318	*Todd Lyght* (DP)	.10
319	Mike Stonebreaker (DP)	.04
320	Randall Cunningham (90)	.08
321	Terance Mathis (90)	.04
322	Gaston Green (90)	.04
323	Johnny Bailey (90)	.04
324	Donnie Elder (90)	.04
325	Dwight Stone (90)	.04
326	*J.J. Birden* (90)	.35
327	Alex Wright (90)	.04
328	Eric Metcalf (90)	.04
329	Andre Rison (TL)	.15
330	Warren Moon (TL)	.10
331	Steve Tasker, Reyna Thompson (DT)	.04
332	Mel Gray (DT)	.04
333	Nick Lowery (DT)	.04
334	Sean Landeta (DT)	.04
335	David Fulcher (DT)	.04
336	Joey Browner (DT)	.04
337	Albert Lewis (DT)	.04
338	Rod Woodson (DT)	.06
339	Shane Conlan (DT)	.04
340	Pepper Johnson (DT)	.04
341	Chris Spielman (DT)	.06
342	Derrick Thomas (DT)	.08
343	Ray Childress (DT)	.04
344	Reggie White (DT)	.08
345	Bruce Smith (DT)	.06
346	Darrell Green	.04
347	Ray Bentley	.04
348	Herschel Walker	.06
349	Rodney Holman	.04
350	Al Toon	.04
351	Harry Hamilton	.04
352	Albert Lewis	.04
353	Renaldo Turnbull	.04
354	Junior Seau	.25
355	Merril Hoge	.04
356	Shane Conlan	.04
357	Jay Schroeder	.04
358	Steve Broussard	.04
359	Mark Bavaro	.04
360	Jim Lachey	.04
361	Greg Townsend	.04
362	Dave Krieg	.04
363	Jessie Hester	.04
364	Steve Tasker	.04
365	Ron Hall	.04
366	Pat Leahy	.04
367	Jim Everett	.06
368	Felix Wright	.04
369	Ricky Proehl	.04
370	Anthony Miller	.05
371	Keith Jackson	.08
372	Pete Stoyanovich	.04
373	Tommy Kane	.04
374	Richard Johnson	.04
375	Randall McDaniel	.04
376	John Stephens	.04
377	Haywood Jeffires	.15
378	Rodney Hampton	.50
379	Tim Grunhard	.04
380	Jerry Rice	1.00
381	Ken Harvey	.04
382	Vaughan Johnson	.04
383	J.T. Smith	.04
384	Carnell Lake	.04
385	Dan Marino	1.75
386	Kyle Clifton	.04
387	Wilber Marshall	.04
388	Pete Holohan	.04
389	Gary Plummer	.04
390	William Perry	.04
391	Mark Robinson	.04
392	Nate Odomes	.06
393	Ickey Woods	.04
394	Reyna Thompson	.04
395	Deion Sanders	.40
396	Harris Barton	.04
397	Sammie Smith	.04
398	Vinny Testaverde	.04
399	Ray Donaldson	.04
400	Tim McKyer	.04
401	Nesby Glasgow	.04
402	Brent Williams	.04
403	Rob Moore	.10
404	Bubby Brister	.05
405	David Fulcher	.04
406	Reggie Cobb	.20
407	Jerome Brown	.04
408	Erik Howard	.04
409	Tony Paige	.04
410	John Elway	.35
411	Charles Mann	.04
412	Luis Sharpe	.04
413	Hassan Jones	.04
414	Frank Minnifield	.04
415	Steve DeBerg	.04
416	Mark Carrier	.04
417	Brian Jordan	.04
418	Reggie Langhorne	.04
419	Don Majkowski	.04
420	Marcus Allen	.05
421	Michael Brooks	.04
422	Vai Sikahema	.04
423	Dermontti Dawson	.04
424	Jacob Green	.04
425	Flipper Anderson	.04
426	Bill Brooks	.04
427	Keith McCants	.04
428	Ken O'Brien	.04
429	Fred Barnett	.10
430	Mark Duper	.04
431	Mark Kelso	.04
432	Leslie O'Neal	.04
433	Ottis Anderson	.05
434	Jesse Sapolu	.04
435	Gary Zimmerman	.04
436	Kevin Porter	.04
437	Anthony Thompson	.04
438	Robert Clark	.04
439	Chris Warren	.20
440	Gerald Williams	.04
441	Jim Skow	.04
442	Rick Donnelly	.04
443	Guy McIntyre	.04
444	Jeff Lageman	.04
445	John Offerdahl	.04
446	Clyde Simmons	.04
447	John Kidd	.04
448	Chip Banks	.04
449	Johnny Meads	.04
450	Rickey Jackson	.04
451	Lee Johnson	.04
452	Michael Irvin	.25
453	Leon Seals	.04
454	Darrell Thompson	.20
455	Everson Walls	.04
456	LeRoy Butler	.06
457	Marcus Dupree	.04
458	Kirk Lowdermilk	.04
459	Chris Singleton	.04
460	Seth Joyner	.04
461	(Rueben Mayes) (Hayes in bio should be Heyward)	.04
462	Ernie Jones	.04
463	Greg Kragen	.04
464	Bennie Blades	.04
465	Mark Bortz	.04
466	Tony Stargell	.04
467	Mike Cofer	.05
468	Randy Grimes	.04
469	Tim Worley	.04
470	Kevin Mack	.04
471	Wes Hopkins	.04
472	Will Wolford	.04
473	Sam Seale	.04
474	Jim Ritcher	.04
475	Jeff Hostetler	.20
476	Mitchell Price	.04
477	Ken Lanier	.04
478	Naz Worthen	.04
479	Ed Reynolds	.04
480	Mark Clayton	.05
481	Matt Bahr	.04
482	Gary Reasons	.04
483	Dave Szott	.04
484	Barry Foster	.45
485	Bruce Reimers	.04
486	Dean Biasucci	.04
487	Cris Carter	.05
488	Albert Bentley	.04
489	Robert Massey	.04
490	Al Smith	.04
491	Greg Lloyd	.08
492	Steve McMichael (Photo on back actually Dan Hampton)	.05
493	*Jeff Wright*	.08
494	Scott Davis	.04
495	Freeman McNeil	.04
496	Simon Fletcher	.04
497	Terry McDaniel	.04
498	Heath Sherman	.04
499	Jeff Jaeger	.04
500	Mark Collins	.04
501	Tim Goad	.04
502	Jeff George	.25
503	Jimmie Jones	.05
504	Henry Thomas	.04
505	Steve Young	.60
506	William Roberts	.04
507	Neil Smith	.04
508	Mike Saxon	.04
509	Johnny Bailey	.04
510	Broderick Thomas	.04
511	Wade Wilson	.04
512	Hart Lee Dykes	.04
513	Hardy Nickerson	.04
514	Tim McDonald	.05
515	Frank Cornish	.04
516	Jarvis Williams	.04
517	Carl Lee	.04
518	Carl Banks	.04
519	Mike Golic	.04
520	Brian Noble	.04
521	James Hasty	.04
522	Bubba Paris	.04
523	*Kevin Walker*	.08
524	William Fuller	.04
525	Eddie Anderson	.04
526	Roger Ruzek	.04
527	Robert Blackmon	.04
528	Vince Buck	.04
529	Lawrence Taylor	.10
530	Reggie Roby	.04
531	Doug Riesenberg	.04
532	Joe Jacoby	.04
533	Kirby Jackson	.04
534	Robb Thomas	.04
535	Don Griffin	.04
536	Andre Waters	.05
537	Marc Logan	.04
538	James Thornton	.04
539	Ray Agnew	.04
540	Frank Stams	.04
541	Brett Perriman	.05
542	Andre Ware	.10
543	Kevin Haverdink	.04
544	*Greg Jackson*	.08
545	Tunch Ilkin	.04
546	Dexter Carter	.04
547	Rod Woodson	.06
548	Donnell Woolford	.04
549	Mark Boyer	.04
550	Jeff Query	.04
551	Burt Grossman	.04
552	Mike Kenn	.04
553	Richard Dent	.04
554	Gaston Green	.04
555	Phil Simms	.10
556	Brent Jones	.05
557	Ronnie Lippett	.04
558	Mike Horan	.04
559	Danny Noonan	.04
560	Reggie White	.15
561	Rufus Porter	.04
562	Aaron Wallace	.04
563	Vance Johnson	.04
564	(Aaron Craver) (No copyright line on back)	.04
565A	*Russell Maryland* (No copyright line on back)	.40
565B	*Russell Maryland*	.40
566	Paul Justin	.04
567	Walter Dean	.04
568	*Herman Moore*	3.00
569	*Bill Musgrave*	.10
570	*Rob Carpenter*	.10
571	*Greg Lewis*	.10
572	*Ed King*	.10
573	*Ernie Mills*	.08
574	*Jake Reed*	1.00
575	*Ricky Watters*	2.00
576	*Derek Russell*	.25
577	*Shawn Moore*	.15
578	*Eric Bieniemy*	.15
579	*Chris Zorich*	.30
580	Scott Miller	.05
581	*Jarrod Bunch*	.10
582	*Ricky Ervins*	.20
583	*Browning Nagle*	.20
584	*Eric Turner*	.20
585	*William Thomas*	.08
586	*Stanley Richard*	.30
587	*Adrian Cooper*	.15
588	*Harvey Williams*	.10
589	*Alvin Harper*	.10
590	John Carney	.04
591	Mark Vander Poel	.04
592	*Mike Pritchard*	.35
593	*Eric Moten*	.08
594	*Moe Gardner*	.10
595	*Wesley Carroll*	.10
596	*Eric Swann*	.10
597	Joe Kelly	.05
598	*Steve Jackson*	.10
599	*Kelvin Pritchett*	.15
600	*Jesse Campbell*	.08
601	*Darryll Lewis* (Misspelled Darryl on card)	.08
602	Howard Griffith	.04
603	Blaise Bryant	.04
604	*Vinnie Clark*	.08
605	*Mel Agee*	.08
606	*Bobby Wilson*	.08
607	Kevin Donnalley	.04
608	*Randal Hill*	.35
609	Stan Thomas	.04
610	Mike Heldt	.04
611	*Brett Favre*	4.00
612	*Lawrence Dawsey*	.25
613	Dennis Gibson	.04
614	Dean Dingman	.04
615	*Bruce Pickens*	.08
616	*Todd Marinovich*	.08
617	Gene Atkins	.04
618	Marcus Dupree (Comeback Player)	.04
619	Warren Moon (Man of the Year)	.10
620	Joe Montana (MVP)	.50
621	Neal Anderson (Team MVP)	.05
622	James Brooks (Team MVP)	.05
623	Thurman Thomas (Team MVP)	.20
624	Bobby Humphrey (Team MVP)	.04
625	Kevin Mack (Team MVP)	.04
626	Mark Carrier (Team MVP)	.04
627	Johnny Johnson (Team MVP)	.08
628	Marion Butts (Team MVP)	.05
629	Steve DeBerg (Team MVP)	.05
630	Jeff George (Team MVP)	.10
631	Troy Aikman (MVP)	.50
632	Dan Marino (MVP)	.25
633	Randall Cunningham (Team MVP)	.08
634	Andre Rison (Team MVP)	.08
635	Pepper Johnson (Team MVP)	.04
636	Pat Leahy (Team MVP)	.04
637	Barry Sanders (MVP)	.50
638	Warren Moon (Team MVP)	.08
639	Sterling Sharpe (MVP)	.25
640	Bruce Armstrong (Team MVP)	.04
641	Bo Jackson (Team MVP)	.10
642	Henry Ellard (Team MVP)	.05
643	Earnest Byner (Team MVP)	.04
644	Pat Swilling (Team MVP)	.04
645	John L. Williams (Team MVP)	.04
646	Rod Woodson (Team MVP)	.06
647	Chris Doleman (Team MVP)	.04
648	Joey Browner (Crunch Crew)	.04
649	Erik McMillan (Crunch Crew)	.04
650	David Fulcher (Crunch Crew)	.04
651A	Ronnie Lott (Front 47, back 42)	.08
651B	Ronnie Lott (Front 47, back 42 is now blacked out)	.05
652	Louis Oliver (Crunch Crew)	.04
653	Mark Robinson (Crunch Crew)	.04
654	Dennis Smith (Crunch Crew)	.04
655	Reggie White (Sack Attack)	.08
656	Charles Haley (Sack Attack)	.04
657	Leslie O'Neal (Sack Attack)	.04
658	Kevin Greene (Sack Attack)	.04
659	Dennis Byrd (Sack Attack)	.04
660	Bruce Smith (Sack Attack)	.08
661	Derrick Thomas (Sack Attack)	.10
662	Steve DeBerg (Top Leader)	.04
663	Barry Sanders (TL)	.50
664	Thurman Thomas (TL)	.20
665	Jerry Rice (TL)	.40
666	Derrick Thomas (Top Leader)	.10
667	Bruce Smith (Top Leader)	.08
668	Mark Carrier (Top Leader)	.04
669	Richard Johnson (Top Leader)	.04
670	Jan Stenerud (Hall of Fame)	.05
671	Stan Jones (Hall of Fame)	.05
672	John Hannah (Hall of Fame)	.05
673	Tex Schramm (Hall of Fame)	.05
674	Earl Campbell (Hall of Fame)	.10
675	Mark Carrier, Emmitt Smith (ROY ROY)	.25
676	Warren Moon (DT)	.10
677	Barry Sanders (DT)	.50
678	Thurman Thomas (DT)	.20
679	Andre Reed (DT)	.06
680	Andre Rison (DT)	.15
681	Keith Jackson (DT)	.05
682	Bruce Armstrong (DT)	.05
683	Jim Lachey (DT)	.04
684	Bruce Matthews (DT)	.04
685	Mike Munchak (DT)	.04
686	Don Mosebar (DT)	.04
1B	Super Bowl (Jeff Hostetler)	.25
2B	Super Bowl (Matt Bahr)	.05
3B	Super Bowl (Ottis Anderson)	.05
4B	Super Bowl (Ottis Anderson)	.05

1991 Score Dream Team Autographs

The 11-card, standard-size set was inserted every 5,000 packs of Series II packs. Each player autographed approximately 500 cards.

		MT
Complete Set (11):		850.00
Common Player:		25.00
676	Warren Moon	100.00
677	Barry Sanders	250.00
678	Thurman Thomas	125.00
679	Andre Reed	100.00
680	Andre Rison	100.00
681	Keith Jackson	50.00
682	Bruce Armstrong	25.00
683	Jim Lachey	25.00
684	Bruce Matthews	25.00
685	Mike Munchak	25.00
686	Don Mosebar	25.00

1991 Score Hot Rookie

1991 Score blister packs contained these random inserts which have card fronts showing action shots

of the players in their collegiate uniforms against a hot pink/yellow background. The fronts are bordered in black. Each card back is numbered and includes a close-up shot of the player, plus a brief career summary.

MT
Complete Set (10): 8.00
Common Player: .80
1 Dan McGwire 2.00
2 Todd Lyght 1.00
3 Mike Dumas .80
4 Pat Harlow .80
5 Nick Bell 1.00
6 Chris Smith .80
7 Mike Stonebreaker .80
8 Mike Croel 1.00
9 Kenny Walker 1.00
10 Rob Carpenter .80

1991 Score Supplemental

Rookies and players who were traded during the regular season are featured in this 110-card update set. The fronts have the same design as the regular cards do, except the borders shade from blue-green to white. The backs have a mug shot and player information in a horizontal format framed by a gold border. Card numbering is done on the back with a "T" suffix.

MT
Complete Set (110): 8.00
Common Player: .04
1 Ronnie Lott .10
2 Matt Millen .04
3 Tim McKyer .04
4 Vince Newsome .04
5 Gaston Green .04
6 Brett Perriman .08
7 Roger Craig .06
8 Pete Holohan .04
9 Tony Zendejas .04
10 Lee Williams .04
11 Mike Stonebreaker .04
12 Felix Wright .04
13 Lonnie Young .04
14 *Hugh Millen* .10
15 Roy Green .04
16 *Greg Davis* .10
17 Dexter Manley .04
18 *Ted Washington* .10
19 Norm Johnson .04
20 Joe Morris .04
21 Robert Perryman .04
22 Mike Iaquaniello .04
23 *Gerald Perry* .10
24 Zeke Mowatt .04
25 *Rich Miano* .10
26 Nick Bell .10
27 *Terry Orr* .15
28 *Matt Stover* .15
29 Bubba Paris .04
30 Ron Brown .04
31 Don Davey .04
32 Lee Rouson .04
33 Terry Hoage .04
34 Tony Covington .04
35 John Rienstra .04
36 *Charles Dimry* .08
37 Todd Marinovich .08
38 Winston Moss .04
39 Vestee Jackson .04
40 Brian Hansen .04
41 Irv Eatman .04
42 Jarrod Bunch .08
43 *Kanavis McGhee* .10
44 Vai Sikahema .04
45 *Charles McRae* .10
46 Quinn Early .04
47 *Jeff Faulkner* .10
48 *William Frizzell* .10
49 John Booty .04
50 Tim Harris .04
51 Derek Russell .10
52 *John Flannery* .10
53 *Tim Barnett* .15
54 *Alfred Williams* .15
55 Dan McGwire .04
56 Ernie Mills .10
57 Stanley Richard .04
58 Huey Richardson .04
59 *Jerome Henderson* .10
60 *Bryan Cox* .40
61 Russell Maryland .25
62 *Reggie Jones* .15
63 *Mo Lewis* .10
64 Moe Gardner .04
65 Wesley Carroll .04
66 *Michael Jackson* .25
67 *Shawn Jefferson* .10
68 Chris Zorich .10
69 Kenny Walker .04
70 *Erric Pegram* .10
71 Alvin Harper .10
72 *Harry Colon* .10
73 Scott Miller .04
74 Lawrence Dawsey .10
75 *Phil Hansen* .15
76 *Roman Phifer* .15
77 Greg Lewis .04
78 *Merton Hanks* .15
79 *James Jones* .10
80 Vinnie Clark .04
81 R.J. Kors .04
82 Mike Pritchard .25
83 Stan Thomas .04
84 Lamar Rogers .04
85 *Erik Williams* .25
86 *Keith Traylor* .10
87 Mike Dumas .04
88 Mel Agee .04
89 Harvey Williams .25
90 Todd Lyght .04
91 Jake Reed .50
92 Pat Harlow .04
93 *Antone Davis* .10
94 *Aeneas Williams* .10
95 Eric Bieniemy .04
96 *John Kasay* .10
97 Robert Wilson .04
98 Ricky Ervins .15
99 Mike Croel .10
100 *David Lang* .15
101 *Esera Tuaolo* .10
102 Randal Hill .20
103 *Jon Vaughn* .25
104 Dave McCloughan .04
105 David Daniels .04
106 Eric Moten .04
107 *Anthony Morgan* .15
108 Ed King .04
109 *Leonard Russell* .10
110 Aaron Craver .08

1991 Score National 10

These 10 cards were distributed at the 12th National Sports Collectors Covention in a cello wrapper. A panel on the card back indicates the cards were created for the convention. A mug shot, card number, biographical information and career summary are also provided on the back. The front has a color action photo of the player, with a player/football pattern above and below the photo.

MT
Complete Set (10): 10.00
Common Player: .75
1 Emmitt Smith 8.00
2 Mark Carrier 1.00
3 Steve Broussard 1.00
4 Johnny Johnson 2.00
5 Steve Christie 1.00
6 Richmond Webb .75
7 James Francis .75
8 Jeff George 2.00
9 Rodney Hampton 3.00
10 Calvin Williams 1.00

1991 Score Young Superstars

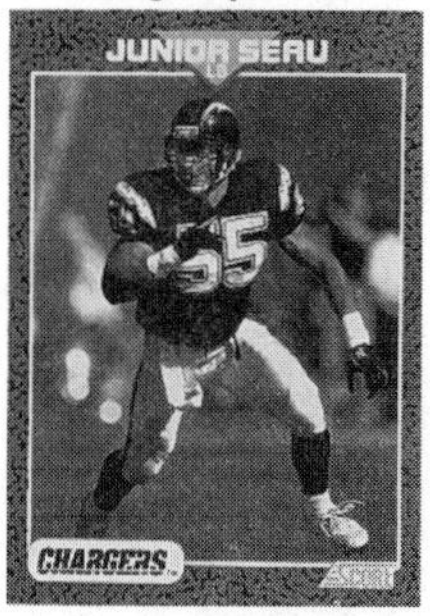

These cards, available in October 1990 via a mail-in offer found on Score wax packs, featured up-and-coming stars of the game. Each front has game-day photography surrounded by black borders and team colors. The card back shows a head shot, a player profile and a scouting report quote.

MT
Complete Set (40): 7.00
Common Player: .10
1 Johnny Bailey .15
2 Johnny Johnson .20
3 Fred Barnett .15
4 Keith McCants .10
5 Brad Baxter .10
6 Dan Owens .10
7 Steve Broussard .15
8 Ricky Proehl .15
9 Marion Butts .20
10 Reggie Cobb .10
11 Dennis Byrd .10
12 Emmitt Smith 3.00
13 Mark Carrier .15
14 Keith Sims .10
15 Dexter Carter .15
16 Chris Singleton .10
17 Steve Christie .10
18 Frank Cornish .10
19 Timm Rosenbach .10
20 Sammie Smith .10
21 Calvin Williams .15
22 Merril Hoge .10
23 Hart Lee Dykes .10
24 Darrell Thompson .10
25 James Francis .10
26 John Elliott .10
27 Jeff George .25
28 Broderick Thomas .15
29 Eric Green .15
30 Steve Walsh .10
31 Harold Green .15
32 Andre Ware .10
33 Richmond Webb .10
34 Junior Seau .40
35 Tim Grunhard .10
36 Tim Worley .10
37 Haywood Jeffires .20
38 Rod Woodson .20
39 Rodney Hampton .20
40 Dave Szott .10

1992 Score

This 550-card set features color action photos surrounded by a solid colored border. The player's position is at the bottom in a dark blue band; his name is at the top in a green band. The back has a mug shot, biography, statistics and profile. Subsets include Draft Picks, Crunch Crew, Rookie of the Year, Little Big Men, Sack Attack, Hall of Famers, and the 90 Plus Club. Two insert sets were also made - Dream Team (25 cards, in foil packs), and Gridiron Stars (45 cards), which were in jumbo packs.

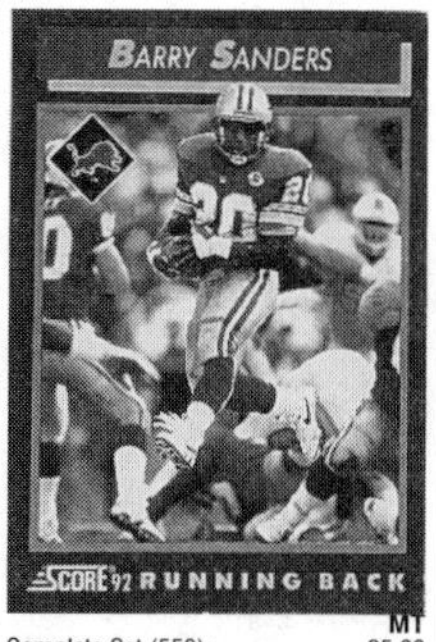

MT
Complete Set (550): 25.00
Common Player: .05
Minor Stars: .10
Pack (17): .30
Wax Box (36): 8.00
1 Barry Sanders 2.00
2 Pat Swilling .05
3 Moe Gardner .05
4 Steve Young 1.50
5 Chris Spielman .05
6 Richard Dent .05
7 Anthony Munoz .05
8 Martin Mayhew .05
9 Terry McDaniel .05
10 Thurman Thomas .40
11 Ricky Sanders .05
12 Steve Atwater .05
13 Tony Tolbert .05
14 Vince Workman .05
15 Haywood Jeffires .05
16 Duane Bickett .05
17 Jeff Uhlenhake .05
18 Tim McDonald .05
19 Cris Carter .10
20 Derrick Thomas .10
21 Hugh Millen .05
22 Bart Oates .05
23 Eugene Robinson .05
24 Jerrol Williams .05
25 Reggie White .10
26 Marion Butts .05
27 Jim Sweeney .05
28 Tom Newberry .05
29 Pete Stoyanovich .05
30 Ronnie Lott .05
31 Simon Fletcher .05
32 Dino Hackett .05
33 Morten Andersen .05
34 Clyde Simmons .05
35 Mark Rypien .05
36 Greg Montgomery .05
37 Nate Lewis .05
38 Henry Ellard .05
39 Luis Sharpe .05
40 Michael Irvin .30
41 Louis Lipps .05
42 John L. Williams .05
43 Broderick Thomas .05
44 Michael Haynes .05
45 Don Majkowski .05
46 William Perry .05
47 David Fulcher .05
48 Tony Bennett .05
49 Clay Matthews .05
50 Warren Moon .10
51 Bruce Armstrong .05
52 Harry Newsome .05
53 Bill Brooks .05
54 Greg Townsend .05
55 Tom Rathman .05
56 Sean Landeta .05
57 Kyle Clifton .05
58 Steve Broussard .05
59 Mark Carrier .05
60 Mel Gray .05
61 Tim Krumrie .05
62 Rufus Porter .05
63 Kevin Mack .05
64 Todd Bowles .05
65 Emmitt Smith 3.00
66 Mike Croel .05
67 Brian Mitchell .05
68 Bennie Blades .05
69 Carnell Lake .05
70 Cornelius Bennett .05
71 Darrell Thompson .05
72 Wes Hopkins .05
73 Jessie Hester .05
74 Irv Eatman .05
75 Mary Cook .05
76 Tim Brown .10
77 Pepper Johnson .05
78 Mark Duper .05
79 Robert Delpino .05
80 Charles Mann .05
81 Brian Jordan .10
82 Wendell Davis .05
83 Lee Johnson .05
84 Ricky Reynolds .05
85 Vaughan Johnson .05
86 Brian Seale .05
87 Sam Seale .05
88 Ed King .05
89 Gaston Green .05
90 Christian Okoye .05
91 Chris Jacke .05
92 Rohn Stark .05
93 Kevin Greene .05
94 Jay Novacek .10
95 Chip Lohmiller .05
96 Cris Dishman .05
97 Ethan Horton .05
98 Pat Harlow .05
99 Mark Ingram .05
100 Mark Carrier .05
101 Deron Cherry .05
102 Sam Mills .05
103 Mark Higgs .05
104 Keith Jackson .05
105 Steve Tasker .05
106 Ken Harvey .05
107 Bryan Hinkle .05
108 Anthony Carter .05
109 Johnny Hector .05
110 Randall McDaniel .05
111 Johnny Johnson .05
112 Shane Conlan .05
113 Ray Horton .05
114 Sterling Sharpe .10
115 Guy McIntyre .05
116 Tom Waddle .05
117 Albert Lewis .05
118 Riki Ellison .05
119 Chris Doleman .05
120 Andre Rison .05
121 Bobby Hebert .05
122 Dan Owens .05
123 Rodney Hampton .10
124 Ron Holmes .05
125 Ernie Jones .05
126 Michael Carter .05
127 Reggie Cobb .05
128 Esera Tuaolo .05
129 Wilber Marshall .05
130 Mike Munchak .05
131 Cortez Kennedy .05
132 Lamar Lathon .05
133 Todd Lyght .05
134 Jeff Feagles .05
135 Burt Grossman .05
136 Mike Cofer .05
137 Frank Warren .05
138 Jarvis Williams .05
139 Eddie Brown .05
140 John Elliott .05
141 Jim Everett .05
142 Hardy Nickerson .05
143 Eddie Murray .05
144 Andre Tippett .05
145 Heath Sherman .05
146 Ronnie Harmon .05
147 Eric Metcalf .05
148 Tony Martin .25
149 Chris Burkett .05
150 Andre Waters .05
151 Ray Donaldson .05
152 Paul Gruber .05
153 Chris Singleton .05
154 Clarence Kay .05
155 Ernest Givins .05
156 Eric Hill .05
157 Jesse Sapolu .05
158 Jack Del Rio .05
159 Erric Pegram .10
160 Joey Browner .05
161 Marcus Allen .10
162 Eric Moten .05
163 Donnell Thompson .05
164 Chuck Cecil .05
165 Matt Millen .05
166 Barry Foster .10
167 Kent Hull .05
168 Tony Jones .05
169 Mike Prior .05
170 Neal Anderson .05
171 Roger Craig .05
172 Felix Wright .05
173 James Francis .05
174 Eugene Lockhart .05
175 Dalton Hilliard .05
176 Nick Lowery .05
177 Tim McKyer .05
178 Lorenzo White .05
179 Jeff Hostetler .10
180 *Jackie Harris* .25
181 Ken Norton .05
182 Flipper Anderson .05
183 Don Warren .05
184 Brad Baxter .05
185 John Taylor .05
186 Harold Green .05
187 James Washington .05
188 Aaron Craver .05
189 Mike Merriweather .05
190 Gary Clark .05
191 Vince Buck .05
192 Cleveland Gary .05
193 Dan Saleaumua .05
194 Gary Zimmerman .05
195 Richmond Webb .05
196 Gary Plummer .05
197 Willie Green .05
198 Chris Warren .30
199 Mike Pritchard .05
200 Art Monk .05
201 Matt Stover .05
202 Tim Grunhard .05
203 Mervyn Fernandez .05
204 Mark Jackson .05
205 Freddie Joe Nunn .05
206 Stan Thomas .05
207 Keith McKeller .05
208 Jeff Lageman .05
209 Kenny Walker .05
210 Dave Krieg .05
211 Dean Clasucci .05
212 Herman Moore 1.00
213 Jon Vaughn .05
214 Howard Cross .05
215 Greg Davis .05
216 Bubby Brister .05
217 John Kasay .05
218 Ron Hall .05
219 Mo Lewis .05
220 Eric Green .05
221 Scott Case .05
222 Sean Jones .05
223 Winston Moss .05
224 Reggie Langhorne .05
225 Greg Lewis .05
226 Todd McNair .05
227 Rod Bernstine .05
228 Joe Jacoby .05
229 Brad Muster .05
230 Nick Bell .05
231 Terry Allen .40
232 Cliff Odom .05
233 Brian Hansen .05
234 William Fuller .05
235 Issiac Holt .05
236 Dexter Carter .05
237 Gene Atkins .05
238 Pat Beach .05
239 Tim McGhee .05
240 Dermontti Dawson .05
241 Dan Fike .05
242 Don Beebe .05
243 Jeff Bostic .05
244 Mark Collins .05
245 Steve Sewell .05
246 Steve Walsh .05
247 Erik Kramer .10
248 Scott Norwood .05
249 Jesse Solomon .05
250 Jerry Ball .05
251 Eugene Daniel .05
252 Michael Stewart .05
253 Fred Barnett .05
254 Rodney Holman .05
255 Stephen Baker .05
256 Don Griffin .05
257 Will Wolford .05
258 Perry Kemp .05
259 Leonard Russell .05
260 Jeff Gossett .05
261 Dwayne Harper .05
262 Vinny Testaverde .05
263 Maurice Hurst .05
264 Tony Casillas .05
265 Louis Oliver .05
266 Jim Morrissey .05
267 Kenneth Davis .05
268 John Alt .05
269 *Michael Zordick* .05
270 Brian Brennan .05
271 Greg Kragen .05
272 Andre Collins .05
273 Dave Meggett .05
274 Scott Fulhage .05
275 Tony Zendejas .05
276 Herschel Walker .05
277 Keith Henderson .05
278 Johnny Bailey .05
279 Vince Newsome .05
280 Chris Hinton .05
281 Robert Blackmon .05
282 James Hasty .05
283 John Offerdahl .05
284 Wesley Carroll .05
285 Lomas Brown .05
286 Neil O'Donnell .25
287 Kevin Porter .05
289 Carlton Bailey .05
290 Leonard Marshall .05
291 John Carney .05
292 Bubba McDowell .05
293 Nate Newton .05
294 Dave Waymer .05
295 Rob Moore .05
296 Earnest Byner .05
297 Jason Staurovsky .05
298 Keith McCants .05
299 Floyd Turner .05
300 Steve Jordan .05
301 Nate Odomes .05
302 Gerald Riggs .05
303 Marvin Washington .05
304 Anthony Thompson .05
305 Steve DeBerg .05
306 Jim Harbaugh .10
307 Larry Brown .05
308 Roger Ruzek .05
309 Jessie Tuggle .05
310 Al Smith .05
311 Mark Kelso .05
312 Lawrence Dawsey .05
313 *Steve Bono* 1.00
314 Greg Lloyd .10
315 Steve Wisniewski .05
316 Gill Fenerty .05
317 Mark Stepnoski .05
318 Derek Russell .05
319 Chris Martin .05
320 Shaun Gayle .05
321 Bob Golic .05
322 Larry Kelm .05
323 *Mike Brim* .05
324 Tommy Kane .05
325 *Mark Schlereth* .05
326 Ray Childress .05
327 *Richard Brown* .05
328 Vincent Brown .05
329 Mike Farr .05
330 Eric Swann .05
331 Bill Fralic .05
332 Rodney Peete .10
333 Jerry Gray .05
334 Ray Berry .05
335 Dennis Smith .05
336 Jeff Herrod .05
337 Tony Mandarich .05
338 Matt Bahr .05
339 Mike Saxon .05
340 Bruce Matthews .05
341 Rickey Jackson .05
342 Eric Allen .05
343 Lonnie Young .05
344 Steve McMichael .05
345 Willie Gault .05
346 Barry Word .05
347 Rich Camarillo .05
348 Bill Romanowski .05
349 Jim Lachey .05
350 Jim Ritcher .05
351 Irving Fryar .05
352 Gary Anderson .05
353 Henry Rolling .05
354 Mark Bortz .05
355 Mark Clayton .05
356 Keith Woodside .05
357 Jonathan Hayes .05
358 Derrick Fenner .05
359 Keith Byars .05
360 Drew Hill .05
361 Harris Barton .05
362 John Kidd .05
363 Aeneas Williams .05
364 Brian Washington .05
365 John Stephens .05
366 Norm Johnson .05
367 Darryl Henley .05
368 William White .05
369 Mark Murphy .05
370 Myron Guyton .05
371 Leon Seals .05
372 Rich Gannon .05
373 Toi Cook .05
374 Anthony Johnson .05
375 Rod Woodson .05
376 Alexander Wright .05
377 Kevin Butler .05
378 Neil Smith .05
379 Gary Anderson .05
380 Reggie Roby .05
381 Jeff Bryant .05
382 Ray Crockett .05
383 Richard Johnson .05
384 Hassan Jones .05
385 Karl Mecklenburg .05
386 Jeff Jaeger .05
387 Keith Willis .05
388 Phil Simms .05
389 Kevin Ross .05
390 Chris Miller .05
391 Brian Noble .05
392 *Jamie Dukes* .05
393 George Jamison .05
394 Rickey Dixon .05
395 Carl Lee .05
396 Jon Hand .05
397 Kirby Jackson .05
398 Pat Terrell .05
399 Howie Long .05
400 Mike Young .05
401 Keith Sims .05
402 Tommy Barnhardt .05
403 Greg McMurty .05
404 Keith Van Horne .05
405 Seth Joyner .05
406 Jim Jeffcoat .05
407 Courtney Hall .05
408 Tony Covington .05
409 Jacob Green .05
410 Charles Haley .05
411 Darryl Talley .05
412 Jeff Cross .05
413 John Elway .40
414 Donald Evans .05
415 Jackie Slater .05
416 John Friesz .05
417 Anthony Smith .05
418 Gill Byrd .05
419 Willie Drewrey .05
420 Jay Hilgenberg .05
421 David Treadwell .05
422 Curtis Duncan .05
423 Sammie Smith .05
424 Henry Thomas .05
425 James Lofton .05
426 Fred Marion .05
427 Bryce Paup .40
428 *Eric Andolsek* .05
429 Reyna Thompson .05
430 Mike Kenn .05
431 Bill Maas .05
432 Quinn Early .05
433 Everson Walls .05
434 Jimmie Jones .05
435 Dwight Stone .05
436 Harry Colon .05
437 Don Mosebar .05
438 Calvin Williams .05
439 Tom Tupa .05
440 Darrell Green .05
441 Eric Thomas .05
442 Terry Wooden .05
443 Brett Perriman .10
444 Todd Marinovich .05
445 Jim Breech .05
446 Eddie Anderson .05
447 Jay Schroeder .05
448 William Roberts .05
449 Brad Edwards .05
450 Tunch Ilkin .05
451 Joe Ivy .05
452 Robert Clark .05
453 Tim Barnett .05
454 Jarrod Bunch .05
455 Tim Harris .05
456 James Brooks .05
457 Trace Armstrong .05
458 Michael Brooks .05
459 Andy Heck .05
460 Greg Jackson .05
461 Vance Johnson .05
462 Kirk Lowdermilk .05
463 Erik McMillan .05
464 Scott Mersereau .05
465 Jeff Wright .05
466 Mike Tomczak .05
467 David Alexander .05
468 Bryan Millard .05
469 John Randle .05
470 Joel Hilgenberg .05
471 *Bennie Thompson* .05
472 Freeman McNeil .05
473 Terry Orr .05
474 Mike Horan .05
475 Leroy Hoard .05
476 *Patrick Rowe* (DP) .05
477 *Siran Stacy* (DP) .05
478 *Amp Lee* (DP) .20
479 *Eddie Blake* (DP) .05
480 *Joe Bowden* (DP) .05
481 *Roderick Milstead* (DP) .05
482 *Keith Hamilton* (DP) .05
483 *Darryl Williams* (DP) .05
484 *Robert Porcher* (DP) .10
485 *Ed Cunningham* (DP) .05
486 *Chris Mims* (DP) .10
487 *Chris Hakel* (DP) .05
488 *Jimmy Smith* (DP) 3.50
489 *Todd Harrison* (DP) .05
490 *Edgar Bennett* (DP) .75
491 *Dexter McNabb* (DP) .05
492 *Leon Searcy* (DP) .05
493 *Tommy Vardell* (DP) .10
494 *Terrell Buckley* (DP) .10
495 *Kevin Turner* (DP) .05
496 *Russ Campbell* (DP) .05
497 *Torrance Small* (DP) .30
498 *Nate Turner* (DP) .05
499 *Cornelius Benton* (DP) .05
500 *Matt Elliott* (DP) .05
501 *Robert Stewart* (DP) .05
502 *Muhammad Shamsid-Deen* (DP) .05
503 *George Williams* (DP) .05
504 *Pumpy Tudors* (DP) .05
505 *Matt LaBounty* (DP) .05
506 *Darryl Hardy* (DP) .05
507 *Derrick Moore* (DP) .50
508 *Willie Clay* (DP) .05
509 *Bob Whitfield* (DP) .05
510 *Ricardo McDonald* (DP) .05
511 *Carlos Huerta* (DP) .05
512 *Selwyn Jones* (DP) .05
513 *Steve Gordon* (DP) .05
514 *Bob Meeks* (DP) .05
515 Bennie Blades (CC) .05
516 Andre Waters (CC) .05
517 Bubba McDowell (CC) .05
518 Kevin Porter (CC) .05
519 Carnell Lake (CC) .05
520 Leonard Russell (ROY) .05
521 Mike Croel (ROY) .05
522 Lawrence Dawsey (ROY) .05
523 Moe Gardner (ROY) .05
524 Steve Broussard (LBM) .05
525 Dave Meggett (LBM) .05
526 Darrell Green (LBM) .05
527 Tony Jones (LBM) .05
528 Barry Sanders (LBM) 1.00
529 Pat Swilling (SA) .05
530 Reggie White (SA) .05
531 William Fuller (SA) .05
532 Simon Fletcher (SA) .05

533	Derrick Thomas (SA)	.05
534	Mark Rypien (MOY)	.05
535	John Mackey (HOF)	.05
536	John Riggins (HOF)	.05
537	Lem Barney (HOF)	.05
538	Shawn McCarthy (90)	.05
539	Al Edwards (90)	.05
540	Alexander Wright (90)	.05
541	Ray Crockett (90)	.05
542	Steve Young (90)	.40
543	Nate Lewis (90)	.05
544	Dexter Carter (90)	.05
545	Reggie Rutland (90)	.05
546	Jon Vaughn (90)	.05
547	Chris Martin (90)	.05
548	Warren Moon (HL)	.05
549	Super Bowl logo	.05
550	Robb Thomas	.05

1992 Score NFL Follies

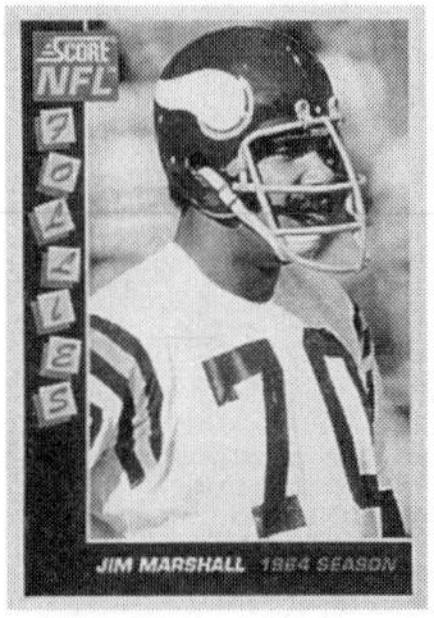

This three-card set was available exclusively through the purchase of NFL Football Card Follies, a tape produced by NFL Films and distributed by Polygram Video. It featured three of the game's wacky and wildest plays. The video was available in video stores nationwide for a suggested retail price of $19.95.

		MT
Complete Set (3):		30.00
Common Player:		8.00
1	Franco Harris	15.00
2	Garo Yepremian	8.00
3	Jim Marshall	8.00

1992 Score Dream Team

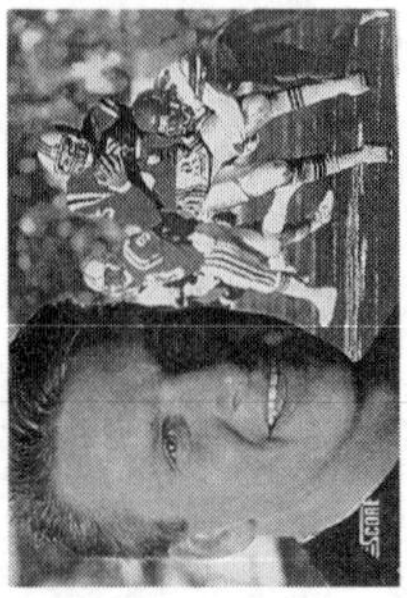

These cards have horizontal fronts which feature a full-bleed color action photo. The team logo is in a diamond in the lower left corner, intersected by color-coded stripes which have the player's name and position (bottom) and set name (left side) in them. The set name is in gold foil. The card back has a portrait shot, team logo, player profile, statistics, biography and card number. Cards were randomly inserted in 1992 Score jumbo packs.

		MT
Complete Set (25):		85.00
Common Player:		1.50
Minor Stars:		3.00
1	Michael Irvin	3.00
2	Haywood Jeffires	3.00
3	Emmitt Smith	20.00
4	Barry Sanders	25.00
5	Marv Cook	1.50
6	Bart Oates	1.50
7	Steve Wisniewski	1.50
8	Randall McDaniel	1.50
9	Jim Lachey	1.50
10	Lomas Brown	1.50
11	Reggie White	4.00
12	Clyde Simmons	1.50
13	Derrick Thomas	3.00
14	Seth Joyner	1.50
15	Darryl Talley	1.50
16	Karl Mecklenburg	1.50
17	Sam Mills	1.50
18	Darrell Green	1.50
19	Steve Atwater	1.50
20	Mark Carrier	1.50
21	Jeff Gossett	1.50
22	Chip Lohmiller	1.50
23	Mel Gray	1.50
24	Steve Tasker	1.50
25	Mark Rypien	1.50

1992 Score Gridiron Stars

Each 1992 Score jumbo pack contained three of these cards, which are devoted to "Gridiron Stars." This is gold foil-stamped along the left side of the card front, which has an action photo of the player, plus his name, position and logo. The numbered card back includes a player profile shot, statistics and a career summary.

		MT
Complete Set (45):		12.00
Common Player:		.25
Minor Stars:		.50
1	Barry Sanders	3.00
2	Mike Croel	.25
3	Thurman Thomas	.50
4	Lawrence Dawsey	.25
5	Brad Baxter	.25
6	Moe Gardner	.25
7	Emmitt Smith	3.00
8	Sammie Smith	.25
9	Rodney Hampton	.50
10	Mark Carrier	.25
11	Mo Lewis	.50
12	Andre Rison	.50
13	Eric Green	.50
14	Richmond Webb	.25
15	Johnny Bailey	.25
16	Mike Pritchard	.25
17	John Friesz	.50
18	Leonard Russell	.25
19	Derrick Thomas	.50
20	Ken Harvey	.25
21	Fred Barnett	.25
22	Aeneas Williams	.25
23	Marion Butts	.25
24	Harold Green	.25
25	Michael Irvin	.50
26	Dan Owens	.25
27	Curtis Duncan	.25
28	Rodney Peete	.25
29	Brian Blades	.25
30	Marv Cook	.25
31	Burt Grossman	.25
32	Michael Haynes	.25
33	Bennie Blades	.25
34	Cornelius Bennett	.25
35	Louis Oliver	.25
36	Rod Woodson	.25
37	Steve Wisniewski	.25
38	Neil Smith	.25
39	Gaston Green	.25
40	Jeff Lageman	.25
41	Chip Lohmiller	.25
42	Tim McDonald	.25
43	John Elliott	.25
44	Steve Atwater	.25
45	Flipper Anderson	.25

1992 Score Young Superstars

Promising stars of the NFL are featured in this 40-card boxed set from Score. Each card front has a glossy, color action photo, framed by two borders - a green one and a purple outer border with black specks inside. The Score logo, player's name and team name also appear on the card front. The back is numbered and includes a mug shot of the player, plus statistics, biographical information, a career summary and a scouting report analyzing the player's skills.

		MT
Complete Set (40):		5.00
Common Player:		.10
1	Michael Irvin	1.00
2	Cortez Kennedy	.30
3	Ken Harvey	.10
4	Bubba McDowell	.10
5	Mark Higgs	.35
6	Andre Rison	.50
7	Lamar Lathon	.10
8	Bennie Blades	.15
9	Anthony Johnson	.10
10	Vince Buck	.10
11	Pat Harlow	.10
12	Mike Croel	.10
13	Myron Guyton	.10
14	Curtis Duncan	.15
15	Michael Haynes	.25
16	Alexander Wright	.10
17	Greg Lewis	.10
18	Chip Lohmiller	.10
19	Nate Lewis	.10
20	Rodney Peete	.15
21	Marv Cook	.15
22	Lawrence Dawsey	.15
23	Pat Terrell	.15
24	John Friesz	.20
25	Tony Bennett	.10
26	Gaston Green	.10
27	Kevin Porter	.10
28	Mike Pritchard	.20
29	Keith Henderson	.10
30	Mo Lewis	.10
31	John Randle	.10
32	Aeneas Williams	.10
33	Floyd Turner	.10
34	Neil Smith	.15
35	Tom Waddle	.10
36	Jeff Lageman	.10
37	Cris Carter	.20
38	Leonard Russell	.25
39	Terry McDaniel	.10
40	Moe Gardner	.10

Values quoted in this guide reflect the retail price of a card — the price a collector can expect to pay when buying a card from a dealer. The wholesale price — that which a collector can expect to receive from a dealer when selling cards — will be significantly lower, depending on desirability and condition.

1993 Score Samples

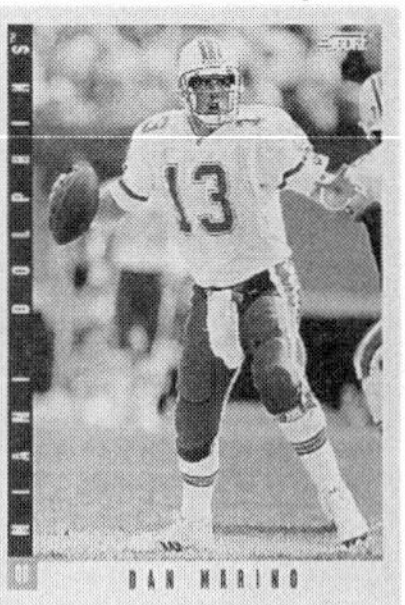

The six-card, regular-size set was issued to preview the base 1993 set. The six cards are virtually identical to the first six cards in the base set, except for a "Promo" stamp on the lower right corner of the card backs.

		MT
Complete Set (6):		5.00
Common Player:		.50
1	Barry Sanders	3.00
2	Moe Gardner	.50
3	Ricky Watters	1.25
4	Todd Lyght	.50
5	Rodney Hampton	.75
6	Curtis Duncan	.50

1993 Score

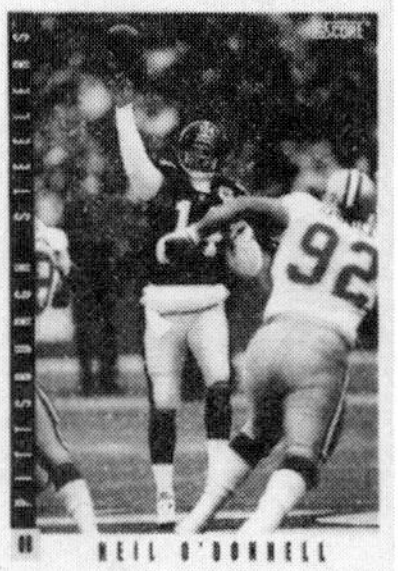

Score's 440-card 1993 set features subsets for Rookies, Super Bowl Highlights, Double Trouble, Rookie of the Year, 90 Plus Club, Highlights, and Hall of Famers. The card fronts have action photos with a white border. The player's team name is in a panel along the side in the appropriate colors, as is the player's name, which is at the bottom of the card. Backs have a profile, mug shot, statistics, biographical information and team logo. Insert sets include Dream Team (26 cards), Franchise (28 cards, one per team), and Men of Autumn (55) - a Score Pinnacle "Men Of Autumn" card which was not included in regular Pinnacle packs.

		MT
Complete Set (440):		15.00
Common Player:		.05
Minor Stars:		.10
Autograph Butkus:		25.00
Pack (15):		.50
Wax Box (36):		15.00
1	Barry Sanders	1.25
2	Moe Gardner	.05
3	Ricky Watters	.25
4	Todd Lyght	.05
5	Rodney Hampton	.10
6	Curtis Duncan	.05
7	Barry Word	.05
8	Reggie Cobb	.05
9	Mike Kenn	.05
10	Michael Irvin	.30
11	Bryan Cox	.05
12	Chris Doleman	.05
13	Rod Woodson	.10
14	Emmitt Smith	2.00
15	Pete Stoyanovich	.05
16	Steve Young	.75
17	Randall McDaniel	.05
18	Cortez Kennedy	.10
19	Mel Gray	.05
20	Barry Foster	.10
21	Tim Brown	.10
22	Todd McNair	.05
23	Anthony Johnson	.05
24	Nate Odomes	.05
25	Brett Favre	2.00
26	Jack Del Rio	.05
27	Terry McDaniel	.05
28	Haywood Jeffires	.05
29	Jay Novacek	.05
30	Wilber Marshall	.05
31	Richmond Webb	.05
32	Steve Atwater	.05
33	James Lofton	.05
34	Harold Green	.05
35	Eric Metcalf	.05
36	Bruce Matthews	.05
37	Albert Lewis	.05
38	Jeff Herrod	.05
39	Vince Workman	.05
40	John Elway	.50
41	Brett Perriman	.05
42	Jon Vaughn	.05
43	Terry Allen	.05
44	Clyde Simmons	.05
45	Bennie Thompson	.05
46	Wendall Davis	.05
47	Bobby Hebert	.05
48	John Offerdahl	.05
49	Jeff Graham	.05
50	Steve Wisniewski	.05
51	Louis Oliver	.05
52	Rohn Stark	.05
53	Cleveland Gary	.05
54	John Randle	.05
55	Jim Everett	.05
56	Donnell Woolford	.05
57	Pepper Johnson	.05
58	Irving Fryar	.05
59	Greg Townsend	.05
60	Chris Burkett	.05
61	Johnny Johnson	.05
62	Ronnie Harmon	.05
63	Don Griffin	.05
64	Wayne Martin	.05
65	John L. Williams	.05
66	Brad Edwards	.05
67	Toi Cook	.05
68	Lawrence Dawsey	.05
69	Johnny Bailey	.05
70	Mike Brim	.05
71	Andre Rison	.10
72	Cornelius Bennett	.05
73	Brad Muster	.05
74	Broderick Thomas	.05
75	Tom Waddle	.05
76	Paul Gruber	.05
77	Jackie Harris	.05
78	Kenneth Davis	.05
79	Norm Johnson	.05
80	Jim Jeffcoat	.05
81	Chris Warren	.10
82	Greg Kragen	.05
83	Ricky Reynolds	.05
84	Hardy Nickerson	.05
85	Brian Mitchell	.05
86	Rufus Porter	.05
87	Greg Jackson	.05
88	Seth Joyner	.05
89	Tim Grunhard	.05
90	Tim Harris	.05
91	Sterling Sharpe	.10
92	Daniel Stubbs	.05
93	Rob Burnett	.05
94	Rich Camarillo	.05
95	Al Smith	.05
96	Thurman Thomas	.10
97	Morten Andersen	.05
98	Reggie White	.10
99	Gill Byrd	.05
100	Pierce Holt	.05
101	Tim McGee	.05
102	Rickey Jackson	.05
103	Vince Newsome	.05
104	Chris Spielman	.05
105	Tim McDonald	.05
106	James Francis	.05
107	Andre Tippett	.05
108	Sam Mills	.05
109	Hugh Millen	.05
110	Brad Baxter	.05
111	Ricky Sanders	.05
112	Marion Butts	.05
113	Fred Barnett	.05
114	Wade Wilson	.05
115	Dave Meggett	.05
116	Kevin Greene	.05
117	Reggie Langhorne	.05
118	Simon Fletcher	.05
119	Tommy Vardell	.05
120	Darion Conner	.05
121	Darren Lewis	.05
122	Charles Mann	.05
123	David Fulcher	.05
124	Tommy Kane	.05
125	Richard Brown	.05
126	Nate Lewis	.05
127	Tony Tolbert	.05
128	Greg Lloyd	.05
129	Herman Moore	.50
130	Robert Massey	.05
131	Chris Jacke	.05
132	Keith Byars	.05
133	William Fuller	.05
134	Rob Moore	.05
135	Duane Bickett	.05
136	Jarrod Bunch	.05
137	Ethan Horton	.05
138	Leonard Russell	.05
139	Darryl Henley	.05
140	Tony Bennett	.05
141	Harry Newsome	.05
142	Kelvin Martin	.05
143	Audray McMillian	.05
144	Chip Lohmiller	.05
145	Henry Jones	.05
146	Rod Bernstine	.05
147	Darryl Talley	.05
148	Clarence Verdin	.05
149	Derrick Thomas	.10
150	Raleigh McKenzie	.05
151	Phil Hansen	.05
152	*Lin Elliott*	.05
153	Chip Banks	.05
154	Shannon Sharpe	.10
155	David Williams	.05
156	Gaston Green	.05
157	Trace Armstrong	.05
158	Todd Scott	.05
159	Stan Humphries	.10
160	Christian Okoye	.05
161	Dennis Smith	.05
162	Derek Kennard	.05
163	Melvin Jenkins	.05
164	Tommy Barnhardt	.05
165	Eugene Robinson	.05
166	Tom Rathman	.05
167	Chris Chandler	.05
168	Steve Broussard	.05
169	Wymon Henderson	.05
170	Bryce Paup	.05
171	Kent Hull	.05
172	Willie Davis	.05
173	Richard Dent	.05
174	Rodney Peete	.05
175	Clay Matthews	.05
176	Erik Williams	.05
177	Mike Cofer	.05
178	Mark Kelso	.05
179	Kurt Gouveia	.05
180	Keith McCants	.05
181	Jim Arnold	.05
182	Sean Jones	.05
183	Chuck Cecil	.05
184	Mark Rypien	.05
185	William Perry	.05
186	Mark Jackson	.05
187	Jim Dombrowski	.05
188	Heath Sherman	.05
189	Bubba McDowell	.05
190	Fuad Reveiz	.05
191	Darren Perry	.05
192	Karl Mecklenburg	.05
193	Frank Reich	.05
194	Tony Casillas	.05
195	Jerry Ball	.05
196	Jessie Hester	.05
197	David Lang	.05
198	Sean Landeta	.05
199	Jerry Gray	.05
200	Mark Higgs	.05
201	Bruce Armstrong	.05
202	Vaughan Johnson	.05
203	Calvin Williams	.05
204	Leonard Marshall	.05
205	Mike Munchak	.05
206	Kevin Ross	.05
207	Daryl Johnston	.05
208	Jay Schroeder	.05
209	Mo Lewis	.05
210	Carlton Haselrig	.05
211	Cris Carter	.10
212	Marv Cook	.05
213	Mark Duper	.05
214	Jackie Slater	.05
215	Mike Prior	.05
216	Warren Moon	.10
217	Mike Saxon	.05
218	Derrick Fenner	.05
219	Brian Washington	.05
220	Jessie Tuggle	.05
221	Jeff Hostetler	.10
222	Deion Sanders	.50
223	Neal Anderson	.05
224	Kevin Mack	.05
225	Tommy Maddox	.05
226	Neil Smith	.05
227	Ronnie Lott	.05
228	Willie Anderson	.05
229	Keith Jackson	.05
230	Pat Swilling	.05
231	Carl Banks	.05
232	Eric Allen	.05
233	Randal Hill	.05
234	Burt Grossman	.05
235	Jerry Rice	.75
236	Santana Dotson	.05
237	Andre Reed	.10
238	Troy Aikman	.75
239	Ray Childress	.05
240	Phil Simms	.05
241	Steve McMichael	.05
242	Browning Nagle	.05
243	Anthony Miller	.05
244	Earnest Byner	.05
245	Jay Hilgenberg	.05
246	Jeff George	.10
247	Marco Coleman	.05
248	Herschel Walker	.05
249	Howie Long	.05
250	Ed McCaffrey	.05
251	Jim Kelly	.10
252	Henry Ellard	.05
253	Joe Montana	1.25
254	Dale Carter	.05
255	John Elliott	.05
256	Gary Clark	.05
257	Carl Pickens	.75
258	Dave Krieg	.05
259	Russell Maryland	.05
260	Randall Cunningham	.10
261	Leslie O'Neal	.05
262	Vinny Testaverde	.05
263	Ricky Ervins	.05
264	Chris Mims	.05
265	Dan Marino	2.00
266	Eric Martin	.05
267	Bruce Smith	.05
268	Jim Harbaugh	.05
269	Steve Emtman	.05
270	Ricky Proehl	.05
271	Vaughn Dunbar	.05
272	Junior Seau	.10
273	Sean Gilbert	.05
274	Jim Lachey	.05
275	Dalton Hilliard	.05
276	David Klingler	.05
277	Robert Jones	.05
278	David Treadwell	.05
279	Tracy Scroggins	.05
280	Terrell Buckley	.05
281	Quentin Coryatt	.05
282	Jason Hanson	.05
283	Desmond Howard	.05
284	Guy McIntyre	.05
285	Gary Zimmerman	.05
286	Marty Carter	.05
287	Jim Sweeney	.05
288	*Arthur Marshall*	.10
289	Eugene Chung	.05
290	Mike Pritchard	.05
291	Jim Ritcher	.05
292	Todd Marinovich	.05
293	Courtney Hall	.05
294	Mark Collins	.05
295	Troy Auzenne	.05
296	Aeneas Williams	.05
297	Andy Heck	.05
298	Shaun Gayle	.05
299	Kevin Fagan	.05
300	Carnell Lake	.05
301	Antone Davis	.05
302	Maurice Hurst	.05
303	Mike Merriweather	.05
304	Reggie Roby	.05
305	Darryl Williams	.05
306	*Jerome Bettis*	1.50
307	*Curtis Conway*	1.00
308	*Drew Bledsoe*	3.00
309	*John Copeland*	.10
310	*Eric Curry*	.10
311	*Lincoln Kennedy*	.10
312	*Dan Williams*	.10
313	*Patrick Bates*	.10
314	*Tom Carter*	.10
315	*Garrison Hearst*	1.50
316	*Joel Hilgenberg*	.05
317	Harris Barton	.05
318	Jeff Lageman	.05
319	*Charles Mincy*	.10
320	Ricardo McDonald	.05
321	Lorenzo White	.05
322	Troy Vincent	.05
323	Bennie Blades	.05
324	Dana Hall	.05
325	Ken Norton	.05
326	Will Wolford	.05
327	Neil O'Donnell	.10
328	Tracy Simien	.05
329	Darrell Green	.05
330	Kyle Clifton	.05
331	*Elbert Shelley*	.05
332	Jeff Wright	.05
333	Mike Johnson	.05
334	John Gesek	.05
335	Michael Brooks	.05
336	George Jamison	.05
337	Johnny Holland	.05
338	Lamar Lathon	.05
339	Bern Brostek	.05
340	Steve Jordan	.05
341	Gene Atkins	.05
342	Aaron Wallace	.05
343	Adrian Cooper	.05
344	Amp Lee	.05
345	Vincent Brown	.05
346	James Hasty	.05
347	Ron Hall	.05
348	Matt Elliott	.05
349	Tim Krumrie	.05
350	Mark Stepnoski	.05
351	Mat Stover	.05
352	James Washington	.05
353	Marc Spindler	.05
354	Frank Warren	.05
355	Vai Sikahema	.05
356	Dan Saleaumua	.05
357	Mark Clayton	.05
358	Brent Jones	.05
359	*Andy Harmon*	.05
360	Anthony Parker	.05
361	Chris Hinton	.05
362	Greg Montgomery	.05
363	Greg McMurtry	.05
364	Craig Heyward	.05
365	David Johnson	.05
366	Bill Romanowski	.05
367	Steve Christie	.05
368	Art Monk	.05
369	Howard Ballard	.05
370	Andre Collins	.05
371	Alvin Harper	.10
372	*Blaise Winter*	.05
373	Al Del Greco	.05
374	Eric Green	.05
375	Chris Mohr	.05
376	Tom Newberry	.05
377	Cris Dishman	.05
378	James Geathers	.05
379	Don Mosebar	.05
380	Andre Ware	.05
381	Marvin Washington	.05
382	Bobby Humphrey	.05
383	Marc Logan	.05
384	Lomas Brown	.05
385	Steve Tasker	.05
386	Chris Miller	.05
387	Tony Paige	.05
388	Charles Haley	.05
389	Rich Moran	.05
390	Mike Sherrard	.05
391	Nick Lowery	.05
392	Henry Thomas	.05
393	Keith Sims	.05
394	Thomas Everett	.05
395	Steve Wallace	.05
396	John Carney	.05
397	Tim Johnson	.05
398	Jeff Gossett	.05
399	Anthony Smith	.05
400	Kelvin Pritchett	.05
401	Dermontti Dawson	.05
402	Alfred Williams	.05
403	Michael Haynes	.05
404	Bart Oates	.05
405	Ken Lanier	.05
406	Vencie Glenn	.05
407	John Taylor	.05
408	Nate Newton	.05
409	Mark Carrier	.05
410	Ken Harvey	.05
411	Troy Aikman (SB)	.40
412	Charles Haley (SB)	.05
413	Warren Moon, Haywood Jeffires (DT)	.05
414	Henry Jones, Mark Kelso (DT)	.05
415	Rickey Jackson, Sam Mills (DT)	.05
416	Clyde Simmons, Reggie White (DT)	.05
417	Dale Carter (RY)	.05
418	Carl Pickens (RY)	.05
419	Vaughn Dunbar (RY)	.05
420	Santana Dotson (RY)	.05
421	Steve Emtman (90-plus)	.05
422	Louis Oliver (90-plus)	.05
423	Carl Pickens (90-plus)	.05
424	Eddie Anderson (90-plus)	.05
425	Deion Sanders (90-plus)	.20
426	Jon Vaughn (90-plus)	.05
427	Darren Lewis (90-plus)	.05
428	Kevin Ross (90-plus)	.05
429	David Brandon (90-plus)	.05
430	Dave Meggett (90-plus)	.05
431	Jerry Rice (H)	.35
432	Sterling Sharpe (H)	.10
433	Art Monk (H)	.05
434	James Lofton (H)	.05
435	Lawrence Taylor	.10
436	Bill Walsh (HF)	.05
437	Chuck Noll (HF)	.05
438	Dan Fouts (HF)	.05
439	Larry Little (HF)	.05
440	Steve Young (MY)	.30

1993 Score Dream Team

The best 13 offensive and 13 defensive players by position are represented in this 1993 Score insert set. Cards were randomly inserted in 1993 Score 35-card packs and were selections made by Score. The horizontal card front has a close-up shot of the player on the right side and an action shot of him on the left against a black panel. The card background is a cloudy sky tinted in brown. The card back has a photo identical to the action photo on the front, except it's big-

ger and fuzzier. A player profile appears at the bottom in a black panel. The back is numbered and also features a team logo.

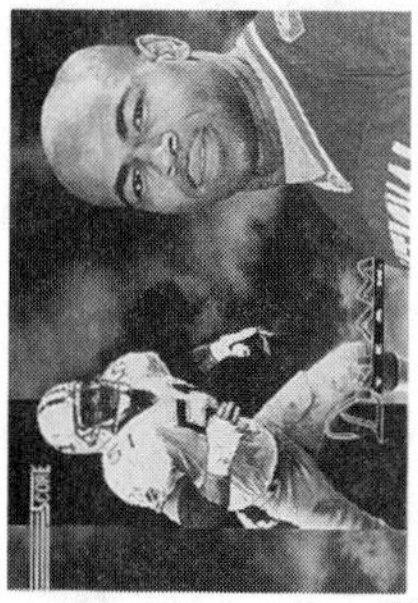

		MT
Complete Set (26):		20.00
Common Player:		.50
Minor Stars:		1.00
1	Steve Young	5.00
2	Emmitt Smith	12.00
3	Barry Foster	1.00
4	Sterling Sharpe	1.00
5	Jerry Rice	5.00
6	Keith Jackson	.50
7	Steve Wallace	.50
8	Richmond Webb	.50
9	Guy McIntyre	.50
10	Carlton Haselrig	.50
11	Bruce Matthews	.50
12	Morten Andersen	.50
13	Rich Camarillo	.50
14	Deion Sanders	3.00
15	Steve Tasker	.50
16	Clyde Simmons	.50
17	Reggie White	1.00
18	Cortez Kennedy	.75
19	Rod Woodson	1.00
20	Terry McDaniel	.50
21	Chuck Cecil	.50
22	Steve Atwater	.50
23	Bryan Cox	.50
24	Derrick Thomas	1.00
25	Wilber Marshall	.50
26	Sam Mills	.50

1993 Score Franchise

A top player from each of the 28 NFL teams has been selected for this insert set. Cards were random inserts in 1993 Score foil packs at a rate of about one every 24 packs. The front has a color action photo and the set's logo; the numbered backs have a close-up shot of the player, plus a profile.

		MT
Complete Set (28):		175.00
Common Player:		2.00
Minor Stars:		4.00
1	Andre Rison	2.00
2	Thurman Thomas	4.00
3	Richard Dent	2.00
4	Harold Green	2.00
5	Eric Metcalf	2.00
6	Emmitt Smith	40.00
7	John Elway	25.00
8	Barry Sanders	40.00
9	Sterling Sharpe	4.00
10	Warren Moon	4.00
11	Jeff Herrod	2.00
12	Derrick Thomas	4.00
13	Steve Wisniewski	2.00
14	Cleveland Gary	2.00
15	Dan Marino	40.00
16	Chris Doleman	2.00
17	Marv Cook	2.00
18	Rickey Jackson	2.00
19	Rodney Hampton	2.00
20	Jeff Lageman	2.00
21	Clyde Simmons	2.00
22	Rich Camarillo	2.00
23	Rod Woodson	4.00
24	Ronnie Harmon	2.00
25	Steve Young	20.00
26	Cortez Kennedy	2.00
27	Reggie Cobb	2.00
28	Mark Rypien	2.00

1993 Score Ore-Ida QB Club

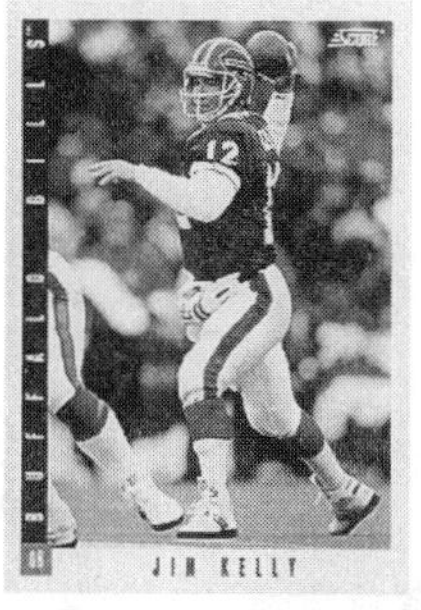

The 18-card, standard-size set was issued with specially marked Ore-Ida Bagel Bites, Twice Baked and Topped Baked Potatoes. Purchasers had to send in six proof-of-purchase seals and $1.50 for two nine-card packs. The cards are indentical in design to cards in the base 1993 set, except for different numbering. Esiason (Jets) and Hostetler (Raiders) are pictured in their new uniforms.

		MT
Complete Set (18):		25.00
Common Player:		.75
1	John Elway	2.00
2	Steve Young	2.00
3	Warren Moon	1.25
4	Randall Cunningham	.75
5	Jeff Hostetler	.75
6	Phil Simms	1.00
7	Jim Everett	.75
8	David Klingler	.75
9	Brett Favre	6.00
10	Troy Aikman	3.50
11	Dan Marino	6.00
12	Mark Rypien	.75
13	Jim Kelly	1.25
14	Jim Harbaugh	1.00
15	Bernie Kosar	.75
16	Boomer Esiason	.75
17	Chris Miller	.75
18	Neil O'Donnell	.75

1994 Score Samples

The nine-card, standrd-size set was issued to preview the 1994 base set and are identical in design to cards in the regular-issued set. The Glyn Milburn card is an example of the Gold Zone insert set.

		MT
Complete Set (9):		3.00
Common Player:		.25
21	Jerome Bettis	1.00
25	Steve Jordan	.25
50	Shannon Sharpe	.40
112	Glyn Milburn (FOIL)	.40
161	Ronnie Lott	.40
257	Derrick Thomas	.50
0	Generic Rookie Card	.25
NNO	Sample Redemption Card	.25
NNO	Score Ad Card	.25

1994 Score

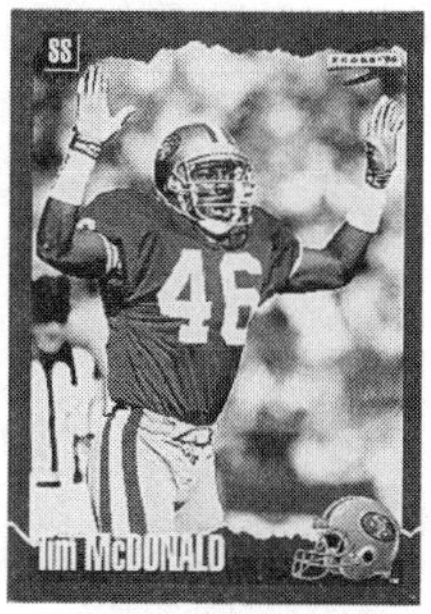

Score's 330-card 1994 set includes Rookie Redemption, Dream Team and Sophomore Showcase insert cards, plus a Gold Zone parallel set. The Gold Zone cards are identical to the regular cards, except they are printed on gold foil; they are inserted one per pack. The card front has a full-color action photo with ragged, torn borders at the top and bottom of the card. The Score logo, player's name and position, and a team helmet are also on the front. Each card back has a mug shot, biographical information, player profile, and statistics. Subsets within the main set are devoted to checklists and 1994 rookies. Nine sample cards, each marked on the back as being a sample, were also made to preview the regular set.

		MT
Complete Set (330):		20.00
Common Player:		.05
Complete Gold Set (330):		100.00
Gold Cards:		2x-4x
Pack (12):		1.00
Wax Box (36):		30.00
1	Barry Sanders	1.00
2	Troy Aikman	.75
3	Sterling Sharpe	.35
4	Deion Sanders	.15
5	Bruce Smith	.10
6	Eric Metcalf	.08
7	John Elway	.50
8	Bruce Matthews	.05
9	Rickey Jackson	.05
10	Cortez Kennedy	.08
11	Jerry Rice	.75
12	Stanley Richard	.05
13	Rod Woodson	.10
14	Eric Swann	.10
15	Eric Allen	.10
16	Richard Dent	.06
17	Carl Pickens	.08
18	Rohn Stark	.05
19	Marcus Allen	.10
20	Steve Wisniewski	.08
21	Jerome Bettis	.15
22	Darrell Green	.05
23	Lawrence Dawsey	.05
24	Larry Centers	.10
25	Steve Jordan	.08
26	Johnny Johnson	.08
27	Phil Simms	.10
28	Bruce Armstrong	.05
29	Willis Roaf	.08
30	Andre Rison	.10
31	Henry Jones	.05
32	Warren Moon	.10
33	Sean Gilbert	.08
34	Ben Coates	.05
35	Seth Joyner	.05
36	Ronnie Harmon	.08
37	Quentin Coryatt	.08
38	Ricky Sanders	.05
39	Gerald Williams	.05
40	Emmitt Smith	2.00
41	Jason Hanson	.05
42	Kevin Smith	.05
43	Irving Fryar	.10
44	Boomer Esiason	.08
45	Darryl Talley	.05
46	Paul Gruber	.05
47	Anthony Smith	.05
48	John Copeland	.05
49	Michael Jackson	.08
50	Shannon Sharpe	.15
51	Reggie White	.15
52	Andre Collins	.05
53	Jack Del Rio	.05
54	John Elliott	.05
55	Kevin Greene	.08
56	Steve Young	.75
57	Erric Pegram	.20
58	Donnell Woolford	.05
59	Darryl Williams	.05
60	Michael Irvin	.35
61	Mel Gray	.05
62	Greg Montgomery	.05
63	Neil Smith	.10
64	Andy Harmon	.05
65	Dan Marino	2.00
66	Leonard Russell	.10
67	Joe Montana	.75
68	John Taylor	.10
69	Cris Dishman	.08
70	Cornelius Bennett	.10
71	Harold Green	.08
72	Anthony Pleasant	.05
73	Dennis Smith	.05
74	Bryce Paup	.05
75	Jeff George	.08
76	Henry Ellard	.05
77	Randall McDaniel	.05
78	Derek Brown	.35
79	Johnny Mitchell	.10
80	Leroy Thompson	.05
81	Junior Seau	.08
82	Kelvin Martin	.08
83	Guy McIntyre	.05
84	Elbert Shelley	.05
85	Louis Oliver	.05
86	Tommy Vardell	.05
87	Jeff Harrod	.05
88	Edgar Bennett	.05
89	Reggie Langhorne	.05
90	Terry Kirby	.20
91	Marcus Robertson	.05
92	Mark Collins	.05
93	Calvin Williams	.08
94	Barry Foster	.15
95	Brent Jones	.05
96	Reggie Cobb	.08
97	Ray Childress	.05
98	Chris Miller	.10
99	John Carney	.05
100	Ricky Proehl	.05
101	Renaldo Turnbull	.08
102	John Randle	.05
103	Willie Anderson	.05
104	*Scottie Graham*	.50
105	Webster Slaughter	.08
106	Tyrone Hughes	.05
107	Ken Norton	.05
108	Jim Kelly	.25
109	Michael Haynes	.15
110	Mark Carrier	.05
111	Eddie Murray	.05
112	Glyn Milburn	.25
113	Jackie Harris	.15
114	Dean Biasucci	.05
115	Tim Brown	.15
116	Mark Higgs	.05
117	Steve Emtman	.05
118	Clay Matthews	.05
119	Clyde Simmons	.05
120	Howard Ballard	.05
121	Ricky Watters	.20
122	William Fuller	.05
123	Robert Brooks	.05
124	Brian Blades	.05
125	Leslie O'Neal	.05
126	Gary Clark	.08
127	Jim Sweeney	.05
128	Vaughan Johnson	.05
129	Gary Brown	.15
130	Todd Lyght	.05
131	Nick Lowery	.05
132	Ernest Givins	.05
133	Lomas Brown	.05
134	Craig Erickson	.05
135	James Francis	.05
136	Andre Reed	.08
137	Jim Everett	.08
138	Nate Odomes	.05
139	Tom Waddle	.05
140	Stevon Moore	.05
141	Rod Bernstine	.05
142	Brett Favre	2.00
143	Roosevelt Potts	.05
144	Chester McGlockton	.05
145	LeRoy Butler	.05
146	Charles Haley	.05
147	Rodney Hampton	.30
148	George Teague	.08
149	Gary Anderson	.05
150	Mark Stepnoski	.05
151	Courtney Hawkins	.05
152	Tim Grunhard	.05
153	David Klingler	.15
154	Erik Williams	.05
155	Herman Moore	.15
156	Daryl Johnston	.05
157	Chris Zorich	.05
158	Shane Conlan	.05
159	Santana Dotson	.05
160	Sam Mills	.08
161	Ronnie Lott	.08
162	Jesse Sapolu	.05
163	Marion Butts	.05
164	Eugene Robinson	.05
165	Mark Schlereth	.05
166	John L. Williams	.05
167	Anthony Miller	.15
168	Rich Camarillo	.05
169	Jeff Lageman	.05
170	Michael Brooks	.05
171	Scott Mitchell	.30
172	Duane Bickett	.05
173	Willie Davis	.05
174	Maurice Hurst	.05
175	Brett Perriman	.05
176	Jay Novacek	.05
177	Terry Allen	.08
178	Pete Metzelaars	.05
179	Erik Kramer	.10
180	Neal Anderson	.05
181	Ethan Horton	.05
182	Tony Bennett	.05
183	Gary Zimmerman	.05
184	Jeff Hostetler	.06
185	Jeff Cross	.05
186	Vincent Brown	.05
187	Herschel Walker	.05
188	Courtney Hall	.05
189	Norm Johnson	.05
190	Hardy Nickerson	.05
191	Greg Townsend	.05
192	Mike Munchak	.05
193	Dante Jones	.05
194	Vinny Testaverde	.08
195	Vance Johnson	.05
196	Chris Jacke	.05
197	Will Wolford	.05
198	Terry McDaniel	.05
199	Bryan Cox	.05
200	Nate Newton	.05
201	Keith Byars	.05
202	Neil O'Donnell	.15
203	Harris Barton	.05
204	Thurman Thomas	.25
205	Jeff Query	.05
206	Russell Maryland	.08
207	Pat Swilling	.05
208	Haywood Jeffires	.05
209	John Alt	.05
210	O.J. McDuffie	.30
211	Keith Sims	.05
212	Eric Martin	.05
213	Kyle Clifton	.05
214	Luis Sharpe	.05
215	Thomas Everett	.05
216	Chris Warren	.05
217	Chris Doleman	.05
218	Tony Jones	.05
219	Karl Mecklenburg	.05
220	Rob Moore	.10
221	Jessie Hester	.05
222	Jeff Jaeger	.05
223	Keith Jackson	.08
224	Mo Lewis	.05
225	Mike Horan	.05
226	Eric Green	.05
227	Jim Ritcher	.05
228	Eric Curry	.05
229	Stan Humphries	.05
230	Mike Johnson	.05
231	Alvin Harper	.10
232	Bennie Blades	.05
233	Cris Carter	.05
234	Morten Anderson	.05
235	Brian Washington	.05
236	Eric Hill	.05
237	Natrone Means	.40
238	Carlton Bailey	.05
239	Anthony Carter	.05
240	Jessie Tuggle	.05
241	Tim Irwin	.05
242	Mark Currier	.05
243	Steve Atwater	.05
244	Sean Jones	.05
245	Bernie Kosar	.05
246	Richmond Webb	.05
247	Dave Meggett	.05
248	Vincent Brisby	.35
249	Fred Barnett	.05
250	Greg Lloyd	.05
251	Tim McDonald	.05
252	Mike Pirtchard	.08
253	Greg Robinson	.10
254	Tony McGee	.05
255	Chris Spielman	.05
256	Keith Loneker	.10
257	Derrick Thomas	.15
258	Wayne Martin	.05
259	Art Monk	.05
260	Andy Heck	.05
261	Chip Lohmiller	.05
262	Simon Fletcher	.05
263	Ricky Reynolds	.05
264	Chris Hinton	.05
265	Ron Moore	.35
266	Raghib Ismail	.15
267	Pete Styanovich	.05
268	Mark Jackson	.05
269	Randall Cunningham	.10
270	Dermontti Dawson	.05
271	Bill Romanowski	.05
272	Tim Johnson	.05
273	Steve Tasker	.05
274	Keith Hamilton	.05
275	Pierce Holt	.05
276	*Heath Shuler*	.25
277	*Marshall Faulk*	3.00
278	*Charles Johnson*	.50
279	*Sam Adams*	.30
280	*Trev Alberts*	.50
281	*Derrick Alexander*	.25
282	*Bryant Young*	.25
283	*Greg Hill*	.50
284	*Darnay Scott*	1.00
285	*Willie McGinest*	.50
286	*Thomas Randolph*	.15
287	*Errict Rhett*	.75
288	*Lamar Smith*	2.50
289	*William Floyd*	.40
290	*Johnnie Morton*	.60
291	*Jamir Miller*	.30
292	*David Palmer*	.50
293	*Dan Wilkinson*	.60
294	*Trent Dilfer*	2.00
295	*Antonio Langham*	.30
296	*Chuck Levy*	.50
297	*John Thierry*	.25
298	*Kevin Lee*	.35
299	*Aaron Glenn*	.25
300	*Charlie Garner*	2.50
301	*Lonnie Johnson*	.15
302	*LeShon Johnson*	.45
303	*Thomas Lewis*	.50
304	*Ryan Yarborough*	.40
305	*Mario Bates*	.20
306	Bills/Cardinals Checklist	.05
307	Bengals/Falcons Checklist	.05
308	Browns/Bears Checklist	.05
309	Broncos/Cowboys Checklist	.05
310	Oilers/Lions Checklist	.05
311	Colts/Packers Checklist	.05
312	Chiefs/Rams Checklist	.05
313	Raiders/Vikings Checklist	.05
314	Dolphins/Saints Checklist	.05
315	Patriots/Giants Checklist	.05
316	Jets/Eagles Checklist	.05
317	Steelers/49ers Checklist	.05
318	Chargers/Bucs Checklist	.05
319	Seahawks/Redskins Checklist	.05
320	Garrison Hearst	.20
321	Drew Bledsoe	.75
322	Tyrone Hughes	.05
323	James Jett	.25
324	Tom Carter	.05
325	Reggie Brooks	.25
326	Dana Stubblefield	.25
327	Jerome Bettis	.15
328	Chris Slade	.15
329	Rick Mirer	.15
330	Emmitt Smith MVP	1.00

1994 Score Gold Zone

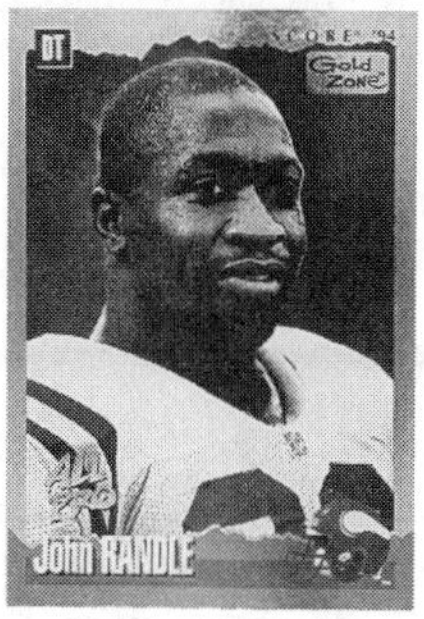

The 330-card, standard-size set is a parallel set with the card fronts having a metallic gold sheen.

	MT
Complete Set (330):	120.00
Common Player:	.30
Veteran Stars:	3x-6x
Young Stars:	2x-4x
RCs:	1.5x-3x

1994 Score Dream Team

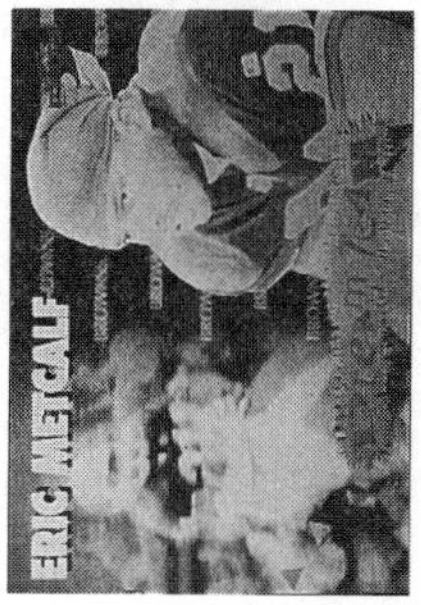

These cards were randomly inserted in 1994 Score packs at a rate of one every 72 packs. The cards have an animating hologram on the front, and feature 18 of the NFL's elite players. The hologram has an action shot and closeup photo of the player on the front, along with his name, Score logo, set logo and his team's name running across the card several times. The backs are numbered with a "DT" prefix and have a Score Football Fifth Anniversary logo, along with the player's 1989 Score card.

		MT
Complete Set (18):		160.00
Common Player:		4.00
Minor Stars:		8.00
1	Troy Aikman	30.00
2	Steve Atwater	4.00
3	Cornelius Bennett	4.00
4	Tim Brown	8.00
5	Michael Irvin	8.00
6	Bruce Matthews	4.00
7	Eric Metcalf	4.00
8	Anthony Miller	4.00
9	Jerry Rice	30.00
10	Andre Rison	8.00
11	Barry Sanders	35.00
12	Deion Sanders	15.00
13	Sterling Sharpe	8.00
14	Neil Smith	4.00
15	Derrick Thomas	8.00
16	Thurman Thomas	8.00
17	Rod Woodson	4.00
18	Steve Young	30.00

1994 Score Rookie Redemption

The 10-card, regular-sized set was inserted every 72 packs as a redemption card. The card fronts have metallic imaging while the backs have a player headshot and season highlights.

		MT
Complete Set (10):		175.00
Common Player:		1.50
Minor Stars:		3.00
1	Heath Shuler	4.00
2	Trent Dilfer	20.00
3	Marshall Faulk	150.00
4	Charlie Garner	20.00
5	LeShon Johnson	3.00
6	Charles Johnson	5.00
7	Errict Rhett	15.00
8	Lake Dawson	1.50
9	Bert Emanuel	4.00
10	Greg Hill	7.00

1994 Score Sophomore Showcase

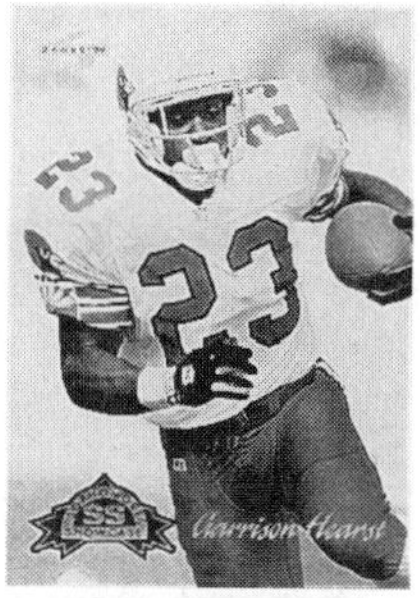

Eighteen of the NFL's top second-year players are featured on these cards, which were random inserts in one out of every four Score jumbo packs. The card front has a full-bleed color photo and the Score logo. The player's name and set logo are stamped in gold foil at the bottom. The card back has the player's name running in a marble-like panel along the left side. There's a closeup shot of the player, along with the set's logo, plus a brief career summary on the other side. Cards are numbered with an "SS" prefix.

		MT
Complete Set (18):		60.00
Common Player:		2.00
1	Jerome Bettis	8.00
2	Rick Mirer	4.00
3	Reggie Brooks	2.00
4	Drew Bledsoe	20.00
5	Ron Moore	2.00
6	Derek Brown	2.00
7	Roosevelt Potts	2.00
8	Terry Kirby	3.00
9	James Jett	2.00
10	Vincent Brisby	5.00
11	Tyrone Hughes	2.00
12	Rocket Ismail	3.00
13	Tony McGee	2.00
14	Garrison Hearst	8.00
15	Eric Curry	2.00
16	Dana Stubblefield	3.00
17	Tom Carter	2.00
18	Chris Slade	3.00

1995 Score Promos

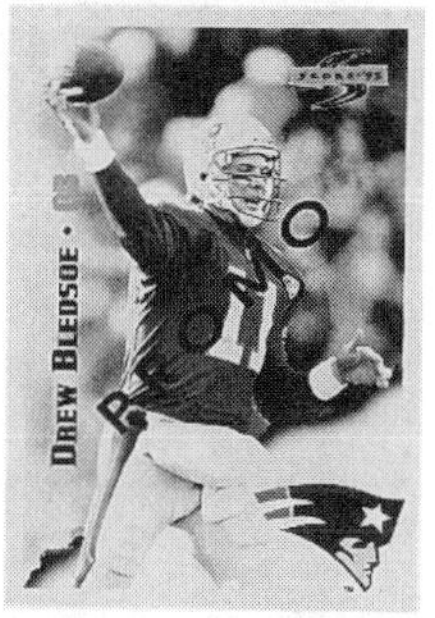

The six-card, regular-size set was distributed in four-card packs as a preview for the 1995 base set. The card fronts have "Promo" stamps.

		MT
Complete Set (6):		10.00
Common Player:		.50
42	Drew Bledsoe	2.50
47	Barry Foster	.50
58	Steve Broussard	.50
211	Star Struck Card (Jerry Rice)	2.50
DT2	Dream Team Card (Troy Aikman)	5.00
NNO	Title Card	.50

1995 Score

Score's 1995 275-card football set includes two subsets (26 Draft Pick cards and 30 Star Struck cards), plus two parallel sets (Red Siege and Artist's Proofs). The regular cards have a color action photo on the front, with the player's name along the left side and his team's logo in the lower right corner. The card back has another color photo, plus a brief career summary and statistics. Red Siege cards (one in three packs) are the same, except they have a red-foil background and have "Red Siege" written on the back. The Artist's Proofs cards (one in 36) have an exclusive stamp on the Red Siege cards. Insert sets include Dream Team, Offense Inc., Pass Time and Reflextions.

		MT
Complete Set (275):		15.00
Common Player:		.05
Comp. Red Siege Set (275):		200.00
Common Red Siege:		.30
Red Siege Cards:		4x-8x
Comp. RS Art. Proof Set (275):		1100.
Common RS Art. Proof:		3.00
RS Art. Proof Cards:		20x-40x
Hobby Pack (12):		1.50
Hobby Wax Box (36):		35.00
Retail Pack (12):		1.00
Retail Wax Box (36):		25.00
1	Steve Young	.50
2	Barry Sanders	1.00
3	Jerry Rice	.75
4	Marshall Faulk	.75
5	Terance Mathis	.05
6	Rod Woodson	.10
7	Seth Joyner	.05
8	Michael Timpson	.05
9	Deion Sanders	.30
10	Emmitt Smith	1.50
11	Cris Carter	.10
12	Jake Reed	.05
13	Reggie White	.10
14	Shannon Sharpe	.10
15	Troy Aikman	.75
16	Andre Reed	.10
17	Tyrone Hughes	.05
18	Sterling Sharpe	.10
19	Jerome Bettis	.30
20	Irving Fryar	.05
21	Warren Moon	.10
22	Ben Coates	.05
23	Frank Reich	.05
24	Henry Ellard	.05
25	Steve Atwater	.05
26	Willie Davis	.05
27	Michael Irvin	.10
28	Harvey Williams	.05
29	Aeneas Williams	.05
30	Errict Rhett	.15
31	Lorenzo White	.05
32	John Elway	.25
33	Rodney Hampton	.10
34	Webster Slaughter	.05
35	Eric Turner	.05
36	Dan Marino	1.50
37	Daryl Johnston	.05
38	Bruce Smith	.05
39	Ron Moore	.05
40	Larry Centers	.05
41	Curtis Conway	.05
42	Drew Bledsoe	.75
43	Quinn Early	.05
44	Marcus Allen	.10
45	Andre Rison	.10
46	*Jeff Blake*	.50
47	Barry Foster	.10
48	Antonio Langham	.05
49	Herman Moore	.10
50	Willie Anderson	.05
51	Rick Mirer	.30
52	Jay Novacek	.05
53	Tim Bowens	.05
54	Carl Pickens	.10
55	Lewis Tillman	.05
56	Lawrence Dawsey	.05
57	Leroy Hoard	.05
58	Steve Broussard	.05
59	Dave Krieg	.05
60	John Taylor	.05
61	Johnny Mitchell	.05
62	Jessie Hester	.05
63	Johnny Bailey	.05
64	Brett Favre	1.50
65	Bryce Paup	.05
66	J.J. Birden	.05
67	Steve Tasker	.05
68	Edgar Bennett	.05
69	Ray Buchanan	.05
70	Brent Jones	.05
71	Dave Meggett	.05
72	Jeff Graham	.05
73	Michael Brooks	.05
74	Ricky Ervins	.05
75	Chris Warren	.05
76	Natrone Means	.30
77	Tim Brown	.10
78	Jim Everett	.05
79	Chris Calloway	.05
80	John L. Williams	.05
81	Chris Chandler	.05
82	Tim McDonald	.05
83	Calvin Williams	.05
84	Tony McGee	.05
85	Erik Kramer	.05
86	Eric Green	.05
87	Nate Newton	.05
88	Leonard Russell	.05
89	Jeff George	.10
90	Raymont Harris	.10
91	Darnay Scott	.40
92	Brian Mitchell	.05
93	Craig Erickson	.05
94	Cortez Kennedy	.10
95	Derrick Alexander	.10
96	Charles Haley	.05
97	Randall Cunningham	.10
98	Haywood Jeffires	.05
99	Ronnie Harmon	.05
100	Dale Carter	.05
101	Dave Brown	.05
102	Michael Haynes	.05
103	Johnny Johnson	.05
104	William Floyd	.10
105	Jeff Hostetler	.05
106	Bernie Parmalee	.10
107	Mo Lewis	.05
108	Bam Morris	.10
109	Vincent Brisby	.05
110	John Randle	.05
111	Steve Walsh	.05
112	Terry Allen	.05
113	Greg Lloyd	.05
114	Merton Hanks	.05
115	Mel Gray	.05
116	Jim Kelly	.10
117	Don Beebe	.05
118	Floyd Turner	.05
119	Neil Smith	.05
120	Keith Byars	.05
121	Rocket Ismail	.05
122	Leslie O'Neal	.05
123	Mike Sherrard	.05
124	Marion Butts	.05
125	Andre Coleman	.05
126	Charles Johnson	.10
127	Derrick Fenner	.05
128	Vinny Testaverde	.05
129	Chris Spielman	.05
130	Bert Emanuel	.25
131	Craig Heyward	.05
132	Anthony Miller	.05
133	Rob Moore	.05
134	Gary Brown	.05
135	David Klingler	.05
136	Sean Dawkins	.10
137	Terry McDaniel	.05
138	Fred Barnett	.05
139	Bryan Cox	.05
140	Andrew Jordan	.05
141	Leroy Thompson	.05
142	Richmond Webb	.05
143	Kimble Anders	.05
144	Mario Bates	.25
145	Irv Smith	.05
146	Carnell Lake	.05
147	Mark Seay	.05
148	Dana Stubblefield	.05
149	Kelvin Martin	.05
150	Pete Metzelaars	.05
151	Roosevelt Potts	.05
152	Bubby Brister	.05
153	Trent Dilfer	.40
154	Ricky Proehl	.05
155	Aaron Glenn	.05
156	Eric Metcalf	.05
157	Kevin Williams	.05
158	Charlie Garner	.05
159	Glyn Milburn	.05
160	Fuad Reveiz	.05
161	Brett Perriman	.05
162	Neil O'Donnell	.05
163	Tony Martin	.05
164	Sam Adams	.05
165	John Friesz	.05
166	Bryant Young	.05
167	Junior Seau	.10
168	Ken Harvey	.05
169	Bill Brooks	.05
170	Eugene Robinson	.05
171	Ricky Sanders	.05
172	Rodney Peete	.05
173	Boomer Esiason	.05
174	Reggie Roby	.05
175	Michael Jackson	.05
176	Gus Frerotte	.10
177	Terry Kirby	.05
178	Jessie Tuggle	.05
179	Courtney Hawkins	.05
180	Heath Shuler	.20
181	Jack Del Rio	.05
182	O.J. McDuffie	.05
183	Ricky Watters	.10
184	Willie Roaf	.05
185	Glenn Foley	.05
186	Blair Thomas	.05
187	Darren Woodson	.05
188	Kevin Greene	.05
189	Jeff Burris	.05
190	Jay Schroeder	.05
191	Stan Humphries	.10
192	Irving Spikes	.10
193	Jim Harbaugh	.05
194	Robert Brooks	.05
195	Greg Hill	.10
196	Herschel Walker	.05
197	Brian Blades	.05
198	Mark Ingram	.05
199	Kevin Turner	.05
200	Lake Dawson	.10
201	Alvin Harper	.05
202	Derek Brown	.05
203	Qadry Ismail	.05
204	Reggie Brooks	.05
205	Steve Young (Starstruck)	.25
206	Emmitt Smith (Starstruck)	.50
207	Stan Humphries (Starstruck)	.10
208	Barry Sanders (Starstruck)	.50
209	Marshall Faulk (Starstruck)	.50
210	Drew Bledsoe (Starstruck)	.50
211	Jerry Rice (Starstruck)	.50
212	Tim Brown (Starstruck)	.10
213	Cris Carter (Starstruck)	.10
214	Dan Marino (Starstruck)	.75
215	Troy Aikman (Starstruck)	.30
216	Jerome Bettis (Starstruck)	.10
217	Deion Sanders (Starstruck)	.10
218	Junior Seau (Starstruck)	.10
219	John Elway (Starstruck)	.10
220	Warren Moon (Starstruck)	.10
221	Sterling Sharpe (Starstruck)	.10
222	Marcus Allen (Starstruck)	.10
223	Michael Irvin (Starstruck)	.10
224	Brett Favre (Starstruck)	.40
225	Rodney Hampton (Starstruck)	.10
226	Dave Brown (Starstruck)	.05
227	Ben Coates (Starstruck)	.05
228	Jim Kelly (Starstruck)	.10
229	Heath Shuler (Starstruck)	.40
230	Herman Moore (Starstruck)	.10
231	Jeff Hostetler (Starstruck)	.05
232	Rick Mirer (Starstruck)	.10
233	Bam Morris (Starstruck)	.10
234	Terance Mathis (Starstruck)	.05
235	Checklist	.05
236	Troy Aikman CL	.20
237	Jerry Rice CL	.20
238	Emmitt Smith CL	.40
239	Steve Young CL	.20
240	Drew Bledsoe CL	.25
241	Marshall Faulk CL	.25
242	Dan Marino CL	.50
243	Junior Seau CL	.05
244	*Ray Zellars*	.10
245	*Rob Johnson*	2.00
246	*Tony Boselli*	.10
247	*Kevin Carter*	.10
248	*Steve McNair*	3.00
249	*Tyrone Wheatley*	.50
250	*Steve Stenstrom*	.10
251	*Stoney Case*	.10
252	*Rodney Thomas*	.10
253	*Michael Westbrook*	1.00
254	*Derrick Alexander*	.10
255	*Kyle Brady*	.10
256	*Kerry Collins*	.10
257	*Rashaan Salaam*	.50
258	*Frank Sanders*	.25
259	*John Walsh*	.10
260	*Sherman Williams*	.10
261	*Ki-Jana Carter*	.30
262	*Jack Jackson*	.10
263	*J.J. Stokes*	.75
264	*Kordell Stewart*	2.50
265	*Dave Barr*	.10
266	*Eddie Goines*	.10
267	*Warren Sapp*	.50
268	*James Stewart*	1.50
269	*Joey Galloway*	1.50
270	*Tyrone Davis*	.10
271	*Napoleon Kaufman*	1.00
272	*Mark Bruener*	.30
273	*Todd Collins*	.10
274	*Billy Williams*	.10
275	*James Stewart*	.10

1995 Score Red Siege

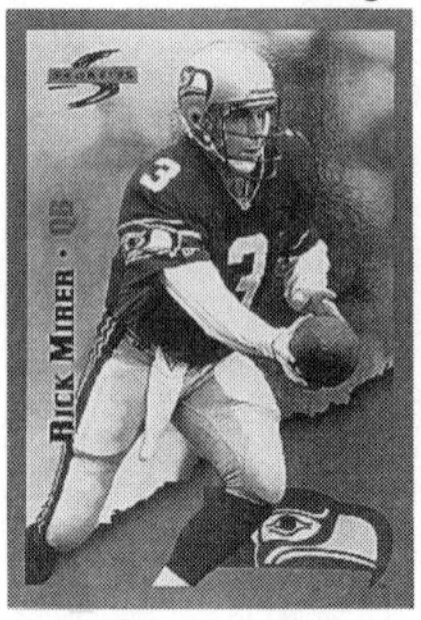

The 275-card, regular-size parallel set, inserted every three packs, have a silver-foil background instead of a white background. A Red Siege logo is printed on the card backs.

	MT
Complete Set (275):	200.00
Common Player:	.30
Veteran Stars:	5x-10x
Young Stars:	4x-8x
RCs:	2.5x-5x

1995 Score Red Siege Artist's Proof

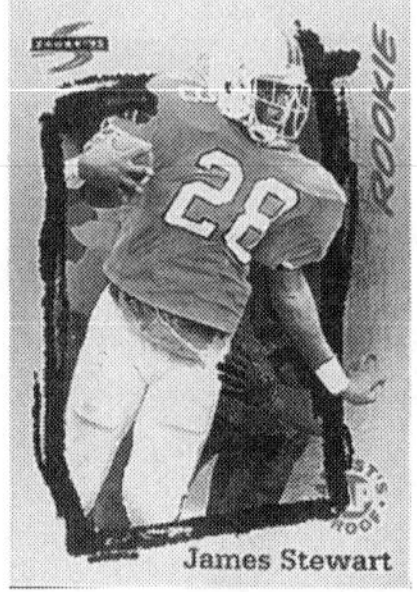

The 275-card, regular-size set, inserted every 36 packs, parallels the Red Siege set with an Artist's Proof stamp on the card front.

	MT
Complete Set (275):	900.00
Common Player:	5.00
Veteran Stars:	30x-50x
Young Stars:	20x-40x
RCs:	12x-25x

1995 Score Dream Team

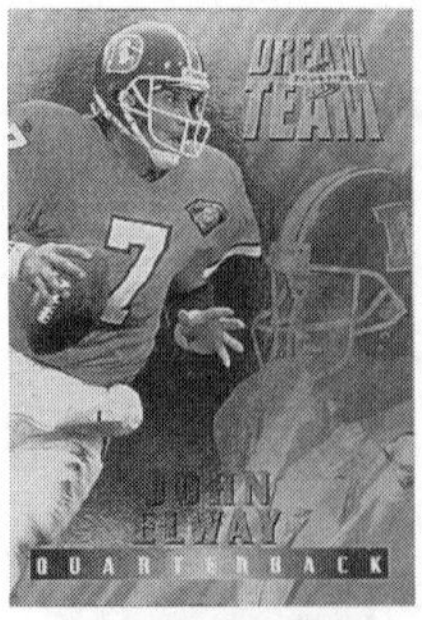

These 1995 Score football inserts were included one per 72 packs, making them the most elusive set. Ten of the league's elite players are featured on gold-foiled cards which have the set logo in the upper right corner. A color action photo and a ghosted image appear on the front. The horizontally-designed back, numbered using a "DT" prefix, has a photo on the top half, with a brief player profile underneath.

		MT
Complete Set (10):		150.00
Common Player:		10.00
1	Steve Young	15.00
2	Troy Aikman	15.00
3	Dan Marino	30.00
4	Drew Bledsoe	15.00
5	Emmitt Smith	30.00
6	Barry Sanders	15.00
7	Jerry Rice	15.00
8	Marshall Faulk	10.00
9	Deion Sanders	10.00
10	John Elway	10.00

1995 Score Offense Inc.

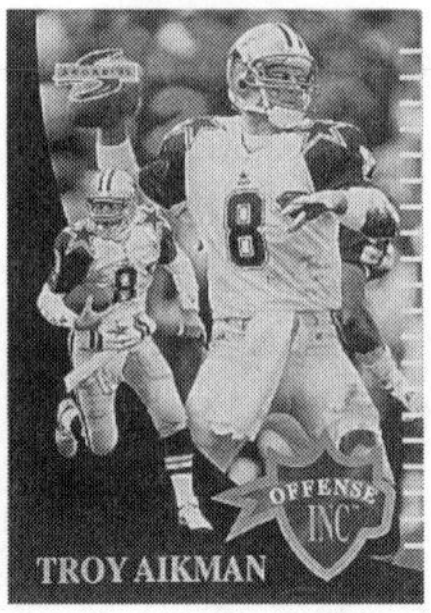

These 1995 Score football insert cards could be found one per 16 packs. The cards feature 30 of the NFL's top offensive players. The card front has a large and small photo of the player, with a foiled set logo shield in the lower right corner. The card back, numbered using an "OF" prefix, reuses the shield, plus a mug shot, a season recap and key statistics from the 1994 season.

		MT
Complete Set (30):		90.00
Common Player:		2.00
1	Steve Young	6.00
2	Emmitt Smith	12.00
3	Dan Marino	12.00
4	Barry Sanders	7.00
5	Jeff Blake	2.00
6	Jerry Rice	6.00
7	Troy Aikman	6.00
8	Brett Favre	12.00
9	Marshall Faulk	2.00
10	Drew Bledsoe	6.00
11	Natrone Means	2.00
12	John Elway	4.00
13	Chris Warren	2.00
14	Michael Irvin	4.00
15	Mario Bates	2.00
16	Warren Moon	2.00
17	Jerome Bettis	4.00
18	Herman Moore	2.00
19	Barry Foster	2.00
20	Jeff George	2.00
21	Cris Carter	2.00
22	Sterling Sharpe	2.00
23	Jim Kelly	2.00
24	Heath Shuler	2.00
25	Marcus Allen	2.00
26	Dave Brown	2.00
27	Rick Mirer	2.00
28	Rodney Hampton	2.00
29	Errict Rhett	2.00
30	Ben Coates	2.00

1995 Score Pass Time

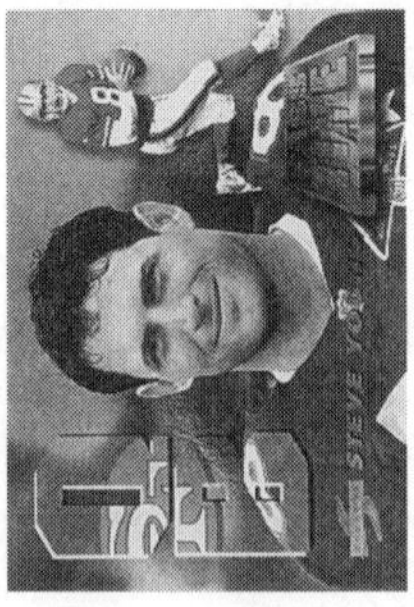

These horizontally-formated insert cards were included one per 18 1995 Score football jumbo packs. Each card front uses gold foil as a background and for the player's name and insert set logo. A larger head-and-shoulders shot and a smaller action photo are the main features. The player's position appears along the left side of the card, with his team logo included within the letters. The card back, numbered using a "PT" prefix, also has two photos, the set logo and a brief career summary.

		MT
Complete Set (18):		160.00
Common Player:		5.00
1	Steve Young	16.00
2	Dan Marino	30.00
3	Drew Bledsoe	16.00
4	Troy Aikman	16.00
5	Glenn Foley	5.00
6	John Elway	12.00
7	Brett Favre	30.00
8	Heath Shuler	5.00
9	Warren Moon	5.00
10	Rick Mirer	5.00
11	Stan Humphries	5.00
12	Jeff Hostetler	5.00
13	Jim Kelly	5.00
14	Randall Cunningham	5.00
15	Jeff Blake	5.00
16	Trent Dilfer	10.00
17	Jeff George	5.00
18	Dave Brown	5.00

1995 Score Reflextions

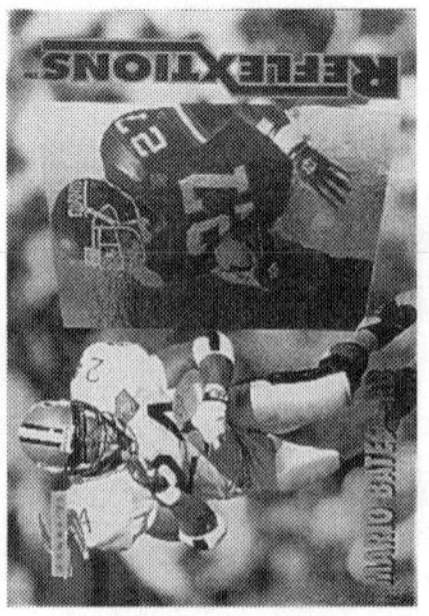

These horizontally-designed insert cards feature two players per card; each is his team's featured player at his position. Only one player's name is listed on the front; his photo is on the left; a photo of his idol is on the right, in a square next to "Reflextions," which is written along the right side. The card back, numbered using an "RF" prefix, has two photos of the players, plus a paragraph which indicates who the second player is. The set logo appears at the top, with the player's team name in a branching extension of the letter X. Cards were randomly included one per 36 hobby packs.

		MT
Complete Set (8):		130.00
Common Player:		5.00
1	Drew Bledsoe, Dan Marino	40.00
2	Charlie Garner, Barry Sanders	20.00
3	Rick Mirer, Warren Moon	5.00
4	Heath Shuler, Steve Young	15.00
5	Marshall Faulk, Emmitt Smith	40.00
6	Derrick Alexander, Jerry Rice	15.00
7	Barry Foster, Bam Morris	5.00
8	Natrone Means, Chris Warren	8.00

1995 Score Pin-Cards

The 40-card, regular-size set features a player from each team and three cards each for the expansion teams (Carolina, Jacksonville) and the new St. Louis Rams. Card No. 40 is a Super Bowl XXX card. Arizona, Atlanta, Carolina, Chicago, Cleveland, Houston, Indianapolis, Jacksonville, Kansas City and Tampa Bay are represented with a team-helmet card with a pin.

		MT
Complete Set (40):		30.00
Common Helmet Card:		.50
Common Player:		.75
1	Jacksonville Jaguars - History	.75
2	Jacksonville Jaguars - Stadium	.75
3	Jacksonville Jaguars - Logo Lore	.75
4	Carolina Panthers - History	.75
5	Carolina Panthers - Stadium	.75
6	Carolina Panthers - Logo Lore	.75
7	St. Louis Rams - History	.75
8	St. Louis Rams - Stadium	.75
9	St. Louis Rams - Logo Lore	.75
10	Drew Bledsoe	2.50
11	Dave Brown	.75
12	Randall Cunningham	.75
13	John Elway	1.25
14	Jim Everett	.75
15	Boomer Esiason	.75
16	Brett Favre	5.00
17	Jeff Hostetler	.75
18	Jim Kelly	1.00
19	David Klingler	.75
20	Dan Marino	5.00
21	Chris Miller	.75
22	Rick Mirer	1.00
23	Warren Moon	1.00
24	Neil O'Donnell	1.00
25	Jerry Rice	2.50
26	Barry Sanders	2.50
27	Junior Seau	1.00
28	Heath Shuler	1.50
29	Emmitt Smith	5.00
30	Arizona Cardinals	.50
31	Atlanta Falcons	.50
32	Carolina Panthers	.75
33	Chicago Bears	.50
34	Cleveland Browns	.75
35	Houston Oilers	.50
36	Indianapolis Colts	.50
37	Jacksonville Jaguars	.75
38	Kansas City Chiefs	.50
39	Tampa Bay Buccaneers	.50
40	Super Bowl XXX Logo	.50

1995 Score Young Stars

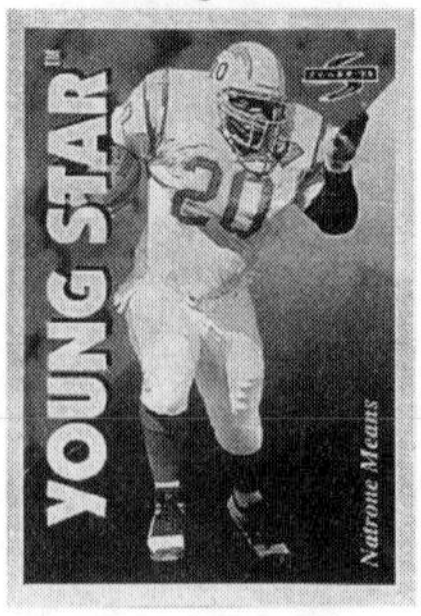

These cards were available at the 1995 NFL Experience Super Bowl Card Show. Pinnacle exchanged the cards for three or five Pinnacle wrappers. The four cards have Gold Zone (limited to 2,000) and Platinum versions (limited to 1,000). The cards are numbered with the "YSG" prefix.

		MT
Complete Set (4):		30.00
Common Player:		5.00
Platinum Cards:		2x
1	Marshall Faulk	8.00
2	Jeff Blake	8.00
3	Drew Bledsoe	12.00
4	Natrone Means	5.00

1995 Summit

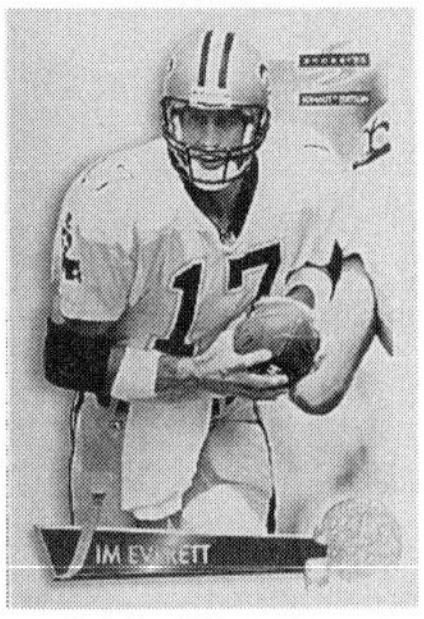

Score's 1995 super-premium effort, Summitt, has 200 cards printed on 24-point stock, making them thicker than normal cards. Each card front has an action photo cutout against a white background. The player's name is stamped in gold foil in a banner at the bottom, alongside his team helmet, also stamped in gold. The horizontally-designed card back has a photo of the player on the left side, with a chart of his 1994 statistics on the right. A parallel set, Ground Zero, was also produced; all cards are reprinted on a prismatic foil. Three insert sets - Rookie Summit, Team Summit and Backfield Stars - were also produced.

		MT
Complete Set (200):		30.00
Common Player:		.10
Minor Stars:		.20
Ground Zero Set (200):		450.00
Ground Zero Cards:		7x-15x
Pack (7):		1.75
Wax Box (24):		30.00
1	Neil O'Donnell	.20
2	Jim Everett	.10
3	Craig Heyward	.10
4	*Jeff Blake*	.50
5	Alvin Harper	.20
6	Heath Shuler	1.00
7	Rodney Hampton	.20
8	Dave Krieg	.10
9	Mark Brunell	1.50
10	Rob Moore	.10
11	Daryl Johnston	.10
12	Marcus Allen	.20
13	Terance Mathis	.10
14	Frank Reich	.10
15	Gus Frerotte	.50
16	John Elway	.50
17	Amp Lee	.10
18	Chris Miller	.10
19	Leroy Hoard	.10
20	Stan Humphries	.20
21	Charlie Garner	.10
22	Jim Kelly	.20
23	Gary Brown	.10
24	Bam Morris	.20
25	Edgar Bennett	.10
26	Erik Kramer	.10
27	Dan Marino	3.00
28	Michael Haynes	.10
29	Lake Dawson	.25
30	Ben Coates	.10
31	Michael Jackson	.10
32	Brett Favre	3.00
33	Calvin Williams	.10

34	Steve Young	1.50
35	Troy Aikman	1.50
36	Greg Hill	.25
37	Leonard Russell	.10
38	Jeff George	.20
39	Herschel Walker	.10
40	Eric Green	.10
41	Haywood Jeffires	.10
42	Terry Kirby	.10
43	Darnay Scott	.50
44	Tim Brown	.20
45	Brian Mitchell	.10
46	Desmond Howard	.10
47	Warren Moon	.10
48	Andre Reed	.10
49	Ricky Proehl	.10
50	Marshall Faulk	.75
51	Lewis Tillman	.10
52	Don Beebe	.10
53	Jerome Bettis	.50
54	Brett Perriman	.20
55	Mario Bates	.30
56	Ronnie Harmon	.10
57	Isaac Bruce	1.00
58	Jackie Harris	.10
59	Dexter Carter	.10
60	Charles Johnson	.25
61	Herman Moore	.40
62	Craig Erickson	.10
63	Kenneth Davis	.10
64	Emmitt Smith	3.00
65	Brent Jones	.10
66	Ricky Watters	.20
67	Henry Ellard	.10
68	Vinny Testaverde	.10
69	Mark Pike	.10
70	Curtis Conway	.30
71	Michael Irvin	.40
72	Jay Novacek	.10
73	Howard Cross	.10
74	Drew Bledsoe	1.50
75	Steve Beuerlein	.10
76	Andre Rison	.20
77	Morten Andersen	.10
78	Trent Dilfer	.40
79	Cris Carter	.20
80	Natrone Means	.75
81	Bernie Parmalee	.30
82	Randall Cunningham	.10
83	Eric Metcalf	.10
84	Rick Mirer	.50
85	Mark Ingram	.10
86	David Klingler	.10
87	Kevin Williams	.10
88	Erric Pegram	.10
89	Keith Byars	.10
90	Sean Dawkins	.20
91	Chris Warren	.25
92	William Floyd	.40
93	Jeff Hostetler	.20
94	Carl Pickens	.20
95	Flipper Anderson	.10
96	Johnny Mitchell	.10
97	Larry Centers	.10
98	Shannon Sharpe	.10
99	Errict Rhett	.30
100	Fred Barnett	.10
101	Harold Green	.10
102	Scott Mitchell	.20
103	Jerry Rice	1.50
104	Shawn Jefferson	.10
105	Glyn Milburn	.10
106	Garrison Hearst	.20
107	John Taylor	.10
108	Keith Cash	.10
109	Robert Brooks	.20
110	Barry Sanders	2.00
111	Ernest Givins	.10
112	Steve Tasker	.10
113	Jeff Graham	.10
114	Chris Chandler	.10
115	Lorenzo Neal	.10
116	Bert Emanuel	.40
117	Mike Sherrard	.10
118	Harvey Williams	.10
119	Reggie Brooks	.10
120	Steve Walsh	.10
121	Leroy Thompson	.10
122	Dave Brown	.10
123	Lorenzo White	.10
124	Steve Bono	.25
125	Irving Fryar	.10
126	Jake Reed	.10
127	Boomer Esiason	.10
128	Rocket Ismail	.10
129	Vincent Brisby	.10
130	Robert Smith	.10
131	Anthony Miller	.10
132	Roosevelt Potts	.10
133	Dave Meggett	.10
134	Junior Seau	.20
135	Neil Smith	.10
136	Charles Haley	.10
137	Rod Woodson	.10
138	Deion Sanders	.75
139	Reggie White	.20
140	John Randle	.10
141	Greg Lloyd	.20
142	Cortez Kennedy	.10
143	Bruce Smith	.10
144	*J.J. Stokes*	1.50
145	*Kyle Brady*	.20
146	*Frank Sanders*	1.00
147	*Michael Westbrook*	1.50
148	*Rob Johnson*	4.00
149	*Tyrone Poole*	.20
150	*Lovell Pinkney*	.20
151	*Tyrone Wheatley*	1.00
152	*Steve McNair*	5.00
153	*Napoleon Kaufman*	4.00
154	*Tamarick Vanover*	1.00
155	*Todd Collins*	.20
156	*Kevin Carter*	.20
157	*Rodney Thomas*	.30
158	*Stoney Case*	.20
159	*Kordell Stewart*	6.00
160	*Tony Boselli*	.20
161	*Sherman Williams*	.20
162	*Christian Fauria*	.20
163	*Ray Zellars*	.20
164	*Ki-Jana Carter*	1.00
165	*Terrell Fletcher*	.20
166	*Curtis Martin*	5.00
167	*Eric Zeier*	.30
168	*Joey Galloway*	3.00
169	*Warren Sapp*	.75
170	*Kerry Collins*	2.00
171	*Mark Bruener*	.30
172	*Chris Sanders*	1.25
173	*Rashaan Salaam*	.50
174	Jerry Rice	.50
175	Marshall Faulk	.75
176	Drew Bledsoe	.75
177	Emmitt Smith	1.25
178	Tim Brown	.20
179	Steve Young	.50
180	Barry Sanders	1.00
181	Michael Irvin	.25
182	Dan Marino	1.25
183	Jeff George	.20
184	Chris Warren	.20
185	Herman Moore	.20
186	Andre Rison	.20
187	Bam Morris	.20
188	Troy Aikman	.50
189	Jim Kelly	.20
190	John Elway	.25
191	Cris Carter	.20
192	Shannon Sharpe	.10
193	Brett Favre	.50
194	Drew Bledsoe	.40
195	John Elway	.20
196	Dan Marino	.50
197	Brett Favre	.30
198	Troy Aikman	.30
199	Steve Young	.30
200	Randall Cunningham, Rick Mirer	.20

1995 Summit Ground Zero

Ground Zero was a 200-card parallel set to the 1995 Score Summit set, and was inserted one per seven packs. Card fronts featured a prismatic silver foil, while card backs contained the words "Ground Zero."

	MT
Complete Set (200):	450.00
Ground Zero Cards:	7x-15x

1995 Summit Backfield Stars

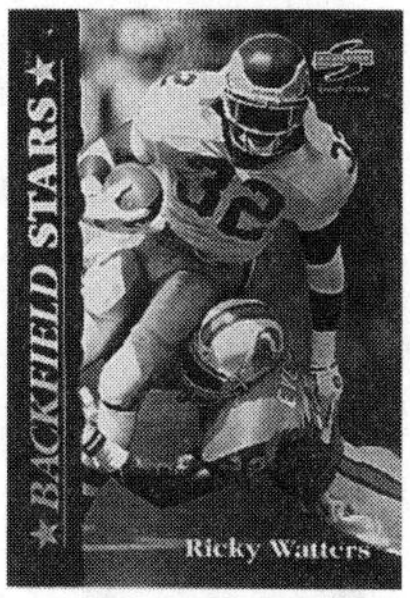

The 1995 Score Summit inserts were included one per 37 packs. They feature 20 of the best running backs on a holographic silver foil printing that gives each runner a dimensional background effect. "Backfield Stars" is written along the left side of the card; the player's name is in the lower right corner. The numbered card back is horizontal and has a player photo on the left, with a brief career summary on the right. The player's name is at the top between two stars.

		MT
Complete Set (20):		110.00
Common Player:		5.00
1	Emmitt Smith	30.00
2	Marshall Faulk	10.00
3	Barry Sanders	20.00
4	Ricky Watters	5.00
5	Rodney Hampton	5.00
6	Chris Warren	5.00
7	Garrison Hearst	5.00
8	Tyrone Wheatley	5.00
9	Rashaan Salaam	5.00
10	Natrone Means	5.00
11	Bam Morris	5.00
12	Jerome Bettis	5.00
13	Errict Rhett	5.00
14	William Floyd	5.00
15	Edgar Bennett	5.00
16	Marcus Allen	5.00
17	Mario Bates	5.00
18	Lorenzo White	5.00
19	Gary Brown	5.00
20	Craig Heyward	5.00

1995 Summit Rookie Summit

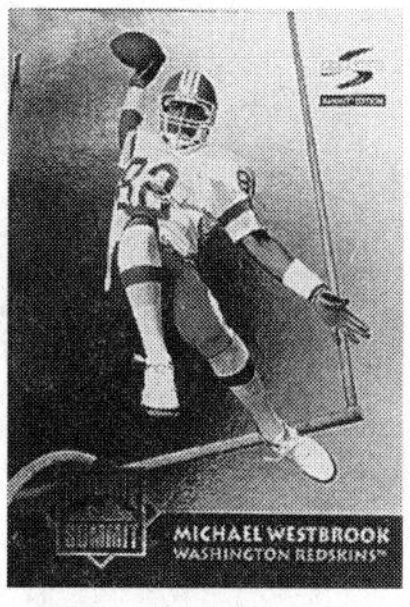

These 1995 Score Summit inserts could be found one per 23 packs. The cards feature exclusive photography taken at Pinnacle's Rookie Photo Shoot before the season began. Each rookie is shown, in his team's NFL uniform, airborne against a goalpost background. Gold Rush foil is used on both sides. The numbered card back has a posed shot of the player in his NFL uniform, with a line describing one of his more recent accomplishments. The "Rookie Summit" logo appears on both sides.

		MT
Complete Set (18):		90.00
Common Player:		3.00
1	Kevin Carter	3.00
2	Sherman Williams	3.00
3	Kordell Stewart	16.00
4	Christian Fauria	3.00
5	J.J. Stokes	6.00
6	Joey Galloway	8.00
7	Michael Westbrook	6.00
8	James Stewart	5.00
9	Stoney Case	3.00
10	Kyle Brady	3.00
11	Terrell Fletcher	3.00
12	Todd Collins	3.00
13	Jimmy Oliver	3.00
14	Napoleon Kaufman	12.00
15	John Walsh	3.00
16	Kerry Collins	7.00
17	Ki-Jana Carter	5.00
18	Terrell Davis	30.00

1995 Summit Team Summit

These cards feature 12 of the league's top players, utilizing spectroetching on a holographic foil card. Cards were randomly included in every 91 packs of 1995 Score Summit football and are numbered.

		MT
Complete Set (12):		160.00
Common Player:		4.00
Minor Stars:		8.00
Inserted 1:91		
1	Dan Marino	20.00
2	Emmitt Smith	20.00
3	Drew Bledsoe	15.00
4	Troy Aikman	15.00
5	Bam Morris	4.00
6	Steve Young	12.00
7	Randall Cunningham	8.00
8	Natrone Means	8.00
9	Barry Sanders	30.00
10	Brett Favre	30.00
11	Errict Rhett	4.00
12	Jerry Rice	15.00

1996 Score

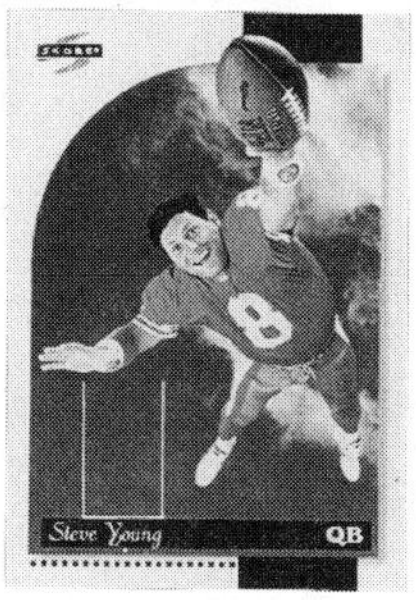

Score's regular 1996 football issue has 275 cards and two parallel sets - Field Force and Artist's Proofs. Each regular card has a color action photo on the front, trimmed to look like a baseball diamond. The player's name and position are in white letters at the bottom in a black bar. The Score logo is in an upper corner. The horizontal back has a mug shot on one side, with the team name under it and a card number in the upper corner. Additional information on the back includes biographical and statistical data and a recap of the player's accomplishments. Field Force cards, found in every sixth pack, are printed on a matte finish. Artist's Proof cards, seeded one per 36 packs, have a gold stamp on a regular issue card. Insert sets include Dream Team, Footsteps, In the Zone, Numbers Game and Settle the Score.

		MT
Complete Set (275):		15.00
Common Player:		.05
Minor Stars:		.10
Comp. Field Force (275):		300.00
Field Force Cards:		6x-12x
Comp. Artist's Proof (275):		800.00
Artist's Proof Cards:		25x-50x
Pack (10):		.75
Wax Box (36):		25.00
1	Emmitt Smith	1.50
2	Flipper Anderson	.05
3	Kordell Stewart	1.00
4	Bruce Smith	.05
5	Marshall Faulk	.75
6	William Floyd	.05
7	Darren Woodson	.05
8	Lake Dawson	.05
9	Terry Allen	.05
10	Ki-Jana Carter	.25
11	Tony Boselli	.05
12	Christian Fauria	.05
13	Jeff George	.05
14	Dan Marino	1.50
15	Rodney Thomas	.30
16	Anthony Miller	.05
17	Chris Sanders	.30
18	Natrone Means	.10
19	Curtis Conway	.05
20	Ben Coates	.05
21	Alvin Harper	.05
22	Frank Sanders	.05
23	Boomer Esiason	.05
24	Lovell Pinkney	.05
25	Troy Aikman	.75
26	Quinn Early	.05
27	Adrian Murrell	.05
28	Chris Spielman	.05
29	Tyrone Wheatley	.05
30	Tim Brown	.05
31	Erik Kramer	.05
32	Warren Moon	.05
33	Jimmy Oliver	.05
34	Herman Moore	.20
35	Quentin Coryatt	.05
36	Heath Shuler	.25
37	Jim Kelly	.05
38	Chris Miller	.05
39	Harvey Williams	.05
40	Vinny Testaverde	.05
41	Steve McNair	.75
42	Jerry Rice	.75
43	Darick Holmes	.05
44	Kyle Brady	.05
45	Greg Lloyd	.05
46	Kerry Collins	.25
47	Willie McGinest	.05
48	Isaac Bruce	.40
49	Carnell Lake	.05
50	Charles Haley	.05
51	Troy Vincent	.05
52	Randall Cunningham	.05
53	Rashaan Salaam	.50
54	Willie Jackson	.05
55	Chris Warren	.15
56	Michael Irvin	.10
57	Mario Bates	.05
58	Warren Sapp	.05
59	John Elway	.25
60	Shannon Sharpe	.05
61	Bam Morris	.05
62	Robert Brooks	.05
63	Rodney Hampton	.05
64	Ken Norton Jr.	.05
65	Bryce Paup	.05
66	Eric Swann	.05
67	Rodney Peete	.05
68	Larry Centers	.05
69	Lamont Warren	.05
70	Jay Novacek	.05
71	Cris Carter	.05
72	Terrell Fletcher	.05
73	Andre Rison	.05
74	Ricky Watters	.05
75	Napoleon Kaufman	.30
76	Reggie White	.05
77	Yancey Thigpen	.40
78	Terry Kirby	.05
79	Deion Sanders	.50
80	Irving Fryar	.05
81	Marcus Allen	.05
82	Carl Pickens	.05
83	Drew Bledsoe	.75
84	Eric Metcalf	.05
85	Robert Smith	.05
86	Tamarick Vanover	.50
87	Henry Ellard	.05
88	Kevin Greene	.05
89	Mark Brunell	.50
90	Terrell Davis	.75
91	Brian Mitchell	.05
92	Aaron Bailey	.05
93	Rocket Ismail	.05
94	Dave Brown	.05
95	Rod Woodson	.05
96	Sean Gilbert	.05
97	Mark Seay	.05
98	Zack Crockett	.05
99	Scott Mitchell	.05
100	Erric Pegram	.05
101	David Palmer	.05
102	Vincent Brisby	.05
103	Brett Perriman	.05
104	Jim Everett	.05
105	Tony Martin	.05
106	Desmond Howard	.05
107	Stan Humphries	.05
108	Bill Brooks	.05
109	Neil Smith	.05
110	Michael Westbrook	.10
111	Herschel Walker	.05
112	Andre Coleman	.05
113	Derrick Alexander	.05
114	Jeff Blake	.60
115	Sherman Williams	.05
116	James Stewart	.05
117	Hardy Nickerson	.05
118	Elvis Grbac	.05
119	Brett Favre	1.50
120	Mike Sherrard	.05
121	Edgar Bennett	.05
122	Calvin Williams	.05
123	Brian Blades	.05
124	Jeff Graham	.05
125	Gary Brown	.05
126	Bernie Parmalee	.05
127	Kimble Anders	.05
128	Hugh Douglas	.05
129	James Stewart	.05
130	Eric Bjornson	.05
131	Ken Dilger	.05
132	Jerome Bettis	.05
133	Cortez Kennedy	.05
134	Bryan Cox	.05
135	Darnay Scott	.05
136	Bert Emanuel	.05
137	Steve Bono	.05
138	Charles Johnson	.05
139	Glyn Milburn	.05
140	Derrick Alexander	.05
141	Dave Meggett	.05
142	Trent Dilfer	.05
143	Eric Zeier	.05
144	Jim Harbaugh	.05
145	Antonio Freeman	.05
146	Orlanda Thomas	.05
147	Russell Maryland	.05
148	Chad May	.05
149	Craig Heyward	.05
150	Aeneas Williams	.05
151	Kevin Williams	.05
152	Charlie Garner	.05
153	J.J. Stokes	.10
154	Stoney Case	.05
155	Mark Chmura	.20
156	Mark Bruener	.05
157	Derek Loville	.05
158	Justin Armour	.05
159	Brent Jones	.05
160	Aaron Craver	.05
161	Terance Mathis	.05
162	Chris Zorich	.05
163	Glenn Foley	.05
164	Johnny Mitchell	.05
165	Junior Seau	.05
166	Willie Davis	.05
167	Rick Mirer	.05
168	Leroy Hoard	.05
169	Greg Hill	.05
170	Steve Tasker	.05
171	Tony Bennett	.05
172	Jeff Hostetler	.05
173	Dave Krieg	.05
174	Mark Carrier	.05
175	Michael Haynes	.05
176	Chris Chandler	.05
177	Ernie Mills	.05
178	Jake Reed	.05
179	Errict Rhett	.50
180	Garrison Hearst	.10
181	Derrick Thomas	.05
182	*Aaron Hayden*	.30
183	Jackie Harris	.05
184	Curtis Martin	1.50
185	Neil O'Donnell	.05
186	Derrick Moore	.05
187	Steve Young	.75
188	Pat Swilling	.05
189	Amp Lee	.05
190	Rob Johnson	.05
191	Todd Collins	.05
192	J.J. Birden	.05
193	O.J. McDuffie	.05
194	Shawn Jefferson	.05
195	Sean Dawkins	.05
196	Fred Barnett	.05
197	Roosevelt Potts	.05
198	Rob Moore	.05
199	Qadry Ismail	.05
200	Barry Sanders	1.00
201	Floyd Turner	.05
202	Wayne Chrebet	.05
203	Andre Reed	.05
204	Tyrone Hughes	.05
205	Keenan McCardell	.05
206	Gus Frerotte	.05
207	Daryl Johnston	.05
208	Haywood Jeffires	.05
209	Steve Atwater	.05
210	Michael Jackson	.05
211	Andre Hastings	.05
212	Joey Galloway	.75
213	Robert Green	.05
214	*Keyshawn Johnson*	2.00
215	*Tony Brackens*	.05
216	*Stepfret Williams*	.05
217	*Mike Alstott*	1.00
218	*Terry Glenn*	1.50
219	*Tim Biakabutuka*	.75
220	*Eric Moulds*	1.50
221	*Jeff Lewis*	.50
222	*Bobby Engram*	.50
223	*Cedric Jones*	.05
224	*Stanley Pritchett*	.05
225	*Kevin Hardy*	.20
226	*Alex Van Dyke*	.30
227	*Willie Anderson*	.05
228	*Regan Upshaw*	.05
229	*Leeland McElroy*	.20
230	*Marvin Harrison*	2.00
231	*Eddie George*	3.00
232	*Lawrence Phillips*	.50
233	Daryl Gardener	.05
234	Alex Molden	.05
235	*Derrick Mayes*	.75
236	John Mobley	.05
237	Isreal Ifeanyi	.05
238	Pete Kendall	.05
239	*Danny Kanell*	.50
240	Jonathan Ogden	.05
241	Reggie Brown	.05
242	Marcus Jones	.05
243	Jon Stark	.05
244	Barry Sanders	.50
245	Brett Favre	.30
246	John Elway	.15
247	Dan Marino	.75
248	Drew Bledsoe	.30
249	Michael Irvin	.05
250	Troy Aikman	.30
251	Emmitt Smith	.75
252	Steve Young	.30
253	Jerry Rice	.30
254	Jeff Blake	.25
255	Tim Brown	.05
256	Bam Morris	.05
257	Rodney Hampton	.05
258	Scott Mitchell	.05
259	Garrison Hearst	.05
260	Larry Centers	.05
261	Neil O'Donnell	.05
262	Orlanda Thomas	.05
263	Hugh Douglas	.05
264	Bill Brooks	.05
265	Harvey Williams	.05
266	Charles Haley	.05
267	Greg Lloyd	.05
268	Daryl Johnston	.05
269	Dan Marino	.30
270	Jeff Blake	.10
271	John Elway	.05
272	Emmitt Smith	.30
273	Brett Favre	.30
274	Jerry Rice	.30
275	Dan Marino, Jeff Blake, John Elway, Emmitt Smith, Brett Favre, Jerry Rice	.50

1996 Score Field Force

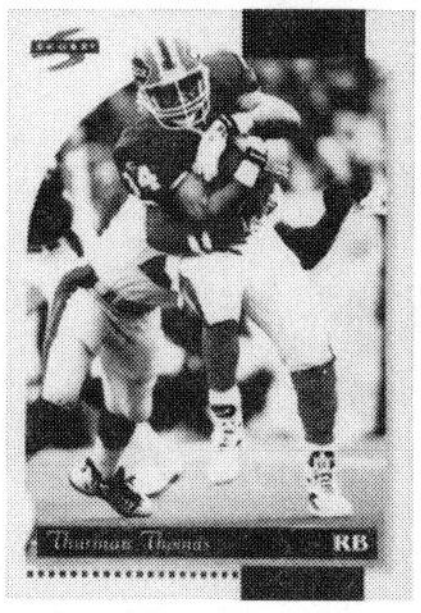

The 275-card, standard-size parallel set, features a matte finish instead of the gloss card-front finish of the base cards. The set was inserted every six packs; 1:3 for jumbo.

	MT
Complete Set (275):	300.00
Common Player:	.40
Veteran Stars:	5x-10x
Young Stars:	4x-8x
RCs:	3x-6x

1996 Score Artist's Proofs

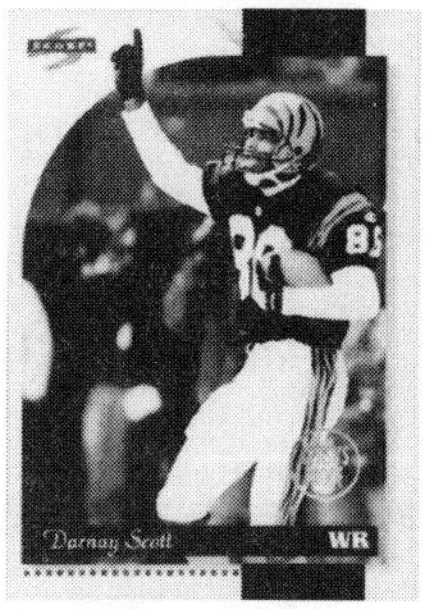

The 275-card, regular-sized parallel set, inserted every 36 packs, features an Artist's Proof logo on the card front. The set is inserted every 18 jumbo packs.

		MT
Complete Set (275):		1000.
Common Player:		4.00
Semistars:		6.00
Veteran Stars:		30x-50x
Young Stars:		20x-40x
RCs:		12x-25x
1	Emmitt Smith	75.00
3	Kordell Stewart	30.00
5	Marshall Faulk	30.00
14	Dan Marino	75.00
25	Troy Aikman	35.00
41	Steve McNair	20.00
42	Jerry Rice	35.00
46	Kerry Collins	30.00
59	John Elway	20.00
79	Deion Sanders	25.00
83	Drew Bledsoe	30.00
90	Terrell Davis	20.00
119	Brett Favre	35.00
184	Curtis Martin	60.00
187	Steve Young	30.00
200	Barry Sanders	50.00
212	Joey Galloway	20.00
214	Keyshawn Johnson	50.00
218	Terry Glenn	35.00
231	Eddie George	50.00
232	Lawrence Phillips	35.00
244	Barry Sanders (SE)	20.00
245	Brett Favre (SE)	20.00
247	Dan Marino (SE)	40.00
248	Drew Bledsoe (SE)	15.00
250	Troy Aikman (SE)	20.00
251	Emmitt Smith (SE)	40.00
252	Steve Young (SE)	15.00
253	Jerry Rice (SE)	20.00
269	Dan Marino (CL)	20.00
273	Brett Favre (CL)	15.00
274	Jerry Rice (CL)	15.00

1996 Score Dream Team

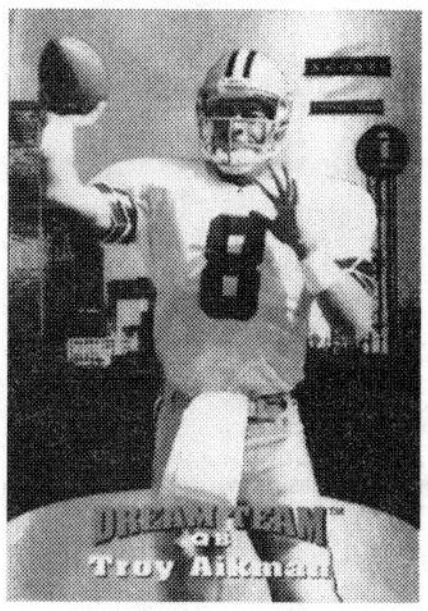

These 1996 Score football inserts feature 10 players who an NFL coach would love to build a team around. The cards were random inserts, one per 72 packs; they are the most exclusive card in 1996 Score.

		MT
Complete Set (10):		120.00
Common Player:		5.00
1	Troy Aikman	15.00
2	Michael Irvin	5.00
3	Emmitt Smith	30.00
4	John Elway	5.00
5	Barry Sanders	15.00
6	Brett Favre	30.00
7	Dan Marino	30.00
8	Drew Bledsoe	15.00
9	Jerry Rice	15.00
10	Steve Young	10.00

1996 Score Footsteps

These 1996 Score football inserts were seeded one per 35 hobby packs. A top rookie from the 1995 season is paired with a top veteran he

most wants to emulate. The 15 dual-player cards are printed with rainbow holographic highlights.

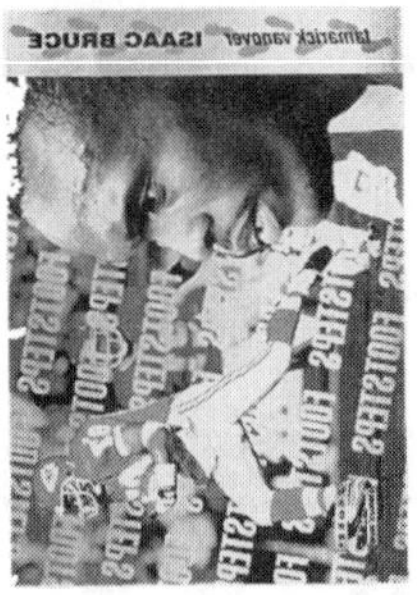

		MT
Complete Set (15):		100.00
Common Player:		2.00
1	Darick Holmes, Errict Rhett	4.00
2	Rashaan Salaam, Natrone Means	6.00
3	Ki-Jana Carter, Barry Sanders	15.00
4	Terrell Davis, Marshall Faulk	12.00
5	Rodney Thomas, Chris Warren	2.00
6	Curtis Martin, Emmitt Smith	25.00
7	Kerry Collins, Troy Aikman	15.00
8	Eric Zeier, Drew Bledsoe	10.00
9	Steve McNair, Brett Favre	15.00
10	Steve Young, Kordell Stewart	15.00
11	J.J. Stokes, Jerry Rice	12.00
12	Joey Galloway, Michael Irvin	5.00
13	Michael Westbrook, Cris Carter	5.00
14	Tamarick Vanover, Isaac Bruce	4.00
15	Orlanda Thomas, Deion Sanders	4.00

1996 Score Numbers Game

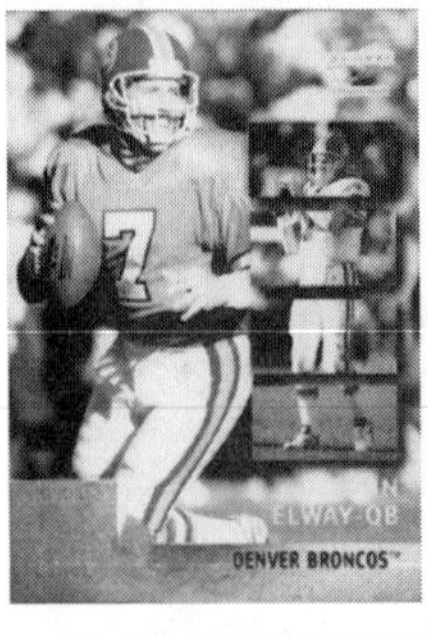

These 25 cards were randomly inserted into every 17 packs of 1996 Score football. The card front has a color action photo on it, with a smaller photo on the right in four pieces. The player's name and position are stamped in gold under this photo. Gold foil stamping is also used for the set icon in the lower left corner. The player's team name is in black letters in the foil band at the bottom. The card back has a color photo of the player, with the rest of the full-bleed photo in black-and-white. The card number is in the upper left corner in a white rectangle; the player's name, position and team name run horizontally down the left side. Four rectangles on the right side each have a tidbit of statistical information.

		MT
Complete Set (25):		90.00
Common Player:		2.00
1	Barry Sanders	7.00
2	Drew Bledsoe	6.00
3	Brett Favre	12.00
4	John Elway	4.00
5	Dan Marino	12.00
6	Michael Irvin	2.00
7	Troy Aikman	6.00
8	Emmitt Smith	12.00
9	Steve Young	6.00
10	Jerry Rice	6.00
11	Chris Sanders	2.00
12	Herman Moore	3.00
13	Frank Sanders	2.00
14	Kordell Stewart	6.00
15	Jeff Blake	5.00
16	Robert Brooks	2.00
17	Marshall Faulk	4.00
18	Carl Pickens	2.00
19	Greg Lloyd	2.00
20	Curtis Conway	2.00
21	Chris Warren	2.00
22	Natrone Means	2.00
23	Deion Sanders	4.00
24	Neil O'Donnell	2.00
25	Ricky Watters	2.00

1996 Score In the Zone

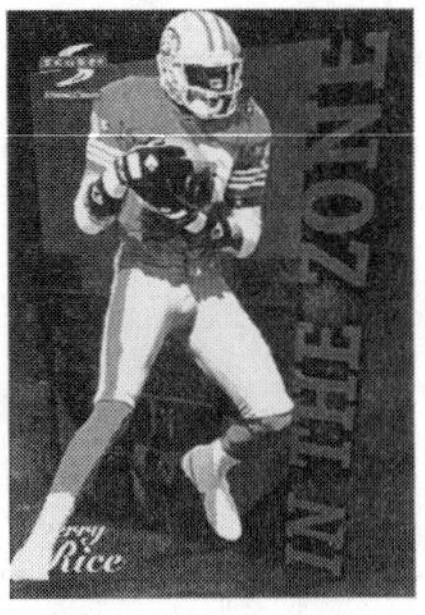

This set features 20 offensive players who excel in getting into the end zone. Cards were exclusive to 1996 Score retail packs, every 33rd pack. The front has a color action photo, with red foil highlights for the set name along the right side and for the stadium background. The player's name is in the lower left corner; the Score logo is in the upper left corner. The numbered back has a color photo, with the player's name, a player profile and a set icon below the card number.

		MT
Complete Set (20):		140.00
Common Player:		2.00
1	Brett Favre	30.00
2	Warren Moon	2.00
3	Erik Kramer	2.00
4	Scott Mitchell	2.00
5	Jeff Blake	8.00
6	Steve Bono	2.00
7	Dan Marino	30.00
8	Troy Aikman	15.00
9	Emmitt Smith	30.00
10	Curtis Martin	20.00
11	Errict Rhett	10.00
12	Terrell Davis	18.00
13	Derek Loville	2.00
14	Rodney Hampton	2.00
15	Cris Carter	2.00
16	Herman Moore	6.00
17	Jerry Rice	15.00
18	Ben Coates	2.00
19	Michael Irvin	2.00
20	Carl Pickens	2.00

1996 Score Settle the Score

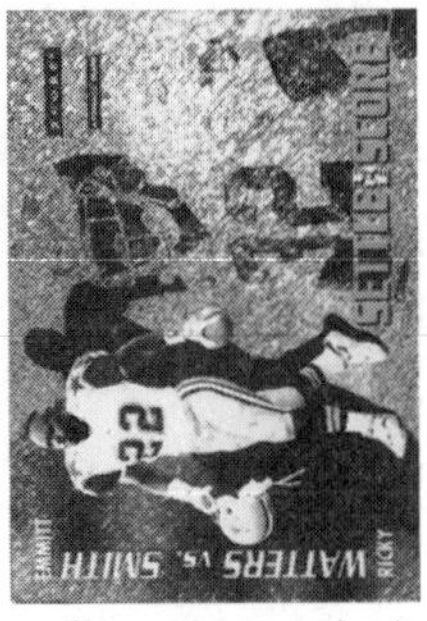

These cards were random inserts in 1996 Score football, one every 36 jumbo packs. Each card features two players on it.

		MT
Complete Set (30):		500.00
Common Player:		5.00
1	Frank Sanders, Charlie Garner	5.00
2	Drew Bledsoe, Neil O'Donnell	12.00
3	Jerry Rice, Craig Heyward	18.00
4	Emmitt Smith, Rod Woodson	35.00
5	Darick Holmes, Dan Marino	35.00
6	Kerry Collins, Steve Young	18.00
7	Rashaan Salaam, Brett Favre	35.00
8	Curtis Conway, Barry Sanders	25.00
9	Troy Aikman, Dan Marino	40.00
10	Dan Marino, Neil O'Donnell	35.00
11	Eric Zeier, Steve McNair	8.00
12	Jeff Blake, Kordell Stewart	18.00
13	Troy Aikman, Heath Shuler	18.00
14	Michael Irvin, Jerry Rice	18.00
15	Emmitt Smith, Ricky Watters	35.00
16	John Elway, Steve Bono	8.00
17	John Elway, Rick Mirer	8.00
18	John Elway, Tim Brown	8.00
19	Barry Sanders, Brett Favre	45.00
20	Barry Sanders, Warren Moon	25.00
21	Brett Favre, Trent Differ	20.00
22	Rodney Thomas, James Stewart	5.00
23	Jim Harbaugh, Drew Bledsoe	14.00
24	Marcus Allen, Harvey Williams	5.00
25	Tamarick Vanover, Joey Galloway	8.00
26	Dan Marino, Drew Bledsoe	40.00
27	Mario Bates, Jerry Rice	18.00
28	Tyrone Wheatley, Michael Westbrook	8.00
29	Napoleon Kaufman, Junior Seau	5.00
30	J.J. Stokes, Isaac Bruce	8.00

1996 Summit

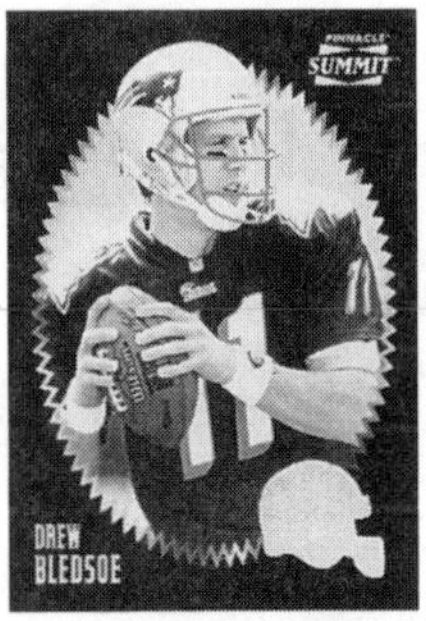

The 200-card, regular-sized set came in seven-card packs and included three subsets: Rookies (35), Quarterhorses (15) and Checklists (4). The card fronts feature the player's name and team helmet in gold foil. The card backs include a headshot of the player with three statistical categories and the card number in the upper left corner. A parallel insert set, Ground Zero, is inserted every six packs and features prismatic foil renditions of the base set. Artist's Proofs, another 200-card parallel set, adds special holographic foil stamps to the base set and are inserted every 35 packs. Other insert sets in Summit are Turf Team, Inspirations, 3rd & Long and its parallel insert set - 3rd & Long Mirage.

		MT
Complete Set (200):		35.00
Common Player:		.10
Minor Stars:		.20
Comp. Ground Zero (200):		400.00
Ground Zero Cards:		6x-12x
Comp. Artist's Proof (200):		1400.
Artist's Proof Cards:		20x-40x
Hobby Pack (7):		3.00
Hobby Wax Box (18):		50.00
1	Troy Aikman	1.25
2	Marshall Faulk	.50
3	Bruce Smith	.10
4	Jerome Bettis	.20
5	Bryan Cox	.10
6	Robert Brooks	.20
7	Dan Marino	2.50
8	Irving Fryar	.10
9	Jerry Rice	1.25
10	Ki-Jana Carter	.20
11	Herman Moore	.30
12	Derrick Thomas	.10
13	Curtis Martin	1.75
14	Jeff Hostetler	.10
15	Errict Rhett	.30
16	Emmitt Smith	2.50
17	Aaron Craver	.10
18	Kyle Brady	.10
19	Tony Martin	.10
20	Vinny Testaverde	.10
21	Charles Haley	.10
22	Rodney Thomas	.10
23	Jim Everett	.10
24	Brian Blades	.10
25	Frank Sanders	.10
26	Bryce Paup	.10
27	Anthony Miller	.10
28	Ken Dilger	.10
29	Orlando Thomas	.10
30	Rodney Hampton	.10
31	Ken Norton Jr.	.10
32	Darren Woodson	.10
33	Antonio Freeman	.10
34	Steve Bono	.10
35	Ben Coates	.10
36	Jeff George	.10
37	Curtis Conway	.10
38	Steve Atwater	.10
39	Fred Barnett	.10
40	Joey Galloway	1.25
41	Jim Kelly	.20
42	Michael Irvin	.20
43	Steve Tasker	.10
44	Warren Moon	.10
45	Hugh Douglas	.10
46	Steve Walsh	.10
47	Kerry Collins	.30
48	Barry Sanders	1.75
49	Steve Young	.75
50	Jim Harbaugh	.10
51	Tyrone Wheatley	.10
52	Boomer Esiason	.10
53	Deion Sanders	.75
54	Steve McNair	1.00
55	Willie McGinest	.10
56	Adrian Murrell	.10
57	Thurman Thomas	.20
58	John Elway	.75
59	William Floyd	.10
60	Eric Zeier	.10
61	Dave Krieg	.10
62	Eric Bjornson	.10
63	Brett Favre	2.50
64	Derrick Alexander	.10
65	Charlie Garner	.10
66	Stan Humphries	.10
67	Bert Emanuel	.10
68	Scott Mitchell	.10
69	Quentin Coryatt	.10
70	Eric Green	.10
71	Jeff Graham	.10
72	Ernie Mills	.10
73	Trent Dilfer	.20
74	Sherman Williams	.10
75	Tamarick Vanover	.50
76	Drew Bledsoe	1.25
77	Jay Novacek	.10
78	Edgar Bennett	.10
79	Tim Brown	.10
80	Greg Lloyd	.10
81	Darick Holmes	.10
82	Carl Pickens	.10
83	Flipper Anderson	.10
84	Bernie Kosar	.10
85	Dave Brown	.10
86	Calvin Williams	.10
87	Michael Westbrook	.20
88	Kevin Williams	.10
89	Chris Sanders	.10
90	Robert Smith	.10
91	Cris Carter	.10
92	Gus Frerotte	.10
93	Larry Centers	.10
94	Eric Metcalf	.10
95	Isaac Bruce	.50
96	Kordell Stewart	1.50
97	Ricky Watters	.20
98	Terrell Fletcher	.10
99	Bernie Parmalee	.10
100	Harvey Williams	.10
101	Hardy Nickerson	.10
102	Jeff Blake	.50
103	Terry Allen	.10
104	Yancey Thigpen	.30
105	Greg Hill	.10
106	Chris Warren	.20
107	Terrell Davis	1.50
108	Mark Brunell	1.00
109	Alvin Harper	.10
110	Marcus Allen	.20
111	Garrison Hearst	.10
112	Derek Loville	.10
113	Craig Heyward	.10
114	Kimble Anders	.10
115	O.J. McDuffie	.10
116	Junior Seau	.20
117	Terry Kirby	.10
118	Erric Pegram	.10
119	Rick Mirer	.10
120	Erik Kramer	.10
121	Brett Perriman	.10
122	Shawn Jefferson	.10
123	J.J. Stokes	.20
124	Kevin Greene	.10
125	Daryl Johnston	.10
126	Mark Chmura	.10
127	James Stewart	.10
128	Mario Bates	.10
129	Rodney Peete	.10
130	Quinn Early	.10
131	Shannon Sharpe	.10
132	Neil Smith	.10
133	Herschel Walker	.10
134	Aaron Bailey	.10
135	Rashaan Salaam	.40
136	Kevin Smith	.10
137	Sean Dawkins	.10
138	Jake Reed	.10
139	Neil O'Donnell	.10
140	Reggie White	.20
141	Vincent Brisby	.10
142	Napoleon Kaufman	.10
143	Brent Jones	.10
144	Mark Seay	.10
145	Heath Shuler	.10
146	Wayne Chrebet	.10
147	*Leeland McElroy*	.30
148	*Tim Biakabutuka*	1.00
149	*John Mobley*	.10
150	*Tony Brackens*	.20
151	*Danny Kanell*	.75
152	*Eddie Kennison*	.40
153	*Jonathan Ogden*	.20
154	*Bobby Engram*	.30
155	*Chris Darkins*	.10
156	*Daryl Gardener*	.10
157	*Keyshawn Johnson*	3.00
158	*Mike Alstott*	1.75
159	*Simeon Rice*	.20
160	*Eric Moulds*	2.50
161	*Stepfret Williams*	.10
162	*Eddie George*	4.00
163	*Duane Clemons*	.10
164	*Amani Toomer*	.20
165	*Rickey Dudley*	.30
166	*Bobby Hoying*	1.00
167	*Lawrence Phillips*	.50
168	*Willie Anderson*	.10
169	*Derrick Mayes*	1.00
170	*Kevin Hardy*	.20
171	*Terry Glenn*	1.75
172	*Stephen Davis*	4.00
173	*Walt Harris*	.20
174	*Marvin Harrison*	3.00
175	*Karim Abdul-Jabbar*	.75
176	*Alex Molden*	.10
177	*Regan Upshaw*	.10
178	*Jerald Moore*	.10
179	*Alex Van Dyke*	.20
180	*Jeff Lewis*	.75
181	*Cedric Jones*	.10
182	Jim Kelly	.10
183	Troy Aikman	.50
184	Jim Harbaugh	.10
185	Neil O'Donnell	.10
186	Steve Young	.30
187	Kerry Collins	.30
188	Scott Mitchell	.10
189	Drew Bledsoe	.50
190	Kordell Stewart	.75
191	Erik Kramer	.10
192	Brett Favre	1.00
193	Warren Moon	.10
194	Jeff Blake	.25
195	Mark Brunell	.50
196	John Elway	.25
197	Checklist (Emmitt Smith)	.30
198	Checklist (Dan Marino)	.30
199	Checklist (Brett Favre)	.30
200	Checklist (Jim Harbaugh)	.10

A player's name in *italic type* indicates a rookie card.

1996 Summit Ground Zero

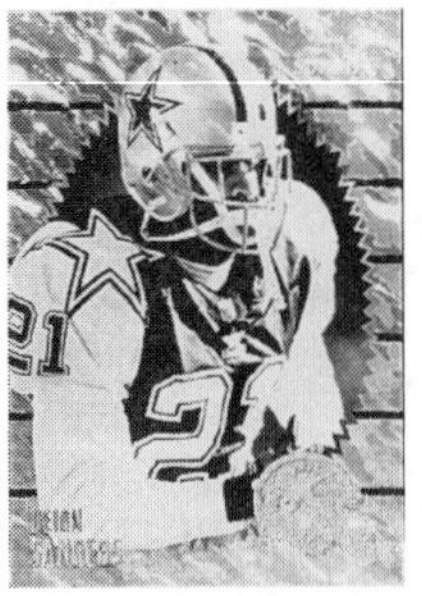

Ground Zero is a 200-card prismatic foil rendition of the regular-issue set. These parallel cards are inserted every six packs.

	MT
Complete Set (200):	400.00
Ground Zero Cards:	6x-12x

1996 Summit Artist's Proofs

Artist's Proofs add a holographic Artist's Proof stamp to all 200 cards in the regular-issue set. These parallel cards are inserted at a rate of one per 35 packs.

	MT
Complete Set (200):	1400.
Artist's Proof Cards:	20x-40x

1996 Summit Premium Stock

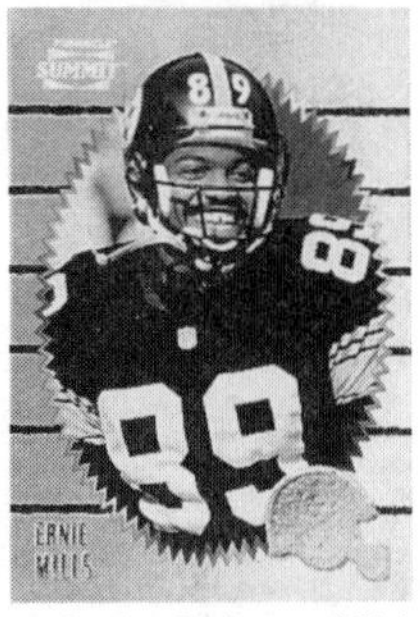

Premium Stock was available in hobby stores and was an upgraded version of Summit Football. In 13-card packs of Premium Stock, the regular-issue set was reprinted in a rainbow holographic foil version. In addition, Turf Team inserts also received special prismatic foil treatment. Other inserts were the same as the regular-issue product.

	MT
Complete Set (200):	50.00
Premium Stock Cards:	1.5x

1996 Summit Inspirations

The 18-card, regular-sized set was inserted in every 17 packs of Summit football. The cards feature foil printing and the production run was limited to 8,000.

		MT
Complete Set (18):		140.00
Common Player:		3.00
1	Jim Harbaugh	3.00
2	Alex Van Dyke	5.00
3	Mike Alstott	5.00
4	Jonathan Ogden	3.00
5	Brett Favre	30.00
6	Tony Brackens	3.00
7	Drew Bledsoe	15.00
8	Danny Kanell	3.00
9	Eric Moulds	5.00
10	John Elway	12.00
11	Eddie George	25.00
12	Karim Abdul-Jabbar	18.00
13	Tim Biakabutuka	10.00
14	Jeff Lewis	3.00
15	Terry Glenn	10.00
16	Jeff Blake	7.00
17	Kevin Hardy	3.00
18	Bobby Engram	7.00

1996 Summit Turf Team

The 16-card, regular-sized set, inserted in hobby packs of Summit football, features spot-embossed technology and is limited to a production run of 4,000.

		MT
Complete Set (16):		350.00
Common Player:		6.00
1	Emmitt Smith	50.00
2	Brett Favre	50.00
3	Curtis Martin	40.00
4	Steve Young	20.00
5	Kerry Collins	12.00
6	Barry Sanders	30.00
7	Dan Marino	50.00
8	Isaac Bruce	12.00
9	Troy Aikman	25.00
10	Marshall Faulk	18.00
11	Joey Galloway	20.00
12	Jeff Blake	6.00
13	Drew Bledsoe	25.00
14	John Elway	20.00
15	Jerry Rice	25.00
16	Michael Irvin	6.00

1996 Summit Third and Long

The 18-card, regular-sized set was inserted in hobby, retail and magazine packs and was limited to a production run of 2,000. The cards are printed on rainbow holographic foil with sequential numbering. An 18-card parallel insert set, Mirage, features a floating football hologram behind the player's image. Mirage is limited to 600 sets.

		MT
Complete Set (18):		500.00
Common Player:		7.50
Minor Stars:		15.00
Production 2,000 Sets		
Mirage Prize Cards:		2x
Production 600 Sets		
1	Michael Irvin	15.00
2	Dan Marino	45.00
3	Keyshawn Johnson	20.00
4	Chris Warren	7.50
5	Rashaan Salaam	7.50
6	Brett Favre	60.00
7	Terry Glenn	15.00
8	Steve Young	20.00
9	Kerry Collins	15.00
10	Emmitt Smith	45.00
11	Marvin Harrison	15.00
12	Jerry Rice	30.00
13	John Elway	45.00
14	Drew Bledsoe	30.00
15	Eddie Kennison	7.50
16	Troy Aikman	30.00
17	Barry Sanders	60.00
18	Terrell Davis	60.00

1996 Summit Hit The Hole

The 16-card, regular-sized set, limited to a production run of 1,000, was randomly inserted in five-card retail packs of 1996 Pinnacle Summit. The set features 16 top offensive players on all-foil printing.

		MT
Complete Set (16):		400.00
Common Player:		10.00
1	Rashaan Salaam	10.00
2	Marshall Faulk	20.00
3	Ricky Watters	10.00
4	Leeland McElroy	10.00
5	Emmitt Smith	70.00
6	Eddie George	50.00
7	Curtis Martin	50.00
8	Lawrence Phillips	25.00
9	Darick Holmes	10.00
10	Barry Sanders	40.00
11	Karim Abdul-Jabbar	35.00
12	Errict Rhett	20.00
13	Terrell Davis	40.00
14	Chris Warren	10.00
15	Rodney Thomas	10.00
16	Tim Biakabutuka	20.00

1997 Score

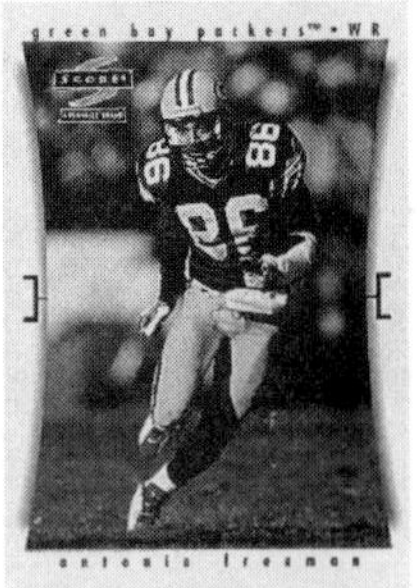

The 330-card set features a player photo in the center on the front, with the team and the player's position printed at the top. The Score logo is in the upper left of the photo, while goalposts appear on the center of each side of the photo. The player's name is printed at the bottom. The base set is paralleled by a Showcase Series and Artist's Proof version.

		MT
Complete Set (330):		15.00
Common Player:		.05
Minor Stars:		.10
Showcase Series:		4x-8x
Artist's Proofs:		20x-40x
Retail Pack (10):		1.00
Retail Wax Box (36):		30.00
Hobby Pack (15):		3.00
Hobby Wax Box (20):		52.00
1	John Elway	.50
2	Drew Bledsoe	.75
3	Brett Favre	1.75
4	Emmitt Smith	1.50
5	Kerry Collins	.25
6	Jerry Rice	.75

7 Kordell Stewart .75
8 Barry Sanders 1.25
9 Dan Marino 1.50
10 Steve Young .50
11 Erik Kramer .05
12 Warren Moon .10
13 Chris Calloway .05
14 Doug Evans .05
15 Darren Woodson .05
16 Alonzo Spellman .05
17 Greg Hill .05
18 Aaron Craver .05
19 Jeff Hostetler .05
20 William Thomas .05
21 Marco Coleman .05
22 Wayne Simmons .05
23 Donnell Woolford .05
24 Vinny Testaverde .10
25 Ed McCaffrey .05
26 Jim Everett .05
27 Gilbert Brown .05
28 Jason Dunn .05
29 Stanley Pritchett .05
30 Joey Galloway .15
31 Amani Toomer .05
32 Chris Penn .05
33 Aeneas Williams .05
34 Bobby Taylor .05
35 Bryan Still .05
36 Ty Law .05
37 Shannon Sharpe .05
38 Marty Carter .05
39 Sam Mills .05
40 William Floyd .05
41 Brad Johnson .05
42 Sean Dawkins .05
43 Michael Irvin .10
44 Jeff George .10
45 Brent Jones .05
46 Mark Brunell .75
47 Rob Moore .05
48 Hardy Nickerson .05
49 Chris Chandler .05
50 Willie Anderson .05
51 Isaac Bruce .15
52 Natrone Means .10
53 Tony Banks .15
54 Marshall Faulk .15
55 Michael Westbrook .05
56 Bruce Smith .05
57 Jamal Anderson .15
58 Jackie Harris .05
59 Sean Gilbert .05
60 Ki-Jana Carter .05
61 Eric Moulds .10
62 James Stewart .05
63 Jeff Blake .10
64 O.J. McDuffie .05
65 Neil Smith .05
66 Kevin Smith .05
67 Terry Allen .05
68 Sean LaChapelle .05
69 Rashaan Salaam .10
70 Jeff Graham .05
71 Mark Carrier .05
72 Allen Aldridge .05
73 Keenan McCardell .05
74 Willie McGinest .05
75 Napoleon Kaufman .10
76 Jerris McPhail .05
77 Eric Swann .05
78 Kimble Anders .05
79 Charles Johnson .05
80 Bryan Cox .05
81 Johnnie Morton .05
82 Andre Rison .05
83 Corey Miller .05
84 Troy Drayton .05
85 Jim Harbaugh .05
86 Wesley Walls .05
87 Bryce Paup .05
88 Curtis Martin 1.00
89 Michael Sinclair .05
90 Chris T. Jones .05
91 Jake Reed .05
92 LeRoy Butler .05
93 Reggie Tongue .05
94 Bert Emanual .05
95 Stan Humphries .05
96 Neil O'Donnell .05
97 Troy Vincent .05
98 Mike Alstott .15
99 Chad Cota .05
100 Marvin Harrison .30
101 Terrell Owens .30
102 Dave Brown .05
103 Harvey Williams .05
104 Desmond Howard .05
105 Carl Pickens .05
106 Kent Graham .05
107 Michael Bates .05
108 Terrell Davis 1.00
109 Marcus Allen .10
110 Ray Zellars .05
111 Chris Warren .05
112 Phillippi Sparks .05
113 Craig Erickson .05
114 Eddie George 1.00
115 Daryl Johnston .05
116 Ricky Watters .10
117 Tedy Bruschi .05
118 Mike Mamula .05
119 Ken Harvey .05
120 John Randle .05
121 Mark Chmura .05
122 Sam Gash .05
123 John Kasay .05
124 Barry Minter .05
125 Raymont Harris .05
126 Derrick Thomas .05
127 Trent Dilfer .10
128 Carnell Lake .05
129 Brian Dawkins .05
130 Tyronne Drakeford .05
131 Daryl Gardener .05
132 Fred Strickland .05
133 Kevin Hardy .05
134 Winslow Oliver .05
135 Herman Moore .15
136 Keith Byars .05
137 Harold Green .05
138 Ty Detmer .05
139 Lamar Thomas .05
140 Elvis Grbac .05
141 Edgar Bennett .05
142 Cornelius Bennett .05
143 Tony Tolbert .05
144 James Hasty .05
145 Ben Coates .05
146 Errict Rhett .10
147 Jason Seahorn .05
148 Michael Jackson .05
149 John Mobley .05
150 Walt Harris .05
151 Terry Kirby .05
152 Devin Wyman .05
153 Ray Crockett .05
154 Quinn Early .05
155 Rodney Thomas .05
156 Mark Seay .05
157 Derrick Alexander .05
158 Lamar Lathon .05
159 Anthony Miller .05
160 Shawn Wooden .05
161 Antonio Freeman .15
162 Cortez Kennedy .05
163 Rickey Dudley .10
164 Tony Carter .05
165 Kevin Williams .05
166 Reggie White .10
167 Tim Bowens .05
168 Roy Barker .05
169 Adrian Murrell .05
170 Anthony Johnson .05
171 Terry Glenn .25
172 Jeff Lewis .05
173 Dorsey Levens .10
174 Willie Jackson .05
175 Willie Clay .05
176 Richmond Webb .05
177 Shawn Lee .05
178 Joe Aska .05
179 Rod Woodson .05
180 Jim Schwantz .05
181 Alfred Williams .05
182 Ferric Collons .05
183 Ken Norton Jr. .05
184 Rick Mirer .10
185 Leeland McElroy .05
186 Rodney Hampton .05
187 Ted Popson .05
188 Fred Barnett .05
189 Junior Seau .10
190 Michael Barrow .05
191 Corey Widmer .05
192 Rodney Peete .05
193 Rod Smith .05
194 Muhsin Muhammad .15
195 Keith Jackson .05
196 Jimmy Smith .05
197 Dave Meggett .05
198 Lawrence Phillips .10
199 Chad Brown .05
200 Darrin Smith .05
201 Larry Centers .05
202 Kevin Greene .05
203 Sherman Williams .05
204 Chris Sanders .05
205 Shawn Jefferson .05
206 Thurman Thomas .10
207 Keyshawn Johnson .30
208 Bryant Young .05
209 Tim Biakabutuka .15
210 Troy Aikman .75
211 Quentin Coryatt .05
212 Karim Abdul-Jabbar .50
213 Brian Blades .05
214 Ray Farmer .05
215 Simeon Rice .05
216 Tyrone Braxton .05
217 Jerome Woods .05
218 Charles Way .05
219 Garrison Hearst .05
220 Bobby Engram .10
221 Billy Davis .05
222 Ken Dilger .05
223 Robert Smith .05
224 John Friesz .05
225 Charlie Garner .05
226 Jerome Bettis .10
227 Darnay Scott .05
228 Terance Mathis .05
229 Brian Williams .05
230 Cris Carter .05
231 Michael Haynes .05
232 Cedric Jones .05
233 Danny Kanell .05
234 Deion Sanders .30
235 Steve Atwater .05
236 Jonathan Ogden .05
237 Lake Dawson .05
238 Eric Allen .05
239 Eddie Kennison .30
240 Irving Fryar .05
241 Michael Strahan .05
242 Steve McNair .40
243 Terrell Buckley .05
244 Merton Hanks .05
245 Jessie Armstead .05
246 Dana Stubblefield .05
247 Brett Perriman .05
248 Mark Collins .05
249 Willie Roaf .05
250 Gus Frerotte .05
251 William Fuller .05
252 Tamarick Vanover .10
253 Scott Mitchell .05
254 Eric Metcalf .05
255 Herschel Walker .05
256 Robert Brooks .05
257 Zach Thomas .15
258 Alvin Harper .05
259 Wayne Chrebet .05
260 Bill Romanowski .05
261 Willie Green .05
262 Dale Carter .05
263 Chris Slade .05
264 J.J. Stokes .05
265 Tim Brown .05
266 Eric Davis .05
267 Mark Carrier .05
268 Tony Martin .05
269 Tyrone Wheatley .05
270 Eugene Robinson .05
271 Curtis Conway .05
272 Michael Timpson .05
273 *Orlando Pace* .50
274 *Tiki Barber* 1.00
275 *Byron Hanspard* .25
276 *Warrick Dunn* 1.25
277 *Rae Carruth* .50
278 *Bryant Westbrook* .30
279 *Antowain Smith* 1.25
280 *Peter Boulware* .05
281 *Reidel Anthony* 1.00
282 *Troy Davis* .20
283 *Jake Plummer* 2.50
284 *Chris Canty* .05
285 *Dwayne Rudd* .05
286 *Ike Hilliard* 1.00
287 *Reinard Wilson* .05
288 *Corey Dillon* 2.50
289 *Tony Gonzalez* .50
290 *Darnell Autry* .50
291 *Kevin Lockett* .20
292 *Darrell Russell* .05
293 *Jim Druckenmiller* 1.00
294 *Scott Mitchell* .05
295 *Joey Kent* .30
296 *Shawn Springs* .50
297 *James Farrior* .50
298 *Sedrick Shaw* .50
299 *Marcus Harris* .05
300 *Danny Wuerffel* .50
301 *Marc Edwards* .20
302 *Michael Booker* .05
303 *David LaFleur* .50
304 *Mike Adams* .05
305 *Pat Barnes* .20
306 *George Jones* .05
307 *Yatil Green* .30
308 Drew Bledsoe .30
309 Troy Aikman .30
310 Terrell Davis .40
311 Jim Everett .05
312 John Elway .20
313 Barry Sanders .50
314 Jim Harbaugh .05
315 Steve Young .20
316 Dan Marino .75
317 Michael Irvin .05
318 Emmitt Smith .75
319 Jeff Hostetler .05
320 Mark Brunell .30
321 Jeff Blake .05
322 Scott Mitchell .05
323 Boomer Esiason .05
324 Jerome Bettis .05
325 Warren Moon .05
326 Neil O'Donnell .05
327 (Jim Kelly) .05
328 Checklist (Dan Marino) .75
329 Checklist (John Elway) .20
330 Checklist (Drew Bledsoe) .30

1997 Score Franchise

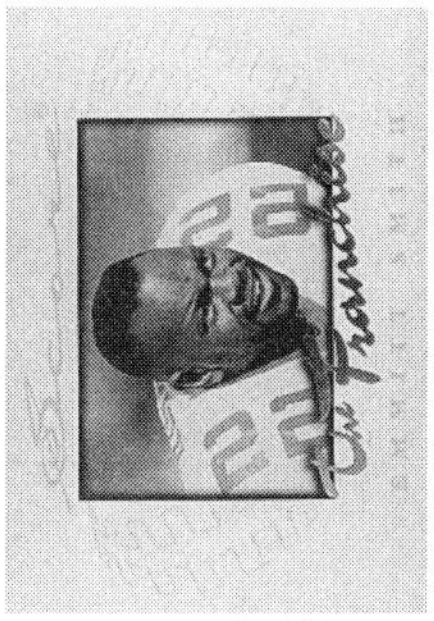

This 16-card set includes the Franchise players from various NFL teams, including Emmitt Smith and Barry Sanders.

MT
Complete Set (16): 200.00
Common Player: 4.00
1 Emmitt Smith 30.00
2 Barry Sanders 25.00
3 Brett Favre 35.00
4 Drew Bledsoe 15.00
5 Jerry Rice 15.00
6 Troy Aikman 15.00
7 Dan Marino 30.00
8 John Elway 10.00
9 Steve Young 10.00
10 Eddie George 18.00
11 Keyshawn Johnson 4.00
12 Terrell Davis 15.00
13 Marshall Faulk 4.00
14 Kerry Collins 6.00
15 Deion Sanders 8.00
16 Joey Galloway 4.00

1997 Score New Breed

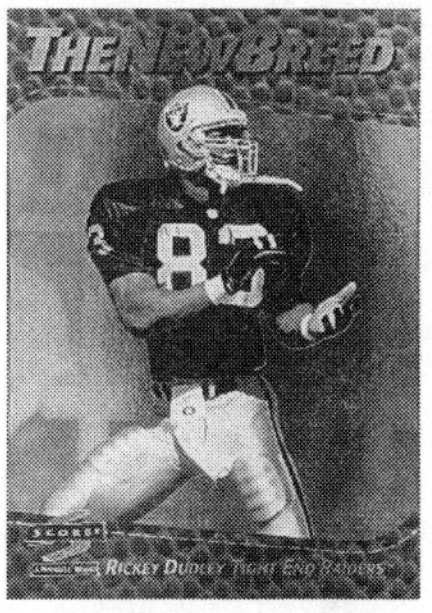

This 18-card set features a player photo superimposed over a holographic background on the card front. "The New Breed" is printed at the top. A football's brown pebble grain is on the top and bottom border of the front. The Score logo is in the lower left, while his name, position and team are printed to the right of the logo. The backs are numbered in the upper left corner.

MT
Complete Set (18): 75.00
Common Player: .75
1 Eddie George 8.00
2 Terrell Davis 8.00
3 Curtis Martin 8.00
4 Tony Banks .75
5 Lawrence Phillips .75
6 Terry Glenn 1.50
7 Jerome Bettis .75
8 Karim Abdul-Jabbar 1.50
9 Napoleon Kaufman .75
10 Isaac Bruce .75
11 Keyshawn Johnson .75
12 Rickey Dudley .75
13 Eddie Kennison 3.00
14 Marvin Harrison 3.00
15 Emmitt Smith 10.00
16 Barry Sanders 10.00
17 Kerry Collins 1.50
18 Brett Favre 12.00

1997 Score The Specialist

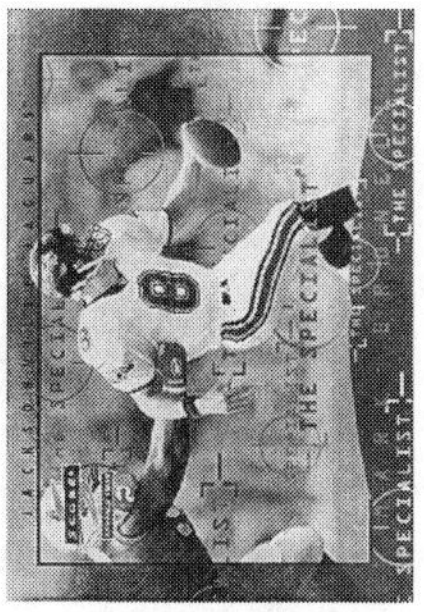

The 18-card chase set features a holographic front, with the player over a background which repeats "The Specialist" many times. The player's name is printed in red at the bottom center. The cards are numbered on the back.

MT
Complete Set (18): 75.00
Common Player: .75
1 Brett Favre 12.00
2 Drew Bledsoe 6.00
3 Mark Brunell 6.00
4 Kerry Collins 1.50
5 John Elway 4.00
6 Barry Sanders 10.00
7 Troy Aikman 6.00
8 Jerry Rice 6.00
9 Dan Marino 10.00
10 Neil O'Donnell .75
11 Scott Mitchell .75
12 Jim Harbaugh .75
13 Emmitt Smith 10.00
14 Steve Young 4.00
15 Dave Brown .75
16 Jeff Blake 2.00
17 Jim Everett .75
18 Kordell Stewart 6.00

1998 Score

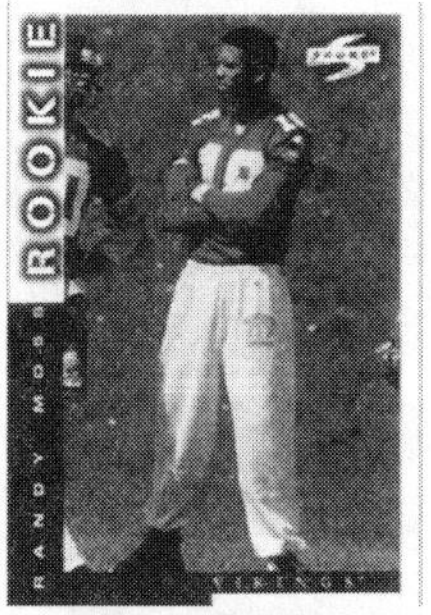

The 270-card base set is made up of 15 Off Season cards, 3 checklists, 20 rookies and 232 veterans. Three parallel sets that include Showcase, Artist's Proofs and One on One. The Showcase set includes only the top 110 players and were inserted 1:7 packs. The Artist's Proof set is made up of the best 50 players in the set and were found 1:35 packs. The last parallel set is the One on One set in which there is only one of each card in the 160-card set. A special hobby exclusive Ryan Leaf autographed card was added with only 200 signed.

MT
Complete Set (270): 50.00
Common Player: .10
Minor Stars: .20
Common Rookie: 1.00
Complete Showcase (110): 120.00
Showcase Cards: 2x-4x
Showcase Rookies: 2x
Inserted 1:7
Complete Artist's Proof (50): 250.00
AP Cards: 5x-10x
Inserted 1:35
Pack: 1.50
Wax Box (24): 30.00
1 John Elway 1.00
2 Kordell Stewart .75
3 Warrick Dunn .75
4 Brad Johnson .30
5 Kerry Collins .20
6 Danny Kanell .10
7 Emmitt Smith 1.50
8 Jamal Anderson .50
9 Jim Harbaugh .20
10 Tony Martin .20
11 Rod Smith .30
12 Dorsey Levens .30
13 Steve McNair .40
14 Derrick Thomas .10
15 Rob Moore .20
16 Peter Boulware .10
17 Terry Allen .20
18 Joey Galloway .30
19 Jerome Bettis .30
20 Carl Pickens .20
21 Napoleon Kaufman .30
22 Troy Aikman 1.00
23 Curtis Conway .20
24 Adrian Murrell .20
25 Elvis Grbac .20
26 Garrison Hearst .30
27 Chris Sanders .10
28 Scott Mitchell .20
29 Junior Seau .20
30 Chris Chandler .20
31 Kevin Hardy .10
32 Terrell Davis 1.50
33 Keyshawn Johnson .30
34 Natrone Means .20
35 Antowain Smith .30
36 Jake Plummer .75
37 Isaac Bruce .20
38 Tony Banks .20
39 Reidel Anthony .20
40 Darren Woodson .10
41 Corey Dillon .50
42 Antonio Freeman .30
43 Eddie George .75
44 Yancey Thigpen .20
45 Tim Brown .20
46 Wayne Chrebet .30
47 Andre Rison .20
48 Michael Strahan .10
49 Deion Sanders .30
50 Eric Moulds .30
51 Mark Brunell .75
52 Rae Carruth .10
53 Warren Sapp .10
54 Mark Chmura .20
55 Darrell Green .10
56 Quinn Early .10
57 Barry Sanders 2.00
58 Neil O'Donnell .20
59 Tony Brackens .10
60 Willie Davis .10
61 Shannon Sharpe .30
62 Shawn Springs .10
63 Tony Gonzalez .10
64 Rodney Thomas .10
65 Terance Mathis .10
66 Brett Favre 2.00
67 Eric Swann .10
68 Kevin Turner .10
69 Tyrone Wheatley .10
70 Trent Dilfer .20
71 Bryan Cox .10
72 Lake Dawson .10
73 Will Blackwell .10
74 Fred Lane .20
75 Ty Detmer .10
76 Eddie Kennison .20
77 Jimmy Smith .30
78 Chris Calloway .10
79 Shawn Jefferson .10
80 Dan Marino 1.50
81 LeRoy Butler .10
82 William Roaf .10
83 Rick Mirer .10
84 Dermontti Dawson .10
85 Errict Rhett .10
86 Lamar Thomas .10
87 Lamar Lathon .10
88 John Randle .10
89 Darryl Williams .10
90 Keenan McCardell .20
91 Erik Kramer .10
92 Ken Dilger .10
93 Dave Meggett .10
94 Jeff Blake .20
95 Ed McCaffrey .20
96 Charles Johnson .20
97 Irving Spikes .10
98 Mike Alstott .30
99 Vincent Brisby .10
100 Michael Westbrook .10
101 Rickey Dudley .10
102 Bert Emanuel .10
103 Daryl Johnston .10
104 Lawrence Phillips .10
105 Eric Bieniemy .10
106 Bryant Westbrook .10
107 Rob Johnson .20
108 Ray Zellars .10
109 Anthony Johnson .10
110 Reggie White .30
111 Wesley Walls .10
112 Amani Toomer .10
113 Gary Brown .10
114 Brian Blades .10
115 Alex Van Dyke .10
116 Michael Haynes .10
117 Jessie Armstead .10
118 James Jett .10
119 Troy Drayton .10
120 Craig Heyward .10
121 Steve Atwater .10
122 Tiki Barber .10
123 Karim Abdul .20
124 Kimble Anders .10
125 Frank Sanders .10
126 David Sloan .10
127 Andre Hastings .10
128 Vinny Testaverde .20
129 Robert Smith .20
130 Horace Copeland .10
131 Larry Centers .10
132 J.J. Stokes .20
133 Ike Hilliard .10
134 Muhsin Muhammad .10
135 Sean Dawkins .10
136 Raymont Harris .10
137 Lamar Smith .10
138 David Palmer .10
139 Steve Young .75
140 Bryan Still .10
141 Keith Byars .10
142 Cris Carter .30
143 Charlie Garner .10
144 Drew Bledsoe 1.00
145 Simeon Rice .10
146 Merton Hanks .10
147 Aeneas Williams .10
148 Rodney Hampton .10
149 Zach Thomas .20
150 Mark Bruener .10
151 Jason Dunn .10
152 Danny Wuerffel .10
153 Jim Druckenmiller .20
154 Greg Hill .10
155 Earnest Byner .10
156 Greg Lloyd .10
157 John Mobley .10
158 Tim Biakabutuka .20
159 Terrell Owens .50
160 O.J. McDuffie .20
161 Glenn Foley .20
162 Derrick Brooks .10
163 Dave Brown .10
164 Ki-Jana Carter .10
165 Bobby Hoying .20
166 Randal Hill .10
167 Michael Irvin .20
168 Bruce Smith .10
169 Troy Davis .10
170 Derrick Mayes .10
171 Henry Ellard .10
172 Dana Stubblefield .10
173 Willie McGinest .10
174 Leeland McElroy .10
175 Edgar Bennett .10
176 Robert Porcher .10
177 Randall Cunningham .30
178 Jim Everett .10
179 Jake Reed .10
180 Quentin Coryatt .10
181 William Floyd .10
182 Jason Sehorn .10
183 Carnell Lake .10
184 Dexter Coakley .10
185 Derrick Alexander .10
186 Johnnie Morton .10
187 Irving Fryar .10
188 Warren Moon .20
189 Todd Collins .10
190 Ken Norton Jr. .10
191 Terry Glenn .20
192 Rashaan Salaam .20
193 Jerry Rice 1.00
194 James Stewart .10
195 David LaFleur .10
196 Eric Green .10
197 Gus Frerotte .20
198 Willie Green .10
199 Marshall Faulk .30
200 Brett Perriman .10
201 Darnay Scott .10
202 Marvin Harrison .20
203 Joe Aska .10
204 Darrien Gordon .10
205 Herman Moore .20
206 Curtis Martin .30
207 Derek Loville .10
208 Dale Carter .10
209 Heath Shuler .10
210 Jonathan Ogden .10
211 Leslie Shepherd .10
212 Tony Boselli .10
213 Eric Metcalf .10
214 Neil Smith .10
215 Anthony Miller .10
216 Jeff George .20
217 Charles Way .10
218 Mario Bates .10
219 Ben Coates .20
220 Michael Jackson .10
221 Thurman Thomas .20
222 Kyle Brady .10
223 Marcus Allen .20
224 Robert Brooks .10
225 Yatil Green .20
226 Byron Hanspard .10
227 Andre Reed .20
228 Chris Warren .10
229 Jackie Harris .10
230 Ricky Watters .20
231 Bobby Engram .10
232 Tamarick Vanover .10
233 *Peyton Manning* 10.00
234 *Curtis Enis* 3.00
235 *Randy Moss* 10.00
236 *Charles Woodson* 2.00
237 *Robert Edwards* 1.00
238 *Jacquez Green* 2.00
239 *Keith Brooking* .50
240 *Jerome Pathon* .50
241 *Kevin Dyson* 2.00
242 *Fred Taylor* 6.00
243 *Tavian Banks* .50
244 *Marcus Nash* .50
245 *Brian Griese* 4.00
246 *Andre Wadsworth* .50
247 *Ahman Green* .75
248 *Joe Jurevicius* .50
249 *Germane Crowell* 2.00
250 *Skip Hicks* .75
251 *Ryan Leaf* 3.00
252 *Hines Ward* .75
253 John Elway .50
254 Mark Brunell .30
255 Brett Favre 1.00
256 Troy Aikman .50
257 Warrick Dunn .30
258 Barry Sanders 1.00
259 Eddie George .30
260 Kordell Stewart .30
261 Emmitt Smith .75
262 Steve Young .25
263 Terrell Davis .75
264 Dorsey Levens .10
265 Dan Marino .75
266 Jerry Rice .50
267 Drew Bledsoe .30
268 Brett Favre 1.00
269 Barry Sanders 1.00
270 Terrell Davis .75

1998 Score Complete Players

Only 10 of the NFL's all-around athletes are included in this set that has three different cards highlighting three specific attributes on special cards with holographic foil stamping. Singles were inserted 1:11 packs.

MT
Complete Set (30): 100.00
Common Player: 2.50
Inserted 1:11
1a Brett Favre 8.00
1b Brett Favre 8.00
1c Brett Favre 8.00
2a John Elway 5.00
2b John Elway 5.00
2c John Elway 5.00
3a Emmitt Smith 6.00
3b Emmitt Smith 6.00
3c Emmitt Smith 6.00
4a Kordell Stewart 2.50
4b Kordell Stewart 2.50
4c Kordell Stewart 2.50

5a Dan Marino 6.00
5b Dan Marino 6.00
5c Dan Marino 6.00
6a Mark Brunell 3.00
6b Mark Brunell 3.00
6c Mark Brunell 3.00
7a Terrell Davis 7.00
7b Terrell Davis 7.00
7c Terrell Davis 7.00
8a Barry Sanders 8.00
8b Barry Sanders 8.00
8c Barry Sanders 8.00
9a Warrick Dunn 2.50
9b Warrick Dunn 2.50
9c Warrick Dunn 2.50
10a Jerry Rice 4.00
10b Jerry Rice 4.00
10c Jerry Rice 4.00

1998 Score Rookie Autographs

The 33-card set includes all of the top rookies from 1998. Each is hand signed and limited to 500.

MT
Complete Set (33): 1600.
Common Player: 20.00
Minor Stars: 40.00
Production 500 Sets
Stephen Alexander 40.00
Tavian Banks 50.00
Charlie Batch 100.00
Keith Brooking 20.00
Thad Busby 20.00
John Dutton 20.00
Tim Dwight 50.00
Kevin Dyson 50.00
Robert Edwards 60.00
Greg Ellis 20.00
Curtis Enis 60.00
Chris Fuamatu-Ma'afala 40.00
Ahman Green 40.00
Jacquez Green 50.00
Brian Griese 70.00
Skip Hicks 50.00
Robert Holcombe 40.00
Tebucky Jones 20.00
Joe Jurevicius 30.00
Ryan Leaf 85.00
Leonard Little 20.00
Alonzo Mayes 20.00
Michael Myers 20.00
Randy Moss 250.00
Marcus Nash 50.00
Jerome Pathon 40.00
Jason Peter 20.00
Anthony Simmons 20.00
Tony Simmons 40.00
Takeo Spikes 30.00
Duane Starks 20.00
Fred Taylor 100.00
Hines Ward 40.00

1998 Score Star Salute

This set highlights the top 20 players in the NFL and puts each of them on a foil board with micro-etching. Singles were issued 1:35 packs.

MT
Complete Set (20): 120.00
Common Player: 4.00
Inserted 1:35
1 Terrell Davis 15.00
2 Barry Sanders 20.00
3 Steve Young 6.00
4 Drew Bledsoe 8.00
5 Kordell Stewart 8.00
6 Emmitt Smith 15.00
7 Dorsey Levens 4.00
8 Corey Dillon 5.00
9 Jerome Bettis 4.00
10 Herman Moore 4.00
11 Brett Favre 20.00
12 Antonio Freeman 5.00
13 Mark Brunell 8.00
14 John Elway 12.00
15 Terry Glenn 4.00
16 Warrick Dunn 7.00
17 Eddie George 8.00
18 Troy Aikman 10.00
19 Deion Sanders 4.00
20 Jerry Rice 10.00

1998 Score Rookie Preview

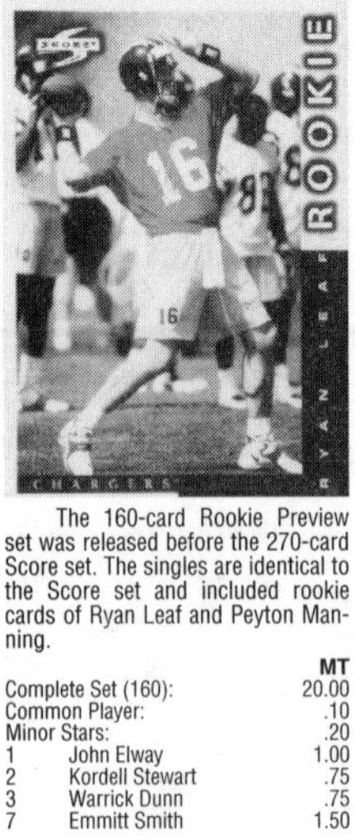

The 160-card Rookie Preview set was released before the 270-card Score set. The singles are identical to the Score set and included rookie cards of Ryan Leaf and Peyton Manning.

MT
Complete Set (160): 20.00
Common Player: .10
Minor Stars: .20
1 John Elway 1.00
2 Kordell Stewart .75
3 Warrick Dunn .75
7 Emmitt Smith 1.50
11 Rod Smith .20
12 Dorsey Levens .20
13 Steve McNair .50
16 Peter Boulware .10
18 Joey Galloway .30
19 Jerome Bettis .20
20 Carl Pickens .20
21 Napoleon Kaufman .30
22 Troy Aikman 1.00
24 Adrian Murrell .10
25 Elvis Grbac .10
27 Chris Sanders .10
28 Scott Mitchell .10
29 Junior Seau .20
30 Chris Chandler .10
31 Kevin Hardy .10
32 Terrell Davis 1.50
35 Antowain Smith .30
36 Jake Plummer .75
37 Isaac Bruce .20
38 Tony Banks .20
40 Darren Woodson .10
41 Corey Dillon .50
42 Antonio Freeman .30
43 Eddie George .75
48 Michael Strahan .10
51 Mark Brunell .75
56 Quinn Early .10
57 Barry Sanders 2.00
58 Neil O'Donnell .10
59 Tony Brackens .10
60 Willie Davis .10
61 Shannon Sharpe .20
62 Shawn Springs .10
63 Tony Gonzalez .10
64 Rodney Thomas .10
65 Terance Mathis .10
66 Brett Favre 2.00
68 Kevin Turner .10
69 Tyrone Wheatley .10
70 Trent Dilfer .20
71 Bryan Cox .10
72 Lake Dawson .10
74 Fred Lane .10
75 Ty Detmer .10
76 Eddie Kennison .10
78 Chris Calloway .10
79 Shawn Jefferson .10
80 Dan Marino 1.50
81 LeRoy Butler .10
82 William Roaf .10
83 Rick Mirer .10
84 Dermontti Dawson .10
86 Lamar Thomas .10
87 Lamar Lathon .10
88 John Randle .10
89 Darryl Williams .10
91 Erik Kramer .10
92 Ken Dilger .10
93 Dave Meggett .10
94 Jeff Blake .20
97 Irving Spikes .10
98 Mike Alstott .30
99 Vincent Brisby .10
101 Rickey Dudley .10
102 Bert Emanuel .10
105 Eric Bieniemy .10
106 Bryant Westbrook .10
108 Ray Zellars .10
110 Reggie White .20
111 Wesley Walls .10
113 Gary Brown .10
114 Brian Blades .10
115 Alex Van Dyke .10
116 Michael Haynes .10
117 Jessie Armstead .10
118 James Jett .10
119 Troy Drayton .10
120 Craig Heyward .10
121 Steve Atwater .10
123 Karim Abdul .20
125 Frank Sanders .10
126 David Sloan .10
127 Andre Hastings .10
130 Horace Copeland .10
135 Sean Dawkins .10
137 Lamar Smith .10
138 David Palmer .10
139 Steve Young .75
140 Bryan Still .10
141 Keith Byars .10
142 Cris Carter .30
144 Drew Bledsoe 1.00
145 Simeon Rice .10
146 Merton Hanks .10
147 Aeneas Williams .10
148 Rodney Hampton .10
149 Zach Thomas .10
150 Mark Bruener .10
151 Jason Dunn .10
155 Earnest Byner .10
156 Greg Lloyd .10
157 John Mobley .10
160 O.J. McDuffie .20
161 Glenn Foley .20
162 Derrick Brooks .10
163 Dave Brown .10
166 Randal Hill .10
167 Michael Irvin .20
168 Bruce Smith .10
170 Derrick Mayes .10
171 Henry Ellard .10
172 Dana Stubblefield .10
173 Willie McGinest .10
175 Edgar Bennett .10
176 Robert Porcher .10
177 Randall Cunningham .30
178 Jim Everett .10
180 Quentin Coryatt .10
181 William Floyd .10
182 Jason Sehorn .10
183 Carnell Lake .10
184 Dexter Coakley .10
185 Derrick Alexander .10
186 Johnnie Morton .10
188 Warren Moon .20
189 Todd Collins .10
190 Ken Norton Jr. .10
191 Terry Glenn .30
193 Jerry Rice 1.00
194 James Stewart .10
196 Eric Green .10
198 Willie Green .10
200 Brett Perriman .10
201 Darnay Scott .10
203 Joe Aska .10
204 Darrien Gordon .10
205 Herman Moore .20
206 Curtis Martin .50
207 Derek Loville .10
208 Dale Carter .10
209 Heath Shuler .20
210 Jonathan Ogden .10
211 Leslie Shepherd .10
212 Tony Boselli .10
213 Eric Metcalf .10
214 Neil Smith .10
215 Anthony Miller .10
216 Jeff George .20
217 Charles Way .10
218 Mario Bates .10
222 Kyle Brady .10
228 Chris Warren .10
229 Jackie Harris .10
233 *Peyton Manning* 8.00
251 *Ryan Leaf* 5.00

1998 Score Rookie Preview Star Salute

Singles from this set were printed on silver foil stock and inserted 1:35 packs.

MT
Complete Set (20): 120.00
Common Player: 4.00
1 Terrell Davis 15.00
2 Barry Sanders 20.00
3 Steve Young 6.00
4 Drew Bledsoe 8.00
5 Kordell Stewart 8.00
6 Emmitt Smith 15.00
7 Dorsey Levens 4.00
8 Corey Dillon 4.00
9 Jerome Bettis 4.00
10 Herman Moore 4.00
11 Brett Favre 20.00
12 Antonio Freeman 4.00
13 Mark Brunell 8.00
14 John Elway 12.00
15 Terry Glenn 4.00
16 Warrick Dunn 7.00
17 Eddie George 8.00
18 Troy Aikman 10.00
19 Deion Sanders 4.00
20 Jerry Rice 10.00

1999 Score

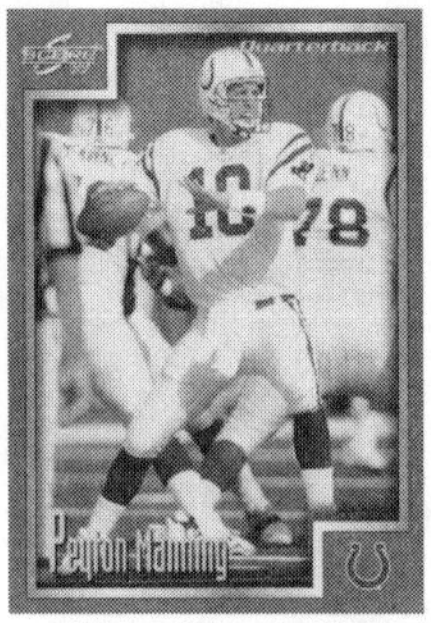

This is a 275-card set that had 55 short-printed cards found 1:3 hobby packs and 1:9 retail packs. The short-prints were of 40 Rookies, 10 All-Pros and 5 Great Combos. The base set is divided into three colors like the first set was in 1989. Red, blue and green borders with the short- prints in green. Inserts include: Showcase, Artist's Proofs, Reprints, Reprint Autographs, Complete Players, Franchise, Future Franchise, Millenium Men, Numbers Game, Rookie Preview Autographs, Scoring Core and Settle the Score.

MT
Complete Set (275): 150.00
Common Player: .10
Minor Stars: .20
Common Rookie (221-260): 1.00
Common All-Pros (261-270): 1.00
Inserted 1:3
Hobby Pack (10): 3.00
Hobby Wax Box (36): 95.00
Retail Pack (10): 1.50
Retail Wax Box (36): 40.00
1 Randy Moss 2.50
2 Randall Cunningham .50
3 Cris Carter .50
4 Robert Smith .20
5 Jake Reed .10
6 Leroy Hoard .10
7 John Randle .10
8 Brett Favre 2.00
9 Antonio Freeman .50
10 Dorsey Levens .20
11 Robert Brooks .20
12 Derrick Mayes .10
13 Mark Chmura .20
14 Darick Holmes .10
15 Vonnie Holliday .20
16 Mike Alstott .50
17 Warrick Dunn .75
18 Trent Dilfer .20
19 Jacquez Green .20
20 Reidel Anthony .20
21 Warren Sapp .10
22 Bert Emanuel .10
23 Curtis Enis .50
24 Curtis Conway .20
25 Bobby Engram .10
26 Erik Kramer .10
27 Moses Moreno .10
28 Edgar Bennett .10
29 Barry Sanders 2.00
30 Charlie Batch .75
31 Herman Moore .50
32 Johnnie Morton .20
33 Germane Crowell .20
34 Terry Fair .10
35 Gary Brown .10
36 Kent Graham .10
37 Kerry Collins .20
38 Charles Way .10
39 Tiki Barber .20
40 Ike Hilliard .10
41 Joe Jurevicius .20
42 Michael Strahan .10
43 Jason Sehorn .10
44 Brad Johnson .50
45 Terry Allen .20
46 Skip Hicks .50
47 Michael Westbrook .20
48 Leslie Shepherd .10
49 Stephen Alexander .10
50 Albert Connell .10
51 Darrell Green .10
52 Jake Plummer 1.00
53 Adrian Murrell .20
54 Frank Sanders .20
55 Rob Moore .20
56 Larry Centers .10
57 Simeon Rice .10
58 Andre Wadsworth .20
59 Duce Staley .10
60 Charles Johnson .10
61 Charlie Garner .10
62 Bobby Hoying .20
63 Darryl Johnston .10
64 Emmitt Smith 1.50
65 Troy Aikman 1.00
66 Michael Irvin .20
67 Deion Sanders .50
68 Chris Warren .20
69 Darren Woodson .10
70 Rod Woodson .10
71 Travis Jervey .10
72 Jerry Rice 1.00
73 Terrell Owens .50
74 Steve Young .75
75 Garrison Hearst .20
76 J.J. Stokes .20
77 Ken Norton .10
78 R.W. McQuarters .10
79 Bryant Young .10
80 Jamal Anderson .50
81 Chris Chandler .20
82 Terrance Mathis .10
83 Tim Dwight .50
84 O.J. Santiago .10
85 Chris Calloway .10
86 Keith Brooking .10
87 Eddie Kennison .10
88 Willie Roaf .10
89 Cameron Cleeland .20
90 Lamar Smith .10
91 Sean Dawkins .10
92 Tim Biakabutuka .20
93 Muhsin Muhammad .10
94 Steve Beuerlein .10
95 Rae Carruth .10
96 Wesley Walls .10
97 Kevin Greene .10
98 Trent Green .50
99 Tony Banks .20
100 Greg Hill .10
101 Robert Holcombe .20
102 Isaac Bruce .30
103 Amp Lee .10
104 Az-Zahir Hakim .20
105 Warren Moon .20
106 Jeff George .20
107 Raghib Ismail .10
108 Kordell Stewart .75
109 Jerome Bettis .20
110 Courtney Hawkins .10
111 Chris Fuamatu-Ma'afala .20
112 Levon Kirkland .10
113 Hines Ward .20
114 Will Blackwell .10
115 Corey Dillon .50
116 Carl Pickens .20
117 Neil O'Donnell .20
118 Jeff Blake .20
119 Darnay Scott .20
120 Takeo Spikes .10
121 Steve McNair .75
122 Frank Wycheck .10
123 Eddie George .75
124 Chris Sanders .10
125 Yancy Thigpen .20
126 Kevin Dyson .20
127 Blaine Bishop .10
128 Fred Taylor 1.00
129 Mark Brunell .75
130 Jimmy Smith .20
131 Keenan McCardell .10
132 Kyle Brady .10
133 Tavian Banks .20
134 James Stewart .10
135 Kevin Hardy .10
136 Jonathan Quinn .10
137 Jermaine Lewis .20
138 Priest Holmes .50
139 Scott Mitchell .20
140 Eric Zeier .10
141 Patrick Johnson .20
142 Ray Lewis .10
143 Terry Kirby .10
144 Ty Detmer .10
145 Irv Smith .10
146 Chris Spielman .10
147 Antonio Langham .10
148 Dan Marino 1.50
149 O.J. McDuffie .20
150 Oronde Gadsden .20
151 Karim Abdul .30
152 Yatil Green .10
153 Zach Thomas .20
154 John Avery .20
155 Lamar Thomas .10
156 Drew Bledsoe .75
157 Terry Glenn .30
158 Ben Coates .20
159 Shawn Jefferson .10
160 Cedric Shaw .10
161 Tony Simmons .20
162 Ty Law .10
163 Robert Edwards .30
164 Curtis Martin .50
165 Keyshawn Johnson .50
166 Vinny Testaverde .20
167 Aaron Glenn .10
168 Wayne Chrebet .30
169 Dedric Ward .10
170 Peyton Manning 1.50
171 Marshall Faulk .50
172 Marvin Harrison .20
173 Jerome Pathon .20
174 Ken Dilger .10
175 E.G. Green .20
176 Doug Flutie .75
177 Thurman Thomas .20
178 Andre Reed .20
179 Eric Moulds .50
180 Antowain Smith .30
181 Bruce Smith .10
182 Rob Johnson .20
183 Terrell Davis 1.50
184 John Elway 1.50
185 Ed McCaffrey .20
186 Rod Smith .20
187 Shannon Sharpe .20
188 Marcus Nash .20
189 Brian Griese .50
190 Neil Smith .10
191 Bubby Brister .20
192 Ryan Leaf .50
193 Natrone Means .50
194 Mikhael Ricks .20
195 Junior Seau .20
196 Jim Harbaugh .20
197 Bryan Still .10
198 Freddie Jones .10
199 Andre Rison .20
200 Elvis Grbac .20
201 Bam Morris .20
202 Rashaan Shehee .10
203 Kimble Anders .10
204 Donnell Bennett .10
205 Tony Gonzalez .20
206 Derrick Alexander .10
207 Jon Kitna .50
208 Ricky Watters .20
209 Joey Galloway .50
210 Ahman Green .20
211 Shawn Springs .10
212 Michael Sinclair .10
213 Napoleon Kaufman .50
214 Tim Brown .20
215 Charles Woodson .50
216 Harvey Williams .10
217 Jon Ritchie .10
218 Rich Gannon .10
219 Rickey Dudley .20
220 James Jett .10
221 *Tim Couch* 15.00
222 *Ricky Williams* 15.00
223 *Donovan McNabb* 12.00
224 *Edgerrin James* 20.00
225 *Torry Holt* 6.00
226 *Daunte Culpepper* 18.00
227 *Akili Smith* 6.00
228 *Champ Bailey* 5.00
229 *Chris Claiborne* 2.50
230 *Chris McAlister* 2.00
231 *Troy Edwards* 5.00
232 *Jevon Kearse* 6.00
233 *Shaun King* 6.00
234 *David Boston* 6.00
235 *Peerless Price* 5.00
236 *Cecil Collins* 6.00
237 *Rob Konrad* 2.00
238 *Cade McNown* 5.00
239 *Shawn Bryson* 1.00
240 *Kevin Faulk* 5.00
241 *Scott Covington* 2.00
242 *James Johnson* 3.00
243 *Mike Cloud* 2.00
244 *Aaron Brooks* 12.00
245 *Sedrick Irvin* 3.00
246 *Amos Zereoue* 5.00
247 *Jermaine Fazande* 1.00
248 *Joe Germaine* 4.00
249 *Brock Huard* 3.00
250 *Craig Yeast* 1.00
251 *Travis McGriff* 2.00
252 *D'Wayne Bates* 2.00
253 *Na Brown* 1.00
254 *Tai Streets* 2.00
255 *Andy Katzenmoyer* 2.00
256 *Kevin Johnson* 6.00
257 *Joe Montgomery* 2.00
258 *Karsten Bailey* 2.00
259 *De'Mond Parker* 2.00
260 *Reg Kelly* 1.00
261 Eddie George 2.00
262 Jamal Anderson 1.00
263 Barry Sanders 5.00
264 Fred Taylor 3.00
265 Keyshawn Johnson 1.00
266 Jerry Rice 3.50
267 Doug Flutie 2.50
268 Deion Sanders 1.00
269 Randall Cunningham 1.00
270 Steve Young 2.50
271 Terrell Davis, John Elway 5.00
272 Marshall Faulk, Peyton Manning 4.00
273 Brett Favre, Antonio Freeman 5.00
274 Troy Aikman, Emmitt Smith 4.00
275 Cris Carter, Randy Moss 6.00

1999 Score Anniversary Showcase Parallel

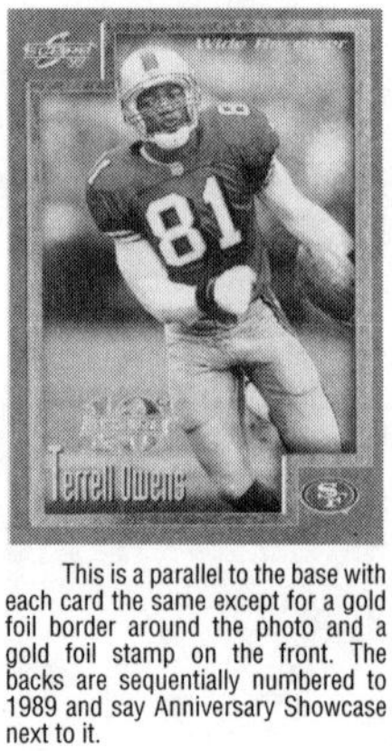

This is a parallel to the base with each card the same except for a gold foil border around the photo and a gold foil stamp on the front. The backs are sequentially numbered to 1989 and say Anniversary Showcase next to it.

MT
Complete Set (275): 450.00
Showcase Cards: 3x-6x
Showcase Rookies: 1.5x
Showcase AP/GC: 2x
Production 1,989 Sets

1999 Score Anniversary Artist Proof Parallel

This is a parallel to the base and each card is sequentially numbered to 10.

MT
Production 10 Sets

1999 Score 1989 Score Reprints

This was a 20-card reprint of the 1989 Score cards that included all of the top rookies and stars from the premiere release. These were only found in hobby product and were sequentially numbered to 1989. The first 150 of each card were autographed.

MT
Complete Set (20): 80.00
Common Player: 3.00
Production 1,989 Sets
1 Barry Sanders 20.00
2 Troy Aikman 10.00
3 John Elway 15.00
4 Cris Carter 8.00
5 Tim Brown 6.00
6 Doug Flutie 5.00
7 Chris Chandler 3.00
8 Thurman Thomas 3.00
9 Steve Young 6.00
10 Dan Marino 12.00
11 Derrick Thomas 3.00
12 Bubby Brister 5.00
13 Jerry Rice 10.00
14 Andre Rison 3.00
15 Randall Cunningham 5.00
16 Vinny Testaverde 3.00
17 Michael Irvin 3.00
18 Rod Woodson 3.00
19 Neil Smith 3.00
20 Deion Sanders 6.00

1999 Score 1989 Score Reprints Autographs

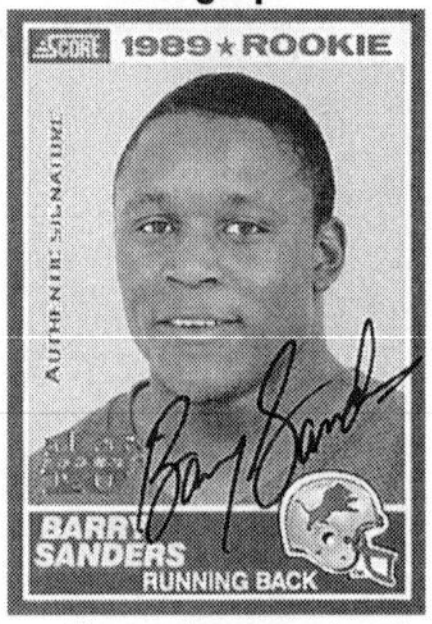

These are the same cards as the Reprint set except for each is autographed and has the words "Authentic Signature" down the side of the fronts of the cards. Only 150 of each were signed.

MT
Complete Set (20): 1700.
Common Player: 40.00
Production 150 Sets
1 Barry Sanders 375.00
2 Troy Aikman 200.00
3 John Elway 300.00
4 Cris Carter 80.00
5 Tim Brown 60.00
6 Doug Flutie 85.00
7 Chris Chandler 40.00
8 Thurman Thomas 40.00
9 Steve Young 85.00
10 Dan Marino 300.00
11 Derrick Thomas 40.00
12 Bubby Brister 60.00
13 Jerry Rice 200.00
14 Andre Rison 40.00
15 Randall Cunningham 75.00
16 Vinny Testaverde 50.00
17 Michael Irvin 40.00
18 Rod Woodson 40.00
19 Neil Smith 40.00
20 Deion Sanders 80.00

Values quoted in this guide reflect the retail price of a card — the price a collector can expect to pay when buying a card from a dealer. The wholesale price — that which a collector can expect to receive from a dealer when selling cards — will be significantly lower, depending on desirability and condition.

1999 Score Complete Players

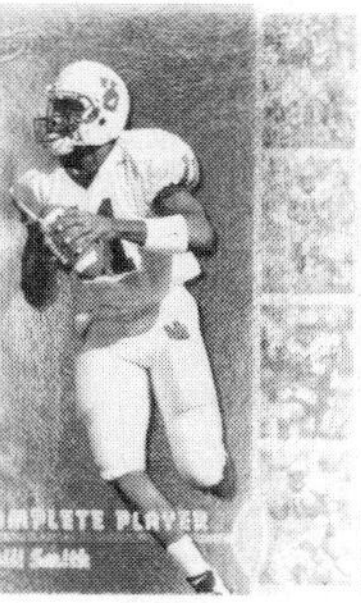

These singles were found in both hobby (1:17) and retail (1:35) product. Each of the 30 cards are printed on foil board with foil stamping and have one large color photo of the player on the front along with four smaller shots in black and white on the side.

		MT
Complete Set (30):		75.00
Common Player:		1.50
Minor Stars:		3.00
Inserted 1:17		
1	Antonio Freeman	1.50
2	Troy Aikman	5.00
3	Jerry Rice	5.00
4	Brett Favre	10.00
5	Cris Carter	3.00
6	Jamal Anderson	1.50
7	John Elway	7.50
8	Mark Brunell	4.00
9	Steve McNair	3.00
10	Kordell Stewart	3.00
11	Drew Bledsoe	4.00
12	Tim Couch	12.00
13	Dan Marino	7.50
14	Akili Smith	5.00
15	Peyton Manning	5.00
16	Jake Plummer	4.00
17	Jerome Bettis	1.50
18	Randy Moss	10.00
19	Keyshawn Johnson	1.50
20	Barry Sanders	10.00
21	Ricky Williams	12.00
22	Emmitt Smith	7.50
23	Corey Dillon	1.50
24	Dorsey Levens	1.50
25	Donovan McNabb	5.00
26	Curtis Martin	1.50
27	Eddie George	3.00
28	Fred Taylor	3.50
29	Steve Young	3.50
30	Terrell Davis	7.50

1999 Score Franchise

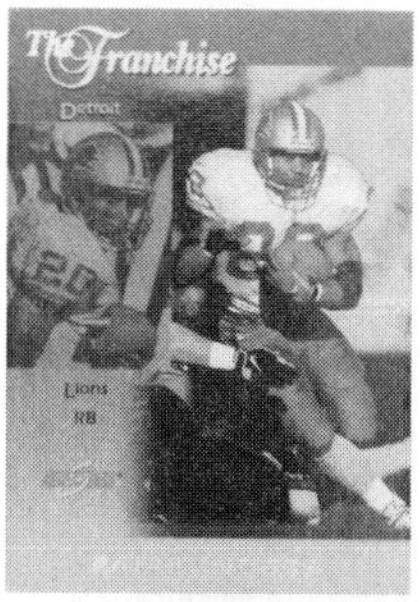

This 31-card set was a retail exclusive (1:35) and picked a star player from each team. Each card is printed on holographic foil board and has a large color photo of the player on the front along with a smaller black and white next to it.

		MT
Complete Set (31):		125.00
Common Player:		2.00
Minor Stars:		4.00
Inserted 1:35		
1	Brett Favre	15.00
2	Randy Moss	15.00
3	Mike Alstott	4.00
4	Barry Sanders	15.00
5	Curtis Enis	4.00
6	Ike Hilliard	2.00
7	Emmitt Smith	10.00
8	Jake Plummer	8.00
9	Brad Johnson	4.00
10	Duce Staley	2.00
11	Jamal Anderson	4.00
12	Steve Young	6.00
13	Eddie Kennison	2.00
14	Isaac Bruce	4.00
15	Muhsin Muhammad	2.00
16	Dan Marino	15.00
17	Drew Bledsoe	7.00
18	Curtis Martin	4.00
19	Doug Flutie	6.00
20	Peyton Manning	10.00
21	Kordell Stewart	5.00
22	Ty Detmer	2.00
23	Corey Dillon	4.00
24	Mark Brunell	7.00
25	Priest Holmes	4.00
26	Eddie George	5.00
27	John Elway	10.00
28	Natrone Means	4.00
29	Tim Brown	2.00
30	Andre Rison	2.00
31	Joey Galloway	4.00

1999 Score Future Franchise

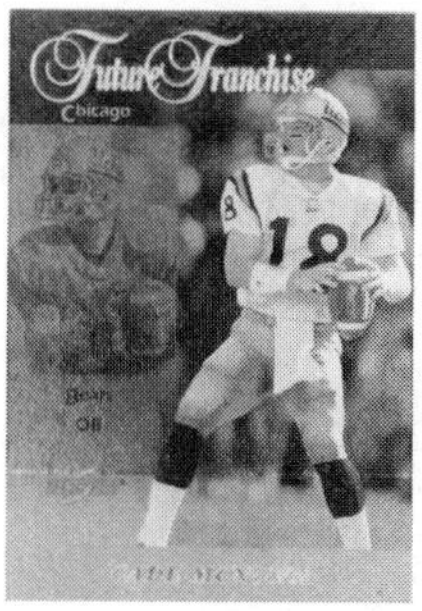

This 31-card set was a hobby exclusive and included a rookie on one side and a star player on the other from the same team. Singles were found 1:35 packs and each were printed on holographic foil board.

		MT
Complete Set (31):		160.00
Common Player:		2.00
Minor Stars:		4.00
Inserted 1:35		
1	Aaron Brooks, Brett Favre	12.00
2	Daunte Culpepper, Randy Moss	15.00
3	Shaun King, Mike Alstott	4.00
4	Sedrick Irvin, Barry Sanders	12.00
5	Cade McNown, Curtis Enis	10.00
6	Joe Montgomery, Ike Hilliard	2.00
7	Wayne McGarity, Emmitt Smith	8.00
8	David Boston, Jake Plummer	6.00
9	Champ Bailey, Brad Johnson	4.00
10	Donovan McNabb, Duce Staley	10.00
11	Reg Kelly, Jamal Anderson	2.00
12	Tai Streets, Steve Young	5.00
13	Ricky Williams, Eddie Kennison	25.00
14	Torry Holt, Isaac Bruce	6.00
15	Mike Rucker, Muhsin Muhammad	2.00
16	James Johnson, Dan Marino	8.00
17	Kevin Faulk, Drew Bledsoe	6.00
18	Randy Thomas, Curtis Martin	4.00
19	Peerless Price, Doug Flutie	5.00
20	Edgerrin James, Peyton Manning	12.00
21	Troy Edwards, Kordell Stewart	5.00
22	Tim Couch, Ty Detmer	25.00
23	Akili Smith, Corey Dillon	10.00
24	Fernando Bryant, Mark Brunell	5.00
25	Chris McAlister, Priest Holmes	4.00
26	Jevon Kearse, Eddie George	5.00
27	Travis McGriff, John Elway	8.00
28	Jermaine Fazande, Natrone Means	2.00
29	Dameane Douglas, Tim Brown	2.00
30	Mike Cloud, Andre Rison	2.00
31	Brock Huard, Joey Galloway	4.00

1999 Score Millenium Men

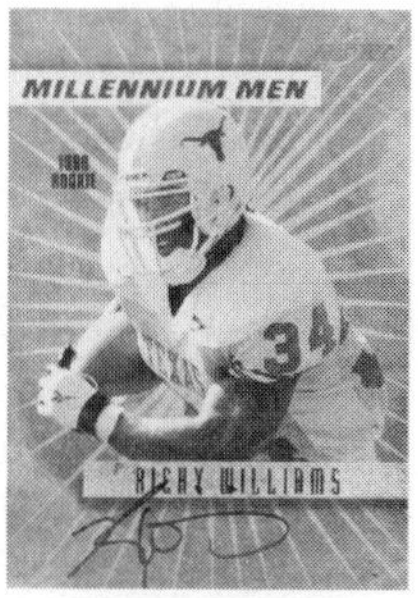

The Millennium Men set has Barry Sanders, representing ten years of NFL excellence with Ricky Williams, representing the outstanding future generation of running backs. Each player has an individual card and a back-to-back single in this 3-card set. Each is sequentially numbered to 1,000 and the first 100 of each are autographed. These were only found in retail product.

		MT
Complete Set (3):		60.00
Common Player:		20.00
Production 1,000 Sets		
1	Barry Sanders	25.00
2	Ricky Williams	20.00
3	Barry Sanders, Ricky Williams	25.00
1AU	Barry Sanders AUTO	375.00
2AU	Ricky Williams AUTO	275.00
3AU	Barry Sanders, Ricky Williams AUTO	500.00

1999 Score Numbers Game

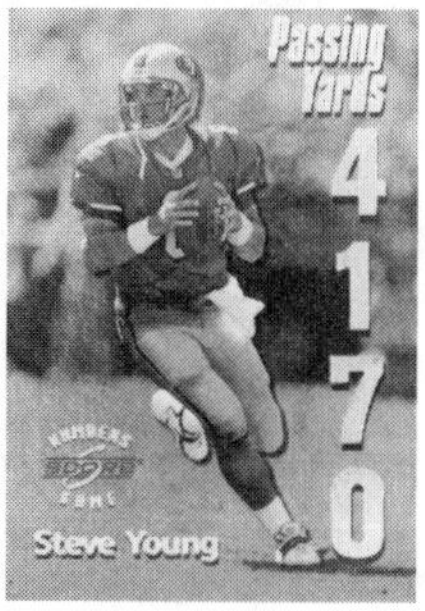

This was a 30-card set that was printed on holographic foil board with gold foil stamping. Each card is sequentially numbered to the player's specific stat.

		MT
Complete Set (30):		75.00
Common Player:		1.50
Numbered to Stat		
1	Brett Favre 4212	7.00
2	Steve Young 4170	3.00
3	Jake Plummer 3737	3.50
4	Drew Bledsoe 3633	3.00
5	Dan Marino 3497	6.00
6	Peyton Manning 3739	6.00
7	Randall Cunningham 3704	1.50
8	John Elway 2806	8.00
9	Doug Flutie 2711	3.00
10	Mark Brunell 2601	3.00
11	Troy Aikman 2330	5.00
12	Terrell Davis 2008	8.00
13	Jamal Anderson 1846	1.50
14	Garrison Hearst 1570	1.50
15	Barry Sanders 1491	12.00
16	Emmitt Smith 1332	7.00
17	Marshall Faulk 1319	3.00
18	Eddie George 1294	4.00
19	Curtis Martin 1287	3.00
20	Fred Taylor 1223	6.00
21	Corey Dillon 1130	3.00
22	Antonio Freeman 1424	3.00
23	Eric Moulds 1368	3.00
24	Randy Moss 1313	12.00
25	Rod Smith 1222	1.50
26	Jerry Rice 1157	7.00
27	Keyshawn Johnson 1131	3.00
28	Terrell Owens 1097	3.00
29	Tim Brown 1012	1.50
30	Cris Carter 1011	3.00

1999 Score Rookie Preview Autographs

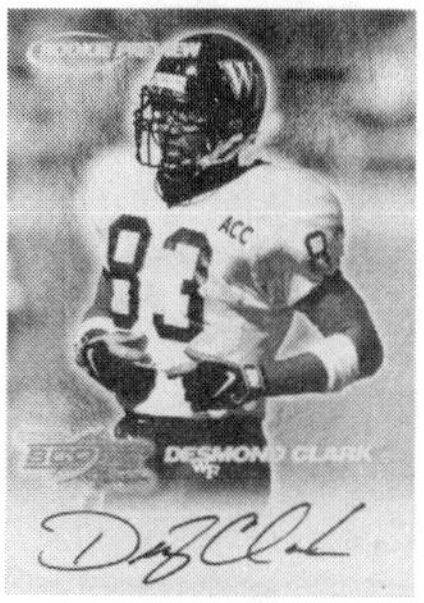

Each of these singles were randomly inserted into hobby packs with each player signing a total of 600 cards. Each card is printed on foil board with the signature on the bottom of the card.

	MT
Common Player:	10.00
Minor Stars:	20.00
Production 600 Sets	
Ricky Williams	150.00
Donovan McNabb	75.00
Edgerrin James	85.00
Torry Holt	50.00
Daunte Culpepper	75.00
Akili Smith	60.00
Champ Bailey	30.00
Chris Claiborne	20.00
Chris McAlister	20.00
Troy Edwards	40.00
Jevon Kearse	35.00
David Boston	50.00
Peerless Price	40.00
Cecil Collins	40.00
Rob Konrad	20.00
Cade McNown	75.00
Shawn Bryson	10.00
Kevin Faulk	50.00
Corby Jones	20.00
James Johnson	30.00
Mike Cloud	20.00
Autrey Denson	25.00
Sedrick Irvin	30.00
Michael Bishop	40.00
Joe Germaine	30.00
De'Mond Parker	20.00
Shaun King	30.00
D'Wayne Bates	20.00
Na Brown	10.00
Tai Streets	25.00
Kevin Johnson	30.00
Jim Kleinsasser	20.00
Darnell McDonald	25.00
Travis McGriff	20.00

1999 Score Scoring Core

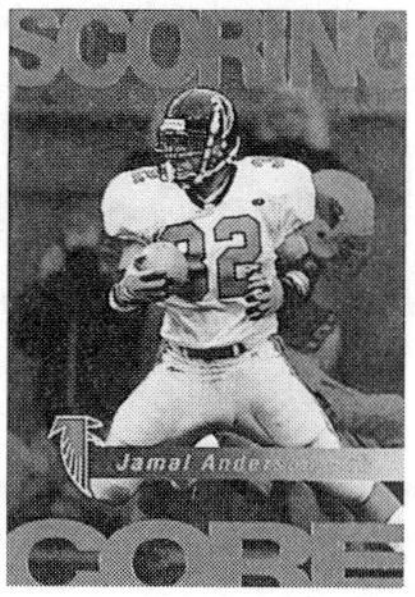

Scoring Core's holographic foil design highlights 30 players who find their way into the end zone. Singles were found 1:17 hobby packs and 1:35 retail.

		MT
Complete Set (30):		75.00
Common Player:		1.50
Minor Stars:		3.00
Inserted 1:17		
1	Antonio Freeman	1.50
2	Troy Aikman	5.00
3	Jerry Rice	5.00
4	Brett Favre	10.00
5	Cris Carter	3.00
6	Jamal Anderson	1.50
7	John Elway	7.50
8	Tim Brown	1.50
9	Mark Brunell	4.00
10	Terrell Owens	3.00
11	Drew Bledsoe	4.00
12	Tim Couch	12.00
13	Dan Marino	7.50
14	Marshall Faulk	1.50
15	Peyton Manning	5.00
16	Jake Plummer	4.00
17	Jerome Bettis	1.50
18	Randy Moss	10.00
19	Charlie Batch	3.00
20	Barry Sanders	10.00
21	Ricky Williams	12.00
22	Emmitt Smith	7.50
23	Joey Galloway	1.50
24	Herman Moore	1.50
25	Natrone Means	1.50
26	Mike Alstott	1.50
27	Eddie George	3.00
28	Fred Taylor	3.50
29	Steve Young	3.50
30	Terrell Davis	7.50

1999 Score Settle the Score

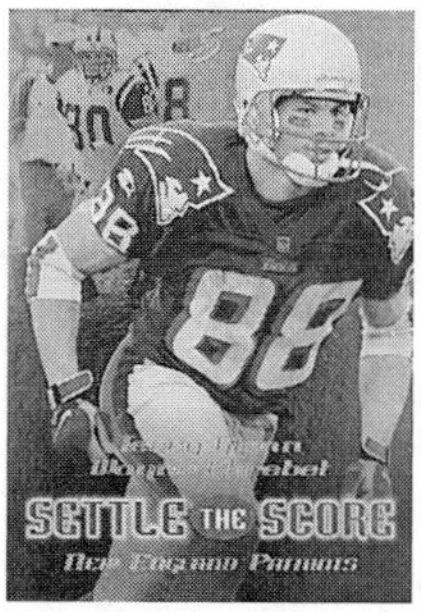

This retail exclusive insert is a dual-sided foil set that matches two players who need to settle the score between each other. Singles were inserted 1:17 packs.

		MT
Complete Set (30):		70.00
Common Player:		1.50
Minor Stars:		3.00
Inserted 1:17 Retail		
1	Randall Cunningham, Brett Favre	10.00
2	Doug Flutie, Dan Marino	7.50
3	Terry Allen, Emmitt Smith	7.50
4	Warrick Dunn, Barry Sanders	10.00
5	Corey Dillon, Eddie George	3.00
6	Drew Bledsoe, Vinny Testaverde	4.00
7	Troy Aikman, Jake Plummer	5.00
8	Jamal Anderson, Terrell Davis	7.50
9	Chris Chandler, John Elway	7.50
10	Mark Brunell, Steve Young	4.00
11	Cris Carter, Herman Moore	1.50
12	Steve McNair, Kordell Stewart	3.00
13	Napoleon Kaufman, Natrone Means	1.50
14	Marshall Faulk, Curtis Martin	1.50
15	Antonio Freeman, Terrell Owens	3.00
16	Wayne Chrebet, Terry Glenn	1.50
17	Garrison Hearst, Dorsey Levens	1.50
18	Jon Kitna, Ryan Leaf	3.00
19	Mike Alstott, Robert Smith	1.50
20	Randy Moss, Jerry Rice	10.00
21	Charlie Batch, Peyton Manning	6.00
22	Jerome Bettis, Fred Taylor	4.00
23	Keyshawn Johnson, Eric Moulds	3.00
24	Tim Couch, Ricky Williams	20.00
25	Isaac Bruce, Carl Pickens	1.50
26	Deion Sanders, Charles Woodson	1.50
27	Tim Brown, Rod Smith	1.50
28	Daunte Culpepper, Donovan McNabb	8.00
29	Joey Galloway, Ed McCaffrey	1.50
30	Karim Abdul, Antowain Smith	1.50

1999 Score Supplemental

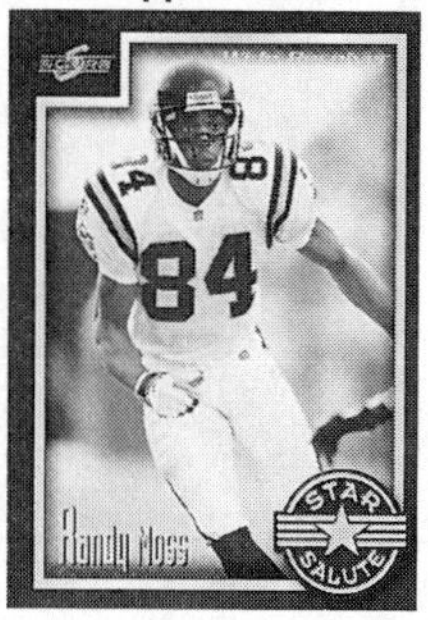

This was a 110-card set that could only be found in factory set form. The set included 24 Mid-Season Updates, 20 Star Salutes and 66 new Rookies. Each set included two insert cards. Inserts included Behind the Numbers, Inscriptions, Quantum Leaf Previews and Zenith Z-Team. SRP was $24.99 per factory set.

		MT
Complete Set (110):		35.00
Common Player:		.10
Minor Stars:		.20
Common Rookie:		.50
1	*Chris Griesen*	2.00
2	*Sherdrick Bonner*	1.00
3	*Joel Makovicka*	2.00
4	*Andy McCullough*	1.00
5	*Jeff Paulk*	1.50
6	*Brandon Stokley*	1.50
7	*Sheldon Jackson*	1.00
8	*Bobby Collins*	2.00
9	*Kamil Loud*	1.00
10	*Antoine Winfield*	1.50
11	*Jerry Azumah*	1.00
12	*James Allen*	3.00
13	*Nick Williams*	1.00
14	*Michael Basnight*	1.00
15	*Damon Griffin*	1.50
16	*Ronnie Powell*	1.50
17	*Darrin Chiaverini*	2.00
18	*Mark Campbell*	1.00
19	*Mike Lucky*	1.00
20	*Wane McGarity*	2.00
21	*Jason Tucker*	3.00
22	*Ebenezer Ekuban*	1.50
23	*Robert Thomas*	1.00
24	*Dat Nguyen*	1.50
25	*Olandis Gary*	5.00
26	*Desmond Clark*	1.00
27	*Andre Cooper*	1.00
28	*Chris Watson*	1.25
29	*Al Wilson*	1.50
30	*Cory Sauter*	1.00
31	*Brock Olivo*	.50
32	*Basil Mitchell*	1.50
33	*Matt Snider*	.50
34	*Antwan Edwards*	1.50
35	*Mike McKenzie*	1.50
36	*Terrence Wilkins*	4.00
37	*Fernando Bryant*	1.00
38	*Larry Parker*	1.00
39	*Autry Denson*	2.00
40	*Jim Kleinsasser*	2.00
41	*Michael Bishop*	2.50
42	*Andy Katzenmoyer*	1.50
43	*Brett Bech*	1.00
44	*Sean Bennett*	1.50
45	*Dan Campbell*	.50
46	*Ray Lucas*	3.00
47	*Scott Dreisbach*	1.50
48	*Cecil Martin*	1.50
49	*Dameane Douglas*	1.00
50	*Jed Weaver*	.50
51	*Jerame Tuman*	1.00
52	*Steve Heiden*	.50
53	*Jeff Garcia*	8.00
54	*Terry Jackson*	1.50
55	*Charlie Rogers*	1.00
56	*Lamar King*	.50
57	*Kurt Warner*	15.00
58	*Dre' Bly*	1.00
59	*Justin Watson*	1.00
60	*Rabih Abdullah*	.50
61	*Martin Gramatica*	1.00
62	*Darnell McDonald*	2.00
63	*Anthony McFarland*	1.00
64	*Larry Brown*	.50
65	*Kevin Daft*	1.50
66	*Mike Sellers*	.50
67	Ken Oxendine	.20
68	Errict Rhett	.20
69	Stoney Case	.10
70	Jonathon Linton	.20
71	Marcus Robinson	1.50
72	Shane Matthews	.20
73	Cade McNown	3.00
74	Akili Smith	3.00
75	Karim Abdul	.20
76	Tim Couch	6.00
77	Kevin Johnson	2.00
78	Ron Rivers	.10
79	Bill Schroeder	.10
80	Edgerrin James	8.00
81	Cecil Collins	2.00
82	Matthew Hatchette	.20
83	Daunte Culpepper	3.00
84	Ricky Williams	6.00
85	Tyrone Wheatley	.20
86	Donovan McNabb	3.00
87	Marshall Faulk	.50
88	Torry Holt	2.00
89	Stephen Davis	.50
90	Brad Johnson	.50
91	Jake Plummer	.50
92	Emmitt Smith	1.00
93	Troy Aikman	1.00
94	John Elway	1.00
95	Terrell Davis	1.00
96	Barry Sanders	1.50
97	Brett Favre	1.50
98	Antonio Freeman	.50
99	Peyton Manning	1.50
100	Fred Taylor	1.00
101	Mark Brunell	.50
102	Dan Marino	1.00
103	Randy Moss	1.50
104	Cris Carter	.50
105	Drew Bledsoe	.75
106	Terry Glenn	.40
107	Keyshawn Johnson	.40
108	Jerry Rice	1.00
109	Steve Young	.75
110	Eddie George	.50

1999 Score Supplemental Behind The Numbers

This 30-card insert included both veterans and rookies. Each single was printed on holographic foil board with foil stamping. Singles were sequentially numbered to 1,000. A parallel Gold version was also issued with each card numbered to the player's jersey number.

		MT
Complete Set (30):		250.00
Common Player:		5.00
Production 1,000 Sets		
1	Kurt Warner	30.00
2	Tim Couch	20.00
3	Randy Moss	20.00
4	Brett Favre	20.00
5	Marvin Harrison	5.00
6	Terry Glenn	5.00
7	John Elway	15.00
8	Troy Aikman	12.00
9	Steve McNair	5.00
10	Kordell Stewart	5.00
11	Drew Bledsoe	8.00
12	Jon Kitna	5.00
13	Dan Marino	15.00
14	Jerry Rice	12.00
15	Edgerrin James	30.00
16	Jake Plummer	8.00
17	Antonio Freeman	5.00
18	Peyton Manning	15.00
19	Keyshawn Johnson	5.00
20	Barry Sanders	20.00
21	Cris Carter	5.00
22	Emmitt Smith	15.00
23	Steve Young	8.00
24	Ricky Williams	20.00
25	Doug Flutie	8.00
26	Mark Brunell	8.00
27	Eddie George	5.00
28	Fred Taylor	12.00
29	Donovan McNabb	12.00
30	Terrell Davis	15.00

1999 Score Supplemental Inscriptions

This 30-card insert included autographs of both past and present players. The never-released 1997 Inscriptions of Barry Sanders was randomly inserted into this product. The rest of the singles were found at one in three boxes.

		MT
Complete Set (30):		1000.
Common Player:		15.00
Minor Stars:		30.00
1	Eric Moulds	30.00
2	Chris Chandler	15.00
3	Thurman Thomas	30.00
4	Tim Brown	30.00
5	Priest Holmes	30.00
6	Wesley Walls	15.00
7	Corey Dillon	30.00
8	Duce Staley	30.00
9	Natrone Means	30.00
10	Isaac Bruce	30.00
11	Joey Galloway	30.00
12	Skip Hicks	30.00
13	Terrell Owens	30.00
14	Eric Moss	15.00
15	Kurt Warner	200.00
16	Johnny Unitas	125.00
17	Bart Starr	150.00
18	Earl Campbell	50.00
19	Jim Brown	150.00
20	Vinny Testaverde	30.00
21	Kordell Stewart	40.00
22	Steve McNair	40.00

23	Stephen Davis	30.00
24	Ricky Williams	125.00
25	Marvin Harrison	40.00
26	Brad Johnson	30.00
27	Dorsey Levens	30.00
28	Jon Kitna	30.00
29	Brian Griese	40.00
30	Tim Biakabutuka	15.00

1999 Score Supplemental Quantum Leaf Previews

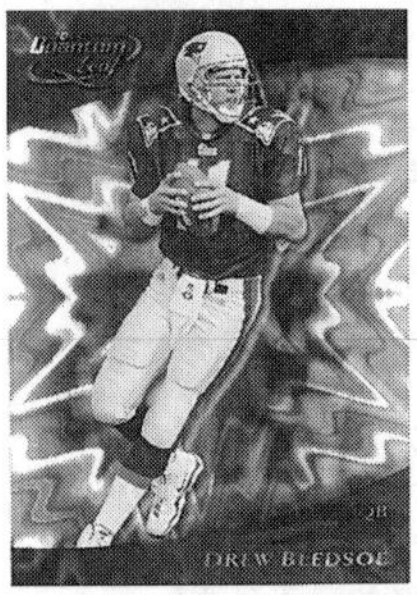

This 18-card insert gave collectors a look at the first 2000 release. Each player was pictured on dot matrix hologram foil and randomly inserted.

		MT
Complete Set (18):		150.00
Common Player:		3.00
1	Barry Sanders	15.00
2	Ricky Williams	15.00
3	Terrell Davis	12.00
4	John Elway	12.00
5	Edgerrin James	25.00
6	Tim Couch	15.00
7	Peyton Manning	12.00
8	Kurt Warner	25.00
9	Randy Moss	15.00
10	Dan Marino	12.00
11	Brett Favre	15.00
12	Eddie George	3.00
13	Marvin Harrison	3.00
14	Jerry Rice	10.00
15	Emmitt Smith	12.00
16	Keyshawn Johnson	3.00
17	Drew Bledsoe	7.00
18	Marshall Faulk	3.00

1999 Score Supplemental Zenith Z-Team

This 20-card insert included the cream of the crop in the NFL. Each was pictured on clear plastic with holographic foil stamping and were sequentially numbered to 100.

		MT
Complete Set (20):		600.00
Common Player:		15.00
Production 100 Sets		
1	Steve Young	20.00
2	Barry Sanders	60.00
3	Fred Taylor	30.00
4	Marshall Faulk	15.00
5	Emmitt Smith	45.00
6	Brett Favre	60.00
7	Troy Aikman	30.00
8	Terrell Davis	45.00
9	Edgerrin James	85.00
10	Drew Bledsoe	20.00
11	Dan Marino	45.00
12	Randy Moss	60.00
13	Ricky Williams	60.00
14	Mark Brunell	20.00
15	Jake Plummer	25.00
16	Jerry Rice	30.00
17	Peyton Manning	45.00
18	Tim Couch	60.00
19	Eddie George	15.00
20	John Elway	45.00

2000 Score

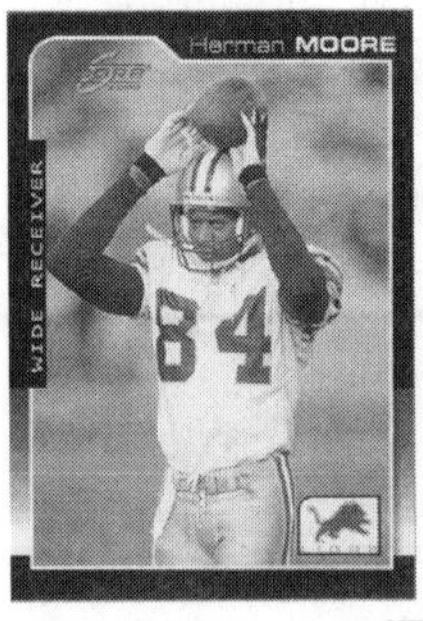

		MT
Complete Set (329):		175.00
Common Player:		.10
Minor Stars:		.20
Common Player (#221-275):		.20
Inserted 1:2		
Common Rookie:		1.50
Inserted 1:4		
Pack (10):		2.00
Wax Box (36):		50.00
1	Michael Pittman	.10
2	Jake Plummer	.50
3	Rob Moore	.20
4	David Boston	.50
5	Frank Sanders	.20
6	Jamal Anderson	.50
7	Chris Chandler	.20
8	Tim Dwight	.50
9	Terance Mathis	.10
10	Shawn Jefferson	.10
11	Ashley Ambrose	.10
12	Peter Boulware	.10
13	Priest Holmes	.50
14	Tony Banks	.30
15	Qadry Ismail	.10
16	Shannon Sharpe	.20
17	Rod Woodson	.10
18	Matt Stover	.10
19	Michael McCrary	.10
20	Doug Flutie	.50
21	Rob Johnson	.30
22	Eric Moulds	.50
23	Peerless Price	.50
24	Jonathon Linton	.20
25	Antowain Smith	.50
26	Jay Riemersma	.10
27	Muhsin Muhammad	.20
28	Tim Biakabutuka	.20
29	Patrick Jeffers	.50
30	Wesley Walls	.20
31	Steve Beuerlein	.30
32	John Kasay	.10
33	Curtis Enis	.50
34	Cade McNown	.75
35	Marcus Robinson	.50
36	Bobby Engram	.10
37	Eddie Kennison	.10
38	Akili Smith	.50
39	Carl Pickens	.20
40	Corey Dillon	.50
41	Darnay Scott	.20
42	Errict Rhett	.20
43	Karim Abdul	.10
44	Tim Couch	1.25
45	Kevin Johnson	.50
46	Darrin Chiaverini	.10
47	Terry Kirby	.10
48	Jason Tucker	.20
49	Raghib Ismail	.10
50	Joey Galloway	.50
51	Michael Irvin	.20
52	Troy Aikman	1.00
53	Emmitt Smith	1.50
54	David LaFleur	.10
55	Trevor Pryce	.10
56	Brian Griese	.50
57	Olandis Gary	.50
58	Terrell Davis	1.50
59	Rod Smith	.30
60	Ed McCaffrey	.30
61	Gus Frerotte	.20
62	Jason Elam	.10
63	Kavika Pittman	.10
64	James Stewart	.30
65	Charlie Batch	.50
66	Johnnie Morton	.20
67	Herman Moore	.30
68	Germane Crowell	.20
69	Barry Sanders	2.00
70	Chris Claiborne	.10
71	Brett Favre	2.00
72	Antonio Freeman	.50
73	Dorsey Levens	.50
74	De'Mond Parker	.20
75	Corey Bradford	.20
76	Basil Mitchell	.10
77	Bill Schroeder	.10
78	Peyton Manning	1.50
79	Marvin Harrison	.50
80	Terrence Wilkins	.20
81	Edgerrin James	2.00
82	E.G. Green	.10
83	Chad Bratzke	.10
84	Mark Brunell	.75
85	Fred Taylor	.75
86	Jimmy Smith	.30
87	Keenan McCardell	.20
88	Kevin Hardy	.10
89	Aaron Beasley	.10
90	Elvis Grbac	.20
91	Derrick Alexander	.10
92	Tony Gonzalez	.20
93	Donnell Bennett	.10
94	Warren Moon	.20
95	Andre Rison	.20
96	James Hasty	.10
97	Dan Marino	1.50
98	Thurman Thomas	.20
99	James Johnson	.10
100	O.J. McDuffie	.20
101	Tony Martin	.10
102	Oronde Gadsden	.20
103	Zach Thomas	.20
104	Sam Madison	.10
105	Jay Fiedler	.20
106	Damon Huard	.50
107	Robert Smith	.50
108	Leroy Hoard	.10
109	Randy Moss	1.75
110	Cris Carter	.50
111	Daunte Culpepper	.75
112	John Randle	.10
113	Randall Cunningham	.50
114	Gary Anderson	.10
115	Drew Bledsoe	.75
116	Terry Glenn	.50
117	Kevin Faulk	.30
118	Terry Allen SP	15.00
119	Adam Vinatieri	.10
120	Ty Law	.10
121	Lawyer Milloy	.10
122	Troy Brown	.10
123	Ben Coates	.20
124	Cameron Cleeland	.20
125	Jeff Blake	.20
126	Ricky Williams	1.25
127	Jake Reed	.20
128	*Jake Delhomme*	2.00
129	Andrew Glover	.10
130	Keith Poole	.10
131	Joe Horn	.10
132	Kerry Collins	.20
133	Joe Montgomery	.10
134	Sean Bennett	.10
135	Amani Toomer	.20
136	Ike Hilliard	.20
137	Joe Jurevicius	.10
138	Tiki Barber	.20
139	Victor Green	.10
140	Ray Lucas	.50
141	Vinny Testaverde	.30
142	Curtis Martin	.50
143	Wayne Chrebet	.30
144	Tyrone Wheatley	.20
145	Rich Gannon	.20
146	Napoleon Kaufman	.50
147	Tim Brown	.30
148	Rickey Dudley	.20
149	Charles Woodson	.50
150	James Jett	.10
151	Duce Staley	.50
152	Charles Johnson	.10
153	Donovan McNabb	.75
154	Troy Vincent	.10
155	Troy Edwards	.50
156	Jerome Bettis	.50
157	Kordell Stewart	.50
158	Richard Huntley	.20
159	Hines Ward	.20
160	Levon Kirkland	.10
161	Ryan Leaf	.30
162	Jim Harbaugh	.20
163	Jermaine Fazande	.20
164	Natrone Means	.20
165	Junior Seau	.20
166	Curtis Conway	.20
167	Freddie Jones	.20
168	Jeff Graham	.10
169	Terrell Owens	.50
170	Jeff Garcia	.50
171	Jerry Rice	1.00
172	Steve Young	.75
173	Garrison Hearst	.30
174	Charlie Garner	.20
175	Fred Beasley	.10
176	Bryant Young	.10
177	Derrick Mayes	.20
178	Sean Dawkins	.20
179	Jon Kitna	.50
180	Ricky Watters	.30
181	Charlie Rogers	.10
182	Kurt Warner	2.50
183	Marshall Faulk	.50
184	Isaac Bruce	.50
185	Az-Zahir Hakim	.20
186	Trent Green	.20
187	Jeff Wilkins	.10
188	Torry Holt	.50
189	London Fletcher	.10
190	Robert Holcombe	.10
191	Todd Lyght	.10
192	Keyshawn Johnson	.50
193	Derrick Brooks	.10
194	Warren Sapp	.20
195	Shaun King	.75
196	Warrick Dunn	.50
197	Mike Alstott	.50
198	Jacquez Green	.20
199	Reidel Anthony	.20
200	Martin Gramatica	.10
201	Donnie Abraham	.10
202	Steve McNair	.60
203	Eddie George	.60
204	Jevon Kearse	.60
205	Frank Wycheck	.10
206	Kevin Dyson	.20
207	Yancey Thigpen	.20
208	Al Del Greco	.10
209	Jeff George	.30
210	Adrian Murrell	.20
211	Brad Johnson	.50
212	Stephen Davis	.50
213	Stephen Alexander	.10
214	Michael Westbrook	.30
215	Darrell Green	.10
216	Champ Bailey	.30
217	Albert Connell	.10
218	Larry Centers	.10
219	Bruce Smith	.10
220	Deion Sanders	.30
221	Ricky Williams	1.00
222	Edgerrin James	2.00
223	Tim Couch	1.00
224	Cade McNown	.75
225	Olandis Gary	.50
226	Torry Holt	.50
227	Donovan McNabb	.75
228	Shaun King	.75
229	Kevin Johnson	.50
230	Kurt Warner	3.00
231	Tony Gonzalez	.20
232	Frank Wycheck	.20
233	Eddie George	.75
234	Mark Brunell	1.00
235	Corey Dillon	.50
236	Peyton Manning	2.00
237	Keyshawn Johnson	.50
238	Rich Gannon	.20
239	Terry Glenn	.20
240	Tony Brackens	.20
241	Edgerrin James	2.00
242	Tim Brown	.30
243	Michael Strahan	.20
244	Kurt Warner	3.00
245	Brad Johnson	.50
246	Aeneas Williams	.20
247	Marshall Faulk	.50
248	Dexter Coakley	.20
249	Warren Sapp	.20
250	Mike Alstott	.50
251	David Sloan	.20
252	Cris Carter	.50
253	Muhsin Muhammad	.30
254	Isaac Bruce	.50
255	Wesley Walls	.20
256	Steve Beuerlein	.30
257	Kurt Warner	3.00
258	Peyton Manning	2.00
259	Brad Johnson	.50
260	Edgerrin James	2.00
261	Curtis Martin	.50
262	Stephen Davis	.50
263	Emmitt Smith	1.50
264	Marvin Harrison	.50
265	Jimmy Smith	.30
266	Randy Moss	2.00
267	Marcus Robinson	.50
268	Kevin Carter	.20
269	Simeon Rice	.20
270	Robert Porcher	.20
271	Jevon Kearse	.60
272	Mike Vanderjagt	.20
273	Olindo Mare	.20
274	Todd Peterson	.20
275	Mike Hollis	.20
276	*Mike Anderson 500*	150.00
277	*Peter Warrick*	7.00
278	*Courtney Brown*	2.00
279	*Plaxico Burress*	4.00
280	*Corey Simon*	2.00
281	*Thomas Jones*	3.00
282	*Travis Taylor*	2.50
283	*Shaun Alexander*	5.00
284	*Patrick Pass 500*	25.00
285	*Chris Redman*	3.00
286	*Chad Pennington*	6.00
287	*Jamal Lewis*	10.00
288	*Brian Urlacher*	5.00
289	*Bubba Franks*	2.00
290	*Dez White*	2.00
291	*Frank Moreau 500*	30.00
292	*Ron Dayne*	8.00
293	*Sylvester Morris*	4.00
294	*R. Jay Soward*	2.00
295	*Deon Dyer*	1.50
296	*Spergon Wynn 500*	25.00
297	*Rondell Mealey*	2.00
298	*Travis Prentice*	2.50
299	*Darrell Jackson*	2.50
300	*Giovanni Carmazzi*	2.00
301	*Anthony Lucas*	1.50
302	*Danny Farmer*	2.00
303	*Dennis Northcutt*	2.00
304	*Troy Walters*	1.50
305	*Laveranues Coles*	2.50
306	*Kwame Cavil*	1.50
307	*Tee Martin*	2.00
308	*J.R. Redmond*	2.00
309	*Tim Rattay*	2.00
310	*Jerry Porter*	2.00
311	*Michael Wiley*	2.00
312	*Reuben Droughns*	1.50
313	*Trung Canidate*	2.00
314	*Shyrone Stith*	1.50
315	*Marc Bulger*	1.50
316	*Tom Brady*	2.00
317	*Doug Johnson*	2.00
318	*Todd Husak*	2.00
319	*Gari Scott*	1.50
320	*Windrell Hayes 500*	25.00
321	*Chris Cole*	1.50
322	*Sammy Morris*	2.00
323	*Trevor Gaylor*	2.00
324	*Jarious Jackson*	2.00
325	*Doug Chapman 500*	30.00
326	*Ron Dugans*	2.00
327	*Ron Dixon 500*	35.00
328	*Joe Hamilton*	2.00
329	*Todd Pinkston*	2.00
330	*Chad Morton*	2.00

2000 Score Final Score Parallel

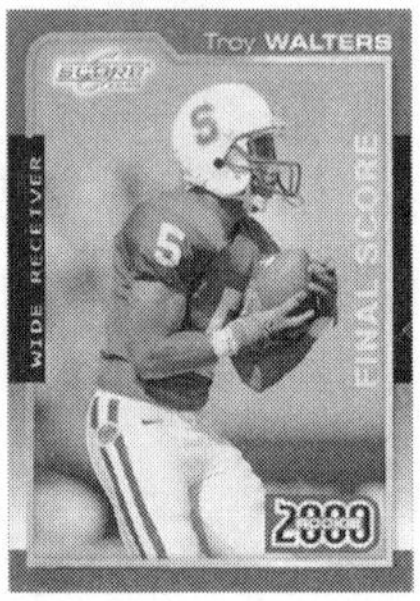

	MT
Cards #'d 25-35:	30x-60x
Subsets #'d 25-35:	15x-30x
Rookies #'d 25-35:	6x-12x
Cards #'d 40-54:	25x-50x
Subsets #'d 40-54:	10x-20x
Rookies #'d 40-54:	5x-10x
Cards #'d to 66:	20x-40x
Subsets #'d to 66:	7x-14x
Rookies #'d to 66:	4x-8x
Card #118 Never Issued	
Production #'d To A 1999 Stat	

2000 Score Scorecard Parallel

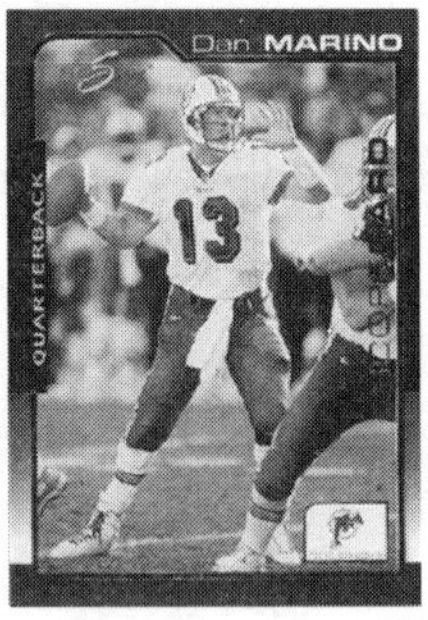

	MT
Complete Set (329):	450.00
Scorecard Cards:	3x-6x
Scorecard Subsets:	2x
Scorecard Rookies:	2x
Card #118 Never Issued	
Production 2,000 Sets	

2000 Score Air Mail

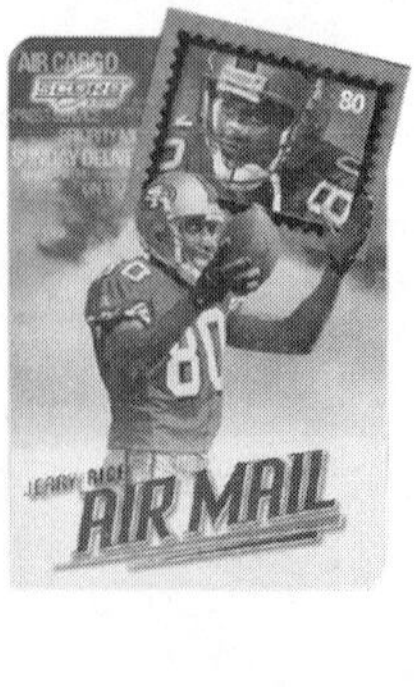

		MT
Complete Set (30):		130.00
Common Player:		2.00
Minor Stars:		4.00
Inserted 1:70		
First Class Cards:		3x-6x
Production 50 Sets		
AM1	Isaac Bruce	4.00
AM2	Cris Carter	4.00
AM3	Tim Dwight	4.00
AM4	Joey Galloway	4.00
AM5	Marvin Harrison	4.00
AM6	Keyshawn Johnson	4.00
AM7	Jon Kitna	4.00
AM8	Steve McNair	4.00
AM9	Eric Moulds	4.00
AM10	Drew Bledsoe	6.00
AM11	John Elway	10.00
AM12	Brett Favre	12.00
AM13	Antonio Freeman	4.00
AM14	Peyton Manning	10.00
AM15	Randy Moss	10.00
AM16	Steve Young	5.00
AM17	Jake Plummer	4.00
AM18	Troy Aikman	8.00
AM19	Mark Brunell	5.00
AM20	Tim Couch	8.00
AM21	Dan Marino	10.00
AM22	Jerry Rice	8.00
AM23	Kevin Johnson	4.00
AM24	Michael Westbrook	2.00
AM25	Kurt Warner	15.00
AM26	Doug Flutie	4.00
AM27	Jimmy Smith	2.00
AM28	Germane Crowell	2.00
AM29	Cade McNown	4.00
AM30	Muhsin Muhammad	2.00

2000 Score Building Blocks

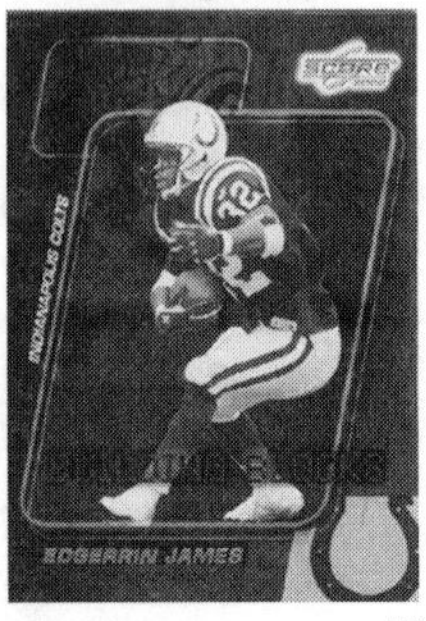

		MT
Complete Set (30):		40.00
Common Player:		.75
Minor Stars:		1.50
Inserted 1:17		
BB1	Cade McNown	1.75
BB2	Peerless Price	.75
BB3	Akili Smith	1.50
BB4	Randy Moss	4.00
BB5	Edgerrin James	5.00
BB6	Kurt Warner	6.00
BB7	Ray Lucas	.75
BB8	Jevon Kearse	1.50
BB9	Torry Holt	1.50
BB10	Ricky Williams	2.50
BB11	Daunte Culpepper	1.50
BB12	Fred Taylor	2.00
BB13	Brian Griese	1.50
BB14	Marcus Robinson	1.50
BB15	David Boston	.75
BB16	James Johnson	.75
BB17	Charlie Batch	1.50
BB18	Jake Plummer	1.50
BB19	Duce Staley	1.50
BB20	Germane Crowell	.75
BB21	Curtis Enis	.75
BB22	Donovan McNabb	1.50
BB23	Tim Couch	2.50
BB24	Stephen Davis	1.50
BB25	Jon Kitna	1.50
BB26	Shaun King	1.75
BB27	Kevin Johnson	1.50
BB28	Peyton Manning	4.00
BB29	Olandis Gary	1.50
BB30	Muhsin Muhammad	.75

2000 Score Complete Players

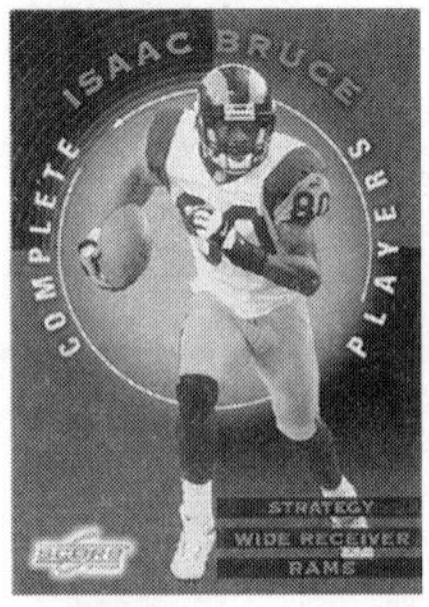

		MT
Complete Set (40):		70.00
Common Player:		.75
Minor Stars:		1.50
Inserted 1:17		
Green Cards:		5x-10x
Inserted 1:359		
Blue Cards:		7x-14x
Inserted 1:718		
CP1	Eric Moulds	1.50
CP2	Tim Couch	2.50
CP3	Marvin Harrison	1.50
CP4	Brett Favre	5.00
CP5	Steve Young	2.00
CP6	Brad Johnson	1.50
CP7	Randy Moss	4.00
CP8	Mark Brunell	2.00
CP9	Steve McNair	1.50
CP10	Donovan McNabb	1.75
CP11	Drew Bledsoe	2.00
CP12	Kurt Warner	6.00
CP13	Dan Marino	4.00
CP14	Muhsin Muhammad	.75
CP15	Jimmy Smith	.75
CP16	Fred Taylor	2.00
CP17	Corey Dillon	1.50
CP18	Peyton Manning	4.00
CP19	Keyshawn Johnson	1.50
CP20	Barry Sanders	5.00
CP21	Brian Griese	1.50
CP22	Emmitt Smith	3.50
CP23	Jerry Rice	3.00
CP24	Joey Galloway	1.50
CP25	Cris Carter	1.50
CP26	Robert Smith	.75
CP27	Eddie George	1.75
CP28	Marshall Faulk	1.50
CP29	Tim Brown	.75
CP30	Terrell Davis	3.50
CP31	Jamal Anderson	1.50
CP32	Edgerrin James	5.00
CP33	Antowain Smith	1.50
CP34	Antonio Freeman	1.50
CP35	Isaac Bruce	1.50
CP36	Stephen Davis	1.50
CP37	Troy Aikman	3.00
CP38	Kevin Johnson	1.50
CP39	Ricky Watters	.75
CP40	Mike Alstott	1.50

2000 Score Franchise

		MT
Complete Set (31):		70.00
Common Player:		1.00
Minor Stars:		2.00
Inserted 1:35 Retail		
F1	Emmitt Smith	5.00
F2	Amani Toomer	1.00
F3	Jake Plummer	2.00
F4	Brad Johnson	2.00
F5	Donovan McNabb	2.50
F6	Jerry Rice	4.00
F7	Jamal Anderson	2.00
F8	Marshall Faulk	2.00
F9	Steve Beuerlein	1.00
F10	Ricky Williams	4.00
F11	Brett Favre	8.00
F12	Barry Sanders	8.00
F13	Randy Moss	8.00
F14	Shaun King	2.50
F15	Cade McNown	2.50
F16	Dan Marino	6.00
F17	Drew Bledsoe	3.00
F18	Curtis Martin	2.00
F19	Peyton Manning	6.00
F20	Eric Moulds	2.00
F21	Mark Brunell	3.00
F22	Akili Smith	2.00
F23	Tim Couch	4.00
F24	Jerome Bettis	2.00
F25	Qadry Ismail	1.00
F26	Eddie George	2.50
F27	Jim Harbaugh	1.00
F28	Terrell Davis	5.00
F29	Elvis Grbac	1.00
F30	Tim Brown	2.00
F31	Jon Kitna	2.00

2000 Score Future Franchise

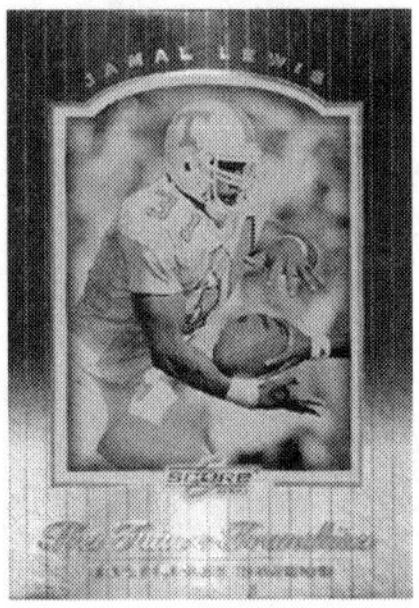

		MT
Complete Set (30):		100.00
Common Player:		1.00
Minor Stars:		2.00
Inserted 1:35 Hobby		
FF1	Michael Wiley, Emmitt Smith	6.00
FF2	Ron Dayne, Amani Toomer	12.00
FF3	Thomas Jones, Jake Plummer	6.00
FF4	Redemption	
FF5	Todd Pinkston, Donovan McNabb	2.50
FF6	Giovanni Carmazzi, Jerry Rice	5.00
7	Mareno Philyaw, Jamal Anderson	2.00
8	Trung Canidate, Marshall Faulk	2.00
9	Deon Grant, Steve Beuerlein	1.00
10	Marc Bulger, Ricky Williams	4.00
11	Bubba Franks, Brett Favre	10.00
12	Reuben Droughns, Barry Sanders	10.00
13	Doug Chapman, Randy Moss	8.00
14	Joe Hamilton, Shaun King	2.50
15	Dez White, Cade McNown	2.50
16	Ben Kelly, Dan Marino	8.00

17 J.R. Redmond, Drew Bledsoe 3.00
18 Chad Pennington, Curtis Martin 8.00
19 Rob Morris, Peyton Manning 7.00
20 Avion Black, Eric Moulds 2.00
21 R. Jay Soward, Mark Brunell 3.00
22 Peter Warrick, Akili Smith 10.00
23 Courtney Brown, Tim Couch 5.00
24 Plaxico Burress, Jerome Bettis 8.00
25 Jamal Lewis, Qadry Ismail 6.00
26 Keith Bulluck, Eddie George 2.00
27 Trevor Gaylor, Jim Harbaugh 1.00
28 Chris Cole, Terrell Davis 7.00
29 Sylvester Morris, Elvis Grbac 2.50
30 Jerry Porter, Tim Brown 2.00
31 Shaun Alexander, Jon Kitna 5.00

2000 Score Numbers Game

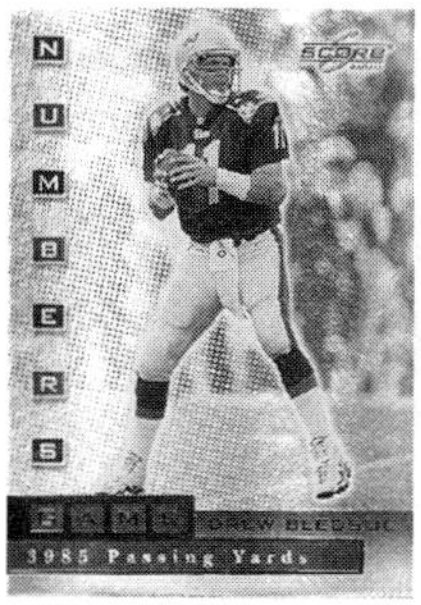

MT
Complete Set (50): 175.00
Common Player: 1.00
Minor Stars: 2.00
Production #'d To Season Stat
1A Kurt Warner 4353 5.00
1B Kurt Warner 325 15.00
2A Steve Beuerlein 4436 1.00
2B Steve Beuerlein 343 2.00
3A Peyton Manning 4135 4.00
3B Peyton Manning 331 12.00
4A Brad Johnson 4005 1.00
4B Brad Johnson 316 3.00
5A Steve McNair 2179 2.00
5B Steve McNair 187 8.00
6A Mark Brunell 3060 2.00
6B Mark Brunell 259 6.00
7A Marvin Harrison 1663 2.00
7B Marvin Harrison 115 6.00
8A Isaac Bruce 1165 2.50
8B Isaac Bruce 77 7.00
9A Cris Carter 1241 2.00
9B Cris Carter 90 7.00
10A Randy Moss 1413 6.00
10B Randy Moss 80 25.00
11A Marcus Robinson 1444 2.00
11B Marcus Robinson 84 8.00
12A Terry Glenn 1147 2.00
12B Terry Glenn 69 7.00
13A Edgerrin James 1553 5.00
13B Edgerrin James 369 15.00
14A Curtis Martin 1464 1.00
14B Curtis Martin 367 3.00
15A Stephen Davis 1405 1.00
15B Stephen Davis 290 3.00
16A Emmitt Smith 1397 4.00
16B Emmitt Smith 329 10.00
17A Marshall Faulk 1381 1.00
17B Marshall Faulk 253 4.00
18A Eddie George 1304 2.00
18B Eddie George 320 4.00
19A Olandis Gary 1159 2.00
19B Olandis Gary 276 5.00
20A Dorsey Levens 1034 1.00
20B Dorsey Levens 279 3.00
21A Robert Smith 1015 1.00
21B Robert Smith 221 3.00
22A Jerome Bettis 1091 1.00
22B Jerome Bettis 299 3.00
23A Corey Dillon 1200 2.00
23B Corey Dillon 263 4.00
24A Drew Bledsoe 3985 2.00
24B Drew Bledsoe 305 6.00
25A Fred Taylor 732 4.00
25B Fred Taylor 159 10.00

2000 Score Rookie Preview Autographs

MT
Complete Set (45): 850.00
Common Player: 10.00
Inserted 1:70 Hobby
Production 300 to 700 Sets
Roll Call Cards: 2x
Production 50 Sets
SR1 Ahmed Plummer 10.00
SR2 Peter Warrick 50.00
SR4 Plaxico Burress 35.00
SR5 Corey Simon 10.00
SR6 Thomas Jones 30.00
SR7 Travis Taylor 25.00
SR8 Shaun Alexander 40.00
SR9 Deon Grant 10.00
SR10 Chris Redman 30.00
SR11 Chad Pennington 50.00
SR12 Jamal Lewis 75.00
SR15 Dez White 15.00
SR16 Ron Dayne 60.00
SR17 Sylvester Morris 30.00
SR18 R. Jay Soward 20.00
SR19 Sherrod Gideon 10.00
SR20 Travis Prentice 25.00
SR21 Darrell Jackson 20.00
SR22 Giovanni Carmazzi 20.00
SR23 Anthony Lucas 10.00
SR24 Danny Farmer 15.00
SR25 Dennis Northcutt 20.00
SR26 Troy Walters 10.00
SR27 Laveranues Coles 20.00
SR28 Kwame Cavil 10.00
SR29 Tee Martin 20.00
SR30 J.R. Redmond 25.00
SR31 Tim Rattay 25.00
SR32 Jerry Porter 15.00
SR33 Michael Wiley 15.00
SR34 Reuben Droughns 10.00
SR35 Trung Canidate 15.00
SR36 Shyrone Stith 10.00
SR37 Marc Bulger 10.00
SR38 Tom Brady 15.00
SR39 Doug Johnson 15.00
SR40 Todd Husak 15.00
SR41 Gari Scott 10.00
SR42 Chafie Fields 10.00
SR43 Sammy Morris 20.00
SR44 Trevor Gaylor 10.00
SR45 Ron Dugans 15.00
SR46 Chris Daniels 10.00
SR47 Joe Hamilton 15.00
SR48 Todd Pinkston 15.00

2000 Score Team 2000

MT
Complete Set (20): 60.00
Common Player: 1.00
Minor Stars: 2.00
Blue Production 1,500 Sets
1:Hobby Box
Gold Cards: 1x
Production #'d To Player's Rookie Year
Randomly Inserted In Retail
Green Cards: 2x-4x
Production 200 Sets
Red Cards: 2x
Production 500 Sets
TM1 Barry Sanders 6.00
TM2 Troy Aikman 4.00
TM3 Cris Carter 2.00
TM4 Emmitt Smith 5.00
TM5 Brett Favre 6.00
TM6 Jimmy Smith 1.00
TM7 Drew Bledsoe 2.50
TM8 Marshall Faulk 2.00
TM9 Steve McNair 2.00
TM10 Marvin Harrison 2.00
TM11 Eddie George 2.25
TM12 Eric Moulds 2.00
TM13 Jake Plummer 2.00
TM14 Antowain Smith 2.00
TM15 Fred Taylor 2.50
TM16 Randy Moss 6.00
TM17 Peyton Manning 5.00
TM18 Ricky Williams 3.00
TM19 Edgerrin James 5.00
TM20 Kurt Warner 8.00

2000 Score Team 2000 Autographs

MT
Common Player: 35.00
Randomly Inserted In Hobby
Production 50 Sets
TM1 Barry Sanders 250.00
TM2 Troy Aikman 150.00
TM3 Cris Carter 70.00
TM4 Emmitt Smith 200.00
TM5 Brett Favre 250.00
TM6 Jimmy Smith 35.00
TM7 Drew Bledsoe 100.00
TM8 Marshall Faulk 70.00
TM9 Steve McNair 70.00
TM10 Marvin Harrison 70.00
TM11 Eddie George 85.00
TM12 Eric Moulds 35.00
TM13 Jake Plummer 70.00
TM14 Antowain Smith 35.00
TM15 Fred Taylor 85.00
TM16 Randy Moss 200.00
TM17 Peyton Manning 200.00
TM18 Ricky Williams 175.00
TM19 Edgerrin James 225.00
TM20 Kurt Warner 275.00

2001 Score Select

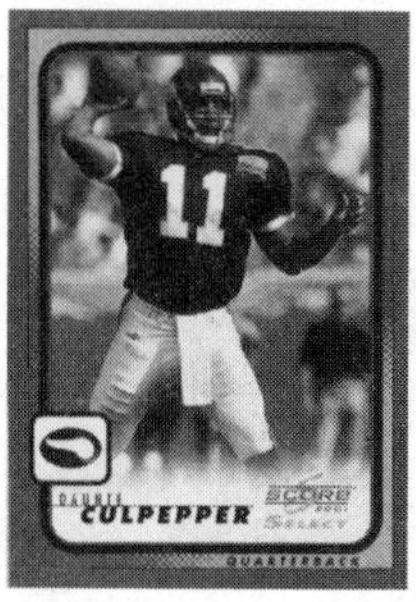

MT
Complete Set (330): 1000.
Common Player: .15
Minor Stars: .30
Common SP (221-270): .50
Production 325 Sets
Common Rookie: 5.00
Production 275 Sets
Pack (5): 5.00
Wax Box (20): 80.00
1 David Boston .50
2 Frank Sanders .15
3 Jake Plummer .50
4 Michael Pittman .15
5 Rob Moore .15
6 Thomas Jones .15
7 Chris Chandler .15
8 Doug Johnson .15
9 Jamal Anderson .50
10 Tim Dwight .50
11 Brandon Stokley .15
12 Chris Redman .50
13 Jamal Lewis 2.00
14 Qadry Ismail .15
15 Ray Lewis .15
16 Rod Woodson .15
17 Shannon Sharpe .15
18 Travis Taylor .15
19 Trent Dilfer .15
20 Elvis Grbac .15
21 Eric Moulds .15
22 Jay Riemersma .15
23 Peerless Price .15
24 Rob Johnson .15
25 Sam Cowart .15
26 Sammy Morris .15
27 Shawn Bryson .15
28 Donald Hayes .15
29 Muhsin Muhammad .15
30 Patrick Jeffers .15
31 Reggie White .50
32 Steve Beuerlein .15
33 Tim Biakabutuka .15
34 Wesley Walls .15
35 Brian Urlacher 1.25
36 Cade McNown .50
37 Dez White .15
38 James Allen .15
39 Marcus Robinson .50
40 Marty Booker .15
41 Akili Smith .50
42 Corey Dillon .50
43 Danny Farmer .15
44 Peter Warrick 1.25
45 Ron Dugans .15
46 Takeo Spikes .15
47 Courtney Brown .15
48 Dennis Northcutt .15
49 JaJuan Dawson .15
50 Kevin Johnson .30
51 Tim Couch .75
52 Travis Prentice .15
53 Anthony Wright .15
54 Emmitt Smith 1.75
55 James McKnight .15
56 Joey Galloway .15
57 Raghib Ismail .15
58 Randall Cunningham .50
59 Troy Aikman 1.25
60 Brian Griese 1.00
61 Ed McCaffrey .50
62 Gus Frerotte .15
63 John Elway 2.00
64 Mike Anderson 1.50
65 Olandis Gary .15
66 Rod Smith .15
67 Terrell Davis 1.25
68 Barry Sanders 2.00
69 Charlie Batch .50
70 Germane Crowell .15
71 Herman Moore .15
72 James Stewart .15
73 Johnnie Morton .15
74 Robert Porcher .15
75 Jim Harbaugh .15
76 Ahman Green .15
77 Antonio Freeman .50
78 Bill Schroeder .15
79 Brett Favre 2.50
80 Bubba Franks .15
81 Dorsey Levens .15
82 E.G. Green .15
83 Edgerrin James 2.00
84 Jerome Pathon .15
85 Ken Dilger .15
86 Marcus Pollard .15
87 Marvin Harrison .50
88 Peyton Manning 2.00
89 Terrence Wilkins .15
90 Fred Taylor .75
91 Hardy Nickerson .15
92 Jimmy Smith .15
93 Keenan McCardell .15
94 Kyle Brady .15
95 Mark Brunell .75
96 Tony Brackens .15
97 Derrick Alexander .15
98 Sylvester Morris .15
99 Tony Gonzalez .15
100 Tony Richardson .15
101 Kimble Anders .15
102 Warren Moon .50
103 Dan Marino 2.00
104 Jay Fiedler .50
105 Lamar Smith .15
106 O.J. McDuffie .15
107 Oronde Gadsden .15
108 Sam Madison .15
109 Thurman Thomas .15
110 Tony Martin .15
111 Zach Thomas .15
112 Cris Carter .50
113 Daunte Culpepper 1.25
114 Matthew Hatchette .15
115 Randy Moss 2.00
116 Robert Smith .50
117 Drew Bledsoe .75
118 J.R. Redmond .15
119 Kevin Faulk .15
120 Michael Bishop .15
121 Terry Glenn .15
122 Troy Brown .15
123 Ty Law .15
124 Aaron Brooks .75
125 Darren Howard .15
126 Jake Reed .15
127 Jeff Blake .15
128 Joe Horn .15
129 La'Roi Glover .15
130 Ricky Williams 1.00
131 Willie Jackson .15
132 Albert Connell .15
133 Amani Toomer .15
134 Ike Hilliard .15
135 Jason Sehorn .15
136 Jessie Armstead .15
137 Kerry Collins .15
138 Michael Strahan .15
139 Ron Dayne 1.25
140 Ron Dixon .15
141 Tiki Barber .15
142 Anthony Becht .15
143 Chad Pennington 1.25
144 Curtis Martin .50
145 Dedric Ward .15
146 Laveranues Coles .50
147 Vinny Testaverde .15
148 Wayne Chrebet .15
149 Andre Rison .15
150 Charles Woodson .15
151 Darrell Russell .15
152 Napoleon Kaufman .15
153 Rich Gannon .15
154 Tim Brown .50
155 Tyrone Wheatley .15
156 Chad Lewis .15
157 Charles Johnson .15
158 Donovan McNabb 1.00
159 Duce Staley .50
160 Hugh Douglas .15
161 Na Brown .15
162 Todd Pinkston .15
163 James Thrash .15
164 Bobby Shaw .15
165 Hines Ward .15
166 Jerome Bettis .50
167 Kordell Stewart .50
168 Levon Kirkland .15
169 Plaxico Burress .50
170 Richard Huntley .15
171 Troy Edwards .15
172 Jeff Graham .15
173 Junior Seau .15
174 Doug Flutie .60
175 Charlie Garner .15
176 Jeff Garcia .50
177 Jerry Rice 1.50
178 Steve Young .75
179 Terrell Owens .15
180 Brock Huard .15
181 Darrell Jackson .50
182 Derrick Mayes .15
183 Ricky Watters .15
184 Shaun Alexander .75
185 Matt Hasselbeck .15
186 John Randle .15
187 Az-Zahir Hakim .15
188 Isaac Bruce .50
189 Kurt Warner 2.50
190 Marshall Faulk .75
191 Torry Holt .50
192 Trent Green .15
193 Derrick Brooks .15
194 Jacquez Green .15
195 John Lynch .15
196 Keyshawn Johnson .50
197 Mike Alstott .50
198 Reidel Anthony .15
199 Shaun King .50
200 Warren Sapp .15
201 Warrick Dunn .50
202 Ryan Leaf .50
203 Carl Pickens .15
204 Derrick Mason .15
205 Eddie George .75
206 Frank Wycheck .15
207 Jevon Kearse .50
208 Neil O'Donnell .15
209 Steve McNair .50
210 Yancey Thigpen .15
211 Andre Reed .15
212 Brad Johnson .50
213 Bruce Smith .15
214 Champ Bailey .50
215 Darrell Green .15
216 Deion Sanders .50
217 Irving Fryar .15
218 Jeff George .15
219 Michael Westbrook .15
220 Stephen Davis .50
221 Terrell Owens AP 2.00
222 Peyton Manning AP 7.00
223 Stephen Davis AP 2.00
224 Marvin Harrison AP 2.00
225 Donovan McNabb AP 3.00
226 Edgerrin James AP 6.00
227 Eric Moulds AP .15
228 Daunte Culpepper AP 4.00
229 Eddie George AP 2.50
230 Cris Carter AP 2.00
231 Rich Gannon AP .15
232 Jeff Garcia AP 2.00
233 Jimmy Smith AP .15
234 Tony Gonzalez AP .15
235 Torry Holt AP 2.00
236 Jevon Kearse AP 2.00
237 Ray Lewis AP .15
238 Warren Sapp AP .15
239 Brian Urlacher AP 4.00
240 Champ Bailey AP .15
241 Peyton Manning LL 7.00
242 Jeff Garcia LL 2.00
243 Elvis Grbac LL .15
244 Daunte Culpepper LL 4.00
245 Brett Favre LL 8.00
246 Edgerrin James LL 6.00
247 Robert Smith LL .15
248 Eddie George LL 2.50
249 Mike Anderson LL 4.00
250 Corey Dillon LL 2.00
251 Torry Holt LL 2.00
252 Rod Smith LL .15
253 Isaac Bruce LL 2.00
254 Terrell Owens LL 2.00
255 Randy Moss LL 7.00
256 La'Roi Glover LL .15
257 Trace Armstrong LL .15
258 Warren Sapp LL .15
259 Hugh Douglas LL .15
260 Jason Taylor LL .15
261 Mike Anderson SS 4.00
262 Jamal Lewis SS 5.00
263 Sylvester Williams SS .15
264 Darrell Jackson SS 2.00
265 Peter Warrick SS 3.00
266 Ron Dayne SS 3.00
267 Shaun Alexander SS 2.00
268 Plaxico Burress SS 2.00
269 Brian Urlacher SS 2.00
270 Courtney Brown SS .15
271 *Michael Vick* 75.00
272 *Drew Brees* 60.00
273 *Chris Weinke* 40.00
274 *Quincy Carter* 25.00
275 *Sage Rosenfels* 15.00
276 *Josh Heupel* 20.00
277 *David Rivers* 5.00
278 *Ben Leard* 10.00
279 *Marques Tuiasosopo* 30.00
280 *Mike McMahon* 15.00
281 *Deuce McAllister* 30.00
282 *LaMont Jordan* 15.00
283 *LaDainian Tomlinson* 60.00
284 *James Jackson* 20.00
285 *Anthony Thomas* 60.00
286 *Travis Henry* 25.00
287 *Travis Minor* 20.00
288 *Rudi Johnson* 15.00
289 *Michael Bennett* 40.00
290 *Kevan Barlow* 15.00
291 *Reggie White* 10.00
292 *Moran Norris* 5.00
293 *Ja'Mar Toombs* 10.00
294 *Heath Evans* 5.00
295 *David Terrell* 40.00
296 *Santana Moss* 30.00
297 *Rod Gardner* 35.00
298 *Quincy Morgan* 20.00
299 *Freddie Mitchell* 25.00
300 *Boo Williams* 5.00
301 *Reggie Wayne* 30.00
302 *Ronney Daniels* 10.00
303 *Bobby Newcombe* 15.00
304 *Vinny Sutherland* 12.00
305 *Cedrick Wilson* 10.00
306 *Robert Ferguson* 20.00
307 *Ken-Yon Rambo* 15.00
308 *Alex Bannister* 15.00
309 *Koren Robinson* 35.00
310 *Chad Johnson* 18.00
311 *Chris Chambers* 18.00
312 *Javon Green* 10.00
313 *Marvin "Snoop" Minnis* 20.00
314 *Scotty Anderson* 10.00
315 *Todd Heap* 12.00
316 *Alge Crumpler* 12.00
317 *Marcellus Rivers* 10.00
318 *Rashon Burns* 5.00
319 *Jamal Reynolds* 12.00
320 *Andre Carter* 12.00
321 *Justin Smith* 12.00
322 *Gerard Warren* 15.00
323 *Tommy Polley* 10.00
324 *Dan Morgan* 15.00
325 *Torrance Marshall* 12.00
326 *Correl Buckhalter* 20.00
327 *Derrick Gibson* 5.00
328 *Adam Archuleta* 12.00
329 *Jamar Fletcher* 12.00
330 *Nate Clements* 10.00
NNO Supplemental Set Exch 50.00

2001 Score Select Behind The Numbers

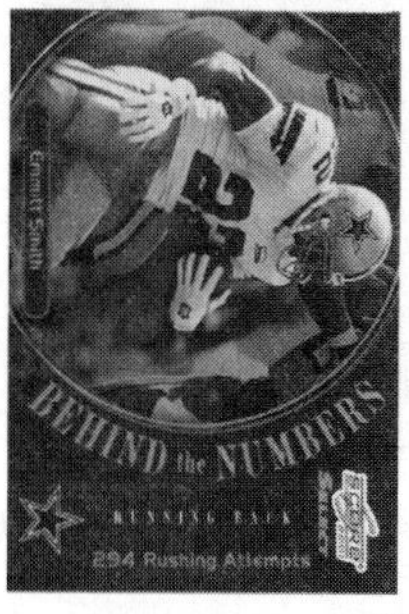

MT
Common Player: 5.00
Numbered to Season Stat
BN1 Brett Favre/338 18.00
BN2 Marshall Faulk/253 7.00
BN3 Michael Vick/87 60.00
BN4 Peyton Manning/357 15.00
BN5 David Terrell/63 25.00
BN6 Randy Moss/77 30.00
BN7 Kurt Warner/235 15.00
BN8 Edgerrin James/387 12.00
BN9 Drew Brees/309 15.00
BN10 Daunte Culpepper/297 10.00
BN11 Jeff Garcia/355 5.00
BN12 Mike Anderson/297 10.00
BN13 Jamal Lewis/309 12.00
BN14 Eddie George/403 7.00
BN15 Michael Bennett/310 12.00
BN16 Emmitt Smith/294 12.00
BN17 Chris Weinke/266 10.00
BN18 Tim Brown/76 10.00
BN19 Eric Moulds/94 5.00
BN20 Marvin Harrison/102 10.00
BN21 Deuce McAllister/105 18.00
BN22 Donovan McNabb/330 8.00
BN23 Fred Taylor/292 5.00
BN24 Santana Moss/45 20.00
BN25 Cris Carter/96 10.00
BN26 Robert Smith/295 5.00
BN27 LaDainian Tomlinson/369 12.00
BN28 Isaac Bruce/87 10.00
BN29 Terrell Owens/97 10.00
BN30 Torry Holt/82 10.00
BN31 Ricky Williams/248 8.00
BN32 Curtis Martin/312 5.00
BN33 Stephen Davis/332 5.00
BN34 Corey Dillon/315 5.00
BN35 Ed McCaffrey/101 7.00
BN36 Steve McNair/248 5.00
BN37 Rudi Johnson/324 8.00
BN38 Antonio Freeman/62 10.00
BN39 Jerry Rice/75 25.00
BN40 Aaron Brooks/113 12.00

A card number in parentheses ( ) indicates the set is unnumbered.

2001 Score Select Complete Players

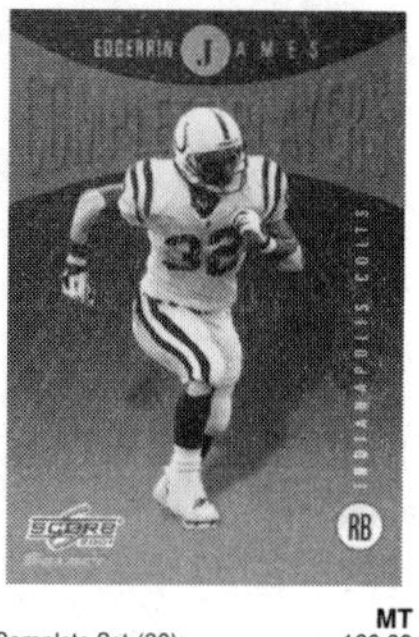

MT
Complete Set (30): 160.00
Common Player: 4.00
Production 550 Sets
CP1 Edgerrin James 10.00
CP2 Marshall Faulk 4.00
CP3 Kurt Warner 12.00
CP4 Daunte Culpepper 7.00
CP5 Donovan McNabb 5.00
CP6 Koren Robinson 6.00
CP7 Peyton Manning 12.00
CP8 Eddie George 4.00
CP9 Fred Taylor 4.00
CP10 Drew Brees 15.00
CP11 Randy Moss 12.00
CP12 Cris Carter 4.00
CP13 Steve Young 4.00
CP14 Marvin Harrison 4.00
CP15 Isaac Bruce 4.00
CP16 Terrell Owens 4.00
CP17 Mike Anderson 8.00
CP18 Jamal Lewis 8.00
CP19 Curtis Martin 4.00
CP20 Ricky Williams 6.00
CP21 Jerry Rice 8.00
CP22 Steve McNair 4.00
CP23 Michael Vick 25.00
CP24 Brett Favre 15.00
CP25 John Elway 12.00
CP26 Dan Marino 12.00
CP27 Barry Sanders 10.00
CP28 Michael Bennett 10.00
CP29 David Terrell 8.00
CP30 Emmitt Smith 8.00

2001 Score Select Franchise Fabrics/Tags

MT
Common Player: 50.00
Production 50 Sets
FT1 Daunte Culpepper 125.00
FT2 Stephen Davis 60.00
FT3 Kurt Warner 200.00
FT4 Ricky Williams 150.00
FT5 Terrell Owens 60.00
FT6 Ricky Watters 50.00
FT7 Rich Gannon 50.00
FT8 Mike Anderson 125.00
FT9 Tony Gonzalez 60.00
FT10 Jerome Bettis 60.00
FT11 Peter Warrick 100.00
FT12 Tim Couch 100.00
FT13 Mark Brunell 100.00
FT14 Edgerrin James 180.00
FT15 Curtis Martin 60.00
FT16 Brett Favre 250.00
FT17 Donovan McNabb 125.00
FT18 Drew Bledsoe 100.00
FT19 Jake Plummer 60.00
FT20 Eric Moulds 60.00
FT21 Lamar Smith 60.00
FT22 Junior Seau 50.00
FT23 Wesley Walls 50.00
FT24 Jamal Anderson 60.00
FT25 Warren Sapp 60.00
FT26 Ron Dayne 125.00
FT27 Jamal Lewis 150.00
FT28 Cade McNown 60.00
FT29 Charlie Batch 60.00
FT30 Eddie George 85.00
FT31 Troy Aikman 175.00

2001 Score Select The Future Franchise

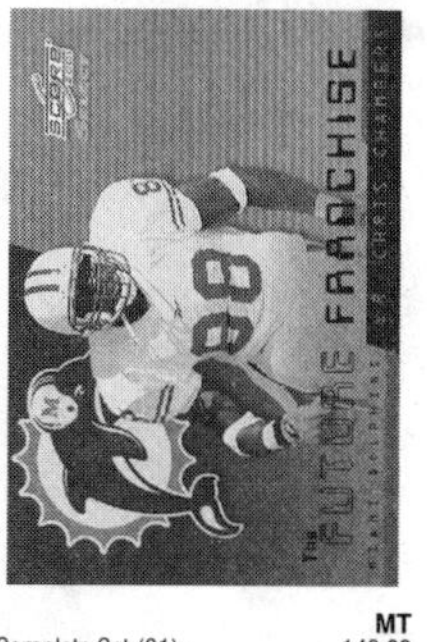

MT
Complete Set (31): 140.00
Common Player: 2.00
Minor Stars: 4.00
Production 550 Sets
FF1 Tim Couch, James Jackson 5.00
FF2 Peter Warrick, Justin Smith 6.00
FF3 Jerome Bettis, Casey Hampton 4.00

FF4	Fred Taylor, Marcus Stroud	5.00
FF5	Eddie George, Dan Alexander	5.00
FF6	Jamal Lewis, Todd Heap	10.00
FF7	Peyton Manning, Reggie Wayne	12.00
FF8	Drew Bledsoe, Jabari Holloway	5.00
FF9	Curtis Martin, Santana Moss	6.00
FF10	Eric Moulds, Travis Henry	5.00
FF11	Lamar Smith, Chris Chambers	4.00
FF12	Tony Gonzalez, Marvin "Snoop" Minnis	4.00
FF13	Rich Gannon, Marques Tuiasosopo	5.00
FF14	Ricky Watters, Koren Robinson	6.00
FF15	Junior Seau, LaDainian Tomlinson	12.00
FF16	Brian Griese, Kevin Kasper	5.00
FF17	Terrell Owens, Kevan Barlow	4.00
FF18	Ricky Williams, Deuce McAllister	7.00
FF19	Kurt Warner, Damione Lewis	12.00
FF20	Muhsin Muhammad, Chris Weinke	7.00
FF21	Jamal Anderson, Michael Vick	25.00
FF22	Brett Favre, Robert Ferguson	15.00
FF23	Randy Moss, Michael Bennett	12.00
FF24	Marcus Robinson, David Terrell	10.00
FF25	Warrick Dunn, Kenyatta Walker	4.00
FF26	James Stewart, Mike McMahon	2.00
FF27	Jake Plummer, Bobby Newcombe	4.00
FF28	Kerry Collins, Jesse Palmer	2.00
FF29	Emmitt Smith, Quincy Carter	10.00
FF30	Stephen Davis, Rod Gardner	6.00
FF31	Donovan McNabb, Freddie Mitchell	6.00

2001 Score Select Rookie Preview

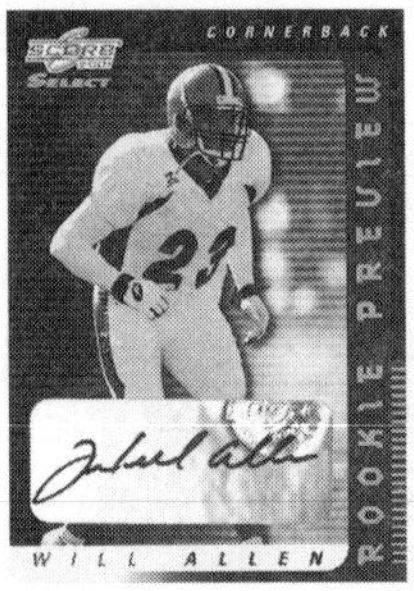
CORNERBACK
ROOKIE PREVIEW
WILL ALLEN

		MT
Common Player:		7.00
RP1	Michael Vick/150	120.00
RP2	Drew Brees/150	70.00
RP3	Chris Weinke/250	30.00
RP4	Quincy Carter	7.00
RP5	Josh Heupel/450	15.00
RP6	David Terrell/150	40.00
RP7	Santana Moss/250	30.00
RP8	Freddie Mitchell/350	20.00
RP9	Reggie Wayne/250	20.00
RP10	Rod Gardner/50	45.00
RP11	Chris Chambers/450	12.00
RP12	Chad Johnson/450	10.00
RP13	Ken-Yon Rambo/550	10.00
RP14	Deuce McAllister/150	35.00
RP15	LaDainian Tomlinson/250	45.00
RP16	Travis Henry/450	15.00
RP17	Anthony Thomas/250	20.00
RP18	Michael Bennett/250	35.00
RP19	LaMont Jordan/350	12.00
RP20	Kevan Barlow/450	10.00
RP21	Reggie White/550	12.00
RP22	Sage Rosenfels/50	20.00
RP23	David Rivers	7.00
RP24	Mike McMahon/450	10.00
RP25	Quincy Morgan/450	12.00
RP26	Boo Williams	7.00
RP27	Vinny Sutherland	7.00
RP28	Alex Bannister/450	10.00
RP29	Marvin "Snoop" Minnis/450	12.00
RP30	Cedrick Wilson/450	7.00
RP31	Torrance Marshall	7.00
RP32	Bobby Newcombe	7.00
RP33	Ja'Mar Toombs	7.00
RP34	Correl Buckhalter/550	12.00
RP35	Andre Carter	7.00
RP36	Jamal Reynolds/350	8.00
RP37	Richard Seymour/350	8.00
RP38	Tommy Polley	7.00
RP39	Jamar Fletcher	7.00
RP40	Fred Smoot	7.00
RP41	Dan Morgan	7.00
RP42	James Jackson/350	12.00
RP43	Rudi Johnson/350	10.00
RP44	Scotty Anderson	7.00
RP45	Travis Minor/750	12.00
RP46	Robert Ferguson/350	12.00
RP47	Ronney Daniels	7.00
RP48	Heath Evans	7.00
RP49	Justin Smith/350	10.00
RP50	Gerard Warren/350	10.00
RP51	Koren Robinson/50	45.00
RP52	T.J. Houshmandzadeh/450	8.00
RP53	Todd Heap/750	7.00
RP54	Javon Green	7.00
RP55	Alge Crumpler/750	7.00
RP56	Derrick Gibson	7.00
RP57	Marcellus Rivers	7.00
RP58	Ken Lucas	7.00
RP59	Nate Clements	7.00
RP60	Will Allen/750	7.00

2001 Score Select Rookie Roll Call Autographs

		MT
Common Player:		15.00
Production 50 Sets		
RP1	Michael Vick	200.00
RP2	Drew Brees	120.00
RP3	Chris Weinke	60.00
RP5	Josh Heupel	60.00
RP6	David Terrell	85.00
RP7	Santana Moss	80.00
RP8	Freddie Mitchell	40.00
RP9	Reggie Wayne	45.00
RP101	Rod Gardner	50.00
RP11	Chris Chambers	25.00
RP12	Chad Johnson	25.00
RP13	Ken-Yon Rambo	20.00
RP14	Deuce McAllister	65.00
RP15	LaDainian Tomlinson	100.00
RP16	Travis Henry	40.00
RP17	Anthony Thomas	50.00
RP18	Michael Bennett	85.00
RP19	LaMont Jordan	25.00
RP20	Kevan Barlow	25.00
RP21	Reggie White	20.00
RP22	Sage Rosenfels	25.00
RP24	Mike McMahon	25.00
RP25	Quincy Morgan	25.00
RP28	Alex Bannister	25.00
RP29	Marvin "Snoop" Minnis	30.00
RP30	Cedrick Wilson	20.00
RP34	Correll Buckhelter	25.00
RP36	Jamal Reynolds	20.00
RP37	Richard Seymour	15.00
RP42	James Jackson	25.00
RP43	Rudi Johnson	20.00
RP45	Travis Minor	30.00
RP46	Robert Ferguson	30.00
RP49	Justin Smith	25.00
RP50	Gerard Warren	25.00
RP51	Koren Robinson	50.00
RP52	T.J. Houshmandzadeh	15.00
RP53	Todd Heap	20.00
RP55	Alge Crumpler	20.00
RP60	Will Allen	15.00

2001 Score Select Settle The Score

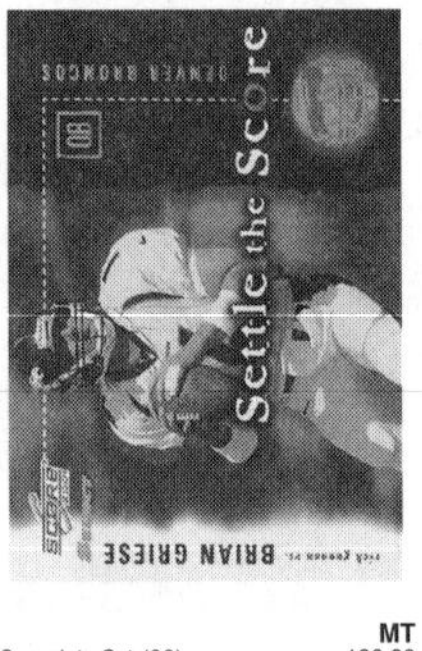
DENVER BRONCOS
Settle the Score
BRIAN GRIESE

		MT
Complete Set (30):		120.00
Common Player:		2.00
Minor Stars:		4.00
Production 550 Sets		
SS1	Kurt Warner, Steve McNair	12.00
SS2	Randy Moss, Isaac Bruce	12.00
SS3	Emmitt Smith, Stephen Davis	8.00
SS4	Marshall Faulk, Robert Smith	5.00
SS5	Eddie George, Ray Lewis	5.00
SS6	Fred Taylor, Jerome Bettis	5.00
SS7	Peyton Manning, Drew Bledsoe	12.00
SS8	Daunte Culpepper, Aaron Brooks	7.00
SS9	Marvin Harrison, Eric Moulds	4.00
SS10	Jerry Rice, Cris Carter	8.00
SS11	Curtis Martin, Edgerrin James	10.00
SS12	Donovan McNabb, Ron Dayne	6.00
SS13	Brett Favre, Warren Sapp	12.00
SS14	Tony Gonzalez, Shannon Sharpe	2.00
SS15	Wayne Chrebet, Keyshawn Johnson	2.00
SS16	Tim Couch, Cade McNown	5.00
SS17	Terrell Davis, Jamal Anderson	8.00
SS18	Mike Anderson, Jamal Lewis	10.00
SS19	Terrell Owens, Antonio Freeman	4.00
SS20	Brian Griese, Rich Gannon	5.00
SS21	Ricky Watters, Charlie Garner	2.00
SS22	Muhsin Muhammad, Ricky Williams	6.00
SS23	Jeff Garcia, Elvis Grbac	4.00
SS24	Rod Smith, Jimmy Smith	2.00
SS25	Brian Urlacher, Ahman Green	6.00
SS26	Darrell Jackson, Sylvester Morris	4.00
SS27	Peter Warrick, Travis Taylor	6.00
SS28	Dan Marino, John Elway	12.00
SS29	Steve Young, Mark Brunell	5.00
SS30	Troy Aikman, Jake Plummer	7.00

2001 Score Select Zenith Z-Team

		MT
Complete Set (38):		400.00
Common Player:		5.00
Minor Stars:		10.00
Production 100 Sets		
ZT1	Michael Vick	60.00
ZT2	Donovan McNabb	15.00
ZT3	Daunte Culpepper	18.00
ZT4	Kurt Warner	30.00
ZT5	Peyton Manning	25.00
ZT6	Brett Favre	30.00
ZT7	Dan Marino	25.00
ZT8	John Elway	25.00
ZT9	Steve Young	12.00
ZT10	Troy Aikman	18.00
ZT11	Chad Pennington	15.00
ZT12	Brian Griese	12.00
ZT13	Drew Brees	35.00
ZT14	David Terrell	25.00
ZT15	Eric Moulds	5.00
ZT16	Marvin Harrison	10.00
ZT17	Randy Moss	25.00
ZT18	Reggie Wayne	12.00
ZT19	Terrell Owens	10.00
ZT20	Jerry Rice	18.00
ZT21	Cris Carter	10.00
ZT22	Isaac Bruce	10.00
ZT23	Peter Warrick	12.00
ZT24	Deuce McAllister	18.00
ZT25	Edgerrin James	20.00
ZT26	Robert Smith	5.00
ZT27	Marshall Faulk	12.00
ZT28	Ricky Williams	15.00
ZT29	Michael Bennett	25.00
ZT30	Emmitt Smith	25.00
ZT31	Eddie George	12.00
ZT32	Jamal Lewis	20.00
ZT33	Ron Dayne	18.00
ZT34	Mike Anderson	18.00
ZT35	Barry Sanders	25.00
ZT36	Stephen Davis	10.00
ZT37	Koren Robinson	15.00
ZT38	LaDainian Tomlinson	30.00

1997 Score Board NFL Rookies

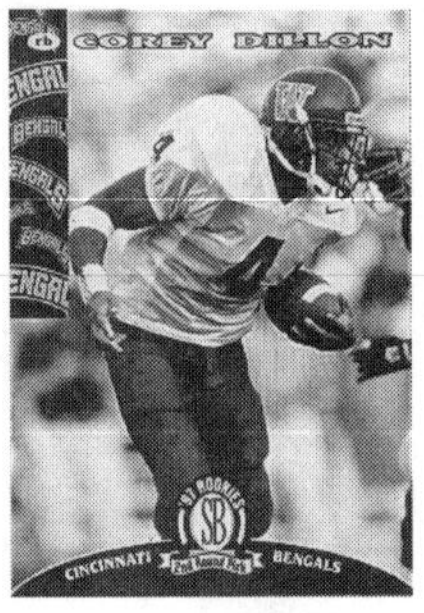
COREY DILLON
CINCINNATI BENGALS

The 100-card set features the player's name at the top, while the logo of the teams that drafted him is included in a black stripe in the upper left corner. The '97 Rookies Score Board logo is in the lower center. The team's name is printed inside a black half oval at the bottom. The black stripe that runs along the left side of the back includes the various logos, player's name, bio and card number. To the right of the stripe is the player's photo, highlights and stats. The set was paralleled by the Dean's List, which was inserted 1:5 packs. Vintage rookie cards and autographed rookie cards of current and ex-NFL players were also randomly inserted.

		MT
Complete Set (100):		10.00
Common Player:		.05
Minor Stars:		.10
Dean's List:		2x-3x
1	Jake Plummer	2.00
2	Tony Gonzalez	.20
3	Trevor Pryce	.05
4	Greg Jones	.05
5	Koy Detmer	1.25
6	Rae Carruth	.75
7	Peter Boulware	.05
8	Warrick Dunn	2.00
9	Antowain Smith	.30
10	Troy Davis	1.00
11	David LaFleur	.30
12	Yatil Green	1.00
13	Michael Booker	.05
14	Shawn Springs	.30
15	Bryant Westbrook	.30
16	Byron Hanspard	.50
17	Darrell Russell	.05
18	Corey Dillon	1.00
19	Tyrus McCloud	.05
20	Reinard Wilson	.05
21	Adam Meadows	.05
22	Tremain Mack	.05
23	Ricky Parker	.05
24	George Jones	.05
25	Terry Battle	.05
26	Will Blackwell	.05
27	Jerald Sowell	.05
28	Isaac Byrd	.05
29	Chris Naeole	.05
30	Kevin Lockett	.05
31	Freddie Jones	.05
32	Pat Barnes	.05
33	Torrian Gray	.05
34	Brian Manning	.05
35	Dedric Ward	.05
36	Pete Monty	.05
37	Sam Madison	.05
38	Sedrick Shaw	.05
39	Mike Logan	.05
40	Albert Connell	.05
41	Canute Curtis	.05
42	Ronde Barber	.05
43	Orlando Pace	.75
44	Edward Perry	.05
45	Tiki Barber	.50
46	Kevin Jackson	.05
47	Jerry Wunsch	.05
48	Michael Hamilton	.05
49	Darnell Autry	.50
50	Jim Druckenmiller	1.25
51	James Farrior	.05
52	Derrick Mason	.25
53	Ty Howard	.05
54	Jason Taylor	.05
55	Reidel Anthony	1.00
56	Bert Berry	.05
57	Marc Edwards	.05
58	James Hamilton	.05
59	Ike Hilliard	1.00
60	Tommy Knight	.05
61	Walter Jones	.05
62	Chad Levitt	.05
63	Pratt Lyons	.05
64	Greg Clark	.05
65	Ryan Phillips	.05
66	Jason Martin	.05
67	Scott Sanderson	.05
68	Alshermond Singleton	.05
69	Duce Staley	.50
70	Jared Tomich	.05
71	Ross Verba	.05
72	Derrick Rodgers	.05
73	Mike Vrabel	.05
74	John Allred	.05
75	Bob Sapp	.05
76	Brad Otton	.05
77	Tarik Glenn	.05
78	Chad Scott	.05
79	Nathan Davis	.05
80	Henri Crockett	.05
81	Tarik Saleh	.05
82	Seth Payne	.05
83	Pete Chryplewicz	.05
84	Reidel Anthony	.50
85	Reinard Wilson	.05
86	Byron Hanspard	.20
87	Shawn Springs	.20
88	David LaFleur	.20
89	Troy Davis	.50
90	Warrick Dunn	1.00
91	Peter Boulware	.05
92	Rae Carruth	.20
93	Tony Gonzalez	.10
94	Jake Plummer	.25
95	Orlando Pace	.25
96	Ike Hilliard	.50
97	Kevin Jackson	.05
98	Jim Druckenmiller	.60
99	Shawn Springs	.20
100	Warrick Dunn	1.00

1997 Score Board NFL Rookies Dean's List

Dean's List is a parallel set of the NFL Rookies base cards. Dean's List cards were inserted one per five packs.

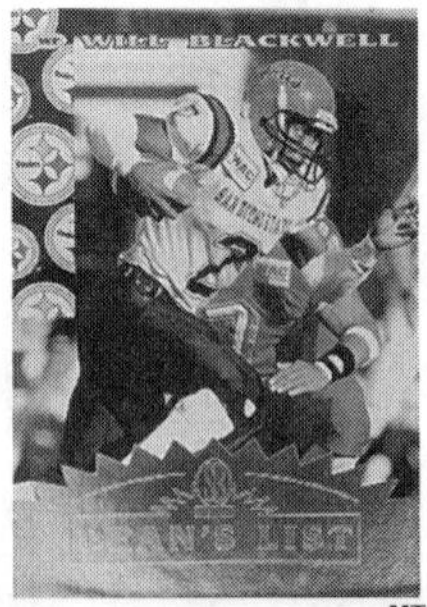
WILL BLACKWELL
DEAN'S LIST

	MT
Dean's List Cards:	2x-3x

Values quoted in this guide reflect the retail price of a card — the price a collector can expect to pay when buying a card from a dealer. The wholesale price — that which a collector can expect to receive from a dealer when selling cards — will be significantly lower, depending on desirability and condition.

1997 Score Board NFL Rookies NFL War Room

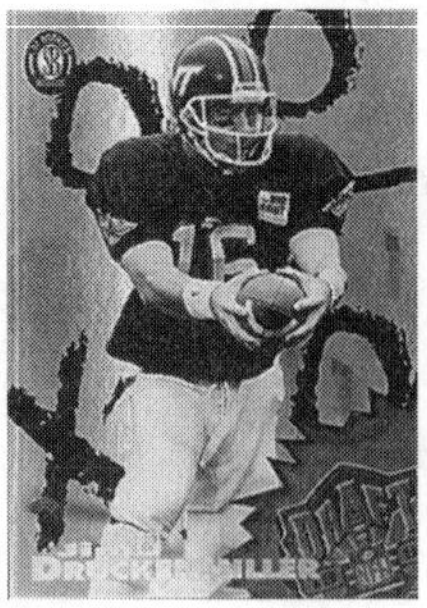
DRUCKENMILLER

The 20-card set was inserted 1:100 packs. It includes comments from NFL insiders on players that were selected on draft day. The cards carry a "W" prefix.

		MT
Complete Set (20):		300.00
Common Player:		10.00
Minor Stars:		20.00
1	Yatil Green	45.00
2	Antowain Smith	20.00
3	Tony Gonzalez	20.00
4	Corey Dillon	10.00
5	Jake Plummer	30.00
6	Peter Boulware	10.00
7	Orlando Pace	30.00
8	Darrell Russell	10.00
9	Reinard Wilson	10.00
10	Shawn Springs	20.00
11	Bryant Westbrook	20.00
12	Rae Carruth	40.00
13	Warrick Dunn	80.00
14	David LaFleur	20.00
15	Byron Hanspard	30.00
16	Michael Booker	10.00
17	Reidel Anthony	45.00
18	Troy Davis	45.00
19	Chris Naeole	10.00
20	Jim Druckenmiller	60.00

1997 Score Board NFL Rookies Varsity Club

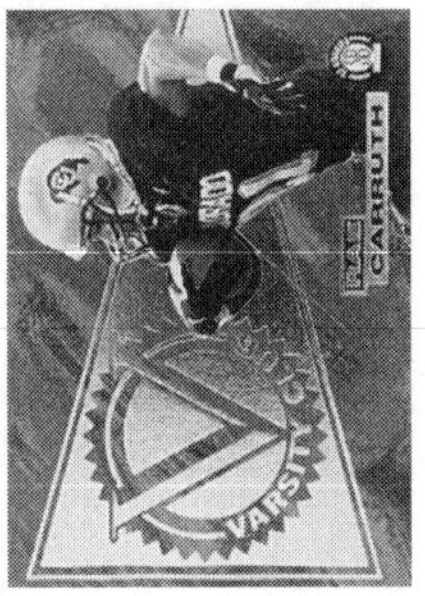
RAE CARRUTH
VARSITY CLUB

Inserted 1:36 packs, the 30-card set features the school pennant and team logo of the player's college or university. The cards are numbered and carry a "V" prefix.

		MT
Complete Set (30):		140.00
Common Player:		2.00
Minor Stars:		4.00
1	Tiki Barber	10.00
2	Sedrick Shaw	2.00
3	Kevin Lockett	2.00
4	Byron Hanspard	10.00
5	David LaFleur	6.00
6	Warrick Dunn	25.00
7	Yatil Green	15.00
8	Corey Dillon	6.00
9	Orlando Pace	10.00
10	Tony Gonzalez	4.00
11	Darrell Russell	2.00
12	Jake Plummer	10.00
13	Peter Boulware	2.00
14	Shawn Springs	6.00
15	Bryant Westbrook	6.00
16	Rae Carruth	12.00
17	Antowain Smith	6.00
18	Reidel Anthony	15.00
19	Michael Booker	2.00
20	Freddie Jones	2.00
21	Pat Barnes	2.00
22	Troy Davis	15.00
23	Walter Jones	2.00
24	Reinard Wilson	2.00
25	George Jones	2.00
26	Terry Battle	2.00
27	Tommy Knight	2.00
28	Tremain Mack	2.00
29	Jim Druckenmiller	20.00
30	Ike Hilliard	15.00

A card number in parentheses ( ) indicates the set is unnumbered.

1997 Score Board Playbook By The Numbers

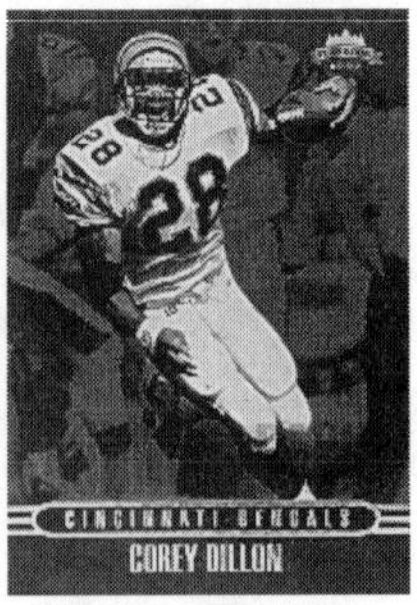
CINCINNATI BENGALS
COREY DILLON

Playbook By The Numbers consists of a 50-card base set. The base set is divided into five subsets: quarterbacks, running backs, wide receivers, defensive players and rookies. The base cards are numbered within their subset. Silver Magnified (sequentially numbered to 2,000; inserted one per two packs) and Gold Magnified (numbered to 200; 1:21) parallel versions were also produced. Three insert sets were included in this product: Standout Numbers, Red Zone Stats and Master Signings.

		MT
Complete Set (50):		30.00
Common Player:		.10
Minor Stars:		.20
Gold Magnified Cards:		10x-20x
Silver Magnified Cards:		3x
Wax Box:		35.00
1	Troy Aikman (Quarterback)	1.00
2	Mark Brunell (Quarterback)	1.00
3	Dan Marino (Quarterback)	2.00
4	Brett Favre (Quarterback)	2.50
5	Kordell Stewart (Quarterback)	1.00
6	Drew Bledsoe (Quarterback)	1.00
7	John Elway (Quarterback)	.75
8	Kerry Collins (Quarterback)	.30
9	Steve Young (Quarterback)	.75
10	Jeff Blake (Quarterback)	.20
1	Emmitt Smith (Running Back)	2.00
2	Terrell Davis (Running Back)	1.00
3	Barry Sanders (Running Back)	1.00
4	Marshall Faulk (Running Back)	.20
5	Robert Smith (Running Back)	.10
6	Curtis Martin (Running Back)	1.00
7	Jerome Bettis (Running Back)	.20
8	Eddie George (Running Back)	1.50
9	Terry Allen (Running Back)	.10
10	Ricky Watters (Running Back)	.20
1	Carl Pickens (Wide Receiver)	.10
2	Michael Irvin (Wide Receiver)	.20
3	Herman Moore (Wide Receiver)	.20
4	Robert Brooks (Wide Receiver)	.10
5	Cris Carter (Wide Receiver)	.10
6	Terry Glenn (Wide Receiver)	.75
7	Tim Brown (Wide Receiver)	.10
8	Jerry Rice (Wide Receiver)	1.00
9	Keyshawn Johnson (Wide Receiver)	.30
10	Isaac Bruce (Wide Receiver)	.20
1	Simeon Rice (Defense)	.10
2	Peter Boulware (Defense)	.10
3	Bruce Smith (Defense)	.10
4	Deion Sanders (Defense)	.50
5	Reggie White (Defense)	.20
6	Darrell Russell (Defense)	.10
7	Greg Lloyd (Defense)	.10
8	Junior Seau (Defense)	.10
9	Shawn Springs (Defense)	.20
10	Cortez Kennedy (Defense)	.10

Post-1980 cards in Near Mint condition will generally sell for about 75% of the quoted Mint value. Excellent-condition cards bring no more than 40%.

1 Tony Gonzalez (Rookie) .30
2 Rae Carruth (Rookie) .50
3 Warrick Dunn (Rookie) 4.00
4 Tiki Barber (Rookie) .40
5 Antowain Smith (Rookie) 2.00
6 Corey Dillon (Rookie) 2.00
7 Troy Davis (Rookie) .40
8 Danny Wuerffel (Rookie) .60
9 Jim Druckenmiller (Rookie) 2.50
10 Pat Barnes (Rookie) .30

1997 Score Board Playbook Red Zone Stats

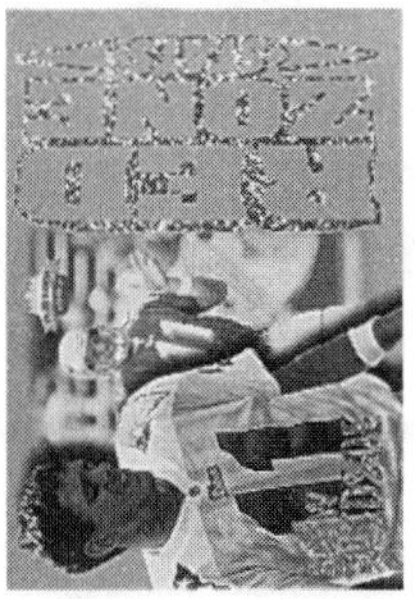

Red Zone Stats is a 10-card insert, seeded one per 20 packs. This insert has Silver Magnified (numbered to 1,000; inserted one per 21 packs) and Gold Magnified (numbered to 100; 1:210) parallel versions. They have a "RZ" prefix.

MT
Complete Set (10): 75.00
Common Player: 2.50
Minor Stars: 5.00
Magnified Gold Cards: 4x-8x
Magnified Silver Cards: 1x
1 Emmitt Smith 15.00
2 Terry Allen 2.50
3 Troy Aikman 10.00
4 Brett Favre 20.00
5 John Elway 8.00
6 Drew Bledsoe 10.00
7 Terrell Davis 10.00
8 Karim Abdul-Jabbar 5.00
9 Curtis Martin 10.00
10 Warrick Dunn 10.00

1997 Score Board Playbook Standout Numbers

Standout Numbers is a 30-card insert which was inserted one per four packs. Standout Numbers also has Silver Magnified (numbered to 2,700, inserted one per three packs) and Gold Magnified (numbered to 270; 1:26) parallel versions. The cards are numbered with a "SN" prefix.

MT
Complete Set (30): 75.00
Common Player: 1.00
Minor Stars: 2.00
Magnified Golds: 2x-4x
Magnified Silvers: 1x
1 Drew Bledsoe 5.00
2 Emmitt Smith 10.00
3 Cris Carter 1.00
4 Brett Favre 12.00
5 Jerome Bettis 2.00
6 Mark Brunell 5.00
7 John Elway 4.00
8 Troy Aikman 5.00
9 Steve Young 4.00
10 Kordell Stewart 5.00
11 Reggie White 2.00
12 Isaac Bruce 2.00
13 Dan Marino 10.00
14 Kevin Greene 1.00
15 Tim Brown 2.00
16 Terry Glenn 3.00
17 Ricky Watters 2.00
18 Carl Pickens 1.00
19 Keyshawn Johnson 2.00
20 Barry Sanders 5.00
21 Marshall Faulk 2.00
22 James Stewart 1.00
23 Jerry Rice 5.00
24 Curtis Martin 5.00
25 Herman Moore 2.00
26 Terry Allen 1.00
27 Eddie George 7.00
28 Warrick Dunn 5.00
29 Marcus Allen 2.00
30 Terrell Davis 5.00

1977 Seahawks Fred Meyer

The 13-card, 7-1/4" x 6" set, distributed by Fred Meyer Department Stores, feature a color action shot with a headshot inset in a lower corner (cards 3, 5, 12, and 13a have no insets). Seahawks quarterback Jim Zorn is represented on two No. 13 cards, one having no inset. All card backs are blank.

NM
Complete Set (14): 75.00
Common Player: 5.00
1 Steve August 5.00
2 Autry Beamon 5.00
3 Terry Beeson 5.00
4 Dennis Boyd 5.00
5 Norm Evans 5.00
6 Sammy Green 5.00
7 Ron Howard 5.00
8 Steve Largent 20.00
9 Steve Myer 5.00
10 Steve Niehaus 5.00
11 Sherman Smith 5.00
12 Don Testerman 5.00
13A Jim Zorn (No inset photo) 12.00
13B Jim Zorn (With inset photo) 12.00

1977 Seahawks Team Issue

The 10-card, 5" x 7" set features black and white headshots of Seattle players with blank backs. A facsimile autograph also appears on each card front.

NM
Complete Set (10): 75.00
Common Player: 5.00
1 Ron Howard 5.00
2 Steve Largent 25.00
3 John Leypoldt 5.00
4 Bob Lurtsema 5.00
5 Steve Myer 5.00
6 Steve Niehaus 5.00
7 Jack Patera (CO) 6.00
8 Sherman Smith 5.00
9 Don Testerman 5.00
10 Jim Zorn 12.00

1978-80 Seahawks Nalley's

The 24-card, 10-3/4" x 9" set was available on the box backs of eight-ounce Nally's potato chip products. The color posed fronts feature a facsimile autograph with Seattle's schedule and player stats on the box sides. Prices are for complete boxes.

NM
Complete Set (24): 750.00
Common Player (1-8): 25.00
Common Player (9-16): 20.00
Common Player (17-24): 15.00
1 Steve Largent 300.00
2 Autry Beamon 25.00
3 Jim Zorn 65.00
4 Sherman Smith 40.00
5 Ron Coder 25.00
6 Terry Beeson 25.00
7 Steve Niehaus 30.00
8 Ron Howard 25.00
9 Steve Myer 20.00
10 Tom Lynch 20.00
11 David Sims 20.00
12 John Yarno 20.00
13 Bill Gregory 25.00
14 Steve Raible 25.00
15 Dennis Boyd 20.00
16 Steve August 20.00
17 Keith Simpson 15.00
18 Michael Jackson 15.00
19 Manu Tuiasosopo 20.00
20 Sam McCullum 20.00
21 Keith Butler 15.00
22 Sam Akins 15.00
23 Dan Doornink 20.00
24 Dave Brown 20.00

1979 Seahawks Police

The 16-card, 2-5/8" x 4-1/8" set, sponsored by Coca-Cola, Kiwanis, the Washington State Crime Prevention Association and local law enforcement, contain "Tips from the Seahawks" on the card backs.

NM
Complete Set (16): 12.00
Common Player: .75
1 Steve August .75
2 Autry Beamon .75
3 Terry Beeson .75
4 Dennis Boyd .75
5 Dave Brown .75
6 Efren Herrera .75
7 Steve Largent 8.00
8 Tom Lynch .75
9 Bob Newton .75
10 Jack Patera (CO) 1.00
11 Sea Gal (Keri Truscan) .75
12 Seahawk (Mascot) .75
13 David Sims .75
14 Sherman Smith .75
15 John Yarno .75
16 Jim Zorn 3.00

1980 Seahawks Police

The 16-card, 2-5/8" x 4-1/8" set, sponsored by local law enforcement, Coca-Cola, Kiwanis, the Washington State Crime Prevention Association and Ernst Home Centers, features "tips from the Seahawks" on the card backs.

NM
Complete Set (16): 10.00
Common Player: .60
1 Sam McCullum .60
2 Dan Doornink .60
3 Sherman Smith .60
4 Efren Herrera .60
5 Bill Gregory .60
6 Keith Simpson .60
7 Manu Tuiasosopo .60
8 Michael Jackson .60
9 Steve Raible .60
10 Steve Largent 6.00
11 Jim Zorn 2.00
12 Nick Bebout .60
13 The Seahawk (mascot) .60
14 Jack Patera (CO) .75
15 Robert Hardy .60
16 Keith Butler .60

1980 Seahawks 7-Up

The 10-card, 2-3/8" x 3-1/4" set features a player closeup on the card fronts with player bio information on the card backs. Quarterback Jim Zorn and receiver Steve Largent do not appear due to their sponsorships with Darigold Dairy.

NM
Complete Set (10): 125.00
Common Player: 12.00
1 Steve August 12.00
2 Terry Beeson 12.00
3 Dan Doornink 12.00
4 Michael Jackson 12.00
5 Tom Lynch 12.00
6 Steve Myer 12.00
7 Steve Raible 20.00
8 Sherman Smith 20.00
9 Manu Tuiasosopo 12.00
10 John Yarno 12.00

1981 Seahawks 7-Up

The 30-card, 3-1/2" x 5-1/2" set features color action shots and facsimile autographs on the card fronts. The card backs contain a brief player bio. As with the 1980 set, Zorn and Largent do not appear because of conflicting sponsorships.

MT
Complete Set (30): 85.00
Common Player: 3.00
1 Sam Adkins 3.00
2 Steve August 3.00
3 Terry Beeson 3.00
4 Dennis Boyd 3.00
5 Dave Brown 4.00
6 Louis Bullard 3.00
7 Keith Butler 3.00
8 Peter Cronan 3.00
9 Dan Doornink 4.00
10 Jacob Green 6.00
11 Bill Gregory 3.00
12 Robert Hardy 3.00
13 Efren Herrera 3.00
14 Michael Jackson 3.00
15 Art Kuehn 3.00
16 Steve Largent 20.00
17 Tom Lynch 3.00
18 Sam McCullum 4.00
19 Steve Myer 3.00
20 Jack Patera (CO) 4.00
21 Steve Raible 3.00
22 The Sea Gals 3.00
23 The Seahawk Mascot 3.00
24 Keith Simpson 3.00
25 Sherman Smith 3.00
26 Manu Tuiasosopo 3.00
27 Herman Weaver 3.00
28 Cornell Webster 3.00
29 John Yarno 3.00
30 Jim Zorn 8.00

1982 Seahawks Police

The 16-card, 2-5/8" x 4-1/8" set, issued by the Washington State Crime Prevention Association, Kiwanis, Coca-Cola, local law enforcement and Ernst Home Centers, includes "Tips from the Seahawks" on the card backs and the set contains the card of team mascot Sea Gal (No. 4). Also, the cards of Sam McCullum and Jack Patera were distributed in lesser quantities.

MT
Complete Set (16): 12.00
Common Player: .40
1 Sam McCullum (SP) 2.00
2 Manu Tuiasosopo .50
3 Sherman Smith .60
4 Karen Godwin (Sea Gal) .40
5 Dave Brown .60
6 Keith Simpson .40
7 Steve Largent 5.00
8 Michael Jackson .40
9 Kenny Easley .75
10 Dan Doornink .40
11 Jim Zorn 2.00
12 Jack Patera (CO SP) 2.00
13 Jacob Green .60
14 Dave Krieg 3.00
15 Steve August .40
16 Keith Butler .40

1982 Seahawks 7-Up

The 15-card, 3-1/2" x 5-1/2" set features color action shots on the card fronts with "Seahawks Fan Mail Courtesy" printed, as well as a facsimile autograph. The card backs include "Tips from the Seahawks" and the cards of Zorn and Largent are included with Darigold logo on the backs.

MT
Complete Set (15): 75.00
Common Player: 3.00
1 Edwin Bailey 3.00
2 Dave Brown 3.00
3 Kenny Easley 5.00
4 Ron Essink 3.00
5 Jacob Green (No facsimile autograph) 5.00
6 Robert Hardy 3.00
7 John Harris 3.00
8 David Hughes 3.00
9 Paul Johns (HOR) 3.00
10 Kerry Justin 3.00
11 Dave Krieg 12.00
12 Steve Largent (Darigold logo or Gold-n-Soft) 20.00
13 Keith Simpson 3.00
14 Manu Tuiasosopo 3.00
15 Jim Zorn (HOR) (Darigold logo or Gold-n-Soft) 8.00

1984 Seahawks GTE

The 12-card, 3-1/2" x 5-1/2" set features a color shot with a headshot inset in a corner, along with a facsimile autograph on the card front. The card backs have a brief player bio.

MT
Complete Set (12): 40.00
Common Player: 2.00
1 Kenny Easley 3.00
2 Jacob Green 3.00
3 John Harris 2.00
4 Norm Johnson 4.00
5 Chuck Knox (CO) 2.00
6 Dave Krieg 7.00
7 Steve Largent 16.00
8 Joe Nash 2.00
9 Keith Simpson 2.00
10 Mike Tice 2.00
11 Curt Warner 7.00
12 Charley Young 3.00

1984 Seahawks Nalley's

The four-card, 10-3/4" x 9" set was available on the box backs of Nalley's potato chips. The box sides contain Seattle's schedule and player bio information. Prices are for complete boxes.

MT
Complete Set (4): 50.00
Common Player: 10.00
1 Kenny Easley 10.00
2 Dave Krieg 15.00
3 Steve Largent 25.00
4 Curt Warner 15.00

1985 Seahawks Police

The 16-card, 2-5/8" x 4-1/8" set was sponsored by Kiwanis, Coca-Cola, KOMO-TV4, McDonald's, the Washington State Crime Prevention Association and local law enforcement. The card backs contain "Tips from the Seahawks."

MT
Complete Set (16): 8.00
Common Player: .40
1 Dave Brown .50
2 Jeff Bryant .50
3 Blair Bush .50
4 Keith Butler .40
5 Dan Doornink .40
6 Kenny Easley 1.00
7 Jacob Green .60
8 John Harris .40
9 Norm Johnson 1.00
10 Chuck Knox (CO) 1.00
11 Dave Krieg 1.50
12 Steve Largent 3.00
13 Joe Nash .50
14 Bruce Scholtz .40
15 Curt Warner 1.25
16 Fredd Young .60

1986 Seahawks Police

The 16-card, 2-5/8" x 4-1/8" set, sponsored by local law enforcement, contain "Tips from the Seahawks" on the card backs.

MT
Complete Set (16): 8.00
Common Player: .40
1 Edwin Bailey .40
2 Dave Brown .50
3 Jeff Bryant .50
4 Blair Bush .50
5 Keith Butler .40
6 Kenny Easley .60
7 Jacob Green .60
8 Michael Jackson .40
9 Chuck Knox (CO) .60
10 Dave Krieg 1.50
11 Steve Largent 3.00
12 Joe Nash .50
13 Bruce Scholtz .40
14 Terry Taylor .40
15 Curt Warner .75
16 Fredd Young .60

1987 Seahawks GTE

The 24-card, 3-5/8" x 5-1/2" set features color fronts with a facsimile player signature. The card backs have a career summary and a greeting from the player with another autograph.

MT
Complete Set (24): 60.00
Common Player: 1.50
1 Edwin Bailey 1.50
2 Brian Bosworth 2.50
3 Dave Brown 2.00
4 Jeff Bryant 2.00
5 Bobby Joe Edmonds 3.00
6 Jacob Green 3.00
7 Michael Jackson 1.50
8 Norm Johnson 3.00
9 Jeff Kemp 2.50
10 Chuck Knox (CO) 3.00
11 Dave Krieg 5.00
12 Steve Largent 10.00
13 Ron Mattes 1.50
14 Bryan Millard 1.50
15 Paul Moyer 1.50
16 Eugene Robinson 2.00
17 Paul Skansi 1.50
18 Kelly Stouffer 2.00
19 Terry Taylor 1.50
20 Mike Tice 1.50
21 Daryl Turner 2.00
22 Curt Warner 4.00
23 John L. Williams 4.00
24 Fredd Young 2.00

1987 Seahawks Police

The 16-card, 2-5/8" x 4-1/8" set features a silver border with a blue/green Seahawks logo. The card backs contain a safety tip.

MT
Complete Set (16): 5.00
Common Player: .35
1 Jeff Bryant .35
2 Kenny Easley .60
3 Bobby Joe Edmonds .35
4 Jacob Green .60
5 Chuck Knox (CO) .60
6 Dave Krieg 1.50
7 Steve Largent 2.50
8 Ron Mattes .35
9 Bryan Millard .35
10 Eugene Robinson .60
11 Bruce Scholtz .35
12 Paul Skansi .35
13 Curt Warner .75
14 John L. Williams 1.00
15 Mike Wilson .35
16 Fredd Young .35

1987 Seahawks Snyder's/Franz

The 12-card, standard-size set was distributed in the Spokane area (Snyder bread) and Portland area (Franz bread). The card fronts contain a color photo with blue borders while the backs feature a player career summary.

MT
Complete Set (12): 60.00
Common Player: 5.00
1 Jeff Bryant 5.00
2 Keith Butler 5.00
3 Randy Edwards 5.00
4 Byron Franklin 5.00
5 Jacob Green 7.00
6 Dave Krieg 10.00
7 Bryan Millard 5.00
8 Paul Moyer 5.00
9 Eugene Robinson 7.00
10 Mike Tice 5.00
11 Daryl Turner 6.00
12 Curt Warner 8.00

1988 Seahawks Domino's

The 50-card, 2-1/2" x 8-1/2" set was distributed in panel strips with coupons for each Domino's pizza ordered. The first panel contained nine-cards and included a 12-1/2" x 8-1/2" team photo. Cards 10-13, 14-17, 18-21, 22-25, 26-29, 30-33, 34-38, 39-42, 43-46 and 47-50 were issued on a weekly basis.

MT
Complete Set (51): 45.00
Common Player: .60
1 Steve Largent 10.00
2 Kelly Stouffer .75
3 Bobby Joe Edmonds 1.00
4 Patrick Hunter .75
5 Ventrella/Valle/Gellos .60
6 Edwin Bailey .60
7 Alonzo Mitz .60
8 Tommy Kane 1.00
9 Chuck Knox (CO) 1.00
10 Curt Warner 2.00
11 Alvin Powell .60
12 Joe Nash .60
13 Brian Blades 3.00
14 Blair Bush .75
15 Melvin Jenkins .60
16 Ruben Rodriguez .60
17 Tommie Agee .60
18 Eugene Robinson .75
19 Dwayne Harper .60
20 Raymond Butler .60
21 Jeff Kemp 1.00
22 Norm Johnson .75
23 Bryan Millard .60
24 Tony Woods 1.00
25 Paul Skansi .60
26 Jacob Green 1.00
27 Randall Morris .60
28 Mike Tice .60
29 Kevin Harmon .60
30 Dave Krieg 2.50
31 Nesby Glasgow .75
32 Bruce Scholtz .60
33 John Spagnola .60
34 Jeff Bryant .75
35 Stan Eisenhooth .60
36 Dave Wyman .60
37 Greg Gaines .60
38 Charlie Jones (NBC ANN) .60
39 Terry Taylor .60
40 Vernon Dean .60
41 Mike Wilson .60
42 Darrin Miller .60
43 John L. Williams 2.50
44 Grant Feasel .60
45 M.L. Johnson .60
46 Ken Clarke .75
47 Brian Bosworth .75
48 Ron Mattes .60
49 Paul Moyer .60
50 Rufus Porter 1.00
NNO Team Photo (Large size) 7.00

Values quoted in this guide reflect the retail price of a card — the price a collector can expect to pay when buying a card from a dealer. The wholesale price — that which a collector can expect to receive from a dealer when selling cards — will be significantly lower, depending on desirability and condition.

1988 Seahawks Police

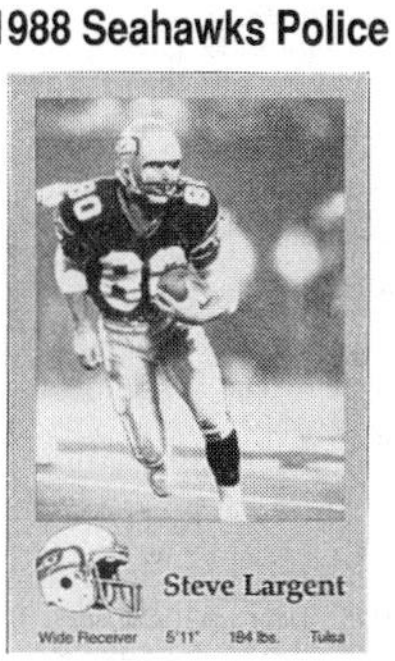

Steve Largent
Wide Receiver 5'11" 184 lbs. Tulsa

The 16-card, 2-5/8" x 4-1/8" set features color photos with gray borders and the backs include safety tips. Terry Taylor's card was pulled from distribution after he was suspended from the team.

MT
Complete Set (16): 10.00
Common Player: .50
1 Brian Bosworth 1.00
2 Jeff Bryant .60
3 Raymond Butler .50
4 Jacob Green 1.00
5 Patrick Hunter .60
6 Norm Johnson .75
7 Chuck Knox (CO) .75
8 Dave Krieg 1.50
9 Steve Largent 2.50
10 Ron Mattes .50
11 Bryan Millard .50
12 Paul Moyer .50
13 Terry Taylor (SP) 2.50
14 Curt Warner 1.00
15 John L. Williams 1.25
16 Fredd Young (SP) 4.50

1988 Seahawks Snyder's/Franz

The 12-card, standard-size set was issued in the Spokane area in Snyder's bread and in the Portland area in Franz bread. The card fronts have a color photo with blue borders.

MT
Complete Set (10): 125.00
Common Player: 12.00
1 Steve August 12.00
2 Terry Beeson 12.00
3 Dan Doornink 15.00
4 Michael Jackson 12.00
5 Tom Lynch 12.00
6 Steve Myer 12.00
7 Steve Raible 20.00
8 Sherman Smith 20.00
9 Manu Tuiasosopo 15.00
10 John Yarno 12.00

1989 Seahawks Oroweat

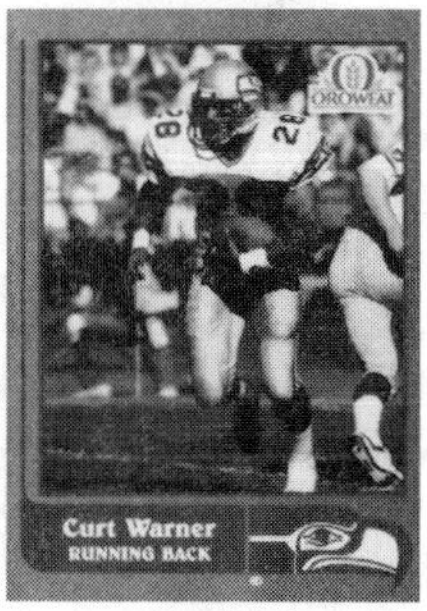

OROWEAT
Curt Warner
RUNNING BACK

The 20-card, standard-size set was produced for Oroweat by Pacific and features silver borders. The horizontal backs contain player bio and stat information with career highlights. Each card was available in Oroweat's Oatnut Bread with a total distribution of 1.5 million.

MT
Complete Set (20): 25.00
Common Player: .60
1 Paul Moyer .60
2 Dave Wyman .60
3 Tony Woods 1.00
4 Kelly Stouffer 1.00
5 Brian Blades 3.00
6 Norm Johnson 1.50
7 Curt Warner 2.00
8 John L. Williams 2.00
9 Edwin Bailey .60
10 Jacob Green 1.00
11 Paul Skansi .60
12 Jeff Bryant .75
13 Bruce Scholtz .60
14 Dave Krieg 3.00
15 Steve Largent 8.00
16 Joe Nash .75
17 Mike Wilson .60
18 Ron Mattes .60
19 Grant Feasel .60
20 Bryan Millard .60

1989 Seahawks Police

The 16-card, 2-5/8" x 4-1/8" set feature light blue borders with color action shots. The card backs contain

safety tips, except for Largent's card, which lists his NFL records.

		MT
Complete Set (16):		5.00
Common Player:		.40
1	Brian Blades	1.00
2	Brian Bosworth	.50
3	Jeff Bryant	.50
4	Jacob Green	.60
5	Chuck Knox (CO)	.60
6	Dave Krieg	1.25
7	Steve Largent	2.00
8	Bryan Millard	.40
9	Rufus Porter	.50
10	Paul Moyer	.40
11	Eugene Robinson	.50
12	Ruben Rodriguez	.40
13	Kelly Stouffer	.50
14	Curt Warner	1.00
15	John L. Williams	1.00
16	Tony Woods	.60

1990 Seahawks Oroweat

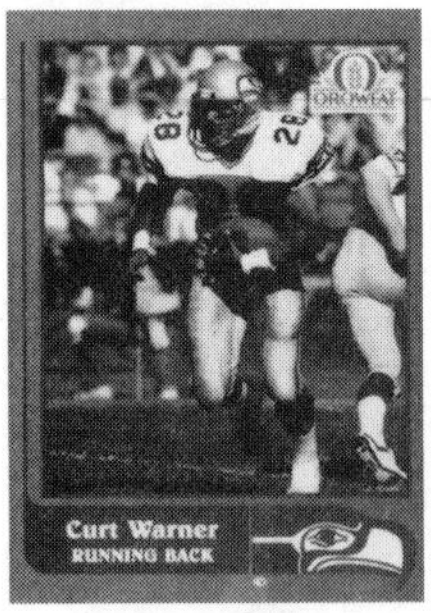
Curt Warner
RUNNING BACK

The 50-card, regular-size set, produced by Pacific, was available in loaves of Oroweat's Oat Nut, Health Nut and Twelve Grain breads. The first 20 cards of the set were issued before the season with the remaining cards issued during the season. No card No. 25 was produced.

		MT
Complete Set (50):		30.00
Common Player (1-20):		.35
Common Player (21-50):		.50
1	Dave Krieg	1.50
2	Rick Donnelly	.35
3	Brian Blades	1.50
4	Cortez Kennedy	1.75
5	John L. Williams	1.50
6	Jeff Chadwick	.35
7	Thom Kaumeyer	.35
8	Bryan Millard	.35
9	Eugene Robinson	.50
10	Jacob Green	.50
11	Willie Bouyer	.35
12	Jeff Bryant	.50
13	Chris Warren	3.00
14	Derrick Fenner	.75
15	Paul Skansi	.35
16	Joe Cain	.35
17	Tommy Kane	.60
18	Tom Flores (GM)	.60
19	Terry Wooden	.50
20	Tony Woods	.60
21	Ricky Andrews	.50
22	Joe Tofflemire	.50
23	Ned Bolcar	.50
24A	Kelly Stouffer	1.00
24B	Melvin Jenkins	.50
26	Norm Johnson	.75
27	Eric Hayes	.50
28	Mike Morris	.50
29	Edwin Bailey	.50
30	Ron Heller	.50
31	Darren Comeaux	.60
32	Andy Heck	.60
33	Ronnie Lee	.50
34	Robert Blackmon	.60
35	Joe Nash	.60
36	Patrick Hunter	.60
37	Darrick Brilz	.50
38	Ron Mattes	.50
39	Nesby Glasgow	.60
40	Dwayne Harper	.50
41	Chuck Knox (CO)	.75
42	Travis McNeal	.60
43	Derek Loville	1.50
44	Dave Wyman	.50
45	Louis Clark	.50
46	Grant Feasel	.50
47	James Jones	.60
48	Rufus Porter	1.00
49	Jeff Kemp	1.00
50	James Jefferson	.60
NNO	Title Card	3.00
		.50

1990 Seahawks Police

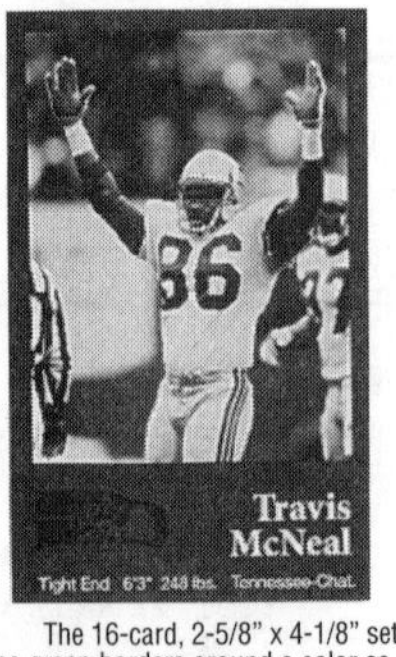
Travis
McNeal
Tight End 6'3" 248 lbs. Tennessee-Chat.

The 16-card, 2-5/8" x 4-1/8" set has green borders around a color action shot with safety tips appearing on the backs.

		MT
Complete Set (16):		5.00
Common Player:		.35
1	Brian Blades	.75
2	Grant Feasel	.35
3	Jacob Green	.75
4	Andy Heck	.50
5	James Jefferson	.50
6	Norm Johnson	.75
7	Cortez Kennedy	1.00
8	Chuck Knox (CO)	.75
9	Dave Krieg	1.00
10	Travis McNeal	.35
11	Bryan Millard	.35
12	Rufus Porter	.50
13	Paul Skansi	.35
14	John L. Williams	.75
15	Tony Woods	.50
16	David Wyman	.35

1991 Seahawks Oroweat

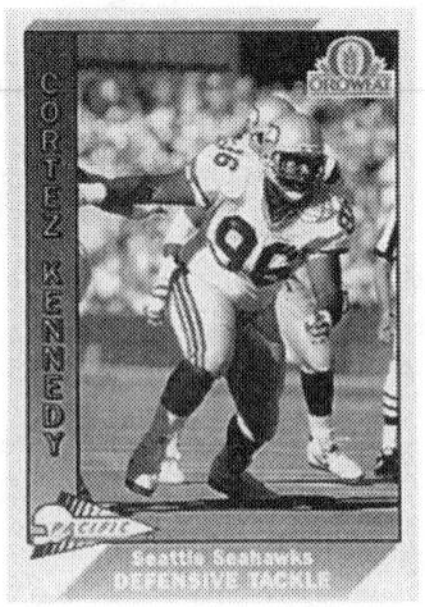
CORTEZ KENNEDY
PACIFIC
Seattle Seahawks
DEFENSIVE TACKLE

The 50-card, standard-size set, produced by Pacific, was distributed in loaves of Oroweat bread and in five-card packs at a Seattle home game. The cards are very similar to Pacific's 1991 inaugural NFL set, except for the Oroweat logo in the upper right corner of the card front.

		MT
Complete Set (50):		30.00
Common Player:		.50
1	Tommy Kane	.50
2	Norm Johnson	.75
3	Robert Blackmon	.50
4	Mike Tice	.50
5	Cortez Kennedy	1.50
6	Bryan Millard	.50
7	Tony Woods	.50
8	Paul Skansi	.50
9	John L. Williams	1.50
10	Terry Wooden	.75
11	Brian Blades	1.25
12	Jacob Green	.75
13	Joe Nash	.75
14	Eugene Robinson	.75
15	Rufus Porter	.75
16	Andy Heck	.50
17	Derrick Fenner	1.00
18	Nesby Glasgow	.50
19	Chris Warren	3.00
20	Dave Krieg	1.50
21	Vann McElroy	.50
22	Jeff Bryant	.50
23	Warren Wheat	.50
24	Marcus Cotton	.50
25	David Wyman	.50
26	Joe Cain	.50
27	Darrick Brilz	.50
28	Eric Hayes	.50
29	Ronnie Lee	.50
30	Louis Clark	.50
31	James Jones	.50
32	Dwayne Harper	.50
33	Grant Feasel	.50
34	Trey Junkin	.50
35	James Jefferson	.50
36	Edwin Bailey	.50
37	Derrick Loville	1.50
38	Travis McNeal	.50
39	Rick Donnelly	.50
40	Rod Stephens	.50
41	Darren Comeaux	.50
42	Brian Davis	.50
43	Bill Hitchcock	.50
44	Jeff Chadwick	.75
45	Patrick Hunter	.75
46	David Daniels	.50
47	Doug Thomas	.50
48	Dan McGwire	.75
49	John Kasay	.75
50	Jeff Kemp	.75
NNO	Title Card	2.50

1992 Seahawks Oroweat

The 50-card, regular-size set, produced by Pacific, was delivered in various loaves of Oroweat bread. The card design is very similar to the base 1992 Pacific set, except for the Oroweat and KIRO Newsradio logos.

		MT
Complete Set (51):		25.00
Common Player:		.50
1	Brian Blades	1.00
2	Patrick Hunter	.75
3	Jeff Bryant	.75
4	Robert Blackmon	.50
5	Joe Cain	.50
6	Grant Feasel	.50
7	Dan McGwire	.50
8	David Wyman	.50
9	Jacob Green	.50
10	Theo Adams	.50
11	Brian Davis	.50
12	Andy Heck	.50
13	Bill Hitchcock	.50
14	Joe Nash	.50
15	Rod Stephens	.50
16	John Hunter	.50
17	Paul Green	.50
18	James Jones	.50
19	Robb Thomas	.75
20	Tony Woods	.50
21	Dedrick Dodge	.50
22	Tracy Johnson	.50
23	Darrick Brilz	.50
24	Joe Tofflemire	.50
25	Louis Clark	.50
26	Rueben Mayes	.75
27	Natu Tuatagaloa	.50
28	Terry Wooden	.75
29	Tommy Kane	.50
30	Stan Gelbaugh	.75
31	Nesby Glasgow	.50
32	Kelly Stouffer	.50
33	Ray Roberts	.50
34	Doug Thomas	.50
35	David Daniels	.50
36	John Kasay	.75
37	Cortez Kennedy	.75
38	Tyrone Rodgers	.50
39	Bryan Millard	.50
40	Eugene Robinson	.75
41	Malcolm Frank	.50
42	Dwayne Harper	.50
43	Ron Heller	.50
44	Rick Tuten	.50
45	Trey Junkin	.50
46	Bob Spitulski	.50
47	Chris Warren	2.00
48	John L. Williams	.75
49	Ronnie Lee	.50
50	Rufus Porter	.75
NNO	Title/Ad Card	1.00

1993 Seahawks Oroweat

The 50-card, standard size set, sponsored by Oroweat and KIRO Newsradio, was produced by Pacific. The cards' design is very similar to Pacific's 1993 base set and were included in various loaves of Oroweat bread.

		MT
Complete Set (50):		25.00
Common Player:		.50
1	Cortez Kennedy	1.00
2	Robb Thomas	.75
3	Rueben Mayes	.75
4	Rick Tuten	.50
5	Tracy Johnson	.50
6	Michael Bates	.50
7	Andy Heck	.50
8	Stan Gelbaugh	.75
9	Dan McGwire	.75
10	Mike Keim	.50
11	Grant Feasel	.50
12	Brian Blades	1.00
13	Tyrone Rodgers	.50
14	Paul Green	.50
15	Rafael Robinson	.50
16	John Kasay	.75
17	Chris Warren	2.00
18	Michael Sinclair	.50
19	John L. Williams	.75
20	Bob Spitulski	.50
21	Eugene Robinson	.75
22	Patrick Hunter	.75
23	Kevin Murphy	.50
24	Dave McCloughan	.50
25	Rick Mirer	5.00
26	Ray Donaldson	.75
27	E.J. Junior	.50
28	Jeff Bryant	.75
29	Ferrell Edmunds	.50
30	Tommy Kane	.75
31	Terry Wooden	.75
32	Doug Thomas	.50
33	Carlton Gray	.50
34	Kelvin Martin	.75
35	Rod Stephens	.50
36	Darrick Brilz	.50
37	Joe Tofflemire	.50
38	James Jefferson	.50
39	Rufus Porter	.75
40	Jeff Blackshear	.50
41	Dwayne Harper	.50
42	Ray Roberts	.50
43	Robert Blackmon	.50
44	Joe Nash	.50
45	Michael McCrary	.50
46	Trey Junkin	.50
47	Natu Tuatagaloa	.50
48	Bill Hitchcock	.50
49	Jon Vaughn	.75
50	Dean Wells	.50

1994 Seahawks Oroweat

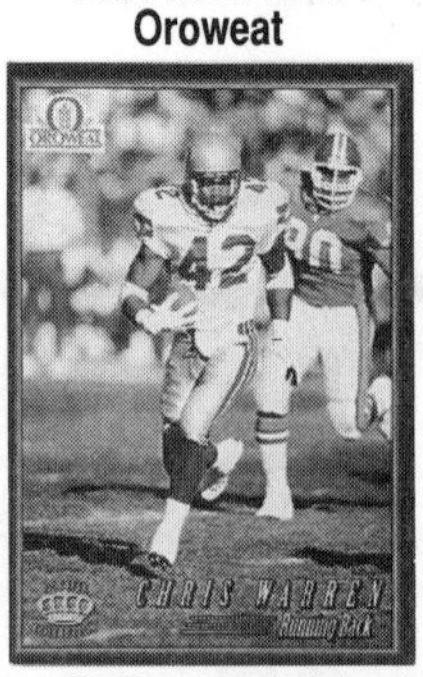
CHRIS WARREN
Running Back

The 50-card, standard-size set, produced by Pacific, was issued in various loaves of Oroweat bread in the Northwest area. The cards are almost identical in design to Pacific's 1994 football set, except for the Oroweat logo in the upper right corner of the card front.

		MT
Complete Set (50):		25.00
Common Player:		.50
1	Brian Blades	.75
2	Terrence Warren	.50
3	Carlton Gray	.50
4	Bob Spitulski	.50
5	Dean Wells	.50
6	Lamar Smith	.50
7	Michael Bates	.50
8	Duane Bickett	.60
9	Cortez Kennedy	1.00
10	Dave McCloughan	.50
11	Tracy Johnson	.50
12	Eugene Robinson	.60
13	Jeff Blackshear	.50
14	Tyrone Rodgers	.50
15	Trey Junkin	.50
16	Ferrell Edmunds	.50
17	Tony Brown	.50
18	Orlando Watters	.50
19	John Kasay	.60
20	Rafael Robinson	.50
21	Kelvin Martin	.60
22	Stan Gelbaugh	.60
23	Steve Smith	.50
24	Ray Donaldson	.60
25	Rufus Porter	.50
26	Patrick Hunter	.60
27	Terry Wooden	.60
28	Sam Adams	.60
29	Mack Strong	.60
30	Chris Warren	1.25
31	Bill Hitchcock	.50
32	David Brandon	.50
33	Michael McCrary	.50
34	Jon Vaughn	.60
35	Paul Green	.50
36	Mike Keim	.50
37	Joe Tofflemire	.50
38	Rick Tuten	.50
39	Rick Mirer	3.00
40	Rod Stephens	.50
41	Robert Blackmon	.50
42	Howard Ballard	.50
43	Michael Sinclair	.50
44	Kevin Mawae	.50
45	Brent Williams	.50
46	Ray Roberts	.50
47	Robb Thomas	.60
48	Antonio Edwards	.50
49	Dan McGwire	.50
50	Joe Nash	.50

1982 Sears-Roebuck

The 12-card, 5" x 7" set, issued by 37 different Sears district stores, closely resembles the Marketcom posters. The card backs contain bio and career highlight information with the Sears Roebuck logo on the card back bottom. Because of the football strike in 1982, many of the cards were not distributed and were either destroyed or thrown out.

		MT
Complete Set (12):		265.00
Common Player:		8.00
1	Ken Anderson	15.00
2	Terry Bradshaw	25.00
3	Earl Campbell	25.00
4	Dwight Clark	8.00
5	Cris Collinsworth	8.00
6	Tony Dorsett	20.00
7	Dan Fouts	18.00
8	Franco Harris	20.00
9	Joe Montana	75.00
10	Walter Payton	40.00
11	Randy White	15.00
12	Kellen Winslow	15.00

1993 Select

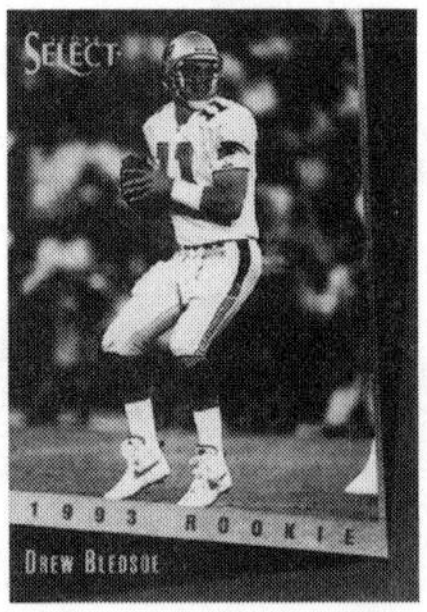
SELECT
1993 ROOKIE
DREW BLEDSOE

Score's 1993 Select set includes 200 cards which are framed on two sides by green. A 10-card insert set, Gridiron Skills, was also produced; cards were randomly inserted in packs.

		MT
Complete Set (200):		40.00
Common Player:		.25
Minor Stars:		.50
Pack (15):		3.00
Wax Box (36):		100.00
1	Steve Young	3.00
2	Andre Reed	.50
3	Deion Sanders	2.00
4	Harold Green	.25
5	Wendell Davis	.25
6	Mike Johnson	.25
7	Troy Aikman	3.00
8	Johnny Mitchell	.25
9	Dale Carter	.25
10	Bruce Matthews	.25
11	Terrell Buckley	.25
12	Steve Emtman	.25
13	Neil Smith	.25
14	Tim Brown	.50
15	Chris Doleman	.25
16	Dan Marino	6.00
17	Terry McDaniel	.25
18	Neal Anderson	.25
19	Phil Simms	.25
20	Jeff Lageman	.25
21	Jerry Rice	3.00
22	Dermontti Dawson	.25
23	Reggie Cobb	.25
24	Junior Seau	.50
25	Darrell Green	.25
26	Chris Warren	.50
27	Randall Cunningham	.50
28	Bruce Smith	.25
29	Bryan Cox	.25
30	David Klingler	.25
31	Chip Lohmiller	.25
32	Eric Metcalf	.25
33	Ken Norton	.25
34	John Elway	3.00
35	Harris Barton	.25
36	Tim Barnett	.25
37	Rodney Hampton	.50
38	Desmond Howard	.25
39	Tom Rathman	.25
40	Derrick Thomas	.50
41	Randal Hill	.25
42	Steve Wisniewski	.25
43	Brett Favre	8.00
44	Darryl Talley	.25
45	Shane Conlan	.25
46	Anthony Miller	.50
47	Randall McDaniel	.25
48	Rod Woodson	.25
49	Eric Martin	.25
50	Ronnie Lott	.25
51	Chris Spielman	.25
52	Vincent Brown	.25
53	Donnell Woolford	.25
54	Richmond Webb	.25
55	Emmitt Smith	6.00
56	Haywood Jeffires	.25
57	Jim Kelly	.50
58	James Francis	.25
59	Steve Wallace	.25
60	Jarrod Bunch	.25
61	Lawrence Dawsey	.25
62	Steve Atwater	.25
63	Art Monk	.50
64	Eric Green	.25
65	Lawrence Taylor	.50
66	Ronnie Harmon	.25
67	Fred Barnett	.25
68	Cortez Kennedy	.25
69	Mark Collins	.25
70	Howie Long	.50
71	Jackie Harris	.25
72	Irving Fryar	.25
73	Jim Everett	.25
74	Troy Vincent	.25
75	Cris Carter	.50
76	Boomer Esiason	.25
77	Sam Mills	.25
78	Lorenzo White	.25
79	Andre Rison	.50
80	Quentin Coryatt	.25
81	Steve McMichael	.25
82	Nick Lowery	.25
83	Michael Irvin	.50
84	Thurman Thomas	.50
85	Bill Romanowski	.25
86	Carl Pickens	2.00
87	Tim McDonald	.25
88	Bernie Kosar	.25
89	Greg Lloyd	.25
90	Barry Sanders	5.00
91	Shannon Sharpe	.50
92	Henry Thomas	.25
93	Barry Foster	.25
94	Antone Davis	.25
95	Stan Humphries	.50
96	Eric Swann	.25
97	Mike Pritchard	.25
98	Reggie White	.50
99	Jeff Hostetler	.25
100	Willie Anderson	.25
101	Gary Clark	.25
102	Morten Andersen	.25
103	Leonard Russell	.25
104	Chris Hinton	.25
105	John Stephens	.25
106	Byron Evans	.25
107	Warren Moon	.50
108	Marv Cook	.25
109	*Carlton Gray*	.25
110	Jay Novacek	.25
111	Gary Anderson	.25
112	Andre Tippett	.25
113	Cornelius Bennett	.25
114	Clyde Simmons	.25
115	Jeff George	.50
116	Audray McMillian	.25
117	Mark Carrier	.25
118	Vaughan Johnson	.25
119	Kevin Greene	.25
120	John Taylor	.25
121	Jerry Ball	.25
122	Pat Swilling	.25
123	*George Teague*	.50
124	Ricky Reynolds	.25
125	Marcus Allen	.50
126	Henry Jones	.25
127	Ricky Watters	.50
128	Leon Searcy	.25
129	Chris Miller	.25
130	Jim Harbaugh	.50
131	Luis Sharpe	.25
132	Simon Fletcher	.25
133	Eric Allen	.25
134	Carlton Haselrig	.25
135	Harvey Williams	.25
136	Leslie O'Neal	.25
137	Sterling Sharpe	.50
138	Tim Harris	.25
139	Mark Rypien	.25
140	Harry Galbreath	.25
141	Sean Gilbert	.25
142	Keith Jackson	.25
143	Mark Clayton	.25
144	Guy McIntyre	.25
145	Jessie Tuggle	.25
146	Leonard Marshall	.25
147	Willie Davis	.25
148	Herman Moore	2.00
149	Charles Haley	.25
150	Amp Lee	.25
151	Gary Zimmerman	.25
152	Bennie Blades	.25
153	Pierce Holt	.25
154	Edgar Bennett	.50
155	Joe Montana	4.00
156	Ted Washington	.25
157	Hardy Nickerson	.25
158	Rohn Stark	.25
159	Brent Jones	.25
160	Eugene Robinson	.25
161	Pepper Johnson	.25
162	Dan Saleaumua	.25
163	Seth Joyner	.25
165	Mike Munchak	.25
166	*Drew Bledsoe*	15.00
167	*Curtis Conway*	3.00
168	*Lincoln Kennedy*	.50
169	*Dana Stubblefield*	1.00
170	*Wayne Simmons*	.50
171	*Garrison Hearst*	5.00
172	*Jerome Bettis*	8.00
173	*Eric Curry*	.50
174	*Natrone Means*	5.00
175	*Glyn Milburn*	.50
176	*Marvin Jones*	.50
177	*O.J. McDuffie*	3.00
178	*Dan Williams*	.50
179	*Rick Mirer*	.75
180	*John Copeland*	.50
181	*Willie Roaf*	.50
182	*Patrick Bates*	.50
183	*Troy Drayton*	.75
184	*Vincent Brisby*	.50
185	*Irv Smith*	.50
186	Marion Butts	.25
187	Wayne Martin	.25
188	Brian Blades	.25
189	Mel Gray	.25
190	Mark Stepnoski	.25
191	Ernest Givins	.25
192	Steve Tasker	.25
193	Tim Grunhard	.25
194	Stanley Richard	.25
195	Jeff Wright	.25
196	Rodney Peete	.25
197	Tunch Ilkin	.25
198	Rich Camarillo	.25
199	Erik Williams	.25
200	Pete Stoyanovich	.25

1993 Select Gridiron Skills

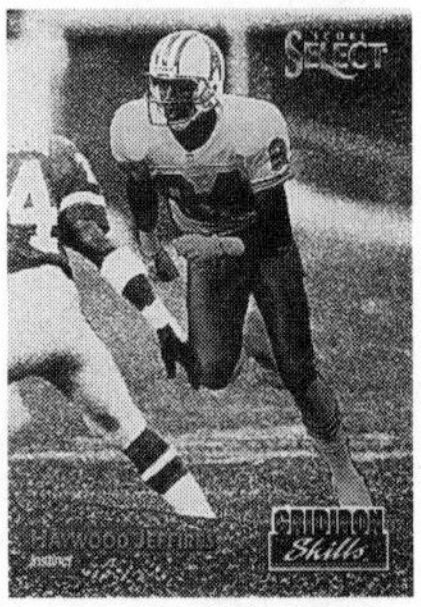
SELECT
Haywood Jeffires
GRIDIRON
Skills

These cards were random inserts in 1993 Score Select foil packs at a rate of about one every 72 packs. Five top wide receivers and five top quarterbacks are represented. The card front has a player action photo against a shiny, metallic-like background. The player's name and position are at the bottom in a red stripe, along with the set logo. The back has a player photo and a description of the skills he brings to the football field. Each card is numbered.

		MT
Complete Set (10):		250.00
Common Player:		5.00
Minor Stars:		10.00
1	Warren Moon	10.00
2	Steve Young	30.00
3	Dan Marino	60.00
4	John Elway	40.00
5	Troy Aikman	30.00
6	Sterling Sharpe	10.00
7	Jerry Rice	30.00
8	Andre Rison	10.00
9	Haywood Jeffires	5.00
10	Michael Irvin	10.00

1993 Select Young Stars

These metallic-like cards, sold as a set in a black box, use FX printing technology. Each card front has a color action photo against a tombstone-like background. The player's name and "Young Stars" are written at the top of the card, above the arch. The Select logo is in the lower left corner. The front and back use team colors in the design. The back has a team helmet in the center, above a player profile. Cards are numbered. There were 5,900 sets produced; each includes a certificate of authenticity which indicates the set's serial number.

		MT
Complete Set (38):		50.00
Common Player:		1.00
1	Brett Favre	10.00
2	Anthony Miller	1.00
3	Rodney Hampton	2.50
4	Cortez Kennedy	1.00
5	Junior Seau	2.50
6	Ricky Watters	2.50
7	Terry Allen	1.50
8	Drew Bledsoe	4.00
9	Rick Mirer	4.00
10	Jeff Graham	1.00
11	Barry Foster	1.00
12	Eric Green	1.00
13	Troy Aikman	10.00
14	Michael Haynes	1.00
15	Johnny Mitchell	1.00
16	Lawrence Dawsey	1.00
17	Mo Lewis	1.00
18	Andre Ware	1.00
19	Neil O'Donnell	2.00
20	Broderick Thomas	1.00

21 Tim Barnett 1.00
22 Fred Barnett 1.00
23 Carl Pickens 3.00
24 Santana Dotson 1.00
25 Sean Gilbert 1.00
26 Quentin Coryatt 1.00
27 Arthur Marshall 1.00
28 Dale Carter 1.00
29 Henry Jones 1.00
30 Terrell Buckley 1.00
31 Tommy Vardell 1.00
32 Russell Maryland 1.00
33 Steve Emtman 1.00
34 Jarrod Bunch 1.00
35 Alfred Williams 1.00
36 Brian Mitchell 1.00
37 Chris Warren 3.00
38 Deion Sanders 4.00

1994 Select Samples

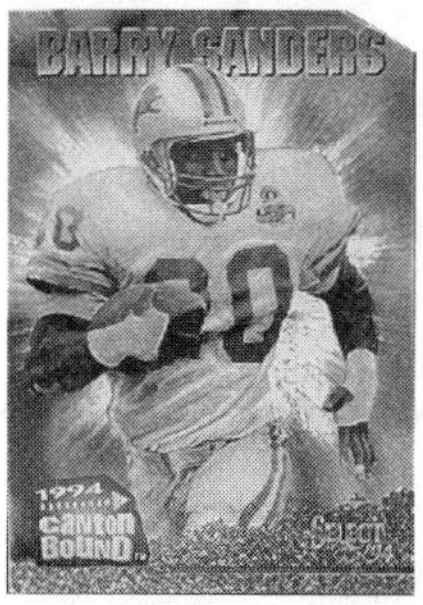

The seven-card, regular-sized set was issued to preview the 1994 Select set. The cards are virtually identical to the base set and include a Canton Bound and Future Force insert sample. The card numbers are the same as the base card counterparts.

MT
Complete Set (7): 10.00
Common Player: 1.00
5 Rod Woodson 1.00
19 Junior Seau 1.50
33 Mark Carrier (DB) 1.00
218 Charlie Garner 1.00
CB4 Barry Sanders 4.00
FF2 Drew Bledsoe 4.00
NNO Title Card 1.00

1994 Select

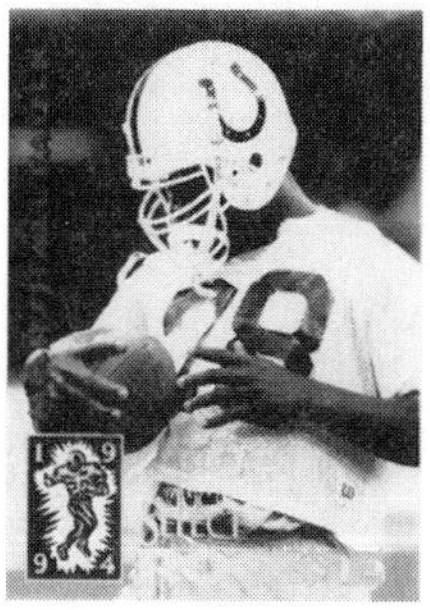

Select consists of a 225-card base set. The cards feature a full-bleed photo and a small, oval-shaped, black and white photo with a gold-foil border on the front. A 25-card rookie subset is included in the base series. Insert sets in Select include Canton Bound (12 cards, 1:48) and Future Force (12 cards, 1:48).

MT
Complete Set (225): 30.00
Common Player: .15
Minor Stars: .30
Pack (12): 4.00
Wax Box (24): 75.00
1 Emmitt Smith 3.00
2 Bruce Smith .15
3 Randall McDaniel .15
4 Drew Bledsoe 2.50
5 Rod Woodson .15
6 Richard Dent .15
7 Norm Johnson .15
8 Jim Everett .15
9 Harold Green .15
10 John Elway 3.00
11 Barry Sanders 4.00
12 Sterling Sharpe .30
13 Marcus Robertson .15
14 Steve Wisniewski .15
15 Irving Fryar .15
16 Tyrone Hughes .15
17 Garrison Hearst 1.00
18 Randall Cunningham .50
19 Junior Seau .30
20 Rick Mirer .30
21 Jerry Rice 2.00
22 Eric Metcalf .15
23 Roosevelt Potts .15
24 Neil Smith .15
25 Jerome Bettis 1.00
26 Keith Hamilton .15
27 Hardy Nickerson .15
28 Steve Tasker .15
29 Johnny Johnson .15
30 Tom Carter .15
31 Andre Rison .30
32 Cortez Kennedy .30
33 Mark Carrier .15
34 Shannon Sharpe .30
35 Eric Swann .15
36 Steve Young 1.50
37 Johnny Mitchell .15
38 Dermontti Dawson .15
39 Mike Johnson .15
40 Troy Aikman 2.00
41 Pierce Holt .15
42 Derrick Thomas .30
43 Reggie Cobb .15
44 Michael Jackson .15
45 Lomas Brown .15
46 Jeff Hostetler .15
47 Pete Stoyanovich .15
48 Reggie White .50
49 Quentin Coryatt .15
50 Cris Carter .75
51 Sean Gilbert .15
52 Chris Slade .15
53 Ronnie Harmon .15
54 Renaldo Turnbull .15
55 Fred Barnett .15
56 John Elliott .15
57 Deion Sanders 1.00
58 John Carney .15
59 Louis Oliver .15
60 Greg Lloyd .15
61 Chris Hinton .15
62 Ron Moore .15
63 Vincent Brown .15
64 Tony McGee .15
65 Erik Williams .15
66 Thurman Thomas .30
67 Neil O'Donnell .30
68 Scott Mitchell .30
69 Keith Byars .15
70 Henry Ellard .15
71 Chris Spielman .15
72 LeRoy Butler .15
73 Tim Brown .30
74 Darrell Green .15
75 Bruce Matthews .15
76 Stan Humphries .30
77 Will Wolford .15
78 John Taylor .15
79 Joe Montana 3.00
80 Chris Warren .30
81 Michael Brooks .15
82 Vance Johnson .15
83 Rob Moore .30
84 Herschel Walker .15
85 Alvin Harper .15
86 Wayne Martin .15
87 Leslie O'Neal .15
88 Willie Anderson .15
89 Tommy Vardell .15
90 Mike Sherrard .15
91 Chris Jacke .15
92 Jim Kelly .30
93 Jeff Graham, Thomas Everett .15
94 Bryan Cox .15
95 Michael Irvin .30
96 Jeff Lageman .15
97 Webster Slaughter .15
98 Eugene Robinson .15
99 Vencie Glenn .15
100 Sean Jones .15
101 Calvin Williams .15
102 Jim Harbaugh .30
103 Eric Curry .15
104 Terry Allen .30
105 Darryl Williams .15
106 Gary Clark .15
107 Marcus Allen .50
108 Chip Lohmiller .15
109 Vaughan Johnson .15
110 Herman Moore .75
111 Barry Foster .15
112 Rocket Ismail .15
113 Erric Pegram .15
114 Anthony Miller .15
115 Shane Conlan .15
116 David Klingler .15
117 Mark Collins .15
118 Tony Bennett .15
119 Donnell Woolford .15
120 Reggie Brooks .15
121 Sam Mills .15
122 Greg Montgomery .15
123 Kevin Greene .15
124 Terry McDaniel .15
125 Henry Jones .15
126 Ricky Watters .30
127 Dan Marino 3.00
128 Steve Atwater .15
129 Ricky Proehl .15
130 Ernest Givins .15
131 John L. Williams .15
132 John Randle .15
133 Jay Novacek .15
134 Boomer Esiason .30
135 Jessie Hester .15
136 Courtney Hawkins .15
137 Ben Coates .30
138 Stevon Moore .15
139 Eric Allen .15
140 Jessie Tuggle .15
141 Marion Butts .15
142 Brett Favre 4.00
143 Andre Reed .30
144 Rodney Hampton .30
145 Keith Sims .15
146 Derek Brown .15
147 Eric Green .15
148 Greg Robinson .15
149 Nate Newton .15
150 Mark Higgs .15
151 Nick Lowery .15
152 Craig Erickson .15
153 Anthony Carter .15
154 Simon Fletcher .15
155 Ronnie Lott .30
156 Gary Brown .15
157 Brent Jones .15
158 Jim Sweeney .15
159 Robert Brooks .15
160 Keith Jackson .15
161 Daryl Johnston .15
162 Tom Waddle .15
163 Eric Martin .15
164 Cornelius Bennett .15
165 Tim McDonald .15
166 Chris Doleman .15
167 Gary Zimmerman .15
168 Al Smith .15
169 Mark Carrier .15
170 Harris Barton .15
171 Ray Childress .15
172 Darryl Talley .15
173 James Jett .15
174 Mark Stepnoski .15
175 Jeff Query .15
176 Charles Haley .15
177 Rod Bernstine .15
178 Richmond Webb .15
179 Rich Camarillo .15
180 Pat Swilling .15
181 Chris Miller .15
182 Mike Pritchard .15
183 Checklist .15
184 Natrone Means .75
185 Erik Kramer .15
186 Clyde Simmons .15
187 Checklist .15
188 Warren Moon .30
189 Michael Haynes .15
190 Terry Kirby .30
191 Brian Blades .15
192 Haywood Jeffires .15
194 Morten Andersen .15
195 Dana Stubblefield .15
196 Ken Norton .15
197 Art Monk .15
198 Seth Joyner .15
199 *Heath Shuler* .40
200 *Marshall Faulk* 6.00
201 *Charles Johnson* .40
202 *Derrick Alexander* .40
203 *Greg Hill* .50
204 *Darnay Scott* 1.50
205 *Willie McGinest* .50
206 *Thomas Randolph* .25
207 *Errict Rhett* 1.00
208 *William Floyd* .50
209 *Johnnie Morton* 1.25
210 *David Palmer* 1.00
211 *Dan Wilkinson* .50
212 *Trent Dilfer* 2.50
213 *Antonio Langham* .50
214 *Chuck Levy* .25
215 *John Thierry* .25
216 *Kevin Lee* .25
217 *Aaron Glenn* .25
218 *Charlie Garner* 1.75
219 *Jeff Burris* .25
220 *LeShon Johnson* .25
221 *Thomas Lewis* .25
222 *Ryan Yarborough* .25
223 *Mario Bates* .50
224 Checklist .15
225 Checklist .15
SR1 Marshall Faulk SR 40.00
SR2 Dan Wilkinson SR 10.00

1994 Select Canton Bound

Canton Bound is a 12-card insert featuring Dufex technology. The set features players destined for the Hall of Fame and was inserted 1:48.

MT
Complete Set (12): 260.00
Common Player: 5.00
Minor Stars: 10.00
Inserted 1:48
1 Emmitt Smith 45.00
2 Sterling Sharpe 10.00
3 Joe Montana 45.00
4 Barry Sanders 60.00
5 Jerry Rice 30.00
6 Ronnie Lott 5.00
7 Reggie White 10.00
8 Steve Young 20.00
9 Jerome Bettis 10.00
10 Bruce Smith 5.00
11 Troy Aikman 30.00
12 Thurman Thomas 10.00

1994 Select Future Force

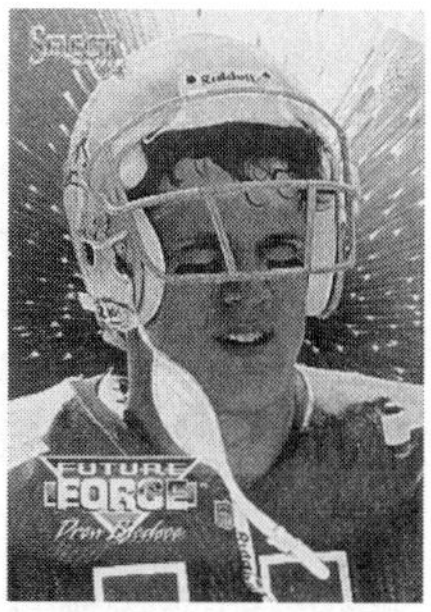

Future Force is a 12-card insert which was seeded 1:48. The cards feature Dufex technology.

MT
Complete Set (12): 75.00
Common Player: 3.00
Minor Stars: 6.00
Inserted 1:48
1 Rick Mirer 6.00
2 Drew Bledsoe 30.00
3 Jerome Bettis 12.00
4 Reggie Brooks 3.00
5 Natrone Means 10.00
6 James Jett 3.00
7 Terry Kirby 6.00
8 Vincent Brisby 3.00
9 Gary Brown 3.00
10 Tyrone Hughes 3.00
11 Dana Stubblefield 6.00
12 Garrison Hearst 12.00

1994 Select Franco Harris

The standard-size Harris card was given away at Pinnacle's party at the 15th National Sports Card Convention. The card front features a metallic Harris image with his signature on the card's back. The card is numbered as "x of 5,000."

MT
Complete Set (1): 25.00
Common Player: 25.00
1 Franco Harris 25.00

1995 Select Certified Promos

This three-card promo set was issued to give collectors and dealers a look at the designs for 1995 Select Certified. It included two base cards and one Gold Team insert.

MT
Complete Set (3): 20.00
Common Player: 5.00
10 Steve Young 5.00
44 Troy Aikman 5.00
7 Dan Marino (Gold Team) 15.00

1995 Select Certified

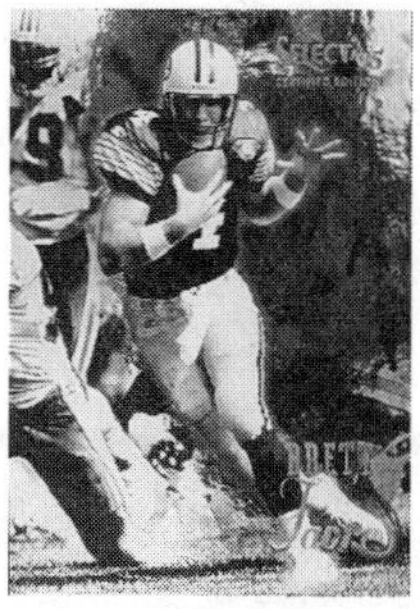

These 1995 Select cards feature 24-point stock and double lamination for each card. The 135-card set includes 29 rookies. Gold foil printing is used for the player's name and the brand logo on the front, which has a full-bleed action photo on it. Each card is also reprinted using a gold mirror mylar foil technology to form a parallel set. These cards were randomly inserted into every fifth pack. Insert sets include Certified Future, Certified Gold Team and The Select Few.

MT
Complete Set (135): 100.00
Common Player: .25
Minor Stars: .50
Comp. Checklist Set (7): 3.00
Pack (6): 6.00
Wax Box (20): 110.00
1 Marshall Faulk 3.00
2 Heath Shuler 1.00
3 Garrison Hearst .50
4 Errict Rhett 1.00
5 Jeff George .50
6 Jerome Bettis 2.00
7 Jim Kelly .50
8 Rick Mirer .50
9 Willie Davis .25
10 Steve Young 3.00
11 Erik Kramer .25
12 Natrone Means 1.00
13 *Jeff Blake* 1.50
14 Neil O'Donnell .50
15 Andre Rison .25
16 Randall Cunningham .25
17 Emmitt Smith 6.00
18 Tim Brown .50
19 Shannon Sharpe .25
20 Boomer Esiason .25
21 Barry Sanders 8.00
22 Rodney Hampton .50
23 Robert Brooks 1.00
24 Jim Everett .25
25 Gary Brown .25
26 Drew Bledsoe 4.00
27 Desmond Howard .25
28 Cris Carter .50
29 Marcus Allen .50
30 Dan Marino 6.00
31 Warren Moon .50
32 Dave Krieg .25
33 Ben Coates .25
34 Terance Mathis .25
35 Mario Bates 1.00
36 Andre Reed .25
37 Dave Brown .25
38 Jeff Graham .25
39 Johnny Mitchell .25
40 Carl Pickens 1.00
41 Jeff Hostetler .25
42 Vinny Testaverde .25
43 Ricky Watters .50
44 Troy Aikman 4.00
45 Bam Morris 1.00
46 John Elway 3.00
47 Junior Seau .50
48 Scott Mitchell .25
49 Jerry Rice 4.00
50 Brett Favre 8.00
51 Chris Warren .50
52 Chris Chandler .25
53 Lorenzo White .25
54 Craig Erickson .25
55 Alvin Harper .25
56 Steve Beuerlein .25
57 Edgar Bennett .25
58 Steve Bono .50
59 Eric Green .25
60 Jake Reed .25
61 Terry Kirby .25
62 Vincent Brisby .25
63 Lake Dawson .50
64 Torrance Small .25
65 Mark Brunell 4.00
66 Haywood Jeffires .25
67 Flipper Anderson .25
68 Ron Moore .25
69 LeShon Johnson .25
70 Rocket Ismail .25
71 Herman Moore 2.00
72 Charlie Garner .25
73 Anthony Miller .25
74 Greg Lloyd .25
75 Michael Irvin 1.00
76 Stan Humphries .50
77 Leroy Hoard .25
78 Deion Sanders 4.00
79 Darnay Scott 1.50
80 Chris Miller .25
81 Curtis Conway .50
82 Trent Dilfer 1.00
83 Bruce Smith .25
84 Reggie Brooks .25
85 Frank Reich .25
86 Henry Ellard .25
87 Eric Metcalf .25
88 Sean Gilbert .25
89 Larry Centers .25
90 Ricky Ervins .25
91 Craig Heyward .25
92 Rod Woodson .25
93 Steve Walsh .25
94 Fred Barnett .25
95 William Floyd 1.00
96 Harvey Williams .25
97 Greg Hill .50
98 Irving Fryar .25
99 Kevin Williams .25
100 Herschel Walker .25
101 Sean Dawkins .25
102 Michael Haynes .25
103 Reggie White .50
104 Robert Smith .25
105 *Todd Collins* .50
106 *Michael Westbrook* 8.00
107 *Frank Sanders* 5.00
108 *Christian Fauria* .50
109 *Stoney Case* 1.50
110 *Jimmy Oliver* .50
111 *Mark Bruener* 1.00
112 *Rodney Thomas* .50
113 *Chris Jones* 2.00
114 *James Stewart* .50
115 *Kevin Carter* 1.00
116 *Eric Zeier* 1.00
117 *Curtis Martin* 20.00
118 *James Stewart* 10.00
119 *Joe Aska* .50
120 *Ken Dilger* 1.00
121 *Tyrone Wheatley* 7.00
122 *Ray Zellars* .50
123 *Kyle Brady* 1.50
124 *Chad May* .50
125 *Napoleon Kaufman* 10.00
126 *Terrell Davis* 30.00
127 *Warren Sapp* 3.00
128 *Sherman Williams* .50
129 *Kordell Stewart* 15.00
130 *Ki-Jana Carter* 1.50
131 *Terrell Fletcher* .50
132 *Rashaan Salaam* 1.00
133 *J.J. Stokes* 2.00
134 *Kerry Collins* 10.00
135 *Joey Galloway* 10.00

1995 Select Certified Mirror Golds

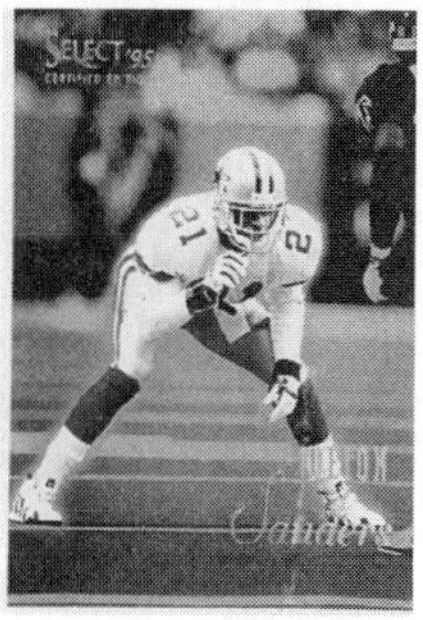

These cards are a parallel set to Select Certified's main set, except they use gold mirror mylar foil technology. Cards were seeded one per five packs.

MT
Complete Set (135): 1200.
Common Player: 2.00
Minor Stars: 4.00
Mirror Gold Cards: 4x-8x
1 Marshall Faulk 10.00
2 Heath Shuler 4.00
3 Garrison Hearst 4.00
4 Errict Rhett 4.00
5 Jeff George 4.00
6 Jerome Bettis 8.00
7 Jim Kelly 4.00
8 Rick Mirer 4.00
9 Willie Davis 2.00
10 Steve Young 25.00
11 Erik Kramer 2.00
12 Natrone Means 4.00
13 Jeff Blake 6.00
14 Neil O'Donnell 2.00
15 Andre Rison 2.00
16 Randall Cunningham 4.00
17 Emmitt Smith 45.00
18 Tim Brown 4.00
19 Shannon Sharpe 2.00
20 Boomer Esiason 2.00
21 Barry Sanders 50.00
22 Rodney Hampton 4.00
23 Robert Brooks 2.00
24 Jim Everett 2.00
25 Gary Brown 2.00
26 Drew Bledsoe 30.00
27 Desmond Howard 2.00
28 Cris Carter 4.00
29 Marcus Allen 4.00
30 Dan Marino 45.00
31 Warren Moon 4.00
32 Dave Krieg 2.00
33 Ben Coates 2.00
34 Terance Mathis 2.00
35 Mario Bates 2.00
36 Andre Reed 2.00
37 Dave Brown 2.00
38 Jeff Graham 2.00
39 Johnny Mitchell 2.00
40 Carl Pickens 4.00
41 Jeff Hostetler 2.00
42 Vinny Testaverde 2.00
43 Ricky Watters 4.00
44 Troy Aikman 30.00
45 Bam Morris 2.00
46 John Elway 45.00
47 Junior Seau 4.00
48 Scott Mitchell 2.00
49 Jerry Rice 30.00
50 Brett Favre 50.00
51 Chris Warren 4.00
52 Chris Chandler 2.00
53 Lorenzo White 2.00
54 Craig Erickson 2.00
55 Alvin Harper 2.00
56 Steve Beuerlein 2.00
57 Edgar Bennett 2.00
58 Steve Bono 4.00
59 Eric Green 2.00
60 Jake Reed 2.00
61 Terry Kirby 2.00
62 Vincent Brisby 2.00
63 Lake Dawson 2.00
64 Torrance Small 2.00
65 Mark Brunell 30.00
66 Haywood Jeffires 2.00
67 Flipper Anderson 2.00
68 Ron Moore 2.00
69 LeShon Johnson 2.00
70 Rocket Ismail 2.00
71 Herman Moore 4.00
72 Charlie Garner 2.00
73 Anthony Miller 2.00
74 Greg Lloyd 2.00
75 Michael Irvin 4.00
76 Stan Humphries 2.00
77 Leroy Hoard 2.00
78 Deion Sanders 25.00
79 Darnay Scott 4.00
80 Chris Miller 2.00
81 Curtis Conway 4.00
82 Trent Dilfer 4.00
83 Bruce Smith 2.00
84 Reggie Brooks 2.00
85 Frank Reich 2.00
86 Henry Ellard 2.00
87 Eric Metcalf 2.00
88 Sean Gilbert 2.00
89 Larry Centers 2.00
90 Ricky Ervins 2.00
91 Craig Heyward 2.00
92 Rod Woodson 2.00
93 Steve Walsh 2.00
94 Fred Barnett 2.00
95 William Floyd 4.00
96 Harvey Williams 2.00
97 Greg Hill 2.00
98 Irving Fryar 2.00
99 Kevin Williams 2.00
100 Herschel Walker 2.00
101 Sean Dawkins 2.00
102 Michael Haynes 2.00
103 Reggie White 4.00
104 Robert Smith 4.00
105 Todd Collins 2.00
106 Michael Westbrook 30.00
107 Frank Sanders 15.00
108 Christian Fauria 4.00
109 Stoney Case 4.00
110 Jimmy Oliver 4.00
111 Mark Bruener 4.00
112 Rodney Thomas 4.00
113 Chris Jones 4.00
114 James Stewart 4.00
115 Kevin Carter 4.00
116 Eric Zeier 4.00
117 Curtis Martin 45.00
118 James Stewart 35.00
119 Joe Aska 4.00
120 Ken Dilger 4.00
121 Tyrone Wheatley 25.00
122 Ray Zellars 4.00
123 Kyle Brady 4.00
124 Chad May 4.00
125 Napoleon Kaufman 30.00
126 Terrell Davis 300.00
127 Warren Sapp 8.00
128 Sherman Williams 4.00
129 Kordell Stewart 50.00
130 Ki-Jana Carter 6.00
131 Terrell Fletcher 4.00
132 Rashaan Salaam 6.00
133 J.J. Stokes 12.00
134 Kerry Collins 15.00
135 Joey Galloway 50.00

1995 Select Certified Checklists

The seven-card, standard-size set was issued one per pack of Select Certified and features members of the Quarterback Club.

MT
Complete Set (7): 4.00
Common Player: .25
1 Drew Bledsoe .75
2 John Elway .40
3 Dan Marino 1.50
4 Brett Favre 1.50
5 Troy Aikman .75
6 Steve Young .60
7 Rick Mirer (UER), Randall Cunningham (Gold Team list incorrect) .25

1995 Select Certified Future

These cards pay tribute to the 10 best rookies in the 1995 season. Each card is done in gold foil background. Cards were random inserts, one per 19 packs of 1995 Score Select Certified product.

MT
Complete Set (10): 120.00
Common Player: 3.00
1 Ki-Jana Carter 6.00
2 Steve McNair 25.00
3 Kerry Collins 6.00
4 Michael Westbrook 6.00
5 Joey Galloway 10.00
6 J.J. Stokes 6.00
7 Rashaan Salaam 6.00
8 Tyrone Wheatley 3.00
9 Todd Collins 3.00
10 Curtis Martin 25.00

1995 Select Certified Gold Team

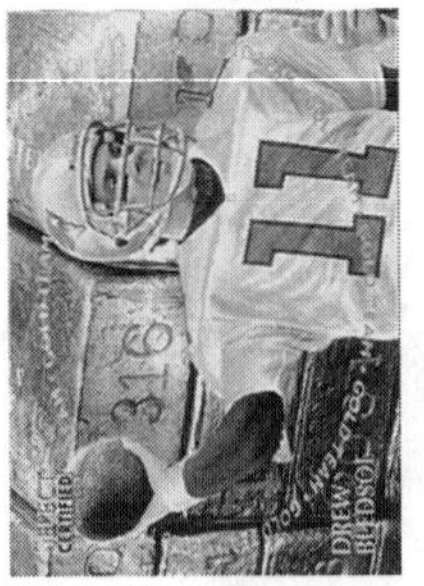

Ten of the NFL's biggest stars are featured on these 1995 Select Certified inserts. The cards use gold Dufex, with textured gold foil highlights on both sides of the card. Gold Team inserts were seeded one per 41 packs.

		MT
Complete Set (10):		400.00
Common Player:		20.00
1	Jerry Rice	35.00
2	Emmitt Smith	70.00
3	Drew Bledsoe	35.00
4	Marshall Faulk	20.00
5	Troy Aikman	35.00
6	Barry Sanders	35.00
7	Dan Marino	70.00
8	Errict Rhett	20.00
9	Brett Favre	70.00
10	Steve McNair	35.00

1995 Select Certified Select Few

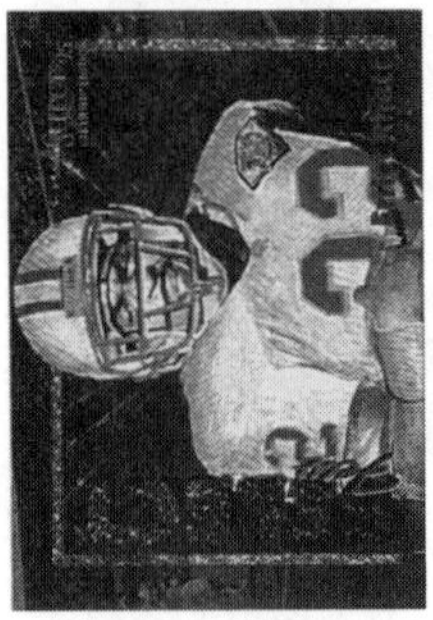

These cards, which appear one per 32 packs of 1995 Select Certified product, showcase 20 top talents. Another version of Select Few appears in a plastic holder and is inserted on the inside of sealed boxes.

		MT
Complete Set (20):		600.00
Common Player:		7.00
Cards are numbered of 2250		
Comp. 1028 Numb. Set (20):		1200.
1028 Numb. Cards:		1x-2x
1	Dan Marino	60.00
2	Emmitt Smith	60.00
3	Marshall Faulk	7.00
4	Barry Sanders	40.00
5	Drew Bledsoe	40.00
6	Brett Favre	60.00
7	Troy Aikman	40.00
8	Jerry Rice	40.00
9	Steve Young	30.00
10	Natrone Means	10.00
11	Bam Morris	7.00
12	Errict Rhett	7.00
13	John Elway	25.00
14	Heath Shuler	10.00
15	Ki-Jana Carter	10.00
16	Kerry Collins	14.00
17	Steve McNair	30.00
18	Rashaan Salaam	10.00
19	Tyrone Wheatley	7.00
20	J.J. Stokes	10.00

1996 Select Promos

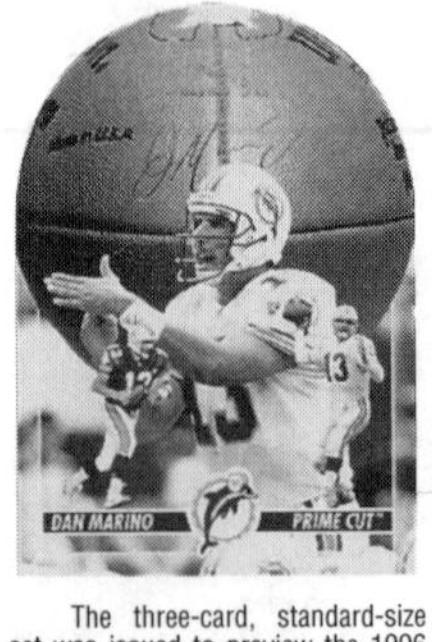

The three-card, standard-size set was issued to preview the 1996 Select card set. Aikman's and Favre's cards are base cards while the Marino card previews the Prime Cut insert.

		MT
Complete Set (3):		8.00
Common Player:		1.50
1	Troy Aikman	1.50
10	Prime Cut card (Dan Marino)	5.00
19	Brett Favre	4.00

1996 Select

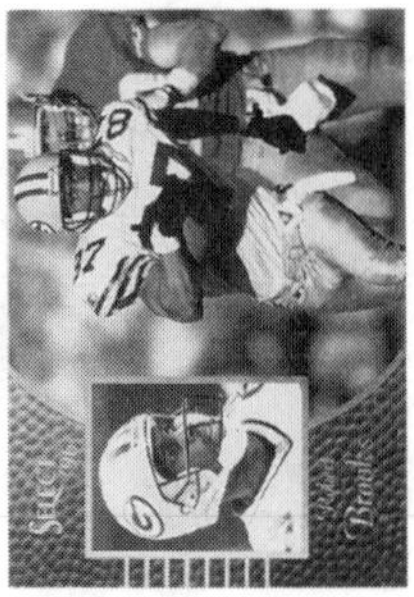

Only hobby shops were able to carry Select football. The 200-card set has five checklists, 30 top rookies, and 15 Fluid and Fleet cards. Each regular card is also featured in a parallel Artist's Proof set, seeded one card per 23 packs. Each regular card front is horizontal, with a gold-foil framed box with a mug shot on the left side, against a pigskin football background. The Select logo above the picture and the player's name below are also in gold foil. The right side of the card has a full-bleed color action photo. The back also uses a football motif for the background, along with a checkerboard pattern with a photo inside it. The Select logo is in one square, as is a team logo. A card number is in the upper right corner in a white square, with a player photo underneath. Statistics run along the bottom of the card. Insert sets are: Building Blocks, Four-midable and Prime Cut.

		MT
Complete Set (200):		25.00
Common Player:		.10
Minor Stars:		.20
Comp. Artist's Proof (200):		1400.
Artist's Proof Cards:		20x-40x
Pack (10):		2.00
Wax Box (24):		45.00
1	Troy Aikman	1.50
2	Marshall Faulk	1.00
3	Kordell Stewart	1.50
4	Larry Centers	.10
5	Tamarick Vanover	1.00
6	Ken Norton Jr.	.10
7	Steve Tasker	.10
8	Dan Marino	3.00
9	Heath Shuler	.50
10	Anthony Miller	.10
11	Mario Bates	.10
12	Natrone Means	.20
13	Darren Woodson	.10
14	Chris Sanders	.50
15	Chris Warren	.20
16	Eric Metcalf	.10
17	Quentin Coryatt	.10
18	Jeff Hostetler	.10
19	Brett Favre	3.00
20	Curtis Martin	2.50
21	Floyd Turner	.10
22	Curtis Conway	.10
23	Orlando Thomas	.10
24	Lee Woodall	.10
25	Darick Holmes	.10
26	Marcus Allen	.10
27	Ricky Watters	.10
28	Herman Moore	.30
29	Rodney Hampton	.10
30	Alvin Harper	.10
31	Jeff Blake	1.00
32	Wayne Chrebet	.10
33	Jerry Rice	1.50
34	Dave Krieg	.10
35	Mark Brunell	.75
36	Terry Allen	.10
37	Emmitt Smith	3.00
38	Bryan Cox	.10
39	Tony Martin	.10
40	John Elway	.50
41	Warren Moon	.10
42	Yancey Thigpen	1.00
43	Jeff George	.20
44	Rodney Thomas	.50
45	Joey Galloway	1.25
46	Jim Kelly	.10
47	Drew Bledsoe	1.50
48	Greg Lloyd	.10
49	Michael Irvin	.20
50	Quinn Early	.10
51	Brent Jones	.10
52	Rashaan Salaam	1.00
53	James Stewart	.10
54	Gus Frerotte	.10
55	Edgar Bennett	.10
56	Lamont Warren	.10
57	Napoleon Kaufman	.20
58	Kevin Williams	.10
59	Irving Fryar	.10
60	Trent Dilfer	.10
61	Eric Zeier	.10
62	Tyrone Wheatley	.10
63	Isaac Bruce	.75
64	Terrell Davis	1.00
65	Lake Dawson	.10
66	Carnell Lake	.10
67	Kerry Collins	.30
68	Kyle Brady	.10
69	Rodney Peete	.10
70	Carl Pickens	.20
71	Robert Smith	.10
72	Rod Woodson	.10
73	Deion Sanders	.75
74	Sean Dawkins	.10
75	William Floyd	.10
76	Barry Sanders	1.50
77	Ben Coates	.10
78	Neil O'Donnell	.10
79	Bill Brooks	.10
80	Steve Bono	.10
81	Jay Novacek	.10
82	Bernie Parmalee	.10
83	Derek Loville	.10
84	Frank Sanders	.20
85	Robert Brooks	.10
86	Jim Harbaugh	.10
87	Rick Mirer	.10
88	Craig Heyward	.10
89	Greg Hill	.10
90	Andre Coleman	.10
91	Shannon Sharpe	.10
92	Hugh Douglas	.10
93	Andre Hastings	.10
94	Bryce Paup	.10
95	Jim Everett	.10
96	Brian Mitchell	.10
97	Jeff Graham	.10
98	Steve McNair	1.00
99	Charlie Garner	.10
100	Willie McGinest	.10
101	Harvey Williams	.10
102	Daryl Johnston	.10
103	Cris Carter	.10
104	J.J. Stokes	.20
105	Garrison Hearst	.20
106	Mark Chmura	.50
107	Derrick Thomas	.10
108	Errict Rhett	.75
109	Terance Mathis	.10
110	Dave Brown	.10
111	Erric Pegram	.10
112	Scott Mitchell	.10
113	Aaron Bailey	.10
114	Stan Humphries	.10
115	Bruce Smith	.10
116	Rob Johnson	.10
117	O.J. McDuffie	.10
118	Brian Blades	.10
119	Steve Atwater	.10
120	Tyrone Hughes	.10
121	Michael Westbrook	.20
122	Ki-Jana Carter	.50
123	Adrian Murrell	.10
124	Steve Young	1.50
125	Charles Haley	.10
126	Vincent Brisby	.10
127	Jerome Bettis	.10
128	Erik Kramer	.10
129	Roosevelt Potts	.10
130	Tim Brown	.10
131	Reggie White	.10
132	Jake Reed	.10
133	Junior Seau	.10
134	Stoney Case	.10
135	Kimble Anders	.10
136	Brett Perriman	.10
137	Todd Collins	.10
138	Sherman Williams	.10
139	Hardy Nickerson	.10
140	Ernie Mills	.10
141	Glyn Milburn	.10
142	Terry Kirby	.10
143	Bert Emanuel	.10
144	Aeneas Williams	.10
145	Aaron Craver	.10
146	Jackie Harris	.10
147	Amp Lee	.10
148	*Aaron Hayden*	.50
149	Antonio Freeman	.10
150	Kevin Greene	.10
151	*Kevin Hardy*	.40
152	*Eric Moulds*	2.00
153	*(Tim Biakabutuka)*	1.00
154	*(Keyshawn Johnson)*	2.50
155	*(Jeff Lewis)*	.50
156	*(Stepfret Williams)*	.10
157	*(Tony Brackens)*	.20
158	*(Mike Alstott)*	1.50
159	*(Willie Anderson)*	.10
160	*(Marvin Harrison)*	3.00
161	*(Regan Upshaw)*	.10
162	*(Bobby Engram)*	.50
163	*(Leeland McElroy)*	.20
164	*(Alex Van Dyke)*	.20
165	*(Stanley Pritchett)*	.10
166	*(Cedric Jones)*	.10
167	*(Terry Glenn)*	1.75
168	*(Eddie George)*	4.00
169	*(Lawrence Phillips)*	.50
170	*(Jonathan Ogden)*	.10
171	*(Danny Kanell)*	.50
172	*(Alex Molden)*	.10
173	*(Daryl Gardener)*	.10
174	*(Derrick Mayes)*	1.00
175	*(Marco Battaglia)*	.10
176	*(Jon Stark)*	.10
177	*(Karim Abdul-Jabbar)*	.75
178	*(Stephen Davis)*	4.00
179	*(Rickey Dudley)*	.30
180	*(Eddie Kennison)*	.30
181	Barry Sanders	.75
182	Brett Favre	.50
183	John Elway	.30
184	Steve Young	.50
185	Michael Irvin	.10
186	Jerry Rice	.50
187	Emmitt Smith	1.00
188	Isaac Bruce	.10
189	Chris Warren	.20
190	Errict Rhett	.40
191	Herman Moore	.10
192	Carl Pickens	.10
193	Cris Carter	.10
194	Terrell Davis	.75
195	Rodney Thomas	.10
196	Dan Marino	.50
197	Drew Bledsoe	.20
198	Emmitt Smith	.50
199	Jerry Rice	.30
200	John Elway, Barry Sanders	.30

Post-1980 cards in Near Mint condition will generally sell for about 75% of the quoted Mint value. Excellent-condition cards bring no more than 40%.

1996 Select Artist's Proofs

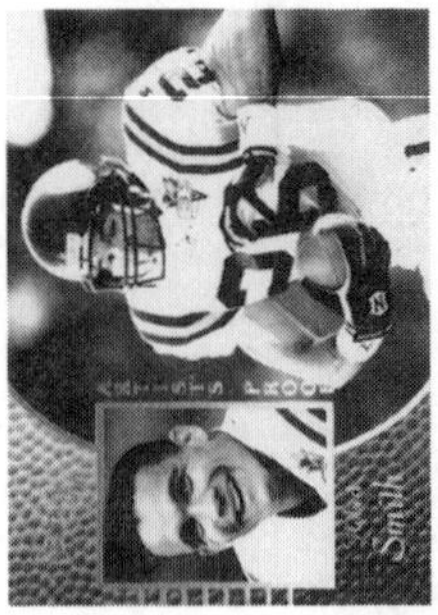

The 200-card, standard-size set parallels the base set, inserted every 23 packs, with Artist's Proof printed in gold foil.

		MT
Complete Set (200):		1600.
Common Player:		5.00
Veteran Stars:		30x-50x
Young Stars:		20x-40x
RCs:		12x-25x
1	Troy Aikman	70.00
2	Marshall Faulk	40.00
3	Kordell Stewart	60.00
8	Dan Marino	125.00
10	Brett Favre	70.00
20	Curtis Martin	90.00
33	Jerry Rice	60.00
37	Emmitt Smith	125.00
40	John Elway	30.00
45	Joey Galloway	50.00
47	Drew Bledsoe	50.00
64	Terrell Davis	50.00
67	Kerry Collins	60.00
73	Deion Sanders	35.00
76	Barry Sanders	60.00
98	Steve McNair	50.00
124	Steve Young	50.00
154	Keyshawn Johnson	60.00
167	Terry Glenn	50.00
168	Eddie George	75.00
169	Lawrence Phillips	50.00
181	Barry Sanders (FF)	30.00
182	Brett Favre (FF)	35.00
184	Steve Young (FF)	25.00
186	Jerry Rice (FF)	30.00
187	Emmitt Smith (FF)	60.00
196	Dan Marino (CL)	35.00
197	Drew Bledsoe (CL)	15.00
198	Emmitt Smith (CL)	35.00
199	Jerry Rice (CL)	20.00
200	Barry Sanders (CL), John Elway	20.00

1996 Select Building Blocks

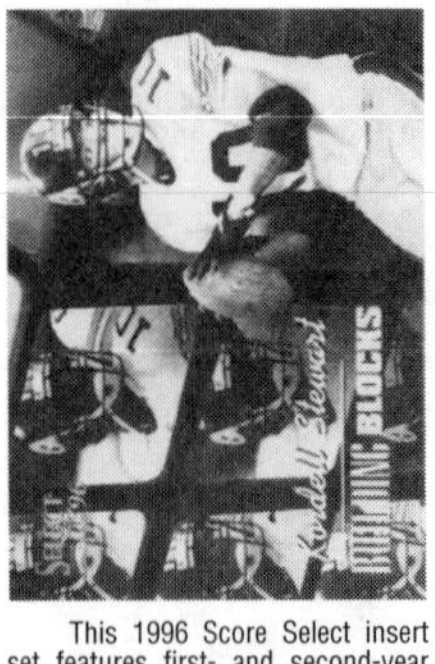

This 1996 Score Select insert set features first- and second-year players who appear to be headed to stardom. The cards, seeded one per 48 packs, use all-foil Dufex print technology. The card front has a color action photo, with a background similar to a television display room; the "screens" have a smaller mug shot taken from the larger action photo. The player's name and "Building Blocks" are written in silver foil in the lower left corner. The vertical back has a color action photo on one half, with a card number in a black rectangle above. The other side has the brand logo, player's name, set name, position and team, and brief player profile.

		MT
Complete Set (20):		180.00
Common Player:		4.00
1	Curtis Martin	25.00
2	Terrell Davis	25.00
3	Darick Holmes	4.00
4	Rashaan Salaam	6.00
5	Ki-Jana Carter	6.00
6	Rodney Thomas	4.00
7	Kerry Collins	8.00
8	Eric Zeier	4.00
9	Steve McNair	15.00
10	Kordell Stewart	20.00
11	J.J. Stokes	6.00
12	Joey Galloway	10.00
13	Michael Westbrook	6.00
14	Mike Alstott	4.00
15	Tony Brackens	4.00
16	Terry Glenn	10.00
17	Kevin Hardy	4.00
18	Leeland McElroy	6.00
19	Tim Biakabutuka	12.00
20	Keyshawn Johnson	15.00

1996 Select Four-midable

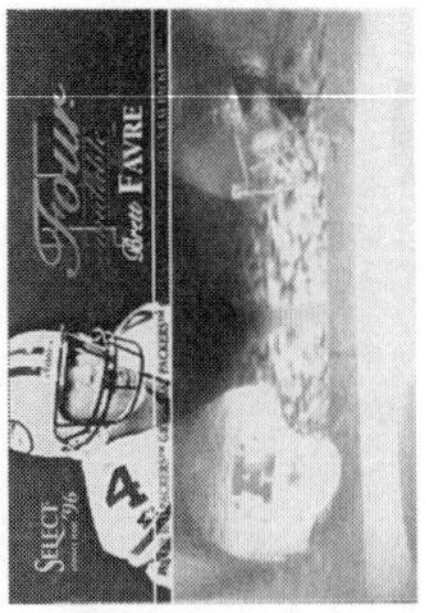

These 1996 Score Select inserts were seeded one per 18 packs. Each card front has a full-motion hologram which features crashing AFC and NFC helmets, as well as a color photo of a player who appeared in the championship games. The hologram is at the bottom; the color photo is in a conference color-coordinated panel at the top. Blue is used for the NFC; red is used for the AFC. The logos are included in the background. The brand name and set name are written in silver foil, as is the player's team name, which is repeated above the hologram. The horizontal back has a color action photo incorporated into a black-and-white stadium scene, plus a black rectangle which recaps the player's championship game performance. A card number is also given.

		MT
Complete Set (16):		70.00
Common Player:		2.00
1	Troy Aikman	10.00
2	Michael Irvin	4.00
3	Emmitt Smith	20.00
4	Deion Sanders	7.00
5	Brett Favre	20.00
6	Robert Brooks	2.00
7	Edgar Bennett	2.00
8	Reggie White	4.00
9	Kordell Stewart	10.00
10	Yancey Thigpen	5.00
11	Neil O'Donnell	2.00
12	Greg Lloyd	2.00
13	Jim Harbaugh	2.00
14	Sean Dawkins	2.00
15	Marshall Faulk	7.00
16	Quentin Coryatt	2.00

1996 Select Prime Cut

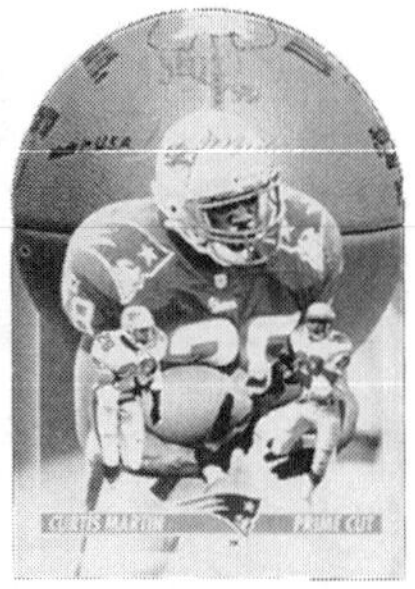

These cards are the highlight inserts in Score's 1996 Select football product. The cards are die-cut and feature 18 of the NFL's most elite players. The top of the card is die-cut around a football which has a facsimile autograph of the player. Below is a larger color action photo, flanked by two smaller ones. The player's name is in a bar at the bottom, along with "Prime Cut" and a team logo in the center. Cards were limited to 1,996 each and were inserted in every 80th pack.

		MT
Complete Set (18):		550.00
Common Player:		5.00
1	Emmitt Smith	70.00
2	Troy Aikman	40.00
3	Michael Irvin	5.00
4	Steve Young	30.00
5	Jerry Rice	40.00
6	Drew Bledsoe	40.00
7	Brett Favre	70.00
8	John Elway	30.00
9	Barry Sanders	40.00
10	Dan Marino	70.00
11	Isaac Bruce	15.00
12	Marshall Faulk	10.00
13	Errict Rhett	10.00
14	Chris Warren	5.00
15	Herman Moore	5.00
16	Deion Sanders	20.00
17	Joey Galloway	20.00
18	Curtis Martin	50.00

1996 Select Certified

The 125-card, regular-sized set was available in six-card packs. The card fronts feature a full mirror background with the color player action shot. The player's name is printed down the right border with in-depth statistics printed on the horizontal card back. Parallel versions of the base set are available in Certified Red (1:5) and Certified Blue (1:50). Mirror Red (1:100), Mirror Blue (1:200) and Mirror Gold (1:300) parallel inserts were also issued. Artist's Proof (1:18), Gold Team (1:38) and Thumbs Up (1:41) were the other inserts and each card was also available in Premium Stock, nine-card packs.

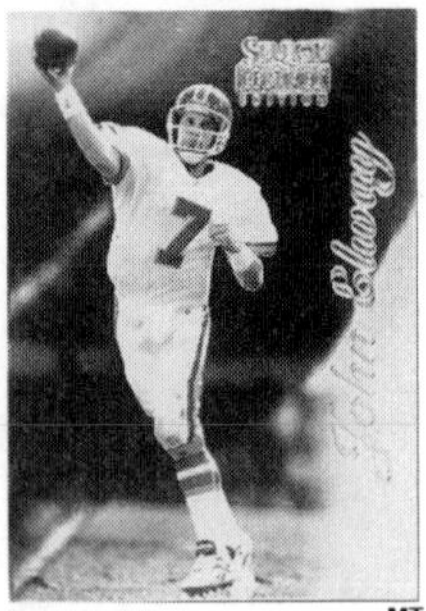

		MT
Complete Set (125):		50.00
Common Player:		.20
Minor Stars:		.40
Artist's Proof Stars:		12x-24x
Artist's Proof Rookies:		6x-12x
Certified Blue Stars:		25x-50x
Certified Blue Rookies:		12x-24x
Mirror Blue Stars:		75x-150x
Mirror Blue Rookies:		40x-80x
Certified Red Stars:		3x-6x
Certified Red Rookies:		2x-4x
Mirror Red Stars:		40x-80x
Mirror Red Rookies:		20x-40x
Mirror Gold Stars:		150x-300x
Mirror Gold Rookies:		75x-150x
Pack (6):		7.50
Wax Box (20):		140.00
1	Isaac Bruce	1.00
2	Rick Mirer	.20
3	Jake Reed	.20
4	Reggie White	.40
5	Harvey Williams	.20
6	Jim Everett	.20
7	Tony Martin	.20
8	Craig Heyward	.20
9	Tamarick Vanover	1.25
10	Hugh Douglas	.20
11	Erik Kramer	.20
12	Charlie Garner	.20
13	Erric Pegram	.20
14	Scott Mitchell	.20
15	Michael Westbrook	.75
16	Robert Smith	.20
17	Kerry Collins	.75
18	Derek Loville	.20
19	Jeff Blake	.40
20	Terry Kirby	.20
21	Bruce Smith	.20
22	Stan Humphries	.20
23	Rodney Thomas	.20
24	Wayne Chrebet	.20
25	Napoleon Kaufman	.20
26	Marshall Faulk	1.00
27	Emmitt Smith	5.00
28	Natrone Means	.20
29	Neil O'Donnell	.20
30	Warren Moon	.40
31	Junior Seau	.40
32	Chris Sanders	.20
33	Barry Sanders	3.00
34	Jeff Graham	.20
35	Kordell Stewart	2.50
36	Jim Harbaugh	.20
37	Chris Warren	.20
38	Cris Carter	.20
39	J.J. Stokes	.75
40	Tyrone Wheatley	.40
41	Terrell Davis	6.00
42	Mark Brunell	1.50
43	Steve Young	2.00
44	Rodney Hampton	.20
45	Drew Bledsoe	2.00
46	Larry Centers	.20
47	Ken Norton Jr.	.20
48	Deion Sanders	2.00
49	Alvin Harper	.20
50	Trent Dilfer	.40
51	Steve McNair	2.00
52	Robert Brooks	.20
53	Edgar Bennett	.20
54	Troy Aikman	2.50
55	Dan Marino	5.00
56	Steve Bono	.20
57	Marcus Allen	.40
58	Rodney Peete	.20
59	Ben Coates	.20
60	Yancey Thigpen	.40
61	Tim Brown	.20
62	Jerry Rice	2.50
63	Quinn Early	.20
64	Ricky Watters	.40
65	Thurman Thomas	.40
66	Greg Lloyd	.20
67	Eric Metcalf	.20
68	Jeff George	.20
69	John Elway	2.00
70	Frank Sanders	.20
71	Curtis Conway	.20
72	Greg Hill	.20
73	Darick Holmes	.20
74	Herman Moore	.40
75	Carl Pickens	.20
76	Eric Zeier	.20
77	Curtis Martin	3.50
78	Rashaan Salaam	1.00
79	Joey Galloway	1.50
80	Jeff Hostetler	.20
81	Jim Kelly	.40
82	Dave Brown	.20
83	Errict Rhett	.75
84	Michael Irvin	.40
85	Brett Favre	5.00
86	Cedric Jones	.20
87	*Jeff Lewis*	2.00

88	*Alex Van Dyke*	.40
89	*Regan Upshaw*	.20
90	*Karim Abdul-Jabbar*	2.50
91	*Marvin Harrison*	10.00
92	*Stephen Davis*	15.00
93	*Terry Glenn*	5.00
94	*Kevin Hardy*	.40
95	*Stanley Pritchett*	.40
96	*Willie Anderson*	.20
97	*Lawrence Phillips*	2.50
98	*Bobby Hoying*	2.50
99	*Amani Toomer*	.40
100	*Eddie George*	15.00
101	*Stepfret Williams*	.20
102	*Eric Moulds*	6.00
103	*Simeon Rice*	.40
104	*John Mobley*	.40
105	*Keyshawn Johnson*	8.00
106	*Daryl Gardener*	.20
107	*Tony Banks*	4.00
108	*Bobby Engram*	.75
109	*Jonathan Ogden*	.40
110	*Eddie Kennison*	.75
111	*Danny Kanell*	1.50
112	*Tony Brackens*	.40
113	*Tim Biakabutuka*	3.00
114	*Leeland McElroy*	1.00
115	*Rickey Dudley*	1.00
116	Troy Aikman	1.00
117	Brett Favre	2.00
118	Drew Bledsoe	1.00
119	Steve Young	1.00
120	Kerry Collins	1.00
121	John Elway	1.00
122	Dan Marino	2.50
123	Kordell Stewart	1.25
124	Jeff Blake	.40
125	Jim Harbaugh	.20

1996 Select Certified Red

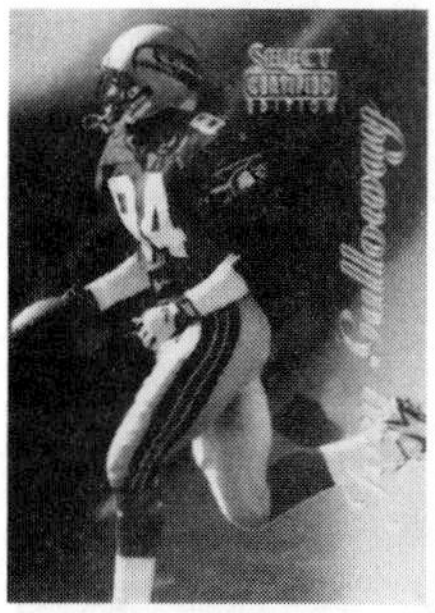

Certified Red parallel cards were a parallel set to the 125-card Select Certified set in 1996. They were inserted every five packs and feature a full red background.

	MT
Complete Set (125):	300.00
Certified Red Cards:	3x-6x

1996 Select Certified Blue

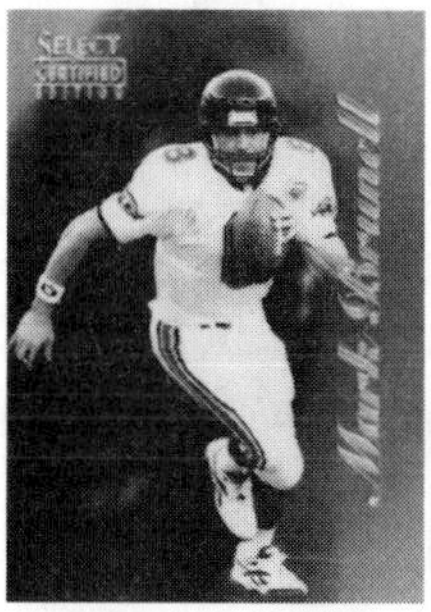

This 125-card set paralleled the 1996 Select Certified set, but pictured each card on a full blue background. Certified Blue inserts were seeded every 50 packs.

	MT
Complete Set (125):	2500.
Certified Blue Cards:	25x-50x

1996 Select Certified Artist's Proofs

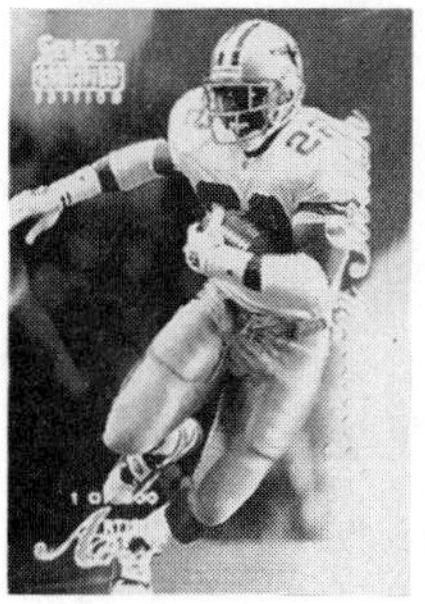

This 125-card set paralleled the 1996 Select Certified set, but includes a holographic Artist's Proof stamp on the front of the card. Artist's Proofs were seeded every 18 packs.

	MT
Complete Set (125):	1200.
Artist's Proof Cards:	12x-24x

1996 Select Certified Mirror Red

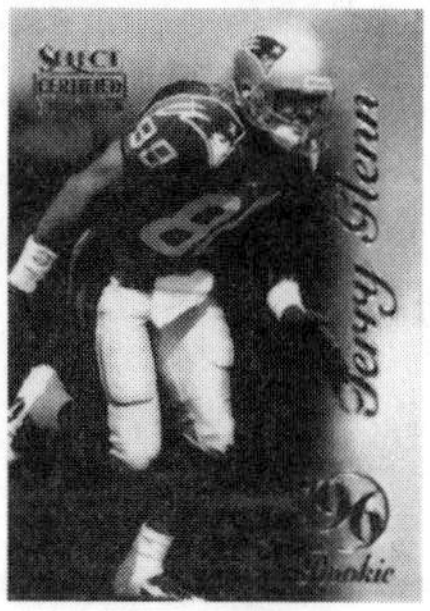

Mirror Red included all 125 cards in 1996 Select Certified, but featured roughly three-fourths of the background in red, with the remaining portion unchanged from regular-issue cards. The entire front then has a mirror effect. Mirror Red inserts were seeded every 100 packs.

	MT
Mirror Red Cards:	40x-80x

1996 Select Certified Mirror Blue

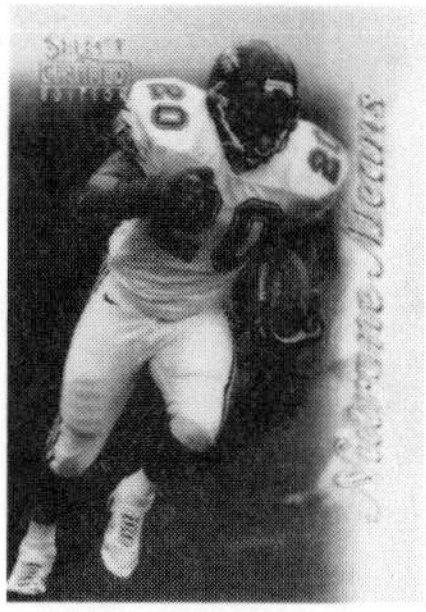

This 125-card set featured a mostly blue background, with the rest still having the regular-issue background color, then a mirror background over the entire front. Mirror Blues parallel the regular-issue set and are seeded every 200 packs.

	MT
Mirror Blue Cards:	75x-150x

1996 Select Certified Mirror Gold

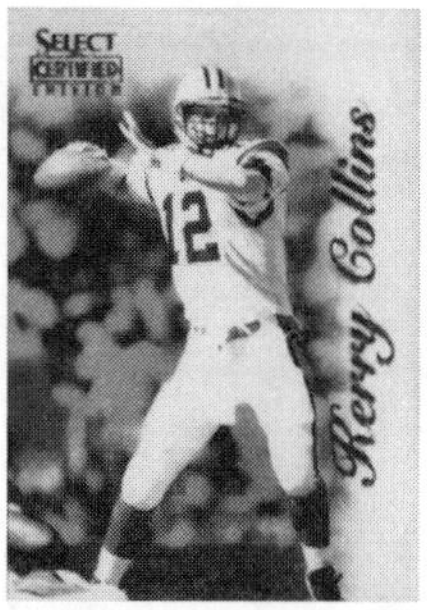

Mirror Golds parallel the 125-card base set and feature most of the background in gold, with the remaining portion in regular-issue card color. The entire front is put through a mirror process that gives it a holographic appearance. Mirror Gold inserts are found every 300 packs.

	MT
Mirror Gold Cards:	150x-300x

1996 Select Certified Gold Team

The Gold Team is an 18-card, regular-sized insert set that was found every 38 packs of 1996 Select Certified. The card fronts feature a full gold action shot while the backs, also in complete gold, are individually numbered.

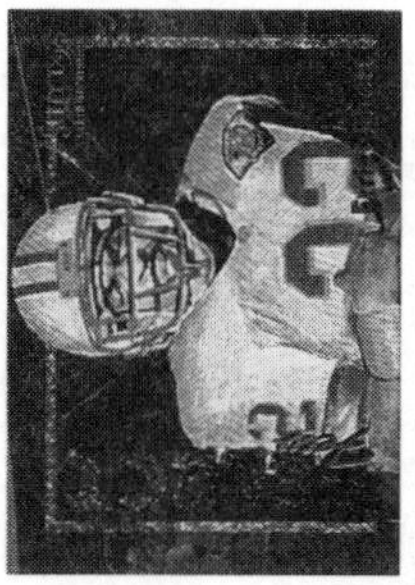

		MT
Complete Set (18):		500.00
Common Player:		8.00
1	Emmitt Smith	60.00
2	Barry Sanders	30.00
3	Dan Marino	60.00
4	Steve Young	25.00
5	Troy Aikman	30.00
6	Jerry Rice	30.00
7	Rashaan Salaam	8.00
8	Marshall Faulk	15.00
9	Drew Bledsoe	30.00
10	Steve McNair	15.00
11	Brett Favre	60.00
12	Terrell Davis	30.00
13	Kordell Stewart	30.00
14	Keyshawn Johnson	15.00
15	Kerry Collins	15.00
16	Curtis Martin	45.00
17	Isaac Bruce	15.00
18	Terry Glenn	25.00

1996 Select Certified Thumbs Up

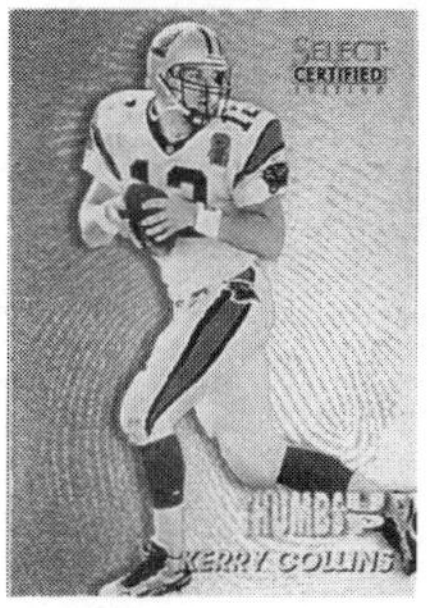

The 24-card, regular-sized set was inserted every 41 packs of Select Certified. The silver card fronts feature an actual thumbprint of the Quarterback Club member pictured. The card backs include another photo and the player's "Thumbs Up Moment" and are individually numbered.

		MT
Complete Set (24):		450.00
Common Player:		8.00
1	Steve Young	30.00
2	Jeff Blake	15.00
3	Dan Marino	60.00
4	Kerry Collins	15.00
5	John Elway	25.00
6	Neil O'Donnell	8.00
7	Brett Favre	60.00
8	Scott Mitchell	8.00
9	Troy Aikman	30.00
10	Jim Harbaugh	8.00
11	Drew Bledsoe	30.00
12	Jeff Hostetler	8.00
13	Marvin Harrison	15.00
14	Tim Biakabutuka	8.00
15	Eddie George	35.00
16	Tony Brackens	8.00
17	Karim Abdul-Jabbar	20.00
18	Daryl Gardener	8.00
19	Alex Van Dyke	8.00
20	Terry Glenn	30.00
21	Eric Moulds	8.00
22	Eddie Kennison	12.00
23	Regan Upshaw	8.00
24	Mike Alstott	10.00

1996 Select Certified Premium Stock

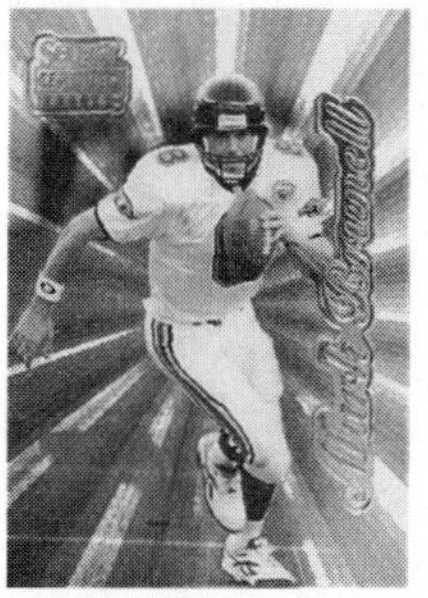

Premium Stock was an enhanced version of Select Certified that was available to the hobby only in jumbo nine-card packs. Premium Stock treated the base cards and the Mirror Red inserts with a micro-etching process, while all other inserts are the same. Packs of Premium Stock contained all of the inserts, but at easier insertion rates than regular packs. The odds in Premium Stock were: Certified Red (1:3), Certified Blue (1:33), Mirror Red (1:66), Mirror Blue (1:133), Mirror Gold (1:199), Artist's Proof (1:12), Gold Team (1:25) and Thumbs Up (1:27).

	MT
Complete Set (125):	100.00
Premium Stock Cards:	2x

1996 Select Certified Premium Stock Etched Mirror Red

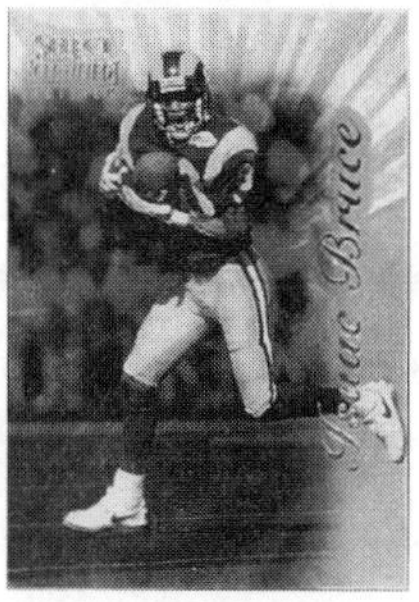

Premium Stock Etched Mirror Red inserts paralleled the 125-card Select Certified set, but were available only in Premium Stock packs at a rate of one per 66 packs. This was the only insert that was changed in Premium Stock versus the regular-issue packs. The fronts of these cards have etched foil similar to the base set for Premium Stock.

	MT
Etched Mirror Red Cards:	150x-300x

1997 Pinnacle Certified

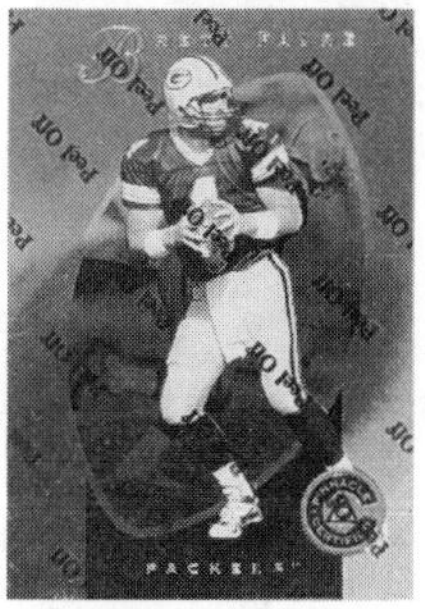

Pinnacle Certified consists of a 150-card base set, four parallels and two inserts. The base cards were printed on silver mirror board. The parallel sets include Certified Red (1:5), Mirror Red (1:99), Mirror Blue (1:199) and Mirror Blue (1:299). The inserts are Certified Team (20 cards, 1:19) and Epix (24 cards, 1:15). All cards in the set have a clear-coat protector.

		MT
Complete Set (150):		75.00
Common Player:		.25
Minor Stars:		.50
Certified Red Cards:		3x-6x
Certified Red Rookies:		2x-3x
Mirror Red Stars:		30x-60x
Mirror Red Rookies:		15x-30x
Mirror Blue Stars:		50x-100x
Mirror Blue Rookies:		25x-50x
Mirror Gold Stars:		100x-200x
Mirror Gold Rookies:		50-100x
Pack (6):		6.00
Wax Box (20):		100.00
1	Emmitt Smith	5.00
2	Dan Marino	5.00
3	Brett Favre	6.00
4	Steve Young	2.00
5	Kerry Collins	.75
6	Troy Aikman	2.50
7	Drew Bledsoe	2.50
8	Eddie George	4.00
9	Jerry Rice	3.00
10	John Elway	2.00
11	Barry Sanders	4.00
12	Mark Brunell	2.50
13	Elvis Grbac	.25
14	Tony Banks	1.50
15	Vinny Testaverde	.25
16	Rick Mirer	.25
17	Carl Pickens	.25
18	Deion Sanders	1.50
19	Terry Glenn	2.50
20	Heath Shuler	.25
21	Dave Brown	.25
22	Keyshawn Johnson	1.00
23	Jeff George	.50
24	Ricky Watters	.50
25	Kordell Stewart	2.50
26	Junior Seau	.25
27	Terrell Owens	2.00
28	Warren Moon	.50
29	Isaac Bruce	.50
30	Steve McNair	2.00
31	Gus Frerotte	.25
32	Trent Dilfer	.50
33	Shannon Sharpe	.25
34	Scott Mitchell	.25
35	Antonio Freeman	.50
36	Jim Harbaugh	.25
37	Natrone Means	.50
38	Marcus Allen	.50
39	Karim Abdul-Jabbar	1.75
40	Tim Biakabutuka	.25
41	Jeff Blake	.50
42	Michael Irvin	.50
43	Herschel Walker	.25
44	Curtis Martin	2.50
45	Eddie Kennison	.50
46	Napoleon Kaufman	.75
47	Larry Centers	.25
48	Jamal Anderson	.50
49	Derrick Alexander	.25
50	Bruce Smith	.25
51	Wesley Walls	.25
52	Rod Smith	.25
53	Keenan McCardell	.25
54	Robert Brooks	.25
55	Willie Green	.25
56	Jake Reed	.25
57	Joey Galloway	.50
58	Eric Metcalf	.25
59	Chris Sanders	.25
60	Jeff Hostetler	.25
61	Kevin Greene	.25
62	Frank Sanders	.25
63	Dorsey Levens	.50
64	Sean Dawkins	.25
65	Cris Carter	.25
66	Andre Hastings	.25
67	Amani Toomer	.25
68	Adrian Murrell	.50
69	Ty Detmer	.25
70	Yancey Thigpen	.25
71	Jim Everett	.25
72	Todd Collins	.25
73	Curtis Conway	.50
74	Herman Moore	.50
75	Neil O'Donnell	.25
76	Rod Woodson	.25
77	Tony Martin	.25
78	Kent Graham	.25
79	Andre Reed	.25
80	Reggie White	.50
81	Thurman Thomas	.50
82	Garrison Hearst	.25
83	Chris Warren	.25
84	Wayne Chrebet	.25
85	Chris T. Jones	.25
86	Anthony Miller	.25
87	Chris Chandler	.25
88	Terrell Davis	3.00
89	Mike Alstott	1.50
90	Terry Allen	.25
91	Jerome Bettis	.50
92	Stan Humphries	.25
93	Andre Rison	.25
94	Marshall Faulk	.50
95	Erik Kramer	.25
96	O.J. McDuffie	.25
97	Robert Smith	.25
98	Keith Byars	.25
99	Rodney Hampton	.25
100	Desmond Howard	.25
101	Lawrence Phillips	.50
102	Michael Westbrook	.25
103	Johnnie Morton	.25
104	Ben Coates	.25
105	J.J. Stokes	.50
106	Terance Mathis	.25
107	Errict Rhett	.25
108	Tim Brown	.25
109	Marvin Harrison	1.00
110	Muhsin Muhammad	.25
111	Bam Morris	.25
112	Mario Bates	.25
113	Jimmy Smith	.25
114	Irving Fryar	.25
115	Tamarick Vanover	.25
116	Brad Johnson	.50
117	Rashaan Salaam	.25
118	Ki-Jana Carter	.25
119	Tyrone Wheatley	.25
120	John Friesz	.25
121	*Orlando Pace*	.50
122	*Jim Druckenmiller*	6.00
123	*Byron Hanspard*	.75
124	*David LaFleur*	1.50
125	*Reidel Anthony*	3.00
126	*Antowain Smith*	4.00
127	*Bryant Westbrook*	.50
128	*Fred Lane*	2.00
129	*Tiki Barber*	4.00
130	*Shawn Springs*	.50
131	*Ike Hilliard*	3.00
132	*James Farrior*	.25
133	*Darrell Russell*	.25
134	*Walter Jones*	.25
135	*Tom Knight*	.25
136	*Yatil Green*	1.00
137	*Joey Kent*	.50
138	*Kevin Lockett*	.25
139	*Troy Davis*	1.00
140	*Darnell Autry*	.50
141	*Pat Barnes*	.75
142	*Rae Carruth*	3.00
143	*Will Blackwell*	.50
144	*Warrick Dunn*	4.00
145	*Corey Dillon*	7.00
146	*Dwayne Rudd*	.25
147	*Reinard Wilson*	.25
148	*Peter Boulware*	.25
149	*Tony Gonzalez*	1.50
150	*Danny Wuerffel*	4.00

1997 Pinnacle Certified Epix

Epix is a 24-card insert which features holographic effects. The set consists of Game, Moment and Season cards that highlight each player's top performances. Orange, Purple and Emerald versions of each card were produced. Epix was inserted 1:15.

		MT
Complete Set (24):		400.00
Common Moment (E1-E8):		12.00
Common Season (E9-E16):		8.00
Common Game (E17-E24):		4.00
1	Emmitt Smith	70.00
2	Troy Aikman	40.00
3	Terrell Davis	40.00
4	Drew Bledsoe	40.00
5	Jeff George	12.00
6	Kerry Collins	12.00
7	Antonio Freeman	12.00
8	Herman Moore	12.00
9	Barry Sanders	35.00
10	Brett Favre	50.00
11	Michael Irvin	8.00
12	Steve Young	20.00
13	Mark Brunell	25.00
14	Jerome Bettis	8.00
15	Deion Sanders	15.00
16	Jeff Blake	8.00
17	Dan Marino	30.00
18	Eddie George	20.00
19	Jerry Rice	15.00
20	John Elway	12.00
21	Curtis Martin	12.00
22	Kordell Stewart	20.00
23	Junior Seau	4.00
24	Reggie White	4.00

1997 Pinnacle Certified Team

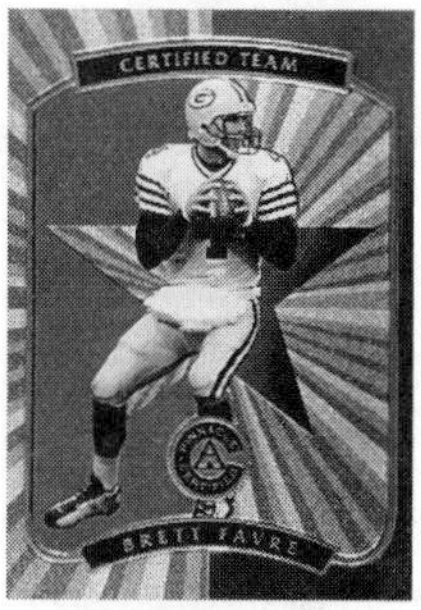

Certified Team is a 20-card insert that was seeded 1:19 in packs of Certified Football. The cards were printed on silver mirror board. Gold (inserted 1:119) and Mirror Gold (25 numbered sets) parallels were also issued.

		MT
Complete Set (20):		250.00
Common Player:		5.00
Inserted 1:19		
Gold Cards:		2x-4x
Inserted 1:119		
Mirror Golds:		20x-40x
Production 25 Sets		
1	Brett Favre	30.00
2	Dan Marino	25.00
3	Emmitt Smith	25.00
4	Eddie George	20.00
5	Jerry Rice	15.00
6	Troy Aikman	15.00
7	Barry Sanders	18.00
8	Terrell Davis	15.00
9	Drew Bledsoe	15.00
10	Curtis Martin	15.00
11	Terry Glenn	7.00
12	Kerry Collins	7.00
13	John Elway	10.00
14	Kordell Stewart	15.00
15	Karim Abdul-Jabbar	8.00
16	Steve Young	10.00
17	Steve McNair	10.00
18	Terrell Owens	5.00
19	Keyshawn Johnson	5.00
20	Mark Brunell	15.00

1997 Pinnacle Totally Certified Platinum Gold

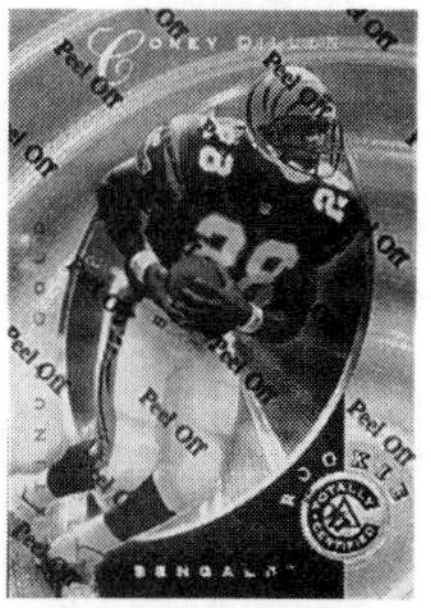

Platinum Gold cards feature a micro-etched holographic mylar finish. Each card is sequentially-numbered to 30 and they were inserted 1:79.

		MT
Platinum Gold Cards:		25x
Platinum Gold Rookies:		7x-14x
Production 30 Sets		
Inserted 1:79		
1	Emmitt Smith	1250.
2	Dan Marino	1250.
3	Brett Favre	1500.
4	Steve Young	500.00
5	Kerry Collins	175.00
6	Troy Aikman	750.00
7	Drew Bledsoe	750.00
8	Eddie George	1000.
9	Jerry Rice	750.00
10	John Elway	600.00

11	Barry Sanders	900.00
12	Mark Brunell	600.00
13	Elvis Grbac	60.00
14	Tony Banks	125.00
15	Vinny Testaverde	60.00
16	Rick Mirer	60.00
17	Carl Pickens	60.00
18	Deion Sanders	400.00
19	Terry Glenn	150.00
20	Heath Shuler	60.00
21	Dave Brown	60.00
22	Keyshawn Johnson	200.00
23	Jeff George	125.00
24	Ricky Watters	125.00
25	Kordell Stewart	750.00
26	Junior Seau	60.00
27	Terrell Owens	375.00
28	Warren Moon	60.00
29	Isaac Bruce	125.00
30	Steve McNair	600.00
31	Gus Frerotte	60.00
32	Trent Dilfer	125.00
33	Shannon Sharpe	60.00
34	Scott Mitchell	60.00
35	Antonio Freeman	200.00
36	Jim Harbaugh	60.00
37	Natrone Means	125.00
38	Marcus Allen	125.00
39	Karim Abdul-Jabbar	150.00
40	Tim Biakabutuka	60.00
41	Jeff Blake	125.00
42	Michael Irvin	125.00
43	Herschel Walker	60.00
44	Curtis Martin	600.00
45	Eddie Kennison	200.00
46	Napoleon Kaufman	200.00
47	Larry Centers	60.00
48	Jamal Anderson	125.00
49	Derrick Alexander	60.00
50	Bruce Smith	60.00
51	Wesley Walls	60.00
52	Rod Smith	60.00
53	Keenan McCardell	60.00
54	Robert Brooks	60.00
55	Willie Green	60.00
56	Jake Reed	60.00
57	Joey Galloway	125.00
58	Eric Metcalf	60.00
59	Chris Sanders	60.00
60	Jeff Hostetler	60.00
61	Kevin Greene	60.00
62	Frank Sanders	60.00
63	Dorsey Levens	200.00
64	Sean Dawkins	60.00
65	Cris Carter	60.00
66	Andre Hastings	60.00
67	Amani Toomer	60.00
68	Adrian Murrell	125.00
69	Ty Detmer	60.00
70	Yancey Thigpen	60.00
71	Jim Everett	60.00
72	Todd Collins	60.00
73	Curtis Conway	60.00
74	Herman Moore	125.00
75	Neil O'Donnell	60.00
76	Rod Woodson	60.00
77	Tony Martin	60.00
78	Kent Graham	60.00
79	Andre Reed	60.00
80	Reggie White	125.00
81	Thurman Thomas	125.00
82	Garrison Hearst	60.00
83	Chris Warren	60.00
84	Wayne Chrebet	60.00
85	Chris T. Jones	60.00
86	Anthony Miller	60.00
87	Chris Chandler	60.00
88	Terrell Davis	750.00
89	Mike Alstott	375.00
90	Terry Allen	60.00
91	Jerome Bettis	125.00
92	Stan Humphries	60.00
93	Andre Rison	60.00
94	Marshall Faulk	125.00
95	Erik Kramer	60.00
96	O.J. McDuffie	60.00
97	Robert Smith	60.00
98	Keith Byars	60.00
99	Rodney Hampton	60.00
100	Desmond Howard	60.00
101	Lawrence Phillips	125.00
102	Michael Westbrook	60.00
103	Johnnie Morton	60.00
104	Ben Coates	60.00
105	J.J. Stokes	60.00
106	Terance Mathis	60.00
107	Errict Rhett	60.00
108	Tim Brown	60.00
109	Marvin Harrison	200.00
110	Muhsin Muhammad	60.00
111	Bam Morris	60.00
112	Mario Bates	60.00
113	Jimmy Smith	60.00
114	Irving Fryar	60.00
115	Tamarick Vanover	60.00
116	Brad Johnson	125.00
117	Rashaan Salaam	60.00
118	Ki-Jana Carter	60.00
119	Tyrone Wheatley	60.00
120	John Friesz	60.00
121	Orlando Pace	75.00
122	Jim Druckenmiller	450.00
123	Byron Hanspard	150.00
124	David LaFleur	200.00
125	Reidel Anthony	300.00
126	Antowain Smith	450.00
127	Bryant Westbrook	75.00
128	Fred Lane	200.00
129	Tiki Barber	300.00
130	Shawn Springs	60.00
131	Ike Hilliard	250.00
132	James Farrior	60.00
133	Darrell Russell	60.00
134	Walter Jones	60.00
135	Tom Knight	60.00
136	Yatil Green	150.00
137	Joey Kent	75.00
138	Kevin Lockett	60.00
139	Troy Davis	150.00
140	Darnell Autry	125.00
141	Pat Barnes	150.00
142	Rae Carruth	250.00
143	Will Blackwell	75.00
144	Warrick Dunn	750.00
145	Corey Dillon	450.00
146	Dwayne Rudd	60.00
147	Reinard Wilson	60.00
148	Peter Boulware	60.00
149	Tony Gonzalez	200.00
150	Danny Wuerffel	300.00

1997 Pinnacle Totally Certified Platinum Red

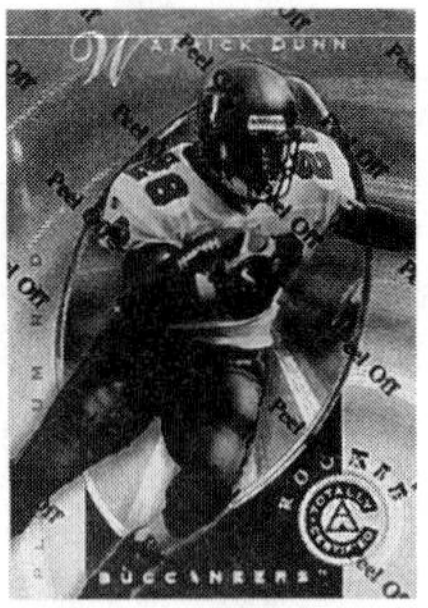

Platinum Red is considered the "base set" for Totally Certified. Each card in the 150-card set is sequentially-numbered to 4,999. The cards feature a micro-etched holographic mylar finish. Platinum Blue (one per pack) and Platinum Gold (1:79) parallels were also included in this series.

		MT
Complete Set (150):		250.00
Common Player:		.75
Minor Stars:		1.50
Common Rookie:		1.00
Reds Sequentially #'d to 4,999		
Pack (3):		7.00
Wax Box (18):		100.00
1	Emmitt Smith	12.00
2	Dan Marino	12.00
3	Brett Favre	15.00
4	Steve Young	7.00
5	Kerry Collins	1.50
6	Troy Aikman	10.00
7	Drew Bledsoe	8.00
8	Eddie George	7.00
9	Jerry Rice	10.00
10	John Elway	12.00
11	Barry Sanders	15.00
12	Mark Brunell	8.00
13	Elvis Grbac	1.50
14	Tony Banks	1.50
15	Vinny Testaverde	1.50
16	Rick Mirer	.75
17	Carl Pickens	1.50
18	Deion Sanders	3.00
19	Terry Glenn	3.00
20	Heath Shuler	.75
21	Dave Brown	.75
22	Keyshawn Johnson	3.00
23	Jeff George	3.00
24	Ricky Watters	1.50
25	Kordell Stewart	5.00
26	Junior Seau	1.50
27	Terrell Owens	3.00
28	Warren Moon	1.50
29	Isaac Bruce	3.00
30	Steve McNair	5.00
31	Gus Frerotte	.75
32	Trent Dilfer	1.50
33	Shannon Sharpe	1.50
34	Scott Mitchell	.75
35	Antonio Freeman	3.00
36	Jim Harbaugh	1.50
37	Natrone Means	1.50
38	Marcus Allen	3.00
39	Karim Abdul-Jabbar	1.50
40	Tim Biakabutuka	1.50
41	Jeff Blake	3.00
42	Michael Irvin	3.00
43	Herschel Walker	.75
44	Curtis Martin	4.00
45	Eddie Kennison	1.50
46	Napoleon Kaufman	3.00
47	Larry Centers	.75
48	Jamal Anderson	3.00
49	Derrick Alexander	.75
50	Bruce Smith	1.50
51	Wesley Walls	.75
52	Rod Smith	1.50
53	Keenan McCardell	1.50
54	Robert Brooks	1.50
55	Willie Green	.75
56	Jake Reed	.75
57	Joey Galloway	3.00
58	Eric Metcalf	.75
59	Chris Sanders	.75
60	Jeff Hostetler	.75
61	Kevin Greene	.75
62	Frank Sanders	1.50
63	Dorsey Levens	3.00
64	Sean Dawkins	.75
65	Cris Carter	3.00
66	Andre Hastings	.75
67	Amani Toomer	1.50
68	Adrian Murrell	1.50
69	Ty Detmer	1.50
70	Yancey Thigpen	1.50
71	Jim Everett	1.50
72	Todd Collins	.75
73	Curtis Conway	1.50
74	Herman Moore	3.00
75	Neil O'Donnell	1.50
76	Rod Woodson	1.50
77	Tony Martin	.75
78	Kent Graham	.75
79	Andre Reed	1.50
80	Reggie White	3.00
81	Thurman Thomas	3.00
82	Garrison Hearst	1.50
83	Chris Warren	1.50
84	Wayne Chrebet	3.00
85	Chris T. Jones	.75
86	Anthony Miller	.75
87	Chris Chandler	1.50
88	Terrell Davis	12.00
89	Mike Alstott	3.00
90	Terry Allen	1.50
91	Jerome Bettis	3.00
92	Stan Humphries	.75
93	Andre Rison	1.50
94	Marshall Faulk	4.00
95	Erik Kramer	.75
96	O.J. McDuffie	1.50
97	Robert Smith	3.00
98	Keith Byars	.75
99	Rodney Hampton	.75
100	Desmond Howard	.75
101	Lawrence Phillips	1.50
102	Michael Westbrook	1.50
103	Johnnie Morton	1.50
104	Ben Coates	1.50
105	J.J. Stokes	1.50
106	Terance Mathis	1.50
107	Errict Rhett	1.50
108	Tim Brown	3.00
109	Marvin Harrison	3.00
110	Muhsin Muhammad	1.50
111	Bam Morris	.75
112	Mario Bates	.75
113	Jimmy Smith	3.00
114	Irving Fryar	1.50
115	Tamarick Vanover	.75
116	Brad Johnson	3.00
117	Rashaan Salaam	.75
118	Ki-Jana Carter	.75
119	Tyrone Wheatley	1.50
120	John Friesz	1.50
121	*Orlando Pace*	2.00
122	*Jim Druckenmiller*	4.00
123	*Byron Hanspard*	4.00
124	*David LaFleur*	2.00
125	*Reidel Anthony*	6.00
126	*Antowain Smith*	7.00
127	*Bryant Westbrook*	2.00
128	*Fred Lane*	4.00
129	*Tiki Barber*	12.00
130	*Shawn Springs*	2.00
131	*Ike Hilliard*	6.00
132	*James Farrior*	1.00
133	*Darrell Russell*	2.00
134	*Walter Jones*	1.00
135	*Tom Knight*	1.00
136	*Yatil Green*	2.00
137	*Joey Kent*	2.00
138	*Kevin Lockett*	1.00
139	*Troy Davis*	2.00
140	*Darnell Autry*	4.00
141	*Pat Barnes*	4.00
142	*Rae Carruth*	2.00
143	*Will Blackwell*	2.00
144	*Warrick Dunn*	10.00
145	*Corey Dillon*	25.00
146	*Dwayne Rudd*	2.00
147	*Reinard Wilson*	1.00
148	*Peter Boulware*	2.00
149	*Tony Gonzalez*	10.00
150	*Danny Wuerffel*	4.00

1996 Sentry Foods Packers-Bears Rivalry

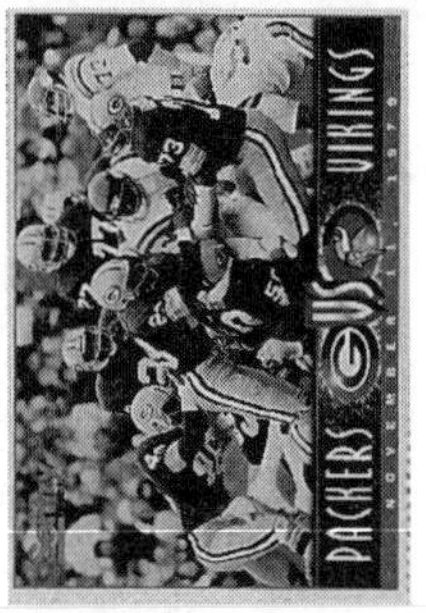

This six-card set was issued through Sentry Foods stores in Wisconsin commemorating the past 23 years of the Green Bay Packers and Chicago Bears rivalry. The set was issued as a perforated sheet with color action photos and both team's helmets at the bottom along with a Sentry Foods logo in the lower left of the horizontal card. The card backs are unnumbered and include the date of the game, highlights and the box score. A full sheet also included coupons below the six cards.

		MT
Complete Set (6):		4.00
Common Player:		.50
1	Dec. 16, 1973 (John Brockington)	.50
2	Sep. 7, 1980 (Chester Marcol)	.50
3	Nov. 5, 1989 (Sterling Sharpe and many Packers celebra ting)	.50
4	Oct. 31, 1994 (Edgar Bennett)	.50
5	Nov. 12, 1995 (Brett Favre handing off to Edgar Bennett)	2.00
6	Oct. 6, 1996 (Packers defense)	.50

1997 Sentry Foods Packers-Vikings

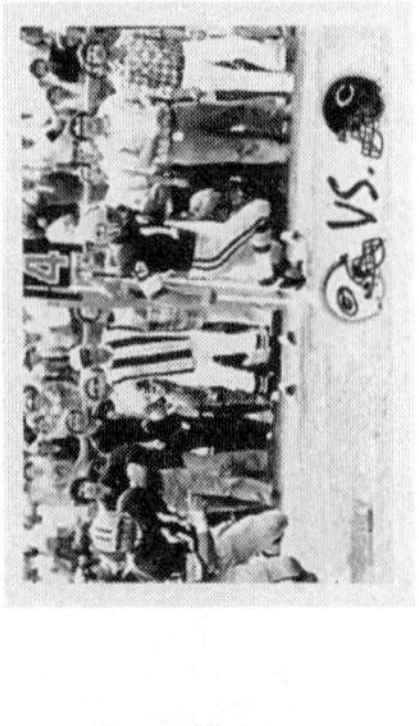

This set was issued as a 10-card perforated sheet and included highlights from the past 30 years of the Green Bay Packers and Minnesota Vikings rivalry. Fronts feature a horizontal game action photo with the Sentry Foods logo in the upper left corner and "Packers vs. Vikings" across the bottom in a strip along with both team's logos. The black-and-white backs have the game's date, Sentry logo, highlights and a box score with a large Packers logo in the background. Cards are unnumbered with the bottom right card in an uncut sheet being an entry form for children to join the Junior Power Pack Club. The sheet was available at participating Sentry stores in Wisconsin.

		MT
Complete Set (9):		6.00
Common Player:		.50
1	Dec. 3, 1967 (Don Chandler kicks)	.50
2	Dec. 10, 1972 (Packer offense)	.50
3	Nov. 26, 1978 (Packer defense stops Chuck Foreman)	.50
4	Nov. 11, 1979 (Packer defense)	.50
5	Oct. 26, 1980 (Lynn Dickey)	.50
6	Nov. 13, 1983 (Packer offense)	.50
7	Dec. 13, 1987 (Paul Ott Carruth)	.50
8	Nov. 26, 1989 (Don Majkowski)	.50
9	Sep. 4, 1994 (Brett Favre handing off to Edgar Bennett)	2.00

1972 7-11 Slurpee Cups

Each of these 60 white plastic cups measures 5-1/4" tall, 3-1/4" in diameter at the mouth and 2" in diameter at the base. The fronts feature a color player portrait with his name and team name. Most of the cups feature a facsimile autograph between the portrait and the player's name. The backs include biographical information, the player's team helmet and the 7-Eleven logo. Another set of 80 cups was released in 1973. The cups are similar except the 1972 cups have a smaller typeface for the player's name (1/16") and do not have "Made in USA" printed on the sides.

		NM
Complete Set (60):		250.00
Common Player:		4.00
1	Donny Anderson	4.00
2	Elvin Bethea	4.00
3	Fred Biletnikoff	8.00
4	Bill Bradley	4.00
5	Terry Bradshaw	25.00
6	Larry Brown	4.00
7	Willie Brown	5.00
8	Norm Bulaich	4.00
9	Dick Butkus	15.00
10	Ray Chester	4.00
11	Bill Curry	4.00
12	Len Dawson	8.00
13	Willie Ellison	4.00
14	Ed Flanagan	4.00
15	Gary Garrison	4.00
16	Gale Gillingham	4.00
17	Joe Greene	8.00
18	Cedrick Hardman	4.00
19	Jim Hart	5.00
20	Ted Hendricks	5.00
21	Winston Hill	4.00
22	Ken Houston	5.00
23	Chuck Howley	4.00
24	Claude Humphrey	4.00
25	Roy Jefferson	4.00
26	Sonny Jurgensen	6.00
27	Leroy Kelly	5.00
28	Paul Krause	4.00
29	George Kunz	4.00
30	Jake Kupp	4.00
31	Ted Kwalick	4.00
32	Willie Lanier	5.00
33	Bob Lilly	6.00
34	Floyd Little	4.00
35	Larry Little	5.00
36	Tom Mack	4.00
37	Milt Morin	4.00
38	Mercury Morris	5.00
39	John Niland	4.00
40	Jim Otto	5.00
41	Steve Owens	4.00
42	Alan Page	5.00
43	Jim Plunkett	5.00
44	Mike Reid	5.00
45	Mel Renfro	5.00
46	Isiah Robertson	4.00
47	Andy Russell	4.00
48	Charlie Sanders	4.00
49	O.J. Simpson	15.00
50	Bubba Smith	5.00
51	Bill Stanfill	4.00
52	Jan Stenerud	5.00
53	Walt Sweeney	4.00
54	Bob Tucker	4.00
55	Jim Tyrer	4.00
56	Rick Volk	4.00
57	Gene Washington	4.00
58	Dave Wilcox	4.00
59	Del Williams	4.00
60	Ron Yary	4.00

1973 7-11 Slurpee Cups

This 80-cup series is similar to the 1972 series except the player's name is printed in larger type (1/8") and the words "Made in USA" are printed down the sides.

		NM
Complete Set (80):		450.00
Common Player:		5.00
1	Dan Abramowicz	6.00
2	Ken Anderson	10.00
3	Jim Beirne	5.00
4	Ed Bell	5.00
5	Bob Berry	5.00
6	Jim Bertelsen	5.00
7	Marlin Briscoe	5.00
8	John Brockington	5.00
9	Larry Brown	6.00
10	Buck Buchanan	7.50
11	Dick Butkus	25.00
12	Larry Carwell	5.00
13	Rich Caster	5.00
14	Bobby Douglass	5.00
15	Pete Duranko	5.00
16	Cid Edwards	5.00
17	Mel Farr	5.00
18	Pat Fischer	5.00
19	Mike Garrett	5.00
20	Walt Garrison	6.00
21	George Goeddeke	5.00
22	Bob Gresham	5.00
23	Jack Ham	10.00
24	Chris Hanburger	5.00
25	Franco Harris	20.00
26	Calvin Hill	6.00
27	J.D. Hill	5.00
28	Marv Hubbard	5.00
29	Scott Hunter	5.00
30	Harold Jackson	6.00
31	Randy Jackson	5.00
32	Bob Johnson	5.00
33	Jim Johnson	7.50
34	Ron Johnson	5.00
35	Leroy Keyes	5.00
36	Greg Landry	6.00
37	Gary Larsen	5.00
38	Frank Lewis	5.00
39	Bob Lilly	10.00
40	Dale Lindsey	5.00
41	Larry Little	7.50
42	Carl (Spider) Lockhart	5.00
43	Mike Lucci	5.00
44	Jim Lynch	5.00
45	Art Malone	5.00
46	Ed Marinaro	6.00
47	Jim Marshall	7.50
48	Ray May	5.00
49	Don Maynard	10.00
50	Don McCauley	5.00
51	Mike McCoy	5.00
52	Tom Mitchell	5.00
53	Tommy Nobis	7.50
54	Dan Pastorini	6.00
55	Mac Percival	5.00
56	Mike Phipps	6.00
57	Ed Podolak	5.00
58	John Reaves	5.00
59	Tim Rossovich	5.00
60	Bo Scott	5.00
61	Ron Sellers	5.00
62	Dennis Shaw	5.00
63	Mike Siani	5.00
64	O.J. Simpson	25.00
65	Bubba Smith	7.50
66	Larry Smith	5.00
67	Jackie Smith	7.50
68	Norm Snead	6.00
69	Jack Snow	5.00
70	Steve Spurrier	20.00
71	Doug Swift	5.00
72	Jack Tatum	7.50
73	Bruce Taylor	5.00
74	Otis Taylor	6.00
75	Bob Trumpy	6.00
76	Jim Turner	5.00
77	Phil Villapiano	5.00
78	Roger Wehrli	5.00
79	Ken Willard	5.00
80	Jack Youngblood	7.50

1983 7-11 Discs

These discs were available at participating 7-Eleven stores in 1983. Each disc, which is numbered on the back as "x of Fifteen," has a portrait and an action picture on the front. The player's team name is at the top of the disc, while his name is at the bottom. His jersey number is on each side. The disc back has the player's career totals, pro honors, a Slurpee logo and the year, 1983.

		MT
Complete Set (15):		30.00
Common Player:		1.00
1	Franco Harris	5.00
2	Dan Fouts	3.00
3	Lee Roy Selmon	1.25
4	Nolan Cromwell	1.25
5	Marcus Allen	5.00
6	Joe Montana	10.00
7	Kellen Winslow	2.00
8	Hugh Green	1.00
9	Ted Hendricks	2.00
10	Danny White	1.50
11	Wes Chandler	1.00
12	Jimmie Giles	1.00
13	Jack Youngblood	2.00
14	Lester Hayes	1.00
15	Vince Ferragamo	1.00

1984 7-11 Discs

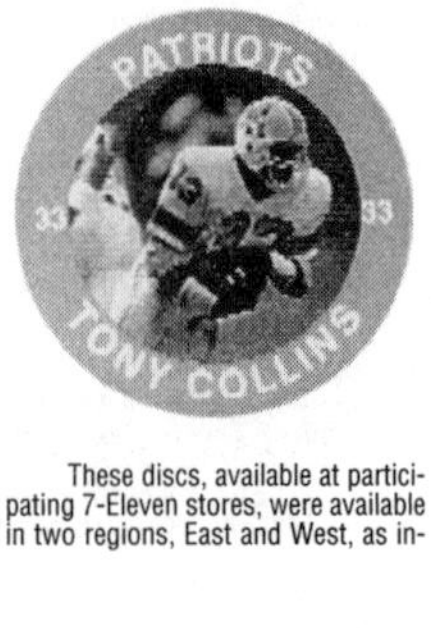

These discs, available at participating 7-Eleven stores, were available in two regions, East and West, as indicated by the card number prefix. The disc has a diameter of 1-3/4" and is designed like the previous year's issue, except the year on the back is 1984.

		MT
Complete Set (40):		60.00
Common Player:		.75
1E	Franco Harris	3.00
2E	Lawrence Taylor	2.00
3E	Mark Gastineau	.75
4E	Lee Roy Selmon	1.00
5E	Ken Anderson	1.50
6E	Walter Payton	4.00
7E	Ken Stabler	1.50
8E	Marcus Allen	2.00
9E	Fred Smerlas	.75
10E	Ozzie Newsome	1.25
11E	Steve Bartkowski	1.00
12E	Tony Dorsett	2.00
13E	John Riggins	1.50
14E	Billy Sims	.75
15E	Dan Marino	9.00
16E	Tony Collins	.75
17E	Curtis Dickey	.75
18E	Ron Jaworski	.75
19E	William Andrews	.75
20E	Joe Theismann	1.50
1W	Franco Harris	2.00
2W	Joe Montana	10.00
3W	Matt Blair	.75
4W	Warren Moon	6.00
5W	Marcus Allen	2.00
6W	John Riggins	1.50
7W	Walter Payton	4.00
8W	Vince Ferragamo	.75
9W	Billy Sims	.75
10W	Ken Anderson	1.25
11W	Lynn Dickey	.75
12W	Tony Dorsett	2.00
13W	Bill Kenney	.75
14W	Ottis Anderson	1.00
15W	Dan Fouts	1.50
16W	Eric Dickerson	3.00
17W	John Elway	6.00
18W	Ozzie Newsome	1.25
19W	Curt Warner	1.00
20W	Joe Theismann	1.50

1981 Shell Posters

The works of three different artists are featured on these 10-7/8" x 13-7/8" posters available at participating Shell Oil stations across the country in 1981. Each poster has a black-and-white drawing of the featured player, as rendered by either K. Atkins, Nick Galloway or Tanenbawm (these signatures are on the corresponding poster fronts). There are, however, some posters which were not signed by the artist (#s 7, 11, 12 and 93). The posters are listed alphabetically by teams, then alphabetically by players. Team sets consist of six posters. A national set of six posters was also made (Payton, Griffin, Logan, Pearson, Campbell and O. Anderson) and was available in markets where a pro team did not exist.

		MT
Complete Set (96):		400.00
Common Player:		4.00
(1)	William Andrews	5.00
(2)	Steve Bartkowski	7.00
(3)	Buddy Curry	3.50
(4)	Wallace Francis	5.00
(5)	Mike Kenn	5.00
(6)	Jeff Van Note	5.00
(7)	Mike Barnes	4.00
(8)	Roger Carr	4.00
(9)	Curtis Dickey	5.00
(10)	Bert Jones	7.00
(11)	Bruce Laird	4.00
(12)	Randy McMillan	5.00
(13)	Brian Baschnagel	4.00
(14)	Vince Evans	5.00
(15)	Gary Fencik	5.00
(16)	Roland Harper	4.00
(17)	Alan Page	9.00
(18)	Walter Payton	10.00
(19)	Ken Anderson	8.00
(20)	Ross Browner	5.00
(21)	Archie Griffin	4.00
(22)	Pat McInally	5.00
(23)	Anthony Munoz	8.00
(24)	Reggie Williams	5.00
(25)	Lyle Alzado	6.00
(26)	Joe DeLamielleure	4.00
(27)	Doug Dieken	4.00
(28)	Dave Logan	4.00
(29)	Reggie Rucker	5.00
(30)	Brian Sipe	5.00
(31)	Benny Barnes	4.00
(32)	Bob Breunig	4.00
(33)	D.D. Lewis	4.00
(34)	Harvey Martin	6.00
(35)	Drew Pearson	4.00
(36)	Rafael Septien	4.00
(37)	Al (Bubba) Baker	5.00
(38)	Dexter Bussey	4.00
(39)	Gary Danielson	5.00
(40)	Freddie Scott	4.00
(41)	Billy Sims	6.00
(42)	Tom Skladany	4.00
(43)	Robert Brazile	6.00
(44)	Ken Burrough	6.00
(45)	Earl Campbell	9.00
(46)	Leon Gray	5.00
(47)	Carl Mauck	5.00
(48)	Ken Stabler	8.00
(49)	Bob Baumhower	5.00
(50)	Jimmy Cefalo	5.00
(51)	A.J. Duhe	5.00
(52)	Nat Moore	6.00
(53)	Ed Newman	4.00
(54)	Uwe Von Schamann	4.00
(55)	Steve Grogan	7.00
(56)	John Hannah	4.50
(57)	Don Hasselbeck	4.00
(58)	Mike Haynes	6.00
(59)	Harold Jackson	5.00
(60)	Steve Nelson	4.00
(61)	Elois Grooms	5.00
(62)	Rickey Jackson	7.50

(63)	Archie Manning	8.00
(64)	Tommy Myers	5.00
(65)	Benny Ricardo	5.00
(66)	George Rogers	6.00
(67)	Harry Carson	7.00
(68)	Dave Jennings	4.00
(69)	Gary Jeter	4.00
(70)	Phil Simms	8.00
(71)	Lawrence Taylor	12.00
(72)	Brad Van Pelt	5.00
(73)	Greg Buttle	5.00
(74)	Bruce Harper	4.00
(75)	Joe Klecko	5.00
(76)	Randy Rasmussen	4.00
(77)	Richard Todd	5.00
(78)	Wesley Walker	6.00
(79)	Ottis Anderson	4.00
(80)	Dan Dierdorf	9.00
(81)	Mel Gray	5.00
(82)	Jim Hart	6.00
(83)	E.J. Junior	5.00
(84)	Pat Tilley	5.00
(85)	Jimmie Giles	5.00
(86)	Charley Hannah	4.00
(87)	Bill Kollar	4.00
(88)	David Lewis	4.00
(89)	Lee Roy Selmon	6.00
(90)	Doug Williams	5.00
(91)	Joe Lavender	4.00
(92)	Mark Moseley	5.00
(93)	Mark Murphy	4.00
(94)	Lemar Parrish	5.00
(95)	John Riggins	9.00
(96)	Joe Washington	5.00

1994 Signature Rookies Fb

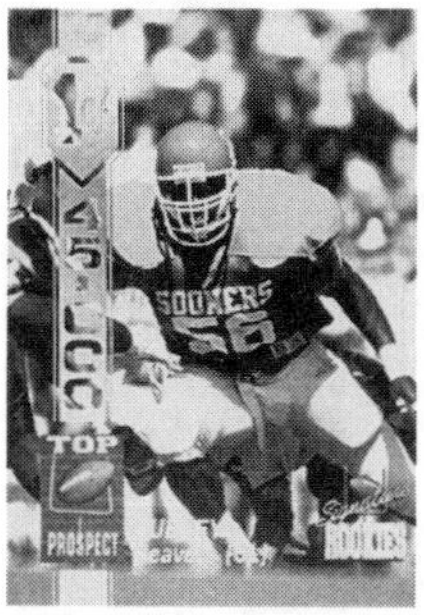

The 60-card, standard-size set featured top NFL prospects in their collegiate uniforms. The player's name and position appear on the bottom edge and the cards are numbered as "x of 45,000" or "Authentic Signature" along the left edge in gold foil. Production was limited to 12,500 boxes. Inserts included Hottest Prospect, Gale Sayers, Charlie Ward and Tony Dorsett.

		MT
Complete Set (60):		8.00
Common Player:		.05
1	Sam Adams	.05
2	Trev Alberts	.05
3	Derrick Alexander	.25
4	Aubrey Beavers	.05
5	Lou Benfatti	.05
6	James Bostic	.05
7	Tim Bowens	.25
8	Rich Braham	.05
9	Isaac Bruce	1.50
10	Vaughn Bryant	.05
11	Brenston Buckner	.05
12	Jeff Burris	.10
13	Carlester Crumpler	.05
14	Lake Dawson	.30
15	Tyronne Drakeford	.05
16	Dan Eichloff	.05
17	Rob Fredrickson	.20
18	Gus Frerotte	.75
19	William Gaines	.05
20	Wayne Gandy	.05
21	Jason Gildon	.05
22	Lemanski Hall	.05
23	Shelby Hill	.05
24	LeShon Johnson	.15
25	Alan Kline	.05
26	Antonio Langham	.10
27	Keith Lyle	.05
28	Van Malone	.05
29	Jamir Miller	.10
30	Byron "Bam" Morris	.50
31	Jeremy Nunley	.05
32	Brad Ottis	.05
33	Joe Panos	.05
34	John Reece	.05
35	Tony Richardson	.05
36	Tim Ruddy	.05
37	Corey Sawyer	.05
38	Malcolm Seabron	.05
39	John Thierry	.05
40	Jason Seahorn	.05
41	Eric Zomalt	.05
42	Toby Wright	.05
43	Willie Jackson	.05
44	Tre Johnson	.05
45	Darren Krein	.05
46	Corey Louchiey	.05
47	Eric Mahlum	.05
48	Chris Maumalanga	.05
49	Jim Miller	.05
50	Aaron Mundy	.05
51	Turhon O'Brannon	.05
52	David Palmer	.10
53	Jim Pyne	.05
54	Errict Rhett	1.25
55	Sam Rogers	.05
56	Jason Winrow	.05
57	Ronnie Woolfork	.05
58	Rob Waldrop	.05
59	Ryan Yarborough	.05
60	Checklist	.05

A player's name in *italic* type indicates a rookie card.

1994 Signature Rookies Signatures

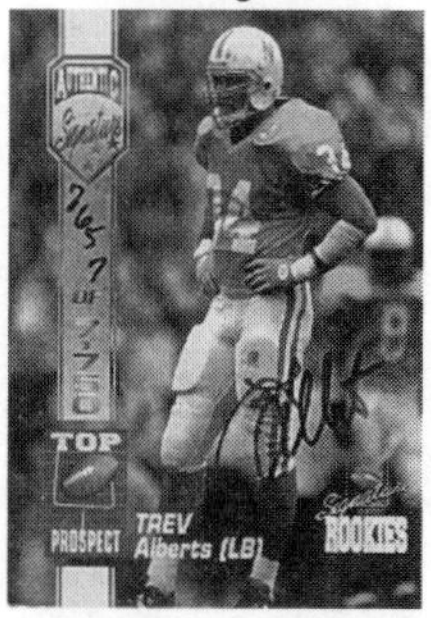

The 59-card, standard-size set was inserted in each six-card pack of Signature Rookies. Each card was numbered as "x of 7,750." Reportedly, 700 Errict Rhett cards are not actually signed by the running back, but that he had an aquaintance autograph the cards for him. Autographed Rhett cards could be sent in to Signature Rookies for verification.

		MT
Complete Set (59):		225.00
Common Autograph:		4.00
1	Sam Adams	4.00
2	Trev Alberts	4.00
3	Derrick Alexander (WR)	6.00
4	Larry Allen	4.00
5	Aubrey Beavers	4.00
6	Lou Benfatti	4.00
7	James Bostic	4.00
8	Tim Bowens	4.00
9	Rich Braham	4.00
10	Isaac Bruce	30.00
11	Vaughn Bryant	4.00
12	Brenston Buckner	4.00
13	Jeff Burris	4.00
14	Carlester Crumpler	6.00
15	Lake Dawson	6.00
16	Tyronne Drakeford	4.00
17	Dan Eichloff	4.00
18	Rob Fredrickson	4.00
19	Gus Frerotte	10.00
20	William Gaines	4.00
21	Wayne Gandy	4.00
22	Jason Gildon	4.00
23	Lemanski Hall	4.00
24	Shelby Hill	4.00
25	Willie Jackson	4.00
26	LeShon Johnson	6.00
27	Tre Johnson	4.00
28	Alan Kline	4.00
29	Darren Krein	4.00
30	Antonio Langham	6.00
31	Corey Louchiey	4.00
32	Keith Lyle	4.00
33	Eric Mahlum	4.00
34	Van Malone	4.00
35	Chris Maumalanga	4.00
36	Jamir Miller	4.00
37	Jim Miller	6.00
38	Byron "Bam" Morris	6.00
39	Aaron Mundy	4.00
40	Jeremy Nunley	4.00
41	Turhonn O'Bannon	4.00
42	Brad Ottis	4.00
43	David Palmer	5.00
44	Joe Panos	4.00
45	Jim Pyne	4.00
46	John Reece	4.00
47	Errict Rhett	10.00
48	Tony Richardson	4.00
49	Sam Rogers	4.00
50	Tim Ruddy	4.00
51	Corey Sawyer	4.00
52	Malcolm Seabron	4.00
53	Jason Sehorn	4.00
54	John Thierry	4.00
55	Jason Winrow	4.00
56	Ronnie Woolford	4.00
57	Toby Wright	4.00
58	Ryan Yarborough	4.00
59	Eric Zomalt	4.00

1994 Signature Rookies Bonus Signatures

The 15-card, standard-size set was hand-numbered out of 7,750 and the player's signature appeared on the bottom edge. Cards were randomly inserted in 1994 Tetrad packs.

		MT
Complete Set (15):		35.00
Common Signature:		3.00
Coupons Replace Some Cards		
1	Jamal Anderson	10.00
2	Myron Bell	3.00
3	Mitch Berger	3.00
4	Jocelyn Borgella	3.00
5	Chris Brantley	3.00
6	Ron Edwards	3.00
7	Rob Holmberg	3.00
8	Fred Lester	3.00
9	Joseph Patton	3.00
10	Eric Ravotti	3.00
11	Jim Reid	3.00
12	Jerry Reynolds	3.00
13	Bracey Walker	3.00
14	Gabe Wilkins	3.00
15	Brant Boyer	3.00

1994 Signature Rookies Tony Dorsett

The two-card, standard-size set, limited to 5,000, are numbered as out of 5,000 autographed 1,000 cards. Dallas Cowboys Hall of Fame running back.

	MT
Complete Set (2):	6.00
Common Player:	3.00
Complete Signature Set (2):	125.00
Tony Dorsett AU/1000	60.00

1994 Signature Rookies Hottest Prospects

The five-card, standard-size set was numbered out of 15,000 and featured the players in their collegiate uniforms. The cards are numbered and carry an "A" prefix.

		MT
Complete Set (5):		10.00
Common Player:		2.00
1	Willie McGinest	3.00
2	Bryant Young	4.00
3	DeWayne Washington	2.00
4	Aaron Taylor	2.00
5	Charles Johnson	2.50

1994 Signature Rookies Gale Sayers

The two-card, standard-size set was randomly inserted into packs and was limited to 5,000 of each card. The former Chicago Bears star autographed 1,000 of the cards.

	MT
Complete Set (2):	8.00
Common Sayers:	4.00
Comp. Signature Set (2):	150.00
Gale Sayers AU/1000	75.00

1994 Signature Rookies Charlie Ward

The five-card, standard-size set highlights Florida State's 1993 Heisman winner and 5,000 of each card was produced. Ward autographed 525 of his cards. The cards are numbered with a "C" prefix.

		MT
Complete Set (5):		4.00
Common Ward:		1.00
Complete Signed Set (5):		150.00
Charlie Ward AU/25		30.00
1	Charlie Ward (In throwing motion)	1.00
2	Charlie Ward (Ready to hand-off)	1.00
3	Charlie Ward (Posed football shot)	1.00
4	Charlie Ward (Holding basketball at waist)	1.00
5	Charlie Ward (holding basketball overhead)	1.00

1995 SR Auto-Phonex

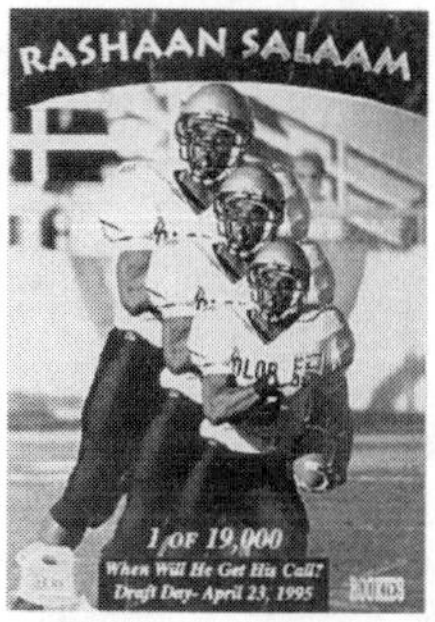

The 40-card, standard-size set features card fronts with triple images of the key player in his collegiate uniform. The player's name appears in gold foil along the bottom edge with "1 of 19,000" printed on the bottom. Each case of Auto-Phonex features Hot Packs, which include an autographed phone card plus five additional autographed cards. J.J. Stokes was featured on the $5 card (1:287) while the $25 card (Kevin Carter) is inserted every 1,437. Ten Warren Sapp $100 cards (1:14,371) and eight $1,000 (Rashaan Salaam and Ki-Jana Carter) were included every 35,928 packs.

		MT
Complete Set (40):		10.00
Common Player:		.10
1	Warren Sapp	.30
2	Kevin Carter	.20
3	Ki-Jana Carter	.75
4	J.J. Stokes	1.00
5	Derrick Alexander	.20
6	Rashaan Salaam	1.25
7	Jamal Willis	.10
8	Frank Sanders	.60
9	Rob Johnson	.10
10	Derrick Brooks	.20
11	Sherman Williams	.30
12	Dave Barr	.10
13	Christian Fauria	.20
14	Stoney Case	.10
15	Rodney Thomas	.60
16	James A. Stewart	.20
17	Ray Zellars	.30
18	Jack Jackson	.10
19	Terrell Davis	1.25
20	Kyle Brady	.20
21	Ruben Brown	.20
22	Brent Moss	.10
23	John Sacca	.10
24	David Dunn	.20
25	Eddie Goines	.10
26	Curtis Martin	1.50
27	Billy Williams	.10
28	Steve Stenstrom	.10
29	Mark Bruener	.30
30	Kelvin Anderson	.10
31	Ellis Johnson	.20
32	Steve Ingram	.10
33	Larry Jones	.10
34	Bobby Taylor	.30
35	Joe Aska	.10
36	Jerrott Willard	.10
37	Chris T. Jones	.30
38	Mark Birchmeier	.10
39	Jimmy Hitchcock	.10
40	Tyrone Davis	.10
NNO	Ki-Jana Carter (CL)	.30

1995 SR Auto-Phonex Phone Card Signatures

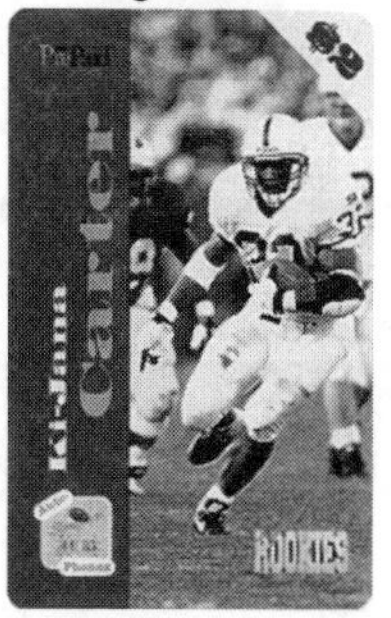

The 40-card, 2-3/8" x 3-1/8" phone card set was inserted in each pack of SR Auto-Phonex. The cards have rounded corners and the common card has $2 of calling time. $5 cards of J.J. Stokes (1:287), $25 cards of Kevin Carter (1:1,437) and $100 cards of Warren Sapp (1:14,371) were also inserted, as were eight $1,000 cards of Ki-Jana Carter and Rashaan Salaam (1:35,928).

		MT
Complete Set (40):		250.00
Common Player:		3.00
1	Warren Sapp	8.00
2	Kevin Carter	4.00
3	Ki-Jana Carter	6.00
4	J.J. Stokes	15.00
5	Derrick Alexander	4.00
6	Rashaan Salaam	8.00
7	Jamal Willis	3.00
8	Frank Sanders	10.00
9	Eric Zeier	6.00
10	Derrick Brooks	4.00
11	Sherman Williams	5.00
12	Dave Barr	3.00
13	Christian Fauria	4.00
14	Stoney Case	3.00
15	Rodney Thomas	6.00
16	James A. Stewart	4.00
17	Ray Zellars	5.00
18	Jack Jackson	3.00
19	Terrell Davis	50.00
20	Kyle Brady	4.00
21	Ruben Brown	4.00
22	Brent Moss	3.00
23	John Sacca	3.00
24	David Dunn	4.00
25	Eddie Goines	3.00
26	Curtis Martin	30.00
27	Billy Williams	3.00
28	Steve Stenstrom	3.00
29	Mark Bruener	6.00
30	Kelvin Anderson	3.00
31	Ellis Johnson	4.00
32	Steve Ingram	3.00
33	Larry Jones	3.00
34	Bobby Taylor	5.00
35	Joe Aska	3.00
36	Jerrott Willard	3.00
37	Chris T. Jones	8.00
38	Mark Birchmeier	3.00
39	Jimmy Hitchcock	3.00
40	Tyrone Davis	3.00
NNO	J.J. Stokes $5 Card	40.00
NNO	Kevin Carter $25 Card	80.00

1995 SR Auto-Phonex Signatures

The 10-card, standard-size set was randomly inserted in Hot Packs and was also available through a mail-in redemption offer. The cards are identical in design to the regular-issue cards, except for the signatures.

		MT
Complete Set (10):		325.00
Common Player:		10.00
3A	Ki-Jana Carter	30.00
6A	Rashaan Salaam	30.00
8A	Frank Sanders	50.00
11A	Sherman Williams	20.00
12A	Dave Barr	10.00
14A	Stoney Case	20.00
16A	James A. Stewart	15.00
17A	Ray Zellars	20.00
20A	Kyle Brady	20.00
23A	John Sacca	10.00

1995 SR Draft Preview

The 80-card, standard-size set was issued in six-card packs for $5, and included an autographed card. Each player signed 7,750 of his own cards, and 39,000 of each card was produced. An international version was also produced, limited to a production total of 13,500, 2,750 of which were signed.

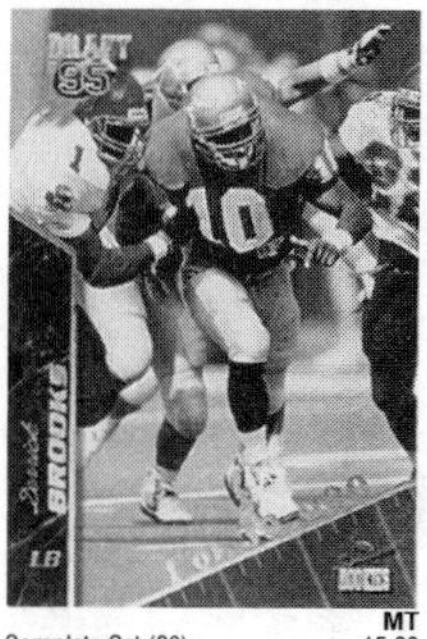

		MT
Complete Set (80):		15.00
Common Player:		.10
International:		1x-2x
1	Derrick Alexander	.15
2	Kelvin Anderson	.10
3	Antonio Armstrong	.10
4	Jamie Asher	.10
5	Joe Aska	.10
6	Dave Barr	.10
7	Brandon Bennett	.10
8	Tony Berti	.10
9	Mark Birchmeier	.10
10	Tony Boselli	.15
11	Derrick Brooks	.15
12	Anthony Brown	.10
13	Ruben Brown	.15
14	Mark Bruener	.30
15	Ontiwaun Carter	.10
16	Stoney Case	.10
17	Byron Chamberlain	.10
18	Shannon Clavelle	.10
19	Jamal Cox	.10
20	Zack Crockett	.15
21	Terrell Davis	1.50
22	Tyrone Davis	.10
23	Lee DeRamus	.10
24	Ken Dilger	.40
25	Hugh Douglas	.50
26	David Dunn	.15
27	Chad Eaton	.10
28	Hicham El-Mashtoub	.10
29	Christian Fauria	.15
30	Terrell Fletcher	.30
31	Antonio Freeman	.10
32	Eddie Goines	.10
33	Roger Graham	.10
34	Carl Greenwood	.10
35	Ed Hervey	.10
36	Jimmy Hitchcock	.10
37	Darius Holland	.10
38	Torey Hunter	.10
39	Steve Ingram	.10
40	Jack Jackson	.10
41	Trezelle Jenkins	.10
42	Ellis Johnson	.15
43	Eric Johnson	.15
44	Rob Johnson	.10
45	Chris T. Jones	.25
46	Larry Jones	.10
47	Shawn King	.10
48	Scotty Lewis	.10
49	Curtis Martin	2.00
50	Oscar McBride	.10
51	Kez McCorvey	.10
52	Bronzell Miller	.10
53	Pete Mitchell	.25
54	Brent Moss	.10
55	Craig Newsome	.15
56	Herman O'Berry	.10
57	Matt O'Dwyer	.10
58	Tyrone Poole	.15
59	Brian Pruitt	.10
60	Cory Raymer	.10
61	John Sacca	.10
62	Frank Sanders	.75
63	J.J. Smith	.10
64	Brendan Stai	.10
65	Steve Stenstrom	.10
66	James O. Stewart	.40
67	Kordell Stewart	1.50
68	Ben Talley	.10
69	Bobby Taylor	.25
70	Johnny Thomas	.10
71	Orlando Thomas	.15
72	Rodney Thomas	.75
73	Zach Wiegert	.15
74	Jerrott Willard	.10
75	Billy Williams	.10
76	Sherman Williams	.25
77	Jamal Willis	.10
78	Dave Wohlabaugh	.10
79	Eric Zeier	.75
80	Checklist	.10

1995 SR Draft Preview Signatures

The 79-card, standard-size parallel set (minus the checklist), was included in each pack of SR Draft Preview. Each player signed 7,750 cards out of the 39,000 produced, and 2,750 out of the 13,500 produced for the international set.

		MT
Complete Set (79):		250.00
Common Player:		2.50
International:		1x-2x
1	Derrick Alexander	3.00
2	Kelvin Anderson	2.50
3	Antonio Armstrong	2.50
4	Jamie Asher	2.50
5	Joe Aska	2.50
6	Dave Barr	2.50
7	Brandon Bennett	2.50
8	Tony Berti	2.50
9	Mark Birchmeier	2.50
10	Tony Boselli	3.00
11	Derrick Brooks	3.00
12	Anthony Brown	2.50
13	Ruben Brown	3.00
14	Mark Bruener	4.00
15	Ontiwaun Carter	2.50
16	Stoney Case	2.50
17	Byron Chamberlain	2.50
18	Shannon Clavelle	2.50
19	Jamal Cox	2.50
20	Zack Crockett	3.00
21	Terrell Davis	30.00
22	Tyrone Davis	2.50
23	Lee DeRamus	2.50
24	Ken Dilger	5.00
25	Hugh Douglas	5.00
26	David Dunn	3.00
27	Chad Eaton	2.50
28	Hicham El-Mashtoub	2.50
29	Christian Fauria	3.00
30	Terrell Fletcher	4.00
31	Antonio Freeman	20.00
32	Eddie Goines	2.50
33	Roger Graham	2.50
34	Carl Greenwood	2.50
35	Ed Hervey	2.50
36	Jimmy Hitchcock	2.50
37	Darius Holland	2.50
38	Torey Hunter	2.50
39	Steve Ingram	2.50
40	Jack Jackson	2.50
41	Trezelle Jenkins	2.50
42	Ellis Johnson	3.00
43	Eric Johnson	3.00
44	Rob Johnson	2.50
45	Chris T. Jones	8.00
46	Larry Jones	2.50
47	Shawn King	2.50
48	Scotty Lewis	2.50
49	Curtis Martin	20.00
50	Oscar McBride	2.50
51	Kez McCorvey	2.50
52	Bronzell Miller	2.50
53	Pete Mitchell	4.00
54	Brent Moss	2.50
55	Craig Newsome	3.00
56	Herman O'Berry	2.50
57	Matt O'Dwyer	2.50
58	Tyrone Poole	3.00
59	Brian Pruitt	2.50
60	Cory Raymer	2.50
61	John Sacca	2.50
62	Frank Sanders	8.00
63	J.J. Smith	2.50
64	Brendan Stai	2.50
65	Steve Stenstrom	2.50
66	James O. Stewart	5.00
67	Kordell Stewart	20.00
68	Ben Talley	2.50
69	Bobby Taylor	4.00
70	Johnny Thomas	2.50
71	Orlando Thomas	3.00
72	Rodney Thomas	5.00
73	Zach Wiegert	3.00
74	Jerrott Willard	2.50
75	Billy Williams	2.50
76	Sherman Williams	4.00
77	Jamal Willis	2.50
78	Dave Wohlabaugh	2.50
79	Eric Zeier	5.00

1995 SR Draft Preview Franchise Rookies

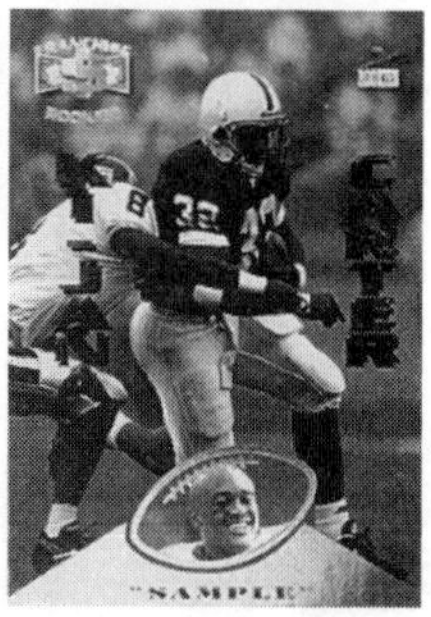

The 10-card, standard-size set was inserted every eight packs of SR Draft Preview. Production was limited to 10,000 sets with each player signing 2,500 of his own card. The cards are numbered with a "R" prefix.

		MT
Complete Set (10):		12.00
Common Player:		.50
1	Kyle Brady	.75
2	Kevin Carter	.50
3	Ki-Jana Carter	3.00
4	Luther Ellis	.50
5	Rashaan Salaam	4.00
6	Warren Sapp	.75
7	James A. Stewart	.50
8	J.J. Stokes	3.00
9	Michael Westbrook	2.00
10	Ray Zellars	.75

1995 SR Draft Preview Franchise Rookies Signatures

The 10-card, standard-size set was limited to 2,500 of each card and is identical in design to the Franchise Rookies insert set with the exception of the player's autograph on the card front. The cards carry a "R" prefix.

		MT
Complete Set (10):		75.00
Common Player:		4.00
1	Kyle Brady	5.00
2	Kevin Carter	4.00
3	Ki-Jana Carter	6.00
4	Luther Ellis	4.00
5	Rashaan Salaam	10.00
6	Warren Sapp (1125)	8.00

7	James A. Stewart	4.00
8	J.J. Stokes	12.00
9	Michael Westbrook	15.00
10	Ray Zellars	4.00

1995 SR Draft Preview International Franchise Duo

The 10-card, regular-size set was inserted every 10 packs and features one draft choice on each side of the card. "International" appears in the silver triangle and the player's name is divided (first and last) on the left and right sides.

		MT
Complete Set (10):		20.00
Common Player:		1.50
1	Ki-Jana Carter, Kevin Carter	3.00
2	Warren Sapp, Derrick Alexander	2.00
3	James A. Stewart, James O. Stewart	2.00
4	Michael Westbrook, J.J. Stokes	2.50
5	Kyle Brady, Kerry Collins	3.00
6	Steve McNair, Kerry Collins	5.00
7	Eric Zeier, Kordell Stewart	5.00
8	Rob Johnson, Stoney Case	1.50
9	Rashaan Salaam, Ki-Jana Carter	3.00
10	Ray Zellars, Sherman Williams	2.00

1995 SR Draft Preview Int'l Franchise Duo Signatures

The 16-card, standard-size set features one draft choice on each side of the card and is a parallel set in design with the International Franchise Duo insert set. Warren Sapp and James A. Stewart, included in the regular-issue set, did not sign and the set skips No. 12.

		MT
Complete Set (16):		700.00
Common Player:		15.00
1	Derrick Alexander (AU/200)	15.00
2	Kyle Brady (AU/242)	20.00
3	Kevin Carter (AU/315)	15.00
4	Ki-Jana Carter (AU/400)	30.00
5	Stoney Case (AU/200)	15.00
6	Kerry Collins (AU/600)	80.00
7	Rob Johnson (AU/309)	35.00
8	Steve McNair (AU/600)	70.00
9	Rashaan Salaam (AU/299)	100.00
10	Kordell Stewart (AU/309)	150.00
11	James O. Stewart (AU/200)	30.00
13	J.J. Stokes (AU/284)	80.00
14	Michael Westbrook (AU/282)	70.00
15	Sherman Williams (AU/312)	20.00
16	Eric Zeier (AU/314)	35.00
17	Ray Zellars (AU/310)	20.00

1995 SR Draft Preview Masters of the Mic

The five-card, standard-size set features some of the top announcers. Each announcer autographed 1,000 of his cards with 30,000 total sets produced. The card backs contain a brief announcer profile. An international version was also produced with the only difference being the silver-foil "International" stamp.

	MT
Complete Set (5):	10.00
Common Player:	2.00
International:	1x-2x

1995 SR Draft Preview Masters of the Mic Signatures

This five-card insert consists of autographed versions of the Masters of the Mic set. Each announcer signed 1,000 cards, which were inserted 1:4. The cards are numbered with a "M" prefix.

		MT
Complete Set (5):		75.00
Common Player:		15.00
1	Todd Christensen	15.00
2	Jerry Glanville	15.00
3	Howie Long	15.00
4	Dick Stockton	15.00
5	Joe Theismann UER	15.00

1995 SR Draft Preview Peripheral Vision

Peripheral Vision was a five-card insert that featured Rashaan Salaam and Ki-Jana Carter, each with two cards of their own as well as sharing the double sided card No. 5. These inserts are numbered "1 of 5,000," and carry a V1-V5 card number. Autographed versions of each card are also available and limited to 100 of each.

		MT
Complete Set (5):		15.00
Common Player:		2.50
Comp. Sign. Set (5):		650.00
Common Signature:		80.00
Signature Stars:		15x-30x
1	Rashaan Salaam	4.00
2	Rashaan Salaam	4.00
3	Ki-Jana Carter	2.50
4	Ki-Jana Carter	2.50
5	Ki-Jana Carter, Rashaan Salaam	3.00

1995 SR Draft Preview Peripheral Vision Signatures

This five-card autographed set was inserted one per 24 packs.

		MT
Complete Set (5):		550.00
Common Player:		80.00
1/2	Rashaan Salaam	80.00
3/4	Ki-Jana Carter	80.00
5/6	Ki-Jana Carter, Rashaan Salaam	250.00
V2	Rashaan Salaam	150.00
V4	Ki-Jana Carter	90.00

1995 SR Draft Preview Old Judge Previews

Inserted 1:24, the cards in this five-card set measure 2" x 3". They are designed to look like the old tobacco cards. The card fronts feature a color photo on a solid background with the words "Old Judge, T-95 Test Issue" printed across the top. The backs contain basic player information.

		MT
Complete Set (5):		20.00
Common Player:		1.50
Signatures:		10x
1	Blake Brockermeyer	1.50
2	Kerry Collins	8.00
3	Steve McNair	8.00
4	J.J. O'Laughlin	1.50
5	John Walsh	1.50

1995 SR Draft Preview Old Judge Previews Signatures

An autographed version of Old Judge Previews, these cards were inserted 1:24. Each player signed 515 cards for this insert.

		MT
Complete Set (5):		200.00
Common Player:		15.00
1	Blake Brockermeyer	15.00
2	Kerry Collins	80.00
3	Steve McNair	80.00
4	J.J. O'Laughlin	15.00
5	John Walsh	15.00

1995 SR Signature Prime Previews

This five-card set was randomly inserted in packs of Basketball Autobilia. The cards are borderless and feature a color photo on both sides. The backs feature biographical information and college stats.

		MT
Complete Set (5):		12.00
Common Player:		1.00
1	Ki-Jana Carter	2.00
2	Kyle Brady	1.00
3	J.J. Stokes	2.50
4	Rashaan Salaam	3.00
5	Steve McNair	5.00

1995 SR Signature Prime

SR Signature Prime consists of a 50-card base set with one parallel and one insert. The base cards feature a borderless color photo on the front. The player's name is printed in gold in a red stripe on the left side of the card. The card backs contain another color photo, biographical information and college stats. The only insert is TD Club (1:1). Both the base set and TD Club have autographed versions as well.

		MT
Complete Set (50):		20.00
Common Player:		.15
Checklist (NNO)		.10
1	Justin Armour	.15
2	Joe Aska	.15
3	Henry Bailey	.15
4	Jay Barker	.15
5	Dave Barr	.15
6	Kevin Bouie	.15
7	Mark Bruener	.40
8	Stoney Case	.15
9	Curtis Ceaser	.15
10	Todd Collins	.75
11	Jerry Colquitt	.15
12	Terrell Davis	4.00
13	David Dunn	.40
14	O'Mar Ellison	.15
15	Christian Fauria	.40
16	Antonio Freeman	3.00
17	Eddie Goines	.15
18	Aaron Hayden	.40
19	William Henderson	.15
20	Kevin Hickman	.15
21	Jack Jackson	.15
22	Travis Jervey	.15
23	Rob Johnson	.40
24	Chris T. Jones	.75
25	Larry Jones	.15
26	Curtis Marsh	.15
27	Curtis Martin	4.00
28	Fred McCrary	.15
29	Mike Miller	.15
30	Shannon Myers	.15
31	Jimmy Oliver	.15
32	Dino Philyaw	.15
33	Lovell Pinkney	.15
34	Michael Roan	.15
35	Chris Sanders	.75
36	Frank Sanders	.75
37	Cory Schlesinger	.40
38	Charlie Simmons	.15
39	David Sloan	.40
40	Steve Stenstrom	.15
41	James A. Stewart	.15
42	Rodney Thomas	.40
43	A.C. Tellison	.15
44	Tamarick Vanover	.75
45	John Walsh	.15
46	Kendell Watkins	.15
47	Charles Way	.40
48	Craig Whelihan	.15
49	Eric Zeier	.40
50	Ray Zellars	.40

1995 SR Signature Prime Signatures

This set consists of autographed versions of the Signature Prime base set. The cards were inserted one per pack and sealed in a protective holder. Each player signed 3,000 of his cards which are numbered in the bottom right corner.

		MT
Complete Set (50):		275.00
Common Player:		4.00
1	Justin Armour	4.00
2	Joe Aska	4.00
3	Henry Bailey	4.00
4	Jay Barker	4.00
5	Dave Barr	4.00
6	Kevin Bouie	4.00
7	Mark Bruener	8.00
8	Stoney Case	4.00
9	Curtis Ceaser	4.00
10	Todd Collins	8.00
11	Jerry Colquitt	4.00
12	Terrell Davis	30.00
13	David Dunn	8.00
14	O'Mar Ellison	4.00
15	Christian Fauria	8.00
16	Antonio Freeman	20.00
17	Eddie Goines	4.00
18	Aaron Hayden	8.00
19	William Henderson	4.00
20	Kevin Hickman	4.00
21	Jack Jackson	4.00
22	Travis Jervey	4.00
23	Rob Johnson	4.00
24	Chris T. Jones	12.00
25	Larry Jones	4.00
26	Curtis Marsh	4.00
27	Curtis Martin	30.00
28	Fred McCrary	4.00
29	Mike Miller	4.00
30	Shannon Myers	4.00
31	Jimmy Oliver	4.00
32	Dino Philyaw	4.00
33	Lovell Pinkney	4.00
34	Michael Roan	4.00
35	Chris Sanders	12.00
36	Frank Sanders	12.00
37	Cory Schlesinger	8.00
38	Charlie Simmons	4.00
39	David Sloan	8.00
40	Steve Stenstrom	4.00
41	James A. Stewart	8.00
42	Rodney Thomas	8.00
43	A.C. Tellison	4.00
44	Tamarick Vanover	12.00
45	John Walsh	4.00
46	Kendell Watkins	4.00
47	Charles Way	4.00
48	Craig Whelihan	4.00
49	Eric Zeier	8.00
50	Ray Zellars	8.00

1995 SR Signature Prime TD Club

TD Club is a 10-card insert, limited to 15,000 cards per player. The fronts feature a player photo against a silver foil background and a "T" prefix.

		MT
Complete Set (10):		12.00
Common Player:		.50
1	Kyle Brady	.50
2	Ki-Jana Carter	1.50
3	Kerry Collins	3.00
4	Joey Galloway	2.00
5	Steve McNair	3.00
6	Rashaan Salaam	2.00
7	James O. Stewart	.75
8	J.J. Stokes	2.00
9	Michael Westbrook	2.00
10	Sherman Williams	.50

1995 SR Signature Prime TD Club Signatures

Each player in the TD Club insert signed 1,000 of their cards for this parallel set. The cards are sequentially numbered carrying a "T" prefix and are sealed in a protective holder.

		MT
Complete Set (10):		300.00
Common Player:		15.00
1	Kyle Brady	15.00
2	Ki-Jana Carter	25.00
3	Kerry Collins	75.00
4	Joey Galloway	40.00
5	Steve McNair	75.00
6	Rashaan Salaam	30.00
7	James O. Stewart	25.00
8	J.J. Stokes	30.00
9	Michael Westbrook	30.00
10	Sherman Williams	15.00

1996 SR Autobilia

SR Autobilia consists of a 55-card base set featuring rookies from the 1995 and 1996 seasons. Instant win cards were randomly inserted in packs. The cards were redeemable for autographs and memorabilia.

		MT
Complete Set (55):		15.00
Common Player:		.10
1	Ruben Brown	.10
2	Kevin Carter	.10
3	Ki-Jana Carter	.25
4	Stoney Case	.10
5	Kerry Collins	.75
6	Terrell Davis	1.00
7	Antonio Freeman	.50
8	Joey Galloway	.75
9	Darick Holmes	.25
10	Jack Jackson	.10
11	Curtis Martin	1.00
12	O.J. McDuffie	.25
13	Steve McNair	.30
14	Byron "Bam" Morris	.50
15	Craig Newsome	.10
16	Errict Rhett	.50
17	Rashaan Salaam	.75
18	Frank Sanders	.25
19	James O. Stewart	.25
20	Kordell Stewart	.75
21	J.J. Stokes	.50
22	Rodney Thomas	.25
23	Tamarick Vanover	.50
24	Michael Westbrook	.50
25	Sherman Williams	.10
26	Eric Zeier	.40
27	Karim Abdul-Jabbar	1.50
28	Mike Alstott	1.00
29	Willie Anderson	.10
30	Tony Banks	1.25
31	Marco Battaglia	.40
32	Tim Biakabutuka	1.50
33	Stephen Davis	.60
34	Chris Doering	.10
35	Daryl Gardener	.10
36	Eddie George	2.50
37	Terry Glenn	2.50
38	Randall Godfrey	.10
39	Marvin Harrison	1.00
40	Aaron Hayden	.25
41	Mercury Hayes	.40
42	Dietrich Jells	.10
43	Cedric Jones	.10
44	Jeff Lewis	.30
45	Derrick Mayes	.75
46	Leland McElroy	1.00
47	Jerald Moore	.40
48	Eric Moulds	.75
49	Kendrick Nord	.10
50	Stanley Pritchett	.25
51	Jon Stark	.10
52	Steve Taneyhill	.10
53	Amani Toomer	.75
54	Stepfret Williams	.50
55	Checklist	.10

1992 SkyBox Impel Impact Prime Time Promos

These unnumbered promotional cards were distributed as a set in January 1992 during the Super Bowl XXVI show. The Earnest Byner card shows him in action on the front, with his name and number above the photo in maroon. A maroon bar along the right side of the card contains his team's name, in white letters. A Prime Time logo appears in the lower left corner. The card back, as does the one for Jim Kelly, says the card is a limited-edition commemorative card and includes an advertisement for Impel's Impact and Prime Time products. The Kelly card front shows him ready to pass. Because the cards were produced before Impel changed its name to SkyBox, subtle card front design changes can be detected on the later-released base brands.

		MT
Complete Set (2):		10.00
Common Player:		3.00
----	Impact (Jim Kelly)	7.50
----	PrimeTime (Earnest Byner)	3.00

1992 SkyBox Impact Promos

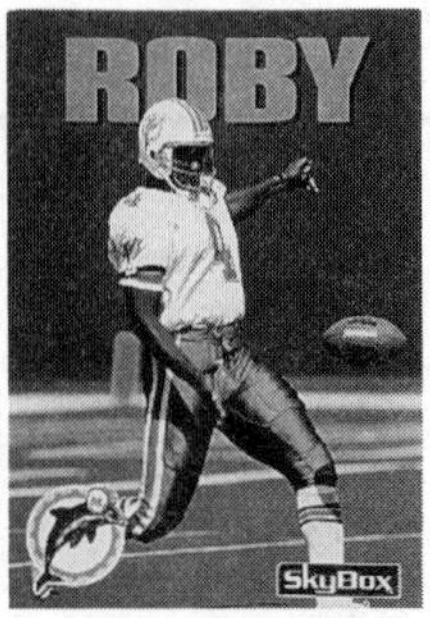

These three cards, available together in a promotional pack, preview the 1992 SkyBox Impact set. The cards' design is similar to the regular issue, except the numbers, which are on the card back. They use 001, 002 and 003.

		MT
Complete Set (3):		6.00
Common Player:		1.00
1	Jim Kelly	5.00
2	Michael Dean Perry	2.00
3	Reggie Roby	1.00

1992 SkyBox Impact

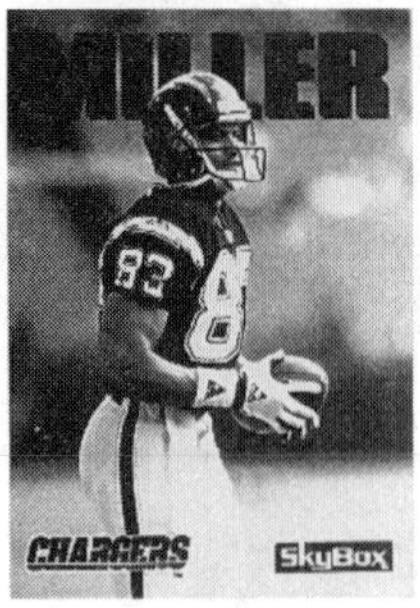

This 350-card set features full-bleed action photos with the players' names printed in block letters across the top. The back has an action photo, career highlights, stats, a biography and the player's position, as diagramed with Xs and Os. Subsets include Team Checklists, High Impact League Leaders, Sudden Impact Hardest Hitters, and Instant Impact Rookies. Insert sets include Major Impact (20 cards featuring top players) and Holograms (two feature Jim Kelly and Lawrence Taylor; the rest are mail-in offers).

		MT
Complete Set (350):		14.00
Common Player:		.05
Pack (12):		.50
Wax Box (36):		14.00
1	Jim Kelly	.25
2	Andre Rison	.25
3	Michael Dean Perry	.05
4	Herman Moore	.50
5	*Fred McAfee*	.15
6	Ricky Proehl	.05
7	Jim Everett	.05
8	Mark Carrier	.05
9	Eric Martin	.05
10	John Elway	1.00
11	Michael Irvin	.25
12	Keith McCants	.05
13	Greg Lloyd	.05
14	Lawrence Taylor	.10
15	Mike Tomczak	.05
16	Cortez Kennedy	.10
17	William Fuller	.05
18	James Lofton	.05
19	Kevin Fagan	.05
20	Bill Brooks	.05
21	Roger Craig	.05
22	Jay Novacek	.10
23	Steve Sewell	.05
24	William Perry	.05
25	Jerry Rice	1.00
26	James Joseph	.05
27	Timm Rosenbach	.05
28	Pat Terrell	.05
29	Jon Vaughn	.08
30	Steve Walsh	.05
31	James Hasty	.05
32	Dwight Stone	.05
33	Derrick Fenner	.05
34	Mark Bortz	.05
35	Dan Saleaumua	.05
36	Sammie Smith	.05
37	Antone Davis	.05
38	Steve Young	1.00
39	Mike Baab	.05
40	Rick Fenney	.05
41	Chris Hinton	.05
42	Bart Oates	.05
43	Bryan Hinkle	.05
44	James Francis	.05
45	Ray Crockett	.05
46	Eric Dickerson	.05
47	Hart Lee Dykes	.05
48	Percy Snow	.05
49	Ron Hall	.05
50	Warren Moon	.25
51	Ed West	.05
52	Clarence Verdin	.05
53	Eugene Lockhart	.05
54	Andre Reed	.15
55	Kevin Ross	.05
56	Al Noga	.05
57	Wes Hopkins	.05
58	Rufus Porter	.05
59	Brian Mitchell	.05
60	Reggie Roby	.05
61	Rodney Peete	.05
62	Jeff Herrod	.05
63	Anthony Smith	.05
64	Brad Muster	.05
65	Jessie Tuggle	.05
66	Al Smith	.05
67	Jeff Hostetler	.20
68	John L. Williams	.05
69	Paul Gruber	.05
70	Cornelius Bennett	.05
71	William White	.05
72	Tom Rathman	.05
73	Boomer Esiason	.10
74	Neil Smith	.05
75	Sterling Sharpe	.10
76	James Jones	.05
77	David Treadwell	.05
78	Flipper Anderson	.05
79	Eric Allen	.05
80	Joe Jacoby	.05
81	Keith Sims	.05
82	Bubba McDowell	.05
83	Ronnie Lippett	.05
84	Cris Carter	.05
85	Chris Burkett	.05
86	Issiac Holt	.05
87	Duane Bickett	.05
88	Leslie O'Neal	.05
89	Gill Fenerty	.05
90	Pierce Holt	.05
91	Willie Drewrey	.05
92	Brian Blades	.05
93	Tony Martin	.05
94	Jessie Hester	.05
95	John Stephens	.05
96	Keith Willis	.05
97	Vai Sikahema	.05
98	Mark Higgs	.15
99	Steve McMichael	.05
100	Deion Sanders	.15
101	Marvin Washington	.05
102	Ken Norton	.05
103	Barry Word	.10
104	Sean Jones	.05
105	Ronnie Harmon	.05
106	Donnell Woolford	.05
107	Ray Agnew	.05
108	Lemuel Stinson	.05
109	Dennis Smith	.05
110	Lorenzo White	.05
111	Craig Heyward	.05
112	Jeff Query	.05
113	Gary Plummer	.05
114	John Taylor	.08
115	Rohn Stark	.05
116	Tom Waddle	.08
117	Jeff Cross	.05
118	Tim Green	.05
119	Anthony Munoz	.05
120	Mel Gray	.05
121	Ray Donaldson	.05
122	Dennis Byrd	.05
123	Carnell Lake	.05
124	Broderick Thomas	.05
125	Charles Mann	.05
126	Darion Conner	.05
127	John Roper	.05
128	Jack Del Rio	.05
129	Rickey Dixon	.05
130	Eddie Anderson	.05
131	Steve Broussard	.05
132	Michael Young	.05
133	Lamar Lathon	.05
134	Rickey Jackson	.05
135	Billy Ray Smith	.05
136	Tony Casillas	.05
137	Ickey Woods	.05
138	Ray Childress	.05
139	Vance Johnson	.05
140	Brett Perriman	.05
141	Calvin Williams	.10
142	Dino Hackett	.05
143	Jacob Green	.05
144	Robert Delpino	.05
145	Marv Cook	.05
146	Dwayne Harper	.05
147	Ricky Ervins	.08
148	Kelvin Martin	.08
149	Leroy Hoard	.05
150	Dan Marino	1.25
151	Richard Johnson	.05
152	Henry Ellard	.05
153	Al Toon	.05
154	Dermontti Dawson	.05
155	Robert Blackmon	.05
156	Howie Long	.05
157	David Fulcher	.05
158	Mike Merriweather	.05
159	Gary Anderson	.05
160	John Friesz	.05
161	Eugene Robinson	.05
162	Brad Baxter	.05
163	Bennie Blades	.05
164	Harold Green	.05
165	Ernest Givins	.05
166	Deron Cherry	.05
167	Carl Banks	.05
168	Keith Jackson	.10
169	Pat Leahy	.05
170	Alvin Harper	.10
171	David Little	.05
172	Anthony Carter	.05
173	Willie Gault	.05
174	Bruce Armstrong	.05
175	Junior Seau	.15
176	Eric Metcalf	.05
177	Tony Mandarich	.05
178	Ernie Jones	.05
179	Albert Bentley	.05
180	Mike Pritchard	.15
181	Bubby Brister	.05
182	Vaughan Johnson	.05
183	Robert Clark	.05
184	Lawrence Dawsey	.05
185	Eric Green	.05
186	Jay Schroeder	.05
187	Andre Tippett	.05
188	Vinny Testaverde	.05
189	Wendell Davis	.05
190	Russell Maryland	.15
191	Chris Singleton	.05
192	Ken O'Brien	.05
193	Merril Hoge	.05
194	*Steve Bono*	.50
195	Earnest Byner	.05
196	Mike Singletary	.05
197	Gaston Green	.05
198	Mark Carrier	.05
199	Harvey Williams	.10
200	Randall Cunningham	.15
201	Cris Dishman	.05
202	Greg Townsend	.05
203	Christian Okoye	.05
204	Sam Mills	.05
205	Kyle Clifton	.05
206	Jim Harbaugh	.08
207	Anthony Thompson	.05
208	Rob Moore	.08
209	Irving Fryar	.05
210	Derrick Thomas	.15
211	Chris Miller	.05
212	Doug Smith	.05
213	Michael Haynes	.20
214	Phil Simms	.10
215	Charles Haley	.05
216	Burt Grossman	.05
217	Rod Bernstine	.05
218	Louis Lipps	.05
219	Dan McGwire	.05
220	Ethan Horton	.05
221	Michael Carter	.05
222	Neil O'Donnell	.10
223	Anthony Miller	.05
224	Eric Swann	.05
225	Thurman Thomas	.40

226 Jeff George .25
227 Joe Montana 1.00
228 Leonard Marshall .05
229 Haywood Jeffires .10
230 Mark Clayton .05
231 Chris Doleman .05
232 Troy Aikman 1.50
233 Gary Anderson .05
234 Pat Swilling .05
235 Ronnie Lott .07
236 Brian Jordan .05
237 Bruce Smith .07
238 Tony Jones .05
239 Tim McKyer .05
240 Gary Clark .05
241 Mitchell Price .05
242 John Kasay .05
243 Stephone Paige .05
244 Jeff Wright .05
245 Shannon Sharpe .15
246 Keith Byars .05
247 Charles Dimry .05
248 Steve Smith .05
249 Erric Pegram .15
250 Bernie Kosar .05
251 Peter Tom Willis .05
252 Mark Ingram .05
253 Keith McKeller .05
254 Lewis Billups .05
255 Alton Montgomery .05
256 Jimmie Jones .05
257 Brent Williams .05
258 Gene Atkins .05
259 Reggie Rutland .05
260 Sam Seale .05
261 Andre Ware .07
262 Fred Barnett .10
263 Randal Hill .10
264 Patrick Hunter .05
265 Johnny Rembert .05
266 Monte Coleman .05
267 Aaron Wallace .05
268 Ferrell Edmunds .05
269 Stan Thomas .05
270 Robb Thomas .05
271 Martin Bayless .05
272 Dean Biasucci .05
273 Keith Henderson .05
274 Vinnie Clark .05
275 Emmitt Smith 2.00
276 Mark Rypien .10
277 Atlanta Falcons Wing and a Prayer .10
278 Buffalo Bills Machine Gun .10
279 Chicago Bears Grizzly .05
280 Cincinnati Bengals Price is Right .05
281 Cleveland Browns Coasting .05
282 Dallas Cowboys Gunned Down .15
283 Denver Broncos The Drive II .15
284 Detroit Lions Lions Roar .05
285 Green Bay Packers Razor Sharpe .15
286 Houston Oilers Oil's Well .10
287 Indianapolis Colts Whew .10
288 Kansas City Chiefs Ambush .10
289 Los Angeles Raiders Lott of Defense .05
290 Los Angeles Rams Ram It .05
291 Miami Dolphins Miami Ice .15
292 Minnesota Vikings Purple Blaze .05
293 New England Patriots Surprise Attack .05
294 New Orlean Saints Marching In .05
295 New York Giants Almost Perfect .05
296 New York Jets Playoff Bound .05
297 Philadelphia Eagles Flying High .05
298 Phoenix Cardinals .05
299 Pittsburgh Steelers Steel Curtain .05
300 San Diego Chargers Lightning .05
301 San Francisco 49ers Instant Rice .15
302 Seattle Seahawks Defense Never Rests .05
303 Tampa Bay Buccaneers Stunned .05
304 Washington Redskins Super .05
305 Jim Kelly (LL) .10
306 Steve Young (LL) .15
307 Thurman Thomas (LL) .20
308 Emmitt Smith (LL) 1.00
309 Haywood Jeffires (LL) .05
310 Michael Irvin (LL) .30
311 William Fuller (LL) .05
312 Pat Swilling (LL) .05
313 Ronnie Lott (LL) .07
314 Deion Sanders (LL) .07
315 Cornelius Bennett .05
316 David Fulcher .05
317 Ronnie Lott .05
318 Pat Swilling .05
319 Lawrence Taylor .07
320 Derrick Thomas .07
321 *Steve Emtman* .15
322 *Carl Pickens* 1.50
323 *David Klingler* .25
324 *Dale Carter* .25
325 *Mike Gaddis* .08
326 *Quentin Coryatt* .35
327 *Darryl Williams* .15
328 *Jeremy Lincoln* .15
329 *Robert Jones* .15
330 *Bucky Richardson* .30
331 *Tony Brooks* .10
332 *Alonzo Spellman* .20
333 *Robert Brooks* 1.00
334 *Marco Coleman* .20
335 *Siran Stacy* .15
336 *Tommy Maddox* .25
337 *Steve Israel* .15
338 *Vaughn Dunbar* .15
339 *Shane Collins* .15
340 *Kevin Smith* .25
341 *Chris Mims* .25
342 *Chester McGlockton* .25
343 *Tracy Scroggins* .25
344 *Howard Dinkins* .10
345 *Levon Kirkland* .10
346 *Terrell Buckley* .30
347 *Marquez Pope* .10
348 *Phillippi Sparks* .10
349 *Joe Bowden* .10
350 *Edgar Bennett* .75

1992 SkyBox Impact Holograms

These holograms were included as random inserts in foil packs (#s H1 and H2) or offered to those who responded to the mail-in offer which made them available (#s H3-H6). The card front has a full-bleed hologram photo, plus the player's last name. The back has a color photo and a career summary.

		MT
Complete Set (6):		15.00
Common Player:		2.00
1	Jim Kelly	3.00
2	Lawrence Taylor	2.50
3	Christian Okoye	2.00
4	Mark Rypien	3.00
5	Pat Swilling	3.00
6	Ricky Ervins	2.00

1992 SkyBox Impact Major Impact

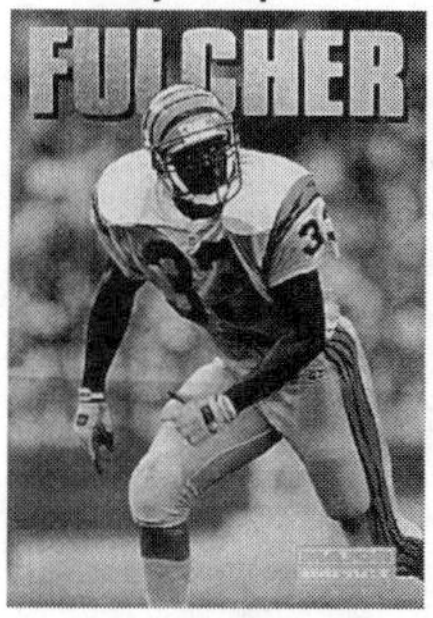

These cards feature 20 players who have a tremendous impact on NFL games. Each borderless card front has a full-bleed color photo and the player's last name stamped in silver-foil block letters across the top. The back has an action shot and career summary. A blue stripe separates these items on the cards for NFC players (11-20), while a red stripe is used for AFC cards (1-10). Cards are numbered with an "M" prefix and were randomly inserted in 1992 SkyBox Impact jumbo packs.

		MT
Complete Set (20):		15.00
Common Player:		.50
Minor Stars:		1.00
1	Cornelius Bennett	.50
2	David Fulcher	.50
3	Haywood Jeffires	.50
4	Ronnie Lott	.50
5	Dan Marino	5.00
6	Warren Moon	1.00
7	Christian Okoye	.50
8	Andre Reed	.50
9	Derrick Thomas	1.00
10	Thurman Thomas	1.00
11	Troy Aikman	2.50
12	Randall Cunningham	1.00
13	Michael Irvin	1.00
14	Jerry Rice	2.50
15	Joe Montana	2.50
16	Mark Rypien	.50
17	Deion Sanders	1.50
18	Emmitt Smith	5.00
19	Pat Swilling	.50
20	Lawrence Taylor	1.00

1992 SkyBox Primetime Previews

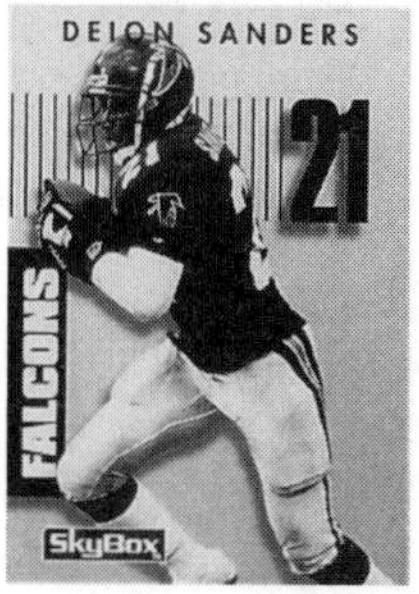

This five-card set allowed collectors to see what the Primetime sets would look like and are exact replicas of the regular-issue cards, except for being numbered A-D, plus a title card. Five-card sets were originally packaged in cello packs.

		MT
Complete Set (5):		10.00
Common Player:		1.00
A	Jerry Rice	4.00
B	Deion Sanders	3.00
C	John Elway	2.00
D	Vaughn Dunbar	1.00
NNO	Title Card (Advertisement)	1.00

1992 SkyBox Primetime

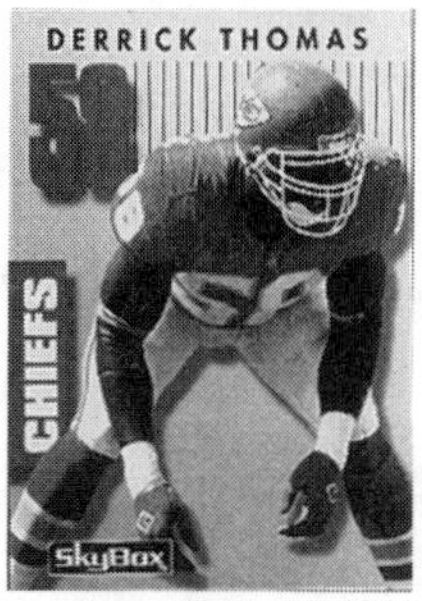

This 360-card set features cards which use cut-out action photos superimposed against a grey background with thin black lines. The player's name is at the top, while his jersey number is included at the bottom in his team's colors. His team name is in a color-coded bar on the left. Half of the card back features an action photo; the rest has stats, a biography and career summary. A team color-coded band with the player's name separates the photo and the remaining information. A 28-card subset, Team MVP, was also made. Insert cards feature Costacos Brothers poster art (15 silver foil cards); a poster checklist; a Kelly hologram; and a Steve Emtman Horse-Power card. Five promo cards were also made and were available in cello packs.

		MT
Complete Set (360):		30.00
Common Player:		.10
Minor Stars:		.20
Pack (12):		.75
Wax Box (36):		25.00

1 Deion Sanders 1.25
2 *Shane Collins* .20
3 *James Patton* .10
4 Reggie Roby .10
5 Merril Hoge .10
6 Vinny Testaverde .10
7 Boomer Esiason .10
8 Troy Aikman 2.50
9 *Tommy Jeter* .10
10 Brent Williams .10
11 Mark Rypien .10
12 Jim Kelly .25
13 Dan Marino 4.00
14 Bill Cowher .10
15 Leslie O'Neal .10
16 Joe Montana 2.50
17 William Fuller .10
18 Paul Gruber .10
19 Bernie Kosar .10
20 Rickey Jackson .10
21 Earnest Byner .10
22 Emmitt Smith 5.00
23 Neal Anderson .10
24 Greg Lloyd .20
25 Ronnie Harmon .10
26 Ray Donaldson .10
27 Kevin Ross .10
28 Irving Fryar .10
29 John Williams .10
30 Chris Hinton .10
31 *Tracy Scroggins* .20
32 Rohn Stark .10
33 David Fulcher .10
34 Thurman Thomas .50
35 Christian Okoye .20
36 *Vaughn Dunbar* .20
37 *Joel Steed* .10
38 James Francis (card number on back is actually 354) .10
39 Dermontti Dawson .10
40 Mark Higgs .10
41 Flipper Anderson .10
42 Ronnie Lott .10
43 Jim Everett .10
44 Burt Grossman .10
45 Charles Haley .10
46 Ricky Proehl .10
47 *Marquez Pope* .10
48 David Treadwell .10
49 William White .10
50 John Elway 1.00
51 Mark Carrier .10
52 Brian Blades .10
53 Keith McKeller .10
54 Art Monk .20
55 Lamar Lathon .10
56 Pat Swilling .10
57 Steve Broussard .10
58 Derrick Thomas .20
59 Keith Jackson .20
60 Leonard Marshall .10
61 Eric Metcalf (card number on back is actually 350) .10
62 Andy Heck .10
63 Mark Carrier .10
64 Neil O'Donnell .10
65 Broderick Thomas .10
66 Erik Kramer .20
67 Joe Montana 1.25
68 Robert Delpino .10
69 *Steve Israel* .10
70 Herman Moore 1.25
71 Jacob Green .10
72 Lorenzo White .10
73 Nick Lowery .10
74 Eugene Robinson .10
75 Carl Banks .10
76 Bruce Smith .10
77 Mark Rypien .10
78 Anthony Munoz .10
79 *Clayton Holmes* .10
80 Jerry Rice 2.50
81 Henry Ellard .10
82 Tim McGee .10
83 Al Toon .10
84 Haywood Jeffires .10
85 Mike Singletary .10
86 Thurman Thomas .25
87 Jessie Hester .10
88 Michael Irvin .50
89 Jack Del Rio .10
90 Seth Joyner (No player photo) .10
91 Jeff Herrod .10
92 Michael Dean Perry .10
93 Louis Oliver .10
94 Dan McGwire .10
95 Cris Carter .20
96 *Dale Carter* .50
97 Cornelius Bennett .10
98 *Edgar Bennett* .50
99 Steve Young 2.50
100 Warren Moon .20
101 Deion Sanders .50
102 Mel Gray .10
103 Mark Murphy .10
104 Jeff George .50
105 Anthony Miller .10
106 Tom Rathman .10
107 *Fred McAfee* .10
108 *Paul Siever* .10
109 Lemuel Stinson .10
110 Vance Johnson .10
111 Jay Schroeder .10
112 Calvin Williams .10
113 Cortez Kennedy .10
114 *Quentin Coryatt* .30
115 Ronnie Lippett .10
116 Brad Baxter .10
117 Bubba McDowell .10
118 Cris Carter .20
119 John Stephens .10
120 James Hasty .10
121 Bubby Brister .10
122 *Robert Jones* .20
123 Sterling Sharpe .20
124 *Jason Hanson* .20
125 Sam Mills .10
126 Ernie Jones .10
127 *Chester McGlockton* .50
128 *Troy Vincent* .20
129 *Chuck Smith* .10
130 Tim McKyer .10
131 Tom Newberry .10
132 *Leonard Wheeler* .10
133 *Patrick Rowe* .10
134 Eric Swann .10
135 *Jeremy Lincoln* .10
136 Brian Noble .10
137 Allen Pinkett .10
138 *Carl Pickens* 1.50
139 Eric Green .10
140 Louis Lipps .10
141 Chris Singleton .10
142 Gary Clark .10
143 Tim Green .10
144 *Dennis Green* .10
145 Gary Anderson .10
146 Miami Dolphins .10
147 Kelvin Martin .10
148 *Mike Holmgren* .10
149 Gaston Green .10
150 *Terrell Buckley* .10
151 *Robert Brooks* 1.50
152 Anthony Smith .10
153 Jay Novacek .10
154 Webster Slaughter .10
155 John Roper .10
156 *Steve Emtman* .20
157 Tony Sacca .10
158 Ray Crockett .10
159 Jerry Rice 1.00
160 *Alonzo Spellman* .20
161 Deion Sanders .50
162 Robert Clark .10
163 Mark Ingram .10
164 *Ricardo McDonald* .10
165 Emmitt Smith 3.00
166 *Tommy Maddox* .20
167 *Tom Myslinski* .10
168 Tony Bennett (No player photo on card) .10
169 Ernest Givins .10
170 Eugene Robinson .10
171 Roger Craig .10
172 Irving Fryar .10
173 Jeff Herrod .10
174 *Chris Mims* .20
175 Bart Oates .10
176 Michael Irvin .50
177 Lawrence Dawsey .10
178 Warren Moon .10
179 Timm Rosenbach .10
180 Bobby Ross .10
181 Chris Burkett .10
182 *Tony Brooks* .10
183 Clarence Verdin .10
184 Bernie Kosar .10
185 Eric Martin .10
186 Jeff Bryant .10
187 Carnell Lake .10
188 *Darren Woodson* .40
189 Dwayne Harper .10
190 Bernie Kosar .10
191 Keith Sims .10
192 Rich Gannon .10
193 Broderick Thomas .10
194 Michael Young .10
195 Cris Dishman .10
196 Wes Hopkins .10
197 Christian Okoye .10
198 David Little .10
199 *Chris Crooms* .10
200 Lawrence Taylor .20
201 *Marc Boutte* .10
202 Mark Carrier .10
203 Keith McCants .10
204 *Dwayne Sabb* .10
205 Brian Mitchell .10
206 Keith Byars .10
207 Jeff Hostetler .20
208 Percy Snow .10
209 Lawrence Taylor .10
210 *Troy Auzenne* .10
211 Warren Moon .10
212 Mike Pritchard .10
213 Eric Dickerson .10
214 Harvey Williams .10
215 Phil Simms (Misspelled Sims on card front) .10
216 *Sean Lumpkin* (Card number on back is actually 002) .10
217 *Marco Coleman* .10
218 *Phillippi Sparks* .10
219 *Gerald Dixon* .10
220 Steve Walsh .10
221 Russell Maryland .10
222 Eddie Anderson .10
223 *Shane Dronett* .10
224 *Todd Collins* .20
225 *Leon Searcy* .10
226 Andre Rison .10
227 James Lofton .10
228 Ken O'Brien .10
230 Nick Bell .10
231 Ben Smith .10
232 Wendell Davis .10
233 *Craig Thompson* .10
234 *Dana Hall* .10
235 *Larry Webster* .10
236 Jerry Rice 1.00
237 Rod Bernstine .10
238 *David Klingler* .20
239 *Greg Skrepenak* .10
240 *Mark Wheeler* .10
241 *Kevin Smith* .20
242 Charles Mann .10
243 Barry Sanders .20
244 *Curtis Whitley* .10
245 Ronnie Harmon .10
246 Brent Jones .10
247 *Robert Harris* .10
248 Ted Marchibroda .10
249 Willie Gault .10
250 *Siran Stacy* .10
251 Dennis Byrd .10
252 *Corey Harris* .10
253 Al Noga .10
254 *David Shula* .10
255 Rob Moore .10
256 Marv Cook .10
257 John Elway .30
258 Harold Green .10
259 Tom Flores .10
260 Andre Reed .10
261 Anthony Thompson .10
262 Issiac Holt .10
263 *Mike Evans* .10
264 *Jimmy Smith* 3.50
265 Anthony Carter .10
266 *Ashley Ambrose* .10
267 *John Fina* (Card number on back is actually 357) .10
268 *Sean Gilbert* .40
269 Ken Norton Jr. .10
270 Barry Word .10
271 Pat Swilling .10
272 Dan Marino 1.50
273 David Fulcher .10
274 William Perry .10
275 Ed West .10
276 Gene Atkins .10
277 Neal Anderson .10
278 Dino Hackett .10
279 Greg Townsend .10
280 Andre Tippett .10
281 *Darryl Williams* .10
282 *Kurt Barber* .10
283 Pat Terrell .10
284 Derrick Thomas .10
285 *Eddie Robinson* .10
286 Howie Long .10
287 Tim McDonald (No player photo) .10
288 Thurman Thomas .10
289 Wendell Davis .10
290 Jeff Cross .10
291 Duane Bickett .10
292 *Tony Smith* .10
293 Jerry Ball .10
294 Jessie Tuggle .10
295 Chris Burkett .10
296 *Eugene Chung* .10
297 Chris Miller .10
298 Albert Bentley .10
299 Richard Johnson .10
300 Randall Cunningham .10
301 *Courtney Hawkins* .10
302 Ray Childress .10
303 Rodney Peete .10
304 Kevin Fagan .10
305 Ronnie Lott .10
306 Michael Carter .10
307 Derrick Thomas .10
308 Jarvis Williams .10
309 Greg Lloyd .10
310 Ethan Horton .10
311 Ricky Ervins .10
312 Bennie Blades .10
313 Troy Aikman 1.00
314 Bruce Armstrong .10
315 Leroy Hoard .10
316 Gary Anderson .10
317 Steve McMichael .10
318 Junior Seau .50
319 *Mark Thomas* .10
320 Fred Barnett .10
321 Mike Merriweather .10
322 Keith Willis .10
323 Brett Perriman .10
324 Michael Haynes .10
325 Jim Harbaugh .10
326 Sammie Smith .10
327 Robert Delpino .10
328 Tony Mandarich .10
329 Mark Bortz .10
330 *Ray Etheridge* .10
331 Jarvis Williams .10
332 Dan Marino 1.50
333 Dwight Stone .10
334 Billy Ray Smith .10
335 Darion Connor .10
336 *Howard Dinkins* .10
337 *Robert Porcher* .50
338 Chris Doleman .10
339 Alvin Harper .20
340 John Taylor .10
341 Ray Agnew .10
342 Jon Vaughn .10
343 *James Brown* .10
344 Michael Irvin .50
345 Neil Smith .10
346 Vaughn Johnson .10
347 Checklist .10
348 Checklist .10
349 Checklist .10
350 Checklist (See also number 61) .10
351 Checklist .10
352 Checklist .10
353 Checklist .10
354 Checklist (See also number 38) .10
355 Checklist .10
356 Checklist .10
357 Checklist (See also number 267) .10
358 Checklist (See also number 138) .10
359 Checklist .10
360 Checklist .10

1992 SkyBox Primetime Poster Cards

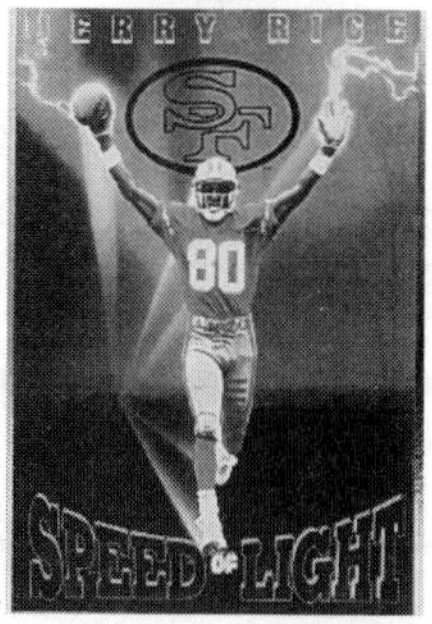

These insert cards feature photos used on posters made by Costacos to capture the essence of the player's nickname, image or city he plays in. The cards, randomly inserted in 1992 SkyBox Primetime foil packs, are identical to their counterparts in SkyBox's regular 1992 Primetime set, except the inserts have silver foil-stamped borders on the front. The cards were estimated to be two per 36-pack box of cards and were found in the 10,000 numbered cases distributed to the hobby only. Card backs have the Primetime logo in the upper left, along with a card number, which uses an "M" prefix, in the upper right. A photo, career summary and team logo also appear.

		MT
Complete Set (16):		55.00
Common Player:		1.25
1	Bernie Kosar	1.50
2	Mark Carrier	1.25
3	Neal Anderson	1.25
4	Thurman Thomas	5.50
5	Deion Sanders	6.00
6	Joe Montana	8.00
7	Jerry Rice	8.00
8	Jarvis Williams	1.25
9	Dan Marino	15.00
10	Derrick Thomas	2.25
11	Christian Okoye	1.25
12	Warren Moon	3.00
13	Michael Irvin	7.50
14	Troy Aikman	8.00
15	Emmitt Smith	15.00
16	Checklist	1.25

1993 SkyBox Premium

SkyBox Premium's 270-card set features silhouetted action photos highlighted by the contrast of the team color, two-tone background. Team logos, the player's name and a foil-stamped SkyBox Premium logo is also on the front. The back has a color action photo, a biography, four-year statistics, and career totals. Card fronts are UV-coated. Insert sets include Costacos Brothers posters (10 cards), Chris Mortensen's PrimeTime Rookies (10 cards) and Thunder and Lightning (nine dual teammate cards).

		MT
Complete Set (270):		45.00
Common Player:		.10
Minor Stars:		.20
Comp. Poster Card Set (10):		5.00
Pack (12):		1.50
Wax Box (36):		50.00
1	Eric Martin	.10
2	Earnest Byner	.10
3	Ricky Proehl	.10
4	Mark Carrier	.10
5	Shannon Sharpe	.20
6	Anthony Thompson	.10
7	*Drew Bledsoe*	7.00
8	*Tom Carter*	.40
9	*Ryan McNeil*	.20
10	Troy Aikman	2.00
11	Robert Jones	.10
12	Rodney Peete	.10
13	Wendell Davis	.10
14	Thurman Thomas	.50
15	John Stephens	.10
16	Rodney Hampton	.25
17	Eric Bieniemy	.10
18	Santana Dotson	.10
19	Jeff George	.20
20	John L. Williams	.10
21	Barry Wood	.10
22	Chris Miller	.10
23	Jeff Hostetler	.20
24	Dwight Stone	.10
25	Brad Baxter	.10
26	Randall Cunningham	.20
27	Mark Higgs	.10
28	Vaughn Dunbar	.10
29	Ricky Ervins	.10

30	Johnny Bailey	.10
31	Michael Jackson	.10
32	Mike Croel	.10
33	Steve Young	2.00
34	*Deon Figures*	.20
35	*Robert Smith*	3.00
36	*Irv Smith*	.20
37	Charles Haley	.10
38	Cris Dishman	.10
39	Barry Sanders	3.00
40	Jim Harbaugh	.10
41	Darryl Talley	.10
42	Jackie Harris	.10
43	Phil Simms	.10
44	Marion Butts	.10
45	Anthony Munoz	.10
46	Steve Emtman	.10
47	Kelvin Martin	.10
48	Joe Montana	3.00
49	Andre Rison	.25
50	Ethan Horton	.10
51	Kevin Greene	.10
52	Browning Nagle	.10
53	Tim Harris	.10
54	Keith Byars	.10
55	Terry Allen	.10
56	Chip Lohmiller	.10
57	Robert Massey	.10
58	Michael Dean Perry	.10
59	Tommy Maddox	.10
60	Jerry Rice	2.00
61	*Lincoln Kennedy*	.10
62	*Jerome Bettis*	2.50
63	*Coleman Rudolph*	.10
64	Emmitt Smith	4.00
65	Curtis Duncan	.10
66	Andre Ware	.10
67	Neal Anderson	.10
68	Jim Kelly	.25
69	Reggie White	.25
70	Dave Meggett	.10
71	Junior Seau	.40
72	Courtney Hawkins	.10
73	Clarence Verdin	.10
74	Tommy Kane	.10
75	Dale Carter	.10
76	Michael Haynes	.10
77	Willie Gault	.10
78	Eric Green	.10
79	Ronnie Lott	.10
80	Vai Sikahema	.10
81	Mark Ingram	.10
82	Anthony Carter	.10
83	Mark Rypien	.10
84	Gary Clark	.10
85	Bernie Kosar	.10
86	Cleveland Gary	.10
87	Tom Rathman	.10
88	*Tony McGee*	.40
89	*Rick Mirer*	.50
90	*John Copeland*	.50
91	Michael Irvin	.20
92	Wilber Marshall	.10
93	Mel Gray	.10
94	Craig Heyward	.10
95	Don Beebe	.10
96	Andre Tippett	.10
97	Derek Brown	.10
98	Ronnie Harmon	.10
99	Derrick Fenner	.10
100	Rodney Culver	.10
101	Cortez Kennedy	.20
102	Marcus Allen	.20
103	Steve Broussard	.10
104	Tim Brown	.25
105	Merril Hoge	.10
106	Chris Burkett	.10
107	Fred Barnett	.10
108	Dan Marino	4.00
109	Chris Doleman	.10
110	Art Monk	.10
111	Ernie Jones	.10
112	Jay Hilgenberg	.10
113	Jim Everett	.10
114	John Taylor	.10
115	*Steve Everett*	.25
116	*Carlton Gray*	.20
117	*Eric Curry*	.50
118	Ken Norton	.10
119	Lorenzo White	.10
120	Pat Swilling	.10
121	William Perry	.10
122	Brett Favre	4.00
123	Jon Vaughn	.10
124	Mark Jackson	.10
125	Stan Humphries	.20
126	Harold Green	.10
127	Anthony Jackson	.10
128	Brian Blades	.10
129	Willie Davis	.10
130	Bobby Hebert	.10
131	Terry McDaniel	.10
132	Jeff Graham	.10
133	Jeff Lageman	.10
134	Andre Waters	.10
135	Steve Walsh	.10
136	Cris Carter	.20
137	Tim McGee	.10
138	Chuck Cecil	.10
139	John Elway	1.00
140	Todd Lyght	.10
141	Brent Jones	.10
142	*Patrick Bates*	.25
143	*Darrien Gordon*	.50
144	*Michael Strahan*	.10
145	Jay Novacek	.10
146	Warren Moon	.25
147	Rodney Holman	.10
148	Anthony Morgan	.10
149	Sterling Sharpe	.20
150	Leonard Russell	.10
151	Lawrence Taylor	.20
152	Leslie O'Neal	.10
153	Carl Pickens	1.00
154	Aaron Cox	.10
155	Ferrell Edmunds	.10
156	Neil O'Donnell	.20
157	Tony Smith	.10
158	James Lofton	.10
159	*George Teague*	.50
160	Boomer Esiason	.20
161	Eric Allen	.10
162	Floyd Turner	.10
163	Esera Tuaolo	.10
164	Darrell Green	.10
165	Steve Beuerlein	.10
166	Vance Johnson	.10
167	Willie Anderson	.10
168	Ricky Watters	.20
169	*Marvin Jones*	.20
170	*Dana Stubblefield*	.75
171	*Willie Roaf*	.25
172	Russell Maryland	.10
173	Ernest Givins	.10
174	Willie Green	.10
175	Bruce Smith	.10
176	Terrell Buckley	.10
177	Scott Zolak	.10
178	Mike Sherrard	.10
179	Lawrence Dawsey	.10
180	Jay Schroeder	.10
181	Quentin Coryatt	.10
182	Harvey Williams	.10
183	*Natrone Means*	3.00
184	Eric Dickerson	.20
185	Gaston Green	.10
186	*Thomas Smith*	.25
187	Johnny Johnson	.10
188	Marco Coleman	.10
189	Wade Wilson	.10
190	Rich Gannon	.10
191	Brian Mitchell	.10
192	Eric Metcalf	.10
193	Robert Delpino	.10
194	Shane Conlan	.10
195	Dexter Carter	.10
196	*Garrison Hearst*	3.00
197	*Chris Slade*	.20
198	*Troy Drayton*	.30
199	*Lin Elliot*	.10
200	Haywood Jeffires	.10
201	Herman Moore	1.00
202	Cornelius Bennett	.10
203	Mark Clayton	.10
204	Marv Cook	.10
205	Stephen Baker	.10
206	Gary Anderson	.10
207	Eddie Brown	.10
208	Will Wolford	.10
209	Derrick Thomas	.20
210	Seth Joyner	.10
211	Mike Pritchard	.10
212	Rod Woodson	.20
213	*Todd Kelly*	.20
214	Rob Moore	.10
215	Keith Jackson	.10
216	Wesley Carroll	.10
217	Steve Jordan	.10
218	Ricky Sanders	.10
219	Tommy Vardell	.10
220	Rod Bernstine	.10
221	Henry Ellard	.10
222	Amp Lee	.10
223	*O.J. McDuffie*	2.00
224	*Carl Simpson*	.20
225	*Dan Williams*	.20
226	Thomas Everett	.10
227	Webster Slaughter	.10
228	Trace Armstrong	.10
229	Kenneth Davis	.10
230	Tony Bennett	.10
231	Reyna Thompson	.10
232	Anthony Miller	.10
233	Reggie Cobb	.10
234	Mark Duper	.10
235	Chris Warren	.30
236	Christian Okoye	.10
237	Irving Fryar	.10
238	Deion Sanders	1.00
239	Barry Foster	.10
240	*Ernest Dye*	.10
241	Calvin Williams	.10
242	Louis Oliver	.10
243	Dalton Hilliard	.10
244	Roger Craig	.10
245	Randall Hill	.10
246	Vinny Testaverde	.10
247	Steve Atwater	.10
248	Jim Price	.10
249	*Martin Harrison*	.20
250	*Curtis Conway*	2.00
251	*Demetrius DuBose*	.20
252	*Leonard Renfro*	.10
253	Alvin Harper	.40
254	Leonard Harris	.10
255	Tom Waddle	.10
256	Andre Reed	.20
257	Sanjay Beach	.10
258	Michael Timpson	.10
259	Nate Lewis	.10
260	Steve DeBerg	.10
261	David Klingler	.10
262	Dan McGwire	.10
263	Dave Krieg	.10
264	Brad Muster	.10
265	Nick Bell	.10
266	Checklist 1	.10
267	Checklist 2	.10
268	Checklist 3	.10
269	Checklist 4	.10
270	Checklist 5	.10

1993 SkyBox Poster Art Cards

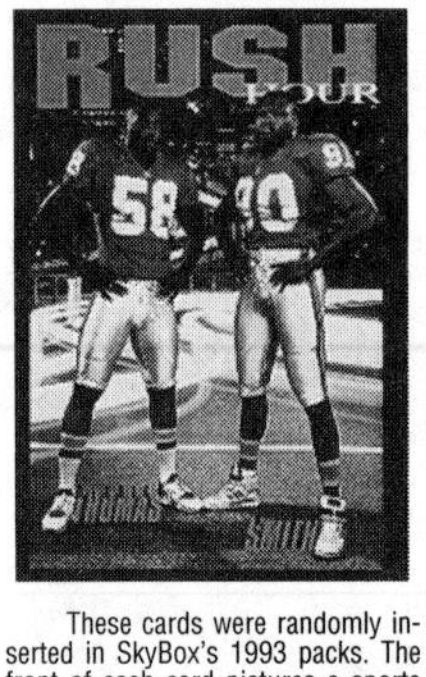

These cards were randomly inserted in SkyBox's 1993 packs. The front of each card pictures a sports poster created by the Costacos Brothers. Each reproduction is framed by a black border. The back has a photo at the top half, with a gold stripe underneath containing the player's name. A team logo and brief career summary are at the bottom against a white background. The cards are numbered with a "CB" prefix.

		MT
Complete Set (10):		7.00
Common Player:		.50
1	Cowboys Defense	.75
2	Cowboys Champs	3.00
3	Barry Foster	1.75
4	Art Monk	.50
5	Jerry Rice	2.00
6	Barry Sanders	2.50
7	Deion Sanders	.75
8	Junior Seau	.75
9	Derrick Thomas, Neil Smith	.75
10	Steve Young	1.25

1993 SkyBox Premium Rookies

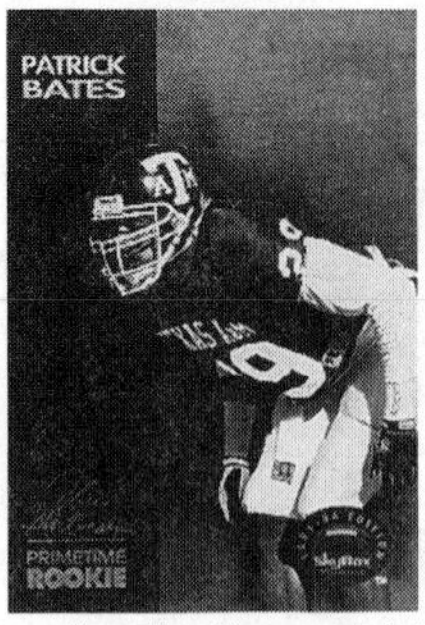

These 10 rookies were selected for this set by Chris Mortensen, of ESPN and The Sporting News. He predicted the players would be "prime timers" in 1993. The card front, which has a gold-and-black metallic background, shows the player in his collegiate uniform. A black stripe at the left contains the player's name, set title and Mortensen's facsimile signature. Mortensen is pictured on the bottom half of the card back, along with his player evaluation and the player's position. The top half has a photo of the player, plus his name, in a gold stripe, and a card number, which uses a "PR" prefix.

		MT
Complete Set (10):		60.00
Common Player:		5.00
1	Patrick Bates	5.00
2	Drew Bledsoe	25.00
3	Darrien Gordon	5.00
4	Garrison Hearst	15.00
5	Marvin Jones	5.00
6	Terry Kirby	5.00
7	Natrone Means	10.00
8	Rick Mirer	7.00
9	Willie Roaf	5.00
10	Dan Williams	5.00

1993 SkyBox Premium Thunder and Lightning

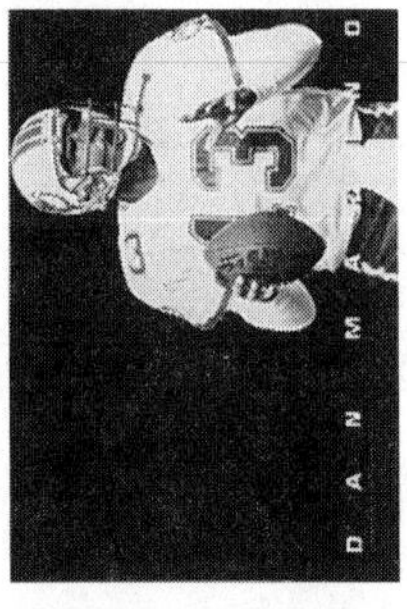

These cards are in a horizontal format and feature two teammates per card, one on each side. The player on the Thunder side is featured against a metallic black-and-gold background. Those on the Lightning side are featured against a black-and-silver metallic background with lightning bolts running through it. The player's name is in white lettering across the bottom. A TL prefix is used to number the cards; the number is on the Lightning side of the card. Cards were random inserts in every ninth 1993 SkyBox Premium 12-card foil pack.

		MT
Complete Set (9):		40.00
Common Player:		3.00
1	Jim Kelly, Thurman Thomas	3.00
2	Brett Favre, Sterling Sharpe	12.00
3	Dan Marino, Keith Jackson	12.00
4	Sam Mills, Vaughan Johnson	3.00
5	Warren Moon, Haywood Jeffires	3.00
6	Troy Aikman, Michael Irvin	10.00
7	Randall Cunningham, Fred Barnett	3.00
8	Steve Young, Jerry Rice	10.00
9	Dennis Smith, Steve Atwater	3.00

1993 SkyBox Celebrity Cycle Protypes

This four-card set includes three actual celebrities and one mystery card, which pictures a Harley-Davidson motorcycle against an American flag background. Backs are blank except for a large red stamp that reads "UNFINISHED SKYBOX PROTOTYPE."

		MT
Complete Set (4):		8.00
Common Player:		1.00
1	Mitch Frerotte	1.00
2	Jerry Glanville (CO)	1.00
3	Kenny Lofton (Cleveland Indians)	5.00
4	Mystery Celebrity Cycle Card	1.00

1993 SkyBox Impact Promos

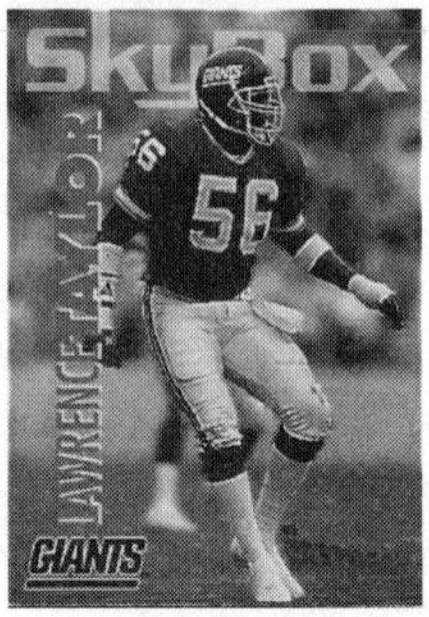

This two-card promotional set was mailed to dealers to promote the 1993 Impact set, and was numbered IP1 and IP2. Cards contain the same design as the regular-issue product. Another version of the Jim Kelly card was distributed at the 1993 Chicago National, but is differentiated by a blue foil stamp commemorating the event.

		MT
Complete Set (2):		3.00
Common Player:		1.00
1	Jim Kelly	2.00
2	Lawrence Taylor	1.00

1993 SkyBox Impact

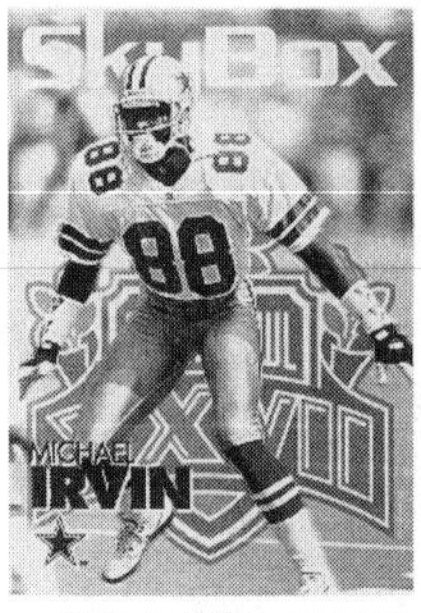

SkyBox's 1993 Impact set has 400 cards featuring full-bleed color action photos; the backgrounds are not in focus, so the player appears to stand out. The player's name and logo are at the bottom; SkyBox is written at the top. The back has a color photo, four-year statistics, a biography and career totals. Subsets include Class of '83, checklists, Rookies First Round and Rookies Second Round. Insert cards include redemption cards for a set of draft picks (29 cards) and a dual-sport card of Magic Johnson/Jim Kelley. SkyBox color foil cards were also created for each player in the 400-card set. Four different foil colors were used; each player is done in one color only. They can be collected to form a 400-card set. Two promo cards, using the same design as the regular 1993 SkyBox Impact set, were also produced.

		MT
Complete Set (400):		15.00
Common Player:		.03
Complete Set Colors (392):		75.00
Color Cards:		2x-4x
Pack (12):		.50
Wax Box (36):		14.00
1	Steve Broussard	.03
2	Michael Haynes	.10
3	Tony Smith	.03
4	Tory Epps	.03
5	Chris Hinton	.03
6	Bobby Hebert	.03
7	Tim McKyer	.03
8	Chris Miller	.03
9	Bruce Pickens	.03
10	Mike Pritchard	.05
11	Andre Rison	.20
12	Deion Sanders	.10
13	Pierce Holt	.03
14	Jessie Tuggle	.03
15	Don Beebe	.03
16	Cornelius Bennett	.03
17	Kenneth Davis	.03
18	Kent Hull	.03
19	Jim Kelly	.25
20	Mark Kelso	.03
21	Keith McKellar	.03
22	Andre Reed	.10
23	Jim Richter	.03
24	Bruce Smith	.04
25	Thurman Thomas	.10
26	Steve Christie	.03
27	Darryl Talley	.03
28	Pete Metzelaars	.03
29	Steve Tasker	.03
30	Henry Jones	.03
31	Neal Anderson	.05
32	Trace Armstrong	.03
33	Mark Bortz	.03
34	Mark Carrier	.03
35	Wendell Davis	.03
36	Richard Dent	.03
37	Jim Harbaugh	.05
38	Steve McMichael	.03
39	Craig Heyward	.03
40	William Perry	.03
41	Donnell Woolford	.03
42	Tom Waddle	.05
43	Anthony Morgan	.03
44	Jim Breech	.03
45	David Klingler	.15
46	Derrick Fenner	.03
47	David Fulcher	.03
48	James Francis	.03
49	Harold Green	.03
50	Carl Pickens	.15
51	Jay Schroeder	.03
52	Alex Gordon	.03
53	Eric Ball	.03
54	Eddie Brown	.03
55	Jay Hilgenberg	.03
56	Michael Jackson	.05
57	Bernie Kosar	.05
58	Kevin Mack	.03
59	Eric Metcalf	.03
60	Michael Dean Perry	.03
61	Tommy Vardell	.05
62	Leroy Hoard	.03
63	Clay Matthews	.03
64	Vinny Testaverde	.05
65	Mark Carrier	.03
66	Troy Aikman	1.00
67	*Lin Elliot*	.08
68	Thomas Everett	.03
69	Alvin Harper	.25
70	Ray Horton	.03
71	Michael Irvin	.10
72	Russell Maryland	.03
73	Jay Novacek	.03
74	Emmitt Smith	2.00
75	Tony Casillas	.03
76	Robert Jones	.03
77	Ken Norton	.03
78	Daryl Johnston	.03
79	Charles Haley	.03
80	*Leon Lett*	.25
81	Steve Atwater	.03
82	Mike Croel	.05
83	John Elway	1.00
84	Simon Fletcher	.03
85	Vance Johnson	.03
86	Shannon Sharpe	.08
87	Rod Bernstine	.03
88	Robert Delpino	.03
89	Karl Mecklenburg	.03
90	Steve Sewell	.03
91	Tommy Maddox	.15
92	*Arthur Marshall*	.25
93	Dennis Smith	.03
94	Derek Russell	.03
95	Bernie Blades	.03
96	Michael Cofer	.03
97	Willie Green	.08
98	Herman Moore	.40
99	Rodney Peete	.05
100	Andre Ware	.03
101	Barry Sanders	1.25
102	Chris Spielman	.03
103	Jason Hanson	.03
104	Mel Gray	.03
105	Pat Swilling	.03
106	Bill Fralic	.03
107	Rodney Herman	.03
108	Brett Favre	2.00
109	Sterling Sharpe	.10
110	Reggie White	.10
111	Terrell Buckley	.15
112	Sanjay Beach	.03
113	Tony Bennett	.03
114	Jackie Harris	.15
115	Bryce Paup	.03
116	Shawn Patterson	.03
117	John Stephens	.03
118	Cris Dishman	.03
119	Ernest Givins	.03
120	Haywood Jeffires	.10
121	Lamar Lathon	.03
122	Warren Moon	.15
123	Lorenzo White	.03
124	Curtis Duncan	.03
125	Webster Slaughter	.03
126	Cody Carlson	.03
127	Leonard Harris	.03
128	Bruce Matthews	.03
129	Ray Childress	.03
130	Al Smith	.03
131	Jeff George	.15
132	Anthony Johnson	.03
133	Steve Emtman	.08
134	Quentin Coryatt	.08
135	Rodney Culver	.03
136	Jessie Hester	.03
137	Aaron Cox	.03
138	Clarence Verdin	.03
139	Joe Montana	1.25
140	Dave Krieg	.03
141	Harvey Williams	.03
142	Derrick Thomas	.15
143	Barry Word	.05
144	Christian Okoye	.03
145	Nick Lowery	.03
146	Dale Carter	.03
147	Willie Davis	.10
148	Tim Barnett	.03
149	Neal Smith	.03
150	Marcus Allen	.06
151	Nick Bell	.04
152	Tim Brown	.35
153	Eric Dickerson	.03
154	Willie Gault	.03
155	Howie Long	.03
156	Gaston Green	.03
157	Chester McGlockton	.03
158	Eddie Anderson	.03
159	Ethan Horton	.03
160	James Lofton	.03
161	Jeff Hostetler	.10
162	Terry McDaniel	.03
163	Flipper Anderson	.03
164	Shane Conlan	.03
165	Jim Everett	.05
166	Henry Ellard	.03
167	Cleveland Gary	.03
168	Todd Lyght	.03
169	Sean Gilbert	.03
170	Jim Price	.03
171	Bill Hawkins	.03
172	Mark Clayton	.03
173	Mark Higgs	.10
174	Dan Marino	2.00
175	Louis Oliver	.03
176	Reggie Roby	.03
177	Bobby Humphrey	.03
178	Troy Vincent	.10
179	Marco Coleman	.05
180	Aaron Craver	.05
181	Keith Jackson	.10
182	Mark Duper	.03
183	Pete Stoyanovich	.03
184	Irving Fryar	.03
185	Brian Cox	.03
186	Terry Allen	.06
187	Anthony Carter	.03
188	Cris Carter	.03
189	Chris Doleman	.03
190	Rich Gannon	.06
191	Sean Salisbury	.03
192	Hassan Jones	.03
193	Steve Jordan	.03
194	Roger Craig	.05
195	Todd Scott	.03
196	Esera Tualo	.03
197	Ray Agnew	.03
198	Marv Cook	.03
199	Tom Hodson	.03
200	Chris Singleton	.03
201	Michael Timpson	.03
202	Jon Vaughn	.03
203	Leonard Russell	.10
204	Scott Zolak	.03
205	Renya Thompson	.03
206	Andre Tippett	.03
207	Morten Andersen	.03
208	Wesley Carroll	.03
209	Vince Buck	.03
210	Rickey Jackson	.03
211	Vaughn Johnson	.03
212	Eric Martin	.03
213	Sam Mills	.03
214	Steve Walsh	.05
215	Wade Wilson	.05
216	Vaughn Dunbar	.03
217	Brad Muster	.03
218	Dalton Hilliard	.03
219	Floyd Turner	.03
220	Stephen Baker	.03
221	Mark Jackson	.03
222	Jarrod Bunch	.05
223	Mark Collins	.03
224	Rodney Hampton	.25
225	Phil Simms	.10
226	Pepper Johnson	.03
227	Dave Meggett	.03
228	Derek Brown	.03
229	Mike Sherrard	.03
230	Lawrence Taylor	.10
231	Leonard Marshall	.03
232	Brad Baxter	.03
233	Dennis Byrd	.03
234	Ronnie Lott	.05
235	Boomer Esiason	.10
236	Browning Nagle	.05
237	Rob Moore	.05
238	Jeff Lageman	.03
239	Johnny Mitchell	.25
240	Chris Burkett	.03
241	Eric Thomas	.03
242	Johnny Johnson	.10
243	Eric Allen	.05
244	Fred Barnett	.05
245	Keith Byars	.03
246	Randall Cunningham	.10
247	Heath Sherman	.03
248	Calvin Williams	.05
249	Erik McMillan	.03
250	Byron Evans	.03
251	Seth Joyner	.03
252	Vai Sikahema	.03
253	Andre Waters	.03
254	Tim Harris	.03
255	Mark Bavaro	.03
256	Clyde Simmons	.03
257	Steve Beuerlein	.10
258	Randal Hill	.05
259	Ernie Jones	.03
260	Robert Massey	.03
261	Rickey Proehl	.05
262	Aeneas Williams	.03
263	Johnny Bailey	.03
264	Cris Chandler	.03
265	Anthony Thompson	.03
266	Gary Clark	.05
267	Chuck Cecil	.03
268	Rich Camarillo	.03
269	Neil O'Donnell	.25
270	Gerald Williams	.03
271	Greg Lloyd	.03
272	Eric Green	.03
273	Merril Hoge	.03
274	Ernie Mills	.03
275	Rod Woodson	.05
276	Gary Anderson	.03
277	Barry Foster	.10
278	Jeff Graham	.03
279	Dwight Stone	.03
280	Kevin Greene	.03
281	Eric Bieniemy	.03
282	Marion Butts	.05
283	Gill Byrd	.03
284	Stan Humphries	.03
285	Anthony Miller	.05
286	Leslie O'Neal	.03
287	Junior Seau	.15
288	Ronnie Harmon	.03
289	Nate Lewis	.03
290	John Kidd	.03
291	Steve Young	1.00
292	John Taylor	.06
293	Jerry Rice	.75
294	Tim McDonald	.03
295	Brent Jones	.03
296	Tom Rathman	.03

297	Dexter Carter	.03
298	Mike Cofer	.03
299	Ricky Watters	.40
300	Mervyn Fernandez	.03
301	Amp Lee	.08
302	Kevin Fagan	.03
303	Roy Foster	.03
304	Bill Romanowski	.03
305	Brian Blades	.03
306	John L. Williams	.03
307	Tommy Kane	.03
308	John Kasay	.03
309	Chris Warren	.10
310	Rufus Porter	.03
311	Cortez Kennedy	.10
312	Dan McGwire	.05
313	Stan Gelbaugh	.03
314	Kelvin Martin	.03
315	Ferrell Edmunds	.03
316	Eugene Robinson	.03
317	Gary Anderson	.03
318	Reggie Cobb	.05
319	Lawrence Dawsey	.03
320	Courtney Hawkins	.03
321	Santana Dotson	.03
322	Ron Hall	.03
323	Keith McCants	.03
324	Martin Mayhew	.03
325	Anthony Munoz	.03
326	Steve DeBerg	.03
327	Vince Workman	.03
328	Earnest Byner	.03
329	Ricky Ervins	.05
330	Jim Lachey	.03
331	Chip Lohmiller	.03
332	Ricky Sanders	.03
333	Brad Edwards	.03
334	Tim McGee	.03
335	Darrell Green	.05
336	Charles Mann	.03
337	Wilber Marshall	.03
338	Brian Mitchell	.03
339	Art Monk	.05
340	Mark Rypien	.08
341	John Elway (C83)	.10
342	Jim Kelly (C83)	.10
343	Dan Marino (C83)	.20
344	Eric Dickerson (C83)	.08
345	Willie Gault (C83)	.05
346	Ken O'Brien (C83)	.05
347	Darrell Green (C83)	.05
348	Richard Dent (C83)	.03
349	Karl Mecklenburg (C83)	.03
350	Henry Ellard (C83)	.03
351	Roger Craig (C83)	.05
352	Charles Mann (C83)	.03
353	Checklist A	.03
354	Checklist B	.03
355	Checklist C	.03
356	Checklist D	.03
357	Checklist E	.03
358	Checklist F	.03
359	Checklist G	.03
360	Checklist (rookies)	.03
361	*Drew Bledsoe*	2.50
362	*Rick Mirer*	.25
363	*Garrison Hearst*	1.00
364	*Marvin Jones*	.15
365	*John Copeland*	.25
366	*Eric Curry*	.25
367	*Curtis Conway*	1.00
368	*Willie Roaf*	.15
369	*Lincoln Kennedy*	.20
370	*Jerome Bettis*	1.00
371	*Dan Williams*	.10
372	*Patrick Bates*	.10
373	*Brad Hopkins*	.10
374	*Steve Everett*	.10
375	*Wayne Simmons*	.10
376	*Tom Carter*	.15
377	*Ernest Dye*	.10
378	*Lester Holmes*	.10
379	*Irv Smith*	.25
380	*Robert Smith*	1.00
381	*Darrien Gordon*	.20
382	*Deon Figures*	.20
383	*O.J. McDuffie*	.75
384	*Dana Stubblefield*	.50
385	*Todd Kelly*	.10
386	*Thomas Smith*	.10
387	*George Teague*	.25
388	*Carlton Gray*	.15
389	*Chris Slade*	.25
390	*Ben Coleman*	.10
391	*Ryan McNeil*	.10
392	*Demetrius DuBose*	.20
393	*Carl Simpson*	.10
394	*Coleman Rudolph*	.10
395	*Tony McGee*	.15
396	*Roger Harper*	.15
397	*Troy Drayton*	.25
398	*Michael Strahan*	.10
399	*Natrone Means*	1.00
400	*Glyn Milburn*	.60

1993 SkyBox Impact Colors

Colors was a 392-card set (400 minus the eight checklists) that came one per pack and were designated by UV coating and a foil Impact logo on the front in one of four colors - gold, silver, blue and red.

		MT
Complete Set (10):		80.00
Common Player:		3.00
1	Patrick Bates	3.00
2	Drew Bledsoe	25.00
3	Darrien Gordon	3.00
4	Garrison Hearst	16.00
5	Marvin Jones	3.00
6	Terry Kirby	5.00
7	Natrone Means	12.00
8	Rick Mirer	14.00
9	Willie Roaf	5.00
10	Dan Williams	3.00

1993 SkyBox Impact Kelly/Magic

SkyBox spokesmen Jim Kelly and Magic Johnson selected a team of their favorite players for this insert set. The cards are foil stamped and indicate which player selected them by either a Kelly's Heroes logo or Magic's Kingdom logo on it, in a small panel along the left which has a player portrait shot. An action photo and the player's name are on the right. Each card has selection by both players on opposite sides. The cards were random inserts in foil packs. The two spokesmen also autographed 500 cards which were offered to those who found individually numbered redemption certificates randomly included among packs. Those who obtained cards 12 and 32, the uniform numbers of Kelly and Johnson, were to receive the autographed cards personally from the players.

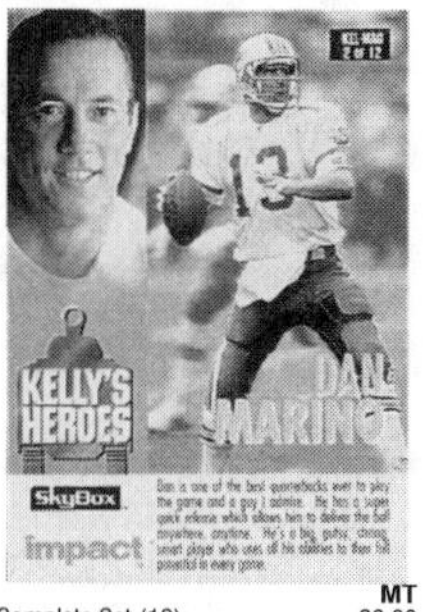

		MT
Complete Set (12):		20.00
Common Player:		1.00
Minor Stars:		2.00
Inserted 1:12		
1	Title card	1.00
2	Dan Marino, Jim Kelly	5.00
3	Jay Novacek, Keith Jackson	1.00
4	Thurman Thomas, Barry Sanders	5.00
5	Barry Sanders, Emmitt Smith	5.00
6	Jerry Rice, Sterling Sharpe	3.00
7	Andre Reed, Jerry Rice	3.00
8	Thurman Thomas, Patrick Swilling	2.00
9	Darryl Talley, Lawrence Taylor	2.00
10	Rod Woodson, Darrell Green	1.00
11	Steve Tasker, Elvis Patterson	1.00
12	Morten Andersen, Chip Lowery	1.00

1993 SkyBox Impact Update

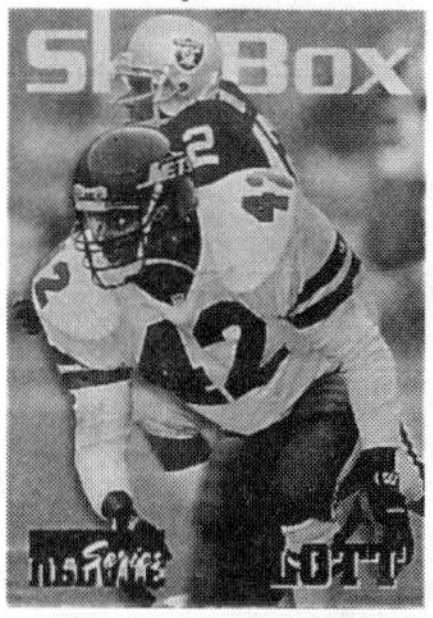

This 20-card set could be obtained by sending five Impact wrappers plus $3.99 for postage and handling. The set focuses on players who switched teams through free agency and pictures the player in his new uniform in front of the player in his old uniform. Cards are numbered and have a "U" prefix.

		MT
Complete Set (20):		10.00
Common Player:		.25
Minor Stars:		.50
1	Pierce Holt	.25
2	Vinny Testaverde	.50
3	Rod Bernstine	.25
4	Reggie White	.50
5	Mark Clayton	.25
6	Joe Montana	5.00
7	Marcus Allen	.50
8	Jeff Hostetler	.25
9	Shane Conlan	.25
10	Brad Muster	.25
11	Mike Sherrard	.25
12	Ronnie Lott	.50
13	Steve Beuerlein	.25
14	Gary Clark	.25
15	Kevin Greene	.25
16	Tim McDonald	.25
17	Wilber Marshall	.25
18	Keith Byars	.25
19	Pat Swilling	.25
20	Boomer Esiason	.25

1993 SkyBox Impact Rookie Redemption

This 29-card set features all of the first round picks from the 1993 NFL Draft, excluding Sean Dawkins (16th), who signed an exclusive contract with Courtside. The set could be obtained either by pulling a redemption card (seeded one per 180 packs) or by a second chance drawing. Cards picture the players in their pro uniforms, with the name running up the left side and the draft position in the lower right corner. Cards are numbered with a "R" prefix.

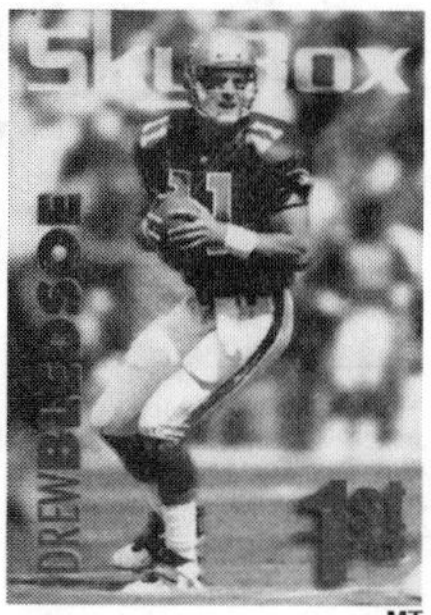

		MT
Complete Set (29):		20.00
Common Player:		.50
Minor Stars:		1.00
1	Title Card/Checklist (Drew Bledsoe)	2.50
2	Drew Bledsoe	5.00
3	Rick Mirer	1.00
4	Garrison Hearst	1.75
5	Marvin Jones	.50
6	John Copeland	.50
7	Eric Curry (UER) (Card front states he was selected in sixth round instead of sixth pick)	.50
8	Curtis Conway	1.25
9	Willie Roaf	.50
10	Lincoln Kennedy	.50
11	Jerome Bettis	1.75
12	Dan Williams	.50
13	Patrick Bates	.50
14	Brad Hopkins	.50
15	Steve Everitt	.50
16	Wayne Simmons	.50
17	Tom Carter	.50
18	Ernest Dye	.50
19	Lester Holmes	.50
20	Irv Smith	.50
21	Robert Smith	1.75
22	Darrien Gordon	.50
23	Deon Figures	.50
24	Leonard Renfro	.50
25	O.J. McDuffie	1.25
26	Dana Stubblefield	1.00
27	Todd Kelly	.50
28	Thomas Smith	.50
29	George Teague	.50
NNO	Rookie Redemption Card Expired	.50

1994 SkyBox Promos

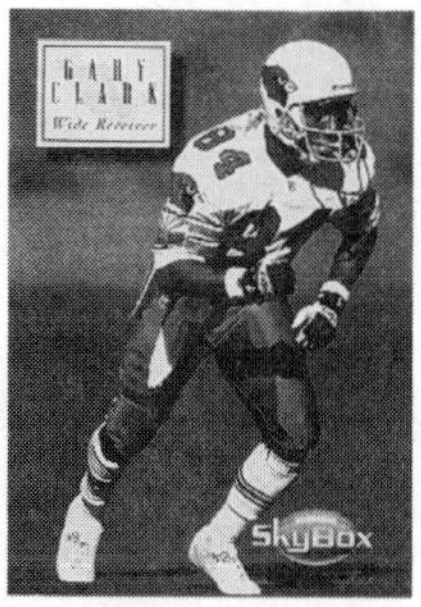

Six different players and a commemorative card were issued for this set, which promotes the 1994 SkyBox Premium set. The cards are numbered S1-S6, with the commemorative card having no number.

		MT
Complete Set (7):		8.00
Common Player:		1.00
1	Tom Carter	1.00
2	Gary Clark	1.00
3	James Jett	1.00
4	Jim Kelly	2.00
5	Ronnie Lott	1.50
6	John Taylor	1.00
NNO	Sample Commemorative Game Card	1.00

1994 SkyBox Premium

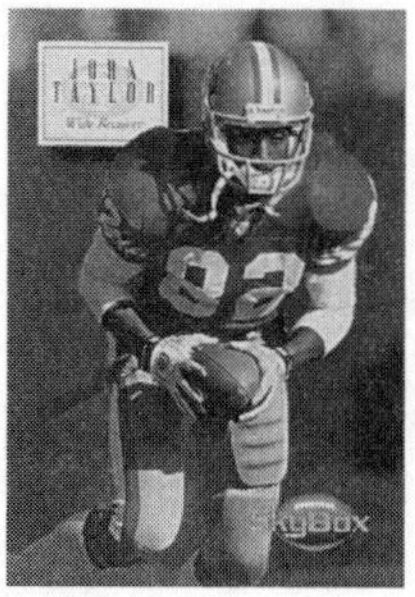

SkyBox released its 1994 premium football set in a single-series, 200-card issue. Cards have a borderless design on the front and show a player against an action background, highlighted with team colors. The flip side presents an up-close photo, biographical information, 1993 season and NFL career stats and a scouting report written by Chris Mortensen. The regular-issue set contains several subsets, including 23 Prime Movers and 40 rookies. SkyBox also had various randomly inserted sets, autographed cards and a sweepstakes game card. Insert sets were entitled SkyTech Stars, SkyBox Revolution and Prime Time Rookies.

		MT
Complete Set (200):		35.00
Common Player:		.10
Minor Stars:		.20
Pack (10):		2.00
Wax Box (36):		55.00
1	Steve Beuerlein	.10
2	Gary Clark	.10
3	Garrison Hearst	1.00
4	Ron Moore	.10
5	Eric Swann	.10
6	Chuck Cecil	.10
7	Seth Joyner	.10
8	Clyde Simmons	.10
9	Andre Rison	.20
10	Deion Sanders	1.00
11	Erric Pegram	.10
12	Steve Broussard	.10
13	Chris Doleman	.10
14	Jeff George	.30
15	Cornelius Bennett	.10
16	Jim Kelly	.20
17	Andre Reed	.10
18	Bruce Smith	.10
19	Darryl Talley	.10
20	Thurman Thomas	.30
21	Mark Carrier	.10
22	Dante Jones	.10
23	Curtis Conway	.30
24	Tim Worley	.10
25	Erik Kramer	.10
26	John Copeland	.10
27	David Klingler	.10
28	Derrick Fenner	.10
29	Harold Green	.10
30	Carl Pickens	.50
31	Tony McGee	.10
32	Steve Everitt	.10
33	Michael Jackson	.10
34	Eric Metcalf	.10
35	Vinny Testaverde	.20
36	Michael Dean Perry	.10
37	Troy Aikman	2.00
38	Alvin Harper	.20
39	Michael Irvin	.60
40	Jay Novacek	.10
41	Emmitt Smith	4.00
42	Charles Haley	.10
43	Daryl Johnston	.10
44	Kevin Williams	.30
45	Rodney Peete	.10
46	John Elway	1.00
47	Shannon Sharpe	.20
48	Rod Bernstine	.10
49	Glyn Milburn	.20
50	Mike Pritchard	.10
51	Anthony Miller	.10
52	Herman Moore	1.50
53	Barry Sanders	3.50
54	Scott Mitchell	.20
55	Pat Swilling	.10
56	Willie Green	.10
57	Edgar Bennett	.10
58	Brett Favre	4.00
59	Sterling Sharpe	.20
60	Reggie White	.20
61	Sean Jones	.10
62	Reggie Cobb	.10
63	Haywood Jeffires	.10
64	Lorenzo White	.10
65	Webster Slaughter	.10
66	Gary Brown	.10
67	Steve Emtman	.10
68	Quentin Coryatt	.10
69	*Sean Dawkins*	.30
70	Jim Harbaugh	.10
71	Tony Bennett	.10
72	Marcus Allen	.20
73	Steve Bono	.20
74	Dale Carter	.10
75	Joe Montana	3.00
76	Neil Smith	.10
77	Derrick Thomas	.20
78	Keith Cash	.10
79	Tim Brown	.20
80	Raghib Ismail	.10
81	Jeff Hostetler	.20
82	Patrick Bates	.10
83	James Jett	.10
84	Jerome Bettis	1.00
85	Chris Miller	.10
86	Marc Boutte	.10
87	Sean Gilbert	.20
88	Keith Jackson	.10
89	Terry Kirby	.20
90	Dan Marino	4.00
91	Brian Cox	.10
92	Bernie Kosar	.10
93	Qadry Ismail	.20
94	Robert Smith	.25
95	Terry Allen	.10
96	Scottie Graham	.30
97	Warren Moon	.20
98	Drew Bledsoe	3.00
99	Ben Coates	.40
100	Leonard Russell	.10
101	Vincent Brisby	.40
102	Marion Butts	.10
103	Morten Andersen	.10
104	Derek Brown	.10
105	Michael Haynes	.10
106	Sam Mills	.10
107	Lorenzo Neal	.10
108	Willie Roaf	.10
109	Jim Everett	.10
110	Michael Brooks	.10
111	Rodney Hampton	.20
112	Dave Brown	.20
113	Dave Meggett	.10
114	Ronnie Lott	.10
115	Boomer Esiason	.10
116	Rob Moore	.10
117	Johnny Johnson	.10
118	Marvin Jones	.10
119	Johnny Mitchell	.10
120	Fred Barnett	.10
121	Randall Cunningham	.20
122	Herschel Walker	.10
123	Calvin Williams	.10
124	Neil O'Donnell	.20
125	Eric Green	.10
126	Leroy Thompson	.10
127	Rod Woodson	.20
128	Barry Foster	.20
129	Deon Figures	.10
130	John L. Williams	.10
131	Chris Mims	.10
132	Darrien Gordon	.10
133	Stan Humphries	.30
134	Natrone Means	1.00
135	Junior Seau	.30
136	Brent Jones	.10
137	Jerry Rice	3.00
138	Dana Stubblefield	.20
139	John Taylor	.10
140	Ricky Watters	.20
141	Steve Young	3.00
142	Ken Norton	.10
143	Brian Blades	.10
144	Cortez Kennedy	.20
145	Kelvin Martin	.10
146	Rick Mirer	.20
147	Chris Warren	.20
148	Eric Curry	.10
149	Santana Dotson	.10
150	Craig Erickson	.10
151	Hardy Nickerson	.10
152	Paul Gruber	.10
153	Reggie Brooks	.20
154	Tom Carter	.10
155	Desmond Howard	.10
156	Ken Harvey	.10
157	*Dan Wilkinson*	.40
158	*Marshall Faulk*	4.00
159	*Heath Shuler*	.50
160	*Willie McGinest*	.50
161	*Trev Alberts*	.20
162	*Trent Dilfer*	3.00
163	*Bryant Young*	.50
164	*Sam Adams*	.20
165	*Antonio Langham*	.20
166	*Jamir Miller*	.20
167	*John Thierry*	.20
168	*Aaron Glenn*	.20
169	*Joe Johnson*	.20
170	*Bernard Williams*	.20
171	*Wayne Gandy*	.20
172	*Aaron Taylor*	.20
173	*Charles Johnson*	.50
174	*DeWayne Washington*	.20
175	*Todd Steussie*	.20
176	*Tim Bowens*	.20
177	*Johnnie Morton*	1.50
178	*Rob Fredrickson*	.20
179	*Shante Carver*	.20
180	*Thomas Lewis*	.20
181	*Greg Hill*	1.00
182	*Henry Ford*	.20
183	*Jeff Burris*	.20
184	*William Floyd*	.50
185	*Derrick Alexander*	.50
186	*Glenn Foley*	1.50
187	*Charlie Garner*	2.50
188	*Errict Rhett*	1.00
189	*Chuck Levy*	.20
190	*Bam Morris*	1.00
191	*Donnell Bennett*	.75
192	*LeShon Johnson*	.50
193	*Mario Bates*	.50
194	*David Palmer*	.50
195	*Darnay Scott*	1.50
196	*Lake Dawson*	.50
197	Checklist	.10
198	Checklist	.10
199	Checklist	.10
200	Checklist for Insert Cards	.10

1994 SkyBox Premium Inside the Numbers

Inside the Numbers is a 20-card set that features a borderless design on gold foil. The set was inserted at a rate of one per retail pack.

		MT
Complete Set (20):		20.00
Common Player:		.40
1	Jim Kelly	.75
2	Ronnie Lott	.75
3	Morten Andersen	.40
4	Reggie White	1.25
5	Terry Kirby	.60
6	Marcus Allen	1.00
7	Thurman Thomas	1.00
8	Joe Montana	8.00
9	Tom Carter	.40
10	Jerome Bettis	2.00
11	Sterling Sharpe	.75
12	Andre Rison	.75
13	Reggie Brooks	.40
14	Hardy Nickerson	.60
15	Ricky Watters	1.00
16	Gary Brown	.40
17	Natrone Means	1.50
18	LeShon Johnson	.60
19	Errict Rhett	.75
20	Trent Dilfer	1.75

1994 SkyBox QB Autograph Exchange Set

SkyBox randomly inserted 500 SkyBox QB Autograph Exchange Cards in its packs, giving collectors a chance to receive a limited, three-card autographed set of Ken Stabler, Jim Kelly and Trent Dilfer. Each set was presented in an individually numbered lucite card holder. Cards were numbered with a "QB" prefix.

		MT
Complete Set (3):		
Common Player:		
1	Ken Stabler	30.00
2	Jim Kelly	30.00
3	Trent Dilfer	20.00

1994 SkyBox Premium Revolution

This insert set provides an up-close look at 15 of the NFL's premium players. Each card front is printed with portrait photography on a pewter foil background. Revolution cards are numbered on the back with an "R" prefix and were inserted one every 20th pack of SkyBox Premium cards. The card back uses the player's team colors for a background, and includes a team logo and a player biography.

		MT
Complete Set (15):		125.00
Common Player:		4.00
Minor Stars:		8.00
1	Jim Kelly	4.00
2	Thurman Thomas	8.00
3	Troy Aikman	18.00
4	Michael Irvin	8.00
5	Emmitt Smith	30.00
6	John Elway	20.00
7	Barry Sanders	18.00
8	Sterling Sharpe	8.00
9	Joe Montana	18.00
10	Jerome Bettis	10.00
11	Dan Marino	30.00
12	Drew Bledsoe	18.00
13	Jerry Rice	18.00
14	Steve Young	15.00
15	Rick Mirer	10.00

1994 SkyBox Premium Rookies

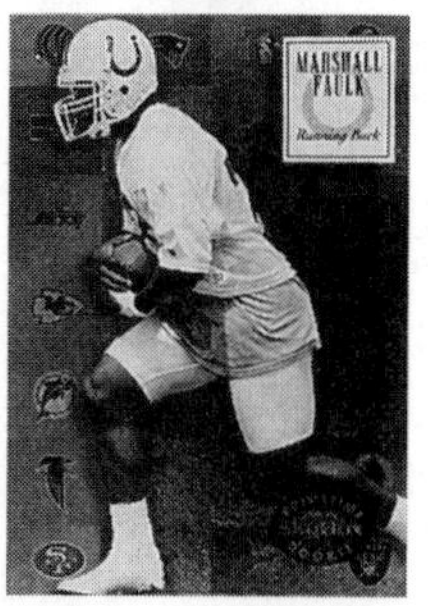

Prime Time Rookies consists of 10 Chris Mortensen-selected rookies who were expected to make the biggest impact in the 1994 season. Cards from this set were randomly inserted at a rate of one every 96th pack of SkyBox Premium cards. Card backs are numbered with a "PT" prefix.

		MT
Complete Set (10):		180.00
Common Player:		10.00
1	Trent Dilfer	15.00
2	Heath Shuler	15.00
3	Marshall Faulk	40.00
4	Charlie Garner	10.00
5	Errict Rhett	15.00
6	Greg Hill	12.00
7	William Floyd	10.00
8	Charles Johnson	10.00
9	Derrick Alexander	10.00
10	David Palmer	10.00

1994 SkyBox Premium SkyTech Stars

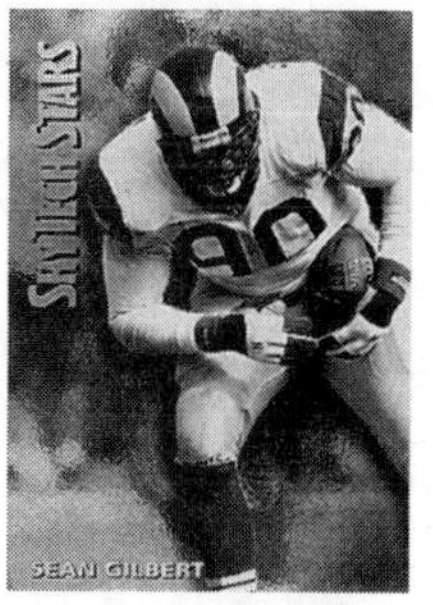

SkyTech Stars were found in one of every six packs of SkyBox Premium cards. The set features 30 selected players printed over a foil background; cards are the same as they appear in the regular set except for the foil printing. Cards are numbered on the back with an "ST" prefix and include a photo, team logo, biography and statistics.

		MT
Complete Set (30):		100.00
Common Player:		2.00
Minor Stars:		4.00
1	Troy Aikman	8.00
2	Emmitt Smith	16.00
3	Michael Irvin	4.00
4	John Elway	7.00
5	Sterling Sharpe	4.00
6	Joe Montana	8.00
7	Drew Bledsoe	8.00
8	Rick Mirer	4.00
9	Junior Seau	4.00
10	Jerome Bettis	4.00
11	Rod Woodson	2.00
12	Tim Brown	2.00

13 Jeff George 4.00
14 Brett Favre 16.00
15 Reggie White 4.00
16 Cortez Kennedy 2.00
17 Ricky Watters 4.00
18 Shannon Sharpe 2.00
19 Reggie Brooks 2.00
20 Heath Shuler 5.00
21 Marshall Faulk 8.00
22 Thurman Thomas 4.00
23 Barry Foster 2.00
24 Sean Gilbert 2.00
25 Jerry Rice 8.00
26 Andre Rison 4.00
27 Barry Sanders 10.00
28 Jim Kelly 4.00
29 Steve Young 8.00
30 Dan Marino 16.00

1994 SkyBox Impact Promos

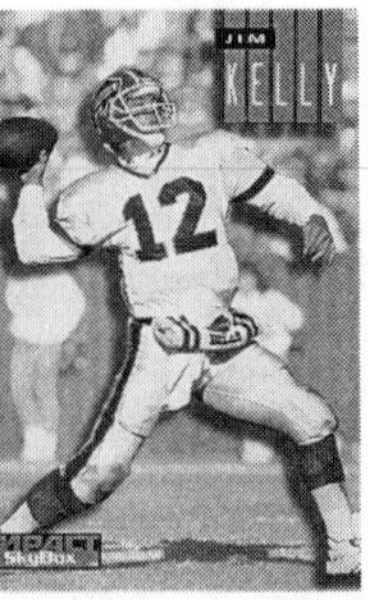

This six-card set was issued to preview the SkyBox Impact set and carried the same card designs as the regular-issue cards. The cards are numbered with an "S" prefix on the back. In addition, the cards were also issued as a 7-1/2" x 8-1/2" unperforated sheet at the 1994 National Sports Collectors Convention.

MT
Complete Set (6): 8.00
Common Player: 1.00
1 Marcus Allen 2.00
2 Chris Doleman 1.00
3 Craig Erickson 1.00
4 Jim Kelly 3.00
5 Reggie Roby 1.00
6 Rod Woodson 1.50

1994 SkyBox Impact

These cards feature a borderless design which shows a player highlighted against a ghosted action background. The set's name is in one of the bottom corners; the player's name is in a top corner. The card back has an oversized action photo, biographical information, stats, a card number and a player profile. There are 30 rookies and five checklists in the set. Insert cards included with the set are: Instant Impact Rookies (one in 30 packs); Ultimate Impact Players (one in 15 packs); and the SkyBox Impact NFL Rookie Exchange Card, found one in every 350 packs. This "IOU" card is redeemable for a limited-edition set of NFL first-round draft choice selections pictured in their NFL uniforms. There were also six promo cards created to preview the regular set. They have the same basic design, except they are numbered with an "S" prefix.

MT
Complete Set (300): 20.00
Common Player: .05
Minor Stars: .10
Pack (12): .75
Wax Box (36): 25.00
1 Johnny Bailey .05
2 Steve Beuerlein .05
3 Gary Clark .05
4 Garrison Hearst .50
5 Ron Moore .05
6 Ricky Proehl .05
7 Eric Swann .05
8 Aeneas Williams .05
9 Robert Massey .05
10 Chuck Cecil .05
11 Ken Harvey .05
12 Michael Haynes .05
13 Tony Smith .05
14 Bobby Hebert .05
15 Mike Pritchard .05
16 Andre Rison .10
17 Deion Sanders .50
18 Pierce Holt .05
19 Erric Pegram .10
20 Jessie Tuggle .05
21 Steve Broussard .05
22 Don Beebe .05
23 Cornelius Bennett .05
24 Kenneth Davis .05
25 Bill Brooks .05
26 Jim Kelly .10
27 Andre Reed .05
28 Bruce Smith .05
29 Darryl Talley .05
30 Thurman Thomas .10
31 Steve Tasker .05
32 Neal Anderson .05
33 Mark Carrier .05
34 Richard Dent .05
35 Jim Harbaugh .10
36 Chris Gedney .05
37 Tom Waddle .05
38 Curtis Conway .50
39 Dante Jones .05
40 Donnell Woolford .05
41 Tim Worley .05
42 John Copeland .05
43 David Klingler .05
44 Derrick Fenner .05
45 Harold Green .05
46 Carl Pickens .50
47 Tony McGee .05
48 Darryl Williams .05
49 Steve Everitt .05
50 Michael Jackson .05
51 Eric Metcalf .05
52 Tommy Vardell .05
53 Vinny Testaverde .05
54 Mark Carrier .05
55 Michael Dean Perry .05
56 Eric Turner .05
57 Troy Aikman 1.00
58 Alvin Harper .10
59 Michael Irvin .10
60 Leon Lett .05
61 Russell Maryland .05
62 Jay Novacek .05
63 Emmitt Smith 2.00
64 Ken Norton Jr. .05
65 Charles Haley .05
66 Daryl Johnston .05
67 Kevin Smith .05
68 James Washington .05
69 Kevin Williams .30
70 Bernie Kosar .05
71 Mike Croel .05
72 John Elway .50
73 Shannon Sharpe .05
74 Rod Bernstine .05
75 Simon Fletcher .05
76 Arthur Marshall .05
77 Glyn Milburn .05
78 Dennis Smith .05
79 Herman Moore .50
80 Rodney Peete .10
81 Barry Sanders 1.25
82 Mel Gray .05
83 Erik Kramer .10
84 Pat Swilling .05
85 Willie Green .05
86 Chris Spielman .05
87 Robert Porcher .05
88 Derrick Moore .05
89 Edgar Bennett .05
90 Tony Bennett .05
91 LeRoy Butler .05
92 Brett Favre 2.00
93 Jackie Harris .05
94 Sterling Sharpe .10
95 Darrell Thompson .05
96 Reggie White .10
97 Terrell Buckley .05
98 Cris Dishman .05
99 Ernest Givins .05
100 Haywood Jeffires .05
101 Warren Moon .10
102 Lorenzo White .05
103 Webster Slaughter .05
104 Ray Childress .05
105 Wilbur Marshall .05
106 Gary Brown .05
107 Mariusu Robertson .05
108 Sean Jones .05
109 Jeff George .10
110 Steve Emtman .05
111 Quentin Coryatt .05
112 *Sean Dawkins* .40
113 Jeff Herrod .05
114 Roosevelt Potts .05
115 Marcus Allen .10
116 Kimble Anders .05
117 Tim Barnett .05
118 J.J. Birden .05
119 Dale Carter .05
120 Willie Davis .05
121 Nick Lowery .05
122 Joe Montana 1.00
123 Kevin Ross .05
124 Neil Smith .05
125 Derrick Thomas .05
126 Keith Cash .05
127 Tim Brown .10
128 Raghib Ismail .05
129 Ethan Horton .05
130 Jeff Hostetler .10
131 Patrick Bates .05
132 Terry McDaniel .05
133 Anthony Smith .05
134 Greg Robinson .05
135 James Jett .05
136 Alexander Wright .05
137 Willie Anderson .05
138 Shane Conlan .05
139 Jim Everett .05
140 Henry Ellard .05
141 Jerome Bettis .25
142 Troy Drayton .05
143 Sean Gilbert .05
144 Chris Miller .05
145 Keith Byars .05
146 Marco Coleman .05
147 Bryan Cox .05
148 Irving Fryar .05
149 Mark Ingram .05
150 Keith Jackson .05
151 Terry Kirby .05
152 Dan Marino 2.00
153 O.J. McDuffie .20
154 Scott Mitchell .10
155 Anthony Carter .05
156 Cris Carter .10
157 Chris Doleman .05
158 Steve Jordan .05
159 Qadry Ismail .05
160 Randall McDaniel .05
161 John Randle .05
162 Robert Smith .20
163 Henry Thomas .05
164 Terry Allen .05
165 *Scottie Graham* .10
166 Drew Bledsoe 1.00
167 Vincent Brown .05
168 Ben Coates .05
169 Leonard Russell .05
170 Andre Tippett .05
171 Vincent Brisby .05
172 Michael Timpson .05
173 Bruce Armstrong .05
174 Morten Andersen .05
175 Derek Brown .05
176 Quinn Early .05
177 Rickey Jackson .05
178 Vaughan Johnson .05
179 Lorenzo Neal .05
180 Sam Mills .05
181 Irv Smith .05
182 Renaldo Turnbull .05
183 Wade Wilson .05
184 Willie Roaf .05
185 Michael Brooks .05
186 Mark Jackson .05
187 Rodney Hampton .10
188 Phil Simms .05
189 Dave Meggett .05
190 Mike Sherrard .05
191 Chris Calloway .05
192 Brad Baxter .05
193 Ronnie Lott .05
194 Boomer Esiason .05
195 Rob Moore .05
196 Johnny Johnson .05
197 Marvin Jones .10
198 Mo Lewis .05
199 Johnny Mitchell .05
200 Brian Washington .05
201 Eric Allen .05
202 Fred Barnett .05
203 Mark Bavaro .05
204 Randall Cunningham .10
205 Vaughn Hebron .05
206 Seth Joyner .05
207 Clyde Simmons .05
208 Herschel Walker .05
209 Calvin Williams .05
210 Neil O'Donnell .10
211 Eric Green .05
212 Leroy Thompson .05
213 Rod Woodson .05
214 Barry Foster .05
215 Jeff Graham .05
216 Kevin Greene .05
217 Deon Figures .05
218 Greg Lloyd .10
219 Marion Butts .05
220 Chris Mims .05
221 Darrien Gordon .05
222 Ronnie Harmon .05
223 Stan Humphries .10
224 Nate Lewis .05
225 Natrone Means .40
226 Anthony Miller .05
227 Leslie O'Neal .05
228 Junior Seau .10
229 Brent Jones .05
230 Tim McDonald .05
231 Tom Rathman .05
232 Jerry Rice 1.00
233 Dana Stubblefield .10
234 John Taylor .05
235 Ricky Watters .10
236 Steve Young 1.00
237 Amp Lee .05
238 Robert Blackmon .05
239 Brian Blades .05
240 Cortez Kennedy .05
241 Kelvin Martin .05
242 Rick Mirer .25
243 Eugene Robinson .05
244 Chris Warren .10
245 John L. Williams .05
246 Jon Vaughn .05
247 Reggie Cobb .05
248 Horace Copeland .05
249 *Derrick Alexander* .25
250 Santana Dotson .05
251 Craig Erickson .05
252 Courtney Hawkins .05
253 Hardy Nickerson .05
254 Vince Workman .05
255 Paul Gruber .05
256 Reggie Brooks .05
257 Tom Carter .05
258 Andre Collins .05
259 Darrell Green .05
260 Desmond Howard .05
261 Tim McGee .05
262 Brian Mitchell .05
263 Art Monk .05
264 John Friesz .05
265 Ricky Sanders .05
266 Checklist A .05
267 Checklist B .05
268 Checklist C .05
269 Checklist D .05
270 Checklist E .05
271 Carolina Panthers .20
272 Jacksonville Jaguars .20
273 *Dan Wilkinson* .10
274 *Marshall Faulk* 3.00
275 *Heath Shuler* .25
276 *Willie McGinest* .25
277 *Trev Alberts* .10
278 *Trent Dilfer* .50
279 *Bryant Young* .40
280 *Sam Adams* .10
281 *Antonio Langham* .10
282 *Jamir Miller* .10
283 *John Thierry* .10
284 *Aaron Glenn* .10
285 *Joe Johnson* .10
286 *Bernard Williams* .10
287 *Wayne Gandy* .10
288 *Aaron Taylor* .10
289 *Charles Johnson* .50
290 *DeWayne Washington* .10
291 *Todd Steussie* .10
292 *Tim Bowens* .10
293 *Johnnie Morton* .50
294 *Rob Fredrickson* .10
295 *Shante Carver* .10
296 *Thomas Lewis* .10
297 *Greg Hill* .50
298 *Henry Ford* .10
299 *Jeff Burris* .10
300 *William Floyd* .50
NNO Carolina Panthers 30.00

1994 SkyBox Impact Instant Impact

Each of these card fronts features a full-bleed color photo against a faded background. The Instant Impact logo is stamped in gold foil in the lower right corner, while the player's name is in the upper left corner in team color-coded boxes. The backs are horizontal and have another action photo, plus a brief player profile. The player's name and team logo are in a color stripe at the top of the card, next to "Instant Impact," which is written in a black box. Cards, numbered with an "R" prefix, were randomly inserted one out of every 30th SkyBox Impact pack.

MT
Complete Set (12): 35.00
Common Player: 2.00
1 Rick Mirer 3.00
2 Jerome Bettis 4.00
3 Reggie Brooks 2.00
4 Terry Kirby 2.00
5 Vincent Brisby 2.00
6 James Jett 2.00
7 Drew Bledsoe 10.00
8 Dana Stubblefield 2.00
9 Natrone Means 4.00
10 Curtis Conway 3.00
11 O.J. McDuffie 3.00
12 Garrison Hearst 5.00

1994 SkyBox Impact Quarterback Update

This 10-card set contains traded and rookie quarterbacks in their new uniforms and are identical to the Impact base card design. The set was available through a redemption offer, as well as a one per pack retail exclusive insert.

MT
Complete Set (11): 5.00
Common Player: .40
1 Warren Moon .60
2 Trent Dilfer .75
3 Jeff George .60
4 Heath Shuler .75
5 Jim Harbaugh .60
6 Rodney Peete .40
7 Chris Miller .40
8 Jim Everett .40
9 Scott Mitchell .60
10 Erik Kramer .40
NNO Checklist .40

1994 SkyBox Impact Rookie Redemption

This redemption set included the first 29 players chosen in the 1994 NFL Draft. The redemption card was randomly inserted into packs of 1994 SkyBox Impact.

MT
Complete Set (30): 25.00
Common Player: .25
Minor Stars: .50
1 Dan Wilkinson .50
2 Marshall Faulk 8.00
3 Heath Shuler 1.00
4 Willie McGinest .50
5 Trev Alberts .25
6 Trent Dilfer 5.00
7 Bryant Young .50
8 Sam Adams .25
9 Antonio Langham .25
10 Jamir Miller .25
11 John Thierry .25
12 Aaron Glenn .50
13 Joe Johnson .25
14 Bernard Williams .25
15 Wayne Gandy .25
16 Aaron Taylor .25
17 Charles Johnson 1.00
18 DeWayne Washington .50
19 Todd Steussie .50
20 Tim Bowens .25
21 Johnnie Morton 1.00
22 Rob Fredrickson .25
23 Shante Carver .25
24 Thomas Lewis .25
25 Greg Hill 1.00
26 Henry Ford .25
27 Jeff Burris .25
28 William Floyd 1.00
29 Derrick Alexander (WR) 1.00
NNO Rookie Redemption Exp. .50

1994 SkyBox Impact Ultimate Impact

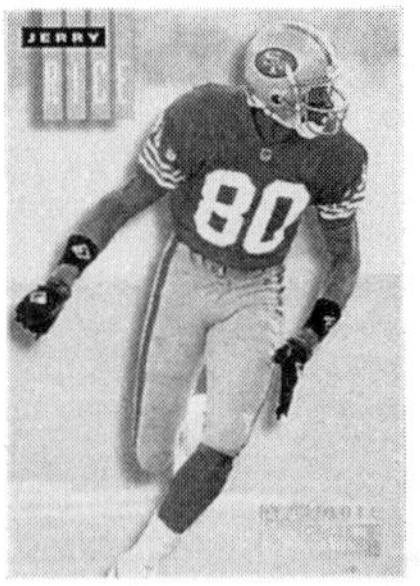

These cards, randomly inserted in every 15th pack of 1994 SkyBox Impact cards, feature 15 top NFL players. Each card front has a color action photo against a borderless background. The player's name is spelled out in boxes at the top. The Ultimate logo is stamped in silver foil in the lower right corner. Each card back is numbered with a "U" prefix and is in a horizontal format. A color action shot takes up more than half of the card. A player profile fills the rest.

MT
Complete Set (15): 75.00
Common Player: 2.00
Minor Stars: 2.00
1 Troy Aikman 10.00
2 Emmitt Smith 20.00
3 Michael Irvin 2.00
4 Joe Montana 10.00
5 Jerry Rice 10.00
6 Sterling Sharpe 2.00
7 Steve Young 10.00
8 Ricky Watters 2.00
9 Barry Sanders 10.00
10 John Elway 12.00
11 Reggie White 2.00
12 Jim Kelly 2.00
13 Thurman Thomas 2.00
14 Dan Marino 20.00
15 Brett Favre 20.00

1995 SkyBox

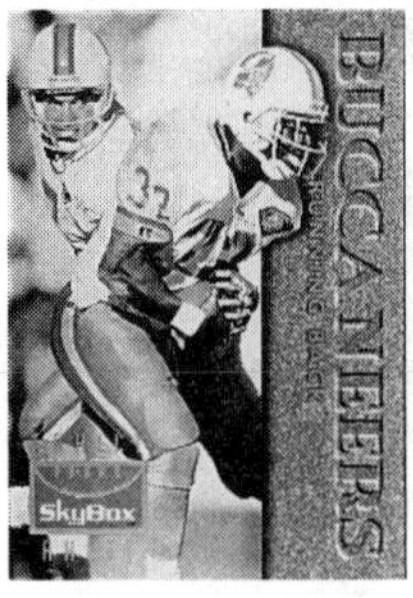

SkyBox Premium football for 1995 includes 200 cards, comprised of 120 veteran players, 40 rookies, 10 Style Points, 10 Mirror Images and four each for the Jacksonville and Carolina expansion teams. Each card has a color action photo of the player on the left, with his team name and position along the right side in a sandpaper-colored panel. The player's name is in the lower left corner, with a gold foil SkyBox logo sandwiched in between. The back has a mug shot, biographical information, 1994 and career stats, and a player profile, all against a background of his team's primary color. Insert sets include Paydirt, QuickStrike, The Promise and Prime Time Rookies. Also, Premium Moments merchandise cards, offering collectors a chance to purchase autographed memorabilia, were included one per hobby pack. In every sixth retail pack, the cards are replaced by a decoder game card called Great Men Make Great Moments Make Great Cards, which could be decoded at special displays at participating hobby shops.

MT
Complete Set (200): 20.00
Common Player: .10
Minor Stars: .20
Pack (10): 1.50
Wax Box (36): 42.00
1 Garrison Hearst .20
2 Dave Krieg .10
3 Rob Moore .10
4 Eric Swann .10
5 Larry Centers .10
6 Jeff George .20
7 Craig Heyward .10
8 Terance Mathis .10
9 Eric Metcalf .10
10 Jim Kelly .20
11 Andre Reed .10
12 Bruce Smith .10
13 Thurman Thomas .20
14 Randy Baldwin .10
15 Don Beebe .10
16 Barry Foster .10
17 Lamar Lathon .10
18 Frank Reich .10
19 Jeff Graham .10
20 Raymont Harris .10
21 Lewis Tillman .10
22 Michael Timpson .10
23 *Jeff Blake* .50
24 Carl Pickens .20
25 Darnay Scott .50
26 Dan Wilkinson .10
27 Derrick Alexander .25
28 Leroy Hoard .10
29 Antonio Langham .10
30 Andre Rison .20
31 Eric Turner .10
32 Troy Aikman 1.00
33 Michael Irvin .30
34 Daryl Johnston .10
35 Emmitt Smith 2.00
36 John Elway .40
37 Glyn Milburn .10
38 Anthony Miller .10
39 Shannon Sharpe .10
40 Scott Mitchell .10
41 Herman Moore .20
42 Barry Sanders 2.00
43 Chris Spielman .10
44 Edgar Bennett .10
45 Robert Brooks .10
46 Brett Favre 2.00
47 Reggie White .20
48 Mel Gray .10
49 Haywood Jeffires .10
50 Webster Slaughter .10
51 Craig Erickson .10
52 Quentin Coryatt .10
53 Sean Dawkins .10
54 Marshall Faulk 1.00
55 Steve Beuerlein .10
56 Reggie Cobb .10
57 Desmond Howard .10
58 Ernest Givins .10
59 Jeff Lageman .10
60 Marcus Allen .20
61 Steve Bono .25
62 Greg Hill .25
63 Derrick Thomas .20
64 Tim Bowens .10
65 Irving Fryar .10
66 Eric Green .10
67 Terry Kirby .10
68 Dan Marino 2.00
69 O.J. McDuffie .10
70 Bernie Parmalee .25
71 Terry Allen .10
72 Cris Carter .20
73 Quadry Ismail .10
74 Warren Moon .20
75 Jake Reed .10
76 Drew Bledsoe 1.00
77 Vincent Brisby .10
78 Ben Coates .10
79 Dave Meggett .10
80 Mario Bates .30
81 Jim Everett .10
82 Michael Haynes .10
83 Tyrone Hughes .10
84 Dave Brown .10
85 Rodney Hampton .10
86 Thomas Lewis .10
87 Herschel Walker .10
88 Mike Sherrard .10
89 Boomer Esiason .10
90 Aaron Glenn .10
91 Johnny Johnson .10
92 Johnny Mitchell .10
93 Ron Moore .10
94 Tim Brown .20
95 Raghib Ismail .10
96 Jeff Hostetler .20
97 Chester McGlockton .10
98 Fred Barnett .10
99 Randall Cunningham .10
100 Charlie Garner .10
101 Ricky Watters .20
102 Calvin Williams .10
103 Charles Johnson .30
104 Bam Morris .10
105 Neil O'Donnell .10
106 Rod Woodson .10
107 Jerome Bettis .30
108 Troy Drayton .10
109 Sean Gilbert .10
110 Chris Miller .10
111 Leonard Russell .10
112 Ronnie Harmon .10
113 Stan Humphries .20
114 Shawn Jefferson .10
115 Natrone Means .20
116 Junior Seau .20
117 William Floyd .40
118 Brent Jones .10
119 Jerry Rice 1.00
120 Deion Sanders 1.00
121 Dana Stubblefield .10
122 Bryant Young .10
123 Steve Young 1.00
124 Brian Blades .10
125 Cortez Kennedy .10
126 Rick Mirer .40
127 Ricky Proehl .10
128 Chris Warren .20
129 Horace Copeland .10
130 Trent Dilfer .50
131 Alvin Harper .20
132 Jackie Harris .10
133 Hardy Nickerson .10
134 Errict Rhett .20
135 Henry Ellard .10
136 Brian Mitchell .10
137 Heath Shuler .75
138 Tydus Winans .10
139 Drew Bledsoe, Brett Favre 1.00
140 Marshall Faulk, William Floyd 1.00
141 Brett Favre, Trent Dilfer .50
142 Dan Marino, Brett Favre 1.00
143 Errict Rhett, Trent Dilfer .50
144 Jerry Rice, Eric Turner .50
145 Andre Rison, Eric Turner .10
146 Barry Sanders, Dave Meggett .50
147 Emmitt Smith, Daryl Johnston .75
148 Steve Young, Brett Favre 1.00
149 Emmitt Smith, Errict Rhett .75
150 Barry Sanders, Marshall Faulk 1.00
151 Jerry Rice, Darnay Scott .50
152 Daryl Johnston, William Floyd .25
153 Dan Marino, Trent Dilfer 1.00
154 John Elway, Heath Shuler .40
155 Natrone Means, Bam Morris .30
156 Dan Wilkinson, Reggie White .10
157 Rodney Hampton, Mario Bates .10
158 Marvin Jones, Junior Seau .10
159 *Ki-Jana Carter* .50
160 *Tony Boselli* .20
161 *Steve McNair* 4.00
162 *Michael Westbrook* 1.50
163 *Kerry Collins* 2.00
164 *Kevin Carter* .20
165 *Mike Mamula* .20
166 *Joey Galloway* 3.00
167 *Kyle Brady* .20
168 *J.J. Stokes* 1.50
169 *Warren Sapp* .75
170 *Rob Johnson* 3.00
171 *Tyrone Wheatley* .75
172 *Napoleon Kaufman* 3.00
173 *James Stewart* 3.00
174 *Joe Aska* .25
175 *Rashaan Salaam* .40
176 *Tyrone Poole* .20
177 *Ty Law* .20
178 *Dino Philyaw* .20
179 *Mark Bruener* .20
180 *Derrick Brooks* .20
181 *Jack Jackson* .20
182 *Ray Zellars* .20
183 *Eddie Goines* .20
184 *Chris Sanders* .40
185 *Charlie Simmons* .20
186 *Lee DeRamus* .20
187 *Frank Sanders* .30
188 *Rodney Thomas* .20

189	*Steve Stenstrom*	.20
190	*Stoney Case*	.25
191	*Tyrone Davis*	.20
192	*Kordell Stewart*	6.00
193	*Christian Fauria*	.25
194	*Todd Collins*	.20
195	*Sherman Williams*	.20
196	*Lovell Pinckney*	.20
197	*Eric Zeier*	.20
198	*Zack Crockett*	.20
199	Checklist A	.10
200	Checklist B	.10

1995 SkyBox Inside the Numbers

Inside the Numbers featured 20 players on a design that was very similar to the regular-issue set. These were seeded at a rate of one per retail pack.

		MT
Complete Set (20):		25.00
Common Player:		.40
1	William Floyd	.75
2	Marshall Faulk	1.50
3	Warren Moon	.75
4	Cris Carter	.75
5	Deion Sanders	1.50
6	Drew Bledsoe	2.50
7	Natrone Means	1.00
8	Herschel Walker	.40
9	Ben Coates	.75
10	Mel Gray	.40
11	Barry Sanders	3.00
12	Steve Young	2.00
13	Rashaan Salaam	2.00
14	Andre Reed	.40
15	Tyrone Hughes	.40
16	Eric Turner	.40
17	Ki-Jana Carter	2.00
18	Dan Marino	5.00
19	Errict Rhett	1.50
20	Jerry Rice	2.50

1995 SkyBox Paydirt

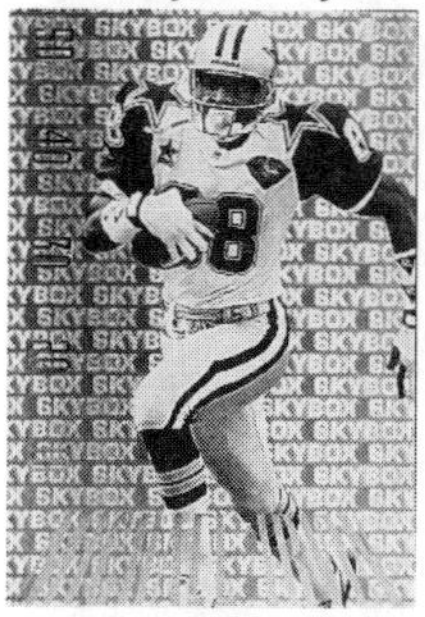

These 1995 SkyBox Premium football inserts feature 30 of the top NFL players who can put the ball in the end zone. Each card front has a color action photo, with the player's name at the bottom in gold foil. Gold foil yard markers run along the left side of the card, which has a prismatic background which alternates between saying SkyBox and Paydirt. The card back is numbered with a "PD" prefix and features a square in the upper right corner with a photo inside, plus a brief description of the player's talents below. "Paydirt" is written along the left side of the card. Cards were random inserts, one every four packs.

		MT
Complete Set (30):		70.00
Common Gold Player:		1.00
Minor Gold Stars:		2.00
Comp. Colors Set (30):		700.00
Colors Cards:		5x-10x
1	Troy Aikman	4.00
2	J.J. Stokes	3.00
3	Ki-Jana Carter	3.00
4	Steve McNair	4.50
5	Jerome Bettis	1.00
6	Tim Brown	1.00
7	Cris Carter	1.00
8	John Elway	3.00
9	Marshall Faulk	2.00
10	Brett Favre	8.00
11	Michael Westbrook	2.50
12	Rodney Hampton	1.00
13	Michael Irvin	2.00
14	Dan Marino	8.00
15	Natrone Means	2.00
16	David Meggett	1.00
17	Joey Galloway	4.00
18	Herman Moore	2.00
19	Bam Morris	1.00
20	Carl Pickens	2.00
21	Errict Rhett	2.00
22	Kerry Collins	2.00
23	Barry Sanders	5.00
24	Deion Sanders	3.00
25	Emmitt Smith	8.00
26	Thurman Thomas	2.00
27	Ricky Watters	1.00
28	Rod Woodson	1.00
29	Chris Warren	2.00
30	Steve Young	4.00

1995 SkyBox The Promise

This 1995 SkyBox Premium insert set features 18 young stars. The cards, included one per 24 packs, have a color action photo on the front, with a large ghosted head shot as the background. The card has a gold metallic effect, and uses gold foil for the insert set name. The back is horizontal and includes a small photo and a brief summary of the player's accomplishments. Cards are numbered with a "P" prefix in the upper right corner.

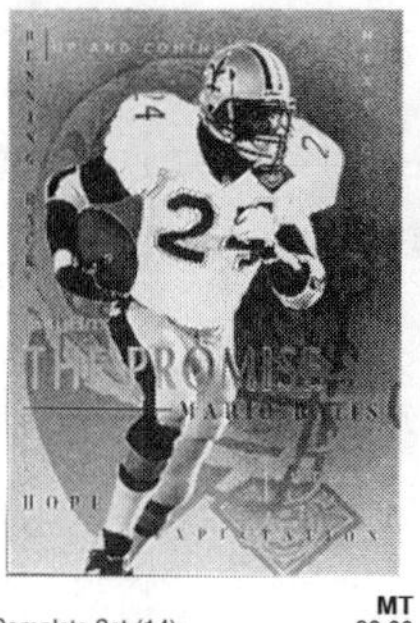

		MT
Complete Set (14):		20.00
Common Player:		2.00
Minor Stars:		4.00
1	Derrick Alexander	4.00
2	Mario Bates	4.00
3	Trent Dilfer	4.00
4	Marshall Faulk	6.00
5	William Floyd	4.00
6	Aaron Glenn	4.00
7	Raymont Harris	4.00
8	Greg Hill	4.00
9	Charles Johnson	4.00
10	Bam Morris	4.00
11	Errict Rhett	2.00
12	Darnay Scott	2.00
13	Heath Shuler	2.00
14	Dan Wilkinson	4.00

1995 SkyBox Quick Strike

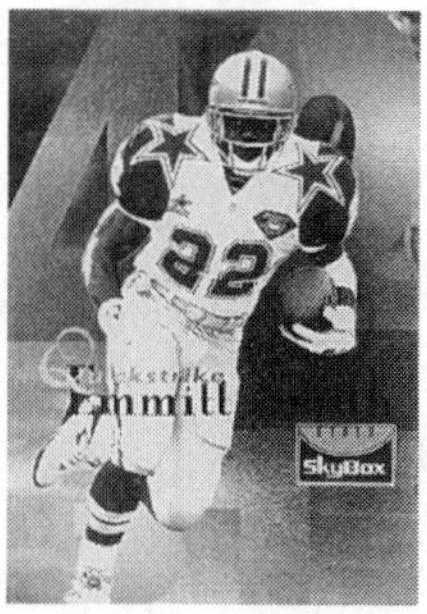

These 1995 SkyBox Premium inserts feature 10 of the NFL's most potent scoring threats. The cards were random inserts, one per 12 packs. The card front has an action photo of the player, against a metallic-like background which has the score of one of his team's wins in which he played a prominent role. The insert set and SkyBox logos are stamped in gold foil. The horizontal back has a photo and a brief summary of the game. Cards are numbered with a "Q" prefix.

		MT
Complete Set (10):		40.00
Common Player:		2.00
1	Chris Warren	2.00
2	Marshall Faulk	3.00
3	William Floyd	2.00
4	Jerry Rice	7.00
5	Eric Turner	2.00
6	Tim Brown	2.00
7	Deion Sanders	2.00
8	Emmitt Smith	14.00
9	Rod Woodson	2.00
10	Steve Young	7.00

1995 SkyBox Rookie Receivers

This eight-card set was inserted as a complete set in every retail box. The cards are identical in design to the rookies in the regular-issue set, except for the numbering which is "X" of 8.

		MT
Complete Set (8):		5.00
Common Player:		.50
1	Michael Westbrook	1.00
2	Joey Galloway	1.50
3	J.J. Stokes	1.00
4	Frank Sanders	.75
5	Chris Sanders	.75
6	Tyrone Davis	.50
7	Jimmy Oliver	.50
NNO	Cover/Checklist Card	.50

1995 SkyBox Prime Time Rookies

These 1995 SkyBox Premium inserts feature 10 rookies who might be destined for greatness in the NFL. These cards were included one per 96 packs and are numbered using a "PT" prefix. The card front has a photo of the player superimposed against a clockface. Gold foil stamping is used for the player's name and insert set name, which appears at the bottom of the card in script. The horizontal back has a photo on one side, and biographical and collegiate information on the other, all against a background of cogs.

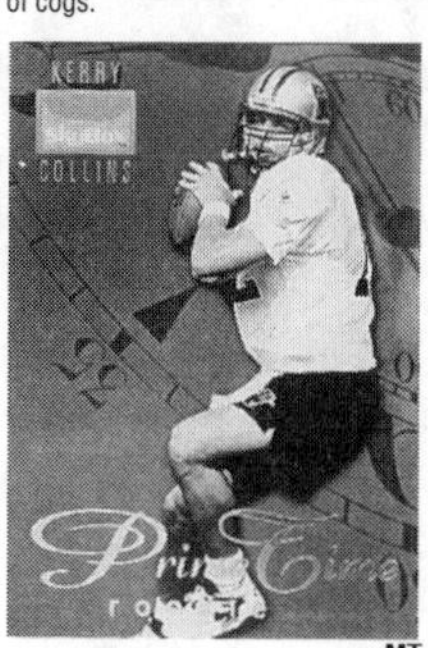

		MT
Complete Set (10):		190.00
Common Player:		10.00
1	Ki-Jana Carter	10.00
2	Kerry Collins	15.00
3	Joey Galloway	20.00
4	Steve McNair	35.00
5	Rashaan Salaam	15.00
6	James Stewart	25.00
7	J.J. Stokes	15.00
8	Rodney Thomas	10.00
9	Michael Westbrook	15.00
10	Tyrone Wheatley	10.00

1995 SkyBox Impact

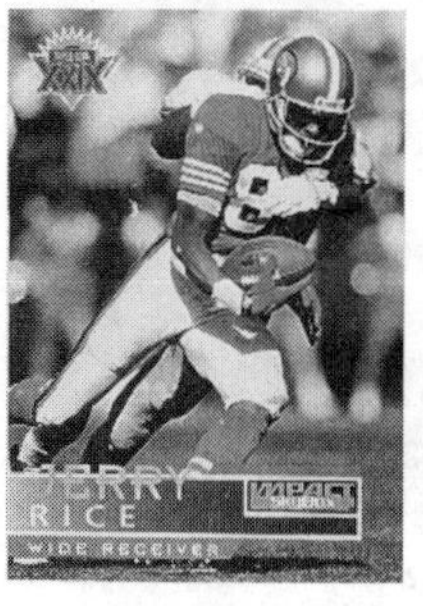

SkyBox Impact's 1995 NFL football set has 200 cards, including 30 top rookies, five cards each for the expansion Jacksonville Jaguars and Carolina Panthers, and subsets such as Specialists and Super Sophs. Each UV-coated front has a full-bleed color action photo, with the player's name and position at the bottom, flanked by a SkyBox logo. The player's first name is stamped in gold foil. The card back is horizontal, with a photo on the right with career stats printed over it. All 49ers cards have a Super Bowl Champion logo on them. The card number is in a black circle in the upper right corner. The left side of the card has the player's name at the top in team color-coded bars. Below follows a team logo and biographical information, then a brief player profile. Insert sets include the hobby-only Future Hall of Famers, Impact Power, Fox More Attitude, and Countdown to Impact. Included in each pack is a SkyBox/NFL on Fox Play Action Match & Win instant win game card, which gave collectors a chance to win tickets and a VIP trip to the 1995-96 NFC Championship Game, NFL on Fox varsity jackets, T-shirts, caps and 1995 SkyBox Premium NFL packs. In addition, there is a redemption for a SkyMotion card, which captures three seconds of actual game action. There are two cards, both of Brett Favre (one running, one passing). One is available through the redemption card (one per 360 packs), the other through an on-wrapper offer.

		MT
Complete Set (200):		15.00
Common Player:		.05
Minor Stars:		.10
Hobby Pack (12):		1.50
Hobby Wax Box (36):		45.00
Retail Pack (12):		1.25
Retail Wax Box (36):		38.00
1	Garrison Hearst	.10
2	Ron Moore	.05
3	Eric Swann	.05
4	Aeneas Williams	.05
5	Jeff George	.05
6	Craig Heyward	.05
7	Terrance Mathis	.05
8	Andre Rison	.10
9	Cornelius Bennett	.05
10	Jim Kelly	.10
11	Andre Reed	.05
12	Bruce Smith	.05
13	Thurman Thomas	.15
14	Frank Reich	.05
15	Lamar Lathon	.05
16	Darrien Connor	.05
17	Randy Baldwin	.05
18	Don Beebe	.05
19	Mark Carrier	.05
20	Jeff Graham	.05
21	Raymont Harris	.15
22	Alonzo Spellman	.05
23	Lewis Tillman	.05
24	Steve Walsh	.05
25	*Jeff Blake*	.50
26	Carl Pickens	.05
27	Darnay Scott	.40
28	Dan Wilkinson	.05
29	Derrick Alexander	.20
30	Leroy Hoard	.05
31	Antonio Langham	.05
32	Vinny Testaverde	.05
33	Eric Turner	.05
34	Troy Aikman	.75
35	Charles Haley	.05
36	Alvin Harper	.05
37	Michael Irvin	.20
38	Daryl Johnston	.05
39	Jay Novacek	.05
40	Leon Lett	.05
41	Emmitt Smith	1.50
42	John Elway	.25
43	Glyn Milburn	.05
44	Anthony Miller	.05
45	Leonard Russell	.05
46	Shannon Sharpe	.10
47	Scott Mitchell	.05
48	Herman Moore	.10
49	Barry Sanders	1.00
50	Chris Spielman	.05
51	Edgar Bennett	.05
52	Robert Brooks	.05
53	Brett Favre	1.50
54	Bryce Paup	.05
55	Sterling Sharpe	.10
56	Reggie White	.10
57	Ray Childress	.05
58	Haywood Jeffires	.05
59	Webster Slaughter	.05
60	Lorenzo White	.05
61	Trev Alberts	.05
62	Quentin Coryatt	.05
63	Sean Dawkins	.15
64	Marshall Faulk	.50
65	Jeff Lageman	.05
66	Steve Beuerlein	.05
67	Desmond Howard	.05
68	Kelvin Martin	.05
69	Reggie Cobb	.05
70	Marcus Allen	.10
71	Greg Hill	.20
72	Joe Montana	.75
73	Neil Smith	.05
74	Derrick Thomas	.10
75	Tim Brown	.10
76	Rocket Ismail	.05
77	Jeff Hostetler	.05
78	Chester McGlockton	.05
79	Harvey Williams	.05
80	Tim Bowens	.05
81	Irving Fryar	.05
82	Keith Jackson	.05
83	Terry Kirby	.05
84	Dan Marino	1.50
85	O.J. McDuffie	.05
86	Bernie Parmalee	.15
87	Terry Allen	.05
88	Cris Carter	.10
89	Quadry Ismail	.05
90	Warren Moon	.10
91	Jake Reed	.05
92	Drew Bledsoe	1.00
93	Vincent Brisby	.05
94	Ben Coates	.05
95	Michael Timpson	.05
96	Jim Everett	.05
97	Michael Haynes	.05
98	Willie Roaf	.05
99	Michael Brooks	.05
100	Dave Brown	.05
101	Rodney Hampton	.05
102	Thomas Lewis	.05
103	Dave Meggett	.05
104	Boomer Esiason	.05
105	Johnny Johnson	.05
106	Johnny Mitchell	.05
107	Rob Moore	.05
108	Fred Barnett	.05
109	Randall Cunningham	.10
110	Charlie Garner	.05
111	Herschel Walker	.05
112	Barry Foster	.05
113	Eric Green	.05
114	Charles Johnson	.20
115	Greg Lloyd	.05
116	Bam Morris	.35
117	Neil O'Donnell	.10
118	Rod Woodson	.05
119	Willie Anderson	.05
120	Jerome Bettis	.25
121	Troy Drayton	.05
122	Sean Gilbert	.05
123	Ronnie Harmon	.05
124	Stan Humphries	.10
125	Shawn Jefferson	.05
126	Natrone Means	.30
127	Leslie O'Neal	.05
128	Junior Seau	.10
129	William Floyd	.25
130	Brent Jones	.05
131	Jerry Rice	.50
132	Deion Sanders	.40
133	Dana Stubblefield	.05
134	Ricky Watters	.05
135	Bryant Young	.05
136	Steve Young	.50
137	Brian Blades	.05
138	Cortez Kennedy	.10
139	Rick Mirer	.30
140	Chris Warren	.05
141	Horace Copeland	.05
142	Trent Dilfer	.30
143	Hardy Nickerson	.05
144	Errict Rhett	.10
145	Henry Ellard	.05
146	Brian Mitchell	.05
147	Heath Shuler	.25
148	Tydus Winans	.05
149	Steve Tasker	.05
150	Jeff Burris	.05
151	Tyrone Hughes	.05
152	Mel Gray	.05
153	Kevin Williams	.05
154	Andre Coleman	.05
155	Corey Sawyer	.05
156	Darrien Gordon	.05
157	Aaron Glenn	.05
158	Eric Metcalf	.05
159	Errict Rhett	.40
160	Marshall Faulk	.75
161	Darnay Scott	.05
162	William Floyd	.10
163	Charlie Garner	.05
164	Heath Shuler	.40
165	Trent Dilfer	.20
166	Willie McGinest	.05
167	Bam Morris	.20
168	Mario Bates	.05
169	*Ki-Jana Carter*	.50
170	*Tony Boselli*	.10
171	*Steve McNair*	2.50
172	*Michael Westbrook*	.75
173	*Kerry Collins*	1.00
174	*Kevin Carter*	.10
175	*Mike Mamula*	.10
176	*Joseph Galloway*	1.50
177	*Kyle Brady*	.10
178	*J.J. Stokes*	.75
179	*Warren Sapp*	.50
180	*Rob Johnson*	2.00
181	*Tyrone Wheatley*	.50
182	*Napoleon Kaufman*	2.00
183	*James Stewart*	1.25
184	*Dino Philyaw*	.10
185	*Rashaan Salaam*	.40
186	*Tyrone Poole*	.10
187	*Ty Law*	.10
188	*Joe Aska*	.10
189	*Mark Bruener*	.10
190	*Derrick Brooks*	.10
191	*Jack Jackson*	.10
192	*Ray Zellars*	.10
193	*Eddie Goines*	.10
194	*Chris Sanders*	.30
195	*Charlie Simmons*	.10
196	*Lee DeRamus*	.10
197	*Frank Sanders*	.30
198	*Rodney Thomas*	.30
199	Checklist A	.05
200	Checklist B	.05
M1	Brett Favre SKY (SkyMotion)	25.00

1995 SkyBox Impact Countdown

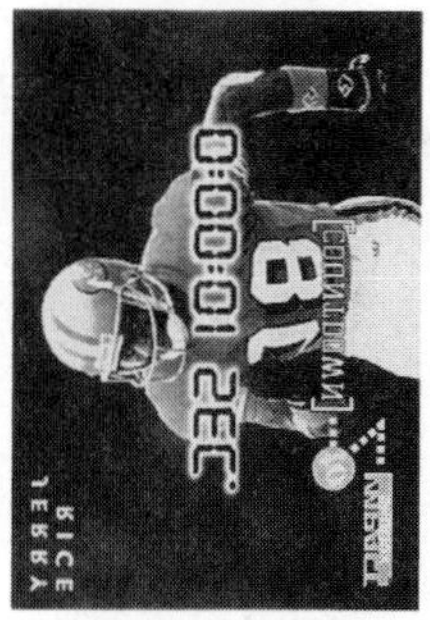

These 10 cards address some of the more unique stats of the NFL's best players in a whole new way. For example, how many minutes did it actually take for Barry Sanders to run for a league-leading 1,883 yards? His insert card, like the rest, will provide the foiled answer on the front. The cards are horizontal, with the set logo and brand logo toward the bottom of the card. The player's name is in the upper right corner. The card back has a photo on one side, and a brief explanation of the unique stat which is being featured. A card number, using a "C" prefix, is in a red circle in the upper right corner.

		MT
Complete Set (10):		60.00
Common Player:		3.00
1	Barry Sanders	10.00
2	Jerry Rice	7.00
3	Steve Young	7.00
4	Troy Aikman	7.00
5	Dan Marino	15.00
6	Emmitt Smith	15.00
7	Junior Seau	3.00
8	Drew Bledsoe	7.00
9	Brett Favre	15.00
10	Deion Sanders	5.00

1995 SkyBox Impact Future Hall of Famers

This 1995 SkyBox Impact insert set presents eight solid candidates who are on their way to the Pro Football Hall of Fame. The cards were random inserts in hobby packs only, one per 60 packs. Cards are numbered using an "HF" prefix; fronts have "Hall of Fame" written on them.

		MT
Complete Set (7):		180.00
Common Player:		15.00
#2 was never made.		
1	Jerry Rice	25.00
3	Steve Young	25.00
4	John Elway	15.00
5	Dan Marino	50.00
6	Emmitt Smith	50.00
7	Barry Sanders	25.00
8	Troy Aikman	25.00

1995 SkyBox Impact Fox More Attitude

These 15 cards include seven young NFL veterans and eight 1995 first-round draft picks who represent a fresh new attitude of SkyBox and the NFL on Fox. Cards were seeded one per nine packs of 1995 SkyBox Impact product. The card front has a color action photo of the player with a football field for a background. "Same Game" and "More Attitude," in foil, are written along the left side of the card, as is the player's name, which is also stamped in foil. The "NFL on Fox" logo is stamped in foil in the lower right corner. The card back has a parallelogram in the center which contains a color photo towards the top, with a summary of the player's attitude underneath. There's biographical information along the left side of the card; a card number in the upper right in a black circle, and the player's name are along the right side. The card number uses an "F" prefix.

		MT
Complete Set (15):		40.00
Common Player:		2.00
1	Ki-Jana Carter	2.00
2	Steve McNair	6.00
3	Michael Westbrook	4.00
4	Kerry Collins	3.00
5	Joseph Galloway	3.00
6	J.J. Stokes	2.00
7	Tyrone Wheatley	3.00
8	Rashaan Salaam	3.00
9	Trent Dilfer	3.00
10	William Floyd	3.00
11	Marshall Faulk	3.00
12	Errict Rhett	3.00
13	Heath Shuler	3.00
14	Drew Bledsoe	7.00
15	Ben Coates	3.00

1995 SkyBox Impact Power

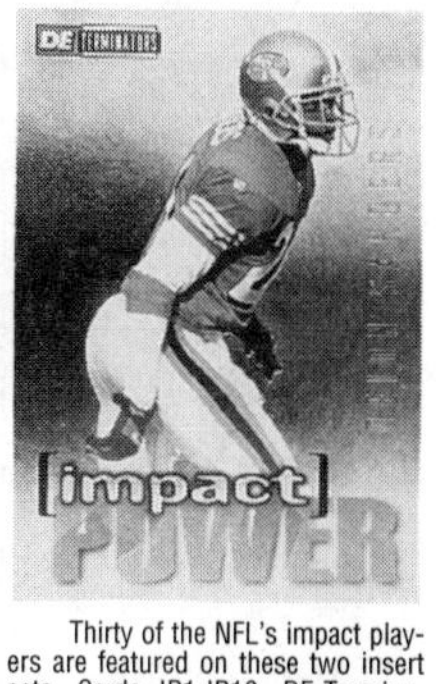

Thirty of the NFL's impact players are featured on these two insert sets. Cards IP1-IP10, DE-Terminators, are devoted to 10 defensive players who make big hits. Cards IP11-IP30, Stars of the Ozone, are devoted to 20 offensive stars who make big plays. There was, however, no card made for IP25. Cards were seeded one per three packs of 1995 SkyBox Impact product. The card fronts for each set are similar; both have foil backgrounds, have the set icon in the upper left corner and have the player's name in foil along the right side of the card. The backs are similar, too. There's a smaller color photo in a box in the upper right corner; a card number, using an "IP" prefix, is in a black circle in the opposite corner. The player's name and "Impact Power" are written along the left side. An assessment of the player's skills is below the photo.

		MT
Complete Set (30):		25.00
Common Player:		.50
Minor Stars:		1.00
IP25 was never made.		
1	Junior Seau	1.00
2	Reggie White	1.00
3	Eric Swann	.50
4	Bruce Smith	.50
5	Rod Woodson	.50
6	Derrick Thomas	1.00
7	Chester McGlockton	.50
8	Cortez Kennedy	.50
9	Deion Sanders	1.50
10	Bryan Cox	.50
11	Jerry Rice	3.00
12	Sterling Sharpe	1.00
13	Tim Brown	1.00
14	Marshall Faulk	1.00
15	Brett Favre	5.00
16	Chris Warren	.50
17	Herman Moore	.50
18	Steve Young	3.00
19	Andre Rison	1.00
20	Thurman Thomas	1.00
21	Marcus Allen	1.00
22	Michael Irvin	1.00
23	Emmitt Smith	5.00
24	John Elway	2.00
26	Barry Sanders	5.00
27	Troy Aikman	3.00
28	Natrone Means	1.00
29	Ben Coates	.50
30	Errict Rhett	1.00

1995 SkyBox Impact Rookie Running Backs

Rookie Running Backs was available as a set and inserted into each retail box. It included eight different rookies, with designs very similar to the rookies in the base set, except for the numbering (1-8), and one unnumbered header card.

		MT
Complete Set (9):		7.00
Common Player:		.50

1	Ki-Jana Carter	1.00
2	Tyrone Wheatley	.50
3	Napoleon Kaufman	.75
4	James O. Stewart	.50
5	Rashaan Salaam	1.25
6	Ray Zellars	.50
7	Rodney Thomas	.75
8	Curtis Martin	3.00
NNO	Cover/Checklist Card	.30

1995 SkyBox Impact Fox Announcers

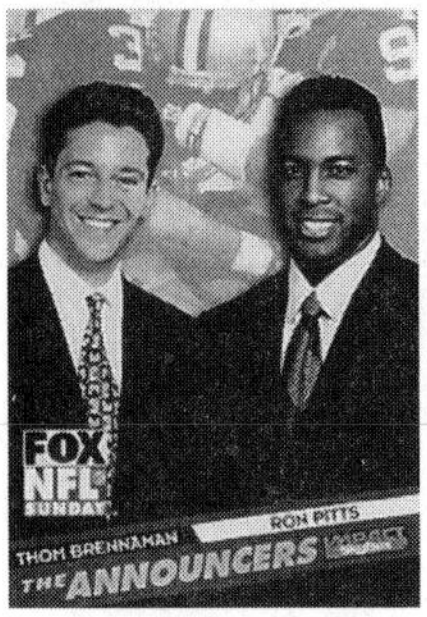

This seven-card set featured FOX's NFL Sunday announcers and was done to promote SyBox's ties to the network. Fronts pictured teams of announcers, while the back contained information about them. There was also an unnumbered header card included.

		MT
Complete Set (8):		10.00
Common Player:		1.00
1	Pat Summerall, John Madden	3.00
2	James Brown, Jimmy Johnson, Terry Bradshaw, Howie Long	3.00
3	Dick Stockton, Matt Millen	1.00
4	Kevin Harlan, Jerry Glanville	1.00
5	Joe Buck, Tim Green	1.00
6	Kenny Albert, Anthony Munoz	1.50
7	Thom Brennaman, Ron Pitts	1.00
NNO	Cover Card	1.00

1996 SkyBox

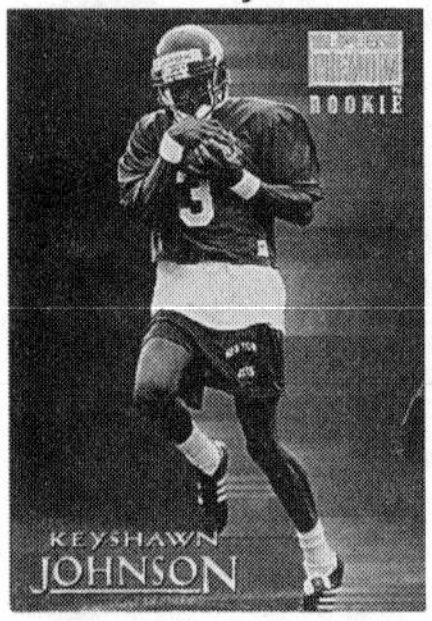

SkyBox Premium was a 250-card set that marked the fifth anniversary of the product. The regular-issue set includes 178 regular player cards, 50 rookies (179-228), 10 Prime Time Rookie Retrospectives (229-238), which are quad cards, 10 Panorama (239-248) and two checklists (249-250). SkyBox Premium was issued in 10-card packs and contains the final two cards in the Brett Favre MVP Series (cards 1, 2, 3 were in Impact), side B of the Favre Lenticular Exchange card, six SkyBox spokesperson autographs and a Rubies parallel set. Inserts include: V, Next Big Thing, Thunder and Lightning, Close-Ups and Prime Time Rookies.

		MT
Complete Set (250):		25.00
Common Player:		.10
Minor Stars:		.20
Comp. Rubie Set (228):		1800.
Rubie Stars:		20x-40x
Rubie Rookies:		15x-30x
Pack (10):		2.50
Wax Box (24):		45.00
1	Larry Centers	.10
2	Boomer Esiason	.10
3	Garrison Hearst	.10
4	Rob Moore	.10
5	Frank Sanders	.20
6	Eric Swann	.10
7	Bert Emanuel	.10
8	Jeff George	.10
9	Craig Heyward	.10
10	Terance Mathis	.10
11	Eric Metcalf	.10
12	Derrick Alexander	.10
13	Leroy Hoard	.10
14	Michael Jackson	.10
15	Vinny Testaverde	.10
16	Eric Turner	.10
17	Darick Holmes	.40
18	Jim Kelly	.20
19	Bryce Paup	.10
20	Andre Reed	.10
21	Bruce Smith	.10
22	Thurman Thomas	.20
23	Tim Tindale	.10
24	Mark Carrier	.10
25	Kerry Collins	.50
26	Willie Green	.10
27	Lamar Lathon	.10
28	Tyrone Poole	.10
29	Curtis Conway	.10
30	Bryan Cox	.10
31	Erik Kramer	.10
32	Nate Lewis	.10
33	Rashaan Salaam	.75
34	Alonzo Spellman	.10
35	Michael Timpson	.10
36	Jeff Blake	.75
37	Ki-Jana Carter	.20
38	David Dunn	.10
39	Carl Pickens	.10
40	Darnay Scott	.10
41	Troy Aikman	1.50
42	Charles Haley	.10
43	Michael Irvin	.10
44	Daryl Johnston	.10
45	Jay Novacek	.10
46	Deion Sanders	1.00
47	Emmitt Smith	2.50
48	Kevin Williams	.10
49	Steve Atwater	.10
50	Terrell Davis	1.25
51	John Elway	.75
52	Anthony Miller	.10
53	Shannon Sharpe	.10
54	Mike Sherrard	.10
55	Scott Mitchell	.10
56	Herman Moore	.50
57	Johnnie Morton	.10
58	Brett Perriman	.10
59	Barry Sanders	1.75
60	Edgar Bennett	.10
61	Robert Brooks	.10
62	Mark Chmura	.25
63	Brett Favre	2.50
64	Antonio Freeman	.10
65	Keith Jackson	.10
66	Reggie White	.20
67	Chris Chandler	.10
68	Mel Gray	.10
69	Steve McNair	1.00
70	Chris Sanders	.40
71	Rodney Thomas	.30
72	Quentin Coryatt	.10
73	Sean Dawkins	.10
74	Ken Dilger	.10
75	Marshall Faulk	.75
76	Jim Harbaugh	.10
77	Lamont Warren	.10
78	Tony Boselli	.10
79	Mark Brunell	1.00
80	Willie Jackson	.10
81	Natrone Means	.10
82	James Stewart	.10
83	Marcus Allen	.10
84	Kimble Anders	.10
85	Steve Bono	.10
86	Lake Dawson	.10
87	Neil Smith	.10
88	Derrick Thomas	.10
89	Tamarick Vanover	.75
90	Fred Barnett	.10
91	Terry Kirby	.10
92	Dan Marino	2.50
93	O.J. McDuffie	.10
94	Bernie Parmalee	.10
95	Richmond Webb	.10
96	Cris Carter	.10
97	Qadry Ismail	.10
98	Scottie Graham	.10
99	Warren Moon	.10
100	Jake Reed	.10
101	Robert Smith	.10
102	Drew Bledsoe	1.25
103	Vincent Brisby	.10
104	Ben Coates	.10
105	Curtis Martin	2.00
106	David Meggett	.10
107	Chris Slade	.10
108	Mario Bates	.10
109	Jim Everett	.10
110	Michael Haynes	.10
111	Tyrone Hughes	.10
112	Renaldo Turnbull	.10
113	Dave Brown	.10
114	Chris Calloway	.10
115	Rodney Hampton	.10
116	Thomas Lewis	.10
117	Tyrone Wheatley	.10
118	Kyle Brady	.10
119	Hugh Douglas	.10
120	Aaron Glenn	.10
121	Jeff Graham	.10
122	Adrian Murrell	.10
123	Neil O'Donnell	.10
124	Tim Brown	.10
125	Nolan Harrison	.10
126	Billy Joe Hobert	.10
127	Jeff Hostetler	.10
128	Napoleon Kaufman	.30
129	Chester McGlockton	.10
130	Harvey Williams	.10
131	Charlie Garner	.10
132	Andy Harmon	.10
133	Chris T. Jones	.10
134	Mike Mamula	.10
135	Rodney Peete	.10
136	Bobby Taylor	.10
137	Ricky Watters	.10
138	Jerome Bettis	.20
139	Greg Lloyd	.10
140	Jim Miller	.10
141	Ernie Mills	.10
142	Kordell Stewart	1.25
143	Yancey Thigpen	.30
144	Rod Woodson	.10
145	Andre Coleman	.10
146	Terrell Fletcher	.10
147	*Aaron Hayden*	.30
148	Stan Humphries	.10
149	Junior Seau	.10
150	Isaac Bruce	.75
151	Kevin Carter	.10
152	Todd Kinchen	.10
153	Leslie O'Neal	.10
154	Mark Rypien	.10
155	William Floyd	.10
156	Merton Hanks	.10
157	Brent Jones	.10
158	Derek Loville	.10
159	Ken Norton	.10
160	Jerry Rice	1.50
161	J.J. Stokes	.75
162	Steve Young	1.00
163	Brian Blades	.10
164	Christian Fauria	.10
165	Joey Galloway	1.00
166	Rick Mirer	.10
167	Chris Warren	.20
168	Trent Dilfer	.10
169	Alvin Harper	.10
170	Jackie Harris	.10
171	Hardy Nickerson	.10
172	Errict Rhett	.50
173	Terry Allen	.10
174	Henry Ellard	.10
175	Gus Frerotte	.10
176	Brian Mitchell	.10
177	Heath Shuler	.10
178	Michael Westbrook	.75
179	*Karim Abdul-Jabbar*	.75
180	*Mike Alstott*	1.50
181	*Willie Anderson*	.10
182	*Marco Battaglia*	.10
183	*Tim Biakabutuka*	1.00
184	*Tony Brackens*	.10
185	*Duane Clemons*	.10
186	*Marcus Coleman*	.10
187	*Ernie Conwell*	.10
188	*Chris Darkins*	.10
189	*Stephen Davis*	4.00
190	*Brian Dawkins*	.10
191	*Rickey Dudley*	.30
192	*Jason Dunn*	.20
193	*Bobby Engram*	.30
194	*Daryl Gardener*	.10
195	*Eddie George*	4.00
196	*Terry Glenn*	2.00
197	*Kevin Hardy*	.30
198	*Walt Harris*	.20
199	*Marvin Harrison*	3.00
200	*Bobby Hoying*	1.00
201	*Isreal Ifeanyi*	.10
202	*DeRon Jenkins*	.10
203	*Keyshawn Johnson*	2.50
204	*Lance Johnstone*	.10
205	*Cedric Jones*	.30
206	*Marcus Jones*	.10
207	*Eddie Kennison*	.50
208	*Jevon Langford*	.10
209	*Dedric Mathis*	.10
210	*Jermaine Mayberry*	.10
211	*Leeland McElroy*	.30
212	*Johnny McWilliams*	.10
213	*Ray Mickens*	.10
214	*John Mobley*	.25
215	*Jerald Moore*	.25
216	*Eric Moulds*	2.00
217	*Mushin Muhammad*	1.00
218	*Jonathan Ogden*	.20
219	*Lawrence Phillips*	.75
220	*Kavika Pittman*	.10
221	*Stanley Pritchett*	.50
222	*Simeon Rice*	.30
223	*Detron Smith*	.10
224	*Bryan Still*	.50
225	*Amani Toomer*	.50
226	*Regan Upshaw*	.10
227	*Alex Van Dyke*	.20
228	*Stepfret Williams*	.10
229	Retrospective (Quentin Coryatt, Chester McGlockton, Carl Pickens, Robert Brooks)	.20
230	Retrospective (Dale Carter, Edgar Bennett, Drew Bledsoe, Garrison Hearst)	.40
231	Retrospective (Natrone Means, Rick Mirer, Jerome Bettis, Robert Smith)	.20
232	Retrospective (O.J. McDuffie, Curtis Conway, Marshall Faulk, Greg Hill)	.20
233	Retrospective (Heath Shuler, Trent Dilfer, William Floyd, Charles Johnson)	.20
234	Retrospective (Errict Rhett, Sean Dawkins, Mario Bates, Ki-Jana Carter)	.20
235	Retrospective (Kerry Collins, Steve McNair, Joey Galloway, Rashaan Salaam)	.40
236	Retrospective (J.J. Stokes, Michael Westbrook, Kyle Brady, Kordell Stewart)	.40
237	Retrospective (Keyshawn Johnson, Eddie George, Leeland McElroy, Lawrence Phillips)	.20
238	Retrospective (Bobby Engram, Rickey Dudley, Eric Moulds, Tim Biakabutuka)	.20
239	Panorama Jan. 14, 1996 (Kordell Stewart, Quentin Coryatt)	.40
240	Panorama Nov. 26, 1995 (Robert Brooks)	.20
241	Panorama Nov. 12, 1995 (Henry Jones, Terance Mathis)	.10
242	Panorama Dec. 9, 1995 (Mark Seay, Alfred Pupunu)	.10
243	Panorama Sept. 17, 1995 (Robert Brooks, Willie Beamon)	.20
244	Panorama Oct. 29, 1995 - 49ers Halloween	.10
245	Panorama Oct. 15, 1995	.10
246	Panorama Dec. 31, 1995 (Zack Crockett, Junior Seau)	.20
247	Panorama Jan. 14, 1996 (Kevin Williams, Doug Evans)	.10
248	Panorama Nov. 19, 1995 (Tim Jacobs, Antonio Freeman)	.20
249	Checklist (1-141)	.10
250	Checklist (141-250)	.10

A player's name in *italic* type indicates a rookie card.

1996 SkyBox Rubies

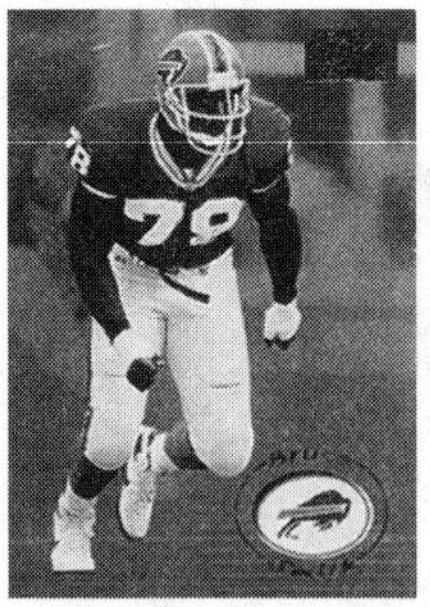

Rubies was a 248-card parallel set (250 minus checklists) that were inserted into hobby boxes under the packs. Rubies awarded collectors that purchased sealed boxes since the person who opened the box would pull a Rubies insert. Rubies are distinguished by ruby foil in place of the gold foil found on common cards.

	MT
Complete Set (228):	1800.
Rubies:	20x-40x

1996 SkyBox V

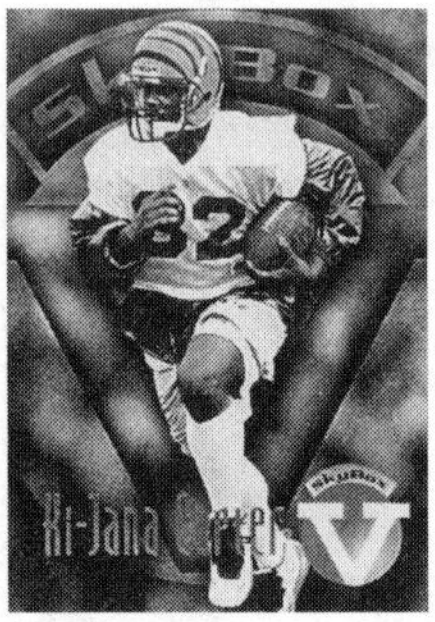

Ten players who changed the game over the last five years are featured in V, which was seeded every 18 packs. This insert celebrates SkyBox's fifth anniversary with die-cut, V-shaped designs.

		MT
Complete Set (10):		40.00
Common Player:		1.50
1	Ki-Jana Carter	3.00
2	Kerry Collins	3.00
3	Trent Dilfer	1.50
4	Joey Galloway	8.00
5	Herman Moore	4.00
6	Errict Rhett	4.00
7	Rashaan Salaam	5.00
8	Deion Sanders	8.00
9	Thurman Thomas	1.50
10	Reggie White	1.50

1996 SkyBox Next Big Thing

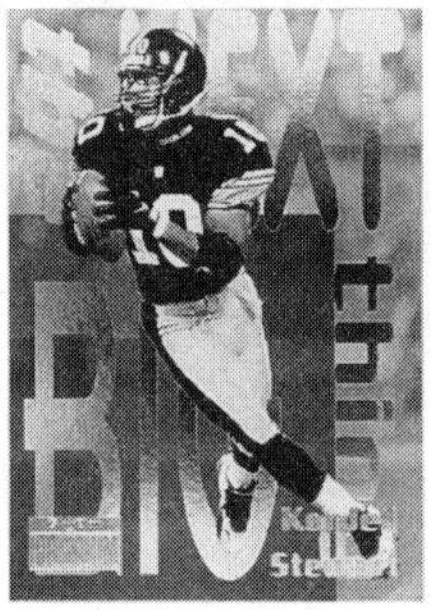

Next Big Thing showcases 15 young players that are expected to produce big things through their careers. Inserted at a one per 40 rate, these inserts feature a multi-colored foil background with the words "Next Big Thing" in bold.

		MT
Complete Set (15):		120.00
Common Player:		4.00
1	Mark Brunell	10.00
2	Rickey Dudley	8.00
3	Bobby Engram	8.00
4	Antonio Freeman	4.00
5	Eddie George	30.00
6	Terry Glenn	15.00
7	Marvin Harrison	12.00
8	Keyshawn Johnson	10.00
9	Napoleon Kaufman	4.00
10	Steve McNair	10.00
11	Alex Molden	4.00
12	Frank Sanders	4.00
13	Kordell Stewart	20.00
14	Amani Toomer	4.00
15	Alex Van Dyke	4.00

1996 SkyBox Thunder and Lightning

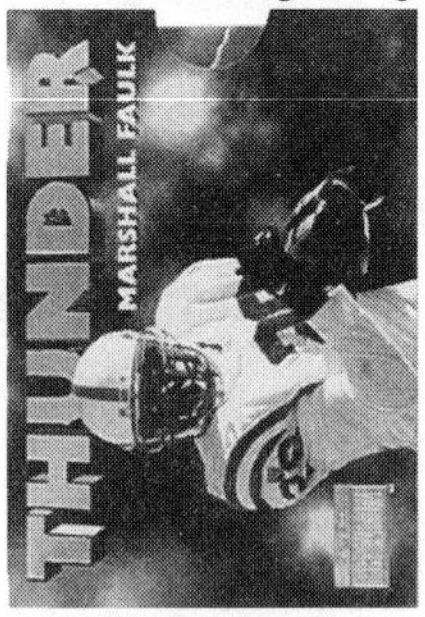

Thunder and Lightning was made up of 20 players featured on 10 different cards (numbered 1-10 a & b) who make lethal 1-2 combinations. Each card is actually a card- within-a-card where the "lightning" player is inserted into the "thunder" card. Thunder and Lightning inserts were found every 72 packs.

		MT
Complete Set (10):		200.00
Common Player:		8.00
1	Emmitt Smith, Troy Aikman	50.00
2	Barry Sanders, Scott Mitchell	25.00
3	Marshall Faulk, Jim Harbaugh	20.00
4	Dan Marino, O.J. McDuffie	40.00
5	Jerry Rice, Steve Young	30.00
6	Jeff Blake, Carl Pickens	8.00
7	Brett Favre, Edgar Bennett	40.00
8	Curtis Martin, Drew Bledsoe	30.00
9	Errict Rhett, Trent Dilfer	8.00
10	Rick Mirer, Chris Warren	8.00

1996 SkyBox Prime-Time Rookies

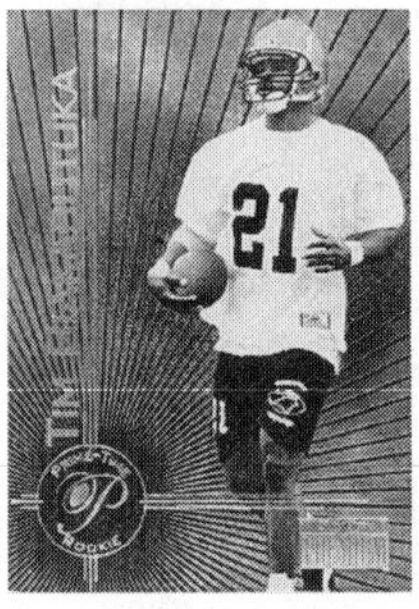

Prime Time Rookies returned to Premium as a hobby-only insert that showcased the top rookies from the 1996 NFL Draft. These inserts were found every 96 packs.

		MT
Complete Set (10):		170.00
Common Player:		12.00
1	Tim Biakabutuka	20.00
2	Rickey Dudley	12.00
3	Bobby Engram	14.00
4	Eddie George	40.00
5	Terry Glenn	35.00
6	Marvin Harrison	20.00
7	Keyshawn Johnson	25.00
8	Leeland McElroy	12.00
9	Eric Moulds	12.00
10	Lawrence Phillips	25.00

1996 SkyBox Close-Ups

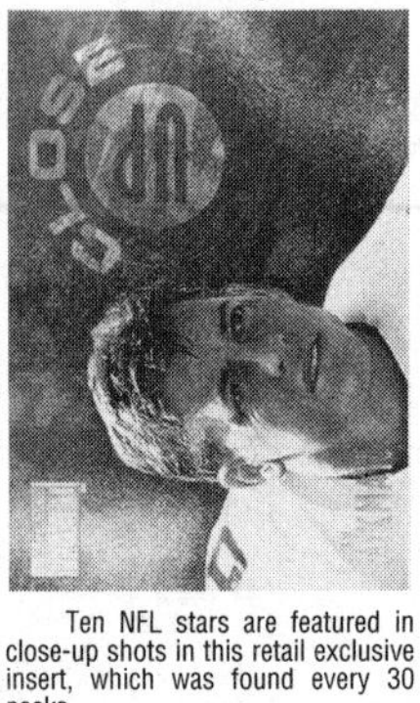

Ten NFL stars are featured in close-up shots in this retail exclusive insert, which was found every 30 packs.

		MT
Complete Set (10):		175.00
Common Player:		7.00
1	Troy Aikman	25.00
2	Drew Bledsoe	25.00
3	Isaac Bruce	12.00
4	Terrell Davis	30.00
5	John Elway	20.00
6	Barry Sanders	25.00
7	Emmitt Smith	50.00
8	Kordell Stewart	20.00
9	Tamarick Vanover	7.00
10	Ricky Watters	7.00

1996 SkyBox Autographs

The six spokesman for Fleer/SkyBox signed cards to be inserted into packs of Premium at a rate of one per 450. Highlighted by Brett Favre, the set also includes Trent Dilfer, Daryl Johnston, Eric Turner, Dave Meggett and William Floyd.

	MT
Complete Set (6):	350.00
Common Player:	20.00
Trent Dilfer	40.00
Brett Favre	250.00
William Floyd	20.00
Daryl Johnston	20.00
Dave Meggett	20.00
Eric Turner	20.00

1996 SkyBox Brett Favre MVP

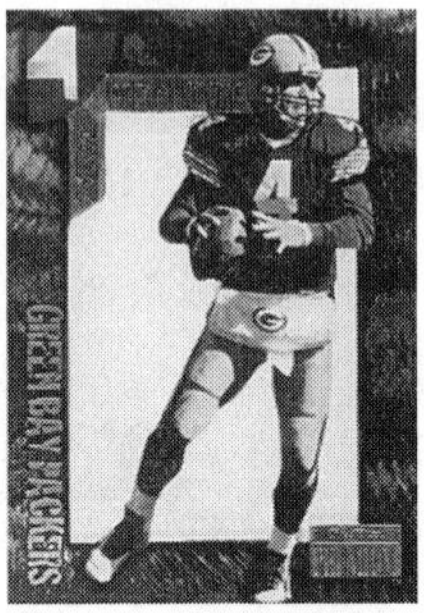

Brett Favre MVP Series was a five-card insert devoted to SkyBox spokesman and NFL MVP Brett Favre. Cards 1-3A were found in Impact, with a one per 480 insert rate, while cards 3B-5 were in packs of Premium, with a one per 240 insertion rate. Each card showed off a different technology, with No. 1 printed on foil, No. 2 printed on acrylic, No. 3 utilizing lenticular technology, No. 4 was die-cut and No. 5 was printed on leather. Card No. 3 required collectors to obtain sides A and B, from Impact and Premium, respectively, to redeem it for the actual lenticular card.

		MT
Complete Set (6):		180.00
Common Player:		30.00
1	Brett Favre Foil	40.00
2	Brett Favre Acrylic	40.00
3a	Brett Favre Exch.A	30.00
3b	Brett Favre Exch.B	40.00
3c	Brett Favre Prize	60.00
4	Brett Favre Die-Cut	30.00
5	Brett Favre Leather	30.00

1996 SkyBox Impact

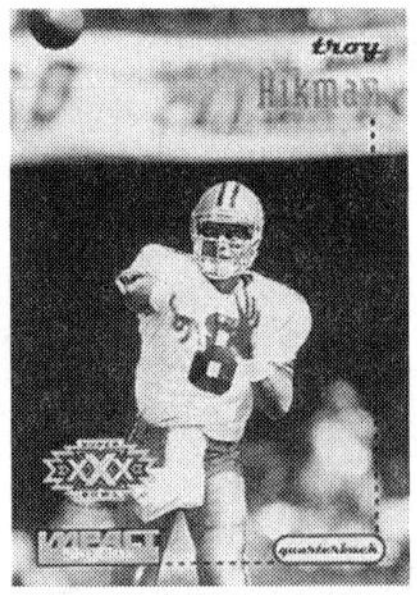

Impact Football was a 200-card set that featured borderless action shots and commentary on card backs by Fox analyst Matt Millen. The set includes 148 veterans, 40 rookies (149-188), five Inspirations (189-193), five Brett Favre Highlights and two checklists. There were five different inserts sets - NFL on Fox, Excelerators, Intimidators, No Surrender and VersaTeam - and three Brett Favre MVP Series cards and a Favre SkyMint Exchange card.

		MT
Complete Set (200):		18.00
Common Player:		.05
Minor Stars:		.10
Pack (10):		1.50
Wax Box (24):		32.00
1	Garrison Hearst	.05
2	Rob Moore	.05
3	Frank Sanders	.05
4	Eric Swann	.05
5	Aeneas Williams	.05
6	Bert Emanuel	.05

7	Jeff George	.05
8	Craig Heyward	.05
9	Terance Mathis	.05
10	Eric Metcalf	.05
11	Leroy Hoard	.05
12	Michael Jackson	.05
13	Andre Rison	.05
14	Vinny Testaverde	.05
15	Eric Turner	.05
16	Darrick Holmes	.05
17	Jim Kelly	.05
18	Bryce Paup	.05
19	Bruce Smith	.05
20	Thurman Thomas	.05
21	Mark Carrier	.05
22	Kerry Collins	.25
23	Derrick Moore	.05
24	Tyrone Poole	.05
25	Curtis Conway	.05
26	Jeff Graham (Jets)	.05
27	Erik Kramer	.05
28	Rashaan Salaam	.50
29	Jeff Blake	.60
30	Ki-Jana Carter	.25
31	Carl Pickens	.05
32	Darnay Scott	.05
33	Troy Aikman	.75
34	Charles Haley	.05
35	Michael Irvin	.10
36	Daryl Johnston	.05
37	Jay Novacek	.05
38	Deion Sanders	.50
39	Emmitt Smith	1.50
40	Steve Atwater	.05
41	Terrell Davis	.75
42	John Elway	.25
43	Anthony Miller	.05
44	Shannon Sharpe	.05
45	Scott Mitchell	.05
46	Herman Moore	.20
47	Brett Perriman	.05
48	Barry Sanders	1.00
49	Edgar Bennett	.05
50	Robert Brooks	.05
51	Mark Chmura	.20
52	Brett Favre	1.50
53	Reggie White	.10
54	Mel Gray	.05
55	Steve McNair	.75
56	Chris Sanders	.25
57	Rodney Thomas	.30
58	Quentin Coryatt	.05
59	Sean Dawkins	.05
60	Ken Dilger	.05
61	Marshall Faulk	.75
62	Jim Harbaugh	.05
63	Tony Boselli	.05
64	Mark Brunell	.50
65	Keenan McCardell	.05
66	James Stewart	.05
67	Marcus Allen	.05
68	Steve Bono	.05
69	Neil Smith	.05
70	Derrick Thomas	.05
71	Tamarick Vanover	.50
72	Bryan Cox (Bears)	.05
73	Irving Fryar (Eagles)	.05
74	Eric Green	.05
75	Dan Marino	1.50
76	O.J. McDuffie	.05
77	Bernie Parmalee	.05
78	Cris Carter	.05
79	Qadry Ismail	.05
80	Warren Moon	.05
81	Jake Reed	.05
82	Robert Smith	.05
83	Drew Bledsoe	.75
84	Ben Coates	.05
85	Curtis Martin	1.25
86	Willie McGinnest	.05
87	David Meggett	.05
88	Mario Bates	.05
89	Quinn Early (Bills)	.05
90	Jim Everett	.05
91	Michael Haynes	.05
92	Renaldo Turnbull	.05
93	Dave Brown	.05
94	Rodney Hampton	.05
95	Thomas Lewis	.05
96	Phillippi Sparks	.05
97	Tyrone Wheatley	.05
98	Kyle Brady	.05
99	Hugh Douglas	.05
100	Mo Lewis	.05
101	Adrian Murrell	.05
102	Tim Brown	.05
103	Jeff Hostetler	.05
104	Raghib Ismail	.05
105	Chester McGlockton	.05
106	Harvey Williams	.05
107	Fred Barnett (Dolphins)	.05
108	William Fuller	.05
109	Charlie Garner	.05
110	Rodney Peete	.05
111	Ricky Watters	.05
112	Calvin Williams	.05
113	Bam Morris	.05
114	Neil O'Donnell (Jets)	.05
115	Erric Pegram	.05
116	Kordell Stewart	1.00
117	Yancey Thigpen	.30
118	Rod Woodson	.05
119	Jerome Bettis (Steelers)	.05
120	Isaac Bruce	.40
121	Troy Drayton	.05
122	Leslie O'Neal	.05
123	*Aaron Hayden*	.30
124	Stan Humphries	.05
125	Natrone Means (Jaguars)	.10
126	Junior Seau	.05
127	William Floyd	.05
128	Brent Jones	.05
129	Derek Loville	.05
130	Ken Norton	.05
131	Jerry Rice	.75
132	J.J. Stokes	.10
133	Steve Young	.75
134	Brian Blades	.05
135	Joey Galloway	.75
136	Cortez Kennedy	.05
137	Rick Mirer	.10
138	Chris Warren	.15
139	Trent Differ	.05
140	Alvin Harper	.05
141	Jackie Harris	.05
142	Hardy Nickerson	.05
143	Errict Rhett	.50
144	Terry Allen	.05
145	Henry Ellard	.05
146	Brian Mitchell	.05
147	Heath Shuler	.25
148	Michael Westbrook	.10
149	*Karim Abdul-Jabbar*	.50
150	*Mike Alstott*	1.50
151	*Marco Battaglia*	.05
152	*Tim Biakabutuka*	.75
153	*Sean Boyd*	.05
154	*Tony Brackens*	.05
155	*Duane Clemons*	.05
156	*Marcus Coleman*	.05
157	*Chris Darkins*	.30
158	*Rickey Dudley*	.30
159	*Jason Dunn*	.20
160	*Bobby Engram*	.10
161	*Daryl Gardener*	.05
162	*Eddie George*	3.00
163	*Terry Glenn*	1.50
164	*Kevin Hardy*	.20
165	*Marvin Harrison*	2.00
166	*Dietrich Jells*	.05
167	*DeRon Jenkins*	.05
168	*Darrius Johnson*	.05
169	*Keyshawn Johnson*	2.00
170	*Lance Johnstone*	.05
171	*Cedric Jones*	.05
172	*Marcus Jones*	.05
173	*Danny Kanell*	.50
174	*Eddie Kennison*	.30
175	*Jevon Langford*	.05
176	*Markco Maddox*	.05
177	*Derrick Mayes*	.75
178	*Leeland McElroy*	.20
179	*Del McGee*	.05
180	*Johnny McWilliams*	.05
181	*Alex Molden*	.05
182	*Eric Moulds*	1.50
183	*Jonathan Ogden*	.05
184	*Lawrence Phillips*	.50
185	*Simeon Rice*	.20
186	*Amani Toomer*	.30
187	*Regan Upshaw*	.05
188	*Jerome Woods*	.05
189	Darrell Green (Inspirations)	.05
190	Daryl Johnston (Inspirations)	.05
191	Sam Mills (Inspirations)	.05
192	Earnest Byner (Inspirations)	.05
193	Herschel Walker (Inspirations)	.05
194	Brett Favre (Highlights)	.25
195	Brett Favre (Highlights)	.25
196	Brett Favre (Highlights)	.25
197	Brett Favre (Highlights)	.25
198	Brett Favre (Highlights)	.25
199	Checklist	.05
200	Checklist	.05

1996 SkyBox Impact Excelerators

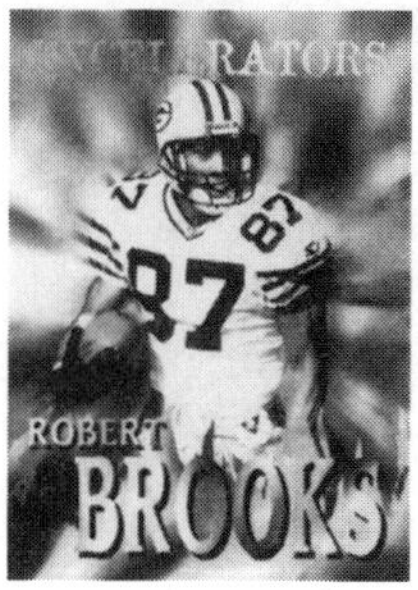

Excelerators included 15 players who have breakaway speed. The word "Excelerators" is written across the top in foil, with the player's name across the bottom, with flames rising up. These inserts were seeded every 12 packs.

		MT
Complete Set (15):		40.00
Common Player:		2.00
1	Robert Brooks	2.00
2	Isaac Bruce	4.00
3	William Floyd	2.00
4	Joey Galloway	6.00
5	Michael Irvin	2.00
6	Napoleon Kaufman	2.00
7	Anthony Miller	2.00
8	Herman Moore	4.00
9	Barry Sanders	8.00
10	Chris Sanders	2.00
11	Kordell Stewart	6.00
12	Rodney Thomas	2.00
13	Tamarick Vanover	2.00
14	Ricky Watters	2.00
15	Michael Westbrook	2.00

1996 SkyBox Impact Intimidators

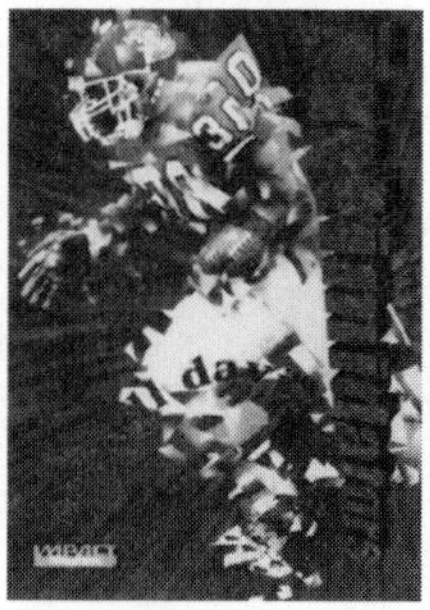

Intimidators was a 10-card insert that displayed the NFL's toughest players against a shattered-looking background. The word "Intimidators" runs down the right side and gets smaller toward the bottom. Intimidators inserts were seeded every 20 packs of Impact.

		MT
Complete Set (10):		45.00
Common Player:		2.00
1	Terrell Davis	6.00
2	Hugh Douglas	2.00
3	Dan Marino	12.00
4	Curtis Martin	10.00
5	Carl Pickens	2.00
6	Errict Rhett	4.00
7	Jerry Rice	6.00
8	Emmitt Smith	12.00
9	Eric Swann	2.00
10	Chris Warren	3.00

1996 SkyBox Impact More Attitude

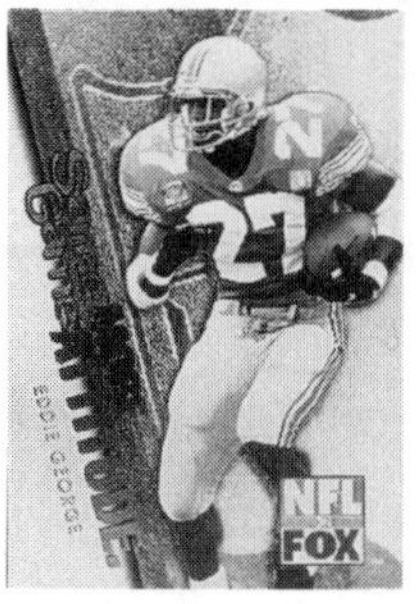

More Attitude was the easiest insert to get in Impact, with an insertion rate of one per three packs. The insert displayed 20 rookies from 1996 in their college uniforms with silver foil backgrounds.

		MT
Complete Set (20):		25.00
Common Player:		.50
1	Karim Abdul-Jabbar	3.00
2	Tim Biakabutuka	2.00
3	Bobby Engram	2.00
4	Daryl Gardener	.50
5	Eddie George	5.00
6	Terry Glenn	4.00
7	Kevin Hardy	.50
8	Marvin Harrison	2.50
9	DeRon Jenkins	.50
10	Keyshawn Johnson	3.00
11	Cedric Jones	.50
12	Eddie Kennison	1.50
13	Jevon Langford	.50
14	Leeland McElroy	1.50
15	Johnny McWilliams	.50
16	Eric Moulds	2.00
17	Lawrence Phillips	1.00
18	Jonathan Ogden	.50
19	Simeon Rice	.50
20	Amani Toomer	1.00

1996 SkyBox Impact No Surrender

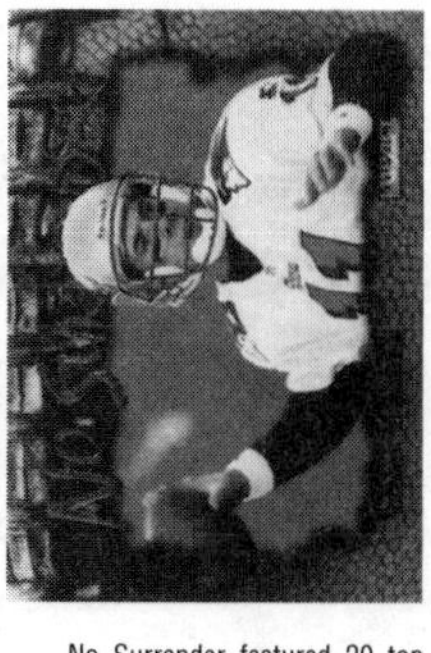

No Surrender featured 20 top players in a horizontal format with the player's image embossed against a football background. The words "No Surrender" are written across the top of the card in red foil. This insert is seeded in every 40 hobby packs.

		MT
Complete Set (20):		150.00
Common Player:		5.00
1	Marcus Allen	5.00
2	Jeff Blake	10.00
3	Drew Bledsoe	15.00
4	Ben Coates	5.00
5	Brett Favre	30.00
6	Terry Glenn	18.00
7	Jim Harbaugh	5.00
8	Kevin Hardy	5.00
9	Keyshawn Johnson	16.00
10	Dan Marino	30.00
11	Leeland McElroy	10.00
12	Steve McNair	14.00
13	Herman Moore	7.00
14	Lawrence Phillips	10.00
15	Errict Rhett	10.00
16	Jerry Rice	15.00
17	Simeon Rice	5.00
18	Barry Sanders	20.00
19	Rodney Thomas	7.00
20	Tyrone Wheatley	5.00

1996 SkyBox Impact Versateam

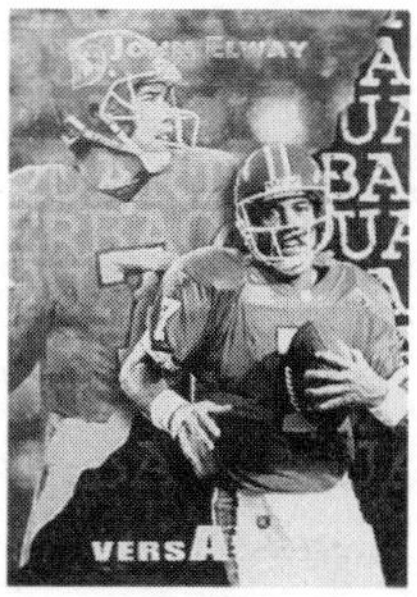

This 10-card insert featured NFL stars that excel at multiple things. The cards, which are found every 120 packs, feature a color action shot of the player over a green tinted background. The background is split diagonally, with half containing the player's position and half with another shot of the player.

		MT
Complete Set (10):		200.00
Common Player:		10.00
1	Tim Brown	10.00
2	Terrell Davis	25.00
3	John Elway	16.00
4	Marshall Faulk	15.00
5	Joey Galloway	25.00
6	Curtis Martin	45.00
7	Deion Sanders	15.00
8	Kordell Stewart	35.00
9	Chris Warren	10.00
10	Steve Young	30.00

1996 SkyBox Impact Rookies

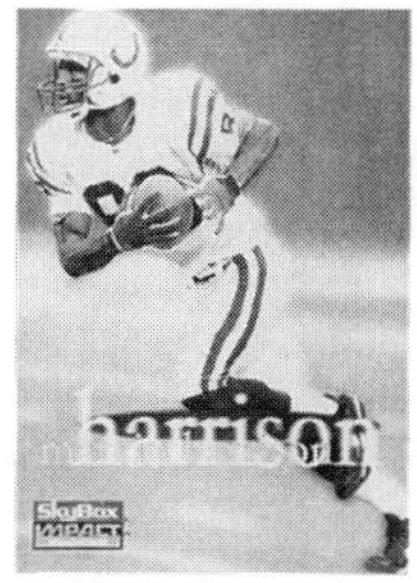

Although released in early 1997, Impact Rookies is generally considered a 1996 product due to its focus on 1996 rookies. The set consists of 150 cards, including 70 1996 rookies, 50 All-Time Impact Rookies, 20 Rookie Sleepers and 10 Rookie Record Holders. Ten-card packs had the following inserts: 1996 All-Rookie Team, Draft Board, Rookie Rewind, 1997 NFL Draft Exchange and 1996 Rookies. In addition, autographed versions of Karim Abdul-Jabbar, Rickey Dudley, Marvin Harrison, Lawrence Phillips, Eddie Kennison and Amani Toomer 1996 Rookies inserts were available through a case topper redemption offer. One redemption card was included in six-box cases, with two per 12-box case and three per 20-box case.

		MT
Complete Set (150):		12.00
Common Player:		.05
Minor Stars:		.10
Pack (10):		1.25
Wax Box (36):		35.00
1	Leeland McElroy	.10
2	Johnny McWilliams	.05
3	Simeon Rice	.10
4	DeRon Jenkins	.05
5	*Jermaine Lewis*	1.00
6	Ray Lewis	.75
7	Jonathan Ogden	.10
8	*Eric Moulds*	1.50
9	*Tim Biakabutuka*	.50
10	*Muhsin Muhammad*	.50
11	Winslow Oliver	.05
12	Bobby Engram	.20
13	Walt Harris	.10
14	Willie Anderson	.05
15	Marco Battaglia	.05
16	Jevon Langford	.05
17	Kavika Pittman	.05
18	Stepfret Williams	.05
19	Tory James	.05
20	*Jeff Lewis*	.50
21	John Mobley	.05
22	Detron Smith	.05
23	*Derrick Mayes*	.75
24	*Eddie George*	2.50
25	*Marvin Harrison*	2.00
26	Dedric Mathis	.05
27	Tony Brackens	.05
28	Kevin Hardy	.10
29	Jerome Woods	.05
30	*Karim Abdul-Jabbar*	.50
31	Daryl Gardener	.05
32	Jerris McPhail	.05
33	Stanley Pritchett	.05
34	*Zach Thomas*	.50
35	Duane Clemons	.05
36	Moe Williams	.05
37	Tedy Bruschi	.05
38	*Terry Glenn*	1.25
39	Alex Molden	.05
40	Ricky Whittle	.05
41	Cedric Jones	.05
42	*Danny Kanell*	.50
43	Amani Toomer	.10
44	Marcus Coleman	.05
45	*Keyshawn Johnson*	1.50
46	Ray Mickens	.05
47	Alex Van Dyke	.10
48	*Rickey Dudley*	.20
49	Lance Johnstone	.05
50	Brian Dawkins	.05
51	Jason Dunn	.05
52	Ray Farmer	.05
53	*Bobby Hoying*	.50
54	Jermaine Mayberry	.05
55	Bryan Still	.05
56	*Tony Banks*	.50
57	Ernie Conwell	.05
58	*Eddie Kennison*	.20
59	Jerald Moore	.10
60	*Lawrence Phillips*	.50
61	Isreal Ifeanyi	.10
62	*Terrell Owens*	2.00
63	Iheanyi Uwaezuoke	.10
64	*Mike Alstott*	1.25
65	Marcus Jones	.05
66	Nilo Silvan	.05
67	Regan Upshaw	.05
68	*Stephen Davis*	2.50
69	Troy Aikman	.50
70	Terry Allen	.05
71	Edgar Bennett	.05
72	Jerome Bettis	.10
73	Drew Bledsoe	.50
74	Tim Brown	.10
75	Mark Brunell	.50
76	Cris Carter	.10
77	Kerry Collins	.10
78	Terrell Davis	1.00
79	John Elway	.50
80	Marshall Faulk	.10
81	Brett Favre	1.00
82	Joey Galloway	.10
83	Rodney Hampton	.05
84	Jim Harbaugh	.05
85	Michael Irvin	.10
86	Chris T. Jones	.05
87	Napoleon Kaufman	.20
88	Jim Kelly	.10
89	Dan Marino	.75
90	Curtis Martin	.30
91	Terance Mathis	.05
92	Steve McNair	.30
93	Anthony Miller	.05
94	Scott Mitchell	.05
95	Herman Moore	.10
96	Brett Perriman	.05
97	Carl Pickens	.10
98	Jerry Rice	.50
99	Andre Rison	.05
100	Rashaan Salaam	.05
101	Barry Sanders	1.00
102	Chris Sanders	.05
103	Deion Sanders	.20
104	Frank Sanders	.05
105	Bruce Smith	.05
106	Emmitt Smith	.75
107	Robert Smith	.10
108	Kordell Stewart	.75
109	J.J. Stokes	.05
110	Yancey Thigpen	.05
111	Thurman Thomas	.05
112	Eric Turner	.05
113	Tamarick Vanover	.05
114	Chris Warren	.05
115	Ricky Watters	.10
116	Michael Westbrook	.05
117	Reggie White	.10
118	Steve Young	.30
119	Jeff Blake	.05
120	Robert Brooks	.05
121	Isaac Bruce	.10
122	Mark Chmura	.05
123	Wayne Chrebet	.10
124	Ben Coates	.05
125	Ken Dilger	.05
126	Bert Emanuel	.05
127	Gus Frerotte	.05
128	Kevin Greene	.05
129	Erik Kramer	.05
130	Greg Lloyd	.05
131	Tony Martin	.05
132	Brian Mitchell	.05
133	Bryce Paup	.05
134	Jake Reed	.05
135	Errict Rhett	.05
136	Yancey Thigpen	.05
137	Tamarick Vanover	.05
138	Chris Warren	.05
139	Marcus Allen	.10
140	Jerome Bettis	.10
141	Tim Brown	.10
142	Mark Carrier	.05
143	Marshall Faulk	.10
144	Tyrone Hughes	.05
145	Dan Marino	.75
146	Curtis Martin	.30
147	Barry Sanders	1.00
148	Orlando Thomas	.10
149	Checklist (1-107)	.05
150	Checklist (108-150/inserts)	.05

1996 SkyBox Impact Rookies All-Rookie Team

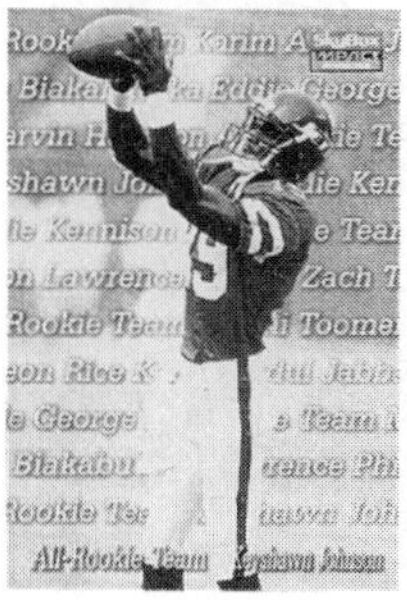

This 10-card insert includes some of the top rookies from the 1996 season. The fronts feature an embossed image of the player on a matte finish, with the words All-Rookie Team and the names of different members of the team printed in the background in white, embossed letters. All-Rookie Team inserts are numbered and inserted every six packs.

		MT
Complete Set (10):		20.00
Common Player:		1.00
1	Karim Abdul-Jabbar	4.00
2	Tim Biakabutuka	2.00
3	Eddie George	6.00
4	Marvin Harrison	3.00
5	Keyshawn Johnson	3.00
6	Eddie Kennison	2.00
7	Lawrence Phillips	3.00
8	Zach Thomas	2.00
9	Amani Toomer	1.00
10	Simeon Rice	1.00

1996 SkyBox Impact Rookies Draft Board

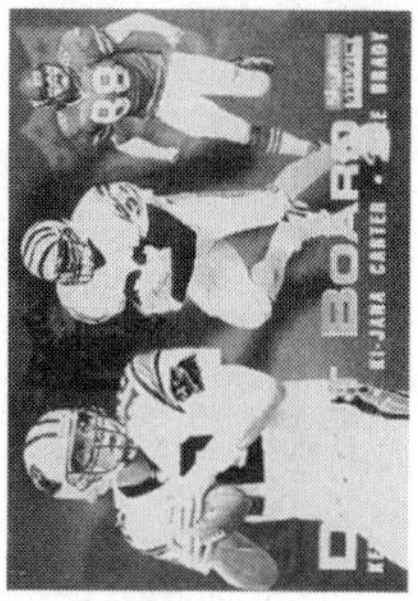

Draft Board has 20 cards that feature multiple players on the front in a horizontal format against a maroon background. The back explains the tie between the players - whether they were all late round picks or attended the same college - and are numbered. Draft Board inserts are found every 24 packs.

		MT
Complete Set (20):		170.00
Common Player:		4.00
1	Terry Glenn, Rickey Dudley, Bobby Hoying	12.00
2	Simeon Rice, Kevin Hardy	4.00
3	Emmitt Smith, Errict Rhett	30.00
4	Deion Sanders, Corey Sawyer, Derrick Brooks	10.00
5	Terry Allen, Marcus Allen	4.00
6	John Mobley, Andre Reed	4.00
7	Drew Bledsoe, Rick Mirer, Mark Brunell	14.00
8	John Elway, Jim Kelly, Dan Marino	30.00
9	Carl Pickens, Anthony Miller	4.00
10	Antonio Freeman, Robert Brooks, Chris T. Jones	4.00
11	Jerome Bettis, Ricky Watters, Tim Brown	4.00
12	Jerry Rice, Herman Moore, Michael Irvin	15.00
13	Terrell Davis, Rodney Hampton, Garrison Hearst	15.00
14	Kerry Collins, Ki-Jana Carter, Kyle Brady	10.00
15	Barry Sanders, Thurman Thomas	15.00
16	Jermaine Lewis, Jeff Lewis, Ray Lewis	4.00
17	Steve Young, Troy Aikman	15.00
18	Curtis Martin, Chris Warren, Jamal Anderson	20.00
19	Kordell Stewart, Rashaan Salaam, Michael Westbrook	8.00
20	Tony Banks, Muhsin Muhammad	6.00

1996 SkyBox Impact Rookies Rookie Rewind

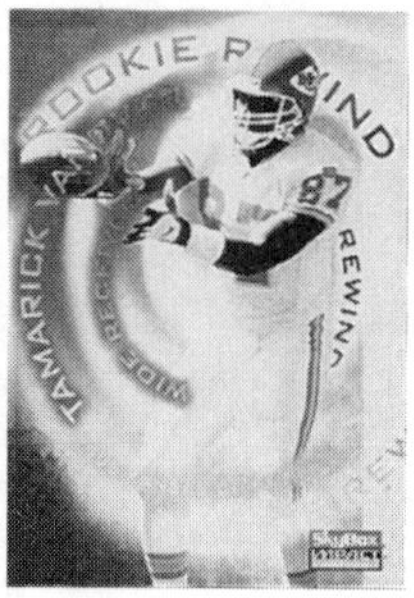

Rookie Rewind looks back on past drafts to reflect their rise to stardom. Ten different players are featured over a swirl background with the words "Rookie Rewind" in gold foil across the bottom. Rookie Rewind inserts were found only in hobby packs and carried an insertion rate of one per 120.

		MT
Complete Set (10):		50.00
Common Player:		1.50
1	Jamal Anderson	3.00
2	Jeff Blake	3.00
3	Robert Brooks	1.50
4	Mark Brunell	8.00
5	Brett Favre	18.00
6	Aaron Hayden	1.50
7	Derek Loville	1.50
8	Emmitt Smith	18.00
9	Robert Smith	1.50
10	Tamarick Vanover	3.00

1996 SkyBox Impact Rookies 1996 Rookies

This insert showcased the top rookies of 1996 on cards that were individually numbered to 1,996. The 10 offensive stars included in this insert are found every 144 packs. Autographed versions of Abdul-Jabbar, Dudley, Harrison, Phillips, Kennison and Toomer were available as case toppers.

		MT
Complete Set (10):		200.00
Common Player:		8.00
1	Karim Abdul-Jabbar	30.00
2	Tim Biakabutuka	8.00
3	Rickey Dudley	8.00
4	Eddie George	45.00
5	Terry Glenn	35.00
6	Marvin Harrison	25.00
7	Keyshawn Johnson	25.00
8	Eddie Kennison	15.00
9	Lawrence Phillips	20.00
10	Amani Toomer	8.00

1996 SkyBox SkyMotion

SkyBox's 1996 SkyMotion set features the video work of NFL films to reproduce 3.5 seconds of game action on each card. No special lights or glasses are needed to get the full effect of the card; all it takes is a flick of the wrist. The cards provide the whole picture of how the play unfolds. The cards are laminated onto paper, enabling SkyBox to print stats and other information on the back for the first time. (Previous cards were plastic, printed on one side only). In addition, there's a Replay parallel set of all 60 cards; these cards feature rounded edges with special foil stamping on the card back. One Replay card is included in each box. Two other insert sets were also made - Big Bang and Team Galaxy.

		MT
Complete Set (60):		150.00
Common Player:		1.50
Minor Stars:		3.00
Gold Cards:		4x-8x
Pack (2):		4.00
Wax Box (24):		80.00
1	Troy Aikman	10.00
2	Marcus Allen	3.00
3	Jeff Blake	5.00
4	Drew Bledsoe	10.00
5	Tim Brown	1.50
6	Isaac Bruce	6.00
7	Mark Brunell	7.00
8	Cris Carter	1.50
9	Kerry Collins	4.00
10	Ben Coates	1.50
11	Curtis Conway	1.50
12	Terrell Davis	10.00
13	Trent Dilfer	1.50
14	Hugh Douglas	1.50
15	John Elway	6.00
16	Marshall Faulk	5.00
17	Brett Favre	15.00
18	William Floyd	1.50
19	Joey Galloway	7.00
20	Jeff George	1.50
21	Rodney Hampton	1.50
22	Jim Harbaugh	1.50
23	*Aaron Hayden*	3.00
24	Jeff Hostetler	1.50
25	Tyrone Hughes	1.50
26	Michael Irvin	3.00
27	Daryl Johnston	1.50
28	Jim Kelly	1.50
29	Greg Lloyd	1.50
30	Dan Marino	15.00
31	Curtis Martin	12.00
32	Chester McGlockton	1.50
33	Steve McNair	6.00
34	Eric Metcalf	1.50
35	Scott Mitchell	1.50
36	Herman Moore	4.00
37	Bryce Paup	1.50
38	Carl Pickens	1.50
39	Errict Rhett	4.00
40	Jerry Rice	10.00
41	Rashaan Salaam	4.00
42	Barry Sanders	10.00
43	Chris Sanders	1.50
44	Deion Sanders	6.00
45	Junior Seau	1.50
46	Heath Shuler	1.50
47	Bruce Smith	1.50
48	Emmitt Smith	15.00
49	Kordell Stewart	8.00
50	Eric Swann	1.50
51	Derrick Thomas	1.50
52	Thurman Thomas	1.50
53	Eric Turner	1.50
54	Tamarick Vanover	6.00
55	Chris Warren	3.00
56	Ricky Watters	1.50
57	Michael Westbrook	4.00
58	Reggie White	3.00
59	Rod Woodson	1.50
60	Steve Young	7.00

1996 SkyBox SkyMotion Gold

Actually called Replay, but referred to in the hobby as Golds, this 60-card parallel set featured rounded edges and special foil stamping on the card back to differentiate it from regular-issue cards. Gold parallels were inserted as a box topper into every other hobby box as a reward to box purchasers.

	MT
Complete Set (60):	1000.
Gold Cards:	4x-8x

1996 SkyBox SkyMotion Big Bang

These 1996 SkyBox SkyMotion inserts have 10 top rookies against a background of exploding fireworks. The cards, using lenticular printing, were seeded one per every packs.

	MT
Complete Set (10):	100.00
Common Player:	4.00
Tim Biakabutuka	10.00
Rickey Dudley	8.00
Eddie George	25.00
Terry Glenn	20.00
Kevin Hardy	4.00
Marvin Harrison	15.00
Keyshawn Johnson	15.00
Leeland McElroy	8.00
Lawrence Phillips	8.00
Simeon Rice	4.00

1996 SkyBox SkyMotion Team Galaxy

These 1996 SkyBox SkyMotion inserts showcase five of the NFL's top stars against a backdrop of planets and footballs. The cards, printed using lenticular printing, were seeded one per 35 packs.

		MT
Complete Set (5):		150.00
Common Player:		20.00
1	Karim Abdul-Jabbar	20.00
2	Brett Favre	50.00
3	Curtis Martin	40.00
4	Jerry Rice	35.00
5	Emmitt Smith	50.00

1997 SkyBox

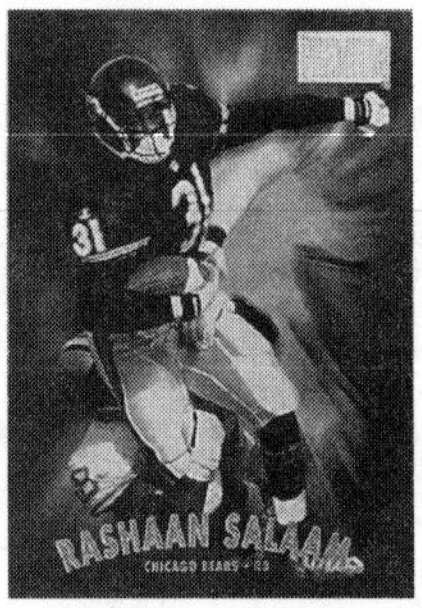

This 250-card base set features 208 veterans, 40 rookies and two checklists. The base cards have a holographic foil design on 20 pt. card stock. The inserts for the set include Rookie Preview, Close Ups, PrimeTime Rookies, Premium Players, Larger Than Life, Autographics and Star Rubies.

		MT
Complete Set (250):		35.00
Common Player:		.10
Minor Stars:		.20
Ruby Cards:		50x-100x
Ruby Rookies:		25x-50x
Pack (8):		2.50
Wax Box (24):		50.00
1	Brett Favre	3.00
2	Michael Bates	.10
3	Jeff Graham	.10
4	Terry Glenn	.30
5	Stephen Davis	.10
6	Wesley Walls	.10
7	Barry Sanders	1.50
8	Chris Sanders	.10
9	O.J. McDuffie	.10
10	Ken Dilger	.10
11	Kimble Anders	.10
12	Keenan McCardell	.10
13	Ki-Jana Carter	.10
14	Gary Brown	.10
15	Andre Rison	.10
16	Edgar Bennett	.10
17	Jerome Bettis	.20
18	Ted Johnson	.10
19	John Friez	.10
20	Tony Brackens	.10
21	Bryan Cox	.10
22	Eric Moulds	.10
23	Johnnie Morton	.10
24	Brad Johnson	.10
25	Bam Morris	.10
26	Anthony Johnson	.10
27	Jim Harbaugh	.10
28	Keyshawn Johnson	.20
29	Cary Blanchard	.10
30	Curtis Conway	.10
31	Herschel Walker	.10
32	Thurman Thomas	.20
33	Frank Sanders	.10
34	Lawrence Phillips	.20
35	Scottie Graham	.10
36	Jim Everett	.10
37	Dale Carter	.10
38	Ashley Ambrose	.10
39	Mark Chmura	.20
40	James Stewart	.10
41	John Mobley	.10
42	Terrell Davis	1.25
43	Ben Coates	.10
44	Jeff George	.10
45	Ty Detmer	.10
46	Isaac Bruce	.20
47	Chris Warren	.10
48	Steve Walsh	.10
49	Bruce Smith	.10
50	Cris Carter	.10
51	Jamal Anderson	.10
52	Tim Biakabutuka	.10
53	Steve Young	.75
54	Eric Turner	.10
55	Jessie Tuggle	.10
56	Chris T. Jones	.10
57	Daryl Johnston	.10
58	Randall Cunningham	.10
59	Trent Dilfer	.20
60	Mark Brunell	1.25
61	Warren Moon	.10
62	Terry Kirby	.10
63	Eddie George	1.75
64	Neil Smith	.10
65	Gilbert Brown	.10
66	Emmitt Smith	2.50
67	Chad Brown	.10
68	Jamie Asher	.10
69	Willie McGinest	.10
70	Tim Brown	.10
71	Quentin Coryatt	.10
72	Mario Bates	.10
73	Fred Barnett	.10
74	Hugh Douglas	.10
75	Eric Swann	.10
76	Chris Chandler	.10
77	Larry Centers	.10
78	Vinny Testaverde	.10
79	Jermaine Lewis	.10
80	Junior Seau	.10
81	Kevin Greene	.10
82	Ricky Watters	.20
83	Anthony Miller	.10
84	Michael Westbrook	.10
85	Charles Way	.10
86	Andre Reed	.10
87	Darrell Green	.10
88	Troy Aikman	1.25
89	Jim Pyne	.10
90	Dan Marino	2.50
91	Elvis Grbac	.10
92	Mel Gray	.10
93	Marcus Allen	.20
94	Terry Allen	.10
95	Karim Abdul-Jabbar	.30
96	Rick Mirer	.10
97	Bert Emanuel	.10
98	John Elway	.75
99	Tony Martin	.10
100	Zach Thomas	.20
101	Harvey Williams	.10
102	Jason Sehorn	.10
103	Lawyer Milloy	.10
104	Thomas Lewis	.10
105	Michael Irvin	.20
106	James Hundon	.10
107	Willie Green	.10
108	Bobby Engram	.10
109	Mike Alstott	.20
110	Greg Lloyd	.10
111	Shannon Sharpe	.10
112	Desmond Howard	.10
113	Jason Elam	.10
114	Qadry Ismail	.10
115	William Thomas	.10
116	Marshall Faulk	.20
117	Tyrone Wheatley	.10
118	Tommy Vardell	.10
119	Rashaan Salaam	.20
120	Brian Mitchell	.10
121	Terance Mathis	.10
122	Dorsey Levens	.20
123	Todd Collins	.20
124	Derrick Alexander	.10
125	Stan Humphries	.10
126	Kordell Stewart	1.25
127	Kent Graham	.10
128	Yancey Thigpen	.10
129	Bryan Still	.10
130	Carl Pickens	.10
131	Ray Lewis	.10
132	Curtis Martin	1.25
133	Kerry Collins	.30
134	Ed McCaffrey	.10
135	Darick Holmes	.10
136	Glyn Milburn	.10
137	Rickey Dudley	.10
138	Terrell Owens	.75
139	Kevin Williams	.10
140	Reggie White	.20
141	Darnay Scott	.10
142	Brett Perriman	.10
143	Neil O'Donnell	.10
144	Natrone Means	.20
145	Jerris McPhail	.10
146	Lamar Lathon	.10
147	Michael Jackson	.10
148	Simeon Rice	.10
149	Greg Hill	.10
150	Erik Kramer	.10
151	Quinn Early	.10
152	Tamarick Vanover	.10
153	Derrick Thomas	.10
154	Nilo Silvan	.10
155	Deion Sanders	.50
156	Lorenzo Neal	.10
157	Steve McNair	1.00
158	Levon Kirkland	.10
159	Bobby Hebert	.10
160	William Floyd	.20
161	Leeland McElroy	.10
162	Chester McGlockton	.10
163	Michael Haynes	.10
164	Aeneas Williams	.10
165	Hardy Nickerson	.10
166	Rodney Woodson	.10
167	Iheanyi Uwaezuoke	.10
168	Chris Slade	.10
169	Herman Moore	.20
170	Rob Moore	.10
171	Andre Hastings	.10
172	Antonio Freeman	.40
173	Tony Boselli	.10
174	Drew Bledsoe	1.25
175	Sam Mills	.10
176	Robert Smith	.10
177	Jimmy Smith	.10
178	Alex Molden	.10
179	Joey Galloway	.20
180	Irving Fryar	.10
181	Wayne Chrebet	.10
182	Dave Brown	.10
183	Robert Brooks	.20
184	Tony Banks	.30
185	Eric Metcalf	.10
186	Napoleon Kaufman	.20
187	Frank Wycheck	.10
188	Donnell Woolford	.10
189	Kevin Turner	.10
190	Eddie Kennison	.40
191	Cortez Kennedy	.10
192	Raymont Harris	.10
193	Ronnie Harmon	.10
194	Kevin Hardy	.10
195	Gus Frerotte	.10
196	Marvin Harrison	.40
197	Jeff Blake	.20
198	Mike Tomczak	.10
199	William Roaf	.10
200	Jerry Rice	1.25
201	Jake Reed	.10
202	Ken Norton	.10
203	Errict Rhett	.20
204	Adrian Murrell	.20
205	Rodney Hampton	.10
206	Scott Mitchell	.10
207	Jason Dunn	.10
208	Ray Zellars	.10
209	*Michael Adams*	.10
210	*John Allred*	.10
211	*Reidel Anthony*	1.50
212	*Darnell Autry*	.30
213	*Tiki Barber*	1.50
214	*Will Blackwell*	.20
215	*Peter Boulware*	.10
216	*Macey Brooks*	.10
217	*Rae Carruth*	1.50
218	*Troy Davis*	.30
219	*Corey Dillon*	4.00
220	*Jim Druckenmiller*	2.50
221	*Warrick Dunn*	2.00
222	*Marc Edwards*	.10
223	*James Farrior*	.10
224	*Tony Gonzalez*	.75
225	*Jay Graham*	.50
226	*Yatil Green*	.30
227	*Byron Hanspard*	.50
228	*Ike Hilliard*	1.25
229	*Leon Johnson*	.10
230	*Damon Jones*	.10
231	*Freddie Jones*	.50
232	*Joey Kent*	.50
233	*David LaFleur*	.75
234	*Kevin Lockett*	.10
235	*Sam Madison*	.10
236	*Brian Manning*	.10
237	*Ronnie McAda*	.10
238	*Orlando Pace*	.50
239	*Jake Plummer*	4.00
240	*Keith Poole*	.10
241	*Darrell Russell*	.10
242	*Sedrick Shaw*	.30
243	*Antowain Smith*	1.50
244	*Shawn Springs*	.50
245	*Duce Staley*	8.00
246	*Dedric Ward*	.50
247	*Bryant Westbrook*	.20
248	*Danny Wuerffel*	.75
249	Checklist	.10
250	Checklist	.10

1997 SkyBox Autographics

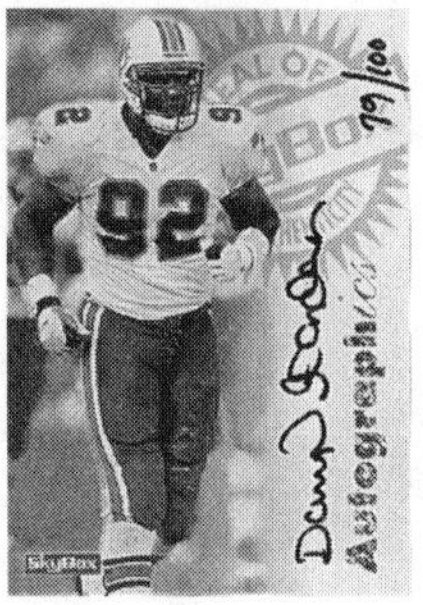

Inserted 1:240 packs, the cards featured signed fronts. In addition, an Autographics Century Marks parallel set was also randomly seeded.

	MT
Common Player:	15.00
Minor Stars:	30.00
Century Marks:	2x
Karim Abdul-Jabbar	80.00
Larry Allen	15.00
Terry Allen	30.00
Mike Alstott	75.00
Darnell Autry	45.00
Tony Banks	75.00
Pat Barnes	30.00
Jeff Blake	30.00
Michael Booker	15.00
Reuben Brown	15.00
Rae Carruth	15.00
Cris Carter	30.00
Ben Coates	30.00
Ernie Conwell	15.00
Terrell Davis	150.00
Ty Detmer	15.00
Ken Dilger	15.00
Corey Dillon	80.00
Jim Druckenmiller	125.00
Rick Dudley	30.00
Brett Favre CM	700.00
Antonio Freeman	50.00
Daryl Gardner	15.00
Chris Gedney	15.00
Eddie George	100.00
Hunter Goodwin	15.00
Marvin Harrison	60.00
Garrison Hearst	30.00
William Henderson	30.00
Michael Jackson	30.00
Tory James	15.00
Rob Johnson	30.00
Chris T. Jones	15.00
Pete Kendall	15.00
Eddie Kennison	60.00
David LaFleur	40.00
Jeff Lewis	30.00
Thomas Lewis	15.00
Keith Lockett	30.00
Brian Manning	15.00
Dan Marino	400.00
Ed McCaffrey	15.00
Keenan McCardell	30.00
Glyn Milburn	15.00
Alex Molden	15.00
Johnnie Morton	15.00
Winslow Oliver	15.00
Jerry Rice	350.00
Rashaan Salaam	30.00
Frank Sanders	15.00
Shannon Sharpe	30.00
Sedrick Shaw	40.00
Alex Smith	15.00
Antowain Smith	80.00
Emmitt Smith	350.00
Jimmy Smith	30.00
Shawn Springs	15.00
James Stewart	15.00
Kordell Stewart	150.00
Rodney Thomas	15.00
Amani Toomer	15.00
Floyd Turner	15.00
Alex Van Dyke	15.00
Mike Vrabel	15.00
Chris Warren	15.00
Charles Way	15.00
Reggie White (Century)	100.00
Rickey Whittle	15.00
Sherman Williams	15.00
John Wittman	15.00

1997 SkyBox Close Ups

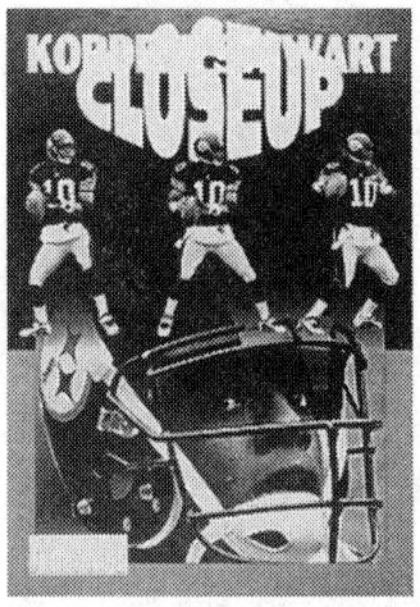

This 18-card insert features head shots of young NFL players. Four more pictures are included on the card. Close Ups were inserted 1:18.

		MT
Complete Set (10):		100.00
Common Player:		3.00
1	Terrell Davis	15.00
2	Troy Aikman	15.00
3	Drew Bledsoe	15.00
4	Steve McNair	10.00
5	Jerry Rice	15.00
6	Kordell Stewart	15.00
7	Kerry Collins	6.00
8	John Elway	10.00
9	Deion Sanders	8.00
10	Joey Galloway	3.00

1997 SkyBox Larger Than Life

Larger Than Life is a 10-card insert featuring the legends of today. Larger Than Life cards were inserted one per 360 packs.

		MT
Complete Set (10):		450.00
Common Player:		15.00
1	Emmitt Smith	75.00
2	Barry Sanders	90.00
3	Curtis Martin	40.00
4	Dan Marino	75.00
5	Keyshawn Johnson	25.00
6	Marvin Harrison	15.00
7	Terry Glenn	20.00
8	Eddie George	60.00
9	Brett Favre	90.00
10	Karim Abdul-Jabbar	20.00

1997 SkyBox Premium Players

Premium Players is a 15-card insert set which was seeded one per 192 packs.

		MT
Complete Set (15):		800.00
Common Player:		8.00
1	Eddie George	85.00
2	Terry Glenn	25.00
3	Karim Abdul-Jabbar	25.00
4	Emmitt Smith	100.00
5	Dan Marino	100.00
6	Brett Favre	120.00
7	Keyshawn Johnson	8.00
8	Curtis Martin	60.00
9	Marvin Harrison	8.00
10	Barry Sanders	75.00
11	Jerry Rice	60.00
12	Terrell Davis	60.00
13	Troy Aikman	60.00
14	Drew Bledsoe	60.00
15	John Elway	40.00

1997 SkyBox PrimeTime Rookies

PrimeTime Rookies is a 10-card insert featuring the top rookies of 1997. This set was inserted one per 96 packs.

		MT
Complete Set (10):		175.00
Common Player:		7.00
1	Jim Druckenmiller	35.00
2	Antowain Smith	25.00
3	Rae Carruth	15.00
4	Yatil Green	15.00
5	Ike Hilliard	15.00
6	Reidel Anthony	20.00
7	Orlando Pace	7.00
8	Peter Boulware	7.00
9	Warrick Dunn	45.00
10	Troy Davis	15.00

1997 SkyBox Reebok Bronze

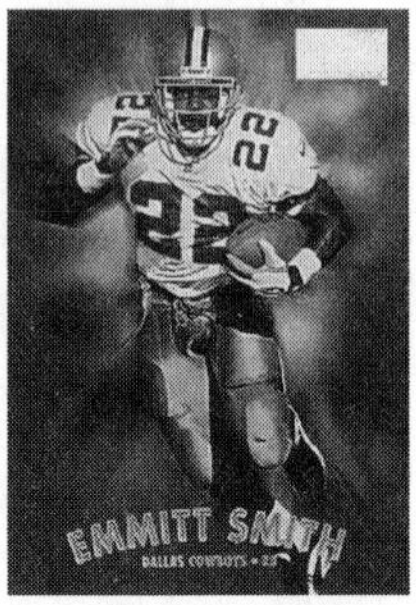

The Reebok Value Added set came in bronze, silver, gold, ruby and emerald versions. The overall insertion rate for the Reebok Value Added set was one per pack.

		MT
Complete Set (15):		4.00
Common Player:		.10
Gold:		4x
Green:		25x-50x
Red:		10x-20x
Silver:		2x
12	Keenan McCardell	.10
37	Dale Carter	.10
38	Ashley Ambrose	.10
43	Ben Coates	.10
66	Emmitt Smith	1.50
95	Karim Abdul-Jabbar	.50
98	John Elway	1.50
110	Greg Lloyd	.10
123	Todd Collins	.10
161	Leeland McElroy	.10
169	Herman Moore	.10
175	Sam Mills	.10
180	Irving Fryar	.10
202	Ken Norton	.10
205	Rodney Hampton	.10

1997 SkyBox Rookie Preview

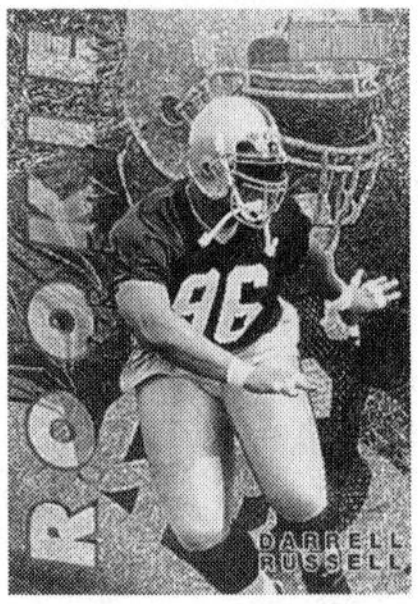

These 15 embossed insert cards feature some of the top rookies of 1997. Rookie Preview cards were inserted 1:6.

		MT
Complete Set (15):		30.00
Common Player:		1.00
1	Reidel Anthony	3.00
2	Tiki Barber	3.00
3	Peter Boulware	1.00
4	Rae Carruth	2.50
5	Jim Druckenmiller	4.50
6	Warrick Dunn	6.00
7	James Farrior	1.00
8	Yatil Green	2.50
9	Byron Hanspard	2.00
10	Ike Hilliard	2.50
11	Orlando Pace	1.50
12	Darrell Russell	1.00
13	Antowain Smith	3.00
14	Shawn Springs	1.50
15	Bryant Westbrook	1.00

A card number in parentheses ( ) indicates the set is unnumbered.

1997 SkyBox Impact

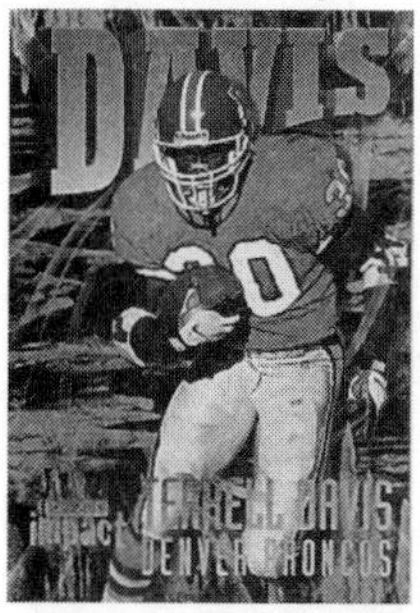

The 250-card set contains 207 player cards, three checklists and 40 rookies. The cards feature the player's photo superimposed over a jagged background, with the player's name printed in 3-D block letters at the top. The player's first and last name and team are printed at the bottom right in gold foil, while the Impact logo is in the lower left. The backs include the player's name, position, quote, Impact stats, bio, stats, photo and team helmet over a team-colored football background. A Rave parallel set was randomly seeded. SkyBox produced less than 150 Rave sets.

	MT
Complete Set (250):	25.00
Common Player:	.05
Minor Stars:	.10
Circa Rave Stars:	40x-80x
Circa Rave Rookies:	20x-40x
Pack (8):	1.75
Wax Box (36):	53.00

1 Carl Pickens .05
2 Ray Lewis .05
3 Darrell Green .05
4 Brett Favre 1.75
5 Todd Collins .05
6 Errict Rhett .10
7 John Elway .50
8 Troy Aikman .75
9 Steve McNair .75
10 Kordell Stewart .75
11 Drew Bledsoe .75
12 Kerry Collins .25
13 Dan Marino 1.50
14 Ricky Watters .10
15 Marvin Harrison .30
16 Simeon Rice .05
17 Qadry Ismail .05
18 Andre Coleman .05
19 Keyshawn Johnson .30
20 Barry Sanders 1.25
21 Rickey Dudley .10
22 Emmitt Smith 1.50
23 Erik Kramer .05
24 Tony Boselli .05
25 Steve Young .50
26 Rod Woodson .05
27 Eddie George 1.00
28 Curtis Martin 1.00
29 Amani Toomer .05
30 Terrell Davis 1.00
31 Jim Everett .05
32 Marcus Allen .10
33 Karim Abdul-Jabbar .50
34 Thurman Thomas .10
35 Cortez Kennedy .05
36 Jerome Bettis .10
37 Kevin Carter .05
38 Gilbert Brown .05
39 Bert Emanuel .05
40 Kyle Brady .05
41 Trent Dilfer .10
42 Garrison Hearst .05
43 Kevin Greene .05
44 Bryan Cox .05
45 Desmond Howard .05
46 Larry Centers .05
47 Quentin Coryatt .05
48 Michael Jackson .05
49 John Randle .05
50 Mark Brunell .75
51 William Thomas .05
52 Glyn Milburn .05
53 Mike Alstott .10
54 Chris Spielman .05
55 Junior Seau .10
56 Brian Blades .05
57 Lamar Lathon .05
58 Derrick Thomas .05
59 Dave Brown .05
60 Frank Wycheck .05
61 Chris Slade .05
62 Neil Smith .05
63 Ashley Ambrose .05
64 Alex Molden .05
65 Edgar Bennett .05
66 Alvin Harper .05
67 Jamal Anderson .15
68 Eddie Kennison .30
69 Ken Norton .05
70 Zach Thomas .20
71 Leeland McElroy .10
72 Terry Allen .05
73 Raymont Harris .05
74 Ken Dilger .05
75 Jason Dunn .05
76 Robert Smith .05
77 William Roaf .05
78 Bruce Smith .05
79 Vinny Testaverde .05
80 Jerry Rice .75
81 Tim Brown .05
82 James Stewart .05
83 Andre Reed .05
84 Herman Moore .15
85 Stan Humphries .05
86 Chris Warren .05
87 Tyrone Wheatley .05
88 Michael Irvin .10
89 Dan Wilkinson .05
90 Tony Banks .20
91 Chester McGlockton .05
92 Reggie White .10
93 Elvis Grbac .05
94 Willie Davis .05
95 Greg Lloyd .05
96 Ben Coates .05
97 Rashaan Salaam .10
98 Eric Swann .05
99 Hugh Douglas .05
100 Henry Ellard .05
101 Rod Smith .05
102 Tim Biakabutuka .10
103 Chad Brown .05
104 Kevin Hardy .05
105 Chris T. Jones .05
106 Antonio Freeman .20
107 Lamont Warren .05
108 Derrick Alexander .05
109 Brett Perriman .05
110 Antonio Langham .05
111 Eric Moulds .05
112 O.J. McDuffie .05
113 Eric Metcalf .05
114 Ray Zellars .05
115 Marco Coleman .05
116 Terry Kirby .05
117 Darren Woodson .05
118 Charles Johnson .05
119 Sam Mills .05
120 Rodney Hampton .05
121 Rick Mirer .10
122 Derrick Brooks .05
123 Greg Hill .05
124 John Mobley .05
125 Chris Sanders .05
126 Kent Graham .05
127 Michael Westbrook .05
128 Harvey Williams .05
129 Keenan McCardell .05
130 Neil O'Donnell .05
131 LeRoy Butler .05
132 Willie McGinest .05
133 Ki-Jana Carter .05
134 Robert Jones .05
135 Jim Harbaugh .05
136 Wesley Walls .05
137 Jackie Harris .05
138 Jermaine Lewis .05
139 Jake Reed .05
140 John Friesz .05
141 Jerris McPhail .05
142 Charlie Garner .05
143 Bryce Paup .05
144 Tony Martin .05
145 Shannon Sharpe .05
146 Terrell Owens .50
147 Curtis Conway .10
148 Jamie Asher .05
149 Lawrence Phillips .10
150 Deion Sanders .30
151 Frank Sanders .05
152 Joey Galloway .20
153 Mel Gray .05
154 Robert Brooks .10
155 Jeff George .05
156 Michael Haynes .05
157 Chris Chandler .05
158 Adrian Murrell .05
159 Tamarick Vanover .05
160 Marshall Faulk .10
161 Thomas Lewis .05
162 Ty Detmer .05
163 Darnay Scott .05
164 Bam Morris .05
165 Scott Mitchell .05
166 Brad Johnson .05
167 Dave Meggett .05
168 Bobby Engram .05
169 Natrone Means .10
170 Eric Pegram .05
171 Leonard Russell .05
172 Muhsin Muhammad .05
173 Aeneas Williams .05
174 Fred Barnett .05
175 William Floyd .05
176 Kimble Anders .05
177 Darick Holmes .05
178 Willie Green .05
179 Rodney Thomas .05
180 Derrick Alexander .05
181 Sean Dawkins .05
182 Dorsey Levens .10
183 Napoleon Kaufman .05
184 Mario Bates .05
185 Yancey Thigpen .05
186 Johnnie Morton .05
187 Gus Frerotte .05
188 Terance Mathis .05
189 Tyrone Hughes .05
190 Wayne Chrebet .05
191 Tony Brackens .05
192 Hardy Nickerson .05
193 Daryl Johnston .05
194 Irving Fryar .05
195 Jeff Blake .15
196 Charles Way .05
197 Brian Mitchell .05
198 Brent Jones .05
199 Mark Chmura .05
200 Terry Glenn .30
201 Cris Carter .05
202 Steve Atwater .05
203 Rob Moore .05
204 Anthony Johnson .05
205 Warren Moon .10
206 Darrien Gordon .05
207 Isaac Bruce .15
208 *Reidel Anthony* 1.00
209 *Darnell Autry* .50
210 *Tiki Barber* 1.50
211 *Pat Barnes* .30
212 *Terry Battle* .10
213 *Michael Booker* .10
214 *Peter Boulware* .20
215 *Chris Canty* .10
216 *Rae Carruth* 1.00
217 *Troy Davis* .30
218 *Corey Dillon* 2.50
219 *Jim Druckenmiller* 2.00
220 *Warrick Dunn* 1.25
221 *James Farrior* .10
222 *Tarik Glenn* .10
223 *Tony Gonzalez* .50
224 *Yatil Green* .30
225 *Byron Hanspard* .30
226 *Ike Hilliard* 1.00
227 *Kenny Holmes* .10
228 *Walter Jones* .10
229 *Tom Knight* .10
230 *David LaFleur* .40
231 *Kenard Lang* .10
232 *Kevin Lockett* .10
233 *Tremain Mack* .10
234 *Sam Madison* .10
235 *Chris Naeole* .10
236 *Orlando Pace* .40
237 *Jake Plummer* 2.50
238 *Dwayne Rudd* .10
239 *Darrell Russell* .25
240 *Jamie Sharper* .10
241 *Sedrick Shaw* .50
242 *Antowain Smith* 1.25
243 *Shawn Springs* .50
244 *Bryant Westbrook* .20
245 *Reinard Wilson* .10
246 *Danny Wuerffel* 1.00
247 *Renaldo Wynn* .10
248 Checklist .05
249 Checklist .05
250 Checklist .05

1997 SkyBox Impact Raves

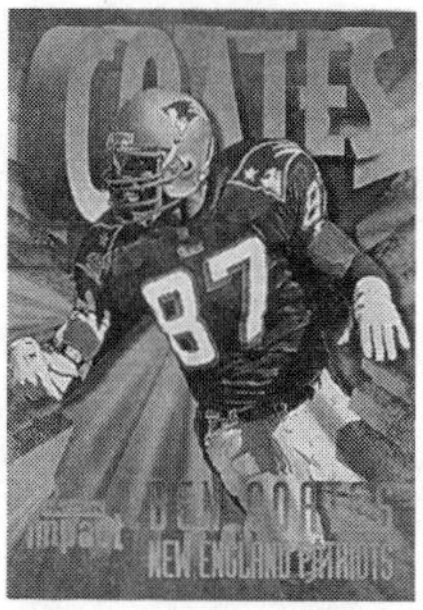

Rave is a parallel of the SkyBox Impact base set. The Rave set parallels 247 cards (not the checklists) and was limited to 150 sets.

	MT
Rave Stars:	40x-80x
Rave Rookies:	20x-40x

1997 SkyBox Impact Boss

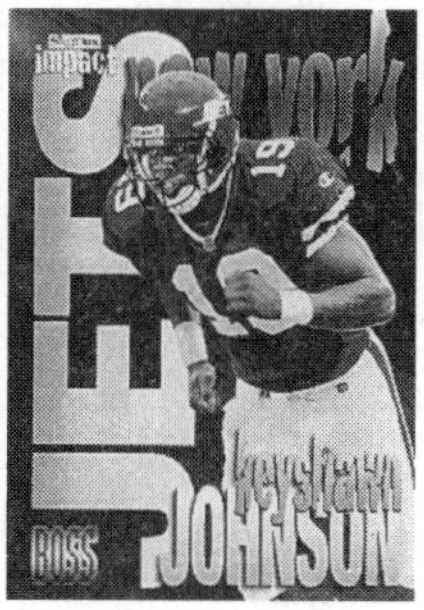

Inserted 1:6 packs, the 20-card set features the player's photo, name and team name embossed on the front. The backs have the player's name, team, position and highlights on the left side, while the Boss logo runs vertically along the right border. The cards are numbered "of 20" in the upper right corner. The Super Boss parallel set was inserted 1:36 packs. The cards are identical to the base Boss, except the cards are printed on foil. The Super Boss logo appears in the lower left of the card front. The Super Boss cards also have an "SB" suffix with the card numbers on the back.

	MT
Complete Set (20):	40.00
Common Player:	1.00
Super Boss Cards:	2x-4x

1 Karim Abdul-Jabbar 2.00
2 Troy Aikman 3.00
3 Tim Biakabutuka 1.00
4 Mark Brunell 3.00
5 Rae Carruth 2.00
6 Kerry Collins 2.00
7 Corey Dillon 2.00
8 Jim Druckenmiller 3.00
9 Warrick Dunn 4.00
10 Brett Favre 6.00
11 Eddie George 4.00
12 Marvin Harrison 1.50
13 Keyshawn Johnson 1.50
14 Eddie Kennison 1.50
15 Dan Marino 5.00
16 Curtis Martin 4.00
17 Steve McNair 3.00
18 Orlando Pace 1.00
19 Barry Sanders 4.00
20 Steve Young 2.00

1997 SkyBox Impact Excelerators

The 12-card set was inserted 1:48 packs. The die-cut cards have the player's photo superimposed over a black and silver background, with a shield in the center. Excelerators is printed in red in the center of the background, while the player's name is printed in silver over the center of the player photo. The SkyBox logo is at the bottom center of the front. The backs have a player photo in the center, with his name and highlights printed inside the shield. The card numbers are printed "of 12."

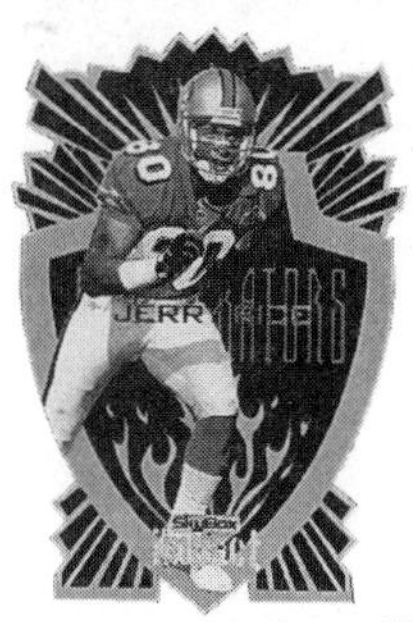

	MT
Complete Set (12):	100.00
Common Player:	3.00

1 Mark Brunell 15.00
2 Rae Carruth 10.00
3 Terrell Davis 20.00
4 Joey Galloway 3.00
5 Marvin Harrison 6.00
6 Keyshawn Johnson 3.00
7 Eddie Kennison 6.00
8 Steve McNair 12.00
9 Jerry Rice 15.00
10 Emmitt Smith 30.00
11 Shawn Springs 6.00
12 Kordell Stewart 15.00

1997 SkyBox Impact Instant Impact

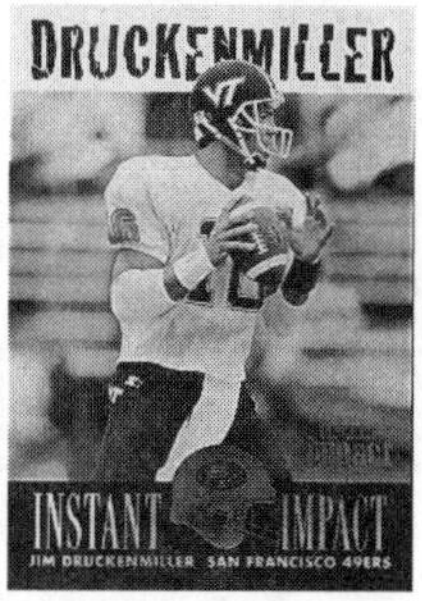

The 15-card set was inserted 1:24 packs. The player's last name is printed in black at the top inside a white stripe. The Impact logo is printed in silver in the lower right of the photo. A black stripe at the bottom includes "Instant Impact," player's name and team in silver foil. The team's helmet is located in the bottom center. The backs have the card number "of 15" printed at the top, while his highlights are printed in the center of the card. The black stripe on the bottom repeats the information from the front, without the silver foil.

	MT
Complete Set (15):	75.00
Common Player:	1.50

1 Reidel Anthony 10.00
2 Darnell Autry 3.00
3 Tiki Barber 3.00
4 Peter Boulware 1.50
5 Troy Davis 3.00
6 Jim Druckenmiller 12.00
7 Warrick Dunn 15.00
8 Yatil Green 8.00
9 Ike Hilliard 4.00
10 Orlando Pace 3.00
11 Darrell Russell 1.50
12 Sedrick Shaw 5.00
13 Shawn Springs 5.00
14 Bryant Westbrook 1.50
15 Danny Wuerffel 12.00

1997 SkyBox Impact Rave Reviews

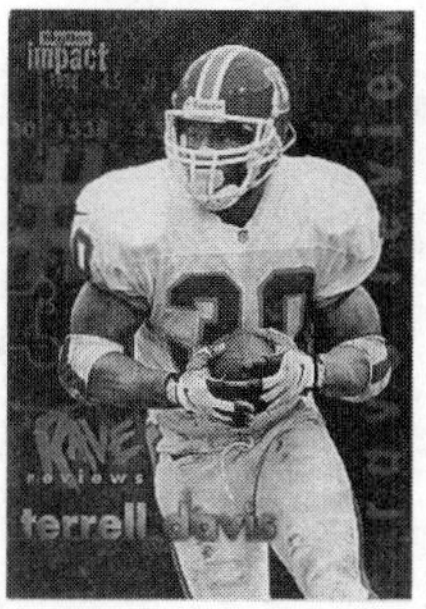

Inserted 1:288 packs, the 12-card set includes a player photo superimposed over a holofoil background of numbers. The Rave Reviews logo is printed above the player's name in the lower left corner. "Rave Review" is printed in holofoil vertically along the right border. The backs have the player's name at the top, with a quote from Ronnie Lott along the left border. The player's photo is on the right. Lott's photo and description, along with the card number "of 12" are printed in the lower left.

	MT
Complete Set (12):	425.00
Common Player:	15.00
Inserted 1:288	

1 Terrell Davis 50.00
2 John Elway 30.00
3 Brett Favre 50.00
4 Joey Galloway 15.00
5 Eddie George 25.00
6 Terry Glenn 15.00
7 Dan Marino 40.00
8 Curtis Martin 20.00
9 Jerry Rice 25.00
10 Barry Sanders 50.00
11 Deion Sanders 15.00
12 Emmitt Smith 40.00

1997 SkyBox Impact Total Impact

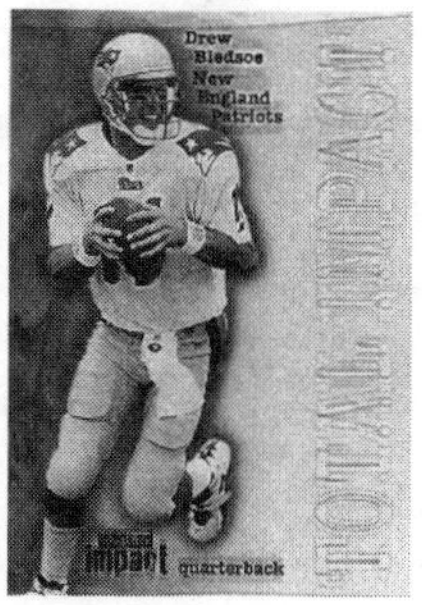

Inserted 1:36 retail packs, the 10-card set is printed on plastic over a white background.

	MT
Complete Set (10):	75.00
Common Player:	5.00

1 Karim Abdul-Jabbar 7.00
2 Troy Aikman 12.00
3 Drew Bledsoe 12.00
4 Isaac Bruce 5.00
5 Kerry Collins 7.00
6 John Elway 10.00
7 Terry Glenn 7.00
8 Lawrence Phillips 5.00
9 Deion Sanders 8.00
10 Kordell Stewart 12.00

1998 SkyBox

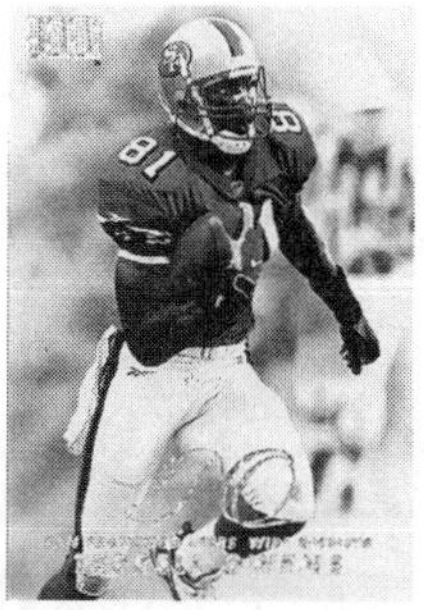

This 250-card included 195 veteran stars, 15 One for the Ages subset cards and 40 rookies seeded one per four packs. Each card featured a borderless design on the front, with the player's name, team, position and SkyBox logo printed in a prismatic gold foil. Backs contain a closeup of the player over a black background. Each card was paralleled in a Star Rubies parallel which was numbered to 50 sets. Insert sets include: Autographics, D'Stroyers, Intimidation Nation, Prime Time Rookies, Rap Show and Soul of the Game.

	MT
Complete Set (250):	225.00
Common Player:	.10
Minor Stars:	.20
Common Rookie (211-250):	1.50
Inserted 1:4	
Star Ruby Cards:	75x-150x
Star Ruby Rookies:	4x-8x
Production 50 Sets	
Pack (8):	3.25
Wax Box (24):	70.00

1 John Elway 1.25
2 Drew Bledsoe 1.25
3 Antonio Freeman .50
4 Merton Hanks .10
5 James Jett .10
6 Ricky Proehl .10
7 Deion Sanders .50
8 Frank Sanders .10
9 Bruce Smith .10
10 Tiki Barber .20
11 Isaac Bruce .20
12 Mark Brunell 1.00
13 Quinn Early .10
14 Terry Glenn .20
15 Darrien Gordon .10
16 Keith Byars .10
17 Terrell Davis 1.25
18 Charlie Garner .10
19 Eddie Kennison .20
20 Keenan McCardell .10
21 Eric Moulds .10
22 Jimmy Smith .20
23 Reidel Anthony .20
24 Rae Carruth .10
25 Michael Irvin .50
26 Dorsey Levens .20
27 Derrick Mayes .10
28 Adrian Murrell .20
29 Dwayne Rudd .10
30 Leslie Shepherd .10
31 Jamal Anderson .20
32 Robert Brooks .10
33 Sean Dawkins .10
34 Cris Dishman .10
35 Rickey Dudley .10
36 Bobby Engram .10
37 Chester McGlockton .10
38 Terrell Owens .20
39 Wayne Chrebet .10
40 Dexter Coakley .10
41 Kerry Collins .20
42 Trent Dilfer .20
43 Bobby Hoying .10
44 Glyn Milburn .10
45 Rob Moore .10
46 Jake Reed .10
47 Dana Stubblefield .10
48 Reggie White .20
49 Natrone Means .20
50 Troy Aikman 1.25
51 Aaron Bailey .10
52 William Floyd .10
53 Eric Metcalf .10
54 Warrick Dunn 1.00
55 Chad Lewis .10
56 Curtis Martin .75
57 Tony Martin .10
58 John Randle .10
59 Jeff Burris .10
60 Larry Centers .10
61 Bert Emanuel .10
62 Sean Gilbert .10
63 David Palmer .10
64 Eric Bieniemy .10
65 Peter Boulware .10
66 Charles Johnson .10
67 Jerris McPhail .10
68 Scott Mitchell .10
69 Chris Sanders .10
70 Ken Dilger .10
71 Brad Johnson .20
72 Danny Kanell .10
73 Fred Lane .20
74 Warren Sapp .10
75 Carl Pickens .20
76 Cris Carter .20
77 Marshall Faulk .20
78 Keyshawn Johnson .20
79 Tony McGee .10
80 Muhsin Muhammad .10
81 Kordell Stewart 1.00
82 Karl Williams .10
83 Willie Davis .10
84 David Dunn .10
85 Marvin Harrison .20
86 Michael Jackson .10
87 John Mobley .10
88 Shawn Springs .10
89 Wesley Walls .10
90 Jermaine Lewis .10
91 Ed McCaffrey .10
92 Chris Calloway .10
93 Lamont Warren .10
94 Ricky Watters .20
95 Tony Banks .20
96 Tony Brackens .10
97 Gary Brown .10
98 Howard Griffith .10
99 Ray Lewis .10
100 Jeff Blake .20
101 Charlie Jones .10
102 Glenn Foley .20
103 Jay Graham .10
104 James McKnight .10
105 Steve McNair .75
106 Chad Scott .10
107 Rod Smith .20
108 Jason Taylor .10
109 Corey Dillon 1.00
110 Eddie George 1.00
111 Jim Harbaugh .20
112 Warren Moon .20
113 Shannon Sharpe .20
114 Darnell Autry .10
115 Brett Favre 2.50
116 Jeff George .20
117 Tony Gonzalez .10
118 Garrison Hearst .20
119 Randal Hill .10
120 Eric Swann .10
121 Jamie Asher .10
122 Tim Brown .20
123 Stephen Davis .10
124 Chris Chandler .10
125 Jerry Rice 1.25
126 Troy Davis .10
127 Ronnie Harmon .10
128 Andre Rison .10
129 Duce Staley .10
130 Charles Way .10
131 Bryant Westbrook .10
132 Mike Alstott .50
133 Gus Frerotte .10
134 Travis Jervey .10
135 Daryl Johnston .10
136 Jake Plummer 1.00
137 Junior Seau .20
138 Robert Smith .20
139 Thurman Thomas .20
140 Karim Abdul-Jabbar .20
141 Jerome Bettis .20
142 Byron Hanspard .10
143 Raymont Harris .10
144 Willie McGinest .10
145 Barry Sanders 2.50
146 Irv Smith .10
147 Michael Strahan .10
148 Frank Wycheck .10
149 Steve Broussard .10
150 Joey Galloway .50
151 Courtney Hawkins .10
152 O.J. McDuffie .10
153 Herman Moore .20
154 Chris Penn .10
155 O.J. Santiago .10
156 Yancey Thigpen .10

157	Jason Sehorn	.10
158	Ben Coates	.10
159	Ernie Conwell	.10
160	Dale Carter	.10
161	Jeff Graham	.10
162	Rob Johnson	.20
163	Damon Jones	.10
164	Mark Chmura	.20
165	Curtis Conway	.20
166	Elvis Grbac	.10
167	Andre Hastings	.10
168	Terry Kirby	.10
169	Aeneas Williams	.10
170	Derrick Alexander	.10
171	Troy Brown	.10
172	Irving Fryar	.10
173	Jerald Moore	.10
174	Andre Reed	.10
175	James Stewart	.20
176	Chris Warren	.10
177	Will Blackwell	.10
178	Erik Kramer	.10
179	Dan Marino	2.00
180	Terance Mathis	.10
181	Johnnie Morton	.10
182	J.J. Stokes	.20
183	Rodney Thomas	.10
184	Steve Young	.75
185	Kimble Anders	.10
186	Napoleon Kaufman	.50
187	Orlando Pace	.10
188	Antowain Smith	.75
189	Emmitt Smith	2.00
190	Terry Allen	.10
191	Mark Bruener	.10
191	Mark Bruener	.10
192	Rodney Harrison	.10
193	Billy Joe Hobert	.10
194	Leon Johnson	.10
195	Freddie Jones	.10
196	Super Bowl	.10
197	Super Bowl	.10
198	Super Bowl	.10
199	Super Bowl	.10
200	Super Bowl	.10
201	Super Bowl	.10
202	Super Bowl	.10
203	Super Bowl	.10
204	Super Bowl	.10
205	Super Bowl	.10
206	Super Bowl	.10
207	Super Bowl	.10
208	Super Bowl	.10
209	Super Bowl	.10
210	Super Bowl	.10
211	*(Robert Edwards)*	8.00
212	*Roland Williams*	1.50
213	*Joe Jurevicius*	3.00
214	*Wilmont Perry*	1.50
215	*Robert Holcombe*	6.00
216	*Larry Shannon*	1.50
217	*Skip Hicks*	6.00
218	*Patrick Johnson*	1.50
219	*Pat Palmer*	1.50
220	*John Dutton*	1.50
221	*Az-Zahir Hakim*	7.00
222	*Mikhael Ricks*	3.00
223	*Rashaan Shehee*	3.00
224	*Ryan Leaf*	10.00
225	*Alvis Whitted*	1.50
226	*Marcus Nash*	6.00
227	*Fred Taylor*	25.00
228	*Hines Ward*	6.00
229	*Chris Fuamatu-Ma'afala*	5.00
230	*Jerome Pathon*	3.00
231	*Peyton Manning*	45.00
232	*Charles Woodson*	10.00
233	*Jon Ritchie*	1.50
234	*Scott Frost*	1.50
235	*John Avery*	6.00
236	*Jonathon Linton*	5.00
237	*Jacquez Green*	8.00
238	*Andre Wadsworth*	3.00
239	*Cam Quayle*	1.50
240	*Randy Moss*	45.00
241	*Raymond Priester*	1.50
242	*Donald Hayes*	1.50
243	*Brian Griese*	15.00
244	*Brian Alford*	1.50
245	*Kevin Dyson*	8.00
246	*Jammi German*	1.50
247	*Cameron Cleeland*	4.00
248	*Curtis Enis*	10.00
249	*Terry Hardy*	1.50
250	*Tony Simmons*	4.00

1998 SkyBox Star Rubies

Star Rubies paralleled all 250 cards in SkyBox. The gold foil stamps of the regular cards were replaced by red foil and backs were numbered to 50.

	MT
Star Ruby Cards:	75x-150x
Star Ruby Rookies:	4x-8x

1998 SkyBox Autographics

A total of 73 different NFL players signed cards for Autographics in 1998. The program ran through Thunder, Metal Universe, SkyBox and E-X2001 products. Regular versions are signed in black ink, while Blue versions are individually numbered to 50. Cards were inserted 1:112 in Thunder, 1:68 in Metal Universe and Premium and 1:48 packs of E-X2001.

	MT
Common Player:	10.00
Minor Stars:	20.00
Inserted 1:48 E-X2001	
Inserted 1:68 Metal Universe	
Inserted 1:68 SkyBox Premium	
Inserted 1:112 Thunder	
Blue Signatures:	2x-4x
Production 50 Sets	
Kevin Abrams	10.00
Mike Alstott	35.00
Jamie Asher	10.00
Jon Avery	40.00
Tavian Banks	45.00
Pat Barnes	10.00
Jerome Bettis	30.00
Eric Bjornson	10.00
Peter Boulware	10.00
Troy Brown	10.00
Mark Breunner	10.00
Mark Brunell	85.00
Rae Carruth	10.00
Ray Crockett	10.00
Germane Crowell	40.00
Stephen Davis	20.00
Troy Davis	10.00
Sean Dawkins	10.00
Trent Dilfer	30.00
Corey Dillon	60.00
Jim Druckenmiller	30.00
Kevin Dyson	35.00
Marc Edwards	10.00
Robert Edwards	60.00
Bobby Engram	10.00
Curtis Enis	70.00
William Floyd	20.00
Glenn Foley	20.00
Chris Fuamatu-Ma'afal	30.00
Joey Galloway	35.00
Jeff George	30.00
Ahman Green	40.00
Jacquez Green	50.00
Yatil Green	20.00
Byron Hanspard	25.00
Marvin Harrison	30.00
Skip Hicks	35.00
Robert Holcombe	40.00
Bobby Hoying	25.00
Travis Jervey	20.00
Rob Johnson	30.00
Freddie Jones	10.00
Eddie Kennison	20.00
Fred Lane	20.00
Ryan Leaf	100.00
Dorsey Levens	30.00
Jeff Lewis	20.00
Jermaine Lewis	20.00
Dan Marino	225.00
Curtis Martin	60.00
Steve Matthews	10.00
Alonzo Mayes	20.00
Keenan McCardell	20.00
Willie McGinnest	10.00
James McKnight	20.00
Glyn Milburn	10.00
Warren Moon	35.00
Randy Moss	250.00
Marcus Nash	35.00
Terrell Owens	40.00
Jason Peter	20.00
Jake Plummer	100.00
John Randle	20.00
Shannon Sharpe	40.00
Jimmy Smith	20.00
Lamar Smith	10.00
Robert Smith	35.00
Duce Staley	20.00
Kordell Stewart	100.00
Fred Taylor	125.00
Rodney Thomas	10.00
Kevin Turner	10.00
Hines Ward	40.00
Charles Way	10.00
Frank Wycheck	10.00

1998 SkyBox D'stroyers

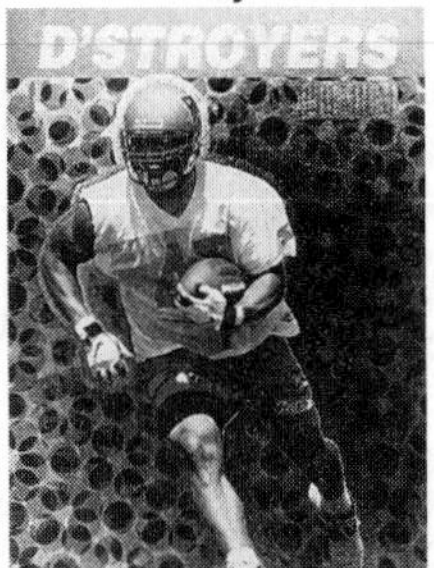

D'Stroyers was a 15-card insert that highlighted top young players in the league. The players were featured over a prismatic foil background and inserted one per six packs.

		MT
Complete Set (15):		35.00
Common Player:		.75
Minor Stars:		1.50
Inserted 1:6		
1	Antowain Smith	3.00
2	Corey Dillon	4.00
3	Charles Woodson	4.00
4	Randy Moss	12.00
5	Deion Sanders	1.50
6	Robert Edwards	5.00
7	Herman Moore	1.50
8	Mark Brunell	6.00
9	Dorsey Levens	.75
10	Curtis Enis	4.00
11	Drew Bledsoe	6.00
12	Steve McNair	3.00
13	Keyshawn Johnson	.75
14	Bobby Hoying	.75
15	Trent Dilfer	1.50

1998 SkyBox Intimidation Nation

Intimidation Nation captured 15 of the top players in the league over a flaming background. This insert was the toughest to find in SkyBox and inserted one per 360 packs.

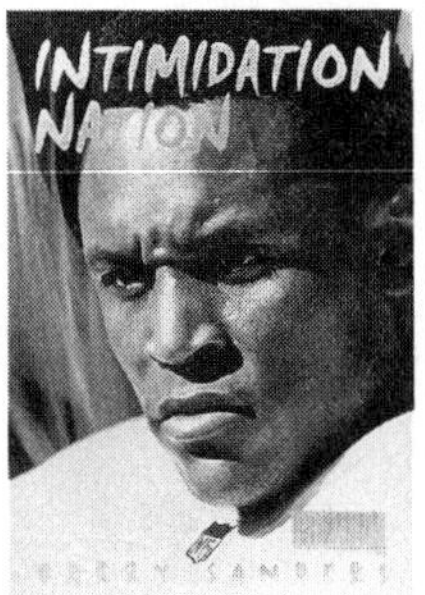

		MT
Complete Set (15):		750.00
Common Player:		20.00
Inserted 1:360		
1	Terrell Davis	75.00
2	Emmitt Smith	100.00
3	Barry Sanders	120.00
4	Brett Favre	120.00
5	Eddie George	45.00
6	Jerry Rice	60.00
7	John Elway	60.00
8	Mark Brunell	50.00
9	Troy Aikman	60.00
10	Peyton Manning	100.00
11	Ryan Leaf	50.00
12	Curtis Martin	20.00
13	Dan Marino	100.00
14	Warrick Dunn	45.00
15	Jake Plummer	45.00

1998 SkyBox Prime Time Rookies

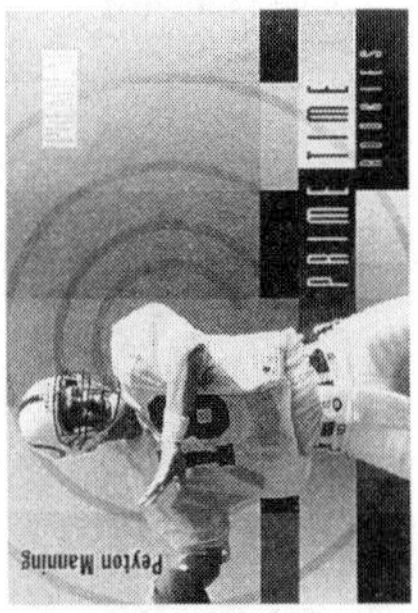

Ten rookies were featured on this horizontal, multi-colored background insert set. The cards featured the rookie on the left side with a bullseye over the background. Prime Time Rookies were seeded one per 96 packs.

		MT
Complete Set (10):		200.00
Common Player:		6.00
Inserted 1:96		
1	Curtis Enis	15.00
2	Robert Edwards	15.00
3	Fred Taylor	25.00
4	Robert Holcombe	12.00
5	Ryan Leaf	20.00
6	Peyton Manning	40.00
7	Randy Moss	60.00
8	Charles Woodson	20.00
9	Andre Wadsworth	6.00
10	Kevin Dyson	6.00

1998 SkyBox Rap Show

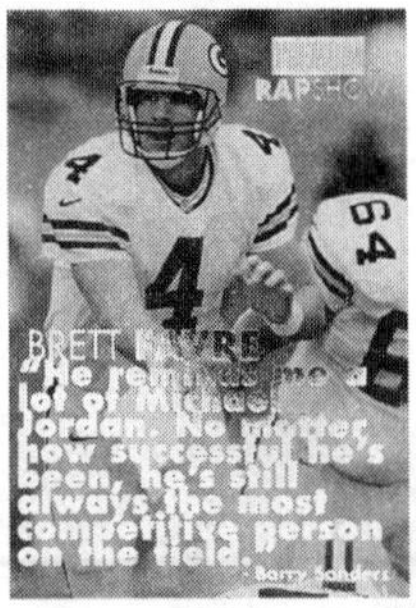

This 15-card insert featured an action shot of the player with a silver foil-stamped quote from one of his peers on the front. Rap Show inserts were seeded per 36 packs.

		MT
Complete Set (15):		150.00
Common Player:		5.00
Minor Stars:		8.00
Inserted 1:36		
1	John Elway	20.00
2	Drew Bledsoe	20.00
3	Corey Dillon	12.00
4	Brett Favre	40.00
5	Barry Sanders	40.00
6	Eddie George	15.00
7	Emmitt Smith	30.00
8	Jake Plummer	15.00
9	Joey Galloway	8.00
10	Ricky Watters	5.00
11	Mike Alstott	8.00
12	Kordell Stewart	15.00
13	Antonio Freeman	8.00
14	Terrell Davis	20.00
15	Warrick Dunn	15.00

1998 SkyBox Soul of the Game

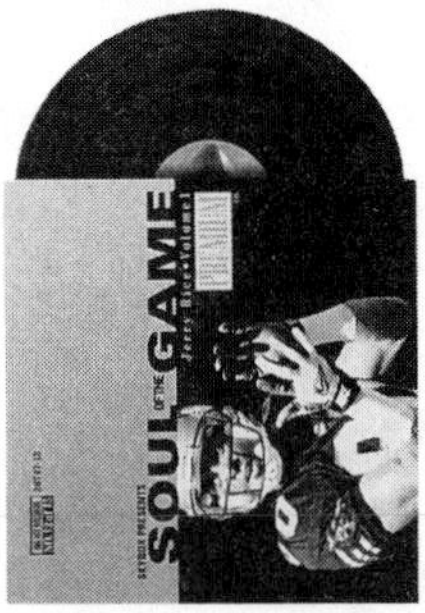

Soul of the Game were horizontal inserts that resembled a record sleeve with the album half out. The cards were one solid piece of plastic and inserted one per 18 packs.

		MT
Complete Set (15):		80.00
Common Player:		3.00
Minor Stars:		5.00
Inserted 1:18		
1	Troy Aikman	15.00
2	Dorsey Levens	3.00
3	Deion Sanders	7.00
4	Antonio Freeman	5.00
5	Dan Marino	20.00
6	Keyshawn Johnson	3.00
7	Terry Glenn	3.00
8	Tim Brown	3.00
9	Curtis Martin	10.00
10	Bobby Hoying	3.00
11	Kordell Stewart	12.00
12	Jerry Rice	15.00
13	Steve McNair	10.00
14	Joey Galloway	5.00
15	Steve Young	10.00

1998 SkyBox Double Vision

Each single in this 32-card set measures 5-1/2" x 7" and has an interactive team color-coded slide on the front. So when you pull the tab the player goes from black and white to color. Along with another color picture of that player with his name, team and position.

		MT
Complete Set (32):		130.00
Common Player:		4.00
Production 5,000 Sets		
1	Dan Marino	12.00
2	John Elway	8.00
3	Troy Aikman	8.00
4	Steve Young	6.00
5	Terrell Davis	12.00
6	Barry Sanders	16.00
7	Jerry Rice	8.00
8	Kordell Stewart	6.00
9	Jake Plummer	6.00
10	Brett Favre	16.00
11	Drew Bledsoe	6.00
12	Tony Banks	4.00
13	Kerry Collins	4.00
14	Steve McNair	6.00
15	Warren Moon	4.00
16	Ryan Leaf	10.00
17	Peyton Manning	16.00
18	Elvis Grbac	4.00
19	Jeff Blake	4.00
20	Brad Johnson	4.00
21	Trent Dilfer	4.00
22	Scott Mitchell	4.00
23	Dan Marino	12.00
24	John Elway	8.00
25	Troy Aikman	8.00
26	Steve Young	6.00
27	Terrell Davis	12.00
28	Barry Sanders	16.00
29	Jerry Rice	8.00
30	Kordell Stewart	6.00
31	Jake Plummer	6.00
32	Brett Favre	16.00

1998 SkyBox Thunder

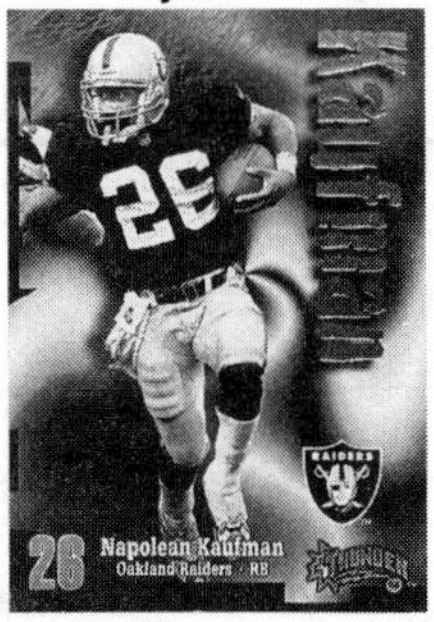

This 250-card set replaced Thunder in 1998 and arrived with 225 veterans and 25 rookies. Thunder was tiered, with 1-100 seeded 4:1 packs, 101-200 seeded 3:1 and 201-250 seeded 1:1. Cards featured a borderless artsy design with the color image of the player over it. The player's last name was foil stamped in large letters down either side. Each card was reprinted in both Rave and Super Rave parallel sets. Thunder also included five insert sets: Boss, Destination: End Zone, Number Crushers, Quick Strike, Autographics and StarBurst.

		MT
Complete Set (250):		50.00
Common Player (1-200):		.10
Minor Stars (1-200):		.20
Common Player (201-250):		.20
Minor Stars (201-250):		.40
Rave Cards (1-200):		40x-80x
Rave Stars (201-250):		20x-40x
Rave Rookies (201-250):		10x-20x
Pack (8):		1.50
Wax Box (36):		50.00
1	Reggie White	.20
2	Elvis Grbac	.10
3	Ed McCaffrey	.10
4	O.J. McDuffie	.10
5	Scott Mitchell	.10
6	Byron Hanspard	.20
7	John Randle	.10
8	Shawn Jefferson	.10
9	Peter Boulware	.10
10	Karl Williams	.10
11	Napoleon Kaufman	.50
12	Barry Minter	.10
13	Cris Dishman	.10
14	James Stewart	.10
15	Marcus Robertson	.10
16	Rodney Harrison	.10
17	Micheal Barrow	.10
18	Michael Sinclair	.10
19	DeWayne Washington	.10
20	Phillippi Sparks	.10
21	Ernie Conwell	.10
22	Ken Dilger	.10
23	Johnnie Morton	.10
24	Eric Swann	.10
25	Curtis Conway	.20
26	Duce Staley	.10
27	Darrell Green	.10
28	Quinn Early	.10
29	LeRoy Butler	.10
30	Winfred Tubbs	.10
31	Darren Woodson	.10
32	Marcus Allen	.20
33	Glenn Foley	.10
34	Tom Knight	.10
35	Sam Shade	.10
36	James McKnight	.10
37	Leeland McElroy	.10
38	Earl Holmes	.10
39	Ryan McNeil	.10
40	Cris Carter	.20
41	Jessie Armstead	.10
42	Bryce Paup	.10
43	Chris Slade	.10
44	Eric Metcalf	.10
45	Jim Harbaugh	.20
46	Terry Kirby	.10
47	Donnie Edwards	.10
48	Darryl Williams	.10
49	Neil Smith	.10
50	Warren Sapp	.10
51	Jason Taylor	.10
52	Irving Fryar	.10
53	Jeff George	.20
54	Yancey Thigpen	.10
55	Ricky Proehl	.10
56	Kevin Greene	.10
57	Joel Steed	.10
58	Larry Allen	.10
59	Thurman Thomas	.20
60	Aaron Glenn	.10
61	Natrone Means	.20
62	Chris Calloway	.10
63	Chuck Smith	.10
64	Chidi Ahanotu	.10
65	Mario Bates	.10
66	Jonathan Ogden	.10
67	Drew Bledsoe	1.00
68	John Mobley	.10
69	Antowain Smith	.60
70	Aeneas Williams	.10
71	Brian Williams	.10
72	Derrick Thomas	.10
73	Ted Johnson	.10
74	Troy Drayton	.10
75	Mike Pritchard	.10
76	Darnay Scott	.10
77	James Jett	.10
78	Dwayne Rudd	.10
79	Marvin Harrison	.20
80	Dermontti Dawson	.10
81	Keith Lyle	.10
82	Steve Atwater	.10
83	Tyrone Wheatley	.10
84	Tony Brackens	.10
85	Dale Carter	.10
86	Robert Porcher	.10
87	Merton Hanks	.10
88	Leon Johnson	.10
89	Simeon Rice	.10
90	Robert Brooks	.10
91	William Thomas	.10
92	Wesley Walls	.10
93	Chester McGlockton	.10
94	Chris Chandler	.10
95	Michael Strahan	.10
96	Ray Zellars	.10
97	Dexter Coakley	.10
98	Rob Johnson	.20
99	Eric Green	.10
100	Darrien Gordon	.10
101	Gary Brown	.10
102	Reidel Anthony	.20
103	Keenan McCardell	.10
104	Leslie O'Neal	.10
105	Bryant Westbrook	.10
106	Derrick Alexander	.10
107	Jeff Blake	.20
108	Ben Coates	.10
109	Shawn Springs	.10
110	Robert Smith	.20
111	Karim Abdul-Jabbar	.20
112	Willie Davis	.10
113	Mark Chmura	.20
114	Terry Allen	.10
115	Will Blackwell	.10
116	Jamal Anderson	.10
117	Dana Stubblefield	.10
118	Trent Dilfer	.20
119	Jermaine Lewis	.10
120	Chad Brown	.10
121	Tamarick Vanover	.10
122	Tony Martin	.10
123	Larry Centers	.10
124	J.J. Stokes	.10
125	Danny Kanell	.10
126	Wayne Chrebet	.10
127	Kerry Collins	.20
128	Tony Banks	.30
129	Randal Hill	.10
130	Jimmy Smith	.10
131	Tim Brown	.20
132	Zach Thomas	.10
133	Rod Smith	.20
134	Frank Wycheck	.10
135	Garrison Hearst	.20
136	Bruce Smith	.10
137	Hardy Nickerson	.10
138	Sean Dawkins	.10
139	Willie McGinest	.10
140	Kimble Anders	.10
141	Michael Westbrook	.10
142	Chris Doleman	.10
143	Ricky Watters	.20
144	Levon Kirkland	.10
145	Rob Moore	.20
146	Eddie Kennison	.20
147	Rickey Dudley	.10
148	Jay Graham	.10
149	Brad Johnson	.30
150	Bobby Hoying	.10
151	Sherman Williams	.10
152	Charles Way	.10
153	Adrian Murrell	.20
154	Chris Sanders	.10
155	Greg Hill	.10
156	Rae Carruth	.20
157	Mike Alstott	.50
158	Terance Mathis	.10
159	Antonio Freeman	.30
160	Junior Seau	.20
161	Chris Warren	.10
162	Shannon Sharpe	.20
163	Derrick Rodgers	.10
164	Charles Johnson	.10
165	Marshall Faulk	.20
166	Jamie Asher	.10
167	Michael Jackson	.10
168	Terrell Owens	.30
169	Jason Sehorn	.10
170	Raymont Harris	.10
171	Jake Reed	.10
172	Kevin Hardy	.10
173	Jerald Moore	.10
174	Michael Irvin	.20
175	Freddie Jones	.10
176	Steve McNair	.50
177	Carnell Lake	.10
178	Troy Brown	.10
179	Hugh Douglas	.10
180	Andre Rison	.20
181	Leslie Shepherd	.10
182	Andre Hastings	.10
183	Fred Lane	.20
184	Andre Reed	.10
185	Darrell Russell	.10
186	Frank Sanders	.10
187	Derrick Brooks	.10
188	Charlie Garner	.10
189	Bert Emanuel	.10
190	Terrell Buckley	.10
191	Carl Pickens	.20
192	Tiki Barber	.30
193	Pete Mitchell	.10
194	Gilbert Brown	.10
195	Isaac Bruce	.30
196	Ray Lewis	.10
197	Warren Moon	.20
198	Tony Gonzalez	.20
199	John Mobley	.10
200	Gus Frerotte	.10
201	Brett Favre	4.00
202	Terrell Davis	2.50
203	Dan Marino	3.50
204	Barry Sanders	4.00
205	Steve Young	1.00
206	Deion Sanders	1.00
207	Kordell Stewart	2.00
208	Eddie George	2.50
209	Jake Plummer	2.00
210	Warrick Dunn	2.00
211	John Elway	2.00
212	Terry Glenn	.40
213	Mark Brunell	2.00
214	Corey Dillon	1.50
215	Joey Galloway	.40
216	Dorsey Levens	.40
217	Troy Aikman	2.00
218	Keyshawn Johnson	.40
219	Jerome Bettis	.40
220	Curtis Martin	1.25
221	Herman Moore	.40
222	Emmitt Smith	3.50
223	Jerry Rice	2.00
224	Drew Bledsoe	2.00
225	Antowain Smith	1.25
226	*Stephen Alexander*	.20
227	*John Avery*	.50
228	*Kevin Dyson*	2.00
229	*Robert Edwards*	.75
230	*Greg Ellis*	.20
231	*Curtis Enis*	3.00
232	*Chris Fuamatu-Ma'afal*	.75
233	*Ahman Green*	.75
234	*Jacquez Green*	2.00
235	*Az-Zahir Hakim*	.75
236	*Skip Hicks*	.75
237	*Joe Jurevicius*	.50
238	*Ryan Leaf*	4.00
239	*Peyton Manning*	20.00
240	*Alonzo Mayes*	.50
241	*R.W. McQuarters*	.20
242	*Randy Moss*	20.00
243	*Marcus Nash*	.50
244	*Jerome Pathon*	.50
245	*Jason Peter*	.50
246	*Brian Simmons*	.50
247	*Takeo Spikes*	.50
248	*Fred Taylor*	8.00
249	*Andre Wadsworth*	.50
250	*Charles Woodson*	3.00

1998 SkyBox Thunder Rave

Rave was a 250-card parallel set to Thunder, and featured prismatic silver foil on the front to distinguish

them from the base cards. Rave parallels were sequentially numbered to 150 on the back in silver foil and were found only in hobby packs.

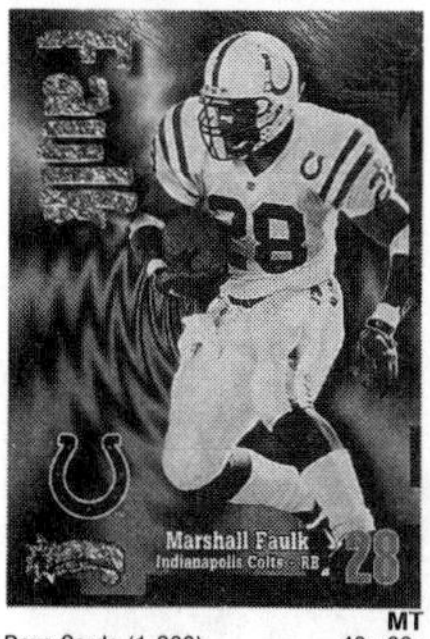
Marshall Faulk
Indianapolis Colts - RB

	MT
Rave Cards (1-200):	40x-80x
Rave Stars (201-250):	20x-40x
Rave Rookies (201-250):	10x-20x

1998 SkyBox Thunder Super Rave

Super Rave was a 250-card parallel set that was found only in hobby packs. Cards were sequentially numbered to 25 sets.

	MT
Super Rave Cards (1-200):	125x-250x
Super Rave Stars (201-250):	100x-200x
Super Rave Rookies (201-250):	20x-40x

1998 SkyBox Thunder Boss

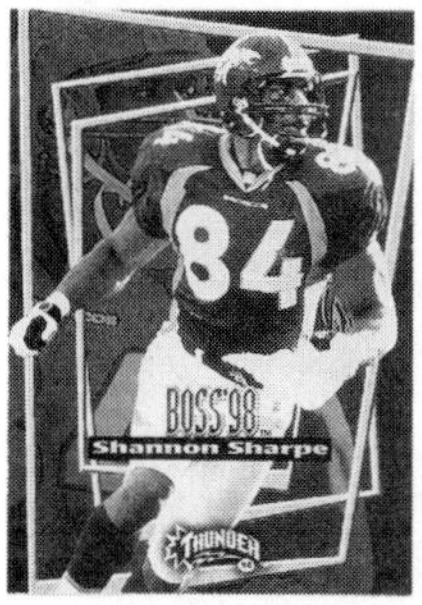
Shannon Sharpe

This insert featured 20 players on an embossed design. Backgrounds on the front were done in team colors with several quardrilaterals added. Boss cards were inserted one per eight packs and numbered with a "B" suffix.

		MT
Complete Set (20):		35.00
Common Player:		.75
Minor Stars:		1.50
1	Troy Aikman	6.00
2	Drew Bledsoe	6.00
3	Tim Brown	.75
4	Antonio Freeman	1.50
5	Joey Galloway	1.50
6	Terry Glenn	1.50
7	Bobby Hoying	.75
8	Michael Irvin	1.50
9	Keyshawn Johnson	.75
10	Dorsey Levens	1.50
11	Curtis Martin	5.00
12	John Mobley	.75
13	Jake Plummer	6.00
14	John Randle	.75
15	Deion Sanders	3.00
16	Junior Seau	.75
17	Shannon Sharpe	.75
18	Bruce Smith	.75
19	Robert Smith	.75
20	Dana Stubblefield	.75

1998 SkyBox Thunder Destination End Zone

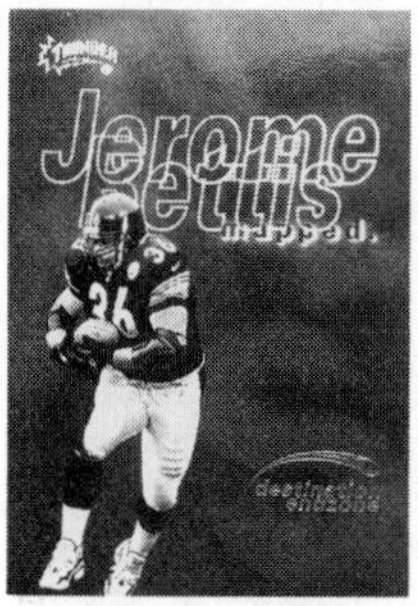
Jerome Bettis

This 15-card insert captured top scorers in the league on a green background. A small image of the player is placed in a bottom corner with his name in silver letters, and the insert name in red foil. These were inserted one per 96 packs and numbered with a "DE" suffix.

		MT
Complete Set (15):		200.00
Common Player:		5.00
1	Jerome Bettis	5.00
2	Mark Brunell	20.00
3	Terrell Davis	25.00
4	Corey Dillon	15.00
5	Warrick Dunn	20.00
6	John Elway	20.00
7	Brett Favre	50.00
8	Eddie George	20.00
9	Dorsey Levens	5.00
10	Curtis Martin	15.00
11	Herman Moore	5.00
12	Barry Sanders	50.00
13	Emmitt Smith	40.00
14	Kordell Stewart	25.00
15	Steve Young	15.00

1998 SkyBox Thunder Number Crushers

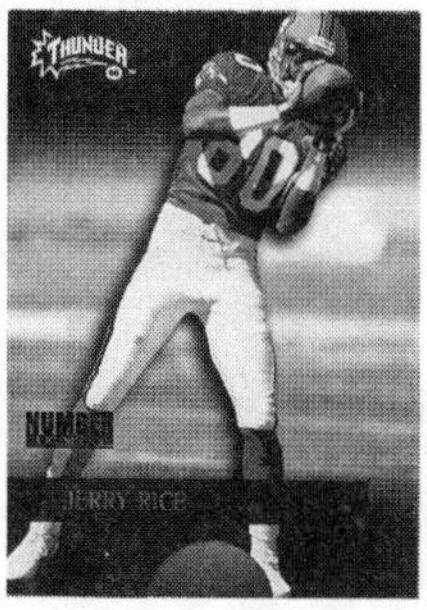
Jerry Rice

Number Crushers was a 10-card insert that featured the player on the front over a gridlike background. Backs were numbered with a "NC" suffix and included a Q&A section with a pull-out card that contained the answers. These were inserted one per 16 packs.

		MT
Complete Set (10):		45.00
Common Player:		2.00
Minor Stars:		4.00
1	Troy Aikman	6.00
2	Jerome Bettis	4.00
3	Tim Brown	2.00
4	Mark Brunell	6.00
5	Dan Marino	12.00
6	Herman Moore	4.00
7	Rob Moore	2.00
8	Jerry Rice	6.00
9	Shannon Sharpe	2.00
10	Emmitt Smith	12.00

1998 SkyBox Thunder Quick Strike

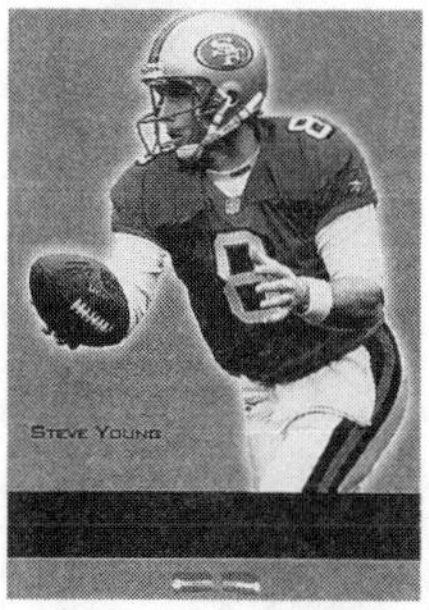
Steve Young

This 12-card, matchbook-like insert featured players over an olive background, with a black strip across the bottom resembling a match strike area. The card opened up to reveal another card of the player, while the back of the matchbook contained only the insert logo. Cards were inserted one per 300 packs and numbered with a "QS" suffix.

		MT
Complete Set (12):		550.00
Common Player:		25.00
1	Terrell Davis	50.00
2	John Elway	50.00
3	Brett Favre	80.00
4	Joey Galloway	25.00
5	Eddie George	50.00
6	Keyshawn Johnson	25.00
7	Dan Marino	70.00
8	Jerry Rice	50.00
9	Barry Sanders	80.00
10	Deion Sanders	30.00
11	Kordell Stewart	50.00
12	Steve Young	40.00

1998 SkyBox Thunder Star Burst

StarBurst was a 10-card insert featuring the player over a gold holofoil background that "bursts" against a regular background tinted in team colors. These were inserted one per 32 packs and numbered with a "SB" suffix.

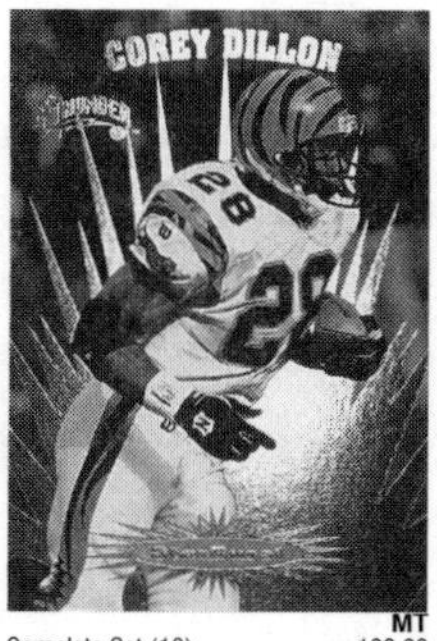
Corey Dillon

		MT
Complete Set (10):		100.00
Common Player:		3.00
1	Tiki Barber	3.00
2	Corey Dillon	8.00
3	Warrick Dunn	10.00
4	Curtis Enis	8.00
5	Ryan Leaf	12.00
6	Peyton Manning	20.00
7	Randy Moss	30.00
8	Jake Plummer	10.00
9	Antowain Smith	6.00
10	Charles Woodson	8.00

1999 SkyBox Dominion

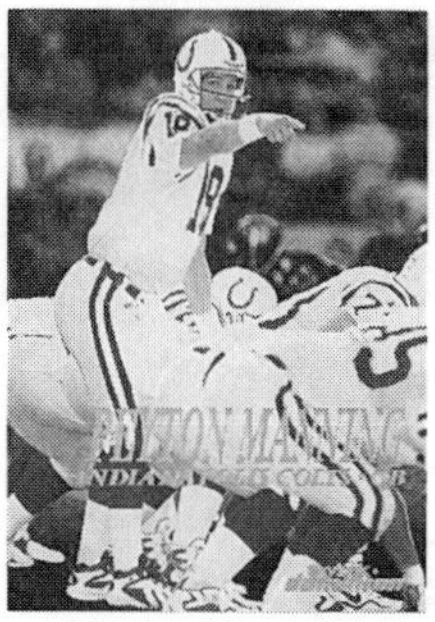
Peyton Manning

This was a 250-card set that included 50 unseeded rookie cards. Each base card included game-action photography with the player's name and team in silver foil. Insert sets included: Atlantattitude, Generation Next, Goal 2 Go, Hats Off and Hats Off Autographs. SRP was $1.89 for nine-card packs.

		MT
Complete Set (250):		45.00
Common Player:		.15
Minor Stars:		.30
Common Rookie:		.50
Pack (9):		2.25
Wax Box (36):		70.00
1	Randy Moss	2.00
2	James Jett	.15
3	Lawyer Milloy	.15
4	Mike Alstott	.50
5	Courtney Hawkins	.15
6	Carl Pickens	.30
7	Marvin Harrison	.50
8	Robert Smith	.50
9	Fred Taylor	1.00
10	Barry Sanders	2.00
11	Tony Gonzalez	.15
12	Leroy Hoard	.15
13	Drew Bledsoe	.75
14	Cam Cleeland	.30
15	Steve Atwater	.15
16	Eric Moulds	.50
17	Herman Moore	.50
18	Rickey Dudley	.15
19	Jeff Blake	.30
20	Eddie George	.50
21	Antonio Freeman	.50
22	Stephen Alexander	.15
23	Larry Centers	.15
24	Chris Chandler	.30
25	James Stewart	.30
26	Randall Cunningham	.50
27	Mark Brunell	.75
28	David Palmer	.15
29	Eric Green	.15
30	Terry Glenn	.50
31	Jerry Rice	1.00
32	Ricky Proehl	.15
33	Tony Banks	.30
34	John Elway	1.50
35	Johnnie Morton	.15
36	Tony Simmons	.30
37	Jon Kitna	.50
38	Trent Green	.30
39	Peyton Manning	1.50
40	Emmitt Smith	1.50
41	Warrick Dunn	.50
42	Jerome Bettis	.50
43	Ricky Watters	.30
44	Raghib Ismail	.15
45	Ryan Leaf	.30
46	Jackie Harris	.15
47	Robert Holcombe	.15
48	Dorsey Levens	.50
49	Duce Staley	.30
50	Brett Favre	2.00
51	Andre Rison	.15
52	Curtis Conway	.30
53	Mark Chmura	.30
54	Doug Flutie	.75
55	Ernie Mills	.15
56	Jeff George	.30
57	Chris Warren	.15
58	Alonzo Mayes	.15
59	Freddie Jones	.15
60	Shannon Sharpe	.30
61	O.J. Santiago	.15
62	Shawn Springs	.15
63	Kent Graham	.15
64	Muhsin Muhammad	.15
65	Keith Poole	.15
66	Chris Spielman	.15
67	Curtis Enis	.30
68	Lamar Smith	.15
69	Charles Johnson	.15
70	Kerry Collins	.30
71	Charlie Batch	.75
72	Keenan McCardell	.30
73	Ty Detmer	.30
74	Mark Bruener	.15
75	Lamar Thomas	.15
76	Kwamie Lassiter	.15
77	Bam Morris	.15
78	Michael Sinclair	.15
79	Darnay Scott	.30
80	Napoleon Kaufman	.50
81	Ed McCaffery	.30
82	Reidel Anthony	.30
83	Kevin Greene	.15
84	Michael Irvin	.30
85	Charles Way	.15
86	Tim Brown	.30
87	Johnny McWilliams	.15
88	Brad Johnson	.50
89	Antonio Langham	.15
90	Bruce Smith	.15
91	Reggie Barlow	.15
92	Ty Law	.15
93	Bobby Engram	.15
94	Kimble Anders	.15
95	Dale Carter	.15
96	Jimmy Smith	.30
97	Marc Edwards	.15
98	Ken Dilger	.15
99	Adrian Murrell	.30
100	Terance Mathis	.15
101	Gary Anderson	.15
102	Garrison Hearst	.30
103	Ahman Green	.30
104	Daryl Johnston	.15
105	O.J. McDuffie	.30
106	Matthew Hatchette	.15
107	Chris Doleman	.15
108	Steve McNair	.50
109	Leon Johnson	.15
110	Terrell Davis	1.50
111	Rob Moore	.30
112	Troy Aikman	1.00
113	John Avery	.30
114	Frank Wycheck	.15
115	Curtis Martin	.50
116	Jim Harbaugh	.30
117	Sean Dawkins	.15
118	Glenn Foley	.30
119	Warren Sapp	.15
120	R.W. McQuarters	.15
121	Yancey Thigpen	.30
122	Frank Sanders	.30
123	Tim Dwight	.50
124	Pete Mitchell	.15
125	Steve Beuerlein	.30
126	Tyrone Davis	.15
127	Jamie Asher	.15
128	Corey Dillon	.50
129	Doug Pederson	.15
130	Deion Sanders	.50
131	J.J. Stokes	.30
132	Jermaine Lewis	.30
133	Gary Brown	.15
134	Derrick Alexander	.15
135	Tony McGee	.15
136	Kyle Brady	.15
137	Mikhael Ricks	.15
138	Germane Crowell	.30
139	Skip Hicks	.30
140	Ben Coates	.30
141	Will Blackwell	.15
142	Al Del Greco	.15
143	Jake Plummer	1.00
144	Marshall Faulk	.50
145	Antowain Smith	.50
146	Corey Fuller	.15
147	Keyshawn Johnson	.50
148	John Randle	.15
149	Terrell Buckley	.15
150	Terry Kirby	.15
151	Robert Brooks	.15
152	Karim Abdul	.30
153	Jason Seahorn	.15
154	Elvis Grbac	.30
155	Andre Reed	.15
156	Ike Hilliard	.15
157	Jamal Anderson	.50
158	Jake Reed	.15
159	Rich Gannon	.15
160	Michael Jackson	.15
161	Bert Emanuel	.15
162	Charles Woodson	.50
163	Ray Lewis	.15
164	Trent Dilfer	.30
165	Oronde Gadsden	.30
166	Wesley Walls	.15
167	Joey Galloway	.50
168	Mo Lewis	.15
169	Darren Woodson	.15
170	Cris Carter	.50
171	Brian Mitchell	.15
172	Tim Biakabutuka	.30
173	Michael Westbrook	.30
174	Dan Marino	1.50
175	Greg Hill	.15
176	Priest Holmes	.50
177	Fred Lane	.15
178	Isaac Bruce	.30
179	Erik Kramer	.15
180	Steve Young	.75
181	Terry Fair	.15
182	Brian Griese	.75
183	Leslie Shepherd	.15
184	Kordell Stewart	.75
185	Charlie Jones	.15
186	Chris Calloway	.15
187	Wayne Chrebet	.30
188	Natrone Means	.30
189	David LaFleur	.15
190	Rod Smith	.30
191	Kevin Dyson	.30
192	Scott Mitchell	.15
193	Andre Wadsworth	.15
194	Vinny Testaverde	.30
195	Az-Zahir Hakim	.30
196	Joe Jurevicius	.15
197	Junior Seau	.30
198	Jason Elam	.15
199	Terrell Owens	.50
200	Jacquez Green	.30
201	*Tim Couch*	8.00
202	*Donovan McNabb*	5.00
203	*Cade McNown*	2.00
204	*Akili Smith*	5.00
205	*Kevin Faulk*	2.00
206	*Sedrick Irvin*	1.50
207	*Edgerrin James*	8.00
208	*Ricky Williams*	8.00
209	*D'Wayne Bates*	1.00
210	*David Boston*	3.00
211	*Torry Holt*	3.00
212	*Peerless Price*	2.00
213	*Daunte Culpepper*	5.00
214	*Troy Edwards*	3.00
215	*Rob Konrad*	1.00
216	*Joe Germaine*	1.00
217	*James Johnson*	1.50
218	*Brock Huard*	1.50
219	*Cecil Collins*	5.00
220	*Jeff Paulk,Eugene Baker*	.50
221	*Marty Booker,Jim Finn*	.50
222	*Scott Covington,Nick Williams*	.50
223	*Kevin Johnson,Darrin Chiaverini*	3.00
224	*Ebenezer Ekuban,Dat Nguyen*	.75
225	*Al Wilson,Chad Plummer*	.50
226	*Chris Claiborne,Aaron Gibson*	.75
227	*Aaron Brooks,De'Mond Parker*	2.50
228	*John Tait,Michael Cloud*	.75
229	*Andy Katzenmoyer,Michael Bishop*	1.50
230	*Joe Montgomery,Dan Campbell*	.75
231	*Na Brown,Cecil Martin*	.50
232	*Amos Zereoue,Jerame Tuman*	1.50
233	*Jermaine Fazande,Steve Heiden*	.50
234	*Karsten Bailey,Charlie Rogers*	.50
235	*Shaun King,Martin Gramatica*	4.00
236	*Jevon Kearse,Kevin Daft*	1.50
237	*Champ Bailey,Tim Alexander*	1.50
238	*Karsten Bailey,Darnell McDonald*	1.00
239	*Lamarr Glenn,Terry Jackson*	.50
240	*Troy Smith,Malcolm Johnson*	.50
241	*Rondel Menendez,Craig Yeast*	.50
242	*Jed Weaver,James Dearth*	.50
243	*Joel Makovicka,Shawn Bryson*	.50
244	*Desmond Clark,Jim Kleinsasser*	.75
245	*Sean Bennett,Autry Denson*	1.00
246	*Billy Miller,Wane McGarity*	.75
247	*Mike Lucky,Justin Swift*	.50
248	*Travis McGriff,Mar Tay Jenkins*	.75
249	*Donald Driver,Larry Parker*	.75
250	*Antoine Winfield,Dre' Bly*	.75

1999 SkyBox Dominion Atlantattitude

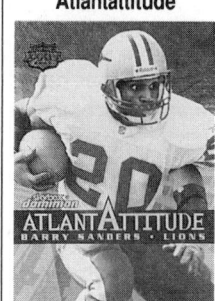

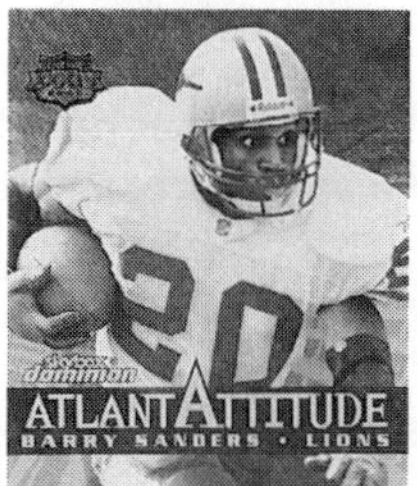
Atlantattitude
Barry Sanders • Lions

This 15-card insert set included players who had the chance to lead their team to Super Bowl XXXIV in Atlanta. Singles were inserted 1:24 packs. Parallel Plus sets (1:240) and Warp Tek (numbered to player's uniform number) were also issued.

		MT
Complete Set (15):		100.00
Common Player:		2.00
Minor Stars:		4.00
Inserted 1:24		
Plus Cards:		3x
Inserted 1:240		
Warp Tek Cards:		
Production to player's uniform number		
1	Charlie Batch	4.00
2	Mark Brunell	5.00
3	Tim Couch	15.00
4	Terrell Davis	10.00
5	Warrick Dunn	4.00
6	Brett Favre	15.00
7	Peyton Manning	10.00
8	Dan Marino	10.00
9	Randy Moss	15.00
10	Jake Plummer	7.00
11	Barry Sanders	15.00
12	Akili Smith	7.00
13	Emmitt Smith	10.00
14	Fred Taylor	7.00
15	Ricky Williams	15.00

1999 SkyBox Dominion Atlantattitude Plus Parallel

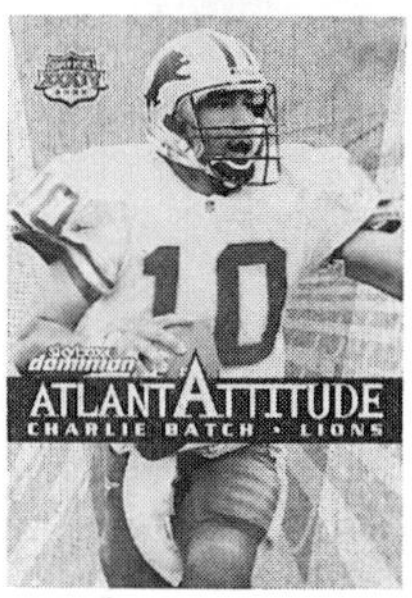
Atlantattitude
Charlie Batch • Lions

This was a 15-card insert set that paralleled the Atlantattitude insert. Singles from this insert were found 1:240 packs.

	MT
Plus Cards:	3x
Inserted 1:240	

1999 SkyBox Dominion Atlantattitude Warp Tek Parallel

This was a 15-card insert set that paralleled the Atlantattitude insert. Each single in this set was sequentially numbered to the player's jersey number.

		MT
Common Player:		50.00
Production to player's uniform number		
1	Charlie Batch 10	135.00
2	Mark Brunell 8	150.00
3	Tim Couch 2	500.00
4	Terrell Davis 30	140.00
5	Warrick Dunn 28	50.00
6	Brett Favre 4	400.00
7	Peyton Manning 18	225.00
8	Dan Marino 13	275.00
9	Randy Moss 84	100.00
10	Jake Plummer 16	150.00
11	Barry Sanders 20	275.00
12	Akili Smith 11	135.00
13	Emmitt Smith 22	175.00
14	Fred Taylor 28	125.00
15	Ricky Williams 34	200.00

1999 SkyBox Dominion Generation Next

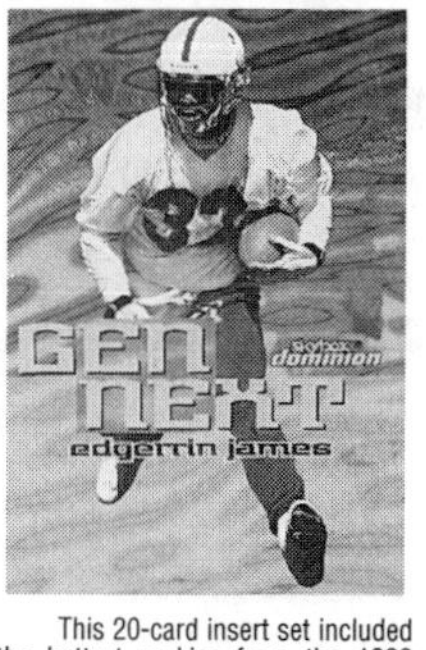
Gen Next
edgerrin james

This 20-card insert set included the hottest rookies from the 1999 season. Singles were inserted 1:3 packs. Two parallel sets were issued: Plus (1:30) and Warp Tek (1:300).

		MT
Complete Set (20):		25.00
Common Player:		.50
Minor Stars:		1.00
Inserted 1:3		
Plus Cards:		3x
Inserted 1:30		
Warp Tek Cards:		5x-10x
Inserted 1:300		
1	D'Wayne Bates	.50
2	David Boston	1.50
3	Cecil Collins	2.50
4	Tim Couch	5.00
5	Daunte Culpepper	2.50
6	Troy Edwards	1.50
7	Kevin Faulk	1.25
8	Joe Germaine	1.00
9	Torry Holt	1.50
10	Brock Huard	1.00
11	Sedrick Irvin	1.00
12	Edgerrin James	4.00
13	James Johnson	1.25
14	Kevin Johnson	1.50
15	Shaun King	1.25
16	Donovan McNabb	2.50
17	Cade McNown	2.50
18	Akili Smith	2.50
19	Ricky Williams	5.00
20	Amos Zereoue	1.25

1999 SkyBox Dominion Generation Next Plus Parallel

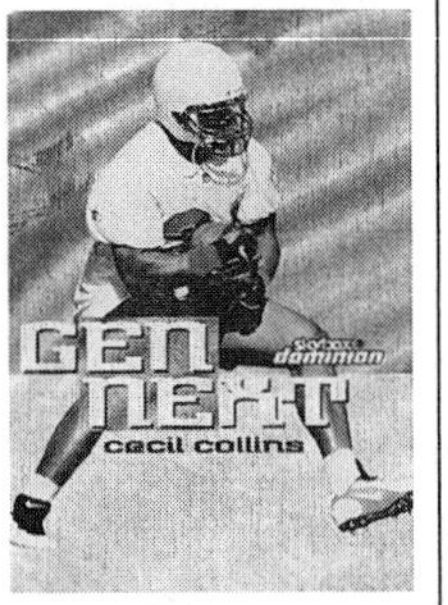

This was a 20-card insert set that paralleled the Generation Next insert. These singles were found 1:30 packs.

	MT
Plus Cards:	3x
Inserted 1:30	

1999 SkyBox Dominion Generation Next Warp Tek Parallel

This was a 20-card insert set that paralleled the Generation Next insert. These singles were found 1:300 packs.

		MT
Warp Tek Cards:		5x-10x
Inserted 1:300		
1	D'Wayne Bates	6.00
2	David Boston	10.00
3	Cecil Collins	8.00
4	Tim Couch	35.00
5	Daunte Culpepper	20.00
6	Troy Edwards	10.00
7	Kevin Faulk	8.00
8	Joe Germaine	6.00
9	Torry Holt	12.00
10	Brock Huard	6.00
11	Sedrick Irvin	8.00
12	Edgerrin James	50.00
13	James Johnson	8.00
14	Kevin Johnson	15.00
15	Shaun King	20.00
16	Donovan McNabb	20.00
17	Cade McNown	20.00
18	Akili Smith	15.00
19	Ricky Williams	35.00
20	Amos Zereoue	8.00

1999 SkyBox Dominion Goal 2 Go

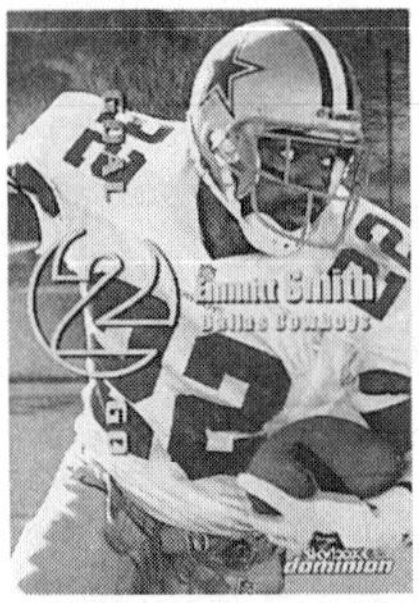

This was a 10-card insert set that pictured two players on the same card with one on each side. Singles were inserted 1:9 packs. A Plus parallel (1:90) and Warp Tek parallel (1:900) were also issued.

		MT
Complete Set (10):		25.00
Common Player:		1.50
Inserted 1:9		
Plus Cards:		3x
Inserted 1:90		
Warp Tek Cards:		10x-20x
Inserted 1:900		
1	Terrell Davis, Jamal Anderson	4.00
2	Brett Favre, Jake Plummer	5.00
3	Randy Moss, Jerry Rice	5.00
4	Warrick Dunn, Barry Sanders	5.00
5	Eddie George, Fred Taylor	1.50
6	Emmitt Smith, Marshall Faulk	4.00
7	Keyshawn Johnson, Terrell Owens	1.50
8	Peyton Manning, Ryan Leaf	4.00
9	Dan Marino, John Elway	4.00
10	Cade McNown, Charlie Batch	3.00

A player's name in *italic type* indicates a rookie card.

1999 SkyBox Dominion Goal 2 Go Plus Parallel

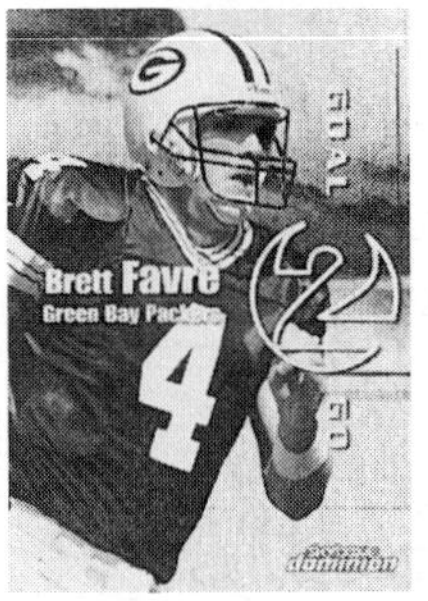

This was a 10-card insert set that paralleled the Goal 2 Go insert. Singles were found 1:90 packs.

	MT
Plus Cards:	3x
Inserted 1:90	

1999 SkyBox Dominion Goal 2 Go Warp Tek Parallel

This was a 10-card insert set that paralleled the Goal 2 Go insert. Singles were inserted 1:900 packs.

		MT
Warp Tek Cards:		10x-20x
Inserted 1:900		
1	Terrell Davis, Jamal Anderson	25.00
2	Brett Favre, Jake Plummer	40.00
3	Randy Moss, Jerry Rice	35.00
4	Warrick Dunn, Barry Sanders	35.00
5	Eddie George, Fred Taylor	20.00
6	Emmitt Smith, Marshall Faulk	25.00
7	Keyshawn Johnson, Terrell Owens	15.00
8	Peyton Manning, Ryan Leaf	35.00
9	Dan Marino, John Elway	35.00
10	Cade McNown, Charlie Batch	35.00

1999 SkyBox Dominion Hats Off

This six-card insert set included swatches of caps worn at the 1999 NFL Draft on April 10, 1999 in New York City by six NFL rookies. Each card has a different amount produced and singles were randomly inserted.

		MT
Complete Set (6):		750.00
Common Player:		100.00
1	Tim Couch 135	200.00
2	Donovan McNabb 130	120.00
3	Akili Smith 85	100.00
4	Ricky Williams 130	200.00
5	Daunte Culpepper 100	120.00
6	Cade McNown 120	120.00

1999 SkyBox Dominion Hats Off Autographs

This is a five-card insert set that parallels the Hats Off insert. Each of these singles was autographed. Tim Couch did not sign in this insert. Each player signed a total of 20 cards.

	MT
Complete Set (5):	2000.
Common Player:	300.00
Production 20 Sets	
Couch did not sign	
Donovan McNabb	450.00
Akili Smith	300.00
Ricky Williams	600.00
Daunte Culpepper	550.00
Cade McNown	300.00

1999 SkyBox Molten Metal

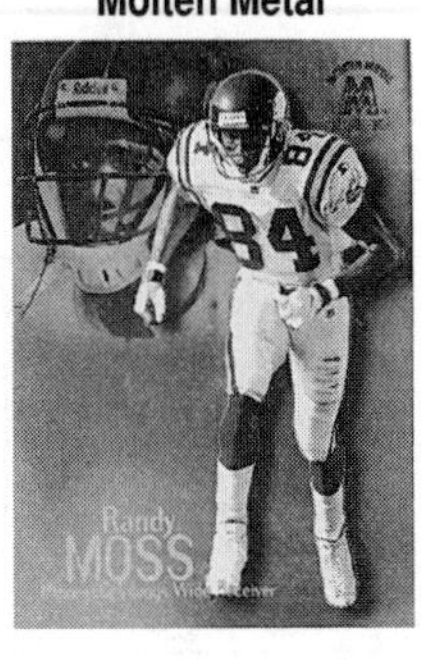

This 151-card set had a 26-card rookie subset that was inserted 1:5 packs. Each of the rookie cards had rounded corners and was printed on actual metal. Insert sets included: Autographics, Gridiron Gods, Patchworks, Perfect Fit and Top Notch. SRP was $2.99 for five-card packs.

		MT
Complete Set (151):		120.00
Common Player:		.25
Minor Stars:		.50
Common Rookie:		2.00
Inserted 1:5		
Pack (5):		4.00
Wax Box (24):		75.00
1	Terrell Davis	4.50
2	Chris Chandler	.50
3	Terry Glenn	1.00
4	Jon Kitna	1.25
5	Bubby Brister	.50
6	Jermaine Lewis	.25
7	Doug Flutie	2.00
8	Napoleon Kaufman	1.00
9	Yancey Thigpen	.50
10	Bobby Engram	.25
11	Barry Sanders	6.00
12	Ben Coates	.50
13	Joey Galloway	1.00
14	Charlie Batch	2.00
15	Jerome Bettis	1.00
16	Brad Johnson	1.00
17	Brian Griese	2.50
18	Jeff Lewis	.25
19	Jake Plummer	2.50
20	Mark Brunell	2.50
21	Robert Smith	1.00
22	Steve Young	2.00
23	Derrick Mayes	.50
24	Wayne Chrebet	.75
25	Rich Gannon	.50
26	Steve McNair	1.25
27	Charles Johnson	.25
28	Stephen Alexander	.25
29	Jeff Blake	.50
30	Tony Gonzalez	.50
31	Eddie Kennison	.25
32	Hines Ward	.50
33	Isaac Bruce	1.00
34	Peyton Manning	4.50
35	Doug Pederson	.25
36	Stephen Davis	1.00
37	Terance Mathis	.25
38	Herman Moore	1.00
39	Fred Taylor	3.00
40	Courtney Hawkins	.25
41	Michael Westbrook	.50
42	Vinny Testaverde	.50
43	Jacquez Green	.50
44	Rocket Ismail	.25
45	Curtis Martin	1.00
46	Tim Brown	.50
47	Kevin Dyson	.50
48	Steve Beuerlein	.50
49	Adrian Murrell	.50
50	Randall Cunningham	1.00
51	Jerry Rice	3.00
52	Tim Biakabutuka	.50
53	Muhsin Muhammad	.50
54	Antonio Freeman	1.00
55	Cris Carter	1.00
56	Lawrence Phillips	.50
57	Michael Irvin	.50
58	Terrell Owens	1.00
59	Warrick Dunn	1.00
60	Leslie Shepherd	.25
61	O.J. McDuffie	.50
62	Byron Hanspard	.25
63	Trent Dilfer	.50
64	Eric Moulds	1.00
65	Scott Mitchell	.25
66	Marc Edwards	.25
67	Dorsey Levens	1.00
68	Dan Marino	4.50
69	Jason Sehorn	.25
70	Junior Seau	.50
71	Reidel Anthony	.50
72	Rob Moore	.50
73	Deion Sanders	1.00
74	Rickey Dudley	.50
75	Keyshawn Johnson	1.00
76	Eddie George	1.25
77	E.G. Green	.50
78	Terry Kirby	.25
79	John Avery	.50
80	Pete Mitchell	.25
81	Natrone Means	.75
82	Mike Alstott	1.00
83	Carl Pickens	.50
84	Karim Abdul	.50
85	Kerry Collins	.50
86	Erik Kramer	.25
87	Robert Holcombe	.50
88	Willie Jackson	.25
89	Marcus Pollard	.25
90	Bam Morris	.25
91	Gary Brown	.25
92	Freddie Jones	.25
93	*Kurt Warner*	20.00
94	Priest Holmes	1.00
95	Duce Staley	1.00
96	Skip Hicks	.50
97	Frank Sanders	.50
98	Corey Dillon	1.00
99	Shannon Sharpe	.75
100	Randy Moss	6.00
101	Sean Dawkins	.25
102	Marshall Faulk	1.00
103	Mark Chmura	.50
104	Keenan McCardell	.50
105	Jimmy Smith	1.00
106	Jim Harbaugh	.50
107	Jamal Anderson	1.00
108	Elvis Grbac	.50
109	Ed McCaffrey	.75
110	Drew Bledsoe	2.50
111	Curtis Conway	.50
112	Billy Joe Tolliver	.25
113	J.J. Stokes	.50
114	Curtis Enis	1.00
115	Antowain Smith	1.00
116	Troy Aikman	3.00
117	Ricky Watters	.50
118	Kordell Stewart	1.00
119	Derrick Alexander	.25
120	Emmitt Smith	4.50
121	Billy Joe Hobert	.25
122	Johnnie Morton	.25
123	Rod Smith	.75
124	Marvin Harrison	1.00
125	Brett Favre	6.00
126	*Craig Yeast*	2.00
127	*Ricky Williams*	12.00
128	*Brandon Stokley*	2.00
129	*Akili Smith*	7.00
130	*Peerless Price*	4.00
131	*Joe Montgomery*	2.00
132	*Cade McNown*	5.00
133	*Donovan McNabb*	10.00
134	*Shaun King*	6.00
135	*J.J. Johnson*	3.00
136	*Kevin Johnson*	5.00
137	*Edgerrin James*	15.00
138	*Terry Jackson*	2.00
139	*Sedrick Irvin*	3.00
140	*Brock Huard*	3.00
141	*Torry Holt*	5.00
142	*Amos Zereoue*	2.00
143	*Kevin Faulk*	3.00
144	*Troy Edwards*	3.00
145	*Donald Driver*	2.00
146	*Daunte Culpepper*	12.00
147	*Tim Couch*	12.00
148	*Cecil Collins*	3.00
149	*David Boston*	5.00
150	*Champ Bailey*	3.00
151	*Olandis Gary*	6.00

1999 SkyBox Molten Metal Gridiron Gods

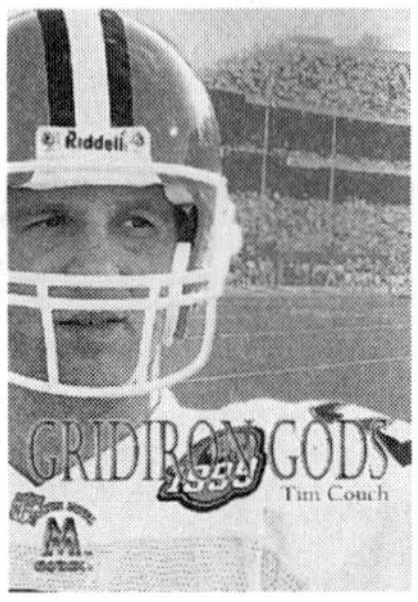

This 20-card insert set included the top players in the NFL. Singles were inserted 1:6 packs. Parallel Silver (1:24), Gold (1:72) and Blue (numbered to 99) sets were also released.

		MT
Complete Set (20):		50.00
Common Player:		2.00
Inserted 1:6		
Silver Cards:		2x
Inserted 1:24		
Gold Cards:		4x
Inserted 1:72		
Blue Cards:		5x-10x
Production 99 Sets		
1	Randy Moss	6.00
2	Keyshawn Johnson	2.00
3	Mike Alstott	2.00
4	Brian Griese	3.00
5	Tim Couch	8.00
6	Troy Aikman	4.00
7	Warrick Dunn	2.00
8	Mark Brunell	3.00
9	Jerry Rice	4.00
10	Dorsey Levens	2.00
11	Fred Taylor	4.00
12	Emmitt Smith	5.00
13	Edgerrin James	12.00
14	Eddie George	2.50
15	Drew Bledsoe	3.00
16	Deion Sanders	2.00
17	Charlie Batch	2.50
18	Kordell Stewart	2.00
19	Brad Johnson	2.00
20	Akili Smith	3.50

1999 SkyBox Molten Metal Gridiron Gods Blue Parallel

This was a 20-card parallel to the Gridiron God insert set. Each of these singles was sequentially numbered to 99.

	MT
Blue Cards:	5x-10x
Production 99 Sets	

1999 SkyBox Molten Metal Gridiron Gods Gold Parallel

This was a 20-card parallel to the Gridiron Gods insert set. These singles were found 1:72 packs.

	MT
Gold Cards:	4x
Inserted 1:72	

A card number in parentheses ( ) indicates the set is unnumbered.

1999 SkyBox Molten Metal Gridiron Gods Silver Parallel

This was a 20-card parallel to the Gridiron Gods insert set. These singles were found 1:24 packs.

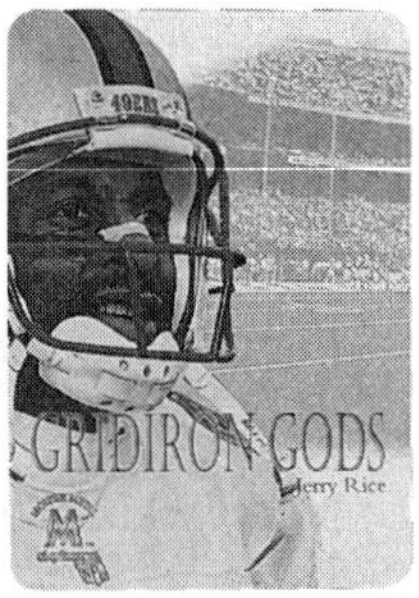

	MT
Silver Cards:	2x
Inserted 1:24	

1999 SkyBox Molten Metal Patchworks

This nine-card insert set included pieces of numbers, names or patches from player-worn jerseys. Singles were inserted 1:360 packs.

		MT
Complete Set (9):		1000.
Common Player:		50.00
Inserted 1:360		
1	Drew Bledsoe	100.00
2	Terrell Davis	125.00
3	Brett Favre	200.00
4	Peyton Manning	200.00
5	Dan Marino	175.00
6	Herman Moore	50.00
7	Randy Moss	250.00
8	Jerry Rice	125.00
9	Steve Young	85.00

1999 SkyBox Molten Metal Perfect Fit

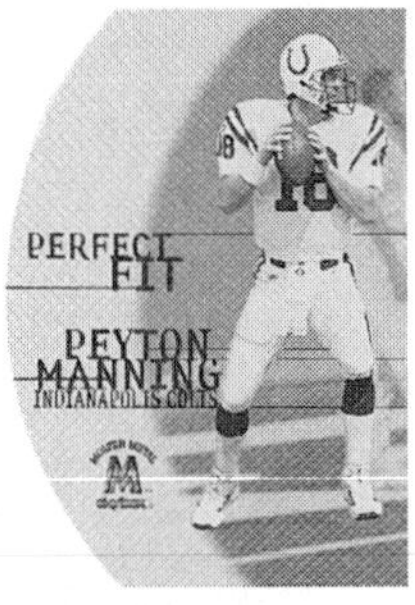

This 10-card insert set included players who make their teams complete. Singles were inserted 1:24 packs. Parallel Silver (1:72), Gold (1:216) and Red (numbered to 25) versions were also released.

		MT
Complete Set (10):		70.00
Common Player:		5.00
Inserted 1:24		
Silver Cards:		2x
Inserted 1:72		
Gold Cards:		4x
Inserted 1:216		
Red Cards:		8x-16x
Production 25 Sets		
1	Barry Sanders	12.00
2	Brett Favre	12.00
3	Dan Marino	10.00
4	Edgerrin James	20.00
5	Emmitt Smith	10.00
6	Fred Taylor	5.00
7	Randy Moss	12.00
8	Terrell Davis	10.00
9	Tim Couch	12.00
10	Peyton Manning	10.00

1999 SkyBox Molten Metal Perfect Fit Gold Parallel

This was a ten-card parallel to the Perfect Fit insert. Singles were found 1:216 packs.

	MT
Gold Cards: 4x	
Inserted 1:216	

1999 SkyBox Molten Metal Perfect Fit Red Parallel

This was a ten-card parallel to the Perfect Fit insert set. Each single was sequentially numbered to 25.

	MT
Red Cards:	8x-16x
Production 25 Sets	

1999 SkyBox Molten Metal Perfect Fit Silver Parallel

This was a ten-card parallel to the Perfect Fit insert set. Singles were inserted 1:72 packs.

	MT
Silver Cards:	2x
Inserted 1:72	

1999 SkyBox Molten Metal Top Notch

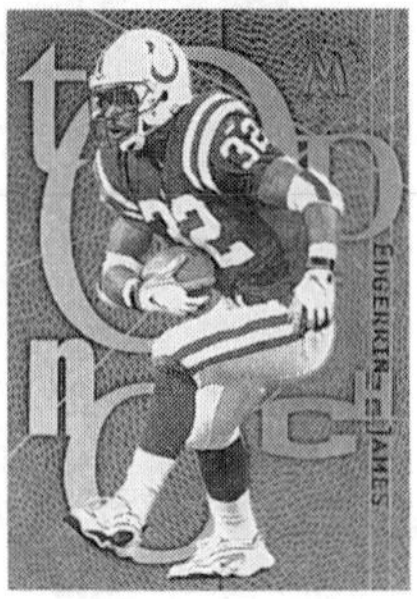

This 15-card insert set included the top players in the NFL. Singles were found 1:12 packs. Parallel Silver (1:36), Gold (1:108) and Green (numbered to 75) versions were also produced.

		MT
Complete Set (15):		60.00
Common Player:		2.00
Inserted 1:12		
Silver Cards:		2x
Inserted 1:36		
Gold Cards:		4x
Inserted 1:108		
Green Cards:		5x-10x
Production 75 Sets		
1	Jake Plummer	5.00
2	Cade McNown	6.00
3	Tim Couch	10.00
4	Emmitt Smith	7.00
5	Charlie Batch	4.00
6	Donovan McNabb	6.00
7	Steve Young	4.00
8	Brian Griese	4.00
9	Doug Flutie	4.00
10	Edgerrin James	15.00
11	Fred Taylor	5.00
12	Keyshawn Johnson	2.00
13	Mark Brunell	4.00
14	Randy Moss	10.00
15	Ricky Williams	10.00

1999 SkyBox Molten Metal Top Notch Gold Parallel

This was a 15-card parallel to the Top Notch insert set. Each of these singles was inserted 1:108 packs.

	MT
Gold Cards:	4x
Inserted 1:108	

1999 SkyBox Molten Metal Top Notch Green Parallel

This was a 15-card parallel to the Top Notch insert set. Singles were sequentially numbered to 75.

	MT
Green Cards:	5x-10x
Production 75 Sets	

1999 SkyBox Molten Metal Top Notch Silver Parallel

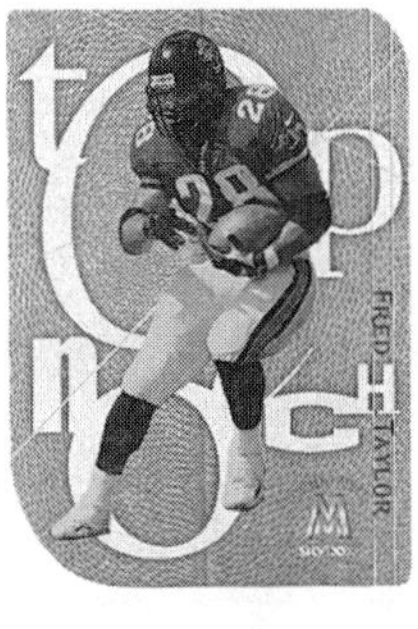

This was a 15-card parallel to the Top Notch insert set. Singles were found 1:36 packs.

	MT
Silver Cards:	2x
Inserted 1:36	

1999 SkyBox Premium

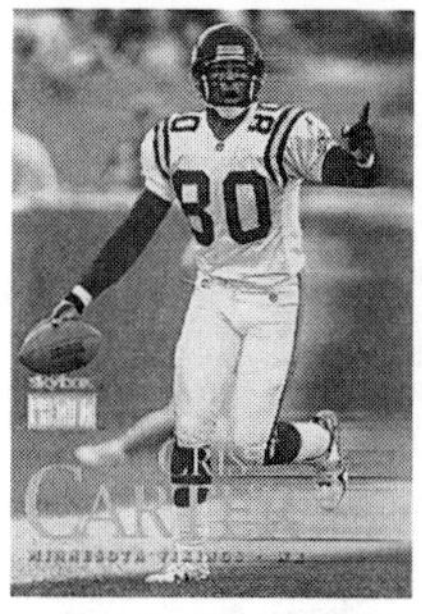

This was a 290-card set that included 40 rookies with two different cards. One version wasn't seeded while the other was found 1:8 packs. The seeded version pictured the rookies in an action photo, while the other version was posed. Insert sets included: Star Rubies, 2000 Men, Autographics, Box Tops, Deja Vu, Genuine Coverage, Prime Time Rookies and Year 2. SRP was $2.69 for eight-card packs.

		MT
Complete Set (290):		325.00
Common Player:		.15
Minor Stars:		.30
Common Rookie:		.50
Common SP:		1.50
SP in Action Photos		
Inserted 1:8		
Hobby Pack (8):		2.75
Hobby Wax Box (24):		60.00
1	Randy Moss	2.50
2	Jamie Asher	.15
3	Joey Galloway	.50
4	Kent Graham	.15
5	Leslie Shepherd	.15
6	Levon Kirkland	.15
7	Marcus Pollard	.15
8	O.J. McDuffie	.15
9	Bill Romanowski	.15
10	Priest Holmes	.50
11	Tim Biakabutuka	.15
12	Duce Staley	.30
13	Isaac Bruce	.30
14	Jay Riemersma	.15
15	Karim Abdul	.15
16	Kevin Dyson	.30
17	Rickey Dudley	.15
18	Rocket Ismail	.15
19	Billy Davis	.15
20	James Jett	.15
21	Jerome Bettis	.50
22	Michael McCrary	.15
23	Michael Westbrook	.30
24	Oronde Gadsden	.30
25	Brad Johnson	.50
26	Shawn Springs	.15
27	Cris Carter	.50
28	Ed McCaffrey	.30
29	Gary Brown	.15
30	Hines Ward	.30
31	Hugh Douglas	.15
32	Jamir Miller	.15
33	Michael Bates	.15
34	Peyton Manning	2.00
35	Tony Banks	.30
36	Charles Way	.15
37	Charlie Batch	1.00
38	Jake Reed	.15
39	Mark Brunell	1.00
40	Skip Hicks	.30
41	Steve Young	.75
42	Wesley Walls	.15
43	Antonio Langham	.15
44	Antowain Smith	.50
45	Brian Griese	1.00
46	Jessie Armstead	.15
47	Thurman Thomas	.30
48	Jeff George	.50
49	Jessie Tuggle	.15
50	Jim Harbaugh	.30
51	Marvin Harrison	.50
52	Randall Cunningham	.50
53	Stephen Alexander	.15
54	Tiki Barber	.30
55	Billy Joe Tolliver	.15
56	Bruce Smith	.15
57	Eddie George	.75
58	Eugene Robinson	.15
59	John Elway	2.00
60	Ken Dilger	.15
61	Rodney Harrison	.15
62	Ty Detmer	.15
63	Andre Reed	.15
64	Dorsey Levens	.50
65	Eddie Kennison	.15
66	Freddie Jones	.15
67	Jacquez Green	.30
68	Jason Elam	.15
69	Marc Edwards	.15
70	Terance Mathis	.15
71	Alonzo Mayes	.15
72	Andre Wadsworth	.15
73	Barry Sanders	2.50
74	Derrick Alexander	.15
75	Garrison Hearst	.30
76	Leon Johnson	.15
77	Mike Alstott	.50
78	Shawn Jefferson	.15
79	Andre Hastings	.15
80	Eric Moulds	.50
81	Ryan Leaf	.50
82	Takeo Spikes	.15
83	Terrell Davis	2.00
84	Tim Dwight	.50
85	Trent Dilfer	.30
86	Vonnie Holliday	.15
87	Antonio Freeman	.30
88	Carl Pickens	.30
89	Chris Chandler	.30
90	Dale Carter	.15
91	La'Roi Glover	.15
92	Natrone Means	.30
93	Reidel Anthony	.30
94	Brett Favre	2.50
95	Bubby Brister	.30
96	Cameron Cleeland	.30
97	Chris Calloway	.15
98	Corey Dillon	.50
99	Greg Hill	.15
100	Vinny Testaverde	.30
101	Trent Green	.30
102	Sam Gash	.15
103	Mikhael Ricks	.15
104	Emmitt Smith	2.00
105	Doug Flutie	.75
106	Deion Sanders	.50
107	Charles Johnson	.15
108	Bam Morris	.15
109	Andre Rison	.30
110	Doug Pederson	.15
111	Marshall Faulk	.50
112	Tim Brown	.30
113	Warren Sapp	.15
114	Bryan Still	.15
115	Chris Penn	.15
116	Jamal Anderson	.50
117	Keyshawn Johnson	.50
118	Ricky Proehl	.15
119	Robert Brooks	.15
120	Tony Gonzalez	.30
121	Ty Law	.15
122	Elvis Grbac	.30
123	Jeff Blake	.30
124	Mark Chmura	.30
125	Junior Seau	.30
126	Mo Lewis	.15
127	Ray Buchanan	.15
128	Robert Holcombe	.30
129	Tony Simmons	.30
130	David Palmer	.15
131	Ike Hilliard	.15
132	Mike Vanderjagt	.15
133	Rae Carruth	.15
134	Sean Dawkins	.15
135	Shannon Sharpe	.30
136	Curtis Conway	.30
137	Darrell Green	.15
138	Germane Crowell	.30
139	J.J. Stokes	.30
140	Kevin Hardy	.15
141	Rob Moore	.30
142	Robert Smith	.50
143	Wayne Chrebet	.30
144	Yancey Thigpen	.30
145	Jerome Pathon	.15
146	John Mobley	.15
147	Kerry Collins	.30
148	Peter Boulware	.15
149	Matthew Hatchette	.15
150	Kordell Stewart	.50
151	Koy Detmer	.15
152	Sedrick Shaw	.15
153	Steve Beuerlein	.30
154	Zach Thomas	.30
155	Adrian Murrell	.30
156	Bobby Engram	.15
157	Bryan Cox	.15
158	Drew Bledsoe	1.00
159	Jerry Rice	1.25
160	Keenan McCardell	.30
161	Steve McNair	.50
162	Terry Fair	.15
163	Derrick Brooks	.15
164	Eric Green	.15
165	Erik Kramer	.15
166	Frank Sanders	.15
167	Fred Taylor	1.25
168	Johnnie Morton	.15
169	R.W. McQuarters	.15
170	Terry Glenn	.50
171	Frank Wycheck	.15
172	John Avery	.30
173	Kevin Turner	.15
174	Larry Centers	.15
175	Michael Irvin	.30
176	Rich Gannon	.30
177	Ricky Watters	.30
178	Rodney Thomas	.15
179	Scott Mitchell	.15
180	Chad Brown	.15
181	John Randle	.15
182	Michael Strahan	.15
183	Muhsin Muhammad	.30
184	Reggie Barlow	.15
185	Rod Smith	.30
186	Dan Marino	2.00
187	Dexter Coakley	.15
188	Jermaine Lewis	.30
189	Jon Kitna	.75
190	Napoleon Kaufman	.50
191	Will Blackwell	.15
192	Aaron Glenn	.15
193	Ben Coates	.30
194	Curtis Enis	.50
195	Herman Moore	.50
196	Jake Plummer	1.25
197	Jimmy Smith	.50
198	Terrell Owens	.50
199	Warrick Dunn	.50
200	Charles Woodson	.50
201	Ahman Green	.30
202	Mark Bruener	.15
203	Ray Lewis	.15
204	Tony Martin	.15
205	Troy Aikman	1.25
206	Curtis Martin	.50
207	Darnay Scott	.30
208	Derrick Mayes	.30
209	Keith Poole	.15
210	Warren Moon	.30
211	*Chris Claiborne*	1.00
211	Chris Claiborne SP	5.00
212	*Ricky Williams*	8.00
212	Ricky Williams SP	30.00
213	*Tim Couch*	8.00
213	Tim Couch SP	30.00
214	*Champ Bailey*	1.50
214	Champ Bailey SP	6.00
215	*Torry Holt*	2.50
215	Torry Holt SP	10.00
216	*Donovan McNabb*	4.00
216	Donovan McNabb SP	15.00
217	*David Boston*	2.50
217	David Boston SP	10.00
218	*Chris McAllister*	1.00
218	Chris McAllister SP	5.00
219	*Michael Bishop*	1.75
219	Michael Bishop SP	7.00
220	*Daunte Culpepper*	6.00
220	Daunte Culpepper SP	20.00
221	*Joe Germaine*	1.50
221	Joe Germaine SP	6.00
222	*Edgerrin James*	10.00
222	Edgerrin James SP	40.00
223	*Jevon Kearse*	2.50
223	Jevon Kearse SP	10.00
224	*Ebenezer Ekuban*	1.00
224	Ebenezer Ekuban SP	3.00
225	*Scott Covington*	.50
225	Scott Covington SP	1.50
226	*Aaron Brooks*	3.00
226	Aaron Brooks SP	10.00
227	*Cecil Collins*	4.00
227	Cecil Collins SP	15.00
228	*Akili Smith*	4.00
228	Akili Smith SP	15.00
229	*Shaun King*	3.00
229	Shaun King SP	12.00
230	*Chad Plummer*	.50
230	Chad Plummer SP	1.50
231	*Peerless Price*	1.75
231	Peerless Price SP	8.00
232	*Antoine Winfield*	1.00
232	Antoine Winfield SP	3.00
233	*Antwan Edwards*	1.00
233	Antwan Edwards SP	3.00
234	*Rob Konrad*	1.00
234	Rob Konrad SP	3.00
235	*Troy Edwards*	2.50
235	Troy Edwards SP	10.00
236	*Terry Jackson*	.50
236	Terry Jackson SP	1.50
237	*Jimmy Kleinsasser*	1.00
237	Jim Kleinsasser SP	5.00
238	*Joe Montgomery*	1.50
238	Joe Montgomery SP	6.00
239	*Desmond Clark*	.50
239	Desmond Clark SP	1.50
240	*Lamar King*	.50
240	Lamar King SP	1.50
241	*Dameane Douglas*	.50
241	Dameane Douglas SP	1.50
242	*Martin Gramatica*	1.25
242	Martin Gramatica SP	6.00
243	*James Finn*	.50
243	James Finn SP	1.50
244	*Andy Katzenmoyer*	1.25
244	Andy Katzenmoyer SP	5.00
245	*Dee Miller*	.50
245	Dee Miller SP	1.50
246	*D'Wayne Bates*	1.00
246	D'Wayne Bates SP	3.00
247	*Amos Zereoue*	2.00
247	Amos Zereoue SP	8.00
248	*Karsten Bailey*	1.00
248	Karsten Bailey SP	3.00
249	*Kevin Johnson*	2.50
249	Kevin Johnson SP	10.00
250	*Cade McNown*	2.50
250	Cade McNown SP	5.00

1999 SkyBox Premium Shining Star Rubies Parallel

This was a 290-card parallel to the base set. Each of the singles was sequentially numbered to 30 except for the seeded rookie cards which were numbered to 15.

	MT
Ruby Cards: 50x-100x	
Ruby Rookies: 15x-30x	
Production 30 Sets	
Ruby SP's: 5x-10x	
Production 15 Sets	

1999 SkyBox Premium 2000 Men

This 15-card insert set included players who looked to be the stars for the next millennium. Each single was sequentially numbered to 100.

		MT
Complete Set (15):		650.00
Common Player:		20.00
Production 100 Sets		
1	Warrick Dunn	20.00
2	Tim Couch	80.00
3	Fred Taylor	40.00
4	Jake Plummer	40.00
5	Jerry Rice	40.00
6	Edgerrin James	80.00
7	Mark Brunell	30.00
8	Peyton Manning	60.00
9	Randy Moss	80.00
10	Terrell Davis	60.00
11	Charlie Batch	30.00
12	Dan Marino	60.00
13	Emmitt Smith	60.00
14	Brett Favre	80.00
15	Barry Sanders	80.00

1999 SkyBox Premium Autographics

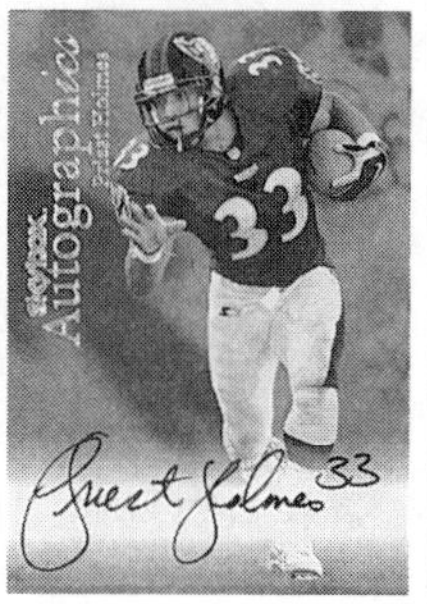

This was a 79-card insert that was found in several SkyBox products. Singles were issued in Dominion, E-X Century, Molten Metal, Metal Universe and SkyBox Premium at 1:68 hobby packs and 1:90 retail packs. Each single had the autograph on the front of the card and each also had a parallel Red version that was sequentially numbered to 50.

	MT
Common Player:	10.00
Minor Stars:	20.00
Inserted 1:68	
Foil Cards:	2x
Production 50 Sets	
Stephen Alexander	20.00
Mike Alstott	40.00
Champ Bailey	30.00
Karsten Bailey	10.00
Charlie Batch	50.00
D'Wayne Bates	20.00
Michael Bishop	35.00
Dre' Bly	10.00
David Boston	50.00
Gary Brown	10.00
Na Brown	10.00
Tim Brown	30.00
Troy Brown	10.00
Mark Bruener	10.00
Mark Brunell	50.00
Shawn Bryson	10.00
Wayne Chrebet	30.00
Chris Claiborne	20.00
Cam Cleeland	10.00
Cecil Collins	75.00
Daunte Culpepper	75.00
Randall Cunningham	40.00
Terrell Davis	85.00
Ty Detmer	10.00
Jared DeVries	10.00
Troy Edwards	50.00
Kevin Faulk	35.00
Marshall Faulk	40.00
Doug Flutie	50.00
Oronde Gadsden	20.00
Joey Galloway	35.00
Eddie George	50.00
Martin Gramatica	20.00
Anthony Gray	10.00
Ahman Green	20.00
Brian Griese	70.00
Howard Griffith	10.00
Marvin Harrison	45.00
Courtney Hawkins	10.00
Vonnie Holliday	10.00
Torry Holt	50.00
Sedrick Irvin	30.00
Edgerrin James	150.00
Patrick Jeffers	30.00
James Johnson	35.00
Kevin Johnson	50.00
Freddie Jones	10.00
Jevon Kearse	35.00
Shaun King	40.00
Jon Kitna	35.00
Rob Konrad	10.00
Dorsey Levens	30.00
Peyton Manning	100.00
Darnell McDonald	20.00
Donovan McNabb	75.00
Cade McNown	75.00
Eric Moss	10.00
Randy Moss	175.00
Eric Moulds	30.00
Marcus Nash	20.00
Terrell Owens	35.00
Jerome Pathon	20.00
Jake Plummer	75.00
Peerless Price	35.00
Mikhael Ricks	10.00
Frank Sanders	20.00
Tony Simmons	10.00
Akili Smith	75.00
Antowain Smith	35.00
L.C. Stevens	10.00
Michael Strahan	10.00
Tai Streets	10.00
Lamar Thomas	10.00
Jerame Tuman	10.00
Kevin Turner	10.00
Tyrone Wheatley	20.00
Ricky Williams	150.00
Frank Wycheck	10.00
Amos Zereoue	40.00

1999 SkyBox Premium Autographics Foil Parallel

This was a 79-card parallel to the Autographics insert set. Each of these singles was printed with red foil and sequentially numbered to 50.

	MT
Foil Cards:	2x
Production 50 Sets	

1999 SkyBox Premium Box Tops

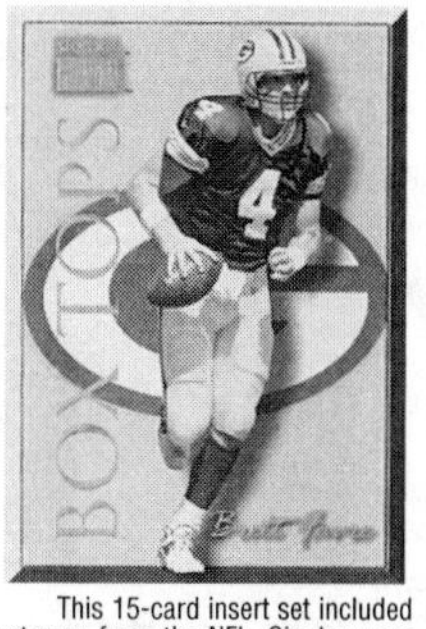

This 15-card insert set included veterans from the NFL. Singles were inserted 1:12 packs.

		MT
Complete Set (15):		45.00
Common Player:		2.00
Inserted 1:12		
1	Terrell Davis	6.00
2	Troy Aikman	4.00
3	Peyton Manning	6.00
4	Mark Brunell	3.00
5	Eddie George	2.50
6	Corey Dillon	2.00
7	Dan Marino	6.00
8	Brett Favre	8.00
9	Barry Sanders	8.00
10	Emmitt Smith	6.00
11	Fred Taylor	4.00
12	Jerry Rice	4.00
13	Jamal Anderson	2.00
14	Joey Galloway	2.00
15	Randy Moss	8.00

1999 SkyBox Premium Deja Vu

This 15-card insert set included a draft pick paired with a veteran who was the same number pick in a previous draft. Singles were inserted 1:36 picks. A parallel die-cut version was also issued with each of those singles sequentially numbered to 99.

		MT
Complete Set (15):		50.00
Common Player:		2.00
Inserted 1:36		
1	Akili Smith, Barry Sanders	12.00
2	Cade McNown, Warrick Dunn	6.00
3	Cecil Collins, Jerris McPhail	6.00
4	Champ Bailey, Curtis Conway	2.00
5	Daunte Culpepper, Michael Irvin	6.00
6	David Boston, Tim Biakabutuka	3.00
7	Donovan McNabb, Marshall Faulk	6.00
8	Edgerrin James, Michael Westbrook	12.00
9	Kevin Faulk, Joey Kent	2.00
10	Kevin Johnson, Jerome Pathon	3.00
11	Ricky Williams, Deion Sanders	12.00
12	Shaun King, Germane Crowell	2.00
13	Tim Couch, Troy Aikman	12.00
14	Torry Holt, Tim Brown	3.00
15	Troy Edwards, Eric Metcalf	3.00

1999 SkyBox Premium Genuine Coverage

This was a six-card insert set that included a piece of a game-worn jersey. Each card had a different amount issued and was randomly inserted.

	MT
Complete Set (6):	600.00
Common Player:	50.00
Drew Bledsoe	85.00
Mark Brunell	85.00
Randall Cunningham	60.00
Brett Favre	175.00
Herman Moore	50.00
Randy Moss	225.00

1999 SkyBox Premium Prime Time Rookies

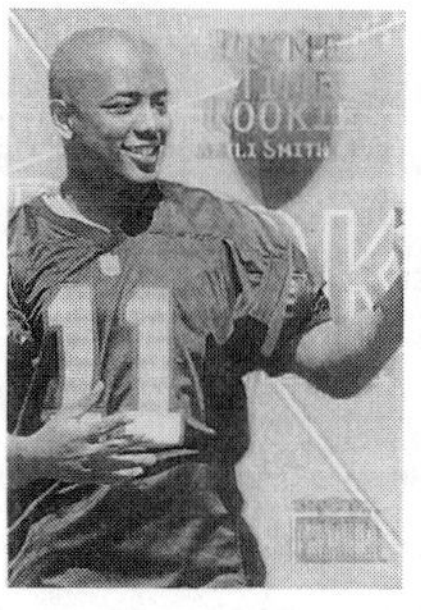

This 15-card insert set included the best rookies from 1999. Singles were found 1:96 packs. A parallel Autograph version was also issued with each of those singles sequentially numbered to 25.

		MT
Complete Set (15):		160.00
Common Player:		5.00
Inserted 1:96		
1	Ricky Williams	30.00
2	Tim Couch	30.00
3	Edgerrin James	30.00
4	Daunte Culpepper	15.00
5	David Boston	10.00
6	Akili Smith	15.00
7	Cecil Collins	15.00
8	Cade McNown	15.00
9	Torry Holt	10.00
10	Donovan McNabb	15.00
11	Kevin Johnson	10.00
12	Shaun King	8.00
13	Champ Bailey	5.00
14	Troy Edwards	10.00
15	Kevin Faulk	8.00

1999 SkyBox Premium Prime Time Rookies Autographs

This was a 15-card parallel to the Prime Time Rookie insert set. Each of these singles was autographed and sequentially numbered to 25.

		MT
Common Player:		100.00
Production 25 Sets		
1	Ricky Williams	400.00
2	Tim Couch	400.00
3	Edgerrin James	550.00
4	Daunte Culpepper	200.00
5	David Boston	150.00
6	Akili Smith	180.00
7	Cecil Collins	100.00
8	Cade McNown	200.00
9	Torry Holt	150.00
10	Donovan McNabb	200.00
11	Kevin Johnson	150.00
12	Shaun King	200.00
13	Champ Bailey	100.00
14	Troy Edwards	150.00
15	Kevin Faulk	100.00

1999 SkyBox Premium Year 2

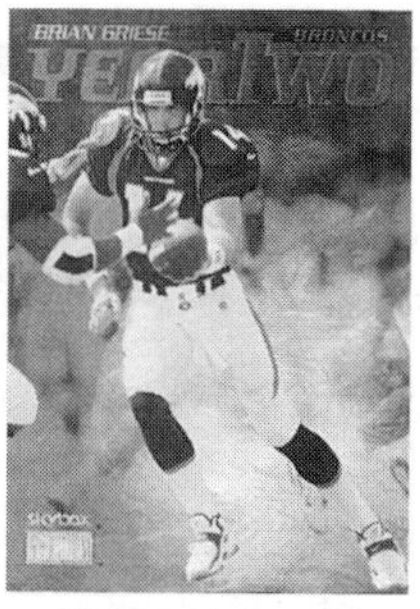

This 15-card insert set included players who were in their second year as a pro. Singles were found 1:6 packs.

		MT
Complete Set (15):		15.00
Common Player:		.75
Minor Stars:		1.50
Inserted 1:6		
1	Ahman Green	.75
2	Terry Fair	.75
3	Charlie Batch	2.00
4	Ryan Leaf	1.50
5	Skip Hicks	1.50
6	John Avery	.75
7	Charles Woodson	1.50
8	Jacquez Green	.75
9	Kevin Dyson	.75
10	Marcus Nash	.75
11	Robert Holcombe	.75
12	Germane Crowell	1.50
13	Curtis Enis	1.50
14	Tim Dwight	1.50
15	Brian Griese	3.00

2000 SkyBox

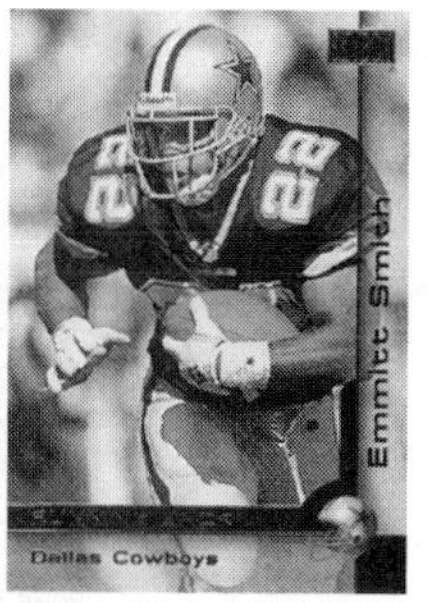

		MT
Complete Set (300):		375.00
Common Player:		.15
Minor Stars:		.30
Common Rookie:		.50
Common SP:		5.00
SP Cards Horizontal Photo		
Production 2,000 Sets		
Pack (10):		3.00
Wax Box (24):		55.00
1	Tim Couch	1.25
2	Edgerrin James	1.50
3	Wesley Walls	.30
4	Brian Griese	.60
5	Herman Moore	.30
6	Mark Brunell	.75
7	John Randle	.15
8	Victor Green	.15
9	Michael Sinclair	.15
10	Jevon Kearse	.60
11	Peter Boulware	.15
12	Kevin Johnson	.50
13	Vonnie Holliday	.15
14	Jason Taylor	.15
15	Cameron Cleeland	.30
16	Jeff Graham	.15
17	Jacquez Green	.30
18	Chris McAlister	.15
19	Takeo Spikes	.15
20	Marvin Harrison	.50
21	Jay Fiedler	.50
22	Jake Reed	.15

23	Jerry Rice	1.00
24	Shaun King	.75
25	Donovan McNabb	.75
26	David Boston	.50
27	Curtis Enis	.50
28	Olandis Gary	.60
29	James Stewart	.50
30	Jimmy Smith	.50
31	Randy Moss	1.75
32	Keyshawn Johnson	.50
33	Kevin Carter	.15
34	Stephen Davis	.50
35	Jay Riemersma	.30
36	Emmitt Smith	1.25
37	E.G. Green	.15
38	Dwayne Rudd	.15
39	Michael Strahan	.15
40	Troy Edwards	.50
41	Derrick Mayes	.30
42	Eddie George	.60
43	Bruce Smith	.15
44	Andre Wadsworth	.15
45	Bobby Engram	.15
46	Byron Chamberlain	.15
47	Antonio Freeman	.50
48	Hardy Nickerson	.15
49	Terry Glenn	.50
50	Wayne Chrebet	.30
51	London Fletcher	.15
52	Michael Westbrook	.30
53	Rob Moore	.30
54	Eddie Kennison	.15
55	Ed McCaffrey	.30
56	Dorsey Levens	.30
57	Andre Rison	.30
58	Willie McGinest	.15
59	Tyrone Wheatley	.30
60	Kurt Warner	2.00
61	Stephen Alexander	.15
62	Jessie Tuggle	.15
63	Jim Miller	.15
64	Luther Elliss	.15
65	Bill Schroeder	.30
66	Elvis Grbac	.30
67	Ty Law	.15
68	Tim Brown	.30
69	Marshall Faulk	.50
70	Champ Bailey	.15
71	Charlie Batch	.50
72	Steve Beuerlein	.30
73	Raghib Ismail	.15
74	Kevin Hardy	.15
75	Zach Thomas	.30
76	Aaron Glenn	.15
77	Jerome Bettis	.50
78	Chris Chandler	.30
79	Marcus Robinson	.50
80	Derrick Alexander	.15
81	Drew Bledsoe	.75
82	Charles Woodson	.30
83	Isaac Bruce	.50
84	Darrell Green	.15
85	Tim Dwight	.50
86	Darnay Scott	.30
87	Chris Claiborne	.15
88	Tony Gonzalez	.30
89	Tony Simmons	.15
90	Rich Gannon	.30
91	Torry Holt	.50
92	Jamal Anderson	.50
93	Akili Smith	.50
94	Germane Crowell	.50
95	Lawyer Milloy	.15
96	Napoleon Kaufman	.50
97	Grant Wistrom	.15
98	Terance Mathis	.15
99	Karim Abdul	.30
100	Kerry Collins	.30
101	Troy Vincent	.15
102	Jermaine Fazande	.30
103	Warren Sapp	.30
104	Tony Banks	.30
105	Darrin Chiaverini	.15
106	Corey Bradford	.15
107	Tony Martin	.15
108	Jeff Blake	.30
109	Torrance Small	.15
110	Freddie Jones	.15
111	Warrick Dunn	.50
112	Tim Biakabutuka	.30
113	Rod Smith	.50
114	Kyle Brady	.15
115	Oronde Gadsden	.15
116	Dedric Ward	.15
117	Mikhael Ricks	.15
118	Bryant Young	.15
119	Michael Bates	.15
120	Junior Seau	.30
121	Bill Romanowski	.15
122	Reggie Barlow	.15
123	Jeff Garcia	.15
124	Peerless Price	.30
125	Jeff George	.30
126	Cornelius Bennett	.15
127	Amani Toomer	.30
128	Charles Johnson	.15
129	Cortez Kennedy	.15
130	Samari Rolle	.15
131	Eric Moulds	.50
132	Joey Galloway	.50
133	Peyton Manning	1.50
134	Robert Smith	.50
135	Jessie Armstead	.15
136	Will Blackwell	.15
137	Jon Kitna	.50
138	Kevin Dyson	.30
139	Jake Plummer	.50
140	Cade McNown	.75
141	Terrell Davis	1.25
142	Johnnie Morton	.15
143	Fred Taylor	.75
144	Ed McDaniel	.15
145	Vinny Testaverde	.50
146	Az-Zahir Hakim	.30
147	Brad Johnson	.50
148	Antowain Smith	.30
149	Rob Konrad	.15
150	Sam Cowart	.15
151	Chris Carter	.50
152	Jason Sehorn	.15
153	Levon Kirkland	.15
154	Shawn Springs	.15
155	Frank Wycheck	.15
156	Troy Aikman	1.00
157	Keenan McCardell	.30
158	Sam Madison	.15
159	Curtis Martin	.50
160	Hines Ward	.15
161	Steve Young	.75
162	Blaine Bishop	.15
163	Shannon Sharpe	.30
164	Michael Pittman	.15
165	Brett Favre	1.75
166	Damon Huard	.30
167	Keith Poole	.15
168	Curtis Conway	.30
169	Derrick Brooks	.15
170	Duce Staley	.50
171	Rob Johnson	.30
172	Pete Gonzalez	.15
173	Ken Dilger	.15
174	Ike Hilliard	.30
175	Bobby Taylor	.15
176	Ricky Watters	.30
177	Steve McNair	.60
178	Patrick Johnson	.15
179	Carl Pickens	.30
180	Terrence Wilkins	.30
181	Rashaan Shehee	.15
182	Ricky Williams	1.25
183	James Jett	.15
184	Terrell Owens	.50
185	John Lynch	.15
186	Muhsin Muhammad	.30
187	Ryan McNeil	.15
188	Jerome Pathon	.15
189	Daunte Culpepper	.75
190	Joe Jurevicius	.15
191	Kordell Stewart	.50
192	Christian Fauria	.15
193	Yancey Thigpen	.15
194	Patrick Jeffers	.50
195	Corey Dillon	.50
196	Tamarick Vanover	.15
197	Doug Flutie	.60
198	Rickey Dudley	.15
199	Charlie Garner	.30
200	Mike Alstott	.50
201	*Courtney Brown*	.60
201S	Courtney Brown SP	6.00
202	*Peter Warrick*	3.00
202S	Peter Warrick SP	30.00
203	*Thomas Jones*	1.20
203S	Thomas Jones SP	12.00
204	*Sylvester Morris*	1.50
204S	Sylvester Morris SP	15.00
205	*Chad Pennington*	2.50
205S	Chad Pennington SP	25.00
206	*Ron Dayne*	3.00
206S	Ron Dayne SP	30.00
207	*Todd Pinkston*	.60
207S	Todd Pinkston SP	6.00
208	*Todd Husak*	.50
208S	Todd Husak SP	5.00
209	*Chris Redman*	1.20
209S	Chris Redman SP	12.00
210	*Jerry Porter*	.60
210S	Jerry Porter SP	6.00
211	*Michael Wiley*	.60
211S	Michael Wiley SP	6.00
212	*J.R. Redmond*	.80
212S	J.R. Redmond SP	8.00
213	*Dennis Northcutt*	.60
213S	Dennis Northcutt SP	6.00
214	*Gari Scott*	.50
214S	Gari Scott SP	5.00
215	*Bashir Yamini*	.50
215S	Bashir Yamini SP	5.00
216	*Danny Farmer*	.60
216S	Danny Farmer SP	6.00
217	*Corey Simon*	.60
217S	Corey Simon SP	6.00
218	*Plaxico Burress*	1.50
218S	Plaxico Burress SP	15.00
219	*Chad Morton*	.60
219S	Chad Morton SP	6.00
220	*Bubba Franks*	.60
220S	Bubba Franks SP	6.00
221	*Shaun Alexander*	2.00
221S	Shaun Alexander SP	20.00
222	*Dez White*	.60
222S	Dez White SP	6.00
223	*Mareno Philyaw*	.50
223S	Mareno Philyaw SP	5.00
224	*Travis Taylor*	.80
224S	Travis Taylor SP	8.00
225	*Brian Urlacher*	2.00
225S	Brian Urlacher SP	20.00
226	*Jamal Lewis*	4.00
226S	Jamal Lewis SP	40.00
227	*Sherrod Gideon*	.50
227S	Sherrod Gideon SP	5.00
228	*Shyrone Stith*	.50
228S	Shyrone Stith SP	5.00
229	*Chris Cole*	.50
229S	Chris Cole SP	5.00
230	*Darrell Jackson*	.80
230S	Darrell Jackson SP	8.00
231	*Quinton Spotwood*	.50
231S	Quinton Spotwood SP	5.00
232	*Tee Martin*	.60
232S	Tee Martin SP	6.00
233	*Tim Rattay*	.60
233S	Tim Rattay SP	6.00
234	*Marc Bulger*	.50
234S	Marc Bulger SP	5.00
235	*Doug Johnson*	.60
235S	Doug Johnson SP	6.00
236	*Joe Hamilton*	.60
236S	Joe Hamilton SP	6.00
237	*Trevor Gaylor*	.60
237S	Trevor Gaylor SP	6.00
238	*Travis Prentice*	1.00
238S	Travis Prentice SP	10.00
239	*R. Jay Soward*	.60
239S	R. Jay Soward SP	6.00
240	*Trung Canidate*	.60
240S	Trung Canidate SP	6.00
241	*Giovanni Carmazzi*	.60
241S	Giovanni Carmazzi SP	6.00
242	*Reuben Droughns*	.50
242S	Reuben Droughns SP	5.00
243	*Curtis Keaton*	.50
243S	Curtis Keaton SP	5.00
244	*Laveranues Coles*	.80
244S	Laveranues Coles SP	8.00
245	*Ron Dugans*	.60
245S	Ron Dugans SP	6.00
246	*Mike Anderson*	4.00
246S	Mike Anderson SP	40.00
247	*Anthony Becht*	.60
247S	Anthony Becht SP	6.00
248	*Raynoch Thompson*	.50
248S	Raynoch Thompson SP	5.00
249	*Rob Morris*	.50
249S	Rob Morris SP	5.00
250	*Chafie Fields*	.50
250S	Chafie Fields SP	5.00

2000 SkyBox Star Rubies Parallel

		MT
Complete Set (250):		125.00
Ruby Cards:		3x-6x
Ruby Rookies:		2x-4x
Inserted 1:12		

2000 SkyBox Star Rubies Extreme Parallel

		MT
Extreme Cards:		25x-50x
Extreme Rookies:		12x-24x
Production 50 Sets		

2000 SkyBox Autographics

		MT
Common Player:		10.00
Minor Stars:		20.00
Inserted 1:72		
Silver Cards:		1.2x
Production 250 Sets		
	Kimble Anders	10.00
	Champ Bailey	20.00
	Charlie Batch	20.00
	Donnell Bennett	10.00
	David Boston	25.00
	Peter Boulware	10.00
	Mark Brunell	35.00
	Wayne Chrebet	20.00
	Stephen Davis	25.00
	Jake Delhomme	20.00
	Corey Dillon	20.00
	Reuben Droughns	20.00
	Deon Dyer	10.00
	Danny Farmer	10.00
	Kevin Faulk	20.00
	Sherrod Gideon	10.00
	Damon Griffith	10.00
	Priest Holmes	20.00
	Raghib Ismail	10.00
	Patrick Jeffers	20.00
	Rob Johnson	20.00
	Terry Kirby	10.00
	Shane Matthews	10.00
	Ed McCaffrey	20.00
	Cade McNown	35.00
	Rondell Mealey	10.00
	Johnnie Morton	10.00
	Terrell Owens	20.00
	Chad Pennington	65.00
	John Randle	10.00
	Jake Reed	10.00
	Marcus Robinson	25.00
	Akili Smith	30.00
	Jimmy Smith	20.00
	R. Jay Soward	20.00
	Kordell Stewart	25.00
	Shyrone Stith	10.00
	Amani Toomer	10.00
	Dedric Ward	10.00
	Dez White	20.00
	Frank Wycheck	10.00

2000 SkyBox Genuine Coverage Common

		MT
Common Player:		20.00
Inserted 1:288		
	David Boston	25.00
	Corey Dillon	25.00
	Tim Dwight	25.00
	Terry Kirby	20.00
	Shane Matthews	20.00
	Rob Moore	20.00
	Johnnie Morton	20.00
	Frank Sanders	20.00

2000 SkyBox Genuine Coverage Hobby

		MT
Common Player:		20.00
Inserted 1:144		
	Shaun Alexander	85.00
	Courtney Brown	35.00
	Ron Dayne	120.00
	Reuben Droughns	20.00
	Bubba Franks	30.00
	Sylvester Morris	35.00
	Chad Pennington	100.00
	Jerry Porter	25.00
	Travis Prentice	40.00
	J.R. Redmond	40.00
	Peter Warrick	120.00

2000 SkyBox Patchworks

		MT
Complete Set (16):		
Common Player:		20.00
	Troy Aikman	60.00
	Jamal Anderson	20.00
	Drew Bledsoe	45.00
	Mark Brunell	45.00
	Tim Couch	45.00
	Brett Favre	100.00
	Eddie George	50.00
	Marvin Harrison	50.00
	Edgerrin James	75.00
	Cade McNown	20.00
	Jake Plummer	20.00
	Jerry Rice	70.00
	Junior Seau	50.00
	Emmitt Smith	75.00
	Fred Taylor	40.00
	Kurt Warner	100.00

2000 SkyBox Preemptive Strike

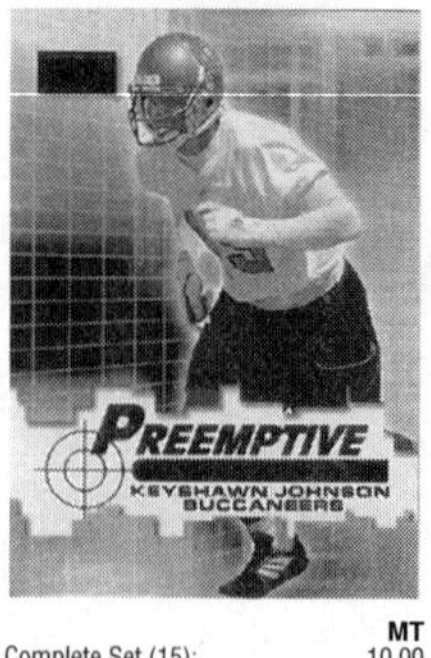

		MT
Complete Set (15):		10.00
Common Player:		.50
Minor Stars:		1.00
Inserted 1:4		
Star Ruby Cards:		5x-10x
Production 100 Sets		
1	Tim Couch	1.75
2	Edgerrin James	3.00
3	Jake Plummer	1.00
4	Akili Smith	1.00
5	Cade McNown	1.25
6	Isaac Bruce	1.00
7	Marvin Harrison	1.00
8	Troy Aikman	2.00
9	Germane Crowell	1.00
10	Cris Carter	1.00
11	Keyshawn Johnson	1.00
12	Donovan McNabb	1.25
13	Charlie Batch	1.00
14	Muhsin Muhammad	.50
15	Marcus Robinson	1.00

2000 SkyBox SkyLines

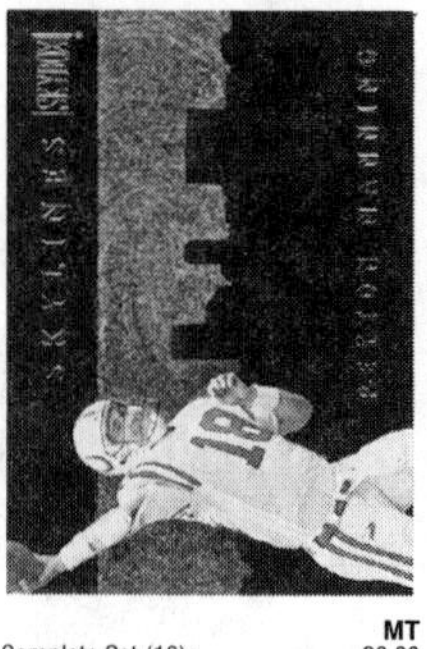

		MT
Complete Set (10):		20.00
Common Player:		1.00
Inserted 1:11		
Star Ruby Cards:		7x-14x
Production 50 Sets		
1	Tim Couch	2.50
2	Edgerrin James	4.00
3	Terrell Davis	3.00
4	Jamal Anderson	1.00
5	Kurt Warner	5.00
6	Charlie Batch	1.00
7	Emmitt Smith	3.00
8	Peyton Manning	4.00
9	Cade McNown	2.00
10	Mark Brunell	2.00

2000 SkyBox Sole Train

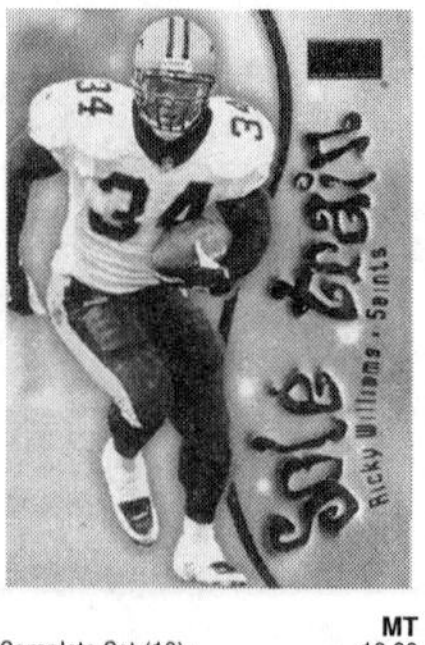

		MT
Complete Set (10):		10.00
Common Player:		1.00
Inserted 1:8		
Star Ruby Cards:		5x-10x
Production 100 Sets		
1	Edgerrin James	3.50
2	Eddie George	1.50
3	Marshall Faulk	1.50
4	Emmitt Smith	2.50
5	Fred Taylor	1.75
6	Stephen Davis	1.00
7	Ricky Williams	2.00
8	Jamal Anderson	1.00
9	Warrick Dunn	1.00
10	Jerome Bettis	1.00

A player's name in *italic type* indicates a rookie card.

2000 SkyBox Sunday's Best

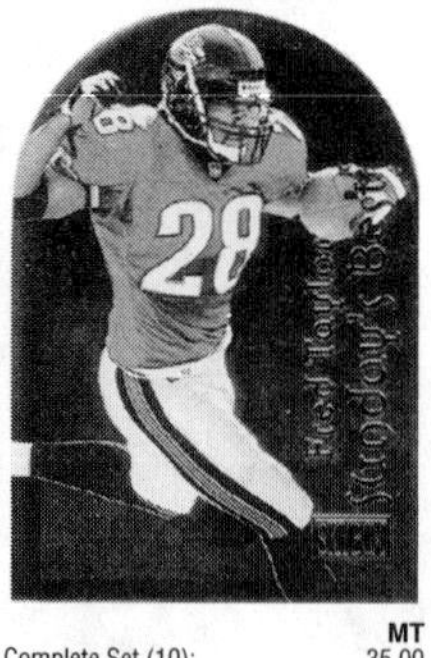

		MT
Complete Set (10):		35.00
Common Player:		2.00
Inserted 1:24		
Star Ruby Cards:		5x-10x
Production 50 Sets		
1	Tim Couch	3.00
2	Edgerrin James	6.00
3	Terrell Davis	4.00
4	Peyton Manning	6.00
5	Marshall Faulk	2.00
6	Brett Favre	6.00
7	Emmitt Smith	4.00
8	Randy Moss	6.00
9	Fred Taylor	2.50
10	Ricky Williams	3.00

2000 SkyBox Superlatives

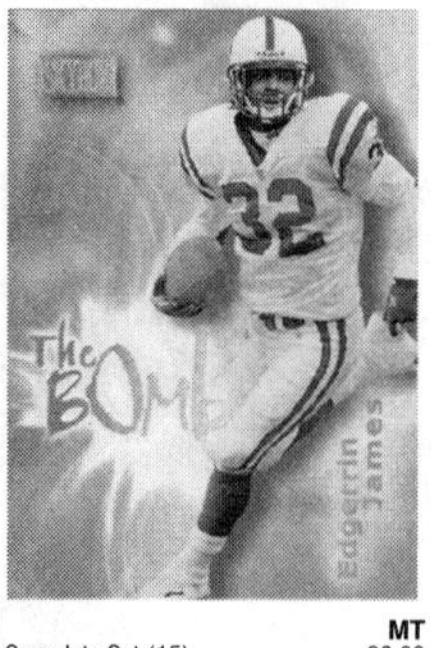

		MT
Complete Set (15):		20.00
Common Player:		.50
Minor Stars:		1.00
Inserted 1:11		
Star Ruby Cards:		7x-14x
Production 50 Sets		
1	Tim Couch	2.50
2	Edgerrin James	5.00
3	Randy Moss	5.00
4	Marshall Faulk	1.00
5	Fred Taylor	2.00
6	Jake Plummer	1.00
7	Vinny Testaverde	.50
8	Troy Aikman	2.50
9	Drew Bledsoe	2.00
10	Stephen Davis	1.00
11	Marvin Harrison	1.00
12	Steve Young	2.00
13	Jimmy Smith	1.00
14	Ricky Williams	2.50
15	Kurt Warner	6.00

2000 SkyBox The Bomb

		MT
Complete Set (10):		30.00
Common Player:		2.00
Inserted 1:24		
Star Ruby Cards:		5x-10x
Production 50 Sets		
1	Tim Couch	3.50
2	Kurt Warner	6.00
3	Edgerrin James	5.00
4	Randy Moss	5.00
5	Keyshawn Johnson	2.00
6	Brett Favre	5.00
7	Peyton Manning	5.00
8	Eddie George	2.50
9	Isaac Bruce	2.00
10	Marvin Harrison	2.00

1992 Slam Thurman Thomas

Thurman Thomas was featured in this 11-card (10 cards, plus one promo) set. Slam reported the production run to be 25,000 total sets and included an autographed (limited to 1,000) edition card for every 25 sets ordered.

		MT
Complete Set (11):		10.00
Common Player:		1.00
1	Thurman Thomas (RB-Willowridge HS)	1.00
2	Thurman Thomas (HS-All American)	1.00
3	Thurman Thomas (Gator Bowl MVP)	1.00
4	Thurman Thomas (RB-Oklahoma State)	1.00
5	Thurman Thomas (All Big 8)	1.00
6	Thurman Thomas (1st Team All-American)	1.00
7	Thurman Thomas (RB-Buffalo)	1.00
8	Thurman Thomas (AFC All-Pro)	1.00
9	Thurman Thomas (AFC Rushing Champion)	1.00
10	Thurman Thomas (NFL Leader-Total Yards)	1.00
P1	Thurman Thomas (Promo 1)	1.00
AU	Thurman Thomas (Autographed)	80.00

1993 Slam Jerome Bettis

Jerome Bettis is featured in this six-card set (five cards, plus a promo) by Slam. Sets arrived with one autographed card, 4 regular issue cards, plus the promo card. There is also a certificate of authenticity that lists the production number out of a total of 5,000 produced.

		MT
Complete Set (6):		12.00
Common Player:		2.00
1	Jerome Bettis (High School All-American)	2.00
2	Jerome Bettis (Freshman Notre Dame)	2.00
3	Jerome Bettis (1991 Notre Dame Co-MVP)	2.00
4	Jerome Bettis (All-American)	2.00
5	Jerome Bettis (10th Pick Overall)	2.00
P1	Jerome Bettis (Promo 1) (FB Notre Dame)	2.00
1AU	Jerome Bettis (High School All-American)	15.00
2AU	Jerome Bettis (Freshman Notre Dame)	15.00
3AU	Jerome Bettis (1991 Notre Dame Co-MVP)	15.00
4AU	Jerome Bettis (All-American)	20.00
5AU	Jerome Bettis (10th Pick Overall)	20.00

1978 Slim Jim

Specially-marked Slim Jim products in 1978 contained a 3" x 5-3/4" panel featuring two football player discs. The discs, featuring a player mug shot, biographical data, an NFLPA logo and "Slim Jim Collection" on the front, were issued by Michael Schechter Associates. MSA is also on the disc front. Each disc has a diameter of 2-3/8" and is perforated so it can be cut out from the panel. The same two players were always on the same panel. They are listed according to the pairs on the panel, starting with 1A and 1B and ending 69-70. Note: The prices for each disc are actually the value of the panel. So, 1A and 1B would be $20, not $40.

		NM
Complete Set (70):		350.00
Common Player:		8.00
1A	Lyle Alzado	20.00
1B	Archie Manning	20.00
2A	Bill Bergey	20.00
2B	John Riggins	20.00
3A	Fred Biletnikoff	20.00
3B	Dan Dierdorf	20.00
4A	John Cappelletti	8.00
4B	Bob Chandler	8.00
5A	Tommy Casanova	8.00
5B	Darryl Stingley	8.00
6A	Billy Joe Dupree	8.00
6B	Nat Moore	8.00
7A	John Dutton	8.00
7B	Paul Krause	8.00
8A	Leon Gray	8.00
8B	Richard Caster	8.00
9A	Mel Gray	8.00
9B	Claude Humphrey	8.00
10A	Joe Greene	12.00
10B	Dexter Bussey	12.00
11A	Jack Gregory	8.00
11B	Billy Johnson	8.00
12A	Steve Grogan	8.00
12B	Jerome Barkum	8.00
13A	John Hannah	10.00
13B	Isaac Curtis	10.00
14A	Jim Hart	9.00
14B	Otis Sistrunk	9.00
15A	Tommy Hart	8.00
15B	Ron Howard	8.00
16A	Wilbur Jackson	8.50
16B	Riley Odoms	8.50
17A	Ron Jaworski	10.00
17B	Mike Thomas	10.00
18A	Larry Little	12.00
18B	Isiah Robertson	12.00
19A	Ron McDole	8.00
19B	Willie Buchanon	8.00
20A	Lydell Mitchell	8.50
20B	Glen Edwards	8.50
21A	Robert Newhouse	8.00
21B	Glenn Doughty	8.00
22A	Alan Page	10.00
22B	Fred Carr	10.00
23A	Walter Payton	55.00
23B	Larry Csonka	55.00
24A	Greg Pruitt	8.00
24B	Doug Buffone	8.00
25A	Ahmad Rashad	12.00
25B	Jeff Van Note	12.00
26A	Golden Richards	10.00
26B	Rocky Bleier	10.00
27A	Clarence Scott	8.00
27B	Joe DeLamielleure	8.00
28A	Lee Roy Selmon	10.00
28B	Charlie Sanders	10.00
29A	Bruce Taylor	8.50
29B	Otis Armstrong	8.50
30A	Emmitt Thomas	8.00

30B	Elvin Bethea	8.00
31A	Brad Van Pelt	8.00
31B	Ted Washington	8.00
32A	Gene Washington	15.00
32B	Charlie Joiner	15.00
33A	Clarence Williams	8.00
33B	Lemar Parrish	8.00
34A	Roger Wehrli	12.00
34B	Gene Upshaw	12.00
35A	Don Woods	8.00
35B	Ron Jessie	8.00

1993 SP

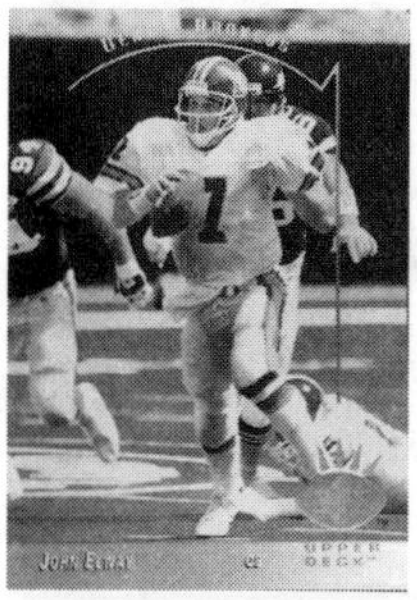

These cards, sold only through hobby dealers, feature gold foil logos, a Premier Prospects subset printing using Light F/X and Electric printing processes, and full-bleed color photos. The borders are team color-coded, too. Gold foil is used for the player's name and set logo. The back has a photo, player stats, biographical information, a card number and a gold-foil Upper Deck hologram. Random foil packs had a card from the 15-card All-Pro insert set. Upper Deck also created a promo card to preview the design for its new set. The card features Kansas City Chiefs quarterback Joe Montana, but it is not identified as a promo card. However, the promo card's number, 19, is different from the number he is assigned in the regular set (#122). The promo card is worth $4.

		MT
Complete Set (270):		150.00
Common Player:		.25
Minor Stars:		.50
Foil Prospects:		1.00
Pack (12):		10.00
Wax Box (24):		225.00
1	*Curtis Conway*	5.00
2	*John Copeland*	1.00
3	*Kevin Williams*	1.00
4	*Dan Williams*	1.00
5	*Patrick Bates*	1.00
6	*Jerome Bettis*	15.00
7	*O.J. McDuffie*	5.00
8	*Robert Smith*	20.00
9	*Drew Bledsoe*	50.00
10	*Irv Smith*	2.00
11	*Marvin Jones*	1.00
12	*Victor Bailey*	1.00
13	*Garrison Hearst*	10.00
14	*Natrone Means*	7.00
15	Todd Kelly	1.00
16	*Rick Mirer*	2.00
17	*Eric Curry*	1.00
18	*Reggie Brooks*	1.00
19	Eric Dickerson	.50
20	*Roger Harper*	.25
21	Michael Haynes	.25
22	Bobby Hebert	.25
23	*Lincoln Kennedy*	.50
24	Chris Miller	.25
25	Mike Pritchard	.25
26	Andre Rison	.75
27	Deion Sanders	2.00
28	Cornelius Bennett	.25
29	Kenneth Davis	.25
30	Henry Jones	.25
31	Jim Kelly	1.00
32	*John Parrella*	.25
33	Andre Reed	.50
34	Bruce Smith	.50
35	*Thomas Smith*	.25
36	Thurman Thomas	1.00
37	Neal Anderson	.25
38	*Myron Baker*	.25
39	Mark Carrier	.25
40	Richard Dent	.50
41	*Chris Gedney*	.25
42	Jim Harbaugh	.50
43	Craig Heyward	.25
44	*Carl Simpson*	.25
45	Alonzo Spellman	.25
46	Derrick Fenner	.25
47	Harold Green	.25
48	David Klingler	.25
49	Ricardo McDonald	.25
50	*Tony McGee*	.50
51	Carl Pickens	1.50
52	*Steve Tovar*	.25
53	Alfred Williams	.25
54	Darryl Williams	.25
55	Jerry Ball	.25
56	*Michael Caldwell*	.25
57	Mark Carrier	.25
58	*Steve Everitt*	.25
59	*Dan Footman*	.25
60	Pepper Johnson	.25
61	Bernie Kosar	.50
62	Eric Metcalf	.50
63	Michael Dean Perry	.50
64	Troy Aikman	3.00
65	Charles Haley	.50
66	Michael Irvin	1.00
67	Robert Jones	.25
68	*Derrick Lassic*	.50
69	Russell Maryland	.50
70	Ken Norton	.25
71	*Darrin Smith*	.50
72	Emmitt Smith	6.00
73	Steve Atwater	.25
74	Rod Bernstine	.25
75	*Jason Elam*	1.00
76	John Elway	3.00
77	Simon Fletcher	.25
78	Tommy Maddox	.25
79	*Glyn Milburn*	1.00
80	Derek Russell	.25
81	Shannon Sharpe	.50
82	Bennie Blades	.25
83	Willie Green	.25
84	*Antonio London*	.25
85	*Ryan McNeil*	.25
86	Herman Moore	1.50
87	Rodney Peete	.50
88	Barry Sanders	6.00
89	Chris Spielman	.25
90	Pat Swilling	.25
91	*Mark Brunell*	25.00
92	Terrell Buckley	.25
93	Brett Favre	6.00
94	Jackie Harris	.25
95	Sterling Sharpe	1.00
96	John Stephens	.25
97	Reggie White	1.00
98	*Wayne Simmons*	.50
99	*George Teague*	.50
100	*Michael Barrow*	.25
101	Cody Carson	.25
102	Ray Childress	.25
103	*Brad Hopkins*	.25
104	Haywood Jeffires	.25
105	Wilber Marshall	.25
106	Warren Moon	1.00
107	Webster Slaughter	.25
108	Lorenzo White	.25
109	John Baylor	.25
110	Duane Bickett	.25
111	Quentin Coryatt	.25
112	Steve Emtman	.25
113	Jeff George	1.00
114	Jessie Hester	.25
115	Anthony Johnson	.25
116	Reggie Langhorne	.25
117	*Roosevelt Potts*	.25
118	Marcus Allen	1.00
119	J.J. Birden	.25
120	Willie Davis	.25
121	*Jaime Fields*	.25
122	Joe Montana	4.00
123	*Will Shields*	.25
124	Neil Smith	.25
125	Derrick Thomas	.50
126	Harvey Williams	.25
127	Tim Brown	1.00
128	*Billy Joe Hobert*	1.50
129	Jeff Hostetler	.50
130	Ethan Horton	.25
131	Raghib Ismail	.25
132	Howie Long	.25
133	Terry McDaniel	.25
134	*Greg Robinson*	.25
135	Anthony Smith	.25
136	Willie Anderson	.25
137	Marc Boutte	.25
138	Shane Conlan	.25
139	*Troy Drayton*	.75
140	Henry Ellard	.25
141	Jim Everett	.50
142	Cleveland Gary	.25
143	Sean Gilbert	.25
144	David Lang	.25
145	Marco Coleman	.25
146	Bryan Cox	.25
147	Irving Fryar	.50
148	Keith Jackson	.25
149	*Terry Kirby*	1.50
150	Dan Marino	6.00
151	Scott Mitchell	.50
152	Troy Vincent	.25
153	Richmond Webb	.25
154	Anthony Carter	.25
155	Cris Carter	1.50
156	Roger Craig	.50
157	Chris Doleman	.25
158	*Qadry Ismail*	4.00
159	Steve Jordan	.25
160	Audray McMillian	.25
161	Gino Torretta	.25
162	Barry Word	.25
163	Vincent Brown	.25
164	Marv Cook	.25
165	*Sam Gash*	.50
166	Pat Harlow	.25
167	Greg McMurtry	.25
168	*Todd Rucci*	.25
169	Leonard Russell	.25
170	*Scott Sisson*	.25
171	*Chris Slade*	.50
172	Morten Andersen	.25
173	*Derek Brown*	.50
174	*Reggie Freeman*	.25
175	Rickey Jackson	.25
176	Eric Martin	.25
177	Wayne Martin	.25
178	Brad Muster	.25
179	*Willie Roaf*	.50
180	Renaldo Turnbull	.25
181	Derek Brown	.25
182	*Marcus Buckley*	.25
183	Jarrod Bunch	.25
184	Rodney Hampton	.50
185	Ed McCaffrey	1.00
186	Kanavis McGhee	.25
187	Phil Simms	.50
188	*Michael Strahan*	.25
189	Lawrence Taylor	1.00
190	Kurt Barber	.25
191	Boomer Esiason	.50
192	Johnny Johnson	.25
193	Ronnie Lott	.50
194	Johnny Mitchell	.25
195	Rob Moore	.50
196	*Adrian Murrell*	6.00
197	Coleman Rudolph	.25
198	Marvin Washington	.25
199	Eric Allen	.25
200	Fred Barnett	.25
201	Randall Cunningham	1.00
202	Byron Evans	.25
203	Lester Holmes	.25
204	Seth Joyner	.25
205	*Leonard Renfro*	.25
206	Heath Sherman	.25
207	Clyde Simmons	.25
208	Johnny Bailey	.25
209	Steve Beuerlein	.25
210	Chuck Cecil	.25
211	*Larry Centers*	1.50
212	Ben Coleman	.25
213	*Ernest Dye*	.25
214	Ken Harvey	.25
215	Randal Hill	.25
216	Ricky Proel	.25
217	*Deon Figures*	.50
218	Barry Foster	.25
219	Eric Green	.25
220	Kevin Greene	.50
221	Carlton Haselrig	.25
222	*Andre Hasting*	1.50
223	Greg Lloyd	.25
224	Neil O'Donnell	.50
225	Rod Woodson	.50
226	Marion Butts	.25
227	*Darren Carrington*	.50
228	*Darrien Gordon*	.50
229	Ronnie Harmon	.25
230	Stan Humphries	.50
231	Anthony Miller	.25
232	Chris Mims	.25
233	Leslie O'Neal	.25
234	Junior Seau	.75
235	Dana Hall	.25
236	*Adrian Hardy*	.25
237	Brent Jones	.25
238	Tim McDonald	.25
239	Tom Rathman	.25
240	Jerry Rice	3.00
241	*Dana Stubblefield*	1.00
242	Ricky Watters	1.00
243	Steve Young	2.50
244	Brian Blades	.25
245	Ferrell Edmunds	.25
246	*Carlton Gray*	.25
247	Cortez Kennedy	.25
248	Kelvin Martin	.25
249	Dan McGwire	.25
250	Jon Vaughn	.25
251	Chris Warren	.50
252	John L. Williams	.25
253	Reggie Cobb	.25
254	*Horace Copeland*	.50
255	Lawrence Dawsey	.25
256	*Demetrius DuBose*	.25
257	Craig Erickson	.50
258	Courtney Hawkins	.25
259	*John Lynch*	3.00
260	Hardy Nickerson	.25
261	*Lamar Thomas*	.50
262	Carl Banks	.25
263	*Tom Carter*	.50
264	Brad Edwards	.25
265	Kurt Gouveia	.25
266	Darrell Green	.25
267	Charles Mann	.25
268	Art Monk	.50
269	Mark Rypien	.25
270	Ricky Sanders	.25

1993 SP All-Pros

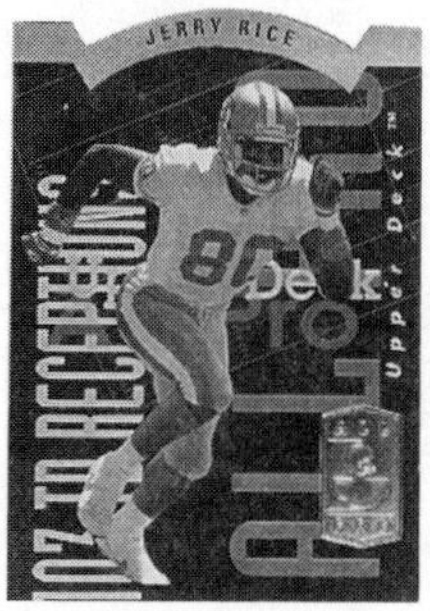

These cards, using a die-cut technique, feature 15 All-Pros, as indicated by the "All-Pro" logo stamped in gold foil on the card front. The front has a color action photo against a black background, plus a statistical category which the player led the league in. His name is in the gold-foil arc at the top of the card. The back has another photo, along with the player's name and team, which run along the left side. Season highlights and a card number, using an "AP" prefix, are also given on the back. The cards were randomly inserted in 1993 Upper Deck SP packs.

		MT
Complete Set (15):		160.00
Common Player:		1.50
Minor Stars:		3.00
Inserted 1:15		
1	Steve Young	12.00
2	Warren Moon	3.00
3	Troy Aikman	15.00
4	Dan Marino	30.00
5	Barry Sanders	30.00
6	Barry Foster	1.50
7	Emmitt Smith	30.00
8	Thurman Thomas	3.00
9	Jerry Rice	15.00
10	Sterling Sharpe	3.00
11	Anthony Miller	1.50
12	Haywood Jeffires	1.50
13	Junior Seau	3.00
14	Reggie White	3.00
15	Derrick Thomas	1.50

1994 SP

This set has reduced in size from the 270 cards in 1993 to 200 in 1994, and also has a smaller print run. The set includes more than 40 rookies in it, too. Each card in the set has a 1994 game-action photograph, including players in their throwback uniforms. A strip down the right side contains the SP logo, fading from dark to light, with an Upper Deck hologram about two-thirds of the way up. The player's name and position is also in this strip. His team name is in the lower right corner. The back has a photo of the player in the top half, with statistics and a biography in the bottom half. A card number and Upper Deck are in the upper corners. The player's name and position are under the photo. Every card in the set is also reprinted using a die-cut design to form a parallel set. One die-cut card was included in each pack. These cards have a silver-foil hologram on the back, rather than a gold-foil hologram, which appears on the regular cards. A 40-card insert set, All-Pro/Future All-Pro, was also produced; cards were randomly included in every fifth pack. These cards were also produced in a die-cut version; they were randomly included in every 75th pack. Two commemorative record-breaker cards, honoring accomplishments by Dan Marino and Jerry Rice, were also produced. One of each card was included in every case made.

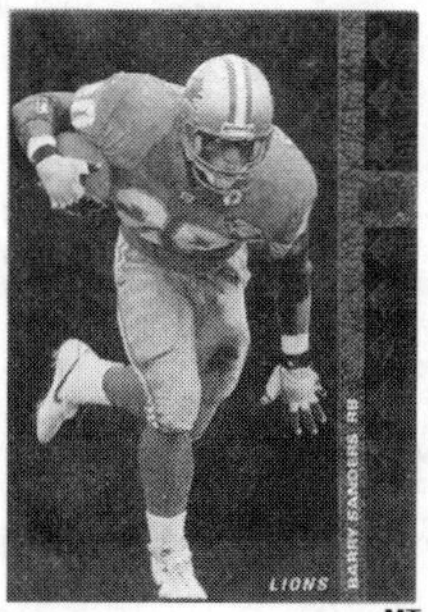

		MT
Complete Set (200):		65.00
Common Player:		.20
Minor Stars:		.40
Foil Prospects:		.75
Die Cut Cards:		1x-3x
Pack (8):		3.25
Wax Box (32):		90.00
1	*Dan Wilkinson*	1.00
2	*Heath Shuler*	1.00
3	*Marshall Faulk*	40.00
4	*Willie McGinest*	1.00
5	*Trent Dilfer*	10.00
6	*Bryant Young*	1.00
7	*Antonio Langham*	.75
8	*John Thierry*	.75
9	*Aaron Glenn*	.75
10	*Charles Johnson*	1.50
11	*DeWayne Washington*	.75
12	*Johnnie Morton*	2.00
13	*Greg Hill*	1.50
14	*William Floyd*	1.25
15	*Derrick Alexander*	1.50
16	*Darnay Scott*	2.00
17	*Errict Rhett*	4.00
18	*Charlie Garner*	10.00
19	*Thomas Lewis*	.75
20	*David Palmer*	.75
21	Andre Reed	.40
22	Thurman Thomas	.50
23	Bruce Smith	.20
24	Jim Kelly	.50
25	Cornelius Bennett	.20
26	*Bucky Brooks*	.40
27	*Jeff Burris*	.40
28	Jim Harbaugh	.40
29	Tony Bennett	.20
30	Quentin Coryatt	.20
31	Floyd Turner	.20
32	Roosevelt Potts	.20
33	Jeff Herrod	.20
34	Irving Fryar	.20
35	Bryan Cox	.20
36	Dan Marino	5.00
37	Terry Kirby	.20
38	Michael Stewart	.20
39	Bernie Kosar	.20
40	*Aubrey Beavers*	.40
41	Vincent Brisby	.75
42	Ben Coates	.20
43	Drew Bledsoe	3.00
44	Marion Butts	.20
45	Chris Slade	.20
46	Michael Timpson	.20
47	Ray Crittenden	.40
48	Rob Moore	.20
49	Johnny Mitchell	.20
50	Art Monk	.40
51	Boomer Esiason	.20
52	Ronnie Lott	.20
53	*Ryan Yarborough*	.75
54	Carl Pickens	1.50
55	David Klingler	.20
56	Harold Green	.20
57	John Copeland	.20
58	(Louis Oliver)	.20
59	*Corey Sawyer*	.20
60	Michael Jackson	.20
61	Mark Rypien	.20
62	Vinny Testaverde	.20
63	Eric Metcalf	.20
64	Eric Turner	.20
65	Haywood Jeffires	.20
66	Michael Barrow	.20
67	Cody Carlson	.20
68	Gary Brown	.20
69	Bucky Richardson	.20
70	Al Smith	.20
71	Eric Green	.20
72	Neil O'Donnell	.40
73	Barry Foster	.20
74	Greg Lloyd	.20
75	Rod Woodson	.40
76	*Bam Morris*	1.00
77	John L. Williams	.20
78	Anthony Miller	.20
79	Mike Pritchard	.20
80	John Elway	2.00
81	Shannon Sharpe	.40
82	Steve Atwater	.20
83	Simon Fletcher	.20
84	Glyn Milburn	.20
85	Mark Collins	.20
86	Keith Cash	.20
87	Willie Davis	.20
88	Joe Montana	3.00
89	Marcus Allen	.40
90	Neil Smith	.20
91	Derrick Thomas	.40
92	Tim Brown	.40
93	Jeff Hostetler	.40
94	Terry McDaniel	.20
95	Raghib Ismail	.20
96	*Rob Fredrickson*	.75
97	Harvey Williams	.20
98	Steve Wisniewski	.20
99	Stan Humphries	.50
100	Natrone Means	1.00
101	Leslie O'Neal	.20
102	Junior Seau	.50
103	Ronnie Harmon	.20
104	Shawn Jefferson	.20
105	Howard Ballard	.20
106	Rick Mirer	1.00
107	Cortez Kennedy	.20
108	Chris Warren	.40
109	Brian Blades	.20
110	*Sam Adams*	.50
111	Gary Clark	.20
112	Steve Beuerlein	.20
113	Ron Moore	.20
114	Eric Swann	.20
115	Clyde Simmons	.20
116	Seth Joyner	.20
117	Troy Aikman	3.00
118	Charles Haley	.20
119	Alvin Harper	.20
120	Michael Irvin	1.00
121	Daryl Johnston	.20
122	Emmitt Smith	5.00
123	*Shante Carver*	.40
124	Dave Brown	.20
125	Rodney Hampton	.40
126	Dave Meggett	.20
127	Chris Calloway	.20
128	Mike Sherrard	.20
129	Carlton Bailey	.20
130	Randall Cunningham	.40
131	William Fuller	.20
132	Eric Allen	.20
133	*Calvin Williams*	.40
134	Herschel Walker	.20
135	*Bernard Williams*	.20
136	Henry Ellard	.20
137	Ethan Horton	.20
138	Desmond Howard	.20
139	Reggie Brooks	.20
140	John Friesz	.20
141	Tom Carter	.20
142	Terry Allen	.20
143	Adrian Cooper	.20
144	Qadry Ismail	.20
145	Warren Moon	.40
146	Henry Thomas	.20
147	*Todd Steussie*	.40
148	Cris Carter	.40
149	Andy Heck	.20
150	Curtis Conway	1.50
151	Erik Kramer	.40
152	Lewis Tillman	.20
153	Dante Jones	.20
154	Alonzo Spellman	.20
155	Herman Moore	2.00
156	Broderick Thomas	.20
157	Scott Mitchell	.40
158	Barry Sanders	4.00
159	Chris Speilman	.20
160	Pat Swilling	.20
161	Bennie Blades	.20
162	Sterling Sharpe	.40
163	Brett Favre	5.00
164	Reggie Cobb	.20
165	Reggie White	.40
166	Sean Jones	.20
167	George Teague	.20
168	LeShon Johnson	.20
169	Courtney Hawkins	.20
170	Jackie Harris	.20
171	Craig Erickson	.20
172	Santana Dotson	.20
173	Eric Curry	.20
174	Hardy Nickerson	.20
175	Derek Brown	.20
176	Jim Everett	.20
177	Michael Haynes	.20
178	Tyrone Hughes	.20
179	Wayne Martin	.20
180	Willie Roaf	.20
181	Irv Smith	.20
182	Jeff George	.50
183	Andre Rison	.40
184	Erric Pegram	.20
185	*Bert Emanuel*	3.00
186	Chris Doleman	.20
187	Ron George	.20
188	Chris Miller	.20
189	Troy Drayton	.20
190	Chris Chandler	.20
191	Jerome Bettis	2.00
192	Jimmie Jones	.20
193	Sean Gilbert	.20
194	Jerry Rice	3.00
195	Brent Jones	.20
196	Deion Sanders	2.50
197	Steve Young	3.00
198	Ricky Watters	.40
199	Dana Stubblefield	.20
200	Ken Norton	.20
RB1	Dan Marino 300 TDs	45.00
RB2	Jerry Rice 127 TDs	25.00

1994 Sp Die-Cuts

This set has reduced in size from the 270 cards in 1993 to 200 in 1994, and also has a smaller print run. The set includes more than 40 rookies in it, too. Each card in the set has a 1994 game-action photograph, including players in their throwback uniforms. A strip down the right side contains the SP logo, fading from dark to light, with an Upper Deck hologram about two-thirds of the way up. The player's name and position is also in this strip. His team name is in the lower right corner. The back has a photo of the player in the top half, with statistics and a biography in the bottom half. A card number and Upper Deck are in the upper corners. The player's name and position are under the photo. Every card in the set is also reprinted using a die-cut design to form a parallel set. One die-cut card was included in each pack. These cards have a silver-foil hologram on the back, rather than a gold-foil hologram, which appears on the regular cards. A 40-card insert set, All-Pro/Future All-Pro, was also produced; cards were randomly included in every fifth pack. These cards were also produced in a die-cut version; they were randomly included in every 75th pack. Two commemorative record-breaker cards, honoring accomplishments by Dan Marino and Jerry Rice, were also produced. One of each card was included in every case made.

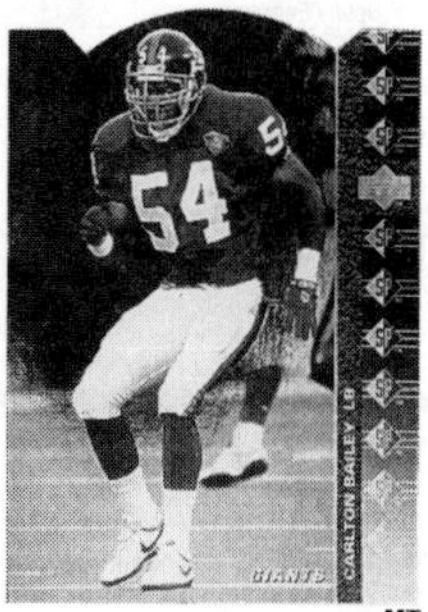

		MT
Complete Set (200):		200.00
Common Player:		.50
Minor Stars:		1.00
Unlisted Stars:		1x-3x
1	*Dan Wilkinson*	3.00
2	*Heath Shuler*	20.00
3	*Marshall Faulk*	50.00
4	*Willie McGinest*	3.00
5	*Trent Dilfer*	15.00
6	*Bryant Young*	4.00
7	*Antonio Langham*	4.00
8	*John Thierry*	1.00
9	*Aaron Glenn*	1.00
10	*Charles Johnson*	8.00
11	*DeWayne Washington*	1.00
12	*Johnnie Morton*	3.00
13	*Greg Hill*	10.00
14	*William Floyd*	15.00
15	*Derrick Alexander*	8.00
16	*Darnay Scott*	8.00
17	*Errict Rhett*	20.00
18	Charlie Garner	8.00
19	*Thomas Lewis*	3.00
20	*David Palmer*	5.00
21	Andre Reed	1.00
22	Thurman Thomas	1.00
23	Bruce Smith	1.00
24	Jim Kelly	1.00
25	Cornelius Bennett	1.00
26	*Bucky Brooks*	3.00
27	*Jeff Burris*	3.00
28	Jim Harbaugh	.50
29	Tony Bennett	.50
30	Quentin Coryatt	.50
31	Floyd Turner	.50
32	Roosevelt Potts	.50
33	Jeff Herrod	.50
34	Irving Fryar	.50
35	Bryan Cox	.50
36	Dan Marino	20.00
37	Terry Kirby	.50
38	Michael Stewart	.50
39	Bernie Kosar	.50
40	*Aubrey Beavers*	1.00
41	Vincent Brisby	3.00
42	Ben Coates	3.00
43	Drew Bledsoe	20.00
44	Marion Butts	.50
45	Chris Slade	.50
46	Michael Timpson	.50
47	Ray Crittenden	1.00
48	Rob Moore	.50
49	Johnny Mitchell	.50
50	Art Monk	1.00
51	Boomer Esiason	.50
52	Ronnie Lott	.50
53	*Ryan Yarborough*	1.00
54	Carl Pickens	.50
55	David Klingler	.50
56	Harold Green	.50
57	John Copeland	.50
58	.20 (Louis Oliver)	.50
59	*Corey Sawyer*	.50
60	Michael Jackson	.50
61	Mark Rypien	.50
62	Vinny Testaverde	.50
63	Eric Metcalf	.50
64	Eric Turner	.50
65	Haywood Jeffires	.50
66	Michael Barrow	.50
67	Cody Carlson	.50
68	Gary Brown	.50
69	Bucky Richardson	.50
70	Al Smith	.50
71	Eric Green	.50
72	Neil O'Donnell	1.00
73	Barry Foster	1.00
74	Greg Lloyd	.50
75	Rod Woodson	1.00
76	*Bam Morris*	10.00
77	John L. Williams	.50
78	Anthony Miller	1.00
79	Mike Pritchard	.50
80	John Elway	5.00
81	Shannon Sharpe	1.00
82	Steve Atwater	.50
83	Simon Fletcher	.50
84	Glyn Milburn	1.00
85	Mark Collins	.50
86	Keith Cash	.50
87	Willie Davis	.50
88	Joe Montana	15.00
89	Marcus Allen	1.00
90	Neil Smith	.50
91	Derrick Thomas	1.00
92	Tim Brown	1.00

93 Jeff Hostetler .50
94 Terry McDaniel .50
95 Raghib Ismail 1.00
96 *Rob Fredrickson* 3.00
97 Harvey Williams .50
98 Steve Wisniewski .50
99 Stan Humphries 1.00
100 Natrone Means 12.00
101 Leslie O'Neal .50
102 Junior Seau 1.00
103 Ronnie Harmon .50
104 Shawn Jefferson .50
105 Howard Ballard .50
106 Rick Mirer 6.00
107 Cortez Kennedy 1.00
108 Chris Warren 1.00
109 Brian Blades .50
110 *Sam Adams* 1.00
111 Gary Clark .50
112 Steve Beuerlein .50
113 Ron Moore 1.00
114 Eric Swann .50
115 Clyde Simmons .50
116 Seth Joyner .50
117 Troy Aikman 8.00
118 Charles Haley .50
119 Alvin Harper 1.00
120 Michael Irvin 4.00
121 Daryl Johnston .50
122 Emmitt Smith 20.00
123 *Shante Carver* 1.00
124 Dave Brown 1.00
125 Rodney Hampton 1.00
126 Dave Meggett .50
127 Chris Calloway .50
128 Mike Sherrard .50
129 Carlton Bailey .50
130 Randall Cunningham 1.00
131 William Fuller .50
132 Eric Allen .50
133 *Calvin Williams* .50
134 Herschel Walker .50
135 *Bernard Williams* .50
136 Henry Ellard .50
137 Ethan Horton .50
138 Desmond Howard .50
139 Reggie Brooks .50
140 John Friesz .50
141 Tom Carter .50
142 Terry Allen .50
143 Adrian Cooper .50
144 Qadry Ismail .50
145 Warren Moon 1.00
146 Henry Thomas .50
147 *Todd Steussie* 1.00
148 Cris Carter 1.00
149 Andy Heck .50
150 Curtis Conway 1.00
151 Erik Kramer .50
152 Lewis Tillman .50
153 Dante Jones .50
154 Alonzo Spellman .50
155 Herman Moore 1.00
156 Broderick Thomas .50
157 Scott Mitchell 1.00
158 Barry Sanders 10.00
159 Chris Spielman .50
160 Pat Swilling .50
161 Bennie Blades .50
162 Sterling Sharpe 1.50
163 Brett Favre 5.00
164 Reggie Cobb .50
165 Reggie White 1.00
166 Sean Jones .50
167 George Teague .50
168 LeShon Johnson 1.00
169 Courtney Hawkins .50
170 Jackie Harris .50
171 Craig Erickson 1.00
172 Santana Dotson .50
173 Eric Curry .50
174 Hardy Nickerson .50
175 Derek Brown .50
176 Jim Everett .50
177 Michael Haynes .50
178 Tyrone Hughes .50
179 Wayne Martin .50
180 Willie Roaf .50
181 Irv Smith .50
182 Jeff George 1.00
183 Andre Rison 1.00
184 Erric Pegram .50
185 *Bert Emanuel* 4.00
186 Chris Doleman .50
187 Ron George .50
188 Chris Miller .50
189 Troy Drayton .50
190 Chris Chandler .50
191 Jerome Bettis 6.00
192 Jimmie Jones .50
193 Sean Gilbert .50
194 Jerry Rice 8.00
195 Brent Jones .50
196 Deion Sanders 8.00
197 Steve Young 8.00
198 Ricky Watters 1.00
199 Dana Stubblefield .50
200 Ken Norton .50

1994 SP All-Pro Holoviews

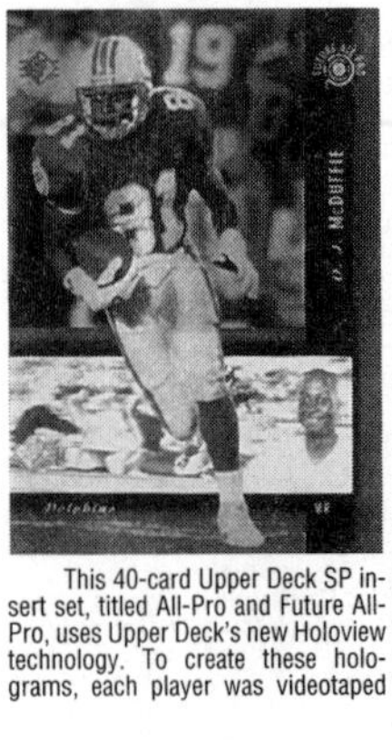

This 40-card Upper Deck SP insert set, titled All-Pro and Future All-Pro, uses Upper Deck's new Holoview technology. To create these holograms, each player was videotaped on a rotating turntable. The individual frames were then synthesized to produce a three-dimensional picture of the player. These cards were inserted into every fifth pack. These insert cards were also reprinted in a version using a die-cut design and rainbow foil. These cards were inserted into packs at a rate of one per every 75 packs.

MT
Complete Set (40): 60.00
Common Player: 1.00
Minor Stars: 2.00
Inserted 1:5
Die-Cut Cards: 2x-4x
Inserted 1:75
1 Jamir Miller 1.00
2 Andre Rison 2.00
3 Bucky Brooks 1.00
4 Thurman Thomas 2.00
5 John Thierry 1.00
6 Dan Wilkinson 1.00
7 Darnay Scott 2.00
8 Antonio Langham 1.00
9 Troy Aikman 6.00
10 Emmitt Smith 10.00
11 John Elway 8.00
12 Barry Sanders 12.00
13 Johnnie Morton 1.00
14 Reggie White 2.00
15 Brett Favre 12.00
16 LeShon Johnson 1.00
17 Joe Montana 6.00
18 Greg Hill 1.00
19 Calvin Jones 1.00
20 Tim Brown 2.00
21 Isaac Bruce 4.00
22 Jerome Bettis 2.00
23 Dan Marino 10.00
24 O.J. McDuffie 2.00
25 Willie McGinest 1.00
26 Mario Bates 1.00
27 Rodney Hampton 1.00
28 Thomas Lewis 1.00
29 Aaron Glenn 1.00
30 Barry Foster 1.00
31 Charles Johnson 2.00
32 Steve Young 5.00
33 Jerry Rice 6.00
34 Bryant Young 1.00
35 William Floyd 1.00
36 Sam Adams 1.00
37 Rick Mirer 2.00
38 Errict Rhett 1.00
39 Reggie Brooks 1.00
40 Heath Shuler 2.00

1994 Sp All-Pro Holoview Die-Cuts

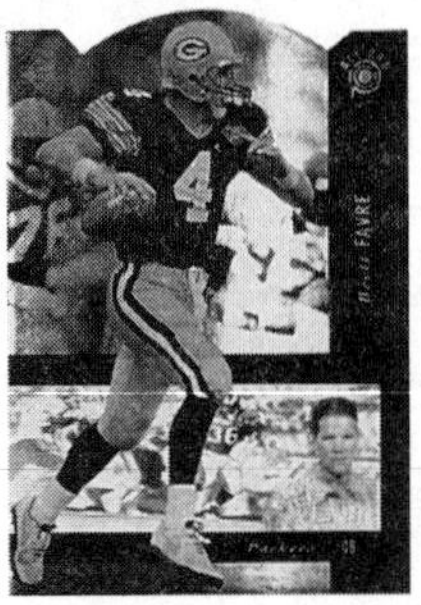

This 40-card Upper Deck SP insert set, titled All-Pro and Future All-Pro, uses Upper Deck's new Holoview technology. To create these holograms, each player was videotaped on a rotating turntable. The individual frames were then synthesized to produce a three-dimensional picture of the player. These cards were inserted into every fifth pack. These insert cards were also reprinted in a version using a die-cut design and rainbow foil. These cards were inserted into packs at a rate of one per every 75 packs.

MT
Complete Set (40): 1600.
Common Player: 15.00
Minor Stars: 30.00
1 Jamir Miller 15.00
2 Andre Rison 15.00
3 Bucky Brooks 15.00
4 Thurman Thomas 30.00
5 John Thierry 15.00
6 Dan Wilkinson 15.00
7 Darnay Scott 50.00
8 Antonio Langham 15.00
9 Troy Aikman 100.00
10 Emmitt Smith 200.00
11 John Elway 80.00
12 Barry Sanders 100.00
13 Johnnie Morton 15.00
14 Reggie White 30.00
15 Brett Favre 200.00
16 LeShon Johnson 15.00
17 Joe Montana 100.00
18 Greg Hill 30.00
19 Calvin Jones 15.00
20 Tim Brown 30.00
21 Isaac Bruce 100.00
22 Jerome Bettis 30.00
23 Dan Marino 200.00
24 O.J. McDuffie 30.00
25 Willie McGinest 15.00
26 Mario Bates 30.00
27 Rodney Hampton 15.00
28 Thomas Lewis 15.00
29 Aaron Glenn 15.00
30 Barry Foster 15.00
31 Charles Johnson 30.00
32 Steve Young 80.00
33 Jerry Rice 100.00
34 Bryant Young 15.00
35 William Floyd 30.00
36 Sam Adams 15.00
37 Rick Mirer 30.00
38 Erric Rhett 50.00
39 Reggie Brooks 15.00
40 Heath Shuler 30.00

1995 Sp

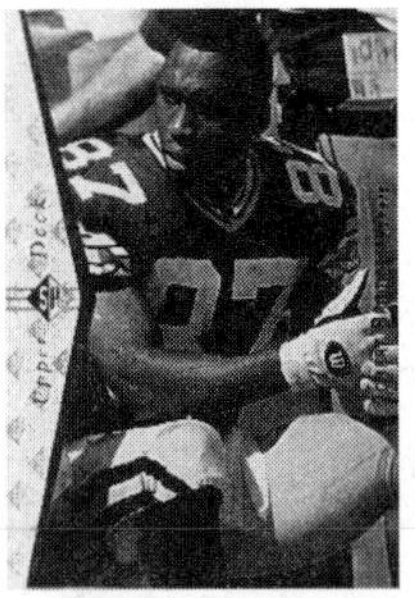

Upper Deck's 1995 SP football contains 200 cards - 180 regular players and 20 Premier Prospects. Each regular card front has a full-bleed color photo on it, with the player's name stamped in copper foil on the right side. Copper foil is also used along the right side for the brand logo and a border between the photo and the logo. A second color photo appears on the card back, which includes biographical information, a career achievement and statistics. "Premier Prospects" are labeled on the fronts as being such. Insert cards in the set include: All-Pros, Holoview F/X and Special FX, and Joe Montana Trilogy (MT17-MT20). A special Dan Marino Record Breaker (DM1) insert and a Montana Tribute card were also produced.

MT
Complete Set (200): 85.00
Common Player: .20
Minor Stars: .40
Pack (8): 6.00
Wax Box (32): 180.00
1 *Ki-Jana Carter* 1.00
2 *Eric Zeier* 2.00
3 *Steve McNair* 10.00
4 *Michael Westbrook* 5.00
5 *Kerry Collins* 4.00
6 *Joey Galloway* 6.00
7 *Kevin Carter* 1.00
8 *Mike Mamula* .40
9 *Kyle Brady* 1.00
10 *J.J. Stokes* 1.50
11 *Tyrone Poole* .40
12 *Rashaan Salaam* .75
13 *Sherman Williams* .50
14 *Luther Elliss* .40
15 *James Stewart* 5.00
16 *Tamarick Vanover* 1.00
17 *Napoleon Kaufman* 5.00
18 *Curtis Martin* 10.00
19 *Tyrone Wheatley* 3.50
20 *Frank Sanders* 2.00
21 *Devin Bush* .40
22 Terance Mathis .20
23 Bert Emanuel .75
24 Eric Metcalf .20
25 Craig Heyward .20
26 Jeff George .40
27 Mark Carrier .20
28 Pete Metzelaars .20
29 Frank Reich .20
30 Sam Mills .20
31 John Kasay .20
32 Willie Green .20
33 Jeff Graham .20
34 Curtis Conway .75
35 Steve Walsh .20
36 Erik Kramer .40
37 Michael Timpson .20
38 Mark Carrier .20
39 Troy Aikman 3.00
40 Michael Irvin .40
41 Charles Haley .20
42 Deion Sanders 2.50
43 Jay Novacek .20
44 Emmitt Smith 6.00
45 Herman Moore 1.00
46 Scott Mitchell .40
47 Bennie Blades .20
48 Johnnie Morton .20
49 Chris Spielman .20
50 Barry Sanders 3.00
51 Edgar Bennett .20
52 Reggie White .40
53 Sean Jones .20
54 Mark Ingram .20
55 Robert Brooks .40
56 Brett Favre 6.00
57 Lovell Pinkney .20
58 Chris Miller .20
59 Isaac Bruce .50
60 Roman Phifer .20
61 Sean Gilbert .20
62 Jerome Bettis 1.00
63 Derrick Alexander .20
64 Cris Carter .40
65 Jake Reed .20
66 Robert Smith .20
67 David Palmer .20
68 Warren Moon .40
69 *Ray Zellars* .40
70 Jim Everett .20
71 Michael Haynes .20
72 Quinn Early .20
73 Willie Roaf .20
74 Mario Bates 1.00
75 Mike Sherrard .20
76 Chris Calloway .20
77 Dave Brown .20
78 Thomas Lewis .20
79 Herschel Walker .20
80 Rodney Hampton .40
81 Fred Barnett .20
82 Calvin Williams .20
83 Randall Cunningham .20
84 Charlie Garner .20
85 Bobby Taylor .20
86 Ricky Watters .40
87 Dave Kreig .20
88 Rob Moore .20
89 Eric Swann .20
90 Clyde Simmons .20
91 Seth Joyner .20
92 Garrison Hearst .40
93 Jerry Rice 3.00
94 Bryant Young .20
95 Brent Jones .20
96 Ken Norton .20
97 William Floyd 1.50
98 Steve Young 3.00
99 *Warren Sapp* 4.00
100 Trent Dilfer 1.00
101 Alvin Harper .40
102 Hardy Nickerson .20
103 Derrick Brooks .20
104 Errict Rhett .40
105 Henry Ellard .20
106 Ken Harvey .20
107 Gus Frerotte 1.00
108 Brian Mitchell .20
109 Terry Allen .20
110 Heath Shuler 1.50
111 Jim Kelly .40
112 Andre Reed .20
113 Bruce Smith .20
114 *Darick Holmes* 1.50
115 Bryce Paup .20
116 Cornelius Bennett .20
117 Carl Pickens .50
118 Darnay Scott 1.25
119 *Jeff Blake* 3.00
120 Steve Tovar .20
121 Tony McGee .20
122 Dan Wilkinson .20
123 Craig Powell .20
124 Vinny Testaverde .20
125 Eric Turner .20
126 Leroy Hoard .20
127 Lorenzo White .20
128 Andre Rison .40
129 Shannon Sharpe .20
130 *Terrell Davis* 15.00
131 Anthony Miller .20
132 Mike Pritchard .20
133 Steve Atwater .20
134 John Elway 2.00
135 Haywood Jeffires .20
136 Gary Brown .20
137 Al Smith .20
138 *Rodney Thomas* .50
139 Ray Childress .20
140 Mel Gray .20
141 Craig Erickson .20
142 Sean Dawkins .20
143 *Ken Dilger* 1.25
144 Ellis Johnson .20
145 Quentin Coryatt .20
146 Marshall Faulk 1.50
147 *Tony Boselli* .40
148 *Rob Johnson* 7.00
149 Desmond Howard .20
150 Steve Beuerlein .20
151 Reggie Cobb .20
152 Jeff Lageman .20
153 Willie Davis .20
154 Marcus Allen .40
155 Neil Smith .20
156 Greg Hill .75
157 Steve Bono .50
158 Derrick Thomas .40
159 Jeff Hostetler .40
160 Harvey Williams .20
161 Raghib Ismail .20
162 Chester McGlockton .20
163 Terry McDaniel .20
164 Tim Brown .40
165 Terry Kirby .20
166 Irving Fryar .20
167 O.J. McDuffie .20
168 Bryan Cox .20
169 Eric Green .20
170 Dan Marino 6.00
171 Ben Coates .20
172 Vincent Brisby .20
173 Chris Slade .20
174 Ty Law .20
175 Vincent Brown .20
176 Drew Bledsoe 3.00
177 Johnny Mitchell .20
178 Boomer Esiason .20
179 *Wayne Chrebet* 8.00
180 Hugh Douglas .20
181 Ron Moore .20
182 Aaron Glenn .20
183 *Mark Bruener* 1.00
184 Neil O'Donnell .40
185 Charles Johnson .75
186 Greg Lloyd .40
187 Rod Woodson .40
188 Bam Morris 1.50
189 *Terrell Fletcher* 1.00
190 Terrance Shaw .20
191 Stan Humphries .40
192 Junior Seau .40
193 Leslie O'Neal .20
194 Natrone Means 2.00
195 *Christian Fauria* .40
196 Rick Mirer 1.00
197 Sam Adams .20
198 Cortez Kennedy .20
199 Eugene Robinson .20
200 Chris Warren .40
NNO Dan Marino Tribute 40.00
NNO Joe Montana Salute 25.00

1995 Sp All-Pros

These All-Pro die-cut cards came in two versions - silver, which was randomly inserted one per every five packs, and gold, which was found one per every 62 packs. The top and bottom of the card are die-cut, with either silver or gold foil; the player's name is at the top, while his team name is at the bottom. All-Pro is written in foil on the left side of the card; the player's position is in foil on the right, along with the brand logo. Card backs, numbered with an "AP" prefix, have a close-up shot of the player, plus a brief summary of the player's achievements.

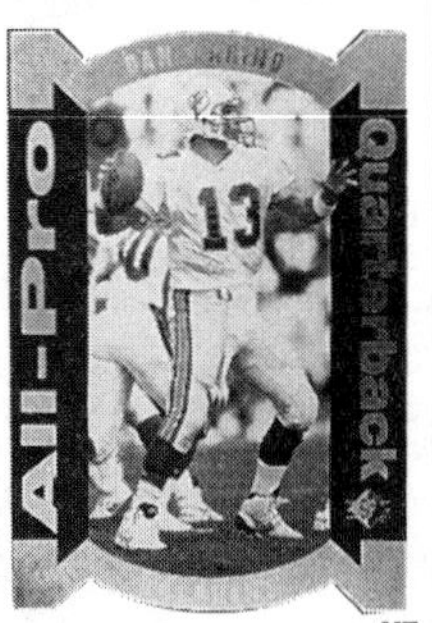

MT
Complete Set (20): 60.00
Common Player: 2.50
Comp. Gold Set (20): 550.00
Gold Cards: 3x-6x
1 Marshall Faulk 5.00
2 Natrone Means 2.50
3 Emmitt Smith 8.00
4 Brett Favre 8.00
5 Michael Westbrook 3.00
6 Jerry Rice 5.00
7 John Elway 4.00
8 Troy Aikman 5.00
9 Rashaan Salaam 4.00
10 Jerome Bettis 2.50
11 Drew Bledsoe 5.00
12 Kerry Collins 3.00
13 Dan Marino 8.00
14 Tyrone Wheatley 3.00
15 Steve McNair 4.00
16 Steve Young 5.00
17 Eric Zeier 3.00
18 Errict Rhett 4.00
19 Michael Irvin 3.00
20 Barry Sanders 5.00

1995 Sp Holoviews

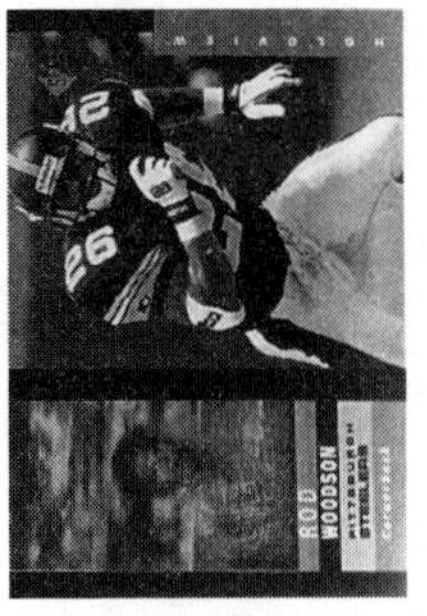

Some of the NFL's top stars and promising rookies are showcased in this 40-card insert set. Cards were randomly included in 1995 Upper Deck football, one per every five packs. The horizontal card front features a glossy color photo on the right side, along with a rectangle which says "Holoview." A hologram of the player up close, plus his name, team name and position, are on the left side. The back is also horizontal and includes an action photo on the left, plus a summary of the player's accomplishments on the right. Cards are numbered using a fraction format - 13/40, etc. Each Holoview was also made in a die-cut version, seeded one per every 75 packs.

MT
Complete Set (40): 125.00
Common Player: 1.00
Minor Stars: 2.00
Inserted 1:5
Die-Cut Cards 3x-6x
Inserted 1:75
1 Joe Montana 10.00
2 Dan Marino 12.00
3 Drew Bledsoe 8.00
4 Ben Coates 1.00
5 Curtis Martin 8.00
6 Kyle Brady 1.00
7 Marshall Faulk 3.00
8 Ki-Jana Carter 2.00
9 Leroy Hoard 1.00
10 James O. Stewart 1.00
11 Mark Bruener 1.00
12 Charles Johnson 1.00
13 Rod Woodson 1.00
14 John Elway 10.00
15 Tim Brown 1.00
16 Napoleon Kaufman 8.00
17 Natrone Means 2.00
18 Jimmy Oliver 1.00
19 Christian Fauria 1.00
20 Joey Galloway 4.00
21 Chris Warren 1.00
22 Kerry Collins 3.00
23 Mario Bates 1.00
24 Jerome Bettis 2.00
25 William Floyd 1.00
26 Jerry Rice 8.00
27 J.J. Stokes 2.00
28 Steve Young 6.00
29 Troy Aikman 8.00
30 Michael Irvin 2.00
31 Emmitt Smith 12.00
32 Rodney Hampton 1.00
33 Heath Shuler 2.00
34 Michael Westbrook 2.00
35 Barry Sanders 15.00
36 Brett Favre 15.00
37 Cris Carter 3.00
38 Warren Moon 2.00
39 James A. Stewart 1.00
40 Errict Rhett 1.00

1995 Sp Holoview Die-Cuts

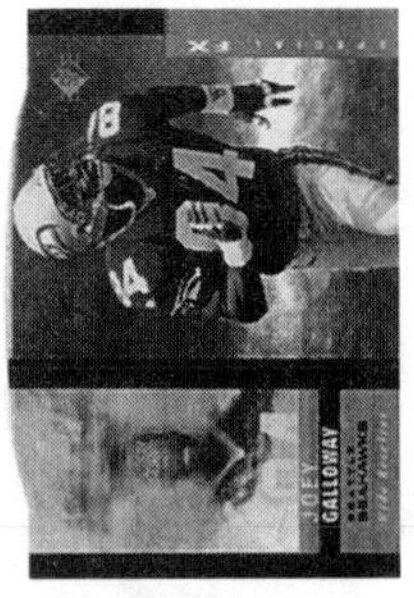

These 40 1995 Upper Deck SP inserts are the same as the regular Holoview insert cards, except they are die-cut around the top of the card. They are seeded one per every 75 packs.

MT
Complete Set (40): 1600.
Common Player: 7.00
1 Joe Montana 70.00
2 Dan Marino 125.00
3 Drew Bledsoe 70.00
4 Ben Coates 7.00
5 Curtis Martin 80.00
6 Kyle Brady 7.00
7 Marshall Faulk 20.00
8 Ki-Jana Carter 14.00
9 Leroy Hoard 7.00
10 James O. Stewart 14.00
11 Mark Bruener 7.00
12 Charles Johnson 7.00
13 Rod Woodson 7.00
14 John Elway 50.00
15 Tim Brown 14.00
16 Napoleon Kaufman 14.00
17 Natrone Means 14.00
18 Jimmy Oliver 7.00
19 Christian Fauria 7.00
20 Joey Galloway 40.00
21 Chris Warren 14.00
22 Kerry Collins 20.00
23 Mario Bates 14.00
24 Jerome Bettis 14.00
25 William Floyd 14.00
26 Jerry Rice 70.00
27 J.J. Stokes 25.00
28 Steve Young 50.00
29 Troy Aikman 70.00
30 Michael Irvin 14.00
31 Emmitt Smith 125.00
32 Rodney Hampton 7.00
33 Heath Shuler 14.00
34 Michael Westbrook 20.00
35 Barry Sanders 70.00
36 Brett Favre 125.00
37 Cris Carter 14.00
38 Warren Moon 14.00
39 James A. Stewart 14.00
40 Errict Rhett 16.00

1995 Sp Championship

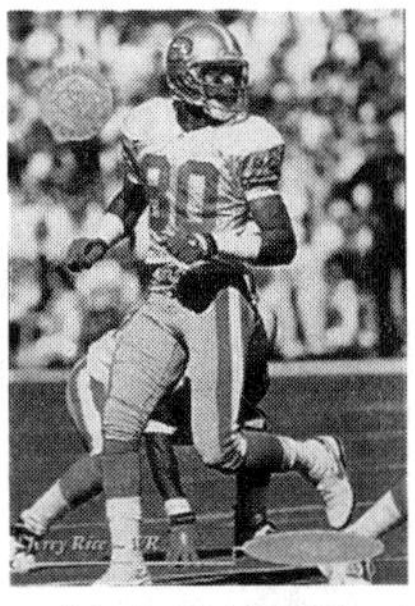

Upper Deck's debut SP Championship series has 225 cards, including 45 Future Champions subset cards. The Championship series of cards is the retail-only spinoff of Upper Deck's hobby-only SP product. All cards, inserts, wrappers and box designs are completely different in the retail and hobby versions. Each card front has a full-bleed color photo on it, plus a brand logo stamped in gold foil. The player's name and position are at the bottom, along with the team name, which is in an oval. Each card in the regular-issue set is also paralleled in a die-cut version that appears one per pack. One per every 15 packs holds a Showcase of the Playoffs insert card. This is a 20-card set of top NFL stars who could make an impact in the playoffs. This insert is also featured in a die-cut version that is seeded one card per every 40 packs.

MT
Complete Set (225): 65.00
Common Player: .15
Minor Stars: .30
Die-Cut Cards: 3x
Die-Cut Rookies: 2x
Inserted 1:1

Pack (6): 3.50
Wax Box (44): 150.00
1 *Frank Sanders* 2.50
2 *Stoney Case* .75
3 *Lorenzo Styles* .30
4 *Todd Collins* .30
5 *Darick Holmes* .60
6 *Brian DeMarco* .30
7 *Tyrone Poole* .30
8 *Kerry Collins* 2.50
9 *Rashaan Salaam* .50
10 *Steve Stenstrom* .30
11 *Ki-Jana Carter* .50
12 *Eric Zeier* .75
13 *Sherman Williams* .30
14 *Terrell Davis* 12.00
15 *David Dunn* .30
16 *Luther Elliss* .30
17 *Craig Newsome* .30
18 *Antonio Freeman* 6.00
19 *Steve McNair* 6.00
20 *Anthony Cook* .30
21 *Rodney Thomas* .30
22 *Ellis Johnson* .50
23 *Ken Dilger* .50
24 *James O. Stewart* 5.00
25 *Pete Mitchell* .30
26 *Tamarick Vanover* .60
27 *Orlanda Thomas* .30
28 *Corey Fuller* .30
29 *Curtis Martin* 7.00
30 *Ty Law* .75
31 *Roell Preston* .75
32 *Mark Fields* .30
33 *Tyrone Wheatley* 2.50
34 *Kyle Brady* .50
35 *Napoleon Kaufman* 5.00
36 *Kordell Stewart* 6.00
37 *Mark Bruener* .75
38 *Terrance Shaw* .30
39 *Terrell Fletcher* .50
40 *J.J. Stokes* 1.00
41 *Christian Fauria* .30
42 *Joey Galloway* 4.00
43 *Kevin Carter* .50
44 *Warren Sapp* 1.00
45 *Michael Westbrook* 3.50
46 Clyde Simmons .15
47 Rob Moore .15
48 Seth Joyner .15
49 Dave Kreig .15
50 Garrison Hearst .40
51 Aeneas Williams .15
52 Terance Mathis .15
53 Bert Emanual .50
54 Chris Doleman .15
55 Craig Heyward .15
56 Jeff George .15
57 Eric Metcalf .15
58 Jim Kelly .30
59 Andre Reed .15
60 Russell Copeland .15
61 Bruce Smith .15
62 Cornelius Bennett .15
63 Jeff Burris .15
64 Mark Carrier .15
65 Pete Metzelaars .15
66 Frank Reich .15
67 Sam Mills .15
68 John Kasay .15
69 Willie Green .15
70 Curtis Conway .15
71 Erik Kramer .15
72 Donnell Woolford .15
73 Mark Carrier .15
74 Jeff Graham .15
75 Raymont Harris .15
76 Carl Pickens .30
77 Darnay Scott .30
78 *Jeff Blake* 1.00
79 Dan Wilkinson .15
80 Tony McGee .15
81 Eric Bienemy .15
82 Vinny Testaverde .15
83 Eric Turner .15
84 Leroy Hoard .15
85 Lorenzo White .15
86 Antonio Langham .15
87 Andre Rison .15
88 Troy Aikman 1.50
89 Michael Irvin .50
90 Charles Haley .15
91 Daryl Johnston .15
92 Jay Novacek .15
93 Emmitt Smith 3.00
94 Shannon Sharpe .15
95 Anthony Miller .15
96 Mike Pritchard .15
97 Glyn Milburn .15
98 Simon Fletcher .15
99 John Elway .75
100 Henry Thomas .15
101 Herman Moore .50
102 Scott Mitchell .15
103 Bennie Blades .15
104 Chris Spielman .15
105 Barry Sanders 2.00
106 Mark Ingram .15
107 Edgar Bennett .15
108 Reggie White .30
109 Sean Jones .15
110 Robert Brooks .30
111 Brett Favre 3.00
112 Chris Chandler .15
113 Haywood Jeffires .15
114 Gary Brown .15
115 Al Smith .15
116 Ray Childress .15
117 Mel Gray .15
118 Jim Harbaugh .15
119 Sean Dawkins .15
120 Roosevelt Potts .15
121 Marshall Faulk 1.00
122 Tony Bennett .15
123 Quentin Coryatt .15
124 Desmond Howard .15
125 Tony Boselli .15
126 Steve Beuerlein .15
127 Jeff Lageman .15
128 *Rob Johnson* 5.00
129 Ernest Givins .15
130 Willie Davis .15
131 Marcus Allen .30
132 Neil Smith .15
133 Greg Hill .50
134 Steve Bono .30
135 Lake Dawson .50
136 Dan Marino 3.00
137 Terry Kirby .15
138 Irvin Fryar .15
139 O.J. McDuffie .15
140 Bryan Cox .15
141 Eric Green .15
142 Cris Carter .15
143 Robert Smith .15
144 John Randle .15
145 Jake Reed .15
146 DeWayne Washington .15
147 Warren Moon .30
148 Dave Meggett .15
149 Ben Coates .15
150 Vincent Brisby .15
151 Willie McGinest .15
152 Chris Slade .15
153 Drew Bledsoe 2.00
154 Eric Allen .15
155 Mario Bates .50
156 Jim Everett .15
157 Renaldo Turnbull .15
158 Tyrone Hughes .15
159 Michael Haynes .15
160 Mike Sherrard .15
161 Dave Brown .15
162 Chris Calloway .15
163 Keith Hamilton .15
164 Rodney Hampton .15
165 Herschel Walker .15
166 Adrian Murrell .50
167 Johnny Mitchell .15
168 Boomer Esiason .15
169 Mo Lewis .15
170 Brad Baxter .15
171 Aaron Glenn .15
172 Jeff Hostetler .15
173 Harvey Williams .15
174 Tim Brown .30
175 Terry McDaniel .15
176 Pat Swilling .15
177 Raghib Ismail .15
178 Randall Cunningham .15
179 Calvin Williams .15
180 Ricky Watters .30
181 Charlie Garner .15
182 Fred Barnett .15
183 Rodney Peete .15
184 Neil O'Donnell .30
185 Charles Johnson .40
186 Rod Woodson .15
187 Bam Morris .75
188 Kevin Greene .15
189 Greg Lloyd .15
190 Chris Miller .15
191 Isaac Bruce 1.50
192 Roman Phifer .15
193 Jerome Bettis .30
194 Carlos Jenkins .15
195 Troy Drayton .15
196 Andre Coleman .15
197 Natrone Means .75
198 Leslie O'Neal .15
199 Junior Seau .30
200 Tony Martin .15
201 Stan Humphries .15
202 Steve Young 2.00
203 Jerry Rice 2.00
204 Brent Jones .15
205 Dana Stubblefield .15
206 Lee Woodall .15
207 Merton Hanks .15
208 Rick Mirer .30
209 Brian Blades .15
210 Chris Warren .30
211 Sam Adams .15
212 Cortez Kennedy .15
213 Eugene Robinson .15
214 Alvin Harper .15
215 Trent Dilfer .50
216 Hardy Nickerson .15
217 Errict Rhett .30
218 Eric Curry .15
219 Jackie Harris .15
220 Henry Ellard .15
221 Terry Allen .15
222 Brian Mitchell .15
223 Ken Harvey .15
224 Gus Frerotte .75
225 Heath Shuler 1.25

1995 Sp Championship Die-Cuts

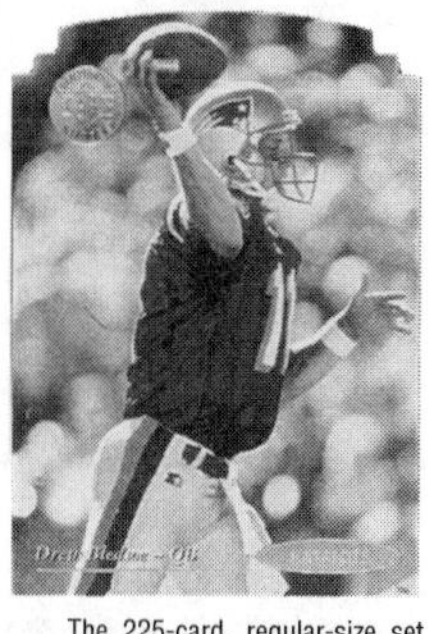

The 225-card, regular-size set was a parallel set to the SP Championship issue, inserted every pack. The cards are essentially identical, except for the die-cut card tops.

MT
Complete Set (225): 150.00
Common Player (1-225): .50
Die-Cut Cards: 2x-4x

1995 Sp Championship Playoff Showcase

These cards feature a color action photo of a player in a box in the center. The set name is in foil at the bottom, along with the player's name and position. A gold-foiled brand logo is above the photo. Card backs are numbered using a "PS" prefix. Cards were randomly included in every 15th pack of 1995 Upper Deck SP Championship product. The inserts were also created in a die-cut version; these cards are seeded one per every 40 packs.

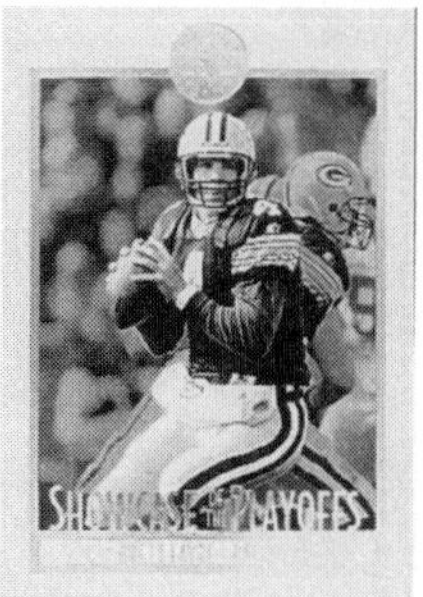

MT
Complete Set (20): 100.00
Common Player: 1.00
Minor Stars: 2.00
Inserted 1:15 275.00
Die-Cut Cards: 2x
Inserted 1:20
1 Troy Aikman 8.00
2 Jerry Rice 8.00
3 Isaac Bruce 2.00
4 Rodney Peete 1.00
5 Rashaan Salaam 2.00
6 Brett Favre 15.00
7 Alvin Harper 1.00
8 Cris Carter 2.00
9 Michael Westbrook 2.00
10 Jeff George 2.00
11 Natrone Means 2.00
12 Dan Marino 12.00
13 Steve Bono 2.00
14 Greg Lloyd 1.00
15 Jim Kelly 2.00
16 Jeff Hostetler 1.00
17 Marshall Faulk 3.00
18 John Elway 10.00
19 Jeff Blake 2.00
20 Andre Rison 1.00

1996 Sp

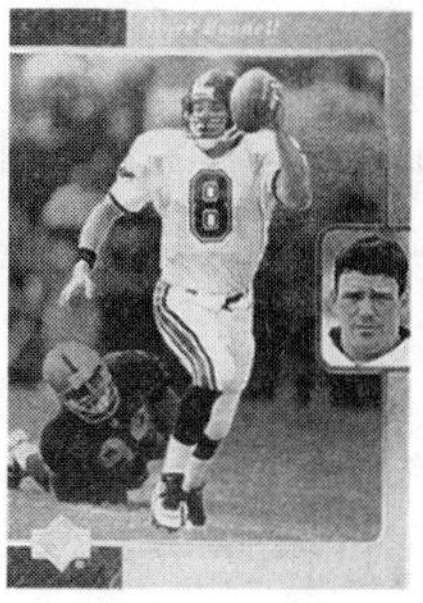

The 188-card, regular-sized set was issued in eight-card packs and included the subset, Premiere Prospects. The release included a five-card SPX Force preview along with an autographed parallel version. Other inserts were: Focus On The Future, Explosive, Holoview and F/X Holoview. The base set cards include an action shot with a player headshot inset along the right border. The player's name appears on the top border with team nickname and position along the bottom.

MT
Complete Set (188): 150.00
Common Player: .20
Minor Stars: .40
Pack (8): 8.00
Wax Box (30): 200.00
1 *Keyshawn Johnson* 12.00
2 *Kevin Hardy* .75
3 *Simeon Rice* .75
4 *Jonathan Ogden* .20
5 *Eddie George* 25.00
6 *Terry Glenn* 8.00
7 *Terrell Owens* 18.00
8 *Tim Biakabutuka* 6.00
9 *Lawrence Phillips* 2.00
10 *Alex Molden* .20
11 *Regan Upshaw* .20
12 *Rickey Dudley* 1.75
13 *Duane Clemons* .20
14 *John Mobley* .20
15 *Eddie Kennison* 1.00
16 *Karim Abdul-Jabbar* 2.00
17 *Eric Moulds* 12.00
18 *Marvin Harrison* 20.00
19 *Stepfret Williams* .20
20 *Stephen Davis* 20.00
21 Deion Sanders 1.50
22 Emmitt Smith 5.00
23 Troy Aikman 2.50
24 Michael Irvin .40
25 Herschel Walker .20
26 Kavika Pittman .20
27 Andre Hastings .20
28 Jerome Bettis .40
29 Mike Tomczak .20
30 Kordell Stewart 2.00
31 Charles Johnson .20
32 Greg Lloyd .20
33 Brett Favre 5.00
34 Mark Chmura .20
35 Edgar Bennett .20
36 Robert Brooks .20
37 Craig Newsome .20
38 Reggie White .40
39 Marshall Faulk 1.50
40 Jim Harbaugh .20
41 Sean Dawkins .20
42 Quentin Coryatt .20
43 Ray Buchanan .20
44 Ken Dilger .20
45 Jerry Rice 2.50
46 J.J. Stokes .40
47 Steve Young 2.00
48 Derek Loville .20
49 Terry Kirby .20
50 Ken Norton .20
51 Tamarick Vanover 1.00
52 Steve Bono .20
53 Marcus Allen .40
54 Neil Smith .20
55 Derrick Thomas .20
56 Dale Carter .20
57 Terance Mathis .20
58 Eric Metcalf .20
59 *Jamal Anderson* 15.00
60 Bert Emanuel .20
61 Craig Heyward .20
62 Cornelius Bennett .20
63 Tony Martin .20
64 Stan Humphries .20
65 Andre Coleman .20
66 Junior Seau .20
67 Terrell Fletcher .20
68 John Carney .20
69 Charlie Jones .20
70 Ricky Watters .40
71 Charlie Garner .20
72 *Bobby Hoying* 2.00
73 Jason Dunn .20
74 Bobby Taylor .20
75 Irving Fryar .20
76 Jim Kelly .20
77 Thurman Thomas .40
78 Darick Holmes .20
79 Bryce Paup .20
80 Bruce Smith .20
81 Andre Reed .20
82 Glyn Milburn .20
83 Brett Perriman .20
84 Herman Moore .75
85 Scott Mitchell .20
86 Barry Sanders 3.00
87 Johnnie Morton .20
88 Dan Marino 5.00
89 O.J. McDuffie .20
90 Stanley Pritchett .20
91 *Zach Thomas* 2.50
92 Daryl Gardner .20
93 Rashaan Salaam .75
94 Erik Kramer .20
95 Curtis Conway .20
96 *Bobby Engram* .75
97 Walt Harris .20
98 Bryan Cox .20
99 John Elway 2.00
100 Terrell Davis 5.00
101 Anthony Miller .20
102 Shannon Sharpe .20
103 Steve Atwater .20
104 *Jeff Lewis* 1.00
105 Joey Galloway 1.50
106 Chris Warren .20
107 Rick Mirer .20
108 Cortez Kennedy .20
109 Michael Sinclair .20
110 John Friesz .20
111 Warren Moon .20
112 Cris Carter .20
113 Jake Reed .20
114 Robert Smith .20
115 John Randle .20
116 Orlanda Thomas .20
117 Jeff Hostetler .20
118 Tim Brown .20
119 Joe Aska .20
120 Napoleon Kaufman .20
121 Terry McDaniel .20
122 Harvey Williams .20
123 Trent Dilfer .20
124 Reggie Brooks .20
125 Alvin Harper .20
126 *Mike Alstott* 10.00
127 Hardy Nickerson .20
128 Mario Bates .20
129 Jim Everett .20
130 Tyrone Hughes .20
131 Michael Haynes .20
132 Eric Allen .20
133 Isaac Bruce 1.50
134 Kevin Carter .20
135 Leslie O'Neal .20
136 *Tony Banks* 15.00
137 Chris Chandler .20
138 Steve McNair 2.00
139 Chris Sanders .20
140 Ronnie Harmon .20
141 Willie Davis .20
142 Michael Westbrook .40
143 Terry Allen .20
144 Brian Mitchell .20
145 Henry Ellard .20
146 Gus Frerotte .20
147 Kerry Collins .50
148 Sam Mills .20
149 Wesley Walls .20
150 Kevin Greene .20
151 *Mushin Muhammad* 10.00
152 Winslow Oliver .20
153 Jeff Blake .50
154 Carl Pickens .20
155 Darnay Scott .20
156 Garrison Hearst .20
157 Marco Battaglia .20
158 Drew Bledsoe 2.00
159 Curtis Martin 4.00
160 Shawn Jefferson .20
161 Ben Coates .20
162 Lawyer Milloy .20
163 Tyrone Wheatley .20
164 Rodney Hampton .20
165 Chris Calloway .20
166 Dave Brown .20
167 *Amani Toomer* 4.00
168 Vinny Testaverde .20
169 Michael Jackson .20
170 Eric Turner .20
171 DeRon Jenkins .20
172 *Jermaine Lewis* 2.00
173 Frank Sanders .20
174 Rob Moore .20
175 Kent Graham .50
176 *Leeland McElroy* .50
177 Larry Centers .25
178 Eric Swann .20
179 Mark Brunell 1.50
180 Willie Jackson .20
181 James O. Stewart .20
182 Natrone Means .20
183 *Tony Brackens* .75
184 Adrian Murrell .20
185 Neil O'Donnell .20
186 Hugh Douglas .20
187 Jeff Graham .20
188 *Alex Van Dyke* .40

1996 Sp Explosive

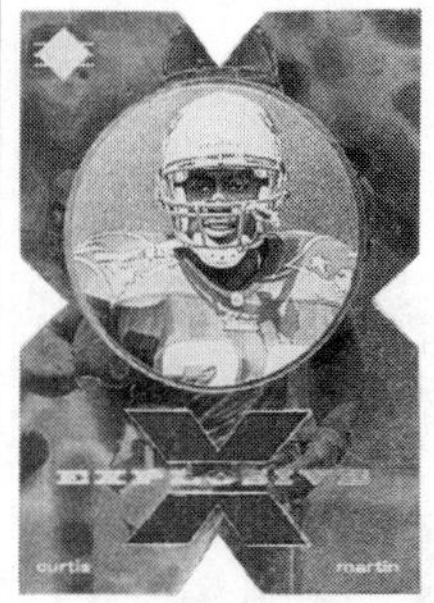

The 20-card, regular-sized, die-cut set was inserted every 360 packs of 1996 Upper Deck SP football. The die-cut cards are in the shape of an "X" and feature a circular headshot of the player over a black-and-white background. The player's first name appears in the lower left corner in lowercase letters with the last name in the right corner, also in lowercase. The card backs are numbered with the "X" prefix.

MT
Complete Set (20): 1700.
Common Player: 25.00
1 Emmitt Smith 250.00
2 Jerry Rice 125.00
3 Rashaan Salaam 25.00
4 Brett Favre 250.00
5 Tim Brown 25.00
6 Tim Biakabutuka 75.00
7 John Elway 100.00
8 Steve Young 100.00
9 Napoleon Kaufman 25.00
10 Troy Aikman 125.00
11 Drew Bledsoe 125.00
12 Carl Pickens 25.00
13 Dan Marino 250.00
14 Eddie George 150.00
15 Joey Galloway 75.00
16 Deion Sanders 75.00
17 Curtis Martin 150.00
18 Marshall Faulk 60.00
19 Keyshawn Johnson 75.00
20 Barry Sanders 160.00

1996 Sp Focus on the Future

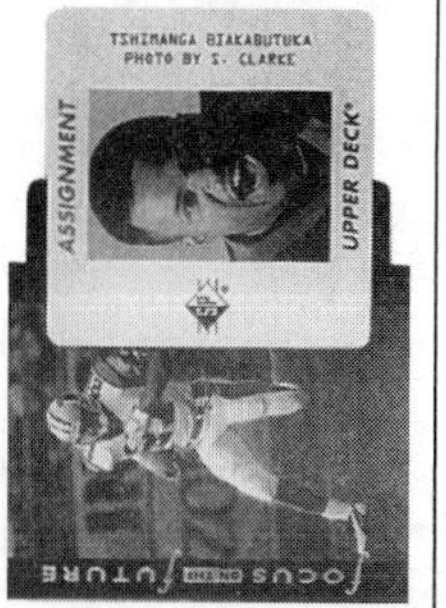

The 30-card, regular-sized, die-cut set was inserted every 30 packs of SP football. The card fronts feature a color player shot over a gold background with a slide film-type addition on the right side. The cel contains a color headshot of the player with the photographer listed along the right border. The card backs are numbered with the "F" prefix.

MT
Complete Set (30): 300.00
Common Player: 6.00
1 Leeland McElroy 6.00
2 Frank Sanders 6.00
3 Darick Holmes 6.00
4 Eric Moulds 12.00
5 Kerry Collins 10.00
6 Tim Biakabutuka 15.00
7 Ki-Jana Carter 6.00
8 Jeff Blake 10.00
9 John Mobley 6.00
10 Johnnie Morton 6.00
11 Eddie George 40.00
12 Steve McNair 20.00
13 Marshall Faulk 8.00
14 Kevin Hardy 6.00
15 Greg Hill 6.00
16 Tamarick Vanover 8.00
17 Karim Abdul-Jabbar 30.00
18 Drew Bledsoe 30.00
19 Curtis Martin 40.00
20 Danny Kanell 6.00
21 Keyshawn Johnson 20.00
22 Napoleon Kaufman 6.00
23 Rickey Dudley 8.00
24 Kordell Stewart 30.00
25 Lawrence Phillips 15.00
26 Isaac Bruce 15.00
27 J.J. Stokes 6.00
28 Joey Galloway 25.00
29 Errict Rhett 8.00
30 Mike Alstott 8.00

1996 Sp Holoview

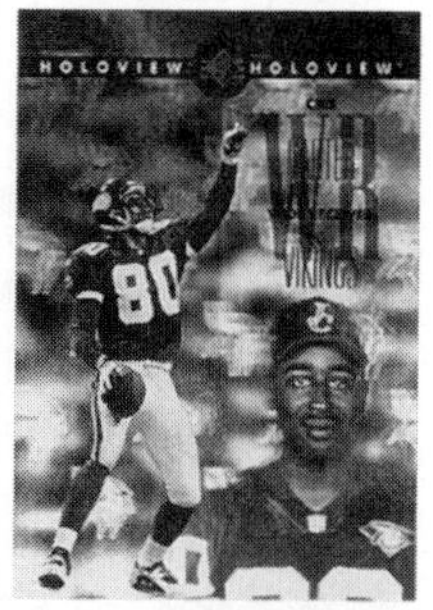

The 48-card, regular-sized set was inserted every seven packs of SP football. The card fronts feature a color player shot over a Holoview image headshot and multiple team logo. The player's name, position and team nickname appears in the upper right quadrant. A 48-card, die-cut parallel version was inserted every 75 packs. The cards also feature the same Holoview image but have a gold top border instead of a team-color top border.

MT
Complete Set (48): 250.00
Common Player: 2.00
Die-Cut Cards: 2x-4x
1 Jerry Rice 12.00
2 Herman Moore 4.00
3 Kerry Collins 4.00
4 Brett Favre 25.00
5 Junior Seau 2.00
6 Troy Aikman 12.00
7 John Elway 8.00
8 Steve Young 8.00
9 Reggie White 4.00
10 Kordell Stewart 12.00
11 Drew Bledsoe 12.00
12 Jeff Blake 4.00
13 Dan Marino 25.00
14 Curtis Martin 15.00
15 Marshall Faulk 6.00
16 Greg Lloyd 2.00
17 Cris Carter 2.00
18 Isaac Bruce 6.00
19 Joey Galloway 8.00
20 Barry Sanders 12.00
21 Emmitt Smith 25.00
22 Edgar Bennett 2.00
23 Rashaan Salaam 4.00
24 Steve McNair 8.00
25 Tamarick Vanover 4.00
26 Deion Sanders 6.00
27 Keyshawn Johnson 6.00
28 Kevin Hardy 2.00
29 Simeon Rice 2.00
30 Lawrence Phillips 6.00
31 Tim Biakabutuka 6.00
32 Terry Glenn 12.00
33 Rickey Dudley 4.00
34 Regan Upshaw 2.00
35 Eddie George 15.00
36 John Mobley 2.00
37 Eddie Kennison 8.00
38 Marvin Harrison 8.00
39 Leeland McElroy 4.00
40 Eric Moulds 4.00
41 Alex Van Dyke 4.00
42 Mike Alstott 5.00
43 Jeff Lewis 2.00
44 Bobby Engram 4.00
45 Derrick Mayes 2.00
46 Karim Abdul-Jabbar 10.00
47 Stepfret Williams 2.00
48 Stephen Davis 4.00

1996 Sp Holoview Die-Cuts

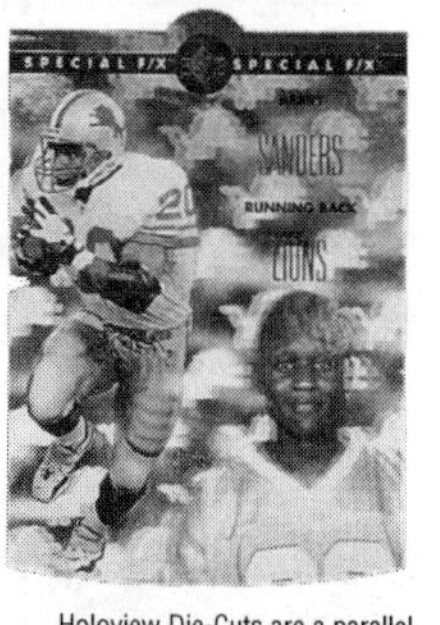

Holoview Die-Cuts are a parallel set to the Holoview Collection, and seeded one per 74 packs. The 48 regular Holoviews are double die-cut on the top and bottom and have gold foil added to them.

MT
Complete Set (48): 1000.
Holoview Die-Cuts: 2x-4x

1996 Sp Spx Force

The five-card, regular-size die-cut set was inserted every 950 packs of 1996 SP football. Each card contained four Holoview images of top players at quarterback, running back, wide receiver and rookies. The fifth card features Holoviews of the top

four at each position (and rookies) and will have an autographed parallel version (1:8,820).

MT
Complete Set (4): 300.00
Common Player: 50.00
Set price does not include Autographs.
1 Keyshawn Johnson, Lawrence Phillips, Terry Glenn, Tim Biakabutuka 50.00
2 Barry Sanders, Emmitt Smith, Marshall Faulk, Curtis Martin 90.00
3 Dan Marino, Brett Favre, Drew Bledsoe, Troy Aikman 100.00
4 Jerry Rice, Herman Moore, Carl Pickens, Isaac Bruce 60.00
5A Keyshawn Johnson AUTO 350.00
5B Dan Marino AUTO 1600.
5C Jerry Rice AUTO 1000.
5D Barry Sanders AUTO 1000.

1996 Spx

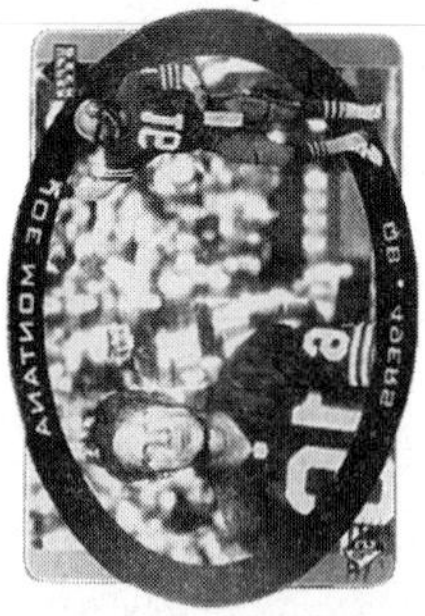

This 50-card die-cut Upper Deck set utilizes Holoview technology on 32-point stock. It combines the top stars of the NFL with the top rookies of the 1995 season. To make a Holoview card, each athlete is videotaped while on a turntable. More than seven seconds - or 200 frames - of videotape are then synthesized to produce a 50-degree, 3D picture. A mug shot also appears in the card, which has an oval (using the team's primary color) that has the player's name at the top and his position and team name below. A small color photo is also on the card front. The card back has a rectangle that includes a color photo, biographical and statistical information, and a recap of his accomplishments. Each card in the regular issue is also reprinted in a Gold parallel set; they are inserted one per every seven packs. Insert cards include a Joe Montana Tribute card (one in 95), a Dan Marino Record Breaker card (one in 81), autographed versions of the Marino and Montana cards (one in 433), and HoloFame Collection.

MT
Complete Set (50): 150.00
Common Player: 1.50
Minor Stars: 3.00
Comp. Gold Set (50): 400.00
Gold Cards: 1x-2x
Marino Auto: 300.00
Montana Auto: 225.00
Pack (1): 3.00
Wax Box (36): 100.00
1 Frank Sanders 3.00
2 Terance Mathis 1.50
3 Todd Collins 3.00
4 Kerry Collins 4.00
5 Carl Pickens 3.00
6 Darnay Scott 3.00
7 Ki-Jana Carter 3.00
8 Eric Zeier 3.00
9 Andre Rison 1.50
10 Sherman Williams 3.00
11 Troy Aikman 8.00
12 Michael Irvin 3.00
13 Emmitt Smith 15.00
14 Shannon Sharpe 1.50
15 John Elway 5.00
16 Barry Sanders 10.00
17 Brett Favre 15.00
18 Rodney Thomas 4.00
19 Marshall Faulk 8.00
20 James O. Stewart 3.00
21 Greg Hill 1.50
22 Tamarick Vanover 3.00
23 Dan Marino 15.00
24 Cris Carter 1.50
25 Warren Moon 1.50
26 Drew Bledsoe 10.00
27 Ben Coates 1.50
28 Curtis Martin 15.00
29 Mario Bates 3.00
30 Tyrone Wheatley 3.00
31 Rodney Hampton 1.50
32 Kyle Brady 1.50
33 Jeff Hostetler 1.50
34 Napoleon Kaufman 4.00
35 Tim Brown 1.50
36 Charles Johnson 3.00
37 Rod Woodson 1.50
38 Natrone Means 4.00
39 J.J. Stokes 7.00
40 Steve Young 8.00
41 Brent Jones 1.50
42 Jerry Rice 8.00
43 Joe Montana 8.00
44 Rick Mirer 3.00
45 Chris Warren 3.00
46 Joey Galloway 10.00
47 Isaac Bruce 3.00
48 Jerome Bettis 3.00
49 Errict Rhett 3.00
50 Michael Westbrook 5.00
UDT-13 (Dan Marino R.B.) 35.00
UDT-19 (Joe Montana Tr.) 25.00

1996 Spx Gold

The 50-card, regular-size set was the parallel gold version of the SPx set.

MT
Complete Set (50): 500.00
Common Player: 4.00
Gold Cards: 2x

1996 Spx Holofame

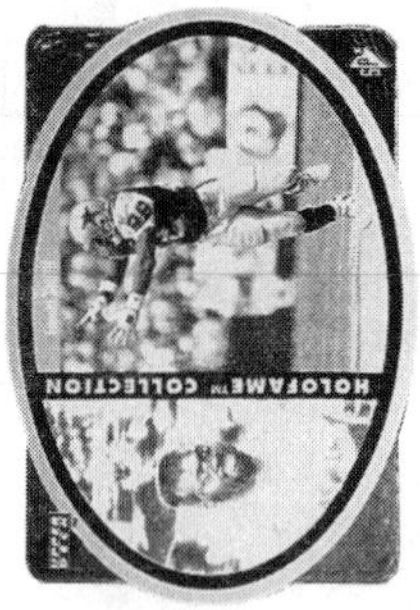

These 1996 Upper Deck SPx insert cards were seeded one per every 24 packs. They showcase players who are likely to be enshrined in the Hall of Fame someday. Cards are numbered using an "Hx" prefix.

MT
Complete Set (10): 150.00
Common Player: 7.00
1 Troy Aikman 15.00
2 Emmitt Smith 30.00
3 Barry Sanders 16.00
4 Steve Young 10.00
5 Jerry Rice 15.00
6 John Elway 12.00
7 Marshall Faulk 10.00
8 Dan Marino 30.00
9 Drew Bledsoe 15.00
10 Natrone Means 7.00

1997 SP Authentic

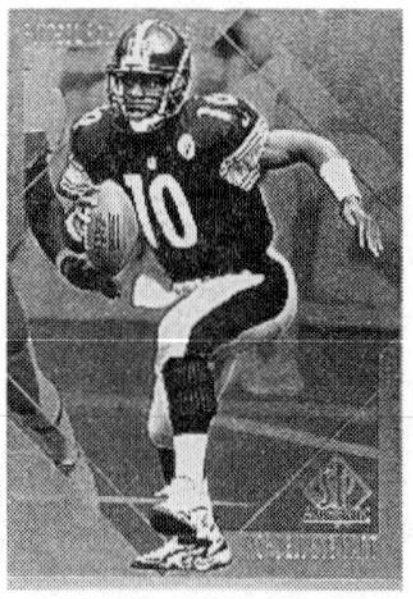

SP Authentic Football is a 198-card set featuring 168 veterans and a subset called Future Watch which contains 30 of the year's top rookies. The front of the cards features an action shot with the player's name in the bottom right corner and team name in the upper left. The card backs feature another action shot and career stats. The inserts include Aikman Power-Deck Audio Cards, ProFiles, Sign of the TImes, Mark of a Legend, Traditions, SP Authentics, and SP Authentics Collection.

MT
Complete Set (198): 150.00
Common Player: .30
Minor Stars: .60
Pack (5): 8.50
Wax Box (24): 200.00
1 *Orlando Pace* 1.00
2 *Darrell Russell* 2.00
3 *Shawn Springs* 2.00
4 *Peter Boulware* .75
5 *Bryant Westbrook* 1.00
6 *Walter Jones* .75
7 *Ike Hilliard* 8.00
8 *James Farrior* .75
9 *Tom Knight* .75
10 *Warrick Dunn* 15.00
11 *Tony Gonzalez* 20.00
12 *Reinard Wilson* 1.00
13 *Yatil Green* 2.00
14 *Reidel Anthony* 6.00
15 *Kenny Holmes* .75
16 *Dwayne Rudd* .75
17 *Renaldo Wynn* .75
18 *David LaFleur* 2.50
19 *Antowain Smith* 10.00
20 *Jim Druckenmiller* 3.00
21 *Rae Carruth* 1.00
22 *Byron Hanspard* 3.00
23 *Jake Plummer* 30.00
24 *Joey Kent* 1.00
25 *Corey Dillon* 35.00
26 *Danny Wuerffel* 2.00
27 *Will Blackwell* 1.00
28 *Troy Davis* 1.00
29 *Darnell Autry* .75
30 *Pat Barnes* 2.00
31 Kent Graham .30
32 Simeon Rice .30
33 Frank Sanders .30
34 Rob Moore .30
35 Eric Swann .30
36 Chris Chandler .30
37 Jamal Anderson .60
38 Terance Mathis .30
39 Bert Emanuel .30
40 Michael Booker .30
41 Vinny Testaverde .30
42 Bam Morris .30
43 Michael Jackson .30
44 Derrick Alexander .30
45 Jamie Sharper .30
46 Kim Herring .30
47 Todd Collins .30
48 Thurman Thomas .60
49 Andre Reed .30
50 Quinn Early .30
51 Bryce Paup .30
52 Marcelius Wiley .30
53 Kerry Collins .75
54 Anthony Johnson .30
55 Tshimanga Biakabutuka .30
56 Muhsin Muhammad .30
57 Sam Mills .30
58 Wesley Walls .30
59 Rick Mirer .30
60 Raymont Harris .30
61 Curtis Conway .60
62 Bobby Engram .30
63 Bryan Cox .30
64 John Allred .30
65 Jeff Blake .60
66 Ki-Jana Carter .30
67 Darnay Scott .30
68 Carl Pickens .30
69 Dan Wilkerson .30
70 Troy Aikman 3.00
71 Emmitt Smith 5.00
72 Michael Irvin .60
73 Deion Sanders 1.50
74 Anthony Miller .30
75 Antonio Anderson .30
76 John Elway 1.75
77 Terrell Davis 3.00
78 Rod Smith .30
79 Shannon Sharpe .30
80 Neil Smith .30
81 Trevor Pryce .30
82 Scott Mitchell .30
83 Barry Sanders 3.00
84 Herman Moore .60
85 Johnnie Morton .30
86 Matt Russell .30
87 Brett Favre 6.00
88 Edgar Bennett .30
89 Robert Brooks .30
90 Antonio Freeman .60
91 Reggie White .60
92 Craig Newsome .30
93 Jim Harbaugh .30
94 Marshall Faulk .60
95 Sean Dawkins .30
96 Marvin Harrison .60
97 Quentin Coryatt .30
98 Tarik Glenn .30
99 Mark Brunell 3.00
100 Natrone Means .30
101 Keenan McCardell .30
102 Jimmy Smith .30
103 Tony Brackens .30
104 Kevin Hardy .30
105 Elvis Grbac .30
106 Marcus Allen .60
107 Greg Hill .30
108 Derrick Thomas .30
109 Dale Carter .30
110 Dan Marino 5.00
111 Karim Abdul-Jabbar 1.75
112 Brian Manning .30
113 Quadry Ismail .30
114 Troy Drayton .30
115 Zach Thomas .60
116 Jason Taylor .30
117 Brad Johnson .60
118 Robert Smith .30
119 John Randle .30
120 Cris Carter .30
121 Jake Reed .30
122 Randall Cunningham .30
123 Drew Bledsoe 3.00
124 Curtis Martin 3.00
125 Terry Glenn 2.50
126 Willie McGinest .30
127 Chris Canty .30
128 Sedrick Shaw .30
129 Heath Shuler .30
130 Mario Bates .30
131 Ray Zellars .30
132 Andre Hastings .30
133 Dave Brown .30
134 Tyrone Wheatley .30
135 Rodney Hampton .30
136 Chris Calloway .30
137 *Tiki Barber* 25.00
138 Neil O'Donnell .30
139 Adrian Murrell .60
140 Wayne Chrebet .30
141 Keyshawn Johnson .60
142 Hugh Douglas .30
143 Jeff George .30
144 Napoleon Kaufman .60
145 Tim Brown .30
146 Desmond Howard .30
147 Rickey Dudley .30
148 Terry McDaniel .30
149 Ty Detmer .30
150 Ricky Watters .60
151 Chris T. Jones .30
152 Irving Fryar .30
153 Mike Mamula .30
154 Jon Harris .30
155 Kordell Stewart 3.00
156 Jerome Bettis .60
157 Charles Johnson .30
158 Greg Lloyd .30
159 George Jones .30
160 Terrell Fletcher .30
161 Stan Humphries .30
162 Tony Martin .30
163 Eric Metcalf .30
164 Junior Seau .30
165 Rod Woodson .30
166 Steve Young 1.75
167 Terry Kirby .30
168 Garrison Hearst .30
169 Jerry Rice 3.00
170 Ken Norton .30
171 Kevin Greene .30
172 Lamar Smith .30
173 Warren Moon .30
174 Chris Warren .30
175 Cortez Kennedy .30
176 Joey Galloway .60
177 Tony Banks 1.25
178 Isaac Bruce .60
179 Eddie Kennison .60
180 Kevin Carter .30
181 Craig Heyward .30
182 Trent Dilfer .60
183 Errict Rhett .30
184 Mike Alstott .60
185 Hardy Nickerson .30
186 Ronde Barber .30
187 Steve McNair 2.00
188 Eddie George 4.50
189 Chris Sanders .30
190 Blaine Bishop .30
191 *Derrick Mason* 10.00
192 Gus Frerotte .30
193 Terry Allen .30
194 Brian Mitchell .30
195 Alvin Harper .30
196 Jeff Hostetler .30
197 Lesley Sheppard .30
198 Stephen Davis .30
A1 Aikman Audio Blue 10.00
A2 Aikman Audio Pro Bowl 25.00
A3 Aikman Audio White/500 100.00

1997 SP Authentic Mark of a Legend

This seven-card collection features autographs from some of the NFL's greatest players. The inserts were seeded 1:168 packs. They have a "ML" prefix.

MT
Complete Set (7): 600.00
Common Player: 50.00
1 Bob Griese 50.00
2 Roger Staubach 150.00
3 Joe Montana 200.00
4 Franco Harris 50.00
5 Gale Sayers 75.00
6 Steve Largent 50.00
7 Tony Dorsett 50.00

1997 SP Authentic ProFiles

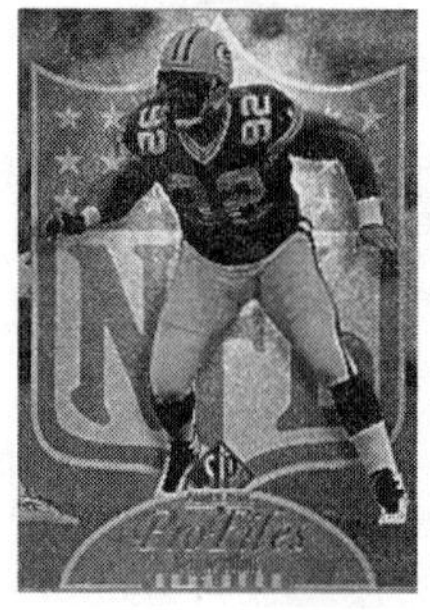

ProFiles is a three-tiered, 40-card insert. The first tier has an action shot of the player with the NFL logo in the background and is inserted 1:5. The second tier card is a die-cut version of tier one and is inserted 1:12. Tier three cards are sequentially numbered to 100.

MT
Complete Set (40): 150.00
Common Player: 1.50
Die-Cut Cards: 2x
Inserted 1:12
Die-Cut 100's: 7x-14x
Production 100 Sets
1 Dan Marino 10.00
2 Kordell Stewart 6.00
3 Emmitt Smith 10.00
4 Brett Favre 12.00
5 Marcus Allen 1.50
6 Jerry Rice 6.00
7 Jeff George 1.50
8 Mark Brunell 6.00
9 Eddie George 8.00
10 Cris Carter 1.50
11 Tshimanga Biakabutuka 1.50
12 Ike Hilliard 4.00
13 Darrell Russell 1.50
14 Jim Druckenmiller 8.00
15 Rae Carruth 4.00
16 Warrick Dunn 12.00
17 Herman Moore 1.50
18 Deion Sanders 3.00
19 Drew Bledsoe 6.00
20 Jeff Blake 1.50
21 Keyshawn Johnson 1.50
22 Curtis Martin 6.00
23 Michael Irvin 1.50
24 Barry Sanders 10.00
25 Carl Pickens 1.50
26 Steve McNair 5.00
27 Terry Allen 1.50
28 Terrell Davis 6.00
29 Lawrence Phillips 1.50
30 Marshall Faulk 1.50
31 Karim Abdul-Jabbar 4.00
32 Steve Young 5.00
33 Tim Brown 1.50
34 Antowain Smith 6.00
35 Kerry Collins 3.00
36 Reggie White 1.50
37 John Elway 5.00
38 Jerome Bettis 1.50
39 Troy Aikman 6.00
40 Junior Seau 1.50

A card number in parentheses ( ) indicates the set is unnumbered.

1997 SP Authentic Sign of the Times

This 30-card insert consists of cards autographed by current NFL players. They were inserted once in 24 packs.

MT
Complete Set (28): 2000.
Common Player: 20.00
Jeff Blake 40.00
Kerry Collins 60.00
Warrick Dunn 125.00
Rae Carruth 30.00
Karim Abdul-Jabbar 40.00
Reidel Anthony 50.00
Terrell Davis 125.00
Joey Galloway 40.00
Marshall Faulk 40.00
Robert Brooks 20.00
Will Blackwell 20.00
Emmitt Smith 325.00
Herman Moore 40.00
Napoleon Kaufman 50.00
Antowain Smith 60.00
Terry Allen 20.00
Tim Brown 30.00
Jerome Bettis 30.00
Rashaan Salaam 20.00
Jim Druckenmiller 50.00
George Jones 20.00
Isaac Bruce 30.00
Tony Gonzalez 20.00
Troy Aikman 200.00
Dan Marino 325.00
Jerry Rice 275.00
Curtis Martin 100.00
Eddie George 125.00

1997 SP Authentic Traditions

Tradition is a six-card insert. The cards feature two autographs, one from an NFL legend and the other from a proven superstar, both from the same team. Tradition was inserted once per 1,440 packs. The cards carry a "TD" prefix.

MT
Complete Set (6): 2800.
Common Player: 150.00
1 Dan Marino, Bob Griese 500.00
2 Troy Aikman, Roger Staubach 450.00
3 Jerry Rice, Joe Montana 1200.
4 Jerome Bettis, Franco Harris 150.00
5 Emmitt Smith, Tony Dorsett 500.00
6 Joey Galloway, Steve Largent 175.00

1997 Spx

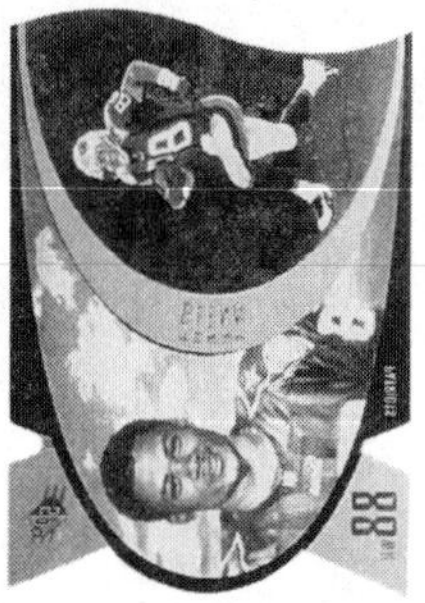

The 50-card, regular-sized, die-cut set was available in one-card packs. The card fronts a hologram panorama-type headshot on the right half of the horizontal card with a color action shot on the left half. The cards are die-cut in the shape of an "X" on the right side.

MT
Complete Set (50): 130.00
Common Player: 1.00
Minor Stars: 2.00
Gold Cards: 3x
Pack (1): 2.50
Wax Box (36): 80.00
1 Jerry Rice 6.00
2 Steve Young 4.00
3 Karim Abdul-Jabbar 3.00
4 Dan Marino 12.00
5 Bobby Engram 2.00
6 Rashaan Salaam 2.00
7 Marvin Harrison 5.00
8 Jim Harbaugh 1.00
9 Marshall Faulk 3.00
10 Eric Moulds 2.00
11 Thurman Thomas 2.00
12 Tamarick Vanover 2.00
13 Steve Bono 1.00
14 Warren Moon 1.00
15 Cris Carter 1.00
16 Carl Pickens 1.00
17 Ki-Jana Carter 1.00
18 Jeff Blake 2.00
19 Tim Biakabutuka 3.00
20 Kerry Collins 5.00
21 Leeland McElroy 2.00
22 Simeon Rice 1.00
23 John Elway 5.00
24 Terrell Davis 8.00
25 Jeff Lewis 1.00
26 Terry Glenn 3.00
27 Curtis Martin 10.00
28 Drew Bledsoe 6.00
29 Lawrence Phillips 3.00
30 Isaac Bruce 3.00
31 Eddie Kennison 2.00
32 Keyshawn Johnson 5.00
33 Stepfret Williams 1.00
34 Emmitt Smith 12.00
35 Troy Aikman 6.00
36 Deion Sanders 4.00
37 Joey Galloway 3.00
38 Rick Mirer 1.00
39 Rickey Dudley 2.00
40 Jeff Hostetler 1.00
41 Junior Seau 1.00
42 Derrick Mayes 1.00
43 Brett Favre 12.00
44 Edgar Bennett 1.00
45 Barry Sanders 8.00
46 Herman Moore 2.00
47 Kordell Stewart 6.00
48 Jerome Bettis 2.00
49 Eddie George 12.00
50 Steve McNair 4.00

1997 Spx Gold

This 50-card set featured the same die-cut design as the base set, but instead of the border being printed in team colors it was printed in gold. Gold parallels were inserted every nine packs.

MT
Complete Set (50): 375.00
Gold Cards: 3x

1997 Spx Holofame

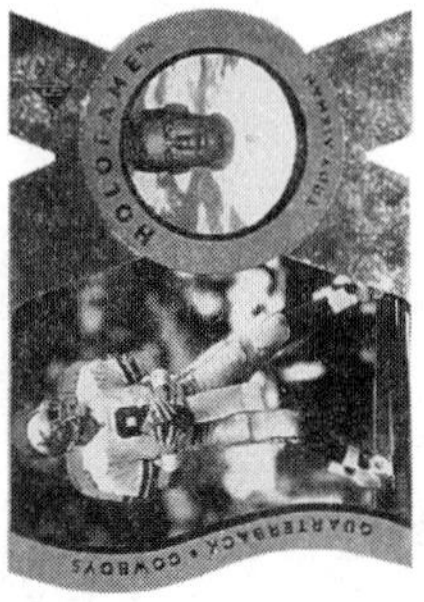

The 10-card, regular-sized set was inserted every 75 packs of Upper Deck's 1997 SPx football. The cards are numbered and carry the "HF" prefix.

MT
Complete Set (20): 600.00
Common Player: 10.00
1 Jerry Rice 45.00
2 Emmitt Smith 90.00
3 Karim Abdul-Jabbar 15.00
4 Brett Favre 90.00
5 Curtis Martin 60.00
6 Eddie Kennison 20.00
7 Troy Aikman 45.00
8 Steve Young 35.00
9 Tim Biakabutuka 10.00
10 Reggie White 10.00
11 Terry Glenn 15.00
12 Lawrence Phillips 10.00
13 Dan Marino 90.00
14 Deion Sanders 25.00
15 Terrell Davis 50.00
16 Marvin Harrison 25.00
17 Eddie George 50.00
18 Marshall Faulk 10.00
19 Keyshawn Johnson 10.00
20 Barry Sanders 45.00

1997 Spx ProMotion

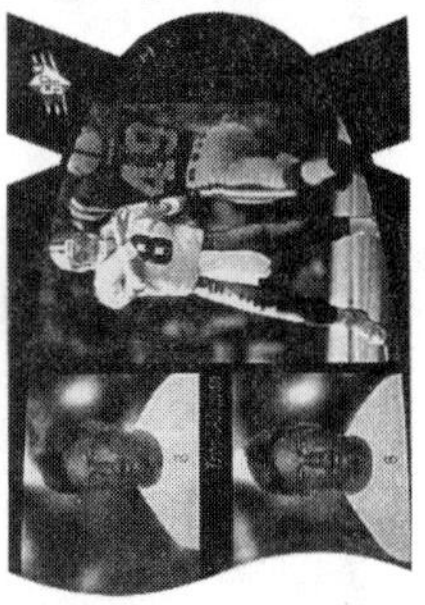

The six-card, regular-sized set was inserted every 433 packs of Upper Deck's 1997 SPx football. They are numbered with a "P" prefix.

MT
Complete Set (6): 500.00
Common Player: 70.00
1 Dan Marino 150.00
2 Joe Montana 100.00
3 Troy Aikman 85.00
4 Barry Sanders 85.00
5 Karim Abdul-Jabbar 70.00
6 Eddie George 100.00

1997 Spx ProMotion Autographs

This insert included autographed versions of each of the six ProMotion inserts. Cards were autographed on the front and sequentially numbered to 100 on the back.

MT
Complete Set (6): 3500.

Common Player: 300.00
1 Dan Marino 1000.
2 Joe Montana 700.00
3 Troy Aikman 600.00
4 Barry Sanders 700.00
5 Karim Abdul-Jabbar 300.00
6 Eddie George 600.00

1998 SP Authentic

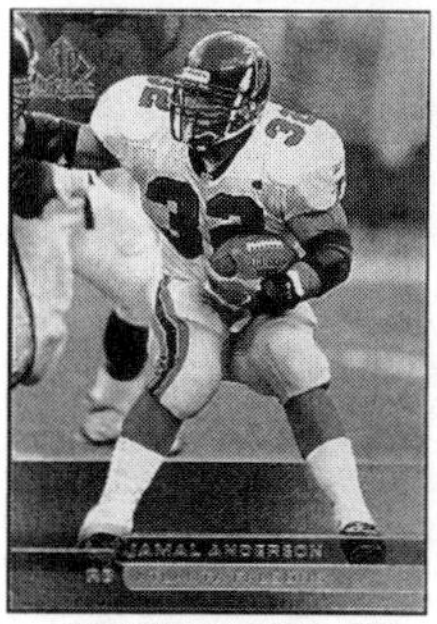

The 126-card regular set features top-notch photography of the league's best players, along with subsets Future Watch and Time Warp. The 30-card Future Watch set is made up of the top rookies from 1998 and each player is sequentially numbered to 2,000. The 12-card Time Warp set pictures today's top stars shown in action during their respective rookie campaigns. This set is also numbered to 2,000. Each single in this set has a parallel Die-Cut card that is numbered to 500.

MT
Complete Set (126): 2250.
Common Player: .25
Minor Stars: .50
Die-Cut Cards: 5x-10x
Production 500 Sets
Common Rookie (1-30): 15.00
Production 2,000 Sets
Die-Cut Rookies: 1x
Production 500 Sets
Common Time Warp (31-42): 5.00
Production 2,000 Sets
Die-Cut Time Warps: 2x
Pack (5): 30.00
Wax Box (24): 625.00
1 *Andre Wadsworth* 20.00
2 *Corey Chavous* 15.00
3 *Keith Brooking* 15.00
4 *Duane Starks* 15.00
5 *Patrick Johnson* 25.00
6 *Jason Peter* 15.00
7 *Curtis Enis* 100.00
8 *Takeo Spikes* 15.00
9 *Greg Ellis* 15.00
10 *Marcus Nash* 30.00
11 *Brian Griese* 275.00
12 *Germane Crowell* 80.00
13 *Vonnie Holliday* 25.00
14 *Peyton Manning* 750.00
15 *Jerome Pathon* 30.00
16 *Fred Taylor* 250.00
17 *John Avery* 30.00
18 *Randy Moss* 500.00
19 *Robert Edwards* 75.00
20 *Tony Simmons* 25.00
21 *Shaun Williams* 15.00
22 *Joe Jurevicius* 20.00
23 *Charles Woodson* 50.00
24 *Tre Thomas* 20.00
25 *Grant Wistrom* 15.00
26 *Ryan Leaf* 125.00
27 *Ahman Green* 160.00
28 *Jacquez Green* 50.00
29 *Kevin Dyson* 50.00
30 *Stephen Alexander* 25.00
31 John Elway 15.00
32 Jerry Rice 15.00
33 Emmitt Smith 20.00
34 Steve Young 10.00
35 Jerome Bettis 7.00
36 Deion Sanders 7.00
37 Andre Rison 5.00
38 Warren Moon 7.00
39 Mark Brunell 10.00
40 Ricky Watters 7.00
41 Dan Marino 20.00
42 Brett Favre 30.00
43 Jake Plummer 1.50
44 Adrian Murrell .25
45 Eric Swann .25
46 Jamal Anderson .75
47 Chris Chandler .25
48 Jim Harbaugh .25
49 Michael Jackson .25
50 Jermaine Lewis .25
51 Rob Johnson .50
52 Antowain Smith .75
53 Thurman Thomas .50
54 Kerry Collins .50
55 Fred Lane .50
56 Rae Carruth .25
57 Erik Kramer .25
58 Curtis Conway .25
59 Corey Dillon 1.00
60 Neil O'Donnell .25
61 Carl Pickens .50
62 Troy Aikman 2.00
63 Emmitt Smith 3.00
64 Deion Sanders .75
65 Terrell Davis 3.00
66 John Elway 2.00
67 Rod Smith .50
68 Scott Mitchell .25
69 Barry Sanders 4.00
70 Herman Moore .50
71 Brett Favre 4.00
72 Dorsey Levens .50
73 Antonio Freeman .75
74 Marshall Faulk .75
75 Marvin Harrison .50
76 Mark Brunell 1.50
77 Keenan McCardell .25
78 Jimmy Smith .50
79 Andre Rison .25
80 Elvis Grbac .25
81 Derrick Alexander .25
82 Dan Marino 3.00
83 Kareem Abdul-Jabbar .50
84 O.J. McDuffie .25
85 Brad Johnson .75
86 Cris Carter .75
87 Robert Smith .50
88 Drew Bledsoe 1.50
89 Terry Glenn .50
90 Ben Coates .25
91 Lamar Smith .25
92 Danny Wuerffel .25
93 Tiki Barber .50
94 Danny Kanell .25
95 Ike Hilliard .25
96 Curtis Martin .75
97 Keyshawn Johnson .75
98 Glenn Foley .25
99 Jeff George .50
100 Tim Brown .50
101 Napoleon Kaufman .75
102 Bobby Hoying .25
103 Charlie Garner .25
104 Irving Fryar .25
105 Kordell Stewart 1.25
106 Jerome Bettis .50
107 Charles Johnson .25
108 Tony Banks .50
109 Isaac Bruce .50
110 Natrone Means .50
111 Junior Seau .50
112 Steve Young 1.00
113 Jerry Rice 2.00
114 Garrison Hearst .50
115 Ricky Watters .50
116 Warren Moon .50
117 Joey Galloway .75
118 Trent Dilfer .50
119 Warrick Dunn 1.50
120 Mike Alstott .75
121 Steve McNair .75
122 Eddie George 1.50
123 Yancey Thigpen .25
124 Gus Frerotte .50
125 Terry Allen .50
126 Michael Westbrook .25

1998 SP Authentic Maximum Impact

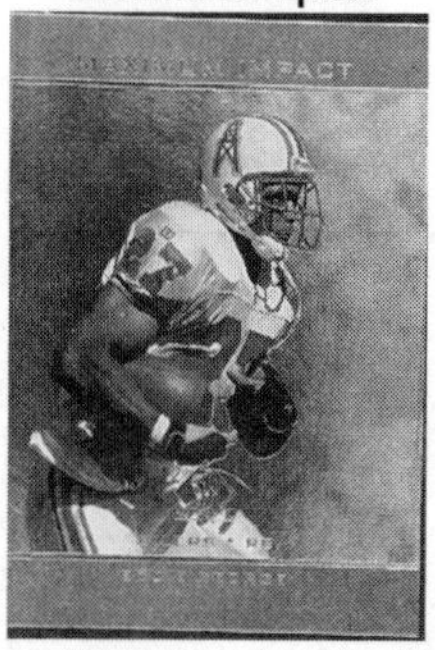

This set was made up of the 30 players who provide the greatest contribution to their team's overall success. Singles were inserted 1:4 packs.

MT
Complete Set (30): 75.00
Common Player: .50
Minor Stars: 1.00
Inserted 1:4
MI1 Brett Favre 6.00
MI2 Warrick Dunn 2.00
MI3 Junior Seau .50
MI4 Steve Young 1.50
MI5 Herman Moore .50
MI6 Antowain Smith 1.00
MI7 John Elway 3.00
MI8 Troy Aikman 3.00
MI9 Dorsey Levens .50
MI10 Kordell Stewart 2.00
MI11 Peyton Manning 8.00
MI12 Eddie George 2.00
MI13 Dan Marino 4.50
MI14 Joey Galloway 1.00
MI15 Mark Brunell 2.00
MI16 Jake Plummer 2.00
MI17 Curtis Enis 4.00
MI18 Corey Dillon 1.50
MI19 Rob Johnson 1.00
MI20 Barry Sanders 6.00
MI21 Deion Sanders 1.25
MI22 Napoleon Kaufman 1.00
MI23 Ryan Leaf 5.00
MI24 Jerry Rice 3.00
MI25 Drew Bledsoe 2.00
MI26 Jerome Bettis 1.00
MI27 Emmitt Smith 4.50
MI28 Tim Brown 1.00
MI29 Curtis Martin 1.25
MI30 Terrell Davis 4.50

1998 SP Authentic Memorabilia

Each card appears in different quanities and could be redeemed for a special piece of autographed memorabilia from the NFL's top rookies.

MT
Common Player: 50.00
Inserted 1:864
M1 Curtis Enis Ball (signed NFL game football) 85.00
M2 Ryan Leaf Ball (signed NFL game football) 125.00
M3 Randy Moss Ball (signed NFL game football) 300.00
M4 Takeo Spikes Ball (signed NFL game football) 50.00
M5 Andre Wadsworth Ball (signed NFL game football) 65.00
M6 Marcus Nash Ball (signed NFL game football) 75.00
M7 Curtis Enis Mini FB (signed mini football) 60.00
M8 Ryan Leaf Mini FB (signed mini football) 90.00
M9 Randy Moss Mini FB (signed mini football) 200.00
M10 Takeo Spikes Mini FB (signed mini football) 50.00
M11 Andre Wadsworth Mini FB (signed mini football) 50.00
M12 Marcus Nash Mini FB (signed mini football) 50.00
M13 Curtis Enis Helmet (signed NFL helmet) 125.00
M14 Ryan Leaf Helmet (signed NFL helmet) 200.00
M15 Randy Moss Helmet (signed NFL helmet) 400.00
M16 Takeo Spikes Helmet (signed NFL helmet) 85.00
M17 Andre Wadsworth Helmet (signed NFL helmet) 85.00
M18 Marcus Nash Helmet (signed NFL helmet) 100.00
M19 Curtis Enis Mini Helmet (signed mini helmet) 60.00
M20 Ryan Leaf Mini Helmet (signed mini helmet) 85.00
M21 Randy Moss Mini Helmet (signed mini helmet) 200.00
M22 Takeo Spikes Mini Helmet (signed mini helmet) 50.00
M23 Andre Wadsworth Mini Helmet (signed mini helmet) 50.00
M24 Marcus Nash Mini Helmet (signed mini helmet) 50.00
M25 "Players Ink" Autograph Collection 50.00
M26 Brett Favre (game-worn authentics ("1-of-1's")) 50.00
M27 Terrell Davis (game-worn authentics ("1-of-1's")) 50.00
M28 Dan Marino (game-worn authentics ("1-of-1's")) 50.00
M29 Jerry Rice (game-worn authentics ("1-of-1's")) 50.00
M30 Mark Brunell (game-worn authentics ("1-of-1's")) 50.00

1998 SP Authentic Player's Ink

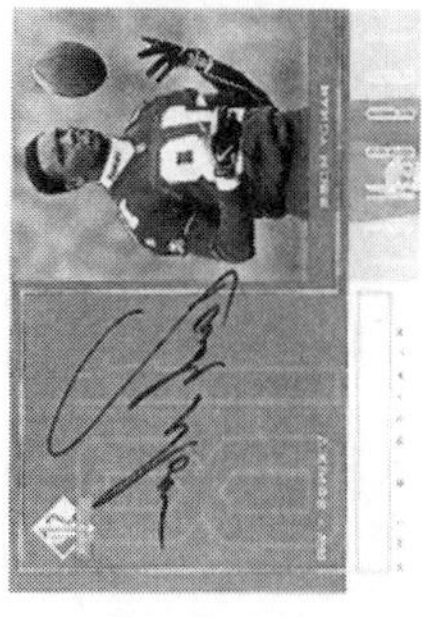

This autographed insert comes in three versions. The base set has the green background, aren't numbered and were inserted 1:23 packs. The first parallel are the Silver cards and each single was sequentially numbered to 100. The last parallel was the Gold version in which each single was numbered to the players jersey number. Some singles were through redemption cards only.

MT
Common Player: 20.00
Inserted 1:23
Silver Cards: 2x
Production 100 Sets
TA Troy Aikman 120.00
BF Brett Favre 240.00
RL Ryan Leaf 75.00
DM Dan Marino 200.00
JR Jerry Rice 120.00
KS Kordell Stewart 100.00
JP Jake Plummer 70.00
KJ Keyshawn Johnson 50.00
SS Shannon Sharpe 40.00
MA Mike Alstott 40.00
BH Bobby Hoying 20.00
RM Randy Moss 250.00
KM Keenan McCardell 20.00
JM Johnnie Morton 20.00
JA Jamal Anderson 50.00
OE Curtis Enis 50.00
MJ Michael Jackson 20.00
AW Andre Wadsworth 30.00
GC Germane Crowell 40.00
BG Brian Griese 80.00
SH Skip Hicks 40.00
MN Marcus Nash 40.00
JP Jerome Pathon 25.00
TS Takeo Spikes 25.00
FT Fred Taylor 100.00
CD Corey Dillon 30.00
RE Robert Edwards 45.00
EG Eddie George 60.00
DL Dorsey Levens 30.00
TV Tamarick Vanover 20.00

1998 SP Authentic Special Forces

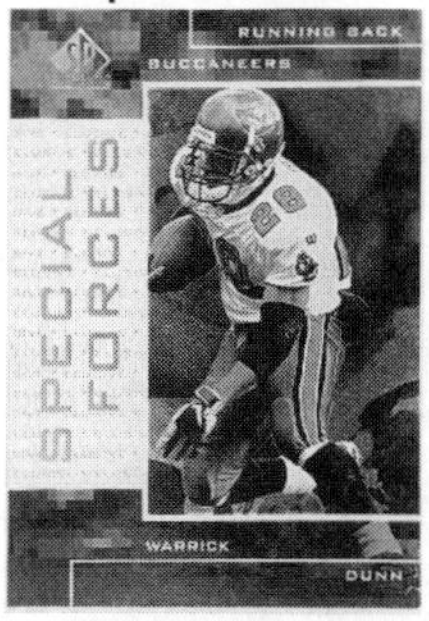

The top specialists in the NFL were showcased in this premium collection set. Each single was sequentially numbered to 1,000.

MT
Complete Set (30): 375.00
Common Player: 3.00
Minor Stars: 6.00
Production 1,000 Sets
S1 Kordell Stewart 12.00
S2 Charles Woodson 15.00
S3 Terrell Davis 20.00
S4 Brett Favre 30.00
S5 Joey Galloway 6.00
S6 Warrick Dunn 10.00
S7 Ryan Leaf 20.00
S8 Drew Bledsoe 12.00
S9 Takeo Spikes 6.00
S10 Barry Sanders 30.00
S11 Troy Aikman 15.00
S12 John Elway 15.00
S13 Jerome Bettis 6.00
S14 Karim Abdul-Jabbar 6.00
S15 Tony Gonzalez 3.00
S16 Steve Young 10.00
S17 Napoleon Kaufman 6.00
S18 Andre Wadsworth 6.00
S19 Herman Moore 6.00
S20 Fred Taylor 25.00
S21 Deion Sanders 6.00
S22 Peyton Manning 45.00
S23 Jerry Rice 15.00
S24 Dan Marino 20.00
S25 Antonio Freeman 6.00
S26 Curtis Enis 12.00
S27 Jake Plummer 10.00
S28 Steve McNair 6.00
S29 Mark Brunell 12.00
S30 Robert Edwards 10.00

1998 SPx

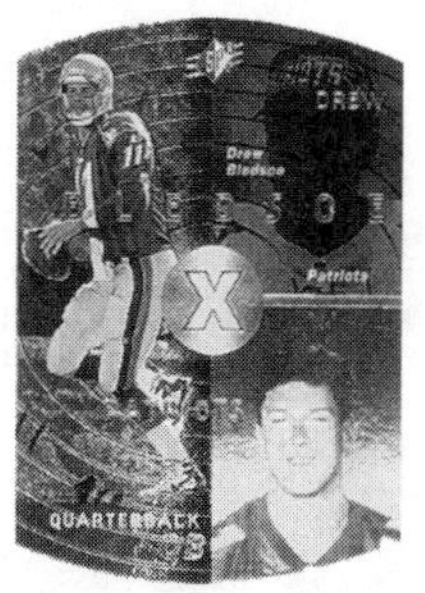

SPx Football features Holoview cards. The 50-card base set utilizes decorative foil and Light F/X on 32-point card stock. Each card features three player photos on the front. SPx Football also has five parallel sets and three inserts. The parallels are Steel Parallel Universe (1:1), Bronze Parallel Universe (1:3), Silver Parallel Universe (1:6), Gold Parallel Universe (1:17) and Grand Finale Parallel Universe (50 total sets). The insert sets are HoloFame (1:54), ProMotion (1:252) and Piece of History (500 total cards). Piece of History cards could be redeemed for a framed, uncut, numbered HoloFame Holoview sheet.

MT
Complete Set (50): 70.00
Common Player: .50
Minor Stars: 1.00
Steel Cards: 1.5x
Bronze Cards: 2x
Silver Cards: 2x-4x
Gold Cards: 4x-8x
Pack (3): 5.00
Wax Box (18): 80.00
1 Jake Plummer 4.00
2 Byron Hanspard 1.00
3 Vinny Testaverde .50
4 Antowain Smith 2.50
5 Kerry Collins 2.00
6 Rae Carruth 1.00
7 Darnell Autry 1.00
8 Rick Mirer .50
9 Jeff Blake 1.00
10 Carl Pickens .50
11 Troy Aikman 3.50
12 Emmitt Smith 5.00
13 Deion Sanders 1.50
14 John Elway 3.00
15 Terrell Davis 3.50
16 Herman Moore 1.00
17 Barry Sanders 5.00
18 Brett Favre 7.00
19 Reggie White 1.00
20 Marshall Faulk 1.00
21 Mark Brunell 2.50
22 Elvis Grbac .50
23 Marcus Allen 1.00
24 Karim Abdul-Jabbar 1.00
25 Dan Marino 6.00
26 Cris Carter .50
27 Drew Bledsoe 3.00
28 Curtis Martin 2.50
29 Heath Shuler .50
30 Ike Hilliard 1.00
31 Keyshawn Johnson 1.00
32 Jeff George .50
33 Napoleon Kaufman 1.00
34 Darrell Russell .50
35 Ricky Watters 1.00
36 Kordell Stewart 3.00
37 Jerome Bettis 1.00
38 Junior Seau .50
39 Steve Young 2.00
40 Jerry Rice 3.00
41 Joey Galloway 1.00
42 Chris Warren .50
43 Orlando Pace 1.00
44 Isaac Bruce 1.00
45 Tony Banks 1.00
46 Trent Dilfer 1.00
47 Warrick Dunn 5.00
48 Steve McNair 2.50
49 Eddie George 3.50
50 Terry Allen .50

1998 SPx Bronze/Gold//Silver/Steel

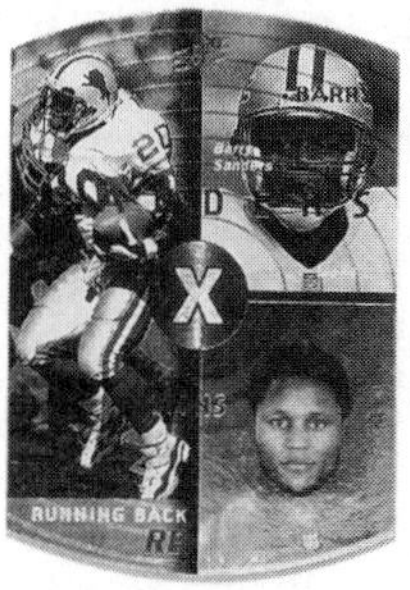

The SPx base set had five parallels, including Steel (1:1), Bronze (1:3), Silver (1:6) and Gold (1:17).

MT
Bronze Cards: 2x
Gold Cards: 4x-8x
Silver Cards: 2x-4x
Steel Cards: 1.5x

1998 SPx Grand Finale

Grand Finale parallels the SPx base set. The all-gold Holoview cards commemorate the final SPx Holoview set. Only 50 sets were produced.

MT
Common Player: 25.00
Minor Stars: 50.00
1 Jake Plummer 175.00
2 Byron Hanspard 100.00
3 Vinny Testaverde 25.00
4 Antowain Smith 125.00
5 Kerry Collins 175.00
6 Rae Carruth 50.00
7 Darnell Autry 50.00
8 Rick Mirer 25.00
9 Jeff Blake 50.00
10 Carl Pickens 25.00
11 Troy Aikman 200.00
12 Emmitt Smith 350.00
13 Deion Sanders 125.00
14 John Elway 200.00
15 Terrell Davis 225.00
16 Herman Moore 50.00
17 Barry Sanders 325.00
18 Brett Favre 450.00
19 Reggie White 50.00
20 Marshall Faulk 50.00
21 Mark Brunell 175.00
22 Elvis Grbac 25.00
23 Marcus Allen 50.00
24 Karim Abdul-Jabbar 100.00
25 Dan Marino 400.00
26 Cris Carter 25.00
27 Drew Bledsoe 200.00
28 Curtis Martin 175.00
29 Heath Shuler 25.00
30 Ike Hilliard 100.00
31 Keyshawn Johnson 50.00
32 Jeff George 25.00
33 Napoleon Kaufman 50.00
34 Darrell Russell 25.00
35 Ricky Watters 50.00
36 Kordell Stewart 200.00
37 Jerome Bettis 50.00
38 Junior Seau 25.00
39 Steve Young 175.00
40 Jerry Rice 225.00
41 Joey Galloway 50.00
42 Chris Warren 25.00
43 Orlando Pace 50.00
44 Isaac Bruce 50.00
45 Tony Banks 100.00
46 Trent Dilfer 50.00
47 Warrick Dunn 250.00
48 Steve McNair 150.00
49 Eddie George 200.00
50 Terry Allen 25.00

1998 SPx HoloFame

HoloFame is a 20-card insert, seeded one per 54 packs. The cards feature top players embossed on Holoview cards with silver decorative foil. Cards are numbered with a "HF" prefix.

MT
Complete Set (20): 325.00
Common Player: 10.00
1 Troy Aikman 30.00
2 Emmitt Smith 50.00
3 John Elway 25.00
4 Terrell Davis 30.00
5 Herman Moore 10.00
6 Reggie White 10.00
7 Brett Favre 60.00
8 Napoleon Kaufman 10.00
9 Dan Marino 50.00
10 Karim Abdul-Jabbar 10.00
11 Cris Carter 10.00
12 Drew Bledsoe 30.00
13 Curtis Martin 25.00
14 Kordell Stewart 30.00
15 Junior Seau 10.00
16 Steve Young 20.00
17 Jerry Rice 30.00
18 Marshall Faulk 10.00
19 Eddie George 30.00
20 Terry Allen 10.00

1998 SPx ProMotion

ProMotion is a 10-card insert (1:252) produced on copper and silver Holoview cards. Cards are numbered with a "P" prefix.

MT
Complete Set (10): 600.00
Common Player: 30.00
1 Troy Aikman 60.00
2 Emmitt Smith 85.00
3 Terrell Davis 60.00
4 Brett Favre 100.00
5 Marcus Allen 30.00
6 Dan Marino 100.00
7 Drew Bledsoe 60.00
8 Ike Hilliard 30.00
9 Warrick Dunn 60.00
10 Eddie George 60.00

1998 SPx Finite

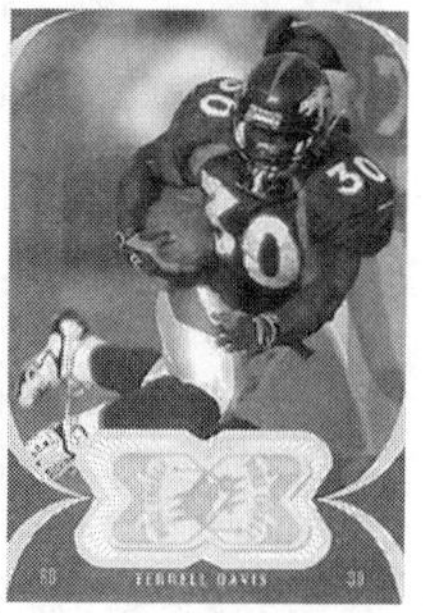

SPx Finite Series One consists of a 190-card base set built from five subsets. The base cards feature silver foil. The set consists of 90 regular cards (numbered to 7,600), 30 Playmakers (5,500), 30 Youth Movement (3,000), 20 Pure Energy (2,500) and 10 Heroes of the Game (1,250). Ten rookie cards were also added to SPx Finite, numbered to 1,998.

MT
Complete Set (370): 2500.
Complete Series 1 (190): 1200.
Complete Series 2 (180): 1300.
Common Player (1-90): 1.00
Minor Stars (1-90): 2.00
Production 7,600 Sets
Common Player (91-120): 1.50
Minor Stars (91-120): 3.00
Production 5,500 Sets
Common Player (121-150): 2.00
Minor Stars (121-150): 4.00
Production 3,000 Sets
Common Player (151-170): 2.50
Minor Stars (151-170): 5.00
Production 2,500 Sets
Common Player (171-180): 6.00
Production 1,250 Sets
Common Player (181-190): 12.00
Production 1,998 Sets
Common Player (191-280): .50
Minor Stars (191-280): 1.00
Common Rookie (191-280): 1.00
Production 10,100 Sets
Production 1,998 for #218,221,239
Common Player (281-310): .75
Minor Stars (281-310): 1.50
Production 7,200 Sets
Common Player (311-340): 1.50
Minor Stars (311-340): 3.00
Production 4,000 Sets
Production 1,700 for #321,338,339
Common Player (341-360): 1.50
Minor Stars (341-360): 3.00
Production 2,700 Sets
Common Player (361-370): 5.00
Production 1,620 Sets
Pack (3): 6.00
Wax Box (18): 105.00
1 Jake Plummer 5.00
2 Eric Swann 1.00
3 Rob Moore 1.00
4 Jamal Anderson 3.00
5 Byron Hanspard 1.00
6 Cornelius Bennett 1.00
7 Michael Jackson 1.00
8 Peter Boulware 1.00
9 Jermaine Lewis 1.00
10 Antowain Smith 3.00
11 Bruce Smith 1.00
12 Bryce Paup 1.00
13 Rae Carruth 1.00
14 Michael Bates 1.00
15 Fred Lane 2.00
16 Darnell Autry 1.00
17 Curtis Conway 2.00
18 Erik Kramer 1.00
19 Corey Dillon 3.50

20	Darnay Scott	1.00
21	Reinard Wilson	1.00
22	Troy Aikman	6.00
23	David LaFleur	1.00
24	Emmitt Smith	8.00
25	John Elway	5.00
26	John Mobley	1.00
27	Terrell Davis	8.00
28	Rod Smith	2.00
29	Bryant Westbrook	1.00
30	Scott Mitchell	1.00
31	Barry Sanders	12.00
32	Dorsey Levens	2.00
33	Antonio Freeman	2.00
34	Reggie White	2.00
35	Marshall Faulk	2.00
36	Marvin Harrison	2.00
37	Ken Dilger	1.00
38	Mark Brunell	5.00
39	Keenan McCardell	1.00
40	Renaldo Wynn	1.00
41	Marcus Allen	2.00
42	Elvis Grbac	1.00
43	Andre Rison	1.00
44	Yatil Green	1.00
45	Zach Thomas	1.00
46	Karim Abdul-Jabbar	2.00
47	John Randle	1.00
48	Brad Johnson	2.00
49	Jake Reed	1.00
50	Danny Wuerffel	1.00
51	Andre Hastings	1.00
52	Drew Bledsoe	5.00
53	Terry Glenn	2.00
54	Ty Law	1.00
55	Danny Kanell	1.00
56	Tiki Barber	2.00
57	Jesse Armstead	1.00
58	Glenn Foley	1.00
59	James Farrior	1.00
60	Wayne Chrebet	2.00
61	Tim Brown	2.00
62	Napoleon Kaufman	3.00
63	Darrell Russell	1.00
64	Bobby Hoying	1.00
65	Irving Fryar	1.00
66	Charlie Garner	1.00
67	Will Blackwell	1.00
68	Kordell Stewart	5.00
69	Levon Kirkland	1.00
70	Tony Banks	2.00
71	Ryan McNeil	1.00
72	Isaac Bruce	2.00
73	Tony Martin	1.00
74	Junior Seau	2.00
75	Natrone Means	2.00
76	Jerry Rice	6.00
77	Garrison Hearst	2.00
78	Terrell Owens	2.00
79	Warren Moon	2.00
80	Joey Galloway	2.00
81	Chad Brown	1.00
82	Warrick Dunn	5.00
83	Mike Alstott	2.00
84	Hardy Nickerson	1.00
85	Steve McNair	3.00
86	Chris Sanders	1.00
87	Darryll Lewis	1.00
88	Gus Frerotte	1.00
89	Terry Allen	1.00
90	Chris Dishman	1.00
91	Kordell Stewart	7.00
92	Jerry Rice	8.00
93	Michael Irvin	3.00
94	Brett Favre	15.00
95	Jeff George	3.00
96	Joey Galloway	3.00
97	John Elway	8.00
98	Troy Aikman	8.00
99	Steve Young	5.00
100	Andre Rison	1.50
101	Ben Coates	1.50
102	Robert Brooks	1.50
103	Dan Marino	12.00
104	Isaac Bruce	3.00
105	Junior Seau	3.00
106	Jake Plummer	7.00
107	Curtis Conway	3.00
108	Jeff Blake	3.00
109	Rod Smith	3.00
110	Barry Sanders	15.00
111	Deion Sanders	4.00
112	Drew Bledsoe	7.00
113	Emmitt Smith	12.00
114	Herman Moore	3.00
115	Dorsey Levens	3.00
116	Jimmy Smith	1.50
117	Tony Martin	1.50
118	Carl Pickens	1.50
119	Keyshawn Johnson	3.00
120	Cris Carter	3.00
121	Warrick Dunn	10.00
122	Marshall Faulk	4.00
123	Trent Dilfer	4.00
124	Napoleon Kaufman	5.00
125	Corey Dillon	7.00
126	Darrell Russell	2.00
127	Danny Kanell	2.00
128	Reidel Anthony	2.00
129	Steve McNair	6.00
130	Ike Hilliard	2.00
131	Tony Banks	4.00
132	Yatil Green	2.00
133	J.J. Stokes	2.00
134	Fred Lane	4.00
135	Bryant Westbrook	2.00
136	Jake Plummer	10.00
137	Byron Hanspard	2.00
138	Rae Carruth	2.00
139	Keyshawn Johnson	4.00
140	Jim Druckenmiller	4.00
141	Amani Toomer	2.00
142	Troy Davis	2.00
143	Antowain Smith	6.00
144	Shawn Springs	2.00
145	Rickey Dudley	2.00
146	Terry Glenn	4.00
147	Johnnie Morton	2.00
148	David LaFleur	2.00
149	Eddie Kennison	4.00
150	Bobby Hoying	2.00
151	Junior Seau	5.00
152	Shannon Sharpe	5.00
153	Bruce Smith	2.50
154	Brett Favre	25.00
155	Emmitt Smith	15.00
156	Keenan McCardell	2.50
157	Kordell Stewart	10.00
158	Troy Aikman	12.00
159	Steve Young	8.00
160	Tim Brown	5.00

161	Eddie George	10.00
162	Herman Moore	5.00
163	Dan Marino	15.00
164	Dorsey Levens	5.00
165	Jerry Rice	12.00
166	Warren Sapp	2.50
167	Robert Smith	5.00
168	Mark Brunell	10.00
169	Terrell Davis	15.00
170	Jerome Bettis	5.00
171	Dan Marino	30.00
172	Barry Sanders	40.00
173	Marcus Allen	6.00
174	Brett Favre	40.00
175	Warrick Dunn	20.00
176	Eddie George	20.00
177	John Elway	20.00
178	Troy Aikman	20.00
179	Cris Carter	6.00
180	Terrell Davis	25.00
181	*Peyton Manning*	300.00
182	*Ryan Leaf*	60.00
183	*Andre Wadsworth*	20.00
184	*Charles Woodson*	35.00
185	*Curtis Enis*	50.00
186	*Grant Wistrom*	12.00
187	*Fred Taylor*	100.00
188	*Takeo Spikes*	25.00
189	*Kevin Dyson*	30.00
190	*Robert Edwards*	40.00
191	Adrian Murrell	1.00
192	Simeon Rice	.50
193	Frank Sanders	.50
194	Chris Chandler	1.00
195	Terrance Mathis	.50
196	*Keith Brooking*	1.50
197	Jim Harbaugh	1.00
198	Errict Rhett	.50
199	*Patrick Johnson*	2.00
200	Rob Johnson	1.00
201	Andre Reed	1.00
202	Thurman Thomas	1.00
203	Kerry Collins	1.00
204	William Floyd	.50
205	Sean Gilbert	.50
206	Bobby Engram	.50
207	Edgar Bennett	.50
208	Walt Harris	.50
209	Carl Pickens	1.00
210	Neil O'Donnell	1.00
211	Tony McGee	.50
212	Deion Sanders	1.50
213	Michael Irvin	1.00
214	*Greg Ellis*	1.50
215	Shannon Sharpe	1.00
216	Neil Smith	.50
217	*Marcus Nash*	4.00
218	*Brian Griese*	85.00
219	Johnnie Morton	.50
220	Herman Moore	1.00
221	*Charlie Batch*	65.00
222	Robert Brooks	.50
223	Mark Chmura	1.00
224	Brett Favre	6.00
225	*Jerome Pathon*	2.00
226	Zack Crockett	.50
227	Dan Footman	.50
228	Jimmy Smith	1.00
229	Bryce Paup	.50
230	James Stewart	.50
231	Derrick Thomas	.50
232	Derrick Alexander	.50
233	Tony Gonzalez	.50
234	Dan Marino	4.50
235	O.J. McDuffie	.50
236	Troy Drayton	.50
237	Cris Carter	1.00
238	Robert Smith	1.00
239	*Randy Moss*	175.00
240	Lamar Smith	.50
241	Sean Dawkins	.50
242	Alex Molden	.50
243	Ben Coates	1.00
244	Ted Johnson	.50
245	Sedrick Shaw	.50
246	Ike Hilliard	.50
247	Jason Sehorn	.50
248	Michael Strahan	.50
249	Keyshawn Johnson	1.00
250	Curtis Martin	1.50
251	Jeff George	1.00
252	Rickey Dudley	.50
253	James Jett	.50
254	Bobby Taylor	.50
255	Rodney Peete	.50
256	William Thomas	.50
257	Jerome Bettis	1.00
258	Charles Johnson	.50
259	*Chris Fuamatu-Ma'afala*	2.50
260	Eddie Kennison	.50
261	*Az-Zahir Hakim*	7.00
262	*Robert Holcombe*	3.00
263	Bryan Still	.50
264	*Mikhael Ricks*	2.00
265	Charlie Jones	.50
266	J.J. Stokes	1.00
267	Marc Edwards	.50
268	Steve Young	2.00
269	Ricky Watters	1.00
270	Cortez Kennedy	.50
271	Shawn Springs	.50
272	Trent Dilfer	1.00
273	Warren Sapp	.50
274	Reidel Anthony	1.00
275	Yancey Thigpen	.50
276	Chris Sanders	.50
277	Eddie George	2.50
278	Leslie Shepherd	.50
279	*Skip Hicks*	4.00
280	Dana Stubblefield	.50
281	John Elway	4.00
282	Brett Favre	8.00
283	Junior Seau	1.50
284	Barry Sanders	8.00
285	Jerry Rice	4.00
286	Antonio Freeman	1.50
287	Peyton Manning	20.00
288	Warrick Dunn	3.00
289	Steve Young	2.00
290	Dan Marino	6.00
291	Jerome Bettis	1.50
292	Ryan Leaf	8.00
293	Deion Sanders	1.50
294	Eddie George	3.00
295	Joey Galloway	1.50
296	Troy Aikman	4.00
297	Andre Wadsworth	1.50
298	Terrell Davis	6.00
299	Steve McNair	2.00
300	Jake Plummer	3.00

301	Emmitt Smith	6.00
302	Isaac Bruce	1.50
303	Kordell Stewart	3.00
304	Dorsey Levens	1.50
305	Antowain Smith	1.75
306	Drew Bledsoe	3.00
307	Marshall Faulk	1.50
308	Herman Moore	1.50
309	Mark Brunell	3.00
310	Charles Woodson	6.00
311	Peyton Manning	30.00
312	Curtis Enis	10.00
313	*Terry Fair*	7.00
314	Andre Wadsworth	5.00
315	*Anthony Simmons*	4.00
316	*Jacquez Green*	12.00
317	Takeo Spikes	4.00
318	*Vonnie Holliday*	7.00
319	*Kyle Turley*	2.00
320	Keith Brooking	4.00
321	Randy Moss	65.00
322	*Shaun Williams*	2.00
323	Greg Ellis	2.00
324	Mikhael Ricks	5.00
325	Charles Woodson	10.00
326	*Corey Chavous*	2.00
327	*Stephen Alexander*	7.00
328	Marcus Nash	7.00
329	*Tre Thomas*	2.00
330	*Duane Starks*	7.00
331	*John Avery*	12.00
332	Kevin Dyson	7.00
333	Fred Taylor	15.00
334	Grant Wistrom	2.00
335	Ryan Leaf	15.00
336	Robert Edwards	12.00
337	*Jason Peter*	4.00
338	Brian Griese	25.00
339	Charlie Batch	25.00
340	Patrick Johnson	4.00
341	John Elway	10.00
342	Curtis Enis	10.00
343	Antonio Freeman	3.00
344	Mark Brunell	6.00
345	Robert Edwards	12.00
346	Ryan Leaf	15.00
347	Steve Young	5.00
348	Jerome Bettis	3.00
349	Antowain Smith	3.00
350	Tim Brown	3.00
351	Peyton Manning	30.00
352	Troy Aikman	8.00
353	Natrone Means	3.00
354	Dan Marino	15.00
355	Junior Seau	1.50
356	Brad Johnson	3.00
357	Jerry Rice	8.00
358	Drew Bledsoe	6.00
359	Fred Taylor	15.00
360	Emmitt Smith	12.00
361	Terrell Davis	20.00
362	Kordell Stewart	10.00
363	Barry Sanders	25.00
364	Jake Plummer	10.00
365	Brett Favre	25.00
366	Curtis Enis	18.00
367	Eddie George	10.00
368	Napoleon Kaufman	5.00
369	Randy Moss	125.00
370	Warrick Dunn	10.00

1998 SPx Finite Radiance

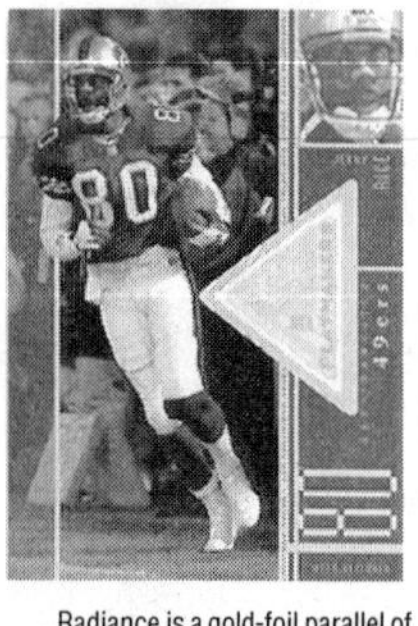

Radiance is a gold-foil parallel of the SPx Finite base set. Regular cards are numbered to 3,800, Playmakers to 2,750, Youth Movement to 1,500, Pure Energy to 1,000 and Heroes of the Game to 100. The ten rookie cards are numbered to 50 in this set.

	MT
Cards (1-90):	2x
Production 3,800 Sets	
Cards (91-120):	2x
Production 2,750 Sets	
Cards (121-150):	2x
Production 1,500 Sets	
Cards (151-170):	2x
Production 1,000 Sets	
Cards (171-180):	5x
Production 100 Sets	
Cards (181-190):	4x
Production 50 Sets	
Cards (191-280):	2x
Production 5,050 Sets	
Production 500 for #218,221,239	
Cards (281-310):	2x
Production 3,600 Sets	
Cards (311-340):	2x
Production 1,885 Sets	
Production 350 for #321,338,339	
Cards (341-360):	2x
Production 900 Sets	
Cards (361-370):	2x
Production 540 Sets	

1998 SPx Finite Spectrum

Spectrum is a rainbow foil version of the SPx Finite base set. Regular cards are numbered to 1,900, Playmakers to 1,375, Youth Movement to 750, Pure Energy to 50 and Heroes of the Game is a 1-of-1 set. The ten rookie cards are also 1-of-1 in this parallel.

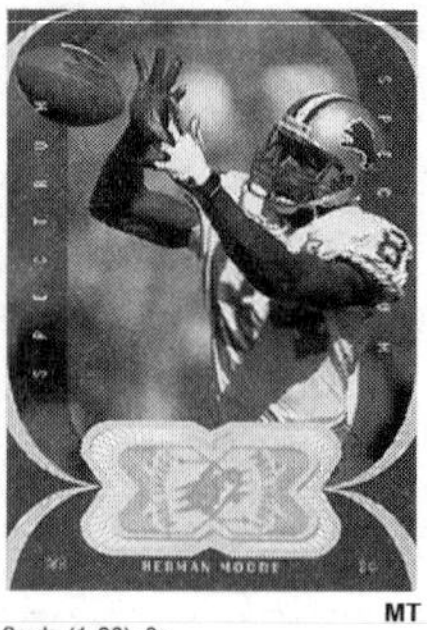

	MT
Cards (1-90): 3x	
Production 1,900 Sets	
Cards (91-120):	3x
Production 1,375 Sets	
Cards (121-150):	4x
Production 750 Sets	
Cards (151-170):	15x-20x
Production 50 Sets	
Cards (171-190):	
Production 1 Set	
Cards (191-280):	4x-8x
Rookies (191-280):	1.5x-3x
Production 325 Sets	
Cards (281-310):	5x-10x
Rookies (281-310):	1.5x-3x
Production 150 Sets	
Cards (311-340):	4x-8x
#321,338,339:	2x-4x
Production 50 Sets	
Cards (341-360):	15x-30x
Rookies (341-360):	6x-12x
Production 25 Sets	
Cards (361-370):	
Production 1 Set	

1999 SP Authentic

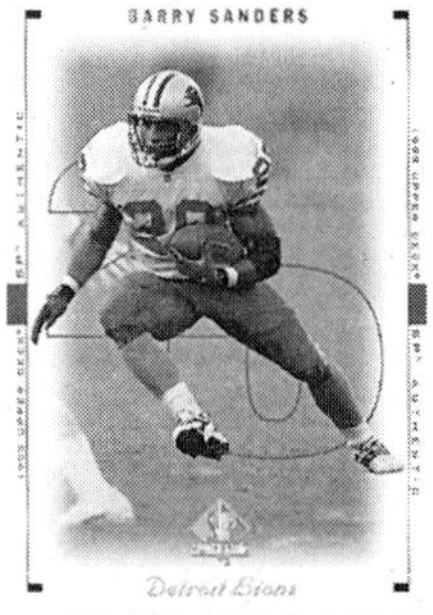

This 145-card set included 55 rookies that were sequentially numbered to 1,999. Parallel sets included Excitement and Excitement Gold. Other insert sets include: Authentic Athletic, Buy Back Autographs, Maximum Impact, New Classics, NFL Headquarters, Player's Ink, Rookie Blitz and Supremacy. SRP was $4.99 for five-card packs.

		MT
Complete Set (145):		2000.
Common Player:		.25
Minor Stars:		.50
Common Rookie:		15.00
Production 1,999 Sets		
Pack (5):		15.00
Wax Box (24):		300.00
1	Jake Plummer	1.50
2	Adrian Murrell	.25
3	Frank Sanders	.50
4	Jamal Anderson	.75
5	Chris Chandler	.50
6	Terance Mathis	.25
7	Priest Holmes	.75
8	Jermaine Lewis	.25
9	Antowain Smith	.75
10	Doug Flutie	1.25
11	Eric Moulds	.75
12	Muhsin Muhammad	.75
13	Tim Biakabutuka	.50
14	Wesley Walls	.50
15	Curtis Enis	.75
16	Bobby Engram	.25
17	Corey Dillon	.75
18	Darnay Scott	.50
19	Terry Kirby	.25
20	Ty Detmer	.25
21	Troy Aikman	2.00
22	Michael Irvin	.50
23	Emmitt Smith	3.00
24	Terrell Davis	3.00
25	Brian Griese	1.50
26	Rod Smith	.75
27	Shannon Sharpe	.75
28	Barry Sanders	4.00
29	Charlie Batch	1.25
30	Herman Moore	.75
31	Johnnie Morton	.25
32	Brett Favre	4.00
33	Antonio Freeman	.75
34	Dorsey Levens	.75
35	Mark Chmura	.50
36	Peyton Manning	3.00
37	Marvin Harrison	.75
38	Mark Brunell	1.25
39	Fred Taylor	2.00
40	Jimmy Smith	.75
41	Elvis Grbac	.50
42	Andre Rison	.50
43	Dan Marino	3.00
44	O.J. McDuffie	.25
45	Yatil Green	.25
46	Randall Cunningham	.75
47	Randy Moss	4.00
48	Robert Smith	.75
49	Cris Carter	.75
50	Drew Bledsoe	1.25
51	Ben Coates	.50
52	Terry Glenn	.75
53	Eddie Kennison	.25
54	Cam Cleeland	.50
55	Ike Hilliard	.50
56	Gary Brown	.25
57	Kerry Collins	.50
58	Vinny Testaverde	.50
59	Keyshawn Johnson	.75
60	Wayne Chrebet	.75
61	Curtis Martin	.75
62	Tim Brown	.50
63	Napoleon Kaufman	.75
64	Charles Woodson	.75
65	Duce Staley	.75
66	Charles Johnson	.25
67	Kordell Stewart	.75
68	Jerome Bettis	.75
69	Marshall Faulk	.75
70	Isaac Bruce	.75
71	Trent Green	.75
72	Jim Harbaugh	.50
73	Junior Seau	.50
74	Natrone Means	.50
75	Steve Young	1.25
76	Jerry Rice	2.00
77	Terrell Owens	.75
78	Lawrence Phillips	.25
79	Joey Galloway	.75
80	Ricky Watters	.50
81	Jon Kitna	1.00
82	Warrick Dunn	.75
83	Trent Dilfer	.50
84	Mike Alstott	.75
85	Eddie George	1.00
86	Steve McNair	1.00
87	Yancey Thigpen	.25
88	Brad Johnson	.75
89	Skip Hicks	.50
90	Michael Westbrook	.50
91	*Ricky Williams*	225.00
92	*Tim Couch*	300.00
93	*Akili Smith*	85.00
94	*Edgerrin James*	275.00
95	*Donovan McNabb*	225.00
96	*Torry Holt*	85.00
97	*Cade McNown*	100.00
98	*Shaun King*	125.00
99	*Daunte Culpepper*	375.00
100	*Brock Huard*	50.00
101	*Chris Claiborne*	20.00
102	*James Johnson*	45.00
103	*Rob Konrad*	20.00
104	*Peerless Price*	50.00
105	*Kevin Faulk*	50.00
106	*Andy Katzenmoyer*	20.00
107	*Troy Edwards*	75.00
108	*Kevin Johnson*	85.00
109	*Mike Cloud*	20.00
110	*David Boston*	75.00
111	*Champ Bailey*	45.00
112	*D'Wayne Bates*	20.00
113	*Joe Germaine*	35.00
114	*Antoine Winfield*	20.00
115	*Fernando Bryant*	15.00
116	*Jevon Kearse*	85.00
117	*Chris McAlister*	20.00
118	*Brandon Stokley*	15.00
119	*Karsten Bailey*	20.00
120	*Daylon McCutcheon*	15.00
121	*Jermaine Fazande*	25.00
122	*Joel Makovicka*	15.00
123	*Ebenezer Ekuban*	20.00
124	*Joe Montgomery*	25.00
125	*Sean Bennett*	25.00
126	*Na Brown*	15.00
127	*De'Mond Parker*	35.00
128	*Sedrick Irvin*	35.00
129	*Terry Jackson*	20.00
130	*Jeff Paulk*	20.00
131	*Cecil Collins*	75.00
132	*Bobby Collins*	15.00
133	*Amos Zereoue*	30.00
134	*Travis McGriff*	20.00
135	*Larry Parker*	15.00
136	*Wane McGarity*	20.00
137	*Cecil Martin*	15.00
138	*Al Wilson*	15.00
139	*Jim Kleinsasser*	25.00
140	*Dat Nguyen*	20.00
141	*Marty Booker*	30.00
142	*Reggie Kelly*	15.00
143	*Scott Covington*	20.00
144	*Antwan Edwards*	20.00
145	*Craig Yeast*	20.00

1999 SP Authentic Excitement Parallel

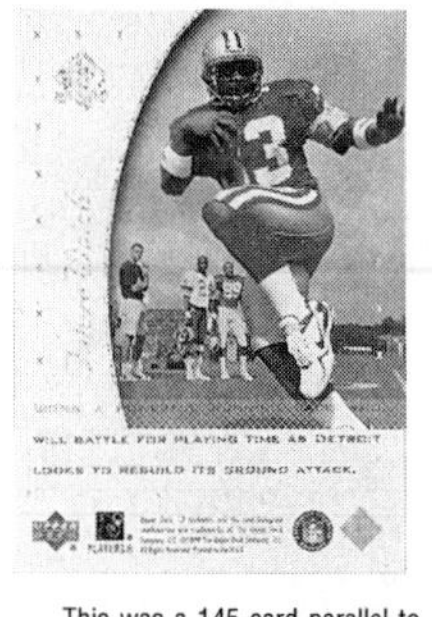

This was a 145-card parallel to the base set. Each single was sequentially numbered to 250 and printed on the front of the cards.

	MT
Excitement Cards:	7x-14x
Excitement Rookies:	1.5x
Production 250 Sets	

1999 SP Authentic Excitement Gold Parallel

This was a 145-card parallel to the base set. Each single was sequentially numbered to 25 and printed on the front of the singles.

	MT
Excitement Cards:	40x-80x
Excitement Rookies:	3x
Production 25 Sets	

1999 SP Authentic Athletic

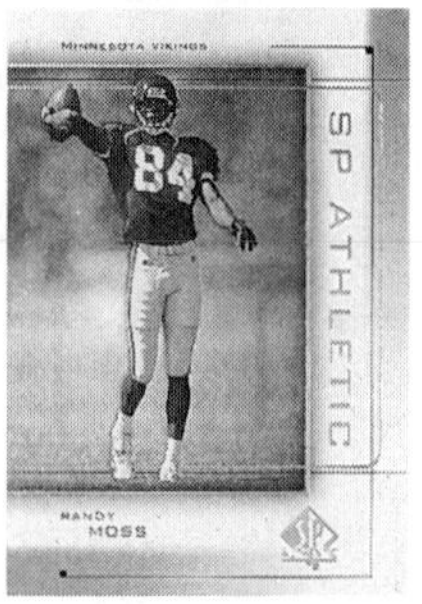

This 10-card insert set included the most exciting and athletic players in the NFL. Singles were inserted 1:10 packs.

		MT
Complete Set (10):		35.00
Common Player:		2.50
Inserted 1:10		
1	Randy Moss	10.00
2	Steve McNair	2.50
3	Jamal Anderson	2.50
4	Curtis Martin	2.50
5	Kordell Stewart	2.50
6	Barry Sanders	10.00
7	Fred Taylor	6.00
8	Doug Flutie	3.50
9	Emmitt Smith	6.00
10	Steve Young	3.50

1999 SP Authentic Maximum Impact

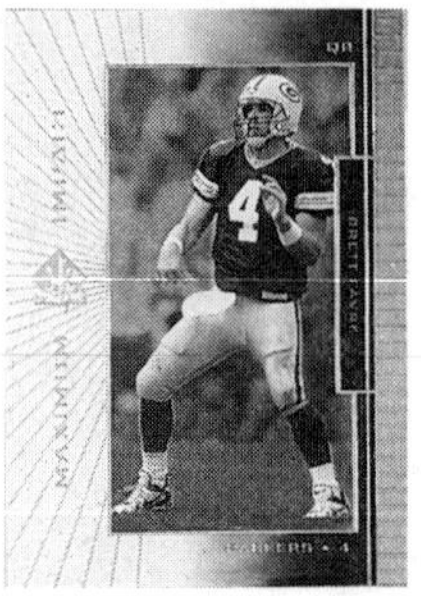

This 10-card insert set included players who provide the greatest contribution to their team's overall success. Singles were inserted 1:4 packs.

		MT
Complete Set (10):		12.00
Common Player:		1.00
Inserted 1:4		
1	Jerry Rice	3.00
2	Eddie George	1.50
3	Marshall Faulk	1.00
4	Keyshawn Johnson	1.00
5	Terrell Davis	4.50
6	Warrick Dunn	1.00
7	Jerome Bettis	1.00
8	Drew Bledsoe	2.00
9	Curtis Martin	1.00
10	Brett Favre	6.00

1999 SP Authentic New Classics

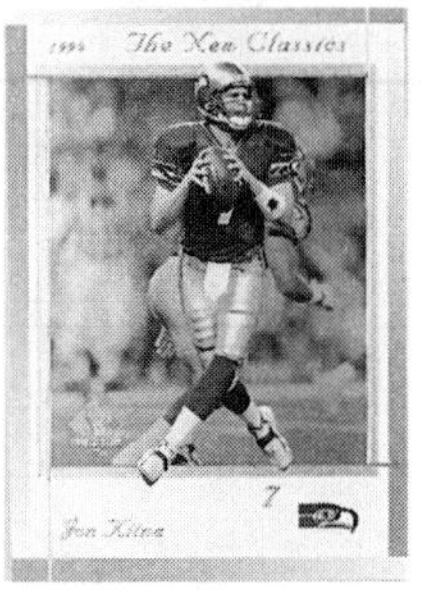

This 10-card insert set included players to watch for the future. Singles were inserted 1:23 packs.

		MT
Complete Set (10):		60.00
Common Player:		3.00
Inserted 1:23		
1	Steve McNair	3.00
2	Jon Kitna	3.00
3	Curtis Enis	3.00
4	Peyton Manning	10.00
5	Fred Taylor	8.00
6	Randy Moss	15.00
7	Donovan McNabb	10.00
8	Terrell Owens	3.00
9	Keyshawn Johnson	3.00
10	Ricky Williams	15.00

1999 SP Authentic NFL Headquarters

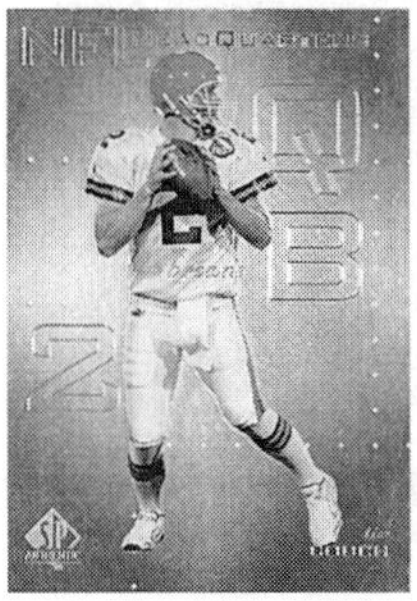

This 10-card insert set included the game's hottest quarterbacks. Singles were inserted 1:10 packs.

		MT
Complete Set (10):		45.00
Common Player:		3.00
Inserted 1:10		
1	Brett Favre	12.00
2	Jake Plummer	5.00
3	Charlie Batch	4.00
4	Akili Smith	6.00
5	Troy Aikman	6.00
6	Drew Bledsoe	5.00
7	Dan Marino	10.00
8	Jon Kitna	3.00
9	Mark Brunell	5.00
10	Tim Couch	12.00

1999 SP Authentic Player's Ink

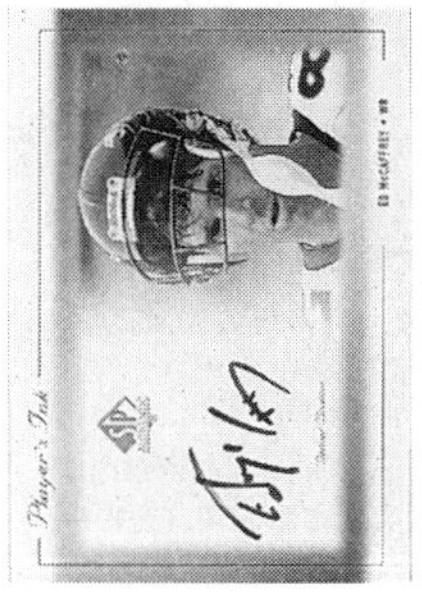

This 40-card insert set included autographs of the top players in the NFL. Many of the rookies were included and singles were inserted 1:23 packs. A parallel Level 2 version was also released and each was sequentially numbered to 100.

		MT
Complete Set (40):		2000.
Common Player:		25.00
Inserted 1:23		
Version 2 Cards:		2x
Production 100 Cards		
TA	Troy Aikman	125.00
JA	Jamal Anderson	25.00
CB	Champ Bailey	25.00
CH	Charlie Batch	35.00
JB	Jerome Bettis	25.00
MB	Michael Bishop	35.00
DR	Drew Bledsoe	75.00
DB	David Boston	45.00
BR	Mark Brunell	75.00
WC	Wayne Chrebet	25.00
CL	Michael Cloud	25.00
TC	Tim Couch	150.00
DC	Daunte Culpepper	60.00
TD	Terrell Davis	100.00
CD	Corey Dillon	35.00
TE	Troy Edwards	45.00
KF	Kevin Faulk	40.00
MF	Marshall Faulk	40.00
DF	Doug Flutie	50.00
AF	Antonio Freeman	25.00
JG	Joey Galloway	25.00
EG	Eddie George	40.00
TH	Torry Holt	45.00
BH	Brock Huard	30.00
EJ	Edgerrin James	200.00
BJ	Brad Johnson	30.00
SK	Shaun King	45.00
PM	Peyton Manning	125.00
DM	Dan Marino	225.00
ED	Ed McCaffrey	25.00
CM	Cade McNown	60.00
NM	Natrone Means	25.00
HM	Herman Moore	25.00
RM	Randy Moss	150.00
EM	Eric Moulds	25.00
TO	Terrell Owens	25.00
JP	Jake Plummer	50.00
JR	Jerry Rice	125.00
SS	Shannon Sharpe	25.00
AS	Akili Smith	60.00

1999 SP Authentic Rookie Blitz

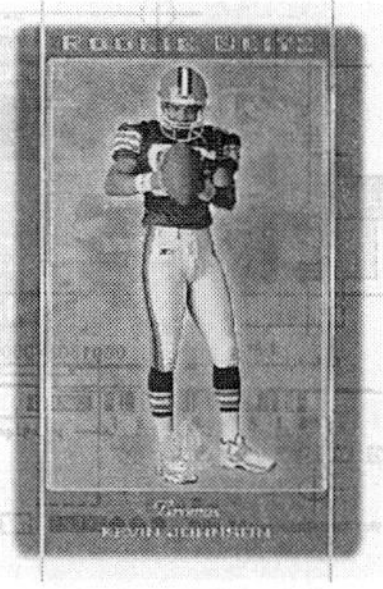

This 19-card insert set included the top rookies from the 1999 season. Singles were inserted 1:11 packs.

		MT
Complete Set (19):		85.00
Common Player:		2.00
Inserted 1:11		
1	Edgerrin James	20.00
2	Tim Couch	15.00
3	Daunte Culpepper	8.00
4	Champ Bailey	3.00
5	Donovan McNabb	8.00
6	Kevin Johnson	6.00
7	Shaun King	6.00
8	Peerless Price	5.00
9	David Boston	6.00
10	Ricky Williams	15.00
11	Akili Smith	8.00
12	Kevin Faulk	4.00
13	D'Wayne Bates	2.00
14	Brock Huard	3.00
15	Rob Konrad	2.00
16	Torry Holt	6.00
17	Troy Edwards	6.00
18	Cade McNown	8.00
19	Cecil Collins	6.00

1999 SP Authentic Supremacy

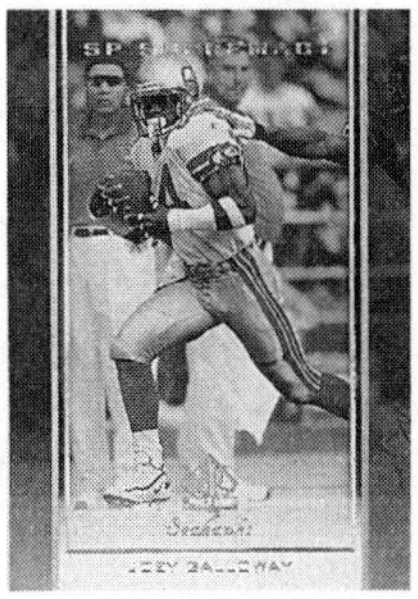

This 12-card insert set included the premier performers in the NFL. Singles were inserted 1:23 packs.

		MT
Complete Set (12):		85.00
Common Player:		3.00
Inserted 1:23		
1	Terrell Davis	10.00
2	Joey Galloway	3.00
3	Dan Marino	10.00
4	Brett Favre	15.00
5	Emmitt Smith	10.00
6	Barry Sanders	15.00
7	Curtis Martin	3.00
8	Jamal Anderson	3.00
9	Jake Plummer	6.00
10	Randy Moss	15.00
11	Tim Couch	15.00
12	Peyton Manning	10.00

1999 SP Authentic Walter Payton

A total of 100 Payton autographed cards were released along with 34 Payton Game-Jersey autographed cards. Each card was randomly inserted.

		MT
WPA	Walter Payton AUTO/100	350.00
WPSP	Walter Payton JER/AUTO 34	3000.

Values quoted in this guide reflect the retail price of a card — the price a collector can expect to pay when buying a card from a dealer. The wholesale price — that which a collector can expect to receive from a dealer when selling cards — will be significantly lower, depending on desirability and condition.

1999 SP Signature

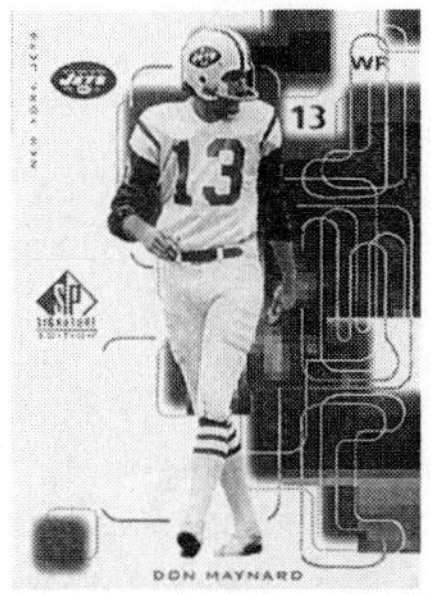

This 180-card release from Upper Deck includes both past and present stars from the NFL. The last 10 cards in the set never made it into the product and were later released to dealers from the manufacture. Inserts include: Autographs and Montana Great Performances.

		MT
Complete Set (180):		450.00
Common Player:		.50
Minor Stars:		1.00
Pack (3):		18.00
Wax Box (12):		180.00
Rookie Pack (2):		40.00
1	Jake Plummer	2.50
2	Mario Bates	.50
3	Adrian Murrell	.50
4	Jamal Anderson	1.50
5	Chris Chandler	1.00
6	Bob Christian	.50
7	O.J. Santiago	.50
8	Jim Harbaugh	1.00
9	Priest Holmes	1.50
10	Ray Lewis	.50
11	Michael Jackson	.50
12	Tony Siragusa	.50
13	Doug Flutie	2.00
14	Antowain Smith	1.25
15	Eric Moulds	1.25
16	William Floyd	.50
17	Fred Lane	.50
18	Muhsin Muhammad	.50
19	Bobby Engram	.50
20	Curtis Enis	1.50
21	Curtis Conway	1.00
22	Corey Dillon	1.50
23	Carl Pickens	1.00
24	Ashley Ambrose	.50
25	Darnay Scott	.50
26	Troy Aikman	3.00
27	Jason Garrett	.50
28	Emmitt Smith	4.50
29	Deion Sanders	1.25
30	John Elway	4.50
31	Terrell Davis	4.50
32	Ed McCaffrey	1.00
33	John Mobley	.50
34	Maa Tanuvasa	.50
35	Ray Crockett	.50
36	Barry Sanders	6.00
37	Herman Moore	1.00
38	Charlie Batch	2.00
39	Robert Porcher	.50
40	Tommy Vardell	.50
41	Brett Favre	6.00
42	Antonio Freeman	1.50
43	Darick Holmes	.50
44	Robert Brooks	.50
45	Peyton Manning	5.00
46	Marshall Faulk	1.25
47	Torrance Small	.50
48	Lamont Warren	.50
49	Zack Crockett	.50
50	Mark Brunell	2.00
51	Pete Mitchell	.50
52	Fred Taylor	4.00
53	Jimmy Smith	1.00
54	Andre Rison	1.00
55	Rich Gannon	.50
56	Donnell Bennett	.50
57	Dan Marino	4.50
58	Karim Abdul	1.00
59	Troy Drayton	.50
60	Jason Taylor	.50
61	Cris Carter	1.25
62	Randy Moss	8.00
63	Robert Smith	1.00
64	Leroy Hoard	.50
65	Randall Cunningham	1.25
66	Derrick Alexander	.50
67	Drew Bledsoe	2.00
68	Robert Edwards	1.25
69	Willie McGinest	.50
70	Chris Slade	.50
71	Terry Glenn	1.00
72	Ty Law	.50
73	Kerry Collins	1.00
74	Sean Dawkins	.50
75	Cameron Cleeland	1.00
76	Sammy Knight	.50
77	Danny Kanell	.50
78	Gary Brown	.50
79	Chris Calloway	.50
80	Curtis Martin	1.25
81	Keyshawn Johnson	1.25
82	Vinny Testaverde	1.00
83	Leon Johnson	.50
84	Kyle Brady	.50
85	Tim Brown	1.00
86	Jeff George	1.00
87	Rickey Dudley	.50
88	Napoleon Kaufman	1.25
89	James Jett	.50
90	Harvey Williams	.50
91	Koy Detmer	.50
92	Duce Staley	.50
93	Charlie Garner	.50
94	Jerome Bettis	1.00
95	Kordell Stewart	1.75
96	Courtney Hawkins	.50
97	Hines Ward	1.00
98	Isaac Bruce	1.00
99	Tony Banks	1.00
100	Greg Hill	.50
101	Keith Lyle	.50
102	Ryan Leaf	2.00
103	Craig Whelihan	.50
104	Charlie Jones	.50
105	Junior Seau	1.00
106	Natrone Means	1.00
107	Rodney Harrison	.50
108	Steve Young	2.00
109	Garrison Hearst	1.00
110	Jerry Rice	3.00
111	Chris Doleman	.50
112	Roy Barker	.50
113	Ricky Watters	1.00
114	Jon Kitna	1.50
115	Joey Galloway	1.25
116	Chad Brown	.50
117	Michael Sinclair	.50
118	Warrick Dunn	1.50
119	Mike Alstott	1.25
120	Bert Emanuel	.50
121	Hardy Nickerson	.50
122	Eddie George	1.50
123	Steve McNair	1.25
124	Yancey Thigpen	.50
125	Frank Wycheck	.50
126	Jackie Harris	.50
127	Terry Allen	1.00
128	Trent Green	1.25
129	Jamie Asher	.50
130	Brian Mitchell	.50
131	Lance Alworth	1.00
132	Fred Biletnikoff	1.25
133	Mel Blount	.50
134	Cliff Branch	.50
135	Harold Carmichael	.50
136	Larry Csonka	1.25
137	Eric Dickerson	1.00
138	Randy Gradishar	.50
139	Joe Greene	1.00
140	Jack Ham	.50
141	Ted Hendricks	.50
142	Charlie Joiner	1.00
143	Ed Jones	.50
144	Billy Kilmer	.50
145	Paul Krause	.50
146	James Lofton	.50
147	Archie Manning	1.00
148	Don Maynard	1.00
149	Ozzie Newsome	.50
150	Jim Otto	.50
151	Lee Roy Selmon	.50
152	Billy Sims	1.00
153	Mike Singletary	1.00
154	Ken Stabler	1.50
155	John Stallworth	1.00
156	Roger Staubach	2.00
157	Charley Taylor	.50
158	Paul Warfield	1.25
159	Kellen Winslow	1.00
160	Jack Youngblood	.50
161	Bill Bergey	.50
162	Raymond Berry	.50
163	Chuck Howley	.50
164	Rocky Bleier	.50
165	Russ Francis	.50
166	Drew Pearson	.50
167	Mercury Morris	.50
168	Dick Anderson	.50
169	Earl Morrall	.50
170	Jim Hart	.50
171	*Ricky Williams*	35.00
172	*Cade McNown*	25.00
173	*Tim Couch*	35.00
174	*Daunte Culpepper*	60.00
175	*Akili Smith*	25.00
176	*Brock Huard*	20.00
177	*Donovan McNabb*	30.00
178	*Michael Bishop*	20.00
179	*Shaun King*	25.00
180	*Tory Holt*	20.00

1999 SP Signature Autographs

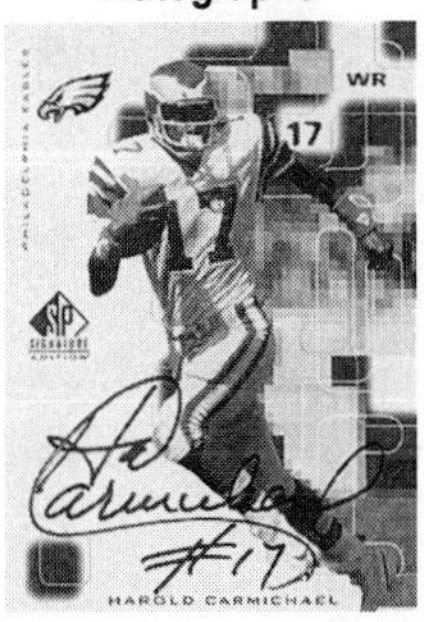

Cards in this insert are the same as the base except for the signature on the front. The backs are different then the regular base card. Singles were inserted one-per-pack. A Gold parallel was produced and inserted 1:59 packs.

		MT
Common Player:		10.00
Minor Stars:		20.00
Inserted 1:1		
Gold Cards:		2x
Inserted 1:59		
KA	Karim Abdul	20.00
TA	Troy Aikman	250.00
DA	Derrick Alexander	10.00
MA	Mike Alstott	50.00
AA	Ashley Ambrose	10.00
AN	Dick Anderson	10.00
TE	Jamie Asher	10.00
DE	Roy Barker	10.00
CB	Charlie Batch	60.00
MB	Mario Bates	10.00
DB	Donnell Bennett	10.00
BB	Bill Bergey	10.00
RY	Raymond Berry	25.00
MI	Michael Bishop	120.00
ML	Mel Blount	20.00
KB	Kyle Brady	10.00
RB	Robert Brooks	20.00
LB	Chad Brown	10.00
GB	Gary Brown	10.00
TB	Tim Brown	35.00
IB	Isaac Bruce	40.00
MK	Mark Brunell	125.00
CY	Chris Calloway	10.00
HC	Harold Carmichael	20.00
CC	Chris Chandler	30.00
BC	Bob Christian	10.00
CL	Cameron Cleeland	20.00
CW	Curtis Conway	20.00
TC	Tim Couch	325.00
CK	Ray Crockett	10.00
ZC	Zack Crockett	10.00
DC	Daunte Culpepper	500.00
NO	Sean Dawkins	10.00
KD	Koy Detmer	10.00
CD	Corey Dillon	35.00
TR	Troy Drayton	10.00
RD	Rickey Dudley	10.00
RE	Robert Edwards	25.00
JE	John Elway	300.00
BT	Bert Emanuel	20.00
BE	Bobby Engram	10.00
CE	Curtis Enis	30.00
MF	Marshall Faulk	40.00
BF	Brett Favre	300.00
WF	William Floyd	10.00
RF	Russ Francis	10.00
AF	Antonio Freeman	75.00
GA	Joey Galloway	70.00
CG	Charlie Garner	20.00
JG	Jason Garrett	10.00
EG	Eddie George	85.00
GE	Jeff George	20.00
GR	Randy Gradishar	10.00
GN	Trent Green	25.00
JH	Jack Ham	20.00
JK	Jackie Harris	10.00
RH	Rodney Harrison	10.00
HT	Jim Hart	20.00
GH	Garrison Hearst	25.00
TH	Ted Hendricks	20.00
HL	Greg Hill	10.00
LH	Leroy Hoard	10.00
DH	Darick Holmes	10.00
PH	Priest Holmes	30.00
WP	Torry Holt	175.00
HY	Chuck Howley	20.00
BH	Brock Huard	100.00
MJ	Michael Jackson	20.00
JJ	James Jett	20.00
KJ	Keyshawn Johnson	50.00
LJ	Leon Johnson	10.00
CJ	Charlie Joiner	20.00
SD	Charlie Jones	20.00
EJ	Ed Jones	20.00
NK	Napoleon Kaufman	50.00
SH	Shaun King	180.00
KI	Jon Kitna	30.00
SK	Sammy Knight	20.00
PK	Paul Krause	20.00
FL	Fred Lane	20.00
TL	Ty Law	10.00
RL	Ray Lewis	10.00
JL	James Lofton	20.00
KL	Keith Lyle	10.00
MG	Archie Manning	30.00
DM	Dan Marino	325.00
NY	Don Maynard	20.00
WM	Willie McGinest	10.00
MN	Donovan McNabb	200.00
QB	Cade McNown	225.00
NM	Natrone Means	30.00
KR	Brian Mitchell	10.00
PT	Pete Mitchell	10.00
JM	John Mobley	10.00
HM	Herman Moore	35.00
MO	Earl Morrall	20.00
MY	Mercury Morris	20.00
RM	Randy Moss	350.00
EM	Eric Moulds	40.00
MM	Muhsin Muhammad	10.00
AM	Adrian Murrell	20.00
HN	Hardy Nickerson	10.00
OZ	Ozzie Newsome	25.00
DP	Drew Pearson	25.00
JP	Jake Plummer	100.00
RP	Robert Porcher	10.00
OJ	O.J. Santiago	10.00
JR	Junior Seau	25.00
LS	Lee Roy Selmon	20.00
MS	Michael Sinclair	10.00
SY	Mike Singletary	25.00
TS	Tony Siragusa	10.00
CS	Chris Slade	10.00
TO	Torrance Small	10.00
AK	Akili Smith	150.00
AS	Antowain Smith	25.00
ES	Emmitt Smith	250.00
JS	Jimmy Smith	30.00
KS	Ken Stabler	40.00
ST	Duce Staley	30.00
SW	John Stallworth	25.00
MT	Maa Tanuvasa	10.00
CT	Charley Taylor	20.00
FT	Fred Taylor	125.00
JT	Jason Taylor	10.00
TV	Tommy Vardell	10.00
HW	Hines Ward	20.00
PW	Paul Warfield	25.00
LW	Lamont Warren	10.00
ND	Ricky Watters	40.00
WH	Craig Whelihan	10.00
HV	Harvey Williams	10.00
RW	Ricky Williams	300.00
KW	Kellen Winslow	25.00
FW	Frank Wycheck	10.00
JY	Jack Youngblood	20.00

1999 SP Signature Montana Great Performances

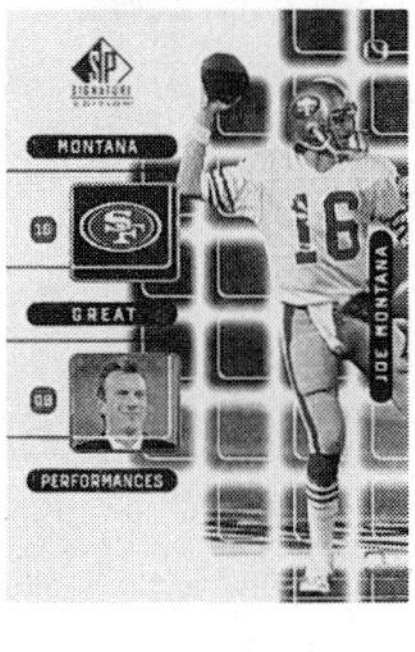

This was a 10-card set that highlights the career of Montana. Singles were randomly inserted. A parallel Autographed version was also produced and found 1:47 packs and a Gold Autographed parallel was made and found 1:880 packs.

		MT
Complete Set (10):		70.00
Common Player:		7.00
Randomly Inserted		
Montana Autographs:		125.00
Inserted 1:47		
Montana Gold Autographs:		600.00
Inserted 1:880		
1	Joe Montana	7.00
2	Joe Montana	7.00
3	Joe Montana	7.00
4	Joe Montana	7.00
5	Joe Montana	7.00
6	Joe Montana	7.00
7	Joe Montana	7.00
8	Joe Montana	7.00
9	Joe Montana	7.00
10	Joe Montana	7.00

1999 SPx

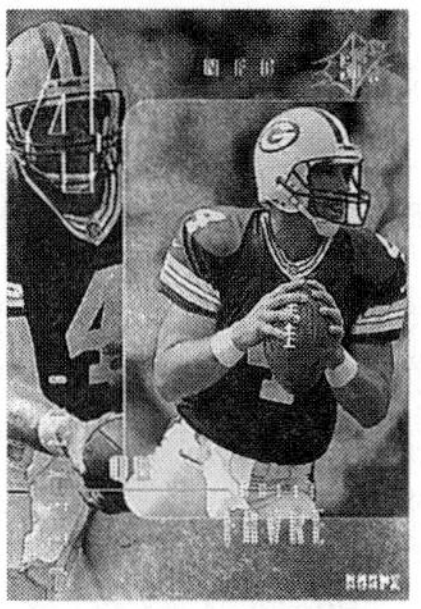

This was a 135-card set that included 45 sequentially numbered rookie cards. A total of 21 of the rookies were numbered to 1,999 and were autographed, 19 rookies were unsigned and numbered to 1,999 and only five were autographed and numbered to 500. Each single had a parallel Radiance and Spectrum single. Other inserts included: Highlight Heroes, Masters, Prolifics, SPxcitement, SPxtreme, Starscape and Winning Materials. SRP was $5.99 for three-card packs.

		MT
Complete Set (135):		3000.
Common Player:		.25
Minor Stars:		.50
Common Rookie:		6.00
Production 1,999 Sets		
Pack (3):		10.00
Wax Box (18):		165.00
1	Jake Plummer	2.00
2	Adrian Murrell	.50
3	Frank Sanders	.50
4	Jamal Anderson	1.00
5	Chris Chandler	.50
6	Terance Mathis	.25
7	Tony Banks	.50
8	Priest Holmes	1.00
9	Jermaine Lewis	.50
10	Antowain Smith	1.00
11	Doug Flutie	1.75
12	Eric Moulds	1.00
13	Tshimanga Biakabutuka	.50
14	Steve Beuerlein	.50
15	Muhsin Muhammad	.25
16	Bobby Engram	.25
17	Curtis Conway	.50
18	Curtis Enis	1.00
19	Corey Dillon	1.00
20	Jeff Blake	.50
21	Carl Pickens	.50
22	Ty Detmer	.25
23	Terry Kirby	.25
24	Leslie Shepherd	.25
25	Troy Aikman	2.50
26	Emmitt Smith	3.50
27	Deion Sanders	1.00
28	Terrell Davis	3.50
29	Rod Smith	.50
30	Bubby Brister	.50
31	Barry Sanders	5.00
32	Herman Moore	1.00
33	Charlie Batch	1.50
34	Brett Favre	5.00
35	Antonio Freeman	1.00
36	Dorsey Levens	1.00
37	Peyton Manning	3.50
38	Marvin Harrison	1.00
39	Jerome Pathon	.25
40	Mark Brunell	2.00
41	Jimmy Smith	.50
42	Fred Taylor	2.50
43	Elvis Grbac	.50
44	Andre Rison	.25
45	Warren Moon	.50
46	Dan Marino	3.50
47	Karim Abdul	.75
48	O.J. McDuffie	.25
49	Randall Cunningham	1.00
50	Robert Smith	1.00
51	Randy Moss	5.00
52	Drew Bledsoe	2.00
53	Terry Glenn	1.00
54	Tony Simmons	.50
55	Danny Wuerffel	.50
56	Cameron Cleeland	.50
57	Kerry Collins	.50
58	Gary Brown	.25
59	Ike Hilliard	.25
60	Vinny Testaverde	.50
61	Curtis Martin	1.00
62	Keyshawn Johnson	1.00
63	Rich Gannon	.25
64	Napoleon Kaufman	1.00

65	Tim Brown	.50
66	Duce Staley	.50
67	Doug Pederson	.25
68	Charles Johnson	.25
69	Kordell Stewart	1.25
70	Jerome Bettis	1.00
71	Trent Green	.75
72	Marshall Faulk	1.00
73	Ryan Leaf	1.25
74	Natrone Means	1.00
75	Jim Harbaugh	.50
76	Steve Young	1.75
77	Garrison Hearst	.50
78	Jerry Rice	2.50
79	Terrell Owens	1.00
80	Ricky Watters	.75
81	Joey Galloway	1.00
82	Jon Kitna	1.25
83	Warrick Dunn	1.25
84	Trent Dilfer	.50
85	Mike Alstott	1.00
86	Steve McNair	1.25
87	Eddie George	1.25
88	Yancey Thigpen	.50
89	Skip Hicks	.75
90	Michael Westbrook	.75
91	*Amos Zereoue*	15.00
92	*Chris Claiborne AUTO 1,999*	20.00
93	*Scott Covington*	8.00
94	*Jeff Paulk*	6.00
95	*Brandon Stokley AUTO 1,999*	15.00
96	*Antoine Winfield*	6.00
97	*Reginald Kelly*	6.00
98	*Jermaine Fazande AUTO 1,999*	30.00
99	*Andy Katzenmoyer*	10.00
100	*Craig Yeast*	6.00
101	*Joe Montgomery*	10.00
102	*Darrin Chiaverini*	6.00
103	*Travis McGriff*	8.00
104	*Jevon Kearse*	60.00
105	*Joel Makovicka AUTO 1,999*	15.00
106	*Aaron Brooks*	125.00
107	*Chris McAlister*	6.00
108	*Jim Kleinsasser*	10.00
109	*Ebenezer Ekuban*	6.00
110	*Karsten Bailey*	6.00
111	*Sedrick Irvin AUTO 1,999*	30.00
112	*D'Wayne Bates AUTO 1,999*	20.00
113	*Joe Germaine AUTO 1,999*	30.00
114	*Cecil Collins AUTO 1,999*	25.00
115	*Michael Cloud*	10.00
116	*James Johnson*	15.00
117	*Champ Bailey AUTO 1,999*	35.00
118	*Rob Konrad*	10.00
119	*Peerless Price AUTO 1,999*	45.00
120	*Kevin Faulk AUTO 1,999*	40.00
121	*Dameane Douglas*	6.00
122	*Kevin Johnson AUTO 1,999*	60.00
123	*Troy Edwards AUTO 1,999*	50.00
124	*Edgerrin James AUTO 1,999*	325.00
125	*David Boston AUTO 1,999*	50.00
126	*Michael Bishop AUTO 1,999*	50.00
127	*Shaun King AUTO SP*	550.00
127A	Shaun King Trade	100.00
128	*Brock Huard AUTO 1,999*	40.00
129	*Torry Holt AUTO 1,999*	80.00
130	*Cade McNown AUTO 500*	250.00
131	*Tim Couch AUTO 500*	500.00
132	*Donovan McNabb AUTO 1,999*	225.00
133	*Akili Smith AUTO 500*	250.00
134	*Daunte Culpepper AUTO 500*	750.00
135	*Ricky Williams AUTO 500*	550.00

1999 SPx Radiance Parallel

This was a 135-card parallel to the base set including unsigned versions of the autographed rookie cards. Each single was printed with a holographic green-foil treatment and was sequentially numbered to 100.

	MT
Radiance Cards (1-90):	15x-30x
Radiance Rookies (1,999):	3x
Radiance Rookies (Auto.):	2x
Radiance Rookies (Auto. 500):	1x
Production 100 Sets	

1999 SPx Spectrum Parallel

This was a 135-card parallel to the base set and each was printed with a holographic red-foil treatment and numbered one-of-one.

MT

Production 1 Set

Post-1980 cards in Near Mint condition will generally sell for about 75% of the quoted Mint value. Excellent-condition cards bring no more than 40%.

1999 SPx Highlight Heroes

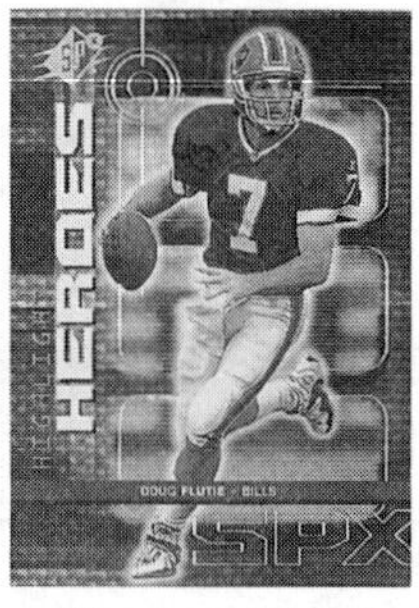

This was a 10-card insert set that included mostly quarterbacks. Singles were inserted 1:9 packs.

		MT
Complete Set (10):		20.00
Common Player:		2.00
Inserted 1:9		
1	Jake Plummer	6.00
2	Doug Flutie	4.00
3	Garrison Hearst	2.00
4	Fred Taylor	6.00
5	Dorsey Levens	2.00
6	Kordell Stewart	3.00
7	Marshall Faulk	2.00
8	Steve Young	4.00
9	Troy Aikman	6.00
10	Jerome Bettis	2.00

1999 SPx Masters

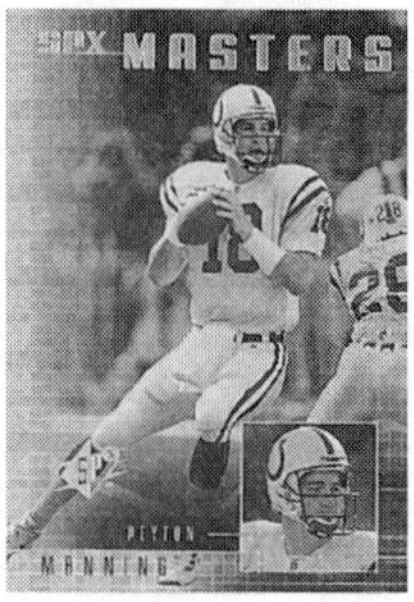

This was a 15-card insert set that included the best players at their respective positions. Singles were inserted 1:17 packs.

		MT
Complete Set (15):		75.00
Common Player:		3.00
Inserted 1:17		
1	Dan Marino	10.00
2	Barry Sanders	12.00
3	Peyton Manning	10.00
4	Joey Galloway	3.00
5	Steve Young	5.00
6	Warrick Dunn	4.00
7	Deion Sanders	3.00
8	Fred Taylor	6.00
9	Charlie Batch	4.00
10	Jamal Anderson	3.00
11	Jake Plummer	6.00
12	Terrell Davis	10.00
13	Eddie George	4.00
14	Mark Brunell	5.00
15	Randy Moss	12.00

1999 SPx Prolifics

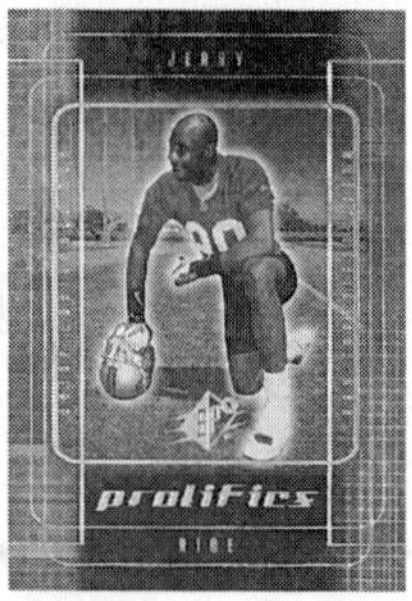

This was a 15-card insert set that included stars who had the ability to score points, yards and wins. Singles were inserted 1:17 packs.

		MT
Complete Set (15):		50.00
Common Player:		3.00
Inserted 1:17		
1	John Elway	10.00
2	Barry Sanders	12.00
3	Jamal Anderson	3.00
4	Terrell Owens	4.00
5	Marshall Faulk	3.00
6	Napoleon Kaufman	3.00
7	Antonio Freeman	3.00
8	Doug Flutie	5.00
9	Vinny Testaverde	3.00
10	Jerry Rice	6.00
11	Eric Moulds	3.00
12	Emmitt Smith	10.00
13	Brett Favre	12.00
14	Randall Cunningham	3.00
15	Keyshawn Johnson	3.00

1999 SPx SPxcitement

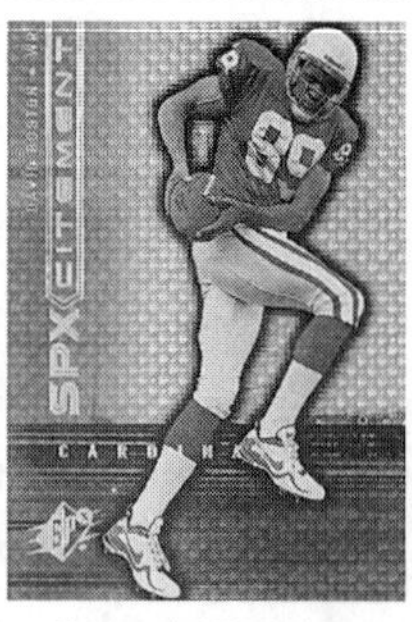

This was a 20-card insert set who featured players who provide non-stop thrills. Singles were inserted 1:3 packs.

		MT
Complete Set (20):		30.00
Common Player:		1.00
Inserted 1:3		
1	Troy Aikman	4.00
2	Edgerrin James	6.00
3	Jerry Rice	4.00
4	Daunte Culpepper	4.00
5	Antowain Smith	1.00
6	Kevin Faulk	2.00
7	Steve McNair	1.00
8	Antonio Freeman	1.00
9	Torry Holt	3.00
10	Napoleon Kaufman	1.00
11	Curtis Martin	1.00
12	Randall Cunningham	1.00
13	Eric Moulds	1.00
14	Priest Holmes	1.00
15	David Boston	3.00
16	Herman Moore	1.00
17	Champ Bailey	1.50
18	Vinny Testaverde	1.00
19	Garrison Hearst	1.00
20	Jon Kitna	1.00

1999 SPx SPxtreme

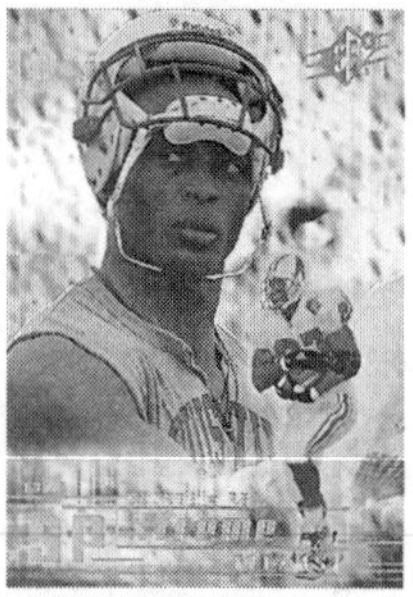

This 20-card insert set highlighted the most collectible stars and saluted their extreme talents to the game. Singles were inserted 1:6 packs.

		MT
Complete Set (20):		45.00
Common Player:		1.50
Inserted 1:6		
1	Emmitt Smith	7.00
2	Brock Huard	2.50
3	David Boston	4.00
4	Edgerrin James	10.00
5	Kevin Faulk	2.50
6	Daunte Culpepper	6.00
7	Charlie Batch	2.50
8	Torry Holt	4.00
9	Andre Rison	1.50
10	Karim Abdul	1.50
11	Kordell Stewart	2.50
12	Curtis Enis	1.50
13	Terrell Owens	1.50
14	Curtis Martin	1.50
15	Ricky Watters	1.50
16	Corey Dillon	1.50
17	Tim Brown	1.50
18	Warrick Dunn	1.50
19	Drew Bledsoe	5.00
20	Eddie George	2.50

1999 SPx Starscape

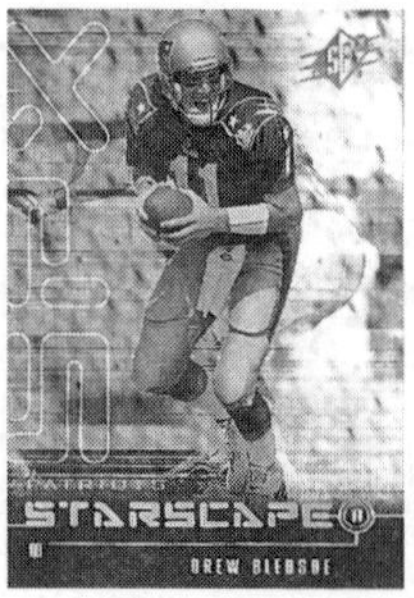

This was a 10-card insert set that featured ten superstars and highlighted their spectacular achievement to date. Singles were inserted 1:9 packs.

		MT
Complete Set (10):		20.00
Common Player:		2.00
Inserted 1:9		
1	Randy Moss	10.00
2	Keyshawn Johnson	2.00
3	Curtis Enis	2.00
4	Jerome Bettis	2.00
5	Mark Brunell	4.00
6	Antowain Smith	2.00
7	Joey Galloway	2.00
8	Drew Bledsoe	4.00
9	Corey Dillon	2.00
10	Steve McNair	2.00

1999 SPx Winning Materials

This 10-card insert set featured two pieces of game-used memorabilia (jersey swatch and football) of the featured player. Singles were inserted 1:252 packs.

		MT
Complete Set (10):		1300.
Common Player:		75.00
Inserted 1:252		
DB	David Boston	75.00
TC	Tim Couch	225.00
DC	Daunte Culpepper	120.00
BF	Brett Favre	250.00
TH	Torry Holt	75.00
DM	Dan Marino	200.00
MC	Donovan McNabb	120.00
CM	Cade McNown	120.00
JR	Jerry Rice	150.00
RW	Ricky Williams	225.00

2000 SP Authentic

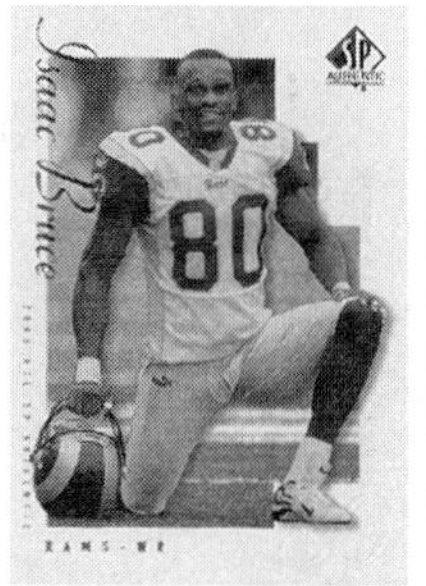

		MT
Complete Set (150):		2000.
Common Player:		.15
Minor Stars:		.30
Common Rookie:		15.00
Production 1,250 Sets		
Pack (5):		5.00
Wax Box (24):		100.00
Common Rookie (151-171):		10.00
Production 1,250 Sets		
1	Jake Plummer	.50
2	David Boston	.50
3	Frank Sanders	.30
4	Chris Chandler	.30
5	Jamal Anderson	.50
6	Shawn Jefferson	.15
7	Tony Banks	.30
8	Shannon Sharpe	.30
9	Rob Johnson	.30
10	Antowain Smith	.30
11	Muhsin Muhammad	.30
12	Steve Beuerlein	.30
13	Cade McNown	.75
14	Curtis Enis	.30
15	Marcus Robinson	.50
16	Akili Smith	.50
17	Corey Dillon	.50
18	Tim Couch	1.25
19	Kevin Johnson	.30
20	Errict Rhett	.30
21	Troy Aikman	1.50
22	Emmitt Smith	1.75
23	Raghib Ismail	.15
24	Joey Galloway	.50
25	Terrell Davis	1.75
26	Olandis Gary	.50
27	Ed McCaffrey	.30
28	Brian Griese	.75
29	Charlie Batch	.50
30	Germane Crowell	.50
31	James O. Stewart	.30
32	Brett Favre	2.50
33	Antonio Freeman	.50
34	Dorsey Levens	.50
35	Peyton Manning	2.00
36	Edgerrin James	2.50
37	Marvin Harrison	.50
38	Mark Brunell	1.00
39	Fred Taylor	1.00
40	Jimmy Smith	.50
41	Elvis Grbac	.30
42	Tony Gonzalez	.30
43	James Johnson	.15
44	Oronde Gadsden	.30
45	Damon Huard	.50
46	Randy Moss	2.00
47	Cris Carter	.50
48	Daunte Culpepper	1.25
49	Drew Bledsoe	1.00
50	Terry Glenn	.50
51	Ricky Williams	1.50
52	Jeff Blake	.30
53	Keith Poole	.15
54	Kerry Collins	.30
55	Amani Toomer	.15
56	Ike Hilliard	.15
57	Wayne Chrebet	.50
58	Curtis Martin	.50
59	Vinny Testaverde	.30
60	Tim Brown	.50
61	Rich Gannon	.30
62	Tyrone Wheatley	.30
63	Duce Staley	.50
64	Donovan McNabb	1.00
65	Troy Edwards	.50
66	Jerome Bettis	.50
67	Kordell Stewart	.60
68	Marshall Faulk	.50
69	Kurt Warner	3.00
70	Isaac Bruce	.50
71	Torry Holt	.50
72	Ryan Leaf	.50
73	Jim Harbaugh	.30
74	Jermaine Fazande	.15
75	Jerry Rice	1.50
76	Terrell Owens	.50
77	Jeff Garcia	.50
78	Ricky Watters	.30
79	Jon Kitna	.50
80	Derrick Mayes	.30
81	Shaun King	1.00
82	Mike Alstott	.50
83	Keyshawn Johnson	.50
84	Warrick Dunn	.50
85	Eddie George	.75
86	Steve McNair	.50
87	Jevon Kearse	.50
88	Brad Johnson	.50
89	Stephen Davis	.50
90	Michael Westbrook	.30
91	*Anthony Lucas*	15.00
92	*Avion Black*	20.00
93	*Dante Hall*	15.00
94	*Darrell Jackson*	45.00
95	*Deltha O'Neal*	20.00
96	*Erron Kinney*	15.00
97	*Doug Chapman*	20.00
98	*Frank Murphy*	15.00
99	*Gari Scott*	15.00
100	*Giovanni Carmazzi*	30.00
101	*JaJuan Dawson*	30.00
102	*Jarious Jackson*	30.00
103	*Rashard Anderson*	20.00
104	*Michael Wiley*	30.00
105	*Spergon Wynn*	35.00
106	*Muneer Moore*	15.00
107	*Ahmed Plummer*	20.00
108	*Chad Morton*	30.00
109	*Rob Morris*	20.00
110	*Ron Dixon*	35.00
111	*Rondell Mealey*	25.00
112	*Sebastian Janikowski*	30.00
113	*Shaun Ellis*	15.00
114	*Rogers Beckett*	15.00
115	*Shyrone Stith*	25.00
116	*Tim Rattay*	45.00
117	*Todd Husak*	30.00
118	*Tom Brady*	85.00
119	*Trevor Gaylor*	25.00
120	*Windrell Hayes*	15.00
121	*Anthony Becht*	35.00
122	*Brian Urlacher*	150.00
123	*Bubba Franks*	25.00
124	*Chad Pennington*	100.00
125	*Chris Redman*	40.00
126	*Corey Simon*	35.00
127	*Curtis Keaton*	25.00
128	*Danny Farmer*	35.00
129	*Dennis Northcutt*	20.00
130	*Dez White*	30.00
131	*J.R. Redmond*	20.00
132	*Jamal Lewis*	125.00
133	*Jerry Porter*	35.00
134	*Joe Hamilton*	45.00
135	*Laveranues Coles*	45.00
136	*R. Jay Soward*	40.00
137	*Reuben Droughns*	25.00
138	*Ron Dayne*	75.00
139	*Ron Dugans*	35.00
140	*Shaun Alexander*	125.00
141	*Sylvester Morris*	40.00
142	*Tee Martin*	35.00
143	*Thomas Jones*	30.00
144	*Todd Pinkston*	35.00
145	*Travis Prentice*	25.00
146	*Travis Taylor*	40.00
147	*Trung Canidate*	35.00
148	*Courtney Brown*	25.00
149	*Plaxico Burress*	85.00
150	*Peter Warrick*	75.00
151	*Billy Volek*	20.00
152	*Bobby Shaw*	20.00
153	*Brad Hoover*	25.00
154	*Brian Finneran*	10.00
155	*Charles Lee*	10.00
156	*Chris Cole*	10.00
157	*Clint Stoerner*	25.00
158	*Doug Johnson*	25.00
159	*Frank Moreau*	25.00
160	*Jake Delhomme*	25.00
161	*KaRon Coleman*	10.00
162	*Kevin McDougal*	10.00
163	*Larry Foster*	15.00
164	*Mike Anderson*	150.00
165	*Patrick Pass*	15.00
166	*Reggie Jones*	25.00
167	*Sammy Morris*	20.00
168	*Shockmain Davis*	10.00
169	*Terrelle Smith*	10.00
170	*Ronney Jenkins*	10.00
171	*Troy Walters*	15.00

Values quoted in this guide reflect the retail price of a card — the price a collector can expect to pay when buying a card from a dealer. The wholesale price — that which a collector can expect to receive from a dealer when selling cards — will be significantly lower, depending on desirability and condition.

2000 SP Authentic Game-Jersey Greats

		MT
Production 175 Sets		300.00
JN	Joe Namath 175	300.00

2000 SP Authentic New Classics

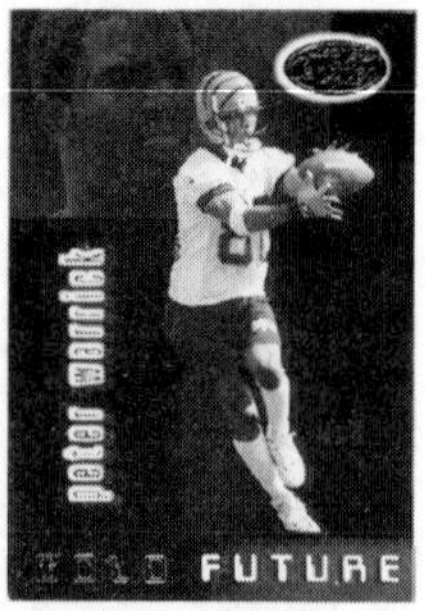

		MT
Complete Set (10):		15.00
Common Player:		1.50
Inserted 1:11		
NC1	Peter Warrick	5.00
NC2	Courtney Brown	1.75
NC3	Trung Candidate	1.50
NC4	Dennis Northcutt	1.75
NC5	J.R. Redmond	2.00
NC6	Daunte Culpepper	2.50
NC7	Edgerrin James	5.00
NC8	Marcus Robinson	1.50
NC9	Shaun King	1.75
NC10	Ricky Williams	2.50

2000 SP Authentic Rookie Fusion

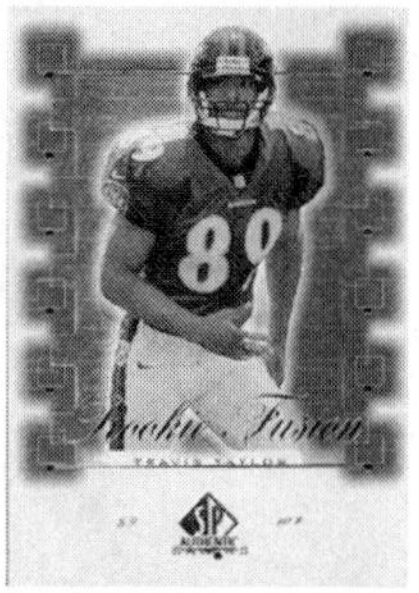

		MT
Complete Set (7):		18.00
Common Player:		3.00
Inserted 1:18		
RF1	Plaxico Burress	4.00
RF2	Chad Pennington	5.00
RF3	Travis Taylor	3.00
RF4	Ron Dayne	6.00
RF5	Thomas Jones	3.50
RF6	Jamal Lewis	8.00
RF7	Sylvester Morris	4.00

2000 SP Authentic Sign of the Times

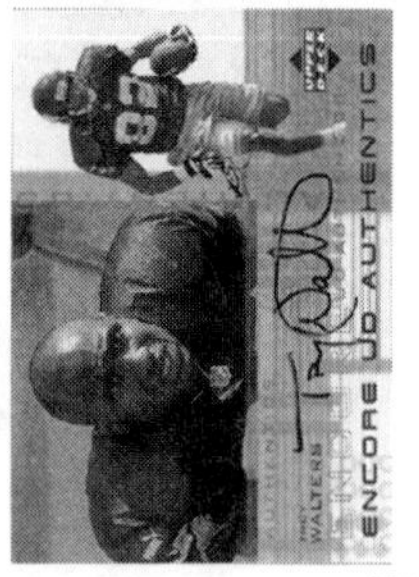

		MT
Common Player:		10.00
Minor Stars:		20.00
Inserted 1:23		
SA	Shaun Alexander	50.00
FB	Mike Alstott	20.00
JA	Jamal Anderson	20.00
CH	Champ Bailey	20.00
CB	Charlie Batch	20.00
BL	Drew Bledsoe	35.00
DB	David Boston	20.00
CO	Courtney Brown	25.00
IB	Isaac Bruce	20.00
MB	Mark Brunell	35.00
PB	Plaxico Burress	25.00
CA	Trung Canidate	10.00
GC	Giovanni Carmazzi	20.00
CC	Cris Carter	25.00
KC	Kwame Cavil	10.00
CR	Chris Chandler	10.00
WC	Wayne Chrebet	20.00
DL	Chris Claiborne	10.00
CL	Chris Coleman	10.00
LC	Laveranues Coles	25.00
KE	Kerry Collins	20.00
TC	Tim Couch	40.00
DC	Daunte Culpepper	60.00
SD	Stephen Davis	20.00
JD	JaJuan Dawson	20.00
RD	Ron Dayne	75.00
TD	Trent Dilfer	20.00
DR	Reuben Droughns	10.00
DU	Ron Dugans	10.00
TE	Troy Edwards	10.00

DF	Danny Farmer	10.00
KF	Kevin Faulk	10.00
MF	Marshall Faulk	25.00
FL	Doug Flutie	25.00
BF	Bubba Franks	20.00
AF	Antonio Freeman	20.00
GF	Gus Frerotte	10.00
JG	Joey Galloway	20.00
OG	Olandis Gary	20.00
TG	Trevor Gaylor	10.00
EG	Eddie George	35.00
SG	Sherrod Gideon	10.00
GO	Tony Gonzalez	20.00
BG	Brian Griese	35.00
JH	Joe Hamilton	20.00
MH	Marvin Harrison	20.00
WH	Windrell Hayes	10.00
TH	Torry Holt	20.00
QI	Qadry Ismail	10.00
DJ	Darrell Jackson	20.00
EJ	Edgerrin James	75.00
BJ	Brad Johnson	20.00
JO	Kevin Johnson	10.00
KJ	Keyshawn Johnson	20.00
RB	Rob Johnson	20.00
TJ	Thomas Jones	25.00
CK	Curtis Keaton	10.00
JK	Jon Kitna	20.00
JL	Jamal Lewis	100.00
AL	Anthony Lucas	10.00
RL	Ray Lucas	20.00
PM	Peyton Manning	100.00
DM	Dan Marino	85.00
TM	Tee Martin	20.00
CM	Cade McNown	25.00
MO	Corey Moore	10.00
HM	Herman Moore	20.00
SM	Sylvester Morris	40.00
RM	Randy Moss	100.00
EM	Eric Moulds	20.00
JN	Joe Namath	125.00
DN	Dennis Northcutt	20.00
TO	Terrell Owens	20.00
CP	Chad Pennington	60.00
JP	Jake Plummer	20.00
PO	Jerry Porter	20.00
TP	Travis Prentice	25.00
TR	Tim Rattay	25.00
RE	Chris Redman	30.00
JR	J.R. Redmond	20.00
SS	Shannon Sharpe	20.00
CS	Corey Simon	20.00
AS	Akili Smith	20.00
RJ	R. Jay Soward	20.00
KS	Kordell Stewart	20.00
JJ	J.J. Stokes	10.00
TT	Travis Taylor	25.00
BU	Brian Urlacher	50.00
TW	Troy Walters	10.00
KW	Kurt Warner	100.00
PW	Peter Warrick	80.00
WA	Ricky Watters	20.00
DW	Dez White	20.00
MW	Michael Wiley	20.00
SY	Steve Young	45.00

2000 SP Authentic SP Athletic

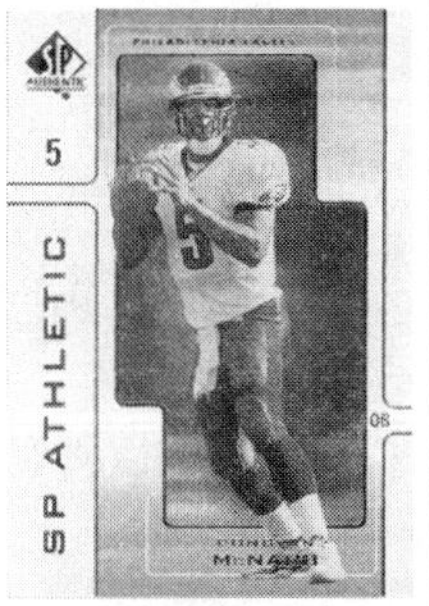

		MT
Complete Set (10):		7.00
Common Player:		1.00
Inserted 1:11		
A1	Marshall Faulk	1.50
A2	Kevin Johnson	1.50
A3	Olandis Gary	1.50
A4	Jeff Garcia	1.50
A5	Akili Smith	1.50
A6	Donovan McNabb	2.00
A7	Rob Johnson	1.00
A8	Marcus Robinson	1.50
A9	Shaun King	1.75
A10	Troy Edwards	1.00

2000 SP Authentic Supremacy

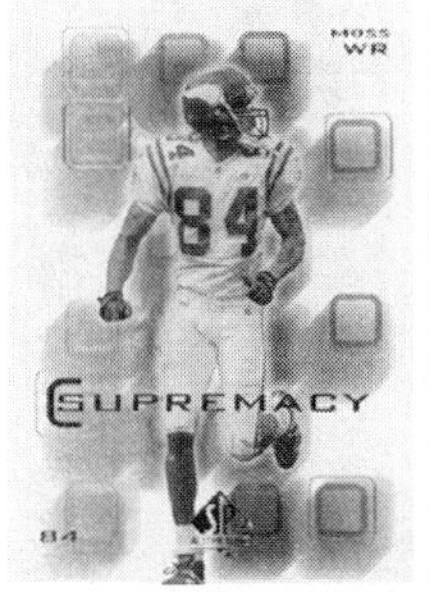

		MT
Complete Set (15):		25.00
Common Player:		1.50
Inserted 1:8		
S1	Mark Brunell	2.00
S2	Terrell Davis	3.50
S3	Jamal Anderson	1.50
S4	Jerry Rice	2.50
S5	Emmitt Smith	3.50
S6	Troy Aikman	2.50
S7	Randy Moss	5.00
S8	Brad Johnson	1.50
S9	Brett Favre	5.00
S10	Keyshawn Johnson	1.50
S11	Fred Taylor	2.00
S12	Kurt Warner	5.00
S13	Tim Couch	2.50
S14	Eddie George	1.75
S15	Drew Bledsoe	2.00

2000 SPx

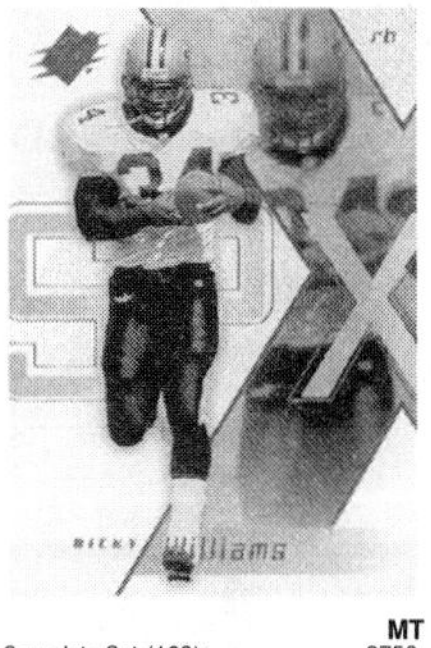

		MT
Complete Set (160):		2750.
Common Player:		.25
Minor Stars:		.50
Common Rookie:		7.00
Production 1,350 Sets		
Common Rookie Jersey:		20.00
Production 2,000 Sets		
Pack (4):		7.00
Wax Box (18):		100.00
1	Jake Plummer	.75
2	David Boston	.75
3	Frank Sanders	.50
4	Chris Chandler	.50
5	Jamal Anderson	.75
6	Shawn Jefferson	.25
7	Qadry Ismail	.25
8	Tony Banks	.50
9	Shannon Sharpe	.50
10	Rob Johnson	.50
11	Eric Moulds	.75
12	Muhsin Muhammad	.50
13	Steve Beuerlein	.50
14	Cade McNown	1.00
15	Marcus Robinson	.75
16	Akili Smith	.75
17	Corey Dillon	.75
18	Darnay Scott	.50
19	Tim Couch	1.50
20	Kevin Johnson	.75
21	Errict Rhett	.50
22	Troy Aikman	1.50
23	Emmitt Smith	2.00
24	Joey Galloway	.75
25	Terrell Davis	2.00
26	Olandis Gary	1.00
27	Brian Griese	1.00
28	Charlie Batch	.75
29	Germane Crowell	.75
30	James O. Stewart	.50
31	Brett Favre	3.00
32	Antonio Freeman	.75
33	Dorsey Levens	.50
34	Peyton Manning	3.00
35	Edgerrin James	3.00
36	Marvin Harrison	.75
37	Mark Brunell	1.25
38	Fred Taylor	1.25
39	Jimmy Smith	.75
40	Keenan McCardell	.50
41	Elvis Grbac	.50
42	Tony Gonzalez	.50
43	Tony Martin	.25
44	Jay Fiedler	.75
45	Damon Huard	.75
46	Randy Moss	3.00
47	Robert Smith	.75
48	Cris Carter	.75
49	Daunte Culpepper	1.50
50	Drew Bledsoe	1.25
51	Terry Glenn	.75
52	Ricky Williams	2.00
53	Jeff Blake	.50
54	Keith Poole	.25
55	Kerry Collins	.50
56	Amani Toomer	.50
57	Ike Hilliard	.50
58	Ray Lucas	.75
59	Curtis Martin	.75
60	Vinny Testaverde	.75
61	Tim Brown	.75
62	Rich Gannon	.50
63	Tyrone Wheatley	.50
64	Napoleon Kaufman	.75
65	Duce Staley	.75
66	Donovan McNabb	1.25
67	Troy Edwards	.50
68	Jerome Bettis	.75
69	Kordell Stewart	.75
70	Marshall Faulk	.75
71	Kurt Warner	3.50
72	Isaac Bruce	.75
73	Torry Holt	.75
74	Ryan Leaf	.75
75	Jim Harbaugh	.50
76	Jerry Rice	1.50
77	Terrell Owens	.75
78	Jeff Garcia	.75
79	Ricky Watters	.50
80	Jon Kitna	.75
81	Derrick Mayes	.50
82	Shaun King	1.25
83	Mike Alstott	.75
84	Keyshawn Johnson	.75
85	Eddie George	1.00
86	Steve McNair	.75
87	Jevon Kearse	.75
88	Brad Johnson	.75
89	Stephen Davis	.75
90	Michael Westbrook	.50
91	*Anthony Lucas*	7.00
92	*Avion Black*	7.00
93	*Corey Moore*	7.00
94	*Chris Cole*	7.00
95	*Chris Hovan*	10.00
96	*Dante Hall*	7.00
97	*Darrell Jackson*	25.00
98	*Deltha O'Neal*	7.00
99	*Doug Chapman*	7.00
100	*Doug Johnson*	20.00
101	*Erron Kinney*	7.00
102	*Frank Moreau*	25.00
103	*Patrick Pass*	10.00
104	*Gari Scott*	7.00
105	*Giovanni Carmazzi*	25.00
106	*JaJuan Dawson*	25.00
107	*James Williams*	7.00
108	*Jarious Jackson*	12.00
109	*John Abraham*	7.00
110	*Keith Bulluck*	7.00
111	*Jonas Lewis*	7.00
112	*Mike Green*	7.00
113	*Ronney Jenkins*	7.00
114	*Michael Wiley*	15.00
115	*Mike Anderson*	60.00
116	*Mareno Philyaw*	7.00
117	*Muneer Moore*	7.00
118	*Paul Smith*	7.00
119	*Raynoch Thompson*	7.00
120	*Rob Morris*	10.00
121	*Ron Dixon*	15.00
122	*Rondell Mealey*	10.00
124	*Shaun Ellis*	7.00
125	*Charles Lee*	10.00
126	*Shyrone Stith*	15.00
127	*Thomas Hamner*	7.00
128	*Tim Rattay*	25.00
129	*Todd Husak*	15.00
130	*Tom Brady*	70.00
131	*Trevor Gaylor*	7.00
132	*Windrell Hayes*	7.00
133	*Anthony Becht*	30.00
134	*Brian Urlacher*	125.00
135	*Bubba Franks*	40.00
136	*Chad Pennington*	100.00
137	*Chris Redman*	60.00
138	*Corey Simon*	30.00
139	*Curtis Keaton*	20.00
140	*Danny Farmer*	20.00
141	*Dennis Northcutt*	20.00
142	*Dez White*	20.00
143	*J.R. Redmond*	20.00
144	*Jamal Lewis*	100.00
145	*Jerry Porter*	30.00
146	*Joe Hamilton*	20.00
147	*Laveranues Coles*	40.00
148	*R. Jay Soward*	20.00
149	*Reuben Droughns*	20.00
150	*Ron Dayne*	75.00
151	*Ron Dugans*	30.00
152	*Shaun Alexander*	100.00
153	*Sylvester Morris*	40.00
154	*Tee Martin*	30.00
155	*Thomas Jones*	30.00
156	*Todd Pinkston*	30.00
157	*Travis Prentice*	30.00
158	*Travis Taylor*	50.00
159	*Trung Canidate*	30.00
160	*Courtney Brown 500*	100.00
161	*Plaxico Burress 500*	175.00

2001 SP Authentic

		MT
Complete Set (190):		25.00
Common Player:		.15
Minor Stars:		.30
Pack (5):		5.00
Wax Box (24):		100.00
1	Jake Plummer	.50
2	Thomas Jones	.30
3	Frank Sanders	.15
4	Jamal Anderson	.50
5	Chris Chandler	.30
6	Tony Martin	.15
7	Jamal Lewis	1.50
8	Elvis Grbac	.30
9	Travis Taylor	.50
10	Peerless Price	.30
11	Rob Johnson	.30
12	Eric Moulds	.50
13	Muhsin Muhammad	.30
14	Isaac Byrd	.15
15	Wesley Walls	.30
16	James Allen	.30
17	Marcus Robinson	.50
18	Brian Urlacher	1.25
19	Jon Kitna	.30
20	Peter Warrick	.60
21	Corey Dillon	.50
22	Kevin Johnson	.30
23	JaJuan Dawson	.15
24	Tim Couch	.75
25	Raghib Ismail	.15
26	Emmitt Smith	1.50
27	Joey Galloway	.50
28	Terrell Davis	1.25
29	Mike Anderson	1.00
30	Brian Griese	.60
31	Ed McCaffrey	.50
32	Charlie Batch	.50
33	James O. Stewart	.30
34	Johnnie Morton	.30
35	Brett Favre	2.50
36	Antonio Freeman	.50
37	Bill Schroeder	.30
38	Ahman Green	.50
39	Peyton Manning	2.00
40	Edgerrin James	1.75
41	Marvin Harrison	.50
42	Mark Brunell	.60
43	Fred Taylor	.60
44	Jimmy Smith	.50
45	Tony Gonzalez	.30
46	Trent Green	.30
47	Oronde Gadsden	.15
48	Jay Fiedler	.50
49	Lamar Smith	.30
50	Randy Moss	2.00
51	Cris Carter	.50
52	Daunte Culpepper	1.25
53	Drew Bledsoe	.60
54	Terry Glenn	.30
55	Antowain Smith	.30
56	Ricky Williams	1.00
57	Joe Horn	.30
58	Aaron Brooks	.50
59	Kerry Collins	.30
60	Tiki Barber	.30
61	Ron Dayne	1.25
62	Vinny Testaverde	.30
63	Wayne Chrebet	.30
64	Curtis Martin	.50
65	Tim Brown	.50
66	Rich Gannon	.30
67	Jerry Rice	1.25
68	Duce Staley	.50
69	Donovan McNabb	1.00
70	Kordell Stewart	.50
71	Jerome Bettis	.50
72	Marshall Faulk	.75
73	Kurt Warner	2.50
74	Isaac Bruce	.50
75	Doug Flutie	.30
76	Junior Seau	.30
77	Jeff Garcia	.50
78	Garrison Hearst	.30
79	Terrell Owens	.50
80	Ricky Watters	.30
81	Matt Hasselbeck	.40
82	Brad Johnson	.30
83	Warrick Dunn	.50
84	Mike Alstott	.50
85	Kevin Dyson	.30
86	Eddie George	.75
87	Steve McNair	.50
88	Champ Bailey	.30
89	Michael Westbrook	.30
90	Stephen Davis	.50
91	*Michael Vick 250*	400.00
92	*Rod Gardner 250*	125.00
93	*Freddie Mitchell 250*	125.00
94	*Koren Robinson 500*	60.00
95	*David Terrell 500*	80.00
96	*Michael Bennett 800*	60.00
97	*Robert Ferguson 800*	20.00
98	*Deuce McAllister 800*	45.00
99	*Travis Henry 800*	40.00
100	*Andre Carter 800*	20.00
101	*Drew Brees 800*	100.00
102	*Santana Moss 500*	60.00
103	*Chris Weinke 390*	70.00
104	*Chad Johnson 160*	60.00
105	*Reggie Wayne 800*	35.00
106	*Kevan Barlow 500*	45.00
107	*Chris Chambers 500*	75.00
108	*Todd Heap 500*	25.00
109	*Anthony Thomas 500*	120.00
110	*James Jackson 500*	30.00
111	*Rudi Johnson 500*	25.00
112	*Mike McMahon 800*	50.00
113	*Josh Heupel 800*	25.00
114	*Travis Minor 500*	40.00
115	*Quincy Morgan 500*	40.00
116	*Dan Morgan 500*	25.00
117	*Jesse Palmer 500*	30.00
118	*Sage Rosenfels 300*	40.00
119	*Marques Tuiasosopo 800*	40.00
120	*LaDainian Tomlinson 500*	120.00
121	*Adam Archuleta 550*	30.00
122	*Alex Bannister 550*	20.00
123	*Alge Crumpler 550*	20.00
124	*Arnold Jackson 550*	15.00
125	*Bobby Newcombe 550*	15.00
126	*Brandon Manumaleuna 550*	12.00
127	*Cedrick Wilson 550*	12.00
128	*Brian Allen 550*	12.00
129	*Dadrian Dee Brown 550*	12.00
130	*Darnerian McCants 550*	12.00
131	*Dave Dickenson 550*	20.00
132	*Derrick Blaylock 550*	12.00
133	*Eddie Berlin 550*	15.00
134	*Francis St. Paul 550*	12.00
135	*Jamar Fletcher 550*	15.00
136	*Josh Booty 550*	20.00
137	*Scotty Anderson 550*	12.00
138	*Ken-Yon Rambo 550*	15.00
139	*Kenyatta Walker 550*	12.00
140	*Kevin Kasper 550*	20.00
141	*Marvin "Snoop" Minnis 550*	35.00
142	*T.J. Houshmandzadeh 550*	15.00
143	*Quincy Carter 550*	85.00
144	*Ronney Daniels 550*	12.00
145	*Sedrick Hodge 550*	12.00
146	*Stevonne (Steve) Smith 550*	12.00
147	*Tim Hasselbeck 550*	15.00
148	*Vinny Sutherland 550*	12.00
149	*Richard Seymour 550*	20.00
150	*Jamie Winborn 550*	15.00
151	*Gerard Warren 800*	12.00
152	*Justin Smith 800*	12.00
153	*David Martin 800*	10.00
154	*Jamal Reynolds 800*	12.00
155	*Dominic Rhodes 800*	45.00
156	*Nate Clements 800*	10.00
157	*Michael Lewis 800*	10.00
158	*Andre King 800*	10.00
159	*Benjamin Gay 800*	30.00
160	*Correll Buckhalter 800*	25.00
161	*Roderick Robinson 800*	10.00
162	*Moran Norris 800*	10.00
163	*Onome Ojo 800*	10.00
164	*Will Allen 800*	10.00
165	*Jonathan Carter 800*	10.00
166	*LaMont Jordan 800*	15.00
167	*DeLawrence Grant 800*	10.00
168	*Derrick Gibson 800*	10.00
169	*A.J. Feeley 800*	10.00
170	*Tim Baker 800*	10.00
171	*Kendrell Bell 800*	40.00
172	*Zeke Moreno 800*	10.00
173	*Carlos Polk 800*	10.00
174	*Ken Lucas 800*	10.00
175	*Heath Evans 800*	10.00
176	*Elvis Joseph 800*	10.00
177	*Damione Lewis 800*	10.00
178	*Tommy Polley 800*	10.00
179	*Fred Smoot 800*	12.00
180	*Jason Brookins 800*	15.00
181	*Nick Goings 800*	12.00
182	*Drew Bennett 800*	15.00
183	*Justin McCareins 800*	10.00
184	*Kabeer Gbaja-Biamila 800*	30.00
185	*Edgerton Hartwell 800*	10.00
186	*Robert Carswell 800*	10.00
187	*Aaron Schobel 800*	10.00
188	*Dan Alexander 800*	12.00
189	*Jamie Winborn 800*	10.00
190	*Karon Riley 800*	10.00

2001 SP Authentic Sign of the Times

		MT
Common Player:		12.00
Inserted 1:47		
MA	Marcus Allen	20.00
TBa	Tiki Barber	12.00
CB	Charlie Batch	15.00
JBl	Jeff Blake	12.00
DB	Drew Bledsoe	25.00
TB	Terry Bradshaw	50.00
DBr	Drew Brees	50.00
JBr	Jim Brown	60.00
TBr	Tim Brown	15.00
WC	Wayne Chrebet	12.00
DC	Daunte Culpepper	40.00
SD	Stephen Davis	15.00
TDa	Terrell Davis	40.00
TDi	Trent Dilfer	12.00
DF	Doug Flutie	18.00
JoG	Joey Galloway	12.00
JGa	Jeff Garcia	30.00
JGe	Jeff George	12.00
AG	Ahman Green	15.00
TH	Torry Holt	15.00
PH	Paul Hornung	25.00
BJ	Brad Johnson	18.00
EJ	Ed "Too Tall" Jones	25.00
JJ	Joe Jurivicius	12.00
JK	Jim Kelly	25.00
HL	Howie Long	35.00
JL	John Lynch	15.00
PM	Peyton Manning	45.00
DM	Dan Marino	75.00
CM	Cade McNown	12.00
JM	Joe Montana	100.00
JMo	Johnnie Morton	12.00
RM	Randy Moss	85.00
JN	Joe Namath	60.00
TO	Terrell Owens	20.00
JPl	Jake Plummer	15.00
JP	Jim Plunkett	18.00
JR	John Riggins	40.00
JS	Junior Seau	15.00
JSe	Jason Sehorn	12.00
AS	Akili Smith	12.00
RS	Roger Staubach	45.00
KS	Kordell Stewart	18.00
CT	Charley Taylor	12.00
VT	Vinny Testaverde	12.00
AT	Amani Toomer	12.00
JU	Johnny Unitas	50.00
BU	Brian Urlacher	30.00
KW	Kurt Warner	70.00
PW	Peter Warrick	18.00
RW	Ricky Williams	30.00
CW	Charles Woodson	12.00
SY	Steve Young	45.00
JY	Jack Youngblood	12.00

2001 SP Authentic Stat Jerseys

		MT
Common Player:		8.00
Inserted 1:23		
SP-TA	Troy Aikman 23	65.00
SP-TA	Troy Aikman 165	30.00
SP-MA	Mike Alstott 1219	10.00
SP-JA	Jesse Armstead 529	8.00
SP-MB	Michael Bennett 55	40.00
SP-MB	Michael Bennett 1681	15.00
SP-DB	Drew Brees 194	45.00
SP-DB	Drew Brees 349	25.00
SP-IB	Isaac Bruce 1471	12.00
SP-MBr	Mark Brunell 236	15.00
SP-TC	Tim Couch 1483	15.00
SP-DC	Daunte Culpepper 40	50.00
SP-DC	Daunte Culpepper 470	20.00
SP-SD	Stephen Davis 1318	8.00
SP-RD	Ron Dayne 770	15.00
SP-WD	Warrick Dunn 422	10.00
SP-WD	Warrick Dunn 1133	8.00
SP-JE	John Elway 300	45.00
SP-BF	Brett Favre 255	45.00
SP-BF	Brett Favre 260	45.00
SP-MF	Marshall Faulk 26	150.00
SP-MF	Marshall Faulk 1359	15.00
SP-JF	Jay Fiedler 225	15.00
SP-DF	Doug Flutie 129	25.00
SP-AF	Antonio Freeman 1424	8.00
SP-BG	Brian Griese 102	30.00
SP-BG	Brian Griese 327	20.00
SP-IH	Ike Hilliard 787	8.00
SP-JK	Jim Kelly 237	30.00
SP-JK	Jim Kelly 403	20.00
SP-RL	Ray Lewis 137	25.00
SP-PM	Peyton Manning 33	85.00
SP-PM	Peyton Manning 87	45.00
SP-PM	Peyton Manning 94	45.00
SP-PM	Peyton Manning 231	30.00
SP-PM	Peyton Manning 440	25.00
SP-DM	Dan Marino 48	100.00
SP-DM	Dan Marino 420	45.00
SP-CM	Curtis Martin 1204	10.00
SP-RM	Randy Moss 43	85.00
SP-RM	Randy Moss 226	35.00
SP-JR	Jerry Rice 1281	20.00
SP-BS	Barry Sanders 99	70.00
SP-BS	Barry Sanders 1000	25.00
SP-WS	Warren Sapp 58	30.00
SP-JS	Junior Seau 1058	8.00
SP-SE	Jason Sehorn 260	12.00
SP-ES	Emmitt Smith 156	70.00
SP-FT	Fred Taylor 1399	12.00
SP-LT	LaDainian Tomlinson 113	60.00
SP-LT	LaDainian Tomlinson 196	50.00
SP-AT	Amani Toomer 1094	8.00
SP-MV	Michael Vick 32	150.00
SP-MV	Michael Vick 1234	40.00
SP-CW	Chris Weinke 16	75.00
SP-CW	Chris Weinke 223	25.00

Post-1980 cards in Near Mint condition will generally sell for about 75% of the quoted Mint value. Excellent-condition cards bring no more than 40%.

2001 SP Game-Used Edition

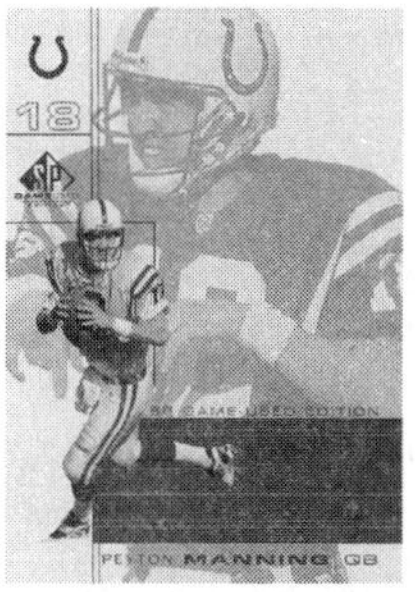

		MT
Complete Set (150):		1800.
Common Player:		.50
Minor Stars:		1.00
Common Rookie Jersey:		25.00
Common Rookie:		10.00
Production 500 Sets		
Pack (3):		30.00
Wax Box (6):		150.00
1	Jake Plummer	2.00
2	David Boston	2.00
3	Frank Sanders	.50
4	Jamal Anderson	2.00
5	Doug Johnson	.50
6	Shawn Jefferson	.50
7	Jamal Lewis	5.00
8	Shannon Sharpe	.50
9	Qadry Ismail	.50
10	Shawn Bryson	.50
11	Rob Johnson	.50
12	Eric Moulds	.50
13	Muhsin Muhammad	.50
14	Brad Hoover	2.00
15	Tim Biakabutuka	.50
16	Cade McNown	2.00
17	Marcus Robinson	2.00
18	Brian Urlacher	4.00
19	Akili Smith	2.00
20	Peter Warrick	4.00
21	Corey Dillon	2.00
22	Kevin Johnson	2.00
23	Rickey Dudley	.50
24	Tim Couch	3.00
25	Tony Banks	.50
26	Emmitt Smith	6.00
27	Carl Pickens	.50
28	Terrell Davis	5.00
29	Mike Anderson	6.00
30	Brian Griese	2.50
31	Ed McCaffrey	2.00
32	Charlie Batch	2.00
33	Germane Crowell	.50
34	James O. Stewart	.50
35	Brett Favre	10.00
36	Antonio Freeman	2.00
37	Ahman Green	.50
38	Peyton Manning	8.00
39	Edgerrin James	7.00
40	Marvin Harrison	2.00
41	Mark Brunell	2.50
42	Fred Taylor	3.00
43	Jimmy Smith	.50
44	Tony Gonzalez	.50
45	Derrick Alexander	.50
46	Oronde Gadsden	.50
47	Ray Lucas	.50
48	Lamar Smith	.50
49	Randy Moss	8.00
50	Cris Carter	2.00
51	Daunte Culpepper	4.00
52	Drew Bledsoe	2.50
53	Terry Glenn	.50
54	Ricky Williams	3.00
55	Jeff Blake	.50
56	Joe Horn	.50
57	Aaron Brooks	2.00
58	Kerry Collins	.50
59	Tiki Barber	.50
60	Ron Dayne	4.00
61	Vinny Testaverde	.50
62	Wayne Chrebet	.50
63	Curtis Martin	2.00
64	Tim Brown	2.00
65	Rich Gannon	.50
66	Tyrone Wheatley	.50
67	Duce Staley	2.00
68	Donovan McNabb	3.00
69	Kordell Stewart	2.00
70	Jerome Bettis	2.00
71	Marshall Faulk	2.50
72	Kurt Warner	8.00
73	Isaac Bruce	2.00
74	Doug Flutie	2.50
75	Curtis Conway	.50
76	Jeff Garcia	2.00
77	Jerry Rice	5.00
78	Charlie Garner	.50
79	Terrell Owens	2.00
80	Ricky Watters	.50
81	Matt Hasselbeck	.50
82	Levon Kirkland	.50
83	Keyshawn Johnson	2.00
84	Brad Johnson	2.00
85	Mike Alstott	2.00
86	Eddie George	2.50
87	Steve McNair	2.00
88	Jeff George	.50
89	Michael Westbrook	2.00
90	Stephen Davis	2.00
91	*Michael Vick*	125.00
92	*Chris Weinke*	60.00
93	*Drew Brees*	100.00
94	*Deuce McAllister*	50.00
95	*Michael Bennett*	60.00
96	*LaDainian Tomlinson*	125.00
97	*Kevan Barlow*	40.00
98	*Travis Minor*	40.00
99	*Rudi Johnson*	30.00
100	*Todd Heap*	30.00
101	*Freddie Mitchell*	50.00
102	*Santana Moss*	50.00
103	*Reggie Wayne*	40.00
104	*Koren Robinson*	50.00
105	*Josh Heupel*	30.00

106	*Rod Gardner*	50.00
107	*Quincy Morgan*	30.00
108	*Chad Johnson*	40.00
109	*Dan Morgan*	40.00
110	*Gerard Warren*	40.00
111	*Chris Chambers*	60.00
112	*James Jackson*	25.00
113	*Jesse Palmer*	30.00
114	*Sage Rosenfels*	40.00
115	*Mike McMahon*	40.00
116	*Marques Tuiasosopo*	50.00
117	*Robert Ferguson*	20.00
118	*Travis Henry*	50.00
119	*Richard Seymour*	25.00
120	*Andre Carter*	40.00
121	*LaMont Jordan*	20.00
122	*Vinny Sutherland*	12.00
123	*Nate Clements*	10.00
124	*David Terrell*	60.00
125	*A.J. Freely*	10.00
126	*David Rivers*	10.00
127	*Marvin "Snoop" Minnis*	25.00
128	*Josh Booty*	15.00
129	*Correl Buckhalter*	25.00
130	*Will Allen*	10.00
131	*Dan Alexander*	20.00
132	*Leonard Davis*	10.00
133	*Anthony Thomas*	75.00
134	*Alge Crumpler*	15.00
135	*Jamal Reynolds*	15.00
136	*Ken-Yon Rambo*	15.00
137	*Bobby Newcombe*	15.00
138	*Alex Bannister*	20.00
139	*Jabari Holloway*	12.00
140	*Jamar Fletcher*	12.00
141	*Adam Archuleta*	12.00
142	*Heath Evans*	10.00
143	*Scotty Anderson*	10.00
144	*Moran Norris*	10.00
145	*Justin Smith*	20.00
146	*Quincy Carter*	30.00
147	*Ronney Daniels*	10.00
148	*Ben Leard*	10.00
149	*Fred Smoot*	15.00
150	*Milton Wynn*	10.00

2001 SP Game-Used Edition Fabric Jersey

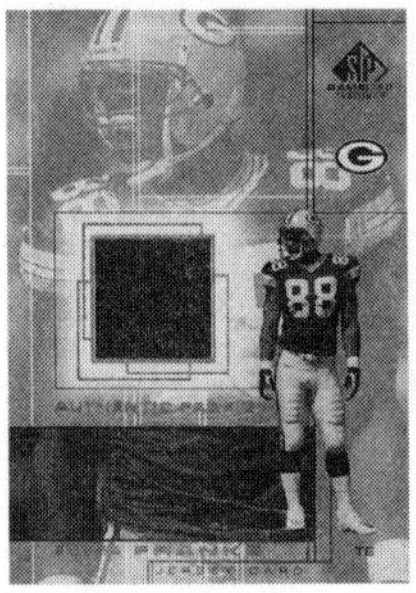

		MT
Common Player:		8.00
Inserted 1:1		
Gold Cards:		2x-4x
Production 25 Sets		
Multi-Colored Swatches:		1.5x
TA	Troy Aikman	45.00
MA	Marcus Allen	20.00
AL	Mike Alstott	12.00
JA	Jamal Anderson	8.00
CB	Champ Bailey	12.00
BA	Tiki Barber	12.00
JB	Jerome Bettis	12.00
DB	Drew Bledsoe	20.00
BO	David Boston	12.00
TB	Terry Bradshaw	65.00
BR	Drew Brees	70.00
IB	Isaac Bruce	12.00
MB	Mark Brunell	20.00
PB	Plaxico Burress	12.00
CC	Chris Chambers	15.00
CH	Chris Chandler	8.00
KC	Kerry Collins	8.00
CO	Curtis Conway	8.00
TC	Tim Couch	20.00
DC	Daunte Culpepper	50.00
SD	Stephen Davis	12.00
TD	Terrell Davis	25.00
RD	Ron Dayne	15.00
CD	Corey Dillon	12.00
WD	Warrick Dunn	12.00
JE	John Elway	60.00
MF	Marshall Faulk	20.00
BF	Brett Favre	50.00
DF	Bubba Franks	8.00
AF	Antonio Freeman	12.00
JG	Jeff Garcia	20.00
TG	Terry Glenn	12.00
AG	Ahman Green	12.00
BG	Brian Griese	20.00
AZ	Az-Zahir Hakim	8.00
IH	Ike Hilliard	8.00
TH	Torry Holt	12.00
EJ	Edgerrin James	60.00
BJ	Brad Johnson	12.00
TJ	Thomas Jones	12.00
SK	Shaun King	12.00
DL	Dorsey Levens	12.00
JL	Jamal Lewis	30.00
RL	Ray Lewis	12.00
PM	Peyton Manning	45.00
MC	Ed McCaffrey	12.00
DM	Deuce McCallister	45.00
FM	Freddie Mitchell	25.00
JM	Joe Montana	85.00
RM	Randy Moss	60.00
EM	Eric Moulds	12.00
TO	Terrell Owens	12.00
WP	Walter Payton	100.00
MP	Michael Pittman	8.00
JP	Jake Plummer	8.00
JR	Jerry Rice	30.00
FS	Frank Sanders	8.00
WS	Warren Sapp	8.00
JS	Junior Seau	8.00
SE	Jason Sehorn	8.00
AS	Akili Smith	12.00
JS	Justin Smith	8.00
RS	Rod Smith	12.00
BS	Bart Starr	75.00
KS	Kordell Stewart	12.00
JJ	J.J. Stokes	8.00
FT	Fran Tarkenton	45.00
FTa	Fred Taylor	20.00
LT	LaDainian Tomlinson	70.00
AT	Amani Toomer	8.00
MT	Marques Tuiasosopo	25.00
JU	Johnny Unitas	60.00
KW	Kurt Warner	40.00
PW	Peter Warrick	15.00
WE	Chris Weinke	40.00
MW	Michael Westbrook	8.00
CW	Charles Woodson	12.00

2001 SP Game-Used Edition Fabric Combo Jersey

		MT
Common Player:		50.00
Production 50 Sets		
2C-JS	Keyshawn Johnson, Warren Sapp	50.00
2C-MJ	Peyton Manning, Edgerrin James	175.00
2C-WH	Kurt Warner, Torry Holt	175.00
2C-FF	Brett Favre, Antonio Freeman	175.00
2C-DC	Ron Dayne, Kerry Collins	50.00
2C-BM	Mark Brunell, Keenan McCardell	50.00
2C-AS	Troy Aikman, Emmitt Smith	75.00
2C-WD	Peter Warrick, Corey Dillon	50.00
2C-SB	Kordell Stewart, Jerome Bettis	50.00
2C-BS	Frank Sanders, David Boston	50.00
2C-WB	Charles Woodson, Tim Brown	50.00
2C-OG	Terrell Owens, Jeff Garcia	50.00
2C-AD	Mike Alstott, Warrick Dunn	50.00
2C-CM	Cris Carter, Randy Moss	175.00
2C-CS	Doug Chapman, Robert Smith	50.00

2001 SP Game-Used Edition Fabric Triple Jersey

		MT
Common Player:		85.00
Production 25 Sets		
3C-FWM	Brett Favre, Kurt Warner, Peyton Manning	300.00
3C-DGJ	Terrell Davis, Eddie George, Edgerrin James	200.00
3C-HHB	Torry Holt, Az-Zahir Hakim, Isaac Bruce	85.00
3C-CMC	Cris Carter, Randy Moss, Daunte Culpepper	250.00
3C-DCB	Ron Dayne, Kerry Collins, Tiki Barber	125.00
3C-LLD	Jamal Lewis, Ray Lewis, Trent Dilfer	125.00

2000 SPx Spectrum Parallel

	MT
Spectrum Cards:	30x-60x
Spectrum Rookies:	1x
Spectrum Rookie Jersey:	1x
Production 25 Sets	

2000 SPx Game Jersey Greats

		MT
Production 400 Sets		
JU	Johnny Unitas 400	300.00

2000 SPx Highlight Heroes

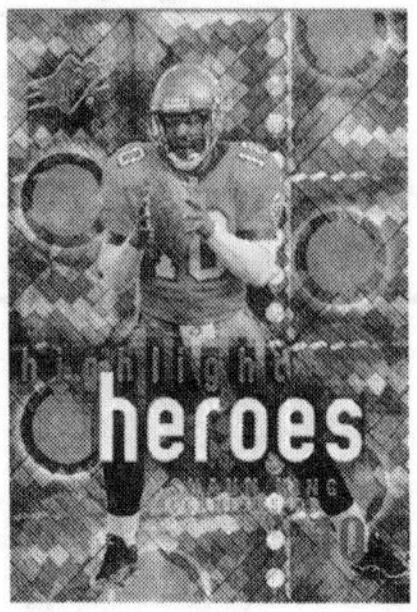

		MT
Complete Set (12):		15.00
Common Player:		1.00
Inserted 1:8		
HH1	Fred Taylor	2.00
HH2	Eddie George	1.50
HH3	Marshall Faulk	1.00
HH4	Shaun King	1.50
HH5	Cris Carter	1.00
HH6	Emmitt Smith	3.50
HH7	Jerry Rice	3.00
HH8	Tim Couch	2.00
HH9	Keyshawn Johnson	1.00
HH10	Troy Aikman	3.00
HH11	Terrell Davis	3.50
HH12	Ricky Williams	2.50

2000 SPx Powerhouse

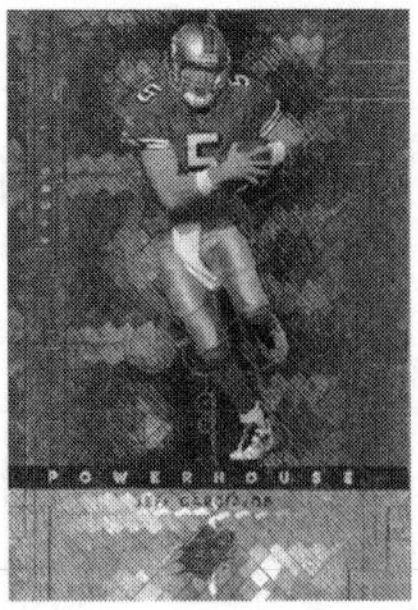

		MT
Complete Set (10):		7.00
Common Player:		.75
Minor Stars:		1.50
Inserted 1:9		
PH1	Akili Smith	1.50
PH2	Kevin Johnson	1.50
PH3	Olandis Gary	1.75
PH4	Jeff Garcia	1.50
PH5	Germane Crowell	.75
PH6	Donovan McNabb	2.00
PH7	Rob Johnson	.75
PH8	Marcus Robinson	1.50
PH9	Shaun King	2.00
PH10	Troy Edwards	.75

2000 SPx Prolifics

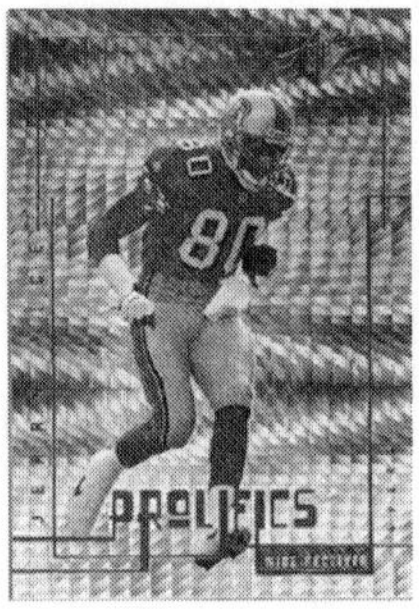

		MT
Complete Set (12):		30.00
Common Player:		2.00
Inserted 1:18		
P1	Stephen Davis	2.00
P2	Terrell Davis	6.00
P3	Jamal Anderson	2.00
P4	Jerry Rice	5.00
P5	Emmitt Smith	6.00
P6	Troy Aikman	5.00
P7	Cris Carter	2.00
P8	Brett Favre	8.00
P9	Mark Brunell	3.00
P10	Tim Couch	3.50
P11	Eddie George	2.50
P12	Marshall Faulk	2.00

2000 SPx SPXcitement

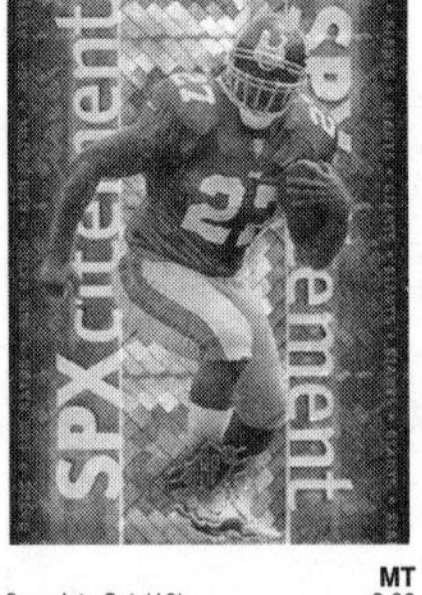

		MT
Complete Set (10):		8.00
Common Player:		.50
Inserted 1:5		
XC1	Plaxico Burress	1.50
XC2	Peter Warrick	3.00
XC3	Todd Pinkston	.50
XC4	Ron Dayne	4.00
XC5	Reuben Droughns	.50
XC6	Danny Farmer	.50
XC7	Bubba Franks	.50
XC8	Laveranues Coles	.50
XC9	Chad Pennington	2.50
XC10	J.R. Redmond	.50

Post-1980 cards in Near Mint condition will generally sell for about 75% of the quoted Mint value. Excellent-condition cards bring no more than 40%.

2000 SPx SPXtreme

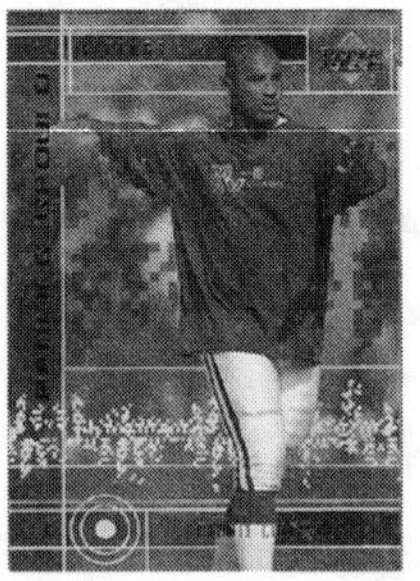

		MT
Complete Set (18):		45.00
Common Player:		2.00
Inserted 1:12		
X1	Isaac Bruce	2.00
X2	Cade McNown	2.50
X3	Daunte Culpepper	3.50
X4	Donovan McNabb	2.50
X5	Brett Favre	8.00
X6	Peyton Manning	8.00
X7	Edgerrin James	8.00
X8	Jon Kitna	2.00
X9	Mark Brunell	3.00
X10	Brad Johnson	2.00
X11	Jevon Kearse	2.00
X12	Curtis Martin	2.00
X13	Steve McNair	2.00
X14	Ricky Williams	4.00
X15	Stephen Davis	2.00
X16	Kurt Warner	10.00
X17	Marvin Harrison	2.00
X18	Randy Moss	8.00

2000 SPx Starscape

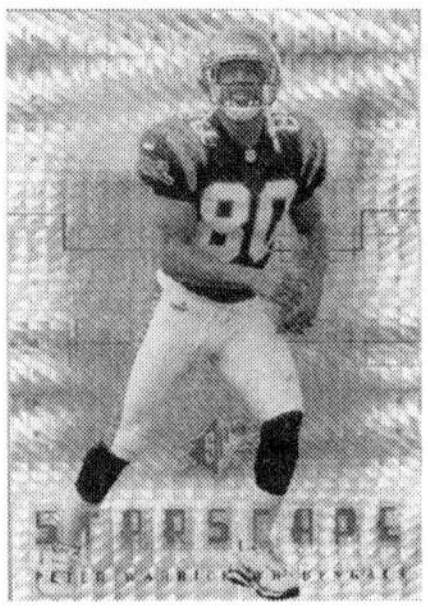

		MT
Complete Set (12):		45.00
Common Player:		2.00
Inserted 1:18		
RS1	Thomas Jones	3.50
RS2	Courtney Brown	2.00
RS3	Peter Warrick	8.50
RS4	Jamal Lewis	12.00
RS5	Sylvester Morris	4.50
RS6	Plaxico Burress	4.50
RS7	Travis Taylor	2.00
RS8	Chad Pennington	7.00
RS9	Ron Dayne	10.00
RS10	Shaun Alexander	6.00
RS11	Giovanni Carmazzi	2.00
RS12	Ron Dugans	2.00

2000 SPx Winning Materials

		MT
Common Player:		20.00
Inserted 1:83		
Autographed Cards:		2x-4x
Production 225 Cards:		
WMSA	Shaun Alexander	40.00
WMCB	Courtney Brown	20.00
WMPB	Plaxico Burress	35.00
WMTC	Trung Canidate	20.00
WMTD	Terrell Davis	45.00
WMRD	Ron Dayne	70.00
WMDR	Reuben Droughns	20.00
WMWD	Warrick Dunn	20.00
WMMF	Marshall Faulk	25.00
WMBF	Brett Favre	60.00
WMDF	Bubba Franks	20.00
WMEG	Eddie George	25.00
WMBG	Brian Griese	25.00
WMTH	Torry Holt	20.00
WMEJ	Edgerrin James	60.00
WMKJ	Keyshawn Johnson	20.00
WMTJ	Thomas Jones	25.00
WMSK	Shaun King	25.00
WMJL	Jamal Lewis	80.00
WMPM	Peyton Manning	60.00
WMTM	Tee Martin	20.00
WMMC	Steve McNair	20.00
WMCM	Cade McNown	25.00
WMSM	Sylvester Morris	35.00
WMRM	Randy Moss	60.00
WMTO	Terrell Owens	20.00
WMCP	Chad Pennington	50.00
WMJP	Jerry Porter	20.00
WMCR	Chris Redman	25.00
WMJR	J.R. Redmond	20.00
WMJR	Jerry Rice	45.00
WMRJ	R. Jay Soward	20.00
WMJJ	J.J. Stokes	20.00
WMKW	Kurt Warner	75.00
WMPW	Peter Warrick	60.00
WMDW	Dez White	20.00

A player's name in *italic type* indicates a rookie card.

2000 SPx Autograph Winning Materials

		MT
Complete Set (18):		
Common Player:		50.00
SA	Shaun Alexander	75.00
CB	Courtney Brown	50.00
TC	Tim Couch	75.00
TD	Terrell Davis	75.00
RD	Ron Dayne	50.00
EG	Eddie George	75.00
BG	Brian Griese	75.00
EJ	Edgerrin James	125.00
KJ	Keyshawn Johnson	75.00
TJ	Thomas Jones	50.00
JL	Jamal Lewis	125.00
PM	Peyton Manning	175.00
TM	Tee Martin	50.00
RM	Randy Moss	175.00
CP	Chad Pennington	100.00
TT	Travis Taylor	50.00
KW	Kurt Warner	175.00
PW	Peter Warrick	75.00

2001 SPx

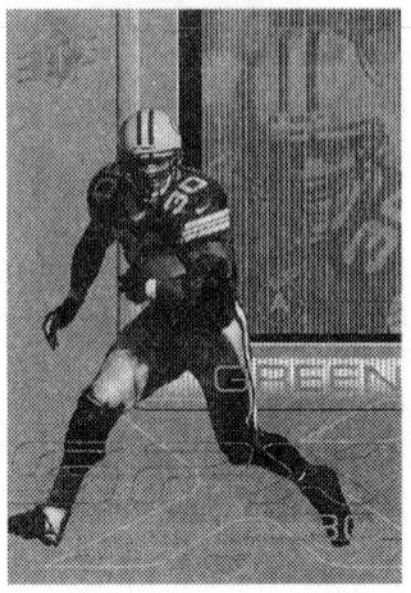

		MT
Complete Set (90):		20.00
Common Player:		.20
Minor Stars:		.40
Common Rookie:		4.00
Pack (4):		7.00
Box (18):		100.00
1	Jake Plummer	.60
2	David Boston	.60
3	Jamal Anderson	.40
4	Chris Chandler	.40
5	Tony Martin	.40
6	Elvis Grbac	.50
7	Qadry Ismail	.20
8	Ray Lewis	.50
9	Rob Johnson	.50
10	Shawn Bryson	.20
11	Eric Moulds	.60
12	Tim Biakabutuka	.20
13	Jeff Lewis	.40
14	Muhsin Muhammad	.20
15	Shane Matthews	.40
16	Marcus Robinson	.60
17	Brian Urlacher	1.50
18	Jon Kitna	.40
19	Peter Warrick	.60
20	Corey Dillon	.60
21	Tim Couch	1.00
22	Travis Prentice	.20
23	Kevin Johnson	.75
24	Raghib Ismail	.20
25	Emmitt Smith	2.00
26	Joey Galloway	.50
27	Terrell Davis	1.50
28	Brian Griese	1.00
29	Rod Smith	.60
30	Ed McCaffrey	.60
31	Charlie Batch	.40
32	Germane Crowell	.20
33	James O. Stewart	.40
34	Brett Favre	3.00
35	Antonio Freeman	.60
36	Ahman Green	.75
37	Peyton Manning	2.50
38	Edgerrin James	2.00
39	Marvin Harrison	.75
40	Mark Brunell	1.00
41	Fred Taylor	1.00
42	Jimmy Smith	.50
43	Tony Gonzalez	.50
44	Trent Green	.50
45	Priest Holmes	.40
46	Lamar Smith	.40
47	Jay Fiedler	.50
48	Oronde Gadsden	.20
49	Daunte Culpepper	1.50
50	Randy Moss	2.50
51	Cris Carter	.75
52	Drew Bledsoe	1.00
53	Troy Brown	.40
54	Ricky Williams	1.25
55	Joe Horn	.40
56	Aaron Brooks	1.00
57	Albert Connell	.20
58	Kerry Collins	.75
59	Tiki Barber	.40
60	Ron Dayne	.40
61	Vinny Testaverde	.60
62	Wayne Chrebet	.50
63	Curtis Martin	.75
64	Tim Brown	.75
65	Jerry Rice	2.00
66	Rich Gannon	.60
67	Duce Staley	.40
68	Donovan McNabb	1.50
69	Kordell Stewart	.50
70	Jerome Bettis	.50
71	Marshall Faulk	1.00
72	Kurt Warner	2.50
73	Isaac Bruce	.75
74	Torry Holt	.75
75	Doug Flutie	1.00
76	Junior Seau	.50
77	Jeff Garcia	1.00
78	Garrison Hearst	.40
79	Terrell Owens	.60
80	Ricky Watters	.40
81	Matt Hasselbeck	.50
82	Brad Johnson	.60
83	Keyshawn Johnson	.75
84	Warrick Dunn	.40
85	Mike Alstott	.40
86	Kevin Dyson	.40
87	Eddie George	1.00
88	Steve McNair	.75
89	Michael Westbrook	.50
90	Stephen Davis	.60
91	*Deuce McAllister*	125.00
92	*Freddie Mitchell*	60.00
93	*Koren Robinson*	12.00
94	*David Terrell*	20.00
95	*Michael Vick*	300.00
96	*Michael Bennett*	60.00
97	*Robert Ferguson*	10.00
98	*Rod Gardner*	12.00
99	*Travis Henry*	40.00
100	*Chad Johnson*	25.00
101	*Drew Brees*	250.00
102	*Santana Moss*	40.00
103	*Chris Weinke*	50.00
104	*Richard Seymour*	20.00
105	*Reggie Wayne*	12.00
106	*Kevan Barlow*	30.00
107	*Chris Chambers*	60.00
108	*Todd Heap*	12.00
109	*Anthony Thomas*	150.00
110	*James Jackson*	20.00
111	*Rudi Johnson*	12.00
112	*Mike McMahon*	50.00
113	*Josh Heupel*	35.00
114	*Travis Minor*	25.00
115	*Quincy Morgan*	10.00
116	*Dan Morgan*	15.00
117	*Jesse Palmer*	25.00
118	*Sage Rosenfels*	25.00
119	*Marques Tuiasosopo*	40.00
120	*Darnerian McCants*	6.00
121	*Marvin "Snoop" Minnis*	10.00
122	*LaDainian Tomlinson*	150.00
123	*Quincy Carter*	20.00
124	*Arnold Jackson*	4.00
125	*Justin McCareins*	6.00
126	*Eddie Berlin*	6.00
127	*Quentin McCord*	4.00
128	*Vinny Sutherland*	6.00
129	*Willie Middlebrooks*	6.00
130	*Dan Alexander*	6.00
131	*Dadrian "Dee" Brown*	6.00
132	*Andre Carter*	6.00
133	*Justin Smith*	6.00
134	*T.J. Houshmandzadeh*	4.00
135	*Andre King*	6.00
136	*Nick Goings*	8.00
137	*Scotty Anderson*	6.00
138	*David Martin*	6.00
139	*Derrick Blaylock*	4.00
140	*Onome Ojo*	4.00
141	*Jonathan Carter*	4.00
142	*Lamont Jordon*	12.00
143	*Dominic Rhodes*	25.00
145	*A.J. Feeley*	8.00
146	*Correll Buckhalter*	12.00
147	*Steve Smith*	6.00
148	*Dave Dickenson*	10.00
149	*Cedrick Wilson*	6.00
150	*Jamie Winborn*	4.00
151	*Alex Bannister*	6.00
152	*Heath Evans*	4.00
153	*Josh Booty*	8.00
154	*Adam Archuleta*	8.00
155	*Francis St. Paul*	4.00
156	*Andre Dyson*	6.00

2001 SPx "Winning Materials"

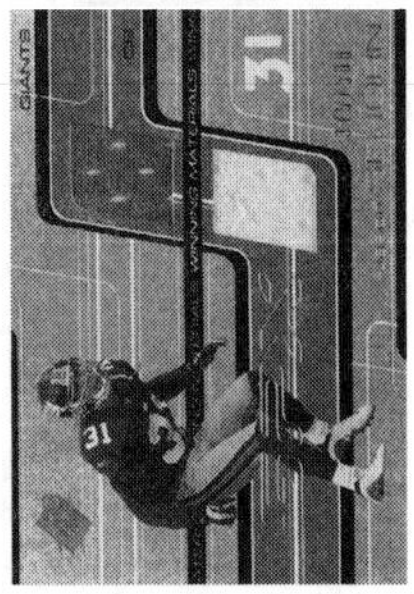

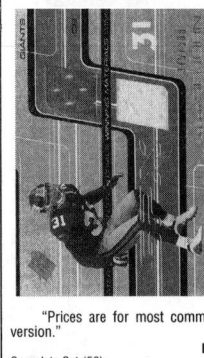

"Prices are for most common version."

	MT
Complete Set (58):	
Common Player:	10.00
WM-TATroy Aikman	25.00
WM-MAMike Alstott	10.00
WM-TBTiki Barber	10.00
WM-KBKevan Barlow	10.00
WM-BEMichael Bennett	25.00
WM-BODavid Boston	15.00
WM-DBDrew Brees	20.00
WM-DB2Drew Brees	20.00
WM-MBMark Brunell	15.00
WM-ACAndre Carter	10.00
WM-CHChris Chambers	25.00
WM-TCTim Couch	20.00
WM-DCDaunte Culpepper	20.00
WM-RDRon Dayne	15.00
WM-MFMarshall Faulk	20.00
WM-BFBrett Favre	40.00
WM-BF2Brett Favre	40.00
WM-RFRobert Ferguson	20.00
WM-JFJay Fiedler	10.00
WM-DFDoug Flutie	15.00
WM-AFAntonio Freeman	10.00
WM-RGRich Gannon	10.00
WM-JGJeff Garcia	15.00
WM-GARod Gardner	10.00
WM-CGCharlie Garner	10.00
WM-EGElvis Grbac	10.00
WM-BGBrian Griese	15.00
WM-HETravis Henry	10.00
WM-JJJames Jackson	10.00
WM-EJEdgerrin James	30.00
WM-TJThomas Jones	10.00
WM-PMPeyton Manning	40.00
WM-DUDeuce McAllister	10.00
WM-FMFreddie Mitchell	10.00
WM-MODan Morgan	10.00

WM-QM	Quincy Morgan	10.00
WM-RM	Randy Moss	20.00
WM-RM2	Randy Moss	20.00
WM-SM	Santana Moss	10.00
WM-TO	Terrell Owen	10.00
WM-PA	Jesse Palmer	10.00
WM-JP	Jake Plummer	10.00
WM-JR	Jerry Rice	25.00
WM-KR	Koren Robinson	10.00
WM-JS	Junior Seau	15.00
WM-SE	Jason Sehorn	10.00
WM-AS	Akili Smith	10.00
WM-FT	Fred Taylor	10.00
WM-DT	David Terrell	10.00
WM-AT	Anthony Thomas	40.00
WM-LT	LaDainian Tomlinson	30.00
WM-LT2	LaDainian Tomlinson	30.00
WM-MT	Marques Tuiasosopo	15.00
WM-MV	Michael Vick	40.00
WM-KW	Kurt Warner	20.00
WM-PW	Peter Warrick	10.00
WM-MA	Reggie Wayne	10.00
WM-CW	Chris Weinke	20.00

1993 Spectrum QB Club Tribute Sheet Promos

The two-sheet, 8-1/2" x 11" set, featuring Aikman and Marino, was issued as a preview for the 1993 Spectrum Quarterback Club Tribute Sheets. Production was limited to 5,000 sheets each.

		MT
Complete Set (2):		10.00
Common Player:		4.00
1	Troy Aikman	4.00
2	Dan Marino	6.00

1993 Spectrum QB Club Tribute Sheets

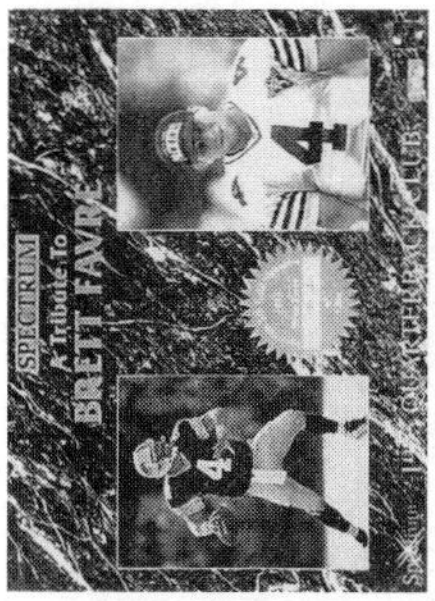

The 12-sheet, 8-1/2" x 11" set featured 12 top quarterbacks with color photos over a black marble background with the player's signature in 24 kt. gold foil. As with the promos, the backs are blank and are limited to a production of 5,000.

		MT
Complete Set (12):		30.00
Common Player:		1.50
1	Troy Aikman	4.00
2	Randall Cunningham	1.50
3	John Elway	3.00
4	Boomer Esiason	1.50
5	Brett Favre	8.00
6	Jim Kelly	2.00
7	Dan Marino	8.00
8	Warren Moon	2.00
9	Phil Simms	1.50
10	Steve Young	3.00
11	AFC Stars (Jeff Hostetler, Bernie Kosar, Neil O'Donnell)	1.50
12	NFC Stars (Jim Everett, Chris Miller, Mark Rypien)	1.50

1993 Spectrum/ Front Row Promos

The five-card, standard-size set was issued as a preview of Spectrum Holdings Group and its purchase of the Front Row trademark. The fronts feature action color shots with the backs containing bio and stat information inset over another player shot. An oval with "For Promotional Use Only" printed inside was featured on the card backs.

		MT
Complete Set (5):		8.00
Common Player:		1.50
1	Eric Curry	1.50
2	Andre Hastings	1.50
3	Qadry Ismail	2.00
4	Lincoln Kennedy	1.50
5	O.J. McDuffie	2.50

1993 Spectrum/ Front Row Tribute Sheet

The 8-1/2" x 11" sheet was issued to promote Spectrum Holdings Group and its purchase of the Front Row trademark. A gold-foil bar edged in purple contains "Outstanding Players of the 1993 Draft" over a black granite-like background. Production run was 5,000 and the backs were blank.

		MT
Complete Set (1):		2.00
Common Panel:		2.00
1	Qadry Ismail, Lincoln Kennedy, O.J. McDuffie, Andre Hastings, Eric Curry	2.00

1992 Sport Decks Promo Aces

These four playing card Aces were produced by Junior Card and Toy Inc. to promote the premier edition of Sport Decks NFL playing cards. One standard-size card was given away during each of the four days of the National Sports Collectors Convention in Atlanta. The front has a color action photo on it against a full-bleed metallic-sheen background. The card number and suit are in the upper left corner; a Team NFL logo is in the upper right corner. These are situated on a metallic bar running across the top. A similar bar runs along the bottom. It contains a team helmet, the player's name and position, and a Sport Decks logo. There were reportedly 6,000 silver-barred cards and 1,000 gold-barred cards made (three times more valuable than the values listed below for silver ones). The card backs are white, with pink and black lettering which provides advertisements, logos and the players who will be featured in the suit corresponding to the pictured player.

		MT
Complete Set (4):		12.00
Common Player:		1.00
AC	Emmitt Smith	6.00
AD	Thurman Thomas	2.00
AH	Dan Marino	5.00
AS	Mark Rypien	1.00

1992 Sport Decks

This 55-card deck of playing cards was produced after Sport Decks debuted the set at the 1992 National Sports Collectors Convention in Atlanta. Each card front has rounded corners and features a full-bleed color action shot. A stripe at the top contains a card number and suit in the upper left corner, with a Team NFL logo in the upper right corner. The bottom stripe contains a team helmet, player's name and position and card number and suit. The back has a white-bordered blue-green football field which has an "Official 1992 Season Football Star Cards" logo in the middle of a goal post.

		MT
Complete Set (55):		5.00
Common Player:		.05
AC	Troy Aikman	.75
2C	Rodney Peete	.07
3C	Cris Carter	.07
4C	Randal Hill	.07
5C	Jeff Hostetler	.07
6C	Flipper Anderson	.05
7C	Chris Miller	.10
8C	Anthony Carter	.07
9C	Timm Rosenbach	.05
10C	Sterling Sharpe	.25
JC	Ricky Ervins	.05
QC	Jerry Rice	.50
KC	Emmitt Smith	1.00
AD	Jim Kelly	.25
2D	John Friesz	.10
3D	Gaston Green	.05
4D	Hugh Millen	.05
5D	Dan McGwire	.05
6D	Eric Green	.05
7D	Christian Okoye	.07
8D	Ronnie Lott	.10
9D	Rob Moore	.07
10D	Mark Clayton	.05
JD	Thurman Thomas	.25
QD	John Elway	.45
KD	Warren Moon	.30
AH	Dan Marino	.75
2H	Anthony Munoz	.10
3H	Nick Bell	.05
4H	Michael Dean Perry	.05
5H	Haywood Jeffires	.05
6H	Bubby Brister	.05
7H	Andre Reed	.07
8H	Anthony Miller	.07
9H	Ken O'Brien	.05
10H	Bernie Kosar	.10
JH	Derrick Thomas	.10
QH	Jeff George	.10
KH	Boomer Esiason	.10
AS	Mark Rypien	.10
2S	Phil Simms	.10
3S	Pat Swilling	.07
4S	Jim Harbaugh	.10
5S	Mike Singletary	.10
6S	Lawrence Taylor	.15
7S	John Taylor	.10
8S	Keith Jackson	.10
9S	Vinny Testaverde	.10
10S	Andre Rison	.20
JS	Michael Irvin	.25
QS	Earnest Byner	.05
KS	Randall Cunningham	.10
JK	Eric Dickerson	.10
JK	Jim Everett	.10
xx	Title card	.05

1994 Sportflics Samples

The seven-card, regular-sized set was issued as a preview for the 1994 Sportflics base set. The upper right corners of the cards are cut off indicating it as a sample. The set is virtually identical in design to the regular-issue set.

		MT
Complete Set (7):		8.00
Common Player:		.50
3	Flipper Anderson (yellow "Anderson" name on back missing shadow)	.50
50	Reggie Brooks (yellow "Brooks" name on back missing shadow)	.50
70	Herman Moore (name on front 1/4" away from year logo)	1.50
145	Chuck Levy (back photo black and white)	.50
180	Jerome Bettis ("TM" by Starflics logo on front)	2.00
HH1	Barry Jones (Head-to-Head production number box on back missing)	2.50
NNO	Sportflics Ad Card (corners intact)	.50

1994 Sportflics

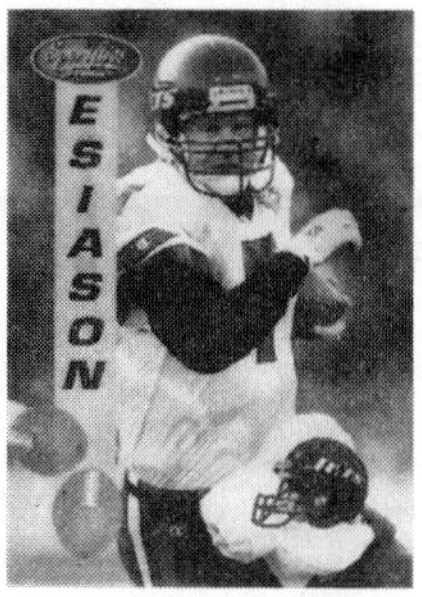

Pinnacle revealed its premier edition of Sportflics 2000 Football in a 184-card set. Each card contains two different shots of the player on the same card. One shot is visible instantly, the second is apparent with a slight turn. Sportflics contained five insert sets. Random cards from Sack Attack, Head to Head, Artist's Proof, Find the Football and Rookie Rivalry were inserted in the five-card packs. Within the primary set itself, there were two subsets, entitled Starflics and The Rookies.

		MT
Complete Set (184):		40.00
Common Player:		.15
Minor Stars:		.30
Comp. Artist Proof (184):		850.00
Artist Proof Cards:		8x-16x
Pack (5):		2.00
Wax Box (36):		50.00
1	Deion Sanders	1.25
2	Leslie O'Neal	.15
3	Willie Anderson	.15
4	Anthony Carter	.15
5	Thurman Thomas, Vincent Brisby	.15
6	Johnny Mitchell	.15
7	Jeff Hostetler	.15
8	Renaldo Turnbull	.15
9	Chris Warren	.40
10	Darrell Green	.15
11	Randall Cunningham	.15
12	Barry Sanders	2.00
13	Jeff Cross	.15
14	Glyn Milburn	.15
15	Willie Davis	.15
16	Tony McGee	.15
17	Gary Clark	.15
18	Michael Jackson	.15
19	Alvin Harper	.15
20	Tim Worley	.15
21	Quentin Coryatt	.15
22	Michael Brooks	.15
23	Boomer Esiason	.15
24	Ricky Watters	.30
25	Craig Erickson	.15
26	Willie Green	.15
27	Brett Favre	3.00
28	John Elway	1.00
29	Steve Beuerlein	.15
30	Emmitt Smith	4.00
31	Troy Aikman	2.00
32	Cody Carlson	.15
33	Brian Mitchell	.15
34	Herschel Walker	.15
35	Bruce Smith	.15
36	Harold Green	.15
37	Erric Pegram	.15
38	Ronnie Harmon	.15
39	Brian Blades	.15
40	Sterling Sharpe	.30
41	Leonard Russell	.15
42	Cleveland Gary	.15
43	Tom Waddle, Lamar Smith	.15
44	Lawrence Dawsey	.15
45	Jerry Rice	2.00
46	Terry Allen	.15
47	Reggie Langhorne	.15
48	Derek Brown	.15
49	Terry Kirby, Lake Dawson	.15
50	Reggie Brooks	.15
51	Calvin Williams	.15
52	Cornelius Bennett	.15
53	Russell Maryland	.15
54	Rob Moore	.15
55	Dana Stubblefield	.15
56	Rod Woodson	.15
57	Rodney Hampton	.30
58	Neil Smith	.15
59	Anthony Smith	.15
60	Neal Anderson	.15
61	Drew Bledsoe	2.00
62	John Copeland	.15
63	David Klingler	.15
64	Phil Simms	.15
65	Vincent Brisby	.15
66	Richard Dent	.15
67	Eric Metcalf	.15
68	Eric Curry	.15
69	Victor Bailey	.15
70	Herman Moore	1.00
71	Steve Jordan	.15
72	Jerome Bettis	.50
73	Natrone Means	.75
74	Webster Slaughter	.15
75	Jackie Harris	.15
76	Michael Irvin	.30
77	Steve Emtman	.15
78	Eugene Robinson	.15
79	Tim Brown	.30
80	Derrick Thomas	.15
81	Vinny Testaverde	.15
82	Mark Jackson	.15
83	Ricky Proehl	.15
84	Stan Humphries	.15
85	Garrison Hearst	1.00
86	Jim Kelly	.30
87	Brent Jones	.15
88	Eric Martin	.15
89	Wilber Marshall	.15
90	Chris Spielman	.15
91	Eric Green	.15
92	Andre Rison	.15
93	Andre Reed	.15
94	Carl Pickens	.75
95	Junior Seau	.30
96	Dwight Stone	.15
97	Mike Sherrard	.15
98	Vincent Brown	.15
99	Cris Carter	.15
100	Mark Higgs	.15
101	Steve Young	2.00
102	Mark Carrier	.15
103	Barry Foster	.15
104	Tommy Vardell	.15
105	Shannon Sharpe	.15
106	Reggie White	.30
107	Ernest Givins	.15
108	Marcus Allen	.30
109	James Jett	.15
110	Keith Jackson	.15
111	Irving Fryar	.15
112	Ronnie Lott	.15
113	Cortez Kennedy	.15
114	Ron Moore	.15
115	Rick Mirer	.75
116	Neil O'Donnell	.30
117	Courtney Hawkins	.15
118	Johnny Johnson	.15
119	Ben Coates	.30
120	Dan Marino	4.00
121	Sean Gilbert	.15
122	Rocket Ismail	.15
123	Joe Montana	2.00
124	Roosevelt Potts	.15
125	Gary Brown	.15
126	Reggie Cobb	.15
127	Marion Butts	.15
128	Scott Mitchell	.15
129	John L. Williams	.15
130	Jeff George	.30
131	Bobby Hebert	.15
132	John Friesz	.15
133	Anthony Miller	.15
134	Jim Harbaugh	.15
135	Erik Kramer	.15
136	Jim Everett	.15
137	Michael Haynes	.15
138	Rod Bernstine	.15
139	Chris Miller	.15
140	Henry Ellard	.15
141	William Fuller	.15
142	Warren Moon	.30
143	*Lamar Smith*	.15
144	*Charlie Garner*	1.50
145	*Chuck Levy*	.15
146	*Dan Wilkinson*	.30
147	*Perry Klein*	.15
148	*William Floyd*	1.00
149	*Lake Dawson*	1.00
150	*David Palmer*	.50
151	*James Bostic*	.15
152	*Marshall Faulk*	6.00
153	*Greg Hill*	1.00
154	*Heath Shuler*	3.00
155	*Errict Rhett*	4.00
156	*Sam Adams*	.15
157	*Charles Johnson*	1.00
158	*Ryan Yarborough*	.15
159	*Thomas Lewis*	.15
160	*Willie McGinest*	.50
161	*Jamir Miller*	.15
162	*Calvin Jones*	.15
163	*Donnell Bennett*	.15
164	*Trev Alberts*	.15
165	*LeShon Johnson*	.15
166	*Johnnie Morton*	1.00
167	*Derrick Alexander*	.50
168	*Jeff Cothran*	.15
169	*Bucky Brooks*	.30
170	*Bert Emanuel*	2.00
171	*Darnay Scott*	3.00
172	*Kevin Lee*	.15
173	*Mario Bates*	2.00
174	*Bryant Young*	.75
175	*Trent Dilfer*	2.00
176	Joe Montana	1.00
177	Emmitt Smith	2.00
178	Troy Aikman	1.00
179	Steve Young	1.00
180	Jerome Bettis	.40
181	John Elway	.50
182	Dan Marino	2.00
183	Brett Favre	1.00
184	Barry Sanders	1.00

1994 Sportflics Head-To-Head

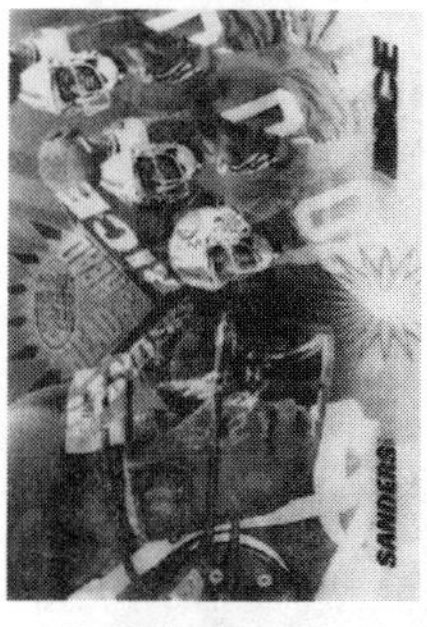

Head-to-Head captured some of the game's fiercest rivalries. Cards show a close-up shot of both players with their helmets on, on opposing sides of the card. The second picture captures the player in action, with three photos to give the illusion of movement. The Sportflics logo is between the helmets on the one shot and, on the second shot it turns into a large Head to Head logo with both players' names. The back shows a close shot of the two, with their name and team name next to them.

		MT
Complete Set (10):		220.00
Common Player:		7.00
1	Barry Sanders, Dante Jones	25.00
2	Emmitt Smith, Carlton Bailey	50.00
3	Rod Woodson, Dan Marino	50.00
4	Jerry Rice, Deion Sanders	25.00
5	Vaughan Johnson, Jerome Bettis	7.00
6	Reggie White, Troy Aikman	25.00
7	Steve Young, Renaldo Turnbull	25.00
8	Sterling Sharpe, Eric Allen	7.00
9	Joe Montana, Anthony Smith	25.00
10	John Elway, Neil Smith	10.00

1994 Sportflics Pride of Texas

The four-card, standard-size set was given away at the National Convention in Houston by Pinnacle. One Dallas Cowboys (Harper), one Houston Oilers (Brown) and two Dallas Stars (Modano, Hatcher). Production was limited to 2,500 of each card. Each card has an "N" prefix.

		MT
Complete Set (4):		15.00
Common Player:		3.00
1	Alvin Harper	3.00
2	Gary Brown	3.00
3	Mike Modano	6.00
4	Derian Hatcher	3.00

1994 Sportflics Rookie Rivalry

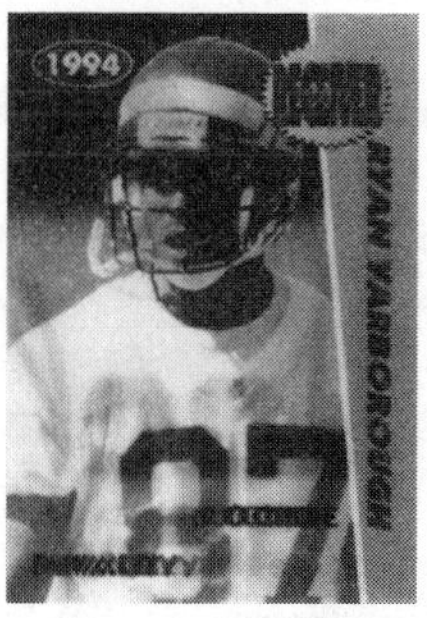

Rookie Rivalry pits two of the league's top prospects against each other. This 12-card insert had an insertion ratio of one per 24 packs and was in hobby packs only.

		MT
Complete Set (10):		65.00
Common Player:		3.00
Minor Stars:		6.00
1	William Floyd, Marshall Faulk	17.00
2	Dan Wilkinson, Sam Adams	3.00
3	Trent Dilfer, Heath Shuler	8.00
4	Jamir Miller, Trev Alberts	3.00
5	Johnnie Morton, Charles Johnson	6.00
6	Chuck Levy, Charles Garner	6.00
7	Thomas Lewis, Derrick Alexander	3.00
8	Darnay Scott, Isaac Bruce	15.00
9	David Palmer, Ryan Yarborough	3.00
10	LeShon Johnson, Donnell Bennett	3.00

1994 Sportflics Artist's Proofs

The 184-card, standard-size set was issued as a parallel version to the base set. "Artist's Proof" is printed on the card fronts.

	MT
Complete Set (184):	900.00
Common Player:	2.00
Artist's Proof Cards:	8x-16x

A card number in parentheses ( ) indicates the set is unnumbered.

1995 Sportflix

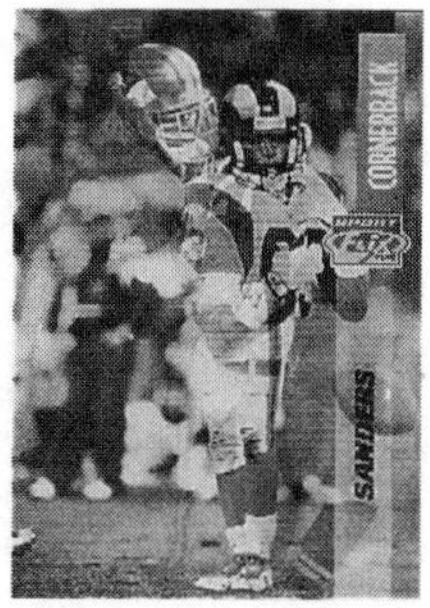

This set marked Pinnacle's debut for Sportflix Football cards. The 175-card set includes more than 30 top rookies, plus a 20-card Game Winners subset. Cards were issued in packs of five, which could also contain one of five different insert cards - Artist's Proof (175-card parallel set, one per every 36 packs), Rolling Thunder, Rookie Lightning, ProMotion and Man 2 Man, which could be found in jumbo packs only. The regular cards feature two different pictures on the front, each visible through the concept of "magic motion" when the card is tilted. The player's name appears along the right side, with the letters increasing in size as the card is tilted. His position and the Sportflix logo are also along the side. The horizontal card back has a photo of the player on one side, flanked by key career statistical totals in the middle and a brief career summary on the opposite side. The player's name is in the upper left corner; the Sportflix logo is in the lower right corner.

		MT
Complete Set (175):		30.00
Common Player:		.10
Minor Stars:		.20
Artist Proof Cards:		15x-30x
Artist Proof Rookies:		6x-12x
Inserted 1:36 Hobby		
Pack (5):		1.50
Wax Box (36):		40.00
1	Troy Aikman	1.00
2	Rodney Hampton	.10
3	Jerry Rice	1.00
4	Reggie White	.30
5	Mark Ingram	.10
6	Chris Spielman	.10
7	Curtis Conway	.20
8	Erik Kramer	.20
9	Emmitt Smith	1.50
10	Alvin Harper	.10
11	Junior Seau	.20
12	Mike Pritchard	.10
13	Ricky Ervins	.10
14	Jim Harbaugh	.20
15	Dan Marino	1.50
16	Marshall Faulk	.50
17	Lorenzo White	.10
18	Cortez Kennedy	.10
19	Rocket Ismail	.10
20	Eric Metcalf	.10
21	Chris Chandler	.20
22	John Elway	1.00
23	Boomer Esiason	.20
24	Herman Moore	.20
25	Deion Sanders	.50
26	Charles Johnson	.20
27	Daryl Johnston	.10
28	Dave Krieg	.10
29	Jim Kelly	.20
30	Warren Moon	.20
31	Lewis Tillman	.10
32	Bruce Smith	.10
33	Jake Reed	.20
34	Craig Heyward	.10
35	Frank Reich	.10
36	Stan Humphries	.10
37	Charles Haley	.10
38	Andre Rison	.20
39	James Jett	.10
40	Jay Novacek	.10
41	Gary Brown	.10
42	Steve Bono	.20
43	Cris Carter	.30
44	Steve Atwater	.10
45	Andre Reed	.20
46	Greg Lloyd	.10
47	Mark Seay	.10
48	Dave Meggett	.10
49	Steve Beuerlein	.10
50	Jeff Graham	.10
51	Barry Sanders	2.00
52	Willie Davis	.10
53	Robert Smith	.30
54	Steve Walsh	.10
55	Michael Irvin	.20
56	Natrone Means	.30
57	Chris Warren	.10
58	Tim Brown	.20
59	Steve Young	.75
60	Jerome Bettis	.30
61	Shannon Sharpe	.20
62	Errict Rhett	.20
63	Scott Mitchell	.20
64	Leroy Hoard	.20
65	Garrison Hearst	.30
66	Terance Mathis	.20
67	Sean Gilbert	.10
68	Fred Barnett	.10
69	Hardy Nickerson	.10
70	Jim Everett	.10
71	Randall Cunningham	.30
72	Carl Pickens	.20
73	Jeff Hostetler	.10
74	Marcus Allen	.30

75	Jeff George	.20
76	Brett Favre	2.00
77	Chris Miller	.10
78	Craig Erickson	.10
79	Herschel Walker	.20
80	Bert Emanuel	.20
81	Leonard Russell	.10
82	Ricky Watters	.20
83	Robert Brooks	.20
84	Dave Brown	.10
85	Henry Ellard	.10
86	Barry Foster	.10
87	Johnny Mitchell	.10
88	Eric Allen	.10
89	Darnay Scott	.20
90	Harvey Williams	.10
91	Neil O'Donnell	.20
92	Drew Bledsoe	1.00
93	Ken Harvey	.10
94	Irving Fryar	.20
95	Rod Woodson	.10
96	Anthony Miller	.10
97	Mario Bates	.20
98	*Jeff Blake*	.50
99	Rick Mirer	.20
100	William Floyd	.20
101	Michael Haynes	.10
102	Flipper Anderson	.10
103	Greg Hill	.20
104	Mark Brunell	1.00
105	Vinny Testaverde	.30
106	Heath Shuler	.20
107	Ron Moore	.10
108	Ernest Givins	.10
109	Mike Sherrard	.10
110	Charlie Garner	.20
111	Trent Dilfer	.30
112	Bam Morris	.20
113	Lake Dawson	.10
114	Brian Blades	.10
115	Brent Jones	.10
116	Ronnie Harmon	.10
117	Eric Green	.10
118	Ben Coates	.20
119	*Ki-Jana Carter*	.30
120	*Steve McNair*	3.00
121	*Michael Westbrook*	1.25
122	*Kerry Collins*	1.50
123	*Joey Galloway*	2.50
124	*Kyle Brady*	.30
125	*J.J. Stokes*	1.50
126	*Tyrone Wheatley*	.30
127	*Rashaan Salaam*	.30
128	*Napoleon Kaufman*	2.50
129	*Frank Sanders*	1.00
130	*Stoney Case*	.20
131	*Todd Collins*	.20
132	*Lovell Pinkney*	.10
133	*Sherman Williams*	.20
134	*Rob Johnson*	2.00
135	*Mark Bruener*	.30
136	*Lee DeRamus*	.10
137	*Chad May*	.20
138	*James Stewart*	.30
139	*Ray Zellars*	.20
140	*Dave Barr*	.20
141	*Kordell Stewart*	5.00
142	*Jimmy Oliver*	.10
143	*Terrell Fletcher*	.30
144	*James Stewart*	2.50
145	*Terrell Davis*	10.00
146	*Joe Aska*	.10
147	*John Walsh*	.20
148	*Tyrone Davis*	.10
149	Emmitt Smith	.75
150	Barry Sanders	1.00
151	Jerry Rice	.50
152	Steve Young	.40
153	Dan Marino	.75
154	Troy Aikman	.50
155	Drew Bledsoe	.50
156	John Elway	.50
157	Brett Favre	1.00
158	Michael Irvin	.10
159	Heath Shuler	.10
160	Warren Moon	.10
161	Jim Kelly	.10
162	Randall Cunningham	.15
163	Jeff Hostetler	.10
164	Dave Brown	.10
165	Neil O'Donnell	.10
166	Rick Mirer	.10
167	Jim Everett	.10
168	Boomer Esiason	.10
169	Dan Marino	.75
170	Drew Bledsoe	.50
171	John Elway	.50
172	Emmitt Smith	.75
173	Steve Young	.40
174	Barry Sanders	1.00
175	Jerry Rice	.50

1995 Sportflix Artist's Proofs

The 175-card, standard-size set was a parallel version of the base set and was inserted every 36 packs. The Artist's Proof logo in gold and black appears on the card front.

	MT
Complete Set (175):	1400.
Common Player:	2.50
Artist's Proof Cards:	15x-30x
Artist's Proof Rookies:	6x-12x

1995 Sportflix Artist's Proof Parallel

	MT
Complete Set (175):	30.00
Common Player:	.10
Minor Stars:	.20
Artist Proof Cards:	15x-30x
Artist Proof Rookies:	6x-12x
Inserted 1:36 Hobby	
Wax Box:	45.00

1995 Sportflix Man 2 Man

These 1995 Pinnacle Sportflix cards were randomly included one per every eight jumbo packs of the base product. Each card front features two players, so 24 are represented in the 12-card set. The cards do not use the "magic motion" concept, but do feature the players superimposed against a football game scene. The player's names are on the front, along with the Sportflix and insert set logos. The card back is numbered 1 of 12, etc., and includes a color photo of each player superimposed against a black-and-white photo of the same shot. Two small paragraphs between the photos offer brief descriptions of the players' skills.

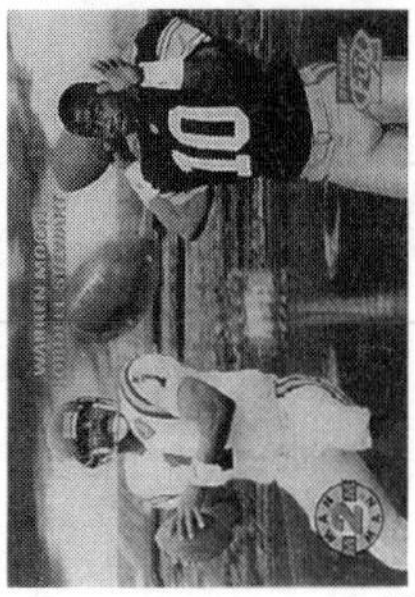

		MT
Complete Set (12):		100.00
Common Player:		5.00
1	Troy Aikman, Dan Marino	20.00
2	Emmitt Smith, Marshall Faulk	20.00
3	Kerry Collins, Drew Bledsoe	14.00
4	Steve Young, Steve McNair	12.00
5	Barry Sanders, Ki-Jana Carter	12.00
6	Heath Shuler, John Elway	8.00
7	Rashaan Salaam, Bam Morris	8.00
8	Ricky Watters, Natrone Means	5.00
9	Jerry Rice, J.J. Stokes	12.00
10	Kordell Stewart, Warren Moon	12.00
11	Brett Favre, Jeff Blake	15.00
12	Michael Westbrook, Joey Galloway	5.00

1995 Sportflix ProMotion

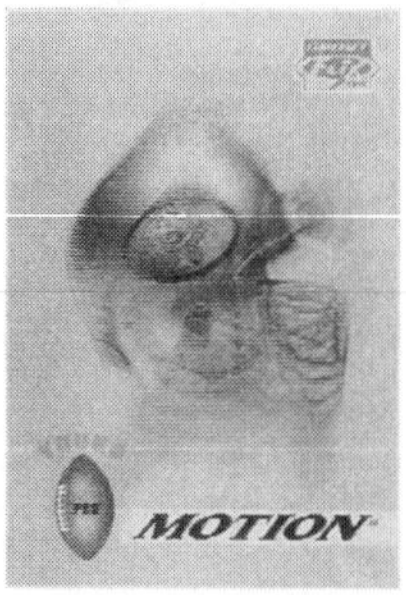

These 1995 Pinnacle Sportflix insert cards showcase the company's unique morphing technology, in which a player turns into, or morphs into, his team logo through 36 frames of action. The Sportflix logo is in the upper right corner; the player's last name appears above a football, which says "Pro" inside and is located alongside the word "Motion." The horizontal card back uses this same design at the bottom; a player photo and brief player profile are also included on the back. Cards are numberd using a "PM" prefix. Cards were randomly included one per every 48 packs.

		MT
Complete Set (12):		180.00
Common Player:		5.00
1	Steve Young	20.00
2	Troy Aikman	18.00
3	Dan Marino	35.00
4	Drew Bledsoe	25.00
5	John Elway	10.00
6	Jim Kelly	5.00
7	Jerry Rice	20.00
8	Michael Irvin	8.00
9	Emmitt Smith	35.00
10	Marshall Faulk	25.00
11	Natrone Means	10.00
12	Ki-Jana Carter	18.00

1995 Sportflix Rolling Thunder

These Rolling Thunder insert cards feature 12 running backs each against a spinning pinwheel background on the front. "Rolling Thunder" is written along the left side of the card; the player's name, which increases in size as the card is tilted, is in the lower left corner. A Sportflix logo is in the upper right corner. The card back, numbered 1 of 12, etc., has a full color photo of the player in the upper portion of the card; the bottom portion contains the bottom half of the photo in a ghosted format, with the insert set name and a brief player profile superimposed over it. A team helmet is also in the upper right corner. Cards were random inserts, one every 12 packs of 1995 Pinnacle Sportflix.

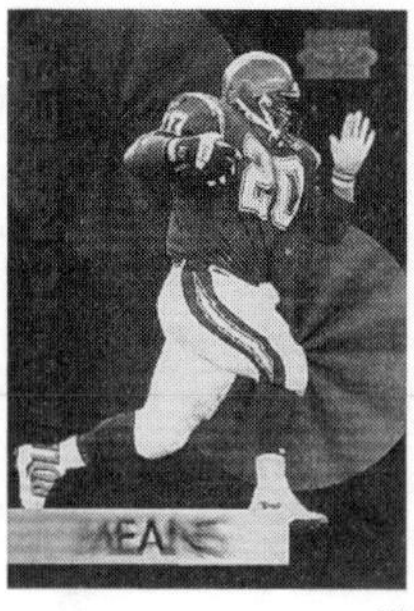

		MT
Complete Set (12):		75.00
Common Player:		3.00
1	Emmitt Smith	18.00
2	Barry Sanders	10.00
3	Marshall Faulk	10.00
4	Ki-Jana Carter	8.00
5	Rashaan Salaam	8.00
6	Tyrone Wheatley	6.00
7	Natrone Means	5.00
8	Jerome Bettis	3.00
9	Errict Rhett	8.00
10	Bam Morris	3.00
11	William Floyd	5.00
12	Mario Bates	3.00

1995 Sportflix Rookie Lightning

These insert cards feature 12 of the top rookies entering the NFL in 1995. Cards were random inserts, one per every 36 packs of 1995 Pinnacle Sportflix. The card front uses the "magic motion" concept to create two different photos when the card is tilted. "Rookie" and "Lightning" alternate along the right side when the card is tilted, while the player's name at the bottom increases in size. The Sportflix logo and the player's position are in the upper left corner. The card back has the set logo and number (1 of 12, etc.) in the upper right corner. The outline of one of the photos from the front is also on the back.

		MT
Complete Set (11):		120.00
Common Player:		7.00
1	Ki-Jana Carter	15.00
2	Steve McNair	20.00
3	Michael Westbrook	10.00
4	Kerry Collins	25.00
5	Joey Galloway	20.00
6	J.J. Stokes	20.00
7	Tyrone Wheatley	7.00
8	Rashaan Salaam	20.00
9	Napoleon Kaufman	12.00
10	Kordell Stewart	25.00
11	James Stewart	7.00

1999 Sports Illustrated

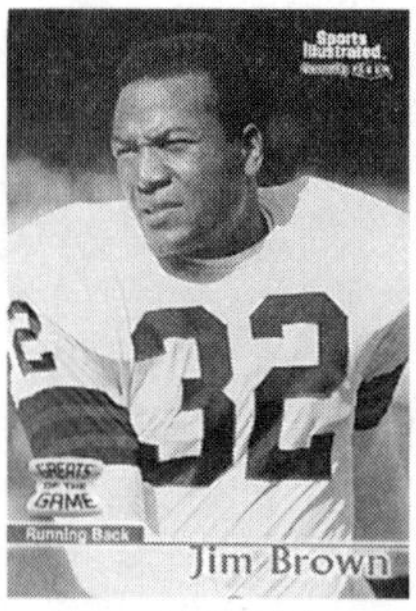

This was a 150-card release that included 90 stars of yesterday and today, 30 Fresh Faces (impact rookies of 1998) and 30 Super Bowl MVP's. Top inserts include: Autographs, Canton Calling and SI Covers.

		MT
Complete Set (150):		100.00
Common Player:		.15
Minor Stars:		.30
Common Rookie:		1.00
Pack (7):		17.00
Wax Box (12):		190.00
1	Bart Starr	.50
2	Bart Starr	.50
3	Joe Namath	.50
4	Len Dawson	.30
5	Chuck Howley	.15
6	Roger Staubach	.50
7	Jake Scott	.15
8	Larry Csonka	.30
9	Franco Harris	.30
10	Fred Biletnikoff	.15
11	Harvey Martin, Randy White	.15
12	Terry Bradshaw	.50
13	Terry Bradshaw	.50
14	Jim Plunkett	.30
15	Joe Montana	1.00
16	Marcus Allen	.50
17	Joe Montana	1.00
18	Richard Dent	.15
19	Phil Simms	.30
20	Doug Williams	.15
21	Jerry Rice	1.00
22	Joe Montana	1.00
23	Ottis Anderson	.30
24	Mark Rypien	.15
25	Troy Aikman	1.00
26	Emmitt Smith	1.50
27	Steve Young	.50
28	Larry Brown	.15
29	Desmond Howard	.15
30	Terrell Davis	1.50
31	Y.A. Tittle	.30
32	Paul Hornung	.50
33	Gale Sayers	.50
34	Garo Yepremian	.15
35	Bert Jones	.30
36	Joe Washington	.15
37	Joe Theismann	.30
38	Roger Craig	.30
39	Mike Singletary	.30
40	Bobby Bell	.15
41	Ken Houston	.15
42	Lenny Moore	.15
43	Mark Moseley	.15
44	Chuck Bednarik	.15
45	Ted Hendricks	.15
46	Steve Largent	.50
47	Bob Lilly	.15
48	Don Maynard	.50
49	John Mackey	.15
50	Anthony Munoz	.15
51	Bobby Mitchell	.15
52	Jim Brown	.50
53	Otto Graham	.50
54	Earl Morrall	.15
55	Danny White	.30
56	Karim Abdul-Jabbar	.50
57	Charlie Garner	.15
58	Jeff Blake	.30
59	Reggie White	.50
60	Derrick Thomas	.15
61	Duce Staley	.15
62	Tim Brown	.30
63	Elvis Grbac	.30
64	Tony Banks	.30
65	Rob Johnson	.30
66	Danny Kanell	.15
67	Marshall Faulk	.50
68	Warrick Dunn	1.25
69	Dan Marino	3.00
70	Jimmy Smith	.50
71	John Elway	2.50
72	Charles Way	.15
73	Ricky Watters	.30
74	Terry Glenn	.50
75	Bobby Hoying	.30
76	Curtis Martin	.50
77	Trent Dilfer	.30
78	Emmitt Smith	3.00
79	Irving Fryar	.15
80	Troy Aikman	2.00
81	Barry Sanders	4.00
82	Brett Favre	4.00
83	Robert Smith	.50
84	Dorsey Levens	.50
85	Cris Carter	.50
86	Jeff George	.30
87	Jerome Bettis	.30
88	Warren Moon	.30
89	Steve Young	.75
90	Fred Lane	.30
91	Jerry Rice	2.00
92	Natrone Means	.50
93	Mike Alstott	.50
94	Kordell Stewart	1.50
95	Jake Plummer	1.75
96	Jamal Anderson	.75
97	Corey Dillon	1.00
98	Deion Sanders	.50
99	Mark Brunell	1.50
100	Garrison Hearst	.50
101	Andre Rison	.15
102	Antowain Smith	.75
103	Drew Bledsoe	1.50
104	Eddie George	1.50
105	Keyshawn Johnson	.50
106	Isaac Bruce	.30
107	Rob Moore	.30
108	Steve McNair	.75
109	Terrell Davis	3.00
110	Carl Pickens	.30
111	Wayne Chrebet	.50
112	Kerry Collins	.30
113	Eric Metcalf	.15
114	Joey Galloway	.50
115	Shannon Sharpe	.30
116	Robert Brooks	.15
117	Glenn Foley	.30
118	Yancey Thigpen	.30
119	Frank Sanders	.30
120	Herman Moore	.50
121	Antonio Freeman	.75
122	Michael Irvin	.30
123	Brad Johnson	.50
124	James Stewart	.15
125	Jim Harbaugh	.30
126	Peyton Manning	12.00
127	Ryan Leaf	6.00
128	Curtis Enis	4.00
129	Fred Taylor	10.00
130	Randy Moss	25.00
131	John Avery	3.00
132	Charles Woodson	5.00
133	Robert Edwards	3.50
134	Charlie Batch	8.00
135	Brian Griese	5.00
136	Skip Hicks	3.00
137	Jacquez Green	3.00
138	Robert Holcombe	2.00
139	Kevin Dyson	3.00
140	Rodney Williams	1.00
141	Ahman Green	2.00
142	Tavian Banks	2.00
143	Donald Hayes	1.00
144	Tony Simmons	3.00
145	Patrick Johnson	2.00
146	Marcus Nash	3.00
147	Germane Crowell	3.00
148	R.W. McQuarters	2.00
149	Jonathan Quinn	2.00
150	Andre Wadsworth	2.00

1999 Sports Illustrated Autographs

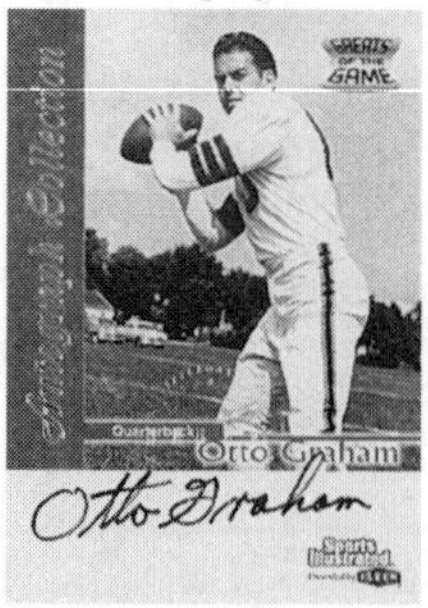

A total of 35 players from the past signed cards in this insert with numbers unknown. Singles were found one-per-pack.

	MT
Complete Set (35):	3000.
Common Player:	10.00
Minor Stars:	20.00
Inserted 1:1	
Ottis Anderson	20.00
Chuck Bednarik	10.00
Bobby Bell	10.00
Terry Bradshaw	400.00
Jim Brown	250.00
Roger Craig	25.00
Len Dawson	175.00
Otto Graham	30.00
Franco Harris	175.00
Ted Hendricks	10.00
Paul Hornung	185.00
Ken Houston	10.00
Bert Jones	10.00
Steve Largent	35.00
Bob Lilly	10.00
John Mackey	10.00
Don Maynard	20.00
Bobby Mitchell	10.00
Joe Montana	425.00
Lenny Moore	10.00
Earl Morrall	10.00
Mark Moseley	10.00
Anthony Munoz	20.00
Joe Namath	450.00
Jim Plunkett	20.00
Gale Sayers	35.00
Mike Singletary	100.00
Bart Starr	400.00
Roger Staubach	200.00
Joe Theismann	85.00
Y.A. Tittle	100.00
Joe Washington	10.00
Danny White	10.00
Doug Williams	100.00
Garo Yepremian	10.00

1999 Sports Illustrated Canton Calling

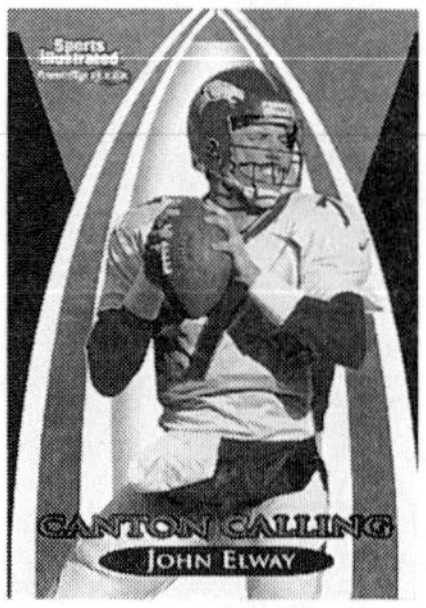

This was an 8-card set that included players who are on their way to the Hall of Fame. Singles were inserted 1:12 packs and a parallel Gold insert was also produced and found 1:120 packs.

		MT
Complete Set (8):		60.00
Common Player:		3.00
Inserted 1:12		
Gold Cards:		3x-6x
Inserted 1:120		
1	Warren Moon	3.00
2	Emmitt Smith	10.00
3	Jerry Rice	8.00
4	Brett Favre	15.00
5	Barry Sanders	15.00
6	Dan Marino	10.00
7	John Elway	10.00
8	Troy Aikman	8.00

Values quoted in this guide reflect the retail price of a card — the price a collector can expect to pay when buying a card from a dealer. The wholesale price — that which a collector can expect to receive from a dealer when selling cards — will be significantly lower, depending on desirability and condition.

1999 Sports Illustrated Covers

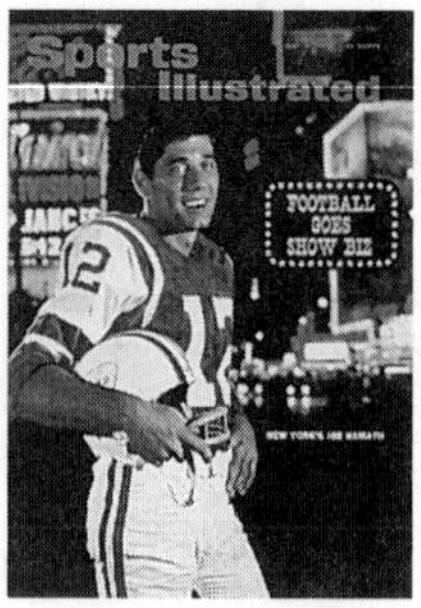

This was a 60-card set that took the best covers from the past and reproduced them on a card. Singles were found one-per-pack.

		MT
Complete Set (60):		30.00
Common Player:		.25
Minor Stars:		.50
Inserted 1:1		
1	Jim Brown	.50
2	Y.A. Tittle	.25
3	Dallas Cowboys	.25
4	Joe Namath	.75
5	Bart Starr	.50
6	Earl Morrall	.25
7	Minnesota Vikings	.25
8	Kansas City Chiefs	.25
9	Len Dawson	.25
10	Monday Night Football	.25
11	Jim Plunkett	.25
12	Garo Yepremian	.25
13	Larry Csonka	.25
14	Terry Bradshaw	.50
15	Franco Harris	.25
16	Bert Jones	.25
17	Harvey Martin, Randy White	.25
18	Roger Staubach	.50
19	Marcus Allen	.50
20	Joe Washington	.25
21	Dan Marino	2.50
22	Joe Theismann	.25
23	Roger Craig	.25
24	Mike Singletary	.25
25	Chicago Bears	.25
26	Phil Simms	.25
27	Vinny Testaverde	.25
28	Doug Williams	.25
29	Jerry Rice	1.50
30	Herschel Walker	.25
31	Joe Montana	1.75
32	Ottis Anderson	.25
33	Rocket Ismail	.25
34	Bruce Smith	.25
35	Thurman Thomas	.25
36	Mark Rypien	.25
37	Jim Harbaugh	.25
38	Randall Cunningham	.25
39	Troy Aikman	1.50
40	Reggie White	.50
41	Junior Seau	.25
42	Emmitt Smith	2.50
43	Natrone Means	.25
44	Ricky Watters	.25
45	Pittsburgh Steelers	.25
46	Steve Young, Troy Aikman	1.00
47	Steve Young	1.00
48	Deion Sanders	.50
49	Elvis Grbac	.25
50	Green Bay Packers	.25
51	Brett Favre	3.00
52	Mark Brunell, Kerry Collins	1.00
53	Antonio Freeman	.75
54	Desmond Howard	.25
55	AFC Central Quarterbacks	.25
56	Warrick Dunn	.50
57	Jerome Bettis	.25
58	John Elway	2.00
59	Brent Jones	.25
60	Terrell Davis	3.00

1976 Sportstix

The 10-sticker, 3-1/2" in diameter set was numbered as a continuation of non-sport issues. The helmet logos on the stickers have been erased and two major errors exist: Drew Pearson's card actually has Gloster Richardson on the card while Fred Biletnikoff's last name is spelled wrong on card No. 32.

		NM
Complete Set (11):		200.00
Common Player:		10.00
31	Carl Eller	20.00
32	Fred Biletnikoff (UER, Misspelled Belitnikoff)	30.00
33	Terry Metcalf	15.00
34	Gary Huff	10.00
35	Steve Bartkowski	20.00
36	Dan Pastorini	15.00
37	Drew Pearson (UER, photo is of Gloster Richardson)	20.00
38	Bert Jones	15.00
39	Otis Armstrong	15.00
40	Don Woods	10.00
C	Dick Butkus	60.00

Post-1980 cards in Near Mint condition will generally sell for about 75% of the quoted Mint value. Excellent-condition cards bring no more than 40%.

1991 Stadium Club

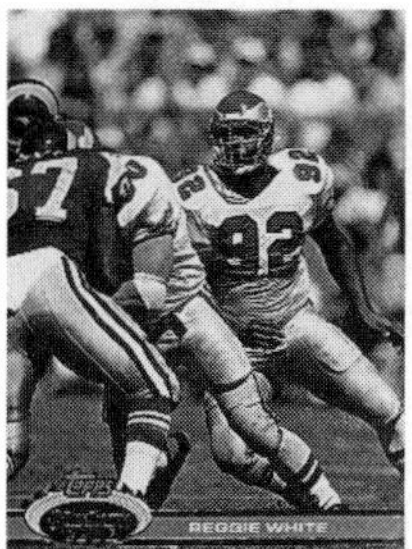

Topps made its premiere edition debut with its 1991 Stadium Club set of 500 cards. The glossy cards feature full-bleed action photos on the front. The player's name is at the bottom in an aqua stripe that is bordered in gold. The back uses a horizontal format with a football field and stadium for a background. A biography, Sporting News Football Analysis Report and miniature replica of the player's Topps rookie card are also included on the back.

		MT
Complete Set (500):		90.00
Common Player:		.20
Minor Stars:		.40
Pack (12):		4.00
Wax Box (36):		100.00
1	Pepper Johnson	.20
2	Emmitt Smith	10.00
3	Deion Sanders	3.00
4	Andre Collins	.20
5	Eric Metcalf	.30
6	Richard Dent	.30
7	Eric Martin	.20
8	Marcus Allen	.50
9	Gary Anderson	.20
10	Joey Browner	.20
11	Lorenzo White	.20
12	Bruce Smith	.20
13	Mark Boyer	.20
14	Mike Piel	.20
15	Albert Bentley	.20
16	Bennie Blades	.20
17	Jason Staurovsky	.20
18	Anthony Toney	.20
19	Dave Krieg	.20
20	*Harvey Williams*	2.00
21	Bubba Paris	.20
22	Tim McGee	.20
23	Brian Noble	.20
24	Vinny Testaverde	.30
25	Doug Widell	.20
26	John Jackson	.20
27	Marion Butts	.20
28	Deron Cherry	.20
29	Don Warren	.20
30	Rod Woodson	.75
31	Mike Baab	.20
32	Greg Jackson	.20
33	Jerry Robinson	.20
34	Dalton Hilliard	.20
35	Brian Jordan	.20
36	James Thornton (Misspelled Thorton on cards back)	.20
37	Michael Irvin	1.00
38	Billy Joe Tolliver	.20
39	Jeff Herrod	.20
40	Scott Norwood	.20
41	Ferrell Edmunds	.20
42	Andre Waters	.20
43	Kevin Glover	.20
44	Ray Berry	.20
45	Timm Rosenbach	.20
46	Reuben Davis	.20
47	Charles Wilson	.20
48	*Todd Marinovich*	.20
49	Harris Barton	.20
50	Jim Breech	.20
51	Ron Holmes	.20
52	Chris Singleton	.20
53	Pat Leahy	.20
54	Tom Newberry	.20
55	Greg Montgomery	.20
56	Robert Blackmon	.20
57	Jay Hilgenberg	.20
58	Rodney Hampton	1.00
59	Brett Perriman	.75
60	*Ricky Watters*	7.00
61	Howie Long	.20
62	Frank Cornish	.20
63	Chris Miller	.20
64	Keith Taylor	.20
65	Tony Paige	.20
66	Gary Zimmerman	.20
67	Mark Royals	.20
68	Ernie Jones	.20
69	David Grant	.20
70	Shane Conlan	.20
71	Jerry Rice	5.00
72	Christian Okoye	.20
73	Eddie Murray	.20
74	Reggie White	.75
75	*Jeff Graham*	2.00
76	Mark Jackson	.20
77	David Grayson	.20
78	Dan Stryzinski	.20
79	Sterling Sharpe	.75
80	Cleveland Gary	.20
81	Johnny Meads	.20
82	Howard Cross	.20
83	Ken O'Brien	.20
84	Brian Blades	.20
85	Ethan Horton	.20
86	Bruce Armstrong	.20
87	*James Washington*	.40
88	Eugene Daniel	.20
89	James Lofton	.20
90	Louis Oliver	.20
91	Boomer Esiason	.30
92	Seth Joyner	.20
93	Mark Carrier	.20
94	*Brett Favre* (Favre misspelled as Farve)	70.00
95	Lee Williams	.20
96	Neal Anderson	.20
97	Brent Jones	.20
98	John Alt	.20
99	Rodney Peete	.20
100	Steve Broussard	.20
101	Cedric Mack	.20
102	Pat Swilling	.20
103	Stan Humphries	2.00
104	Darrell Thompson	.20
105	Reggie Langhorne	.20
106	Kenny Davidson	.20
107	Jim Everett	.30
108	Keith Millard	.20
109	Garry Lewis	.20
110	Jeff Hostetler	1.00
111	Lamar Lathon	.20
112	Johnny Bailey	.20
113	Cornelius Bennett	.20
114	Travis McNeal	.20
115	Jeff Lageman	.20
116	*Nick Bell*	.20
117	Calvin Williams	.50
118	Shawn Lee	.20
119	Anthony Munoz	.20
120	Jay Novacek	.40
121	Kevin Fagan	.20
122	Leo Goeas	.20
123	Vance Johnson	.20
124	Brent Williams	.20
125	Clarence Verdin	.20
126	Luis Sharpe	.20
127	Darrell Green	.20
128	Barry Word	.20
129	Steve Walsh	.40
130	Bryan Hinkle	.20
131	Ed West	.20
132	Jeff Campbell	.20
133	Dennis Byrd	.20
134	Nate Odomes	.20
135	Trace Armstrong	.20
136	Jarvis Williams	.20
137	Warren Moon	1.00
138	*Eric Moten*	.20
139	Tony Woods	.20
140	Phil Simms	.20
141	Ricky Reynolds	.20
142	Frank Stams	.20
143	Kevin Mack	.20
144	Wade Wilson	.20
145	Shawn Collins	.20
146	Roger Craig	.20
147	Jeff Feagles	.20
148	Norm Johnson	.20
149	Terrance Mathis	2.00
150	Reggie Cobb	.20
151	Chip Banks	.20
152	Darryl Pollard	.20
153	Karl Mecklenburg	.20
154	Ricky Proehl	.20
155	Pete Stoyanovich	.20
156	John Stephens	.20
157	Ron Morris	.20
158	Steve DeBerg	.20
159	Mike Munchak	.20
160	Brett Maxie	.20
161	Don Beebe	.20
162	Martin Mayhew	.20
163	Merril Hoge	.20
164	Kelvin Pritchett	.20
165	Jim Jeffcoat	.20
166	Myron Guyton	.20
167	Ickey Woods	.20
168	Andre Ware	.20
169	Gary Plummer	.20
170	Henry Ellard	.20
171	Scott Davis	.20
172	Randall McDaniel	.20
173	*Randal Hill*	1.00
174	Anthony Bell	.20
175	Gary Anderson	.20
176	Byron Evans	.20
177	Tony Mandarich	.20
178	Jeff George	2.00
179	Art Monk	.40
180	Mike Kenn	.20
181	Sean Landeta	.20
182	Shaun Gayle	.20
183	Michael Carter	.20
184	Robb Thomas	.20
185	Richmond Webb	.20
186	Carnell Lake	.20
187	Rueben Mayes	.20
188	Issiac Holt	.20
189	Leon Seals	.20
190	Al Smith	.20
191	Steve Atwater	.20
192	Greg McMurtry	.20
193	Al Toon	.20
194	Cortez Kennedy	.40
195	Gill Byrd	.20
196	Carl Zander	.20
197	Robert Brown	.20
198	Buford McGee	.20
199	Mervyn Fernandez	.20
200	Mike Dumas	.20
201	*Rob Burnett*	.40
202	Brian Mitchell	.20
203	Randall Cunningham	.50
204	Sammie Smith	.20
205	Ken Clarke	.20
206	Floyd Dixon	.20
207	Ken Norton	.20
208	Tony Siragusa	.20
209	Louis Lipps	.20
210	Chris Martin	.20
211	Jamie Mueller	.20
212	Dave Waymer	.20
213	Donnell Woolford	.20
214	Paul Gruber	.20
215	Ken Harvey	.20
216	*Henry Jones*	.40
217	Tommy Barnhardt	.20
218	Arthur Cox	.20
219	Pat Terrell	.20
220	Curtis Duncan	.20
221	Jeff Jaeger	.20
222	Scott Stephen	.20
223	Rob Moore	.20
224	Chris Hinton	.20
225	Marv Cook	.20
226	Patrick Hunter	.20
227	Earnest Byner	.20
228	Troy Aikman	4.00
229	Kevin Walker	.20
230	Keith Jackson	.20
231	*Russell Maryland*	.75
232	Charles Haley	.20
233	Nick Lowery	.20
234	Erik Howard	.20
235	Leonard Smith	.20
236	Tim Irwin	.20
237	Simon Fletcher	.20
238	Thomas Everett	.20
240	Leroy Hoard	.20
241	Wayne Haddix	.20
242	Gary Clark	.20
243	Eric Andolsek	.20
244	Jim Wahler	.20
245	Vaughan Johnson	.20
246	Kevin Butler	.20
247	Steve Tasker	.20
248	LeRoy Butler	.20
250	*Eric Turner*	1.00
251	Kevin Ross	.20
252	Stephen Baker	.20
253	Harold Green	.20
254	Rohn Stark	.20
255	Joe Nash	.20
256	Jesse Sapolu	.20
257	Willie Gault	.20
258	Jerome Brown	.20
259	Ken Willis	.20
260	Courtney Hall	.20
261	Hart Lee Dykes	.20
262	William Fuller	.20
263	Stan Thomas	.20
264	Dan Marino	6.00
265	Ron Cox	.20
266	Eric Green	.50
267	Anthony Carter	.20
268	Jerry Ball	.20
269	Ron Hall	.20
270	Dennis Smith	.20
271	Eric Hill	.20
272	*Dan McGwire*	.20
273	Lewis Billups	.20
274	Rickey Jackson	.20
275	Jim Sweeney	.20
276	Pat Beach	.20
277	Kevin Porter	.20
278	Mike Sherrard	.20
279	Andy Heck	.20
280	Ron Brown	.20
281	Lawrence Taylor	.50
282	Anthony Pleasant	.20
283	Wes Hopkins	.20
284	Jim Lachey	.20
285	Tim Harris	.20
286	Tony Epps	.20
287	Wendell Davis	.20
288	Bubba McDowell	.20
289	Reggie Roby, Bubby Brister	.20
290	*Chris Zorich*	1.00
291	Mike Merriweather	.20
292	Burt Grossman	.20
293	Eric McMillan	.20
294	John Elway	2.00
295	Toi Cook	.20
297	Matt Bahr	.20
298	Chris Spielman	.20
299	Freddie Joe Nunn (Troy Aikman and Emmitt Smith shown in background)	.30
300	Jim C. Jenson	.20
301	David Fulcher (Rookie card should be '88, not '89)	.20
302	Tommy Hodson	.20
303	Stephone Page	.20
304	Greg Townsend	.20
305	Dean Biasucci	.20
306	Jimmie Jones	.20
307	Eugene Marve	.20
308	Flipper Anderson	.20
309	Darryl Talley	.20
310	*Mike Croel*	.40
311	Thane Gash	.20
312	Perry Kemp	.20
313	Heath Sherman	.20
314	Mike Singletary	.20
315	Chip Lohmiller	.20
316	Tunch Ilkin	.20
317	Junior Seau	2.00
318	Mike Gann	.20
319	Tim McDonald	.20
320	Kyle Clifton	.20
321	Dan Owens	.20
322	Tim Grunhard	.20
323	Stan Brock	.20
324	Rodney Holman	.20
325	Mark Ingram	.20
326	*Browning Nagle*	.40
327	Joe Montana	5.00
328	Carl Lee	.20
329	John L. Williams	.20
330	David Griggs	.20
331	Clarence Kay	.20
332	Irving Fryar	.20
333	Doug Smith	.20
334	Kent Hull	.20
335	Mike Wilcher	.20
336	Ray Donaldson	.20
337	Mark Carrier (Rookie card should be '90, not '89)	.20
338	Kelvin Martin	.20
339	Keith Byars	.20
340	Wilber Marshall	.20
341	Ronnie Lott	.20
342	Blair Thomas	.20
343	Ronnie Harmon	.20
344	Brian Brennan	.20
345	*Charles McRae*	.20
346	Michael Cofer	.20
347	Keith Willis	.20
348	Bruce Kozerski	.20
349	Dave Meggett	.20
350	John Taylor	.20
351	Johnny Holland	.20
352	Steve Christie	.20
353	*Ricky Ervins*	1.00
354	Robert Massey	.20
355	Derrick Thomas	.50
356	Tommy Kane	.20
357	Melvin Bratton	.20
358	Bruce Matthews	.20
359	Mark Duper	.20
360	Jeff Wright	.20
361	Barry Sanders	6.00
362	Chuck Webb	.20
363	Darryl Grant	.20
364	William Roberts	.20
365	Reggie Rutland	.20
366	Clay Matthews	.20
367	Anthony Miller	.20
368	Mike Prior	.20
369	Jessie Tuggle	.20
370	Brad Muster	.20
371	Jay Schroeder	.20
372	Greg Lloyd	.20
373	Mike Cofer	.20
374	James Brooks	.20
375	Danny Noonan (Misspelled Noonen on card back)	.20
376	Latin Berry	.20
377	Brad Baxter	.20
378	Godfrey Myles	.20
379	Morten Andersen	.20
380	Keith Woodside	.20
381	Bobby Humphrey	.20
382	Mike Golic	.20
383	Keith McCants	.20
384	Anthony Thompson	.20
385	Mark Clayton	.20
386	Neil Smith	.20
387	Bryan Millard	.20
388	Mel Gray (Wrong Mel Gray pictured on card back)	.20
389	Ernest Givins	.20
390	Reyna Thompson	.20
391	*Eric Bieniemy*	.40
392	Jon Hand	.20
393	Mark Rypien	.20
394	Bill Romanowski	.20
395	Thurman Thomas	1.50
396	Jim Harbaugh	.20
397	Don Mosebar	.20
398	Andre Rison	.50
399	Mike Johnson	.20
400	Dermontti Dawson	.20
401	Herschel Walker	.30
402	Joe Prokop	.20
403	Eddie Brown	.20
404	Nate Newton	.20
405	Damone Johnson	.20
406	Jessie Hester	.20
407	Jim Arnold	.20
408	Ray Agnew	.20
409	Michael Brooks	.20
410	Keith Sims	.20
411	Carl Banks	.20
412	Jonathan Hayes	.20
413	Richard Johnson	.20
414	*Darryll Lewis*	.20
415	Jeff Bryant	.20
416	Leslie O'Neal	.20
417	Andre Reed	.30
418	Charles Mann	.20
419	Keith DeLong	.20
420	Bruce Hill	.20
421	Matt Brock	.20
422	Johnny Johnson	.30
423	Mark Bortz	.20
424	Ben Smith	.20
425	Jeff Cross	.20
426	Irv Pankey	.20
427	Hassan Jones	.20
428	Andre Tippett	.20
429	Tim Worley	.20
430	Daniel Stubbs	.20
431	Max Montoya	.20
432	Jumbo Elliott	.20
433	Duane Bickett	.20
434	*Nate Lewis*	.50
435	*Leonard Russell*	1.00
436	Hoby Brenner	.20
437	Ricky Sanders	.20
438	Pierce Holt	.20
439	Derrick Fenner	.20
440	Drew Hill	.20
441	Will Wolford	.20
442	Albert Lewis	.20
443	James Francis	.20
444	Chris Jackie (Jacke)	.20
445	Mike Farr	.20
446	Stephen Braggs	.20
447	Michael Haynes	1.00
448	Freeman McNeil (2008 pounds, sic)	.20
449	Kevin Donnalley	.20
450	John Offerdahl	.20
451	Eric Allen	.20
452	Keith McKeller	.20
453	Kevin Greene	.20
454	Ronnie Lippett	.20
455	Ray Childress	.20
456	Mike Saxon	.20
457	Mark Robinson	.20
458	Greg Kragen	.20
459	Steve Jordan	.20
460	John Johnson	.20
461	Sam Mills	.20
462	Bo Jackson	.40
463	Mark Collins	.20
464	Percy Snow	.20
465	Jeff Bostic	.20
466	Jacob Green	.20
467	Dexter Carter	.20
468	Rich Camarillo	.20
469	Bill Brooks	.20
470	John Carney	.20
471	Don Majkowski	.20
472	Ralph Tamm	.20
473	Fred Barnett	1.00
474	Jim Covert	.20
475	Kenneth Davis	.20
476	Jerry Gray	.20
477	Broderick Thomas	.20
478	Chris Doleman	.20
479	Haywood Jeffires	.40
480	Craig Heyward	.20
481	Markus Koch	.20
482	Tim Krumrie	.20
483	Robert Clark	.20
484	Mike Rozier	.20
485	Danny Villa	.20
486	Gerald Williams	.20
487	Steve Wisniewski	.20
488	J.B. Brown	.20
489	Eugene Robinson	.20
490	Ottis Anderson	.20
491	Tony Stargell	.20
492	Jack Del Rio	.20
493	Lamar Rogers	.20
494	Ricky Nattiel	.20
495	Dan Saleaumua	.20
496	Checklist Card	.20
497	Checklist Card	.20
498	Checklist Card	.20
499	Checklist Card	.20
500	Checklist Card	.20

1992 Stadium Club Promo Sheet

This nine-card promotional sheet was distributed at the 13th National Sports Collector's Convention in 1992. The sheet pictures the cards in a larger-than-the-finished- product format, but has a gold foil line framing the card that reveals the standard sized card. Sheet backs have a large logo promoting the event.

		MT
Complete Set (1):		10.00
Common Player:		10.00
NNO	Promo Sheet (Barry Sanders, Gene Atkins, Louis Oliver, Paul Gruber, Emmitt Smith, Steve Jordan, Warren Moon, Seth Joyner, Ronnie Lott)	10.00

1992 Stadium Club

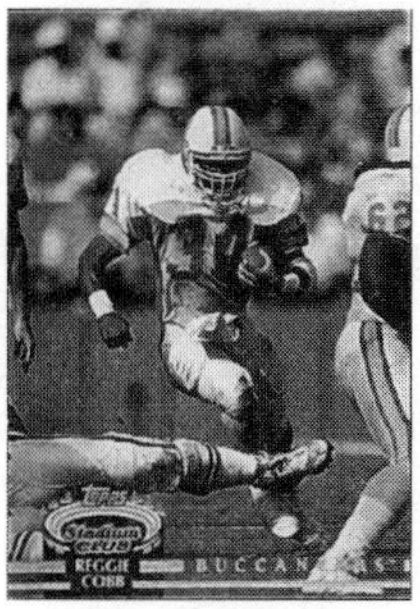

This three-card series contains 700 cards. Each glossy card has a full-bleed color photo on the front, with a Stadium Club logo and player's name at the bottom. The team name is between two gold foil stripes. The back is done horizontally and includes a career summary, Sporting News Skills Rating System report and a miniature version of the player's Topps rookie card. The set has 30 Members Choice cards (#s 291-310 and 601-610), which are labeled on the card fronts.

		MT
Complete Set (700):		150.00
Complete Series 1 (300):		15.00
Complete Series 2 (300):		15.00
Complete Hi Series (100):		125.00
Common Player:		.10
Common Player (601-700):		.30
Series 1 or 2 Pack (12):		.90
Series 1 or 2 Wax Box (36):		24.00
Series 3 Pack (12):		14.00
Series 3 Wax Box (36):		475.00
1	Mark Rypien	.10
2	*Carlton Bailey*	.15
3	Kevin Glover	.10
4	Vance Johnson	.10
5	Jim Jeffcoat	.10
6	Dan Saleaumua	.10
7	Darion Conner	.10
8	Don Maggs	.10
9	Richard Dent	.15
10	Mark Murphy	.10
11	Wesley Carroll	.10
12	Chris Burkett	.10
13	Steve Wallace	.10
14	Jacob Green	.10
15	Roger Ruzek	.10
16	J.B. Brown	.10
17	Dave Meggett	.10
18	David Johnson	.10
19	Rich Gannon	.10
20	Kevin Mack	.10
21	Reggie Cobb	.10
22	Nate Lewis	.10
23	Doug Smith	.10
24	Irving Fryar	.10
25	Anthony Thompson	.10
26	Duane Bickett	.10
27	Don Majkowski	.10
28	Mark Schlereth	.10
29	Melvin Jenkins	.10
30	Michael Haynes	.15
31	Greg Lewis	.10
32	Kenneth Davis	.10
33	Derrick Thomas	.20
34	David Williams	.10
35	Neal Anderson	.10
36	Andre Collins	.10
37	Jesse Solomon	.10
38	Barry Sanders	3.00
39	Jeff Gossett	.10
40	Rickey Jackson	.10
41	Ray Berry	.10
42	Leroy Hoard	.10
43	Eric Thomas	.10
44	Brian Washington	.10
45	Pat Terrell	.10
46	Eugene Robinson	.10
47	Luis Sharpe	.10
48	Jerome Brown	.10
49	Mark Collins	.10
50	Johnny Holland	.10
51	Tony Paige	.10
52	Willie Green	.10
53	Steve Atwater	.10
54	Brad Muster	.10
55	Cris Dishman	.10
56	Sam (Eddie Anderson)	.10
57	Sam Mills	.10
58	Donald Evans	.10
59	Jon Vaughn	.10
60	Marion Butts	.10
61	Rodney Holman	.10
62	*Dwayne White*	.10
63	Martin Mayhew	.10
64	Jonathan Hayes	.10
65	Andre Rison	.15
66	Calvin Williams	.10
67	James Washington	.10
68	Tim Harris	.10
69	Jim Richter	.10
70	Johnny Johnson	.10
71	John Offerdahl	.10
72	Herschel Walker	.10
73	Perry Kemp	.10
74	Erik Howard	.10
75	Lamar Lathon	.10
76	Greg Kragen	.10
77	Jay Schroeder	.10
78	Jim Arnold	.10
79	Chris Miller	.10
80	Deron Cherry	.10
81	Jim Harbaugh	.20
82	Gill Fenerty	.10
83	Fred Stokes	.10
84	Roman Phifer	.10
85	Clyde Simmons	.10
86	Vince Newsome	.10
87	Lawrence Dawsey	.10
88	Eddie Brown	.10
89	Greg Montgomery	.10
90	Jeff Lageman	.10
91	Terry Wooden	.10
92	Nate Newton	.10
93	David Richards	.10
94	Derek Russell	.10
95	Steve Jordan	.10
96	Hugh Millen	.10
97	Mark Duper	.10
98	Sean Landeta	.10
99	James Thornton	.10
100	Darrell Green	.10
101	Harris Barton	.10
102	John Alt	.10
103	Mike Farr	.10
104	Bob Golic	.10
105	Gene Atkins	.10
106	Gary Anderson	.10
107	Norm Johnson	.10
108	Eugene Daniel	.10
109	Kent Hull	.10
110	John Elway	1.00
111	Rich Camarillo	.10
112	Charles Wilson	.10
113	Matt Bahr	.10
114	Mark Carrier	.10
115	Richmond Webb	.10
116	Charles Mann	.10
117	Tim McGee	.10
118	Wes Hopkins	.10
119	Mo Lewis	.10
120	Warren Moon	.25
121	Damone Johnson	.10
122	Kevin Gogan	.10
123	Joey Browner	.10
124	Tommy Kane	.10
125	Vincent Brown	.10
126	Barry Word	.10
127	Michael Brooks	.10
128	Jumbo Elliot	.10
129	Marcus Allen	.25
130	Tom Waddle	.10
131	Jim Dombrowski	.10
132	Aeneas Williams	.10
133	Clay Matthews	.10
134	Thurman Thomas	.50
135	Dean Biasucci	.10
136	Moe Gardner	.10
137	James Campen	.10
138	Tim Johnson	.10
139	Erik Kramer	.15
140	Keith McCants	.10
141	John Carney	.10
142	Tunch Ilkin	.10
143	Louis Oliver	.10
144	Bill Maas	.10
145	Wendell Davis	.10
146	Pepper Johnson	.10
147	Howie Long	.10
148	Brett Maxie	.10
149	Tony Casillas	.10
150	Michael Carter	.10
151	Byron Evans	.10
152	Lorenzo White	.10
153	Larry Kelm	.10
154	Andy Heck	.10
155	Harry Newsome	.10
156	Chris Singleton	.10
157	Mike Kenn	.10
158	Jeff Faulkner	.10
159	Ken Lanier	.10
160	Darryl Talley	.10
161	*Louie Aguiar*	.10
162	Danny Copeland	.10
163	Kevin Porter	.10
164	Trace Armstrong	.10
165	Dermontti Dawson	.10
166	*Fred McAfee*	.10
167	Ronnie Lott	.10
168	Tony Mandarich	.10
169	Howard Cross	.10
170	Vestee Jackson	.10
171	Jeff Herrod	.10
172	*Randy Hilliard*	.10
173	Robert Wilson	.10
174	*Joe Walter*	.10
175	Chris Spielman	.10
176	Darryl Henley	.10
177	Jay Hilgenberg	.10
178	John Kidd	.10
179	Doug Widell	.10
180	Seth Joyner	.10
181	Nick Bell	.10
182	Don Griffin	.10
183	Johnny Meads	.10
184	Jeff Bostic	.10
185	Johnny Hector	.10
186	Jessie Tuggle	.10
187	Robb Thomas	.10
188	Shane Conlan	.10
189	*Michael Zordich*	.10
190	Emmitt Smith	5.00
191	Robert Blackmon	.10
192	Carl Lee	.10
193	Harry Galbreath	.10
194	Ed King	.10
195	Stan Thomas	.10
196	Andre Waters	.10
197	Pat Harlow	.10
198	Zefross Moss	.10
199	Bobby Hebert	.10
200	Doug Riesenberg	.10
201	Mike Croel	.10
202	Jeff Jaeger	.10
203	Gary Plummer	.10
204	Chris Jacke	.10
205	Neil O'Donnell	.50

206 Mark Bortz .10
207 Tim Barnett .10
208 Jerry Ball .10
209 Chip Lohmiller .10
210 Jim Everett .10
211 Tim McKyer .10
212 Aaron Craver .10
213 John L. Williams .10
214 Simon Fletcher .10
215 Walter Reeves .10
216 Terance Mathis .10
217 Mike Pitts .10
218 Bruce Matthews .10
219 Howard Ballard .10
220 Leonard Russell .10
221 Michael Stewart .10
222 Mike Merriweather .10
223 Ricky Sanders .10
224 Ray Horton .10
225 Michael Jackson .10
226 Bill Romanowski .10
227 Steve McMichael .10
228 Chris Martin .10
229 Tim Green .10
230 Karl Mecklenburg .10
231 Felix Wright .10
232 Charles McRae .10
233 Pete Stoyanovich .10
234 Stephen Baker .10
235 Herman Moore 1.50
236 Terry McDaniel .10
237 Dalton Hilliard .10
238 Gill Byrd .10
239 Leron Seals .10
240 Rod Woodson .15
241 Curtis Duncan .10
242 Keith Jackson .10
243 Mark Stepnoski .10
244 Art Monk .15
245 Matt Stover .10
246 John Roper .10
247 Rodney Hampton .40
248 Steve Wisniewski .10
249 Bryan Millard .10
250 Todd Lyght .10
251 Marvin Washington .10
252 Eric Swann .10
253 Bruce Kozerski .10
254 Jon Hand .10
255 Scott Fulhage .10
256 Chuck Cecil .10
257 Eric Martin .10
258 Eric Metcalf .10
259 T.J. Turner .10
260 Kirk Lowdermilk .10
261 Keith McKeller .10
262 Wymon Henderson .10
263 David Alexander .10
264 George Jamison .10
265 Ken Norton .10
266 Jim Lachey .10
267 *Bo Orlando* .10
268 Nick Lowery .10
269 Keith Van Horne .10
270 Dwight Stone .10
271 Kerith DeLong .10
272 James Francis .10
273 Greg McMurtry .10
274 Ethan Horton .10
275 Stan Brock .10
276 Ken Harvey .10
277 Ronnie Harmon .10
278 Mike Pritchard .10
279 Kyle Clifton .10
280 Anthony Johnson .10
281 Esera Tuaolo .10
282 Vernon Turner .10
283 David Griggs .10
284 Dino Hackett .10
285 Carwell Gardner .10
286 Ron Hall .10
287 Reggie White .20
288 S.C. Checklist 1-100 .10
289 S.C. Checklist 101-200 .10
290 S.C. Checklist 201-300 .10
291 Mark Clayton .10
292 Pat Swilling .10
293 Ernest Givins .10
294 Broderick Thomas .10
295 John Friesz .15
296 Cornelius Bennett .10
297 Anthony Carter .10
298 Earnest Byner .10
299 Michael Irvin .50
300 Cortez Kennedy .10
301 Barry Sanders 2.00
302 Mike Croel .10
303 Emmitt Smith 3.00
304 Leonard Russell .10
305 Neal Anderson .10
306 Derrick Thomas .15
307 Mark Rypien .10
308 Reggie White .20
309 Rod Woodson .15
310 Rodney Hampton .20
311 Carnell Lake .10
312 Robert Delpino .10
313 Brian Blades .10
314 Marc Spindler .10
315 Scott Norwood .10
316 Frank Warren .10
317 David Treadwell .10
318 Steve Broussard .10
319 Lorenzo Lynch .10
320 Ray Agnew .10
321 Derrick Walker .10
322 *Vinson Smith* .10
323 Gary Clark .10
324 Charles Haley .10
325 Keith Byars .10
326 Winston Moss .10
327 *Paul McJulien* .10
328 Tony Covington .10
329 Mark Carrier .10
330 Mark Tuinei .10
331 *Tracy Simien* .10
332 Jeff Wright .10
333 Bryan Cox .10
334 Lonnie Young .10
335 Clarence Verdin .10
336 Dan Fike .10
337 Steve Sewell .10
338 Gary Zimmerman .10
339 Barney Bussey .10
340 William Perry .10
341 Jeff Hostetler .15
342 Doug Smith .10
343 Cleveland Gary .10
344 Todd Marinovich .10
345 Rich Moran .10
346 Tony Woods .10
347 Vaughan Johnson .10
348 Marv Cook .10
349 Pierce Holt .10
350 Gerald Williams .10
351 Kevin Butler .10
352 William White .10
353 Henry Rolling .10
354 James Joseph .10
355 Vinny Testaverde .10
356 Scott Radecic .10
357 Lee Johnson .10
358 Steve Tasker .10
359 David Lutz .10
360 Audrey McMillan .10
361 Brad Baxter .10
362 Mark Dennis .10
363 Erric Pegram .15
364 Sean Jones .10
365 William Roberts .10
366 Steve Young 1.75
367 Joe Jacoby .10
368 *Richard Brown* .10
369 Keith Kartz .10
370 Freddie Joe Nunn .10
371 Darren Comeaux .10
372 Larry Brown .10
373 Haywood Jeffires .10
374 Tom Newberry .10
375 *Steve Bono* 1.25
376 Kevin Ross .10
377 Kelvin Pritchett .10
378 Jessie Hester .10
379 Mitchell Price .10
380 Barry Foster .10
381 Reyna Thompson .10
382 Cris Carter .20
383 Lemuel Stinson .10
384 Rod Bernstine .10
385 James Lofton .10
386 Kevin Murphy .10
387 Greg Townsend .10
388 *Edgar Bennett* .75
389 Rob Moore .10
390 Eugene Lockhart .10
391 Bern Brostek .10
392 Craig Heyward .10
393 Ferrell Edmunds .10
394 John Kasay .10
395 Jesse Sapolu .10
396 Jim Breech .10
397 Neil Smith .10
398 Bryce Paup .40
399 Tony Tolbert .10
400 Bubby Brister .10
401 Dennis Smith .10
402 Dan Owens .10
403 Steve Beuerlein .10
404 Rick Tuten .10
405 Eric Allen .10
406 Eric Hill .10
407 Don Warren .10
408 Greg Jackson .10
409 Chris Doleman .10
410 Anthony Munoz .10
411 Michael Young .10
412 Cornelius Bennett .10
413 Ray Childress .10
414 Kevin Call .10
415 Burt Grossman .10
416 Scott Miller .10
417 Tim Newton .10
418 Robert Young .10
419 *Tommy Vardell* .15
420 Michael Walter .10
421 *Chris Port* .10
422 *Carlton Haselrig* .10
423 Rodney Peete .10
424 Scott Stephen .10
425 Chris Warren 1.00
426 *Scott Galbraith* .10
427 Fuad Reveiz .10
428 Irv Eatman .10
429 David Szott .10
430 Brent Williams .10
431 Mike Horan .10
432 Brent Jones .10
433 Paul Gruber .10
434 Carlos Huerta .10
435 Scott Case .10
436 Greg Davis .10
437 Ken Clarke .10
438 Alfred Williams .10
439 Jim Jensen .10
440 Louis Lipps .10
441 Larry Roberts .10
442 James Jones .10
443 Don Mosebar .10
444 Quinn Early .10
445 Robert Brown .10
446 Tom Thayer .10
447 Michael Irvin .40
448 Jarrod Bunch .10
449 Riki Ellison .10
450 Joe Phillips .10
451 Ernest Givins .10
452 Glenn Parker .10
453 Brett Perriman .25
454 *Jayice Pearson* .10
455 Mark Jackson .10
456 *Siran Stacy* .10
457 Rufus Porter .10
458 Michael Ball .10
459 Craig Taylor .10
460 *George Thomas* .10
461 Alvin Wright .10
462 Ron Hallstrom .10
463 *Mike Mooney* .10
464 Dexter Carter .10
465 *Marty Carter* .10
466 Pat Swilling .10
467 Mike Golic .10
468 Reggie Roby .10
469 Randall McDaniel .10
470 John Stephens .10
471 *Ricardo McDonald* .10
472 Wilber Marshall .10
473 Jim Sweeney .10
474 Ernie Jones .10
475 Bennie Blades .10
476 Don Beebe .10
477 Grant Feasel .10
478 Ernie Mills .10
479 Tony Jones .10
480 Jeff Uhlenhake .10
481 Gaston Green .10
482 John Taylor .10
483 Anthony Smith .10
484 Tony Bennett .10
485 *David Brandon* .10
486 Shawn Jefferson .10
487 Christian Okoye .10
488 Leonard Marshall .10
489 Jay Novacek .10
490 Harold Green .10
491 Bubba McDowell .10
492 Gary Anderson .10
493 *Terrell Buckley* .20
494 *Jamie Dukes* .10
495 Morten Andersen .10
496 Henry Thomas .10
497 Bill Lewis .10
498 Jeff Cross .10
499 Hardy Nickerson .10
500 Henry Ellard .10
501 *Joe Bowden* .10
502 Brian Noble .10
503 Mike Cofer .10
504 Jeff Bryant .10
505 Lomas Brown .10
506 Chip Banks .10
507 Keith Taylor .10
508 Mark Kelso .10
509 *Dexter McNabb* .10
510 *Gene Chilton* .10
511 George Thornton .10
512 Jeff Criswell .10
513 Brad Edwards .10
514 Ron Heller .10
515 Tim Brown .20
516 *Keith Hamilton* .30
517 Mark Higgs .10
518 Tommy Barnhardt .10
519 Brian Jordan .10
520 Ray Crockett .10
521 Karl Wilson .10
522 Ricky Reynolds .10
523 Max Montoya .10
524 David Little .10
525 *Alonzo Mitz* .10
526 Darryll Lewis .10
527 Keith Henderson .10
528 Leroy Butler .10
529 Rob Burnett .10
530 Chris Chandler .10
531 Maury Buford .10
532 Mark Ingram .10
533 Mike Saxon .10
534 Bill Fralic .10
535 *Craig Patterson* .10
536 John Randle .10
537 Dwayne Harper .10
538 *Chris Hakel* .10
539 Maurice Hurst .10
540 Warren Powers .10
541 Will Wolford .10
542 Dennis Gibson .10
543 Jackie Slater .10
544 Floyd Turner .10
545 Guy McIntyre .10
546 Eric Green .10
547 Rohn Stark .10
548 William Fuller .10
549 Alvin Harper .20
550 Mark Clayton .10
551 *Natu Tuatagaloa* .10
552 Fred Barnett .10
553 *Bob Whitfield* .10
554 Courtney Hall .10
555 Brian Mitchell .10
556 Patrick Hunter .10
557 Rick Bryan .10
558 Anthony Carter .10
559 Jim Wahler .10
560 Joe Morris .10
561 Tony Zendejas .10
562 Mervyn Fernandez .10
563 Jamie Williams .10
564 Darrell Thompson .10
565 Adrian Cooper .10
566 Chris Goode .10
567 *Jeff Davidson* .10
568 James Hasty .10
569 *Chris Mims* .50
570 *Ray Seals* .15
571 Myron Guyton .10
572 Todd McNair .10
573 Andre Tippett .10
574 Kirby Jackson .10
575 Mel Gray .10
576 Stephone Paige .10
577 Scott Davis .10
578 John Gesek .10
579 Earnest Byner .10
580 John Friesz .10
581 Al Smith .10
582 Flipper Anderson .10
583 *Amp Lee* .25
584 Greg Lloyd .15
585 Cortez Kennedy .10
586 Keith Sims .10
587 Terry Allen .50
588 David Fulcher .10
589 Chris Hinton .10
590 Tim McDonald .10
591 Bruce Armstrong .10
592 Sterling Sharpe .20
593 Tom Rathman .10
594 Bill Brooks .10
595 Broderick Thomas .10
596 Jim Wilks .10
597 Tyrone Braxton .10
598 Checklist 301-400 .10
599 Checklist 401-500 .10
600 Checklist 501-600 .10
601 Andre Reed (MC) .50
602 Troy Aikman (MC) 3.00
603 Dan Marino (MC) 6.00
604 Randall Cunningham (MC) .50
605 Jim Kelly (MC) 1.00
606 Deion Sanders (MC) 2.00
607 Junior Seau (MC) 1.00
608 Jerry Rice (MC) 3.00
609 Bruce Smith (MC) .50
610 Lawrence Taylor (MC) .50
611 *Todd Collins* .50
612 *Ty Detmer* 2.00
613 Browning Nagle .30
614 Tony Sacca .30
615 Boomer Esiason .30
616 Billy Joe Tolliver .30
617 Leslie O'Neal .30
618 *Mark Wheeler* .30
619 Eric Dickerson .50
620 Phil Simms .30
621 *Troy Vincent* 1.00
622 *Jason Hanson* .50
623 Andre Reed .50
624 Russell Maryland .50
625 *Steve Emtman* 1.00
626 *Sean Gilbert* 1.50
627 *Dana Hall* 1.00
628 Dan McGwire .30
629 Lewis Billups .30
630 *Darryl Williams* .50
631 *Dwayne Sabb* .50
632 Mark Royals .30
633 Cary Conklin .30
634 Al Toon .30
635 Junior Seau 1.50
636 *Greg Skrepenak* .30
637 Deion Sanders 3.00
638 Steve DeOssie .30
639 Randall Cunningham .50
640 Jim Kelly 1.00
641 *Michael Brandon* .30
642 *Clayton Holmes* .30
643 Webster Slaughter .30
644 Ricky Proehl .30
645 Jerry Rice 5.00
646 Carl Banks .30
647 J.J. Birden .30
648 *Tracy Scroggins* 1.00
649 *Alonzo Spellman* 1.00
650 Joe Montana 5.00
651 *Courtney Hawkins* 1.00
652 *Corey Widmer* .30
653 *Robert Brooks* 7.00
654 *Darren Woodson* 1.00
655 Derrick Bengals .30
656 Steve Christie .30
657 *Chester McGlockton* 3.00
658 *Steve Israel* .30
659 *Robert Harris* .30
660 Dan Marino 10.00
661 Ed McCaffrey 2.50
662 *Johnny Mitchell* 1.00
663 Timm Rosenbach .30
664 Anthony Miller .30
665 Merril Hoge .30
666 *Eugene Chung* .30
667 Rueben Mayes .30
668 Martin Bayless .30
669 *Ashley Ambrose* .30
670 Michael Cofer .30
671 *Shane Dronett* .30
672 Bernie Kosar .50
673 Mike Singletary .50
674 *Mike Lodish* .30
675 *Phillippi Sparks* .50
676 Joel Steed .30
677 Kevin Fagan .30
678 Randal Hill .30
679 Ken O'Brien .30
680 Lawrence Taylor .50
681 Harvey Williams .50
682 *Quentin Coryatt* 1.00
683 Brett Favre 85.00
684 *Robert Jones* 1.00
685 Michael Dean Perry .50
686 Bruce Smith .50
687 *Troy Auzenne* .30
688 *Thomas McLemore* .30
689 *Dale Carter* 1.50
690 *Marc Boutte* .30
691 Jeff George 2.00
692 *Dion Lambert* .30
693 *Vaughn Dunbar* .30
694 *Derek Brown* .30
695 Troy Aikman 5.00
696 *John Fina* .30
697 *Kevin Smith* 1.00
698 *Corey Miller* .30
699 *Lance Olberding* .30
700 Checklist 601-700 .50

1992 Stadium Club No.1 Draft Picks

This four-card insert set features three former #1 draft picks, plus Rocket Ismail. Cards were randomly inserted in 1992 Topps Stadium Club Series II packs, and are numbered on the back. Each card front has a full-bleed photo, along with the player's name, Stadium Club logo and #1 symbol at the bottom. A football in the top upper right has the year the player was selected in it. The card back has a closeup shot of the player, a player biography and set logo.

MT
Complete Set (4): 30.00
Common Player: 7.00
1 Jeff George 10.00
2 Russell Maryland 7.00
3 Steve Emtman 7.00
4 Raghib Ismail 7.00

1992 Stadium Club QB Legends

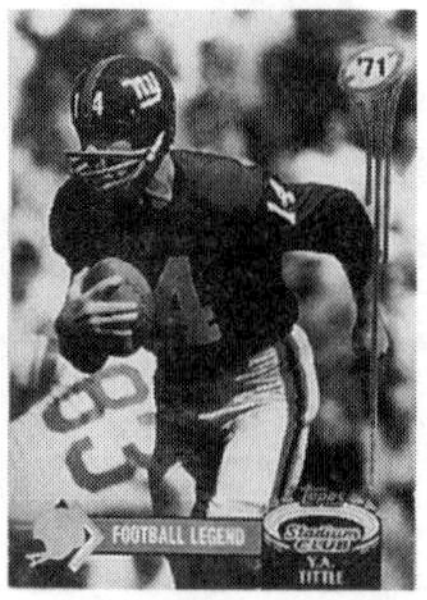

These cards, featuring six Hall of Fame quarterbacks, were random inserts in 1992 Topps Stadium Club Series II packs, one per every 72 packs. The card front has a color action photo, along with the player's name and Stadium Club logo at the bottom. The set's name is given in a blue bar at the bottom, too, adjacent to a gold foil football helmet on the left. A lime green football appears in the upper right corner, with the year the player was inducted into the Hall of Fame inside it. The football is edged in gold foil and has three gold-foil stripes running down from it. The horizontal backs have a green and black background which includes a player photo, career statistics, a mini version of the player's first Topps card, and the player's facsimile autograph stamped in gold foil. Each card back is also numbered.

MT
Complete Set (6): 15.00
Common Player: 3.00
1 Y.A. Tittle 3.00
2 Bart Starr 4.00
3 John Unitas 4.00
4 George Blanda 3.00
5 Roger Staubach 5.00
6 Terry Bradshaw 5.00

1993 Stadium Club Promo Sheet

This nine-card promo sheet was distributed at the 1993 National Sports Collectors Convention in Chicago. Similar to the 1992 sheet, the photos are shown larger than normal and contain a gold line that reveals the true standard size card. Sheet backs contain a large logo celebrating the event.

MT
Complete Set (1): 8.00
Common Player: 8.00
NNO Promo Sheet (Johnny Bailey, Vai Sikahema, Richard Dent, Sterling Sharpe, Tommy Barnhardt, Cris Carter, Cortez Kennedy, Christian Okoye, Reggie Cobb) 8.00

1993 Stadium Club

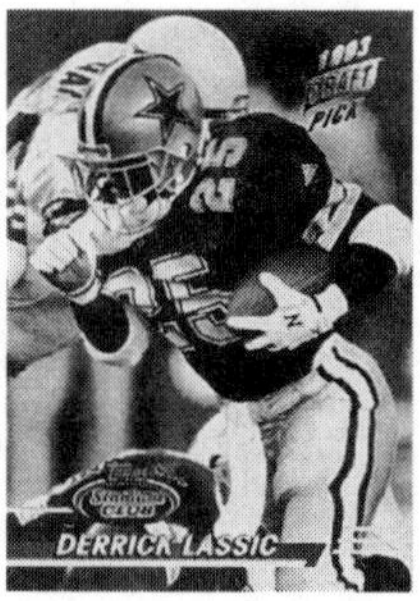

1993 Stadium Club football cards were issued in two 250-card series. Each card front has a full-bleed color photo and the player's name is foil stamped in gold at the bottom in a green stripe. The backs have statistics, a Football News Skills Rating Systems review and a miniature version of the player's Topps rookie card. A high-number series (#s 501-550) was also issued and includes Members Choice cards, Draft Picks, 1st-Year Players and Key Acquisitions. Super Team cards were randomly inserted into packs, one per every 24 packs. If the team pictured on a Super Team card wins a division title, conference championship or the Super Bowl, the card can be redeemed for special prizes. Other insert cards include First Day Production (silver foil) and Master Photo winner cards, which can be redeemed for a group of three Stadium Club Master Photos.

MT
Complete Set (550): 50.00
Complete Series 1 (250): 25.00
Complete Series 2 (250): 15.00
Complete High Series (50): 10.00
Common Player: .10
Minor Stars: .20
First Day Cards: 10x-20x
First Day Rookies: 5x-10x
Series 1 Pack (15): 2.50
Series 1 Wax Box (24): 50.00
Series 2 or 3 Pack (15): 1.50
Series 2 or 3 Wax Box (24): 25.00
1 Sterling Sharpe .50
2 Chris Burkett .10
3 Santana Dotson .10
4 Michael Jackson .10
5 Neal Anderson .10
6 Bryan Cox .10
7 Dennis Gibson .10
8 Jeff Graham .10
9 Roger Ruzek .10
10 Duane Bickett .10
11 Charles Mann .10
12 Tommy Maddox .15
13 Vaughn Dunbar .10
14 Gary Plummer .10
15 Chris Miller .10
16 Chris Warren .75
17 Alvin Harper .20
18 Eric Dickerson .10
19 Mike Jones .10
20 Ernest Givins .10
21 *Natrone Means* 2.00
22 Doug Riesenberg .10
23 Barry Word .10
24 Sean Salisbury .10
25 Derrick Fenner .10
26 David Howard .10
27 Mark Kelso .10
28 Todd Lyght .10
29 Dana Hall .10
30 Eric Metcalf .10
31 Jason Hanson .10
32 Dwight Stone .10
33 Johnny Mitchell .20
34 Reggie Roby .10
35 Terrell Buckley .15
36 Steve McMichael .10
37 Marty Carter .10
38 Seth Joyner .10
39 Rohn Stark .10
40 *Eric Curry* .50
41 Tommy Barnhardt .10
42 Karl Mecklenburg .10
43 Darion Conner .10
44 Ronnie Harmon .10
45 Cortez Kennedy .20
46 Tim Brown .10
47 Bill Lewis .10
48 Randall McDaniel .10
49 Curtis Duncan .10
50 Troy Aikman 3.00
51 David Klingler .20
52 Brent Jones .10
53 Dave Krieg .10
54 Bruce Smith .10
55 Vincent Brown .10
56 *O.J. McDuffie* 2.25
57 Cleveland Gary .10
58 *Larry Centers* .75
59 Pepper Johnson .10
60 Dan Marino 4.00
61 Robert Porcher .10
62 Jim Harbaugh .10
63 Sam Mills .10
64 Gary Anderson .10
65 Neil O'Donnell .50
66 Keith Byars .10
67 Jeff Herrod .10
68 Marion Butts .10
69 Terry McDaniel .10
70 John Elway 1.00
71 Steve Broussard .10
72 Kelvin Martin .10
73 *Tom Carter* .20
74 Bryce Paup .10
75 Jim Kelly .50
76 Bill Romanowski .10
77 Andre Collins .10
78 Mike Farr .10
79 Henry Ellard .10
80 Dale Carter .10
81 Johnny Bailey .10
82 *Garrison Hearst* 2.50
83 Brent Williams .10
84 Richard McDonald .10
85 Emmitt Smith 4.00
86 Vai Sikahema .10
87 Jackie Harris .20
88 Alonzo Spellman .10
89 Mark Wheeler .10
90 Dalton Hilliard .10
91 Mark Higgs .20
92 Aaron Wallace .10
93 Earnest Byner .10
94 Stanley Richard .10
95 Cris Carter .10
96 *Bobby Houston* .20
97 Craig Heyward .10
98 Bernie Kosar .10
99 Mike Croel .10
100 Deion Sanders 1.00
101 Warren Moon .20
102 Christian Okoye .10
103 Ricky Watters .50
104 Eric Swann .10
105 Rodney Hampton .20
106 Daryl Johnston .10
107 Andre Reed .20
108 *Jerome Bettis* 2.50
109 Eugene Daniel .10
110 Leonard Russell .15
111 Darryl Williams .10
112 Rod Woodson .10
113 Boomer Esiason .20
114 James Hasty .10
115 Marc Boutte .10
116 Tom Waddle .10
117 Lawrence Dawsey .10
118 Mark Collins .10
119 Willie Gault .10
120 Barry Sanders 2.50
121 Leroy Hoard .10
122 Anthony Munoz .10
123 Jesse Sapolu .10
124 Art Monk .10
125 Randal Hill .10
126 John Offerdahl .10
127 Carlos Jenkins .10
128 Al Smith .10
129 Michael Irvin .50
130 Kenneth Davis .10
131 *Curtis Conway* 2.00
132 Steve Atwater .10
133 Neil Smith .10
134 *Steve Everitt* .20
135 Chris Mims .10
136 Rickey Jackson .10
137 Edgar Bennett .60
138 Mike Pritchard .10
139 Richard Dent .10
140 Barry Foster .10
141 Eugene Robinson .10
142 Jackie Slater .10
143 Paul Gruber .10
144 Rob Moore .20
145 *Robert Smith* 3.00
146 Lorenzo White .10
147 Tommy Vardell .10
148 Dave Meggett .10
149 Vince Workman .10
150 Terry Allen .15
151 Howie Long .10
152 Charles Haley .10
153 Pete Metzelaars .10
154 *John Copeland* .50
155 Aeneas Williams .10
156 Ricky Sanders .10
157 Andre Ware .10
158 Tony Paige .10
159 Jerome Henderson .10
160 Harold Green .10
161 Wymon Henderson .10
162 Andre Rison .20
163 Donald Evans .10
164 Todd Scott .10
165 Steve Emtman .20
166 William Fuller .10
167 Michael Dean Perry .10
168 Randall Cunningham .20

169	Toi Cook	.10
170	Browning Nagle	.10
171	Darryl Henley	.10
172	*George Teague*	.40
173	Derrick Thomas	.20
174	Jay Novacek	.10
175	Mark Carrier	.10
176	Kevin Fagan	.10
177	Nate Lewis	.10
178	Courtney Hawkins	.20
179	Robert Blackmon	.10
180	*Rick Mirer*	.50
181	Mike Lodish	.10
182	Jarrod Bunch	.10
183	Anthony Smith	.10
184	Brian Noble	.10
185	Eric Bieniemy	.10
186	Keith Jackson	.20
187	Eric Martin	.10
188	Vance Johnson	.10
189	Kevin Mack	.10
190	Rich Camarillo	.10
191	Ashley Ambrose	.10
192	Ray Childress	.10
193	Jim Arnold	.10
194	Ricky Ervins	.10
195	Gary Anderson	.10
196	Eric Allen	.10
197	Roger Craig	.10
198	Jon Vaughn	.10
199	Tim McDonald	.10
200	Broderick Thomas	.10
201	Jessie Tuggle	.10
202	Alonzo Mitz	.10
203	Harvey Williams	.10
204	Russell Maryland	.10
205	Marvin Washington	.10
206	Jim Everett	.10
207	Trace Armstrong	.10
208	Steve Young	2.00
209	Tony Woods	.10
210	Brett Favre	4.00
211	Nate Odomes	.10
212	Ricky Proehl	.10
213	Jim Dombrowski	.10
214	Anthony Carter	.10
215	Tracy Simien	.10
216	Clay Matthews	.10
217	*Patrick Bates*	.35
218	Jeff George	.25
219	David Fulcher	.10
220	Phil Simms	.15
221	Eugene Chung	.10
222	Reggie Cobb	.10
223	Jim Sweeney	.10
224	Greg Lloyd	.10
225	Sean Jones	.10
226	*Marvin Jones*	.40
227	Bill Brooks	.10
228	Moe Gardner	.10
229	Louis Oliver	.10
230	Flipper Anderson	.10
231	Marc Spindler	.10
232	Jerry Rice	2.00
233	Chip Lohmiller	.10
234	Nolan Harrison	.10
235	Heath Sherman	.10
236	Reyna Thompson	.10
237	Derrick Walker	.10
238	Rufus Porter	.10
239	Checklist 1-125	.10
240	Checklist 126-250	.10
241	John Elway	.40
242	Troy Aikman	1.25
243	Steve Emtman	.15
244	Ricky Watters	.50
245	Barry Foster	.20
246	Dan Marino	1.50
247	Reggie White	.15
248	Thurman Thomas	.60
249	Broderick Thomas	.10
250	Joe Montana	2.00
251	Tim Goad	.10
252	Joe Nash	.10
253	Anthony Johnson	.10
254	Carl Pickens	1.00
255	Steve Beuerlein	.15
256	*Anthony Newman*	.10
257	Corey Miller	.10
258	Steve DeBerg	.10
259	Johnny Holland	.10
260	Jerry Ball	.10
261	*Siupeli Malamala*	.15
262	Steve Wisniewski	.10
263	Kelvin Pritchett	.10
264	Chris Gardocki	.10
265	Henry Thomas	.10
266	*Arthur Marshall*	.40
267	Quinn Early	.10
268	Jonathan Hayes	.10
269	Erric Pegram	.40
270	Clyde Simmons	.10
271	Eric Moten	.10
272	Brian Mitchell	.10
273	Adrian Cooper	.10
274	Gaston Green	.10
275	John Taylor	.10
276	Jeff Uhlenhake	.10
277	Phil Hansen	.10
278	*Kevin Williams*	.50
279	Robert Massey	.10
280a	*Drew Bledsoe*	5.00
280b	*Drew Bledsoe Err.*	10.00
281	Walter Reeves	.10
282	*Carlton Gray*	.20
283	Derek Brown	.10
284	Martin Mayhew	.10
285	Sean Gilbert	.10
286	Jessie Hester	.10
287	Mark Clayton	.10
288	Blair Thomas	.10
289	J.J. Birden	.10
290	Shannon Sharpe	.20
291	*Richard Fain*	.15
292	Gene Atkins	.10
293	Burt Grossman	.10
294	Chris Doleman	.10
295	Pat Swilling	.10
296	Mike Kenn	.10
297	Merril Hoge	.10
298	Don Mosebar	.10
299	Kevin Smith	.10
300	Darrell Green	.10
301	*Dan Footman*	.20
302	Vestee Jackson	.10
303	Carwell Gardner	.10
304	Amp Lee	.10
305	Bruce Matthews	.10
306	Antone Davis	.10
307	Dean Biasucci	.10
308	Maurice Hurst	.10
309	John Kasay	.10
310	Lawrence Taylor	.15
311	Ken Harvey	.10
312	Willie Davis	.15
313	Tony Bennett	.15
314	Jay Schroeder	.10
315	Darren Perry	.10
316	*Troy Drayton*	1.00
317	*Dan Williams*	.20
318	Michael Haynes	.15
319	Renaldo Turnbull	.10
320	Junior Seau	.15
321	Ray Crockett	.10
322	Will Furrer	.10
323	Byron Evans	.10
324	Jim McMahon	.10
325	Robert Jones	.10
326	Eric Davis	.10
327	Jeff Cross	.10
328	Kyle Clifton	.10
329	Haywood Jeffires	.15
330	Jeff Hostetler	.15
331	Darryl Talley	.10
332	Keith McCants	.10
333	Mo Lewis	.10
334	Matt Stover	.10
335	Ferrell Edmunds	.10
336	Matt Brock	.10
337	Ernie Mills	.10
338	Shane Dronett	.10
339	Brad Muster	.10
340	Jesse Solomon	.10
341	John Randle	.10
342	Chris Spielman	.10
343	David Whitmore	.10
344	Glenn Parker	.10
345	Marco Coleman	.10
346	Kenneth Gant	.10
347	Cris Dishman	.10
348	Kenny Walker	.10
349	*Roosevelt Potts*	.45
350	Reggie White	.30
351	Gerald Robinson	.10
352	Mark Rypien	.15
353	Stan Humphries	.15
354	Chris Singleton	.10
355	Herschel Walker	.10
356	Ron Hall	.10
357	Ethan Horton	.10
358	Anthony Pleasant	.10
359	*Thomas Smith*	.20
360	Audray McMillian	.10
361	D.J. Johnson	.10
362	Ron Heller	.10
363	Bern Brostek	.10
364	Ronnie Lott	.10
365	Reggie Johnson	.15
366	*Lin Elliott*	.15
367	Lemuel Stinson	.10
368	William White	.10
369	Ernie Jones	.10
370	Tom Rathman	.10
371	Tommy Kane	.10
372	David Brandon	.10
373	Lee Johnson	.10
374	Wade Wilson	.10
375	Nick Lowery	.10
376	Bubba McDowell	.10
377	*Wayne Simmons*	.15
378	Calvin Williams	.10
379	Courtney Hall	.10
380	Troy Vincent	.10
381	Tim McGee	.10
382	*Russell Freeman*	.15
383	Steve Tasker	.10
384	*Michael Strahan*	.15
385	Greg Skrepenak	.10
386	Jake Reed	.10
387	Pete Stoyanovich	.10
388	*Levon Kirkland*	.15
389	Mel Gray	.10
390	Brian Washington	.10
391	Don Griffin	.10
392	Desmond Howard	.50
393	Luis Sharpe	.10
394	Mike Johnson	.10
395	Andre Tippett	.10
396	Donnell Woolford	.10
397	*Demetrius DuBose*	.20
398	Pat Terrell	.10
399	Todd McNair	.10
400	Ken Norton	.10
401	Keith Hamilton	.10
402	Andy Heck	.10
403	Jeff Gossett	.10
404	Dexter McNabb	.10
405	Richmond Webb	.10
406	Irving Fryar	.10
407	Brian Hansen	.10
408	David Little	.10
409	*Glyn Milburn*	.25
410	Doug Dawson	.10
411	Scott Mersereau	.10
412	Don Beebe	.10
413	Vaughan Johnson	.10
414	Jack Del Rio	.10
415	*Darrien Gordon*	.20
416	Mark Schlereth	.10
417	Lomas Brown	.10
418	William Thomas	.10
419	James Francis	.10
420	Quentin Coryatt	.15
421	Tyji Armstrong	.10
422	Hugh Millen	.10
423	*Adrian White*	.15
424	Eddie Anderson	.10
425	Mark Ingram	.10
426	Ken O'Brien	.10
427	Simon Fletcher	.10
428	Tim McKyer	.10
429	Leonard Marshall	.10
430	Eric Green	.10
431	Leonard Harris	.10
432	*Darin Jordan*	.15
433	Erik Howard	.10
434	David Lang	.10
435	Eric Turner	.10
436	Michael Cofer	.10
437	Jeff Bryant	.10
438	Charles McRae	.10
439	Henry Jones	.10
440	Joe Montana	3.00
441	Morten Andersen	.10
442	Jeff Jaeger	.10
443	Leslie O'Neal	.10
444	Leroy Butler	.10
445	Steve Jordan	.10
446	Brad Edwards	.10
447	J.B. Brown	.10
448	Kerry Cash	.10
449	Mark Tuinei	.10
450	Rodney Peete	.10
451	Sheldon White	.10
452	Wesley Carroll	.10
453	Brad Baxter	.10
454	Mike Pitts	.10
455	Greg Montgomery	.10
456	Kenny Davidson	.10
457	Scott Fulhage	.10
458	Greg Townsend	.10
459	Rod Bernstine	.10
460	Gary Clark	.10
461	Hardy Nickerson	.10
462	Sean Landeta	.10
463	Rob Burnett	.10
464	Fred Barnett	.15
465	John L. Williams	.10
466	Anthony Miller	.15
467	Roman Phifer	.10
468	Rich Moran	.10
469	*Willie Roaf*	.50
470	William Perry	.15
471	Marcus Allen	.15
472	Carl Lee	.10
473	Kurt Gouveia	.10
474	Jarvis Williams	.10
475	Alfred Williams	.10
476	Mark Stepnoski	.10
477	Steve Wallace	.10
478	Pat Harlow	.10
479	Chip Banks	.10
480	Cornelius Bennett	.10
481	*Ryan McNeil*	.20
482	Norm Johnson	.10
483	Dermontti Dawson	.10
484	Dwayne White	.10
485	Derek Russell	.10
486	Lionel Washington	.10
487	Eric Hill	.10
488	*Michael Barrow*	.15
489	Checklist 251-375	.10
490	Checklist 376-500	.10
491	Emmitt Smith (MC)	2.00
492	Derrick Thomas (MC)	.15
493	Deion Sanders (MC)	.50
494	Randall Cunningham (MC)	.15
495	Sterling Sharpe (MC)	.20
496	Barry Sanders (MC)	1.25
497	Thurman Thomas	.50
498	Brett Favre (MC)	1.50
499	Vaughan Johnson (MC)	.10
500	Steve Young (MC)	1.00
501	Marvin Jones	.20
502	*Reggie Brooks*	.20
503	Eric Curry	.10
504	Drew Bledsoe	2.00
505	Glyn Milburn	.50
506	Jerome Bettis	1.00
507	Robert Smith	.75
508	Dana Stubblefield	.50
509	Tom Carter	.50
510	Rick Mirer	.50
511	Russell Copeland	1.00
512	*Deon Figures*	.30
513	*Tony McGee*	.50
514	*Derrick Lassic*	.30
515	Everett Lindsay	.10
516	*Derek Brown*	1.00
517	Harold Alexander	.10
518	Tom Scott	.10
519	*Elvis Grbac*	4.00
520	*Terry Kirby*	1.00
521	Doug Pelfrey	.10
522	*Horace Copeland*	.75
523	*Irv Smith*	.20
524	*Lincoln Kennedy*	.40
525	Jason Elam	.10
526	*Qadry Ismail*	.75
527	Artie Smith	.10
528	*Tyrone Hughes*	1.00
529	Lance Gunn	.10
530	*Vincent Brisby*	1.00
531	Patrick Robinson	.10
532	Raghib Ismail	.50
533	Willie Beamon	.10
534	*Vaughn Hebron*	.25
535	Darren Drozdov	.10
536	*James Jett*	.75
537	*Michael Bates*	.50
538	Tom Rouen	.10
539	Michael Husted	.10
540	*Greg Robinson*	.50
541	Carl Banks	.10
542	Kevin Greene	.10
543	Scott Mitchell	.50
544	Michael Brooks	.10
545	Shane Conlan	.10
546	Vinny Testaverde	.10
547	Robert Delpino	.10
548	Bill Fralic	.10
549	Carlton Bailey	.10
550	Johnny Johnson	.10
NNO	Jerry Rice	15.00

1993 Stadium Club First Day Cards

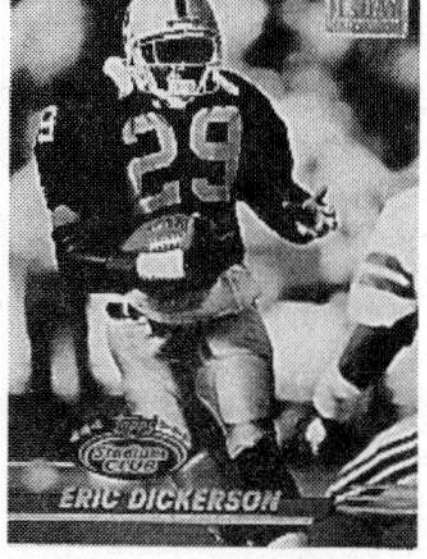

1993 Stadium Club football cards were issued in two 250-card series. Each card front has a full-bleed color photo and the player's name is foil stamped in gold at the bottom in a green stripe. The backs have statistics, a Football News Skills Rating Systems review and a miniature version of the player's Topps rookie card. A high-number series (#s 501-550) was also issued and includes Members Choice cards, Draft Picks, 1st-Year Players and Key Acquisitions. Super Team cards were randomly inserted into packs, one per every 24 packs. If the team pictured on a Super Team card wins a division title, conference championship or the Super Bowl, the card can be redeemed for special prizes. Other insert cards include First Day Production (silver foil) and Master Photo winner cards, which can be redeemed for a group of three Stadium Club Master Photos.

		MT
Complete Set (550):		2000.
Complete Series 1 (250):		1100.
Complete Series 2 (250):		600.00
Complete Hi Series (50):		300.00
Common Player:		2.00
Minor Stars:		5.00
Unlisted Stars:		10x-30x
1	Sterling Sharpe	10.00
2	Chris Burkett	2.00
3	Santana Dotson	2.00
4	Michael Jackson	2.00
5	Neal Anderson	2.00
6	Bryan Cox	2.00
7	Dennis Gibson	2.00
8	Jeff Graham	2.00
9	Roger Ruzek	2.00
10	Duane Bickett	2.00
11	Charles Mann	2.00
12	Tommy Maddox	2.00
13	Vaughn Dunbar	2.00
14	Gary Plummer	2.00
15	Chris Miller	2.00
16	Chris Warren	10.00
17	Alvin Harper	10.00
18	Eric Dickerson	5.00
19	Mike Jones	2.00
20	Ernest Givins	2.00
21	*Natrone Means*	15.00
22	Doug Riesenberg	2.00
23	Barry Word	2.00
24	Sean Salisbury	2.00
25	Derrick Fenner	2.00
26	David Howard	2.00
27	Mark Kelso	2.00
28	Todd Lyght	2.00
29	Dana Hall	2.00
30	Eric Metcalf	5.00
31	Jason Hanson	2.00
32	Dwight Stone	2.00
33	Johnny Mitchell	5.00
34	Reggie Roby	2.00
35	Terrell Buckley	2.00
36	Steve McMichael	2.00
37	Marty Carter	2.00
38	Seth Joyner	2.00
39	Rohn Stark	2.00
40	*Eric Curry*	8.00
41	Tommy Barnhardt	2.00
42	Karl Mecklenburg	2.00
43	Darion Conner	2.00
44	Ronnie Harmon	2.00
45	Cortez Kennedy	5.00
46	Tim Brown	5.00
47	Bill Lewis	2.00
48	Randall McDaniel	2.00
49	Curtis Duncan	2.00
50	Troy Aikman	90.00
51	David Klingler	5.00
52	Brent Jones	2.00
53	Dave Krieg	2.00
54	Bruce Smith	2.00
55	Vincent Brown	2.00
56	*O.J. McDuffie*	40.00
57	Cleveland Gary	2.00
58	*Larry Centers*	8.00
59	Pepper Johnson	2.00
60	Dan Marino	125.00
61	Robert Porcher	2.00
62	Jim Harbaugh	2.00
63	Sam Mills	2.00
64	Gary Anderson	2.00
65	Neil O'Donnell	8.00
66	Keith Byars	2.00
67	Jeff Herrod	2.00
68	Marion Butts	2.00
69	Terry McDaniel	2.00
70	John Elway	25.00
71	Steve Broussard	2.00
72	Kelvin Martin	2.00
73	*Tom Carter*	6.00
74	Bryce Paup	2.00
75	Jim Kelly	10.00
76	Bill Romanowski	2.00
77	Andre Collins	2.00
78	Mike Farr	2.00
79	Henry Ellard	2.00
80	Dale Carter	2.00
81	Johnny Bailey	2.00
82	*Garrison Hearst*	30.00
83	Brent Williams	2.00
84	Richard McDonald	2.00
85	Emmitt Smith	125.00
86	Vai Sikahema	2.00
87	Jackie Harris	2.00
88	Alonzo Spellman	2.00
89	Mark Wheeler	2.00
90	Dalton Hilliard	2.00
91	Mark Higgs	2.00
92	Aaron Wallace	2.00
93	Earnest Byner	2.00
94	Stanley Richard	2.00
95	Cris Carter	5.00
96	*Bobby Houston*	2.00
97	Craig Heyward	2.00
98	Bernie Kosar	5.00
99	Mike Croel	2.00
100	Deion Sanders	20.00
101	Warren Moon	10.00
102	Christian Okoye	2.00
103	Ricky Watters	10.00
104	Eric Swann	2.00
105	Rodney Hampton	10.00
106	Daryl Johnston	2.00
107	Andre Reed	5.00
108	*Jerome Bettis*	60.00
109	Eugene Daniel	2.00
110	Leonard Russell	2.00
111	Darryl Williams	2.00
112	Rod Woodson	5.00
113	Boomer Esiason	5.00
114	James Hasty	2.00
115	Marc Boutte	2.00
116	Tom Waddle	2.00
117	Lawrence Dawsey	2.00
118	Mark Collins	2.00
119	Willie Gault	2.00
120	Barry Sanders	80.00
121	Leroy Hoard	2.00
122	Anthony Munoz	2.00
123	Jesse Sapolu	2.00
124	Art Monk	5.00
125	Randal Hill	5.00
126	John Offerdahl	2.00
127	Carlos Jenkins	2.00
128	Al Smith	2.00
129	Michael Irvin	30.00
130	Kenneth Davis	2.00
131	*Curtis Conway*	15.00
132	Steve Atwater	2.00
133	Neil Smith	2.00
134	*Steve Everitt*	5.00
135	Chris Mims	2.00
136	Rickey Jackson	2.00
137	Edgar Bennett	2.00
138	Mike Pritchard	2.00
139	Richard Dent	2.00
140	Barry Foster	10.00
141	Eugene Robinson	2.00
142	Jackie Slater	2.00
143	Paul Gruber	2.00
144	Rob Moore	5.00
145	*Robert Smith*	40.00
146	Lorenzo White	2.00
147	Tommy Vardell	2.00
148	Dave Meggett	5.00
149	Vince Workman	2.00
150	Terry Allen	2.00
151	Howie Long	2.00
152	Charles Haley	2.00
153	Pete Metzelaars	2.00
154	*John Copeland*	5.00
155	Aeneas Williams	2.00
156	Ricky Sanders	2.00
157	Andre Ware	2.00
158	Tony Paige	2.00
159	Jerome Henderson	2.00
160	Harold Green	2.00
161	Wymon Henderson	2.00
162	Andre Rison	5.00
163	Donald Evans	2.00
164	Todd Scott	2.00
165	Steve Emtman	2.00
166	William Fuller	2.00
167	Michael Dean Perry	2.00
168	Randall Cunningham	10.00
169	Toi Cook	2.00
170	Browning Nagle	2.00
171	Darryl Henley	2.00
172	*George Teague*	6.00
173	Derrick Thomas	10.00
174	Jay Novacek	2.00
175	Mark Carrier	2.00
176	Kevin Fagan	2.00
177	Nate Lewis	2.00
178	Courtney Hawkins	2.00
179	Robert Blackmon	2.00
180	*Rick Mirer*	6.00
181	Mike Lodish	2.00
182	Jarrod Bunch	2.00
183	Anthony Smith	2.00
184	Brian Noble	2.00
185	Eric Bieniemy	2.00
186	Keith Jackson	2.00
187	Eric Martin	2.00
188	Vance Johnson	2.00
189	Kevin Mack	2.00
190	Rich Camarillo	2.00
191	Ashley Ambrose	2.00
192	Ray Childress	2.00
193	Jim Arnold	2.00
194	Ricky Ervins	2.00
195	Gary Anderson	2.00
196	Eric Allen	2.00
197	Roger Craig	2.00
198	Jon Vaughn	2.00
199	Tim McDonald	2.00
200	Broderick Thomas	2.00
201	Jessie Tuggle	2.00
202	Alonzo Mitz	2.00
203	Harvey Williams	2.00
204	Russell Maryland	2.00
205	Marvin Washington	2.00
206	Jim Everett	2.00
207	Trace Armstrong	2.00
208	Steve Young	50.00
209	Tony Woods	2.00
210	Brett Favre	125.00
211	Nate Odomes	2.00
212	Ricky Proehl	2.00
213	Jim Dombrowski	2.00
214	Anthony Carter	2.00
215	Tracy Simien	2.00
216	Clay Matthews	2.00
217	*Patrick Bates*	5.00
218	Jeff George	8.00
219	David Fulcher	2.00
220	Phil Simms	5.00
221	Eugene Chung	2.00
222	Reggie Cobb	2.00
223	Jim Sweeney	2.00
224	Greg Lloyd	2.00
225	Sean Jones	2.00
226	*Marvin Jones*	5.00
227	Bill Brooks	2.00
228	Moe Gardner	2.00
229	Louis Oliver	2.00
230	Flipper Anderson	2.00
231	Marc Spindler	2.00
232	Jerry Rice	100.00
233	Chip Lohmiller	2.00
234	Nolan Harrison	2.00
235	Heath Sherman	2.00
236	Reyna Thompson	2.00
237	Derrick Walker	2.00
238	Rufus Porter	2.00
239	Checklist 1-125	2.00
240	Checklist 126-250	2.00
241	John Elway	10.00
242	Troy Aikman	35.00
243	Steve Emtman	2.00
244	Ricky Watters	7.00
245	Barry Foster	5.00
246	Dan Marino	90.00
247	Reggie White	5.00
248	Thurman Thomas	8.00
249	Broderick Thomas	2.00
250	Joe Montana	70.00
251	Tim Goad	2.00
252	Joe Nash	2.00
253	Anthony Johnson	2.00
254	Carl Pickens	2.00
255	Steve Beuerlein	2.00
256	*Anthony Newman*	2.00
257	Corey Miller	2.00
258	Steve DeBerg	2.00
259	Johnny Holland	2.00
260	Jerry Ball	2.00
261	*Siupeli Malamala*	2.00
262	Steve Wisniewski	2.00
263	Kelvin Pritchett	2.00
264	Chris Gardocki	2.00
265	Henry Thomas	2.00
266	*Arthur Marshall*	5.00
267	Quinn Early	2.00
268	Jonathan Hayes	2.00
269	Erric Pegram	2.00
270	Clyde Simmons	2.00
271	Eric Moten	2.00
272	Brian Mitchell	2.00
273	Adrian Cooper	2.00
274	Gaston Green	2.00
275	John Taylor	5.00
276	Jeff Uhlenhake	2.00
277	Phil Hansen	2.00
278	*Kevin Williams*	20.00
279	Robert Massey	2.00
280	*Drew Bledsoe*	150.00
281	Walter Reeves	2.00
282	*Carlton Gray*	5.00
283	Derek Brown	2.00
284	Martin Mayhew	2.00
285	Sean Gilbert	2.00
286	Jessie Hester	2.00
287	Mark Clayton	2.00
288	Blair Thomas	2.00
289	J.J. Birden	2.00
290	Shannon Sharpe	6.00
291	*Richard Fain*	2.00
292	Gene Atkins	2.00
293	Burt Grossman	2.00
294	Chris Doleman	2.00
295	Pat Swilling	2.00
296	Mike Kenn	2.00
297	Merril Hoge	2.00
298	Don Mosebar	2.00
299	Kevin Smith	2.00
300	Darrell Green	2.00
301	*Dan Footman*	2.00
302	Vestee Jackson	2.00
303	Carwell Gardner	2.00
304	Amp Lee	2.00
305	Bruce Matthews	2.00
306	Antone Davis	2.00
307	Dean Biasucci	2.00
308	Maurice Hurst	2.00
309	John Kasay	2.00
310	Lawrence Taylor	5.00
311	Ken Harvey	2.00
312	Willie Davis	2.00
313	Tony Bennett	2.00
314	Jay Schroeder	2.00
315	Darren Perry	2.00
316	*Troy Drayton*	10.00
317	*Dan Williams*	5.00
318	Michael Haynes	2.00
319	Renaldo Turnbull	2.00
320	Junior Seau	8.00
321	Ray Crockett	2.00
322	Will Furrer	2.00
323	Byron Evans	2.00
324	Jim McMahon	2.00
325	Robert Jones	2.00
326	Eric Davis	2.00
327	Jeff Cross	2.00
328	Kyle Clifton	2.00
329	Haywood Jeffires	5.00
330	Jeff Hostetler	5.00
331	Darryl Talley	2.00
332	Keith McCants	2.00
333	Mo Lewis	2.00
334	Matt Stover	2.00
335	Ferrell Edmunds	2.00
336	Matt Brock	2.00
337	Ernie Mills	2.00
338	Shane Dronett	2.00
339	Brad Muster	2.00
340	Jesse Solomon	2.00
341	John Randle	2.00
342	Chris Spielman	2.00
343	David Whitmore	2.00
344	Glenn Parker	2.00
345	Marco Coleman	2.00
346	Kenneth Gant	2.00
347	Cris Dishman	2.00
348	Kenny Walker	2.00
349	*Roosevelt Potts*	5.00
350	Reggie White	5.00
351	Gerald Robinson	2.00
352	Mark Rypien	2.00
353	Stan Humphries	5.00
354	Chris Singleton	2.00
355	Herschel Walker	5.00
356	Ron Hall	2.00
357	Ethan Horton	2.00
358	Anthony Pleasant	2.00
359	*Thomas Smith*	5.00
360	Audray McMillian	2.00
361	D.J. Johnson	2.00
362	Ron Heller	2.00
363	Bern Brostek	2.00
364	Ronnie Lott	5.00
365	Reggie Johnson	2.00
366	*Lin Elliott*	2.00
367	Lemuel Stinson	2.00
368	William White	2.00
369	Ernie Jones	2.00
370	Tom Rathman	2.00
371	Tommy Kane	2.00
372	David Brandon	2.00
373	Lee Johnson	2.00
374	Wade Wilson	2.00
375	Nick Lowery	2.00
376	Bubba McDowell	2.00
377	*Wayne Simmons*	2.00
378	Calvin Williams	2.00
379	Courtney Hall	2.00
380	Troy Vincent	2.00
381	Tim McGee	2.00
382	*Russell Freeman*	2.00
383	Steve Tasker	2.00
384	*Michael Strahan*	2.00
385	Greg Skrepenak	2.00
386	Jake Reed	2.00
387	Pete Stoyanovich	2.00
388	*Levon Kirkland*	2.00
389	Mel Gray	2.00
390	Brian Washington	2.00
391	Don Griffin	2.00
392	Desmond Howard	5.00
393	Luis Sharpe	2.00
394	Mike Johnson	2.00
395	Andre Tippett	2.00
396	Donnell Woolford	2.00
397	*Demetrius DuBose*	5.00

398	Pat Terrell	2.00
399	Todd McNair	2.00
400	Ken Norton	2.00
401	Keith Hamilton	2.00
402	Andy Heck	2.00
403	Jeff Gossett	2.00
404	Dexter McNabb	2.00
405	Richmond Webb	2.00
406	Irving Fryar	2.00
407	Brian Hansen	2.00
408	David Little	2.00
409	*Glyn Milburn*	10.00
410	Doug Dawson	2.00
411	Scott Mersereau	2.00
412	Don Beebe	2.00
413	Vaughan Johnson	2.00
414	Jack Del Rio	2.00
415	*Darrien Gordon*	5.00
416	Mark Schlereth	2.00
417	Lomas Brown	2.00
418	William Thomas	2.00
419	James Francis	2.00
420	Quentin Coryatt	2.00
421	Tyji Armstrong	2.00
422	Hugh Millen	2.00
423	*Adrian White*	2.00
424	Eddie Anderson	2.00
425	Mark Ingram	2.00
426	Ken O'Brien	2.00
427	Simon Fletcher	2.00
428	Tim McKyer	2.00
429	Leonard Marshall	2.00
430	Eric Green	2.00
431	Leonard Harris	2.00
432	*Darin Jordan*	2.00
433	Erik Howard	2.00
434	David Lang	2.00
435	Eric Turner	2.00
436	Michael Cofer	2.00
437	Jeff Bryant	2.00
438	Charles McRae	2.00
439	Henry Jones	2.00
440	Joe Montana	100.00
441	Morten Andersen	2.00
442	Jeff Jaeger	2.00
443	Leslie O'Neal	2.00
444	Leroy Butler	2.00
445	Steve Jordan	2.00
446	Brad Edwards	2.00
447	J.B. Brown	2.00
448	Kerry Cash	2.00
449	Mark Tuinei	2.00
450	Rodney Peete	2.00
451	Sheldon White	2.00
452	Wesley Carroll	2.00
453	Brad Baxter	2.00
454	Mike Pitts	2.00
455	Greg Montgomery	2.00
456	Kenny Davidson	2.00
457	Scott Fulhage	2.00
458	Greg Townsend	2.00
459	Rod Bernstine	2.00
460	Gary Clark	2.00
461	Hardy Nickerson	2.00
462	Sean Landeta	2.00
463	Rob Burnett	2.00
464	Fred Barnett	2.00
465	John L. Williams	2.00
466	Anthony Miller	5.00
467	Roman Phifer	2.00
468	Rich Moran	2.00
469	*Willie Roaf*	5.00
470	William Perry	2.00
471	Marcus Allen	10.00
472	Carl Lee	2.00
473	Kurt Gouveia	2.00
474	Jarvis Williams	2.00
475	Alfred Williams	2.00
476	Mark Stepnoski	2.00
477	Steve Wallace	2.00
478	Pat Harlow	2.00
479	Chip Banks	2.00
480	Cornelius Bennett	5.00
481	*Ryan McNeil*	2.00
482	Norm Johnson	2.00
483	Dermontti Dawson	2.00
484	Dwayne White	2.00
485	Derek Russell	2.00
486	Lionel Washington	2.00
487	Eric Hill	2.00
488	*Michael Barrow*	2.00
489	Checklist 251-375	2.00
490	Checklist 376-500	2.00
491	Emmitt Smith (MC)	75.00
492	Derrick Thomas (MC)	5.00
493	Deion Sanders (MC)	10.00
494	Randall Cunningham (MC)	5.00
495	Sterling Sharpe (MC)	5.00
496	Barry Sanders (MC)	40.00
497	Thurman Thomas	10.00
498	Brett Favre (MC)	14.00
499	Vaughan Johnson (MC)	2.00
500	Steve Young (MC)	15.00
501	Marvin Jones	2.00
502	*Reggie Brooks*	6.00
503	Eric Curry	2.00
504	Drew Bledsoe	75.00
505	Glyn Milburn	5.00
506	Jerome Bettis	15.00
507	Robert Smith	5.00
508	Dana Stubblefield	10.00
509	Tom Carter	2.00
510	Rick Mirer	20.00
511	Russell Copeland	2.00
512	*Deon Figures*	8.00
513	*Tony McGee*	5.00
514	*Derrick Lassic*	2.00
515	Everett Lindsay	2.00
516	*Derek Brown*	10.00
517	Harold Alexander	2.00
518	Tom Scott	2.00
519	*Elvis Grbac*	10.00
520	*Terry Kirby*	10.00
521	Doug Pelfrey	2.00
522	*Horace Copeland*	6.00
523	*Irv Smith*	6.00
524	*Lincoln Kennedy*	5.00
525	Jason Elam	2.00
526	*Qadry Ismail*	20.00
527	Artie Smith	2.00
528	*Tyrone Hughes*	20.00
529	Lance Gunn	2.00
530	*Vincent Brisby*	30.00
531	Patrick Robinson	2.00
532	Raghib Ismail	5.00
533	Willie Beamon	2.00
534	*Vaughn Hebron*	5.00
535	Darren Drozdov	2.00
536	*James Jett*	7.00
537	*Michael Bates*	5.00
538	Tom Rouen	2.00
539	Michael Husted	2.00
540	*Greg Robinson*	2.00
541	Carl Banks	2.00
542	Kevin Greene	2.00
543	Scott Mitchell	5.00
544	Michael Brooks	2.00
545	Shane Conlan	2.00
546	Vinny Testaverde	2.00
547	Robert Delpino	2.00
548	Bill Fralic	2.00
549	Carlton Bailey	2.00
550	Johnny Johnson	2.00

1993 Stadium Club Master Photos I

Master Photos were available through redemption cards inserted every 24 packs of Stadium Club. The redemption cards offered three Master Photos, with the entire set containing 12 players. The fronts were larger than the normal cards, but contained a gold border to reveal a standard sized card. Backs were full of text and statistics, with the player's name printed in a strip down the middle.

		MT
Complete Set (12):		15.00
Common Player:		.75
Minor Stars:		1.50
1	Barry Foster	.75
2	Barry Sanders	6.00
3	Reggie Cobb	.75
4	Cortez Kennedy	.75
5	Steve Young	3.00
6	Ricky Watters	1.50
7	Rob Moore	1.50
8	Derrick Thomas	1.50
9	Jeff George	1.50
10	Sterling Sharpe	1.50
11	Bruce Smith	.75
12	Deion Sanders	2.00

1993 Stadium Club Master Photos II

Similar to the Series I Master Photos, every 24 packs of Series II also had redemption cards that could be redeemed for three Master Photos. There were also redemption cards for complete sets. This 12-card set was 5" x 7" and contained larger than normal cards that contain gold borders to reveal the standard sized cards.

		MT
Complete Set (12):		10.00
Common Player:		.75
Minor Stars:		1.50
1	Morten Andersen	.75
2	Ken Norton Jr	.75
3	Clyde Simmons	.75
4	Roman Phifer	.75
5	Greg Townsend	.75
6	Darryl Talley	.75
7	Herschel Walker	.75
8	Reggie White	1.50
9	Jesse Solomon	.75
10	Joe Montana	5.00
11	John Taylor	.75
12	Cornelius Bennett	.75

1993 Stadium Club Super Teams

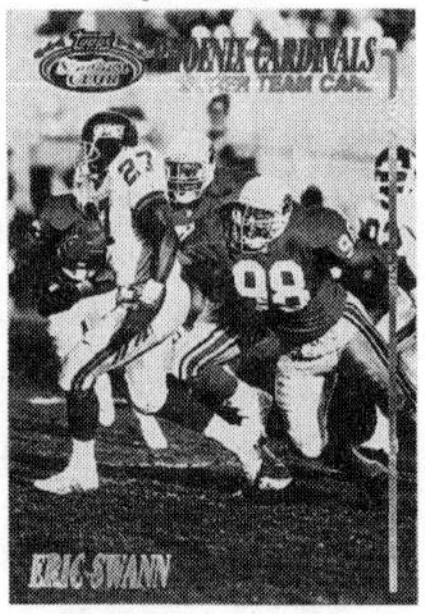

Twenty-eight different NFL teams had Super Team cards that were inserted into Stadium Club Series II Football. Team cards featuring division winners (Cowboys, 49ers, Lions, Bills, Oilers, Chiefs), conference championship teams (Cowboys, Bills) or Super Bowl XXVII winner (Cowboys) were redeemable for prizes. Division winners could get embossed, gold foil Stadium Club cards of that team with a division winner logo. Conference Champion cards were redeemable for 12 special embossed gold Master Photos of that team. Super Bowl cards were redeemable for a 500-card complete set of Stadium Club cards with a Super Bowl logo.

		MT
Complete Set (28):		75.00
Common Player:		2.00
Minor Stars:		4.00
Inserted 1:24		
1	Jim Harbaugh	4.00
2	David Klingler	2.00
3	Jim Kelly	4.00
4	John Elway	10.00
5	Bernie Kosar	2.00
6	Reggie Cobb	2.00
7	Eric Swann	2.00
8	Stan Humphries	2.00
9	Derrick Thomas	4.00
10	Steve Emtman	2.00
11	Emmitt Smith	20.00
12	Dan Marino	12.00
13	Randall Cunningham	4.00
14	Deion Sanders	4.00
15	Steve Young	8.00
16	Lawrence Taylor	4.00
17	Brad Baxter	2.00
18	Barry Sanders	15.00
19	Warren Moon	4.00
20	Brett Favre	15.00
21	Brent Williams	2.00
22	Howie Long	2.00
23	Cleveland Gary	2.00
24	Mark Rypien	2.00
25	Sam Mills	2.00
26	Cortez Kennedy	2.00
27	Barry Foster	2.00
28	Terry Allen	2.00

1993 Stadium Club Super Teams Division Winners

Super Team Division Winners were available to those collectors who had the Cowboys, 49ers, Lions, Bills, Oilers and Chiefs team cards and redeemed them for the team set. The cards are similar to the base cards, but contain a logo reading "Division Winner" on the front.

		MT
Complete Bag Bills (13):		8.00
Complete Bag Chiefs (13):		10.00
Complete Bag Cowboys (13):		15.00
Complete Bag 49ers (13):		12.00
Complete Bag Lions (13):		8.00
Complete Bag Oilers (13):		8.00
Common Player:		.50
B27	Mark Kelso	.50
B54	Bruce Smith	1.00
B75	Jim Kelly	1.25
B107	Andre Reed	1.00
B153	Pete Metzelaars	.50
B211	Nate Odomes	.50
B227	Bill Brooks	.50
B331	Darryl Talley	.50
B383	Steve Tasker	.50
B412	Don Beebe	.50
B439	Henry Jones	.50
B480	Cornelius Bennett	.75
F29	Dana Hall	.50
F52	Brent Jones	.75
F76	Bill Romanowski	.50
F103	Ricky Watters	1.25
F176	Kevin Fagan	.50
F199	Tim McDonald	.50
F208	Steve Young	3.00
F232	Jerry Rice	3.00
F275	John Taylor	.75
F326	Eric Davis	.50
F370	Tom Rathman	.50
L7	Dennis Gibson	.50
L31	Jason Hanson	.50
L61	Robert Porcher	.50
L120	Barry Sanders	3.00
L231	Marc Spindler	.50
L263	Kelvin Pritchett	.50
L295	Pat Swilling	.75
L321	Ray Crockett	.50
L342	Chris Spielman	.50
L368	William White	.50
L389	Mel Gray	.75
L450	Rodney Peete	.50
O20	Ernest Givins	.75
O101	Warren Moon	1.25
O128	Al Smith	.50
O146	Lorenzo White	.75
O166	William Fuller	.50
O192	Ray Childress	.75
O225	Sean Jones	.50
O305	Bruce Mathews	.50
O329	Haywood Jeffires	.75
O347	Cris Dishman	.50
O376	Bubba McDowell	.50
O455	Greg Montgomery	.50
CH80	Dale Carter	.75
CH133	Neil Smith	.75
CH173	Derrick Thomas	1.00
CH203	Harvey Williams	.75
CH215	Tracy Simien	.50
CH268	Jonathan Hayes	.50
CH289	J.J. Birden	.75
CH312	Willie Davis	.75
CH375	Nick Lowery	.50
CH399	Todd McNair	.50
CH440	Joe Montana	3.00
CH471	Marcus Allen	.75
CO17	Alvin Harper	.75
CO50	Troy Aikman	3.00
CO85	Emmitt Smith	5.00
CO106	Daryl Johnston	.75
CO129	Michael Irvin	1.50
CO152	Charles Haley	.75
CO174	Jay Novacek	.75
CO204	Russell Maryland	.50
CO278	Kevin Williams (WR)	1.00
CO299	Kevin Smith	.50
CO325	Robert Jones	.50
CO400	Ken Norton Jr	.50
DW3	Bills Super Team DW (Jim Kelly)	1.00
DW9	Chiefs Super Team DW (Derrick Thomas)	1.00
DW11	Cowboys Super Team DW (Emmitt Smith)	3.00
DW15	49ers Super Team DW (Steve Young)	1.75
DW18	Lions Super Team DW (Barry Sanders)	1.75
DW19	Oilers Super Team DW (Warren Moon)	1.00

1993 Stadium Club Super Teams Conference Winners

Super Team Division Winners were available to those collectors who redeemed their 1993 Super Team cards of Cowboys or Bills. Collectors received a 12-card set stamped with a gold foil conference logo, as well as a Master Photo set of the team. The cards are similar to base cards in Stadium Club, except for the conference champions logo on the front.

		MT
Complete Bag Bills (13):		7.00
Complete Bag Cowboys (13):		15.00
Common Player:		.50
B27	Mark Kelso	.50
B54	Bruce Smith	1.00
B75	Jim Kelly	1.25
B107	Andre Reed	1.00
B153	Pete Metzelaars	.50
B211	Nate Odomes	.50
B227	Bill Brooks	.50
B331	Darryl Talley	.50
B383	Steve Tasker	.50
B412	Don Beebe	.50
B439	Henry Jones	.50
B480	Cornelius Bennett	.75
CO17	Alvin Harper	.75
CO50	Troy Aikman	3.00
CO85	Emmitt Smith	5.00
CO106	Daryl Johnston	.75
CO129	Michael Irvin	1.50
CO152	Charles Haley	.75
CO174	Jay Novacek	.75
CO204	Russell Maryland	.50
CO278	Kevin Williams (WR)	1.50
CO299	Kevin Smith	.50
CO325	Robert Jones	.50
CO400	Ken Norton Jr.	.50
CW3	Cowboys Super Team CW (Emmitt Smith)	3.00
CW11	Bills Super Team CW (Jim Kelly)	1.00

1993 Stadium Club Super Team Master Photos

Super Team Master Photos were available to those collectors with either a Bills or Cowboys Super Team card. Along with a specially stamped team set, collectors also received these 5" x 7", uncropped Master Photos. The sets arrived in a bag and had blank backs and either a gold foil "N" for NFC or "A" for AFC edged by stars beneath the player photo.

		MT
Complete Bag Bills (12):		10.00
Complete Bag Cowboys (12):		20.00
Common Player:		.75
B1	Don Beebe	.75
B2	Cornelius Bennett	1.00
B3	Bill Brooks	.75
B4	Henry Jones	.75
B5	Jim Kelly	1.50
B6	Mark Kelso	.75
B7	Pete Metzelaars	.75
B8	Nate Odomes	.75
B9	Andre Reed	1.25
B10	Bruce Smith	1.25
B11	Darryl Talley	.75
B12	Steve Tasker	.75
CO1	Troy Aikman	4.00
CO2	Charles Haley	1.00
CO3	Alvin Harper	1.00
CO4	Michael Irvin	2.00
CO5	Daryl Johnston	1.00
CO6	Robert Jones	.75
CO7	Russell Maryland	.75
CO8	Ken Norton Jr	.75
CO9	Jay Novacek	1.00
CO10	Emmitt Smith	7.50
CO11	Kevin Smith	.75
CO12	Kevin Williams (WR)	2.00

1993 Stadium Club Super Teams Super Bowl

Collectors holding the Cowboys Super Team card from 1993 Stadium Club could redeem that card for a 500-card Stadium Club set stamped with a gold foil Super Bowl XXVIII logo stamped on the front. The set arrived with the redeemed Super Team Cowboys card that also has a Super Bowl logo.

		MT
Complete Set (501):		75.00
Common Player:		.15
Semistars:		.30
SB3	Cowboys Super Team SB (Emmitt Smith)	4.00

1993 Stadium Club Members Only Parallel

Only Stadium Club members could purchase this 579-card set from Topps that included the entire 550-card Stadium Club set, along with 28 Super Teams and a signed Jerry Rice Record Breaker card. Production was limited to 10,000 factory sets, with each costing $199. The cards are identical to the regular-issue cards, except for a gold-foil "Members Only" logo.

		MT
Complete Set (579):		200.00
Common Player (1-550):		.20
Semistars:		.40
NNO	Jerry Rice (RB Auto) (signed card)	50.00

1994 Stadium Club

Stadium Club Football Series I contains 270 cards, including several new subsets, like Chalk Talk, Chain Gang, Great Expectations and Topps Best cards. Chalk Talk (221-229) offers players that frequently move the chains. Chalk Talk cards (71-74) display photographs on the fronts and illustrations on the backs. Great Expectations (182-190) highlight the best rookies of 1993, while Topps Best utilizes Topps Finest technology to showcase the top players at each position. Topps Stadium Club Football also has a three-card insert set called Dynasty and Destiny, as well as 1st Day Production and Super Team cards. Stadium Club cards have a borderless, high-gloss look on the front with the players name centered on the bottom. The backs feature a shot of the player and statistics. Series II also had 270 cards (#s 271-540) and three insert sets. 1st Day Production cards were once again offered in Series II packs. Two new insert sets - Ring Leaders and Frequent Scorers - were also produced. A 90-card High series was also issued, featuring rookies and veterans in their NFL 75th anniversary throwback uniforms. Each card is also available in a parallel 1st Day Issue set, seeded one per every 12 packs. Three insert sets were also made, utilizing Finest's chromium technology. The sets are Bowman's Best Black (veteran stars), Bowman's Best Blue (Rookies) and Bowman's Best Mirror Images (veteran and a rookie on the same card). These three insert types were each seeded at a rate of one per every three packs. A parallel Bowman's Refractors set of the 45 cards was also made; they were seeded one per every 12 packs. In addition, each 24th pack contained one of six Expansion Team Redemption cards - offense, defense or special teams - for the Carolina Panthers and Jacksonville Jaguars. The cards entitled the finders to a 22-card Topps Finest set of the players for the team depicted on the redemption card, or both teams.

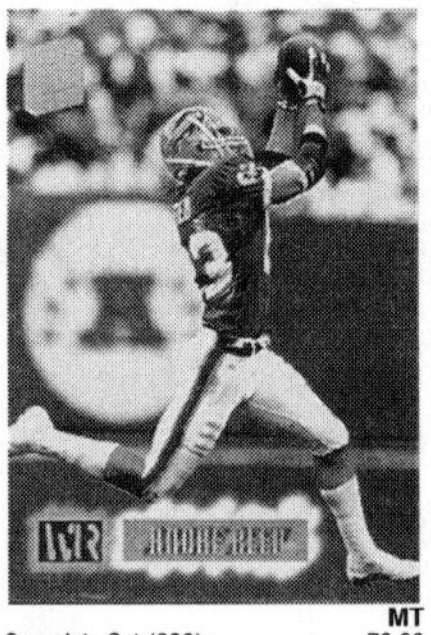

		MT
Complete Set (630):		70.00
Complete Series 1 (270):		30.00
Complete Series 2 (270):		25.00
Complete High Series (90):		15.00
Common Player:		.10
Minor Stars:		.20
First Day Cards:		8x-16x
First Day Rookies:		5x-10x
Inserted 1:24		
Series 1 Pack (12):		2.00
Series 1 Wax Box (24):		38.00
Series 2 Pack (12):		2.00
Series 2 Wax Box (24):		38.00
Series 3 Pack (10):		3.50
Series 3 Wax Box (24):		65.00
1	*Dan Wilkinson*	.20
2	Chip Lohmiller	.10
3	Roosevelt Potts	.10
4	Martin Mayhew	.10
5	Shane Conlan	.10
6	*Sam Adams*	.20
7	Mike Kenn	.10
8	Tim Goad	.10
9	Tony Jones	.10
10	Ron Moore	.25
11	Mark Bortz	.10
12	Darren Carrington	.10
13	Eric Martin	.10
14	Eric Allen	.10
15	*Aaron Glenn*	.25
16	Bryan Cox	.10
17	Levon Kirkland	.10
18	Qadry Ismail	.20
19	Shane Dronett	.10
20	Chris Spielman	.10
21	*Rob Fredrickson*	.20
22	Wayne Simmons	.10
23	*Glenn Montgomery*	.20
24	*Jason Sehorn*	.20
25	Nick Lowery	.10
26	Dennis Brown	.10
27	Kenneth Davis	.10
28	*Shante Carver*	.25
29	*Ryan Yarborough*	.20
30	Cortez Kennedy	.20
31	Anthony Pleasant	.10
32	Jessie Tuggle	.10
33	Herschel Walker	.20
34	Andre Collins	.10
35	*William Floyd*	.50
36	Harold Green	.10
37	Courtney Hawkins	.10
38	Curtis Conway	.20
39	Ben Coates	.20
40	Natrone Means	.50
41	Eric Hill	.10
42	Keith Kartz	.10
43	Alexander Wright	.10
44	William Roaf	.10
45	Vencie Glenn	.10
46	Ronnie Lott, David Lutz	.10
47	George Koonce, Kelvin Martin	.10
48	Rod Woodson	.20
49	Tim Grunhard	.10
50	Cody Carlson	.10
51	*Bryant Young*	.75
52	Jay Novacek	.10
53	Darryl Talley	.10
54	Gary Anderson, Harry Colon	.10
55	David Meggett	.10
56	*Aubrey Beavers*	.25
57	James Folston	.10
58	Willie Davis	.10
59	Jason Elam	.10
60	Eric Metcalf	.10
61	Bruce Armstrong	.10
62	Ron Heller	.10
63	LeRoy Butler	.10
64	Terry Obee	.10
65	Kurt Gouveia	.10
66	Pierce Holt	.10
67	David Alexander	.10
68	*Deral Boykin*	.20
69	Carl Pickens	.10
70	Broderick Thomas	.10
71	Barry Sanders	1.25
72	Qadry Ismail	.20
73	Thurman Thomas	.25
74	Junior Seau, Bob Dahl	.10
75	Vinny Testaverde	.10
76	Tyrone Hughes	.10
77	Nate Newton	.10
78	Eric Swann	.10
79	Brad Baxter	.10
80	Dana Stubblefield	.10
81	John Elliott	.10
82	Steve Wisniewski	.10
83	Eddie Robinson	.10
84	*Isaac Davis*	.20
85	Cris Carter	.20
86	Mel Gray	.10
87	Cornelius Bennett	.10
88	Neil O'Donnell	.20
89	Jon Hand	.10
90	John Elway	.75
91	Bill Hitchcock	.10
92	Neil Smith	.10
93	*Joe Johnson*	.20
94	Edgar Bennett	.10
95	Vincent Brown	.10
96	Tommy Vardell	.10
97	Donnell Woolford	.10
98	Lincoln Kennedy	.10
99	O.J. McDuffie	.50
100	*Heath Shuler*	.50
101	Jerry Rice	1.00
102	Erik Williams	.10
103	Randall McDaniel	.10
104	Dermontti Dawson	.10
105	Nate Newton	.10
106	Harris Barton	.10
107	Shannon Sharpe	.20
108	Sterling Sharpe	.20
109	Steve Young	1.00
110	Emmitt Smith	2.00
111	Thurman Thomas	.20
112	Kyle Clifton	.10
113	Desmond Howard	.20
114	Quinn Early	.10
115	David Klingler	.10
116	Bern Brostek	.10
117	Gary Clark	.10
118	Courtney Hall	.10
119	*Joe King*	.10
120	Quentin Coryatt	.10
121	*Johnnie Morton*	.50
122	Andre Reed	.20
123	Eric Davis	.10
124	Jack Del Rio	.10
125	Greg Lloyd	.10
126	Bubba McDowell	.10
127	Mark Jackson	.10
128	Jeff Jaeger	.10
129	Chris Warren	.20
130	Tom Waddle	.10
131	Tony Smith	.10
132	Todd Collins	.10
133	Mark Bavaro	.10
134	Joe Phillips	.10
135	Chris Jacke	.10
136	Glyn Milburn	.20
137	Keith Jackson	.10
138	Steve Tovar	.10
139	Tim Johnson	.10
140	Brian Washington	.10
141	Troy Drayton	.10
142	*DeWayne Washington*	.25
143	Erik Williams	.10
144	Eric Turner	.10
145	John Taylor	.20
146	Richard Cooper	.10
147	*Van Malone*	.10
148	*Tim Ruddy*	.20
149	Henry Jones	.10
150	Tim Brown	.20
151	Stan Humphries	.20
152	Harry Newsome	.10
153	Craig Erickson	.20
154	Gary Anderson	.10
155	Ray Childress	.10
156	Howard Cross	.10
157	Heath Sherman	.10
158	Terrell Buckley	.10
159	J.B. Brown	.10
160	Joe Montana	2.50
161	David Wyman	.10
162	Norm Johnson	.10
163	Rod Stephens	.10
164	*Willie McGinest*	.50
165	Barry Sanders	2.50
166	Marc Logan	.10
167	Anthony Newman	.10
168	Russell Maryland	.10
169	Luis Sharpe	.10
170	Jim Kelly	.25
171	*Tre' Johnson*	.10
172	Johnny Mitchell	.10
173	*David Palmer*	.50
174	Bob Dahl	.10
175	Aaron Wallace	.10
176	Chris Gardocki	.10
177	Hardy Nickerson	.10
178	Jeff Query	.10
179	Leslie O'Neal	.10
180	Kevin Greene	.10
181	Alonzo Spellman	.10
182	Reggie Brooks	.10
183	Dana Stubblefield	.10
184	Tyrone Hughes	.10
185	Drew Bledsoe	1.00
186	Ron Moore	.20
187	Jason Elam	.10
188	Rick Mirer	.50
189	William Roaf	.10
190	Jerome Bettis	.50

191	Brad Hopkins	.10
192	Derek Brown	.10
193	Nolan Harrison	.10
194	Jon Randle	.10
195	Carlton Bailey	.10
196	Kevin Williams	.25
197	*Greg Hill*	1.00
198	Mark McMillian	.10
199	Brad Edwards	.10
200	Dan Marino	4.00
201	Ricky Watters	.20
202	George Teague	.10
203	Steve Beuerlein	.10
204	*Jeff Burris*	.20
205	Steve Atwater	.10
206	*John Thierry*	.50
207	Patrick Hunter	.10
208	*Wayne Gandy*	.10
209	Derrick Moore	.10
210	Phil Simms	.10
211	Kirk Lowdermilk	.10
212	Patrick Robinson	.10
213	Kevin Mitchell	.10
214	Jonathan Hayes	.10
215	Michael Dean Perry	.10
216	John Fina	.10
217	Anthony Smith	.10
218	Paul Gruber	.10
219	Carnell Lake	.10
220	Carl Lee	.10
221	Steve Christie	.10
222	Greg Montgomery	.10
223	Reggie Brooks	.10
224	Derrick Thomas	.20
225	Eric Metcalf	.10
226	Michael Haynes	.10
227	Bobby Hebert	.10
228	Tyrone Hughes	.10
229	Donald Frank	.10
230	Vaughan Johnson	.10
231	Eric Thomas	.10
232	Ernest Givins	.10
233	Charles Haley	.10
234	Darrell Green	.10
235	Harold Alexander	.10
236	Dwayne Sabb	.10
237	Harris Barton	.10
238	Randall Cunningham	.20
239	Ray Buchanan	.10
240	Sterling Sharpe	.20
241	Chris Mims	.10
242	Mark Carrier	.10
243	Ricky Proehl	.10
244	Michael Brooks	.10
245	Sean Gilbert	.10
246	David Lutz	.10
247	Kelvin Martin	.10
248	*Scottie Graham*	.50
249	Irving Fryar	.10
250	Ricardo McDonald	.10
251	Marvcus Patton	.10
252	*Errict Rhett*	1.00
253	Winston Moss	.10
254	Rod Vernstine	.10
255	Terry Wooden	.10
256	*Antonio Langham*	.50
257	Tommy Barnhardt	.10
258	Marvin Washington	.10
259	Bo Orlando	.10
260	Marcus Allen	.20
261	*Mario Bates*	.25
262	Marco Coleman	.10
263	Doug Riesenberg	.10
264	Jesse Sapolu	.10
265	Dermontti Dawson	.10
266	*Fernando Smith*	.20
267	David Szott	.10
268	Steve Christie	.10
269	Bruce Matthews	.10
270	Michael Irvin	.50
271	Seth Joyner	.10
272	Santana Dotson	.10
273	Vincent Brisby	.50
274	Rohn Stark	.10
275	John Copeland	.10
276	Toby Wright	.10
277	David Griggs	.10
278	*Aaron Taylor*	.20
279	Chris Doleman	.10
280	Reggie Brooks	.10
281	Willie Anderson	.10
282	Alvin Harper	.20
283	Chris Hinton	.10
284	Kelvin Pritchett	.10
285	Russell Copeland	.10
286	Dwight Stone	.10
287	Jeff Gossett	.10
288	Larry Allen	.10
289	Kevin Mawae	.10
290	Mark Collins	.10
291	Chris Zorich	.10
292	Vince Buck	.10
293	Gene Atkins	.10
294	Webster Slaughter	.10
295	Steve Young	1.50
296	Dan Williams	.10
297	Jesse Armstead	.10
298	Victor Bailey	.10
299	John Carney	.10
300	Emmitt Smith	4.00
301	*Bucky Brooks*	.50
302	Mo Lewis	.10
303	Eugene Daniel	.10
304	Tyji Armstrong	.10
305	Eugene Chung	.10
306	Raghib Ismail	.20
307	Sean Jones	.10
308	Rick Cunningham	.10
309	Ken Harvey	.10
310	Jeff George	.20
311	Jon Vaughn	.10
312	Roy Barker	.10
313	Michael Barrow	.10
314	Ryan McNeil	.10
315	Pete Stoyanovich	.10
316	Darryl Williams	.10
317	Renaldo Turnbull	.10
318	Eric Green	.10
319	Nate Lewis	.10
320	Mike Flores	.10
321	Derek Russell	.10
322	Marcus Spears	.10
323	Corey Miller	.10
324	Derrick Thomas	.20
325	Steve Everitt	.10
326	Brent Jones	.10
327	*Marshall Faulk*	8.00
328	Don Beebe	.10
329	Harry Swayne	.10
330	Boomer Esiason	.10
331	Don Mosebar	.10

332	*Isaac Bruce*	5.00
333	Rickey Jackson	.10
334	Daryl Johnston	.10
335	Lorenzo Lynch	.10
336	Brian Blades	.10
337	Michael Timpson	.10
338	Reggie Cobb	.10
339	Joe Walter	.10
340	Barry Foster	.20
341	Richmond Webb	.10
342	Pat Swilling	.10
343	Shaun Gayle	.10
344	Reggie Roby	.10
345	Chris Calloway	.10
346	Doug Dawson	.10
347	Rob Burnett	.10
348	Dana Hall	.10
349	Horace Copeland	.10
350	Shannon Sharpe	.20
351	Rich Miano	.10
352	Henry Thomas	.10
353	Dan Saleaumua	.10
354	Kevin Ross	.10
355	Morten Andersen	.10
356	Anthony Blaylock	.10
357	Stanley Richard	.10
358	Albert Lewis	.10
359	Darren Woodson	.10
360	Drew Bledsoe	2.00
361	Eric Mahlum	.10
362	*Trent Dilfer*	3.00
363	William Roberts	.10
364	Robert Brooks	.10
365	Jason Hanson	.10
366	Troy Vincent	.10
367	William Thomas	.10
368	Lonnie Johnson	.10
369	*Jamir Miller*	.20
370	Michael Jackson	.10
371	*Charlie Ward*	1.25
372	Shannon Sharpe	.20
373	Jackie Slater	.10
374	Steve Young	.20
375	Bobby Wilson	.10
376	Paul Frase	.10
377	Dale Carter	.10
378	Robert Delpino	.10
379	*Bert Emanuel*	2.00
380	Rick Mirer	.50
381	Carlos Jenkins	.10
382	Gary Brown	.10
383	Doug Pelfrey	.10
384	Dexter Carter	.10
385	Chris Miller	.10
386	*Charles Johnson*	1.00
387	James Joseph	.10
388	Darrin Smith	.10
389	James Jett	.10
390	Junior Seau	.20
391	Chris Slade	.10
392	Jim Harbaugh	.10
393	Herman Moore	.75
394	Thomas Randolph	.10
395	Lamar Thomas	.10
396	Reggie Rivers	.10
397	Larry Centers	.10
398	Chad Brown	.10
399	Terry Kirby	.20
400	Bruce Smith	.10
401	*Keenan McCardell*	2.50
402	Tim McDonald	.10
403	Robert Smith	.10
404	Matt Brock	.10
405	Tony McGee	.10
406	Ethan Horton	.10
407	Michael Haynes	.10
408	Steve Jackson	.10
409	Erik Kramer	.10
410	Jerome Bettis	1.00
411	D.J. Johnson	.10
412	John Alt	.10
413	Jeff Lageman	.10
414	Rick Tuten	.10
415	Jeff Robinson	.10
416	*Kevin Lee*	.20
417	*Thomas Lewis*	.20
418	Kerry Cash	.10
419	*Chuck Levy*	.20
420	Mark Ingram	.10
421	Dennis Gibson	.10
422	Tyronne Drakeford	.10
423	James Washington	.10
424	Dante Jones	.10
425	Eugene Robinson	.10
426	Johnny Johnson	.10
427	Brian Mitchell	.10
428	Charles Mincy	.10
429	Mark Carrier	.10
430	Vince Workman	.10
431	James Francis	.10
432	Clay Matthews	.10
433	Randall McDaniel	.10
434	Brad Ottis	.10
435	Bruce Smith	.10
436	Cortez Kennedy	.20
437	John Randle	.10
438	Neil Smith	.10
439	Cornelius Bennett	.10
440	Junior Seau	.20
441	Derrick Thomas	.20
442	Rod Woodson	.20
443	Terry McDaniel	.10
444	Tim McDonald	.10
445	Mark Carrier	.10
446	Irv Smith	.10
447	Steve Wallace	.10
448	Cris Dishman	.10
449	Bill Brooks	.10
450	Jeff Hostetler	.10
451	Brenston Buckner	.10
452	Ken Ruettgers	.10
453	Marc Boutte	.10
454	John Offerdahl	.10
455	Allen Aldridge	.10
456	Steve Emtman	.10
457	Andre Rison	.20
458	Shawn Jefferson	.10
459	*Todd Steussie*	.20
460	Scott Mitchell	.20
461	Tom Carter	.10
462	*Donnell Bennett*	.20
463	James Jones	.10
464	Antone Davis	.10
465	Jim Everett	.10
466	Tony Tolbert	.10
467	Merril Hoge	.10
468	Michael Bates	.10
469	Phil Hansen	.10
470	Rodney Hampton	.20
471	Aeneas Williams	.10
472	Al Del Greco	.10

473	Todd Lyght	.10
474	Joel Steed	.10
475	Merton Hanks	.10
476	Tony Stargell	.10
477	Greg Robinson	.10
478	Roger Duffy	.10
479	Simeon Fletcher	.10
480	Reggie White	.20
481	Lee Johnson	.10
482	Wayne Martin	.10
483	Thurman Thomas	.20
484	Warren Moon	.20
485	Sam Rogers	.10
486	Erric Pegram	.10
487	Will Wolford	.10
488	Duane Young	.10
489	Keith Hamilton	.10
490	Haywood Jeffires	.10
491	Trace Armstrong	.10
492	J.J. Birden	.10
493	Ricky Ervins	.10
494	Robert Blackmon	.10
495	William Perry	.10
496	Robert Massey	.10
497	Jim Jeffcoat	.10
498	Pat Harlow	.10
499	Jeff Cross	.10
500	Jerry Rice	1.25
501	*Darnay Scott*	2.00
502	Clyde Simmons	.10
503	Henry Rolling	.10
504	James Hasty	.10
505	Leroy Thompson	.10
506	Darrell Thompson	.10
507	Tim Bowens	.10
508	Gerald Perry	.10
509	Mike Croel	.10
510	Sam Mills	.10
511	Steve Young	.50
512	Hardy Nickerson	.10
513	Cris Carter	.20
514	Boomer Esiason	.10
515	Bruce Smith	.10
516	Emmitt Smith	2.00
517	Eugene Robinson	.10
518	Gary Brown	.10
519	Jerry Rice	.75
520	Troy Aikman	1.00
521	Marcus Allen	.20
522	Junior Seau	.20
523	Sterling Sharpe	.20
524	Dana Stubblefield	.10
525	Tom Carter	.10
526	Pete Metzelaars	.10
527	Russell Freeman	.10
528	Keith Cash	.10
529	Willie Drewrey	.10
530	Randal Hill	.10
531	Pepper Johnson	.10
532	Rob Moore	.20
533	Todd Kelly	.10
534	Keith Byars	.10
535	Mike Fox	.10
536	Brett Favre	4.00
537	Terry McDaniel	.10
538	Darren Perry	.10
539	Maurice Hurst	.10
540	Troy Aikman	2.00
541	Junior Seau	.20
542	Steve Broussard	.10
543	Lorenzo White	.10
544	Terry McDaniel	.10
545	Henry Thomas	.10
546	Tyrone Hughes	.10
547	Mark Collins	.10
548	Gary Anderson	.10
549	Darrell Green	.10
550	Jerry Rice	1.50
551	Cornelius Bennett	.10
552	Aeneas Williams	.10
553	Eric Metcalf	.10
554	John Elliott	.10
555	Mo Lewis	.10
556	Darren Carrington	.10
557	Kevin Greene	.10
558	John Elway	.50
559	Eugene Robinson	.10
560	Drew Bledsoe	2.00
561	Fred Barnett	.10
562	*Bernie Parmalee*	1.00
563	Bryce Paup	.10
564	Donnell Woolford	.10
565	Terance Mathis	.10
566	Santana Dotson	.10
567	Randall McDaniel	.10
568	Stanley Richard	.10
569	Brian Blades	.10
570	Jerome Bettis	1.00
571	Neil Smith	.10
572	Andre Reed	.20
573	Michael Bankston	.10
574	Dana Stubblefield	.10
575	Rod Woodson	.20
576	Ken Harvey	.10
577	Andre Rison	.20
578	Darion Conner	.10
579	Michael Strahan	.10
580	Barry Sanders	2.00
581	Pepper Johnson	.10
582	Lewis Tillman	.10
583	Jeff George	.20
584	Michael Haynes	.10
585	Herschel Walker	.20
586	Tim Brown	.20
587	Jim Kelly	.20
588	Ricky Watters	.20
589	Randall Cunningham	.20
590	Troy Aikman	2.00
591	Ken Norton	.10
592	Cortez Kennedy	.10
593	Ricky Ervins	.10
594	Cris Carter	.20
595	Sterling Sharpe	.20
596	John Randle	.10
597	Shannon Sharpe	.20
598	*Ray Crittenden*	.20
599	Barry Foster	.25
600	Deion Sanders	1.00
601	Seth Joyner	.10
602	Chris Warren	.20
603	Tom Rathman	.10
604	Brett Favre	3.00
605	Marshall Faulk	2.00
606	Terry Allen	.10
607	Ben Coates	.50
608	Brian Washington	.10
609	Henry Ellard	.10
610	David Meggett	.10
611	Stan Humphries	.10
612	Warren Moon	.20
613	Marcus Allen	.20

614	Ed McDaniel	.10
615	Joe Montana	2.00
616	Jeff Hostetler	.10
617	Johnny Johnson	.10
618	Andre Coleman	.10
619	Willie Davis	.10
620	Rick Mirer	.50
621	Dan Marino	3.00
622	Rob Moore	.20
623	*Byron Morris*	.50
624	Natrone Means	.50
625	Steve Young	1.00
626	Jim Everett	.10
627	Michael Brooks	.10
628	Dermontti Dawson	.10
629	Reggie White	.20
630	Emmitt Smith	2.50

1994 Stadium Club First Day Cards

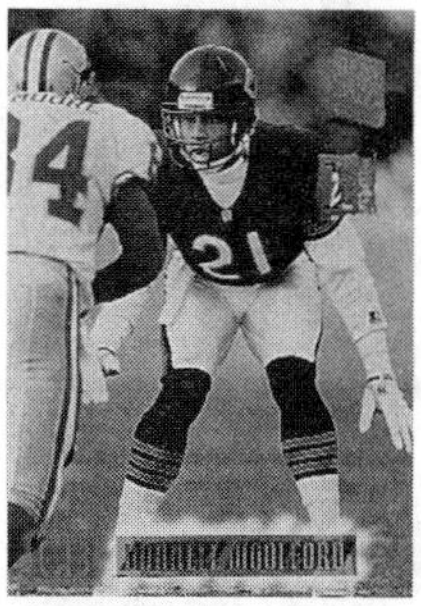

First Day Issues parallel cards were inserted one per 12 packs, and parallel the 630-card base set. The cards are distinguished by a gold foil "First Day" stamp on front.

	MT
Complete Set (630):	3000.
Complete Series 1 (270):	1200.
Complete Series 2 (270):	1200.
Complete High Series (90):	600.00
Common Player:	2.00
Minor Stars:	5.00
Unlisted Stars:	12x-25x

1	*Dan Wilkinson*	10.00
2	Chip Lohmiller	2.00
3	Roosevelt Potts	2.00
4	Martin Mayhew	2.00
5	Shane Conlan	2.00
6	*Sam Adams*	8.00
7	Mike Kenn	2.00
8	Tim Goad	2.00
9	Tony Jones	2.00
10	Ron Moore	8.00
11	Mark Bortz	2.00
12	Darren Carrington	2.00
13	Eric Martin	2.00
14	Eric Allen	2.00
15	*Aaron Glenn*	6.00
16	Bryan Cox	2.00
17	Levon Kirkland	2.00
18	Qadry Ismail	5.00
19	Shane Dronett	2.00
20	Chris Spielman	2.00
21	*Rob Fredrickson*	8.00
22	Wayne Simmons	2.00
23	*Glenn Montgomery*	5.00
24	*Jason Sehorn*	5.00
25	Nick Lowery	2.00
26	Dennis Brown	2.00
27	Kenneth Davis	2.00
28	*Shante Carver*	5.00
29	*Ryan Yarborough*	7.00
30	Cortez Kennedy	5.00
31	Anthony Pleasant	2.00
32	Jessie Tuggle	2.00
33	Herschel Walker	5.00
34	Andre Collins	2.00
35	*William Floyd*	40.00
36	Harold Green	2.00
37	Courtney Hawkins	2.00
38	Curtis Conway	5.00
39	Ben Coates	5.00
40	Natrone Means	45.00
41	Eric Hill	2.00
42	Keith Kartz	2.00
43	Alexander Wright	2.00
44	William Roaf	2.00
45	Vencie Glenn	2.00
46	Ronnie Lott, David Lutz	2.00
47	George Koonce, Kelvin Martin	2.00
48	Rod Woodson	5.00
49	Tim Grunhard	2.00
50	Cody Carlson	2.00
51	*Bryant Young*	18.00
52	Jay Novacek	2.00
53	Darryl Talley	2.00
54	Gary Anderson, Harry Colon	2.00
55	David Meggett	2.00
56	*Aubrey Beavers*	5.00
57	James Folston	2.00
58	Willie Davis	2.00
59	Jason Elam	2.00
60	Eric Metcalf	2.00
61	Bruce Armstrong	2.00
62	Ron Heller	2.00
63	LeRoy Butler	2.00
64	Terry Obee	2.00
65	Kurt Gouveia	2.00
66	Pierce Holt	2.00
67	David Alexander	2.00
68	*Deral Boykin*	2.00
69	Carl Pickens	2.00
70	Broderick Thomas	2.00
71	Barry Sanders	25.00
72	Qadry Ismail	5.00
73	Thurman Thomas	8.00
74	Junior Seau, Bob Dahl	2.00
75	Vinny Testaverde	2.00
76	Tyrone Hughes	2.00
77	Nate Newton	2.00
78	Eric Swann	2.00
79	Brad Baxter	2.00
80	Dana Stubblefield	2.00

81	John Elliott	2.00
82	Steve Wisniewski	2.00
83	Eddie Robinson	2.00
84	*Isaac Davis*	5.00
85	Cris Carter	5.00
86	Mel Gray	2.00
87	Cornelius Bennett	2.00
88	Neil O'Donnell	5.00
89	Jon Hand	2.00
90	John Elway	20.00
91	Bill Hitchcock	2.00
92	Neil Smith	2.00
93	*Joe Johnson*	2.00
94	Edgar Bennett	2.00
95	Vincent Brown	5.00
96	Tommy Vardell	2.00
97	Donnell Woolford	2.00
98	Lincoln Kennedy	2.00
99	O.J. McDuffie	10.00
100	*Heath Shuler*	12.00
101	Jerry Rice	25.00
102	Erik Williams	2.00
103	Randall McDaniel	2.00
104	Dermontti Dawson	2.00
105	Nate Newton	2.00
106	Harris Barton	2.00
107	Shannon Sharpe	5.00
108	Sterling Sharpe	5.00
109	Steve Young	25.00
110	Emmitt Smith	45.00
111	Thurman Thomas	7.00
112	Kyle Clifton	2.00
113	Desmond Howard	2.00
114	Quinn Early	2.00
115	David Klingler	2.00
116	Bern Brostek	2.00
117	Gary Clark	2.00
118	Courtney Hall	2.00
119	*Joe King*	2.00
120	Quentin Coryatt	2.00
121	*Johnnie Morton*	6.00
122	Andre Reed	5.00
123	Eric Davis	2.00
124	Jack Del Rio	2.00
125	Greg Lloyd	2.00
126	Bubba McDowell	2.00
127	Mark Jackson	2.00
128	Jeff Jaeger	2.00
129	Chris Warren	5.00
130	Tom Waddle	2.00
131	Tony Smith	2.00
132	Todd Collins	2.00
133	Mark Bavaro	2.00
134	Joe Phillips	2.00
135	Chris Jacke	2.00
136	Glyn Milburn	5.00
137	Keith Jackson	2.00
138	Steve Tovar	2.00
139	Tim Johnson	2.00
140	Brian Washington	2.00
141	Troy Drayton	2.00
142	*DeWayne Washington*	5.00
143	Erik Williams	2.00
144	Eric Turner	2.00
145	John Taylor	5.00
146	Richard Cooper	2.00
147	*Van Malone*	2.00
148	*Tim Ruddy*	2.00
149	Henry Jones	2.00
150	Tim Brown	5.00
151	Stan Humphries	5.00
152	Harry Newsome	2.00
153	Craig Erickson	5.00
154	Gary Anderson	2.00
155	Ray Childress	2.00
156	Howard Cross	2.00
157	Heath Sherman	2.00
158	Terrell Buckley	2.00
159	J.B. Brown	2.00
160	Joe Montana	60.00
161	David Wyman	2.00
162	Norm Johnson	2.00
163	Rod Stephens	2.00
164	*Willie McGinest*	5.00
165	Barry Sanders	50.00
166	Marc Logan	2.00
167	Anthony Newman	2.00
168	Russell Maryland	2.00
169	Luis Sharpe	2.00
170	Jim Kelly	8.00
171	*Tre' Johnson*	2.00
172	Johnny Mitchell	2.00
173	*David Palmer*	6.00
174	Bob Dahl	2.00
175	Aaron Wallace	2.00
176	Chris Gardocki	2.00
177	Hardy Nickerson	2.00
178	Jeff Query	2.00
179	Leslie O'Neal	2.00
180	Kevin Greene	2.00
181	Alonzo Spellman	2.00
182	Reggie Brooks	2.00
183	Dana Stubblefield	2.00
184	Tyrone Hughes	2.00
185	Drew Bledsoe	35.00
186	Ron Moore	5.00
187	Jason Elam	2.00
188	Rick Mirer	15.00
189	William Roaf	2.00
190	Jerome Bettis	15.00
191	Brad Hopkins	2.00
192	Derek Brown	2.00
193	Nolan Harrison	2.00
194	Jon Randle	2.00
195	Carlton Bailey	2.00
196	Kevin Williams	5.00
197	*Greg Hill*	25.00
198	Mark McMillian	2.00
199	Brad Edwards	2.00
200	Dan Marino	90.00
201	Ricky Watters	5.00
202	George Teague	2.00
203	Steve Beuerlein	2.00
204	*Jeff Burris*	8.00
205	Steve Atwater	2.00
206	*John Thierry*	5.00
207	Patrick Hunter	2.00
208	*Wayne Gandy*	2.00
209	Derrick Moore	2.00
210	Phil Simms	2.00
211	Kirk Lowdermilk	2.00
212	Patrick Robinson	2.00
213	Kevin Mitchell	2.00
214	Jonathan Hayes	2.00
215	Michael Dean Perry	2.00
216	John Fina	2.00
217	Anthony Smith	2.00
218	Paul Gruber	2.00
219	Carnell Lake	2.00
220	Carl Lee	2.00
221	Steve Christie	2.00

222	Greg Montgomery	2.00
223	Reggie Brooks	2.00
224	Derrick Thomas	5.00
225	Eric Metcalf	2.00
226	Michael Haynes	2.00
227	Bobby Hebert	2.00
228	Tyrone Hughes	2.00
229	Donald Frank	2.00
230	Vaughan Johnson	2.00
231	Eric Thomas	2.00
232	Ernest Givins	2.00
233	Charles Haley	2.00
234	Darrell Green	2.00
235	Harold Alexander	2.00
236	Dwayne Sabb	2.00
237	Harris Barton	2.00
238	Randall Cunningham	6.00
239	Ray Buchanan	2.00
240	Sterling Sharpe	10.00
241	Chris Mims	2.00
242	Mark Carrier	2.00
243	Ricky Proehl	2.00
244	Michael Brooks	2.00
245	Sean Gilbert	2.00
246	David Lutz	2.00
247	Kelvin Martin	2.00
248	*Scottie Graham*	5.00
249	Irving Fryar	2.00
250	Ricardo McDonald	2.00
251	Marvcus Patton	2.00
252	*Errict Rhett*	40.00
253	Winston Moss	2.00
254	Rod Vernstine	2.00
255	Terry Wooden	2.00
256	*Antonio Langham*	10.00
257	Tommy Barnhardt	2.00
258	Marvin Washington	2.00
259	Bo Orlando	2.00
260	Marcus Allen	5.00
261	*Mario Bates*	30.00
262	Marco Coleman	2.00
263	Doug Riesenberg	2.00
264	Jesse Sapolu	2.00
265	Dermontti Dawson	2.00
266	*Fernando Smith*	2.00
267	David Szott	2.00
268	Steve Christie	2.00
269	Bruce Matthews	2.00
270	Michael Irvin	20.00
271	Seth Joyner	2.00
272	Santana Dotson	2.00
273	Vincent Brisby	10.00
274	Rohn Stark	2.00
275	John Copeland	2.00
276	Toby Wright	2.00
277	David Griggs	2.00
278	*Aaron Taylor*	2.00
279	Chris Doleman	2.00
280	Reggie Brooks	2.00
281	Willie Anderson	2.00
282	Alvin Harper	5.00
283	Chris Hinton	2.00
284	Kelvin Pritchett	2.00
285	Russell Copeland	2.00
286	Dwight Stone	2.00
287	Jeff Gossett	2.00
288	Larry Allen	2.00
289	Kevin Mawae	2.00
290	Mark Collins	2.00
291	Chris Zorich	2.00
292	Vince Buck	2.00
293	Gene Atkins	2.00
294	Webster Slaughter	2.00
295	Steve Young	35.00
296	Dan Williams	2.00
297	Jesse Armstead	2.00
298	Victor Bailey	2.00
299	John Carney	2.00
300	Emmitt Smith	90.00
301	*Bucky Brooks*	5.00
302	Mo Lewis	2.00
303	Eugene Daniel	2.00
304	Tyji Armstrong	2.00
305	Eugene Chung	2.00
306	Raghib Ismail	5.00
307	Sean Jones	2.00
308	Rick Cunningham	2.00
309	Ken Harvey	2.00
310	Jeff George	5.00
311	Jon Vaughn	2.00
312	Roy Barker	2.00
313	Michael Barrow	2.00
314	Ryan McNeil	2.00
315	Pete Stoyanovich	2.00
316	Darryl Williams	2.00
317	Renaldo Turnbull	2.00
318	Eric Green	2.00
319	Nate Lewis	2.00
320	Mike Flores	2.00
321	Derek Russell	2.00
322	Marcus Spears	2.00
323	Corey Miller	2.00
324	Derrick Thomas	5.00
325	Steve Everitt	2.00
326	Brent Jones	2.00
327	*Marshall Faulk*	100.00
328	Don Beebe	2.00
329	Harry Swayne	2.00
330	Boomer Esiason	2.00
331	Don Mosebar	2.00
332	*Isaac Bruce*	60.00
333	Rickey Jackson	2.00
334	Daryl Johnston	2.00
335	Lorenzo Lynch	2.00
336	Brian Blades	2.00
337	Michael Timpson	2.00
338	Reggie Cobb	2.00
339	Joe Walter	2.00
340	Barry Foster	7.00
341	Richmond Webb	2.00
342	Pat Swilling	2.00
343	Shaun Gayle	2.00
344	Reggie Roby	2.00
345	Chris Calloway	2.00
346	Doug Dawson	2.00
347	Rob Burnett	2.00
348	Dana Hall	2.00
349	Horace Copeland	2.00
350	Shannon Sharpe	5.00
351	Rich Miano	2.00
352	Henry Thomas	2.00
353	Dan Saleaumua	2.00
354	Kevin Ross	2.00
355	Morten Andersen	2.00
356	Anthony Blaylock	2.00
357	Stanley Richard	2.00
358	Albert Lewis	2.00
359	Darren Woodson	2.00
360	Drew Bledsoe	60.00
361	Eric Mahlum	2.00
362	*Trent Dilfer*	35.00

363	William Roberts	2.00
364	Robert Brooks	2.00
365	Jason Hanson	2.00
366	Troy Vincent	2.00
367	William Thomas	2.00
368	Lonnie Johnson	2.00
369	*Jamir Miller*	5.00
370	Michael Jackson	2.00
371	*Charlie Ward*	20.00
372	Shannon Sharpe	5.00
373	Jackie Slater	2.00
374	Steve Young	5.00
375	Bobby Wilson	2.00
376	Paul Frase	2.00
377	Dale Carter	2.00
378	Robert Delpino	2.00
379	*Bert Emanuel*	25.00
380	Rick Mirer	20.00
381	Carlos Jenkins	2.00
382	Gary Brown	2.00
383	Doug Pelfrey	2.00
384	Dexter Carter	2.00
385	Chris Miller	2.00
386	*Charles Johnson*	25.00
387	James Joseph	2.00
388	Darrin Smith	2.00
389	James Jett	2.00
390	Junior Seau	5.00
391	Chris Slade	2.00
392	Jim Harbaugh	2.00
393	Herman Moore	15.00
394	Thomas Randolph	2.00
395	Lamar Thomas	2.00
396	Reggie Rivers	2.00
397	Larry Centers	2.00
398	Chad Brown	2.00
399	Terry Kirby	5.00
400	Bruce Smith	2.00
401	Keenan McCardell	25.00
402	Tim McDonald	2.00
403	Robert Smith	2.00
404	Matt Brock	2.00
405	Tony McGee	2.00
406	Ethan Horton	2.00
407	Michael Haynes	2.00
408	Steve Jackson	2.00
409	Erik Kramer	2.00
410	Jerome Bettis	20.00
411	D.J. Johnson	2.00
412	John Alt	2.00
413	Jeff Lageman	2.00
414	Rick Tuten	2.00
415	Jeff Robinson	2.00
416	*Kevin Lee*	5.00
417	*Thomas Lewis*	8.00
418	Kerry Cash	2.00
419	*Chuck Levy*	2.00
420	Mark Ingram	2.00
421	Dennis Gibson	2.00
422	Tyronne Drakeford	2.00
423	James Washington	2.00
424	Dante Jones	2.00
425	Eugene Robinson	2.00
426	Johnny Johnson	2.00
427	Brian Mitchell	2.00
428	Charles Mincy	2.00
429	Mark Carrier	2.00
430	Vince Workman	2.00
431	James Francis	2.00
432	Clay Matthews	2.00
433	Randall McDaniel	2.00
434	Brad Ottis	2.00
435	Bruce Smith	2.00
436	Cortez Kennedy	5.00
437	John Randle	2.00
438	Neil Smith	2.00
439	Cornelius Bennett	2.00
440	Junior Seau	5.00
441	Derrick Thomas	5.00
442	Rod Woodson	5.00
443	Terry McDaniel	2.00
444	Tim McDonald	2.00
445	Mark Carrier	2.00
446	Irv Smith	2.00
447	Steve Wallace	2.00
448	Cris Dishman	2.00
449	Bill Brooks	2.00
450	Jeff Hostetler	2.00
451	Brenston Buckner	2.00
452	Ken Ruettgers	2.00
453	Marc Boutte	2.00
454	John Offerdahl	2.00
455	Allen Aldridge	2.00
456	Steve Emtman	2.00
457	Andre Rison	5.00
458	Shawn Jefferson	2.00
459	*Todd Steussie*	2.00
460	Scott Mitchell	5.00
461	Tom Carter	2.00
462	*Donnell Bennett*	5.00
463	James Jones	2.00
464	Antone Davis	2.00
465	Jim Everett	2.00
466	Tony Tolbert	2.00
467	Merril Hoge	2.00
468	Michael Bates	2.00
469	Phil Hansen	2.00
470	Rodney Hampton	5.00
471	Aeneas Williams	2.00
472	Al Del Greco	2.00
473	Todd Lyght	2.00
474	Joel Steed	2.00
475	Merton Hanks	2.00
476	Tony Stargell	2.00
477	Greg Robinson	2.00
478	Roger Duffy	2.00
479	Simon Fletcher	2.00
480	Reggie White	5.00
481	Lee Johnson	2.00
482	Wayne Martin	2.00
483	Thurman Thomas	8.00
484	Warren Moon	6.00
485	Sam Rogers	2.00
486	Erric Pegram	2.00
487	Will Wolford	2.00
488	Duane Young	2.00
489	Keith Hamilton	2.00
490	Haywood Jeffires	2.00
491	Trace Armstrong	2.00
492	J.J. Birden	2.00
493	Ricky Ervins	2.00
494	Robert Blackmon	2.00
495	William Perry	2.00
496	Robert Massey	2.00
497	Jim Jeffcoat	2.00
498	Pat Harlow	2.00
499	Jeff Cross	2.00
500	Jerry Rice	45.00
501	*Darnay Scott*	40.00
502	Clyde Simmons	2.00
503	Henry Rolling	2.00
504	James Hasty	2.00
505	Leroy Thompson	2.00
506	Darrell Thompson	2.00
507	Tim Bowens	2.00
508	Gerald Perry	2.00
509	Mike Croel	2.00
510	Sam Mills	2.00
511	Steve Young	20.00
512	Hardy Nickerson	2.00
513	Cris Carter	5.00
514	Boomer Esiason	2.00
515	Bruce Smith	2.00
516	Emmitt Smith	50.00
517	Eugene Robinson	2.00
518	Gary Brown	2.00
519	Jerry Rice	20.00
520	Troy Aikman	20.00
521	Marcus Allen	5.00
522	Junior Seau	5.00
523	Sterling Sharpe	5.00
524	Dana Stubblefield	2.00
525	Tom Carter	2.00
526	Pete Metzelaars	2.00
527	Russell Freeman	2.00
528	Keith Cash	2.00
529	Willie Drewrey	2.00
530	Randal Hill	2.00
531	Pepper Johnson	2.00
532	Rob Moore	5.00
533	Todd Kelly	2.00
534	Keith Byars	2.00
535	Mike Fox	2.00
536	Brett Favre	90.00
537	Terry McDaniel	2.00
538	Darren Perry	2.00
539	Maurice Hurst	2.00
540	Troy Aikman	45.00
541	Junior Seau	7.00
542	Steve Broussard	2.00
543	Lorenzo White	2.00
544	Terry McDaniel	2.00
545	Henry Thomas	2.00
546	Tyrone Hughes	2.00
547	Mark Collins	2.00
548	Gary Anderson	2.00
549	Darrell Green	2.00
550	Jerry Rice	45.00
551	Cornelius Bennett	2.00
552	Aeneas Williams	2.00
553	Eric Metcalf	2.00
554	John Elliott	2.00
555	Mo Lewis	2.00
556	Darren Carrington	2.00
557	Kevin Greene	2.00
558	John Elway	20.00
559	Eugene Robinson	2.00
560	Drew Bledsoe	45.00
561	Fred Barnett	2.00
562	*Bernie Parmalee*	30.00
563	Bryce Paup	2.00
564	Donnell Woolford	2.00
565	Terance Mathis	2.00
566	Santana Dotson	2.00
567	Randall McDaniel	2.00
568	Stanley Richard	2.00
569	Brian Blades	2.00
570	Jerome Bettis	20.00
571	Neil Smith	2.00
572	Andre Reed	5.00
573	Michael Bankston	2.00
574	Dana Stubblefield	2.00
575	Rod Woodson	5.00
576	Ken Harvey	2.00
577	Andre Rison	5.00
578	Darion Conner	2.00
579	Michael Strahan	2.00
580	Barry Sanders	35.00
581	Pepper Johnson	2.00
582	Lewis Tillman	2.00
583	Jeff George	6.00
584	Michael Haynes	2.00
585	Herschel Walker	5.00
586	Tim Brown	5.00
587	Jim Kelly	6.00
588	Ricky Watters	5.00
589	Randall Cunningham	5.00
590	Troy Aikman	45.00
591	Ken Norton	2.00
592	Cortez Kennedy	5.00
593	Ricky Ervins	2.00
594	Cris Carter	5.00
595	Sterling Sharpe	10.00
596	John Randle	2.00
597	Shannon Sharpe	5.00
598	*Ray Crittenden*	5.00
599	Barry Foster	6.00
600	Deion Sanders	35.00
601	Seth Joyner	2.00
602	Chris Warren	5.00
603	Tom Rathman	2.00
604	Brett Favre	25.00
605	Marshall Faulk	45.00
606	Terry Allen	2.00
607	Ben Coates	10.00
608	Brian Washington	2.00
609	Henry Ellard	2.00
610	David Meggett	2.00
611	Stan Humphries	5.00
612	Warren Moon	5.00
613	Marcus Allen	5.00
614	Ed McDaniel	2.00
615	Joe Montana	60.00
616	Jeff Hostetler	2.00
617	Johnny Johnson	2.00
618	Andre Coleman	2.00
619	Willie Davis	2.00
620	Rick Mirer	20.00
621	Dan Marino	90.00
622	Rob Moore	2.00
623	*Byron Morris*	40.00
624	Natrone Means	40.00
625	Steve Young	30.00
626	Jim Everett	2.00
627	Michael Brooks	2.00
628	Dermontti Dawson	2.00
629	Reggie White	5.00
630	Emmitt Smith	75.00

1994 Stadium Club Bowman Black

These 17 insert cards, featuring NFL veterans, were included in 1994-95 Stadium Club Football High series packs, one per every three packs. The cards utilize Finest chromium technology and have a black tint to them. "Bowman's Best" is written on the front. The back has a card number, close-up shot and summaries of the player's stats and skills. Refractor versions were also made for each Blue card; they were seeded one per every 12 packs.

		MT
	Complete Set (17):	90.00
	Common Player:	1.00
	Comp. Refr. Set (17):	275.00
	Refractor Cards:	1x-3x
1	Jerry Rice	6.00
2	Deion Sanders	4.00
3	Reggie White	1.00
4	Dan Marino	10.00
5	Natrone Means	2.00
6	Rick Mirer	2.00
7	Michael Irvin	2.00
8	John Elway	4.00
9	Junior Seau	1.00
10	Drew Bledsoe	5.00
11	Sterling Sharpe	1.00
12	Brett Favre	10.00
13	Troy Aikman	5.00
14	Barry Sanders	7.00
15	Steve Young	5.00
16	Emmitt Smith	10.00
17	Joe Montana	5.00

1994 Stadium Club Bowman Blue

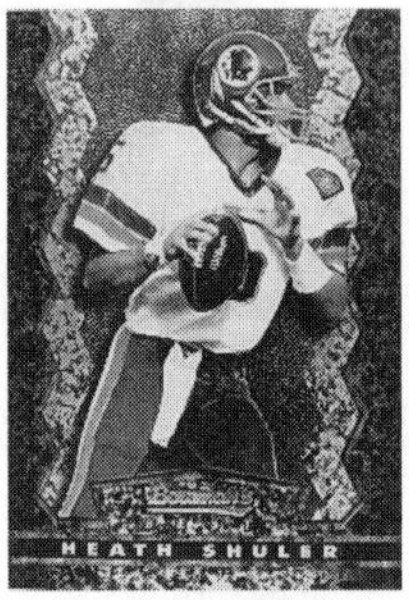

These 1994-95 Topps Stadium Club High Series inserts feature 17 of the NFL's most promising rookies. Cards, which use the Finest chromium technology, were seeded one per three packs. The cards are similar in design to the Bowman Black inserts, except these have a blue tint to them. There were also Refractors made for each Blue card; they are seeded one per every 12 packs.

		MT
	Complete Set (17):	40.00
	Common Player:	1.00
	Comp. Refr. Set (17):	125.00
	Refractor Cards:	1x-3x
1	Marshall Faulk	6.00
2	Derrick Alexander	1.00
3	Darnay Scott	2.00
4	Gus Frerotte	2.00
5	Jeff Blake	6.00
6	Charles Johnson	2.00
7	Thomas Lewis	1.00
8	Charlie Garner	1.00
9	Aaron Glenn	1.00
10	William Floyd	2.00
11	Antonio Langham	1.00
12	Errict Rhett	3.00
13	Heath Shuler	3.00
14	Jeff Burris	1.00
15	Dan Wilkinson	1.00
16	Rob Fredrickson	1.00
17	Tim Bowens	1.00

1994 Stadium Club Bowman Mirror Images

These cards match a top NFL veteran with a promising rookie. The horizontal front, using Finest chromium technology, shows both players, with their names underneath. The cards were random inserts in 1994-95 Topps Stadium High Series packs, one per every three packs. Refractor versions were also made; they could be found one per every 12 packs.

		MT
	Complete Set (11):	45.00
	Common Player:	1.00
	Comp. Refrac. Set (11):	130.00
	Refractor Cards:	1x-3x
18	Deion Sanders, Aaron Glenn	3.00
19	Barry Sanders, Marshall Faulk	7.00
20	Darryl Johnston, William Floyd	2.00
21	Reggie White, Tim Bowens	1.00
22	Troy Aikman, Heath Shuler	6.00
23	Donnell Woolford, Antonio Langham	1.00
24	Rodney Hampton, Errict Rhett	6.00
25	Tyrone Hughes, Jeff Burris	1.00
26	Henry Thomas, Dan Wilkinson	1.00
27	Jerry Rice, Derrick Alexander	5.00
28	Emmitt Smith, Bam Morris	10.00

A card number in parentheses ( ) indicates the set is unnumbered.

1994 Stadium Club Dynasty and Destiny

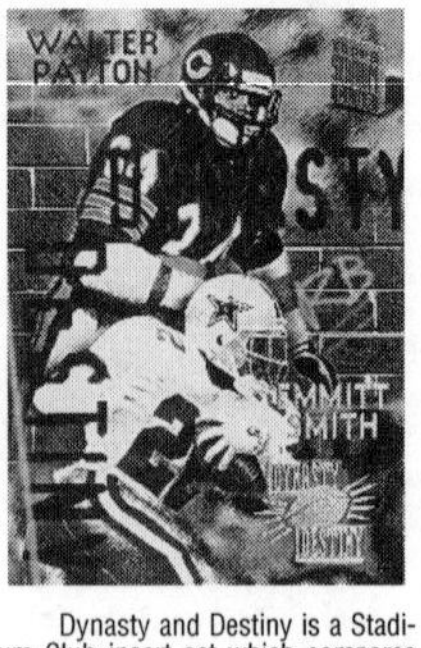

Dynasty and Destiny is a Stadium Club insert set which compares former NFL players who are or will be Hall of Fame members with current players. Three cards appeared in Series I and three more followed in Series II. Each card front shows both players, with their names, the set name and Stadium Club logo stamped in gold foil. Destiny and Dynasty are also written on the card front. The back, numbered 1 of 6, etc., compares statistics for both players from their first year in the league and their career totals. Mug shots are also given.

		MT
	Complete Set (6):	25.00
	Common Player:	5.00
1	Walter Payton, Emmitt Smith	12.00
2	Steve Largent, Tom Waddle	5.00
3	Randy White, Cortez Kennedy	5.00
4	Dan Fouts, Troy Aikman	8.00
5	Mike Singletary, Junior Seau	5.00
6	Ozzie Newsome, Shannon Sharpe	5.00

1994 Stadium Club Expansion Team Redemption

This 44-card Finest set was available through redemption cards in Stadium Club Series III, seeded one per 24 packs. The set introduced the two new expansion teams - Jacksonville Jaguars and Carolina Panthers - with three redemption cards per franchise, labeled offense, defense and special teams, which could be redeemed for that group of players in their new uniforms. There was also a complete set redemption card found every 336 packs. The deadline for redemptions was February 20, 1996.

		MT
	Jaguars Prize Set (22):	20.00
	Panthers Prize Set (22):	25.00
	Common Jaguar (J1-J22):	.75
	Common Panther (P1-P22):	.75
	Comp. Trade Card Set (6):	3.00
J1	James O. Stewart	2.00
J2	Kelvin Pritchett	.75
J3	Mike Dumas	.75
J4	Brian DeMarco	.75
J5	James Williams	.75
J6	Ernest Givins	.75
J7	Harry Colon	.75
J8	Derek Brown	.75
J9	Santo Stephens	.75
J10	Jeff Lageman	.75
J11	Bryan Barker	.75
J12	Dave Widell	.75
J13	Willie Jackson	1.00
J14	Vinnie Clark	.75
J15	Mickey Washington	.75
J16	Le'Shai Maston	.75
J17	Darren Carrington	.75
J18	Steve Beuerlein	.75
J19	Mark Williams	.75
J20	Keith Goganious	.75
J21	Shawn Bouwens	.75
J22	Chris Hudson	.75
P1	Kerry Collins	8.00
P2	Rod Smith	.75
P3	Willie Green	.75
P4	Greg Kragen	.75
P5	Blake Brockermeyer	.75
P6	Bob Christian	.75
P7	Carlton Bailey	.75
P8	Bubba McDowell	.75
P9	Matt Elliott	.75
P10	Tyrone Poole	1.00
P11	John Kasay	.75
P12	Gerald Williams	.75
P13	Derrick Moore	.75
P14	Don Beebe	.75
P15	Sam Mills	.75
P16	Darion Conner	.75
P17	Eric Guliford	.75
P18	Mike Fox	.75
P19	Pete Metzelaars	.75
P20	Frank Reich	1.00
P21	Mark Carrier	.75
P22	Vince Workman	.75
NNO	Jacksonville Jaguars Defense Redemption Card	.50
NNO	Jacksonville Jaguars Offense Redemption Card	.50
NNO	Jacksonville Jaguars Special Teams Redemption Card	.50
NNO	Carolina Panthers Defense Redemption Card	.50
NNO	Carolina Panthers Offense Redemption Card	.50
NNO	Carolina Panthers Special Teams Redemption Card	.50
NNO	Carolina Panthers Complete Set Redemption	.50

1994 Stadium Club Frequent Scorers

These Stadium Club Series II inserts feature 10 different players, each having five different point cards, worth six points each. Collectors can receive a Finest quality upgrade set of the player by sending in 30 Frequent Scorer point cards of him. The point cards were included one per every three packs.

		MT
	Complete Set (10):	150.00
	Common Player:	6.00
1	Chris Warren	9.00
2	Marshall Faulk	25.00
3	Drew Bledsoe	25.00
4	Dan Marino	35.00
5	Vinny Testaverde	6.00
6	Jeff George	9.00
7	Steve Young	20.00
8	Dave Meggett	6.00
9	Stan Humphries	9.00
10	Rick Mirer	15.00

1994 Stadium Club Ring Leaders

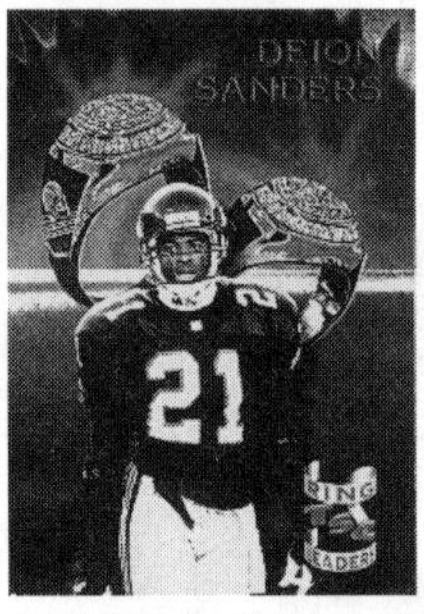

These Stadium Club Series II inserts feature active players who have played in a Pro Bowl and have led the league in a statistical category. Topps used a "Power Matrix" technology that "makes the cards shine beyond belief." These cards were randomly included in every 24th pack.

		MT
	Complete Set (12):	50.00
	Common Player:	4.00
1	Emmitt Smith	20.00
2	Steve Young	10.00
3	Deion Sanders	7.00
4	Warren Moon	4.00
5	Thurman Thomas	4.00
6	Jerry Rice	10.00
7	Sterling Sharpe	4.00
8	Barry Sanders	12.00
9	Reggie White	4.00
10	Michael Irvin	4.00
11	Ronnie Lott	4.00
12	Herschel Walker	4.00

1994 Stadium Club Super Teams

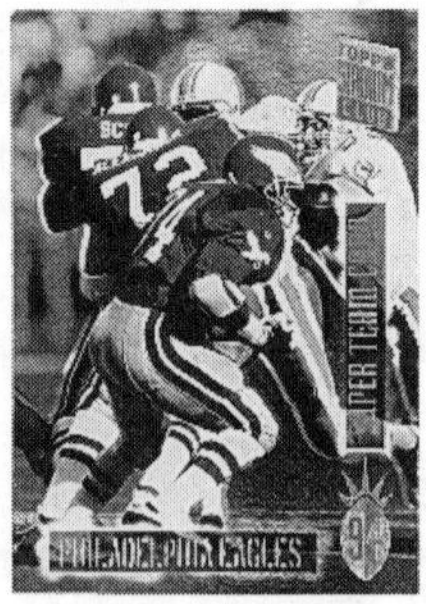

Stadium Club Football also inserted Super Team cards into one of every 24 packs. The cards feature a wide-angle action shot of the team. If the team pictured won the Super Bowl, conference title or division championship, the Super Team card could be redeemed for additional cards that formed a parallel set but had either Super Bowl logo, conference championship logo or division winner logo, respectively.

		MT
	Complete Set (28):	125.00
	Common Player:	2.00
1	Cardinals	2.00
2	Falcons	2.00
3	Bills	2.00
4	Bears	2.00
5	Bengals	2.00
6	Browns	2.00
7	Cowboys	10.00
8	Broncos	6.00
9	Lions	6.00
10	Packers	10.00
11	Oilers	2.00
12	Colts	2.00
13	Chiefs	7.00
14	Raiders	2.00
15	Rams	2.00
16	Dolphins	5.00
17	Vikings	5.00
18	Patriots	6.00
19	Saints	2.00
20	Giants	2.00
21	Jets	2.00
22	Eagles	2.00
23	Steelers	4.00
24	Chargers	6.00
25	49ers	12.00
26	Seahawks	4.00
27	Buccaneers	2.00
28	Redskins	2.00

1994 Stadium Club Super Teams Division Winners

Collectors who had Super Team cards of the Cowboys, 49ers, Vikings, Chargers, Steelers and Dolphins could redeem the cards for a 10-card team bag set via mail. The cards were essentially the same as regular-issue cards, except for a division winner gold foil logo.

		MT
	Complete Bag Chargers (11):	5.00
	Complete Bag Cowboys (11):	12.00
	Complete Bag Dolphins (11):	10.00
	Complete Bag 49ers (11):	12.00
	Complete Bag Vikings (11):	6.00
	Complete Bag Steelers (11):	6.00
	Common Player:	.40
7DW	Cowboys Super Team DW (Emmitt Smith, Troy Aikman)	2.50
16DW	Dolphins Super Team DW (Irving Fryar)	.75
17DW	DW Vikings Super Team DW (Cris Carter)	.75
23DW	Steelers Super Team DW (Neil O'Donnell)	.75
24DW	Chargers Super Team DW (Natrone Means)	.75
25DW	49ers Super Team DW (Jerry Rice, Steve Young, Ricky Watters)	1.50
D16	Bryan Cox	.40
D56	Aubrey Beavers	.40
D99	O.J. McDuffie	1.00
D200	Dan Marino	4.00
D249	Irving Fryar	.60
D262	Marco Coleman	.40
D341	Richmond Webb	.40
D399	Terry Kirby	.60
D507	Tim Bowens	.60
D562	Bernie Parmalee	1.50
F35	William Floyd	2.00
F51	Bryant Young	1.25
F80	Dana Stubblefield	1.00
F201	Ricky Watters	.60
F295	Steve Young	2.50
F326	Brent Jones	.60
F402	Tim McDonald	.40
F475	Merton Hanks	.40
F500	Jerry Rice	2.50
F600	Deion Sanders	1.50
V18	Qadry Ismail	1.00
V85	Cris Carter	.60
V124	Jack Del Rio	.40
V142	DeWayne Washington	.60
V173	David Palmer	.60
V194	John Randle	.40
V352	Henry Thomas	.40
V433	Randall McDaniel	.40
V459	Todd Steussie	.60
V484	Warren Moon	1.00
CH12	Darren Carrington	.40
CH40	Natrone Means	.75
CH84	Isaac Davis	.40
CH151	Stan Humphries	1.00
CH179	Leslie O'Neal	.60
CH299	John Carney	.40
CH357	Stanley Richard	.40
CH390	Junior Seau	1.00
CH421	Dennis Gibson	.40
CH458	Shawn Jefferson	.60
CO52	Jay Novacek	.60
CO168	Russell Maryland	.40
CO233	Charles Haley	.60
CO270	Michael Irvin	1.00
CO282	Alvin Harper	.60
CO300	Emmitt Smith	4.00
CO334	Daryl Johnston	.60
CO359	Darren Woodson	.40
CO423	James Washington	.40
CO540	Troy Aikman	2.50

1994 Stadium Club Super Teams Master Photos

Super Team cards of the AFC and NFC Champions - the Chargers and 49ers - were redeemable for this 10-card team bag set of Master Photos of that respective team. The Master Photos were essentially the same as the base cards, but were printed on an oversized card, with a white border around the photo, and they have a conference winner gold foil logo.

		MT
	Complete Bag Chargers (11):	7.50
	Complete Bag 49ers (11):	15.00
	Common Player:	.50
24CW	Chargers Super Team CW (Natrone Means)	.75
25CW	49ers Super Team CW (Jerry Rice, Steve Young, Ricky Watters)	1.50
F35	William Floyd	2.50
F51	Bryant Young	1.50

F80 Dana Stubblefield 1.25
F201 Ricky Watters .75
F295 Steve Young 3.00
F326 Brent Jones .75
F402 Tim McDonald .75
F475 Merton Hanks .50
F500 Jerry Rice 3.00
F600 Deion Sanders 1.75
CH12 Darren Carrington .50
CH40 Natrone Means 1.00
CH84 Isaac Davis .50
CH151 Stan Humphries 1.25
CH179 Leslie O'Neal .75
CH299 John Carney .50
CH357 Stanley Richard .50
CH390 Junior Seau 1.25
CH421 Dennis Gibson .50
CH458 Shawn Jefferson .75

1994 Stadium Club Super Teams Super Bowl

Super Team cards of the Super Bowl XXIX Champion 49ers could be redeemed for a 540-card parallel set to the regular-issue Stadium Club set. The cards are essentially the same as regular-issue cards, except for a "Super Bowl XXIX" logo on the front. The sets also came with a 49ers Super Team card that also had a "Super Bowl XXIX" logo on the front.

		MT
Complete Set (541):		60.00
Common Player:		.10
SB25	49ers Super Team SB (Jerry Rice, Steve Young, Ricky Watters)	2.00

1994 Stadium Club Members Only Parallel

Stadium Club Members Only parallel sets were only available directly from Topps to Stadium Club members. The sets include all base cards and inserts, and are essentially the same as regular-issue cards, except for a special "Members Only" logo on the front.

		MT
Complete Fact. Set (722):		250.00
Common Player (1-630):		.25
Common Player (DD1-DD6):		.25
Common Player (RL1-RL12):		.50
Common Player (ST1-ST28):		.25
DD1	Emmitt Smith, Walter Payton	8.00
DD2	Steve Largent, Tom Waddle	.25
DD3	Randy White, Cortez Kennedy	.40
DD4	Troy Aikman, Dan Fouts	5.00
DD5	Junior Seau, Mike Singletary	.40
DD6	Shannon Sharpe, Ozzie Newsome	.25
RL1	Emmitt Smith	12.00
RL2	Steve Young	6.00
RL3	Deion Sanders	4.00
RL4	Warren Moon	.75
RL5	Thurman Thomas	.75
RL6	Jerry Rice	8.00
RL7	Sterling Sharpe	.75
RL8	Barry Sanders	8.00
RL9	Reggie White	.75
RL10	Michael Irvin	.75
RL11	Ronnie Lott	.50
RL12	Herschel Walker	.50
ST1	Steve Beuerlein	.25
ST2	Drew Hill	.25
ST3	Jim Kelly	.40
ST4	Joe Cain	.25
ST5	Derrick Fenner	.25
ST6	Tommy Vardell	.25
ST7	Emmitt Smith	12.00
ST8	John Elway	4.00
ST9	Barry Sanders	8.00
ST10	Brent Favre	8.00
ST11	Gary Brown	.25
ST12	Zefross Moss	.25
ST13	Joe Montana	8.00
ST14	Howie Long	.40
ST15	Jerome Bettis	2.50
ST16	Irving Fryar	.40
ST17	Cris Carter	.40
ST18	Drew Bledsoe	6.00
ST19	Rickey Jackson	.25
ST20	Phil Simms	.40
ST21	Boomer Esiason	.40
ST22	Herschel Walker	.40
ST23	Neil O'Donnell	1.00
ST24	Natrone Means	2.50
ST25	Jerry Rice, Steve Young	8.00
ST26	Rick Mirer	2.50
ST27	Craig Erickson	.25
ST28	Reggie Brooks	.25

1994 Stadium Club Members Only 50

This 50-card set was exclusively available to Stadium Club members and contained 45 regular Stadium Club cards and five Finest cards. The words "Topps Stadium Club Members Only" appear in gold foil in one of the top corners.

		MT
Complete Set (50):		25.00
Common Player:		.25
1	Jerry Rice	4.00
2	Erik Williams	.25
3	Nate Newton	.25
4	Jesse Sapolu	.25
5	Randall McDaniel	.25
6	Harris Barton	.25
7	Jay Novacek	.40
8	Michael Irvin	.75
9	Steve Young	2.50
10	Jerome Bettis	1.50
11	Daryl Johnston	.40
12	Neil Smith	.40
13	Cortez Kennedy	.40
14	Ray Childress	.25
15	Leslie O'Neal	.40
16	Derrick Thomas	.40
17	Junior Seau	.75
18	Greg Lloyd	.40
19	Rod Woodson	.40
20	Nate Odomes	.25
21	Dennis Smith	.25
22	Steve Atwater	.25
23	Reggie White	.75
24	John Randle	.25
25	Sean Gilbert	.25
26	Richard Dent	.40
27	Rickey Jackson	.25
28	Hardy Nickerson	.25
29	Renaldo Turnbull	.25
30	Deion Sanders	2.00
31	Eric Allen	.25
32	Tim McDonald	.25
33	Mark Carrier (DB)	.25
34	Tim Brown	.75
35	Richmond Webb	.25
36	Keith Sims	.25
37	Bruce Matthews	.25
38	Steve Wisniewski	.25
39	Howard Ballard	.25
40	Shannon Sharpe	.40
41	Anthony Miller	.40
42	John Elway	2.50
43	Thurman Thomas	.75
44	Marcus Allen	.60
45	Andre Rison	.40
46	Drew Bledsoe	.25
47	Willie Roaf	.25
48	Reggie Brooks	.40
49	Dana Stubblefield	.40
50	Rick Mirer	1.25

1995 Stadium Club

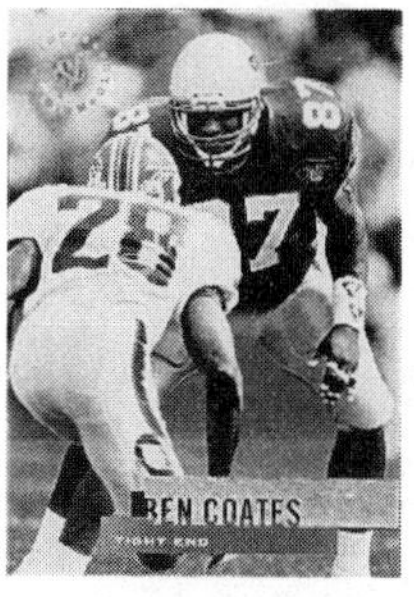

Topps released its 1995 Stadium Club issue in two 225-card series. Series I has 180 regular cards of the top NFL players, plus 15 Draft Picks and 30 Extreme Corps subset cards. Series II has two subsets also - Xpansion Team and Draft Pixs. Each regular card front has full-bleed photography and is stamped with textured foil. Regular cards are stamped with gold; subset cards are emblazoned with rainbow and silver foil. Card backs have a second full-bleed photo, biographical data, 1994 and career stats, Skills Ratings and Trench Talk, an assessment of the player's strengths and career highlights. In addition, hobbyists can see the winners of Stadium Club's Extreme Fans contest from 1994. Four different fans can be found on the back of each regular card holding up one of the Skills Ratings cards. Series I inserts include Power Surge, Metalists, Nemeses, and Nightmares (hobby only). Series II inserts include MVPs, Power Surge, Ground Attack and Nightmares II (hobby only.) Also, as a special to Series II jumbo and rack packs, parallel sets have been created for the Draft Pix and Extreme Corps cards. These double foil-stamped (green and gold vs. the regular rainbow and silver) theme cards use diffraction foil and are in every jumbo and rack pack.

		MT
Complete Set (450):		100.00
Comp. Series 1 (225):		60.00
Comp. Series 2 (225):		40.00
Common Player:		.10
Minor Stars:		.20
Ser. 1 Hobby Pack (12):		1.50
Ser. 1 Hobby Wax Box (24):		30.00
Ser. 2 Hobby Pack (12):		2.50
Ser. 2 Hobby Wax Box (24):		45.00
Ser. 1 or 2 Ret. Pack (12):		1.50
Ser. 1 or 2 Ret. Wax Box (24):		35.00
1	Steve Young	1.00
2	Stan Humphries	.25
3	Chris Boniol	.20
4	Darren Perry	.10
5	Vinny Testaverde	.10
6	Aubrey Beavers	.10
7	DeWayne Washington	.10
8	Marion Butts	.10
9	George Koonce	.10
10	Joe Cain	.10
11	Mike Johnson	.10
12	Dale Carter	.10
13	Greg Biekert	.10
14	Aaron Pierce	.10
15	Aeneas Williams	.10
16	Steve Grant	.20
17	Henry Jones	.10
18	James Williams	.10
19	Andy Harmon	.10
20	Anthony Miller	.10
21	Kevin Ross	.10
22	Erik Howard	.10
23	Brian Blades	.10
24	Trent Dilfer	.50
25	Roman Phifer	.10
26	Bruce Kozerski	.10
27	Henry Ellard	.10
28	Rich Camarillo	.10
29	Richmond Webb	.10
30	George Teague	.10
31	Antonio Langham	.10
32	Barry Foster	.10
33	Bruce Armstrong	.10
34	Tim McDonald	.10
35	James Harris	.10
36	Lomas Brown	.10
37	Jay Novacek	.10
38	John Thierry	.10
39	John Elliott	.10
40	Terry McDaniel	.10
41	Shawn Lee	.10
42	Shane Dronett	.10
43	Cornelius Bennett	.10
44	Steve Bono	.20
45	Byron Evans	.10
46	Eugene Robinson	.10
47	Tony Bennett	.10
48	Michael Bankston	.10
49	William Roaf	.10
50	Bobby Houston	.10
51	Ken Harvey	.10
52	Bruce Matthews	.10
53	Lincoln Kennedy	.10
54	Todd Lyght	.10
55	Paul Gruber	.10
56	Corey Sawyer	.10
57	Myron Guyton	.10
58	John Jackson	.10
59	Sean Jones	.10
60	Pepper Johnson	.10
61	Steve Walsh	.10
62	Corey Miller	.10
63	Fuad Reveiz	.10
64	Rickey Jackson	.10
65	Scott Mitchell	.10
66	Michael Irvin	.30
67	Andre Reed	.10
68	Mark Seay	.10
69	Keith Byars	.10
70	Marcus Allen	.20
71	Shannon Sharpe	.20
72	Eric Hill	.10
73	James Washington	.10
74	Greg Jackson	.10
75	Chris Warren	.20
76	Will Wolford	.10
77	Anthony Smith	.10
78	Cris Dishman	.10
79	Carl Pickens	.10
80	Tyrone Hughes	.10
81	Chris Miller	.10
82	Clay Matthews	.10
83	Lonnie Marts	.10
84	Jerome Henderson	.10
85	Ben Coates	.10
86	Deon Figures	.10
87	Anthony Pleasant	.10
88	Guy McIntyre	.10
89	Jake Reed	.10
90	Rodney Hampton	.10
91	Santana Dotson	.10
92	Jeff Blackshear	.10
93	Willie Clay	.10
94	Nate Newton	.10
95	Bucky Brooks	.10
96	Lamar Lathon	.10
97	Tim Grunhard	.10
98	Harris Barton	.10
99	Brian Mitchell	.10
100	Natrone Means	.75
101	Sean Dawkins	.10
102	Chris Slade	.10
103	Tom Rathman	.10
104	Fred Barnett	.10
105	Gary Brown	.10
106	Leonard Russell	.10
107	Alfred Williams	.10
108	Kelvin Martin	.10
109	Alexander Wright	.10
110	O.J. McDuffie	.10
111	Mario Bates	.40
112	Tony Casillas	.10
113	Michael Timpson	.10
114	Robert Brooks	.10
115	Rob Burnett	.10
116	Mark Collins	.10
117	Chris Calloway	.10
118	Courtney Hawkins	.10
119	Marvcus Patton	.10
120	Greg Lloyd	.10
121	Ryan McNeil	.10
122	Gary Plummer	.10
123	Dwayne Sabb	.10
124	Jessie Hester	.10
125	Terance Mathis	.10
126	Steve Atwater	.10
127	Lorenzo Lynch	.10
128	James Francis	.10
129	John Fina	.10
130	Emmitt Smith	3.00
131	Bryan Cox	.10
132	Robert Blackmon	.10
133	Kenny Davidson	.10
134	Eugene Daniel	.10
135	Vince Buck	.10
136	Leslie O'Neal	.10
137	James Jett	.10
138	Johnny Johnson	.10
139	Michael Zordich	.10
140	Warren Moon	.25
141	William White	.10
142	Carl Banks	.10
143	Marty Carter	.10
144	Keith Hamilton	.10
145	Alvin Harper	.20
146	Corey Harris	.10
147	Elijah Alexander	.25
148	Darrell Green	.10
149	*Yancey Thigpen*	1.50
150	Deion Sanders	.75
151	Burt Grossman	.10
152	J.B. Brown	.10
153	Johnny Bailey	.10
154	Harvey Williams	.10
155	*Jeff Blake*	.50
156	Al Smith	.10
157	Chris Doleman	.10
158	Garrison Hearst	.20
159	Bryce Paup	.10
160	Herman Moore	.20
161	Cortez Kennedy	.10
162	Marquez Pope	.10
163	Quinn Early	.10
164	Broderick Thomas	.10
165	Jeff Herrod	.10
166	Robert Jones	.10
167	Mo Lewis	.10
168	Ray Crittenden	.10
169	Raymont Harris	.20
170	Bruce Smith	.10
171	Dana Stubblefield	.10
172	Charles Haley	.10
173	Charles Johnson	.40
174	Shawn Jefferson	.10
175	Leroy Hoard	.10
176	Bernie Parmalee	.30
177	Scottie Graham	.10
178	Edgar Bennett	.10
179	Aubrey Matthews	.10
180	Don Beebe	.10
181	Eric Swann (Extreme Corps)	.10
182	Jeff George (Extreme Corps)	.20
183	Jim Kelly (Extreme Corps)	.20
184	Sam Mills (Extreme Corps)	.10
185	Mark Carrier (Extreme Corps)	.10
186	Dan Wilkinson (Extreme Corps)	.10
187	Eric Turner (Extreme Corps)	.10
188	Troy Aikman (Extreme Corps)	2.50
189	John Elway (Extreme Corps)	1.00
190	Barry Sanders (Extreme Corps)	2.50
191	Brett Favre (Extreme Corps)	4.00
192	Michael Barrow (Extreme Corps)	.10
193	Marshall Faulk (Extreme Corps)	1.00
194	Steve Beuerlein (Extreme Corps)	.10
195	Neil Smith (Extreme Corps)	.10
196	Jeff Hostetler (Extreme Corps)	.20
197	Jerome Bettis (Extreme Corps)	.75
198	Dan Marino (Extreme Corps)	4.00
199	Cris Carter (Extreme Corps)	.20
200	Drew Bledsoe (Extreme Corps)	2.50
201	Jim Everett (Extreme Corps)	.20
202	Dave Brown (Extreme Corps)	.10
203	Boomer Esiason (Extreme Corps)	.10
204	Randall Cunningham (Extreme Corps)	.20
205	Rod Woodson (Extreme Corps)	.10
206	Junior Seau (Extreme Corps)	.20
207	Jerry Rice (Extreme Corps)	2.50
208	Rick Mirer (Extreme Corps)	1.00
209	Errict Rhett (Extreme Corps)	.30
210	Heath Shuler (Extreme Corps)	.50
211	*Bobby Taylor* (Draft Picks)	.20
212	*Jesse James* (Draft Picks)	.20
213	*Devin Bush* (Draft Picks)	.20
214	*Luther Elliss* (Draft Picks)	.20
215	*Kerry Collins* (Draft Picks)	2.00
216	*Derrick Alexander* (Draft Picks)	.20
217	*Rashaan Salaam* (Draft Picks)	.50
218	*J.J. Stokes* (Draft Picks)	2.00
219	*Todd Collins* (Draft Picks)	.20
220	*Ki-Jana Carter* (Draft Picks)	.50
221	*Kyle Brady* (Draft Picks)	1.00
222	*Kevin Carter* (Draft Picks)	.20
223	*Tony Boselli* (Draft Picks)	.20
224	*Scott Gragg* (Draft Picks)	.20
225	*Warren Sapp* (Draft Picks)	1.50
226	Ricky Reynolds	.10
227	Roosevelt Potts	.10
228	Jessie Tuggle	.10
229	Anthony Newman	.10
230	Randall Cunningham	.10
231	Jason Elam	.10
232	Darnay Scott	.50
233	Tom Carter	.10
234	Michael Barrow	.10
235	Steve Tasker	.10
236	Howard Cross	.10
237	Charles Wilson	.10
238	Rob Fredrickson	.10
239	Russell Maryland	.10
240	Dan Marino	3.00
241	Rafael Robinson	.10
242	Ed McDaniel	.10
243	Brett Perriman	.20
244	Chuck Levy	.10
245	Errict Rhett	1.50
246	Tracy Simien	.10
247	Steve Everitt	.10
248	John Jurkovic	.10
249	Johnny Mitchell	.10
250	Mark Carrier	.10
251	Merton Hanks	.10
252	Joe Johnson	.10
253	Andre Coleman	.10
254	Ray Buchanan	.10
255	Jeff George	.20
256	Shane Conlan	.10
257	Gus Frerotte	.50
258	Doug Pelfrey	.10
259	Glenn Montgomery	.10
260	John Elway	.50
261	Larry Centers	.10
262	Calvin Williams	.10
263	Gene Atkins	.10
264	Tim Brown	.20
265	Leon Lett	.10
266	Martin Mayhew	.10
267	Arthur Marshall	.10
268	Maurice Hurst	.10
269	Greg Hill	.40
270	Junior Seau	.20
271	Rick Mirer	.40
272	Jack Del Rio	.10
273	Lewis Tillman	.10
274	Renaldo Turnbull	.10
275	Dan Footman	.10
276	John Taylor	.10
277	Russell Copeland	.10
278	Tracy Scroggins	.10
279	Lou Benfatti	.10
280	Rod Woodson	.10
281	Troy Drayton	.10
282	Quentin Coryatt	.10
283	Craig Heyward	.10
284	Jeff Cross	.10
285	Hardy Nickerson	.10
286	Dorsey Levens	.75
287	Derek Russell	.10
288	Seth Joyner	.10
289	Kimble Anders	.10
290	Drew Bledsoe	1.00
291	Bryant Young	.10
292	Chris Zorich	.10
293	Michael Strahan	.10
294	Kevin Greene	.10
295	Aaron Glenn	.10
296	Jimmy Spencer	.10
297	Eric Turner	.10
298	William Thomas	.10
299	Dan Wilkinson	.10
300	Troy Aikman	1.00
301	Terry Wooden	.10
302	Heath Shuler	1.00
303	Jeff Burris	.10
304	Mark Stepnoski	.10
305	Chris Mims	.10
306	Todd Steussie	.10
307	Johnnie Morton	.10
308	Darryl Talley	.10
309	Nolan Harrison	.10
310	Dave Brown	.10
311	Brent Jones	.10
312	Curtis Conway	.10
313	Ronald Humphrey	.10
314	Richie Anderson	.10
315	Jim Everett	.10
316	Willie Davis	.10
317	Ed Cunningham	.10
318	Willie McGinest	.10
319	Sean Gilbert	.10
320	Brett Favre	3.00
321	Bennie Thompson	.10
322	Neil O'Donnell	.20
323	Vince Workman	.10
324	Terry Kirby	.10
325	Simon Fletcher	.10
326	Ricardo McDonald	.10
327	Duane Young	.10
328	Jim Harbaugh	.10
329	D.J. Johnson	.10
330	Boomer Esiason	.10
331	Donnell Woolford	.10
332	Mike Sherrard	.10
333	Tyrone Legette	.10
334	Larry Brown	.10
335	William Floyd	.40
336	Reggie Brooks	.10
337	Patrick Bates	.10
338	Jim Jeffcoat	.10
339	Ray Childress	.10
340	Cris Carter	.20
341	Charlie Garner	.10
342	Bill Hitchcock	.10
343	Levon Kirkland	.10
344	Robert Porcher	.10
345	Darryl Williams	.10
346	Vincent Brisby	.10
347	Kenyon Rasheed	.10
348	Floyd Turner	.10
349	Bob Whitefield	.10
350	Jerome Bettis	.40
351	Brad Baxter	.10
352	Darrin Smith	.10
353	Lamar Thomas	.10
354	Lorenzo Neal	.10
355	Erik Kramer	.10
356	Dwayne Harper	.10
357	Doug Evans	.10
358	Jeff Feagles	.10
359	Ray Crockett	.10
360	Neil Smith	.10
361	Troy Vincent	.10
362	Don Griffin	.10
363	Michael Brooks	.10
364	Carlton Gray	.10
365	Thomas Smith	.10
366	Ken Norton	.10
367	Tony McGee	.10
368	Eric Metcalf	.10
369	Mel Gray	.10
370	Barry Sanders	2.50
371	Raghib Ismail	.10
372	Chad Brown	.20
373	Qadry Ismail	.10
374	Anthony Prior	.10
375	Kevin Lee	.10
376	Robert Young	.10
377	Kevin Williams	.10
378	Tydus Winans	.10
379	Ricky Watters	.20
380	Jim Kelly	.20
381	Eric Swann	.10
382	Mike Pritchard	.10
383	Derek Brown	.10
384	Dennis Gibson	.10
385	Byron Morris	.10
386	Reggie White	.20
387	Jeff Graham	.10
388	Marshall Faulk	1.00
389	Joe Phillips	.10
390	Jeff Hostetler	.10
391	Irving Fryar	.10
392	Stevon Moore	.10
393	Bert Emanuel	.40
394	Leon Searcy	.10
395	Robert Smith	.10
396	Michael Bates	.10
397	Thomas Lewis	.10
398	Joe Bowden	.10
399	Steve Tovar	.10
400	Jerry Rice	1.25
401	Toby Wright	.10
402	Daryl Johnston	.10
403	Vincent Brown	.10
404	Marvin Washington	.10
405	Chris Spielman	.10
406	Willie Jackson	.10
407	Harry Boatswain	.10
408	Kelvin Pritchett	.10
409	Dave Widell	.10
410	Frank Reich	.10
411	Corey Mayfield	.10
413	Keith Goganious	.10
414	John Kasay	.10
415	Ernest Givins	.10
416	Randy Baldwin	.10
417	Shawn Bouwens	.10
418	Mike Fox	.10
419	Mark Carrier	.10
420	Steve Beuerlein	.10
421	Steve Lofton	.10
422	Jeff Lageman	.10
423	Paul Butcher	.10
424	Mark Brunell	3.00
425	Vernon Turner	.10
426	Tim McKyer	.10
427	James Williams	.10
428	Tommy Barnhardt	.10
429	Rogerick Green	.10
430	Desmond Howard	.10
431	Darion Conner	.10
432	Reggie Clark	.10
433	Eric Guliford	.10
434	*Rob Johnson*	3.00
435	Sam Mills	.10
436	*Kordell Stewart*	6.00
437	*James Stewart*	3.00
438	*Zach Wiegert*	.10
439	*Ellis Johnson*	.10
440	*Matt O'Dwyer*	.10
441	*Anthony Cook*	.10
442	*Ron Davis*	.10
443	*Chris Hudson*	.10
444	*Hugh Douglas*	.20
445	*Tyrone Poole*	.10
446	*Korey Stringer*	.10
447	*Ruben Brown*	.10
448	*Brian DeMarco*	.10
449	*Michael Westbrook*	1.50
450	*Steve McNair*	5.00

1995 Stadium Club Ground Attack

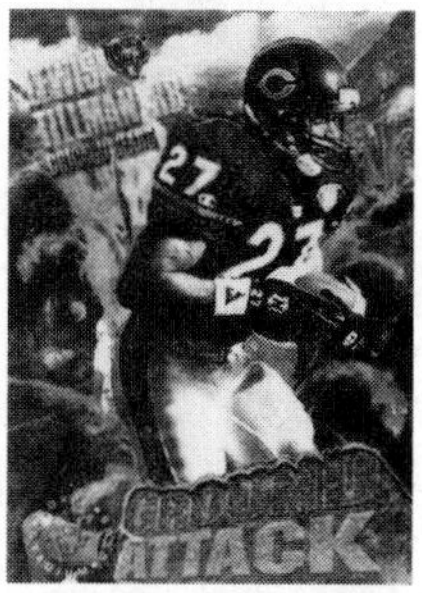

These 1995 Topps Stadium Club Series II inserts feature 10 of the NFL's best backfield combinations together on one card. Etched foil is used on both sides. Cards were random inserts, one per every 14 retail and one per every 18 hobby packs.

		MT
Complete Set (15):		45.00
Common Player:		1.50
Minor Stars:		3.00
Inserted 1:18 Hobby		
1	Emmitt Smith, Daryl Johnston	10.00
2	Edgar Bennett, Brett Favre	12.00
3	Bernie Parmalee, Irving Spikes	1.50
4	John Elway, Glyn Milburn	10.00
5	Chris Warren, Rick Mirer	1.50
6	Marcus Allen, Greg Hill	3.00
7	Errict Rhett, Vince Workman	3.00
8	Byron Morris, Eric Pegram	1.50
9	Mario Bates, Derek Brown	1.50
10	William Floyd, Steve Young	6.00
11	Charlie Garner, Randall Cunningham	3.00
12	Lewis Tillman, Raymont Harris	1.50
13	Harvey Williams, Jeff Hostetler	1.50
14	Larry Centers, Garrison Hearst	3.00
15	Marshall Faulk, Roosevelt Potts	3.00

1995 Stadium Club Metalists

These cards, Topps' first ever laser-cut cards, feature eight players who have won multiple awards in their distinguished careers. The laser process allows for more precise and detailed cutting on the inside of the cards, giving them a unique look which is patterned after the color photo on the front. "Metalists" is written at the top of the card; the player's name is written along the bottom. The brand logo is also on the card front. The back, numbered using an "M" prefix, has the laser-cut image on one side, flanked by a brief recap of the awards the player won. Cards were seeded one per every 18 retail packs

and one per every 24 hobby packs of 1995 Topps Stadium Club Series I product.

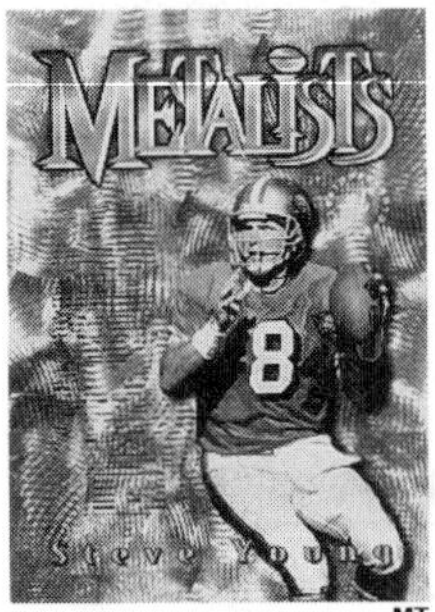

		MT
Complete Set (8):		75.00
Common Player:		5.00
1	Jerry Rice	15.00
2	Barry Sanders	15.00
3	John Elway	7.00
4	Dana Stubblefield	5.00
5	Emmitt Smith	25.00
6	Deion Sanders	7.00
7	Marshall Faulk	7.00
8	Steve Young	8.00

1995 Stadium Club MVPs

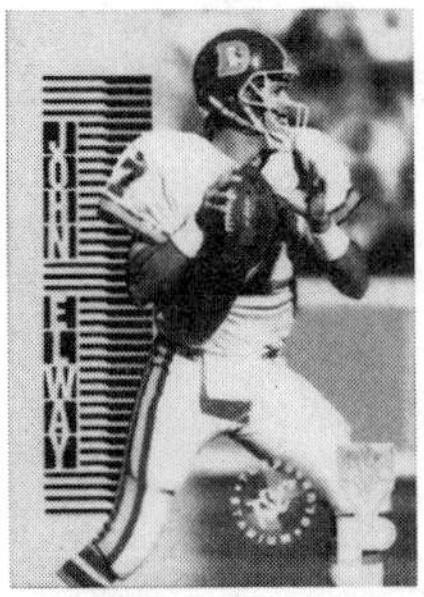

These eight cards celebrate the achievements of several players who have become the best of the best in the NFL while on their way to the Hall of Fame. The cards, seeded one per every 18 retail and one per every 24 hobby packs of 1995 Topps Stadium Club Series II product, are laser cut and highlight gold foil stamping on chromium stock. The player's name is laser cut along the left side of the card. Foil stamping is used for the MVP logo at the bottom of the card.

		MT
Complete Set (8):		40.00
Common Player:		2.00
1	Jerry Rice	5.00
2	Boomer Esiason	2.00
3	Randall Cunningham	2.00
4	Marcus Allen	2.00
5	John Elway	4.00
6	Dan Marino	10.00
7	Emmitt Smith	10.00
8	Steve Young	4.00

1995 Stadium Club Nemeses

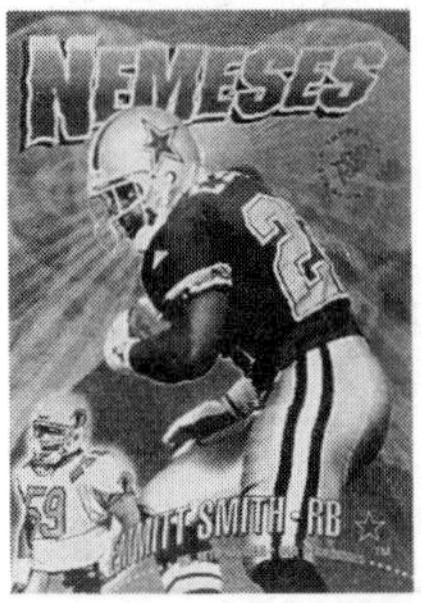

Fifteen cards highlighting football's top rivalries make up this 1995 Topps Stadium Club Series I insert set. Complete with etched foil on both sides, the cards match up two players who are known for their classic confrontations, one on each side. Nemeses is written at the top of the card; the player's name, position and team helmet are at the bottom. The cards were seeded one per every 24th pack.

		MT
Complete Set (15):		130.00
Common Player:		5.00
1	Barry Sanders, Jack Del Rio	15.00
2	Reggie White, Lomas Brown	5.00
3	Terry McDaniel, Anthony Miller	5.00
4	Brett Favre, Chris Spielman	25.00
5	Junior Seau, Chris Warren	5.00
6	Cortez Kennedy, Steve Wisniewski	5.00
7	Rod Woodson, Tim Brown	5.00
8	Troy Aikman, Michael Brooks	15.00
9	Bruce Smith, Bruce Armstrong	5.00
10	Jerry Rice, Donnell Woolford	15.00
11	Emmitt Smith, Seth Joyner	25.00
12	Dan Marino, Cornelius Bennett	25.00
13	Marshall Faulk, Bryan Cox	8.00
14	Stan Humphries, Greg Lloyd	5.00
15	Michael Irvin, Deion Sanders	5.00

1995 Stadium Club Nightmares

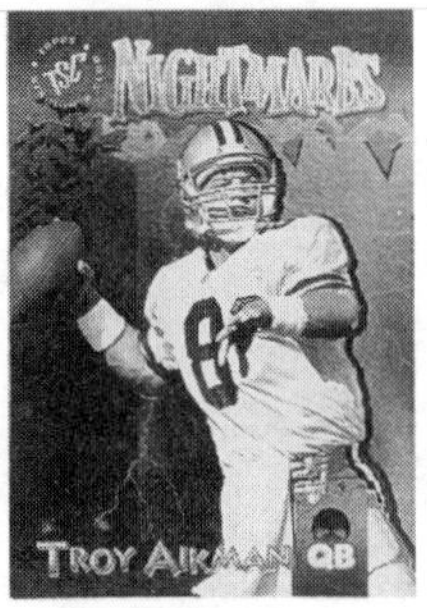

This 30-card series was released as two 15-card insert sets; cards 1-15 were in 1995 Topps Stadium Club Series I hobby packs only (1 in 24), while 16-30 were in Series II hobby packs (1 in 18). "Biting" commentary on each player is provided by Vampirella, Topps' original "bad girl" comic character, who describes how the player terrorizes his opponents. The Series II Nightmare cards, which premiere artwork from the "Vampirella Gallery" release, feature a new etched foil design.

		MT
Complete Set (30):		200.00
Comp. Series 1 (15):		130.00
Comp. Series 2 (15):		70.00
Common Player:		4.00
1	Drew Bledsoe	15.00
2	Barry Sanders	15.00
3	Reggie White	4.00
4	Michael Irvin	4.00
5	Jerry Rice	15.00
6	Jerome Bettis	4.00
7	Dan Marino	25.00
8	Bruce Smith	4.00
9	Steve Young	15.00
10	Junior Seau	4.00
11	Emmitt Smith	25.00
12	Deion Sanders	10.00
13	Rod Woodson	4.00
14	Marshall Faulk	7.00
15	Troy Aikman	15.00
16	Stan Humphries	4.00
17	Chris Warren	4.00
18	Jack Del Rio	4.00
19	Randall Cunningham	4.00
20	Natrone Means	4.00
21	Dana Stubblefield	4.00
22	Jim Kelly	4.00
23	Cris Carter	4.00
24	Cornelius Bennett	4.00
25	Errict Rhett	10.00
26	Terry McDaniel	4.00
27	Rodney Hampton	4.00
28	Brett Favre	25.00
29	Bryan Cox	4.00
30	John Elway	10.00

1995 Stadium Club Power Surge

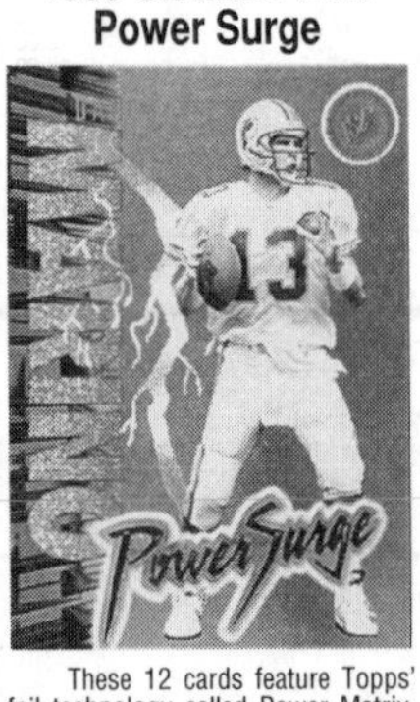

These 12 cards feature Topps' foil technology called Power Matrix. The cards, random inserts in 1995 Topps Stadium Club Series I packs, showcase the NFL's best players when the game is on the line. Cards were inserted one per every 18 packs.

		MT
Complete Set (24):		125.00
Comp. Series 1 (12):		75.00
Comp. Series 2 (12):		50.00
Common Player:		4.00
P1	Steve Young	10.00
P2	Natrone Means	8.00
P3	Cris Carter	4.00
P4	Junior Seau	6.00
P5	Barry Sanders	15.00
P6	Michael Irvin	6.00
P7	John Elway	8.00
P8	Emmitt Smith	20.00
P9	Greg Lloyd	4.00
P10	Jerry Rice	13.00
P11	Marshall Faulk	6.00
P12	Drew Bledsoe	10.00
PS1	Dan Marino	20.00
PS2	Ken Harvey	4.00
PS3	Chris Warren	6.00
PS4	Henry Ellard	4.00
PS5	Marshall Faulk	6.00
PS6	Irving Fryar	4.00
PS7	Kevin Ross	4.00
PS8	Vince Workman	4.00
PS9	Ray Buchanan	4.00
PS10	Tony Martin	4.00
PS11	D.J. Johnson	4.00
PS12	Steve Young	10.00

1995 Stadium Club Members Only Parallel

The 550-card, standard-size set was a parallel issue to the base 1995 Stadium Club issue and was released in two, 275-card series, available only through the Members Only Club. Just 2,000 sets were produced and were available for $99.95 for each series in a factory box that also included parallels of each insert. The cards are differentiated with the base cards by a gold-foil Members Only stamp. Each complete set order also came with three-pin set and a replica game ticket of the 1995 Pro Football Hall of Fame game between Jacksonville and Carolina.

		MT
Complete Set (550):		300.00
Common Player (1-450):		.20
Common Player (GA1-GA15):		.35
Common Player (ME1-ME8):		35.00
Common Player (MV1-MV8):		.35
Common Player (NE1-NE15):		.35
Common Player (NM1-NM30):		.35
Common Player (P1-P12/PS1-PS12):		.35
P1	Steve Young	3.00
P2	Natrone Means	.50
P3	Cris Carter	.50
P4	Junior Seau	.50
P5	Barry Sanders	4.00
P6	Michael Irvin	1.00
P7	John Elway	2.50
P8	Emmitt Smith	8.00
P9	Greg Lloyd	.35
P10	Jerry Rice	4.00
P11	Marshall Faulk	3.00
P12	Drew Bledsoe	3.00
GA1	Emmitt Smith	8.00
GA2	Brett Favre	4.00
GA4	John Elway	2.50
GA5	Rick Mirer	.50
GA6	Greg Hill	.50
GA7	Errict Rhett	3.00
GA8	Byron "Bam" Morris	.35
GA9	Derek Brown (RB)	.35
GA10	Steve Young	3.00
GA11	Charlie Garner	.35
GA12	Lewis Tillman	.35
GA13	Harvey Williams	.35
GA14	Garrison Hearst	.75
GA15	Marshall Faulk	3.00
ME1	Jerry Rice	4.00
ME2	Barry Sanders	4.00
ME3	John Elway	2.50
ME4	Dana Stubblefield	.50
ME5	Emmitt Smith	8.00
ME6	Deion Sanders	2.50
ME7	Marshall Faulk	3.00
ME8	Steve Young	3.00
MV1	Jerry Rice	4.00
MV2	Boomer Esiason	.35
MV3	Randall Cunningham	.35
MV4	Marcus Allen	.50
MV5	John Elway	2.50
MV6	Dan Marino	8.00
MV7	Emmitt Smith	8.00
MV8	Steve Young	3.00
NE1	Barry Sanders, Jack Del Rio	4.00
NE2	Reggie White, Lomas Brown	.50
NE3	Terry McDaniel, Anthony Miller	.35
NE4	Brett Favre, Chris Spielman	4.00
NE5	Junior Seau, Chris Warren	.50
NE6	Cortez Kennedy, Steve Wisniewski	.35
NE7	Rod Woodson, Tim Brown	.50
NE8	Troy Aikman, Michael Brooks	4.00
NE9	Bruce Smith, Bruce Armstrong	.50
NE10	Jerry Rice, Donnell Woolford	4.00
NE11	Emmitt Smith, Seth Joyner	8.00
NE12	Dan Marino, Cornelius Bennett	8.00
NE13	Marshall Faulk, Bryan Cox	3.00
NE14	Stan Humphries, Greg Lloyd	.50
NE15	Michael Irvin, Deion Sanders	.75
NM1	Drew Bledsoe	3.00
NM2	Barry Sanders	4.00
NM3	Reggie White	.50
NM4	Michael Irvin	1.00
NM5	Jerry Rice	4.00
NM6	Jerome Bettis	.50
NM7	Dan Marino	8.00
NM8	Bruce Smith	.35
NM9	Steve Young	3.00
NM10	Junior Seau	.50
NM11	Emmitt Smith	8.00
NM12	Deion Sanders	2.50
NM13	Rod Woodson	.50
NM14	Marshall Faulk	3.00
NM15	Troy Aikman	4.00
NM16	Stan Humphries	.50
NM17	Chris Warren	.50
NM18	Jack Del Rio	.35
NM19	Randall Cunningham	.35
NM20	Natrone Means	.50
NM21	Dana Stubblefield	.35
NM22	Jim Kelly	.50
NM23	Cris Carter	.50
NM24	Cornelius Bennett	.35
NM25	Errict Rhett	3.00
NM26	Terry McDaniel	.35
NM27	Rodney Hampton	.50
NM28	Brett Favre	4.00
NM29	Bryan Cox	.35
NM30	John Elway	2.50
PS1	Dan Marino	8.00
PS2	Ken Harvey	.35
PS3	Chris Warren	.50
PS4	Henry Ellard	.35
PS5	Marshall Faulk	3.00
PS6	Irving Fryar	.35
PS7	Kevin Ross	.35
PS8	Vince Workman	.35
PS9	Ray Buchanan	.35
PS10	Tony Martin	.50
PS11	D.J. Johnson	.35
PS12	Steve Young	3.00

1995 Stadium Club Members Only 50

The 50-card, standard-size boxed set featured the 44 starting players from the 1995 Pro Bowl and five Finest cards of the top rookies from the 1994 class. The remaining card was of Jerry Rice and Emmitt Smith who were elected to start in the Pro Bowl, but missed it due to injuries. The set was available to Members Only club members.

		MT
Complete Set (50):		20.00
Common Player:		.25
1	Tim Brown	.40
2	Richmond Webb	.25
3	Keith Sims	.25
4	Dermontti Dawson	.25
5	Duval Love	.25
6	Bruce Armstrong	.25
7	Ben Coates	.40
8	Andre Reed	.40
9	John Elway	.25
10	Marshall Faulk	.25
11	Natrone Means	.40
12	Charles Haley	.25
13	John Randle	.25
14	Leon Lett	.25
15	William Fuller	.25
16	Ken Harvey	.25
17	Chris Spielman	.25
18	Bryce Paup	.40
19	Deion Sanders	1.50
20	Aeneas Williams	.25
21	Darren Woodson	.25
22	Merton Hanks	.25
23	Michael Irvin	.75
24	William Roaf	.25
25	Nate Newton	.25
26	Mark Stepnoski	.25
27	Randall McDaniel	.25
28	Lomas Brown	.25
29	Brent Jones	.40
30	Cris Carter	.40
31	Steve Young	2.00
32	Barry Sanders	4.00
33	Jerome Bettis	.75
34	Bruce Smith	.40
35	Michael Dean Perry	.25
36	Cortez Kennedy	.40
37	Leslie O'Neal	.40
38	Derrick Thomas	.40
39	Junior Seau	.75
40	Greg Lloyd	.40
41	Rod Woodson	.40
42	Terry McDaniel	.25
43	Eric Turner	.25
44	Carnell Lake	.25
45	Jerry Rice, Emmitt Smith	6.00
46	William Floyd	1.00
47	Tim Bowens	.40
48	Heath Shuler	1.50
49	Bryant Young	.75
50	Marshall Faulk	2.50

1996 Stadium Club

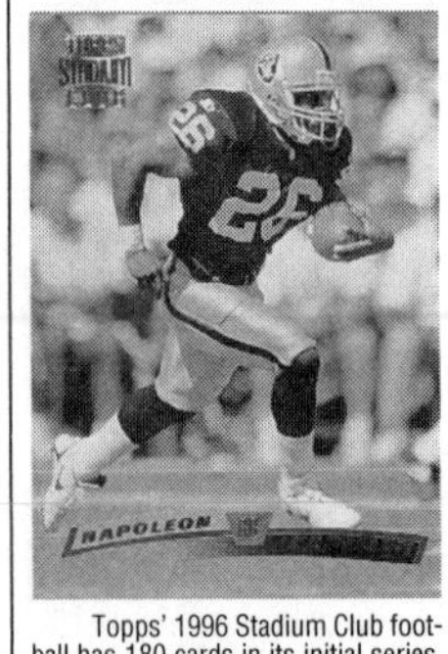

Topps' 1996 Stadium Club football has 180 cards in its initial series. Insert sets include Contact Prints, Dot Matrix Parallel, Pro Bowl Embossed, Laser Sites, Cut Backs, and three versions of Extreme Player cards (bronze, silver and gold). Series II also has 180 cards in it, featuring 45 of the league's top rookies and traded players in their new uniforms. All regular cards in both series have etched gold foil and are UV coated. Series II inserts include Photo Gallery, New Age, TSC Matrix Parallel, NFL Playoff Box, Fusion Laser Cut (hobby exclusive) and Brace Yourself (retail only). Interactive game cards (Sunday Night Box, in Series I, and NFL Playoff Box, in Series II) were seeded in packs (one in 12 and 1 in 24 packs, respectively). Those who find the cards were eligible to win prizes based on the final scores of selected games.

		MT
Complete Set (360):		80.00
Complete Series 1 (180):		40.00
Complete Series 2 (180):		40.00
Common Player:		.10
Minor Stars:		.20
Dot Matrix:		10x
Match Proofs:		100x
Ser. 1 Pack (10):		2.00
Ser. 1 Wax Box (24):		40.00
Ser. 2 Pack (10):		2.00
Ser. 2 Wax Box (24):		40.00
1	Kyle Brady (TSC Matrix Parallel Set)	.10
2	Mickey Washington	.10
3	Seth Joyner	.10
4	Vinny Testaverde	.10
5	Thomas Randolph	.10
6	Heath Shuler (TSC Matrix Parallel Set)	.20
7	Ty Law	.10
8	Blake Brockermeyer	.10
9	Darryll Lewis	.10
10	Jeff Blake (TSC Matrix Parallel Set)	.75
11	Tyrone Hughes (TSC Matrix Parallel Set)	.10
12	Horace Copeland	.10
13	Roman Phifer	.10
14	Eugene Robinson	.10
15	Anthony Miller (TSC Matrix Parallel Set)	.10
16	Robert Smith	.10
17	Chester McGlockton	.10
18	Marty Carter	.10
19	Scott Mitchell (TSC Matrix Parallel Set)	.10
20	O.J. McDuffie	.10
21	Stan Humphries (TSC Matrix Parallel Set)	.10
22	Eugene Daniel	.10
23	Devin Bush	.10
24	Darick Holmes	.10
25	Ricky Watters (TSC Matrix Parallel Set)	.10
26	J.J. Stokes (TSC Matrix Parallel Set)	.20
27	George Koonce	.10
28	Tamarick Vanover (TSC Matrix Parallel Set)	.75
29	Yancey Thigpen (TSC Matrix Parallel Set)	.50
30	Troy Aikman (TSC Matrix Parallel Set)	1.25
31	Rashaan Salaam (TSC Matrix Parallel Set)	.50
32	Anthony Cook	.10
33	Tim McKyer	.10
34	Dale Carter	.10
35	Marvin Washington	.10
36	Terry Allen	.10
37	Keith Goganious	.10
38	Pepper Johnson	.10
39	Dave Brown	.10
40	Levon Kirkland	.10
41	Ken Dilger	.10
42	Harvey Williams (TSC Matrix Parallel Set)	.10
43	Robert Blackmon	.10
44	Kevin Carter	.10
45	Warren Moon (TSC Matrix Parallel Set)	.10
46	Allen Aldridge	.10
47	Terance Mathis (TSC Matrix Parallel Set)	.10
48	Junior Seau (TSC Matrix Parallel Set)	.10
49	William Fuller	.10
50	Lee Woodall (TSC Matrix Parallel Set)	.10
51	Aeneas Williams (TSC Matrix Parallel Set)	.10
52	Thomas Smith	.10
53	Chris Slade	.10
54	Eric Allen (TSC Matrix Parallel Set)	.10
55	David Sloan	.10
56	Hardy Nickerson	.10
57	Michael Irvin (TSC Matrix Parallel Set)	.20
58	Corey Sawyer	.10
59	Eric Green	.10
60	Reggie White (TSC Matrix Parallel Set)	.10
61	Isaac Bruce (TSC Matrix Parallel Set)	.75
62	Darrell Green	.10
63	Aaron Glenn	.10
64	Mark Brunell (TSC Matrix Parallel Set)	1.00
65	Mark Carrier	.10
66	Mel Gray	.10
67	Phillippi Sparks	.10
68	Ernie Mills	.10
69	Rick Mirer (TSC Matrix Parallel Set)	.10
70	Neil Smith (TSC Matrix Parallel Set)	.10
71	Terry McDaniel	.10
72	Terrell Davis (TSC Matrix Parallel Set)	2.00
73	Alonzo Spellman	.10
74	Jessie Tuggle	.10
75	Terry Kirby	.10
76	David Palmer	.10
77	Calvin Williams	.10
78	Shaun Gayle	.10
79	Bryant Young	.10
80	Jim Harbaugh (TSC Matrix Parallel Set)	.10
81	Michael Jackson (TSC Matrix Parallel Set)	.10
82	David Meggett (TSC Matrix Parallel Set)	.10
83	Henry Thomas	.10
84	Jim Kelly (TSC Matrix Parallel Set)	.10
85	Frank Sanders (TSC Matrix Parallel Set)	.10
86	Daryl Johnston	.10
87	Alvin Harper	.10
88	John Copeland	.10
89	Mark Chmura (TSC Matrix Parallel Set)	.25
90	Jim Everett (TSC Matrix Parallel Set)	.10
91	Bobby Houston	.10
92	Willie Jackson	.10
93	Carlton Bailey	.10
94	Todd Lyght	.10
95	Ken Harvey	.10
96	Erric Pegram	.10
97	Anthony Smith	.10
98	Kimble Anders	.10
99	Steve McNair (TSC Matrix Parallel Set)	.75
100	Jeff George (TSC Matrix Parallel Set)	.20
101	Michael Timpson	.10
102	Brent Jones	.10
103	Mike Mamula	.10
104	Jeff Cross	.10
105	Craig Newsome	.10
106	Howard Cross	.10
107	Terry Wooden	.10
108	Randall McDaniel	.10
109	Andre Reed	.10
110	Steve Atwater	.10
111	Larry Centers	.10
112	Tony Bennett	.10
113	Drew Bledsoe (TSC Matrix Parallel Set)	1.25
114	Terrell Fletcher	.10
115	Warren Sapp	.10
116	Deion Sanders (TSC Matrix Parallel Set)	.75
117	Bryce Paup (TSC Matrix Parallel Set)	.10
118	Mario Bates	.10
119	Steve Tovar	.10
120	Barry Sanders (TSC Matrix Parallel Set)	2.00
121	Tony Boselli	.10
122	Michael Barrow	.10
123	Sam Mills (TSC Matrix Parallel Set)	.10
124	Tim Brown (TSC Matrix Parallel Set)	.10
125	Darren Perry	.10
126	Brian Blades	.10
127	Tyrone Wheatley	.10
128	Derrick Thomas (TSC Matrix Parallel Set)	.10
129	Edgar Bennett	.10
130	Cris Carter (TSC Matrix Parallel Set)	.10
131	Steve Grant	.10
132	Kevin Williams	.10
133	Darnay Scott	.20
134	Rod Stephens	.10
135	Ken Norton (TSC Matrix Parallel Set)	.10
136	*Tim Biakabutuka* (Draft Pick)	1.00
137	*Willie Anderson* (Draft Pick)	.10
138	*Lawrence Phillips* (Draft Pick)	.75
139	*Jonathan Ogden* (Draft Pick)	.10
140	*Simeon Rice* (Draft Pick)	.25
141	*Alex Van Dyke* (Draft Pick)	.20
142	*Jerome Woods* (Draft Pick)	.10
143	*Eric Moulds* (Draft Pick)	2.00
144	*Mike Alstott* (Draft Pick)	1.50
145	*Marvin Harrison* (Draft Pick)	3.00
146	*Duane Clemons* (Draft Pick)	.10
147	*Regan Upshaw* (Draft Pick)	.10
148	*Eddie Kennison* (Draft Pick)	.50
149	*John Mobley* (Draft Pick)	.10
150	*Keyshawn Johnson* (Draft Pick)	2.50
151	*Marco Battaglia* (Draft Pick)	.10
152	*Rickey Dudley* (Draft Pick)	.50
153	*Kevin Hardy* (Draft Pick)	.20
154	Curtis Martin (Shining Moments)	2.00
155	Dan Marino (Shining Moments)	2.00
156	Rashaan Salaam (Shining Moments)	.50
157	Joey Galloway (Shining Moments)	.75
158	John Elway (Shining Moments)	.40
159	Marshall Faulk (Shining Moments)	.50
160	Jerry Rice (Shining Moments)	1.00
161	Darren Bennett (Shining Moments)	.10
162	Tamarick Vanover (Shining Moments)	.50
163	Orlando Thomas (Shining Moments)	.10
164	Jim Kelly (Shining Moments)	.10
165	Larry Brown (Shining Moments)	.10
166	Errict Rhett (Shining Moments)	.40
167	Warren Moon (Shining Moments)	.10
168	Hugh Douglas (Shining Moments)	.10
169	Jim Everett (Shining Moments)	.10
170	AFC Championship Game (Shining Moments)	.10
171	Larry Centers (Shining Moments)	.10
172	Marcus Allen (Golden Moments)	.10
173	Morten Andersen (Golden Moments)	.10
174	Brett Favre (Golden Moments)	2.00

175	Jerry Rice (Golden Moments)	.75
176	Glyn Milburn (Golden Moments)	.10
177	Thurman Thomas (Golden Moments)	.10
178	Michael Irvin (Golden Moments)	.10
179	Barry Sanders (Golden Moments)	2.00
180	Dan Marino (Golden Moments)	2.00
181	Joey Galloway	1.00
182	Dwayne Harper	.10
183	Antonio Langham	.10
184	Chris Zorich	.10
185	Willie McGinest	.10
186	Wayne Chrebet	.10
187	Dermontti Dawson	.10
188	Charlie Garner	.10
189	Quentin Coryatt	.10
190	Rodney Hampton	.10
191	Kelvin Pritchett	.10
192	Willie Green	.10
193	Garrison Hearst	.10
194	Tracy Scroggins	.10
195	Raghib Ismail	.10
196	Michael Westbrook	.30
197	Troy Drayton	.10
198	Rob Fredrickson	.10
199	Sean Lumpkin	.10
200	John Elway	.75
201	Bernie Parmalee	.10
202	Chris Chandler	.10
203	Lake Dawson	.10
204	Orlando Thomas	.10
205	Carl Pickens	.20
206	Kurt Schulz	.10
207	Clay Matthews	.10
208	Winston Moss	.10
209	Sean Dawkins	.10
210	Emmitt Smith	2.50
211	Mark Carrier	.10
212	Clyde Simmons	.10
213	Derrick Brooks	.10
214	William Floyd	.20
215	Aaron Hayden	.10
216	Brian DeMarco	.10
217	Ben Coates	.10
218	Renaldo Turnbull	.10
219	Adrian Murrell	.10
220	Marcus Allen	.20
221	Brett Maxie	.10
222	Trev Alberts	.10
223	Darren Woodson	.10
224	Brian Mitchell	.10
225	Michael Haynes	.10
226	Sean Jones	.10
227	Eric Zeier	.10
228	Herman Moore	.30
229	Shane Conlan	.10
230	Chris Warren	.20
231	Dana Stubblefield	.10
232	Andre Coleman	.10
233	Kordell Stewart	1.25
234	Ray Crockett	.10
235	Craig Heyward	.10
236	Mike Fox	.10
237	Derek Brown	.10
238	Thomas Lewis	.10
239	Hugh Douglas	.10
240	Tom Carter	.10
241	Toby Wright	.10
242	Jason Belser	.10
243	Rodney Peete	.10
244	Napoleon Kaufman	.10
245	Merton Hanks	.10
246	Harry Colon	.10
247	Greg Hill	.10
248	Vincent Brisby	.10
249	Eric Hill	.10
250	Brett Favre	2.50
251	Leroy Hoard	.10
252	Eric Guliford	.10
253	Stanley Richard	.10
254	Carlos Jenkins	.10
255	D'Marco Farr	.10
256	Carlton Gray	.10
257	Derek Loville	.10
258	Ray Buchanan	.10
259	Jake Reed	.10
260	Dan Marino	2.50
261	Brad Baxter	.10
262	Pat Swilling	.10
263	Andy Harmon	.10
264	Harold Green	.10
265	Shannon Sharpe	.10
266	Erik Kramer	.10
267	Lamar Lathon	.10
268	Stevon Moore	.10
269	Tony Martin	.10
270	Bruce Smith	.10
271	James Washington	.10
272	Tyrone Poole	.10
273	Eric Swann	.10
274	Dexter Carter	.10
275	Greg Lloyd	.10
276	Michael Zordich	.10
277	Steve Wisniewski	.10
278	Chris Calloway	.10
279	Irv Smith	.10
280	Steve Young	1.00
281	James Stewart	.10
282	Blaine Bishop	.10
283	Rob Moore	.10
284	Eric Metcalf	.10
285	Kerry Collins	.30
286	Dan Wilkinson	.10
287	Curtis Conway	.10
288	Jay Novacek	.10
289	Henry Ellard	.10
290	Curtis Martin	2.00
291	Brett Perriman	.10
292	Jeff Lageman	.10
293	Trent Dilfer	.10
294	Cortez Kennedy	.10
295	Jeff Hostetler	.10
296	Mark Fields	.10
297	Qadry Ismail	.10
298	Steve Bono	.10
299	Tony Tolbert	.10
300	Jerry Rice	1.25
301	Marvcus Patton	.10
302	Robert Brooks	.20
303	Terry Ray	.10
304	John Thierry	.10
305	Errict Rhett	.30
306	Ricardo McDonald	.10
307	Antonio London	.10
308	Lonnie Johnson	.10
309	Mark Collins	.10
310	Marshall Faulk	.50
311	Anthony Pleasant	.10
312	Howard Griffith	.10
313	Roosevelt Potts	.10
314	Jim Flanigan	.10
315	'Omar Ellison	.10
316	Boomer Esiason	.10
317	Leslie O'Neal	.10
318	Jerome Bettis	.20
319	Larry Brown	.10
320	Neil O'Donnell	.10
321	Andre Rison	.10
322	Cornelius Bennett	.10
323	Quinn Early	.10
324	Bryan Cox	.10
325	Irving Fryar	.10
326	Eddie Robinson	.10
327	Chris Doleman	.10
328	Sean Gilbert	.10
329	Steve Walsh	.10
330	Kevin Greene	.10
331	Chris Spielman	.10
332	Jeff Graham	.10
333	*Anthony Dorsett Jr.*	.20
334	*Amani Toomer*	.50
335	*Walt Harris*	.50
336	*Ray Mickens*	.10
337	*Danny Kanell*	.50
338	*Daryl Gardener*	.10
339	*Jonathan Ogden*	.50
340	*Eddie George*	5.00
341	*Jeff Lewis*	.75
342	*Terrell Owens*	3.50
343	*Brian Dawkins*	.10
344	Tim Biakabutuka	.50
345	Marvin Harrison	1.50
346	*Lawyer Milloy*	.10
347	Eric Moulds	1.00
348	Alex Van Dyke	.20
349	*John Mobley*	.10
350	*Kevin Hardy*	.10
351	*Ray Lewis*	8.00
352	Lawrence Phillips	.30
353	*Stepfret Williams*	.10
354	*Bobby Engram*	.50
355	*Leeland McElroy*	.30
356	*Marco Battaglia*	.10
357	Rickey Dudley	.20
358	*Bobby Hoying*	.75
359	*Cedric Jones*	.10
360	Keyshawn Johnson	1.00

1996 Stadium Club Dot Matrix

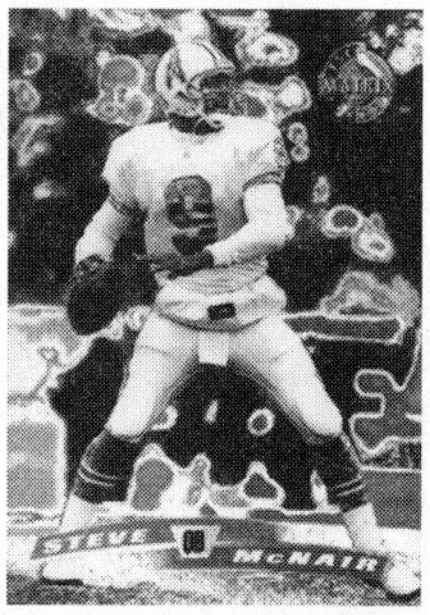

Ninety of the cards from Topps' 1996 Stadium Club set have been duplicated for a parallel insert set. Forty-five cards from Series I have been selected, using dot matrix foil for the design. There were also 45 Series II cards chosen; these cards also have holographic foil in the design. Cards were seeded one per every 12 packs in the corresponding series. The TSC logo is on the card front.

		MT
Complete Set (90):		85.00
Common Player:		1.00
1	Kyle Brady	1.00
6	Heath Shuler	1.00
10	Jeff Blake	6.00
11	Tyrone Hughes	1.00
15	Anthony Miller	1.00
19	Scott Mitchell	1.00
21	Stan Humphries	1.00
25	Ricky Watters	1.00
26	J.J. Stokes	6.00
28	Tamarick Vanover	7.00
29	Yancey Thigpen	5.00
30	Troy Aikman	12.00
31	Rashaan Salaam	5.00
42	Harvey Williams	1.00
45	Warren Moon	1.00
47	Terance Mathis	1.00
48	Junior Seau	1.00
50	Lee Woodall	1.00
51	Aeneas Williams	1.00
54	Eric Allen	1.00
57	Michael Irvin	2.00
60	Reggie White	3.00
61	Isaac Bruce	5.00
64	Mark Brunell	5.00
69	Rick Mirer	2.00
70	Neil Smith	1.00
72	Terrell Davis	15.00
80	Jim Harbaugh	1.00
81	Michael Jackson	1.00
82	David Meggett	1.00
84	Jim Kelly	2.00
85	Frank Sanders	1.00
89	Mark Chmura	1.00
90	Jim Everett	1.00
99	Steve McNair	10.00
100	Jeff George	1.00
113	Drew Bledsoe	10.00
116	Deion Sanders	10.00
117	Bryce Paup	1.00
120	Barry Sanders	20.00
123	Sam Mills	1.00
124	Tim Brown	1.00
128	Derrick Thomas	1.00
130	Cris Carter	1.00
135	Ken Norton	1.00
181	Joey Galloway	10.00
182	Chris Zorich	1.00
185	Willie McGinest	1.00
186	Wayne Chrebet	1.00
190	Rodney Hampton	1.00
196	Michael Westbrook	5.00
200	John Elway	10.00
204	Orlando Thomas	1.00
205	Carl Pickens	2.00
210	Emmitt Smith	25.00
213	Derrick Brooks	1.00
217	Ben Coates	1.00
220	Marcus Allen	2.00
224	Brian Mitchell	1.00
227	Eric Zeier	1.00
228	Herman Moore	4.00
230	Chris Warren	2.00
233	Kordell Stewart	12.00
235	Craig Heyward	1.00
239	Hugh Douglas	1.00
240	Tom Carter	1.00
243	Rodney Peete	1.00
244	Napoleon Kaufman	1.00
250	Brett Favre	25.00
260	Dan Marino	25.00
265	Shannon Sharpe	1.00
266	Erik Kramer	1.00
267	Lamar Lathon	1.00
270	Bruce Smith	1.00
275	Greg Lloyd	1.00
280	Steve Young	10.00
282	Blaine Bishop	1.00
284	Eric Metcalf	1.00
285	Kerry Collins	15.00
286	Dan Wilkinson	1.00
287	Curtis Conway	1.00
288	Jay Novacek	1.00
290	Curtis Martin	20.00
293	Trent Dilfer	1.00
295	Jeff Hostetler	1.00
298	Steve Bono	1.00
300	Jerry Rice	12.00
302	Robert Brooks	2.00
305	Errict Rhett	3.00
310	Marshall Faulk	5.00

1996 Stadium Club Match Proofs

Match Proofs are a parallel set that runs through all 270 cards from Series I and II. This parallel set features identical fronts, but has different backs than regular-issue cards. Production of Match Proofs was limited to only 100 sets.

	MT
Proof Cards:	20x-40x

1996 Stadium Club Brace Yourself

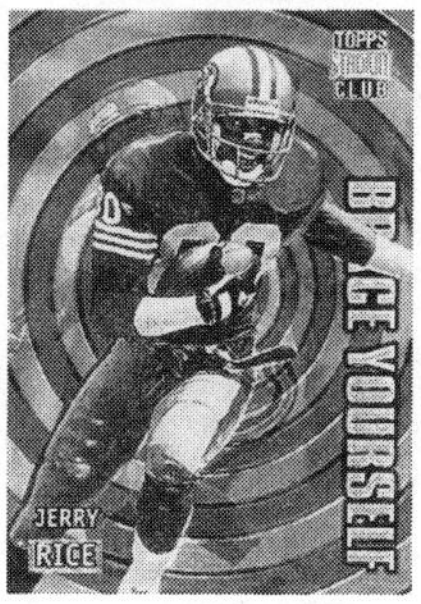

These cards are Stadium Club's retail-only inserts in Series II. Each card features a gridiron great on an embossed, holographic foil card. The front has a photo in the middle, with a bull's-eye as the background. The TSC logo is in the upper right corner; the player's name is in the lower left corner. "Brace Yourself" is written along the right side. The card back repeats the bull's-eye pattern as the background, with the player's name, team name, position and card number (using a "BY" prefix) toward the top. The middle of the card comments about the player's talents. Cards were seeded one per every 24 packs.

		MT
Complete Set (10):		125.00
Common Player:		3.00
1	Dan Marino	30.00
2	Marshall Faulk	10.00
3	Greg Lloyd	3.00
4	Steve Young	20.00
5	Emmitt Smith	30.00
6	Junior Seau	3.00
7	Chris Warren	3.00
8	Jerry Rice	20.00
9	Troy Aikman	20.00
10	Barry Sanders	20.00

1996 Stadium Club Contact Prints

These 10 cards were included in 1996 Topps Stadium Club Series I packs, one per every 12 packs. The cards feature a bone-jarring hit on the front in color, against a contact sheet which shows several smaller black-and-white prints of cards from the set as the background. "Contact Print" is in red foil along the left side of the card; "Takedown" is in blue foil along the bottom. The TSC logo is stamped in the upper right corner of the horizontally-designed front. The horizontal back has a closeup photo of one of the players featured on the front, along with an extended cutline on the right side about the photo on the front. The name of the featured player is in white letters at the top; the name of the player being hit is in smaller white letters next to it. "Takedown" is written along the bottom of the card, with a card number (using a "CP" prefix) next to it.

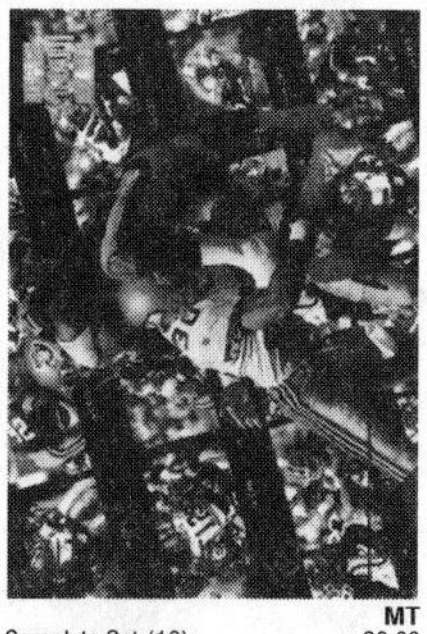

		MT
Complete Set (10):		20.00
Common Player:		2.00
1	Ken Norton	2.00
2	Chris Zorich	2.00
3	Corey Harris	2.00
4	Sam Mills	2.00
5	Bryce Paup	2.00
6	Rob Fredrickson	2.00
7	Darnell Walker	2.00
8	Derrick Thomas	2.00
9	Hardy Nickerson	2.00
10	Reggie White	3.00

1996 Stadium Club Cut Backs

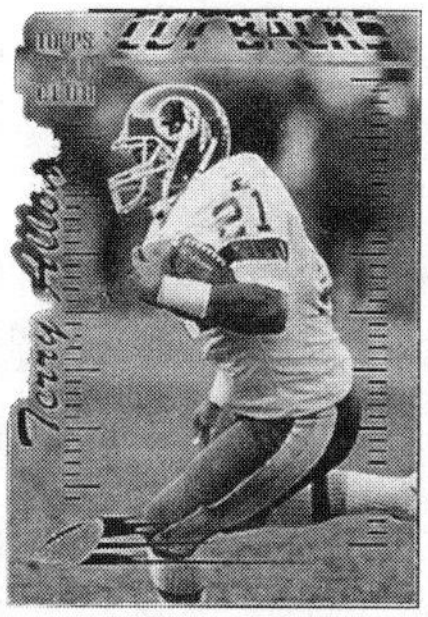

These eight cards were randomly included in 1996 Topps Stadium Club Series I hobby packs only, one per every 36 packs. Speedster running backs such as Curtis Martin and Barry Sanders are featured on these precisely-cut laser designed cards.

		MT
Complete Set (8):		60.00
Common Player:		3.00
1	Emmitt Smith	25.00
2	Barry Sanders	18.00
3	Curtis Martin	18.00
4	Chris Warren	5.00
5	Errict Rhett	10.00
6	Rodney Hampton	3.00
7	Ricky Watters	3.00
8	Terry Allen	3.00

1996 Stadium Club Fusion

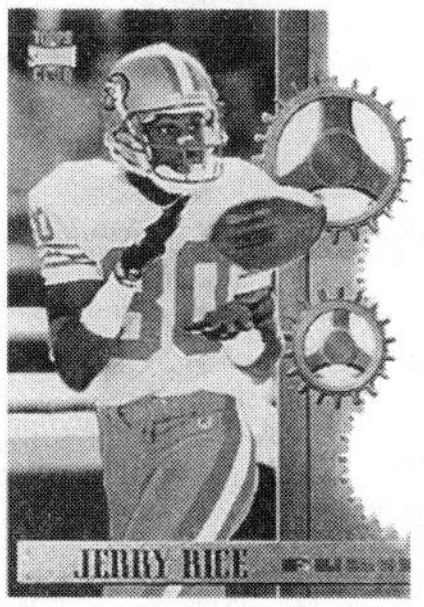

These cards were found exclusively in 1996 Topps Stadium Club Series II packs, one per every 24 packs. Cards, which are laser cut along one side, are intended to be "fused" together to match up a pair of teammates, forming a larger image. Eight different dynamic duos are spotlighted in this set.

		MT
Complete Set (16):		135.00
Common Player:		4.00
1A	Steve Young	16.00
1B	Jerry Rice	20.00
2A	Drew Bledsoe	20.00
2B	Curtis Martin	25.00
3A	Trent Dilfer	4.00
3B	Errict Rhett	8.00
4A	Jeff Hostetler	4.00
4B	Tim Brown	4.00
5A	Brett Favre	30.00
5B	Robert Brooks	4.00
6A	Jim Harbaugh	4.00
6B	Marshall Faulk	10.00
7A	Erik Kramer	4.00
7B	Rashaan Salaam	8.00
8A	Scott Mitchell	4.00
8B	Barry Sanders	25.00

1996 Stadium Club Laser Sites

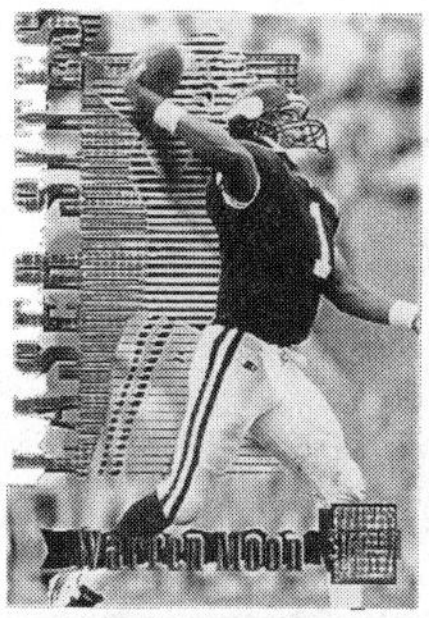

These eight cards were inserted one per every 36 hobby packs of 1996 Topps Stadium Club Series I football. Each card has an intricate laser cut design, polished off with diffraction foil stamping. Eight top quarterbacks were selected for the set.

		MT
Complete Set (8):		70.00
Common Player:		3.00
1	Brett Favre	25.00
2	Dan Marino	25.00
3	Steve Young	13.00
4	Troy Aikman	13.00
5	Jim Harbaugh	3.00
6	Scott Mitchell	3.00
7	Erik Kramer	3.00
8	Warren Moon	3.00

1996 Stadium Club Namath Finest

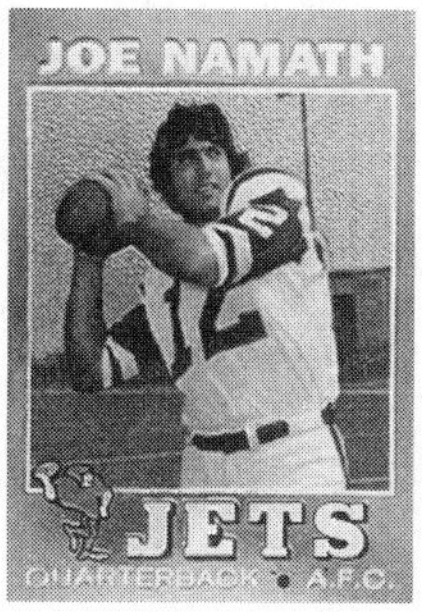

Following on the heels of the Joe Namath reprints in 1996 Topps packs, Finest and Finest Refractor versions of these 10 cards were included in 1996 Topps Stadium Club Series I packs. Finest cards were seeded one per every 24 packs; Refractor versions were one per every 96 packs. Cards are labeled on the back as being part of a reprint set, with a number (1 of 10, etc.) also included. The Refractors are also labeled on the back as being such.

		MT
Complete Set (10):		100.00
Common Player:		10.00
Comp. Refractor Set (10):		300.00
Refractors:		3x
1	1965	15.00
2	1966	10.00
3	1967	10.00
4	1968	10.00
5	1969	10.00
6	1970	10.00
7	1971	10.00
8	1972	10.00
9	1972	10.00
10	1973	10.00

1996 Stadium Club Namath Finest Refractors

This 10-card insert is a parallel to the Finest Namath Reprints, with Refractor versions seeded every 96 packs. Namath Reprints first appeared in Topps Football and were then reprinted in Finest technology for Stadium Club Series I packs. The insert showcases some of Namath's top cards throughout his career.

	MT
Complete Set (10):	300.00
Refractors:	3x

A card number in parentheses ( ) indicates the set is unnumbered.

1996 Stadium Club New Age

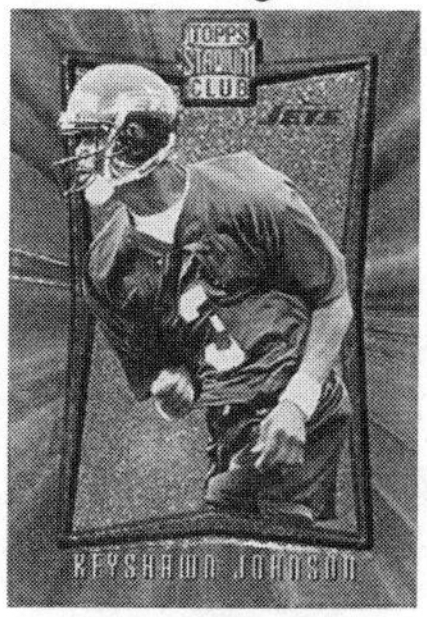

These cards were seeded one per every 24 packs of 1996 Topps Stadium Club Series II product. Twenty 1996 NFL draft picks and first-year rookies are spotlighted on the cards, which use etched dot matrix technology for the front. The front also has a color photo in the middle with a frame around it. A team logo is in the upper left corner of the frame. A TSC logo is at the top of the card; the player's name is along the bottom. The card back has a rectangle in the middle which has the player's name, team name and position toward the top, just below a card number (which uses an "NA" prefix). Inside the rectangle is a recap of the player's collegiate accomplishments. "New Age" is at the top of the card.

		MT
Complete Set (20):		100.00
Common Player:		3.00
1	Alex Van Dyke	5.00
2	Lawrence Phillips	10.00
3	Tim Biakabutuka	10.00
4	Reggie Brown	3.00
5	Duane Clemons	3.00
6	Marco Battaglia	3.00
7	Cedric Jones	3.00
8	Jerome Woods	3.00
9	Eric Moulds	10.00
10	Kevin Hardy	3.00
11	Rickey Dudley	5.00
12	Regan Upshaw	3.00
13	Eddie Kennison	6.00
14	Jonathan Ogden	3.00
15	John Mobley	3.00
16	Mike Alstott	10.00
17	Alex Molden	3.00
18	Marvin Harrison	15.00
19	Simeon Rice	3.00
20	Keyshawn Johnson	15.00

1996 Stadium Club Photo Gallery

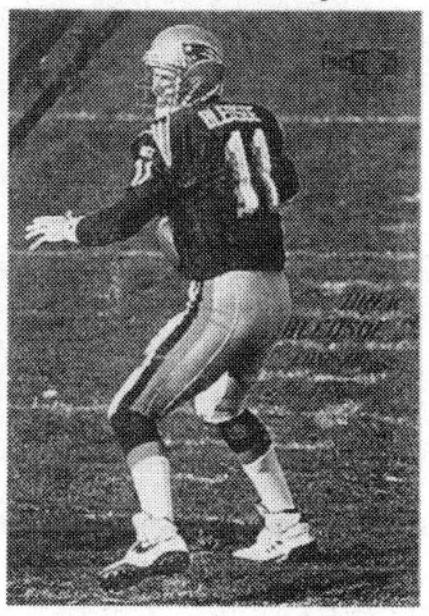

These cards were seeded one per every 18 packs of 1996 Topps Stadium Club Series II product. Each card features a customized design that complements the outstanding photography, and is printed on smooth cast-coated stock with an exclusive Topps high gloss laminate. The Photo Gallery logo, player's name, opponent, and game date from when the picture was taken are stamped in red, blue or silver foil on the front. The card back has the player's team name and position listed at the top, with the player's name below. The date of the game is under his name, with a recap of the game below, on one side. A color photo is on the other side. The card number, using a "PG" prefix, is in the lower left corner.

		MT
Complete Set (21):		150.00
Common Player:		2.00
1	Emmitt Smith	25.00
2	Jeff Blake	5.00
3	Junior Seau	2.00
4	Robert Brooks	2.00
5	Barry Sanders	18.00
6	Drew Bledsoe	13.00
7	Joey Galloway	10.00
8	Marshall Faulk	8.00
9	Mark Brunell	10.00
10	Jerry Rice	13.00
11	Rashaan Salaam	6.00
12	Troy Aikman	13.00
13	Steve Young	10.00
14	Tim Brown	2.00
15	Brett Favre	25.00

16	Kerry Collins	5.00
17	John Elway	10.00
18	Curtis Martin	18.00
19	Deion Sanders	10.00
20	Dan Marino	25.00
21	Chris Warren	2.00

1996 Stadium Club Pro Bowl

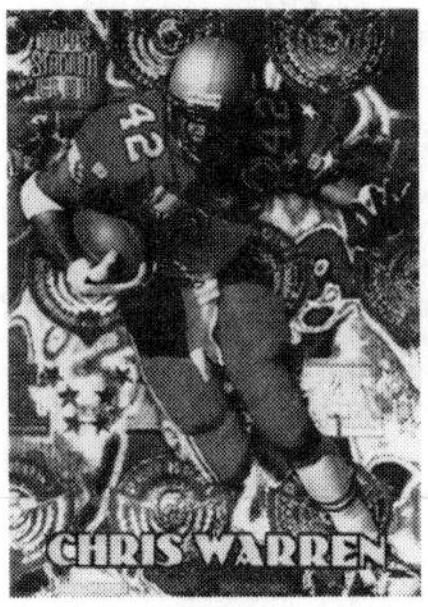

These 20 embossed cards were seeded one per every 24 retail packs of 1996 Topps Stadium Club Series I product. The cards used etched Power Matrix technology. Twenty participants in the 1996 Pro Bowl game are featured in the set.

		MT
Complete Set (20):		150.00
Common Player:		3.00
Minor Stars:		6.00
Inserted 1:24 Retail		
1	Brett Favre	30.00
2	Bruce Smith	3.00
3	Ricky Watters	6.00
4	Yancey Thigpen	6.00
5	Barry Sanders	30.00
6	Jim Harbaugh	3.00
7	Michael Irvin	6.00
8	Chris Warren	3.00
9	Dana Stubblefield	3.00
10	Jeff Blake	6.00
11	Emmitt Smith	20.00
12	Bryce Paup	3.00
13	Steve Young	10.00
14	Kevin Greene	3.00
15	Jerry Rice	15.00
16	Curtis Martin	10.00
17	Reggie White	6.00
18	Derrick Thomas	3.00
19	Cris Carter	6.00
20	Greg Lloyd	3.00

1996 Stadium Club Members Only Parallel

This set is a complete parallel of the 1996 Stadium Club set. It was sold through Topps' Members Only Club. This issue was available in factory set form and included all the base set and insert cards. Club members could purchase the entire set or an individual series. Each card featured a special Members Only stamp.

		MT
Complete Set (476):		300.00
Common Player (1-360):		.20
Common Player (C1-C8):		.35
Common Player (F1A-F8B):		.35
Common Player (N1-N10):		1.00
Common Player (BY1-BY10):		.35
Common Player (CP1-CP10):		.35
Common Player (NA1-NA20):		.35
Common Player (PB1-PB20):		.35
Common Player (PG1-PG20):		.50
Semistars Inserts:		.50
Stars Inserts:		.75
Stars:		2x to 4x
*RCs:		2x
C1	Emmitt Smith	8.00
C2	Barry Sanders	5.00
C3	Curtis Martin	4.00
C4	Chris Warren	.50
C5	Errict Rhett	.50
C6	Rodney Hampton	.35
C7	Ricky Watters	.50
C8	Terry Allen	.50
F1A	Steve Young	3.00
F1B	Jerry Rice	4.00
F2A	Drew Bledsoe	4.00
F2B	Curtis Martin	4.00
F3A	Trent Dilfer	.50
F3B	Errict Rhett	.50
F4A	Jeff Hostetler	.35
F4B	Tim Brown	.50
F5A	Brett Favre	10.00
F5B	Robert Brooks	.75
F6A	Jim Harbaugh	.50
F6B	Marshall Faulk	.75
F7A	Rashaan Salaam	.75
F7B	Erik Kramer	.35
F8A	Scott Mitchell	.35
F8B	Barry Sanders	5.00
N1	Joe Namath 1965	1.00
N2	Joe Namath 1966	1.00
N3	Joe Namath 1967	1.00
N4	Joe Namath 1968	1.00
N5	Joe Namath 1969	1.00
N6	Joe Namath 1970	1.00
N7	Joe Namath 1971	1.00
N8	Joe Namath 1972	1.00
N9	Joe Namath 1972	1.00
N10	Joe Namath 1973	1.00
BY1	Dan Marino	8.00
BY2	Marshall Faulk	.75
BY3	Greg Lloyd	.35
BY4	Steve Young	3.00
BY5	Emmitt Smith	8.00
BY6	Junior Seau	.50
BY7	Chris Warren	.50
BY8	Jerry Rice	4.00
BY9	Troy Aikman	4.00
BY10	Barry Sanders	5.00
CP1	Ken Norton, Drew Bledsoe	3.00
CP2	Chris Zorich, Barry Sanders	3.00
CP3	Corey Harris, Harvey Williams	.35
CP4	Sam Mills, Thurman Thomas	.75
CP5	Bryce Paup, Derrick Moore	.35
CP6	Rob Fredrickson, Chris Warren	.50
CP7	Darnell Walker, Bernie Parmalee	.35
CP8	Derrick Thomas, Gus Frerotte	.50
CP9	Hardy Nickerson, Robert Smith	.35
CP10	Reggie White, Dave Brown	.75
NA1	Alex Van Dyke	.50
NA2	Lawrence Phillips	1.00
NA3	Tim Biakabutuka	1.00
NA4	Reggie Brown	.35
NA5	Duane Clemons	.35
NA6	Marco Battaglia	.35
NA7	Cedric Jones	.35
NA8	Jerome Woods	.35
NA9	Eric Moulds	1.00
NA10	Kevin Hardy	.35
NA11	Rickey Dudley	.50
NA12	Regan Upshaw	.35
NA13	Eddie Kennison	2.50
NA14	Jonathan Ogden	.35
NA15	John Mobley	.35
NA16	Mike Alstott	1.50
NA17	Alex Molden	.35
NA18	Marvin Harrison	2.50
NA19	Simeon Rice	.35
NA20	Keyshawn Johnson	2.50
PB1	Brett Favre	10.00
PB2	Bruce Smith	.50
PB3	Ricky Watters	.50
PB4	Yancey Thigpen	.50
PB5	Barry Sanders	5.00
PB6	Jim Harbaugh	.50
PB7	Michael Irvin	.75
PB8	Chris Warren	.50
PB9	Dana Stubblefield	.35
PB10	Jeff Blake	.50
PB11	Emmitt Smith	8.00
PB12	Bryce Paup	.35
PB13	Steve Young	3.00
PB14	Kevin Greene	.35
PB15	Jerry Rice	4.00
PB16	Curtis Martin	4.00
PB17	Reggie White	.75
PB18	Derrick Thomas	.50
PB19	Cris Carter	.50
PB20	Greg Lloyd	.35
PG1	Emmitt Smith	8.00
PG2	Jeff Blake	.50
PG3	Junior Seau	.50
PG4	Robert Brooks	.75
PG5	Barry Sanders	5.00
PG6	Drew Bledsoe	4.00
PG7	Joey Galloway	.75
PG8	Marshall Faulk	.75
PG9	Mark Brunell	4.00
PG10	Jerry Rice	4.00
PG11	Rashaan Salaam	.75
PG12	Troy Aikman	4.00
PG13	Steve Young	3.00
PG14	Tim Brown	.50
PG15	Brett Favre	10.00
PG16	Kerry Collins	3.00
PG17	John Elway	3.00
PG18	Curtis Martin	4.00
PG19	Deion Sanders	2.00
PG20	Dan Marino	8.00
PG21	Chris Warren	.50

1996 Stadium Club Sunday Night Redemption

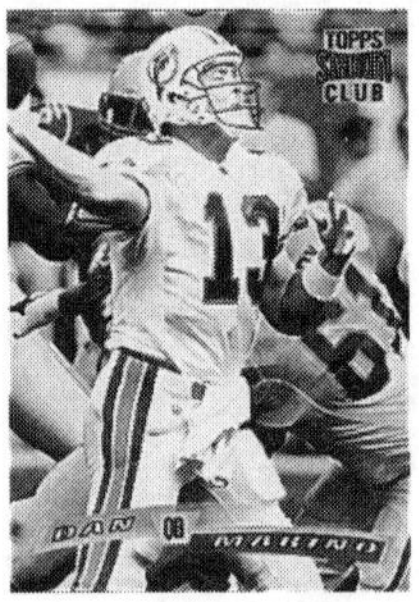

Sunday Night Redemption cards were inserted in Stadium Club Series One packs (1:24 hobby and retail; 1:20 jumbo). The cards were designated for a certain week of the NFL season and if the score of that week's Sunday night game matched the two numbers on the card, collectors could mail the card in and receive two jumbo Finest cards featuring players in that week's game.

		MT
Complete Set (32):		250.00
Common Player:		5.00
1A	Rodney Hampton	5.00
1B	Jim Kelly	8.00
2A	Dan Marino	25.00
2B	Frank Sanders	5.00
3A	Trent Dilfer	7.00
3B	John Elway	12.00
4A	Eric Metcalf	5.00
4B	Ricky Watters	6.00
5A	Terry Allen	6.00
5B	Keyshawn Johnson	8.00
6A	Jeff Blake	8.00
6B	Steve McNair	10.00
7A	Marshall Faulk	8.00
7B	Eric Zeier	5.00
9A	Drew Bledsoe	15.00
9B	Bruce Smith	5.00
10A	Jim Everett	5.00
10B	Steve Young	12.00
11A	Dave Brown	5.00
11B	Kerry Collins	12.00
12A	Tim Brown	6.00
12B	Cris Carter	6.00
13A	Isaac Bruce	8.00
13B	Brett Favre	30.00
14A	Curtis Martin	15.00
14B	Junior Seau	6.00
15A	Warren Moon	6.00
15B	Barry Sanders	18.00
16A	Mark Brunell	15.00
16B	Chris Warren	5.00
17A	Terrell Davis	15.00
17B	Stan Humphries	5.00

1997 Stadium Club

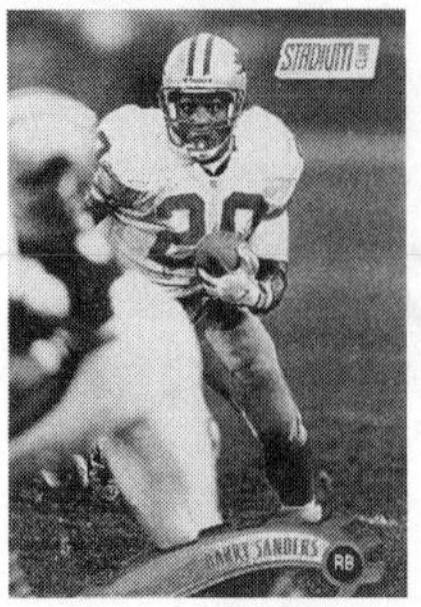

The 170-card Series I set included a full-bleed photo on the front, with the Stadium Club logo at the top and a "wave" on the bottom that included the player's name and position. The backs included an action shot, with the player's name, bio and highlights on the left side in a "ripped out" area. The stats appear in a box in the lower right, along with one highlight. There are three parallel sets. Printing Plates (cyan, yellow, magenta and black plates of each card for a total of 640 cards) were inserted in Home Team Advantage packs. One-of-a-Kind parallel cards were seeded 1:48 packs, while First Day Issue parallel cards were found 1:24 retail packs. Series II also had 170 cards and the same three parallel sets. The base set did include a 20-card Transaction subset, featuring important off-season moves.

		MT
Complete Set (340):		60.00
Complete Series 1 (170):		30.00
Complete Series 2 (170):		30.00
Common Player:		.10
Minor Stars:		.20
First Day Stars:		20x-40x
First Day Rookies:		10x-20x
One of a Kind Stars:		30x-60x
One of a Kind Rookies:		15x-30x
Hobby Ser 1/2 Pack (9):		3.00
Hobby Ser 1/2 Wax Box (24):		60.00
Retail Set 1/2 Pack (6):		2.00
Retail Set 1/2 Wax Box (36):		65.00
1	Junior Seau	.20
2	Michael Irvin	.20
3	Marcus Allen	.20
4	Dale Carter	.10
5	*Darnell Autry*	.40
6	Isaac Bruce	.20
7	Darrell Green	.10
9	Steve Atwater	.10
10	Kordell Stewart	1.50
11	Tony Brackens	.10
12	Gus Frerotte	.10
13	Henry Ellard	.10
14	Charles Way	.10
15	*Jim Druckenmiller*	2.00
16	Orlando Thomas	.10
17	Terrell Davis	1.25
18	Jim Schwantz	.10
19	Derrick Thomas	.10
20	Curtis Martin	1.50
21	Deion Sanders	.50
22	Bruce Smith	.10
23	Jake Reed	.10
24	Leeland McElroy	.10
25	Jerome Bettis	.20
26	Neil Smith	.10
27	Terry Allen	.10
28	Gilbert Brown	.10
29	Steve McNair	.75
30	Kerry Collins	.30
31	Thurman Thomas	.20
32	Kenny Holmes	.10
33	Karim Abdul-Jabbar	.30
34	Steve Young	1.00
35	Jerry Rice	1.25
36	Jeff George	.10
37	Errict Rhett	.20
38	Mike Alstott	.20
39	Tim Brown	.10
40	Keyshawn Johnson	.20
41	Jim Harbaugh	.10
42	Kevin Hardy	.10
43	Kevin Greene	.10
44	Eric Metcalf	.10
45	Troy Aikman	1.25
46	Marshall Faulk	.20
47	Shannon Sharpe	.10
48	Warren Moon	.10
49	Mark Brunell	1.25
50	Dan Marino	3.00
51	*Byron Hanspard*	1.00
52	Chris Chandler	.10
53	Wayne Chrebet	.10
54	Antonio Langham	.10
55	Barry Sanders	2.00
56	Curtis Conway	.10
57	Ricky Watters	.20
58	William Thomas	.10
59	Chris Warren	.10
60	Terry Glenn	.30
61	*Peter Boulware*	.10
62	Chad Cota	.10
63	Eddie Kennison	.50
64	Lamar Smith	.10
65	Brett Favre	3.00
66	Michael Westbrook	.10
67	Larry Centers	.10
68	Trent Dilfer	.20
69	Stevon Moore	.10
70	John Elway	1.00
71	Bryce Paup	.10
72	Quentin Coryatt	.10
73	Rashaan Salaam	.20
74	Thomas Lewis	.10
75	Drew Bledsoe	1.25
76	Cris Carter	.10
77	Joe Bowden	.10
78	Allen Aldridge	.10
79	Zach Thomas	.30
80	Emmitt Smith	3.00
81	Daryl Johnston	.10
82	Vinny Testaverde	.10
83	James Stewart	.10
84	Edgar Bennett	.10
85	*Shawn Springs*	.30
86	Elvis Grbac	.10
87	Levon Kirkland	.10
88	Jeff Graham	.10
89	Terrell Fletcher	.10
90	Eddie George	2.00
91	Jessie Tuggle	.10
92	Terrell Owens	.75
93	Wayne Martin	.10
94	Dwayne Harper	.10
95	Mark Collins	.10
96	Marvcus Patton	.10
97	Napoleon Kaufman	.10
98	Keenan McCardell	.10
99	Ty Detmer	.10
100	Reggie White	.20
101	William Floyd	.10
102	Scott Mitchell	.10
103	Robert Blackmon	.10
104	Dan Wilkinson	.10
105	Warren Sapp	.10
106	Raymont Harris	.10
107	Brian Mitchell	.10
108	Tyrone Poole	.10
109	Derrick Alexander	.10
110	David Palmer	.10
111	James Farrior	.10
112	Daryl Gardener	.10
113	Marty Carter	.10
114	Lawrence Phillips	.20
115	Wesley Walls	.10
116	John Friesz	.10
117	Roman Phifer	.10
118	Jason Sehorn	.10
119	Henry Thomas	.10
120	Natrone Means	.20
121	Ty Law	.10
122	*Tony Gonzalez*	1.00
123	Kevin Williams	.10
124	Regan Upshaw	.10
125	Antonio Freeman	.30
126	Jessie Armstead	.10
127	*Pat Barnes*	.30
128	Charlie Garner	.10
129	Irving Fryar	.10
130	Rickey Dudley	.10
131	Rodney Harrison	.10
132	Brent Jones	.10
133	Neil O'Donnell	.10
134	Darryll Lewis	.10
135	Jason Belser	.10
136	Mark Chmura	.10
137	Seth Joyner	.10
138	Herschel Walker	.10
139	Santana Dotson	.10
140	Carl Pickens	.10
141	Terance Mathis	.10
142	Walt Harris	.10
143	John Mobley	.10
144	Gabe Northern	.10
145	Herman Moore	.20
146	Michael Jackson	.10
147	Chris Sanders	.10
148	LeShon Johnson	.10
149	Darrell Russell	.10
150	Winslow Oliver	.10
151	Tamarick Vanover	.10
152	Tony Martin	.10
153	Lamar Lathon	.10
154	Stanley Richard	.10
155	Derrick Brooks	.10
156	*Warrick Dunn*	2.50
157	Tim McDonald	.10
158	Keith Lyle	.10
159	Terry McDaniel	.10
160	Andre Hastings	.10
161	Phillippi Sparks	.10
162	Tedy Bruschi	.10
163	*Bryant Westbrook*	.20
164	Victor Green	.10
165	Jimmy Smith	.10
166	Greg Biekert	.10
167	Frank Sanders	.10
168	Chris Doleman	.10
169	Phil Hansen	.10
170	Walter Jones	.10
171	Mark Carrier	.10
172	Greg Hill	.10
173	Erik Kramer	.10
174	Chris Spielman	.10
175	Tom Knight	.10
176	Sam Mills	.10
177	Robert Smith	.10
178	Dorsey Levens	.20
179	Chris Slade	.10
180	Troy Vincent	.10
181	Mario Bates	.10
182	Ed McCaffrey	.10
183	Mike Mamula	.10
184	Chad Hennings	.10
185	Stan Humphries	.10
186	Reinard Wilson	.10
187	Kevin Carter	.10
188	Qadry Ismail	.10
189	Cortez Kennedy	.10
190	Eric Swann	.10
191	*Corey Dillon*	5.00
192	Renaldo Wynn	.10
193	Bobby Hebert	.10
194	Fred Barnett	.10
195	Ray Lewis	.10
196	Robert Jones	.10
197	Brian Williams	.10
198	Willie McGinest	.10
199	*Jake Plummer*	5.00
200	Aeneas Williams	.10
201	Ashley Ambrose	.10
202	Cornelius Bennett	.10
203	Mo Lewis	.10
204	James Hasty	.10
205	Carnell Lake	.10
206	Heath Shuler	.10
207	Dana Stubblefield	.10
208	Corey Miller	.10
209	*Ike Hilliard*	1.50
210	Bryant Young	.10
211	Hardy Nickerson	.10
212	Blaine Bishop	.10
213	Marcus Robertson	.10
214	Tony Bennett	.10
215	Kent Graham	.10
216	Steve Bono	.10
217	*Will Blackwell*	.50
218	Tyrone Braxton	.10
219	Eric Moulds	.20
220	Rod Woodson	.10
221	Anthony Johnson	.10
222	Willie Davis	.10
223	Darrin Smith	.10
224	Rick Mirer	.10
225	Marvin Harrison	.50
226	Dixon Edwards	.10
227	Joe Aska	.10
228	*Yatil Green*	.50
229	William Fuller	.10
230	Eddie Robinson	.10
231	Brian Blades	.10
232	Michael Sinclair	.10
233	Ken Harvey	.10
234	Harvey Williams	.10
235	Simeon Rice	.10
236	Chris T. Jones	.10
237	Bert Emanuel	.10
238	Corey Sawyer	.10
239	Chris Calloway	.10
240	Jeff Blake	.20
241	Alonzo Spellman	.10
242	Bryan Cox	.10
243	*Antowain Smith*	2.50
244	Tim Biakabutuka	.20
245	Ray Crockett	.10
246	Dwayne Rudd	.10
247	Glyn Milburn	.10
248	Gary Plummer	.10
249	O.J. McDuffie	.10
250	Willie Clay	.10
251	Jim Everett	.10
252	Eugene Daniel	.10
253	Jessie Armstead	.10
254	Mel Gray	.10
255	Ken Norton	.10
256	Johnnie Morton	.10
257	Courtney Hawkins	.10
258	Ricardo McDonald	.10
259	Todd Lyght	.10
260	Michael Barrow	.10
261	Aaron Glenn	.10
262	Clay Matthews	.10
263	*Troy Davis*	.30
264	Eric Hill	.10
265	Darrien Gordon	.10
266	Lake Dawson	.10
267	John Randle	.10
268	Lamar Thomas	.10
269	Mickey Washington	.10
270	Amani Toomer	.10
271	Steve Grant	.10
272	Adrian Murrell	.20
273	Derrick Witherspoon	.10
274	Michael Zordich	.10
275	Ben Coates	.10
277	Jim Schwantz	.10
278	Aaron Hayden	.10
279	Ryan McNeil	.10
280	LeRoy Butler	.10
281	Craig Newsome	.10
282	Bill Romanowski	.10
283	Michael Bankston	.10
284	Kevin Smith	.10
285	Byron Morris	.10
286	Darnay Scott	.10
287	*David LaFleur*	.50
288	Randall Cunningham	.20
289	Eric Davis	.10
290	Todd Collins	.10
291	Steve Tovar	.10
292	Jermaine Lewis	.10
293	Alfred Williams	.10
294	Brad Johnson	.20
295	Charles Johnson	.10
296	Ted Johnson	.10
297	Merton Hanks	.10
298	Andre Coleman	.10
299	Keith Jackson	.10
300	Terry Kirby	.10
301	Tony Banks	.30
302	Terrance Shaw	.10
303	Bobby Engram	.10
304	Hugh Douglas	.10
305	Lawyer Milloy	.10
306	James Jett	.10
307	*Joey Kent*	.50
308	Rodney Hampton	.10
309	DeWayne Washington	.10
310	Kevin Lockett	.10
311	Ki-Jana Carter	.10
312	Jeff Lageman	.10
313	Don Beebe	.10
314	Willie Williams	.10
315	Tyrone Wheatley	.10
316	Leslie O'Neal	.10
317	Quinn Early	.10
318	Sean Gilbert	.10
319	Tim Bowens	.10
320	Sean Dawkins	.10
321	Ken Dilger	.10
322	George Koonce	.10
323	Jevon Langford	.10
324	Mike Caldwell	.10
325	*Orlando Pace*	.50
326	Garrison Hearst	.10
327	Mike Tomczak	.10
328	Rob Moore	.10
329	Andre Reed	.10
330	Kimble Anders	.10
331	Qadry Ismail	.10
333	Dave Brown	.10
334	Bennie Blades	.10
335	Jamal Anderson	.20
336	John Lynch	.10
337	Tyrone Hughes	.10
338	Ronnie Harmon	.10
339	*Rae Carruth*	1.25
340	Robert Brooks	.10

1997 Stadium Club First Day

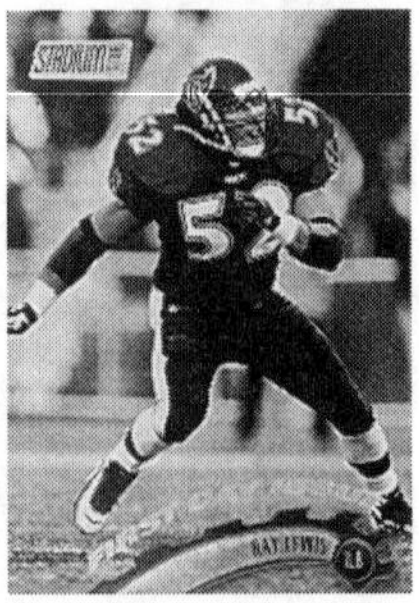

First Day Issue is a retail-only parallel of the Stadium Club Series base set which was inserted one per 24 packs. Each card was marked with a gold foil logo with the parallel name on the front of the card.

	MT
First Day Stars:	20x-40x
First Day Rookies:	10x-20x

1997 Stadium Club One of a Kind

One of a Kind is a hobby-only parallel which was seeded one per 48 packs. Each card is marked with a special security stamp. All 340 cards from Series I and II are paralleled.

	MT
One of a Kind Stars:	30x-60x
One of a Kind Rookies:	15x-30x

1997 Stadium Club Aerial Assault

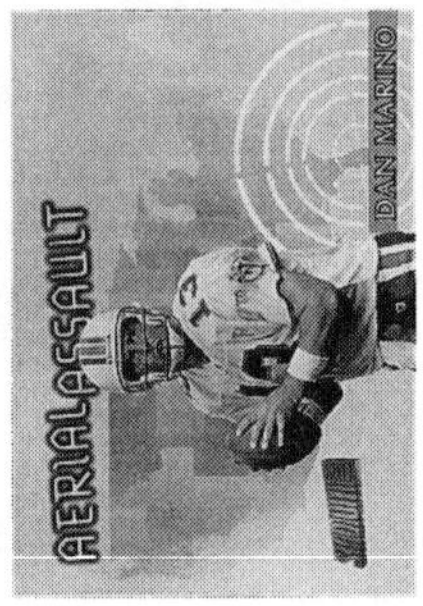

The 10-card set was inserted 1:12 packs. A player photo is superimposed over a holographic background of the United States, with the team's city targeted. "Aerial Assault" is printed at the top left, while the Stadium Club logo and the player's name are in the lower right. The backs, which are numbered with an "AA" prefix, has the player photo on the left, with the player's name, team and 1996 passing stats all to the right.

		MT
Complete Set (10):		40.00
Common Player:		1.50
1	Dan Marino	10.00
2	Mark Brunell	5.00
3	Troy Aikman	5.00
4	Ty Detmer	1.50
5	John Elway	3.00
6	Drew Bledsoe	5.00
7	Steve Young	3.00
8	Vinny Testaverde	1.50
9	Kerry Collins	3.00
10	Brett Favre	12.00

1997 Stadium Club Bowman's Best Previews

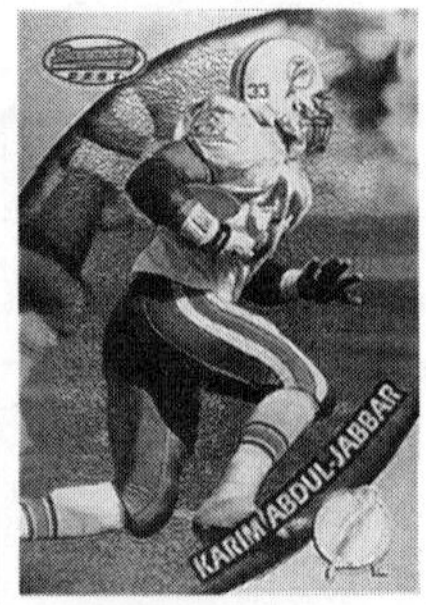

The 15-card set was a sneak peek at the 1997 set. The cards were inserted at a 1:24 rate. The foil cards have a Bowman's Best logo in the up-

per left, with the player's name and team logo in the lower right. The backs, which are numbered with a "BBP" prefix, have the player photo on the left, with his name, bio, stats and highlights on the right. A Refractor parallel version was seeded 1:96 packs, while an Atomic Refractor version was found 1:192 packs.

	MT
Complete Set (15):	110.00
Common Player:	3.00
Refractors:	2x-3x
Atomic Refractors:	3x-6x
1 Dan Marino	20.00
2 Terry Allen	3.00
3 Jerome Bettis	3.00
4 Kevin Greene	3.00
5 Junior Seau	3.00
6 Brett Favre	25.00
7 Isaac Bruce	6.00
8 Michael Irvin	3.00
9 Kerry Collins	6.00
10 Karim Abdul-Jabbar	6.00
11 Keenan McCardell	3.00
12 Ricky Watters	3.00
13 Mark Brunell	12.00
14 Jerry Rice	12.00
15 Drew Bledsoe	12.00

1997 Stadium Club Bowman's Best Rookie Preview

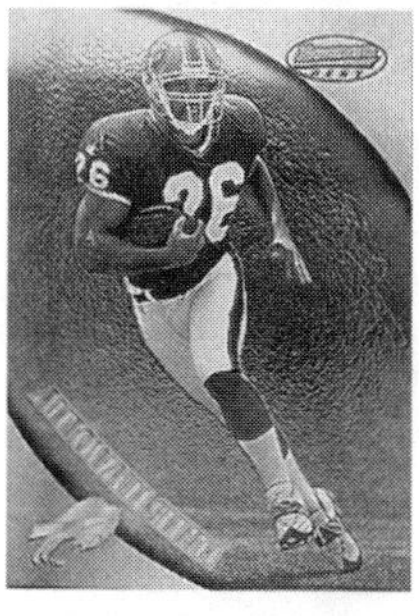

These 15 chromium cards feature top rookies from 1997. The cards were inserted 1:24, with Refractor (1:96) and Atomic Refractor (1:192) versions also available. Cards are numbered with a "BBP" prefix.

	MT
Complete Set (15):	100.00
Common Player:	3.00
Refractors	2x-3x
Atomic Refractors:	3x-6x
1 Orlando Pace	3.00
2 David LaFleur	6.00
3 James Farrior	3.00
4 Tony Gonzalez	6.00
5 Ike Hilliard	6.00
6 Antowain Smith	15.00
7 Tom Knight	3.00
8 Troy Davis	6.00
9 Yatil Green	6.00
10 Jim Druckenmiller	20.00
11 Bryant Westbrook	3.00
12 Darrell Russell	3.00
13 Rae Carruth	10.00
14 Shawn Springs	3.00
15 Peter Boulware	3.00

1997 Stadium Club Co-Signers

Seventy-two NFL players autographed these two-sided cards. There are 108 Co-Signers matchups. Co-Signers were found one per 63 Series I packs and one per 68 Series II packs.

	MT
Common Player (1-36):	75.00
Common Player (37-72):	50.00
Common Player (73-108):	25.00
1 Karim Abdul-Jabbar, Eddie George	400.00
2 Trace Armstrong, Alonzo Spellman	75.00
3 Steve Atwater, Kevin Hardy	75.00
4 Fred Barnett, Lake Dawson	75.00
5 Blaine Bishop, Darrell Green	75.00
6 Jeff Blake, Gus Frerotte	150.00
7 Steve Bono, Cris Carter	125.00
8 Tim Brown, Isaac Bruce	150.00
9 Wayne Chrebet, Mickey Washington	75.00
10 Curtis Conway, Eddie Kennison	150.00
11 Eric Davis, Jason Sehorn	75.00
12 Terrell Davis, Thurman Thomas	180.00
13 Ken Dilger, Kent Graham	75.00
14 Stephen Grant, Marvcus Patton	75.00
15 Keith Hamilton, Mike Tomczak	75.00
16 Rodney Hampton, David Meggett	75.00
17 Merton Hanks, Aeneas Williams	75.00
18 No Card	
19 Brent Jones, Wesley Walls	75.00
20 Carnell Lake, Tim McDonald	75.00
21 Thomas Lewis, Keith Lyle	75.00
22 Leeland McElroy, Jeff Lageman	75.00
23 Ray Mickens, Willie Davis	75.00
24 Herman Moore, Desmond Howard	150.00
25 Stevon Moore, William Thomas	75.00
26 Adrian Murrell, Levon Kirkland	125.00
27 Simeon Rice, Winslow Oliver	75.00
28 Bill Romanowski, Gary Plummer	75.00
29 Junior Seau, Chris Spielman	75.00
30 Chris Slade, Kevin Greene	75.00
31 Derrick Thomas, Chris T. Jones	75.00
32 Orlando Thomas, Bobby Engram	75.00
33 Amani Toomer, Thomas Randolph	75.00
34 Steve Tovar, Ellis Johnson	75.00
35 Herschel Walker, Anthony Johnson	75.00
36 Darren Woodson, Aaron Glenn	75.00
37 Karim Abdul-Jabbar, Thurman Thomas	125.00
38 Blaine Bishop, Tim McDonald	50.00
39 Jeff Blake, Derrick Thomas	80.00
40 No Card	
41 Cris Carter, Marvin Harrison	125.00
42 Curtis Conway, Wesley Walls	50.00
43 Willie Davis, Amani Toomer	50.00
44 Lake Dawson, Ray Mickens	50.00
45 Ken Dilger, Ellis Johnson	50.00
46 Bobby Engram, Thomas Lewis	50.00
47 Gus Frerotte, Chris T. Jones	75.00
48 Eddie George, Terrell Davis	250.00
49 Aaron Glenn, Eric Davis	50.00
50 Kent Graham, Steve Tovar	50.00
51 Darrell Green, Carnell Lake	50.00
52 Kevin Greene, Steve Atwater	50.00
53 Rodney Hampton, Anthony Johnson	50.00
54 Kevin Hardy, Merton Hanks	50.00
55 Desmond Howard, Tim Brown	80.00
56 Eddie Kennison, Brent Jones	100.00
57 Levon Kirkland, Simeon Rice	50.00
58 Jeff Lageman, Adrian Murrell	75.00
59 Keith Lyle, Wayne Chrebet	50.00
60 David Meggett, Herschel Walker	50.00
61 Herman Moore, Isaac Bruce	125.00
62 Winslow Oliver, Leeland McElroy	50.00
63 Marvcus Patton, Keith Hamilton	50.00
64 Gary Plummer, Junior Seau	50.00
65 Thomas Randolph, Fred Barnett	50.00
66 Alonzo Spellman, Stephen Grant	50.00
67 Chris Spielman, Stevon Moore	50.00
68 William Thomas, Bill Romanowski	50.00
69 Mike Tomczak, Trace Armstrong	50.00
70 Mickey Washington, Orlando Thomas	50.00
71 Aeneas Williams, Chris Slade	50.00
72 Darren Woodson, Jason Sehorn	50.00
73 Trace Armstrong, Keith Hamilton	25.00
74 Isaac Bruce, Desmond Howard	75.00
75 Terrell Davis, Karim Abdul-Jabbar	250.00
76 Tim Brown, Herman Moore	100.00
77 Derrick Thomas, Gus Frerotte	40.00
78 Thurman Thomas, Eddie George	150.00
79 Steve Atwater, Chris Slade	25.00
80 Merton Hanks, Kevin Greene	25.00
81 Marvin Harrison, Steve Bono	75.00
82 Anthony Johnson, David Meggett	25.00
83 Stephen Grant, Mike Tomczak	25.00
84 Herschel Walker, Rodney Hampton	25.00
85 Aeneas Williams, Kevin Hardy	25.00
86 Anthony Johnson, David Meggett	25.00
87 Brent Jones, Curtis Conway	25.00
88 Carnell Lake, Blaine Bishop	25.00
89 Tim McDonald, Darrell Green	25.00
90 Trace Armstrong, Keith Hamilton	25.00
91 Winslow Oliver, Levon Kirkland	25.00
92 Simeon Rice, Jeff Lageman	25.00
93 Wesley Walls, Eddie Kennison	40.00
94 Adrian Murrell, Leeland McElroy	40.00
95 Winslow Oliver, Levon Kirkland	25.00
96 Marvcus Patton, Alonzo Spellman	25.00
97 No Card	
98 Ray Mickens, Thomas Randolph	25.00
99 Junior Seau, Bill Romanowski	25.00
100 Marvcus Patton, Alonzo Spellman	25.00
101 Derrick Thomas, Gus Frerotte	40.00
102 Orlando Thomas, Keith Lyle	25.00
103 Thurman Thomas, Eddie George	150.00
104 Wayne Chrebet, Thomas Lewis	25.00
105 Steve Tovar, Ken Dilger	25.00
106 Ellis Johnson, Kent Graham	25.00
107 Wesley Walls, Eddie Kennison	40.00
108 Aeneas Williams, Kevin Hardy	25.00

1997 Stadium Club Grid Kids

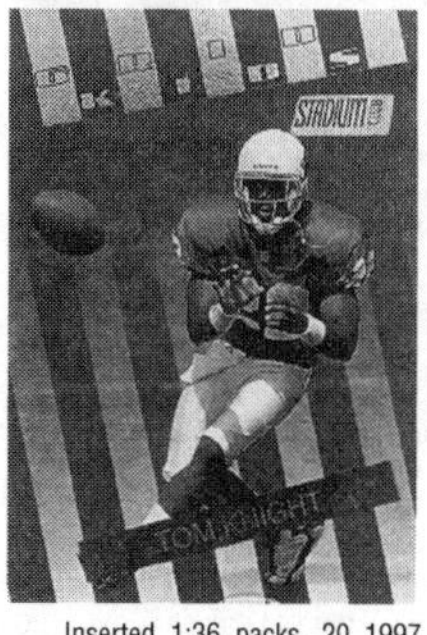

Inserted 1:36 packs, 20 1997 NFL Draft picks are showcased in their game uniforms in the set. The cards are numbered with a "GK" prefix.

	MT
Complete Set (20):	150.00
Common Player:	3.00
Minor Stars:	6.00
1 Orlando Pace	6.00
2 Darrell Russell	3.00
3 Shawn Springs	6.00
4 Peter Boulware	3.00
5 Bryant Westbrook	6.00
6 Darnell Autry	8.00
7 Ike Hilliard	10.00
8 James Farrior	3.00
9 Jake Plummer	18.00
10 Tony Gonzalez	8.00
11 Yatil Green	10.00
12 Corey Dillon	15.00
13 Dwayne Rudd	3.00
14 Renaldo Wynn	3.00
15 David LaFleur	8.00
16 Antowain Smith	12.00
17 Jim Druckenmiller	15.00
18 Rae Carruth	10.00
19 Tom Knight	3.00
20 Byron Hanspard	8.00

1997 Stadium Club Never Compromise

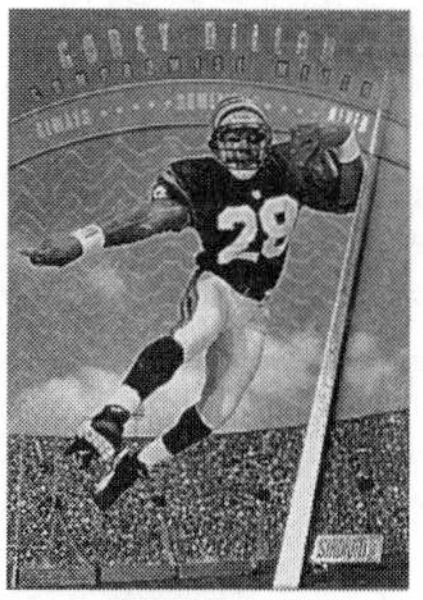

This 40-card insert features 10 veterans and 30 rookies. The cards could be found every 12 packs. They are numbered with a "NC" prefix.

	MT
Complete Set (40):	225.00
Common Player:	1.50
Minor Stars:	3.00
1 Orlando Pace	3.00
2 Corey Dillon	15.00
3 Tony Gonzalez	3.00
4 Tom Knight	1.50
5 Deion Sanders	10.00
6 Dwayne Rudd	1.50
7 Warrick Dunn	25.00
8 Kenny Holmes	1.50
9 Will Blackwell	1.50
10 Shawn Springs	1.50
11 Rae Carruth	8.00
12 Edgar Bennett	1.50
13 Walter Jones	1.50
14 Reidel Anthony	8.00
15 Troy Davis	3.00
16 Mark Brunell	15.00
17 Pat Barnes	6.00
18 Reggie White	3.00
19 Darrell Russell	1.50
20 Ike Hilliard	3.00
21 Emmitt Smith	30.00
22 David LaFleur	6.00
23 Yatil Green	3.00
24 Barry Sanders	20.00
25 Bryant Westbrook	1.50
26 Lawrence Phillips	1.50
27 Peter Boulware	1.50
28 Joey Kent	3.00
29 Kevin Lockett	1.50
30 Derrick Thomas	1.50
31 Antowain Smith	15.00
32 James Farrior	1.50
33 Kordell Stewart	15.00
34 Byron Hanspard	6.00
35 Jim Druckenmiller	15.00
36 Reinard Wilson	1.50
37 Darnell Autry	6.00
38 Steve Young	10.00
39 Renaldo Wynn	1.50
40 Jake Plummer	15.00

1997 Stadium Club Offensive Strikes

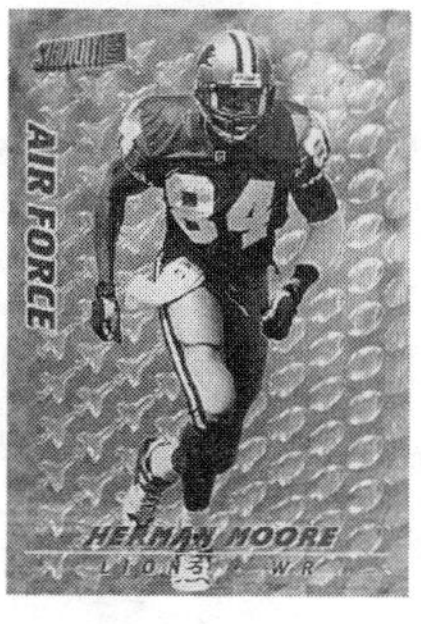

Inserted 1:12 packs, the top five running backs and wide receivers from 1996 are featured in this set. The cards are borderless foilboard.

	MT
Complete Set (10):	45.00
Common Player:	1.50
AF1 Jerry Rice (Air Force)	5.00
AF2 Carl Pickens (Air Force)	1.50
AF3 Shannon Sharpe (Air Force)	1.50
AF4 Herman Moore (Air Force)	1.50
AF5 Terry Glenn (Air Force)	3.00
GC1 Barry Sanders (Ground Control)	8.00
GC2 Curtis Martin (Ground Control)	5.00
GC3 Emmitt Smith (Ground Control)	10.00
GC4 Terrell Davis (Ground Control)	5.00
GC5 Eddie George (Ground Control)	8.00

1997 Stadium Club Triumvirate

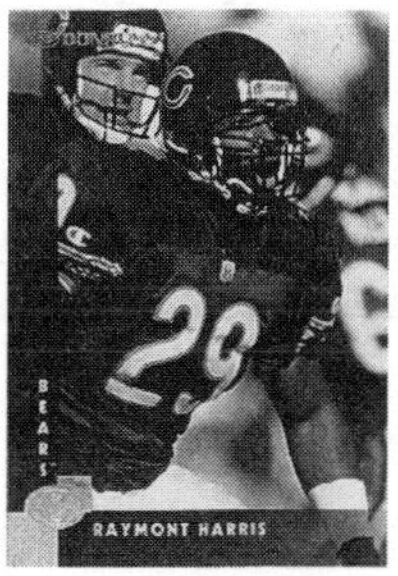

Exclusive to retail packs, the laser-cut cards featured a trio of leading NFL offensive teammates fused together. There are six different complete cards made up of three players per, each player card is seeded at a 1:36 pack ratio. Refractor versions were found 1:96, while Atomic Refractor versions were seeded 1:192.

	MT
Complete Set (18):	200.00
Common Player:	5.00
Refractors:	2x-4x
Atomic Refractors:	3x-6x
T1A Emmitt Smith	30.00
T1B Troy Aikman	15.00
T1C Michael Irvin	5.00
T2A Curtis Martin	15.00
T2B Drew Bledsoe	15.00
T2C Terry Glenn	7.00
T3A Barry Sanders	20.00
T3B Scott Mitchell	5.00
T3C Herman Moore	5.00
T4A William Floyd	5.00
T4B Steve Young	10.00
T4C Jerry Rice	15.00
T5A Terrell Davis	15.00
T5B John Elway	10.00
T5C Shannon Sharpe	5.00
T6A Edgar Bennett	5.00
T6B Brett Favre	30.00
T6C Antonio Freeman	8.00

1997 Stadium Club Triumvirate II

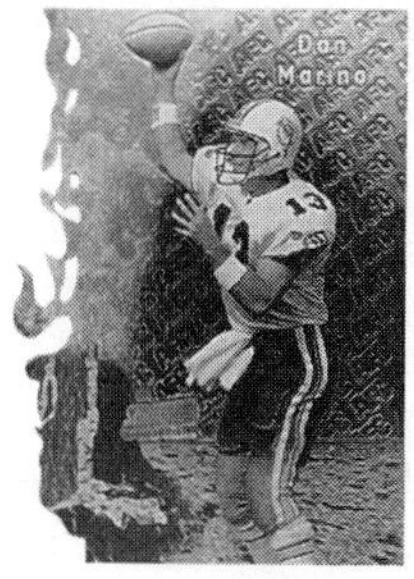

This 18-card, laser-cut insert consists of six trios of players, whose cards can be fit together. Triumvirate was seeded 1:36, with Refractor (1:144) and Atomic Refractor (1:288) also created.

	MT
Complete Set (18):	200.00
Common Player:	5.00
Refractors:	2x-3x
Atomic Refractors: 3x-6x	
T1A John Elway	10.00
T1B Drew Bledsoe	15.00
T1C Dan Marino	25.00
T2A Troy Aikman	15.00
T2B Brett Favre	30.00
T2C Steve Young	10.00
T3A Terrell Davis	15.00
T3B Eddie George	20.00
T3C Curtis Martin	15.00
T4A Emmitt Smith	25.00
T4B Ricky Watters	5.00
T4C Barry Sanders	20.00
T5A Shannon Sharpe	5.00
T5B Terry Glenn	5.00
T5C Carl Pickens	5.00
T6A Jake Plummer	10.00
T6B Orlando Pace	5.00
T6C Jim Druckenmiller	15.00

1998 Stadium Club

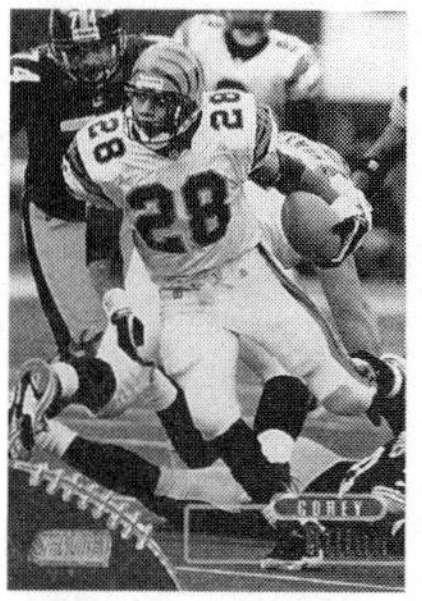

Stadium Club was issued in a single-series, 195-card set in 1998, with a 30-card Star Rookies subset seeded one per two packs (1:1 jumbo pack). Cards featured a borderless design with embossed, holographic foil on 20-point stock. Stadium Club was paralleled in three different sets, with each exclusive to specific packs: First Day Issue (retail), One of a Kind (hobby) and Printing Plates (Home Team Advantage). Inserts include: Chrome, Chrome Refractors, Co-Signers (hobby), Double Threat, Leading Legends (retail), Prime Rookies, Triumvirates (hobby) and SuperChrome Oversized cards.

	MT
Complete Set (195):	85.00
Common Player:	.15
Minor Stars:	.30
Common Rookie (166-195):	1.50
Inserted 1:2	
One Of A Kind Cards:	30x-60x
One Of A Kind Rookies:	3x-6x
Inserted 1:32 Hobby	
Production 150 Sets	
First Day Issue Cards:	20x-40x
First Day Issue Rookies:	2x-4x
Inserted 1:47 Retail	
Production 200 Sets	
Pack (9):	3.00
Wax Box (24):	60.00
1 Barry Sanders	3.00
2 Tony Martin	.15
3 Fred Lane	.30
4 Darren Woodson	.15
5 Andre Reed	.30
6 Blaine Bishop	.15
7 Robert Brooks	.30
8 Tony Banks	.30
9 Charles Way	.15
10 Mark Brunell	1.25
11 Darrell Green	.15
12 Aeneas Williams	.15
13 Rob Johnson	.30
14 Deion Sanders	.50
15 Marshall Faulk	.30
16 Stephen Boyd	.15
17 Adrian Murrell	.30
18 Wayne Chrebet	.15
19 Michael Sinclair	.15
20 Dan Marino	2.00
21 Willie Davis	.15
22 Chris Warren	.30
23 John Mobley	.15
24 Shannon Sharpe	.30
25 Thurman Thomas	.30
26 Corey Dillon	1.00
27 Zach Thomas	.30
28 James Jett	.15
29 Eric Metcalf	.15
30 Drew Bledsoe	1.25
31 Scott Greene	.15
32 Simeon Rice	.15
33 Robert Smith	.30
34 Keenan McCardell	.15
35 Jessie Armstead	.15
36 Jerry Rice	1.50
37 Eric Green	.15
38 Terrell Owens	.50
39 Tim Brown	.30
40 Vinny Testaverde	.15
41 Brian Stablein	.15
42 Bert Emanuel	.15
43 Terry Glenn	.30
44 Chad Cota	.15
45 Jermaine Lewis	.15
46 Derrick Thomas	.15
47 O.J. McDuffie	.15
48 Frank Wycheck	.15
49 Steve Broussard	.15
50 Terrell Davis	2.00
51 Napoleon Kaufman	.50
52 Dan Wilkinson	.15
53 Kerry Collins	.30
54 Frank Sanders	.15
55 Jeff Burris	.15
56 Michael Westbrook	.15
57 Michael McCrary	.15
58 Bobby Hoying	.15
59 Jerome Bettis	.30
60 Amp Lee	.15
61 Levon Kirkland	.15
62 Dana Stubblefield	.15
63 Terance Mathis	.15
64 Mark Chmura	.30
65 Bryant Westbrook	.15
66 Rod Smith	.30
67 Derrick Alexander	.15
68 Jason Taylor	.15
69 Eddie George	1.25
70 Elvis Grbac	.15
71 Junior Seau	.30
72 Marvin Harrison	.30
73 Neil O'Donnell	.15
74 Johnnie Morton	.15
75 John Randle	.15
76 Danny Kanell	.15
77 Charlie Garner	.15
78 J.J. Stokes	.30
79 Troy Aikman	1.50
80 Gus Frerotte	.15
81 Jake Plummer	1.25
82 Andre Hastings	.15
83 Steve Atwater	.15
84 Larry Centers	.15
85 Kevin Hardy	.15
86 Willie McGinest	.15
87 Joey Galloway	.30
88 Charles Johnson	.15
89 Warrick Dunn	1.25
90 Derrick Rodgers	.15
91 Aaron Glenn	.15
92 Shawn Jefferson	.15
93 Antonio Freeman	.30
94 Jake Reed	.15
95 Reidel Anthony	.30
96 Cris Dishman	.15
97 Jason Sehorn	.15
98 Herman Moore	.30
99 John Elway	1.50
100 Brad Johnson	.30
101 Jeff George	.30
102 Emmitt Smith	2.00
103 Steve McNair	.75
104 Ed McCaffrey	.15
105 Errict Rhett	.15
106 Dorsey Levens	.30
107 Michael Jackson	.15
108 Carl Pickens	.15
109 James Stewart	.30
110 Karim Abdul-Jabbar	.30
111 Jim Harbaugh	.15
112 Yancey Thigpen	.15
113 Chad Brown	.15
114 Chris Sanders	.15
115 Cris Carter	.30
116 Glenn Foley	.30
117 Ben Coates	.15
118 Jamal Anderson	.30
119 Steve Young	.75
120 Scott Mitchell	.15
121 Rob Moore	.15
122 Bobby Engram	.15
123 Rod Woodson	.15
124 Terry Allen	.15
125 Warren Sapp	.15
126 Irving Fryar	.15
127 Isaac Bruce	.30
128 Rae Carruth	.15
129 Sean Dawkins	.15
130 Andre Rison	.15
131 Kevin Greene	.15
132 Warren Moon	.30
133 Keyshawn Johnson	.30
134 Jay Graham	.15
135 Mike Alstott	.50
136 Peter Boulware	.15
137 Doug Evans	.15
138 Jimmy Smith	.30
139 Kordell Stewart	1.25
140 Tamarick Vanover	.15
141 Chris Slade	.15
142 Freddie Jones	.15
143 Erik Kramer	.15
144 Ricky Watters	.30
145 Chris Chandler	.15
146 Garrison Hearst	.30
147 Trent Dilfer	.30
148 Bruce Smith	.15
149 Brett Favre	3.00
150 Will Blackwell	.15
151 Rickey Dudley	.15
152 Natrone Means	.30
153 Curtis Conway	.30
154 Tony Gonzalez	.15
155 Jeff Blake	.30
156 Michael Irvin	.30
157 Curtis Martin	.75
158 Tim McDonald	.15
159 Wesley Walls	.15
160 Michael Strahan	.15
161 Reggie White	.30
162 Jeff Graham	.15
163 Ray Lewis	.15
164 Antowain Smith	.75

166	*Ryan Leaf*	6.00
167	*Jerome Pathon*	1.50
168	*Duane Starks*	1.50
169	*Brian Simmons*	1.50
170	*Patrick Johnson*	1.50
171	*Keith Brooking*	1.50
172	*Kevin Dyson*	4.00
173	*Robert Edwards*	6.00
174	*Grant Wistrom*	1.50
175	*Curtis Enis*	5.00
176	*John Avery*	4.00
177	*Jason Peter*	1.50
178	*Brian Griese*	8.00
179	*Tavian Banks*	4.00
180	*Andre Wadsworth*	2.50
181	*Skip Hicks*	4.00
182	*Hines Ward*	4.00
183	*Greg Ellis*	2.00
184	*Robert Holcombe*	4.00
185	*Joe Jurevicius*	2.00
186	*Takeo Spikes*	2.00
187	*Ahman Green*	8.00
188	*Jacquez Green*	4.00
189	*Randy Moss*	25.00
190	*Charles Woodson*	5.00
191	*Fred Taylor*	10.00
192	*Marcus Nash*	2.00
193	*Germane Crowell*	5.00
194	*Tim Dwight*	4.00
195	*Peyton Manning*	25.00

1998 Stadium Club First Day Issue

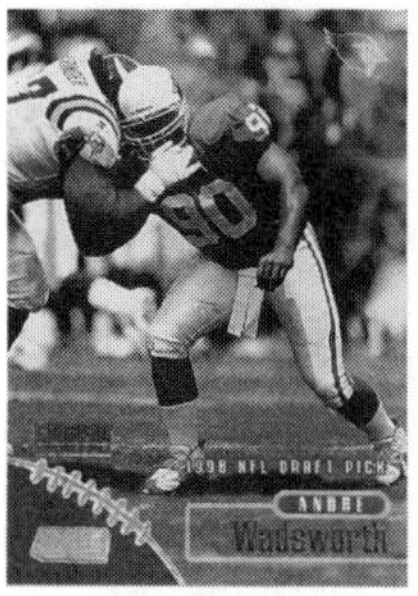

First Day Issue cards paralleled the 195-card regular-issue set, but are distinguished by a gold foil "First Day Issue" stamp on the front. These parallels were exclusive to retail packs, are numbered to 200 in gold foil on the back and inserted one per 47 packs.

	MT
First Day Issue Cards:	20x-40x
First Day Issue Rookies:	2x-4x

1998 Stadium Club One of a Kind

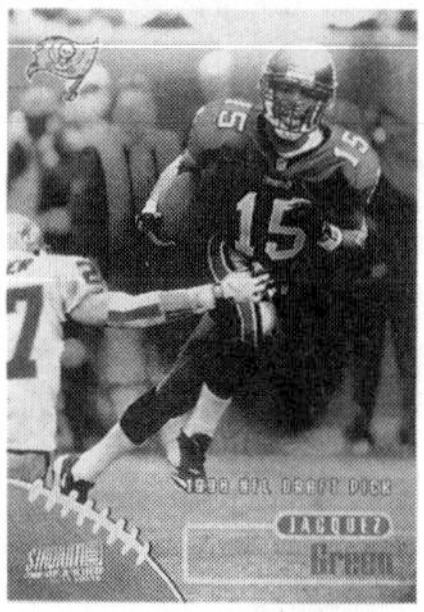

One of a Kind cards paralleled the 195-card base set in Stadium Club, but added a darkened, foil finish the the front, with the insert name below the Stadium Club logo in the lower left corner. These parallel cards were exclusive to hobby packs, numbered on the back to 150 in gold foil and inserted one per 32 packs.

	MT
One of a Kind Cards:	30x-60x
One of a Kind Rookies:	3x-6x

1998 Stadium Club Chrome

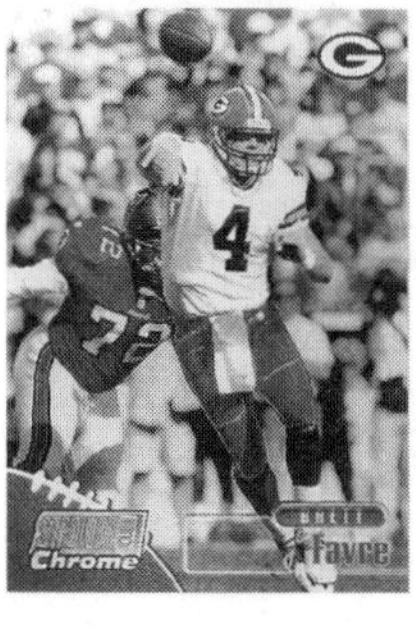

This 20-card insert was seeded one per 12 packs of Stadium Club. Cards previewed the upcoming Chrome set, however with a different design. While normal Chrome cards were patterned after Topps cards, these inserts were chromium versions of the Stadium Club base cards. Chrome inserts were numbered with a "SCC" prefix and also had Refractor versions seeded one per 48 packs.

		MT
Complete Set (20):		100.00
Common Player:		2.00
Minor Stars:		4.00
Inserted 1:12		
Refractors:		2x
Inserted 1:48		
1	John Elway	6.00
2	Mark Brunell	6.00
3	Jerome Bettis	4.00
4	Steve Young	5.00
5	Herman Moore	4.00
6	Emmitt Smith	10.00
7	Warrick Dunn	6.00
8	Dan Marino	10.00
9	Kordell Stewart	8.00
10	Barry Sanders	15.00
11	Tim Brown	2.00
12	Dorsey Levens	4.00
13	Eddie George	6.00
14	Jerry Rice	8.00
15	Terrell Davis	8.00
16	Napoleon Kaufman	5.00
17	Troy Aikman	8.00
18	Drew Bledsoe	8.00
19	Antonio Freeman	4.00
20	Brett Favre	15.00

1998 Stadium Club Co-Signers

This 12-card hobby exclusive insert featured eight total players with both autographs on the same side of the card. Each arrived with a gold foil Topps "Certified Autograph Issue" stamp. Cards 1-4 were inserted 1:9,400 hobby and 1:5,640 jumbos, 5-8 were inserted 1:3,133 hobby and 1:1,880 jumbos and 9-12 were inserted one per 261 hobby and 1:141 jumbo packs. Co-Signers were numbered with a "CO" prefix.

		MT
Complete Set (12):		3000.
Common Player:		50.00
CO1	Peyton Manning, Ryan Leaf	550.00
CO2	Dan Marino, Kordell Stewart	550.00
CO3	Eddie George, Corey Dillon	250.00
CO4	Dorsey Levens, Mike Alstott	225.00
CO5	Ryan Leaf, Dan Marino	400.00
CO6	Peyton Manning, Kordell Stewart	350.00
CO7	Eddie George, Mike Alstott	150.00
CO8	Dorsey Levens, Corey Dillon	125.00
CO9	Peyton Manning, Dan Marino	200.00
CO10	Ryan Leaf, Kordell Stewart	100.00
CO11	Eddie George, Dorsey Levens	70.00
CO12	Mike Alstott, Corey Dillon	50.00

1998 Stadium Club Double Threat

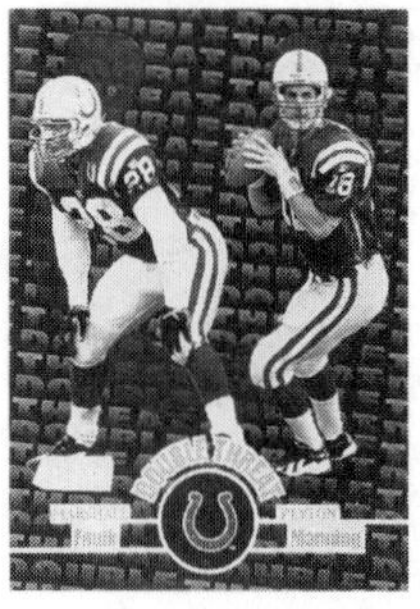

This 10-card insert features two top tandems from 10 different NFL teams. Each player takes up half the card and contains the insert name printed repeatedly across the background along with the team logo. Double Threat inserts are seeded one per eight packs and are numbered with a "DT" prefix.

		MT
Complete Set (10):		50.00
Common Player:		1.50
Inserted 1:8		
1	Marshall Faulk, Peyton Manning	15.00
2	Curtis Conway, Curtis Enis	6.00
3	Drew Bledsoe, Robert Edwards	7.00
4	Warrick Dunn, Jacquez Green	6.00
5	John Elway, Marcus Nash	7.00
6	Mark Brunell, Fred Taylor	8.00
7	Eddie George, Kevin Dyson	6.00
8	Michael Jackson, Patrick Johnson	1.50
9	Terry Glenn, Tony Simmons	1.50
10	Natrone Means, Ryan Leaf	7.00

1998 Stadium Club Leading Legends

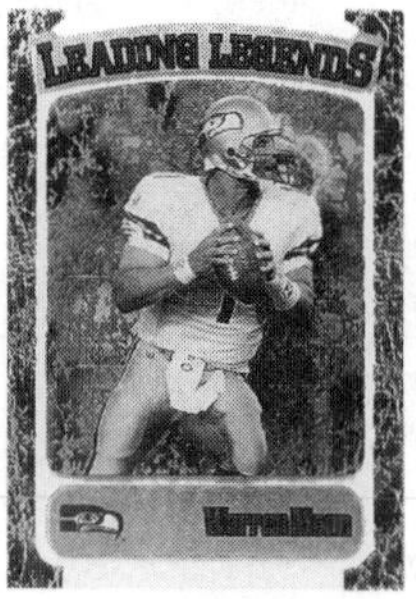

Leading Legends was a retail-exclusive insert that displayed the NFL's current record-holders among quarterbacks, wide receivers and running backs. The cards are printed on plastic with a gold foil background and card back. These were inserted one per 12 packs and unnumbered.

		MT
Complete Set (10):		40.00
Common Player:		2.00
Inserted 1:12 Retail		
1	Jerry Rice	5.00
2	Bruce Smith	2.00
3	Reggie White	3.00
4	Warren Moon	2.00
5	Dan Marino	7.00
6	John Elway	5.00
7	Emmitt Smith	7.00
8	Brett Favre	10.00
9	Steve Young	4.00
10	Barry Sanders	10.00

1998 Stadium Club Prime Rookies

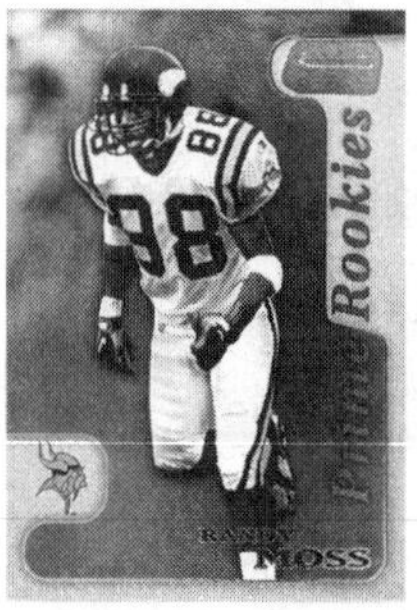

This 10-card insert displayed the top draft picks in 1998 on a silver foil finish, with the insert name running up the right side. Prime Rookies were inserted one per eight packs and numbered with a "PR" prefix.

		MT
Complete Set (10):		50.00
Common Player:		1.50
Inserted 1:8		
1	Ryan Leaf	6.00
2	Andre Wadsworth	3.00
3	Fred Taylor	8.00
4	Kevin Dyson	4.00
5	Charles Woodson	6.00
6	Robert Edwards	5.00
7	Grant Wistrom	1.50
8	Curtis Enis	6.00
9	Randy Moss	20.00
10	Peyton Manning	15.00

1998 Stadium Club Super Chrome

SuperChrome featured 3-1/4" x 4-9/16" versions of the 20-card Chrome insert. These were inserted one per hobby box, with Refractor versions every 12 Home Team Advantage/ Hobby Collector Pack boxes.

		MT
Complete Set (20):		100.00
Common Player:		2.00
Minor Stars:		4.00
Refractors:		2x
1	John Elway	6.00
2	Mark Brunell	6.00
3	Jerome Bettis	4.00
4	Steve Young	5.00
5	Herman Moore	4.00
6	Emmitt Smith	10.00
7	Warrick Dunn	6.00
8	Dan Marino	10.00
9	Kordell Stewart	8.00
10	Barry Sanders	15.00
11	Tim Brown	2.00
12	Dorsey Levens	4.00
13	Eddie George	6.00
14	Jerry Rice	8.00
15	Terrell Davis	8.00
16	Napoleon Kaufman	5.00
17	Troy Aikman	8.00
18	Drew Bledsoe	8.00
19	Antonio Freeman	4.00
20	Brett Favre	15.00

1998 Stadium Club Triumvirate Luminous

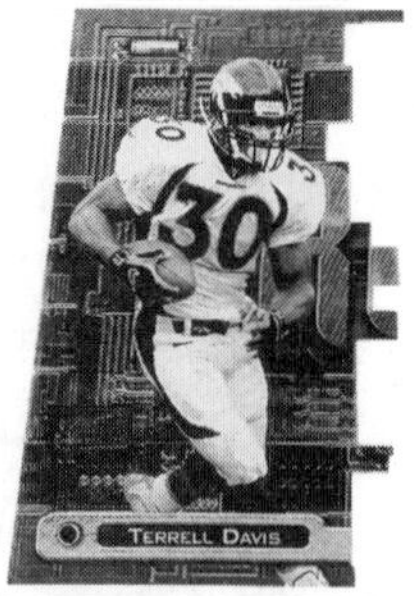

Triumvirate was a 15-card, hobby-only insert in 1998. It featured three teammates on die-cut, fit-together cards numbered with a "T" prefix and either an A, B or C suffix. Regular, Luminous versions were seeded one per 24 packs, Luminescent versions were one per 96 and Illuminators were one per 192 packs.

		MT
Complete Set (15):		100.00
Common Player:		3.00
Minor Stars:		6.00
Inserted 1:24 Hobby		
Luminescent Cards:		2x
Inserted 1:96 Hobby		
Illuminator Cards:		5x
Inserted 1:192 Hobby		
T1A	Terrell Davis	10.00
T1B	John Elway	10.00
T1C	Shannon Sharpe	3.00
T2A	Barry Sanders	20.00
T2B	Scott Mitchell	3.00
T2C	Herman Moore	6.00
T3A	Dorsey Levens	6.00
T3B	Brett Favre	20.00
T3C	Antonio Freeman	6.00
T4A	Emmitt Smith	15.00
T4B	Troy Aikman	10.00
T4C	Michael Irvin	6.00
T5A	Napoleon Kaufman	6.00
T5B	Jeff George	3.00
T5C	Tim Brown	3.00

1999 Stadium Club

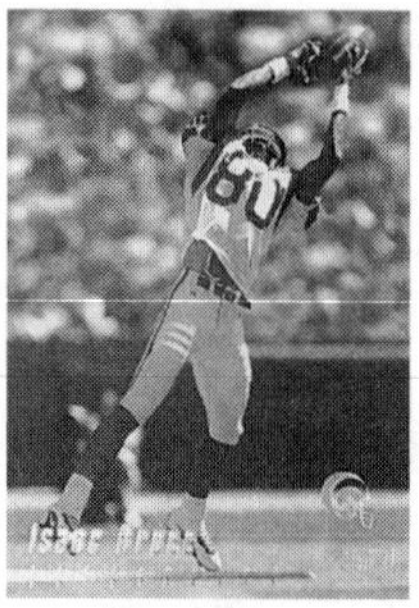

This was a 200-card set that included two subsets consisting of 25 Transactions and 25 Draft Picks found 1:3 packs. Each card was embossed and printed full-bleed on 20-point stock with a holographic foil logo. Two parallel sets were issued: First Day and One of a Kind. Other inserts included: Chrome Previews, Co-Signers, Emperors of the Zone, Lone Star Autographs, 3x3 Luminous and Never Compromise. SRP was $2.00 for six-card packs.

		MT
Complete Set (200):		85.00
Common Player:		.15
Minor Stars:		.30
Common Rookie:		1.00
Inserted 1:3		
Pack (6):		2.50
Wax Box (24):		50.00
1	Dan Marino	2.00
2	Andre Reed	.15
3	Michael Westbrook	.30
4	Isaac Bruce	.50
5	Curtis Martin	.50
6	Courtney Hawkins	.15
7	Charles Way	.15
8	Terrell Owens	.50
9	Warrick Dunn	.50
10	Jake Plummer	1.50
11	Chad Brown	.15
12	Yancey Thigpen	.30
13	Lamar Thomas	.15
14	Keenan McCardell	.30
15	Shannon Sharpe	.30
16	Robert Brooks	.30
17	Cameron Cleeland	.30
18	Derrick Thomas	.15
19	Mark Brunell	1.00
20	Jamal Anderson	.50
21	Germane Crowell	.30
22	Rod Smith	.30
23	Ty Law	.15
24	Cris Carter	.50
25	Terrell Davis	2.00
26	Takeo Spikes	.15
27	Tim Biakabutuka	.15
28	Jermaine Lewis	.30
29	Adrian Murrell	.30
30	Doug Flutie	.75
31	Curtis Enis	.50
32	Skip Hicks	.30
33	Steve McNair	.75
34	Charles Woodson	.50
35	Jessie Armstead	.15
36	Shawn Springs	.15
37	Levon Kirkland	.15
38	Freddie Jones	.30
39	Warren Sapp	.15
40	Emmitt Smith	2.00
41	Reidel Anthony	.30
42	Tony Simmons	.30
43	Andre Hastings	.15
44	Byron Morris	.15
45	Jimmy Smith	.30
46	Antonio Freeman	.50
47	Herman Moore	.50
48	Muhsin Muhammed	.30
49	Chris Chandler	.30
50	John Elway	2.00
51	Aeneas Williams	.15
52	Bobby Engram	.15
53	Billy Davis	.15
54	Zach Thomas	.30
55	Mike Alstott	.50
56	Junior Seau	.30
57	Aaron Glenn	.15
58	Darrell Green	.15
59	Thurman Thomas	.30
60	Troy Aikman	1.50
61	Bill Romanowski	.15
62	Wesley Walls	.15
63	Andre Wadsworth	.15
64	Robert Smith	.50
65	Elvis Grbac	.30
66	Terry Fair	.15
67	Ben Coates	.30
68	Bert Emanuel	.15
69	Jacquez Green	.30
70	Barry Sanders	3.00
71	James Jett	.15
72	Gary Brown	.15
73	Stephen Alexander	.15
74	Wayne Chrebet	.50
75	Drew Bledsoe	1.00
76	John Lynch	.15
77	Jake Reed	.30
78	Marvin Harrison	.50
79	Johnnie Morton	.15
80	Brett Favre	3.00
81	Charlie Batch	1.00
82	Antowain Smith	.50
83	O.J. Santiago	.15
84	Larry Centers	.15
85	John Mobley	.15
86	Ernie Mills	.15
87	Jeff Blake	.30
88	Curtis Conway	.30
89	Bruce Smith	.15
90	Peyton Manning	2.00
91	Ray Lewis	.15
92	Ray Buchanan	.15
93	Tim Dwight	.50
94	O.J. McDuffie	.30
95	Vonnie Holliday	.30
96	Jon Kitna	.75
97	Trent Dilfer	.30
98	Jerome Bettis	.50
99	Dedric Ward	.15
100	Fred Taylor	1.50
101	Ike Hilliard	.15
102	Frank Wycheck	.15
103	Eric Moulds	.50
104	Rob Moore	.30
105	Ed McCaffrey	.50
106	Carl Pickens	.30
107	Priest Holmes	.50
108	Kevin Hardy	.15
109	Terry Glenn	.50
110	Keyshawn Johnson	.50
111	Karim Abdul	.30
112	Stephen Boyd	.15
113	Ahman Green	.30
114	Duce Staley	.50
115	Vinny Testaverde	.30
116	Napoleon Kaufman	.50
117	Frank Sanders	.15
118	Peter Boulware	.15
119	Kevin Greene	.15
120	Steve Young	.75
121	Darnay Scott	.30
122	Deion Sanders	.50
123	Corey Dillon	.50
124	Randall Cunningham	.50
125	Eddie George	.75
126	Derrick Alexander	.15
127	Mark Chmura	.30
128	Michael Sinclair	.15
129	Rickey Dudley	.30
130	Joey Galloway	.50
131	Michael Strahan	.15
132	Ricky Proehl	.15
133	Natrone Means	.30
134	Dorsey Levens	.50
135	Andre Rison	.30
136	John Avery	.30
137	John Randle	.15
138	Terance Mathis	.15
139	Erik Kramer	.15
140	Jerry Rice	1.50
141	Michael Irvin	.30
142	Oronde Gadsden	.30
143	Jerome Pathon	.15
144	Ricky Watters	.50
145	J.J. Stokes	.30
146	Kordell Stewart	.75
147	Tim Brown	.30
148	Garrison Hearst	.50
149	Tony Gonzalez	.30
150	Randy Moss	3.00
151	*Daunte Culpepper*	10.00
152	*Amos Zereoue*	4.00
153	*Champ Bailey*	3.00
154	*Peerless Price*	4.00
155	*Edgerrin James*	20.00
156	*Joe Germaine*	3.00
157	*David Boston*	5.00
158	*Kevin Faulk*	4.00
159	*Troy Edwards*	5.00
160	*Akili Smith*	8.00
161	*Kevin Johnson*	5.00
162	*Rob Konrad*	3.00
163	*Shaun King*	6.00
164	*James Johnson*	4.00
165	*Donovan McNabb*	8.00
166	*Torry Holt*	5.00
167	*Michael Cloud*	2.00
168	*Sedrick Irvin*	3.00
169	*Cade McNown*	5.00
170	*Ricky Williams*	15.00
171	*Karsten Bailey*	1.00
172	*Cecil Collins*	8.00
173	*Brock Huard*	3.00
174	*D'Wayne Bates*	2.00
175	*Tim Couch*	15.00
176	Transactions (Torrance Small)	.15
177	Transactions (Warren Moon)	.30
178	Transactions (Raghib Ismail)	.15
179	Transactions (Marshall Faulk)	.50
180	Transactions (Trent Green)	.50
181	Transactions (Sean Dawkins)	.15
182	Transactions (Pete Mitchell)	.15
183	Transactions (Jeff Graham)	.15
184	Transactions (Eddie Kennison)	.15
185	Transactions (Kerry Collins)	.30
186	Transactions (Eric Green)	.15
187	Transactions (Kyle Brady)	.15
188	Transactions (Tony Martin)	.15
189	Transactions (Jim Harbaugh)	.30
190	Transactions (Carnell Lake)	.15
191	Transactions (Steve Atwater)	.15
192	Transactions (Dale Carter)	.15
193	Transactions (Charles Johnson)	.15
194	Transactions (Tony Banks)	.15
195	Transactions (Jeff George)	.30
196	Transactions (Scott Mitchell)	.15
197	Transactions (Chris Calloway)	.15
198	Transactions (Rich Gannon)	.15
199	Transactions (Leslie Shepherd)	.15
200	Transactions (Brad Johnson)	.50

1999 Stadium Club First Day Issue Parallel

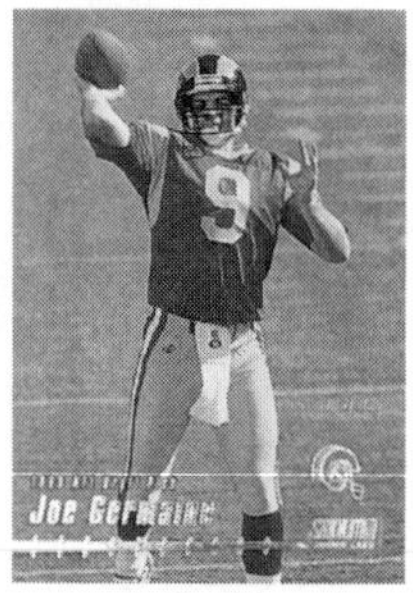

This 200-card insert set was a parallel to the base set and was a retail exclusive. Each single had the "First Day Issue" foil stamp on the fronts. Singles were sequentially numbered to 150 and found 1:38 packs.

	MT
First Day Cards:	10x-20x
First Day Rookies:	2x-4x
Production 150 Sets	
Inserted 1:38 Retail	

1999 Stadium Club One of a Kind Parallel

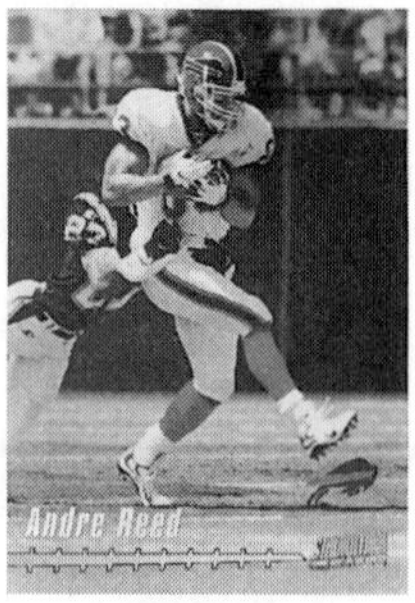

This was a 200-card insert set that was a hobby exclusive and paralleled the base set. Singles were sequentially numbered to 150 and inserted 1:48 packs.

	MT
One of a Kind Cards:	10x-20x
One of a Kind Rookies:	2x-4x
Production 150 Sets	
Inserted 1:48 Hobby	

A player's name in *italic type* indicates a rookie card.

1999 Stadium Club Chrome Preview

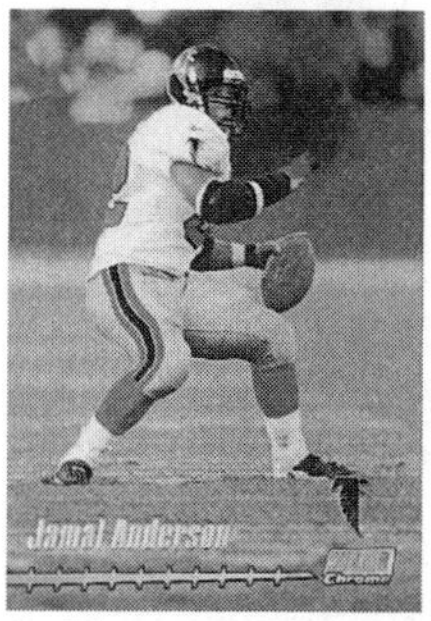

This was a 20-card insert set that included the hottest players from the Stadium Club set and pictured them with chromium stock. Singles were inserted 1:24 packs. A parallel Refractor version was made and inserted 1:96 packs. A Jumbo version was issued and found one-per-box and a Jumbo Refractor version was issued one every twelve boxes.

		MT
Complete Set (20):		100.00
Common Player:		3.00
Inserted 1:24		
Refractors:		2x
Inserted 1:96		
Jumbos:		1x
Inserted 1:box		
Jumbo Refractors:		3x
Inserted 1:12 boxes		
1	Randy Moss	12.00
2	Terrell Davis	8.00
3	Peyton Manning	8.00
4	Fred Taylor	6.00
5	John Elway	8.00
6	Steve Young	4.00
7	Brett Favre	12.00
8	Jamal Anderson	3.00
9	Barry Sanders	12.00
10	Dan Marino	8.00
11	Jerry Rice	6.00
12	Emmitt Smith	8.00
13	Randall Cunningham	3.00
14	Troy Aikman	6.00
15	Akili Smith	6.00
16	Donovan McNabb	6.00
17	Edgerrin James	12.00
18	Torry Holt	4.00
19	Ricky Williams	12.00
20	Tim Couch	12.00

1999 Stadium Club Co-Signers

This six-card insert set was a hobby exclusive and showcased six different double-autographed cards. Both players and their autographs were pictured on the same side of the card. Each single included the gold foil Topps "Certified Autograph Issue" stamp. Cards #1 and #2 were inserted 1:2,854 packs and cards #3-#6 were issued 1:1,189.

		MT
Complete Set (6):		1500.
Common Player:		150.00
Inserted 1:2,854 (1-3)		
Inserted 1:1,189 (4-6)		
1	Ricky Williams, Terrell Davis	325.00
2	Edgerrin James, Terrell Davis	325.00
3	Tim Couch, Dan Marino	325.00
4	Tim Couch, Peyton Manning	300.00
5	Randy Moss, Jerry Rice	300.00
6	Vinny Testaverde, Dan Marino	150.00

1999 Stadium Club Emperors of the Zone

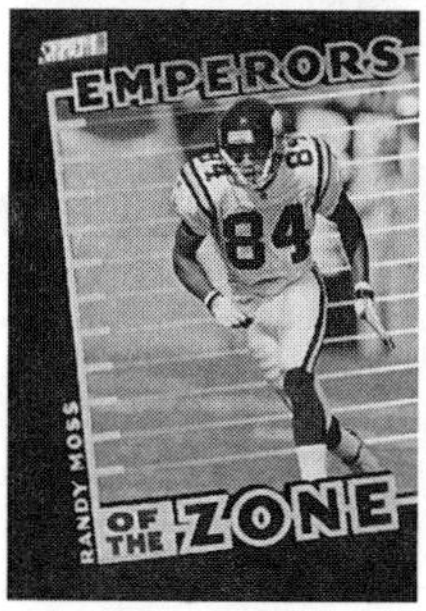

This 10-card insert set included the best touchdown producers in the NFL. Each was featured on a solid black styrene card with silver foil. Singles were inserted 1:12 packs.

		MT
Complete Set (10):		30.00
Common Player:		1.00
Inserted 1:12		
1	Ricky Williams	6.00
2	Brett Favre	6.00
3	Donovan McNabb	3.00
4	Peyton Manning	4.00
5	Terrell Davis	4.00
6	Jamal Anderson	1.00
7	Edgerrin James	6.00
8	Fred Taylor	4.00
9	Tim Couch	6.00
10	Randy Moss	6.00

1999 Stadium Club Lone Star Autographs

This 11-card insert set included autographs from some of the top players in the NFL. Each single included the Topps "Certified Autograph Issue" stamp. Singles were found 1:697 packs.

		MT
Complete Set (11):		1000.
Common Player:		30.00
Inserted 1:697		
1	Randy Moss	200.00
2	Jerry Rice	150.00
3	Peyton Manning	175.00
4	Vinny Testaverde	30.00
5	Tim Couch	200.00
6	Dan Marino	175.00
7	Edgerrin James	200.00
8	Fred Taylor	100.00
9	Garrison Hearst	30.00
10	Antonio Freeman	50.00
11	Torry Holt	75.00

1999 Stadium Club 3 X 3 Luminous

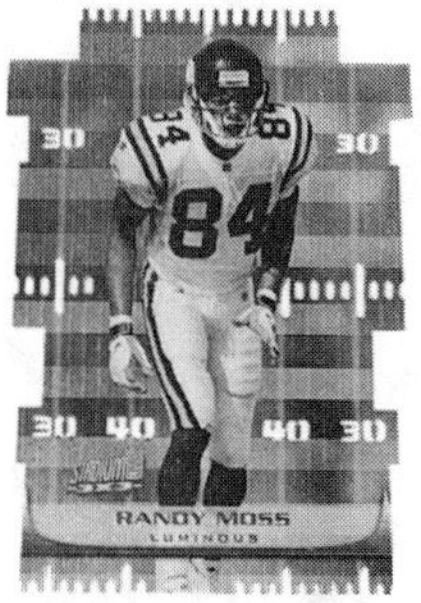

This 15-card insert set featured three stars on three different technologies, Luminous, Luminescent and Illuminator, with each combination arranged by position and conference. Each single is featured on a laser-cut design where the collector could fuse three players together to form one oversized card. Luminous singles were found 1:36 packs. The Luminescent parallel singles were found 1:144 packs and the Illuminator cards were inserted 1:288 packs.

		MT
Complete Set (15):		85.00
Common Player:		3.00
Inserted 1:36		
Luminescent Cards:		3x
Inserted 1:144		
Illuminator Cards:		4x
Inserted 1:288		
1A	Brett Favre	12.00
1B	Troy Aikman	6.00
1C	Jake Plummer	6.00
2A	Jamal Anderson	3.00
2B	Emmitt Smith	8.00
2C	Barry Sanders	12.00
3A	Antonio Freeman	3.00
3B	Randy Moss	12.00
3C	Jerry Rice	6.00
4A	Peyton Manning	8.00
4B	John Elway	8.00
4C	Dan Marino	8.00
5A	Fred Taylor	6.00
5B	Terrell Davis	8.00
5C	Curtis Martin	3.00

1999 Stadium Club Never Compromise

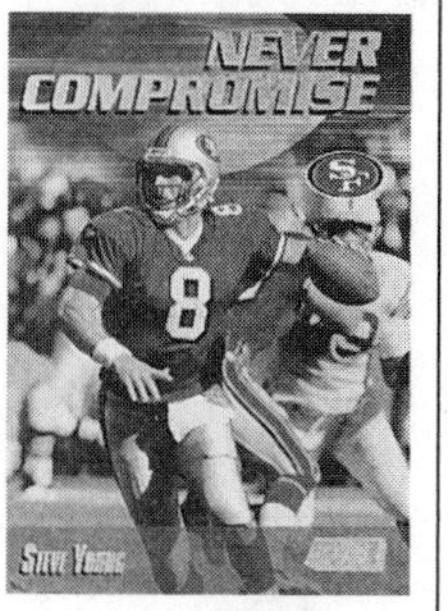

This 30-card insert set was divided into three different subsets. The Rookies featured ten hot newcomers, The ten Stars included current NFL stars at the pinnacle of their success and the Legends featured ten Canton-bound season veterans whose play should enshrine them in the Hall of Fame. They were inserted 1:12 packs.

		MT
Complete Set (30):		80.00
Common Player:		1.00
Minor Stars:		2.00
Inserted 1:12		
1	Tim Couch	8.00
2	David Boston	2.50
3	Daunte Culpepper	4.00
4	Donovan McNabb	4.00
5	Ricky Williams	8.00
6	Troy Edwards	2.50
7	Akili Smith	4.00
8	Torry Holt	2.50
9	Cade McNown	4.00
10	Edgerrin James	8.00
11	Randy Moss	8.00
12	Peyton Manning	6.00
13	Eddie George	2.00
14	Fred Taylor	4.00
15	Jamal Anderson	1.00
16	Joey Galloway	2.00
17	Terrell Davis	6.00
18	Keyshawn Johnson	2.00
19	Antonio Freeman	2.00
20	Jake Plummer	4.00
21	Steve Young	2.50
22	Barry Sanders	8.00
23	Dan Marino	6.00
24	Emmitt Smith	6.00
25	Brett Favre	8.00
26	Randall Cunningham	2.00
27	John Elway	6.00
28	Drew Bledsoe	3.00
29	Jerry Rice	4.00
30	Troy Aikman	4.00

1999 Stadium Club Chrome

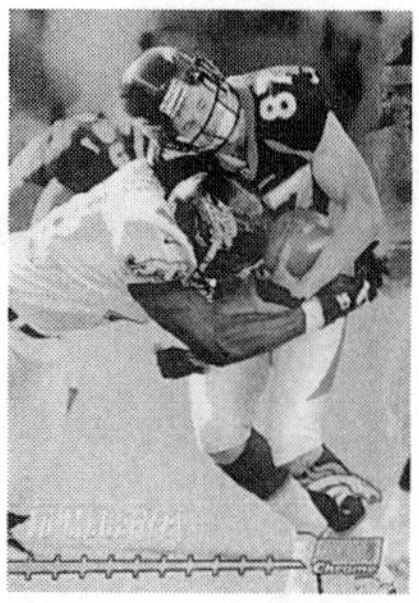

This was a 150-card set that utilized Chrome technology and each single was printed on 23-point stock. Parallel sets included First Day Issues and Refractors. Other inserts included: Clear Shots, Eyes of the Game, Never Compromise and True Colors. SRP was $4.00 for five-card packs.

		MT
Complete Set (150):		100.00
Common Player:		.25
Minor Stars:		.50
Common Rookie:		2.00
Pack (5):		4.00
Wax Box (24):		85.00
1	Dan Marino	3.00
2	Andre Reed	.50
3	Michael Westbrook	.50
4	Isaac Bruce	1.00
5	Curtis Martin	1.00
6	Terrell Owens	1.00
7	Warrick Dunn	1.00
8	Jake Plummer	1.50
9	Chad Brown	.25
10	Yancey Thigpen	.50
11	Keenan McCardell	.50
12	Shannon Sharpe	.50
13	Cameron Cleeland	.50
14	Mark Brunell	1.50
15	Jamal Anderson	1.00
16	Germane Crowell	.50
17	Rod Smith	.75
18	Cris Carter	1.00
19	Terrell Davis	3.00
20	Tim Biakabutuka	.50
21	Jermaine Lewis	.25
22	Adrian Murrell	.25
23	Doug Flutie	1.25
24	Curtis Enis	1.00
25	Skip Hicks	.50
26	Steve McNair	1.25
27	Charles Woodson	1.00
28	Freddie Jones	.25
29	Warren Sapp	.25
30	Emmitt Smith	3.00
31	Reidel Anthony	.50
32	Tony Simmons	.50
33	Andre Hastings	.25
34	Byron Morris	.25
35	Jimmy Smith	1.00
36	Antonio Freeman	1.00
37	Herman Moore	1.00
38	Muhsin Muhammed	.50
39	Chris Chandler	.50
40	John Elway	3.00
41	Bobby Engram	.25
42	Keith Poole	.25
43	Mike Alstott	1.00
44	Junior Seau	.50
45	Thurman Thomas	.50
46	Troy Aikman	2.00
47	Wesley Walls	.50
48	Robert Smith	1.00
49	Elvis Grbac	.50
50	Ben Coates	.50
51	Bert Emanuel	.25
52	Jacquez Green	.50
53	Barry Sanders	4.00
54	James Jett	.25
55	Gary Brown	.25
56	Stephen Alexander	.25
57	Wayne Chrebet	1.00
58	Drew Bledsoe	1.50
59	Jake Reed	.50
60	Marvin Harrison	1.00
61	Johnnie Morton	.25
62	Brett Favre	4.00
63	Charlie Batch	1.25
64	Antowain Smith	1.00
65	Ernie Mills	.25
66	Jeff Blake	.50
67	Curtis Conway	.50
68	Bruce Smith	.25
69	Peyton Manning	3.00
70	Tim Dwight	1.00
71	O.J. McDuffie	.50
72	Jon Kitna	1.00
73	Trent Dilfer	.50
74	Jerome Bettis	1.00
75	Dedric Ward	.25
76	Fred Taylor	2.00
77	Ike Hilliard	.50
78	Frank Wycheck	.25
79	Eric Moulds	1.00
80	Rob Moore	.75
81	Ed McCaffrey	.75
82	Carl Pickens	.50
83	Priest Holmes	1.00
84	Terry Glenn	1.00
85	Keyshawn Johnson	1.00
86	Karim Abdul	.50
87	Ahman Green	.50
88	Duce Staley	1.00
89	Vinny Testaverde	.50
90	Napoleon Kaufman	1.00
91	Frank Sanders	.50
92	Steve Young	1.25
93	Darnay Scott	.50
94	Deion Sanders	1.00
95	Corey Dillon	1.00
96	Randall Cunningham	1.00
97	Eddie George	1.25
98	Derrick Alexander	.25
99	Mark Chmura	.50
100	Rickey Dudley	.50
101	Joey Galloway	1.00
102	Ricky Proehl	.25
103	Natrone Means	.75
104	Dorsey Levens	1.00
105	Andre Rison	.50
106	John Avery	.50
107	Terance Mathis	.25
108	Rae Carruth	.25
109	Jerry Rice	2.00
110	Michael Irvin	.50
111	Oronde Gadsden	.50
112	Jerome Pathon	.25
113	Ricky Watters	.50
114	J.J. Stokes	.50
115	Kordell Stewart	1.00
116	Tim Brown	.50
117	Tony Gonzalez	.50
118	Randy Moss	4.00
119	*Daunte Culpepper*	12.00
120	*Amos Zereoue*	3.00
121	*Champ Bailey*	4.00
122	*Peerless Price*	4.00
123	*Edgerrin James*	20.00
124	*Joe Germaine*	3.00
125	*David Boston*	6.00
126	*Kevin Faulk*	4.00
127	*Troy Edwards*	6.00
128	*Akili Smith*	8.00
129	*Kevin Johnson*	6.00
130	*Rob Konrad*	2.00
131	*Shaun King*	8.00
132	*James Johnson*	4.00
133	*Donovan McNabb*	10.00
134	*Torry Holt*	6.00
135	*Michael Cloud*	2.00
136	*Sedrick Irvin*	3.00
137	*Cade McNown*	5.00
138	*Ricky Williams*	10.00
139	*Karsten Bailey*	2.00
140	*Cecil Collins*	2.00
141	*Brock Huard*	4.00
142	*D'Wayne Bates*	2.00
143	*Tim Couch*	10.00
144	Raghib Ismail	.25
145	Marshall Faulk	1.00
146	Trent Green	.50
147	Tony Martin	.25
148	Jim Harbaugh	.25
149	Rich Gannon	.25
150	Brad Johnson	.75

1999 Stadium Club Chrome First Day Parallel

This was a 150-card parallel to the base set. Each single included the "First Day Issue" stamp and was sequentially numbered to 100. They were inserted 1:59 packs. A parallel Refractor version was also released and each of those was sequentially numbered to 25 and inserted 1:235 packs.

	MT
First Day Cards:	15x-30x
First Day Rookies:	4x-8x
Inserted 1:59	
Production 100 Sets	

1999 Stadium Club Chrome Refractors Parallel

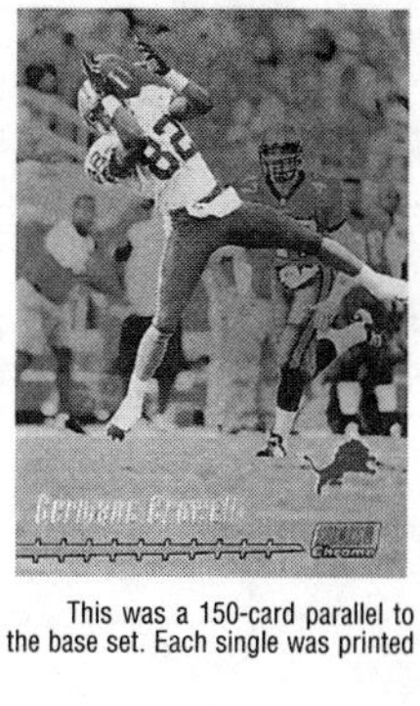

This was a 150-card parallel to the base set. Each single was printed with iridescent technology and inserted 1:12 packs.

	MT
Refractor Cards:	3x-6x
Refractor Rookies:	2x
Inserted 1:12	

1999 Stadium Club Chrome Clear Shots

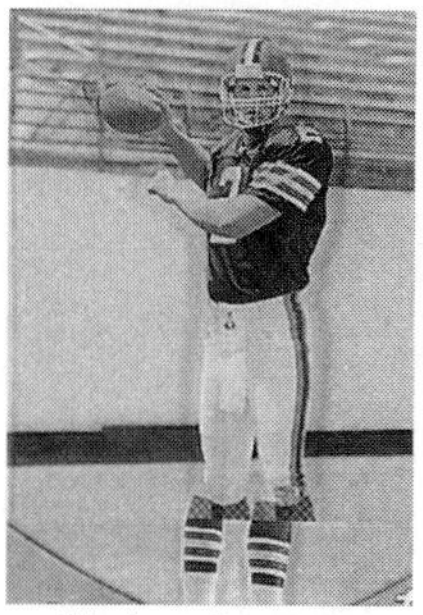

This nine-card insert set was an exclusive to the Stadium Club Chrome product. Each single was printed on a clear polycarbonate stock and was die cut. Singles were inserted 1:22 packs. A Refractor version was also released with each of those singles inserted 1:110 packs.

		MT
Complete Set (9):		45.00
Common Player:		2.00
Inserted 1:22		
Refractor Cards:		3x
Inserted 1:110		
1	David Boston	4.00
2	Edgerrin James	20.00
3	Chris Claiborne	2.00
4	Torry Holt	4.00
5	Tim Couch	12.00
6	Donovan McNabb	7.00
7	Akili Smith	5.00
8	Champ Bailey	3.00
9	Troy Edwards	4.00

1999 Stadium Club Chrome Eyes of the Game

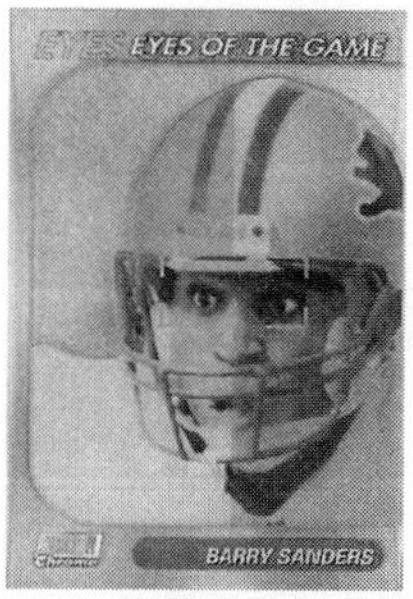

This seven-card insert set was an exclusive insert to Stadium Club Chrome Football. A mix of rookies and veterans was included in this set. Singles were inserted 1:20 packs. A parallel Refractor version was also issued and found 1:100 packs.

		MT
Complete Set (7):		45.00
Common Player:		5.00
Inserted 1:20		
Refractor Cards:		3x
Inserted 1:100		
1	Tim Couch	10.00
2	Ricky Williams	10.00
3	Barry Sanders	10.00
4	Brett Favre	10.00
5	Terrell Davis	5.00
6	Peyton Manning	10.00
7	Randy Moss	10.00

1999 Stadium Club Chrome Never Compromise

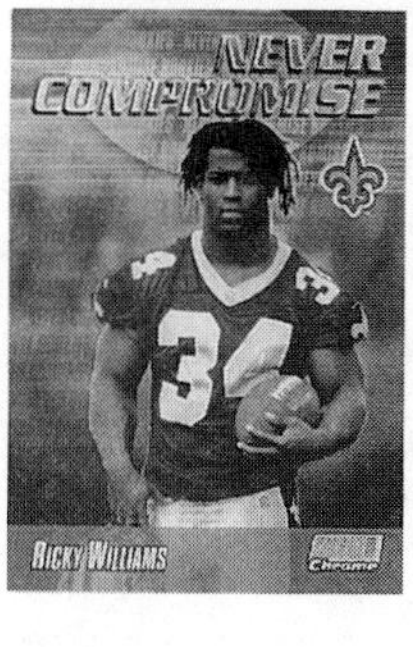

This 40-card insert set included 20 rookies and 20 veterans. Singles were inserted 1:6 packs. A parallel Refractor version was issued and inserted 1:30 packs.

		MT
Complete Set (40):		150.00
Common Player:		1.50
Minor Stars:		3.00
Inserted 1:6		
Refractor Cards:		3x
Inserted 1:30		
1	Tim Couch	10.00
2	David Boston	3.00
3	Daunte Culpepper	6.00
4	Donovan McNabb	6.00
5	Ricky Williams	10.00
6	Troy Edwards	3.00
7	Akili Smith	5.00
8	Torry Holt	4.00
9	Cade McNown	6.00
10	Edgerrin James	15.00
11	Cecil Collins	3.00
12	Peerless Price	1.50
13	Kevin Johnson	4.00
14	Champ Bailey	3.00
15	Kevin Faulk	3.00
16	D'Wayne Bates	1.50
17	Shaun King	6.00
18	Sedrick Irvin	3.00
19	James Johnson	3.00
20	Rob Konrad	1.50
21	Randy Moss	12.00
22	Peyton Manning	12.00
23	Eddie George	4.00
24	Fred Taylor	6.00
25	Jamal Anderson	1.50
26	Joey Galloway	1.50
27	Terrell Davis	8.00
28	Keyshawn Johnson	1.50
29	Antonio Freeman	1.50
30	Jake Plummer	5.00
31	Steve Young	4.00
32	Barry Sanders	12.00
33	Dan Marino	10.00
34	Emmitt Smith	10.00
35	Brett Favre	12.00
36	Randall Cunningham	1.50
37	John Elway	10.00
38	Drew Bledsoe	5.00
39	Jerry Rice	6.00
40	Troy Aikman	6.00

1999 Stadium Club Chrome True Colors

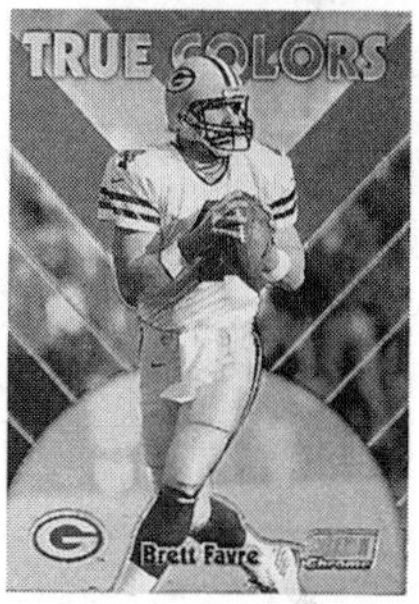

This was a 10-card insert set that was an exclusive to the Stadium Club Chrome product. Singles were inserted 1:24 packs. A parallel Refractor version was also released and found 1:120 packs.

		MT
Complete Set (10):		65.00
Common Player:		5.00
Inserted 1:24		
Refractor Cards:		3x
Inserted 1:120		
1	Doug Flutie	5.00
2	Steve Young	5.00
3	Jake Plummer	7.00
4	Jerry Rice	8.00
5	Randy Moss	12.00
6	Fred Taylor	8.00
7	Peyton Manning	12.00
8	Dan Marino	10.00
9	Brett Favre	12.00
10	Terrell Davis	8.00

2000 Stadium Club

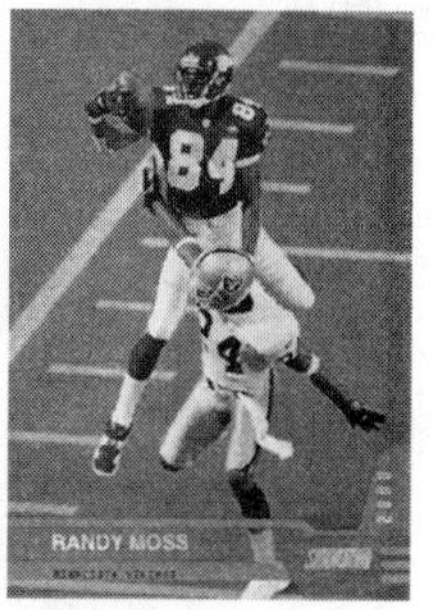

		MT
Complete Set (175):		85.00
Common Player:		.15
Minor Stars:		.30
Common Rookie:		1.50
Inserted 1:4		
Pack (7):		3.00
Wax Box (24):		55.00
1	Peyton Manning	1.75
2	Pete Mitchell	.15
3	Napoleon Kaufman	.50

4 Mikhael Ricks .15
5 Mike Alstott .50
6 Brad Johnson .50
7 Tony Gonzalez .30
8 Germane Crowell .30
9 Marcus Robinson .50
10 Stephen Davis .50
11 Terance Mathis .15
12 Jake Plummer .50
13 Qadry Ismail .15
14 Cade McNown .75
15 Zach Thomas .30
16 Curtis Martin .50
17 Torrance Small .15
18 Steve McNair .60
19 Jim Harbaugh .30
20 Keyshawn Johnson .50
21 Antonio Freeman .50
22 Ed McCaffrey .30
23 Elvis Grbac .30
24 Peerless Price .50
25 Jerome Bettis .50
26 Yancey Thigpen .30
27 *Jake Delhomme* 1.50
28 Keith Poole .15
29 Carl Pickens .30
30 Jerry Rice 1.00
31 Rob Moore .30
32 Reidel Anthony .30
33 Jimmy Smith .50
34 Ray Lucas .30
35 Troy Aikman 1.00
36 Steve Beuerlein .30
37 Charlie Batch .50
38 Derrick Mayes .30
39 Tim Brown .30
40 Eddie George .60
41 O.J. McDuffie .30
42 Ike Hilliard .30
43 Bill Schroeder .30
44 Jim Miller .15
45 Chris Chandler .30
46 Fred Taylor .75
47 Ricky Watters .30
48 Tyrone Wheatley .30
49 Bruce Smith .30
50 Marshall Faulk .50
51 Terry Kirby .15
52 Champ Bailey .30
53 Troy Edwards .50
54 Doug Flutie .60
55 Charles Johnson .15
56 Michael Westbrook .30
57 Frank Wycheck .15
58 Drew Bledsoe .75
59 Terrence Wilkins .30
60 Ricky Williams 1.25
61 Rod Smith .30
62 Errict Rhett .30
63 Vinny Testaverde .30
64 Jacquez Green .30
65 Curtis Conway .30
66 Wayne Chrebet .50
67 Albert Connell .30
68 Kordell Stewart .50
69 Bert Emanuel .15
70 Randy Moss 1.75
71 Akili Smith .60
72 Brian Griese .60
73 Frank Sanders .30
74 Wesley Walls .15
75 Michael Pittman .15
76 Steve Young .60
77 Jevon Kearse .60
78 Az-Zahir Hakim .30
79 James Stewart .30
80 Brett Favre 2.00
81 Dan Marino 1.50
82 Joe Horn .15
83 Mark Brunell .75
84 Eddie Kennison .15
85 Deion Sanders .50
86 Priest Holmes .50
87 Terry Glenn .50
88 Olandis Gary .60
89 Patrick Jeffers .50
90 Emmitt Smith 1.50
91 J.J. Stokes .15
92 Warrick Dunn .50
93 Damon Huard .50
94 Herman Moore .50
95 Corey Dillon .50
96 Joey Galloway .50
97 Jamal Anderson .50
98 Junior Seau .30
99 Robert Smith .50
100 Edgerrin James 2.00
101 Derrick Alexander .15
102 Johnnie Morton .15
103 Sean Dawkins .15
104 Derrick Brooks .15
105 Rickey Dudley .15
106 Keenan McCardell .30
107 Kerry Collins .30
108 Kevin Johnson .50
109 Eric Moulds .50
110 Terrell Davis 1.50
111 Shawn Jefferson .15
112 Donovan McNabb .75
113 Torry Holt .50
114 Marvin Harrison .50
115 Amani Toomer .30
116 Tony Martin .15
117 Curtis Enis .50
118 Tiki Barber .30
119 Freddie Jones .15
120 Muhsin Muhammad .30
121 Shaun King .75
122 Isaac Bruce .50
123 Duce Staley .60
124 Hardy Nickerson .15
125 Corey Bradford .30
126 Kevin Hardy .15
127 Hines Ward .30
128 Charlie Garner .30
129 Warren Sapp .30
130 Tim Couch 1.25
131 Kevin Dyson .30
132 Raghib Ismail .15
133 Tim Dwight .50
134 Darnay Scott .30
135 Jeff George .30
136 Dorsey Levens .30
137 Jeff Blake .30
138 Jon Kitna .50
139 Rich Gannon .30
140 Cris Carter .50
141 Jeff Graham .15
142 James Johnson .30
143 Tim Biakabutuka .30
144 Bobby Engram .15
145 Tony Banks .30
146 Shannon Sharpe .30
147 Antowain Smith .50
148 Terrell Owens .50
149 Rob Johnson .30
150 Kurt Warner 2.00
151 *Thomas Jones* 7.00
152 *Chad Pennington* 10.00
153 *Ron Dayne* 12.00
154 *Tee Martin* 4.00
155 *Reuben Droughns* 3.00
156 *Jerry Porter* 4.00
157 *R. Jay Soward* 4.00
158 *Sylvester Morris* 4.00
159 *Todd Pinkston* 1.50
160 *Courtney Brown* 4.00
161 *Travis Taylor* 5.00
162 *Ron Dugans* 3.00
163 *Laveranues Coles* 3.00
164 *Joe Hamilton* 3.00
165 *Curtis Keaton* 1.50
166 *Bubba Franks* 3.50
167 *Dennis Northcutt* 3.50
168 *Chris Redman* 4.00
169 *Travis Prentice* 3.00
170 *Shaun Alexander* 7.00
171 *Jamal Lewis* 7.00
172 *Peter Warrick* 10.00
173 *J.R. Redmond* 4.00
174 *Trung Canidate* 2.50
175 *Plaxico Burress* 6.00

2000 Stadium Club All-Pro Competition

MT
Complete Set (6): 600.00
Common Player: 50.00
Production 50 Sets
HTA Only
APC1 Jevon Kearse, Warren Sapp 75.00
APC2 Marshall Faulk, Edgerrin James 175.00
APC3 Keyshawn Johnson, Randy Moss 175.00
APC4 Frank Wycheck, Wesley Walls 50.00
APC5 Stephen Davis, Eddie George 100.00
APC6 Cris Carter, Isaac Bruce 85.00

2000 Stadium Club All-Pro Relics

MT
Complete Set (18): 700.00
Common Player: 25.00
Inserted 1:353
SB Steve Beuerlein 35.00
PB Peter Boulware 25.00
IB Isaac Bruce 40.00
CC Cris Carter 65.00
SD Stephen Davis 40.00
MF Marshall Faulk 65.00
EG Eddie George 85.00
KH Kevin Hardy 25.00
EJ Edgerrin James 125.00
KJ Keyshawn Johnson 40.00
JK Jevon Kearse 50.00
TL Todd Lyght 25.00
RM Randy Moss 125.00
MM Muhsin Muhammad 25.00
HN Hardy Nickerson 25.00
WS Warren Sapp 30.00
WW Wesley Walls 30.00
FW Frank Wycheck 25.00

2000 Stadium Club All-Pro Relics Autographs

MT
Common Player: 100.00
Inserted 1:5,474
Production 50 Sets
APA1 Eddie George 125.00
APA2 Edgerrin James 200.00
APA4 Stephen Davis 100.00
APA5 Isaac Bruce 100.00

2000 Stadium Club Beam Team

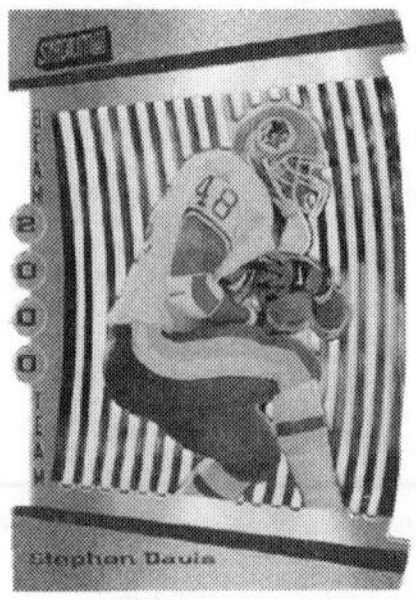

MT
Complete Set (30): 150.00
Common Player: 2.50
Minor Stars: 5.00
Inserted 1:171
Production 500 Sets
BT1 Brett Favre 15.00
BT2 Stephen Davis 5.00
BT3 Germane Crowell 2.50
BT4 Jevon Kearse 5.00
BT5 Edgerrin James 15.00
BT6 Randy Moss 15.00
BT7 Isaac Bruce 5.00
BT8 Charlie Garner 2.50
BT9 Eddie George 6.00
BT10 Kurt Warner 20.00
BT11 Raghib Ismail 2.50
BT12 Doug Flutie 6.00
BT13 Jimmy Smith 5.00
BT14 Eric Moulds 5.00
BT15 Marvin Harrison 5.00
BT16 Ricky Watters 2.50
BT17 Marcus Robinson 5.00
BT18 Mark Brunell 7.00
BT19 Tim Dwight 5.00
BT20 Peyton Manning 15.00
BT21 Patrick Jeffers 2.50
BT22 Az-Zahir Hakim 2.50
BT23 Fred Taylor 8.00
BT24 Tim Biakabutuka 2.50
BT25 Marshall Faulk 5.00
BT26 Shannon Sharpe 2.50
BT27 Tony Gonzalez 2.50
BT28 Steve McNair 5.00
BT29 Antonio Freeman 5.00
BT30 Keyshawn Johnson 5.00

2000 Stadium Club Capture the Action

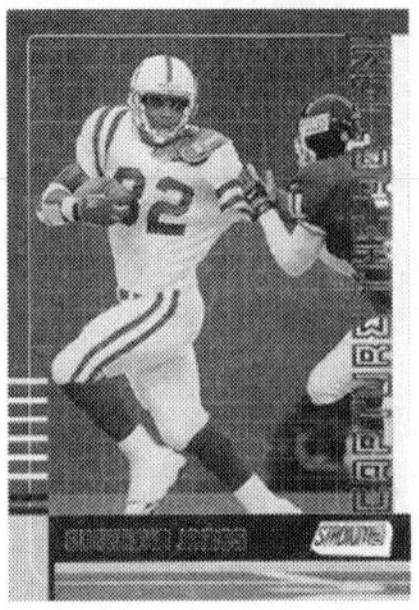

MT
Complete Set (30): 45.00
Common Player: .75
Minor Stars: 1.50
Inserted 1:8
Game View Cards: 4x-8x
Inserted 1:454
Production 100 Sets
CA1 Brett Favre 5.00
CA2 Drew Bledsoe 2.00
CA3 Dan Marino 4.00
CA4 Peyton Manning 4.00
CA5 Kurt Warner 5.00
CA6 Brad Johnson 1.50
CA7 Steve Beuerlein .75
CA8 Troy Aikman 3.00
CA9 Edgerrin James 4.00
CA10 Marshall Faulk 1.50
CA11 Stephen Davis 1.50
CA12 Eddie George 2.00
CA13 Emmitt Smith 4.00
CA14 Curtis Martin 1.50
CA15 Ricky Williams 2.50
CA16 Jimmy Smith 1.50
CA17 Marvin Harrison 1.50
CA18 Muhsin Muhammad .75
CA19 Keyshawn Johnson 1.50
CA20 Marcus Robinson 1.50
CA21 Antonio Freeman 1.50
CA22 Randy Moss 5.00
CA23 Tim Brown 1.50
CA24 Eric Moulds 1.50
CA25 Isaac Bruce 1.50
CA26 Zach Thomas .75
CA27 Warren Sapp .75
CA28 Jevon Kearse 1.50
CA29 Junior Seau .75
CA30 Kevin Carter .75

2000 Stadium Club Co-Signers

MT
Complete Set (6): 750.00
Common Player: 75.00
Inserted 1:2,270
CS1 Peyton Manning, Kurt Warner 400.00
CS2 Edgerrin James, Marshall Faulk 200.00
CS3 Stephen Davis, Eddie George 125.00
CS4 Jimmy Smith, Cris Carter 75.00
CS5 Marvin Harrison, Isaac Bruce 75.00
CS6 Jon Kitna, Cade McNown 85.00

2000 Stadium Club Goal to Go

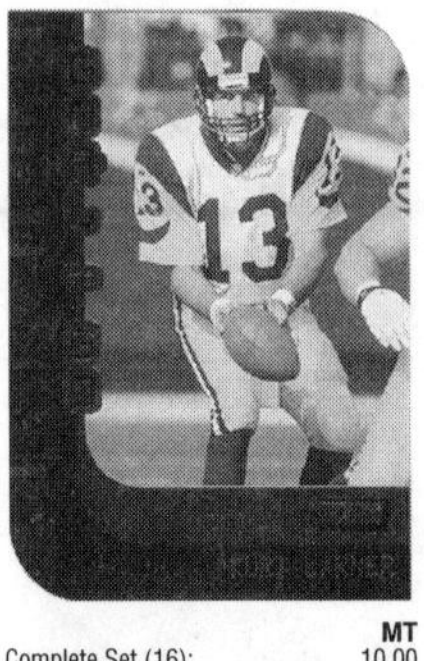

MT
Complete Set (16): 10.00
Common Player: .50
Minor Stars: 1.00
Inserted 1:8
G1 Cris Carter 1.00
G2 Stephen Davis 1.00
G3 Marvin Harrison 1.00
G4 Edgerrin James 2.50
G5 Zach Thomas .50
G6 Terrell Davis 2.00
G7 Leroy Hoard .50
G8 Kurt Warner 3.00
G9 Tony Gonzalez .50
G10 James Stewart .50
G11 Isaac Bruce 1.00
G12 Emmitt Smith 2.00
G13 Dorsey Levens 1.00
G14 Jevon Kearse 1.00
G15 Eddie George 1.50
G16 Warren Sapp .50

2000 Stadium Club Lone Star Autographs

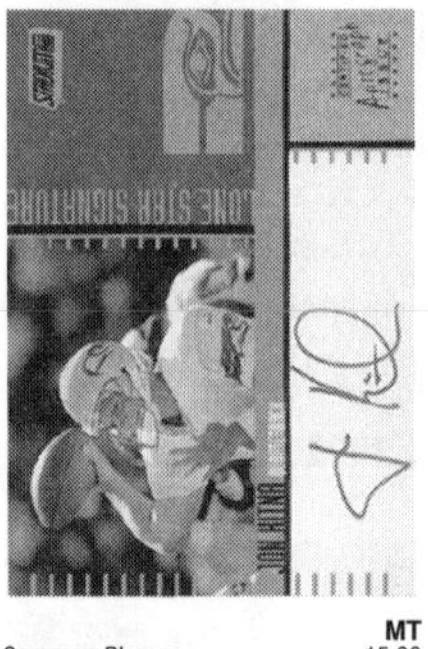

MT
Common Player: 15.00
Inserted 1:202
Card #17 Never Released
LS1 Edgerrin James 85.00
LS2 Stephen Davis 20.00
LS3 Marshall Faulk 25.00
LS4 Eddie George 45.00
LS5 Isaac Bruce 25.00
LS6 Jimmy Smith 15.00
LS7 Cris Carter 25.00
LS8 Kurt Warner 85.00
LS9 Marvin Harrison 25.00
LS10 Kevin Carter 15.00
LS11 Ron Dayne 85.00
LS12 Chad Pennington 60.00
LS13 Sylvester Morris 25.00
LS14 Thomas Jones 45.00
LS15 Shaun Alexander 45.00
LS16 Chris Redman 25.00
LS18 Peter Warrick 100.00
LS19 Jon Kitna 15.00
LS20 Cade McNown 40.00
LS21 Az-Zahir Hakim 15.00
LS22 Amani Toomer 15.00
LS23 Wesley Walls 15.00
LS24 Marcus Robinson 40.00
LS25 Zach Thomas 25.00
LS26 Tony Gonzalez 25.00
LS27 Muhsin Muhammad 25.00
LS28 Ed McCaffrey 25.00
LS29 Eric Moulds 25.00
LS30 Peyton Manning 100.00
LS31 Joe Montana 300.00

2000 Stadium Club Tunnel Vision

MT
Complete Set (8): 12.00
Common Player: 1.00
Inserted 1:Box
TV1 Edgerrin James 3.00
TV2 Brett Favre 3.00
TV3 Marshall Faulk 1.00
TV4 Emmitt Smith 2.00
TV5 Peyton Manning 3.00
TV6 Eddie George 1.50
TV7 Kurt Warner 4.00
TV8 Fred Taylor 1.75

2001 Stadium Club

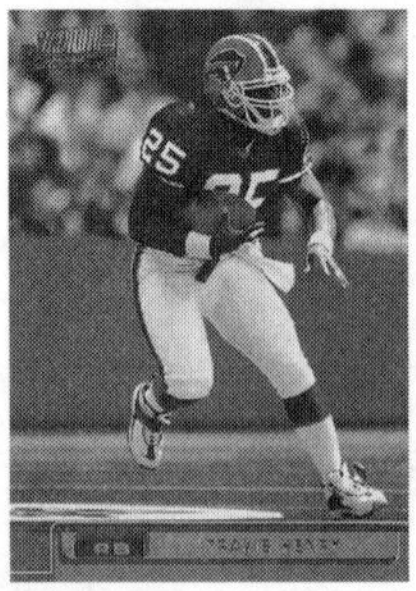

MT
Complete Set (175): 125.00
Common Player: .15
Minor Stars: .30
Common Rookie: 1.00
Inserted 1:4
Pack (6): 3.00
Wax Box (24): 55.00
1 Peyton Manning 1.50
2 Akili Smith .30
3 Brian Griese .60
4 Wayne Chrebet .15
5 Oronde Gadsden .15
6 Marvin Harrison .50
7 Charles Johnson .15
8 Jay Fiedler .50
9 Kerry Collins .15
10 Troy Aikman 1.00
11 Donovan McNabb .75
12 Ike Hilliard .15
13 Warrick Dunn .15
14 Derrick Alexander .15
15 Jake Plummer .50
16 Corey Dillon .50
17 Ahman Green .15
18 Keenan McCardell .15
19 Derrick Mason .15
20 Jerry Rice 1.25
21 Emmitt Smith 1.50
22 Dedric Ward .15
23 Jamal Anderson .50
24 Charlie Garner .15
25 Vinny Testaverde .15
26 Shaun Alexander .60
27 Terry Glenn .15
28 Cade McNown .50
29 Germane Crowell .15
30 Jeff Graham .15
31 Rich Gannon .15
32 Jevon Kearse .50
33 Shannon Sharpe .15
34 Marcus Robinson .50
35 Rod Smith .15
36 Curtis Martin .50
37 Robert Smith .50
38 Marshall Faulk .60
39 Tony Richardson .15
40 Travis Prentice .15
41 Edgerrin James 1.50
42 Duce Staley .50
43 Keyshawn Johnson .50
44 Joe Horn .15
45 Shawn Bryson .15
46 Ray Lewis .15
47 Fred Taylor .75
48 Jeff George .15
49 Sean Dawkins .15
50 Daunte Culpepper 1.00
51 Chris Chandler .15
52 Tim Couch .75
53 Trent Dilfer .15
54 Steve McNair .50
55 Kordell Stewart .50
56 Aaron Brooks .50
57 Michael Pittman .15
58 Bill Schroeder .15
59 Junior Seau .15
60 Kurt Warner 1.75
61 Drew Bledsoe .60
62 Steve Beuerlein .15
63 Mike Anderson 1.25
64 Brad Johnson .50
65 Tim Brown .50
66 Qadry Ismail .15
67 Doug Flutie .60
68 Terrell Owens .50
69 Raghib Ismail .15
70 Charlie Batch .50
71 Jerome Pathon .15
72 Peter Warrick 1.00
73 Hines Ward .15
74 Ron Dayne 1.00
75 Lamar Smith .15
76 Amani Toomer .15
77 Joey Galloway .50
78 James Allen .15
79 Isaac Bruce .50
80 David Boston .50
81 James Thrash .15
82 Tony Gonzalez .15
83 Jason Taylor .15
84 Ricky Watters .15
85 Terance Mathis .15
86 Troy Brown .15
87 Mark Brunell .75
88 Rob Johnson .15
89 Freddie Jones .15
90 Eddie George .60
91 Tiki Barber .15
92 Donald Hayes .15
93 Muhsin Muhammad .15
94 Johnnie Morton .15
95 Warren Sapp .15
96 Bobby Shaw .15
97 Randy Moss 1.50
98 Jerome Bettis .50
99 Antonio Freeman .50
100 Jamal Lewis 1.25
101 Andre Rison .15
102 Kevin Faulk .15
103 Jon Kitna .50
104 Shawn Jefferson .15
105 Kevin Johnson .50
106 Torry Holt .50
107 Cris Carter .50
108 Chad Lewis .15
109 Stephen Davis .50
110 Jeff Blake .15
111 Elvis Grbac .15
112 Ed McCaffrey .50
113 Tim Biakabutuka .15
114 Trent Green .15
115 Jeff Garcia .50
116 Jacquez Green .15
117 Shaun King .50
118 Jimmy Smith .15
119 James Stewart .15
120 Brian Urlacher 1.00
121 Tyrone Wheatley .15
122 J.R. Redmond .15
123 Eric Moulds .15
124 Ricky Williams .50
125 Brett Favre 2.00
126 *Koren Robinson* 5.00
127 *Richard Seymour* 1.50
128 *Jamal Reynolds* 2.00
129 *Kevin Kasper* 2.00
130 *LaMont Jordan* 2.50
131 *Reggie Wayne* 4.00
132 *Travis Henry* 4.00
133 *Alge Crumpler* 2.00
134 *Quincy Carter* 4.00
135 *Michael Bennett* 8.00
136 *Jamie Winborn* 1.00
137 *Josh Heupel* 6.00
138 *Will Allen* 1.50
139 *Scotty Anderson* 1.00
140 *LaDainian Tomlinson* 10.00
141 *Freddie Mitchell* 4.00
142 *Gerard Warren* 2.00
143 *Chad Johnson* 2.50
144 *Todd Heap* 2.00
145 *Leonard Davis* 1.00
146 *Kevan Barlow* 2.00
147 *Correl Buckhalter* 2.00
148 *Fred Smoot* 2.00
149 *Steve Smith* 1.00
150 *David Terrell* 6.00
151 *Chris Chambers* 2.50
152 *Mike McMahon* 2.00
153 *Rudi Johnson* 2.00
154 *Marques Tuiasosopo* 4.00
155 *Deuce McAllister* 6.00
156 *Marcus Stroud* 2.00
157 *Bobby Newcombe* 2.00
158 *Rod Gardner* 5.00
159 *Drew Brees* 10.00
160 *Jesse Palmer* 2.00
161 *Derrick Gibson* 1.00
162 *James Jackson* 3.00
163 *Dan Morgan* 2.00
164 *Michael Vick* 12.00
165 *Marvin "Snoop" Minnis* 3.00
166 *Anthony Thomas* 10.00
167 *Andre Carter* 2.00
168 *Travis Minor* 3.00
169 *Quincy Morgan* 2.50
170 *Justin Smith* 2.50
171 *Tay Cody* 1.00
172 *Santana Moss* 6.00
173 *Sage Rosenfels* 2.50
174 *Robert Ferguson* 3.00
175 *Chris Weinke* 6.00

2001 Stadium Club All-Pro Autos

MT
Complete Set (6): 175.00
Common Player: 25.00
SPA-DC Daunte Culpepper 50.00
SPA-SD Stephen Davis 25.00
SPA-EG Eddie George 50.00
SPA-TG Tony Gonzalez 25.00
SPA-MH Marvin Harrison 25.00
SPA-EJ Edgerrin James 75.00

2001 Stadium Club All-Pro Relics

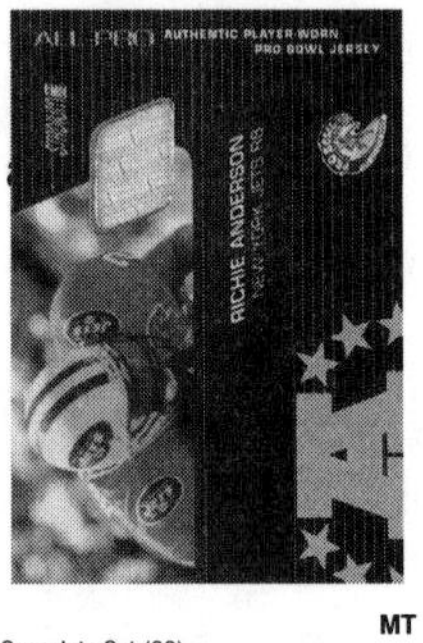

MT
Complete Set (33):
Common Player: 8.00
SP-DA Donnie Abraham 8.00
SP-SA Stephen Alexander 10.00
SP-LA Larry Allen 8.00
SP-RA Richie Anderson 8.00
SP-JA Jessie Armstead 8.00
SP-TA Trace Armstrong 8.00
SP-CB Champ Bailey 15.00
SP-RB Ruben Brown 8.00
SP-CC Cris Carter 15.00
SP-JC Jeff Christy 8.00
SP-MC Marco Coleman 8.00
SP-DC Daunte Culpepper 25.00
SP-HD Hugh Douglas 8.00
SP-LE Luther Elliss 8.00
SP-ENG Eddie George 25.00
SP-LG La'Roi Glover 8.00
SP-TG Tony Gonzalez 10.00
SP-MG Martin Grammatica 8.00
SP-RG Robert Griffith 8.00
SP-MH Marvin Harrison 15.00
SP-DH Desmond Howard 8.00
SP-EJ Edgerrin James 30.00
SP-JK Jevon Kearse 10.00
SP-BM Brock Marion 8.00
SP-KM Keith Mitchell 8.00
SP-JO Jonathan Ogden 8.00
SP-TO Terrell Owens 15.00
SP-WS Warren Sapp 10.00
SP-JS Jimmy Smith 8.00
SP-RS Rod Smith 8.00
SP-JT Jeremiah Trotter 8.00
SP-TV Troy Vincent 8.00
SP-RW Rod Woodson 10.00

2001 Stadium Club Common Threads

MT
Complete Set (6): 100.00
Common Player: 20.00
CT-CR Daunte Culpepper, David Rivers 30.00
CT-GT Eddie George, LaDainian Tomlinson 30.00
CT-JB Edgerrin James, Kevan Barlow 40.00
CT-DM Corey Dillon, Travis Minor 20.00
CT-MJ Eric Moulds, Chad Johnson 20.00
CT-HW Marvin Harrison, Reggie Wayne 30.00

2001 Stadium Club Common Threads Autographs

MT
Complete Set (6): 275.00
Common Player: 30.00
CTA-CR Daunte Culpepper, David Rivers 75.00
CTA-GT Eddie George, LaDainian Tomlinson 75.00
CTA-JB Edgerrin James, Kevan Barlow 75.00
CTA-DM Corey Dillon, Travis Minor 40.00
CTA-MJ Eric Moulds, Chad Johnson 30.00

CTA-HW	Marvin Harrison, Reggie Wayne	50.00

2001 Stadium Club Co-Signers

		MT
Common Player:		60.00
CO-FJ	Edgerrin James, Marshall Faulk	125.00
CO-MO	Randy Moss, Terrell Owens	100.00
CO-FB	Brett Favre, Aaron Brooks	200.00
CO-CG	Daunte Culpepper, Jeff Garcia	60.00
CO-AL	Mike Anderson, Jamal Lewis	60.00

2001 Stadium Club Highlight Reels

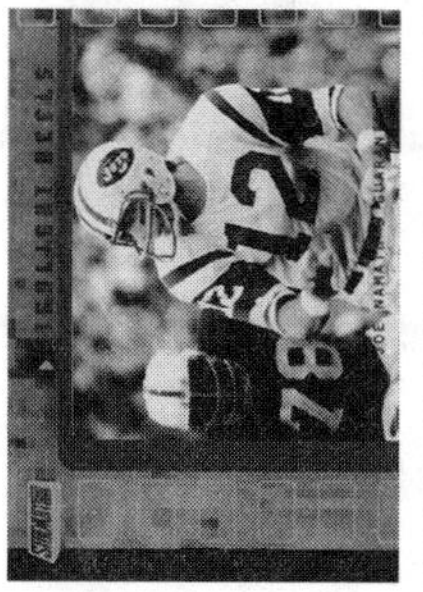

		MT
Complete Set (5):		15.00
Common Player:		2.00
Inserted 1:8		
HR-AA	Alan Ameche	2.00
HR-JE	John Elway	5.00
HR-BG	Bob Griese	3.00
HR-JN	Joe Namath	6.00
HR-BS	Bart Starr	5.00

2001 Stadium Club Jersey All-Pro

		MT
Common Player:		10.00
Inserted 1:44		
SP-DA	Donnie Abraham	15.00
SP-SA	Stephen Alexander	15.00
SP-LA	Larry Allen	10.00
SP-RA	Richie Anderson	10.00
SP-JA	Jessie Armstead	12.00
SP-TA	Trace Armstrong	12.00
SP-CB	Champ Bailey	20.00
SP-RB	Ruben Brown	10.00
SP-CC	Cris Carter	30.00
SP-JC	Jeff Christy	10.00
SP-MC	Marco Coleman	12.00
SP-DC	Daunte Culpepper	30.00
SP-HD	Hugh Douglas	10.00
SP-LE	Luther Ellis	12.00
SP-EGE	Eddie George	30.00
SP-LG	La'Roi Glover	12.00
SP-TG	Tony Gonzalez	15.00
SP-MG	Martin Gramatica	12.00
SP-RG	Robert Griffith	10.00
SP-MH	Marvin Harrison	20.00
SP-DH	Desmond Howard	15.00
SP-EJ	Edgerrin James	50.00
SP-JK	Jevon Kearse	20.00
SP-BM	Brock Marion	10.00
SP-KM	Keith Mitchell	10.00
SP-JO	Jonathan Ogden	10.00
SP-TO	Terrell Owens	15.00
SP-WS	Warren Sapp	15.00
SP-JS	Jimmy Smith	12.00
SP-RS	Rod Smith	12.00
SP-JT	Jeremiah Trotter	10.00
SP-TV	Troy Vincent	10.00
SP-RW	Rod Woodson	15.00

2001 Stadium Club In Focus

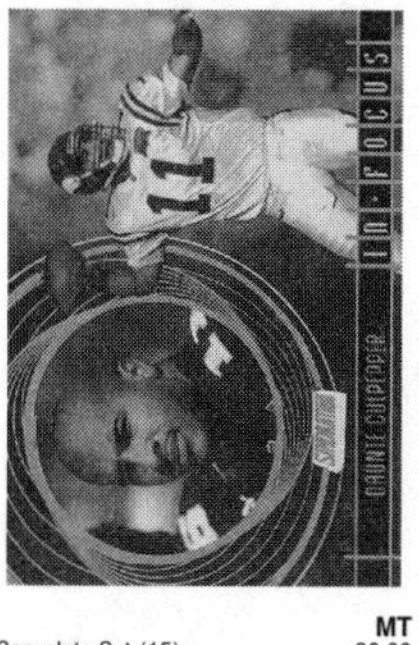

		MT
Complete Set (15):		20.00
Common Player:		1.00
Inserted 1:8		
IF1	Peyton Manning	5.00
IF2	Marshall Faulk	1.50
IF3	Torry Holt	1.00
IF4	Daunte Culpepper	2.50
IF5	Edgerrin James	4.00
IF6	Marvin Harrison	1.00
IF7	Jeff Garcia	1.00
IF8	Robert Smith	1.00
IF9	Randy Moss	4.00
IF10	Mike Anderson	2.50
IF11	Corey Dillon	1.00
IF12	Rod Smith	1.00
IF13	Brett Favre	6.00
IF14	Eddie George	1.50
IF15	Terrell Owens	1.00

2001 Stadium Club Lone Star Signatures

		MT
Common Player:		10.00
Inserted 1:84		
LS-DA	Dan Alexander	25.00
LS-MA	Mike Anderson	35.00
LS-KB	Kevan Barlow	10.00
LS-JB	Josh Booty	10.00
LS-DB	Drew Brees	70.00
LS-DC	Daunte Culpepper	40.00
LS-SD	Stephen Davis	20.00
LS-MF	Marshall Faulk	25.00
LS-EG	Eddie George	25.00
LS-MH	Marvin Harrison	20.00
LS-TH	Travis Henry	25.00
LS-JH	Joe Horn	10.00
LS-EJ	Edgerrin James	50.00
LS-DM	Deuce McAllister	40.00
LS-QM	Quincy Morgan	20.00
LS-TO	Terrell Owens	20.00
LS-JP	Jesse Palmer	10.00
LS-DT	David Terrell	40.00
LS-AT	Anthony Thomas	35.00
LS-LT	LaDainian Tomlinson	70.00
LS-MV	Michael Vick	150.00
LS-KW	Kenyatta Walker	10.00
LS-RW	Reggie Wayne	30.00

2001 Stadium Club Stepping Up

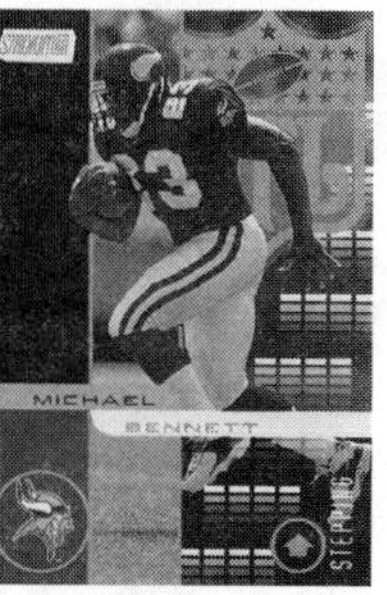

		MT
Complete Set (15):		35.00
Common Player:		1.25
SU1	David Terrell	4.00
SU2	LaDainian Tomlinson	7.00
SU3	Michael Vick	12.00
SU4	Koren Robinson	3.00
SU5	Michael Bennett	5.00
SU6	Chad Johnson	1.25
SU7	Drew Brees	7.00
SU8	Reggie Wayne	2.50
SU9	Freddie Mitchell	2.50
SU10	Chris Weinke	3.50
SU11	Rod Gardner	3.00
SU12	Chris Chambers	1.25
SU13	Deuce McAllister	4.00
SU14	Santana Moss	3.00
SU15	Robert Ferguson	1.50

1963 Stancraft Playing Cards

This 54-card set, titled "Official NFL All-Time Greats," commemorates the opening of the Pro Football Hall of Fame in Canton, Ohio. Each of the cards, designed as playing cards, features an artistic drawing of the player, with his name, position, team name and years played below the picture, which is done in brown ink. The Aces and Jokers, however, have NFL logos on them instead of artwork. Two styles were used for the card backs - an NFL logo in the center surrounded by the 14 NFL team logos in a checkerboard pattern, all against a red background, or a green background with the 14 team helmets contained within it. Cards, 2-1/4" x 3-1/2" with rounded corners, came in a plastic box.

		NM
Complete Set (54):		125.00
Common Player:		1.50
AC	NFL Logo	1.50
2C	Johnny Blood McNally	2.00
3C	Bobby Mitchell	3.00
4C	Bill Howton	1.50
5C	Wilbur Fats Henry	2.00
6C	Tony Canedeo	2.00
7C	Bulldog Turner	3.00
8C	Charlie Trippi	2.00
9C	Tommy Mason	1.50
10C	Earl "Dutch" Clark	2.00
JC	Y.A. Tittle	5.00
QC	Lou Groza	5.00
KC	Bobby Layne	6.00
AD	NFL Logo	1.50
2D	Frankie Albert	1.50
3D	Del Shofner	1.50
4D	Ollie Matson	4.00
5D	Mike Ditka	8.00
6D	Otto Graham	6.00
7D	Chuck Bednarik	4.00
8D	Jim Taylor	3.00
9D	Mel Hein	2.00
10D	Eddie Price	1.50
JD	Sonny Randle	1.50
QD	Joe Perry	4.00
KD	Bob Waterfield	5.00
AH	NFL Logo	1.50
2H	Paul Hornung	5.00
3H	Johnny Unitas	10.00
4H	Doak Walker	5.00
5H	Tom Fears	3.00
6H	Jim Thorpe	10.00
7H	Gino Marchetti	3.00
8H	Claude Buddy Young	1.50
9H	Jim Benton	2.00
10H	Jim Brown	12.00
JH	George Halas	1.50
QH	Sammy Baugh	4.00
KH	Bill Dudley	2.50
1S	NFL Logo	1.50
2S	Eddie LeBaron	2.00
3S	Don Hutson	3.50
4S	Clarke Hinkle	2.00
5S	Charley Conerly	2.50
6S	Earl (Curly) Lambeau	2.00
7S	Sid Luckman	5.00
8S	Pete Pihos	2.00
9S	Dante Lavelli	2.00
10S	Norm Van Brocklin	4.00
JS	Cloyce Box	1.50
QS	Joe Schmidt	3.00
KS	Elroy Hirsch	3.00
xx	Joker (NFL logo)	2.00
xx	Joker (NFL logo)	2.00
1D	NFL Logo	1.50
2D	Frankie Albert	1.50
3D	Del Shofner	1.50
4D	Ollie Matson	4.00
5D	Mike Ditka	8.00
6D	Otto Graham	6.00
7D	Chuck Bednarik	4.00
8D	Jim Taylor	3.00
9D	Mel Hein	2.00
10D	Eddie Price	1.50
11D	Sonny Randle	1.50
12D	Joe Perry	4.00
13D	Bob Waterfield	5.00
1H	NFL Logo	1.50
2H	Paul Hornung	5.00
3H	Johnny Unitas	10.00
4H	Doak Walker	5.00
5H	Tom Fears	3.00
6H	Jim Thorpe	10.00
7H	Gino Marchetti	3.00
8H	Claude Buddy Young	1.50
9H	Jim Benton	2.00
10H	Jim Brown	12.00
11H	George Halas	1.50
12H	Sammy Baugh	4.00
13H	Bill Dudley	2.50
1S	NFL Logo	1.50
2S	Eddie LeBaron	2.00
3S	Don Hutson	3.50
4S	Clarke Hinkle	2.00
5S	Charley Conerly	2.50
6S	Earl Curly Lambeau	2.00
7S	Sid Luckman	5.00
8S	Pete Pihos	2.00
9S	Dante Lavelli	2.00
10S	Norm Van Brocklin	4.00
11S	Cloyce Box	1.50
12S	Joe Schmidt	3.00
13S	Elroy Hirsch	3.00

1991 Star Pics Promos

Star Pics issued these cards to promote their 1991 set. They were distributed in two-card panels and inserted in an issue of Pro Football Weekly. The card fronts feature a color photo with a football border. The backs are green and include basic player information and a close-up photo.

		MT
Complete Set (4):		4.00
Common Player:		1.00
1	Mark Carrier DB	1.00
2	Aaron Craver	1.00
3	Dan McGwire	1.00
4	Eric Turner	1.00

1991 Star Pics Fb

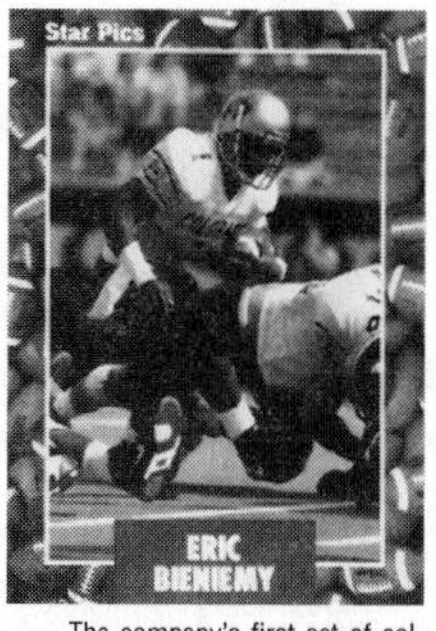

The company's first set of college prospects was released in June 1991. The set features 44 out of 55 first- and second-round picks from the 1991 draft. All 91 players in the set -- the roster of which was set before the draft -- were selected. Subsets include the nine-card flashback issue (NFL players in college uniforms) and Top Pick Agents, featuring player representatives. At least one in 50 sets contained a randomly- inserted autograph. (Key: FL - flashback, A - agent). Two promo panels, each featuring two standard-size cards, were also produced to preview the regular 1991 set's design. The players paired together were 1) Mark Carrier, $1, and 2) Aaron Craver, $1, and 3) Dan McGwire, $1, and 4) Eric Turner, $1.

		MT
Complete Set (112):		6.00
Common Player:		.05
Common Autograph:		6.00
Autograph Cards:		20x-40x
NFL Autographs:		200x-400x
1	1991 NFL Draft Overview	.05
2	Barry Sanders (FL)	.10
3	Nick Bell	.10
4	Kevin Pritchett	.05
5	Huey Richardson	.05
6	Mike Croel	.10
7	Paul Justin	.05
8	Ivory Lee Brown	.05
9	Herman Moore	1.25
10	Derrick Thomas (FL)	.15
11	Keith Taylor	.05
12	Joe Johnson	.05
13	Dan McGwire	.10
14	Harvey Williams	.50
15	Eric Moten	.05
16	Steve Zucker	.05
17	Randal Hill	.20
18	Browning Nagle	.05
19	Stan Thomas	.05
20	Emmitt Smith (FL)	.50
21	Ted Washington	.05
22	Lamar Rogers	.05
23	Kenny Walker	.05
24	Howard Griffith	.05
25	Reggie Johnson	.05
26	Lawrence Dawsey	.05
27	Joe Garten	.05
28	Moe Gardner	.05
29	Michael Stonebreaker	.05
30	Jeff George (FL)	.15
31	Leigh Steinberg (A)	.05
32	John Flannery	.05
33	Pat Harlow	.05
34	Kanavis McGhee	.05
35	Michael Dumas	.05
36	Godfrey Myles	.05
37	Shawn Moore	.05
38	Jeff Graham	.50
39	Ricky Watters	1.00
40	Andre Ware (FL)	.05
41	Henry Jones	.10
42	Eric Turner	.30
43	Bob Wolf (A)	.05
44	Randy Baldwin	.05
45	Morris Lewis	.05
46	Jerry Evans	.05
47	Derek Russell	.05
48	Merton Hanks	.40
49	Kevin Donnalley	.05
50	Troy Aikman (FL)	.30
51	William Thomas	.05
52	Chris Thome	.05
53	Ricky Ervins	.10
54	Jake Reed	.25
55	Jerome Henderson	.05
56	Mark Vander Poel	.05
57	Bernard Ellison	.05
58	Jack Mills (A)	.05
59	Jarrod Bunch	.05
60	Mark Carrier (FL)	.05
61	Rocen Keeton	.05
62	Louis Riddick	.05
63	Bobby Wilson	.05
64	Steve Jackson	.05
65	Brett Favre	2.50
66	Ernie Mills	.20
67	Joe Valerio	.05
68	Chris Smith	.05
69	Ralph Cindrich	.05
70	Christian Okoye (FL)	.05
71	Charles McRae	.05
72	Jon Vaughn	.05
73	Eric Swann	.30
74	Bill Musgrave	.05
75	Eric Bieniemy	.20
76	Pat Tyrance	.05
77	Vince Clark	.05
78	Eugene Williams	.05
79	Rob Carpenter	.05
80	Deion Sanders (FL)	.25
81	Roman Phifer	.10
82	Greg Lewis	.05
83	John Johnson	.05
84	Richard Howell (A)	.05
85	Jesse Campbell	.05
86	Stanley Richard	.05
87	Alfred Williams	.05
88	Mike Pritchard	.25
89	Mel Agee	.05
90	Aaron Craver	.05
91	Tim Barnett	.05
92	Wesley Carroll	.05
93	Kevin Scott	.05
94	Darren Lewis	.05
95	Tim Bruton	.05
96	Tim James	.05
97	Darryl Lewis	.05
98	Shawn Jefferson	.20
99	Mitch Donahue	.05
100	Marvin Demoff (A)	.05
101	Adrian Cooper	.05
102	Bruce Pickens	.05
103	Scott Zolak	.05
104	Phil Hansen	.05
105	Ed King	.05
106	Mike Jones	.05
107	Alvin Harper	.50
108	Robert Young	.05
109	Offensive Top Prospects	.05
110	Defensive Top Prospects	.05

1992 Star Pics Fb

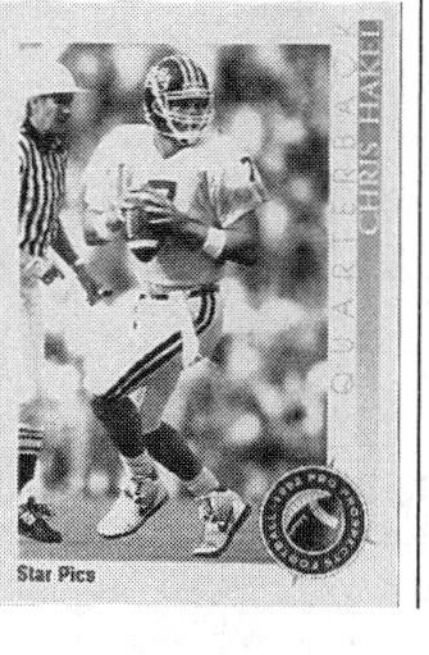

The top collegiate pro prospects are featured in this 100-card set from Star Pics. Each card front has a glossy color action photo on the front, with a white border. The player's name and position run vertically along the left side of the card. A Star Pics logo appears in the lower right corner. The card back has a mug shot of the player, and summarizes his collegiate accomplishments. A scouting report, which lists the player's strengths and weaknesses, is also given. A card number appears in the upper left corner. Cards were sold as a factory set, or in 10-card packs. Subsets in the main set included five Flashback cards (#s 10, 20, 30, 50 and 70) and 10 StarStat cards. Two StarStat cards (#s 1 and 65) were included in the factory sets. The eight others were random inserts in packs.

		MT
Complete Set (100):		6.00
Common Player:		.05
Common Autograph:		6.00
Autograph Cards:		20x-40x
NFL Autographs:		100x-200x
1	Steve Emtman	.10
2	Chris Hakel	.05
3	Phillippi Sparks	.05
4	Howard Dinkins	.05
5	Robert Brooks	.75
6	Chris Pederson	.05
7	Bucky Richardson	.10
8	Keith Goganious	.05
9	Robert Porcher	.05
10	Andre Rison	.20
11	Jason Hanson	.30
12	Tommy Vardell	.10
13	Kurt Barber	.05
14	Bernard Dafney	.05
15	Levon Kirkland	.05
16	Corey Widmer	.05
17	Santana Dotson	.10
18	Chris Holder	.05
19	Elbert Turner	.05
20	Mike Croel	.10
21	Darren Perry	.05
22	Troy Vincent	.10
23	Quentin Coyratt	.40
24	John Brown III	.05
25	John Ray	.05
26	Vaughn Dunbar	.10
27	Stacey Dillard	.05
28	Alonzo Spellman	.20
29	Darren Woodson	.10
30	Pat Swilling	.10
31	Eddie Robinson	.05
32	Tyji Armstrong	.05
33	Bill Johnson	.05
34	Eugene Chung	.05
35	Ricardo McDonald	.05
36	Sean Lumpkin	.05
37	Greg Skrepenak	.05
38	Ashley Ambrose	.05
39	Kevin Smith	.05
40	Todd Collins	.05
41	Shane Dronett	.05
42	Ronnie West	.05
43	Darryl Williams	.05
44	Rodney Blackshear	.05
45	Dion Lambert	.05
46	Mike Saunders	.05
47	Keo Coleman	.05
48	Dana Hall	.10
49	Arthur Marshall	.05
50	Leonard Russell	.05
51	Matt Rodgers	.05
52	Shane Collins	.05
53	Courtney Hawkins	.10
54	Chuck Smith	.05
55	Joe Bowden	.05
56	Gene McGuire	.05
57	Tracy Scroggins	.10
58	Mark D'Onofrio	.05
59	Jimmy Smith	1.00
60	Carl Pickens	1.50
61	Robert Harris	.05
62	Erick Anderson	.05
63	Doug Rigby	.05
64	Keith Hamilton	.05
65	Vaughn Dunbar	.10
66	Willie Clay	.05
67	Robert Jones	.05
68	Leon Searcy Jr.	.05
69	Elliot Pilton	.05
70	Thurman Thomas	.20
71	Mark Wheeler	.05
72	Jeremy Lincoln	.10
73	Tony McCoy	.05
74	Charles Davenport	.05
75	Patrick Rowe	.05
76	Tommy Jeter	.05
77	Rod Smith	.05
78	Johnny Mitchell	.25
79	Corey Barlow	.05
80	Scottie Graham	.15
81	Mark Bounds	.05
82	Chester McGlockton	.10
83	Ray Roberts	.05
84	Dale Carter	.10
85	James Patton	.05
86	Tyrone Legette	.05
87	Leodis Flowers	.05
88	Rico Smith	.05
89	Kevin Turner	.10
90	Steve Emtman	.10
91	Rodney Culver	.10
92	Chris Mims	.15
93	Carlos Snow	.05
94	Corey Harris	.10
95	Nate Williams	.05
96	Timothy Roberts	.05
97	Steve Israel	.05
98	Tony Smith	.05
99	Dwayne Sabb	.05
100	Checklist	.05

1992 Star Pics StarStat Bonus Fb

Eight top collegiate NFL prospects are featured in this insert set. Cards were random inserts in 10-card foil StarPaks and compare the players' collegiate statistics to those of NFL greats. Fronts have the "StarStats" logo on them; backs have the card number. Two additional StarStat cards, for Steve Emtman and Vaughn Dunbar, were also made and were included in the 1992 Star Pics factory set.

		MT
Complete Set (8):		8.00
Common Player:		.50
1	Dale Carter	1.00
2	Carl Pickens	6.00
3	Alonzo Spellman	1.00
4	Jimmy Smith	1.25
5	Quentin Coryatt	2.00
6	Troy Vincent	.50
7	Darryl Williams	.50
8	Courtney Hawkins	.50

1989 Star-Cal Decals

The 54-card, 3" x 4-1/2" sticker set featured players from six NFL teams, and was licensed by the NFL and the NFL Players' Association. The cards have rounded edges with a silver logo (First Edition 1989) in the upper left corner. Each decal also came with a pennant-shaped mini team banner decal in the player's team colors.

		MT
Complete Set (54):		80.00
Common Player:		1.00
1	Raul Allegre	1.00
2	Carl Banks	1.00
3	Cornelius Bennett	1.50
4	Brian Blades	1.50
5	Kevin Butler	1.00
6	Harry Carson	1.00
7	Anthony Carter	1.00
8	Michael Carter	1.00
9	Shane Conlan	1.00
10	Roger Craig	1.50
11	Richard Dent	1.25
12	Chris Doleman	1.00
13	Tony Dorsett	4.00
14	Dave Duerson	1.00
15	Charles Haley	1.50
16	Dan Hampton	1.00
17	Al Harris	1.00
18	Mark Jackson	1.00
19	Vance Johnson	1.00
20	Steve Jordan	1.00
21	Clarence Kay	1.00
22	Jim Kelly	4.00
23	Tommy Kramer	1.00
24	Ronnie Lott	2.00
25	Lionel Manuel	1.00
26	Guy McIntyre	1.00
27	Steve McMichael	1.25
28	Karl Mecklenburg	1.25
29	Orson Mobley	1.00
30	Joe Montana	20.00
31	Joe Morris	1.00
32	Joe Nash	1.00
33	Ricky Nattiel	1.00
34	Chuck Nelson	1.00
35	Darrin Nelson	1.00
36	Karl Nelson	1.00
37	Scott Norwood	1.00
38	Bart Oates	1.00
39	Rufus Porter	1.00
40	Andre Reed	2.00
41	Phil Simms	2.00
42	Mike Singletary	1.50
43	Fred Smerlas	1.00
44	Bruce Smith	2.00
45	Kelly Stouffer	1.00
46	Scott Studwell	1.00
47	Matt Suhey	1.00
48	Steve Tasker	1.00
49	Keena Turner	1.00
50	John L. Williams	1.25
51	Wade Wilson	1.00
52	Sammy Winder	1.00
53	Tony Woods	1.00
54	Eric Wright	1.00

1990 Star-Cal Decals Prototypes

The four-card, 3" x 4-1/2" set was issued as a preview to the 1990 94-card decal set.

		MT
Complete Set (4):		5.00
Common Player:		1.00
1	Jeff Hostetler	1.00
2	Mike Kenn	1.00
3	Freeman McNeil	1.00
4	Steve Young	3.00

1990 Star-Cal Decals

The 94-card, 3" x 4-1/2" decal set was similar to the 1989 release, complete with facsimile autographs. Six players each from 12 of the league's top teams are featured. Each player decal was issued with a pennant-shaped mini team banner (3-1/2" x 2"). The set is also known as the Grid-Star decal set.

		MT
Complete Set (94):		160.00
Common Player:		1.00
1	Eric Allen	1.00
2	Marcus Allen	2.00
3	Flipper Anderson	1.00
4A	Neal Anderson (printed name in black letters)	1.00
4B	Neal Anderson (printed name in white letters)	1.00
5A	Carl Banks (printed name in black letters)	1.00
5B	Carl Banks (printed name in white letters)	1.00
6	Mark Bavaro	1.00
7	Cornelius Bennett	1.50
8	Brian Blades	1.00
9	Joey Browner	1.00
10	Keith Byars	1.00
11A	Anthony Carter (printed name in black letters)	1.00

11B	Anthony Carter (printed name in white letters)	1.00
12	Cris Carter	2.00
13	Michael Carter	1.00
14	Gary Clark	1.00
15	Mark Collins	1.00
16	Shane Conlan	1.00
17	Jim Covert	1.00
18A	Roger Craig (printed name black letters)	1.50
18B	Roger Craig (printed name white letters)	1.50
19	Richard Dent	1.25
20	Chris Doleman	1.00
21	Dave Duerson	1.00
22	Henry Ellard	1.50
23A	John Elway (printed name in black letters)	6.00
23B	John Elway (printed name in white letters)	8.00
24	Jim Everett	1.25
25	Mervyn Fernandez	1.00
26	Willie Gault	1.25
27	Bob Golic	1.00
28	Darrell Green	1.25
29	Kevin Greene	1.25
30	Charles Haley	1.25
31	Jay Hilgenberg	1.00
32	Pete Holohan	1.00
33	Kent Hull	1.00
34	Bobby Humphrey	1.00
35A	Bo Jackson (printed name in black letters)	2.00
35B	Bo Jackson (printed name in white letters)	2.00
36	Keith Jackson	1.25
37	Mark Jackson	1.25
38	Joe Jacoby	1.00
39	Vance Johnson	1.00
40	Jim Kelly	3.00
41	Bernie Kosar	1.25
42	Greg Kragen	1.00
43	Jeff Lageman	1.00
44	Pat Leahy	1.00
45	Howie Long	1.25
46A	Ronnie Lott (serial numbered 11419)	1.50
46B	Ronnie Lott (serial numbered 11414)	1.50
47	Kevin Mack	1.00
48	Charles Mann	1.00
49	Leonard Marshall	1.00
50	Clay Matthews	1.25
51	Eric McMillan	1.00
52	Karl Mecklenburg	1.25
53	Dave Meggett (UER) (name misspelled Megget)	1.25
54A	Eric Metcalf (serial numbered 11414)	2.00
54B	Eric Metcalf (serial numbered 11424)	1.50
55	Keith Millard	1.00
56	Frank Minnifield	1.00
57A	Joe Montana (printed name in black letters autograph covers only left leg)	12.00
57B	Joe Montana (printed name in black letters autograph covers both legs)	15.00
57C	Joe Montana (printed name in white letters autograph covers only left leg)	20.00
58	Joe Nash	1.00
59	Ken O'Brien	1.25
60	Rufus Porter	1.00
61	Andre Reed	1.50
62	Mark Rypien	1.25
63	Gerald Riggs	1.00
64	Mickey Shuler	1.00
65	Clyde Simmons	1.25
66A	Phil Simms (printed name in black letters)	1.50
66B	Phil Simms (printed name in white letters)	1.50
67A	Mike Singletary (printed name in black letters)	1.50
67B	Mike Singletary (printed name in white letters)	1.50
68	Jackie Slater	1.00
69	Bruce Smith	1.50
70A	Kelly Stouffer (serial numbered 11414)	1.00
70B	Kelly Stouffer (serial numbered 11427)	1.00
71	John Taylor	1.25
72	Lawyer Tillman	1.00
73	Al Toon	1.25
74A	Herschel Walker (printed name in black letters)	1.50
74B	Herschel Walker (printed name in white letters)	1.50
75	Reggie White	2.00
76A	John L. Williams (printed name in black letters autograph below knees)	1.00
76B	John L. Williams (printed name in black letters autograph above knees)	1.00
76C	John L. Williams (printed name in white letters autograph below knees)	1.00
77	Tony Woods	1.00
78	Gary Zimmerman	1.00

1988 Starline Prototypes

The four-card, regular-size set was never issued to the public and just 75 sets were produced. Each card in the set features a color photo with a blue border.

		MT
Complete Set (4):		500.00
Common Player:		75.00
1	John Elway	150.00
2	Bernie Kosar	75.00
3	Joe Montana	275.00
4	Phil Simms	75.00

1961 Steelers Jay Publishing

The 12-card, 5" x 7" set features black and white photos with blank backs and were issued in 12-card packs for 25 cents.

		NM
Complete Set (12):		30.00
Common Player:		2.50
1	Preston Carpenter	2.50
2	Dean Derby	2.50
3	Buddy Dial	2.50
4	John Henry Johnson	2.50
5	Bobby Layne	2.50
6	Gene Lipscomb	2.50
7	Bill Mack	2.50
8	Fred Mautino	2.50
9	Lou Michaels	2.50
10	Buddy Parker (CO)	2.50
11	Myron Pottios	2.50
12	Tom Tracy	2.50

1963 Steelers IDL

The 26-card, 4" x 5" set features black and white photos with white borders and an IDL logo in the bottom left corner. The backs are blank.

		NM
Complete Set (26):		75.00
Common Player:		3.00
1	Frank Atkinson	3.00
2	Jim Bradshaw	3.00
3	Ed Brown	3.00
4	John Burrell	3.00
5	Preston Carpenter	3.00
6	Lou Cordileone	3.00
7	Buddy Dial	3.00
8	Bob Ferguson	3.00
9	Glenn Glass	3.00
10	Dick Haley	3.00
11	Dick Hoak	3.00
12	John Henry Johnson	3.00
13	Brady Keys	3.00
14	Joe Krupa	3.00
15	Ray Lemek	3.00
16	Bill Mack	3.00
17	Lou Michaels	3.00
18	Bill Nelsen	3.00
19	Buzz Nutter	3.00
20	Myron Pottios	3.00
21	John Reger	3.00
22	Mike Sandusky	3.00
23	Ernie Stautner	3.00
24	George Tarasovic	3.00
25	Clendon Thomas	3.00
26	Tom Tracy	3.00

1968 Steelers KDKA

The 15-card, 2-3/8" x 4-1/8" set featured multiple players on each horizontal card front by position.

		NM
Complete Set (15):		30.00
Common Player:		2.50
1	Centers: (John Knight, Ray Mansfield)	2.50
2	Coaches: (Bill Austin (Head), Fletcher, Torgeson, McLaughlin, Taylor, Heinrich, DePasqua, Berlin (trainer))	2.50
3	Defensive Backs: (Bob Hohn, Paul Martha, Marv Woodson)	2.50
4	Defensive Backs: (John Foruria, Clendon Thomas, Bob Morgan)	2.50
5	Defensive Linemen: (Ben McGhee, Chuck Hinton, Dick Arndt, Ken Kortas, Lloyd Voss)	2.50
6	Flankers: (Roy Jefferson, Ken Hebert (End-Kicker))	2.50
7	Fullbacks: (Earl Gros, Bill Asbury)	2.50
8	Guards: (Larry Granger, Sam Davis, Bruce Van Dyke)	2.50
9	Linebackers: (Andy Russell, Bill Saul, John Campbell, Ray May)	2.50
10	Quarterbacks: (Dick Shiner, Kent Nix)	2.50
11	Rookies: (Ken Hebert, Ernie Ruple, Mike Taylor)	2.50
12	Running Backs: (Dick Hoak, Don Shy, Jim Butler)	2.50
13	Split Ends: (J.R. Wilburn, Dick Compton)	2.50
14	Tackles: (Fran O'Brien, Mike Haggerty, John Brown)	2.50
15	Tight Ends: (John Hilton, Chet Anderson)	2.50

1972 Steelers Photo Sheets

The eight-card, 2" x 3" set was issued in 10" x 8" sheets. The card fronts feature a black and white photo with the Steelers helmet appearing in the lower left corner. The backs are blank.

		NM
Complete Set (8):		30.00
Common Player:		1.50
1	Ralph Anderson, Jim Clack, Bobby Maples, Henry Davis, Jon Kolb, Ray Mansfield, Sam Davis, Chuck Allen	1.50
2	Jim Brumfield, Chuck Beatty, Bobby Walden, Frank Lewis, Lee Calland, Warren Bankston, Mel Blount, John Rowser	1.50
3	Bud Carson (CO), Bob Fry (CO), Dick Hoak (CO), Babe Parilli (CO), George Perles (CO), Lou Riecke (CO), Charley Sumner (CO), Lionel Taylor (CO)	1.50
4	Jack Ham, Ben McGee, Brian Stenger, Lloyd Voss, Bruce Van Dyke, L.C. Greenwood, Gerry Mullins, John Brown	1.50
5	Joe Greene, Bert Askson (UER), Mel Holmes, Dwight White, Bob Adams, Larry Brown, Dave Smith, John McMakin (Misspelled Burt)	1.50
6	Chuck Noll (CO), Jon Staggers, Terry Hanratty, Roy Gerela, Terry Bradshaw, Bob Leahy, Joe Gilliam, Rocky Bleier	1.50
7	Dick Post, Franco Harris, Dennis Meyer, Lorenzo Brinkley, Steve Furness, Gordon Gravelle, Rick Sharp, Dave Kalina	1.50
8	Mike Wagner, Ron Shanklin, Preston Pearson, Glen Edwards, Al Young, John Fuqua, Andy Russell, Steve Davis	1.50

1978 Steelers Team Issue

This set consists of eight 8" x 10" sheets which feature eight black-and-white photos each. Each player photo measures 2" x 3". The sheets are blank-backed and unnumbered.

		NM
Complete Set (8):		80.00
Common Panel:		10.00
1	B. Carr, Reggie Harrison RB, Mel Blount, Doug Becker, Tom Brzoza, Loren Toews, Mike Webster, Dennis Winston	12.00
2	Jack Deloplaine, Wentford Gains, Sidney Thornton, Rick Moser, Randy Reutershan, Nat Terry, Frank Lewis, Brad Wagner	10.00
3	Willie Fry, Steve Furness, Tom Beasley, Ted Petersen, Gary Dunn, L.C. Greenwood, Fred Anderson, Lance Reynolds	12.00
4	Dave LaCrosse, Jon Kolb, Robin Cole, Sam Davis G, Jack Lambert, Jack Ham, Brad Cousina, John Hicks	12.00
5	Gerry Mullins, Dave Pureifory, Ray Pinney, Joe Greene, John Banaszak, Steve Courson, Dwight White, Larry Brown	12.00
6	Chuck Noll CO, Craig Colquitt, Roy Gerela, Terry Bradshaw, Mike Kruczek, Cliff Stoudt, Rocky Bleier, Tony Dungy	18.00
7	John Stallworth, Theo Bell, Randy Grossman, Andre Keys, Jim Smith, L. McCarthey, Lynn Swann, Bennie Cunningham	15.00
8	Mike Wagner, R. Scott, Glen Edwards, Alvin Maxson, Ron Johnson DB, Larry Anderson, Donnie Shell, Franco Harris	12.00

1981 Steelers Police

The 16-card, 2-5/8" x 4-1/8" set was sponsored by the Steelers, Kiwanis, Coca-Cola and local law enforcement. The card fronts feature an action shot with the player's name, position, uniform number, height and weight. The card backs have "Steeler's Tips."

		MT
Complete Set (16):		25.00
Common Player:		.75
9	Matt Bahr	1.25
12	Terry Bradshaw (Passing)	10.00
31	Donnie Shell (Referee back)	1.50
32	Franco Harris (Running with ball)	6.00
47	Mel Blount (Running without ball)	3.00
52	Mike Webster (Standing)	1.50
57	Sam Davis	.75
58	Jack Lambert (Facing left)	5.00
9	Jack Ham (Sportsmanship back)	3.00
64	Steve Furness	.75
68	L.C. Greenwood	2.00
75	Joe Greene	5.00
76	John Banaszak	.75
79	Larry Brown (Chin 7/16" from bottom)	.75
82	John Stallworth (Running with ball)	2.50
88	Lynn Swann (Double coverage back)	6.00

1982 Steelers Police

The 16-card, 2-5/8" x 4-1/8" set is virtually identical in design with the 1981 set. The cards are sponsored by Coca-Cola, local law enforcement, Kiwanis and the Steelers. The card backs contain "Steeler's Tips."

		MT
Complete Set (16):		12.00
Common Player:		.40
12	Terry Bradshaw (Portrait)	5.00
31	Donnie Shell (Double Coverage back)	.60
32	Franco Harris (Portrait)	2.50
44	Frank Pollard	.40
47	Mel Blount (Running with ball)	1.50
52	Mike Webster (Portrait)	.75
58	Jack Lambert (Facing forward)	2.50
59	Jack Ham (Teamwork back)	1.50
65	Tom Beasley	.40
67	Gary Dunn	.40
74	Ray Pinney	.40
79	Larry Brown (Chin 5/16" from bottom)	.40
82	John Stallworth (Posed shot)	1.25
88	Lynn Swann (Sportsmanship back)	3.00
89	Bennie Cunningham	.50
90	Bob Kohrs	.40

1983 Steelers Police

The 17-card, 2-5/8" x 4-1/8" set is similar to the Police sets from 1981 and 1982. Card No. 2 has two variations of the spelling of coach Chuck Noll's last name.

		MT
Complete Set (16):		8.00
Common Player:		.25
1	Walter Abercrombie	.35
2	Gary Anderson (K)	.50
3	Mel Blount	.75
4	Terry Bradshaw	3.00
5	Robin Cole	.25
6	Steve Courson	.25
7	Bennie Cunningham	.35
8	Franco Harris	2.00
9	Greg Hawthorne	.25
10	Jack Lambert	1.00
11A	Chuck Noll (CO ERRM) (Misspelled Knoll)	5.00
11B	Chuck Noll (CO COR)	1.00
12	Donnie Shell	.35
13	John Stallworth	1.00
14	Mike Webster	.75
15	Dwayne Woodruff	.25
16	Rick Woods	.25

1984 Steelers Police

The 16-card, 2-5/8" x 4-1/8" set, sponsored by McDonald's, Kiwanis, the Steelers and local law enforcement, features action shots with "Steeler Tips" on the card backs. The cards are similar to the previous Police sets, except for the McDonald's and Kiwanis logos on the card fronts.

		MT
Complete Set (16):		8.00
Common Player:		.40
1	Gary Anderson (K)	.60
16	Mark Malone	.60
19	David Woodley	.60
30	Frank Pollard	.40
32	Franco Harris	2.00
34	Walter Abercrombie	.50
49	Dwayne Woodruff	.40
52	Mike Webster	.75
57	Mike Merriweather	.60
58	Jack Lambert	1.50
67	Gary Dunn	.40
73	Craig Wolfley	.40
82	John Stallworth	1.50
83	Louis Lipps	1.00
92	Keith Gary	.40
92	Keith Willis	.50

1985 Steelers Police

The 16-card, 2-5/8" x 4-1/8" set was sponsored by local law enforcement, Giant Eagle, the Steelers and Kiwanis. The card backs have "Steeler Tips."

		MT
Complete Set (16):		5.00
Common Player:		.40
1	Gary Anderson K (Kickoff back)	.50
16	Mark Malone (Playbook back)	.50
21	Eric Williams	.40
30	Frank Pollard (Second Effort back)	.40
31	Donnie Shell (Zone back)	.50
34	Walter Abercrombie (Teamwork back)	.50
49	Dwayne Woodruff (Turnover back)	.40
50	David Little	.50
52	Mike Webster (Offside back)	.75
53	Bryan Hinkle (Blindside back)	.40
56	Robin Cole (Timeout back)	.40
57	Mike Merriweather (Blitz back)	.60
82	John Stallworth (Captains back)	1.50
83	Louis Lipps (Pride back)	.60
93	Keith Willis (QB Sack card)	.40
NNO	Chuck Noll CO (Coach back)	1.25

1986 Steelers Police

The 15-card, 2-5/8" x 4-1/8" set was issued by Kiwanis, Giant Eagle, local law enforcement and the Steelers. The card fronts are virtually identical to the 1985 set, with the Giant Eagle and Kiwanis logos found in the top corners and brief bio information located along the bottom edge. The card backs contain "Steeler Tips."

		MT
Complete Set (15):		5.00
Common Player:		.35
1	Gary Anderson (K) (Field Goal back)	.60
16	Mark Malone (Quarterback back)	.60
24	Rich Erenberg	.50
30	Frank Pollard (Running Back back)	.50
31	Donnie Shell (Interception back)	.60
34	Walter Abercrombie (Penalty back)	.50
49	Dwayne Woodruff	.35
52	Mike Webster (Possession back)	.75
53	Bryan Hinkle (Prevent back)	.35
56	Robin Cole (Equipmen back)	.35
57	Mike Merriweather (Linebacker back)	.50
62	Tunch Ilkin	.50
64	Edmund Nelson	.35
67	Gary Dunn (Defensive Holding back)	.35
82	John Stallworth (Victory back)	1.00
83	Louis Lipps (Receiver back)	.75

1987 Steelers Police

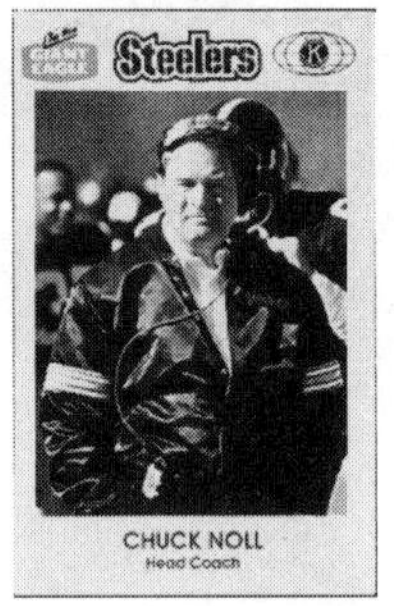

The 16-card, 2-5/8" x 4-1/8" set has basically the same design as the 1985 and 1986 sets, complete with Kiwanis and Giant Eagle logos and "Steeler Tips."

		MT
Complete Set (16):		5.00
Common Player:		.35
1	Walter Abercrombie (Option Pass back)	.50
2	Gary Anderson (K) (Extra Point back)	.60
3	Bubby Brister	.90
4	Gary Dunn (Neutral Zone back)	.35
5	Preston Gothard	.35
6	Bryan Hinkle (Outside Linebackers back)	.50
7	Earnest Jackson	.50
8	Louis Lipps (Corner Pattern back)	.75
9	Mark Malone (Adverse Conditions back)	.60
10	Mike Merriweather (Instant Replay back)	.50
11	Chuck Noll (CO) (Referee back)	.75
12	John Rienstra	.35
13	Donnie Shell (Defense back)	.60
14	John Stallworth (Crackback Block back)	1.00
15	Mike Webster (Sportsmanship back)	.75
16	Keith Willis (Down back)	.35

1988 Steelers Police

The 16-card, 2-5/8" x 4-1/8" set is similar in design to the previous mid-1980s Steelers Police set as it is sponsored by Giant Eagle and Kiwanis and features "Steeler Tips" on the card backs. The Steelers helmet on the card backs have three white diamonds as opposed to the previous three years' helmets which had two black diamonds.

		MT
Complete Set (16):		5.00
Common Player:		.35
1	Gary Anderson (K)	.60
2	Bubby Brister	.75
3	Thomas Everett	.60
4	Delton Hall	.35
5	Bryan Hinkle	.35
6	Tunch Ilkin	.35
7	Earnest Jackson	.50
8	Louis Lipps	.60
9	David Little	.35
10	Mike Merriweather	.50
11	Frank Pollard	.50
12	John Rienstra	.35
13	Mike Webster	.75
14	Keith Willis	.35
15	Craig Wolfley	.35
16	Rod Woodson	1.50

1989 Steelers Police

The 16-card, 2-5/8" x 4-1/8" set is virtually identical to previous Police sets with sponsorships by Kiwanis and Giant Eagle. The card backs contain "Steeler Tips '89."

		MT
Complete Set (16):		5.00
Common Player:		.40
1	Gary Anderson	.60
6	Bubby Brister	.60
18	Harry Newsome	.40
24	Rodney Carter	.40
26	Rod Woodson	1.00
27	Thomas Everett	.60
33	Merril Hoge	.40
53	Bryan Hinkle	.40
54	Hardy Nickerson	.75
62	Tunch Ilkin	.40
63	Dermontti Dawson	.60
74	Terry Long	.40
78	Tim Johnson	.40
83	Louis Lipps	.75
97	Aaron Jones	.40
98	Gerald Williams	.40

1990 Steelers Police

The 16-card, 2-5/8" x 4-1/8" set features identical front designs as previous Police sets, with the Kiwanis and Giant Eagle logos. The card backs have "Steelers '90 Tips."

		MT
Complete Set (16):		5.00
Common Player:		.35
1	Gary Anderson (K)	.35
2	Bubby Brister	.60
3	Thomas Everett	.35
4	Merril Hoge	.35
5	Tunch Ilkin	.35
6	Carnell Lake	.50
7	Louis Lipps	.75
8	David Little	.35
9	Greg Lloyd	.75
10	Mike Mularkey	.35
11	Hardy Nickerson	.75
12	Chuck Noll (CO)	.75
13	John Rienstra	.35
14	Keith Willis	.35
15	Rod Woodson	.90
16	Tim Worley	.50

1991 Steelers Police

The 16-card, 2-5/8" x 4-1/8" set features front and back designs which are similar to previous Police sets. The card backs contain "Steelers Tips '91" while the Giant Eagle and Kiwanis logos appear on both sides.

		MT
Complete Set (16):		5.00
Common Player:		.35
1	Gary Anderson (K)	.35
2	Bubby Brister	.60
3	Dermontti Dawson	.35
4	Eric Green	.75
5	Bryan Hinkle	.35
6	Merril Hoge	.50
7	John Jackson	.35
8	D.J. Johnson	.35
9	Carnell Lake	.50
10	Louis Lipps	.60
11	Greg Lloyd	1.00
12	Mike Mularkey	.35
13	Chuck Noll (CO)	.75
14	Dan Stryzinski	.35
15	Gerald Williams	.35
16	Rod Woodson	.90

1992 Steelers Police

The 16-card, 2-5/8" x 4-3/16" set was sponsored by Kiwanis and Giant Eagle and featured a color shot on the card front. The player's height, weight and position appear below his name with "Steelers Tips '92" and the Steelers' 60th anniversary logo featured on the card backs.

		MT
Complete Set (16):		5.00
Common Player:		.35
1	Gary Anderson (K)	.35
2	Bubby Brister	.50
3	Bill Cowher (CO)	.75
4	Dermontti Dawson	.35
5	Eric Green	.50
6	Carlton Haselrig	.35
7	Merril Hoge	.35
8	John Jackson	.35
9	Carnell Lake	.50
10	Louis Lipps	.60
11	Greg Lloyd	.75
12	Neil O'Donnell	1.00
13	Tom Ricketts	.35
14	Gerald Williams	.35
15	Jerrol Williams	.35
16	Rod Woodson	.75

1993 Steelers Police

The 16-card, 2-1/2" x 4" set, sponsored by Giant Eagle and Kiwanis, features a color action shot on the card front with "Steelers Tips '93" on the back. The Kiwanis and Giant Eagle logos appear on both the card front and back.

		MT
Complete Set (16):		5.00
Common Player:		.30
1	Gary Anderson (K)	.30
2	Adrian Cooper	.30
3	Bill Cowher (CO)	.50
4	Dermontti Dawson	.30
5	Donald Evans	.30
6	Eric Green	.50
7	Bryan Hinkle	.30

8	Merril Hoge	.30
9	Garry Howe	.30
10	Greg Lloyd	.75
11	Neil O'Donnell	1.00
12	Jerry Olsavsky	.30
13	Leon Searcy	.30
14	Dwight Stone	.30
15	Gerald Williams	.30
16	Rod Woodson	.75

1995 Steelers Eat'n Park

The four-strip card set was issued by Eat'n Park during a four-week window and each strip contained three peel-off player cards. The card fronts feature a color image over a silver background. Each strip was sold for 99 cents.

		MT
Complete Set (4):		5.00
Common Player:		1.00
1	Darren Perry, Rod Woodson, Greg Lloyd	1.50
2	Ray Seals, Carnell Lake, Kevin Greene	1.00
3	Dermontti Dawson, Erric Pegram, Mark Bruener	1.00
4	Kordell Stewart, Yancey Thigpen, Neil O'Donnell	2.50

1995 Steelers Giant Eagle Coins

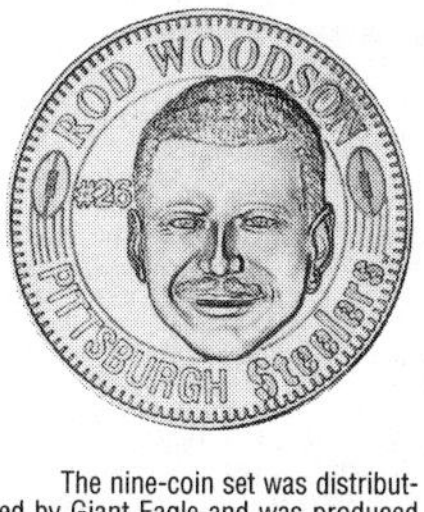

The nine-coin set was distributed by Giant Eagle and was produced by Classic Pro Line. The coins were available in packs with cards for $1.89. The coins/cards were issued over a nine-week period beginning Sept. 3. The coin fronts have the player's face while the backs have the Pittsburgh team logo.

		MT
Complete Set (9):		10.00
Common Player:		1.00
1	Mel Blount	1.00
2	Bill Cowher (CO)	1.00
3	Joe Greene	1.50
4	Kevin Greene	1.00
5	Franco Harris	1.50
6	Jack Lambert	1.50
7	Greg Lloyd	1.50
8	Byron "Bam" Morris	1.00
9	Rod Woodson	1.50

1995 Steelers Giant Eagle ProLine

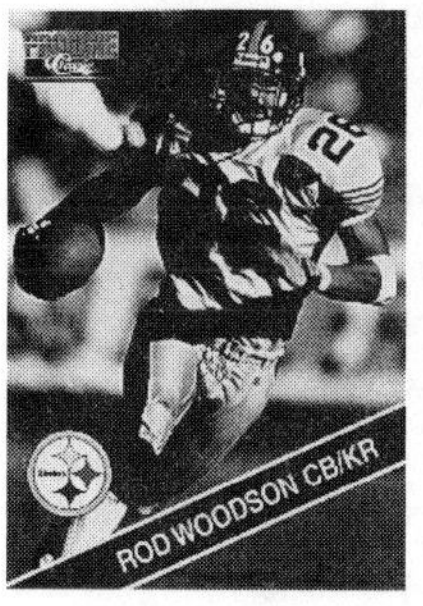

The nine-card, standard-size set, issued by Giant Eagle and produced by Classic Pro Line, was distributed in packs with the nine-coin set. The card fronts feature a color action shot with the Steelers logo appearing in the lower left corner. The card backs have a checklist of the nine players.

		MT
Complete Set (9):		8.00
Common Player:		.75
1	Kevin Greene	.75
2	Franco Harris	1.00
3	Greg Lloyd	1.00
4	Joe Greene	1.00
5	Byron "Bam" Morris	.75
6	Jack Lambert	1.00
7	Rod Woodson	1.00
8	Mel Blount	.75
9	Bill Cowher (CO)	.75

1996 Steelers Kids Club

The Steelers sponsored this four-card set. The cards feature color photography and black and yellow borders.

		MT
Complete Set (4):		5.00
Common Player:		1.00
1	Bill Cowher CO	1.50
2	Greg Lloyd	1.00
3	Kordell Stewart	3.00
4	Rod Woodson	1.00

1979 Stop 'N' Go

These 18 3D cards were available at Stop 'N' Go markets in 1979. Each front has a 3D effect player photo on the front, along with his team's helmet at the top. His name and team name are in a panel at the bottom of the card; "NFL 3-D Football Stars" is written at the top. The back of the card is numbered 1 of 18, etc., and includes yearly stats, plus summaries of the player's professional and collegiate accomplishments. The Stop 'N' Go logo is also on the card back. The cards measure 2-1/8" x 3-1/4".

		NM
Complete Set (18):		45.00
Common Player:		1.25
1	Gregg Bingham	1.25
2	Ken Burrough	1.50
3	Preston Pearson	1.50
4	Sam Cunningham	2.00
5	Robert Newhouse	2.00
6	Walter Payton	13.00
7	Robert Brazile	1.50
8	Rocky Bleier	2.50
9	Toni Fritsch	1.25
10	Jack Ham	3.00
11	Jay Saldi	1.25
12	Roger Staubach	15.00
13	Franco Harris	8.00
14	Otis Armstrong	2.00
15	Lyle Alzado	2.00
16	Billy Johnson	1.50
17	Elvin Bethea	1.50
18	Joe Greene	5.00

1980 Stop 'N' Go

These 3D cards were available with beverage purchases at participating Stop 'N' Go markets in 1980. The card design is similar to the previous year's design, except the card front has a star on each side of the panel at the bottom where the player's name is. The card back is somewhat different, however, with the main difference being the 1979 statistics and a 1980 copyright logo.

		NM
Complete Set (48):		50.00
Common Player:		.75
1	John Jefferson	1.00
2	Herbert Scott	.75
3	Pat Donovan	.75
4	William Andrews	1.25
5	Frank Corral	.75
6	Fred Dryer	1.50
7	Franco Harris	5.00
8	Leon Gray	.75
9	Gregg Bingham	.75
10	Louis Kelcher	.75
11	Robert Newhouse	1.25
12	Preston Pearson	1.00
13	Wallace Francis	1.00
14	Pat Haden	2.00
15	Jim Youngblood	.75
16	Rocky Bleier	1.50
17	Gifford Nielsen	.75
18	Elvin Bethea	1.00
19	Charlie Joiner	3.00
20	Tony Hill	1.00
21	Drew Pearson	1.25
22	Alfred Jenkins	1.00
23	Dave Elmendorf	.75
24	Jack Reynolds	1.25
25	Joe Greene	3.00
26	Robert Brazile	1.00
27	Mike Reinfeldt	.75
28	Bob Griese	4.50
29	Harold Carmichael	1.50
30	Ottis Anderson	4.00
31	Ahmad Rashad	3.50
32	Archie Manning	1.50
33	Ricky Bell	1.00
34	Jay Saldi	.75
35	Ken Burrough	1.00
36	Don Woods	.75
37	Henry Childs	.75
38	Wilbur Jackson	.75
39	Steve DeBerg	1.50
40	Ron Jessie	.75
41	Mel Blount	2.50
42	Cliff Branch	1.50
43	Chuck Muncie	1.25
44	Ken MacAfee	.75
45	Charley Young	1.00
46	Cody Jones	.75
47	Jack Ham	2.00
48	Ray Guy	1.50

1976 Sunbeam NFL Die Cuts

The 28-card, standard-sized set is die-cut so that each card can stand up when perforated. The team's helmet, name and player drawing appear on the card fronts while the backs have a brief team history with the Sunbeam logo. The cards were printed on white or gray stock, with or without the Sunbeam logo.

		NM
Complete Set (29):		200.00
Common Player:		8.00
1	Atlanta Falcons	8.00
2	Baltimore Colts	8.00
3	Buffalo Bills	8.00
4	Chicago Bears	8.00
5	Cincinnati Bengals	8.00
6	Cleveland Browns	8.00
7	Dallas Cowboys	10.00
8	Denver Broncos	8.00
9	Detroit Lions	8.00
10	Green Bay Packers	10.00
11	Houston Oilers	8.00
12	Kansas City Chiefs	8.00
13	Los Angeles Rams	8.00
14	Miami Dolphins	10.00
15	Minnesota Vikings	8.00
16	New England Patriots	8.00
17	New Orleans Saints	8.00
18	New York Giants	8.00
19	New York Jets	8.00
20	Oakland Raiders	10.00
21	Philadelphia Eagles	8.00
22	Pittsburgh Steelers	8.00
23	St. Louis Cardinals	8.00
24	San Diego Chargers	8.00
25	San Francisco 49ers	10.00
26	Seattle Seahawks	8.00
27	Tampa Bay Buccaneers	8.00
28	Washington Redskins	10.00
NNO	NFL Logo (Blankbacked)	8.00

1976 Sunbeam SEC Die Cuts

The 20-card, standard-size set was die-cut so when each card was perforated, it could stand up. The set is similar in design to the NFL set of the same year, except with SEC teams. The card fronts feature the school's logo with the backs containing the school's 1976 schedule. The cards were distributed in Sunbeam bread packages.

		NM
Complete Set (20):		125.00
Common Player:		5.00
1	Alabama Crimson Tide (Team Profile)	10.00
2	Alabama Crimson Tide (Schedule)	10.00
3	Auburn War Eagle (Team Profile)	6.00
4	Auburn War Eagle (Schedule)	6.00
5	Florida Gators (Team Profile)	7.00
6	Florida Gators (Schedule)	7.00
7	Georgia Bulldogs (Team Profile)	6.00
8	Georgia Bulldogs (Schedule)	6.00
9	Kentucky Wildcats (Team Profile)	6.00
10	Kentucky Wildcats (Schedule)	6.00
11	Louisiana St. Tigers (Team Profile)	6.00
12	Louisiana St. Tigers (Schedule)	6.00
13	Miss. St. Bulldogs (Team Profile)	5.00
14	Miss. St. Bulldogs (Schedule)	5.00
15	Ole Miss Rebels (Team Profile)	5.00
16	Ole Miss Rebels (Schedule)	5.00
17	Tennessee Volunteers (Team Profile)	7.00
18	Tennessee Volunteers (Schedule)	7.00
19	Vanderbilt Commodores (Team Profile)	5.00
20	Vanderbilt Commodores (Schedule)	5.00

1972 Sunoco Stamps

Each NFL team is represented by 24 players in this 624-stamp set - 12 offensive and 12 defensive players have been chosen. The stamps measure 1-5/8" x 2-3/8" and were given away in perforated sheets of nine at participating Sun Oil Co. gas stations. Each stamp, featuring an oval with a player photo inside against a corresponding team color-coded background, is unnumbered. Two albums were issued to hold the stamps - a 56-page "NFL Action '72" album and a 128-page album. The albums had specific spots for each sticker, as indicated by a square providing the player's name, uniform number, age, height, weight and college he attended. There were 16 additional perforated sheets inside the album, too. The stamps could be placed inside the album by using the tabs which were provided with the album, instead of licking them.

		NM
Complete Set (624):		125.00
Common Player:		.10
(1)	Ken Burrow	.15
(2)	Bill Sandeman	.10
(3)	Andy Maurer	.10
(4)	Jeff Van Note	.20
(5)	Malcolm Snider	.10
(6)	George Kunz	.25
(7)	Jim Mitchell	.10
(8)	Wes Chesson	.10
(9)	Bob Berry	.20
(10)	Dick Shiner	.10
(11)	Jim Butler	.10
(12)	Art Malone	.10
(13)	Claude Humphrey	.25
(14)	John Small	.10
(15)	Glen Condren	.10
(16)	John Zook	.20
(17)	Don Hansen	.10
(18)	Tommy Nobis	1.25
(19)	Greg Brezina	.20
(20)	Ken Reaves	.10
(21)	Tom Hayes	.10
(22)	Tom McCauley	.10
(23)	Bill Bell	.15
(24)	Bill Lothridge	.20
(25)	Ed Hinton	.10
(26)	Bob Vogel	.10
(27)	Glenn Ressler	.10
(28)	Bill Curry	.30
(29)	John Williams	.10
(30)	Dan Sullivan	.10
(31)	Tom Mitchell	.10
(32)	John Mackey	1.50
(33)	Ray Perkins	2.00
(34)	John Unitas	6.00
(35)	Tom Matte	.30
(36)	Norm Bulaich	.25
(37)	Bubba Smith	1.00
(38)	Bill Newsome	.10
(39)	Fred Miller	.10
(40)	Roy Hinton	.10
(41)	Ray May	.10
(42)	Ted Hendricks	1.50
(43)	Charlie Stukes	.10
(44)	Rex Kern	.30
(45)	Jerry Logan	.10
(46)	Rick Volk	.20
(47)	David Lee	.15
(48)	Jim O'Brien	.25
(49)	J.D. Hill	.20
(50)	Willie Young	.10
(51)	Jim Reilly	.10
(52)	Bruce Jarvis	.15
(53)	Levert Carr	.10
(54)	Donnie Green	.10
(55)	Jan White	.20
(56)	Marlin Briscoe	.40
(57)	Dennis Shaw	.15
(58)	O.J. Simpson	12.00
(59)	Wayne Patrick	.10
(60)	John Leypoldt	.10
(61)	Al Cowlings	.75
(62)	Jim Dunaway	.20
(63)	Bob Tatarek	.10
(64)	Cal Snowden	.10
(65)	Paul Guidry	.10
(66)	Edgar Chandler	.20
(67)	Al Andrews	.10
(68)	Robert James	.10
(69)	Alvin Wyatt	.10
(70)	John Pitts	.10
(71)	Pete Richardson	.15
(72)	Spike Jones	.10
(73)	Dick Gordon	.20
(74)	Randy Jackson	.10
(75)	Glen Holloway	.10
(76)	Rick Coady	.10
(77)	Jim Cadile	.10
(78)	Steve Wright	.10
(79)	Bob Wallace	.10
(80)	George Farmer	.15
(81)	Bobby Douglass	.40
(82)	Don Shy	.10
(83)	Cyril Pinder	.10
(84)	Mac Percival	.10
(85)	Willie Holman	.10
(86)	George Seals	.15
(87)	Bill Staley	.10
(88)	Ed O'Bradovich	.20
(89)	Doug Buffone	.10
(90)	Dick Butkus	3.00
(91)	Ross Brupbacher	.20
(92)	Charlie Ford	.10
(93)	Joe Taylor	.10
(94)	Ron Smith	.20
(95)	Jerry Moore	.10
(96)	Bobby Joe Green	.15
(97)	Chip Myers	.10
(98)	Rufus Mayes	.10
(99)	Howard Fest	.10
(100)	Bob Johnson	.30
(101)	Pat Matson	.10
(102)	Vern Holland	.10
(103)	Bruce Coslet	.75
(104)	Bob Trumpy	1.00
(105)	Virgil Carter	.20
(106)	Fred Willis	.10
(107)	Jess Phillips	.10
(108)	Horst Muhlmann	.15
(109)	Royce Berry	.10
(110)	Mike Reid	.50
(111)	Steve Chomyszak	.10
(112)	Ron Carpenter	.10
(113)	Al Beauchamp	.15
(114)	Bill Bergey	.50
(115)	Ken Avery	.10
(116)	Lemar Parrish	.40
(117)	Ken Riley	.40
(118)	Sandy Durko	.10
(119)	Dave Lewis	.10
(120)	Paul Robinson	.20
(121)	Fair Hooker	.20
(122)	Doug Dieken	.10
(123)	John Demarie	.10
(124)	Jim Copeland	.10
(125)	Gene Hickerson	.10
(126)	Bob McKay	.10
(127)	Milt Morin	.20
(128)	Frank Pitts	.10
(129)	Mike Phipps	.50
(130)	Leroy Kelly	1.50
(131)	Bo Scott	.20
(132)	Don Cockroft	.10
(133)	Ron Snidow	.10
(134)	Walter Johnson	.10
(135)	Jerry Sherk	.30
(136)	Jack Gregory	.10
(137)	Jim Houston	.10
(138)	Dale Lindsey	.10
(139)	Bill Andrews	.25
(140)	Clarence Scott	.20
(141)	Ernie Kellerman	.10
(142)	Walt Sumner	.10
(143)	Mike Howell	.10
(144)	Reece Morrison	.10
(145)	Bob Hayes	1.00
(146)	Ralph Neely	.20
(147)	John Niland	.10
(148)	Dave Manders	.20
(149)	Blaine Nye	.10
(150)	Rayfield Wright	.20
(151)	Billy Truax	.10
(152)	Lance Alworth	3.00
(153)	Roger Staubach	10.00
(154)	Duane Thomas	.50
(155)	Walt Garrison	.30
(156)	Mike Clark	.10
(157)	Larry Cole	.10
(158)	Jethro Pugh	.20
(159)	Bob Lilly	2.00
(160)	George Andrie	.20
(161)	Dave Edwards	.10
(162)	Lee Roy Jordan	.90
(163)	Chuck Howley	.30
(164)	Herb Adderley	1.00
(165)	Mel Renfro	.75
(166)	Cornell Green	.30
(167)	Cliff Harris	.20
(168)	Ron Widby	.10
(169)	Jerry Simmons	.10
(170)	Roger Shoals	.10
(171)	Larron Jackson	.10
(172)	George Goeddeke	.10
(173)	Mike Schnitker	.10
(174)	Mike Current	.10
(175)	Billy Masters	.15
(176)	Jack Gehrke	.10
(177)	Don Horn	.20
(178)	Floyd Little	1.00
(179)	Bobby Anderson	.30
(180)	Jim Turner	.20
(181)	Rich Jackson	.10
(182)	Paul Smith	.10
(183)	Dave Costa	.10
(184)	Lyle Alzado	1.00
(185)	Olen Underwood	.10
(186)	Fred Forsberg	.10
(187)	Chip Myrtle	.10
(188)	Leroy Mitchell	.10
(189)	Billy Thompson	.20
(190)	Charlie Greer	.10
(191)	George Saimes	.20
(192)	Billy Van Heusen	.10
(193)	Earl McCullouch	.20
(194)	Jim Yarbrough	.10
(195)	Chuck Walton	.15
(196)	Ed Flanagan	.10
(197)	Frank Gallagher	.10
(198)	Rockne Freitas	.10
(199)	Charlie Sanders	.25
(200)	Larry Walton	.10
(201)	Greg Landry	.40
(202)	Altie Taylor	.20
(203)	Steve Owens	.40
(204)	Errol Mann	.10
(205)	Joe Robb	.10
(206)	Dick Evey	.10
(207)	Jerry Rush	.10
(208)	Larry Hand	.15
(209)	Paul Naumoff	.20
(210)	Mike Lucci	.20
(211)	Wayne Walker	.10
(212)	Lem Barney	1.00
(213)	Dick LeBeau	.20
(214)	Mike Weger	.10
(215)	Wayne Rasmussen	.10
(216)	Herman Weaver	.10
(217)	John Spilis	.10
(218)	Francis Peay	.10
(219)	Bill Lueck	.10
(220)	Ken Bowman	.10
(221)	Gale Gillingham	.20
(222)	Dick Himes	.10
(223)	Rich McGeorge	.10
(224)	Carroll Dale	.20
(225)	Bart Starr	3.50
(226)	Scott Hunter	.30
(227)	John Brockington	.30
(228)	Dave Hampton	.20
(229)	Clarence Williams	.10
(230)	Mike McCoy	.20
(231)	Bob Brown	.20
(232)	Alden Roche	.10
(233)	Dave Robinson	.25
(234)	Jim Carter	.20
(235)	Fred Carr	.20
(236)	Ken Ellis	.15
(237)	Doug Hart	.10
(238)	Al Randolph	.10
(239)	Al Matthews	.10
(240)	Tim Webster	.10
(241)	Jim Beirne	.10
(242)	Bob Young	.10
(243)	Elbert Drungo	.10
(244)	Sam Walton	.20
(245)	Alvin Reed	.10
(246)	Charlie Joiner	1.50
(247)	Dan Pastorini	.30
(248)	Charlie Johnson	.30
(249)	Lynn Dickey	.40
(250)	Woody Campbell	.10
(251)	Robert Holmes	.20
(252)	Mark Moseley	.30
(253)	Pat Holmes	.10
(254)	Mike Tilleman	.10
(255)	Leo Brooks	.10
(256)	Elvin Bethea	.30
(257)	George Webster	.30
(258)	Garland Boyette	.10
(259)	Ron Pritchard	.15
(260)	Zeke Moore	.10
(261)	Willie Alexander	.10
(262)	Ken Houston	1.00
(263)	John Charles	.10
(264)	Linzy Cole	.10
(265)	Elmo Wright	.25
(266)	Jim Tyrer	.20
(267)	Ed Buddle	.20
(268)	Jack Rudnay	.10
(269)	Mo Moorman	.10
(270)	Dave Hill	.10
(271)	Morris Stroud	.10
(272)	Otis Taylor	.40
(273)	Len Dawson	3.00
(274)	Ed Podolak	.30
(275)	Wendell Hayes	.10
(276)	Jan Stenerud	1.25
(277)	Marvin Upshaw	.10
(278)	Curley Culp	.30
(279)	Buck Buchanan	1.00
(280)	Aaron Brown	.10
(281)	Bobby Bell	1.25
(282)	Willie Lanier	1.50
(283)	Jim Lynch	.20
(284)	Jim Marsalis	.20
(285)	Emmitt Thomas	.20
(286)	Jim Kearney	.10
(287)	Johnny Robinson	.40
(288)	Jerrel Wilson	.10
(289)	Jack Snow	.35
(290)	Charlie Cowan	.10
(291)	Tom Mack	.50
(292)	Ken Iman	.10
(293)	Joe Scibelli	.10
(294)	Harry Schuh	.10
(295)	Rob Klein	.20
(296)	Lance Rentzel	.35
(297)	Roman Gabriel	.60
(298)	Les Josephson	.20
(299)	Willie Ellison	.20
(300)	David Ray	.10
(301)	Jack Youngblood	1.25
(302)	Merlin Olsen	1.75
(303)	Phil Olsen	.10
(304)	Coy Bacon	.10
(305)	Jim Purnell	.10
(306)	Marlin McKeever	.20
(307)	Isiah Robertson	.30
(308)	Jim Nettles	.10
(309)	Gene Howard	.10
(310)	Kermit Alexander	.20
(311)	Dave Elmendorf	.10
(312)	Pat Studstill	.20
(313)	Paul Warfield	1.50
(314)	Doug Crusan	.10
(315)	Bob Kuechenberg	.50
(316)	Bob DeMarco	.20
(317)	Larry Little	1.00
(318)	Norm Evans	.20
(319)	Marv Fleming	.20
(320)	Howard Twilley	.30
(321)	Bob Griese	2.50
(322)	Jim Klick	.60
(323)	Larry Csonka	2.00
(324)	Garo Yepremian	.30
(325)	Jim Riley	.10
(326)	Manny Fernandez	.30
(327)	Bob Heinz	.10
(328)	Bill Stanfill	.30
(329)	Doug Swift	.10
(330)	Nick Buoniconti	1.00
(331)	Mike Kolen	.10
(332)	Tim Foley	.30
(333)	Curtis Johnson	.10
(334)	Dick Anderson	.40
(335)	Jake Scott	.50
(336)	Larry Seiple	.10
(337)	Gene Washington	.20
(338)	Grady Alderman	.10
(339)	Ed White	.25
(340)	Mick Tingelhoff	.20
(341)	Milt Sunde	.10
(342)	Ron Yary	.50
(343)	John Beasley	.10
(344)	John Henderson	.10
(345)	Fran Tarkenton	4.00
(346)	Clint Jones	.20
(347)	Dave Osborn	.20
(348)	Fred Cox	.20
(349)	Carl Eller	.50
(350)	Gary Larsen	.10
(351)	Alan Page	1.00
(352)	Jim Marshall	1.00
(353)	Roy Winston	.20
(354)	Lonnie Warwick	.10
(355)	Wally Hilgenberg	.10
(356)	Bobby Bryant	.15
(357)	Ed Sharockman	.10
(358)	Charlie West	.10
(359)	Paul Krause	.60
(360)	Bob Lee	.20
(361)	Randy Vataha	.40
(362)	Mike Montler	.10
(363)	Halvor Hagen	.10
(364)	Jon Morris	.10
(365)	Len St. Jean	.10
(366)	Tom Neville	.10
(367)	Tom Beer	.15
(368)	Ron Sellers	.20
(369)	Jim Plunkett	1.00
(370)	Carl Garrett	.20
(371)	Jim Nance	.30
(372)	Charlie Gogolak	.20
(373)	Ike Lassiter	.10
(374)	Dave Rowe	.10
(375)	Julius Adams	.20
(376)	Dennis Wirgowski	.10
(377)	Ed Weisacosky	.10
(378)	Jim Cheyunski	.10
(379)	Steve Kiner	.10
(380)	Larry Carwell	.10
(381)	John Outlaw	.10
(382)	Rickie Harris	.10
(383)	Don Webb	.10
(384)	Tom Janik	.10
(385)	Al Dodd	.20
(386)	Don Morrison	.10
(387)	Jake Kupp	.10
(388)	John Didion	.10
(389)	Del Williams	.10
(390)	Glen Ray Hines	.10
(391)	Dave Parks	.20
(392)	Dan Abramowicz	.40
(393)	Archie Manning	2.00
(394)	Bob Gresham	.10
(395)	Virgil Robinson	.10
(396)	Charlie Durkee	.10
(397)	Richard Neal	.10
(398)	Bob Pollard	.10
(399)	Dave Long	.10
(400)	Joe Owens	.10
(401)	Carl Cunningham	.10
(402)	Jim Flanigan	.15
(403)	Wayne Colman	.10
(404)	D'Artagnan Martin	.10
(405)	Delles Howell	.10
(406)	Hugo Hollas	.10
(407)	Doug Wyatt	.10
(408)	Julian Fagan	.10
(409)	Don Hermann	.10
(410)	Willie Young	.10
(411)	Bob Hyland	.10
(412)	Greg Larson	.10
(413)	Doug Van Horn	.10
(414)	Charlie Harper	.10
(415)	Bob Tucker	.25
(416)	Joe Morrison	.20
(417)	Randy Johnson	.20
(418)	Tucker Frederickson	.30
(419)	Ron Johnson	.30
(420)	Pete Gogolak	.20
(421)	Henry Reed	.10
(422)	Jim Kanicki	.10
(423)	Roland Lakes	.10
(424)	John Douglas	.10
(425)	Ron Hornsby	.10
(426)	Jim Files	.10
(427)	Willie Williams	.10
(428)	Otto Brown	.10
(429)	Scott Eaton	.10
(430)	Carl Lockhart	.20
(431)	Tom Blanchard	.20
(432)	Rocky Thompson	.20
(433)	Rich Caster	.30
(434)	Randy Rasmussen	.10
(435)	John Schmitt	.10
(436)	Dave Herman	.20
(437)	Winston Hill	.20
(438)	Pete Lammons	.20
(439)	Don Maynard	2.00
(440)	Joe Namath	10.00
(441)	Emerson Boozer	.30
(442)	John Riggins	4.00
(443)	George Nock	.10
(444)	Bobby Howfield	.10
(445)	Gerry Philbin	.10
(446)	John Little	.10
(447)	Chuck Hinton	.10
(448)	Mark Lomas	.10

(449)	Ralph Baker	.10
(450)	Al Atkinson	.10
(451)	Larry Grantham	.20
(452)	John Dockery	.10
(453)	Earlie Thomas	.10
(454)	Phil Wise	.10
(455)	W.K. Hicks	.10
(456)	Steve O'Neal	.15
(457)	Drew Buie	.10
(458)	Art Shell	2.00
(459)	Gene Upshaw	2.00
(460)	Jim Otto	.75
(461)	Geprge Buehler	.10
(462)	Bob Brown	.40
(463)	Ray Chester	.40
(464)	Fred Biletnikoff	2.00
(465)	Daryle Lamonica	.60
(466)	Marv Hubbard	.20
(467)	Clarence Davis	.20
(468)	George Blanda	2.00
(469)	Tony Cline	.10
(470)	Art Thoms	.10
(471)	Tom Keating	.20
(472)	Ben Davidson	1.00
(473)	Phil Villapiano	.40
(474)	Dan Conners	.10
(475)	Duane Benson	.10
(476)	Nemiah Wilson	.10
(477)	Willie Brown	1.00
(478)	George Atkinson	.20
(479)	Jack Tatum	.40
(480)	Jerry DePoyster	.10
(481)	Harold Jackson	.50
(482)	Wade Key	.10
(483)	Henry Allison	.10
(484)	Mike Evans	.10
(485)	Steve Smith	.20
(486)	Harold Carmichael	1.25
(487)	Ben Hawkins	.20
(488)	Pete Liske	.40
(489)	Rick Arrington	.10
(490)	Lee Bouggess	.10
(491)	Tom Woodeshick	.20
(492)	Tom Dempsey	.50
(493)	Richard Harris	.20
(494)	Don Hultz	.10
(495)	Ernie Calloway	.15
(496)	Mel Tom	.10
(497)	Steve Zabel	.20
(498)	Tim Rossovich	.20
(499)	Ron Porter	.10
(500)	Al Nelson	.10
(501)	Nate Ramsey	.10
(502)	Leroy Keyes	.40
(503)	Bill Bradley	.50
(504)	Tom McNeill	.10
(505)	Dave Smith	.10
(506)	Jon Kolb	.10
(507)	Gerry Mullins	.10
(508)	Ray Mansfield	.10
(509)	Bruce Van Dyke	.10
(510)	John Brown	.10
(511)	Ron Shanklin	.30
(512)	Terry Bradshaw	7.50
(513)	Terry Hanratty	.40
(514)	Preston Pearson	.40
(515)	John Fuqua	.20
(516)	Roy Gerela	.10
(517)	L.C. Greenwood	.75
(518)	Joe Greene	2.50
(519)	Lloyd Voss	.10
(520)	Dwight White	.20
(521)	Jack Ham	2.50
(522)	Chuck Allen	.10
(523)	Brian Stenger	.10
(524)	Andy Russell	.75
(525)	John Rowser	.10
(526)	Mel Blount	2.00
(527)	Mike Wagner	.20
(528)	Bobby Walden	.10
(529)	Mel Gray	.30
(530)	Bob Reynolds	.10
(531)	Dan Dierdorf	.60
(532)	Wayne Mulligan	.10
(533)	Clyde Williams	.10
(534)	Ernie McMillan	.10
(535)	Jackie Smith	1.00
(536)	John Gilliam	.20
(537)	Jim Hart	.50
(538)	Pete Beathard	.40
(539)	Johnny Roland	.30
(540)	Jim Bakken	.30
(541)	Ron Yankowski	.10
(542)	Fred Heron	.15
(543)	Bob Rowe	.10
(544)	Chuck Walker	.10
(545)	Larry Stallings	.20
(546)	Jamie Rivers	.10
(547)	Mike McGill	.10
(548)	Miller Farr	.10
(549)	Roger Wehrli	.30
(550)	Larry Willingham	.10
(551)	Larry Wilson	1.00
(552)	Chuck Latourette	.10
(553)	Billy Parks	.20
(554)	Terry Owens	.25
(555)	Doug Wilkerson	.10
(556)	Carl Mauck	.10
(557)	Walt Sweeney	.10
(558)	Russ Washington	.10
(559)	Pettis Norman	.20
(560)	Gary Garrison	.20
(561)	John Hadl	.60
(562)	Mike Montgomery	.10
(563)	Mike Garrett	.30
(564)	Dennis Partee	.10
(565)	Deacon Jones	1.00
(566)	Ron East	.10
(567)	Kevin Hardy	.10
(568)	Steve DeLong	.20
(569)	Rick Redman	.10
(570)	Bob Babich	.15
(571)	Pete Barnes	.10
(572)	Bob Howard	.10
(573)	Joe Beauchamp	.10
(574)	Bryant Salter	.10
(575)	Chris Fletcher	.10
(576)	Jerry LeVias	.20
(577)	Dick Witcher	.10
(578)	Len Rohde	.12
(579)	Randy Beisler	.10
(580)	Forrest Blue	.20
(581)	Woody Peoples	.10
(582)	Cas Banaszek	.10
(583)	Ted Kwalick	.40
(584)	Gene Washington	.50
(585)	John Brodie	1.25
(586)	Ken Willard	.40
(587)	Vic Washington	.20
(588)	Bruce Gossett	.10
(589)	Tommy Hart	.15
(590)	Charlie Krueger	.20
(591)	Earl Edwards	.10
(592)	Cedric Hardman	.20
(593)	Dave Wilcox	.25
(594)	Frank Nunley	.10
(595)	Skip Vanderbundt	.10
(596)	Jimmy Johnson	.60
(597)	Bruce Taylor	.30
(598)	Mel Phillips	.10
(599)	Rosey Taylor	.20
(600)	Steve Spurrier	2.50
(601)	Charley Taylor	1.50
(602)	Jim Snowden	.10
(603)	Ray Schoenke	.10
(604)	Len Hauss	.20
(605)	John Wilbur	.10
(606)	Walt Rock	.10
(607)	Jerry Smith	.20
(608)	Roy Jefferson	.20
(609)	Bill Kilmer	1.00
(610)	Larry Brown	1.00
(611)	Charlie Harraway	.20
(612)	Curt Knight	.10
(613)	Ron McDole	.10
(614)	Manuel Sistrunk	.10
(615)	Diron Talbert	.20
(616)	Verlon Biggs	.10
(617)	Jack Pardee	.75
(618)	Myron Pottios	.20
(619)	Chris Hanburger	.50
(620)	Pat Fischer	.20
(621)	Mike Bass	.10
(622)	Richie Petitbon	.20
(623)	Brig Owens	.10
(624)	Mike Bragg	.15

1972 Sunoco Stamps Update

These unnumbered 1-5/8" x 2-3/8" stamps are identical to the 1972 Sunoco stamps, but were not listed in the album which was produced to house the stamps. They were issued as team sheets later in the year.

		NM
Complete Set (82):		75.00
Common Player:		1.00
(1)	Clarence Ellis	1.00
(2)	Dave Hampton	1.50
(3)	Dennis Havig	1.00
(4)	John James	1.00
(5)	Joe Profit	1.00
(6)	Lonnie Hepburn	1.00
(7)	Dennis Nelson	1.00
(8)	Mike McBath	1.00
(9)	Walt Patulski	1.00
(10)	Bob Asher	1.00
(11)	Steve DeLong	1.00
(12)	Tony McGee	1.00
(13)	James Osborne	1.00
(14)	Jim Seymour	1.00
(15)	Tommy Casanova	1.50
(16)	Neil Craig	1.00
(17)	Essex Johnson	1.25
(18)	Sherman White	1.00
(19)	Bob Briggs	1.00
(20)	Thom Darden	1.25
(21)	Marv Bateman	1.00
(22)	Toni Fritsch	1.00
(23)	Calvin Hill	3.00
(24)	Pat Toomay	1.25
(25)	Pete Duranko	1.00
(26)	Marv Montgomery	1.00
(27)	Rod Sherman	1.00
(28)	Bob Kowalkowski	1.00
(29)	Jim Mitchell	1.00
(30)	Larry Woods	1.00
(31)	Willie Buchanon	1.50
(32)	Leland Glass	1.00
(33)	MacArthur Lane	1.50
(34)	Chester Marcol	1.00
(35)	Ron Widby	1.00
(36)	Ken Burrough	1.50
(37)	Calvin Hunt	1.00
(38)	Ron Saul	1.00
(39)	Greg Simpson	1.00
(40)	Mike Sensibaugh	1.00
(41)	Dave Chapple	1.00
(42)	Jim Langer	6.00
(43)	Mike Eischeid	1.00
(44)	John Gilliam	1.25
(45)	Ron Acks	1.00
(46)	Bob Gladieux	1.00
(47)	Honoe Jackson	1.00
(48)	Reggie Rucker	1.50
(49)	Pat Studstill	1.00
(50)	Bob Windsor	1.00
(51)	Joe Federspiel	1.00
(52)	Bob Newland	4.00
(53)	Pete Athas	1.00
(54)	Charlie Evans	1.00
(55)	Jack Gregory	1.00
(56)	John Mendenhall	1.00
(57)	Ed Bell	1.00
(58)	John Elliott	1.00
(59)	Chris Farasopoulos	1.00
(60)	Bob Svihus	1.00
(61)	Steve Tannen	1.00
(62)	Cliff Branch	3.00
(63)	Gus Otto	1.00
(64)	Otis Sistrunk	1.25
(65)	Charlie Smith	1.00
(66)	John Reaves	1.00
(67)	Larry Watkins	1.00
(68)	Henry Davis	1.00
(69)	Ben McGee	1.00
(70)	Donny Anderson	1.25
(71)	Walker Gillette	1.00
(72)	Martin Imhoff	1.00
(73)	Bobby Moore (aka Ahmad Rashad)	8.00
(74)	Norm Thompson	1.00
(75)	Lionel Aldridge	1.00
(76)	Dave Costa	1.00
(77)	Cid Edwards	1.00
(78)	Tim Rossovich	1.00
(79)	Dave Williams	1.00
(80)	Johnny Fuller	1.00
(81)	Terry Hermeling	1.00
(82)	Paul Laaveg	1.00

A card number in parentheses ( ) indicates the set is unnumbered.

1995 Superior Pix Promos

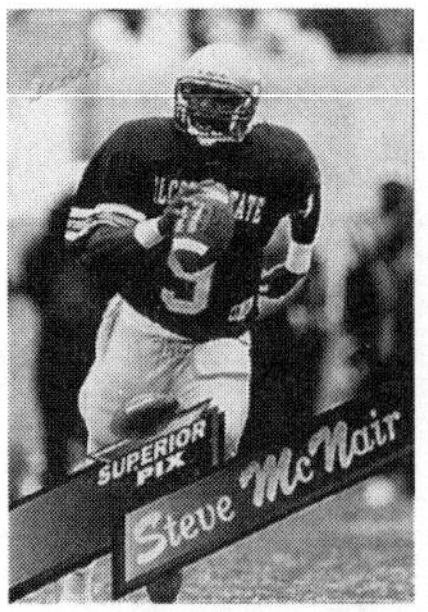

This four-card preview of the 1995 Superior Pix set was distributed through mail and at the 1995 National. The cards are identical to the Superior Pix set except that the promo cards have the National logo on the back.

		MT
Complete Set (4):		8.00
Common Player:		1.00
1	Steve McNair	3.00
2	Kerry Collins	2.00
3	Tyrone Wheatley	1.00
4	Joey Galloway	2.00

1995 Superior Pix

Superior Pix consists of a 110-card base set, an autographed variant and four insert sets. The base cards include the words "95 Draft" printed in gold foil on the front. The inserts include Deep Threat (five cards, 1:9), Instant Impact (five cards, 1:18), Open Field (five cards, 1:18) and Top Defender (five cards, 1:9).

		MT
Complete Set (110):		10.00
Common Player:		.05
1	Ki-Jana Carter	.25
2	Tony Boselli	.25
3	Steve McNair	1.50
4	Michael Westbrook	.50
5	Kerry Collins	1.50
6	Terrell Davis	2.00
7	Kevin Bouie	.05
8	Brian Williams	.05
9	Kez McCorvey	.05
10	Kyle Brady	.25
11	Rob Johnson	.50
12	Carl Greenwood	.05
13	Mark Fields	.05
14	Andrew Greene	.05
15	Orlando Thomas	.05
16	Don Sasa	.05
17	Brent Moss	.05
18	Jamal Willis	.05
19	Michael Hendricks	.05
20	Rashaan Salaam	.50
21	John Sacca	.05
22	Cory Raymer	.05
23	Kirby Dar Dar	.05
24	Lee DeRamus	.05
25	Joey Galloway	.75
26	Mike Frederick	.05
27	Todd Collins	.50
28	Stoney Case	.05
29	Devin Bush	.05
30	Chad May	.05
31	Darick Holmes	.25
32	Johnny Thomas	.05
33	Luther Ellis	.05
34	Tyrone Wheatley	.25
35	Terry Connealy	.05
36	Ruben Brown	.05
37	Kelvin Anderson	.05
38	Tony Berti	.05
39	Steve Ingram	.05
40	Kevin Carter	.25
41	Dave Wohlabaugh	.05
42	Mike Morton	.05
43	Steve Stenstrom	.05
44	Zach Wiegert	.05
45	Rodney Thomas	.10
46	Eddie Goines	.05
47	Kenny Gales	.05
48	Jamal Ellis	.05
49	Demetrius Edwards	.05
50	Justin Armour	.05
51	Billy Williams	.05
52	Ed Hervey	.05
53	Antonio Armstrong	.05
54	Oliver Gibson	.05
55	David Dunn	.10
56	Tyrone Davis	.05
57	Craig Newsome	.05
58	William Strong	.05
59	Sherman Williams	.05
60	James O. Stewart	.25
61	Bryan Schwartz	.05
62	Frank Sanders	.25
63	Barrett Robbins	.05
64	Bronzell Miller	.05
65	Curtis Martin	2.00
66	Chris T. Jones	.50
67	Dave Barr	.05
68	Anthony Brown	.05
69	Ken Dilger	.25
70	Warren Sapp	.25
71	James A. Stewart	.05
72	Corey Fuller	.05
73	Christian Fauria	.25
74	Brian DeMarco	.05
75	J.J. Stokes	.50
76	Hicham El-Mashtoub	.05
77	Anthony Cook	.05
78	Mark Bruener	.25
79	Blake Brockemeyer	.05
80	Derrick Brooks	.05
81	Joe Aska	.05
82	Lance Brown	.05
83	Pete Mitchell	.05
84	Kordell Stewart	2.00
85	Bobby Taylor	.25
86	Jimmy Hitchcock	.05
87	Jack Jackson	.05
88	Ray Zellars	.05
89	Darius Holland	.05
90	Derrick Alexander	.25
91	Torey Hunter	.05
92	Scotty Lewis	.05
93	Carl Reeves	.05
94	Terrell Fletcher	.05
95	Ontiwaun Carter	.05
96	Trezelle Jenkins	.05
97	Mark Birchmeier	.05
98	Len Raney	.05
99	Ronald Cherry	.05
100	Tyrone Wheatley	.25
101	John Jones	.05
102	Zack Crockett	.05
103	Larry Jones	.05
104	Michael McCoy	.05
105	Ellis Johnson	.05
106	Jerrott Willard	.05
107	Jason James	.05
108	J.J. Smith	.05
109	Mike Mamula	.05
110	Checklist	.05

1995 Superior Pix Autographs

This set is a parallel of the Superior Pix base set. Each player autographed a number of their cards. The card fronts have "authentic signature" printed on them and are individually numbered. They were inserted one per pack.

		MT
Complete Set (109):		300.00
Common Player:		2.00
1	Ki-Jana Carter/1000	20.00
2	Tony Boselli/4000	3.00
3	Steve McNair/3000	15.00
4	Michael Westbrook/4000	7.00
5	Kerry Collins/3000	15.00
6	Terrell Davis/5000	18.00
7	Kevin Bouie	2.00
8	Brian Williams	2.00
9	Kez McCorvey/6500	2.00
10	Kyle Brady/3500	3.00
11	Rob Johnson/3000	8.00
12	Carl Greenwood	2.00
13	Mark Fields/5000	2.00
14	Andrew Greene/5000	2.00
15	Orlando Thomas/6000	2.00
16	Don Sasa/6500	2.00
17	Brent Moss	2.00
18	Jamal Willis	2.00
19	Michael Hendricks	2.00
20	Rashaan Salaam/3500	7.00
21	John Sacca	2.00
22	Cory Raymer/6000	2.00
23	Kirby Dar Dar	2.00
24	Lee DeRamus/6500	2.00
25	Joey Galloway/4000	10.00
26	Mike Frederick/6000	2.00
27	Todd Collins/5000	3.00
28	Stoney Case/4000	2.00
29	Devin Bush/5000	2.00
30	Chad May/4000	2.00
31	Darrick Holmes/5500	8.00
32	Johnny Thomas/6500	2.00
33	Luther Ellis/5000	2.00
34	Tyrone Wheatley/5000	3.00
35	Terry Connealy/6500	2.00
36	Ruben Brown/3500	2.00
37	Kelvin Anderson	2.00
38	Tony Berti	2.00
39	Steve Ingram	2.00
40	Kevin Carter/4000	3.00
41	Dave Wohlabaugh/6500	2.00
42	Mike Morton/4000	2.00
43	Steve Stenstrom/5000	2.00
44	Zach Wiegert/5000	2.00
45	Rodney Thomas/5000	3.00
46	Eddie Goines	2.00
47	Kenny Gales/6500	2.00
48	Jamal Ellis/6500	2.00
49	Demetrius Edwards/6500	2.00
50	Justin Armour/5000	2.00
51	Billy Williams	2.00
52	Ed Hervey	2.00
53	Antonio Armstrong	2.00
54	Oliver Gibson	2.00
55	David Dunn/5000	3.00
56	Tyrone Davis	2.00
57	Craig Newsome/4000	2.00
58	William Strong	2.00
59	Sherman Williams/3500	2.00
60	James O. Stewart/4000	3.00
61	Bryan Schwartz/6000	2.00
62	Frank Sanders/5000	7.00
63	Barrett Robbins/6000	2.00
64	Bronzell Miller	2.00
65	Curtis Martin/4000	18.00
66	Chris T. Jones/4000	7.00
67	Dave Barr/5000	2.00
68	Anthony Brown/6500	2.00
69	Ken Dilger/6000	3.00
70	Warren Sapp/4000	3.00
71	James A. Stewart	2.00
72	Corey Fuller/5000	2.00
73	Christian Fauria/5000	3.00
74	Brian DeMarco/6000	2.00
75	J.J. Stokes/1000	16.00
76	Hicham El-Mashtoub	2.00
77	Anthony Cook/6000	2.00
78	Mark Bruener/4000	3.00
79	Blake Brockermeyer/4000	2.00
80	Derrick Brooks/4000	2.00
81	Joe Aska/4000	2.00
82	Lance Brown/6500	2.00
83	Pete Mitchell/6500	2.00
84	Kordell Stewart/6500	15.00
85	Bobby Taylor/4000	3.00
86	Jimmy Hitchcock	2.00
87	Jack Jackson/5000	2.00
88	Ray Zellars/4000	3.00
89	Darius Holland	2.00
90	Derrick Alexander/4000	3.00
91	Torey Hunter/6000	2.00
92	Scotty Lewis/6500	2.00
93	Carl Reeves	2.00
94	Terrell Fletcher/6000	3.00
95	Ontiwaun Carter/6500	2.00
96	Trezelle Jenkins/5000	2.00
97	Mark Birchmeier	2.00
98	Len Raney	2.00
99	Ronald Cherry/6500	2.00
100	Tyrone Wheatley/6500	3.00
101	John Jones	2.00
102	Zack Crockett/6000	2.00
103	Larry Jones/4000	2.00
104	Michael McCoy	2.00
105	Ellis Johnson/3500	2.00
106	Jerrott Willard/5000	2.00
107	Jason James	2.00
108	J.J. Smith	2.00
109	Mike Mamula/4000	2.00

1995 Superior Pix Deep Threat

This five-card insert (1:9) features the top wide receiver prospects from the 1995 Draft. The card fronts have a player photo on a prism background, with the words "1995 Draft Pix Series" at the top.

		MT
Complete Set (5):		8.00
Common Player:		1.00
1	Michael Westbrook	2.00
2	Joey Galloway	2.50
3	J.J. Stokes	2.00
4	Kyle Brady	1.00
5	Frank Sanders	2.00

1995 Superior Pix Instant Impact

Instant Impact is a five-card insert (1:18). The fronts have a split blue/silver/green foil background.

		MT
Complete Set (5):		8.00
Common Player:		.75
1	Steve McNair	3.00
2	Kerry Collins	3.00
3	Tyrone Wheatley	.75
4	Joey Galloway	1.50
5	Tony Boselli	.75

1995 Superior Pix Open Field

Open Field features the top running back prospects from the 1995 Draft on a split-color prism background. This five-card set was inserted 1:18.

		MT
Complete Set (5):		5.00
Common Player:		.75
1	Ki-Jana Carter	1.25
2	Tyrone Wheatley	.75
3	James O. Stewart	1.25
4	Rashaan Salaam	1.50
5	Ray Zellars	.75

1995 Superior Pix Top Defender

The top defensive linemen from the 1995 Draft are featured in this five-card set (1:9). The players are pictured on a blue and gold wood grain background.

		MT
Complete Set (5):		4.00
Common Player:		1.00
1	Kevin Carter	1.00
2	Derrick Alexander	1.00
3	Warren Sapp	1.00
4	Derrick Brooks	1.00
5	Mike Mamula	1.00

1991 Surge WLAF Police

The 39-card, 2-3/8" x 3-1/2" set, sponsored by American Airlines, features players from the WLAF Sacramento Surge team. The card fronts feature a color photo with an American Airlines logo appearing along the top border. The lower right corner contains a triangle with the Surge helmet. The card backs give bio information and a safety tip.

		MT
Complete Set (39):		20.00
Common Player:		.60
1	Mike Adams	.75
2	Sam Archer	.60
3	John Buddenberg	.60
4	Jon Burman	.60
5	Tony Burse	.75
6	Ricardo Cartwright	.60
7	Greg Coauette	.60
8	Paco Craig	.60
9	John Dominic	.60
10	Mike Elkins	1.00
11	Oliver Erhorn	.60
12	Mel Farr	1.00
13	Victor Floyd	.60
14	Byron Forsythe	.60
15	Paul Frazier	.60
16	Tom Gerhart	.60
17	Mike Hall	.60
18	Anthony Henton	.60
19	Nate Hill	.60
20	Kubanai Kalombo	.60
21	Shawn Knight	1.00
22	Sean Kugler	.60
23	Matti Lindholm	.60
24	Art Malone	.75
25	Robert McWright	.60
26	Tim Moore	.60
27	Pete Najarian	.60
28	Mark Nua	.60
29	Carl Parker	.60
30	Leon Perry	.60
31	Juha Salo	.60
32	Saute Sapolu	.60
33	Paul Soltis	.60
34	Richard Stephens	.60
35	Kay Stephenson (CO)	.75
36	Kendall Trainor	.75
37	Mike Wallace	.60
38	Curtis Wilson	.60
39	Rick Zumwalt	.60

1988 Swell Football Greats

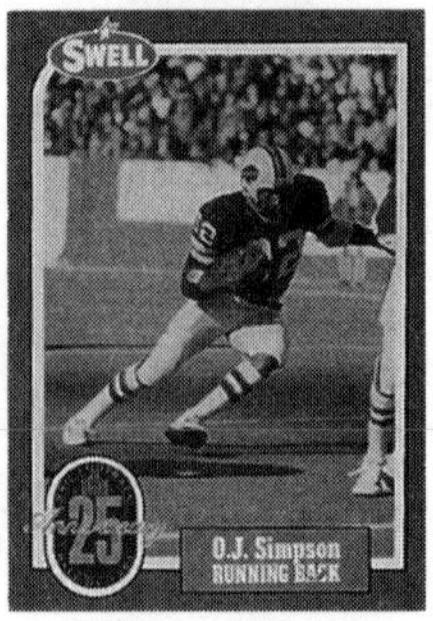

Swell's first set picturing members of the Pro Football Hall of Fame featured 144 players, coaches and executives. The set was released in 10-card wax packs and in complete sets in August 1988. A separate checklist was included. The standard-size cards feature full-color photos or sepia-toned black-and-white photos (in the case of older players) enclosed in a blue border. A red Swell logo is seen in the upper left corner; the Hall of Fame's 25th Anniversary logo is in the lower left, and the player's name and position is in white type in a red box in the lower right corner. Card backs feature blue borders and the player's biographical notes and career statistics in a white rectangle. Cards are printed on white cardboard stock. There have been some reports of small nicks and notches along the tops of some of the cards in the factory-issued sets.

		MT
Complete Set (144):		15.00
Common Player:		.10
1	Pete Rozell	.30
2	Joe Namath	1.50
3	Frank Gatski	.10
4	O.J. Simpson	2.00
5	Roger Staubach	1.50
6	Herb Adderly	.10
7	Lance Alworth	.25
8	Doug Atkins	.10
9	Red Badgro	.10
10	Cliff Battles	.10
11	Sammy Baugh	.35
12	Raymond Berry	.15
13	Charles Bidwell, Sr.	.10
14	Chuck Bednarik	.15
15	Bert Bell	.10
16	Bobby Bell	.10
17	George Blanda	.25
18	Jim Brown	1.00
19	Paul Brown	.15
20	Roosevelt Brown	.10
21	Ray Flaherty	.10
22	Len Ford	.15
23	Dan Fortmann	.10
24	Bill George	.10
25	Art Donovan	.10
26	John (Paddy) Driscoll	.10
27	Jimmy Conzelman	.10
28	Willie Davis	.10
29	Earl "Dutch" Clark	.10
30	George Connor	.10
31	Guy Chamberlain	.10
32	Jack Christiansen	.10
33	Tony Canadeo	.15
34	Joe Carr	.10
35	Willie Brown	.10
36	Dick Butkus	.35
37	Bill Dudley	.10
38	Turk Edwards	.10
39	Weeb Ewbank	.20
40	Tom Fears	.10
41	Otto Graham	.40
42	Red Grange	.50
43	Frank Gifford	.60
44	Sid Gillman	.10
45	Forrest Gregg	.10
46	Lou Groza	.25
47	Joe Guyon	.10
48	George Halas	.20
49	Ed Healy	.10
50	Mel Hein	.10
51	Pete Henry	.15
52	Arnie Herber	.10
53	Bill Hewitt	.10
54	Clark Hinkle	.10
55	Elroy Hirsch	.25
56	Robert Hubbard	.10
57	Sam Huff	.10
58	Lamar Hunt	.15
59	Don Hutson	.20
60	Deacon Jones	.10
61	Sonny Jurgensen	.15
62	Walt Kiesling	.10
63	Frank Kinard	.10
64	Curley Lambeau	.10
65	Dick Lane	.10
66	Yale Lary	.10
67	Dante Lavelli	.10
68	Bobby Lane	.20
69	Alphonse Leemans	.10
70	Bob Lilly	.15
71	Vince Lombardi	.35
72	Sid Luckman	.20
73	William Roy Lyman	.10
74	Tim Mara	.10

75	Gino Marchetti	.15
76	George Preston Marshall	.10
77	Ollie Matson	.15
78	George McAfee	.10
79	Mike McCormack	.10
80	Hugh McElhenny	.15
81	John McNally	.15
82	Mike Michalske	.10
83	Wayne Millner	.10
84	Bobby Mitchell	.10
85	Ron Mix	.15
86	Lenny Moore	.15
87	Marion Motley	.15
88	George Musso	.10
89	Bronko Nagurski	.35
90	Earle Neale	.10
91	Ernie Nevers	.20
92	Ray Nitschke	.20
93	Leo Nomellini	.10
94	Merlin Olsen	.15
95	Jim Otto	.10
96	Steve Owen	.10
97	Clarence Parker	.10
98	Jim Parker	.10
99	Joe Perry	.15
100	Pete Pihos	.10
101	Hugh Ray	.10
102	Dan Reeves	.10
103	Jim Ringo	.10
104	Andy Robustelli	.10
105	Art Rooney	.10
106	Gale Sayers	.50
107	Joe Schmidt	.10
108	Bart Starr	.75
109	Ernie Stautner	.15
110	Ken Strong	.10
111	Joe Stydahar	.15
112	Charley Taylor	.15
113	Jim Taylor	.15
114	Jim Thorpe	.75
115	Y.A. Tittle	.35
116	George Trafton	.10
117	Charley Trippi	.10
118	Emlen Tunnell	.10
119	Clyde Turner	.10
120	Johnny Unitas	1.75
121	Norm Van Brocklin	.20
122	Steve Van Buren	.10
123	Paul Warfield	.10
124	Bob Waterfield	.20
125	Arnie Weinmeister	.10
126	Bill Willis	.10
127	Larry Wilson	.10
128	Alex Wojciechowicz	.10
129	Doak Walker	.25
130	Willie Lanier	.10
131	Paul Hornung	.25
132	Ken Houston	.10
133	Fran Tarkenton	.50
134	Don Maynard	.15
135	Larry Csonka	.30
136	Joe Greene	.15
137	Len Dawson	.15
138	Gene Upshaw	.10
139	Jim Langer	.10
140	John Henry Johnson	.10
141	Fred Biletnikoff	.15
142	Mike Ditka	.50
143	Jack Ham	.15
144	Alan Page	.15

1989 Swell Football Greats

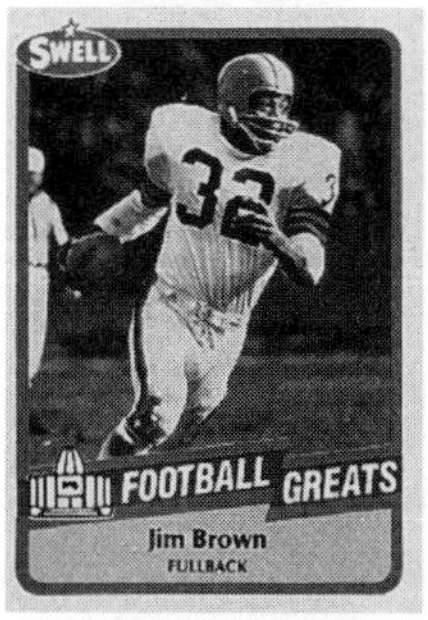

The 1989 edition of Swell Football Greats again included every member of the Pro Football Hall of Fame inducted through 1989. Swell had released its initial set of HOFers in 1988. The standard-size cards featured white borders with red striping. The Swell logo is in the upper left corner, and a blue flag carries the "Football Greats" slogan across the bottom of the card, just above the player's name and position. Most of the photos are in color. Those that feature early greats are sepia-toned. Backs are printed in two colors and contain biographical notes and career highlights as well as the year of Hall of Fame induction. Cards, which were released in late August 1989, were issued in wax packs of 10 cards each. Collector's Sets were also released by Swell, which is a division of the Philadelphia Chewing Gum Corp. One variation exists in the set: In the upper right corner of card #27, Sid Luckman. The scarcer error card shows "Sid" and the first part of "Chicago" printed in white. This was air-brushed out in later versions. The set has so little collector interest, however, that the error has no real additional value.

		MT
	Complete Set (150):	15.00
	Common Player:	.10
1	Terry Bradshaw	1.00
2	Bert Bell	.10
3	Joe Carr	.10
4	Earl "Dutch" Clark	.10
5	Harold "Red" Grange	.60
6	Wilbur "Pete" Henry	.10
7	Mel Hein	.10
8	Cal Hubbard	.10
9	George Halas	.30
10	Don Hutson	.15
11	Curley Lambeau	.10
12	Tim Mara	.10
13	George Preston Marshall	.10
14	John McNally	.10
15	Bronko Nagurski	.40
16	Ernie Nevers	.15
17	Jim Thorpe	.50
18	Ed Healy	.10
19	Clarke Hinkle	.10
20	Link Lyman	.10
21	Mike Michalske	.10
22	George Trafton	.10
23	Guy Chamberlain	.15
24	John "Paddy" Driscoll	.10
25	Dan Fortmann	.10
26	Otto Graham	.40
27A	Sid Luckman	.35
27B	Sid Luckman (corrected)	1.25
28	Steve Van Buren	.15
29	Bob Waterfield	.20
30	Bill Dudley	.15
31	Joe Guyon	.10
32	Arnie Herber	.10
33	Walt Kiesling	.10
34	Jimmy Conzelman	.10
35	Art Rooney	.10
36	Willie Wood	.10
37	Art Shell	.25
38	Sammy Baugh	.45
39	Mel Blount	.10
40	Lamar Hunt	.15
41	Norm Van Brocklin	.30
42	Y.A. Tittle	.35
43	Andy Robustelli	.10
44	Vince Lombardi	.35
45	Frank Kinard	.10
46	Bill Hewitt	.10
47	Jim Brown	1.00
48	Pete Pihos	.10
49	Hugh McElhenny	.15
50	Tom Fears	.15
51	Jack Christiansen	.10
52	Ernie Stautner	.15
53	Joe Perry	.15
54	Leo Nomellini	.15
55	Earl "Greasy" Neale	.10
56	Turk Edwards	.10
57	Alex Wojciechowicz	.10
58	Charley Trippi	.10
59	Marion Motley	.20
60	Wayne Miller	.10
61	Elroy Hirsch	.10
62	Art Donovan	.10
63	Cliff Battles	.10
64	Emlen Tunnell	.15
65	Joe Stydahar	.10
66	Ken Strong	.10
67	Dan Reeves	.10
68	Bobby Layne	.30
69	Paul Brown	.20
70	Charles Bidwell, Sr.	.10
71	Chuck Bednarik	.15
72	Bulldog Turner	.10
73	Hugh "Shorty" Ray	.10
74	Steve Owen	.10
75	George McAfee	.10
76	Forrest Gregg	.15
77	Frank Gifford	.50
78	Jim Taylor	.10
79	Len Ford	.10
80	Ray Flaherty	.10
81	Lenny Moore	.15
82	Dante Lavelli	.10
83	George Connor	.15
84	Roosevelt Grier	.10
85	Dick Lane	.10
86	Lou Groza	.30
87	Bill George	.10
88	Tony Canadeo	.10
89	Joe Schmidt	.10
90	Jim Parker	.10
91	Wayne Millner	.10
92	Raymond Berry	.20
93	Ollie Matson	.15
94	Gino Marchetti	.10
95	Larry Wilson	.10
96	Ray Nitschke	.25
97	Tuffy Leemans	.10
98	Weeb Ewbank	.10
99	Lance Alworth	.30
100	Bill Willis	.10
101	Bart Starr	.35
102	Gale Sayers	.35
103	Herb Adderly	.10
104	Johnny Unitas	1.00
105	Ron Mix	.10
106	Yale Lary	.10
107	Red Badgro	.10
108	Jim Otto	.10
109	Bob Lilly	.15
110	Deacon Jones	.15
111	Doug Atkins	.10
112	Jim Ringo	.10
113	Willie Davis	.10
114	George Blanda	.35
115	Bobby Bell	.10
116	Merlin Olsen	.15
117	George Musso	.10
118	Sam Huff	.15
119	Paul Warfield	.25
120	Bobby Mitchell	.10
121	Sonny Jurgensen	.25
122	Sid Gilman	.10
123	Arnie Weinmeister	.10
124	Charley Taylor	.10
125	Mike McCormack	.10
126	Willie Brown	.10
127	O.J. Simpson	1.50
128	Pete Rozelle	.25
129	Joe Namath	1.25
130	Frank Gatski	.10
131	Willie Lanier	.10
132	Ken Houston	.10
133	Paul Hornung	.25
134	Roger Staubach	1.25
135	Len Dawson	.15
136	Larry Csonka	.30
137	Doak Walker	.20
138	Fran Tarkenton	.60
139	Don Maynard	.15
140	Jim Langer	.15
141	John Henry Johnson	.10
142	Joe Greene	.20
143	Jack Ham	.10
144	Mike Ditka	.75
145	Alan Page	.10
146	Fred Biletnikoff	.15
147	Gene Upshaw	.10
148	Dick Butkus	.50
149	Checklist 1 & 2	.10
150	Checklist 3 & 4	.10

1990 Swell Football Greats

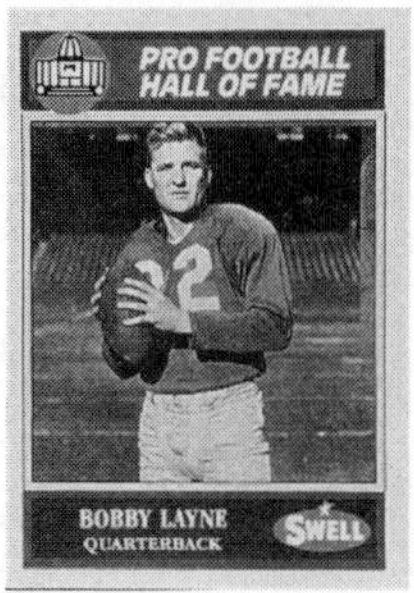

Swell, which had released two straight sets of Pro Football Hall of Famers, returned with this 160-card set, also featuring HOFers. Produced by the Philadelphia Gum Co., the set includes 155 HOFers, two checklists, and three Hall of Fame cards. Cards are standard size, with a white border and blue and yellow lines. As in previous issues, some cards of the older players may have sepia-toned, rather than full-color, photos.

		MT
	Complete Set (160):	15.00
	Common Player:	.10
1	Terry Bradshaw	1.00
2	Bert Bell	.10
3	Joe Carr	.10
4	Dutch Clark	.15
5	Red Grange	.40
6	Pete Henry	.10
7	Mel Hein	.10
8	Cal Hubbard	.10
9	George Halas	.25
10	Don Hutson	.15
11	Curly Lambeau	.15
12	Tim Mara	.10
13	G. Preston Marshall	.10
14	John McNally	.10
15	Bronko Nagurski	.35
16	Ernie Nevers	.15
17	Jim Thorpe	.75
18	Ed Healy	.10
19	Clark Hinkle	.10
20	Link Lyman	.10
21	Mike Michalske	.10
22	George Trafton	.10
23	Guy Chamberlain	.10
24	Paddy Driscoll	.10
25	Dan Fortmann	.10
26	Otto Graham	.50
27	Sid Luckman	.40
28	Steve Van Buren	.15
29	Bob Waterfield	.25
30	Bill Dudley	.10
31	Joe Guyon	.10
32	Arnie Herber	.10
33	Walt Kiesling	.10
34	Jimmy Conzelman	.10
35	Art Rooney	.15
36	Willie Wood	.10
37	Art Shell	.15
38	Sammy Baugh	.40
39	Mel Blount	.10
40	Lamar Hunt	.15
41	Norm Van Brocklin	.25
42	Y.A. Tittle	.30
43	Andy Robustelli	.10
44	Vince Lombardi	.25
45	Bruiser Kinard	.10
46	Bill Hewitt	.10
47	Jim Brown	1.00
48	Pete Pihos	.10
49	Hugh McElhenny	.15
50	Tom Fears	.10
51	Jack Christiansen	.10
52	Ernie Stautner	.10
53	Joe Perry	.15
54	Leo Nomellini	.10
55	Greasy Neale	.10
56	Turk Edwards	.10
57	Alex Wojciechowicz	.20
58	Charlie Trippi	.10
59	Marion Motley	.15
60	Wayne Miller	.10
61	Elroy Hirsch	.20
62	Art Donovan	.10
63	Cliff Battles	.10
64	Emlen Tunnell	.10
65	Joe Stydahar	.10
66	Ken Strong	.10
67	Dan Reeves	.15
68	Bobby Layne	.25
69	Paul Brown	.20
70	Charles Bidwell, Sr.	.10
71	Chuck Bednarik	.15
72	Bulldog Turner	.10
73	Shorty Ray	.10
74	Steve Owen	.10
75	George McAfee	.10
76	Forrest Gregg	.10
77	Frank Gifford	.40
78	Jim Taylor	.15
79	Len Ford	.10
80	Ray Flaherty	.10
81	Lenny Moore	.15
82	Dante Lavelli	.10
83	George Connor	.15
84	Roosevelt Brown	.10
85	Dick Lane	.10
86	Lou Groza	.20
87	Bill George	.10
88	Tony Canadeo	.10
89	Joe Schmidt	.15
90	Jim Parker	.10
91	Raymond Berry	.15
92	Ace Parker	.10
93	Ollie Matson	.15
94	Gino Marchetti	.10
95	Larry Wilson	.10
96	Ray Nitschke	.15
97	Tuffy Leemans	.10
98	Weeb Ewbank	.15
99	Lance Alworth	.20
100	Bill Willis	.10
101	Bart Starr	.30
102	Gale Sayers	.30
103	Herb Adderly	.10
104	Johnny Unitas	1.00
105	Ron Mix	.10
106	Yale Lary	.10
107	Red Badgro	.10
108	Jim Otto	.10
109	Bob Lilly	.15
110	Deacon Jones	.15
111	Doug Atkins	.10
112	Jim Ringo	.15
113	Willie Davis	.10
114	George Blanda	.35
115	Bobby Bell	.10
116	Merlin Olsen	.15
117	George Musso	.10
118	Sam Huff	.10
119	Paul Warfield	.15
120	Bobby Mitchell	.10
121	Sonny Jurgensen	.15
122	Sid Gilman	.10
123	Arnie Weinmeister	.10
124	Charley Taylor	.10
125	Mike McCormack	.10
126	Willie Brown	.10
127	O.J. Simpson	1.50
128	Pete Rozelle	.25
129	Joe Namath	1.25
130	Frank Gatski	.10
131	Willie Lanier	.15
132	Ken Houston	.10
133	Paul Hornung	.25
134	Roger Staubach	1.00
135	Len Dawson	.15
136	Larry Csonka	.25
137	Doak Walker	.15
138	Fran Tarkenton	.40
139	Don Maynard	.10
140	Jim Langer	.10
141	John H. Johnson	.10
142	Joe Greene	.20
143	Jack Ham	.10
144	Mike Ditka	.50
145	Alan Page	.10
146	Fred Biletnikoff	.15
147	Gene Upshaw	.10
148	Dick Butkus	.30
149	Buck Buchanan	.10
150	Franco Harris	.30
151	Tom Landry	.35
152	Ted Hendricks	.10
153	Bob St. Clair	.10
154	Jack Lambert	.20
155	Bob Griese	.20
156	Admission Coupon	.10
157	Enshrinement Day	.10
158	Hall of Fame	.10
159	Checklist 1 & 2	.10
160	Checklist 3 & 4	.10

T

1962 Tang Team Photos

The 14-card, 8" x 10" set features a team photo with the players' names along the bottom border. The backs are blank. The set was available for 50 cents back in 1962 with a Tang seal. Reprints have been made in recent years.

		NM
	Complete Set (14):	100.00
	Common Player:	8.00
1	Baltimore Colts	8.00
2	Chicago Bears	8.00
3	Cleveland Browns	8.00
4	Dallas Cowboys	15.00
5	Detroit Lions	8.00
6	Green Bay Packers	15.00
7	Los Angeles Rams	8.00
8	Minnesota Vikings	12.00
9	New York Giants	8.00
10	Philadelphia Eagles	8.00
11	Pittsburgh Steelers	12.00
12	St. Louis Cardinals	8.00
13	San Francisco 49ers	12.00
14	Washington Redskins	12.00

1981 TCMA Greats

These standard-size cards were issued by TCMA in 1981. Each card front has a color photo of a player from the 1950s or '60s, framed by a white border. The card back is white and uses black ink to provide a career summary, biographical information, a TCMA copyright and a card number. Some cards, however, went unnumbered and command values about 2 times more than their numbered counterparts.

		MT
	Complete Set (78):	25.00
	Common Player:	.25
1	Alex Karras	1.00
2	Fran Tarkenton	3.00
3	John Unitas	4.50
4	Bobby Layne	2.00
5	Roger Staubach	6.00
6	Joe Namath	6.00
7	1954 New York Giants	.50
8	Jimmy Brown	6.00
9	Ray Wietecha	.25
10	R.C. Owens	.25
11	Alex Webster	.35
12	Jim Otto	1.00
13	Jim Taylor	1.00
14	Kyle Rote	.75
15	Roger Ellis	.25
16	Nick Pietrosante	.35
17	Milt Plum	.30
18	Eddie LeBaron	.50
19	Jimmy Patton	.25
20	Yale Lary	1.00
21	Leo Nomellini	1.25
22	Johnny Olszewski	.25
23	Ernie Koy	.35
24	Bill Wade	.35
25	Billy Wells	.25
26	Ron Waller	.25
27	Pat Summerall	.60
28	Joe Schmidt	1.25
29	Bob St. Clair	.75
30	Dick Lynch	.35
31	Tommy McDonald	.50
32	Earl Morrall	.50
33	Jim Martin	.25
34	Dick Modzelewski	.30
35	Dick LeBeau	.35
36	Dick Post	.25
37	Les Richter	.35
38	Andy Robustelli	.75
39	Pete Retzlaff	.35
40	Fred Biletnikoff	1.50
41	Timmy Brown	.35
42	Babe Parilli	.35
43	Lance Alworth	1.75
44	Sammy Baugh	1.75
45	Paul (Tank) Younger	.35
46	Chuck Bednarik	1.50
47	Art Donovan	1.25
48	Len Dawson	2.00
49	Don Maynard	1.25
50	Joe Morrison	.35
51	John Eliott	.25
52	Jim Ringo	.85
53	Max McGee	.35
54	Art Powell	.35
55	Galen Fiss	.25
56	Jack Stroud	.25
57	Bake Turner	.35
58	Mike McCormack	.75
59	L.G. Dupre	.35
60	Bill McPeak	.25
61	Art Spinney	.25
62	Fran Rogel	.25
63	Ollie Matson	1.25
64	Doak Walker	1.25
65	Lenny Moore	1.25
66	George Shaw, Bert Rechichar	.25
67	Kyle Rote, Jim Lee Howell, Ray Krause	.35
68	Andy Robustelli, Roosevelt Grier, Dick Modzelewski, Jim Katcavage	.65
69	Tucker Frederickson, Ernie Koy	.35
70	Gino Marchetti	1.00
71	Earl Morrall, Allie Sherman	.50
72	Roosevelt Brown	.75
73	Howard Cassady (Hopalong)	.35
74	Don Chandler	.35
75	Joe Childress	.25
76	Rick Casares	.35
77	Charley Conerly	1.00
78	1958 Giants QB's (Don Heinrich, Tom Dublinski, Charlie Conerly)	.50

1987 TCMA Update

This set, produced by TCMA's successor (CMC), is a reissue of TCMA's 1981 set, but 12 additional cards were added. The extra cards were numbered from were the first issue ended, at 79. The copyright on the card back is CMC 1987.

		MT
	Complete Set (12):	20.00
	Common Player:	.75
79	Fred Dryer	1.00
80	Ed Marinaro	1.00
81	O.J. Simpson	10.00
82	Joe Theismann	2.50
83	Roman Gabriel	1.00
84	Terry Metcalf	.75
85	Lyle Alzado	1.50
86	Jake Scott	.75
87	Cliff Branch	1.50
88	Rocky Bleier	1.00
89	Cliff Harris	.75
90	Archie Manning	2.00

1960 Texans 7-Eleven

The standard-sized cards feature a black and white photo of the player with his name, position and team along the bottom edge. The horizontal card backs have player highlights in typewriter-style print. Even though there are 11 cards checklisted, there may have been more in the unnumbered set.

		NM
	Complete Set (11):	400.00
	Common Player:	35.00
1	Max Boydston	35.00
2	Mel Branch	35.00
3	Chris Burford	35.00
4	Ray Collins (UER) (No team name on front)	35.00
5	Cotton Davidson	35.00
6	Abner Haynes	60.00
7	Sherrill Headrick	35.00
8	Bill Krisher	35.00
9	Paul Miller	35.00
10	Johnny Robinson	60.00
11	Jack Spikes	35.00

A card number in parentheses ( ) indicates the set is unnumbered.

1992 Thunderbolts Arena

Area Temps sponsored this set featuring the Cleveland Thunderbolts of the Arena Football League. The 24 cards are printed on plain white card stock. The fronts feature a black and white player photo framed by a purple line. The backs contain basic player information. Both sides feature the Area Temps logo. The cards are unnumbered.

		MT
	Complete Set (24):	20.00
	Common Player:	.60
1	Eric Anderson	.60
2	Robert Banks	.60
3	Bobby Bounds	.60
4	Marvin Bowman	.60
5	George Cooper	.60
6	Michael Denbrock ACO	.60
7	Chris Drennan	.60
8	Dennis Fitzgerald ACO	.60
9	John Fletcher	.60
10	Andre Giles	.60
11	Chris Harkness	.60
12	Major Harris	5.00
13	Luther Johnson	.60
14	Marvin Mattox	.60
15	Cedric McKinnon	.60
16	Cleo Miller ACO	.75
17	Tony Missick	.60
18	Anthony Newsom	.60
19	Phil Poirier	.60
20	Alvin Powell	.60
21	Ray Puryear	.60
22	Dave Whinham CO	.60
23	Brian Williams	.60
24	Kennedy Wilson	.60

1961 Titans Jay Publishing

The 12-card, 5" x 7" set features black and white photos of the New York Titans, an original AFL team that eventually became the New York Jets. The cards were originally packaged 12 to a pack and sold for 25 cents. The backs are blank.

		NM
	Complete Set (12):	75.00
	Common Player:	5.00
1	Al Dorow	5.00
2	Larry Grantham	6.00
3	Mike Hagler	5.00
4	Mike Hudock	5.00
5	Bob Jewett	5.00
6	Jack Klotz	5.00
7	Don Maynard	20.00
8	John McMullan	5.00
9	Bob Mischak	5.00
10	Art Powell	10.00
11	Bob Reifsnyder	6.00
12	Sid Youngelman	6.00

1995 Tombstone Pizza

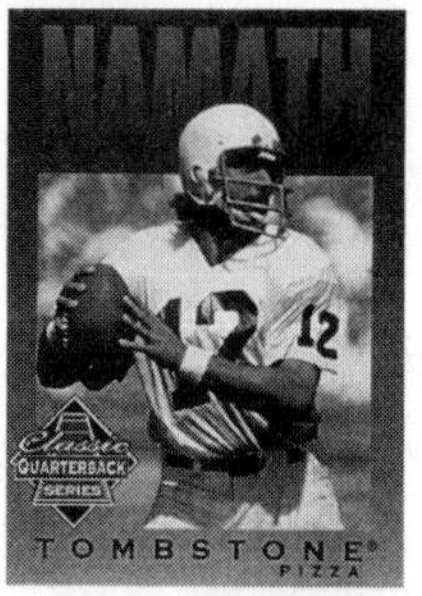

The 12-card, standard-size set was randomly inserted in specially marked Tombstone pizzas. The entire set was available for $1 and three Tombstone proof of purchase seals. The card fronts feature a color photo with the quarterback's last name along the top border in large print. The card backs include career statistics and a player quote.

		MT
	Complete Set (12):	20.00
	Common Player:	1.00
1	Ken Anderson	1.00
2	Terry Bradshaw	4.00
3	Len Dawson	1.50
4	Dan Fouts	1.50
5	Bob Griese	2.00
6	Billy Kilmer	1.00
7	Joe Namath	6.00
8	Jim Plunkett	1.00
9	Ken Stabler	2.50
10	Bart Starr	2.00
11	Joe Theismann	1.00
12	Johnny Unitas	3.00

1995 Tombstone Pizza Autographs

The 12-card, standard-size set was a parallel to the base Classic Quarterback Series. Each quarterback signed 10,000 of his own cards.

		MT
	Complete Set (12):	300.00
	Common Player:	15.00
1	Ken Anderson	15.00
2	Terry Bradshaw	45.00
3	Len Dawson	25.00
4	Dan Fouts	25.00
5	Bob Griese	25.00

6 Billy Kilmer 15.00
7 Joe Namath 60.00
8 Jim Plunkett 15.00
9 Ken Stabler 35.00
10 Bart Starr 35.00
11 Joe Theismann 15.00
12 Johnny Unitas 40.00

1996 Tombstone Pizza Quarterback Club Caps

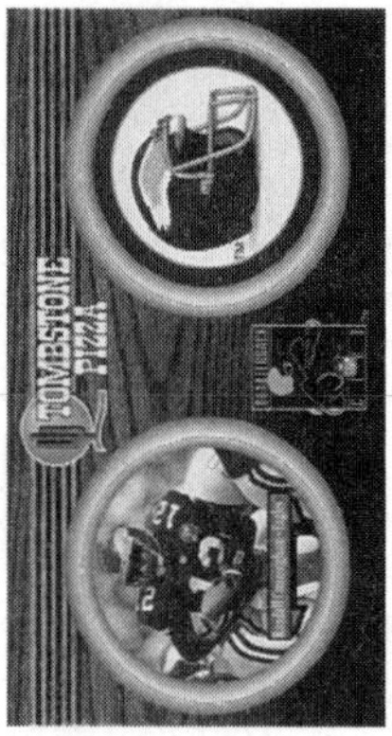

The 14-card, 1-5/8" cap set was distributed by Tombstone Pizza and produced by Pinnacle. The caps were issued on a punch-out board (8-1/2" x 11"). A black plastic slammer was also included with the set.

MT
Complete Set (14): 15.00
Common Player: .50
1 Steve Young 1.00
2 Emmitt Smith 2.50
3 Junior Seau .50
4 Barry Sanders 1.25
5 Jerry Rice 1.25
6 Dan Marino 2.50
7 Jim Kelly .60
8 Michael Irvin .60
9 Brett Favre 1.25
10 Marshall Faulk 1.00
11 John Elway .75
12 Randall Cunningham .50
13 Drew Bledsoe 1.00
14 Troy Aikman 1.25

1950 Topps Felt Backs

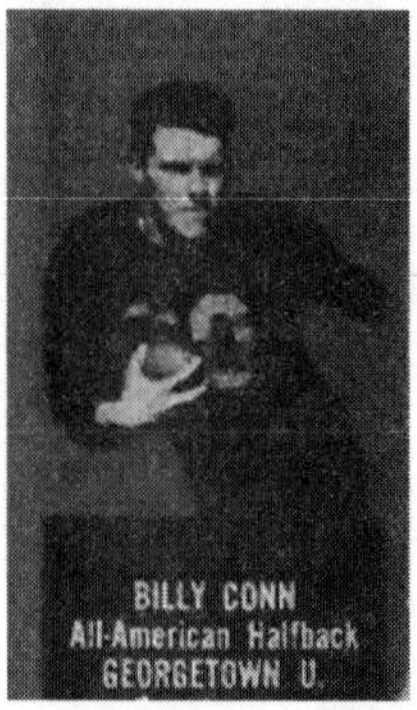
BILLY CONN
All-American Halfback
GEORGETOWN U.

These 7/8" x 1-7/16" cards feature several top collegiate players of the era on the front; a mug shot has the player's name, position and college under it. The card back is felt and includes his college's team pennant. Cards come with either brown or yellow backgrounds; yellow backgrounds are generally twice the listed values. The following cards come in both versions: 5, 6, 9, 13, 30, 35, 36, 39, 46, 51, 52, 54, 55, 57, 61, 66, 71, 75, 76, 78, 84, 86, 87, 92, and 100.

NM
Complete Set (100): 4800.
Common Player: 40.00
Lou Allen 40.00
Morris Bailey 40.00
George Bell 40.00
Lindy Berry 40.00
Mike Boldin 40.00
Bernie Botula 40.00
Bob Bowlby 40.00
Bob Bucher 40.00
Al Burnett 40.00
Don Burson 40.00
Paul Campbell 40.00
Herb Carey 40.00
Bimbo Cecconi 40.00
Bill Chauncey 40.00
Dick Clark 40.00
Tom Coleman 40.00
Billy Conn 40.00
John Cox 40.00
Lou Creekmur 45.00
Glen Davis 50.00
Warren Davis 40.00
Bob Deuber 40.00
Ray Dooney 45.00
Tom Dublinski 40.00
Jeff Fleischman 40.00
Jack Friedland 40.00
Bob Fuchs 40.00
Arnold Galiffa 40.00
Dick Gilman 40.00
Frank Gitschier 40.00
Gene Glick 40.00
Bill Gregus 45.00
Harold Hagan 40.00
Charles Hall 40.00
Leon Hart 60.00
Bob Hester 40.00
George Hughes 40.00
Levi Jackson 40.00
Jackie Jensen 125.00
Charlie Justice 100.00
Gary Kerkorian 40.00
Bernie Krueger 40.00
Bill Kuhn 40.00
Dean Laun 40.00
Chet Leach 40.00
Bobby Lee 40.00
Roger Lehew 40.00
Glenn Lippman 40.00
Melvin Lyle 40.00
Len Makowski 40.00
Al Malekoff 40.00
Jim Martin 50.00
Frank Mataya 40.00
Ray Matthews 45.00
Dick McKissack 40.00
Frank Miller 40.00
John Miller 40.00
Ed Modzelewski 45.00
Don Mouser 40.00
James Murphy 40.00
Ray Nagle 45.00
Leo Nomellini 140.00
James O'Day 40.00
Joe Paterno 375.00
Andy Pavich 40.00
Pete Perini 40.00
Jim Powers 40.00
Dave Rakestraw 45.00
Herb Rich 40.00
Fran Rogel 40.00
Darrell Royal 80.00
Steve Sawle 40.00
Nick Sebeck 40.00
Herb Seidell 40.00
Charles Shaw 40.00
Emil Sitko 40.00
Ed (Butch) Songin 45.00
Mariano Stalloni 40.00
Ernie Stautner 135.00
Don Stehley 40.00
Gil Stevenson 45.00
Bishop Strickland 40.00
Harry Szulborski 40.00
Wally Teninga 40.00
Clayton Tonnemaker 40.00
Deacon Dan Towler 55.00
Bert Turek 40.00
Harry Ulinski 40.00
Leon Van Billingham 40.00
Langdon Viracola 40.00
Leo Wagner 40.00
Doak Walker 150.00
Jim Ward 40.00
Art Weiner 45.00
Dick Weiss 40.00
Froggie Williams 40.00
Robert (Red) Wilson 45.00
Roger (Red) Wilson 40.00
Carl Wren 40.00
Pete Zinaich 40.00

1951 Topps

Referred to as the 1951 Topps "Magic" set, this 1951 issue was Topps' first major football card set. The 75-card set featured the nation's top college players. The backs of the cards include a football trivia question with the answer concealed under a scratch-off area.

NM
Complete Set (75): 1000.
Common Player: 16.00
1 *Jimmy Monahan* 25.00
2 *Bill Wade* 45.00
3 Bill Reichardt 16.00
4 *Babe Parilli* 35.00
5 Billie Burkhalter 16.00
6 Ed Weber 16.00
7 Tom Scott 16.00
8 Frank Guthridge 16.00
9 John Karras 16.00
10 *Vic Janowicz* 100.00
11 Lloyd Hill 16.00
12 *Jim Weatherall* 20.00
13 Howard Hansen 16.00
14 Lou D'Achille 16.00
15 Johnny Turco 16.00
16 Jerrell Price 16.00
17 John Coatta 16.00
18 Bruce Patton 16.00
19 *Marion Campbell* 32.00
20 Blaine Earon 16.00
21 Dewey McConnell 16.00
22 Ray Beck 16.00
23 Jim Prewett 16.00
24 Bob Steele 16.00
25 Art Betts 16.00
26 Walt Trillhaase 16.00
27 Gil Bartosh 16.00
28 Bob Bestwick 16.00
29 Tom Rushing 16.00
30 *Bert Rechichar* 32.00
31 Bill Owens 16.00
32 Mike Goggins 16.00
33 John Petitbon 16.00
34 Byron Townsend 16.00
35 Ed Rotticci 16.00
36 Steve Wadiak 16.00
37 *Bobby Marlow* 17.00
38 Bill Fuchs 16.00
39 Ralph Staub 16.00
40 Bill Vesprini 16.00
41 Zack Jordan 16.00
42 Bob Smith 16.00
43 Charles Hanson 16.00
44 Glenn Smith 16.00
45 Armand Kitto 16.00
46 Vinnie Drake 16.00
47 Bill Putich 16.00
48 *George Young* 40.00
49 Don McRae 16.00
50 Frank Smith 16.00
51 Dick Hightower 16.00
52 Clyde Pickard 16.00
53 Bob Reynolds 16.00
54 Dick Gregory 16.00
55 Dale Samuels 16.00
56 Gale Galloway 16.00
57 Vic Pujo 16.00
58 Dave Waters 16.00
59 Joe Ernest 16.00
60 Elmer Costa 16.00
61 Nick Liotta 16.00
62 John Dottley 16.00
63 Hi Faubion 16.00
64 David Harr 16.00
65 Bill Matthews 16.00
66 Carroll McDonald 16.00
67 Dick Dewing 16.00
68 Joe Johnson 16.00
69 Arnold Burwitz 16.00
70 Ed Dobrowolski 16.00
71 Joe Dudeck 16.00
72 *John Bright* 20.00
73 Harold Loehlein 16.00
74 Lawrence Hairston 16.00
75 *Bob Carey* 20.00

1955 Topps All-American

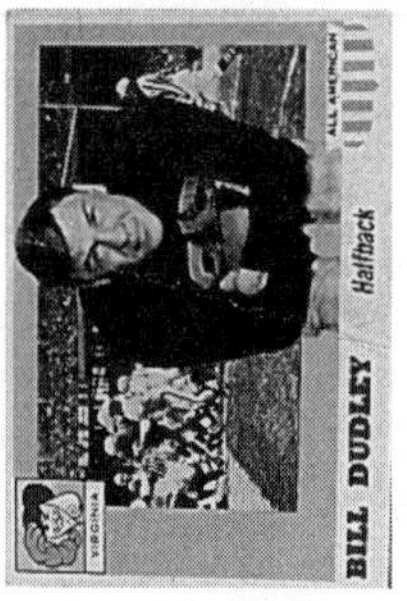
BILL DUDLEY
Halfback

This was the last Topps set to have college stars. The 100-card All-American set includes past and contemporary college stars. Cards measure 2-5/8" x 3-5/8" and feature a horizontal format. A number of the cards were short-printed in this set. Because the set featured many stars of the past, this set includes the only "regular issue" cards of several Hall of Famers (though technically these cards shouldn't qualify as "regular issue" cards since they weren't released during the player's career). Some of these rookie cards include Red Grange, Mel Hein, Jim Thorpe, Ernie Nevers, Bruiser Kinard, Ace parker, Don Hutson and Pete Henry. The only card issued of the Four Horsemen also appears in this set. The second (and last) "regular issue" cards of these players appear in this set: Knute Rockne, Ken Strong, Turk Edwards, and Alex Wojciechowicz. This set also includes the last cards of Bill Dudley, Otto Graham, Whizzer White (his second-year card, which actually should be his rookie card, since the 1954 Bowman card showed not Byron "Whizzer" White but Wilford White) and Sid Luckman. Two variations exist in the set. The backs on #14 Gaynell Tinsley and #21 Whizzer White were switched. The corrected versions are more plentiful than the errors. (Key: SP - short-printed)

NM
Complete Set (100): 3500.
Common Player: 15.00
SP Cards: 17.50
Glassine Pack (9): 2000.
Cello Pack (20): 3100.
1 *Herman Hickman* 90.00
2 John Kimbrough 15.00
3 Ed Weir 15.00
4 Ernie Pinckert 15.00
5 Bobby Grayson 15.00
6 *Niles Kinnick* 70.00
7 Andy Bershak 15.00
8 George Cafego 15.00
9 Tom Hamilton (SP) 35.00
10 Bill Dudley 30.00
11 Bobby Dodd (SP) 35.00
12 Otto Graham 175.00
13 Aaron Rosenberg 15.00
14 Gaynell "Gus" Tinsley (Whizzer White back) 25.00
14a Gaynell "Gus" Tinsley 25.00
15 Ed Kaw (SP) 35.00
16 Knute Rockne 325.00
17 Bob Reynolds 15.00
18 Pudge Heffelfinger (SP) 35.00
19 *Bruce A. Smith* 25.00
20 Sammy Baugh 200.00
21 *Whizzer White* (SP, Gaynell Tinsley back) 70.00
21a Whizzer White (SP) 70.00
22 Brick Muller 15.00
23 *Dick Kazmaier* 20.00
24 Ken Strong 30.00
25 Casimir Myslinski (SP) 35.00
26 *Larry Kelley* (SP) 35.00
27 Red Grange 350.00
28 *Mel Hein* (SP) 40.00
29 Leo Nomellini (SP) 50.00
30 Wes E. Fesler 15.00
31 *George Sauer Sr.* 20.00
32 Hank Foldberg 15.00
33 Bob Higgins 15.00
34 *Davey O'Brien* 25.00
35 *Tom Harmon* (SP) 50.00
36 Turk Edwards (SP) 40.00
37 Jim Thorpe 375.00
38 *Amos Alonzo Stagg* 60.00
39 Jerome Holland 15.00
40 Donn Moomaw 15.00
41 Joseph Alexander (SP) 35.00
42 J. Edward Tryon (SP) 35.00
43 George Savitsky 15.00
44 Ed Garbisch 15.00
45 Elmer Oliphant 15.00
46 Arnold Lassman 15.00
47 Bo McMillan 15.00
48 Ed Widseth 15.00
49 Don Zimmerman 15.00
50 Ken Kavanaugh 15.00
51 Duane Purvis (SP) 35.00
52 John Lujack 50.00
53 John F. Green 15.00
54 Edwin Dooley (SP) 35.00
55 Frank Merritt (SP) 35.00
56 *Ernie Nevers* 50.00
57 Vic Hanson (SP) 35.00
58 Ed Franco 15.00
59 *Doc Blanchard* 45.00
60 Dan Hill 15.00
61 Charles Brickley (SP) 35.00
62 Harry Newman 15.00
63 Charlie Justice 30.00
64 Benny Friedman 15.00
65 Joe Donchess (SP) 35.00
66 *Bruiser Kinard* 20.00
67 Frankie Albert 15.00
68 Four Horsemen (SP) 475.00
69 *Frank Sinkwich* 18.00
70 Bill Daddio 15.00
71 Bob Wilson 15.00
72 Chub Peabody 15.00
73 Hugh Governali 15.00
74 Gene McEver 15.00
75 Hugh Gallarneau 15.00
76 *Angelo Bertelli* 18.00
77 Bowden Wyatt (SP) 35.00
78 *Jay Berwanger* 20.00
79 Pug Lund 15.00
80 Bennie Oosterbaan 15.00
81 Cotton Warburton 15.00
82 Alex Wojciechowicz 25.00
83 Ted Coy (SP) 35.00
84 *Ace Parker* (SP) 40.00
85 Sid Luckman 85.00
86 Albie Booth (SP) 35.00
87 Adolph Schultz (SP) 35.00
88 Ralph G. Kercheval 15.00
89 Marshall Goldberg 15.00
90 Charlie O'Rourke 15.00
91 Bob Odell 15.00
92 Biggie Munn 15.00
93 Willie Heston (SP) 35.00
94 Joe Bernard (SP) 35.00
95 Red Cagle (SP) 35.00
96 Bill Hollenbeck (SP) 35.00
97 *Don Hutson* (SP) 225.00
98 *Beattie Feathers* (SP) 75.00
99 Don Witmire (SP) 35.00
100 *Wilbur "Fats" Henry* 150.00

1956 Topps

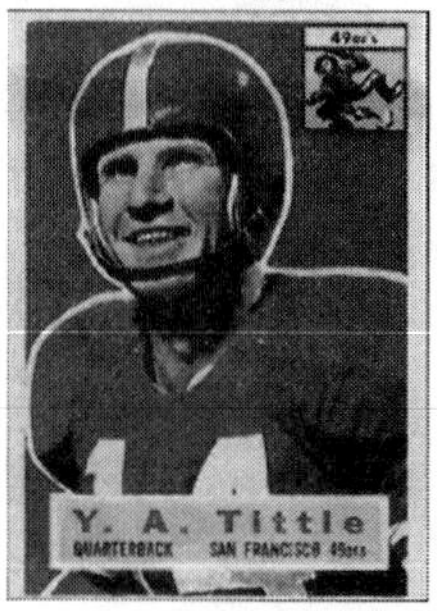
Y. A. Tittle
QUARTERBACK SAN FRANCISCO 49ers

This set of 120 cards plus an unnumbered (and probably short-printed) checklist was oversized, measuring 2-5/8" x 3-5/8". This was Topps' first set to feature only professional football players. Most notable about this set was the inclusion of the first team cards by any company (cards of the Chicago Cardinals and Washington Redskins players, however, were short-printed). Rookies in this set include Hall of Famers Roosevelt Brown, Joe Schmidt, Bill George and Lenny Moore, plus Rosey Grier. Second-year cards in this set are those of Alan Ameche, Art Donovan and Mike McCormack.

NM
Complete Set (120): 1500.
Common Player: 5.00
SP Cards: 30.00
Team Cards: 17.00
Checklist: 375.00
Wax Pack Dark Gr. (6): 400.00
1 Jack Carson 75.00
2 Gordon Soltau 5.00
3 Frank Varrichione 5.00
4 Eddie Bell 5.00
5 *Alex Webster* 15.00
6 Norm Van Brocklin 30.00
7 Green Bay Packers 17.00
8 Lou Creekmur 5.00
9 Lou Groza 25.00
10 Tom Bienemann 30.00
11 George Blanda 50.00
12 Alan Ameche 10.00
13 Vic Janowicz 40.00
14 Dick Moegle 5.00
15 Fran Rogel 5.00
16 Harold Giancanelli 5.00
17 Emlen Tunnell 15.00
18 Tank Younger 5.00
19 Bill Howton 8.00
20 Jack Christiansen 15.00
21 Darrell Brewster 5.00
22 Chicago Cardinals 100.00
23 Ed Brown 5.00
24 Joe Campanella 5.00
25 Leon Heath 30.00
26 San Francisco 49ers 17.00
27 Dick Flanagan 5.00
28 Chuck Bednarik 25.00
29 Kyle Rote 15.00
30 Les Richter 5.00
31 Howard Ferguson 5.00
32 Dorne Dibble 5.00
33 Kenny Konz 5.00
34 Dave Mann 30.00
35 Rick Casares 5.00
36 Art Donovan 25.00
37 Chuck Drazenovich 30.00
38 Joe Arenas 5.00
39 Lynn Chandnois 5.00
40 Philadelphia Eagles 17.00
41 *Roosevelt Brown* 40.00
42 Tom Fears 15.00
43 Gary Knafelc 5.00
44 *Joe Schmidt* 45.00
45 Cleveland Browns 17.00
46 Len Teeuws 30.00
47 *Bill George* 35.00
48 Baltimore Colts 17.00
49 Eddie LeBaron 40.00
50 Hugh McElhenny 25.00
51 Ted Marchibroda 5.00
52 Adrian Burk 5.00
53 Frank Gifford 60.00
54 Charley Toogood 5.00
55 Tobin Rote 8.00
56 Bill Stits 5.00
57 Don Colo 5.00
58 Ollie Matson 75.00
59 Harlon Hill 5.00
60 *Lenny Moore* 85.00
61 Washington Redskins 85.00
62 Billy Wilson 5.00
63 Pittsburgh Steelers 17.00
64 Bob Pellegrini 5.00
65 Ken MacAfee 5.00
66 Willard Sherman 5.00
67 Roger Zatkoff 5.00
68 Dave Middleton 5.00
69 Ray Renfro 5.00
70 Don Stonesifer 30.00
71 *Stan Jones* 30.00
72 Jim Mutscheller 5.00
73 Volney Peters 30.00
74 Leo Nomellini 20.00
75 Ray Mathews 5.00
76 Dick Bielski 5.00
77 Charley Conerly 25.00
78 Elroy Hirsch 25.00
79 *Bill Forester* 8.00
80 Jim Doran 5.00
81 Fred Morrison 5.00
82 Jack Simmons 30.00
83 Bill McColl 5.00
84 Bert Rechichar 5.00
85 Joe Scudero 30.00
86 Y.A. Tittle 40.00
87 Ernie Stautner 20.00
88 Norm Willey 5.00
89 Bob Schnelker 5.00
90 Dan Towler 8.00
91 John Martinkovic 5.00
92 Detroit Lions 17.00
93 George Ratterman 5.00
94 Chuck Ulrich 30.00
95 Bobby Watkins 5.00
96 Buddy Young 5.00
97 Billy Wells 30.00
98 Bob Toneff 5.00
99 Bill McPeak 5.00
100 Bobby Thompson 5.00
101 *Roosevelt Grier* 30.00
102 Ron Waller 5.00
103 Bobby Dillon 5.00
104 Leon Hart 8.00
105 Mike McCormack 15.00
106 John Olszewski 30.00
107 Bill Wightkin 5.00
108 *George Shaw* 8.00
109 Dale Atkeson 30.00
110 Joe Perry 20.00
111 Dale Dodrill 5.00
112 Tom Scott 5.00
113 New York Giants 17.00
114 Los Angeles Rams 17.00
115 Al Carmichael 5.00
116 Bobby Layne 40.00
117 Ed Modzelewski 5.00
118 Lamar McHan 30.00
119 Chicago Bears 17.00
120 *Billy Vessels* 35.00

1957 Topps

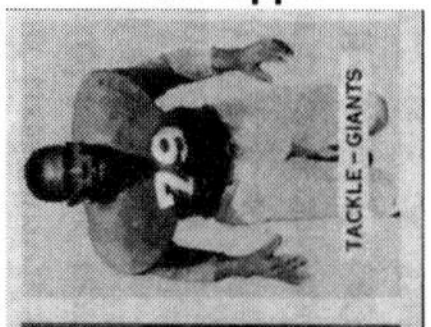
TACKLE - GIANTS

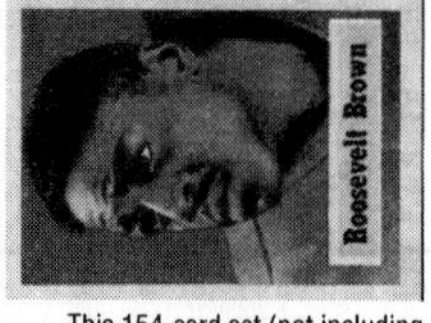
Roosevelt Brown

This 154-card set (not including the unnumbered checklist) has a horizontal format with two different pictures of the player on each side -- a head shot and a posed action shot. Issued in two series, the second series is more difficult to obtain than the first. Rookie cards in this set include Night Train Lane, Ray Berry, Earl Morrall, Bart Starr, John Unitas and Paul Hornung. Second-year cards include Roosevelt Brown, Pat Summerall, John Henry Johnson, Bob St. Clair, Lenny Moore and Len Ford (this is also his last regular-issued card). The final regular-issue card of Elroy Hirsch is also in this set. One variation does exist: The scarce card #58 of Willard Sherman has no team name on the front. The corrected version reads "Los Angeles Rams." It's believed that a number of the high series cards are short-printed, including Starr, Unitas and Hornung.

NM
Complete Set (155): 2400.
Common Player (1-88): 4.50
Common Player (89-154): 6.50
Checklist: 700.00
Series 1 Wax Pack (6): 400.00
Series 2 Wax Pack (6): 800.00
1 Eddie LeBaron 30.00
2 *Pete Retzlaff* 8.00
3 Mike McCormack 10.00
4 Lou Baldacci 4.50
5 Gino Marchetti 14.00
6 Leo Nomellini 13.00
7 Bobby Watkins 6.00
8 Dave Middleton 6.00
9 Bobby Dillon 6.00
10 Les Richter 6.00
11 Roosevelt Brown 13.00
12 *Lavern Torgeson* 6.00
13 Dick Bielski 4.50
14 Pat Summerall 13.00
15 *Jack Butler* 7.00
16 John Henry Johnson 13.00
17 Art Spinney 4.50
18 Bob St. Clair 10.00
19 Perry Jeter 4.50
20 Lou Creekmur 4.50
21 Dave Hanner 4.50
22 Norm Van Brocklin 25.00
23 *Don Chandler* 6.50
24 Al Dorow 4.50
25 Tom Scott 4.50
26 Ollie Matson 16.00
27 Fran Rogel 4.50
28 Lou Groza 20.00
29 Billy Vessels 4.50
30 Y.A. Tittle 32.50
31 George Blanda 45.00
32 Bobby Layne 30.00
33 Bill Howton 4.50
34 Bill Wade 4.50
35 Emlen Tunnell 12.00
36 Leo Elter 4.50
37 *Clarence Peaks* 6.00
38 Don Stonesifer 4.50
39 George Tarasovic 4.50
40 Darrell Brewster 4.50
41 Bert Rechichar 4.50
42 Billy Wilson 4.50
43 Ed Brown 4.50
44 Gene Gedman 4.50
45 Gary Knafelc 4.50
46 Elroy Hirsch 20.00
47 Don Heinrich 4.50
48 Gene Brito 4.50
49 Chuck Bednarik 15.00
50 Dave Mann 4.50
51 Bill McPeak 4.50
52 Kenny Konz 4.50
53 Alan Ameche 8.00
54 Gordon Soltau 4.50
55 Rick Casares 4.50
56 Charlie Ane 4.50
57 Al Carmichael 4.50
58A Willard Sherman ERR (no team name on front) 300.00
58B Willard Sherman COR (Rams) 5.00
59 Kyle Rote 8.00
60 Chuck Drazenovich 4.50
61 Bobby Walston 4.50
62 John Olszewski 4.50
63 Ray Mathews 4.50
64 Maurice Bassett 4.50
65 Art Donovan 20.00
66 Joe Arenas 4.50
67 Harlon Hill 4.50
68 Yale Lary 10.00
69 Bill Forester 4.50
70 Bob Boyd 4.50
71 Andy Robustelli 13.00
72 *Sam Baker* 7.00
73 Bob Pellegrini 4.50
74 Leo Sanford 4.50
75 Sid Watson 4.50
76 Ray Renfro 4.50
77 Carl Taseff 4.50
78 Clyde Conner 4.50
79 J.C. Caroline 4.50
80 *Howard Cassady* 10.00
81 Tobin Rote 6.00
82 Ron Waller 4.50
83 *Jim Patton* 7.00
84 Volney Peters 4.50
85 *Dick Lane* 40.00
86 Royce Womble 4.50
87 *Duane Putnam* 6.00
88 Frank Gifford 85.00
89 Steve Meilinger 6.50
90 Buck Lansford 6.50
91 Lindon Crow 6.50
92 Ernie Stautner 15.00
93 *Preston Carpenter* 10.00
94 *Raymond Berry* 125.00
95 Hugh McElhenny 25.00
96 Stan Jones 12.00
97 Dorne Dibble 6.50
98 Joe Scudero 6.50
99 Eddie Bell 6.50
100 Joe Childress 6.50
101 Elbert Nickel 6.50
102 Walt Michaels 6.50
103 Jim Mutscheller 6.50
104 *Earl Morrall* 50.00
105 Larry Strickland 6.50
106 Jack Christiansen 15.00
107 Fred Cone 6.50
108 *Bud McFadin* 10.00
109 Charley Conerly 25.00
110 Tom Runnels 6.50
111 Ken Keller 6.50
112 James Root 6.50
113 Ted Marchibroda 6.50
114 Don Paul 6.50
115 George Shaw 6.50
116 Dick Moegle 6.50
117 Don Bingham 6.50
118 Leon Hart 10.00
119 *Bart Starr* 400.00
120 Paul Miller 6.50
121 Alex Webster 10.00
122 Ray Wietecha 6.50
123 Johnny Carson 6.50
124 *Tommy McDonald* 14.00

125 *Jerry Tubbs* 10.00
126 Jack Scarbath 6.50
127 Ed Modzelewski 6.50
128 Lenny Moore 45.00
129 Joe Perry 25.00
130 Bill Wightkin 6.50
131 Jim Doran 6.50
132 Howard Ferguson 6.50
133 Tom Wilson 6.50
134 Dick James 6.50
135 Jimmy Harris 6.50
136 Chuck Ulrich 6.50
137 Lynn Chandnois 6.50
138 *Johnny Unitas* 450.00
139 Jim Ridlon 6.50
140 Zeke Bratkowski 10.00
141 Ray Krouse 6.50
142 John Martinkovic 6.50
143 Jim Cason 6.50
144 Ken MacAfee 6.50
145 *Sid Youngelman* 10.00
146 Paul Larson 6.50
147 Len Ford 15.00
148 Bob Toneff 6.50
149 Ronnie Knox 6.50
150 *Jim David* 10.00
151 *Paul Hornung* 400.00
152 Tank Younger 6.50
153 Bill Svoboda 6.50
154 Fred Morrison 40.00

1958 Topps

This 132-card set features an oval photo of the player on the front and a bright red background on the back. The card set also includes team cards, which had been missing from the previous year's set. Rookies here include Jim Brown and Sonny Jurgensen. Second-year cards are those of Bart Starr, Jim Ringo (his rookie was in '55), Bill George, and Ray Berry. This set also includes the last Topps card of Jack Christiansen.

NM
Complete Set (132): 1300.
Common Player: 3.75
Wax Pack (6): 465.00
1 *Gene Filipski* 14.00
2 Bobby Layne 25.00
3 Joe Schmidt 9.00
4 Bill Barnes 3.75
5 *Milt Plum* 8.00
6 Billie Howton 2.00
7 Howard Cassady 4.00
8 James Dooley 2.00
9 Cleveland Browns Team 6.50
10 Lenny Moore 15.00
11 Pete Brewster 3.75
12 Alan Ameche 5.00
13 Jim David 3.75
14 Jim Mutscheller 3.75
15 Andy Robustelli 9.00
16 Gino Marchetti 9.00
17 Ray Renfro 2.00
18 Yale Lary 8.50
19 Gary Glick 3.75
20 *Jon Arnett* 8.00
21 Bob Boyd 3.75
22 Johnny Unitas 115.00
23 Zeke Bratkowski 4.00
24 Sid Youngelman 3.75
25 Leo Elter 3.75
26 Ken Konz 3.75
27 Washington Redskins Team 7.00
28 C. Brettschneider 3.75
29 Chicago Bears Team 7.00
30 Alex Webster 4.00
31 Al Carmichael 3.75
32 Bobby Dillon 3.75
33 Steve Meilinger 3.75
34 Sam Baker 2.00
35 Chuck Bednarik 15.00
36 Vic Zucco 3.75
37 George Tarasovic 3.75
38 Bill Wade 3.75
39 Dick Stanfell 3.75
40 Jerry Norton 3.75
41 San Francisco 49ers Team 7.00
42 Emlen Tunnell 9.00
43 Jim Doran 3.75
44 Ted Marchibroda 3.75
45 Chet Hanulak 3.75
46 Dale Dodrill 3.75
47 John Carson 3.75
48 Dick Deschaine 3.75
49 Billy Wells 3.75
50 Larry Morris 3.75
51 Jack McClairen 3.75
52 Lou Groza 15.00
53 Rick Casares 3.75
54 Don Chandler 3.75
55 Duane Putnam 3.75
56 Gary Knafelc 3.75
57 Earl Morrall 10.00
58 *Ron Kramer* 4.00
59 Mike McCormack 8.00
60 Gern Nagler 3.75
61 New York Giants Team 7.00
62 *Jim Brown* 400.00
63 *Joe Marconi* 4.00
64 *R.C. Owens* 4.00
65 *Jimmy Carr* 4.00
66 Bart Starr 95.00
67 Tom Wilson 3.75
68 Lamar McHan 2.00
69 Chicago Cardinals Team 7.00
70 Jack Christiansen 8.00
71 *Don McElhenny* 4.00
72 Ron Waller 3.75
73 Frank Gifford 50.00
74 Bert Rechichar 3.75
75 John H. Johnson 10.00
76 Jack Butler 3.75
77 Frank Varrichione 3.75
78 Ray Mathews 3.75
79 Marv Matsuzak 3.75
80 Harlon Hill 3.75
81 Lou Creekmur 3.75
82 Woody Lewis 3.75
83 Don Heinrich 2.00
84 Charley Conerly 15.00
85 Los Angeles Rams Team 7.00
86 Y.A. Tittle 30.00
87 Bob Walston 3.75
88 Earl Putnam 3.75
89 Leo Nomellini 8.50
90 *Sonny Jurgensen* 100.00
91 Don Paul 3.75
92 Paige Cothren 3.75
93 Joe Perry 13.00
94 Tobin Rote 4.00
95 Billy Wilson 3.75
96 Green Bay Packers Team 7.00
97 Torgy Torgeson 3.75
98 Milt Davis 3.75
99 Larry Strickland 3.75
100 *Matt Hazeltine* 4.00
101 Walt Yowarski 3.75
102 Roosevelt Brown 8.00
103 Jim Ringo 8.00
104 Joe Krupa 3.75
105 Les Richter 3.75
106 Art Donovan 15.00
107 John Olszewski 3.75
108 Ken Keller 3.75
109 Philadelphia Eagles Team 5.50
110 Baltimore Colts Team 7.00
111 Dick Bielski 3.75
112 Eddie LeBaron 4.00
113 Gene Brito 3.75
114 *William Galimore* 12.00
115 Detroit Lions Team 7.00
116 Pittsburgh Steelers Team 7.00
117 L.G. Dupre 3.75
118 Babe Parilli 4.00
119 Bill George 8.00
120 Raymond Berry 30.00
121 Jim Podoley 3.75
122 Hugh McElhenny 15.00
123 Ed Brown 3.75
124 Dicky Moegle 3.75
125 Tom Scott 3.75
126 Tom McDonald 4.00
127 Ollie Matson 15.00
128 Preston Carpenter 3.75
129 George Blanda 35.00
130 Gordy Soltau 3.75
131 *Dick Nolan* 4.00
132 *Don Bosseler* 16.00

1959 Topps

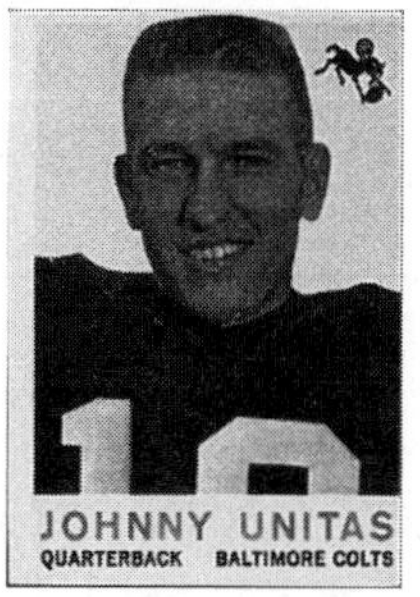
JOHNNY UNITAS
QUARTERBACK BALTIMORE COLTS

This 176-card set, featuring alternating blue and red letters for player names, was issued in two series, with the first being more valuable than the second. Team cards also included checklists on the back of each, and pennant cards were included and numbered as part of the set. This set showcases the rookie cards of Max McGee, Sam Huff, Alex Karras, John David Crow, Jerry Kramer, Jim Parker, Bobby Mitchell, and Jim Taylor (actually not the HOFer; see below). Second-year cards in the set are those of Paul Hornung and Jim Brown. Card #155, Jim Taylor, does not show the HOF running back for the Packers, as the card reads; instead, it shows Chicago Cardinal linebacker Jim Taylor. This mistake was repeated the following year, meaning a card actually depicting Taylor did not appear until 1961.

NM
Complete Set (176): 1000.
Common Player (1-88): 2.50
Common Player (89-176): 2.00
Team Cards: 5.00
Series 1 Wax Pack (6): 350.00
Series 2 Wax Pack (6): 300.00
1 Johnny Unitas 100.00
2 Gene Brito 2.50
3 Detroit Lions Team Card 5.00
4 *Max McGee* 20.00
5 Hugh McElhenny 12.00
6 Joe Schmidt 8.00
7 Kyle Rote 5.00
8 Clarence Peaks 2.50
9 Pittsburgh Steelers Pennant Card 5.00
10 Jim Brown 125.00
11 Ray Mathews 2.50
12 Bobby Dillon 2.50
13 Joe Childress 2.50
14 Terry Barr 2.50
15 *Del Shofner* 4.50
16 Bob Pellegrini 2.50
17 Baltimore Colts Team Card 5.00
18 Preston Carpenter 2.50
19 Leo Nomellini 7.00
20 Frank Gifford 30.00
21 Charlie Ane 2.50
22 Jack Butler 2.50
23 Bart Starr 55.00
24 Chicago Cardinals Pennant Card 2.50
25 Bill Barnes 2.50
26 Walt Michaels 2.50
27 Clyde Conner 2.50
28 Paige Cothren 2.50
29 Roosevelt Grier 5.00
30 Alan Ameche 5.00
31 Philadelphia Eagles Team Card 5.00
32 Dick Nolan 2.00
33 R.C. Owens 2.50
34 Dale Dodrill 2.50
35 Gene Gedman 2.50
36 *Gene Lipscomb* 8.00
37 Ray Renfro 2.50
38 Cleveland Brown Pennant Card 2.50
39 Bill Forester 2.50
40 Bobby Layne 25.00
41 Pat Summerall 8.50
42 Jerry Mertens 2.50
43 Steve Myhra 2.50
44 John Henry Johnson 7.00
45 Woody Lewis 2.50
46 Green Bay Packers Team Card 5.00
47 Don Owens 2.50
48 Ed Beatty 2.50
49 Don Chandler 2.00
50 Ollie Matson 12.00
51 *Sam Huff* 40.00
52 Tom Miner 2.50
53 New York Giants Pennant Card 2.50
54 Kenny Konz 2.50
55 Raymond Berry 15.00
56 Howard Ferguson 2.50
57 Chuck Ulrich 2.50
58 Bob St. Clair 5.00
59 *Don Burroughs* 3.00
60 Lou Groza 15.00
61 San Francisco 49ers Team Card 5.00
62 Andy Nelson 2.50
63 Hal Bradley 2.50
64 Dave Hanner 2.50
65 Chuck Connerly 11.00
66 Gene Cronin 2.50
67 Duane Putnam 2.50
68 Baltimore Colts Pennant Card 2.50
69 Ernie Stautner 8.00
70 Jon Arnett 3.00
71 Ken Panfil 2.50
72 Matt Hazeltine 2.50
73 Harley Sewell 2.50
74 Mike McCormack 5.00
75 Jim Ringo 5.00
76 Los Angeles Rams Team Card 5.00
77 *Bob Gain* 3.00
78 Buzz Nutter 2.50
79 Jerry Norton 2.50
80 Joe Perry 12.00
81 Carl Brettschneider 2.50
82 Paul Hornung 60.00
83 Philadelphia Eagles Pennant Card 2.50
84 Les Richter 2.00
85 Howard Cassady 2.00
86 Art Donovan 8.00
87 Jim Patton 2.50
88 Pete Retzlaff 3.50
89 Jim Mutscheller 2.00
90 Zeke Bratkowski 3.00
91 Washington Redskins Team Card 5.00
92 Art Hunter 2.00
93 Gern Nagler 2.00
94 Chuck Weber 2.00
95 *Lew Carpenter* 2.50
96 Stan Jones 5.00
97 Ralph Guglielmi 2.00
98 Green Bay Packer Pennant Card 2.50
99 Ray Wietecha 2.00
100 Lenny Moore 10.00
101 *Jim Ray Smith* 3.00
102 *Abe Woodson* 5.00
103 *Alex Karras* 40.00
104 Chicago Bears Team Card 5.00
105 *Johnny Crow* 10.00
106 *Joe Fortunato* 5.00
107 Babe Parilli 3.00
108 Proverb Jacobs 2.00
109 Gino Marchetti 8.00
110 Bill Wade 2.00
111 San Francisco 49ers Pennant Card 2.50
112 Karl Rubke 2.00
113 Dave Middleton 2.00
114 Roosevelt Brown 5.00
115 John Olszewski 2.00
116 *Jerry Kramer* 25.00
117 *King Hill* 3.50
118 Chicago Cardinals Team Card 5.00
119 Frank Varrichione 2.00
120 Rick Casares 2.00
121 George Strugar 2.00
122 *Bill Glass* 2.50
123 Don Bosseler 2.00
124 John Reger 2.50
125 *Jim Ninowski* 3.00
126 Los Angeles Rams Pennant Card 2.50
127 Willard Sherman 2.00
128 Bob Schnelker 2.00
129 Ollie Spencer 2.00
130 Y.A. Tittle 25.00
131 Yale Lary 6.00
132 *Jim Parker* 20.00
133 New York Giants Team Card 5.00
134 Jim Schrader 2.00
135 M.C. Reynolds 2.00
136 Mike Sandusky 2.00
137 Ed Brown 2.00
138 Al Barry 2.00
139 Detroit Lions Pennant Card 2.50
140 *Bobby Mitchell* 35.00
141 Larry Morris 2.00
142 *Jim Phillips* 3.00
143 Jim David 2.00
144 Joe Krupa 2.00
145 Willie Galimore 3.00
146 Pittsburgh Steelers Team Card 5.00
147 Andy Robustelli 7.50
148 Bill Wilson 2.00
149 Leo Sanford 2.00
150 Eddie LeBaron 5.00
151 Bill McColl 2.00
152 Buck Lansford 2.00
153 Chicago Bears Pennant Card 2.50
154 Leo Sugar 2.00
155 *Jim Taylor* 17.00
156 Lindon Crow 2.00
157 Jack McClairen 2.00
158 *Vince Costello* 2.50
159 Stan Wallace 2.00
160 *Mel Triplett* 3.00
161 Cleveland Browns Team Card 5.00
162 Dan Currie 2.00
163 L.G. Dupre 2.00
164 John Morrow 2.00
165 Jim Podoley 2.00
166 *Bruce Bosley* 2.50
167 Harlon Hill 2.00
168 Washington Redskins Pennant Card 2.50
169 Junior Wren 2.00
170 Tobin Rote 2.50
171 Art Spinney 2.00
172 Chuck Drazenovich 2.00
173 *Bobby Joe Conrad* 5.00
174 Jesse Richardson 2.00
175 Sam Baker 2.00
176 *Tom Tracy* 8.00

1960 Topps

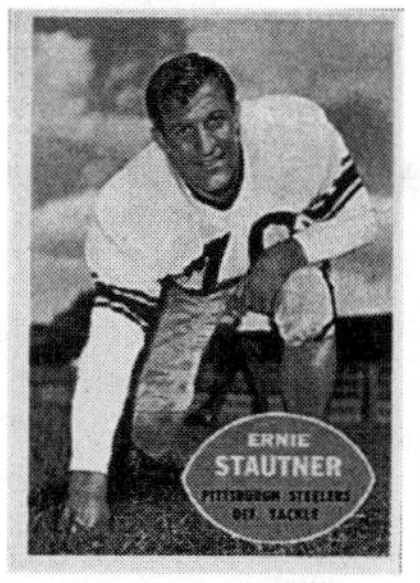
ERNIE
STAUTNER
PITTSBURGH STEELERS
DEF. TACKLE

This 132-card set by Topps, featuring NFL players only (Fleer picked up teams from the AFL in its 1960 set), showcased the inclusion of the expansion Dallas Cowboys. Cards are again numbered alphabetically according to city name. Card backs had a "Football Funnies" quiz which revealed the answer underneath a scratch-off area. This set marks the rookie cards of HOFer Forrest Gregg, future announcer Tom Brookshier, and former Jets coach Joe Walton. Second-year cards in the set include Jim Parker, Doug Atkins (his rookie card was six years prior to his second-year card), Bobby Mitchell, and Sam Huff. There are three errors in the set. Card #52, Jim Taylor, shows not the HOF running back of the Packers, as advertised; it again shows Cardinals linebacker Jim Taylor. This mistake was made in the 1959 set as well. The other errors are reversed negatives; on the card of #97, Frank Varrichione, and on card #20, Doug Atkins.

NM
Complete Set (132): 625.00
Common Player: 1.75
Team Cards: 5.00
Wax Pack (6): 400.00
1 Johnny Unitas 80.00
2 Alan Ameche 5.00
3 Lenny Moore 7.00
4 Raymond Berry 7.00
5 Jim Parker 7.00
6 George Preas 1.75
7 Art Spinney 1.75
8 *Bill Pellington* 2.50
9 *Johnny Sample* 2.50
10 Gene Lipscomb 3.50
11 Baltimore Colts Team Card (Checklist 67-132) 5.00
12 Ed Brown 1.75
13 Rick Casares 1.75
14 Willie Galimore 1.75
15 Jim Dooley 1.75
16 Harlon Hill 1.75
17 Stan Jones 4.50
18 Bill George 4.50
19 *Erich Barnes* 3.00
20 Doug Atkins 5.50
21 Chicago Bears Team Card (Checklist 1-66) 5.00
22 Milt Plum 2.50
23 Jim Brown 85.00
24 Sam Baker 1.75
25 Bobby Mitchell 10.00
26 Ray Renfro 1.75
27 Billy Howton 1.75
28 Jim Ray Smith 1.75
29 *Jim Shofner* 3.50
30 Bob Gain 1.75
31 Cleveland Browns Team Card (Checklist 1-66) 5.00
32 Don Heinrich 1.75
33 Ed Modzelewski 1.75
34 Fred Cone 1.75
35 L.G. Dupre 1.75
36 Dick Bielski 1.75
37 Charlie Ane 1.75
38 Jerry Tubbs 1.75
39 Doyle Nix 1.75
40 Ray Krouse 1.75
41 Earl Morrall 5.00
42 Hopalong Cassady 1.75
43 Dave Middleton 1.75
44 *Jim Gibbons* 2.50
45 Darris McCord 1.75
46 Joe Schmidt 5.50
47 Terry Barr 1.75
48 Yale Lary 5.00
49 Gil Mains 1.75
50 Detroit Lions Team Card (Checklist 1-66) 5.00
51 Bart Starr 40.00
52 Jim Taylor 8.00
53 Lew Carpenter 1.75
54 Paul Hornung 35.00
55 Max McGee 3.00
56 *Forrest Gregg* 28.00
57 Jim Ringo 5.50
58 Bill Forester 1.75
59 Dave Hanner 1.75
60 Green Bay Packers Team Card (Checklist 67-132) 5.00
61 Bill Wade 1.75
62 *Frank Ryan* 8.00
63 Ollie Matson 8.00
64 Jon Arnett 1.75
65 Del Shofner 1.75
66 Jim Phillips 1.75
67 Art Hunter 1.75
68 Les Richter 1.75
69 *Lou Michaels* 3.00
70 John Baker 1.75
71 Los Angeles Rams Team Card (Checklist 1-66) 5.00
72 Charley Conerly 10.00
73 Mel Triplett 1.75
74 Frank Gifford 45.00
75 Alex Webster 1.75
76 Bob Schnelker 1.75
77 Pat Summerall 7.00
78 Roosevelt Brown 5.50
79 Jimmy Patton 1.75
80 Sam Huff 15.00
81 Andy Robustelli 6.00
82 New York Giants Team Card (Checklist 1-66) 5.00
83 Clarence Peaks 1.75
84 Bill Barnes 1.75
85 Pete Retzlaff 1.75
86 Bobby Walston 1.75
87 Chuck Bednarik 7.00
88 Bob Pellagrini 1.75
89 *Tom Brookshier* 6.00
90 Marion Campbell 1.75
91 Jesse Richardson 1.75
92 Philadelphia Eagles Team Card (Checklist 1-66) 5.00
93 Bobby Layne 23.00
94 John Henry Johnson 5.50
95 Tom Tracy 1.75
96 Preston Carpenter 1.75
97 Frank Varrichione 1.75
98 John Nisby 1.75
99 Dean Derby 1.75
100 George Tarasovic 1.75
101 Ernie Stautner 6.00
102 Pittsburgh Steelers Team Card (Checklist 67-132) 5.00
103 King Hill 1.75
104 Mal Hammack 1.75
105 John Crow 3.50
106 Bobby Joe Conrad 1.75
107 Woodley Lewis 1.75
108 Don Gillis 1.75
109 Carl Brettschneider 1.75
110 Leo Sugar 1.75
111 Frank Fuller 1.75
112 St. Louis Cardinals Team Card (Checklist 67-132) 5.00
113 Y.A. Tittle 22.00
114 Joe Perry 7.00
115 *J.D. Smith* 3.00
116 Hugh McElhenny 8.00
117 Billy Wilson 1.75
118 Bob St. Clair 3.50
119 Matt Hazeltine 1.75
120 Abe Woodson 1.75
121 Leo Nomellini 5.00
122 San Francisco 49ers Team Card (Checklist 67-132) 5.00
123 Ralph Gugliemi 1.75
124 Don Bosseler 1.75
125 Johnny Olszewski 1.75
126 Bill Anderson 1.75
127 *Joe Walton* 3.50
128 Jim Schrader 1.75
129 Ralph Felton 1.75
130 Gary Glick 1.75
131 Bob Toneff 1.75
132 Washington Redskins 25.00

1960 Topps Team Emblem Stickers

One of each of these 33 metallic inserts was included in a wax pack of 1960 Topps football cards. The team emblem stickers are unnumbered and included NFL teams (1-13) and college teams (14-33). This was Topps' first football insert set. Future Topps inserts in the early '60s would also include college teams. These sticker fronts are bordered in black and show either a blue, silver or gold background. The stickers measure about 2" x 3".

NM
Complete Set (33): 175.00
Common Pro Team: 6.00
Common College Team: 4.50
(1) Baltimore Colts 6.00
(2) Chicago Bears 6.00
(3) Cleveland Browns 6.00
(4) Dallas Cowboys 8.00
(5) Detroit Lions 8.00
(6) Green Bay Packers 6.00
(7) Los Angeles Rams 6.00
(8) New York Giants 6.00
(9) Philadelphia Eagles 6.00
(10) Pittsburgh Steelers 6.00
(11) St. Louis Cardinals 6.00
(12) San Francisco 49ers 6.00
(13) Washington Redskins 8.00
(14) Air Force 4.50
(15) Army 4.50
(16) California 4.50
(17) Dartmouth 4.50
(18) Duke 4.50
(19) LSU 4.50
(20) Michigan 4.50
(21) Mississippi 4.50
(22) Navy 4.50
(23) Notre Dame 15.00
(24) SMU 4.50
(25) USC 4.50
(26) Syracuse 4.50
(27) Tennessee 4.50
(28) Texas 4.50
(29) UCLA 4.50
(30) Minnesota 4.50
(31) Washington 4.50
(32) Wisconsin 4.50
(33) Yale 4.50

1961 Topps

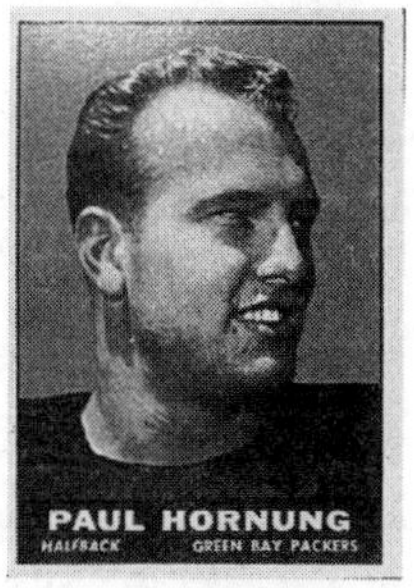
PAUL HORNUNG
HALFBACK GREEN BAY PACKERS

This set of 198 cards was the last full Topps set to include both AFL players and NFL players. The AFL segment of the set (133-197) does not include team checklists. Cards are similar to the 1961 Topps baseball issue and feature a ruboff game on the back. The set is once again numbered in order of teams - alphabetically by city. Rookies in this set include John Brodie, Don Maynard, Jim Otto and Tom Flores. Second-year cards include Alex Karras, Henry Jordan, Sonny Jurgensen (three years after his rookie card debuted), Abner Haynes, Jack Kemp and Ron Mix. This set included the last regular-issue cards of Alan Ameche, Charley Conerly, Kyle Rote, Chuck Bednarik and Tom Brookshier. Card #41 could actually be considered Packer running back Jim Taylor's rookie card. His rookie and second- year cards Topps printed in 1959 and 1960 actually depicted Cardinal linebacker Jim Taylor instead of HOFer Jim Taylor.

NM
Complete Set (198): 1100.
Common Player: 2.00
Series 1 Wax Pack (5): 410.00
Series 2 Wax Pack (5): 410.00
1 Johnny Unitas 90.00
2 Lenny Moore 7.00
3 Alan Ameche 4.00
4 Raymond Berry 7.00
5 Jim Mutscheller 2.00
6 Jim Parker 4.50
7 Gino Marchetti 5.50
8 Gene Lipscomb 3.00
9 Baltimore Colts 4.00
10 Bill Wade 2.00
11 *Johnny Morris* 6.00
12 Rick Casares 2.00
13 Harlon Hill 2.00
14 Stan Jones 4.50
15 Doug Atkins 5.00
16 Bill George 4.50
17 J.C. Caroline 2.00
18 Chicago Bears 4.00
19 Big Time Football comes to Texas (Eddie LeBaron) 3.25
20 Eddie LeBaron 3.00
21 Don McElhenny 2.00
22 L.G. Dupre 2.00
23 Jim Doran 2.00
24 Billy Howton 2.00
25 Buzz Guy 2.00
26 *Jack Patera* 2.00
27 Tom Frankauser 2.00
28 Dallas Cowboys 10.00
29 Jim Ninowski 2.00
30 *Dan Lewis* 2.00
31 *Nick Pietrosante* 3.00
32 *Gail Cogdill* 2.00
33 Jim Gibbons 2.00
34 Jim Martin 2.00
35 Alex Karras 20.00
36 Joe Schmidt 5.00
37 Detroit Lions 4.00
38 Set Scoring Record (Paul Hornung) 10.00
39 Bart Starr 40.00
40 Paul Hornung 28.00
41 Jim Taylor 24.00
42 Max McGee 2.00
43 *Boyd Dowler* 5.00
44 Jim Ringo 4.25
45 *Henry Jordan* 15.00
46 Bill Forester 2.00
47 Green Bay Packers 4.00
48 Frank Ryan 2.00
49 Jon Arnett 2.00
50 Ollie Matson 6.50
51 Jim Phillips 2.00
52 Del Shofner 2.00
53 Art Hunter 2.00
54 Gene Brito 2.00
55 Lindon Crow 2.00
56 Los Angeles Rams 4.00
57 25-TD Passes (Johnny Unitas) 15.00
58 Y.A. Tittle 22.00
59 *John Brodie* 40.00
60 J.D. Smith 2.00
61 R.C. Owens 2.00
62 Clyde Conner 2.00
63 Bob St. Clair 4.00

64	Leo Nomellini	5.00
65	Abe Woodson	2.00
66	San Francisco 49ers	4.00
67	Checklist	50.00
68	Milt Plum	2.00
69	Ray Renfro	2.00
70	Bobby Mitchell	7.00
71	Jim Brown	85.00
72	Mike McCormack	4.00
73	Jim Ray Smith	2.00
74	Sam Baker	2.00
75	Walt Michaels	2.00
76	Cleveland Browns	4.00
77	(Jim Brown IA)	35.00
78	George Shaw	2.00
79	Hugh McElhenny	6.00
80	Clancy Osborne	2.00
81	Dave Middleton	2.00
82	Frank Youso	2.00
83	Don Joyce	2.00
84	Ed Culpepper	2.00
85	Charley Conerly	8.00
86	Mel Triplett	2.00
87	Kyle Rote	4.00
88	Roosevelt Brown	4.50
89	Ray Wietecha	2.00
90	Andy Robustelli	6.00
91	Sam Huff	7.50
92	Jim Patton	2.00
93	New York Giants	4.00
94	Leads Giants for 13th Year (Chas Conerly)	5.00
95	Sonny Jurgensen	20.00
96	Tommy McDonald	2.00
97	Billy Barnes	2.00
98	Bobby Waltson	2.00
99	Pete Retzlaff	2.00
100	Jim McCusker	2.00
101	Chuck Bednarik	7.00
102	Tom Brookshier	3.00
103	Philadelphia Eagles	4.00
104	Bobby Layne	20.00
105	John Henry Johnson	5.00
106	Tom Tracy	2.00
107	*Buddy Dial*	3.00
108	*Jim Orr*	3.50
109	Mike Sandusky	2.00
110	John Reger	2.00
111	Junior Wren	2.00
112	Pittsburgh Steelers	4.00
113	Sets New Passing Record (Bobby Layne)	7.00
114	John Roach	2.00
115	*Sam Etcheverry*	2.00
116	John David Crow	3.00
117	Mal Hammack	2.00
118	*Sonny Randle*	2.00
119	Leo Sugar	2.00
120	Jerry Norton	2.00
121	St. Louis Cardinals	4.00
122	Checklist	35.00
123	Ralph Guglielmi	2.00
124	Dick James	2.00
125	Don Bosseler	2.00
126	Joe Walton	2.00
127	Bill Anderson	2.00
128	*Vince Promuto*	2.25
129	Bob Toneff	2.00
130	Jim Paluck	2.00
131	Washington Redskins	4.00
132	Wins NFL Passing Title (Milt Plum)	3.00
133	Abner Haynes	3.50
134	Mel Branch	2.00
135	Jerry Cornelison	2.00
136	Bill Krisher	2.00
137	Paul Miller	2.00
138	Jack Spikes	2.00
139	*Johnny Robinson*	6.00
140	*Cotton Davidson*	4.00
141	Dave Smith	2.00
142	Bill Groman	2.00
143	Rich Michael	2.00
144	Mike Dukes	2.00
145	George Blanda	26.00
146	Billy Cannon	4.00
147	Dennit Morris	2.00
148	Jacky Lee	2.00
149	Al Dorrow	2.00
150	*Don Maynard*	50.00
151	*Art Powell*	6.00
152	Sid Youngelman	2.00
153	Bob Mischak	2.00
154	Larry Grantham	2.00
155	Tom Saidock	2.00
156	Roger Donnahoo	2.00
157	Lavern Torczon	2.00
158	*Archie Matsos*	2.00
159	Elbert Dubenion	3.00
160	*Wray Carlton*	2.00
161	Rich McCabe	2.00
162	Ken Rice	2.00
163	Art Baker	2.00
164	Tom Rychiec	2.00
165	Mack Yoho	2.00
166	Jack Kemp	150.00
167	Paul Lowe	3.25
168	Ron Mix	9.00
169	Paul Maguire	3.00
170	Volney Peters	2.00
171	Ernie Wright	2.00
172	Ron Nery	2.00
173	*Dave Kocourek*	2.00
174	Jim Colclough	2.00
175	Babe Parilli	3.25
176	Billy Lott	2.00
177	Fred Bruney	2.00
178	Ross O'Hanley	2.00
179	Walt Cudzik	2.00
180	Charles Leo	2.00
181	Bob Dee	2.00
182	*Jim Otto*	40.00
183	Eddie Macon	2.00
184	Dick Christy	2.00
185	Alan Miller	2.00
186	*Tom Flores*	25.00
187	Joe Cannavino	2.00
188	Don Manoukian	2.00
189	Bob Coolbaugh	2.00
190	*Lionel Taylor*	7.00
191	Bud McFadin	2.00
192	Goose Gonsoulin	2.00
193	Frank Tripucka	2.75
194	*Gene Mingo*	3.00
195	Eldon Danenhauer	2.00
196	Bob McNamara	2.00
197	Dave Rolle	2.00
198	Checklist	90.00

1961 Topps Stickers

This set of 48 stickers was included one per pack in the 1961 Topps football set. Stickers are unnumbered and are grouped according to NFL (1-15), AFL (16-24), and colleges (25-48). The stickers were issued with tabs that could be peeled off. For the sticker to be considered Mint, tabs would have to be intact.

		NM
Complete Set (48):		175.00
Common Pro Team:		6.00
Common College Team:		3.50
(1)	NFL Emblem	6.00
(2)	Baltimore Colts	6.00
(3)	Chicago Bears	6.00
(4)	Cleveland Browns	6.00
(5)	Dallas Cowboys	8.00
(6)	Detroit Lions	6.00
(7)	Green Bay Packers	8.00
(8)	Los Angeles Rams	6.00
(9)	Minnesota Vikings	6.00
(10)	New York Giants	6.00
(11)	Philadelphia Eagles	6.00
(12)	Pittsburgh Steelers	6.00
(13)	San Francisco 49ers	6.00
(14)	St. Louis Cardinals	6.00
(15)	Washington Redskins	8.00
(16)	AFL Emblem	8.00
(17)	Boston Patriots	6.00
(18)	Buffalo Bills	8.00
(19)	Dallas Texans	8.00
(20)	Denver Broncos	6.00
(21)	Houston Oilers	6.00
(22)	Oakland Raiders	8.00
(23)	San Diego Chargers	6.00
(24)	Titans of New York	6.00
(25)	Air Force	3.50
(26)	Alabama	6.00
(27)	Arkansas	3.50
(28)	Army	5.00
(29)	Baylor	3.50
(30)	California	3.50
(31)	Georgia Tech	3.50
(32)	Illinois	3.50
(33)	Kansas	3.50
(34)	Kentucky	3.50
(35)	Miami	3.50
(36)	Michigan	6.00
(37)	Missouri	3.50
(38)	Navy	5.00
(39)	Oregon	3.50
(40)	Penn State	6.00
(41)	Pittsburgh	3.50
(42)	Purdue	3.50
(43)	USC	6.00
(44)	Stanford	3.50
(45)	TCU	3.50
(46)	Virginia	3.50
(47)	Washington	3.50
(48)	Washington State	3.50

1962 Topps

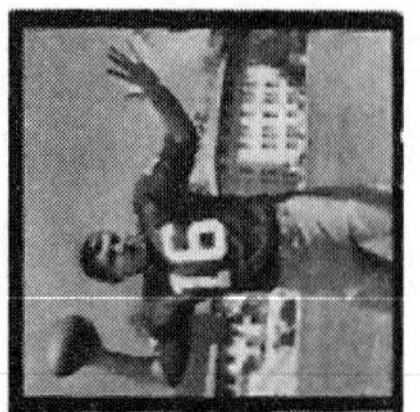

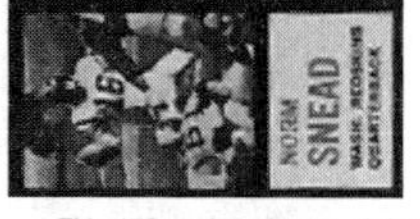
NORM SNEAD
WASHINGTON REDSKINS QUARTERBACK

This 176-card set is one of the decade's toughest to complete in mint condition because of the easily-scuffed black borders. Like many of the Topps sets of this era, a good number of the cards in the set are short-printed, probably because the number of cards in the set didn't exactly match the amount that would fit onto printing sheets. Cards are again grouped by teams, which are listed in alphabetical order by city. This was the first time in five years Topps tried a horizontal format; Topps would try it again in 1966. Rookies in this set include Mike Ditka, Ernie Davis (his only regular-issue card), Roman Gabriel, Fran Tarkenton, Bill Kilmer and Norm Snead. Second-year cards in the set include Don Meredith (his first Topps card) and John Brodie. Last-year cards in the set include Max McGee and Hall of Famers Joe Perry, Ollie Matson and Bobby Layne. The last Topps cards of Frank Gifford and Andy Robustelli are also included. (Key: SP - short printed)

		NM
Complete Set (176):		1700.
Common Player:		3.50
SP Cards:		7.50
Wax Pack (FB Bucks):		36.00
Wax Pack (Pro Stars):		385.00
1	Johnny Unitas	125.00
2	Lenny Moore	9.00
3	*Alex Hawkins* (SP)	8.00
4	Joe Perry	9.00
5	Raymond Berry (SP)	20.00
6	Steve Myhra	3.50
7	Tom Gilburg (SP)	7.50
8	Gino Marchetti	7.50
9	Bill Pellington	3.50
10	Andy Nelson	3.50
11	Wendell Harris (SP)	7.50
12	Baltimore Colts Team	3.50
13	Billy Wade (SP)	7.50
14	Willie Galimore	3.50
15	Johnny Morris (SP)	7.50
16	Rick Casares	3.50
17	*Mike Ditka*	225.00
18	Stan Jones	4.50
19	Roger LeClerc	3.50
20	Angelo Coia	3.50
21	Doug Atkins	7.50
22	Bill George	5.00
23	*Richie Petitbon*	5.00
24	Ron Bull (SP)	8.00
25	Chicago Bears Team	3.50
26	Howard Cassady	3.50
27	Ray Renfro (SP)	7.50
28	Jim Brown	125.00
29	Rick Kreitling	3.50
30	Jim Ray Smith	3.50
31	John Morrow	3.50
32	Lou Groza	12.00
33	Bob Gain	3.50
34	Bernie Parrish	3.50
35	Jim Shofner	3.50
36	*Ernie Davis* (SP)	110.00
37	Cleveland Browns Team	3.50
38	Eddie LeBaron	3.50
39	Don Meredith (SP)	80.00
40	J.W. Lockett (SP)	7.50
41	*Don Perkins*	7.50
42	Billy Howton	3.50
43	Dick Bielski	3.50
44	*Mike Connelly*	3.00
45	Jerry Tubbs (SP)	7.50
46	Don Bishop (SP)	7.50
47	Dick Moegle	3.50
48	Bobby Plummer (SP)	7.50
49	Dallas Cowboys Team	10.00
50	Milt Plum	3.50
51	Dan Lewis	3.50
52	Nick Pietrosante (SP)	7.50
53	Gail Cogdill	3.50
54	Jim Gibbons	3.50
55	Jim Martin	3.50
56	Yale Lary	7.50
57	Darris McCord	3.50
58	Alex Karras	15.00
59	Joe Schmidt	7.50
60	Dick Lane	6.00
61	John Lomakoski (SP)	7.50
62	Detroit Lions Team (SP)	15.00
63	Bart Starr (SP)	70.00
64	Paul Hornung (SP)	50.00
65	Tom Moore (SP)	7.50
66	Jim Taylor (SP)	30.00
67	Max McGee (SP)	7.50
68	Jim Ringo (SP)	15.00
69	*Fuzzy Thurston* (SP)	15.00
70	Forrest Gregg	7.50
71	Boyd Dowler	3.50
72	Henry Jordan (SP)	6.50
73	Bill Forester (SP)	7.50
74	Earl Gros (SP)	7.50
75	Green Bay Packers (SP)	20.00
76	Checklist (SP)	80.00
77	Zeke Bratkowski (SP)	7.50
78	Jon Arnett (SP)	7.50
79	Ollie Matson (SP)	20.00
80	Dick Bass (SP)	7.50
81	Jim Phillips	3.50
82	*Carroll Dale*	4.00
83	Frank Varrichione	3.50
84	Art Hunter	3.50
85	*Danny Villanueva*	3.50
86	Les Richter (SP)	7.50
87	Lindon Crow	3.50
88	*Roman Gabriel* (SP)	50.00
89	Los Angeles Rams (SP)	15.00
90	*Fran Tarkenton* (SP)	200.00
91	Jerry Reichow (SP)	7.50
92	Hugh McElhenny (SP)	20.00
93	Mel Triplett (SP)	7.50
94	*Tommy Mason* (SP)	7.50
95	Dave Middleton (SP)	7.50
96	Frank Youso (SP)	7.50
97	Mike Mercer (SP)	7.50
98	Rip Hawkins (SP)	7.50
99	Cliff Livingston (SP)	7.50
100	*Roy Winston* (SP)	7.50
101	Minnesota Vikings Team (SP)	20.00
102	Y.A. Tittle	30.00
103	Joe Walton	3.50
104	Frank Gifford	40.00
105	Alex Webster	3.50
106	Del Shofner	3.50
107	Don Chandler	3.50
108	Andy Robustelli	7.50
109	Jim Katcavage	3.50
110	Sam Huff (SP)	20.00
111	Erich Barnes	3.50
112	Jimmy Patton	3.50
113	Jerry Hillebrand (SP)	7.50
114	New York Giants Team	3.50
115	Sonny Jurgensen	20.00
116	Tommy McDonald	3.50
117	Ted Dean (SP)	7.50
118	Clarence Peaks	3.50
119	Bobby Walston	3.50
120	Pete Retzlaff (SP)	7.50
121	Jim Schrader (SP)	7.50
122	J.D. Smith	3.50
123	King Hill	3.50
124	Maxie Baughan	3.50
125	Pete Case (SP)	7.50
126	Philadelphia Eagles Team	3.50
127	Bobby Layne	25.00
128	Tom Tracy	3.50
129	John Henry Johnson	7.00
130	Buddy Dial (SP)	7.50
131	Preston Carpenter	3.50
132	Lou Michaels (SP)	7.50
133	Gene Lipscomb (SP)	8.00
134	Ernie Stautner (SP)	15.00
135	John Reger (SP)	7.50
136	Myron Pottios	3.50
137	Bob Ferguson (SP)	7.50
138	Pittsburgh Steelers Team	3.50
139	Sam Etcheverry	3.50
140	John David Crow (SP)	7.50
141	Bobby Joe Conrad (SP)	7.50
142	*Prentice Gautt* (SP)	8.00
143	Frank Mestnik	3.50
144	Sonny Randle	3.50
145	Gerry Perry	3.50
146	Jerry Norton	3.50
147	Jimmy Hill	3.50
148	Bill Stacy	3.50
149	Fate Echols (SP)	7.50
150	St. Louis Cardinals Team	3.50
151	*Bill Kilmer*	25.00
152	John Brodie	15.00
153	J.D. Smith	3.50
154	C.R. Roberts (SP)	7.50
155	Monty Stickles	3.50
156	Clyde Conner	3.50
157	Bob St. Clair	7.50
158	*Tommy Davis*	3.50
159	Leo Nomellini	5.50
160	Matt Hazeltine	3.50
161	Abe Woodson	3.50
162	Dave Baker	3.50
163	San Francisco 49ers Team	3.50
164	*Norm Snead* (SP)	30.00
165	Dick James	3.50
166	Bobby Mitchell	8.00
167	Sam Horner	3.50
168	Bill Barnes	3.50
169	Bill Anderson	3.50
170	Fred Dugan	3.50
171	John Aveni (SP)	7.50
172	Bob Toneff	3.50
173	Jim Kerr	3.50
174	Leroy Jackson (SP)	7.50
175	Washington Redskins Team	3.50
176	Checklist	100.00

1962 Topps Bucks

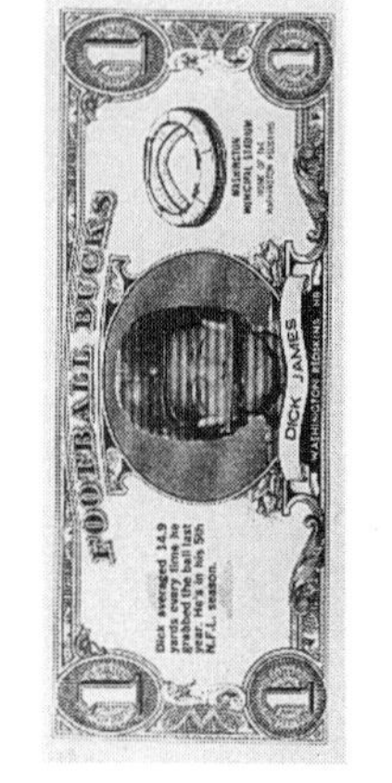
FOOTBALL BUCKS
DICK JAMES

This 48-card set was issued one per wax pack in the 1962 Topps football issue. The 1-1/4" x 4-1/4" "cards" have a dollar bill motif with the player's head in the middle and his name underneath. Backs show the same motif, with the NFL and team logo encircled. The Topps Bucks were printed on white paper.

		NM
Complete Set (48):		400.00
Common Player:		4.50
1	J.D. Smith	4.50
2	Bart Starr	25.00
3	Dick James	4.50
4	Alex Webster	6.00
5	Paul Hornung	18.00
6	John David Crow	6.00
7	Jimmy Brown	60.00
8	Don Perkins	4.50
9	Bobby Walston	4.50
10	Jim Phillips	4.50
11	Y.A. Tittle	20.00
12	Sonny Randle	4.50
13	Jerry Reichow	4.50
14	Yale Lary	7.00
15	Buddy Dial	4.50
16	Ray Renfro	4.50
17	Norm Snead	4.50
18	Leo Nemellini	6.00
19	Hugh McElhenny	8.00
20	Eddie LeBaron	4.50
21	Bill Howton	4.50
22	Bobby Mitchell	9.00
23	Nick Pietrosante	4.50
24	John Unitas	30.00
25	Raymond Berry	9.00
26	Billy Kilmer	7.00
27	Lenny Moore	8.00
28	Tommy McDonald	4.50
29	Del Shofner	4.50
30	Jim Taylor	12.00
31	Joe Schmidt	7.00
32	Bill George	6.00
33	Fran Tarkenton	65.00
34	Willie Galimore	4.50
35	Bobby Layne	17.00
36	Max McGee	4.50
37	Jon Arnett	4.50
38	Lou Groza	10.00
39	Frank Varrichione	4.50
40	Milt Plum	4.50
41	Prentice Gault	4.50
42	Billy Wade	6.00
43	Gino Marchetti	7.00
44	John Brodie	10.00
45	Sonny Jurgensen	10.00
46	Clarence Peaks	4.50
47	Mike Ditka	20.00
48	John Henry Johnson	7.00

1963 Topps

Topps' 170-card set of NFL players features teams grouped in alphabetical order by city name. As with many Topps sets in this era, numerous cards were short-printed because the number of cards didn't match the size of Topps' printing sheets, meaning some were produced in more quantities than others. Rookies in this set include Hall of Famers Deacon Jones, Bob Lilly, Willie Wood, and Ray Nitschke. Other important rookie cards include Jim Marshall and Charlie Johnson. The set also features the second-year cards of Roman Gabriel, Mike Ditka, Fran Tarkenton and Bill Kilmer. Last-year cards here include Eddie LeBaron, Fuzzy Thurston, Hugh McElhenny, Ernie Stautner and Leo Nomellini. The final Topps cards of such players as Night Train Lane, Yale Lary, Joe Schmidt, Y.A. Tittle, Rosey Grier, Sam Huff, John Henry Johnson and Bob St. Clair are also in this set. (Key: SP - short printed)

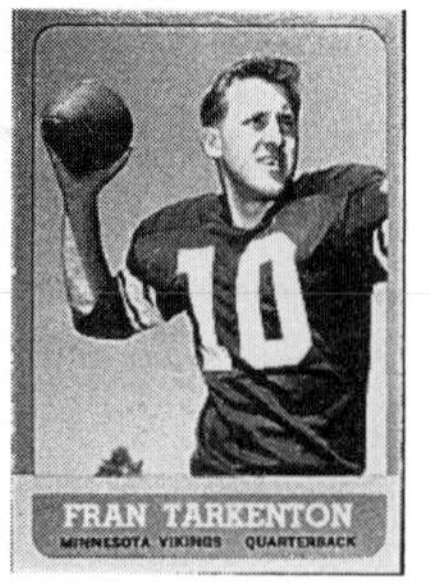
FRAN TARKENTON
MINNESOTA VIKINGS QUARTERBACK

		NM
Complete Set (170):		1300.
Common Player:		2.00
Wax Pack (5):		350.00
1	Johnny Unitas	100.00
2	Lenny Moore	7.00
3	Jimmy Orr	2.00
4	Raymond Berry	7.00
5	Jim Parker	5.00
6	Alex Sandusky	2.00
7	Dick Szymanski	2.00
8	Gino Marchetti	5.00
9	*Billy Ray Smith*	3.00
10	Bill Pellington	2.00
11	*Bob Boyd*	2.00
12	Baltimore Colts Team (SP)	8.50
13	Frank Ryan (SP)	6.00
14	Jim Brown (SP)	200.00
15	Ray Renfro (SP)	4.50
16	Rich Kreitling (SP)	4.50
17	Mike McCormack (SP)	9.00
18	Jim Ray Smith (SP)	4.50
19	Lou Groza (SP)	17.00
20	Bill Glass (SP)	4.50
21	Galen Fiss (SP)	4.50
22	*Don Fleming* (SP)	6.00
23	Bob Gain (SP)	4.50
24	Cleveland Browns (SP)	8.50
25	Milt Plum	2.00
26	Dan Lewis	2.00
27	Nick Pietrosante	2.00
28	Gail Cogdill	2.00
29	Harley Sewell	2.00
30	Jim Gibbons	2.00
31	Carl Brettschneider	2.00
32	Dick Lane	3.50
33	Yale Lary	4.00
34	*Roger Brown*	3.00
35	Joe Schmidt	4.75
36	Detroit Lions Team (SP)	8.50
37	Roman Gabriel	7.00
38	Zeke Bratkowski	2.00
39	Dick Bass	2.00
40	Jon Arnett	2.00
41	Jim Phillips	2.00
42	Frank Varrichione	2.00
43	Danny Villanueva	2.00
44	*Deacon Jones*	50.00
45	Lindon Crow	2.00
46	Marlin McKeever	2.00
47	*Ed Meador*	2.50
48	Los Angeles Rams Team	4.00
49	Y.A. Tittle (SP)	40.00
50	Del Shofner (SP)	3.50
51	Alex Webster (SP)	6.00
52	Phil King (SP)	4.50
53	Jack Stroud (SP)	4.50
54	Darrell Dess (SP)	4.50
55	Jim Katcavage (SP)	4.50
56	Roosevelt Grier (SP)	8.00
57	Erich Barnes (SP)	4.50
58	Jim Patton (SP)	4.50
59	Sam Huff (SP)	14.00
60	New York Giants Team	4.00
61	Bill Wade	2.00
62	Mike Ditka	60.00
63	Johnny Morris	2.00
64	Roger LeClerc	2.00
65	Roger Davis	2.00
66	Joe Marconi	2.00
67	Herman Lee	2.00
68	Doug Atkins	5.00
69	Joe Fortunato	2.00
70	Bill George	4.75
71	Richie Petitbon	5.00
72	Chicago Bears Team (SP)	8.50
73	Eddie LeBaron (SP)	6.00
74	Don Meredith (SP)	50.00
75	Don Perkins (SP)	6.00
76	Amos Marsh (SP)	4.50
77	Bill Howton (SP)	4.50
78	Andy Cverko (SP)	4.50
79	Sam Baker (SP)	4.50
80	Jerry Tubbs (SP)	4.50
81	Don Bishop (SP)	4.50
82	*Bob Lilly*	125.00
83	Jerry Norton (SP)	4.50
84	Dallas Cowboys	16.00
85	Checklist	25.00
86	Bart Starr	40.00
87	Jim Taylor	16.00
88	Boyd Dowler	2.00
89	Forrest Gregg	5.25
90	Fuzzy Thurston	3.00
91	Jim Ringo	4.75
92	Ron Kramer	2.00
93	Hank Jordan	2.00
94	Bill Forester	2.00
95	*Willie Wood*	27.00
96	*Ray Nitschke*	80.00
97	Green Bay Packers Team	4.00
98	Fran Tarkenton	50.00
99	Tommy Mason	2.00
100	Mel Triplett	2.00
101	Jerry Reichow	2.00
102	Frank Youso	2.00
103	Hugh McElhenny	7.00
104	Gerry Huth	2.00
105	Ed Sharockman	2.00
106	Rip Hawkins	2.00
107	*Jim Marshall*	25.00
108	Jim Prestel	2.00
109	Minnesota Vikings Team	4.00
110	Sonny Jurgensen (SP)	22.00
111	*Timmy Brown* (SP)	8.00
112	Tommy McDonald (SP)	4.50
113	Clarence Peaks (SP)	4.50
114	Pete Retzlaff (SP)	4.50
115	Jim Schrader (SP)	4.50
116	Jim McCusker (SP)	4.50
117	Don Burroughs (SP)	4.50
118	Maxie Buaghan (SP)	4.50
119	Riley Gunnels (SP)	4.50
120	Jimmy Carr (SP)	4.50
121	Philadelphia Eagles (SP)	8.50
122	Ed Brown (SP)	4.50
123	John Henry Johnson	12.00
124	Buddy Dial (SP)	4.50
125	Red Mack (SP)	4.50
126	Preston Carpenter (SP)	4.50
127	Ray Lemek (SP)	4.50
128	Buzz Nutter (SP)	4.50
129	Ernie Stautner (SP)	12.00
130	Lou Michaels (SP)	4.50
131	*Clendon Thomas* (SP)	6.00
132	Tom Bettis (SP)	4.50
133	Pittsburgh Steelers (SP)	8.50
134	John Brodie	10.00
135	J.D. Smith	2.00
136	Bill Kilmer	5.00
137	*Bernie Casey*	4.50
138	Tommy Davis	2.00
139	Ted Connolly	2.00
140	Bob St. Clair	5.00
141	Abe Woodson	2.00
142	Matt Hazeltine	2.00
143	Leo Nomellini	5.50
144	Dan Colchico	2.00
145	San Francisco 49ers (SP)	8.50
146	*Charlie Johnson*	8.00
147	John David Crow	2.00
148	Bobby Joe Conrad	2.00
149	Sonny Randle	2.00
150	Prentice Gautt	2.00
151	Taz Anderson	2.00
152	*Ernie McMillan*	2.00
153	Jimmy Hill	2.00
154	Bill Koman	2.00
155	*Larry Wilson*	25.00
156	Don Owens	2.00
157	St. Louis Cardinals (SP)	8.50
158	Norm Snead (SP)	8.00
159	*Bobby Mitchell* (SP)	14.00
160	Billy Barnes (SP)	4.50
161	Fred Dugan (SP)	4.50
162	Don Bosseler (SP)	4.50
163	John Nisby (SP)	4.50
164	Riley Mattson (SP)	4.50
165	Bob Toneff (SP)	4.50
166	Rod Breedlove (SP)	4.50
167	Dick James (SP)	4.50
168	Claud Crabb (SP)	4.50
169	Washington Redskins Team (SP)	8.50
170	Checklist	60.00

1964 Topps

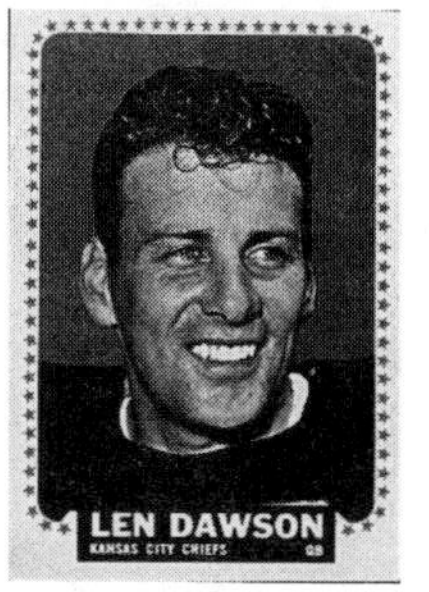
LEN DAWSON
KANSAS CITY CHIEFS QB

Considered to be one of the toughest sets of the decade, this 176-card set was Topps' first to feature only American Football League players. Because of the awkward size of the set and the inability to print the cards on two sheets, some of the cards in the set are short-printed. Cards are numbered by city and by player. This set contains the rookie cards of Daryle Lamonica, Buck Buchanan, John Hadi, and Hall of Famers Bobby Bell and Matt Snell. Second-year cards in the set include Nick Buoniconti, Len Dawson and Lance Alworth. An interesting error exists in the set: Bo Roberson, #151, has a helmet with the Raiders logo at the bottom of the card. Helmets were not part of the card design, and logos were always airbrushed. (Key: SP - short printed)

		NM
Complete Set (176):		1500.
Common Player:		3.00
SP Cards:		6.00
Wax Pack (5):		420.00

Wax Pack (8): 550.00
1 Tommy Addison (SP) 30.00
2 *Houston Antwine* 4.00
3 Nick Buoniconti 12.00
4 Ron Burton (SP) 6.00
5 Gino Cappelletti 6.00
6 Jim Colclough (SP) 6.00
7 Bob Dee (SP) 6.00
8 Larry Eisenhauer 3.00
9 Dick Felt (SP) 6.00
10 Larry Garron 3.00
11 Art Graham 3.00
12 Ron Hall 3.00
13 Charles Long 3.00
14 Don McKinnon 3.00
15 Don Oakes (SP) 6.00
16 Ross O'Hanley (SP) 6.00
17 Babe Parilli (SP) 6.00
18 Jesse Richardson (SP) 6.00
19 Jack Rudolph (SP) 6.00
20 *Don Webb* 4.00
21 Boston Patriots Team 4.50
22 Ray Abbruzzese 3.00
23 *Stew Barber* 4.00
24 Dave Behrman 3.00
25 Al Bemiller 3.00
26 Elbert Dubenion (SP) 6.00
27 *Jim Dunaway* (SP) 10.00
28 Booker Edgerson (SP) 6.00
29 Cookie Gilchrist (SP) 15.00
30 Jack Kemp (SP) 200.00
31 *Daryle Lamonica* 60.00
32 Bill Miller 3.00
33 *Herb Paterra* 4.00
34 Ken Rice (SP) 6.00
35 Ed Rutkowski 3.00
36 *George Saimes* 4.00
37 Tom Sestak 3.00
38 Billy Shaw (SP) 6.00
39 Mike Stratton 3.00
40 Gene Sykes 3.00
41 John Tracey (SP) 6.00
42 Sid Youngelman (SP) 6.00
43 Buffalo Bills Team 4.50
44 Eldon Danenhauer (SP) 6.00
45 Jim Fraser (SP) 6.00
46 Chuck Gavin (SP) 6.00
47 Goose Gonsoulin (SP) 6.00
48 *Ernie Barnes* 4.00
49 Tom Janik 3.00
50 *Billy Joe* 4.00
51 *Ike Lassiter* 4.00
52 John McCormick (SP) 6.00
53 Lewis Bud McFadin (SP) 3.00
54 Gene Mingo (SP) 3.00
55 Charlie Mitchell 3.00
56 John Nocera (SP) 6.00
57 Tom Nomina 3.00
58 Harold Olson (SP) 6.00
59 Bob Scarpitto 3.00
60 John Sklopan 3.00
61 Mickey Slaughter 3.00
62 Don Stone 3.00
63 Jerry Sturm 3.00
64 Lionel Taylor (SP) 12.00
65 Denver Broncos Team (SP) 17.00
66 *Scott Appleton* 4.00
67 Tony Banfield (SP) 6.00
68 George Blanda (SP) 60.00
69 Billy Cannon 4.50
70 Doug Cline (SP) 6.00
71 Gary Cutsinger (SP) 6.00
72 Willard Dewveall (SP) 6.00
73 Don Floyd (SP) 6.00
74 Freddy Gick (SP) 6.00
75 Charlie Hennigan (SP) 10.00
76 Ed Husmann (SP) 6.00
77 Bobby Jancik (SP) 6.00
78 Jacky Lee (SP) 6.00
79 Bob McLeod (SP) 6.00
80 Rich Michael (SP) 6.00
81 *Larry Onesti* 4.00
82 Checklist 50.00
83 Bob Schmidt (SP) 6.00
84 Walt Suggs (SP) 6.00
85 Bob Talamini (SP) 6.00
86 Charley Tolar (SP) 6.00
87 *Don Trull* 5.00
88 Houston Oilers Team 4.50
89 Fred Arbanas 3.00
90 *Bobby Bell* 35.00
91 Mel Branch (SP) 6.00
92 *Buck Buchanan* 35.00
93 *Ed Budde* 6.00
94 Chris Burford (SP) 6.00
95 *Walt Corey* 6.00
96 Len Dawson (SP) 75.00
97 *Dave Grayson* 4.00
98 Abner Haynes 4.00
99 Sherrill Headrick (SP) 6.00
100 E.J. Holub 3.00
101 Bobby Hunt 3.00
102 Frank Jackson (SP) 6.00
103 Curtis McClinton 3.00
104 Jerry Mays (SP) 6.00
105 Johnny Robinson (SP) 6.75
106 Jack Spikes (SP) 6.00
107 Smokey Stover (SP) 6.00
108 *Jim Tyrer* 6.00
109 Duane Wood (SP) 6.00
110 Kansas City Chiefs Team 4.50
111 Dick Christy (SP) 6.00
112 Dan Ficca (SP) 6.00
113 Larry Grantham 3.00
114 Curley Johnson (SP) 7.00
115 Gene Heeter 3.00
116 Jack Klotz 3.00
117 *Pete Liske* 4.00
118 Bob McAdam 3.00
119 Dee Mackey (SP) 6.00
120 Bill Mathis (SP) 6.00
121 Don Maynard 30.00
122 Dainard Paulson (SP) 6.00
123 *Gerry Philbin* 4.00
124 Mark Smolinski (SP) 6.00
125 *Matt Snell* 15.00
126 Mike Taliaferro 3.00
127 *Bake Turner* (SP) 12.00
128 Jeff Ware 3.00
129 Clyde Washington 3.00
130 *Dick Wood* 4.00
131 New York Jets Team 4.50
132 Dalva Allen (SP) 6.00
133 Dan Birdwell 3.00
134 *Dave Costa* 4.00
135 Dobiue Craig 3.00
136 Clem Daniels 3.00
137 Cotton Davidson (SP) 6.00
138 Claude Gibson 3.00
139 Tom Flores 15.00
140 Wayne Hawkins (SP) 6.00
141 Ken Herock 3.00
142 Jon Jelacic (SP) 6.00
143 Joe Krakoski 3.00
144 Archie Matsos (SP) 6.00
145 Mike Mercer 3.00
146 Alan Miller (SP) 6.00
147 Bob Mischak (SP) 6.00
148 Jim Otto (SP) 25.00
149 Clancy Osborne (SP) 6.00
150 Art Powell (SP) 9.00
151 Bo Roberson 3.00
152 Fred Williamson (SP) 10.00
153 Oakland Raiders Team 4.50
154 *Chuck Allen* (SP) 10.00
155 Lance Alworth 40.00
156 George Blair 3.00
157 Earl Faison 3.00
158 Sam Gruniesen 3.00
159 *John Hadl* 35.00
160 Dick Harris (SP) 6.00
161 Emil Karas (SP) 6.00
162 Dave Kocourek (SP) 6.00
163 Ernie Ladd 3.00
164 Keith Lincoln 6.00
165 Paul Lowe (SP) 10.00
166 Charles McNeil 3.00
167 Jacque MacKinnon (SP) 6.00
168 Ron Mix (SP) 15.00
169 Don Norton (SP) 6.00
170 Don Rogers (SP) 6.00
171 Tobin Rote (SP) 10.00
172 Henry Schmidt (SP) 6.00
173 Bud Whitehead 3.00
174 Ernie Wright (SP) 6.00
175 San Diego Chargers Team 4.50
176 Checklist (SP) 150.00

1964 Topps Pennant Stickers

These 24 peel-off stickers (they measure about 2" x 4-1/2") were inserted one per wax pack of the 1964 Topps football cards. The unnumbered pennants covered AFL teams and major college teams. Since stickers were folded to fit into the backs, all of them are found with a crease.

NM
Complete Set (24): 240.00
AFL Team: 12.00
College Team: 7.00
(1) Boston Patriots 12.00
(2) Buffalo Bills 12.00
(3) Denver Broncos 12.00
(4) Houston Oilers 12.00
(5) K.C. Chiefs 12.00
(6) New York Jets 12.00
(7) Oakland Raiders 12.00
(8) San Diego Chargers 12.00
(9) Air Force 7.00
(10) Army 7.00
(11) Dartmouth 7.00
(12) Duke 7.00
(13) Michigan 7.00
(14) Minnesota 7.00
(15) Mississippi 7.00
(16) Navy 7.00
(17) Notre Dame 15.00
(18) SMU 7.00
(19) USC 7.00
(20) Syracuse 7.00
(21) Texas 7.00
(22) Washington 7.00
(23) Wisconsin 7.00
(24) Yale 7.00

1965 Topps

Topps' second set featuring only AFL players is easily the most valued set of the decade for several reasons - the oversized (about 2-1/2" x 5") cards are attractive; it includes Joe Namath's rookie card; and Topps' unorthodox printing method created an abundance of certain cards, but a scarcity of others - all throughout the 176-card set, too, not just in one sequentially-numbered series. There may be a variation on Namath's rookie card as well. There's a report of a card showing Broadway Joe with a butterfly tattoo on his arm; on other cards, this tattoo is airbrushed off. It's uncertain how many, or even if, this variation exists. Besides Namath, other rookies in this set include Fred Biletnikoff, Willie Brown, and Ben Davidson. Second-year cards include those of Daryle Lamonica, Bobby Bell, Buck Buchanon, Matt Snell and John Hadl. (Key: SP - short printed)

NM
Complete Set (176): 3800.
Common Player: 6.50
SP Cards: 11.50
Wax Pack (5): 640.00
1 Tommy Addison (SP) 35.00
2 Houston Antwine (SP) 11.50
3 Nick Buoniconti (SP) 24.00
4 Ron Burton (SP) 11.50
5 Gino Cappelletti (SP) 20.00
6 Jim Colclough 6.50
7 Bob Dee (SP) 11.50
8 Larry Eisenhauer 6.50
9 J.D. Garrett 6.50
10 Larry Garron 6.50
11 Art Graham (SP) 11.50
12 Ron Hall 6.50
13 Charles Long 6.50
14 *Jon Morris* 10.00
15 Bill Neighbors (SP) 11.50
16 Ross O'Hanley 6.50
17 Babe Parilli (SP) 11.50
18 Tony Romeo (SP) 11.50
19 Jack Rudolph (SP) 11.50
20 Bob Schmidt 6.50
21 Don Webb (SP) 11.50
22 Jim Whalen (SP) 11.50
23 Stew Barber 6.50
24 Glenn Bass (SP) 11.50
25 Al Bemiller (SP) 11.50
26 Wray Carlton (SP) 11.50
27 Tom Day 6.50
28 Elbert Dubenion (SP) 11.50
29 Jim Dunaway 6.50
30 *Pete Gogolak* (SP) 19.00
31 Dick Hudson (SP) 11.50
32 Harry Jacobs (SP) 11.50
33 Billy Joe (SP) 11.50
34 *Tom Keating* (SP) 17.00
35 Jack Kemp (SP) 200.00
36 Daryle Lamonica (SP) 40.00
37 Paul Maguire (SP) 20.00
38 *Ron McDole* (SP) 15.00
39 George Saimes (SP) 11.50
40 Tom Sestak (SP) 11.50
41 Billy Shaw (SP) 11.50
42 Mike Stratton (SP) 11.50
43 John Tracey (SP) 11.50
44 Ernie Warlick 6.50
45 Odell Barry 6.50
46 *Willie Brown* (SP) 65.00
47 Gerry Bussell (SP) 11.50
48 Eldon Danehauer (SP) 11.50
49 Al Denson (SP) 11.50
50 *Hewritt Dixon* (SP) 19.00
51 Cookie Gilchrist (SP) 25.00
52 Goose Gonsoulin (SP) 11.50
53 Abner Haynes (SP) 18.00
54 Jerry Hopkins (SP) 11.50
55 Ray Jacobs (SP) 11.50
56 Jacky Lee (SP) 11.50
57 John McCormick 6.50
58 Bob McCullough (SP) 11.50
59 John McGeever 6.50
60 Charlie Mitchell (SP) 11.50
61 Jim Perkins (SP) 11.50
62 Bob Scarpitto (SP) 11.50
63 Mickey Slaughter (SP) 11.50
64 Jerry Sturm (SP) 11.50
65 Lionel Taylor (SP) 20.00
66 Scott Appleton (SP) 11.50
67 Johnny Baker (SP) 11.50
68 Sonny Bishop (SP) 11.50
69 George Blanda (SP) 90.00
70 Sid Blanks (SP) 11.50
71 Ode Burrell (SP) 11.50
72 Doug Cline (SP) 11.50
73 Willard Dewveall 6.50
74 *Larry Elkins* 10.00
75 Don Floyd (SP) 11.50
76 Freddy Glick 6.50
77 Tom Goode (SP) 11.50
78 Charlie Hennigan (SP) 18.00
79 Ed Husmann 6.50
80 Bobby Jancik (SP) 11.50
81 Bud McFadin (SP) 11.50
82 Bob McLeod (SP) 11.50
83 Jim Norton (SP) 11.50
84 Walt Suggs 6.50
85 Bob Talamini 6.50
86 Charley Tolar (SP) 11.50
87 Checklist 1-88 (SP) 145.00
88 Don Trull (SP) 11.50
89 Fred Arbanas (SP) 11.50
90 *Pete Beathard* (SP) 22.00
91 Bobby Bell (SP) 25.00
92 Mel Branch (SP) 11.50
93 Tommy Brooker (SP) 11.50
94 Buck Buchanan (SP) 25.00
95 Ed Budde (SP) 11.50
96 Chris Burford (SP) 11.50
97 Walt Corey 6.50
98 Jerry Cornelison 6.50
99 Len Dawson (SP) 80.00
100 Jon Gilliam (SP) 11.50
101 Sherrill Headrick (SP) 11.50
102 Dave Hill (SP) 11.50
103 E.J. Holub (SP) 11.50
104 Bobby Hunt (SP) 11.50
105 Frank Jackson (SP) 11.50
106 Jerry Mays 6.50
107 Curtis McClinton (SP) 11.50
108 Bobby Ply (SP) 11.50
109 Johnny Robinson (SP) 11.50
110 Jim Tyrer (SP) 11.50
111 Bill Baird (SP) 11.50
112 *Ralph Baker* (SP) 15.00
113 Sam DeLuca (SP) 11.50
114 Larry Grantham (SP) 11.50
115 Gene Heeter (SP) 11.50
116 *Winston Hill* (SP) 20.00
117 *John Huarte* (SP) 30.00
118 Cosmo Iacavazzi (SP) 11.50
119 Curley Johnson (SP) 11.50
120 Dee Mackey 6.50
121 Don Maynard 35.00
122 *Joe Namath* (SP) 1650.
123 Dainard Paulson 6.50
124 Gerry Philbin (SP) 11.50
125 *Sherman Plunkett* 19.00
126 Mark Smolinski 6.50
127 Matt Snell (SP) 25.00
128 Mike Taliaferro (SP) 11.50
129 Bake Turner (SP) 15.00
130 Clyde Washington (SP) 11.50
131 *Verlon Biggs* (SP) 15.00
132 Dalva Allen 6.50
133 *Fred Biletnikoff* (SP) 200.00
134 Billy Cannon (SP) 20.00
135 Dave Costa (SP) 11.50
136 Clem Daniels (SP) 11.50
137 *Ben Davidson* (SP) 50.00
138 Cotton Davidson (SP) 11.50
139 Tom Flores (SP) 27.00
140 Claude Gibson 6.50
141 Wayne Hawkins 6.50
142 Archie Matsos (SP) 11.50
143 Mike Mercer (SP) 11.50
144 Bob Mischak (SP) 11.50
145 Jim Otto 25.00
146 Art Powell (SP) 13.00
147 Warren Powers (SP) 11.50
148 Ken Rice (SP) 11.50
149 Bo Roberson (SP) 11.50
150 *Harry Schuh* 12.00
151 Larry Todd (SP) 11.50
152 Fred Williamson (SP) 20.00
153 J.R. Williamson 6.50
154 Chuck Allen 6.50
155 Lance Alworth 65.00
156 Frank Buncom 6.50
157 *Steve DeLong* (SP) 17.00
158 Earl Faison (SP) 11.50
159 Kenny Graham (SP) 11.50
160 George Gross (SP) 11.50
161 John Hadl (SP) 28.00
162 Emil Karas (SP) 11.50
163 Dave Kocourek (SP) 11.50
164 Ernie Ladd (SP) 20.00
165 Keith Lincoln (SP) 20.00
166 Paul Lowe (SP) 20.00
167 Jacque MacKinnon 6.50
168 Ron Mix 20.00
169 Don Norton (SP) 11.50
170 Bob Petrich 6.50
171 Rick Redman (SP) 11.50
172 Pat Shea 6.50
173 *Walt Sweeney* (SP) 15.00
174 *Dick Westmoreland* 12.00
175 Ernie Wright (SP) 11.50
176 Checklist 89-176 (SP) 200.00

1965 Topps Rub-Offs

This 36-card, unnumbered set was included one per pack in wax packs of 1965 Topps football. The set, which measures two by three inches, includes the eight American Football League teams plus 28 college team emblems. Similar in design to the 1961 Topps baseball rub-offs, the fronts carried a team logo and team name in reverse type, while the backs carried instructions on how to use the rub-offs.

NM
Complete Set (36): 400.00
Common AFL Team: 15.00
Common College Team: 10.00
(1) Boston Patriots 15.00
(2) Buffalo Bills 20.00
(3) Denver Broncos 25.00
(4) Houston Oilers 20.00
(5) Kansas City Chiefs 15.00
(6) New York Jets 20.00
(7) Oakland Raiders 35.00
(8) San Diego Chargers 15.00
(9) Alabama 15.00
(10) Air Force Academy 10.00
(11) Arkansas 15.00
(12) Army 15.00
(13) Boston College 10.00
(14) Duke 15.00
(15) Illinois 10.00
(16) Kansas 15.00
(17) Kentucky 10.00
(18) Maryland 10.00
(19) Miami 15.00
(20) Minnesota 15.00
(21) Mississippi 10.00
(22) Navy 15.00
(23) Nebraska 15.00
(24) Notre Dame 35.00
(25) Penn State 15.00
(26) Purdue 10.00
(27) Southern California 10.00
(28) Southern Methodist 15.00
(29) Stanford 10.00
(30) Syracuse 10.00
(31) Texas 10.00
(32) Texas Christian 15.00
(33) Virginia 10.00
(34) Washington 15.00
(35) Wisconsin 10.00
(36) Yale 10.00

1966 Topps

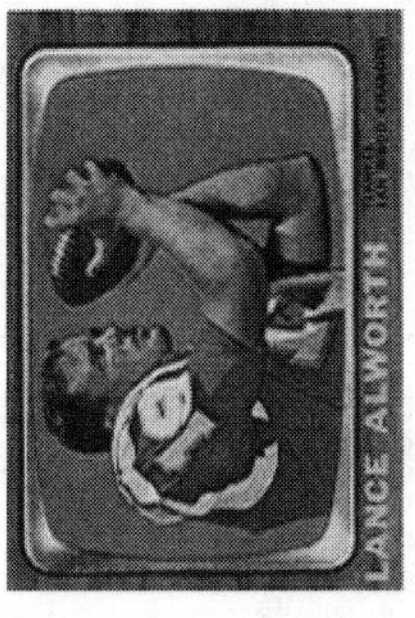

This set, which shows AFL players only (Topps' third straight) is quite popular with collectors. It uses a TV motif. Cards were once again grouped in alphabetical order by city name, then by the player's last name. Joe Namath's second-year card is the set's biggest selling player card, but "card" #15, the Funny Ring checklist, is a very difficult find and is easily the most expensive card in the set. Other key cards include rookie cards of Otis Taylor, Jim Turner and George Sauer Jr., second-year cards of Fred Biletnikoff and Ben Davidson, and cards showing Hall of Famers George Blanda, Bobby Bell, Len Dawson, Don Maynard, Ron Mix, Jim Otto and Lance Alworth. A Jack Kemp card is the set's third most expensive card; other high-priced cards are checklists, which are hard to find in mint.

NM
Complete Set (132): 1300.
Common Player: 4.00
Wax Pack (5+1): 305.00
1 Tom Addison 20.00
2 Houston Antwine 4.00
3 Nick Buoniconti 9.00
4 Gino Cappelletti 6.00
5 Bob Dee 4.00
6 Larry Garron 4.00
7 Art Graham 4.00
8 Ron Hall 4.00
9 Charles Long 4.00
10 Jon Morris 4.00
11 Don Oakes 4.00
12 Babe Parilli 4.00
13 Don Webb 4.00
14 Jim Whalen 4.00
15 Funny Ring CL 275.00
16 Stew Barber 4.00
17 Glenn Bass 4.00
18 Dave Behrman 4.00
19 Al Bemiller 4.00
20 *Butch Byrd* 5.00
21 Wray Carlton 4.00
22 Tom Day 4.00
23 Elbert Dubenion 4.00
24 Jim Dunaway 4.00
25 Dick Hudson 4.00
26 Jack Kemp 170.00
27 Daryle Lamonica 10.00
28 Tom Sestak 4.00
29 Billy Shaw 4.00
30 Mike Stratton 4.00
31 Eldon Danenhauer 4.00
32 Cookie Gilchrist 7.00
33 Goose Gonsoulin 4.00
34 *Wendell Hayes* 8.00
35 Abner Haynes 4.00
36 Jerry Hopkins 4.00
37 Ray Jacobs 4.00
38 Charlie Janerette 4.00
39 Ray Kubala 4.00
40 John McCormick 4.00
41 Leroy Moore 4.00
42 Bob Scarpitto 4.00
43 Mickey Slaughter 4.00
44 Jerry Sturm 4.00
45 Lionel Taylor 6.50
46 Scott Appleton 4.00
47 Johnny Baker 4.00
48 George Blanda 40.00
49 Sid Blanks 4.00
50 Danny Brabham 4.00
51 Ode Burrell 4.00
52 Gary Cutsinger 4.00
53 Larry Elkins 4.00
54 Don Floyd 4.00
55 *Willie Frazier* 6.00
56 Freddy Glick 4.00
57 Charles Hennigan 5.00
58 Bobby Jancik 4.00
59 Rich Michael 4.00
60 Don Trull 4.00
61 Checklist 40.00
62 Fred Arbanas 4.00
63 Pete Beathard 5.00
64 Bobby Bell 8.00
65 Ed Budde 4.00
66 Chris Burford 4.00
67 Len Dawson 35.00
68 Jon Gilliam 4.00
69 Sherrill Headrick 4.00
70 E.J. Holub 4.00
71 Bobby Hunt 4.00
72 Curtis McClinton 4.00
73 Jerry Mays 5.00
74 Johnny Robinson 5.00
75 *Otis Taylor* 17.00
76 Tom Erlandson 4.00
77 *Norman Evans* 8.00
78 Tom Goode 4.00
79 Mike Hudock 4.00
80 Frank Jackson 4.00
81 Billy Joe 4.00
82 Dave Kocourek 4.00
83 Bo Roberson 4.00
84 Jack Spikes 4.00
85 *Jim Warren* 8.00
86 *Willie West* 5.00
87 Dick Westmoreland 4.00
88 Eddie Wilson 4.00
89 Dick Wood 4.00
90 Verlon Biggs 4.00
91 Sam DeLuca 4.00
92 Winston Hill 4.00
93 Dee Mackey 4.00
94 Bill Mathis 4.00
95 Don Maynard 25.00
96 Joe Namath 340.00
97 Dainard Paulson 4.00
98 Gerry Philbin 4.00
99 Sherman Plunkett 4.00
100 Paul Rochester 4.00
101 *George Sauer Jr.* 12.00
102 Matt Snell 7.00
103 *Jim Turner* 6.00
104 Fred Biletnikoff 50.00
105 Bill Budness 4.00
106 Billy Cannon 6.00
107 Clem Daniels 4.00
108 Ben Davidson 10.00
109 Cotton Davidson 4.00
110 Claude Gibson 4.00
111 Wayne Hawkins 4.00
112 Ken Herock 4.00
113 Bob Mischak 4.00
114 Gus Otto 4.00
115 Jim Otto 15.00
116 Art Powell 6.00
117 Harry Schuh 4.00
118 Chuck Allen 4.00
119 Lance Alworth 30.00
120 Frank Buncom 4.00
121 Steve DeLong 4.50
122 John Farris 4.00
123 Ken Graham 4.00
124 Sam Gruneison 4.00
125 John Hadl 8.00
126 Walt Sweeney 4.00
127 Keith Lincoln 4.00
128 Ron Mix 9.00
129 Don Norton 4.00
130 Pat Shea 4.00
131 Ernie Wright 4.00
132 Checklist 90.00

1966 Topps Funny Rings

The 24-card, 1-1/4" x 3" set was issued in each pack of 1966 Topps Football. The card fronts feature a ring that can be punched out and folded to make a ring. The backs are blank.

NM
Complete Set (24): 500.00
Common Player: 25.00
1 Funny Ring - Kiss Me 25.00
2 Funny Ring - Bloodshot Eye 25.00
3 Funny Ring - Big Mouth 25.00
4 Funny Ring - Toothache 25.00
5 Funny Ring - Fish eats Fish 25.00
6 Funny Ring - Mrs. Skull 25.00
7 Funny Ring - Hot Dog 25.00
8 Funny Ring - Head with Nail 25.00
9 Funny Ring - Ah 25.00
10 Funny Ring - Apple with Worm 25.00
11 Funny Ring - Snake 25.00
12 Funny Ring - Yicch 25.00
13 Funny Ring - If You Can Read This 25.00
14 Funny Ring - Nuts to You 25.00
15 Funny Ring - Get Lost 25.00
16 Funny Ring - You Fink 25.00
17 Funny Ring - Hole in Shoe 25.00
18 Funny Ring - Head with One Eye 25.00
19 Funny Ring - Mr. Ugly 25.00
20 Funny Ring - Mr. Fang 25.00
21 Funny Ring - Mr. Fright 25.00
22 Funny Ring - Mr. Boo 25.00
23 Funny Ring - Mr. Glug 25.00
24 Funny Ring - Mr. Blech 25.00

1967 Topps

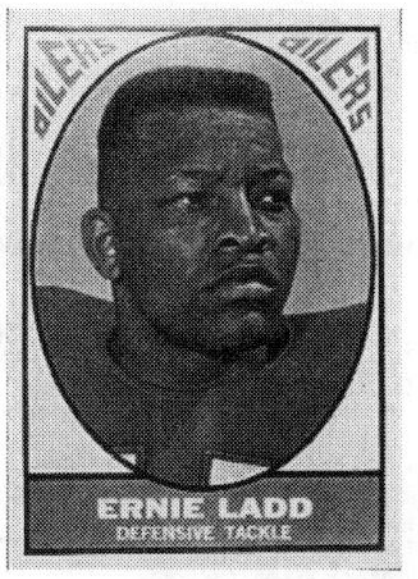

This 132-card set is the last AFL-only set issued by Topps. Best-known for the inclusion of Joe-Namath's second-year card, the set also features another Jack Kemp card. Wahoo McDaniels' only card is also in this set. Cards are grouped according to each of the nine AFL teams. It's very difficult to find an unmarked checklist; consequently, prices are pretty high on those two cards.

NM
Complete Set (132): 650.00
Common Player: 2.50
Wax Pack (5): 255.00
1 John Huarte 10.00
2 Babe Parilli 2.50
3 Gino Cappelletti 3.00
4 Larry Garron 2.50
5 Tom Addison 2.50
6 Jon Morris 2.50
7 Houston Antwine 2.50
8 Don Oakes 2.50
9 Larry Eisenhauer 2.50
10 Jim Hunt 2.50
11 Jim Whalen 2.50
12 Art Graham 2.50
13 Nick Buoniconti 6.00
14 Bob Dee 2.50
15 Keith Lincoln 4.00
16 Tom Flores 5.50
17 Art Powell 3.00
18 Stew Barber 2.50
19 Wray Carlton 2.50
20 Elbert Dubenion 2.50
21 Jim Dunanaway 2.50
22 Dick Hudson 2.50
23 Harry Jacobs 2.50
24 Jack Kemp 100.00
25 Ron McDole 2.50
26 George Saimes 2.50
27 Tom Sestak 2.50
28 Billy Shaw 2.50
29 Mike Stratton 2.50
30 *Nemiah Wilson* 3.00
31 John McCormick 2.50
32 Rex Mirich 2.50
33 Dave Costa 2.50
34 Goose Gonsoulin 2.50
35 Abner Haynes 3.50
36 Wendell Hayes 2.50
37 Archie Matsos 2.50
38 John Bramlett 2.50
39 Jerry Sturm 2.50
40 Max Leetzow 2.50
41 Bob Scarpitto 2.50
42 Lionel Taylor 3.50
43 Al Denson 2.50
44 *Miller Farr* 3.50
45 Don Trull 1.50
46 Jacky Lee 2.50
47 Bobby Jancik 2.50
48 Ode Burrell 2.50
49 Larry Elkins 2.50
50 W.K. Hicks 2.50
51 Sid Blanks 2.50
52 Jim Norton 2.50
53 *Bobby Maples* 3.00
54 Bob Talamini 2.50
55 Walter Suggs 2.50
56 Gary Cutsinger 2.50
57 Danny Brabham 2.50
58 Ernie Ladd 4.00
59 Checklist 40.00
60 Pete Beathard 2.50
61 Len Dawson 20.00
62 Bobby Hunt 2.50
63 Bert Coan 2.50
64 Curtis McClinton 2.50
65 Johnny Robinson 2.50
66 E.J. Holub 2.50
67 Jerry Mays 2.50
68 Jim Tyrer 2.50
69 Bobby Bell 5.50
70 Fred Arbanas 2.50
71 Buck Buchanan 5.50
72 Chris Burford 2.50
73 Otis Taylor 4.00
74 Cookie Gilchrist 5.00
75 Earl Faison 2.50

76	George Wilson Jr.	2.50
77	Rick Norton	2.50
78	Frank Jackson	2.50
79	Joe Auer	2.50
80	Willie West	2.50
81	Jim Warren	2.50
82	*Wahoo McDaniel*	30.00
83	Ernie Park	2.50
84	Bill Neighbors	2.50
85	Norm Evans	2.50
86	Tom Nomina	2.50
87	Rich Zecher	2.50
88	Dave Kocourek	2.50
89	Bill Baird	2.50
90	Ralph Baker	2.50
91	Verlon Biggs	2.50
92	Sam DeLuca	2.50
93	Larry Grantham	2.50
94	Jim Harris	2.50
95	Winston Hill	2.50
96	Bill Mathis	2.50
97	Don Maynard	20.00
98	Joe Namath	185.00
99	Gerry Philbin	2.50
100	Paul Rochester	2.50
101	George Sauer	3.50
102	Matt Snell	3.50
103	Daryle Lamonica	6.00
104	Glenn Bass	2.50
105	Jim Otto	6.00
106	Fred Biletnikoff	30.00
107	Cotton Davidson	2.50
108	Larry Todd	2.50
109	Billy Cannon	3.00
110	Clem Daniels	2.50
111	Dave Grayson	2.50
112	*Kent McCloughan*	2.50
113	Bob Svihus	2.50
114	Isaac Lassiter	2.50
115	Harry Schuh	2.50
116	Ben Davidson	6.00
117	Tom Day	2.50
118	Scott Appleton	2.50
119	*Steve Tensi*	3.00
120	John Hadl	5.00
121	Paul Lowe	3.00
122	Jim Allison	2.50
123	Lance Alworth	25.00
124	Jacque MacKinnon	2.50
125	Ron Mix	5.50
126	Bob Petrich	2.50
127	Howard Kingdig	2.50
128	Steve DeLong	2.50
129	Chuck Allen	2.50
130	Frank Buncom	2.50
131	*Speedy Duncan*	5.00
132	Checklist	60.00

1967 Topps Comic Pennants

The 31-card, standard-size sticker set was issued in packs of 1967 Topps and is considered to be scarce - the set was probably discontinued before the end of the shipping. The cards contain juvenile humor (Denver girls look like Broncos). The cards are numbered in the upper right corner.

		NM
Complete Set (31):		600.00
Common Player:		20.00
1	Navel Academy	20.00
2	City College of Useless Knowledge	20.00
3	Notre Dame (Hunchback of)	40.00
4	Psychedelic State	20.00
5	Minneapolis Mini-skirts	20.00
6	School of Art - Go, Van Gogh	20.00
7	Washington Is Dead	25.00
8	School of Hard Knocks	20.00
9	Alaska (If I See Her ...)	20.00
10	Confused State	20.00
11	Yale Locks Are Tough to Pick	20.00
12	University of Transylvania	20.00
13	Down With Teachers	20.00
14	Cornell Caught Me Cheating	20.00
15	Houston Oilers (You're a Fink)	25.00
16	Harvard (Flunked Out)	25.00
17	Diskotech	20.00
18	Dropout U	20.00
19	Air Force (Gas Masks)	20.00
20	Nutstu U	20.00
21	Michigan State Pen	20.00
22	Denver Broncos (Girls Look Like)	25.00
23	Buffalo Bills (Without Paying My)	25.00
24	Army of Dropouts	20.00
25	Miami Dolphins (Bitten by Two)	30.00
26	Kansas City (Has Too Few Workers And Too Many) Chiefs	20.00
27	Boston Patriots (Banned In)	20.00
28	(Fat People) in Oakland (Are Usually Icebox) Raiders	30.00
29	(I'd Go) West (If I'd Just) Point (In The Right Direction)	20.00
30	New York Jets (Skies Are Crowded With)	25.00
31	San Diego Chargers (Police Will Press)	20.00

1968 Topps

Topps' first set to clear 200 cards in number was also its first set in five years to feature NFL players as well as AFL players. Released in two series, the second series is a little tougher to find. First-series cards show blue printing on the backs, while second series issues have green. The 219-card set features a special design for cards of players from the Super Bowl teams, the Oakland Raiders and Green Bay Packers. Cards of players from these teams show players in a horizontal format set against a stylized football backdrop. Remaining cards are in a vertical format. Each carries a player photo inside a white frame with the players name, position and team in an oval at the card bottom. A number of second-series card backs can be pieced together to show a picture of Bart Starr or Len Dawson (10 cards per player). Puzzle-piece card backs are found on cards 141, 145, 146, 148, 151-53, 155, 163, 168, 170, 172, 186, 195 and 197. One error in the set is on #12, Kent McCloughan. The back spells his name "McCloughlan." Another mix-up occurs on card #70, Dick Van Raaphorst's card. The back lists his name as "Van Raap Horst." Also, there are two different checklist cards; the back of one is blue, the back of the other is green. Rookies in this set include Bob Griese, Jim Hart, Craig Morton, Joe Kapp, Jim Grabowski, Jack Snow, and Donny Anderson. Other valuable cards include Bart Starr, Don Meredith, Joe Namath, Gale Sayers, John Unitas, Dick Butkis, George Blanda, Jack Kemp, and Fran Tarkenton. This set featured the final regular-issue cards of Hall of Famers Mike Ditka and Jim Taylor.

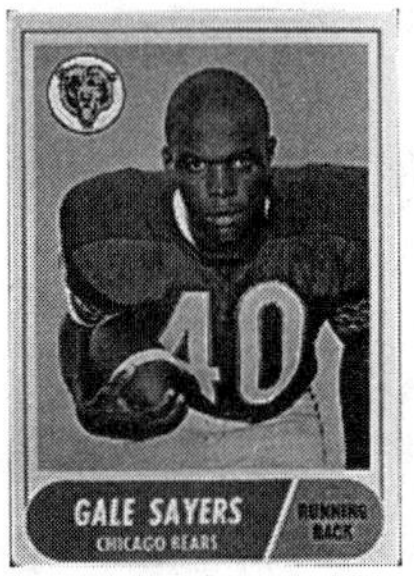

		NM
Complete Set (219):		575.00
Common Player (1-131):		.80
Common Player (132-219):		1.50
Series 1 Wax Pack (5):		130.00
Series 1 Wax Box (24):		2275.
Series 2 Wax Pack (5):		175.00
Series 2 Wax Box (24):		3125.
1	Bart Starr	35.00
2	Dick Bass	.80
3	Grady Alderman	1.25
4	Obert Logan	1.25
5	*Ernie Koy*	1.50
6	Don Hultz	1.25
7	Earl Gros	1.25
8	Jim Bakken	.80
9	George Mira	.80
10	Carl Kammerer	1.25
11	Willie Frazier	.80
12	Kent McCloughan	1.25
13	George Sauer	1.50
14	Jack Clancy	.80
15	Jim Tyrer	.80
16	Bobby Maples	1.25
17	Bo Hickey	1.25
18	Frank Buncom	1.25
19	Keith Lincoln	1.50
20	Jim Whalen	.80
21	Junior Coffey	1.25
22	Billy Ray Smith	1.25
23	Johnny Morris	1.50
24	Ernie Green	1.25
25	Don Meredith	21.00
26	Wayne Walker	.80
27	Carroll Dale	.80
28	Bernie Casey	.80
29	*Dave Osborn*	1.50
30	Ray Poage	1.25
31	Homer Jones	.80
32	Sam Baker	.80
33	Bill Saul	1.25
34	Ken Willard	.80
35	Bobby Mitchell	4.00
36	Gary Garrison	1.50
37	Billy Cannon	1.50
38	Ralph Baker	1.25
39	*Howard Twilley*	3.50
40	Wendell Hayes	.80
41	Jim Norton	1.25
42	Tom Beer	1.25
43	Chris Burford	.80
44	Steve Barber	1.25
45	Leroy Mitchell	1.25
46	Dan Grimm	1.25
47	Jerry Logan	1.25
48	Andy Livingston	1.25
49	Paul Warfield	10.00
50	Don Perkins	1.25
51	Ron Kramer	.80
52	Bob Jeter	1.50
53	*Les Josephson*	1.50
54	Bobby Walden	1.50
55	Checklist	15.00
56	Walter Roberts	1.25
57	Henry Carr	.80
58	Gary Ballman	.80
59	J.R. Wilburn	1.25
60	*Jim Hart*	8.00
61	Jimmy Johnson	.80
62	Chris Harburger	1.50
63	John Hadl	3.00
64	Hewritt Dixon	1.25
65	Joe Namath	80.00
66	Jim Warren	1.25
67	Curtis McClinton	.80
68	Bob Talamini	.80
69	Steve Tensi	1.25
70	Dick Van Raaphorst	1.25
71	Art Powell	1.50
72	*Jim Nance*	3.50
73	Bob Riggle	1.25
74	John Mackey	3.50
75	Gale Sayers	50.00
76	Gene Hickerson	1.25
77	Dan Reeves	10.00
78	Tom Nowatzke	1.25
79	Elijah Pitts	.80
80	Lamar Lundy	1.25
81	Paul Flatley	1.25
82	Dave Whitsell	1.25
83	Spider Lockhart	.80
84	Dave Lloyd	1.25
85	Roy Jefferson	.80
86	Jackie Smith	5.00
87	John David Crow	1.50
88	Sonny Jurgensen	6.50
89	Ron Mix	3.50
90	Clem Daniels	.80
91	Cornell Gordon	1.25
92	Tom Goode	1.25
93	Bobby Bell	3.50
94	Walt Suggs	1.25
95	Eric Crabtree	1.25
96	Sherrill Headrick	.80
97	Wray Carlton	.80
98	Gino Cappelletti	1.50
99	Tommy McDonald	.80
100	Johnny Unitas	25.00
101	Richie Petitbon	1.25
102	Erich Barnes	.80
103	Bob Hayes	3.00
104	Milt Plum	1.50
105	Boyd Dowler	.80
106	Ed Meador	.80
107	Fred Cox	.80
108	*Steve Stonebreaker*	1.50
109	Aaron Thomas	1.25
110	Norm Snead	1.50
111	*Paul Martha*	1.50
112	Jerry Stovall	.80
113	Kay McFarland	1.25
114	Pat Richter	1.25
115	Rick Redman	1.25
116	Tom Keating	1.25
117	Matt Snell	2.50
118	Dick Westmoreland	1.25
119	Jerry Mays	.80
120	Sid Blanks	1.25
121	Al Denson	1.25
122	Bobby Hunt	1.25
123	Mike Mercer	1.25
124	Nick Buoniconti	3.00
125	*Ron Vanderkelen*	.80
126	Ordell Braase	1.25
127	Dick Butkus	36.00
128	Gary Collins	.80
129	Mel Renfro	1.50
130	Alex Karras	6.00
131	Herb Adderley	3.00
132	Roman Gabriel	3.50
133	Bill Brown	1.50
134	Kent Kramer	1.50
135	Tucker Frederickson	1.50
136	Nate Ramsey	1.50
137	Marv Woodson	1.50
138	Ken Gray	1.50
139	John Brodie	7.00
140	Jerry Smith	1.50
141	Brad Hubbert	1.50
142	George Blanda	23.00
143	*Pete Lammons*	1.50
144	Doug Moreau	1.50
145	E.J. Holub	1.50
146	Ode Burrell	1.50
147	Bob Scarpitto	1.50
148	Andre White	1.50
149	Jack Kemp	60.00
150	Art Graham	1.50
151	Tommy Nobis	4.00
152	*Willie Richardson*	1.50
153	Jack Concannon	1.50
154	Bill Glass	1.50
155	*Craig Morton*	12.00
156	Pat Studstill	1.50
157	Ray Nitschke	5.00
158	Roger Brown	1.50
159	Joe Kapp	5.00
160	Jim Taylor	10.00
161	Fran Tarkenton	20.00
162	Mike Ditka	25.00
163	*Andy Russell*	5.00
164	Larry Wilson	4.00
165	Tommy Davis	1.50
166	Paul Krause	1.35
167	Leslie Duncan	1.50
168	Fred Biletnikoff	11.00
169	Don Maynard	10.00
170	Frank Emanuel	1.50
171	Len Dawson	13.00
172	Miller Farr	1.50
173	*Floyd Little*	20.00
174	Lonnie Wright	1.50
175	Paul Costa	1.50
176	Don Trull	1.50
177	Jerry Simmons	1.50
178	Tom Matte	1.50
179	Bennie McRae	1.50
180	Jim Kanicki	1.50
181	Bob Lilly	7.00
182	Tom Watkins	1.50
183	*Jim Grabowski*	2.00
184	*Jack Snow*	4.50
185	*Gary Cuozzo*	1.50
186	Billy Kilmer	4.00
187	Jim Katcavage	1.50
188	Floyd Peters	1.50
189	Bill Nelsen	1.50
190	Bobby J. Conrad	1.50
191	Kermit Alexander	1.50
192	Charley Taylor	6.00
193	Lance Alworth	13.00
194	Daryle Lamonica	5.00
195	Al Atkinson	1.50
196	*Bob Griese*	85.00
197	Buck Buchanan	4.00
198	Pete Beathard	1.50
199	Nemiah Wilson	1.50
200	Ernie Wright	1.50
201	George Saimes	1.50
202	John Charles	1.50
203	Randy Johnson	1.50
204	Tony Lorick	1.50
205	Dick Evey	1.50
206	Leroy Kelly	7.50
207	Lee Roy Jordan	5.00
208	Jim Gibbons	1.50
209	*Donny Anderson*	4.00
210	Maxie Baughan	1.50
211	Joe Morrison	1.50
212	Jim Snowden	1.50
213	Lenny Lyles	1.50
214	Bobby Joe Green	1.50
215	Frank Ryan	1.35
216	Cornell Green	1.50
217	Karl Sweetan	1.50
218	Dave Williams	1.50
219	Checklist (blue)	20.00

1968 Topps Posters

Sixteen players from both the AFL and NFL are included in this set. Posters, printed on paper, measure about 5" x 7" and were issued in gum packs, similar to the Topps baseball posters of the same year. A full-color posed action shot is on the front, with the players, name, team and position shown in an oval at the bottom of the front. Backs are blank.

		NM
Complete Set (16):		50.00
Common Player:		1.50
1	Johnny Unitas	9.00
2	Leroy Kelly	1.50
3	Bob Hayes	1.50
4	Bart Starr	5.00
5	Charley Taylor	1.50
6	Fran Tarkenton	4.50
7	Jim Bakken	1.50
8	Gale Sayers	6.00
9	Gary Cuozzo	1.50
10	Les Josephson	1.50
11	Jim Nance	1.50
12	Brad Hubbert	1.50
13	Keith Lincoln	1.50
14	Don Maynard	2.00
15	Len Dawson	3.00
16	Jack Clancy	1.50

1968 Topps Stand-Ups

These 22 unnumbered card-size (2-1/2" x 3-1/2") issues were meant to be punched and folded in order to make them stand. Cards lose much of their value if they're not complete; obviously, not too many complete sets have been found. Cards show a head shot of the player, with his name beneath the photo. Backs are blank. Cards are listed below in alphabetical order.

		NM
Complete Set (22):		225.00
Common Player:		5.00
(1)	Sid Blanks	5.00
(2)	John Brodie	12.00
(3)	Jack Concannon	5.00
(4)	Roman Gabriel	7.00
(5)	Art Graham	5.00
(6)	Jim Grabowski	5.00
(7)	John Hadl	7.00
(8)	Jim Hart	7.00
(9)	Homer Jones	5.00
(10)	Sonny Jurgensen	15.00
(11)	Alex Karras	9.00
(12)	Billy Kilmer	7.00
(13)	Daryle Lamonica	5.00
(14)	Floyd Little	5.00
(15)	Curtis McClinton	5.00
(16)	Don Meredith	35.00
(17)	Joe Namath	85.00
(18)	Bill Nelsen	5.00
(19)	Dave Osborn	5.00
(20)	Willie Richardson	5.00
(21)	Frank Ryan	5.00
(22)	Norm Snead	5.00

1968 Topps Test Teams

These were printed in an extremely limited number by Topps. Cards are a bit oversize -- about 2-1/2" x 4-5/8" -- and show a posed shot of the entire team on the front. A nameplate is beneath the picture, and a "frame" features footballs in each of the corners. The back is a guide to the photo, complete with little footballs to indicate each row. Cards were issued in alphabetical order by city name, and are numbered on the back.

		NM
Complete Set (25):		2700.
Common Team:		100.00
1	Atlanta Falcons	100.00
2	Baltimore Colts	100.00
3	Buffalo Bills	100.00
4	Chicago Bears	135.00
5	Cleveland Browns	100.00
6	Dallas Cowboys	135.00
7	Denver Broncos	135.00
8	Detroit Lions	100.00
9	Green Bay Packers	135.00
10	Houston Oilers	100.00
11	Kansas City Chiefs	100.00
12	Los Angeles Rams	100.00
13	Miami Dolphins	135.00
14	Minnesota Vikings	100.00
15	New England Patriots	100.00
16	New Orleans Saints	100.00
17	New York Giants	135.00
18	New York Jets	135.00
19	Oakland Raiders	135.00
20	Philadelphia Eagles	100.00
21	Pittsburgh Steelers	135.00
22	St. Louis Cardinals	100.00
23	San Diego Chargers	100.00
24	San Francisco 49ers	135.00
25	Washington Redskins	100.00

1968 Topps Team Patch/Stickers

These patches, inserted into packs of Topps test team cards, feature team logos for each NFL team. One test team card and a sticker were in each pack; the stickers were supposed to be the main item inside, according to the wrapper. The stickers measure 2-1/2" x 3-1/2".

		NM
Complete Set (44):		1600.
Common Sticker:		10.00
1	1 and 2	15.00
2	3 and 4	10.00
3	5 and 6	12.00
4	7 and 8	10.00
5	9 and 0	10.00
6	A and B	12.00
7	C and D	10.00
8	E and F	10.00
9	G and H	12.00
10	I and W	10.00
11	J and X	10.00
12	Atlanta Falcons	60.00
13	Baltimore Colts	65.00
14	Chicago Bears	80.00
15	Cleveland Browns	60.00
16	Dallas Cowboys	140.00
17	Detroit Lions	60.00
18	Green Bay Packers	80.00
19	Los Angeles Rams	60.00
20	Minnesota Vikings	65.00
21	New Orleans Saints	60.00
22	New York Giants	75.00
23	K and L	10.00
24	M and O	12.00
25	N and P	10.00
26	Q and R	10.00
27	S and T	12.00
28	U and V	10.00
29	Y and Z	10.00
30	Philadelphia Eagles	60.00
31	Pittsburgh Steelers	80.00
32	St. Louis Cardinals	60.00
33	San Francisco 49ers	75.00
34	Washington Redskins	120.00
35	Boston Patriots	60.00
36	Buffalo Bills	75.00
37	Denver Broncos	120.00
38	Houston Oilers	75.00
39	Kansas City Chiefs	60.00
40	Miami Dolphins	110.00
41	New York Jets	75.00
42	Oakland Raiders	140.00
43	San Diego Chargers	60.00
44	Cincinnati Bengals	70.00

1969 Topps

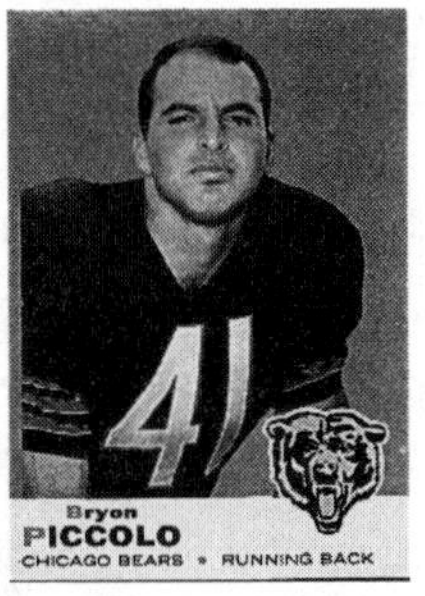

This 263-card set was printed in two series and in two different styles. The first series cards (1-132) have no borders, while the second series has white borders. In the borderless version, a player photo is set against a brightly colored background. A large team logo is in the lower right hand corner, and a player name and position and team name are in a white box at the card bottom. Second-series cards are of identical design, except for a white border around the player photo. This development is not pleasing for collectors searching for the first series in mint condition, since the lack of borders makes it tough to find any in superb condition. The variation in the set is the checklist card, #132, which is found with and without borders, depending on the series in which it was printed. Another variation in the set involved card #18, Tom Beer. In some versions of the card, the "B" in his last name is slightly raised above the rest of the name on the card front. Versions of each have been reported. The key card in this set is Brian Piccolo's rookie card; this and his Four In One issue are the only cards on which he appears. Other rookies in this set include Larry Csonka, Lance Rentzel, and Mike Curtis. Hall of Famers Doug Atkins and Bobby Mitchell were featured on their final regular-issue cards.

		NM
Complete Set (263):		550.00
Common Player (1-132):		1.00
Common Player (133-263):		1.15
Series 1 Wax Pack (12):		225.00
Series 1 Wax Box (24):		4025.
Series 2 Wax Pack (12):		190.00
Series 2 Wax Box (24):		3425.
1	LeRoy Kelly	12.00
2	Paul Flatley	1.00
3	Jim Cadile	1.00
4	Erich Barnes	1.00
5	Willie Richardson	1.00
6	Bob Hayes	3.00
7	Bob Jeter	1.00
8	Jim Colclough	1.00
9	Sherrill Headrick	1.00
10	Jim Dunaway	1.00
11	Bill Munson	1.00
12	Jack Pardee	1.75
13	Jim Lindsey	1.00
14	Dave Whitsell	1.00
15	Tucker Frederickson	1.00
16	Alvin Haymond	1.00
17	Andy Russell	1.00
18	Tom Beer	1.00
19	Bobby Maples	1.00
20	Len Dawson	8.00
21	Willis Crenshaw	1.00
22	Tommy Davis	1.00
23	Rickie Harris	1.00
24	Jerry Simmons	1.00
25	Johnny Unitas	25.00
26	*Brian Piccolo*	75.00
27	Bob Matheson	1.00
28	Howard Twilley	1.00
29	Jim Turner	1.00
30	*Pete Banaszak*	1.50
31	*Lance Rentzel*	1.50
32	Bill Triplett	1.00
33	Boyd Dowler	1.00
34	Merlin Olsen	5.00
35	Joe Kapp	1.50
36	*Dan Abramowicz*	3.00
37	Spider Lockhart	1.00
38	Tom Day	1.00
39	Art Graham	1.00
40	Bob Cappadona	1.00
41	Gary Ballman	1.00
42	Clendon Thomas	1.00
43	Jackie Smith	3.00
44	Dave Wilcox	1.00
45	Jery Smith	1.00
46	Dan Grimm	1.00
47	Tom Matte	1.00
48	John Stofa	1.00
49	Rex Mirich	1.00
50	Milloer Farr	1.00
51	Gale Sayers	50.00
52	Bill Nelsen	1.00
53	Bob Lilly	6.00
54	Wayne Walker	1.00
55	Ray Nitschke	5.00
56	Ed Meador	1.00
57	Lonnie Warwick	1.00
58	Wendell Hayes	1.00
59	*Dick Anderson*	3.00
60	Don Maynard	6.00
61	Tony Lorick	1.00
62	Pete Gogolak	1.00
63	Nate Ramsey	1.00
64	Dick Shiner	1.00
65	Larry Wilson	3.25
66	Ken Willard	1.00
67	Charley Taylor	5.50
68	Billy Cannon	1.50
69	Lance Alworth	8.00
70	Jim Nance	1.00
71	Nick Rassas	1.00
72	Lenny Lyles	1.00
73	Bennie McRae	1.00
74	Bill Glass	1.00
75	Don Meredith	20.00
76	Dick LeBeau	1.00
77	Carroll Dale	1.00
78	Ron McDole	1.00
79	Charley King	1.00
80	Checklist 1-132	14.00
81	Dick Bass	1.00
82	Roy Winston	1.00
83	Don McCall	1.00
84	Jim Katcavage	1.00
85	Norm Snead	3.00
86	Earl Gros	1.00
87	Don Brumm	1.00
88	Sonny Bishop	1.00
89	Fred Arbanas	1.00
90	Karl Noonan	1.00
91	Dick Witcher	1.00
92	Vince Promuto	1.00
93	Tommy Nobis	3.00
94	Jerry Hill	1.00
95	*Ed O'Bradovich*	1.75
96	Ernie Kellerman	1.00
97	Chuck Howley	1.00
98	Hewritt Dixon	1.00
99	Ron Mix	3.25
100	Joe Namath	80.00
101	Billy Gambrell	1.00
102	Elijah Pitts	1.00
103	Billy Truax	1.00
104	Ed Sharockman	1.00
105	Doug Atkins	3.25
106	Greg Larson	1.00
107	Israel Lang	1.00
108	Houston Antwine	1.00
109	Paul Guidry	1.00
110	Al Denson	1.00
111	Roy Jefferson	1.00
112	Chuck LaTourette	1.00
113	Jimmy Johnson	1.00
114	Bobby Mitchell	4.00
115	Randy Johnson	1.00
116	Lou Michaels	1.00
117	Rudy Kuechenberg	1.00
118	Walt Suggs	1.00
119	Goldie Sellers	1.00
120	*Larry Csonka*	80.00
121	Jim Houston	1.00
122	Craig Baynham	1.00
123	Alex Karras	6.00
124	Jim Grabowski	1.25
125	Roman Gabriel	3.00
126	Larry Bowie	1.00
127	Dave Parks	1.00
128	Ben Davidson	2.00
129	Steve DeLong	1.00
130	Fred Hill	1.00
131	Ernie Koy	1.00
132	Checklist 133-263	15.00
133	Dick Hoak	1.15
134	*Larry Stallings*	1.50
135	*Clifton McNeil*	1.50
136	Walter Rock	1.15
137	Billy Lothridge	1.15
138	Bob Vogel	1.15
139	Dick Butkus	25.00
140	Frank Ryan	1.50
141	Larry Garron	1.15
142	George Saimes	1.15
143	Frank Buncom	1.15
144	Don Perkins	1.50
145	Johnny Robinson	1.15
146	Lee Roy Caffey	1.15
147	Bernie Casey	1.15
148	Billy Martin	1.15
149	Gene Howard	1.15
150	Fran Tarkenton	20.00
151	Eric Crabtree	1.15
152	W.K. Hicks	1.15
153	Bobby Bell	4.00
154	Sam Baker	1.15
155	Marv Woodson	1.15
156	Dave Williams	1.15
157	Bruce Bosley	1.15
158	Carl Kammerer	1.15
159	Jim Burson	1.15

160	Roy Hilton	1.15
161	Bob Griese	30.00
162	Bob Talamini	1.15
163	Jim Otto	3.75
164	Ron Bull	1.15
165	Walter Johnson	1.50
166	Lee Roy Jordan	3.50
167	Mike Lucci	1.15
168	Willie Wood	3.50
169	Maxie Baughan	1.15
170	Bill Brown	1.15
171	John Hadl	3.00
172	Gino Cappelletti	1.75
173	George Byrd	1.15
174	Steve Stonebreaker	1.15
175	Joe Morrison	1.15
176	Joe Scarpati	1.15
177	Bobby Walden	1.15
178	Roy Shivers	1.15
179	Kermit Alexander	1.15
180	Pat Richter	1.15
181	Pete Perreault	1.15
182	Pete Duranko	1.15
183	Leroy Mitchell	1.15
184	Jim Simon	1.15
185	Billy Ray Smith	1.15
186	Jack Concannon	1.15
187	Ben Davis	1.15
188	Mike Clark	1.15
189	Jim Gobbons	1.15
190	Dave Robinson	1.15
191	Otis Taylor	2.00
192	Nick Buoniconti	2.75
193	Matt Snell	2.00
194	Bruce Gossett	1.15
195	Mick Tingelhoff	1.50
196	Earl Leggett	1.15
197	Pete Case	1.15
198	*Tom Woodeshick*	1.50
199	Ken Kortas	1.15
200	Jim Hart	3.00
201	Fred Biletnikoff	10.00
202	Jacque MacKinnon	1.15
203	Jim Whalen	1.15
204	Matt Hazeltine	1.15
205	Charlie Gogolak	1.15
206	Ray Ogden	1.15
207	John Mackey	3.75
208	Rosey Taylor	1.15
209	Gene Hickerson	1.15
210	*Dave Edwards*	1.50
211	Tom Sestak	1.15
212	Ernie Wright	1.15
213	Dave Costa	1.15
214	Tom Vaughn	1.15
215	Bart Starr	25.00
216	Les Josephson	1.15
217	Fred Cox	1.15
218	Mike Tilleman	1.15
219	Darrell Dess	1.15
220	Dave Lloyd	1.15
221	Pete Beathard	1.00
222	Buck Buchanan	3.50
223	Frank Emanuel	1.15
224	Paul Martha	1.15
225	Johnny Roland	1.15
226	Gary Lewis	1.15
227	Sonny Jurgensen	7.00
228	Jim Butler	1.15
229	*Mike Curtis*	4.00
230	Richie Petitbon	1.50
231	George Sauer Jr.	1.15
232	George Blanda	20.00
233	Gary Garrison	1.15
234	Gary Collins	1.15
235	Craig Morton	4.00
236	Tom Nowatzke	1.15
237	Donny Anderson	1.15
238	Deacon Jones	4.00
239	Grady Alderman	1.15
240	Bill Kilmer	3.00
241	Mike Taliaferro	1.15
242	Stew Barber	1.15
243	Bobby Hunt	1.15
244	Homer Jones	1.15
245	Bob Brown	1.15
246	Bill Asbury	1.15
247	Charley Johnson	1.75
248	Chris Hanburger	1.15
249	John Brodie	8.00
250	Earl Morrall	2.00
251	Floyd Little	5.00
252	*Jerrell Wilson*	1.50
253	Jim Keyes	1.15
254	Mel Renfro	1.50
255	Herb Adderley	4.00
256	Jack Snow	1.15
257	Charlie Durkee	1.15
258	Charlie Harper	1.15
259	J.R. Wilburn	1.15
260	Charlie Krueger	1.15
261	Pete Jacquess	1.15
262	Gerry Philbin	1.15
263	Daryle Lamonica	12.00

1969 Topps Four In Ones

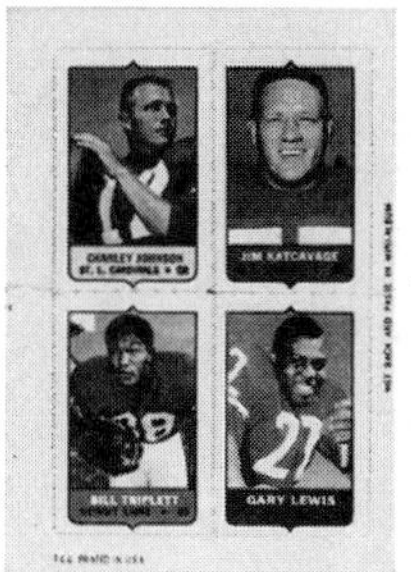
CHARLEY JOHNSON
JIM KATCAVAGE
BILL TRIPLETT
GARY LEWIS

Issued one per pack in the 1969 Topps football wax packs, each "card" contained four perforated cards of NFL players which could be punched out and inserted into each team's mini-album. The cards are unnumbered, but appear here in alphabetical order according to the last name of the player who appears in the upper left corner of the card. One variation does exist: Cards #27 and 28 show the same four players, but Charlie Johnson on #27 has a red logo while #28 gives him a white one. Bill Triplett on #27 has a white logo, while #28 is red. Both seem to have been issued in equal quantities. Most of the cards in this set are of the key players, including Brian Piccolo and Larry Csonka rookies. A few of the lesser-known NFL players appeared in this set only and not the regular 1969 set (and vice versa). An important note: the entire card is priced here. The small, individual cards have very little value when separated from the rest of the card, as is the case with Topps' 1980-81 basketball issue.

		NM
Complete Set (66):		185.00
Common Card:		1.00
(1)	Grady Alderman, Jerry Smith, Gale Sayers, Dick LeBeau	6.00
(2)	Jim Allison, Frank Buncom, Frank Emanuel, George Sauer Jr.	1.00
(3)	Lance Alworth, Don Maynard, Ron McDole, Billy Cannon	3.00
(4)	Dick Anderson, Mike Taliaferro, Fred Biletnikoff, Otis Taylor	2.25
(5)	Ralph Baker, Les Duncan, Eric Crabtree, Bobby Bell	1.00
(6)	Gary Ballman, Jerry Hill, Roy Jefferson, Boyd Dowler	1.00
(7)	Tom Beer, Miller Farr, Jim Colclough, Steve DeLong	1.00
(8)	Sonny Bishop, Pete Banaszak, Paul Guidry, Tom Day	1.00
(9)	Bruce Bosley, J.R. Wilburn, Tom Nowatzke, Jim Simon	1.00
(10)	Larry Bowie, Willis Crenshaw, Tommy Davis, Paul Flatley	1.00
(11)	Nick Buoniconti, George Saimes, Jacque MacKinnon, Pete Duranko	1.00
(12)	Jim Burson, Dan Abramowicz, Ed O'Bradovich, Dick Witcher	1.00
(13)	Reg Carolan, Larry Garron, W.K. Hicks, Pete Jacques	1.00
(14)	Bert Coan, John Hadl, Dan Birdwell, Sam Brunelli	1.00
(15)	Hewritt Dixon, Goldie Sellers, Joe Namath, Howard Twilley	20.00
(16)	Charlie Durkee, Clinton McNeil, Maxie Baughan, Fran Tarkenton	6.00
(17)	Pete Gogolak, Ron Bull, Chuck LaTourette, Willie Richardson	1.00
(18)	Bob Griese, Jim Lemoine, Dave Grayson, Walt Sweeney	4.00
(19)	Jim Hart, Darrell Dess, Kermit Alexander, Mick Tingelhoff	1.00
(20)	Alvin Haymond, Elijah Pitts, Billy Ray Smith, Ken Willard	1.00
(21)	Gene Hickerson, Donny Anderson, Dick Butkus, Mike Lucci	4.00
(22)	Fred Hill, Ernie Koy, Tommy Nobis, Bennie McRae	1.00
(23)	Dick Hoak, Roman Gabriel, Ed Sharockman, Dave Williams	1.00
(24)	Jim Houston, Roy Shivers, Carroll Dale, Bill Asbury	1.00
(25)	Gene Howard, Joe Morrison, Billy Martin, Ben Davis	1.00
(26)	Chuck Howley, Brian Piccolo, Chris Hanburger, Erich Barnes	14.00
(27)	Charlie Johnson, Jim Katcavage, Gary Lewis, Bill Triplett (red white)	4.00
(28)	Charlie Johnson, Jim Katcavage, Gary Lewis, Bill Triplett (white red)	4.00
(29)	Walter Johnson, Tucker Frederickson, Dave Lloyd, Bobby Walden	1.00
(30)	Sonny Jurgensen, Dick Bass, Paul Martha, Dave Parks	3.00
(31)	Leroy Kelly, Ed Meador, Bart Starr, Ray Ogden	6.00
(32)	Charlie King, Bob Cappadona, Fred Arbanas, Ben Davidson	1.00
(33)	Daryle Lamonica, Carl Cunningham, Bobby Hunt, Stew Barber	1.00
(34)	Israel Lang, Bob Lilly, Jim Butler, John Brodie	4.00
(35)	Jim Lindsey, Ray Nitschke, Rickie Harris, Bob Vogel	1.00
(36)	Billy Lothridge, Herb Adderly, Charlie Gogolak, John Mackey	2.00
(37)	Bobby Maples, Karl Noonan, Houston Antwine, Wendell Hayes	1.00
(38)	Don Meredith, Gary Collins, Homer Jones, Marv Woodson	6.00
(39)	Rex Mirich, Art Graham, Jim Turner, John Stofa	1.00
(40)	Leroy Mitchell, Sid Blanks, Paul Rochester, Pete Perreault	1.00
(41)	Jim Nance, Jim Dunaway, Larry Csonka, Ron Mix	2.00
(42)	Bill Nelsen, Bill Munson, Nate Ramsey, Mike Curtis	1.00
(43)	Jim Otto, Dave herman, Dave Costa, Dennis Randall	1.00
(44)	Jack Pardee, Norm Snead, Craig Baynham	1.00
(45)	Richie Petitbon, John Robinson, Mike Clark, Jack Snow	1.00
(46)	Nick Rassas, Tom Matte, Lance Rentzel, Bobby Mitchell	1.00
(47)	Pat Richter, Dave Whitsell, Joe Kapp, Bill Glass	1.00
(48)	Johnny Roland, Craig Morton, Bill Brown, Sam Baker	1.00
(49)	Andy Russell, Randy Johnson, Bob Matheson, Alex Karras	2.00
(50)	Joe Scarpati, Walter Rock, Jack Concannon, Bernie Casey	1.00
(51)	Tom Sestak, Ernie Wright, Doug Moreau, Matt Snell	1.00
(52)	Jerry Simmons, Bob Hayes, Doug Atkins, Spider Lockhart	1.00
(53)	Jackie Smith, Jim Grabowski, Jim Johnson, Charley Taylor	2.00
(54)	Larry Stallings, Roosevelt Taylor, Jim Gibbons, Bob Brown	1.00
(55)	Mike Stratton, Marion Rushing, Soloman Brannan, Jim Keyes	1.00
(56)	Walt Suggs, Len Dawson, Sherrill Headrick, Al Denson	2.00
(57)	Bob Talamini, George Blanda, Jim Whalen, Jack Kemp	22.00
(58)	Clendon Thomas, Don McCall, Earl Morrall, Lonnie Warwick	1.00
(59)	Don Trull, Gerry Philbin, Gary Garrison, Buck Buchanan	1.00
(60)	John Unitas, Les Josephson, Fred Cox, Mel Renfro	9.00
(61)	Wayne Walker, Tony Lorick, Dave Wilcox, Merlin Olsen	2.00
(62)	Willie West, Ken Herock, George Byrd, Gino Cappelletti	1.00
(63)	Jerrel Wilson, John Bramlett, Pete Beathard, Floyd Little	1.00
(64)	Larry Wilson, Lou Michaels, Billy Gambrell, Earl Gros	1.00
(65)	Willie Wood, Steve Stonebreaker, Vince Promuto, Jim Cadie	1.00
(66)	Tom Woodeshick, Greg Larson, Billy Kilmer, Don Perkins	1.50

1969 Topps mini-albums

The 26 team booklets were intended as stamp books for the 1969 Topps Four In Ones. You punched out the four players on the card and stuck them into this 2-1/2" x 3-1/2" book, right over the picture of the player. The booklets are numbered on the back and arranged in alphabetical order by city name. Aside from its condition, in order for a book to be considered mint, there must be no stamps in it.

		NM
Complete Set (26):		50.00
Common Booklet:		2.00
1	Atlanta Falcons	2.00
2	Baltimore Colts	2.00
3	Chicago Bears	4.00
4	Cleveland Browns	2.00
5	Dallas Cowboys	5.00
6	Detroit Lions	2.00
7	Green Bay Packers	5.00
8	Los Angeles Rams	2.00
9	Minnesota Vikings	2.00
10	New Orleans Saints	2.00
11	New York Giants	4.00
12	Philadelphia Eagles	2.00
13	Pittsburgh Steelers	4.00
14	St. Louis Cardinals	2.00
15	San Francisco 49ers	4.00
16	Washington Redskins	2.00
17	Boston Patriots	4.00
18	Buffalo Bills	4.00
19	Cincinnati Bengals	2.00
20	Denver Broncos	5.00
21	Houston Oilers	4.00
22	Kansas City Chiefs	4.00
23	Miami Dolphins	4.00
24	New York Jets	4.00
25	Oakland Raiders	5.00
26	San Diego Chargers	2.00

1970 Topps

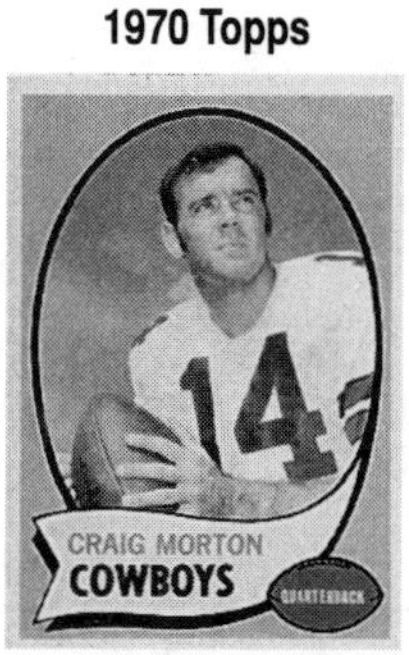
CRAIG MORTON
COWBOYS
QUARTERBACK

The 1970 Topps set, which included 263 cards, was printed in two series. The second series is a little tougher to find than the first, since it was printed in lesser quantities. One variation that appears in the set is #113, Lance Rentzel. His name appears in red on the "common" card; on the hard-to-find variation, his name appears in black. Card #132, the second-series checklist card, was double- printed, a common practice for Topps during its multi-series production days. The set is best known for its inclusion of the O.J. Simpson rookie card, but other rookies in the set are Leroy Brown, Jan Stenerud, Alan Page, Bob Trumpy, Bubba Smith, Bill Bergey, Calvin Hill and Fred Dryer.

		NM
Complete Set (263):		450.00
Common Player (1-132):		.50
Common Player (133-263):		.75
Series 1 Wax Pack (10+):		230.00
Series 1 Wax Box (24):		4150.
Series 2 Wax Pack (10):		85.00
Series 2 Wax Box (24):		1675.
1	Len Dawson	15.00
2	Doug Hart	.50
3	Verlon Biggs	.50
4	*Ralph Neely*	.75
5	Harmon Wages	.50
6	Dan Conners	.50
7	Gino Cappelletti	1.00
8	Erich Barnes	.75
9	Checklist 1-132	7.50
10	Bob Griese	15.00
11	Ed Flanagan	.50
12	George Seals	.50
13	Harry Jacobs	.50
14	Mike Haffner	.50
15	Bob Vogel	.50
16	Bill Peterson	.50
17	Spider Lockhart	.50
18	Billy Truax	.50
19	Jim Beirne	.50
20	Leroy Kelly	4.00
21	Dave Lloyd	.50
22	Mike Tilleman	.50
23	Gary Garrison	.50
24	*Larry Brown*	7.00
25	*Jan Stenerud*	12.00
26	Rolf Krueger	.50
27	Roland Lakes	.50
28	Dick Hoak	.50
29	*Gene Washington* (Vikings)	.75
30	Bart Starr	20.00
31	Dave Grayson	.50
32	Jerry Rush	.50
33	Len St. Jean	.50
34	Randy Edmunds	.50
35	Matt Snell	1.50
36	Paul Costa	.50
37	Mike Pyle	.50
38	Roy Hilton	.50
39	Steve Tensi	.50
40	Tommy Nobis	2.00
41	Pete Case	.50
42	Andy Rice	.50
43	*Elvin Bethea*	3.50
44	Jack Snow	.50
45	Mel Renfro	1.00
46	Andy Livingston	.50
47	Gary Ballman	.50
48	Bob DeMarco	.50
49	Steve DeLong	.50
50	Daryle Lamonica	3.50
51	*Jim Lynch*	.75
52	*Mel Farr*	.75
53	Bob Long	.50
54	John Elliott	.50
55	Ray Nitschke	4.00
56	Jim Shorter	.50
57	Dave Wilcox	.50
58	Eric Crabtree	.50
59	*Alan Page*	40.00
60	Jim Nance	.50
61	Glen Ray Hines	.50
62	John Mackey	3.00
63	Ron McDole	.50
64	Tom Beier	.50
65	Bill Nelsen	.65
66	Paul Flatley	.50
67	Sam Brunelli	.50
68	Jack Pardee	1.50
69	Brig Owens	.50
70	Gale Sayers	35.00
71	Lee Roy Jordan	2.00
72	*Harold Jackson*	8.00
73	John Hadl	2.50
74	Dave Parks	.50
75	*Lem Barney*	15.00
76	Johnny Roland	.50
77	Ed Budde	.50
78	Ben McGee	.50
79	Ken Bowman	.50
80	Fran Tarkenton	20.00
81	*Gene Washington*	4.00
82	Larry Grantham	.50
83	Bill Brown	.50
84	John Charles	.50
85	Fred Biletnikoff	7.00
86	Royce Berry	.50
87	Bob Lilly	4.50
88	Earl Morrall	2.00
89	Jerry LeVias	.50
90	*O.J. Simpson*	80.00
91	Mike Howell	.50
92	Ken Gray	.50
93	Chris Hanburger	.50
94	*Larry Seiple*	.75
95	*Rich Jackson*	.75
96	Rockne Freitas	.50
97	*Dick Post*	.75
98	Ben Hawkins	.50
99	Ken Reaves	.50
100	Roman Gabriel	2.50
101	Dave Rowe	.50
102	Dave Robinson	.50
103	Otis Taylor	1.50
104	Jim Turner	.50
105	Joe Morrison	.50
106	Dick Evey	.50
107	Ray Mansfield	.50
108	Grady Alderman	.50
109	Bruce Gossett	.50
110	*Bob Trumpy*	5.00
111	Jim Hunt	.50
112	Larry Stallings	.50
113	Lance Rentzel (red)	1.50
113a	Lance Rentzel (black)	1.50
114	*Bubba Smith*	25.00
115	Norm Snead	1.00
116	Jim Otto	2.50
117	*Bo Scott*	.75
118	Rick Redman	.50
119	George Byrd	.50
120	*George Webster*	2.00
121	Chuck Walton	.50
122	Dave Costa	.50
123	Al Dodd	.50
124	Len Hauss	.50
125	Deacon Jones	3.50
126	Randy Johnson	.50
127	Ralph Heck	.50
128	*Emerson Boozer*	2.50
129	Johnny Robinson	.65
130	John Brodie	6.00
131	*Gale Gillingham*	1.00
132	Checklist 133-263 (DP)	8.00
133	Chuck Walker	.75
134	Bennie McRae	.75
135	Paul Warfield	6.00
136	Dan Darragh	.75
137	*Paul Robinson*	1.00
138	Ed Philpott	.75
139	Craig Morton	2.00
140	*Tom Dempsey*	5.00
141	Al Nelson	.75
142	Tom Matte	.75
143	Dick Schafrath	.75
144	Willie Brown	4.00
145	Charley Taylor	4.50
146	John Huard	.75
147	Dave Osborn	.75
148	Gene Mingo	.75
149	Larry Hand	.75
150	Joe Namath	50.00
151	*Tom Mack*	7.00
152	Kenny Graham	.75
153	Don Herrmann	.75
154	Bobby Bell	3.75
155	Hoyle Granger	.75
156	*Claude Humphrey*	1.25
157	Clifton McNeil	.75
158	Mick Tingelhoff	1.00
159	*Don Horn*	1.00
160	Larry Wilson	3.00
161	Tom Neville	.75
162	Larry Csonka	25.00
163	*Doug Buffone*	.75
164	Cornell Green	.75
165	*Haven Moses*	2.50
166	Bill Kilmer	2.50
167	*Tim Rossovich*	.75
168	*Bill Bergey*	5.00
169	Gary Collins	.75
170	Floyd Little	3.00
171	Tom Keating	.75
172	Pat Fischer	.75
173	Walt Sweeney	.75
174	Greg Larson	.75
175	Carl Eller	3.00
176	George Sauer	.75
177	Jim Hart	2.00
178	Bob Brown	.75
179	*Mike Garrett*	4.00
180	Johnny Unitas	22.00
181	Tom Regner	.75
182	Bob Jeter	.75
183	Gail Cogdill	.75
184	Earl Gros	.75
185	Dennis Partee	.75
186	Charlie Krueger	.75
187	Martin Baccaglio	.75
188	Charlie Long	.75
189	Bob Hayes	3.00
190	Dick Butkus	13.00
191	Al Bemiller	.75
192	Dick Westmoreland	.75
193	Joe Scarpati	.75
194	Ron Snidow	.75
195	*Earl McCullough*	1.00
196	Jake Kupp	.75
197	Bob Lurtsema	.75
198	Mike Current	.75
199	Charlie Smith	.75
200	Sonny Jurgensen	6.50
201	Mike Curtis	.75
202	Aaron Brown	.75
203	Richie Petitbon	1.00
204	Walt Suggs	.75
205	Roy Jefferson	.75
206	*Russ Washington*	1.00
207	*Woody Peoples*	1.00
208	Dave Williams	.75
209	*John Zook*	1.00
210	Tom Woodeshick	.75
211	Howard Fest	.75
212	Jack Concannon	.75
213	Jim Marshall	2.75
214	Jon Morris	.75
215	Dan Abramowicz	.75
216	Paul Martha	.75
217	Ken Willard	.75
218	Walter Rock	.75
219	Garland Boyette	.75
220	Buck Buchanan	3.75
221	Bill Munson	.75
222	*David Lee*	1.00
223	Karl Noonan	.75
224	Harry Schuh	.75
225	Jackie Smith	1.25
226	Gerry Philbin	.75
227	Ernie Koy	.75
228	Chuck Howley	.75
229	Billy Shaw	.75
230	Jerry Hillebrand	.75
231	*Bill Thompson*	1.50
232	Carroll Dale	.75
233	Gene Hickerson	.75
234	Jim Butler	.75
235	*Greg Cook*	1.50
236	Lee Roy Caffey	.75
237	Merlin Olsen	4.50
238	Fred Cox	.75
239	Nate Ramsey	.75
240	Lance Alworth	6.00
241	Chuck Hinton	.75
242	Jerry Smith	.75
243	Tony Baker	.75
244	Nick Buoniconti	2.50
245	Jim Johnson	.75
246	Willie Richardson	.75
247	*Fred Dryer*	15.00
248	Bobby Maples	.75
249	Alex Karras	5.50
250	Joe Kapp	2.00
251	Ben Davidson	2.50
252	Mike Stratton	.75
253	Les Josephson	.75
254	Don Maynard	6.00
255	Houston Antwine	.75
256	*Mac Percival*	1.00
257	George Goeddeke	.75
258	Homer Jones	.75
259	Bob Berry	.75
260	*Calvin Hill*	10.00
261	Willie Wood	3.00
262	Ed Weisacosky	.75
263	Jim Tyrer	3.00

1970 Topps Super Glossy

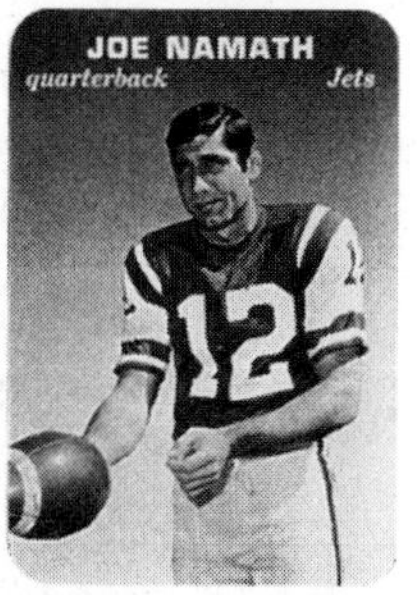
JOE NAMATH
quarterback
Jets

A collector favorite, this 33-card set is among the decade's most expensive subsets. These were found in the second series of 1970 Topps football wax packs and had full-color action-pose glossy fronts, heavy white cardboard stock, and rounded corners. The only information on the white backs is the player's name, team, position and card number.

		NM
Complete Set (33):		300.00
Common Player:		3.00
1	Tommy Nobis	3.00
2	John Unitas	27.50
3	Tom Matte	3.00
4	Mac Percival	3.00
5	Leroy Kelly	3.00
6	Mel Renfro	3.00
7	Bob Hayes	3.00
8	Earl McCullouch	3.00
9	Bart Starr	22.00
10	Willie Wood	7.00
11	Jack Snow	3.00
12	Joe Kapp	5.00
13	Dave Osborn	3.00
14	Dan Abramowicz	3.00
15	Fran Tarkenton	22.00
16	Tom Woodeshick	3.00
17	Roy Jefferson	3.00
18	Jackie Smith	3.00
19	Jim Johnson	3.00
20	Sonny Jurgensen	12.00
21	Houston Antwine	3.00
22	O.J. Simpson	60.00
23	Greg Cook	3.00
24	Floyd Little	4.00
25	Rich Jackson	3.00
26	George Webster	3.00
27	Len Dawson	9.00
28	Bob Griese	14.00
29	Joe Namath	70.00
30	Matt Snell	3.00
31	Daryle Lamonica	4.00
32	Fred Biletnikoff	7.00
33	Dick Post	3.00

1970 Topps posters

This 24-poster set was included one per pack in the first series of 1970 Topps football wax packs. The posters, which measure about 8" x 10", were folded several times; it's very difficult to find any in top condition.

		NM
Complete Set (24):		50.00
Common Player:		1.00
1	Gale Sayers	4.50
2	Bobby Bell	3.00
3	Roman Gabriel	3.25
4	Jim Tyrer	1.00
5	Willie Brown	3.00
6	Carl Eller	3.00
7	Tom Mack	1.50
8	Deacon Jones	3.00
9	Johnny Robinson	1.00
10	Jan Stenerud	2.00
11	Dick Butkus	5.00
12	Lem Barney	1.00
13	David Lee	1.00
14	Larry Wilson	2.00

15	Gene Hickerson	1.00
16	Lance Alworth	3.00
17	Merlin Olsen	3.00
18	Bob Trumpy	2.00
19	Bob Lilly	3.00
20	Mick Tingelhoff	1.50
21	Calvin Hill	2.00
22	Paul Warfield	3.00
23	Chuck Howley	1.00
24	Bob Brown	1.00

1970 Topps Supers

A 35-card set issued three per pack with a stick of gum, the cards featured an action pose of an NFL star with a facsimile autograph. No other identification is on the front. Card backs show the reverse of the player's regular 1970 card. These were printed on heavy white cardboard stock and measure about 3-1/8" x 5-1/4". The final seven in the set were apparently short-printed (possibly added late) and are much harder to find than the first 28 cards.

		NM
Complete Set (35):		300.00
Common Player:		2.75
1	Fran Tarkenton	16.00
2	Floyd Little	3.00
3	Bart Starr	16.00
4	Len Dawson	8.50
5	Dick Post	2.75
6	Sonny Jurgensen	8.50
7	Deacon Jones	5.00
8	Leroy Kelly	2.75
9	Larry Wilson	2.75
10	Greg Cook	2.75
11	Carl Eller	4.50
12	Lem Barney	2.75
13	Lance Alworth	7.00
14	Dick Butkus	12.00
15	John Unitas	25.00
16	Roy Jefferson	2.75
17	Bobby Bell	5.00
18	John Brodie	9.00
19	Dan Abramowicz	2.75
20	Matt Snell	2.75
21	Tom Matte	2.75
22	Gale Sayers	20.00
23	Tom Woodeshick	2.75
24	O.J. Simpson	50.00
25	Roman Gabriel	5.00
26	Jim Nance	2.75
27	Joe Morrison	2.75
28	Calvin Hill	2.75
29	Tommy Nobis	6.50
30	Bob Hayes	6.50
31	Joe Kapp	6.50
32	Daryle Lamonica	6.50
33	Joe Namath	65.00
34	George Webster	6.50
35	Bob Griese	15.00

1971 Topps

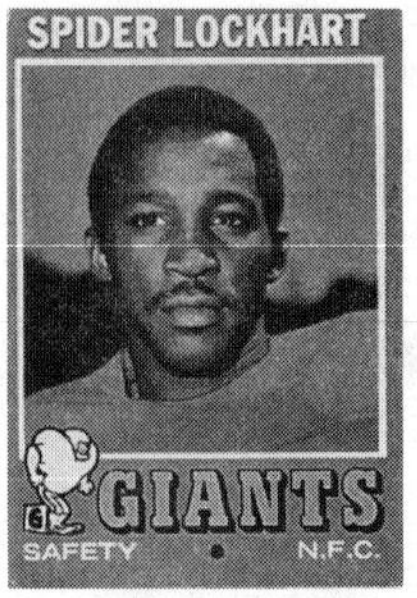

This 263-card set was released in two series, with the first containing cards #1-132 and the second with cards #133-263. The second-series checklist (card #106) is double-printed. There aren't any subsets in the 1971 issue, but the NFC players are designated by red borders and AFC players have blue borders. All-stars have blue borders. This, incidentally, is the last Topps set that would not contain some type of subset. Hall of Famers with rookie cards in this set include Terry Bradshaw, Joe Greene, Willie Lanier, and Ken Houston. Other rookies include Duane Thomas, Ron Johnson, Mercury Morris, Garo Yepremian, Mark Mosley, and Charlie Sanders.

		NM
Complete Set (263):		500.00
Common Player (1-132):		.50
Common Player (133-263):		.75
Series 1 Wax Pack (10+):		230.00
Series 1 Wax Box (24):		4150.
Series 2 Wax Pack (10+):		265.00
Series 2 Wax Box (24):		4850.
1	Johnny Unitas	30.00
2	Jim Butler	.50
3	*Marty Schottenheimer*	20.00
4	Joe O'Donnell	.50
5	Tom Dempsey	1.00
6	Chuck Allen	.50
7	Ernie Kellerman	.50
8	*Walt Garrison*	2.50
9	Bill Van Heusen	.50
10	Lance Alworth	5.00
11	*Greg Landry*	5.00
12	Larry Krause	.50
13	Buck Buchanan	2.50
14	*Roy Gerela*	1.00
15	Clifton McNeil	.50
16	Bob Brown	.50
17	Lloyd Mumphord	.50
18	Gary Cuozzo	.50
19	Don Maynard	5.00
20	Larry Wilson	2.50
21	Charlie Smith	.50
22	Ken Avery	.50
23	Billy Walik	.50
24	Jim Johnson	2.00
25	Dick Butkus	20.00
26	Charley Taylor	4.25
27	Checklist 1-132	8.00
28	*Lionel Aldridge*	1.00
29	Billy Lothridge	.50
30	*Terry Hanratty*	1.25
31	Lee Roy Jordan	2.00
32	*Rick Volk*	.75
33	Howard Kindig	.50
34	*Carl Garrett*	1.00
35	Bobby Bell	2.50
36	Gene Hickerson	.50
37	Dave Parks	.50
38	Paul Martha	.50
39	George Blanda	15.00
40	Tom Woodeshick	.50
41	Alex Karras	4.00
42	Rick Redman	.50
43	Zeke Moore	.50
44	Jack Snow	.50
45	Larry Csonka	12.00
46	Karl Kassulke	.50
47	Jim Hart	2.00
48	Al Atkinson	.50
49	*Horst Muhlmann*	.75
50	Sonny Jurgensen	6.00
51	*Ron Johnson*	2.50
52	Cas Banaszek	.50
53	Bubba Smith	8.00
54	*Bobby Douglass*	1.50
55	Willie Wood	2.50
56	Bake Turner	.50
57	Mike Morgan	.50
58	George Byrd	.50
59	Don Horn	.50
60	Tommy Nobis	2.00
61	Jan Stenerud	3.00
62	*Altie Taylor*	.75
63	Gary Pettigrew	.50
64	Spike Jones	.50
65	*Duane Thomas*	2.50
66	*Marty Domres*	.75
67	Dick Anderson	.50
68	Ken Iman	.50
69	Miller Farr	.50
70	Daryle Lamonica	2.50
71	Alan Page	8.00
72	Pat Matson	.50
73	Emerson Boozer	1.00
74	Pat Fischer	.50
75	Gary Collins	.50
76	*John Fuqua*	1.00
77	Bruce Gossett	.50
78	Ed O'Bradovich	.50
79	*Bob Tucker*	1.50
80	Mike Curtis	.50
81	Rich Jackson	.50
82	Tom Janik	.50
83	Gale Gillingham	.50
84	Jim Mitchell	.50
85	Charlie Johnson	1.00
86	Edgar Chandler	.50
87	Cyril Pinder	.50
88	Johnny Robinson	.50
89	Ralph Neely	.50
90	Dan Abramowicz	.50
91	*Mercury Morris*	6.00
92	Steve DeLong	.50
93	Larry Stallings	.50
94	Tom Mack	2.50
95	Hewritt Dixon	.50
96	Fred Cox	.50
97	Chris Hanburger	.50
98	Gerry Philbin	.50
99	Ernie Wright	.50
100	John Brodie	5.00
101	Tucker Frederickson	.50
102	Bobby Walden	.50
103	Dick Gordon	.50
104	Walter Johnson	.50
105	Mike Lucci	.50
106	Checklist 133-263	6.00
107	Ron Berger	.50
108	Dan Sullivan	.50
109	*George Kunz*	2.00
110	Floyd Little	2.50
111	Zeke Bratkowski	.50
112	Haven Moses	.50
113	*Ken Houston*	20.00
114	*Willie Lanier*	20.00
115	Larry Brown	2.00
116	Tim Rossovich	.50
117	Errol Linden	.50
118	Mel Renfro	1.25
119	Mike Garrett	1.00
120	Fran Tarkenton	20.00
121	*Garo Yepremian*	3.00
122	Glen Condren	.50
123	Johnny Roland	.50
124	Dave Herman	.50
125	Merlin Olsen	4.00
126	Doug Buffone	.50
127	Earl McCullouch	.50
128	Spider Lockhart	.50
129	Ken Willard	.50
130	Gene Washington (MN)	.50
131	*Mike Phipps*	1.75
132	Andy Russell	.50
133	Ray Nitschke	4.50
134	Jerry Logan	.75
135	*MacArthur Lane*	2.00
136	Jim Turner	.75
137	Kent McCloughan	.75
138	Paul Guidry	.75
139	Otis Taylor	1.50
140	*Virgil Carter*	1.00
141	Joe Dawkins	.75
142	Steve Preece	.75
143	*Mike Bragg*	.75
144	Bob Lilly	4.50
145	Joe Kapp	1.25
146	Al Dodd	.75
147	Nick Buoniconti	2.50
148	Speedy Duncan	.75
149	*Cedrick Hardman*	1.00
150	Gale Sayers	30.00
151	Jim Otto	3.00
152	Billy Truax	.75
153	John Elliott	.75
154	Dick LeBeau	.75
155	Bill Bergey	1.75
156	*Terry Bradshaw*	175.00
157	Leroy Kelly	4.50
158	Paul Krause	2.00
159	Ted Vactor	.75
160	Bob Griese	12.00
161	Ernie McMillan	.75
162	Donny Anderson	.75
163	John Pitts	.75
164	Dave Costa	.75
165	Gene Washington (SF)	1.50
166	John Zook	.55
167	Pete Gogolak	.75
168	Erich Barnes	.55
169	Alvin Reed	.75
170	Jim Nance	.75
171	Craig Morton	2.00
172	Gary Garrison	.75
173	Joe Scarpati	.75
174	Adrian Young	.75
175	John Mackey	2.50
176	Mac Percival	.75
177	*Preston Pearson*	4.00
178	Fred Biletnikoff	6.00
179	*Mike Battle*	1.00
180	Len Dawson	7.00
181	Les Josephson	.75
182	Royce Berry	.75
183	Herman Weaver	.75
184	Norm Snead	1.25
185	Sam Brunelli	.75
186	*Jim Kiick*	4.00
187	Austin Denney	.75
188	*Roger Wehrli*	3.00
189	Dave Wilcox	.75
190	Bob Hayes	2.00
191	Joe Morrison	.75
192	Manny Sistrunk	.75
193	*Don Cockroft*	1.50
194	Lee Bouggess	.75
195	Bob Berry	.75
196	Ron Sellers	.75
197	George Webster	.75
198	Hoyle Granger	.75
199	Bob Vogel	.75
200	Bart Starr	22.00
201	Mike Mercer	.75
202	Dave Smith	.75
203	Lee Roy Caffey	.75
204	Mick Tingelhoff	.75
205	Matt Snell	1.50
206	Jim Tyrer	.75
207	Willie Brown	3.50
208	*Bob Johnson*	1.50
209	Deacon Jones	3.00
210	*Charlie Sanders*	4.50
211	*Jake Scott*	5.00
212	*Bob Anderson*	2.00
213	Charlie Krueger	.75
214	Jim Bakken	.75
215	Harold Jackson	2.50
216	Bill Brundige	.75
217	Calvin Hill	2.00
218	Claude Humphrey	.75
219	Glen Ray Hines	.75
220	Bill Nelsen	.75
221	Roy Hilton	.75
222	Don Herrmann	.75
223	John Bramlett	.75
224	Ken Ellis	.75
225	Dave Osborn	.75
226	*Edd Hargett*	.75
227	Gene Mingo	.75
228	Larry Grantham	.75
229	Dick Post	.75
230	Roman Gabriel	3.00
231	Mike Eischeid	.75
232	Jim Lynch	.75
233	*Lemar Parrish*	3.00
234	Cecil Turner	.75
235	*Dennis Shaw*	1.00
236	Mel Farr	.75
237	Curt Knight	.75
238	Chuck Howley	.75
239	*Bruce Taylor*	1.00
240	Jerry LeVias	.75
241	Bob Lurtsema	.75
242	Earl Morrall	2.00
243	Kermit Alexander	.75
244	Jackie Smith	1.00
245	*Joe Greene*	50.00
246	Harmon Wages	.75
247	Errol Mann	.75
248	Mike McCoy	.75
249	*Milt Morin*	1.00
250	Joe Namath	50.00
251	Jackie Burkett	.75
252	Steve Chomyszak	.75
253	Ed Sharockman	.75
254	*Robert Holmes*	1.00
255	John Hadl	2.00
256	Cornell Gordon	.75
257	*Mark Moseley*	5.00
258	Gus Otto	.75
259	Mike Taliaferro	.75
260	O.J. Simpson	25.00
261	Paul Warfield	7.00
262	Jack Concannon	.75
263	Tom Matte	3.00

1971 Topps Game Cards

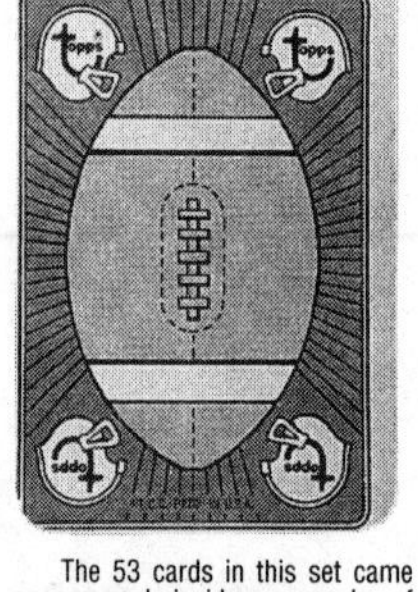

The 53 cards in this set came one per pack inside wax packs of 1971 Topps football cards. Intended for use in a card game, these cards are similar to playing cards and carry a head "Action" shot of the player, his name and team in a diagonal stripe across the front, and a play (such as "Interception," "Touchdown" and "Fumble") on the top and bottom. Card backs are light blue and show the Topps logo inside a football helmet surrounding a football. The set has 52 "playing cards" plus a "first down/field marker" for use with the game. Six of the cards in the series were double-printed: Dick Butkus, Bob Berry, Joe Namath, Andy Russell, Tom Woodeshick, and Bart Starr. (Key: DP -- double-printed)

		NM
Complete Set (53):		125.00
Common Player:		.50
1	Dick Butkus (DP)	4.00
2	Bob Berry (DP)	.50
3	Joe Namath (DP)	17.00
4	Mike Curtis	.50
5	Jim Nance	.50
6	Ron Berger	.50
7	O.J. Simpson	20.00
8	Haven Moses	.50
9	Tommy Nobis	.50
10	Gale Sayers	9.00
11	Virgil Carter	.50
12	Andy Russell (DP)	.50
13	Bill Nelsen	.50
14	Gary Collins	.50
15	Duane Thomas	.50
16	Bob Hayes	.80
17	Floyd Little	.80
18	Sam Brunelli	.50
19	Charlie Sanders	.50
20	Mike Lucci	.50
21	Gene Washington (SF)	.80
22	Willie Wood	3.00
23	Jerry LeVias	.50
24	Charlie Johnson	.80
25	Len Dawson	3.00
26	Bobby Bell	2.00
27	Merlin Olsen	3.00
28	Roman Gabriel	2.00
29	Bob Griese	4.00
30	Larry Csonka	4.00
31	Dave Osborn	.50
32	Gene Washington (MN)	.50
33	Dan Abramowicz	.50
34	Tom Dempsey	.50
35	Fran Tarkenton	9.00
36	Clifton McNeil	.50
37	Johnny Unitas	12.00
38	Matt Snell	.50
39	Daryle Lamonica	.80
40	Hewritt Dixon	.50
41	Tom Woodeshick (DP)	.50
42	Harold Jackson	.50
43	Terry Bradshaw	20.00
44	Ken Avery	.50
45	MacArthur Lane	.50
46	Larry Wilson	2.00
47	John Hadl	1.00
48	Lance Alworth	2.00
49	John Brodie	4.00
50	Bart Starr (DP)	6.00
51	Sonny Jurgensen	6.00
52	Larry Brown	.50
53	Field Marker	.50

1971 Topps Pin-Ups

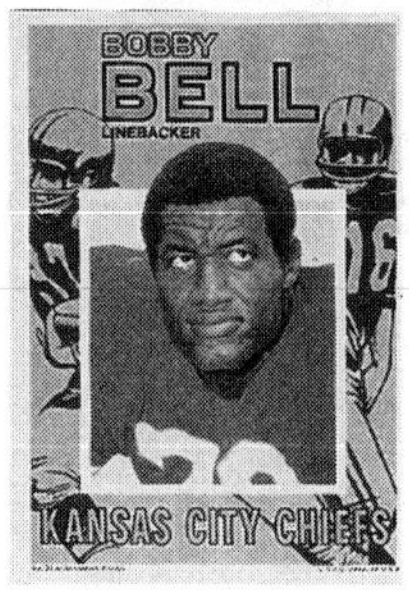

These mini-posters (about 5" x 7") were folded twice and inserted into wax packs. The front features a head shot of the player, with his name in bold capitals above the photo and his team in smaller type at the bottom. Backs showed a football field with side markers, as well as the accompanying instructions. Because these posters were folded, it's very difficult, if not impossible, to find any in Mint condition.

		NM
Complete Set (32):		40.00
Common Player:		.65
1	Gene Washington	.75
2	Andy Russell	.65
3	Harold Jackson	.65
4	Joe Namath	12.00
5	Fran Tarkenton	5.00
6	Dave Osborn	.65
7	Bob Griese	2.50
8	Roman Gabriel	1.00
9	Jerry LeVias	.65
10	Bart Starr	5.00
11	Bob Hayes	1.00
12	Gale Sayers	5.50
13	O.J. Simpson	7.50
14	Sam Brunelli	.65
15	Jim Nance	.65
16	Bill Nelsen	.65
17	Sonny Jurgensen	2.50
18	John Brodie	2.50
19	Lance Alworth	1.50
20	Larry Wilson	1.00
21	Daryle Lamonica	.75
22	Dan Abramowicz	.65
23	Gene Washington (Minn)	.65
24	Bobby Bell	1.50
25	Merlin Olsen	2.00
26	Charlie Sanders	.65
27	Virgil Carter	.65
28	Dick Butkus	7.00
29	Johnny Unitas	7.00
30	Tommy Nobis	.75
31	Floyd Little	.65
32	Larry Brown	.65

1972 Topps

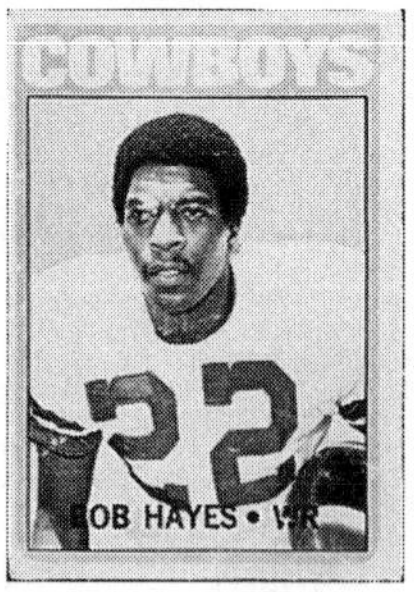

The 1972 set, a 351-card edition, was Topps' last to be issued in series form. The first series includes cards #1-132; the second - somewhat harder to find than the first - includes cards #133-263; and the final series - the difficult series - shows cards #264-351. Because of the difficulty in acquiring a complete set, this is easily the most expensive Topps set of the 1970s. Subsets in this issue include statistical leaders, playoffs, All-Pros and In Action cards. Rookies in the set include John Riggins, Archie Manning, Jim Plunkett, John Brockington, Ted Hendricks, L.C. Greenwood, Lyle Alzado, Dan Pastorini, Gene Upshaw, Roger Staubach, Charlie Joiner and Steve Spurrier. (Key: IA - in action, AP - All Pro)

		NM
Complete Set (351):		2300.
Common Player (1-132):		.50
Common Player (133-263):		.75
Comm Player (264-351):		20.00
Series 1 Wax Pack (10):		57.00
Series 1 Wax Box (24):		985.00
Series 2 Wax Pack (10):		87.00
Series 2 Wax Box (24):		1500.
Series 3 Wax Pack (10):		315.00
Series 3 Wax Box (24):		5200.
1	AFC rushing leaders (Floyd Little, Larry Csonka)	3.50
2	NFC rushing leaders (John Brockington, Steve Owens, Willie Ellison)	1.00
3	AFC passing leaders (Bob Griese, Len Dawson)	2.00
4	NFC passing leaders (Roger Staubach, Bill Kilmer)	4.00
5	AFC receiving leaders (Fred Biletnikoff, Otis Taylor, Randy Vataha)	1.00
6	NFC receiving leaders (Bob Tucker, Ted Kwalick, Harold Jackson, Roy Jefferson)	1.00
7	AFC scoring leaders (Garo Yepremian, Jan Stenerud)	1.50
8	NFC scoring leaders (Curt Knight, Errol Mann, Bruce Gossett)	1.00
9	Jim Kiick	1.25
10	Otis Taylor	1.25
11	Bobby Joe Green	.50
12	Ken Ellis	.50
13	*John Riggins*	32.00
14	Dave Parks	.50
15	John Hadl	1.50
16	Ron Hornsby	.50
17	Chip Myers	.50
18	Bill Kilmer	1.50
19	Fred Hoaglin	.50
20	Carl Eller	1.50
21	Steve Zabel	.50
22	*Vic Washington*	.75
23	Len St. Jean	.50
24	Bill Thompson	.50
25	*Steve Owens*	2.50
26	*Ken Burrough*	1.50
27	Mike Clark	.50
28	Willie Brown	3.00
29	Checklist 1-132	6.00
30	Marlin Briscoe	.50
31	Jerry Logan	.50
32	Donny Anderson	.50
33	Rich McGeorge	.50
34	Charlie Durkee	.50
35	Willie Lanier	4.00
36	Chris Farasopoulos	.50
37	Ronnie Shanklin	.50
38	*Forrest Blue*	1.25
39	Ken Reaves	.50
40	Roman Gabriel	2.00
41	Mac Percival	.50
42	Lem Barney	3.00
43	Nick Buoniconti	1.75
44	Charlie Gogolak	.50
45	*Bill Bradley*	2.00
46	Joe Jones	.50
47	Dave Williams	.50
48	Pete Athas	.50
49	Virgil Carter	.50
50	Floyd Little	2.00
51	Curt Knight	.50
52	Bobby Maples	.50
53	Charlie West	.50
54	*Marv Hubbard*	1.25
55	*Archie Manning*	15.00
56	*Jim O'Brien*	1.00
57	Wayne Patrick	.50
58	Ken Bowman	.50
59	Roger Wehrli	.50
60	Charlie Sanders	1.00
61	Jan Stenerud	2.00
62	Willie Ellison	.50
63	Walt Sweeney	.50
64	Ron Smith	.50
65	*Jim Plunkett*	15.00
66	Herb Adderly	2.50
67	*Mike Reid*	4.00
68	*Richard Caster*	1.50
69	Dave Wilcox	.50
70	Leroy Kelly	2.50
71	*Bob Lee*	1.00
72	Verlon Biggs	.50
73	Henry Allison	.50
74	Steve Ramsey	.50
75	Claude Humphrey	.50
76	*Bob Grim*	1.00
77	John Fuqua	.50
78	Ken Houston	4.00
79	Checklist 133-263	4.50
80	Bob Griese	8.00
81	Lance Rentzel	.50
82	*Ed Podolak*	1.75
83	Ike Hill	.50
84	George Farmer	.50
85	*John Brockington*	4.00
86	Jim Otto	2.00
87	Richard Neal	.50
88	Jim Hart	1.50
89	Bob Babich	.50
90	Gene Washington (S.F.)	.75
91	John Zook	.50
92	Bobby Duhon	.50
93	*Ted Hendricks*	20.00
94	Rockne Freitas	.50
95	Larry Brown	1.50
96	Mike Phipps	1.00
97	Julius Adams	.50
98	Dick Anderson	.50
99	Fred Willis	.50
100	Joe Namath	35.00
101	*L.C. Greenwood*	20.00
102	Mark Nordquist	.50
103	Robert Holmes	.50
104	*Ron Yary*	3.50
105	Bob Hayes	1.75
106	*Lyle Alzado*	14.00
107	Bob Berry	.50
108	*Phil Villapiano*	2.00
109	Dave Elmendorf	.50
110	Gale Sayers	22.00
111	Jim Tyrer	.50
112	*Mel Gray*	4.00
113	Gerry Philbin	.50
114	Bob James	.50
115	Garo Yepremian	1.00
116	Dave Robinson	.50
117	Jeff Queen	.50
118	Norm Snead	.50
119	Jim Nance (IA)	.50
120	Terry Bradshaw (IA)	15.00
121	Jim Kiick (IA)	.50
122	Roger Staubach (IA)	20.00
123	Bo Scott (IA)	.50
124	John Brodie (IA)	2.00
125	Rick Volk (IA)	.50
126	John Riggins (IA)	8.00
127	Bubba Smith (IA)	1.75
128	Roman Gabriel (IA)	1.00
129	Calvin Hill (IA)	.50
130	Bill Nelsen (IA)	.50
131	Tom Matte (IA)	.50
132	Bob Griese (IA)	3.50
133	AFC semi-final	1.50
134	NFC semi-final (Duane Thomas)	1.50
135	AFC semi-final (Don Nottingham)	1.50
136	NFC semi-final	1.50
137	AFC Championship	2.50
138	NFC Championship	2.50
139	Super Bowl	5.00
140	Larry Csonka	7.00
141	Rick Volk	.75
142	Roy Jefferson	.75
143	*Raymond Chester*	1.50
144	Bobby Douglass	.75
145	Bob Lilly	4.00
146	Harold Jackson	2.00
147	Pete Gogolak	.75
148	Art Malone	.75
149	Ed Flanagan	.75
150	Terry Bradshaw	45.00
151	MacArthur Lane	.75
152	Jack Snow	.75
153	Al Beauchamp	.75
154	Bob Anderson	.75
155	*Ted Kwalick*	1.75
156	*Dan Pastorini*	2.00
157	*Emmitt Thomas*	1.50
158	*Randy Vataha*	1.25
159	Al Atkinson	.75
160	O.J. Simpson	15.00
161	Jackie Smith	1.00
162	Ernie Kellerman	.75
163	Dennis Partee	.75
164	Jake Kupp	.75
165	Johnny Unitas	20.00
166	Clint Jones	.75
167	Paul Warfield	6.00
168	Roland McDole	.75
169	Daryle Lamonica	2.25
170	Dick Butkus	10.00
171	Jim Butler	.75
172	Mike McCoy	.75
173	Dave Smith	.75
174	Greg Landry	1.50
175	Tom Dempsey	.75
176	John Charles	.75
177	Bobby Bell	2.50
178	Don Horn	.75
179	Bob Trumpy	2.00
180	Duane Thomas	1.25
181	Merlin Olsen	3.50
182	Dave Herman	.75
183	Jim Nance	.75
184	Pete Beathard	.75
185	Bob Tucker	.75
186	*Gene Upshaw*	14.00
187	Bo Scott	.75
188	*J.D. Hill*	1.25
189	Bruce Gossett	.75
190	Bubba Smith	3.50
191	Edd Hargett	1.00
192	Gary Garrison	.75
193	Jake Scott	1.25
194	Fred Cox	.75
195	Sonny Jurgensen	4.50

196 *Greg Brezina* 1.00
197 Ed O'Bradovich .75
198 John Rowser .75
199 Altie Taylor .75
200 *Roger Staubach* 160.00
201 *Leroy Keyes* 1.50
202 Garland Boyette .75
203 Tom Beer .75
204 Buck Buchanan 2.50
205 Larry Wilson 2.50
206 *Scott Hunter* 1.00
207 Ron Johnson .75
208 Sam Brunelli .75
209 Deacon Jones 2.50
210 Fred Biletnikoff 5.00
211 Bill Nelson .75
212 George Nock .75
213 Dan Abramowicz .75
214 Irv Goode .75
215 *Isiah Robertson* 2.00
216 Tom Matte .75
217 Pat Fischer .75
218 Gene Washington .75
219 Paul Robinson .75
220 John Brodie 4.00
221 *Manny Fernandez* 2.00
222 Errol Mann .75
223 Dick Gordon .75
224 Calvin Hill 1.75
225 Fran Tarkenton 16.00
226 Jim Turner .75
227 Jim Mitchell .75
228 Pete Liske .75
229 Carl Garrett .75
230 Joe Greene 17.00
231 Gale Gillingham .75
232 *Norm Bulaich* 1.25
233 Spider Lockhart .75
234 Ken Willard .75
235 George Blanda 11.00
236 Wayne Mulligan .75
237 Dave Lewis .75
238 Dennis Shaw .75
239 Fair Hooker .75
240 *Larry Little* 17.00
241 Mike Garrett 1.00
242 Glen Ray Hines .75
243 Myron Pottios .75
244 *Charlie Joiner* 25.00
245 Len Dawson 6.50
246 W.K. Hicks .75
247 Les Josephson .75
248 Lance Alworth 6.00
249 Frank Nunley .75
250 Mel Farr (IA) .75
251 Johnny Unitas (IA) 8.00
252 George Farmer (IA) .75
253 Duane Thomas (IA) .75
254 John Hadl (IA) 1.00
255 Vic Washington (IA) .75
256 Don Horn (IA) .75
257 L.C. Greenwood (IA) 3.00
258 Bob Lee (IA) .75
259 Larry Csonka (IA) 3.50
260 Mike McCoy (IA) .75
261 Greg Landry (IA) .75
262 Ray May (IA) .75
263 Bobby Douglass (IA) .75
264 Charlie Sanders (AP) 22.00
265 Ron Yary (AP) 27.50
266 Rayfield Wright (AP) 20.00
267 Larry Little (AP) 40.00
268 John Niland (AP) 20.00
269 Forrest Blue (AP) 20.00
270 Otis Taylor (AP) 20.00
271 Paul Warfield (AP) 60.00
272 Bob Griese (AP) 75.00
273 John Brockington (AP) 20.00
274 Floyd Little (AP) 27.00
275 Garo Yepremian (AP) 30.00
276 Jerrel Wilson (AP) 20.00
277 Carl Eller (AP) 30.00
278 Bubba Smith (AP) 40.00
279 Alan Page (AP) 40.00
280 Bob Lilly (AP) 45.00
281 Ted Hendricks (AP) 45.00
282 Dave Wilcox (AP) 20.00
283 Willie Lanier (AP) 27.50
284 Jim Johnson (AP) 20.00
285 Willie Brown (AP) 27.50
286 Bill Bradley (AP) 20.00
287 Ken Houston (AP) 27.50
288 Mel Farr 20.00
289 Kermit Alexander 20.00
290 *John Gilliam* 25.00
291 *Steve Spurrier* 100.00
292 Walter Johnson 20.00
293 Jack Pardee 20.00
294 Checklist 264-351 80.00
295 Winston Hill 20.00
296 Hugo Hollas 20.00
297 *Ray May* 25.00
298 Jim Bakken 20.00
299 Larry Carwell 20.00
300 Alan Page 50.00
301 Walt Garrison 25.00
302 Mike Lucci 20.00
303 Nemiah Wilson 20.00
304 Carroll Dale 20.00
305 Jim Kanicki 20.00
306 Preston Pearson 25.00
307 Lemar Parrish 20.00
308 Earl Morrall 22.00
309 Tommy Nobis 25.00
310 Rich Jackson 20.00
311 Doug Cunningham 20.00
312 Jim Marsalis 20.00
313 Jim Beirne 20.00
314 Tom McNeill 20.00
315 Milt Morin 20.00
316 *Rayfield Wright* 24.00
317 Jerry LeVias 20.00
318 *Travis Williams* 27.50
319 Edgar Chandler 20.00
320 Bob Wallace 20.00
321 Delles Howell 20.00
322 Emerson Boozer 20.00
323 *George Atkinson* 22.00
324 Mike Montler 20.00
325 Randy Johnson 20.00
326 Mike Curtis 20.00
327 Miller Farr 20.00
328 Horst Muhlmann 20.00
329 *John Niland* 25.00
330 Andy Russell 20.00
331 Mercury Morris 35.00
332 Jim Johnson 20.00
333 Jerrel Wilson 20.00
334 Charley Taylor 40.00
335 Dick LeBeau 20.00
336 Jim Marshall 25.00
337 Tom Mack 25.00
338 Steve Spurrier (IA) 50.00
339 Floyd Little (IA) 25.00
340 Len Dawson (IA) 40.00
341 Dick Butkus (IA) 70.00
342 Larry Brown (IA) 27.50
343 Joe Namath (IA) 335.00
344 Jim Turner (IA) 20.00
345 Doug Cunningham (IA) 20.00
346 Edd Hargett (IA) 20.00
347 Steve Owens (IA) 21.00
348 George Blanda (IA) 45.00
349 Ed Podolak (IA) 20.00
350 Rich Jackson (IA) 20.00
351 Ken Willard (IA) 35.00

1973 Topps

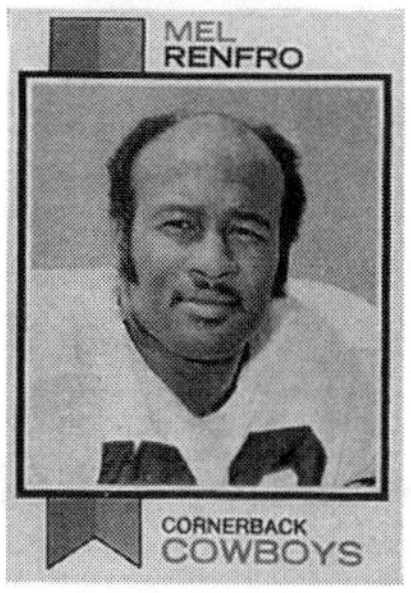

This issue might have been Topps' most important of the decade for a number of reasons. The 1973 set was Topps' first of 10 consecutive football sets at 528 cards, and its first major set that was issued all at once instead of in a series. This coincides with its cutback in baseball cards (787 to 660) and emphasis on football and basketball; it also signaled the end of Topps' high-series release. Subsets in the 1973 release include the usual statistical leaders and playoffs, plus three cards depicting childhood photos of NFL stars. Rookies in this set include Ken Anderson, Lydell Mitchell, Franco Harris, Jack Ham, Art Shell, Ken Riley, Jack Tatum, Dan Dierdorf, Jim Langer, Jack Youngblood and Ken Stabler. Though he went on to play several more years with the Rams and Jets, Joe Namath's final regular-issue card appears in this set. Like Earl Campbell several years later, he apparently was unable to reach a contract agreement after this season. One other item of note: this set has a few of the most unique player names of any football issue: Chip Glass, Happy Feller, and the immortal Remi Prudhomme.

NM
Complete Set (528): 425.00
Common Player: .40
Wax Pack (10+ BTC): 82.00
Wax Box (24): 1450.
Wax Pack (15+ BTC): 105.00
Wax Box (24): 1900.
1 Rushing Leaders (Larry Brown, O.J. Simpson) 6.00
2 Passing Leaders (Norm Snead, Earl Morrall) .75
3 Receiving Leaders (Harold Jackson, Fred Biletnikoff) 1.00
4 Scoring Leaders (Chester Marcol, Bobby Howfield) .75
5 Interception Leaders (Bill Bradley, Mike Sensibaugh) .75
6 Punting Leaders (Dave Chapple, Jerrell Wilson) .75
7 Bob Trumpy 1.25
8 Mel Tom .40
9 Clarence Ellis .40
10 John Niland .40
11 Randy Jackson .40
12 Greg Landry 1.00
13 Cid Edwards .40
14 Phil Olsen .40
15 Terry Bradshaw 25.00
16 *Al Cowlings* 2.00
17 Walker Gillette .40
18 Bob Atkins .40
19 *Diron Talbert* 1.00
20 *Jim Johnson* 1.00
21 Howard Twilley .40
22 Dick Enderle .40
23 Wayne Colman .40
24 John Schmitt .40
25 George Blanda 7.50
26 Milt Morin .40
27 Mike Current .40
28 *Rex Kern* .60
29 MacArthur Lane .40
30 Alan Page 3.00
31 Randy Vataha .40
32 Jim Kearney .40
33 Steve Smith .40
34 *Ken Anderson* 20.00
35 Calvin Hill 1.00
36 Andy Maurer .40
37 Joe Taylor .40
38 Deacon Jones 2.50
39 Mike Weger .40
40 Roy Gerela .40
41 Les Josephson .40
42 Dave Washington .40
43 *Bill Curry* 1.00
44 Fred Heron .40
45 John Brodie 4.00
46 Roy Winston .40
47 Mike Bragg .40
48 Mercury Morris 1.25
49 Jim Files .40
50 Gene Upshaw 3.50
51 Hugo Hollas .40
52 Rod Sherman .40
53 Ron Snidow .40
54 Steve Tannen .40
55 Jim Carter .40
56 *Lydell Mitchell* 3.00
57 *Jack Rudnay* .60
58 Halvor Hagen .40
59 Tom Dempsey .40
60 Fran Tarkenton 15.00
61 Lance Alworth 3.50
62 Vern Holland .40
63 Steve DeLong .40
64 Art Malone .40
65 Isiah Robertson .40
66 Jerry Rush .40
67 Bryant Salter .40
68 Checklist 1-132 4.00
69 J.D. Hill .40
70 Forrest Blue .40
71 Myron Pottios .40
72 *Norm Thompson* .60
73 Paul Robinson .40
74 Larry Grantham .40
75 Manny Fernandez .40
76 Kent Nix .40
77 *Art Shell* 20.00
78 George Saimes .40
79 Don Cockroft .40
80 Bob Tucker .40
81 *Don McCauley* 1.00
82 Bob Brown .40
83 Larry Carwell .40
84 Mo Moorman .40
85 John Gilliam .40
86 Wade Key .40
87 Ross Brupbacher .40
88 Dave Lewis .40
89 *Franco Harris* 50.00
90 Tom Mack .40
91 Mike Tilleman .40
92 Carl Mauck .40
93 Larry Hand .40
94 Dave Foley .40
95 Frank Nunley .40
96 John Charles .40
97 Jim Bakken .40
98 Pat Fischer .40
99 Randy Rasmussen .40
100 Larry Csonka 5.00
101 *Mike Siani* .75
102 Tom Roussel .40
103 *Clarence Scott* .75
104 Charlie Johnson .60
105 Rick Volk .40
106 Willie Young .40
107 Emmitt Thomas .40
108 Jon Morris .40
109 Clarence Williams .40
110 Rayfield Wright .40
111 Norm Bulaich .40
112 Mike Eischeid .40
113 Speedy Thomas .40
114 Glen Holloway .40
115 *Jack Ham* 25.00
116 Jim Nettles .40
117 Errol Mann .40
118 John Mackey 2.00
119 George Kunz .40
120 Bob James .40
121 Garland Boyette .40
122 Mel Phillips .40
123 Johnny Roland .40
124 Doug Swift .40
125 Archie Manning 2.50
126 Dave Herman .40
127 Carleton Oats .40
128 Bill Van Heusen .40
129 Rich Jackson .40
130 Len Hauss .40
131 *Billy Parks* .75
132 Ray May .40
133 NFC Semi-Final (Roger Staubach) 3.00
134 AFC Semi-Final 1.50
135 NFC Semi-Final .75
136 AFC Semi-Final (Bob Griese, Larry Csonka) 2.00
137 NFC Championship (Bill Kilmer, Larry Brown) 1.50
138 AFC Championship .75
139 Super Bowl 1.50
140 *Dwight White* 2.00
141 Jim Marsalis .40
142 Doug Van Horn .40
143 Al Matthews .40
144 Bob Windsor .40
145 *Dave Hampton* .75
146 Horst Muhlmann .40
147 *Wally Hilgenberg* 1.00
148 Ron Smith .40
149 *Coy Bacon* 1.50
150 Winston Hill .40
151 *Ron Jessie* 1.25
152 Ken Iman .40
153 Ron Saul .40
154 *Jim Braxton* .75
155 Bubba Smith 3.00
156 Gary Cuozzo .40
157 Charlie Krueger .40
158 *Tim Foley* .75
159 Lee Roy Jordan 2.00
160 Bob Brown .40
161 Margene Adkins .40
162 Ron Widby .40
163 Jim Houston .40
164 Joe Dawkins .40
165 L.C. Greenwood 3.50
166 Richmond Flowers .40
167 *Curley Culp* 2.00
168 Len St. Jean .40
169 Walter Rock .40
170 Bill Bradley .40
171 *Ken Riley* 2.50
172 Rich Coady .40
173 Don Hansen .40
174 Lionel Aldridge .40
175 Don Maynard 3.00
176 Dave Osborn .40
177 Jim Bailey .40
178 John Pitts .40
179 Dave Parks .40
180 *Chester Marcol* .75
181 Len Rohde .40
182 Jeff Staggs .40
183 Gene Hickerson .40
184 Charlie Evans .40
185 Mel Renfro 1.00
186 Marvin Upshaw .40
187 George Atkinson .40
188 Norm Evans .40
189 Steve Ramsey .40
190 Dave Chapple .40
191 Gerry Mullins .40
192 John Didion .40
193 Bob Gladieux .40
194 Don Hultz .40
195 Mike Lucci .40
196 John Wilbur .40
197 George Farmer .40
198 *Tommy Casanova* 1.25
199 Russ Washington .40
200 Claude Humphrey .40
201 Pat Hughes .40
202 Zeke Moore .40
203 Chip Glass .40
204 Glenn Ressler .40
205 Willie Ellison .40
206 John Leypoldt .40
207 Johnny Fuller .40
208 Bill Hayhoe .40
209 Ed Bell .40
210 Willie Brown 2.00
211 Carl Eller 1.50
212 Mark Nordquist .40
213 Larry Willingham .40
214 Nick Buoniconti 1.75
215 John Hadl 1.25
216 *Jethro Pugh* 1.50
217 Leroy Mitchell .40
218 Billy Newsome .40
219 John McMakin .40
220 Larry Brown 1.25
221 Clarence Scott .40
222 Paul Naumoff .40
223 Ted Fritsch .40
224 Checklist 133-264 4.00
225 Dan Pastorini 1.00
226 Joe Beauchamp .40
227 Pat Matson .40
228 Tony McGee .40
229 Mike Phipps .40
230 Harold Jackson 1.25
231 Willie Williams .40
232 Spike Jones .40
233 Jim Tyrer .40
234 Roy Hilton .40
235 Phil Villapiano .40
236 Charley Taylor 4.00
237 Malcolm Snider .40
238 Vic Washington .40
239 Grady Alderman .40
240 Dick Anderson .40
241 Ron Yankowski .40
242 Billy Masters .40
243 Herb Adderly 2.25
244 David Ray .40
245 John Riggins 9.00
246 *Mike Wagner* 2.00
247 Don Morrison .40
248 Earl McCullouch .40
249 Dennis Wirgowski .40
250 Chris Hanburger .40
251 *Pat Sullivan* 2.00
252 Walt Sweeney .40
253 Willie Alexander .40
254 Doug Dressler .40
255 Walter Johnson .40
256 Ron Hornsby .40
257 Ben Hawkins .40
258 Donnie Green .40
259 Fred Hoaglin .40
260 Jerrill Wilson .40
261 Horace Jones .40
262 Woody Peoples .40
263 Jim Hill .40
264 John Fuqua .40
265 Childhood Photo: (Donny Anderson) .50
266 Childhood Photo: (Roman Gabriel) 1.00
267 Childhood Photo: (Mike Garrett) .50
268 Rufus Mayes .60
269 Chip Myrtle .40
270 *Bill Stanfill* 1.00
271 Clint Jones .40
272 Miller Farr .40
273 Harry Schuh .40
274 Bob Hayes 1.25
275 Bobby Douglass .40
276 Gus Hollomon .40
277 Del Williams .40
278 Julius Adams .40
279 Herman Weaver .40
280 Joe Greene 6.00
281 Wes Chesson .40
282 Charlie Harraway .40
283 Paul Guidry .40
284 Terry Owens .40
285 Jan Stenerud 1.50
286 Pete Athas .40
287 Dale Lindsey .40
288 *Jack Tatum* 7.00
289 Floyd Little 1.50
290 Bob Johnson .40
291 Tommy Hart .40
292 Tom Mitchell .40
293 *Walt Patulski* .90
294 Jim Skaggs .40
295 Bob Griese 7.00
296 Mike McCoy .40
297 Mel Gray 1.00
298 Bobby Bryant .40
299 *Blaine Nye* .60
300 Dick Butkus 6.00
301 Charlie Cowan .40
302 Mark Lomas .40
303 Josh Ashton .40
304 Happy Feller .40
305 Ronnie Shanklin .40
306 Wayne Rasmussen .40
307 Jerry Smith .40
308 Ken Reaves .40
309 Ron East .40
310 Otis Taylor 1.00
311 John Garlington .40
312 Lyle Alzado 3.50
313 Remi Prudhomme .40
314 Cornelius Johnson .40
315 Lemar Parrish .40
316 Jim Kiick .40
317 Steve Zabel .40
318 Alden Roche .40
319 Tom Blanchard .40
320 Fred Biletnikoff 4.00
321 Ralph Neely .40
322 *Dan Dierdorf* 20.00
323 Richard Caster .40
324 Gene Howard .40
325 Elvin Bethea .40
326 Carl Garrett .40
327 Ron Billingsley .40
328 Charlie West .40
329 Tom Neville .40
330 Ted Kwalick .40
331 Rudy Redmond .40
332 Henry Davis .40
333 John Zook .40
334 Jim Turner .40
335 Len Dawson 3.50
336 *Bob Chandler* 1.25
337 Al Beauchamp .40
338 Tom Matte .40
339 Paul Laaveg .40
340 Ken Ellis .40
341 *Jim Langer* 13.00
342 Ron Porter .40
343 *Jack Youngblood* 15.00
344 Cornell Green .40
345 Marv Hubbard .40
346 Bruce Taylor .40
347 Sam Havrilak .40
348 Walt Sumner .40
349 Steve O'Neal .40
350 Ron Johnson .40
351 Rockne Freitas .40
352 Larry Stallings .40
353 Jim Cadile .40
354 Ken Burrough .40
355 Jim Plunkett 4.00
356 Dave Long .40
357 Ralph Anderson .40
358 Checklist 265-396 4.00
359 Gene Washington .40
360 Dave Wilcox .40
361 Paul Smith .40
362 Alvin Wyatt .40
363 Charlie Smith .40
364 Royce Berry .40
365 Dave Elmendorf .40
366 Scott Hunter .40
367 *Bob Kuechenberg* 3.00
368 Pete Gogolak .40
369 Dave Edwards .40
370 Lem Barney 2.50
371 Verlon Biggs .40
372 *John Reaves* .60
373 Ed Podolak .40
374 Chris Farasopoulos .40
375 Gary Garrison .40
376 Tom Funchess .40
377 Bobby Joe Green .40
378 Don Brumm .40
379 Jim O'Brien .40
380 Paul Krause 1.25
381 Leroy Kelly 2.00
382 Ray Mansfield .40
383 Dan Abramowicz .40
384 *John Outlaw* .60
385 Tommy Nobis 1.50
386 Tom Domres .40
387 Ken Willard .40
388 Mike Stratton .40
389 Fred Dryer 3.00
390 Jake Scott .40
391 Rich Houston .40
392 Virgil Carter .40
393 Tody Smith .40
394 Ernie Calloway .40
395 Charlie Sanders .40
396 Fred Willis .40
397 Curt Knight .40
398 Nemiah Wilson .40
399 Carroll Dale .40
400 Joe Namath 30.00
401 Wayne Mulligan .40
402 Jim Harrison .40
403 Tim Rossovich .40
404 David Lee .40
405 Frank Pitts .40
406 Jim Marshall 1.50
407 Bob Brown .40
408 John Rowser .40
409 Mike Montler .40
410 Willie Lanier 2.00
411 Bill Bell .40
412 Cedrick Hardman .40
413 Bob Anderson .40
414 *Earl Morrall* 1.25
415 Ken Houston 1.75
416 Jack Snow .40
417 Dick Cunningham .40
418 Greg Larson .40
419 Mike Bass .40
420 Mike Reid 2.00
421 Walt Garrison .40
422 Pete Liske .40
423 Jim Yarbrough .40
424 Rich McGeorge .40
425 Bobby Howfield .40
426 Pete Banaszak .40
427 Willie Holman .40
428 Dale Hackbart .40
429 Fair Hooker .40
430 Ted Hendricks 4.00
431 Mike Garrett .40
432 Glen Ray Hines .40
433 Fred Cox .40
434 Bobby Walden .40
435 Bobby Bell 2.00
436 David Rowe .40
437 Bob Berry .40
438 Bill Thompson .40
439 Jim Beirne .40
440 Larry Little 3.00
441 Rocky Thompson .40
442 Brig Owens .40
443 Richard Neal .40
444 Al Nelson .40
445 Chip Myers .40
446 Ken Bowman .40
447 Jim Purnell .40
448 Altie Taylor .40
449 Linzy Cole .40
450 Bob Lilly 4.00
451 Charlie Ford .40
452 Milt Sunde .40
453 Doug Wyatt .40
454 *Don Nottingham* .75
455 Johnny Unitas 18.00
456 *Frank Lewis* 1.50
457 Roger Wehrli .40
458 Jim Cheyunski .40
459 *Jerry Sherk* 1.00
460 Gene Washington .40
461 Jim Otto 2.25
462 Ed Budde .40
463 Jim Mitchell .40
464 Emerson Boozer .40
465 Garo Yepremian .40
466 Pete Duranko .40
467 Charlie Joiner 6.00
468 Spider Lockhart .40
469 Marty Domres .40
470 John Brockington 1.00
471 Ed Flanagan .40
472 Roy Jefferson .40
473 Julian Fagan .40
474 Bill Brown .40
475 Roger Staubach 40.00
476 Jan White .40
477 Pat Holmes .40
478 Bob DeMarco .40
479 Merlin Olsen 3.50
480 Andy Russell .40
481 Steve Spurrier 8.00
482 Nate Ramsey .40
483 Dennis Partee .40
484 Jerry Simmons .40
485 Donny Anderson .40
486 Ralph Baker .40
487 *Ken Stabler* 60.00
488 Ernie McMillan .40
489 Ken Burrow .40
490 *Jack Gregory* .60
491 Larry Seiple .40
492 Mick Tingelhoff .40
493 Craig Morton 1.50
494 Cecil Turner .40
495 Steve Owens .50
496 Richie Harris .40
497 Buck Buchanan 2.00
498 Checklist 397-528 4.00
499 Bill Kilmer 1.50
500 O.J. Simpson 15.00
501 Bruce Gossett .40
502 Art Thoms .40
503 Larry Kaminski .40
504 Larry Smith .40
505 Bruce Van Dyke .40
506 Alvin Reed .40
507 Delles Howell .40
508 Leroy Keyes .40
509 Bo Scott .40
510 Ron Yary 1.00
511 Paul Warfield 5.00
512 Mac Percival .40
513 Essex Johnson .40
514 Jackie Smith 1.00
515 Norm Snead .40
516 Charlie Stukes .40
517 *Reggie Rucker* 1.50
518 Bill Sandeman .40
519 Mel Farr .40
520 Raymond Chester .40
521 *Fred Carr* 1.00
522 Jerry LeVias .40
523 Jim Strong .40
524 Roland McDole .40
525 Dennis Shaw .40
526 Dave Manders .40
527 Skip Vanderbundt .40
528 *Mike Sensibaugh* 1.25

1973 Topps Team Checklists

This was the first time Topps issued separate team checklists in its 528-card sets, a practice that would end with the 1974 set. The cards showed an anonymous action shot at the top of the card, with a Topps logo in a football helmet facing the team name. The checklist was beneath all that, and showed the card number, name, uniform number and position (as it would in 1974). Card backs carried pieces to a puzzle of either Larry Brown or Joe Namath; or they carried a message that read, "Collect all 26 Team Checklists and complete your Joe Namath & Larry Brown Puzzles."

NM
Complete Set (26): 35.00
Common Team: 1.50
1 Atlanta Falcons 1.50
2 Baltimore Colts 1.50
3 Buffalo Bills 1.50
4 Chicago Bears 1.50
5 Cincinnati Bengals 1.50
6 Cleveland Browns 1.50
7 Dallas Cowboys 1.50
8 Denver Broncos 1.50
9 Detroit Lions 1.50
10 Green Bay Packers 1.50
11 Houston Oilers 1.50
12 Kansas City Chiefs 1.50
13 Los Angeles Rams 1.50
14 Miami Dolphins 1.50
15 Minnesota Vikings 1.50
16 New England Patriots 1.50
17 New Orleans Saints 1.50
18 New York Giants 1.50
19 New York Jets 1.50
20 Oakland Raiders 1.50
21 Philadelphia Eagles 1.50
22 Pittsburgh Steelers 1.50
23 St. Louis Cardinals 1.50
24 San Diego Chargers 1.50
25 San Francisco 49ers 1.50
26 Washington Redskins 1.50

1974 Topps

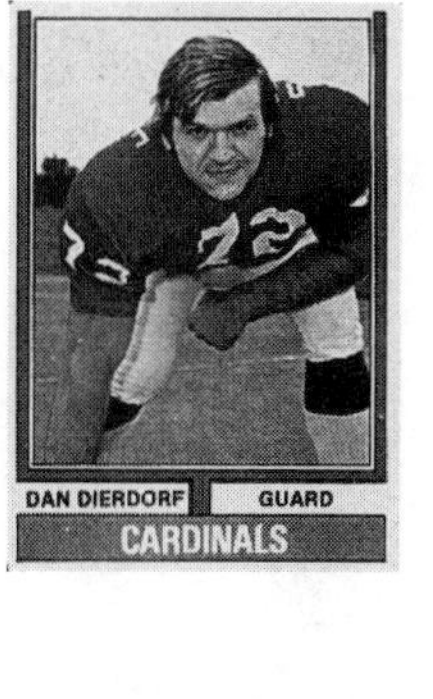

This was Topps' second 528-card set, and marked the second and last time team checklists would be issued unnumbered and separate from the set. Rookies in this set include Ahmad Rashad, Greg Pruitt, Chuck Foreman, Harold Carmichael, Ray Guy, John Matuszak, Conrad Dobler, Ed Marinaro, Darryl Stingley, Lynn Dickey, Billy Joe DuPree, D.D. Lewis, John Hannah, Terry Metcalf, Joe Ferguson and Bert Jones. In addition, this set features the last regularly-issued card of Johnny Unitas. All Pro cards showing individual players are found on cards 121-144. Other subsets include statistical leader and playoff cards. There is one error in the set, on card #265, Bob Lee. The back of the card lists his team as the Atlanta Hawks instead of the Falcons.

	NM
Complete Set (528):	325.00
Common Player:	.35
Wax Pack (10+ BTC):	32.50
Wax Box (24):	560.00

		NM
1	O.J. Simpson	20.00
2	Blaine Nye	.35
3	Don Hansen	.35
4	Ken Bowman	.35
5	Carl Eller	1.00
6	Jerry Smith	.35
7	Ed Podolak	.35
8	Mel Gray	.35
9	Pat Matson	.35
10	Floyd Little	1.25
11	Frank Pitts	.35
12	*Vern Den Herder*	.75
13	John Fuqua	.35
14	Jack Tatum	1.50
15	Winston Hill	.35
16	John Beasley	.35
17	David Lee	.35
18	Rich Coady	.35
19	Ken Willard	.35
20	Coy Bacon	.35
21	Ben Hawkins	.35
22	Paul Guidry	.35
23	Norm Snead	.75
24	Jim Yarbrough	.35
25	*Jack Reynolds*	2.25
26	Josh Ashton	.35
27	Donnie Green	.35
28	Bob Hayes	1.00
29	John Zook	.35
30	Bobby Bryant	.35
31	Scott Hunter	.35
32	Dan Dierdorf	5.00
33	Curt Knight	.35
34	*Elmo Wright*	.60
35	Essex Johnson	.35
36	Walt Sumner	.35
37	Marv Montgomery	.35
38	Tim Foley	.35
39	Mike Siani	.35
40	Joe Greene	6.00
41	Bobby Howfield	.35
42	Del Williams	.35
43	Don McCauley	.35
44	Randy Jackson	.35
45	Ron Smith	.35
46	Gene Washington	.50
47	Po James	.35
48	Soloman Freelon	.35
49	Bob Windsor	.35
50	John Hadl	1.00
51	Greg Larson	.35
52	Steve Owens	.35
53	Jim Cheyunski	.35
54	Rayfield Wright	.35
55	Dave Hampton	.35
56	Ron Widby	.35
57	Milt Sunde	.35
58	Bill Kilmer	1.25
59	Bobby Bell	1.50
60	Jim Bakken	.50
61	Rufus Mayes	.35
62	Vic Washington	.35
63	Gene Washington	.35
64	Clarence Scott	.35
65	Gene Upshaw	2.00
66	Larry Seiple	.35
67	John McMakin	.35
68	Ralph Baker	.35
69	Lydell Mitchell	1.00
70	Archie Manning	1.75
71	George Farmer	.35
72	Ron East	.35
73	Al Nelson	.35
74	Pat Hughes	.35
75	Fred Willis	.35
76	Larry Walton	.35
77	Tom Neville	.35
78	Ted Kwalick	.35
79	Walt Patulski	.35
80	John Niland	.35
81	Ted Fritsch	.35
82	Paul Krause	1.00
83	Jack Snow	.35
84	Mike Bass	.35
85	Jim Tyrer	.35
86	Ron Yankowski	.35
87	Mike Phipps	.35
88	Al Beauchamp	.35
89	*Riley Odoms*	2.00
90	MacArthur Lane	.35
91	Art Thoms	.35
92	Marlin Briscoe	.35
93	Bruce Van Dyke	.35
94	Tom Myers	.35
95	Calvin Hill	.75
96	Bruce Laird	.35
97	Tony McGee	.35
98	Len Rohde	.35
99	Tom McNeill	.35
100	Delles Howell	.35
101	Gary Garrison	.35
102	Dan Goich	.35
103	Len St. Jean	.35
104	Zeke Moore	.35
105	*Ahmad Rashad*	15.00
106	Mel Renfro	1.00
107	Jim Mitchell	.35
108	Ed Budde	.35
109	Harry Schuh	.35
110	*Greg Pruitt*	4.00
111	Ed Flanagan	.35
112	Larry Stallings	.35
113	*Chuck Foreman*	4.00
114	Royce Berry	.35
115	Gale Gillingham	.35
116	Charlie Johnson	.75
117	Checklist 1-132	2.50
118	Bill Butler	.35
119	Roy Jefferson	.35
120	Bobby Douglass	.35
121	*Harold Carmichael*	15.00
122	George Kuntz (AP)	.35
123	Larry Little (AP)	1.50
124	Forrest Blue (AP)	.35
125	Ron Yary (AP)	.75
126	Tom Mack (AP)	.35
127	Bob Tucker (AP)	.35
128	Paul Warfield (AP)	4.00
129	Fran Tarkenton (AP)	10.00
130	O.J. Simpson (AP)	15.00
131	Larry Csonka (AP)	3.50
132	Bruce Gossett (AP)	.35
133	Bill Stanfill (AP)	.35
134	Alan Page (AP)	2.25
135	Paul Smith (AP)	.35
136	Claude Humphrey (AP)	.35
137	Jack Ham (AP)	7.00
138	Lee Roy Jordan (AP)	1.50
139	Phil Villapiano (AP)	.35
140	Ken Ellis (AP)	.35
141	Willie Brown (AP)	1.25
142	Dick Anderson (AP)	.35
143	Bill Bradley (AP)	.35
144	Jerrel Wilson (AP)	.35
145	Reggie Rucker	.60
146	Marty Domres	.35
147	Bob Kowalkowski	.35
148	*John Matuszak*	4.00
149	*Mike Adamle*	.75
150	Johnny Unitas	16.00
151	Charlie Ford	.35
152	*Bob Klein*	.60
153	Jim Merlo	.35
154	Willie Young	.35
155	Donny Anderson	.35
156	Brig Owens	.35
157	Bruce Jarvis	.35
158	Ron Carpenter	.35
159	Don Cockroft	.35
160	Tommy Nobis	1.25
161	Craig Morton	1.25
162	Jon Staggers	.35
163	Mike Eischeid	.35
164	*Jerry Sisemore*	.60
165	Cedric Hardman	.35
166	Bill Thompson	.35
167	Jim Lynch	.35
168	Bob Moore	.35
169	Glen Edwards	.35
170	Mercury Morris	1.00
171	Julius Adams	.35
172	Cotton Speyrer	.35
173	Bill Munson	.35
174	Benny Johnson	.35
175	*Burgess Owens*	.60
176	Cid Edwards	.35
177	Doug Buffone	.35
178	Charlie Cowan	.35
179	Bob Newland	.35
180	Ron Johnson	.35
181	Bob Rowe	.35
182	Len Hauss	.35
183	*Joe DeLamielleure*	2.00
184	*Sherman White*	.75
185	Fair Hooker	.35
186	Nick Mike-Mayer	.35
187	Ralph Neely	.35
188	Rich McGeorge	.35
189	*Ed Marinaro*	4.50
190	Dave Wilcox	.35
191	Joe Owens	.35
192	Bill Van Heusen	.35
193	Jim Kearney	.35
194	*Otis Sistrunk*	3.00
195	Ronnie Shanklin	.35
196	Bill Lenkaitis	.35
197	Tom Drougas	.35
198	Larry Hand	.35
199	Mack Alston	.35
200	Bob Griese	5.00
201	Earlie Thomas	.35
202	Carl Gersbach	.35
203	Jim Harrison	.35
204	Jake Kupp	.35
205	Merlin Olsen	3.50
206	Spider Lockhart	.35
207	Walter Gillette	.35
208	Verlon Biggs	.35
209	Bob James	.35
210	Bob Trumpy	1.00
211	Jerry Sherk	.35
212	Andy Maurer	.35
213	Fred Carr	.35
214	Mick Tingelhoff	.35
215	Steve Spurrier	7.00
216	Richard Harris	.35
217	Charlie Greer	.35
218	Buck Buchanan	2.00
219	*Ray Guy*	10.00
220	Franco Harris	20.00
221	*Darryl Stingley*	2.50
222	Rex Kern	.35
223	Toni Fritsch	.35
224	Levi Johnson	.35
225	Bob Kuechenberg	.60
226	Elvin Bethea	.35
227	*Al Woodall*	.50
228	Terry Owens	.35
229	Bivian Lee	.35
230	Dick Butkus	6.00
231	*Jim Bertelsen*	.60
232	*John Mendenhall*	.50
233	*Conrad Dobler*	2.50
234	J.D. Hill	.35
235	Ken Houston	1.50
236	Dave Lewis	.35
237	John Garlington	.35
238	Bill Sandeman	.35
239	Alden Roche	.35
240	John Gilliam	.35
241	Bruce Taylor	.35
242	Vern Winfield	.35
243	Bobby Maples	.35
244	Wendell Hayes	.35
245	George Blanda	7.00
246	Dwight White	.35
247	Sandy Durko	.35
248	Tom Mitchell	.35
249	Chuck Walton	.35
250	Bob Lilly	4.00
251	Doug Swift	.35
252	*Lynn Dickey*	3.00
253	*Jerome Barkum*	1.50
254	Clint Jones	.35
255	Billy Newsome	.35
256	Bob Asher	.35
257	Joe Scibelli	.35
258	Tom Blanchard	.35
259	Norm Thompson	.35
260	Larry Brown	1.00
261	Paul Seymour	.35
262	Checklist 133-264	2.50
263	*Doug Dieken*	.75
264	Lemar Parrish	.35
265	Bob Lee	.35
266	Bob Brown	.35
267	Roy Winston	.35
268	Randy Beisler	.35
269	Joe Dawkins	.35
270	Tom Dempsey	.35
271	Jack Rudnay	.35
272	Art Shell	6.00
273	Mike Wagner	.75
274	Rick Cash	.35
275	Greg Landry	1.00
276	Glenn Ressler	.35
277	*Billy Joe DuPree*	4.00
278	Norm Evans	.35
279	Billy Parks	.35
280	John Riggins	6.00
281	Lionel Aldridge	.35
282	Steve O'Neal	.35
283	Craig Clemons	.35
284	Willie Williams	.35
285	Isiah Robertson	.35
286	Dennis Shaw	.35
287	Bill Brundige	.35
288	John Leypoldt	.35
289	John DeMarie	.35
290	Mike Reid	1.25
291	Greg Brezina	.35
292	*Willie Buchanon*	1.00
293	Dave Osborn	.35
294	Mel Phillips	.35
295	Haven Moses	.35
296	Wade Key	.35
297	Marvin Upshaw	.35
298	Ray Mansfield	.35
299	Edgar Chandler	.35
300	Marv Hubbard	.35
301	Herman Weaver	.35
302	Jim Bailey	.35
303	*D.D. Lewis*	1.50
304	Ken Burrough	.35
305	Jake Scott	.35
306	Randy Rasmussen	.35
307	Pettis Norman	.35
308	Carl Johnson	.35
309	Joe Taylor	.35
310	Pete Gogolak	.35
311	Tony Baker	.35
312	John Richardson	.35
313	Dave Robinson	.35
314	*Reggie McKenzie*	2.50
315	*Isaac Curtis*	3.00
316	Tom Darden	.35
317	Ken Reaves	.35
318	Malcolm Snider	.35
319	*Jeff Siemon*	1.50
320	Dan Abramowicz	.35
321	Lyle Alzado	2.50
322	John Reaves	.35
323	Morris Stroud	.35
324	Bobby Walden	.35
325	Randy Vataha	.35
326	Nemiah Wilson	.35
327	Paul Naumoff	.35
328	Rushing Leaders (O.J. Simpson, John Brockington)	5.00
329	Passing Leaders (Ken Stabler, Roger Staubach)	4.00
330	Receiving Leaders (Fred Willis, Harold Carmichael)	1.25
331	Scoring Leaders (Roy Gerela, David Ray)	.60
332	Interception Leaders (Dick Anderson, Mike Wagner, Bobby Bryant)	.60
333	Punting Leaders (Jerrell Wilson, Tom Wittum)	.60
334	Dennis Nelson	.35
335	Walt Garrison	.35
336	Tody Smith	.35
337	Ed Bell	.35
338	Bryant Salter	.35
339	Wayne Colman	.35
340	Garo Yepremian	.35
341	Bob Newton	.35
342	*Vince Clements*	.50
343	Ken Iman	.35
344	Jim Tolbert	.35
345	Chris Hanburger	.35
346	Dave Foley	.35
347	Tommy Casanova	.60
348	John James	.35
349	Clarence Williams	.35
350	Leroy Kelly	1.00
351	*Stu Voigt*	.75
352	Skip Vanderbundt	.35
353	Pete Duranko	.35
354	John Outlaw	.35
355	Jan Stenerud	1.25
356	Barry Pearson	.35
357	Brian Dowling	.50
358	Dan Conners	.35
359	Bob Bell	.35
360	Rick Volk	.35
361	Pat Toomay	.35
362	Bob Gresham	.35
363	John Schmitt	.35
364	Mel Rogers	.35
365	Manny Fernandez	.35
366	Ernie Jackson	.35
367	*Gary Huff*	1.00
368	Bob Grim	.35
369	Ernie McMillan	.35
370	Dave Elmendorf	.35
371	Mike Bragg	.35
372	John Skorupan	.35
373	Howard Fest	.35
374	*Jerry Tagge*	1.00
375	Art Malone	.35
376	Bob Babich	.35
377	Jim Marshall	1.25
378	Bob Hoskins	.35
379	Don Zimmerman	.35
380	Ray May	.35
381	Emmitt Thomas	.35
382	Terry Hanratty	.35
383	*John Hannah*	15.00
384	George Atkinson	.35
385	Ted Hendricks	3.00
386	Jim O'Brien	.35
387	Jethro Pugh	.35
388	Elbert Drungo	.35
389	Richard Caster	.35
390	Deacon Jones	2.25
391	Checklist 265-396	2.50
392	Jess Phillips	.35
393	Gary Lyle	.35
394	Jim Files	.35
395	Jim Hart	1.50
396	Dave Chapple	.35
397	Jim Langer	2.50
398	John Wilbur	.35
399	Dwight Harrison	.35
400	John Brockington	.60
401	Ken Anderson	6.50
402	Mike Tilleman	.35
403	Charlie Hall	.35
404	Tommy Hart	.35
405	Norm Bulaich	.35
406	Jim Turner	.35
407	Mo Moorman	.35
408	Ralph Anderson	.35
409	Jim Otto	2.00
410	Andy Russell	.35
411	Glenn Doughty	.35
412	Altie Taylor	.35
413	Marv Bateman	.35
414	Willie Alexander	.35
415	Bill Zapalac	.35
416	Russ Washington	.35
417	Joe Federspiel	.35
418	Craig Cotton	.35
419	Randy Johnson	.35
420	Harold Jackson	1.00
421	Roger Wehrli	.35
422	Charlie Harraway	.35
423	Spike Jones	.35
424	Bob Johnson	.35
425	Mike McCoy	.35
426	Dennis Havig	.35
427	Bob McKay	.35
428	Steve Zabel	.35
429	Horace Jones	.35
430	Jim Johnson	1.00
431	Roy Gerela	.35
432	Tom Graham	.35
433	Curley Culp	.35
434	Ken Mendenhall	.35
435	Jim Plunkett	3.00
436	Julian Fagan	.35
437	Mike Garrett	.35
438	Bobby Joe Green	.35
439	Jack Gregory	.35
440	Charlie Sanders	.35
441	Bill Curry	.35
442	Bob Pollard	.35
443	David Ray	.35
444	*Terry Metcalf*	4.50
445	Pat Fischer	.35
446	Bob Chandler	.35
447	Bill Bergey	1.00
448	Walter Johnson	.35
449	*Charlie Young*	1.50
450	Chester Marcol	.35
451	Ken Stabler	20.00
452	Preston Pearson	.75
453	Mike Current	.35
454	Ron Bolton	.35
455	Mark Lomas	.35
456	Raymond Chester	.35
457	Jerry LeVias	.35
458	Skip Butler	.35
459	*Mike Livingston*	.75
460	AFC Semi-finals	.75
461	NFC Semi-finals (Roger Staubach)	3.00
462	Playoff Championship (Ken Stabler, Fran Tarkenton)	2.50
463	Super Bowl	2.00
464	Wayne Mulligan	.35
465	Horst Muhlmann	.35
466	Milt Morin	.35
467	Don Parish	.35
468	Richard Neal	.35
469	Ron Jessie	.35
470	Terry Bradshaw	20.00
471	Fred Dryer	2.50
472	Jim Carter	.35
473	Ken Burrow	.35
474	*Wally Chambers*	1.00
475	Dan Pastorini	.75
476	Don Morrison	.35
477	Carl Mauck	.35
478	*Larry Cole*	.75
479	Jim Kiick	.35
480	Willie Lanier	1.50
481	Don Herrmann	.35
482	George Hunt	.35
483	Bob Howard	.35
484	Myron Pottios	.35
485	Jackie Smith	1.00
486	Vern Holland	.35
487	Jim Braxton	.35
488	Joe Reed	.35
489	Wally Hilgenberg	.35
490	Fred Biletnikoff	3.50
491	Bob DeMarco	.35
492	Mark Nordquist	.35
493	Larry Brooks	.35
494	Pete Athas	.35
495	Emerson Boozer	.35
496	L.C. Greenwood	1.50
497	Rockne Freitas	.35
498	Checklist 397-528	2.50
499	Joe Schmiesing	.35
500	Roger Staubach	28.00
501	Al Cowlings	1.00
502	*Sam Cunningham*	2.00
503	Dennis Partee	.35
504	John Didion	.35
505	Nick Buoniconti	1.25
506	Carl Garrett	.35
507	Doug Van Horn	.35
508	Jamie Rivers	.35
509	Jack Youngblood	3.50
510	Charley Taylor	2.50
511	Ken Riley	.60
512	*Joe Ferguson*	2.50
513	Bill Lueck	.35
514	Ray Brown	.35
515	Fred Cox	.35
516	Joe Jones	.35
517	Larry Schreiber	.35
518	Dennis Wirgowski	.35
519	Leroy Mitchell	.35
520	Otis Taylor	.75
521	Henry Davis	.35
522	Bruce Barnes	.35
523	Charlie Smith	.35
524	*Bert Jones*	5.00
525	Lem Barney	2.00
526	*John Fitzgerald*	.50
527	Tom Funchess	.35
528	Steve Tannen	.60

1974 Topps Team Checklists

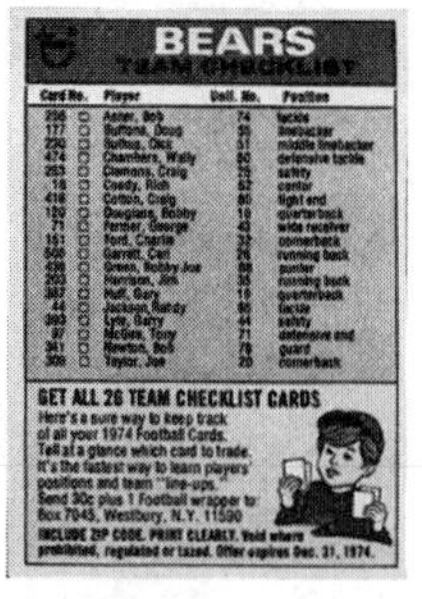

These unnumbered checklists were issued in wax packs of 1974 Topps cards. At the bottom of the card was an ad for a sendaway offer where collectors could buy the entire run of checklists through Topps. The back of the card carried instructions for a game that could be played with football cards. This was the last time Topps would issue team checklists separate from the rest of the set.

		NM
Complete Set (26):		35.00
Common Team:		1.50
(1)	Atlanta Falcons	1.50
(2)	Baltimore Colts	1.50
(3)	Buffalo Bills	1.50
(4)	Chicago Bears	1.50
(5)	Cincinnati Bengals	1.50
(6)	Cleveland Browns	1.50
(7)	Dallas Cowboys	1.50
(8)	Denver Broncos	1.50
(9)	Detroit Lions	1.50
(10)	Green Bay Packers	1.50
(11)	Houston Oilers	1.50
(12)	Kansas City Chiefs	1.50
(13)	Los Angeles Rams	1.50
(14)	Miami Dolphins	1.50
(15)	Minnesota Vikings	1.50
(16)	New England Patriots	1.50
(17)	New Orleans Saints	1.50
(18)	New York Giants	1.50
(19)	New York Jets	1.50
(20)	Oakland Raiders	1.50
(21)	Philadelphia Eagles	1.50
(22)	Pittsburgh Steelers	1.50
(23)	St. Louis Cardinals	1.50
(24)	San Diego Chargers	1.50
(25)	San Francisco 49ers	1.50
(26)	Washington Redskins	1.50

1975 Topps

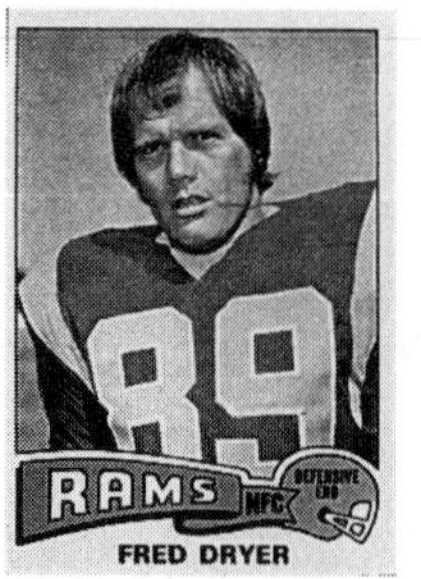

The 528-card 1975 issue was arguably Topps' most attractive offering of the decade. Its clean design and white borders leaves room for the photo, player's name, a pennant with the team name, and the player's position in a green helmet. Most notable for the inclusion of the Dan Fouts rookie card, other rookies in this set are Mel Blount, Rocky Bleier, Drew Pearson, Lynn Swann, James Harris, Otis Armstrong, Lawrence McCutcheon and Joe Theismann. One feature of this set is the larger number of separate All-Pro cards, numbered 201-225. Each shows two star players. Other subsets include Statistical Leaders, Record Breakers, Highlights and Playoff Action. George Blanda has two "honorary" cards in this set, numbers 7 and 8. The first shows him in a black jersey and lists his career highlights on the back; the second shows him in a white Oakland jersey and documents his career statistics. No team checklists were issued for this set.

	NM
Complete Set (528):	325.00
Common Player:	.30
Wax Pack (10):	33.00
Wax Box (36):	840.00

		NM
1	Rushing Leaders (Lawrence McCutcheon, Otis Armstrong)	1.75
2	Passing Leaders (Sonny Jurgensen, Ken Anderson)	1.50
3	Receiving Leaders (Charley Young, Lydell Mitchell)	.60
4	Scoring Leaders (Chester Marcol, Roy Gerela)	.60
5	Interception Leaders (Ray Brown, Emmitt Thomas)	.60
6	Punting Leaders (Tom Blanchard, Ray Guy)	.60
7	George Blanda (highlights, black jersey)	5.00
8	George Blanda (career, white jersey)	5.00
9	Ralph Baker	.30
10	Don Woods	.30
11	Bob Asher	.30
12	*Mel Blount*	25.00
13	Sam Cunningham	.60
14	Jackie Smith	.30
15	Greg Landry	.75
16	Buck Buchanan	1.50
17	Haven Moses	.30
18	Clarence Ellis	.30
19	Jim Carter	.30
20	Charley Taylor	2.25
21	Jess Phillips	.30
22	Larry Seiple	.30
23	Doug Dieken	.30
24	Ron Saul	.30
25	Isaac Curtis	.75
26	*Gary Larsen*	.75
27	Bruce Jarvis	.30
28	Steve Zabel	.30
29	John Mendenhall	.30
30	Rick Volk	.30
31	Checklist 1-132	2.50
32	Dan Abramowicz	.30
33	Bubba Smith	2.00
34	David Ray	.30
35	Dan Dierdorf	2.00
36	Randy Rasmussen	.30
37	Bob Howard	.30
38	Gary Huff	.30
39	*Rocky Bleier*	15.00
40	Mel Gray	.30
41	Tony McGee	.30
42	Larry Hand	.30
43	Wendell Hayes	.30
44	*Doug Wilkerson*	.50
45	Paul Smith	.30
46	Dave Robinson	.30
47	Bivian Lee	.30
48	*Jim Mandich*	.50
49	Greg Pruitt	1.00
50	Dan Pastorini	.60
51	Ron Pritchard	.30
52	Dan Conners	.30
53	Fred Cox	.30
54	Tony Greene	.30
55	Craig Morton	1.00
56	Jerry Sisemore	.30
57	Glenn Doughty	.30
58	Larry Schreiber	.30
59	*Charlie Waters*	4.00
60	Jack Youngblood	1.50
61	Bill Lenkaitis	.30
62	Greg Brezina	.30
63	Bob Pollard	.30
64	Mack Alston	.30
65	*Drew Pearson*	12.00
66	Charlie Stukes	.30
67	Emerson Boozer	.30
68	Dennis Partee	.30
69	Bob Newton	.30
70	Jack Tatum	.30
71	Frank Lewis	.30
72	Bob Young	.30
73	Julius Adams	.30
74	Paul Naumoff	.30
75	Otis Taylor	.60
76	Dave Hampton	.30
77	Mike Current	.30
78	Brig Owens	.30
79	Bobby Scott	.30
80	Harold Carmichael	4.00
81	Bill Stanfill	.30
82	Bob Babich	.30
83	Vic Washington	.30
84	Mick Tingelhoff	.30
85	Bob Trumpy	1.00
86	Earl Edwards	.30
87	Ron Hornsby	.30
88	Don McCauley	.30
89	Jimmy Johnson	.30
90	Andy Russell	.30
91	Cornell Green	.30
92	Charlie Cowan	.30
93	Jon Staggers	.30
94	Billy Newsome	.30
95	Willie Brown	1.25
96	Carl Mauck	.30
97	Doug Buffone	.30
98	Preston Pearson	.60
99	Jim Bakken	.30
100	Bob Griese	5.00
101	Bob Windsor	.30
102	Rockne Freitas	.30
103	Jim Marsalis	.30
104	Bill Thompson	.30
105	Ken Burrow	.30
106	Diron Talbert	.30
107	Joe Federspiel	.30
108	Norm Bulaich	.30
109	Bob DeMarco	.30
110	Tom Wittum	.30
111	Larry Hefner	.30
112	Tody Smith	.30
113	Stu Voigt	.30
114	Horst Muhlmann	.30
115	Ahmad Rashad	5.00
116	Joe Dawkins	.30
117	George Kunz	.30
118	D.D. Lewis	.30
119	Levi Johnson	.30
120	Len Dawson	3.50
121	Jim Bertelsen	.30
122	Ed Bell	.30
123	Art Thoms	.30
124	Joe Beauchamp	.30
125	Jack Ham	5.00
126	Carl Garrett	.30
127	Roger Finnie	.30
128	Howard Twilley	.30
129	Bruce Barnes	.30
130	Nate Wright	.30

131	Jerry Tagge	.30
132	Floyd Little	1.25
133	John Zook	.30
134	Len Hauss	.30
135	Archie Manning	1.50
136	Po James	.30
137	Walt Sumner	.30
138	Randy Beisler	.30
139	Willie Alexander	.30
140	Garo Yepremian	.30
141	Chip Myers	.30
142	Jim Braxton	.30
143	Doug Van Horn	.30
144	Stan White	.30
145	Roger Staubach	25.00
146	Herman Weaver	.30
147	Marvin Upshaw	.30
148	Bob Klein	.30
149	Earlie Thomas	.30
150	John Brockington	.30
151	Mike Siani	.30
152	Sam Davis	.30
153	Mike Wagner	.30
154	Larry Stallings	.30
155	Wally Chambers	.30
156	Randy Vataha	.30
157	Jim Marshall	1.00
158	Jim Turner	.30
159	Walt Sweeney	.30
160	Ken Anderson	3.50
161	Ray Brown	.30
162	John Didion	.30
163	Tom Dempsey	.30
164	Clarence Scott	.30
165	Gene Washington	.30
166	Willie Rodgers	.30
167	Doug Swift	.30
168	Rufus Mayes	.30
169	Marv Bateman	.30
170	Lydell Mitchell	.30
171	Ron Smith	.30
172	Bill Munson	.30
173	Bob Grim	.30
174	Ed Budde	.30
175	Bob Lilly	3.50
176	*Jim Youngblood*	2.00
177	Steve Tannen	.30
178	Rich McGeorge	.30
179	Jim Tyrer	.30
180	Forrest Blue	.30
181	Jerry LeVias	.30
182	*Joe Gilliam*	.60
183	*Jim Otis*	1.25
184	Mel Tom	.30
185	Paul Seymour	.30
186	George Webster	.30
187	Pete Duranko	.30
188	Essex Johnson	.30
189	Bob Lee	.30
190	Gene Upshaw	1.50
191	Tom Myers	.30
192	Don Zimmerman	.30
193	John Garlington	.30
194	Skip Butler	.30
195	Tom Mitchell	.30
196	Jim Langer	1.50
197	Ron Carpenter	.30
198	Dave Foley	.30
199	Bert Jones	1.50
200	Larry Brown	.75
201	All Pro Receivers (Charley Taylor, Fred Biletnikoff)	2.00
202	All Pro Tackles (Russ Washington, Rayfield Wright)	.50
203	All Pro Guards (Tom Mack, Larry Little)	1.00
204	All Pro Centers (Jeff Van Note, Jack Rudnay)	.50
205	All Pro Guards (Gale Gillingham, John Hannah)	1.00
206	All Pro Tackles (Winston Hill, Dan Dierdorf)	.50
207	All Pro Tight Ends (Riley Odoms, Charley Young)	.50
208	All Pro Quarterbacks (Fran Tarkenton, Ken Stabler)	3.00
209	All Pro Backs (Lawrence McCutcheon, O.J. Simpson)	5.00
210	All Pro Backs (Otis Armstrong, Terry Metcalf)	.50
211	All Pro Receivers (Isaac Curtis, Mel Gray)	.50
212	All Pro Kickers (Roy Gerela, Chester Marcol)	.50
213	All Pro Ends (Elvin Bethea, Jack Youngblood)	.50
214	All Pro Tackles (Otis Sistrunk, Alan Page)	.50
215	All Pro Tackles (Merlin Olsen, Mike Reid)	1.25
216	All Pro Ends (Carl Eller, Lyle Alzado)	1.00
217	All Pro Linebackers (Ted Hendricks, Phil Villapiano)	1.00
218	All Pro Linebackers (Willie Lanier, Lee Roy Jordan)	1.00
219	All Pro Linebackers (Andy Russell, Isiah Robertson)	.50
220	All Pro Cornerbacks (Emmitt Thomas, Nate Wright)	.50
221	All Pro Cornerbacks (Lemar Parrish, Willie Buchanon)	.50
222	All Pro Safeties (Ken Houston, Dick Anderson)	1.00
223	All Pro Safeties (Cliff Harris, Jack Tatum)	1.00
224	All Pro Punters (Tom Wittum, Ray Guy)	.50
225	All Pro Returners (Greg Pruitt, Terry Metcalf)	.50
226	Ted Kwalick	.30
227	Spider Lockhart	.30
228	Mike Livingston	.30
229	Larry Cole	.30
230	Gary Garrison	.30
231	Larry Brooks	.30
232	Bobby Howfield	.30
233	Fred Carr	.30
234	Norm Evans	.30
235	Dwight White	.30
236	Conrad Dobler	.30
237	Garry Lyle	.30
238	Darryl Stingley	1.00
239	Tom Graham	.30
240	Chuck Foreman	1.00
241	Ken Riley	.30
242	Don Morrison	.30
243	Lynn Dickey	.75
244	Don Cockroft	.30
245	Claude Humphrey	.30
246	John Skorupan	.30
247	Raymond Chester	.30
248	Cas Banaszek	.30
249	Art Malone	.30
250	Ed Flanagan	.30
251	Checklist 133-264	2.50
252	Nemiah Wilson	.30
253	Ron Jessie	.30
254	Jim Lynch	.30
255	Bob Tucker	.30
256	Terry Owens	.30
257	John Fitzgerald	.30
258	Jack Snow	.30
259	Garry Puetz	.30
260	Mike Phipps	.30
261	Al Matthews	.30
262	Bob Kuechenberg	.30
263	Ron Yankowski	.30
264	Ron Shanklin	.30
265	Bobby Douglass	.30
266	Josh Ashton	.30
267	Bill Van Heusen	.30
268	Jeff Siemon	.30
269	Bob Newland	.30
270	Gale Gillingham	.30
271	Zeke Moore	.30
272	Mike Tilleman	.30
273	John Leypoldt	.30
274	Ken Mendenhall	.30
275	Norm Snead	.30
276	Bill Bradley	.30
277	Jerry Smith	.30
278	Clarence Davis	.30
279	Jim Yarbrough	.30
280	Lemar Parrish	.30
281	Bobby Bell	1.50
282	*Lynn Swann*	45.00
283	John Hicks	.30
284	Coy Bacon	.30
285	Lee Roy Jordan	1.25
286	Willie Buchanon	.30
287	Al Woodall	.30
288	Reggie Rucker	.30
289	John Schmitt	.30
290	Carl Eller	1.00
291	Jake Scott	.30
292	Donny Anderson	.30
293	Charley Wade	.30
294	John Tanner	.30
295	Charley Johnson	.30
296	Tom Blanchard	.30
297	Curley Culp	.30
298	*Jeff Van Note*	1.25
299	Bob James	.30
300	Franco Harris	12.00
301	Tim Berra	.30
302	Bruce Gossett	.30
303	Berlon Biggs	.30
304	Bob Kowalkowski	.30
305	Marv Hubbard	.30
306	Ken Avery	.30
307	Mike Adamle	.30
308	Don Herrmann	.30
309	Chris Fletcher	.30
310	Roman Gabriel	1.25
311	Billy Joe DuPree	1.00
312	Fred Dryer	2.00
313	John Riggins	5.00
314	Bob McKay	.30
315	Ted Hendricks	1.50
316	Bobby Bryant	.30
317	Don Nottingham	.30
318	John Hannah	4.00
319	Rich Coady	.30
320	Phil Villapiano	.30
321	Jim Plunkett	2.00
322	Lyle Alzado	1.25
323	Ernie Jackson	.30
324	Billy Parks	.30
325	Willie Lanier	1.50
326	John James	.30
327	Joe Ferguson	1.00
328	*Ernie Holmes*	1.00
329	Bruce Laird	.30
330	Chester Marcol	.30
331	Dave Wilcox	.30
332	Pat Fischer	.30
333	Steve Owens	.30
334	Royce Berry	.30
335	Russ Washington	.30
336	Walker Gillette	.30
337	Mark Nordquist	.30
338	*James Harris*	1.00
339	Warren Koegel	.30
340	Emmitt Thomas	.30
341	Walt Garrison	.30
342	Thom Darden	.30
343	Mike Eischeid	.30
344	Ernie McMillan	.30
345	Nick Buoniconti	1.00
346	George Farmer	.30
347	Sam Adams	.30
348	Larry Cipa	.30
349	Bob Moore	.30
350	*Otis Armstrong*	4.00
351	George Blanda (RH)	2.50
352	Fred Cox (RH)	.60
353	Tom Dempsey (RH)	.60
354	Ken Houston (RH)	.60
355	O.J. Simpson (RH)	7.00
356	Ron Smith (RH)	.60
357	Bob Atkins	.30
358	Pat Sullivan	.30
359	Joe DeLamielleure	.60
360	*L. McCutcheon*	2.50
361	David Lee	.30
362	Mike McCoy	.30
363	Skip Vanderbundt	.30
364	Mark Moseley	.75
365	Lem Barney	1.50
366	Doug Dressler	.30
367	*Dan Fouts*	50.00
368	Bob Hyland	.30
369	John Outlaw	.30
370	Roy Gerela	.30
371	Isiah Robertson	.30
372	Jerome Barkum	.30
373	Ed Podolak	.30
374	Milt Morin	.30
375	John Niland	.30
376	Checklist 265-396	2.50
377	Ken Iman	.30
378	Manny Fernandez	.30
379	Dave Gallagher	.30
380	Ken Stabler	14.00
381	Mack Herron	.30
382	Bill McClard	.30
383	Ray May	.30
384	Don Hansen	.30
385	Elvin Bethea	.30
386	Joe Scibelli	.30
387	Neal Craig	.30
388	Marty Domres	.30
389	Ken Ellis	.30
390	Charley Young	.30
391	Tommy Hart	.30
392	Moses Denson	.30
393	Larry Walton	.30
394	Dave Green	.30
395	Ron Johnson	.30
396	Ed Bradley	.30
397	J.T. Thomas	.30
398	Jim Bailey	.30
399	Barry Pearson	.30
400	Fran Tarkenton	8.50
401	Jack Rudnay	
402	Rayfield Wright	.30
403	Roger Wehrli	.30
404	Vern Den Herder	.30
405	Fred Biletnikoff	3.00
406	Ken Grandberry	.30
407	Bob Adams	.30
408	Jim Merlo	.30
409	John Pitts	.30
410	Dave Osborn	.30
411	Dennis Havig	.30
412	Bob Johnson	.30
413	Ken Burrow	.30
414	Jim Cheyunski	.30
415	MacArthur Lane	.30
416	*Joe Theismann*	25.00
417	*Mike Boryla*	.50
418	Bruce Taylor	.30
419	Chris Hanburger	.30
420	Tom Mack	.30
421	Errol Mann	.30
422	Jack Gregory	.30
423	Harrison Davis	.30
424	Burgess Owens	.30
425	Joe Greene	4.00
426	Morris Stroud	.30
427	John DeMarie	.30
428	Mel Renfro	.75
429	Cid Edwards	.30
430	Mike Reid	1.00
431	Jack Mildren	.30
432	Jerry Simmons	.30
433	Ron Yary	.30
434	Howard Stevens	.30
435	Ray Guy	1.75
436	Tommy Nobis	1.00
437	Solomon Freelon	.30
438	J.D. Hill	.30
439	Toni Linhart	.30
440	Dick Anderson	.30
441	Guy Morriss	.30
442	Bob Hoskins	.30
443	John Hadl	1.00
444	Roy Jefferson	.30
445	Charlie Sanders	.30
446	Pat Curran	.30
447	David Knight	.30
448	Bob Brown	.30
449	Pete Gogolak	.30
450	Terry Metcalf	1.00
451	Bill Bergey	.75
452	(Dan Abramowicz) (HL)	.60
453	Otis Armstrong (HL)	1.00
454	Cliff Branch (HL)	1.50
455	John James (HL)	.60
456	Lydell Mitchell (HL)	.60
457	Lemar Parrish (HL)	.60
458	Ken Stabler (HL)	4.00
459	Lynn Swann (HL)	7.00
460	Emmitt Thomas (HL)	.60
461	Terry Bradshaw	15.00
462	Jerrel Wilson	.30
463	Walter Johnson	.30
464	Golden Richards	.30
465	Tommy Casanova	.30
466	Randy Jackson	.30
467	Ron Bolton	.30
468	Joe Owens	.30
469	Wally Hilgenberg	.30
470	Riley Odoms	.50
471	Otis Sistrunk	.30
472	Eddie Ray	.30
473	Reggie McKenzie	.75
474	Elbert Drungo	.30
475	Mercury Morris	.75
476	Dan Dickel	.30
477	Merritt Kersey	.30
478	Mike Holmes	.30
479	Clarence Williams	.30
480	Bill Kilmer	.50
481	Altie Taylor	.30
482	Dave Elmendorf	.30
483	Bob Rowe	.30
484	Pete Athas	.30
485	Winston Hill	.30
486	Bo Mathews	.30
487	Earl Thomas	.30
488	Jan Stenerud	1.25
489	Steve Holden	.30
490	*Cliff Harris*	4.00
491	*Boobie Clark*	.50
492	Joe Taylor	.30
493	Tom Neville	.30
494	Wayne Colman	.30
495	Jim Mitchell	.30
496	Paul Krause	.75
497	Jim Otto	2.00
498	John Rowser	.30
499	Larry Little	1.00
500	O.J. Simpson	12.00
501	*John Dutton*	1.50
502	Pat Hughes	.30
503	Malcolm Snider	.30
504	Fred Willis	.30
505	Harold Jackson	.90
506	Mike Bragg	.30
507	Jerry Sherk	.30
508	Mirro Roder	.30
509	Tom Sullivan	.30
510	Jim Hart	1.00
511	Cedrick Hardman	.30
512	Blaine Nye	.30
513	Elmo Wright	.30
514	Herb Orvis	.30
515	Richard Caster	.30
516	*Doug Kotar*	.50
517	Checklist 397-528	2.50
518	Jesse Freitas	.30
519	Ken Houston	1.25
520	Alan Page	1.75
521	Tim Foley	.30
522	Bill Olds	.30
523	Bobby Maples	.30
524	*Cliff Branch*	10.00
525	Merlin Olsen	3.00
526	AFC Champions (Terry Bradshaw, Franco Harris)	2.50
527	NFC Champions (Chuck Foreman)	1.00
528	Super Bowl (Terry Bradshaw)	4.00

1975 Topps Team Checklists

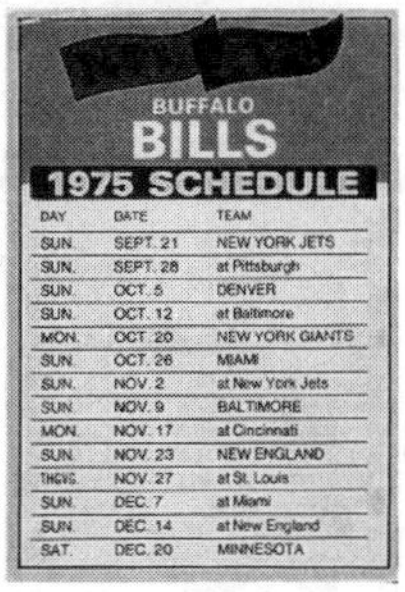

Each of the 26 NFL teams is represented in this set, which was available as a mail-in offer from Topps as an uncut sheet. Each card is standard size, and shows the team's 1975 schedule on the front. The card back is unnumbered and contains a checklist for the players in the team set.

		NM
Complete Set (26):		195.00
Common Player:		8.00
(1)	Atlanta Falcons	8.50
(2)	Baltimore Colts	8.00
(3)	Buffalo Bills	8.00
(4)	Chicago Bears	9.00
(5)	Cincinnati Bengals	8.00
(6)	Cleveland Browns	9.00
(7)	Dallas Cowboys	10.00
(8)	Denver Broncos	10.00
(9)	Detroit Lions	8.00
(10)	Green Bay Packers	8.00
(11)	Houston Oilers	8.00
(12)	Kansas City Chiefs	8.00
(13)	Los Angeles Rams	8.00
(14)	Miami Dolphins	10.00
(15)	Minnesota Vikings	9.00
(16)	New England Patriots	8.00
(17)	New York Giants	9.00
(18)	New York Jets	9.00
(19)	New Orleans Saints	8.00
(20)	Oakland Raiders	10.00
(21)	Philadelphia Eagles	8.00
(22)	Pittsburgh Steelers	9.00
(23)	St. Louis Cardinals	8.00
(24)	San Diego Chargers	8.00
(25)	San Francisco 49ers	9.00
(26)	Washington Redskins	10.00

1976 Topps

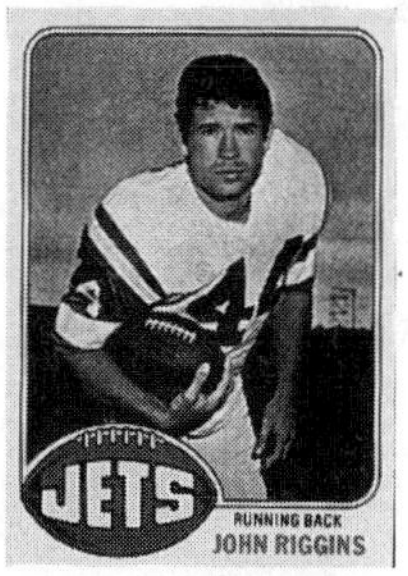

This is the most valuable of the 528-card sets issued by Topps, primarily because of the inclusion of Walter Payton's rookie card. Other rookies in this set include Steve Bartkowski, Harvey Martin, Russ Francis, Randy White, Jack Lambert, Randy Gradishar, Steve Grogan, and Ron Jaworski. The set also features the second-year card of Dan Fouts. Hall of Famers (and future Hall of Famers) showing up in the 1976 Topps issue include Payton, Fouts, Martin, White, Lambert, Willie Lanier, Fred Biletnikoff, Ray Guy, Alan Page, Bob Griese, Franco Harris, O.J. Simpson, John Riggins, Len Dawson, Paul Warfield, George Blanda, Roger Staubach, Ken Stabler, Larry Csonka, Charley Taylor and Fran Tarkenton. (Key: AP - All Pro)

		NM
Complete Set (528):		350.00
Common Player:		.25
Team Cards:		1.25
Wax Pack (10):		36.00
Wax Box (36):		940.00
1	George Blanda	5.00
2	Neil Colzie	.50
3	Chuck Foreman	.50
4	Jim Marshall	.50
5	Terry Metcalf	.50
6	O.J. Simpson	3.00
7	Fran Tarkenton	3.00
8	Charley Taylor	1.00
9	Ernie Holmes	.25
10	Ken Anderson (AP)	2.00
11	Bobby Bryant	.25
12	Jerry Smith	.25
13	David Lee	.25
14	*Robert Newhouse*	1.25
15	Vern Den Herder	.25
16	John Hannah	2.00
17	J.D. Hill	.25
18	James Harris	.25
19	Willie Buchanon	.25
20	Charley Young (AP)	.25
21	Jim Yarbrough	.25
22	Ronnie Coleman	.25
23	Don Cockroft	.25
24	Willie Lanier	1.00
25	Fred Biletnikoff	3.00
26	Ron Yankowski	.25
27	Spider Lockhart	.25
28	Bob Johnson	.25
29	J.T. Thomas	.25
30	Ron Yary (AP)	.25
31	*Brad Dusek*	.50
32	Raymond Chester	.25
33	Larry Little	.75
34	*Pat Leahy*	1.00
35	*Steve Bartkowski*	4.00
36	Tom Myers	.25
37	Bill Van Heusen	.25
38	Russ Washington	.25
39	Tom Sullivan	.25
40	Curley Culp (AP)	.25
41	Johnnie Gray	.25
42	Bob Klein	.25
43	Lem Barney	1.00
44	*Harvey Martin*	4.00
45	Reggie Rucker	.25
46	Neil Clabo	.25
47	Ray Hamilton	.25
48	Joe Ferguson	.75
49	Ed Podolak	.25
50	Ray Guy (AP)	1.50
51	Glen Edwards	.25
52	Jim LeClair	.25
53	Mike Barnes	.25
54	*Nat Moore*	4.00
55	Bill Kilmer	.75
56	Larry Stallings	.25
57	Jack Gregory	.25
58	Steve Mike-Mayer	.25
59	Virgil Livers	.25
60	Jerry Sherk (AP)	.25
61	Guy Morriss	.25
62	Barty Smith	.25
63	Jerome Barkum	.25
64	Ira Gordon	.25
65	Paul Krause	.60
66	John McMakin	.25
67	Checklist 1-132	2.00
68	Charley Johnson	.25
69	Tommy Nobis	.75
70	Lydell Mitchell	.25
71	Vern Holland	.25
72	Tim Foley	.25
73	Golden Richards	.25
74	Bryant Salter	.25
75	Terry Bradshaw	14.00
76	Ted Hendricks	1.25
77	*Rich Saul*	.35
78	John Smith	.25
79	Altie Taylor	.25
80	Cedrick Hardman (AP)	.25
81	Ken Payne	.25
82	Zeke Moore	.25
83	Alvin Maxson	.25
84	Wally Hilgenberg	.25
85	John Niland	.25
86	Mike Sensibaugh	.25
87	Ron Johnson	.25
88	Winston Hill	.25
89	Charlie Joiner	2.00
90	Roger Wehrli (AP)	.75
91	Mike Bragg	.25
92	Dan Dickel	.25
93	Earl Morrall	.75
94	Pat Toomay	.25
95	Gary Garrison	.25
96	Ken Geddes	.25
97	Mike Current	.25
98	Bob Avellini	.35
99	Dave Pureifory	.25
100	Franco Harris (AP)	7.00
101	Randy Logan	.25
102	John Fitzgerald	.25
103	*Gregg Bingham*	.40
104	Jim Plunkett	1.50
105	Carl Eller	.75
106	Larry Walton	.25
107	Clarence Scott	.25
108	Skip Vanderbundt	.25
109	Boobie Clark	.25
110	Tom Mack (AP)	.25
111	Bruce Laird	.25
112	*Dave Dalby*	.60
113	John Leypoldt	.25
114	Barry Pearson	.25
115	Larry Brown	.60
116	Jackie Smith	.25
117	Pat Hughes	.25
118	Al Woodall	.25
119	John Zook	.25
120	Jake Scott (AP)	.25
121	Rich Glover	.25
122	Ernie Jackson	.25
123	Otis Armstrong	1.00
124	Bob Grim	.25
125	Jeff Siemon	.25
126	Harold Hart	.25
127	John DeMarie	.25
128	Dan Fouts	10.00
129	Jim Kearney	.25
130	John Dutton (AP)	.40
131	Calvin Hill	.50
132	Toni Fritsch	.25
133	Ron Jessie	.25
134	Don Nottingham	.25
135	Lemar Parrish	.25
136	*Russ Francis*	4.00
137	Joe Reed	.25
138	C.L. Whittington	.25
139	Otis Sistrunk	.25
140	Lynn Swann (AP)	15.00
141	Jim Carter	.25
142	Mike Montler	.25
143	Walter Johnson	.25
144	Doug Kotar	.25
145	Roman Gabriel	1.00
146	Billy Newsome	.25
147	Ed Bradley	.25
148	*Walter Payton*	250.00
149	Johnny Fuller	.25
150	Alan Page (AP)	1.50
151	Frank Grant	.25
152	Dave Green	.25
153	Nelson Munsey	.25
154	Jim Mandich	.25
155	Lawrence McCutcheon	.75
156	Steve Ramsey	.25
157	Ed Flanagan	.25
158	*Randy White*	25.00
159	Gerry Mullins	.25
160	Jan Stenerud (AP)	.75
161	Steve Odom	.25
162	Roger Finnie	.25
163	Norm Snead	.25
164	Jeff Van Note	.40
165	Bill Bergey	.60
166	Allen Carter	.25
167	Steve Holden	.25
168	Sherman White	.25
169	Bob Berry	.25
170	Ken Houston (AP)	1.00
171	Bill Olds	.25
172	Larry Seiple	.25
173	Cliff Branch	3.00
174	Reggie McKenzie	.25
175	Dan Pastorini	.50
176	Paul Naumoff	.25
177	Checklist 133-265	2.00
178	Durwood Keeton	.25
179	Earl Thomas	.25
180	L.C. Greenwood (AP)	.85
181	John Outlaw	.25
182	Frank Nunley	.25
183	*Dave Jennings*	1.00
184	McArthur Lane	.25
185	Chester Marcol	.25
186	J.J. Jones	.25
187	Tom DeLeone	.25
188	Steve Zabel	.25
189	Ken Johnson	.25
190	Rayfield Wright (AP)	.25
191	Brent McClanahan	.25
192	Pat Fischer	.25
193	*Roger Carr*	1.00
194	Manny Fernandez	.25
195	Roy Gerela	.25
196	Dave Elmendorf	.25
197	Bob Kowalkowski	.25
198	Phil Villapiano	.25
199	Will Wynn	.25
200	*Terry Metcalf*	.50
201	Passing Leaders: (Ken Anderson, Fran Tarkenton)	2.00
202	Receiving Leaders: (Reggie Rucker, Lydell Mitchell, Chuck Foreman)	.50
203	Rushing Leaders: (O.J. Simpson, Jim Otis)	3.00
204	Scoring Leaders: (O.J. Simpson, Chuck Foreman)	3.00
205	Interception Leaders: (Mel Blount, Paul Krause)	.75
206	Punting Leaders: (Ray Guy, Herman Weaver)	.50
207	Ken Ellis	.25
208	Ron Saul	.25
209	Toni Linhart	.25
210	Jim Langer (AP)	1.25
211	Jeff Wright	.25
212	Moses Denson	.25
213	Earl Edwards	.25
214	Walker Gillette	.25
215	Bob Trumpy	.50
216	Emmitt Thomas	.25
217	Lyle Alzado	1.25
218	Carl Garrett	.25
219	Van Green	.25
220	*Jack Lambert* (AP)	28.00
221	Spike Jones	.25
222	John Hadl	.75
223	*Billy Johnson*	2.50
224	Tony McGee	.25
225	Preston Pearson	.50
226	Isiah Robertson	.25
227	Errol Mann	.25
228	Paul Seal	.25
229	*Roland Harper*	.75
230	*Ed White*	.75
231	Joe Theismann	6.50
232	Jim Cheyunski	.25
233	Bill Stanfill	.25
234	Marv Hubbard	.25
235	Tommy Casanova	.25
236	Bob Hyland	.25
237	Jesse Freitas	.25
238	Norm Thompson	.25
239	Charlie Smith	.25
240	John James (AP)	.25
241	Alden Roche	.25
242	Gordon Jolley	.25
243	Larry Ely	.25
244	Richard Caster	.25
245	Joe Greene	3.25
246	Larry Schreiber	.25
247	Terry Schmidt	.25
248	Jerrel Wilson	.25
249	Marty Domres	.25
250	Isaac Curtis (AP)	.25
251	Harold McLinton	.25
252	Fred Dryer	2.00
253	Bill Lenkaitis	.25
254	Don Hardeman	.25
255	Bob Griese	4.00
256	*Oscar Roan*	.40
257	*Randy Gradishar*	3.00
258	*Bob Thomas*	.50
259	Joe Owens	.25
260	Cliff Harris (AP)	1.00
261	Frank Lewis	.25
262	Mike McCoy	.25
263	*Rickey Young*	.60
264	*Brian Kelley*	.40
265	Charlie Sanders	.25

266	Jim Hart	1.00
267	Gregg Gantt	.25
268	John Ward	.25
269	Al Beauchamp	.25
270	Jack Tatum (AP)	.25
271	Jim Lash	.25
272	Diron Talbert	.25
273	Checklist 265-396	2.00
274	Steve Spurrier	4.00
275	Greg Pruitt	.60
276	Jim Mitchell	.25
277	Jack Rudnay	.25
278	*Freddie Solomon*	1.00
279	Frank LeMaster	.25
280	Wally Chambers (AP)	.25
281	Mike Collier	.25
282	Clarence Williams	.25
283	Mitch Hoopes	.25
284	Ron Bolton	.25
285	Harold Jackson	.75
286	Greg Landry	.60
287	Tony Greene	.25
288	Howard Stevens	.25
289	Roy Jefferson	.25
290	Jim Bakken (AP)	.25
291	Doug Sutherland	.25
292	Marvin Cobb	.25
293	Mack Alston	.25
294	Rod McNeil	.25
295	Gene Upshaw	1.00
296	Dave Gallagher	.25
297	Larry Ball	.25
298	Ron Howard	.25
299	*Don Strock*	1.50
300	O.J. Simpson (AP)	10.00
301	Ray Mansfield	.25
302	Larry Marshall	.25
303	Dick Himes	.25
304	*Ray Wersching*	.40
305	John Riggins	4.00
306	Bob Parsons	.25
307	Ray Brown	.25
308	Len Dawson	3.00
309	Andy Maurer	.25
310	Jack Youngblood (AP)	1.00
311	Essex Johnson	.25
312	Stan White	.25
313	Drew Pearson	4.00
314	Rockne Freitas	.25
315	Mercury Morris	.60
316	Willie Alexander	.25
317	Paul Warfield	3.00
318	Bob Chandler	.25
319	Bobby Walden	.25
320	Riley Odoms (AP)	.25
321	Mike Boryla	.25
322	Bruce Van Dyke	.25
323	Pete Banaszak	.25
324	Darryl Stingley	.50
325	John Mendenhall	.25
326	Dan Dierdorf	1.50
327	Bruce Taylor	.25
328	Don McCauley	.25
329	John Reaves	.25
330	Chris Hanburger (AP)	.25
331	NFC Champions (Roger Staubach)	3.00
332	AFC Champions (Franco Harris)	2.00
333	Super Bowl X (Terry Bradshaw)	2.25
334	Godwin Turk	.25
335	Dick Anderson	.25
336	Woody Green	.25
337	Pat Curran	.25
338	Council Rudolph	.25
339	Joe Lavender	.25
340	John Gilliam (AP)	.25
341	*Steve Furness*	.75
342	D.D. Lewis	.25
343	Duane Carrell	.25
344	Jon Morris	.25
345	John Brockington	.25
346	Mike Phipps	.25
347	*Lyle Blackwood*	.60
348	Julius Adams	.25
349	Terry Hermeling	.25
350	*Rolland Lawrence* (AP)	.50
351	Glenn Doughty	.25
352	Doug Swift	.25
353	Mike Strachan	.25
354	Craig Morton	.50
355	George Blanda	5.00
356	Garry Puetz	.25
357	Carl Mauck	.25
358	Walt Patulski	.25
359	Stu Voigt	.25
360	Fred Carr (AP)	.25
361	Po James	.25
362	Otis Taylor	.50
363	Jeff West	.25
364	Gary Huff	.25
365	Dwight White	.25
366	Dan Ryczek	.25
367	*Jon Keyworth*	.50
368	Mel Renfro	.60
369	*Bruce Coslet*	1.00
370	Len Hauss (AP)	.25
371	Rick Volk	.25
372	Howard Twilley	.25
373	*Cullen Bryant*	.60
374	Bob Babich	.25
375	Herman Weaver	.25
376	*Steve Grogan*	8.00
377	Bubba Smith	1.50
378	Burgess Owens	.25
379	Alvin Matthews	.25
380	Art Shell	2.00
381	Larry Brown	.25
382	Horst Muhlmann	.25
383	Ahmad Rashad	2.50
384	Bobby Maples	.25
385	Jim Marshall	.90
386	Joe Dawkins	.25
387	Dennis Partee	.25
388	Eddie McMillan	.25
389	Randy Johnson	.25
390	Bob Kuechenberg (AP)	.25
391	Rufus Mayes	.25
392	Lloyd Mumphord	.25
393	Ike Harris	.25
394	Dave Hampton	.25
395	Roger Staubach	15.00
396	Doug Buffone	.25
397	Howard Fest	.25
398	Wayne Mulligan	.25
399	Bill Bradley	.25
400	Chuck Foreman (AP)	.60
401	Jack Snow	.25
402	Bob Howard	.25
403	John Matuszak	1.00
404	Bill Munson	.25
405	Andy Russell	.25
406	Skip Butler	.25
407	Hugh McKinnis	.25
408	Bob Penchion	.25
409	Mike Bass	.25
410	George Kunz (AP)	.25
411	Ron Pritchard	.25
412	Barry Smith	.25
413	Norm Bulaich	.25
414	Marv Bateman	.25
415	Ken Stabler	8.00
416	Conrad Dobler	.25
417	Bob Tucker	.25
418	Gene Washington	.25
419	Ed Marinaro	1.00
420	Jack Ham (AP)	3.25
421	Jim Turner	.25
422	Chris Fletcher	.25
423	Carl Barzilauskas	.25
424	*Robert Brazile*	2.50
425	Harold Carmichael	1.50
426	*Ron Jaworski*	4.00
427	*Ed "Too Tall" Jones*	20.00
428	Larry McCarren	.25
429	*Mike Thomas*	.50
430	Joe DeLamielleure (AP)	.25
431	Tom Blanchard	.25
432	Ron Carpenter	.25
433	Levi Johnson	.25
434	Sam Cunningham	.25
435	Garo Yapremian	.25
436	Mike Livingston	.25
437	Larry Csonka	3.00
438	Doug Dieken	.25
439	Bill Lueck	.25
440	Tom MacLeod (AP)	.25
441	Mick Tingelhoff	.25
442	Terry Hanratty	.25
443	Mike Siani	.25
444	Dwight Harrison	.25
445	Jim Otis	.25
446	Jack Reynolds	.25
447	*Jean Fugett*	.40
448	Dave Beverly	.25
449	*Bernard Jackson*	1.00
450	Charley Taylor	2.00
451	Atlanta Falcons Team	1.50
452	Baltimore Colts Team	1.50
453	Buffalo Bills Team	1.50
454	Chicago Bears Team	1.50
455	Cincinnati Bengals Team	1.50
456	Cleveland Browns Team	1.50
457	Dallas Cowboys Team	1.50
458	Denver Broncos Team	1.50
459	Detroit Lions Team	1.50
460	Green Bay Packers Team	1.50
461	Houston Oilers Team	1.50
462	Kansas City Chiefs Team	1.50
463	Los Angeles Rams Team	1.50
464	Miami Dolphins Team	1.50
465	Minnesota Vikings Team	1.50
466	New England Patriots Team	1.50
467	New Orleans Saints Team	1.50
468	New York Giants Team	1.50
469	New York Jets Team	1.50
470	Oakland Raiders Team	1.50
471	Philadelphia Eagles Team	1.50
472	Pittsburgh Steelers Team	1.50
473	St. Louis Cardinals Team	1.50
474	San Diego Chargers Team	1.50
475	San Francisco 49ers Team	1.50
476	Seattle Seahawks Team	1.50
477	Tampa Bay Bucaneers Team	1.50
478	Washington Redskins Team	1.50
479	Fred Cox	.25
480	Mel Blount (AP)	5.00
481	John Bunting	.25
482	Ken Mendenhall	.25
483	Will Harrell	.25
484	Marlin Briscoe	.25
485	Archie Manning	1.00
486	Tody Smith	.25
487	George Hunt	.25
488	Roscoe Word	.25
489	Paul Seymour	.25
490	Lee Roy Jordan (AP)	1.00
491	Chip Myers	.25
492	Norm Evans	.25
493	Jim Bertelsen	.25
494	Mark Moseley	.50
495	George Buehler	.25
496	Charlie Hall	.25
497	Marvin Upshaw	.25
498	*Tom Banks*	.50
499	Randy Vataha	.25
500	Fran Tarkenton (AP)	7.00
501	Mike Wagner	.25
502	Art Malone	.25
503	Fred Cook	.25
504	Rich McGeorge	.25
505	Ken Burrough	.25
506	Nick Mike-Mayer	.25
507	Checklist 397-528	2.00
508	Steve Owens	.25
509	*Brad Van Pelt*	.75
510	Ken Riley (AP)	.25
511	Art Thoms	.25
512	Ed Bell	.25
513	Tom Wittum	.25
514	Jim Braxton	.25
515	Nick Buoniconti	.60
516	*Brian Sipe*	2.00
517	Jim Lynch	.25
518	Prentice McCray	.25
519	Tom Dempsey	.25
520	Mel Gray (AP)	.25
521	Nate Wright	.25
522	Rocky Bleier	3.00
523	Dennis Johnson	.25
524	Jerry Sisemore	.25
525	Bert Jones	1.00
526	Perry Smith	.25
527	Blaine Nye	.25
528	Bob Moore	.50

1976 Topps Team Checklists

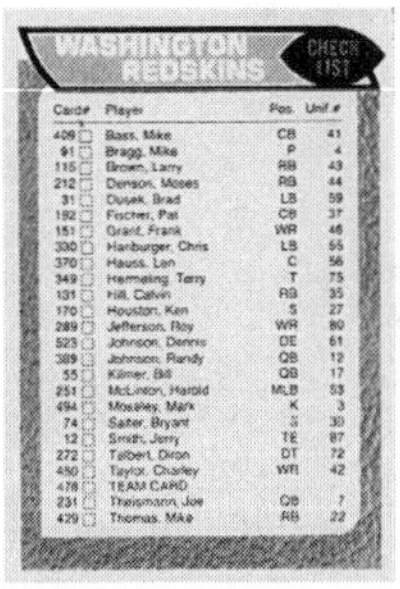

The 30-card, standard-size set includes team checklist for each of the 28 NFL teams and two checklists. The set was available in uncut sheets from Topps and was unnumbered. The cards parallel the team checklists in the base sets (451-478), but come in thinner stock.

		NM
Complete Set (30):		130.00
Common Player:		5.00
1	Atlanta Falcons	5.00
2	Baltimore Colts	5.00
3	Buffalo Bills	5.00
4	Chicago Bears	7.50
5	Cincinnati Bengals	5.00
6	Cleveland Browns	5.00
7	Dallas Cowboys	10.00
8	Denver Broncos	5.00
9	Detroit Lions	5.00
10	Green Bay Packers	5.00
11	Houston Oilers	5.00
12	Kansas City Chiefs	5.00
13	Los Angeles Rams	5.00
14	Miami Dolphins	7.50
15	Minnesota Vikings	5.00
16	New England Patriots	5.00
17	New York Giants	5.00
18	New York Jets	5.00
19	New Orleans Saints	5.00
20	Oakland Raiders	7.50
21	Philadelphia Eagles	5.00
22	Pittsburgh Steelers	7.50
23	St. Louis Cardinals	5.00
24	San Diego Chargers	5.00
25	San Francisco 49ers	7.50
26	Seattke Seahawks	5.00
27	Tampa Bay Buccaneers	5.00
28	Washington Redskins	7.50
29	Checklist 1-132	5.00
30	Checklist 133-264	5.00

1977 Topps

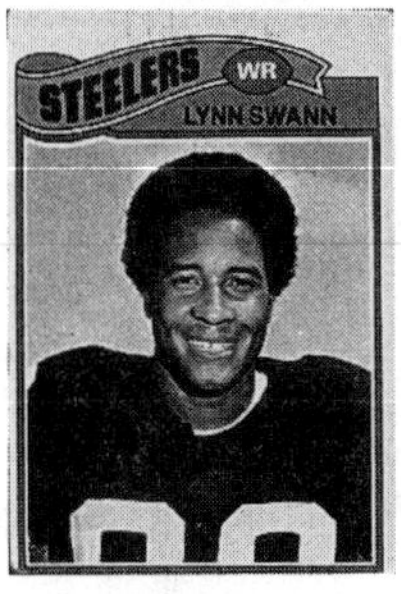

Known primarily for containing Steve Largent's rookie issue, this set of 528 cards also has the second-year card of Walter Payton. Other rookie cards included in the set are Pat Haden, Jim Zorn, John Cappeletti, Richard Todd, Harry Carson, Chuck Muncie, Archie Griffin and Dave Casper. All-Pro designations were once again placed on the regular-issued card. Of the subsets, the "Record" run appears in the middle of the set; AFC/NFC championship and the Super Bowl card are the last three in the set; and the statistical leader cards are the first six. This was the last year in which team checklists were issued; future cards would show team leaders with the checklists.

		NM
Complete Set (528):		230.00
Common Player:		.20
Wax Pack (10):		17.50
Wax Box (36):		440.00
Wax Pack (14):		22.50
Wax Box (36):		580.00
1	Passing Leaders: (James Harris, Ken Stabler)	1.75
2	Receiving Leaders: (Drew Pearson, MacArthur Lane)	.50
3	Rushing Leaders: (Walter Payton, O.J. Simpson)	9.00
4	Scoring Leaders: (Mark Moseley, Toni Linhart)	.35
5	Interception Leaders: (Monte Jackson, Ken Riley)	.35
6	Punting Leaders: (John James, Marv Bateman)	.35
7	Mike Phipps	.20
8	Rick Volk	.20
9	Steve Furness	.20
10	Isaac Curtis	.20
11	Nate Wright	.20
12	Jean Fugett	.20
13	Ken Mendenhall	.20
14	Sam Adams	.20
15	Charlie Waters	1.00
16	Bill Stanfill	.20
17	John Holland	.20
18	*Pat Haden*	3.00
19	Bob Young	.20
20	Wally Chambers (AP)	.20
21	Lawrence Gaines	.20
22	Larry McCarren	.20
23	Horst Muhlmann	.20
24	Phil Villapiano	.20
25	Greg Pruitt	.20
26	Ron Howard	.20
27	Craig Morton	.75
28	Rufus Mayes	.20
29	*Lee Roy Selmon*	7.00
30	Ed White (AP)	.20
31	Harold McLinton	.20
32	Glenn Doughty	.20
33	Bob Kuechenberg	.20
34	Duane Carrell	.20
35	Riley Odoms	.20
36	Bobby Scott	.20
37	Nick Mike-Mayer	.20
38	Bill Lenkaitis	.20
39	Roland Harper	.20
40	Tommy Hart (AP)	.20
41	Mike Sensibaugh	.20
42	Rusty Jackson	.20
43	Levi Johnson	.20
44	Mike McCoy	.20
45	Roger Staubach	10.00
46	Fred Cox	.20
47	Bob Babich	.20
48	Reggie McKenzie	.20
49	Dave Jennings	.20
50	*Mike Haynes* (AP)	5.00
51	Larry Brown	.20
52	Marvin Cobb	.20
53	Fred Cook	.20
54	Freddie Solomon	.30
55	John Riggins	2.50
56	John Bunting	.20
57	Ray Wersching	.20
58	Mike Livingston	.20
59	Billy Johnson	.50
60	Mike Wagner (AP)	.20
61	Waymond Bryant	.20
62	Jim Otis	.20
63	Ed Galigher	.20
64	Randy Vataha	.20
65	*Jim Zorn*	4.00
66	John Keyworth	.20
67	Checklist 1-132	1.50
68	Henry Childs	.20
69	Thom Darden	.20
70	George Kunz (AP)	.20
71	Lenvil Elliott	.20
72	Curtis Johnson	.20
73	Doug Van Horn	.20
74	Joe Theismann	4.00
75	Dwight White	.20
76	Scott Laidlaw	.20
77	Monte Johnson	.20
78	Dave Beverly	.20
79	Jim Mitchell	.20
80	Jack Youngblood (AP)	.75
81	Mel Gray	.20
82	Dwight Harrison	.20
83	John Hadl	.50
84	*Matt Blair*	2.00
85	Charlie Sanders	.20
86	Noah Jackson	.20
87	Ed Marinaro	.40
88	Bob Howard	.20
89	John McDaniel	.20
90	Dan Dierdorf (AP)	1.25
91	Mark Moseley	.35
92	Cleo Miller	.20
93	Andre Tillman	.20
94	Bruce Taylor	.20
95	Bert Jones	1.00
96	*Anthony Davis*	1.00
97	Don Goode	.20
98	*Ray Rhodes*	5.00
99	*Mike Webster*	8.00
100	O.J. Simpson (AP)	5.00
101	*Doug Plank*	.75
102	Efren Herrera	.20
103	Charlie Smith	.20
104	Carlos Brown	.20
105	Jim Marshall	.70
106	Paul Naumoff	.20
107	Walter White	.20
108	*John Cappelletti*	2.50
109	Chip Myers	.20
110	Ken Stabler (AP)	8.00
111	Joe Ehrmann	.20
112	Rick Engles	.20
113	Jack Dolbin	.20
114	Ron Bolton	.20
115	Mike Thomas	.20
116	Mike Fuller	.20
117	John Hill	.20
118	*Richard Todd*	1.00
119	*Duriel Harris*	.50
120	John James (AP)	.20
121	Lionel Antoine	.20
122	John Skorupan	.20
123	Skip Butler	.20
124	Bob Tucker	.20
125	Paul Krause	.50
126	Dave Hampton	.20
127	Tom Wittum	.20
128	Gary Huff	.20
129	Emmitt Thomas	.20
130	Drew Pearson (AP)	2.00
131	Ron Saul	.20
132	Steve Niehaus	.20
133	Fred Carr	.20
134	Norm Bulaich	.20
135	Bob Trumpy	.40
136	Greg Landry	.20
137	George Buehler	.20
138	Reggie Rucker	.20
139	Julius Adams	.20
140	Jack Ham (AP)	2.50
141	Wayne Morris	.20
142	Marv Bateman	.20
143	Bobby Maples	.20
144	Harold Carmichael	1.00
145	Bob Avellini	.20
146	*Harry Carson*	7.00
147	Lawrence Pillers	.20
148	Ed Williams	.20
149	Dan Pastorini	.40
150	Ron Yary (AP)	.20
151	Joe Lavender	.20
152	Pat McInally	.75
153	Lloyd Mumphord	.20
154	Cullen Bryant	.20
155	Willie Lanier	.75
156	Gene Washington	.30
157	Scott Hunter	.20
158	Jim Merlo	.20
159	Randy Grossman	.20
160	Blaine Nye (AP)	.20
161	Ike Harris	.20
162	Doug Dieken	.20
163	Guy Morriss	.20
164	Bob Parsons	.20
165	Steve Grogan	2.00
166	John Brockington	.20
167	Charlie Joiner	1.50
168	Ron Carpenter	.20
169	Jeff Wright	.20
170	Chris Hanburger (AP)	.20
171	*Roosevelt Leaks*	.40
172	Larry Little	.60
173	John Matuszak	.20
174	Joe Ferguson	.50
175	Brad Van Pelt	.30
176	*Dexter Bussey*	.30
177	*Steve Largent*	50.00
178	Dewey Selmon	.20
179	Randy Gradishar	1.00
180	Mel Blount (AP)	3.00
181	Dan Neal	.20
182	Rich Szaro	.20
183	Mike Boryla	.20
184	Steve Jones	.20
185	Paul Warfield	2.00
186	*Greg Buttle*	.40
187	Rich McGeorge	.20
188	*Leon Gray*	.50
189	John Shinners	.20
190	Toni Linhart (AP)	.20
191	Robert Miller	.20
192	Jake Scott	.20
193	Jon Morris	.20
194	Randy Crowder	.20
195	Lynn Swann	10.00
196	Marsh White	.20
197	*Rod Perry*	.30
198	Willie Hall	.20
199	Mike Hartenstine	.20
200	Jim Bakken (AP)	.20
201	Atlanta Falcons Team	1.00
202	Baltimore Colts Team	1.00
203	Buffalo Bills Team	1.00
204	Chicago Bears Team	1.00
205	Cincinnati Bengals Team	1.00
206	Cleveland Browns Team	1.00
207	Dallas Cowboys Team	1.00
208	Denver Broncos Team	1.00
209	Detroit Lions Team	1.00
210	Green Bay Packers Team	1.00
211	Houston Oilers Team	1.00
212	Kansas City Chiefs Team	1.00
213	Los Angeles Rams Team	1.00
214	Miami Dolphins Team	1.00
215	Minnesota Vikings Team	1.00
216	New England Patriots Team	1.00
217	New Orleans Saints Team	1.00
218	New York Giants Team	1.00
219	New York Jets Team	1.00
220	Oakland Raiders Team	1.00
221	Philadelphia Eagles Team	1.00
222	Pittsburgh Steelers Team	1.00
223	St. Louis Cardinals Team	1.00
224	San Diego Chargers Team	1.00
225	San Francisco 49ers Team	1.00
226	Seattle Seahawks Team	1.00
227	Tampa Bay Bucaneers Team	1.00
228	Washington Redskins Team	1.00
229	Sam Cunningham	.20
230	Alan Page (AP)	1.25
231	Eddie Brown	.20
232	Stan White	.20
233	Vern Den Herder	.20
234	Clarence Davis	.20
235	Ken Anderson	1.75
236	Karl Chandler	.20
237	Will Harrell	.20
238	Clarence Scott	.20
239	Bo Rather	.20
240	Robert Brazile (AP)	.40
241	Bob Bell	.20
242	Rolland Lawrence	.20
243	Tom Sullivan	.20
244	Larry Brunson	.20
245	Terry Bradshaw	7.00
246	Rich Saul	.20
247	Cleveland Elam	.20
248	Don Woods	.20
249	Bruce Laird	.20
250	Coy Bacon (AP)	.20
251	Russ Francis	.60
252	Jim Braxton	.20
253	Perry Smith	.20
254	Jerome Barkum	.20
255	Garo Yepremian	.20
256	Checklist 133-264	1.50
257	*Tony Galbreath*	.50
258	Troy Archer	.20
259	Brian Sipe	1.00
260	Billy Joe DuPree (AP)	.50
261	Bobby Walden	.20
262	Larry Marshall	.20
263	Ted Fritsch	.20
264	Larry Hand	.20
265	Tom Mack	.30
266	Ed Bradley	.20
267	Pat Leahy	.75
268	Louis Carter	.20
269	*Archie Griffin*	5.00
270	Art Shell (AP)	1.50
271	Stu Voigt	.20
272	Prentice McCray	.20
273	MacArthur Lane	.20
274	Dan Fouts	5.00
275	Charley Young	.20
276	*Wilbur Jackson*	.50
277	John Hicks	.20
278	Nat Moore	.60
279	Virgil Livers	.20
280	Curley Culp (AP)	.20
281	Rocky Bleier	1.00
282	John Zook	.20
283	Tom DeLeone	.20
284	*Danny White*	5.00
285	Otis Armstrong	.40
286	Larry Walton	.20
287	Jim Carter	.20
288	Don McCauley	.20
289	Frank Grant	.20
290	Roger Wehrli (AP)	.20
291	Mick Tinglehoff	.20
292	Bernard Jackson	.20
293	*Tom Owen*	.30
294	Mike Esposito	.20
295	Fred Biletnikoff	2.00
296	*Revie Sorey*	.30
297	John McMakin	.20
298	Dan Ryczek	.20
299	Wayne Moore	.20
300	Franco Harris (AP)	4.00
301	*Rick Upchurch*	2.00
302	Jim Stienke	.20
303	Charlie Davis	.20
304	Don Cockroft	.20
305	Ken Burrough	.20
306	Clark Gaines	.20
307	Bobby Douglass	.20
308	Ralph Perretta	.20
309	Wally Hilgenberg	.20
310	*Monte Jackson* (AP)	.40
311	*Chris Bahr*	.50
312	Jim Cheyunski	.20
313	Mike Patrick	.20
314	Ed "Too Tall" Jones	5.00
315	Bill Bradley	.20
316	Benny Malone	.20
317	Paul Seymour	.20
318	Jim Laslavic	.20
319	Frank Lewis	.20
320	Ray Guy (AP)	.75
321	Allen Ellis	.20
322	Conrad Dobler	.30
323	Chester Marcol	.20
324	Doug Kotar	.20
325	Lemar Parrish	.20
326	Steve Holden	.20
327	Jeff Van Note	.20
328	Howard Stevens	.20
329	Brad Dusek	.20
330	Joe DeLamielleure (AP)	.20
331	Jim Plunkett	1.00
332	Checklist 265-396	1.50
333	Lou Piccone	.20
334	Ray Hamilton	.20
335	Jan Stenerud	.60
336	Jeris White	.20
337	*Sherman Smith*	.35
338	Dave Green	.20
339	Terry Schmidt	.20
340	*Sammie White* (AP)	1.25
341	*Jon Kolb*	.30
342	Randy White	7.00
343	Bob Klein	.20
344	Bob Kowalkowski	.20
345	Terry Metcalf	.30
346	Joe Danelo	.20
347	Ken Payne	.20
348	Neal Craig	.20
349	Dennis Johnson	.20
350	Bill Bergey (AP)	.50
351	Raymond Chester	.20
352	Bob Matheson	.20
353	Mike Kadish	.20
354	*Mark Van Eeghen*	.75
355	L.C. Greenwood	.60
356	Sam Hunt	.50
357	Darrell Austin	.20
358	Jim Turner	.20
359	Ahmad Rashad	2.00
360	Walter Payton (AP)	35.00
361	Mark Arneson	.20
362	Jerrel Wilson	.20
363	Steve Bartkowski	1.00
364	John Watson	.20
365	Ken Riley	.20
366	Gregg Bingham	.20
367	Golden Richards	.20
368	Clyde Powers	.20
369	Diron Talbert	.20
370	Lydell Mitchell	.30
371	Bob Jackson	.20
372	Jim Mandich	.20
373	Frank LeMaster	.20
374	Benny Ricardo	.20
375	Lawrence McCutcheon	.30
376	Lynn Dickey	.50
377	Phil Wise	.20
378	Tony McGee	.20
379	Norm Thompson	.20
380	*Dave Casper* (AP)	5.00
381	Glen Edwards	.20
382	Bob Thomas	.20
383	Bob Chandler	.20
384	Rickey Young	.20
385	Carl Eller	.60
386	Lyle Alzado	1.00
387	John Leypoldt	.20
388	Gordon Bell	.20
389	Mike Bragg	.20
390	Jim Langer (AP)	1.00
391	Vern Holland	.20
392	Nelson Munsey	.20
393	Mack Mitchell	.20
394	Tony Adams	.20
395	Preston Pearson	.35
396	Emanuel Zanders	.20
397	Vince Papale	.20
398	*Joe Fields*	.30
399	Craig Clemons	.20
400	Fran Tarkenton (AP)	6.00
401	Andy Johnson	.20
402	Willie Buchanon	.20
403	Pat Curran	.20
404	Ray Jarvis	.20
405	Joe Greene	2.00
406	Bill Simpson	.20
407	Ronnie Coleman	.20
408	J.K. McKay	.20
409	Pat Fischer	.20
410	John Dutton (AP)	.20
411	Boobie Clark	.20
412	*Pat Tilley*	1.00
413	Don Strock	.30
414	Brian Kelley	.20
415	Gene Upshaw	1.00
416	Mike Montler	.20
417	Checklist 397-528	1.50
418	John Gilliam	.20
419	Brent McClanahan	.20

420	Jerry Sherk (AP)	.20
421	Roy Gerela	.20
422	Tim Fox	.20
423	John Ebersole	.20
424	James Scott	.20
425	*Delvin Williams*	.75
426	Spike Jones	.20
427	Harvey Martin	1.25
428	Don Herrmann	.20
429	Calvin Hill	.40
430	Isiah Robertson (AP)	.20
431	Tony Greene	.20
432	Bob Johnson	.20
433	Lem Barney	.90
434	Eric Torkelson	.20
435	John Mendenhall	.20
436	Larry Seiple	.20
437	Art Kuehn	.20
438	John Vella	.20
439	Greg Latta	.20
440	Roger Carr (AP)	.20
441	Doug Sutherland	.20
442	Mike Kruczek	.20
443	Steve Zabel	.20
444	*Mike Pruitt*	1.00
445	Harold Jackson	.60
446	George Jakowenko	.20
447	John Fitzgerald	.20
448	Terry Joyce	.20
449	Jim LeClair	.20
450	Ken Houston (AP)	.75
451	Record: (Steve Grogan)	.40
452	Record: (Jim Marshall)	.40
453	Record: (O.J. Simpson)	5.00
454	Record: (Tarkenton)	3.00
455	Record: (Jim Zorn)	.40
456	Robert Pratt	.20
457	Walker Gillette	.20
458	Charlie Hall	.20
459	Robert Newhouse	.30
460	John Hannah (AP)	1.25
461	Ken Reaves	.20
462	Herman Weaver	.20
463	James Harris	.20
464	Howard Twilley	.20
465	Jeff Siemon	.20
466	John Outlaw	.20
467	*Chuck Muncie*	1.50
468	Bob Moore	.20
469	Robert Woods	.20
470	Cliff Branch (AP)	1.50
471	Johnnie Gray	.20
472	Don Hardeman	.20
473	Steve Ramsey	.20
474	Steve Mike-Mayer	.20
475	Gary Garrison	.20
476	Walter Johnson	.20
477	Neil Clabo	.20
478	Len Hauss	.20
479	Darryl Stingley	.40
480	Jack Lambert (AP)	7.00
481	Mike Adamle	.20
482	David Lee	.20
483	Tom Mullen	.20
484	Claude Humphrey	.20
485	Jim Hart	.60
486	Bobby Thompson	.20
487	Jack Rudnay	.20
488	Rich Sowells	.20
489	Reuben Gant	.20
490	Cliff Harris (AP)	.75
491	Bob Brown	.20
492	Don Nottingham	.20
493	Ron Jessie	.20
494	Otis Sistrunk	.30
495	Bill Kilmer	.60
496	Oscar Roan	.20
497	Bill Van Heusen	.20
498	Randy Logan	.20
499	John Smith	.20
500	Chuck Foreman (AP)	.50
501	J.T. Thomas	.20
502	Steve Schubert	.20
503	Mike Barnes	.20
504	J.V. Cain	.20
505	Larry Csonka	2.00
506	Elvin Bethea	.20
507	Ray Easterling	.20
508	Joe Reed	.20
509	Steve Odom	.20
510	Tommy Casanova (AP)	.20
511	Dave Dalby	.20
512	Richard Caster	.20
513	Fred Dryer	1.50
514	Jeff Kinney	.20
515	Bob Griese	4.00
516	*Butch Johnson*	.75
517	Gerald Irons	.20
518	Don Calhoun	.20
519	Jack Gregory	.20
520	Tom Banks (AP)	.20
521	Bobby Bryant	.20
522	Reggie Harrison	.20
523	Terry Hermeling	.20
524	David Taylor	.20
525	*Brian Baschnagel*	.50
526	AFC Championship: (Ken Stabler)	.40
527	NFC Championship	.40
528	Super Bowl XI	1.50

1977 Topps Holsum Packers/Vikings

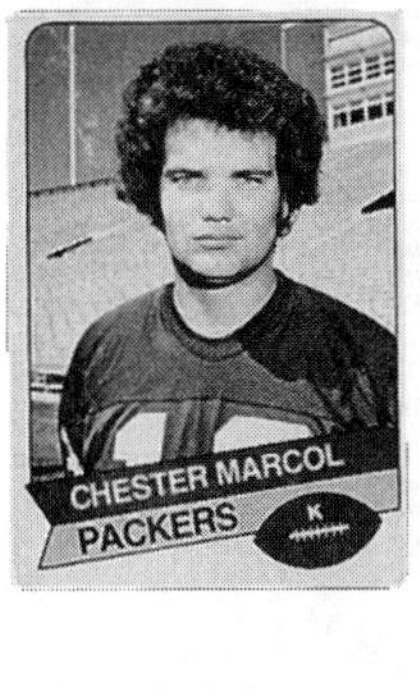

The 22-card, standard-size set featuring 11 Green Bay players (1-11) and 11 Minnesota players (12-22) was issued in Holsum Bread packages. For an unapparent reason, Holsum did not print its name or logo anywhere on the cards.

		NM
Complete Set (22):		45.00
Common Player:		1.00
1	Lynn Dickey	3.00
2	John Brockington	2.00
3	Will Harrell	1.00
4	Ken Payne	1.00
5	Rich McGeorge	1.00
6	Steve Odom	1.00
7	Jim Carter	1.00
8	Fred Carr	1.00
9	Willie Buchanon	2.00
10	Mike McCoy	1.00
11	Chester Marcol	1.00
12	Chuck Foreman	4.00
13	Ahmad Rashad	7.00
14	Sammie White	3.00
15	Stu Voigt	1.00
16	Fred Cox	1.00
17	Carl Eller	4.00
18	Alan Page	6.00
19	Jeff Siemon	1.00
20	Bobby Bryant	1.00
21	Paul Krause	3.00
22	Ron Yary	2.00

1977 Topps Mexican

The 528-card, standard-size set is the Spanish parallel set to the standard 1977 Topps set. All text on the card fronts and backs is in Spanish. The wrappers are also deemed collectible as they depict various NFL stars.

		NM
Complete Set (528):		6000.
Common Player:		8.00
Common Checklist:		12.00
Semistars:		10.00
Pack (2):		
Wax Box (36):		
1	Passing Leaders (James Harris, Ken Stabler)	100.00
2	Receiving Leaders (Drew Pearson, MacArthur Lane)	15.00
3	Rushing Leaders (Walter Payton, O.J. Simpson)	180.00
4	Scoring Leaders (Mark Moseley, Toni Linhart)	25.00
18	Pat Haden	30.00
29	Lee Roy Selmon (UER) (Misspelled Leroy)	75.00
45	Roger Staubach	100.00
50	Mike Haynes (AP)	25.00
55	John Riggins	30.00
65	Jim Zorn	30.00
74	Joe Theismann	40.00
80	Jack Youngblood (AP)	15.00
90	Dan Dierdorf (AP)	20.00
95	Bert Jones	15.00
96	Anthony Davis	20.00
98	Ray Rhodes	25.00
99	Mike Webster	50.00
100	O.J. Simpson (AP)	100.00
108	John Cappelletti	20.00
110	Ken Stabler (AP)	100.00
130	Drew Pearson (AP)	25.00
140	Jack Ham (AP)	30.00
144	Harold Carmichael	15.00
146	Harry Carson	40.00
165	Steve Grogan	20.00
167	Charlie Joiner	20.00
173	John Matuszak	20.00
177	Steve Largent	550.00
179	Randy Gradishar	15.00
180	Mel Blount (AP)	30.00
185	Paul Warfield	30.00
195	Lynn Swann	100.00
230	Alan Page (AP)	20.00
235	Ken Anderson	20.00
245	Terry Bradshaw	100.00
259	Brian Sipe	15.00
269	Archie Griffin	50.00
270	Art Shell (AP)	15.00
274	Dan Fouts	60.00
281	Rocky Bleier	30.00
284	Danny White	50.00
295	Fred Biletnikoff	30.00
300	Franco Harris (AP)	50.00
314	Ed "Too Tall" Jones	75.00
320	Ray Guy (AP)	15.00
331	Jim Plunkett	15.00
342	Randy White	60.00
359	Ahmad Rashad	20.00
360	Walter Payton (AP)	400.00
380	Dave Casper (AP)	40.00
386	Lyle Alzado	15.00
400	Fran Tarkenton (AP)	60.00
405	Joe Greene	30.00
412	Pat Tilley	20.00
415	Gene Upshaw	20.00
427	Harvey Martin	20.00
433	Lem Barney	15.00
444	Mike Pruitt	20.00
450	Ken Houston (AP)	20.00
453	O.J. Simpson (RB)	70.00
454	Most Yardage, Passing, Lifetime (Fran Tarkenton) (RB)	35.00
455	Most Passing Yards Season, Rookie (Jim Zorn) (RB)	25.00
460	John Hannah (AP)	15.00
467	Chuck Muncie	15.00
470	Cliff Branch (AP)	30.00
480	Jack Lambert (AP)	60.00
505	Larry Csonka	45.00
515	Bob Griese	45.00
526	AFC Championship (Ken Stabler)	75.00
527	NFC Championship	75.00
528	Super Bowl XI	200.00

A player's name in *italic type* indicates a rookie card.

1977 Topps Team Checklists

The 30-card, standard-size set contains a 28 team checklist and two checklist cards and was available through Topps as an uncut sheet. The cards are identical to the checklists in the base set, except for the thinner stock.

		NM
Complete Set (30):		120.00
Common Player:		5.00
1	Atlanta Falcons	5.00
2	Baltimore Colts	5.00
3	Buffalo Bills	5.00
4	Chicago Bears	8.00
5	Cincinnati Bengals	5.00
6	Cleveland Browns	5.00
7	Dallas Cowboys	10.00
8	Denver Broncos	5.00
9	Detroit Lions	5.00
10	Green Bay Packers	8.00
11	Houston Oilers	5.00
12	Kansas City Chiefs	5.00
13	Los Angeles Rams	5.00
14	Miami Dolphins	8.00
15	Minnesota Vikings	5.00
16	New England Patriots	5.00
17	New York Giants	5.00
18	New York Jets	5.00
19	New Orleans Saints	5.00
20	Oakland Raiders	8.00
21	Philadelphia Eagles	5.00
22	Pittsburgh Steelers	8.00
23	St. Louis Cardinals	5.00
24	San Diego Chargers	5.00
25	San Francisco 49ers	8.00
26	Seattle Seahawks	5.00
27	Tampa Bay Buccaneers	5.00
28	Washington Redskins	8.00
NN01	Checklist 1-132	5.00
NN02	Checklist 133-264	5.00

1978 Topps

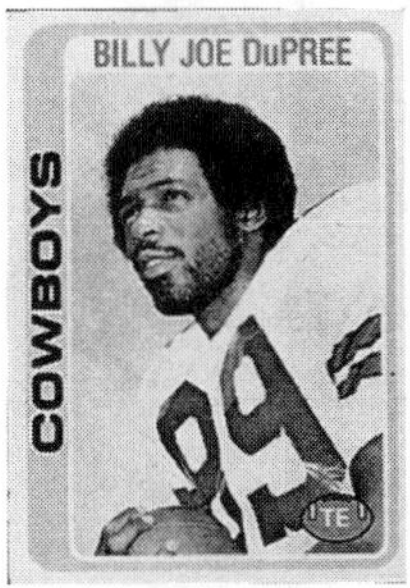

Topps' fourth 528-card set featured a colorful design, with the team name in white inside a solid border of color down the left side of the card. The subsets in the 1978 set include highlights, conference leader cards, and team leader cards (the last cards in the set; the team leader cards are arranged alphabetically by city name). This is the first time Topps pictured the actual team leaders on its team cards. The set is most notable for the inclusion of the Dorsett rookie card, the Largent second-year card, and the Payton third-year card. Other rookies in the set include Johnny Rodgers, Joe Klecko, John Stallworth, Wesley Walker, Stanley Morgan and Pete Johnson. (Key: AP - All Pro)

		NM
Complete Set (528):		140.00
Common Player:		.15
Wax Pack (14):		10.00
Wax Box (36):		240.00
1	Gary Huff (HL)	.25
2	Craig Morton (HL)	.25
3	Walter Payton (HL)	6.00
4	O.J. Simpson (HL)	3.00
5	Fran Tarkenton (HL)	2.00
6	Bob Thomas (HL)	.25
7	Joe Pisarcik	.15
8	Skip Thomas	.15
9	Roosevelt Leaks	.15
10	Ken Houston (AP)	.75
11	Tom Blanchard	.15
12	Jim Turner	.15
13	Tom DeLeone	.15
14	Jim LeClair	.15
15	Bob Avellini	.15
16	Tony McGee	.15
17	James Harris	.15
18	Terry Nelson	.15
19	Rocky Bleier	.75
20	Joe DeLamielleure (AP)	.15
21	Richard Caster	.15
22	*A.J. Duhe*	1.00
23	John Outlaw	.15
24	Danny White	1.50
25	Larry Csonka	1.50
26	David Hill	.15
27	Mark Arneson	.15
28	Jack Tatum	.15
29	Norm Thompson	.15
30	Sammie White	.30
31	Dennis Johnson	.15
32	Robin Earl	.15
33	Don Cockroft	.15
34	Bob Johnson	.15
35	John Hannah	.75
36	Scott Hunter	.15
37	Ken Burrough	.15
38	Wilbur Jackson	.15
39	Rich McGeorge	.15
40	Lyle Alzado (AP)	.75
41	John Ebersole	.15
42	*Gary Green*	.15
43	Art Kuehn	.15
44	Glen Edwards	.15
45	Lawrence McCutcheon	.15
46	Duriel Harris	.15
47	Rich Szaro	.15
48	Mike Washington	.15
49	Stan White	.15
50	Dave Casper (AP)	1.00
51	Len Hauss	.15
52	James Scott	.15
53	Brian Sipe	.60
54	Gary Shirk	.15
55	Archie Griffin	.60
56	Mike Patrick	.15
57	Mario Clark	.15
58	Jeff Siemon	.15
59	Steve Mike-Mayer	.15
60	Randy White (AP)	2.50
61	Darrell Austin	.15
62	Tom Sullivan	.15
63	*Johnny Rodgers*	1.75
64	Ken Reaves	.15
65	Terry Bradshaw	6.00
66	Fred Steinfort	.15
67	Curley Culp	.15
68	Ted Hendricks	.75
69	Raymond Chester	.15
70	Jim Langer (AP)	.75
71	Calvin Hill	.30
72	Mike Hartenstine	.15
73	Gerald Irons	.15
74	Billy Brooks	.15
75	John Mendenhall	.15
76	Andy Johnson	.15
77	Tom Wittum	.15
78	Lynn Dickey	.25
79	Carl Eller	.40
80	Tom Mack	.15
81	Clark Gaines	.15
82	Lem Barney	.75
83	Mike Montler	.15
84	Jon Kolb	.15
85	Bob Chandler	.15
86	Robert Newhouse	.15
87	Frank LeMaster	.15
88	Jeff West	.15
89	Lyle Blackwood	.15
90	Gene Upshaw (AP)	.15
91	Frank Grant	.50
92	Tom Hicks	.15
93	Mike Pruitt	.35
94	Chris Bahr	.15
95	Russ Francis	.35
96	Norris Thomas	.15
97	*Gary Barbaro*	.40
98	Jim Merlo	.15
99	Karl Chandler	.15
100	Fran Tarkenton	4.00
101	Abdul Salaam	.15
102	Marv Kellum	.15
103	Herman Weaver	.15
104	Roy Gerela	.15
105	Harold Jackson	.50
106	Dewey Selmon	.15
107	Checklist 1-132	1.00
108	Clarence Davis	.15
109	Robert Pratt	.15
110	Harvey Martin (AP)	.60
111	Brad Dusek	.15
112	Greg Latta	.15
113	Tony Peters	.15
114	Jim Braxton	.15
115	Ken Riley	.15
116	Steve Nelson	.15
117	Rick Upchurch	.35
118	Spike Jones	.15
119	Doug Kotar	.15
120	Bob Griese (AP)	3.00
121	Burgess Owens	.15
122	Rolf Benirschke	.60
123	Haskel Stanback	.15
124	J.T. Thomas	.15
125	Ahmad Rashad	1.25
126	Rick Kane	.15
127	Elvin Bethea	.15
128	Dave Dalby	.15
129	Mike Barnes	.15
130	Isiah Robertson	.15
131	Jim Plunkett	.75
132	Allan Ellis	.15
133	Mike Bragg	.15
134	Bob Jackson	.15
135	Coy Bacon	.15
136	John Smith	.15
137	Chuck Muncie	.35
138	Johnnie Gray	.15
139	Jimmy Robinson	.15
140	Tom Banks	.15
141	*Marvin Powell*	.40
142	Jerrell Wilson	.15
143	Ron Howard	.15
144	*Rob Lytle*	.35
145	L.C. Greenwood	.50
146	Morris Owens	.15
147	Joe Reed	.15
148	Mike Kadish	.15
149	Phil Villapiano	.15
150	Lydell Mitchell	.15
151	Randy Logan	.15
152	Mike Williams	.15
153	Jeff Van Note	.15
154	Steve Schubert	.15
155	Bill Kilmer	.50
156	Boobie Clark	.15
157	Charlie Hall	.15
158	*Raymond Clayborn*	.60
159	Jack Gregory	.15
160	Cliff Harris (AP)	.50
161	Joe Fields	.15
162	Don Nottingham	.15
163	Ed White	.15
164	Toni Fritsch	.15
165	Jack Lambert	3.00
166	NFC Champions (Roger Staubach)	1.50
167	AFC Champions: (Rob Lytle)	.30
168	Super Bowl XII (Tony Dorsett)	2.50
169	*Neal Colzie*	.20
170	Cleveland Elam (AP)	.15
171	David Lee	.15
172	Jim Otis	.15
173	Archie Manning	.75
174	Jim Carter	.15
175	Jean Fugett	.15
176	Willie Parker	.15
177	Haven Moses	.15
178	Horace King	.15
179	Bob Thomas	.15
180	Monte Jackson	.15
181	Steve Zabel	.15
182	John Fitzgerald	.15
183	Mike Livingston	.15
184	Larry Poole	.15
185	Isaac Curtis	.15
186	Chuck Ramsey	.15
187	Bob Klein	.15
188	Ray Rhodes	.15
189	Otis Sistrunk	.15
190	Bill Bergey	.30
191	Sherman Smith	.15
192	Dave Green	.15
193	Carl Mauck	.15
194	Reggie Harrison	.15
195	Roger Carr	.15
196	Steve Bartkowski	.75
197	Ray Wershing	.15
198	Willie Buchanon	.15
199	Neil Clabo	.15
200	Walter Payton (AP)	20.00
201	Sam Adams	.15
202	Larry Gordon	.15
203	Pat Tilley	.15
204	Mack Mitchell	.15
205	Ken Anderson	1.25
206	Scott Dierking	.15
207	Jack Rudnay	.15
208	Jim Stienke	.15
209	Bill Simpson	.15
210	Errol Mann	.15
211	Bucky Dilts	.15
212	Reuben Gant	.15
213	*Thomas Henderson*	.50
214	Steve Furness	.15
215	John Riggins	2.00
216	*Keith Krepfle*	.35
217	*Fred Dean*	1.25
218	Emanuel Zanders	.15
219	Don Testerman	.15
220	George Kunz	.15
221	Darryl Stingley	.25
222	Ken Sanders	.15
223	Gary Huff	.15
224	Gregg Bingham	.15
225	Jerry Sherk	.15
226	Doug Plank	.15
227	Ed Taylor	.15
228	Emery Moorehead	.15
229	*Reggie Williams*	2.50
230	Claude Humphrey	.15
231	*Randy Cross*	2.50
232	Jim Hart	.50
233	Bobby Bryant	.15
234	Larry Brown	.15
235	Mark Van Eeghen	.15
236	Terry Hermeling	.15
237	Steve Odom	.15
238	Jan Stenerud	.50
239	Andre Tillman	.15
240	*Tom Jackson* (AP)	4.00
241	Ken Mendenhall	.15
242	Tim Fox	.15
243	Don Herrmann	.15
244	Eddie McMillan	.15
245	Greg Pruitt	.30
246	J.K. McKay	.15
247	Larry Keller	.15
248	Dave Jennings	.15
249	Bo Harris	.15
250	Revie Sorey	.15
251	Tony Greene	.15
252	Butch Johnson	.35
253	Paul Naumoff	.15
254	Rickey Young	.15
255	Dwight White	.15
256	Joe Lavender	.15
257	Checklist 133-264	1.00
258	Ronnie Coleman	.15
259	Charlie Smith	.15
260	Ray Guy (AP)	.50
261	David Taylor	.15
262	Bill Lenkaitis	.15
263	Jim Mitchell	.15
264	Delvin Williams	.15
265	Jack Youngblood	.60
266	Chuck Crist	.15
267	Richard Todd	.30
268	*Dave Logan*	.35
269	Rufus Mayes	.15
270	Brad Van Pelt	.15
271	Chester Marcol	.15
272	J.V. Cain	.15
273	Larry Seiple	.15
274	Brent McClanahan	.15
275	Mike Wagner	.15
276	Diron Talbert	.15
277	Brian Baschnagel	.15
278	Ed Podolak	.15
279	Don Goode	.15
280	John Dutton	.15
281	Don Calhoun	.15
282	Monte Johnson	.15
283	Ron Jessie	.15
284	Jon Morris	.15
285	Riley Odoms	.15
286	Marv Bateman	.15
287	*Joe Klecko*	2.00
288	Oliver Davis	.15
289	John McDaniel	.15
290	Roger Staubach	8.00
291	Brian Kelley	.15
292	Mike Hogan	.15
293	John Leypoldt	.15
294	Jack Novak	.15
295	Joe Greene	1.50
296	John Hill	.15
297	Danny Buggs	.15
298	Ted Albrecht	.15
299	Nelson Munsey	.15
300	Chuck Foreman	.40
301	Dan Pastorini	.30
302	Tommy Hart	.15
303	Dave Beverly	.15
304	*Tony Reed*	.30
305	Cliff Branch	1.00
306	Clarence Duren	.15
307	Randy Rasmussen	.15
308	Oscar Roan	.15
309	Lenvil Elliott	.15
310	Dan Dierdorf (AP)	1.00
311	Johnny Perkins	.15
312	*Rafael Septien*	.30
313	Terry Beeson	.15
314	Lee Roy Selmon	.50
315	*Tony Dorsett*	35.00
316	Greg Landry	.30
317	Jake Scott	.15
318	Dan Peiffer	.15
319	John Bunting	.15
320	*John Stallworth*	20.00
321	Bob Howard	.15
322	Larry Little	.50
323	Reggie McKenzie	.15
324	Duane Carrell	.15
325	Ed Simonini	.15
326	John Vella	.15
327	*Wesley Walker*	3.50
328	Jon Keyworth	.15
329	Ron Bolton	.15
330	Tommy Casanova	.15
331	Passing Leaders: (Bob Griese, Roger Staubach)	3.50
332	Receiving Leaders: (Lydell Mitchell, Ahmad Rashad)	.25
333	Rushing Leaders: (Mark Van Eeghen, Walter Payton)	2.25
334	Scoring Leaders: (Errol Mann, Walter Payton)	2.25
335	Interception Leaders: (Lyle Blackwood, Rolland Lawrence)	.25
336	Punting Leaders: (Ray Guy, Tom Blanchard)	.25
337	Robert Brazile	.15
338	Charlie Joiner	1.00
339	Joe Ferguson	.30
340	Bill Thompson	.15
341	Sam Cunningham	.15
342	Curtis Johnson	.15
343	Jim Marshall	.50
344	Charlie Sanders	.15
345	Willie Hall	.15
346	Pat Haden	.75
347	Jim Bakken	.15
348	Bruce Taylor	.15
349	Barty Smith	.15
350	Drew Pearson	1.00
351	Mike Webster	2.00
352	Bobby Hammond	.15
353	Dave Mays	.15
354	Pat McInally	.15
355	Toni Linhart	.15
356	Larry Hand	.15
357	Ted Fritsch	.15
358	Larry Marshall	.15
359	Waymond Bryant	.15
360	*Louie Kelcher*	.35
361	*Stanley Morgan*	4.00
362	*Bruce Harper*	.30
363	Bernard Jackson	.15
364	Walter White	.15
365	Ken Stabler	6.00
366	Fred Dryer	1.00
367	Ike Harris	.15
368	Norm Bulaich	.15
369	Merv Krakau	.15
370	John James	.15
371	*Bennie Cunningham*	.30
372	Doug Van Horn	.15
373	Thom Darden	.15
374	*Eddie Edwards*	.15
375	Mike Thomas	.15
376	Fred Cook	.15
377	Mike Phipps	.15
378	Paul Krause	.15
379	Harold Carmichael	.75
380	Mike Haynes (AP)	1.00
381	Wayne Morris	.15
382	Greg Buttle	.15
383	Jim Zorn	.50
384	Jack Dolbin	.15
385	Charlie Waters	.50
386	Dan Ryczek	.15
387	*Joe Washington*	1.00
388	Checklist 265-396	1.00
389	James Hunter	.15
390	Billy Johnson	.15
391	Jim Allen	.15
392	George Buehler	.15
393	Harry Carson	1.25
394	Cleo Miller	.15
395	Gary Burley	.15
396	Mark Moseley	.25
397	Virgil Livers	.15
398	Joe Ehrmann	.15
399	Freddie Solomon	.15
400	O.J. Simpson	5.00
401	Julius Adams	.15
402	Artimus Parker(	.15
403	Gene Washington	.15
404	Herman Edwards	.15
405	Craig Morton	.50
406	Alan Page	.75
407	Larry McCarren	.15
408	Tony Galbreath	.15
409	Roman Gabriel	.60
410	Efren Herrera (AP)	.15
411	*Jim Smith*	.60
412	Bill Bryant	.15
413	Doug Dieken	.15
414	Marvin Cobb	.15
415	Fred Biletnikoff	1.50
416	Joe Theismann	2.50
417	Roland Harper	.15
418	Derrel Luce	.15
419	Ralph Perretta	.15
420	*Louis Wright*	1.00
421	Prentice McCray	.15
422	Garry Puetz	.15
423	*Alfred Jenkins*	.50
424	Paul Seymour	.15
425	Garo Yepremian	.15
426	Emmitt Thomas	.15
427	Dexter Bussey	.15
428	John Sanders	.15
429	Ed "Too Tall" Jones	2.00
431	Frank Lewis	.15
432	Jerry Golsteyn	.15
433	Clarence Scott	.15
434	*Pete Johnson*	.50
435	Charley Young	.15
436	Harold McLinton	.15
437	Noah Jackson	.15
438	Bruce Laird	.15
439	John Matuszak	.15
440	Nat Moore (AP)	.35
441	Leon Gray	.15
442	Jerome Barkum	.15
443	Steve Largent	15.00
444	John Zook	.15
445	Preston Pearson	.30
446	Conrad Dobler	.15
447	Wilbur Summers	.15
448	Lou Piccone	.15
449	Ron Jaworski	.60
450	Jack Ham (AP)	1.50
451	Mick Tingelhoff	.15
452	Clyde Powers	.15
453	John Cappelletti	.50
454	Dick Ambrose	.15
455	Lemar Parrish	.15

456	Ron Saul	.15
457	Bob Parsons	.15
458	Glenn Doughty	.15
459	Don Woods	.15
460	Art Shell (AP)	1.00
461	Sam Hunt	.15
462	Lawrence Pillers	.15
463	Henry Childs	.15
464	Roger Wehrli	.15
465	Otis Armstrong	.30
466	*Bob Baumhower*	.75
467	Ray Jarvis	.15
468	Guy Morriss	.15
469	Matt Blair	.35
470	Bill Joe DuPree	.35
471	Roland Hooks	.15
472	Joe Danelo	.15
473	Reggie Rucker	.15
474	Vern Holland	.15
475	Mel Blount	1.25
476	Eddie Brown	.15
477	Bo Rather	.15
478	Don McCauley	.15
479	Glen Walker	.15
480	Randy Gradishar (AP)	.90
481	Dave Rowe	.15
482	Pat Leahy	.40
483	Mike Fuller	.15
484	David Lewis	.15
485	Steve Grogan	.75
486	Mel Gray	.15
487	*Eddie Payton*	.30
488	Checklist 397-528	1.00
489	Stu Voigt	.15
490	Rolland Lawrence (AP)	.15
491	Nick Mike-Mayer	.15
492	Troy Archer	.15
493	Benny Malone	.15
494	Golden Richards	.15
495	Chris Hanburger	.15
496	Dwight Harrison	.15
497	*Gary Fencik*	.75
498	Rich Saul	.15
499	Dan Fouts	5.00
500	Franco Harris (AP)	2.50
501	Atlanta Falcons Team: (Haskel Stanback, Alfred Jenkins, Claude Humphrey, Jeff Merrow, Rolland Lawrence)	.50
502	Baltimore Colts Team: (Lydell Mitchell, Lyle Blackwood, Fred Cook)	.50
503	Buffalo Bills Team: (Bob Chandler, O.J. Simpson, Tony Greene, Sherman White)	2.00
504	Chicago Bears Team: (James Scott, Allan Ellis, Ron Rydalch, Walter Payton)	1.75
505	Cincinnati Bengals Team: (Billy Brooks, Lemar Parrish, Reggie Williams, Gary Burley, Pete Johnson)	.75
506	Cleveland Browns Team: (Reggie Rucker, Thom Darden, Mack Mitchell, Greg Pruitt)	.50
507	Dallas Cowboys Team: (Drew Pearson, Cliff Harris, Harvey Martin, Tony Dorsett)	2.00
508	Denver Broncos Team: (Otis Armstrong, Haven Moses, Bill Thompson, Rick Upchurch)	.50
509	Detroit Lions Team: (Horace King, David Hill, James Hunter, Ken Sanders)	.50
510	Green Bay Packers Team: (Barty Smith, Steve Odom, Steve Luke, M.C. McCoy, Dave Pureifory, Dave Roller)	.50
511	Houston Oilers Team: (Ronnie Coleman, Ken Burrough, Mike Reinfeldt, James Young)	.50
512	Kansas City Chiefs Team: (Ed Podolak, Walter White, Gary Barbaro, Wilbur Young)	.50
513	Los Angeles Rams Team: (Lawrence McCutcheon, Harold Jackson, Bill Simpson, Jack Youngblood)	.50
514	Miami Dolphins Team: (Benny Malone, Nat Moore, Curtis Johnson, A.J. Duhe)	.50
515	Minnesota Vikings Team: (Chuck Foreman, Sammie White, Bobby Bryant, Carl Eller)	.50
516	New England Patriots Team: (Sam Cunningham, Darryl Stingley, Mike Haynes, Tony McGee)	.50
517	New Orleans Saints Team: (Chuck Muncie, Don Herrmann, Chuck Crist, Elois Grooms)	.50
518	New York Giants Team: (Bobby Hammond, Jimmy Robinson, Bill Bryant, John Mendenhall)	.50
519	New York Jets Team: (Clark Gaines, Wesley Walker, Burgess Owens, Joe Klecko)	.75
520	Oakland Raiders Team: (Mark Van Eeghen, Dave Casper, Jack Tatum, Neal Colzie)	.50
521	Philadelphia Eagles Team: (Mike Hogan, Harold Carmichael, Herman Edwards, John Sanders, Lem Burnham)	.50
522	Pittsburgh Steelers Team: (Jim Smith, Mel Blount, Steve Furness, Franco Harris)	1.00
523	St. Louis Cardinals Team: (Terry Metcalf, Mel Gray, Roger Wehrli, Mike Dawson)	.50
524	San Diego Chargers Team: (Rickey Young, Charlie Joiner, Mike Fuller, Gary Johnson)	.50
525	San Francisco 49ers Team: (Delvin Williams, G. Washington, Mel Phillips, Dave Washington, Cleveland Elam)	.50
526	Seattle Seahawks Team: (Steve Largent, Autry Beamon, Walter Packer, Sherman Smith)	1.50
527	Tampa Bay Buccaneers Team: (Morris Owens, Isaac Hagins, Mike Washington, Lee Roy Selmon)	.50
528	Washington Redskins Team: (Jean Fugett, Ken Houston, Dennis Johnson, Mike Thomas)	1.00

1978 Topps Holsum

The 33-card, standard-size set was produced by Topps and distributed with loaves of Holsum Bread. For whatever reason, the cards do not have the Holsum name or logo printed anywhere on the card. As with the 1977 Packers/Vikings Holsum set, an uncut sheet was offered by Topps at an archives auction in 1989.

		NM
Complete Set (33):		250.00
Common Player:		3.00
1	Rolland Lawrence	3.00
2	Walter Payton	80.00
3	Lydell Mitchell	4.00
4	Joe DeLamielleure	3.00
5	Ken Anderson	10.00
6	Greg Pruitt	4.00
7	Harvey Martin	5.00
8	Tom Jackson	5.00
9	Chester Marcol	3.00
10	Jim Carter	3.00
11	Will Harrell	3.00
12	Greg Landry	4.00
13	Billy Johnson	4.00
14	Jan Stenerud	5.00
15	Lawrence McCutcheon	4.00
16	Bob Griese	20.00
17	Chuck Foreman	4.00
18	Sammie White	4.00
19	Jeff Siemon	3.00
20	Mike Haynes	4.00
21	Archie Manning	6.00
22	Brad Van Pelt	3.00
23	Richard Todd	4.00
24	Dave Casper	4.00
25	Bill Bergey	4.00
26	Franco Harris	20.00
27	Mel Gray	4.00
28	Louie Kelcher	3.00
29	O.J. Simpson	30.00
30	Jim Zorn	4.00
31	Lee Roy Selmon	6.00
32	Ken Houston	6.00
33	Checklist Card	8.00

1979 Topps

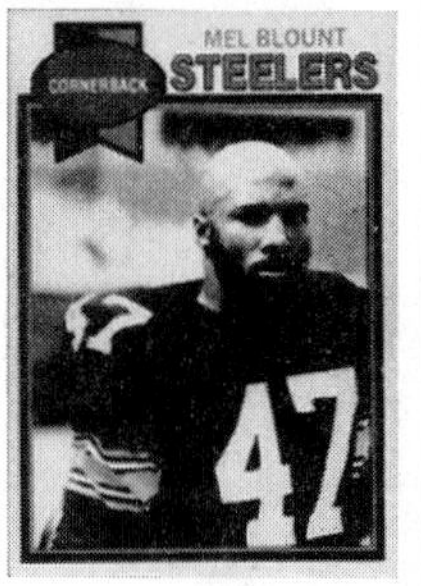

Topps' fifth 528-card set was similar in design to its 1973 set, which also showed a small flag. This set, though, showed only the lower half of the flag in solid color, and showed the player's position in a football superimposed over the flag. The team name appeared in any one of a number of colors in capital letters above the photo. Subsets in this year's issue include conference leaders and playoff results. This set is notable for the inclusion of the only four cards Topps issued depicting running back Earl Campbell. Topps was apparently unable to reach a contract agreement with Campbell after this season - possibly similar to the Joe Namath situation after 1973. In addition to Campbell, other rookie cards in this set include Doug Williams, Steve DeBerg, Wilbert Montgomery, Tony Hill, James Jefferson, Ozzie Newsome, and James Lofton. This set also contains the second-year card of Tony Dorsett. (Key: AP - All Pro)

		NM
Complete Set (528):		140.00
Common Player:		.15
Wax Pack (12):		9.00
Wax Box (36):		235.00
1	Passing Leaders (Roger Staubach, Terry Bradshaw)	5.00
2	Receiving Leaders (Rickey Young, Steve Largent)	.75
3	Rushing Leaders (Walter Payton, Earl Campbell)	7.00
4	Scoring Leaders (Frank Corral, Pat Leahy)	.25
5	Interception Leaders (Willie Buchanon, Ken Stone, Thom Darden)	.25
6	Punting Leaders (Tom Skladany, Pat McInally)	.25
7	Johnny Perkins	.15
8	Charles Phillips	.15
9	Derrel Luce	.15
10	John Riggins	1.50
11	Chester Marcol	.15
12	Bernard Jackson	.15
13	Dave Logan	.15
14	Bo Harris	.15
15	Alan Page	.75
16	John Smith	.15
17	Dwight McDonald	.15
18	John Cappelletti	.25
19	Pittsburgh Steelers Team (Franco Harris, Larry Anderson, Tim Dungy, L.C. Greenwood)	.75
20	Bill Bergey (AP)	.25
21	Jerome Barkum	.15
22	Larry Csonka	1.25
23	Joe Ferguson	.25
24	Ed "Too Tall" Jones	1.00
25	Dave Jennings	.15
26	Horace King	.15
27	Steve Little	.15
28	Morris Bradshaw	.15
29	Joe Ehrmann	.15
30	Ahmad Rashad (AP)	.75
31	Joe Lavender	.15
32	Dan Neal	.15
33	Johnny Evans	.15
34	Pete Johnson	.15
35	Mike Haynes (AP)	.40
36	Tim Mazzetti	.15
37	*Mike Barber*	.20
38	San Francisco 49ers Team (O.J. Simpson, Freddie Solomon, Chuck Crist, Cedrick Hardman)	1.75
39	Bill Gregory	.15
40	Randy Gradishar (AP)	.50
41	Richard Todd	.25
42	Henry Marshall	.15
43	John Hill	.15
44	Sidney Thornton	.15
45	Ron Jessie	.15
46	Bob Baumhower	.15
47	Johnnie Gray	.15
48	*Doug Williams*	2.00
49	Don McCauley	.15
50	Ray Guy (AP)	.30
51	Bob Klein	.15
52	Golden Richards	.15
53	Mark Miller	.15
54	John Sanders	.15
55	Gary Burley	.15
56	Steve Nelson	.15
57	Buffalo Bills Team (Miller, Frank Lewis, Mario Clark, Lucius Sanford)	.50
58	Bobby Bryant	.15
59	Rick Kane	.15
60	Larry Little	.35
61	Ted Fritsch	.15
62	Larry Mallory	.15
63	Marvin Powell	.15
64	Jim Hart	.30
65	Joe Greene (AP)	1.25
66	Walter White	.15
67	Gregg Bingham	.15
68	Errol Mann	.15
69	Bruce Laird	.15
70	Drew Pearson	.75
71	Steve Bartkowski	.60
72	Ted Albrecht	.15
73	Charlie Hall	.15
74	Pat McInally	.15
75	*Al Baker* (AP)	1.00
76	New England Patriots Team (Sam Cunningham, Stanley Morgan, Mike Haynes, Tony McGee)	.50
77	*Steve DeBerg*	4.00
78	John Yarno	.15
79	Stu Voight	.15
80	Frank Corral (AP)	.15
81	Troy Archer	.15
82	Bruce Harper	.15
83	Tom Jackson	.75
84	Larry Brown	.15
85	*Wilbert Montgomery*	1.00
86	Butch Johnson	.15
87	Mike Kadish	.15
88	Ralph Perretta	.15
89	David Lee	.15
90	Mark Van Eeghen	.15
91	John McDaniel	.15
92	Gary Fencik	.15
93	Mack Mitchell	.15
94	Cincinnati Bengals Team (Pete Johnson, Isaac Curtis, Dick Jauron, Ross Browner)	.50
95	Steve Grogan	.50
96	Garo Yepremian	.15
97	Barty Smith	.15
98	Frank Reed	.15
99	Jim Clark	.15
100	Chuck Foreman	.30
101	Joe Klecko	.75
102	Pat Tilley	.15
103	Conrad Dobler	.15
104	Craig Colquitt	.15
105	Dan Pastorini	.20
106	Rod Perry (AP)	.15
107	Nick Mike-Mayer	.15
108	John Matuszak	.15
109	David Taylor	.15
110	Billy Joe DuPree (AP)	.15
111	Harold McLinton	.15
112	Virgil Livers	.15
113	Cleveland Browns Team (Greg Pruitt, Reggie Rucker, Thom Darden, Mack Mitchell)	.50
114	Checklist 1-132	1.00
115	Ken Anderson	1.25
116	Bill Lenkaitis	.15
117	Bucky Dilts	.15
118	Tony Greene	.15
119	Bobby Hammond	.15
120	Nat Moore	.15
121	Pat Leahy (AP)	.30
122	James Harris	.15
123	Lee Roy Selmon	.25
124	Bennie Cunningham	.15
125	Matt Blair (AP)	.15
126	Jim Allen	.15
127	Alfred Jenkins	.15
128	Arthur Whittington	.15
129	Norm Thompson	.15
130	Pat Haden	.40
131	Freddie Solomon	.15
132	Chicago Bears Team (Walter Payton, James Scott, Gary Fencik, Alan Page)	2.00
133	Mark Moseley	.15
134	Cleo Miller	.15
135	*Ross Browner*	.30
136	Don Calhoun	.15
137	David Whitehurst	.15
138	Terry Beeson	.15
139	Ken Stone	.15
140	Brad Van Pelt AP	.15
141	Wesley Walker (AP)	.75
142	Jan Stenerud	.50
143	Henry Childs	.15
144	Otis Armstrong	.25
145	Dwight White	.15
146	Steve Wilson	.15
147	Tom Skladany (AP)	.15
148	Lou Piccone	.15
149	Monte Johnson	.15
150	Joe Washington	.20
151	Philadelphia Eagles Team (Wilbert Montgomery, Harold Carmichael, Herman Edwards, Dennis Harrison)	.60
152	Fred Dean	.25
153	Rolland Lawrence	.15
154	Brian Baschnagel	.15
155	Joe Theismann	1.50
156	Marvin Cobb	.15
157	Dick Ambrose	.15
158	Mike Patrick	.15
159	Gary Shirk	.15
160	Tony Dorsett	8.00
161	Greg Buttle	.15
162	A.J. Duhe	.15
163	Mick Tingelhoff	.15
164	Ken Burrough	.15
165	Mike Wagner	.15
166	AFC Championship (Franco Harris)	1.00
167	NFC Championship	.30
168	Super Bowl XII (Franco Harris)	1.25
169	Oakland Raiders Team (Mark Van Eeghen, Dave Casper, Charles Phillips, Ted Hendricks)	.60
170	O.J. Simpson	4.00
171	Doug Nettles	.15
172	Dan Dierdorf (AP)	.75
173	Dave Beverly	.15
174	Jim Zorn	.35
175	Mike Thomas	.15
176	John Outlaw	.15
177	Jim Turner	.15
178	Freddie Scott	.15
179	Mike Phipps	.15
180	Jack Youngblood (AP)	.50
181	Sam Hunt	.15
182	*Tony Hill*	1.00
183	Gary Barbaro	.15
184	Archie Griffin	.40
185	Jerry Sherk	.15
186	Bobby Jackson	.15
187	Don Woods	.15
188	New York Giants Team (Doug Kotar, Jimmy Robinson, Terry Jackson, George Martin)	.15
189	Raymond Chester	.15
190	Joe DeLamielleure (AP)	.15
191	Tony Galbreath	.15
192	Robert Brazile (AP)	.15
193	Neil O'Donoghue	.15
194	Mike Webster	.75
195	Ed Simonini	.15
196	Denny Malone	.15
197	Tom Wittum	.15
198	Steve Largent (AP)	8.00
199	Tommy Hart	.15
200	Fran Tarkenton	4.00
201	Leon Gray (AP)	.15
202	Leroy Harris	.15
203	Eric Williams	.15
204	Thom Darden (AP)	.15
205	Ken Riley	.15
206	Clark Gaines	.15
207	Kansas City Chiefs Team (Tony Reed, Tim Gray, Art Still)	.50
208	Joe Danelo	.15
209	Glen Walker	.15
210	Art Shell	1.00
211	Jon Keyworth	.15
212	Herman Edwards	.15
213	John Fitzgerald	.15
214	Jim Smith	.15
215	Coy Bacon	.15
216	Dennis Johnson	.15
217	*John Jefferson*	3.00
218	Gary Weaver	.15
219	Tom Blanchard	.15
220	Bert Jones	.50
221	Stanley Morgan	1.50
222	James Hunter	.15
223	Jim O'Bradovich	.15
224	Carl Mauck	.15
225	Chris Bahr	.15
226	New York Jets Team (Kevin Long, Wesley Walker, Bobby Jackson, Burgess Owens, Joe Klecko)	.60
227	Roland Harper	.15
228	Randy Dean	.15
229	Bob Jackson	.15
230	Sammie White	.25
231	Mike Dawson	.15
232	Checklist 133-264	1.00
233	Ken MacAfee	.15
234	Jon Kolb (AP)	.15
235	Willie Hall	.15
236	Ron Saul (AP)	.15
237	Haskel Stanback	.15
238	Zenon Andrusyshyn	.15
239	Norris Thomas	.15
240	Rick Upchurch	.30
241	Robert Pratt	.15
242	Julius Adams	.15
243	Rich McGeorge	.15
244	Seattle Seahawks Team (Sherman Smith, Steve Largent, Cornell Webster, Bill Gregory)	1.00
245	Blair Bush	.15
246	Billy Johnson	.15
247	Randy Rasmussen	.15
248	Brian Kelley	.15
249	Mike Pruitt	.15
250	Harold Carmichael (AP)	.60
251	Mike Hartenstine	.15
252	Robert Newhouse	.15
253	Gary Danielson	.30
254	Mike Fuller	.15
255	L.C. Greenwood (AP)	.40
256	Lemar Parrish	.15
257	Ike Harris	.15
258	*Ricky Bell*	1.00
259	Willie Parker	.15
260	Gene Upshaw	.50
261	Glenn Doughty	.15
262	Steve Zabel	.15
263	Atlanta Falcons Team (Bubba Bean, Wallace Francis, Rolland Lawrence, Greg Brezina)	1.00
264	Ray Wersching	.15
265	Lawrence McCutcheon	.15
266	Willie Buchanon (AP)	.15
267	Matt Robinson	.15
268	Reggie Rucker	.15
269	Doug Van Horn	.15
270	Lydell Mitchell	.15
271	Vern Holland	.15
272	Eason Ramson	.15
273	Steve Towle	.15
274	Jim Marshall	.40
275	Mel Blount	1.00
276	Bob Kuziel	.15
277	James Scott	.15
278	Tony Reed	.15
279	Dave Green	.15
280	Toni Linhart	.15
281	Andy Johnson	.15
282	Los Angeles Rams Team (Cullen Bryant, Willie Miller, Rod Perry, Pat Thomas, Larry Brooks)	1.00
283	Phil Villapiano	.15
284	Dexter Bussey	.15
285	Craig Morton	.50
286	Guy Morriss	.15
287	Lawrence Pillers	.15
288	Gerald Irons	.15
289	Scott Perry	.15
290	Randy White	2.00
291	Jack Gregory	.15
292	Bob Chandler	.15
293	Rich Szaro	.15
294	Sherman Smith	.15
295	Tom Banks (AP)	.15
296	Revie Sorey (AP)	.15
297	Ricky Thompson	.15
298	Ron Yary	.15
299	Lyle Blackwood	.15
300	Franco Harris	2.00
301	Houston Oilers Team (Earl Campbell, Ken Burrough, Willie Alexander, Elvin Bethea)	3.00
302	Scott Bull	.15
303	Dewey Selmon	.15
304	Jack Rudnay	.15
305	Fred Biletnikoff	1.25
306	Jeff West	.15
307	Shafer Suggs	.15
308	*Ozzie Newsome*	15.00
309	Boobie Clark	.15
310	*James Lofton*	15.00
311	Joe Pisarcik	.15
312	Bill Simpson (AP)	.15
313	Haven Moses	.15
314	Jim Merlo	.15
315	Preston Pearson	.15
316	Larry Tearry	.15
317	Tom Dempsey	.15
318	Greg Latta	.15
319	Washington Redskins Team (John Riggins, John McDaniel, Jake Scott, Coy Bacon)	.75
320	Jack Ham (AP)	1.25
321	Harold Jackson	.30
322	George Roberts	.15
323	Ron Jaworski	.40
324	Jim Otis	.15
325	Roger Carr	.15
326	Jack Tatum	.15
327	Derrick Gaffney	.15
328	Reggie Williams	.50
329	Doug Dieken	.15
330	Efren Herrera	.15
331	Record: (Campbell)	5.50
332	Record: (Tony Galbreath)	.25
333	Record: (Bruce Harper)	.25
334	Record: (John James)	.25
335	Record: (Walter Payton)	3.00
336	Record: (Rickey Young)	.15
337	Jeff Van Note	.15
338	San Diego Chargers Team (Lydell Mitchell, John Jefferson, Mike Fuller, Fred Dean)	.60
339	*Stan Walters* (AP)	.20
340	Louis Wright (AP)	.15
341	Horace Ivory	.15
342	Andre Tillman	.15
343	Greg Coleman	.15
344	*Doug English* (AP)	.60
345	Ted Hendricks	.50
346	Rich Saul	.15
347	Mel Gray	.15
348	Toni Fritsch	.15
349	Cornell Webster	.15
350	Ken Houston	.50
351	Ron Johnson	.15
352	Doug Kotar	.15
353	Brian Sipe	.40
354	Billy Brooks	.15
355	John Dutton	.15
356	Don Goode	.15
357	Detroit Lions Team (Dexter Bussey, David Hill, Jim Allen, Al Baker)	1.00
358	Reuben Gant	.15
359	Bob Parsons	.15
360	Cliff Harris (AP)	.35
361	Raymond Clayborn	.20
362	Scott Dierking	.15
363	Bill Bryan	.15
364	Mike Livingston	.15
365	Otis Sistrunk	.15
366	Charley Young	.15
367	Keith Wortman	.15
368	Checklist 265-396	1.00
369	Mike Michel	.15
370	Delvin Williams	.15
371	Steve Furness	.15
372	Emery Moorehead	.15
373	Clarence Scott	.15
374	Rufus Mayes	.15
375	Chris Hanberger	.15
376	Baltimore Colts Team (Joe Washington, Roger Carr, Norm Thompson, John Dutton)	.50
377	Bob Avellini	.15
378	Jeff Siemon	.15
379	Roland Hooks	.15
380	Russ Francis	.15
381	Roger Wehrli	.15
382	Joe Fields	.15
383	Archie Manning	.50
384	Rob Lytle	.15
385	Thomas Henderson	.15
386	Morris Owens	.15
387	Dan Fouts	4.00
388	Chuck Crist	.15
389	Ed O'Neil	.15
390	*Earl Campbell* (AP)	30.00
391	Randy Grossman	.15
392	Monte Jackson	.15
393	John Mendenhall	.15
394	Miami Dolphins Team (Delvin Williams, Duriel Harris, Tim Foley, Vern Den Herder)	.50
395	Isaac Curtis	.15
396	Mike Bragg	.15
397	Doug Plank	.15
398	Mike Barnes	.15
399	Calvin Hill	.20
400	Roger Staubach (AP)	8.00
401	Doug Beaudoin	.15
402	Chuck Ramsey	.15
403	Mike Hogan	.15
404	Mario Clark	.15
405	Riley Odoms	.15
406	Carl Eller	.30
407	Green Bay Packers Team (Terdell Middleton, James Lofton, Willie Buchanon, Ezra Johnson)	2.75
408	Mark Arenson	.15
409	*Vince Ferragamo*	.60
410	Cleveland Elam	.15
411	*Donnie Shell*	3.00
412	Ray Rhodes	.15
413	Don Cockroft	.15
414	Don Bass	.15
415	Cliff Branch	.75
416	Diron Talbert	.15
417	Tom Hicks	.15
418	Roosevelt Leaks	.15
419	Charlie Joiner	.75
420	Lyle Alzado (AP)	.75
421	Sam Cunningham	.15
422	Larry Keller	.15
423	Jim Mitchell	.15
424	Randy Logan	.15
425	Jim Langer	.40
426	Gary Green	.15
427	Luther Blue	.15
428	Dennis Johnson	.15
429	Danny White	.75
430	Roy Gerela	.15
431	Jimmy Robinson	.15
432	Minnesota Vikings Team (Chuck Foreman, Ahmad Rashad, Bobby Bryant, Mark Mullaney)	.50
433	Oliver Davis	.15
434	Lenvill Elliott	.15
435	Willie Miller	.15
436	Brad Dusek	.15
437	Bob Thomas	.15
438	Ken Mendenhall	.15
439	Clarence Davis	.15
440	Bob Griese	2.00
441	Tony McGee	.15
442	Ed Taylor	.15
443	Ron Howard	.15
444	Wayne Morris	.15
445	Charlie Waters	.35
446	Rick Danmeier	.15
447	Paul Naumoff	.15
448	Keith Krepfle	.15
449	Rusty Jackson	.15
450	John Stallworth	3.00
451	New Orleans Saints Team (Tony Galbreath, Henry Childs, Tom Myers, Elex Price)	.50
452	Ron Mikolajczyk	.15
453	Fred Dryer	.75
454	Jim LeClair	.15
455	Greg Pruitt	.25
456	Jake Scott	.15
457	Steve Schubert	.15
458	George Kunz	.15

#	Player	Value
459	Mike Williams	.15
460	Dave Casper (AP)	.15
461	Sam Adams	.15
462	Abdul Salaam	.15
463	Terdell Middleton	.15
464	Mike Wood	.15
465	Bill Thompson (AP)	.15
466	Larry Gordon	.15
467	Benny Ricardo	.15
468	Reggie McKenzie	.15
469	Dallas Cowboys Team (Tony Dorsett, Tony Hill, Benny Barnes, Harvey Martin, Randy White)	1.00
470	Rickey Young	.15
471	Charlie Smith	.15
472	Al Dixon	.15
473	Tom DeLeone	.15
474	Louis Breeden	.15
475	Jack Lambert	2.00
476	Terry Hermeling	.15
477	J.K. McKay	.15
478	Stan White	.15
479	Terry Nelson	.15
480	Walter Payton (AP)	12.00
481	Dave Dalby	.15
482	Burgess Owens	.15
483	Rolf Benirschke	.15
484	Jack Dolbin	.15
485	John Hannah (AP)	.60
486	Checklist 397-528	1.00
487	Greg Landry	.20
488	St. Louis Cardinals Team (Jim Otis, Pat Tilley, Ken Stone, Mike Dawson)	.50
489	Paul Krause	.15
490	John James	.15
491	Merv Krakau	.15
492	Dan Doornink	.15
493	Curtis Johnson	.15
494	Rafael Septien	.15
495	Jean Fugett	.15
496	Frank LeMaster	.15
497	Allan Ellis	.15
498	*Billy Waddy*	.20
499	Hank Bauer	.15
500	Terry Bradshaw (AP)	5.50
501	Larry McCarren	.15
502	Fred Cook	.15
503	Chuck Muncie	.20
504	Herman Weaver	.15
505	Eddie Edwards	.15
506	Tony Peters	.15
507	Denver Broncos Team (Lonnie Perrin, Riley Odoms, Steve Foley, Bernard Jackson, Lyle Alzado)	.50
508	Jimbo Elrod	.15
509	David Hill	.15
510	Harvey Martin	.35
511	Terry Miller	.15
512	*June Jones*	1.00
513	Randy Cross	.30
514	Duriel Harris	.15
515	Harry Carson	.75
516	Tim Fox	.15
517	John Zook	.15
518	Bob Tucker	.15
519	Kevin Long	.15
520	Ken Stabler	4.00
521	John Bunting	.15
522	Rocky Bleier	.75
523	Noah Jackson	.15
524	Cliff Parsley	.15
525	Louie Kelcher (AP)	.15
526	Tampa Bay Bucaneers (Ricky Bell, Morris Owens, Cedric Brown, Lee Roy Selmon)	.60
527	Bob Brudzinski	.15
528	Danny Buggs	.15

1980 Topps

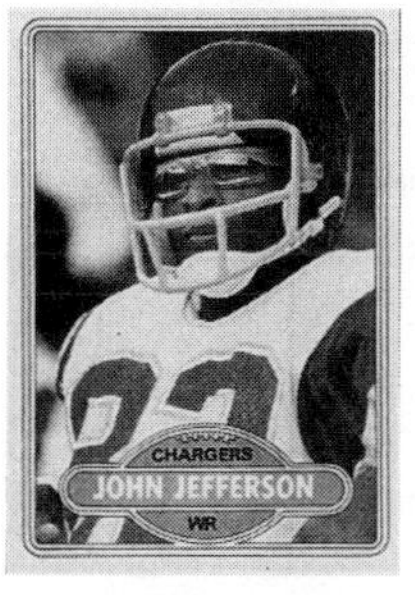

The cards in this set feature a football at the bottom of the card with the team name and position on either side of the player's name. The 528-card set has subsets featuring, as usual, record breakers and the previous year's playoff decisions. Rookies in this set include Ottis Anderson, Tommy Kramer, Phil Simms and Wes Chandler. (Key: AP - All Pro)

#	Player	NM
	Complete Set (528):	65.00
	Common Player:	.08
	Wax Pack (12):	3.25
	Wax Box (36):	70.00
1	Record: (O. Anderson)	1.00
2	Record: (Harold Carmichael)	.15
3	Record: (Dan Fouts)	1.00
4	Record: (Paul Krause)	.15
5	Record: (Rick Upchurch)	.15
6	Record: (Garo Yepremian)	.15
7	Harold Jackson	.25
8	Mike Williams	.08
9	Calvin Hill	.15
10	Jack Ham	1.00
11	Dan Melville	.08
12	Matt Robinson	.08
13	Billy Campfield	.08
14	Phil Tabor	.08
15	Randy Hughes	.08
16	Andre Tillman	.08
17	Isaac Curtis	.08
18	Charley Hannah	.08
19	Washington Redskins Team (John Riggins, Danny Buggs, Joe Lavender, Coy Bacon)	.50
20	Jim Zorn	.30
21	Brian Baschnagel	.08
22	Jon Keyworth	.08
23	Phil Villapiano	.08
24	Richard Osborne	.08
25	Rich Saul (AP)	.08
26	Doug Beaudoin	.08
27	Cleveland Elam	.08
28	Charlie Joiner	.65
29	Dick Ambrose	.08
30	*Mike Reinfeldt* (AP)	.11
31	*Matt Bahr*	1.75
32	Keith Krepfle	.08
33	Herbert Scott	.08
34	Doug Kotar	.08
35	Bob Griese	1.75
36	*Jerry Butler*	.40
37	Rolland Lawrence	.08
38	Gary Weaver	.08
39	Kansas City Chiefs Team (Ted McKnight, J.T. Smith, Gary Barbaro, Art Still)	.40
40	Chuck Muncie	.08
41	Mike Hartenstine	.08
42	Sammie White	.20
43	Ken Clark	.08
44	Clarence Harmon	.08
45	Bert Jones	.30
46	Mike Washington	.08
47	Joe Fields	.08
48	Mike Wood	.08
49	Oliver Davis	.08
50	Stan Walters (AP)	.08
51	Riley Odoms	.08
52	Steve Pisarkiewicz	.08
53	Tony Hill	.40
54	Scott Perry	.08
55	*George Martin*	.40
56	George Roberts	.08
57	Seattle Seahawks Team (Sherman Smith, Steve Largent, Dave Brown, Manu Tuiasosopo)	.75
58	Billy Johnson	.08
59	Reuben Johnson	.08
60	*Dennis Harrah* (AP)	.20
61	Rocky Bleier	.35
62	Sam Hunt	.08
63	Allan Ellis	.08
64	Ricky Thompson	.08
65	Ken Stabler	1.50
66	Dexter Bussey	.08
67	Ken Mendenhall	.08
68	Woodrow Lowe	.08
69	Thom Darden	.08
70	Randy White (AP)	1.50
71	Ken MacAfee	.08
72	Ron Jaworski	.30
73	*William Andrews*	1.00
74	Jimmy Robinson	.08
75	Roger Wehrli (AP)	.08
76	Miami Dolphins Team (Larry Csonka, Nat Moore, Neal Colzie, Gerald Small, Vern Den Herder)	.50
77	Jack Rudnay	.08
78	James Lofton	4.00
79	Robert Brazile	.08
80	Russ Francis	.08
81	Ricky Bell	.30
82	Bob Avellini	.08
83	Bobby Jackson	.08
84	Mike Bragg	.08
85	Cliff Branch	.50
86	Blair Bush	.08
87	Sherman Smith	.08
88	Glen Edwards	.08
89	Don Cockroft	.08
90	Louis Wright (AP)	.15
91	Randy Grossman	.08
92	*Carl Hariston*	.75
93	Archie Manning	.40
94	New York Giants Team (Billy Taylor, Earnest Gray, George Martin)	.30
95	Preston Pearson	.08
96	Rusty Chambers	.08
97	Greg Coleman	.08
98	Charley Young	.08
99	*Matt Cavanaugh*	.30
100	Jesse Baker	.08
101	Doug Plank	.08
102	Checklist 1-132	.65
103	*Luther Bradley*	.11
104	Bob Kuziel	.08
105	Craig Morton	.35
106	Sherman White	.08
107	*Jim Breech*	.75
108	Hank Bauer	.08
109	Tom Blanchard	.08
110	Ozzie Newsome (AP)	4.00
111	Steve Furness	.08
112	Frank LeMaster	.08
113	Dallas Cowboys Team (Tony Dorsett, Tony Hill, Harvey Martin)	.75
114	Doug Van Horn	.08
115	Delvin Williams	.08
116	Lyle Blackwood	.08
117	Derrick Gaffney	.08
118	Cornell Webster	.08
119	Sam Cunningham	.08
120	Jim Youngblood (AP)	.08
121	Bob Thomas	.08
122	*Jack Thompson*	.15
123	Randy Cross	.08
124	Karl Lorch	.08
125	Mel Gray	.08
126	John James	.08
127	Terdell Middleton	.08
128	Leroy Jones	.08
129	Tom DeLeone	.08
130	John Stallworth (AP)	1.00
131	*Jimmie Giles*	.08
132	Philadelphia Eagles Team (Wilbert Montgomery, Harold Carmichael, Brenard Wilson, Carl Hairston)	.30
133	Gary Green	.08
134	John Dutton	.08
135	Harry Carson (AP)	.50
136	Bob Kuechenberg	.08
137	Ike Harris	.08
138	*Tommy Kramer*	1.00
139	Sam Adams	.08
140	Doug English (AP)	.15
141	Steve Schubert	.08
142	Rusty Jackson	.08
143	Reese McCall	.08
144	Scott Dierking	.08
145	Ken Houston (AP)	.50
146	Bob Martin	.08
147	Sam McCullum	.08
148	Tom Banks	.08
149	Willie Buchanon	.08
150	Greg Pruitt	.20
151	Denver Broncos Team (Otis Armstrong, Rick Upchurch, Steve Foley, Brison Manor)	.30
152	Don Smith	.08
153	Pete Johnson	.08
154	Charlie Smith	.08
155	Mel Blount	.75
156	John Mendenhall	.08
157	Danny White	.50
158	*Jimmy Cefalo*	.30
159	Richard Bishop (AP)	.08
160	Walter Payton (AP)	8.00
161	Dave Dalby	.08
162	Preston Dennard	.08
163	Johnnie Gray	.08
164	Russell Erxleben	.08
165	Toni Fritsch (AP)	.08
166	Terry Hermeling	.08
167	Roland Hooks	.08
168	Roger Carr	.08
169	San Diego Chargers Team (Clarence Williams, John Jefferson, Woodrow Lowe, Ray Preston, Wilbur Young)	.30
170	*Ottis Anderson* (AP)	5.00
171	Brian Sipe	.30
172	Leonard Thompson	.08
173	Tony Reed	.08
174	Bob Tucker	.08
175	Joe Greene	1.00
176	Jack Dolbin	.08
177	Chuck Ramsey	.08
178	Paul Hofer	.08
179	Randy Logan	.08
180	David Lewis (AP)	.08
181	Duriel Harris	.08
182	June Jones	.50
183	Larry McCarren	.08
184	Ken Johnson	.08
185	Charlie Waters	.30
186	Noah Jackson	.08
187	Reggie Williams	.25
188	New England Patriots Team (Sam Cunningham, Harold Jackson, Raymond Clayborn, Tony McGee)	.30
189	Carl Eller	.35
190	Ed White (AP)	.08
191	Mario Clark	.08
192	Roosevelt Leaks	.08
193	Ted McKnight	.08
194	Danny Buggs	.08
195	*Lester Hayes*	1.50
196	Clarence Scott	.08
197	New Orleans Saints Team (Chuck Muncie, Wes Chandler, Tom Myers, Elois Grooms, Don Reese)	.30
198	Richard Caster	.08
199	Louie Giammona	.08
200	Terry Bradshaw	2.75
201	Ed Newman	.08
202	Fred Dryer	.50
203	Dennis Franks	.08
204	*Bob Breunig*	.40
205	Alan Page	.50
206	Earnest Gray	.15
207	Minnesota Vikings Team (Rickey Young, Ahmad Rashad, Tommy Hannon, Nate Wright, Mark Mullaney)	.40
208	Horace Ivory	.08
209	Isaac Hagins	.08
210	Gary Johnson (Chargers, AP)	.08
211	Kevin Long	.08
212	Bill Thompson	.08
213	Don Bass	.08
214	*George Starke*	.20
215	Efren Herrera	.08
216	Theo Bell	.08
217	Monte Jackson	.08
218	Reggie McKenzie	.08
219	Bucky Dilts	.08
220	Lyle Alzado	.50
221	Tim Foley	.08
222	Mark Arneson	.08
223	Fred Quillan	.08
224	Benny Ricardo	.08
225	*Phil Simms*	15.00
226	Chicago Bears Team (Walter Payton, Brian Baschnagel, Gary Fencik, Terry Schmidt, Jon Osborne)	1.00
227	Max Runager	.08
228	Barty Smith	.08
229	Jay Saldi	.08
230	John Hannah (AP)	.50
231	Tim Wilson	.08
232	Jeff Van Note	.08
233	Henry Marshall	.08
234	Diron Talbert	.08
235	Garo Yepremian	.08
236	Larry Brown	.08
237	Clarence Williams	.08
238	Burgess Owens	.08
239	Vince Ferragamo	.25
240	Rickey Young	.08
241	Dave Logan	.08
242	Larry Gordon	.08
243	Terry Miller	.08
244	Baltimore Colts Team (Joe Washington, Fred Cook)	.30
245	Steve DeBerg	1.75
246	Checklist 133-264	.65
247	Greg Latta	.08
248	Raymond Clayborn	.08
249	Jim Clack	.08
250	Drew Pearson	.50
251	John Bunting	.08
252	Rob Lytle	.08
253	Jim Hart	.25
254	John McDaniel	.08
255	Dave Pear (AP)	.08
256	Donnie Shell	.50
257	Dan Doornink	.08
258	*Wallace Francis*	.35
259	Dave Beverly	.08
260	Lee Roy Selmon (AP)	.25
261	Doug Dieken	.08
262	Gary David	.08
263	Bob Rush	.08
264	Buffalo Bills Team (Curtis Brown, Frank Lewis, Keith Moody, Sherman White)	.30
265	Greg Landry	.20
266	Jan Stenerud	.40
267	Tom Hicks	.08
268	Pat McInally	.08
269	Tim Fox	.08
270	Harvey Martin	.30
271	Dan Lloyd	.08
272	Mike Barber	.08
273	*Wendell Tyler*	.60
274	Jeff Komlo	.08
275	*Wes Chandler*	2.50
276	Brad Dusek	.08
277	Charlie Johnson	.08
278	Dennis Swilley	.08
279	Johnny Evans	.08
280	Jack Lambert (AP)	1.25
281	Vern Den Herder	.08
282	Tampa Bay Bucaneers Team (Ricky Bell, Isaac Hagins, Lee Roy Selmon)	.30
283	Bob Klein	.08
284	Jim Turner	.08
285	Marvin Powell (AP)	.08
286	Aaron Kyle	.08
287	Dan Neal	.08
288	Wayne Morris	.08
289	Steve Bartkowski	.35
290	Dave Jennings	.08
291	John Smith	.08
292	Bill Gregory	.08
293	Frank Lewis	.08
294	Fred Cook	.08
295	David Hill (AP)	.08
296	Wade Key	.08
297	Sidney Thornton	.08
298	Charlie Hall	.08
299	Joe Lavender	.08
300	*Tom Rafferty*	.15
301	*Mike Renfro*	.15
302	Wilbur Jackson	.08
303	Green Bay Packers Team (Terdell Middleton, James Lofton, Johnnie Gray, Robert Barber, Ezra Johnson)	1.00
304	Henry Childs	.08
305	Russ Washington (AP)	.08
306	Jim LeClair	.08
307	Tommy Hart	.08
308	Gary Barbaro	.08
309	Billy Taylor	.08
310	Ray Guy	.25
311	Don Hasselbeck	.08
312	Doug Williams	.75
313	Nick Mike-Mayer	.08
314	Don McCauley	.08
315	Wesley Walker	.40
316	Dan Dierdorf	.50
317	*Dave Brown*	.30
318	Leroy Harris	.08
319	Pittsburgh Steelers Team (Franco Harris, John Stallworth, Jack Lambert, Steve Furness, L.C. Greenwood)	.75
320	Mark Moseley (AP)	.08
321	Mark Dennard	.08
322	Terry Nelson	.08
323	Tom Jackson	.50
324	Rick Kane	.08
325	Jerry Sherk	.08
326	Ray Preston	.08
327	Golden Richards	.08
328	Randy Dean	.08
329	Rick Danmeier	.08
330	Tony Dorsett	4.50
331	Passing Leaders (Dan Fouts, Roger Staubach)	2.00
332	Receiving Leaders (Joe Washington, Ahmad Rashad)	.15
333	Sack Leaders (Jesse Baker, Al Baker, Jack Youngblood)	.15
334	Scoring Leaders (John Smith, Jack Moseley)	.15
335	Interception Leaders (Mike Reinfeldt, Lemar Parrish)	.15
336	Punting Leaders (Bob Grupp, Dave Jennings)	.15
337	Freddie Solomon	.08
338	Cincinnati Bengals Team (Pete Johnson, Don Bass, Dick Jauron, Gary Burley)	.30
339	Ken Stone	.08
340	Greg Buttle (AP)	.08
341	Bob Baumhower	.08
342	Billy Waddy	.08
343	Cliff Parsley	.08
344	Walter White	.08
345	Mike Thomas	.08
346	Neil O'Donoghue	.08
347	Freddie Scott	.08
348	Joe Ferguson	.20
349	Doug Nettles	.08
350	Mike Webster (AP)	.50
351	Ron Saul	.08
352	Julius Adams	.08
353	Rafael Septien	.08
354	Cleo Miller	.08
355	Keith Simpson (AP)	.08
356	Johnny Perkins	.08
357	Jerry Sisemore	.08
358	Arthur Wittington	.08
359	St. Louis Cardinals Team (Ottis Anderson, Pat Tilley, Ken Stone, Bob Pollard)	.60
360	Rick Upchurch	.08
361	Kim Bokamper	.20
362	Roland Harper	.08
363	Pat Leahy	.08
364	Louis Breeden	.08
365	John Jefferson	.75
366	Jerry Eckwood	.08
367	David Whitehurst	.08
368	Willie Parker	.08
369	Ed Simonini	.08
370	Jack Youngblood (AP)	.40
371	*Don Warren*	1.50
372	Andy Johnson	.08
373	D.D. Lewis	.08
374	*Beasley Reece*	.30
375	L.C. Greenwood	.30
376	Cleveland Browns Team (Mike Pruitt, Dave Logan, Thom Darden, Jerry Sherk)	.30
377	Herman Edwards	.08
378	*Rob Carpenter*	.25
379	Herman Weaver	.08
380	Gary Fencik (AP)	.11
381	Don Strock	.08
382	Art Shell	.50
383	Tim Mazzetti	.08
384	Bruce Harper	.08
385	Al Baker	.08
386	Conrad Dobler	.08
387	Stu Voight	.08
388	Ken Anderson	.75
389	Pat Tilley	.08
390	John Riggins	1.25
391	Checklist 265-396	.65
392	Fred Dean (AP)	.15
393	*Benny Barnes*	.15
394	Los Angeles Rams Team (Wendell Tyler, Preston Dennard, Nolan Cromwell, Jim Youngblood)	.30
395	Brad Van Pelt	.08
396	Eddie Hare	.08
397	John Sciarra	.15
398	Bob Jackson	.08
399	John Yarno	.08
400	Franco Harris (AP)	1.75
401	Ray Wersching	.08
402	Virgil Livers	.08
403	Raymond Chester	.08
404	Leon Gray	.08
405	Richard Todd	.20
406	Larry Little	.25
407	Ted Fritsch	.08
408	Larry Mucker	.08
409	Jim Allen	.08
410	Randy Grandishar	.40
411	Atlanta Falcons Team (William Andrews, Wallace Francis, Rolland Lawrence, Don Smith)	.30
412	Louie Kelcher	.08
413	Robert Newhouse	.08
414	Gary Shirk	.08
415	Mike Haynes (AP)	.25
416	Craig Colquitt	.08
417	Lou Piccone	.08
418	*Clay Matthews*	3.00
419	Marvin Cobb	.08
420	Harold Carmichael (AP)	.50
421	Uwe Von Schamann	.08
422	Mike Phipps	.08
423	*Nolan Cromwell*	1.00
424	Glenn Doughty	.08
425	Bob Young (AP)	.08
426	Tony Galbreath	.08
427	Luke Prestridge	.08
428	Terry Beeson	.08
429	Jack Tatum	.08
430	Lemar Parrish (AP)	.08
431	Chester Marcol	.08
432	Houston Oilers Team (Dan Pastorini, Ken Burrough, Mike Reinfeldt, Jesse Baker)	.30
433	John Fitzgerald	.08
434	Gary Jeter	.40
435	Steve Grogan	.40
436	Jon Kolb	.08
437	Jim O'Bradovich	.08
438	Gerald Irons	.08
439	Jeff West	.08
440	Wilbert Montgomery	.30
441	Norris Thomas	.08
442	James Scott	.08
443	Curtis Brown	.08
444	Ken Fantetti	.08
445	Pat Haden	.30
446	Carl Mauck	.08
447	Bruce Laird	.08
448	Otis Armstrong	.20
449	Gene Upshaw	.30
450	Steve Largent (AP)	4.50
451	Benny Malone	.08
452	Steve Nelson	.08
453	Mark Cotney	.08
454	Joe Danelo	.08
455	Billy Joe DuPree	.15
456	Ron Johnson	.08
457	Archie Griffin	.25
458	Reggie Rucker	.08
459	Claude Humphrey	.08
460	Lydell Mitchell	.08
461	Steve Towle	.08
462	Revie Sorey	.08
463	Tom Skladany	.08
464	Clark Gaines	.08
465	Frank Corral	.08
466	*Steve Fuller*	.25
467	Ahmad Rashad (AP)	.75
468	Oakland Raiders Team (Mark Van Eghen, Cliff Branch, Lester Hayes, Willie Jones)	.30
469	Brian Peets	.08
470	*Pat Donovan* (AP)	.20
471	Ken Burrough	.08
472	Don Calhoun	.08
473	Bill Bryan	.08
474	Terry Jackson	.08
475	Joe Theismann	1.50
476	Jim Smith	.08
477	Joe DeLamielleure	.08
478	Mike Pruitt (AP)	.08
479	Steve Mike-Mayer	.08
480	Bill Bergey	.15
481	Mike Fuller	.08
482	Bob Parsons	.08
483	Billy Brooks	.08
484	Jerome Barkum	.08
485	Larry Csonka	1.00
486	John Hill	.08
487	Mike Dawson	.08
488	Detroit Lions Team (Dexter Bussey, Freddie Scott, Jim Allen, Luther Bradley, Al Baker)	.30
489	Ted Hendricks	.50
490	Dan Pastorini	.15
491	Stanley Morgan	.75
492	AFC Championship (Rocky Bleier)	.20
493	NFC Championship (Vince Ferragamo)	.20
494	Super Bowl XIV	.50
495	Dwight White	.08
496	Haven Moses	.08
497	Guy Morriss	.08
498	Dewey Selmon	.08
499	*Dave Butz*	1.50
500	Chuck Foreman	.20
501	Chris Bahr	.08
502	Mark Miller	.08
503	Tony Greene	.08
504	Bruce Kelley	.08
505	Joe Washington	.15
506	Butch Johnson	.08
507	New York Jets Team (Clark Gaines, Wesley Walker, Burgess Owens, Joe Klecko)	.30
508	Steve Little	.08
509	Checklist 397-528	.65
510	Mark Van Eeghen	.08
511	Gary Danielson	.08
512	Manu Tuiasosopo	.08
513	*Paul Coffman*	.40
514	Cullen Bryant	.08
515	Nat Moore	.08
516	Bill Lenkaitis	.08
517	*Lynn Cain*	.25
518	Gregg Bingham	.08
519	Ted Albrecht	.08
520	Dan Fouts (AP)	2.00
521	Bernard Jackson	.08
522	Coy Bacon	.08
523	*Tony Franklin*	.25
524	Bo Harris	.08
525	Bob Grupp (AP)	.08
526	San Francisco 49ers Team (Paul Hofer, Freddie Solomon, James Owens, Dwaine Board)	.30
527	Steve Wilson	.08
528	Bennie Cunningham	.08

1980 Topps Super

Printed on heavy white card-board stock, these oversize (around 5" x 7") cards featured 30 NFL stars. The front displays a color photo of the player and his name appears in a gold plaque atop the card; the back lists his name, position and team with the Topps logo in the center of the card. This is a set similar to the 1980 Topps Superstar Photo Baseball set.

#	Player	NM
	Complete Set (30):	15.00
	Common Player:	.30
1	Franco Harris	1.00
2	Bob Griese	1.00
3	Archie Manning	.30
4	Harold Carmichael	.30
5	Wesley Walker	.30
6	Richard Todd	.30
7	Dan Fouts	.90
8	Ken Stabler	.60
9	Jack Youngblood	.30
10	Jim Zorn	.30
11	Tony Dorsett	1.50
12	Lee Roy Selmon	.30
13	Russ Francis	.30
14	John Stallworth	.30
15	Terry Bradshaw	1.50
16	Joe Theismann	1.00
17	Ottis Anderson	.30
18	John Jefferson	.30
19	Jack Ham	.30
20	Joe Greene	.30
21	Chuck Muncie	.30
22	Ron Jaworski	.30
23	John Hannah	.30
24	Randy Gradishar	.30
25	Jack Lambert	.30
26	Ricky Bell	.30
27	Drew Pearson	.30
28	Rick Upchurch	.30
29	Brad Van Pelt	.30
30	Walter Payton	3.50

1981 Topps

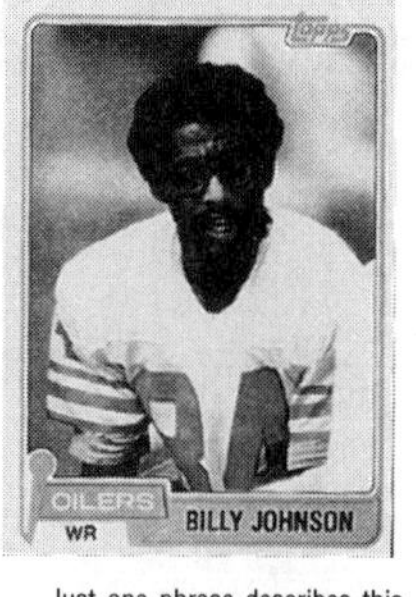

Just one phrase describes this set: Joe Montana rookie. Other rookie cards in this set include Mark Gastineau, Art Monk, Billy Sims,

Kellen Winslow, Joe Cribbs, Dwight Clark, Curtis Dickey and Charles White. The 528-card set is bordered in white. Around the photos is black piping which leads to a colored scroll at the bottom of the card showing the team and player. Super Action cards in this set - included along with the player's regular card - show the major stars in action. (Key: SA - Super Action, AP - All Pro)

MT
Complete Set (528): 250.00
Common Player: .08
Wax Pack (12-1979 Wr.): 12.25
Wax Box (36-12 card): 320.00
Wax Pack (15): 16.00
Wax Box (36-15 card): 400.00
1 Passing Leaders .10
2 Receiving Leaders .50
3 Sack Leaders .10
4 Scoring Leaders .10
5 Interception Leaders .10
6 Punting Leaders .10
7 Don Calhoun .08
8 Jack Tatum .08
9 Reggie Rucker .08
10 Mike Webster (AP) .25
11 *Vince Evans* 1.00
12 Ottis Anderson .75
13 Leroy Harris .08
14 Gordon King .08
15 Harvey Martin .15
16 Johnny Lam Jones .15
17 Ken Greene .08
18 Frank Lewis .08
19 Seattle Seahawks Team .65
20 Lester Hayes (AP) .25
21 Uwe Von Schamann .08
22 Joe Washington .08
23 Louie Kelcher .08
24 Willie Miller .08
25 Steve Grogan .25
26 John Hill .08
27 Stan White .08
28 William Andrews (SA) .08
29 Clarence Scott .08
30 Leon Gray (AP) .08
31 Craig Colquitt .08
32 Doug Williams .25
33 Bob Breunig .08
34 Billy Taylor .08
35 Harold Carmichael .50
36 Ray Wersching .08
37 Dennis Johnson .08
38 Archie Griffin .15
39 Los Angeles Rams Team (Cullen Bryant, Billy Waddy, Nolan Cromwell, Jack Youngblood) .08
40 Gary Fencik (AP) .08
41 Lynn Dickey .15
42 Steve Bartkowski (SA) .08
43 Art Shell .50
44 Wilbur Jackson .08
45 Frank Corral .08
46 Ted McKnight .08
47 Joe Klecko .15
48 Don Doornink .08
49 Doug Dieken .08
50 *Jerry Robinson* (AP) .50
51 Wallace Francis .08
52 Dave Preston .08
53 Jay Saldi .08
54 Rush Brown .08
55 Phil Simms 5.00
56 Nick Mike-Mayer .08
57 Washington Redskins Team 2.00
58 Mike Renfro .08
59 Ted Brown (SA) .08
60 Steve Nelson (AP) .08
61 Sidney Thornton .08
62 Kent Hill .08
63 Don Bessillieu .10
64 Fred Cook .08
65 Raymond Chester .08
66 Rick Kane .08
67 Mike Fuller .08
68 Dewey Selmon .08
69 *Charles White* 1.00
70 Jeff Van Note (AP) .08
71 Robert Newhouse .08
72 *Roynell Young* .20
73 Lynn Cain (SA) .08
74 Mike Friede .08
75 Earl Cooper .08
76 New Orleans Saints Team .15
77 Rick Danmeier .08
78 Darrol Ray .08
79 Gregg Bingham .08
80 John Hannah (AP) .40
81 Jack Thompson .08
82 Rick Upchurch .08
83 Mike Butler .08
84 Don Warren .25
85 Mark Van Eeghen .08
86 *J.T. Smith* 1.00
87 Herman Weaver .08
88 Terry Bradshaw (SA) 1.00
89 Charlie Hall .08
90 Donnie Shell .30
91 Ike Harris .08
92 Charlie Johnson .08
93 Rickey Watts .08
94 New England Patriots Team .15
95 Drew Pearson .60
96 Neil O'Donoghue .08
97 Conrad Dobler .08
98 Jewerl Thomas .08
99 Mike Barber .08
100 *Billy Sims* (AP) 1.50
101 Vern Den Herder .08
102 Greg Landry .15
103 Joe Cribbs (SA) .15
104 *Mark Murphy* .20
105 Chuck Muncie .08
106 Alfred Jackson .08
107 Chris Bahr .08
108 Gordon Jones .08
109 *Willie Harper* .10
110 Dave Jennings (AP) .08
111 Bennie Cunningham .08
112 Jerry Sisemore .08
113 Cleveland Browns Team .20
114 Rickey Young .08
115 Ken Anderson .75
116 Randy Gradishar .20
117 *Eddie Lee Ivery* .20
118 Wesley Walker .20
119 Chuck Foreman .20
120 Nolan Cromwell (AP) .20
121 Curtis Dickey (SA) .08
122 Wayne Morris .08
123 Greg Stemrick .08
124 Coy Bacon .08
125 Jim Zorn .20
126 Henry Childs .08
127 Checklist 1-132 .25
128 Len Walterscheid .08
129 Johnny Evans .08
130 Gary Barbaro (AP) .08
131 Jim Smith .08
132 New York Jets Team .15
133 Curtis Brown .08
134 D.D Lewis .08
135 Jim Plunkett .50
136 Nat Moore .08
137 Don McCauley .08
138 Tony Dorsett (SA) .75
139 Julius Adams .08
140 Ahmad Rashad (AP) .50
141 Rich Saul .08
142 Ken Fantetti .08
143 Kenny Johnson .08
144 Clark Gaines .08
145 Mark Moseley .08
146 *Vernon Perry* .15
147 Jerry Sherk .08
148 Freddie Solomon .08
149 Jerry Sherk .08
150 *Kellen Winslow* (AP) 10.00
151 Green Bay Packers Team .25
152 Ross Browner .08
153 Dan Fouts (SA) .60
154 Woody Peoples .08
155 Jack Lambert 1.00
156 Mike Dennis .08
157 Rafael Septien .08
158 Archie Manning .20
159 Don Hasselbeck .08
160 Alan Page (AP) .50
161 Arthur Whittington .08
162 Billy Waddy .08
163 Horace Belton .08
164 Luke Prestridge .08
165 Joe Theismann .75
166 Morris Towns .08
167 Dave Brown .08
168 Ezra Johnson .08
169 Tampa Bay Bucaneers Team .10
170 Joe DeLamielleure (AP) .08
171 Earnest Gray (SA) .08
172 Mike Thomas .08
173 Jim Haslett .08
174 *David Woodley* .10
175 Al Bubba Baker .20
176 *Nesby Glasgow* .20
178 Ton Brahaney .08
179 Herman Edwards .08
180 *Junior Miller* (AP) .20
181 Richard Wood .08
182 Lenvil Elliott .08
183 Sammie White .20
184 Russell Erxieben .08
185 Ed "Too Tall" Jones .75
186 Ray Guy (SA) .08
187 Haven Moses .08
188 New York Giants Team .20
189 David Whitehurst .08
190 John Jefferson (AP) .20
191 Terry Beeson .08
192 *Dan Ross* .25
193 Dave Williams .08
194 *Art Monk* 12.00
195 Roger Wehrli .08
196 Rickey Feacher .08
197 Miami Dolphins Team (Tony Nathan, Gerald Small, Kim Bokamper, A.J. Duhe) .08
198 Carl Roaches .08
199 Cilly Campfield .08
200 Ted Hendricks (AP) .15
201 *Fred Smerlas* .75
202 Walter Payton (SA) 2.00
203 Luther Bradley .08
204 Herbert Scott .08
205 Jack Youngblood .25
206 Danny Pittman .08
207 Houston Oilers Team (Carl Roaches, Mike Barber, Jack Tatum, Jesse Baker, Robert Brazile) .08
208 Vagas Ferguson .08
209 Mark Dennard .08
210 Lemar Parrish (AP) .08
211 Bruce Harper .08
212 Ed Simonini .08
213 *Nick Lowery* 1.00
214 *Kevin House* .20
215 *Mike Kenn* 1.50
216 *Joe Montana* 175.00
217 Joe Senser .08
218 Lester Hayes (SA) .08
219 Gene Upshaw .20
220 Franco Harris 1.50
221 Ron Bolton .08
222 Charles Alexander .08
223 Matt Robinson .08
224 Ray Oldham .08
225 George Martin .08
226 Buffalo Bills Team .20
227 Tony Franklin .08
228 George Cumby .08
229 Butch Johnson .08
230 Mike Haynes (AP) .08
231 Rob Carpenter .08
232 Steve Fuller .08
233 John Sawyer .08
234 Kenny King (SA) .08
235 Jack Ham .60
236 Jimmy Rogers .08
237 Bob Parsons .08
238 *Marty Lyons* .50
239 Pat Tilley .08
240 Dennis Harrah (AP) .08
241 Thom Darden .08
242 Rolf Benirschke .08
243 Gerald Small .08
244 Atlanta Falcons Team .15
245 Roger Carr .08
246 Sherman White .08
247 Ted Brown .08
248 Matt Cavanaugh .08
249 John Dutton .08
250 Bill Bergey (AP) .15
251 Jim Allen .08
252 Mike Nelms (SA) .08
253 Tom Blanchard .08
254 Ricky Thompson .08
255 John Matuszak .08
256 Randy Grossman .08
257 Ray Griffin .08
258 Lynn Cain .08
259 Checklist 133-164 .25
260 Mike Pruitt (AP) .08
261 Chris Ward .08
262 Fred Steinfort .08
263 James Owens .08
264 Chicago Bears Team 1.50
265 Dan Fouts 1.50
266 Arnold Morgado .08
267 John Jefferson (SA) .08
268 Bill Lenkaitis .08
269 James Jones .08
270 Brad Van Pelt .08
271 Steve Largent 1.75
272 Elvin Bethea .08
273 Cullen Bryant .08
274 Gary Danielson .08
275 Tony Galbreath .08
276 Dave Butz .20
277 Steve Mike-Mayer .08
278 Ron Johnson .08
279 Tom DeLeone .08
280 Ron Jaworski .20
281 Mel Gray .08
282 San Diego Chargers Team .15
283 Mark Brammer .08
284 Alfred Jenkins (SA) .08
285 Greg Buttle .08
286 Randy Hughes .08
287 Delvin Williams .08
288 Brian Baschnagel .08
289 Gary Jeter .08
290 Stanley Morgan (AP) .50
291 Gerry Ellis .08
292 Al Richardson .08
293 Jimmie Giles .08
294 Dave Jennings (SA) .08
295 Wilbert Montgomery .15
296 Dave Pureifory .08
297 Greg Hawthorne .08
298 Dick Ambrose .08
299 Terry Hermeling .08
300 Danny White .40
301 Ken Burrough .08
302 Paul Hofer .08
303 Denver Broncos Team .15
304 Eddie Payton .08
305 Isaac Curtis .08
306 Benny Ricardo .08
307 Riley Odoms .08
308 Bob Chandler .08
309 Larry Heater .08
310 *Art Still* (AP) .50
311 Harold Jackson .20
312 Charlie Joiner (SA) .25
313 Jeff Nixon .08
314 Aundra Thompson .08
315 Richard Todd .10
316 *Dan Hampton* 4.00
317 Doug Marsh .08
318 Louie Giammona .08
319 San Francisco 49ers Team .50
320 Manu Tuiasosopo .08
321 Rich Milot .08
322 Mike Guman .08
323 Bob Kuechenberg .08
324 Tom Skladany .08
325 Dave Logan .08
326 Bruce Laird .08
327 James Jones (SA) .08
328 Joe Danelo .08
329 *Kenny King* .08
330 Pat Donovan (Ap) .08
331 Record: (Earl Cooper) .10
332 Record: (John Jefferson) .10
333 Record: (Kenny King) .10
334 Record: (Rod Martin) .10
335 Record: (Jim Plunkett) .10
336 Record: (Bill Thompson) .10
337 John Cappelletti .10
338 Detroit Lions Team .20
339 Don Smith .08
340 Rod Perry (AP) .08
341 David Lewis .08
342 *Mark Gastineau* .75
343 Steve Largent (SA) .85
344 Charley Young .08
345 Toni Fritsch .08
346 Matt Blair .08
347 Don Bass .08
348 Jim Jensen .20
349 Karl Lorch .08
350 Brian Sipe (AP) .20
351 Theo Bell .08
352 Sam Adams .08
353 Paul Coffman .08
354 Eric Harris .08
355 Tony Hill .20
356 J.T. Turner .08
357 Frank LeMaster .08
358 Jim Jodat .08
359 Oakland Raiders Team .25
360 *Joe Cribbs* (AP) 1.00
361 James Lofton (SA) 1.00
362 Dexter Bussey .08
363 Bobby Jackson .08
364 Steve DeBerg 1.00
365 Ottis Anderson 1.50
366 Tom Myers .08
367 John James .08
368 Reese McCall .08
369 Jack Reynolds .08
370 Gary Jonson (AP) .08
371 Jimmy Cefalo .08
372 Horace Ivory .08
373 Garo Yepremian .08
374 Brian Kelley .08
375 Terry Bradshaw 2.50
376 Dallas Cowboys Team .50
377 Randy Logan .08
378 Tim Wilson .08
379 Archie Manning (SA) .08
380 Revie Sorey (AP) .08
381 Randy Holloway .08
382 Henry Lawrence .08
383 Pat McInally .08
384 Kevin Long .08
385 Louis Wright .08
386 Leonard Thompson .08
387 Jan Stenerud .20
388 *Raymond Butler* .20
389 Checklist 265-396 .08
390 Steve Bartkowski (Ap) .20
391 Clarence Harmon .08
392 Wilbert Montgomery (SA) .08
393 Billy Joe DuPree .20
394 Kansas City Chiefs Team (Ted McKnight, Henry Marshall, Gary Barbaro, Art Still) .08
395 Earnest Gray .08
396 Ray Hamilton .08
397 Brenard Wilson .08
398 Calvin Hill .10
399 Robin Cole .08
400 Walter Payton (AP) 4.50
401 Jim Hart .20
402 Ron Yary .08
403 Cliff Branch .40
404 Roland Hooks .08
405 Ken Stabler 1.00
406 Chuck Ramsey .08
407 Mike Nelms .08
408 Ron Jaworski (SA) .08
409 James Hunter .20
410 Lee Roy Selmon .20
411 Baltimore Colts Team (Curtis Dickey, Roger Carr, Bruce Laird, Mike Barnes) .08
412 Henry Marshall .08
413 Preston Pearson .08
414 Richard Bishop .08
415 Greg Pruitt .08
416 Matt Bahr .20
417 Tony Mullady .08
418 Glen Edwards .08
419 Sam McCullum .08
420 Stan Walters (AP) .08
421 George Roberts .08
422 *Dwight Clark* 4.00
423 *Pat Thomas* .10
424 Bruce Harper (SA) .08
425 Craig Morton .20
426 Derrick Gaffney .08
427 Pete Johnson .08
428 Wes Chandler .50
429 Burgess Owens .08
430 James Lofton (AP) 3.50
431 Tony Reed .08
432 Minnesota Vikings Team .40
433 *Ron Springs* .10
434 Tim Fox .08
435 Ozzie Newsome 3.00
436 Steve Furness .08
437 Will Lewis .08
438 Mike Hartenstine .08
439 John Bunting .08
440 *Eddie Murray* 2.00
441 Mike Pruitt (SA) .08
442 Larry Swider .08
443 Steve Freeman .08
444 Bruce Hardy .20
445 Pat Haden .20
446 *Curtis Dickey* .20
447 Doug Wilkerson .08
448 Alfred Jenkins .08
449 Dave Dalby .08
450 Robert Brazile (AP) .08
451 Bobby Hammond .08
452 Raymond Clayborn .08
453 Jim Miller .08
454 Roy Simmons .08
455 Charlie Waters .20
456 Ricky Bell .08
457 Ahmad Rashad (SA) .25
458 Don Cockroft .08
459 Keith Krepfle .08
460 Marvin Powell (AP) .08
461 Tommy Kramer .25
462 Jim LeClair .08
463 Freddie Scott .08
464 Rob Lytle .08
465 Johnnie Gray .08
466 *Doug France* .15
467 *Carlos Carson* .20
468 St. Louis Cardinals Team .20
469 Efren Herrera .08
470 Randy White (AP) .75
471 Richard Caster .08
472 Andy Johnson .08
473 Billy Sims (SA) .25
474 Joe Lavender .08
475 Harry Carson .40
476 John Stallworth .75
477 Bob Thomas .08
478 Keith Wright .08
479 Ken Stone .08
480 Carl Hariston (AP) .08
481 Reggie McKenzie .08
482 Bob Griese 1.00
483 Mike Bragg .08
484 Scott Dierking .08
485 David Hill .08
486 Brian Sipe (SA) .08
487 Rod Martin .25
488 Cincinnati Bengals Team (Pete Johnson, Dan Ross, Louis Breeden, Eddie Edwards) .08
489 Preston Dennard .08
490 John Smith (AP) .08
491 Mike Reinfeldt .08
492 NFC Championship (Ron Jaworski) .08
493 AFC Championship (Jim Plunkett) .08
494 Super Bowl XV (Jim Plunkett, King) .40
495 Joe Greene 1.00
496 Charlie Joiner .60
497 Rolland Lawrence .08
498 Bubba Baker (SA) .08
499 Brad Dusek .08
500 Tony Dorsett 2.50
501 Robin Earl .08
502 Theotis Brown .08
503 Joe Ferguson .15
504 Bealsey Reece .08
505 Lyle Alzado .20
506 *Tony Nathan* .40
507 Philadelphia Eagles Team (Wilbert Montgomery, Charlie Smith, Brenard Wilson, Claude Humphrey) .08
508 Herb Orvis .08
509 Clarence Williams .08
510 Ray Guy (AP) .25
511 Jeff Komlo .08
512 Freddie Solomon (SA) .08
513 Tim Mazzetti .08
514 Elvis Peacock .08
515 Russ Francis .08
516 Roland Harper .08
517 Checklist 397-528 .25
518 Billy Johnson .08
519 Dan Dierdorf .40
520 Fred Dean (AP) .08
521 Jerry Butler .08
522 Ron Saul .08
523 Charlie Smith .08
524 Kellen Winslow (SA) 3.00
525 Bert Jones .20
526 Pittsburgh Steelers Team .75
527 Duriel Harris .08
528 William Andrews .25

1981 Topps Red Border Stickers

These stickers came in their own little containers and measure 1-15/16" x 2-9/16". Each of the 28 NFL teams is represented in the set, which features red borders on the front, framing a color photo. The player's name and position are also listed. The sticker back has the sticker number, player name, position and team, biographical information and instructions on how to apply the sticker.

MT
Complete Set (28): 20.00
Common Player: .40
1 Steve Bartkowski 1.00
2 Bert Jones 1.00
3 Joe Cribbs .60
4 Walter Payton 5.00
5 Ross Browner .40
6 Brian Sipe .75
7 Tony Dorsett 2.50
8 Randy Gradishar .60
9 Billy Sims 1.00
10 James Lofton 1.75
11 Mike Barber .40
12 Art Still .40
13 Jack Youngblood .75
14 Dave Woodley .50
15 Ahmad Rashad 1.25
16 Russ Francis .50
17 Archie Manning .75
18 Dave Jennings .40
19 Richard Todd .50
20 Lester Hayes .60
21 Ron Jaworski .50
22 Franco Harris 2.00
23 Ottis Anderson 1.00
24 John Jefferson .50
25 Freddie Solomon .40
26 Steve Largent 3.50
27 Lee Roy Selmon .75
28 Art Monk 8.00

1981 Topps Stickers

These stickers, which measure 1-15/16" x 2-9/16", are numbered alphabetically by teams within divisions. The front has a color photo with a white frame, plus the sticker number. That number is also on the back, along with the player's name, position, team and instructions on how to apply the sticker. A sticker album was also made available as a mail-in offer. The album cover features a Buffalo Bills player.

MT
Complete Set (262): 25.00
Common Player: .05
1 AFC Passing Leader (Brian Sipe) .10
2 AFC Passing Yardage Leader (Dan Fouts) .50
3 AFC Receiving Yardage Leader (John Jefferson) .08
4 AFC Kickoff Return Yardage Leader (Bruce Harper) .05
5 AFC Punt Return Yardage Leader (J.T. Smith) .05
6 AFC Punting Leader (Luke Prestidge) .05
7 AFC Interceptions Leader (Lester Hayes) .05
8 AFC Sacks Leader (Gary Johnson) .05
9 Bert Jones .15
10 Fred Cook .05
11 Roger Carr .10
12 Greg Landry .08
13 Raymond Butler .08
14 Bruce Laird .05
15 Ed Simonini .05
16 Curtis Dickey .10
17 Joe Cribbs .10
18 Joe Ferguson .15
19 Ben Williams .05
20 Jerry Butler .08
21 Roland Hooks .05
22 Fred Smerlas .08
23 Frank Lewis .05
24 Mark Brammer .05
25 Dave Woodley .08
26 Nat Moore .10
27 Uwe Von Schamann .05
28 Vern Den Herder .05
29 Tony Nathan .10
30 Duriel Harris .08
31 Don McNeal .05
32 Delvin Williams .05
33 Stanley Morgan .15
34 John Hannah .15
35 Horace Ivory .05
36 Steve Nelson .05
37 Steve Grogan .15
38 Vagas Ferguson .15
39 John Smith .05
40 Mike Haynes .12
41 Mark Gastineau .15
42 Wesley Walker .15
43 Joe Klecko .10
44 Chris Ward .05
45 Johnny Lam Jones .08
46 Marvin Powell .08
47 Richard Todd .15
48 Greg Buttle .08
49 Eddie Edwards .05
50 Dan Ross .08
51 Ken Anderson .50
52 Ross Browner .08
53 Dan Bass .08
54 Jim LeClair .05
55 Pete Johnson .08
56 Anthony Munoz 1.25
57 Brian Sipe .12
58 Mike Pruitt .10
59 Greg Pruitt .15
60 Thom Darden .05
61 Ozzie Newsome .40
62 Dave Logan .05
63 Lyle Alzado .15
64 Reggie Rucker .08
65 Robert Brazile .08
66 Mike Barber .08
67 Carl Roaches .10
68 Ken Stabler .30
69 Gregg Bingham .08
70 Mike Renfro .08
71 Leon Gray .05
72 Rob Carpenter .10
73 Franco Harris .50
74 Jack Lambert .30
75 Jim Smith .05
76 Mike Webster .15
77 Sidney Thornton .05
78 Joe Greene .40
79 John Stallworth .20
80 Tyrone McGriff .05
81 Randy Gradishar .12
82 Haven Moses .08
83 Riley Odoms .10
84 Matt Robinson .05
85 Craig Morton .12
86 Rulon Jones .05
87 Rick Upchurch .10
88 Jim Jensen .05
89 Art Still .12
90 J.T. Smith .12
91 Steve Fuller .05
92 Gary Barbaro .05
93 Ted McKnight .05
94 Bob Grupp .05
95 Henry Marshall .05
96 Mike Williams .05
97 Jim Plunkett .25
98 Lester Hayes .12
99 Cliff Branch .20
100 John Matuszak .10
101 Matt Millen .10
102 Kenny King .05
103 Ray Guy .15
104 Ted Hendricks .20
105 John Jefferson .12
106 Fred Dean .12
107 Dan Fouts .35
108 Charlie Joiner .25
109 Kellen Winslow 1.25
110 Gary Johnson .08
111 Mike Thomas .05
112 Louie Kelcher .12
113 Jim Zorn .12
114 Terry Beeson .05
115 Jacob Green .35
116 Steve Largent 1.25
117 Dan Doornink .05
118 Manu Tuiasosopo .05
119 John Sawyer .05
120 Jim Jodat .05
121 Walter Payton (All-Pro) 2.00
122 Brian Sipe (All-Pro) .25
123 Joe Cribbs (All-Pro) .25
124 James Lofton (All-Pro) .60
125 John Jefferson (All-Pro) .25
126 Leon Gray (All-Pro) .15
127 Joe DeLamielleure (All-Pro) .20
128 Mike Webster (All-Pro) .30
129 John Hannah (All-Pro) .30
130 Mike Kenn (All-Pro) .20
131 Kellen Winslow (All-Pro) 1.50
132 Lee Roy Selmon (All-Pro) .30
133 Randy White (All-Pro) .30
134 Gary Johnson (All-Pro) .15
135 Art Still (All-Pro) .20
136 Robert Brazile (All-Pro) .20
137 Nolan Cromwell (All-Pro) .20
138 Ted Hendricks (All-Pro) .50
139 Lester Hayes (All-Pro) .25
140 Randy Gradishar (All-Pro) .35
141 Lemar Parrish (All-Pro) .20
142 Donnie Shell (All-Pro) .20
143 NFC Passing Leader (Ron Jaworski) .12
144 NFC Passing Leader (Archie Manning) .20
145 NFC Rushing Yardage Leader (Walter Payton) .75
146 NFC Rushing Touchdowns Leader (Billy Sims) .25
147 NFC Receiving Yardage Leader (James Lofton) .25
148 NFC Punting Leader (Dave Jennings) .05
149 NFC Interceptions Leader (Nolan Cromwell) .08
150 NFC Sacks Leader (Al (Bubba) Baker) .08
151 Tony Dorsett .50
152 Harvey Martin .15
153 Danny White .25
154 Pat Donovan .05
155 Drew Pearson .15
156 Robert Newhouse .10
157 Randy White .40
158 Butch Johnson .10
159 Dave Jennings .05
160 Brad Van Pelt .05
161 Phil Simms .40
162 Mike Friede .05
163 Billy Taylor .08
164 Gary Jeter .08
165 George Martin .05

166 Earnest Gray .05
167 Ron Jaworski .15
168 Bill Bergey .10
169 Wilbert Montgomery .08
170 Charlie Smith .05
171 Jerry Robinson .08
172 Herman Edwards .05
173 Harold Carmichael .15
174 Claude Humphrey .10
175 Ottis Anderson .30
176 Jim Hart .15
177 Pat Tilley .08
178 Rush Brown .05
179 Tom Brahaney .05
180 Dan Dierdorf .25
181 Wayne Morris .05
182 Doug Marsh .05
183 Art Monk 3.00
184 Clarence Harmon .05
185 Lemar Parrish .12
186 Joe Theismann .35
187 Joe Lavender .05
188 Wilbur Jackson .05
189 Dave Butz .05
190 Coy Bacon .05
191 Walter Payton 1.50
192 Alan Page .15
193 Vince Evans .20
194 Roland Harper .08
195 Dan Hampton .80
196 Gary Fencik .08
197 Mike Hartenstine .05
198 Robin Earl .05
199 Billy Sims .25
200 Leonard Thompson .05
201 Jeff Komlo .08
202 Al (Bubba) Baker .10
203 Ed Murray .15
204 Dexter Bussey .05
205 Tom Ginn .05
206 Freddie Scott .08
207 James Lofton .50
208 Mike Butler .05
209 Lynn Dickey .12
210 Gerry Ellis .05
211 Edd Lee Ivery .10
212 Ezra Johnson .05
213 Paul Coffman .08
214 Aundra Thompson .05
215 Ahmad Rashad .25
216 Tommy Kramer .08
217 Matt Blair .08
218 Sammie White .08
219 Ted Brown .08
220 Joe Senser .08
221 Rickey Young .08
222 Randy Holloway .05
223 Lee Roy Selmon .15
224 Doug Williams .10
225 Ricky Bell .10
226 David Lewis .05
227 Gordon Jones .08
228 Dewey Selmon .08
229 Jimmie Giles .10
230 Mike Washington .05
231 William Andrews .15
232 Jeff Van Note .08
233 Steve Bartkowski .15
234 Junior Miller .08
235 Lynn Cain .08
236 Joel Williams .05
237 Alfred Jenkins .08
238 Kenny Johnson .05
239 Jack Youngblood .20
240 Elvis Peacock .08
241 Cullen Bryant .10
242 Dennis Harrah .05
243 Billy Waddy .05
244 Nolan Cromwell .10
245 Doug France .05
246 Johnnie Johnson .08
247 Archie Manning .25
248 Tony Galbreath .10
249 Wes Chandler .15
250 Stan Brock .05
251 Ike Harris .05
252 Russell Erxleben .05
253 Jimmy Rogers .05
254 Tom Myers .05
255 Dwight Clark .75
256 Earl Cooper .05
257 Steve DeBerg .25
258 Randy Cross .10
259 Freddie Solomon .08
260 Jim Miller .05
261 Charley Young .08
262 Bobby Leopold .05

1982 Topps

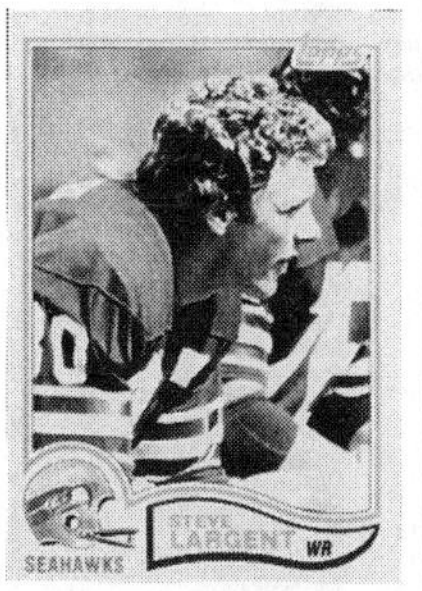

Topps' last 528-card set was issued in 1982, and the design was nearly a duplicate of the 1975 football set. Football helmets featuring the team's helmet design appeared on these cards for the first time. Also included in this set were in-action cards of top stars and a subset featuring NFL brother tandems. Cards are numbered alphabetically by team and by the last name of the player. Notable rookies in this set include Cris Collinsworth, Anthony Munoz, Freeman McNeil, George Rogers, Ronnie Lott, Lawrence Taylor and Neil Lomax. (Key: AP - All Pro, IA - In Action)

MT
Complete Set (528): 90.00
Common Player: .05
Wax Pack (15): 5.00
Wax Box (36): 120.00
1 Ken Anderson (RB) .50
2 Dan Fouts (RB) .50
3 LeRoy Irvin (RB) .10
4 Stump Mitchell (RB) .10
5 George Rogers (RB) .15
6 Dan Ross (RB) .10
7 AFC Championship (Ken Anderson, Pete Johnson) .15
8 NFC Championship (Earl Cooper) .15
9 Super Bowl XVI (Anthony Munoz) .75
10 Baltimore Colts Team .15
11 Raymond Butler .05
12 Roger Carr .05
13 Curtis Dickey .05
14 Zachary Dixon .05
15 Nesby Glasgow .05
16 Bert Jones .10
17 Bruce Laird .05
18 Reese McCall .05
19 Randy McMillan .05
20 Ed Simonini .05
21 Buffalo Bills Team .15
22 Mark Brammer .05
23 Curtis Brown .05
24 Jerry Butler .05
25 Mario Clark .05
26 Joe Cribbs .15
27 Joe Cribbs (IA) .05
28 Joe Ferguson .15
29 Jim Haslett .05
30 Frank Lewis (AP) .05
31 Frank Lewis (IA) .05
32 Shane Nelson .05
33 Charles Romes .05
34 Bill Simpson .05
35 Fred Smerlas .05
36 Cincinnati Bengals Team .15
37 Charles Alexander .05
38 Ken Anderson (AP) .50
39 Ken Anderson (IA) .20
40 Jim Breech .05
41 Jim Breech (IA) .05
42 Louis Breeden .05
43 Ross Browner .05
44 *Cris Collinsworth* 1.00
45 Cris Collinsworth IA (IA) .50
46 Isaac Curtis .05
47 Pete Johnson .05
48 Pete Johnson (IA) .05
49 Steve Kreider .05
50 Pat McInnaly (AP) .05
51 *Anthony Munoz* (AP) 7.00
52 Dan Ross .05
53 David Verser .05
54 Reggie Williams .05
55 Cleveland Browns Team .20
56 Lyle Alzado .20
57 Dick Ambrose .05
58 Ron Bolton .05
59 Steve Cox .05
60 Joe DeLamielleure .05
61 Tom DeLeone .05
62 Doug Dieken .05
63 Ricky Feacher .05
64 Don Goode .05
65 Robert L. Jackson .05
66 Dave Logan .05
67 Ozzie Newsome 1.50
68 Ozzie Newsome (IA) .75
69 Greg Pruitt .10
70 Mike Pruitt .05
71 Mike Pruitt (IA) .05
72 Reggie Rucker .05
73 Clarence Scott .05
74 Brian Sipe .10
75 Charles White .10
76 Denver Broncos Team .15
77 Rubin Carter .05
78 Steve Foley .05
79 Randy Gradishar .25
80 Tom Jackson .25
81 Craig Morton .25
82 Craig Morton (IA) .10
83 Riley Odoms .05
84 Rick Parros .05
85 Dave Preston .05
86 Tony Reed .05
87 Bob Swenson .05
88 Bill Thompson .05
89 Rick Upchurch .05
90 *Steve Watson* (AP) .25
91 Steve Watson (IA) .10
92 Houston Oilers Team .15
93 Mike Barber .05
94 Elvin Bethea .05
95 Gregg Bingham .05
96 Robert Brazile (AP) .05
97 Ken Burrough .05
98 Toni Fritsch .05
99 Leon Gray .05
100 *Gifford Nielsen* .15
101 Vernon Perry .05
102 Mike Reinfeldt .05
103 Mike Renfro .05
104 Carl Roaches (AP) .05
105 Ken Stabler 1.00
106 Greg Stemrick .05
107 J.C. Wilson .05
108 Tim Wilson .05
109 Kansas City Chiefs Team .15
110 Gary Barbaro (AP) .05
111 Brad Budde (AP) .05
112 *Joe Delaney* (AP) .25
113 Joe Delaney (IA) .10
114 Steve Fuller .05
115 Gary Green .05
116 James Hadnot .05
117 Eric Harris .05
118 Billy Jackson .05
119 Bill Kenney .05
120 Nick Lowery (AP) 1.50
121 Nick Lowery (IA) .60
122 Henry Marshall .05
123 J.T. Smith .25
124 Art Still .05
125 Miami Dolphins Team .15
126 Bob Baumhower (AP) .05
127 Glenn Blackwood .05
128 Jimmy Cefalo .05
129 A.J. Duhe .05
130 Andra Franklin .10
131 Duriel Harris .05
132 Nat Moore .05
133 Tony Nathan .05
134 Ed Newman .05
135 Earnie Rhone .05
136 Don Strock .05
137 Tommy Vigorito .05
138 Uwe Von Schamann .05
139 Uwe Von Schamann (IA) .05
140 David Woodley .05
141 New England Patriots Team .10
142 Julius Adams .05
143 Richard Bishop .05
144 Matt Cavanaugh .05
145 Raymond Clayborn .05
146 *Tony Collins* .20
147 Vagas Ferguson .05
148 Tim Fox .05
149 Steve Grogan .25
150 John Hannah (AP) .25
151 John Hannah (IA) .10
152 Don Hasselbeck .05
153 Mike Haynes .05
154 Harold Jackson .10
155 Andy Johnson .05
156 Stanley Morgan .10
157 Stanley Morgan (IA) .10
158 Steve Nelson .05
159 Rod Shoate .05
160 New York Jets Team .25
161 Dan Alexander .05
162 Mike Augustyniak .05
163 Jerome Barkum .05
164 Greg Buttle .05
165 Scott Dierking .05
166 Joe Fields .05
167 Mark Gastineau (AP) .20
168 Mark Gastineau (IA) .10
169 Bruce Harper .05
170 Johnny Lam Jones .05
171 Joe Klecko (AP) .10
172 Joe Klecko (IA) .05
173 Pat Leahy .05
174 Pat Leahy (IA) .05
175 Marty Lyons .10
176 *Freeman McNeil* 1.00
177 Marvin Powell AP .05
178 Chuck Ramsey .05
179 Darrol Ray .05
180 Abdul Salaam .05
181 Richard Todd .10
182 Richard Todd (IA) .05
183 Wesley Walker .20
184 Chris Ward .05
185 Oakland Raiders Team .15
186 Cliff Branch .25
187 Bob Chandler .05
188 Ray Guy .25
189 Lester Hayes (AP) .05
190 Ted Hendricks (AP) .05
191 Monte Jackson .05
192 Derrick Jensen .05
193 Kenny King .05
194 Rod Martin .05
195 John Matuszak .05
196 *Matt Millen* 1.25
197 Derrick Ramsey .05
198 Art Shell .40
199 Mark Van Eeghen .05
200 Arthur Whittington .05
201 *Marc Wilson* .20
202 Pittsburgh Steelers Team .50
203 Mel Blount (AP) .75
204 Terry Bradshaw 1.50
205 Terry Bradshaw (IA) .75
206 Craig Colquitt .05
207 Bennie Cunningham .05
208 Russell Davis .05
209 Gary Dunn .05
210 Jack Ham .75
211 Franco Harris .75
212 Franco Harris (IA) .50
213 Jack Lambert (AP) .75
214 Jack Lambert (IA) .50
215 *Mark Malone* .20
218 Jim Smith .05
219 John Stallworth .60
220 John Stallworth (IA) .30
221 David Trout .05
222 Mike Webster (AP) .20
223 San Diego Chargers Team .15
224 Rolf Bernirschke .05
225 Rolf Benirschke (IA) .05
226 *James Brooks* 1.00
227 Willie Buchanon .05
228 Wes Chandler .15
229 Wes Chandler (IA) .10
230 Dan Fouts 1.00
231 Dan Fouts (IA) .50
232 Gary Johnson (AP) .05
233 Charlie Joiner .40
234 Charlie Joiner (IA) .20
235 Louie Kelcher .05
236 Chuck Muncie (AP) .05
237 Chuck Muncie (IA) .05
238 George Roberts .05
239 Ed White .05
240 Doug Wilkerson (AP) .05
241 Kellen Winslow (AP) 2.00
242 Kellen Winslow IA (IA) 1.00
243 Seattle Seahawks Team .20
244 Theotis Brown .05
245 Don Doornink .05
246 John Harris .05
247 Efren Herrera .05
248 David Hughes .05
249 Steve Largent 1.75
250 Steve Largent (IA) .90
251 Sam McCullum .05
252 Sherman Smith .05
253 Manu Tuiasosopo .05
254 John Yarno .05
255 Jim Zorn .10
256 Jim Zorn (IA) .05
257 (Joe Montana, Ken Anderson) 2.00
258 Receiving Leaders (Kellen Winslow, Dwight Clark) .50
259 Sack Leaders (Joe Klecko, Curtis Greer) .10
260 Scoring Leaders (Jim Breech, Nick Lowery, Ed Murray, Rafael Septien) .10
261 Interception Leaders (John Harris, Everson Walls) .20
262 Punting Leaders (Pat McInally, Tom Skladany) .10
263 Brothers: (Chris Bahr, Matt Bahr) .10
264 Brothers: (Lyle Blackwood, Glenn Blackwood) .10
265 Brothers: (Pete Brock, Stan Brock) .10
266 Brothers: (Archie Griffin, Ray Griffin) .10
267 Brothers: (John Hannah, Charley Hannah) .20
268 Brothers: (Monte Jackson, Terry Jackson) .10
269 Brothers: (Eddie Payton, Walter Payton) 1.00
270 Brothers: (Dewey Selmon, Lee Roy Selmon) .10
271 Atlanta Falcons Team .15
272 Williams Andrews .05
273 William Anderws (IA) .05
274 Steve Bartkowski .25
275 Steve Bartkowski (IA) .05
276 Bobby Butler .05
277 Lynn Cain .05
278 Wallace Francis .05
279 Alfred Jackson .05
280 John James .05
281 Alfred Jenkins (AP) .05
282 Alfred Jenkins (IA) .05
283 Kenny Johnson .05
284 Mike Kenn (AP) .25
285 Fulton Kuykendall .05
286 Mike Luckhurst .05
287 Mick Luckhurst (IA) .05
288 Junior Miller .05
289 Al Richardson .05
290 R.C. Thielemann .05
291 Jeff Van Note .05
292 Chicago Bears Team .75
293 Brian Baschnagel .05
294 Robin Earl .05
295 Vince Evans .20
296 Gary Fencik (AP) .05
297 Dan Hampton 1.00
298 Noah Jackson .05
299 Ken Margerum .05
300 Jim Osborne .05
301 Bob Parsons .05
302 Walter Payton 4.00
303 Walter Payton IA (IA) 2.00
304 Revie Sorey .05
305 *Matt Suhey* .25
306 Rickey Watts .05
307 Dallas Cowboys Team .60
308 Bob Breunig .05
309 *Doug Cosbie* .25
310 Pat Donovan (AP) .05
311 Tony Dorsett (AP) 1.00
312 Tony Dorsett (IA) .60
313 Michael Downs .05
314 Billy Joe DuPree .15
315 John Dutton .05
316 Tony Hill .05
317 Butch Johnson .05
318 Ed "Too Tall" Jones (AP) .60
319 James Jones .05
320 Harvey Martin .15
321 Drew Pearson .40
322 Herbert Scott (AP) .05
323 Rafael Septien (AP) .05
324 Rafael Septien (IA) .05
325 Ron Springs .05
326 *Dennis Thurman* .10
327 *Everson Walls* .50
328 Everson Walls (IA) .25
329 Danny White .25
330 Danny White (IA) .10
331 Randy White (AP) .60
332 Randy White (IA) .25
333 Detroit Lions Team .15
334 Jim Allen .05
335 Al Bubba Baker .05
336 Dexter Bussey .05
337 Doug English (AP) .05
338 Ken Fantetti .05
339 William Gay .05
340 David Hill .05
341 *Eric Hipple* .05
342 Rick Kane .05
343 Ed Murray .40
344 Ed Murray (IA) .20
345 Ray Oldham .05
346 Dave Pureifory .05
347 Freddie Scott .05
348 Freddie Scott (IA) .05
349 Billy Sims (AP) .30
350 Billy Sims (IA) .15
351 Tom Skladany (AP) .05
352 Leonard Thompson .05
353 Stan White .05
354 Green Bay Packers Team .40
355 Paul Coffman .05
356 George Cumby .05
357 Lynn Dickey .10
358 Lynn Dickey (IA) .05
359 Gerry Ellis .05
360 Maurice Harvey .05
361 Harlan Huckleby .05
362 John Jefferson .20
363 Mark Lee .05
364 James Lofton (AP) 1.75
365 James Lofton (IA) .75
366 Jan Stenerud .25
367 Jan Stenerud (IA) .10
368 Rich Wingo .05
369 Los Angeles Rams Team .20
370 Frank Corral .05
371 Nolan Cromwell (AP) .25
372 Nolan Cromwell (IA) .10
373 Preston Dennard .05
374 Mike Fanning .05
375 Doug France .05
376 Mike Guman .05
377 Pat Haden .25
378 Dennis Harrah .05
379 *Drew Hill* 2.00
380 *LeRoy Irvin* .40
381 Cody Jones .05
382 Rod Perry .05
383 Rich Saul (AP) .05
384 Pat Thomas .05
385 Wendell Tyler .08
386 Wendell Tyler (IA) .05
387 Billy Waddy .05
388 Jack Youngblood .25
389 Minnesota Vikings Team .15
390 Matt Blair (AP) .05
391 Ted Brown .08
392 Ted Brown (IA) .05
393 Rick Danmeier .05
394 Tommy Kramer .25
395 Mark Mullaney .05
396 Eddie Payton .05
397 Ahmad Rashad .40
398 Joe Senser .08
399 Joe Senser (IA) .05
400 Sammy White .05
401 Sammy White (IA) .05
402 Ron Yary .05
403 Rickey Young .05
404 New Orleans Saints Team .50
405 Russell Erxieben .05
406 Elois Grooms .05
407 Jack Holmes .05
408 Archie Manning .25
409 Derland Moore .05
410 *George Rogers* 1.00
411 George Rogers (IA) .40
412 Toussaint Tyler .05
413 *Dave Waymer* .20
414 Wayne Wilson .05
415 New York Giants Team .15
416 *Scott Brunner* .10
417 Rob Carpenter .05
418 Harry Carson (AP) .25
419 Bill Currier .05
420 Joe Danelo .05
421 Joe Danelo (IA) .05
422 *Mark Haynes* .35
423 Terry Jackson .05
424 Dave Jennings .05
425 Gary Jeter .05
426 Brian Kelley .07
427 George Martin .05
428 Curtis McGriff .05
429 Bill Neill .05
430 Johnny Perkins .05
431 Beasley Reece .07
432 Gary Shirk .05
433 Phil Simms 1.50
434 *Lawrence Taylor* (AP) 30.00
435 Lawrence Taylor IA (IA) 10.00
436 Brad Van Pelt .05
437 Philadelphia Eagles Team .15
438 John Bunting .05
439 Billy Campfield .05
440 Harold Carmichael .25
441 Harold Carmichael (IA) .10
442 Herman Edwards .05
443 Tony Franklin .05
444 Tony Franklin (IA) .05
445 Carl Hariston .05
446 Dennis Harrison .05
447 Ron Jaworski .15
448 Charlie Johnson .05
449 Keith Krepfle .05
450 Frank LeMaster .05
451 Randy Logan .05
452 Wilbert Montgomery .07
453 Wilbert Montgomery (IA) .05
454 Hubert Oliver .05
455 Jerry Robinson .05
456 Jerry Robinson (IA) .05
457 Jerry Sisemore .05
458 Charlie Smith .05
459 Stan Walters .05
460 Brenard Wilson .05
461 Roynell Young (AP) .05
462 St. Louis Cardinals Team .25
463 Ottis Anderson 1.00
464 Ottis Anderson (IA) .60
465 Carl Birdsong .05
466 Rush Brown .05
467 Mel Gray .05
468 Ken Greene .05
469 Jim Hart .15
470 *E.J. Junior* .60
471 *Neil Lomax* .75
472 *Stump Mitchell* .40
473 Wayne Morris .05
474 Neil O'Donoghue .05
475 Pat Tilley .05
476 Pat Tilley (IA) .05
477 San Francisco 49ers Team .40
478 Dwight Clark 1.00
479 Dwight Clark (IA) .40
480 Earl Cooper .05
481 Randy Cross (AP) .05
482 Johnny Davis .05
483 Fred Dean .05
484 Fred Dean (IA) .05
485 *Dwight Hicks* .25
486 *Ronnie Lott* (AP) 15.00
487 Ronnie Lott IA (IA) 6.00
488 Joe Montana (AP) 30.00
489 Joe Montana IA (IA) 10.00
490 Ricky Patton .05
491 Jack Reynolds .05
492 Freddie Solomon .05
493 Ray Wersching .05
494 Charley Young .05
495 Tampa Bay Bucaneers Team .15
496 Cedric Brown .05
497 Neal Colzie .05
498 Jerry Eckwood .05
499 Jimmy Giles (AP) .05
500 *Hugh Green* .60
501 Kevin House .05
502 Kevin House (IA) .05
503 Cecil Johnson .05
504 James Owens .05
505 Lee Roy Selmon (AP) .15
506 Mike Washington .05
507 *James Wilder* .65
508 Doug Williams .25
509 Washington Redskins Team .75
510 Perry Brooks .05
511 Dave Butz .05
512 Wilbur Jackson .05
513 Joe Lavender .05
514 Terry Metcalf .15
515 Art Monk 4.00
516 Frank Pollard, Mark Moseley .05
517 Donnie Shell, Mark Murphy (AP) .05
518 Mike Neims (AP) .05
519 Lemar Parrish .05
520 John Riggins 1.00
521 Joe Theismann 1.00
522 Ricky Thompson .05
523 Don Warren .15
524 Joe Washington .05
525 Checklist 1-132 .25
526 Checklist 133-264 .25
527 Checklist 265-396 .25
528 Checklist 397-528 .25

1982 Topps "Coming Soon" Stickers

These stickers were inserted in 1982 Topps football card packs. They are 1-15/16" x 2-9/16", making them the same size as Topps' regular 1982 stickers. They also share the same card numbers, which is why the set is skip-numbered. The card number is on the back, along with the words "Coming Soon!" The fronts of the stickers are gold-bordered foil stickers.

MT
Complete Set (16): 5.00
Common Player: .10
5 MVP Super Bowl XVI (Joe Montana) 2.00
6 NFC Championship .10
9 Super Bowl XVI (Joe Montana) 1.50
71 Tommy Kramer .30
73 George Rogers .30
75 Tom Skladany .10
139 Nolan Cromwell .30
143 Jack Lambert .50
144 Lawrence Taylor 1.75
150 Billy Sims .40
154 Ken Anderson .50
159 John Hannah .40
160 Anthony Munoz .75
220 Ken Anderson .50
221 Dan Fouts .50
222 Frank Lewis .10

1982 Topps Stickers

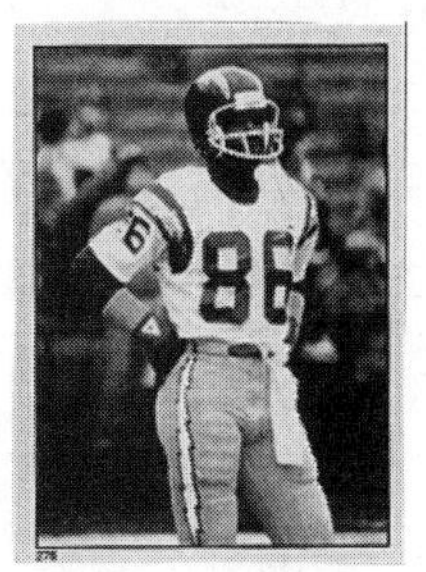

These stickers follow the same format as the 1981 stickers, complete with an album featuring Joe Montana on the cover. However, these stickers have yellow borders and a 1982 copyright date on the back. Foil stickers were also produced again (#s 1-10, 70-77, 139-160, 220-227). Stickers 1 and 2 combine as a puzzle to form a picture of the San Francisco 49ers; 3 and 4 show Super Bowl theme art.

MT
Complete Set (288): 30.00
Common Player: .05
1 Super Bowl XVI (49er Team) .35
2 Super Bowl XVI (49er Team) .15
3 Super Bowl XVI (Theme Art Trophy) .15
4 Super Bowl XVI (Theme Art Trophy) .15
5 MVP Super Bowl XVI (Joe Montana) 3.50
6 1981 NFC Champions 49ers .15
7 1981 AFC Champions (Ken Anderson) .25
8 Super Bowl XVI (Ken Anderson) .25
9 Super Bowl XVI (Joe Montana) 3.00
10 Super Bowl XVI (line blocking) .15
11 Steve Bartkowski .15
12 William Andrews .10
13 Lynn Cain .08
14 Wallace Francis .08
15 Alfred Jackson .08
16 Alfred Jenkins .10
17 Mike Kenn .08
18 Junior Miller .10
19 Vince Evans .10
20 Walter Payton 1.25
21 Dave Williams .05
22 Brian Baschnagel .05
23 Rickey Watts .05
24 Ken Margerum .08
25 Revie Sorey .05
26 Gary Fencik .05
27 Matt Suhey .05
28 Danny White .20
29 Tony Dorsett .50
30 Drew Pearson .25
31 Rafael Septien .08
32 Pat Donovan .05
33 Herbert Scott .05
34 Ed "Too Tall" Jones .20

35	Randy White	.25
36	Tony Hill	.08
37	Eric Hipple	.08
38	Billy Sims	.25
39	Dexter Bussey	.05
40	Freddie Scott	.08
41	David Hill	.05
42	Ed Murray	.10
43	Tom Skladany	.05
44	Doug English	.08
45	Al (Bubba) Baker	.12
46	Lynn Dickey	.12
47	Gerry Ellis	.05
48	Harlan Huckleby	.05
49	James Lofton	.40
50	John Jefferson	.08
51	Paul Coffman	.05
52	Jan Stenerud	.20
53	Rich Wingo	.05
54	Wendell Tyler	.10
55	Preston Dennard	.05
56	Billy Waddy	.05
57	Frank Corral	.05
58	Jack Youngblood	.15
59	Pat Thomas	.05
60	Rod Perry	.08
61	Nolan Cromwell	.10
62	Tommy Kramer	.10
63	Rickey Young	.08
64	Ted Brown	.05
65	Ahmad Rashad	.25
66	Sammie White	.08
67	Joe Senser	.05
68	Ron Yary	.08
69	Matt Blair	.08
70	NFC Passing Leader (Joe Montana)	3.50
71	NFC Passing Yardage Leader (Tommy Kramer)	.20
72	NFC Receiving Yardage Leader (Alfred Jenkins)	.15
73	NFC Rushing Yardage Leader (George Rogers)	.25
74	NFC Rushing Touchdowns Leader (Wendell Tyler)	.30
75	NFC Punting Leader (Tom Skladany)	.15
76	NFC Interceptions Leader (Everson Walls)	.35
77	MFC Sacks Leader (Curtis Greer)	.15
78	Archie Manning	.25
79	Dave Waymer	.05
80	George Rogers	.20
81	Jack Holmes	.05
82	Toussaint Tyler	.05
83	Wayne Wilson	.05
84	Russell Erxleben	.05
85	Elois Grooms	.05
86	Phil Simms	.20
87	Scott Brunner	.10
88	Rob Carpenter	.08
89	Johnny Perkins	.05
90	Dave Jennings	.05
91	Harry Carson	.12
92	Lawrence Taylor	2.50
93	Beasley Reece	.05
94	Mark Haynes	.05
95	Ron Jaworski	.12
96	Wilbert Montgomery	.08
97	Hubert Oliver	.05
98	Harold Carmichael	.10
99	Jerry Robinson	.08
100	Stan Walters	.05
101	Charlie Johnson	.05
102	Roynell Young	.05
103	Tony Franklin	.05
104	Neil Lomax	.15
105	Jim Hart	.15
106	Ottis Anderson	.20
107	Stump Mitchell	.12
108	Pat Tilley	.08
109	Rush Brown	.05
110	E.J. Junior	.05
111	Ken Greene	.05
112	Mel Gray	.08
113	Joe Montana	2.50
114	Ricky Patton	.05
115	Earl Cooper	.05
116	Dwight Clark	.25
117	Freddie Solomon	.08
118	Randy Cross	.10
119	Fred Dean	.08
120	Ronnie Lott	1.75
121	Dwight Hicks	.08
122	Doug Williams	.15
123	Jerry Eckwood	.08
124	James Owens	.08
125	Kevin House	.08
126	Jimmie Giles	.05
127	Charley Hannah	.05
128	Lee Roy Selmon	.15
129	Hugh Green	.12
130	Joe Theismann	.30
131	Joe Washington	.08
132	John Riggins	.25
133	Art Monk	.50
134	Ricky Thompson	.05
135	Don Warren	.08
136	Perry Brooks	.05
137	Mike Nelms	.05
138	Mark Moseley	.05
139	Nolan Cromwell (All-Pro)	.20
140	Dwight Hicks (All-Pro)	.15
141	Ronnie Lott (All-Pro)	2.00
142	Harry Carson (All-Pro)	.20
143	Jack Lambert (All-Pro)	.40
144	Lawrence Taylor (All-Pro)	2.50
145	Mel Blount (All-Pro)	.30
146	Joe Klecko (All-Pro)	.15
147	Randy White (All-Pro)	.35
148	Doug English (All-Pro)	.10
149	Fred Dean (All-Pro)	.20
150	Billy Sims (All-Pro)	.25
151	Tony Dorsett (All-Pro)	.75
152	James Lofton (All-Pro)	.75
153	Alfred Jenkins (All-Pro)	.20
154	Ken Anderson (All-Pro)	.35
155	Kellen Winslow (All-Pro)	.50
156	Marvin Powell (All-Pro)	.10
157	Randy Cross (All-Pro)	.20
158	Mike Webster (All-Pro)	.30
159	John Hannah (All-Pro)	.30
160	Anthony Munoz (All-Pro)	1.25
161	Curtis Dickey	.08
162	Randy McMillan	.08
163	Roger Carr	.08
164	Raymond Butler	.05
165	Reese McCall	.05
166	Ed Simonini	.05
167	Herb Oliver	.05
168	Nesby Glasgow	.05
169	Joe Ferguson	.08
170	Joe Cribbs	.08
171	jerry Butler	.08
172	Frank Lewis	.08
173	Mark Brammer	.05
174	Fred Smerlas	.10
175	Jim Haslett	.05
176	Charles Alexander	.05
177	Bill Simpson	.05
178	Ken Anderson	.20
179	Charles Alexander	.05
180	Pete Johnson	.05
181	Isaac Curtis	.05
182	Cris Collinsworth	.50
183	Pat McInally	.08
184	Anthony Munoz	.50
185	Louis Breeden	.05
186	Jim Breech	.10
187	Brian Sipe	.10
188	Charles White	.10
189	Mike Pruitt	.08
190	Reggie Rucker	.12
191	Dave Logan	.05
192	Ozzie Newsome	.30
193	Dick Ambrose	.05
194	Joe DeLamielleure	.05
195	Ricky Feacher	.05
196	Craig Morton	.12
197	Dave Preston	.05
198	Rick Parros	.05
199	Rick Upchurch	.08
200	Steve Watson	.10
201	Riley Odoms	.08
202	Randy Gradishar	.10
203	Steve Foley	.05
204	Ken Stabler	.30
205	Gifford Nielsen	.08
206	Tim Wilson	.05
207	Ken Burrough	.10
208	Mike Renfro	.10
209	Greg Stemrick	.05
210	Robert Brazile	.08
211	Gregg Bingham	.08
212	Steve Fuller	.08
213	Bill Kenney	.08
214	Joe Delaney	.20
215	Henry Marshall	.05
216	Nick Lowery	.10
217	Art Still	.08
218	Gary Green	.05
219	Gary Barbaro	.05
220	AFC PAssing Leader (Ken Anderson)	.35
221	AFC PAssing Yardage Leader (Dan Fouts)	.50
222	AFC Receiving Yardage Leader (Frank Lewis)	.20
223	AFC Kickoff Return Yardage Leader (James Brooks)	.75
224	AFC Rushing Touchdowns Leader (Chuck Muncie)	.20
225	AFC Punting Leader (Pat McInally)	.20
226	AFC Interceptions Leader (John Harris)	.20
227	AFC Sacks Leader (Joe Klecko)	.20
228	Dave Woodley	.08
229	Tony Nathan	.08
230	Andra Franklin	.05
231	Nat Moore	.08
232	Duriel Harris	.08
233	Uwe Von Schamann	.05
234	Bob Baumhower	.10
235	Glenn Blackwood	.10
236	Tommy Vigorito	.05
237	Steve Grogan	.12
238	Matt Cavanaugh	.08
239	Tony Collins	.08
240	Vagas Ferguson	.10
241	John Smith	.05
242	Stanley Morgan	.10
243	John Hannah	.15
244	Steve Nelson	.05
245	Don Hasselback	.05
246	Richard Todd	.12
247	Bruce Harper	.05
248	Wesley Walker	.12
249	Jerome Barkum	.08
250	Marvin Powell	.08
251	Mark Gastineau	.15
252	Joe Klecko	.08
253	Darrol Ray	.05
254	Marty Lyons	.08
255	Marc Wilson	.10
256	Kenny King	.08
257	Mark Van Eeghen	.08
258	Cliff Branch	.12
259	Bob Chandler	.08
260	Ray Guy	.15
261	Ted Hendricks	.20
262	Lester Hayes	.20
263	Terry Bradshaw	.60
264	Franco Harris	.35
265	John Stallworth	.15
266	Jim Smith	.05
267	Mike Webster	.12
268	Jack Lambert	.20
269	Mel Blount	.15
270	Donnie Shell	.12
271	Bennie Cunningham	.08
272	Dan Fouts	.40
273	Chuck Muncie	.10
274	James Brooks	.65
275	Charlie Joiner	.20
276	Wes Chandler	.12
277	Kellen Winslow	.25
278	Doug Wilkerson	.05
279	Gary Johnson	.08
280	Rolf Benirschke	.05
281	Jim Zorn	.12
282	Theotis Brown	.08
283	Dan Doornink	.05
284	Steve Largent	1.25
285	Sam McCullum	.08
286	Efren Herrera	.05
287	Manu Tuiasosopo	.05
288	John Harris	.05

1983 Topps

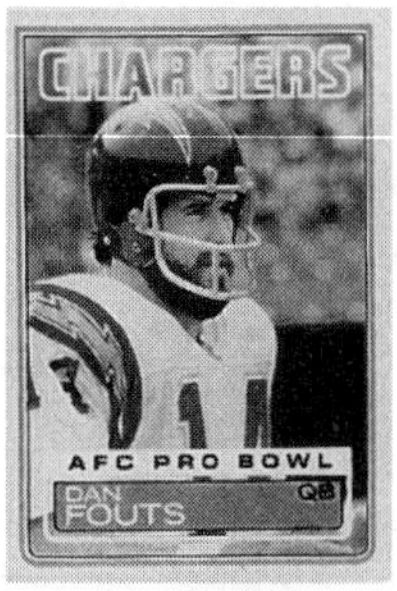

Presumably adjusting for an increase in the size of its baseball card set, Topps cut the number of cards in its annual football card set in 1983 from 528 to 396. Because Topps still printed the cards on four sheets, one-third of the cards were double-printed - accounting for some of the apparent price discrepancies in the list below. Cards in the set are bordered in white and feature the team name in white block letters at the top of the card. The player's name and position are found in a white rectangle near the bottom. All-Pro designations are found above this box. This set is notable for several rookies: Gerald Riggs, Jim McMahon, Mike Singletary, Roy Green and Marcus Allen. It also features Lawrence Taylor's second-year card. Cards are again listed alphabetically by city name and by player name. (Key: PB - Pro Bowl)

		MT
	Complete Set (396):	50.00
	Common Player:	.05
	Wax Pack (13+1):	3.00
	Wax Box (36):	65.00
1	Ken Anderson (RB)	.25
2	Tony Dorsett (RB)	.40
3	Dan Fouts (RB)	.20
4	Joe Montana (RB)	2.00
5	Mark Moseley (RB)	.10
6	Mike Nelms (RB)	.10
7	Darrol Ray (RB)	.10
8	John Riggins (RB)	.25
9	Fulton Walker (RB)	.10
10	NFC Championship (John Riggins)	.10
11	AFC Championship	.10
12	Super Bowl XVII (John Riggins)	.25
13	Atlanta Falcons Team (William Andrews)	.10
14	William Andrews (PB)	.05
15	Steve Bartkowski	.25
16	Bobby Butler	.05
17	Buddy Curry	.05
18	Alfred Jackson	.05
19	Alfred Jenkins	.05
20	Kenny Johnson	.05
21	Mike Kenn (PB)	.05
22	Mick Luckhurst	.05
23	Junior Miller	.05
24	Al Richardson	.05
25	*Gerald Riggs*	.75
26	R.C. Thielemann (PB)	.05
27	Jeff Van Note (PB)	.05
28	Walter Payton (TL)	.75
29	Brian Baschnagel	.05
30	Dan Hampton (PB)	.50
31	Mike Hartenstine	.05
32	Noah Jackson	.05
33	*Jim McMahon*	3.00
34	Emery Moorehead	.05
35	Bob Parsons	.05
36	Walter Payton	2.00
37	Terry Schmidt	.05
38	*Mike Singletary*	7.00
39	Matt Suhey	.05
40	Rickey Watts	.05
41	*Otis Wilson*	.15
42	Tony Dorsett (TL)	.25
43	Bob Breunig (PB)	.05
44	Doug Cosbie	.05
45	Pat Donovan (PB)	.05
46	Tony Dorsett (PB)	.75
47	Tony Hill	.05
48	Butch Johnson	.05
49	Ed "Too Tall" Jones (PB)	.20
50	Harvey Martin	.10
51	Drew Pearson	.25
52	Rafael Septien	.05
53	Ron Springs	.05
54	Dennis Thurman	.05
55	Everson Walls (PB)	.40
56	Danny White (PB)	.15
57	Randy White (PB)	.60
58	Detroit Lions Team (Billy Sims)	.05
59	Al "Bubba" Baker	.10
60	Dexter Bussey	.05
61	Gary Danielson	.05
62	Keith Dorney (PB)	.05
63	Doug English (PB)	.05
64	Ken Fantetti	.05
65	Alvin Hall	.05
66	David Hill	.05
67	Eric Hipple	.05
68	Ed Murray	.10
69	Freddie Scott	.05
70	Billy Sims (PB)	.10
71	Tom Skladany	.05
72	Leonard Thompson	.05
73	Bobby Watkins	.05
74	Green Bay Packers Team (Eddie Lee Ivery)	.10
75	John Anderson	.05
76	Paul Coffman (PB)	.05
77	Lynn Dickey	.05
78	Mike Douglass	.05
79	Eddie Lee Ivery	.05
80	John Jefferson (PB)	.10
81	Ezra Johnson	.05
82	Mark Lee	.05
83	James Lofton (PB)	1.00
84	Larry McCarren (PB)	.05
85	Jan Stenerud	.10
86	Los Angeles Rams Team (Wendell Tyler)	.10
87	Bill Bain	.05
88	Nolan Cromwell (PB)	.05
89	Preston Dennard	.05
90	Vince Ferragamo	.05
91	Mike Guman	.05
92	Kent Hill (PB)	.05
93	Mike Lansford	.05
94	Rod Perry	.05
95	Pat Thomas	.05
96	Jack Youngblood	.15
97	Minnesota Vikings Team (Ted Brown)	.10
98	Matt Blair (PB)	.05
99	Ted Brown	.05
100	Greg Coleman	.05
101	Randy Holloway	.05
102	Tommy Kramer	.10
103	Doug Martin	.05
104	Mark Mullaney	.05
105	Joe Senser	.05
106	Willie Teal	.05
107	Sammy White	.05
108	Rickey Young	.05
109	New Orleans Saints Team (George Rogers)	.10
110	*Stan Brock*	.40
111	Bruce Clark	.05
112	Russell Erxleben	.05
113	Russell Gary	.05
114	Jeff Groth	.05
115	John Hill	.05
116	Derland Moore	.05
117	George Rogers (PB)	.20
118	Ken Stabler	.75
119	Wayne Wilson	.05
120	New York Giants Team (Butch Woolfolk)	.10
121	Scott Brunner	.05
122	Rob Carpenter	.05
123	Harry Carson (PB)	.10
124	Joe Danelo	.05
125	Earnest Gray	.05
126	Mark Haynes (PB)	.05
127	Terry Jackson	.05
128	Dave Jennings (PB)	.05
129	Brian Kelley	.05
130	George Martin	.05
131	Tom Mullady	.05
132	Johnny Perkins	.05
133	Lawrence Taylor (PB)	5.00
134	Brad Van Pelt	.05
135	Butch Woolfolk	.05
136	Philadelphia Eagles Team (Wilbert Montgomery)	.10
137	Harold Carmichael	.25
138	Herman Edwards	.05
139	Tony Franklin	.05
140	Carl Hairston	.05
141	Dennis Harrison (PB)	.05
142	Ron Jaworski	.10
143	Frank LeMaster	.05
144	Wilbert Montgomery	.07
145	Guy Morriss	.05
146	Jerry Robinson	.05
147	Max Runager	.05
148	Ron Smith	.05
149	John Spagnola	.05
150	Stan Walters	.05
151	Roynell Young	.05
152	St. Louis Cardinals Team (Ottis Anderson)	.20
153	Ottis Anderson	.40
154	Carl Birdsong	.05
155	Dan Dierdorf	.15
156	*Roy Green*	.75
157	Elois Grooms	.05
158	Neil Lomax	.10
159	Wayne Morris	.05
160	James Robbins	.05
161	*Luis Sharpe*	.20
162	Pat Tilley	.05
163	San Francisco 49ers Team (Jeff Moore)	.15
164	Dwight Clark (PB)	.40
165	Randy Cross (PB)	.05
166	Russ Francis	.05
167	Dwight Hicks (PB)	.05
168	Ronnie Lott (PB)	3.00
169	Joe Montana	7.00
170	Jeff Moore	.05
171	*Renaldo Nehemiah*	.10
172	Freddie Solomon	.05
173	Ray Wersching	.05
174	Tampa Bay Buccaneers Team (James Wilder)	.10
175	Cedric Brown	.05
176	Bill Capece	.05
177	Neal Colzie	.05
178	Jimmie Giles (PB)	.07
179	Hugh Green (PB)	.07
180	Kevin House	.05
181	James Owens	.05
182	Lee Roy Selmon (PB)	.07
183	Mike Washington	.05
184	James Wilder	.10
185	Doug Williams	.10
186	Washington Redskins Team (John Riggins)	.25
187	Jeff Bostic	.05
188	Charlie Brown (PB)	.05
189	Vernon Dean	.05
190	*Joe Jacoby*	.75
191	*Dexter Manley*	.25
192	Rich Milot	.05
193	Art Monk	1.00
194	Mark Mosely (PB)	.05
195	Mike Nelms (PB)	.05
196	Neal Olkewicz	.05
197	Tony Peters (PB)	.05
198	John Riggins	.60
199	Joe Theismann (PB)	.60
200	Don Warren	.05
201	Jeris White	.05
202	Passing Leaders (Joe Theismann, Ken Anderson)	.20
203	Receiving Leaders (Dwight Clark, Kellen Winslow)	.10
204	Rushing Leaders (Tony Dorsett, Freeman McNeil)	.40
205	Scoring Leaders (Marcus Allen, Wendell Tyler)	.80
206	Interception Leaders (Everson Walls)	.10
207	Punting Leaders (Carl Birdsong, Luke Prestridge)	.10
208	Baltimore Colts Team (Randy McMillan)	.10
209	Matt Bouza	.05
210	Johnnie Cooks	.05
211	Curtis Dickey	.05
212	Nesby Glasgow	.05
213	Derrick Hatchett	.05
214	Randy McMillan	.05
215	*Mike Pagel*	.10
216	*Rohn Stark*	.20
217	Donnell Thompson	.05
218	Leo Wisniewski	.05
219	Buffalo Bills Team (Joe Cribbs)	.10
220	Curtis Brown	.05
221	Jerry Butler	.05
222	Greg Cater	.05
223	Joe Cribbs	.10
224	Joe Ferguson	.10
225	Roosevelt Leaks	.05
226	Frank Lewis	.05
227	Eugene Marve	.05
228	Fred Smerlas (PB)	.08
229	Ben Williams (PB)	.05
230	Cincinnati Bengals Team (Pete Johnson)	.10
231	Charles Alexander	.05
232	Ken Anderson (PB)	.25
233	Jim Breech	.05
234	Ross Browner	.05
235	Cris Collinsworth (PB)	.25
236	Isaac Curtis	.05
237	Pete Johnson	.05
238	Steve Kreider	.05
239	Max Montoya	.05
240	Anthony Munoz (PB)	1.50
241	Ken Riley	.05
242	Dan Ross (PB)	.07
243	Reggie Williams	.05
244	Cleveland Browns Team (Mike Pruitt)	.10
245	*Chip Banks* (PB)	.25
246	Tom Cousineau	.05
247	Joe DeLamielleure	.05
248	Doug Dieken	.05
249	*Hanford Dixon*	.15
250	Ricky Feacher	.05
251	Lawrence Johnson	.05
252	Dave Logan	.05
253	Paul McDonald	.05
254	Ozzie Newsome	.60
255	Mike Pruitt	.05
256	Clarence Scott	.05
257	Brian Sipe	.10
258	Dwight Walker	.05
259	Charles White	.05
260	Denver Broncos Team (Gerald Wilhite)	.10
261	Steve DeBerg	.50
262	Randy Gradishar (PB)	.07
263	Rulon Jones	.05
264	Rick Karlis	.05
265	Don Latimer	.05
266	Rick Parros	.05
267	Luke Prestridge (PB)	.07
268	Rick Upchurch (PB)	.07
269	Steve Watson	.05
270	Gerald Wilhite	.05
271	Houston Oilers Team (Gifford Nielson)	.10
272	Harold Bailey	.05
273	Jesse Baker	.05
274	Gregg Bingham	.05
275	Robert Brazile (PB)	.07
276	Donnie Craft	.05
277	Daryl Hunt	.05
278	Archie Manning	.10
279	Gifford Nielsen	.05
280	Mike Renfro	.05
281	Carl Roaches	.05
282	Kansas City Chiefs Team (Joe Delaney)	.10
283	Gary Barbaro (PB)	.07
284	Joe Delaney	.05
285	*Jeff Gossett*	.60
286	Gary Green (PB)	.05
287	Eric Harris	.05
288	Billy Jackson	.05
289	Bill Kenney	.05
290	Nick Lowery	.60
291	Henry Marshall	.05
292	Art Still (PB)	.05
293	Marcus Allen (TL)	2.00
294	*Marcus Allen* (PB)	25.00
295	Lyle Alzado	.25
296	Chris Bahr	.05
297	Cliff Branch	.25
298	*Todd Christensen*	2.00
299	Ray Guy	.10
300	Frank Hawkins	.05
301	Lester Hayes (PB)	.15
302	Ted Hendricks (PB)	.15
303	Kenny King	.05
304	Rod Martin	.05
305	Matt Millen	.15
306	Burgess Owens	.05
307	Jim Plunkett	.25
308	Miami Dolphins Team (Andra Franklin)	.10
309	Bob Baumhower (PB)	.07
310	Glenn Blackwood	.05
311	Lyle Blackwood	.05
312	A.J. Duhe	.05
313	Andra Franklin (PB)	.07
314	Duriel Harris	.05
315	Bob Kuechenberg (PB)	.07
316	Don McNeal	.05
317	Tony Nathan	.05
318	Ed Newman (PB)	.05
319	Earnie Rhone	.05
320	Joe Rose	.05
321	Don Strock	.07
322	Uwe Von Schamann	.05
323	David Woodley	.05
324	New England Patriots Team (Tony Collins)	.10
325	Julius Adams	.05
326	Pete Brock	.05
327	*Rich Camarillo*	.25
328	Tony Collins	.25
329	Steve Grogan	.25
330	John Hannah (PB)	.25
331	Don Hasselbeck	.05
332	Mike Haynes (PB)	.05
333	Roland James	.05
334	Stanley Morgan	.75
335	Steve Nelson	.05
336	Kenneth Sims	.05
337	Mark Van Eeghen	.05
338	New York Jets Team (Freeman McNeil)	.10
339	Greg Buttle	.05
340	Joe Fields (PB)	.05
341	Mark Gastineau (PB)	.08
342	Bruce Harper	.05
343	Bobby Jackson	.05
344	Bobby Jones	.05
345	Johnny "Lam" Jones	.07
346	Joe Klecko	.10
347	Marty Lyons	.05
348	Freeman McNeil (PB)	.60
349	Lance Mehl	.05
350	Marvin Powell (PB)	.05
351	Darrol Ray	.05
352	Abdul Salaam	.05
353	Richard Todd	.10
354	Wesley Walker (PB)	.25
355	Pittsburgh Steelers Team (Franco Harris)	.25
356	*Gary Anderson*	.75
357	Mel Blount	.25
358	Terry Bradshaw	.75
359	Larry Brown (PB)	.05
360	Bennie Cunningham	.05
361	Gary Dunn	.05
362	Franco Harris	.75
363	Jack Lambert (PB)	.60
364	Frank Pollard	.05
365	Donnie Shell (PB)	.08
366	John Stallworth (PB)	.25
367	Loren Toews	.05
368	Mike Webster (PB)	.10
369	*Dwayne Woodruff*	.10
370	San Diego Chargers Team (Chuck Muncie)	.10
371	Rolf Benirschke (PB)	.05
372	James Brooks	.75
373	Wes Chandler (PB)	.05
374	Dan Fouts (PB)	.75
375	Tim Fox	.05
376	Gary Johnson (PB)	.05
377	Charlie Joiner	.25
378	Louie Kelcher	.05
379	Chuck Muncie (PB)	.07
380	Cliff Thrift	.05
381	Doug Wilkerson (PB)	.05
382	Kellen Winslow (PB)	.75
383	Seattle Seahawks Team (Sherman Smith)	.10
384	*Kenny Easley* (PB)	.40
385	*Jacob Green*	.50
386	John Harris	.05
387	Mike Jackson	.05
388	*Norm Johnson*	.50
389	Steve Largent	.85
390	Keith Simpson	.05
391	Sherman Smith	.05
392	Jeff West	.05
393	Jim Zorn	.05
394	Checklist 1-132	.25
395	Checklist 133-264	.25
396	Checklist 265-396	.25

1983 Topps Sticker Inserts

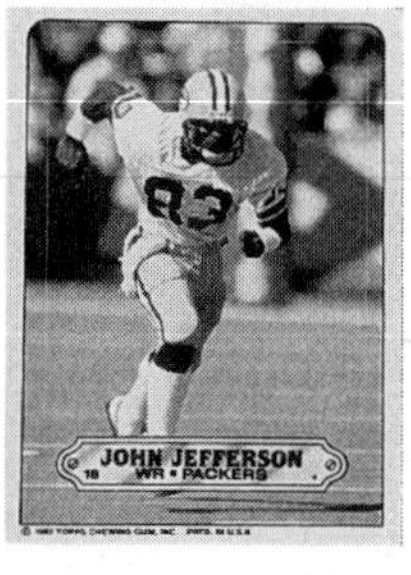

These 33 different inserts, which came in each wax pack of 1983 Topps football cards, pictured an NFL star on the front and a piece to one of three different puzzles on the backs. A gold plaque at the bottom of the card identifies the player.

		MT
	Complete Set (33):	20.00
	Common Player:	.35
1	Marcus Allen	5.00
2	Ken Anderson	.50
3	Ottis Anderson	.35
4	William Andrews	.35
5	Terry Bradshaw	1.25
6	Wes Chandler	.35
7	Dwight Clark	.50
8	Cris Collinsworth	.35
9	Joe Cribbs	.35
10	Nolan Cromwell	.35
11	Tony Dorsett	1.50
12	Dan Fouts	1.00
13	Mark Gastineau	.35
14	Jimmie Giles	.35
15	Franco Harris	1.00
16	Ted Hendricks	.60
17	Tony Hill	.35
18	John Jefferson	.35
19	James Lofton	1.00
20	Freeman McNeil	.50
21	Joe Montana	6.00
22	Mark Moseley	.35
23	Ozzie Newsome	1.00
24	Walter Payton	3.00
25	John Riggins	1.00
26	Billy Sims	.35
27	John Stallworth	.50
28	Lawrence Taylor	3.00
29	Joe Theismann	1.25
30	Richard Todd	.35
31	Wesley Walker	.35
32	Danny White	.35
33	Kellen Winslow	.50

1983 Topps Stickers

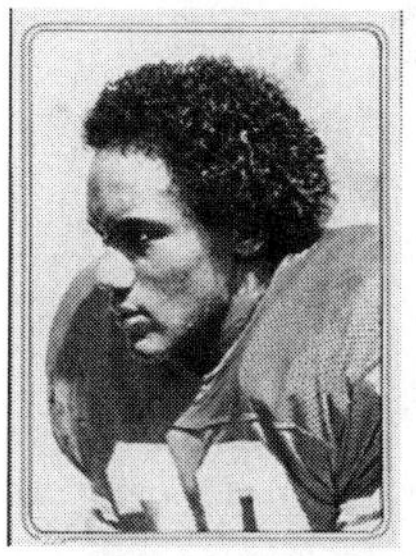

These stickers are similar to those issued in previous years, but can be identified by the rounded frame around the picture on the front and the reference on the back to the 1983 sticker album which was produced. Once again, Topps included foil stickers in the set (#s 1-4, 73-80, 143-152 and 264-271. Foil stickers 1-2 are right and left sides of Franco Harris; 3 and 4 portray Walter Payton.

		MT
Complete Set (330):		30.00
Common Player:		.05
1	Franco Harris	.50
2	Franco Harris	.50
3	Walter Payton	1.25
4	Walter Payton	1.25
5	John Riggins	.35
6	Tony Dorsett	.40
7	Mark Van Eeghen	.05
8	Chuck Muncie	.08
9	Wilbert Montgomery	.08
10	Greg Pruitt	.08
11	Sam Cunningham	.10
12	Ottis Anderson	.20
13	Mike Pruitt	.08
14	Dexter Bussey	.05
15	Mike Pagel	.05
16	Curtis Dickey	.08
17	Randy McMillan	.08
18	Raymond Butler	.05
19	Nesby Glasgow	.05
20	Zachary Dixon	.05
21	Matt Bouza	.05
22	Johnie Cooks	.05
23	Curtis Brown	.05
24	Joe Cribbs	.10
25	Roosevelt Leaks	.08
26	Jerry Butler	.08
27	Frank Lewis	.08
28	Fred Smerlas	.05
29	Ben Williams	.05
30	Joe Ferguson	.15
31	Isaac Curtis	.08
32	Cris Collinsworth	.15
33	Anthony Munoz	.20
34	Max Montoya	.05
35	Ross Browner	.08
36	Reggie Williams	.05
37	Ken Riley	.10
38	Pete Johnson	.08
39	Ken Anderson	.20
40	Charles White	.10
41	Dave Logan	.05
42	Doug Dieken	.05
43	Ozzie Newsome	.20
44	Tom Cousineau	.05
45	Bob Golic	.08
46	Brian Sipe	.10
47	Paul McDonald	.05
48	Mike Pruitt	.10
49	Luke Prestridge	.05
50	Randy Gradishar	.10
51	Rulon Jones	.05
52	Rick Parros	.05
53	Steve DeBerg	.15
54	Tom Jackson	.10
55	Rick Upchurch	.08
56	Steve Watson	.08
57	Robert Brazile	.10
58	Willie Tullis	.05
59	Archie Manning	.15
60	Gifford Nielsen	.08
61	Harold Bailey	.05
62	Carl Roaches	.08
63	Gregg Bingham	.05
64	Daryl Hunt	.05
65	Gary Green	.05
66	Gary Barbaro	.08
67	Bill Kenney	.08
68	Joe Delaney	.10
69	Henry Marshall	.05
70	Nick Lowery	.10
71	Jeff Gossett	.05
72	Art Still	.10
73	AFC Passing Leader (Ken Anderson)	.40
74	AFC PAssing Yardage Leader (Dan Fouts)	.50
75	AFC Receiving Yardage Leader (Wes Chandler)	.25
76	AFC Kickoff Return Yardage Leader (James Brooks)	.40
77	AFC Punt Return Yardage Leader (Rick Upchurch)	.30
78	AFC Punting Leader (Luke Prestridge)	.15
79	AFC Sacks Leader (Jesse Baker)	.15
80	AFC Rushing Yardage Leader (Freeman McNeil)	.30
81	Ray Guy	.15
82	Jim Plunkett	.15
83	Lester Hayes	.08
84	Kenny King	.05
85	Cliff Branch	.12
86	Todd Christensen	.12
87	Lyle Alzado	.15
88	Ted Hendricks	.20
89	Rod Martin	.10
90	Dave Woodley	.10
91	Ed Newman	.05
92	Earnie Rhone	.05
93	Don McNeal	.05
94	Glenn Blackwood	.08
95	Andra Franklin	.08
96	Nat Moore	.12
97	Lyle Blackwood	.08
98	A.J. Duhe	.10
99	Tony Collins	.08
100	Stanley Morgan	.10
101	Pete Brock	.05
102	Steve Nelson	.05
103	Steve Grogan	.15
104	Mark Van Eeghen	.08
105	Don Hasselbeck	.05
106	John Hannah	.15
107	Mike Haynes	.15
108	Wesley Walker	.10
109	Marvin Powell	.08
110	Joe Klecko	.08
111	Bobby Jackson	.05
112	Richard Todd	.10
113	Lance Mehl	.08
114	Johnny Lam Jones	.10
115	Mark Gastineau	.10
116	Freeman McNeil	.15
117	Franco Harris	.30
118	Mike Webster	.15
119	Mel Blount	.15
120	Donnie Shell	.10
121	Terry Bradshaw	.75
122	John Stallworth	.15
123	Jack Lambert	.25
124	Dwayne Woodruff	.05
125	Bennie Cunningham	.05
126	Charlie Joiner	.20
127	Kellen Winslow	.20
128	Rolf Benirschke	.05
129	Louis Kelcher	.08
130	Chuck Muncie	.08
131	Wes Chandler	.10
132	Gary Johnson	.08
133	James Brooks	.15
134	Dan Fouts	.35
135	Jacob Green	.10
136	Michael Jackson	.05
137	Jim Zorn	.12
138	Sherman Smith	.08
139	Keith Simpson	.05
140	Steve Largent	1.25
141	John Harris	.08
142	Jeff West	.08
143	Ken Anderson (top)	.45
144	Ken Anderson (bottom)	.45
145	Tony Dorsett (top)	.40
146	Tony Dorsett (bottom)	.40
147	Dan Fouts (top)	.40
148	Dan Fouts (bottom)	.40
149	Joe Montana (top)	2.00
150	Joe Montana (bottom)	2.00
151	Mark Moseley (top)	.15
152	Mark Moseley (bottom)	.15
153	Richard Todd	.10
154	Butch Johnson	.10
155	Bill (Gary) Hogeboom	.08
156	A.J. Duhe	.08
157	Kurt Sohn	.05
158	Drew Pearson	.10
159	John Riggins	.35
160	Pat Donovan	.15
161	John Hannah	.15
162	Jeff Van Note	.05
163	Randy Cross	.10
164	Marvin Powell	.08
165	Kellen Winslow	.25
166	Dwight Clark	.20
167	Wes Chandler	.08
168	Tony Dorsett	.40
169	Freeman McNeil	.12
170	Ken Anderson	.25
171	Mark Moseley	.08
172	Mark Gastineau	.08
173	Gary Johnson	.05
174	Randy White	.30
175	Ed "Too Tall" Jones	.12
176	Hugh Green	.08
177	Harry Carson	.05
178	Lawrence Taylor	.30
179	Lester Hayes	.08
180	Mark Haynes	.05
181	Dave Jennings	.05
182	Nolan Cromwell	.08
183	Tony Peters	.05
184	Jimmy Cefalo	.05
185	A.J. Duhe	.10
186	John Riggins	.35
187	Charlie Brown	.05
188	Mike Nelms	.05
189	Mark Murphy	.05
190	Fulton Walker	.05
191	Marcus Allen	2.50
192	Chip Banks	.08
193	Charlie Brown	.05
194	Bob Crable	.05
195	Vernon Dean	.05
196	Jim McMahon	.75
197	James Robbins	.08
198	Luis Sharpe	.08
199	Rohn Stark	.05
200	Lester Williams	.05
201	Leo Wisniewski	.05
202	Butch Woolfolk	.30
203	Mike Kenn	.10
204	R.C. Thielemann	.05
205	Buddy Curry	.05
206	Steve Bartkowski	.15
207	Alfred Jenkins	.08
208	Don Smith	.05
209	Alfred Jenkins	.08
210	Fulton Kuykendall	.05
211	William Andrews	.10
212	Gary Fencik	.08
213	Walter Payton	1.50
214	Mike Singletary	1.50
215	Otis Wilson	.08
216	Matt Suhey	.05
217	Dan Hampton	.20
218	Emery Moorehead	.05
219	Mike Hartenstine	.05
220	Danny White	.20
221	Drew Pearson	.10
222	Rafael Septien	.05
223	Ed "Too Tall" Jones	.15
224	Everson Walls	.10
225	Randy White	.20
226	Harvey Martin	.10
227	Tony Hill	.08
228	John Jefferson	.30
229	Billy Sims	.20
230	Leonard Thompson	.05
231	Ed Murray	.05
232	Doug English	.05
233	Ken Fantetti	.05
234	Tom Skladany	.05
235	Freddie Scott	.05
236	Eric Hipple	.08
237	David Hill	.05
238	John Jefferson	.08
239	Paul Coffman	.05
240	Ezra Johnson	.05
241	Mike Douglass	.05
242	Mark Lee	.08
243	John Anderson	.10
244	Jan Stenerud	.15
245	Lynn Dickey	.10
246	James Lofton	.30
247	Vince Ferragamo	.12
248	Preston Dennard	.05
249	Jack Youngblood	.15
250	Mike Guman	.05
251	LeRoy Irvin	.08
252	Mike Lansford	.05
253	Kent Hill	.05
254	Nolan Cromwell	.05
255	Doug Martin	.05
256	Greg Coleman	.05
257	Ted Brown	.05
258	Mark Mullaney	.05
259	Joe Senser	.08
260	Randy Holloway	.05
261	Matt Blair	.08
262	Sammie White	.10
263	Tommy Kramer	.10
264	NFC Passing Leader (Joe Theismann)	.40
265	NFC Passing Yardage Leader (Joe Montana)	1.50
266	NFC Receiving Yardage Leader (Dwight Clark)	.25
267	NFC Kickoff Return Yardage Leader (Mike Nelms)	.10
268	NFC Punting Leader (Carl Birdsong)	.10
269	NFC Interceptions Leader (Everson Walls)	.20
270	NFC Sacks Leader (Doug Martin)	.15
271	NFC Rushing Yardage Leader (Tony Dorsett)	.40
272	Russell Erxleben	.05
273	Stan Brock	.05
274	Jeff Groth	.05
275	Bruce Clark	.05
276	Ken Stabler	.30
277	George Rogers	.10
278	Derland Moore	.08
279	Wayne Wilson	.05
280	Lawrence Taylor	.35
281	Harry Carson	.10
282	Brian Kelley	.05
283	Brad Van Pit	.05
284	Earnest Gray	.05
285	Dave Jennings	.05
286	Rob Carpenter	.05
287	Scott Brunner	.05
288	Ron Jaworski	.15
289	Jerry Robinson	.08
290	Frank LeMaster	.05
291	Wilbert Montgomery	.08
292	Tony Franklin	.05
293	Harold Carmichael	.15
294	John Spagnola	.05
295	Herman Edwards	.05
296	Ottis Anderson	.15
297	Carl Birdsong	.05
298	Doug Marsh	.05
299	Neil Lomax	.12
300	Rush Brown	.05
301	Pat Tilley	.08
302	Wayne Morris	.08
303	Dan Dierdorf	.20
304	Roy Green	.30
305	Joe Montana	1.75
306	Randy Cross	.10
307	Freddie Solomon	.08
308	Jack Reynolds	.10
309	Ronnie Lott	.50
310	Renaldo Nehemiah	.15
311	Russ Francis	.08
312	Dwight Clark	.20
313	Doug Williams	.12
314	Bill Capece	.05
315	Mike Washington	.05
316	Hugh Green	.10
317	Kevin House	.08
318	Lee Roy Selmon	.12
319	Neal Colzie	.10
320	Jimmie Giles	.08
321	Cedric Brown	.05
322	Tony Peters	.05
323	Neal Olkewicz	.05
324	Dexter Manley	.05
325	Joe Theismann	.30
326	Rich Milot	.05
327	Mark Moseley	.08
328	Art Monk	.40
329	Mike Nelms	.08
330	John Riggins	.35

Values quoted in this guide reflect the retail price of a card — the price a collector can expect to pay when buying a card from a dealer. The wholesale price — that which a collector can expect to receive from a dealer when selling cards — will be significantly lower, depending on desirability and condition.

1983 Topps Sticker Boxes

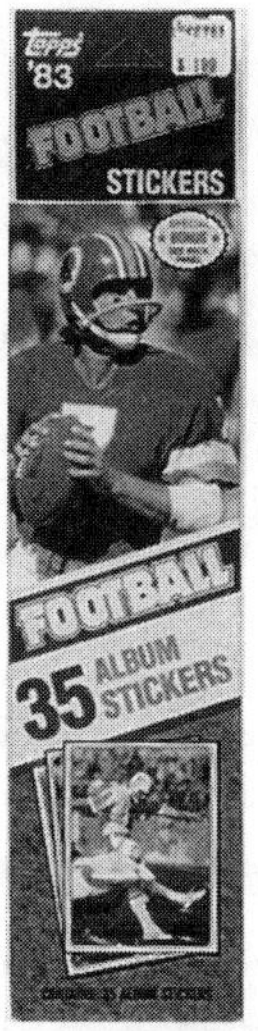

These boxes contained 35 stickers inside, but also had two 2-1/2" x 3-1/2" on them; an offensive player was on each box. The cards are not numbered, and there was no issue for #10, but the box is numbered with a tab. The prices below are for an uncut box.

		MT
Complete Set (12):		15.00
Common Player:		.75
1	Pat Donovan, Mark Gastineau	.75
2	Wes Chandler, Nolan Cromwell	1.25
3	Marvin Powell, Ed "Too Tall" Jones	1.25
4	Ken Anderson, Tony Peters	1.25
5	Freeman McNeil, Lawrence Taylor	2.00
6	Mark Moseley, Dave Jennings	.75
7	Dwight Clark, Mark Haynes	1.50
8	Jeff Van Note, Harry Carson	.75
9	Tony Dorsett, Hugh Green	2.00
11	Randy Cross, Gary Johnson	1.00
12	Kellen Winslow, Lester Hayes	1.25
13	John Hannah, Randy White	2.00

1984 Topps

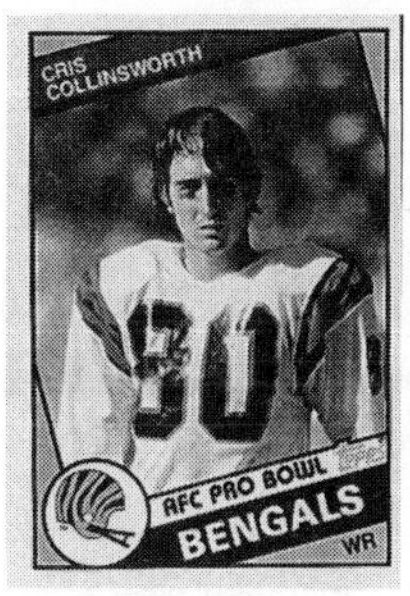

Topps' most sought-after NFL set of the decade is notable for its excellent array of rookies: Dickerson, Elway, Marino, Curt Warner, Mark Duper, Willie Gault and Roger Craig are among them. This is one of the better-designed sets of the decade as well. The 396-card set is numbered alphabetically by city and by player name; AFC teams are listed first, while NFC teams are listed after the NFL leaders. Team leader cards, which had for years shown team leaders in several categories, this year showed just one leader. Card fronts show an angled photo in a yellow stripe. The team logo and name appear at the bottom also at an angle. The Pro Bowl designation appears above the team name. Instant Replay cards issued in this set in addition to the player's regular card featured NFL stars in action poses. The score on the Super Bowl card (#9) is incorrect: instead of 28-9, it should read 38-9. (Key: PB - Pro Bowl, IR - Instant Replay)

		MT
Complete Set (396):		230.00
Common Player:		.05
Wax Pack (15):		18.00
Wax Box (36):		510.00
1	Eric Dickerson (RB)	.75
2	Ali Haji-Sheikh (RB)	.10
3	Franco Harris (RB)	.25
4	Mark Moseley (RB)	.15
5	John Riggins (RB)	.25
6	Jan Stenerud (RB)	.10
7	AFC Championship	.10
8	NFC Championship	.10
9	Super Bowl XVIII	.25
10	Indianapolis Colts Team: (Curtis Dickey)	.10
11	*Raul Allegre*	.10
12	Curtis Dickey	.05
13	*Ray Donaldson*	.10
14	Nesby Glasgow	.05
15	*Chris Hinton* (PB)	1.50
16	*Vernon Maxwell*	.15
17	Randy McMillan	.05
18	Mike Pagel	.05
19	Rohn Stark	.05
20	Leo Wisniewski	.05
21	Buffalo Bills Team: (Joe Cribbs)	.10
22	Jerry Butler	.05
23	Joe Danelo	.05
24	Joe Ferguson	.10
25	Steve Freeman	.05
26	Roosevelt Leaks	.05
27	Frank Lewis	.05
28	Eugene Marve	.05
29	Booker Moore	.05
30	Fred Smerlas (PB)	.07
31	Ben Williams	.05
32	Cincinnati Bengals Team: (Cris Collinsworth)	.10
33	Charles Alexander	.05
34	Ken Anderson	.25
35	Ken Anderson (IR)	.10
36	Jim Breech	.05
37	Cris Collinsworth (PB)	.10
38	Cris Collinsworth (IR)	.06
39	Isaac Curtis	.05
40	Eddie Edwards	.05
41	*Ray Horton*	.20
42	Pete Johnson	.05
43	Steve Kreider	.05
44	Max Montoya	.05
45	Anthony Munoz (PB)	.75
46	Reggie Williams	.05
47	Cleveland Browns Team: (Mike Pruitt)	.10
48	Matt Bahr	.05
49	Chip Banks (PB)	.15
50	Tom Cousineau	.05
51	Joe DeLamielleure	.05
52	Doug Dieken	.05
53	*Bob Golic*	.50
54	Bobby Jones	.05
55	Dave Logan	.05
56	Clay Matthews	1.00
57	Paul McDonald	.05
58	Ozzie Newsome	.50
59	Ozzie Newsome (IR)	.20
60	Mike Pruitt	.05
61	Steve Watson	.05
62	*Barney Chavous*	.20
63	*John Elway*	100.00
64	Steve Foley	.05
65	Tom Jackson	.15
66	Rick Karlis	.05
67	Luke Prestridge	.05
68	Zack Thomas	.05
69	Rick Upchurch	.05
70	Steve Watson	.05
71	*Sammy Winder*	.25
72	Louis Wright (PB)	.05
73	Houston Oilers Team: (Tim Smith)	.10
74	Jesse Baker	.05
75	Gregg Bingham	.05
76	Robert Brazile	.07
77	Steve Brown	.05
78	Chris Dressel	.05
79	Doug France	.05
80	Florian Kempf	.05
81	Carl Roaches	.05
82	*Tim Smith*	.15
83	Willie Tullis	.05
84	Kansas City Chiefs Team: (Carlos Carson)	.10
85	Mike Bell	.05
86	Theotis Brown	.05
87	Carlos Carson (PB)	.10
88	Carlos Carson (IR)	.06
89	*Deron Cherry* (PB)	.75
90	Gary Green (PB)	.05
91	Billy Jackson	.05
92	Bill Kenney	.05
93	Bill Kenney (IR)	.05
94	Nick Lowery	.25
95	Henry Marshall	.05
96	Art Still	.07
97	Los Angeles Raiders Team: (Todd Christensen)	.10
98	Marcus Allen	4.00
99	Marcus Allen IR (IR)	2.00
100	Lyle Alzado	.20
101	Lyle Alzado (IR)	.08
102	Chris Bahr	.05
103	Malcolm Barnwell	.05
104	Cliff Branch	.25
105	Todd Christensen (PB)	.50
106	Todd Christensen (IR)	.20
107	Ray Guy	.20
108	Frank Hawkins	.05
109	Lester Hayes (PB)	.07
110	Ted Hendricks (PB)	.20
111	*Howie Long* (PB)	6.00
112	Rod Martin (PB)	.05
113	*Vann McElroy* (PB)	.15
114	Jim Plunkett	.15
115	Greg Pruitt (PB)	.05
116	Miami Dolphins Team: (Mark Duper)	.10
117	Bobb Baumhower (PB)	.05
118	*Doug Betters* (PB)	.10
119	A.J. Duhe	.05
120	*Mark Duper* (PB)	1.50
121	Andre Franklin (Andra)	.05
122	William Judson	.05
123	*Dan Marino* (PB)	110.00
124	Dan Marino IR (IR)	15.00
125	Nat Moore	.05
126	Ed Newman (PB)	.05
127	*Reggie Roby*	.60
128	Gerald Small	.05
129	*Dwight Stephenson*	.75
130	Uwe Von Schamann	.05
131	New England Patriots Team: (Tony Collins)	.10
132	Rich Camarillo (PB)	.05
133	Tony Collins (PB)	.05
134	Tony Collins (IR)	.05
135	Bob Cryder	.05
136	Steve Grogan	.10
137	John Hannah (PB)	.15
138	*Brian Holloway* (PB)	.15
139	Roland James	.05
140	Stanley Morgan	.25
141	Rick Sanford	.05
142	Mosi Tatupu	.05
143	*Andre Tippett*	1.00
144	New York Jets Team: (Wesley Walker)	.10
145	Jerome Barkum	.05
146	Mark Gastineau (PB)	.07
147	Mark Gastineau (IR)	.05
148	Bruce Harper	.05
149	Johnny "Lam" Jones	.05
150	Joe Klecko (PB)	.07
151	Pat Leahy	.05
152	Freeman McNeil	.20
153	Lance Mehl	.05
154	Marvin Powell (PB)	.07
155	Darrol Ray	.05
156	Pat Ryan	.05
157	Kirk Springs	.05
158	Wesley Walker	.15
159	Pittsburgh Steelers Team: (Franco Harris)	.25
160	*Walter Abercrombie*	.15
161	Gary Anderson (PB)	.05
162	Terry Bradshaw	1.00
163	Craig Colquitt	.05
164	Bennie Cunningham	.05
165	Franco Harris	.75
166	Franco Harris (IR)	.30
167	Jack Lambert (PB)	.60
168	Jack Lambert (IR)	.25
169	Frank Pollard	.05
170	Donnie Shell	.05
171	Mike Webster (PB)	.25
172	Keith Willis	.15
173	Rick Woods	.05
174	San Diego Chargers Team: (Kellen Winslow)	.20
175	Rolf Benirschke	.05
176	James Brooks	.20
177	Maury Buford	.05
178	Wes Chandler (PB)	.05
179	Dan Fouts (PB)	.75
180	Dan Fouts (IR)	.50
181	Charlie Joiner	.25
182	Linden King	.05
183	Chuck Muncie	.05
184	*Billy Ray Smith*	.25
185	Danny Walters	.05
186	Kellen Winslow (PB)	.60
187	Kellen Winslow (IR)	.25
188	Seattle Seahawks Team: (Curt Warner)	.10
189	Steve August	.05
190	Dave Brown	.05
191	Zachary Dixon	.05
192	Kenny Easley	.10
193	Jacob Green	.15
194	Norm Johnson	.05
195	*Dave Krieg*	3.50
196	Steve Largent	.80
197	Steve Largent (IR)	.60
198	*Curt Warner* (PB)	.50
199	Curt Warner (IR)	.20
200	Jeff West	.05
201	Charley Young	.05
202	Passing Leaders: (Dan Marino, Steve Bartkowski) (LL)	4.00
203	Receiving Leaders: (Todd Christensen, Charlie Brown, Earnest Gray, Roy Green)	.10
204	Rushing Leaders: (Curt Warner, Eric Dickerson)	.40
205	Scoring Leaders: (Gary Anderson, Mark Moseley)	.10
206	Interception Leaders: (Vann McElroy, Ken Riley, Mark Murphy)	.10
207	Punting Leaders: (Rich Camarillo, Greg Coleman)	.10
208	Atlanta Falcons Team: (William Andrews)	.10
209	William Andrews (PB)	.05
210	William Andrews (IR)	.05
211	*Stacey Bailey*	.15
212	Steve Bartkowski	.15
213	Steve Barkowski (IR)	.05
214	Ralph Giacomarro	.05
215	Billy Johnson (PB)	.07
216	Mike Kenn (PB)	.05
217	Mick Luckhurst	.05
218	Gerald Riggs	.10
219	R.C. Thielemann (PB)	.05
220	Jeff Van Note	.05
221	Walter Payton (TL)	.75
222	*Jim Covert*	.75
223	Leslie Frazier	.05
224	*Willie Gault*	.50
225	Mike Hartenstine	.05
226	Noah Jackson	.05
227	Jim McMahon	1.50
228	Walter Payton (PB)	2.00
229	Walter Payton IR (IR)	1.00
230	*Mike Richardson*	.10
231	Terry Schmidt	.05
232	Mike Singletary (PB)	1.75
233	Matt Suhey	.05
234	Bob Thomas	.05
235	Dallas Cowboys Team: (Tony Dorsett)	.25
236	Bob Breunig	.05
237	Doug Cosbie (PB)	.05
238	Tony Dorsett (PB)	.60
239	Tony Dorsett (IR)	.25
240	John Dutton	.05
241	Tony Hill	.05
242	Ed "Too Tall" Jones (PB)	.20
243	Drew Pearson	.20
244	Rafael Septien	.05
245	Ron Springs	.05
246	Dennis Thurman	.05
247	Everson Walls (PB)	.15
248	Danny White	.25
249	Randy White (PB)	.60
250	Detroit Lions Team: (Billy Sims)	.10
251	*Jeff Chadwick*	.25

252	Garry Cobb	.05
253	Doug English (PB)	.05
254	William Gay	.05
255	Eric Hipple	.05
256	*James Jones*	.25
257	Bruce McNorton	.05
258	Ed Murray	.05
259	Ulysses Norris	.05
260	Billy Sims	.15
261	Billy Sims (IR)	.08
262	Leonard Thompson	.05
263	Green Bay Packers Team: (James Lofton)	.25
264	John Anderson	.05
265	Paul Coffman (PB)	.05
266	Lynn Dickey	.07
267	Gerry Ellis	.05
268	John Jefferson	.07
269	John Jefferson (IR)	.05
270	Ezra Johnson	.05
271	Tim Lewis	.05
272	James Lofton (PB)	1.50
273	James Lofton (IR)	.75
274	Larry McCarren (PB)	.05
275	Jan Stenerud	.25
276	Eric Dickerson (TL)	.75
277	Mike Barber	.05
278	Jim Collins	.05
279	Nolan Cromwell (PB)	.05
280	*Eric Dickerson* (PB)	7.00
281	Eric Dickerson IR (IR)	2.00
282	George Farmer	.05
283	Vince Ferragamo	.10
284	Kent Hill (PB)	.05
285	John Misko	.05
286	*Jackie Slater* (PB)	2.00
287	Jack Youngblood	.05
288	Minnesota Vikings Team: (Darrin Nelson)	.10
289	Ted Brown	.05
290	Greg Coleman	.05
291	Steve Dils	.05
292	Tony Galbreath	.05
293	Tommy Kramer	.10
294	Doug Martin	.05
295	*Darrin Nelson*	.25
296	Benny Ricardo	.05
297	John Swain	.05
298	John Turner	.05
299	New Orleans Saints Team: (George Rogers)	.10
300	*Morten Andersen*	3.00
301	Russell Erxleben	.05
302	Jeff Groth	.05
303	*Rickey Jackson* (PB)	3.00
304	Johnnie Poe	.05
305	George Rogers	.10
306	Richard Todd	.10
307	Jim Wilks	.05
308	Dave Wilson	.05
309	Wayne Wilson	.05
310	New York Giants Team: (Earnest Gray)	.10
311	Leon Bright	.05
312	Scott Brunner	.05
313	Rob Carpenter	.05
314	Harry Carson (PB)	.20
315	Earnest Gray	.05
316	Ali Haji-Sheikh (PB)	.05
317	Mark Haynes (PB)	.08
318	Dave Jennings	.05
319	Brian Kelley	.05
320	Phil Simms	1.00
321	Lawrence Taylor (PB)	3.00
322	Lawrence Taylor IR (IR)	2.00
323	Brad Van Pelt	.05
324	Butch Woolfolk	.05
325	Philadelphia Eagles Team: (Mike Quick)	.15
326	Harold Carmichael	.20
327	Herman Edwards	.05
328	Michael Haddix	.10
329	Dennis Harrison	.05
330	Ron Jaworski	.10
331	Wilbert Montgomery	.07
332	Hubert Oliver	.05
333	*Mike Quick* (PB)	.75
334	Jerry Robinson	.05
335	Max Runager	.05
336	Michael Williams	.05
337	St. Louis Cardinals Team: (Ottis Anderson)	.15
338	Ottis Anderson	.50
339	Al "Bubba" Baker	.05
340	Carl Birdsong (PB)	.05
341	David Galloway	.05
342	Roy Green (PB)	.25
343	Roy Green (IR)	.10
344	*Curtis Greer*	.10
345	Neil Lomax	.10
346	Doug Marsh	.05
347	Stump Mitchell	.05
348	*Lionel Washington*	.50
349	San Francisco 49ers Team: (Dwight Clark)	.15
350	Dwaine Board	.05
351	Dwight Clark	.25
352	Dwight Clark (IR)	.10
353	*Roger Craig*	5.00
354	Fred Dean	.05
355	Fred Dean (IR)	.10
356	Dwight Hicks (PB)	.05
357	Ronnie Lott (PB)	1.50
358	Joe Montana (PB)	9.00
359	Joe Montana IR (IR)	4.00
360	Freddie Solomon	.05
361	Wendell Tyler	.05
362	Ray Wersching	.05
363	*Eric Wright*	.15
364	Tampa Bay Buccaneers Team: (Kevin House)	.10
365	Gerald Carter	.05
366	Hugh Green (PB)	.07
367	Kevin House	.05
368	Michael Morton	.05
369	James Owens	.05
370	Booker Reese	.05
371	Lee Roy Selmon (PB)	.07
372	Jack Thompson	.05
373	James Wilder	.10
374	Steve Wilson	.05
375	Washington Redskins Team: (John Riggins)	.20
376	Jeff Bostic (PB)	.05
377	Charlie Brown (PB)	.05
378	Charlie Brown (IR)	.05
379	Dave Butz (PB)	.05
380	*Darrell Green*	2.00
381	*Russ Grimm* (PB)	.50
382	Joe Jacoby (PB)	.05
383	Dexter Manley	.05
384	Art Monk	1.00
385	Mark Moseley	.05
386	Mark Murphy (PB)	.05
387	Mike Nelms	.05
388	John Riggins	.60
389	John Riggins (IR)	.25
390	Joe Theismann (PB)	.50
391	Joe Theismann (IR)	.25
392	Don Warren	.05
393	Joe Washington	.05
394	Checklist 1-132	.25
395	Checklist 133-264	.25
396	Checklist 265-396	.25

1984 Topps NFL Stars

This 11-card set was included, one per pack, in the 1984 Topps football card wax packs. Styled almost exactly as the 1985 NFL Stars set a year later, the glossy cards included an action photo of the player bordered in blue, plus the NFL logo and the player name at the bottom of the card. Cards were printed on heavy white cardboard stock.

		MT
Complete Set (11):		6.00
Common Player:		.25
1	Curt Warner	.40
2	Eric Dickerson	2.50
3	Dan Marino	2.00
4	Steve Bartkowski	.25
5	Todd Christensen	.25
6	Roy Green	.25
7	Charlie Brown	.25
8	Earnest Gray	.25
9	Mark Gastineau	.25
10	Fred Dean	.25
11	Lawrence Taylor	.40

1984 Topps Play Cards

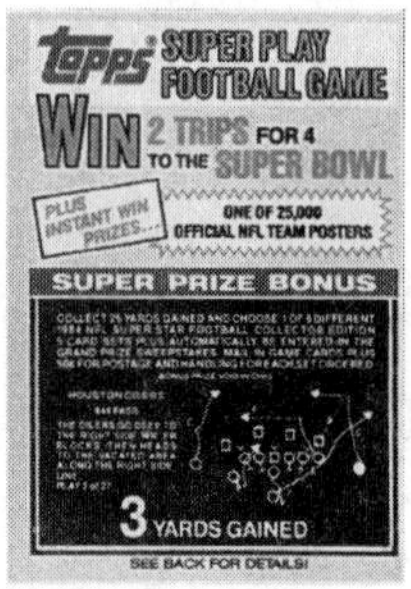

The 27-card, standard-size set was inserted in each pack of 1984 Topps Football. The card fronts describe prizes for the collectors and game rules, as well as the number of yards gained. Collectors had to collect at least 25 yards for five 1984 Glossy inserts. The card backs of the Play Cards contain game rules.

		MT
Complete Set (27):		15.00
Common Player:		.60
1	Houston Oilers (2 yards gained)	.60
2	Houston Oilers (3 yards gained)	.60
3	Cleveland Browns (4 yards gained)	.60
4	Cleveland Browns (5 yards gained)	.60
5	Cincinnati Bengals (6 yards gained)	.60
6	Pittsburgh Steelers (7 yards gained)	.75
7	New Orleans Saints (8 yards gained)	.75
8	New York Giants (2 yards gained)	.60
9	Washington Redskins (3 yards gained)	.75
10	Green Bay Packers (4 yards gained)	.60
11	Atlanta Falcons (5 yards gained)	.60
12	Detroit Lions (6 yards gained)	.60
13	New England Patriots (7 yards gained)	.60
14	New York Jets (8 yards gained)	.75
15	Buffalo Bills (2 yards gained)	.60
16	Kansas City Chiefs (3 yards gained)	.60
17	Miami Dolphins (4 yards gained)	.75
18	San Diego Chargers (5 yards gained)	.60
19	Seattle Seahawks (6 yards gained)	.60
20	Seattle Seahawks (7 yards gained)	.60
21	Dallas Cowboys (8 yards gained)	1.00
22	St. Louis Cardinals (2 yards gained)	.60
23	Chicago Bears (3 yards gained)	.60
24	San Francisco 49ers (4 yards gained)	1.00
25	Philadelphia Eagles (5 yards gained)	.60
26	Minnesota Vikings (6 yards gained)	.60
27	Los Angeles Rams (7 yards gained)	.75

A player's name in *italic* type indicates a rookie card.

1984 Topps Glossy Send-In

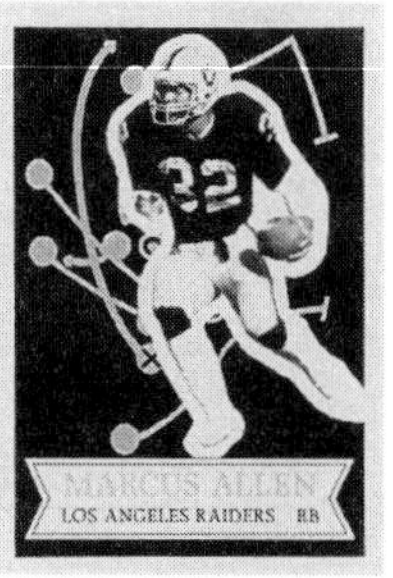

This 30-card set was available only through a mail-in offer. Cards show an action pose of the player on the front with a blackboard diagram as a background. His name, team and position are at the bottom. Backs identify the player, set and card number.

		MT
Complete Set (30):		14.00
Common Player:		.25
1	Marcus Allen	1.25
2	John Riggins	.40
3	Walter Payton	2.00
4	Tony Dorsett	1.00
5	Franco Harris	.75
6	Curt Warner	.40
7	Eric Dickerson	2.50
8	Mike Pruitt	.25
9	Ken Anderson	.25
10	Dan Fouts	.50
11	Terry Bradshaw	.75
12	Joe Theismann	.40
13	Joe Montana	2.00
14	Danny White	.25
15	Kellen Winslow	.25
16	Wesley Walker	.25
17	Drew Pearson	.25
18	James Lofton	.25
19	Cris Collinsworth	.25
20	Dwight Clark	.25
21	Mark Gastineau	.25
22	Lawrence Taylor	.40
23	Randy White	.25
24	Ed "Too Tall" Jones	.25
25	Jack Lambert	.25
26	Fred Dean	.25
27	Jan Stenerud	.40
28	Bruce Harper	.25
29	Todd Christensen	.25
30	Greg Pruitt	.25

1984 Topps Stickers

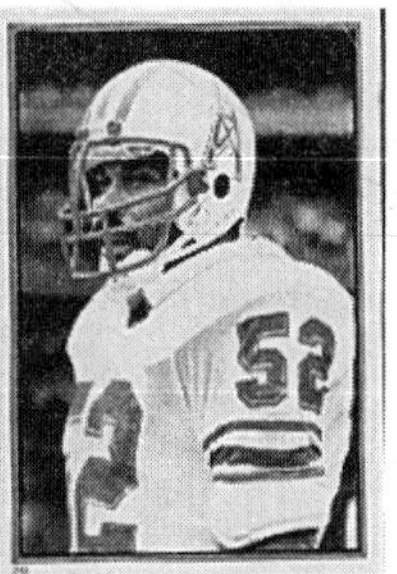

Topps has followed its same format for these stickers, except some of the stickers come in pairs, which are listed in parentheses. Those without are full stickers, comprising the entire card. An album, featuring Charlie Joiner on the front and Dan Fouts on the back, was also issued, as were foil stickers.

		MT
Complete Set (283):		35.00
Common Player:		.05
1	Super Bowl XVIII (Plunkett/Allen)	.35
2	Super Bowl XVIII (Plunkett/Allen)	.15
3	Super Bowl XVIII (Plunkett/Allen)	.15
4	Super Bowl XVIII (Plunkett/Allen)	.15
5	Marcus Allen (Super Bowl MVP)	.75
6	Walter Payton	1.00
7	Mike Richardson (157)	.03
8	Jim McMahon (158)	.10
9	Mike Hartenstine (159)	.05
10	Mike Singletary	.20
11	Willie Gault	.10
12	Terry Schmidt (162)	.05
13	Emery Moorehead (163)	.05
14	Leslie Frazier (164)	.06
15	Jack Thompson (165)	.05
16	Booker Reese (166)	.05
17	James Wilder (166)	.05
18	Lee Roy Selmon (167)	.08
19	Hugh Green	.06
20	Gerald Carter (170)	.05
21	Steve Wilson (171)	.05
22	Michael Morton (172)	.05
23	Kevin House	.05
24	Ottis Anderson	.12
25	Lionel Washington (175)	.08
26	Pat Tilley (176)	.05
27	Curtis Greer (177)	.05
28	Roy Green	.08
29	Carl Birdsong	.05
30	Neil Lomax (180)	.06
31	Lee Nelson (181)	.05
32	Stump Mitchell (182)	.04
33	Tony Hill (183)	.05
34	Everson Walls (184)	.05
35	Danny White (185)	.08
36	Tony Dorsett	.40
37	Ed "Too Tall" Jones	.12
38	Rafael Septien (188)	.05
39	Doug Crosbie (189)	.05
40	Drew Pearson (190)	.06
41	Randy White	.20
42	Ron Jaworski	.10
43	Anthony Griggs (193)	.05
44	Hubert Oliver (194)	.05
45	Wilbert Montgomery (195)	.05
46	Dennis Harrison	.05
47	Mike Quick	.08
48	Jerry Robinson (198)	.04
49	Michael Williams (199)	.05
50	Herman Edwards (200)	.05
51	Steve Bartkowski (201)	.06
52	Mick Luckhurst (202)	.05
53	Mike Pitts (203)	.05
54	William Andrews	.10
55	R.C. Thielemann	.05
56	Buddy Curry (206)	.05
57	Billy Johnson (207)	.04
58	Ralph Giacomaro (208)	.05
59	Mike Kenn	.08
60	Joe Montana	1.75
61	Fred Dean (211)	.05
62	Dwight Clark (212)	.10
63	Wendell Tyler (213)	.05
64	Dwight Hicks	.05
65	Ronnie Lott	.25
66	Roger Craig (216)	.40
67	Fred Solomon (217)	.05
68	Ray Wersching (218)	.05
69	Brad Van Pelt (219)	.05
70	Butch Woolfolk (220)	.05
71	Terry Kinard (221)	.05
72	Lawrence Taylor	.35
73	Ali Haji-Sheikh	.05
74	Mark Haynes (224)	.05
75	Rob Carpenter (225)	.05
76	Earnest Gray (226)	.05
77	Harry Carson	.10
78	Billy Sims	.15
79	Ed Murray (229)	.05
80	William Gay (230)	.05
81	Leonard Thompson (231)	.05
82	Doug English	.08
83	Eric Hipple	.08
84	Ken Fantetti (234)	.05
85	Bruce McNorton (235)	.05
86	James Jones (236)	.05
87	Lynn Dickey (237)	.06
88	Ezra Johnson (238)	.05
89	Jan Stenerud (239)	.08
90	James Lofton	.20
91	Larry McCarren	.05
92	John Jefferson (242)	.05
93	Mike Douglass (243)	.05
94	Gerry Ellis (244)	.05
95	Paul Coffman	.05
96	Eric Dickerson	1.00
97	Jackie Slater (247)	.20
98	Carl Ekern (248)	.05
99	Vince Ferragamo (249)	.06
100	Kent Hill	.05
101	Nolan Cromwell	.08
102	Jack Youngblood (252)	.10
103	John Misko (253)	.05
104	Mike Barber (254)	.07
105	Jeff Bostic (255)	.05
106	Mark Murphy (256)	.05
107	Joe Jacoby (257)	.05
108	John Riggins	.25
109	Joe Theismann	.30
110	Russ Grimm (260)	.05
111	Neal Olkewicz (261)	.07
112	Charlie Brown (262)	.05
113	Dave Butz	.08
114	George Rogers	.10
115	Jim Kovach (265)	.05
116	Dave Wilson (266)	.05
117	Johnnie Poe (267)	.05
118	Russell Erxleben	.05
119	Rickey Jackson	.50
120	Jeff Groth (270)	.05
121	Richard Todd (271)	.06
122	Wayne Wilson (272)	.05
123	Steve Dils (273)	.05
124	Benny Ricardo (274)	.05
125	John Turner (275)	.05
126	Ted Brown	.05
127	Greg Coleman	.05
128	Darrin Nelson (278)	.05
129	Scott Studwell (279)	.06
130	Tommy Kramer (280)	.06
131	Doug Martin	.05
132	Nolan Cromwell (144, All-Pro)	7.50
133	Carl Birdsong (145, All-Pro)	.10
134	Deron Cherry (146, All-Pro)	.20
135	Ronnie Lott (147, All-Pro)	.30
136	Lester Hayes (148, All-Pro)	.10
137	Lawrence Taylor (149, All-Pro)	.30
138	Jack Lambert (150, All-Pro)	.20
139	Chip Banks (151, All-Pro)	.10
140	Lee Roy Selmon (152, All-Pro)	.15
141	Fred Smerlas (153, All-Pro)	.10
142	Doug English (154, All-Pro)	.10
143	Doug Betters (155, All-Pro)	.10
144	Dan Marino (132, All-Pro)	3.00
145	Ali Haji-Sheikh (133, All-Pro)	.10
146	Eric Dickerson (134, All-Pro)	.65
147	Curt Warner (135, All-Pro)	.15
148	James Lofton (136, All-Pro)	.25
149	Todd Christensen (All-Pro)	.15
150	Cris Collinsworth (All-Pro)	.20
151	Mike Kenn (139, All-Pro)	.10
152	Russ Grimm (140, All-Pro)	.10
153	Jeff Bostic (141, All-Pro)	.10
154	John Hannah (142, All-Pro)	.15
155	Anthony Munoz (143, All-Pro)	.20
156	Ken Anderson	.35
157	Pete Johnson (7)	.05
158	Reggie Williams (8)	.06
159	Isaac Curtis (9)	.05
160	Anthony Munoz	.20
161	Cris Collinsworth	.15
162	Charles Alexander (12)	.05
163	Ray Horton (13)	.10
164	Steve Keider (14)	.05
165	Ben Williams (15)	.05
166	Frank Lewis (16)	.08
167	Roosevelt Leaks (17)	.05
168	Joe Ferguson	.08
169	Fred Smerlas	.08
170	Joe Danelo (20)	.05
171	Chris Keating (21)	.05
172	Jerry Butler (22)	.05
173	Eugene Marve	.05
174	Louis Wright	.08
175	Barney Chavous (25)	.10
176	Zack Thomas (26)	.05
177	Luke Prestridge (27)	.05
178	Steve Watson	.08
179	John Elway	5.00
180	Steve Foley (30)	.05
181	Sammy Winder (31)	.10
182	Rick Upchurch (32)	.05
183	Bobby Jones (33)	.08
184	Matt Bahr (34)	.05
185	Doug Dieken (35)	.05
186	Mike Pruitt	.08
187	Chip Banks	.10
188	Tom Cousineau (38)	.05
189	Paul McDonald (39)	.05
190	Clay Matthews (40)	.08
191	Ozzie Newsome	.20
192	Dan Fouts	.40
193	Chuck Muncie (43)	.05
194	Linden King (44)	.05
195	Charlie Joiner (45)	.08
196	Wes Chandler	.08
197	Kellen Winslow	.20
198	James Brooks (48)	.10
199	Mike Green (49)	.05
200	Rolf Benirschke (58)	.05
201	Henry Marshall (51)	.05
202	Nick Lowery (52)	.06
203	Jerry Blanton (53)	.05
204	Bill Kenney	.08
205	Carlos Carson	.08
206	Billy Jackson (56)	.05
207	Art Still (57)	.05
208	Theotis Brown (58)	.05
209	Deron Cherry	.25
210	Curtis Dickey	.08
211	Nesby Glasgow (61)	.05
212	Mike Pagel (62)	.05
213	Ray Donaldson (63)	.05
214	Raul Allegre	.05
215	Chris Hinton	.30
216	Rohn Stark (66)	.08
217	Randy McMillan (67)	.08
218	Vernon Maxwell (68)	.05
219	A.J. Duhe (69)	.10
220	Andra Franklin (70)	.05
221	Ed Newman (71)	.05
222	Dan Marino	7.50
223	Doug Betters	.08
224	Bob Baumhower (74)	.05
225	Reggie Roby (75)	.08
226	Dwight Stephenson (76)	.08
227	Mark Duper	.40
228	Mark Gastineau	.15
229	Freeman McNeil (79)	.08
230	Bruce Harper (80)	.05
231	Wesley Walker (81)	.06
232	Marvin Powell	.08
233	Joe Klecko	.08
234	Johnny Lam Jones (84)	.05
235	Lance Mehl (85)	.05
236	Pat Ryan (86)	.05
237	Florian Kempf (87)	.05
238	Carl Roaches (88)	.05
239	Gregg Bigham (89)	.05
240	Tim Smith	.05
241	Jesse Baker	.05
242	Doug France (92)	.08
243	Chris Dressel (93)	.05
244	Willie Tullis (94)	.05
245	Robert Brazile	.08
246	Tony Collins	.08
247	Brian Holloway (97)	.05
248	Stanley Morgan (98)	.06
249	Rick Sanford (99)	.05
250	John Hannah	.15
251	Rich Camarillo	.08
252	Andre Tippett (102)	.08
253	Steve Grogan (103)	.08
254	Clayton Weishuhn (104)	.05
255	Jim Plunkett (105)	.08
256	Rod Martin (106)	.08
257	Lester Hayes (107)	.05
258	Marcus Allen	.50
259	Todd Christensen	.10
260	Ted Hendricks (110)	.08
261	Greg Pruitt (111)	.05
262	Howie Long (112)	.50
263	Vann McElroy	.05
264	Curt Warner	.25
265	Jacob Green (115)	.06
266	Bruce Scholtz (116)	.05
267	Steve Largent (117)	.50
268	Kenny Easley	.10
269	Dave Krieg	.35
270	Dave Brown (120)	.05
271	Zachary Dixon (121)	.05
272	Norm Johnson (122)	.05
273	Terry Bradshaw (123)	.30
274	Keith Willis (124)	.05
275	Gary Anderson (125)	.05
276	Franco Harris	.35
277	Mike Webster	.15
278	Calvin Sweeney (128)	.05
279	Rick Woods (129)	.05
280	Bennie Cunningham (130)	.08
281	Jack Lambert	.15
282	Curt Warner (283)	.35
283	Todd Christensen (282)	.15

1984 Topps USFL

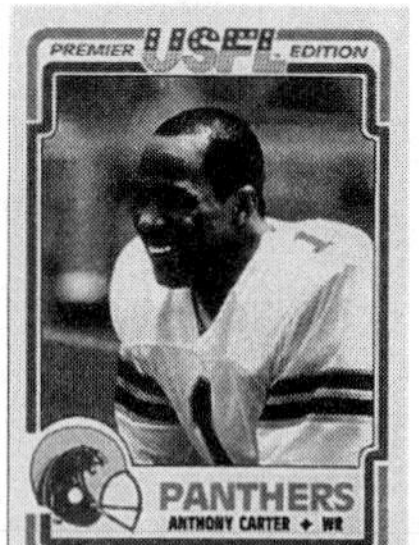

This 132-card set was Topps' first issue of United States Football League cards, and it's proven to be the most valuable set Topps issued in the 1980s. Several key rookie cards can be found in this set, including Jim Kelly, Herschel Walker, Reggie White, Anthony Carter, Bobby Hebert, Kelvin Bryant and Mike Rozier. Issued as a factory set, cards were printed on white cardboard stock. Bordered in red and blue piping over white space with the USFL logo and "Premier Edition" at the top of the card, a team helmet appears at lower left with the team name in red and the player name in black over a yellow background below the photo. Cards were numbered alphabetically by city name and by the player's last name.

		MT
Complete Set (132):		375.00
Common Player:		1.50
1	Luther Bradley	1.50
2	Frank Corral	1.50
3	Trumaine Johnson	1.50
4	Greg Landry	1.50
5	Kit Lathrop	1.50
6	Kevin Long	1.50
7	Tim Spencer	1.50
8	Stan White	1.50
9	Buddy Aydelette	1.50
10	Tom Banks	1.50
11	Fred Bohannon	1.50
12	Joe Cribbs	1.50
13	Joey Jones	1.50
14	Scott Norwood	1.50
15	Jim Smith	1.50
16	Cliff Stoudt	1.50
17	Vince Evans	2.00
18	Vagas Ferguson	1.50
19	John Gillen	1.50
20	Kris Haines	1.50
21	Glenn Hyde	1.50
22	Mark Keel	1.50
23	Garry Lewis	1.50
24	Doug Plank	1.50
25	Neil Balholm	1.50
26	David Dumars	1.50
27	David Martin	1.50
28	Craig Penrose	1.50
29	Dave Stalls	1.50
30	*Harry Sydney*	1.00
31	Vincent White	1.50
32	George Yarno	1.50
33	Kiki DeAyala	1.50
34	Sam Harrell	1.50
35	Mike Hawkins	1.50
36	*Jim Kelly*	100.00
37	Mark Rush	1.50
38	*Ricky Sanders*	10.00
39	Paul Bergmann	1.50
40	Tom Dinkel	1.50
41	Wyatt Henderson	1.50
42	*Vaughan Johnson*	5.00
43	Willie McClendon	1.50
44	Matt Robinson	1.50
45	George Achica	1.50
46	Mark Adickes	1.50
47	Howard Carson	1.50
48	Kevin Nelson	1.50
49	Jeff Partridge	1.50
50	JoJo Townsell	1.50
51	Eddie Weaver	1.50
52	*Steve Young*	250.00
53	Derrick Crawford	1.50
54	Walter Lewis	1.50
55	Phil McKinnely	1.50
56	Vic Minore	1.50
57	Gary Shirk	1.50
58	*Reggie White*	100.00
59	*Anthony Carter*	15.00
60	John Corker	1.50
61	David Greenwood	1.50
62	*Bobby Hebert*	10.00
63	Derek Holloway	1.50
64	Ken Lacy	1.50
65	Tyrone McGriff	1.50
66	Ray Pinney	1.50
67	Gary Barbaro	1.50
68	Sam Bowers	1.50
69	Clarence Collins	1.50
70	Willie Harper	1.50
71	Jim LeClair	1.50
72	Bob Leopold	1.50
73	Brian Sipe	2.00
74	*Herschel Walker*	25.00
75	Junior Ah You	1.50
76	*Marcus Dupree*	2.00
77	Marcus Marek	1.50
78	Tim Mazzetti	1.50
79	Mike Robinson	1.50
80	Dan Ross	1.50
81	Mark Schellen	1.50
82	Johnnie Walton	1.50
83	Gordon Banks	1.50
84	Fred Besana	1.50

85 Dave Browning 1.50
86 Eric Jordan 1.50
87 Frank Manumaleuga 1.50
88 *Gary Plummer* 4.00
89 Stan Talley 1.50
90 Arthur Whittington 1.50
91 Terry Beeson 1.50
92 *Mel Gray* 2.00
93 Mike Katolin 1.50
94 Dewey McClain 1.50
95 Sidney Thorton 1.50
96 Doug Williams 2.50
97 *Kelvin Bryant* 2.50
98 John Bunting 1.50
99 *Irv Eatman* 2.00
100 Scott Fitzkee 1.50
101 Chuck Fusina 1.50
102 *Sean Landeta* 3.00
103 David Trout 1.50
104 Scott Woerner 1.50
105 Glenn Carano 1.50
106 Ron Crosby 1.50
107 Jerry Holmes 1.50
108 Bruce Huther 1.50
109 *Mike Rozier* 4.00
110 Larry Swider 1.50
111 Danny Buggs 1.50
112 Putt Choate 1.50
113 Rich Garza 1.50
114 Joey Hackett 1.50
115 Rick Neuheisel 1.50
116 Mike St. Clair 1.50
117 *Gary Anderson* 4.00
118 Zenon Andrusyshyn 1.50
119 Doug Beaudoin 1.50
120 Mike Butler 1.50
121 Willie Gillespie 1.50
122 Fred Nordgren 1.50
123 John Reaves 1.50
124 Eric Truvillon 1.50
125 Reggie Collier 1.50
126 Mike Guess 1.50
127 Mike Hohensee 1.50
128 *Craig James* 4.00
129 Eric Robinson 1.50
130 Billy Taylor 1.50
131 Joey Walters 1.50
132 Checklist 1-132 1.50

1985 Topps

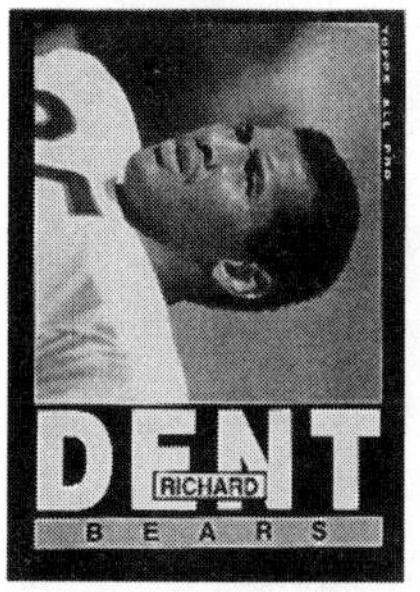

This was Topps' most radical card design in football cards in decades. Player photos were mounted horizontally in this 396-card set, with black borders surrounding the photo. The player's last name appeared in large white letters across the bottom of the card, with his first name in smaller letters in the middle of his last name. The team name appeared in smaller, darker type in the upper left corner. Cards in this issue were numbered alphabetically according to city name and conference, with NFC teams listed first and AFC teams listed after the league leader cards. This set includes rookie cards of Richard Dent, Henry Ellard, Joe Morris, Warren Moon, Mark Clayton, Tony Eason, Ken O'Brien and Louis Lipps. (Key: AP - All Pro)

MT
Complete Set (396): 80.00
Common Player: .05
Wax Pack (15): 4.75
Wax Box (36): 120.00
1 Record: (Mark Clayton) .60
2 Record: (Eric Dickerson) .50
3 Record: (Charlie Joiner) .15
4 (Dan Marino RB) 8.00
5 Record: (Art Monk) .30
6 (Walter Payton RB) 1.00
7 NFC Championship: (Matt Suhey) .10
8 AFC Championship: (Bennett) .10
9 Super Bowl XIX: (Wendell Tyler) .15
10 Atlanta Falcons Team: (Gerald Riggs) .10
11 William Andrews .05
12 Stacey Bailey .05
13 Steve Bartkowski .15
14 *Rick Bryan* .25
15 Alfred Jackson .05
16 Kenny Johnson .05
17 Mike Ken (AP) .05
18 *Mike Pitts* .25
19 Gerald Riggs .05
20 Sylvester Stamps .05
21 R.C. Theilemann .05
22 Chicago Bears Team: .75
23 *Todd Bell* (AP) .12
24 *Richard Dent* (AP) 4.00
25 Gary Fencik .05
26 Dave Finzer .05
27 Leslie Frazier .05
28 Steve Fuller .05
29 Willie Gault .40
30 Dan Hampton (AP) .60
31 Jim McMahon .60
32 *Steve McMichael* 1.00
33 Walter Payton (AP) 1.75
34 Mike Singletary .75
35 Matt Suhey .05
36 Bob Thomas .05
37 Dallas Cowboys Team: (Tony Dorsett) .25
38 *Bill Bates* 1.00
39 Doug Cosbie .05
40 Tony Dorsett .60
41 Michael Downs .05
42 Mike Hegman .05
43 Tony Hill .05
44 *Gary Hogeboom* .10
45 *Jim Jeffcoat* .50
46 Ed "Too Tall" Jones .25
47 Mike Renfro .05
48 Rafael Septien .05
49 Dennis Thurman .05
50 Everson Walls .05
51 Danny White .20
52 Randy White .40
53 Detroit Lions Team .10
54 Jeff Chadwick .05
55 *Mike Cofer* .25
56 Gary Danielson .05
57 Keith Dorney .05
58 Doug English .05
59 William Gay .05
60 Ken Jenkins .05
61 James Jones .05
62 Ed Murray .05
63 Billy Sims .12
64 Leonard Thompson .05
65 Bobby Watkins .05
66 Green Bay Packers Team: (Lynn Dickey) .10
67 Paul Coffman .05
68 Lynn Dickey .05
69 Mike Douglass .05
70 Tom Flynn .05
71 Eddie Lee Ivery .05
72 Ezra Johnson .05
73 Mark Lee .05
74 Tim Lewis .05
75 James Lofton .50
76 Bucky Scribner .05
77 Los Angeles Rams Team: (Eric Dickerson) .40
78 Nolan Cromwell .05
79 Eric Dickerson (AP) 1.00
80 *Henry Ellard* 5.00
81 Kent Hill .05
82 LeRoy Irvin .05
83 Jeff Kemp .35
84 Mike Lansford .05
85 Barry Redden .05
86 Jackie Slater .40
87 *Doug Smith* .50
88 Jack Youngblood .15
89 Minnesota Vikings Team .10
90 Alfred Anderson .15
91 Ted Brown .05
92 Greg Coleman .05
93 Tommy Hannon .05
94 Tommy Kramer .10
95 *Leo Lewis* .20
96 Doug Martin .05
97 Darrin Nelson .05
98 Jan Stenerud (AP) .20
99 Sammy White .05
100 New Orleans Saints Team .10
101 Morten Anderson .75
102 *Hoby Brenner* .15
103 Bruce Clark .05
104 Hokie Gajan .05
105 *Brian Hansen* .15
106 Rickey Jackson 1.00
107 George Rogers .15
108 Dave Wilson .05
109 Tyrone Young .05
110 New York Giants Team .10
111 *Carl Banks* 1.00
112 *Jim Burt* .40
113 Rob Carpenter .05
114 Harry Carson .15
115 Earnest Gray .05
116 Ali Haji-Sheikh .05
117 Mark Haynes (AP) .05
118 Bobby Johnson .05
119 *Lionel Manuel* .12
120 *Joe Morris* .75
121 *Zeke Mowatt* .10
122 *Jeff Rutledge* .20
123 Phil Simms .60
124 Lawrence Taylor (AP) 1.25
125 Philadelphia Eagles Team: (Wilbert Montgomery) .10
126 Greg Brown .05
127 Ray Ellis .05
128 Dennis Harrison .05
129 *Wes Hopkins*, Marvin Harvey .50
130 Mike Horan .05
131 *Kenny Jackson* .15
132 Ron Jaworski .12
133 Paul McFadden .05
134 Wilbert Montgomery .05
135 Mike Quick .12
136 John Spagnola .05
137 St. Louis Cardinals Team .10
138 Ottis Anderson .30
139 Al "Bubba" Baker .05
140 Roy Green .15
141 Curtis Greer .05
142 E.J. Junior (AP) .05
143 Neil Lomax .05
144 Stump Mitchell .05
145 Neil O'Donoghue .05
146 Pat Tilley .05
147 Lionel Washington .15
148 San Francisco 49ers 1.00
149 Dwaine Board .05
150 Dwight Clark .20
151 Roger Craig 1.25
152 Randy Cross (AP) .05
153 Fred Dean .05
154 Keith Fahnhorst .05
155 Dwight Hicks .05
156 Ronnie Lott .50
157 Joe Montana 7.00
158 Renaldo Nehemiah .05
159 Fred Quillan .05
160 Jack Reynolds .05
161 Freddie Solomon .05
162 *Keena Turner* .50
163 Wendell Tyler .05
164 Ray Wersching .05
165 Carlton Williamson .05
166 Tampa Bay Buccaneers Team: (Steve DeBerg) .10
167 Gerald Carter .05
168 Mark Cotney .05
169 Steve DeBerg .40
170 Sean Farrell .05
171 Hugh Green .05
172 Kevin House .05
173 David Logan .05
174 Michael Morton .05
175 Lee Roy Selmon .05
176 James Wilder .05
177 Washington Redskins Team: (John Riggins) .20
178 Charlie Brown .05
179 *Monte Coleman* .75
180 Vernon Dean .05
181 Darrell Green .65
182 Russ Grimm .15
183 Joe Jacoby .05
184 Dexter Manley .05
185 Art Monk 1.00
186 Mark Moseley .05
187 Calvin Muhammad .05
188 Mike Nelms .05
189 John Riggins .50
190 Joe Theismann .50
191 Joe Washington .05
192 Passing Leaders: (Joe Montana, Dan Marino) 13.00
193 Receiving Leaders: (Ozzie Newsome, Art Monk) .35
194 Rushing Leaders: (Earnest Jackson, Eric Dickerson) .40
195 Scoring Leaders: (Gary Anderson, Ray Wersching) .10
196 Interception Leaders: (Kenny Easley, Tom Flynn) .10
197 Punting Leaders: (Jim Arnold, Brian Hansen) .10
198 Buffalo Bills Team: (Greg Bell) .10
199 *Greg Bell* .85
200 Preston Dennard .05
201 Joe Ferguson .10
202 Byron Franklin .05
203 Steve Freeman .05
204 Jim Haslett .05
205 Charles Romes .05
206 Fred Smerlas .05
207 *Darryl Talley* 2.00
208 Van Williams .05
209 Cincinnati Bengals Team: (Ken Anderson, Larry Kinnebrew) .10
210 Ken Anderson .20
211 Jim Breech .05
212 Louis Breeden .05
213 James Brooks .25
214 Ross Browner .05
215 Eddie Edwards .05
216 M.L. Harris .05
217 Bobby Kemp .05
218 *Larry Kinnebrew* .10
219 Anthony Munoz (AP) .40
220 Reggie Williams .05
221 Cleveland Browns Team: (Boyce Green) .10
222 Matt Bahr .05
223 Chip Banks .05
224 Reggie Camp .05
225 Tom Cousineau .05
226 Joe DeLamielleure .05
227 Ricky Feacher .05
228 Boyce Green .05
229 Al Gross .05
230 Clay Matthews .50
231 Paul McDonald .05
232 Ozzie Newsome (AP) .35
233 Mike Pruitt .05
234 Don Rogers .05
235 Denver Broncos (John Elway, Sammy Winder) .70
236 Rubin Carter .05
237 Barney Chavous .05
238 John Elway 15.00
239 Steve Foley .05
240 Mike Harden .05
241 Tom Jackson .15
242 Butch Johnson .05
243 Rulon Jones .05
244 Rick Karlis .05
245 Steve Watson .05
246 Gerald Wilhite .05
247 Sammy Winder .05
248 Houston Oilers Team: (Larry Moriarty) .10
249 Jesse Baker .05
250 Carter Hartwig .05
251 *Warren Moon* 20.00
252 *Larry Moriarty* .10
253 *Mike Munchak* .50
254 Carl Roaches .05
255 Tim Smith .05
256 Willie Tullis .05
257 Jamie Williams .05
258 Indianapolis Colts Team: (Art Schlichter) .10
259 Raymond Butler .05
260 Johnie Cooks .05
261 Eugene Daniel .05
262 Curtis Dickey .05
263 Chris Hinton .20
264 Vernon Maxwell .05
265 Randy McMillan .05
266 Art Schlichter .15
267 Rohn Stark .15
268 Leo Wisniewski .05
269 Kansas City Chiefs Team: (Bill Kenney) .10
270 Jim Arnold .05
271 Mike Bell .05
272 Todd Blackledge .15
273 Carlos Carson .05
274 Deron Cherry .25
275 *Herman Heard* .10
276 Bill Kenney .05
277 Nick Lowery .30
278 *Bill Maas* .30
279 Henry Marshall .05
280 Art Still .05
281 Los Angeles Raiders Team: (Marcus Allen) .30
282 Marcus Allen 2.00
283 Lyle Alzado .20
284 Chris Bahr .05
285 Malcolm Barnwell .05
286 Cliff Branch .15
287 Todd Christensen .05
288 Ray Guy .15
289 Lester Hayes .05
290 Mike Haynes (AP) .05
291 Henry Lawrence .05
292 Howie Long 2.00
293 Rod Martin (AP) .05
294 Vann McElroy .05
295 Matt Millen .05
296 *Bill Pickel* .15
297 Jim Plunkett .20
298 *Dokie Williams* .10
299 Marc Wilson .05
300 Miami Dolphins Team: (Mark Duper) .15
301 Bob Baumhower .05
302 Doug Betters .05
303 Glenn Blackwood .05
304 Lyle Blackwood .05
305 Kim Bokamper .05
306 Charles Bowser .05
307 Jimmy Cefalo .05
308 *Mark Clayton* (AP) 1.00
309 A.J. Duhe .05
310 Mark Duper .50
311 Andra Franklin .05
312 Bruce Hardy .05
313 Pete Johnson .05
314 Dan Marino (AP) 30.00
315 Tony Nathan .05
316 Ed Newman .05
317 Reggie Roby (AP) .15
318 Dwight Stephenson (AP) .05
319 Uwe Von Schamann .05
320 New England Patriots Team: (Tony Collins) .10
321 Raymond Clayborn .05
322 Tony Collins .05
323 *Tony Eason* .30
324 Tony Franklin .05
325 *Irving Fryar* 4.00
326 John Hannah (AP) .20
327 Brian Holloway .05
328 *Craig James* .50
329 Stanley Morgan .20
330 Steve Nelson (AP) .05
331 Derrick Ramsey .05
332 Stephen Starring .05
333 Mosi Tatupu .05
334 Andre Tippett .50
335 New York Jets Team: (Mark Gastineau, Ferguson) .10
336 Russell Carter .05
337 Mark Gastineau (AP) .05
338 Bruce Harper .05
339 Bobby Humphery .05
340 Johnny "Lam" Jones .05
341 Joe Klecko .05
342 Pat Leahy .05
343 Marty Lyons .05
344 Freeman McNeil .20
345 Lance Mehl .05
346 *Ken O'Brien* .50
347 Marvin Powell .05
348 Pat Ryan .05
349 *Mickey Shuler* .40
350 Wesley Walker .15
351 Pittsburgh Steelers Team (Mark Malone) .10
352 Walter Abercrombie .05
353 Gary Anderson .05
354 Robin Cole .05
355 Bennie Cunningham .05
356 Rich Erenberg .05
357 Jack Lambert .40
358 *Louis Lipps* .50
359 Mark Malone .05
360 *Mike Merriweather* .60
361 Frank Pollard .05
362 Donnie Shell .05
363 John Stallworth .15
364 Sam Washington .05
365 Mike Webster .20
366 Dwayne Woodruff .05
367 San Diego Chargers Team .10
368 Rolf Benirschke .05
369 *Gill Byrd* 1.00
370 Wes Chandler .05
371 Bobby Duckworth .05
372 Dan Fouts .60
373 Mike Green .05
374 *Pete Holohan* .60
375 Earnest Jackson .20
376 Lionel James .20
377 Charlie Joiner .30
378 Billy Ray Smith .05
379 Kellen Winslow .30
380 Seattle Seahawks Team (Dave Krieg) .10
381 Dave Brown .05
382 Jeff Bryant .05
383 Dan Doornink .05
384 Kenny Easley (AP) .05
385 Jacob Green .05
386 David Hughes .05
387 Norm Johnson .05
388 Dave Krieg .75
389 Steve Largent .80
390 *Joe Nash* .20
391 Daryl Turner .05
392 Curt Warner .15
393 *Fredd Young* .20
394 Checklist 1-132 .15
395 Checklist 133-264 .15
396 Checklist 265-396 .15

1985 Topps Box Bottoms

The bottoms of 1985 Topps wax pack boxes featured these cards, which are numbered using a letter instead of a number. The design is the same as a regular 1985 Topps card, except the front border is red and "Topps Superstars" is printed at the top. The backs are identical to the regular cards' backs except for the letters used as card numbers.

MT
Complete Set (16): 15.00
Common Player: .30
A Marcus Allen 1.50
B Ottis Anderson .30
C Mark Clayton 1.00
D Eric Dickerson 1.00
E Tony Dorsett .75
F Dan Fouts .75
G Mark Gastineau .30
H Charlie Joiner .50
I James Lofton .75
J Neil Lomax .30
K Dan Marino 6.00
L Art Monk .75
M Joe Montana 6.00
N Walter Payton 2.50
O John Stallworth .30
P Lawrence Taylor .75

1985 Topps Star Set

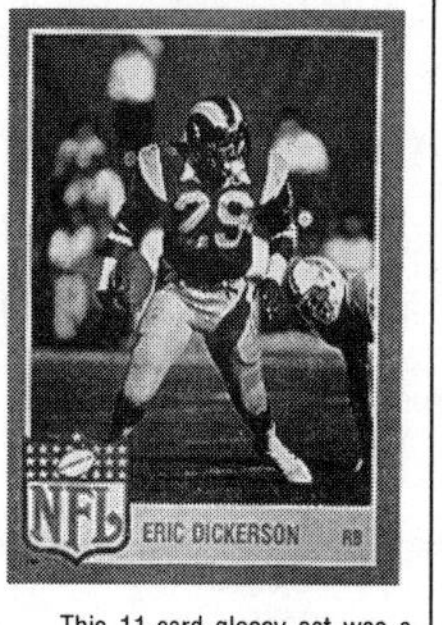

This 11-card glossy set was a follow-up to the 1984 insert set. Cards were printed on heavy white cardboard stock, with red borders surrounding an action picture of each player. Cards were issued one per wax pack with the 1985 cards. Card backs were printed in blue and red and show pretty much the same design, front and back, as the 1984 insert set, but with smaller type indicating the year of issue on the back. This was the second and final year of Topps' production of United States Football League cards. The 132-card set was issued as a factory set. Cards were numbered alphabetically according to city and according to the player's last name. Printed on white cardboard stock, fronts show a bright red border with a white and blue stripe across the middle; the USFL logo appears in the upper right corner. The team name appears in heavy red type at the bottom of the card, and the player's name and position is in a yellow football above the team name. Card backs show a goalpost design in blue and red. The set includes rookies Doug Flutie, Gary Clark and Gerald McNeill; plus Herschel Walker's second-year card.

MT
Complete Set (11): 6.50
Common Player: .25
1 Mark Clayton .25
2 Eric Dickerson 1.75
3 John Elway 1.00
4 Mark Gastineau .25
5 Ronnie Lott .40
6 Dan Marino 1.25
7 Joe Montana 1.50
8 Walter Payton 1.50
9 John Riggins .35
10 John Stallworth .25
11 Lawrence Taylor .35

1985 Topps "Coming Soon" Stickers

These stickers say "Coming Soon" on the backs and share identical card numbers with their counterparts in Topps' regular 1985 sticker set; thus, the checklist is skip-numbered. These stickers, which were random inserts in 1985 Topps football packs, measure 2-1/8" x 3" each but, unlike many of the regular stickers, feature only one player per sticker. The stickers have a colored photo on the front with a color frame and white border surrounding it.

MT
Complete Set (30): 5.00
Common Player: .08
6 Ken Anderson .30
15 Greg Bell .15
24 John Elway .75
33 Ozzie Newsome .25
42 Charlie Joiner .25
51 Bill Kenney .15
60 Randy McMillan .08
69 Dan Marino 2.00
77 Mark Clayton .50
78 Mark Gastineau .08
87 Warren Moon 2.00
96 Tony Eason .15
105 Marcus Allen .50
114 Steve Largent .60
123 John Stallworth .20
156 Walter Payton 1.00
165 James Wilder .12
174 Neil Lomax .15
183 Tony Dorsett .35
192 Mike Quick .15
201 William Andrews .10
210 Joe Montana 2.50
214 Dwight Clark .35
219 Lawrence Taylor .35
228 Billy Sims .15
237 James Lofton .30
246 Eric Dickerson .50
255 John Riggins .25
268 George Rogers .12
281 Tommy Kramer .08

1985 Topps Stickers

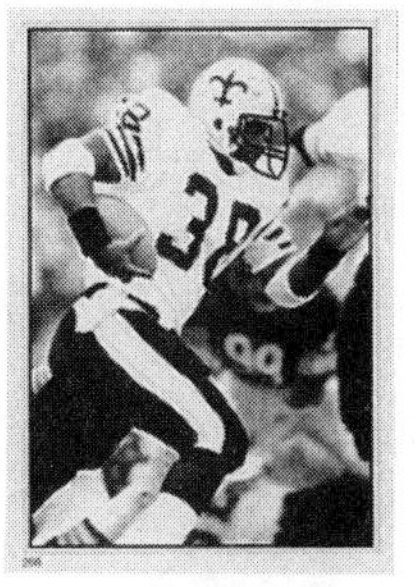

These stickers are different than those issued in previous years, because no foil stickers were produced. However, there were stickers issued in pairs on some cards; they are noted as being partners by the parenthesis which follows the player's name in the checklist. Charlie Joiner, Art Monk, Joe Montana, Dan Marino, Walter Payton and Eric Dickerson are all featured on the album cover; the 49ers team is on the back.

MT
Complete Set (285): 20.00
Common Player: .05
1 Super Bowl XIX 1.50
2 Super Bowl XIX 1.00
3 Super Bowl XIX .10
4 Super Bowl XIX .10
5 Super Bow XIX .08
6 Ken Anderson .30
7 M.L. Harris (157) .05
8 Eddie Edwards (157) .05
9 Louis Breeden (159) .05
10 Larry Kinnebrew .05
11 Isaac Curtis (161) .06
12 James Brooks (162) .12
13 Jim Breech (163) .05
14 Boomer Esiason (164) .75
15 Greg Bell .10
16 Fred Smerlas (166) .05
17 Joe Ferguson (167) .06
18 Ken Johnson (168) .05
19 Darryl Talley (169) .25
20 Preston Dennard (170) .05
21 Charles Romes (171) .05
22 Jim Haslett (172) .05
23 Byron Franklin .05
24 John Elway 1.25
25 Rulon Jones (175) .05
26 Butch Johnson (176) .05
27 Rick Karlis (177) .05
28 Sammy Winder .05
29 Tom Jackson (179) .10
30 Mike Harden (180) .05
31 Steve Watson (181) .05
32 Steve Foley (182) .05
33 Ozzie Newsome .25
34 Al Gross (184) .05
35 Paul McDonald (185) .05
36 Matt Bahr (186) .07
37 Charles White (187) .06
38 Don Rogers (188) .05
39 Mike Pruitt (189) .05
40 Reggie Camp (190) .05
41 Boyce Green .05
42 Charlie Joiner .20
43 Dan Fouts (193) .25
44 Keith Ferguson (194) .05
45 Pete Holohan (195) .05
46 Earnest Jackson .08
47 Wes Chandler (197) .06
48 Gill Byrd (198) .15
49 Kellen Winslow (199) .15
50 Billy Ray Smith (200) .06
51 Bill Kenney .08
52 Herman Heard (202) .05
53 Art Still (203) .05
54 Nick Lowery (204) .05
55 Deron Cherry (205) .08
56 Jenry Marshall (206) .05
57 Mike Bell (207) .05
58 Todd Blackledge (208) .05
59 Carlos Carson .08
60 Randy McMillan .05
61 Donnell Thompson (211) .05
62 Raymond Butler (212) .05
63 Ray Donaldson (213) .05
64 Art Schlichter .15
65 Rohn Stark (215) .05
66 Johnie Cooks (216) .05
67 Mike Pagel (217) .05
68 Eugene Daniel (218) .05
69 Dan Marino 2.00
70 Pete Johnson (220) .05
71 Tony Nathan (221) .05
72 Glenn Blackwood (222) .05
73 Woody Bennett (223) .05
74 Dwight Stephenson (224) .05
75 Mark Duper (225) .10
76 Doug Betters (226) .05
77 Mark Clayton .50
78 Mark Gastineau .08
79 Johnny Lam Jones (229) .05
80 Mickey Shuler (230) .05
81 Tony Paige (231) .15
82 Freeman McNeil .15
83 Russell Carter (233) .06
84 Wesley Walker (234) .06
85 Bruce Harper (235) .15
86 Ken O'Brien (236) 1.75
87 Warren Moon .05
88 Jesse Baker (238) .05
89 Carl Roaches (239) .05
90 Carter Hartwig (240) .05
91 Larry Moriarty (241) .05
92 Robert Brazile (242) .05
93 Oliver Luck (243) .05

94	Willie Tullis (244)	.05
95	Tim Smith	.05
96	Tony Eason	.12
97	Stanley Morgan (247)	.10
98	Mosi Tatupu (248)	.05
99	Raymond Clayborn (249)	.08
100	Andre Tippett	.10
101	Craig James (251)	.15
102	Derrick Ramsey (252)	.05
103	Tony Collins (253)	.05
104	Tony Franklin (254)	.05
105	Marcus Allen	.40
106	Chris Bahr (256)	.05
107	Marc Wilson (257)	.05
108	Howie Long (258)	.10
109	Bill Pickel (259)	.05
110	Mike Haynes (260)	.08
111	Malcolm Barnwell (261)	.05
112	Rod Martin (262)	.05
113	Todd Christensen	.10
114	Steve Largent	.75
115	Curt Warner (265)	.08
116	Kenny Easley (266)	.05
117	Jacob Green (267)	.05
118	Daryl Turner	.08
119	Norm Johnson (269)	.05
120	Dave Krieg (270)	.10
121	Eric Lane (271)	.05
122	Jeff Bryant (272)	.05
123	John Stallworth	.12
124	Donnie Shell (274)	.05
125	Gary Anderson (275)	.05
126	Mark Malone (276)	.05
127	Sam Washington (277)	.05
128	Frank Pollard (278)	.05
129	Mike Merriweather (279)	.10
130	Walter Abercrombie (280)	.05
131	Louis Lipps	.30
132	Mark Clayton (144)	.35
133	Randy Cross (145)	.06
134	Eric Dickerson (146)	.35
135	John Hannah (147)	.10
136	Mike Kenn (148)	.05
137	Dan Marino (149)	1.50
138	Art Monk (151)	.15
139	Anthony Munoz (151)	.10
140	Ozzie Newsome (152)	.10
141	Walter Payton (153)	.40
142	Jan Stenerud (154)	.08
143	Dwight Stephenson (155)	.05
144	Todd Bell (132)	.05
145	Richard Dent (133)	.50
146	Kenny Easley (134)	.05
147	Mark Gastineau (135)	.06
148	Dan Hampton (136)	.10
149	Mark Haynes (137)	.05
150	Mike Haynes (138)	.06
151	E.J. Junior (139)	.05
152	Rod Martin (140)	.10
153	Steve Nelson (141)	.05
154	Reggie Roby (142)	.05
155	Lawrence Taylor (143)	.15
156	Walter Payton	.60
157	Dan Hampton (7)	.08
158	Willie Gault (8)	.06
159	Matt Suhey (9)	.05
160	Richard Dent	1.00
161	Mike Singletary (11)	.10
162	Gary Fencik (12)	.05
163	Jim McMahon (13)	.10
164	Bob Thomas (14)	.05
165	James Wilder	.08
166	Steve DeBerg (16)	.08
167	Mark Cotney (17)	.05
168	Adger Armstrong (18)	.05
169	Gerald Carter (19)	.05
170	David Logan (20)	.05
171	Hugh Green (21)	.05
172	Lee Roy Selmon (22)	.06
173	Kevin House	.10
174	Neil Lomax	.12
175	Ottis Anderson (25)	.10
176	Al (Bubba) Baker (26)	.05
177	E.J. Junior (27)	.08
178	Roy Green	.10
179	Pat Tilley (29)	.05
180	Stump Mitchell (30)	.05
181	Lionel Washington (31)	.05
182	Curtis Greer (32)	.05
183	Tony Dorsett	.25
184	Gary Hogeboom (34)	.06
185	Jim Jeffcoat (35)	.06
186	Danny White (36)	.08
187	Michael Downs (37)	.05
188	Doug Cosbie (38)	.08
189	Tony Hill (39)	.05
190	Rafael Septien (40)	.05
191	Randy White	.15
192	Mike Quick	.08
193	Ray Ellis (43)	.05
194	John Spagnola (44)	.05
195	Dennis Harrison (45)	.05
196	Wilbert Montgomery	.08
197	Greg Brown (47)	.05
198	Ron Jaworski (48)	.08
199	Paul McFadden (49)	.05
200	Wes Hopkins (50)	.05
201	William Andrews	.10
202	Mike Pitts (52)	.05
203	Steve Bartkowski (53)	.08
204	Gerald Riggs (54)	.08
205	Alfred Jackson (55)	.05
206	Don Smith (56)	.05
207	Mike Kenn (57)	.05
208	Kenny Johnson (58)	.05
209	Stacey Bailey	.05
210	Joe Montana	1.25
211	Wendell Tyler (61)	.05
212	Keena Turner (62)	.08
213	Ray Wersching (63)	.05
214	Dwight Clark	.15
215	Dwaine Board (65)	.05
216	Roger Craig (66)	.15
217	Ronnie Lott (67)	.15
218	Freddie Solomon (68)	.08
219	Lawrence Taylor	.25
220	Zeke Mowatt (70)	.05
221	Harry Carson (71)	.06
222	Rob Carpenter (72)	.05
223	Bobby Johnson (73)	.05
224	Joe Morris (74)	.07
225	Mark Haynes (75)	.05
226	Lionel Manuel (76)	.05
227	Phil Simms	.15
228	Billy Simms	.12
229	Leonard Thompson (79)	.03
230	James Jones (80)	.05
231	Ed Murray (81)	.05
232	William Gay	.05
233	Gary Danielson (83)	.05
234	Curtis Green (84)	.05
235	Bobby Watkins (85)	.05
236	Doug English (86)	.05
237	James Lofton	.20
238	Eddie Lee Ivery (88)	.06
239	Mike Douglas (89)	.05
240	Gerry Ellis (90)	.05
241	Tim Lewis (91)	.08
242	Paul Coffman (92)	.05
243	Tom Flynn (93)	.05
244	Ezra Johnson (94)	.05
245	Lynn Dickey	.08
246	Eric Dickerson	.60
247	Jack Youngblood (97)	.08
248	Doug Smith (98)	.05
249	Jeff Kemp (99)	.05
250	Kent Hill	.05
251	Mike Lansford (101)	.05
252	Henry Ellard (102)	.35
253	LeRoy Irvin (103)	.06
254	Ron Brown (104)	.20
255	John Riggins	.06
256	Dexter Manley (106)	.10
257	Darrell Green (107)	.15
258	Joe Theismann (108)	.05
259	Mark Moseley (109)	.05
260	Clint Didier (110)	.05
261	Vernon Dean (111)	.05
262	Calvin Muhammad (112)	.05
263	Art Monk	.20
264	Bruce Clark	.08
265	Hoby Brenner (115)	.05
266	Dave Wilson (116)	.06
267	Hokie Gajan (117)	.05
268	George Rogers	.10
269	Rickey Jackson (119)	.08
270	Brian Hansen (120)	.04
271	Dave Waymer (121)	.05
272	Richard Todd (122)	.05
273	Jan Stenerud	.15
274	Ted Brown (124)	.05
275	Leo Lewis (125)	.05
276	Scott Studwell (126)	.05
277	Alfred Anderson (127)	.05
278	Rufus Bess (128)	.05
279	Darrin Nelson (129)	.05
280	Greg Coleman (130)	.05
281	Tommy Kramer	.08
282	Joe Montana (283)	1.25
283	Dan Marino (282)	1.00
284	Brian Hansen (285)	.05
285	Jim Arnold (284)	.05

1985 Topps USFL

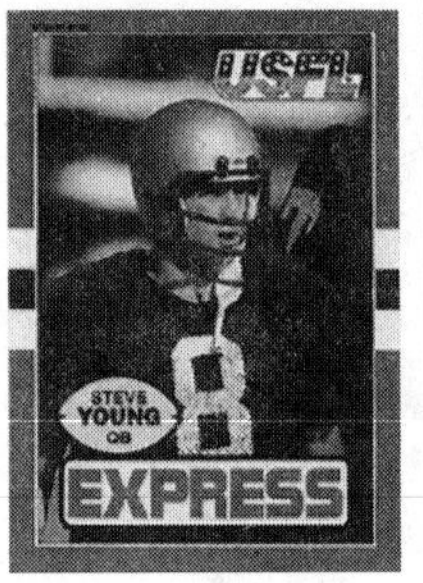

This was the second and final year of Topps' production of United States Football League cards. The 132-card set was issued as a factory set. Cards were numbered alphabetically according to city and according to the player's last name. Printed on white cardboard stock, fronts show a bright red border with a white and blue stripe across the middle; the USFL logo appears in the upper right corner. The team name appears in heavy red type at the bottom of the card, and the player's name and position are in a yellow football above the team name. Card backs show a goal-post design in blue and red. The set includes rookies of Doug Flutie, Gary Clark and Gerald McNeil, plus Herschel Walker's second-year card.

		MT
Complete Set (132):		175.00
Common Player:		.35
1	Case DeBruijn	.35
2	Mike Katolin	.35
3	Bruce Laird	.35
4	Kit Lathrop	.35
5	Kevin Long	.35
6	Karl Lorch	.35
7	Dave Tipton	.35
8	Doug Williams	.40
9	Luis Zendejas	.35
10	Kelvin Bryant	.75
11	Willie Collier	.35
12	Irv Eatman	.50
13	Scott Fitzkee	.35
14	*William Fuller*	6.00
15	Chuck Fusina	.35
16	Pete Kugler	.35
17	Garcia Lane	.35
18	Mike Lush	.35
19	*Sam Mills*	8.00
20	Buddy Aydelette	.35
21	Joe Cribbs	.50
22	David Dumars	.35
23	Robin Earl	.35
24	Joey Jones	.35
25	Leon Perry	.35
26	Dave Pureifory	.35
27	Bill Roe	.35
28	*Doug Smith*	2.00
29	Cliff Stoudt	.35
30	Jeff Delaney	.35
31	Vince Evans	.50
32	*Leonard Harris*	2.00
33	Bill Johnson	.35
34	Marc Lewis	.35
35	David Martin	.35
36	Bruce Thornton	.35
37	Craig Walls	.35
38	Vincent White	.35
39	Luther Bradley	.35
40	Pete Catan	.35
41	Kiki DeAyala	.35
42	Tony Fritsch	.35
43	Sam Harrell	.35
44	*Richard Johnson*	1.50
45	Jim Kelly	40.00
46	*Gerald McNeil*	1.50
47	*Clarence Verdin*	2.00
48	Dale Walters	.35
49	*Gary Clark*	15.00
50	Tom Dinkel	.35
51	Mike Edwards	.35
52	Brian Franco	.35
53	Bob Gruber	.35
54	Robbie Mahfouz	.35
55	Mike Rozier	1.75
56	Brian Sipe	.50
57	J.T. Turner	.35
58	Howard Carson	.35
59	*Wymon Henderson*	.60
60	Kevin Nelson	.35
61	Jeff Partridge	.35
62	Ben Rudolph	.35
63	JoJo Townsell	.35
64	Eddie Weaver	.35
65	Steve Young	80.00
66	*Tony Zendejas*	.75
67	Mossy Cade	.35
68	*Leonard Coleman*	.50
69	John Corker	.35
70	Derrick Crawford	.35
71	Art Kuehn	.35
72	Walter Lewis	.35
73	Tyrone McGriff	.35
74	Tim Spencer	.35
75	Reggie White	30.00
76	*Gizmo Williams*	2.00
77	Sam Bowers	.35
78	*Maurice Carthon*	1.25
79	Clarence Collins	.35
80	*Doug Flutie*	70.00
81	Freddie Gilbert	.35
82	Kerry Justin	.35
83	Dave Lapham	.35
84	Rick Partridge	.35
85	*Roger Ruzek*	1.00
86	Herschel Walker	6.00
87	Gordon Banks	.35
88	Monte Bennett	.35
89	*Albert Bentley*	3.00
90	Novo Bojovic	.35
91	Dave Browning	.35
92	Anthony Carter	4.00
93	Bobby Hebert	3.00
94	Ray Pinney	.35
95	Stan Talley	.35
96	Ruben Vaughan	.35
97	Curtis Bledsoe	.35
98	Reggie Collier	.35
99	Jerry Doerger	.35
100	Jerry Golsteyn	.35
101	Bob Niziolek	.35
102	Joel Patten	.35
103	Ricky Simmons	.35
104	Joey Walters	.35
105	Marcus Dupree	.35
106	Jeff Gossett	.50
107	Frank Lockett	.35
108	Marcus Marek	.35
109	Kenny Neil	.35
110	Robert Pennywell	.35
111	Matt Robinson	.35
112	Dan Ross	.35
113	Doug Woodward	.35
114	Danny Buggs	.35
115	Putt Choate	.35
116	Greg Fields	.35
117	Ken Hartley	.35
118	Nick Mike-Mayer	.35
119	Rick Neuheisel	.35
120	Peter Raeford	.35
121	Gary Worthy	.35
122	Gary Anderson	3.00
123	Zenon Andrusyshyn	.35
124	Greg Boone	.35
125	Mike Butler	.35
126	Mike Clark	.35
127	Willie Gillespie	.35
128	James Harrell	.35
129	Marvin Harvey	.35
130	John Reaves	.35
131	Eric Truvillion	.35
132	Checklist 1-132	.50

1985 Topps USFL New Jersey Generals

This nine-card sheet features members of the USFL's New Jersey Generals. The panel is 7-1/2" x 10-1/2"; individual cards would be the standard size if they were cut out of the panel. The card front has an action photo of the player, along with his name, team name and team logo. The back is numbered and includes biographical and statistical information, plus a brief player profile. The card stock is gray; the print is yellow and red on the back.

		MT
Complete Set (9):		35.00
Common Player:		2.00
1	Walt Michaels	2.00
2	Sam Bowers	2.00
3	Clarence Collins	2.00
4	Doug Flutie	20.00
5	Gregory Johnson	2.00
6	Jim LeClair	3.00
7	Bobby Leopold	2.00
8	Herschel Walker	15.00
9	Membership card (schedule on back)	2.00

1986 Topps

Topps' 1986 offering was 396 cards for the fourth straight year. Cards showed a green background with diagonal white stripes; a photo of the player was enclosed in one of several colorful borders. The player's name is found at the bottom of the card; his team is at right. All-Pro cards show a small designation just above the player's name. Team cards show a yellow border. Cards were numbered according to the team's finish the previous season. Rookies in this set include William Perry, Al Toon, Jerry Rice, Keith Millard, Bernie Kosar, and Boomer Esiason. (Key: AP - All Pro)

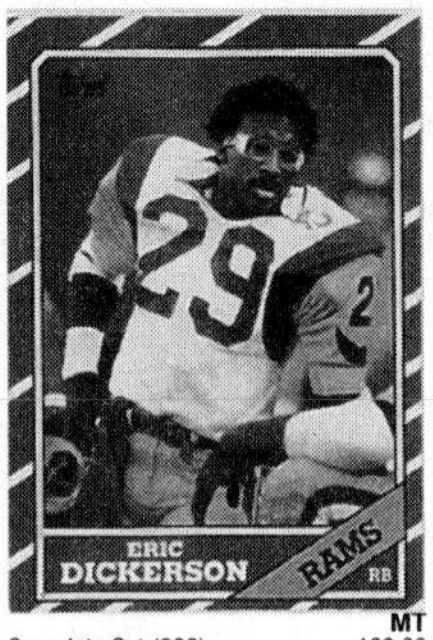

		MT
Complete Set (396):		180.00
Common Player:		.05
Wax Pack (15):		14.00
Wax Box (36):		390.00
1	Marcus Allen	.65
2	Eric Dickerson	.30
3	Lionel James	.30
4	Steve Largent	.30
5	George Martin	.10
6	Stephone Paige	.10
7	Walter Payton	.75
8	Super Bowl XX	.20
9	Chicago Bears Team (Walter Payton)	.75
10	Jim McMahon	.30
11	Walter Payton (AP)	2.00
12	Matt Suhey	.05
13	Willie Gault	.10
14	*Dennis McKinnon*	.25
15	Emery Moorhead	.05
16	Jim Covert (AP)	.10
17	*Jay Hilgenberg* (AP)	.50
18	*Kevin Butler*	1.00
19	Richard Dent (AP)	1.00
20	*William Perry*	.80
21	Steve McMichael	.50
22	Dan Hampton	.25
23	Otis Wilson	.05
24	Mike Singletary	.60
25	*Wilber Marshall*	1.00
26	Leslie Frazier	.05
27	*Dave Duerson*	.35
28	Gary Fencik	.10
29	New England Patriots Team (Craig James)	.10
30	Tony Eason	.20
31	Steve Grogan	.15
32	Craig James	.10
33	Tony Collins	.05
34	Irving Fryar	1.50
35	Brian Holloway (AP)	.10
36	John Hannah (AP)	.20
37	Tony Franklin	.05
38	Garin Veris	.10
39	Andre Tippett (AP)	.20
40	Steve Nelson	.05
41	Raymond Clayborn	.05
42	*Fred Marion*	.10
43	Rich Camarillo	.05
44	Miami Dolphins Team (Dan Marino)	2.00
45	Dan Marino (AP)	12.00
46	Tony Nathan	.10
47	Ron Davenport	.10
48	Mark Duper	.30
49	Mark Clayton	.50
50	Nat Moore	.05
51	Bruce Hardy	.05
52	Roy Foster	.05
53	Dwight Stephenson	.05
54	*Fuad Reveiz*	.20
55	Bob Baumhower	.10
56	Mike Charles	.05
57	Hugh Green	.05
58	Glenn Blackwood	.05
59	Reggie Roby	.05
60	Los Angeles Raiders Team (Marcus Allen)	.25
61	Marc Wilson	.10
62	Marcus Allen (AP)	1.25
63	Dokie Williams	.05
64	Todd Christensen	.05
65	Chris Bahr	.05
66	Fulton Walker	.05
67	Howie Long	.50
68	Bill Pickel	.05
69	Ray Guy	.15
70	*Greg Townsend*	1.00
71	Rod Martin	.05
72	Matt Millen	.05
73	Mike Haynes (AP)	.10
74	Lester Hayes	.05
75	Vann McElroy	.05
76	Los Angeles Rams Team (Eric Dickerson)	.15
77	Dieter Brock	.10
78	Eric Dickerson	1.00
79	Henry Ellard	1.00
80	*Ron Brown*	.30
81	Tony Hunter	.10
82	Kent Hill (AP)	.05
83	Doug Smith	.05
84	Dennis Harrah	.05
85	Jackie Slater	.25
86	Mike Lansford	.05
87	Gary Jeter	.05
88	Mike Wilcher	.05
89	Jim Collins	.05
90	LeRoy Irvin	.10
91	Gary Green	.05
92	Nolan Cromwell	.05
93	Dale Hatcher	.05
94	New York Jets Team (Freeman McNeil)	.10
95	Ken O'Brien	.35
96	Freeman McNeil	.20
97	*Tony Paige*	.50
98	Johnny "Lam" Jones	.05
99	Wesley Walker	.10
100	Kurt Sohn	.05
101	*Al Toon*	1.00
102	Mickey Shuler	.05
103	Marvin Powell	.10
104	Pat Leahy	.05
105	Mark Gastineau	.25
106	Joe Klecko (AP)	.10
107	Marty Lyons	.05
108	Lance Mehl	.05
109	Bobby Jackson	.05
110	Dave Jennings	.05
111	Denver Broncos Team (Sammy Winder)	.10
112	John Elway	10.00
113	Sammy Winder	.10
114	Gerald Wilhite	.10
115	Steve Watson	.10
116	*Vance Johnson*	.50
117	Rick Karlis	.05
118	Rulon Jones	.10
119	*Karl Mecklenburg* (AP)	2.50
120	Louis Wright	.05
121	Mike Harden	.05
122	*Dennis Smith*	.50
123	Steve Foley	.05
124	Dallas Cowboys Team (Tony Hill)	.10
125	Danny White	.20
126	Tony Dorsett	.50
127	Timmy Newsome	.05
128	Mike Renfro	.05
129	Tony Hill	.10
130	Doug Cosbie (AP)	.10
131	Rafael Septien	.10
132	Ed "Too Tall" Jones	.25
133	Randy White	.25
134	Jim Jeffcoat	.20
135	Everson Walls (AP)	.05
136	Dennis Thurman	.05
137	New York Giants Team (Joe Morris)	.10
138	Phil Simms	.40
139	Joe Morris	.20
140	*George Adams*	.05
141	Lionel Manuel	.05
142	Bobby Johnson	.05
143	*Phil McConkey*	.20
144	*Mark Bavaro*	1.00
145	Zeke Mowatt	.05
146	Brad Benson	.10
147	*Bart Oates*	.60
148	*Leonard Marshall* (AP)	.50
149	Jim Burt	.10
150	George Martin	.05
151	Lawrence Taylor (AP)	.75
152	Harry Carson (AP)	.15
153	Elvis Patterson	.10
154	Sean Landeta	.10
155	San Francisco 49ers Team (Roger Craig)	.25
156	Joe Montana	6.00
157	Roger Craig	.75
158	Wendell Tyler	.10
159	Carl Monroe	.05
160	Dwight Clark	.25
161	*Jerry Rice*	120.00
162	Randy Cross	.05
163	Keith Fahnhorst	.05
164	Jeff Stover	.05
165	*Michael Carter*	.50
166	Dwaine Board	.05
167	Eric Wright	.05
168	Ronnie Lott	.75
169	Carlton Williamson	.05
170	Washington Redskins Team (Dave Butz)	.10
171	Joe Theismann	.40
172	*Jay Schroeder*	.50
173	George Rogers	.15
174	Ken Jenkins	.05
175	Art Monk (AP)	.75
176	*Gary Clark*	2.00
177	Joe Jacoby	.05
178	Russ Grimm	.05
179	Mark Moseley	.10
180	Dexter Manely	.15
181	*Charles Mann*	1.00
182	Vernon Dean	.05
183	*Raphel Cherry*	.15
184	Curtis Jordan	.05
185	Cleveland Browns Team (Bernie Kosar)	.40
186	Gary Danielson	.05
187	*Bernie Kosar*	2.00
188	*Kevin Mack*	.50
189	*Earnest Byner*	1.00
190	Glen Young	.05
191	Ozzie Newsome	.30
192	Mike Baab	.05
193	Cody Risien	.10
194	Bob Golic	.10
195	Reggie Camp	.05
196	Chip Banks	.10
197	Tom Cousineau	.10
198	*Frank Minnifield*	.30
199	Al Gross	.10
200	Seattle Seahawks Team (Curt Warner)	.10
201	Dave Krieg	.25
202	Curt Warner	.10
203	Steve Largent (AP)	.65
204	Norm Johnson	.05
205	Daryl Turner	.05
206	Jacob Green	.05
207	Joe Nash	.05
208	Jeff Bryant	.05
209	Randy Edwards	.10
210	Fredd Young	.10
211	Kenny Easley	.05
212	John Harris	.05
213	Green Bay Packers Team (Paul Coffman)	.10
214	Lynn Dickey	.15
215	Gerry Ellis	.05
216	Eddie Lee Ivery	.05
217	Jessie Clark	.05
218	James Lofton	.60
219	Paul Coffman	.05
220	Alphonso Carreker	.05
221	Ezra Johnson	.05
222	Mike Douglass	.05
223	Tim Lewis	.05
224	*Mark Murphy*	.05
225	Passing Leaders (Joe Montana, Ken O'Brien)	1.00
226	Receiving Leaders (Lionel James, Roger Craig)	.15
227	Rushing Leaders (Marcus Allen, Gerald Riggs)	.25
228	Scoring Leaders (Gary Anderson, Kevin Butler)	.05
229	Interception Leaders (Eugene Daniel, Albert Lewis, Everson Walls)	.05
230	San Diego Chargers Team (Dan Fouts)	.20
231	Dan Fouts	.60
232	Lionel James	.10
233	*Gary Anderson*	1.00
234	*Tim Spencer*	.10
235	Wes Chandler	.10
236	Charlie Joiner	.25
237	Kellen Winslow	.25
238	*Jim Lachey*	.50
239	Bob Thomas	.05
240	Jeffery Dale	.05
241	Ralf Mojsiejenko	.05
242	Detroit Lions Team (Eric Hipple)	.10
243	Eric Hipple	.05
244	Billy Sims	.15
245	James Jones	.05
246	*Pete Mandley*	.15
247	Leonard Thompson	.05
248	*Lomas Brown*	.50
249	Ed Murray	.05
250	Curtis Green	.05
251	William Gay	.05
252	Jimmy Williams	.05
253	Bobby Watkins	.05
254	Cincinnati Bengals Team (Boomer Esiason)	.75
255	*Boomer Esiason*	4.00
256	James Brooks	.35
257	Larry Kinnebrew	.10
258	Cris Collinsworth	.05
259	Mike Martin	.05
260	*Eddie Brown*	.50
261	Anthony Munoz	.25
262	Jim Breech	.05
263	Ross Browner	.10
264	Carl Zander	.05
265	James Griffin	.05
266	Robert Jackson	.05
267	Pat McInally	.10
268	Philadelphia Eagles Team (Ron Jaworski)	.10
269	Ron Jaworski	.15
270	Earnest Jackson	.05
271	Mike Quick	.10
272	John Spagnola	.05
273	Mark Dennard	.05
274	Paul McFadden	.05
275	*Reggie White*	12.00
276	Greg Brown	.05
277	Herman Edwards	.05
278	Roynell Young	.10
279	Wes Hopkins (AP)	.05
280	Pittsburgh Steelers Team (Walter Abercrombie)	.10
281	Mark Malone	.05
282	Frank Pollard	.05
283	Walter Abercrombie	.10
284	Louis Lipps	.40
285	John Stallworth	.15
286	Mike Webster	.20
287	Gary Anderson (AP)	.25
288	Keith Willis	.05
289	Mike Merriweather	.10
290	Dwayne Woodruff	.05
291	Donnie Shell	.10
292	Minnesota Vikings Team (Tommy Kramer)	.10
293	Tommy Kramer	.10
294	Darrin Nelson	.05
295	Ted Brown	.05
296	Buster Rhymes	.15
297	*Anthony Carter*	2.00
298	*Steve Jordan*	1.00
299	*Keith Millard*	.50
300	*Joey Browner*	.75
301	John Turner	.05
302	Greg Coleman	.05
303	Kansas City Chiefs Team (Todd Blackledge)	.10
304	Bill Kenney	.05
305	Herman Heard	.05
306	*Stephon Paige*	.75
307	Carlos Carson	.05
308	Nick Lowery	.20
309	Mike Bell	.05
310	Bill Maas	.05
311	Art Still	.10
312	*Albert Lewis*	1.25
313	Deron Cherry (AP)	.20
314	Indianapolis Colts Team (Rohn Stark)	.10
315	Mike Pagel	.05
316	Randy McMillian	.05
317	*Albert Bentley*	.40
318	George Wonsley	.10
319	Robbie Martin	.05
320	Pat Beach	.05
321	Chris Hinton	.10
322	*Duane Bickett*	.50
323	Eugene Daniel	.05
324	*Cliff Odom*	.15
325	Rohn Stark (AP)	.05
326	St. Louis Cardinals Team (Stump Mitchell)	.10
327	Neil Lomax	.15
328	Stump Mitchell	.05
329	Ottis Anderson	.20
330	J.T. Smith	.05
331	Pat Tilley	.05
332	Roy Green	.05
333	Lance Smith	.05
334	Curtis Greer	.05
335	*Freddie Joe Nunn*	.35
336	E.J. Junior	
337	*Lonnie Young*	.20
338	New Orleans Saints Team (Wayne Wilson)	.10
339	*Bobby Hebert*	.75
340	Dave Wilson	.05
341	Wayne Wilson	.05
342	Hoby Brenner	.05
343	Stan Brock	.05

344 Morten Andersen .35
345 Bruce Clark .05
346 Rickey Jackson .60
347 Dave Waymer .05
348 Brian Hansen
349 Houston Oilers Team (Warren Moon) .60
350 Warren Moon 4.00
351 *Mike Rozier* .30
352 Butch Woolfolk .05
353 Drew Hill .30
354 *Willie Drewrey* .20
355 Tim Smith .05
356 Mike Munchak .30
357 *Ray Childress* 1.50
358 Frank Bush .05
359 Steve Brown .05
360 Atlanta Falcons Team (Gerald Riggs) .10
361 Dave Archer .05
362 Gerald Riggs .10
363 William Andrews .05
364 Billy Johnson .05
365 Arthur Cox .05
366 Mike Kenn .05
367 *Bill Fralic* .75
368 Mick Luckhurst .05
369 Rick Bryan .05
370 Bobby Butler .05
371 Rick Donnelly .05
372 Tampa Bay Buccaneers Team (James Wilder) .10
373 Steve DeBerg .25
374 *Steve Young* 35.00
375 James Wilder .05
376 Kevin House .05
377 Gerald Carter .05
379 Sean Farrell .05
380 Donald Igwebuike .05
381 David Logan .05
382 *Jeremiah Castille* .12
383 Buffalo Bills Team (Greg Bell) .10
384 *Bruce Mathison* .15
385 Joe Cribbs .05
386 Greg Bell .15
387 Jerry Butler .05
388 *Andre Reed* 5.00
389 *Bruce Smith* 5.00
390 Fred Smerlas .05
391 Darryl Talley .50
392 Jim Haslett .05
393 Charles Romes .05
394 Checklist 1-132 .15
395 Checklist 133-264 .15
396 Checklist 265-396 .15

1986 Topps Box Bottoms

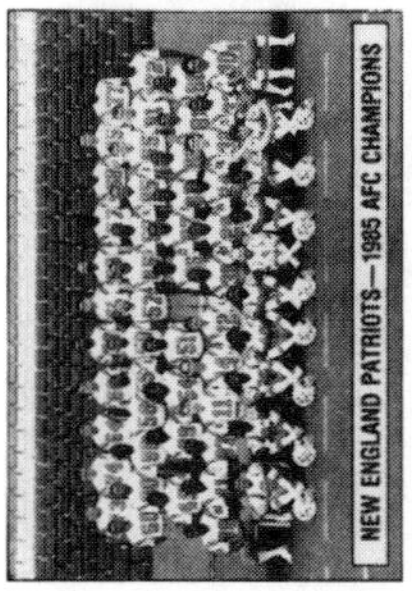

These four cards were featured on the sides of 1986 Topps wax pack boxes, one per box. The cards, which are standard size, feature the top four teams in the NFL in 1985 - the two Super Bowl participants and their opponents in the conference championship games. The team is pictured on the front; the back identifies those in the picture.

MT
Complete Set (4): 5.00
Common Player: 1.00
A Chicago Bears 2.50
B New England Patriots 1.00
C Los Angeles Rams 1.00
D Miami Dolphins 2.50

1986 Topps 1000 Yard Club

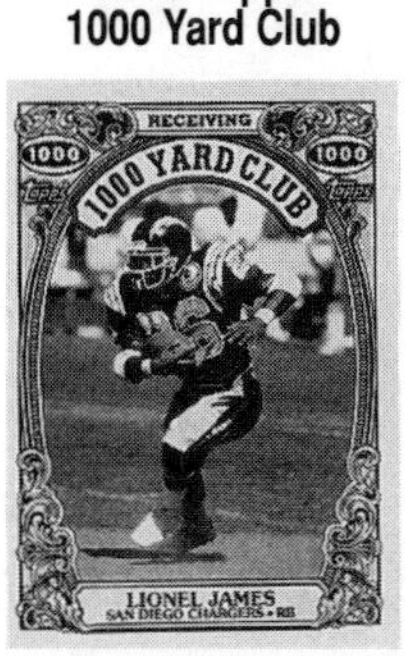

Issued one card per wax pack with the 1986 regular-issue cards, this 26-card set shows each player who gained 1,000 yards rushing or receiving the previous year. The card order was determined by the number of yards gained, with Marcus Allen, 1985's leading ground-gainer, ending up first. (San Francisco's Roger Craig gained 1,000 yards rushing and receiving the previous year, but only his rushing yardage is listed). Printed on heavy white cardboard stock, card fronts show an ornate arch design in light green. Backs are printed in red and orange.

MT
Complete Set (26): 6.00
Common Player: .10
1 Marcus Allen .40
2 Gerald Riggs .20
3 Walter Payton 1.00
4 Joe Morris .30
5 Freeman McNeil .20
6 Tony Dorsett .50
7 James Wilder .10
8 Steve Largent 1.00
9 Mike Quick .10
10 Eric Dickerson 1.25
11 Craig James .10
12 Art Monk .20
13 Wes Chandler .10
14 Drew Hill .10
15 James Lofton .20
16 Louis Lipps .20
17 Cris Collinsworth .10
18 Tony Hill .10
19 Kevin Mack .10
20 Curt Warner .20
21 George Rogers .10
22 Roger Craig .40
23 Earnest Jackson .10
24 Lionel James .10
25 Stump Mitchell .10
26 Earnest Byner .10

1986 Topps Stickers

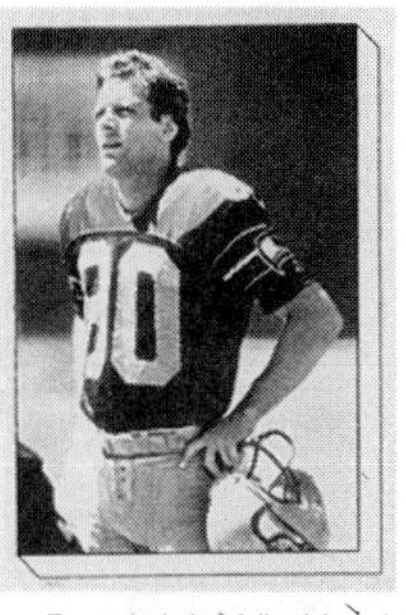

Topps included foil stickers in its sticker set again in 1986, and followed the format it used for previous issues. The stickers use a shadow box for the frame on the front, around a color photo. A card number appears on both sides. The back has its information printed in brown ink against a white background. Some stickers were issued in pairs, as indicated by the parenthesis after the player's name in the checklist. The All-Pro players are foil stickers (#s 132-143), as are #s 282-285. The Chicago Bears are featured on the covers of the corresponding album which was issued to hold the stickers; Walter Payton is on the front.

MT
Complete Set (285): 20.00
Common Player: .05
1 Walter Payton (left) .60
2 Walter Payton (right) .60
3 Richard Dent (left) .10
4 Richard Dent (right) .10
5 Richard Dent (Super Bowl MVP) .40
6 Walter Payton 1.00
7 William Perry .12
8 Jim McMahon (158) .10
9 Richard Dent (159) .10
10 Jim Covert (160) .05
11 Dan Hampton (161) .08
12 Mike Singletary (162) .08
13 Jay Hilgenberg (163) .06
14 Otis Wilson (164) .04
15 Jimmie Giles .05
16 Kevin House (166) .03
17 Jeremiah Castille (167) .03
18 James Wilder .05
19 Donald Igwebuike (169) .05
20 David Logan (170) .05
21 Jeff Davis (171) .05
22 Frank Garcia (172) .05
23 Steve Young (173) 1.00
24 Stump Mitchell .08
25 E.J. Junior .08
26 J.T. Smith (176) .05
27 Pat Tilley (177) .05
28 Neil Lomax (178) .06
29 Leonard Smith (179) .05
30 Ottis Anderson (180) .08
31 Curtis Greer (181) .05
32 Roy Green (182) .06
33 Tony Dorsett .30
34 Tony Hill (184) .05
35 Doug Cosbie (185) .06
36 Everson Walls .08
37 Randy White (187) .10
38 Rafael Septien (188) .05
39 Mike Renfro (189) .05
40 Danny White (190) .05
41 Ed "Too Tall" Jones (191) .10
42 Earnest Jackson .08
43 Mike Quick .08
44 Wes Hopkins (194) .05
45 Reggie White (195) .75
46 Greg Brown (196) .05
47 Paul McFadden (197) .05
48 John Spagnola (198) .05
49 Ron Jaworski (199) .05
50 Herman Hunter (200) .05
51 Gerald Riggs .10
52 Mike Pitts (202) .05
53 Buddy Curry (203) .05
54 Billy Johnson .12
55 Rick Donnelly (205) .05
56 Rick Bryan (206) .08
57 Bobby Butler (207) .05
58 Mike Luckhurst (208) .05
59 Mike Kenn (209) .05
60 Roger Craig .25
61 Joe Montana 1.75
62 Michael Carter (212) .10
63 Eric Wright (213) .05
64 Dwight Clark (214) .10
65 Ronnie Lott (215) .12
66 Carlton Williamson (216) .05
67 Wendell Tyler (217) .08
68 Dwaine Board (218) .05
69 Joe Morris .12
70 Leonard Marshall (220) .05
71 Lionel Manuel (221) .05
72 Harry Carson .10
73 Phil Simms (223) .10
74 Sean Landeta (224) .05
75 Lawrence Taylor (225) .15
76 Elvis Patterson (226) .05
77 George Adams (227) .05
78 James Jones .08
79 Leonard Thompson .05
80 William Graham (230) .05
81 Mark Nichols (231) .05
82 William Gay (232) .05
83 Jimmy Williams (233) .05
84 Billy Sims (234) .12
85 Bobby Watkins (235) .05
86 Ed Murray (236) .05
87 James Lofton .25
88 Jessie Clark (238) .05
89 Tim Lewis (239) .05
90 Eddie Lee Ivery .08
91 Phillip Epps (241) .05
92 Ezra Johnson (242) .05
93 Mike Douglass (243) .05
94 Paul Coffman (244) .05
95 Randy Scott (245) .03
96 Eric Dickerson .45
97 Dale Hatcher .05
98 Ron Brown (248) .06
99 LeRoy Irvin (249) .05
100 Ken Hill (250) .05
101 Dennis Harrah (251) .05
102 Jackie Slater (252) .08
103 Mike Wilcher (253) .05
104 Doug Smith (254) .05
105 Art Monk .25
106 Joe Jacoby (256) .05
107 Russ Grimm (257) .05
108 George Rogers .10
109 Dexter Manley (259) .05
110 Jay Schroeder (260) .12
111 Gary Clark (261) .50
112 Curtis Jordan (262) .05
113 Charles Mann (263) .08
114 Morten Andersen .08
115 Rickey Jackson .10
116 Glen Redd (266) .05
117 Bobby Hebert (267) .20
118 Hoby Brenner (268) .05
119 Brian Hansen (269) .05
120 Dave Waymer (270) .05
121 Bruce Clark (271) .05
122 Wayne Wilson (272) .05
123 Joey Browner .05
124 Darrin Nelson (274) .08
125 Keith Millard (275) .15
126 Anthony Carter .35
127 Buster Rhymes (277) .04
128 Steve Jordan (278) .20
129 Greg Coleman (279) .05
130 Ted Brown (280) .05
131 John Turner (281) .05
132 Harry Carson (144, All-Pro) .20
133 Deron Cherry (145, All-Pro) .10
134 Richard Dent (146, All-Pro) .20
135 Mike Haynes (147, All-Pro) .12
136 Wes Hopkins (148, All-Pro) .10
137 Joe Klecko (149, All-Pro) .10
138 Leonard Marshall (150, All-Pro) .10
139 Karl Mecklenburg (151, All-Pro) .12
140 Rohn Stark (152, All-Pro) .10
141 Lawrence Taylor (153, All-Pro) .25
142 Andre Tippett (154, All-Pro) .12
143 Everson Walls (155, All-Pro) .12
144 Marcus Allen (132, All-Pro) .35
145 Gary Anderson (133, All-Pro) .10
146 Doug Cosbie (134, All-Pro) .15
147 Jim Covert (135, All-Pro) .15
148 John Hannah (136, All-Pro) .15
149 Jay Hilgenberg (137, All-Pro) .12
150 Ken Hil (138, All-Pro) .10
151 Brian Holloway (139, All-Pro) .10
152 Steve Largent (140, All-Pro) .75
153 Dan Marino (141, All-Pro) 1.50
154 Art Monk (142, All-Pro) .25
155 Walter Payton (143, All-Pro) .75
156 Anthony Munoz .15
157 Boomer Esiason .40
158 Cris Collinsworth (8) .06
159 Eddie Edwards (9) .05
160 James Griffin (10) .05
161 Jim Breech (11) .05
162 Eddie Brown (12) .05
163 Ross Browner (13) .05
164 James Brooks (14) .07
165 Greg Bell .05
166 Jerry Butler (16) .05
167 Don Wilson (17) .05
168 Andre Reed .75
169 Jim Haslett (19) .05
170 Bruce Mathison (20) .05
171 Bruce Smith (21) .40
172 Joe Cribbs (22) .05
173 Charles Romes (23) .05
174 Karl Mecklenburg .08
175 Rulon Jones .05
176 John Elway (26) .40
177 Sammy Winder (27) .10
178 Louis Wright (28) .05
179 Steve Watson (29) .05
180 Dennis Smith (30) .05
181 Mike Harden (31) .05
182 Vance Johnson (32) .10
183 Kevin Mack .10
184 Chip Banks (34) .05
185 Bob Golic (35) .05
186 Earnest Byner .35
187 Ozzie Newsome (37) .12
188 Bernie Kosar (38) .60
189 Don Rogers (39) .05
190 Al Gross (40) .05
191 Clarence Weathers (41) .08
192 Lionel James .08
193 Dan Fouts .40
194 Wes Chandler (44) .06
195 Kellen Winslow (45) .10
196 Gary Anderson (46) .07
197 Charlie Joiner (47) .08
198 Ralf Mojsiejenko (48) .05
199 Bob Thomas (49) .05
200 Tim Spencer (50) .05
201 Deron Cherry .10
202 Bill Maas (52) .05
203 Herman Heard (53) .05
204 Carlos Carson .08
205 Nick Lowery (55) .08
206 Bill Kenney (56) .05
207 Albert Lewis (57) .25
208 Art Still (58) .05
209 Stephone Paige (59) .25
210 Rohn Stark .05
211 Chris Hinton .10
212 Albert Bentley (62) .10
213 Eugene Daniel (63) .05
214 Pat Beach (64) .05
215 Cliff Odom (65) .05
216 Duane Bickett (66) .20
217 George Wonsley (67) .05
218 Randy McMillan (68) .05
219 Dan Marino 1.50
220 Dwight Stephenson (70) .08
221 Roy Foster (71) .05
222 Mark Clayton .20
223 Mark Duper (73) .10
224 Fuad Reveiz (74) .05
225 Reggie Roby (75) .05
226 Tony Nathan (76) .05
227 Ron Davenport (77) .05
228 Freeman McNeil .10
229 Joe Klecko .08
230 Mark Gastineau (80) .05
231 Ken O'Brien (81) .06
232 Lance Mehl (82) .05
233 Al Toon (83) .20
234 Mickey Shuler (84) .05
235 Pat Leahy (85) .05
236 Wesley Walker (86) .06
237 Drew Hill .10
238 Warren Moon (88) .40
239 Mike Rozier (89) .10
240 Mike Munchak .10
241 Tim Smith (91) .05
242 Butch Woolfolk (92) .05
243 Willie Drewrey (93) .05
244 Keith Bostic (94) .05
245 Jesse Baker (95) .05
246 Craig James .15
247 John Hannah .12
248 Tony Eason (98) .06
249 Andre Tippett (99) .06
250 Tony Collins (100) .05
251 Brian Holloway (101) .05
252 Irving Fryar (102) .10
253 Raymond Clayborn (103) .05
254 Steve Nelson (104) .05
255 Marcus Allen .25
256 Mike Haynes (106) .08
257 Todd Christensen (107) .06
258 Howie Long .12
259 Lester Hayes (109) .05
260 Rod Martin (110) .08
261 Dokie Williams (111) .08
262 Chris Bahr (112) .05
263 Bill Pickel (113) .05
264 Curt Warner .10
265 Steve Largent .60
266 Fredd Young (116) .06
267 Dave Krieg (117) .08
268 Daryl Turner (118) .05
269 John Harris (119) .05
270 Randy Edwards (120) .05
271 Kenny Easley (121) .05
272 Jacob Green (122) .05
273 Gary Anderson .05
274 Mike Webster (124) .07
275 Walter Abercombie (125) .08
276 Louis Lipps .10
277 Frank Pollard (127) .05
278 Mike Merriweather (128) .05
279 Mark Malone (129) .05
280 Donnie Shell (130) .08
281 John Stallworth (131) .06
282 Marcus Allen (284) .50
283 Ken O'Brien (285) .15
284 Kevin Butler (282) .15
285 Roger Craig (283) .35

1987 Topps

Topps' fifth straight 396-card set was bordered in white and carried two flags at the top of the card - one indicating the team, the other indicating the player name. His position was listed in the border above the name. Cards were numbered in order of the team's finish the previous year. This set, which seems to be one of the hottest sets since the '84 issue, includes such rookies as Randall Cunningham, Jim Everett, Reuben Mayes, John Offerdahl, Ernest Givins and Tim Harris. This set also features the last regular-issue card of all-time rushing leader Walter Payton. Three errors have been found in the set: On the back of card #274, Rueben Mayes, the statistical heading reads "Comp" for completions, when it should read "yards." The statistical heading was apparently intended for a quarterback instead of a running back. Also, the back of card #288, John Stallworth, is missing statistics from the years 1982-86. Finally, the reverse of Ross Browner's card (#263) contains a reference to the Bengals' 1982 Super Bowl win. The Bengals, however, lost to the 49ers that year. Not only that, the card also lists the Super Bowl date as 1-10-82 when it was actually played 1-24-82. (Key: AP - All Pro)

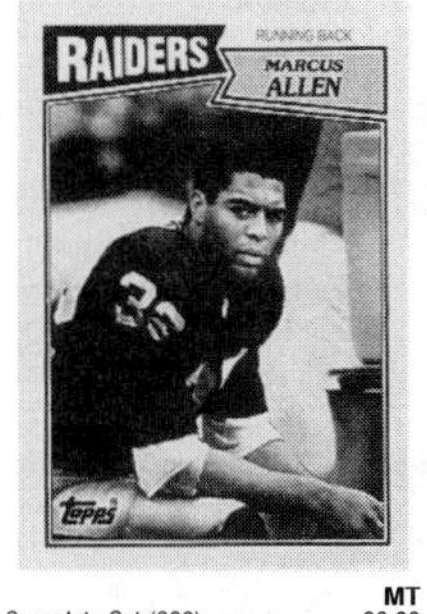

MT
Complete Set (396): 30.00
Common Player: .05
Wax Pack (15+1): 60.00
Wax Box (36): .07
1 Super Bowl XXI .15
2 Todd Christensen .05
3 Dave Jennings .05
4 Charlie Joiner .10
5 Steve Largent .25
6 Dan Marino 2.00
7 Donnie Shell .05
8 Phil Simms .15
9 Giants team (Mark Bavaro) .07
10 Phil Simms .35
11 Joe Morris (AP) .12
12 *Maurice Carthon* .15
13 Lee Rouson .05
14 Bobby Johnson .05
15 Lionel Manuel .05
16 Phil McConkey .05
17 Mark Bavaro (AP) .60
18 Zeke Mowatt .05
19 Raul Allegre .05
20 Sean Landeta .05
21 Brad Benson .05
22 Jim Burt .05
23 Leonard Marshall .40
24 Carl Banks .50
25 Harry Carson .12
26 Lawrence Taylor (AP) .50
27 *Terry Kinard* .20
28 *Pepper Johnson* 1.00
29 *Erik Howard* .15
30 Broncos team (Gerald Wilhite) .07
31 John Elway 4.00
32 Gerald Wilhite .05
33 Sammy Winder .05
34 Ken Bell .05
35 Steve Watson .05
36 Rick Karlis .05
37 Keith Bishop .05
38 Rulon Jones .05
39 Karl Mecklenburg (AP) .75
40 Louis Wright .05
41 Mike Harden .05
42 Dennis Smith .40
43 Bears team (Walter Payton) .50
44 Jim McMahon .25
45 *Doug Flutie* 8.00
46 Walter Payton 1.25
47 Matt Suhey .05
48 Willie Gault .15
49 *Dennis Gentry* .25
50 Kevin Butler .25
51 Jim Covert (AP) .05
52 Jay Hilgenberg .25
53 Dan Hampton .20
54 Steve McMichael .15
55 William Perry .15
56 Richard Dent .50
57 Otis Wilson .05
58 Mike Singletary (AP) .50
59 Wilber Marshall .50
60 Mike Richardson .05
61 Dave Duerson .15
62 Gary Fencik .05
63 Redskins team (George Rogers) .07
64 Jay Schroeder .35
65 George Rogers .05
66 *Kelvin Bryant* .25
67 Ken Jenkins .05
68 Gary Clark .50
69 Art Monk .50
70 *Clint Didier* .15
71 Steve Cox .05
72 Joe Jacoby .05
73 Russ Grimm .05
74 Charles Mann .30
75 Dave Butz .05
76 Dexter Manley (AP) .05
77 Darrell Green (AP) .30
78 Curtis Jordan .05
79 Browns team .07
80 Bernie Kosar .50
81 Curtis Dickey .05
82 Kevin Mack .20
83 Herman Fontenot .05
84 *Brian Brennan* .20
85 Ozzie Newsome .25
86 Jeff Gossett .05
87 Cody Risien (AP) .05
88 Reggie Camp .05
89 Bob Golic .05
90 Carl Hairston .05
91 Chip Banks .05
92 Frank Minnifield .05
93 Hanford Dixon (AP) .05
94 *Gerald McNeil* .20
95 Dave Puzzuoli .05
96 Patriots team (Andre Tippett) .07
97 Tony Eason .05
98 Craig James .05
99 Tony Collins .05
100 Mosi Tatupu .05
101 Stanley Morgan .15
102 Irving Fryar .65
103 Stephen Starring .05
104 Tony Franklin (AP) .05
105 Rich Camarillo .05
106 Garin Veris .05
107 Andre Tippett (AP) .12
108 Don Blackmon .05
109 *Ronnie Lippett* .30
110 Raymond Clayborn .05
111 49ers team (Roger Craig) .12
112 Joe Montana 4.00
113 Roger Craig .30
114 Joe Cribbs .05
115 Jerry Rice (AP) 10.00
116 Dwight Clark .15
117 Ray Wersching .05
118 Max Runager .05
119 Jeff Stover .05
120 Dwaine Board .05
121 *Tim McKyer* .30
122 *Don Griffin* .40
123 Ronnie Lott (AP) .30
124 Tom Holmoe .05
125 *Charles Haley* 3.00
126 Jets team (Mark Gastineau) .05
127 Ken O'Brien .20
128 Pat Ryan .05
129 Freeman McNeil .15
130 *Johnny Hector* .30
131 Al Toon (AP) .50
132 Wesley Walker .12
133 Mickey Shuler .05
134 Pat Leahy .05
135 Mark Gastineau .05
136 Joe Klecko .05
137 Marty Lyons .05
138 Bob Crable .05
139 Lance Mehl .05
140 Dave Jennings .05
141 *Harry Hamilton* .15
142 Lester Lyles .05
143 Bobby Humphery .05
144 Rams team (Eric Dickerson) .15
145 *Jim Everett* 3.00
146 Eric Dickerson (AP) .50
147 Barry Redden .05
148 Ron Brown .15
149 Kevin House .05
150 Henry Ellard .60
151 Doug Smith .05
152 Dennis Harrah (AP) .05
153 Jackie Slater .15
154 Gary Jeter .05
155 Carl Ekern .05
156 Mike Wilcher .05
157 *Jerry Gray* .25
158 LeRoy Irvin .15
159 Nolan Cromwell .05
160 Chiefs team (Todd Blackledge) .07
161 Bill Kenney .05
162 Stephone Paige .25
163 Henry Marshall .05
164 Carlos Carson .05
165 Nick Lowery .15
166 *Irv Eatman* .10
167 Brad Budde .05
168 Art Still .05
169 Bill Maas (AP) .05
170 *Lloyd Burruss* .20
171 Deron Cherry (AP) .15
172 Seahawks team (Curt Warner) .07
173 Dave Krieg .20
174 Curt Warner .05
175 *John L. Williams* 1.00
176 *Bobby Joe Edmonds* .20
177 Steve Largent .60
178 Bruce Scholtz .05
179 Norm Johnson .05
180 Jacob Green .05
181 Fredd Young .05
182 Dave Brown .05
183 Kenny Easley .05
184 Bengals team (James Brooks) .07
185 Boomer Esiason .75
186 James Brooks .12
187 Larry Kinnebrew .05
188 Cris Collinsworth .15
189 Eddie Brown .35
190 *Tim McGee* 1.00
191 Jim Breech .05
192 Anthony Munoz .20
193 Max Montoya .05
194 Eddie Edwards .05
195 Ross Browner .05
196 Emanuel King .05
197 Louis Breeden .05
198 Vikings team (Darrin Nelson) .07
199 Tommy Kramer .05
200 Darrin Nelson .05
201 Allen Rice .05
202 Anthony Carter .30
203 Leo Lewis .05
204 Steve Jordan .40
205 Chuck Nelson .05
206 Greg Coleman .05
207 *Gary Zimmerman* .30
208 Doug Martin .05
209 Keith Millard .20
210 *Issiac Holt* .15
211 Joey Browner .20
212 Rufus Bess .05
213 Raiders team (Marcus Allen) .15
214 Jim Plunkett .15
215 Marcus Allen .90
216 *Napoleon McCallum* .12
217 Dokie Williams .05
218 Todd Christensen .05
219 Chris Bahr .05
220 Howie Long .25
221 Bill Pickel .05
222 *Sean Jones* 1.50
223 Lester Hayes .05

224	Mike Haynes	.05
225	Vann McElroy	.05
226	Fulton Walker	.05
227	Passing Leaders (Tommy Kramer, Dan Marino)	.50
228	Receiving Leaders (Jerry Rice, Todd Christensen)	.50
229	Rushing leaders (Eric Dickerson, Curt Warner)	.25
230	Scoring leaders (Kevin Butler, Tony Franklin)	.07
231	Interception leaders (Ronnie Lott, Deron Cherry)	.07
232	Dolphins team (Reggie Roby)	.07
233	Dan Marino (AP)	8.00
234	*Lorenzo Hampton*	.12
235	Tony Nathan	.05
236	Mark Duper	.12
237	Mark Clayton	.50
238	Nat Moore	.05
239	Bruce Hardy	.05
240	Reggie Roby	.05
241	Roy Foster	.05
242	Dwight Stephenson (AP)	.05
243	Hugh Green	.05
244	*John Offerdahl*	.50
245	Mark Brown	.05
246	Doug Betters	.05
247	Bob Baumhower	.05
248	Falcons team (Gerald Riggs)	.07
249	Dave Archer	.15
250	Gerald Riggs	.10
251	William Andrews	.05
252	Charlie Brown	.05
253	Arthur Cox	.05
254	Rick Donnelly	.05
255	Bill Fralic (AP)	.30
256	*Mike Gann*	.10
257	Rick Bryan	.05
258	Bret Clark	.05
259	Mike Pitts	.05
260	Cowboys team (Tony Dorsett)	.15
261	Danny White	.15
262	*Steve Pelluer*	.10
263	Tony Dorsett	.40
264	*Herschel Walker*	2.50
265	Timmy Newsome	.05
266	Tony Hill	.05
267	*Mike Sherrard*	.20
268	Jim Jeffcoat	.05
269	Ron Fellows	.05
270	Bill Bates	.20
271	Michael Downs	.05
272	Saints team (Bobby Hebert)	.12
273	Dave Wilson	.05
274	*Rueben Mayes*	.30
275	Hoby Brenner	.05
276	*Eric Martin*	.75
277	Morten Andersen	.35
278	Brian Hansen	.05
279	Rickey Jackson	.50
280	Dave Waymer	.05
281	Bruce Clark	.05
282	James Geathers	.20
283	Steelers team (Walter Abercrombie)	.07
284	Mark Malone	.05
285	Earnest Jackson	.05
286	Walter Abercrombie	.05
287	Louis Lipps	.15
288	John Stallworth	.15
289	Gary Anderson	.05
290	Keith Willis	.05
291	Mike Merriweather	.05
292	Lupe Sanchez	.05
293	Donnie Shell	.05
294	Eagles team (Keith Byars)	.30
295	Mike Reichenbach	.05
296	*Randall Cunningham*	6.00
297	*Keith Byars*	1.00
298	Mike Quick	.05
299	Kenny Jackson	.05
300	*John Teltschik*	.10
301	Reggie White (AP)	3.00
302	Ken Clarke	.05
303	Greg Brown	.05
304	Roynell Young	.05
305	*Andre Waters*	.50
306	Oilers team (Warren Moon)	.35
307	Warren Moon	2.25
308	Mike Rozier	.10
309	Drew Hill	.25
310	*Ernest Givins*	1.00
311	Lee Johnson	.10
312	Kent Hill	.05
313	*Dean Steinkuhler*	.30
314	Ray Childress	.60
315	*John Grimsley*	.25
316	Jesse Baker	.05
317	Lions team (Eric Hipple)	.07
318	*Chuck Long*	.12
319	James Jones	.05
320	Garry James	.05
321	Jeff Chadwick	.05
322	Leonard Thompson	.05
323	Pete Mandley	.05
324	Jimmie Giles	.05
325	Herman Hunter	.05
326	Keith Ferguson	.05
327	Devon Mitchell	.05
328	Cardinals team (Neil Lomax)	.07
329	Neil Lomax	.05
330	Stump Mitchell	.05
331	Earl Ferrell	.05
332	*Vai Sikahema*	.60
333	*Ron Wolfley*	.15
334	J.T. Smith	.05
335	Roy Green	.05
336	Al Baker	.05
337	Freddie Joe Nunn	.05
338	Cedrick Mack	.05
339	Chargers team (Gary Anderson)	.07
340	Dan Fouts	.50
341	Gary Anderson	.25
342	Wes Chandler	.05
343	Kellen Winslow	.20
344	Ralf Mojsiejenko	.05
345	Rolf Benirschke	.05
346	*Lee Williams*	.75
347	*Leslie O'Neal*	2.00
348	Billy Ray Smith	.05
349	Gill Byrd	.30
350	Packers team (Paul Ott Caruth)	.05
351	Randy Wright	.05
352	*Kenneth Davis*	.75
353	Gerry Ellis	.05
354	James Lofton	.50
355	Phillip Epps	.05
356	Walter Stanley	.25
357	Eddie Lee Ivery	.05
358	*Tim Harris*	.50
359	Mark Lee	.05
360	Mossy Cade	.05
361	Bills team (Jim Kelly)	1.25
362	*Jim Kelly*	6.00
363	Robb Riddick	.05
364	Greg Bell	.10
365	Andre Reed	1.00
366	*Pete Metzelaars*	.35
367	Sean McNanie	.05
368	Fred Smerlas	.05
369	Bruce Smith	1.00
370	Darryl Talley	.25
371	Charles Romes	.05
372	Colts team (Rohn Stark)	.07
373	Jack Trudeau	.25
374	Gary Hogeboom	.05
375	Randy McMillan	.05
376	Albert Bentley	.10
377	Matt Bouza	.05
378	*Bill Brooks*	2.00
379	Rohn Stark (AP)	.05
380	Chris Hinton	.05
381	Ray Donaldson	.05
382	*Jon Hand*	.25
383	Buccaneers team (James Wilder)	.07
384	Steve Young	5.00
385	James Wilder	.05
386	Frank Garcia	.05
387	Gerald Carter	.05
388	Phil Freeman	.05
389	Calvin Magee	.05
390	Donald Igwebuike	.05
391	David Logan	.05
392	Jeff Davis	.05
393	Chris Washington	.05
394	Checklist 1-132	.10
395	Checklist 133-264	.10
396	Checklist 265-396	.10

1987 Topps Box Bottoms

These cards can be distinguished from Topps' regular cards by the yellow borders around the photo on the front. Plus, the cards were on the bottom of 1987 Topps wax pack boxes, and would have to be cut out to measure the standard-size Topps cards. It's better to leave them intact. The cards also use a letter for numbering, instead of a number.

		MT
Complete Set (16):		10.00
Common Player:		.30
A	Mark Bavaro	.40
B	Todd Christensen	.50
C	Eric Dickerson	.65
D	John Elway	1.50
E	Rulon Jones	.30
F	Dan Marino	3.00
G	Karl Mecklenburg	.30
H	Joe Montana	3.00
I	Joe Morris	.50
J	Walter Payton	1.25
K	Jerry Rice	3.50
L	Phil Simms	.50
M	Lawrence Taylor	.60
N	Al Toon	.35
O	Curt Warner	.40
P	Reggie White	1.25

1987 Topps 1000 Yard Club

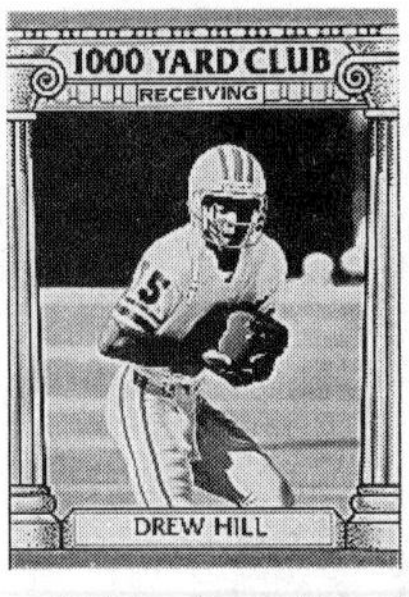

Printed on heavy white cardboard stock, 1,000 Yard Club cards were found inside wax packs of 1987 Topps football cards. Each card pictures a player who gained 1,000 or more yards rushing or receiving. Cards feature a parthenon design on the front in blue; backs are light blue and carry a game-by-game yardage summary for each player.

		MT
Complete Set (24):		4.50
Common Player:		.15
1	Eric Dickerson	.75
2	Jerry Rice	.75
3	Joe Morris	.30
4	Stanley Morgan	.15
5	Curt Warner	.20
6	Reuben Mayes	.25
7	Walter Payton	.90
8	Gerald Riggs	.20
9	Mark Duper	.15
10	Gary Clark	.15
11	George Rogers	.15
12	Al Toon	.25
13	Todd Christensen	.15
14	Mark Clayton	.15
15	Bill Brooks	.25
16	Drew Hill	.15
17	James Brooks	.15
18	Steve Largent	.60
19	Art Monk	.15
20	Ernest Givins	.20
21	Cris Collingsworth	.20
22	Wesley Walker	.15
23	J.T. Smith	.15
24	Mark Bavaro	.15

1987 Topps Stickers

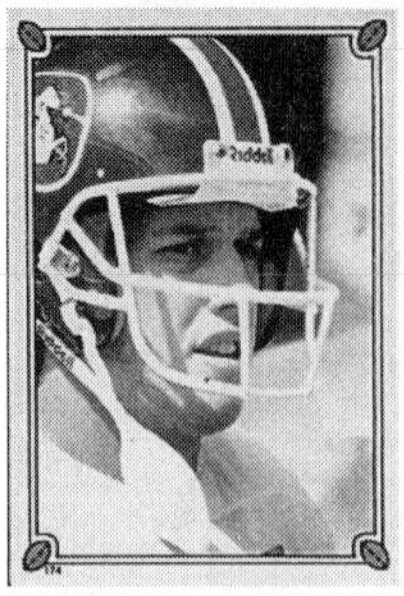

Each of these stickers is 2-1/8" x 3" and features a new design element from previous years' issues - four footballs are included in the frame around the picture on the front, one for each corner. A sticker number appears on both sides. All-Pro foils were again produced, as were stickers in pairs; they are matched up as indicated by the number in parenthesis. The backs have red ink on a white background. The album cover this time features artwork devoted to the New York Giants.

		MT
Complete Set (285):		15.00
Common Player:		.05
1	Phil Simms (Super Bowl MVP)	.40
2	Super Bowl XXI (upper left)	.15
3	Super Bowl XXI (upper right)	.15
4	Super Bowl XXI (lower left)	.15
5	Super Bowl XXI (lower right)	.15
6	Mike Singletary	.12
7	Jim Covert (156)	.50
8	Willie Gault (157)	.06
9	Jim McMahon (158)	.08
10	Doug Flutie (159)	1.00
11	Richard Dent (160)	.08
12	Kevin Butler (161)	.05
13	Wilber Marshall (162)	.08
14	Walter Payton	.60
15	Calvin Magee	.05
16	David Logan (165)	.05
17	Jeff Davis (166)	.05
18	Gerald Carter (167)	.05
19	James Wilder	.05
20	Chris Washington (168)	.05
21	Phil Freeman (169)	.05
22	Frank Garcia (170)	.05
23	Donald Igwebuike (171)	.05
24	Al (Bubba) Baker (175)	.08
25	Vai Sikhema (176)	.05
26	Leonard Smith (177)	.05
27	Ron Wolgley (178)	.05
28	J.T. Smith	.08
29	Roy Green (179)	.06
30	Cedric Mack (180)	.05
31	Neil Lomax (181)	.06
32	Stump Mitchell	.08
33	Herschel Walker	.50
34	Danny White (184)	.06
35	Michael Downs (185)	.05
36	Randy White (186)	.08
37	Eugene Lockhart (188)	.05
38	Mike Sherrard (189)	.20
39	Jim Jeffcoat (190)	.05
40	Tony Hill (191)	.06
41	Tony Dorsett	.35
42	Keith Byars (192)	.30
43	Andre Waters (193)	.06
44	Kenny Jackson (194)	.05
45	John Teltschick (195)	.05
46	Roynell Young (196)	.05
47	Randall Cunningham (197)	.60
48	Mike Reichenbach (198)	.05
49	Reggie White	.40
50	Mike Quick	.08
51	Bill Fralic (201)	.05
52	Sylvester Stamps (202)	.05
53	Bret Clark (203)	.05
54	William Andrews (204)	.05
55	Buddy Curry (205)	.05
56	Dave Archer (206)	.10
57	Rick Bryan (207)	.05
58	Gerald Riggs	.12
59	Charlie Brown	.05
60	Joe Montana	2.00
61	Jerry Rice	1.50
62	Carlton Williamson (212)	.05
63	Roger Craig (213)	.12
64	Ronnie Lott (214)	.15
65	Dwight Clark (215)	.15
66	Jeff Stover (216)	.05
67	Charles Haley (217)	.20
68	Ray Wersching (218)	.05
69	Lawrence Taylor	.30
70	Joe Morris	.12
71	Carl Banks (221)	.10
72	Mark Bavaro (222)	.06
73	Harry Carson (223)	.05
74	Phil Simms (224)	.10
75	Jim Burt (225)	.05
76	Brad Benson (226)	.05
77	Leonard Marshall (227)	.05
78	Jeff Chadwick	.05
79	Devon Mitchell (228)	.05
80	Chuck Long (229)	.06
81	Demetrious Johnson (230)	.05
82	Herman Hunter (231)	.05
83	Kieth Ferguson (232)	.05
84	Gary James (233)	.05
85	Leonard Thompson (234)	.05
86	James Jones	.08
87	Kenneth Davis	.35
88	Brian Noble (237)	.07
89	Al Del Greco (238)	.05
90	Mark Lee (239)	.05
91	Randy Wright	.25
92	Tim Harris (240)	.25
93	Phillip Epps (241)	.05
94	Walter Stanley (242)	.10
95	Eddie Lee Ivery (243)	.05
96	Doug Smith (247)	.05
97	Jerry Gray (248)	.05
98	Jim Everett (250)	.06
99	Jim Everett (250)	.60
100	Jackie Slater (251)	.06
101	Vince Newsome (252)	.10
102	LeRoy Irvin (253)	.10
103	Henry Ellard	.10
104	Eric Dickerson	.60
105	George Rogers (256)	.06
106	Darrell Green (257)	.07
107	Art Monk (258)	.07
108	Neal Olkewicz (260)	.05
109	Russ Grimm (261)	.05
110	Dexter Manley (262)	.05
111	Kelvin Bryant (263)	.05
112	Jay Schroeder	.15
113	Gary Clark	.15
114	Rickey Jackson	.08
115	Eric Martin (264)	.07
116	Dave Waymer (265)	.05
117	Morten Andersen (266)	.06
118	Bruce Clark (167)	.08
119	Hoby Brenner (269)	.07
120	Brian Hansen (270)	.05
121	Dave Wilson (271)	.05
122	Rueben Mayes	.10
123	Tommy Kramer	.08
124	Mark Malone (124)	.05
125	Anthony Carter (275)	.10
126	Keith Millard (276)	.08
127	Steve Jordan	.12
128	Chuck Nelson (277)	.06
129	Issiac Holt (278)	.05
130	Darrin Nelson (279)	.05
131	Gary Zimmerman (280)	.05
132	Mark Bavaro (146, All-Pro)	.10
133	Jim Covert (147, All-Pro)	.10
134	Eric Dickerson (148, All-Pro)	.35
135	Bill Fralic (149, All-Pro)	.10
136	Tony Franklin (150, All-Pro)	.10
137	Dennis Harrah (151, All-Pro)	.10
138	Dan Marino (152, All-Pro)	1.25
139	Joe Morris (153, All-Pro)	.25
140	Jerry Rice (154, All-Pro)	1.00
141	Cody Risien (155, All-Pro)	.10
142	Dwight Stephenson (282, All-Pro)	.12
143	Al Toon (283, All-Pro)	.20
144	Deron Cherry (284, All-Pro)	.12
145	Hanford Dixon (285, All-Pro)	.10
146	Darrell Green (132, All-Pro)	.15
147	Ronnie Lott (133, All-Pro)	.20
148	Bill Maas (134, All-Pro)	.10
149	Dexter Manley (135, All-Pro)	.10
150	Karl Mecklenburg (136, All-Pro)	.12
151	Mike Singletary (137, All-Pro)	.20
152	Rohn Stark (138, All-Pro)	.10
153	Lawrence Taylor (139, All-Pro)	.30
154	Andre Tippett (140, All-Pro)	.12
155	Reggie White (141, All-Pro)	.35
156	Boomer Esiason (7)	.15
157	Anthony Munoz (8)	.12
158	Tim McGee (9)	.20
159	Max Montoya (10)	.05
160	Jim Breech (11)	.05
161	Tim Krumrie (12)	.05
162	Eddie Brown (13)	.06
163	James Brooks	.10
164	Cris Collinsworth	.12
165	Charles Romes (16)	.05
166	Robb Riddick (17)	.05
167	Eugene Marve (18)	.05
168	Chris Burkett (20)	.10
169	Bruce Smith (21)	.12
170	Greg Bell (22)	.05
171	Pete Metzelaars (23)	.05
172	Jim Kelly	1.50
173	Andre Reed	.30
174	John Elway	.60
175	Mike Harden (24)	.05
176	Gerald Willhite (25)	.05
177	Rulon Jones (26)	.05
178	Ricky Hunley (27)	.05
179	Mark Jackson (29)	.05
180	Rich Karlis (30)	.05
181	Sammy Winder (31)	.08
182	Karl Mecklenburg	.08
183	Bernie Kosar	.35
184	Kevin Mack (34)	.05
185	Bob Golic (35)	.05
186	Ozzie Newsome (36)	.08
187	Brian Brennan	.05
188	Gerald McNeil (37)	.05
189	Hanford Dixon (38)	.05
190	Cody Risien (39)	.05
191	Chris Rockins (40)	.05
192	Gill Byrd (42)	.05
193	Kellen Winslow (43)	.08
194	Billy Ray Smith (44)	.05
195	Wes Chandler (45)	.08
196	Leslie O'Neal (46)	.25
197	Ralf Mojsiejenko (47)	.05
198	Lee Williams (48)	.20
199	Gary Anderson	.08
200	Dan Fouts	.30
201	Stephone Paige (51)	.08
202	Irv Eatman (52)	.05
203	Bill Kenney (53)	.05
204	Dino Hackett (54)	.08
205	Carlos Carson (55)	.05
206	Art Still (56)	.06
207	Lloyd Burruss (57)	.05
208	Deron Cherry	.08
209	Bill Maas	.05
210	Gary Hogeboom	.08
211	Rohn Stark	.05
212	Cliff Odom (62)	.05
213	Randy McMillan (63)	.05
214	Chris Hinton (64)	.05
215	Matt Bouza (65)	.05
216	Ray Donaldson (66)	.05
217	Bill Brooks (67)	.08
218	Jack Trudeau (68)	.06
219	Mark Duper	.15
220	Dan Marino	1.50
221	Dwight Stephenson (71)	.08
222	Mark Clayton (72)	.10
223	Roy Foster (73)	.05
224	John Offerdahl (74)	.20
225	Lorenzo Hampton (75)	.05
226	Reggie Roby (76)	.05
227	Tony Nathan (77)	.08
228	Johnny Hector (79)	.08
229	Wesley Walker (80)	.06
230	Mark Gastineau (81)	.10
231	Ken O'Brien (82)	.05
232	Dave Jennings (83)	.05
233	Mickey Shuler (84)	.05
234	Joe Klecko (85)	.05
235	Freeman McNeil	.10
236	Al Toon	.08
237	Warren Moon (88)	.35
238	Dean Steinkuhler (89)	.08
239	Mike Rozier (90)	.06
240	Ray Childress (92)	.08
241	Tony Zendejas (93)	.05
242	John Grimsley (94)	.05
243	Jesse Baker (95)	.05
244	Ernest Givins	.30
245	Drew Hill	.10
246	Tony Franklin	.05
247	Steve Grogan (96)	.06
248	Garin Veris (97)	.05
249	Stanley Morgan (98)	.06
250	Fred Morgan (98)	.05
251	Raymond Clayborn (100)	.07
252	Mosi Tatupu (101)	.05
253	Tony Eason (102)	.05
254	Andre Tippett	.08
255	Todd Christensen	.08
256	Howie Long (105)	.06
257	Marcus Allen (106)	.12
258	Vann McElroy (107)	.05
259	Dokie Williams	.05
260	Mike Haynes (108)	.08
261	Sean Jones	.10
262	Jim Plunkett (110)	.07
263	Chris Bahr (111)	.05
264	Dave Krieg (115)	.08
265	Jacob Green (116)	.05
266	Norm Johnson (117)	.05
267	Fredd Young (118)	.05
268	Steve Largent	.50
269	Dave Brown (119)	.05
270	Kenny Easley (120)	.05
271	Bobby Joe Edmonds (121)	.05
272	Curt Warner	.15
273	Mike Merriweather	.08
274	Mark Malone (124)	.05
275	Bryan Hinkle (125)	.05
276	Earnest Jackson (126)	.05
277	Keith Willis (128)	.05
278	Walter Abercrombie (129)	.06
279	Donnie Shell (130)	.08
280	John Stallworth (131)	.06
281	Louis Lipps	.08
282	Eric Dickerson (142)	.30
283	Dan Marino (143)	1.00
284	Tony Franklin (144)	.08
285	Todd Christensen	.12

1987 Topps American/United Kingdom

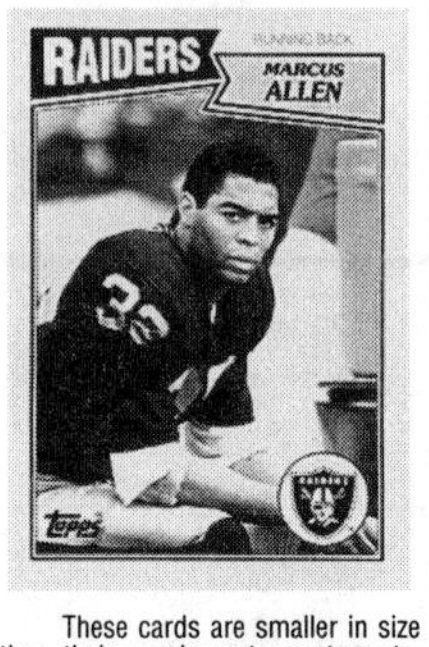

These cards are smaller in size than their regular set counterparts, measuring 2-1/8" x 3". The cards, which were made available in the United Kingdom, also have different photos. However, the basic design remains similar to Topps' 1986 regular issue. The back has a football term explained inside a football (Talking Football), plus a card number. A special collector's box was also produced to house the set. The box had a set checklist on its side. Cards 76-87 form a team action puzzle on one side and William Perry on the other.

		MT
Complete Set (88):		40.00
Common Player:		.10
1	Phil Simms	.65
2	Joe Morris	.35
3	Mark Bavaro	.25
4	Sean Landeta	.10
5	Lawrence Taylor	2.00
6	John Elway	4.00
7	Sammy Winder	.10
8	Rulon Jones	.10
9	Karl Mecklenburg	.15
10	Walter Payton	4.00
11	Dennis Gentry	.10
12	Kevin Butler	.10
13	Jim Covert	.10
14	Richard Dent	.35
15	Mike Singletary	.50
16	Jay Schroeder	.50
17	George Rogers	.25
18	Gary Clark	.50
19	Art Monk	.50
20	Dexter Manley	.10
21	Darrell Green	.35
22	Bernie Kosar	1.00
23	Cody Risien	.10
24	Hanford Dixon	.10
25	Tony Eason	.25
26	Stanley Morgan	.25
27	Tony Franklin	.10
28	Andre Tippett	.25
29	Joe Montana	8.00
30	Jerry Rice	8.00
31	Ronnie Lott	.75
32	Ken O'Brien	.25
33	Freeman McNeil	.15
34	Al Toon	.25
35	Wesley Walker	.25
36	Eric Dickerson	1.50
37	Dennis Harrah	.10
38	Bill Maas	.10
39	Deron Cherry	.25
40	Curt Warner	.20
41	Bobby Joe Edmonds	.25
42	Steve Largent	2.00
43	Boomer Esiason	2.00
44	James Brooks	.25
45	Cris Collinsworth	.25
46	Tim McGee	.35
47	Tommy Kramer	.25
48	Marcus Allen	1.00
49	Todd Christensen	.35
50	Sean Jones	.35
51	Dan Marino	8.00
52	Mark Duper	.25
53	Mark Clayton	.30
54	Dwight Stephenson	.25
55	Gerald Riggs	.25
56	Bill Fralic	.25
57	Tony Dorsett	1.50
58	Herschel Walker	1.50
59	Rueben Mayes	.25
60	Lupe Sanchez	.10
61	Reggie White	2.50
62	Warren Moon	3.00
63	Ernest Givins	1.50
64	Drew Hill	.25
65	Jeff Chadwick	.25
66	Herman Hunter	.10
67	Vai Sikhema	.25
68	J.T. Smith	.10
69	Dan Fouts	1.00
70	Lee Williams	.50
71	Randy Wright	.25
72	Jim Kelly	7.00
73	Bruce Smith	.75
74	Bill Brooks	.35
75	Rohn Stark	.10
76	Team Action	.10
77	Team Action	.10
78	Team Action	.10
79	Team Action	.10
80	Team Action	.10
81	Team Action	.10
82	Team Action	.10
83	Team Action	.10
84	Team Action	.10
85	Team Action	.10
86	Team Action	.10
87	Team Action	.10
88	Checklist Card	.10

1988 Topps

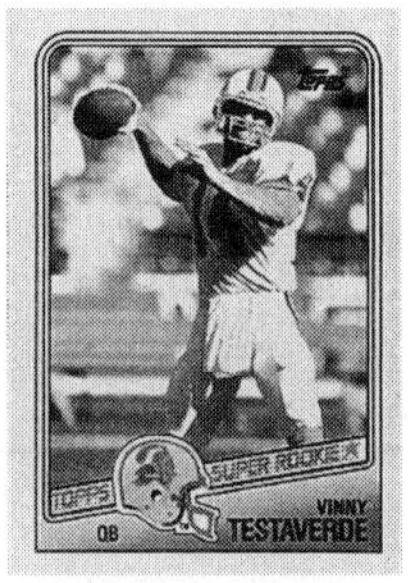

This set, issued in August 1988, was issued by teams in order of finish. These standard-size cards again showed the team helmets on front and All-Pro and Super Rookie designations (this was Topps' first year using Super Rookie labels). This set is noteworthy for the inclusion of Bo Jackson's rookie football card. (Key: AP - All Pro, SP - Super Rookie)

		MT
Complete Set (396):		12.00
Common Player:		.05
Wax Pack (15):		.85
Wax Box (36):		14.00
1	Super Bowl XXII	.10

2 Vencie Glenn .05
3 Steve Largent .15
4 Joe Montana .80
5 Walter Payton .30
6 Jerry Rice .70
7 Redskins team (Kelvin Bryant) .05
8 Doug Williams .05
9 George Rogers .05
10 Kelvin Bryant .05
11 Timmy Smith, Kent Hill (SR) .05
12 Art Monk, Ray Childress .25
13 Gary Clark .50
14 *Ricky Sanders* .50
15 Steve Cox .05
16 Joe Jacoby .05
17 Charles Mann .15
18 Dave Butz .05
19 Darrell Green (AP) .05
20 Dexter Manley .05
21 Barry Wilburn .05
22 Broncos team (Sammy Winder) .05
23 John Elway (AP) .75
24 Sammy Winder .05
25 Vance Johnson .20
26 *Mark Jackson* .70
27 *Ricky Nattiel* (SR) .12
28 Clarence Kay .05
29 Rich Karlis .05
30 Keith Bishop .05
31 Mike Horan .05
32 Rulon Jones .05
33 Karl Mecklenburg .12
34 Jim Ryan .05
35 Mark Haynes .05
36 Mike Harden .05
37 49ers team (Roger Craig) .05
38 Joe Montana 1.50
39 Steve Young 1.00
40 Roger Craig .20
41 *Tom Rathman* .50
42 Joe Cribbs .05
43 Jerry Rice (AP) 2.00
44 Mike Wilson .05
45 *Ron Heller* .15
46 Ray Wersching .05
47 Michael Carter .05
48 Dwaine Board .05
49 Michael Walter .05
50 Don Griffin .05
51 Ronnie Lott .30
52 Charlie Haley .30
53 Dana McLemore .05
54 Saints Team (Bobby Hebert) .05
55 Bobby Hebert .30
56 Rueben Mayes .05
57 *Dalton Hilliard* .25
58 Eric Martin .30
59 John Tice .10
60 Brad Edelman .05
61 Morten Andersen (AP) .15
62 Brian Hansen .05
63 *Mel Gray* .60
64 Rickey Jackson .30
65 *Sam Mills* .50
66 *Pat Swilling* .50
67 Dave Waymer .05
68 Bears Team (Willie Gault) .05
69 Jim McMahon .15
70 *Mike Tomczak* .25
71 *Neal Anderson* .75
72 Willie Gault .10
73 Dennis Gentry .05
74 Dennis McKinnon .05
75 Kevin Butler .05
76 Jim Covert .05
77 Jay Hilgenberg .05
78 Steve McMichael .05
79 William Perry .05
80 Richard Dent .20
81 Ron Rivera .05
82 Mike Singletary (AP) .20
83 Dan Hampton .10
84 Dave Duerson .05
85 Browns team (Bernie Kosar) .05
86 Bernie Kosar .05
87 Earnest Byner .40
88 Kevin Mack .10
89 *Webster Slaughter* .75
90 Gerald McNeil .05
91 Brian Brennan .05
92 Ozzie Newsome .20
93 Cody Risien .05
94 Bob Golic .05
95 Carl Hairston .05
96 *Mike Johnson* .20
97 Clay Matthews .05
98 Frank Minnifield .05
99 Hanford Dixon (AP) .05
100 Dave Puzzuoli .05
101 *Felix Wright* .15
102 Oilers team (Warren Moon) .20
103 Warren Moon .75
104 Mike Rozier .05
105 *Alonzo Highsmith* (SR) .15
106 Drew Hill .20
107 Ernest Givins .40
108 *Curtis Duncan* .50
109 *Tony Zendejas* .12
110 Mike Munchak (AP) .12
113 *Al Smith* .35
114 Keith Bostic .05
115 Jeff Donaldson .05
116 Colts team (Eric Dickerson) .15
117 Jack Trudeau .05
118 Eric Dickerson (AP) .30
119 Albert Bentley .05
120 Matt Bouza .05
121 Bill Brooks .35
122 Dean Biasucci .12
123 Chris Hinton .05
124 Ray Donaldson .05
125 *Ron Solt* .10
126 Donnell Thompson .05
127 Barry Krauss .05
128 Duane Bickett .10
129 *Mike Prior* .15
130 Seahawks team (Curt Warner) .05
131 Dave Krieg .15
132 Curt Warner .05
133 John L. Williams .25
134 Bobby Joe Edmonds .05
135 Steve Largent .30
136 Raymond Butler .05
137 Norm Johnson .05
138 Ruben Rodriguez .05
139 Blair Bush .05
140 Jacob Green .05
141 Joe Nash .05
142 Jeff Bryant .05
143 Fredd Young (AP) .05
144 *Brian Bosworth* (SR) .15
145 Kenny Easley (AP) .05
146 Vikings team (Tommy Kramer) .05
147 *Wade Wilson* .50
148 Tommy Kramer .05
149 Darrin Nelson .05
150 *D.J. Dozier* (SR) .12
151 Anthony Carter .25
152 Leo Lewis .05
153 Steve Jordan .20
154 Gary Zimmerman .05
155 Chuck Nelson .05
156 *Henry Thomas* (SR) .50
157 *Chris Doleman* .60
158 *Scott Studwell* .12
159 *Jesse Solomon* .10
160 Joey Browner (AP) .15
161 Neal Guggemos .05
162 Steelers team (Louis Lipps) .05
163 Mark Malone .05
164 Walter Abercrombie .05
165 Earnest Jackson .05
166 Frank Pollard .05
167 *Dwight Stone* .30
168 Gary Anderson .05
169 *Harry Newsome* .10
170 Keith Willis .05
171 Keith Gray .05
172 *David Little* .12
173 Mike Merriweather .05
174 Dwayne Woodruff .05
175 Patriots team (Irving Fryar) .05
176 Steve Grogan .10
177 Tony Eason .05
178 Tony Collins .05
179 Mosi Tatupu .05
180 Stanley Morgan .05
181 Irving Fryar .30
182 Stephen Starring .05
183 Tony Franklin .05
184 Rich Camarillo .05
185 Garin Veris .05
186 Andre Tippett (AP) .05
187 Ronnie Lippett .05
188 Fred Marion .05
189 Dolphins team (Dan Marino) .50
190 Dan Marino 1.50
191 *Troy Stradford* (SR) .10
192 Lorenzo Hampton .05
193 Mark Duper .10
194 Mark Clayton .25
195 Reggie Roby .05
196 Dwight Stephenson (AP) .05
197 T.J. Turner .05
198 John Bosa (SR) .05
199 Jackie Shipp .05
200 John Offerdahl .05
201 Mark Brown .05
202 Paul Lankford .05
203 Chargers Team (Kellen Winslow) .05
204 Tim Spencer .05
205 Gary Anderson .10
206 Curtis Adams .05
207 Lionel James .05
208 Chip Banks .05
209 Kellen Winslow .15
210 Ralf Mojsiejenko .05
211 Jim Lachey .15
212 Lee Williams .15
213 Billy Ray Smith .05
214 *Vencie Glenn* .25
215 NFL Passing Leaders (Bernie Kosar, Joe Montana) .50
216 NFL Receiving Leaders (Al Toon, J.T. Smith) .05
217 NFL Rushing Leaders (Charles White, Eric Dickerson) .15
218 NFL Scoring Leaders (Jim Breech, Jerry Rice) .30
219 NFL Interception Leaders (Keith Bostic, Mark Kelso, Mike Prior, Barry Wilburn) .05
220 Bills team (Jim Kelly) .30
221 Jim Kelly 1.00
222 *Ronnie Harmon* .50
223 Robb Riddick .05
224 Andre Reed .50
225 *Chris Burkett* .50
226 Pete Metzelaars .05
227 Bruce Smith (AP) .50
228 Darryl Talley .12
229 Eugene Marve .05
230 *Cornelius Bennett* 1.00
231 *Mark Kelso* .20
232 *Shane Conlan* (SR) .50
233 Eagles team (Randall Cunningham) .25
234 Randall Cunningham .50
235 Keith Byars .50
236 Anthony Toney .05
237 Mike Quick .05
238 Kenny Jackson .05
239 John Spagnola .05
240 Paul McFadden .05
241 Reggie White (AP) .60
242 Ken Clarke .05
243 Mike Pitts .05
244 *Clyde Simmons* .50
245 *Seth Joyner* .85
246 Andre Waters .12
247 *Jerome Brown* (SR) .30
248 Cardinals team (Stump Mitchell) .05
249 Neil Lomax .05
250 Stump Mitchell .05
251 Earl Ferrell .05
252 Vai Sikahema .05
253 J.T. Smith (AP) .05
254 Roy Green .10
255 Robert Awalt (SR) .05
256 Freddie Joe Nunn .05
257 *Leonard Smith* .10
258 Travis Curtis .05
259 Cowboys team (Herschel Walker) .15
260 Danny White .10
261 Herschel Walker .25
262 Tony Dorsett .20
263 Doug Cosbie .05
264 *Roger Ruzek* .12
265 Darryl Clack .05
266 Ed "Too Tall" Jones .15
267 Jim Jeffcoat .05
268 Everson Walls .05
269 Bill Bates .05
270 Michael Downs .05
271 Giants team (Mark Bavaro) .05
272 Phil Simms .30
273 Joe Morris .05
274 Lee Rouson .05
275 George Adams .05
276 Lionel Manuel .05
277 Mark Bavaro (AP) .05
278 Raul Allegre .05
279 Sean Landeta .05
280 Erik Howard .05
281 Leonard Marshall .05
282 Carl Banks (AP) .15
283 Pepper Johnson .15
284 Harry Carson .10
285 Lawrence Taylor .25
286 Terry Kinard .05
287 Rams team (Jim Everett) .15
288 Jim Everett .40
289 Charles White (AP) .05
290 Ron Brown .05
291 Henry Ellard .25
292 Mike Lansford .05
293 Dale Hatcher .05
294 Doug Smith .05
295 Jackie Slater (AP) .05
296 Jim Collins .05
297 Jerry Gray .05
298 LeRoy Irvin .05
299 Nolan Cromwell .05
300 *Kevin Greene* 1.00
301 Jets team (Ken O'Brien) .05
302 Ken O'Brien .15
303 Freeman McNeil .05
304 Johnny Hector .05
305 Al Toon .20
306 JoJo Townsell .05
307 Mickey Shuler .05
308 Pat Leahy .05
309 Roger Vick .05
310 Alex Gordon .05
311 Troy Benson .05
312 Bob Crable .05
313 Harry Hamilton .05
314 Packers team (Phil Epps) .05
315 Randy Wright .05
316 Kenneth Davis .35
317 Phillip Epps .05
318 Walter Stanley .05
319 Frankie Neal .05
320 Don Bracken .05
321 *Brian Noble* .15
322 *Johnny Holland* (SR) .15
323 Tim Harris .35
324 Mark Murphy .05
325 Raiders team (Bo Jackson) .50
326 Marc Wilson .05
327 *Bo Jackson* (SR) 2.00
328 Marcus Allen .30
329 James Lofton .20
330 Todd Christensen .05
331 Chris Bahr .05
332 Stan Talley .05
333 Howie Long .10
334 Sean Jones .05
335 Matt Millen .05
336 Stacey Toran .05
337 Vann McElroy .05
338 Greg Townsend .15
339 Bengals team (Boomer Esiason) .15
340 Boomer Esiason .50
341 Larry Kinnebrew .05
342 Stanford Jennings .05
343 Eddie Brown .05
344 Jim Breech .05
345 Anthony Munoz (AP) .12
346 Scott Fulhage .05
347 *Tim Krumrie* .20
348 Reggie Williams .05
349 *David Fulcher* .30
350 Buccaneers team (James Wilder) .05
351 Frank Garcia .05
352 *Vinny Testaverde* (SR) 4.00
353 James Wilder .05
354 Jeff Smith .05
355 Gerald Carter .05
356 Calvin Magee .05
357 Donald Igwebuike .05
358 Ron Holmes .05
359 Chris Washington .05
360 Ervin Randle .05
361 Chiefs team (Bill Kenney) .05
362 Bill Kenney .05
363 *Christian Okoye* (SR) .25
364 Paul Palmer .05
365 Stephone Paige .12
366 Carlos Carson .05
367 Kelly Goodburn .05
368 Bill Maas (AP) .05
369 Mike Bell .05
370 *Dino Hackett* .15
371 Deron Cherry .05
372 Lions team (James Jones) .05
373 Chuck Long .05
374 Garry James .05
375 James Jones .05
376 Pete Mandley .05
377 Gary Lee (SR) .05
378 Ed Murray .05
379 Jim Arnold .05
380 Dennis Gibson (SR) .05
381 Mike Cofer .05
382 James Griffin .05
383 Falcons team (Gerald Riggs) .05
384 Scott Campbell .05
385 Gerald Riggs .05
386 Floyd Dixon .05
387 Rick Donnelly (AP) .05
388 Bill Fralic (AP) .05
389 Major Everett .05
390 Mike Gann .05
391 *Tony Casillas* .25
392 Rick Bryan .05
393 John Rade .05
394 Checklist 1-132 .05
395 Checklist 133-264 .05
396 Checklist 265-396 .05

1988 Topps Box Bottoms

The bottoms of 1988 Topps wax pack boxes had these cards, which honor award-winning achievements by professional players while they were in college. Two players are featured on each card. The cards are numbered on the back using a letter and include a summary of the player's collegiate accomplishment. The cards are standard size.

		MT
Complete Set (16):		5.00
Common Player:		.20
A	Vinny Testaverde	.50
B	Dean Steinkuhler	.20
C	George Rogers	.20
D	Kenneth Sims	.20
E	Cornelius Bennett	.50
F	Bo Jackson	1.00
G	Ross Browner	.35
H	Doug Flutie	1.00
I	Herschel Walker	.50
J	Jim Plunkett	.50
K	Charles White	.25
L	Brad Budde	.20
M	Marcus Allen	.50
N	Mike Rozier	.25
O	Tony Dorsett	.75
P	Checklist	.20

1988 Topps 1000 Yard Club

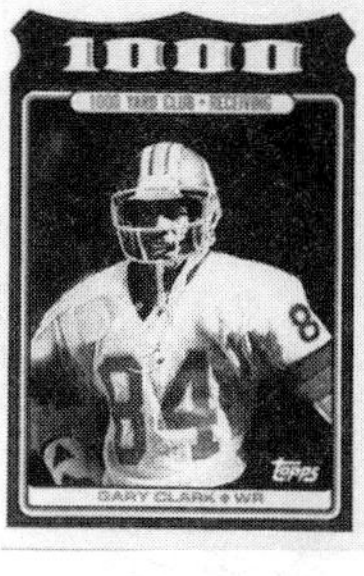

One card from this 28-card set was again issued in a wax pack of Topps football cards. The standard-size glossy cards on thick white cardboard stock feature "1000" in bold green border around a full-color action photo. Backs feature a game-by-game recap of the runner or receiver's yardage.

		MT
Complete Set (28):		4.50
Common Player:		.10
1	Charles White	.10
2	Eric Dickerson	.75
3	J.T. Smith	.10
4	Jerry Rice	.75
5	Gary Clark	.10
6	Carlos Carson	.10
7	Drew Hill	.10
8	Curt Warner	.10
9	Al Toon	.10
10	Mike Rozier	.10
11	Ernest Givins	.10
12	Anthony Carter	.10
13	Reuben Mayes	.10
14	Steve Largent	.75
15	Herschel Walker	.75
16	James Lofton	.10
17	Gerald Riggs	.10
18	Mark Bavaro	.10
19	Roger Craig	.50
20	Webster Slaughter	.10
21	Henry Ellard	.10
22	Mike Quick	.10
23	Stump Mitchell	.10
24	Eric Martin	.10
25	Mark Clayton	.10
26	Chris Burkett	.10
27	Marcus Allen	.30
28	Andre Reed	.10

1988 Topps Stickers

These stickers can be distinguished from Topps' previous efforts by the two frames used on the front to border the color photograph. An inner frame of yellow footballs is adjacent to an outer red frame of the picture. Each sticker measures 2-1/8" x 3" and is numbered on both sides. All-Pro stickers were produced as foil stickers again, and pairs of stickers were also made, as indicated by parentheses. Stickers 2-5 form a puzzle of Doug Williams featured in action during Super Bowl XXII. Williams is also featured on the back of the album cover which was produced to hold the stickers; the Redskins in action are featured on the front.

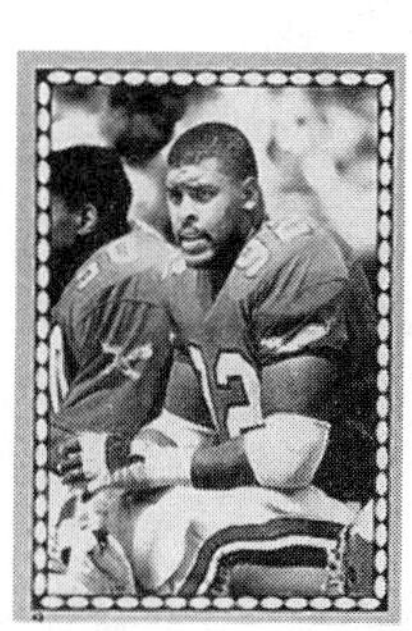

		MT
Complete Set (285):		15.00
Common Player:		.05
1	Doug Williams (Super Bowl XXII MVP)	.20
2	Super Bowl XXII	.08
3	Super Bowl XXII	.08
4	Super Bowl XXII	.08
5	Super Bowl XXII	.08
6	Neal Anderson (234)	.25
7	Willie Gault (224)	.08
8	Dennis Gentry (219)	.05
9	Dave Duerson (197)	.05
10	Steve McMichael (266)	.05
11	Dennis McKinnon (230)	.05
12	Mike Singletary (209)	.08
13	Jim McMahon	.12
14	Richard Dent	.10
15	Vinny Testaverde (167)	.20
16	Gerald Carter (187)	.05
17	Jeff Smith (185)	.05
18	Chris Washington (212)	.05
19	Bobby Futrell (231)	.05
20	Calvin Magee (182)	.05
21	Ron Holmes (169)	.05
22	Ervin Randle	.05
23	James Wilder	.08
24	Neil Lomax	.08
25	Robert Awalt (161)	.05
26	Leonard Smith (177)	.05
27	Stump Mitchell (178)	.05
28	Vai Sikahema (280)	.06
29	Freddie Joe Nunn (222)	.05
30	Earl Ferrell (223)	.05
31	Roy Green (157)	.10
32	J.T. Smith	.10
33	Michael Downs	.05
34	Herschel Walker	.30
35	Roger Ruzek (269)	.05
36	Ed "Too Tall" Jones (245)	.07
37	Everson Walls (252)	.05
38	Bill Bates (213)	.05
39	Doug Cosbie (179)	.05
40	Eugene Lockhart (186)	.05
41	Danny White (205)	.07
42	Randall Cunningham	.40
43	Reggie White	.30
44	Anthony Toney (256)	.05
45	Mike Quick (248)	.08
46	John Spagnola (235)	.05
47	Clyde Simmons (275)	.20
48	Andre Waters (261)	.05
49	Keith Byars (265)	.08
50	Jerome Brown (240)	.15
51	John Rade	.05
52	Rick Donnelly	.05
53	Scott Campbell (160)	.05
54	Floyd Dixon (246)	.05
55	Gerald Riggs (236)	.06
56	Bill Fralic (267)	.08
57	Mike Gann (165)	.05
58	Tony Casillas (168)	.15
59	Rick Bryan (257)	.05
60	Jerry Rice	1.00
61	Ronnie Lott	.25
62	Ray Wersching (220)	.05
63	Charles Haley (281)	.06
64	Joe Montana (190)	.75
65	Joe Cribbs (221)	.05
66	Mike Wilson (203)	.05
67	Roger Craig (251)	.12
68	Michael Walter (162)	.05
69	Mark Bavaro	.08
70	Carl Banks	.10
71	George Adams (274)	.03
72	Phil Simms (216)	.15
73	Lawrence Taylor (181)	.12
74	Joe Morris (198)	.06
75	Lionel Manuel (204)	.05
76	Sean Landeta (210)	.05
77	Harry Carson (159)	.05
78	Chuck Long (166)	.05
79	James Jones (159)	.08
80	Gary James (158)	.05
81	Gary Lee (176)	.05
82	Jim Arnold (260)	.05
83	Dennis Gibson (232)	.05
84	Mike Cofer (242)	.05
85	Pete Mandley	.05
86	James Griffin	.05
87	Randy Wright (206)	.05
88	Phillip Epps (191)	.05
89	Brian Noble (249)	.10
90	Johnny Holland (258)	.10
91	Dave Brown (156)	.05
92	Brent Fullwood (207)	.05
93	Kenneth Davis (194)	.08
94	Tim Harris	.15
95	Walter Stanley	.08
96	Charles White	.15
97	Jackie Slater	.08
98	Jim Everett (271)	.12
99	Mike Lansford (200)	.05
100	Henry Ellard (199)	.06
101	Dale Hatcher (170)	.05
102	Jim Collins (268)	.05
103	Jerry Gray (214)	.05
104	LeRoy Irvin (276)	.05
105	Darrell Green	.12
106	Doug Williams	.10
107	Gary Clark (247)	.10
108	Charles Mann (171)	.10
109	Art Monk (270)	.12
110	Barry Wilburn (196)	.05
111	Alvin Walton (188)	.05
112	Dexter Manley (233)	.05
113	Kelvin Bryant (180)	.04
114	Morten Andersen	.10
115	Rueben Mayes (244)	.06
116	Brian Hansen (279)	.05
117	Dalton Hilliard (241)	.10
118	Rickey Jackson (195)	.06
119	Eric Martin (189)	.06
120	Mel Gray (278)	.05
121	Bobby Hebert (215)	.08
122	Pat Swilling	.40
123	Anthony Carter	.12
124	Wade Wilson (225)	.20
125	Darrin Nelson (250)	.05
126	D.J. Dozier (239)	.06
127	Chris Doleman	.30
128	Henry Thomas (255)	.05
129	Jesse Solomon (211)	.05
130	Neal Guggemos (243)	.05
131	Joey Browner (208)	.06
132	Carl Banks (152, All-Pro)	.10
133	Joey Browner (145, All-Pro)	.10
134	Hanford Dixon (149, All-Pro)	.10
135	Rick Donnelly (147, All-Pro)	.10
136	Kenny Easley (155, All-Pro)	.15
137	Darrell Green (151, All-Pro)	.15
138	Bill Maas (148, All-Pro)	.10
139	Mike Singletary (153, All-Pro)	.15
140	Bruce Smith (154, All-Pro)	.20
141	Andre Tippett (146, All-Pro)	.10
142	Reggie White (150, All-Pro)	.20
143	Fredd Young (144, All-Pro)	.10
144	Morten Andersen (143, All-Pro)	.10
145	Mark Bavaro (133, All-Pro)	.10
146	Eric Dickerson (141, All-Pro)	.30
147	John Elway (134, All-Pro)	.75
148	Bill Fralic (138, All-Pro)	.10
149	Mike Munchak (135, All-Pro)	.10
150	Anthony Munoz (142, All-Pro)	.15
151	Jerry Rice (137, All-Pro)	1.00
152	Jackie Slater (132, All-Pro)	.12
153	J.T. Smith (139, All-Pro)	.10
154	Dwight Stephenson (140, All-Pro)	.12
155	Charles White (136, All-Pro)	.12
156	Larry Kinnebrew (91)	.05
157	Stanford Jennings (31)	.05
158	Eddie Brown (80)	.05
159	Scott Fulhage (77)	.05
160	Boomer Esiason (53)	.12
161	Tim Krumrie (25)	.05
162	Anthony Munoz (68)	.08
163	Jim Breech	.05
164	Reggie Williams	.08
165	Andre Reed (57)	.20
166	Cornelius Bennett (78)	.30
167	Ronnie Harmon (15)	.15
168	Shane Conlan (58)	.15
169	Chris Burkett (21)	.06
170	Mark Kelso (101)	.08
171	Robb Riddick (108)	.05
172	Bruce Smith	.15
173	Jim Kelly	.60
174	Jim Ryan	.06
175	John Elway	.60
176	Sammy Winder (81)	.05
177	Karl Mecklenburg (26)	.05
178	Mark Haynes (27)	.05
179	Rulon Jones (39)	.05
180	Ricky Nattiel (113)	.08
181	Vance Johnson (73)	.05
182	Mike Harden (20)	.05
183	Frank Minnifield	.05
184	Bernie Kosar	.25
185	Earnest Byner (17)	.12
186	Webster Slaughter (40)	.15
187	Brian Brennan (16)	.05
188	Carl Hairston (111)	.05
189	Mike Johnson (119)	.05
190	Clay Matthews (64)	.06
191	Kevin Mack (88)	.06
192	Kellen Winslow	.12
193	Billy Ray Smith	.08
194	Gary Anderson (93)	.06
195	Chip Banks (118)	.05
196	Elvis Patterson (110)	.05
197	Lee Williams (9)	.07
198	Curtis Adams (74)	.05
199	Vencie Glenn (100)	.05
200	Ralf Mojsiejenko (99)	.05
201	Carlos Carson	.05
202	Bill Maas	.05
203	Christian Okoye (66)	.15
204	Deron Cherry (75)	.08
205	Dino Hackett (41)	.05
206	Mike Bell (87)	.05
207	Stephone Paige (92)	.06
208	Bill Kenney (131)	.06
209	Paul Palmer (12)	.05
210	Jack Trudeau (76)	.06
211	Albert Bentley (129)	.06
212	Bill Brooks (18)	.06
213	Dean Biasucci (38)	.05
214	Cliff Odom (103)	.05
215	Barry Krauss (121)	.05
216	Mike Prior (72)	.06
217	Eric Dickerson	.35
218	Duane Bickett	.08
219	Dwight Stephenson (8)	.08
220	John Offerdahl (62)	.10
221	Troy Stradford (65)	.06
222	John Bosa (29)	.04
223	Jackie Shipp (30)	.05
224	Paul Lankford (7)	.05
225	Mark Duper (124)	.08
226	Dan Marino	1.50
227	Mark Clayton	.15
228	Bob Crable	.05
229	Al Toon	.08
230	Freeman McNeil (11)	.06

231 Johnny Hector (19) .05
232 Pat Leahy (83) .05
233 Ken O'Brien (112) .05
234 Alex Gordon (6) .05
235 Harry Hamilton (46) .05
236 Mickey Shuler (55) .05
237 Mike Rozier .08
238 Al Smith .15
239 Ernest Givins (126) .15
240 Warren Moon (50) .25
241 Drew Hill (117) .10
242 Alonzo Highsmith (84) .15
243 Mike Munchak (130) .06
244 Keith Bostic (115) .05
245 Sean Jones (36) .08
246 Stanley Morgan (54) .06
247 Garin Veris (107) .05
248 Stephen Starring (45) .05
249 Steve Grogan (89) .06
250 Irving Fryar (125) .10
251 Rich Camarillo (67) .05
252 Ronnie Lippett (37) .05
253 Andre Tippett .08
254 Fred Marion .05
255 Howie Long (128) .10
256 James Lofton (44) .12
257 Vance Mueller (59) .05
258 Jerry Robinson (90) .05
259 Todd Christensen (79) .06
260 Vann McElroy (82) .05
261 Greg Townsend (48) .10
262 Bo Jackson .85
263 Marcus Allen .30
264 Curt Warner .10
265 Jacob Green (49) .06
266 Norm Johnson (10) .05
267 Brian Bosworth (56) .05
268 Bobby Joe Edmonds (102) .05
269 Dave Krieg (35) .07
270 Kenny Easley (109) .06
271 Steve Largent (98) .30
272 Fredd Young .05
273 David Little .05
274 Frank Pollard (71) .05
275 Dwight Stone (47) .08
276 Mike Merriweather (104) .06
277 Earnest Jackson .05
278 Delton Hall (120) .05
279 Gary Anderson (116) .05
280 Harry Newsome (28) .08
281 Dwayne Woodruff (63) .05
282 J.T. Smith (283) .05
283 Charles White (282) .05
284 Reggie White (285) .15
285 Morten Andersen (284) .10

1988 Topps Sticker Backs

These cards were left after collectors would remove the 1988 Topps stickers from their card. Each card measures 2-1/8" x 3" and features a prominent offensive player. The sticker has "Superstar" written at the top, above the color player photo. His name and card number appear at the bottom in a stat box, using 1 of 67, etc.

MT
Complete Set (67): 5.00
Common Player: .05
1 Doug Williams .10
2 Gary Clark .15
3 John Elway .50
4 Sammy Winder .05
5 Vance Johnson .07
6 Joe Montana 1.50
7 Roger Craig .15
8 Jerry Rice 1.00
9 Rueben Mayes .05
10 Eric Martin .10
11 Neal Anderson .30
12 Willie Gault .10
13 Bernie Kosar .25
14 Kevin Mack .05
15 Webster Slaughter .15
16 Warren Moon .40
17 Mike Rozier .10
18 Drew Hill .10
19 Eric Dickerson .30
20 Bill Brooks .05
21 Curt Warner .15
22 Steve Largent .40
23 Darrin Nelson .05
24 Anthony Carter .15
25 Earnest Jackson .05
26 Weegie Thompson .05
27 Stephen Starring .05
28 Stanley Morgan .10
29 Dan Marino 1.50
30 Troy Stadford .10
31 Mark Clayton .15
32 Curtis Adams .05
33 Kellen Winslow .15
34 Jim Kelly .60
35 Ronnie Harmon .25
36 Chris Burkett .15
37 Randall Cunningham .35
38 Anthony Toney .05
39 Mike Quick .10
40 Neil Lomax .10
41 Stump Mitchell .10
42 J.T. Smith .10
43 Herschel Walker .25
44 Herschel Walker .25
45 Joe Morris .12
46 Mark Bavaro .12
47 Charles White .15
48 Henry Ellard .10
49 Ken O'Brien .10
50 Freeman McNeil .10
51 Al Toon .12
52 Kenneth Davis .10
53 Walter Stanley .10
54 Marcus Allen .30
55 James Lofton .25
56 Boomer Esiason .20
57 Larry Kinnebrew .05
58 Eddie Brown .10
59 James Wilder .07
60 Gerald Carter .05
61 Christian Okoye .20
62 Carlos Carson .05
63 James Jones .05
64 Pete Mandley .05
65 Gerald Riggs .10
66 Floyd Dixon .05
67 Checklist Card .10

1989 Topps

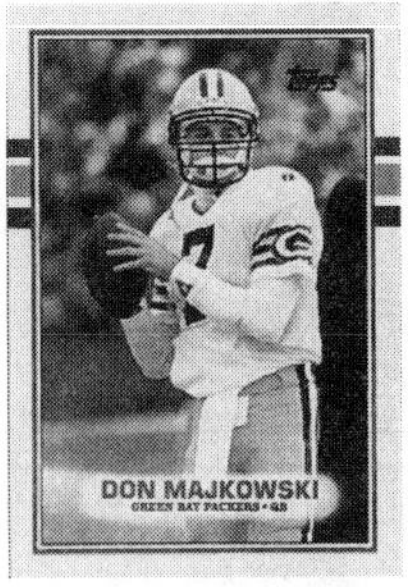

Topps released its seventh straight 396-card set in late August 1989. Cards are standard size, with white borders and a multicolored stripe about three-quarters from the bottom. Player names and teams are at the bottom of the card in an opaque circle. Card backs feature a dark green on yellow design. There are a few errors in the set: Card #24, Eddie Brown, lists his birthday as 12/18 and it's actually 12/17; card #27, Boomer Esiason, has him a native of East Islip, when it should be West Islip; the front of card #56, Mark Kelso, reads "BILL" instead of "BILLS"; on Jay Hilgenberg's card, a "g" is missing from "Chicago" on the card front. The back of Mark Rypien's card (#253) lists 14 as his 1988 completion total, while it should read 114. Card #125, Robert Delpino, correctly shows his team designation as "Rams" on the front, but lists "Los Angeles Raiders" on the back; card #247, Karl Mecklenberg, lists him as being drafted in the second round when it should be the 12th. Rodney Holman's card also features a problem with the card front: there are six different variations of "BENGALS". One has a small space between the "B" and "E"; the second has the "B" a little above the rest of the line of type; the third has it just a little below; the fourth shows just the "B" with no other letters behind it; another shows the "B" partially superimposed over the "E"; another shows "CINCINNATI B" without the rest of "Bengals"; and the last one is the correct version. Rookies in this set include Sterling Sharpe, Don Majkowski, Ickey Woods, John Stephens, John Taylor, Erik McMillan, Keith Jackson and Tom Newberry. (Key: AP - All Pro, SR - Super Rookie)

MT
Complete Set (396): 15.00
Common Player: .05
Wax Pack (15+1): .60
Wax Box (36): 12.50
1 Super Bowl XXIII .50
2 Tim Brown .70
3 Eric Dickerson .12
4 Steve Largent .12
5 Dan Marino .60
6 49ers Team (Joe Montana) .30
7 Jerry Rice (AP) 1.25
8 Roger Craig (AP) .05
9 Ronnie Lott .15
10 Michael Carter .05
11 Charles Haley .05
12 Joe Montana 1.50
13 *John Taylor* 1.00
14 Michael Walter .05
15 *Mike Cofer* .10
16 Tom Rathman .05
17 *Danny Stubbs* .12
18 Keena Turner .05
19 Tim McKyer .05
20 Larry Roberts .05
21 Jeff Fuller .05
22 Bubba Paris .05
23 Bengals Team (Boomer Esiason) .05
24 Eddie Brown (AP) .05
25 Boomer Esiason (AP) .30
26 Tim Krumrie (AP) .05
27 Ickey Woods (SR) .05
28 Anthony Munoz .05
29 Tim McGee .05
30 Max Montoya .05
31 David Grant .05
32 *Rodney Holman* .25
33 David Fulcher .05
34 Jim Skow .05
35 James Brooks .05
36 Reggie Williams .05
37 *Eric Thomas* .10
38 Stanford Jennings .05
39 Jim Breech .05
40 Bills Team (Jim Kelly) .15
41 Shane Conlan (AP) .15
42 Scott Norwood (AP) .05
43 Cornelius Bennett .30
44 Bruce Smith (AP) .15
45 *Thurman Thomas* (SR) 2.00
46 Jim Kelly .50
47 John Kidd .05
48 *Kent Hull* .15
49 Art Still .05
50 Fred Smerlas .05
51 Derrick Burroughs .05
52 Andre Reed .30
53 Robb Riddick .05
54 Chris Burkett .05
55 Ronnie Harmon .20
56 Mark Kelso .05
57 Bears Team (Thomas Sanders) .05
58 Mike Singletary (AP) .10
59 Jay Hilgenberg (AP) .05
60 Richard Dent .05
61 Ron Rivera .05
62 Jim McMahon .05
63 Mike Tomczak .12
64 Neal Anderson .30
65 Dennis Gentry .05
66 Dan Hampton .05
67 David Tate .05
68 *Thomas Sanders* .10
69 Steve McMichael .05
70 Dennis McKinnon .05
71 *Brad Muster* .20
72 *Vestee Jackson* .10
73 Dave Duerson .05
74 Vikings Team (Keith Millard) .05
75 Joey Browner (AP) .05
76 *Carl Lee* (AP) .10
77 Gary Zimmerman (AP) .05
78 *Hassan Jones* .10
79 Anthony Carter .05
80 Ray Berry .05
81 Steve Jordan .05
82 Issiac Holt .05
83 Wade Wilson .05
84 Chris Doleman .20
85 Alfred Anderson .05
86 Keith Millard .05
87 Darrin Nelson .05
88 D.J. Dozier .05
89 Scott Studwell .05
90 Oilers Team (Tony Zendejas) .05
91 *Bruce Matthews* (AP) .30
92 Curtis Duncan .20
93 Warren Moon .40
94 *Johnny Meads* .10
95 Drew Hill .05
96 Alonzo Highsmith .05
97 Mike Munchak .05
98 Mike Rozier .05
99 Tony Zendejas .05
100 Jeff Donaldson .05
101 Ray Childress .05
102 Sean Jones .05
103 Ernest Givins .20
104 *William Fuller* .40
105 *Allen Pinkett* .15
106 Eagles Team (Randall Cunningham) .10
107 *Keith Jackson* (AP) .50
108 Reggie White (AP) .25
109 Clyde Simmons .25
110 John Teltschik .05
111 Wes Hopkins .05
112 Keith Byars .05
113 Jerome Brown .05
114 Mike Quick .05
115 Randall Cunningham .40
116 Anthony Toney .05
117 Ron Johnson .05
118 Terry Hoage .05
119 Seth Joyner .25
120 *Eric Allen* .40
121 *Cris Carter* 2.00
122 Rams Team (Greg Bell) .05
123 *Tom Newberry* (AP) .15
124 Pete Holohan .05
125 *Robert Delpino* .35
126 Carl Ekern .05
127 Greg Bell .05
128 Mike Lansford .05
129 Jim Everett .15
130 Mike Wilcher .05
131 Jerry Gray .05
132 Dale Hatcher .05
133 Doug Smith .05
134 Kevin Greene .15
135 Jackie Slater .05
136 *Aaron Cox* .12
137 Henry Ellard .05
138 Browns Team (Bernie Kosar) .05
139 Frank Minnifield (AP) .05
140 Webster Slaughter .25
141 Bernie Kosar .20
142 Charles Buchanan .05
143 Clay Matthews .05
144 *Reggie Langhorne* .30
145 Hanford Dixon .05
146 Brian Brennan .05
147 Earnest Byner .05
148 *Michael Dean Perry* 1.00
149 Kevin Mack .05
150 Matt Bahr .05
151 Ozzie Newsome .20
152 Saints Team (Craig Heyward) .05
153 Morten Andersen .05
154 Pat Swilling .25
155 Sam Mills .05
156 Lonzell Hill .05
157 Dalton Hilliard .05
158 *Craig Heyward* .50
159 *Vaughan Johnson* .30
160 Reuben Mayes .05
161 *Gene Atkins* .10
162 Bobby Hebert .20
163 Rickey Jackson .05
164 Eric Martin .05
165 Giants Team (Joe Morris) .05
166 Lawrence Taylor (AP) .15
167 Bart Oates .05
168 Carl Banks .05
169 Eric Moore .05
170 *Sheldon White* .12
171 *Mark Collins* .12
172 Phil Simms .15
173 Jim Burt .10
174 *Stephen Baker* .25
175 Mark Bavaro .05
176 Pepper Johnson .05
177 Lionel Manuel .05
178 Joe Morris .05
179 *John Elliott* .15
180 Gary Reasons .05
181 Seahawks Team (Dave Krieg) .05
182 *Brian Blades* (SR) .75
183 Steve Largent .25
184 *Rufus Porter* .15
185 Ruben Rodriguez .05
186 Curt Warner .05
187 Paul Moyer .05
188 Dave Krieg .05
189 Jacob Green .05
190 John L. Williams .05
191 *Eugene Robinson* .15
192 Brian Bosworth .05
193 Patriots Team (Tony Eason) .05
194 *John Stephens* (SR) .20
195 *Robert Perryman* .10
196 Andre Tippett .05
197 Fred Marion .05
198 Doug Flutie .75
199 Stanley Morgan .05
200 *Johnny Rembert* .10
201 Tony Eason .05
202 Marvin Allen .05
203 Raymond Clayborn .05
204 Irving Fryar .05
205 Colts Team (Chris Chandler) .05
206 Eric Dickerson (AP) .20
207 Chris Hinton (AP) .05
208 Duane Bickett .05
209 *Chris Chandler* 2.00
210 Jon Hand .05
211 Ray Donaldson .05
212 Dean Biasucci .05
213 Bill Brooks .05
214 *Chris Goode* .10
215 *Clarence Verdin* .20
216 Albert Bentley .05
217 Passing Leaders (Wade Wilson, Boomer Esiason) .05
218 Receiving Leaders (Henry Ellard, Al Toon) .05
219 Rushing Leaders (Herschel Walker, Eric Dickerson) .15
220 Scoring Leaders (Mike Cofer, Scott Norwood) .05
221 Interception Leaders (Scott Case, Erik McMillan) .05
222 Jets Team (Ken O'Brien) .05
223 Erik McMillan (SR) .10
224 *James Hasty* (SR) .12
225 Al Toon .05
226 *John Booty* .12
227 Johnny Hector .05
228 Ken O'Brien .05
229 Marty Lyons .05
230 Mickey Shuler .05
231 Robin Cole .05
232 Freeman McNeil .05
233 Marion Barber .05
234 JoJo Townsell .05
235 Wesley Walker .05
236 Roger Vick .05
237 Pat Leahy .05
238 Broncos Team (John Elway) .10
239 Mike Horan (AP) .05
240 Tony Dorsett .25
241 John Elway .50
242 Mark Jackson .05
243 Sammy Winder .05
244 Rich Karlis .05
245 Vance Johnson .05
246 *Steve Sewell* .10
247 Karl Mecklenburg .05
248 Rulon Jones .05
249 *Simon Fletcher* .30
250 Redskins Team (Doug Williams) .05
251 *Chip Lohmiller* (SR) .30
252 Jamie Morris (SR) .05
253 *Mark Rypien* (SR) .40
254 Barry Wilburn .05
255 Mark May .10
256 Wilbur Marshall .05
257 Charles Mann .05
258 Gary Clark .15
259 Doug Williams .05
260 Art Monk .15
261 Kelvin Bryant .05
262 Dexter Manley .05
263 Ricky Sanders .05
264 Raiders Team (Marcus Allen) .05
265 *Tim Brown* (AP) 1.50
266 Jay Schroeder .05
267 Marcus Allen .12
268 Mike Haynes .05
269 Bo Jackson .75
270 *Steve Beuerlein* 1.00
271 Vann McElroy .05
272 Willie Gault .05
273 Howie Long .05
274 Greg Townsend .05
275 Mike Wise .05
276 Cardinals Team (Neil Lomax) .05
277 Luis Sharpe .05
278 Scott Dill .05
279 Vai Sikahema .05
280 Ron Wolfley .05
281 David Galloway .05
282 *Jay Novacek* .75
283 Neil Lomax .05
284 Robert Awalt .05
285 Cedric Mack .05
286 Freddie Joe Nunn .05
287 J.T. Smith .05
288 Stump Mitchell .05
289 Roy Green .05
290 Dolphins Team (Dan Marino) .25
291 *Jarvis Williams* (SR) .10
292 Troy Stradford .05
293 Dan Marino 2.00
294 T.J. Turner .05
295 John Offerdahl .05
296 *Ferrell Edmunds* .15
297 Scott Schwedes .05
298 Lorenzo Hampton .05
299 Jim Jensen .05
300 Brian Sochia .05
301 Reggie Roby .05
302 Mark Clayton .05
303 Chargers Team (Tim Spencer) .05
304 Lee Williams .05
305 *Gary Plummer* .15
306 Gary Anderson .05
307 Gill Byrd .05
308 Jamie Holland .05
309 Billy Ray Smith .05
310 Lionel James .05
311 *Mark Vlasic* .20
312 Curtis Adams .05
313 *Anthony Miller* 1.00
314 Steelers Team (Frank Pollard) .05
315 *Bubby Brister* .50
316 David Little .05
317 Tunch Ilkin .05
318 Louis Lipps .05
319 *Warren Williams* .10
320 Dwight Stone .05
321 *Merril Hoge* .20
322 *Thomas Everett* .25
323 *Rod Woodson* .75
324 Gary Anderson .05
325 Buccaneer Team (Ron Hall) .05
326 Donnie Elder .05
327 Vinny Testaverde .15
328 Harry Hamilton .05
329 James Wilder .05
330 Lars Tate .05
331 *Mark Carrier* .65
332 Bruce Hill .05
333 *Paul Gruber* .12
334 Ricky Reynolds .05
335 Eugene Marve .05
336 Falcons Team (J. Williams) .05
337 *Aundray Bruce* (SR) .10
338 John Rade .05
339 *Scott Case* .10
340 Robert Moore .05
341 *Chris Miller* .60
342 Gerald Riggs .05
343 Gene Lang .05
344 Marcus Cotton .05
345 Rick Donnelly .05
346 *John Settle* .10
347 Bill Fralic .05
348 Chiefs Team (Dino Hackett) .05
349 Steve DeBerg .05
350 Mike Stensrud .05
351 Dino Hackett .05
352 Deron Cherry .05
353 Christian Okoye .12
354 Bill Maas .05
355 Carlos Carson .05
356 Albert Lewis .05
357 Paul Palmer .05
358 Nick Lowery .05
359 Stephone Paige .05
360 Lions Team (Chuck Long) .05
361 *Chris Spielman* (SR) .30
362 Jim Arnold .05
363 Devon Mitchell .05
364 Mike Cofer .05
365 *Bennie Blades* .15
366 James Jones .05
367 Garry James .05
368 Pete Mandley .05
369 Keith Ferguson .05
370 Dennis Gibson .05
371 Packers Team (Johnny Holland) .05
372 Brent Fullwood .05
373 Don Majkowski .20
374 Timothy Harris .05
375 *Keith Woodside* .10
376 Mark Murphy .05
377 Dave Brown .05
378 *Perry Kemp* .10
379 *Sterling Sharpe* 1.50
380 *Chuck Cecil* .25
381 Walter Stanley .05
382 Cowboys Team (Steve Pelleur) .05
383 *Michael Irvin* (SR) 1.50
384 Bill Bates .05
385 Herschel Walker .15
386 Darryl Clack .05
387 Danny Noonan .05
388 Eugene Lockhart .05
389 Ed "Too Tall" Jones .05
390 Steve Pelluer .05
391 Ray Alexander .05
392 *Nate Newton* .20
393 Garry Cobb .05
394 Checklist 1-132 .05
395 Checklist 133-264 .05
396 Checklist 265-396 .05

1989 Topps Box Bottoms

The 16-card, standard-size set featured the weekly offensive and defensive award winners for the 1988 season. The cards were included four to the bottom of each box of 1989 football. Two players (offensive and defensive) are on each card.

MT
Complete Set (16): 5.00
Common Player: .25
A Neal Anderson, Terry Hoage .25
B Boomer Esiason, Jacob Green .50
C Wesley Walker, Gary Jeter .25
D Jim Everett, Danny Noonan .25
E Neil Lomax, Dexter Manley .25
F Kelvin Bryant, Kevin Greene .25
G Roger Craig, Tim Harris .50
H Dan Marino, Carl Banks 2.00
I Drew Hill, Robin Cole .25
J Neil Lomax, Lawrence Taylor .50
K Roy Green, Tim Krumrie .25
L Bobby Hebert, Aundray Bruce .25
M Ickey Woods, Lawrence Taylor .50
N Louis Lipps, Greg Townsend .25
O Curt Warner, Tim Harris .25
P Dave Krieg, Kevin Greene .35

1989 Topps 1000 Yard Club

These standard-size cards, printed on heavy white cardboard stock and featuring a full-color action shot of each NFL player who gained more tha 1,000 yards rushing or receiving during the 1988 season, were included in wax packs of 1989 Topps football cards. Fronts feature a yellow-and-blue ribbon from the upper right corner, across the top and leading to a "1000 Yard Club" medal at lower left. The photo and medal are bordered in red, with the player's name in white and his position in black also in the border. Card backs are in orange, with an ornate "1000 Yard Club" medal and ribbon reaching from the card number at upper left to the bottom center of the card. Statistics mark the game-by-game progress of the runner-receiver's season.

MT
Complete Set (24): 4.00
Common Player: .10
1 Eric Dickerson .60
2 Herschel Walker .60
3 Roger Craig .40
4 Henry Ellard .10
5 Jerry Rice .60
6 Eddie Brown .10
7 Anthony Carter .10
8 Greg Bell .10
9 John Stephens .10
10 Ricky Sanders .10
11 Drew Hill .10
12 Mark Clayton .10
13 Gary Anderson .10
14 Neal Anderson .20
15 Roy Green .10
16 Eric Martin .10
17 Joe Morris .10
18 Al Toon .10
19 Ickey Woods .20
20 Bruce Hill .10
21 Lionel Manuel .10
22 Curt Warner .10
23 John Settle .10
24 Mike Rozier .10

1989 Topps Traded

This 132-card set was released in March of 1990. It was a boxed set through only hobby dealers, similar to the baseball "Traded" sets that Topps had been issuing since 1981. The set includes 1989 rookies, players not included in the regular '89 set and players that had been traded (now shown with their new team).

MT
Complete Set (132): 18.00
Common Player: .05
1 *Eric Ball* .10
2 Tony Mandarich .05
3 *Shawn Collins* .10
4 *Ray Bentley* .10
5 Tony Casillas .10
6 *Al Del Greco* .10
7 *Dan Saleaumua* .10
8 Keith Bishop .05
9 *Rodney Peete* .40
10 *Lorenzo White* .25
11 *Steve Smith* .25
12 Pete Mandley .05
13 Mervyn Fernandez .05
14 *Flipper Anderson* .30
15 *Louis Oliver* .15
16 Rick Fenney .05
17 Gary Jeter .05
18 Greg Cox .05
19 *Bubba McDowell* .15
20 Ron Heller .05
21 *Tim McDonald* .25
22 *Jerrol Williams* .10
23 *Marion Butts* .40
24 Steve Young 1.00
25 Mike Merriweather .05
26 Richard Johnson .05
27 Gerald Riggs .05
28 Dave Waymer .05
29 Isaac Holt .05
30 *Deion Sanders* 1.75
31 Todd Blackledge .05
32 *Jeff Cross* .30
33 *Steve Wisniewski* .20
34 Ron Brown .05
35 *Ron Bernstine* .35
36 *Jeff Uhlenhake* .08
37 *Donnell Woolford* .12
38 *Bob Gagliano* .12
39 Ezra Johnson .05
40 Ron Jaworski .05
41 *Lawyer Tillman* .10
42 *Lorenzo Lynch* .10
43 Mike Alexander .10
44 *Tim Worley* .15
45 Guy Bingham .05
46 *Cleveland Gary* .25
47 Danny Peebles .05
48 Clarence Weathers .05
49 *Jeff Lageman* .10
50 *Eric Metcalf* .65
51 *Myron Guyton* .10
52 *Steve Atwater* .20
53 John Foucade .05
54 Randall McDaniel .12
55 *Al Noga* .15
56 *Sammie Smith* .10
57 Jesse Solomon .05
58 *Greg Kragen* .10
59 *Don Beebe* .50
60 Hart Lee Dykes .05
61 *Trace Armstrong* .15
62 Steve Pelluer .05
63 Barry Krauss .05
64 Kevin Murphy .05
65 *Steve Tasker* .30
66 *Jessie Small* .10
67 *Dave Meggett* .25
68 Dean Hamel .05
69 Jim Covert .05
70 *Troy Aikman* 3.00
71 Raul Allegre .05
72 *Chris Jacke* .15
73 Leslie O'Neal .25
74 *Keith Taylor* .10
75 *Steve Walsh* .50
76 Tracy Rocker .05

77	*Robert Massey*	.12
78	Bryan Wagner	.05
79	Steve DeOssie	.05
80	*Carnell Lake*	.12
81	*Frank Reich*	.50
82	*Tyrone Braxton*	.10
83	*Barry Sanders*	12.00
84	*Pete Stoyanovich*	.20
85	Paul Palmer	.05
86	*Billy Joe Tolliver*	.10
87	*Eric Hill*	.08
88	Gerald McNeil	.05
89	Bill Hawkins	.05
90	*Derrick Thomas*	.75
91	*Jim Harbaugh*	1.00
92	Brian Williams	.05
93	Jack Trudeau	.05
94	Leonard Smith	.05
95	Gary Hogeboom	.05
96	*A.J. Johnson*	.10
97	Jim McMahon	.05
98	*David Williams*	.12
99	Rohn Stark	.05
100	Sean Landeta	.05
101	*Tim Johnson*	.08
102	*Andre Rison*	.50
103	Earnest Byner	.05
104	*Don McPherson*	.08
105	*Zefross Moss*	.08
106	*Frank Stams*	.10
107	*Courtney Hall*	.10
108	*Marc Logan*	.15
109	James Lofton	.15
110	*Lewis Tillman*	.50
111	Irv Pankey	.05
112	Ralf Mojsiejenko	.05
113	*Bobby Humphrey*	.08
114	Chris Burkett	.05
115	*Greg Lloyd*	.40
116	Matt Millen	.05
117	Carl Zander	.05
118	*Wayne Martin*	.25
119	Mike Saxon	.05
120	Herschel Walker	.12
121	*Andy Heck*	.08
122	Mark Robinson	.05
123	*Keith Van Horne*	.08
124	Ricky Hunley	.05
125	*Timm Rosenbach*	.15
126	Steve Grogan	.05
127	*Stephen Braggs*	.08
128	Terry Long	.05
129	Evan Cooper	.05
130	Robert Lyles	.05
131	Mike Webster	.05
132	Checklist	.05

1989 Topps American/United Kingdom

This boxed set of 33 cards was distributed in the United Kingdom using a design similar to Topps' regular 1989 set. However, the card stock for the back is not grey, like it is for the regular cards; these ones have white backs. The set's checklist is included on the box; card numbers do not match those in the regular set.

		MT
Complete Set (33):		35.00
Common Player:		1.00
1	Anthony Carter	1.00
2	Jim Kelly	2.50
3	Bernie Kosar	1.50
4	John Elway	4.00
5	Andre Tippett	1.00
6	Henry Ellard	1.50
7	Eddie Brown	1.00
8	Gary Anderson	1.00
9	Eric Martin	1.00
10	Ickey Woods	1.00
11	Mike Singletary	1.00
12	Phil Simms	1.50
13	Brian Bosworth	1.00
14	Mark Clayton	1.25
15	Eric Dickerson	1.50
16	John Stephens	1.00
17	Neal Anderson	1.00
18	Al Toon	1.00
19	Lionel Manuel	.75
20	Joe Montana	7.00
21	Reggie White	2.00
22	Randall Cunningham	1.75
23	Lawrence Taylor	1.50
24	Jim Everett	1.25
25	Neil Lomax	1.00
26	Herschel Walker	1.25
27	Roger Craig	1.25
28	Greg Bell	1.00
29	Ricky Sanders	1.00
30	Joe Morris	1.00
31	Curt Warner	1.00
32	Boomer Esiason	1.50
33	Dan Marino	7.00

1990 Topps

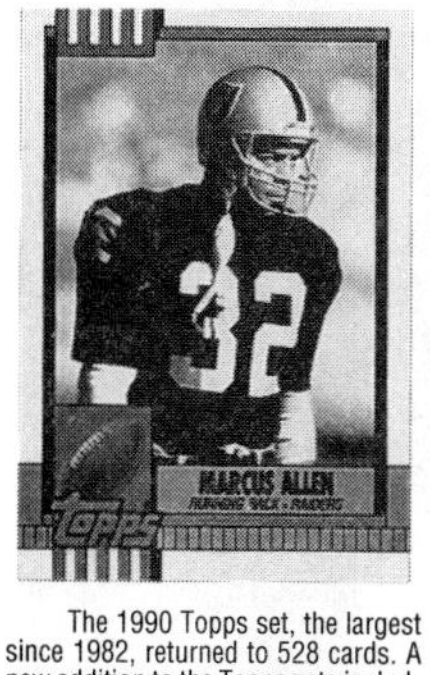

The 1990 Topps set, the largest since 1982, returned to 528 cards. A new addition to the Topps sets included 25 1990 draft pick cards; other subsets included four 1989 record breakers, four league leader cards and a Super Bowl card. Each wax pack included one of 31 glossy 1,000 Yard Club insert cards featuring players who gained 1,000 yards or more during the 1989 NFL season. Because NFL Properties denied Topps a license, cards have no free-standing team logos. A 196-card Bowman football set, also scheduled to be issued in 1990, was also scratched. Variations include cards #28, 193, 229 and 501-528 - all the Topps horizontal issues - which originally appeared without the small black vertical "hashmarks" running below the red border and underneath the Topps logo. These were corrected very early; no premium value has been put on them, but they should fetch 35-50 cents over the regular card price. Also, Topps issued "corrected" cards, presumably both in wax and in factory sets, that do not have the "unauthorized" tagline. These are thought to be scarcer than the unauthorized cards. (Key: RB - Record Breaker).

		MT
Complete Set (528):		10.00
Common Player:		.04
Wax Pack (15+1):		.50
Wax Box (36):		8.50
1	Joe Montana (RB)	.50
2	Flipper Anderson (RB)	.04
3	Troy Aikman (RB)	.50
4	Kevin Butler (RB)	.04
5	Super Bowl XXIV	.04
6	*Dexter Carter*	.20
7	Matt Millen	.04
8	Jerry Rice	.75
9	Ronnie Lott	.10
10	John Taylor	.20
11	Guy McIntyre	.04
12	Roger Craig	.04
13	Joe Montana	1.00
14	*Brent Jones*	.75
15	Tom Rathman	.04
16	Harris Barton	.04
17	Charles Haley	.04
18	*Pierce Holt*	.20
19	Michael Carter	.04
20	Chet Brooks	.04
21	Eric Wright	.04
22	Mike Cofer	.04
23	Jim Fahnhorst	.04
24	Keena Turner	.04
25	Don Griffin	.04
26	*Kevin Fagan*	.08
27	Bubba Paris	.04
28	Rushing Leaders	.15
29	Steve Atwater	.04
30	Tyrone Braxton	.04
31	Ron Holmes	.04
32	Bobby Humphrey	.04
33	Greg Kragen	.04
34	David Treadwell	.04
35	Karl Mecklenburg	.04
36	Dennis Smith	.04
37	John Elway	.40
38	Vance Johnson	.04
39	Simon Fletcher	.04
40	Jim Juriga	.04
41	Mark Jackson	.04
42	Melvin Bratton	.04
43	*Wymon Henderson*	.10
44	Ken Ball	.04
45	Sammy Winder	.04
46	Alphonso Carreker	.04
47	Orson Mobley	.04
48	*Rodney Hampton*	1.00
49	Dave Meggett	.12
50	Myron Guyton	.10
51	Phil Simms	.10
52	Lawrence Taylor	.10
53	Carl Banks	.04
54	Pepper Johnson	.04
55	Leonard Marshall	.04
56	Mark Collins	.04
57	Erik Howard	.04
58	*Eric Dorsey*	.10
59	Ottis Anderson	.04
60	Mark Bavaro	.04
61	*Odessa Turner*	.12
62	Gary Reasons	.04
63	Maurice Carthon	.04
64	Lionel Manuel	.04
65	Sean Landeta	.04
66	Perry Williams	.04
67	*Pat Terrell*	.12
68	Flipper Anderson	.15
69	Jackie Slater	.04
70	Tom Newberry	.04
71	Jerry Gray	.04
72	Henry Ellard	.04
73	Doug Smith	.04
74	Kevin Greene	.04
75	Jim Everett	.04
76	Mike Lansford	.04
77	Greg Bell	.04
78	Pete Holohan	.04
79	Robert Delpino	.04
80	Mike Wilcher	.04
81	Mike Piel	.04
82	Mel Owens	.04
83	*Michael Stewart*	.10
84	*Ben Smith*	.10
85	Keith Jackson	.25
86	Reggie White	.15
87	Eric Allen	.04
88	Jerome Brown	.04
89	Robert Drummond	.04
90	Anthony Toney	.04
91	Keith Byars	.04
92	Cris Carter	.30
93	Randall Cunningham	.20
94	Ron Johnson	.04
95	Mike Quick	.04
96	Clyde Simmons	.04
97	Mike Pitts	.04
98	Izel Jenkins	.04
99	Seth Joyner	.04
100	Mike Schad	.04
101	Wes Hopkins	.04
102	Kirk Lowdermilk	.04
103	Rick Fenney	.04
104	Randall McDaniel	.04
105	Herschel Walker	.04
106	Al Noga	.04
107	Gary Zimmerman	.04
108	Chris Doleman	.04
109	Keith Millard	.04
110	Carl Lee	.04
111	Joey Browner	.04
112	Steve Jordan	.04
113	*Reggie Rutland*	.10
114	Wade Wilson	.04
115	Anthony Carter	.04
116	Rich Karlis	.04
117	Hassan Jones	.04
118	Henry Thomas	.04
119	Scott Studwell	.04
120	Ralf Mojsiejenko	.04
121	Earnest Byner	.04
122	Gerald Riggs	.04
123	Tracy Rocker	.04
124	A.J. Johnson	.04
125	Charles Mann	.04
126	Art Monk	.04
127	Rickey Sanders	.04
128	Gary Clark	.15
129	Jim Lachey	.04
130	*Martin Mayhew*	.15
131	Ravin Caldwell	.04
132	Don Warren	.04
133	Mark Rypien	.25
134	*Ed Simmons*	.10
135	Darryl Grant	.04
136	Darryl Green	.04
137	Chip Lommiller	.04
138	*Tony Bennett*	.35
139	Tony Mandarich	.04
140	Sterling Sharpe	.75
141	Tim Harris	.04
142	Don Majkowski	.04
143	Rich Moran	.04
144	Jeff Query	.04
145	Brent Fullwood	.04
146	Chris Jacke	.04
147	Keith Woodside	.04
148	Perry Kemp	.04
149	Herman Fontenot	.04
150	Dave Brown	.04
151	Brian Noble	.04
152	Johnny Holland	.04
153	Mark Murphy	.04
154	Bob Nelson	.04
155	*Darrell Thompson*	.25
156	Lawyer Tillman	.04
157	Eric Metcalf	.12
158	Webster Slaughter	.04
159	Frank Minnifield	.04
160	Brian Brennan	.04
161	Thane Gash	.04
162	Robert Banks	.04
163	Bernie Kosar	.04
164	David Grayson	.04
165	Kevin Mack	.04
166	Mike Johnson	.04
167	Tim Manoa	.04
168	Ozzie Newsome	.10
169	Felix Wright	.04
170	Al Baker	.04
171	Reggie Langhorne	.04
172	Clay Matthews	.04
173	Andrew Stewart	.04
174	*Barry Foster*	.10
175	Tim Worley	.04
176	Tim Johnson	.04
177	Carnell Lake	.04
178	Greg Lloyd	.04
179	Rod Woodson	.15
180	Tunch Ilkin	.04
181	Dermontti Dawson	.04
182	Gary Anderson	.04
183	Bubby Brister	.10
184	Louis Lipps	.04
185	Merril Hoge	.04
186	Mike Mularkey	.04
187	Derek Hill	.04
188	Rodney Carter	.04
189	Dwayne Carter	.04
190	Keith Willis	.04
191	Jerry Olsavsky	.04
192	Mark Stock	.04
193	Sacks Leaders	.04
194	Leonard Smith	.04
195	Darryl Talley	.04
196	Mark Kelso	.04
197	Kent Hull	.04
198	*Nate Odomes*	.30
199	Pete Metzelaars	.04
200	Don Beebe	.15
201	Ray Bentley	.04
202	Steve Tasker	.10
203	Scott Norwood	.04
204	Andre Reed	.20
205	Bruce Smith	.04
206	Thurman Thomas	.50
207	Jim Kelly	.35
208	Cornelius Bennett	.04
209	Shane Conlan	.04
210	Larry Kinnebrew	.04
211	*Jeff Alm*	.10
212	Robert Lyles	.04
213	Bubba McDowell	.04
214	Mike Munchak	.04
215	Bruce Matthews	.04
216	Warren Moon	.25
217	Drew Hill	.04
218	Ray Childress	.04
219	Steve Brown	.04
220	Alonzo Highsmith	.04
221	Allen Pinkett	.04
222	Sean Jones	.04
223	Johnny Meads	.04
224	John Grimsley	.10
225	*Haywood Jeffires*	.50
226	Curtis Duncan	.04
227	*Greg Montgomery*	.10
228	Ernest Givins	.04
229	Passing Leaders	.20
230	Robert Massey	.04
231	John Fourcade	.04
232	Dalton Hilliard	.04
233	Vaughan Johnson	.04
234	Hoby Brenner	.04
235	Pat Swilling	.04
236	Kevin Haverdink	.04
237	Bobby Hebert	.15
238	Sam Mills	.04
239	Eric Martin	.04
240	Lonzell Hill	.04
241	Steve Trapilo	.04
242	Rickey Jackson	.04
243	Craig Heyward	.04
244	Rueben Mayes	.04
245	Morten Andersen	.04
246	*Percy Snow*	.10
247	Pete Mandley	.04
248	Derrick Thomas	.30
249	Dan Saleaumua	.04
250	*Todd McNair*	.15
251	Leonard Griffin	.04
252	Jonathan Hayes	.04
253	Christian Okoye	.04
254	Albert Lewis	.04
255	Nick Lowery	.04
256	Kevin Ross	.04
257	Steve DeBerg	.04
258	Stephone Paige	.04
259	*James Saxon*	.10
260	Herman Heard	.04
261	Deron Cherry	.04
262	Dino Hackett	.04
263	Neil Smith	.20
264	Steve Pelluer	.04
265	Eric Thomas	.04
266	Eric Ball	.04
267	Leon White	.04
268	Tim Krumrie	.04
269	Jason Buck	.04
270	Boomer Esiason	.20
271	Carl Zander	.04
272	Eddie Brown	.04
273	David Fulcher	.04
274	Tim McGee	.04
275	James Brooks	.04
276	*Rickey Dixon*	.10
277	Ickey Woods	.04
278	Anthony Munoz	.04
279	Rodney Holman	.04
280	Mike Alexander	.04
281	Mervyn Fernandez	.04
282	Steve Wisniewski	.04
283	Steve Smith	.04
284	Howie Long	.04
285	Bo Jackson	.45
286	Mike Dyal	.04
287	Thomas Benson	.04
288	Willie Gault	.04
289	Marcus Allen	.04
290	Greg Townsend	.04
291	Steve Beuerlein	.30
292	Scott Davis	.04
293	*Eddie Anderson*	.10
294	Terry McDaniel	.04
295	Tim Brown	.45
296	Bob Golic	.04
297	*Jeff Jaeger*	.12
298	*Jeff George*	1.00
299	Chip Banks	.04
300	Andre Rison	.25
301	Rohn Stark	.04
302	Keith Taylor	.04
303	Jack Trudeau	.04
304	Chris Hinton	.04
305	Ray Donaldson	.04
306	*Jeff Herrod*	.10
307	Clarence Verdin	.04
308	Jon Hand	.04
309	Bill Brooks	.04
310	Albert Bentley	.04
311	Mike Prior	.04
312	Pat Beach	.04
313	Eugene Daniel	.04
314	Duane Bickett	.04
315	Dean Biasucci	.04
316	*Richmond Webb*	.25
317	Jeff Cross	.04
318	Louis Oliver	.04
319	Sammie Smith	.04
320	Pete Stoyanovich	.04
321	John Offerdahl	.04
322	Ferrell Edmunds	.04
323	Dan Marino	.75
324	Andre Brown	.04
325	Reggie Roby	.04
326	Jarvis Williams	.04
327	Roy Foster	.04
328	Mark Clayton	.04
329	Brian Sochia	.04
330	Mark Duper	.04
331	T.J. Turner	.04
332	Jeff Uhlenhake	.04
333	Jim Jensen	.04
334	*Cortez Kennedy*	.25
335	Andy Heck	.04
336	Rufus Porter	.04
337	Brian Blades	.15
338	Dave Krieg	.04
339	John L. Williams	.04
340	David Wyman	.04
341	*Paul Skansi*	.10
342	Eugene Robinson	.04
343	Joe Nash	.04
344	Jacob Green	.04
345	Jeff Bryant	.04
346	Ruben Rodriguez	.04
347	Norm Johnson	.04
348	Darren Comeaux	.04
349	*Andre Ware*	.20
350	Richard Johnson	.04
351	Rodney Peete	.10
352	Barry Sanders	1.25
353	Chris Spielman	.04
354	Eddie Murray	.04
355	Jerry Ball	.04
356	Mel Gray	.04
357	*Eric Williams*	.10
358	*Robert Clark*	.10
359	Jason Phillips	.04
360	*Terry Taylor*	.08
361	Bennie Blades	.04
362	Michael Cofer	.04
363	Jim Arnold	.04
364	*Marc Spindler*	.10
365	Jim Covert	.04
366	Jim Harbaugh	.20
367	Neal Anderson	.15
368	Mike Singletary	.04
369	John Roper	.04
370	Steve McMichael	.04
371	Dennis Gentry	.04
372	Brad Muster	.04
373	Ron Morris	.04
374	James Thornton	.04
375	Kevin Butler	.04
376	Richard Dent	.04
377	Dan Hampton	.04
378	Jay Hilgenberg	.04
379	Donnell Woolford	.04
380	Trace Armstrong	.04
381	*Junior Seau*	1.00
382	Rod Bernstine	.15
383	Marion Butts	.15
384	Burt Grossman	.04
385	Darrin Nelson	.04
386	Leslie O'Neal	.04
387	Billy Joe Tolliver	.04
388	Courtney Hall	.04
389	Lee Williams	.04
390	Anthony Miller	.30
391	Gill Byrd	.04
392	Wayne Walker	.04
393	Billy Ray Smith	.04
394	Vencie Glenn	.04
395	Tim Spencer	.04
396	Gary Plummer	.04
397	Arthur Cox	.04
398	Jamie Holland	.04
399	*Keith McCants*	.10
400	Kevin Murphy	.04
401	Danny Peebles	.04
402	Mark Robinson	.04
403	Broderick Thomas	.04
404	Ron Hall	.04
405	Mark Carrier	.04
406	Paul Gruber	.04
407	Vinny Testaverde	.10
408	Bruce Hill	.04
409	Lars Tate	.04
410	Harry Hamilton	.04
411	Ricky Reynolds	.04
412	Donald Igwebuike	.04
413	Reuben Davis	.04
414	William Howard	.04
415	*Winston Moss*	.10
416	*Chris Singleton*	.10
417	Hart Lee Dykes	.04
418	Steve Grogan	.04
419	Bruce Armstrong	.04
420	Robert Perryman	.04
421	Andre Tippett	.04
422	Sammy Martin	.04
423	Stanley Morgan	.04
424	Cedric Jones	.04
425	Sean Farrell	.04
426	Marc Wilson	.04
427	John Stephens	.04
428	Eric Sievers	.04
429	*Maurice Hurst*	.10
430	Johnny Rembert	.04
431	Receiving Leaders	.25
432	Eric Hill	.04
433	Gary Hogeboom	.04
434	Timm Rosenbach	.04
435	Tim McDonald	.04
436	Rich Camarillo	.04
437	Luis Sharpe	.04
438	J.T. Smith	.04
439	Roy Green	.04
440	*Ernie Jones*	.15
441	Robert Awalt	.04
442	Vai Sikahema	.04
443	Joe Wolf	.04
444	Stump Mitchell	.04
445	David Galloway	.04
446	Ron Wolfley	.04
447	Freddie Joe Nunn	.04
448	*Blair Thomas*	.15
449	Jeff Lageman	.04
450	Tony Eason	.04
451	Eric McMillan	.04
452	Jim Sweeney	.04
453	Ken O'Brien	.04
454	Johnny Hector	.04
455	JoJo Townsell	.04
456	Roger Vick	.04
457	Dennis Hasty	.04
458	*Dennis Byrd*	.25
459	Ron Stallworth	.04
460	Mickey Shuler	.04
461	Bobby Humphery	.04
462	Kyle Clifton	.04
463	Al Toon	.04
464	Freeman McNeil	.04
465	Pat Leahy	.04
466	Scott Case	.04
467	Shawn Collins	.04
468	Floyd Dixon	.04
469	Deion Sanders	.35
470	Tony Casillas	.04
471	*Michael Haynes*	.50
472	Chris Miller	.25
473	John Settle	.04
474	Aundray Bruce	.04
475	Gene Lang	.04
476	*Tim Gordon*	.10
477	Scott Fulhage	.04
478	Bill Fralic	.04
479	*Jessie Tuggle*	.25
480	Marcus Cotton	.04
481	Steve Walsh	.04
482	Troy Aikman	1.25
483	Ray Horton	.04
484	*Tony Tolbert*	.20
485	Steve Folsom	.04
486	*Ken Norton Jr.*	.50
487	*Kelvin Martin*	.25
488	Jack Del Rio	.04
489	*Daryl Johnston*	1.00
490	Bill Bates	.04
491	Jim Jeffcoat	.04
492	Vince Albritton	.04
493	Eugene Lockhart	.04
494	Mike Saxon	.04
495	James Dixon	.04
496	Willie Broughton	.04
497	Checklist 1-132	.04
498	Checklist 133-264	.04
499	Checklist 265-396	.04
500	Checklist 397-528	.04
501	Bears Team	.04
502	Bengals Team	.04
503	Bills Team	.04
504	Broncos Team	.04
505	Browns Team	.04
506	Buccaneers Team	.04
507	Cardinals Team	.04
508	Chargers Team	.04
509	Chiefs Team	.04
510	Colts Team	.04
511	Cowboys Team	.65
512	Dolphins Team	.04
513	Eagles Team	.04
514	Falcons Team	.04
515	49ers Team	.20
516	Giants Team	.04
517	Jets Team	.04
518	Lions Team	.04
519	Oilers Team	.10
520	Packers Team	.04
521	Patriots Team	.04
522	Raiders Team	.12
523	Rams Team	.04
524	Redskins Team	.04
525	Saints Team	.04
526	Seahawks Team	.04
527	Steelers Team	.04
528	Vikings Team	.04

1990 Topps Box Bottoms

These standard-size cards were included on the bottoms of 1990 Topps wax pack boxes. Each card has two photos on it; an offensive and defensive NFL Player of the Week from the 1989 season is featured. The back uses letters instead of card numbers and explains why the player was selected as the league's best performer for the week. The card design is similar to that which was used for Topps' regular 1990 set.

		MT
Complete Set (16):		6.00
Common Player:		.30
A	Jim Kelly, Dave Grayson	.50
B	Henry Ellard, Derrick Thomas	.50
C	Joe Montana, Vince Newsome	1.50
D	Bubby Brister, Tim Harris	.30
E	Christian Okoye, Keith Millard	.30
F	Warren Moon, Jerome Brown	.50
G	John Elway, Mike Merriweather	1.00
H	Webster Slaughter, Pat Swilling	.35
I	Rich Karlis, Lawrence Taylor	.35
J	Dan Marino, Greg Kragen	1.00
K	Boomer Esiason, Brent Williams	.35
L	Flipper Anderson, Pierce Holt	.30
M	Richard Johnson, David Fulcher	.30
N	John Taylor, Mike Prior	.50
O	Mark Rypien, Brett Faryniarz	.35
P	Greg Bell, Chris Doleman	.30

1990 Topps 1000 Yard Club

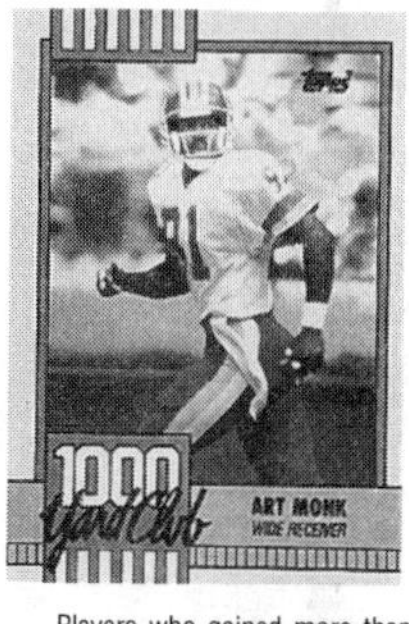

Players who gained more than 1,000 yards rushing or receiving during the 1989 NFL season are honored in this 30-card insert set. Cards were randomly included in 1990 Topps packs, one per pack. The front has a color picture, his and the set's name, plus the Topps' logo. Each back recaps each game from the 1989 season to show how the player reached the 1,000-yard milestone. The cards, numbered 1-30, are numbered according by yardage totals, with the leading yard gainer being #1, and so forth. The design for the card front is similar to the regular 1990 Topps football card design.

		MT
Complete Set (30):		3.50
Common Player:		.05
1	Jerry Rice	.50
2	Christian Okoye	.15
3	Barry Sanders	1.00
4	Sterling Sharpe	.40
5	Mark Carrier	.15
6	Henry Ellard	.05
7	Andre Reed	.25
8	Neal Anderson	.25
9	Dalton Hilliard	.05
10	Anthony Miller	.20
11	Thurman Thomas	.25
12	James Brooks	.15
13	Webster Slaughter	.05
14	Gary Clark	.05
15	Tim McGee	.05
16	Art Monk	.15
17	Bobby Humphrey	.25
18	Flipper Anderson	.10
19	Ricky Sanders	.10
20	Greg Bell	.05
21	Vance Johnson	.05
22	Richard Johnson	.05
23	Eric Martin	.05
24	John Taylor	.25
25	Mervyn Fernandez	.10
26	Anthony Carter	.10
27	Brian Blades	.10
28	Roger Craig	.20
29	Ottis Anderson	.20
30	Mark Clayton	.07

1990 Topps Traded

Like its predecessor, the Topps football update again pictured rookies and traded players on white cardboard stock. The issue was sold as a

boxed set and was available only through hobby shops.

		MT
Complete Set (132):		15.00
Common Player:		.03
1	Gerald McNeil	.03
2	Andre Rison	.15
3	Steve Walsh	.10
4	Lorenzo White	.10
5	Max Montoya	.05
6	William Roberts	.03
7	Alonzo Highsmith	.10
8	Chris Hinton	.10
9	Stanley Morgan	.10
10	Mickey Shuler	.03
11	Bobby Humphrey	.03
12	Gary Anderson	.03
13	Mike Tomczak	.03
14	Anthony Pleasant	.03
15	Walter Stanley	.03
16	Greg Bell	.10
17	*Tony Martin*	2.00
18	Terry Kinard	.03
19	Cris Carter	.50
20	James Wilder	.03
21	Jerry Kauric	.03
22	Irving Fryer	.03
23	Ken Harvey	.03
24	James Williams	.15
25	Ron Cox	.03
26	Andre Ware	.50
27	*Emmitt Smith*	10.00
28	Junior Seau	.50
29	Mark Carrier	.50
30	Rodney Hampton	.50
31	*Rob Moore*	1.25
32	Bern Brostek	.10
33	Dexter Carter	.40
34	Blair Thomas	.65
35	Harold Green	.30
36	Darrell Thompson	.20
37	Eric Green	.25
38	Renaldo Turnbull	.20
39	*Leroy Hoard*	.50
40	Anthony Thompson	.25
41	Jeff George	.50
42	Alexander Wright	.15
43	Richmond Webb	.25
44	Cortez Kennedy	.75
45	Ray Agnew	.10
46	Percy Snow	.15
47	Chris Singleton	.10
48	James Francis	.20
49	Tony Bennett	.10
50	*Reggie Cobb*	.20
51	Barry Foster	.10
52	Ben Smith	.10
53	Anthony Smith	.10
54	Steve Christie	.10
55	Johnny Bailey	.20
56	Alan Grant	.03
57	Eric Floyd	.03
58	Robert Blackmon	.03
59	Brent Williams	.03
60	Raymond Clayborn	.03
61	Dave Duerson	.07
62	Derrick Fenner	.50
63	Ken Willis	.03
64	*Brad Baxter*	.25
65	Tony Paige	.03
66	Jay Schroeder	.15
67	Jim Breech	.03
68	Barry Word	.50
69	Anthony Dilweg	.10
70	*Rich Gannon*	5.00
71	*Stan Humphries*	.50
72	Jay Novacek	.50
73	Tommy Kane	.03
74	Everson Walls	.03
75	Mike Rozier	.10
76	Robb Thomas	.03
77	*Terance Mathis*	2.00
78	Leroy Irvin	.03
79	Jeff Donaldson	.03
80	Ethan Horton	.03
81	J.B. Brown	.03
82	Joe Kelly	.03
83	John Carney	.03
84	Dan Stryzinski	.03
85	John Kidd	.03
86	Al Smith	.03
87	Travis McNeal	.03
88	Reyna Thompson	.10
89	Rick Donnelly	.03
90	Marv Cook	.03
91	Mike Farr	.03
92	Daniel Stubbs	.03
93	Jeff Campbell	.20
94	Tim McKyer	.10
95	Ian Beckles	.03
96	Lemuel Stinson	.03
97	Frank Cornish	.03
98	Riki Ellison	.03
99	Jamie Mueller	.03
100	Brian Hansen	.03
101	Warren Powers	.03
102	Howard Cross	.03
103	Tim Grunhard	.03
104	*Johnny Johnson*	.20
105	*Calvin Williams*	.65
106	Keith McCants	.15
107	Lamar Lathon	.10
108	Steve Broussard	.35
109	Glenn Parker	.07
110	Alton Montgomery	.07
111	Jim McMahon	.07
112	Aaron Wallace	.25
113	Keith Sims	.07
114	Ervin Randle	.03
115	Walter Wilson	.03
116	Terry Wooden	.07
117	Bernard Cook	.03
118	Tony Stargell	.07
119	Jimmie Jones	.07
120	Andre Collins	.03
121	*Ricky Proehl*	.40
122	Darion Conner	.07
123	Jeff Rutledge	.03
124	Heath Sherman	.25
125	Tommie Agee	.03
126	Tory Epps	.03
127	Tom Hodson	.25
128	Jessie Hester	.03
129	Alfred Oglesby	.03
130	Chris Chandler	.03
131	*Fred Barnett*	.50
132	Checklist	.03

A player's name in *italic type* indicates a rookie card.

1991 Topps

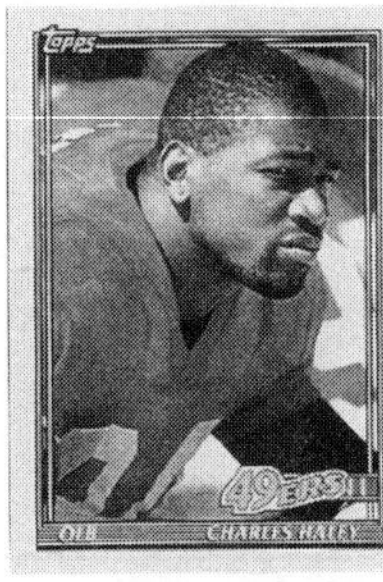

Topps' largest-ever football set was issued in August 1991. The style of the cards is the same as in 1991 Topps baseball and hockey. Subsets include highlights, all-pros, draft picks and super rookies. (Key: HL - highlight, LL - league leader)

		MT
Complete Set (660):		13.00
Complete Factory Set (660):		17.00
Common Player:		.04
Pack (16):		.20
Wax Box (36):		5.00
1	Super Bowl XXV	.08
2	Roger Craig (HL)	.04
3	Derrick Thomas (HL)	.12
4	Pete Stoyanovich (HL)	.04
5	Ottis Anderson (HL)	.04
6	Jerry Rice (HL)	.30
7	Warren Moon (HL)	.10
8	Warren Moon, Jim Everett (LL)	.10
9	Thurman Thomas, Barry Sanders (LL)	.50
10	Haywood Jeffires, Jerry Rice (LL)	.25
11	Richard Johnson, Mark Carrier (LL)	.04
12	Derrick Thomas, Charles Haley (LL)	.10
13	Jumbo Elliott	.04
14	Leonard Marshall	.04
15	William Roberts	.04
16	Lawrence Taylor	.10
17	Mark Ingram	.04
18	Rodney Hampton	.75
19	Carl Banks	.04
20	Ottis Anderson	.04
21	Mark Collins	.04
22	Pepper Johnson	.04
23	Dave Meggett	.04
24	Reyna Thompson	.04
25	Mike Fox	.04
26	Maurice Carthon	.04
27	Jeff Hostetler	.25
28	*Greg Jackson*	.10
29	Sean Landeta	.04
30	Bart Oates	.04
31	Phil Simms	.10
32	Erik Howard	.04
33	Myron Guyton	.04
34	Mark Bavaro	.04
35	Jarrod Bunch	.15
36	*Will Wolford*	.04
37	Ray Bentley	.04
38	Nate Odomes	.04
39	Scott Norwood	.04
40	Darryl Talley	.04
41	Carwell Gardner	.04
42	James Lofton	.04
43	Shane Conlan	.04
44	Steve Tasker	.04
45	James Williams	.04
46	Kent Hull	.04
47	Al Edwards	.04
48	Frank Reich	.04
49	Leon Seals	.04
50	Keith McKeller	.04
51	Thurman Thomas	.50
52	Leonard Smith	.04
53	Andre Reed	.15
54	Kenneth Davis	.04
55	*Jeff Wright*	.12
56	Jamie Mueller	.04
57	Jim Ritcher	.04
58	Bruce Smith	.04
59	*Ted Washington*	.10
60	Guy McIntyre	.04
61	Michael Carter	.04
62	Pierce Holt	.04
63	Darryl Pollard	.04
64	Mike Sherrard	.04
65	Dexter Carter	.04
66	Bubba Paris	.04
67	Harry Sydney	.04
68	Tom Rathman	.04
69	Jesse Sapolu	.04
70	Mike Cofer (S.F.)	.04
71	Keith DeLong	.04
72	Joe Montana	1.00
73	Bill Romanowski	.04
74	John Taylor	.15
75	Brent Jones	.04
76	Harris Barton	.04
77	Charles Haley	.04
78	Eric Davis	.04
79	Kevin Fagan	.04
80	Jerry Rice	1.00
81	Dave Waymer	.04
82	*Todd Marinovich*	.25
83	Steve Smith	.04
84	Tim Brown	.12
85	Ethan Horton	.04
86	Marcus Allen	.04
87	Terry McDaniel	.04
88	Thomas Benson	.04
89	Roger Craig	.04
90	Don Mosebar	.04
91	Aaron Wallace	.04
92	Eddie Anderson	.04
93	Willie Gault	.04
94	Howie Long	.04
95	Jay Schroeder	.04
96	Ronnie Lott	.10
97	Bob Golic	.04
98	Bo Jackson	.35

99	Bo Jackson	.35
100	Max Montoya	.04
101	Scott Davis	.04
102	Greg Townsend	.04
103	Garry Lewis	.04
104	Mervyn Fernandez	.04
105	Steve Wisniewski	.04
106	Jeff Jaeger	.04
107	*Nick Bell*	.20
108	*Mark Dennis*	.08
109	Jarvis Williams	.04
110	Mark Clayton	.04
111	Harry Galbreath	.04
112	Dan Marino	2.00
113	Louis Oliver	.04
114	Pete Stoyanovich	.04
115	Ferrell Edmunds	.04
116	Jeff Cross	.04
117	Richmond Webb	.04
118	Jim Jensen	.04
119	Keith Sims	.04
120	Mark Duper	.04
121	*Shawn Lee*	.12
122	Reggie Roby	.04
123	Jeff Uhlenhake	.04
124	Sammie Smith	.04
125	John Offerdahl	.04
126	Hugh Green	.04
127	Tony Paige	.04
128	David Griggs	.04
129	J.B. Brown	.04
130	*Harvey Williams*	.50
131	John Alt	.04
132	Albert Lewis	.04
133	Robb Thomas	.04
134	Neil Smith	.04
135	Stephone Paige	.04
136	Nick Lowery	.04
137	Steve DeBerg	.04
138	*Rich Baldinger*	.10
139	Percy Snow	.04
140	Kevin Porter	.04
141	Chris Martin	.04
142	Deron Cherry	.04
143	Derrick Thomas	.30
144	Tim Grunhard	.04
145	Todd McNair	.04
146	David Szott	.04
147	Dan Saleaumua	.04
148	Jonathan Hayes	.04
149	Christian Okoye	.04
150	Dino Hackett	.04
151	*Bryan Barker*	.10
152	Kevin Ross	.04
153	Barry Word	.15
154	Stan Thomas	.04
155	Brad Muster	.04
156	Donnell Woolford	.04
157	Neal Anderson	.10
158	Jim Covert	.04
159	Jim Harbaugh	.10
160	Shaun Gayle	.04
161	William Perry	.04
162	Ron Morris	.04
163	Mark Bortz	.04
164	James Thornton	.04
165	Ron Rivera	.04
166	Kevin Butler	.04
167	Jay Hilgenberg	.04
168	Peter Tom Willis	.04
169	Johnny Bailey	.04
170	Ron Cox	.04
171	Keith Van Horne	.04
172	Mark Carrier	.04
173	Richard Dent	.04
174	Wendell Davis	.10
175	Trace Armstrong	.04
176	Mike Singletary	.04
177	*Chris Zorich*	.35
178	Gerald Riggs	.04
179	Jeff Bostic	.04
180	*Kurt Gouvela*	.15
181	Stan Humphries	.15
182	Chip Lohmiller	.04
183	*Raleigh McKenzie*	.10
184	Alvin Walton	.04
185	Ernest Byner	.04
186	Markus Koch	.04
187	Art Monk	.04
188	Ed Simmons	.04
189	*Bobby Wilson*	.10
190	Charles Mann	.04
191	Darrell Green	.04
192	Mark Rypien	.15
193	Ricky Sanders	.04
194	Jim Lachey	.04
195	Martin Mayhew	.04
196	Gary Clark	.15
197	Wilber Marshall	.04
198	Darryl Grant	.04
199	Don Warren	.04
200	*Ricky Ervins*	.20
201	Eric Allen	.04
202	Anthony Toney	.04
203	Ben Smith	.04
204	David Alexander	.04
205	Jerome Brown	.04
206	Mike Golic	.04
207	Roger Ruzek	.04
208	Andre Waters	.04
209	Fred Barnett	.15
210	Randall Cunningham	.15
211	Mike Schad	.04
212	Reggie White	.15
213	Mike Bellamy	.04
214	*Jeff Feagles*	.08
215	Wes Hopkins	.04
216	Clyde Simmons	.04
217	Keith Byars	.04
218	Seth Joyner	.04
219	Byron Evans	.04
220	Keith Jackson	.15
221	Calvin Williams	.15
222	Mike Dumas	.04
223	Ray Childress	.04
224	Ernest Givins	.04
225	Lamar Lathon	.04
226	Greg Montgomery	.04
227	Mike Munchak	.04
228	Al Smith	.04
229	Bubba McDowell	.04
230	Haywood Jeffires	.15
231	Drew Hill	.04
233	Warren Moon	.25
234	*Doug Smith*	.10
235	*Cris Dishman*	.15
236	Teddy Garcia	.04
237	Richard Johnson	.04
238	Bruce Matthews	.04
239	Gerald McNeil	.04
240	Johnny Meads	.04

241	Curtis Duncan	.04
242	Sean Jones	.04
243	Lorenzo White	.10
244	*Rob Carpenter*	.12
245	Bruce Reimers	.04
246	Ickey Woods	.04
247	Lewis Billups	.04
248	Boomer Esiason	.15
249	Tim Krumrie	.04
250	David Fulcher	.04
251	Jim Breech	.04
252	Mitchell Price	.04
253	Carl Zander	.04
254	*Barney Bussey*	.10
255	Leon White	.04
256	Eddie Brown	.04
257	James Francis	.04
258	Harold Green	.15
259	Anthony Munoz	.04
260	James Brooks	.04
261	*Kevin Walker*	.12
262	Bruce Kozerski	.04
263	David Grant	.04
264	Tim McGee	.04
265	Rodney Holman	.04
266	*Dan McGwire*	.15
267	Andy Heck	.04
268	Dave Krieg	.04
269	David Wyman	.04
270	Robert Blackmon	.04
271	Grant Feasel	.04
272	*Patrick Hunter*	.12
273	Travis McNeal	.04
274	John L. Williams	.04
275	Tony Woods	.04
276	Derrick Fenner	.10
277	Jacob Green	.04
278	Brian Blades	.04
279	Eugene Robinson	.04
280	Terry Wooden	.04
281	Jeff Bryant	.04
282	Norm Johnson	.04
283	Joe Nash	.04
284	Rick Donnelly	.04
285	Chris Warren	.75
286	Tommy Kane	.04
287	Cortez Kennedy	.30
288	*Ernie Mills*	.15
289	Dermontti Dawson	.04
290	Tunch Ilkin	.04
291	Tim Worley	.04
293	Gary Anderson (Pit.)	.04
294	Chris Calloway	.04
295	Carnell Lake	.04
296	Dan Stryzinski	.04
297	Rod Woodson	.04
298	*John Jackson*	.10
299	Bubby Brister	.04
300	Thomas Everett	.04
301	Merril Hoge	.04
302	Eric Green	.10
303	Greg Lloyd	.04
304	Gerald Williams	.04
305	Bryan Hinkle	.04
306	Keith Willis	.04
307	Louis Lipps	.04
308	Donald Evans	.04
309	David Johnson	.04
310	*Wesley Carroll*	.10
311	Eric Martin	.04
312	Brett Maxie	.04
313	Rickey Jackson	.04
314	Robert Massey	.04
315	Pat Swilling	.04
316	Morten Andersen	.04
317	*Toi Cook*	.10
318	Sam Mills	.04
319	Steve Walsh	.04
320	*Tommy Barnhardt*	.10
321	Vince Buck	.04
322	Joel Hilgenberg	.04
323	Rueben Mayes	.04
325	Renaldo Turnbull	.04
326	Vaughan Johnson	.04
327	Gill Fenerty	.04
328	Stan Brock	.04
329	Dalton Hilliard	.04
330	Hoby Brenner	.04
331	Craig Heyward	.04
332	Jon Hand	.04
333	Duane Bickett	.04
334	Jessie Hester	.04
335	Rohn Stark	.04
336	Zefross Moss	.04
337	Bill Brooks	.04
338	Clarence Verdin	.04
339	Mike Prior	.04
340	Chip Banks	.04
341	Dean Biasucci	.04
342	Ray Donaldson	.04
343	Jeff Herrod	.04
344	Donnell Thompson	.04
345	Chris Goode	.04
346	Eugene Daniel	.04
347	Pat Beach	.04
348	Keith Taylor	.04
349	Jeff George	.30
350	*Tony Siragusa*	.10
351	Randy Dixon	.04
352	Albert Bentley	.04
353	*Russell Maryland*	.50
354	Mike Saxon	.04
355	Godfrey Myles	.08
356	*Mark Stepnoski*	.12
357	*James Washington*	.12
358	Jay Novacek	.25
359	Kelvin Martin	.04
360	Emmitt Smith	2.00
361	Jim Jeffcoat	.04
362	Alexander Wright	.10
363	James Dixon	.04
364	Daniel Stubbs	.04
365	Jack Del Rio	.04
366	Jack Del Rio	.10
367	*Mark Tuinei*	.10
368	Michael Irvin	.25
369	*John Gesek*	.10
370	Ken Willis	.04
371	Troy Aikman	1.00
372	Jimmie Jones	.04
373	Nate Newton	.04
374	Issiac Holt	.04
375	*Alvin Harper*	.30
376	Todd Kalis	.04
377	Wade Wilson	.04
378	Joey Browner	.04
379	Chris Doleman	.04
380	Hassan Jones	.04
381	Henry Thomas	.04

382	Darrell Fullington	.04
383	Steve Jordan	.04
384	Gary Zimmerman	.04
385	Ray Berry	.04
386	Cris Carter	.04
387	Mike Merriweather	.04
388	Carl Lee	.04
389	Keith Millard	.04
390	Reggie Rutland	.04
391	Anthony Carter	.04
392	Mark Dusbabek	.04
393	Kirk Lowerdermilk	.04
394	Al Noga	.04
395	Herschel Walker	.04
396	Randall McDaniel	.04
397	*Herman Moore*	3.50
398	John Jackson, Eddie Murray	.04
399	Lomas Brown	.04
400	Marc Spindler	.04
401	Bennie Blades	.04
402	Kevin Glover	.04
403	*Aubrey Matthews*	.10
404	Michael Cofer (Det.)	.04
405	Robert Clark	.04
406	Eric Clark	.04
407	William White	.04
408	Rodney Peete	.04
409	Mel Gray	.04
410	Jim Arnold	.04
411	Jeff Campbell	.04
412	Chris Spielman	.04
413	Jerry Ball	.04
414	Dan Owens	.04
415	Barry Sanders	1.25
416	Andre Ware	.12
417	*Stanley Richard*	.30
418	Gill Byrd	.04
419	John Kidd	.04
420	Sam Seale	.04
421	Gary Plummer	.04
422	Anthony Miller	.04
423	Ronnie Harmon	.04
424	Frank Cornish	.04
425	Marion Butts	.04
426	Leo Goeas	.04
427	Junior Seau	.30
428	Courtney Hall	.04
429	Leslie O'Neal	.04
430	Martin Bayless	.04
431	John Carney	.04
432	Lee Williams	.04
433	Arthur Cox	.04
434	Burt Grossman	.04
435	*Nate Lewis*	.25
436	Rod Bernstine	.04
437	*Henry Rolling*	.10
438	Billy Joe Tolliver	.04
439	*Vince Clark*	.10
440	Brian Noble	.04
441	Charles Wilson	.04
442	Don Majkowski	.04
443	Tim Harris	.04
444	Scott Stephen	.04
445	Perry Kemp	.04
446	Darrell Thompson	.15
447	Chris Jacke	.04
448	Mark Murphy	.04
449	Ed West	.04
450	LeRoy Butler	.04
451	Keith Woodside	.04
452	Tony Bennett	.04
453	Mark Lee	.04
454	*James Campen*	.08
455	Robert Brown	.04
456	Sterling Sharpe	.10
457	Tony Mandarich	.08
458	Johnny Holland	.04
459	*Matt Brock*	.12
460	Esera Tuaolo	.08
461	Freeman McNeil	.04
462	Terance Mathis	.10
463	Rob Moore	.20
464	Darrell Davis	.04
465	Chris Burkett	.04
466	Jeff Criswell	.04
467	Tony Stargell	.04
468	Ken O'Brien	.04
469	Erik McMillan	.04
470	Jeff Lageman	.04
471	Pat Leahy	.04
472	Dennis Byrd	.04
473	Jim Sweeney	.04
474	Brad Baxter	.15
475	Joe Kelly	.04
476	Al Toon	.04
477	Joe Prokop	.04
478	Mark Boyer	.04
479	Kyle Clifton	.04
480	James Hasty	.04
481	*Browning Nagle*	.25
482	Gary Anderson (T.B.)	.04
483	Mark Carrier (T.B.)	.04
484	Ricky Reynolds	.04
485	Bruce Hill	.04
486	Steve Christie	.04
487	Paul Gruber	.04
488	Jess Anderson	.04
489	Reggie Cobb	.30
490	Harry Hamilton	.04
491	Vinny Testaverde	.10
492	*Mark Royals*	.08
493	Keith McCants	.04
494	Ron Hall	.04
495	Ian Beckles	.04
496	Mark Robinson	.04
497	Reuben Davis	.04
498	Wayne Haddix	.04
499	Kevin Murphy	.04
500	Eugene Marve	.04
501	Broderick Thomas	.04
502	*Eric Swann*	.20
503	Ernie Jones	.04
504	Rich Camarillo	.04
505	Tim McDonald	.04
506	Freddie Joe Nunn	.04
507	*Tim Jorden*	.08
508	Johnny Johnson	.30
509	Eric Hill	.04
510	Derek Kennard	.04
511	Ricky Proehl	.12
512	Bill Lewis	.04
513	Roy Green	.04
514	Anthony Bell	.04
515	Timm Rosenbach	.04
516	*Jim Wahler*	.10
517	Anthony Thompson	.04
518	Ken Harvey	.04
519	Luis Sharpe	.04
520	Walter Reeves	.04

521	Lonnie Young	.04
522	Rod Saddler	.04
523	*Todd Lyght*	.15
524	Alvin Wright	.04
525	Flipper Anderson	.04
526	Jackie Slater	.04
527	Damone Johnson	.04
528	Cleveland Gary	.04
529	Mike Piel	.04
530	Buford McGee	.04
531	Michael Stewart	.04
532	Jim Everett	.04
533	Mike Wilcher	.04
534	Irv Pankey	.04
535	Bern Brostek	.04
536	Henry Ellard	.04
537	Doug Smith	.04
538	Larry Kelm	.04
539	Pat Terrell	.04
541	Jerry Gray	.04
542	Kevin Greene	.04
543	*Duval Love*	.10
544	Frank Stams	.04
545	*Mike Croel*	.20
546	Mark Jackson	.04
547	Greg Kragen	.04
548	Karl Mecklenburg	.04
549	Simon Fletcher	.04
550	Bobby Humphrey	.04
551	Ken Lanier	.04
552	Vance Johnson	.04
553	Ron Holmes	.04
554	John Elway	.40
555	Melvin Bratton	.04
556	Dennis Smith	.04
557	Ricky Nattiel	.04
558	Clarence Kay	.04
559	Michael Brooks	.04
560	Mike Horan	.04
561	Warren Powers	.04
562	Keith Karts	.04
563	Shannon Sharpe	.10
564	Wymon Henderson	.04
565	Steve Atwater	.04
566	David Treadwell	.04
567	*Bruce Pickens*	.10
568	Jessie Tuggle	.04
569	Chris Hinton	.04
570	Keith Jones	.04
571	Bill Fralic	.04
572	Mike Rozier	.04
573	Scott Fulhage	.04
574	Floyd Dixon	.04
575	Andre Rison	.25
576	Darion Conner	.04
577	Brian Jordan	.15
578	Michael Haynes	.35
579	Oliver Barnett	.04
580	Shawn Collins	.04
581	Tim Green	.04
582	Deion Sanders	.35
583	Mike Kenn	.04
584	Mike Gann	.04
585	Chris Miller	.04
586	Tory Epps	.04
587	Steve Broussard	.04
588	Gary Wilkins	.04
589	*Eric Turner*	.30
590	Thane Gash	.04
591	Clay Matthews	.04
592	Mike Johnson	.04
593	Raymond Clayborn	.04
594	Leroy Hoard	.10
595	Reggie Langhorne	.04
596	Mike Baab	.04
597	Anthony Pleasant	.04
598	David Grayson	.04
599	*Rob Burnett*	.12
600	Frank Minnifield	.04
601	Gregg Rakoczy	.04
602	Eric Metcalf	.04
603	Paul Farren	.04
604	Brian Brennan	.04
605	Tony Jones	.04
606	Stephen Braggs	.04
607	Kevin Mack	.04
608	*Pat Harlow*	.10
609	Marv Cook	.04
610	John Stephens	.04
611	Ed Reynolds	.04
612	Tim Goad	.04
613	Chris Singleton	.04
614	Bruce Armstrong	.04
615	Tom Hodson	.04
616	Sammy Martin	.04
617	Andre Tippett	.04
618	Johnny Rembert	.04
619	Maurice Hurst	.04
620	Vincent Brown	.04
621	Ray Agnew	.04
622	Ronnie Lippett	.04
623	Greg McMurtry	.04
624	Brent Williams	.04
625	Jason Staurovsky	.04
626	Marvin Allen	.04
627	Hart Lee Dykes	.04
628	Falcons Team	.04
629	Bills Team	.04
630	Bears Team	.04
631	Bengals Team	.04
632	Browns Team	.04
633	Cowboys Team	.04
634	Broncos Team	.04
635	Lions Team	.04
636	Packers Team	.04
637	Oilers Team	.10
638	Colts Team	.15
639	Chiefs Team	.04
640	Raiders Team (Tom Newberry)	.04
641	Rams Team	.04
642	Dolphins Team	.04
643	Vikings Team	.04
644	Patriots Team	.04
645	Saints Team	.04
646	Giants Team	.04
647	Jets Team	.04
648	Eagles Team	.08
649	Cardinals Team	.04
650	Steelers Team	.04
651	Chargers Team	.04
652	49ers Team	.04
653	Seahawks Team	.04
654	Buccaneers Team	.04
655	Redskins Team	.04
656	Checklist	.04
657	Checklist	.04
658	Checklist	.04
659	Checklist	.04
660	Checklist	.04

1991 Topps 1000 Yard Club

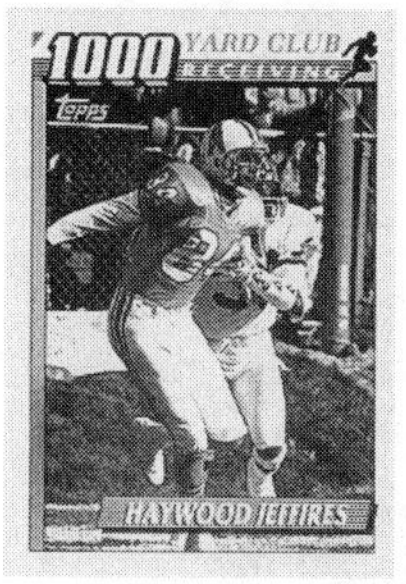

The 18 players featured in this insert set were receivers and running backs who gained more than 1,000 yards during the 1990 NFL season. Each card front has a color action photo, with the "1000 Yard Club" logo at the top. The photo has a red border at the top, while the player's name is at the bottom in an orange stripe. There is no border at the bottom or on the right, but the left side of the card has a red and purple border. The card back gives the player's game-by-game totals in blue and pink against a white background. A card number is in the upper right corner.

		MT
	Complete Set (18):	6.00
	Common Player:	.25
1	Jerry Rice	1.50
2	Barry Sanders	1.75
3	Thurman Thomas	.75
4	Henry Ellard	.25
5	Marion Butts	.75
6	Earnest Byner	.25
7	Andre Rison	.50
8	Bobby Humphrey	.25
9	Gary Clark	.35
10	Sterling Sharpe	1.25
11	Flipper Anderson	.25
12	Neal Anderson	.35
13	Haywood Jeffires	.45
14	Stephone Paige	.35
15	Drew Hill	.25
16	Barry Word	.35
17	Anthony Carter	.30
18	James Brooks	.25

1992 Topps

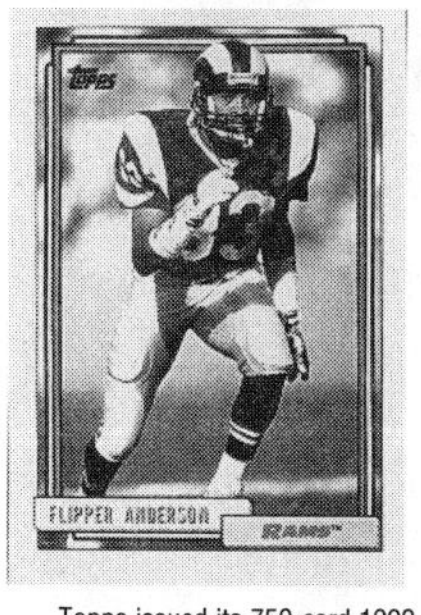

Topps issued its 759-card 1992 set in three series - 330, 330 and 99 cards. The fronts have action photos inside team color-coded frames bordered by white. The backs have a biography, statistics, a photo of the team's stadium and a player profile. Topps Gold cards were also produced for each card; these gold-foil versions were inserted one per foil pack.

		MT
	Complete Set (759):	35.00
	Complete Series 1 (330):	15.00
	Complete Series 2 (330):	10.00
	Complete Hi Series (99):	10.00
	Common Player:	.05
	Minor Stars:	.10
	Complete Gold Set (759):	125.00
	Complete Gold Series 1 (330):	55.00
	Complete Gold Series 2 (330):	50.00
	Complete Gold Hi Series (99):	20.00
	Common Gold:	.15
	Unlisted Stars:	2x-4x
	Series 1 or 2 Pack (15):	.40
	Series 1 or 2 Wax Box (36):	12.00
	Series 3 Pack (15):	.75
	Series 3 Wax Box (36):	22.00
1	Tim McGee	.05
2	Rich Camarillo	.05
3	Anthony Johnson	.05
4	Lary Kelm	.05
5	Irving Fryar	.05
6	Joey Browner	.05
7	Michael Walter	.05
8	Cortez Kennedy	.15
9	Reyna Thompson	.05
10	John Friesz	.05
11	Leroy Hoard	.05
12	Steve McMichael	.05
13	Marvin Washington	.05
14	Clyde Simmons	.05
15	Stephone Paige	.05
16	Mike Utley	.20
17	Tunch Ilkin	.05
18	Lawrence Dawsey	.05
19	Vance Johnson	.05
20	Bryce Paup	.05
21	Jeff Wright	.05
22	Gill Fenerty	.05
23	Lamar Lathon	.05
24	Danny Copeland	.05
25	Marcus Allen	.05
26	Tim Green	.05
27	Pete Stoyanovich	.05
28	Alvin Harper	.10
29	Roy Foster	.05
30	Eugene Daniel	.05
31	Luis Sharpe	.05
32	Terry Wooden	.05
33	Jim Breech	.05
34	*Randy Hilliard*	.10
35	Roman Phifer	.05
36	Erik Howard	.05
37	Chris Singleton	.05
38	Matt Stover	.05
39	Tim Irwin	.05
40	Karl Mecklenburg	.05
41	Joe Phillips	.05
42	Bill Jones	.05
43	Mark Carrier	.05
44	George Jamison	.05
45	Rob Taylor	.05
46	Jeff Jaeger	.05
47	Don Majkowski	.05
48	Al Edwards	.05
49	Curtis Duncan	.05
50	Sam Mills	.05
51	Terance Mathis	.05
52	Brian Mitchell	.05
53	Mike Pritchard	.20
54	Calvin Williams	.12
55	Hardy Nickerson	.05
56	Nate Newton	.05
57	Steve Wallace	.05
58	John Offerdahl	.05
59	Aeneas Williams	.05
60	Lee Johnson	.05
61	*Ricardo McDonald,* Jeff Feagles	.12
62	David Richards	.05
63	Paul Gruber	.05
64	Greg McMurtry	.05
65	Jay Hilgenberg	.05
66	Tim Grunhard	.05
67	*Dwayne White*	.08
68	Don Beebe	.05
69	Simon Fletcher	.05
70	Warren Moon	.20
71	Chris Jacke	.05
72	Steve Wisniewski	.05
73	Mike Coffer	.05
74	Tim Johnson	.05
75	T.J. Turner	.05
76	Scott Case	.05
77	Michael Jackson	.10
78	Jon Hand	.05
79	Stan Brock	.05
80	Robert Blackmon	.05
81	David Johnson	.05
82	Damone Johnson	.05
83	Marc Spindler	.05
84	Larry Brown	.05
85	Ray Berry	.05
86	Andre Waters	.05
87	Carlos Huerta	.05
88	Brad Muster	.05
89	Chuck Cecil	.05
90	Nick Lowery	.05
91	Cornelius Bennett	.05
92	Jessie Tuggle	.05
93	*Mark Schlereth*	.10
94	Vestee Jackson	.05
95	Eric Bieniemy	.05
96	Jeff Hostetler	.15
97	Ken Lanier	.05
98	Wayne Haddix	.05
99	Lorenzo White	.05
100	Mervyn Fernandez	.05
101	Brent Williams	.05
102	Ian Beckles	.05
103	Harris Barton	.05
104	*Edgar Bennett*	.50
105	Mike Pitts	.05
106	Fuad Reveiz	.05
107	Vernon Turner	.05
108	*Tracy Hayworth*	.10
109	Checklist 1-110	.05
110	Tom Waddle	.15
111	Fred Stokes	.05
112	Howard Ballard	.05
113	David Szott	.05
114	Tim McKyer	.05
115	Kyle Clifton	.05
116	Tony Bennett	.05
117	Joel Hilgenberg	.05
118	Dwayne Harper	.05
119	Mike Baab	.05
120	Mark Clayton	.05
121	Eric Swann	.05
122	Neil O'Donnell	.10
123	Mike Munchak	.05
124	Howie Long	.05
125	John Elway	.50
126	Joe Prokop	.05
127	Pepper Johnson	.05
128	Richard Dent	.05
129	*Robert Porcher*	.15
130	Earnest Byner	.05
131	Kent Hull	.05
132	Mike Merriweather	.05
133	Scott Fulhage	.05
134	Kevin Porter	.05
135	Tony Casillas	.05
136	Dean Biasucci	.05
137	Ben Smith	.05
138	Bruce Kozerski	.05
139	Jeff Campbell	.05
140	Kevin Greene	.05
141	Gary Plummer	.05
142	Vincent Brown	.05
143	Ron Hall	.05
144	*Louis Aguiar*	.10
145	Mark Duper	.05
146	Jesse Sapolu	.05
147	Jeff Gossett	.05
148	Brian Noble	.05
149	Derek Russell	.15
150	*Carlton Bailey*	.15
151	Kelly Goodburn	.05
152	Audrey McMillian	.05
153	Neal Anderson	.10
154	Bill Maas	.05
155	Rickey Jackson	.05
156	Chris Miller	.05
157	Darren Comeaux	.05
158	David Williams	.05
159	Rich Gannon	.10
160	Kevin Mack	.05
161	Jim Arnold	.05
162	Reggie White	.15
163	Leonard Russell	.25
164	Doug Smith	.05
165	Tony Mandarich	.05
166	Greg Lloyd	.05
167	Jumbo Elliott	.05
168	Jonathan Hayes	.05
169	Jim Ritcher	.05
170	Mike Kenn	.05
171	James Washington	.05
172	Tim Harris	.05
173	James Thornton	.05
174	*John Brandes*	.10
175	*Fred McAfee*	.15
176	Henry Rolling	.05
177	Tony Paige	.05
178	Jay Schroeder	.05
179	Jeff Herrod	.05
180	Emmitt Smith	2.50
181	Wymon Henderson	.05
182	Rob Moore	.05
183	Robert Wilson	.05
184	*Michael Zordich*	.10
185	Jim Harbaugh	.05
186	Vince Workman	.05
187	Ernest Givins	.05
188	Herschel Walker	.05
189	Dan Fike	.05
190	Seth Joyner	.05
191	Steve Young	1.00
192	Dennis Gibson	.05
193	Darryl Talley	.05
194	Emile Harry	.05
195	Bill Fralic	.05
196	Michael Stewart	.05
197	James Francis	.05
198	Jerome Henderson	.05
199	John L. Williams	.05
200	Rod Woodson	.05
201	Mike Farr	.05
202	Greg Montgomery	.05
203	Andre Collins	.05
204	Scott Miller	.05
205	Clay Matthews	.05
206	Ethan Horton	.05
207	Rich Miano	.05
208	*Chris Mims*	.30
209	Anthony Morgan	.05
210	Rodney Hampton	.10
211	Chris Hinton	.05
212	Esera Tuaolo	.05
213	Shane Conlan	.05
214	John Carney	.05
215	Kenny Walker	.05
216	Scott Radecic	.05
217	Chris Martin	.05
218	Checklist 111-220	.05
219	Weseley Carroll	.05
220	Bill Romanowski	.05
221	Reggie Cobb	.15
222	Alfred Anderson	.05
223	Cleveland Gary	.05
224	*Eddie Blake*	.10
225	Chris Spielman	.05
226	John Roper	.05
227	*George Thomas*	.10
228	Jeff Faulkner	.05
229	Chip Lohmiller	.05
230	Hugh Millen	.05
231	Ray Horton	.05
232	James Campen	.05
233	Howard Cross	.05
234	Keith McKeller	.05
235	Dino Hackett	.05
236	Jerome Brown	.05
237	Andy Heck	.05
238	Jerome Brown	.05
239	Bruce Matthews	.05
240	Jeff Lageman	.05
241	Bobby Hebert	.05
242	Gary Anderson	.05
243	Mark Bortz	.05
244	Rich Moran	.05
245	Jeff Uhlenhake	.05
246	Ricky Sanders	.05
247	Clarence Kay	.05
248	Ed King	.05
249	Eddie Anderson	.05
250	*Amp Lee*	.35
251	Norm Johnson	.05
252	Michael Carter	.05
253	Felix Wright	.05
254	Leon Seals	.05
255	Nate Lewis	.05
256	Kevin Call	.05
257	Darryl Henley	.05
258	Jon Vaughn	.10
259	Matt Bahr, David Alexander	.05
260	Johnny Johnson	.15
261	Ken Norton	.05
262	Wendell Davis	.05
263	Eugene Robinson	.05
264	David Treadwell	.05
265	Michael Haynes	.25
266	Robb Thomas	.05
267	Nate Odomes	.05
268	Martin Mayhew	.05
269	Perry Kemp	.05
270	Jerry Ball	.05
271	*Tommy Vardell*	.20
272	Ernie Mills	.05
273	Mo Lewis	.05
274	Roger Ruzek	.05
275	Steve Smith	.05
276	*Bo Orlando*	.10
277	Louis Oliver	.05
278	Toi Cook	.05
279	Eddie Brown	.05
280	Keith McCants	.05
281	Rob Burnett	.05
282	Keith DeLong	.05
283	Stan Thomas	.05
284	Robert Brown	.05
285	John Alt	.05
286	Randy Dixon	.05
287	Siran Stacy	.20
288	Ray Agnew	.05
289	Darion Conner	.15
290	Kirk Lowdermilk	.05
291	Greg Jackson	.05
292	Ken Harvey	.05
293	Jacob Green	.10
294	Mark Tuinei	.05
295	Mark Rypien	.15
296	*Gerald Robinson*	.08
297	Broderick Thompson	.05
298	Doug Widell	.05
299	Carwell Gardner	.10
300	Barry Sanders	1.25
301	Eric Metcalf	.05
302	Erick Thomas	.05
303	*Terrell Buckley*	.25
304	Byron Evans	.05
305	Johnny Hector	.05
306	Steve Broussard	.05
307	Gene Atkins	.05
308	Terry McDaniel	.05
309	Charles McRae	.05
310	Jim Lachey	.05
311	Pat Harlow	.05
312	Kevin Butler	.05
313	Scott Stephen	.05
314	Dermontti Dawson	.05
315	Johnny Meads	.05
316	Checklist 221-330	.05
317	Aaron Craver	.05
318	Michael Brooks	.05
319	Guy McIntyre	.05
320	Thurman Thomas	.25
321	Courtney Hall	.05
322	Dan Saleaumua	.05
323	*Vinson Smith*	.10
324	Steven Jordan	.05
325	Walter Reeves	.05
326	Erik Kramer	.05
327	Duane Bickett	.05
328	Tom Newberry	.05
329	John Kasay	.05
330	Dave Meggett	.05
331	Kevin Ross	.05
332	*Keith Hamilton*	.15
333	Dwight Stone	.05
334	Mel Gray	.05
335	Harry Galbreath	.05
336	William Perry	.05
337	Brian Blades	.05
338	Randall McDaniel	.05
339	*Pat Coleman*	.12
340	Michael Irvin	.25
341	Checklist 331-440	.05
342	Chris Mohr	.05
343	Greg Davis	.05
344	Dave Cadigan	.05
345	Art Monk	.05
346	Tim Goad	.05
347	Vinnie Clark	.05
348	David Fulcher	.05
349	Craig Heward	.05
350	Ronnie Lott	.05
351	Dexter Carter	.05
352	Mark Jackson	.05
353	Brian Jordan	.05
354	Ray Donaldson	.05
355	Jim Price	.05
356	Rod Bernstine	.05
357	*Tony Mayberry*	.10
358	*Richard Brown*	.10
360	Haywood Jeffires	.15
361	Henry Thomas	.05
362	Jeff Graham	.12
363	Don Warren	.05
364	Scott Davis	.05
365	Harlon Barnett	.05
366	Mark Collins	.05
367	Rick Tuten	.05
368	*Lonnie Marts*	.15
369	Dennis Smith	.05
370	Steve Tasker	.05
371	Robert Massey	.05
372	Ricky Reynolds	.05
373	Alvin Wright	.05
374	Kelvin Martin	.05
375	Vince Buck	.05
376	John Kidd	.05
378	Bryan Cox	.05
379	*Jamie Dukes*	.08
380	Anthony Munoz	.05
381	*Mark Gunn*	.10
382	Keith Henderson	.05
383	Charles Wilson	.05
384	*Shawn McCarthy*	.10
385	Ernie Jones	.05
386	Nick Bell	.10
387	Derrick Walker	.05
388	Mark Stepnoski	.05
389	Broderick Thomas	.05
390	Reggie Roby	.05
391	Bubba McDowell	.05
392	Eric Martin	.05
393	*Toby Cashton*	.10
394	Bern Brostek	.05
395	Christian Okoye	.05
396	Frank Minnifield	.05
397	Mike Golic	.05
398	Grant Feasel	.05
399	Michael Ball	.05
400	Mike Croel	.05
401	Maury Buford	.05
402	Jeff Bostic	.05
403	Sean Landeta	.05
404	Terry Allen	.35
405	Donald Evans	.05
406	Don Mosebar	.05
407	D.J. Dozier	.05
408	Bruce Pickens	.05
409	Jim Dombrowski	.05
410	Deron Cherry	.05
411	Richard Johnson	.05
412	Alexander Wright	.05
413	Tom Rathman	.05
414	Mark Dennis	.05
415	Phil Hansen	.05
416	Lonnie Young	.05
417	Burt Grossman	.05
418	Tony Covington	.05
419	John Stephens	.05
420	Jim Everett	.05
421	Johnny Holland	.05
422	*Mike Barber*	.12
423	Carl Lee	.05
424	*Craig Patterson*	.10
425	Greg Townsend	.05
426	Brett Perriman	.05
427	Morten Andersen	.05
428	John Gesek	.05
429	Bryan Barker	.05
430	John Taylor	.05
431	Donnell Woolford	.05
432	Ron Holmes	.05
433	Lee Williams	.05
434	Alfred Oglesby	.05
435	Jarrod Bunch	.05
436	*Carlton Haselrig*	.10
437	Rufus Porter	.05
438	Rohn Stark	.05
439	Tony Jones	.05
440	Andre Rison	.25
441	Eric Hill	.05
442	Jesse Solomon	.05
443	Jackie Slater	.05
444	Donnie Elder	.05
445	Brett Maxie	.05
446	Max Montoya	.05
447	Will Wolford	.05
448	Craig Taylor	.05
449	Jimmie Jones	.05
450	Anthony Carter	.05
451	*Brian Bollinger*	.08
452	Checklist 441-550	.05
453	Brad Edwards	.05
454	*Gene Chilton*	.08
455	Eric Allen	.05
456	William Roberts	.05
457	Eric Green	.05
458	Irvin Eatman	.05
459	Derrick Thomas	.15
460	Tommy Kane	.05
461	LeRoy Butler	.05
462	Oliver Barnett	.05
463	Anthony Smith	.05
464	Chris Dishman	.05
465	Pat Terrell	.05
466	Greg Kragen	.05
467	Rodney Peete	.05
468	Willie Drewrey	.05
469	Jim Wilks	.05
470	Vince Newsome	.05
471	Chris Gardocki	.05
472	Chris Chandler	.05
473	George Thornton	.05
474	Albert Lewis	.05
475	Kevin Glover	.05
476	*Joe Bowden*	.10
477	Harry Sydney	.05
478	Bob Golic	.05
479	Tony Zendejas	.05
480	Brad Baxter	.05
481	Steve Beuerlein	.15
482	Mark Higgs	.10
483	Drew Hill	.05
484	Bryan Millard	.05
485	Mark Kelso	.05
486	David Grant	.05
487	Gary Zimmerman	.05
488	Leonard Marshall	.05
489	Keith Jackson	.15
490	Sterling Sharpe	.10
491	Ferrell Edmunds	.05
492	Wilber Marshall	.05
493	Charles Haley	.05
494	Riki Ellison	.05
495	Bill Brooks	.05
496	Bill Hawkins	.05
497	Erik Williams	.05
498	*Leon Searcy*	.10
499	Mike Horan	.05
500	Pat Swilling	.05
501	Maurice Hurst	.05
502	William Fuller	.05
503	Tim Newton	.05
504	Lorenzo Lynch	.05
505	Tim Barnett	.05
506	Tom Thayer	.05
507	Chris Burkett	.05
508	Ronnie Harmon	.05
509	James Brooks	.05
510	Bennie Blades	.05
511	Roger Craig	.05
512	Tony Woods	.05
513	Greg Lewis	.05
514	Eric Pegram	.15
515	Elvis Patterson	.05
516	Jeff Cross	.05
517	Myron Guyton	.05
518	Jay Novacek	.15
519	*Leo Barker*	.10
520	Keith Byars	.05
521	Dalton Hilliard	.05
522	Ted Washington	.05
523	*Dexter McNabb*	.10
524	Frank Reich	.05
525	Henry Ellard	.05
526	Barry Foster	.05
527	Barry Word	.15
528	Gary Anderson	.05
529	Reggie Rutland	.05
530	Stephen Baker	.05
531	John Flannery	.05
532	Steve Wright	.05
533	Eric Sanders	.05
534	*Bob Whitfield*	.15
535	Gaston Green	.05
536	Anthony Pleasant	.05
537	Jeff Bryant	.05
538	Jarvis Williams	.05
539	Jim Morrissey	.05
540	Andre Tippett	.05
541	Gill Byrd	.05
542	Raleigh McKenzie	.05
543	Jim Sweeney	.05
544	David Lutz	.05
545	Wayne Martin	.05
546	Karl Wilson	.05
547	Pierce Holt	.05
548	Doug Smith	.05
549	*Nolan Harrison*	.10
550	Freddie Joe Nunn	.05
551	Eric Moore	.05
552	Cris Carter	.05
553	Kevin Gogan	.05
554	Harold Green	.05
555	Kenneth Davis	.05
556	Travis McNeal	.05
557	Jim Jensen	.05
558	Willie Green	.20
559	*Scott Galbraith*	.12
560	Louis Lipps	.05
561	Matt Brock	.05
562	Mike Prior	.05
563	Checklist 551-660	.05
564	Robert Delpino	.05
565	Vinny Testaverde	.05
566	Willie Gault	.05
567	Quinn Early	.05
568	Eric Moten	.05
569	Lance Smith	.05
570	Darrell Green	.05
571	Moe Gardner	.05
572	Steve Atwater	.05
573	Ray Childress	.05
574	Dave Krieg	.05
575	Bruce Armstrong	.05
576	Fred Barnett	.15
577	Don Griffin	.05
578	*David Brandon*	.10
579	Robert Young	.05
580	Keith Van Horne	.05
581	Jeff Criswell	.05
582	Lewis Tillman	.05
583	Bubby Brister	.05
584	Aaron Wallace	.05
585	Chris Doleman	.05
586	*Marty Carter*	.15
587	Chris Warren	.25
588	David Griggs	.05
589	Darrell Thompson	.05
590	Marion Butts	.05
591	Scott Norwood	.05
592	Lomas Brown	.05
593	Daryl Johnston	.05
594	*Alonzo Mitz*	.10
595	Tommy Barnhardt	.05
596	Tim Jorden	.05
597	Neil Smith	.05
598	Todd Marinovich	.12
599	Sean Jones	.05
600	Clarence Verdin	.05
601	Trace Armstrong	.05
602	*Steve Bono*	.50
603	Mark Ingram	.05
604	Flipper Anderson	.05
605	James Jones	.05
606	Al Noga	.05
607	Rick Bryan	.05
608	Eugene Lockhart	.05
609	Charles Mann	.05
610	James Hasty	.05
612	Tim Brown	.35
613	David Little	.05
614	Keith Sims	.05
615	Kevin Murphy	.05
616	Ray Crockett	.05
617	Jim Jeffcoat	.05
618	Patrick Hunter	.05
619	Keith Kartz	.05
620	Peter Tom Willis	.05
621	Vaughan Johnson	.05
622	Shawn Jefferson	.05
623	Anthony Thompson	.05
624	John Rienstra	.05
625	Don Maggs	.05
626	Todd Lyght	.05
627	Brent Jones	.05
628	Todd McNair	.05
629	Winston Moss	.05
630	Mark Carrier	.05
631	Dan Owens	.05
632	Sammie Smith	.05
633	James Lofton	.05
634	*Paul McJulien*	.10
635	Tony Tolbert	.05
636	Carnell Lake	.05
637	Gary Clark	.05
638	Brian Washington	.05
639	Jessie Hester	.05
640	Doug Riesenberg	.05
641	*Joe Walter*	.10
642	John Rade	.05
643	Wes Hopkins	.05
644	Kelly Stouffer	.05
645	Marv Cook	.05
646	Ken Clarke	.05
647	Bobby Humphrey	.05
648	Tim McDonald	.05
649	*Donald Frank*	.12
650	Richmond Webb	.05
651	Lemuel Stinson	.05
652	Merton Hanks	.05
653	Frank Warren	.05
654	Thomas Benson	.05
655	Al Smith	.05
656	Steve DeBerg	.05
657	*Jayice Pearson*	.10
658	Joe Morris	.05
659	Fred Strickland	.05
660	Kelvin Pritchett	.05
661	Lewis Billups	.05
662	Todd Collins	.05
663	Corey Miller	.05
664	Levon Kirkland	.05
665	Jerry Rice	1.00
666	Mike Lodish	.05
667	Chuck Smith	.05
668	Lance Olberding	.05
669	*Kevin Smith*	.30
670	*Dale Carter*	.30
671	*Sean Gilbert*	.30
672	Ken O'Brien	.05
673	Ricky Proehl	.05
674	Junior Seau	.05
675	Courtney Hawkins	.05
676	Eddie Robinson	.05
677	Tom Jeter	.05
678	Jeff George	.05
679	Cary Conklin	.05
680	Rueben Mayes	.05
681	Sean Lumpkin	.05
682	Dan Marino	1.50
683	*Ed McDaniel*	.25
684	Greg Skrepenak	.05
685	Tracy Scroggins	.05
686	*Tommy Maddox*	.30
687	Mike Singletary	.05
688	Patrick Rowe	.05
689	Phillipi Sparks	.05
690	Joel Steed	.05
691	Kevin Fagan	.05
692	Deion Sanders	.05
693	Bruce Smith	.05
694	*David Klingler*	.10
695	Clayton Holmes	.05
696	Brett Favre	2.50
697	Marc Boutte	.05
698	Dwayne Sabb	.05
699	Ed McCaffrey	.05
700	Randall Cunningham	.05
701	*Quentin Coryatt*	.30
702	Bernie Kosar	.05
703	*Vaughn Dunbar*	.15
704	Browning Nagle	.05
705	Mark Wheeler	.05
706	Paul Siever	.05
707	Anthony Miller	.05
708	Corey Widmer	.05
709	Eric Dickerson	.05
710	Martin Bayless	.05
711	Jason Hanson	.05
712	Michael Dean Perry	.05
713	Billy Joe Toliver	.05
714	Chad Hennings	.05
715	*Bucky Richardson*	.30
716	Steve Israel	.05
717	Robert Harris	.05
718	Timm Rosenbach	.05
719	Joe Montana	1.00
720	*Derek Brown*	.15
721	*Robert Brooks*	1.50
722	Boomer Esiason	.05
723	Troy Auzenne	.05
724	John Fina	.05
725	Chris Crooms	.05
726	Eugene Chung	.05
727	Darren Woodson	.05

728	Leslie O'Neal	.05
729	Dan McGwire	.05
730	Al Toon	.05
731	Michael Brandon	.05
732	Steve DeOssie	.05
733	Jim Kelly	.30
734	Webster Slaughter	.05
735	Tony Smith	.05
736	Shane Collins	.05
737	Randal Hill	.05
738	Chris Holder	.05
739	Russell Maryland	.05
740	*Carl Pickens*	.75
741	Andre Reed	.05
742	*Steve Emtman*	.15
743	Carl Banks	.05
744	Troy Aikman	1.00
745	Mark Royals	.05
746	J.J. Birden	.05
747	Michael Cofer	.05
748	Darryl Ashmore	.05
749	Dion Lambert	.05
750	Phil Simms	.05
751	Reggie E. White	.05
752	Harvey Williams	.05
753	Ty Detmer	.05
754	Tony Brooks	.05
755	Steve Christie	.05
756	Lawrence Taylor	.05
757	Merril Hoge	.05
758	Robert Jones	.05
759	Checklist 661-792	.05

1992 Topps Gold

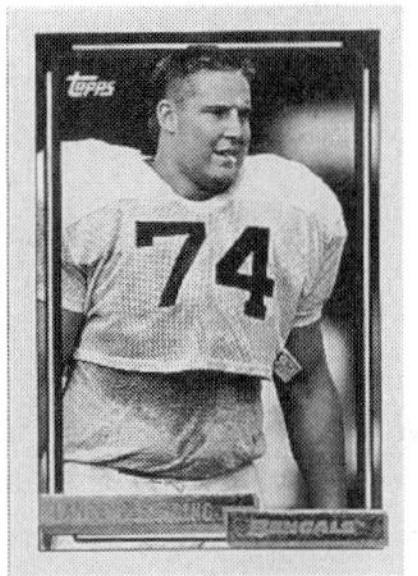

The 759-card, standard-sized set was a parallel to the base set and was inserted once every pack; three every rack pack, and 20 per 660-card factory set. The cards listed below replaced the seven checklist cards. Ten gold cards were also included with each 99-card Hi Series.

		MT
Complete Set (759):		130.00
Complete Series 1 (330):		60.00
Complete Series 2 (330):		50.00
Complete Hi Series (99):		20.00
Common Player:		.20
Veteran Stars:		1.5x-3x
Young Stars:		2x
RCs:		1.25x-2.5x
109	Freeman McNeil	.40
218	David Daniels	.40
316	Chris Hakel	.40
341	Ottis Anderson	.40
452	Shawn Moore	.40
563	Mike Mooney	.40
759	Curtis Whitley	.40

1992 Topps No. 1 Draft Picks

The four-card, standard-size set features No. 1 draft picks from 1990, 1991 and 1992, as well as Notre Dame standout Raghib "Rocket" Ismail. The cards were randomly inserted in 1992 Hi Series packs and the entire set was included with the 99-card Hi Series factory set.

		MT
Complete Set (4):		4.00
Common Player:		1.00
1	Jeff George	1.50
2	Russell Maryland	1.00
3	Steve Emtman	1.00
4	Rocket Ismail	1.25

1992 Topps 1000 Yard Club

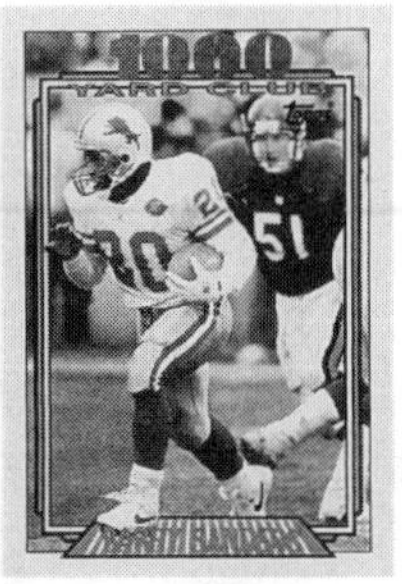

Receivers and running backs who gained more than 1,000 yards during the 1991 NFL season are featured in this 20-card insert set. The white-bordered card front has a color action photo, along with the set's name at the top. The player's name is at the bottom in a green-and-white striped bar. The player's name and 1000 on the front are in red foil. The back has a game-by-game summary in a lime green panel against a background designed like a football field. Each card back is also numbered.

		MT
Complete Set (20):		15.00
Common Player:		.50
1	Emmitt Smith	6.00
2	Barry Sanders	4.00
3	Michael Irvin	2.00
4	Thurman Thomas	2.00
5	Gary Clark	.75
6	Haywood Jeffires	.75
7	Michael Haynes	1.50
8	Drew Hill	.50
9	Mark Duper	.75
10	James Lofton	1.00
11	Rodney Hampton	2.50
12	Mark Clayton	.75
13	Erric Pegram	1.00
14	Art Monk	1.00
15	Earnest Byner	.50
16	Gaston Green	.50
17	Christian Okoye	.50
18	Irving Fryar	.65
19	John Taylor	.75
20	Brian Blades	.50

1993 Topps

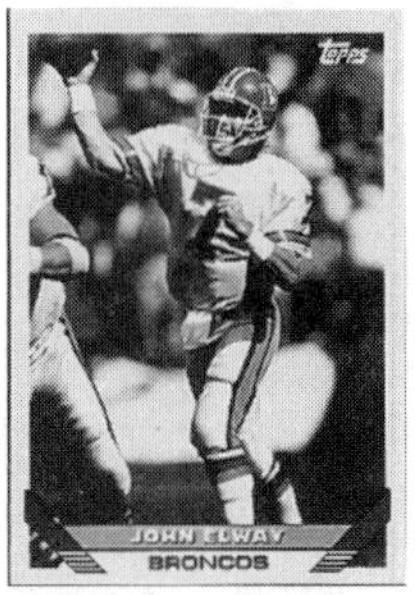

Topps issued its 1993 set in two 330-card series. Subsets include Franchise Players (9 cards), Team Leaders (28), Record Breakers (2), League Leaders (5), Draft Picks (30) and Field Generals (10). The card front has a color action photo surrounded by white borders. The player's name and team are at the bottom between team color-coded diagonal bars. The back has a mug shot, statistics, career summary and biography against a team color-coded background. Each pack contains one Topps Gold card. Topps Black Gold cards were also made and inserted one per every 48 packs.

		MT
Complete Set (660):		25.00
Comp. Factory Set (673):		35.00
Complete Series 1 (330):		15.00
Complete Series 2 (330):		10.00
Common Player:		.05
Minor Stars:		.10
Complete Gold Set (660):		90.00
Complete Gold Series 1 (330):		50.00
Complete Gold Series 2 (330):		40.00
Common Gold:		.20
Minor Gold Stars:		.40
Unlisted Gold Stars:		2x-4x
Series 1 or 2 Pack (15):		.50
Series 1 or 2 Wax Box (36):		14.00

1	Art Monk	.05
2	Jerry Rice	.50
3	Stanley Richard	.05
4	Ron Hall	.05
5	Daryl Johnston	.10
6	Wendell Davis	.05
7	Vaughn Dunbar	.10
8	Mike Jones	.05
9	Anthony Johnson	.05
10	Chris Miller	.05
11	Kyle Clifton	.05
12	*Curtis Conway*	1.00
13	Lionel Washington	.05
14	Reggie Johnson	.05
15	David Little	.05
16	Nick Lowery	.05
17	Darryl Williams	.05
18	Brent Jones	.05
19	Bruce Matthews	.05
20	Heath Sherman, John Kasay	.05
22	*Troy Drayton*	.35
23	Eric Metcalf	.05
24	Andre Tippett	.05
25	Rodney Hampton	.35
26	Henry Jones	.05
27	Jim Everett	.05
28	Steve Jordan	.05
29	LeRoy Butler	.05
30	Troy Vincent	.15
31	Nate Lewis	.05
32	Rickey Jackson	.05
33	Darion Conner	.05
34	*Tom Carter*	.25
35	Jeff George	.20
36	*Larry Centers*	.30
37	Reggie Cobb	.15
38	Mike Saxon	.05
39	Brad Baxter	.05
40	Reggie White	.12
41	Haywood Jeffires	.15
42	Alfred Williams	.05
43	Aaron Wallace	.05
44	Tracy Simien	.05
45	Pat Harlow	.05
46	D.J. Johnson	.05
47	Don Griffin	.05
48	Flipper Anderson	.05
49	Keith Kartz	.05
50	Bernie Kosar	.05
51	Kent Hull	.05
52	Erik Howard	.05
53	Pierce Holt	.05
54	Dwayne Harper	.05
55	Bennie Blades	.05
56	Mark Duper	.05
57	Brian Noble	.05
58	Jeff Feagles	.05
59	Michael Haynes	.20
60	Junior Seau	.15
61	Gary Anderson	.05
62	Jon Hand	.05
63	*Lin Elliott*	.10
64	*Dana Stubblefield*	.50
65	Vaughan Johnson	.05
66	Mo Lewis	.05
67	Aeneas Williams	.05
68	David Fulcher	.05
69	Chip Lohmiller	.05
70	Greg Townsend	.05
71	Simon Fletcher	.05
72	Sean Salisbury	.05
73	Christian Okoye	.05
74	Jim Arnold	.05
75	Bruce Smith	.05
76	Fred Barnett	.15
77	Bill Romanowski	.05
78	Dermontti Dawson	.05
79	Bern Brostek	.05
80	Warren Moon	.15
81	Bill Fralic	.05
82	Lomas Brown	.05
83	Duane Bickett	.05
84	Neil Smith	.05
85	Reggie White	.05
86	Tim McDonald	.05
87	Leslie O'Neal	.05
88	Steve Young	.50
89	Paul Gruber	.05
90	Wilber Marshall	.05
91	Trace Armstrong	.05
92	*Bobby Houston*	.10
93	George Thornton	.05
94	Keith McCants	.05
95	Ricky Sanders	.05
96	Jackie Harris	.20
97	Todd Marinovich	.12
98	Henry Thomas	.05
99	Jeff Wright	.05
100	John Elway	.50
101	*Garrison Hearst*	1.00
102	Roy Foster	.05
103	David Lang	.05
104	Matt Stover	.05
105	Lawrence Taylor	.10
106	Pete Stoyanovich	.05
107	Jessie Tuggle	.05
108	William White	.05
109	*Andy Harmon*	.12
110	John L. Williams	.05
111	Jon Vaughn	.05
112	John Alt	.05
113	Chris Jacke	.05
114	Jim Breech	.05
115	Eric Martin	.05
116	Derrick Walker	.05
117	Ricky Ervins	.12
118	Roger Craig	.05
119	Jeff Gossett	.05
120	Emmitt Smith	2.00
121	Bob Whitfield	.05
122	Alonzo Spellman	.05
123	David Klingler	.15
124	Tommy Maddox	.10
125	Robert Porcher	.05
126	Edgar Bennett	.15
127	Harvey Williams	.15
128	*Dave Brown*	1.00
129	Johnny Mitchell	.25
130	*Drew Bledsoe*	3.00
131	Zefross Moss	.05
132	Nate Odomes	.05
133	Rufus Porter	.05
134	Jackie Slater	.05
135	Steve Young	.50
136	Chris Calloway	.05
137	Steve Atwater	.05
138	Mark Carrier	.05
139	Marvin Washington	.05
140	Barry Foster	.05
141	Ricky Reynolds	.05
142	Bubba McDowell	.05
143	*Dan Footman*	.15
144	Richmond Webb	.05
145	Mike Pritchard	.12
146	Chris Spielman	.05
147	Dave Krieg	.05
148	Nick Bell	.15
149	Vincent Brown	.05
150	Seth Joyner	.05
151	Tommy Kane	.05
152	*Carlton Gray*	.25
153	Harry Newsome	.05
154	Rohn Stark	.05
155	Shannon Sharpe	.05
156	Charles Haley	.05
157	Cornelius Bennett	.05
158	Doug Riesenberg	.05
159	Amp Lee	.10
160	Sterling Sharpe	.40
161	Alonzo Mitz	.05
162	Pat Terrill	.05
163	Mark Schlereth	.05
164	Gary Anderson	.05
165	Quinn Early	.05
166	*Jerome Bettis*	1.25
167	Lawrence Dawsey	.05
168	Derrick Thomas	.15
169	Rodney Peete	.10
170	Jim Kelly	.25
171	Deion Sanders	.25
172	Richard Dent	.05
173	Emmitt Smith	.75
174	Barry Sanders	.50
175	Sterling Sharpe	.25
176	Cleveland Gary	.05
177	Terry Allen	.10
178	Vaughan Johnson	.05
179	Rodney Hampton	.10
180	Randall Cunningham	.05
181	Ricky Proehl	.05
182	Jerry Rice	.20
183	Reggie Cobb	.05
184	Earnest Byner	.05
185	Jeff Lageman	.05
186	Carlos Jenkins	.05
187	Cardinals Draft Picks	.50
188	Todd Lyght	.05
189	*Carl Simpson*	.12
190	Barry Sanders	1.25
191	Jim Harbaugh	.10
192	Roger Ruzek	.05
193	Brent Williams	.05
194	Chip Banks	.05
195	Mike Croel	.05
196	Marion Butts	.05
197	James Washington	.05
198	John Offerdahl	.05
199	Tom Rathman	.05
200	Joe Montana	1.25
201	Pepper Johnson	.05
202	Cris Dishman	.05
203	*Adrian White*	.10
204	*Reggie Brooks*	.25
205	Cortez Kennedy	.10
206	Robert Massey	.05
207	Toi Cook	.05
208	Harry Sydney	.05
209	*Lincoln Kennedy*	.15
210	Randall McDaniel	.05
211	Eugene Daniel	.05
212	Rob Burnett	.05
213	Steve Broussard	.05
214	Brian Washington	.05
215	*Leonard Renfro*	.12
216	Audray McMillian, Henry Jones	.05
217	Sterling Sharpe, Anthony Miller	.20
218	Clyde Simmons, Leslie O'Neal	.05
219	Emmitt Smith, Barry Foster	.50
220	Steve Young, Warren Moon	.12
221	Mel Gray	.05
222	Luis Sharpe	.05
223	Eric Moten	.05
224	Albert Lewis	.05
225	Alvin Harper	.30
226	Steve Wallace	.05
227	Mark Higgs	.15
228	Eugene Lockhart	.05
229	Sean Jones	.05
230	Buccaneers Draft Picks	.15
231	Jimmy Williams	.05
232	*Demetrius DuBose*	.15
233	John Roper	.05
234	Keith Hamilton	.05
235	Donald Evans	.05
236	Kenneth Davis	.05
237	*John Copeland*	.30
238	Leonard Russell	.12
239	Ken Harvey	.05
240	Dale Carter	.10
241	Anthony Pleasant	.05
242	Darrell Green	.05
243	*Natrone Means*	1.00
244	Rob Moore	.10
245	Chris Doleman	.05
246	J.B. Brown	.05
247	Ray Crockett	.05
248	John Taylor	.10
249	Russell Maryland	.05
250	Brett Favre	2.00
251	Carl Pickens	.50
252	Andy Heck	.05
253	Jerome Henderson	.05
254	Deion Sanders	.15
255	Steve Emtman	.10
256	Calvin Williams	.05
257	Sean Gilbert	.05
258	Don Beebe	.05
259	*Robert Smith*	1.00
260	Rogert Blackmon	.05
261	Jim Kelly	.10
262	Harold Green	.05
263	Clay Matthews	.05
264	John Elway	.10
265	Warren Moon	.10
266	Jeff George	.10
267	Derrick Thomas	.05
268	Howie Long	.05
269	Dan Marino	.60
270	Jon Vaughn	.05
271	Chris Burkett	.05
272	Barry Foster	.10
273	Marion Butts	.05
274	Chris Warren	.05
275	Giants Draft Picks	.15
276	Tony Casillas	.05
277	Jarrod Bunch	.05
278	Eric Green	.05
279	Stan Brock	.05
280	Chester McGlockton	.05
281	Ricky Watters	.40
282	Dan Saleaumua	.05
283	Rich Camarillo	.05
284	Cris Carter	.05
285	*Rick Mirer*	.25
286	Matt Brock	.05
287	Burt Grossman	.05
288	Andre Collins	.05
289	Mark Jackson	.05
290	Dan Marino	2.00
291	Cornelius Bennett	.05
292	Steve Atwater	.05
293	Bryan Cox	.05
294	Sam Mills	.05
295	Pepper Johnson	.05
296	Seth Joyner	.05
297	Chris Spielman	.05
298	Junior Seau	.05
299	Cortez Kennedy	.05
300	Broderick Thomas	.05
301	Todd McNair	.05
302	Nate Newton	.05
303	Mike Waltr	.05
304	Clyde Simmons	.05
305	Ernie Mills	.05
306	Steve Wisniewski	.05
307	*Coleman Rudolph*	.10
308	Thurman Thomas	.50
309	Reggie Roby	.05
310	Eric Swann	.05
311	Mark Wheeler	.05
312	Jeff Herrod	.05
313	Leroy Hoard	.05
314	*Patrick Bates*	.10
315	Earnest Byner	.05
316	Dave Meggett	.05
317	*George Teague*	.25
318	Ray Childress	.05
319	Mike Kenn	.05
320	Jason Hanson	.05
321	Gary Clark	.10
322	Chris Gardocki	.05
323	Ken Norton	.05
324	*Eric Curry*	.30
325	Byron Evans	.05
326	*O.J. McDuffie*	1.00
327	Dwight Stone	.05
328	Tommy Barnhardt	.05
329	Checklist 1-165	.05
330	Checklist 166-330	.05
331	Erik Williams	.05
332	Phil Hansen	.05
333	*Martin Harrison*	.15
334	Mark Ingram	.05
335	Mark Rypien	.08
336	Anthony Miller	.05
337	Antone Davis	.05
338	Mike Munchak	.05
339	Wayne Martin	.05
340	Joe Montana	1.50
341	*Deon Figures*	.15
342	Ed McDaniel	.05
343	Chris Burkett	.05
344	Tony Smith	.05
345	James Lofton	.05
346	Courtney Hawkins	.05
347	Dennis Smith	.05
348	Anthony Morgan	.05
349	Chris Goode	.05
350	Phil Simms	.10
351	Patrick Hunter	.05
352	Brett Perriman	.07
353	Corey Miller	.05
354	Harry Galbreath	.05
355	Mark Carrier	.05
356	Troy Drayton	.05
357	Greg Davis	.05
358	Tim Krumrie	.05
359	Tim McDonald	.05
360	Webster Slaughter	.05
361	Steve Christie	.05
362	Courtney Hall	.05
363	Charles Mann	.05
364	Vestee Jackson	.05
365	Robert Jones	.05
366	Rich Miano	.06
367	Morten Andersen	.06
368	Jeff Graham	.05
369	Martin Mayhew	.05
370	Anthony Carter	.05
371	Greg Kragen	.05
372	Ron Cox	.05
373	Perry Williams	.05
374	Willie Gault	.05
375	Chris Warren	.15
376	Reyna Thompson	.05
377	Bennie Thompson	.05
378	Kevin Mack	.05
379	Clarence Verdin	.05
380	Marc Boutte	.05
381	*Marvin Jones*	.15
382	Greg Jackson	.05
383	Steve Bono	.50
384	Terrell Buckley	.10
385	Garrison Hearst	.50
386	Mike Brim	.05
387	Jesse Sapolu	.05
388	Carl Lee	.05
389	Jeff Cross	.05
390	Karl Mecklenburg	.05
391	Chad Hennings	.05
392	Oliver Barnett	.05
393	Dalton Hilliard	.06
394	Broderick Thompson	.05
395	Raghib Ismail	.25
396	John Kidd	.05
397	Eddie Anderson	.05
398	Lamar Lathon	.05
399	Darren Perry	.05
400	Drew Bledsoe	2.00
401	Ferrell Edmunds	.05
402	Lomas Brown	.05
403	Drew Hill	.05
404	David Whitmore	.05
405	Mike Johnson	.05
406	Paul Gruber	.05
407	Kirk Lowdermilk	.05
408	Curtis Conway	.50
409	Bryce Paup	.05
410	Boomer Esiason	.08
411	Jay Schroeder	.06
412	*Anthony Newman*	.08
413	Ernie Jones	.05
414	Carlton Bailey	.05
415	Kenneth Gant	.05
416	Todd Scott	.05
417	Anthony Smith	.05
418	Erik McMillan	.05
419	Ronnie Harmon	.06
420	Andre Reed	.07
421	Wymon Henderson	.05
422	Carnell Lake	.05
423	Al Noga	.05
424	Curtis Duncan	.05
425	Mike Gann	.05
426	Eugene Robinson	.05
427	Scott Mersereau	.05
428	Chris Singleton	.05
429	Gerald Robinson	.05
430	Pat Swilling	.05
431	Ed McCaffrey	.05
432	Neal Anderson	.06
433	Joe Phillips	.05
434	Jerry Ball	.05
435	Tyrone Stowe	.05
436	Dana Stubblefield	.25
437	Eric Curry	.10
438	Derrick Fenner	.05
439	Mark Clayton	.06
440	Quentin Coryatt	.10
441	*Willie Roaf*	.10
442	Earnest Dye	.05
443	Jeff Jaeger	.05
444	Stan Humphries	.05
445	Johnny Johnson	.07
446	Larry Brown	.05
447	Kurt Gouveia	.05
448	*Qadry Ismail*	.25
449	Dan Footman	.05
450	Tom Waddle	.05
451	Kelvin Martin	.05
452	Kanavis McGhee	.05
453	Herman Moore	.50
454	Jesse Solomon	.05
455	Shane Conlan	.05
456	Joel Steed	.05
457	Charles Arbuckle	.05
458	Shane Dronett	.05
459	Steve Tasker	.05
460	Herschel Walker	.07
461	Willie Davis	.10
462	Al Smith	.05
463	O.J. McDuffie	.50
464	Kevin Fagan	.05
465	Hardy Nickerson	.05
466	Leonard Marshall	.05
467	John Baylor	.05
468	Jay Novacek	.06
469	*Wayne Simmons*	.10
470	Tommy Vardell	.06
471	Cleveland Gary	.05
472	Mark Collins	.05
473	Craig Heyward	.05
474	John Copeland	.08
475	Jeff Hostetler	.08
476	Brian Mitchell	.05
477	Natrone Means	.75
478	Brad Muster	.05
479	David Lutz	.05
480	Andre Rison	.30
481	Michael Zordich	.05
482	Jim McMahon	.06
483	Carlton Gray	.05
484	Chris Mohr	.05
485	Ernest Givins	.05
486	Tony Tolbert	.05
487	Vai Sikahema	.05
488	Larry Webster	.05
489	James Hasty	.05
490	Reggie White	.10
491	*Reggie Rivers*	.25
492	Roman Phifer	.05
493	Levon Kirkland	.05
494	Demetrius DuBose	.10
495	William Perry	.05
496	Clay Matthews	.05
497	Aaron Jones	.05
498	Jack Trudeau	.05
499	Michael Brooks	.05
500	Jerry Rice	.60
501	Lonnie Marts	.05
502	Tim McGee	.05
503	Kelvin Pritchett	.05
504	Bobby Hebert	.06
505	Audray McMillian	.05
506	Chuck Cecil	.05
507	Leonard Renfro	.05
508	Ethan Horton	.05
509	Kevin Smith	.06
510	Louis Oliver	.05
511	John Stephens	.05
512	Browning Nagle	.07
513	Ricardo McDonald	.05
514	Leslie O'Neal	.05
515	Lorenzo White	.07
516	*Thomas Smith*	.10
517	Tony Woods	.05
518	Darryl Henley	.05
519	Robert Delpino	.05
520	Rod Woodson	.07
521	Phillippi Sparks	.05
522	Jessie Hester	.05
523	Shaun Gayle	.05
524	Brad Edwards	.05
525	Randall Cunningham	.10
526	Marv Cook	.05
527	Dennis Gibson	.05
528	Erric Pegram	.25
529	Terry McDaniel	.05
530	Troy Aikman	1.25
531	Irving Fryar	.06
532	Blair Thomas	.05
533	Jim Wilks	.05
534	Michael Jackson	.06
535	Eric Davis	.05
536	James Campen	.05
537	Steve Beuerlein	.10
538	Robert Smith	.15
539	J.J. Birden	.05
540	Broderick Thomas	.05
541	Darryl Talley	.05
542	*Russell Freeman*	.10
543	David Alexander	.05
544	Chris Mims	.07
545	Coleman Rudolph	.05
546	Steve McMichael	.05
547	David Williams	.05
548	Chris Hinton	.05
549	Jim Jeffcoat	.05
550	Howie Long	.05
551	*Roosevelt Potts*	.25
552	Bryan Cox	.05
553	David Richards	.05
554	Reggie Brooks	.40
555	Neil O'Donnell	.25
556	Irv Smith	.05
557	Henry Ellard	.05
558	Steve DeBerg	.05
559	Jim Sweeney	.05
560	Harold Green	.05
561	Darrell Thompson	.05
562	Vinny Testaverde	.08
563	Bubby Brister	.06
564	Sean Landeta	.05
565	Neil Smith	.05
566	Craig Erickson	.05
567	Jim Ritcher	.05
568	Don Mosebar	.05
569	John Gesek	.05
570	Gary Plummer	.05
571	Norm Johnson	.05
572	Ron Heller	.05
573	Carl Simpson	.05
574	Greg Montgomery	.05
575	Dana Hall	.05
576	Vencie Glenn	.05
577	Dean Biasucci	.05
578	Rod Bernstine	.05
579	Randal Hill	.07
580	Sam Mills	.05
581	Santana Dotson	.05
582	Greg Lloyd	.06
583	Eric Thomas	.05
584	Henry Rolling	.05
585	Tony Bennett	.05
586	Sheldon White	.05
587	Mark Kelso	.05
588	Marc Spindler	.05
589	Greg McMurtry	.05
590	Art Monk	.07
591	Marco Coleman	.05
592	Tony Jones	.05
593	Melvin Jenkins	.05
594	Kevin Ross	.05
595	William Fuller	.05
596	James Joseph	.05
597	*Lamar McGriggs*	.15
598	Gill Byrd	.05
599	Alexander Wright	.05
600	Rick Mirer	.10
601	Richard Dent	.05
602	Thomas Everett	.05
603	Jack Del Rio	.05
604	Jerome Bettis	.75
605	Ronnie Lott	.06
606	Marty Carter	.05
607	*Arthur Marshall*	.30
608	Lee Johnson	.05
609	Bruce Armstrong	.05
610	Ricky Proehl	.05

611 Will Wolford .05
612 Mike Prior .05
613 George Jamison .05
614 Gene Atkins .05
615 Merril Hoge .05
616 Desmond Howard .25
617 Jarvis Williams .05
618 Marcus Allen .07
619 Gary Brown .25
620 Bill Brooks .05
621 Eric Allen .05
622 *Todd Kelly* .10
623 Michael Dean Perry .05
624 David Braxton .05
625 Mike Sherrard .05
626 Jeff Bryant .05
627 Eric Bieniemy .06
628 Tim Brown .06
629 Troy Auzenne .05
630 Michael Irvin .35
631 Maurice Hurst .05
632 Duane Bickett .05
633 George Teague .08
634 Vince Workman .05
635 Renaldo Turnbull .05
636 Johnny Bailey .05
637 *Dan Williams* .15
638 James Thornton .05
639 Terry Allen .06
640 Kevin Greene .05
641 Tony Zendejas .05
642 *Scott Kowalkowski* .10
643 Jeff Query .05
644 Brian Blades .05
645 Keith Jackson .08
646 Monte Coleman .05
647 Guy McIntyre .05
648 Barry Word .05
649 *Steve Everitt* .10
650 Patrick Bates .10
651 Marcus Robertson .05
652 John Carney .05
653 Derek Brown .06
654 Carwell Gardner .05
655 Moe Gardner .05
656 Andre Ware .06
657 Keith Van Horne .05
658 Hugh Millen .05
659 Checklist 3 of 4 .05
660 Checklist 4 of 4 .05

1993 Topps Gold

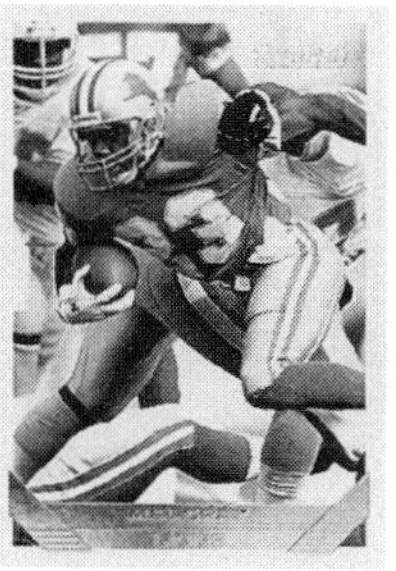

The 660-card, standard-size set was inserted in each pack (Three per rack pack, five per jumbo) and was a parallel to the 1993 base Topps set. The four checklist cards were replaced by the player cards listed below.

	MT
Complete Set (660):	90.00
Complete Series 1 (330):	50.00
Complete Series 2 (330):	40.00
Common Player:	.15
Veteran Stars:	1.5x-3x
Young Stars:	1.25x-2.5x
RCs:	1.25x-2.5x
329 Terance Mathis	1.00
330 Alex Wojchiechowicz	.50
659 Pat Chaffey	.50
660 Milton Mack	.50

1993 Topps Black Gold

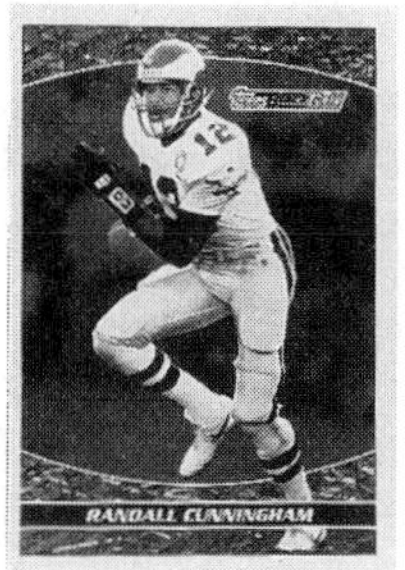

These cards feature an action photo against a curved, screened gold-foil background with white borders. The player's name is in a black stripe at the bottom; the set name is also on the card front. The numbered backs are in a horizontal format and include a player profile shot and a career summary against a blue-green background. Cards were randomly included in every 48th pack of 1993 Topps football; cards 1-22 were in Series I packs, while 23-44 were in Series II packs. "You Just Won" cards were also available in Series I packs, good for mail-in offers for cards 1-11, 12-22 and 1-22. Series II packs had offers for cards 23-33, 34-44, 23-44 and the entire set (1-44). Winners then became eligible to win one of 500 uncut sheets of the set.

	MT
Complete Set (44):	35.00
Complete Series 1 (22):	15.00
Complete Series 2 (22):	20.00
Common Player:	.50
Minor Stars:	1.00

1 Kelvin Martin .50
2 Audray McMillian .50
3 Terry Allen .50
4 Vai Sikahema .50
5 Clyde Simmons .50
6 Lorenzo White .50
7 Michael Irvin 2.00
8 Troy Aikman 5.00
9 Mark Kelso .50
10 Cleveland Gary .50
11 Greg Montgomery .50
12 Jerry Rice 5.00
13 Rod Woodson 1.00
14 Leslie O'Neal .50
15 Harold Green .50
16 Randall Cunningham 1.00
17 Ricky Watters 2.00
18 Andre Rison 1.00
19 Eugene Robinson .50
20 Wayne Martin .50
21 Chris Warren 1.00
22 Anthony Miller .50
23 Steve Young 3.00
24 Tim Harris .50
25 Emmitt Smith 8.00
26 Sterling Sharpe 1.00
27 Henry Jones .50
28 Warren Moon 1.00
29 Barry Foster .50
30 Dale Carter .50
31 Mel Gray .50
32 Barry Sanders 5.00
33 Dan Marino 8.00
34 Fred Barnett .50
35 Deion Sanders 3.00
36 Simon Fletcher .50
37 Donnell Woolford .50
38 Reggie Cobb .50
39 Brett Favre 8.00
40 Thurman Thomas 1.00
41 Rodney Hampton .50
42 Eric Martin .50
43 Pete Stoyanovich .50
44 Herschel Walker .50

1993 Topps FantaSports

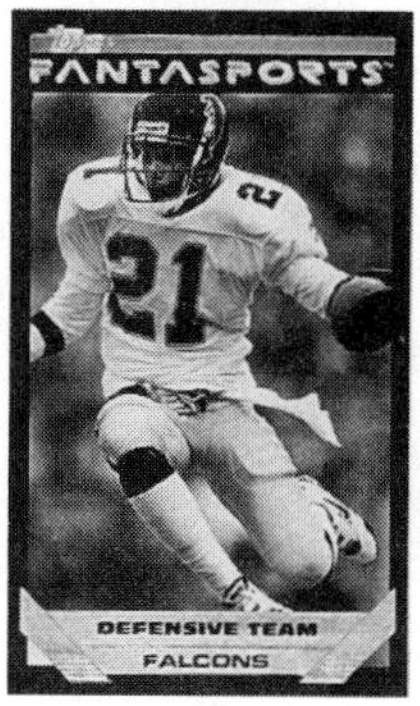

The 200-card, 3" x 5" set is an interactive fantasy game in which the players are rated on a three-year basis. For $159, the collector could purchase the entire set which also included entry into the fantasy league, a stat book, worksheets and instructions. The collector who earned the best fantasy score over 18 games won four tickets to Super Bowl XXVIII. The game was test-marketed in four cities: Buffalo, Houston, Kansas City and Washington, D.C. "FantaSports" appears in gold foil on the top black border. The cards are arranged by position.

	MT
Complete Set (200):	120.00
Common Player:	.25

1 Chris Miller .25
2 Jim Kelly 1.00
3 Jim Harbaugh .75
4 David Klingler .25
5 Bernie Kosar .50
6 Troy Aikman 8.00
7 John Elway 5.00
8 Tommy Maddox .25
9 Rodney Peete .50
10 Andre Ware .50
11 Brett Favre 20.00
12 Warren Moon 1.00
13 Jeff George 1.00
14 Dave Krieg .50
15 Joe Montana 8.00
16 Todd Marinovich .25
17 Jim Everett .50
18 Dan Marino 20.00
19 Sean Salisbury .25
20 Drew Bledsoe 8.00
21 Dave Brown .75
22 Phil Simms .50
23 Boomer Esiason .50
24 Browning Nagle .25
25 Randall Cunningham .50
26 Neil O'Donnell .50
27 Stan Humphries 1.00
28 Steve Young 5.00
29 Rick Mirer 3.00
30 Mark Rypien .50
31 Kenneth Davis .25
32 Thurman Thomas 1.50
33 Steve Broussard .25
34 Neal Anderson .50
35 Craig Heyward .25
36 Derrick Fenner .25
37 Harold Green .25
38 Leroy Hoard .25
39 Kevin Mack .25
40 Eric Metcalf 1.00
41 Tommy Vardell .25
42 Daryl Johnston .75
43 Emmitt Smith 20.00
44 Barry Sanders 8.00
45 Edgar Bennett .75
46 Lorenzo White .50
47 Anthony Johnson .25
48 Todd McNair .25
49 Christian Okoye .25
50 Harvey Williams .75
51 Barry Word .25
52 Nick Bell .25
53 Eric Dickerson .75
54 Jerome Bettis 5.00
55 Cleveland Gary .25
56 Mark Higgs .25
57 Tony Paige .25
58 Terry Allen .75
59 Roger Craig .50
60 Robert Smith 1.25
61 Leonard Russell .50
62 Jon Vaughn .25
63 Vaughn Dunbar .25
64 Dalton Hilliard .25
65 Jarrod Bunch .25
66 Rodney Hampton .75
67 Dave Meggett .25
68 Brad Baxter .25
69 Heath Sherman .25
70 Vai Sikahema .25
71 Johnny Bailey .25
72 Larry Centers .75
73 Garrison Hearst 3.00
74 Barry Foster .25
75 Eric Bieniemy .25
76 Marion Butts .25
77 Ronnie Harmon .25
78 Natrone Means 4.00
79 Amp Lee .25
80 Tom Rathman .25
81 Ricky Watters 1.00
82 Chris Warren 1.00
83 John L. Williams .25
84 Gary Anderson (RB) .25
85 Reggie Cobb .25
86 Vince Workman .25
87 Reggie Brooks .75
88 Earnest Byner .25
89 Ricky Ervins .25
90 Michael Haynes .50
91 Mike Pritchard .75
92 Andre Rison .75
93 Don Beebe .50
94 Andre Reed .50
95 Curtis Conway 3.00
96 Wendell Davis .25
97 Tom Waddle .25
98 Carl Pickens 1.00
99 Michael Jackson .50
100 Alvin Harper .75
101 Michael Irvin 1.00
102 Vance Johnson .25
103 Mel Gray .50
104 Sterling Sharpe 1.00
105 Curtis Duncan .25
106 Ernest Givins .50
107 Haywood Jeffires .50
108 Tim Brown 1.00
109 Willie Gault .25
110 Flipper Anderson .25
111 Henry Ellard .75
112 Mark Duper .50
113 O.J. McDuffie 2.00
114 Anthony Carter .50
115 Cris Carter 1.00
116 Mike Farr .25
117 Quinn Early .50
118 Eric Martin .25
119 Chris Calloway .25
120 Mark Jackson .25
121 Rob Moore .50
122 Fred Barnett .50
123 Calvin Williams .50
124 Gary Clark .50
125 Randal Hill .50
126 Ricky Proehl .25
127 Jeff Graham .50
128 Ernie Mills .50
129 Dwight Stone .25
130 Nate Lewis .25
131 Jerry Rice 8.00
132 John Taylor .50
133 Tommy Kane .25
134 Kelvin Martin .25
135 Lawrence Dawsey .50
136 Courtney Hawkins .50
137 Art Monk .50
138 Pete Metzelaars .25
139 Jay Novacek .50
140 Reggie Johnson .25
141 Shannon Sharpe .75
142 Jackie Harris .50
143 Troy Drayton .25
144 Keith Jackson .50
145 Steve Jordan .25
146 Johnny Mitchell .50
147 Eric Green .50
148 Derrick Walker .25
149 Brent Jones .50
150 Ron Hall .25
151 Norm Johnson .25
152 Jim Breech .25
153 Matt Stover .25
154 Lin Elliott .25
155 Jason Hanson .25
156 Chris Jacke .25
157 Nick Lowery .25
158 Pete Stoyanovich .25
159 Roger Ruzek .25
160 Gary Anderson (K) .25
161 John Kasay .25
162 Chip Lohmiller .25
163 Chris Gardocki .25
164 Mike Saxon .25
165 Jim Arnold .25
166 Rohn Stark .25
167 Jeff Gossett .25
168 Reggie Roby .25
169 Harry Newsome .25
170 Tommy Barnhardt .25
171 Jeff Feagles .25
172 Rick Camarillo .25
173 Falcons Defense (Deion Sanders) 4.00
174 Bills Defense (Cornelius Bennett) .50
175 Bears Defense (Mark Carrier) (DB) .50
176 Bengals Defense (Darryl Williams) .25
177 Browns Defense (Michael Dean Perry) .50
178 Cowboys Defense (Russell Maryland) .50
179 Broncos Defense (Steve Atwater) .25
180 Lions Defense (Bennie Blades) .25
181 Packers Defense (Reggie White) 1.00
182 Oilers Defense (Cris Dishman) .25
183 Colts Defense (Steve Emtman) .25
184 Chiefs Defense (Derrick Thomas) 1.00
185 Raiders Defense (Howie Long) .50
186 Rams Defense (Sean Gilbert) .50
187 Dolphins Defense (John Offerdahl) .25
188 Vikings Defense (Chris Doleman) .25
189 Patriots Defense (Andre Tippett) .25
190 Saints Defense (Sam Mills) .25
191 Giants Defense (Lawrence Taylor) .75
192 Jets Defense (James Hasty) .25
193 Eagles Defense (Clyde Simmons) .50
194 Cardinals Defense (Eric Swann) .50
195 Steelers Defense (Greg Lloyd) .75
196 Chargers Defense (Junior Seau) 1.25
197 49ers Defense (Kevin Fagan) .25
198 Seahawks Defense (Cortez Kennedy) .75
199 Buccaneers Defense (Broderick Thomas) .25
200 Redskins Defense (Darrell Green) .50

1994 Topps

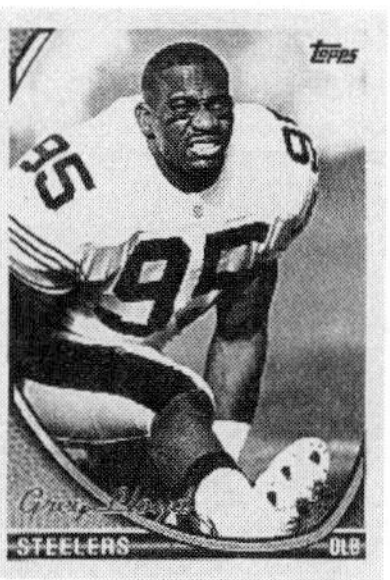

Topps issued its 1994 set in two 330-card series, along with its parallel Special Effects set. Two insert sets, Finest and Spectralight All-Pros, were also made. The regular cards have a front with a full-color action photo, bordered by a gold-foil border and white frame. The Topps logo appears on the front, too, along with the player's name, which is stamped in gold foil. The card back has a player photo, biographical and statistical information, a card number and a player profile. Subsets within the main set included Career Active Leaders, Draft Picks, Tools of the Game, and Measures of Greatness. Special Effects cards were issued one per pack.

	MT
Complete Set (660):	45.00
Complete Series 1 (330):	22.00
Complete Series 2 (330):	22.00
Common Player:	.05
Special Effects Set (660):	300.00
SE Cards:	3x-6x
Series 1 or 2 Pack (12):	1.00
Series 1 or 2 Wax Box (36):	30.00

1 Emmitt Smith 2.00
2 Russell Copeland .08
3 Jesse Sapolu .05
4 David Scott .05
5 Rodney Hampton .30
6 Bubba McDowell .05
7 Bryce Paup .05
8 Winston Moss .05
9 Brett Perriman .05
10 Rod Woodson .10
11 John Randle .05
12 David Wyman .05
13 Jeff Cross .05
14 Richard Cooper .05
15 Johnny Mitchell .10
16 David Alexander .05
17 Ronnie Harmon .07
18 Tyrone Stowe .05
19 Chris Zorich .05
20 Rob Burnett .05
21 Harold Alexander .05
22 Rod Stephens .05
23 Mark Wheeler .05
24 Dwayne Sabb .05
25 Troy Drayton .15
26 Kurt Gouveia .05
27 Warren Moon .15
28 Jeff Query .05
29 *Chuck Levy* .40
30 Bruce Smith .10
31 Doug Riesenberg .05
32 Willie Drewrey .05
33 Nate Newton .07
34 James Jett .20
35 George Teague .20
36 Marc Spindler .05
37 Jack Del Rio .05
38 Dale Carter .05
39 Steve Atwater .07
40 Herschel Walker .07
41 James Hasty .05
42 Seth Joyner .10
43 Keith Jackson .10
44 Tommy Vardell .05
45 Antonio Langham .05
46 Derek Brown .25
47 John Wojciechowski .05
48 Horace Copeland .15
49 Luis Sharpe .05
50 Pat Harlow .05
51 *David Palmer* .65
52 Tony Smith .05
53 Tim Johnson .05
54 Anthony Newman .05
55 Terry Wooden .05
56 Derrick Fenner .05
57 Mike Fox .05
58 Brad Hopkins .05
59 Daryl Johnson .08
60 Steve Young .75
61 *Scottie Graham* .35
62 Nolan Harrison .05
63 David Richards .05
64 Chris Mohr .05
65 Hardy Nickerson .05
66 Heath Sherman .05
67 Irving Fryar .10
68 Ray Buchanan .05
69 Jay Taylor .05
70 Shannon Sharpe .15
71 Vinny Testaverde .05
72 Renaldo Turnbull .05
73 Dwight Stone .05
74 *Willie McGinnest* .50
75 Darrell Green .07
76 Kyle Clifton .05
77 Leo Goeas .05
78 Ken Ruettgers .05
79 Craig Heyward .05
80 Andre Rison .20
81 Chris Mims .15
82 Gary Clark .07
83 Ricardo McDonald .05
84 Patrick Hunter .05
85 Bruce Matthews .05
86 Russell Maryland .06
87 Gary Anderson .05
88 Brad Edwards .05
89 Carlton Bailey .05
90 Qadry Ismail .50
91 Terry McDaniel .05
92 Willie Green .05
93 Cornelius Bennett .05
94 Paul Gruber .05
95 Pete Stoyanovich .08
96 Merton Hanks .05
97 Tre' Johnson .05
98 Jonathan Hayes .05
99 Jason Elam .15
100 Jerome Bettis .50
101 Ronnie Lott .08
102 Maurcie Hurst .05
103 Kirk Lowdermilk .05
104 Tony Jones .05
105 Steve Beuerlein .08
106 Isaac Davis .05
107 Vaughan Johnson .05
108 Terrell Buckley .05
109 Pierce Holt .05
110 Alonzo Spellman .05
111 Patrick Robinson .05
112 Cortez Kennedy .10
113 Kevin Williams .50
114 Danny Copeland .05
115 Chris Doleman .05
116 Jerry Rice .45
117 Neil Smith .08
118 Emmitt Smith .75
119 Eugene Robinson, Nate Odomes .05
120 Steve Young .60
121 Carnell Lake .05
122 Ernest Givins .05
123 Henry Jones .05
124 Michael Brooks .05
125 Jason Hanson .07
126 Andy Harmon .05
127 *Errict Rhett* .75
128 Harris Barton .05
129 Greg Robinson .05
130 Derrick Thomas .10
131 Keith Kartz .05
132 Lincoln Kennedy .08
133 Leslie O'Neal .05
134 Tim Goad .05
135 Rohn Stark .05
136 O.J. McDuffie .40
137 Donnell Woolford .05
138 *Jamir Miller* .50
139 Eric Thomas .05
140 Willie Roaf .08
141 Wayne Gandy .05
142 Mike Brim .05
143 Kelvin Martin .08
144 Edgar Bennett .07
145 Michael Dean Perry .05
146 Shante Carver .05
147 Jesse Armstead .05
148 Mo Elewonibi .05
149 Dana Stubblefield .35
150 Cody Carlson .05
151 Vencie Glenn .05
152 Levon Kirkland .05
153 Derrick Moore .15
154 John Fina .05
155 Jeff Hostetler .15
156 Courtney Hawkins .20
157 Todd Collins .05
158 Neil Smith .05
159 Simon Fletcher .08
160 Dan Marino 2.00
161 *Sam Adams* .25
162 Marvin Washington .05
163 John Copeland .05
164 Eugene Robinson .05
165 Mark Carrier .05
166 Mike Kenn .05
167 Tyrone Hughes .05
168 Darren Carrington .05
169 Shane Conlan .05
170 Ricky Proehl .05
171 Jeff Herrod .05
172 Mark Carrier .05
173 George Koonce .05
174 Desmond Howard .08
175 David Meggett .05
176 Charles Haley .06
177 Steve Wisniewski .05
178 Dermontti Dawson .05
179 Tim McDonald .08
180 Broderick Thomas .05
181 Bernard Dafney .05
182 Bo Orlando .10
183 Andre Reed .10
184 Randall Cunningham .15
185 Chris Spielman .05
186 Keith Byars .05
187 Ben Coates .05
188 Tracy Simien .05
189 Carl Pickens .10
190 Reggie White .15
191 Norm Johnson .05
192 Brian Washington .05
193 Stan Humphries .05
194 Fred Stokes .05
195 Dan Williams .05
196 John Elway .40
197 Eric Allen .10
198 Hardy Nickerson .05
199 Jerome Bettis .25
200 Troy Aikman 1.00
201 Thurman Thomas .40
202 Cornelius Bennett .05
203 Michael Irvin .20
204 Jim Kelly .20
205 Junior Seau .10
206 *Heath Shuler* .25
207 Howard Cross .05
208 Pat Swilling .05
209 Pete Metzelaars .05
210 Tony McGee .05
211 Neil O'Donnell .08
212 Eugene Chung .05
213 J.B. Brown .05
214 Marcus Allen .15
215 Harry Newsome .05
216 *Greg Hill* .50
217 *Ryan Yarborough* .30
218 Marty Carter .05
219 Bern Brostek .05
220 Boomer Esiason .07
221 Vince Buck .05
222 Jim Jeffcoat .05
223 Bob Dahl .05
224 Marion Butts .06
225 Ron Moore .50
226 Robert Blackmon .05
227 Curtis Conway .30
228 Jon Hand .05
229 Shane Dronett .05
230 Erik Williams .05
231 Dennis Brown .05
232 Ray Childress .05
233 *Johnnie Morton* .50
234 Kent Hull .05
235 John Elliott .05
236 Ron Heller .05
237 J.J. Birden .05
238 Thomas Randolph .05
239 Chip Lohmiller .07
240 Tim Brown .10
241 Steve Tovar .05
242 Moe Gardner .05
243 Vincent Brown .05
244 Tony Zendejas .05
245 Eric Allen .08
246 *Joe King* .05
247 Mo Lewis .05
248 Rod Bernstine .07
249 Tom Waddle .05
250 Junior Seau .10
251 Eric Metcalf .05
252 Cris Carter .08
253 Bill Hitchcock .05
254 Zefross Moss .05
255 Morten Andersen .07
256 Keith Rucker .05
257 Chris Jacke .05
258 Richmond Webb .07
259 Herman Moore .10
260 Phil Simms .10
261 Mark Tuninei .05
262 Don Beebe .05
263 Marc Logan .05
264 Willie Davis .05
265 David Klingler .15
266 Martin Mayhew .05
267 Mark Bavaro .05
268 Greg Lloyd .05
269 Al Del Greco .05
270 Reggie Brooks .20
271 Greg Townsend .05
272 Rohn Stark .05
273 Marcus Allen .05
274 Ronnie Lott .05
275 Dan Marino .65
276 Sean Gilbert .07
277 LeRoy Butler .07
278 Troy Auzenne .05
279 Eric Swann .05
280 Quentin Coryatt .06
281 Anthony Pleasant .05
282 Brad Baxter .05
283 Carl Lee .05
284 Courtney Hall .08
285 Quinn Early .05
286 Eddie Robinson .05
287 Marco Coleman .05
288 Harold Green .05
289 Santana Dotson .05
290 Robert Porcher .05
291 Joe Phillips .05
292 Mark McMillian .05
293 Eric Davis .05
294 Mark Jackson .05
295 Darryl Talley .05
296 Curtis Duncan .05
297 Bruce Armstrong .05
298 Eric Hill .05
299 Andre Collins .05
300 Jay Novacek .08
301 Roosevelt Potts .15
302 Eric Martin .05
303 Chris Warren .05
304 Deral Boykin .05
305 Jessie Tuggle .05
306 Glyn Milburn .25
307 Terry Obee .05
308 Eric Turner .05
309 *DeWayne Washington* .25
310 Sterling Sharpe .35
311 Jeff Gossett .05
312 John Carney .05
313 *Aaron Glenn* .20

314	Nick Lowery	.05
315	Thurman Thomas	.15
316	Troy Aikman	.65
317	Thurman Thomas	.10
318	Michael Irvin	.15
319	Steve Beuerlein	.07
320	Jerry Rice	.75
321	Alexander Wright	.05
322	Michael Bates	.05
323	Greg Davis	.05
324	Mark Bortz	.05
325	Kevin Greene	.05
326	Wayne Simmons	.05
327	Wayne Martin	.05
328	Michael Irvin	.30
329	Checklist 1	.05
330	Checklist 2	.05
331	Doug Pelfrey	.05
332	Myron Quyton	.05
333	Howard Ballard	.05
334	Ricky Ervins	.05
335	Steve Emtman	.05
336	Eric Curry	.05
337	*Bert Emanuel*	1.00
338	Darryl Ashmore	.05
339	Stevon Moore	.05
340	Garrison Hearst	.50
341	Vance Johnson	.05
342	Anthony Johnson	.05
343	Merril Hoge	.05
344	William Thomas	.05
345	Scott Mitchell	.15
346	Jim Everett	.05
347	Ray Crockett	.05
348	Bryan Cox	.07
349	*Charles Johnson*	.50
350	Randall McDaniel	.05
351	Michael Barrow	.05
352	Darrell Thompson	.05
353	Kevin Gogan	.05
354	Brad Daluiso	.05
355	Mark Collins	.05
356	*Bryant Young*	.30
357	Steve Christie	.05
358	Derek Kennard	.05
359	Jon Vaughn	.05
360	Drew Bledsoe	1.00
361	Randy Baldwin	.05
362	Kevin Ross	.05
363	Reuben Davis	.05
364	Chris Miller	.05
365	Tim McGee	.05
366	Tony Woods	.05
367	Dean Biasucci	.05
368	George Jamison	.05
369	Lorenzo Lynch	.05
370	Johnny Johnson	.05
371	Greg Kragen	.05
372	Vinson Smith	.05
373	Vince Workman	.05
374	*Allen Aldridge*	.20
375	Terry Kirby	.30
376	*Mario Bates*	.20
377	Dixon Edwards	.05
378	Leon Searcy	.05
379	Eric Guliford	.05
380	Gary Brown	.05
381	Phil Hansen	.05
382	Keith Hamilton	.05
383	John Alt	.05
384	John Taylor	.05
385	Reggie Cobb	.05
386	*Rob Fredrickson*	.30
387	Pepper Johnson	.05
388	*Kevin Lee*	.35
389	Stanley Richard	.05
390	Jackie Slater	.05
391	Darrick Brilz	.05
392	John Gesek	.05
393	Kelvin Pritchett	.05
394	Aeneas Williams	.05
395	*Henry Ford*	.25
396	*Eric Mahlum*	.20
397	Tom Rouen	.05
398	Vinnie Clark	.05
399	Jim Sweeney	.05
400	Troy Aikman	2.25
401	Toi Cook	.05
402	Dan Saleaumua	.05
403	Andy Heck	.05
404	Deon Figures	.10
405	Henry Thomas	.05
406	Glen Montgomery	.05
407	*Trent Dilfer*	2.00
408	Eddie Murray	.05
409	Gene Atkins	.05
410	Mike Sherrard	.05
411	Don Mosebar	.05
412	Thomas Smith	.05
413	Ken Norton	.05
414	Robert Brooks	.05
415	Jeff Lageman	.05
416	Tony Siragusa	.05
417	Brian Blades	.05
418	Matt Stover	.05
419	Jesse Solomon	.05
420	Reggie Roby	.05
421	Shawn Jefferson	.05
422	Marc Boutte	.05
423	William White	.05
424	Clyde Simmons	.05
425	Anthony Miller	.08
426	Brent Jones	.05
427	Tim Grunhard	.05
428	Alfred Williams	.05
429	Roy Barker	.05
430	Dante Jones	.05
431	Leroy Thompson	.05
432	Marcus Robertson	.05
433	*Thomas Lewis*	.50
434	Sean Jones	.05
435	Michael Haynes	.05
436	Albert Lewis	.05
437	*Tim Bowens*	.30
438	Marvcus Patton	.05
439	Rich Miano	.05
440	Craig Erickson	.05
441	*Larry Allen*	.20
442	*Fernando Smith*	.20
443	D.J. Johnson	.05
444	Leonard Russell	.05
445	*Marshall Faulk*	3.00
446	Najee Mustafaa	.05
447	Brian Hansen	.05
448	*Isaac Bruce*	4.00
449	Kevin Scott	.05
450	Natrone Means	.40
451	Tracy Rogers	.05
452	Mike Croel	.05
453	Anthony Edwards	.05
454	*Brenston Buckner*	.20
455	Tom Carter	.05
456	Burt Grossman	.05
457	Jimmy Spencer	.05
458	Raghib Ismail	.20
459	Fred Strickland	.05
460	*Jeff Burris*	.30
461	Adrian Hardy	.05
462	Lamar McGriggs	.05
463	Webster Slaughter	.05
464	Demetrius DuBose	.05
465	Dave Brown	.20
466	Kenneth Gant	.05
467	Erik Kramer	.05
468	Mark Ingram	.05
469	Roman Phifer	.05
470	Steve Young	.12
471	Nick Lowery	.08
472	Irving Fryar	.08
473	Art Monk	.08
474	Mel Gray	.08
475	Reggie White	.08
476	Eric Ball	.05
477	Dwayne Harper	.05
478	Will Shields	.05
479	Roger Harper	.05
480	Rick Mirer	.50
481	Vincent Brisby	.20
482	John Jurkovic	.05
483	Michael Jackson	.05
484	Ed Cunningham	.05
485	*Brad Ottis*	.15
486	Sterling Palmer	.05
487	Tony Bennett	.05
488	Mike Pritchard	.05
489	*Bucky Brooks*	.35
490	Troy Vincent	.05
491	Eric Green	.05
492	*Van Malone*	.25
493	*Marcus Spears*	.25
494	Brian Williams	.05
495	Robert Smith	.15
496	Haywood Jeffires	.07
497	Darrin Smith	.05
498	Tommy Barnhardt	.05
499	Anthony Smith	.05
500	Ricky Watters	.05
501	Antone Davis	.05
502	David Braxton	.05
503	*Donnell Bennett*	.50
504	Donald Evans	.05
505	Lewis Tillman	.05
506	Lance Smith	.05
507	*Aaron Taylor*	.20
508	Ricky Sanders	.05
509	Dennis Smith	.05
510	Barry Foster	.30
511	Stan Brock	.05
512	Henry Rolling	.05
513	Walter Reeves	.05
514	John Booty	.05
515	Kenneth Davis	.05
516	Cris Dishman	.05
517	Bill Lewis	.05
518	Jeff Bryant	.05
519	Brian Mitchell	.05
520	Joe Montana	1.00
521	Keith Sims	.05
522	Harry Colon	.05
523	Leon Lett	.05
524	Carlos Jenkins	.05
525	Victor Bailey	.15
526	Harvey Williams	.05
527	Irv Smith	.10
528	*Jason Sehorn*	.20
529	*John Thierry*	.25
530	Brett Favre	2.00
531	*Sean Dawkins*	.30
532	Erric Pegram	.05
533	Jimmy Williams	.05
534	Michael Timpson	.05
535	Willie Anderson	.05
536	John Parrella	.05
537	Freddie Joe Nunn	.05
538	Doug Dawson	.05
539	Michael Stewart	.05
540	John Elway	.65
541	Ronnie Lott	.05
542	Barry Sanders	.50
543	Andre Reed	.08
544	Deion Sanders	.10
545	Dan Marino	.75
546	Carlton Bailey	.08
547	Emmitt Smith	1.00
548	Alvin Harper	.08
549	Eric Metcalf	.08
550	Jerry Rice	.50
551	Derrick Thomas	.08
552	Mark Collins	.08
553	Eric Turner	.08
554	Sterling Sharpe	.12
555	Steve Young	.20
556	*Darnay Scott*	1.00
557	Joel Steed	.05
558	Dennis Gibson	.05
559	Charles Mincy	.05
560	Rickey Jackson	.05
561	Dave Cadigan	.05
562	Rick Tuten	.05
563	Mike Caldwell	.05
564	*Todd Steussie*	.30
565	Kevin Smith	.05
566	Arthur Marshall	.05
567	Aaron Wallace	.05
568	Calvin Williams	.05
569	Todd Kelly	.05
570	Barry Sanders	1.25
571	Shaun Gayle	.05
572	Will Wolford	.05
573	Ethan Norton	.05
574	Chris Slade	.15
575	Jeff Wright	.05
576	*Toby Wright*	.20
577	Lamar Thomas	.05
578	Chris Singleton	.05
579	Ed West	.05
580	Jeff George	.08
581	*Kevin Mitchell*	.15
582	Chad Brown	.05
583	Rich Camarillo	.05
584	Gary Zimmerman	.05
585	Randal Hill	.05
586	Keith Cash	.05
587	Sam Mills	.05
588	Shawn Lee	.05
589	Kent Graham	.12
590	Steve Everitt	.05
591	Rob Moore	.05
592	*Kevin Mawae*	.20
593	Jerry Ball	.05
594	Larry Brown	.05
595	Tim Krumrie	.05
596	*Aubrey Beavers*	.30
597	Chris Hinton	.05
598	Greg Montgomery	.05
599	Jimmie Jones	.05
600	Jim Kelly	.20
601	*Joe Johnson*	.25
602	Tim Irwin	.05
603	Steve Jackson	.05
604	James Williams	.05
605	Blair Thomas	.05
606	Daman Hughes	.05
607	Russell Freeman	.05
608	Andre Hastings	.10
609	Ken Harvey	.05
610	Jim Harbaugh	.05
611	Emmitt Smith	.80
612	Andre Rison	.10
613	Steve Young	.20
614	Anthony Miller	.10
615	Barry Sanders	.50
616	Bernie Kosar	.05
617	Chris Gardocki	.05
618	*William Floyd*	.30
619	Matt Brock	.05
620	*Dan Wilkinson*	.45
621	Tony Meola	.05
622	Tony Tolbert	.05
623	Mike Zandofsky	.05
624	William Fuller	.05
625	Steve Jordan	.05
626	Mike Johnson	.05
627	Ferrell Edmunds	.05
628	Gene Williams	.05
629	Willie Beamon	.05
630	Gerald Perry	.05
631	John Baylor	.05
632	Carwell Gardner	.05
633	Thomas Everett	.08
634	Lamar Lathon	.05
635	Michael Bankston	.05
636	Ray Crittenden	.05
637	Kimble Anders	.05
638	Robert Delpino	.05
639	Darren Perry	.05
640	Byron Evans	.05
641	Mark Higgs	.05
642	Lorenzo Neal	.05
643	Henry Ellard	.05
644	Trace Armstrong	.05
645	Greg McMurtry	.05
646	Steve McMichael	.05
647	Terance Mathis	.05
648	Eric Bieniemy	.05
649	Bobby Houston	.05
650	Alvin Harper	.05
651	*James Folston*	.15
652	Mel Gray	.05
653	Adrian Cooper	.05
654	Dexter Carter	.05
655	Don Griffin	.05
656	Corey Weimer	.05
657	Lee Johnson	.05
658	Nate Odomes	.05
659	Checklist 3	.05
660	Checklist 4	.05

1994 Topps Special Effects

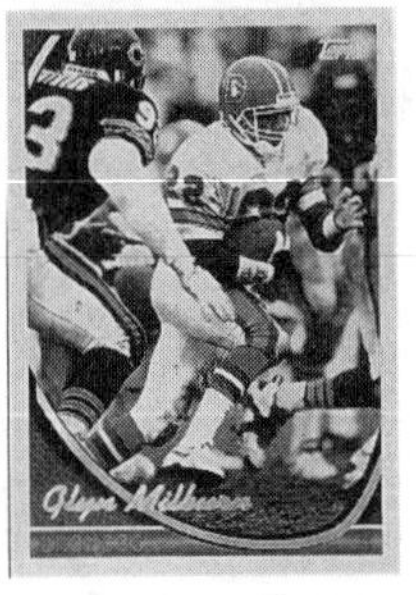

The 660-card, regular-sized set was issued as a parallel to the 1994 base set. The cards were inserted every two packs (and rack packs) and feature a clear plastic prismatic coating with a holographic stripe.

	MT
Complete Set (660):	350.00
Complete Series 1 (330):	175.00
Complete Series 2 (330):	175.00
Common Player:	.30
Veteran Stars:	3.5x-7x
Young Stars:	2.5x-5x
RCs:	2x-4x

1994 Topps All-Pro

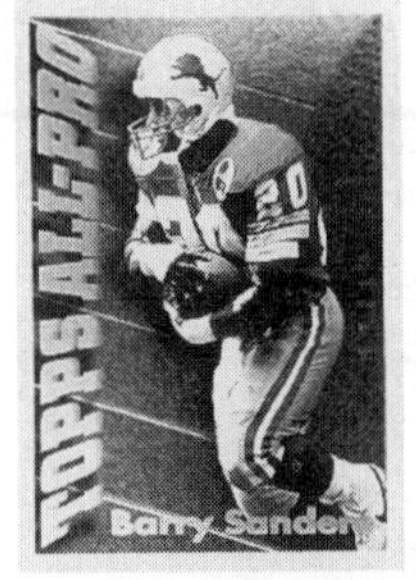

These 1994 Topps football inserts were included at a rate of one per every 36 Series II packs. Topps introduces its new Spectralight foil process for these cards, which feature 25 of the NFL's top stars. Each card is printed on a foil-stamped, foil-backed card.

		MT
Complete Set (25):		45.00
Common Player:		1.00
Minor Stars:		2.00
1	Michael Irvin	2.00
2	Erik Williams	1.00
3	Steve Wisniewski	1.00
4	Dermontti Dawson	1.00
5	Nate Newton	1.00
6	Harris Barton	1.00
7	Shannon Sharpe	2.00
8	Jerry Rice	10.00
9	Troy Aikman	10.00
10	Barry Sanders	12.00
11	Jerome Bettis	5.00
12	Jason Hanson	1.00
13	Eric Metcalf	1.00
14	Reggie White	2.00
15	Cortez Kennedy	1.00
16	Michael Dean Perry	1.00
17	Bruce Smith	1.00
18	Darryl Talley	1.00
19	Hardy Nickerson	1.00
20	Derrick Thomas	2.00
21	Mark Collins	1.00
22	Eric Allen	1.00
23	Tim McDonald	1.00
24	Marcus Robertson	1.00
25	Greg Montgomery	1.00

1994 Topps 1000/3000

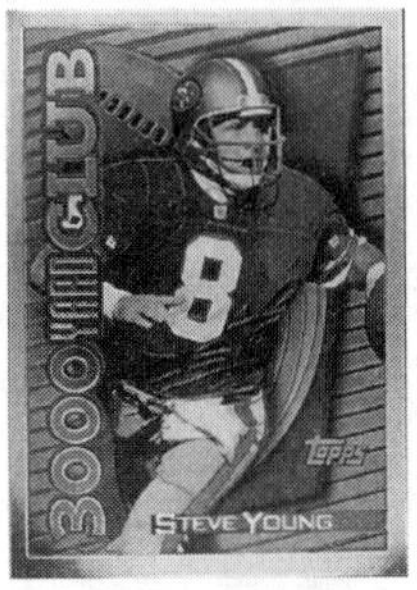

These cards were found one in every 32 packs of 1994 Topps football cards. They feature 20 receivers and running backs who gained 1,000 yards in 1993, plus 12 quarterbacks who threw for more than 3,000 yards. Each card front has the set name running along the left side of the card. The player's name and Topps' logo are in the bottom left corner. The back has an action photo and game-by-game recap of the player's 1993 season. Cards are numbered 1 of 32, etc.

		MT
Complete Set (32):		75.00
Common Player:		1.00
Minor Stars:		2.00
1	Jerry Rice	7.00
2	Chris Warren	2.00
3	Leonard Russell	1.00
4	Gary Brown	1.00
5	Tim Brown	2.00
6	Erric Pegram	1.00
7	Irving Fryar	1.00
8	Anthony Miller	1.00
9	Reggie Langhorne	1.00
10	Thurman Thomas	2.00
11	Reggie Brooks	1.00
12	Andre Rison	2.00
13	Ron Moore	1.00
14	Michael Irvin	2.00
15	Barry Sanders	8.00
16	Cris Carter	2.00
17	Rodney Hampton	2.00
18	Jerome Bettis	2.00
19	Sterling Sharpe	2.00
20	Emmitt Smith	14.00
21	John Elway	5.00
22	Brett Favre	14.00
23	Jim Kelly	2.00
24	Warren Moon	2.00
25	Phil Simms	1.00
26	Craig Erickson	1.00
27	Neil O'Donnell	1.00
28	Steve Young	5.00
29	Steve Beuerlein	1.00
30	Troy Aikman	7.00
31	Jeff Hostetler	1.00
32	Boomer Esiason	1.00

1994 Topps Archives 1956

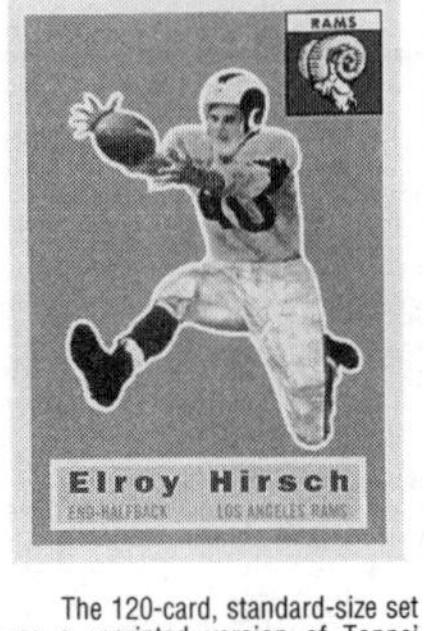

The 120-card, standard-size set was a reprinted version of Topps' 1956 set (the checklist was not reprinted). The cards were sold in 12-card packs for $2 with whatever errors the originals had left in. The cards backs were printed in red and black on gray stock.

		MT
Complete Set (120):		20.00
Common Player:		.10
1	Johnny Carson	.10
2	Gordon Soltau	.10
3	Frank Varrichione	.10
4	Eddie Bell	.10
5	Alex Webster	.20
6	Norm Van Brocklin	2.00
7	Green Bay Packers Team Card	.30
8	Lou Creekmur	.20
9	Lou Groza	1.50
10	Tom Bienemann	.10
11	George Blanda	1.50
12	Alan Ameche	.40
13	Vic Janowicz	.40
14	Dick Moegle	.20
15	Fran Rogel	.10
16	Harold Giancanelli	.10
17	Emlen Tunnell	.60
18	Paul (Tank) Younger	.30
19	Bill Howton	.20
20	Jack Christiansen	.75
21	Darrell Brewster	.10
22	Chicago Cardinals Team Card	.30
23	Ed Brown	.20
24	Joe Campanella	.10
25	Leon Heath	.10
26	San Francisco 49ers Team Card	.30
27	Dick Flanagan	.10
28	Chuck Bednarik	1.00
29	Kyle Rote	.60
30	Les Richter	.20
31	Howard Ferguson	.10
32	Dorne Dibble	.10
33	Kenny Konz	.10
34	Dave Mann	.10
35	Rick Casares	.20
36	Art Donovan	1.00
37	Chuck Drazenovich	.10
38	Joe Arenas	.10
39	Lynn Chandnois	.10
40	Philadelphia Eagles Team Card	.30
41	Roosevelt Brown	.60
42	Tom Fears	.75
43	Gary Knafelc	.10
44	Joe Schmidt	1.00
45	Cleveland Browns Team Card (UER) (Card back does not credit the Browns with being Champs in 1955)	.60
46	Len Teeuws	.10
47	Bill George	.60
48	Baltimore Colts Team Card	.30
49	Eddie LeBaron	.40
50	Hugh McElhenny	1.25
51	Ted Marchibroda	.20
52	Adrian Burk	.10
53	Frank Gifford	3.50
54	Charley Toogood	.10
55	Tobin Rote	.20
56	Bill Stits	.10
57	Don Colo	.10
58	Ollie Matson	1.00
59	Harlon Hill	.10
60	Lenny Moore	2.00
61	Washington Redskins Team Card	.30
62	Billy Wilson	.20
63	Pittsburgh Steelers Team Card	.30
64	Bob Pellegrini	.10
65	Ken MacAfee	.20
66	Willard Sherman	.10
67	Roger Zatkoff	.10
68	Dave Middleton	.10
69	Ray Renfro	.20
70	Don Stonesifer	.10
71	Stan Jones	.60
72	Jim Mutscheller	.10
73	Volney Peters	.10
74	Leo Nomellini	.75
75	Ray Mathews	.10
76	Dick Bielski	.10
77	Charley Conerly	1.00
78	Elroy Hirsch	1.00
79	Bill Forester	.20
80	Jim Doran	.10
81	Fred Morrison	.10
82	Jack Simmons	.10
83	Bill McColl	.10
84	Bert Rechichar	.10
85	Joe Scudero	.10
86	Y.A. Tittle	3.00
87	Ernie Stautner	1.00
88	Norm Willey	.10
89	Bob Schnelker	.10
90	Dan Towler	.30
91	John Martinkovic	.10
92	Detroit Lions Team Card	.30
93	George Ratterman	.10
94	Chuck Ulrich	.10
95	Bobby Watkins	.10
96	Buddy Young	.30
97	Billy Wells	.10
98	Bob Toneff	.10
99	Bill McPeak	.10
100	Bobby Thomason	.10
101	Roosevelt Grier	.60
102	Ron Waller	.10
103	Bobby Dillon	.10
104	Leon Hart	.30
105	Mike McCormack	.60
106	John Olszewski	.10
107	Bill Wightkin	.10
108	George Shaw	.20
109	Dale Atkeson	.10
110	Joe Perry	1.00
111	Dale Dodrill	.10
112	Tom Scott	.10
113	New York Giants Team Card	.30
114	Los Angeles Rams Team Card (UER) (Back incorrect, Rams were not 1955 champs)	.30
115	Al Carmichael	.10
116	Bobby Layne	3.00
117	Ed Modzelewski	.20
118	Lamar McHan	.10
119	Chicago Bears Team Card	.30
120	Billy Vessels	.50

1994 Topps Archives 1956 Gold

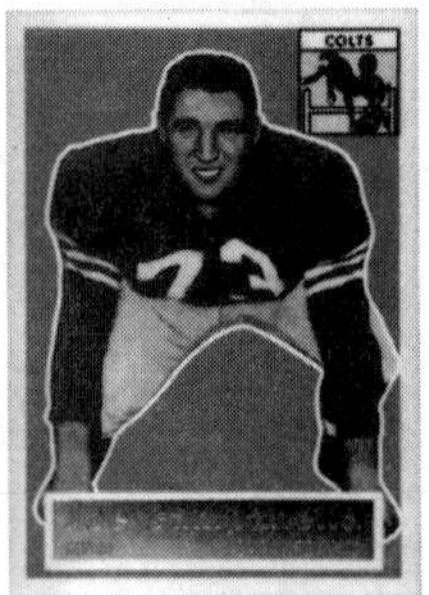

The 120-card, standard-size set was issued as a gold parallel to the base 1956 reprint set and were randonly inserted into packs of 1956/57 packs.

	MT
Complete Set (120):	50.00
Common Player:	.25
Gold Cards:	1.25x-2.5x

1994 Topps Archives 1957

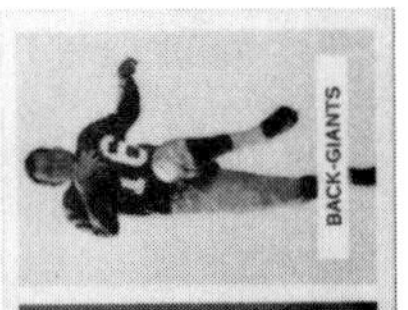

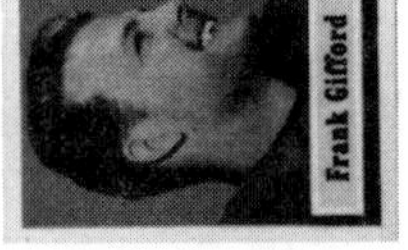

The 154-card, standard-size set was reprinted by Topps (except for the checklist) and was available in 12-card packs for $2. Any errors with the original 1957 set were not changed. The card backs were printed in red and black on gray card stock. Gold versions (3x) were also produced by Topps.

		MT
Complete Set (154):		20.00
Common Player:		.10
1	Eddie LeBaron	.30
2	Pete Retzlaff	.20
3	Mike McCormack	.50
4	Lou Baldacci	.10
5	Gino Marchetti	1.00
6	Leo Nomellini	.75
7	Bobby Watkins	.10
8	Dave Middleton	.10
9	Bobby Dillon	.10
10	Les Richter	.20
11	Roosevelt Brown	.50
12	Lavern Torgeson	.10
13	Dick Bielski	.10
14	Pat Summerall	1.00
15	Jack Butler	.10
16	John Henry Johnson	.75
17	Art Spinney	.10
18	Bob St. Clair	.50
19	Perry Jeter	.10
20	Lou Creekmur	.30
21	Dave Hanner	.10
22	Norm Van Brocklin	1.50
23	Don Chandler	.10
24	Al Dorow	.10
25	Tom Scott	.10
26	Ollie Matson	1.00
27	Fran Rogel	.10
28	Lou Groza	1.50
29	Billy Vessels	.20
30	Y.A. Tittle	2.00
31	George Blanda	1.50
32	Bobby Layne	2.00
33	Bill Howton	.20
34	Bill Wade	.20
35	Emlen Tunnell	.75
36	Leo Elter	.10
37	Clarence Peaks	.20
38	Don Stonesifer	.10
39	George Tarasovic	.10
40	Darrell Brewster	.10
41	Bert Rechichar	.10
42	Billy Wilson	.20
43	Ed Brown	.20
44	Gene Gedman	.10
45	Gary Knafelc	.10
46	Elroy Hirsch	1.00
47	Don Heinrich	.10
48	Gene Brito	.10
49	Chuck Bednarik	1.00
50	Dave Mann	.10
51	Bill McPeak	.10
52	Kenny Konz	.10
53	Alan Ameche	.40
54	Gordon Soltau	.10
55	Rick Casares	.30

56	Charlie Ane	.10
57	Al Carmichael	.10
58	Willard Sherman	.10
59	Kyle Rote	.50
60	Chuck Drazenovich	.10
61	Bobby Walston	.10
62	John Olszewski	.10
63	Ray Mathews	.10
64	Maurice Bassett	.10
65	Art Donovan	1.00
66	Joe Arenas	.10
67	Harlon Hill	.10
68	Yale Lary	.60
69	Bill Forester	.20
70	Bob Boyd	.10
71	Andy Robustelli	1.00
72	Sam Baker	.20
73	Bob Pellegrini	.10
74	Leo Sanford	.10
75	Sid Watson	.10
76	Ray Renfro	.20
77	Carl Taseff	.10
78	Clyde Conner	.10
79	J.C. Caroline	.10
80	Howard Cassady	.30
81	Tobin Rote	.20
82	Ron Waller	.10
83	Jim Patton	.20
84	Volney Peters	.10
85	Dick Lane	.60
86	Royce Womble	.10
87	Duane Putnam	.10
88	Frank Gifford	3.00
89	Steve Meilinger	.10
90	Buck Lansford	.10
91	Lindon Crow	.10
92	Ernie Stautner	.75
93	Preston Carpenter	.20
94	Raymond Berry	1.50
95	Hugh McElhenny	1.00
96	Stan Jones	.50
97	Dorne Dibble	.10
98	Joe Scudero	.10
99	Eddie Bell	.10
100	Joe Childress	.10
101	Elbert Nickel	.10
102	Walt Michaels	.20
103	Jim Mutscheller	.10
104	Earl Morrall	.40
105	Larry Strickland	.10
106	Jack Christiansen	.75
107	Fred Cone	.10
108	Bud McFadin	.10
109	Charley Conerly	1.00
110	Tom Runnels	.10
111	Ken Keller	.10
112	James Root	.10
113	Ted Marchibroda	.30
114	Don Paul	.10
115	George Shaw	.20
116	Dick Moegle	.20
117	Don Bingham	.10
118	Leon Hart	.20
119	Bart Starr	4.00
120	Paul Miller	.10
121	Alex Webster	.20
122	Ray Wietecha	.10
123	Johnny Carson	.10
124	Tommy McDonald	.30
125	Jerry Tubbs	.10
126	Jack Scarbath	.10
127	Ed Modzelewski	.10
128	Lenny Moore	1.00
129	Joe Perry	1.00
130	Bill Wightkin	.10
131	Jim Doran	.10
132	Howard Ferguson (UER) (Name misspelled Furgeson on front)	.10
133	Tom Wilson	.10
134	Dick James	.10
135	Jimmy Harris	.10
136	Chuck Ulrich	.10
137	Lynn Chandnois	.10
138	Johnny Unitas	5.00
139	Jim Ridlon	.10
140	Zeke Bratkowski	.20
141	Ray Krouse	.10
142	John Martinkovic	.10
143	Jim Cason	.10
144	Ken MacAfee	.20
145	Sid Youngelman	.10
146	Paul Larson	.10
147	Len Ford	1.00
148	Bob Toneff	.10
149	Ronnie Knox	.10
150	Jim David	.10
151	Paul Hornung	4.00
152	Paul (Tank) Younger	.30
153	Bill Svoboda	.10
154	Fred Morrison	.30

1994 Topps Archives 1957 Gold

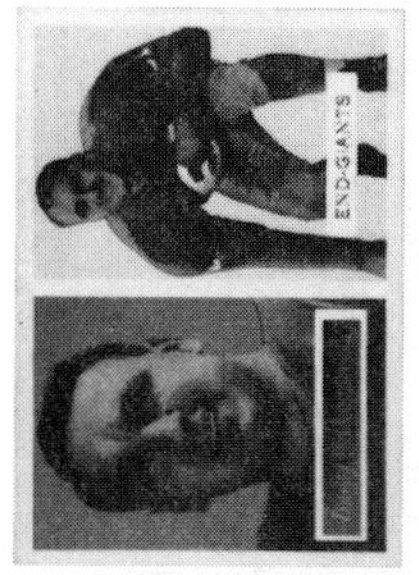

The 154-card, standard-size set was issued as a gold parallel to the base 1957 reprint issue. The cards were randomly inserted into 1956/57 packs.

		MT
Complete Set (154):		50.00
Common Player:		.25
Gold Cards:		1.25x-2.5x

1995 Topps

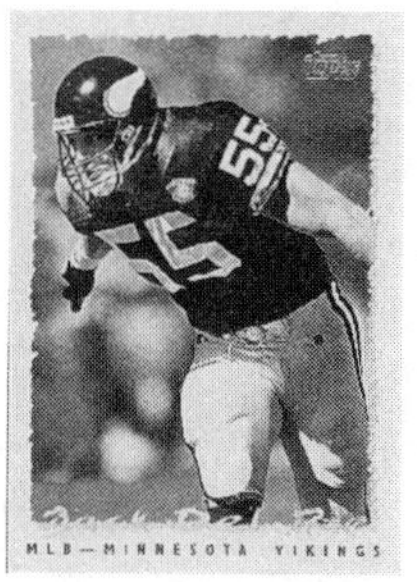
MLB—MINNESOTA VIKINGS

Topps released its 1995 football set in two series - 248 cards in Series I and 220 in Series II. Each card is UV-coated and gold-foil stamped. Top free agents, hot draft picks, expansion team players, and Steve Young tribute cards are among the subsets in the set. 1,000 and 3,000 Yard Club theme cards are also part of the main set. A new addition to the regular cards is that Topps spotlights the player's achievements; if he led the conference in a statistical category, the stat is printed in red on the back (with a diamond added if he tied). Also on the horizontal card back, which is team color coordinated, are a closeup shot, stats, biographical information and a brief player profile. Inserts in Series I are Topps Finest, Finest Refractors, Hit List, Sensational Sophomores, Power Boosters and Yesteryear. An Instant Winner card was also randomly inserted at a rate of one per every 1,980 packs; the card entitles the finder to a complete 27-card Finest set with Finest Protectors. Series II inserts include: Air Raid, Finest Refractors, ProFiles, Power Boosters, Finest, and All-Pro.

		MT
Complete Set (468):		45.00
Comp. Series 1 (248):		25.00
Comp. Series 2 (220):		20.00
Common Player:		.05
Minor Stars:		.10
Ser. 1 or 2 Hob. Pack (12):		1.50
Ser. 1 or 2 Hob. Wax Box (36):		40.00
Ser. 1 or 2 Ret. Pack (12):		1.00
Ser. 1 or 2 Ret. Wax Box (36):		30.00
1	Barry Sanders (1,000 Yard Club)	.50
2	Chris Warren (1,000 Yard Club)	.05
3	Jerry Rice (1,000 Yard Club)	.50
4	Emmitt Smith (1,000 Yard Club)	1.00
5	Henry Ellard (1,000 Yard Club)	.05
6	Natrone Means (1,000 Yard Club)	.25
7	Terance Mathis (1,000 Yard Club)	.05
8	Tim Brown (1,000 Yard Club)	.05
9	Andre Reed (1,000 Yard Club)	.05
10	Marshall Faulk (1,000 Yard Club)	.20
11	Irving Fryar (1,000 Yard Club)	.05
12	Cris Carter (1,000 Yard Club)	.05
13	Michael Irvin (1,000 Yard Club)	.10
14	Jake Reed (1,000 Yard Club)	.05
15	Ben Coates (1,000 Yard Club)	.05
16	Herman Moore (1,000 Yard Club)	.05
17	Carl Pickens (1,000 Yard Club)	.05
18	Fred Barnett (1,000 Yard Club)	.05
19	Sterling Sharpe (1,000 Yard Club)	.05
20	Anthony Miller (1,000 Yard Club)	.05
21	Thurman Thomas (1,000 Yard Club)	.10
22	Andre Rison (1,000 Yard Club)	.10
23	Brian Blades (1,000 Yard Club)	.05
24	Rodney Hampton (1,000 Yard Club)	.05
25	Terry Allen (1,000 Yard Club)	.05
26	Jerome Bettis (1,000 Yard Club)	.25
27	Errict Rhett (1,000 Yard Club)	.40
28	Rob Moore (1,000 Yard Club)	.05
29	Shannon Sharpe (1,000 Yard Club)	.05
30	Drew Bledsoe (3,000 Yard Club)	.50
31	Dan Marino (3,000 Yard Club)	1.00
32	Warren Moon (3,000 Yard Club)	.10
33	Steve Young (3,000 Yard Club)	.25
34	Brett Favre (3,000 Yard Club)	1.00
35	Jim Everett (3,000 Yard Club)	.05
36	Jeff George (3,000 Yard Club)	.05
37	John Elway (3,000 Yard Club)	.25
38	Jeff Hostetler (3,000 Yard Club)	.05
39	Randall Cunningham (3,000 Yard Club)	.10
40	Stan Humphries (3,000 Yard Club)	.05
41	Jim Kelly (3,000 Yard Club)	.10
42	Tommy Barnhardt	.05
43	Bob Whitfield	.05
44	William Thomas	.05
45	Glyn Milburn	.05
46	Steve Christie	.05
47	Kevin Mawae	.05
48	Vencie Glenn	.05
49	Eric Curry	.05
50	Jeff Hostetler	.05
51	Tyronne Stowe	.05
52	Steve Jackson	.05
53	Ben Coleman	.05
54	Brad Baxter	.05
55	Darryl Williams	.05
56	Troy Drayton	.05
57	George Teague	.05
58	Calvin Williams	.05
59	Jeff Cross	.05
60	Leroy Hoard	.05
61	John Carney	.05
62	Daryl Johnston	.05
63	Jim Jeffcoat	.05
64	Matt Stover	.05
65	Leroy Butler	.05
66	Curtis Conway	.05
67	O.J. McDuffie	.05
68	Robert Massey	.05
69	Ed McDaniel	.05
70	William Floyd	.25
71	Willie Davis	.05
72	William Roberts	.05
73	Chester McGlockton	.05
74	D.J. Johnson	.05
75	Rondell Jones	.05
76	Morten Andersen	.05
77	Glenn Parker	.05
78	William Fuller	.05
79	Ray Buchanan	.05
80	Maurice Hurst	.05
81	Wayne Gandy	.05
82	Marcus Turner	.05
83	Greg Davis	.05
84	Terry Wooden	.05
85	Thomas Everett	.05
86	Steve Broussard	.05
87	Tom Carter	.05
88	Glenn Montgomery	.05
89	Larry Allen	.05
90	Donnell Woolford	.05
91	John Alt	.05
92	Phil Hansen	.05
93	Seth Joyner	.05
94	Michael Brooks	.05
95	Randall McDaniel	.05
96	Tydus Winans	.05
97	Rob Fredrickson	.05
98	Ray Crockett	.05
99	Courtney Hall	.05
100	Merton Hanks	.05
101	Aaron Glenn	.05
102	Roosevelt Potts	.05
103	Leon Lett	.05
104	Jessie Tuggle	.05
105	Martin Mayhew	.05
106	William Roaf	.05
107	Todd Lyght	.05
108	Ernest Givins	.05
109	Tony McGee	.05
110	Barry Sanders	1.25
111	Dermontti Dawson	.05
112	Rick Tuten	.05
113	Vincent Brisby	.05
114	Charlie Garner	.05
115	Irving Fryar	.05
116	Stevon Moore	.05
117	Matt Darby	.05
118	Howard Cross	.05
119	John Gesek	.05
120	Jack Del Rio	.05
121	Marcus Allen	.10
122	Torrance Small	.05
123	Chris Mims	.05
124	Don Mosebar	.05
125	Carl Pickens	.05
126	Tom Rouen	.05
127	Garrison Hearst	.10
128	Charles Johnson	.25
129	Derek Brown	.05
130	Troy Aikman	.75
131	Troy Vincent	.05
132	Ken Ruettgers	.05
133	Michael Jackson	.05
134	Dennis Gibson	.05
135	Brett Perriman	.05
136	Jeff Graham	.05
137	Chad Brown	.05
138	Ken Norton	.05
139	Chris Slade	.05
140	Dave Brown	.05
141	Bert Emanuel	.25
142	Renaldo Turnbull	.05
143	Jim Harbaugh	.05
144	Michael Barrow	.05
145	Vincent Brown	.05
146	Bryant Young	.05
147	Boomer Esiason	.05
148	Sean Gilbert	.05
149	Greg Truitt	.05
150	Rod Woodson	.05
151	Robert Porcher	.05
152	Joe Phillips	.05
153	Gary Zimmerman	.05
154	Bruce Smith	.05
155	Randall Cunningham	.10
156	Fred Strickland	.05
157	Derrick Alexander	.25
158	James Williams	.05
159	Scott Dill	.05
160	Tim Bowens	.05
161	Floyd Turner	.05
162	Ronnie Harmon	.05
163	Wayne Martin	.05
164	John Randle	.05
165	Larry Centers	.05
166	Larry Brown	.05
167	Albert Lewis	.05
168	Michael Strahan	.05
169	Reggie Brooks	.05
170	Craig Heyward	.05
171	Pat Harlow	.05
172	Eugene Robinson	.05
173	Shane Conlan	.05
174	Bennie Blades	.05
175	Neil O'Donnell	.05
176	Steve Tovar	.05
177	Donald Evans	.05
178	Brent Jones	.05
179	Ray Childress	.05
180	Reggie White	.05
181	David Alexander	.05
182	Greg Hill	.25
183	Vinny Testaverde	.05
184	Jeff Burris	.05
185	Hardy Nickerson	.05
186	Terry Kirby	.05
187	Kirk Lowdermilk	.05
188	Eric Swann	.05
189	Chris Zorich	.05
190	Simon Fletcher	.05
191	Qadry Ismail	.05
192	Heath Shuler	.50
193	Michael Haynes	.05
194	Mike Sherrard	.05
195	Nolan Harrison	.05
196	Marcus Robertson	.05
197	Kevin Williams	.05
198	Moe Gardner	.05
199	Rick Mirer	.40
200	Junior Seau	.10
201	Byron Morris	.10
202	Willie McGinest	.05
203	Chris Spielman	.05
204	Darnay Scott	.40
205	Jesse Sapolu	.05
206	Marvin Washington	.05
207	Anthony Newman	.05
208	Cortez Kennedy	.10
209	Quentin Coryatt	.05
210	Neil Smith	.05
211	Keith Sims	.05
212	Sean Jones	.05
213	Tony Jones	.05
214	Lewis Tillman	.05
215	Darren Woodson	.05
216	Jason Hanson	.05
217	John Taylor	.05
218	Shawn Lee	.05
219	Kevin Greene	.05
220	Jerry Rice	.75
221	*Ki-Jana Carter*	.30
222	*Tony Boselli*	.10
223	*Michael Westbrook*	1.00
224	*Kerry Collins*	1.00
225	*Kevin Carter*	.10
226	*Kyle Brady*	.10
227	*J.J. Stokes*	1.00
228	*Derrick Alexander*	.10
229	*Warren Sapp*	.75
230	*Ruben Brown*	.10
231	*Hugh Douglas*	.10
232	*Luther Elliss*	.10
233	*Rashaan Salaam*	.30
234	*Tyrone Poole*	.10
235	*Korey Stringer*	.10
236	*Devin Bush*	.10
237	*Cory Raymer*	.10
238	*Zach Wiegert*	.10
239	*Ron Davis*	.10
240	*Todd Collins*	.10
241	*Bobby Taylor*	.10
242	*Patrick Riley*	.10
243	*Scott Gragg*	.10
244	*Marvcus Patton*	.05
245	Alvin Harper	.05
246	Ricky Watters	.10
247	Checklist 1 of 2	.05
248	Checklist 2 of 2	.05
249	Terance Mathis	.05
250	Mark Carrier	.05
251	Elijah Alexander	.05
252	George Koonce	.05
253	Tony Bennett	.05
254	Steve Wisniewski	.05
255	Bernie Parmalee	.20
256	Dwayne Sabb	.05
257	Lorenzo Neal	.05
258	Corey Miller	.05
259	Fred Barnett	.05
260	Greg Lloyd	.05
261	Robert Blackmon	.05
262	Ken Harvey	.05
263	Eric Hill	.05
264	Russell Copeland	.05
265	*Jeff Blake*	.30
266	Carl Banks	.05
267	Jay Novacek	.05
268	Mel Gray	.05
269	Kimble Anders	.05
270	Cris Carter	.10
271	Johnny Mitchell	.05
272	Shawn Jefferson	.05
273	Doug Brien	.05
274	Sean Landeta	.05
275	Scott Mitchell	.10
276	Charles Wilson	.05
277	Anthony Smith	.05
278	Anthony Miller	.05
279	Steve Walsh	.05
280	Drew Bledsoe	.75
281	Jamir Miller	.05
282	Robert Brooks	.10
283	Sean Lumpkin	.05
284	Bryan Cox	.05
285	Byron Evans	.05
286	Chris Doleman	.05
287	Anthony Pleasant	.05
288	Steve Grant	.05
289	Doug Riesenberg	.05
290	Natrone Means	.40
291	Henry Thomas	.05
292	Mike Pritchard	.05
293	Courtney Hawkins	.05
294	Bill Bates	.05
295	Jerome Bettis	.20
296	Russell Maryland	.05
297	Stanley Richard	.05
298	William White	.05
299	Dan Wilkinson	.05
300	Steve Young	.75
301	Gary Brown	.05
302	Jake Reed	.05
303	Carlton Gray	.05
304	Levon Kirkland	.05
305	Shannon Sharpe	.05
306	Luis Sharpe	.05
307	Marshall Faulk	.50
308	Stan Humphries	.10
309	Chris Calloway	.05
310	Tim Brown	.10
311	Steve Everitt	.05
312	Raymont Harris	.05
313	Tim McDonald	.05
314	Trent Dilfer	.25
315	Jim Everett	.05
316	Ray Crittenden	.05
317	Jim Kelly	.10
318	Andre Reed	.05
319	Chris Miller	.05
320	Bobby Houston	.05
321	Charles Haley	.05
322	James Francis	.05
323	Bernard Williams	.05
324	Michael Bates	.05
325	Brian Mitchell	.05
326	Mike Johnson	.05
327	Eric Bieniemy	.05
328	Aubrey Beavers	.05
329	Dale Carter	.05
330	Emmitt Smith	2.00
331	Darren Perry	.05
332	Marquez Pope	.05
333	Clyde Simmons	.05
334	Corey Croom	.05
335	Thomas Randolph	.05
336	Harvey Williams	.05
337	Michael Timpson	.05
338	Eugene Daniel	.05
339	Shane Dronett	.05
340	Eric Turner	.05
341	Eric Metcalf	.05
342	Leslie O'Neal	.05
343	Mark Wheeler	.05
344	Mark Pike	.05
345	Brett Favre	2.00
346	Johnny Bailey	.05
347	Henry Ellard	.05
348	Chris Gardocki	.05
349	Henry Jones	.05
350	Dan Marino	2.00
351	Lake Dawson	.20
352	Mark McMillian	.05
353	Deion Sanders	.40
354	Antonio London	.05
355	Cris Dishman	.05
356	Ricardo McDonald	.05
357	Dexter Carter	.05
358	Kevin Smith	.05
359	*Yancey Thigpen*	.30
360	Chris Warren	.10
361	Quinn Early	.05
362	John Mangum	.05
363	Santana Dotson	.05
364	Raghib Ismail	.05
365	Aeneas Williams	.05
366	Dan Williams	.05
367	Sean Dawkins	.05
368	Pepper Johnson	.05
369	Roman Phifer	.05
370	Rodney Hampton	.05
371	Darrell Green	.05
372	Michael Zordich	.05
373	Andre Coleman	.05
374	Wayne Simmons	.05
375	Michael Irvin	.20
376	Clay Matthews	.05
377	Dewayne Washington	.05
378	Keith Byars	.05
379	Todd Collins	.25
380	Mark Collins	.05
381	Joel Steed	.05
382	Bart Oates	.05
383	Al Smith	.05
384	Rafael Robinson	.05
385	Mo Lewis	.05
386	Aubrey Matthews	.05
387	Corey Sawyer	.05
388	Bucky Brooks	.05
389	Erik Kramer	.05
390	Tyrone Hughes	.05
391	Terry McDaniel	.05
392	Craig Erickson	.05
393	Mike Flores	.05
394	Harry Swayne	.05
395	Irving Spikes	.05
396	Lorenzo Lynch	.05
397	Antonio Langham	.05
398	Edgar Bennett	.05
399	Thomas Lewis	.05
400	John Elway	.30
401	Jeff George	.10
402	Errict Rhett	.75
403	Bill Romanowski	.05
404	Alexander Wright	.05
405	Warren Moon	.10
406	Eddie Robinson	.05
407	John Copeland	.05
408	Robert Jones	.05
409	Steve Bono	.15
410	Cornelius Bennett	.05
411	Ben Coates	.05
412	Dana Stubblefield	.05
413	Darryl Talley	.05
414	Brian Blades	.05
415	Herman Moore	.20
416	Nick Lowery	.05
417	Donnell Bennett	.05
418	Van Malone	.05
419	Pete Stoyanovich	.05
420	Joe Montana	1.00
421	Steve Young (Steve Young Subset Cards)	.30
422	Steve Young (Steve Young Subset Cards)	.30
423	Steve Young (Steve Young Subset Cards)	.30
424	Steve Young (Steve Young Subset Cards)	.30
425	Steve Young (Steve Young Subset Cards)	.30
426	Rod Stephens	.05
427	*Ellis Johnson* (Draft Picks)	.10
428	*Kordell Stewart* (Draft Picks)	4.00
429	*James Stewart* (Draft Picks)	1.50
430	*Steve McNair* (Draft Picks)	3.00
431	*Brian DeMarco* (Draft Picks)	.10
432	*Matt O'Dwyer* (Draft Picks)	.10
433	*Lorenzo Styles* (Draft Picks)	.10
434	*Anthony Cook* (Draft Picks)	.20
435	*Jesse James* (Draft Picks)	.10
436	*Darryl Pounds* (Draft Picks)	.10
437	Derrick Graham (Carolina Panther Team)	.05
438	Vernon Turner (Carolina Panther Team)	.05
439	Carlton Bailey (Carolina Panther Team)	.05
440	Darion Conner (Carolina Panther Team)	.05
441	Randy Baldwin (Carolina Panther Team)	.05
442	Tim McKyer (Carolina Panther Team)	.05
443	Sam Mills (Carolina Panther Team)	.05
444	Bob Christian (Carolina Panther Team)	.05
445	Steve Lofton (Carolina Panther Team)	.05
446	Lamar Lathon (Carolina Panther Team)	.05
447	Tony Smith (Carolina Panther Team)	.05
448	Don Beebe (Carolina Panther Team)	.05
449	Barry Foster (Carolina Panther Team)	.05
450	Frank Reich (Carolina Panther Team)	.05
451	Pete Metzelaars (Carolina Panther Team)	.05
452	Reggie Cobb (Jacksonville Jaguar Expansion Team)	.05
453	Jeff Lageman (Jacksonville Jaguar Expansion Team)	.05
454	Derek Brown (Jacksonville Jaguar Expansion Team)	.05
455	Desmond Howard (Jacksonville Jaguar Expansion Team)	.05
456	Vinnie Clark (Jacksonville Jaguar Expansion Team)	.05
457	Keith Goganious (Jacksonville Jaguar Expansion Team)	.05
458	Shawn Bouwens (Jacksonville Jaguar Expansion Team)	.05
459	*Rob Johnson* (Jacksonville Jaguar Expansion Team)	2.00
460	Steve Beuerlein (Jacksonville Jaguar Expansion Team)	.05
461	Mark Brunell (Jacksonville Jaguar Expansion Team)	1.00
462	Harry Colon (Jacksonville Jaguar Expansion Team)	.05
463	Chris Hudson (Jacksonville Jaguar Expansion Team)	.05
464	Darren Carrington (Jacksonville Jaguar Expansion Team)	.05
465	Ernest Givins (Jacksonville Jaguar Expansion Team)	.05
466	Kelvin Pritchett (Jacksonville Jaguar Expansion Team)	.05
467	Checklist 3 of 4	.05
468	Checklist 4 of 4	.05

1995 Topps Air Raid

These 10 1995-96 Topps football inserts utilize the dynamic Power Matrix technology to highlight the best NFL wide receiver/quarterback tandems. The cards were random inserts in every 24th pack of Series II product, retail packs only.

		MT
Complete Set (10):		60.00
Common Player:		3.00
1	Steve Young, Jerry Rice	10.00
2	Warren Moon, Cris Carter	3.00
3	Jeff George, Terance Mathis	3.00
4	Dave Brown, Mike Sherrard	3.00
5	Drew Bledsoe, Ben Coates	10.00
6	John Elway, Shannon Sharpe	7.00
7	Jeff Blake, Carl Pickens	3.00
8	Dan Marino, Irving Fryar	20.00
9	Randall Cunningham, Fred Barnett	3.00
10	Troy Aikman, Michael Irvin	8.00

1995 Topps All-Pros

Twenty-two players who personify the best in the game are captured on these all-silver foil cards, exclusive inserts in 1995-96 Topps Seires II hobby packs. The cards are seeded one per every eight packs.

		MT
Complete Set (22):		25.00
Common Player:		1.00
1	Jerry Rice	4.00
2	Lomas Brown	1.00
3	Nate Newton	1.00
4	Dermontti Dawson	1.00
5	Keith Sims	1.00
6	Richmond Webb	1.00
7	Shannon Sharpe	1.00
8	Michael Irvin	1.00
9	Steve Young	4.00
10	Barry Sanders	6.00
11	Marshall Faulk	5.00
12	Bruce Smith	1.00
13	Dana Stubblefield	1.00
14	John Randle	1.00
15	Reggie White	1.00

16 Greg Lloyd 1.00
17 Junior Seau 1.00
18 Cornelius Bennett 1.00
19 Rod Woodson 1.00
20 Deion Sanders 3.00
21 Darren Woodson 1.00
22 Merton Hanks 1.00

1995 Topps Expansion Team Boosters

The 20-card, standard-size set was randomly inserted every 36 Series II packs and is a parallel version of the expansion subset in Series II. The cards are printed on 28-point stock with diffraction foil.

MT
Complete Set (30): 75.00
Common Player: 2.50
437 Derrick Graham 2.50
438 Vernon Turner 2.50
439 Carlton Bailey 2.50
440 Darion Conner 2.50
441 Randy Baldwin 2.50
442 Tim McKyer 2.50
443 Sam Mills 3.50
444 Bob Christian 2.50
445 Steve Lofton 2.50
446 Lamar Lathon 2.50
447 Tony Smith (RB) 3.50
448 Don Beebe 3.50
449 Barry Foster 2.50
450 Frank Reich 3.50
451 Pete Metzelaars 2.50
452 Reggie Cobb 2.50
453 Jeff Lageman 2.50
454 Derek Brown (TE) 2.50
455 Desmond Howard 5.00
456 Vinnie Clark 2.50
457 Keith Goganious 2.50
458 Shawn Bowens 2.50
459 Rob Johnson 4.00
460 Steve Beuerlein 2.50
461 Mark Brunell 8.00
462 Harry Colon 2.50
463 Chris Hudson 2.50
464 Darren Carrington 2.50
465 Ernest Givins 3.50
466 Kelvin Pritchett 2.50

1995 Topps Finest Inserts

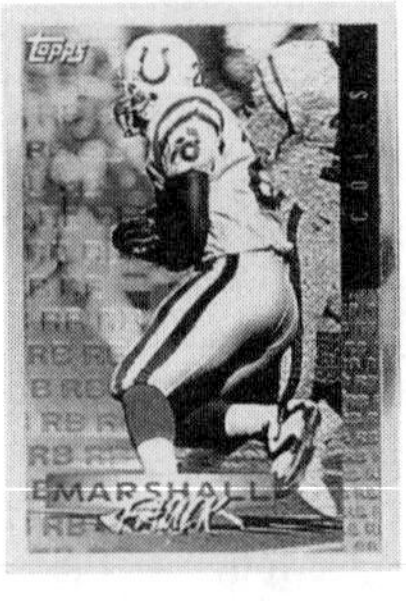

Topps added a little mystery to its 1995-96 football set when it created its Series I Finest insert cards. The cards, seeded one per every 36 packs, have black opaque protectors over them instead of the clear protectors. This means that collectors have to peel off the protector to see what card they have. They will, however, be able to determine what position the player plays; three different card backs, which are visible, were made - for quarterbacks, wide receivers and running backs. The card could even be a Refractor version; this is a parallel set which has cards seeded one per every 36 hobby packs or 432 retail packs. In addition, an Instant Winner card was inserted at a rate of one per every 1,980 packs. The card entitles the finder to a complete 27-card set with clear Finest protectors.

MT
Complete Set (27): 90.00
Common Player: 1.50
Minor Stars: 3.00
Complete Refractor Set (27): 300.00
Refractors: 1x-2x
Troy Aikman 8.00
Stan Humphries 1.50
Dan Marino 16.00
Brett Favre 16.00
Steve Young 6.00
Jim Kelly 3.00
John Elway 6.00
Warren Moon 3.00
Drew Bledsoe 8.00
Barry Sanders 10.00
Natrone Means 3.00
Ricky Watters 3.00
Chris Warren 1.50
Marshall Faulk 3.00
Jerome Bettis 1.50
Rodney Hampton 1.50
Errict Rhett 3.00
Emmitt Smith 16.00
Jerry Rice 8.00
Andre Reed 1.50
Irving Fryar 1.50
Herman Moore 1.50
Tim Brown 1.50
Terance Mathis 1.50
Henry Ellard 1.50
Michael Irvin 3.00
Cris Carter 1.50

1995 Topps Finest Boosters

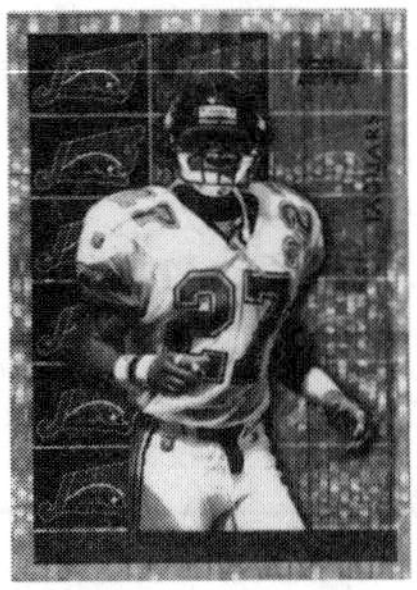

These cards were random inserts in 1995 Topps Series II packs. They are numbered B166-B187.

MT
Complete Set (22): 100.00
Common Player: 2.00
Comp. Refractor Set (22): 200.00
Refractors: 1x-2x
166 Barry Sanders 12.00
167 Bryant Young 2.00
168 Boomer Esiason 2.00
169 Terance Mathis 2.00
170 Troy Aikman 10.00
171 Junior Seau 2.00
172 Rodney Hampton 2.00
173 Jim Everett 2.00
174 Dan Marino 18.00
175 Steve Young 10.00
176 Cris Carter 2.00
177 Eric Swann 2.00
178 Rick Mirer 4.00
179 Jerome Bettis 4.00
180 Emmitt Smith 18.00
181 Jim Kelly 2.00
182 John Elway 6.00
183 Dana Stubblefield 2.00
184 Drew Bledsoe 10.00
185 Jerry Rice 10.00
186 Michael Irvin 4.00
187 Bruce Smith 2.00

1995 Topps Florida Hot Bed

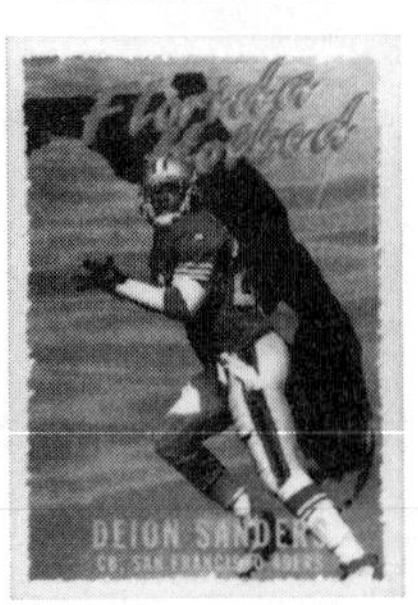

The 15-card standard-size set was inserted in each retail pack amd features top players who attended a Florida college. The card fronts depict a map outline of Florida with "Florida Hot Bed" printed in orange at the top. The player and team name are in gold foil near the card bottom. The card backs are numbered with the "FH" prefix and contain a player headshot with a commentary on his NFL career over a water background.

MT
Complete Set (15): 25.00
Common Player: 1.00
1 Deion Sanders 4.00
2 Brian Blades 1.00
3 Errict Rhett 5.00
4 Kevin Williams 1.00
5 Cortez Kennedy 1.00
6 Corey Sawyer 1.00
7 Russell Maryland 1.00
8 Emmitt Smith 10.00
9 Vinny Testaverde 1.00
10 William Floyd 1.50
11 Brett Perriman 1.00
12 Nate Newton 1.00
13 Jim Kelly 1.50
14 LeRoy Butler 1.00
15 Michael Irvin 1.50

1995 Topps Hit List

Hit List features 20 of the hardest most feared defenders in the league. Topps uses a stone-crushing design for the cards, which were inserts in 1995-96 Topps football Series I packs. They are seeded one per every four packs, making them the most common of the inserts.

MT
Complete Set (20): 10.00
Common Player: .50
Minor Stars: 1.00
1 Pepper Johnson .50
2 Elijah Alexander .50
3 Joe Cain .50
4 Andre Collins .50
5 Chris Spielman .50
6 Bryan Cox .50
7 Ed McDaniel .50
8 Jack Del Rio .50
9 Jeff Herrod .50
10 Greg Lloyd 1.00
11 Reggie White 1.50
12 Robert Jones .50
13 Eric Turner .50
14 Vincent Brown .50
15 Kevin Greene .50
16 Bruce Smith 1.00
17 Hardy Nickerson .50
18 Seth Joyner .50
19 Darryl Talley .50
20 Junior Seau 1.50

1995 Topps 1000/3000 Boosters

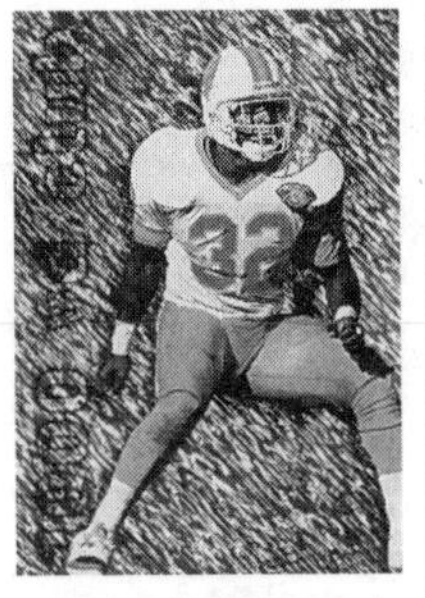

This Power Boosters set is a parallel set of the 1,000- and 3,000-Yard Club subset cards found in Topps 1995 Series I. Each card is "boosted" up to 28-point stock on a dynamic full foil board stock. A Power Boosters card replaces two regular cards in every 36th pack.

MT
Complete Set (41): 140.00
Common Player: 3.00
1 Barry Sanders 12.00
2 Chris Warren 3.00
3 Jerry Rice 10.00
4 Emmitt Smith 20.00
5 Henry Ellard 3.00
6 Natrone Means 3.00
7 Terance Mathis 3.00
8 Tim Brown 3.00
9 Andre Reed 3.00
10 Marshall Faulk 5.00
11 Irving Fryar 3.00
12 Cris Carter 3.00
13 Michael Irvin 3.00
14 Jake Reed 3.00
15 Ben Coates 3.00
16 Herman Moore 3.00
17 Carl Pickens 3.00
18 Fred Barnett 3.00
19 Sterling Sharpe 3.00
20 Anthony Miller 3.00
21 Thurman Thomas 3.00
22 Andre Rison 3.00
23 Brian Blades 3.00
24 Rodney Hampton 3.00
25 Terry Allen 3.00
26 Jerome Bettis 3.00
27 Errict Rhett 3.00
28 Rob Moore 3.00
29 Shannon Sharpe 3.00
30 Drew Bledsoe 10.00
31 Dan Marino 20.00
32 Warren Moon 3.00
33 Steve Young 7.00
34 Brett Favre 20.00
35 Jim Everett 3.00
36 Jeff George 3.00
37 John Elway 7.00
38 Jeff Hostetler 3.00
39 Randall Cunningham 3.00
40 Stan Humphries 3.00
41 Jim Kelly 3.00

1995 Topps Profiles

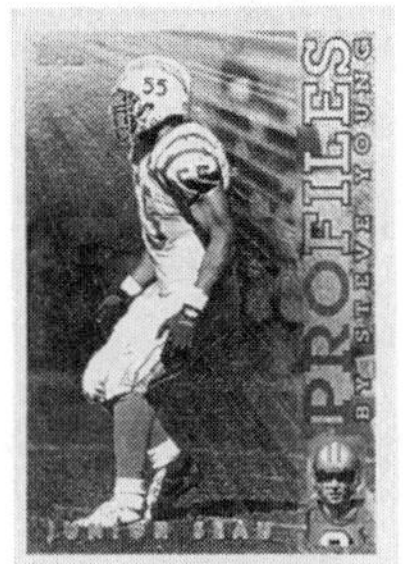

Topps' spokesman, San Francisco 49ers quarterback Steve Young, lends his insights and unique observations of 15 key players for this 1995-96 Topps Series II insert set. These all-silver foil cards are inserted at a rate of one per every 12th pack.

MT
Complete Set (15): 35.00
Common Player: 1.00
1 Emmitt Smith 10.00
2 Chris Spielman 1.00
3 Rod Woodson 1.00
4 Deion Sanders 3.00
5 Junior Seau 1.00
6 Byron Evans 1.00
7 Jerome Bettis 1.00
8 Charles Haley 1.00
9 Jerry Rice 5.00
10 Barry Sanders 7.00
11 Hardy Nickerson 1.00
12 Natrone Means 1.00
13 Darren Woodson 1.00
14 Reggie White 1.00
15 Troy Aikman 4.00

1995 Topps Sensational Sophomores

Ten of the hottest 1994 rookies, including Rookie of the Year Marshall Faulk, comprise this 1995-96 Topps Series I insert set. The cards, printed with Dot Matrix technology, are inserted at a rate of one per every 24 packs and are found exclusively in retail packs.

MT
Complete Set (10): 20.00
Common Player: 1.00
1 Marshall Faulk 4.00
2 Heath Shuler 2.00
3 Tim Bowens 1.00
4 Bryant Young 2.00
5 Dan Wilkinson 2.00
6 Errict Rhett 1.00
7 Andre Coleman 1.00
8 Aaron Glenn 1.00
9 Trent Dilfer 3.00
10 Byron Morris 2.00

1995 Topps Yesteryear

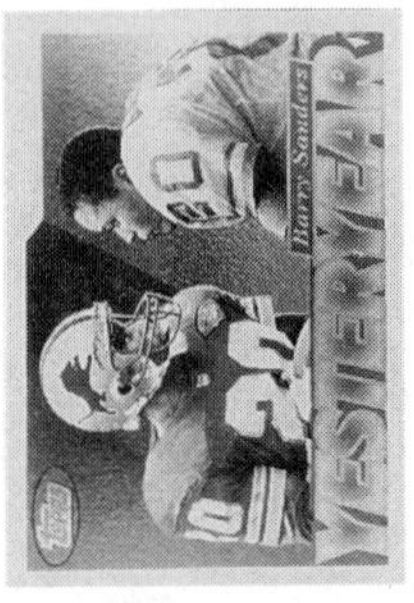

The 15 players who make up this 1995-96 Topps football Series I insert set have not only survived the test but have risen to the top. Each card, printed using Finest technology, features past and present photos and compares the player's rookie season to the previous one. Cards were random inserts, one per every 72 hobby packs.

MT
Complete Set (15): 75.00
Common Player: 2.00
1 Stan Humphries 2.00
2 Dan Marino 20.00
3 Irving Fryar 2.00
4 Warren Moon 2.00
5 Steve Young 8.00
6 Kevin Greene 2.00
7 Jeff Hostetler 2.00
8 Jack Del Rio 2.00
9 Reggie White 2.00
10 Jerry Rice 10.00
11 Bruce Smith 2.00
12 Rod Woodson 2.00
13 Deion Sanders 7.00
14 Barry Sanders 10.00
15 Brett Favre 20.00

1995 Topps Factory Jaguars

The 473-card standard-size set was issued to honor the Jaguars debut season. The cards parallel the base set and each card has a foil Jaguars stamp. Reportedly, just 4,000 sets were produced.

MT
Complete Set (473): 50.00
Common Player: .10
Veteran Stars: .75x-1.5x
Young Stars: .6x-1.25x

1995 Topps Factory Panthers

The 473-card standard-size set was issued to commemorate the Panthers debut season. The set parallels the base set with card having a foil Carolina stamp. Reportedly, there were just 4,000 sets produced.

MT
Complete Set (473): 50.00
Common Player: .10
Veteran Stars: .75x-1.5x
Young Stars: .6x-1.25x

Post-1980 cards in Near Mint condition will generally sell for about 75% of the quoted Mint value. Excellent-condition cards bring no more than 40%.

1996 Topps Promos

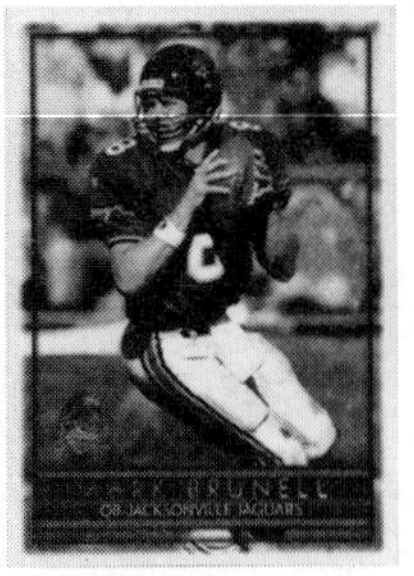

This six-card promo set was sent to dealers and media to provide a sneak peak at the designs for 1996 Topps Football. It arrived in a clear, cello pack containing all six cards.

MT
Complete Set (6): 15.00
Common Player: 1.50
35 Quentin Coryatt 1.50
50 Kerry Collins 5.00
60 Mark Brunell 5.00
73 Mark Carrier 1.50
145 Mel Gray 1.50
405 Ben Coates 1.50

1996 Topps

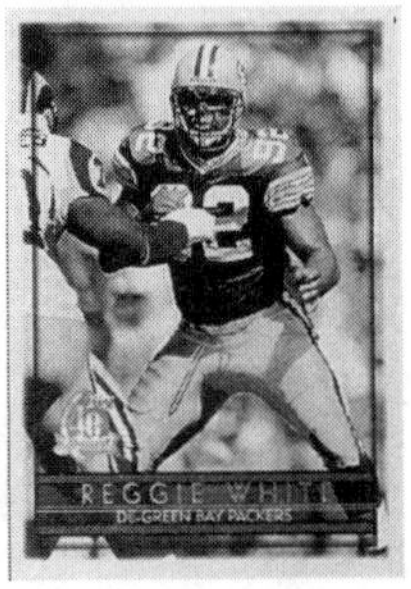

Topps 1996 set marks the 40th year the company has been in football. To commemorate that milestone, Broadway Joe Namath, the New York Jets quarterback, who guaranteed a victory in the Super Bowl in 1969, guarantees this set is Topps best ever. As a tribute to Namath, Topps features him in a 10-card insert set which reprints his 10 Topps cards (1 in 18 packs). He also reviews 10 active NFL quarterbacks for his "Broadway's Reviews" insert set. A 40th Anniversary insert set features 40 of today's top stars pictured on original Topps card designs (one for every year). Other inserts include Turf Warriors, Hobby Masters, a Sweepstakes card (1 in 108 packs), which entitles the finder to one of the 40 sets made during the last 40 years, or all 40, if you're the grand prize winner). The regular 1996 Topps set has 440 cards in it. Each front has a color photo on it, with the player's name, position and team at the bottom between two parallel bars. Topps 40th Anniversary logo is also stamped on each card.

MT
Complete Set (440): 35.00
Common Player: .05
Minor Stars: .10
Pack (11): 1.50
Wax Box (36): 45.00
1 Troy Aikman 1.00
2 Kevin Greene .05
3 Robert Brooks .05
4 Eugene Daniel .05
5 Rodney Peete .05
6 James Hasty .05
7 Tim McDonald .05
8 Darick Holmes .05
9 Morten Andersen .05
10 Junior Seau .05
11 Brett Perriman .05
12 Eric Green .05
13 Jim Flanigan .05
14 Cortez Kennedy .05
15 Orlando Thomas .05
16 Anthony Miller .05
17 Sean Gilbert .05
18 Rob Fredrickson .05
19 Willie Green .05
20 Jeff Blake .50
21 Trent Dilfer .05
22 Chris Chandler .05
23 Renaldo Turnbull .05
24 David Meggett .05
25 Heath Shuler .40
26 Michael Jackson .05
27 Thomas Randolph .05
28 Keith Goganious .05
29 Seth Joyner .05
30 Wayne Chrebet .05
31 Craig Newsome .05
32 William Fuller .05
33 Merton Hanks .05
34 Dale Carter .05
35 Quentin Coryatt .05
36 Robert Jones .05
37 Eric Metcalf .05
38 Byron Morris .05
39 Bill Brooks .05
40 Barry Sanders 2.00
41 Michael Haynes .05
42 Joey Galloway .50
43 Robert Smith .05
44 John Thierry .05
45 Bryan Cox .05
46 Anthony Parker .05
47 Harvey Williams .05
48 Terrell Davis 3.00
49 Darnay Scott .10
50 Kerry Collins .25
51 Cris Dishman .05
52 Dwayne Harper .05
53 Warren Sapp .05
54 Will Moore .05
55 Earnest Byner .05
56 Aaron Glenn .05
57 Michael Westbrook .50
58 Vencie Glenn .05
59 Rob Moore .05
60 Mark Brunell .75
61 Craig Heyward .05
62 Eric Allen .05
63 Bill Romanowski .05
64 Dana Stubblefield .05
65 Steve Bono .05
66 George Koonce .05
67 Larry Brown .05
68 Warren Moon .05
69 Erric Pegram .05
70 Jim Kelly .05
71 Jason Belser .05
72 Henry Thomas .05
73 Mark Carrier .05
74 Terry Wooden .05
75 Terry McDaniel .05
76 O.J. McDuffie .05
77 Dan Wilkinson .05
78 Blake Brockermeyer .05
79 Michael Barrow .05
80 Dave Brown .05
81 Todd Lyght .05
82 Henry Ellard .05
83 Jeff Lageman .05
84 Anthony Pleasant .05
85 Aeneas Williams .05
86 Vincent Brisby .05
87 Terrell Fletcher .05
88 Brad Baxter .05
89 Shannon Sharpe .05
90 Errict Rhett .20
91 Michael Zordich .05
92 Dan Saleaumua .05
93 Devin Bush .05
94 Wayne Simmons .05
95 Tyrone Hughes .05
96 John Randle .05
97 Tony Tolbert .05
98 Yancey Thigpen .40
99 J.J. Stokes .50
100 Marshall Faulk .40
101 Barry Minter .05
102 Glenn Foley .05
103 Chester McGlockton .05
104 Carlton Gray .05
105 Terry Kirby .05
106 Darryll Lewis .05
107 Thomas Smith .05
108 Mike Fox .05
109 Antonio Langham .05
110 Drew Bledsoe 1.00
111 Troy Drayton .05
112 Marvcus Patton .05
113 Tyrone Wheatley .05
114 Desmond Howard .05
115 Johnny Mitchell .05
116 Dave Krieg .05
117 Natrone Means .15
118 Herman Moore .20
119 Darren Woodson .05
120 Ricky Watters .05
121 Emmitt Smith (1,000 Yard Club) 1.00
122 Barry Sanders (1,000 Yard Club) .50
123 Curtis Martin (1,000 Yard Club) .75
124 Chris Warren (1,000 Yard Club) .05
125 Terry Allen (1,000 Yard Club) .05
126 Ricky Watters (1,000 Yard Club) .05
127 Errict Rhett (1,000 Yard Club) .40
128 Rodney Hampton (1,000 Yard Club) .05
129 Terrell Davis (1,000 Yard Club) .50
130 Harvey Williams (1,000 Yard Club) .05
131 Craig Heyward (1,000 Yard Club) .05
132 Marshall Faulk (1,000 Yard Club) .40
133 Rashaan Salaam (1,000 Yard Club) .25
134 Garrison Hearst (1,000 Yard Club) .05
135 Edgar Bennett (1,000 Yard Club) .05
136 Thurman Thomas (1,000 Yard Club) .05
137 Brian Washington .05
138 Derek Loville .05
139 Curtis Conway .05
140 Isaac Bruce .25
141 Ricardo McDonald .05
142 Bruce Armstrong .05
143 Will Wolford .05
144 Thurman Thomas .10
145 Mel Gray .05
146 Napoleon Kaufman .20
147 Terry Allen .05
148 Chris Calloway .05
149 Harry Colon .05
150 Pepper Johnson .05
151 Marco Coleman .05
152 Shawn Jefferson .05
153 Larry Centers .05
154 Lamar Lathon .05
155 Mark Chmura .20
156 Dermontti Dawson .05
157 Alvin Harper .05
158 Randall McDaniel .05
159 Allen Aldridge .05
160 Chris Warren .10
161 Jessie Tuggle .05
162 Sean Lumpkin .05
163 Bobby Houston .05

164	Dexter Carter	.05
165	Erik Kramer	.05
166	Brock Marion	.05
167	Toby Wright	.05
168	John Copeland	.05
169	Sean Dawkins	.05
170	Tim Brown	.05
171	Darion Conner	.05
172	Aaron Hayden	.05
173	Charlie Garner	.05
174	Anthony Cook	.05
175	Derrick Thomas	.05
176	Willie McGinest	.05
177	Thomas Lewis	.05
178	Sherman Williams	.05
179	Cornelius Bennett	.05
180	Frank Sanders	.05
181	Leroy Hoard	.05
182	Bernie Parmalee	.05
183	Sterling Palmer	.05
184	Kelvin Pritchett	.05
185	Kordell Stewart	1.00
186	Brent Jones	.05
187	Robert Blackmon	.05
188	Adrian Murrell	.05
189	Edgar Bennett	.05
190	Rashaan Salaam	.50
191	Ellis Johnson	.05
192	Andre Coleman	.05
193	Will Shields	.05
194	Derrick Brooks	.05
195	Carl Pickens	.10
196	Carlton Bailey	.05
197	Terance Mathis	.05
198	Carlos Jenkins	.05
199	Derrick Alexander	.05
200	Deion Sanders	.40
201	Glyn Milburn	.05
202	Chris Sanders	.25
203	Raghib Ismail	.05
204	Fred Barnett	.05
205	Quinn Early	.05
206	Henry Jones	.05
207	Herschel Walker	.05
208	James Washington	.05
209	Lee Woodall	.05
210	Neil Smith	.05
211	Tony Bennett	.05
212	Ernie Mills	.05
213	Clyde Simmons	.05
214	Chris Slade	.05
215	Tony Boselli	.05
216	Ryan McNeil	.05
217	Rob Burnett	.05
218	Stan Humphries	.05
219	Rick Mirer	.05
220	Troy Vincent	.05
221	Sean Jones	.05
222	Marty Carter	.05
223	Boomer Esiason	.05
224	Charles Haley	.05
225	Sam Mills	.05
226	Greg Biekert	.05
227	Bryant Young	.05
228	Ken Dilger	.05
229	Levon Kirkland	.05
230	Brian Mitchell	.05
231	Hardy Nickerson	.05
232	Elvis Grbac	.05
233	Kurt Schulz	.05
234	Chris Doleman	.05
235	Tamarick Vanover	.50
236	Jesse Campbell	.05
237	William Thomas	.05
238	Shane Conlan	.05
239	Jason Elam	.05
240	Steve McNair	.50
241	Jerry Rice (1,000 Yard Club)	.50
242	Isaac Bruce (1,000 Yard Club)	.30
243	Herman Moore (1,000 Yard Club)	.05
244	Michael Irvin (1,000 Yard Club)	.05
245	Robert Brooks (1,000 Yard Club)	.05
246	Brett Perriman (1,000 Yard Club)	.05
247	Cris Carter (1,000 Yard Club)	.05
248	Tim Brown (1,000 Yard Club)	.05
249	Yancey Thigpen (1,000 Yard Club)	.20
250	Jeff Graham (1,000 Yard Club)	.05
251	Carl Pickens (1,000 Yard Club)	.05
252	Tony Martin (1,000 Yard Club)	.05
253	Eric Metcalf (1,000 Yard Club)	.05
254	Jake Reed (1,000 Yard Club)	.05
255	Quinn Early (1,000 Yard Club)	.05
256	Anthony Miller (1,000 Yard Club)	.05
257	Joey Galloway (1,000 Yard Club)	.25
258	Bert Emanuel (1,000 Yard Club)	.05
259	Terance Mathis (1,000 Yard Club)	.05
260	Curtis Conway (1,000 Yard Club)	.05
261	Henry Ellard (1,000 Yard Club)	.05
262	Mark Carrier (1,000 Yard Club)	.05
263	Brian Blades (1,000 Yard Club)	.05
264	William Roaf	.05
265	Ed McDaniel	.05
266	Nate Newton	.05
267	Brett Maxie	.05
268	Anthony Smith	.05
269	Mickey Washington	.05
270	Jerry Rice	1.00
271	Shaun Gayle	.05
272	Gilbert Brown	.05
273	Mark Bruener	.05
274	Eugene Robinson	.05
275	Marvin Washington	.05
276	Keith Sims	.05
277	Ashley Ambrose	.05
278	Garrison Hearst	.05
279	Donnell Woolford	.05
280	Cris Carter	.05
281	Curtis Martin	1.50
282	Scott Mitchell	.05
283	Stevon Moore	.05
284	Roman Phifer	.05
285	Ken Harvey	.05
286	Rodney Hampton	.05
287	Willie Davis	.05
288	Yonel Jourdain	.05
289	Brian DeMarco	.05
290	Reggie White	.05
291	Kevin Williams	.05
292	Gary Plummer	.05
293	Terrance Shaw	.05
294	Calvin Williams	.05
295	Eddie Robinson	.05
296	Tony McGee	.05
297	Clay Matthews	.05
298	Joe Cain	.05
299	Tim McKyer	.05
300	Greg Lloyd	.05
301	Steve Wisniewski	.05
302	Ray Buchanan	.05
303	Lake Dawson	.05
304	Kevin Carter	.05
305	Phillippi Sparks	.05
306	Emmitt Smith	2.00
307	Ruben Brown	.05
308	Tom Carter	.05
309	William Floyd	.05
310	Jim Everett	.05
311	Vincent Brown	.05
312	Dennis Gibson	.05
313	Lorenzo Lynch	.05
314	Corey Harris	.05
315	James Stewart	.05
316	Kyle Brady	.05
317	Irving Fryar	.05
318	Jake Reed	.05
319	Vinny Testaverde	.05
320	John Elway	.30
321	Tracy Scroggins	.05
322	Chris Spielman	.05
323	Horace Copeland	.05
324	Chris Zorich	.05
325	Mike Mamula	.05
326	Henry Ford	.05
327	Steve Walsh	.05
328	Stanley Richard	.05
329	Mike Jones	.05
330	Jim Harbaugh	.05
331	Darren Perry	.05
332	Ken Norton	.05
333	Kimble Anders	.05
334	Harold Green	.05
335	Tyrone Poole	.05
336	Mark Fields	.05
337	Darren Bennett	.05
338	Mike Sherrard	.05
339	Terry Ray	.05
340	Bruce Smith	.05
341	Daryl Johnston	.05
342	Vinnie Clark	.05
343	Mike Caldwell	.05
344	Vinson Smith	.05
345	Mo Lewis	.05
346	Brian Blades	.05
347	Rod Stephens	.05
348	David Palmer	.05
349	Blaine Bishop	.05
350	Jeff George	.05
351	George Teague	.05
352	Jeff Hostetler	.05
353	Michael Strahan	.05
354	Eric Davis	.05
355	Jerome Bettis	.05
356	Irv Smith	.05
357	Jeff Herrod	.05
358	Jay Novacek	.05
359	Bryce Paup	.05
360	Neil O'Donnell	.05
361	Eric Swann	.05
362	Corey Sawyer	.05
363	Ty Law	.05
364	Bo Orlando	.05
365	Marcus Allen	.05
366	Mark McMillian	.05
367	Mark Carrier	.05
368	Jackie Harris	.05
369	Steve Atwater	.05
370	Steve Young	1.00
371	Brett Favre (3,000 Yard Club)	.75
372	Scott Mitchell (3,000 Yard Club)	.05
373	Warren Moon (3,000 Yard Club)	.05
374	Jeff George (3,000 Yard Club)	.05
375	Jim Everett (3,000 Yard Club)	.05
376	John Elway (3,000 Yard Club)	.15
377	Erik Kramer (3,000 Yard Club)	.05
378	Jeff Blake (3,000 Yard Club)	.25
379	Dan Marino (3,000 Yard Club)	1.00
380	Dave Krieg (3,000 Yard Club)	.05
381	Drew Bledsoe (3,000 Yard Club)	.50
382	Stan Humphries (3,000 Yard Club)	.05
383	Troy Aikman (3,000 Yard Club)	.50
384	Steve Young (3,000 Yard Club)	.50
385	Jim Kelly (3,000 Yard Club)	.05
386	Steve Bono (3,000 Yard Club)	.05
387	David Sloan	.05
388	Jeff Graham	.05
389	Hugh Douglas	.05
390	Dan Marino	1.50
391	Winston Moss	.05
392	Darrell Green	.05
393	Mark Stepnoski	.05
394	Bert Emanuel	.05
395	Eric Zeier	.05
396	Willie Jackson	.05
397	Qadry Ismail	.05
398	Michael Brooks	.05
399	D'Marco Farr	.05
400	Brett Favre	2.00
401	Carnell Lake	.05
402	Pat Swilling	.05
403	Steve Grant	.05
404	Steve Tasker	.05
405	Ben Coates	.05
406	Steve Tovar	.05
407	Tony Martin	.05
408	Grant Hill	.05
409	Eric Guliford	.05
410	Michael Irvin	.05
411	Eric Hill	.05
412	Mario Bates	.05
413	Brian Stablein	.05
414	*Marcus Jones*	.05
415	*Reggie Brown*	.05
416	*Lawrence Phillips*	.50
417	*Alex Van Dyke*	.10
418	*Daryl Gardener*	.05
419	*Mike Alstott*	1.50
420	*Kevin Hardy*	.10
421	*Rickey Dudley*	.20
422	*Jerome Woods*	.05
423	*Eric Moulds*	1.50
424	*Cedric Jones*	.05
425	*Simeon Rice*	.40
426	*Marvin Harrison*	2.00
427	*Tim Biakabutuka*	.75
428	*Duane Clemons*	.05
429	*Alex Molden*	.05
430	*Keyshawn Johnson*	2.00
431	*Willie Anderson*	.05
432	*John Mobley*	.05
433	*Leeland McElroy*	.20
434	*Regan Upshaw*	.05
435	*Eddie George*	3.00
436	*Jonathan Ogden*	.10
437	*Eddie Kennison*	.50
438	*Jermain Mayberry*	.05
439	Checklist	.05
440	Checklist	.05

1996 Topps Broadway's Reviews

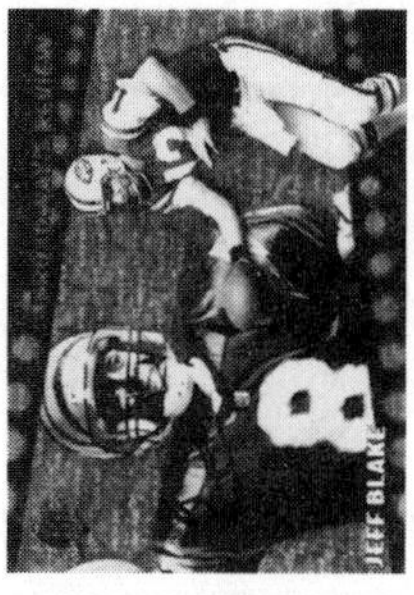

JEFF BLAKE

These 1996 Topps football inserts feature 10 of today's top quarterbacks pictured with an archive photo of Joe Namath. The horizontally-designed card front is designed like a filmstrip. The card back has Namath's review of the player, written by the Hall of Famer himself. Cards were seeded one per every 12 packs.

		MT
Complete Set (10):		30.00
Common Player:		1.50
1	Kerry Collins	3.00
2	Drew Bledsoe	4.00
3	Jeff Blake	1.50
4	Brett Favre	7.00
5	Scott Mitchell	1.50
6	Troy Aikman	4.00
7	Steve Young	3.00
8	Jim Harbaugh	1.50
9	John Elway	2.50
10	Dan Marino	7.00

1996 Topps 40th Anniversary

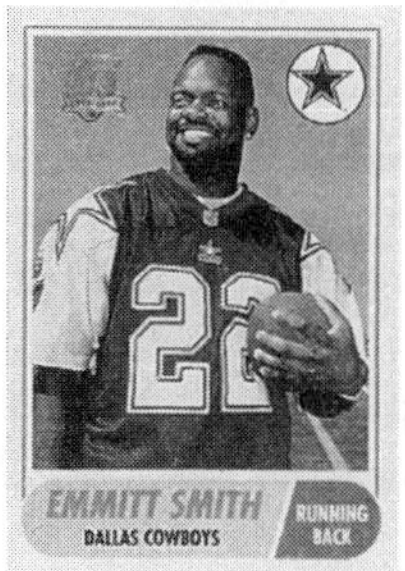

EMMITT SMITH
DALLAS COWBOYS
RUNNING BACK

Forty of today's top NFL stars are featured on these 1996 Topps football cards, which utilize Topps original designs from its first 40 years of producing cards. Each player in the set represents a different year, using a classic pose from that set. The cards, seeded one per every six packs, have Topps 40th Anniversary logo stamped in gold foil on the front.

		MT
Complete Set (40):		70.00
Common Player:		1.00
Minor Stars:		2.00
1	Jim Harbaugh '56	1.00
2	Greg Lloyd '57	1.00
3	Barry Sanders '58	5.00
4	Merton Hanks '59	1.00
5	Herman Moore '60	2.00
6	Tim Brown '61	1.00
7	Brett Favre '62	10.00
8	Cris Carter '63	1.00
9	Curtis Martin '64	7.00
10	Bryce Paup '65	1.00
11	Steve Bono '66	1.00
12	Blaine Bishop '67	1.00
13	Emmitt Smith '68	10.00
14	Carnell Lake '69	1.00
15	Marshall Faulk '70	4.00
16	Mike Morris '71	1.00
17	Shannon Sharpe '72	1.00
18	Steve Young '73	4.00
19	Jeff George '74	2.00
20	Junior Seau '75	1.00
21	Chris Warren '76	2.00
22	Heath Shuler '77	2.00
23	Jeff Blake '78	3.00
24	Reggie White '79	2.00
25	Jeff Hostetler '80	1.00
26	Errict Rhett '81	2.00
27	Rodney Hampton '82	1.00
28	Jerry Rice '83	5.00
29	Jim Everett '84	1.00
30	Isaac Bruce '85	3.00
31	Dan Marino '86	10.00
32	Marcus Allen '87	2.00
33	Erik Kramer '88	1.00
34	John Elway '89	2.00
35	Ricky Watters '90	1.00
36	Troy Aikman '91	5.00
37	Drew Bledsoe '92	5.00
38	Scott Mitchell '93	1.00
39	Rashaan Salaam '94	2.00
40	Kerry Collins '95	2.00

1996 Topps Hobby Masters

These 20 cards, a hobby only insert, feature the game's top 10 superstars, as chosen by hobbyists. The cards, seeded one per every 36 packs of 1996 Topps football hobby, use 28-point foil board. The card front has a color action photo in the middle, with a closeup shot as the background. "Hobby Masters" is written towards the bottom of the card, along with the player's name, position and a team logo. Topps 40th Anniversary logo is also on the front.

		MT
Complete Set (20):		150.00
Common Player:		2.00
Minor Stars:		4.00
1	Brett Favre	25.00
2	Emmitt Smith	25.00
3	Drew Bledsoe	12.00
4	Marshall Faulk	10.00
5	Steve Young	12.00
6	Barry Sanders	18.00
7	Troy Aikman	12.00
8	Jerry Rice	12.00
9	Michael Irvin	4.00
10	Dan Marino	25.00
11	Chris Warren	4.00
12	Reggie White	2.00
13	Jeff Blake	4.00
14	Greg Lloyd	2.00
15	Curtis Martin	18.00
16	Junior Seau	2.00
17	Kerry Collins	4.00
18	Deion Sanders	7.00
19	Joey Galloway	10.00
20	John Elway	6.00

1996 Topps Namath Reprint

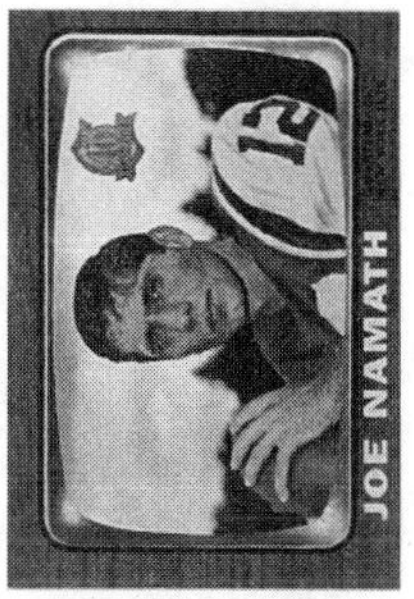

JOE NAMATH

"Broadway Joe" Namath's 10 Topps cards are reprinted for this 1996 Topps football insert set, including his 1965 Topps rookie card, one of the most valuable modern-day football cards. The cards were seeded at a ratio of one per every 18 packs.

		MT
Complete Set (10):		50.00
Common Player:		5.00
1	1965	10.00
2	1966	5.00
3	1967	5.00
4	1968	5.00
5	1969	5.00
6	1970	5.00
7	1971	5.00
8	1972	5.00
9	1972	5.00
10	1973	5.00

Values quoted in this guide reflect the retail price of a card — the price a collector can expect to pay when buying a card from a dealer. The wholesale price — that which a collector can expect to receive from a dealer when selling cards — will be significantly lower, depending on desirability and condition.

1996 Topps Turf Warriors

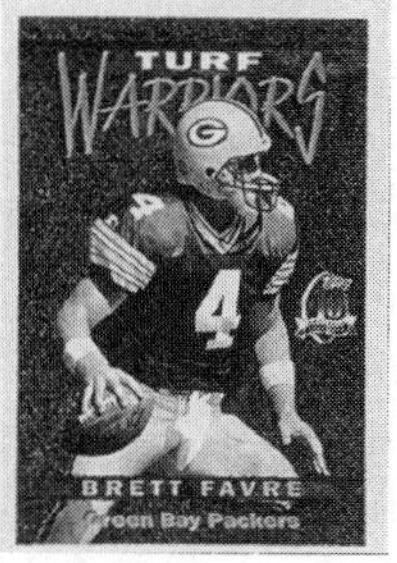

TURF WARRIORS
BRETT FAVRE
Green Bay Packers

This insert features 22 players on coated cards with an astro-turf type surface. Turf Warriors are inserted every 36 packs of Topps Football.

		MT
Complete Set (22):		120.00
Common Player:		3.00
1	Bryce Paup	3.00
2	Ben Coates	3.00
3	Jim Harbaugh	3.00
4	Brian Mitchell	3.00
5	Brett Favre	20.00
6	Junior Seau	3.00
7	Michael Irvin	3.00
8	Steve Young	10.00
9	Terry McDaniel	3.00
10	Curtis Martin	16.00
11	Greg Lloyd	3.00
12	Cris Carter	3.00
13	Emmitt Smith	20.00
14	Reggie White	3.00
15	Marshall Faulk	6.00
16	Jerry Rice	14.00
17	Shannon Sharpe	3.00
18	Dan Marino	20.00
19	Ken Norton	3.00
20	Barry Sanders	12.00
21	Neil Smith	3.00
22	Troy Aikman	12.00

1996 Topps Chrome

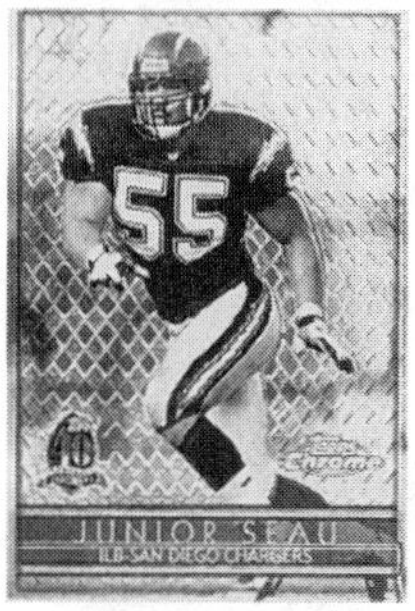

JUNIOR SEAU
LB SAN DIEGO CHARGERS

Chrome Football includes 165 of the best cards from Topps Football and adds its chromium finish. Among the cards in Chrome are Draft Picks, 1000 Yard Club and 3000 Yard Club subsets. Four-card packs included Tide Turners and 40th Anniversary inserts, as well as Refractor versions of the entire set and all inserts.

		MT
Complete Set (165):		250.00
Common Player:		.25
Common Rookies (150-164):		1.00
Minor Stars:		.50
Pack (4):		10.00
Wax Box (24):		225.00
1	Troy Aikman	3.00
2	Kevin Greene	.25
3	Robert Brooks	.25
4	Junior Seau	.50
5	Brett Perriman	.25
6	Cortez Kennedy	.25
7	Orlando Thomas	.25
8	Anthony Miller	.25
9	Jeff Blake	1.00
10	Trent Dilfer	1.00
11	Heath Shuler	.25
12	Michael Jackson	.25
13	Merton Hanks	.25
14	Dale Carter	.25
15	Eric Metcalf	.25
16	Barry Sanders	6.00
17	Joey Galloway	1.00
18	Bryan Cox	.25
19	Harvey Williams	.25
20	Terrell Davis	6.00
21	Darnay Scott	.25
22	Kerry Collins	.75
23	Warren Sapp	.25
24	Michael Westbrook	.25
25	Mark Brunell	3.00
26	Craig Heyward	.25
27	Eric Allen	.25
28	Dana Stubblefield	.25
29	Steve Bono	.25
30	Larry Brown	.25
31	Warren Moon	.50
32	Jim Kelly	.50
33	Terry McDaniel	.25
34	Dan Wilkinson	.25
35	Dave Brown	.25
36	Todd Lyght	.25
37	Aeneas Williams	.25
38	Shannon Sharpe	.50
39	Errict Rhett	.50
40	Yancey Thigpen	.50
41	J.J. Stokes	.25
42	Marshall Faulk	1.00
43	Chester McGlockton	.25
44	Darryll Lewis	.25
45	Drew Bledsoe	3.00
46	Tyrone Wheatley	.25
47	Herman Moore	1.00
48	Darren Woodson	.25
49	Ricky Watters	.50
50	Emmitt Smith TYC	2.50
51	Barry Sanders TYC	2.00
52	Curtis Martin TYC	1.50
53	Chris Warren TYC	.25
54	Errict Rhett TYC	.25
55	Rodney Hampton TYC	.25
56	Terrell Davis TYC	3.00
57	Marshall Faulk TYC	.50
58	Rashaan Salaam TYC	.25
59	Curtis Conway	.50
60	Isaac Bruce	1.00
61	Thurman Thomas	.50
62	Terry Allen	.25
63	Lamar Lathon	.25
64	Mark Chmura	.50
65	Chris Warren	.25
66	Jessie Tuggle	.25
67	Erik Kramer	.25
68	Tim Brown	.50
69	Derrick Thomas	.25
70	Willie McGinest	.25
71	Frank Sanders	.25
72	Bernie Parmalee	.25
73	Kordell Stewart	3.00
74	Brent Jones	.25
75	Edgar Bennett	.25
76	Rashaan Salaam	.50
77	Carl Pickens	.50
78	Terance Mathis	.25
79	Deion Sanders	1.50
80	Glyn Milburn	.25
81	Lee Woodall	.25
82	Neil Smith	.25
83	Stan Humphries	.25
84	Rick Mirer	.25
85	Troy Vincent	.25
86	Sam Mills	.25
87	Brian Mitchell	.25
88	Hardy Nickerson	.25
89	Tamarick Vanover	.50
90	Steve McNair	3.00
91	Jerry Rice TYC	1.50
92	Isaac Bruce TYC	.50
93	Herman Moore TYC	.50
94	Cris Carter TYC	.25
95	Tim Brown TYC	.25
96	Carl Pickens TYC	.25
97	Joey Galloway TYC	.50
98	Jerry Rice	3.00
99	Cris Carter	.50
100	Curtis Martin	3.00
101	Scott Mitchell	.25
102	Ken Harvey	.25
103	Rodney Hampton	.25
104	Reggie White	.50
105	Eddie Robinson	.25
106	Greg Lloyd	.25
107	Phillippi Sparks	.25
108	Emmitt Smith	5.00
109	Tom Carter	.25
110	Jim Everett	.25
111	James Stewart	.25
112	Kyle Brady	.25
113	Irving Fryar	.25
114	Vinny Testaverde	.25
115	John Elway	3.00
116	Chris Spielman	.25
117	Mike Mamula	.25
118	Jim Harbaugh	.50
119	Ken Norton	.25
120	Bruce Smith	.25
121	Daryl Johnston	.25
122	Blaine Bishop	.25
123	Jeff George	.50
124	Jeff Hostetler	.25
125	Jerome Bettis	.50
126	Jay Novacek	.25
127	Bryce Paup	.25
128	Neil O'Donnell	.25
129	Marcus Allen	1.00
130	Steve Young	2.00
131	Brett Favre TYC	3.00
132	Scott Mitchell TYC	.25
133	John Elway TYC	2.00
134	Jeff Blake TYC	.50
135	Dan Marino TYC	3.00
136	Drew Bledsoe TYC	1.50
137	Troy Aikman TYC	1.50
138	Steve Young TYC	1.00
139	Jim Kelly TYC	.25
140	Jeff Graham	.25
141	Hugh Douglas	.25
142	Dan Marino	6.00
143	Darrell Green	.25
144	Eric Zeier	.25
145	Brett Favre	6.00
146	Carnell Lake	.25
147	Ben Coates	.25
148	Tony Martin	.25
149	Michael Irvin	.50
150	*Lawrence Phillips*	15.00
151	*Alex Van Dyke*	1.00
152	*Kevin Hardy*	1.00
153	*Rickey Dudley*	6.00
154	*Eric Moulds*	30.00
155	*Simeon Rice*	1.00
156	*Marvin Harrison*	60.00
157	*Tim Biakabutuka*	15.00
158	*Duane Clemons*	1.00
159	*Keyshawn Johnson*	50.00
160	*John Mobley*	1.00
161	*Leeland McElroy*	2.00
162	*Eddie George*	75.00
163	*Jonathan Ogden*	1.00
164	*Eddie Kennison*	5.00
165	Checklist	.25

Post-1980 cards in Near Mint condition will generally sell for about 75% of the quoted Mint value. Excellent-condition cards bring no more than 40%.

1996 Topps Chrome Refractors

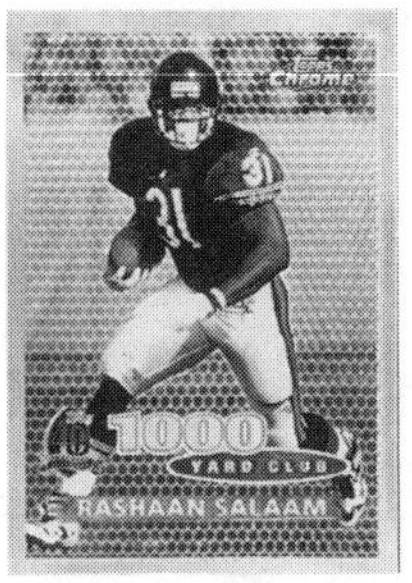

Topps Chrome Refractors are a parallel of the Topps Chrome base set. Refractors were inserted one per 12 packs.

		MT
Complete Set (165):		1500.
Common Player:		3.00
Common Rookies (150-164):		6.00
Minor Stars:		6.00
1	Troy Aikman	45.00
2	Kevin Greene	3.00
3	Robert Brooks	3.00
4	Junior Seau	6.00
5	Brett Perriman	3.00
6	Cortez Kennedy	3.00
7	Orlando Thomas	3.00
8	Anthony Miller	3.00
9	Jeff Blake	10.00
10	Trent Dilfer	10.00
11	Heath Shuler	3.00
12	Michael Jackson	3.00
13	Merton Hanks	3.00
14	Dale Carter	3.00
15	Eric Metcalf	3.00
16	Barry Sanders	90.00
17	Joey Galloway	10.00
18	Bryan Cox	3.00
19	Harvey Williams	3.00
20	Terrell Davis	90.00
21	Darnay Scott	3.00
22	Kerry Collins	6.00
23	Warren Sapp	3.00
24	Michael Westbrook	3.00
25	Mark Brunell	40.00
26	Craig Heyward	3.00
27	Eric Allen	3.00
28	Dana Stubblefield	3.00
29	Steve Bono	3.00
30	Larry Brown	3.00
31	Warren Moon	6.00
32	Jim Kelly	6.00
33	Terry McDaniel	3.00
34	Dan Wilkinson	3.00
35	Dave Brown	3.00
36	Todd Lyght	3.00
37	Aeneas Williams	3.00
38	Shannon Sharpe	6.00
39	Errict Rhett	6.00
40	Yancey Thigpen	6.00
41	J.J. Stokes	3.00
42	Marshall Faulk	10.00
43	Chester McGlockton	3.00
44	Darryll Lewis	3.00
45	Drew Bledsoe	45.00
46	Tyrone Wheatley	3.00
47	Herman Moore	10.00
48	Darren Woodson	3.00
49	Ricky Watters	6.00
50	Emmitt Smith TYC	30.00
51	Barry Sanders TYC	30.00
52	Curtis Martin TYC	20.00
53	Chris Warren TYC	3.00
54	Errict Rhett TYC	3.00
55	Rodney Hampton TYC	3.00
56	Terrell Davis TYC	40.00
57	Marshall Faulk TYC	6.00
58	Rashaan Salaam TYC	3.00
59	Curtis Conway	6.00
60	Isaac Bruce	10.00
61	Thurman Thomas	6.00
62	Terry Allen	3.00
63	Lamar Lathon	3.00
64	Mark Chmura	6.00
65	Chris Warren	3.00
66	Jessie Tuggle	3.00
67	Erik Kramer	3.00
68	Tim Brown	6.00
69	Derrick Thomas	3.00
70	Willie McGinest	3.00
71	Frank Sanders	3.00
72	Bernie Parmalee	3.00
73	Kordell Stewart	60.00
74	Brent Jones	3.00
75	Edgar Bennett	3.00
76	Rashaan Salaam	6.00
77	Carl Pickens	6.00
78	Terance Mathis	3.00
79	Deion Sanders	20.00
80	Glyn Milburn	3.00
81	Lee Woodall	3.00
82	Neil Smith	3.00
83	Stan Humphries	3.00
84	Rick Mirer	3.00
85	Troy Vincent	3.00
86	Sam Mills	3.00
87	Brian Mitchell	3.00
88	Hardy Nickerson	3.00
89	Tamarick Vanover	6.00
90	Steve McNair	40.00
91	Jerry Rice TYC	18.00
92	Isaac Bruce TYC	6.00
93	Herman Moore TYC	6.00
94	Cris Carter TYC	3.00
95	Tim Brown TYC	3.00
96	Carl Pickens TYC	3.00
97	Joey Galloway TYC	6.00
98	Jerry Rice	30.00
99	Cris Carter	6.00
100	Curtis Martin	40.00
101	Scott Mitchell	3.00
102	Ken Harvey	3.00
103	Rodney Hampton	3.00
104	Reggie White	6.00
105	Eddie Robinson	3.00
106	Greg Lloyd	3.00
107	Phillippi Sparks	3.00
108	Emmitt Smith	75.00
109	Tom Carter	3.00
110	Jim Everett	3.00
111	James Stewart	3.00
112	Kyle Brady	3.00
113	Irving Fryar	3.00
114	Vinny Testaverde	3.00
115	John Elway	40.00
116	Chris Spielman	3.00
117	Mike Mamula	3.00
118	Jim Harbaugh	6.00
119	Ken Norton	3.00
120	Bruce Smith	3.00
121	Daryl Johnston	3.00
122	Blaine Bishop	3.00
123	Jeff George	6.00
124	Jeff Hostetler	3.00
125	Jerome Bettis	6.00
126	Jay Novacek	3.00
127	Bryce Paup	3.00
128	Neil O'Donnell	3.00
129	Marcus Allen	10.00
130	Steve Young	30.00
131	Brett Favre TYC	35.00
132	Scott Mitchell TYC	3.00
133	John Elway TYC	25.00
134	Jeff Blake TYC	6.00
135	Dan Marino TYC	35.00
136	Drew Bledsoe TYC	18.00
137	Troy Aikman TYC	18.00
138	Steve Young TYC	12.00
139	Jim Kelly TYC	3.00
140	Jeff Graham	3.00
141	Hugh Douglas	3.00
142	Dan Marino	80.00
143	Darrell Green	3.00
144	Eric Zeier	3.00
145	Brett Favre	90.00
146	Carnell Lake	3.00
147	Ben Coates	3.00
148	Tony Martin	3.00
149	Michael Irvin	6.00
150	Lawrence Phillips	75.00
151	Alex Van Dyke	6.00
152	Kevin Hardy	6.00
153	Rickey Dudley	20.00
154	Eric Moulds	125.00
155	Simeon Rice	6.00
156	Marvin Harrison	175.00
157	Tim Biakabutuka	40.00
158	Duane Clemons	6.00
159	Keyshawn Johnson	175.00
160	John Mobley	6.00
161	Leeland McElroy	10.00
162	Eddie George	200.00
163	Jonathan Ogden	6.00
164	Eddie Kennison	20.00
165	Checklist	3.00

1996 Topps Chrome 40th Anniversary

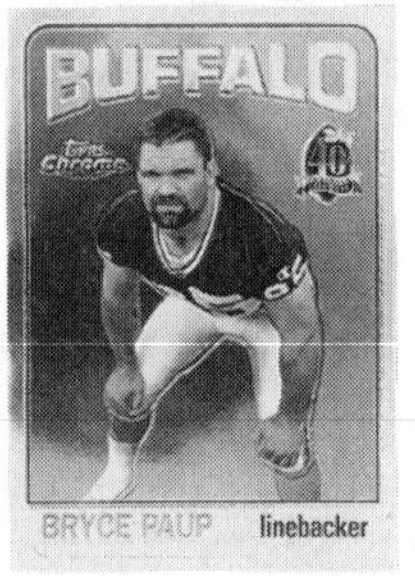

Originally found in Topps, this 40-card insert was printed with a Chrome finish and inserted every eight packs. 40th Anniversary insert celebrated 40 years of Topps football with today's players in classic poses and original card designs from 1955 to 1995.

		MT
Complete Set (40):		140.00
Common Player:		2.00
Refractors:		2x-3x
1	Jim Harbaugh (1956)	2.00
2	Greg Lloyd (1957)	2.00
3	Barry Sanders (1958)	20.00
4	Merton Hanks (1959)	2.00
5	Herman Moore (1960)	2.00
6	Tim Brown (1961)	2.00
7	Brett Favre (1962)	20.00
8	Cris Carter (1963)	2.00
9	Curtis Martin (1964)	10.00
10	Bryce Paup (1965)	2.00
11	Steve Bono (1966)	2.00
12	Blaine Bishop (1967)	2.00
13	Emmitt Smith (1968)	15.00
14	Carnell Lake (1969)	2.00
15	Marshall Faulk (1970)	4.00
16	Bam Morris (1971)	2.00
17	Shannon Sharpe (1972)	2.00
18	Steve Young (1973)	8.00
19	Jeff George (1974)	2.00
20	Junior Seau (1975)	2.00
21	Chris Warren (1976)	2.00
22	Heath Shuler (1977)	2.00
23	Jeff Blake (1978)	5.00
24	Reggie White (1979)	2.00
25	Jeff Hostetler (1980)	2.00
26	Errict Rhett (1981)	2.00
27	Rodney Hampton (1982)	2.00
28	Jerry Rice (1983)	10.00
29	Jim Everett (1984)	2.00
30	Isaac Bruce (1985)	5.00
31	Dan Marino (1986)	15.00
32	Marcus Allen (1987)	2.00
33	Erik Kramer (1988)	2.00
34	John Elway (1989)	12.00
35	Ricky Watters (1990)	2.00
36	Troy Aikman (1991)	10.00
37	Drew Bledsoe (1992)	10.00
38	Scott Mitchell (1993)	2.00
39	Rashaan Salaam (1994)	4.00
40	Kerry Collins (1995)	4.00

1996 Topps Chrome 40th Anniversary Refractors

Each card in Chrome's 40th Anniversary insert was also printed in a Refractor version. Refractors of this insert are found every 24 packs.

	MT
Complete Set (40):	375.00
Refractors:	2x-3x

1996 Topps Chrome Tide Turners

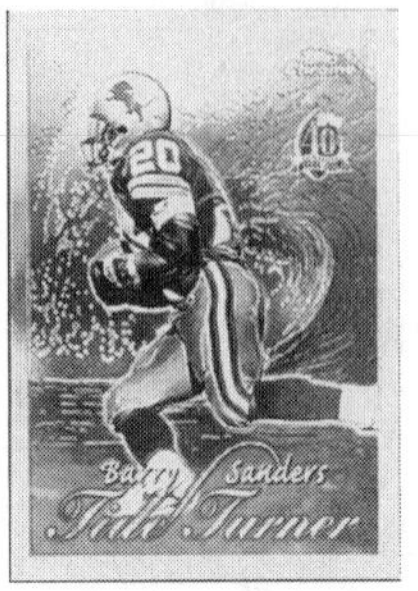

Tide Turners was a 10-card insert that was exclusively produced for Chrome. It featured top playmakers in the NFL and was inserted every 12 packs.

		MT
Complete Set (15):		70.00
Common Player:		1.50
Refractors:		4x-6x
1	Rashaan Salaam	3.00
2	Warren Moon	1.50
3	Marshall Faulk	4.00
4	Jeff Blake	3.00
5	Curtis Martin	10.00
6	Eric Metcalf	1.50
7	Errict Rhett	3.00
8	Scott Mitchell	1.50
9	Ricky Watters	3.00
10	Jerry Rice	8.00
11	Emmitt Smith	15.00
12	Erik Kramer	1.50
13	Jim Harbaugh	1.50
14	Barry Sanders	18.00
15	John Elway	6.00

1996 Topps Chrome Tide Turners Refractors

This 10-card set is a parallel to the regular Tide Turners inserts. It includes Topps' popular Refractor finish and was inserted every 48 packs.

	MT
Complete Set (15):	280.00
Refractors:	4x-6x

1996 Topps Gilt Edge

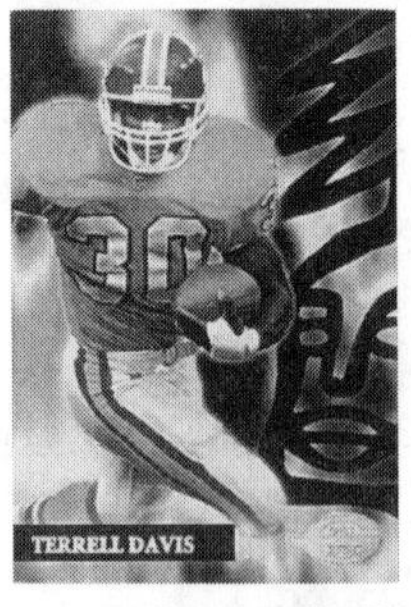

As part of its sponsorship of the first-ever NFL Pro Bowl Experience card show held in conjunction with the Pro Bowl Game in February 1996, Topps issued this 90-card hobby exclusive set. The cards feature 84 members from the Pro Bowl rosters, plus five players who had Pro Bowl-caliber seasons and a checklist. Each card utilizes Topps gilt edge technology, which places gold gilt edging around every card. A gilt edge logo replaces the Topps logo on each card front too, which has a color action photo and one of the set's icons on it. The card back has biographical and statistical information at the top, with a set icon in the background. A recap of the player's 1995 accomplishments, a team logo and a close-up shot round out the back's design. In addition, a parallel version of the set was created using platinum gilt edging. These cards were seeded one per pack, as were Gilt Edge Pro Bowl Skills insert cards.

		MT
Complete Set (90):		25.00
Common Player:		.15
Minor Stars:		.30
Platinum Cards:		2x-4x
Pack (9):		1.25
Wax Box (20):		20.00
1	Brett Favre	4.00
2	Kevin Glover	.15
3	Nate Newton	.15
4	Randall McDaniel	.15
5	William Roaf	.15
6	Lomas Brown	.15
7	Jay Novacek	.15
8	Emmitt Smith	4.00
9	Barry Sanders	2.50
10	Jerry Rice	2.00
11	Herman Moore	.50
12	Larry Centers	.15
13	Chester McGlockton	.15
14	Dan Saleaumua	.15
15	Bruce Smith	.15
16	Neil Smith	.15
17	Junior Seau	.30
18	Bryce Paup	.15
19	Greg Lloyd	.30
20	Terry McDaniel	.15
21	Dale Carter	.15
22	Carnell Lake	.15
23	Steve Atwater	.15
24	Elbert Shelley	.15
25	Brian Mitchell	.15
26	Jeff Feagles	.15
27	Morten Andersen	.15
28	Dan Marino	4.00
29	Dermontti Dawson	.15
30	Steve Wisniewski	.15
31	Bruce Matthews	.15
32	Bruce Armstrong	.15
33	Richmond Webb	.15
34	Ben Coates	.15
35	Marshall Faulk	1.50
36	Chris Warren	.30
37	Carl Pickens	.30
38	Tim Brown	.15
39	Kimble Anders	.15
40	John Randle	.15
41	Eric Swann	.15
42	Reggie White	.30
43	Charles Haley	.15
44	Ken Norton	.15
45	Lee Woodall	.15
46	Ken Harvey	.15
47	Aeneas Williams	.15
48	Eric Davis	.15
49	Darren Woodson	.15
50	Merton Hanks	.15
51	Steve Tasker	.15
52	Glyn Milburn	.15
53	Jason Elam	.15
54	Darren Bennett	.15
55	Steve Young	2.00
56	Bart Oates	.15
57	Larry Allen	.15
58	Mark Tuinei	.15
59	Mark Chmura	.15
60	Michael Irvin	.30
61	Ricky Watters	.30
62	Cortez Kennedy	.15
63	Leslie O'Neal	.15
64	Bryan Cox	.15
65	Derrick Thomas	.15
66	Darryll Lewis	.15
67	Blaine Bishop	.15
68	Dana Stubblefield	.15
69	William Fuller	.15
70	Jessie Tuggle	.15
71	William Thomas	.15
72	Eric Allen	.15
73	Tim McDonald	.15
74	Jim Harbaugh	.30
75	Mark Stepnoski	.15
76	Keith Sims	.15
77	Gary Zimmerman	.15
78	Shannon Sharpe	.15
79	Anthony Miller	.15
80	Curtis Martin	3.00
81	Troy Aikman	2.00
82	Cris Carter	.30
83	Jeff Blake	1.00
84	Yancey Thigpen	1.00
85	Isaac Bruce	1.00
86	Sam Mills	.15
87	Terrell Davis	3.00
88	Larry Brown	.15
89	Joey Galloway	2.00
90	Checklist	.15

1996 Topps Gilt Edge Platinum

The 90-card, standard size parallel set was included in each pack. The card edges have a platinum "gilt edging" instead of gold.

	MT
Complete Set (90):	90.00
Common Player:	.40
Veteran Stars:	1.5x-3x
Young Stars:	1.25x-2.5x

1996 Topps Gilt Edge Definitive Edge

This 15-card skills insert set features top players on cards using five different designs; each design is used to cover three themes - Fire, Volcano and Fury; Warrior, Chieftan and Guardian; Strength, Courage and Endurance; Hurricane, Speed and Lightning; and Illusion, Mischief and Tricks. Nine of the players chosen for the set were also chosen to play in the Pro Bowl Game. One skills card was inserted in every pack.

		MT
Complete Set (15):		30.00
Common Player:		.25
1	Bruce Smith (Strength)	.25
2	Brett Favre (Courage)	8.00
3	Marcus Allen (Endurance)	.25
4	Junior Seau (Hurricane)	.25
5	Deion Sanders (Speed)	2.00
6	Jerry Rice (Lightning)	4.00
7	Steve Young (Fire)	4.00
8	Drew Bledsoe (Volcano)	3.00
9	Michael Irvin (Fury)	.50
10	Reggie White (Warrior)	.25
11	Dan Marino (Chieftan)	8.00
12	John Alt (Guardian)	.25
13	Barry Sanders (Illusion)	5.00
14	Orlando Thomas (Mischief)	.25
15	Kordell Stewart (Tricks)	4.00

1996 Topps Laser

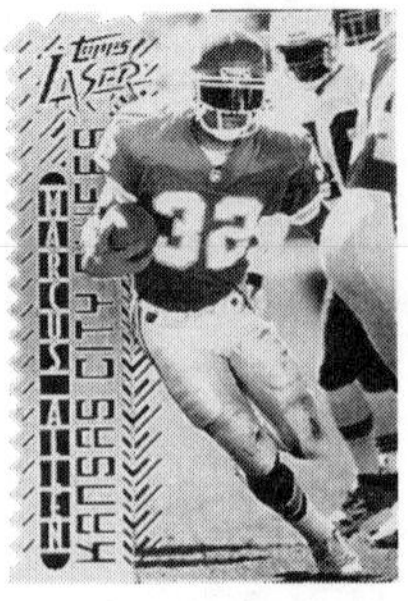

After its debut in baseball, Topps Laser Football arrived in four-card packs with 128 cards in the regular issue set. Laser featured surgically precise cutting across the entire card surface, with silver stamped AFC cards and gold stamped NFC cards. Laser was released in a single series and included three insert sets, called Bright Spots, 1996 Draft Picks and Stadium Stars.

		MT
Complete Set (128):		70.00
Common Player:		.25
Minor Stars:		.50
Pack (4):		4.00
Wax Box (24):		80.00
1	Marshall Faulk	.50
2	Alonzo Spellman	.25
3	Frank Sanders	.25
4	Anthony Pleasant	.25
5	Scott Mitchell	.25
6	Robert Brooks	.50
7	Robert Jones	.25
8	Phillippi Sparks	.25
9	Rodney Peete	.25
10	Kordell Stewart	3.00
11	Ken Norton	.25
12	Brian Mitchell	.25
13	Ben Coates	.25
14	Quinn Early	.25
15	Emmitt Smith	6.00
16	Steve Bono	.25
17	Anthony Miller	.25
18	Mel Gray	.25
19	Neil O'Donnell	.25
20	Tim Brown	.50
21	Terrell Fletcher	.25
22	John Randle	.25
23	Fred Barnett	.25
24	Craig Heyward	.25
25	Ki-Jana Carter	.50
26	Eric Allen	.25
27	Warren Sapp	.25
28	Terry Wooden	.25
29	Darion Conner	.25
30	Mark Brunell	2.00
31	Vinny Testaverde	.25
32	Chris Calloway	.25
33	Steve Walsh	.25
34	Ken Dilger	.25
35	Bryan Cox	.25
36	Rob Moore	.25
37	Henry Thomas	.25
38	Henry Ellard	.25
39	Mark Chmura	.25
40	Jerry Rice	3.00
41	Michael Irvin	.50
42	Willie McGinest	.25
43	Steve McNair	3.00
44	Tamarick Vanover	2.00
45	Cris Carter	.25
46	Levon Kirkland	.25
47	Terry McDaniel	.25
48	Jessie Tuggle	.25
49	O.J. McDuffie	.25
50	Bruce Smith	.25
51	Tyrone Hughes	.25
52	Tony Martin	.25
53	Hardy Nickerson	.25
54	Garrison Hearst	.25
55	Sam Mills	.25
56	Mark Carrier	.25
57	Quentin Coryatt	.25
58	Neil Smith	.25
59	Michael Westbrook	2.00
60	Greg Lloyd	.25
61	Jeff Hostetler	.25
62	Wayne Chrebet	.25
63	Herschel Walker	.25
64	Pepper Johnson	.25
65	John Elway	3.00
66	Reggie White	.50
67	James Stewart	.25
68	Bernie Parmalee	.25
69	Robert Smith	.25
70	Drew Bledsoe	3.00
71	Marvcus Patton	.25
72	Stan Humphries	.25
73	Darnay Scott	.50
74	Jim Kelly	.50
75	Terance Mathis	.25
76	Erik Kramer	.25
77	Marcus Allen	.50
78	Ernie Mills	.25
79	Harvey Williams	.25
80	Brett Favre	6.00
81	Seth Joyner	.25
82	Tyrone Poole	.25
83	Troy Aikman	3.00
84	Warren Moon	.50
85	Isaac Bruce	1.00
86	Errict Rhett	.50
87	Rick Mirer	.25
88	Anthony Smith	.25
89	Bert Emanuel	.25
90	Junior Seau	.50
91	Terry Allen	.25
92	Brent Jones	.25
93	Adrian Murrell	.25
94	Dave Brown	.25
95	Bryce Paup	.25
96	Jim Everett	.25
97	Brian Washington	.25
98	Jim Harbaugh	.25
99	Shannon Sharpe	.25
100	Dan Marino	6.00
101	Curtis Martin	4.00
102	Ricky Watters	.50
103	Yancey Thigpen	.50
104	Trent Dilfer	.50
105	Joey Galloway	3.00
106	Edgar Bennett	.25
107	Willie Jackson	.25
108	Mark Collins	.25
109	Rashaan Salaam	.50
110	Eric Metcalf	.25
111	Terrell Davis	4.00
112	Darryll Lewis	.25
113	Ken Harvey	.25
114	Rob Fredrickson	.25
115	Rodney Hampton	.25
116	Chris Slade	.25
117	Jeff George	.25
118	Lamar Lathon	.25
119	Curtis Conway	.25
120	Barry Sanders	3.00
121	Eric Zeier	.25
122	Jeff Blake	2.00
123	Derrick Thomas	.25
124	Tyrone Wheatley	.25
125	Steve Young	3.00
126	Napoleon Kaufman	.25
127	David Meggett	.25
128	Kerry Collins	.75

1996 Topps Laser Bright Spots

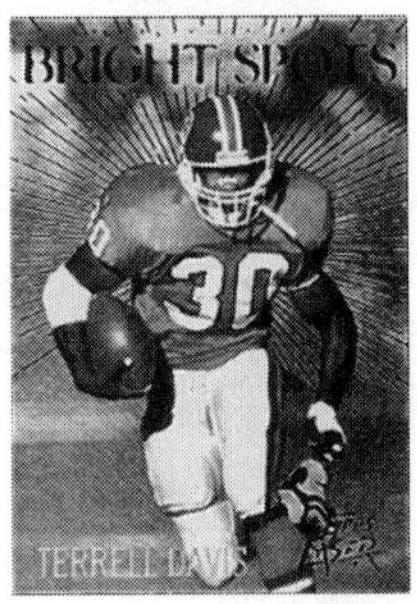

Bright Spots included 16 top young players on full-bleed, double-diffraction foil-stamped cards. Bright Spots were seeded every 24 packs of Laser.

		MT
Complete Set (16):		175.00
Common Player:		6.00
1	Curtis Martin	30.00
2	Tom Carter	6.00
3	Dave Brown	6.00
4	Wayne Chrebet	6.00
5	Rashaan Salaam	10.00
6	Mark Brunell	15.00
7	Elvis Grbac	6.00
8	Errict Rhett	6.00
9	Isaac Bruce	10.00
10	Kerry Collins	10.00
11	Mario Bates	6.00
12	Joey Galloway	20.00
13	Napoleon Kaufman	6.00
14	Tamarick Vanover	6.00
15	Marshall Faulk	8.00
16	Terrell Davis	30.00

1996 Topps Laser Draft Picks

Sixteen different 1996 draft picks can be found in this insert. Draft Picks inserts are laser cut with double-diffraction foil and inserted every 12 packs.

		MT
Complete Set (16):		90.00
Common Player:		5.00
1	Keyshawn Johnson	16.00
2	Lawrence Phillips	10.00
3	Bobby Hoying	5.00
4	Marco Battaglia	5.00
5	Kevin Hardy	5.00
6	Jerome Woods	5.00
7	Ray Mickens	5.00
8	John Mobley	5.00
9	Marvin Harrison	15.00
10	Walt Harris	5.00
11	Duane Clemons	5.00
12	Regan Upshaw	5.00
13	Brian Dawkins	5.00
14	Bobby Engram	10.00
15	Eddie Kennison	8.00
16	Jeff Lewis	5.00

1996 Topps Laser Stadium Stars

Stadium Stars included 16 of the top players in the NFL on cards that have a laser-sculpted cover that reveals a full-bleed card of the player

underneath. These book-like inserts are seeded every 48 packs.

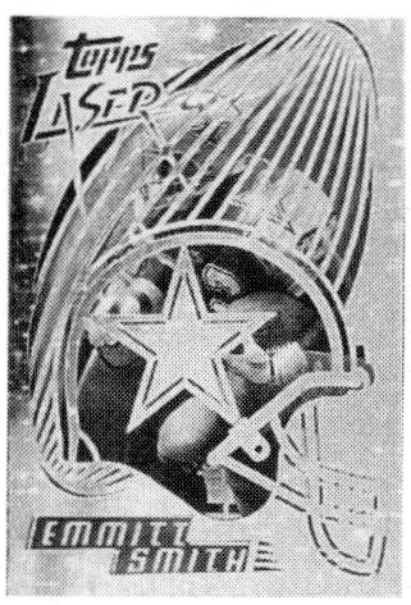

		MT
Complete Set (16):		350.00
Common Player:		10.00
1	Barry Sanders	50.00
2	Jim Harbaugh	10.00
3	Tim Brown	10.00
4	Jim Everett	10.00
5	Brett Favre	80.00
6	Junior Seau	10.00
7	Greg Lloyd	10.00
8	Cris Carter	10.00
9	Emmitt Smith	80.00
10	Dan Marino	80.00
11	Jeff Blake	20.00
12	Darrell Green	10.00
13	John Elway	30.00
14	Marcus Allen	10.00
15	Steve Young	35.00
16	Drew Bledsoe	50.00

1997 Topps

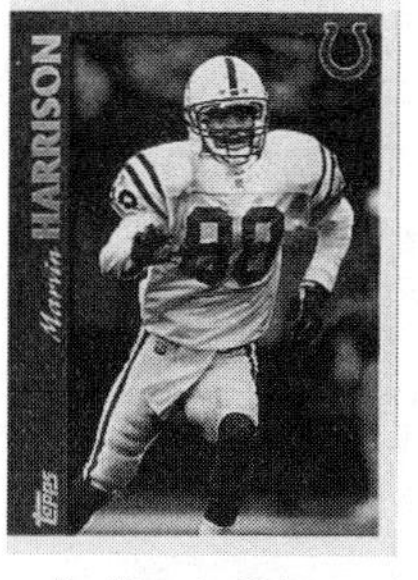

The 415-card set features a colored border on the left of the card front. In that border are the Topps' logo in gold foil in the lower left and the player's name in the upper left. The team's logo is in the upper right. A white border surrounds the three remaining sides. The backs have the player's name, team, position, bio, stats and highlights. A "Minted in Canton" parallel, which features a special gold foil stamp, was randomly seeded in packs.

		MT
Complete Set (415):		40.00
Common Player:		.05
Minor Stars:		.10
Minted Canton Cards:		5x-10x
Pack (11):		1.30
Wax Box (36):		42.00
1	Brett Favre	2.50
2	Lawyer Milloy	.05
3	Tim Biakabutuka	.10
4	Clyde Simmons	.05
5	Deion Sanders	.50
6	Anthony Miller	.05
7	Marquez Pope	.05
8	Mike Tomczak	.05
9	William Thomas	.05
10	Marshall Faulk	.20
11	John Randle	.05
12	Jim Kelly	.10
13	Steve Bono	.05
14	Rod Stephens	.05
15	Stan Humphries	.05
16	Terrell Buckley	.05
17	Ki-Jana Carter	.10
18	Marcus Robertson	.05
19	Corey Harris	.05
20	Rashaan Salaam	.10
21	Rickey Dudley	.05
22	Jamir Miller	.05
23	Martin Mayhew	.05
24	Jason Sehorn	.05
25	Isaac Bruce	.20
26	Johnnie Morton	.05
27	Antonio Langham	.05
28	Cornelius Bennett	.05
29	Joe Johnson	.05
30	Keyshawn Johnson	.40
31	Willie Green	.05
32	Craig Newsome	.05
33	Brock Marion	.05
34	Corey Fuller	.05
35	Ben Coates	.05
36	Ty Detmer	.05
37	Charles Johnson	.05
38	Willie Jackson	.05
39	Tyronne Drakeford	.05
40	Gus Frerotte	.05
41	Robert Blackmon	.05
42	Andre Coleman	.05
43	Mario Bates	.05
44	Chris Calloway	.05
45	Terry McDaniel	.05
46	Anthony Davis	.05
47	Stanley Pritchett	.05
48	Ray Buchanan	.05
49	Chris Chandler	.05
50	Ashley Ambrose	.05
51	Tyrone Braxton	.05
52	Pepper Johnson	.05
53	Frank Sanders	.05
54	Clay Matthews	.05
55	Bruce Smith	.05
56	Jermaine Lewis	.05
57	Mark Carrier	.05
58	Jeff Graham	.05
59	Keith Lyle	.05
60	Trent Dilfer	.10
61	Trace Armstrong	.05
62	Jeff Herrod	.05
63	Tyrone Wheatley	.05
64	Torrance Small	.05
65	Chris Warren	.05
66	Terry Kirby	.05
67	Erric Pegram	.05
68	Sean Gilbert	.05
69	Greg Biekert	.05
70	Ricky Watters	.10
71	Chris Hudson	.05
72	Tamarick Vanover	.10
73	Orlando Thomas	.05
74	Jimmy Spencer	.05
75	John Mobley	.05
76	Henry Thomas	.05
77	Santana Dotson	.05
78	Boomer Esiason	.05
79	Bobby Hebert	.05
80	Kerry Collins	.25
81	Bobby Engram	.05
82	Kevin Smith	.05
83	Rick Mirer	.10
84	Ted Johnson	.05
85	Derrick Alexander	.05
86	Hugh Douglas	.05
87	Rodney Harrison	.05
88	Roman Phifer	.05
89	Warren Moon	.10
90	Thurman Thomas	.10
91	Michael McCrary	.05
92	Dana Stubblefield	.05
93	Andre Hastings	.05
94	William Fuller	.05
95	Jeff Hostetler	.05
96	Danny Kanell	.05
97	Mark Fields	.05
98	Eddie Robinson	.05
99	Daryl Gardener	.05
100	Drew Bledsoe	1.00
101	Winslow Oliver	.05
102	Raymont Harris	.05
103	LeShon Johnson	.05
104	Byron Morris	.05
105	Herman Moore	.20
106	Keith Jackson	.05
107	Chris Penn	.05
108	Robert Griffith	.05
109	Jeff Burris	.05
110	Troy Aikman	1.00
111	Allen Aldridge	.05
112	Mel Gray	.05
113	Aaron Bailey	.05
114	Michael Strahan	.05
115	Adrian Murrell	.05
116	Chris Mims	.05
117	Robert Jones	.05
118	Derrick Brooks	.05
119	Tom Carter	.05
120	Carl Pickens	.05
121	Tony Brackens	.05
122	O.J. McDuffie	.05
123	Napoleon Kaufman	.05
124	Chris T. Jones	.05
125	Kordell Stewart	.75
126	Ray Zellars	.05
127	Jessie Tuggle	.05
128	Greg Kragen	.05
129	Brett Perriman	.05
130	Steve Young	.50
131	Willie Clay	.05
132	Kimble Anders	.05
133	Eugene Daniel	.05
134	Jevon Langford	.05
135	Shannon Sharpe	.05
136	Wayne Simmons	.05
137	Leeland McElroy	.05
138	Mike Caldwell	.05
139	Eric Moulds	.10
140	Eddie George	1.00
141	Jamal Anderson	.30
142	Michael Timpson	.05
143	Tony Tolbert	.05
144	Robert Smith	.05
145	Mike Alstott	.10
146	Gary Jones	.05
147	Terrance Shaw	.05
148	Carlton Gray	.05
149	Kevin Carter	.05
150	Darrell Green	.05
151	David Dunn	.05
152	Ken Norton	.05
153	Chad Brown	.05
154	Pat Swilling	.05
155	Irving Fryar	.05
156	Michael Haynes	.05
157	Shawn Jefferson	.05
158	Steve Grant	.05
159	James Stewart	.05
160	Derrick Thomas	.05
161	Tim Bowens	.05
162	Dixon Edwards	.05
163	Michael Barrow	.05
164	Antonio Freeman	.10
165	Terrell Davis	1.25
166	Henry Ellard	.05
167	Daryl Johnston	.05
168	Bryan Cox	.05
169	Chad Cota	.05
170	Vinny Testaverde	.05
171	Andre Reed	.05
172	Larry Centers	.05
173	Craig Heyward	.05
174	Glyn Milburn	.05
175	Hardy Nickerson	.05
176	Corey Miller	.05
177	Bobby Houston	.05
178	Marco Coleman	.05
179	Winston Moss	.05
180	Tony Banks	.30
181	Jeff Lageman	.05
182	Jason Belser	.05
183	James Jett	.05
184	Wayne Martin	.05
185	David Meggett	.05
186	Terrell Owens	.50
187	Willie Williams	.05
188	Eric Turner	.05
189	Chuck Smith	.05
190	Simeon Rice	.05
191	Kevin Greene	.05
192	Lance Johnston	.05
193	Marty Carter	.05
194	Ricardo McDonald	.05
195	Michael Irvin	.10
196	George Koonce	.05
197	Robert Porcher	.05
198	Mark Collins	.05
199	Louis Oliver	.05
200	John Elway	.50
201	Jake Reed	.05
202	Rodney Hampton	.05
203	Aaron Glenn	.05
204	Mike Mamula	.05
205	Terry Allen	.05
206	John Lynch	.05
207	Todd Lyght	.05
208	Dean Wells	.05
209	Aaron Hayden	.05
210	Blaine Bishop	.05
211	Bert Emanuel	.05
212	Mark Carrier	.05
213	Dale Carter	.05
214	Jimmy Smith	.05
215	Jim Harbaugh	.05
216	Jeff George	.05
217	Anthony Newman	.05
218	Ty Law	.05
219	Brent Jones	.05
220	Emmitt Smith	2.00
221	Bennie Blades	.05
222	Alfred Williams	.05
223	Eugene Robinson	.05
224	Fred Barnett	.05
225	Errict Rhett	.20
226	Leslie O'Neal	.05
227	Michael Sinclair	.05
228	Marvcus Patton	.05
229	Darrien Gordon	.05
230	Jerome Bettis	.10
231	Troy Vincent	.05
232	Ray Mickens	.05
233	Lonnie Johnson	.05
234	Charles Way	.05
235	Chris Sanders	.05
236	Bracey Walker	.05
237	Dave Krieg	.05
238	Kent Graham	.05
239	Ray Lewis	.05
240	Cris Carter	.05
241	Elvis Grbac	.05
242	Eric Davis	.05
243	Harvey Williams	.05
244	Eric Allen	.05
245	Bryant Young	.05
246	Terrell Fletcher	.05
247	Darren Perry	.05
248	Ken Harvey	.05
249	Marvin Washington	.05
250	Marcus Allen	.10
251	Darrin Smith	.05
252	James Francis	.05
253	Michael Jackson	.05
254	Ryan McNeil	.05
255	Mark Chmura	.10
256	Keenan McCardell	.05
257	Tony Bennett	.05
258	Irving Spikes	.05
259	Jason Dunn	.05
260	Joey Galloway	.25
261	Eddie Kennison	.40
262	Lonnie Marts	.05
263	Thomas Lewis	.05
264	Tedy Bruschi	.05
265	Steve Atwater	.05
266	Dorsey Levens	.20
267	Kurt Schulz	.05
268	Rob Moore	.05
269	Walt Harris	.05
270	Steve McNair	.75
271	Bill Romanowski	.05
272	Sean Dawkins	.05
273	Don Beebe	.05
274	Fernando Smith	.05
275	Willie McGinest	.05
276	Levon Kirkland	.05
277	Tony Martin	.05
278	Warren Sapp	.05
279	Lamar Smith	.05
280	Mark Brunell	1.00
281	Jim Everett	.05
282	Victor Green	.05
283	Mike Jones	.05
284	Charlie Garner	.05
285	Karim Abdul-Jabbar	.75
286	Michael Westbrook	.10
287	Lawrence Phillips	.10
288	Amani Toomer	.05
289	Neil Smith	.05
290	Barry Sanders	1.25
291	Willie Davis	.05
292	Bo Orlando	.05
293	Alonzo Spellman	.05
294	Eric Hill	.05
295	Wesley Walls	.05
296	Todd Collins	.05
297	Stevon Moore	.05
298	Eric Metcalf	.05
299	Darren Woodson	.05
300	Jerry Rice	1.00
301	Scott Mitchell	.05
302	Ray Crockett	.05
303	Jim Schwantz	.05
304	Steve Tovar	.05
305	Terance Mathis	.05
306	Earnest Byner	.05
307	Chris Spielman	.05
308	Curtis Conway	.10
309	Chris Dishman	.05
310	Marvin Harrison	.40
311	Sam Mills	.05
312	Brent Alexander	.05
313	Shawn Wooden	.05
314	DeWayne Washington	.05
315	Terry Glenn	.25
316	Winfred Tubbs	.05
317	Dave Brown	.05
318	Neil O'Donnell	.05
319	Anthony Parker	.05
320	Junior Seau	.10
321	Brian Mitchell	.05
322	Regan Upshaw	.05
323	Darryl Williams	.05
324	Chris Doleman	.05
325	Rod Woodson	.05
326	Derrick Witherspoon	.05
327	Chester McGlockton	.05
328	Mickey Washington	.05
329	Greg Hill	.05
330	Reggie White	.10
331	John Copeland	.05
332	Doug Evans	.05
333	Lamar Lathon	.05
334	Mark Maddox	.05
335	Natrone Means	.10
336	Corey Widmer	.05
337	Terry Wooden	.05
338	Merton Hanks	.05
339	Cortez Kennedy	.05
340	Tyrone Hughes	.05
341	Tim Brown	.05
342	John Jurkovic	.05
343	Carnell Lake	.05
344	Stanley Richard	.05
345	Darryll Lewis	.05
346	Dan Wilkinson	.05
347	Broderick Thomas	.05
348	Brian Williams	.05
349	Eric Swann	.05
350	Dan Marino	2.00
351	Anthony Johnson	.05
352	Joe Cain	.05
353	Quinn Early	.05
354	Seth Joyner	.05
355	Garrison Hearst	.05
356	Edgar Bennett	.05
357	Brian Washington	.05
358	Kevin Hardy	.05
359	Quentin Coryatt	.05
360	Tim McDonald	.05
361	Brian Blades	.05
362	Courtney Hawkins	.05
363	Ray Farmer	.05
364	Jesse Armstead	.05
365	Curtis Martin	1.25
366	Zach Thomas	.30
367	Frank Wycheck	.05
368	Darnay Scott	.05
369	Percy Ellsworth	.05
370	Desmond Howard	.05
371	Aeneas Williams	.05
372	Bryce Paup	.05
373	Michael Bates	.05
374	Brad Johnson	.05
375	Jeff Blake	.25
376	Donnell Woolford	.05
377	Mo Lewis	.05
378	Phillippi Sparks	.05
379	Michael Bankston	.05
380	LeRoy Butler	.05
381	Tyrone Poole	.05
382	Wayne Chrebet	.05
383	Chris Slade	.05
384	Checklist 1 of 2	.05
385	Checklist 2 of 2	.05
386	*Will Blackwell*	.75
387	*Tom Knight*	.10
388	*Darnell Autry*	.30
389	*Bryant Westbrook*	.50
390	*David LaFleur*	1.50
391	*Antowain Smith*	3.00
392	*Kevin Lockett*	.75
393	*Rae Carruth*	2.00
394	*Renaldo Wynn*	.10
395	*Jim Druckenmiller*	4.00
396	*Kenny Holmes*	.10
397	*Shawn Springs*	.75
398	*Troy Davis*	.40
399	*Dwayne Rudd*	.10
400	*Orlando Pace*	.75
401	*Byron Hanspard*	.50
402	*Corey Dillon*	6.00
403	*Walter Jones*	.10
404	*Reidel Anthony*	3.00
405	*Peter Boulware*	.10
406	*Reinard Wilson*	.10
407	*Pat Barnes*	.30
408	*Yatil Green*	.40
409	*Joey Kent*	.75
410	*Ike Hilliard*	2.50
411	*Jake Plummer*	6.00
412	*Darrell Russell*	.10
413	*James Farrior*	.10
414	*Tony Gonzalez*	1.50
415	*Warrick Dunn*	3.00

1997 Topps Career Best

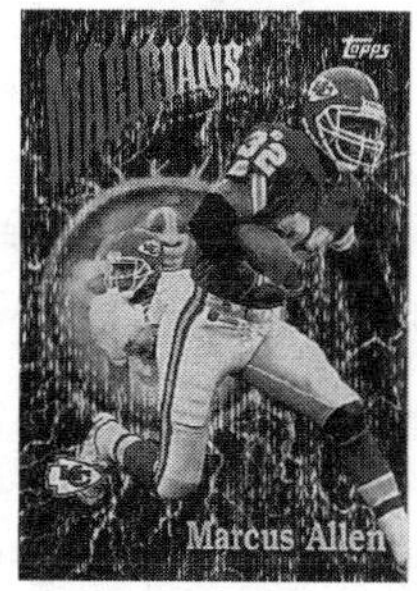

This chase set includes Dan Marino, two cards of Marcus Allen, Reggie White and Jerry Rice.

		MT
Complete Set (5):		50.00
Common Player:		7.00
1	Dan Marino	25.00
2	Marcus Allen	7.00
3	Marcus Allen	7.00
4	Reggie White	7.00
5	Jerry Rice	12.00

1997 Topps Hall of Fame Autograph

This four-card insert featured autographs from the four current Hall of Fame inductees and carried an "HF" prefix on the card back. The Haynes and Webster cards were inserted one per 436 hobby packs (1:120 jumbo), Mara was inserted one per 872 hobby packs (1:240 jumbo) and the Shula card was seeded one per 290 hobby packs (1:80 jumbo).

		MT
Complete Set (4):		200.00
Common Player:		25.00
1	Don Shula	80.00
2	Wellington Mara	75.00
3	Mike Webster	25.00
4	Mike Haynes	30.00

1997 Topps Hall Bound

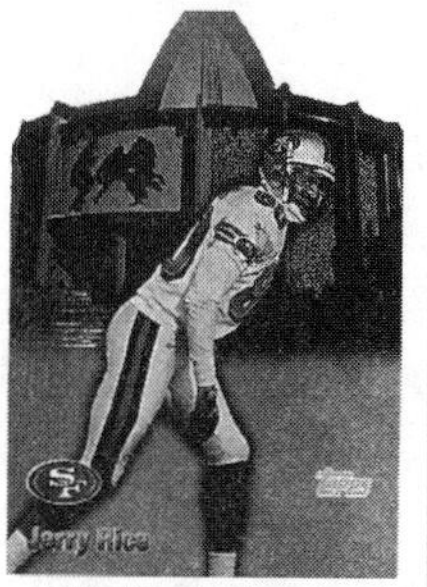

This 15-card set was inserted 1:36 hobby packs. The embossed cards were produced on die-cut mirror board. Card are numbered with a "HB" prefix.

		MT
Complete Set (15):		100.00
Common Player:		3.00
1	Jerry Rice	12.00
2	Rod Woodson	3.00
3	Marcus Allen	3.00
4	Reggie White	3.00
5	Emmitt Smith	20.00
6	Junior Seau	3.00
7	Troy Aikman	12.00
8	Bruce Smith	3.00
9	John Elway	8.00
10	Brett Favre	25.00
11	Thurman Thomas	3.00
12	Deion Sanders	6.00
13	Dan Marino	20.00
14	Steve Young	8.00
15	Barry Sanders	12.00

1997 Topps High Octane

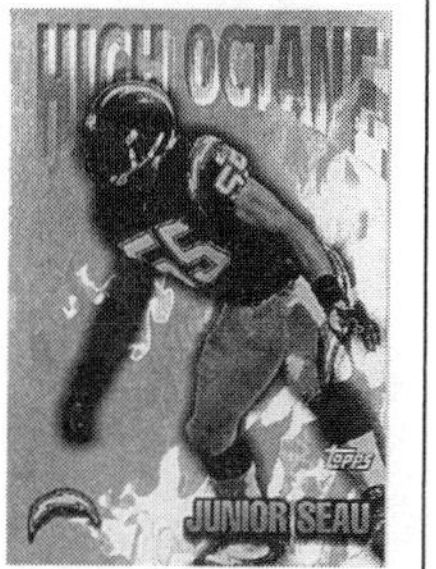

Inserted 1:36 packs, the 15-card chase set includes "High Octane" at the top front of the cards, with the player's photo superimposed over a uniluster back. The team's logo is in the lower left, with the player's name in the lower right. The backs, which are numbered with an "HO" prefix, have the player's bio on the upper left, with his photo in the upper right. Four bar graphs are included in the center, with his highlights in the lower left.

		MT
Complete Set (15):		120.00
Common Player:		3.00
1	Brett Favre	25.00
2	Jerome Bettis	3.00
3	Jerry Rice	12.00
4	Junior Seau	3.00
5	Emmitt Smith	20.00
6	Herman Moore	3.00
7	Shannon Sharpe	3.00
8	Curtis Martin	12.00
9	Eddie George	12.00
10	Barry Sanders	12.00
11	John Elway	8.00
12	Steve Young	8.00
13	Drew Bledsoe	12.00
14	Troy Aikman	12.00
15	Dan Marino	20.00

1997 Topps Mystery Finest

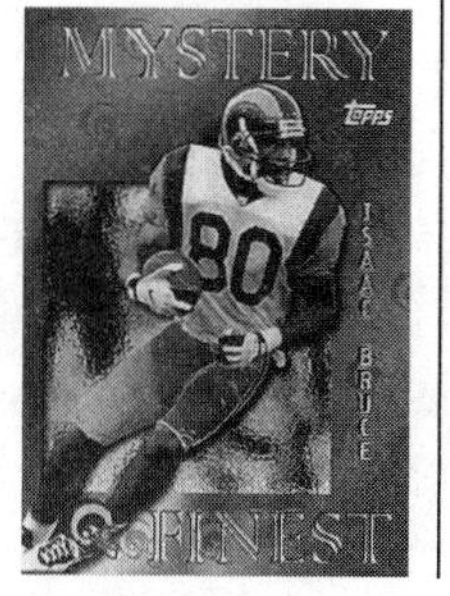

The Mystery Finest chase set features 20 Pro Bowl players pictured three different ways, in their team's away jersey (bronze card, 1:36 packs), the team's home uniform (silver card, 1:108) and their Pro Bowl jersey (gold card, 1:324). Bronze Refractor parallels are found 1:144, silver Refractors are located 1:432 and a Gold Refractor is seeded 1:1,296 packs. Cards are numbered with a "M" prefix.

		MT
Complete Set (20):		130.00
Common Player:		3.00
Bronze Refractors:		2x-3x
Silver Cards:		2x
Silver Refractors:		5x
Gold Cards:		8x
Gold Refractors:		12x-24x
1	Barry Sanders	12.00
2	Mark Brunell	12.00
3	Terrell Davis	12.00
4	Isaac Bruce	6.00
5	Jerry Rice	12.00
6	Drew Bledsoe	12.00
7	Carl Pickens	3.00
8	Steve Young	8.00
9	Cris Carter	3.00
10	John Elway	8.00
11	Junior Seau	3.00
12	Herman Moore	3.00
13	Vinny Testaverde	3.00
14	Jerome Bettis	3.00
15	Troy Aikman	12.00
16	Reggie White	3.00
17	Kerry Collins	5.00
18	Curtis Martin	12.00
19	Shannon Sharpe	3.00
20	Brett Favre	25.00

1997 Topps Season's Best

The 25-card chase set was seeded 1:16 packs. The set honors players in five different categories, rushing leaders (Thunder and Lightning), passing experts (Air Command), receiving specialists (Special Delivery), sack masters (Demolition Men) and all-purpose yardage gainers (Magicians).

		MT
Complete Set (25):		75.00
Common Player:		.75
Minor Stars:		1.50
1	Mark Brunell (Air Command)	8.00
2	Vinny Testaverde (Air Command)	.75
3	Drew Bledsoe (Air Command)	8.00
4	Brett Favre (Air Command)	16.00
5	Jeff Blake (Air Command)	1.50
6	Barry Sanders (Thunder & Lightning)	10.00
7	Terrell Davis (Thunder & Lightning)	8.00
8	Jerome Bettis (Thunder & Lightning)	1.50
9	Ricky Watters (Thunder & Lightning)	.75
10	Eddie George (Thunder & Lightning)	10.00
11	Brian Mitchell (Magicians)	.75
12	Tyrone Hughes (Magicians)	.75
13	Eric Metcalf (Magicians)	.75
14	Glyn Milburn (Magicians)	.75
15	Ricky Watters (Magicians)	.75
16	Kevin Greene (Demolition Men)	.75
17	Lamar Lathon (Demolition Men)	.75
18	Bruce Smith (Demolition Men)	.75
19	Michael Sinclair (Demolition Men)	.75
20	Derrick Thomas (Demolition Men)	.75
21	Jerry Rice (Special Delivery)	8.00
22	Herman Moore (Special Delivery)	.75
23	Carl Pickens (Special Delivery)	.75
24	Cris Carter (Special Delivery)	.75
25	Brett Perriman (Special Delivery)	.75

1997 Topps Underclassmen

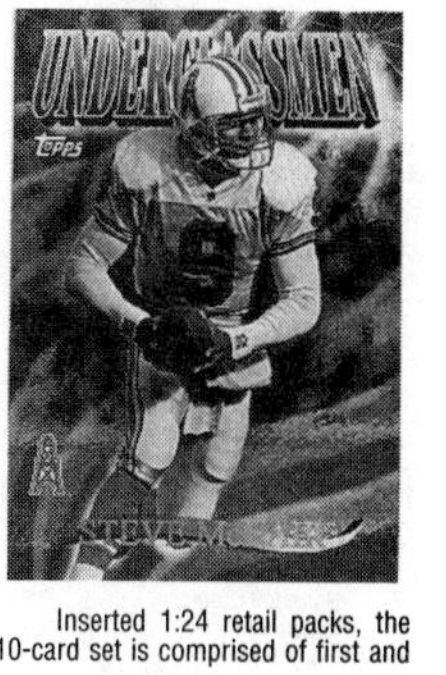

Inserted 1:24 retail packs, the 10-card set is comprised of first and

second year players. The "Underclassmen" logo is at the top center, with the player's photo superimposed over a multicolored holographic background. The player's name is printed in holographic foil at the bottom center. The backs, which are numbered with an "U" prefix, have the player's photo, name, bio, highlights and stats.

		MT
Complete Set (10):		75.00
Common Player:		2.50
Minor Stars:		5.00
1	Kerry Collins	5.00
2	Karim Abdul-Jabbar	10.00
3	Simeon Rice	2.50
4	Keyshawn Johnson	5.00
5	Eddie George	15.00
6	Eddie Kennison	5.00
7	Terry Glenn	12.00
8	Kevin Hardy	2.50
9	Steve McNair	8.00
10	Kordell Stewart	10.00

1997 Topps Chrome

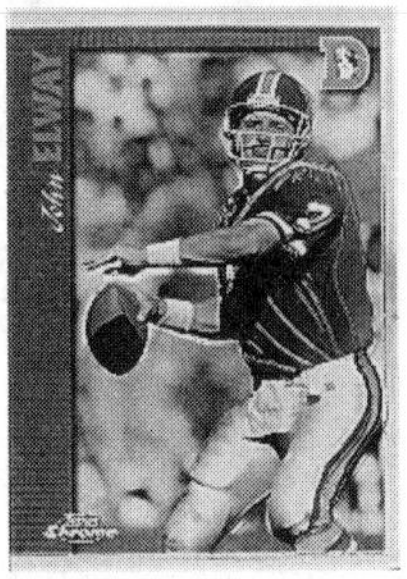

Chrome Football is a 165-card set created with Topps chromium technology and a Topps Chrome logo added to regular Topps cards. Chrome arrived with a full parallel set of Refractors and four inserts also from Topps: Draft Year, Underclassmen, Season's Best and Career Best.

		MT
Complete Set (165):		200.00
Common Player:		.40
Common Player (143-163):		1.00
Minor Stars:		.75
Pack (4):		8.00
Wax Box (24):		160.00
1	Brett Favre	6.00
2	Tim Biakabutuka	.40
3	Deion Sanders	1.50
4	Marshall Faulk	1.00
5	John Randle	.40
6	Stan Humphries	.40
7	Ki-Jana Carter	.75
8	Rashaan Salaam	.40
9	Rickey Dudley	.75
10	Isaac Bruce	1.00
11	Keyshawn Johnson	1.00
12	Ben Coates	.40
13	Ty Detmer	.40
14	Gus Frerotte	.40
15	Mario Bates	.40
16	Chris Calloway	.40
17	Frank Sanders	.40
18	Bruce Smith	.40
19	Jeff Graham	.40
20	Trent Dilfer	1.00
21	Tyrone Wheatley	.40
22	Chris Warren	.40
23	Terry Kirby	.40
24	*Tony Gonzalez*	15.00
25	Ricky Watters	.75
26	Tamarick Vanover	.40
27	Kerry Collins	2.00
28	Bobby Engram	.40
29	Derrick Alexander	.40
30	Hugh Douglas	.40
31	Thurman Thomas	.75
32	Drew Bledsoe	3.00
33	LeShon Johnson	.40
34	Byron Morris	.40
35	Herman Moore	1.00
36	Troy Aikman	3.00
37	Mel Gray	.40
38	Adrian Murrell	.75
39	Carl Pickens	.40
40	Tony Brackens	.40
41	O.J. McDuffie	.40
42	Napoleon Kaufman	1.00
43	Chris T. Jones	.40
44	Kordell Stewart	3.00
45	Steve Young	2.00
46	Shannon Sharpe	.40
47	Leeland McElroy	.40
48	Eric Moulds	.40
49	Eddie George	4.00
50	Jamal Anderson	.75
51	Robert Smith	.75
52	Mike Alstott	1.50
53	Darrell Green	.40
54	Irving Fryar	.40
55	Derrick Thomas	.40
56	Antonio Freeman	1.00
57	Terrell Davis	3.00
58	Henry Ellard	.40
59	Daryl Johnston	.40
60	Bryan Cox	.40
61	Vinny Testaverde	.40
62	Andre Reed	.40
63	Larry Centers	.40
64	Hardy Nickerson	.40
65	Tony Banks	1.50
66	David Meggett	.40
67	Simeon Rice	.40
68	*Warrick Dunn*	15.00
69	Michael Irvin	.75
70	John Elway	4.00
71	Jake Reed	.40
72	Rodney Hampton	.40
73	Aaron Glenn	.40
74	Terry Allen	.40
75	Blaine Bishop	.40
76	Bert Emanuel	.40
77	Mark Carrier	.40
78	Jimmy Smith	.40
79	Jim Harbaugh	.40
80	Brent Jones	.40
81	Emmitt Smith	5.00
82	Fred Barnett	.40
83	Errict Rhett	.40
84	Michael Sinclair	.40
85	Jerome Bettis	1.00
86	Chris Sanders	.40
87	Kent Graham	.40
88	Cris Carter	.40
89	Harvey Williams	.40
90	Eric Allen	.40
91	Bryant Young	.40
92	Marcus Allen	1.00
93	Michael Jackson	.40
94	Mark Chmura	.75
95	Keenan McCardell	.40
96	Joey Galloway	1.00
97	Eddie Kennison	1.00
98	Steve Atwater	.40
99	Dorsey Levens	1.00
100	Rob Moore	.40
101	Steve McNair	3.00
102	Sean Dawkins	.40
103	Don Beebe	.40
104	Willie McGinest	.40
105	Tony Martin	.40
106	Mark Brunell	3.00
107	Karim Abdul-Jabbar	1.00
108	Michael Westbrook	.40
109	Lawrence Phillips	.75
110	Barry Sanders	6.00
111	Willie Davis	.40
112	Wesley Walls	.40
113	Todd Collins	.40
114	Jerry Rice	3.00
115	Scott Mitchell	.40
116	Terance Mathis	.40
117	Chris Spielman	.40
118	Curtis Conway	.40
119	Marvin Harrison	1.00
120	Terry Glenn	2.00
121	Dave Brown	.40
122	Neil O'Donnell	.40
123	Junior Seau	.75
124	Reggie White	.75
125	Lamar Lathon	.40
126	Natrone Means	.75
127	Tim Brown	.40
128	Eric Swann	.40
129	Dan Marino	6.00
130	Anthony Johnson	.40
131	Edgar Bennett	.40
132	Kevin Hardy	.40
133	Brian Blades	.40
134	Curtis Martin	3.00
135	Zach Thomas	.75
136	Darnay Scott	.40
137	Desmond Howard	.40
138	Aeneas Williams	.40
139	Bryce Paup	.40
140	Brad Johnson	.75
141	Jeff Blake	1.00
142	Wayne Chrebet	.40
143	*Will Blackwell*	2.00
144	*Tom Knight*	1.00
145	*Darnell Autry*	2.00
146	*Bryant Westbrook*	2.00
147	*David LaFleur*	4.00
148	*Antowain Smith*	12.00
149	*Rae Carruth*	7.00
150	*Jim Druckenmiller*	8.00
151	*Shawn Springs*	1.00
152	*Troy Davis*	3.00
153	*Orlando Pace*	2.00
154	*Byron Hanspard*	7.00
155	*Corey Dillon*	25.00
156	*Reidel Anthony*	8.00
157	*Peter Boulware*	2.00
158	*Reinard Wilson*	1.00
159	*Pat Barnes*	1.25
160	*Joey Kent*	2.00
161	*Ike Hilliard*	8.00
162	*Jake Plummer*	25.00
163	*Darrell Russell*	1.00
164	Checklist 1	.40
165	Checklist 2	.40

1997 Topps Chrome Refractors

Refractors are a parallel of the Topps Chrome base set. They were inserted one per 12 packs.

		MT
Complete Set (165):		2400.
Common Player:		4.00
Common Player (143-163):		6.00
Minor Stars:		8.00
1	Brett Favre	90.00
2	Tim Biakabutuka	4.00
3	Deion Sanders	20.00
4	Marshall Faulk	8.00
5	John Randle	4.00
6	Stan Humphries	4.00
7	Ki-Jana Carter	8.00
8	Rashaan Salaam	4.00
9	Rickey Dudley	8.00
10	Isaac Bruce	8.00
11	Keyshawn Johnson	8.00
12	Ben Coates	4.00
13	Ty Detmer	4.00
14	Gus Frerotte	4.00
15	Mario Bates	4.00
16	Chris Calloway	4.00
17	Frank Sanders	4.00
18	Bruce Smith	4.00
19	Jeff Graham	4.00
20	Trent Dilfer	8.00
21	Tyrone Wheatley	4.00
22	Chris Warren	4.00
23	Terry Kirby	4.00
24	Tony Gonzalez	25.00
25	Ricky Watters	8.00
26	Tamarick Vanover	4.00
27	Kerry Collins	8.00
28	Bobby Engram	4.00
29	Derrick Alexander	4.00
30	Hugh Douglas	4.00
31	Thurman Thomas	8.00
32	Drew Bledsoe	45.00
33	LeShon Johnson	4.00
34	Byron Morris	4.00
35	Herman Moore	8.00
36	Troy Aikman	45.00
37	Mel Gray	4.00
38	Adrian Murrell	8.00
39	Carl Pickens	4.00
40	Tony Brackens	4.00
41	O.J. McDuffie	4.00
42	Napoleon Kaufman	15.00
43	Chris T. Jones	4.00
44	Kordell Stewart	40.00
45	Steve Young	30.00
46	Shannon Sharpe	4.00
47	Leeland McElroy	4.00
48	Eric Moulds	4.00
49	Eddie George	50.00
50	Jamal Anderson	8.00
51	Robert Smith	8.00
52	Mike Alstott	20.00
53	Darrell Green	4.00
54	Irving Fryar	4.00
55	Derrick Thomas	4.00
56	Antonio Freeman	20.00
57	Terrell Davis	50.00
58	Henry Ellard	4.00
59	Daryl Johnston	4.00
60	Bryan Cox	4.00
61	Vinny Testaverde	4.00
62	Andre Reed	4.00
63	Larry Centers	4.00
64	Hardy Nickerson	4.00
65	Tony Banks	8.00
66	David Meggett	4.00
67	Simeon Rice	4.00
68	Warrick Dunn	175.00
69	Michael Irvin	8.00
70	John Elway	45.00
71	Jake Reed	4.00
72	Rodney Hampton	4.00
73	Aaron Glenn	4.00
74	Terry Allen	4.00
75	Blaine Bishop	4.00
76	Bert Emanuel	4.00
77	Mark Carrier	4.00
78	Jimmy Smith	4.00
79	Jim Harbaugh	4.00
80	Brent Jones	4.00
81	Emmitt Smith	75.00
82	Fred Barnett	4.00
83	Errict Rhett	4.00
84	Michael Sinclair	4.00
85	Jerome Bettis	8.00
86	Chris Sanders	4.00
87	Kent Graham	4.00
88	Cris Carter	8.00
89	Harvey Williams	4.00
90	Eric Allen	4.00
91	Bryant Young	4.00
92	Marcus Allen	8.00
93	Michael Jackson	4.00
94	Mark Chmura	8.00
95	Keenan McCardell	4.00
96	Joey Galloway	8.00
97	Eddie Kennison	8.00
98	Steve Atwater	4.00
99	Dorsey Levens	8.00
100	Rob Moore	4.00
101	Steve McNair	25.00
102	Sean Dawkins	4.00
103	Don Beebe	4.00
104	Willie McGinest	4.00
105	Tony Martin	4.00
106	Mark Brunell	40.00
107	Karim Abdul-Jabbar	8.00
108	Michael Westbrook	4.00
109	Lawrence Phillips	4.00
110	Barry Sanders	90.00
111	Willie Davis	4.00
112	Wesley Walls	4.00
113	Todd Collins	4.00
114	Jerry Rice	45.00
115	Scott Mitchell	4.00
116	Terance Mathis	4.00
117	Chris Spielman	4.00
118	Curtis Conway	4.00
119	Marvin Harrison	8.00
120	Terry Glenn	10.00
121	Dave Brown	4.00
122	Neil O'Donnell	4.00
123	Junior Seau	8.00
124	Reggie White	8.00
125	Lamar Lathon	4.00
126	Natrone Means	8.00
127	Tim Brown	4.00
128	Eric Swann	4.00
129	Dan Marino	75.00
130	Anthony Johnson	4.00
131	Edgar Bennett	4.00
132	Kevin Hardy	4.00
133	Brian Blades	4.00
134	Curtis Martin	25.00
135	Zach Thomas	8.00
136	Darnay Scott	4.00
137	Desmond Howard	4.00
138	Aeneas Williams	4.00
139	Bryce Paup	4.00
140	Brad Johnson	8.00
141	Jeff Blake	8.00
142	Wayne Chrebet	4.00
143	Will Blackwell	8.00
144	Tom Knight	6.00
145	Darnell Autry	8.00
146	Bryant Westbrook	8.00
147	David LaFleur	20.00
148	Antowain Smith	100.00
149	Rae Carruth	35.00
150	Jim Druckenmiller	70.00
151	Shawn Springs	6.00
152	Troy Davis	12.00
153	Orlando Pace	10.00
154	Byron Hanspard	30.00
155	Corey Dillon	175.00
156	Reidel Anthony	50.00
157	Peter Boulware	6.00
158	Reinard Wilson	6.00
159	Pat Barnes	10.00
160	Joey Kent	6.00
161	Ike Hilliard	30.00
162	Jake Plummer	250.00
163	Darrell Russell	6.00
164	Checklist 1	4.00
165	Checklist 2	4.00

1997 Topps Chrome Draft Year

Draft Year is a 15-card insert highlighting two players from the last 15 draft classes. Each side features one of the best players to emerge from that particular draft. Draft Year was inserted 1:48. The Refractor versions were found once in every 144 packs.

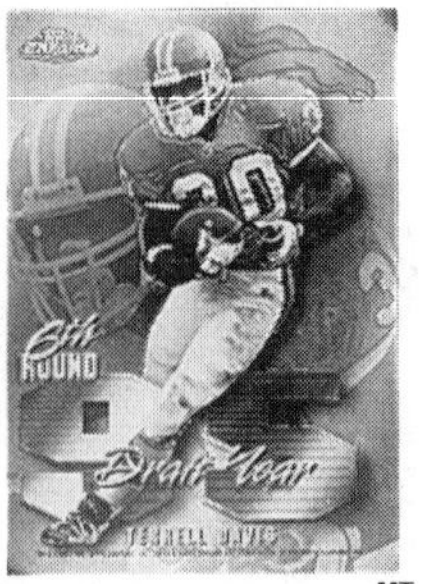

		MT
Complete Set (15):		250.00
Common Player:		5.00
Minor Stars:		10.00
Refractors:		2x
DR1	Dan Marino, John Elway (1983)	40.00
DR2	Reggie White, Steve Young (1984)	15.00
DR3	Bruce Smith, Jerry Rice (1985)	20.00
DR4	Ronnie Harmon, Pat Swilling (1986)	5.00
DR5	Jim Harbaugh, Vinny Testaverde (1987)	5.00
DR6	Michael Irvin, Tim Brown (1988)	10.00
DR7	Troy Aikman, Barry Sanders (1989)	30.00
DR8	Emmitt Smith, Junior Seau (1990)	40.00
DR9	Brett Favre, Ricky Watters (1991)	45.00
DR10	Carl Pickens, Desmond Howard (1992)	5.00
DR11	Mark Brunell, Drew Bledsoe (1993)	30.00
DR12	Marshall Faulk, Isaac Bruce (1994)	10.00
DR13	Terrell Davis, Curtis Martin (1995)	30.00
DR14	Eddie George, Terry Glenn (1996)	35.00
DR15	Ike Hilliard, Shawn Springs (1997)	5.00

1997 Topps Chrome Season's Best

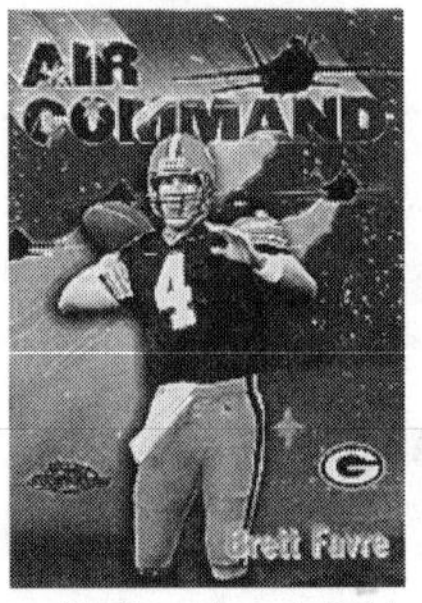

The 25-card Season's Best insert has five different subsets. Each of the five subsets consists of five cards featuring the season's top performers. Air Command features top quarterbacks, Thunder & Lightning has the top rushers, Magicians showcases the top total yardage gainers, Demolition Men highlights the top sack artists and Special Delivery has the top wide receivers. There are also five Career best cards for each category. Season's Best was inserted 1:12 with Refractors found 1:36.

		MT
Complete Set (25):		80.00
Common Player:		1.00
Minor Stars:		2.00
Refractors:		2x-3x
1	Mark Brunell (Air Command)	10.00
2	Vinny Testaverde (Air Command)	1.00
3	Drew Bledsoe (Air Command)	10.00
4	Brett Favre (Air Command)	20.00
5	Jeff Blake (Air Command)	2.00
6	Barry Sanders (Thunder & Lightning)	12.00
7	Terrell Davis (Thunder & Lightning)	10.00
8	Jerome Bettis (Thunder & Lightning)	2.00
9	Ricky Watters (Thunder & Lightning)	2.00
10	Eddie George (Thunder & Lightning)	15.00
11	Brian Mitchell (Magicians)	1.00
12	Tyrone Hughes (Magicians)	1.00
13	Eric Metcalf (Magicians)	1.00
14	Glyn Milburn (Magicians)	1.00
15	Ricky Watters (Magicians)	2.00
16	Kevin Greene (Demolition Men)	1.00
17	Lamar Lathon (Demolition Men)	1.00
18	Bruce Smith (Demolition Men)	1.00
19	Michael Sinclair (Demolition Men)	1.00
20	Derrick Thomas (Demolition Men)	1.00
21	Jerry Rice (Special Delivery)	10.00
22	Herman Moore (Special Delivery)	4.00
23	Carl Pickens (Special Delivery)	1.00
24	Cris Carter (Special Delivery)	1.00
25	Brett Perriman (Special Delivery)	1.00

1997 Topps Chrome Underclassmen

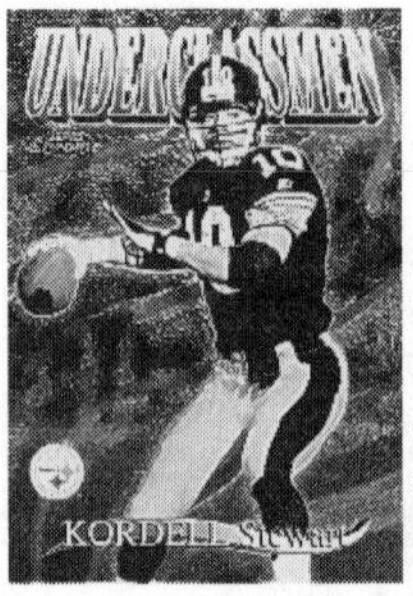

Underclassmen is a 10-card insert highlighting the top second and third year players. The set is inserted 1:8, with Refractor versions found 1:36. Cards are numbered with a "U" prefix.

		MT
Complete Set (10):		50.00
Common Player:		2.00
Refractors:		2x-3x
1	Kerry Collins	4.00
2	Karim Abdul-Jabbar	5.00
3	Simeon Rice	2.00
4	Keyshawn Johnson	3.00
5	Eddie George	14.00
6	Eddie Kennison	4.00
7	Terry Glenn	4.00
8	Kevin Hardy	2.00
9	Steve McNair	8.00
10	Kordell Stewart	10.00

1997 Topps Gallery

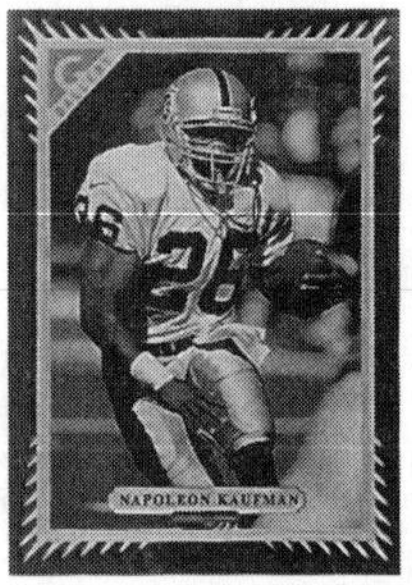

This 135-card base set features top player photos framed by a foil design. The Players Private Issue parallel set includes foil stamping and was inserted 1:12. Insert sets included Photo Gallery, Gallery of Heroes, Critics Choice and Peter Max Serigraphs.

		MT
Complete Set (135):		55.00
Common Player:		.20
Minor Stars:		.40
Private Issue Cards:		20x-40x
Private Issue Rookies:		10x-20x
Pack (6):		2.25
Wax Box (24):		50.00
1	Orlando Pace	.50
2	Darrell Russell	.20
3	Shawn Springs	.50
4	Peter Boulware	.20
5	Bryant Westbrook	.40
6	Walter Jones	.20
7	*Ike Hilliard*	2.00
8	James Farrior	.20
9	Tom Knight	.20
10	*Warrick Dunn*	4.00
11	*Tony Gonzalez*	2.00
12	Reinard Wilson	.20
13	*Yatil Green*	.50
14	*Reidel Anthony*	3.00
15	Kenny Holmes	.20
16	Dwayne Rudd	.20
17	Renaldo Wynn	.20
18	*David LaFleur*	.75
19	*Antowain Smith*	3.00
20	*Jim Druckenmiller*	4.00
21	*Rae Carruth*	2.00
22	*Byron Hanspard*	.75
23	*Jake Plummer*	8.00
24	*Corey Dillon*	7.00
25	*Darnell Autry*	.50
26	*Kevin Lockett*	.20
27	*Troy Davis*	.75
28	Mike Alstott	.40
29	Napoleon Kaufman	.40
30	Terrell Davis	2.50
31	Byron Morris	.20
32	Dana Stubblefield	.20
33	Ki-Jana Carter	.40
34	Hugh Douglas	.20
35	Natrone Means	.40
36	Marshall Faulk	.40
37	Tyrone Wheatley	.20
38	Tony Banks	.50
39	Marvin Harrison	1.50
40	Eddie George	3.50
41	Eddie Kennison	.40
42	Ray Mickens	.20
43	Mike Mamula	.20
44	Tamarick Vanover	.20
45	Rashaan Salaam	.40
46	Trent Dilfer	.40
47	John Mobley	.20
48	Gus Frerotte	.20
49	Isaac Bruce	.50
50	Mark Brunell	2.50
51	Jamal Anderson	.40
52	Keyshawn Johnson	1.50
53	Curtis Conway	.20
54	Zach Thomas	.75
55	Simeon Rice	.20
56	Lawrence Phillips	.40
57	Ty Detmer	.20
58	Bobby Engram	.20
59	Joey Galloway	.75
60	Curtis Martin	2.50
61	Kevin Hardy	.20
62	Eric Moulds	.20
63	Michael Westbrook	.20
64	Robert Smith	.20
65	Karim Abdul-Jabbar	.50
66	Errict Rhett	.40
67	Ray Lewis	.20
68	Terry Glenn	.50
69	Leeland McElroy	.20
70	Kerry Collins	.50
71	Steve McNair	2.00
72	Kordell Stewart	2.00
73	Terry Allen	.20
74	Michael Irvin	.40
75	John Elway	1.50
76	Lamar Lathon	.20
77	Rob Moore	.20
78	Irving Fryar	.20
79	Jim Everett	.20
80	Steve Young	1.50
81	Bryan Cox	.20
82	Dale Carter	.20
83	Chris Warren	.20
84	Shannon Sharpe	.20
85	Reggie White	.40
86	Deion Sanders	1.00
87	Hardy Nickerson	.20
88	Edgar Bennett	.20
89	Kent Graham	.20
90	Dan Marino	4.00
91	Kevin Greene	.20
92	Derrick Thomas	.20
93	Carl Pickens	.20
94	Neil O'Donnell	.20
95	Drew Bledsoe	2.50
96	Michael Haynes	.20
97	Tony Martin	.20
98	Scott Mitchell	.20
99	Rodney Hampton	.20
100	Brett Favre	5.00
101	Darrell Green	.20
102	Rod Woodson	.20
103	Chris Spielman	.20
104	Jake Reed	.20
105	Jerry Rice	2.50
106	Jeff Hostetler	.20
107	Anthony Johnson	.20
108	Keenan McCardell	.20
109	Ben Coates	.20
110	Emmitt Smith	4.00
111	LeRoy Butler	.20
112	Steve Atwater	.20
113	Ricky Watters	.40
114	Jim Harbaugh	.20
115	Marcus Allen	.40
116	Levon Kirkland	.20
117	Jessie Tuggle	.20
118	Ken Norton	.20
119	Thurman Thomas	.40
120	Junior Seau	.40
121	Tim Brown	.20
122	Michael Jackson	.20
123	Eric Metcalf	.20
124	Herman Moore	.40
125	Bruce Smith	.20
126	Cris Carter	.20
127	Dave Brown	.20
128	Jeff Blake	.40
129	Robert Blackmon	.20
130	Barry Sanders	2.50
131	Blaine Bishop	.20
132	Jerome Bettis	.40
133	Stan Humphries	.20
134	Vinny Testaverde	.20
135	Troy Aikman	2.50

1997 Topps Gallery Critics Choice

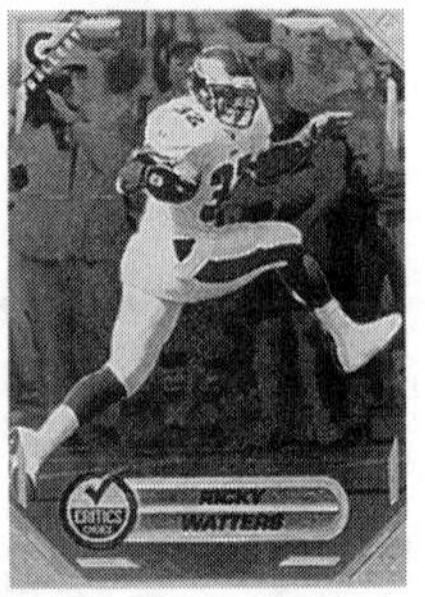

Critics Choice is a 20-card insert featuring player action shots. The cards were inserted 1:24. Cards are numbered and carry a "CC" prefix.

		MT
Complete Set (20):		220.00
Common Player:		4.00
Minor Stars:		8.00
Inserted 1:24		
1	Barry Sanders	30.00
2	Jeff Blake	4.00

3	Vinny Testaverde	8.00
4	Ricky Watters	8.00
5	John Elway	20.00
6	Drew Bledsoe	15.00
7	Kordell Stewart	15.00
8	Mark Brunell	15.00
9	Troy Aikman	15.00
10	Brett Favre	30.00
11	Kevin Hardy	4.00
12	Shannon Sharpe	4.00
13	Emmitt Smith	20.00
14	Rob Moore	4.00
15	Eddie George	15.00
16	Herman Moore	8.00
17	Terry Glenn	8.00
18	Jim Harbaugh	4.00
19	Terrell Davis	25.00
20	Junior Seau	4.00

1997 Topps Gallery Gallery of Heroes

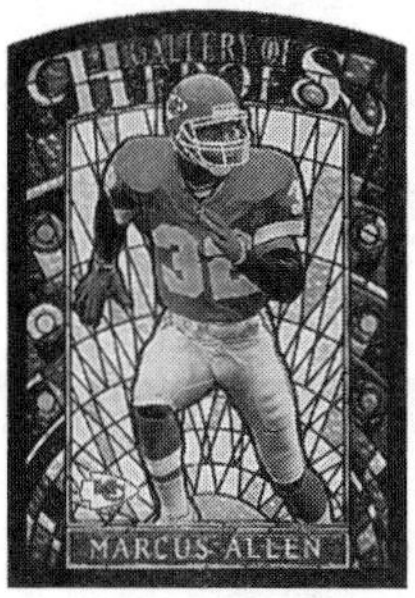

This 15-card insert features a player shot on a transparent, luminous card that looks like a stained glass window. They were inserted 1:36. Cards are numbered with a "GH" prefix.

		MT
Complete Set (15):		240.00
Common Player:		12.00
1	Desmond Howard	12.00
2	Marcus Allen	12.00
3	Kerry Collins	16.00
4	Troy Aikman	25.00
5	Jerry Rice	25.00
6	Drew Bledsoe	25.00
7	John Elway	18.00
8	Mark Brunell	25.00
9	Junior Seau	12.00
10	Brett Favre	45.00
11	Dan Marino	40.00
12	Barry Sanders	30.00
13	Reggie White	12.00
14	Emmitt Smith	40.00
15	Steve Young	18.00

1997 Topps Gallery Peter Max

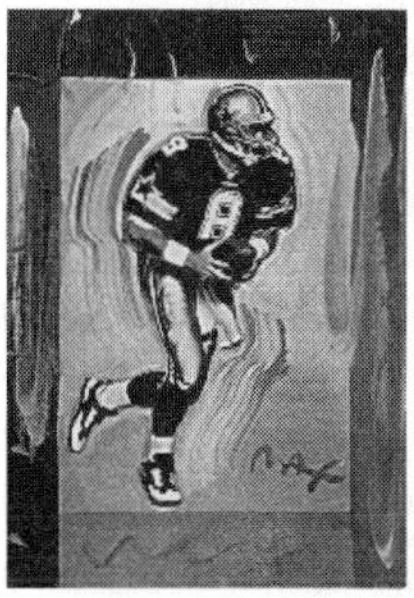

This 10-card insert combines player pictures with colorful art. This insert can be found 1:24. A limited number of the cards were autographed by the artist, Peter max. Cards are numbered and carry a "PM" prefix.

		MT
Complete Set (10):		125.00
Common Player:		4.00
Autographs:		10x-20x
1	Brett Favre	25.00
2	Jerry Rice	15.00
3	Emmitt Smith	20.00
4	John Elway	10.00
5	Barry Sanders	18.00
6	Reggie White	4.00
7	Steve Young	10.00
8	Troy Aikman	15.00
9	Drew Bledsoe	15.00
10	Dan Marino	20.00

Values quoted in this guide reflect the retail price of a card — the price a collector can expect to pay when buying a card from a dealer. The wholesale price — that which a collector can expect to receive from a dealer when selling cards — will be significantly lower, depending on desirability and condition.

1997 Topps Gallery Photo Gallery

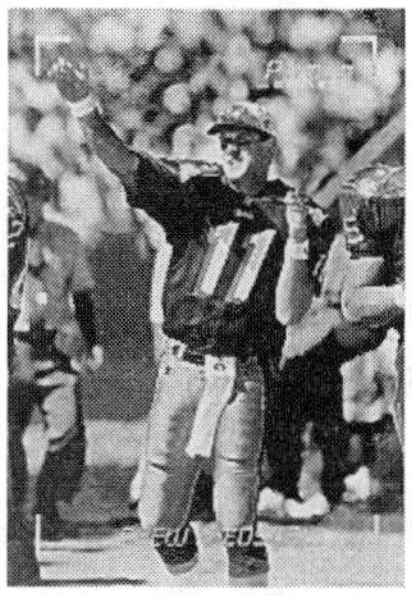

Photo Gallery features top players and double foil stamping. The 15-card set was inserted 1:24. Cards are numbered with a "PG" prefix.

		MT
Complete Set (15):		200.00
Common Player:		3.00
1	Eddie George	25.00
2	Drew Bledsoe	20.00
3	Brett Favre	35.00
4	Emmitt Smith	30.00
5	Dan Marino	30.00
6	Terrell Davis	20.00
7	Kevin Greene	3.00
8	Troy Aikman	20.00
9	Curtis Martin	20.00
10	Barry Sanders	20.00
11	Junior Seau	3.00
12	Deion Sanders	10.00
13	Steve Young	15.00
14	Reggie White	3.00
15	Jerry Rice	20.00

1997 Topps Stars

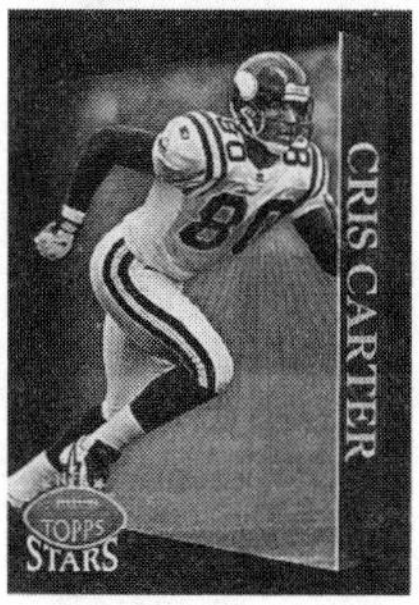

The 125-card set includes 100 NFL stars and 25 1997 NFL draft picks. Each card features diffraction and matte gold foil stamping. The Always Mint parallel set was seeded 1:18 packs. Topps Stars was offered exclusively to Topps Home Team Advantage members.

		MT
Complete Set (125):		50.00
Common Player:		.10
Minor Stars:		.20
Foil Stars:		15x-30x
Foil Rookies:		10x-20x
Pack (7):		4.00
Wax Box (24):		75.00
1	Brett Favre	4.00
2	Michael Jackson	.10
3	Simeon Rice	.10
4	Thurman Thomas	.20
5	Karim Abdul-Jabbar	.50
6	Marvin Harrison	.20
7	John Elway	2.00
8	Carl Pickens	.20
9	Rod Woodson	.10
10	Kerry Collins	.30
11	Cortez Kennedy	.10
12	William Fuller	.10
13	Michael Irvin	.20
14	Tyrone Braxton	.10
15	Steve Young	1.25
16	Keith Lyle	.10
17	Blaine Bishop	.10
18	Jeff Hostetler	.10
19	Levon Kirkland	.10
20	Barry Sanders	3.00
21	Deion Sanders	1.00
22	Jamal Anderson	.20
23	Eric Davis	.10
24	Hardy Nickerson	.10
25	LeRoy Butler	.10
26	Mark Brunell	1.75
27	Aeneas Williams	.10
28	Curtis Martin	1.50
29	Wayne Chrebet	.10
30	Jerry Rice	1.75
31	Jake Reed	.10
32	Wayne Martin	.10
33	Derrick Alexander	.10
34	Isaac Bruce	.20
35	Terrell Davis	2.00
36	Jerome Bettis	.20
37	Keenan McCardell	.10
38	Derrick Thomas	.10
39	Jason Sehorn	.10
40	Keyshawn Johnson	.20
41	Jeff Blake	.20
42	Terry Allen	.10
43	Ben Coates	.10
44	William Thomas	.10
45	Bryce Paup	.10
46	Bryant Young	.10
47	Eric Swann	.10
48	Tim Brown	.20
49	Tony Martin	.10
50	Eddie George	2.00
51	Sam Mills	.10
52	Terry McDaniel	.10
53	Darren Woodson	.10
54	Ashley Ambrose	.10
55	Drew Bledsoe	1.75
56	Larry Centers	.10
57	Ty Detmer	.20
58	Merton Hanks	.10
59	Charles Johnson	.10
60	Dan Marino	3.50
61	Joey Galloway	.20
62	Junior Seau	.20
63	Brett Perriman	.10
64	Wesley Walls	.10
65	Chad Brown	.10
66	Henry Ellard	.10
67	Keith Jackson	.10
68	John Randle	.10
69	Chester McGlockton	.10
70	Emmitt Smith	3.50
71	Vinny Testaverde	.20
72	Steve Atwater	.10
73	Irving Fryar	.10
74	Gus Frerotte	.10
75	Terry Glenn	.30
76	Anthony Johnson	.10
77	Jimmy Smith	.10
78	Terrell Buckley	.10
79	Kimble Anders	.10
80	Cris Carter	.20
81	David Meggett	.10
82	Shannon Sharpe	.20
83	Adrian Murrell	.20
84	Herman Moore	.20
85	Bruce Smith	.10
86	Lamar Lathon	.10
87	Ken Harvey	.10
88	Curtis Conway	.20
89	Alfred Williams	.10
90	Troy Aikman	1.75
91	Carnell Lake	.10
92	Michael Sinclair	.10
93	Ricky Watters	.20
94	Kevin Greene	.10
95	Reggie White	.20
96	Tyrone Hughes	.10
97	Dale Carter	.10
98	Rob Moore	.10
99	Tony Tolbert	.10
100	Willie McGinest	.10
101	*Orlando Pace*	.20
102	*Yatil Green*	.75
103	*Antowain Smith*	5.00
104	*David LaFleur*	1.50
105	*Jake Plummer*	12.00
106	*Will Blackwell*	.50
107	*Dwayne Rudd*	.20
108	*Corey Dillon*	10.00
109	*Pat Barnes*	.50
110	*Peter Boulware*	.20
111	*Tony Gonzalez*	2.00
112	*Renaldo Wynn*	.20
113	*Darrell Russell*	.20
114	*Bryant Westbrook*	.20
115	*James Farrior*	.20
116	*Joey Kent*	.20
117	*Rae Carruth*	2.00
118	*Jim Druckenmiller*	3.00
119	*Byron Hanspard*	.75
120	*Ike Hilliard*	2.00
121	*Kevin Lockett*	.20
122	*Tom Knight*	.20
123	*Shawn Springs*	.20
124	*Troy Davis*	.75
125	*Darnell Autry*	.30

1997 Topps Stars Future Pro Bowlers

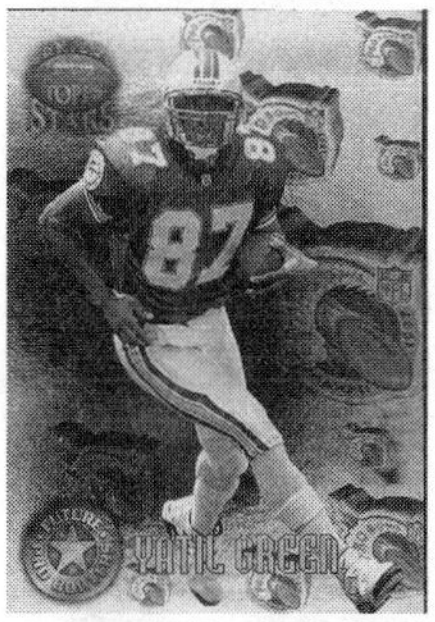

Inserted 1:12 packs, the 15-card set features a player photo superimposed over a backdrop of Pro Bowl 1997 logos. The Topps Stars logo is in the upper left, while the Future Pro Bowlers logo is in the lower left. The player's name is to the right of the logo. The cards are numbered on the back with a prefix of "FPB".

		MT
Complete Set (15):		60.00
Common Player:		2.00
1	Ike Hilliard	3.00
2	Tom Knight	2.00
3	David LaFleur	3.00
4	Byron Hanspard	4.00
5	Kevin Lockett	2.00
6	Rae Carruth	6.00
7	Jim Druckenmiller	10.00
8	Darnell Autry	4.00
9	Joey Kent	2.00
10	Peter Boulware	2.00
11	Orlando Pace	4.00
12	Troy Davis	6.00
13	Antowain Smith	10.00
14	Bryant Westbrook	2.00
15	Yatil Green	3.00

A card number in parentheses ( ) indicates the set is unnumbered.

1997 Topps Stars Hall of Fame Rookie Reprints

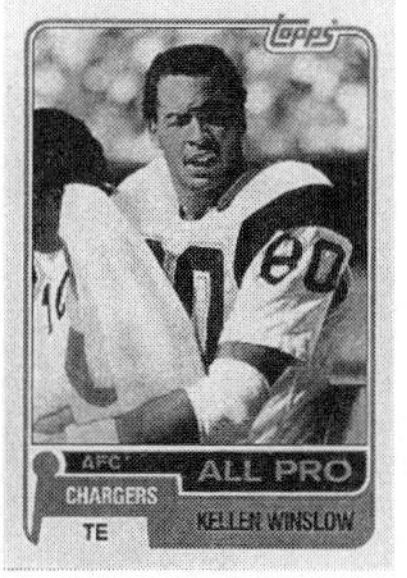

The 10-card set was inserted 1:64 packs, while autographed versions were found 1:128 packs.

		MT
Complete Set (10):		60.00
Common Player:		5.00
Autographs:		3x-6x
1	George Blanda	5.00
2	Dick Butkus	10.00
3	Len Dawson	5.00
4	Jack Ham	5.00
5	Sam Huff	5.00
6	Deacon Jones	5.00
7	Ray Nitschke	5.00
8	Gale Sayers	10.00
9	Randy White	5.00
10	Kellen Winslow	5.00

1997 Topps Stars Pro Bowl Memories

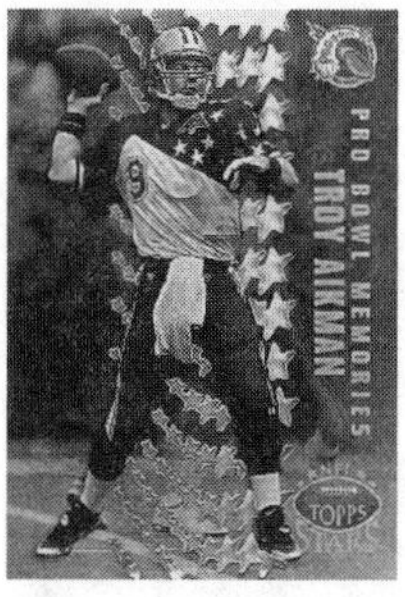

The 10-card set was inserted 1:24 packs. The cards are laser cut through the middle with stars, which start small on the left and grow larger as the stars move to the right. The Pro Bowl logo is in the upper left, while "Pro Bowl Memories" and the player's name are printed vertically along the right border in the middle. The Topps Stars logo is in the lower right. The backs are numbered with a "PBM" prefix.

		MT
Complete Set (10):		100.00
Common Player:		3.00
1	Barry Sanders	25.00
2	Jeff Blake	6.00
3	Ken Harvey	3.00
4	Brett Favre	30.00
5	Jerry Rice	15.00
6	John Elway	15.00
7	Marshall Faulk	3.00
8	Steve Young	10.00
9	Mark Brunell	15.00
10	Troy Aikman	15.00

1997 Topps Stars Pro Bowl Stars

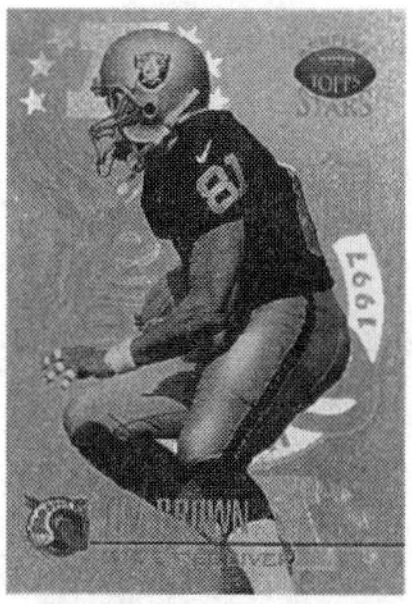

The 30-card set was inserted 1:24 packs. The card fronts feature a player photo superimposed over a unfluster background of the Pro Bowl 1997 logo and the NFC or AFC logo. The Topps Stars logo is in the upper left, while the Pro Bowl logo is in the lower left, with the player's name and position to the right. The backs are numbered with a prefix of "PB".

		MT
Complete Set (30):		125.00
Common Player:		4.00
Minor Stars:		8.00
Inserted 1:24		
1	Brett Favre	30.00
2	Mark Brunell	15.00
3	Kerry Collins	8.00
4	Drew Bledsoe	15.00
5	Barry Sanders	30.00
6	Terrell Davis	25.00
7	Terry Allen	4.00
8	Jerome Bettis	8.00
9	Ricky Watters	4.00
10	Curtis Martin	10.00
11	Emmitt Smith	20.00
12	Kimble Anders	4.00
13	Jerry Rice	15.00
14	Carl Pickens	4.00
15	Herman Moore	8.00
16	Tony Martin	4.00
17	Isaac Bruce	8.00
18	Tim Brown	4.00
19	Wesley Walls	4.00
20	Shannon Sharpe	4.00
21	Dana Stubblefield	4.00
22	Reggie White	8.00
23	Bruce Smith	4.00
24	Bryant Young	4.00
25	Junior Seau	4.00
26	Kevin Greene	4.00
27	Derrick Thomas	4.00
28	Chad Brown	4.00
29	Deion Sanders	10.00
30	Rod Woodson	4.00

1998 Topps

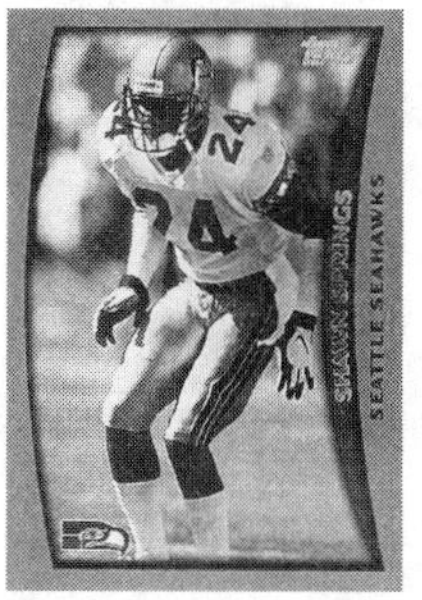

Topps was issued in a single-series 360-card set in 1998. It contained a 30-card 1998 NFL Draft Picks subset that was seeded one per three packs. Cards utilize a gold border around the color shot of the player, with the Topps logo in the upper right, team logo in the lower left and the player's name and team printed up the right side. Backs are horizontal and add another shot of the player, along with statistics and bio information. Inserts in Topps include: Season's Best, Measures of Greatness, Myster Finest, Gridiron Gods (hobby), Hidden Gems (retail), Autographs (hobby) and Generation 2000.

		MT
Complete Set (360):		70.00
Common Player:		.10
Minor Stars:		.20
Pack (11):		2.50
Wax Box (36):		80.00
1	Barry Sanders	2.00
2	Derrick Rodgers	.10
3	Chris Calloway	.10
4	Bruce Armstrong	.10
5	Horace Copeland	.10
6	Chad Brown	.10
7	Ken Harvey	.10
8	Levon Kirkland	.10
9	Glenn Foley	.10
10	Corey Dillon	.50
11	Sean Dawkins	.10
12	Curtis Conway	.20
13	Chris Chandler	.10
14	Kerry Collins	.20
15	Jonathan Ogden	.10
16	Sam Shade	.10
17	Vaughn Hebron	.10
18	Quentin Coryatt	.10
19	Jerris McPhail	.10
20	Warrick Dunn	1.00
21	Wayne Martin	.10
22	Chad Lewis	.10
23	Danny Kanell	.10
24	Shawn Springs	.10
25	Emmitt Smith	1.75
26	Todd Lyght	.10
27	Donnie Edwards	.10
28	Charlie Jones	.10
29	Willie McGinest	.10
30	Steve Young	.75
31	Darrell Russell	.10
32	Gary Anderson	.10
33	Stanley Richard	.10
34	Leslie O'Neal	.10
35	Dermontti Dawson	.10
36	Jeff Brady	.10
37	Kimble Anders	.10
38	Glyn Milburn	.10
39	Greg Hill	.10
40	Freddie Jones	.10
41	Bobby Engram	.10
42	Aeneas Williams	.10
43	Antowain Smith	.75
44	Reggie White	.20
45	Rae Carruth	.10
46	Leon Johnson	.10
47	Bryant Young	.10
48	Jamie Asher	.10
49	Hardy Nickerson	.10
50	Jerome Bettis	.20
51	Michael Strahan	.10
52	John Randle	.10
53	Kevin Hardy	.10
54	Eric Bjornson	.10
55	Morten Andersen	.10
56	Larry Centers	.10
57	Bryce Paup	.10
58	John Mobley	.10
59	Michael Bates	.10
60	Tim Brown	.20
61	Doug Evans	.10
62	Will Shields	.10
63	Jeff Graham	.10
64	Henry Jones	.10
65	Steve Broussard	.10
66	Blaine Bishop	.10
67	Ernie Conwell	.10
68	Heath Shuler	.10
69	Eric Metcalf	.10
70	Terry Glenn	.20
71	James Hasty	.10
72	Robert Porcher	.10
73	Keenan McCardell	.10
74	Tyrone Hughes	.10
75	Troy Aikman	1.00
76	Peter Boulware	.10
77	Rob Johnson	.20
78	Erik Kramer	.10
79	Kevin Smith	.10
80	Andre Rison	.10
81	Jim Harbaugh	.20
82	Chris Hudson	.10
83	Ray Zellars	.10
84	Jeff George	.20
85	Willie Davis	.10
86	Jason Gildon	.10
87	Robert Brooks	.10
88	Chad Cota	.10
89	Simeon Rice	.10
90	Mark Brunell	.75
91	Jay Graham	.10
92	Scott Greene	.10
93	Jeff Blake	.20
94	Jason Belser	.10
95	Derrick Alexander	.10
96	Ty Law	.10
97	Charles Johnson	.10
98	James Jett	.10
99	Darrell Green	.10
100	Brett Favre	2.00
101	George Jones	.10
102	Derrick Mason	.10
103	Sam Adams	.10
104	Lawrence Phillips	.10
105	Randal Hill	.10
106	John Mangum	.10
107	Natrone Means	.20
108	Bill Romanowski	.10
109	Terance Mathis	.10
110	Bruce Smith	.10
111	Pete Mitchell	.10
112	Duane Clemons	.10
113	Willie Clay	.10
114	Eric Allen	.10
115	Troy Drayton	.10
116	Derrick Thomas	.10
117	Charles Way	.10
118	Wayne Chrebet	.10
119	Bobby Hoying	.10
120	Michael Jackson	.10
121	Gary Zimmerman	.10
122	Yancey Thigpen	.10
123	Dana Stubblefield	.10
124	Keith Lyle	.10
125	Marco Coleman	.10
126	Karl Williams	.10
127	Stephen Davis	.10
128	Chris Sanders	.10
129	Cris Dishman	.10
130	Jake Plummer	1.00
131	Darryl Williams	.10
132	Merton Hanks	.10
133	Torrance Small	.10
134	Aaron Glenn	.10
135	Chester McGlockton	.10
136	William Thomas	.10
137	Kordell Stewart	1.00
138	Jason Taylor	.10
139	Lake Dawson	.10
140	Carl Pickens	.10
141	Eugene Robinson	.10
142	Ed McCaffrey	.10
143	Lamar Lathon	.10
144	Ray Buchanan	.10
145	Thurman Thomas	.20
146	Andre Reed	.10
147	Wesley Walls	.10
148	Rob Moore	.10
149	Darren Woodson	.10
150	Eddie George	1.00
151	Michael Irvin	.20
152	Johnnie Morton	.10
153	Ken Dilger	.10
154	Tony Boselli	.10
155	Randall McDaniel	.10
156	Mark Fields	.10
157	Phillippi Sparks	.10
158	William Roaf	.10
159	Troy Vincent	.10
160	Cris Carter	.20
161	Amp Lee	.10
162	Will Blackwell	.10
163	Chad Scott	.10
164	Henry Ellard	.10
165	Robert Jones	.10
166	Garrison Hearst	.10
167	James McKnight	.10
168	Rodney Harrison	.10
169	Adrian Murrell	.20
170	Rod Smith	.10
171	Desmond Howard	.10
172	Ben Coates	.10
173	David Palmer	.10
174	Zach Thomas	.10
175	Dale Carter	.10
176	Mark Chmura	.10
177	Elvis Grbac	.10
178	Jason Hanson	.10
179	Walt Harris	.10
180	Ricky Watters	.20
181	Ray Lewis	.10
182	Lonnie Johnson	.10
183	Marvin Harrison	.20
184	Dorsey Levens	.20
185	Tony Gonzalez	.10
186	Andre Hastings	.10
187	Kevin Turner	.10
188	Mo Lewis	.10
189	Jason Sehorn	.10
190	Drew Bledsoe	1.00
191	Michael Sinclair	.10
192	William Floyd	.10
193	Kenny Holmes	.10
194	Marvcus Patton	.10
195	Warren Sapp	.10
196	Junior Seau	.20

197	Ryan McNeil	.10
198	Tyrone Wheatley	.10
199	Robert Smith	.10
200	Terrell Davis	1.50
201	Brett Perriman	.10
202	Tamarick Vanover	.10
203	Stephen Boyd	.10
204	Zack Crockett	.10
205	Sherman Williams	.10
206	Neil Smith	.10
207	Jermaine Lewis	.10
208	Kevin Williams	.10
209	Byron Hanspard	.20
210	Warren Moon	.20
211	Tony McGee	.10
212	Raymont Harris	.10
213	Eric Davis	.10
214	Darrien Gordon	.10
215	James Stewart	.10
216	Derrick Mayes	.10
217	Brad Johnson	.10
218	Karim Abdul-Jabbar	.20
219	Hugh Douglas	.10
220	Terry Allen	.10
221	Rhett Hall	.10
222	Terrell Fletcher	.10
223	Carnell Lake	.10
224	Darryll Lewis	.10
225	Chris Slade	.10
226	Michael Westbrook	.10
227	Willie Williams	.10
228	Tony Banks	.20
229	Keyshawn Johnson	.20
230	Mike Alstott	.20
231	Tiki Barber	.20
232	Jake Reed	.10
233	Eric Swann	.10
234	Eric Moulds	.10
235	Vinny Testaverde	.10
236	Jessie Tuggle	.10
237	Ryan Wetnight	.10
238	Tyrone Poole	.10
239	Bryant Westbrook	.10
240	Steve McNair	.75
241	Jimmy Smith	.10
242	DeWayne Washington	.10
243	Robert Harris	.10
244	Rod Woodson	.10
245	Reidel Anthony	.20
246	Jessie Armstead	.10
247	O.J. McDuffie	.10
248	Carlton Gray	.10
249	LeRoy Butler	.10
250	Jerry Rice	1.00
251	Frank Sanders	.10
252	Todd Collins	.10
253	Fred Lane	.10
254	David Dunn	.10
255	Micheal Barrow	.10
256	Luther Ellis	.10
257	Scott Mitchell	.10
258	David Meggett	.10
259	Rickey Dudley	.10
260	Isaac Bruce	.20
261	Tony Martin	.10
262	Leslie Shepherd	.10
263	Derrick Thomas	.10
264	Greg Lloyd	.10
265	Terrell Buckley	.10
266	Antonio Freeman	.20
267	Tony Brackens	.10
268	Mark McMillian	.10
269	Dexter Coakley	.10
270	Dan Marino	1.75
271	Bryan Cox	.10
272	Leeland McElroy	.10
273	Jeff Burris	.10
274	Eric Green	.10
275	Darnay Scott	.10
276	Greg Clark	.10
277	Mario Bates	.10
278	Eric Turner	.10
279	Neil O'Donnell	.10
280	Herman Moore	.20
281	Gary Brown	.10
282	Terrell Owens	.20
283	Frank Wycheck	.10
284	Trent Dilfer	.20
285	Curtis Martin	.75
286	Ricky Proehl	.10
287	Steve Atwater	.10
288	Aaron Bailey	.10
289	William Henderson	.10
290	Marcus Allen	.20
291	Tom Knight	.10
292	Quinn Early	.10
293	Michael McCrary	.10
294	Bert Emanuel	.10
295	Tom Carter	.10
296	Kevin Glover	.10
297	Marshall Faulk	.20
298	Harvey Williams	.10
299	Chris Warren	.10
300	John Elway	.75
301	Eddie Kennison	.20
302	Gus Frerotte	.10
303	Regan Upshaw	.10
304	Kevin Gogan	.10
305	Napoleon Kaufman	.30
306	Charlie Garner	.10
307	Shawn Jefferson	.10
308	Tommy Vardell	.10
309	Mike Hollis	.10
310	Irving Fryar	.10
311	Shannon Sharpe	.10
312	Byron Morris	.10
313	Jamal Anderson	.10
314	Chris Gedney	.10
315	Chris Spielman	.10
316	Derrick Alexander	.10
317	O.J. Santiago	.10
318	Anthony Miller	.10
319	Ki-Jana Carter	.10
320	Deion Sanders	.40
321	Joey Galloway	.20
322	J.J. Stokes	.10
323	Rodney Thomas	.10
324	John Lynch	.10
325	Mike Pritchard	.10
326	Terrance Shaw	.10
327	Ted Johnson	.10
328	Ashley Ambrose	.10
329	Checklist	.10
330	Checklist	.10
331	*Jerome Pathon*	2.00
332	*Ryan Leaf*	6.00
333	*Duane Starks*	1.50
334	*Brian Simmons*	1.00
335	*Keith Brooking*	2.00
336	*Robert Edwards*	4.00
337	*Curtis Enis*	4.00
338	*John Avery*	3.00
339	*Fred Taylor*	10.00
340	*Germane Crowell*	5.00
341	*Hines Ward*	2.00
342	*Marcus Nash*	1.00
343	*Jacquez Green*	3.00
344	*Joe Jurevicius*	2.00
345	*Greg Ellis*	1.00
346	*Brian Griese*	8.00
347	*Tavian Banks*	2.00
348	*Robert Holcombe*	3.00
349	*Skip Hicks*	2.00
350	Ahman Green	2.00
351	*Takeo Spikes*	1.00
352	*Randy Moss*	20.00
353	*Andre Wadsworth*	1.00
354	*Jason Peter*	1.00
355	*Grant Wistrom*	1.00
356	*Charles Woodson*	4.00
357	*Kevin Dyson*	3.00
358	*Patrick Johnson*	1.00
359	*Tim Dwight*	4.00
360	*Peyton Manning*	20.00

1998 Topps Autographs

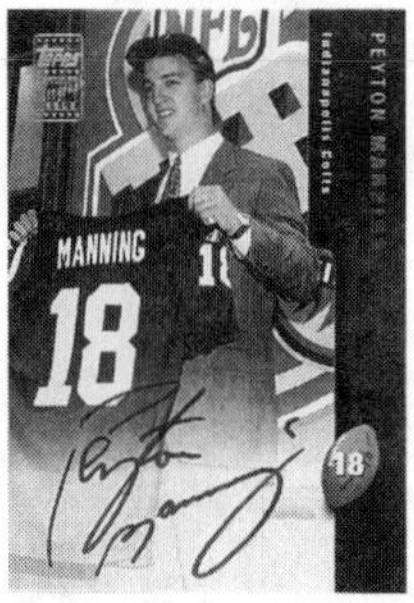

This hobby-only insert featured autographs from 15 top players, with eight veterans, two rookies and the five 1997 NFL Hall of Fame inductees. Each card has a gold foil "Topps Certified Autograph Issue" stamp and was inserted one per 260 hobby packs. Cards are numbered with a "A" prefix.

		MT
Complete Set (15):		650.00
Common Player:		30.00
1	Randy Moss	220.00
2	Mike Alstott	40.00
3	Jake Plummer	70.00
4	Corey Dillon	50.00
5	Kordell Stewart	70.00
6	Eddie George	60.00
7	Jason Sehorn	30.00
8	Joey Galloway	30.00
9	Ryan Leaf	75.00
10	Peyton Manning	150.00
11	Dwight Stephenson	30.00
12	Anthony Munoz	30.00
13	Mike Singletary	30.00
14	Tommy McDonald	30.00
15	Paul Krause	30.00

1998 Topps Generation 2000

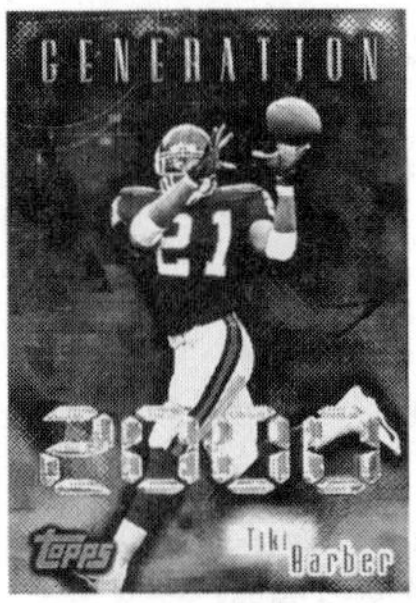

Generation 2000 showcases 15 of football's top young players who should lead the game into the year 2000. The inserts have the word "Generation" across the top and "2000" printed in silver, embossed foil across the bottom. These were numbered with a "GE" prefix and inserted one per 18 packs.

		MT
Complete Set (15):		60.00
Common Player:		2.00
Minor Stars:		4.00
1	Warrick Dunn	10.00
2	Tony Gonzalez	2.00
3	Corey Dillon	8.00
4	Antowain Smith	6.00
5	Mike Alstott	4.00
6	Kordell Stewart	8.00
7	Peter Boulware	2.00
8	Jake Plummer	10.00
9	Tiki Barber	4.00
10	Terrell Davis	12.00
11	Steve McNair	6.00
12	Curtis Martin	8.00
13	Napoleon Kaufman	6.00
14	Terrell Owens	2.00
15	Eddie George	8.00

A player's name in *italic type* indicates a rookie card.

1998 Topps Gridiron Gods

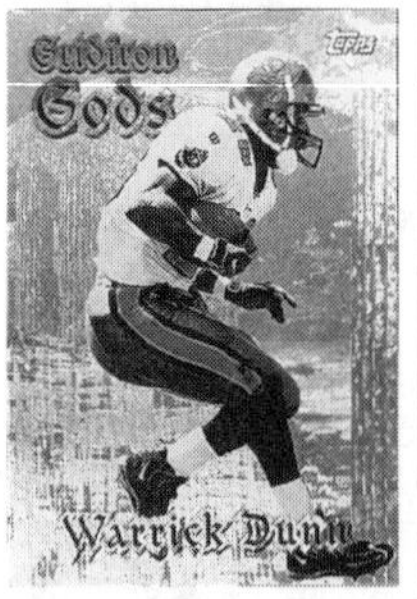

This hobby exclusive insert captures 15 players on uniluster technology, which is a silver etched, holofoil looking background. Cards are numbered with a "G" prefix and inserted one per 36 packs.

		MT
Complete Set (15):		100.00
Common Player:		2.00
Minor Stars:		4.00
1	Barry Sanders	15.00
2	Jerry Rice	10.00
3	Herman Moore	4.00
4	Drew Bledsoe	10.00
5	Kordell Stewart	10.00
6	Tim Brown	2.00
7	Eddie George	8.00
8	Dorsey Levens	4.00
9	Warrick Dunn	8.00
10	Brett Favre	15.00
11	Terrell Davis	12.00
12	Steve Young	7.00
13	Jerome Bettis	4.00
14	Mark Brunell	8.00
15	John Elway	8.00

1998 Topps Hidden Gems

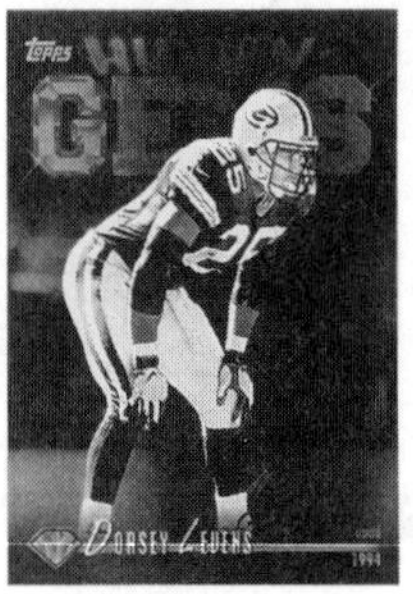

Hidden Gems were exclusive to retail packs and inserted one per 15. This 15-card set is printed on a plastic-like surface and numbered with a "HG" prefix.

		MT
Complete Set (15):		20.00
Common Player:		.50
1	Andre Reed	1.00
2	Kevin Greene	.50
3	Tony Martin	.50
4	Shannon Sharpe	1.00
5	Terry Allen	1.00
6	Brett Favre	8.00
7	Ben Coates	1.00
8	Michael Sinclair	.50
9	Keenan McCardell	.50
10	Brad Johnson	1.00
11	Mark Brunell	4.00
12	Dorsey Levens	1.00
13	Terrell Davis	8.00
14	Curtis Martin	2.00
15	Derrick Rodgers	.50

1998 Topps Measures Of Greatness

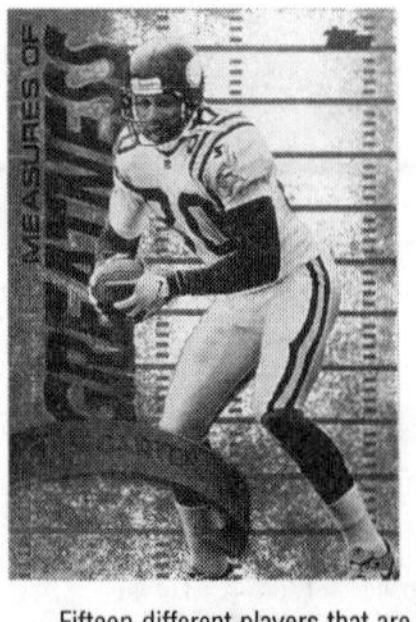

Fifteen different players that are bound for the Hall of Fame are featured in this insert printed on micro dyna-etch technology. The silver foil fronts that feature markings of a football field includes the insert name up the left side, with the player's name in a banner below it. Cards are numbered with a "MG" prefix and inserted one per 36 packs.

		MT
Complete Set (15):		70.00
Common Player:		2.00
Minor Stars:		4.00
1	John Elway	8.00
2	Marcus Allen	4.00
3	Jerry Rice	10.00
4	Tim Brown	2.00
5	Warren Moon	2.00
6	Bruce Smith	2.00
7	Troy Aikman	10.00
8	Reggie White	4.00
9	Irving Fryar	2.00
10	Barry Sanders	15.00
11	Cris Carter	2.00
12	Emmitt Smith	12.00
13	Dan Marino	12.00
14	Rod Woodson	2.00
15	Brett Favre	15.00

1998 Topps Mystery Finest

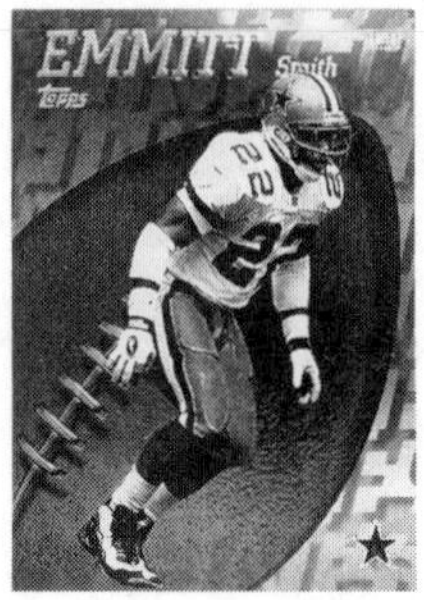

This 20-card insert arrives with black opaque protectors over the front and four different players on the back. Collectors needed to peel the fronts in order to determine which of the four players it was. Mystery Finest cards are numbered with a "M" prefix and inserted one per 36 packs. Refractor versions were also available and seeded one per 144 packs.

		MT
Complete Set (20):		125.00
Common Player:		2.00
Minor Stars:		4.00
Refractors:		3x
1	Steve Young	7.00
2	Dan Marino	17.00
3	Brett Favre	20.00
4	Drew Bledsoe	10.00
5	Mark Brunell	8.00
6	Troy Aikman	10.00
7	Kordell Stewart	10.00
8	John Elway	10.00
9	Barry Sanders	20.00
10	Jerome Bettis	4.00
11	Eddie George	10.00
12	Emmitt Smith	17.00
13	Curtis Martin	5.00
14	Warrick Dunn	10.00
15	Dorsey Levens	4.00
16	Terrell Davis	12.00
17	Herman Moore	4.00
18	Jerry Rice	10.00
19	Tim Brown	2.00
20	Yancey Thigpen	2.00

1998 Topps Season's Best

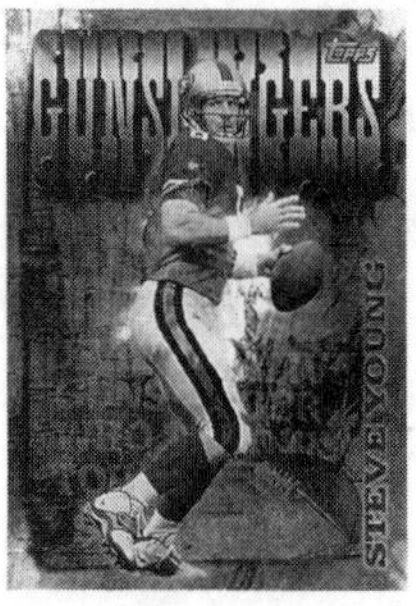

Season's Best includes 30 of the NFL's statistical leaders in six different categories on prismatic foilboard. Power & Speed are rushing leaders, Gunslingers are quarterbacks, Prime Targets are receiving leaders, Heavy Hitters are sack leaders, Quick Six are all-purpose yardage and Career Best are all-time leaders. These are numbered with a "SB" prefix and inserted one per 12 packs.

		MT
Complete Set (30):		90.00
Common Player:		1.00
Minor Stars:		2.00
1	Terrell Davis	8.00
2	Barry Sanders	10.00
3	Jerome Bettis	2.00
4	Dorsey Levens	2.00
5	Eddie George	5.00
6	Brett Favre	10.00
7	Mark Brunell	6.00
8	Jeff George	1.00
9	Steve Young	4.00
10	John Elway	6.00
11	Herman Moore	2.00
12	Rob Moore	1.00
13	Yancey Thigpen	1.00
14	Cris Carter	1.00
15	Tim Brown	1.00
16	Bruce Smith	1.00
17	Michael Sinclair	1.00
18	John Randle	1.00
19	Dana Stubblefield	1.00
20	Michael Strahan	1.00
21	Tamarick Vanover	1.00
22	Darrien Gordon	1.00
23	Michael Bates	1.00
24	David Meggett	1.00
25	Jermaine Lewis	1.00
26	Terrell Davis	8.00
27	Jerry Rice	8.00
28	Barry Sanders	10.00
29	John Randle	1.00
30	John Elway	6.00

1998 Topps Action Flats

This was the debut issue of Action Flats with a checklist of eight of the NFL's most celebrated star and rookie players in dynamic action poses. Each figure came with an exclusive special edition foil-stamped trading card that was different than their card in the Topps set. SRP was $2.99 for this product.

	MT
Complete Set (8):	25.00
Common Player:	3.00
Troy Aikman	3.00
John Elway	3.00
Brett Favre	4.00
Ryan Leaf	3.00
Peyton Manning	5.00
Dan Marino	3.00
Jerry Rice	3.00
Barry Sanders	4.00

1998 Topps Chrome

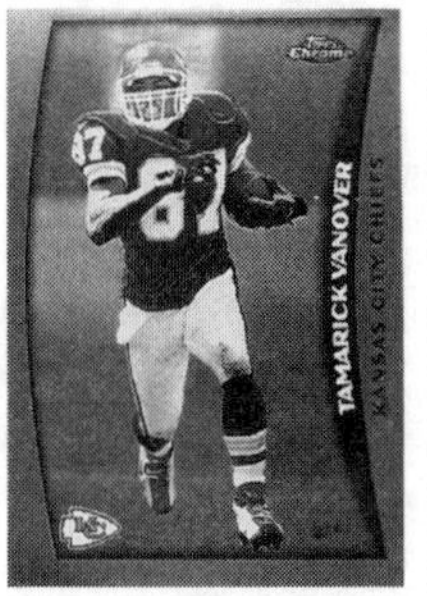

Topps Chrome includes 165 cards from Topps reprinted with a chromium finish. The Topps logo is replaced on both the front and the back by a Topps Chrome logo. Cards are renumbered and reordered within the checklist for the mostpart. Each card was also available in a Refractor versions, while the three inserts - Hidden Gems, Measures of Greatness and Season's Best - are also reprinted from Topps and available in both regular and Refractor versions.

		MT
Complete Set (165):		275.00
Common Player:		.40
Common Rookie:		3.00
Minor Stars:		.75
Refractor Cards:		6x-12x
Refractor Rookies:		2x-4x
Pack (4):		7.00
Wax Box (24):		150.00
1	Barry Sanders	6.00
2	*Duane Starks*	3.00
3	J.J. Stokes	.40
4	Joey Galloway	.75
5	Deion Sanders	1.50
6	Anthony Miller	.40
7	Jamal Anderson	1.00
8	Shannon Sharpe	.40
9	Irving Fryar	.40
10	Curtis Martin	1.50
11	Shawn Jefferson	.40
12	Charlie Garner	.75
13	*Robert Edwards*	5.00
14	Napoleon Kaufman	1.50
15	Gus Frerotte	.40
16	John Elway	3.00
17	*Jerome Pathon*	3.00
18	Marshall Faulk	.75
19	Michael McCrary	.40
20	Marcus Allen	.75
21	Trent Dilfer	.75
22	Frank Wycheck	.40
23	Terrell Owens	.75
24	Herman Moore	.75
25	Neil O'Donnell	.40
26	Darnay Scott	.40
27	*Keith Brooking*	3.00
28	Eric Green	.40
29	Dan Marino	5.00
30	Antonio Freeman	.75
31	Tony Martin	.40
32	Isaac Bruce	.75
33	Rickey Dudley	.40
34	Scott Mitchell	.40
35	*Randy Moss*	65.00
36	Fred Lane	.75
37	Frank Sanders	.40
38	Jerry Rice	3.00
39	O.J. McDuffie	.40
40	Jessie Armstead	.40
41	Reidel Anthony	.40
42	Steve McNair	2.00
43	Jake Reed	.40
44	*Charles Woodson*	15.00
45	Tiki Barber	.40
46	Mike Alstott	.75
47	Keyshawn Johnson	.75
48	Tony Banks	.75
49	Michael Westbrook	.40
50	Chris Slade	.40
51	Terry Allen	.40
52	Karim Abdul-Jabbar	.75
53	Brad Johnson	.75
54	Tony McGee	.40
55	*Kevin Dyson*	15.00
56	Warren Moon	.75
57	Byron Hanspard	.40
58	Jermaine Lewis	.40
59	Neil Smith	.40
60	Tamarick Vanover	.40
61	Terrell Davis	3.00
62	Robert Smith	.75
63	Junior Seau	.75
64	Warren Sapp	.40
65	Michael Sinclair	.40
66	*Ryan Leaf*	15.00
67	Drew Bledsoe	3.00
68	Jason Sehorn	.40
69	Andre Hastings	.40
70	Tony Gonzalez	.75
71	Dorsey Levens	.75
72	Ray Lewis	.40
73	*Grant Wistrom*	3.00
74	Elvis Grbac	.40
75	Mark Chmura	.75
76	Zach Thomas	.40
77	Ben Coates	.40
78	Rod Smith	.40
79	*Andre Wadsworth*	6.00
80	Garrison Hearst	.40
81	Will Blackwell	.40
82	Cris Carter	.40
83	Mark Fields	.40
84	Ken Dilger	.40
85	Johnnie Morton	.40
86	Michael Irvin	.75
87	Eddie George	3.00
88	Rob Moore	.40
89	*Takeo Spikes*	3.00
90	Wesley Walls	.40
91	Andre Reed	.40
92	Thurman Thomas	.75
93	Ed McCaffrey	.40
94	Carl Pickens	.40
95	Jason Taylor	.40
96	Kordell Stewart	3.00
97	*Greg Ellis*	1.00
98	Aaron Glenn	.40
99	Jake Plummer	3.00
100	Checklist	.40
101	Chris Sanders	.40
102	Michael Jackson	.40
103	Bobby Hoying	.40
104	Wayne Chrebet	.40
105	Charles Way	.40
106	Derrick Thomas	.40
107	Troy Drayton	.40
108	*Robert Holcombe*	8.00
109	Pete Mitchell	.40
110	Bruce Smith	.40
111	Terance Mathis	.40
112	Lawrence Phillips	.40
113	Brett Favre	6.00
114	Darrell Green	.40
115	Charles Johnson	.40
116	Jeff Blake	.75
117	Mark Brunell	3.00
118	Simeon Rice	.40
119	Robert Brooks	.40
120	*Jacquez Green*	12.00
121	Willie Davis	.40
122	Jeff George	.75
123	Andre Rison	.40
124	Erik Kramer	.40
125	Peter Boulware	.40
126	*Marcus Nash*	10.00
127	Troy Aikman	3.00
128	Keenan McCardell	.40
129	Bryant Westbrook	.40
130	Terry Glenn	.75
131	Blaine Bishop	.40
132	Tim Brown	.75
133	*Brian Griese*	30.00
134	John Mobley	.40
135	Larry Centers	.40
136	Eric Bjornson	.40
137	Kevin Hardy	.40
138	John Randle	.40
139	Michael Strahan	.40
140	Jerome Bettis	.75
141	Rae Carruth	.40
142	Reggie White	.75
143	Antowain Smith	1.50
144	Aeneas Williams	.40
145	Bobby Engram	.40
146	*Germane Crowell*	15.00
147	Freddie Jones	.40
148	Kimble Anders	.40
149	Steve Young	2.00
150	Willie McGinest	.40
151	Emmitt Smith	5.00
152	*Fred Taylor*	35.00
153	Danny Kanell	.40
154	Warrick Dunn	3.00
155	Kerry Collins	.75
156	Chris Chandler	.40
157	Curtis Conway	.75
158	*Curtis Enis*	15.00
159	Corey Dillon	2.00
160	Glenn Foley	.75
161	Marvin Harrison	.75
162	Chad Brown	.40
163	Derrick Rodgers	.40
164	Levon Kirkland	.40
165	*Peyton Manning*	80.00

1998 Topps Chrome Refractors

All 165 cards in Topps Chrome were reprinted in Refractor versions and inserted one per 12 packs.

	MT
Refractor Cards:	6x-12x
Refractor Rookies:	2x-4x

A card number in parentheses ( ) indicates the set is unnumbered.

1998 Topps Chrome Hidden Gems

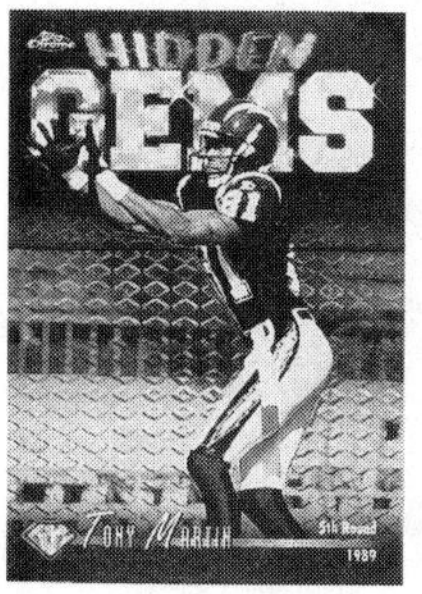

This 15-card set was reprinted from Topps in a chromium version and inserted one per 12 packs. Cards are numbered with "HG" prefix, while Refractors are seeded one per 24 packs.

		MT
Complete Set (15):		40.00
Common Player:		1.50
Minor Stars:		3.00
Refractors:		2x
1	Andre Reed	1.50
2	Kevin Greene	1.50
3	Tony Martin	1.50
4	Shannon Sharpe	1.50
5	Terry Allen	1.50
6	Brett Favre	15.00
7	Ben Coates	1.50
8	Michael Sinclair	1.50
9	Keenan McCardell	1.50
10	Brad Johnson	3.00
11	Mark Brunell	7.00
12	Dorsey Levens	3.00
13	Terrell Davis	10.00
14	Curtis Martin	4.00
15	Derrick Rodgers	1.50

1998 Topps Chrome Measures of Greatness

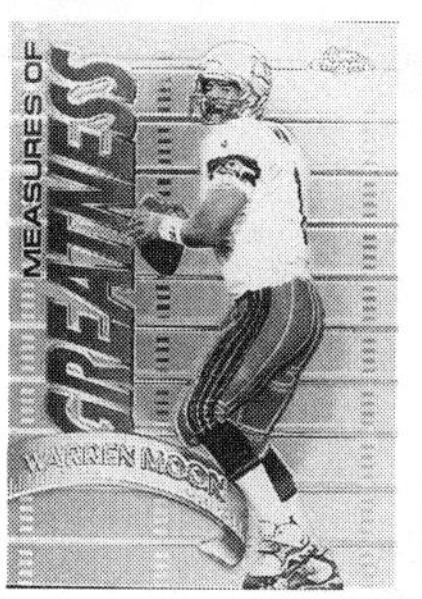

This 15-card set is reprinted from Topps in a chromium version and seeded one per 12 packs. The cards are numbered with a "HG" prefix, while Refractor versions are seeded one per 48 packs.

		MT
Complete Set (15):		80.00
Common Player:		1.50
Minor Stars:		3.00
Refractors:		3x
1	John Elway	7.00
2	Marcus Allen	3.00
3	Jerry Rice	8.00
4	Tim Brown	1.50
5	Warren Moon	1.50
6	Bruce Smith	1.50
7	Troy Aikman	8.00
8	Reggie White	3.00
9	Irving Fryar	1.50
10	Barry Sanders	15.00
11	Cris Carter	1.50
12	Emmitt Smith	12.00
13	Dan Marino	12.00
14	Rod Woodson	1.50
15	Brett Favre	15.00

1998 Topps Chrome Season's Best

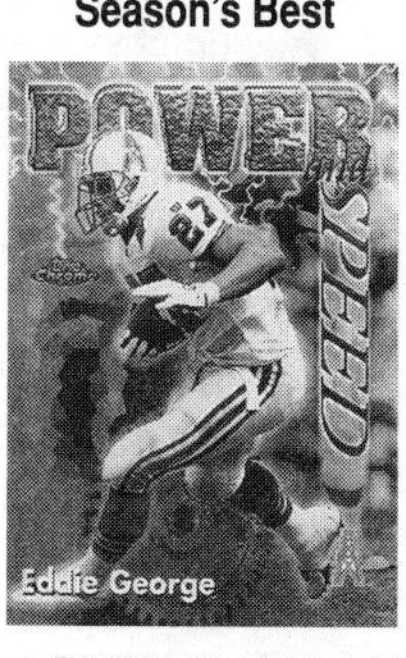

This 30-card insert was reprinted from Topps in a chromium version and inserted one per eight packs. The set is broken up with five cards in six different categories, including Power & Speed, Gunslingers, Prime Targets, Heavy Hitters, Quick Six and Career Best. Season's Best cards are numbered with a "SB" prefix and Refractor versions are seeded one per 24 packs.

		MT
Complete Set (30):		90.00
Common Player:		.50
Minor Stars:		1.00
Refractors:		2x
1	Terrell Davis	10.00
2	Barry Sanders	15.00
3	Jerome Bettis	1.00
4	Dorsey Levens	1.00
5	Eddie George	6.00
6	Brett Favre	15.00
7	Mark Brunell	5.00
8	Jeff George	1.00
9	Steve Young	4.00
10	John Elway	7.00
11	Herman Moore	1.00
12	Rob Moore	.50
13	Yancey Thigpen	.50
14	Cris Carter	1.00
15	Tim Brown	1.00
16	Bruce Smith	.50
17	Michael Smith	.50
18	John Randle	.50
19	Dana Stubblefield	.50
20	Michael Strahan	.50
21	Tamarick Vanover	.50
22	Darrien Gordon	.50
23	Michael Bates	.50
24	David Meggett	.50
25	Jermaine Lewis	.50
26	Terrell Davis	10.00
27	Jerry Rice	6.00
28	Barry Sanders	15.00
29	John Randle	.50
30	John Elway	7.00

1998 Topps Gold Label

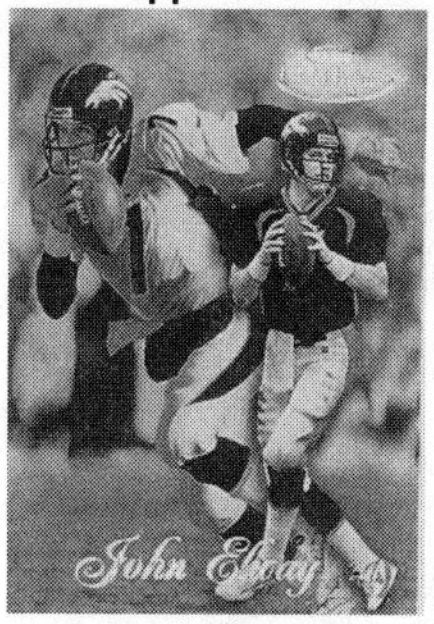

Each card in this set was printed on 35 point spectra-reflective rainbow stock and was gold foiled-stamped with the player's name and the Gold Label logo. The backs of the cards reveal all relevant statistics, including career totals and career bests as well as insightful player commentary. Each card has a parallel Class 2 and a Class 3 card. The Class 2 cards have the name and logo in silver foil and were inserted 1:2 packs. The Class 3 singles were in prismatic gold foil and found 1:4 packs.

		MT
Complete Set (100):		85.00
Common Player:		.25
Minor Stars:		.50
Class 2 Cards:		2x
Class 2 Rookies:		1.5x
Name In Silver Foil		
Inserted 1:2		
Class 3 Cards:		3x
Class 3 Rookies:		2x
Name In Prismatic Gold Foil		
Inserted 1:4		
Hobby Pack (5):		5.00
Hobby Wax Box (24):		110.00
Retail Pack (3):		3.00
Retail Wax Box (36):		90.00
1	John Elway	4.00
2	Rob Moore	.25
3	Jamal Anderson	1.50
4	*Patrick Johnson*	1.50
5	Troy Aikman	4.00
6	Antowain Smith	1.50
7	Wesley Walls	.25
8	*Curtis Enis*	5.00
9	Jimmy Smith	.50
10	Terrell Davis	6.00
11	Marshall Faulk	1.00
12	*Germane Crowell*	6.00
13	*Marcus Nash*	4.00
14	Deion Sanders	1.00
15	Dorsey Levens	.50
16	Corey Dillon	1.50
17	*Fred Taylor*	12.00
18	Derrick Thomas	.25
19	*Kevin Dyson*	4.00
20	*Peyton Manning*	20.00
21	Warren Sapp	.25
22	*Robert Holcombe*	3.00
23	Joey Galloway	1.00
24	Garrison Hearst	.50
25	Brett Favre	8.00
26	Aeneas Williams	.25
27	Danny Kanell	.25
28	Robert Smith	.50
29	Brad Johnson	1.00
30	Dan Marino	6.00
31	Elvis Grbac	.50
32	Terry Allen	.25
33	Frank Sanders	.25
34	Peter Boulware	.25
35	Tim Brown	.50
36	Thurman Thomas	.50
37	Rae Carruth	.25
38	Michael Irvin	.50
39	*Brian Griese*	12.00
40	Kordell Stewart	3.00
41	Johnnie Morton	.25
42	Robert Brooks	.25
43	Keenan McCardell	.25
44	Ben Coates	.50
45	Jerry Rice	4.00
46	*Tony Simmons*	2.50
47	Irving Fryar	.25
48	*Jerome Pathon*	2.00
49	Steve McNair	1.50
50	Warrick Dunn	3.00
51	*Skip Hicks*	4.00
52	*Andre Wadsworth*	2.00
53	Chris Chandler	.50
54	Curtis Conway	.50
55	Eddie George	3.00
56	Jeff Blake	.50
57	*Greg Ellis*	1.50
58	Scott Mitchell	.25
59	Antonio Freeman	1.00
60	Drew Bledsoe	4.00
61	Mark Brunell	3.00
62	Andre Rison	.50
63	Cris Carter	1.00
64	Jake Reed	.25
65	Napoleon Kaufman	1.50
66	Terry Glenn	1.00
67	Jason Sehorn	.25
68	Rickey Dudley	.25
69	Junior Seau	.50
70	Jerome Bettis	1.00
71	J.J. Stokes	.50
72	Warren Moon	.50
73	Isaac Bruce	.50
74	Mike Alstott	1.00
75	Steve Young	2.50
76	*Jacquez Green*	4.00
77	Gus Frerotte	.25
78	Michael Jackson	.25
79	Carl Pickens	.50
80	Bruce Smith	.25
81	Shannon Sharpe	.50
82	Herman Moore	.50
83	Reggie White	1.00
84	Marvin Harrison	.75
85	Jake Plummer	3.00
86	Karim Abdul-Jabbar	.75
87	John Randle	.25
88	*Robert Edwards*	6.00
89	Jeff George	.50
90	Emmitt Smith	6.00
91	Terrell Owens	1.50
92	Trent Dilfer	1.00
93	Darrell Green	.25
94	Andre Reed	.25
95	*Ryan Leaf*	7.00
96	Rod Smith	.50
97	O.J. McDuffie	.25
98	*John Avery*	4.00
99	Charles Way	.25
100	Barry Sanders	8.00

1998 Topps Gold Label Black Label

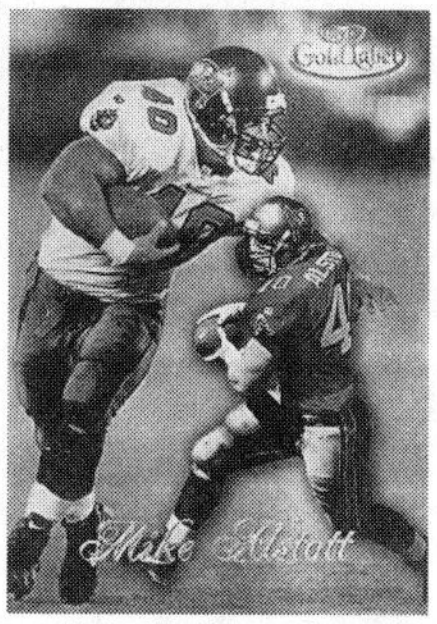

Each of the three versions in this set are the same as in the base Gold Label set except for the logo is in black. Class 1 singles have the name in gold foil and are found 1:8 packs. Class 2 cards are in silver foil and inserted 1:16 packs. Class 3 singles are in prismatic gold foil and inserted 1:32 packs.

	MT
Class 1 Cards:	5x
Class 1 Rookies:	3x
Name In Gold Foil	
Inserted 1:8	
Class 2 Cards:	8x
Class 2 Rookies:	5x
Name In Silver Foil	
Inserted 1:16	
Class 3 Cards:	12x
Class 3 Rookies:	7x
Name In Prismatic Gold Foil	
Inserted 1:32	

1998 Topps Gold Label Red Label

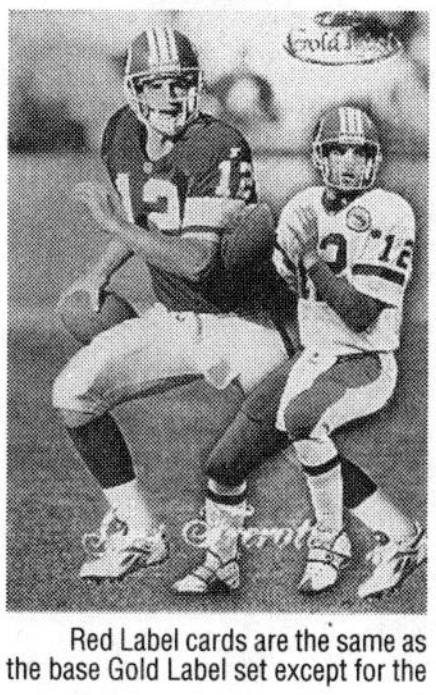

Red Label cards are the same as the base Gold Label set except for the logo is in red foil and each card is sequentially numbered. Class 1 singles have the name in gold foil (1:94) and are numbered to 100. Class 2 singles are in silver foil (1:187) and numbered to 50. Class 3 cards are in prismatic gold foil (1:375) and numbered to 25.

	MT
Class 1 Cards:	20x-40x
Class 1 Rookies:	10x-20x
Name In Gold Foil	
Inserted 1:94	
Production 100 Sets	
Class 2 Cards:	25x-50x
Class 2 Rookies:	12x-25x
Name In Silver Foil	
Inserted 1:187	
Production 50 Sets	
Class 3 Cards:	50x-100x
Class 3 Rookies:	25x-50x
Name In Prismatic Gold Foil	
Inserted 1:375	
Production 25 Sets	

1998 Topps Season Opener

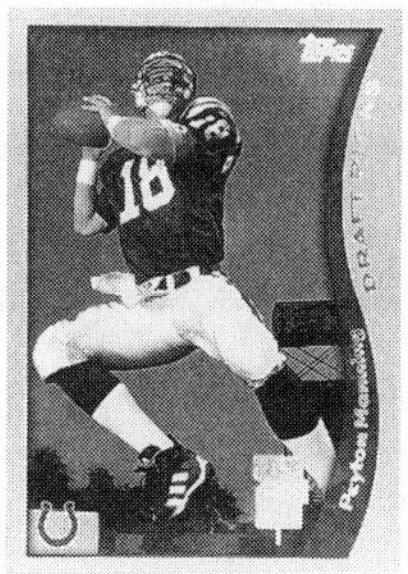

Topps Season Opener was a retail exclusive product comprised of 165 cards that paralleled Topps. While Topps cards were printed with a gold border, Season Opener cards used a silver border and a silver "Season Opener '98" stamp on a goal post to distinguish them. Packs contained seven cards and one Season Opener Sweepstakes card, with which collectors could win a trip to the Pro Bowl in Honolulu, Hawaii.

		MT
Complete Set (165):		160.00
Common Player:		.10
Minor Stars:		.20
Common Rookie:		2.50
Pack (8):		5.00
Wax Box (36):		150.00
1	*Peyton Manning*	40.00
2	*Jerome Pathon*	4.00
3	*Duane Starks*	2.50
4	*Brian Simmons*	2.50
5	*Keith Brooking*	2.50
6	*Robert Edwards*	4.00
7	*Curtis Enis*	7.00
8	*John Avery*	3.00
9	*Fred Taylor*	10.00
10	*Germane Crowell*	10.00
11	*Hines Ward*	4.00
12	*Marcus Nash*	2.50
13	*Jacquez Green*	8.00
14	*Joe Jurevicius*	2.50
15	*Greg Ellis*	2.50
16	*Brian Griese*	15.00
17	*Tavian Banks*	3.00
18	*Robert Holcombe*	3.00
19	*Skip Hicks*	4.00
20	*Ahman Green*	10.00
21	*Takeo Spikes*	2.50
22	*Randy Moss*	35.00
23	*Andre Wadsworth*	4.00
24	*Jason Peter*	2.50
25	*Grant Wistrom*	2.50
26	*Charles Woodson*	7.00
27	*Kevin Dyson*	7.00
28	*Patrick Johnson*	4.00
29	*Tim Dwight*	7.00
30	*Ryan Leaf*	8.00
31	Chad Brown	.10
32	Levon Kirkland	.10
33	Corey Dillon	.50
34	Curtis Conway	.20
35	Chris Chandler	.10
36	Warrick Dunn	.75
37	Danny Kanell	.10
38	Emmitt Smith	1.50
39	Steve Young	.75
40	Kimble Anders	.10
41	Freddie Jones	.10
42	Bobby Engram	.10
43	Aeneas Williams	.10
44	Antowain Smith	.40
45	Reggie White	.20
46	Rae Carruth	.10
47	Jamie Asher	.10
48	Hardy Nickerson	.10
49	Jerome Bettis	.20
50	Michael Strahan	.10
51	John Randle	.10
52	Larry Centers	.10
53	Tim Brown	.20
54	Terry Glenn	.20
55	Keenan McCardell	.10
56	Troy Aikman	1.00
57	Peter Boulware	.10
58	Erik Kramer	.10
59	Andre Rison	.10
60	Jeff George	.20
61	Robert Brooks	.10
62	Simeon Rice	.10
63	Mark Brunell	1.00
64	Jeff Blake	.20
65	Brett Favre	2.00
66	Lawrence Phillips	.10
67	Randal Hill	.10
68	Terance Mathis	.10
69	Bruce Smith	.10
70	Troy Drayton	.10
71	Derrick Thomas	.10
72	Charles Way	.10
73	Bobby Hoying	.10
74	Michael Jackson	.10
75	Chris Sanders	.10
76	Cris Dishman	.10
77	Jake Plummer	1.00
78	Kordell Stewart	.75
79	Carl Pickens	.20
80	Ed McCaffrey	.30
81	Ray Buchanan	.10
82	Thurman Thomas	.20
83	Andre Reed	.10
84	Wesley Walls	.10
85	Rob Moore	.20
86	Eddie George	.75
87	Michael Irvin	.20
88	Johnnie Morton	.10
89	Cris Carter	.30
90	Garrison Hearst	.20
91	Rod Smith	.20
92	Ben Coates	.10
93	Zach Thomas	.20
94	Dale Carter	.10
95	Mark Chmura	.20
96	Elvis Grbac	.10
97	Ray Lewis	.10
98	Lonnie Johnson	.10
99	Darrell Green	.10
100	Marvin Harrison	.20
101	Dorsey Levens	.20
102	Tony Gonzalez	.10
103	Andre Hastings	.10
104	Jason Sehorn	.10
105	Drew Bledsoe	1.00
106	Junior Seau	.20
107	Robert Smith	.20
108	Terrell Davis	1.50
109	Neil Smith	.10
110	Jermaine Lewis	.10
111	Warren Moon	.20
112	Brad Johnson	.20
113	Karim Abdul-Jabbar	.20
114	Terry Allen	.20
115	Chris Slade	.10
116	Michael Westbrook	.10
117	Tony Banks	.20
118	Mike Alstott	.20
119	Jake Reed	.10
120	Bryant Westbrook	.10
121	Steve McNair	.75
122	Jimmy Smith	.20
123	Reidel Anthony	.10
124	Jessie Armstead	.10
125	O.J. McDuffie	.10
126	Jerry Rice	1.00
127	Frank Sanders	.10
128	Fred Lane	.20
129	Scott Mitchell	.10
130	Rickey Dudley	.10
131	Isaac Bruce	.20
132	Tony Martin	.10
133	Leslie Shepherd	.10
134	Derrick Thomas	.10
135	Antonio Freeman	.20
136	Dan Marino	1.50
137	Eric Green	.10
138	Darnay Scott	.10
139	Herman Moore	.20
140	Terrell Owens	.30
141	Trent Dilfer	.20
142	Marshall Faulk	.20
143	John Elway	1.00
144	Gus Frerotte	.10
145	Napoleon Kaufman	.40
146	Charlie Garner	.10
147	Irving Fryar	.10
148	Shannon Sharpe	.20
149	Jamal Anderson	.30
150	Chris Spielman	.10
151	Deion Sanders	.40
152	Joey Galloway	.20
153	J.J. Stokes	.10
154	Quinn Early	.10
155	Michael McCrary	.10
156	Willie McGinest	.10
157	Kevin Hardy	.10
158	Michael Barrow	.10
159	John Mobley	.10
160	Michael Sinclair	.10
161	Warren Sapp	.10
162	Michael Bates	.10
163	Pete Mitchell	.10
164	Barry Sanders	2.00
165	Checklist	.10

1998 Topps Stars

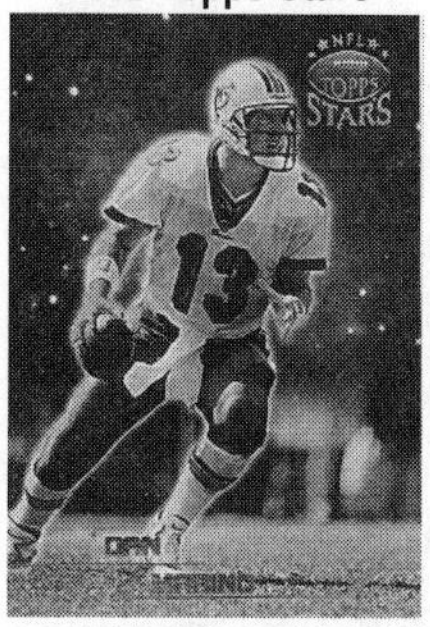

Each borderless card is printed on 20-point stock and uses luminous diffraction technology with matte gold-foil stamping. Every card in this product is sequentially numbered. The Red and Bronze set are both considered base sets and are each numbered to 8,799. Three parallel sets include Silver, Gold and Gold Rainbow. The Silver singles were numbered to 3,999, the Gold cards are to 1,999 and inserted 1:2 packs, and the Gold Rainbow cards were numbered to 99 and found 1:41 packs.

		MT
Complete Set (150):		125.00
Common Red Player:		.20
Minor Red Stars:		.40
Common Red Rookie:		1.00
Production 8,799 Sets		
Bronze Cards:		1x
Production 8,799 Sets		
Silver Cards:		1.5x
Production 3,999 Sets		
Gold Cards:		3x
Gold Rookies:		2x
Production 1,999 Sets		
Inserted 1:2		
Gold Rainbow Cards:		15x-30x
Gold Rainbow Rookies:		5x-10x
Production 99 Sets		
Inserted 1:41		
Pack (6):		3.00
Wax Box (24):		70.00
1	John Elway	2.50
2	*Duane Starks*	1.50
3	Bruce Smith	.20
4	Jeff Blake	.40
5	Carl Pickens	.40
6	Shannon Sharpe	.40
7	*Jerome Pathon*	2.00
8	Jimmy Smith	.40
9	Elvis Grbac	.20
10	Mark Brunell	2.00
11	Karim Abdul-Jabbar	.75
12	Terry Glenn	.75
13	Larry Centers	.20
14	Jeff George	.40
15	Terry Allen	.20
16	Charles Johnson	.20
17	Chris Spielman	.20
18	*Ahman Green*	2.50
19	*Kevin Dyson*	4.00
20	Dan Marino	4.00
21	*Andre Wadsworth*	1.50
22	Chris Chandler	.20
23	Kerry Collins	.40
24	Erik Kramer	.20
25	Warrick Dunn	2.00
26	Michael Irvin	.40
27	Herman Moore	.40
28	Dorsey Levens	.40
29	Cris Carter	.40
30	Drew Bledsoe	2.00
31	Kevin Greene	.20
32	Charles Way	.20
33	Bobby Hoying	.20
34	Tony Banks	.40
35	Steve Young	1.50
36	Trent Dilfer	.40
37	Warren Sapp	.20
38	*Skip Hicks*	2.00
39	Michael Jackson	.20
40	Curtis Martin	1.00
41	Thurman Thomas	.40
42	Corey Dillon	1.50
43	*Brian Griese*	10.00
44	Marshall Faulk	.75
45	Isaac Bruce	.40
46	*Fred Taylor*	12.00
47	Andre Rison	.20
48	O.J. McDuffie	.20
49	*John Avery*	2.00
50	Terrell Davis	4.00
51	*Robert Edwards*	3.00
52	Keyshawn Johnson	.40
53	Rickey Dudley	.20
54	*Hines Ward*	2.00
55	Irving Fryar	.20
56	Freddie Jones	.20
57	Michael Sinclair	.20
58	Darnay Scott	.20
59	*Tim Dwight*	3.00
60	Tim Brown	.40
61	Ray Lewis	.20
62	*Curtis Enis*	4.00
63	Emmitt Smith	4.00
64	Scott Mitchell	.20
65	Antonio Freeman	.75
66	*Randy Moss*	15.00
67	*Peyton Manning*	15.00
68	Danny Kanell	.20
69	Charlie Garner	.20
70	Mike Alstott	.75
71	*Grant Wistrom*	1.00
72	*Jacquez Green*	3.50
73	Gus Frerotte	.20
74	Peter Boulware	.20
75	Jerry Rice	2.50
76	Antowain Smith	1.00
77	*Brian Simmons*	1.00
78	Rod Smith	.40
79	Marvin Harrison	.40
80	*Ryan Leaf*	7.00
81	Keenan McCardell	.20
82	Derrick Thomas	.20
83	Zach Thomas	.40
84	Ben Coates	.20
85	Rob Moore	.20
86	Wayne Chrebet	.20
87	Napoleon Kaufman	.75
88	Levon Kirkland	.20
89	Junior Seau	.40
90	Eddie George	2.00
91	Warren Moon	.40
92	*Anthony Simmons*	1.00
93	Steve McNair	1.25
94	Frank Sanders	.20
95	Joey Galloway	.75
96	Jamal Anderson	.75
97	Rae Carruth	.20
98	Curtis Conway	.40
99	*Greg Ellis*	1.00
100	Kordell Stewart	2.00
101	*Germane Crowell*	4.00
102	Mark Chmura	.40
103	Robert Smith	.40
104	Andre Hastings	.20
105	Reggie White	.40
106	Jessie Armstead	.20
107	Kevin Hardy	.20
108	*Robert Holcombe*	2.00
109	Garrison Hearst	.40
110	Jerome Bettis	.40
111	Reidel Anthony	.40
112	Michael Westbrook	.20
113	*Patrick Johnson*	1.00
114	Andre Reed	.20
115	*Charles Woodson*	4.00
116	*Takeo Spikes*	1.50
117	*Marcus Nash*	2.00
118	*Tavian Banks*	2.00
119	Tony Gonzalez	.40
120	Jake Plummer	2.00
121	*Tony Simmons*	2.50

122 Aaron Glenn .20
123 Ricky Watters .40
124 Kimble Anders .20
125 Barry Sanders 5.00
126 Terance Mathis .20
127 Wesley Walls .20
128 Bobby Engram .20
129 Johnnie Morton .20
130 Brett Favre 5.00
131 Brad Johnson .40
132 John Randle .20
133 Chris Sanders .20
134 *Joe Jurevicius* 2.00
135 Deion Sanders 1.00
136 Terrell Owens 1.00
137 Darrell Green .20
138 Jermaine Lewis .20
139 James Stewart .20
140 Troy Aikman 2.50
141 Hardy Nickerson .20
142 Blaine Bishop .20
143 *Keith Brooking* 2.00
144 *Jason Peter* 1.00
145 Jake Reed .20
146 Jason Sehorn .20
147 Robert Brooks .20
148 J.J. Stokes .40
149 Michael Strahan .20
150 Glenn Foley .40

1998 Topps Stars Galaxy

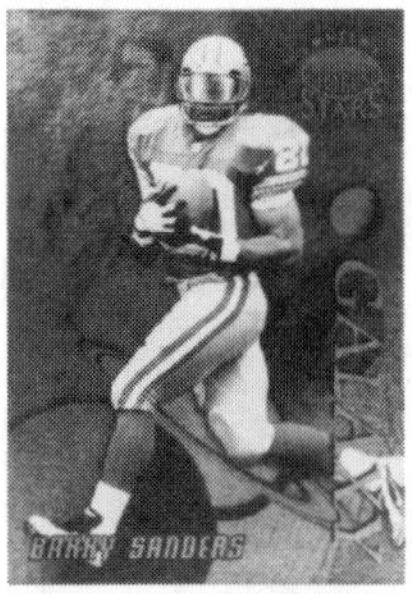

Each single in this set has the bronze foil, was sequentially numbered to 100 and inserted 1:611 packs. Silver foil cards were numbered to 75 and found 1:814 packs. Gold foil cards were numbered to 50 and inserted 1:1,222. Gold Rainbow singles were the toughest to find with only five printed and inserted 1:12,215.

MT
Complete Set (10): 750.00
Common Bronze Player: 25.00
Production 100 Sets
Inserted 1:611
Silver Cards: 1.5x
Production 75 Sets
Inserted 1:814
Gold Cards: 2x
Production 50 Sets
Inserted 1:1,222
G1 Brett Favre 200.00
G2 Barry Sanders 200.00
G3 Bruce Smith 25.00
G4 Herman Moore 50.00
G5 Tim Brown 50.00
G6 Steve Young 75.00
G7 Cris Carter 50.00
G8 John Elway 100.00
G9 Mark Brunell 100.00
G10 Terrell Davis 150.00

1998 Topps Stars Luminaries

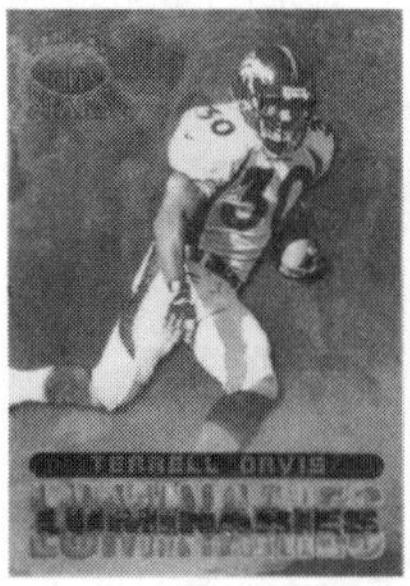

Each card in this set has bronze foil stamping and is sequentially numbered to 100. Singles were tough to pull from packs at 1:407. The Silver parallel set has the foil stamping in silver and is numbered to 75 and was inserted 1:543 packs. The Gold parallel was numbered to 50 and inserted 1:814 packs. The last parallel set was the Gold Rainbow that was limited to five of each and found 1:8,144.

MT
Complete Set (15): 850.00
Common Bronze Player: 25.00
Production 100 Sets
Inserted 1:407
Silver Cards: 1.5x
Production 75 Sets
Inserted 1:543
Gold Cards: 2x
Production 50 Sets
Inserted 1:814

L1 Brett Favre 120.00
L2 Steve Young 45.00
L3 John Elway 100.00
L4 Barry Sanders 120.00
L5 Terrell Davis 100.00
L6 Eddie George 50.00
L7 Herman Moore 25.00
L8 Tim Brown 25.00
L9 Jerry Rice 60.00
L10 Junior Seau 25.00
L11 Bruce Smith 25.00
L12 John Randle 25.00
L13 Peyton Manning 100.00
L14 Ryan Leaf 50.00
L15 Curtis Enis 35.00

1998 Topps Stars Rookie Reprints

Topps reprinted eight NFL Hall of Famers' rookie cards and inserted them 1:24 packs. Each card also has a parallel Autograph card with the odds at 1:153 packs.

MT
Complete Set (8): 30.00
Common Player: 2.00
Inserted 1:24
Autographs: 10x
Inserted 1:153
1 Walter Payton 10.00
2 Don Maynard 4.00
3 Charlie Joiner 4.00
4 Fred Biletnikoff 4.00
5 Paul Hornung 4.00
6 Gale Sayers 6.00
7 John Hannah 2.00
8 Paul Warfield 4.00

1998 Topps Stars Supernova

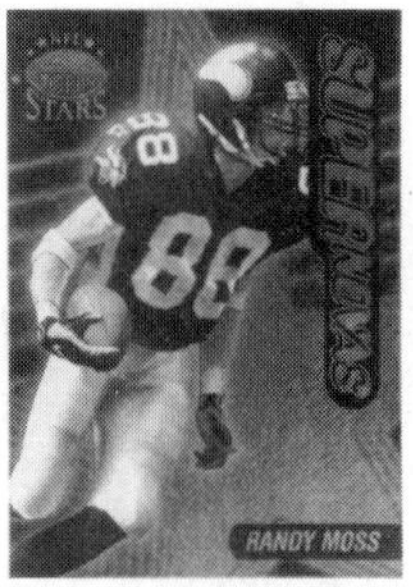

Each single in this set has the bronze foil, was sequentially numbered to 100 and inserted 1:611 packs. Silver foil cards were numbered to 75 and found 1:814 packs. Gold foil cards were numbered to 50 and inserted 1:1,222. Gold Rainbow singles were the toughest to find with only five printed and inserted 1:12,215.

MT
Complete Set (10): 750.00
Common Bronze Player: 25.00
Production 100 Sets
Inserted 1:611
Silver Cards: 1.5x
Production 75 Sets
Inserted 1:814
Gold Cards: 2x
Production 50 Sets
Inserted 1:1,222
S1 Ryan Leaf 50.00
S2 Curtis Enis 60.00
S3 Kevin Dyson 45.00
S4 Randy Moss 200.00
S5 Peyton Manning 100.00
S6 Duane Starks 25.00
S7 Grant Wistrom 25.00
S8 Charles Woodson 60.00
S9 Fred Taylor 100.00
S10 Andre Wadsworth 45.00

Rookie cards are italicized. Pricing for cards from 1980 and older is for Near Mint condition. 1981 cards and newer are priced as Mint.

1999 Topps

Each card in this 357-card set was printed on 16-pt. stock, with green borders and gold foil stamping. Included are 27 rookies that were seeded 1:5 packs. Other subsets include 10 Season Highlights and five Cleveland Browns Expansion Draft cards. Top inserts include: MVP Promotion, All Matrix, Autographs, Hall of Fame Autographs, Mystery Chrome, Picture Perfect, Record Numbers and Season's Best.

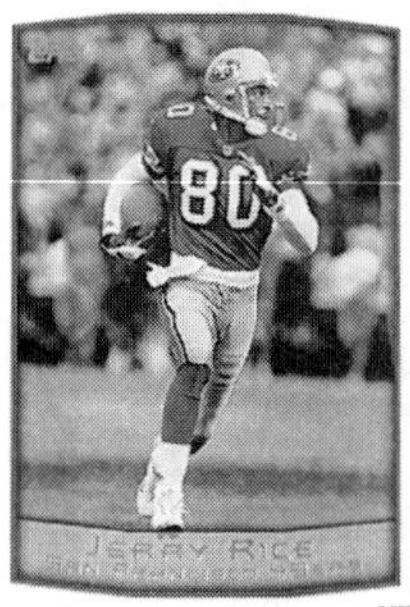

MT
Complete Set (357): 75.00
Common Player: .10
Minor Stars: .20
Common Rookie: 1.00
Inserted 1:5
Pack (11): 1.25
Wax Box (36): 48.00
Jumbo Pack (40): 5.00
Jumbo Wax Box (12): 55.00
Season Opener Pack (7): 1.00
Season Opener Wax Box (24): 20.00
1 Terrell Davis 1.50
2 Adrian Murrell .10
3 Ernie Mills .10
4 Jimmy Hitchcock .10
5 Charlie Garner .10
6 Blaine Bishop .10
7 Junior Seau .20
8 Andre Rison .20
9 Jake Reed .10
10 Cris Carter .40
11 Torrance Small .10
12 Ronald McKinnon .10
13 Tyrone Davis .10
14 Warren Moon .20
15 Joe Johnson .10
16 Bert Emanuel .10
17 Brad Culpepper .10
18 Henry Jones .10
19 Jonathan Ogden .10
20 Terrell Owens .40
21 Derrick Mason .10
22 Jon Ritchie .10
23 Eric Metcalf .10
24 Kevin Carter .10
25 Fred Taylor 1.00
26 DeWayne Washington .10
27 William Thomas .10
28 Raghib Ismail .10
29 Jason Taylor .10
30 Doug Flutie .50
31 Michael Sinclair .10
32 Yancey Thigpen .10
33 Darnay Scott .10
34 Amani Toomer .10
35 Edgar Bennett .10
36 LeRoy Butler .10
37 Jessie Tuggle .10
38 Andrew Glover .10
39 Tim McDonald .10
40 Marshall Faulk .40
41 Ray Mickens .10
42 Kimble Anders .10
43 Trent Green .40
44 Dermontti Dawson .10
45 Greg Ellis .10
46 Hugh Douglas .10
47 Amp Lee .10
48 Lamar Thomas .10
49 Curtis Conway .20
50 Emmitt Smith 1.50
51 Elvis Grbac .10
52 Tony Simmons .20
53 Darrin Smith .10
54 Donovin Darius .10
55 Corey Chavous .10
56 Phillippi Sparks .10
57 Luther Elliss .10
58 Tim Dwight .40
59 Andre Hastings .10
60 Dan Marino 1.50
61 Micheal Barrow .10
62 Corey Fuller .10
63 Bill Romanowski .10
64 Derrick Rodgers .10
65 Natrone Means .30
66 Peter Boulware .10
67 Brian Mitchell .10
68 Cornelius Bennett .10
69 Dedric Ward .10
70 Drew Bledsoe .75
71 Freddie Jones .10
72 Derrick Thomas .10
73 Willie Davis .10
74 Larry Centers .10
75 Mark Brunell .75
76 Chuck Smith .10
77 Desmond Howard .10
78 Sedrick Shaw .10
79 Tiki Barber .10
80 Curtis Martin .40
81 Barry Minter .10
82 Skip Hicks .20
83 O.J. Santiago .10
84 Ed McCaffrey .30
85 Terrell Buckley .10
86 Charlie Jones .10
87 Pete Mitchell .10
88 La'Roi Glover .10
89 Eric Davis .10
90 John Elway 1.50
91 Kavika Pittman .10
92 Fred Lane .10
93 Warren Sapp .10
94 Lorenzo Bromell .10
95 Lawyer Milloy .10
96 Aeneas Williams .10
97 Michael McCrary .10
98 Rickey Dudley .10
99 Bryce Paup .10
100 Jamal Anderson .50
101 D'Marco Farr .10
102 Johnnie Morton .10
103 Jeff Graham .10
104 Sam Cowart .10
105 Bryant Young .10
106 Jermaine Lewis .10
107 Chad Bratzke .10
108 Jeff Burris .10
109 Roell Preston .10
110 Vinny Testaverde .20
111 Ruben Brown .10
112 Darryll Lewis .10
113 Billy Davis .10
114 Bryant Westbrook .10
115 Stephen Alexander .10
116 Terrell Fletcher .10
117 Terry Glenn .30
118 Rod Smith .20
119 Carl Pickens .20
120 Tim Brown .20
121 Mikhael Ricks .10
122 Jason Gildon .10
123 Charles Way .10
124 Rob Moore .20
125 Jerome Bettis .30
126 Kerry Collins .20
127 Bruce Smith .10
128 James Hasty .10
129 Ken Norton Jr. .10
130 Charles Woodson .40
131 Tony McGee .10
132 Kevin Turner .10
133 Jerome Pathon .10
134 Garrison Hearst .30
135 Craig Newsome .10
136 Hardy Nickerson .10
137 Ray Lewis .10
138 Derrick Alexander .10
139 Phil Hansen .10
140 Joey Galloway .50
141 Oronde Gadsden .20
142 Herman Moore .30
143 Bobby Taylor .10
144 Mario Bates .10
145 Kevin Dyson .20
146 Aaron Glenn .10
147 Ed McDaniel .10
148 Terry Allen .20
149 Ike Hilliard .10
150 Steve Young .50
151 Eugene Robinson .10
152 John Mobley .10
153 Kevin Hardy .10
154 Lance Johnstone .10
155 Willie McGinest .10
156 Gary Anderson .10
157 Dexter Coakley .10
158 Mark Fields .10
159 Steve McNair .50
160 Corey Dillon .50
161 Zach Thomas .30
162 Kent Graham .10
163 Tony Parrish .10
164 Sam Gash .10
165 Kyle Brady .10
166 Donnell Bennett .10
167 Tony Martin .10
168 Michael Bates .10
169 Bobby Engram .10
170 Jimmy Smith .20
171 Vonnie Holliday .20
172 Simeon Rice .10
173 Kevin Greene .10
174 Mike Alstott .40
175 Eddie George .50
176 Michael Jackson .10
177 Neil O'Donnell .10
178 Sean Dawkins .10
179 Courtney Hawkins .10
180 Michael Irvin .20
181 Thurman Thomas .20
182 Cameron Cleeland .20
183 Ellis Johnson .10
184 Will Blackwell .10
185 Ty Law .10
186 Merton Hanks .10
187 Dan Wilkinson .10
188 Andre Wadsworth .20
189 Troy Vincent .10
190 Frank Sanders .20
191 Stephen Boyd .10
192 Jason Elam .10
193 Kordell Stewart .50
194 Ted Johnson .10
195 Glyn Milburn .10
196 Gary Brown .10
197 Travis Hall .10
198 John Randle .10
199 Jay Riemersma .10
200 Barry Sanders 2.00
201 Chris Spielman .10
202 Rod Woodson .10
203 Darrell Russell .10
204 Tony Boselli .10
205 Darren Woodson .10
206 Muhsin Muhammad .10
207 Jim Harbaugh .10
208 Isaac Bruce .30
209 Mo Lewis .10
210 Dorsey Levens .30
211 Frank Wycheck .10
212 Napoleon Kaufman .40
213 Walt Harris .10
214 Leon Lett .10
215 Karim Abdul .20
216 Carnell Lake .10
217 Byron Morris .10
218 John Avery .20
219 Chris Slade .10
220 Robert Smith .20
221 Mike Pritchard .10
222 Ty Detmer .10
223 Randall Cunningham .40
224 Alonzo Mayes .10
225 Jake Plummer 1.00
226 Derrick Mayes .10
227 Jeff Brady .10
228 John Lynch .10
229 Steve Atwater .10
230 Warrick Dunn .50
231 Shawn Jefferson .10
232 Erik Kramer .10
233 Ken Dilger .10
234 Ryan Leaf .40
235 Ray Buchanan .10
236 Kevin Williams .10
237 Ricky Watters .20
238 Dwayne Rudd .10
239 Duce Staley .10
240 Charlie Batch .50
241 Tim Biakabutuka .20
242 Tony Gonzalez .20
243 Bryan Still .10
244 Donnie Edwards .10
245 Troy Aikman 1.00
246 Az-Zahir Hakim .20
247 Curtis Enis .40
248 Chris Chandler .20
249 James Jett .10
250 Brett Favre 2.00
251 Keith Poole .10
252 Ricky Proel .10
253 Shannon Sharpe .20
254 Robert Jones .10
255 Chad Brown .10
256 Ben Coates .20
257 Jacquez Green .20
258 Jessie Armstead .10
259 Dale Carter .10
260 Antowain Smith .40
261 Mark Chmura .20
262 Michael Westbrook .20
263 Marvin Harrison .20
264 Darrien Gordon .10
265 Rodney Harrison .10
266 Charles Johnson .10
267 Roman Pfifer .10
268 Reidel Anthony .20
269 Jerry Rice 1.00
270 Eric Moulds .50
271 Rodney Porcher .10
272 Deion Sanders .40
273 Germane Crowell .20
274 Randy Moss 2.00
275 Antonio Freeman .40
276 Trent Dilfer .30
277 Eric Turner .10
278 Jeff George .20
279 Levon Kirkland .10
280 O.J. McDuffie .10
281 Takeo Spikes .10
282 Jim Flanigan .10
283 Chris Warren .10
284 J.J. Stokes .20
285 Bryan Cox .10
286 Sam Madison .10
287 Priest Holmes .40
288 Keenan McCardell .10
289 Michael Strahan .10
290 Robert Edwards .30
291 Tommy Vardell .10
292 Wayne Chrebet .40
293 Chris Calloway .10
294 Wesley Walls .10
295 Derrick Brooks .10
296 Trace Armstrong .10
297 Brian Simmons .10
298 Darrell Green .10
299 Robert Brooks .10
300 Peyton Manning 1.50
301 Dana Stubblefield .10
302 Shawn Springs .10
303 Leslie Shepherd .10
304 Ken Harvey .10
305 Jon Kitna .50
306 Terance Mathis .10
307 Andre Reed .20
308 Jackie Harris .10
309 Rich Gannon .10
310 Keyshawn Johnson .50
311 Victor Green .10
312 Eric Allen .10
313 Terry Fair .10
314 Season Highlights (Jason Elam) .10
315 Season Highlights (Garrison Hearst) .10
316 Season Highlights (Jake Plummer) .50
317 Season Highlights (Randall Cunningham) .20
318 Season Highlights (Randy Moss) 1.00
319 Season Highlights (Jamal Anderson) .20
320 Season Highlights (John Elway) .75
321 Season Highlights (Doug Flutie) .20
322 Season Highlights (Emmitt Smith) .50
323 Season Highlights (Terrell Davis) .75
324 Jerris McPhail .10
325 Damon Gibson .10
326 Jim Pyne .10
327 Antonio Langham .10
328 Freddie Solomon .10
329 *Ricky Williams* 10.00
330 *Daunte Culpepper* 12.00
331 *Chris Claiborne* 1.75
332 *Amos Zereoue* 3.00
333 *Chris McAlister* 1.00
334 *Kevin Faulk* 4.00
335 *James Johnson* 2.50
336 *Mike Cloud* 1.75
337 *Jevon Kearse* 4.00
338 *Akili Smith* 8.00
339 *Edgerrin James* 15.00
340 *Cecil Collins* 8.00
341 *Donovan McNabb* 8.00
342 *Kevin Johnson* 5.00
343 *Torry Holt* 5.00
344 *Rob Konrad* 1.00
345 *Tim Couch* 10.00
346 *David Boston* 5.00
347 *Karsten Bailey* 1.75
348 *Troy Edwards* 5.00
349 *Sedrick Irvin* 1.75
350 *Shaun King* 6.00
351 *Peerless Price* 3.00
352 *Brock Huard* 2.50
353 *Cade McNown* 4.00
354 *Champ Bailey* 2.50
355 *D'Wayne Bates* 1.00
356 Checklist .10
357 Checklist .10

1999 Topps All Matrix

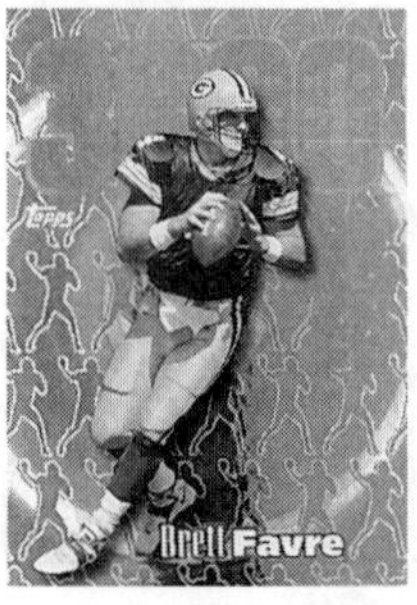

This 30-card insert is divided into three different subsets. 1200 Yard Club (10 running backs who rushed for 1200 yards or more), 3000 Yard Club (quarterbacks with rocket-arms) and '99 Rookie Rush (9 players from the 1999 NFL draft). Each is printed on dot matrix cards and were inserted 1:14 packs.

MT
Complete Set (30): 120.00
Common Player: 1.00
Minor Stars: 2.00
Inserted 1:14
1 1200 Yard Club (Fred Taylor) 6.00
2 1200 Yard Club (Ricky Watters) 2.00
3 1200 Yard Club (Curtis Martin) 3.00
4 1200 Yard Club (Eddie George) 4.00
5 1200 Yard Club (Marshall Faulk) 2.00
6 1200 Yard Club (Emmitt Smith) 8.00
7 1200 Yard Club (Barry Sanders) 12.00
8 1200 Yard Club (Garrison Hearst) 2.00
9 1200 Yard Club (Jamal Anderson) 2.00
10 1200 Yard Club (Terrell Davis) 10.00
11 3000 Yard Club (Chris Chandler) 1.00
12 3000 Yard Club (Steve McNair) 3.00
13 3000 Yard Club (Vinny Testaverde) 1.00
14 3000 Yard Club (Trent Green) 2.00
15 3000 Yard Club (Dan Marino) 8.00
16 3000 Yard Club (Drew Bledsoe) 5.00
17 3000 Yard Club (Randall Cunningham) 2.00
18 3000 Yard Club (Jake Plummer) 6.00
19 3000 Yard Club (Peyton Manning) 10.00
20 3000 Yard Club (Steve Young) 4.00
21 3000 Yard Club (Brett Favre) 12.00
22 99 Rookie Rush (Tim Couch) 15.00
23 99 Rookie Rush (Edgerrin James) 8.00
24 99 Rookie Rush (David Boston) 4.00
25 99 Rookie Rush (Akili Smith) 5.00
26 99 Rookie Rush (Troy Edwards) 2.00
27 99 Rookie Rush (Torry Holt) 3.00
28 99 Rookie Rush (Donovan McNabb) 5.00
29 99 Rookie Rush (Daunte Culpepper) 6.00
30 99 Rookie Rush (Ricky Williams) 15.00

1999 Topps Autographs

This 10-card set was a hobby exclusive that included 8 current stars and 2 top draft picks. Singles were found 1:509 packs except for the Ricky Williams single which was harder to find at 1:18,372.

MT
Complete Set (10): 900.00
Common Player: 25.00
Inserted 1:509
#A5 Inserted 1:18,372
1 Randy Moss 200.00
2 Wayne Chrebet 35.00
3 Tim Couch 150.00
4 Joey Galloway 35.00
5 Ricky Williams 425.00
6 Doug Flutie 50.00
7 Terrell Owens 50.00
8 Marshall Faulk 35.00
9 Rod Smith 25.00
10 Dan Marino 150.00

1999 Topps Hall of Fame Autographs

The five inductees into the Hall of Fame for 1999 are included in this autographed set. Singles were inserted 1:1,832 packs.

MT
Complete Set (5): 185.00
Common Player: 25.00
Inserted 1:1,832
1 Eric Dickerson 50.00
2 Billy Shaw 25.00
3 Lawrence Taylor 80.00
4 Tom Mack 25.00
5 Ozzie Newsome 40.00

1999 Topps Mystery Chrome

Each card in this 20-card set is printed on chrome technology and inserted 1:36 packs. A parallel Refractor version was also made and inserted 1:144 packs.

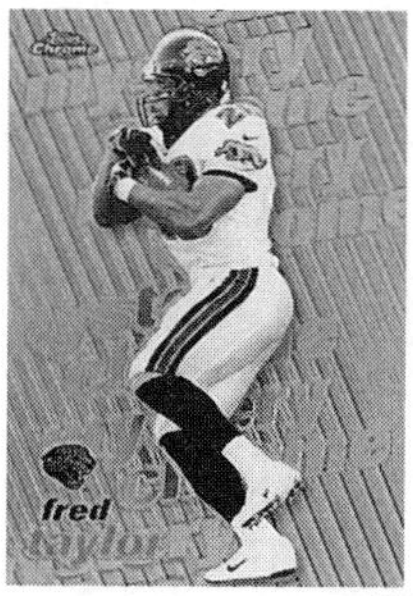

	MT
Complete Set (20):	135.00
Common Player:	3.00
Inserted 1:36	
Mystery Chrome Refractor:	3x
Inserted 1:144	

1	Terrell Davis	15.00
2	Steve Young	6.00
3	Fred Taylor	10.00
4	Chris Claiborne	3.00
5	Terrell Davis	15.00
6	Randall Cunningham	5.00
7	Charlie Batch	7.00
8	Fred Taylor	10.00
9	Vinny Testaverde	3.00
10	Jamal Anderson	3.00
11	Randy Moss	20.00
12	Keyshawn Johnson	5.00
13	Vinny Testaverde	3.00
14	Chris Chandler	3.00
15	Fred Taylor	10.00
16	Ricky Williams	25.00
17	Chris Chandler	3.00
18	John Elway	15.00
19	Randy Moss	20.00
20	Troy Edwards	6.00

1999 Topps Picture Perfect

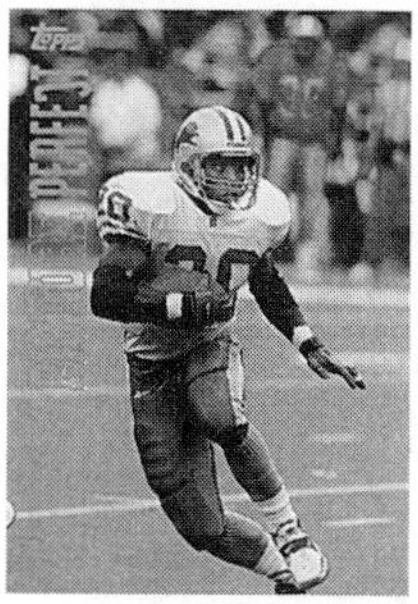

Each card in this 10-card set has an intentional error for collectors to find. A hint is printed on the back of each card and singles were inserted 1:14 packs.

	MT
Complete Set (10):	25.00
Common Player:	1.00
Inserted 1:14	

1	Steve Young	1.00
2	Brett Favre	6.00
3	Terrell Davis	4.00
4	Peyton Manning	4.00
5	Jake Plummer	3.00
6	Fred Taylor	3.00
7	Barry Sanders	6.00
8	Dan Marino	4.00
9	John Elway	4.00
10	Randy Moss	6.00

1999 Topps Record Numbers

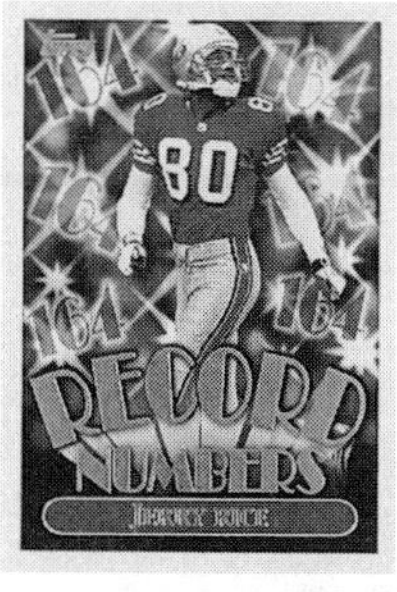

This set features 10 NFL Record Holders on a white stock card with silver foil. Singles were inserted 1:18 packs.

	MT
Complete Set (10):	35.00
Common Player:	1.00
Inserted 1:18	

1	Randy Moss	7.00
2	Terrell Davis	5.00
3	Emmitt Smith	5.00
4	Barry Sanders	7.00
5	Dan Marino	5.00
6	Brett Favre	7.00
7	Doug Flutie	2.00
8	Jerry Rice	3.50
9	Peyton Manning	4.00
10	Jason Elam	1.00

1999 Topps Season's Best

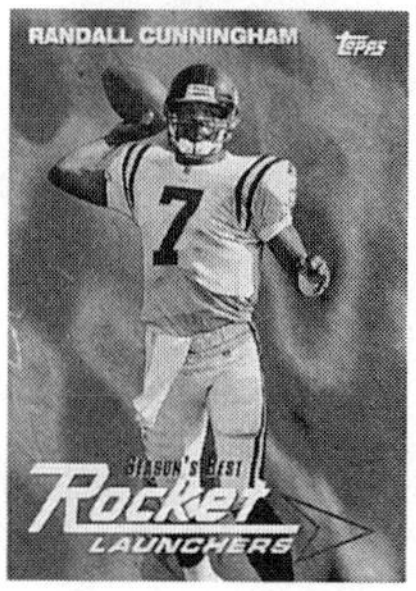

Thirty dominate players show their mettle in six categories printed on metallic foilboard. The following categories are: Bull Rushers (Running Backs), Rocket Launchers (Quarterbacks), Deep Threats (Wide Receivers), Power Packed (Defensive stars), Strike Force (Special Teams) and Career Best (top players). Singles were found 1:18 packs.

	MT
Complete Set (30):	100.00
Common Player:	1.00
Minor Stars:	2.00
Inserted 1:18	

1	Bull Rushers (Terrell Davis)	12.00
2	Bull Rushers (Jamal Anderson)	2.00
3	Bull Rushers (Garrison Hearst)	2.00
4	Bull Rushers (Barry Sanders)	15.00
5	Bull Rushers (Emmitt Smith)	10.00
6	Rocket Launchers (Randall Cunningham)	2.00
7	Rocket Launchers (Brett Favre)	15.00
8	Rocket Launchers (Steve Young)	5.00
9	Rocket Launchers (Jake Plummer)	8.00
10	Rocket Launchers (Peyton Manning)	12.00
11	Deep Threats (Antonio Freeman)	2.00
12	Deep Threats (Eric Moulds)	2.00
13	Deep Threats (Randy Moss)	15.00
14	Deep Threats (Rod Smith)	1.00
15	Deep Threats (Jimmy Smith)	1.00
16	Power Packed (Michael Sinclair)	1.00
17	Power Packed (Kevin Greene)	1.00
18	Power Packed (Michael Strahan)	1.00
19	Power Packed (Michael McCrary)	1.00
20	Power Packed (Hugh Douglas)	1.00
21	Strike Force (Deion Sanders)	3.00
22	Strike Force (Terry Fair)	1.00
23	Strike Force (Jacquez Green)	2.00
24	Strike Force (Corey Harris)	1.00
25	Strike Force (Tim Dwight)	3.00
26	Career Best (Dan Marino)	10.00
27	Career Best (Barry Sanders)	15.00
28	Career Best (Jerry Rice)	8.00
29	Career Best (Bruce Smith)	1.00
30	Career Best (Darrien Gordon)	1.00

1999 Topps Chrome

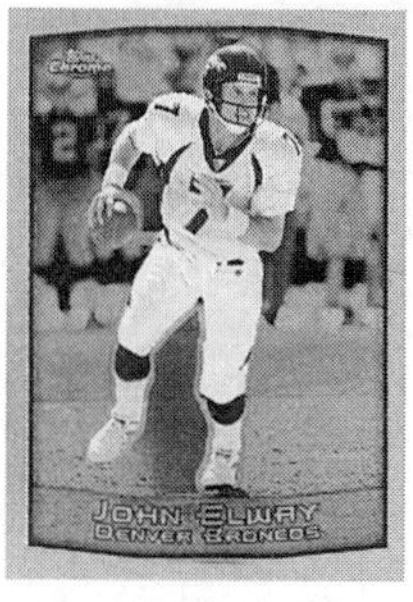

This 165-card set is the same as the regular Topps set except for each card is printed on a chromium card. For the first time in Topps Chrome the rookies were seeded 1:8 packs. Top inserts include: Refractors, All-Etch, Hall of Fame, Record Numbers and Season's Best. Each of the inserts also has a parallel Refractor version.

	MT
Complete Set (165):	700.00
Common Player:	.25
Minor Stars:	.50
Common Rookie:	6.00
Inserted 1:8	
Pack (4):	6.00
Wax Box (24):	120.00

1	Randy Moss	5.00
2	Keyshawn Johnson	1.00
3	Priest Holmes	1.25
4	Warren Moon	.50
5	Joey Galloway	1.00
6	Zach Thomas	.50
7	Cameron Cleeland	.50
8	Jim Harbaugh	.50
9	Napoleon Kaufman	1.00
10	Fred Taylor	2.50
11	Mark Brunell	2.00
12	Shannon Sharpe	.50
13	Jacquez Green	.50
14	Adrian Murrell	.50
15	Cris Carter	1.00
16	Marshall Faulk	1.00
17	Drew Bledsoe	2.00
18	Curtis Martin	1.25
19	Johnnie Morton	.25
20	Doug Flutie	1.50
21	Carl Pickens	.50
22	Jerome Bettis	1.00
23	Derrick Alexander	.25
24	Antowain Smith	1.00
25	Barry Sanders	5.00
26	Reidel Anthony	.50
27	Wayne Chrebet	1.00
28	Terance Mathis	.25
29	Shawn Springs	.25
30	Emmitt Smith	3.50
31	Robert Smith	1.00
32	Charles Johnson	.50
33	Mike Alstott	1.00
34	Ike Hilliard	.25
35	Ricky Watters	.75
36	Charles Woodson	1.00
37	Rod Smith	.50
38	Pete Mitchell	.25
39	Derrick Thomas	.50
40	Dan Marino	3.50
41	Darnay Scott	.50
42	Jake Reed	.50
43	Chris Chandler	.50
44	Dorsey Levens	1.00
45	Kordell Stewart	1.25
46	Eddie George	1.25
47	Corey Dillon	1.00
48	Rich Gannon	.25
49	Chris Spielman	.25
50	Jerry Rice	2.50
51	Trent Dilfer	.75
52	Mark Chmura	.50
53	Jimmy Smith	.50
54	Isaac Bruce	.50
55	Karim Abdul	.75
56	Sedrick Shaw	.25
57	Jake Plummer	2.50
58	Tony Gonzalez	.50
59	Ben Coates	.50
60	John Elway	3.50
61	Bruce Smith	.25
62	Tim Brown	.50
63	Tim Dwight	1.00
64	Yancey Thigpen	.50
65	Terrell Owens	1.00
66	Kyle Brady	.25
67	Tony Martin	.25
68	Michael Strahan	.25
69	Deion Sanders	1.00
70	Steve Young	1.50
71	Dale Carter	.25
72	Ty Law	.25
73	Frank Wycheck	.25
74	Marshall Faulk	1.00
75	Vinny Testaverde	.50
76	Chad Brown	.25
77	Natrone Means	.75
78	Bert Emanuel	.25
79	Kerry Collins	.50
80	Randall Cunningham	1.00
81	Garrison Hearst	1.00
82	Curtis Enis	1.00
83	Steve Atwater	.25
84	Kevin Greene	.25
85	Steve McNair	1.25
86	Andre Reed	.50
87	J.J. Stokes	.50
88	Eric Moulds	1.00
89	Marvin Harrison	.75
90	Troy Aikman	2.50
91	Herman Moore	.75
92	Michael Irvin	.50
93	Frank Sanders	.50
94	Duce Staley	.50
95	James Jett	.25
96	Ricky Proehl	.25
97	Andre Rison	.50
98	Leslie Shepherd	.25
99	Trent Green	.75
100	Terrell Davis	3.50
101	Freddie Jones	.25
102	Skip Hicks	1.00
103	Jeff Graham	.25
104	Rob Moore	.50
105	Torrance Small	.25
106	Antonio Freeman	1.00
107	Robert Brooks	.25
108	Jon Kitna	1.25
109	Curtis Conway	.50
110	Brett Favre	5.00
111	Warrick Dunn	1.25
112	Elvis Grbac	.50
113	Corey Fuller	.25
114	Rickey Dudley	.25
115	Jamal Anderson	1.00
116	Terry Glenn	.75
117	Raghib Ismail	.25
118	John Randle	.25
119	Chris Calloway	.25
120	Peyton Manning	3.50
121	Keenan McCardell	.25
122	O.J. McDuffie	.50
123	Ed McCaffrey	.50
124	Charlie Batch	1.25
125	Jason Elam (Season Highlights)	.25
126	Randy Moss (Season Highlights)	2.50
127	John Elway (Season Highlights)	1.50
128	Emmitt Smith (Season Highlights)	1.50
129	Terrell Davis (Season Highlights)	1.50
130	Jerris McPhail	.25
131	Damon Gibson	.25
132	Jim Pyne	.25
133	Antonio Langham	.25
134	Freddie Solomon	.25
135	*Ricky Williams*	50.00
136	*Daunte Culpepper*	70.00
137	*Chris Claiborne*	8.00
138	*Amos Zereoue*	10.00
139	*Chris McAlister*	6.00
140	*Kevin Faulk*	15.00
141	*James Johnson*	12.00
142	*Mike Cloud*	8.00
143	*Jevon Kearse*	25.00
144	*Akili Smith*	25.00
145	*Edgerrin James*	80.00
146	*Cecil Collins*	10.00
147	*Donovan McNabb*	40.00
148	*Kevin Johnson*	20.00
149	*Torry Holt*	30.00
150	*Rob Konrad*	8.00
151	*Tim Couch*	50.00
152	*David Boston*	20.00
153	*Karsten Bailey*	8.00
154	*Troy Edwards*	15.00
155	*Sedrick Irvin*	10.00
156	*Shaun King*	25.00
157	*Peerless Price*	12.00
158	*Brock Huard*	15.00
159	*Cade McNown*	15.00
160	*Champ Bailey*	12.00
161	*D'Wayne Bates*	6.00
162	*Joe Germaine*	10.00
163	*Andy Katzenmoyer*	8.00
164	*Antoine Winfield*	6.00
165	Checklist	.25

1999 Topps Chrome Refractors Parallel

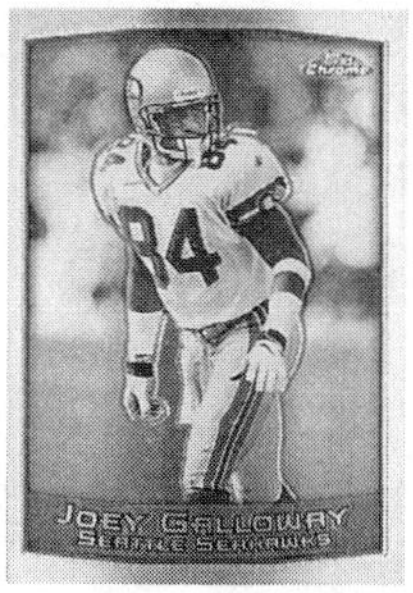

This is a parallel to the base with each single having a mirror shine to them. Singles were inserted 1:12 packs and rookies were found 1:32 packs.

	MT
Complete Set (165):	1800.
Refractor Cards:	6x-12x
Inserted 1:12	
Refractor Rookies:	2x
Inserted 1:32	

1999 Topps Chrome All Etch

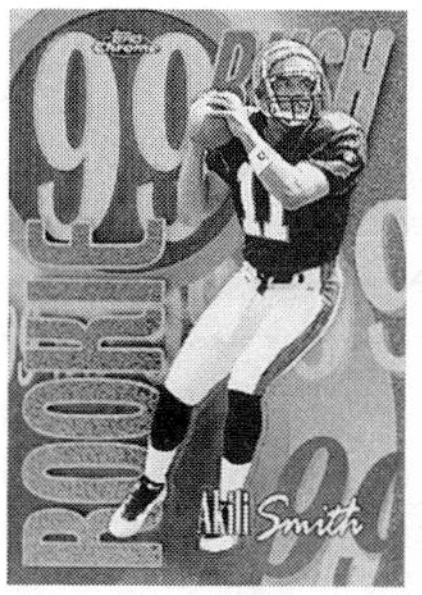

This 30-card insert is divided into three tiers with 1,200 Yard Club, 3,000 Yard Club and '99 Rookie Rush. Singles were inserted 1:24 packs and a Refractor version was also produced and found 1:120 packs.

	MT
Complete Set (30):	170.00
Common Player:	3.00
Minor Stars:	6.00
Inserted 1:24	
Refractors:	2x
Inserted 1:120	

1	Fred Taylor (1200 Yard Club)	12.00
2	Ricky Watters (1200 Yard Club)	3.00
3	Curtis Martin (1200 Yard Club)	6.00
4	Eddie George (1200 Yard Club)	6.00
5	Marshall Faulk (1200 Yard Club)	3.00
6	Emmitt Smith (1200 Yard Club)	18.00
7	Barry Sanders (1200 Yard Club)	25.00
8	Garrison Hearst (1200 Yard Club)	3.00
9	Jamal Anderson (1200 Yard Club)	3.00
10	Terrell Davis (1200 Yard Club)	18.00
11	Chris Chandler (3000 Yard Club)	3.00
12	Steve McNair (3000 Yard Club)	6.00
13	Vinny Testaverde (3000 Yard Club)	3.00
14	Trent Green (3000 Yard Club)	3.00
15	Dan Marino (3000 Yard Club)	18.00
16	Drew Bledsoe (3000 Yard Club)	10.00
17	Randall Cunningham (3000 Yard Club)	6.00
18	Jake Plummer (3000 Yard Club)	12.00
19	Peyton Manning (3000 Yard Club)	18.00
20	Steve Young (3000 Yard Club)	8.00
21	Brett Favre (3000 Yard Club)	25.00
22	Tim Couch (99 Rookie Rushers)	30.00
23	Edgerrin James (99 Rookie Rushers)	15.00
24	David Boston (99 Rookie Rushers)	8.00
25	Akili Smith (99 Rookie Rushers)	10.00
26	Troy Edwards (99 Rookie Rushers)	8.00
27	Torry Holt (99 Rookie Rushers)	8.00
28	Donovan McNabb (99 Rookie Rushers)	10.00
29	Daunte Culpepper (99 Rookie Rushers)	10.00
30	Ricky Williams (99 Rookie Rushers)	30.00

1999 Topps Chrome Hall of Fame

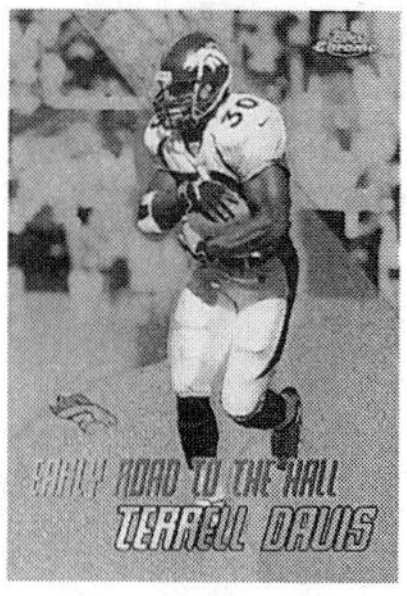

This is a 30-card set of players that are gunning for a spot in Canton, Ohio. The set is divided into three categories (Hall Bound, Early Road to the Hall and Hall Hopefuls) each with a different card design. Hall Bound showcases veterans, Early Road to the Hall features young stars and Hall Hopefuls contains '99 draft picks. Singles were found 1:29 packs and Refractors were sequentially numbered to 100.

	MT
Complete Set (30):	200.00
Common Player:	3.00
Minor Stars:	6.00
Inserted 1:29	
Refractors:	4x
Inserted 1:485	
Production 100 Sets	

1	Akili Smith (Hall Hopefuls)	10.00
2	Troy Edwards (Hall Hopefuls)	8.00
3	Donovan McNabb (Hall Hopefuls)	10.00
4	Cade McNown (Hall Hopefuls)	10.00
5	Ricky Williams (Hall Hopefuls)	30.00
6	David Boston (Hall Hopefuls)	8.00
7	Daunte Culpepper (Hall Hopefuls)	10.00
8	Edgerrin James (Hall Hopefuls)	15.00
9	Torry Holt (Hall Hopefuls)	8.00
10	Tim Couch (Hall Hopefuls)	30.00
11	Terrell Davis (Early Road To)	18.00
12	Fred Taylor (Early Road To)	12.00
13	Antonio Freeman (Early Road To)	3.00
14	Jamal Anderson (Early Road To)	3.00
15	Randy Moss (Early Road To)	25.00
16	Joey Galloway (Early Road To)	3.00
17	Eddie George (Early Road To)	3.00
18	Jake Plummer (Early Road To)	12.00
19	Curtis Martin (Early Road To)	3.00
20	Peyton Manning (Early Road To)	18.00
21	Barry Sanders (Hall Bound)	25.00
22	Steve Young (Hall Bound)	8.00
23	Cris Carter (Hall Bound)	3.00
24	Emmitt Smith (Hall Bound)	18.00
25	John Elway (Hall Bound)	18.00
26	Drew Bledsoe (Hall Bound)	10.00
27	Troy Aikman (Hall Bound)	12.00
28	Brett Favre (Hall Bound)	25.00
29	Jerry Rice (Hall Bound)	12.00
30	Dan Marino (Hall Bound)	18.00

1999 Topps Chrome Record Numbers

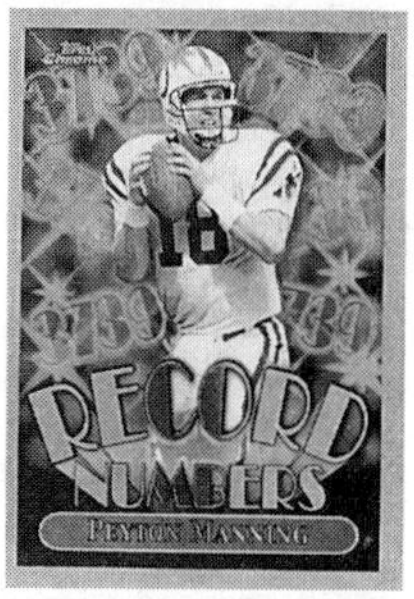

This was a 10-card insert set that included the top players in the game. Singles were inserted 1:72 packs. A parallel Refractor version was also released and found 1:360 packs.

	MT
Complete Set (10):	120.00
Common Player:	4.00
Inserted 1:72	
Refractors:	2x
Inserted 1:360	

1	Randy Moss	25.00
2	Terrell Davis	18.00
3	Emmitt Smith	18.00
4	Barry Sanders	25.00
5	Dan Marino	18.00
6	Brett Favre	25.00
7	Doug Flutie	8.00
8	Jerry Rice	12.00
9	Peyton Manning	15.00
10	Jason Elam	4.00

1999 Topps Chrome Season's Best

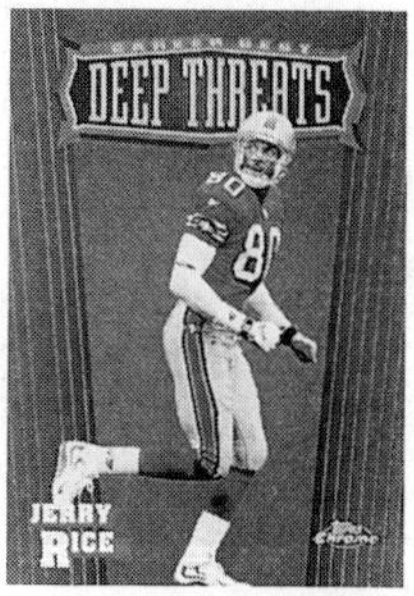

The 30-card set is divided into six categories. Bull Rushers, Rocket Launchers, Deep Threats, Power Packed, Strike Force and Career Best. Each has a different design and was inserted 1:24 packs. A Refractor version was also produced and inserted 1:120 packs.

	MT
Complete Set (30):	125.00
Common Player:	3.00
Minor Stars:	6.00
Inserted 1:24	
Refractors:	2x
Inserted 1:120	

1	Terrell Davis (Bull Rushers)	18.00
2	Jamal Anderson (Bull Rushers)	6.00
3	Garrison Hearst (Bull Rushers)	6.00
4	Barry Sanders (Bull Rushers)	25.00
5	Emmitt Smith (Bull Rushers)	18.00
6	Randall Cunningham (Rocket Launchers)	6.00
7	Brett Favre (Rocket Launchers)	25.00
8	Steve Young (Rocket Launchers)	8.00
9	Jake Plummer (Rocket Launchers)	12.00
10	Peyton Manning (Rocket Launchers)	18.00
11	Antonio Freeman (Deep Threats)	6.00
12	Eric Moulds (Deep Threats)	6.00
13	Randy Moss (Deep Threats)	25.00
14	Rod Smith (Deep Threats)	3.00
15	Jimmy Smith (Deep Threats)	3.00
16	Michael Sinclair (Power Packed)	3.00
17	Kevin Greene (Power Packed)	3.00
18	Michael Strahan (Power Packed)	3.00
19	Michael McCrary (Power Packed)	3.00

20 Hugh Douglas (Power Packed) 3.00
21 Deion Sanders (Strike Force) 6.00
22 Terry Fair (Strike Force) 3.00
23 Jacquez Green (Strike Force) 3.00
24 Corey Harris (Strike Force) 3.00
25 Tim Dwight (Stike Force) 6.00
26 Dan Marino (Career Best) 18.00
27 Barry Sanders (Career Best) 25.00
28 Jerry Rice (Career Best) 12.00
29 Bruce Smith (Career Best) 3.00
30 Darrien Gordon (Career Best) 3.00

1999 Topps Collection

This was a 357-card set that paralleled the regular Topps issue. Each single in this set included the "Topps Collection" gold foil stamp on the fronts of the cards. They were issued in factory set form and SRP was $29.00.

MT
Complete Set (357): 50.00
Common Player: .10
Minor Stars: .20
Common Rookie: 2.00
1 Terrell Davis 1.50
2 Adrian Murrell .10
3 Ernie Mills .10
4 Jimmy Hitchcock .10
5 Charlie Garner .10
6 Blaine Bishop .10
7 Junior Seau .20
8 Andre Rison .20
9 Jake Reed .20
10 Cris Carter .50
11 Torrance Small .10
12 Ronald McKinnon .10
13 Tyrone Davis .10
14 Warren Moon .20
15 Joe Johnson .10
16 Bert Emanuel .20
17 Brad Culpepper .10
18 Henry Jones .10
19 Jonathan Ogden .10
20 Terrell Owens .50
21 Derrick Mason .10
22 Jon Ritchie .10
23 Eric Metcalf .10
24 Kevin Carter .10
25 Fred Taylor 1.00
26 DeWayne Washington .10
27 William Thomas .10
28 Raghib Ismail .10
29 Jason Taylor .10
30 Doug Flutie .50
31 Michael Sinclair .10
32 Yancey Thigpen .20
33 Darnay Scott .20
34 Amani Toomer .10
35 Edgar Bennett .10
36 LeRoy Butler .10
37 Jessie Tuggle .10
38 Andrew Glover .10
39 Tim McDonald .10
40 Marshall Faulk .50
41 Ray Mickens .10
42 Kimble Anders .10
43 Trent Green .20
44 Dermontti Dawson .10
45 Greg Ellis .10
46 Hugh Douglas .10
47 Amp Lee .10
48 Lamar Thomas .10
49 Curtis Conway .20
50 Emmitt Smith 1.50
51 Elvis Grbac .20
52 Tony Simmons .20
53 Darrin Smith .10
54 Donovin Darius .10
55 Corey Chavous .10
56 Phillippi Sparks .10
57 Luther Elliss .10
58 Tim Dwight .50
59 Andre Hastings .10
60 Dan Marino 1.50
61 Michael Barrow .10
62 Corey Fuller .10
63 Bill Romanowski .10
64 Derrick Rodgers .10
65 Natrone Means .20
66 Peter Boulware .10
67 Brian Mitchell .10
68 Cornelius Bennett .10
69 Dedric Ward .10
70 Drew Bledsoe .75
71 Freddie Jones .10
72 Derrick Thomas .20
73 Willie Davis .10
74 Larry Centers .10
75 Mark Brunell .75
76 Chuck Smith .10
77 Desmond Howard .10
78 Sedrick Shaw .10
79 Tiki Barber .20
80 Curtis Martin .50
81 Barry Minter .10
82 Skip Hicks .20
83 O.J. Santiago .10
84 Ed McCaffrey .30
85 Terrell Buckley .10
86 Charlie Jones .10
87 Pete Mitchell .10
88 La'Roi Glover .10
89 Eric Davis .10
90 John Elway 1.50
91 Kavika Pittman .10
92 Fred Lane .20
93 Warren Sapp .20
94 Lorenzo Bromell .10
95 Lawyer Milloy .10
96 Aeneas Williams .10
97 Michael McCrary .10
98 Rickey Dudley .20
99 Bryce Paup .10
100 Jamal Anderson .50
101 D'Marco Farr .10
102 Johnnie Morton .10
103 Jeff Graham .10
104 Sam Cowart .10
105 Bryant Young .10
106 Jermaine Lewis .10
107 Chad Bratzke .10
108 Jeff Burris .10
109 Roell Preston .10
110 Vinny Testaverde .30
111 Ruben Brown .10
112 Darryll Lewis .10
113 Billy Davis .10
114 Bryant Westbrook .10
115 Stephen Alexander .10
116 Terrell Fletcher .10
117 Terry Glenn .50
118 Rod Smith .30
119 Carl Pickens .20
120 Tim Brown .30
121 Mikhael Ricks .10
122 Jason Gildon .10
123 Charles Way .10
124 Rob Moore .20
125 Jerome Bettis .50
126 Kerry Collins .20
127 Bruce Smith .20
128 James Hasty .10
129 Ken Norton Jr. .10
130 Charles Woodson .50
131 Tony McGee .10
132 Kevin Turner .10
133 Jerome Pathon .10
134 Garrison Hearst .30
135 Craig Newsome .10
136 Hardy Nickerson .10
137 Ray Lewis .10
138 Derrick Alexander .10
139 Phil Hansen .10
140 Joey Galloway .50
141 Oronde Gadsden .20
142 Herman Moore .30
143 Bobby Taylor .10
144 Mario Bates .10
145 Kevin Dyson .20
146 Aaron Glenn .10
147 Ed McDaniel .10
148 Terry Allen .20
149 Ike Hilliard .20
150 Steve Young .75
151 Eugene Robinson .10
152 John Mobley .10
153 Kevin Hardy .10
154 Lance Johnstone .10
155 Willie McGinest .10
156 Gary Anderson .10
157 Dexter Coakley .10
158 Mark Fields .10
159 Steve McNair .75
160 Corey Dillon .50
161 Zach Thomas .20
162 Kent Graham .10
163 Tony Parrish .10
164 Sam Gash .10
165 Kyle Brady .10
166 Donnell Bennett .10
167 Tony Martin .20
168 Michael Bates .10
169 Bobby Engram .10
170 Jimmy Smith .50
171 Vonnie Holliday .10
172 Simeon Rice .10
173 Kevin Greene .10
174 Mike Alstott .50
175 Eddie George .75
176 Michael Jackson .10
177 Neil O'Donnell .20
178 Sean Dawkins .10
179 Courtney Hawkins .10
180 Michael Irvin .20
181 Thurman Thomas .20
182 Cameron Cleeland .20
183 Ellis Johnson .10
184 Will Blackwell .10
185 Ty Law .10
186 Merton Hanks .10
187 Dan Wilkinson .10
188 Andre Wadsworth .10
189 Troy Vincent .10
190 Frank Sanders .20
191 Stephen Boyd .10
192 Jason Elam .10
193 Kordell Stewart .50
194 Ted Johnson .10
195 Glyn Milburn .10
196 Gary Brown .10
197 Travis Hall .10
198 John Randle .10
199 Jay Riemersma .10
200 Barry Sanders 2.00
201 Chris Spielman .10
202 Rod Woodson .10
203 Darrell Russell .10
204 Tony Boselli .10
205 Darren Woodson .10
206 Muhsin Muhammed .20
207 Jim Harbaugh .20
208 Isaac Bruce .50
209 Mo Lewis .10
210 Dorsey Levens .50
211 Frank Wycheck .10
212 Napoleon Kaufman .50
213 Walt Harris .10
214 Leon Lett .10
215 Karim Abdul .20
216 Carnell Lake .10
217 Byron Morris .10
218 John Avery .20
219 Chris Slade .10
220 Robert Smith .50
221 Mike Pritchard .10
222 Ty Detmer .10
223 Randall Cunningham .50
224 Alonzo Mayes .10
225 Jake Plummer .75
226 Derrick Mayes .20
227 Jeff Brady .10
228 John Lynch .10
229 Steve Atwater .10
230 Warrick Dunn .50
231 Shawn Jefferson .10
232 Erik Kramer .10
233 Ken Dilger .10
234 Ryan Leaf .50
235 Ray Buchanan .10
236 Kevin Williams .10
237 Ricky Watters .30
238 Dwayne Rudd .10
239 Duce Staley .50
240 Charlie Batch .75
241 Tim Biakabutuka .20
242 Tony Gonzalez .30
243 Bryan Still .10
244 Donnie Edwards .10
245 Troy Aikman 1.00
246 Az-Zahir Hakim .20
247 Curtis Enis .50
248 Chris Chandler .20
249 James Jett .10
250 Brett Favre 2.00
251 Keith Poole .10
252 Ricky Proehl .10
253 Shannon Sharpe .20
254 Robert Jones .10
255 Chad Brown .10
256 Ben Coates .20
257 Jacquez Green .20
258 Jessie Armstead .10
259 Dale Carter .10
260 Antowain Smith .30
261 Mark Chmura .20
262 Michael Westbrook .20
263 Marvin Harrison .50
264 Darrien Gordon .10
265 Rodney Harrison .10
266 Charles Johnson .10
267 Roman Pfifer .10
268 Reidel Anthony .20
269 Jerry Rice 1.00
270 Eric Moulds .50
271 Robert Porcher .10
272 Deion Sanders .30
273 Germane Crowell .30
274 Randy Moss 2.00
275 Antonio Freeman .50
276 Trent Dilfer .20
277 Eric Turner .10
278 Jeff George .30
279 Levon Kirkland .10
280 O.J. McDuffie .20
281 Takeo Spikes .10
282 Jim Flanigan .10
283 Chris Warren .10
284 J.J. Stokes .20
285 Bryan Cox .10
286 Sam Madison .10
287 Priest Holmes .50
288 Keenan McCardell .20
289 Michael Strahan .10
290 Robert Edwards .30
291 Tommy Vardell .10
292 Wayne Chrebet .30
293 Chris Calloway .10
294 Wesley Walls .20
295 Derrick Brooks .10
296 Trace Armstrong .10
297 Brian Simmons .10
298 Darrell Green .10
299 Robert Brooks .10
300 Peyton Manning 1.75
301 Dana Stubblefield .10
302 Shawn Springs .10
303 Leslie Shepherd .10
304 Ken Harvey .10
305 Jon Kitna .50
306 Terance Mathis .10
307 Andre Reed .20
308 Jackie Harris .10
309 Rich Gannon .20
310 Keyshawn Johnson .50
311 Victor Green .10
312 Eric Allen .10
313 Terry Fair .10
314 Jason Elam .10
315 Garrison Hearst .10
316 Jake Plummer .30
317 Randall Cunningham .20
318 Randy Moss 1.00
319 Jamal Anderson .25
320 John Elway .75
321 Doug Flutie .30
322 Emmitt Smith .75
323 Terrell Davis .75
324 Jerris McPhail .10
325 Damon Gibson .10
326 Jim Pyne .10
327 Antonio Langham .10
328 Freddie Solomon .10
329 *Ricky Williams* 10.00
330 *Daunte Culpepper* 10.00
331 *Chris Claiborne* 2.00
332 *Amos Zereoue* 2.00
333 *Chris McAlister* 2.00
334 *Kevin Faulk* 3.00
335 *James Johnson* 3.00
336 *Mike Cloud* 2.00
337 *Jevon Kearse* 5.00
338 *Akili Smith* 6.00
339 *Edgerrin James* 20.00
340 *Cecil Collins* 3.00
341 *Donovan McNabb* 8.00
342 *Kevin Johnson* 6.00
343 *Torry Holt* 6.00
344 *Rob Konrad* 2.00
345 *Tim Couch* 12.00
346 *David Boston* 5.00
347 *Karsten Bailey* 2.00
348 *Troy Edwards* 5.00
349 *Sedrick Irvin* 2.00
350 *Shaun King* 8.00
351 *Peerless Price* 4.00
352 *Brock Huard* 3.00
353 *Cade McNown* 3.50
354 *Champ Bailey* 3.00
355 *D'Wayne Bates* 2.00
356 Checklist .10
357 Checklist .10

1999 Topps Gold Label

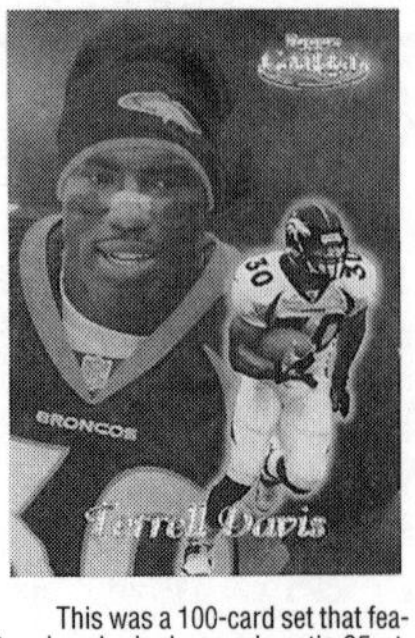

This was a 100-card set that featured each single on prismatic 35-pt. spectral-reflective rainbow stock with the player's name and the Gold Label logo in gold foil. Each player had two other singles with a different photo on the foreground of each card. Each of those cards then had a parallel Black and Red Class issue. The Race to Gold insert also has a Black and Red Class parallels. SRP was $3.99 for four-card packs.

MT
Complete Set (100): 100.00
Common Player: .25
Minor Stars: .50
Common Rookie: 1.00
Class 2 Cards: 2x
Class 2 Rookies: 1x
Inserted 1:2
Class 3 Cards: 3x
Class 3 Rookies: 1.5x
Inserted 1:4
Pack (4): 4.00
Wax Box (24): 85.00
1 Terrell Davis 3.00
2 Jake Plummer 2.00
3 *Michael Cloud* 2.00
4 *D'Wayne Bates* 2.00
5 Jamal Anderson 1.00
6 *Cecil Collins* 6.00
7 Keyshawn Johnson 1.00
8 Jerome Bettis 1.00
9 Ricky Watters .50
10 Brett Favre 4.00
11 *Joe Germaine* 3.00
12 Eddie George 1.00
13 *Jevon Kearse* 4.00
14 Skip Hicks .50
15 *James Johnson* 3.00
16 Terry Glenn 1.00
17 *Troy Edwards* 4.00
18 *Karsten Bailey* 1.00
19 Trent Dilfer .50
20 Barry Sanders 4.00
21 Vinny Testaverde .50
22 Ed McCaffrey .75
23 Shannon Sharpe .50
24 Robert Smith 1.00
25 Emmitt Smith 3.00
26 Rob Moore .50
27 J.J. Stokes .50
28 *Champ Bailey* 3.00
29 Napoleon Kaufman .75
30 Fred Taylor 2.00
31 Corey Dillon 1.00
32 *Sedrick Irvin* 2.50
33 *Chris McAlister* 1.00
34 Warrick Dunn 1.00
35 Isaac Bruce 1.00
36 *Peerless Price* 3.00
37 Dorsey Levens 1.00
38 Wayne Chrebet .75
39 Randall Cunningham 1.00
40 Dan Marino 3.00
41 Chris Chandler .25
42 Mark Brunell 1.50
43 *Kevin Johnson* 4.00
44 Natrone Means .50
45 Jerome Pathon .25
46 *Daunte Culpepper* 10.00
47 *Akili Smith* 5.00
48 Keenan McCardell .50
49 Steve McNair 1.00
50 Randy Moss 4.00
51 Terance Mathis .25
52 Eric Moulds 1.00
53 Raghib Ismail .25
54 *Cade McNown* 4.00
55 Kordell Stewart 1.25
56 *Rob Konrad* 2.00
57 Andre Rison .50
58 Curtis Conway .50
59 *Chris Claiborne* 2.00
60 Jerry Rice 2.00
61 Peyton Manning 3.00
62 Jimmy Smith 1.00
63 Doug Flutie 1.25
64 Frank Sanders .50
65 Antowain Smith .50
66 Curtis Enis 1.00
67 Charlie Batch 1.50
68 Marvin Harrison 1.00
69 Garrison Hearst .75
70 *Ricky Williams* 12.00
71 *Torry Holt* 4.00
72 Mike Alstott 1.00
73 Drew Bledsoe 1.50
74 O.J. McDuffie .50
75 *Donovan McNabb* 6.00
76 Curtis Martin 1.00
77 Priest Holmes 1.00
78 Antonio Freeman 1.00
79 Herman Moore 1.00
80 *Tim Couch* 12.00
81 Troy Aikman 2.00
82 *David Boston* 4.00
83 Tim Brown .50
84 *Kevin Faulk* 3.00
85 Cris Carter 1.00
86 Marshall Faulk 1.00
87 *Shaun King* 4.00
88 Terrell Owens 1.00
89 Carl Pickens .50
90 Steve Young 1.25
91 Rod Smith .75
92 Michael Irvin .50
93 Ike Hilliard .25
94 Jon Kitna 1.25
95 *Brock Huard* 3.00
96 Joey Galloway 1.00
97 *Amos Zereoue* 3.00
98 Duce Staley .75
99 John Elway 3.00
100 *Edgerrin James* 15.00

1999 Topps Gold Label Black Label

Each of the three Classes has a parallel Black Label card. The player's name and Topps Gold Label logo are in black foil. Class 1 singles were found 1:8 packs, Class 2 singles at 1:16 and Class 3 cards at 1:32.

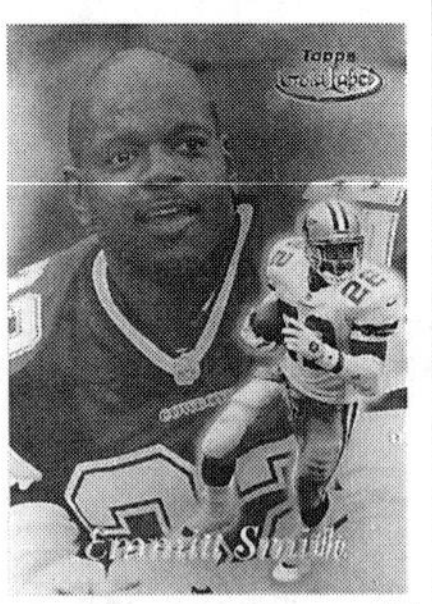

MT
Class 1 Cards: 4x
Class 1 Rookies: 1.5x
Inserted 1:8
Class 2 Cards: 8x
Class 2 Rookies: 3x
Inserted 1:16
Class 3 Cards: 12x
Class 3 Rookies: 5x
Inserted 1:32

1999 Topps Gold Label Red Label

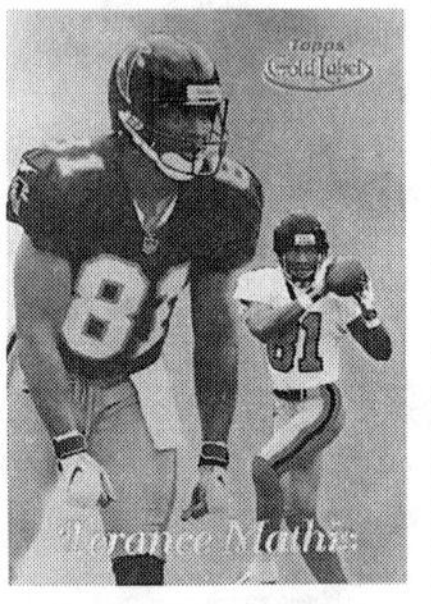

Each of the three Classes has a parallel Red Label card. The player's name and Topps Gold Label logo are in red foil. Class 1 singles were found 1:79 packs and were sequentially numbered to 100. Class 2 singles were inserted 1:157 and were numbered to 50. Class 3 singles were inserted 1:314 and numbered to 25.

MT
Class 1 Cards: 10x-20x
Class 1 Rookies: 4x-8x
Inserted 1:79
Production 100 Sets
Class 2 Cards: 15x-30x
Class 2 Rookies: 6x-12x
Inserted 1:157
Production 50 Sets
Class 3 Cards: 25x-50x
Class 3 Rookies: 10x-20x
Inserted 1:314
Production 25 Sets

1999 Topps Gold Label Race to Gold

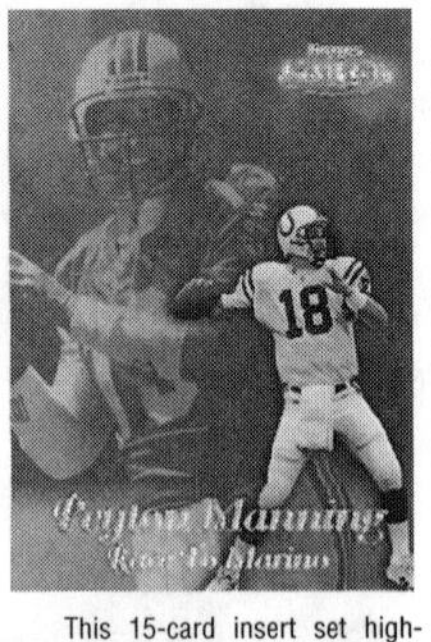

This 15-card insert set highlighted three players: Dan Marino, Walter Payton and Jerry Rice. Each player had five cards and was pictured with a current player who had the best chance of breaking a record that the original player owned. Singles were inserted 1:12 packs. Each single had a parallel Black Label version that was inserted 1:48 packs. Each also had a parallel Red Label version with #1-#5 inserted 1:11,867 and numbered to 13. Cards #6-#10 were found 1:4,638 and numbered to 34. Cards #11-#15 were found 1:1,968 and numbered to 80.

MT
Complete Set (15): 65.00
Common Player: 1.50
Minor Stars: 3.00
Inserted 1:12
Black Label Cards: 2x
Inserted 1:48
Red Label Cards (1-5): 20x-40x
Inserted 1:11,867
Red Label Cards (6-10): 12x-24x
Inserted 1:4,638
Red Label Cards (11-15): 5x-10x
Inserted 1:1,968
1 Brett Favre 12.00
2 Peyton Manning 10.00
3 Drew Bledsoe 5.00
4 Randall Cunningham 3.00
5 Jake Plummer 6.00
6 Emmitt Smith 8.00
7 Terrell Davis 8.00
8 Barry Sanders 12.00
9 Eddie George 4.00
10 Curtis Martin 3.00
11 Antonio Freeman 3.00
12 Eric Moulds 3.00
13 Joey Galloway 3.00
14 Rod Smith 1.50
15 Randy Moss 12.00

1999 Topps Season Opener

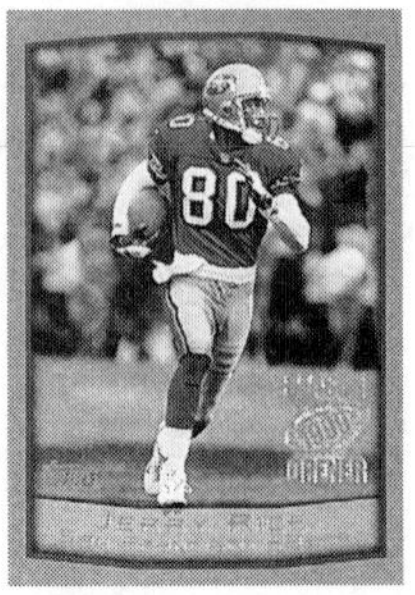

Topps Season Opener Football was a retail exclusive 165-card set that used the same photos as the regular Topps set but had blue borders and a Season Opener stamp in silver foil rather than green borders in the regular issue.

MT
Complete Set (165): 60.00
Common Player: .10
Minor Stars: .20
Common Rookie: 1.50
Pack (6): 2.00
Wax Box (24): 50.00
1 Jerry Rice 1.00
2 Emmitt Smith 1.50
3 Curtis Martin .30
4 Ed McCaffrey .20
5 Oronde Gadsden .20
6 Byron Morris .20
7 Michael Irvin .20
8 Shannon Sharpe .20
9 Levon Kirkland .10
10 Fred Taylor 1.00
11 Andre Reed .20
12 Chad Brown .10
13 Skip Hicks .20
14 Tim Dwight .30
15 Michael Sinclair .10
16 Carl Pickens .20
17 Derrick Alexander .10
18 Kevin Green .10
19 Duce Staley .20
20 Dan Marino 1.50
21 Frank Sanders .20
22 Ricky Proehl .10
23 Frank Wycheck .10
24 Andre Rison .20
25 Natrone Means .20
26 Steve McNair .30
27 Vonnie Holliday .20
28 Charles Woodson .30
29 Rob Moore .20
30 John Elway 1.50
31 Derrick Thomas .20
32 Jake Plummer .75
33 Mike Alstott .30
34 Keenan McCardell .20
35 Mark Chmura .20
36 Keyshawn Johnson .30
37 Priest Holmes .30
38 Antonio Freeman .30
39 Ty Law .10
40 Jamal Anderson .30
41 Courtney Hawkins .10
42 James Jett .10
43 Aaron Glenn .10
44 Jimmy Smith .20
45 Michael McCrary .10
46 Junior Seau .20
47 Bill Romanowski .10
48 Mark Brunell .75
49 Yancey Thigpen .20
50 Steve Young .75
51 Cris Carter .30
52 Vinny Testaverde .20
53 Zach Thomas .20
54 Kordell Stewart .50
55 Tim Biakabutuka .10
56 J.J. Stokes .10
57 Jon Kitna .30
58 Jacquez Green .20
59 Marvin Harrison .20
60 Barry Sanders 2.00
61 Darrell Green .10
62 Terance Mathis .10
63 Ricky Watters .20
64 Chris Chandler .20
65 Cameron Cleeland .20
66 Rod Smith .20
67 Freddie Jones .10
68 Adrian Murrell .20
69 Terrell Owens .30
70 Troy Aikman 1.00
71 John Mobley .10
72 Corey Dillon .30
73 Rickey Dudley .10
74 Randall Cunningham .30
75 Muhsin Muhammed .10
76 Stephen Boyd .10
77 Tony Gonzalez .20
78 Deion Sanders .30
79 Ben Coates .20

80	Brett Favre	2.00
81	Shawn Springs	.10
82	Dorsey Levens	.30
83	Ray Buchanan	.10
84	Charlie Batch	.50
85	John Randle	.10
86	Eddie George	.50
87	Ray Lewis	.10
88	Johnnie Morton	.10
89	Kevin Hardy	.10
90	O.J. McDuffie	.20
91	Herman Moore	.30
92	Tim Brown	.30
93	Bert Emanuel	.10
94	Elvis Grbac	.20
95	Peter Boulware	.10
96	Curtis Conway	.20
97	Doug Flutie	.50
98	Jake Reed	.10
99	Ike Hilliard	.10
100	Randy Moss	2.00
101	Warren Sapp	.10
102	Bruce Smith	.10
103	Joey Galloway	.30
104	Napoleon Kaufman	.30
105	Warrick Dunn	.30
106	Wayne Chrebet	.30
107	Robert Brooks	.10
108	Antowain Smith	.30
109	Trent Differ	.20
110	Peyton Manning	1.50
111	Isaac Bruce	.20
112	John Lynch	.10
113	Terry Glenn	.30
114	Garrison Hearst	.30
115	Jerome Bettis	.30
116	Darnay Scott	.10
117	Lamar Thomas	.10
118	Chris Spielman	.10
119	Robert Smith	.20
120	Drew Bledsoe	.75
121	Reidel Anthony	.10
122	Wesley Walls	.10
123	Eric Moulds	.30
124	Terrell Davis	1.50
125	Dale Carter	.10
126	Charles Johnson	.10
127	Steve Atwater	.10
128	Jim Harbaugh	.20
129	Tony Martin	.10
130	Kerry Collins	.20
131	Trent Green	.30
132	Marshall Faulk	.30
133	Raghib Ismail	.10
134	Warren Moon	.30
135	Jerris McPhail	.10
136	Damon Gibson	.10
137	Jim Pyne	.10
138	Antonio Langham	.10
139	Freddie Solomon	.10
140	Randy Moss SH	1.00
141	John Elway SH	.75
142	Doug Flutie SH	.25
143	Emmitt Smith SH	.75
144	Terrell Davis SH	.75
145	*Troy Edwards*	3.00
146	*Torry Holt*	3.00
147	*Tim Couch*	12.00
148	*Sedrick Irvin*	2.00
149	*Ricky Williams*	12.00
150	*Peerless Price*	3.00
151	*Mike Cloud*	1.50
152	*Kevin Faulk*	3.00
153	*Kevin Johnson*	2.50
154	*James Johnson*	2.50
155	*Edgerrin James*	15.00
156	*D'Wayne Bates*	2.00
157	*Donovan McNabb*	5.00
158	*David Boston*	3.00
159	*Daunte Culpepper*	10.00
160	*Champ Bailey*	2.00
161	*Cecil Collins*	2.00
162	*Cade McNown*	3.00
163	*Brock Huard*	2.00
164	*Akili Smith*	4.00
165	Checklist	.10

1999 Topps Season Opener Autographs

Only two players signed in this insert and were inserted 1:7,126 packs.

		MT
Complete Set (2):		475.00
Common Player:		200.00
Inserted 1:7,126		
1	Tim Couch	275.00
2	Peyton Manning	200.00

1999 Topps Stars

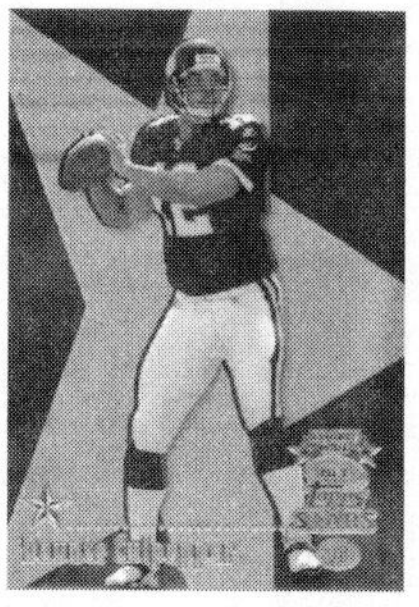

Each card in this 140-card set was printed on 24-pt. stock with foil stamping, flood gloss and metallic ink. Each of the base cards had a star on the front. A parallel Two Star, Three Star and Four Star were released and each of the four issues had a parallel version. Insert sets include: Autographs, New Dawn, Pro Bowl Jersey Redemption, Rookie Relics, Rookie Reprints, Stars of the Game and Zone of Their Own. SRP was $3.00 for six-card packs.

		MT
Complete Set (140):		65.00
Common Player:		.20
Minor Stars:		.40
Common Rookie:		.75
Pack (6):		3.00
Wax Box (24):		65.00
1	*Champ Bailey*	1.50
2	*Akili Smith*	3.00
3	Randy Moss	3.00
4	*Cade McNown*	2.50
5	*Torry Holt*	3.00
6	*Troy Edwards*	2.50
7	*David Boston*	2.50
8	*Edgerrin James*	10.00
9	*Daunte Culpepper*	6.00
10	*Tim Couch*	7.00
11	*Ricky Williams*	7.00
12	Fred Taylor	1.50
13	Barry Sanders	3.00
14	Emmitt Smith	2.00
15	Jerry Rice	1.50
16	Jake Plummer	1.25
17	Terrell Owens	.75
18	Eric Moulds	.75
19	Dan Marino	2.00
20	Steve McNair	.75
21	*Donovan McNabb*	4.00
22	Curtis Martin	.75
23	Peyton Manning	2.00
24	Garrison Hearst	.40
25	Eddie George	.75
26	Antonio Freeman	.75
27	Doug Flutie	1.00
28	*Kevin Faulk*	1.50
29	Brett Favre	3.00
30	Randall Cunningham	.75
31	Mark Brunell	1.25
32	Keyshawn Johnson	.75
33	Terrell Davis	2.00
34	Drew Bledsoe	1.25
35	Jerome Bettis	.75
36	Charlie Batch	1.00
37	Steve Young	1.00
38	Jamal Anderson	.75
39	Troy Aikman	1.50
40	John Elway	2.00
41	*Amos Zereoue*	1.00
42	J.J. Stokes	.40
43	Antowain Smith	.75
44	Jimmy Smith	.75
45	*Shaun King*	4.00
46	*Jevon Kearse*	2.50
47	*Sedrick Irvin*	1.00
48	Rod Smith	.50
49	*Kevin Johnson*	2.50
50	Joey Galloway	.75
51	*Michael Cloud*	1.00
52	*D'Wayne Bates*	1.00
53	*Peerless Price*	2.00
54	Herman Moore	.50
55	*Rob Konrad*	1.00
56	*James Johnson*	1.50
57	*Cecil Collins*	1.50
58	Wayne Chrebet	.75
59	Cris Carter	.75
60	Tim Brown	.50
61	Frank Wycheck	.20
62	Charles Woodson	.75
63	*Antoine Winfield*	.75
64	Ryan Leaf	.50
65	Ricky Watters	.40
66	Yancey Thigpen	.20
67	Michael Westbrook	.40
68	Vinny Testaverde	.40
69	Kordell Stewart	.75
70	Duce Staley	.75
71	Shannon Sharpe	.40
72	Junior Seau	.40
73	Bruce Smith	.20
74	Frank Sanders	.20
75	Warren Sapp	.20
76	Robert Smith	.75
77	Andre Reed	.40
78	Darnay Scott	.40
79	Adrian Murrell	.40
80	Ricky Proehl	.20
81	Zach Thomas	.40
82	Deion Sanders	.75
83	Andre Rison	.40
84	Jake Reed	.40
85	Carl Pickens	.40
86	John Randle	.20
87	Jerome Pathon	.20
88	*Brock Huard*	1.50
89	Elvis Grbac	.40
90	Curtis Enis	.75
91	Rickey Dudley	.20
92	Amani Toomer	.20
93	Robert Brooks	.20
94	Derrick Alexander	.20
95	Reidel Anthony	.40
96	Mark Chmura	.40
97	Trent Dilfer	.40
98	*Ebenezer Ekuban*	.40
99	Tony Banks	.40
100	Terry Glenn	.75
101	Andre Hastings	.20
102	Ike Hilliard	.40
103	Michael Irvin	.40
104	Napoleon Kaufman	.75
105	Dorsey Levens	.75
106	Ed McCaffrey	.50
107	Natrone Means	.40
108	Skip Hicks	.40
109	James Jett	.20
110	Priest Holmes	.75
111	Tim Dwight	.75
112	Curtis Conway	.40
113	Jeff Blake	.40
114	Karim Abdul	.40
115	*Karsten Bailey*	1.25
116	Chris Chandler	.40
117	Germane Crowell	.40
118	Warrick Dunn	.75
119	Bert Emanuel	.20
120	*Jermaine Fazande*	1.25
121	*Joe Germaine*	1.25
122	Tony Gonzalez	.40
123	Jacquez Green	.40
124	Marvin Harrison	.75
125	Corey Dillon	.75
126	Ben Coates	.40
127	*Chris Claiborne*	1.00
128	Isaac Bruce	.75
129	Mike Alstott	.75
130	*Andy Katzenmoyer*	1.00
131	Jon Kitna	.75
132	Keenan McCardell	.40
133	Johnnie Morton	.20
134	O.J. McDuffie	.40
135	*Chris McAlister*	1.00
136	Terance Mathis	.20
137	Thurman Thomas	.20
138	Jermaine Lewis	.20
139	Rob Moore	.20
140	Brad Johnson	.75

1999 Topps Stars Parallel

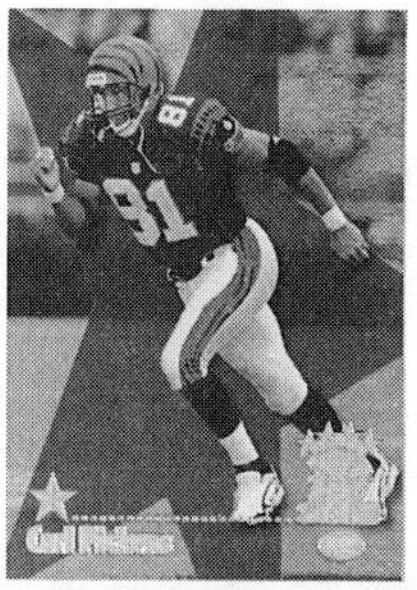

This was a parallel to the base set. Each of the singles in this set were sequentially numbered to 299.

		MT
Parallel Cards:		5x-10x
Parallel Rookies:		2x-4x
Production 299 Sets		
1	*Champ Bailey*	1.50
2	*Akili Smith*	3.00
3	Randy Moss	3.00
4	*Cade McNown*	4.00
5	*Torry Holt*	3.00
6	*Troy Edwards*	2.50
7	*David Boston*	2.50
8	*Edgerrin James*	10.00
9	*Daunte Culpepper*	4.00
10	*Tim Couch*	7.00
11	*Ricky Williams*	7.00
12	Fred Taylor	1.50
13	Barry Sanders	3.00
14	Emmitt Smith	2.00
15	Jerry Rice	1.50
16	Jake Plummer	1.25
17	Terrell Owens	.75
18	Eric Moulds	.75
19	Dan Marino	2.00
20	Steve McNair	.75
21	*Donovan McNabb*	4.00
22	Curtis Martin	.75
23	Peyton Manning	2.00
24	Garrison Hearst	.40
25	Eddie George	.75
26	Antonio Freeman	.75
27	Doug Flutie	1.00
28	*Kevin Faulk*	1.50
29	Brett Favre	3.00
30	Randall Cunningham	.75
31	Mark Brunell	1.25
32	Keyshawn Johnson	.75
33	Terrell Davis	2.00
34	Drew Bledsoe	1.25
35	Jerome Bettis	.75
36	Charlie Batch	1.00
37	Steve Young	1.00
38	Jamal Anderson	.75
39	Troy Aikman	1.50
40	John Elway	2.00
41	*Amos Zereoue*	1.00
42	J.J. Stokes	.40
43	Antowain Smith	.75
44	Jimmy Smith	.75
45	*Shaun King*	4.00
46	*Jevon Kearse*	2.50
47	*Sedrick Irvin*	1.00
48	Rod Smith	.50
49	*Kevin Johnson*	2.50
50	Joey Galloway	.75
51	*Michael Cloud*	1.00
52	*D'Wayne Bates*	1.00
53	*Peerless Price*	2.00
54	Herman Moore	.50
55	*Rob Konrad*	1.00
56	*James Johnson*	1.50
57	*Cecil Collins*	1.50
58	Wayne Chrebet	.75
59	Cris Carter	.75
60	Tim Brown	.50
61	Frank Wycheck	.20
62	Charles Woodson	.75
63	*Antoine Winfield*	.75
64	Ryan Leaf	.50
65	Ricky Watters	.40
66	Yancey Thigpen	.20
67	Michael Westbrook	.40
68	Vinny Testaverde	.40
69	Kordell Stewart	.40
70	Duce Staley	.75
71	Shannon Sharpe	.40
72	Junior Seau	.40
73	Bruce Smith	.20
74	Frank Sanders	.20
75	Warren Sapp	.20
76	Robert Smith	.75
77	Andre Reed	.40
78	Darnay Scott	.40
79	Adrian Murrell	.40
80	Ricky Proehl	.20
81	Zach Thomas	.40
82	Deion Sanders	.75
83	Andre Rison	.40
84	Jake Reed	.40
85	Carl Pickens	.40
86	John Randle	.20
87	Jerome Pathon	.20
88	*Brock Huard*	1.50
89	Elvis Grbac	.40
90	Curtis Enis	.75
91	Rickey Dudley	.20
92	Amani Toomer	.20
93	Robert Brooks	.20
94	Derrick Alexander	.20
95	Reidel Anthony	.40
96	Mark Chmura	.40
97	Trent Dilfer	.40
98	*Ebenezer Ekuban*	.75
99	Tony Banks	.40
100	Terry Glenn	.75
101	Andre Hastings	.20
102	Ike Hilliard	.40
103	Michael Irvin	.40
104	Napoleon Kaufman	.75
105	Dorsey Levens	.75
106	Ed McCaffrey	.50
107	Natrone Means	.40
108	Skip Hicks	.40
109	James Jett	.20
110	Priest Holmes	.75
111	Tim Dwight	.75
112	Curtis Conway	.40
113	Jeff Blake	.40
114	Karim Abdul	.40
115	*Karsten Bailey*	1.25
116	Chris Chandler	.40
117	Germane Crowell	.40
118	Warrick Dunn	.75
119	Bert Emanuel	.20
120	*Jermaine Fazande*	1.25
121	*Joe Germaine*	1.25
122	Tony Gonzalez	.40
123	Jacquez Green	.40
124	Marvin Harrison	.75
125	Corey Dillon	.75
126	Ben Coates	.40
127	*Chris Claiborne*	1.00
128	Isaac Bruce	.75
129	Mike Alstott	.75
130	*Andy Katzenmoyer*	1.00
131	Jon Kitna	.75
132	Keenan McCardell	.40
133	Johnnie Morton	.20
134	O.J. McDuffie	.40
135	*Chris McAlister*	1.00
136	Terance Mathis	.20
137	Thurman Thomas	.40
138	Jermaine Lewis	.20
139	Rob Moore	.20
140	Brad Johnson	.75

1999 Topps Stars Two Star Parallel

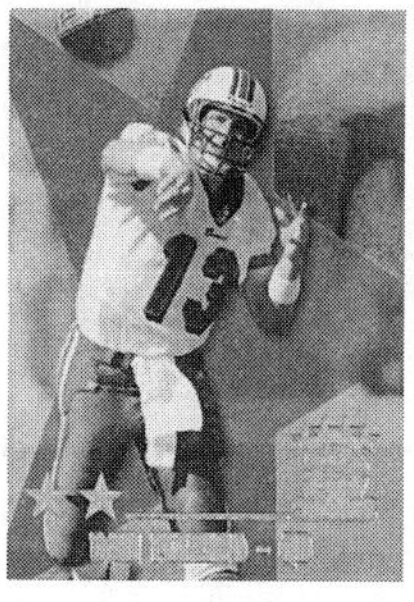

This was a 60-card partial parallel to the base set. Each of the singles had two stars on the front and were inserted 1:1.5 packs.

	MT
Complete Set (60):	50.00
Two Star Cards:	1x

1999 Topps Stars Two Star Parallel

This was a parallel to the Two Star set. Singles from this insert were sequentially numbered to 249 and inserted 1:42 packs.

	MT
Complete Set (60):	500.00
Two Star Cards:	5x-10x
Two Star Rookies:	2x-4x
Production 249 Sets	

1999 Topps Stars Three Star Parallel

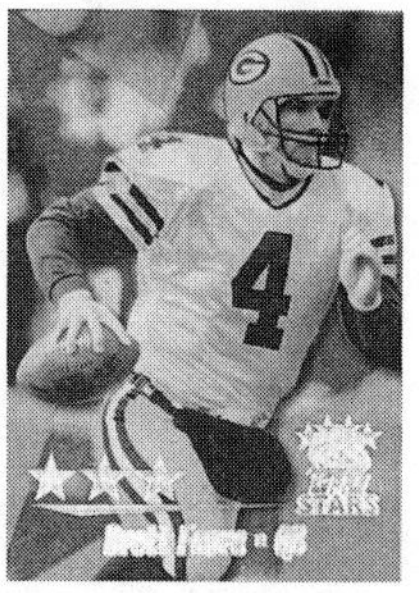

This was a 40-card partial parallel to the base set. Each single had three stars on the front and was inserted one-per-pack.

	MT
Complete Set (40):	35.00
Three Star Cards:	1x
Inserted 1:1	

1999 Topps Stars Three Star Parallel

This was a parallel to the Three Star insert. Each of the singles were sequentially numbered to 199 and inserted 1:79 packs.

	MT
Complete Set (40):	500.00
Three Star Cards:	6x-12x
Three Star Rookies:	3x-6x
Production 199 Sets	

1999 Topps Stars Four Star Parallel

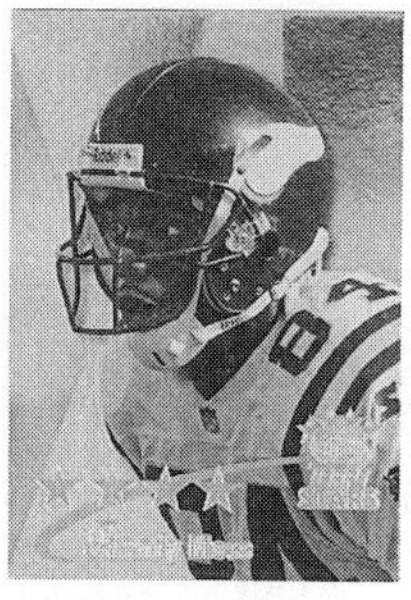

This was a 10-card partial parallel to the base set. Each single had four stars across the front. Singles were inserted 1:4 packs.

	MT
Complete Set (10):	25.00
Four Star Cards:	1x
Inserted 1:4	

1999 Topps Stars Four Star Parallel

This was a parallel to the Four Star insert set. Each single was sequentially numbered to 99 and inserted 1:634 packs.

	MT
Complete Set (10):	150.00
Four Star Cards:	6x-12x
Four Star Rookies:	3x-6x
Production 99 Sets	

1999 Topps Stars Autographs

This six-card insert set included autographs from the 1999 #1 overall draft pick Tim Couch and the 1998 Rookie of the Year Randy Moss. The first three cards in the set had a blue background and were inserted 1:419 packs. Cards #4 and #5 had a red background and were inserted 1:629. The last single had a gold background and was inserted 1:2,528 packs.

		MT
Complete Set (6):		375.00
Common Player:		25.00
Blue Inserted 1:419		
Gold Inserted 1:2,528		
Red Inserted 1:629		
1	Tim Couch B	125.00
2	Torry Holt B	35.00
3	David Boston B	25.00
4	Fred Taylor R	60.00
5	Marshall Faulk R	50.00
6	Randy Moss G	150.00

1999 Topps Stars New Dawn

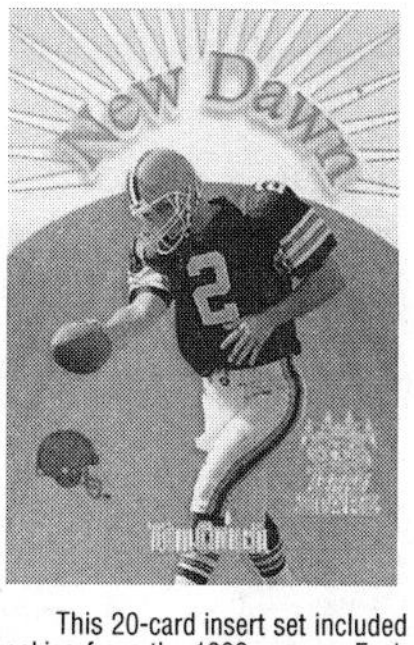

This 20-card insert set included rookies from the 1999 season. Each was printed on 24-pt. stock, with super-premium select metallization treatment and foil stamping. The cards were sequentially numbered to 1,000 and inserted 1:31 packs.

		MT
Complete Set (20):		100.00
Common Player:		1.50
Minor Stars:		3.00
Inserted 1:31		
Production 1,000 Sets		
1	Tim Couch	12.00
2	Kevin Faulk	4.00
3	Troy Edwards	6.00
4	Champ Bailey	4.00
5	Peerless Price	4.00
6	Kevin Johnson	7.00
7	Edgerrin James	20.00
8	Daunte Culpepper	8.00
9	Torry Holt	6.00
10	Donovan McNabb	8.00
11	Shaun King	8.00
12	Michael Cloud	1.50
13	Cade McNown	8.00
14	David Boston	6.00
15	James Johnson	4.00
16	Karsten Bailey	1.50
17	Sedrick Irvin	3.00
18	Akili Smith	7.00
19	D'Wayne Bates	1.50
20	Ricky Williams	12.00

1999 Topps Stars Rookie Relics

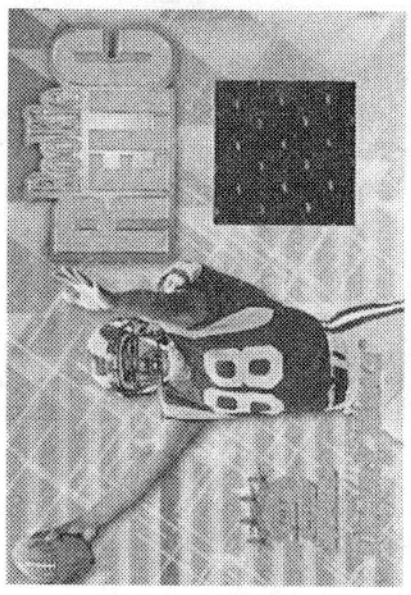

This three-card insert set included rookie Torry Holt and rookies Kurt Warner and Donovan McNabb through redemption cards. Each single included a piece of a game- worn jersey and singles were inserted 1:209 packs.

		MT
Complete Set (3):		225.00
Common Player:		50.00
Inserted 1:209		
1	Kurt Warner	150.00
2	Torry Holt	50.00
3	Donovan McNabb	50.00

1999 Topps Stars Rookie Reprints

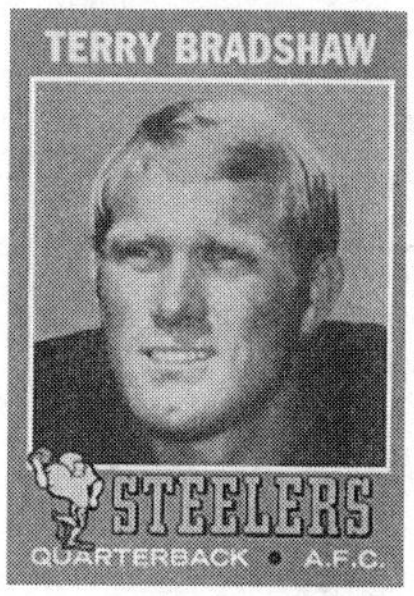

This two-card insert set included reprints of Terry Bradshaw and Roger Staubach's rookie cards. Singles were inserted 1:16 packs. Autographed version were also released at 1:629 packs.

		MT
Complete Set (2):		10.00
Common Player:		5.00
Inserted 1:16		
	Terry Bradshaw	5.00
	Roger Staubach	5.00

1999 Topps Stars Stars of the Game

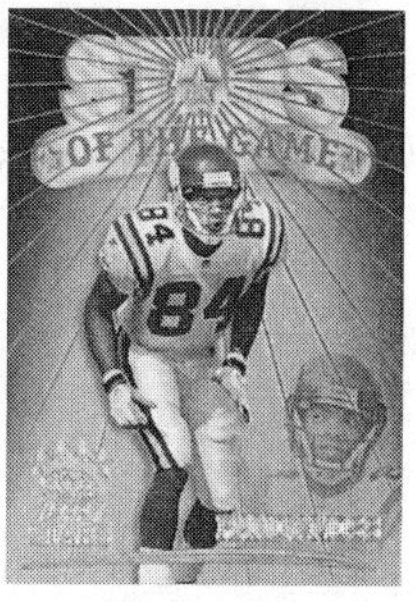

Each single in this 10-card insert set were printed on 24-pt. stock with foil stamping. Each was sequentially numbered to 1,999 and inserted 1:31 packs.

		MT
Complete Set (10):		100.00
Common Player:		2.50
Inserted 1:31		
Production 1,999 Sets		
1	Jamal Anderson	2.50
2	Dan Marino	10.00
3	Barry Sanders	12.00
4	Brett Favre	12.00
5	Emmitt Smith	10.00

6 Fred Taylor 6.00
7 John Elway 10.00
8 Randy Moss 12.00
9 Peyton Manning 10.00
10 Terrell Davis 8.00

1999 Topps Stars Zone of Their Own

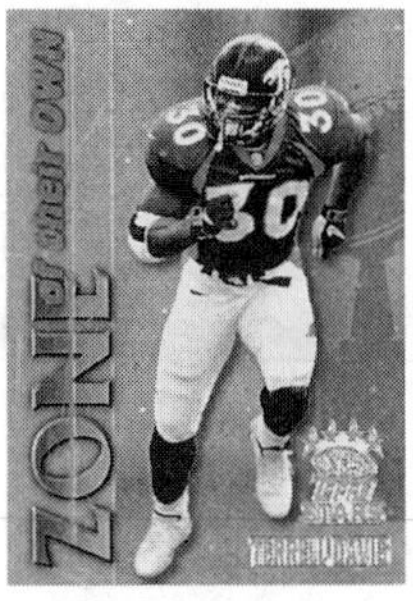

This 10-card insert set included stars who have won individual awards and team titles. Each was printed on 24 pt. stock, foil stamped and sequentially numbered to 1,999. Singles were found 1:31 packs.

MT
Complete Set (10): 60.00
Common Player: 2.50
Inserted 1:31
Production 1,999 Sets
1 Randy Moss 12.00
2 Eddie George 4.00
3 Tim Brown 2.50
4 Curtis Martin 2.50
5 Brett Favre 12.00
6 Barry Sanders 12.00
7 Warrick Dunn 2.50
8 Terrell Davis 8.00
9 Ricky Williams 10.00
10 Doug Flutie 5.00

2000 Topps

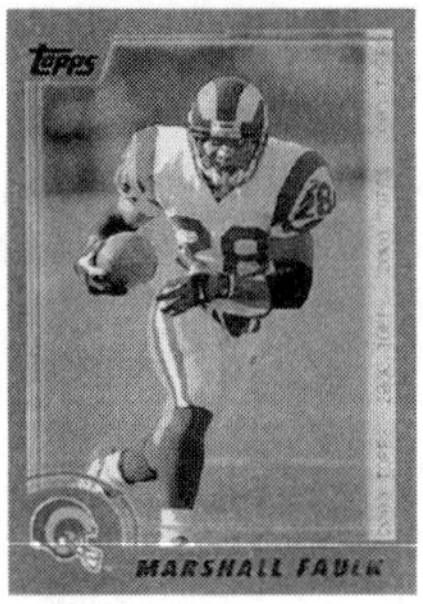

MT
Complete Set (400): 125.00
Common Player: .15
Minor Stars: .30
Common Rookie: 1.50
Inserted 1:5
Pack (10): 1.50
Wax Box (36): 45.00
1 Kurt Warner 2.50
2 Darrell Russell .15
3 Tai Streets .15
4 Bryant Young .15
5 Kent Graham .15
6 Shawn Jefferson .15
7 Wesley Walls .30
8 Jessie Armstead .15
9 Dedric Ward .15
10 Emmitt Smith 1.50
11 James Stewart .30
12 Frank Sanders .30
13 Ray Buchanan .15
14 Olindo Mare .15
15 Andre Reed .30
16 Curtis Conway .30
17 Patrick Jeffers .50
18 Greg Hill .15
19 Johnny Unitas .50
20 Brett Favre 2.00
21 Jerome Pathon .15
22 Jason Tucker .30
23 Charles Johnson .15
24 Brian Mitchell .15
25 Billy Miller .15
26 Jay Fiedler .15
27 Marcus Pollard .15
28 De'Mond Parker .15
29 Leslie Shepherd .15
30 Fred Taylor .75
31 Michael Pittman .15
32 Ricky Watters .30
33 Derrick Brooks .15
34 Junior Seau .30
35 Troy Vincent .15
36 Eric Allen .15
37 Pete Mitchell .15
38 Tony Simmons .15
39 Az-Zahir Hakim .30
40 Dan Marino 1.50
41 Mac Cody .15
42 Scott Dreisbach .15
43 Al Wilson .15
44 Luther Broughton .15
45 Wane McGarity .15
46 Stephen Boyd .15
47 Michael Strahan .15
48 Chris Chandler .30
49 Tony Martin .15
50 Edgerrin James 2.00
51 John Randle .15
52 Warrick Dunn .50
53 Elvis Grbac .30
54 Champ Bailey .30
55 Kyle Brady .15
56 John Lynch .15
57 Kevin Carter .15
58 Mike Pritchard .15
59 *Deon Mitchell* .30
60 Randy Moss 1.75
61 Jermaine Fazande .30
62 Donovan McNabb .75
63 Richard Huntley .30
64 Rich Gannon .30
65 Aaron Glenn .15
66 Amani Toomer .30
67 Andre Hastings .15
68 Ricky Williams 1.25
69 Sam Madison .15
70 Drew Bledsoe .75
71 Eric Moulds .50
72 Justin Armour .15
73 Jamal Anderson .50
74 Mario Bates .15
75 Sam Gash .15
76 Macey Brooks .15
77 Tremain Mack .15
78 David LaFleur .15
79 Dexter Coakley .15
80 Cris Carter .50
81 Byron Chamberlain .15
82 David Sloan .15
83 *Mike Devlin* .30
84 Jimmy Smith .30
85 Derrick Alexander .15
86 Damon Huard .50
87 Jake Reed .15
88 Darrell Green .15
89 Derrick Mason .15
90 Curtis Martin .50
91 Donnie Abraham .15
92 D'Marco Farr .15
93 Ahman Green .30
94 Shane Matthews .15
95 Torrance Small .15
96 Duce Staley .50
97 Jon Ritchie .15
98 Victor Green .15
99 Kerry Collins .30
100 Peyton Manning 1.50
101 Ben Coates .30
102 Thurman Thomas .30
103 Cornelius Bennett .15
104 Terance Mathis .15
105 Adrian Murrell .15
106 Donald Hayes .15
107 Terry Kirby .15
108 James Allen .15
109 Ty Law .15
110 Tim Brown .30
111 Chad Bratzke .15
112 Deion Sanders .50
113 James Johnson .30
114 Tony Richardson .15
115 Tony Brackens .15
116 Ken Dilger .15
117 Albert Connell .30
118 Neil O'Donnell .15
119 *Selucio Sanford* .30
120 Steve Young .75
121 Tony Horne .15
122 Charlie Rogers .15
123 J.J. Stokes .30
124 Kenny Bynum .15
125 Jeff Graham .15
126 Ike Hilliard .30
127 Ray Lucas .50
128 Terry Glenn .50
129 Rickey Dudley .30
130 Joey Galloway .50
131 Brian Dawkins .15
132 Rob Moore .30
133 Bob Christian .15
134 *Anthony Wright* 5.00
135 Antowain Smith .50
136 Kevin Johnson .50
137 Scott Covington .15
138 D'Wayne Bates .15
139 Sam Cowart .15
140 Isaac Bruce .50
141 Tony McGee .15
142 Dale Carter .15
143 Matt Hasselbeck .30
144 Torry Holt .50
145 Daunte Culpepper .75
146 Yatil Green .15
147 Chris Howard .15
148 Irving Fryar .15
149 Derrick Mayes .30
150 Warren Sapp .30
151 Ricky Proehl .15
152 Eric Kresser .15
153 Jeff Garcia .50
154 Freddie Jones .30
155 Michael Cloud .15
156 Wayne Chrebet .30
157 Joe Montgomery .15
158 Shannon Sharpe .30
159 Eddie Kennison .15
160 Eddie George .60
161 Jay Riemersma .15
162 Peter Boulware .15
163 Aeneas Williams .15
164 Jim Miller .15
165 Jamir Miller .15
166 Tim Biakabutuka .30
167 Kordell Stewart .50
168 Charlie Garner .30
169 Germane Crowell .30
170 Stephen Davis .50
171 Jeff George .30
172 Mark Brunell .75
173 Stephen Alexander .15
174 Mike Alstott .50
175 Terry Allen .30
176 Ed McCaffrey .30
177 Bobby Engram .15
178 Andre Cooper .15
179 Kevin Faulk .30
180 Errict Rhett .30
181 Jammi German .15
182 Oronde Gadsden .30
183 Jevon Kearse .50
184 Herman Moore .30
185 Terrence Wilkins .15
186 Raghib Ismail .15
187 Patrick Johnson .15
188 Simeon Rice .15
189 Mo Lewis .15
190 Qadry Ismail .15
191 Terry Jackson .15
192 Rashaan Shehee .15
193 Charles Woodson .50
194 Akili Smith .50
195 Yancey Thigpen .30
196 Michael Westbrook .30
197 Donnell Bennett .15
198 Sedrick Irvin .15
199 Keenan McCardell .30
200 Marshall Faulk .50
201 Jeff Blake .30
202 Rob Johnson .30
203 Vinny Testaverde .30
204 Andy Katzenmoyer .15
205 Michael Basnight .15
206 Lance Schulters .15
207 Shaun King .75
208 Bill Schroeder .15
209 Skip Hicks .15
210 Jake Plummer .50
211 Leroy Hoard .15
212 Reggie Barlow .15
213 E.G. Green .15
214 Fred Lane .15
215 Antonio Freeman .50
216 Grant Wistrom .15
217 Kevin Dyson .30
218 Mikhael Ricks .15
219 Rod Woodson .15
220 Tim Dwight .50
221 Darnay Scott .30
222 Curtis Enis .50
223 Sean Bennett .15
224 Napoleon Kaufman .50
225 Jonathon Linton .30
226 Jim Harbaugh .30
227 Hardy Nickerson .15
228 Todd Lyght .15
229 Dorsey Levens .50
230 Steve Beuerlein .30
231 Marty Booker .15
232 Andre Wadsworth .15
233 James Hasty .15
234 Shawn Bryson .15
235 Larry Centers .15
236 Charlie Batch .50
237 Steve McNair .60
238 Darrin Chiaverini .15
239 Jerome Bettis .50
240 Muhsin Muhammad .30
241 Terrell Fletcher .15
242 Jon Kitna .50
243 Frank Wycheck .15
244 Tony Gonzalez .30
245 Ron Rivers .15
246 Olandis Gary .50
247 Jermaine Lewis .15
248 Joe Jurevicius .15
249 Richie Anderson .15
250 Marcus Robinson .50
251 Shawn Springs .15
252 William Floyd .15
253 *Bobby Shaw* .30
254 Glyn Milburn .15
255 Brian Griese .50
256 Donnie Edwards .15
257 Joe Horn .15
258 Cameron Cleeland .30
259 Glenn Foley .15
260 Corey Dillon .50
261 Troy Brown .15
262 Stoney Case .15
263 Kevin Williams .15
264 London Fletcher .15
265 O.J. McDuffie .15
266 Jonathan Quinn .15
267 Trent Dilfer .30
268 Dameyune Craig .30
269 Terrell Owens .50
270 Tim Couch 1.25
271 Dameane Douglas .15
272 Moses Moreno .15
273 Bruce Smith .15
274 Peerless Price .50
275 Sam Garnes .15
276 Natrone Means .30
277 Na Brown .15
278 Dave Moore .15
279 Chris Sanders .15
280 Troy Aikman 1.00
281 Cecil Collins .30
282 Matthew Hatchette .15
283 Bill Romanowski .15
284 Basil Mitchell .15
285 Tony Banks .30
286 *Jake Delhomme* 2.00
287 Keyshawn Johnson .50
288 Dexter McLeon .15
289 Corey Bradford .30
290 Terrell Davis 1.50
291 Johnnie Morton .30
292 Kevin Lockett .15
293 Robert Smith .50
294 Jeff Lewis .15
295 Wali Rainer .15
296 Troy Edwards .50
297 Keith Poole .15
298 Priest Holmes .50
299 David Boston .50
300 Marvin Harrison .50
301 Levon Kirkland .15
302 Robert Holcombe .15
303 Autry Denson .15
304 Kevin Hardy .15
305 Rod Smith .30
306 Robert Porcher .15
307 Cade McNown .75
308 Craig Yeast .15
309 Doug Flutie .50
310 Jerry Rice 1.00
311 Brad Johnson .50
312 Tiki Barber .30
313 Will Blackwell .15
314 Sean Dawkins .15
315 Jacquez Green .30
316 Zach Thomas .30
317 Gus Frerotte .15
318 Chris Warren .15
319 Carl Pickens .30
320 Tyrone Wheatley .30
321 Kurt Warner 1.25
322 Dan Marino .75
323 Cris Carter .30
324 Brett Favre 1.00
325 Marshall Faulk .30
326 Jevon Kearse .30
327 Edgerrin James 1.00
328 Emmitt Smith .75
329 Andre Reed .15
330 Kevin Dyson, Frank Wycheck .15
331 Olindo Mare .15
332 Marcus Coleman .15
333 James Johnson .15
334 Ray Lucas .30
335 Dedric Ward .15
336 Richie Cunningham .15
337 James Hasty .15
338 Sedrick Shaw .15
339 Kurt Warner 1.25
340 Marshall Faulk .30
341 Brian Shay .50
342 L.C. Stevens .50
343 Corey Thomas .50
344 Scott Milanovich .50
345 Pat Barnes .50
346 Danny Wuerffel .50
347 Kevin Daft .50
348 *Ron Powlus* 1.50
349 Tony Graziani .50
350 *Norman Miller* .50
351 Cory Sauter .50
352 *Marcus Crandell* .50
353 *Sean Morey* .50
354 Jeff Ogden .50
355 Ted White .50
356 *Jim Kubiak* .50
357 *Aaron Stecker* .50
358 Ronnie Powell .50
359 *Matt Lytle* .50
360 *Kendrick Nord* .50
361 *Tim Rattay* 2.00
362 *Rob Morris* 1.50
363 *Chris Samuels* 2.00
364 *Todd Husak* 1.50
365 *Ahmed Plummer* 1.50
366 *Frank Murphy* 1.50
367 *Michael Wiley* 3.00
368 *Giovanni Carmazzi* 2.00
369 *Anthony Becht* 2.00
370 *John Abraham* 1.50
371 *Shaun Alexander* 6.00
372 *Thomas Jones* 4.00
373 *Courtney Brown* 2.00
374 *Curtis Keaton* 1.50
375 *Jerry Porter* 2.00
376 *Corey Simon* 2.00
377 *Dez White* 2.00
378 *Jamal Lewis* 12.00
379 *Ron Dayne* 10.00
380 *R. Jay Soward* 2.00
381 *Tee Martin* 2.00
382 *Shaun Ellis* 1.50
383 *Brian Urlacher* 6.00
384 *Reuben Droughns* 2.00
385 *Travis Taylor* 2.50
386 *Plaxico Burress* 5.00
387 *Chad Pennington* 8.00
388 *Sylvester Morris* 5.00
389 *Ron Dugans* 2.00
390 *Joe Hamilton* 2.00
391 *Chris Redman* 4.00
392 *Trung Canidate* 2.00
393 *J.R. Redmond* 2.50
394 *Danny Farmer* 2.00
395 *Todd Pinkston* 2.00
396 *Dennis Northcutt* 2.00
397 *Laveranues Coles* 2.50
398 *Bubba Franks* 2.00
399 *Travis Prentice* 3.00
400 *Peter Warrick* 10.00

2000 Topps MVP Promotion Parallel

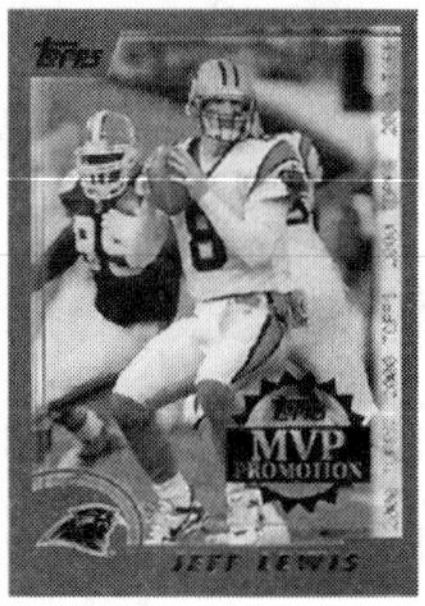

MT
MVP Cards: 25x-50x
MVP Rookies: 5x-10x
Inserted 1:234
1 Kurt Warner 2.50
2 Darrell Russell .15
3 Tai Streets .15
4 Bryant Young .15
5 Kent Graham .15
6 Shawn Jefferson .15
7 Wesley Walls .30
8 Jessie Armstead .15
9 Dedric Ward .15
10 Emmitt Smith 1.50
11 James Stewart .30
12 Frank Sanders .30
13 Ray Buchanan .15
14 Olindo Mare .15
15 Andre Reed .30
16 Curtis Conway .30
17 Patrick Jeffers .50
18 Greg Hill .15
19 John Unitas .50
20 Brett Favre 2.00
21 Jerome Pathon .15
22 Jason Tucker .30
23 Charles Johnson .15
24 Brian Mitchell .15
25 Billy Miller .15
26 Jay Fiedler .15
27 Marcus Pollard .15
28 De'Mond Parker .15
29 Leslie Shepherd .15
30 Fred Taylor .75
31 Michael Pittman .15
32 Ricky Watters .30
33 Derrick Brooks .15
34 Junior Seau .30
35 Troy Vincent .15
36 Eric Allen .15
37 Pete Mitchell .15
38 Tony Simmons .15
39 Az-Zahir Hakim .30
40 Dan Marino 1.50
41 Mac Cody .15
42 Scott Dreisbach .15
43 Al Wilson .15
44 Luther Broughton .15
45 Wane McGarity .15
46 Stephen Boyd .15
47 Michael Strahan .15
48 Chris Chandler .30
49 Tony Martin .15
50 Edgerrin James 2.00
51 John Randle .15
52 Warrick Dunn .50
53 Elvis Grbac .30
54 Champ Bailey .30
55 Kyle Brady .15
56 John Lynch .15
57 Kevin Carter .15
58 Mike Pritchard .15
59 *Deon Mitchell* .30
60 Randy Moss 1.75
61 Jermaine Fazande .30
62 Donovan McNabb .75
63 Richard Huntley .30
64 Rich Gannon .30
65 Aaron Glenn .15
66 Amani Toomer .30
67 Andre Hastings .15
68 Ricky Williams 1.25
69 Sam Madison .15
70 Drew Bledsoe .75
71 Eric Moulds .50
72 Justin Armour .15
73 Jamal Anderson .50
74 Mario Bates .15
75 Sam Gash .15
76 Macey Brooks .15
77 Tremain Mack .15
78 David LaFleur .15
79 Dexter Coakley .15
80 Cris Carter .50
81 Byron Chamberlain .15
82 David Sloan .15
83 *Mike Devlin* .30
84 Jimmy Smith .30
85 Derrick Alexander .15
86 Damon Huard .50
87 Jake Reed .15
88 Darrell Green .15
89 Derrick Mason .15
90 Curtis Martin .50
91 Donnie Abraham .15
92 D'Marco Farr .15
93 Ahman Green .30
94 Shane Matthews .15
95 Torrance Small .15
96 Duce Staley .50
97 Jon Ritchie .15
98 Victor Green .15
99 Kerry Collins .30
100 Peyton Manning 1.50
101 Ben Coates .30
102 Thurman Thomas .30
103 Cornelius Bennett .15
104 Terance Mathis .15
105 Adrian Murrell .15
106 Donald Hayes .15
107 Terry Kirby .15
108 James Allen .15
109 Ty Law .15
110 Tim Brown .30
111 Chad Bratzke .15
112 Deion Sanders .50
113 James Johnson .30
114 Tony Richardson .15
115 Tony Brackens .15
116 Ken Dilger .15
117 Albert Connell .30
118 Neil O'Donnell .15
119 *Selucio Sanford* .30
120 Steve Young .75
121 Tony Horne .15
122 Charlie Rogers .15
123 J.J. Stokes .30
124 Kenny Bynum .15
125 Jeff Graham .15
126 Ike Hilliard .30
127 Ray Lucas .50
128 Terry Glenn .50
129 Rickey Dudley .30
130 Joey Galloway .50
131 Brian Dawkins .15
132 Rob Moore .30
133 Bob Christian .15
134 *Anthony Wright* .75
135 Antowain Smith .50
136 Kevin Johnson .50
137 Scott Covington .15
138 D'Wayne Bates .15
139 Sam Cowart .15
140 Isaac Bruce .50
141 Tony McGee .15
142 Dale Carter .15
143 Matt Hasselbeck .30
144 Torry Holt .50
145 Daunte Culpepper .75
146 Yatil Green .15
147 Chris Howard .15
148 Irving Fryar .15
149 Derrick Mayes .30
150 Warren Sapp .30
151 Ricky Proehl .15
152 Eric Kresser .15
153 Jeff Garcia .50
154 Freddie Jones .30
155 Michael Cloud .15
156 Wayne Chrebet .30
157 Joe Montgomery .15
158 Shannon Sharpe .30
159 Eddie Kennison .15
160 Eddie George .60
161 Jay Riemersma .15
162 Peter Boulware .15
163 Aeneas Williams .15
164 Jim Miller .15
165 Jamir Miller .15
166 Tim Biakabutuka .30
167 Kordell Stewart .50
168 Charlie Garner .30
169 Germane Crowell .30
170 Stephen Davis .50
171 Jeff George .30
172 Mark Brunell .75
173 Stephen Alexander .15
174 Mike Alstott .50
175 Terry Allen .30
176 Ed McCaffrey .30
177 Bobby Engram .15
178 Andre Cooper .15
179 Kevin Faulk .30
180 Errict Rhett .30
181 Jammi German .15
182 Oronde Gadsden .30
183 Jevon Kearse .50
184 Herman Moore .30
185 Terrence Wilkins .15
186 Raghib Ismail .15
187 Patrick Johnson .15
188 Simeon Rice .15
189 Mo Lewis .15
190 Qadry Ismail .15
191 Terry Jackson .15
192 Rashaan Shehee .15
193 Charles Woodson .50
194 Akili Smith .50
195 Yancey Thigpen .30
196 Michael Westbrook .30
197 Donnell Bennett .15
198 Sedrick Irvin .15
199 Keenan McCardell .30
200 Marshall Faulk .50
201 Jeff Blake .30
202 Rob Johnson .30
203 Vinny Testaverde .30
204 Andy Katzenmoyer .15
205 Michael Basnight .15
206 Lance Schulters .15
207 Shaun King .75
208 Bill Schroeder .15
209 Skip Hicks .15
210 Jake Plummer .50
211 Leroy Hoard .15
212 Reggie Barlow .15
213 E.G. Green .15
214 Fred Lane .15
215 Antonio Freeman .50
216 Grant Wistrom .15
217 Kevin Dyson .30
218 Mikhael Ricks .15
219 Rod Woodson .15
220 Tim Dwight .50
221 Darnay Scott .30
222 Curtis Enis .50
223 Sean Bennett .15
224 Napoleon Kaufman .50
225 Jonathon Linton .30
226 Jim Harbaugh .30
227 Hardy Nickerson .15
228 Todd Lyght .15
229 Dorsey Levens .50
230 Steve Beuerlein .30
231 Marty Booker .15
232 Andre Wadsworth .15
233 James Hasty .15
234 Shawn Bryson .15
235 Larry Centers .15
236 Charlie Batch .50
237 Steve McNair .60
238 Darrin Chiaverini .15
239 Jerome Bettis .50
240 Muhsin Muhammad .30
241 Terrell Fletcher .15
242 Jon Kitna .50
243 Frank Wycheck .15
244 Tony Gonzalez .30
245 Ron Rivers .15
246 Olandis Gary .50
247 Jermaine Lewis .15
248 Joe Jurevicius .15
249 Richie Anderson .15
250 Marcus Robinson .50
251 Shawn Springs .15
252 William Floyd .15
253 *Bobby Shaw* .30
254 Glyn Milburn .15
255 Brian Griese .50
256 Donnie Edwards .15
257 Joe Horn .15
258 Cameron Cleeland .30
259 Glenn Foley .15
260 Corey Dillon .50
261 Troy Brown .15
262 Stoney Case .15
263 Kevin Williams .15
264 London Fletcher .15
265 O.J. McDuffie .15
266 Jonathan Quinn .15
267 Trent Dilfer .30
268 Dameyune Craig .30
269 Terrell Owens .50
270 Tim Couch 1.25
271 Dameane Douglas .15
272 Moses Moreno .15
273 Bruce Smith .15
274 Peerless Price .50
275 Sam Garnes .15
276 Natrone Means .30
277 Na Brown .15
278 Dave Moore .15
279 Chris Sanders .15
280 Troy Aikman 1.00
281 Cecil Collins .30
282 Matthew Hatchette .15
283 Bill Romanowski .15
284 Basil Mitchell .15
285 Tony Banks .30
286 *Jake Delhomme* 2.00
287 Keyshawn Johnson .50
288 Dexter McLeon .15
289 Corey Bradford .30
290 Terrell Davis 1.50
291 Johnnie Morton .30
292 Kevin Lockett .15
293 Robert Smith .50
294 Jeff Lewis .15
295 Wali Rainer .15
296 Troy Edwards .50
297 Keith Poole .15
298 Priest Holmes .50
299 David Boston .50
300 Marvin Harrison .50
301 Levon Kirkland .15
302 Robert Holcombe .15
303 Autry Denson .15
304 Kevin Hardy .15
305 Rod Smith .30
306 Robert Porcher .15
307 Cade McNown .75
308 Craig Yeast .15
309 Doug Flutie .50
310 Jerry Rice 1.00
311 Brad Johnson .50
312 Tiki Barber .30
313 Will Blackwell .15
314 Sean Dawkins .15
315 Jacquez Green .30
316 Zach Thomas .30
317 Gus Frerotte .15
318 Chris Warren .15
319 Carl Pickens .30
320 Tyrone Wheatley .30
321 Kurt Warner 1.25
322 Dan Marino .75
323 Cris Carter .30
324 Brett Favre 1.00

325	Marshall Faulk	.30
326	Jevon Kearse	.30
327	Edgerrin James	1.00
328	Emmitt Smith	.75
329	Andre Reed	.15
330	Kevin Dyson, Frank Wycheck	.15
331	Olindo Mare	.15
332	Marcus Coleman	.15
333	James Johnson	.15
334	Ray Lucas	.30
335	Dedric Ward	.15
336	Richie Cunningham	.15
337	James Hasty	.15
338	Sedrick Shaw	.15
339	Kurt Warner	1.25
340	Marshall Faulk	.30
341	Brian Shay	.50
342	L.C. Stevens	.50
343	Corey Thomas	.50
344	Scott Milanovich	.50
345	Pat Barnes	.50
346	Danny Wuerffel	.50
347	Kevin Daft	.50
348	*Ron Powlus*	1.50
349	Tony Graziani	.50
350	*Norman Miller*	.50
351	Cory Sauter	.50
352	*Marcus Crandell*	.50
353	*Sean Morey*	.50
354	Jeff Ogden	.50
355	Ted White	.50
356	*Jim Kubiak*	.50
357	*Aaron Stecker*	.50
358	Ronnie Powell	.50
359	*Matt Lytle*	.50
360	*Kendrick Nord*	.50
361	*Tim Rattay*	4.00
362	*Rob Morris*	1.50
363	*Chris Samuels*	2.00
364	*Todd Husak*	2.00
365	*Ahmed Plummer*	1.50
366	*Frank Murphy*	1.50
367	*Michael Wiley*	3.00
368	*Giovanni Carmazzi*	6.00
369	*Anthony Becht*	2.00
370	*John Abraham*	1.50
371	*Shaun Alexander*	7.00
372	*Thomas Jones*	8.00
373	*Courtney Brown*	5.00
374	*Curtis Keaton*	1.50
375	*Jerry Porter*	3.50
376	*Corey Simon*	2.00
377	*Dez White*	3.00
378	*Jamal Lewis*	7.00
379	*Ron Dayne*	15.00
380	*R. Jay Soward*	4.00
381	*Tee Martin*	3.00
382	*Shaun Ellis*	1.50
383	*Brian Urlacher*	3.00
384	*Reuben Droughns*	2.50
385	*Travis Taylor*	5.00
386	*Plaxico Burress*	10.00
387	*Chad Pennington*	10.00
388	*Sylvester Morris*	4.00
389	*Ron Dugans*	3.00
390	*Joe Hamilton*	2.50
391	*Chris Redman*	4.00
392	*Trung Canidate*	3.00
393	*J.R. Redmond*	4.00
394	*Danny Farmer*	2.00
395	*Todd Pinkston*	2.00
396	*Dennis Northcutt*	3.00
397	*Laveranues Coles*	3.00
398	*Bubba Franks*	3.00
399	*Travis Prentice*	3.00
400	*Peter Warrick*	15.00

2000 Topps Collection

	MT
Complete Set (400):	50.00
Collection Cards: 1x	
Collection Rookies: 1x	

1 Kurt Warner
2 Darrell Russell
3 Tai Streets
4 Bryant Young
5 Kent Graham
6 Shawn Jefferson
7 Wesley Walls
8 Jessie Armstead
9 Dedric Ward
10 Emmitt Smith
11 James Stewart
12 Frank Sanders
13 Ray Buchanan
14 Olindo Mare
15 Andre Reed
16 Curtis Conway
17 Patrick Jeffers
18 Greg Hill
19 Johnny Unitas
20 Brett Favre
21 Jerome Pathon
22 Jason Tucker
23 Charles Johnson
24 Brian Mitchell
25 Billy Miller
26 Jay Fiedler
27 Marcus Pollard
28 De'Mond Parker
29 Leslie Shepherd
30 Fred Taylor
31 Michael Pittman
32 Ricky Watters
33 Derrick Brooks
34 Junior Seau
35 Troy Vincent
36 Eric Allen
37 Pete Mitchell
38 Tony Simmons
39 Az-Zahir Hakim
40 Dan Marino
41 Mac Cody
42 Scott Dreisbach
43 Al Wilson
44 Luther Broughton
45 Wane McGarity
46 Stephen Boyd
47 Michael Strahan
48 Chris Chandler
49 Tony Martin
50 Edgerrin James
51 John Randle
52 Warrick Dunn
53 Elvis Grbac
54 Champ Bailey
55 Kyle Brady
56 John Lynch
57 Kevin Carter
58 Mike Pritchard
59 Deon Mitchell
60 Randy Moss
61 Jermaine Fazande
62 Donovan McNabb
63 Richard Huntley
64 Rich Gannon
65 Aaron Glenn
66 Amani Toomer
67 Andre Hastings
68 Ricky Williams
69 Sam Madison
70 Drew Bledsoe
71 Eric Moulds
72 Justin Armour
73 Jamal Anderson
74 Mario Bates
75 Sam Gash
76 Macey Brooks
77 Tremain Mack
78 David LaFleur
79 Dexter Coakley
80 Cris Carter
81 Byron Chamberlain
82 David Sloan
83 Mike Devlin
84 Jimmy Smith
85 Derrick Alexander
86 Damon Huard
87 Jake Reed
88 Darrell Green
89 Derrick Mason
90 Curtis Martin
91 Donnie Abraham
92 D'Marco Farr
93 Ahman Green
94 Shane Matthews
95 Torrance Small
96 Duce Staley
97 Jon Ritchie
98 Victor Green
99 Kerry Collins
100 Peyton Manning
101 Ben Coates
102 Thurman Thomas
103 Cornelius Bennett
104 Terance Mathis
105 Adrian Murrell
106 Donald Hayes
107 Terry Kirby
108 James Allen
109 Ty Law
110 Tim Brown
111 Chad Bratzke
112 Deion Sanders
113 James Johnson
114 Tony Richardson
115 Tony Brackens
116 Ken Dilger
117 Albert Connell
118 Neil O'Donnell
119 Selucio Sanford
120 Steve Young
121 Tony Horne
122 Charlie Rogers
123 J.J. Stokes
124 Kenny Bynum
125 Jeff Graham
126 Ike Hillard
127 Ray Lucas
128 Terry Glenn
129 Rickey Dudley
130 Joey Galloway
131 Brian Dawkins
132 Rob Moore
133 Bob Christian
134 Anthony Wright
135 Antowain Smith
136 Kevin Johnson
137 Scott Covington
138 D'Wayne Bates
139 Sam Cowart
140 Isaac Bruce
141 Tony McGee
142 Dale Carter
143 Matt Hasselbeck
144 Torry Holt
145 Daunte Culpepper
146 Yatil Green
147 Chris Howard
148 Irving Fryar
149 Derrick Mayes
150 Warren Sapp
151 Ricky Proehl
152 Eric Kresser
153 Jeff Garcia
154 Freddie Jones
155 Michael Cloud
156 Wayne Chrebet
157 Joe Montgomery
158 Shannon Sharpe
159 Eddie Kennison
160 Eddie George
161 Jay Riemersma
162 Craig da Luz
163 Aeneas Williams
164 Jim Miller
165 Jamir Miller
166 Tim Biakabutuka
167 Kordell Stewart
168 Charlie Garner
169 Germane Crowell
170 Stephen Davis
171 Jeff George
172 Mark Brunell
173 Stephen Alexander
174 Mike Alstott
175 Terry Allen
176 Ed McCaffrey
177 Bobby Engram
178 Andre Cooper
179 Kevin Faulk
180 Errict Rhett
181 Jammi German
182 Oronde Gadsden
183 Jevon Kearse
184 Herman Moore
185 Terrence Wilkins
186 Raghib Ismail
187 Patrick Johnson
188 Simeon Rice
189 Mo Lewis
190 Qadry Ismail
191 Terry Jackson
192 Rashaan Shehee
193 Charles Woodson
194 Akili Smith
195 Yancey Thigpen
196 Michael Westbrook
197 Donnell Bennett
198 Sedrick Irvin
199 Keenan McCardell
200 Marshall Faulk
201 Jeff Blake
202 Rob Johnson
203 Vinny Testaverde
204 Andy Katzenmoyer
205 Michael Basnight
206 Lance Schulters
207 Shaun King
208 Bill Schroeder
209 Skip Hicks
210 Jake Plummer
211 Leroy Hoard
212 Reggie Barlow
213 E.G. Green
214 Fred Lane
215 Antonio Freeman
216 Grant Wistrom
217 Kevin Dyson
218 Mikhael Ricks
219 Rod Woodson
220 Tim Dwight
221 Darnay Scott
222 Curtis Enis
223 Sean Bennett
224 Napoleon Kaufman
225 Jonathon Linton
226 Jim Harbaugh
227 Hardy Nickerson
228 Todd Lyght
229 Dorsey Levens
230 Steve Beuerlein
231 Marty Booker
232 Andre Wadsworth
233 James Hasty
234 Shawn Bryson
235 Larry Centers
236 Charlie Batch
237 Steve McNair
238 Darrin Chiaverini
239 Jerome Bettis
240 Muhsin Muhammad
241 Terrell Fletcher
242 Jon Kitna
243 Frank Wycheck
244 Tony Gonzalez
245 Ron Rivers
246 Olandis Gary
247 Jermaine Lewis
248 Joe Jurevicius
249 Richie Anderson
250 Marcus Robinson
251 Shawn Springs
252 William Floyd
253 Bobby Shaw
254 Glyn Milburn
255 Brian Griese
256 Donnie Edwards
257 Joe Horn
258 Cameron Cleeland
259 Glenn Foley
260 Corey Dillon
261 Troy Brown
262 Stoney Case
263 Kevin Williams
264 London Fletcher
265 O.J. McDuffie
266 Jonathan Quinn
267 Trent Dilfer
268 Dameyune Craig
269 Terrell Owens
270 Tim Couch
271 Dameane Douglas
272 Moses Moreno
273 Bruce Smith
274 Peerless Price
275 Sam Garnes
276 Natrone Means
277 Na Brown
278 Dave Moore
279 Chris Sanders
280 Troy Aikman
281 Cecil Collins
282 Matthew Hatchette
283 Bill Romanowski
284 Basil Mitchell
285 Tony Banks
286 Jake Delhomme
287 Keyshawn Johnson
288 Dexter McLeon
289 Corey Bradford
290 Terrell Davis
291 Johnnie Morton
292 Kevin Lockett
293 Robert Smith
294 Jeff Lewis
295 Wali Rainer
296 Troy Edwards
297 Keith Poole
298 Priest Holmes
299 David Boston
300 Marvin Harrison
301 Levon Kirkland
302 Robert Holcombe
303 Autry Denson
304 Kevin Hardy
305 Rod Smith
306 Robert Porcher
307 Cade McNown
308 Craig Yeast
309 Doug Flutie
310 Jerry Rice
311 Brad Johnson
312 Tiki Barber
313 Will Blackwell
314 Sean Dawkins
315 Jacquez Green
316 Zach Thomas
317 Gus Frerotte
318 Chris Warren
319 Carl Pickens
320 Tyrone Wheatley
321 Kurt Warner
322 Dan Marino
323 Cris Carter
324 Brett Favre
325 Marshall Faulk
326 Jevon Kearse
327 Edgerrin James
328 Emmitt Smith
329 Andre Reed
330 Kevin Dyson, Frank Wycheck
331 Olindo Mare
332 Marcus Coleman
333 James Johnson
334 Ray Lucas
335 Dedric Ward
336 Richie Cunningham
337 James Hasty
338 Sedrick Shaw
339 Kurt Warner
340 Marshall Faulk
341 Brian Shay
342 L.C. Stevens
343 Corey Thomas
344 Scott Milanovich
345 Pat Barnes
346 Danny Wuerffel
347 Kevin Daft
348 Ron Powlus
349 Tony Graziani
350 Norman Miller
351 Cory Sauter
352 Marcus Crandell
353 Sean Morey
354 Jeff Ogden
355 Ted White
356 Jim Kubiak
357 Aaron Stecker
358 Ronnie Powell
359 Matt Lytle
360 Kendrick Nord
361 *Tim Rattay*
362 *Rob Morris*
363 *Chris Samuels*
364 *Todd Husak*
365 *Ahmed Plummer*
366 *Frank Murphy*
367 *Michael Wiley*
368 *Giovanni Carmazzi*
369 *Anthony Becht*
370 *John Abraham*
371 *Shaun Alexander*
372 *Thomas Jones*
373 *Courtney Brown*
374 *Curtis Keaton*
375 *Jerry Porter*
376 *Corey Simon*
377 *Dez White*
378 *Jamal Lewis*
379 *Ron Dayne*
380 *R. Jay Soward*
381 *Tee Martin*
382 *Shaun Ellis*
383 *Brian Urlacher*
384 *Reuben Droughns*
385 *Travis Taylor*
386 *Plaxico Burress*
387 *Chad Pennington*
388 *Sylvester Morris*
389 *Ron Dugans*
390 *Joe Hamilton*
391 *Chris Redman*
392 *Trung Canidate*
393 *J.R. Redmond*
394 *Danny Farmer*
395 *Todd Pinkston*
396 *Dennis Northcutt*
397 *Laveranues Coles*
398 *Bubba Franks*
399 *Travis Prentice*
400 *Peter Warrick*

2000 Topps Autographs

		MT
Complete Set (15):		750.00
Common Player:		20.00
Minor Stars:		40.00
Inserted 1:1,015		
Production 250-700		
SA	Shaun Alexander	50.00
SD	Stephen Davis	40.00
RD	Ron Dayne	85.00
MF	Marshall Faulk	50.00
MH	Marvin Harrison	40.00
EJ	Edgerrin James	85.00
TJ	Thomas Jones	60.00
JK	Jon Kitna	20.00
PM	Peyton Manning	125.00
SM	Sylvester Morris	20.00
CP	Chad Pennington	75.00
JS	Jimmy Smith	20.00
ZT	Zach Thomas	20.00
KW	Kurt Warner	150.00
PW	Peter Warrick	85.00

2000 Topps Chrome Previews

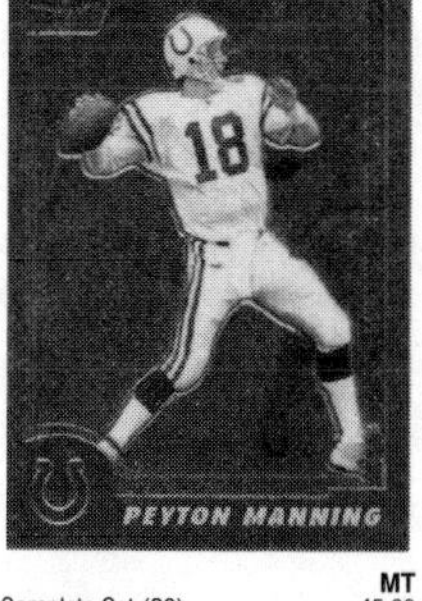

		MT
Complete Set (20):		45.00
Common Player:		1.00
Minor Stars:		2.00
Inserted 1:18		
CP1	Kurt Warner	7.00
CP2	Shaun King	2.50
CP3	Brad Johnson	2.00
CP4	Daunte Culpepper	2.50
CP5	Brett Favre	6.00
CP6	Eddie George	2.50
CP7	Dan Marino	5.00
CP8	Randy Moss	6.00
CP9	Troy Aikman	4.00
CP10	Peyton Manning	5.00
CP11	Fred Taylor	2.50
CP12	Ricky Williams	3.00
CP13	Jimmy Smith	1.00
CP14	Jerry Rice	4.00
CP15	Marshall Faulk	2.00
CP16	Marvin Harrison	2.00
CP17	Stephen Davis	2.00
CP18	Isaac Bruce	2.00
CP19	Emmitt Smith	5.00
CP20	Edgerrin James	6.00

2000 Topps Combos

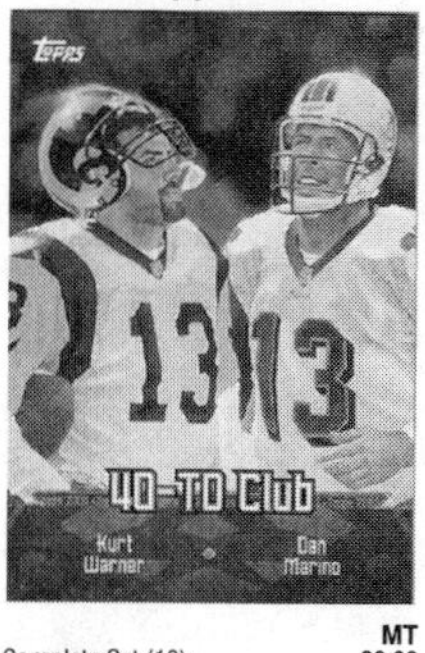

		MT
Complete Set (10):		20.00
Common Player:		1.50
Inserted 1:12		
TC1	Johnny Unitas, Peyton Manning	5.00
TC2	Cris Carter, Randy Moss	5.00
TC3	Ricky Williams, Edgerrin James	6.00
TC4	Marvin Harrison, Jimmy Smith	1.50
TC5	Isaac Bruce, Joey Galloway	1.50
TC6	Donovan McNabb, Tim Couch, Shaun King, Daunte Culpepper, Cade McNown, Akili Smith	4.00
TC7	Stephen Davis, Fred Taylor	2.50
TC8	Marshall Faulk, Eddie George	1.50
TC9	Emmitt Smith, Troy Aikman	4.00
TC10	Kurt Warner, Dan Marino	7.00

2000 Topps Hall of Fame Autographs

		MT
Complete Set (5):		450.00
Common Player:		50.00
Inserted 1:3,551		
HOF1	Joe Montana	300.00
HOF2	Howie Long	80.00
HOF3	Ronnie Lott	60.00
HOF4	Dan Rooney	50.00
HOF5	Dave Wilcox	50.00

2000 Topps Johnny Unitas Reprints

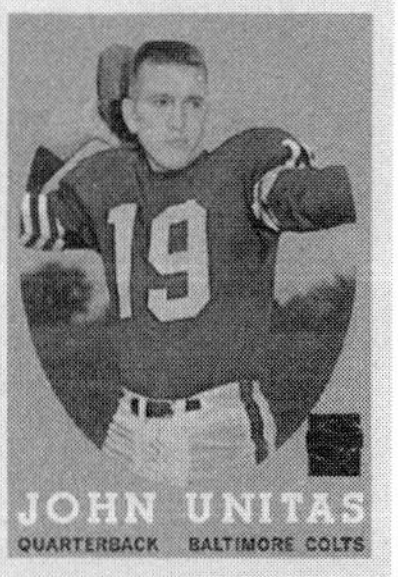

		MT
Complete Set (18):		75.00
Common Player:		5.00
Inserted 1:19 Hobby		
Chrome Cards:		2x
Inserted 1:72 Hobby		
Autographs:		40x
Inserted 1:13,678 Hobby		
R1	Johnny Unitas	5.00
R2	Johnny Unitas	5.00
R3	Johnny Unitas	5.00
R4	Johnny Unitas	5.00
R5	Johnny Unitas	5.00
R6	Johnny Unitas	5.00
R7	Johnny Unitas	5.00
R8	Johnny Unitas	5.00
R9	Johnny Unitas	5.00
R10	Johnny Unitas	5.00
R11	Johnny Unitas	5.00
R12	Johnny Unitas	5.00
R13	Johnny Unitas	5.00
R14	Johnny Unitas	5.00
R15	Johnny Unitas	5.00
R16	Johnny Unitas	5.00
R17	Johnny Unitas	5.00
R18	Johnny Unitas	5.00

2000 Topps Jumbos

		MT
Complete Set (8):		20.00
Common Player:		1.50
1:Hobby Box		
1	Peyton Manning	4.00
2	Marshall Faulk	1.50
3	Dan Marino	4.00
4	Randy Moss	5.00
5	Kurt Warner	6.00
6	Eddie George	2.00
7	Brett Favre	5.00
8	Edgerrin James	5.00

2000 Topps Own The Game

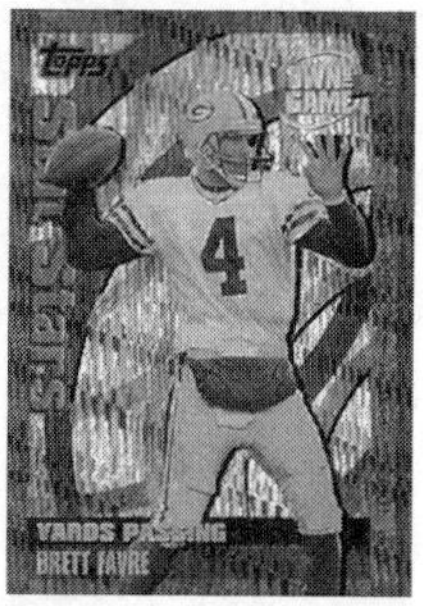

		MT
Complete Set (30):		40.00
Common Player:		1.00
Minor Stars:		2.00
Inserted 1:12		
OTG1	Steve Beuerlein	1.00
OTG2	Kurt Warner	7.00
OTG3	Peyton Manning	5.00
OTG4	Brett Favre	6.00
OTG5	Brad Johnson	2.00
OTG6	Edgerrin James	6.00
OTG7	Curtis Martin	2.00
OTG8	Stephen Davis	2.00
OTG9	Emmitt Smith	5.00
OTG10	Marshall Faulk	2.00
OTG11	Eddie George	2.50
OTG12	Duce Staley	2.00
OTG13	Charlie Garner	1.00
OTG14	Marvin Harrison	2.00
OTG15	Jimmy Smith	1.00
OTG16	Randy Moss	6.00
OTG17	Marcus Robinson	2.00
OTG18	Tim Brown	2.00
OTG19	Germane Crowell	1.00
OTG20	Muhsin Muhammad	1.00
OTG21	Cris Carter	2.00
OTG22	Michael Westbrook	1.00
OTG23	Amani Toomer	1.00
OTG24	Keyshawn Johnson	2.00
OTG25	Isaac Bruce	2.00
OTG26	Kurt Warner	7.00
OTG27	Stephen Davis	2.00
OTG28	Edgerrin James	6.00
OTG29	Cris Carter	2.00
OTG30	Marvin Harrison	2.00

2000 Topps Pro Bowl Jerseys

	MT
Complete Set (24):	1000.
Common Player:	20.00
Minor Stars:	40.00
Inserted 1:271	
Mike Alstott	50.00
Jessie Armstead	20.00
Steve Beuerlein	40.00
Tony Brackens	20.00
Mark Brunell	75.00
Cris Carter	50.00
Kevin Carter	20.00
Corey Dillon	50.00
Rich Gannon	40.00
Eddie George	60.00
Tony Gonzalez	40.00
Kevin Hardy	20.00
Marvin Harrison	50.00
Keyshawn Johnson	50.00
Olindo Mare	20.00
Bruce Matthews	20.00
Muhsin Muhammad	40.00
Darrell Russell	20.00
Warren Sapp	40.00
Emmitt Smith	100.00
Michael Strahan	20.00
Zach Thomas	40.00
Kurt Warner	125.00
Rod Woodson	20.00

2000 Topps Rookie Photo Shoot Autographs

		MT
Common Player:		100.00
Inserted 1:5,761		
SA	Shaun Alexander	250.00
AB	Anthony Becht	100.00
CB	Courtney Brown	125.00
PB	Plaxico Burress	175.00
TC	Trung Canidate	100.00
LC	Laveranues Coles	125.00
RD	Ron Dayne	350.00
RDR	Reuben Droughns	100.00
RDU	Ron Dugans	100.00
DF	Danny Farmer	100.00
DFR	Bubba Franks	100.00
JH	Joe Hamilton	100.00
TJ	Thomas Jones	150.00
CK	Curtis Keaton	100.00
JL	Jamal Lewis	500.00
TM	Tee Martin	100.00
SM	Sylvester Morris	175.00
DN	Dennis Northcutt	100.00
CP	Chad Pennington	300.00
TP	Todd Pinkston	100.00
JP	Jerry Porter	100.00
TPR	Travis Prentice	125.00
CR	Chris Redman	150.00
JR	J.R. Redmond	125.00
CSA	Chris Samuels	100.00
CS	Corey Simon	100.00
TT	Travis Taylor	125.00
BU	Brian Urlacher	250.00
PW	Peter Warrick	350.00
DW	Dez White	100.00

A player's name in *italic type* indicates a rookie card.

2000 Topps Super Bowl MVP Autograph Relic

		MT
Inserted 1:1,287		
SB1	Kurt Warner	300.00

2000 Topps Chrome

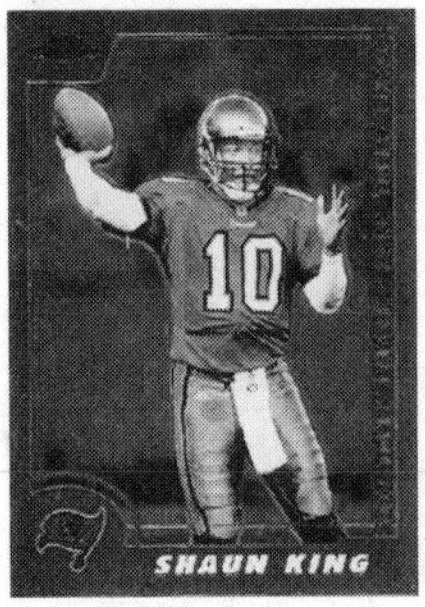

	MT
Complete Set (270):	1350.
Common Player:	.25
Minor Stars:	.50
Common Europe:	1.00
Common Rookie:	15.00
Production 1,650 Sets	
Pack (4):	4.50
Wax Box (24):	85.00

1	Daunte Culpepper	1.50
2	Troy Edwards	1.00
3	Terrell Owens	1.00
4	Ricky Proehl	.25
5	Shaun King	1.50
6	Jeff George	.50
7	Champ Bailey	.50
8	Amani Toomer	.25
9	Stephen Boyd	.25
10	Thurman Thomas	.50
11	Patrick Jeffers	.75
12	Jake Plummer	1.00
13	Peter Boulware	.25
14	Darrin Chiaverini	.25
15	Olandis Gary	1.25
16	Peyton Manning	3.00
17	Joe Horn	.25
18	Wayne Chrebet	.50
19	Freddie Jones	.25
20	Kurt Warner	4.00
21	Mike Alstott	1.00
22	Stephen Davis	1.00
23	Tim Brown	.75
24	Damon Huard	.75
25	Terry Glenn	1.00
26	Ricky Williams	2.50
27	Tim Dwight	1.00
28	Jay Riemersma	.25
29	Carl Pickens	.50
30	Brett Favre	4.00
31	Oronde Gadsden	.25
32	Steve McNair	1.00
33	Michael Pittman	.25
34	Emmitt Smith	2.50
35	Mark Brunell	1.50
36	Ed McCaffrey	.75
37	Tyrone Wheatley	.25
38	Sean Dawkins	.25
39	Jevon Kearse	1.00
40	Tai Streets	.25
41	Keyshawn Johnson	1.00
42	Germane Crowell	.75
43	Yatil Green	.25
44	*Anthony Wright*	15.00
45	Jerry Rice	2.00
46	Az-Zahir Hakim	.50
47	Stephen Alexander	.25
48	Zach Thomas	.50
49	Tony Simmons	.25
50	Jessie Armstead	.25
51	Kordell Stewart	1.00
52	Cade McNown	1.50
53	Tony Gonzalez	.75
54	John Randle	.25
55	Donovan McNabb	1.50
56	Warrick Dunn	1.00
57	Dorsey Levens	1.00
58	Errict Rhett	.25
59	Priest Holmes	.75
60	Terrell Davis	2.50
61	Natrone Means	.50
62	Brad Johnson	1.00
63	Rickey Dudley	.25
64	Billy Miller	.25
65	Randy Moss	3.00
66	Joe Montgomery	.25
67	Johnnie Morton	.25
68	Peerless Price	1.00
69	Raghib Ismail	.25
70	David Boston	1.00
71	Fred Taylor	1.75
72	Jermaine Fazande	.50
73	Elvis Grbac	.50
74	Derrick Mayes	.25
75	Yancey Thigpen	.25
76	Ike Hilliard	.50
77	Muhsin Muhammad	.50
78	Shawn Jefferson	.25
79	Rod Smith	.75
80	Darnay Scott	.50
81	Cameron Cleeland	.50
82	Steve Young	1.50
83	E.G. Green	.25
84	Robert Smith	1.00
85	Jermaine Lewis	.25
86	Tim Biakabutuka	.25
87	Jerome Pathon	.25
88	Kent Graham	.25
89	Bruce Smith	.25
90	Isaac Bruce	1.00
91	Curtis Enis	1.00
92	D'Marco Farr	.25
93	Keith Poole	.25
94	Troy Aikman	2.00
95	Rich Gannon	.50
96	Michael Westbrook	.50
97	Albert Connell	.50
98	James Johnson	.25
99	Jeff Blake	.50
100	Joey Galloway	1.00
101	Rob Moore	.50
102	Chris Chandler	.50
103	Fred Lane	.25
104	Eddie Kennison	.25
105	Kevin Hardy	.25
106	Napoleon Kaufman	1.00
107	Kevin Dyson	.50
108	Keenan McCardell	.50
109	Drew Bledsoe	1.50
110	Kevin Johnson	.75
111	Terance Mathis	.25
112	Gus Frerotte	.25
113	Matthew Hatchette	.25
114	Herman Moore	.75
115	Curtis Martin	1.00
116	Jacquez Green	.25
117	Jake Reed	.25
118	Antonio Freeman	1.00
119	Jim Miller	.25
120	Frank Sanders	.25
121	Brian Griese	1.00
122	Troy Brown	.25
123	Jeff Graham	.25
124	Marshall Faulk	1.00
125	Vinny Testaverde	.50
126	Frank Wycheck	.25
127	Kerry Collins	.50
128	Jay Fiedler	1.00
129	Cris Carter	1.00
130	Jason Tucker	.25
131	Antowain Smith	1.00
132	Tony Banks	.75
133	Terrence Wilkins	.75
134	Tony Martin	.25
135	Richard Huntley	.25
136	J.J. Stokes	.50
137	Ricky Watters	.50
138	Pete Mitchell	.25
139	Jimmy Smith	1.00
140	Doug Flutie	1.00
141	Corey Bradford	.25
142	Curtis Conway	.25
143	Moses Moreno	.25
144	Torry Holt	1.00
145	Warren Sapp	.25
146	Duce Staley	1.00
147	Mikhael Ricks	.25
148	Edgerrin James	3.00
149	Charlie Batch	1.00
150	Rob Johnson	.50
151	Jamal Anderson	1.00
152	Tim Couch	2.50
153	O.J. McDuffie	.50
154	Charles Woodson	.50
155	*Jake Delhomme*	2.50
156	Eddie George	1.25
157	Jim Harbaugh	.25
158	Jon Kitna	1.00
159	Derrick Alexander	.25
160	Marvin Harrison	1.00
161	James Stewart	.50
162	Qadry Ismail	.25
163	Wesley Walls	.25
164	Steve Beuerlein	.50
165	Marcus Robinson	1.00
166	Bill Schroeder	.25
167	Charles Johnson	.25
168	Charlie Garner	.25
169	Eric Moulds	1.00
170	Jerome Bettis	1.00
171	Tai Streets	.25
172	Akili Smith	1.25
173	Jonathon Linton	.50
174	Corey Dillon	1.00
175	Junior Seau	.50
176	Jonathan Quinn	.25
177	Bobby Engram	.25
178	Shannon Sharpe	.50
179	Michael Basnight	.25
180	Sedrick Irvin	.25
181	*Sammy Morris*	30.00
182	*Ron Dixon*	25.00
183	*Trevor Gaylor*	20.00
184	*Chris Cole*	15.00
185	*Deltha O'Neal*	15.00
186	*Sebastian Janikowski*	25.00
187	*Kwame Cavil*	15.00
188	*Chad Morton*	20.00
189	*Terrelle Smith*	15.00
190	*Frank Moreau*	20.00
191	Kurt Warner	2.00
192	Dan Marino	1.50
193	Cris Carter	.50
194	Brett Favre	1.75
195	Marshall Faulk	.50
196	Jevon Kearse	.50
197	Edgerrin James	1.75
198	Emmitt Smith	1.25
199	Andre Reed	.25
200	Kevin Dyson, Frank Wycheck	.25
201	Olindo Mare	.25
202	Marcus Coleman	.25
203	James Johnson	.25
204	Ray Lucas	.25
205	Dedric Ward	.25
206	Richie Cunningham	.25
207	James Hasty	.25
208	Sedrick Shaw	.25
209	Kurt Warner	2.00
210	Marshall Faulk	.50
211	Brian Shay	1.00
212	L.C. Stevens	1.00
213	Corey Thomas	1.00
214	Scott Milanovich	1.00
215	Pat Barnes	1.00
216	Danny Wuerffel	1.00
217	Kevin Daft	1.00
218	*Ron Powlus*	2.50
219	Eric Kresser	1.00
220	Norman Miller	1.00
221	Cory Sauter	1.00
222	Marcus Crandell	1.00
223	Sean Morey	1.00
224	Jeff Ogden	1.00
225	Ted White	1.00
226	Jim Kubiak	1.00
227	Aaron Stecker	1.00
228	Ronnie Powell	1.00
229	Matt Lytle	1.00
230	Kendrick Nord	1.00
231	*Tim Rattay*	25.00
232	*Rob Morris*	15.00
233	*Chris Samuels*	25.00
234	*Todd Husak*	25.00
235	*Ahmed Plummer*	15.00
236	*Frank Murphy*	15.00
237	*Michael Wiley*	20.00
238	*Giovanni Carmazzi*	25.00
239	*Anthony Becht*	20.00
240	*John Abraham*	15.00
241	*Shaun Alexander*	75.00
242	*Thomas Jones*	50.00
243	*Courtney Brown*	25.00
244	*Curtis Keaton*	15.00
245	*Jerry Porter*	20.00
246	*Corey Simon*	25.00
247	*Dez White*	20.00
248	*Jamal Lewis*	150.00
249	*Ron Dayne*	120.00
250	*R. Jay Soward*	20.00
251	*Tee Martin*	25.00
252	*Shaun Ellis*	15.00
253	*Brian Urlacher*	75.00
254	*Reuben Droughns*	15.00
255	*Travis Taylor*	30.00
256	*Plaxico Burress*	60.00
257	*Chad Pennington*	85.00
258	*Sylvester Morris*	60.00
259	*Ron Dugans*	20.00
260	*Joe Hamilton*	20.00
261	*Chris Redman*	50.00
262	*Trung Canidate*	20.00
263	*J.R. Redmond*	30.00
264	*Danny Farmer*	20.00
265	*Todd Pinkston*	25.00
266	*Dennis Northcutt*	25.00
267	*Laveranues Coles*	30.00
268	*Bubba Franks*	25.00
269	*Travis Prentice*	40.00
270	*Peter Warrick*	100.00

2000 Topps Chrome Refractors Parallel

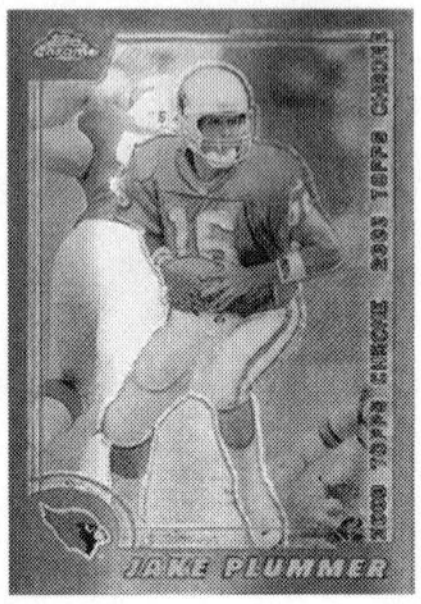

	MT
Refractor Cards:	4x-8x
Inserted 1:12	
Refractor Rookies:	2x
Production 150 Sets	

2000 Topps Chrome Combos

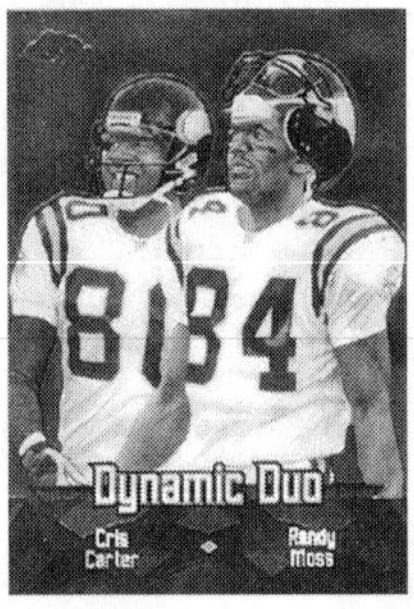

		MT
Complete Set (10):		35.00
Common Player:		2.00
Inserted 1:20		
Refractors:		4x
Inserted 1:200		
TC1	Johnny Unitas, Peyton Manning	6.00
TC2	Cris Carter, Randy Moss	5.00
TC3	Ricky Williams, Edgerrin James	6.00
TC4	Marvin Harrison, Jimmy Smith	2.00
TC5	Isaac Bruce, Joey Galloway	2.00
TC6	Donovan McNabb, Tim Couch, Shaun King, Cade McNown, Daunte Culpepper, Akili Smith	6.00
TC7	Stephen Davis, Fred Taylor	3.00
TC8	Marshall Faulk, Eddie George	2.00
TC9	Emmitt Smith, Troy Aikman	4.00
TC10	Kurt Warner, Dan Marino	8.00

Values quoted in this guide reflect the retail price of a card — the price a collector can expect to pay when buying a card from a dealer. The wholesale price — that which a collector can expect to receive from a dealer when selling cards — will be significantly lower, depending on desirability and condition.

2000 Topps Chrome Own the Game

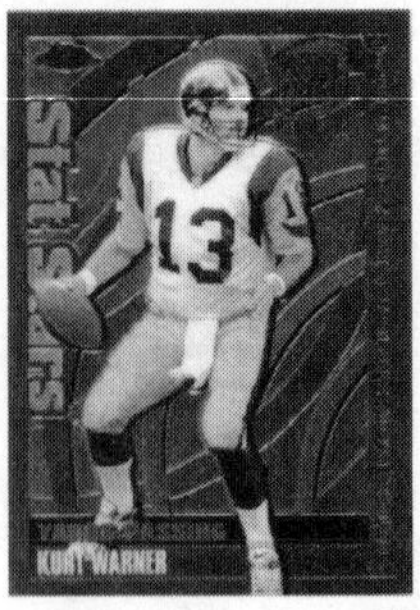

		MT
Complete Set (30):		55.00
Common Player:		1.00
Minor Stars:		2.00
Inserted 1:12		
Refractors:		4x
Inserted 1:120		
OTG1	Steve Beuerlein	1.00
OTG2	Kurt Warner	8.00
OTG3	Peyton Manning	6.00
OTG4	Brett Favre	7.00
OTG5	Brad Johnson	2.00
OTG6	Edgerrin James	6.00
OTG7	Curtis Martin	2.00
OTG8	Stephen Davis	2.00
OTG9	Emmitt Smith	5.00
OTG10	Marshall Faulk	2.00
OTG11	Eddie George	2.50
OTG12	Duce Staley	2.00
OTG13	Charlie Garner	1.00
OTG14	Marvin Harrison	2.00
OTG15	Jimmy Smith	2.00
OTG16	Randy Moss	6.00
OTG17	Marcus Robinson	2.00
OTG18	Tim Brown	1.00
OTG19	Germane Crowell	1.00
OTG20	Muhsin Muhammad	1.00
OTG21	Cris Carter	2.00
OTG22	Michael Westbrook	1.00
OTG23	Amani Toomer	1.00
OTG24	Keyshawn Johnson	2.00
OTG25	Isaac Bruce	2.00
OTG26	Kurt Warner	8.00
OTG27	Stephen Davis	2.00
OTG28	Edgerrin James	6.00
OTG29	Cris Carter	2.00
OTG30	Marvin Harrison	2.00

2000 Topps Chrome Johnny Unitas Reprints

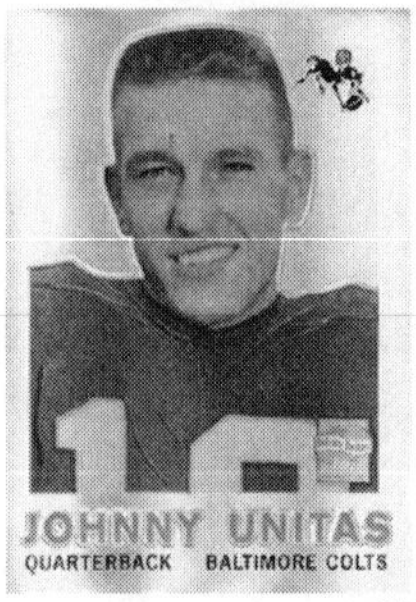

		MT
Complete Set (18):		100.00
Common Player:		6.00
Inserted 1:14		
R1	Johnny Unitas	10.00
R2	Johnny Unitas	6.00
R3	Johnny Unitas	6.00
R4	Johnny Unitas	6.00
R5	Johnny Unitas	6.00
R6	Johnny Unitas	6.00
R7	Johnny Unitas	6.00
R8	Johnny Unitas	6.00
R9	Johnny Unitas	6.00
R10	Johnny Unitas	6.00
R11	Johnny Unitas	6.00
R12	Johnny Unitas	6.00
R13	Johnny Unitas	6.00
R14	Johnny Unitas	6.00
R15	Johnny Unitas	6.00
R16	Johnny Unitas	6.00
R17	Johnny Unitas	6.00
R18	Johnny Unitas	6.00

2000 Topps Chrome Preseason Picks

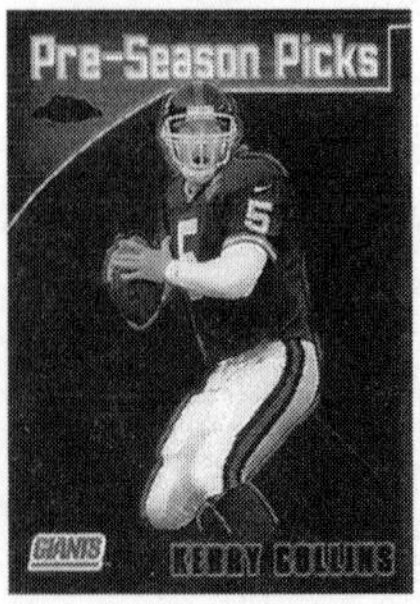

		MT
Complete Set (31):		75.00
Common Player:		1.25
Minor Stars:		2.50
Inserted 1:22		
Refractors:		4x
Inserted 1:220		
P1	Jake Plummer	2.50
P2	Troy Aikman	5.00
P3	Kerry Collins	1.25
P4	Donovan McNabb	3.00
P5	Stephen Davis	2.50
P6	Cade McNown	3.00
P7	Charlie Batch	2.50
P8	Brett Favre	10.00
P9	Randy Moss	10.00
P10	Shaun King	3.00
P11	Tim Couch	5.00
P12	Jamal Anderson	2.50
P13	Steve Beuerlein	1.25
P14	Ricky Williams	5.00
P15	Kurt Warner	10.00
P16	Jerry Rice	5.00
P17	Eric Moulds	2.50
P18	Peyton Manning	8.00
P19	Zach Thomas	1.25
P20	Drew Bledsoe	4.00
P21	Curtis Martin	2.50
P22	Tony Banks	1.25
P23	Akili Smith	2.50
P24	Jimmy Smith	2.50
P25	Jerome Bettis	2.50
P26	Eddie George	3.00
P27	Terrell Davis	6.00
P28	Tony Gonzalez	1.25
P29	Tim Brown	1.25
P30	Junior Seau	1.25
P31	Jon Kitna	2.50

2000 Topps Gallery

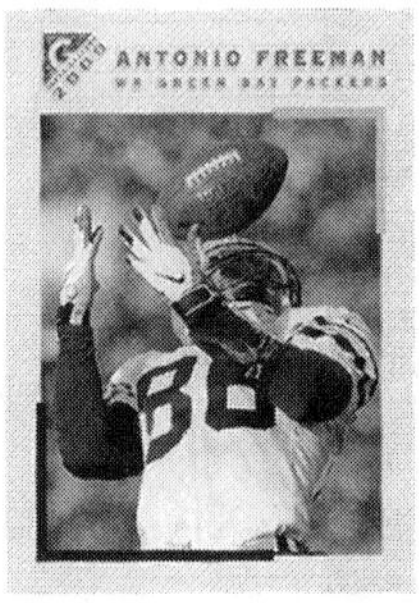

	MT
Complete Set (175):	80.00
Common Player:	.15
Minor Stars:	.30
Common Subset (126-150):	.75
Common Rookie:	1.00
Inserted 1:1	
Pack (6):	3.00
Wax Box (24):	55.00

1	Marshall Faulk	.50
2	Kordell Stewart	.50
3	Priest Holmes	.50
4	James Johnson	.30
5	Charlie Garner	.30
6	Jeff Blake	.30
7	Joey Galloway	.50
8	Terrell Davis	2.00
9	Jerome Bettis	.50
10	Bobby Engram	.15
11	Muhsin Muhammad	.30
12	Marcus Robinson	.50
13	Kerry Collins	.50
14	Jake Plummer	.50
15	J.J. Stokes	.30
16	Tim Couch	1.50
17	Napoleon Kaufman	.50
18	Az-Zahir Hakim	.30
19	Jimmy Smith	.50
20	Eddie George	.75
21	Jacquez Green	.30
22	Champ Bailey	.30
23	Wesley Walls	.30
24	Eric Moulds	.50
25	Corey Dillon	.50
26	Freddie Jones	.15
27	Jevon Kearse	.75
28	Ray Lucas	.50
29	Germane Crowell	.30
30	Randy Moss	2.00
31	Patrick Jeffers	.50
32	Zach Thomas	.30
33	Shannon Sharpe	.30
34	Derrick Mayes	.30
35	Antonio Freeman	.50
36	Terance Mathis	.15
37	Herman Moore	.50
38	Tony Banks	.30
39	Jerry Rice	1.50
40	Troy Aikman	1.50
41	Rickey Dudley	.15
42	Troy Edwards	.50
43	Curtis Martin	.50
44	Eddie Kennison	.15
45	Mark Brunell	1.00
46	Shaun King	1.00
47	Duce Staley	.50
48	Darnay Scott	.30
49	Sean Dawkins	.15
50	Edgerrin James	2.50
51	Olandis Gary	.75
52	Peerless Price	.50
53	Akili Smith	.75
54	Charlie Batch	.50
55	Tim Biakabutuka	.30
56	Rob Moore	.30
57	Keenan McCardell	.30
58	Dan Marino	2.00
59	Tony Gonzalez	.30
60	Stephen Davis	.50
61	Ricky Watters	.30
62	Frank Wycheck	.30
63	Kevin Johnson	.50
64	Isaac Bruce	.50
65	Andre Reed	.15
66	Jamal Anderson	.50
67	Dorsey Levens	.50
68	Raghib Ismail	.15
69	Albert Connell	.30
70	Brett Favre	2.50
71	Wayne Chrebet	.50
72	Jon Kitna	.50
73	Brian Griese	.60
74	Rob Johnson	.30
75	Qadry Ismail	.15
76	Derrick Alexander	.15
77	Tim Dwight	.50
78	Ike Hilliard	.30
79	Frank Sanders	.30
80	Fred Taylor	1.00
81	Robert Smith	.50
82	Vinny Testaverde	.50
83	Steve Young	1.00
84	Tyrone Wheatley	.30
85	Mikhael Ricks	.15
86	Tony Martin	.15
87	Carl Pickens	.30
88	Warrick Dunn	.50
89	Emmitt Smith	2.00
90	Keyshawn Johnson	.50
91	James Stewart	.50
92	Doug Flutie	.75
93	Torry Holt	.50
94	Jeff Graham	.15
95	Steve McNair	.60
96	Errict Rhett	.30
97	Terrell Owens	.50
98	Terry Glenn	.50
99	Steve Beuerlein	.30
100	Kurt Warner	2.50
101	Jeff George	.30
102	Deion Sanders	.50
103	Johnnie Morton	.15
104	Antowain Smith	.50
105	O.J. McDuffie	.30
106	Rod Smith	.30
107	Jim Harbaugh	.30
108	Marvin Harrison	.50
109	Curtis Enis	.50
110	Drew Bledsoe	1.00
111	Mike Alstott	.50
112	Amani Toomer	.30
113	Elvis Grbac	.30
114	Tim Brown	.30
115	Cris Carter	.50
116	Donovan McNabb	1.00
117	Chris Chandler	.30
118	Kevin Dyson	.30
119	Rich Gannon	.30
120	Ricky Williams	1.50
121	Brad Johnson	.50
122	Cade McNown	1.00
123	Ed McCaffrey	.30
124	Michael Westbrook	.30
125	Peyton Manning	2.00
126	Brett Favre	4.00
127	Emmitt Smith	3.00
128	Tim Brown	.75
129	Troy Aikman	2.50
130	Jimmy Smith	.75
131	Dan Marino	3.00
132	Cris Carter	1.00
133	Jerry Rice	2.50
134	Steve Young	1.50
135	Marshall Faulk	1.00
136	Eddie George	1.25
137	Drew Bledsoe	1.50
138	Randy Moss	4.00
139	Germane Crowell	.75
140	Akili Smith	1.25
141	Tim Couch	2.50
142	Marcus Robinson	1.00
143	Daunte Culpepper	1.50
144	Jevon Kearse	1.00
145	Edgerrin James	4.00
146	Tony Gonzalez	.75
147	Cade McNown	1.50
148	Fred Taylor	1.50
149	Donovan McNabb	1.50
150	Ricky Williams	2.50
151	*Jamal Lewis*	10.00
152	*Tee Martin*	1.50
153	*Plaxico Burress*	3.50
154	*Chad Pennington*	6.00
155	*Curtis Keaton*	1.00
156	*Thomas Jones*	3.00
157	*Courtney Brown*	1.50
158	*Ron Dayne*	8.00
159	*Shaun Alexander*	5.00
160	*Travis Taylor*	2.00
161	*Sylvester Morris*	3.50
162	*Giovanni Carmazzi*	1.50
163	*Laveranues Coles*	2.00
164	*Chris Redman*	3.00
165	*Bubba Franks*	1.50
166	*R. Jay Soward*	1.50
167	*Reuben Droughns*	1.00
168	*Todd Pinkston*	1.50
169	*Trung Canidate*	1.50
170	*Danny Farmer*	1.00
171	*Ron Dugans*	1.50
172	*Dennis Northcutt*	1.50
173	*J.R. Redmond*	2.00
174	*Travis Prentice*	2.50
175	*Peter Warrick*	7.00

2000 Topps Gallery Player's Private Issue Parallel

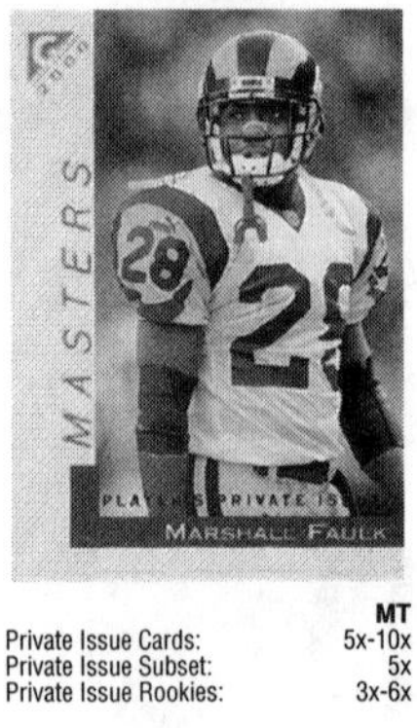

	MT
Private Issue Cards:	5x-10x
Private Issue Subset:	5x
Private Issue Rookies:	3x-6x

Inserted 1:16
Production 250 Sets

1	Marshall Faulk	.50
2	Kordell Stewart	.50
3	Priest Holmes	.50
4	James Johnson	.30
5	Charlie Garner	.30
6	Jeff Blake	.30
7	Joey Galloway	.50
8	Terrell Davis	2.00
9	Jerome Bettis	.50
10	Bobby Engram	.15
11	Muhsin Muhammad	.30
12	Marcus Robinson	.50
13	Kerry Collins	.30
14	Jake Plummer	.50
15	J.J. Stokes	.30
16	Tim Couch	1.50
17	Napoleon Kaufman	.50
18	Az-Zahir Hakim	.30
19	Jimmy Smith	.50
20	Eddie George	.75
21	Jacquez Green	.30
22	Champ Bailey	.30
23	Wesley Walls	.30
24	Eric Moulds	.50
25	Corey Dillon	.50
26	Freddie Jones	.15
27	Jevon Kearse	.75
28	Ray Lucas	.50
29	Germane Crowell	.30
30	Randy Moss	2.00
31	Patrick Jeffers	.50
32	Zach Thomas	.30
33	Shannon Sharpe	.30
34	Derrick Mayes	.30
35	Antonio Freeman	.50
36	Terance Mathis	.15
37	Herman Moore	.50
38	Tony Banks	.30
39	Jerry Rice	1.50
40	Troy Aikman	1.50
41	Rickey Dudley	.15
42	Troy Edwards	.50
43	Curtis Martin	.50
44	Eddie Kennison	.15
45	Mark Brunell	1.00
46	Shaun King	1.00
47	Duce Staley	.50
48	Darnay Scott	.30
49	Sean Dawkins	.15
50	Edgerrin James	2.50
51	Olandis Gary	.75
52	Peerless Price	.50
53	Akili Smith	.75
54	Charlie Batch	.50
55	Tim Biakabutuka	.30
56	Rob Moore	.30
57	Keenan McCardell	.30
58	Dan Marino	2.00
59	Tony Gonzalez	.30
60	Stephen Davis	.50
61	Ricky Watters	.30
62	Frank Wycheck	.30
63	Kevin Johnson	.50
64	Isaac Bruce	.50
65	Andre Reed	.15
66	Jamal Anderson	.50
67	Dorsey Levens	.50
68	Raghib Ismail	.15
69	Albert Connell	.30
70	Brett Favre	2.50
71	Wayne Chrebet	.50
72	Jon Kitna	.50
73	Brian Griese	.60
74	Rob Johnson	.30
75	Qadry Ismail	.15
76	Derrick Alexander	.15
77	Tim Dwight	.50
78	Ike Hilliard	.30
79	Frank Sanders	.30
80	Fred Taylor	1.00
81	Robert Smith	.50
82	Vinny Testaverde	.50
83	Steve Young	1.00
84	Tyrone Wheatley	.30
85	Mikhael Ricks	.15
86	Tony Martin	.15
87	Carl Pickens	.30
88	Warrick Dunn	.50
89	Emmitt Smith	2.00
90	Keyshawn Johnson	.50
91	James Stewart	.50
92	Doug Flutie	.75
93	Torry Holt	.50
94	Jeff Graham	.15
95	Steve McNair	.60
96	Errict Rhett	.30
97	Terrell Owens	.50
98	Terry Glenn	.50
99	Steve Beuerlein	.30
100	Kurt Warner	2.50
101	Jeff George	.30
102	Deion Sanders	.50
103	Johnnie Morton	.15
104	Antowain Smith	.50
105	O.J. McDuffie	.30
106	Rod Smith	.30
107	Jim Harbaugh	.30
108	Marvin Harrison	.50
109	Curtis Enis	.50
110	Drew Bledsoe	1.00
111	Mike Alstott	.50
112	Amani Toomer	.30
113	Elvis Grbac	.30
114	Tim Brown	.30
115	Cris Carter	.50
116	Donovan McNabb	1.00
117	Chris Chandler	.30
118	Kevin Dyson	.30
119	Rich Gannon	.30
120	Ricky Williams	1.50
121	Brad Johnson	.50
122	Cade McNown	1.00
123	Ed McCaffrey	.30
124	Michael Westbrook	.30
125	Peyton Manning	2.00
126	Brett Favre	4.00
127	Emmitt Smith	3.00
128	Tim Brown	.75
129	Troy Aikman	2.50
130	Jimmy Smith	.75
131	Dan Marino	3.00
132	Cris Carter	1.00
133	Jerry Rice	2.50
134	Steve Young	1.50
135	Marshall Faulk	1.50
136	Eddie George	1.25
137	Drew Bledsoe	1.50
138	Randy Moss	4.00
139	Germane Crowell	.75
140	Akili Smith	1.25
141	Tim Couch	2.50
142	Marcus Robinson	1.00
143	Daunte Culpepper	1.50
144	Jevon Kearse	1.00
145	Edgerrin James	4.00
146	Tony Gonzalez	.75
147	Cade McNown	1.50
148	Fred Taylor	1.50
149	Donovan McNabb	1.50
150	Ricky Williams	2.50
151	*Jamal Lewis*	5.00
152	*Tee Martin*	2.50
153	*Plaxico Burress*	8.00
154	*Chad Pennington*	8.00
155	*Curtis Keaton*	1.00
156	*Thomas Jones*	5.00
157	*Courtney Brown*	3.00
158	*Ron Dayne*	10.00
159	*Shaun Alexander*	5.00
160	*Travis Taylor*	4.00
161	*Sylvester Morris*	3.00
162	*Giovanni Carmazzi*	4.00
163	*Laveranues Coles*	2.00
164	*Chris Redman*	3.00
165	*Bubba Franks*	2.50
166	*R. Jay Soward*	3.00
167	*Reuben Droughns*	2.00
168	*Todd Pinkston*	1.00
169	*Trung Canidate*	2.00
170	*Danny Farmer*	1.00
171	*Ron Dugans*	2.00
172	*Dennis Northcutt*	2.50
173	*J.R. Redmond*	3.00
174	*Travis Prentice*	2.50
175	*Peter Warrick*	10.00

2000 Topps Gallery Autographs

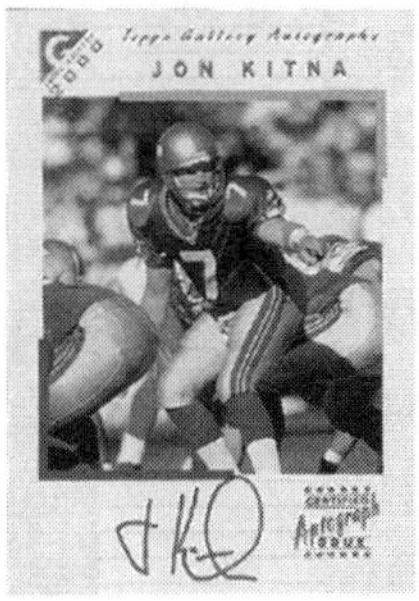

		MT
Complete Set (7):		275.00
Common Player:		20.00
Inserted 1:218		
MF	Marshall Faulk	45.00
TJ	Thomas Jones	45.00
JK	Jon Kitna	20.00
JL	Jamal Lewis	45.00
SM	Sylvester Morris	25.00
ZT	Zach Thomas	20.00
PW	Peter Warrick	100.00

2000 Topps Gallery Exhibitions

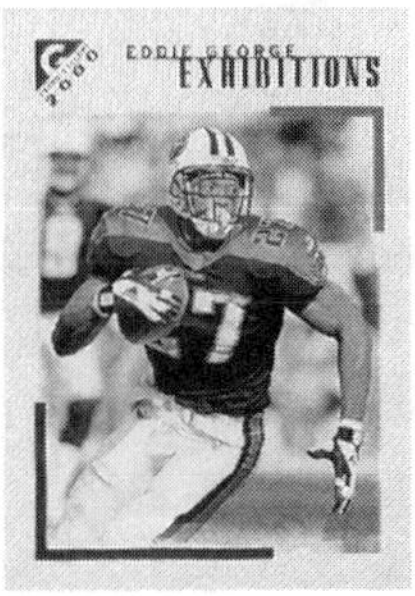

		MT
Complete Set (15):		50.00
Common Player:		2.00
Inserted 1:32		
GE1	Marshall Faulk	3.00
GE2	Muhsin Muhammad	2.00
GE3	Marvin Harrison	3.00
GE4	Stephen Davis	3.00
GE5	Eddie George	4.00
GE6	Antonio Freeman	3.00
GE7	Isaac Bruce	3.00
GE8	Jevon Kearse	3.00
GE9	Curtis Martin	3.00
GE10	Troy Aikman	6.00
GE11	Fred Taylor	4.00
GE12	Edgerrin James	8.00
GE13	Randy Moss	8.00
GE14	Steve Beuerlein	2.00
GE15	Kurt Warner	8.00

Post-1980 cards in Near Mint condition will generally sell for about 75% of the quoted Mint value. Excellent-condition cards bring no more than 40%.

2000 Topps Gallery Gallery of Heroes

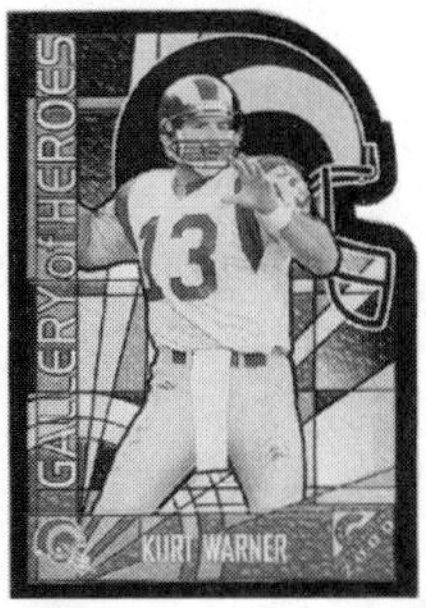

		MT
Complete Set (10):		50.00
Common Player:		3.00
Inserted 1:24		
GH1	Emmitt Smith	8.00
GH2	Troy Aikman	6.00
GH3	Brett Favre	10.00
GH4	Edgerrin James	10.00
GH5	Peyton Manning	10.00
GH6	Randy Moss	10.00
GH7	Marshall Faulk	3.00
GH8	Jerry Rice	6.00
GH9	Kurt Warner	10.00
GH10	Eddie George	4.00

2000 Topps Gallery Heritage

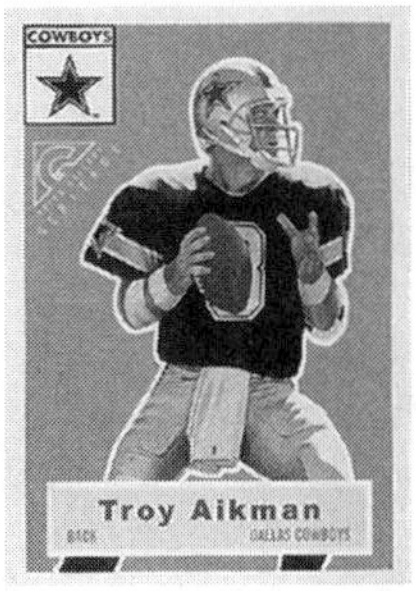

		MT
Complete Set (10):		40.00
Common Player:		2.00
Inserted 1:12		
Proof Cards:		2x
Inserted 1:48		
H1	Marshall Faulk	2.00
H2	Troy Aikman	5.00
H3	Randy Moss	8.00
H4	Brett Favre	8.00
H5	Jerry Rice	5.00
H6	Dan Marino	6.00
H7	Peyton Manning	8.00
H8	Emmitt Smith	6.00
H9	Edgerrin James	8.00
H10	Kurt Warner	8.00

2000 Topps Gallery Proof Positive

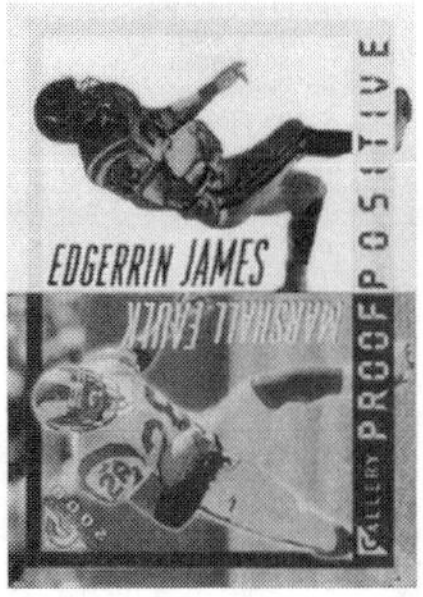

		MT
Complete Set (10):		50.00
Common Player:		3.00
Inserted 1:48		
P1	Dan Marino, Kurt Warner	20.00
P2	Eddie George, Ricky Williams	6.00
P3	Jerry Rice, Keyshawn Johnson	8.00
P4	Bruce Smith, Jevon Kearse	3.00
P5	Marshall Faulk, Edgerrin James	10.00
P6	Marvin Harrison, Marcus Robinson	4.00
P7	Emmitt Smith, Stephen Davis	8.00
P8	Isaac Bruce, Randy Moss	10.00
P9	Steve Young, Mark Brunell	5.00
P10	Drew Bledsoe, Peyton Manning	10.00

A player's name in *italic type* indicates a rookie card.

2000 Topps Gold Label

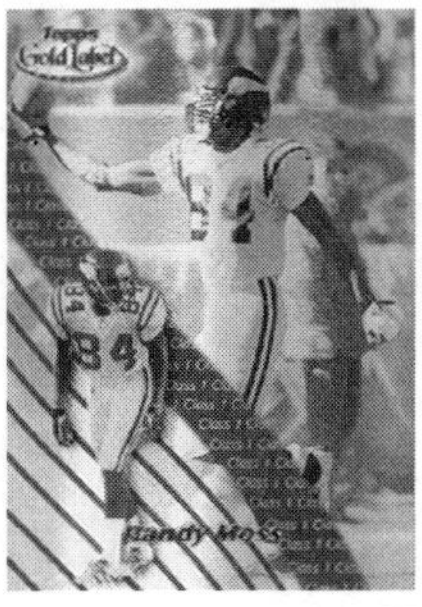

		MT
Complete Set (100):		45.00
Common Player:		.15
Minor Stars:		.30
Common Rookie:		1.00
Pack (5):		5.00
Wax Box (24):		75.00
1	Eric Moulds	.50
2	Muhsin Muhammad	.30
3	Patrick Jeffers	.50
4	Joey Galloway	.50
5	Edgerrin James	2.00
6	Germane Crowell	.50
7	Ed McCaffrey	.30
8	Dorsey Levens	.50
9	Marcus Robinson	.50
10	Tony Gonzalez	.30
11	Robert Smith	.50
12	Rich Gannon	.30
13	Jerry Rice	1.25
14	Mike Alstott	.50
15	Brad Johnson	.30
16	Emmitt Smith	1.75
17	Marvin Harrison	.50
18	Duce Staley	.50
19	Terry Glenn	.50
20	Terrell Owens	.50
21	Antonio Freeman	.50
22	Curtis Enis	.30
23	Michael Westbrook	.30
24	Cris Carter	.50
25	Tim Brown	.30
26	Terrell Davis	1.75
27	Fred Taylor	1.00
28	Amani Toomer	.15
29	Donovan McNabb	1.00
30	Charlie Garner	.30
31	Kurt Warner	2.50
32	Antowain Smith	.30
33	Torry Holt	.50
34	Jake Plummer	.50
35	Steve Beuerlein	.30
36	Raghib Ismail	.15
37	Brett Favre	2.50
38	Mark Brunell	1.00
39	Qadry Ismail	.15
40	Carl Pickens	.30
41	James Stewart	.50
42	Drew Bledsoe	1.00
43	Keenan McCardell	.30
44	Jerome Bettis	.50
45	Jon Kitna	.50
46	Warrick Dunn	.50
47	Jevon Kearse	.50
48	Jamal Anderson	.50
49	Shaun King	1.00
50	Ricky Williams	1.50
51	Elvis Grbac	.30
52	Corey Dillon	.50
53	Brian Griese	.75
54	Steve Young	1.00
55	Tyrone Wheatley	.50
56	Daunte Culpepper	1.25
57	Troy Aikman	1.25
58	Peyton Manning	2.00
59	Stephen Davis	.50
60	Keyshawn Johnson	.50
61	Doug Flutie	.75
62	Ike Hilliard	.15
63	Jeff Blake	.30
64	Tony Banks	.30
65	Tim Couch	1.25
66	Charlie Batch	.50
67	Rob Johnson	.30
68	Cade McNown	.75
69	Steve McNair	.50
70	Eddie George	.75
71	Isaac Bruce	.50
72	Ricky Watters	.30
73	Kordell Stewart	.60
74	Wayne Chrebet	.50
75	Curtis Martin	.50
76	Jimmy Smith	.50
77	Randy Moss	2.00
78	Akili Smith	.50
79	Marshall Faulk	.50
80	Kerry Collins	.30
81	*Ron Dayne*	5.00
82	*Chad Pennington*	3.50
83	*Sylvester Morris*	2.50
84	*Thomas Jones*	2.00
85	*Shaun Alexander*	3.00
86	*Chris Redman*	2.00
87	*Courtney Brown*	1.25
88	*Jerry Porter*	1.00
89	*Ron Dugans*	1.00
90	*Jamal Lewis*	6.00
91	*Travis Prentice*	1.50
92	*Travis Taylor*	1.50
93	*R. Jay Soward*	1.00
94	*Peter Warrick*	4.00
95	*Trung Canidate*	1.00
96	*Tee Martin*	1.25
97	*Bubba Franks*	1.25
98	*Plaxico Burress*	2.50
99	*J.R. Redmond*	1.25
100	*Dennis Northcutt*	1.00

A card number in parentheses ( ) indicates the set is unnumbered.

2000 Topps Gold Label Class 2 Parallel

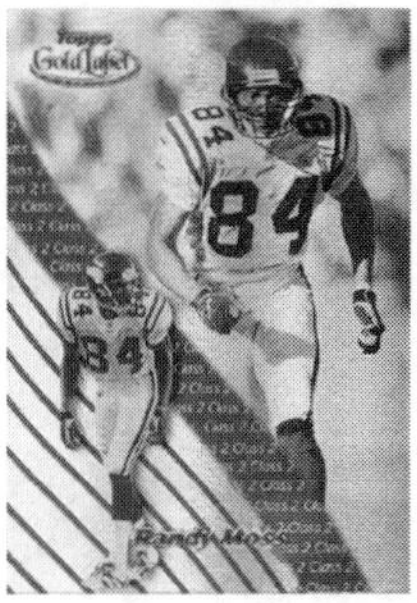

	MT
Class 2 Cards:	1x

2000 Topps Gold Label Class 3 Parallel

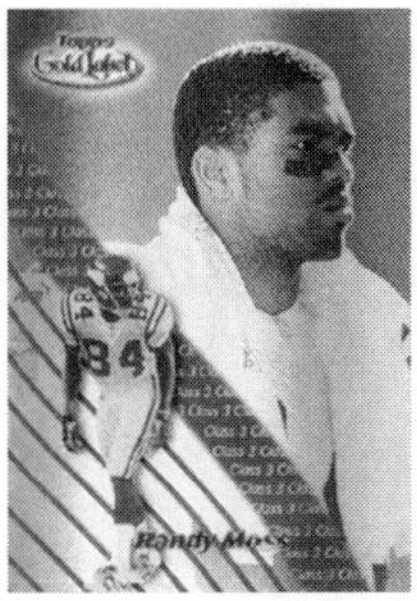

	MT
Class 3 Cards:	1x

2000 Topps Gold Label Premium Parallel

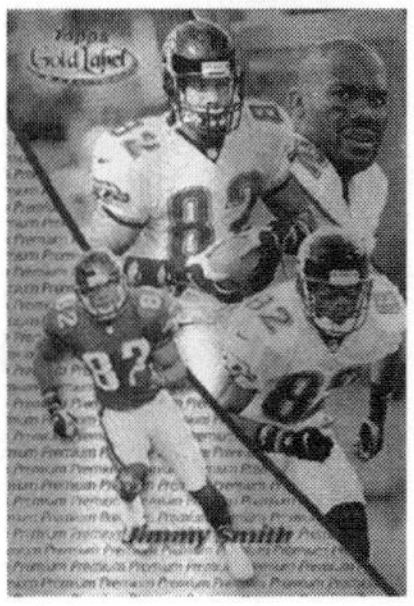

	MT
Complete Set (100):	200.00
Premium Cards:	3x-6x
Premium Rookies:	3x
Production 1,000 Sets	

2000 Topps Gold Label After Burners

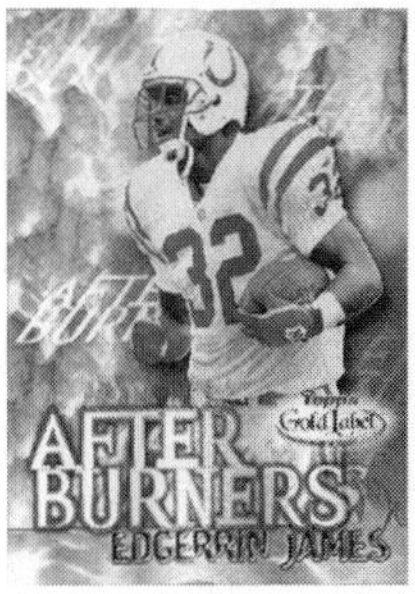

		MT
Complete Set (14):		35.00
Common Player:		2.00
Minor Stars:		4.00
Inserted 1:23		
A1	Brett Favre	12.00
A2	Corey Dillon	4.00
A3	Drew Bledsoe	5.00
A4	Cris Carter	4.00
A5	Jimmy Smith	2.00
A6	Edgerrin James	10.00
A7	Fred Taylor	5.00
A8	Tim Brown	2.00
A9	Marshall Faulk	4.00
A10	Steve Beuerlein	2.00
A11	Antonio Freeman	4.00
A12	Peyton Manning	10.00
A13	Mike Alstott	4.00
A14	Mark Brunell	5.00

2000 Topps Gold Label Bullion

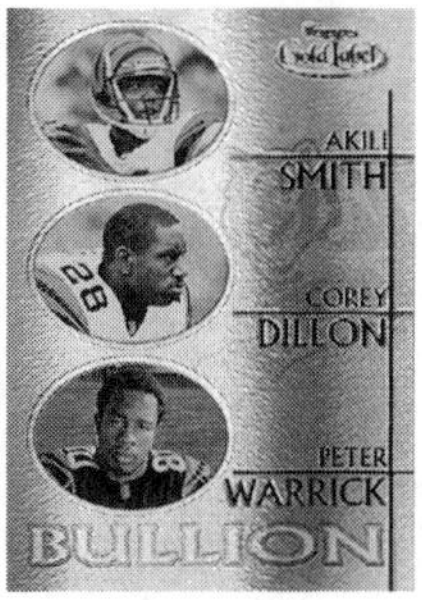

		MT
Complete Set (10):		50.00
Common Player:		2.50
Inserted 1:32		
B1	Daunte Culpepper, Randy Moss, Cris Carter	12.00
B2	Edgerrin James, Peyton Manning, Marvin Harrison	12.00
B3	Brad Johnson, Stephen Davis, Michael Westbrook	2.50
B4	Fred Taylor, Mark Brunell, Jimmy Smith	4.00
B5	Emmitt Smith, Troy Aikman, Joey Galloway	8.00
B6	Akili Smith, Corey Dillon, Peter Warrick	6.00
B7	Marshall Faulk, Kurt Warner, Isaac Bruce	10.00
B8	Steve McNair, Eddie George, Jevon Kearse	4.00
B9	Warren Sapp, Shaun King, Keyshawn Johnson	4.00
B10	Dorsey Levens, Brett Favre, Antonio Freeman	12.00

2000 Topps Gold Label Graceful Giants

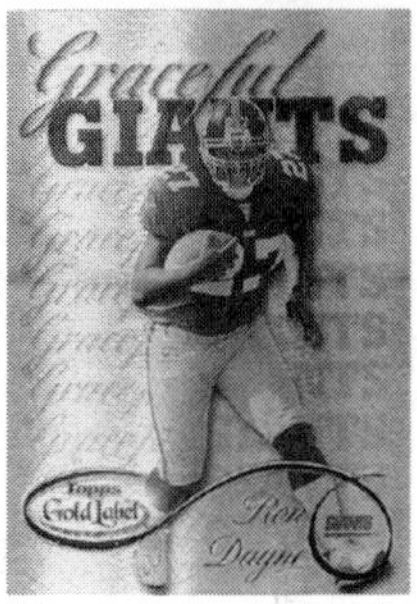

		MT
Complete Set (20):		45.00
Common Player:		2.00
Minor Stars:		4.00
Inserted 1:16		
G1	Eddie George	4.00
G2	Randy Moss	12.00
G3	Keyshawn Johnson	4.00
G4	Warrick Dunn	4.00
G5	Jevon Kearse	4.00
G6	Sylvester Morris	5.00
G7	Ron Dayne	8.00
G8	Wayne Chrebet	2.00
G9	Steve McNair	4.00
G10	Courtney Brown	4.00
G11	Jacquez Green	2.00
G12	Daunte Culpepper	6.00
G13	Tony Gonzalez	2.00
G14	Mike Alstott	4.00
G15	Plaxico Burress	5.00
G16	Drew Bledsoe	6.00
G17	Travis Prentice	4.00
G18	Jerome Bettis	4.00
G19	Ricky Williams	7.00
G20	Jamal Lewis	10.00

2000 Topps Gold Label Holiday Match-Ups Fall

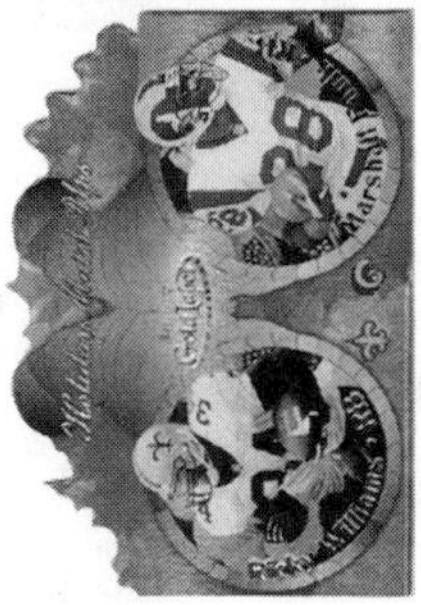

	MT
Complete Set (14):	35.00
Common Player:	2.00
Inserted 1:6	

T1	Randy Moss, Troy Aikman	10.00
T2	Drew Bledsoe, Germane Crowell	3.00
T3	Chris Chandler, Tim Brown	2.00
T4	Rob Johnson, Mike Alstott	2.00
T5	Cade McNown, Wayne Chrebet	2.00
T6	Courtney Brown, Jamal Lewis	8.00
T7	Terrell Davis, Jon Kitna	6.00
T8	Tony Gonzalez, Junior Seau	2.00
T9	Zach Thomas, Peyton Manning	10.00
T10	Ricky Williams, Marshall Faulk	3.50
T11	Duce Staley, Brad Johnson	2.00
T12	Jerome Bettis, Corey Dillon	2.00
T13	Steve McNair, Mark Brunell	3.50
T14	Ron Dayne, Thomas Jones	7.00

2000 Topps Gold Label Holiday Match-Ups Winter

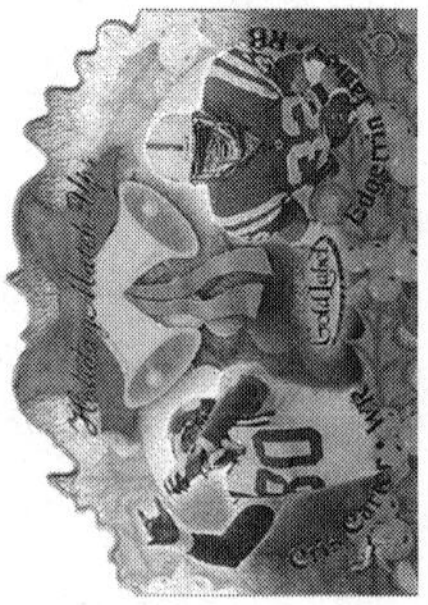

		MT
Complete Set (14):		25.00
Common Player:		1.25
Minor Stars:		2.50
Inserted 1:6		
C1	Jimmy Smith, Kerry Collins	2.50
C2	Charlie Garner, Ed McCaffrey	1.25
C3	Antowain Smith, Shaun Alexander	2.50
C4	Jake Plummer, Michael Westbrook	2.50
C5	Steve Beuerlein, Rich Gannon	1.25
C6	Curtis Enis, Charlie Batch	2.50
C7	Akili Smith, Donovan McNabb	3.00
C8	Sylvester Morris, Jamal Anderson	3.00
C9	O.J. McDuffie, Terry Glenn	1.25
C10	Cris Carter, Edgerrin James	8.00
C11	Curtis Martin, Travis Taylor	2.50
C12	Plaxico Burress, Jeff Graham	4.00
C13	Kurt Warner, Jeff Blake	10.00
C14	Shaun King, Brett Favre	10.00

2000 Topps Gold Label Rookie Autographs

		MT
Complete Set (20):		400.00
Common Player:		15.00
Inserted 1:56		
SA	Shaun Alexander	40.00
CB	Courtney Brown	20.00
PB	Plaxico Burress	30.00
TC	Trung Canidate	15.00
RD	Ron Dayne	70.00
RDU	Ron Dugans	15.00
DF	Bubba Franks	15.00
TJ	Thomas Jones	25.00
JL	Jamal Lewis	80.00
TM	Tee Martin	20.00
SM	Sylvester Morris	30.00
DN	Dennis Northcutt	15.00
CP	Chad Pennington	50.00
JP	Jerry Porter	15.00
TP	Travis Prentice	25.00
CR	Chris Redman	30.00
JR	J.R. Redmond	25.00
RS	R. Jay Soward	15.00
TT	Travis Taylor	20.00
PW	Peter Warrick	60.00

Values quoted in this guide reflect the retail price of a card — the price a collector can expect to pay when buying a card from a dealer. The wholesale price — that which a collector can expect to receive from a dealer when selling cards — will be significantly lower, depending on desirability and condition.

2000 Topps Season Opener

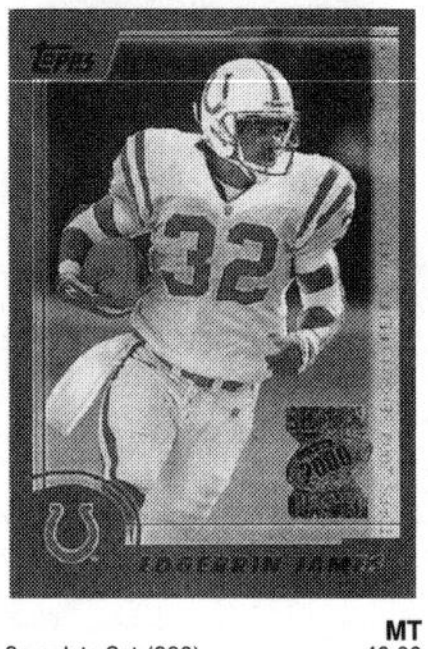

		MT
Complete Set (220):		40.00
Common Player:		.10
Minor Stars:		.20
Common Rookie:		.50
Pack (7):		1.00
Wax Box (36):		25.00
1	Tyrone Wheatley	.20
2	Carl Pickens	.20
3	Zach Thomas	.10
4	Jacquez Green	.10
5	Sean Dawkins	.10
6	Brad Johnson	.30
7	Jerry Rice	.60
8	Doug Flutie	.30
9	Cade McNown	.50
10	Rod Smith	.10
11	Kevin Hardy	.10
12	Marvin Harrison	.30
13	David Boston	.30
14	Priest Holmes	.10
15	Keith Poole	.10
16	Troy Edwards	.30
17	Robert Smith	.30
18	Kevin Lockett	.10
19	Johnnie Morton	.10
20	Terrell Davis	.75
21	Corey Bradford	.10
22	Keyshawn Johnson	.30
23	Tony Banks	.20
24	Matthew Hatchette	.10
25	Troy Aikman	.60
26	Natrone Means	.10
27	Peerless Price	.30
28	Bruce Smith	.20
29	Tim Couch	.75
30	Terrell Owens	.30
31	O.J. McDuffie	.10
32	Troy Brown	.10
33	Corey Dillon	.30
34	Cameron Cleeland	.10
35	Brian Griese	.40
36	Shawn Springs	.10
37	Marcus Robinson	.30
38	Jermaine Lewis	.10
39	Olandis Gary	.40
40	Tony Gonzalez	.20
41	Frank Wycheck	.20
42	Jon Kitna	.20
43	Muhsin Muhammad	.20
44	Jerome Bettis	.30
45	Darrin Chiaverini	.10
46	Steve McNair	.30
47	Charlie Batch	.30
48	Steve Beuerlein	.20
49	Dorsey Levens	.20
50	Jim Harbaugh	.10
51	Jonathon Linton	.10
52	Napoleon Kaufman	.20
53	Curtis Enis	.30
54	Darnay Scott	.20
55	Tim Dwight	.30
56	Mikhael Ricks	.10
57	Kevin Dyson	.10
58	Antonio Freeman	.30
59	E.G. Green	.10
60	Jake Plummer	.30
61	Bill Schroeder	.10
62	Shaun King	.50
63	Michael Basnight	.10
64	Vinny Testaverde	.20
65	Rob Johnson	.20
66	Jeff Blake	.20
67	Marshall Faulk	.30
68	Keenan McCardell	.10
69	Michael Westbrook	.20
70	Yancey Thigpen	.10
71	Akili Smith	.40
72	Charles Woodson	.20
73	Qadry Ismail	.10
74	Patrick Johnson	.10
75	Raghib Ismail	.10
76	Terrence Wilkins	.20
77	Herman Moore	.30
78	Jevon Kearse	.30
79	Oronde Gadsden	.10
80	Errict Rhett	.10
81	Ed McCaffrey	.20
82	Mike Alstott	.20
83	Stephen Alexander	.10
84	Mark Brunell	.50
85	Jeff George	.20
86	Stephen Davis	.30
87	Germane Crowell	.10
88	Charlie Garner	.10
89	Kordell Stewart	.30
90	Tim Biakabutuka	.20
91	Jim Miller	.10
92	Eddie George	.40
93	Joe Montgomery	.10
94	Wayne Chrebet	.10
95	Freddie Jones	.10
96	Ricky Proehl	.10
97	Warren Sapp	.20
98	Derrick Mayes	.10
99	Daunte Culpepper	.50
100	Torry Holt	.30
101	Isaac Bruce	.30
102	Kevin Johnson	.30
103	Antowain Smith	.30
104	Rob Moore	.20
105	Joey Galloway	.20
106	Rickey Dudley	.20
107	Terry Glenn	.30
108	Ike Hilliard	.10
109	Jeff Graham	.10
110	J.J. Stokes	.10
111	Steve Young	.50
112	Albert Connell	.10
113	Tony Brackens	.10
114	James Johnson	.10
115	Tim Brown	.20
116	Terance Mathis	.10
117	Peyton Manning	1.00
118	Kerry Collins	.20
119	Duce Staley	.30
120	Torrance Small	.10
121	Curtis Martin	.30
122	Damon Huard	.20
123	Derrick Alexander	.10
124	Jimmy Smith	.20
125	Cris Carter	.30
126	Jamal Anderson	.30
127	Eric Moulds	.30
128	Drew Bledsoe	.50
129	Ricky Williams	.75
130	Andre Hastings	.10
131	Amani Toomer	.10
132	Rich Gannon	.10
133	Richard Huntley	.10
134	Donovan McNabb	.50
135	Jermaine Fazande	.10
136	Randy Moss	1.00
137	Champ Bailey	.20
138	Elvis Grbac	.10
139	Warrick Dunn	.30
140	John Randle	.10
141	Edgerrin James	1.25
142	Tony Martin	.10
143	Chris Chandler	.20
144	Stephen Boyd	.10
145	Az-Zahir Hakim	.10
146	Tony Simmons	.10
147	Pete Mitchell	.10
148	Junior Seau	.20
149	Ricky Watters	.20
150	Michael Pittman	.10
151	Fred Taylor	.50
152	Charles Johnson	.10
153	Jason Tucker	.10
154	Brett Favre	1.25
155	Patrick Jeffers	.30
156	Curtis Conway	.10
157	Frank Sanders	.10
158	James Stewart	.10
159	Emmitt Smith	.75
160	Jessie Armstead	.10
161	Wesley Walls	.20
162	Kent Graham	.10
163	Kurt Warner	1.50
164	Shawn Jefferson	.10
165	Jammi German	.10
166	Jay Riemersma	.10
167	Fred Lane	.10
168	Jamir Miller	.10
169	David LaFleur	.10
170	David Sloan	.10
171	Jerome Pathon	.10
172	Sam Madison	.10
173	Tiki Barber	.10
174	Yatil Green	.10
175	Checklist	.10
176	Kurt Warner	.75
177	Brett Favre	.50
178	Marshall Faulk	.20
179	Jevon Kearse	.20
180	Edgerrin James	.50
181	Troy Aikman	.30
182	Terrell Davis	.40
183	Steve Beuerlein	.10
184	Tim Brown	.10
185	Randy Moss	.50
186	Drew Bledsoe	.25
187	Curtis Martin	.10
188	Shannon Sharpe	.10
189	Brett Favre	.50
190	Brad Johnson	.10
191	Tony Gonzalez	.10
192	Jon Kitna	.10
193	Peyton Manning	.50
194	Mark Brunell	.25
195	Cade McNown	.25
196	Jim Harbaugh	.10
197	Shaun King	.25
198	Kurt Warner	.75
199	Eddie George	.20
200	Ricky Williams	.40
201	*Curtis Keaton*	.50
202	*Tee Martin*	1.25
203	*Thomas Jones*	3.00
204	*Giovanni Carmazzi*	1.50
205	*Courtney Brown*	1.75
206	*Shaun Alexander*	3.00
207	*Travis Taylor*	2.00
208	*Dennis Northcutt*	1.25
209	*Trung Canidate*	1.00
210	*Jamal Lewis*	3.00
211	*R. Jay Soward*	1.25
212	*Sylvester Morris*	1.75
213	*Ron Dugans*	1.25
214	*Chris Redman*	2.00
215	*Plaxico Burress*	2.50
216	*Peter Warrick*	5.00
217	*Travis Prentice*	1.75
218	*Ron Dayne*	5.00
219	*J.R. Redmond*	1.50
220	*Chad Pennington*	4.00

2000 Topps Season Opener Autograph Cards

		MT
Complete Set (4):		
Common Player:		
1	Kurt Warner	100.00
2	Marvin Harrison	25.00
3	Stephen Davis	25.00
4	Joe Montana	150.00

2000 Topps Season Opener Auto. Super Bowl Memorabilia

		MT
Complete Set (5):		
Common Player:		
1	Deacon Jones	25.00
2	Gayle Sayers	75.00
3	Warren Moon	25.00
4	Fred Biletnikoff	25.00
5	Anthony Munoz	25.00

2000 Topps Season Opener Football Fever

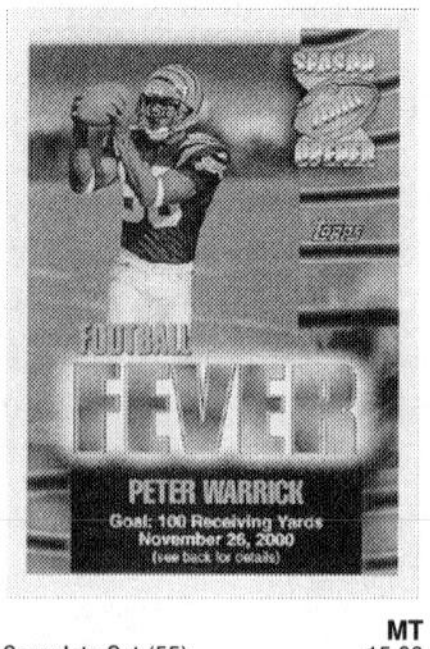

		MT
Complete Set (55):		15.00
Common Player:		.15
Minor Stars:		.30
Three Cards Per Player For #F1-F5		
Four Cards Per Player For #F6-F15		
Inserted 1:1		
F1	Brett Favre	1.00
F2	Kurt Warner	1.25
F3	Brad Johnson	.30
F4	Peyton Manning	.75
F5	Drew Bledsoe	.40
F6	Terrell Davis	.60
F7	Edgerrin James	1.00
F8	Stephen Davis	.30
F9	Fred Taylor	.40
F10	Jamal Lewis	.75
F11	Marvin Harrison	.30
F12	Isaac Bruce	.30
F13	Jimmy Smith	.30
F14	Randy Moss	.75
F15	Peter Warrick	1.25

2000 Topps Stars

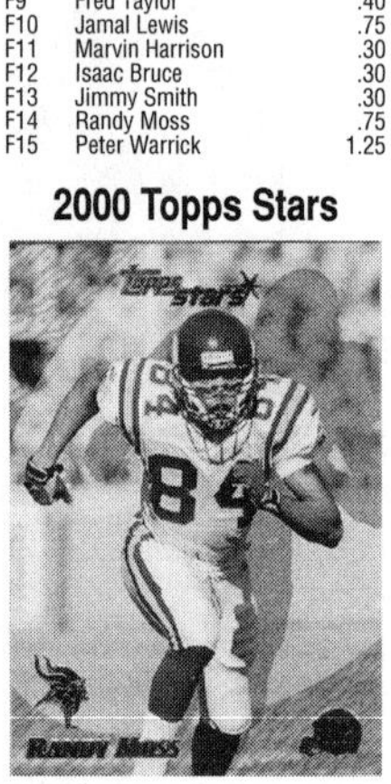

		MT
Complete Set (175):		50.00
Common Player:		.15
Minor Stars:		.30
Common Rookie:		.30
Pack (6):		3.00
Wax Box (24):		55.00
1	Keyshawn Johnson	.50
2	Marcus Robinson	.50
3	Antonio Freeman	.50
4	Jake Plummer	.50
5	Zach Thomas	.30
6	Kordell Stewart	.50
7	Mike Alstott	.50
8	Fred Taylor	1.00
9	J.J. Stokes	.30
10	Emmitt Smith	1.75
11	Derrick Mayes	.30
12	Stephen Davis	.50
13	Jamal Anderson	.50
14	Antowain Smith	.30
15	Steve Beuerlein	.30
16	Olandis Gary	.60
17	Rickey Dudley	.15
18	Sean Dawkins	.15
19	Mark Brunell	1.00
20	Brett Favre	2.50
21	Jim Harbaugh	.30
22	Darnay Scott	.30
23	Herman Moore	.50
24	Drew Bledsoe	1.00
25	Priest Holmes	.50
26	Albert Connell	.30
27	Ike Hilliard	.15
28	Charlie Garner	.30
29	Jimmy Smith	.50
30	Randy Moss	2.50
31	Peerless Price	.30
32	Terrell Davis	1.75
33	Troy Edwards	.50
34	Kevin Dyson	.30
35	O.J. McDuffie	.15
36	Troy Aikman	1.50
37	Frank Sanders	.30
38	Bobby Engram	.15
39	Tyrone Wheatley	.30
40	Ricky Williams	1.50
41	Warrick Dunn	.50
42	Elvis Grbac	.30
43	Dorsey Levens	.50
44	Curtis Conway	.30
45	Johnnie Morton	.30
46	Ed McCaffrey	.30
47	Kevin Johnson	.50
48	Muhsin Muhammad	.50
49	Terance Mathis	.15
50	Eddie George	.75
51	Daunte Culpepper	1.00
52	Jeff Graham	.15
53	Jon Kitna	.50
54	Marvin Harrison	.50
55	Steve McNair	.60
56	Jeff Blake	.30
57	Carl Pickens	.30
58	Germane Crowell	.50
59	Rob Moore	.30
60	Marshall Faulk	.50
61	Jerome Bettis	.50
62	Michael Westbrook	.30
63	Keenan McCardell	.30
64	Shannon Sharpe	.30
65	Rod Smith	.50
66	Curtis Enis	.50
67	Vinny Testaverde	.50
68	Freddie Jones	.30
69	Jevon Kearse	.60
70	Jerry Rice	1.50
71	Champ Bailey	.30
72	Peyton Manning	2.50
73	Rich Gannon	.30
74	Cris Carter	.50
75	Doug Flutie	.75
76	Corey Dillon	.50
77	Tony Gonzalez	.30
78	Shaun King	1.00
79	Terrell Owens	.50
80	Dan Marino	2.00
81	Curtis Martin	.50
82	Patrick Jeffers	.50
83	Brian Griese	.75
84	Akili Smith	.75
85	Charlie Batch	.50
86	Tim Dwight	.50
87	Robert Smith	.50
88	Duce Staley	.50
89	Jacquez Green	.30
90	Steve Young	1.00
91	Tony Martin	.15
92	Az-Zahir Hakim	.30
93	Tim Brown	.50
94	Donovan McNabb	1.00
95	Chris Chandler	.30
96	Tim Couch	1.50
97	Tim Biakabutuka	.30
98	Terry Glenn	.50
99	Wayne Chrebet	.30
100	Kurt Warner	2.75
101	Qadry Ismail	.15
102	Torry Holt	.50
103	Ray Lucas	.50
104	James Johnson	.30
105	Errict Rhett	.15
106	James Stewart	.50
107	Tony Banks	.30
108	Amani Toomer	.30
109	Isaac Bruce	.50
110	Brad Johnson	.50
111	Kerry Collins	.30
112	Eric Moulds	.50
113	Raghib Ismail	.15
114	Keith Poole	.15
115	Rob Johnson	.30
116	Deion Sanders	.50
117	Ricky Watters	.30
118	Cade McNown	1.00
119	Joey Galloway	.50
120	Edgerrin James	2.50
121	Jim Brown	1.00
122	Steve Largent	1.00
123	Joe Montana	3.00
124	Deacon Jones	.30
125	Ronnie Lott	.30
126	Mark Brunell	.50
127	Rich Gannon	.15
128	Tony Gonzalez	.15
129	Randy Moss	1.25
130	Kurt Warner	1.50
131	Marvin Harrison	.30
132	Jimmy Smith	.30
133	Edgerrin James	1.25
134	Corey Dillon	.30
135	Peyton Manning	1.25
136	Brad Johnson	.30
137	Steve Beuerlein	.15
138	Emmitt Smith	.75
139	Marshall Faulk	.30
140	Mike Alstott	.30
141	Deacon Jones	.15
142	Joe Montana	2.00
143	Jim Brown	.50
144	Steve Largent	.50
145	Ronnie Lott	.15
146	Chad Pennington	2.00
147	Peter Warrick	2.50
148	Plaxico Burress	2.00
149	Thomas Jones	1.75
150	Jamal Lewis	1.75
151	*Travis Taylor*	1.50
152	*Shaun Alexander*	2.50
153	*Dez White*	1.00
154	*Thomas Jones*	2.50
155	*Curtis Keaton*	.50
156	*Courtney Brown*	1.25
157	*Danny Farmer*	.50
158	*Trung Canidate*	.75
159	*R. Jay Soward*	1.00
160	*Jamal Lewis*	2.50
161	*Todd Pinkston*	1.00
162	*Reuben Droughns*	.75
163	*Ron Dugans*	1.00
164	*Ron Dayne*	4.00
165	*Laveranues Coles*	1.00
166	*Sylvester Morris*	1.75
167	*Peter Warrick*	4.00
168	*Dennis Northcutt*	1.00
169	*Tee Martin*	1.00
170	*Brian Urlacher*	1.00
171	*Chris Redman*	1.50
172	*Chad Pennington*	3.00
173	*J.R. Redmond*	1.25
174	*Travis Prentice*	1.25
175	*Plaxico Burress*	2.00

2000 Topps Stars Green Parallel

		MT
Green Cards:		5x-10x
Production 299 Sets (1-125)		
Green Cards:		15x-30x
Green Rookies:		8x-16x
Production 99 Sets (126-175)		
1	Keyshawn Johnson	.50
2	Marcus Robinson	.50
3	Antonio Freeman	.50
4	Jake Plummer	.50
5	Zach Thomas	.30
6	Kordell Stewart	.50
7	Mike Alstott	.50
8	Fred Taylor	1.00
9	J.J. Stokes	.30
10	Emmitt Smith	1.75
11	Derrick Mayes	.30
12	Stephen Davis	.50
13	Jamal Anderson	.50
14	Antowain Smith	.30
15	Steve Beuerlein	.30
16	Olandis Gary	.60
17	Rickey Dudley	.15
18	Sean Dawkins	.15
19	Mark Brunell	1.00
20	Brett Favre	2.50
21	Jim Harbaugh	.30
22	Darnay Scott	.30
23	Herman Moore	.50
24	Drew Bledsoe	1.00
25	Priest Holmes	.50
26	Albert Connell	.30
27	Ike Hilliard	.15
28	Charlie Garner	.30
29	Jimmy Smith	.50
30	Randy Moss	2.50
31	Peerless Price	.30
32	Terrell Davis	1.75
33	Troy Edwards	.50
34	Kevin Dyson	.30
35	O.J. McDuffie	.15
36	Troy Aikman	1.50
37	Frank Sanders	.30
38	Bobby Engram	.15
39	Tyrone Wheatley	.30
40	Ricky Williams	1.50
41	Warrick Dunn	.50
42	Elvis Grbac	.30
43	Dorsey Levens	.50
44	Curtis Conway	.30
45	Johnnie Morton	.30
46	Ed McCaffrey	.30
47	Kevin Johnson	.50
48	Muhsin Muhammad	.50
49	Terance Mathis	.15
50	Eddie George	.75
51	Daunte Culpepper	1.00
52	Jeff Graham	.15
53	Jon Kitna	.50
54	Marvin Harrison	.50
55	Steve McNair	.60
56	Jeff Blake	.30
57	Carl Pickens	.30
58	Germane Crowell	.50
59	Rob Moore	.30
60	Marshall Faulk	.50
61	Jerome Bettis	.50
62	Michael Westbrook	.30
63	Keenan McCardell	.30
64	Shannon Sharpe	.30
65	Rod Smith	.50
66	Curtis Enis	.50
67	Vinny Testaverde	.50
68	Freddie Jones	.30
69	Jevon Kearse	.60
70	Jerry Rice	1.50
71	Champ Bailey	.30
72	Peyton Manning	2.50
73	Rich Gannon	.30
74	Cris Carter	.50
75	Doug Flutie	.75
76	Corey Dillon	.50
77	Tony Gonzalez	.30
78	Shaun King	1.00
79	Terrell Owens	.50
80	Dan Marino	2.00
81	Curtis Martin	.50
82	Patrick Jeffers	.50
83	Brian Griese	.75
84	Akili Smith	.75
85	Charlie Batch	.50
86	Tim Dwight	.50
87	Robert Smith	.50
88	Duce Staley	.50
89	Jacquez Green	.30
90	Steve Young	1.00
91	Tony Martin	.15
92	Az-Zahir Hakim	.30
93	Tim Brown	.50
94	Donovan McNabb	1.00
95	Chris Chandler	.30
96	Tim Couch	1.50
97	Tim Biakabutuka	.30
98	Terry Glenn	.50
99	Wayne Chrebet	.30
100	Kurt Warner	2.75
101	Qadry Ismail	.15
102	Torry Holt	.50
103	Ray Lucas	.50
104	James Johnson	.30
105	Errict Rhett	.15
106	James Stewart	.50
107	Tony Banks	.30
108	Amani Toomer	.30
109	Isaac Bruce	.50
110	Brad Johnson	.50
111	Kerry Collins	.30
112	Eric Moulds	.50
113	Raghib Ismail	.15
114	Keith Poole	.15
115	Rob Johnson	.30
116	Deion Sanders	.50
117	Ricky Watters	.30
118	Cade McNown	1.00
119	Joey Galloway	.50
120	Edgerrin James	2.50
121	Jim Brown	1.00
122	Steve Largent	1.00
123	Joe Montana	3.00
124	Deacon Jones	.30
125	Ronnie Lott	.30
126	Mark Brunell	.50
127	Rich Gannon	.15
128	Tony Gonzalez	.15
129	Randy Moss	1.25
130	Kurt Warner	1.50
131	Marvin Harrison	.30
132	Jimmy Smith	.30
133	Edgerrin James	1.25
134	Corey Dillon	.30
135	Peyton Manning	1.25
136	Brad Johnson	.30
137	Steve Beuerlein	.15
138	Emmitt Smith	.75
139	Marshall Faulk	.30
140	Mike Alstott	.30
141	Deacon Jones	.15
142	Joe Montana	2.00
143	Jim Brown	.50
144	Steve Largent	.50
145	Ronnie Lott	.15
146	Chad Pennington	2.00
147	Peter Warrick	2.50
148	Plaxico Burress	2.00
149	Thomas Jones	1.75
150	Jamal Lewis	1.75
151	*Travis Taylor*	1.50
152	*Shaun Alexander*	2.50
153	*Dez White*	1.00
154	*Thomas Jones*	2.50
155	*Curtis Keaton*	.50

156	*Courtney Brown*	1.25
157	*Danny Farmer*	.50
158	*Trung Canidate*	.75
159	*R. Jay Soward*	1.00
160	*Jamal Lewis*	2.50
161	*Todd Pinkston*	1.00
162	*Reuben Droughns*	.75
163	*Ron Dugans*	1.00
164	*Ron Dayne*	4.00
165	*Laveranues Coles*	1.00
166	*Sylvester Morris*	1.75
167	*Peter Warrick*	4.00
168	*Dennis Northcutt*	1.00
169	*Tee Martin*	1.00
170	*Brian Urlacher*	1.00
171	*Chris Redman*	1.50
172	*Chad Pennington*	3.00
173	*J.R. Redmond*	1.25
174	*Travis Prentice*	1.25
175	*Plaxico Burress*	3.00

2000 Topps Stars All-Pro Relics

		MT
Common Player:		20.00
Inserted 1:85		
MA	Mike Alstott	40.00
MB	Mitch Berger	20.00
SB	Steve Beuerlein	30.00
PB	Peter Boulware	20.00
SB	Stephen Boyd	20.00
TB	Tony Brackens	20.00
DB	Derrick Brooks	20.00
CB	Chad Brown	20.00
IS	Isaac Bruce	40.00
MB	Mark Brunell	50.00
CC	Cris Carter	45.00
KC	Kevin Carter	20.00
DC	Dexter Coakley	20.00
SD	Stephen Davis	40.00
BD	Brian Dawkins	20.00
CD	Corey Dillon	40.00
LE	Luther Elliss	20.00
MF	Marshall Faulk	40.00
RG	Rich Gannon	25.00
SG	Sam Gash	20.00
EG	Eddie George	50.00
TG	Tony Gonzalez	30.00
KH	Kevin Hardy	20.00
MH	Marvin Harrison	40.00
EJ	Edgerrin James	85.00
BJ	Brad Johnson	40.00
KJ	Keyshawn Johnson	40.00
TJ	Tre' Johnson	20.00
JK	Jevon Kearse	40.00
CK	Cortez Kennedy	20.00
CL	Carnell Lake	20.00
TL	Todd Lyght	20.00
TM	Tremain Mack	20.00
SM	Sam Madison	20.00
OM	Olindo Mare	20.00
BM	Bruce Matthews	20.00
KM	Kevin Mawae	20.00
MM	Michael McCrary	20.00
RM	Randall McDaniel	20.00
GM	Glyn Milburn	20.00
LM	Lawyer Milloy	20.00
RM	Randy Moss	85.00
MM	Muhsin Muhammad	30.00
HN	Hardy Nickerson	20.00
OP	Orlando Pace	20.00
RP	Robert Porcher	20.00
TP	Trevor Pryce	20.00
WR	William Roaf	20.00
DR	Darrell Russell	20.00
WS	Warren Sapp	30.00
LS	Lance Schulters	20.00
LS	Leon Searcy	20.00
DS	David Sloan	20.00
DS	Detron Smith	20.00
ES	Emmitt Smith	65.00
JS	Jimmy Smith	30.00
MS	Michael Strahan	20.00
AZT	Zach Thomas	30.00
TT	Tom Tupa	20.00
WW	Wesley Walls	30.00
KW	Kurt Warner	85.00
CW	Charles Woodson	30.00
RW	Rod Woodson	20.00
FW	Frank Wycheck	20.00

2000 Topps Stars Autographs

		MT
Complete Set (12):		500.00
Common Player:		12.00
Inserted 1:411		
CC	Cris Carter	35.00
KC	Kevin Carter	12.00
RD	Ron Dayne	85.00
DG	Darrell Green	12.00
FH	Franco Harris	45.00
EJ	Edgerrin James	85.00
DJ	Deacon Jones	25.00
SL	Steve Largent	45.00
RL	Ronnie Lott	30.00
JM	Joe Montana	180.00
CR	Chris Redman	35.00
KW	Kurt Warner	100.00

2000 Topps Stars Pro-Bowl Powerhouse

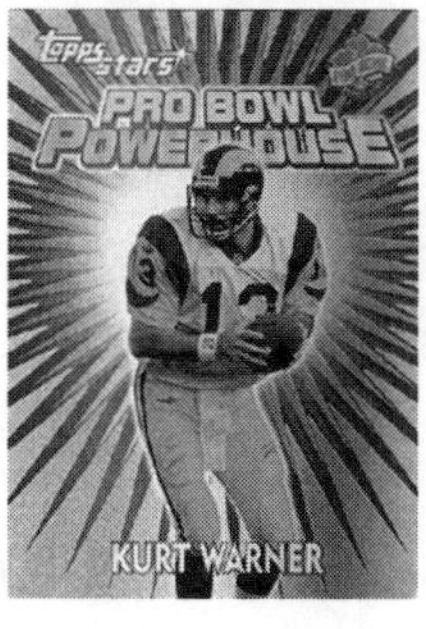

		MT
Complete Set (15):		18.00
Common Player:		.50
Inserted 1:12		
PB1	Kurt Warner	5.00
PB2	Warren Sapp	.50
PB3	Marvin Harrison	1.00
PB4	Kevin Carter	.50
PB5	Jimmy Smith	1.00
PB6	Stephen Davis	1.00
PB7	Edgerrin James	4.00
PB8	Tony Gonzalez	.50
PB9	Sam Madison	.50
PB10	Mike Alstott	1.00
PB11	Marshall Faulk	1.00
PB12	Jevon Kearse	1.00
PB13	Kevin Hardy	.50
PB14	Peyton Manning	4.00
PB15	Randy Moss	4.00

2000 Topps Stars Progression

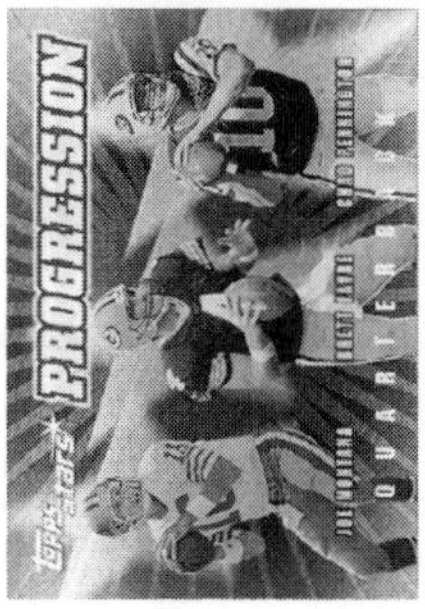

		MT
Complete Set (5):		12.00
Common Player:		2.00
Inserted 1:15		
P1	Joe Montana, Brett Favre, Chad Pennington	7.00
P2	Deacon Jones, Jevon Kearse, Courtney Brown	2.00
P3	Ronnie Lott, John Lynch, Deon Grant	2.00
P4	Steve Largent, Randy Moss, Peter Warrick	5.00
P5	Jim Brown, Edgerrin James, Thomas Jones	3.00

2000 Topps Stars Walk of Fame

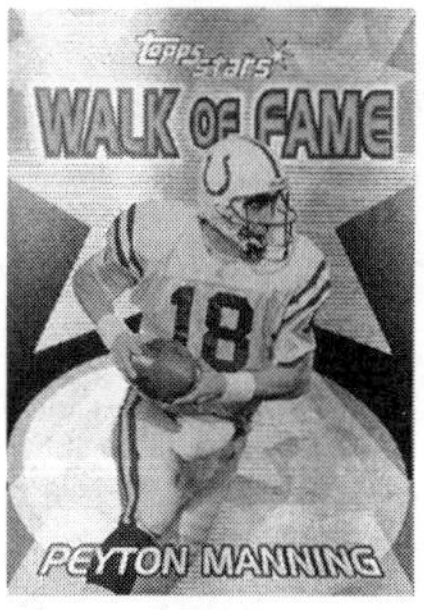

		MT
Complete Set (15):		20.00
Common Player:		1.00
Inserted 1:8		
W1	Randy Moss	4.00
W2	Kurt Warner	5.00
W3	Jimmy Smith	1.00
W4	Cris Carter	1.00
W5	Brett Favre	4.00
W6	Ricky Williams	2.50
W7	Marvin Harrison	1.00
W8	Fred Taylor	1.50
W9	Eddie George	1.25
W10	Edgerrin James	4.00
W11	Jevon Kearse	1.00
W12	Emmitt Smith	2.75
W13	Marshall Faulk	1.00
W14	Terrell Davis	2.75
W15	Peyton Manning	4.00

2001 Topps

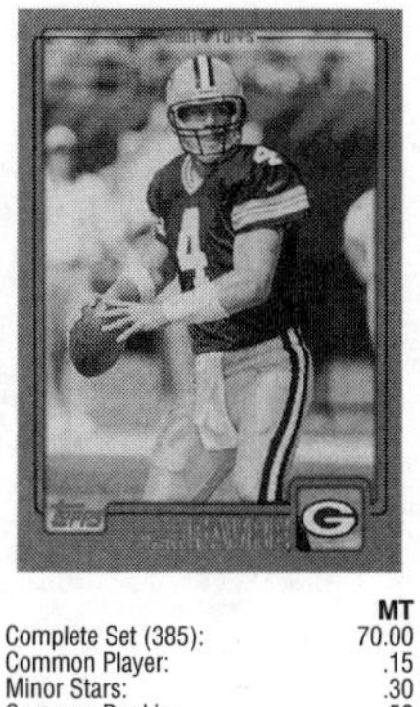

		MT
Complete Set (385):		70.00
Common Player:		.15
Minor Stars:		.30
Common Rookie:		.50
Pack (10):		1.50
Wax Box (36):		45.00
1	Marshall Faulk	.60
2	Lawyer Milloy	.15
3	Rich Gannon	.30
4	Rod Smith	.30
5	David Boston	.50
6	Jeremy McDaniel	.15
7	Joey Galloway	.50
8	Ron Dixon	.15
9	Terrell Fletcher	.15
10	Deion Sanders	.50
11	Jevon Kearse	.50
12	Charles Woodson	.30
13	Brian Walker	.15
14	Mike Peterson	.15
15	Marcus Robinson	.50
16	Duane Starks	.15
17	KaRon Coleman	.15
18	Randy Moss	1.50
19	Reggie Jones	.30
20	Derrick Brooks	.15
21	Eddie George	.60
22	Wayne Chrebet	.50
23	Kevin Hardy	.15
24	Bill Schroeder	.30
25	Doug Flutie	.60
26	Tim Dwight	.30
27	Eddie Kennison	.15
28	Reggie Kelly	.15
29	Ricky Watters	.30
30	Stephen Alexander	.15
31	Az-Zahir Hakim	.30
32	Henri Crockett	.15
33	Joe Horn	.50
34	Danny Farmer	.15
35	Shannon Sharpe	.30
36	Brad Hoover	.50
37	David Patten	.15
38	Kevin Faulk	.30
39	Freddie Jones	.30
40	Michael Westbrook	.30
41	Jacquez Green	.15
42	Torrance Small	.15
43	Terrence Wilkins	.30
44	Brett Favre	2.00
45	Tony Banks	.30
46	Johnnie Morton	.30
47	Jimmy Smith	.50
48	Jerry Rice	1.25
49	Jeff George	.50
50	Ray Lewis	.50
51	Joe Johnson	.30
52	Raghib Ismail	.15
53	Muhsin Muhammad	.30
54	Ken Dilger	.15
55	Ike Hilliard	.30
56	Joey Porter	.15
57	Shaun Alexander	.50
58	Jeff Garcia	.50
59	Jay Fiedler	.30
60	Wane McGarity	.15
61	Steve Beuerlein	.30
62	Tywan Mitchell	.15
63	Travis Prentice	.50
64	Robert Griffith	.15
65	Napoleon Kaufman	.30
66	Randall Godfrey	.15
67	Junior Seau	.30
68	Willie Jackson	.15
69	Larry Foster	.15
70	Brandon Stokley	.30
71	Hugh Douglas	.15
72	James Thrash	.30
73	Vinny Testaverde	.30
74	Leslie Shepherd	.15
75	Terrell Davis	1.50
76	Jake Plummer	.50
77	Corey Dillon	.50
78	Ron Dayne	1.00
79	Brock Huard	.50
80	Todd Husak	.30
81	Richard Huntley	.30
82	Shaun Ellis	.15
83	Kyle Brady	.15
84	Corey Bradford	.15
85	Eric Moulds	.50
86	Brian Finneran	.15
87	Antonio Freeman	.50
88	Terry Glenn	.50
89	Tai Streets	.30
90	Chris Sanders	.15
91	Sylvester Morris	.50
92	Peter Warrick	1.00
93	Chris Greisen	.15
94	Cade McNown	.50
95	Jerome Pathon	.15
96	John Randle	.30
97	Curtis Conway	.30
98	Keyshawn Johnson	.50
99	Trent Green	.50
100	Mike Anderson	1.50
101	Jeff Blake	.30
102	Tee Martin	.30
103	Darrell Jackson	.30
104	Mark Brunell	.60
105	Charlie Batch	.50
106	Wesley Walls	.15
107	Edgerrin James	1.25
108	Robert Wilson	.15
109	Donovan McNabb	.75
110	Champ Bailey	.30
111	Isaac Bruce	.50
112	Michael Strahan	.15
113	Dennis Edwards	.15
114	Randall Cunningham	.30
115	Germane Crowell	.50
116	Jermaine Jewis	.15
117	Dennis McKinley	.15
118	Ryan Leaf	.50
119	Samari Rolle	.15
120	Daunte Culpepper	1.00
121	Tim Couch	.75
122	Greg Biekert	.15
123	Warrick Dunn	.50
124	Richie Anderson	.15
125	Trace Armstrong	.15
126	Bernardo Harris	.15
127	Kwame Cavil	.15
128	James Allen	.50
129	Anthony Becht	.15
130	Tiki Barber	.30
131	Brad Johnson	.30
132	Tyrone Wheatley	.50
133	Kurt Warner	2.00
134	Desmond Howard	.15
135	Thomas Jones	.50
136	Peyton Manning	1.50
137	Tony Richardson	.15
138	Chris Chandler	.30
139	Plaxico Burress	.50
140	J.R. Redmond	.50
141	Fred Taylor	.75
142	Akili Smith	.50
143	Sammy Morris	.50
144	Jessie Armstead	.15
145	Charlie Garner	.30
146	Steve McNair	.50
147	Charles Johnson	.15
148	Troy Aikman	1.00
149	Kevin Johnson	.30
150	Brian Urlacher	1.00
151	Travis Taylor	.50
152	Aaron Shea	.15
153	Michael Cloud	.15
154	Donald Driver	.15
155	Chad Pennington	1.00
156	Troy Edwards	.15
157	Reidel Anthony	.15
158	Michael Bishop	.30
159	Mo Lewis	.15
160	Damon Huard	.30
161	James McKnight	.15
162	Craig Yeast	.15
163	Michael Pittman	.30
164	Robert Smith	.30
165	Terrelle Smith	.15
166	Jeremiah Trotter	.15
167	Amani Toomer	.30
168	JaJuan Dawson	.30
169	Tim Biakabutuka	.30
170	Oronde Gadsden	.30
171	Ray Lucas	.30
172	Jermaine Fazande	.30
173	Todd Bouman	.15
174	Frank Wycheck	.30
175	Hines Ward	.30
176	Ahman Green	.30
177	Kaseem Sinceno	.15
178	Jamal Anderson	.50
179	Jay Riemersma	.15
180	Jarious Jackson	.15
181	Andre Rison	.30
182	Jerome Bettis	.50
183	Blaine Bishop	.15
184	Dorsey Levens	.50
185	James Stewart	.50
186	Chad Lewis	.30
187	Justin Watson	.15
188	Warren Sapp	.30
189	Rod Woodson	.15
190	Ricky Williams	.75
191	Marty Booker	.15
192	MarTay Jenkins	.15
193	Peerless Price	.50
194	Tony Gonzalez	.30
195	Jon Kitna	.50
196	Stephen Davis	.50
197	Curtis Martin	.50
198	Matt Hasselbeck	.50
199	Patrick Johnson	.15
200	Emmitt Smith	1.50
201	Doug Johnson	.50
202	Autry Denson	.30
203	Troy Brown	.15
204	Jeff Graham	.15
205	Corey Simon	.30
206	Jamel White	.15
207	Jeff Lewis	.30
208	Frank Sanders	.30
209	Al Wilson	.15
210	Jason Sehorn	.15
211	Shaun King	.50
212	Torry Holt	.50
213	Kordell Stewart	.50
214	Keenan McCardell	.30
215	Dedric Ward	.15
216	Michael Wiley	.30
217	Rob Johnson	.50
218	Jamal Lewis	1.50
219	Herman Moore	.30
220	Ron Dugans	.15
221	Jason Taylor	.15
222	Charles Lee	.15
223	J.J. Stokes	.30
224	Albert Connell	.30
225	Keith Poole	.15
226	Elvis Grbac	.30
227	Shawn Jefferson	.15
228	Jackie Harris	.15
229	Derrick Alexander	.15
230	Darnell Autry	.30
231	Bobby Shaw	.30
232	Aaron Brooks	.50
233	Cris Carter	.50
234	Desmond Clark	.15
235	Spergon Wynn	.30
236	Qadry Ismail	.15
237	Sam Cowart	.15
238	Zach Thomas	.30
239	Drew Bledsoe	.60
240	Ronney Jenkins	.15
241	Keith Mitchell	.15
242	Laveranues Coles	.50
243	Marcus Pollard	.15
244	Darren Sharper	.15
245	Donald Hayes	.30
246	Brian Griese	.60
247	Frank Moreau	.15
248	Bruce Smith	.15
249	Fred Beasley	.15
250	Mike Alstott	.50
251	Trent Dilfer	.30
252	Terance Mathis	.15
253	Shawn Bryson	.15
254	Dennis Northcutt	.30
255	Brandon Bennett	.15
256	Stacey Mack	.15
257	Tim Brown	.30
258	Duce Staley	.50
259	Sean Dawkins	.15
260	Ricky Proehl	.15
261	Chris Fuamatu-Ma'afala	.15
262	La'Roi Glover	.15
263	Bubba Franks	.30
264	Kevin Lockett	.15
265	Lamar Smith	.50
266	Priest Holmes	.30
267	Macey Brooks	.15
268	Anthony Wright	.50
269	Ed McCaffrey	.30
270	Joe Jurevicius	.30
271	Terrell Owens	.50
272	Tony Simmons	.15
273	Itula Mili	.15
274	Chad Morton	.15
275	Marvin Harrison	.50
276	Jason Gildon	.15
277	Derrick Mason	.50
278	Greg Clark	.15
279	Casey Crawford	.15
280	Kerry Collins	.30
281	Terrell Owens	.30
282	Marshall Faulk	.30
283	Mike Anderson	.75
284	Cris Carter	.30
285	Corey Dillon	.30
286	Daunte Culpepper	.50
287	Peyton Manning	.75
288	Torry Holt	.30
289	Marvin Harrison	.30
290	Edgerrin James	.75
291	Takeo Spikes	.15
292	John Lynch	.15
293	Sam Madison	.15
294	Stephen Boyd	.15
295	Tony Siragusa	.15
296	Robert Porcher	.15
297	Donnell Bennett	.15
298	Hardy Nickerson	.15
299	Jonathan Quinn	.15
300	Rob Morris	.15
301	E.G. Green	.15
302	David Sloan	.15
303	Jason Tucker	.15
304	Darrin Chiaverini	.15
305	Wali Rainer	.15
306	Jerry Azumah	.15
307	Jonathon Linton	.15
308	Dameyune Craig	.15
309	Courtney Brown	.30
310	Jammi German	.15
311	*Michael Vick*	6.00
312	*Jamar Fletcher*	.75
313	*Will Allen*	.50
314	*Jamal Reynolds*	.50
315	*Quincy Morgan*	1.50
316	*Eric Kelly*	.50
317	*Michael Stone*	.50
318	*Rod Gardner*	3.00
319	*Ken-Yon Rambo*	.75
320	*Eric Westmoreland*	.50
321	*Steve Smith*	.75
322	*George Layne*	.50
323	*Justin McCareins*	.75
324	*Adam Archuleta*	.75
325	*Justin Smith*	1.25
326	*David Terrell*	4.00
327	*Correll Buckhelter*	.75
328	*Drew Brees*	5.00
329	*Chris Barnes*	.75
330	*Santana Moss*	4.00
331	*Josh Heupel*	3.50
332	*Cedrick Wilson*	.75
333	*Gerard Warren*	1.50
334	*Jamie Henderson*	.50
335	*Onomo Ojo*	.75
336	*Marcus Stroud*	.50
337	*Quincy Carter*	2.00
338	*Koren Robinson*	3.00
339	*Ryan Pickett*	.50
340	*Chad Johnson*	1.50
341	*Nate Clements*	.50
342	*Jesse Palmer*	1.00
343	*Marvin "Snoop" Minnis*	1.75
344	*Reggie Wayne*	2.50
345	*Kevin Kasper*	.50
346	*Will Peterson*	.50
347	*Marques Tuiasosopo*	2.50
348	*Sage Rosenfels*	1.50
349	*Dan Alexander*	.75
350	*LaDainian Tomlinson*	5.00
351	*Dan Morgan*	.50
352	*Scotty Anderson*	.75
353	*Deuce McAllister*	4.00
354	*Todd Heap*	.50
355	*Tony Dixon*	.50
356	*Chris Chambers*	1.50
357	*Eddie Berlin*	.75
358	*Anthony Thomas*	5.00
359	*James Jackson*	1.75
360	*Richard Seymour*	.50
361	*Andre Carter*	.50
362	*Bobby Newcombe*	.75
363	*Robert Ferguson*	1.75
364	*Jonathan Carter*	.75
365	*Damione Lewis*	.50
366	*Darnerian McCants*	.75
367	*Tim Hasselbeck*	.75
368	*Derrick Gibson*	.50
369	*Rudi Johnson*	1.25
370	*Alge Crumpler*	.75
371	*Derrick Blaylock*	.75
372	*Moran Norris*	.75
373	*Travis Minor*	1.50
374	*LaMont Jordan*	1.50
375	*Kevan Barlow*	1.50
376	*Freddie Mitchell*	2.00
377	*Shaun Rogers*	.50
378	*Tay Cody*	.50
379	*Travis Henry*	2.50
380	*Chris Weinke*	3.50
381	*Willie Middlebrooks*	.50
382	*Rashard Casey*	.75
383	*Mike McMahon*	1.50
384	*Michael Bennett*	5.00
385	*Jabari Holloway*	.75

2001 Topps Collection

	MT
Complete Set (385):	70.00
Collection Cards:	1x

2001 Topps Own The Game Perfect Spiral

		MT
Complete Set (7):		
Common Player:		
PS1	Brian Griese	1.50
PS2	Peyton Manning	4.00
PS3	Jeff Garcia	1.00
PS4	Daunte Culpepper	2.50
PS5	Brett Favre	5.00
PS6	Kurt Warner	5.00
PS7	Donovan McNabb	2.00

2001 Topps All-Pro Autograph Relics

		MT
Complete Set (5):		
Common Player:		50.00
TPA-DC	Daunte Culpepper	150.00
TPA-EJ	Edgerrin James	150.00
TPA-RL	Ray Lewis	75.00
TPA-DM	Derrick Mason	50.00
TPA-JS	Jimmy Smith	50.00

2001 Topps Autographs

		MT
Complete Set (21):		
Common Player:		15.00
TA-KB	Kevan Barlow	15.00
TA-JB	Josh Booty	15.00
TA-DB	Drew Brees	50.00
TA-CC	Chris Chambers	50.00
TA-DC	Daunte Culpepper	50.00
TA-MF	Marshall Faulk	40.00
TA-DH	Donald Hayes	15.00
TA-JH	Joe Horn	15.00
TA-CJ	Chad Johnson	15.00
TA-DM	Derrick Mason	15.00
TA-DJM	Deuce McAllister	100.00
TA-TM	Travis Minor	15.00
TA-SM	Santana Moss	25.00
TA-EM	Eric Moulds	15.00
TA-JP	Jesse Palmer	15.00
TA-ES	Emmitt Smith	125.00
TA-JS	Jimmy Smith	15.00
TA-JT	James Thrash	15.00
TA-BU	Brian Urlacher	75.00
TA-MV	Michael Vick	100.00
TA-TW	Terrence Wilkins	15.00

2001 Topps Combos

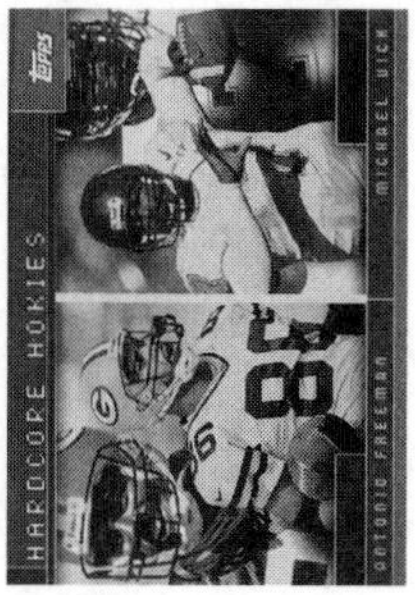

		MT
Complete Set (19):		25.00
Common Player:		2.00
Inserted 1:8		
TC1	Edgerrin James, Santana Moss	5.00
TC2	Torry Holt, Koren Robinson	2.50
TC3	Jamal Lewis, Travis Henry	4.00
TC4	Curtis Martin, Kevan Barlow	2.00
TC5	Cris Carter, Ken-Yon Rambo	2.00
TC6	Troy Aikman, Freddie Mitchell	3.00
TC7	Brian Griese, David Terrell	3.00
TC8	Tyrone Wheatley, Anthony Thomas	2.00
TC9	Warrick Dunn, Travis Minor	2.00
TC10	Peter Warrick, Marvin "Snoop" Minnis	3.00
TC11	Warren Sapp, Dan Morgan	2.00
TC12	Tony Gonzalez, Andre Carter	2.00
TC13	Antonio Freeman, Michael Vick	8.00
TC14	Ron Dayne, Michael Bennett	4.00
TC15	Mike Alstott, Drew Brees	5.00
TC16	Ahman Green, Correll Buckhelter	2.00
TC17	Brad Johnson, Chris Weinke	3.00
TC18	Eric Moulds, Fred Smoot	2.00
TC19	Ray Lewis, Reggie Wayne	2.00

2001 Topps Hall of Fame Autographs

		MT
Complete Set (6):		
Common Player:		
TA-DJ	Deacon Jones	50.00
TA-ML	Marv Levy	50.00
TA-MM	Mike Munchak	50.00
TA-JS	Jackie Slater	50.00
TA-RY	Ron Yary	50.00
TA-JY	Jack Youngblood	50.00

2001 Topps King Of Kings

		MT
Complete Set (8):		450.00
Common Player:		25.00
Inserted 1:580		
K-CD	Corey Dillon	40.00
K-DM	Dan Marino	125.00
K-RM	Randy Moss	125.00
K-TO	Terrell Owens	25.00
K-WP	Walter Payton	150.00
K-JR	Jerry Rice	75.00
K-ES	Emmitt Smith	100.00
K-FT	Fred Taylor	50.00

A player's name in *italic type* indicates a rookie card.

2001 Topps Own The Game All the Way

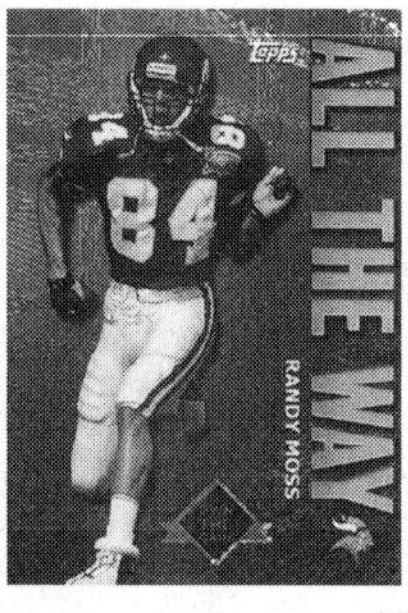

		MT
Complete Set (10):		
Common Player:		.50
AW1	Marvin Harrison	1.00
AW2	Muhsin Muhammad	1.00
AW3	Torry Holt	1.00
AW4	Rod Smith	1.00
AW5	Randy Moss	4.00
AW6	Cris Carter	1.00
AW7	Ed McCaffrey	.50
AW8	Isaac Bruce	1.00
AW9	Terrell Owens	1.00
AW10	Tony Gonzalez	.50

2001 Topps Own The Game Ground Warriors

		MT
Complete Set (7):		
Common Player:		.50
GW1	Edgerrin James	3.50
GW2	Robert Smith	1.00
GW3	Marshall Faulk	1.50
GW4	Mike Anderson	3.00
GW5	Eddie George	1.50
GW6	Corey Dillon	1.00
GW7	Fred Taylor	1.50

2001 Topps Own The Game Intimidators

		MT
Complete Set (3):		
Common Player:		.50
TI1	La'Roi Glover	.50
TI2	Darren Sharper	.50
TI3	Mike Peterson	.50

2001 Topps Own The Game Showtime

		MT
Complete Set (3):		
Common Player:		.50
TS1	Derrick Mason	1.00
TS2	Az-Zahir Hakim	1.00
TS3	Jermaine Lewis	.50

2001 Topps Originals

		MT
Complete Set (4):		400.00
Common Player:		100.00
Inserted 1:1,159		
TO-DM	Dan Marino	150.00
TO-WP	Walter Payton	150.00
TO-JR	Jerry Rice	100.00
TO-ES	Emmitt Smith	125.00

2001 Topps Pro-Bowl Jerseys

		MT
Complete Set (11):		180.00
Common Player:		12.00
Inserted 1:425		
TP-MA	Mike Alstott	25.00
TP-RG	Rich Gannon	20.00
TP-JG	Jeff Garcia	30.00
TP-TH	Torry Holt	25.00
TP-CL	Chad Lewis	12.00
TP-RL	Ray Lewis	25.00
TP-JL	John Lynch	20.00
TP-DM	Derrick Mason	20.00
TP-EM	Eric Moulds	30.00
TP-JS	Junior Seau	20.00
TP-JT	Jason Taylor	12.00

2001 Topps Super Bowl Bunting

		MT
Complete Set (6):		130.00
Common Player:		25.00
Inserted 1:4,702		
SBB1	Kerry Collins	25.00
SBB2	Trent Dilfer	25.00
SBB3	Ike Hilliard	25.00
SBB4	Shannon Sharpe	25.00
SBB5	Ron Dayne	25.00
SBB6	Jason Sehorn	25.00

A card number in parentheses ( ) indicates the set is unnumbered.

2001 Topps Team Topps Legends Autographs

		MT
Complete Set (9):		
Common Player:		
TTR21	Billy Kilmer	20.00
TTR7	Art Donovan	30.00
TTF7	Art Donovan	30.00
TTF13	Joe Namath	75.00
TTR15	Mike Singletary	30.00
TTR12	Don Maynard	30.00
TTF12	Don Maynard	30.00
TTR20	Tom Dempsey	20.00
TTF20	Tom Dempsey	20.00

2001 Topps Walter Payton Reprints

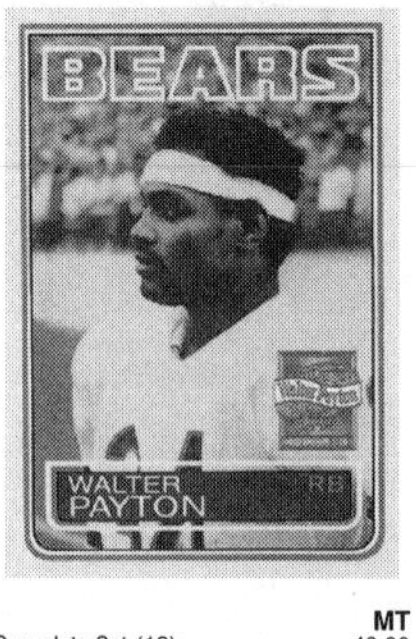

		MT
Complete Set (12):		40.00
Common Player:		4.00
Inserted 1:12		
WP1	Walter Payton 1976	10.00
WP2	Walter Payton 1977	4.00
WP3	Walter Payton 1978	4.00
WP4	Walter Payton 1979	4.00
WP5	Walter Payton 1980	4.00
WP6	Walter Payton 1981	4.00
WP7	Walter Payton 1982	4.00
WP8	Walter Payton 1983	4.00
WP9	Walter Payton 1984	4.00
WP10	Walter Payton 1985	4.00
WP11	Walter Payton 1986	4.00
WP12	Walter Payton 1987	4.00

2001 Topps Chrome

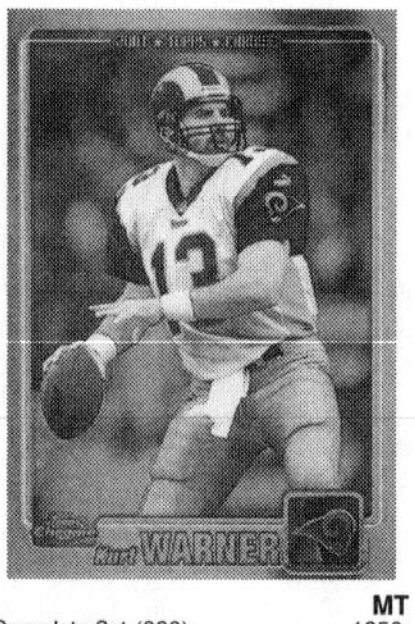

		MT
Complete Set (320):		1250.
Common Player:		.25
Minor Stars:		.50
Common Rookies:		7.00
Inserted 1:12		
Production 999 Sets		
Pack (4):		3.50
Wax Box (24):		70.00
1	Randy Moss	3.00
2	Desmond Howard	.25
3	Shawn Bryson	.25
4	Lamar Smith	.75
5	Peter Warrick	2.00
6	Hines Ward	.50
7	J.R. Redmond	.50
8	Reidel Anthony	.25
9	Rich Gannon	.75
10	Ed McCaffrey	1.00
11	Jamel White	.25
12	Michael Pittman	.50
13	Rob Johnson	.50
14	Tim Couch	1.25
15	Stephen Alexander	.25
16	Ricky Watters	.75
17	Kerry Collins	.75
18	Ricky Williams	1.50
19	Joey Galloway	1.00
20	Chris Chandler	.50
21	Marty Booker	.25
22	Mark Brunell	1.25
23	Antonio Freeman	.75
24	Richie Anderson	.25
25	Amani Toomer	.50
26	Trent Green	.75
27	Terrell Fletcher	.25
28	Kevin Lockett	.25
29	Ron Dixon	.50
30	Charlie Batch	1.00
31	Oronde Gadsden	.50
32	Dorsey Levens	.75
33	Jamal Lewis	2.50
34	Craig Yeast	.25
35	Muhsin Muhammad	.75
36	Willie Jackson	.50
37	Isaac Bruce	1.00
38	Frank Wycheck	.50
39	Troy Brown	.25
40	Anthony Wright	.75
41	Zach Thomas	.50
42	Qadry Ismail	.50
43	Jake Plummer	1.00
44	Keenan McCardell	.50
45	Charles Johnson	.25
46	Brett Favre	4.00
47	Jacquez Green	.25
48	Matt Hasselbeck	1.00
49	Tiki Barber	.75
50	Jeff Garcia	1.00
51	Shawn Jefferson	.25
52	Kevin Johnson	.75
53	Terrence Wilkins	.50
54	Mike Anderson	2.50
55	Tim Brown	1.00
56	Champ Bailey	.75
57	Jimmy Smith	.75
58	Trent Dilfer	.50
59	James Allen	.50
60	David Boston	1.00
61	Jeremiah Trotter	.25
62	Freddie Jones	.50
63	Deion Sanders	1.00
64	Darrell Jackson	.75
65	David Patten	.25
66	Jeremy McDaniel	.25
67	Jay Fiedler	1.00
68	Chad Lewis	.75
69	Raghib Ismail	.50
70	Cade McNown	1.00
71	Jevon Kearse	1.00
72	Jermaine Fazande	.50
73	Junior Seau	.75
74	Rod Smith	.75
75	Jermaine Lewis	.25
76	Dennis Northcutt	.75
77	Charlie Garner	.75
78	Charles Woodson	1.00
79	Wayne Chrebet	1.00
80	Ahman Green	.75
81	Donald Hayes	.50
82	Terance Mathis	.50
83	Warrick Dunn	1.00
84	Chris Sanders	.25
85	Albert Connell	.25
86	Robert Griffith	.25
87	Germane Crowell	.75
88	Tony Banks	.75
89	Travis Taylor	1.00
90	Akili Smith	1.00
91	Michael Westbrook	.75
92	Doug Flutie	1.25
93	Ike Hilliard	.50
94	Terry Glenn	.75
95	Leslie Shepherd	.25
96	Az-Zahir Hakim	.50
97	La'Roi Glover	.25
98	Peyton Manning	3.00
99	Jackie Harris	.25
100	Edgerrin James	2.50
101	Peerless Price	.75
102	Jamal Anderson	1.00
103	Keyshawn Johnson	1.00
104	Derrick Mason	.75
105	J.J. Stokes	.50
106	Kevin Faulk	.50
107	Tony Richardson	.25
108	James Stewart	.75
109	Tim Biakabutuka	.50
110	Jon Kitna	1.00
111	Thomas Jones	.75
112	Steve McNair	1.00
113	Sean Dawkins	.25
114	Jerome Bettis	1.00
115	Donovan McNabb	1.50
116	Bill Schroeder	.50
117	Rod Woodson	.25
118	James McKnight	.25
119	Daunte Culpepper	2.00
120	Todd Husak	.25
121	Shaun King	1.00
122	Tyrone Wheatley	.50
123	Curtis Martin	1.00
124	Terrell Davis	2.00
125	Steve Beuerlein	.50
126	Brad Johnson	.75
127	Joe Horn	.75
128	Fred Taylor	1.25
129	Brian Urlacher	2.00
130	Ray Lewis	1.00
131	Marshall Faulk	1.25
132	Curtis Conway	.50
133	Jason Sehorn	.25
134	Jerome Pathon	.25
135	Derrick Alexander	.50
136	Jerry Rice	2.00
137	Jeff George	.75
138	Johnnie Morton	.50
139	Eric Moulds	1.00
140	Duce Staley	1.00
141	Vinny Testaverde	.75
142	Eddie George	1.25
143	Shaun Alexander	1.25
144	Drew Bledsoe	1.25
145	Emmitt Smith	2.50
146	Marvin Harrison	1.00
147	Frank Sanders	.50
148	Aaron Shea	.25
149	Cris Carter	1.00
150	Tony Gonzalez	.75
151	Marcus Robinson	1.00
152	Danny Farmer	.50
153	Warren Sapp	.50
154	Kurt Warner	3.00
155	Jessie Armstead	.25
156	Lawyer Milloy	.25
157	Brian Griese	1.25
158	Jason Taylor	.50
159	Jeff Lewis	.25
160	Travis Prentice	.75
161	Tim Dwight	.75
162	Kyle Brady	.25
163	Bubba Franks	.50
164	James Thrash	.50
165	Bobby Shaw	.25
166	Ron Dayne	2.00
167	Mike Alstott	1.00
168	Bruce Smith	.50
169	Jeff Graham	.25
170	Jeff Blake	.75
171	Laveranues Coles	.75
172	Herman Moore	.75
173	Shannon Sharpe	.50
174	Corey Dillon	1.00
175	Ken Dilger	.25
176	Eddie Kennison	.50
177	Andre Rison	.50
178	Stephen Davis	1.00
179	Torry Holt	1.00
180	Samari Rolle	.25
181	Michael Strahan	.25
182	Plaxico Burress	1.00
183	Darnell Autry	.25
184	Wesley Walls	.50
185	Elvis Grbac	.75
186	Marcus Pollard	.25
187	Keith Poole	.25
188	Ryan Leaf	1.00
189	Terrell Owens	1.00
190	Dedric Ward	.25
191	Donald Driver	.25
192	Larry Foster	.25
193	Priest Holmes	.75
194	Sammy Morris	.75
195	Reggie Jones	.50
196	Kordell Stewart	1.00
197	Sylvester Morris	1.00
198	Aaron Brooks	1.00
199	Tai Streets	.50
200	Chad Pennington	2.00
201	Terrell Owens	.75
202	Marshall Faulk	.75
203	Mike Anderson	1.25
204	Cris Carter	.75
205	Corey Dillon	.75
206	Daunte Culpepper	.75
207	Peyton Manning	1.50
208	Torry Holt	.75
209	Marvin Harrison	.75
210	Edgerrin James	1.25
211	Sam Madison	.25
212	Jonathan Quinn	.25
213	Rob Morris	.25
214	E.G. Green	.25
215	David Sloan	.25
216	Jason Tucker	.25
217	Wali Rainer	.25
218	Jerry Azumah	.25
219	Dameyune Craig	.25
220	Jammi German	.25
221	*LaDainian Tomlinson*	80.00
222	*Quincy Morgan*	25.00
223	*Steve Smith*	10.00
224	*Santana Moss*	30.00
225	*Koren Robinson*	30.00
226	*Kevin Kasper*	15.00
227	*Jamie Henderson*	10.00
228	*Adam Archuleta*	15.00
229	*Drew Brees*	80.00
230	*Michael Stone*	7.00
231	*Jamar Fletcher*	12.00
232	*Eric Westmoreland*	10.00
233	*Chris Barnes*	12.00
234	*Gerard Warren*	20.00
235	*Marvin "Snoop" Minnis*	30.00
236	*Chris Chambers*	40.00
237	*Darnerian McCants*	10.00
238	*Kevan Barlow*	25.00
239	*Mike McMahon*	20.00
240	*Jabari Holloway*	10.00
241	*Travis Henry*	30.00
242	*Derrick Blaylock*	10.00
243	*Tim Hasselbeck*	15.00
244	*Andre Carter*	12.00
245	*Sage Rosenfels*	20.00
246	*Cedrick Wilson*	12.00
247	*Scotty Anderson*	10.00
248	*Ken-Yon Rambo*	15.00
249	*Marques Tuiasosopo*	30.00
250	*Reggie Wayne*	30.00
251	*Onomo Ojo*	12.00
252	*James Jackson*	25.00
253	*Moran Norris*	7.00
254	*Rashard Casey*	12.00
255	*Rudi Johnson*	20.00
256	*Willie Middlebrooks*	10.00
257	*Freddie Mitchell*	35.00
258	*Deuce McAllister*	40.00
259	*Chad Johnson*	20.00
260	*David Terrell*	40.00
261	*Jamal Reynolds*	15.00
262	*Michael Vick*	100.00
263	*Marcus Stroud*	12.00
264	*Dan Alexander*	15.00
265	*Jonathan Carter*	12.00
266	*Bobby Newcombe*	15.00
267	*Eddie Berlin*	12.00
268	*LaMont Jordan*	20.00
269	*Michael Bennett*	50.00
270	*Shaun Rogers*	7.00
271	*Travis Minor*	20.00
272	*Jesse Palmer*	15.00
273	*Derrick Gibson*	7.00
274	*Chris Weinke*	40.00
275	*Nate Clements*	10.00
276	*Eric Kelly*	7.00
277	*Justin Smith*	20.00
278	*Ryan Pickett*	7.00
279	*Anthony Thomas*	80.00
280	*Will Allen*	12.00
281	*Quincy Carter*	50.00
282	*Richard Seymour*	12.00
283	*Dan Morgan*	12.00
284	*Tay Cody*	7.00
285	*Alge Crumpler*	15.00
286	*Robert Ferguson*	20.00
287	*Will Peterson*	7.00
288	*Tony Dixon*	7.00
289	*Correl Buckhalter*	20.00
290	*Rod Gardner*	40.00
291	*Justin McCareins*	10.00
292	*Josh Heupel*	30.00
293	*Todd Heap*	15.00
294	*Damione Lewis*	12.00
295	*George Layne*	10.00
296	*Jamie Winborn*	10.00
297	*Billy Baber*	7.00
298	*T.J. Houshmandzadeh*	12.00
299	*Aaron Schobel*	7.00
300	*Gary Baxter*	7.00
301	*DeLawrence Grant*	7.00
302	*Morlon Greenwood*	10.00
303	*Shad Meier*	10.00
304	*Torrance Marshall*	15.00
305	*David Martin*	10.00
306	*Anthony Henry*	7.00
307	*Derrick Burgess*	7.00
308	*Andre Dyson*	7.00
309	*Ryan Helming*	7.00
310	*Fred Smoot*	15.00
311	*Arthur Love*	7.00
312	*John Capel*	15.00
313	*Brandon Spoon*	15.00
314	*Tony Stewart*	7.00
315	*Andre King*	10.00
316	*Quentin McCord*	10.00
317	*Zeke Moreno*	7.00
318	*Francis St. Paul*	10.00
319	*Richmond Flowers*	10.00
320	*Derek Combs*	12.00

2001 Topps Chrome All the Way

		MT
Complete Set (10):		3000.00
Common Player:		3.00
AW1	Marvin Harrison	3.00
AW2	Muhsin Muhammad	3.00
AW3	Torry Holt	3.00
AW4	Rod Smith	3.00
AW5	Randy Moss	7.00
AW6	Cris Carter	3.00
AW7	Ed McCaffrey	3.00
AW8	Isaac Bruce	3.00
AW9	Terrell Owens	3.00
AW10	Tony Gonzalez	3.00

2001 Topps Chrome Combos

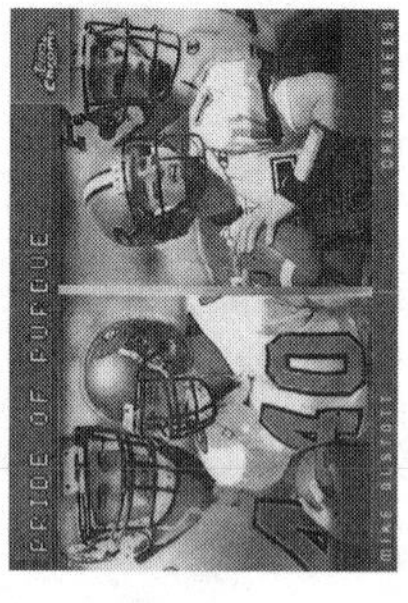

		MT
Complete Set (19):		45.00
Common Player:		2.00
Inserted 1:12		
TC1	Edgerrin James, Santana Moss	5.00
TC2	Torry Holt, Koren Robinson	3.00
TC3	Jamal Lewis, Travis Henry	5.00
TC4	Curtis Martin, Kevan Barlow	2.00
TC5	Cris Carter, Ken-Yon Rambo	2.00
TC6	Troy Aikman, Freddie Mitchell	6.00
TC7	Brian Griese, David Terrell	4.00
TC8	Tyrone Wheatley, Anthony Thomas	3.00
TC9	Warrick Dunn, Travis Minor	2.00
TC10	Peter Warrick, Marvin "Snoop" Minnis	4.00
TC11	Warren Sapp, Dan Morgan	2.00
TC12	Tony Gonzalez, Andre Carter	2.00
TC13	Antonio Freeman, Michael Vick	12.00
TC14	Ron Dayne, Michael Bennett	6.00
TC15	Mike Alstott, Drew Brees	7.00
TC16	Ahman Green, Correl Buckhalter	3.00
TC17	Brad Johnson, Chris Weinke	4.00
TC18	Eric Moulds, Fred Smoot	2.00
TC19	Ray Lewis, Reggie Wayne	3.00

2001 Topps Chrome Ground Warriors

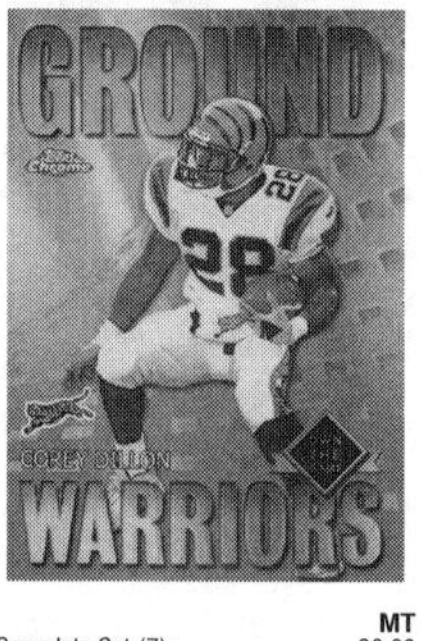

		MT
Complete Set (7):		30.00
Common Player:		3.00
GW1	Edgerrin James	7.00
GW2	Robert Smith	3.00
GW3	Marshall Faulk	7.00
GW4	Mike Anderson	5.00
GW5	Eddie George	5.00
GW6	Corey Dillon	5.00
GW7	Fred Taylor	

2001 Topps Chrome Intimidators

		MT
Complete Set (2):		5.00
Common Player:		
TI1	La'Roi Glover	3.00
TI2	Darren Sharper	3.00

2001 Topps Chrome King Of Kings

		MT
Common Player:		45.00
Inserted 1:734		
K-CD	Corey Dillon 375	45.00
K-DM	Dan Marino 125	150.00
K-RM	Randy Moss EX	125.00
K-TO	Terrell Owens 269	45.00
K-WP	Walter Payton 75	250.00
K-JR	Jerry Rice 125	100.00
K-ES	Emmitt Smith 150	125.00
K-FT	Fred Taylor 250	60.00

2001 Topps Chrome Own the Game

		MT
Complete Set (7):		
Common Player:		2.00
PS1	Brian Griese	2.00
PS2	Peyton Manning	8.00
PS3	Jeff Garcia	2.00
PS4	Daunte Culpepper	5.00
PS5	Brett Favre	10.00
PS6	Kurt Warner	8.00
PS7	Donovan McNabb	4.00

2001 Topps Chrome Pro Bowl Jerseys

		MT
Common Player:		15.00
Inserted 1:299		
TP-MA	Mike Alstott 400	40.00
TP-RG	Rich Gannon 325	25.00
TP-JG	Jeff Garcia 250	50.00
TP-TH	Torry Holt 400	40.00
TP-CL	Chad Lewis 400	15.00
TP-RL	Ray Lewis 375	35.00
TP-JL	John Lynch 325	25.00
TP-DM	Derrick Mason 400	25.00
TP-EM	Eric Moulds 375	40.00
TP-JS	Junior Seau 375	35.00
TP-JT	Jason Taylor 400	20.00

2001 Topps Chrome Rookie Reprint Jerseys

		MT
Common Player:		150.00
Inserted 1:2,729		
TO-DM	Dan Marino 125	250.00
TO-WP	Walter Payton 75	375.00
TO-JR	Jerry Rice 100	150.00
TO-ES	Emmitt Smith 150	180.00

2001 Topps Chrome Showtime

		MT
Complete Set (3):		6.00
Common Player:		
TS1	Derrick Mason	2.00
TS2	Az-Zahir Hakim	2.00
TS3	Jermaine Lewis	4.00

2001 Topps Chrome Walter Payton Reprints

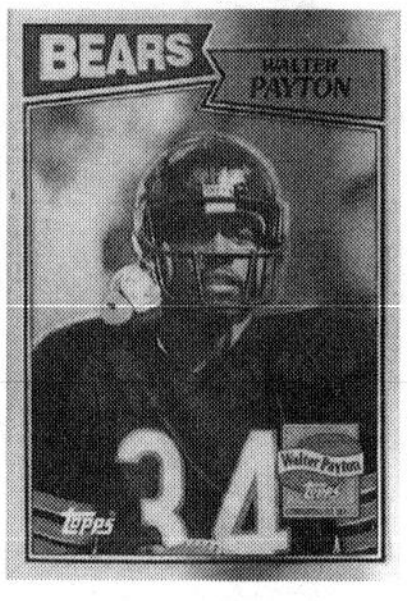

		MT
Complete Set (12):		70.00
Common Player:		8.00
Inserted 1:20		
WP1	Walter Payton 1976-#148	12.00
WP2	Walter Payton 1977-#360	8.00
WP3	Walter Payton 1978-#200	8.00
WP4	Walter Payton 1979-#480	8.00
WP5	Walter Payton 1980-#160	8.00
WP6	Walter Payton 1981-#400	8.00
WP7	Walter Payton 1982-#302	8.00
WP8	Walter Payton 1983-#36	8.00
WP9	Walter Payton 1984-#228	8.00
WP10	Walter Payton 1985-#33	8.00
WP11	Walter Payton 1986-#11	8.00
WP12	Walter Payton 1987-#46	8.00

2001 Topps Chrome Walter Payton Reprint Relic

		MT
Inserted 1:1,204		
WPR	Walter Payton Jersey	150.00

Post-1980 cards in Near Mint condition will generally sell for about 75% of the quoted Mint value. Excellent-condition cards bring no more than 40%.

2001 Topps Debut

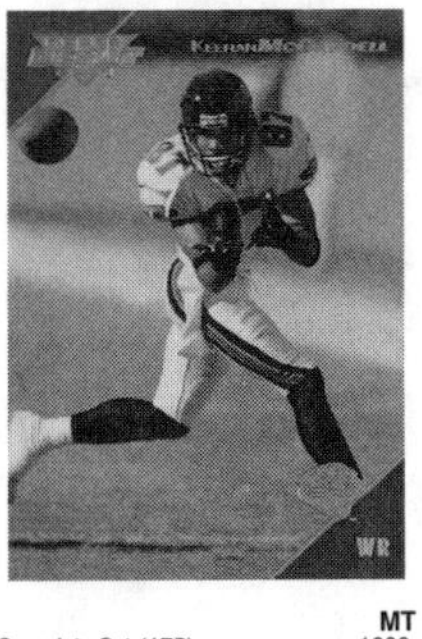

	MT
Complete Set (175):	1000.
Common Player:	.25
Minor Stars:	.50
Common Rookie #101-110:	30.00
Inserted 1:183	
Production 499 Sets	
Common Rookie #111-150:	8.00
Inserted 1:23	
Production 999 Sets	
Common Rookie #151-175:	7.00
Inserted 1:25	
Production 1,499 Sets	
Pack (4):	4.00
Wax Box (24):	70.00

1	Marshall Faulk	.75
2	Ricky Watters	.50
3	Bill Schroeder	.25
4	Muhsin Muhammad	.50
5	Peter Warrick	1.25
6	Marvin Harrison	.75
7	Stephen Davis	.50
8	Cris Carter	.75
9	Charlie Batch	.50
10	David Boston	.50
11	Ike Hilliard	.25
12	Steve McNair	.50
13	Kordell Stewart	.50
14	Travis Prentice	.50
15	Sammy Morris	.75
16	Vinny Testaverde	.50
17	Tyrone Wheatley	.50
18	Jeff Garcia	.75
19	Brett Favre	2.25
20	Jake Plummer	.75
21	Cade McNown	.75
22	Rob Johnson	.50
23	Tim Couch	.75
24	Jerome Bettis	.50
25	Ricky Williams	1.00
26	Darrell Jackson	.50
27	Troy Brown	.25
28	Jamal Lewis	1.75
29	Isaac Bruce	.75
30	Lamar Smith	.50
31	Qadry Ismail	.25
32	Elvis Grbac	.50
33	Shaun Alexander	.75
34	Peyton Manning	1.75
35	Curtis Martin	.75
36	Jamal Anderson	.75
37	Mark Brunell	1.00
38	Emmitt Smith	1.50
39	Chad Lewis	.50
40	Randy Moss	1.75
41	Kurt Warner	2.00
42	Terrence Wilkins	.50
43	Corey Dillon	.75
44	Brian Griese	.75
45	Jon Kitna	.50
46	Eric Moulds	.75
47	Steve Beuerlein	.50
48	James Allen	.75
49	Amani Toomer	.50
50	Daunte Culpepper	1.25
51	Michael Pittman	.50
52	Warrick Dunn	.75
53	Terrell Owens	.75
54	Donald Hayes	.50
55	Keenan McCardell	.50
56	Tony Gonzalez	.50
57	Freddie Jones	.50
58	Charlie Garner	.50
59	Shawn Jefferson	.25
60	Brian Urlacher	1.25
61	Donovan McNabb	1.00
62	Az-Zahir Hakim	.50
63	James Thrash	.50
64	Hines Ward	.50
65	Shawn Bryson	.25
66	Wayne Chrebet	.50
67	Kevin Johnson	.50
68	Eddie George	.75
69	Derrick Alexander	.25
70	Tim Brown	.50
71	Jay Fiedler	.50
72	Aaron Brooks	.75
73	Torry Holt	.50
74	Edgerrin James	1.75
75	Shannon Sharpe	.50
76	Oronde Gadsden	.50
77	Rod Smith	.50
78	Rich Gannon	.50
79	Fred Taylor	1.00
80	Derrick Mason	.50
81	Joe Horn	.50
82	Robert Smith	.50
83	James Stewart	.50
84	Jeff George	.50
85	Troy Aikman	1.25
86	Charles Johnson	.25
87	Ahman Green	.50
88	Shaun King	.50
89	Ray Lewis	.50
90	Trent Dilfer	.50
91	Drew Bledsoe	1.00
92	Jimmy Smith	.50
93	Ed McCaffrey	.50
94	Kerry Collins	.50
95	Terry Glenn	.50
96	Ron Dayne	1.25
97	Keyshawn Johnson	.75
98	Antonio Freeman	.50
99	Tiki Barber	.50
100	Mike Anderson	1.75
101	*Drew Brees*	100.00
102	*Chris Weinke*	65.00
103	*LaDainian Tomlinson*	100.00
104	*Michael Bennett*	80.00
105	*Anthony Thomas*	125.00
106	*LaMont Jordan*	35.00
107	*David Terrell*	70.00
108	*Michael Vick*	150.00
109	*Deuce McAllister*	75.00
110	*James Jackson*	30.00
111	*Mike McMahon*	30.00
112	*Cedrick Wilson*	8.00
113	*Ken Lucas*	8.00
114	*Fred Smoot*	30.00
115	*Alge Crumpler*	10.00
116	*Sage Rosenfels*	35.00
117	*Rashard Casey*	10.00
118	*David Allen*	10.00
119	*Bobby Newcombe*	25.00
120	*Jesse Palmer*	25.00
121	*Tommy Polley*	8.00
122	*Kevan Barlow*	30.00
123	*Scotty Anderson*	8.00
124	*Travis Minor*	30.00
125	*Marvin "Snoop" Minnis*	35.00
126	*Moran Norris*	10.00
127	*Quinton Caver*	10.00
128	*Chad Johnson*	25.00
129	*Boo Williams*	8.00
130	*Brian Natkin*	8.00
131	*Orlando Huff*	8.00
132	*Derrick Gibson*	15.00
133	*Tony Driver*	30.00
134	*Torrence Marshall*	12.00
135	*Alex Bannister*	10.00
136	*Morlon Greenwood*	8.00
137	*Ennis Davis*	10.00
138	*Mike Cerimele*	10.00
139	*David Rivers*	8.00
140	*Dustin McClintock*	8.00
141	*Tay Cody*	10.00
142	*Arthur Love*	8.00
143	*Sly Johnson*	8.00
144	*Dan Alexander*	10.00
145	*Will Allen*	10.00
146	*Andre Dyson*	10.00
147	*Margin Hooks*	8.00
148	*Adam Archuleta*	20.00
149	*Sedrick Hodge*	8.00
150	*Kendrell Bell*	8.00
151	*Reggie Wayne*	12.00
152	*Rod Gardner*	18.00
153	*Chris Chambers*	10.00
154	*Jamal Reynolds*	7.00
155	*Ben Hamilton*	8.00
156	*Dan Morgan*	10.00
157	*Quincy Morgan*	12.00
158	*Travis Henry*	18.00
159	*Ken-Yon Rambo*	7.00
160	*Josh Heupel*	20.00
161	*Marcus Stroud*	8.00
162	*Marques Tuiasosopo*	12.00
163	*Reggie Germany*	10.00
164	*Freddie Milons*	8.00
165	*Jabari Holloway*	10.00
166	*Ben Leard*	7.00
167	*Bhawoh Jue*	7.00
168	*Freddie Mitchell*	15.00
169	*Vinny Sutherland*	7.00
170	*Jeff Backus*	7.00
171	*Correll Buckhelter*	10.00
172	*Mario Fatafehi*	7.00
173	*Jeff Chaney*	7.00
174	*Koren Robinson*	18.00
175	*Santana Moss*	25.00

2001 Topps Gallery

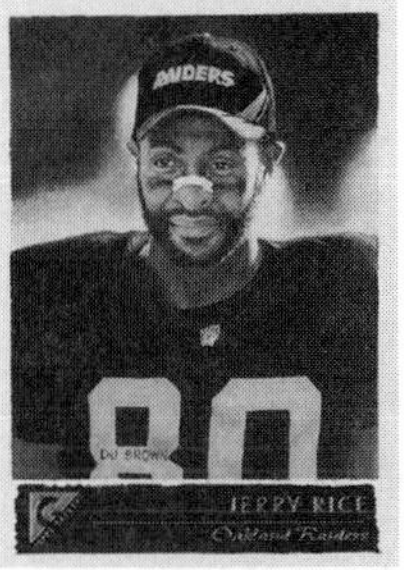

	MT
Complete Set (144):	85.00
Common Player:	.15
Minor Stars:	.30
Common Rookies:	.75
Inserted 1:1	
Pack (6):	3.00
Wax Box (24):	50.00

1	Donovan McNabb	1.00
2	Jamal Anderson	.50
3	Steve McNair	.50
4	Peyton Manning	2.00
5	Curtis Martin	.50
6	Joey Galloway	.50
7	Daunte Culpepper	1.25
8	Corey Dillon	.50
9	Brad Johnson	.30
10	Doug Flutie	.75
11	Jerome Bettis	.50
12	Elvis Grbac	.50
13	Aaron Brooks	.75
14	Ray Lewis	.50
15	Tim Dwight	.50
16	Robert Smith	.30
17	Jake Plummer	.50
18	Jay Fiedler	.50
19	Fred Taylor	.75
20	Jerry Rice	1.25
21	Shaun King	.50
22	Cade McNown	.50
23	Drew Bledsoe	.75
24	Ricky Watters	.30
25	Muhsin Muhammad	.30
26	Shawn Jefferson	.15
27	Tiki Barber	.50
28	Derrick Alexander	.30
29	Stephen Davis	.50
30	James Stewart	.30
31	Terrell Owens	.50
32	Ed McCaffrey	.50
33	Jeff Graham	.15
34	Jamal Lewis	1.50
35	Edgerrin James	1.75
36	Tim Couch	.75
37	Marshall Faulk	.75
38	Ike Hilliard	.30
39	Ahman Green	.50
40	Tim Biakabutuka	.30
41	Akili Smith	.50
42	David Boston	.50
43	Eddie George	.75
44	Hines Ward	.30
45	Chad Lewis	.30
46	Brian Urlacher	1.25
47	Eric Moulds	.50
48	Ricky Williams	1.00
49	Warrick Dunn	.50
50	Kerry Collins	.30
51	Isaac Bruce	.50
52	Jimmy Smith	.30
53	Emmitt Smith	1.50
54	Cris Carter	.50
55	Jeff Garcia	.50
56	Mike Anderson	1.50
57	Lamar Smith	.50
58	Brett Favre	2.50
59	Steve Beuerlein	.30
60	Terry Glenn	.30
61	Tyrone Wheatley	.30
62	Charlie Batch	.50
63	Chris Chandler	.30
64	Sylvester Morris	.50
65	Joe Horn	.30
66	Kevin Johnson	.30
67	Rob Johnson	.30
68	Jeff George	.30
69	Keyshawn Johnson	.50
70	Wayne Chrebet	.30
71	Randy Moss	2.00
72	Marvin Harrison	.50
73	Peter Warrick	.50
74	Darrell Jackson	.30
75	Derrick Mason	.50
76	Oronde Gadsden	.30
77	Charles Johnson	.15
78	James Allen	.30
79	Torry Holt	.50
80	Troy Brown	.15
81	Amani Toomer	.30
82	Junior Seau	.30
83	Troy Aikman	1.25
84	Mark Brunell	.75
85	Brian Griese	.60
86	Charlie Garner	.30
87	Rich Gannon	.30
88	Jeff Blake	.30
89	Donald Hayes	.15
90	Germane Crowell	.30
91	Tony Gonzalez	.30
92	Jon Kitna	.30
93	Vinny Testaverde	.30
94	Kordell Stewart	.50
95	Keenan McCardell	.30
96	Kurt Warner	2.00
97	Bill Schroeder	.30
98	Rod Smith	.50
99	Tim Brown	.30
100	Trent Dilfer	.30
101	*Michael Vick*	12.00
102	*Koren Robinson*	3.00
103	*LaDainian Tomlinson*	7.00
104	*Todd Heap*	1.25
105	*Correll Buckhelter*	1.50
106	*Freddie Mitchell*	2.50
107	*Josh Booty*	.75
108	*Chris Chambers*	1.50
109	*Chris Weinke*	5.00
110	*Steve Smith*	.75
111	*Travis Minor*	1.50
112	*Ken-Yon Rambo*	1.25
113	*Marques Tuiasosopo*	2.50
114	*Bobby Newcombe*	1.00
115	*Drew Brees*	7.00
116	*LaMont Jordan*	1.50
117	*Reggie Germany*	1.00
118	*Reggie Wayne*	2.50
119	*Dan Alexander*	1.00
120	*Alge Crumpler*	1.00
121	*Robert Ferguson*	1.50
122	*Rod Gardner*	3.00
123	*Mike McMahon*	1.25
124	*Kevan Barlow*	2.00
125	*Marvin "Snoop" Minnis*	2.00
126	*Sage Rosenfels*	1.50
127	*Jesse Palmer*	1.25
128	*Michael Bennett*	6.00
129	*Rudi Johnson*	1.25
130	*Deuce McAllister*	4.00
131	*Santana Moss*	3.00
132	*Josh Heupel*	2.00
133	*Quincy Morgan*	2.00
134	*Quincy Carter*	4.00
135	*Anthony Thomas*	3.50
136	*James Jackson*	1.75
137	*Kevin Kasper*	1.25
138	*Alex Bannister*	1.25
139	*David Terrell*	4.00
140	*Chad Johnson*	1.50
141	Walter Payton	.15
142	Bart Starr	.15
143	Sonny Jurgensen	.15
144	Jim Brown	.15
145A	(Joe Namath HTA)	7.00
145B	Joe Namath RETAIL	20.00
NNO	Joe Namath BUCKS	5.00

2001 Topps Gallery Autographs

		MT
Common Player:		15.00
Inserted 1:84		
MA	Mike Anderson	30.00
AB	Aaron Brooks	25.00
TB	Tim Brown	25.00
WC	Wayne Chrebet	15.00
DC	Daunte Culpepper	50.00
TD	Tim Dwight	15.00
JG	Jeff Garcia	25.00
EG	Eddie George	45.00
JL	Jamal Lewis	30.00

2001 Topps Gallery Gallery Heritage

		MT
Complete Set (9):		20.00
Common Player:		1.50
Inserted 1:12		
GH1	Johnny Unitas	4.00
GH2	Bart Starr	4.00
GH3	Y.A. Tittle	2.00
GH4	Chuck Bednarik	1.50
GH5	Randy Moss	4.00
GH6	Jerry Rice	2.50
GH7	Peyton Manning	4.00
GH8	Brett Favre	5.00
GH9	Marshall Faulk	1.75

2001 Topps Gallery Gallery Heritage Autographed Relics

		MT
Complete Set (5):		
Common Player:		
Too uncommon to price		
GRA BF	Brett Favre	
GRA FG	Frank Gifford	
GRA RM	Randy Moss	
GRA JR	Jerry Rice	
GRA BS	Bart Starr	

2001 Topps Gallery Gallery Heritage Relics

		MT
Common Player:		25.00
Inserted 1:211		
GR BF	Brett Favre	45.00
GR FG	Frank Gifford	25.00
GR RM	Randy Moss	40.00
GR JR	Jerry Rice	30.00
GR BS	Bart Starr	30.00

2001 Topps Gallery Originals

		MT
Complete Set (10):		140.00
Common Player:		12.00
Inserted 1:50		
GO DA	Dan Alexander	12.00
GO KB	Kevan Barlow	12.00
GO CC	Cris Carter	25.00
GO RC	Rashard Casey	12.00
GO CD	Corey Dillon	20.00
GO RG	Rod Gardner	20.00
GO CJ	Chad Johnson	12.00
GO PM	Peyton Manning	45.00
GO WS	Warren Sapp	12.00
GO KW	Kurt Warner	40.00

2001 Topps Gallery Star Gallery

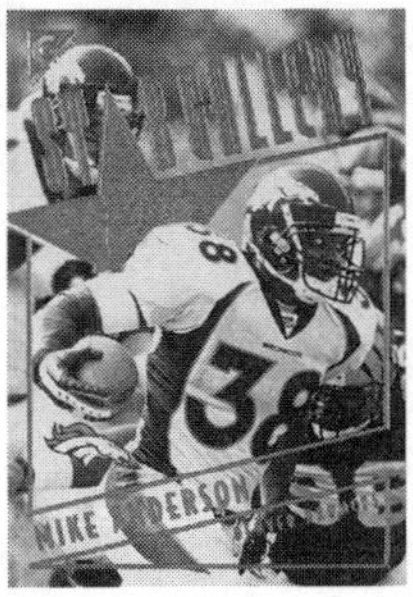

		MT
Complete Set (10):		12.00
Common Player:		1.00
Inserted 1:8		
SG1	Daunte Culpepper	2.00
SG2	Jamal Lewis	2.50
SG3	Peyton Manning	3.00
SG4	Edgerrin James	2.50
SG5	Randy Moss	3.00
SG6	Marshall Faulk	1.25
SG7	Mike Anderson	2.50
SG8	Eddie George	1.25
SG9	Donovan McNabb	1.50
SG10	Cris Carter	1.00

2001 Topps Gallery Team Topps Legends Autographs

		MT
Complete Set (5):		
Common Player:		
TTR13	Jim Brown	100.00
TTF3	John Riggins	25.00
TTR9	Otis Sistrunk	25.00
TTF18	Fred Biletnikoff	75.00
TTF2	Dick Butkus	

Values quoted in this guide reflect the retail price of a card — the price a collector can expect to pay when buying a card from a dealer. The wholesale price — that which a collector can expect to receive from a dealer when selling cards — will be significantly lower, depending on desirability and condition.

2001 Topps Heritage

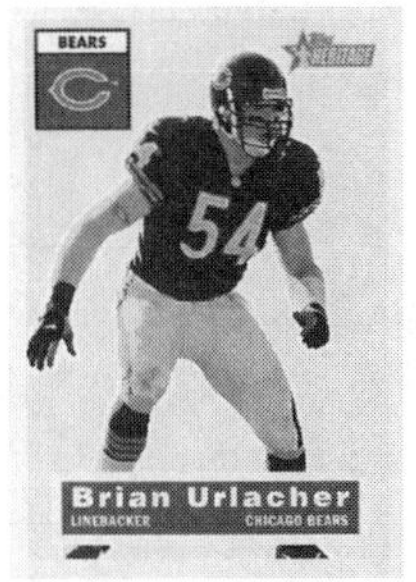

	MT
Complete Set (146):	275.00
Common Player:	.30
Minor Stars:	.60
Common Rookie:	2.00
Inserted 1:23	
Production 1,956 Sets	
Pack (8):	3.00
Wax Box (24):	60.00

1	Ray Lewis	.60
2	Peter Warrick	1.50
3	James Stewart	.60
4	Junior Seau	.60
5	Jeff George	.60
6	Amani Toomer	.30
7	Elvis Grbac	.60
8	David Boston	.75
9	Jimmy Smith	.60
10	Warrick Dunn	.75
11	Hines Ward	.60
12	Joe Horn	.60
13	Stephen Davis	.75
14	Tyrone Wheatley	.75
15	Brian Urlacher	1.50
16	Fred Taylor	1.00
17	Jerry Rice	1.75
18	Keyshawn Johnson	.75
19	Jay Fiedler	.60
20	Jamal Anderson	.75
21	Emmitt Smith	2.00
22	Tiki Barber	.75
23	Daunte Culpepper	1.50
24	Torry Holt	.75
25	Peyton Manning	2.50
26	Eddie George	1.00
27	Jamal Lewis	2.50
28	Ricky Williams	1.25
29	Ahman Green	.60
30	Ed McCaffrey	.60
31	Curtis Martin	.75
32	Isaac Bruce	.75
33	Doug Flutie	1.00
34	Steve McNair	.75
35	Donovan McNabb	1.25
36	Keenan McCardell	.60
37	Charlie Batch	.75
38	Cade McNown	.75
39	Terrell Owens	.75
40	Brad Johnson	.75
41	Robert Smith	.75
42	Muhsin Muhammad	.60
43	Kurt Warner	2.75
44	Lamar Smith	.75
45	Brian Griese	.75
46	Trent Dilfer	.60
47	Jeff Garcia	.75
48	Derrick Mason	.60
49	Drew Bledsoe	1.00
50	Marshall Faulk	1.00
51	Corey Dillon	.75
52	Tony Gonzalez	.60
53	Chad Lewis	.60
54	Shaun Alexander	.75
55	Edgerrin James	2.50
56	Eric Moulds	.75
57	Aaron Brooks	.75
58	Zach Thomas	.60
59	Jerome Bettis	.75
60	Shannon Sharpe	.60
61	Kerry Collins	.60
62	Ricky Watters	.60
63	Tim Couch	1.00
64	Marvin Harrison	.75
65	Tim Brown	.75
66	Mark Brunell	1.00
67	Wayne Chrebet	.60
68	Terry Glenn	.75
69	Mike Anderson	2.50
70	Randy Moss	2.50
71	Freddie Jones	.60
72	Ike Hilliard	.60
73	Derrick Alexander	.30
74	Travis Prentice	.75
75	Brett Favre	3.00
76	Rod Smith	.60
77	Troy Aikman	1.50
78	Cris Carter	.75
79	Rich Gannon	.60
80	Charlie Garner	.60
81	Michael Pittman	.60
82	Jeff Graham	.30
83	Albert Connell	.60
84	Bill Schroeder	.60
85	Jeff Blake	.60
86	Jon Kitna	.60
87	Qadry Ismail	.30
88	Joey Galloway	.75
89	Charles Johnson	.30
90	Troy Brown	.30
91	Johnnie Morton	.60
92	Chris Chandler	.60
93	Donald Hayes	.60
94	Shaun King	.75
95	Vinny Testaverde	.60
96	James Allen	.75
97	Jake Plummer	.75
98	Antonio Freeman	.60
99	Sean Dawkins	.30
100	Ron Dayne	1.50
101	Rob Johnson	.60
102	Kordell Stewart	.75
103	Akili Smith	.75
104	Shawn Jefferson	.30
105	Germane Crowell	.60
106	Kevin Johnson	.75
107	Steve Beuerlein	.60
108	Marcus Robinson	.75
109	Peerless Price	.60
110	Jerome Pathon	.30
111	*Sage Rosenfels*	6.00
112	*Quincy Morgan*	5.00
113	*Chad Johnson*	6.00
114	*Josh Heupel*	15.00
115	*Anthony Thomas*	40.00
116	*Drew Brees*	30.00
117	*Kevan Barlow*	7.00
118	*Chris Chambers*	20.00
119	*Mike McMahon*	6.00
120	*Todd Heap*	5.00
121	*Leonard Davis*	4.00
122	*Richard Seymour*	4.00
123	*Robert Ferguson*	7.00
124	*Andre Carter*	4.00
125	*Jesse Palmer*	5.00
126	*Travis Minor*	7.00
127	*Rudi Johnson*	6.00
128	*Rod Gardner*	12.00
129	*Marvin "Snoop" Minnis*	8.00
130	*Koren Robinson*	12.00
131	*Chris Weinke*	15.00
132	*James Jackson*	7.00
133	*Michael Vick*	50.00
134	*Marques Tuiasosopo*	10.00
135	*Michael Bennett*	20.00
136	*LaDainian Tomlinson*	25.00
137	*Freddie Mitchell*	10.00
138	*Deuce McAllister*	15.00
139	*Quincy Carter*	10.00
140	*Santana Moss*	20.00
141	*David Terrell*	20.00
142	*Reggie Wayne*	10.00
143	*Justin Smith*	2.00
144	*Gerard Warren*	5.00
145	*Travis Henry*	10.00
146	*Dan Morgan*	7.00

2001 Topps Heritage Classic Renditions

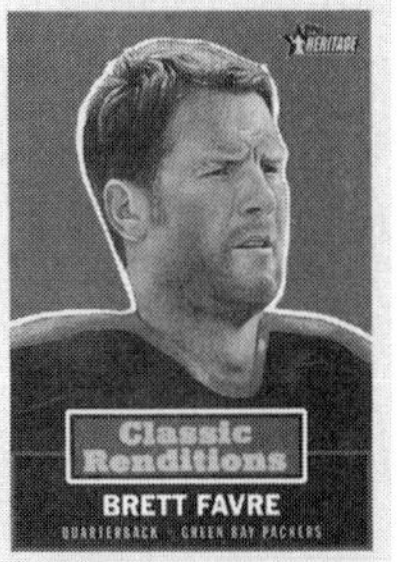

		MT
Complete Set (10):		15.00
Common Player:		.50
Inserted 1:8		
CR1	Donovan McNabb	1.50
CR2	Brett Favre	6.00
CR3	Edgerrin James	4.00
CR4	Peyton Manning	4.00
CR5	Marvin Harrison	.50
CR6	Kurt Warner	5.00
CR7	Marshall Faulk	1.00
CR8	Brian Urlacher	2.00
CR9	Jeff Garcia	1.00
CR10	Terrell Owens	.50

2001 Topps Heritage Classic Renditions Autographs

		MT
Complete Set (3):		
Common Player:		150.00
CRA BF	Brett Favre	200.00
CRA EJ	Edgerrin James	150.00
CRA BU	Brian Urlacher	150.00

2001 Topps Heritage Gridiron Collection Relics

		MT
Complete Set (12):		
Common Player:		15.00
GC1	Daunte Culpepper	25.00
GC2	Eddie George	25.00
GC3	Edgerrin James	40.00
GC4	Tony Gonzalez	15.00
GC5	Marvin Harrison	20.00
GC6	Jimmy Smith	15.00
GC7	Sam Cowart	15.00
GC8		15.00
GC9	Rod Woodson	20.00
GC10	Mo Lewis	15.00
GC11	Charles Woodson	20.00
GC12	Derrick Brooks	15.00

2001 Topps Heritage New Age Performers

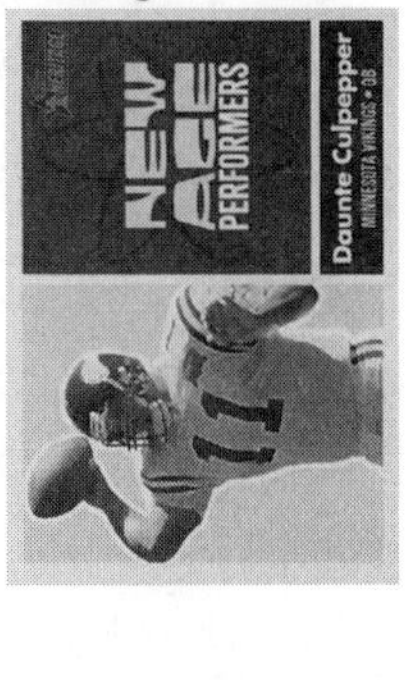

MT
Complete Set (15): 15.00
Common Player: .75
Minor Stars: 1.50
Inserted 1:8
NA1 Marshall Faulk 1.75
NA2 Jerry Rice 2.50
NA3 Marvin Harrison 1.50
NA4 Peyton Manning 5.00
NA5 Torry Holt .75
NA6 Isaac Bruce 1.50
NA7 Eddie George 1.75
NA8 Daunte Culpepper 2.00
NA9 Edgerrin James 4.00
NA10 Randy Moss 5.00
NA11 Jeff Garcia 1.50
NA12 Mike Anderson 4.00
NA13 Terrell Owens 1.50
NA14 Rod Smith .75
NA15 Cris Carter 1.50

2001 Topps Heritage Real One Autographs

MT
Complete Set (21):
Common Player: 20.00
Red sigs 2X
THRO EJEdgerrin James 30.00
THRO MAMike Anderson 20.00
THRO EMEric Moulds 20.00
THRO RWRicky Williams 30.00
THRO MHMarvin Harrison 30.00
THRO DCDaunte Culpepper 40.00
THRO WCWayne Chrebet 20.00
THRO JSJimmy Smith 20.00
THRO BUBrian Urlacher 50.00
THRO SDStephen Davis 20.00
THRO JLJamal Lewis 30.00
THRO TOTerrell Owens 20.00
THRO ABAaron Brooks 25.00
101 Roosevelt Grier 25.00
58 Ollie Matson 20.00
60 Lenny Moore 20.00
41 Roosevelt Brown 25.00
78 Elroy "Crazy Legs" Hirsch 25.00
28 Chuck Bednarik 25.00
86 Y.A. Tittle 25.00
44 Joe Schmidt 20.00

2001 Topps Heritage Souvenir Seating Relics

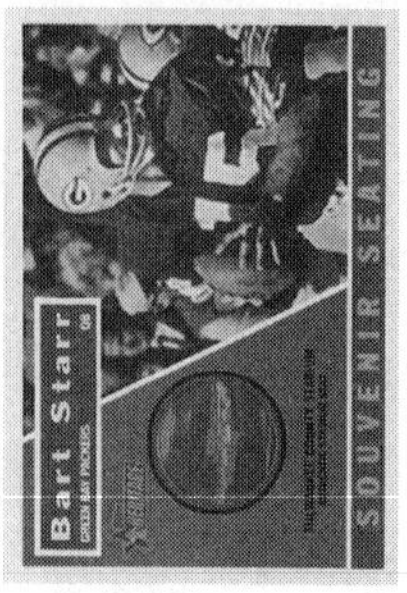

MT
Complete Set (10):
Common Player: 10.00
S1 10.00
S2 10.00
S3 Bart Starr 25.00
S4 10.00
S5 Johnny Unitas 25.00
S6 Raymond Berry 10.00
S7 Lenny Moore 10.00
S8 Jim Brown 25.00
S9 10.00
S10 Chuck Bednarik 10.00

2001 Topps Heritage Team Topps Legends Autographs

MT
Complete Set (13):
Common Player: 20.00
TTR17 Johnny Unitas 40.00
TTR4 Tommy McDonald 20.00
TTR19 Paul Hornung 40.00
TTF10 Chuck Foreman 20.00
TTR16 Cliff Branch 20.00
TTF20 Tom Dempsey 20.00
TTF12 Don Maynard 20.00
TTR12 Don Maynard 20.00
TTR21 Billy Kilmer 20.00
TTF21 Billy Kilmer 20.00
TTF5 John Hannah 20.00
TTR6 Terry Metcalf 20.00
TTF9 Otis Sistrunk 20.00

Values quoted in this guide reflect the retail price of a card — the price a collector can expect to pay when buying a card from a dealer. The wholesale price — that which a collector can expect to receive from a dealer when selling cards — will be significantly lower, depending on desirability and condition.

2001 Topps Heritage Then and Now

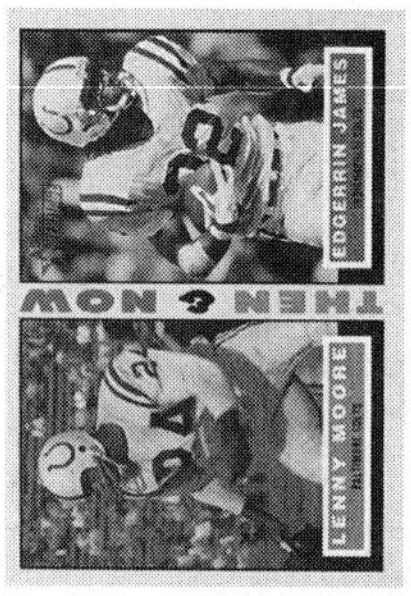

Autographs too uncommon to price.

MT
Complete Set (3): 2.50
Common Player: .50
Inserted 1:8
TN-BL Chuck Bednarik, Ray Lewis .50
TN-MJ Lenny Moore, Edgerrin James 2.00
TN-TG Y.A. Tittle, Jeff Garcia .50

2001 Topps Heritage 1956 Players

MT
Complete Set (15):
Common Player: 2.00
THRO AAAlan Ameche 2.00
THRO CBChuck Bednarik 3.00
THRO RBRoosevelt Brown 2.00
THRO CCCharley Conerly 2.00
THRO ADArt Donovan 2.00
THRO TFTom Fears 2.00
THRO FGFrank Gifford 3.00
THRO RGRoosevelt Grier 2.00
THRO EHElroy "Crazy Legs" Hirsch 4.00
THRO BHBill Howton 2.00
THRO BLBobby Layne 2.00
THRO LMLenny Moore 2.00
THRO YTY.A. Tittle 3.00
THRO ETEmlen Tunnell 3.00
THRO NVNorm Van Brocklin 3.00

2001 Topps Heritage 1956 Topps All-Stars

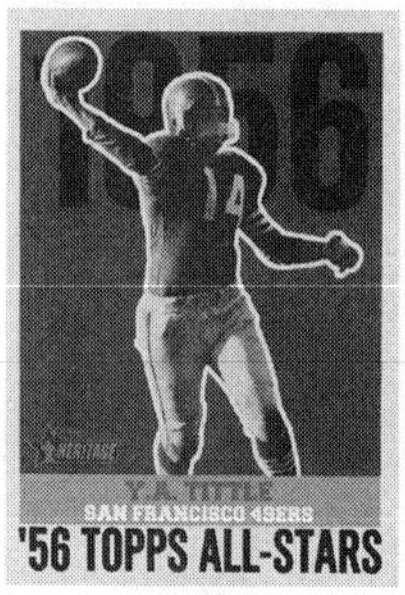

MT
Complete Set (3): 2.00
Common Player: .75
Inserted 1:12
HA-CB Chuck Bednarik .75
HA-LM Lenny Moore .75
HA-YT Y.A. Tittle .75

2001 Topps Reserve

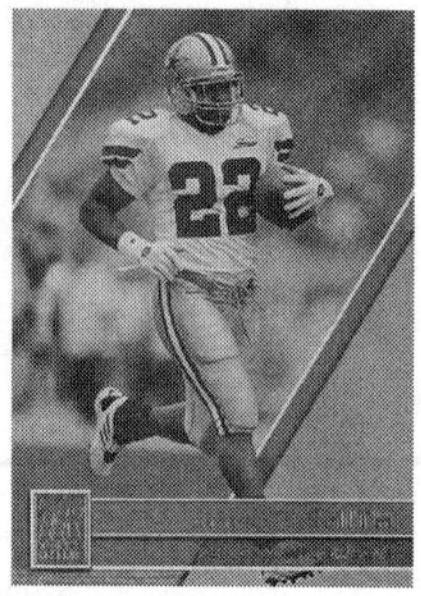

MT
Complete Set (150): 325.00
Common Player: .30
Minor Stars: .60
Common Rookie: 5.00
Inserted 1:5
Wax Box (10): 115.00
1 Jeff Garcia 1.50
2 Joe Horn .30
3 Jeff George .30
4 Ed McCaffrey .60
5 Keenan McCardell .60
6 Jerome Bettis 1.00
7 Jake Plummer .60
8 Doug Flutie 1.50
9 Wayne Chrebet .60
10 Brett Favre 5.00
11 Emmitt Smith 3.00
12 Derrick Mason .60
13 Lamar Smith .60
14 Brian Urlacher 2.50
15 Kurt Warner 4.00
16 Jerry Rice 3.00
17 Tony Gonzalez .60
18 Jeff Blake .60
19 Warrick Dunn 1.00
20 Vinny Testaverde .60
21 Peyton Manning 4.00
22 Drew Bledsoe 1.50
23 Tim Dwight .30
24 Brad Johnson 1.00
25 Peter Warrick 1.00
26 Steve McNair 1.00
27 James Thrash .30
28 Kordell Stewart 1.00
29 Randy Moss 4.00
30 Brian Griese 1.50
31 Curtis Martin 1.00
32 Ike Hilliard .30
33 Torry Holt 1.00
34 James Allen .30
35 Jay Fiedler .60
36 Junior Seau .60
37 Troy Brown .30
38 Ricky Williams 2.00
39 Charlie Garner .60
40 Eddie George 1.50
41 Stephen Davis .60
42 Tim Couch 1.50
43 Jimmy Smith .60
44 Trent Green .60
45 Rod Smith .60
46 Isaac Bruce 1.00
47 Oronde Gadsden .30
48 Keyshawn Johnson 1.00
49 Jeff Graham .30
50 Mark Brunell 1.50
51 Cade McNown .60
52 Terry Glenn .60
53 Derrick Alexander .60
54 Ron Dayne 1.00
55 Shaun Alexander 2.00
56 Chris Chandler .30
57 Rob Johnson .60
58 Germane Crowell .60
59 Cris Carter 1.00
60 Ahman Green 1.00
61 Marshall Faulk 1.50
62 Plaxico Burress .30
63 Duce Staley .60
64 Keron Johnson .60
65 Muhsin Muhammad .60
66 Elvis Grbac .60
67 Fred Taylor 1.50
68 Marcus Robinson 1.00
69 Edgerrin James 3.00
70 Kerry Collins .60
71 Daunte Culpepper 2.50
72 Matt Hasselbeck .60
73 Akili Smith .30
74 Aaron Brooks 1.50
75 Tim Biakabutuka .30
76 Ray Lewis 1.00
77 David Boston 1.00
78 Donovan McNabb 2.50
79 Marvin Harrison 1.00
80 Rich Gannon 1.00
81 Tony Richardson .30
82 Peerless Price .30
83 Jamal Anderson .60
84 Mike Anderson 2.00
85 Terrell Owens 1.00
86 Antonio Freeman .60
87 Charlie Batch .60
88 Jamal Lewis 2.50
89 Jon Kitna .30
90 Joey Galloway .60
91 Tyrone Wheatley .60
92 Jeff Lewis .30
93 Eric Moulds .60
94 Shawn Jefferson .30
95 Tiki Barber .60
96 Tim Brown 1.00
97 Corey Dillon 1.00
98 Tony Banks .60
99 James Stewart .60
100 Amani Toomer .60
101 *Freddie Mitchell* 10.00
102 *James Jackson* 6.00
103 *Michael Bennett* 12.00
104 *LaDainian Tomlinson* 20.00
105 *Gerard Warren* 5.00
106 *Dan Morgan* 5.00
107 *Alge Crumpler* 5.00
108 *Mike McMahon* 10.00
109 *Justin Smith* 5.00
110 *Chris Weinke* 10.00
111 *Rudi Johnson* 5.00
112 *Rod Gardner* 10.00
113 *Koren Robinson* 10.00
114 *Andre Carter* 5.00
115 *Kevan Barlow* 8.00
116 *Jesse Palmer* 6.00
117 *Anthony Thomas* 25.00
118 *Michael Vick* 30.00
119 *Sage Rosenfels* 6.00
120 *Chad Johnson* 5.00
121 *Robert Ferguson* 5.00
122 *Quincy Carter* 12.00
123 *Travis Minor* 6.00
124 *Travis Henry* 8.00
125 *Reggie Wayne* 10.00
126 *David Terrell* 15.00
127 *Josh Heupel* 6.00
128 *Deuce McAllister* 10.00
129 *Todd Heap* 5.00
130 *Drew Brees* 20.00
131 *Marvin "Snoop" Minnis* 8.00
132 *Marques Tuiasosopo* 10.00
133 *Santana Moss* 10.00
134 *Quincy Morgan* 6.00
135 *Chris Chambers* 12.00
136 *Richard Seymour* 5.00
137 *LaMont Jordan* 5.00
138 *Eddie Berlin* 5.00
139 *Correll Buckhalter* 8.00
140 *Justin McCareins* 5.00
141 *Vinny Sutherland* 5.00
142 *Chris Taylor* 5.00
143 *Scotty Anderson* 5.00
144 *Nate Clements* 5.00
145 *Darnerian McCants* 5.00
146 *Dan Alexander* 5.00
147 *A.J. Feeley* 5.00
148 *Chris Barnes* 5.00
149 *Dee Brown* 5.00
150 *Milton Wynn* 5.00

2001 Topps Reserve Autographs

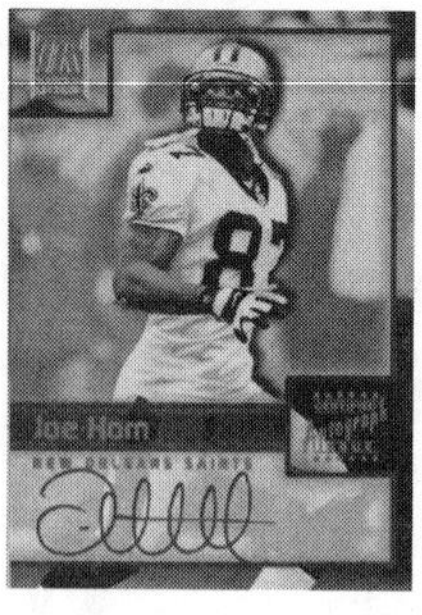

MT
Common Player: 10.00
Inserted 1:9 H; 1:37 R
TR-MA Mike Anderson 25.00
TR-KB Kevan Barlow 15.00
TR-MB Michael Bennett 25.00
TR-JB Josh Booty 10.00
TR-DB Drew Brees 50.00
TR-AB Aaron Brooks 20.00
TR-CC Chris Chambers 25.00
TR-DC Daunte Culpepper 40.00
TR-RG Rod Gardner 20.00
TR-DH Donald Hayes 10.00
TR-TH Travis Henry 15.00
TR-JH Joe Horn 10.00
TR-JJ James Jackson 15.00
TR-WJ Willie Jackson 10.00
TR-CJ Chad Johnson 15.00
TR-JL Jamal Lewis 20.00
TR-DM Derrick Mason 10.00
TR-DMODan Morgan 10.00
TR-QM Quincy Morgan 15.00
TR-SMOSammy Morris 10.00
TR-SM Santana Moss 20.00
TR-EM Eric Moulds 15.00
TR-JP Jesse Palmer 15.00
TR-KR Koren Robinson 20.00
TR-BS Bill Schroeder 10.00
TR-JS Jimmy Smith 15.00
TR-LS Lamar Smith 10.00
TR-TS Tai Streets 10.00
TR-DT David Terrell 25.00
TR-JT James Thrash 10.00
TR-LT LaDainian Tomlinson 40.00
TR-MV Michael Vick 75.00
TR-RWAReggie Wayne 20.00
TR-CW Chris Weinke 25.00
TR-RW Ricky Williams 25.00

2001 Topps Reserve Autographed Mini-Helmets

MT
Complete Set (32):
Common Player: 20.00
Dan Alexander 20.00
Kevan Barlow 20.00
Michael Bennett 40.00
Josh Booty 20.00
Drew Brees 60.00
Quincy Carter 25.00
Chris Chambers 50.00
Rod Gardner 40.00
Travis Henry 20.00
Josh Heupel 20.00
James Jackson 20.00
Chad Johnson 20.00
LaMont Jordan 20.00
Deuce McAllister 60.00
Justin McCareins 20.00
Travis Minor 20.00
Dan Morgan 20.00
Quincy Morgan 20.00
Santana Moss 20.00
Bobby Newcombe 20.00
Jesse Palmer 20.00
Ken-Yon Rambo 20.00
Koren Robinson 20.00
Steve Smith 20.00
Vinny Sutherland 20.00
David Terrell 50.00
Anthony Thomas 80.00
LaDainian Tomlinson 50.00
Michael Vick 80.00
Gerard Warr 20.00
Reggie Wayne 20.00
Chris Weinke 50.00

2001 Topps Reserve Jersey Relics

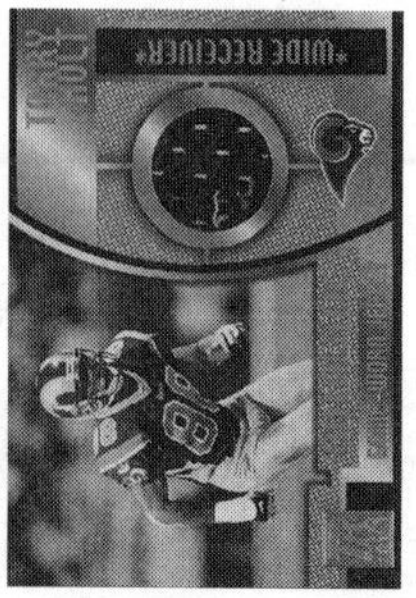

MT
Common Player: 10.00
TRR-SASam Adams 10.00
TRR-MAMike Alstott 10.00
TRR-BBBlaine Bishop 10.00
TRR-DBDerrick Brooks 12.00
TRR-MBMark Brunell 10.00
TRR-THTorry Holt 10.00
TRR-MLMo Lewis 10.00
TRR-SMSam Madison 12.00
TRR-SRSamari Rolle 10.00
TRR-SSShannon Sharpe 10.00
TRR-DSDarren Sharper 12.00
TRR-KWKurt Warner 10.00
TRR-SWSteve Wisniewski 10.00
TRR-CWCharles Woodson 15.00
TRR-FWFrank Wycheck 10.00

2001 Topps Reserve Rookie Premiere Jersey Relics

MT
Common Player: 10.00
Inserted 1:23 H; 1:66 R
TRR-JJJames Jackson 12.00
TRR-RJRudi Johnson 10.00
TRR-MMCMike McMahon 15.00
TRR-MMMarvin "Snoop" Minnis 15.00
TRR-TMTravis Minor 12.00
TRR-DMDan Morgan 10.00
TRR-QMQuincy Morgan 12.00
TRR-MTMarques Tuiasosopo 15.00

2001 Topps Reserve Veteran Game-Worn Relics

MT
Complete Set (4):
Common Player: 20.00
TRR-MAMike Alstott 20.00
TRR-MBMark Brunell 20.00
TRR-THTorry Holt 20.00
TRR-SSShannon Sharpe 20.00

2001 Topps XFL

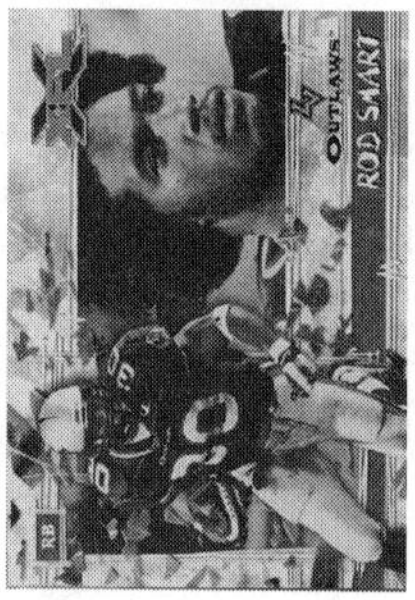

MT
Complete Set (100): 25.00
Common Player: .20
Minor Stars: .40
Pack (8): 2.00
Wax Box (24): 35.00
1 Mike Pawlawski 1.50
2 Todd Doxzon .20
3 James Bostic .75
4 Jim Druckenmiller 1.00
5 Mario Bailey .20
6 Mike Cawley .20
7 Dino Philyaw .40
8 Aaron Bailey .20
9 Juan Johnson .50
10 Kaipo McGuire .20
11 Toya Jones .20
12 Todd Floyd .20
13 Jaimie Baisley .20
14 Brian Shay .50
15 Eric England .20
16 Curtis Alexander .20
17 Tim Lester .75
18 Dialleo Burks .40
19 Charles Puleri .75
20 Zechariah Lord .20
21 Chrys Chukwuma .20
22 Rickey Brady .20
23 Rashaan Salaam 1.50
24 Jermaine Copeland 1.00
25 Butler B'ynote .20
26 Tommy Maddox 1.75
27 Mike Furrey .20
28 Ed Smith .20
29 Pat Barnes 1.00
30 James Hundon .20
31 John Avery 1.75
32 James Willis .20
33 Larry Ryans .20
34 Vaughn Dunbar .40
35 John Williams .20
36 Casey Weldon 1.00
37 Roell Preston .50
38 Jeff Brohm 1.00
39 Rashaan Shehee .40
40 Kevin Swayne .20
41 Ben Snell .20
42 James Williams .20
43 Corte McGuffey .20
44 Charles Jordan .40
45 Frank Leatherwood .20
46 Dwayne Sabb .20
47 Shannon Culver .20
48 Brent Moss .40
49 Zola Davis .20
50 Ryan Clement .50
51 Tyji Armstrong .40
52 Paul Failla .20
53 Michael Blair .20
54 Corey Ivey .20
55 Darryl Hobbs .20
56 Paul Lacoste .20
57 Damon Gourdine .20
58 Wendell Davis .20
59 Joe Cummings .20
60 Stephen Fisher .20
61 Stepfret Williams .75
62 Brandon Sanders .20
63 Michael Black .20
64 Scott Milanovich .75
65 Brian Roche .20
66 Darnell McDonald .75
67 Marcus Hinton .20
68 Quincy Jackson .20
69 Roosevelt Potts .40
70 Rod Smart 2.00
71 Keith Elias .20
72 Latario Rachel .20
73 Mike Sutton .20
74 Kirby Dar Dar .40
75 Derrick Clark .20
76 Antonio Edwards .20
77 Marcus Crandell .20
78 Jerry Crafts .20
79 Brian Roberson .20
80 Las Vegas vs. New York .20
81 Orlando vs. Chicago .20
82 San Francisco vs. Los Angeles .40
83 Memphis vs. Birmingham .20
Kat .20
Rose .20
Dana .20
Lisa Michelle .20
Kiushin .20
Youn .20
Sunni .20
Cicely .20
Tanisha .20
Krissy .20
TK .20
Jensi .20
Jenny .20
Karla .20
Jenny .20
Susanne .20
100 Checklist .20

2001 Topps XFL Endzone Autographs

MT
Complete Set (18): 175.00
Common Player: 10.00
Inserted 1:28 Hobby
Mike Archie 12.00
Michael Black 12.00
Rickey Brady 12.00
Chris Brantley 10.00
Chrys Chukwuma 12.00
Jeremaine Copeland 25.00
Todd Doxzon 10.00
Keith Elias 10.00
Paul Failla 10.00
Mike Furrey 12.00
LeShon Johnson 15.00
Tim Lester 15.00
Tommy Maddox 25.00
Ken Oxendine 12.00
Dino Philyaw 12.00
Roell Preston 15.00
Wally Richardson 18.00
Rashaan Shehee 15.00

2001 Topps XFL Football Relics

MT
Complete Set (8): 175.00
Common Player: 25.00
Inserted 1:34
John Avery 40.00
Pat Barnes 25.00
James Bostic 25.00
Jeff Brohm 35.00
Chuck Clements 25.00
Scott Milanovich 25.00
Charles Puleri 25.00
Rashaan Salaam 30.00

2001 Topps XFL Jersey Relics

MT
Complete Set (8): 120.00
Common Player: 15.00
Inserted 1:34
John Avery 30.00
Pat Barnes 15.00
James Bostic 15.00
Jeff Brohm 25.00
Chuck Clements 15.00
Scott Milanovich 15.00
Charles Puleri 15.00
Rashaan Salaam 20.00

2001 Topps XFL Loaded Cannon

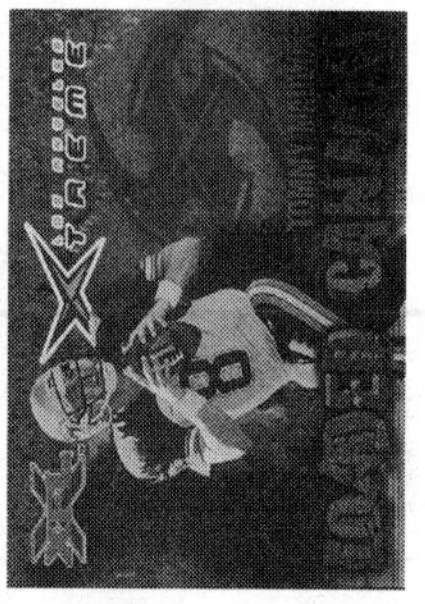

MT
Complete Set (8): 25.00
Common Player: 4.00
Inserted 1:8
1 Tommy Maddox 7.00
2 Casey Weldon 6.00
3 Marcus Crandell 4.00
4 Jeff Brohm 5.00
5 Ryan Clement 4.00
6 Mike Pawlawski 4.00
7 Charles Puleri 4.00
8 Tim Lester 5.00

1977 Touchdown Club

These 50 black-and-white cards were issued as a set in 1977 to honor several Hall-of-Fame caliber retired players. Each front has photo of the player in uniform, with his name below the photo. A black frame borders the photo and his name. The card back has the player's name and number at the top, with his position listed just below them. A brief career summary, listing the player's main honors and accomplishments, is also given. "Touchdown, 1977" is written at the bottom. All of the information on the back is contained within a black box. The set was designed for collectors who wanted the players' autographs; a list of their home addresses was included with the set.

		NM
Complete Set (50):		50.00
Common Player:		.75
1	Red Grange	5.00
2	George Halas	2.00
3	Benny Friedman	.75
4	Cliff Battles	1.00
5	Mike Michalske	.75
6	George McAfee	1.00
7	Beattie Feathers	1.25
8	Ernie Caddel	.75
9	George Musso	1.00
10	Sid Luckman	2.25
11	Cecil Isbell	.75
12	Bronko Nagurski	3.00
13	Hunk Anderson	.80
14	Dick Farman	.80
15	Aldo Forte	.90
16	Ki Aldrich	.80
17	Jim Lee Howell	.75
18	Ray Flaherty	.75
19	Hampton Pool	.80
20	Alex Wojchiechowicz	1.00
21	Bill Osmanski	.75
22	Hank Soar	.75
23	Dutch Clark	1.00
24	Joe Muha	.75
25	Don Hutson	1.50
26	Jim Poole	.85
27	Charley Malone	.75
28	Charlie Trippi	1.25
29	Andy Farkas	.75
30	Clarke Hinkle	1.00
31	Gary Famiglietti	.75
32	Bulldog Turner	1.25
33	Sammy Baugh	3.00
34	Pat Harder	.75
35	Tuffy Leemans	1.00
36	Ken Strong	1.00
37	Barney Poole	.75
38	Bruiser Kinard	1.00
39	Buford Ray	.75
40	Ace Parker	1.25
41	Buddy Parker	.75
42	Mel Hein	1.00
43	Ed Danowski	.75
44	Bill Dudley	1.25
45	Paul Stenn	.80
46	George Connor	1.00
47	George Connor	.75
48	Armand Niccolai	.75
49	Tony Canadeo	1.25
50	Bill Willis	1.50

1989 TV-4NFL Quarterbacks

The 20-card, 2-7/16" x 3-1/8" set features borderless portrait drawings by artist J.C. Ford. The card backs contain career highlights. The set was issued by a television station in Great Britain and were distributed to promote American football in the U.K.

		MT
Complete Set (20):		25.00
Common Player:		.75
1	Dutch Clark	.75
2	Sammy Baugh	1.50
3	Bob Waterfield	.75
4	Sid Luckman	.75
5	Otto Graham	1.00
6	Bobby Layne	.75
7	Norm Van Brocklin	.75
8	George Blanda	.75
9	Y.A. Tittle	1.00
10	Johnny Unitas	3.00
11	Bart Starr	1.25
12	Sonny Jurgensen	1.25
13	Joe Namath	2.50
14	Fran Tarkenton	1.50
15	Roger Staubach	2.50
16	Terry Bradshaw	3.00
17	Dan Fouts	1.25
18	Joe Montana	5.00
19	John Elway	2.00
20	Dan Marino	5.00

U

1992 Ultimate WLAF

The 200-card, WLAF set features color photos with another color action photo on the card back, along with stats, bio information and a highlight. Each nine-pack of cards contained a game card in which the collector who spelled W-O-R-L-D won one million dollars. The final 20 cards are subsets which deal with playing the game (180-192) and collecting cards (193-200).

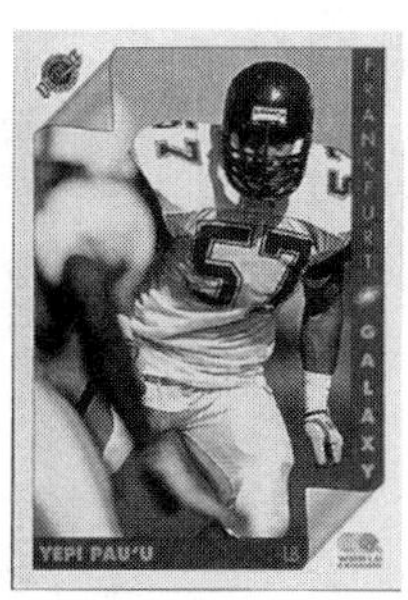

		MT
Complete Set (200):		5.00
Common Player:		.05
1	Barcelona Dragons '91 Team Statistics (Thomas Woods)	.10
2	Demetrius Davis	.15
3	Tim Egerton	.05
4	Scott Erney	.05
5	'91 Rushing Attempt Leader (Tony Baker)	.15
6	Anthony Greene	.05
7	Mike Hinnant (UER) (No position on front)	.05
8	Erik Naposki	.05
9	Paul Palmer	.15
10	Gene Taylor	.05
11	Thomas Woods	.05
12	Tony Rice	.25
13	Terry O'Shea	.05
14	Brett Wiese	.05
15	Kicking Leader (Phillip Alexander)	.05
16	Rushing/Scoring Leader (Eric Wilkerson)	.10
17	Barcelona Dragons Team Picture	.05
18	Barcelona Dragons Checklist	.05
19	Birmingham Fire '91 Team Statistics	.05
20	Eric Jones	.05
21	Steve Avery	.05
22	Willie Bouyer	.05
23	'91 Interception Leader (Anthony Parker)	.20
24	Elroy Harris	.05
25	James Henry	.05
26	Johnny Holland	.10
27	Mark Hopkins	.05
28	Arthur Hunter	.05
29	'91 Sacking Leader (Danny Lockett)	.10
30	Kirk Maggio	.05
31	John Miller	.05
32	Ricky Shaw	.05
33	Phil Ross	.05
34	Mike Norseth	.05
35	Birmingham Fire Checklist	.05
36	Frankfurt Galaxy '91 Team Statistics	.05
37	Anthony Wallace	.05
38	Lew Barnes	.05
39	Richard Buchanan	.05
40	Yepi Pau'u	.05
41	Pat McGuirk (UER) (Played for Raleigh-Durham in 1991)	.05
42	Tony Baker	.15
43	1992 TV Schedule 1	.05
44	Tim Broady	.05
45	Lonnie Finch	.05
46	Chad Fortune	.05
47	Harry Jackson	.05
48	Jason Johnson	.05
49	Pat Moorer	.05
50	Mike Perez	.15
51	Mark Seals	.05
52	Cedric Stallworth	.05
53	Tom Whelihan	.05
54	Joe Johnson	.30
55	Frankfurt Galaxy Checklist	.05
56	London Monarchs '91 Team Statistics (Stan Gelbaugh)	.10
57	Stan Gelbaugh	.35
58	Jeff Alexander	.05
59	Dana Brinson	.05
60	Marlon Brown	.05
61	Dedrick Dodge	.05
62	Judd Garrett	.10
63	Greg Horne	.05
64	Jon Horton	.05
65	Danny Lockett	.10
66	Andre Riley	.05
67	Charlie Young	.10
68	David Smith	.05
69	Irvin Smith	.05
70	Rickey Williams	.05
71	Roland Smith	.05
72	William Kirksey	.05
73	Phillip Alexander	.05
74	London Monarchs Team Picture	.10
75	London Monarchs Checklist	.05
76	Montreal Machine '91 Team Statistics	.05
77	Rollin Putzier	.05
78	Adam Bob	.05
79	K.D. Dunn	.05
80	Darryl Holmes	.05
81	Ricky Johnson	.05
82	Michael Finn	.05
83	Chris Mohr	.15
84	Don Murray	.05
85	Bjorn Nittmo	.10
86	Michael Proctor	.10
87	Broderick Sargent	.05
88	Richard Shelton	.05
89	Emanuel King	.10
90	Pete Mandley	.15
91	Kris McCall	.05
92	1992 TV Schedule 2	.05
93	Montreal Machine Checklist	.05
94	NY/NJ Knights '91 Team Statistics	.05
95	Andre Alexander	.05
96	Pat Marlatt	.05
97	Cecil Fletcher	.05
98	Lonnie Turner	.05
99	Monty Gilbreath	.05
100	Tony Jones (UER) (Should be DB, not WR)	.05
101	Kip Lewis	.05
102	Bob Lilljedahl	.05
103	Mark Moore	.05
104	Falanda Newton	.05
105	Anthony Parker (UER) (Played for Chiefs in 1991, not Bears; was released by the Bears)	.20
106	Kendall Trainor	.10
107	Eric Wilkerson	.05
108	Tony Woods	.20
109	Reggie Slack	.10
110	Joey Banes	.05
111	Ron Sancho	.10
112	Mike Husar	.05
113	NY/NJ Knights Checklist	.05
114	Orlando Thunder '91 Team Statistics	.05
115	Byron Williams (UER) (Waived by Orlando and picked up by NY-NJ)	.05
116	Charlie Baumann	.15
117	Kevin Bell	.10
118	Rodney Lossow	.05
119	Myron Jones	.05
120	Bruce Lasane	.05
121	Eric Mitchel	.10
122	Billy Owens	.05
123	1992 TV Schedule 3	.05
124	Chris Roscoe	.05
125	Tommie Stowers	.05
126	Wayne Dickson (UER) (Not a rookie, he played for Orlando in 1991)	.05
127	Scott Mitchell	1.25
128	Karl Dunbar	.05
129	'91 Punt Return Leader (Dana Brinson)	.05
130	Orlando Thunder Checklist	.05
131	Sacramento Surge Team Statistics	.05
132	1992 TV Schedule 4	.05
133	Mike Adams	.05
134	Greg Coauette	.05
135	Mel Farr Jr. (Should be TE, not FB)	.10
136	Victor Floyd	.05
137	Paul Frazier	.05
138	Tom Gerhart	.05
139	Pete Najarian	.05
140	John Nies	.05
141	Carl Parker	.05
142	Saute Sapolu	.05
143	George Bethune	.05
144	David Archer	.35
145	John Buddenberg	.05
146	'91 Receiving Yardage Leader (Jon Horton) (UER) (Incorrect stats on back)	.05
147	Sacramento Surge Checklist	.05
148	San Antonio Riders '91 Team Statistics	.05
149	Ricky Blake	.10
150	Jim Gallery	.05
151	Jason Garrett	.75
152	John Garrett	.10
153	Broderick Graves	.05
154	Bill Hess	.05
155	Mike Johnson	.05
156	Lee Morris	.05
157	Dwight Pickens	.05
158	Kent Sullivan	.05
159	Ken Watson	.05
160	Ronnie Williams	.05
161	Titus Dixon	.05
162	Mike Kiselak	.05
163	Greg Lee	.05
164	'91 Receiving Leader (Judd Garrett) (Had 71 receptions in 1991, not 18; game high was 12, not 13)	.10
165	San Antonio Riders Checklist	.05
166	Tenth Week Summaries	.05
167	Randy Bethel	.05
168	Melvin Patterson	.05
169	Eric Harmon	.05
170	Patrick Jackson	.05
171	Tim James	.05
172	George Koonce	.15
173	Babe Laufenberg	.25
174	Amir Rasul	.05
175	'91 Passing Leader (Stan Gelbaugh)	.25
176	Jason Wallace	.05
177	Walter Wilson	.05
178	Power Meter Info	.15
179	Ohio Glory Checklist	.05
180	The Football Field (Jim Kelly)	.20
181	Moving the Ball (Jim Kelly)	.20
182	Defense/Back Field Cornerbacks and Safeties (Lawrence Taylor)	.20
183	Defense/Linebackers (Lawrence Taylor)	.20
184	Defense/Defensive Line - Defensive Tackles and Ends (Lawrence Taylor)	.20
185	Offensive/Offensive Line - Centers, Guards, Tackles and Tight Ends (Jim Kelly)	.05
186	Offense/Receivers (Lawrence Taylor)	.20
187	Offense/Running Backs (Jim Kelly)	.20
188	Offensive/Quarterback (Jim Kelly)	.20
189	Special Teams	.10
190	Rules and Regulations - WL Rules that differ from NFL 1990 Rules	.05
191	Defensive Overview - Scoring Touchdowns and Extra Points	.05
192	Offensive Overview - Scoring, Field Goals and Safeties	.05
193	How to Collect - What is a Set (Lawrence Taylor)	.20
194	How to Collect - What is a Wax Pack (Lawrence Taylor)	.20
195	How to Collect - Premier Editions (Lawrence Taylor)	.20
196	How to Collect - What Creates Value (Lawrence Taylor)	.20
197	How to Collect - Rookie Cards (Jim Kelly)	.20
198	How to Collect - Grading Your Cards (Jim Kelly)	.20
199	How to Collect - Storing Your Cards (Jim Kelly)	.20
200	How to Collect - Trading Your Cards (Jim Kelly)	.20

1992 Ultimate WLAF Logo Holograms

The 10-card, standard-size set features holograms of each of the WLAF teams, which were randomly inserted in Ultimate packs.

		MT
Complete Set (10):		5.00
Common Player:		1.00
1	Barcelona Dragons	1.00
2	Birmingham Fire	1.00
3	Frankfurt Galaxy	1.00
4	London Monarchs	1.00
5	Montreal Machine	1.00
6	NY/NJ Knights	1.00
7	Ohio Glory	1.00
8	Orlando Thunder	1.00
9	Sacramento Surge	1.00
10	San Antonio Riders	1.00

1991 Ultra

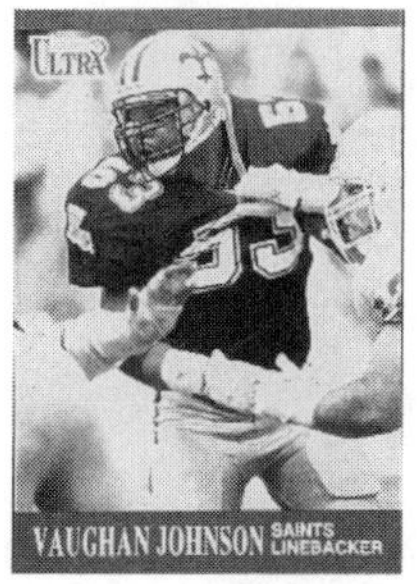

This 300-card set features cards with color action photos with silver borders above and below the photo. The player's name, team and position is in white at the bottom. Backs have silver borders at the top and bottom, with a yellow-to-orange-to-green background. A mug shot is positioned between two smaller action photos on the back. A Rookie Prospect subset was also included; cards are numbered from 279-298. Two 10-card insert sets were also created - Ultra All-Stars and Ultra Performances. The All-Star cards were randomly inserted in 1991 packs which were sold in black boxes; the Performances cards were inserts in packs in green boxes.

		MT
Complete Set (300):		12.00
Common Player:		.05
Minor Stars:		.10
Pack (15):		.40
Wax Box (36):		10.00
1	Don Beebe	.05
2	Shane Conlan	.05
3	Pete Metzelaars	.05
4	Jamie Mueller	.05
5	Scott Norwood	.05
6	Andre Reed	.10
7	Leon Seals	.05
8	Bruce Smith	.05
9	Leonard Smith	.05
10	Thurman Thomas	.25
11	Lewis Billups	.05
12	Jim Breech	.05
13	James Brooks	.05
14	Eddie Brown	.05
15	Boomer Esiason	.10
16	David Fulcher	.05
17	Rodney Holman	.05
18	Bruce Kozerski	.05
19	Tim Krumrie	.05
20	Tim McGee	.05
21	Anthony Munoz	.05
22	Leon White	.05
23	Ickey Woods	.05
24	Carl Zander	.05
25	Brian Brennan	.05
26	Thane Gash	.05
27	Leroy Hoard	.05
28	Mike Johnson	.05
29	Reggie Langhorne	.05
30	Kevin Mack	.05
31	Clay Matthews	.05
32	Eric Metcalf	.05
33	Steve Atwater	.05
34	Melvin Bratton	.05
35	John Elway	.40
36	Bobby Humphrey	.05
37	Mark Jackson	.05
38	Vance Johnson	.05
39	Ricky Nattiel	.05
40	Steve Sewell	.05
41	Dennis Smith	.05
42	David Treadwell	.05
43	Mike Young	.05
44	Ray Childress	.05
45	Cris Dishman	.05
46	William Fuller	.05
47	Ernest Givins	.05
48	John Grimsley	.05
49	Drew Hill	.05
50	Haywood Jeffires	.05
51	Sean Jones	.05
52	Johnny Meads	.05
53	Warren Moon	.10
54	Al Smith	.05
55	Lorenzo White	.05
56	Albert Bentley	.05
57	Duane Bickett	.05
58	Bill Brooks	.05
59	Jeff George	.30
60	Mike Prior	.05
61	Rohn Stark	.05
62	Jack Trudeau	.05
63	Clarence Verdin	.05
64	Steve DeBerg	.05
65	Emile Harry	.05
66	Albert Lewis	.05
67	Nick Lowery	.05
68	Todd McNair	.05
69	Christian Okoye	.05
70	Stephone Paige	.05
71	Kevin Porter	.05
72	Derrick Thomas	.10
73	Robb Thomas	.05
74	Barry Word	.05
75	Marcus Allen	.10
76	Eddie Anderson	.05
77	Tim Brown	.10
78	Mervyn Fernandez	.05
79	Willie Gault	.05
80	Ethan Horton	.05
81	Howie Long	.05
82	Vance Mueller	.05
83	Jay Schroeder	.05
84	Steve Smith	.05
85	Greg Townsend	.05
86	Mark Clayton	.05
87	Jim C. Jensen	.05
88	Dan Marino	1.00
89	Tim McKyer	.05
90	John Offerdahl	.05
91	Louis Oliver	.05
92	Reggie Roby	.05
93	Sammie Smith	.05
94	Hart Lee Dykes	.05
95	Irving Fryar	.05
96	Tommy Hodson	.05
97	Maurice Hurst	.05
98	John Stephens	.05
99	Andre Tippett	.05
100	Mark Boyer	.05
101	Kyle Clifton	.05
102	James Hasty	.05
103	Erik McMillan	.05
104	Rob Moore	.05
105	Joe Mott	.05
106	Ken O'Brien	.05
107	Ron Stallworth	.05
108	Al Toon	.05
109	Gary Anderson	.05
110	Bubby Brister	.05
111	Thomas Everett	.05
112	Merril Hoge	.05
113	Louis Lipps	.05
114	Greg Lloyd	.05
115	Hardy Nickerson	.05
116	Dwight Stone	.05
117	Rod Woodson	.10
118	Tim Worley	.05
119	Rod Bernstine	.05
120	Marion Butts	.05
121	Gill Byrd	.05
122	Arthur Cox	.05
123	Burt Grossman	.05
124	Ronnie Harmon	.05
125	Anthony Miller	.05
126	Leslie O'Neal	.05
127	Gary Plummer	.05
128	Sam Seale	.05
129	Junior Seau	.30
130	Broderick Thompson	.05
131	Billy Joe Tolliver	.05
132	Brian Blades	.05
133	Jeff Bryant	.05
134	Derrick Fenner	.05
135	Jacob Green	.05
136	Andy Heck	.05
137	Patrick Hunter	.05
138	Norm Johnson	.05
139	Tommy Kane	.05
140	Dave Krieg	.05
141	John L. Williams	.05
142	Terry Wooden	.05
143	Steve Broussard	.05
144	Keith Jones	.05
145	Brian Jordan	.05
146	Chris Miller	.05
147	John Rade	.05
148	Andre Rison	.10
149	Mike Rozier	.05
150	Deion Sanders	.40
151	Neal Anderson	.05
152	Trace Armstrong	.05
153	Kevin Butler	.05
154	Mark Carrier	.05
155	Richard Dent	.05
156	Dennis Gentry	.05
157	Jim Harbaugh	.10
158	Brad Muster	.05
159	William Perry	.05
160	Mike Singletary	.05
161	Lemuel Stinson	.05
162	Troy Aikman	1.00
163	Michael Irvin	.30
164	Mike Saxon	.05
165	Emmitt Smith	2.00
166	Jerry Ball	.05
167	Michael Cofer	.05
168	Rodney Peete	.10
169	Barry Sanders	1.25
170	Robert Brown	.05
171	Anthony Dilweg	.05
172	Tim Harris	.05
173	Johnny Holland	.05
174	Perry Kemp	.05
175	Don Majkowski	.05
176	Brian Noble	.05
177	Jeff Query	.05
178	Sterling Sharpe	.10
179	Charles Wilson	.05
180	Keith Woodside	.05
181	Flipper Anderson	.05
182	Bern Brostek	.05
183	Pat Carter	.05
184	Aaron Cox	.05
185	Henry Ellard	.05
186	Jim Everett	.05
187	Cleveland Gary	.05
188	Jerry Gray	.05
189	Kevin Greene	.05
190	Mike Wilcher	.05
191	Alfred Anderson	.05
192	Joey Browner	.05
193	Anthony Carter	.05
194	Chris Doleman	.05
195	Rick Fenney	.05
196	Darrell Fullington	.05
197	Rich Gannon	.05
198	Hassan Jones	.05
199	Steve Jordan	.05
200	Mike Merriweather	.05
201	Al Noga	.05
202	Herschel Walker	.05
203	Wade Wilson	.05
204	Morten Andersen	.05
205	Gene Atkins	.05
206	Toi Cook	.05
207	Craig Heyward	.05
208	Dalton Hilliard	.05
209	Vaughan Johnson	.05
210	Eric Martin	.05
211	Brett Perriman	.10
212	Pat Swilling	.05
213	Steve Walsh	.05
214	Ottis Anderson	.05
215	Carl Banks	.05
216	Maurice Carthon	.05
217	Mark Collins	.05
218	Rodney Hampton	.25
219	Erik Howard	.05
220	Mark Ingram	.05
221	Pepper Johnson	.05
222	Dave Meggett	.05
223	Phil Simms	.05
224	Lawrence Taylor	.10
225	Lewis Tillman	.05
226	Everson Walls	.05
227	Fred Barnett	.05
228	Jerome Brown	.05
229	Keith Byars	.05
230	Randall Cunningham	.10
231	Byron Evans	.05
232	Wes Hopkins	.05
233	Keith Jackson	.05
234	Heath Sherman	.05
235	Anthony Toney	.05
236	Reggie White	.10
237	Rich Camarillo	.05
238	Ken Harvey	.05
239	Eric Hill	.05
240	Johnny Johnson	.05
241	Ernie Jones	.05
242	Tim McDonald	.05
243	Timm Rosenbach	.05
244	Jay Taylor	.05
245	Dexter Carter	.05
246	Mike Cofer	.05
247	Kevin Fagan	.05
248	Don Griffin	.05
249	Charles Haley	.05
250	Brent Jones	.05
251	Joe Montana	1.00
252	Darryl Pollard	.05
253	Tom Rathman	.05
254	Jerry Rice	1.00
255	John Taylor	.05
256	Steve Young	1.00
257	Gary Anderson	.05
258	Mark Carrier	.05
259	Chris Chandler	.05
260	Reggie Cobb	.05
261	Reuben Davis	.05
262	Willie Drewrey	.05
263	Ron Hall	.05
264	Eugene Marve	.05
265	Winston Moss	.05
266	Vinny Testaverde	.05
267	Broderick Thomas	.05
268	Jeff Bostic	.05
269	Earnest Byner	.05
270	Gary Clark	.05
271	Darrell Green	.05
272	Jim Lachey	.05
273	Wilber Marshall	.05
274	Art Monk	.10
275	Gerald Riggs	.05
276	Mark Rypien	.05
277	Ricky Sanders	.05
278	Alvin Walton	.05
279	*Nick Bell*	.05
280	*Eric Bieniemy*	.10
281	*Jarrod Bunch*	.05
282	*Mike Croel*	.10
283	*Brett Favre*	3.50
284	*Moe Gardner*	.10
285	*Pat Harlow*	.05
286	*Randal Hill*	.25
287	*Todd Marinovich*	.10
288	*Russell Maryland*	.10
289	*Dan McGwire*	.10
290	*Ernie Mills*	.10
291	*Herman Moore*	3.50
292	*Godfrey Myles*	.05
293	*Browning Nagle*	.05
294	*Mike Pritchard*	.30
295	*Esera Tuaolo*	.05
296	*Mark Vander Poel*	.05
297	*Ricky Watters*	2.00
298	*Chris Zorich*	.20
299	Checklist Card (Randall Cunningham, Emmitt Smith)	.10
300	Checklist Card (Randall Cunningham, Emmitt Smith)	.10

1991 Ultra All-Stars

These cards, random inserts in 1991 Fleer Ultra packs, feature 10 top NFL players. Each card front has a shield with a head shot of the player, plus two smaller action photos against a gold background. A green stripe at the bottom contains the player's name, team and position. Each

back has a career summary in a white box, bordered with a gold frame. Cards, which are numbered 1 of 10, etc., were randomly inserted in packs that were sold in black boxes.

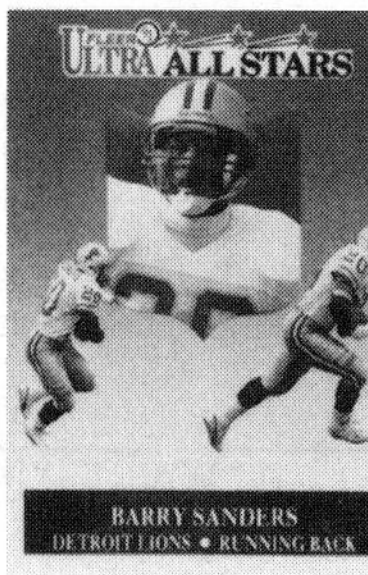

	MT
Complete Set (10):	12.00
Common Player:	.50
Minor Stars:	1.00
1 Barry Sanders	5.00
2 Keith Jackson	.50
3 Bruce Smith	.50
4 Randall Cunningham	1.00
5 Dan Marino	6.00
6 Charles Haley	.50
7 John L. Williams	.50
8 Darrell Green	.50
9 Stephone Paige	.50
10 Kevin Greene	1.00

1991 Ultra Performances

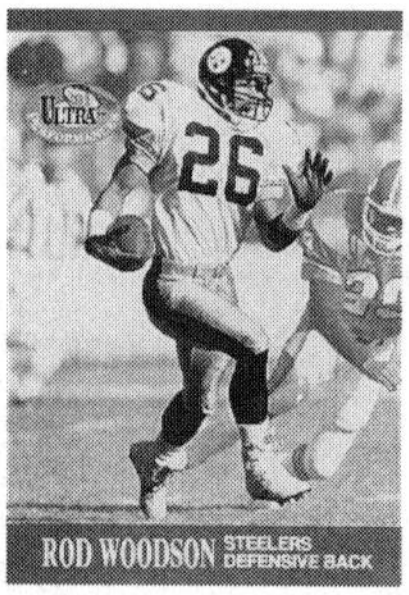

Each card in this 10-card set features a color action photo on the front, with silver stripes as borders at the top and bottom. The player is pictured against a washed-out background with other players in it. The back has a player profile inside a black-and-silver border, plus a card number (1 of 10, etc.). These cards were random inserts in Fleer Ultra packs sold in green boxes.

	MT
Complete Set (10):	25.00
Common Player:	.50
Minor Stars:	1.00
1 Emmitt Smith	10.00
2 Andre Rison	1.00
3 Derrick Thomas	1.00
4 Joe Montana	6.00
5 Warren Moon	1.00
6 Mike Singletary	.50
7 Thurman Thomas	1.00
8 Rod Woodson	.50
9 Jerry Rice	6.00
10 Reggie White	1.00

1991 Ultra Update

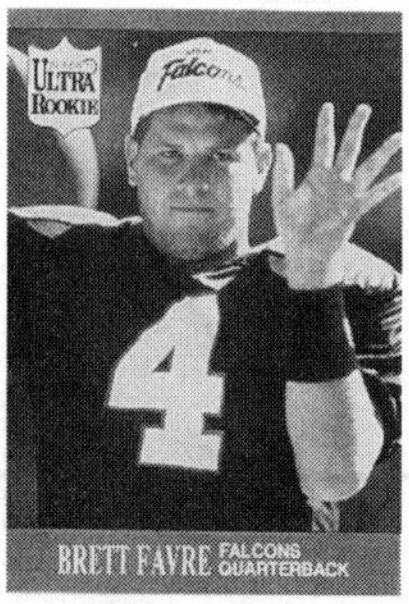

This 100-card set features top rookies and players who were traded during the 1991 season. Cards backs are numbered with a U prefix and have a mug shot of the player in a shield, surrounded by two smaller action shots. Fronts have an "Ultra Rookie" logo for the rookies.

	MT
Complete Set (100):	35.00
Common Player:	.10
Minor Stars:	.20
1 Brett Favre	25.00
2 Moe Gardner	.10
3 Tim McKyer	.10
4 *Bruce Pickens*	.10
5 Mike Pritchard	.30
6 Cornelius Bennett	.10
7 *Phil Hansen*	.10
8 *Henry Jones*	.10
9 Mark Kelso	.10
10 James Lofton	.10
11 *Anthony Morgan*	.20
12 Stan Thomas	.10
13 Chris Zorich	.30
14 Reggie Rembert	.10
15 *Alfred Williams*	.10
16 *Michael Jackson*	1.00
17 *Ed King*	.10
18 Joe Morris	.10
19 Vince Newsome	.10
20 Tony Casillas	.10
21 Russell Maryland	.20
22 Jay Novacek	.20
23 Mike Croel	.10
24 Gaston Green	.10
25 *Kenny Walker*	.10
26 *Melvin Jenkins*	.10
27 Herman Moore	7.00
28 *Kelvin Pritchett*	.10
29 Chris Spielman	.10
30 Vinnie Clark	.10
31 Allen Rice	.10
32 Vai Sikahema	.10
33 Esera Tuaolo	.10
34 *Mike Dumas*	.10
35 *John Flannery*	.10
36 Allen Pinkett	.10
37 *Tim Barnett*	.20
38 Dan Saleaumua	.10
39 *Harvey Williams*	1.00
40 Nick Bell	.10
41 Roger Craig	.10
42 Ronnie Lott	.10
43 Todd Marinovich	.10
44 Robert Delpino	.10
45 *Todd Lyght*	.20
46 Robert Young	.10
47 *Aaron Craver*	.20
48 *Mark Higgs*	.20
49 Vestee Jackson	.10
50 Carl Lee	.10
51 Felix Wright	.10
52 Darrell Fullington	.10
53 Pat Harlow	.10
54 Eugene Lockhart	.10
55 *Hugh Millen*	.20
56 *Leonard Russell*	.25
57 *Jon Vaughn*	.10
58 Quinn Early	.10
59 Bobby Hebert	.10
60 Rickey Jackson	.10
61 Sam Mills	.10
62 Jarrod Bunch	.10
63 John Elliott	.10
64 Jeff Hostetler	.20
65 *Ed McCaffrey*	12.00
66 *Kanavis McGhee*	.10
67 *Mo Lewis*	.10
68 Browning Nagle	.10
69 Blair Thomas	.10
70 *Antone Davis*	.10
71 *Brad Goebel*	.10
72 Jim McMahon	.10
73 Clyde Simmons	.10
74 Randal Hill	.25
75 *Eric Swann*	.50
76 Tom Tupa	.10
77 *Jeff Graham*	1.50
78 Eric Green	.10
79 *Neil O'Donnell*	2.00
80 Huey Richardson	.10
81 Eric Bieniemy	.10
82 John Friesz	.10
83 *Eric Moten*	.10
84 *Stanley Richard*	.20
85 Todd Bowles	.10
86 *Merton Hanks*	.75
87 Tim Harris	.10
88 Pierce Holt	.10
89 *Ted Washington*	.10
90 *John Kasay*	.10
91 Dan McGwire	.10
92 *Lawrence Dawsey*	.20
93 *Charles McRae*	.10
94 Jesse Solomon	.10
95 Robert Wilson	.10
96 *Ricky Ervins*	.20
97 Charles Mann	.10
98 *Bobby Wilson*	.10
99 Jerry Rice PV (PV)	2.00
100 Checklist	.10

1992 Ultra

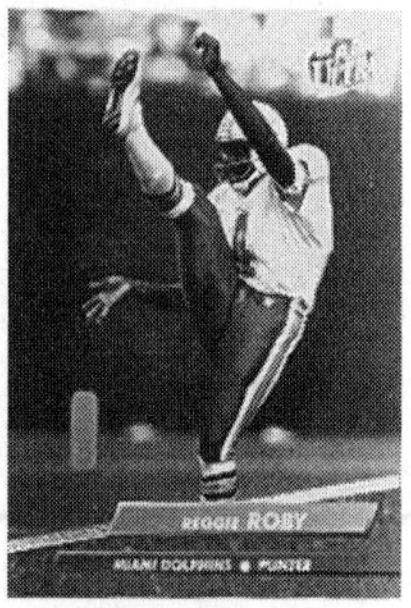

This 450-card set features full-bleed color action photos on the card fronts. The player's name is below a gold-foil stripe at the bottom, along with his team's name and position in bars color-coded according to his team's colors. The back is horizontal and shows a close-up and action shot of the player against a color-coded football field design. Statistics and the player's name are superimposed onto the card. A green marbleized area contains the player's team logo and biography. Subsets include Draft Picks (#s 417-446) and checklists (#s 447-450). Insert sets include Award Winners (10 cards, randomly in foil packs), and Signature Series sets for Chris Miller (10, in foil packs) and Reggie White (10, in foil packs).

	MT
Complete Set (450):	20.00
Common Player:	.05
Pack (15):	.50
Wax Box (36):	15.00
1 Steve Broussard	.05
2 Rick Bryan	.05
3 Scott Case	.05
4 Darrion Conner	.05
5 Bill Fralic	.05
6 Moe Gardner	.05
7 Tim Green	.05
8 Michael Haynes	.40
9 Chris Hinton	.05
10 Mike Kenn	.05
11 Tim McKver	.05
12 Chris Miller	.15
13 Erric Pegram	.15
14 Mike Pritchard	.20
15 Andre Rison	.30
16 Jessie Tuggle	.05
17 *Carlton Bailey*	.25
18 Howard Ballard	.05
19 Cornelius Bennett	.05
20 Shane Conlan	.05
21 Kenneth Davis	.05
22 Kent Hull	.05
23 Mark Kelso	.05
24 James Lofton	.05
25 Keith McKeller	.05
26 Nate Odomes	.05
27 Jim Ritcher	.05
28 Leon Seals	.05
29 Darryl Talley	.05
30 Steve Tasker	.05
31 Thurman Thomas	.50
32 Will Wolford	.05
33 Jeff Wright	.05
34 Neal Anderson	.20
35 Trace Armstrong	.05
36 Mark Carrier	.05
37 Wendell Davis	.05
38 Richard Dent	.05
39 Shaun Gayle	.05
40 Jim Harbaugh	.05
41 Jay Hilgenberg	.05
42 Darren Lewis	.05
43 Steve McMichael	.05
44 Anthony Morgan	.05
45 Brad Muster	.05
46 William Perry	.05
47 John Roper	.05
48 Lemuel Stinson	.05
49 Tom Waddle	.15
50 Donnell Woolford	.05
51 *Leo Barker*	.10
52 Eddie Brown	.05
53 James Francis	.05
54 David Fulcher	.05
55 David Grant	.05
56 Harold Green	.05
57 Rodney Holman	.05
58 Lee Johnson	.05
59 Tim Krumrie	.05
60 Tim McGee	.05
61 *Alonzo Mitz*	.10
62 Anthony Munoz	.05
63 Alfred Williams	.05
64 Stephen Braggs	.05
65 *Richard Brown*	.10
66 *Randy Hilliard*	.10
67 Leroy Hoard	.05
68 Michael Jackson	.15
69 Mike Johnson	.05
70 James Jones	.05
71 Tony Jones	.05
72 Ed King	.05
73 Kevin Mack	.05
74 Clay Matthews	.05
75 Eric Metcalf	.05
76 Vince Newsome	.05
77 Steve Beuerlein	.20
78 Larry Brown	.05
79 Tony Casillas	.05
80 Alvin Harper	.50
81 Issiac Holt	.05
82 Ray Horton	.05
83 Michael Irvin	.40
84 Daryl Johnston	.20
85 Kelvin Martin	.05
86 Ken Norton	.05
87 Jay Novacek	.20
88 Emmitt Smith	5.00
89 *Vinson Smith*	.15
90 Mark Stepnoski	.05
91 Tony Tolbert	.05
92 Alexander Wright	.05
93 Steve Atwater	.05
94 Tyrone Braxton	.05
95 Michael Brooks	.05
96 Mike Croel	.05
97 John Elway	.75
98 Simon Fletcher	.05
99 Gaston Green	.05
100 Mark Jackson	.05
101 Keith Kartz	.05
102 Greg Kragen	.05
103 Greg Lewis	.05
104 Karl Mecklenburg	.05
105 Derek Russell	.25
106 Steve Sewell	.05
107 Dennis Smith	.05
108 David Treadwell	.05
109 Kenny Walker	.05
110 Michael Young	.05
111 Jerry Ball	.05
112 Bennie Blades	.05
113 Lomas Brown	.05
114 *Scott Conover*	.15
116 Mel Gray	.05
117 Willie Green	.15
118 Erik Kramer	.05
119 Dan Owens	.05
120 Rodney Peete	.05
121 Brett Perriman	.05
122 Barry Sanders	3.00
123 Chris Spielman	.05
124 Marc Spindler	.05
125 Willie White	.05
126 Tony Bennett	.05
127 Matt Brock	.05
128 Leroy Butler	.05
129 Chuck Cecil	.05
130 Johnny Holland	.05
131 Perry Kemp	.05
132 Don Majkowski	.05
133 Tony Mandarich	.05
134 Brian Noble	.05
135 Bryce Paup	.05
136 Sterling Sharpe	.30
137 Darrell Thompson	.05
138 Mike Tomczak	.05
139 Vince Workman	.05
140 Ray Childress	.05
141 Cris Dishman	.05
142 Curtis Duncan	.05
143 William Fuller	.05
144 Ernest Givins	.05
145 Haywood Jeffires	.15
146 Sean Jones	.05
147 Lamar Lathon	.05
148 Bruce Matthews	.05
149 Bubba McDowell	.05
150 Johnny Meads	.05
151 Warren Moon	.40
152 Mike Munchak	.05
153 *Bo Orlando*	.30
154 Al Smith	.05
155 Doug Smith	.05
156 Lorenzo White	.05
157 Chip Banks	.05
158 Duane Bickett	.05
159 Bill Brooks	.05
160 Jon Hand	.05
161 Jeff Herrod	.05
162 Jessie Hester	.05
163 Scott Radecic	.05
164 Rohn Stark	.05
165 Clarence Verdin	.05
166 Eugene Daniel	.05
167 John Alt	.05
168 Tim Barnett	.05
169 Tim Grunhard	.05
170 Dino Hackett	.05
171 Jonathan Hayes	.05
172 Bill Maas	.05
173 Chris Martin	.05
174 Christian Okoye	.05
175 Stephone Paige	.05
176 *Jayice Pearson*	.10
177 Kevin Porter	.05
178 Kevin Ross	.05
179 Dan Saleaumua	.05
180 Tracy Simien	.05
181 Neil Smith	.05
182 Derrick Thomas	.35
183 Robb Thomas	.05
184 Barry Wood	.15
185 Marcus Allen	.08
186 Eddie Anderson	.05
187 Nick Bell	.15
188 Tim Brown	.30
189 Mervyn Fernandez	.05
190 Jeff Gossett	.05
192 Ethan Horton	.05
193 Jeff Jaeger	.05
194 Howie Long	.05
195 Ronnie Lott	.05
196 Todd Marinovich	.15
197 Don Mosebar	.05
198 Jay Schroeder	.05
199 Anthony Smith	.05
200 Greg Townsend	.05
201 Lionel Washington	.05
202 Steve Wisniewski	.05
203 Willie Anderson	.05
204 Robert Delpino	.05
205 Henry Ellard	.05
206 Jim Everett	.05
207 Kevin Greene	.05
208 Darryl Henley	.05
209 Damone Johnson	.05
210 Larry Kelm	.05
211 Todd Lyght	.05
212 Jackie Slater	.05
213 Michael Stewart	.05
214 Pat Terrell	.05
215 Robert Young	.05
216 Mark Clayton	.05
217 Bryan Cox	.05
218 Jeff Cross	.05
219 Mark Duper	.05
220 Harry Galbreath	.05
221 David Griggs	.05
222 Mark Higgs	.10
224 John Offerdahl	.05
225 Louis Oliver	.05
226 Tony Paige	.05
227 Reggie Roby	.05
228 Pete Stoyanovich	.05
229 Richmond Webb	.05
230 Terry Allen	.60
231 Ray Berry	.05
232 Anthony Carter	.05
233 Cris Carter	.05
234 Chris Doleman	.05
235 Rich Gannon	.10
236 Steve Jordan	.05
237 Carl Lee	.05
238 Randall McDaniel	.05
239 Mike Merriweather	.05
240 Harry Newsome	.05
241 John Randle	.05
242 Henry Thomas	.05
243 Bruce Armstrong	.05
244 Vincent Brown	.05
245 Marv Cook	.05
246 Irving Fryar	.05
247 Pat Harlow	.05
248 Maurice Hurst	.05
249 Eugene Lockhart	.05
250 Greg McMurtry	.05
251 Hugh Millen	.05
252 Leonard Russell	.35
253 Chris Singleton	.05
254 Andre Tippett	.05
255 Jon Vaughn	.10
256 Morten Andersen	.05
257 Gene Atkins	.05
258 Wesley Carroll	.05
259 Jim Dombrowski	.05
260 Quinn Early	.05
261 Bobby Hebert	.05
262 Joel Hilgenberg	.05
263 Rickey Jackson	.05
264 Vaughan Johnson	.05
265 Eric Martin	.05
266 Brett Maxie	.05
267 *Fred McAfee*	.20
268 Sam Mills	.05
269 Pat Swilling	.05
270 Floyd Turner	.05
271 Steve Walsh	.05
272 Stephen Baker	.05
273 Jarrod Bunch	.05
274 Mark Collins	.05
275 John Elliott	.05
276 Myron Guyton	.05
277 Rodney Hampton	.50
278 Jeff Hostetler	.25
279 Mark Ingram	.05
280 Pepper Johnson	.05
281 Sean Landeta	.05
282 Leonard Marshall	.05
283 Kanavis McGhee	.05
284 Dave Meggett	.05
285 Bart Oates	.05
286 Phil Simms	.10
287 Reyna Thompson	.05
288 Lewis Tillman	.05
289 Brad Baxter	.05
290 *Mike Brim*	.10
291 Chris Burkett	.05
292 Kyle Clifton	.05
293 James Hasty	.05
294 Joe Kelly	.05
295 Jeff Lageman	.05
296 Mo Lewis	.05
297 Erik McMillan	.05
298 Scott Mersereau	.05
299 Rob Moore	.05
300 Tony Stargell	.05
301 Jim Sweeney	.05
302 Marvin Washington	.05
303 Lonnie Young	.05
304 Eric Allen	.05
305 Fred Barnett	.15
306 Keith Byars	.05
307 Byron Evans	.05
308 Wes Hopkins	.05
309 Keith Jackson	.15
310 James Joseph	.05
311 Seth Joyner	.05
312 Roger Ruzek	.05
313 Clyde Simmons	.05
314 William Thomas	.05
315 Reggie White	.35
316 Calvin Williams	.15
317 Rich Camarillo	.05
318 Jeff Faulkner	.05
319 Ken Harvey	.05
320 Eric Hill	.05
321 Johnny Johnson	.10
322 Ernie Jones	.05
323 Tim McDonald	.05
324 Freddie Joe Nunn	.05
325 Luis Sharpe	.05
326 Eric Swann	.05
327 Aeneas Williams	.05
328 *Mike Zordich*	.15
329 Gary Anderson	.05
330 Bubby Brister	.05
331 Barry Foster	.50
332 Eric Green	.05
333 Bryan Hinkle	.05
334 Tunch Ilkin	.05
335 Carnell Lake	.05
336 Louis Lipps	.05
337 David Little	.05
338 Greg Lloyd	.05
339 Neil O'Donnell	.60
340 Rod Woodson	.08
341 Rod Bernstine	.05
342 Marion Butts	.08
343 Gill Byrd	.05
344 John Friesz	.05
345 Burt Grossman	.05
346 Courtney Hall	.05
347 Ronnie Harmon	.05
348 Shawn Jefferson	.05
349 Nate Lewis	.08
350 *Craig McEwen*	.10
351 Eric Moten	.05
352 Gary Plummer	.05
353 Henry Rolling	.05
354 Broderick Thompson	.05
355 Derrick Walker	.05
356 Harris Barton	.05
357 *Steve Bono*	.75
358 Todd Bowles	.05
359 Dexter Carter	.05
360 Michael Carter	.05
361 Keith DeLong	.05
362 Charles Haley	.05
363 Merton Hanks	.05
364 Tim Harris	.05
365 Brent Jones	.05
366 Guy McIntyre	.05
367 Tom Rathman	.05
368 Bill Romanowski	.05
369 Jesse Sapolu	.05
370 John Taylor	.05
371 Steve Young	2.00
372 Robert Blackmon	.05
373 Brian Blades	.05
374 Jacob Green	.05
375 Dwayne Harper	.05
376 Andy Heck	.05
377 Tommy Kane	.05
378 John Kassay	.05
379 Cortez Kennedy	.25
380 Bryan Millard	.05
381 Rufus Porter	.05
382 Eugene Robinson	.05
383 John L. Williams	.05
384 Terry Wooden	.05
385 Gary Anderson	.05
386 Ian Beckles	.05
387 Mark Carrier	.05
388 Reggie Cobb	.10
389 Tony Covington	.05
390 Lawrence Dawsey	.05
391 Ron Hall	.05
392 Keith McCants	.05
393 Charles McRae	.05
394 Tim Newton	.05
395 Jesse Solomon	.05
396 Vinny Testaverde	.05
397 Broderick Thomas	.05
398 Robert Wilson	.05
399 Earnest Byner	.05
400 Gary Clark	.05
401 Andre Collins	.05
402 Brad Edwards	.05
403 Kurt Gouveia	.05
404 Darrell Green	.05
405 Joe Jacoby	.05
407 Chip Lohmiller	.05
408 Charles Mann	.05
409 Wilber Marshall	.05
410 Brian Mitchell	.05
411 Art Monk	.05
412 Mark Rypien	.15
413 Ricky Sanders	.05
414 *Mark Schlereth*	.15
415 Fred Stokes	.05
416 Bobby Wilson	.05
417 *Corey Barlow*	.15
418 *Edgar Bennett*	.50
419 *Eddie Blake*	.15
420 *Terrell Buckley*	.30
421 *Willie Clay*	.15
422 *Rodney Culver*	.25
423 *Ed Cunningham*	.15
424 *Mark D'Onofrio*	.15
425 *Matt Darby*	.10
426 *Charles Davenport*	.10
427 *Will Furrer*	.20
428 *Keith Goganious*	.10
429 *Mario Bailey*	.10
430 *Chris Hakel*	.10
431 *Keith Hamilton*	.25
432 *Aaron Pierce*	.10
433 *Amp Lee*	.35
434 *Scott Lockwood*	.15
435 *Ricardo McDonald*	.15
436 *Dexter McNabb*	.15
437 *Chris Mims*	.40
438 *Mike Mooney*	.15
439 *Ray Roberts*	.15
440 *Patrick Rowe*	.15
441 *Leon Searcy*	.15
442 *Siran Stacy*	.20
443 *Kevin Turner*	.30
444 *Tommy Vardell*	.25
445 *Bob Whitfield*	.20
446 *Darryl Williams*	.25
447 Checklists	.05
448 Checklists	.05
449 Checklists	.05
450 Checklists	.05

1992 Ultra Award Winners

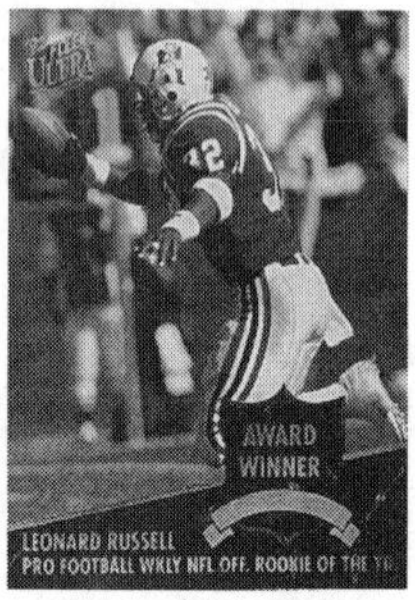

Each of the 10 players in this insert set had award-winning performances during the 1991 season. The front has a full-bleed photo of the player, along with a black marble-like strip at the bottom which contains the player's name and the award he won in gold foil. A black "Award Winner" logo is also superimposed in the lower right corner. The card back has a portrait of the player inside a shield, with his name in a banner above a career summary. Cards were randomly inserted in 1992 Fleer Ultra foil packs and are numbered 1 of 10, etc.

	MT
Complete Set (10):	20.00
Common Player:	1.50
1 Mark Rypien	1.75
2 Cornelius Bennett	1.50
3 Pat Swilling	1.50
4 Lawrence Dawsey	1.75
5 Thurman Thomas	4.00
6 Michael Irvin	5.00
7 Mike Croel	1.50
8 Barry Sanders	8.00
9 Anthony Munoz	1.50
10 Leonard Russell	2.00

1992 Ultra Chris Miller

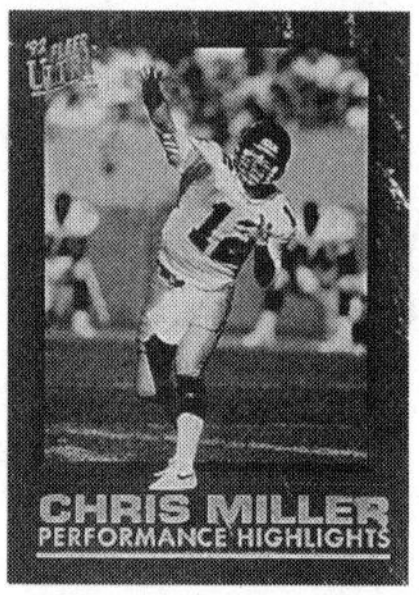

These 10 cards were randomly inserted in 1992 Fleer Ultra foil packs as part of Fleer's signature series. Each card front has a player action photo inside an inner black and outer maroon marbleized border. Miller's name and "Performance Highlights" are in gold foil letters at the bottom. The back has a player portrait shot and career summary against a rose-colored background, plus a card number. Cards 11-12 were available only through a mail-in offer from Fleer; 10 1992 Fleer Ultra wrappers and $2 were required. In addition, Miller signed more than 2,000 cards.

	MT
Complete Set (10):	6.00
Common Miller:	.60
Autograph:	50.00

A player's name in *italic type* indicates a rookie card.

1992 Ultra Reggie White

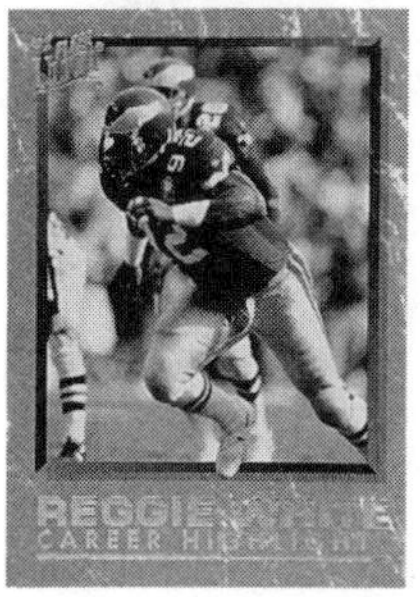

These cards, part of Fleer's signature series, were random inserts in 1992 Fleer Ultra foil packs. Each card front has a color action photo bordered by green and gray marble frames. White's name and "Career Highlights" are in gold foil at the bottom. The back has a career summary and head shot against a gray marble-like background, plus a card number. Cards 11-12 were availble only through a mail-in program to Fleer for 10 1992 Fleer Ultra wrappers and $2. These cards have rose-colored backs. White signed more than 2,000 randomly-inserted cards.

	MT
Complete Set (10):	10.00
Common White:	1.00
Autograph:	75.00

1993 Ultra

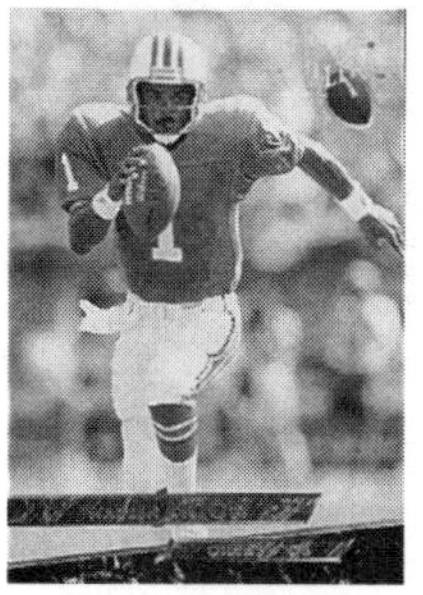

Fleer's 1993 Ultra set consists of 500 cards featuring UV coating and action photos. Insert sets include NFL Award Winners (10 cards), NFL League Leaders (10), All-Rookie Series (10), Stars (10), Touchdown Kings (10) and a Michael Irvin "Performance Highlights" set (10).

		MT
Complete Set (500):		60.00
Common Player:		.10
Minor Stars:		.20
Pack (15):		3.00
Wax Box (36):		90.00
1	Vinnie Clark	.10
2	Darion Connor	.10
3	Eric Dickerson	.20
4	Moe Gardner	.10
5	Tim Green	.10
6	*Roger Harper*	.10
7	Michael Haynes	.10
8	Bobby Hebert	.10
9	Chris Hinton	.10
10	Pierce Holt	.10
11	Mike Kenn	.10
12	*Lincoln Kennedy*	.20
13	Chris Miller	.10
14	Mike Pritchard	.10
15	Andre Rison	.20
16	Deion Sanders	1.50
17	Tony Smith	.10
18	Jessie Tuggle	.10
19	Howard Ballard	.10
20	Don Beebe	.10
21	Cornelius Bennett	.10
22	Bill Brooks	.10
23	Kenneth Davis	.10
24	Phil Hansen	.10
25	Henry Jones	.10
26	Jim Kelly	.50
27	Nate Odomes	.10
28	*John Parrella*	.10
29	Andre Reed	.20
30	Frank Reich	.10
31	Jim Ritcher	.10
32	Bruce Smith	.10
33	*Thomas Smith*	.20
34	Darryl Talley	.10
35	Steve Tasker	.10
36	Thurman Thomas	.50
37	Jeff Wright	.10
38	Neal Anderson	.10
39	Trace Armstrong	.10
40	Mark Carrier	.10
41	*Curtis Conway*	1.50
42	Wendell Davis	.10
43	Richard Dent	.10
44	Shaun Gayle	.10
45	Jim Harbaugh	.10
46	Craig Heyward	.10
47	Darren Lewis	.10
48	Steve McMichael	.10
49	William Perry	.10
50	*Carl Simpson*	.10
51	Alonzo Spellman	.10
52	Keith Van Horne	.10
53	Tom Waddle	.10
54	Donnell Woolford	.10
55	*John Copeland*	.50
56	Derrick Fenner	.10
57	James Francis	.10
58	Harold Green	.10
59	David Klingler	.10
60	Tim Krumrie	.10
61	Ricardo McDonald	.10
62	*Tony McGee*	.75
63	Carl Pickens	1.50
64	Lamar Rogers	.10
65	Jay Schroeder	.10
66	Daniel Stubbs	.10
67	*Steve Tovar*	.10
68	Alfred Williams	.10
69	Darryl Williams	.10
70	Jerry Ball	.10
71	David Brandon	.10
72	Rob Burnett	.10
73	Mark Carrier	.10
74	*Steve Everett*	.20
75	*Dan Footman*	.10
76	Leroy Hoard	.10
77	Michael Jackson	.10
78	Mike Johnson	.10
79	Bernie Kosar	.20
80	Clay Mathews	.10
81	Eric Metcalf	.10
82	Michael Dean Perry	.10
83	Vinny Testaverde	.20
84	Tommy Vardell	.10
85	Troy Aikman	3.00
86	Larry Brown	.10
87	Tony Casillas	.10
88	Thomas Everett	.10
89	Charles Haley	.10
90	Alvin Harper	.20
91	Michael Irvin	.50
92	Jim Jeffcoat	.10
93	Daryl Johnston	.10
94	Robert Jones	.10
95	*Leon Lett*	.50
96	Russell Maryland	.10
97	Nate Newton	.10
98	Ken Norton	.10
99	Jay Novacek	.10
100	*Darrin Smith*	.50
101	Emmitt Smith	5.00
102	Kevin Smith	.10
103	Mark Stepnoski	.10
104	Tony Tolbert	.10
105	*Kevin Williams*	.30
106	Steve Atwater	.10
107	Rod Bernstine	.10
108	Mike Croel	.10
109	Robert Delpino	.10
110	Shane Dronett	.10
111	John Elway	1.50
112	Simon Fletcher	.10
113	Greg Kragen	.10
114	Tommy Maddox	.10
115	*Arthur Marshall*	.20
116	Karl Mecklenburg	.10
117	*Glyn Milburn*	1.00
118	*Reggie Rivers*	.10
119	Shannon Sharpe	.20
120	Dennis Smith	.10
121	Kenny Walker	.10
122	*Dan Williams*	.10
123	Bennie Blades	.10
124	Lomas Brown	.10
125	Bill Fralic	.10
126	Mel Gray	.10
127	Willie Green	.10
128	Jason Hanson	.10
129	*Antonio London*	.10
130	*Ryan McNeil*	.10
131	Herman Moore	2.00
132	Rodney Peete	.10
133	Brett Perriman	.10
134	Kelvin Pritchett	.10
135	Barry Sanders	3.00
136	Tracy Scroggins	.10
137	Chris Spielman	.10
138	Pat Swilling	.10
139	Andre Ware	.10
140	Edgar Bennett	1.00
141	Tony Bennett	.10
142	Matt Brock	.10
143	Terrell Buckley	.10
144	LeRoy Butler	.10
145	Mark Clayton	.10
146	Brett Favre	5.00
147	Jackie Harris	.20
148	Johnny Holland	.10
149	Bill Maas	.10
150	Brian Noble	.10
151	Bryce Paup	.10
152	Ken Ruettgers	.10
153	Sterling Sharpe	.20
154	*Wayne Simmons*	.10
155	John Stephens	.10
156	*George Teague*	.50
157	Reggie White	.20
158	*Michael Barrow*	.20
159	Cody Carlson	.10
160	Ray Childress	.10
161	Cris Duncan	.10
162	Curtis Duncan	.10
163	William Fuller	.10
164	Ernest Givins	.10
165	*Brad Hopkins*	.10
166	Haywood Jeffires	.10
167	Lamar Lathon	.10
168	Wilber Marshall	.10
169	Bruce Matthews	.10
170	Bubba McDowell	.10
171	Warren Moon	.20
172	Mike Munchak	.10
173	Eddie Robinson	.10
174	Al Smith	.10
175	Lorenzo White	.10
176	Lee Williams	.10
177	Chip Banks	.10
178	John Baylor	.10
179	Duane Bickett	.10
180	Kerry Cash	.10
181	Quentin Coryatt	.10
182	Rodney Culver	.10
183	Steve Emtman	.10
184	Jeff George	.50
185	Jeff Herrod	.10
186	Jessie Hester	.10
187	Anthony Jackson	.10
188	Reggie Langhorne	.10
189	*Roosevelt Potts*	.20
190	Rohn Stark	.10
191	Clarence Verdin	.10
192	Will Wolford	.10
193	Marcus Allen	.20
194	John Alt	.10
195	Tim Barnett	.10
196	J.J. Birden	.10
197	Dale Carter	.10
198	Willie Davis	.10
199	*Jamie Fields*	.10
200	Dave Krieg	.10
201	Nick Lowery	.10
202	*Charles Mincy*	.10
203	Joe Montana	3.00
204	Christian Okoye	.10
205	Dan Saleaumua	.10
206	*Will Shields*	.10
207	Tracy Simien	.10
208	Neil Smith	.10
209	Derrick Thomas	.20
210	Harvey Williams	.10
211	Barry Word	.10
212	Eddie Anderson	.10
213	*Patrick Bates*	.20
214	Nick Bell	.10
215	Tim Brown	.20
216	Willie Gault	.10
217	Gaston Green	.10
218	*Billy Jo Hobert*	.75
219	Ethan Horton	.10
220	Jeff Hostetler	.20
221	James Lofton	.10
222	Howie Long	.10
223	Todd Marinovich	.10
224	Terry McDaniel	.10
225	Winston Moss	.10
226	Anthony Smith	.10
227	Greg Townsend	.10
228	Aaron Wallace	.10
229	Lionel Washington	.10
230	Steve Wisniewski	.10
231	Willie Anderson	.10
232	*Jerome Bettis*	2.00
234	Shane Conlan	.10
235	*Troy Drayton*	.50
236	Henry Ellard	.10
237	Jim Everett	.10
238	Cleveland Gary	.10
239	Sean Gilbert	.10
240	Darryl Henley	.10
241	David Lang	.10
242	Todd Lyght	.10
243	*Anthony Newman*	.10
244	Roman Phiefer	.10
245	Gerald Robinson	.10
246	Henry Rolling	.10
247	Jackie Slater	.10
248	Keith Byars	.10
249	Marco Coleman	.10
250	Bryan Cox	.10
251	Jeff Cross	.10
252	Irving Fryar	.10
253	Mark Higgs	.10
254	*Dwight Hollier*	.10
255	Mark Ingram	.10
256	Keith Jackson	.10
257	*Terry Kirby*	1.00
258	Dan Marino	5.00
259	*O.J. McDuffie*	1.50
260	John Offerdahl	.10
261	Louis Oliver	.10
262	Pete Stoyanovich	.10
263	Troy Vincent	.10
264	Richmond Webb	.10
265	Jarvis Williams	.10
266	Terry Allen	.10
267	Anthony Carter	.10
268	Cris Carter	.20
269	Roger Craig	.10
270	Jack Del Rio	.10
271	Chris Doleman	.10
272	*Qadry Ismail*	1.00
273	Steve Jordan	.10
274	Randall McDaniel	.10
275	Audray McMillian	.10
276	John Randle	.10
277	Sean Salisbury	.10
278	Todd Scott	.10
279	*Robert Smith*	2.50
280	Henry Thomas	.10
281	Ray Agnew	.10
282	Bruce Armstrong	.10
283	*Drew Bledsoe*	5.00
284	*Vincent Brisby*	.50
285	Vincent Brown	.10
286	Eugene Chung	.10
287	Marv Cook	.10
288	Pat Harlow	.10
289	Jerome Henderson	.10
290	Greg McMurty	.10
291	Leonard Russell	.10
292	Chris Singleton	.10
293	*Chris Slade*	.20
294	Andre Tippett	.10
295	Brent Williams	.10
296	Scott Zolak	.10
297	Morten Andersen	.10
298	Gene Atkins	.10
299	Mike Buck	.10
300	Toi Cook	.10
301	Jim Dombrowski	.10
302	Vaughn Dunbar	.10
303	Quinn Early	.10
304	Joel Hilgenberg	.10
305	Dalton Hilliard	.10
306	Ricky Jackson	.10
307	Vaughan Johnson	.10
308	Reginald Jones	.10
309	Eric Martin	.10
310	Wayne Martin	.10
311	Sam Mills	.10
312	Brad Muster	.10
313	*Willie Roaf*	.20
314	*Irv Smith*	.20
315	Wade Wilson	.10
316	Carlton Bailey	.10
317	Michael Brooks	.10
318	Derek Brown	.10
319	*Marcus Buckley*	.10
320	Jarrod Bunch	.10
321	Mark Collins	.10
322	Eric Dorsey	.10
323	Rodney Hampton	.20
324	Mark Jackson	.10
325	Pepper Johnson	.10
326	Ed McCaffrey	.10
327	Dave Meggett	.10
328	Bart Oates	.10
329	Mike Sherrard	.10
330	Phil Simms	.10
331	*Michael Strahan*	.10
332	Lawrence Taylor	.20
333	Brad Baxter	.10
334	Chris Burkett	.10
335	Kyle Clifton	.10
336	Boomer Esiason	.10
337	James Hasty	.10
338	Johnny Johnson	.10
339	*Marvin Jones*	.20
340	Jeff Lageman	.10
341	Mo Lewis	.10
342	Ronnie Lott	.10
343	Leonard Marshall	.10
344	Johnny Mitchell	.10
345	Rob Moore	.10
346	Browning Nagle	.10
347	*Coleman Rudolph*	.10
348	Blair Thomas	.10
349	Eric Thomas	.10
350	Brian Washington	.10
351	Marvin Washington	.10
352	Eric Allen	.10
353	*Victor Bailey*	.20
354	Fred Barnett	.10
355	Mark Bavaro	.10
356	Randall Cunningham	.20
357	Byron Evans	.10
358	*Andy Harmon*	.10
359	Tim Harris	.10
360	*Lester Holmes*	.10
361	Seth Joyner	.10
362	Keith Millard	.10
363	*Leonard Renfro*	.10
364	Heath Sherman	.10
365	Vai Sikahema	.10
366	Clyde Simmons	.10
367	William Thomas	.10
368	Herschel Walker	.10
369	Andre Waters	.10
370	Calvin Williams	.10
371	Johnny Bailey	.10
372	Steve Beuerlein	.10
373	Rich Camarillo	.10
374	Chuck Cecil	.10
375	Chris Chandler	.10
376	Gary Clark	.10
377	*Ben Coleman*	.10
378	*Earnest Dye*	.10
379	Ken Harvey	.10
380	*Garrison Hearst*	1.75
381	Randal Hill	.10
382	Robert Massey	.10
383	Freddie Joe Nunn	.10
384	Ricky Proehl	.10
385	Luis Sharpe	.10
386	Tyronne Stowe	.10
387	Eric Swann	.10
388	Aeneas Williams	.10
389	*Chad Brown*	.50
390	Dermontti Dawson	.10
391	Donald Evans	.10
392	*Deon Figures*	.50
393	Barry Foster	.20
394	Jeff Graham	.10
395	Eric Green	.10
396	Kevin Greene	.10
397	Carlton Haselrig	.10
398	*Andre Hastings*	.75
399	D.J. Johnson	.10
400	Carnell Lake	.10
401	Greg Lloyd	.10
402	Neil O'Donnell	.40
403	Darren Perry	.10
404	Mike Tomczak	.10
405	Rod Woodson	.20
406	Eric Bieneimy	.10
407	Marion Butts	.10
408	Gill Byrd	.10
409	*Darren Carrington*	.20
410	*Darrien Gordon*	.75
411	Burt Grossman	.10
412	Courtney Hall	.10
413	Ronnie Harmon	.10
414	Stan Humphries	.20
415	Nate Lewis	.10
416	*Natrone Means*	1.25
417	Anthony Miller	.10
418	Chris Mims	.10
419	Leslie O'Neal	.10
420	Gary Plummer	.10
421	Stanley Richard	.10
422	Junior Seau	.20
423	Harry Swayne	.10
424	Jerrol Williams	.10
425	Harris Barton	.10
426	Steve Bono	1.00
427	Kevin Fagan	.10
428	Don Griffin	.10
429	Dana Hall	.10
430	*Adrian Hardy*	.10
431	Brent Jones	.10
432	*Todd Kelly*	.10
433	Amp Lee	.10
434	Tim McDonald	.10
435	Guy McIntyre	.10
436	Tom Rathman	.10
437	Jerry Rice	3.00
438	Bill Romanowski	.10
439	*Dana Stubblefield*	1.00
440	John Taylor	.10
441	Steve Wallace	.10
442	Mike Walter	.10
443	Ricky Watters	.50
444	Steve Young	3.00
445	Robert Blackmon	.10
446	Brian Blades	.10
447	Jeff Bryant	.10
448	Ferrell Edmunds	.10
449	*Carlton Gray*	.20
450	Dwayne Harper	.10
451	Andy Heck	.10
452	Tommy Kane	.10
453	Cortez Kennedy	.20
454	Kelvin Martin	.10
455	Dan McGwire	.10
456	*Rick Mirer*	.50
457	Rufus Porter	.10
458	Ray Roberts	.10
459	Eugene Robinson	.10
460	Chris Warren	1.00
461	John L. Williams	.10
462	Gary Anderson	.10
463	Tyji Armstrong	.10
464	Reggie Cobb	.10
465	*Eric Curry*	.50
466	Lawrence Dawsey	.10
467	Steve DeBerg	.10
468	Santana Dotson	.10
469	*Demetrius DuBose*	.20
470	Paul Gruber	.10
471	Ron Hall	.10
472	Courtney Hawkins	.10
473	Hardy Nickerson	.10
474	Ricky Reynolds	.10
475	Broderick Thomas	.10
476	Mark Wheeler	.10
477	Jimmy Williams	.10
478	Carl Banks	.10
479	*Reggie Brooks*	.75
480	Earnest Byner	.10
481	*Tom Carter*	.20
482	Andre Collins	.10
483	Brad Edwards	.10
484	Ricky Ervins	.10
485	Kurt Gouveia	.10
486	Darrell Green	.10
487	Desmond Howard	.20
488	Jim Lachey	.10
489	Chip Lohmiller	.10
490	Charles Mann	.10
491	Tim McGee	.10
492	Brian Mitchell	.10
493	Art Monk	.10
494	Mark Rypien	.10
495	Ricky Sanders	.10
496	Checklist	.10
497	Checklist	.10
498	Checklist	.10
499	Checklist	.10
500	Checklist	.10

1993 Ultra All-Rookies

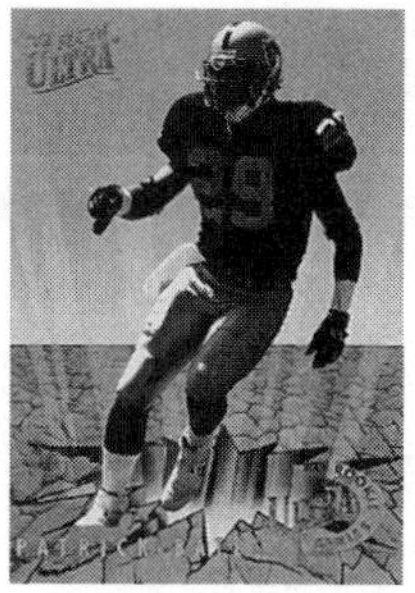

Ten first-year players are featured on these cards, which were random inserts in 1993 Fleer Ultra 14- and 19-card packs. Each front has a color action photo against an orange background. The player's name and set title are stamped in gold foil at the bottom. The back, in a horizontal format, has a close-up shot of the player, plus career highlights, all against an orange-to-yellow background. Card backs are numbered 1 of 10, etc..

		MT
Complete Set (10):		75.00
Common Player:		2.00
Minor Stars:		4.00
1	Patrick Bates	2.00
2	Jerome Bettis	15.00
3	Drew Bledsoe	30.00
4	Curtis Conway	7.00
5	Garrison Hearst	10.00
6	Qadry Ismail	4.00
7	Marvin Jones	2.00
8	Glyn Milburn	4.00
9	Rick Mirer	5.00
10	Kevin Williams	5.00

1993 Ultra Award Winners

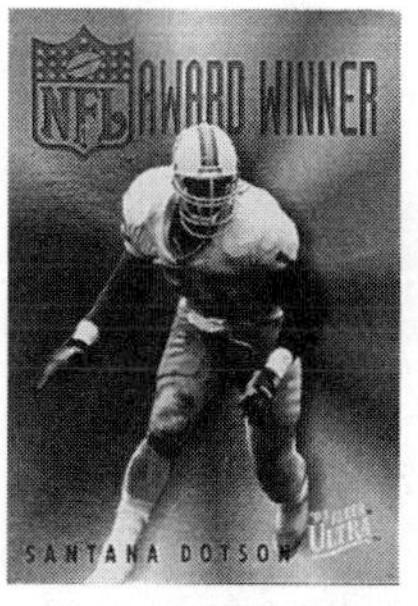

These cards were randomly inserted in 1993 Fleer Ultra 14- and 19-card foil packs. The players who are featured delivered award-winning performances during the 1992 season, such as MVP and Rookie of the Year. Fronts have full-bleed photos on a borderless, gold metallic background. The set's name is at the top, while the player's name is at the bottom. The back has a gold metallic background, with sun rays radiating towards the sides. The player's name and award he won are stamped in silver foil on the back, which also includes his career highlighs and another photo, plus a card number (1 of 10 etc.).

		MT
Complete Set (10):		75.00
Common Player:		3.00
Minor Stars:		6.00
1	Troy Aikman	30.00
2	Dale Carter	3.00
3	Chris Doleman	3.00
4	Santana Dotson	3.00
5	Barry Foster	6.00
6	Jason Hanson	3.00
7	Cortez Kennedy	3.00
8	Carl Pickens	10.00
9	Steve Tasker	3.00
10	Steve Young	25.00

1993 Ultra Michael Irvin

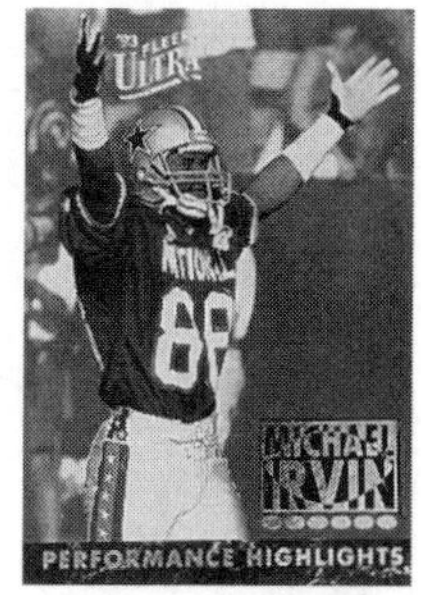

This "Performance Highlights" set features 10 cards devoted to Dallas Cowboys wide receiver Michael Irvin. Each borderless card front features a color action photo and a black marble-like stripe which contains the set subtitle and logo in silver foil. Each back has a color photo, plus career highlights in silver foil letters on a blue-screen panel with a silver foil frame. A black marble-like stripe creates a border at the card bottom. Cards are numbered 1 of 10, etc., and were random inserts in 1993 Fleer Ultra packs.

	MT
Complete Set (10):	10.00
Common Irvin:	1.00
Autograph Irvin:	80.00
Mail-In Irvin (11-12):	1.50

1993 Ultra League Leaders

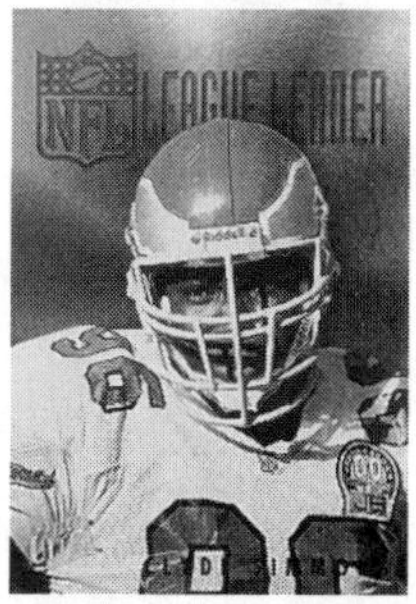

Players who led the league in certain statistical categories are featured on these cards, which were random inserts in 1993 Fleer Ultra 14- and 19-card packs. The card fronts are borderless and have an action shot against a silver metallic background. The player's name is at the bottom; the set title is at the top. The back has a silver metallic background with rays radiating toward the sides. The player's name and set title are stamped in silver foil at the top. The category the player led the league in, and a career summary, follow. The cards are numbered 1 of 10, etc.

		MT
Complete Set (10):		90.00
Common Player:		3.00
Minor Stars:		6.00
1	Haywood Jeffires	3.00
2	Henry Jones	3.00
3	Audray McMillian	3.00
4	Warren Moon	6.00
5	Leslie O'Neal	3.00
6	Deion Sanders	12.00
7	Sterling Sharpe	6.00
8	Clyde Simmons	3.00
9	Emmitt Smith	60.00
10	Thurman Thomas	10.00

1993 Ultra Ultra Stars

Ten of the NFL's premiere players are featured on these cards, which were randomly inserted in 1993 Fleer Ultra 19-card foil packs only. Each front has an action shot of the player superimposed against a ghosted U.S. flag. A grey marble stripe appears at the bottom, along with the player's name, set title and spiraling football, which are stamped in gold foil. Each back has a close-up shot of the player on one side, plus career highlights on the other. The cards are numbered 1 of 10, etc..

		MT
Complete Set (10):		110.00
Common Player:		5.00
Minor Stars:		10.00
1	Brett Favre	50.00
2	Barry Foster	5.00
3	Michael Irvin	10.00
4	Cortez Kennedy	5.00
5	Deion Sanders	15.00
6	Junior Seau	10.00
7	Derrick Thomas	5.00
8	Ricky Watters	10.00
9	Reggie White	10.00
10	Steve Young	30.00

1993 Ultra Touchdown Kings

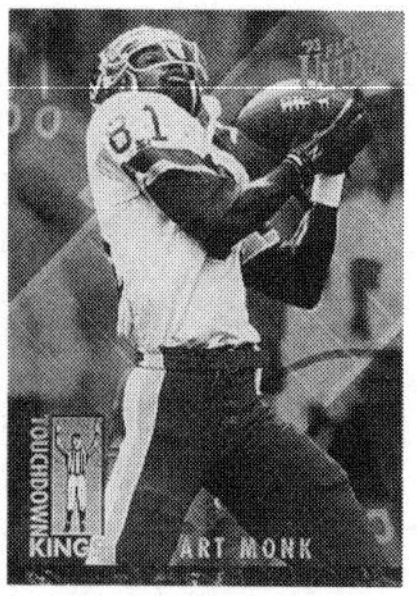

Ten of the NFL's top offensive players are featured on these cards, which were random inserts in 1993 Fleer Ultra 14-card foil packs only. Each front has an action photo of the player superimposed against a ghost-ed football field and diagrammed plays. The player's name and set title are stamped in gold foil at the bottom, which has a green marble-like border. Each back is white with a player photo and stats against a background of play diagrams. The cards are numbered 1 of 10, etc..

		MT
Complete Set (10):		85.00
Common Player:		2.00
Minor Stars:		4.00
1	Rodney Hampton	2.00
2	Dan Marino	15.00
3	Art Monk	2.00
4	Joe Montana	12.00
5	Jerry Rice	10.00
6	Andre Rison	4.00
7	Barry Sanders	20.00
8	Sterling Sharpe	4.00
9	Emmitt Smith	15.00
10	Thurman Thomas	4.00

1994 Ultra

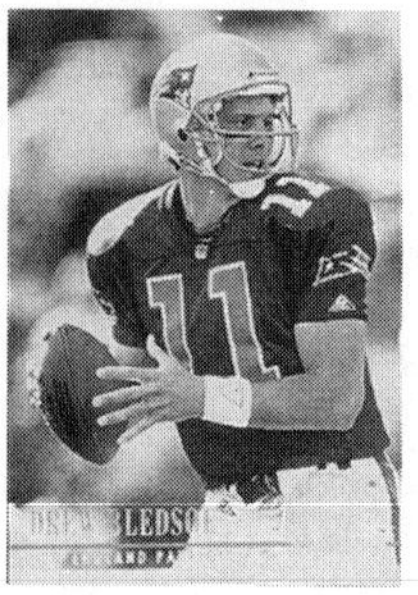

Fleer Ultra Football contains 525 cards using a new design and includes loads of inserts. The first series had six new insert sets, plus a 10-card Rick Mirer highlight set. It also had new enhancements, like gold foil stamping on both sides and four different photos per card. The Series I inserts included: Award Winners (5); Second Year Standouts (15); First Rounders (20), with the cream of the 1994 Draft; Ultra Achievements (10), honoring veteran stars; Touchdown Kings (9) and Ultra Stars (9). Series II inserts included Hot Numbers (15), Scoring Power (6), and Wave of the Future (6).

		MT
Complete Set (525):		50.00
Complete Series 1 (325):		30.00
Complete Series 2 (200):		20.00
Common Player:		.10
Minor Stars:		.20
Series 1 Pack (12):		1.75
Series 1 Wax Box (36):		50.00
Series 2 Pack (12):		1.75
Series 2 Wax Box (36):		50.00
1	Steve Beuerlein	.10
2	Gary Clark	.10
3	Randal Hill	.10
4	Seth Joyner	.10
5	*Jamir Miller*	.20
6	Ron Moore	.20
7	Luis Sharpe	.10
8	Clyde Simmons	.10
9	Eric Swann	.10
10	Aeneas Williams	.10
11	Chris Doleman	.10
12	*Bert Emanuel*	.75
13	Moe Gardner	.10
14	Jeff George	.20
15	Roger Harper	.10
16	Pierce Holt	.10
17	Lincoln Kennedy	.10
18	Erric Pegram	.10
19	Andre Rison	.20
20	Deion Sanders	.75
21	Jessie Tuggle	.10
22	Cornelius Bennett	.10
23	Bill Brooks	.10
24	*Jeff Burris*	.20
25	Kent Hull	.10
26	Henry Jones	.10
27	Jim Kelly	.20
28	Marcus Patton	.10
29	Andre Reed	.15
30	Bruce Smith	.10
31	Thomas Smith	.10
32	Thurman Thomas	.20
33	Jeff Wright	.10
34	Trace Armstrong	.10
35	Mark Carrier	.10
36	Dante Jones	.10
37	Erik Kramer	.10
38	Terry Obee	.10
39	Alonzo Spellman	.10
40	*John Thierry*	.20
41	Tom Waddle	.10
42	Donnell Woolford	.10
43	Tim Worley	.10
44	Chris Zorich	.10
45	John Copeland	.10
46	Harold Green	.10
47	David Klingler	.10
48	Ricardo McDonald	.10
49	Tony McGee	.10
50	Louis Oliver	.10
51	Carl Pickens	.75
52	*Darnay Scott*	.75
53	Steve Tovar	.10
54	*Dan Wilkinson*	.20
55	Darryl Williams	.10
56	*Derrick Alexander*	.50
57	Michael Jackson	.10
58	Tony Jones	.10
59	*Antonio Langham*	.20
60	Eric Metcalf	.10
61	Stevon Moore	.10
62	Michael Dean Perry	.10
63	Anthony Pleasant	.10
64	Vinny Testaverde	.10
65	Eric Turner	.10
66	Tommy Vardell	.10
67	Troy Aikman	1.50
68	Larry Brown	.10
69	*Shante Carver*	.20
70	Charles Haley	.10
71	Michael Irvin	.20
72	Leon Lett	.10
73	Nate Newton	.10
74	Jay Novacek	.10
75	Darrin Smith	.10
76	Emmitt Smith	3.00
77	Tony Tolbert	.10
78	Erik Williams	.10
79	Kevin Williams	.60
80	Steve Atwater	.10
81	Rod Bernstine	.10
82	Ray Crockett	.10
83	Mike Croel	.10
84	Shane Dronett	.10
85	Jason Elam	.10
86	John Elway	.50
87	Simon Fletcher	.10
88	Glyn Milburn	.10
89	Anthony Miller	.10
90	Shannon Sharpe	.10
91	Gary Zimmerman	.10
92	Bennie Blades	.10
93	Lomas Brown	.10
94	Mel Gray	.10
95	Jason Hanson	.10
96	Ryan McNeil	.10
97	Scott Mitchell	.15
98	Herman Moore	.75
99	*Johnnie Morton*	.50
100	Robert Porcher	.10
101	Barry Sanders	2.00
102	Chris Spielman	.10
103	Pat Swilling	.10
104	Edgar Bennett	.10
105	Terrell Buckley	.10
106	Reggie Cobb	.10
107	Brett Favre	3.00
108	Sean Jones	.10
109	Ken Ruettgers	.10
110	Sterling Sharpe	.20
111	Wayne Simmons	.10
112	*Aaron Taylor*	.15
113	George Teague	.10
114	Reggie White	.20
115	Micheal Barrow	.10
116	Gary Brown	.10
117	Cody Carlson	.10
118	Ray Childress	.10
119	Cris Dishman	.10
120	*Henry Ford*	.15
121	Haywood Jeffires	.10
122	Bruce Matthews	.10
123	Bubba McDowell	.10
124	Marcus Robertson	.10
125	Eddie Robinson	.10
126	Webster Slaughter	.10
127	*Trev Alberts*	.20
128	Tony Bennett	.10
129	Ray Buchanan	.10
130	Quentin Coryatt	.10
131	Eugene Daniel	.10
132	Steve Emtman	.10
133	*Marshall Faulk*	6.00
134	Jim Harbaugh	.10
135	Roosevelt Potts	.10
136	Rohn Stark	.10
137	Marcus Allen	.20
138	*Donnell Bennett*	.20
139	Dale Carter	.10
140	Tony Casillas	.10
141	Mark Collins	.10
142	Willie Davis	.10
143	Tim Grunhard	.10
144	*Greg Hill*	.75
145	Joe Montana	2.50
146	Tracy Simien	.10
147	Neil Smith	.10
148	Derrick Thomas	.20
149	Tim Brown	.20
150	*James Folston*	.15
151	*Rob Fredrickson*	.20
152	Jeff Hostetler	.15
153	Raghib Ismail	.15
154	James Jett	.15
155	Terry McDaniel	.10
156	Winston Moss	.10
157	Greg Robinson	.10
158	Anthony Smith	.10
159	Steve Wisniewski	.10
160	Willie Anderson	.10
161	Jerome Bettis	.75
162	*Isaac Bruce*	4.00
163	Shane Conlan	.10
164	*Wayne Gandy*	.10
165	Sean Gilbert	.10
166	Todd Lyght	.10
167	Chris Miller	.10
168	Anthony Newman	.10
169	Roman Phifer	.10
170	Jackie Slater	.10
171	Gene Atkins	.10
172	*Aubrey Beavers*	.20
173	*Tim Bowens*	.20
174	J.B. Brown	.10
175	Marco Coleman	.10
176	Bryan Cox	.10
177	Irving Fryar	.10
178	Terry Kirby	.20
179	Dan Marino	3.00
180	Troy Vincent	.10
181	Richmond Webb	.10
182	Terry Allen	.10
183	Cris Carter	.20
184	Jack Del Rio	.10
185	Vencie Glenn	.10
186	Randall McDaniel	.10
187	Warren Moon	.20
188	*David Palmer*	.50
189	John Randle	.10
190	Todd Scott	.10
191	*Todd Steussie*	.20
192	Henry Thomas	.10
193	*DeWayne Washington*	.20
194	Bruce Armstrong	.10
195	Harlon Barnett	.10
196	Drew Bledsoe	2.00
197	Vincent Brisby	.20
198	Vincent Brown	.10
199	Marion Butts	.10
200	Ben Coates	.50
201	Todd Collins	.10
202	Maurice Hurst	.10
203	*Willie McGinest*	.40
204	Ricky Reynolds	.10
205	Chris Slade	.10
206	*Mario Bates*	.30
207	Derek Brown	.10
208	Vince Buck	.10
209	Quinn Early	.10
210	Jim Everett	.10
211	Michael Haynes	.10
212	Tyrone Hughes	.10
213	*Joe Johnson*	.20
214	Vaughan Johnson	.10
215	William Roaf	.10
216	Renaldo Turnbull	.10
217	Michael Brooks	.10
218	Dave Brown	.20
219	Howard Cross	.10
220	Stacey Dillard	.10
221	John Elliott	.10
222	Keith Hamilton	.10
223	Rodney Hampton	.20
224	*Thomas Lewis*	.20
225	David Meggett	.10
226	Corey Miller	.10
227	*Thomas Randolph*	.20
228	Mike Sherrard	.10
229	Kyle Clifton	.10
230	Boomer Esiason	.15
231	*Aaron Glenn*	.20
232	James Hasty	.10
233	Bobby Houston	.10
234	Johnny Johnson	.10
235	Mo Lewis	.10
236	Ronnie Lott	.15
237	Rob Moore	.10
238	Marvin Washington	.10
239	*Ryan Yarborough*	.20
240	Eric Allen	.10
241	Victor Bailey	.10
242	Fred Barnett	.10
243	Mark Bavaro	.10
244	Randall Cunningham	.20
245	Byron Evans	.10
246	William Fuller	.10
247	Andy Harmon	.10
248	William Perry	.10
249	Herschel Walker	.20
250	*Bernard Williams*	.20
251	Dermontti Dawson	.10
252	Deon Figures	.10
253	Barry Foster	.20
254	Kevin Greene	.10
255	*Charles Johnson*	1.00
256	Levon Kirkland	.10
257	Greg Lloyd	.10
258	Neil O'Donnell	.20
259	Darren Perry	.10
260	Dwight Stone	.10
261	Rod Woodson	.20
262	John Carney	.10
263	*Isaac Davis*	.20
264	Courtney Hall	.10
265	Ronnie Harmon	.10
266	Stan Humphries	.20
267	Vance Johnson	.10
268	Natrone Means	.50
269	Chris Mims	.10
270	Leslie O'Neal	.10
271	Stanley Richard	.10
272	Junior Seau	.20
273	Harris Barton	.10
274	Dennis Brown	.10
275	Eric Davis	.10
276	*William Floyd*	.50
277	John Johnson	.10
278	Tim McDonald	.10
279	Ken Norton	.10
280	Jerry Rice	1.50
281	Jesse Sapolu	.10
282	Dana Stubblefield	.10
283	Ricky Watters	.20
284	*Bryant Young*	.75
285	Steve Young	1.50
286	*Sam Adams*	.20
287	Brian Blades	.10
288	Ferrell Edmunds	.10
289	Patrick Hunter	.10
290	Cortez Kennedy	.20
291	Rick Mirer	.75
292	Nate Odomes	.10
293	Ray Roberts	.10
294	Eugene Robinson	.10
295	Rod Stephens	.10
296	Chris Warren	.20
297	Marty Carter	.10
298	Horace Copeland	.10
299	Eric Curry	.10
300	Santana Dotson	.10
301	Craig Erickson	.20
302	Paul Gruber	.10
303	Courtney Hawkins	.10
304	Martin Mayhew	.10
305	Hardy Nickerson	.10
306	*Errict Rhett*	1.00
307	Vince Workman	.10
308	Reggie Brooks	.10
309	Tom Carter	.10
310	Andre Collins	.10
311	Brad Edwards	.10
312	Kurt Gouveia	.10
313	Darrell Green	.10
314	Ethan Horton	.10
315	Desmond Howard	.10
316	*Tre Johnson*	.20
317	Sterling Palmer	.10
318	*Heath Shuler*	.50
319	Tyronne Stowe	.10
320	NFL 75th Anniversary	.10
321	Checklist	.10
322	Checklist	.10
323	Checklist	.10
324	Checklist	.10
325	Checklist	.10
326	Garrison Hearst	1.00
327	Eric Hill	.10
328	Seth Joyner	.10
329	Jim McMahon	.10
330	Jamir Miller	.10
331	Ricky Proehl	.10
332	Clyde Simmons	.10
333	Chris Doleman	.10
334	Bert Emanuel	.40
335	Jeff George	.20
336	D.J. Johnson	.10
337	Terance Mathis	.10
338	Clay Matthews	.10
339	Tony Smith	.10
340	Don Beebe	.10
341	*Bucky Brooks*	.20
342	Jeff Burris	.20
343	Kenneth Davis	.10
344	Phil Hansen	.10
345	Pete Metzelaars	.10
346	Darryl Talley	.10
347	Joe Cain	.10
348	Curtis Conway	.60
349	Shaun Gayle	.10
350	Chris Gedney	.10
351	Erik Kramer	.10
352	Vinson Smith	.10
353	John Thierry	.10
354	Lewis Tillman	.10
355	Mike Brim	.10
356	Derrick Fenner	.10
357	James Francis	.10
358	Louis Oliver	.10
359	Darnay Scott	1.00
360	Dan Wilkinson	.20
361	Alfred Williams	.10
362	Derrick Alexander	.20
363	Rob Burnett	.10
364	Mark Carrier	.10
365	Steve Everitt	.10
366	Leroy Hoard	.10
367	Pepper Johnson	.10
368	Antonio Langham	.20
369	Shante Carver	.10
370	Alvin Harper	.20
371	Daryl Johnston	.10
372	Russell Maryland	.10
373	Kevin Smith	.10
374	Mark Stepnoski	.10
375	Darren Woodson	.10
376	Allen Aldridge	.10
377	Ray Crockett	.10
378	Karl Mecklenburg	.10
379	Anthony Miller	.10
380	Mike Pritchard	.10
381	Leonard Russell	.10
382	Dennis Smith	.10
383	Anthony Carter	.10
384	Van Malone	.10
385	Robert Massey	.10
386	Scott Mitchell	.10
387	Johnnie Morton	.40
388	Brett Perriman	.10
389	Tracy Scroggins	.10
390	Robert Brooks	.30
391	LeRoy Butler	.10
392	Reggie Cobb	.10
393	Sean Jones	.10
394	George Koonce	.10
395	Steve McMichael	.10
396	Bryce Paup	.10
397	Aaron Taylor	.10
398	Henry Ford	.10
399	Ernest Givins	.10
400	*Jeremy Nunley*	.15
401	Bo Orlando	.10
402	Al Smith	.10
403	*Barron Wortham*	.15
404	Trev Alberts	.20
405	Tony Bennett	.10
406	Kerry Cash	.10
407	*Sean Dawkins*	1.00
408	Marshall Faulk	3.00
409	Jim Harbaugh	.10
410	Jeff Herrod	.10
411	Kimble Anders	.10
412	Donnell Bennett	.10
413	J.J. Birden	.10
414	Mark Collins	.10
415	Lake Dawson	.30
416	Greg Hill	.75
417	Charles Mincy	.10
418	Greg Biekert	.10
419	Rob Fredrickson	.10
420	Nolan Harrison	.10
421	Jeff Jaeger	.10
422	Albert Lewis	.10
423	Chester McGlockton	.10
424	Tom Rathman	.10
425	Harvey Williams	.10
426	Isaac Bruce	2.00
427	Troy Drayton	.10
428	Wayne Gandy	.10
429	Fred Stokes	.10
430	Robert Young	.10
431	Gene Atkins	.10
432	Aubrey Beavers	.10
433	Tim Bowens	.10
434	Keith Byars	.10
435	Jeff Cross	.10
436	Mark Ingram	.10
437	Keith Jackson	.10
438	Michael Stewart	.10
439	Chris Hinton	.10
440	Qadry Ismail	.15
441	Carlos Jenkins	.10
442	Warren Moon	.20
443	David Palmer	.20
444	Jake Reed	.10
445	Robert Smith	.40
446	Todd Steussie	.10
447	DeWayne Washington	.10
448	Marion Butts	.10
449	Tim Goad	.10
450	Myron Guyton	.10
451	*Kevin Lee*	.20
452	Willie McGinest	.20
453	Ricky Reynolds	.10
454	Michael Timpson	.10
455	Morten Andersen	.10
456	Jim Everett	.10
457	Michael Haynes	.10
458	Joe Johnson	.10
459	Wayne Martin	.10
460	Sam Mills	.10
461	Irv Smith	.10
462	Carlton Bailey	.10
463	Chris Calloway	.10
464	Mark Jackson	.10
465	Thomas Lewis	.20
466	Thomas Randolph	.10
467	*Stevie Anderson*	.15
468	Brad Baxter	.10
469	Aaron Glenn	.10
470	Jeff Lageman	.10
471	Johnny Mitchell	.10
472	Art Monk	.15
473	William Fuller	.10
474	*Charlie Garner*	2.50
475	Vaughn Hebron	.10
476	Bill Romanowski	.10
477	William Thomas	.10
478	Greg Townsend	.10
479	Bernard Williams	.10
480	Calvin Williams	.10
481	Eric Green	.10
482	Charles Johnson	.50
483	Carnell Lake	.10
484	*Bam Morris*	.50
485	John L. Williams	.10
486	Darren Carrington	.10
487	*Andre Coleman*	.20
488	Isaac Davis	.10
489	Dwane Harper	.10
490	Tony Martin	.10
491	Mark Seay	.40
492	Richard Dent	.10
493	William Floyd	.75
494	Rickey Jackson	.10
495	Brent Jones	.10
496	Ken Norton	.10
497	Gary Plummer	.10
498	Deion Sanders	1.50
499	John Taylor	.20
500	*Lee Woodall*	.20
501	Bryant Young	.30
502	Sam Adams	.20
503	Howard Ballard	.10
504	Michael Bates	.10
505	Trev Alberts, Robert Blackmon	.10
506	John Kasay	.10
507	Kelvin Martin	.10
508	Kevin Mawae	.10
509	Rufus Porter	.10
510	Lawrence Dawsey	.10
511	*Trent Dilfer*	2.00
512	Thomas Everett	.10
513	Jackie Harris	.10
514	Errict Rhett	1.50
515	Henry Ellard	.10
516	John Friesz	.10
517	Ken Harvey	.10
518	Ethan Horton	.10
519	Tre Johnson	.10
520	Jim Lachey	.10
521	Heath Shuler	1.50
522	Tony Woods	.10
523	Checklist	.10
524	Checklist	.10
525	Checklist	.10

1994 Ultra Achievement Awards

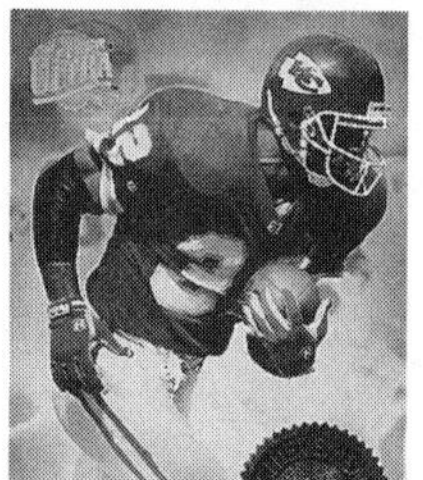

Ultra Achievement Awards featured NFL veteran stars with long records of significant accomplishments. Sterling Sharpe's record breaking reception record is an example of the achievements captured in this 10-card set.

		MT
Complete Set (10):		10.00
Common Player:		.50
1	Marcus Allen	.50
2	John Elway	1.00
3	Dan Marino	4.00
4	Joe Montana	3.00
5	Jerry Rice	2.00
6	Barry Sanders	2.00
7	Sterling Sharpe	.50
8	Emmitt Smith	4.00
9	Thurman Thomas	.50
10	Reggie White	.50

1994 Ultra Award Winners

Award Winners were found in random packs of 1994 Ultra Football. It showcases the AFC/NFC Offensive Rookies of the Year, Super Bowl MVP, Defensive Player of the Year, and the NFL Defensive Rookie of the Year. Each card shows the player on a three-photo background.

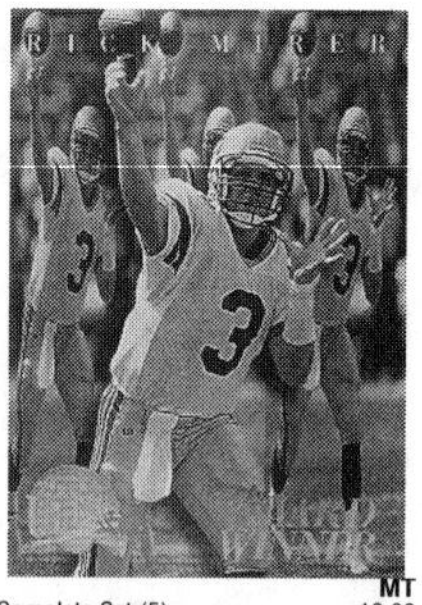

		MT
Complete Set (5):		10.00
Common Player:		1.00
1	Jerome Bettis	2.00
2	Rick Mirer	1.50
3	Emmitt Smith	5.00
4	Dana Stubblefield	1.00
5	Rod Woodson	1.00

1994 Ultra First Rounders

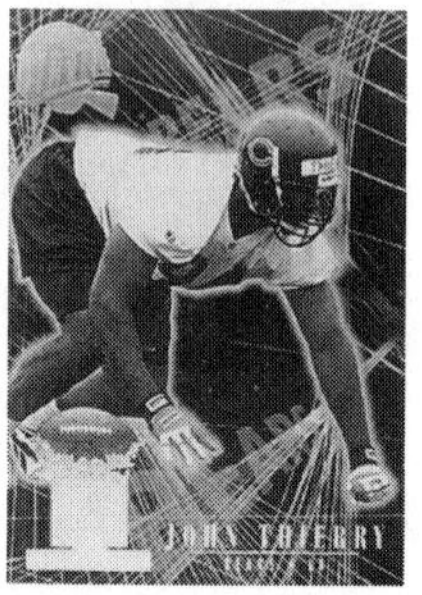

First Rounders could be found in 14, 17 and 20-card foil packs of Fleer Ultra Football. This 20-card set features the top selections in the '94 draft cast onto a cobweb- looking background, with a First Rounder stamp in the bottom left corner.

		MT
Complete Set (20):		15.00
Common Player:		.50
1	Sam Adams	.50
2	Trev Alberts	.50
3	Shante Carver	.50
4	Marshall Faulk	3.00
5	William Floyd	2.00
6	Rob Fredrickson	.50
7	Wayne Gandy	.50
8	Aaron Glenn	.50
9	Charles Johnson	.50
10	Joe Johnson	.50
11	Antonio Langham	.50
12	Willie McGinest	.50
13	Jamir Miller	.50
14	Johnnie Morton	.50
15	Heath Shuler	1.00
16	John Thierry	.50
17	DeWayne Washington	.50
18	Dan Wilkinson	.50
19	Bernard Williams	.50
20	Bryant Young	1.00

1994 Ultra Flair Hot Numbers

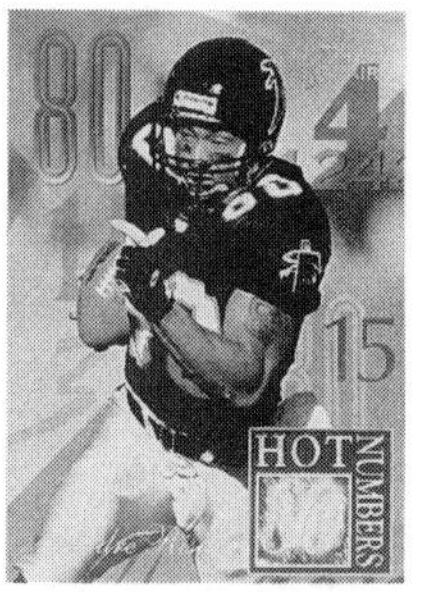

These cards feature the super premium quality of Fleer Flair, including double-thick card stock, polyester lamination and six- color printing. The Hot Number inserts, randomly included in Fleer Ultra Series II packs, showcase 15 running backs, quarterbacks and receivers who pile up yardage. Each card front has an action shot over a team-colored, swirling background. Different dates and numbers that are important to the pictured player appear within the background. Player names are written across the bottom in gold foil, with the Flair logo in the upper right corner. In the bottom right corner a large box, outlined in black, displays "Hot Numbers," with the player's uniform number inside the box. Card backs, numbered 1 of 15, etc., have another photo and career summary.

		MT
Complete Set (15):		25.00
Common Player:		.50
1	Troy Aikman	4.00
2	Jerome Bettis	1.00
3	Tim Brown	.50
4	John Elway	2.00
5	Rodney Hampton	.50
6	Michael Irvin	.75
7	Dan Marino	5.00
8	Joe Montana	4.00
9	Jerry Rice	3.00
10	Andre Rison	.50
11	Barry Sanders	3.00
12	Sterling Sharpe	.50
13	Emmitt Smith	5.00
14	Thurman Thomas	.75
15	Steve Young	3.00

1994 Ultra Flair Scoring Power

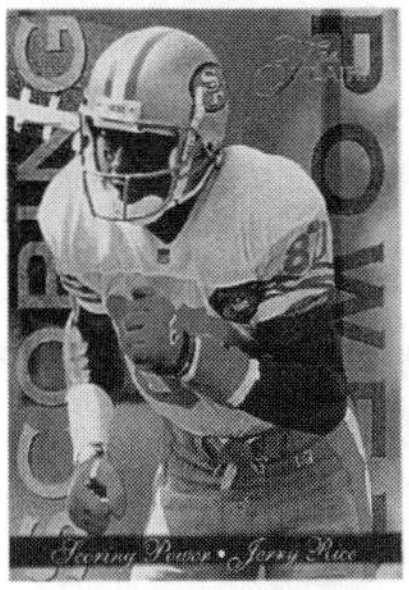

Each of these six insert cards contains a football background with the words "Scoring Power" running up and down opposite sides of the card. A black strip across the bottom of each card contains the player's name, and the words "Scoring Power." The inserts, randomly included in 1994 Fleer Ultra Series II packs, feature highly productive quarterbacks, running backs and wide receivers. The Fleer Flair logo is on each card front. Card backs have gold foil stamping, a photo, a career summary and a card number (1 of 6, etc.).

		MT
Complete Set (6):		20.00
Common Player:		3.00
1	Marcus Allen	3.00
2	Natrone Means	5.00
3	Jerry Rice	5.00
4	Andre Rison	3.00
5	Emmitt Smith	8.00
6	Ricky Watters	3.00

1994 Ultra Flair Wave of the Future

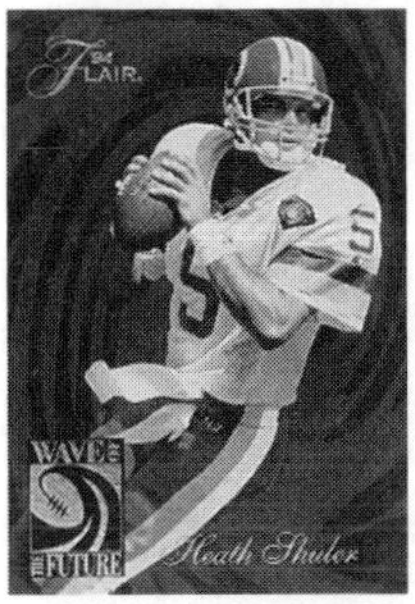

These 1994 Fleer Ultra Series II inserts, randomly included in packs, feature six top rookies from the 1994 season. Players are pictured in their NFL uniforms over an iridescent, swirling background. The player's name, Flair logo and set logo are stamped in gold foil on the card front. The card back has a photo, career summary and a number (1 of 6, etc.).

		MT
Complete Set (6):		10.00
Common Player:		1.00
1	Trent Dilfer	1.50
2	Marshall Faulk	3.00
3	Greg Hill	1.00
4	Charles Johnson	1.00
5	Heath Shuler	1.50
6	Dan Wilkinson	1.00

Values quoted in this guide reflect the retail price of a card — the price a collector can expect to pay when buying a card from a dealer. The wholesale price — that which a collector can expect to receive from a dealer when selling cards — will be significantly lower, depending on desirability and condition.

1994 Ultra Rick Mirer

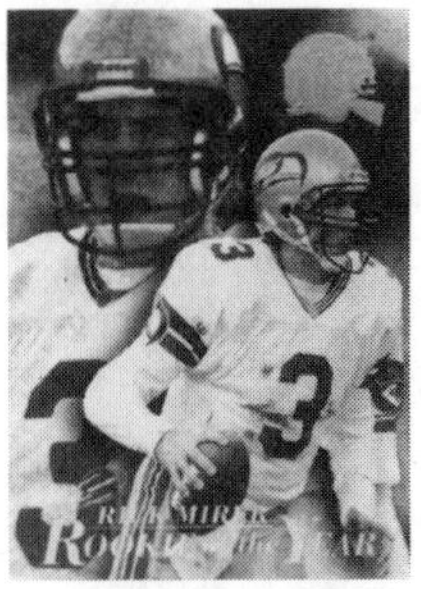

Rick Mirer "Rookie of the Year" is a 10-card set inserted into Ultra packs. It highlights his rookie season and gives a brief history of Mirer.

	MT
Complete Set (10):	5.00
Common Mirer:	.50
Mirer Auto:	50.00

1994 Ultra Second Year Standouts

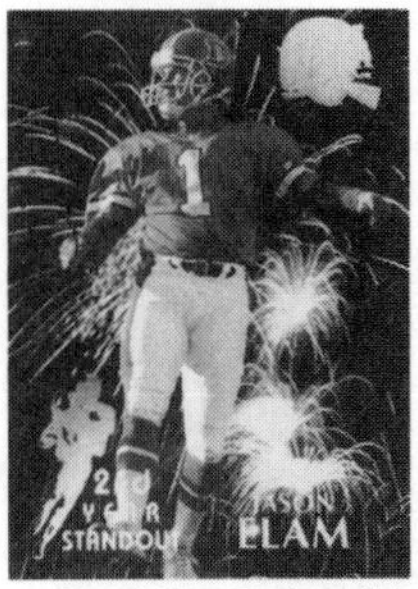

Second Year Standouts highlight high-profile 1993 rookies starting their second season. This 15-card set was inserted into foil packs of Ultra Football. Each card displays the second year standout with fireworks going off in the background.

		MT
Complete Set (15):		15.00
Common Player:		1.00
1	Jerome Bettis	1.50
2	Drew Bledsoe	5.00
3	Reggie Brooks	1.00
4	Tom Carter	1.00
5	Eric Curry	1.00
6	Jason Elam	1.00
7	Tyrone Hughes	1.00
8	James Jett	1.00
9	Terry Kirby	1.50
10	Natrone Means	1.00
11	Rick Mirer	1.00
12	Ron Moore	1.00
13	William Roaf	1.00
14	Chris Slade	1.00
15	Dana Stubblefield	1.00

1994 Ultra Ultra Stars

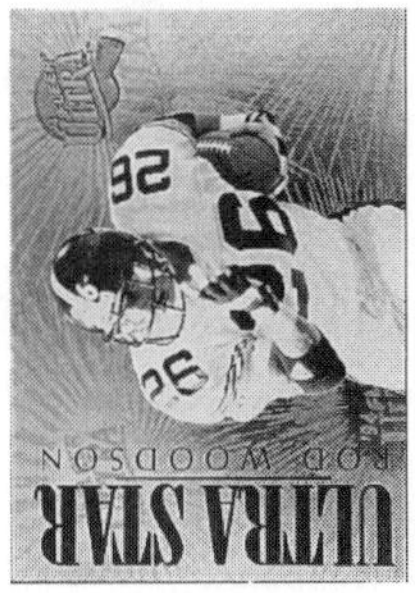

This nine-card set was found in only 17-card packs of Ultra Football. It includes some of the brightest stars in the NFL. Ultra Stars are also quite scarce and are printed on 100% etched-foil.

		MT
Complete Set (9):		125.00
Common Player:		5.00
1	Troy Aikman	25.00
2	Jerome Bettis	10.00
3	Tim Brown	5.00
4	Michael Irvin	10.00
5	Rick Mirer	5.00
6	Jerry Rice	25.00
7	Barry Sanders	25.00
8	Emmitt Smith	35.00
9	Rod Woodson	5.00

A player's name in *italic type* indicates a rookie card.

1994 Ultra Touchdown Kings

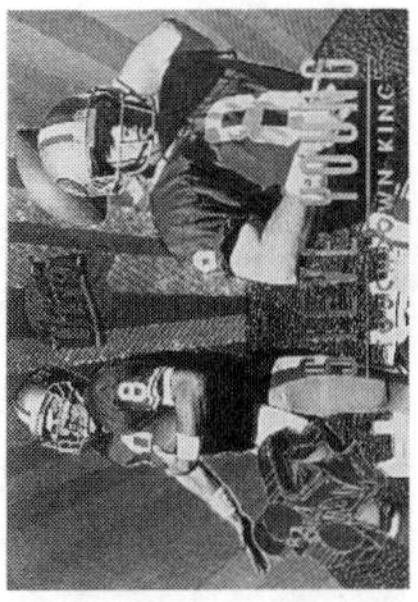

Touchdown Kings are a 100% foil-etched shot of a nine players who have proven scoring ability. Since they were randomly inserted exclusively into 14 and 20-card packs of Ultra Football, they are the rarest insert set. Each card shows two shots of the featured player on a horizontal background

		MT
Complete Set (9):		85.00
Common Player:		3.00
Minor Stars:		6.00
1	Marcus Allen	6.00
2	Dan Marino	20.00
3	Joe Montana	15.00
4	Jerry Rice	15.00
5	Andre Rison	3.00
6	Sterling Sharpe	6.00
7	Emmitt Smith	20.00
8	Ricky Watters	6.00
9	Steve Young	10.00

1995 Ultra

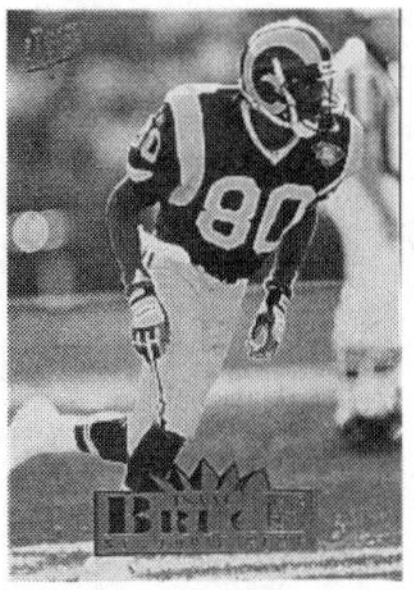

Fleer released its 550-card 1995 Ultra set in two series - a 350-card Series I, plus a 200-card Ultra Extra set. Card fronts have a full-bleed color action photo, with the player name stamped in a square at the bottom, with a mountain range design. The card back has a number in the upper left corner and features two smaller color photos and a ghosted image on a horizontal background. The player's name and position are stamped in gold. A team helmet and 1994 and career statistic lines are also given. All regular and insert cards are on 40-percent thicker stock. A Gold Medallion parallel set, featuring 100-percent gold-foil embossed backgrounds, was also created for each regular and insert card. Cards were include one per pack. Ultra Extra is composed of subsets: 60 Rookies, 60 Player Updates, 60 Extra Stars, six Rollout cards and 12 Extra Effort cards. Series I insert sets include: Award Winners (1 in 5 packs), First Rounders (1 in 7), Touchdown Kings (1 in 7 12-card packs), Rising Stars (1 in 37), Ultra Stars (1 in 7 17-card packs), Ultra Achievement (1 in 7) and Second Year Standouts (1 in 5). Ultra Extra inserts include: 30 Ultrabilties cards (10 each for Guns, Bolts and Blasts; 1 in 5 packs), Big Finish (1 in 20, hobby exclusive packs), Ultra Magna Force (1 in 20, retail exclusive), and All-Rookie Team (1 in 55). Also found in Ultra Extra are Gold Medallion Hot Packs (1 in 72), which contain all Gold Medallion cards, and All-Rookie Team Hot Packs (1 per 360), which contain a complete set of All-Rookie Team inserts.

		MT
Complete Set (550):		70.00
Comp. Series 1 (350):		35.00
Comp. Series 2 (200):		35.00
Common Player:		.10
Minor Stars:		.20
Comp. Gold Med. Set (550):		350.00
Comp. Gold Med. Series 1 (350):		200.00
Comp. Gold Med. Series 2 (200):		150.00
Gold Medallion Cards: 3x-6x		
Series 1 Pack (12):		1.50
Series 1 Wax Box (36):		45.00
Series 2 Pack (12):		2.50
Series 2 Wax Box (36):		60.00
1	Michael Bankston	.10
2	Larry Centers	.10
3	Garrison Hearst	.20
4	Eric Hill	.10
5	Seth Joyner	.10
6	Lorenzo Lynch	.10
7	Jamir Miller	.20
8	Clyde Simmons	.10
9	Eric Swann	.10
10	Aeneas Williams	.10
11	Devin Bush	.20
12	Ron Davis	.10
13	Chris Doleman	.10
14	Bert Emanuel	.40
15	Jeff George	.20
16	Roger Harper	.10
17	Craig Heyward	.10
18	Pierce Holt	.10
19	D.J. Johnson	.10
20	Terance Mathis	.10
21	Chuck Smith	.10
22	Jessie Tuggle	.10
23	Cornelius Bennett	.10
24	Reuben Brown	.20
25	Jeff Burris	.10
26	Matt Darby	.10
27	Phil Hansen	.10
28	Henry Jones	.10
29	Jim Kelly	.20
30	Mark Maddox	.20
31	Andre Reed	.20
32	Bruce Smith	.10
33	Don Beebe	.10
34	*Kerry Collins*	2.00
35	Darion Conner	.10
36	Pete Metzelaars	.10
37	Sam Mills	.10
38	Tyrone Poole	.20
39	Joe Cain	.10
40	Mark Carrier	.10
41	Curtis Conway	.10
42	Jeff Graham	.10
43	Raymont Harris	.10
44	Erik Kramer	.10
45	*Rashaan Salaam*	.50
46	Lewis Tillman	.10
47	Donnell Woolford	.10
48	Chris Zorich	.10
49	*Jeff Blake*	.50
50	Mike Brim	.10
51	*Ki-Jana Carter*	1.50
52	James Francis	.10
53	Carl Pickens	.20
54	Darnay Scott	.75
55	Steve Tovar	.10
56	Dan Wilkinson	.10
57	Alfred Williams	.10
58	Darryl Williams	.10
59	Derrick Alexander	.20
60	Rob Burnett	.10
61	Steve Everitt	.10
62	Leroy Hoard	.10
63	Michael Jackson	.10
64	Pepper Johnson	.10
65	Tony Jones	.10
66	Antonio Langham	.10
67	Anthony Pleasant	.10
68	Craig Powell	.20
69	Vinny Testaverde	.20
70	Eric Turner	.10
71	Troy Aikman	1.50
72	Charles Haley	.10
73	Michael Irvin	.20
74	Daryl Johnston	.10
75	Robert Jones	.10
76	Leon Lett	.10
77	Russell Maryland	.10
78	Jay Novacek	.10
79	Darrin Smith	.10
80	Emmitt Smith	3.00
81	Kevin Smith	.10
82	Erik Williams	.10
83	Kevin Williams	.10
84	*Sherman Williams*	.20
85	Darren Woodson	.10
86	Elijah Alexander	.20
87	Steve Atwater	.10
88	Ray Crockett	.10
89	Shane Dronett	.10
90	Jason Elam	.10
91	John Elway	.60
92	Simon Fletcher	.10
93	Glyn Milburn	.10
94	Anthony Miller	.10
95	Leonard Russell	.10
96	Shannon Sharpe	.20
97	Bennie Blades	.10
98	Lomas Brown	.10
99	Willie Clay	.10
100	Luther Elliss	.20
101	Mike Johnson	.10
102	Robert Massey	.10
103	Scott Mitchell	.10
104	Herman Moore	.50
105	Brett Perriman	.10
106	Robert Porcher	.10
107	Barry Sanders	2.50
108	Chris Spielman	.10
109	Edgar Bennett	.10
110	Robert Brooks	.10
111	LeRoy Butler	.10
112	Brett Favre	3.00
113	Sean Jones	.10
114	John Jurkovic	.10
115	George Koonce	.10
116	Wayne Simmons	.10
117	George Teague	.10
118	Reggie White	.20
119	Micheal Barrow	.10
120	Gary Brown	.10
121	Cody Carlson	.10
122	Ray Childress	.10
123	Cris Dishman	.10
124	Bruce Matthews	.10
125	*Steve McNair*	4.00
126	Marcus Robertson	.10
127	Webster Slaughter	.10
128	Al Smith	.10
129	Tony Bennett	.10
130	Ray Buchanan	.10
131	Quentin Coryatt	.10
132	Sean Dawkins	.10
133	Marshall Faulk	1.00
134	Stephen Grant	.10
135	Jim Harbaugh	.10
136	Jeff Herrod	.10
137	Ellis Johnson	.20
138	Tony Siragusa	.10
139	Steve Beuerlein	.10
140	*Tony Boselli*	.20
141	Darren Carrington	.10
142	Reggie Cobb	.10
143	Kelvin Martin	.10
144	Kelvin Pritchett	.10
145	Joel Smeenge	.10
146	*James Stewart*	2.50
147	Marcus Allen	.20
148	Kimble Anders	.10
149	Dale Carter	.10
150	Mark Collins	.10
151	Willie Davis	.10
152	Lake Dawson	.20
153	Greg Hill	.20
154	Trezelle Jenkins	.10
155	Darren Mickell	.10
156	Tracy Simien	.10
157	Neil Smith	.10
158	William White	.10
159	Joe Aska	.20
160	Greg Biekert	.10
161	Tim Brown	.20
162	Rob Fredrickson	.10
163	*Andrew Glover*	.20
164	Jeff Hostetler	.20
165	Raghib Ismail	.10
166	*Napoleon Kaufman*	1.00
167	Terry McDaniel	.10
168	Chester McGlockton	.10
169	Anthony Smith	.10
170	Harvey Williams	.10
171	Steve Wisniewski	.10
172	Gene Atkins	.10
173	Aubrey Beavers	.10
174	Tim Bowens	.10
175	Bryan Cox	.10
176	Jeff Cross	.10
177	Irving Fryar	.10
178	Dan Marino	3.00
179	O.J. McDuffie	.10
180	Billy Milner	.10
181	Bernie Parmalee	.20
182	Troy Vincent	.10
183	Richmond Webb	.10
184	Derrick Alexander	.20
185	Cris Carter	.20
186	Jack Del Rio	.10
187	Qadry Ismail	.10
188	Ed McDaniel	.10
189	Randall McDaniel	.10
190	Warren Moon	.20
191	John Randle	.10
192	Jake Reed	.10
193	Fuad Reveiz	.10
194	Korey Stringer	.20
195	DeWayne Washington	.10
196	Bruce Armstrong	.10
197	Drew Bledsoe	1.50
198	Vincent Brisby	.10
199	Vincent Brown	.10
200	Marion Butts	.10
201	Ben Coates	.10
202	Myron Guyton	.10
203	Maurice Hurst	.10
204	Mike Jones	.10
205	Ty Law	.20
206	Willie McGinest	.10
207	Chris Slade	.10
208	Mario Bates	.40
209	Quinn Early	.10
210	Jim Everett	.20
211	Mark Fields	.10
212	Michael Haynes	.10
213	Tyrone Hughes	.10
214	Joe Johnson	.10
215	Wayne Martin	.10
216	William Roaf	.10
217	Irv Smith	.10
218	Jimmy Spencer	.10
219	Winfred Tubbs	.10
220	Renaldo Turnbull	.10
221	Michael Brooks	.10
222	Dave Brown	.10
223	Chris Calloway	.10
224	Howard Cross	.10
225	John Elliott	.10
226	Keith Hamilton	.10
227	Rodney Hampton	.20
228	Thomas Lewis	.10
229	Thomas Randolph	.10
230	Mike Sherrard	.10
231	Michael Strahan	.10
232	*Tyrone Wheatley*	1.50
233	Brad Baxter	.10
234	*Kyle Brady*	.50
235	Kyle Clifton	.10
236	*Hugh Douglas*	.20
237	Boomer Esiason	.20
238	Aaron Glenn	.10
239	Bobby Houston	.10
240	Johnny Johnson	.10
241	Mo Lewis	.10
242	Johnny Mitchell	.10
243	Marvin Washington	.10
244	Fred Barnett	.10
245	Randall Cunningham	.20
246	William Fuller	.10
247	Charlie Garner	.10
248	Andy Harmon	.10
249	Greg Jackson	.10
250	*Mike Mamula*	.20
251	Bill Romanowski	.10
252	Bobby Taylor	.20
253	William Thomas	.10
254	Calvin Williams	.10
255	Michael Zordich	.10
256	Chad Brown	.10
257	*Mark Bruener*	.50
258	Dermontti Dawson	.10
259	Barry Foster	.10
260	Kevin Greene	.10
261	Charles Johnson	.40
262	Carnell Lake	.10
263	Greg Lloyd	.10
264	Bam Morris	.20
265	Neil O'Donnell	.20
266	Darren Perry	.10
267	Ray Seals	.10
268	*Kordell Stewart*	3.00
269	John L. Williams	.10
270	Rod Woodson	.20
271	Jerome Bettis	.20
272	Isaac Bruce	1.00
273	*Kevin Carter*	.20
274	Shane Conlan	.10
275	Troy Drayton	.10
276	Sean Gilbert	.10
277	Todd Lyght	.10
278	Chris Miller	.10
279	Anthony Newman	.10
280	Roman Phifer	.10
281	Robert Young	.10
282	John Carney	.10
283	Andre Coleman	.10
284	Courtney Hall	.10
285	Ronnie Harmon	.10
286	Dwayne Harper	.10
287	Stan Humphries	.20
288	Shawn Jefferson	.10
289	Tony Martin	.10
290	Natrone Means	.20
291	Chris Mims	.10
292	Leslie O'Neal	.10
293	Junior Seau	.20
294	Mark Seay	.10
295	Eric Davis	.10
296	William Floyd	.20
297	Merton Hanks	.10
298	Brent Jones	.10
299	Ken Norton	.10
300	Gary Plummer	.10
301	Jerry Rice	1.50
302	Deion Sanders	.75
303	Jesse Sapolu	.10
304	*J.J. Stokes*	2.00
305	Dana Stubblefield	.10
306	John Taylor	.10
307	Steve Wallace	.10
308	Lee Woodall	.10
309	Bryant Young	.10
310	Steve Young	1.50
311	Sam Adams	.10
312	Howard Ballard	.10
313	Robert Blackman	.10
314	Brian Blades	.10
315	*Joey Galloway*	2.50
316	Carlton Gray	.10
317	Cortez Kennedy	.10
318	Rick Mirer	.20
319	Eugene Robinson	.10
320	Chris Warren	.20
321	Terry Wooden	.10
322	Derrick Brooks	.20
323	Lawrence Dawsey	.10
324	Trent Dilfer	.75
325	Santana Dotson	.10
326	Thomas Everett	.10
327	Paul Gruber	.10
328	Jackie Harris	.10
329	Courtney Hawkins	.10
330	Martin Mayhew	.10
331	Hardy Nickerson	.10
332	Errict Rhett	1.50
333	*Warren Sapp*	1.00
334	Charles Wilson	.10
335	Reggie Brooks	.10
336	Tom Carter	.10
337	Henry Ellard	.10
338	Ricky Ervins	.10
339	Darrell Green	.10
340	Ken Harvey	.10
341	Brian Mitchell	.10
342	Cory Raymer	.20
343	Heath Shuler	1.00
344	*Michael Westbrook*	1.50
345	Tony Woods	.10
346	Checklist	.10
347	Checklist	.10
348	Checklist	.10
349	Checklist	.10
350	Checklist	.10
351	Checklist	.10
352	Checklist	.10
353	Dave Krieg	.10
354	Rob Moore	.10
355	J.J. Birden	.10
356	Eric Metcalf	.10
357	Bryce Paup	.10
358	Willie Green	.10
359	Derrick Moore	.10
360	Michael Timpson	.10
361	Eric Bieniemy	.10
362	Keenan McCardell	.10
363	Andre Rison	.20
364	Lorenzo White	.10
365	Deion Sanders	1.00
366	Wade Wilson	.10
367	Aaron Craver	.10
368	Michael Dean Perry	.10
369	*Rod Smith*	15.00
370	Henry Thomas	.10
371	Mark Ingram	.10
372	Chris Chandler	.10
373	Mel Gray	.10
374	Flipper Anderson	.10
375	Craig Erickson	.10
376	Mark Brunell	1.50
377	Ernest Givens	.10
378	Randy Jordan	.10
379	Webster Slaughter	.10
380	*Tamarick Vanover*	1.50
381	Gary Clark	.10
382	Steve Emtman	.10
383	Eric Green	.10
384	Louis Oliver	.10
385	Robert Smith	.10
386	David Meggett	.10
387	Eric Allen	.10
388	Wesley Walls	.10
389	Herschel Walker	.10
390	Ronald Moore	.10
391	Adrian Murrell	.20
392	Charles Wilson	.10
393	Derrick Fenner	.10
394	Pat Swilling	.10
395	Kelvin Martin	.10
396	Rodney Peete	.10
397	Ricky Watters	.20
398	Erric Pegram	.10
399	Leonard Russell	.10
400	Alexander Wright	.10
401	Darrien Gordon	.10
402	Alfred Pupunu	.10
403	Elvis Grbac	.10
404	Derek Loville	.20
405	Steve Broussard	.10
406	Ricky Proehl	.10
407	Bobby Joe Edmonds	.10
408	Alvin Harper	.10
409	Dave Moore	.10
410	Terry Allen	.10
411	Gus Frerotte	.50
412	*Leslie Shepherd*	.20
413	*Stoney Case*	.75
414	*Frank Sanders*	1.50
415	*Roell Preston*	.20
416	*Lorenzo Styles*	.20
417	*Justin Armour*	.20
418	*Todd Collins*	.20
419	*Darick Holmes*	1.50
420	Kerry Collins	1.00
421	*Tyrone Poole*	.20
422	Rashaan Salaam	.30
423	*Todd Sauerbrun*	.20
424	Ki-Jana Carter	1.50
425	*David Dunn*	.20
426	*Earnest Hunter*	.20

427	*Eric Zeier*	1.00
428	*Eric Bjorson*	.20
429	*Sherman Williams*	.20
430	*Terrell Davis*	8.00
431	*Luther Elliss*	.20
432	*Kez McCorvey*	.20
433	*Antonio Freeman*	2.00
434	*Craig Newsome*	.20
435	Steve McNair	2.00
436	*Chris Sanders*	1.50
437	*Zack Crockett*	.20
438	*Ellis Johnson*	.20
439	*Tony Boselli*	.20
440	James Stewart	.30
441	*J.J. Smith*	.20
442	Tamarick Vanover	1.50
443	*Derrick Alexander*	.20
444	*Chad May*	.20
445	*James Stewart*	.50
446	*Ty Law*	.20
447	*Curtis Martin*	4.00
448	*Will Moore*	.20
449	*Mark Fields*	.20
450	*Ray Zellars*	.20
451	*Charles Way*	.20
452	Tyrone Wheatley	1.00
453	*Kyle Brady*	.20
454	*Wayne Chrebet*	1.00
455	Hugh Douglas	.20
456	*Chris Jones*	1.00
457	*Mike Mamula*	.20
458	*Fred McCrary*	.20
459	*Bobby Taylor*	.20
460	Mark Bruener	.40
461	Kordell Stewart	2.00
462	*Kevin Carter*	.20
463	*Lovell Pinckney*	.20
464	*Johnny Thomas*	.20
465	*Terrell Fletcher*	.50
466	*Jimmy Oliver*	.20
467	J.J. Stokes	1.00
468	*Christian Fauria*	.20
469	Joey Galloway	2.00
470	*Derrick Brooks*	.20
471	Warren Sapp	.20
472	Michael Westbrook	.75
473	Garrison Hearst	.20
474	Jeff George	.20
475	Terance Mathis	.10
476	Andre Reed	.10
477	Bruce Smith	.10
478	Lamar Lathon	.10
479	Curtis Conway	.20
480	Jeff Blake	1.50
481	Carl Pickens	.20
482	Eric Turner	.10
483	Troy Aikman	.75
484	Michael Irvin	.20
485	Emmitt Smith	1.50
486	John Elway	.20
487	Shannon Sharpe	.10
488	Herman Moore	.20
489	Barry Sanders	1.00
490	Brett Favre	1.00
491	Reggie White	.20
492	Haywood Jeffires	.10
493	Sean Dawkins	.10
494	Marshall Faulk	1.00
495	Desmond Howard	.10
496	Steve Bono	.20
497	Derrick Thomas	.20
498	Irving Fryar	.10
499	Terry Kirby	.10
500	Dan Marino	1.75
501	O.J. McDuffie	.10
502	Cris Carter	.10
503	Warren Moon	.20
504	Jake Reed	.10
505	Drew Bledsoe	.75
506	Ben Coates	.10
507	Jim Everett	.10
508	Rodney Hampton	.10
509	Mo Lewis	.10
510	Tim Brown	.20
511	Jeff Hostetler	.20
512	Raghib Ismail	.10
513	Chester McGlockton	.10
514	Fred Barnett	.10
515	Greg Lloyd	.10
516	Bam Morris	.20
517	Rod Woodson	.10
518	Jerome Bettis	.20
519	Isaac Bruce	.75
520	Stan Humphries	.20
521	Natrone Means	.20
522	Junior Seau	.20
523	William Floyd	.20
524	Jerry Rice	.75
525	Steve Young	.75
526	Cortez Kennedy	.10
527	Rick Mirer	.20
528	Chris Warren	.20
529	Trent Dilfer	.20
530	Errict Rhett	.75
531	Darrell Green	.10
532	Heath Shuler	.50
533	Stoney Case	.10
534	Eric Zeier	.50
535	Kerry Collins	1.00
536	Steve McNair	1.50
537	Kordell Stewart	2.00
538	*Rob Johnson*	3.00
539	Eric Ball	.10
540	Darrick Brownlow	.10
541	Paul Butcher	.10
542	Carlester Crumpler	.10
543	Maurice Douglas	.10
544	Keith Elias	.10
545	Kenneth Gant	.10
546	Corey Harris	.10
547	Andre Hastings	.10
548	Thomas Holmco	.10
549	Lenny McGill	.10
550	Mark Pike	.10

1995 Ultra Gold Medallion

Ultra Gold Medallions paralleled the regular-issue set with the same photo, but a gold foil background. Gold Medallions were found at a rate of one per pack.

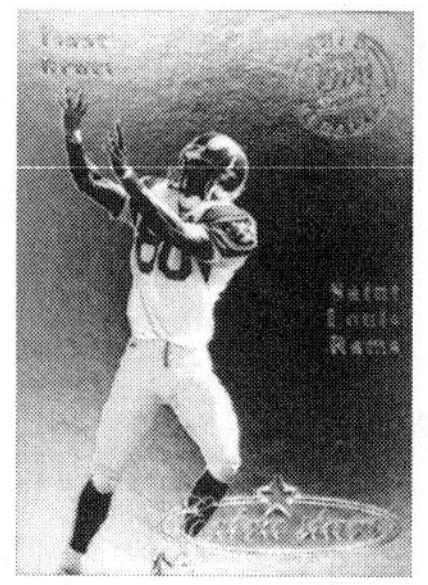

	MT
Complete Set (550):	350.00
Complete Series 1 (350):	200.00
Complete Series 2 (200):	150.00
Gold Medallion Cards:	3x-6x

1995 Ultra Achievements

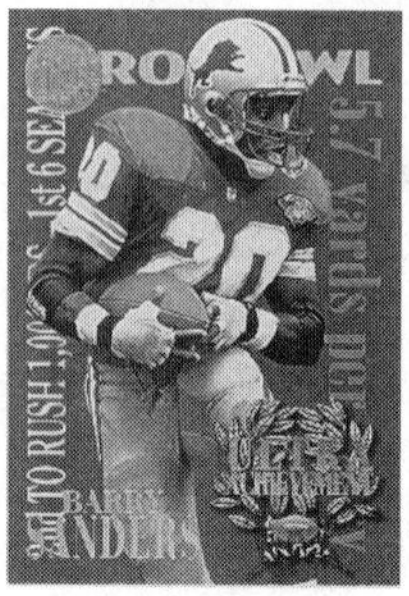

These 1995 Fleer Ultra Series I inserts feature 10 of the league's top performers. Cards were randomly included one per every seven packs. The card front has a color action photo, with the player's name and Ultra Achievement and Ultra logos stamped in gold. Running inside the card format are the player's achievements from the 1994 season. The card back, numbered 1 of 10, etc., has another color photo, with a box superimposed over the photo to provide a summary of the player's season recap. The achievements listed along the front borders repeat on the back.

		MT
Complete Set (10):		10.00
Common Player:		.50
Comp. Gold Set (10):		30.00
Gold Cards:		1x-2x
1	Drew Bledsoe	3.00
2	Cris Carter	.50
3	Ben Coates	.50
4	Mel Gray	.50
5	Jerry Rice	2.00
6	Barry Sanders	3.00
7	Deion Sanders	1.50
8	Herschel Walker	.50
9	DeWayne Washington	.50
10	Steve Young	2.00

1995 Ultra All-Rookie Team

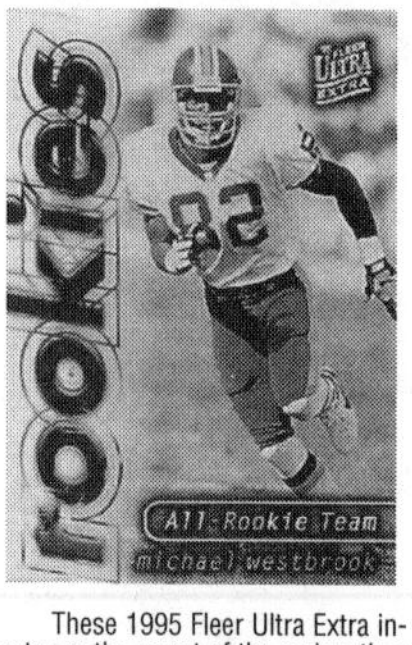

These 1995 Fleer Ultra Extra inserts are the rarest of the series; they can be found one in every 55 packs. The cards are acetate and feature the top 10 rookies from the 1995 season. "Rookies" is written along one border of the card.

		MT
Complete Set (10):		160.00
Common Player:		10.00
Hot Pack Cards Half Price		
1	Michael Westbrook	15.00
2	Terrell Davis	40.00
3	Curtis Martin	30.00
4	Joey Galloway	20.00
5	Rashaan Salaam	10.00
6	J.J. Stokes	15.00
7	Napoleon Kaufman	20.00
8	Mike Mamula	10.00
9	Kyle Brady	10.00
10	Hugh Douglas	10.00

1995 Ultra Award Winners

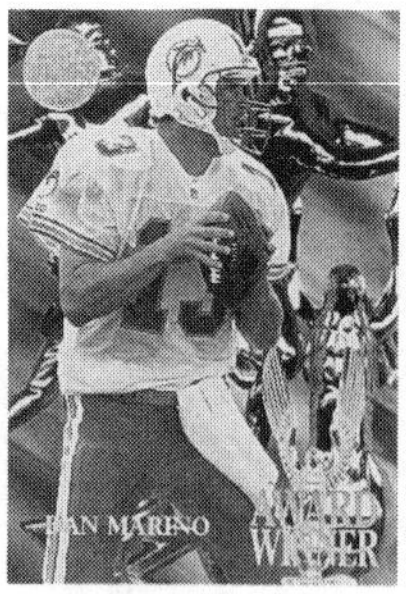

These 1995 Fleer Ultra Series I inserts could be found one per every five packs. They feature six players who captured postseason awards after the 1994 season ended. The card front has a color photo of the player superimposed over a collage of the award he won. His name and the Ultra and Award Winner logos are stamped in gold. The player's name is also in gold on the back, which is numbered 1 of 6, etc. The back has a player photo on one half of the card, with a recap of why he won the specific award. The award trophy collage is again used for the background.

		MT
Complete Set (6):		10.00
Common Player:		.50
Comp. Gold Set (6):		20.00
Gold Cards:		1x-2x
1	Tim Bowens	.50
2	Marshall Faulk	1.25
3	Dan Marino	3.00
4	Barry Sanders	2.00
5	Deion Sanders	1.00
6	Steve Young	1.25

1995 Ultra First Rounders

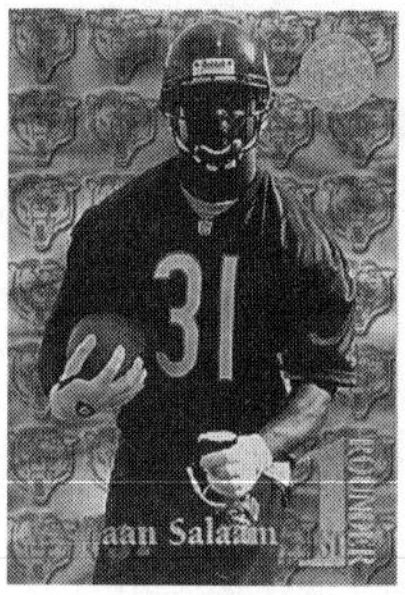

These 1995 Fleer Ultra Series I inserts feature 20 of the top selections from the 1995 draft. The cards could be found one per every seven packs. The card front uses gold stamping for the Fleer Ultra and insert set logos, plus the player's name. A player photo is superimposed against a background collage of his team's logo. The back, numbered 1 of 20, etc., has the same collage as a background, plus a smaller player photo and a draft analysis of the player. His name also appears in gold at the top of the card.

		MT
Complete Set (20):		35.00
Common Player:		.50
Comp. Gold Set (20):		75.00
Gold Cards:		1x-2x
1	Derrick Alexander	.50
2	Tony Boselli	1.00
3	Kyle Brady	1.00
4	Mark Bruener	.50
5	Devin Bush	.50
6	Kevin Carter	.50
7	Ki-Jana Carter	3.00
8	Kerry Collins	2.00
9	Mark Fields	.50
10	Joe Galloway	5.00
11	Napoleon Kaufman	2.00
12	Ty Law	.50
13	Mike Mamula	.50
14	Steve McNair	6.00
15	Rashaan Salaam	3.00
16	Warren Sapp	1.00
17	James Stewart	1.00
18	J.J. Stokes	2.00
19	Michael Westbrook	2.00
20	Tyrone Wheatley	1.00

1995 Ultra Magna Force

These 1995 Fleer Ultra Extra inserts feature 20 top NFL stars and were random inserts in retail packs only, one every 20 packs.

		MT
Complete Set (20):		110.00
Common Player:		2.00
1	Emmitt Smith	20.00
2	Jerry Rice	10.00
3	Drew Bledsoe	10.00
4	Marshall Faulk	10.00
5	Heath Shuler	3.00
6	Carl Pickens	3.00
7	Ben Coates	2.00
8	Terry Allen	2.00
9	Terance Mathis	2.00
10	Fred Barnett	2.00
11	O.J. McDuffie	2.00
12	Garrison Hearst	3.00
13	Deion Sanders	6.00
14	Reggie White	3.00
15	Herman Moore	3.00
16	Brett Favre	20.00
17	William Floyd	3.00
18	Curtis Martin	20.00
19	Joey Galloway	12.00
20	Tyrone Wheatley	4.00

1995 Ultra Overdrive

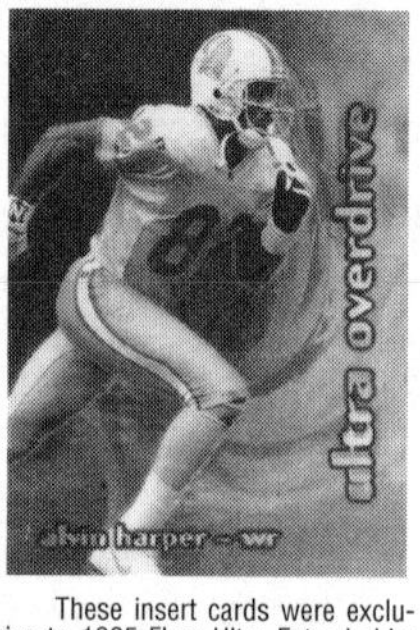

These insert cards were exclusive to 1995 Fleer Ultra Extra hobby packs, one per every 20 packs. The card fronts have a metallic shine to them, with a color action photo in the center. Ultra Overdrive appears along the right border. The player's name and position are in the lower left corner. The card back, numbered one of twenty, etc., features a ghosted image of an action photo, with a square around the player's head, which is in color. A brief player profile is also given.

		MT
Complete Set (20):		100.00
Common Player:		2.00
1	Barry Sanders	10.00
2	Troy Aikman	10.00
3	Natrone Means	3.00
4	Steve Young	10.00
5	Errict Rhett	2.00
6	Terrell Davis	14.00
7	Michael Westbrook	2.00
8	Michael Irvin	3.00
9	Chris Warren	3.00
10	Tim Brown	2.00
11	Jerome Bettis	2.00
12	Ricky Watters	2.00
13	Derrick Thomas	2.00
14	Bruce Smith	2.00
15	Rashaan Salaam	4.00
16	Jeff Blake	2.00
17	Alvin Harper	2.00
18	Shannon Sharpe	2.00
19	Eric Swann	2.00
20	Andre Rison	2.00

1995 Ultra Rising Stars

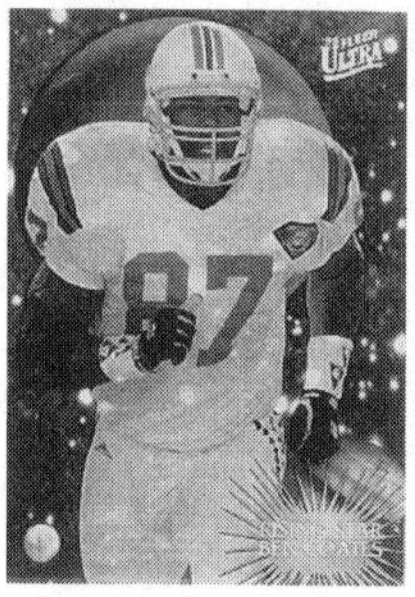

These inserts were randomly included one in every 37 packs, making them the scarcest of the 1995 Fleer Ultra Series I inserts. These nine cards, numbered 1 of 9, etc., are printed on acetate with an "ultra crystal" planetary design. The front has a color photo, with the player, set and insert set names in gold foil. The back, numbered 1 of 9, etc., also uses gold for the player name. He is pictured again as the background, with a brief career summary superimposed over it.

		MT
Complete Set (9):		60.00
Common Player:		3.00
Comp. Gold Set (9):		120.00
Gold Cards:		1x-2x
1	Jerome Bettis	3.00
2	Jeff Blake	7.00
3	Drew Bledsoe	15.00
4	Ben Coates	3.00
5	Marshall Faulk	8.00
6	Brett Favre	25.00
7	Natrone Means	6.00
8	Bam Morris	6.00
9	Eric Turner	3.00

A player's name in *italic type* indicates a rookie card.

1995 Ultra Second Year Standouts

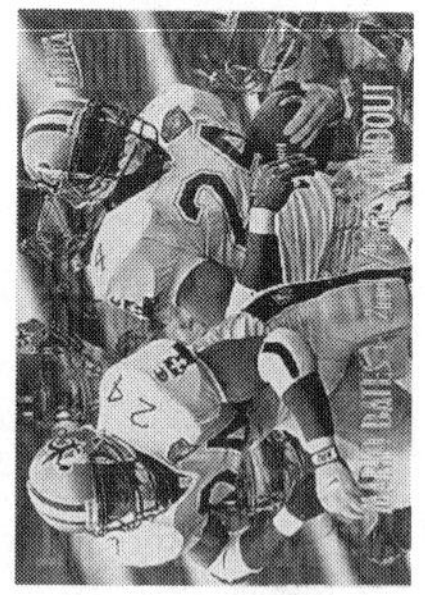

This horizontally-designed insert set was featured in 1995 Fleer Ultra Series I packs, one per every five packs. The front uses gold stamping for the set and insert set logos, plus the name of the player, who is pictured twice. A team helmet collage is used for the background. The back, also horizontal, is numbered 1 of 15, etc., and features one of the players chosen as a top sophomore in the NFL. A color photo and brief recap of the player's rookie season accomplishments are also on the back. His name is in gold. The background says "2nd Year Standout" in a repeated pattern.

		MT
Complete Set (15):		15.00
Common Player:		.50
Comp. Gold Set (15):		30.00
Gold Cards:		1x-2x
1	Derrick Alexander	.50
2	Mario Bates	.50
3	Tim Bowens	.50
4	Bert Emanuel	1.25
5	Marshall Faulk	4.00
6	William Floyd	2.00
7	Rob Fredrickson	.50
8	Antonio Langham	.50
9	Bam Morris	2.00
10	Errict Rhett	3.00
11	Darnay Scott	.50
12	Heath Shuler	2.00
13	DeWayne Washington	.50
14	Dan Wilkinson	.50
15	Bryant Young	.50

1995 Ultra Ultra Stars

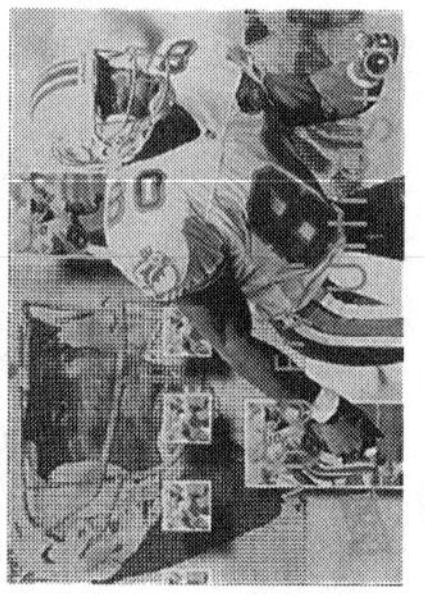

These 1995 Fleer Ultra Series I inserts were included one per every seven 17-card packs. They feature 10 of the NFL's top players. The horizontal card front has a larger photo of the player, against a collage of the same photo in different sizes and color patterns. Silver stamping is used for the player's name and set and insert set logos. The back, numbered 1 of 10, etc., uses silver foil and a horizontal format. A color photo is on one half of the card; a brief career summary comprises the other.

		MT
Complete Set (10):		15.00
Common Player:		.50
Comp. Gold Med. Set (10):		30.00
Gold Med. Cards:		1x-2x
1	Tim Brown	.50
2	Marshall Faulk	2.00
3	Irving Fryar	.50
4	Dan Marino	4.00
5	Natrone Means	.50
6	Jerry Rice	2.00
7	Barry Sanders	3.00
8	Deion Sanders	1.50
9	Emmitt Smith	4.00
10	Rod Woodson	.50

1995 Ultra Touchdown Kings

These 1995 Fleer Ultra Series I inserts feature 10 of the NFL's top touchdown scorers from 1994. The cards were random inserts, one every seventh 12-card packs. The front uses gold stamping for the player's name and insert and set logos. A TD with a crown on top of it appears in the lower right corner. A color player photo is superimposed against a crystal-like "TD"/football background. The card back, numbered 1 of 10, etc., has a color photo on one side; a recap of the player's scoring accomplishments from 1994 are on the other. Gold foil stamping is used for the number and player's name.

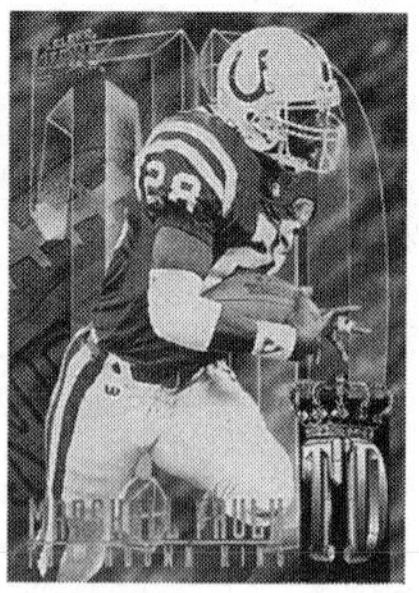

		MT
Complete Set (10):		10.00
Common Player:		.50
Comp. Gold Set (10):		20.00
Gold Cards:		1x-2x
1	Marshall Faulk	2.00
2	Terance Mathis	.50
3	Natrone Means	.50
4	Herman Moore	.50
5	Carl Pickens	1.00
6	Jerry Rice	2.00
7	Andre Rison	.50
8	Emmitt Smith	3.00
9	Chris Warren	.50
10	Steve Young	2.00

1995 Ultra Ultrabilities

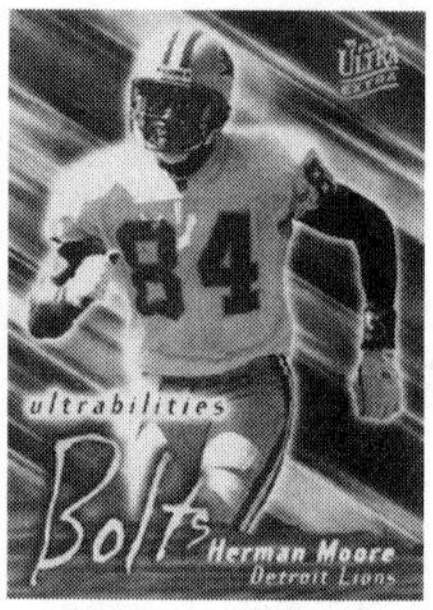

These 1995 Fleer Ultra Extra inserts could be found one per every five packs. The 30 cards are broken into three subsets of 10 cards each - Guns (quarterbacks), Bolts (receivers and running backs) and Blasts (hard-hitting defensive players and running backs). The respective subset name is on the card front in gold foil, along with the word Ultrabilities. The background is orange; the player's name is in white in a colored panel at the bottom. Each card back is numbered 1 of 30, etc., and includes a mug shot of the player, plus a ghosted image of him in action. A brief player profile is also provided. Near a team logo in the upper left corner is the player's name, in his team's primary uniform color. A word describing a key element of the player's skills is written along the right side of the card.

		MT
Complete Set (30):		65.00
Common Player:		1.00
1	Dan Marino (Guns)	10.00
2	Steve Young (Guns)	6.00
3	Drew Bledsoe (Guns)	6.00
4	Jeff Blake (Guns)	2.00
5	Troy Aikman (Guns)	6.00
6	John Elway (Guns)	4.00
7	Trent Dilfer (Guns)	3.00
8	Steve Bono (Guns)	2.00
9	Brett Favre (Guns)	10.00
10	Kerry Collins (Guns)	2.00
11	Barry Sanders (Bolts)	6.00
12	Errict Rhett (Bolts)	1.00
13	Emmitt Smith (Bolts)	10.00
14	Chris Warren (Bolts)	2.00
15	Irving Fryar (Bolts)	1.00
16	Charlie Garner (Bolts)	1.00
17	Joey Galloway (Bolts)	8.00
18	Eric Metcalf (Bolts)	1.00
19	Herman Moore (Bolts)	2.00
20	Robert Smith (Bolts)	1.00
21	Natrone Means (Blasts)	3.00
22	Derrick Thomas (Blasts)	1.00
23	Bruce Smith (Blasts)	1.00
24	Hugh Douglas (Blasts)	1.00
25	Mike Mamula (Blasts)	1.00
26	Jerome Bettis (Blasts)	2.00
27	Bam Morris (Blasts)	3.00
28	Tim Bowens (Blasts)	1.00
29	William Floyd (Blasts)	3.00
30	Daryl Johnston (Blasts)	1.00

1996 Ultra

Fleer's 1996 Ultra football set is packed with rookies - 55 in all - featured as cards in a subset and two insert sets. The 15-card subset has the rookies in their college uniforms, with their new NFL team logos. Insert sets

featuring rookies include a 30-card Ultra Rookies set and a 10-card All-Rookie Team set. Two other subsets were also produced for the 200-card set - First Impressions and Secret Weapons. The other insert card sets are Mr. Momentum, Sledgehammer, and Pulsating. Similar to last year's format, both NFC and AFC cards feature unique designs, with NFC players' last names printed against a blue background while a red background is used for AFC stars. 1995 Pro Bowl player cards have a special Pro Bowl designation. Each regular card has a full-bleed color action photo on the front. The back also has a color action photo, plus a ghosted image which has a recap of the player's 1995 season. Above the recap and along the top are 1995 and career totals; the player's name, team logo and biographical information are below. A card number is in the upper left corner of the horizontally-designed card back.

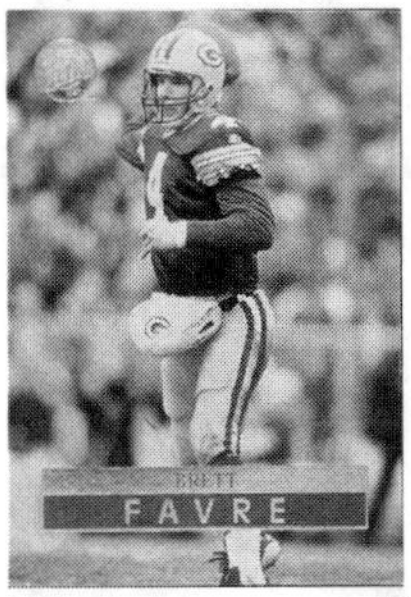

		MT
Complete Set (200):		35.00
Common Player:		.10
Minor Stars:		.20
Pack (12):		2.50
Wax Box (24):		50.00
1	Larry Centers	.10
2	Garrison Hearst	.20
3	Rob Moore	.20
4	Eric Swann	.10
5	Aeneas Williams	.10
6	Bert Emanuel	.10
7	Jeff George	.20
8	Craig Heyward	.10
9	Terance Mathis	.10
10	Eric Metcalf	.10
11	Cornelius Bennett	.10
12	Darick Holmes	.20
13	Jim Kelly	.50
14	Bryce Paup	.10
15	Bruce Smith	.20
16	Mark Carrier	.10
17	Kerry Collins	.50
18	Lamar Lathon	.10
19	Derrick Moore	.10
20	Tyrone Poole	.10
21	Curtis Conway	.20
22	Jeff Graham	.10
23	Raymont Harris	.10
24	Erik Kramer	.10
25	Rashaan Salaam	.50
26	Jeff Blake	.50
27	Ki-Jana Carter	.20
28	Carl Pickens	.20
29	Darnay Scott	.20
30	Dan Wilkinson	.10
31	Leroy Hoard	.10
32	Michael Jackson	.10
33	Andre Rison	.10
34	Vinny Testaverde	.50
35	Eric Turner	.10
36	Troy Aikman	1.50
37	Charles Haley	.10
38	Michael Irvin	.20
39	Daryl Johnston	.10
40	Jay Novacek	.10
41	Deion Sanders	.75
42	Emmitt Smith	2.00
43	Steve Atwater	.10
44	Terrell Davis	4.00
45	John Elway	2.00
46	Anthony Miller	.10
47	Shannon Sharpe	.50
48	Scott Mitchell	.20
49	Herman Moore	.50
50	Johnnie Morton	.10
51	Brett Perriman	.10
52	Barry Sanders	3.00
53	Chris Spielman	.10
54	Edgar Bennett	.10
55	Robert Brooks	.20
56	Mark Chmura	.20
57	Brett Favre	3.00
58	Reggie White	.50
59	Mel Gray	.10
60	Haywood Jeffires	.10
61	Steve McNair	1.25
62	Chris Sanders	.20
63	Rodney Thomas	.20
64	Quentin Coryatt	.10
65	Sean Dawkins	.10
66	Ken Dilger	.10
67	Marshall Faulk	.50
68	Jim Harbaugh	.20
69	Tony Boselli	.10
70	Mark Brunell	1.50
71	Desmond Howard	.10
72	Jimmy Smith	.50
73	James Stewart	.10
74	Marcus Allen	.50
75	Steve Bono	.20
76	Lake Dawson	.10
77	Neil Smith	.10
78	Derrick Thomas	.20
79	Tamarick Vanover	.20
80	Bryan Cox	.10
81	Irving Fryar	.10
82	Eric Green	.10
83	Dan Marino	2.00
84	O.J. McDuffie	.20
85	Bernie Parmalee	.10
86	Cris Carter	.50
87	Qadry Ismail	.10
88	Warren Moon	.20
89	Jake Reed	.20
90	Robert Smith	.50
91	Drew Bledsoe	1.50
92	Vincent Brisby	.10
93	Ben Coates	.50
94	Curtis Martin	1.25
95	Willie McGinest	.10
96	David Meggett	.10
97	Mario Bates	.20
98	Quinn Early	.10
99	Jim Everett	.20
100	Michael Haynes	.10
101	Renaldo Turnbull	.10
102	Dave Brown	.10
103	Rodney Hampton	.20
104	Mike Sherrard	.10
105	Phillippi Sparks	.10
106	Tyrone Wheatley	.20
107	Hugh Douglas	.10
108	Boomer Esiason	.20
109	Aaron Glenn	.10
110	Mo Lewis	.10
111	Johnny Mitchell	.10
112	Tim Brown	.50
113	Jeff Hostetler	.10
114	Raghib Ismail	.10
115	Chester McGlockton	.10
116	Harvey Williams	.10
117	Fred Barnett	.10
118	William Fuller	.10
119	Charlie Garner	.20
120	Ricky Watters	.50
121	Calvin Williams	.10
122	Kevin Greene	.10
123	Greg Lloyd	.10
124	Bam Morris	.20
125	Neil O'Donnell	.20
126	Erric Pegram	.10
127	Kordell Stewart	2.00
128	Yancey Thigpen	.50
129	Rod Woodson	.10
130	Jerome Bettis	.50
131	Isaac Bruce	.50
132	Troy Drayton	.10
133	Sean Gilbert	.10
134	Chris Miller	.10
135	Andre Coleman	.10
136	Ronnie Harmon	.10
137	Aaron Hayden	.20
138	Stan Humphries	.20
139	Natrone Means	.50
140	Junior Seau	.20
141	William Floyd	.10
142	Merton Hanks	.10
143	Brent Jones	.10
144	Derek Loville	.10
145	Jerry Rice	1.50
146	J.J. Stokes	.50
147	Steve Young	1.25
148	Brian Blades	.10
149	Joey Galloway	1.00
150	Cortez Kennedy	.10
151	Rick Mirer	.20
152	Chris Warren	.20
153	Derrick Brooks	.10
154	Trent Dilfer	.50
155	Alvin Harper	.10
156	Jackie Harris	.10
157	Hardy Nickerson	.10
158	Errict Rhett	.20
159	Terry Allen	.20
160	Henry Ellard	.10
161	Brian Mitchell	.10
162	Heath Shuler	.20
163	Michael Westbrook	.20
164	*Tim Biakabutuka*	1.25
165	*Tony Brackens*	.20
166	*Rickey Dudley*	.75
167	*Bobby Engram*	.30
168	*Daryl Gardener*	.10
169	*Eddie George*	4.00
170	*Terry Glenn*	2.00
171	*Kevin Hardy*	.20
172	*Keyshawn Johnson*	2.50
173	*Cedric Jones*	.10
174	*Leeland McElroy*	.30
175	*Jonathan Ogden*	.20
176	*Lawrence Phillips*	.75
177	*Simeon Rice*	.20
178	*Regan Upshaw*	.10
179	Justin Armour (First Impressions)	.10
180	Kyle Brady (First Impressions)	.10
181	Devin Bush (First Impressions)	.10
182	Kevin Carter (First Impressions)	.10
183	Wayne Chrebet (First Impressions)	.50
184	Napoleon Kaufman (First Impressions)	.75
185	Frank Sanders (First Impressions)	.20
186	Warren Sapp (First Impressions)	.10
187	Eric Zeier (First Impressions)	.10
188	Ray Zellars (First Impressions)	.10
189	Bill Brooks (Secret Weapons)	.10
190	Chris Calloway (Secret Weapons)	.10
191	Zack Crockett (Secret Weapons)	.10
192	Antonio Freeman (Secret Weapons)	1.00
193	Tyrone Hughes (Secret Weapons)	.10
194	Daryl Johnston (Secret Weapons)	.10
195	Tony Martin (Secret Weapons)	.10
196	Keenan McCardell (Secret Weapons)	.10
197	Glyn Milburn (Secret Weapons)	.10
198	David Palmer (Secret Weapons)	.10
199	Checklist	.10
200	Checklist	.10

1996 Ultra All-Rookie Die Cuts

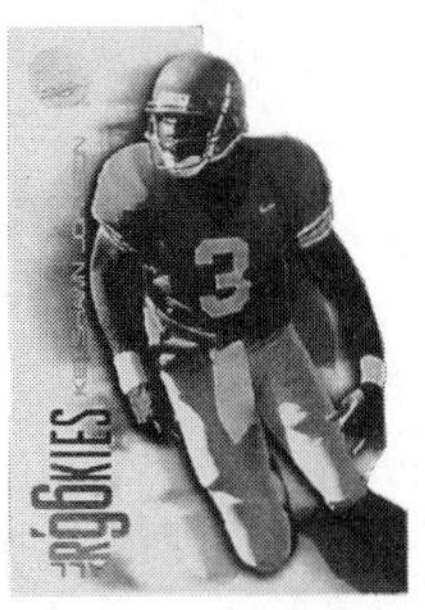

These 10 cards feature the top picks in the 1996 NFL Draft. The cards, which use a die-cut design, show the player in his college uniform. Red-foil stamping is used for "All Rookies," which is written along the left side of the card, below the player's name and foil-stamped Ultra logo. The card back has a ghosted player action photo on one side, with a smaller color action photo on the other. The player's name is at the top, next to a card number (1 of 10, etc.). Below the photo is a recap of the skills the player showed while he was in college. "All Rookies" is also stamped in red foil on the back. Cards were randomly inserted in 1996 Fleer Ultra packs, one every 180 packs.

		MT
Complete Set (10):		150.00
Common Player:		6.00
Minor Stars:		12.00
Inserted 1:180		
1	Bobby Engram	12.00
2	Daryl Gardener	6.00
3	Eddie George	50.00
4	Terry Glenn	20.00
5	Kevin Hardy	6.00
6	Keyshawn Johnson	30.00
7	Cedric Jones	6.00
8	Leeland McElroy	6.00
9	Jonathan Ogden	6.00
10	Simeon Rice	6.00

1996 Ultra Mr. Momentum

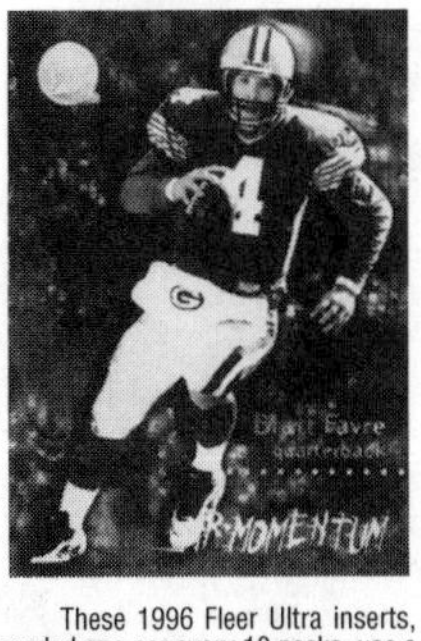

These 1996 Fleer Ultra inserts, seeded one per every 10 packs, use a holographic foil background to showcase players who jump start their teams. Gold foil stamping is used for the player's name, position, brand logo and "Mr. Momentum." The card back has a color photo in the background, with a card number (1 of 20, etc.) in the upper left corner. The player's name, team name and team logo are underneath. In the middle of the card is a recap of the player's 1995 season, and how he can sway the outcome of a game.

		MT
Complete Set (20):		45.00
Common Player:		1.00
Minor Stars:		2.00
Inserted 1:10		
1	Robert Brooks	1.00
2	Isaac Bruce	2.00
3	Terrell Davis	8.00
4	John Elway	6.00
5	Marshall Faulk	2.00
6	Brett Favre	8.00
7	Joey Galloway	2.00
8	Dan Marino	6.00
9	Curtis Martin	4.00
10	Herman Moore	2.00
11	Carl Pickens	1.00
12	Jerry Rice	4.00
13	Barry Sanders	8.00
14	Chris Sanders	1.00
15	Deion Sanders	2.00
16	Kordell Stewart	4.00
17	Tamarick Vanover	1.00
18	Chris Warren	1.00
19	Ricky Watters	2.00
20	Steve Young	3.00

1996 Ultra Pulsating

These 1996 Fleer Ultra inserts feature 10 of the NFL's most thrilling players. The special foil-enhanced cards were seeded one per every 20 packs. Gold foil stamping is used on the card front for the player's name, brand logo and a gold bar at the bottom, which has the word "Pulsating" etched into it. The back has a wavy pattern to it, similar to the foil design on the front. A color photo is in the card's center, with a wavy-lined recap of the player's 1995 season below. Gold foil is used for the player's name at the top, next to a card number (1 of 10, etc.).

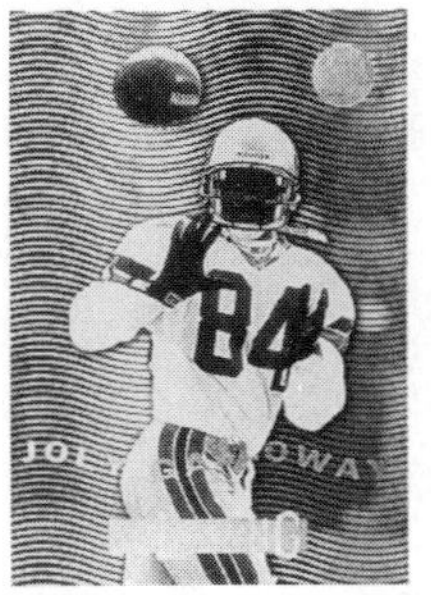

		MT
Complete Set (10):		40.00
Common Player:		1.00
Minor Stars:		2.00
Inserted 1:20		
1	Isaac Bruce	2.00
2	Brett Favre	10.00
3	Joey Galloway	2.00
4	Curtis Martin	4.00
5	Rashaan Salaam	1.00
6	Barry Sanders	10.00
7	Deion Sanders	3.00
8	Emmitt Smith	8.00
9	Kordell Stewart	5.00
10	Chris Warren	1.00

1996 Ultra Rookies

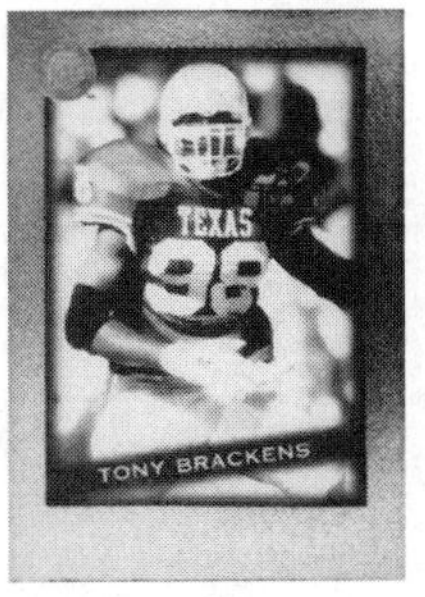

Thirty of the NFL's top 1996 draft picks are featured on these 1996 Fleer Ultra inserts. The cards, seeded one per every three packs, have gold foil borders around a color action photo on the front. The Ultra logo and "Ultra Rookies" are incorporated into the border. A color stripe at the bottom has the player's name inside. The back has a square in the center containing another color photo, with biographical information below. Ultra Rookies is written at the top of the card, with the player's name and card number (1 of 30, etc.) in a color band below.

		MT
Complete Set (30):		45.00
Common Player:		1.00
Minor Stars:		2.00
Inserted 1:3		
1	Karim Abdul-Jabbar	4.00
2	Mike Alstott	4.00
3	Marco Battaglia	1.00
4	Tim Biakabutuka	2.00
5	Sean Boyd	1.00
6	Tony Brackens	1.00
7	Duane Clemons	1.00
8	Bobby Engram	2.00
9	Daryl Gardener	1.00
10	Eddie George	10.00
11	Terry Glenn	4.00
12	Kevin Hardy	1.00
13	Marvin Harrison	3.00
14	Dietrich Jells	1.00
15	Keyshawn Johnson	6.00
16	Lance Johnstone	1.00
17	Cedric Jones	1.00
18	Marcus Jones	1.00
19	Danny Kanell	2.00
20	Markco Maddox	1.00
21	Derrick Mayes	2.00
22	Leeland McElroy	1.00
23	Dell McGee	1.00
24	Alex Molden	1.00
25	Eric Moulds	5.00
26	Jonathan Ogden	1.00
27	Lawrence Phillips	2.00
28	Simeon Rice	1.00
29	Regan Upshaw	1.00
30	Jerome Woods	1.00

1996 Ultra Sledgehammer

These embossed cards, seeded one per every 15th 1996 Fleer Ultra hobby packs, feature the NFL's power players on both sides of the ball. The embossed front has a raised color action photo on it, with Sledgehammer written along the left side of the card. A logo appears in the lower left corner, framed in gold foil. The player's name is near the bottom in a white stripe; the brand logo is in the upper right corner. The card back has another color photo, with a colored square on it that summarizes the player's skills. The player's team name is written in his team's colors at the top, opposite a card number (1 of 10, etc.). The player's name appears toward the bottom of the card.

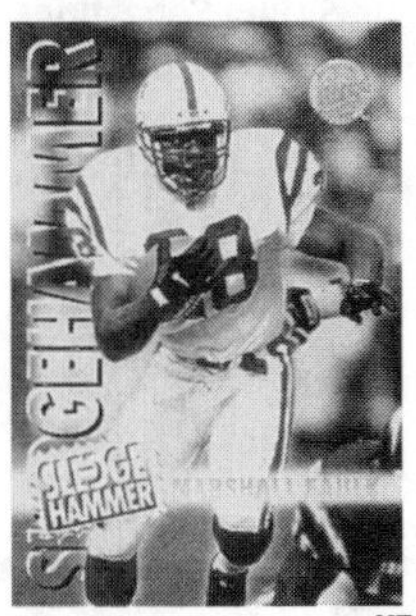

		MT
Complete Set (10):		45.00
Common Player:		2.00
Minor Stars:		4.00
Inserted 1:15 Hobby		
1	Jeff Blake	4.00
2	Terrell Davis	15.00
3	Hugh Douglas	2.00
4	Marshall Faulk	5.00
5	Michael Irvin	4.00
6	Steve McNair	7.00
7	Natrone Means	4.00
8	Errict Rhett	2.00
9	Emmitt Smith	10.00
10	Rodney Thomas	2.00

1996 Ultra Sensations

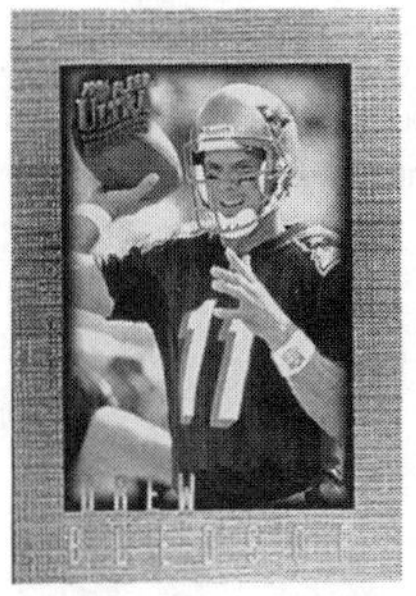

Ultra Sensations was a Series II product, but didn't resemble the Series I release. Instead it went a new direction with 100 cards that appeared in five different versions. Forty percent of the print run had gold borders, 30 percent blue, 20 percent marbleized gold, nine percent pewter and one percent holographic gold foil. The only differentiation between any of the versions was a thick border around the entire card. Ultra Sensations included two inserts: Creative Chaos and Random Rookies.

		MT
Complete Gold Set (100):		20.00
Common Player:		.10
Minor Stars:		.20
Blue Cards:		1.5x
Marbleized Gold Cards:		2x
Pewter Cards:		4x
Holographic Gold Cards:		15x
Pack (10):		2.50
Wax Box (24):		45.00
1	*Leeland McElroy*	.30
2	Frank Sanders	.10
3	Eric Swann	.10
4	Jeff George	.10
5	Terrance Mathis	.10
6	Eric Metcalf	.10
7	Michael Jackson	.10
8	Eric Turner	.10
9	Jim Kelly	.10
10	Bryce Paup	.10
11	Bruce Smith	.10
12	Thurman Thomas	.20
13	*Tim Biakabutuka*	1.00
14	Kerry Collins	.30
15	*Muhsin Muhammad*	1.00
16	Winslow Oliver	.10
17	Curtis Conway	.10
18	Bryan Cox	.10
19	*Bobby Engram*	1.00
20	Erik Kramer	.10
21	Rashaan Salaam	.30
22	Jeff Blake	.30
23	Ki-Jana Carter	.20
24	Carl Pickens	.10
25	Troy Aikman	1.25
26	Michael Irvin	.20
27	Daryl Johnston	.10
28	Deion Sanders	.75
29	Emmitt Smith	2.50
30	Terrell Davis	1.75
31	John Elway	1.00
32	Anthony Miller	.10
33	John Mobley	.10
34	Scott Mitchell	.10
35	Herman Moore	.20
36	Barry Sanders	1.25
37	Edgar Bennett	.10
38	Robert Brooks	.10
39	Brett Favre	2.50
40	Reggie White	.20
41	*Eddie George*	3.00
42	Steve McNair	.75
43	Chris Sanders	.10
44	Quentin Coryatt	.10
45	Marshall Faulk	.30
46	Jim Harbaugh	.10
47	*Marvin Harrison*	2.00
48	Mark Brunell	1.00
49	Natrone Means	.10
50	Andre Rison	.10
51	Marcus Allen	.20
52	Steve Bono	.10
53	Greg Hill	.10
54	Tamarick Vanover	.30
55	*Karim Abdul-Jabbar*	.50
56	Dan Marino	2.50
57	O.J. McDuffie	.10
58	*Zach Thomas*	1.00
59	Cris Carter	.10
60	Warren Moon	.10
61	Jake Reed	.10
62	Drew Bledsoe	1.25
63	Ben Coates	.10
64	*Terry Glenn*	1.50
65	Curtis Martin	.75
66	Mario Bates	.10
67	Michael Haynes	.10
68	Dave Brown	.10
69	Rodney Hampton	.10
70	Amani Toomer	.10
71	Tyrone Wheatley	.10
72	*Keyshawn Johnson*	2.00
73	Neil O'Donnell	.10
74	Tim Brown	.10
75	*Rickey Dudley*	.30
76	Napoleon Kaufman	.10
77	Chester McGlockton	.10
78	Charlie Garner	.10
79	Chris T. Jones	.10
80	Ricky Watters	.20
81	Jerome Bettis	.20
82	Kordell Stewart	1.25
83	Rod Woodson	.10
84	Aaron Hayden	.10
85	Stan Humphries	.10
86	Junior Seau	.10
87	*Tony Banks*	1.00
88	Isaac Bruce	.50
89	*Lawrence Phillips*	.50
90	Derek Loville	.10
91	Jerry Rice	1.25
92	J.J. Stokes	.40
93	Steve Young	1.00
94	Joey Galloway	1.00
95	Rick Mirer	.10
96	Chris Warren	.10
97	Trent Dilfer	.10
98	Errict Rhett	.30
99	Terry Allen	.10
100	Michael Westbrook	.20

1996 Ultra Sensations Creative Chaos

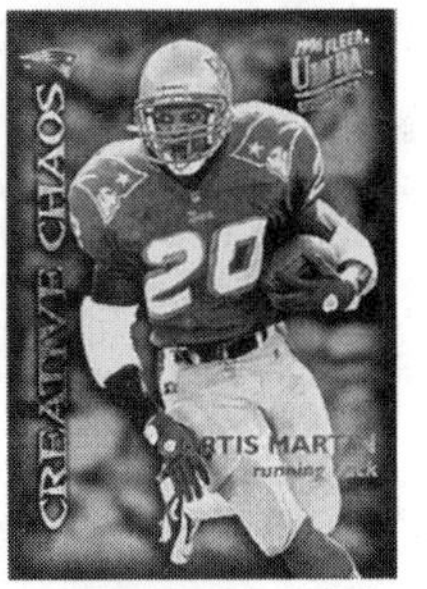

Creative Chaos featured 10 players on double-sided cards that matched each player, resulting in 100 total cards. These inserts were included in every 12 packs.

		MT
Complete Set (100):		600.00
Common Player:		4.00
Minor Stars:		8.00
1	Emmitt Smith, Emmitt Smith	20.00
1	Emmitt Smith, Brett Favre	18.00
1	Emmitt Smith, Curtis Martin	16.00
1	Emmitt Smith, Chris Warren	12.00
1	Emmitt Smith, Deion Sanders	13.00
1	Emmitt Smith, Steve Young	14.00
1	Emmitt Smith, Jerry Rice	15.00
1	Emmitt Smith, Terrell Davis	15.00
1	Emmitt Smith, Carl Pickens	12.00
1	Emmitt Smith, Marshall Faulk	13.00
2	Brett Favre, Emmitt Smith	18.00
2	Brett Favre, Brett Favre	16.00
2	Brett Favre, Curtis Martin	14.00
2	Brett Favre, Chris Warren	10.00
2	Brett Favre, Deion Sanders	11.00
2	Brett Favre, Steve Young	12.00
2	Brett Favre, Jerry Rice	13.00
2	Brett Favre, Terrell Davis	13.00
2	Brett Favre, Carl Pickens	10.00
2	Brett Favre, Marshall Faulk	11.00
3	Curtis Martin, Emmitt Smith	16.00

3	Curtis Martin, Brett Favre	14.00
3	Curtis Martin, Curtis Martin	12.00
3	Curtis Martin, Chris Warren	8.00
3	Curtis Martin, Deion Sanders	9.00
3	Curtis Martin, Steve Young	10.00
3	Curtis Martin, Jerry Rice	11.00
3	Curtis Martin, Terrell Davis	11.00
3	Curtis Martin, Carl Pickens	8.00
3	Curtis Martin, Marshall Faulk	9.00
4	Chris Warren, Emmitt Smith	12.00
4	Chris Warren, Brett Favre	10.00
4	Chris Warren, Curtis Martin	8.00
4	Chris Warren, Chris Warren	4.00
4	Chris Warren, Deion Sanders	4.00
4	Chris Warren, Steve Young	4.00
4	Chris Warren, Jerry Rice	8.00
4	Chris Warren, Terrell Davis	8.00
4	Chris Warren, Carl Pickens	4.00
4	Chris Warren, Marshall Faulk	4.00
5	Deion Sanders, Emmitt Smith	13.00
5	Deion Sanders, Brett Favre	11.00
5	Deion Sanders, Curtis Martin	9.00
5	Deion Sanders, Chris Warren	4.00
5	Deion Sanders, Deion Sanders	8.00
5	Deion Sanders, Steve Young	8.00
5	Deion Sanders, Jerry Rice	8.00
5	Deion Sanders, Terrell Davis	8.00
5	Deion Sanders, Carl Pickens	4.00
5	Deion Sanders, Marshall Faulk	4.00
6	Steve Young, Emmitt Smith	14.00
6	Steve Young, Brett Favre	12.00
6	Steve Young, Curtis Martin	10.00
6	Steve Young, Chris Warren	4.00
6	Steve Young, Deion Sanders	4.00
6	Steve Young, Steve Young	4.00
6	Steve Young, Jerry Rice	8.00
6	Steve Young, Terrell Davis	9.00
6	Steve Young, Carl Pickens	4.00
6	Steve Young, Marshall Faulk	4.00
7	Jerry Rice, Emmitt Smith	15.00
7	Jerry Rice, Brett Favre	13.00
7	Jerry Rice, Curtis Martin	11.00
7	Jerry Rice, Chris Warren	8.00
7	Jerry Rice, Deion Sanders	8.00
7	Jerry Rice, Steve Young	8.00
7	Jerry Rice, Jerry Rice	10.00
7	Jerry Rice, Terrell Davis	10.00
7	Jerry Rice, Carl Pickens	8.00
7	Jerry Rice, Marshall Faulk	8.00
8	Terrell Davis, Emmitt Smith	15.00
8	Terrell Davis, Brett Favre	13.00
8	Terrell Davis, Curtis Martin	11.00
8	Terrell Davis, Chris Warren	8.00
8	Terrell Davis, Deion Sanders	8.00
8	Terrell Davis, Steve Young	9.00
8	Terrell Davis, Jerry Rice	10.00
8	Terrell Davis, Terrell Davis	10.00
8	Terrell Davis, Carl Pickens	8.00
8	Terrell Davis, Marshall Faulk	8.00
9	Carl Pickens, Emmitt Smith	12.00
9	Carl Pickens, Brett Favre	10.00
9	Carl Pickens, Curtis Martin	8.00
9	Carl Pickens, Chris Warren	4.00
9	Carl Pickens, Deion Sanders	4.00
9	Carl Pickens, Steve Young	4.00
9	Carl Pickens, Jerry Rice	8.00
9	Carl Pickens, Terrell Davis	8.00
9	Carl Pickens, Carl Pickens	4.00
9	Carl Pickens, Marshall Faulk	4.00
10	Marshall Faulk, Emmitt Smith	13.00
10	Marshall Faulk, Brett Favre	11.00
10	Marshall Faulk, Curtis Martin	9.00
10	Marshall Faulk, Chris Warren	4.00
10	Marshall Faulk, Deion Sanders	4.00
10	Marshall Faulk, Steve Young	4.00
10	Marshall Faulk, Jerry Rice	8.00
10	Marshall Faulk, Terrell Davis	8.00
10	Marshall Faulk, Carl Pickens	4.00
10	Marshall Faulk, Marshall Faulk	4.00

1996 Ultra Sensations Random Rookies

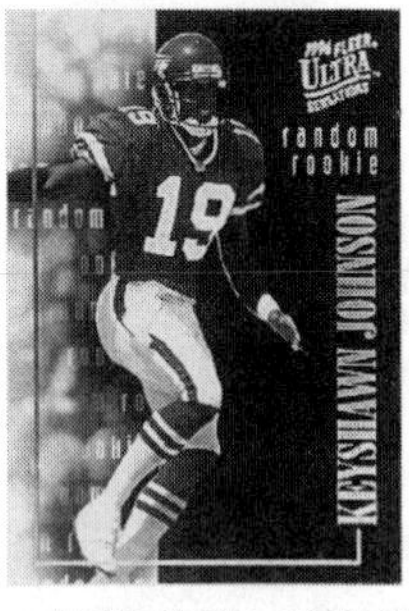

Random Rookies arrived with 80 percent of the print run in silver foil and 20 percent in gold foil. The set included 10 cards, with the first five in hobby and the second five in retail packs. Random Rookies were seeded one every 48 packs.

		MT
Complete Set (10):		60.00
Common Player:		2.00
Gold Cards:		2x-3x
1	Keyshawn Johnson	10.00
2	Eddie George	25.00
3	Leeland McElroy	4.00
4	Eric Moulds	2.00
5	Lawrence Phillips	8.00
6	Marvin Harrison	10.00
7	Tim Biakabutuka	8.00
8	Terry Glenn	20.00
9	Rickey Dudley	6.00
10	Tony Banks	8.00

1997 Ultra

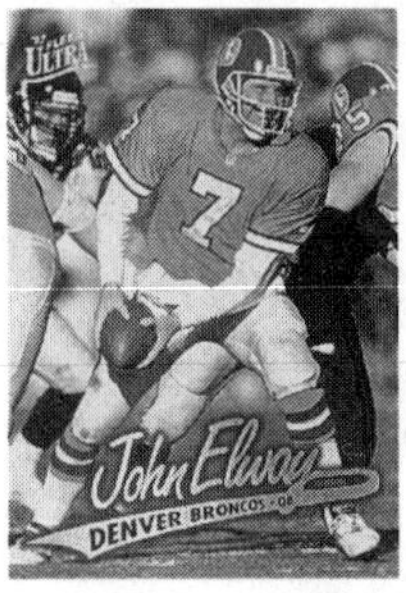

The 350-card set featured 346 cards and four checklists. The fronts showcase a full-bleed photo with the Ultra logo in the upper left. The player's name is written in script at the bottom center, while the team and his position are printed beneath the name. The backs include two photos, with his name, bio and stats beginning in the center and continuing to the bottom. The Gold Medallion parallel cards were inserted one per pack, while the Platinum Medallion parallel cards were exclusive in hobby packs and found 1:100 packs. Inserts in Series I include Blitzkrieg, Play of the Game, Rookies, Starring Role, Sunday School and Talent Show. Inserts in Series II include First Rounders, Rising Stars, Specialists, Comeback Kids, The Main Event, Ultra All-Rookie Team, Ultra Specialists, Ultra Stars, Million Dollar Moments, Memorabilia Offer Card, Lucky 13 Redemption Cards and REEBOK Chase Promotion.

		MT
Complete Set (350):		90.00
Complete Series 1 (200):		30.00
Complete Series 2 (150):		60.00
Common Player:		.10
Minor Stars:		.20
Gold Cards:		2x-4x
Platinum Stars:		40x-80x
Platinum Rookies:		20x-40x
Ser. 1, 2 Pack (10):		2.50
Ser. 1, 2 Wax Box (24):		55.00
1	Brett Favre	2.50
2	Ricky Watters	.20
3	Dan Marino	2.00
4	Bryan Still	.10
5	Chester McGlockton	.10
6	Tim Biakabutuka	.20
7	Dave Brown	.10
8	Mike Alstott	.20
9	O.J. McDuffie	.10
10	Mark Brunell	1.25
11	Michael Bates	.10
12	Tyrone Wheatley	.10
13	Eddie George	1.50
14	Kevin Greene	.10
15	Jerris McPhail	.10
16	Harvey Williams	.10
17	Eric Swann	.10
18	Carl Pickens	.10
19	Darrell Davis	.10
20	Charles Way	.10
21	Jamie Asher	.10
22	Qadry Ismail	.10
23	Lawrence Phillips	.20
24	John Friez	.10
25	Dorsey Levens	.20
26	Willie McGinest	.10
27	Chris T. Jones	.10
28	Cortez Kennedy	.10
29	Raymont Harris	.10
30	William Roaf	.10
31	Ted Johnson	.10
32	Tony Martin	.10
33	Jim Everett	.10
34	Ray Zellars	.10
35	Derrick Alexander	.10
36	Leonard Russell	.10
37	William Thomas	.10
38	Karim Abdul-Jabbar	.50
39	Kevin Turner	.10
40	Robert Brooks	.10
41	Kent Graham	.10
42	Tony Brackens	.10
43	Rodney Hampton	.10
44	Drew Bledsoe	1.25
45	Barry Sanders	1.50
46	Tim Brown	.10
47	Reggie White	.20
48	Terry Allen	.10
49	Jim Harbaugh	.10
50	John Elway	.75
51	William Floyd	.10
52	Michael Jackson	.10
53	Larry Centers	.10
54	Emmitt Smith	2.00
55	Bruce Smith	.10
56	Terrell Owens	.50
57	Deion Sanders	.50
58	Neil O'Donnell	.10
59	Kordell Stewart	1.00
60	Bobby Engram	.10
61	Keenan McCardell	.10
62	Ben Coates	.10
63	Curtis Martin	1.75
64	Hugh Douglas	.10
65	Eric Moulds	.20
66	Derrick Thomas	.20
67	Bam Morris	.10
68	Bryan Cox	.10
69	Rob Moore	.10
70	Michael Haynes	.10
71	Brian Mitchell	.10
72	Alex Molden	.10
73	Steve Young	.75
74	Andre Reed	.10
75	Michael Westbrook	.20
76	Eric Metcalf	.10
77	Tony Banks	.30
78	Ken Dilger	.10
79	John Henry Mills	.10
80	Ashley Ambrose	.10
81	Jason Dunn	.10
82	Trent Dilfer	.20
83	Wayne Chrebet	.10
84	Ty Detmer	.10
85	Aeneas Williams	.10
86	Frank Wycheck	.10
87	Jessie Tuggle	.10
88	Steve McNair	1.00
89	Chris Slade	.10
90	Anthony Johnson	.10
91	Simeon Rice	.10
92	Mike Tomczak	.10
93	Sean Jones	.10
94	Wesley Walls	.10
95	Thurman Thomas	.20
96	Scott Mitchell	.10
97	Desmond Howard	.10
98	Chris Warren	.10
99	Glyn Milburn (RB)	.10
100	Vinny Testaverde	.10
101	James Stewart	.10
102	Iheanyi Uwaezuoke	.10
103	Stan Humphries	.10
104	Terance Mathis	.10
105	Thomas Lewis	.10
106	Eddie Kennison	.40
107	Rashaan Salaam	.20
108	Curtis Conway	.10
109	Chris Sanders	.10
110	Marcus Allen	.20
111	Gilbert Brown	.10
112	Jason Sehorn	.10
113	Zach Thomas	.20
114	Bobby Hebert	.10
115	Herman Moore	.20
116	Ray Lewis	.10
117	Darnay Scott	.10
118	Jamal Anderson	.20
119	Keyshawn Johnson	.40
120	Adrian Murrell	.10
121	Sam Mills	.10
122	Irving Fryar	.10
123	Ki-Jana Carter	.10
124	Gus Frerotte	.10
125	Terry Glenn	.50
126	Quentin Coryatt	.10
127	Robert Smith	.10
128	Jeff Blake	.20
129	Natrone Means	.20
130	Isaac Bruce	.30
131	Lamar Lathon	.10
132	Johnnie Morton	.10
133	Jerry Rice	1.25
134	Errict Rhett	.20
135	Junior Seau	.20
136	Joey Galloway	.40
137	Napoleon Kaufman	.10
138	Troy Aikman	1.25
139	Kevin Hardy	.10
140	Jimmy Smith	.10
141	Edgar Bennett	.10
142	Hardy Nickerson	.10
143	Greg Lloyd	.10
144	Dale Carter (WR)	.10
145	Jake Reed	.10
146	Cris Carter	.10
147	Todd Collins	.10
148	Mel Gray	.10
149	Lawyer Milloy	.10
150	Kimble Anders	.10
151	Darick Holmes	.10
152	Bert Emanuel	.10
153	Marshall Faulk	.20
154	Frank Sanders	.10
155	Leeland McElroy	.20
156	Rickey Dudley	.20
157	Tamarick Vanover	.20
158	Kerry Collins	.40
159	Jeff Graham	.10
160	Jerome Bettis	.20
161	Greg Hill	.10
162	John Mobley	.10
163	Michael Irvin	.20
164	Marvin Harrison	.40
165	Jim Schwantz	.10
166	Jermaine Lewis	.10
167	Levon Kirkland	.10
168	Nilo Silvan	.10
169	Ken Norton	.10
170	Yancey Thigpen	.10
171	Antonio Freeman	.20
172	Terry Kirby	.10
173	Brad Johnson	.10
174	*Reidel Anthony*	1.50
175	*Tiki Barber*	1.50
176	*Pat Barnes*	.50
177	*Michael Booker*	.20
178	*Peter Boulware*	.20
179	*Rae Carruth*	1.00
180	*Troy Davis*	.50
181	*Corey Dillon*	4.00
182	*Jim Druckenmiller*	1.00
183	*Warrick Dunn*	2.00
184	*James Farrior*	.20
185	*Yatil Green*	.50
186	*Walter Jones*	.20
187	*Tom Knight*	.20
188	*Sam Madison*	.20
189	*Tyrus McCloud*	.20
190	*Orlando Pace*	.50
191	*Jake Plummer*	4.00
192	*Dwayne Rudd*	.20
193	*Darrell Russell*	.20
194	*Sedrick Shaw*	.50
195	*Shawn Springs*	.50
196	*Bryant Westbrook*	.50
197	*Danny Wuerffel*	.75
198	*Reinard Wilson*	.20
199	Checklist	.10
200	Checklist	.10
201	Rick Mirer	.10
202	Torrance Small	.10
203	Ricky Proehl	.10
204	Will Blackwell	.30
205	Warrick Dunn	.50
206	Rob Johnson	.20
207	Jim Schwantz	.10
208	*Ike Hilliard*	1.00
209	Chris Canty	.10
210	Chris Boniol	.10
211	Jim Druckenmiller	.75
212	*Tony Gonzalez*	1.00
213	Scottie Graham	.10
214	*Byron Hanspard*	.50
215	Gary Brown	.10
216	Darrell Russell	.10
217	Sedrick Shaw	.50
218	Boomer Esiason	.10
219	Peter Boulware	.10
220	Willie Green	.10
221	Dietrich Jells	.10
222	Freddie Jones	.30
223	Eric Metcalf	.10
224	John Henry Mills	.10
225	Michael Timpson	.10
226	Danny Wuerffel	.50
227	Daimon Shelton	.10
228	Henry Ellard	.10
229	Flipper Anderson	.10
230	Hunter Goodwin	.10
231	Jay Graham	.50
232	*Duce Staley*	15.00
233	Lamar Thomas	.10
234	Rod Woodson	.10
235	Zack Crockett	.10
236	Ernie Mills	.10
237	Kyle Brady	.10
238	Jesse Campbell	.10
239	Anthony Miller	.10
240	Michael Haynes	.10
241	Qadry Ismail	.10
242	Tom Knight	.10
243	Brian Manning	.10
244	Derrick Mayes	.10
245	Jamie Sharper	.10
246	Sherman Williams	.10
247	Yatil Green	.30
248	Howard Griffith	.10
249	Brian Blades	.10
250	Mark Chmura	.20
251	Chris Darkins	.10
252	Willie Davis	.10
253	Quinn Early	.10
254	Marc Edwards	.10
255	Charlie Jones	.10
256	Jake Plummer	2.00
257	Heath Shuler	.10
258	Fred Barnett	.10
259	Koy Detmer	.20
260	Michael Booker	.10
261	Chad Brown	.10
262	Garrison Hearst	.20
263	Leon Johnson	.10
264	*Antowain Smith*	2.00
265	*Darnell Autry*	.40
266	Craig Heyward	.10
267	Walter Jones	.10
268	Dexter Coakley	.30
269	Mercury Hayes	.10
270	Brett Perriman	.10
271	Chris Spielman	.10
272	Kevin Greene	.10
273	Kevin Lockett	.10
274	Troy Davis	.30
275	Brent Jones	.10
276	Chris Chandler	.10
277	Bryant Westbrook	.20
278	Desmond Howard	.10
279	Tyrone Hughes	.10
280	Kez McCorvey	.10
281	Stephen Davis	.10
282	Steve Everitt	.10
283	Andre Hastings	.10
284	*Marcus Robinson*	15.00
285	Donnell Woolford	.10
286	Mario Bates	.10
287	Corey Dillon	1.25
288	Jackie Harris	.10
289	Lorenzo Neal	.10
290	Anthony Pleasant	.10
291	Andre Rison	.10
292	Amani Toomer	.10
293	Eric Turner	.10
294	Elvis Grbac	.10
295	Cris Dishman	.10
296	Tom Carter	.10
297	Mark Carrier	.10
298	Orlando Pace	.20
299	Jay Riemersma	.10
300	Daryl Johnston	.10
301	Joey Kent	.30
302	Ronnie Harmon	.10
303	Raghib Ismail	.10
304	Terrell Davis	1.25
305	Sean Dawkins	.10
306	Jeff George	.20
307	David Palmer	.10
308	Dwayne Rudd	.10
309	J.J. Stokes	.20
310	James Farrior	.10
311	William Fuller	.10
312	George Jones	.20
313	John Allred	.10
314	Tony Graziani	.10
315	Jeff Hostetler	.10
316	Keith Poole	.10
317	Neil Smith	.10
318	Steve Tasker	.10
319	Mike Vrabel	.10
320	Pat Barnes	.30
321	James Hundon	.10
322	O.J. Santiago	.10
323	Billy Davis	.10
324	Shawn Springs	.20
325	Reinard Wilson	.10
326	Charles Johnson	.10
327	Michael Barrow	.10
328	*Derrick Mason*	3.00
329	Muhsin Muhammad	.10
330	*David LaFleur*	.50
331	Reidel Anthony	.75
332	Tiki Barber	1.00
333	Ray Buchanan	.10
334	John Elway	.75
335	Alvin Harper	.10
336	Damon Jones	.10
337	*Dedric Ward*	3.00
338	Jim Everett	.10
339	Jon Harris	.10
340	Warren Moon	.10
341	Rae Carruth	.50
342	John Mobley	.10
343	Tyrone Poole	.10
344	Mike Cherry	.10
345	Horace Copeland	.10
346	Deon Figures	.10
347	Antowuan Wyatt	.10
348	Tommy Vardell	.10
349	Checklist	.10
350	Checklist	.10

1997 Ultra Gold

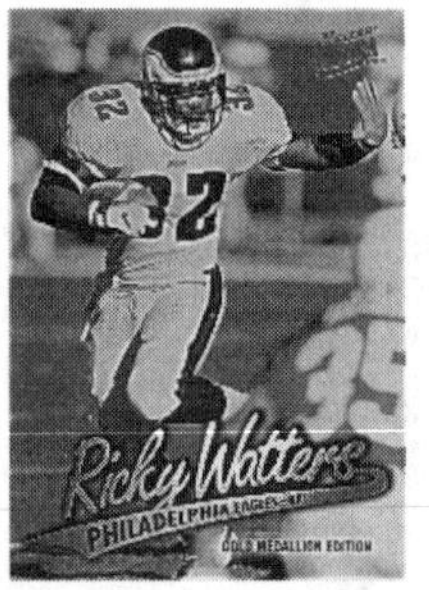

Gold Medallions ran parallel to the Ultra Football set, and included 198 cards from Series I and 148 cards from Series II (the two checklist cards in each series were not issued in Gold Medallion versions). The foil on the front of the card was printed in gold versus the silver foil used on regular-issue cards. In addition, the words "Gold Medallion Edition" were printed across the front bottom right of the cards, while card backs carried a "G" prefix on the card number. Gold Medallion parallels were issued at a rate of one per pack in both Series.

	MT
Gold Stars:	2x-4x
Gold Rookies:	2x

1997 Ultra Platinum

Platinum Medallions were a parallel set to the Ultra Football set and included 198 cards from Series I and 148 cards from Series II (the two checklist cards in each series were not issued in Platinum Medallion versions). A prismatic foil is used on the front of the card versus the silver foil used on regular-issue cards. In addition, the words "Platinum Medallion Edition" were printed across the front bottom right of the cards, while card backs carried a "P" prefix on the card number. Platinum Medallion parallels were issued at a rate of one per 100 hobby packs in both Series.

	MT
Platinum Stars:	40x-80x
Platinum Rookies:	20x-40x

1997 Ultra All-Rookie Team

This 12-card insert features the top rookies of 1997. An action shot of the players is set on a golden plaque. The cards were inserted once per 18 packs in Series II.

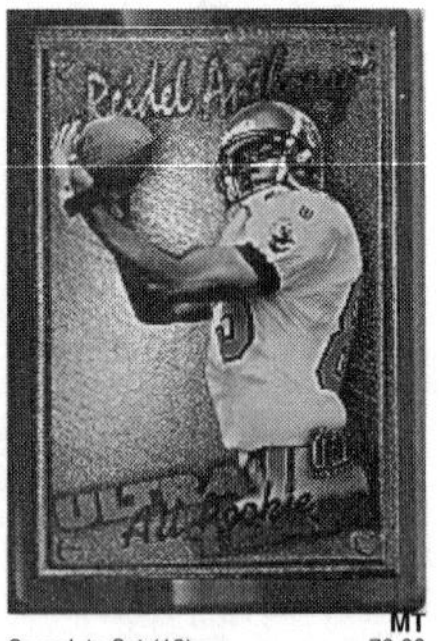

		MT
Complete Set (12):		70.00
Common Player:		3.00
Minor Stars:		6.00
1	Antowain Smith	10.00
2	Jay Graham	3.00
3	Ike Hilliard	6.00
4	Warrick Dunn	18.00
5	Tony Gonzalez	3.00
6	David LaFleur	3.00
7	Reidel Anthony	8.00
8	Rae Carruth	6.00
9	Byron Hanspard	3.00
10	Joey Kent	3.00
11	Kevin Lockett	3.00
12	Jake Plummer	8.00

1997 Ultra Blitzkrieg

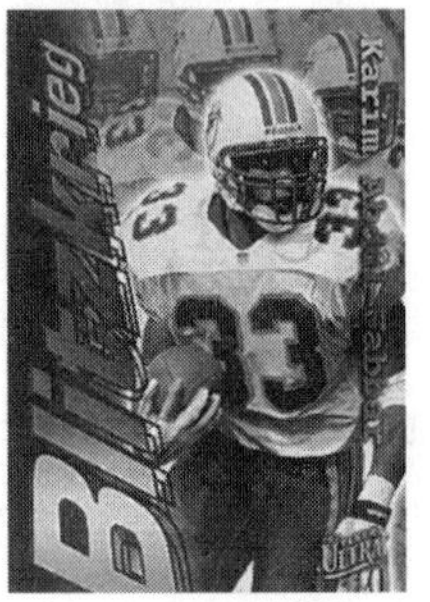

Inserted 1:6 packs, the 18-card set featured "Blitzkrieg" printed along the left border of the card. The player's photo is superimposed over a multiple-photo background. The player's name is printed vertically along the upper right border. The Ultra logo is in the lower right. The backs have the player's photo on the left, with his name in the upper right. His highlights appear to the right of the photo. The card number, which is labeled "of 18," is printed in the lower right. The Ultra Blitzkrieg die-cut parallel set was inserted 1:36 packs. The die-cut was featured on the left border. This insert was only available in Series I.

		MT
Complete Set (18):		90.00
Common Player:		2.00
Die-Cut Cards:		2x-3x
1	Eddie George	8.00
2	Terry Glenn	4.00
3	Karim Abdul-Jabbar	5.00
4	Emmitt Smith	12.00
5	Dan Marino	12.00
6	Brett Favre	15.00
7	Keyshawn Johnson	2.00
8	Curtis Martin	8.00
9	Marvin Harrison	4.00
10	Barry Sanders	8.00
11	Jerry Rice	8.00
12	Terrell Davis	8.00
13	Troy Aikman	8.00
14	Drew Bledsoe	8.00
15	John Elway	6.00
16	Kordell Stewart	8.00
17	Kerry Collins	4.00
18	Steve Young	6.00

1997 Ultra Comeback Kids

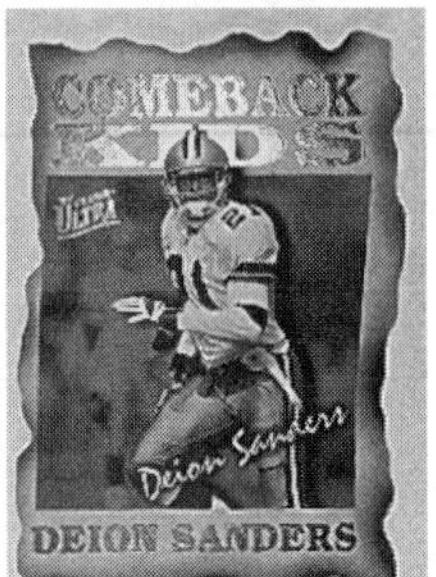

Comeback Kids contains 10 cards featuring the NFL's top go-to players. The cards are designed as die-cut wanted posters. They were inserted 1:8 in Series II.

		MT
Complete Set (10):		35.00
Common Player:		1.25
1	Dan Marino	10.00
2	Barry Sanders	7.00
3	Jerry Rice	5.00
4	John Elway	4.00
5	Steve Young	3.00
6	Deion Sanders	2.00
7	Mark Brunell	5.00
8	Tim Biakabutuka	1.25
9	Tony Banks	2.00
10	Terry Allen	1.25

1997 Ultra First Rounders

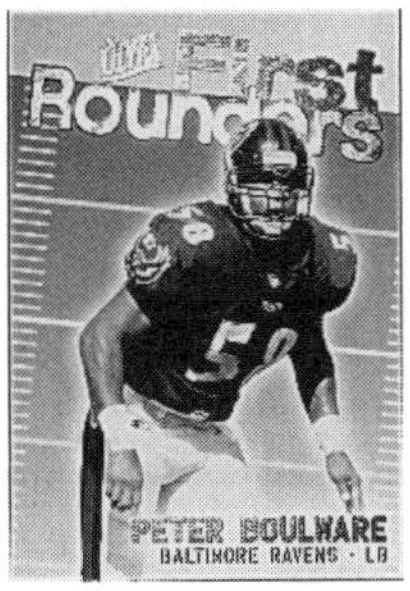
First Rounders
PETER BOULWARE
BALTIMORE RAVENS · LB

This 12-card insert features first-round draft picks who made an immediate impression in 1997. The card fronts feature an action shot of the player against a gridiron background. The insertion rate was 1:4 in Series II.

		MT
Complete Set (12):		18.00
Common Player:		.50
Minor Stars:		1.00
1	Antowain Smith	3.00
2	Rae Carruth	2.00
3	Peter Boulware	.50
4	Shawn Springs	1.00
5	Bryant Westbrook	.50
6	Orlando Pace	1.00
7	Jim Druckenmiller	5.00
8	Yatil Green	2.00
9	Reidel Anthony	2.00
10	Ike Hilliard	2.00
11	Darrell Russell	.50
12	Warrick Dunn	6.00

1997 Ultra Play of the Game

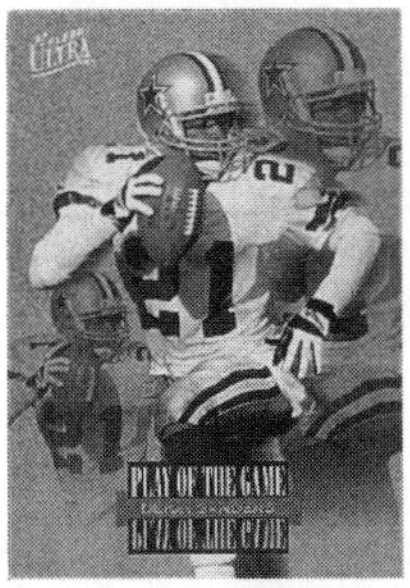
PLAY OF THE GAME

The 10-card set was inserted 1:8 packs in Series I. The front features three player photos. The back has information on a specific game that the player excelled in.

		MT
Complete Set (10):		30.00
Common Player:		1.00
1	Deion Sanders	3.00
2	Jerry Rice	7.00
3	Michael Westbrook	1.00
4	Steve McNair	5.00
5	Marshall Faulk	2.00
6	Terrell Davis	7.00
7	Mark Brunell	7.00
8	Isaac Bruce	2.00
9	Tony Banks	1.00
10	Jamal Anderson	2.00

1997 Ultra Reebok Bronze

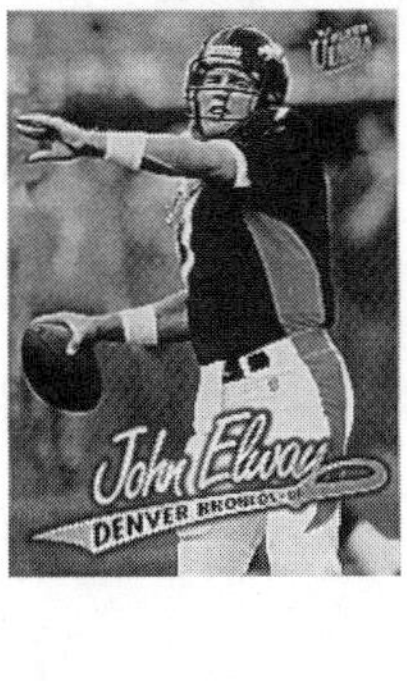
John Elway
DENVER BRONCOS

The Reebok Chase Promotion consisted of parallel versions of 15 basic cards. The parallels featured a Reebok logo on the back and came in three tiers of scarcity (bronze, silver, and gold). The cards were inserted one per pack in Series II.

	MT
Complete Bronze Set (15):	3.00
Common Bronze Player:	.20
Gold Cards:	3x
Green Cards:	15x-30x
Red Cards:	8x-16x
Silver Cards: 1x	
Torrance Small	.20
Jim Schwantz	.20
Chris Boniol	.20
Eric Metcalf	.20
Jesse Campbell	.20
Qadry Ismail	.20
Brett Perriman	.20
Chris Spielman	.20
Desmond Howard	.20
Steve Everitt	.20
Lorenzo Neal	.20
Neil Smith	.20
Steve Tasker	.20
John Elway	.75
Tyrone Poole	.20

1997 Ultra Rising Stars

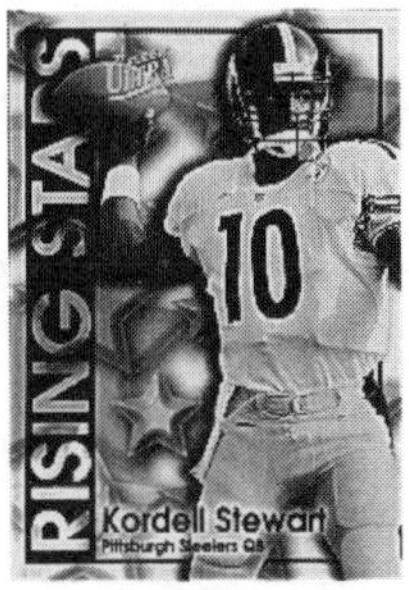
RISING STARS
Kordell Stewart
Pittsburgh Steelers QB

Rising Stars were inserted 1:4 in Series II. The 10 cards feature a soon-to-be star player. The front has an action shot with a star-filled background.

		MT
Complete Set (10):		10.00
Common Player:		.50
Minor Stars:		1.00
1	Keyshawn Johnson	1.00
2	Terrell Davis	3.00
3	Kordell Stewart	3.00
4	Kerry Collins	1.00
5	Joey Galloway	1.00
6	Steve McNair	2.00
7	Jamal Anderson	.50
8	Michael Westbrook	.50
9	Marshall Faulk	.50
10	Isaac Bruce	1.00

1997 Ultra Rookies

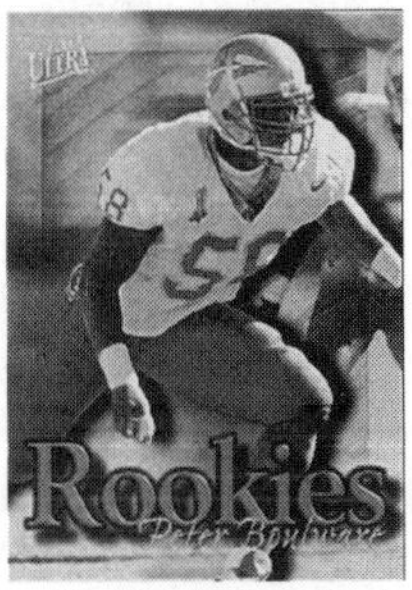
Rookies
Peter Boulware

The 12-card set was inserted 1:4 packs. The player is featured in his college photo on the front and superimposed over a purple and blue background. "Rookies" is printed in green at the bottom, with his name in silver foil in the lower right. The backs, which are numbered "of 12," features "Rookies" in the upper left and his highlights below. His photo and name are printed along the right side. The Ultra Rookies parallel version was seeded 1:18 packs. The parallel cards feature a sculpted-embossed player image over a matte finish background. Rookies were only available in Series I.

		MT
Complete Set (12):		20.00
Common Player:		.75
Gold Embossed:		2x-3x
1	Darnell Autry	2.00
2	Orlando Pace	1.50
3	Peter Boulware	.75
4	Shawn Springs	1.50
5	Bryant Westbrook	.75
6	Rae Carruth	2.00
7	Jim Druckenmiller	6.00
8	Yatil Green	1.00
9	James Farrior	.75
10	Dwayne Rudd	.75
11	Darrell Russell	.75
12	Warrick Dunn	3.00

1997 Ultra Specialists

This 18-card insert features top players on a die-cut card that looks like a manilla file folder. The cards were inserted 1:6 in Series II. Ultra Specialists parallels the regular insert. Inserted 1:36, the die-cut folders open up to reveal an oversized photo. Ultra Specialists also appeared only in Series II.

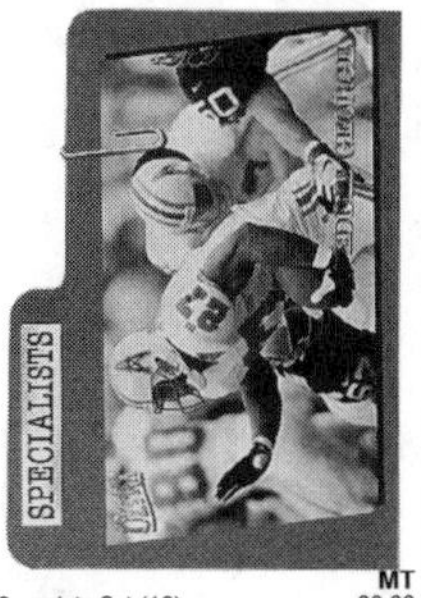
SPECIALISTS

		MT
Complete Set (18):		80.00
Common Player:		2.00
Ultra Specialists:		3x
1	Eddie George	8.00
2	Terry Glenn	3.00
3	Karim Abdul-Jabbar	3.00
4	Emmitt Smith	10.00
5	Brett Favre	12.00
6	Mark Brunell	6.00
7	Curtis Martin	6.00
8	Kerry Collins	2.00
9	Marvin Harrison	2.00
10	Jerry Rice	6.00
11	Tony Martin	2.00
12	Terrell Davis	6.00
13	Troy Aikman	6.00
14	Drew Bledsoe	6.00
15	John Elway	4.00
16	Kordell Stewart	6.00
17	Keyshawn Johnson	2.00
18	Steve Young	4.00

1997 Ultra Starring Role

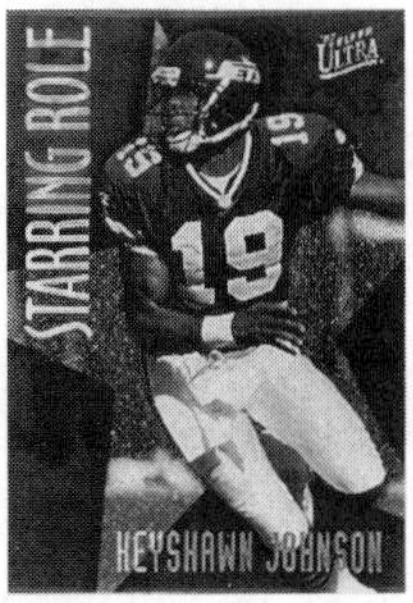
STARRING ROLE
KEYSHAWN JOHNSON

The 10-card set was inserted 1:288 packs. The acrylic die-cut cards feature a silver-foil stamp on the front. The insert was featured in Series I.

		MT
Complete Set (10):		500.00
Common Player:		20.00
1	Emmitt Smith	90.00
2	Barry Sanders	70.00
3	Curtis Martin	50.00
4	Dan Marino	90.00
5	Keyshawn Johnson	20.00
6	Marvin Harrison	30.00
7	Terry Glenn	30.00
8	Eddie George	70.00
9	Brett Favre	100.00
10	Karim Abdul-Jabbar	30.00

1997 Ultra Ultra Stars

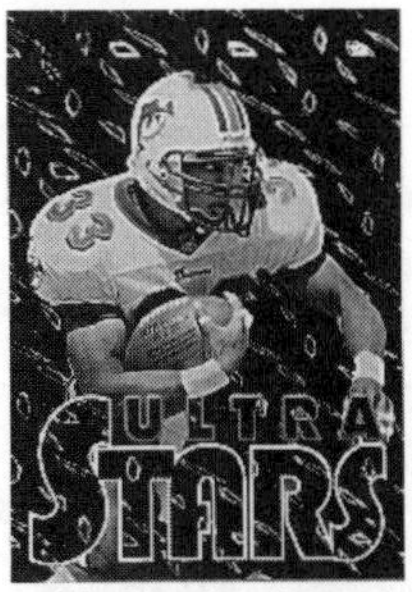
ULTRA
STARS

This 10-card set features top players on a pattern holofoil background. Inserted 1:288 and found in Series II.

		MT
Complete Set (10):		425.00
Common Player:		30.00
1	Emmitt Smith	60.00
2	Barry Sanders	75.00
3	Curtis Martin	35.00
4	Dan Marino	60.00
5	Mark Brunell	35.00
6	Marvin Harrison	30.00
7	Terry Glenn	40.00
8	Eddie George	50.00
9	Brett Favre	75.00
10	Karim Abdul-Jabbar	30.00

1997 Ultra Sunday School

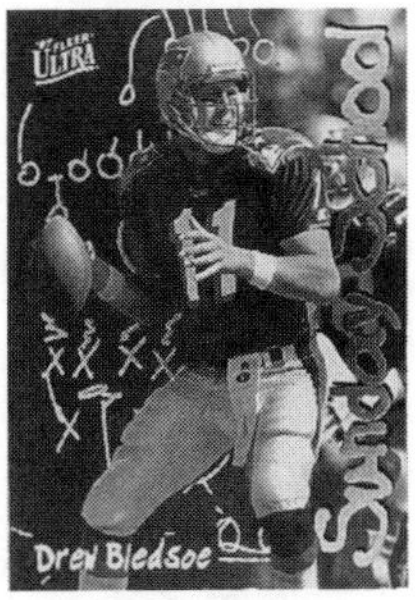
Drew Bledsoe

Inserted 1:8 packs, the 10-card chase set features a player photo superimposed over a black background on the left side of the card. Also included in the background is a play diagramed in silver foil. The player's name is printed in silver foil in the lower left, while the Sunday School logo is printed vertically along the right border. The backs, numbered "of 10," have the player's photo on the left side, with his name, highlights and card number to the right of it. Only in Series I.

		MT
Complete Set (10):		40.00
Common Player:		1.00
1	Marvin Harrison	3.00
2	Barry Sanders	7.00
3	Troy Aikman	7.00
4	Drew Bledsoe	7.00
5	John Elway	5.00
6	Kordell Stewart	6.00
7	Kerry Collins	2.00
8	Steve Young	5.00
9	Deion Sanders	4.00
10	Joey Galloway	1.00

1997 Ultra Talent Show

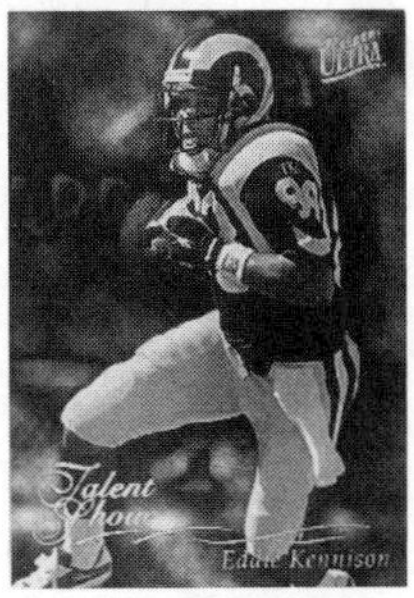
Talent Show
Eddie Kennison

Inserted 1:4 packs, this 10-card set features the player photo superimposed over a multicolored background. The Talent Show logo appears in gold in the lower left, with the player's name in the lower right. The back, numbered "of 10," features a full-bleed photo of the player. Printed along the left border inside a box is the player's name, his highlights and card number. This insert appeared in Series I.

		MT
Complete Set (10):		12.00
Common Player:		.75
1	Joey Galloway	2.00
2	Steve McNair	3.00
3	Marshall Faulk	1.00
4	Isaac Bruce	1.50
5	Michael Westbrook	.75
6	Zach Thomas	1.25
7	Jamal Anderson	.75
8	Mike Alstott	.75
9	Mark Brunell	4.00
10	Eddie Kennison	2.50

1997 Ultra The Main Event

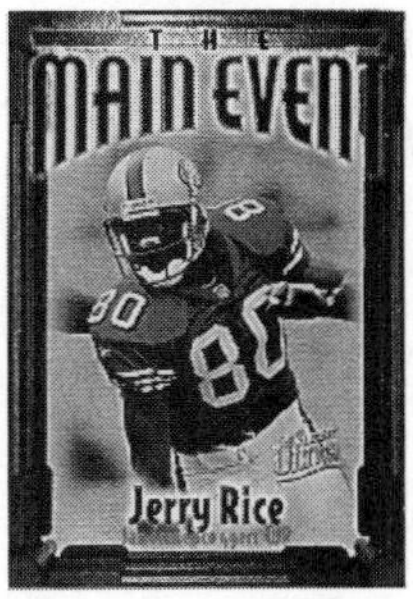
THE
MAIN EVENT
Jerry Rice

This 10-card insert features headline making players. The cards are printed on canvas stock and resemble a top view of a boxing ring. The Main Event was inserted 1:8 in Series II.

		MT
Complete Set (10):		25.00
Common Player:		1.25
1	Dan Marino	8.00
2	Barry Sanders	7.00
3	Jerry Rice	4.00
4	Drew Bledsoe	4.00
5	John Elway	3.00
6	Troy Aikman	4.00
7	Deion Sanders	2.00
8	Joey Galloway	1.25
9	Steve McNair	3.00
10	Marshall Faulk	1.25

1998 Ultra

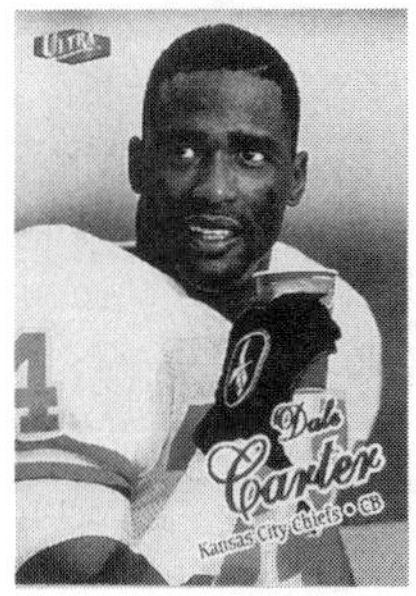
Dale Carter
Kansas City Chiefs · CB

Ultra Football was released in two series in 1998 and contained a total of 425 cards. Series I had 197 veterans, three checklists and a 25-card 1998 Rookies subset seeded one per three packs. Series II had 132 player cards, 25 '98 Greats, three checklists and 40 rookies seeded one per three packs. Cards featured a full color shot of the player, with his name embossed foil writing in the lower right corner. Every card appears in three different parallels - Gold Medallion, Platinum Medallion and Masterpieces. Inserts in Series I include: Canton Classics, Flair Showcase Preview, Next Century, Sensational Sixty, Shots and Touchdown Kings. Inserts in Series II include: Rush Hour, Damage, Inc., Caught in the Draft, Indefensible and Exclamation Points.

		MT
Complete Set (425):		250.00
Complete Series 1 (225):		150.00
Complete Series 2 (200):		100.00
Common Player:		.15
Minor Stars:		.30
Common Rookie (201-225):		2.00
Common Rookie (386-425):		1.00
Inserted 1:3		
Gold Cards:		2x-4x
Inserted 1:1 Hobby		
Gold Rookies:		1.5x
Inserted 1:24 Hobby		
Platinum Cards:		40x-80x
Production 98 Sets		
Platinum Rookies:		4x-8x
Production 66 Sets		
Series 1 Pack (10):		6.00
Series 1 Wax Box (24):		125.00
Series 2 Pack (10):		2.00
Series 2 Wax Box (24):		40.00
1	Barry Sanders	2.50
2	Brett Favre	2.50
3	Napoleon Kaufman	.50
4	Robert Smith	.30
5	Terry Allen	.15
6	Vinny Testaverde	.15
7	William Floyd	.15
8	Carl Pickens	.15
9	Antonio Freeman	.30
10	Ben Coates	.15
11	Elvis Grbac	.15
12	Kerry Collins	.30
13	Orlando Pace	.15
14	Steve Broussard	.15
15	Terance Mathis	.15
16	Tiki Barber	.30
17	Cris Carter	.15
18	Derrick Alexander	.15
19	Eric Metcalf	.15
20	Jeff George	.30
21	Leslie Shepherd	.15
22	Natrone Means	.30
23	Scott Mitchell	.15
24	Adrian Murrell	.15
25	Gilbert Brown	.15
26	Jimmy Smith	.15
27	Mark Bruener	.15
28	Troy Aikman	1.00
29	Warrick Dunn	1.50
30	Jay Graham	.15
31	Craig Whelihan	.15
32	Ed McCaffrey	.15
33	Jamie Asher	.15
34	John Randle	.15
35	Michael Jackson	.15
36	Rickey Dudley	.15
37	Sean Dawkins	.15
38	Andre Rison	.15
39	Bert Emanuel	.15
40	Jeff Blake	.30
41	Curtis Conway	.15
42	Eddie Kennison	.30
43	James McKnight	.15
44	Rae Carruth	.15
45	Tito Wooten	.15
46	Cris Dishman	.15
47	Ernie Conwell	.15
48	Fred Lane	.15
49	Jamal Anderson	.15
50	Lake Dawson	.15
51	Michael Strahan	.15
52	Reggie White	.30
53	Trent Dilfer	.30
54	Troy Brown	.15
55	Wesley Walls	.15
56	Chidi Ahanotu	.15
57	Dwayne Rudd	.15
58	Jerry Rice	1.25
59	Johnnie Morton	.15
60	Sherman Williams	.15
61	Steve McNair	.75
62	Yancey Thigpen	.15
63	Chris Chandler	.15
64	Dexter Coakley	.15
65	Horace Copeland	.15
66	Jerald Moore	.15
67	Leon Johnson	.15
68	Mark Chmura	.30
69	Michael Barrow	.15
70	Muhsin Muhammad	.15
71	Terry Glenn	.30
72	Tony Brackens	.15
73	Chad Scott	.15
74	Glenn Foley	.15
75	Keenan McCardell	.15
76	Peter Boulware	.15
77	Reidel Anthony	.30
78	William Henderson	.15
79	Tony Martin	.15
80	Tony Gonzalez	.15
81	Charlie Jones	.15
82	Chris Gedney	.15
83	Chris Calloway	.15
84	Dale Carter	.15
85	Ki-Jana Carter	.15
86	Shawn Springs	.15
87	Antowain Smith	.75
88	Eric Turner	.15
89	John Mobley	.15
90	Ken Dilger	.15
91	Bobby Hoying	.15
92	Curtis Martin	1.00
93	Drew Bledsoe	1.00
94	Gary Brown	.15
95	Marvin Harrison	.30
96	Todd Collins	.15
97	Chris Warren	.15
98	Danny Kanell	.15
99	Tony McGee	.15
100	Rod Smith	.15
101	Frank Sanders	.15
102	Irving Fryar	.15
103	Marcus Allen	.30
104	Marshall Faulk	.30
105	Bruce Smith	.15
106	Charlie Garner	.15
107	Jim Harbaugh	.30
108	Randal Hill	.15
109	Ricky Proehl	.15
110	Rob Moore	.15
111	Shannon Sharpe	.15
112	Warren Moon	.15
113	Zach Thomas	.15
114	Dan Marino	2.00
115	Duce Staley	.15
116	Eric Swann	.15
117	Kenny Holmes	.15
118	Merton Hanks	.15
119	Raymont Harris	.15
120	Terrell Davis	1.25
121	Thurman Thomas	.30
122	Wayne Martin	.15
123	Charles Way	.15
124	Chuck Smith	.15
125	Corey Dillon	1.00
126	Darnell Autry	.15
127	Isaac Bruce	.30
128	Joey Galloway	.30
129	Kimble Anders	.15
130	Aeneas Williams	.15
131	Andre Hastings	.15
132	Chad Lewis	.15
133	J.J. Stokes	.15
134	John Elway	1.00
135	Karim Abdul-Jabbar	.30
136	Ken Harvey	.15
137	Robert Brooks	.15
138	Rodney Thomas	.15
139	James Stewart	.15
140	Billy Joe Hobert	.15
141	Frank Wycheck	.15
142	Jake Plummer	1.50
143	Jerris McPhail	.15
144	Kordell Stewart	1.25
145	Terrell Owens	.30
146	Willie Green	.15
147	Anthony Miller	.15
148	Courtney Hawkins	.15
149	Larry Centers	.15
150	Gus Frerotte	.15
151	O.J. McDuffie	.15
152	Ray Zellars	.15
153	Terry Kirby	.15
154	Tommy Vardell	.15
155	Willie Davis	.15
156	Chris Canty	.15
157	Byron Hanspard	.15
158	Chris Penn	.15
159	Damon Jones	.15
160	Derrick Mayes	.15
161	Emmitt Smith	2.00
162	Keyshawn Johnson	.15
163	Mike Alstott	.50
164	Tom Carter	.15
165	Tony Banks	.30
166	Bryant Westbrook	.15
167	Chris Sanders	.15
168	Deion Sanders	.50
169	Garrison Hearst	.15
170	Jason Taylor	.15
171	Jerome Bettis	.30
172	John Lynch	.15
173	Troy Davis	.15
174	Freddie Jones	.15
175	Herman Moore	.30
176	Jake Reed	.15
177	Mark Brunell	1.00
178	Ray Lewis	.15
179	Stephen Davis	.15
180	Tim Brown	.15
181	Willie McGinest	.15
182	Andre Reed	.15
183	Darrien Gordon	.15
184	David Palmer	.15
185	James Jett	.15
186	Junior Seau	.15
187	Zack Crockett	.15
188	Brad Johnson	.30
189	Charles Johnson	.15
190	Eddie George	1.25
191	Jermaine Lewis	.15
192	Michael Irvin	.30
193	Reggie Brown	.15
194	Steve Young	.50
195	Warren Sapp	.15
196	Wayne Chrebet	.15

197	David Dunn	.15
198	(Dorsey Levens CL)	.15
199	(Troy Aikman CL)	.30
200	(John Elway CL)	.30
201	*Peyton Manning*	40.00
202	*Ryan Leaf*	12.00
203	*Charles Woodson*	8.00
204	*Andre Wadsworth*	3.00
205	*Brian Simmons*	3.00
206	*Curtis Enis*	10.00
207	*Randy Moss*	40.00
208	*Germane Crowell*	10.00
209	*Greg Ellis*	2.00
210	*Kevin Dyson*	8.00
211	*Skip Hicks*	4.00
212	*Alonzo Mayes*	2.00
213	*Robert Edwards*	4.00
214	*Fred Taylor*	10.00
215	*Robert Holcombe*	3.00
216	*John Dutton*	2.00
217	*Vonnie Holliday*	3.00
218	*Tim Dwight*	5.00
219	*Tavian Banks*	3.00
220	*Marcus Nash*	3.00
221	*Jason Peter*	2.00
222	*Michael Myers*	2.00
223	*Takeo Spikes*	2.00
224	*Kivuusama Mays*	2.00
225	*Jacquez Green*	7.00
226	Doug Flutie	2.50
227	Ike Hillard	.15
228	Craig Heyward	.15
229	Kevin Hardy	.15
230	Jason Dunn	.15
231	Billy Davis	.15
232	Chester McGlockton	.15
233	Sean Gilbert	.15
234	Bert Emanuel	.15
235	Keith Byars	.15
236	Tyrone Wheatley	.15
237	Ricky Proehl	.15
238	Michael Bates	.15
239	Derrick Alexander	.15
240	Harvey Williams	.15
241	Mike Pritchard	.15
242	Paul Justin	.15
243	Jeff Hostetler	.15
244	Eric Moulds	.30
245	Jeff Burris	.15
246	Gary Brown	.15
247	Antwuan Wyatt	.15
248	Dan Wilkinson	.15
249	Chris Warren	.15
250	Lawrence Phillips	.15
251	Eric Metcalf	.15
252	Pat Swilling	.15
253	Lamar Smith	.15
254	Quinn Early	.15
255	Carlester Crumpler	.15
256	Eric Bieniemy	.15
257	Aaron Bailey	.15
258	Gabe Wilkins	.15
259	Rod Woodson	.15
260	Ricky Whittle	.15
261	Iheanyi Uwaezuoke	.15
262	Heath Shuler	.15
263	Darren Sharper	.15
264	John Henry Mills	.15
265	Marco Battaglia	.15
266	Yancey Thigpen	.15
267	Irv Smith	.15
268	Jamie Sharper	.15
269	Marcus Robinson	5.00
270	Dorsey Levens	.15
271	Qadry Ismail	.15
272	Desmond Howard	.15
273	Webster Slaughter	.15
274	Eugene Robinson	.15
275	Bill Romanowski	.15
276	Vincent Brisby	.15
277	Errict Rhett	.15
278	Albert Connell	.15
279	Thomas Lewis	.15
280	John Farquhar	.15
281	Marc Edwards	.15
282	Tyrone Davis	.50
283	Eric Allen	.15
284	Aaron Glenn	.15
285	Roosevelt Potts	.15
286	Kez McCorvey	.15
287	Joey Kent	.15
288	Jim Druckenmiller	.30
289	Sean Dawkins	.15
290	Edgar Bennett	.15
291	Vinny Testaverde	.30
292	Chris Slade	.15
293	Lamar Lathon	.15
294	Jackie Harris	.15
295	Jim Harbaugh	.30
296	Rob Fredrickson	.15
297	Ty Detmer	.15
298	Karl Williams	.15
299	Troy Drayton	.15
300	Curtis Martin	.75
301	Tamarick Vanover	.15
302	Lorenzo Neal	.15
303	John Hall	.15
304	Kevin Greene	.15
305	Bryan Still	.15
306	Neil Smith	.15
307	Mark Rypien	.15
308	Shawn Jefferson	.15
309	Aaron Taylor	.15
310	Sedrick Shaw	.15
311	O.J. Santiago	.15
312	Kevin Abrams	.15
313	Dana Stubblefield	.15
314	Daryl Johnston	.15
315	Yatil Green	.15
316	Jeff Graham	.15
317	Mario Bates	.15
318	Adrian Murrell	.30
319	Larry Brown	.15
320	Jahine Arnold	.15
321	Justin Armour	.15
322	Ricky Watters	.30
323	Lamont Warren	.15
324	Mack Strong	.15
325	Darnay Scott	.15
326	Brian Mitchell	.15
327	Rob Johnson	.30
328	Kent Graham	.15
329	Hugh Douglas	.15
330	Simeon Rice	.15
331	Corey Holliday	.15
332	Randall Cunningham	.75
333	Steve Atwater	.15
334	Latario Rachel	.15
335	Tony Martin	.15
336	Leroy Hoard	.15
337	Howard Griffith	.15
338	Kevin Lockett	.15
339	William Floyd	.15
340	Jerry Ellison	.15
341	Kyle Brady	.15
342	Michael Westbrook	.15
343	Kevin Turner	.15
344	David LaFleur	.15
345	Robert Jones	.15
346	Dave Brown	.15
347	Kevin Williams	.15
348	Amani Toomer	.15
349	Amp Lee	.15
350	Bryce Paup	.15
351	DeWayne Washington	.15
352	Mercury Hayes	.15
353	Scottie Graham	.15
354	Ray Crockett	.15
355	Ted Washington	.15
356	Pete Mitchell	.15
357	Billy Jenkins	.15
358	(Troy Aikman CL)	.50
359	(Drew Bledsoe CL)	.50
360	(Steve Young CL)	.40
361	Antonio Freeman	.30
362	Antowain Smith	.50
363	Barry Sanders	3.00
364	Bobby Hoying	.15
365	Brett Favre	3.00
366	Corey Dillon	.75
367	Dan Marino	2.00
368	Drew Bledsoe	1.50
369	Eddie George	1.25
370	Emmitt Smith	2.00
371	Herman Moore	.30
372	Jake Plummer	1.00
373	Jerome Bettis	.30
374	Jerry Rice	1.50
375	Joey Galloway	.30
376	John Elway	1.50
377	Kordell Stewart	1.00
378	Mark Brunell	1.00
379	Keyshawn Johnson	.15
380	Steve Young	1.00
381	Steve McNair	.75
382	Terrell Davis	2.00
383	Tim Brown	.15
384	Troy Aikman	1.50
385	Warrick Dunn	1.00
386	Ryan Leaf	10.00
387	*Tony Simmons*	3.00
388	*Chris Howard*	1.00
389	*John Avery*	2.00
390	*Shaun Williams*	1.00
391	*Anthony Simmons*	2.00
392	*Rashaan Shehee*	2.00
393	Robert Holcombe	1.50
394	*Larry Shannon*	1.00
395	Skip Hicks	2.00
396	*Rod Rutledge*	1.00
397	*Donald Hayes*	2.00
398	Curtis Enis	4.00
399	*Mikhael Ricks*	3.00
400	*Brian Griese*	25.00
401	*Michael Pittman*	3.00
402	Jacquez Green	3.00
403	*Jerome Pathon*	3.00
404	*Ahman Green*	12.00
405	Marcus Nash	1.50
406	Randy Moss	30.00
407	*Terry Fair*	3.00
408	*Jammi German*	2.00
409	*Stephen Alexander*	2.00
410	*Grant Wistrom*	1.00
411	*Charlie Batch*	20.00
412	Fred Taylor	15.00
413	*Patrick Johnson*	2.00
414	Robert Edwards	2.00
415	*Keith Brooking*	2.00
416	Peyton Manning	30.00
417	*Duane Starks*	2.00
418	Andre Wadsworth	2.00
419	*Brian Alford*	2.00
420	*Brian Kelly*	1.00
421	*Joe Jurevicius*	2.00
422	*Tebucky Jones*	1.00
423	*R.W. McQuarters*	2.00
424	Kevin Dyson	3.00
425	Charles Woodson	6.00

1998 Ultra Gold Medallion

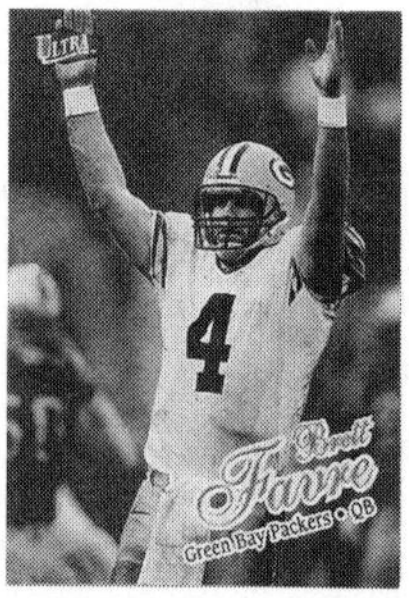

All 425 cards in Ultra Series I and II were paralleled in Gold Medallion versions. The cards featured a gold tint to the front and were numbered with a "G" suffix. Throughout both series, they were inserted in hobby packs only at a rate of one per pack, except for the rookie subsets in both series which were seeded one per 24 packs.

	MT
Gold Medallion Cards:	2x-4x
Gold Medallion Rookies:	1.5x

1998 Ultra Platinum Medallion

All 425 cards in Ultra Series I and II were also available in Platinum Medallion versions. These cards added a platinum tint to the background, showed the player image in black and white and added silver prismatic writing to the player's name. All cards were hobby-only with cards all regular cards sequentially numbered to 98, while the 25-card rookie subset in Series I and the 40-card rookie subset in Series II are numbered to only 66.

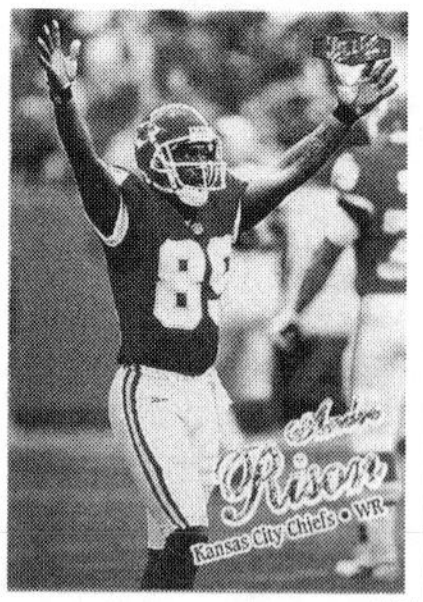

	MT
Platinum Medallion Cards:	50x-100x
Platinum Medallion Rookies:	4x-8x

1998 Ultra Canton Classics

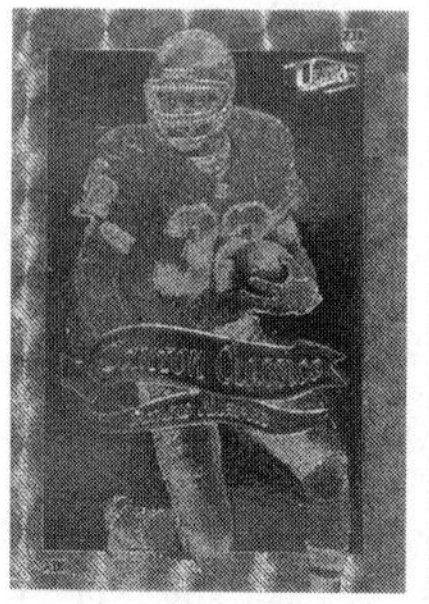

Canton Classics features 10 future Hall of Famers on cards enhanced with 23 karat gold coating and embossing, with an etched border. Backs are numbered with a "CC" suffix and feature an off-color shot of the player again along with some career highlights. These were inserted one per 288 packs.

		MT
Complete Set (10):		375.00
Common Player:		20.00
1	Terrell Davis	50.00
2	Brett Favre	70.00
3	John Elway	35.00
4	Barry Sanders	70.00
5	Eddie George	30.00
6	Jerry Rice	35.00
7	Emmitt Smith	50.00
8	Dan Marino	50.00
9	Troy Aikman	35.00
10	Marcus Allen	20.00

1998 Ultra Caught in the Draft

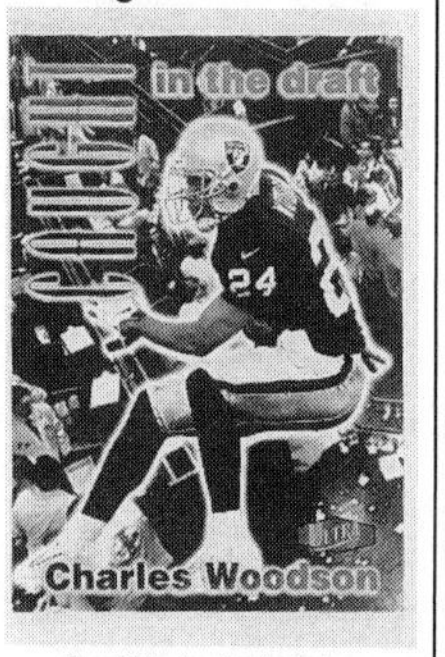

Caught in the Draft singles were found in Series II packs and inserted 1:24. Only rookies who made an impact in '98 were included.

		MT
Complete Set (15):		100.00
Common Player:		3.00
Inserted 1:24		
1	Andre Wadsworth	3.00
2	Curtis Enis	7.00
3	Germane Crowell	5.00
4	Peyton Manning	20.00
5	Tavian Banks	5.00
6	Fred Taylor	15.00
7	John Avery	5.00
8	Randy Moss	30.00
9	Robert Edwards	6.00
10	Charles Woodson	8.00
11	Ryan Leaf	8.00
12	Ahman Green	5.00
13	Robert Holcombe	4.00
14	Jacquez Green	5.00
15	Skip Hicks	5.00

1998 Ultra Damage Inc.

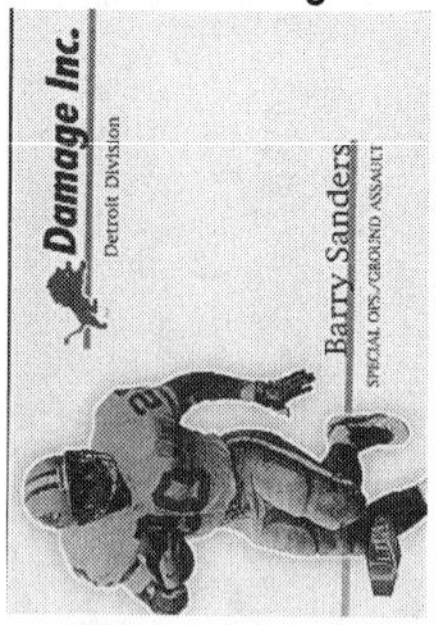

Each single in this set has a business card look to it. Singles were found in Series II packs at 1:72.

		MT
Complete Set (15):		250.00
Common Player:		5.00
Inserted 1:72		
1	Terrell Davis	30.00
2	Joey Galloway	8.00
3	Kordell Stewart	15.00
4	Troy Aikman	20.00
5	Barry Sanders	40.00
6	Ryan Leaf	15.00
7	Antonio Freeman	8.00
8	Keyshawn Johnson	5.00
9	Eddie George	15.00
10	Warrick Dunn	15.00
11	Drew Bledsoe	20.00
12	Peyton Manning	40.00
13	Antowain Smith	8.00
14	Brett Favre	40.00
15	Emmitt Smith	30.00

1998 Ultra Exclamation Points

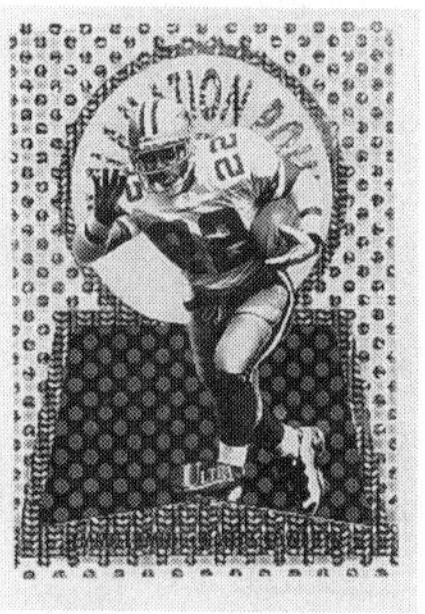

Exclamation Point cards can be found in Series II packs at 1:288. Each single in this 15-card set is printed on plastic and has a pattern holofoil front.

		MT
Complete Set (15):		550.00
Common Player:		15.00
Inserted 1:288		
1	Terrell Davis	50.00
2	Brett Favre	60.00
3	John Elway	50.00
4	Barry Sanders	60.00
5	Peyton Manning	60.00
6	Jerry Rice	30.00
7	Emmitt Smith	50.00
8	Dan Marino	50.00
9	Kordell Stewart	25.00
10	Mark Brunell	25.00
11	Ryan Leaf	30.00
12	Corey Dillon	20.00
13	Antowain Smith	15.00
14	Curtis Martin	15.00
15	Deion Sanders	15.00

1998 Ultra Flair Showcase Preview

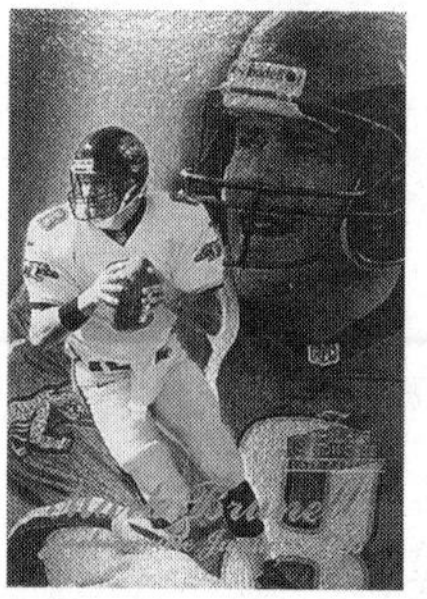

This 10-card insert previewed the upcoming Flair Showcase set. Cards featured the designs of 1998 Flair Showcase and included the logo. They were inserted one per 144 packs of Series I.

		MT
Complete Set (10):		250.00
Common Player:		10.00
1	Kordell Stewart	30.00
2	Mark Brunell	20.00
3	Terrell Davis	30.00
4	Brett Favre	60.00
5	Steve McNair	10.00
6	Curtis Martin	10.00
7	Warrick Dunn	30.00
8	Emmitt Smith	45.00
9	Dan Marino	45.00
10	Corey Dillon	20.00

1998 Ultra Indefensible

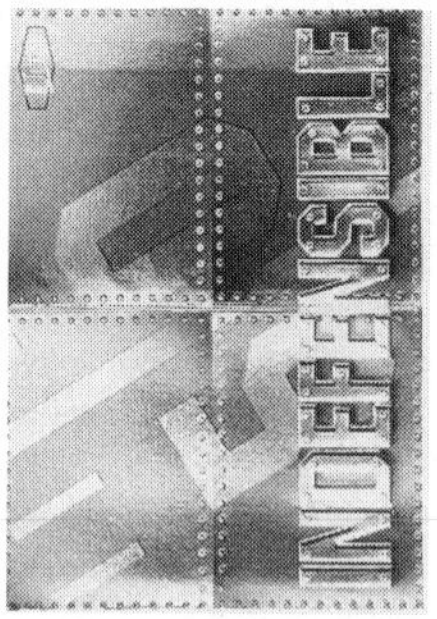

Each card in this 10-card set folds out from its original size and has embossed graphics on the front. Singles were inserted 1:144 packs.

		MT
Complete Set (10):		200.00
Common Player:		10.00
Inserted 1:144		
1	Jake Plummer	20.00
2	Mark Brunell	20.00
3	Terrell Davis	40.00
4	Jerry Rice	25.00
5	Barry Sanders	50.00
6	Curtis Martin	10.00
7	Warrick Dunn	20.00
8	Emmitt Smith	40.00
9	Dan Marino	40.00
10	Corey Dillon	15.00

1998 Ultra Next Century

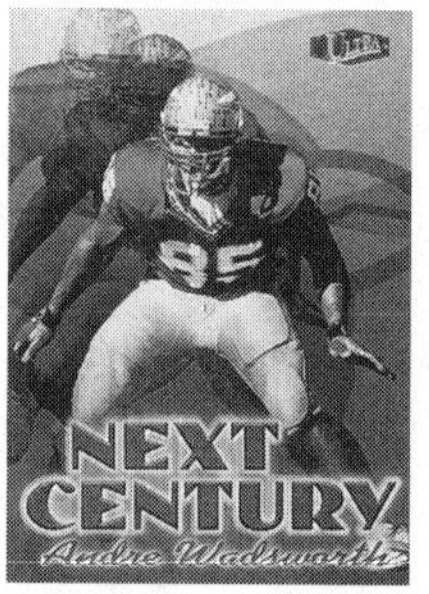

This 15-card insert featured top rookies from 1998 on cards printed on 100 percent gold foil and sculpture embossing. Next Century inserts were numbered with a "NC" suffix and inserted one per 72 packs.

		MT
Complete Set (15):		200.00
Common Player:		5.00
1	Ryan Leaf	20.00
2	Peyton Manning	40.00
3	Charles Woodson	20.00
4	Randy Moss	50.00
5	Curtis Enis	20.00
6	Ahman Green	10.00
7	Peter Warrick	5.00
8	Andre Wadsworth	10.00
9	Germane Crowell	5.00
10	Robert Edwards	12.00
11	Tavian Banks	12.00
12	Takeo Spikes	5.00
13	Jacquez Green	12.00
14	Brian Simmons	6.00
15	Alonzo Mayes	5.00

1998 Ultra Rush Hour

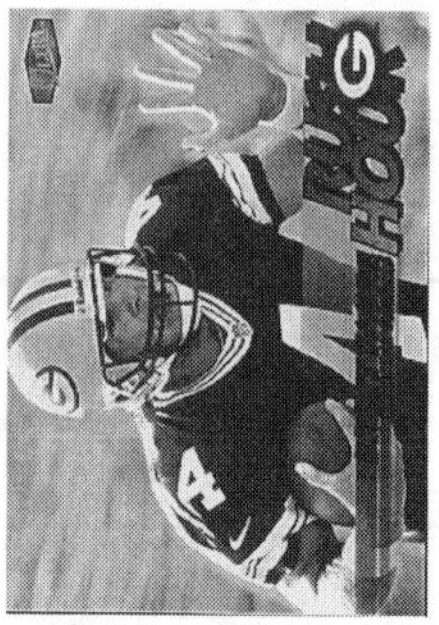

Rush Hour singles were found in Series II packs at a rate of 1:6. Fleer included both veterans and rookies from '98 in this 20-card set.

		MT
Complete Set (20):		35.00
Common Player:		1.00
Minor Stars:		2.00
Inserted 1:6		
1	Robert Edwards	4.00
2	John Elway	4.00
3	Mike Alstott	2.00
4	Robert Holcombe	2.00
5	Mark Brunell	3.00
6	Deion Sanders	2.00
7	Curtis Martin	2.50
8	Curtis Enis	3.00
9	Dorsey Levens	1.00
10	Fred Taylor	6.00
11	John Avery	3.00
12	Eddie George	3.00
13	Jake Plummer	3.00
14	Andre Wadsworth	1.00
15	Fred Lane	1.00
16	Corey Dillon	2.50
17	Brett Favre	8.00
18	Kordell Stewart	3.00
19	Steve McNair	3.00
20	Warrick Dunn	3.00

1998 Ultra Sensational Sixty

This 60-card insert was available only in retail packs at a rate of one per pack. These were numbered with a "SS" suffix and found in Series I.

		MT
Complete Set (60):		45.00
Common Player:		.50
Minor Stars:		1.00
Inserted 1:1 Retail		
1	Karim Abdul-Jabbar	1.00
2	Troy Aikman	2.00
3	Terry Allen	.50
4	Mike Alstott	1.00
5	Tony Banks	1.00
6	Jerome Bettis	1.00
7	Drew Bledsoe	1.50
8	Peter Boulware	.50
9	Robert Brooks	.50
10	Tim Brown	.50
11	Isaac Bruce	1.00
12	Mark Brunell	1.50
13	Cris Carter	1.00
14	Kerry Collins	1.00
15	Curtis Conway	.50
16	Terrell Davis	3.00
17	Troy Davis	.50
18	Trent Dilfer	1.00
19	Corey Dillon	1.25
20	Warrick Dunn	1.50
21	John Elway	2.00
22	Bert Emanuel	.50
23	Brett Favre	4.00
24	Antonio Freeman	1.00
25	Gus Frerotte	.50
26	Joey Galloway	1.00
27	Eddie George	1.50
28	Jeff George	1.00
29	Elvis Grbac	.50
30	Marvin Harrison	1.00
31	Bobby Hoying	.50
32	Michael Irvin	1.00
33	Brad Johnson	1.00
34	Keyshawn Johnson	1.00
35	Dan Marino	3.00
36	Curtis Martin	1.00
37	Tony Martin	.50
38	Keenan McCardell	.50
39	Steve McNair	1.00
40	Warren Moon	1.00
41	Herman Moore	1.00
42	Johnnie Morton	.50
43	Terrell Owens	1.00
44	Carl Pickens	.50
45	Jake Plummer	1.50
46	Jerry Rice	2.00
47	Andre Rison	.50
48	Barry Sanders	4.00
49	Deion Sanders	1.00
50	Junior Seau	.50
51	Shannon Sharpe	1.00
52	Antowain Smith	1.00
53	Emmitt Smith	3.00
54	Jimmy Smith	.50
55	Robert Smith	1.00
56	Kordell Stewart	1.50
57	Jeff Blake	.50
58	Charles Way	.50
59	Reggie White	1.00
60	Steve Young	1.25

1998 Ultra Shots

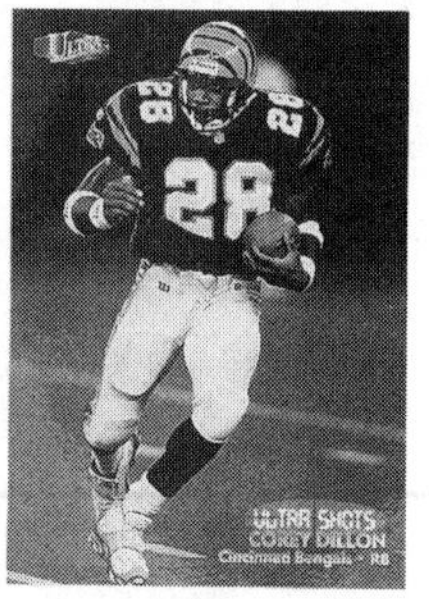

Shots was a 20-card insert that allowed photographers to discuss the shot that is captured on the card front. These were numbered with a "US" suffix and inserted one per six packs of Series I.

		MT
Complete Set (20):		45.00
Common Player:		1.50
Minor Stars:		3.00
1	Deion Sanders	3.00
2	Corey Dillon	4.00
3	Mike Alstott	3.00
4	Jake Plummer	4.00
5	Antowain Smith	3.00
6	Kordell Stewart	4.00
7	Curtis Martin	3.00
8	Bobby Hoying	1.50

9	Kerry Collins	3.00
10	Herman Moore	3.00
11	Terry Glenn	3.00
12	Eddie George	4.00
13	Drew Bledsoe	4.00
14	Steve McNair	3.00
15	Jerry Rice	4.00
16	Trent Dilfer	1.50
17	Joey Galloway	3.00
18	Dan Marino	8.00
19	Barry Sanders	10.00
20	Warrick Dunn	4.00

1998 Ultra Top 30 Parallel Set

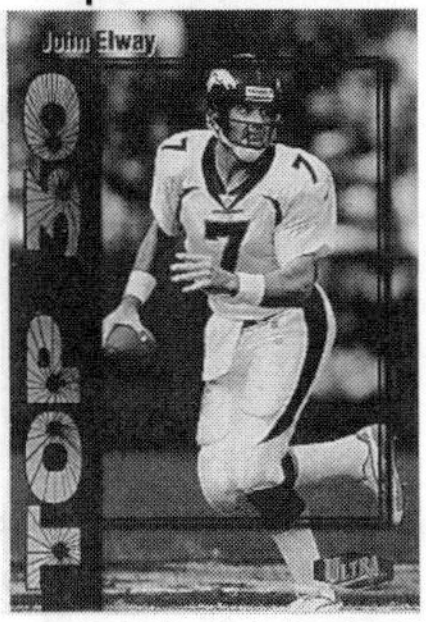

This retail exclusive insert could be found in Retail Series II packs at a rate of 1:1.

		MT
Complete Set (30):		30.00
Common Player:		.25
1	Warrick Dunn	.75
2	Troy Aikman	2.00
3	Trent Dilfer	.50
4	Tony Banks	.50
5	Tim Brown	.50
6	Terrell Davis	3.00
7	Steve McNair	.75
8	Steve Young	1.50
9	Mark Brunell	1.50
10	Kordell Stewart	1.00
11	Keyshawn Johnson	.75
12	John Elway	3.00
13	Joey Galloway	.50
14	Jerry Rice	2.00
15	Jerome Bettis	.50
16	Jake Plummer	1.50
17	Emmitt Smith	3.00
18	Eddie George	.75
19	Drew Bledsoe	1.50
20	Dan Marino	3.00
21	Curtis Martin	1.00
22	Curtis Conway	.25
23	Cris Carter	.50
24	Corey Dillon	.75
25	Carl Pickens	.25
26	Brett Favre	4.00
27	Bobby Hoying	.25
28	Barry Sanders	4.00
29	Antowain Smith	.50
30	Antonio Freeman	.50

1998 Ultra Touchdown Kings

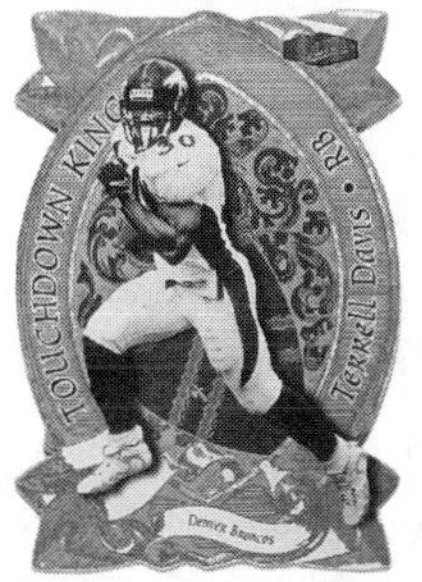

This die-cut insert showcased 15 players on an embossed design. Cards were numbered on the back with a "TK" suffix and inserted one per 24 packs of Series I.

		MT
Complete Set (15):		100.00
Common Player:		3.00
Minor Stars:		6.00
1	Terrell Davis	12.00
2	Joey Galloway	6.00
3	Kordell Stewart	10.00
4	Corey Dillon	8.00
5	Barry Sanders	20.00
6	Cris Carter	3.00
7	Antonio Freeman	6.00
8	Mike Alstott	6.00
9	Eddie George	10.00
10	Warrick Dunn	10.00
11	Drew Bledsoe	10.00
12	Karim Abdul-Jabbar	6.00
13	Mark Brunell	10.00
14	Brett Favre	20.00
15	Emmitt Smith	15.00

1999 Ultra

Ultra Football is a 300-card set with 50 short-printed cards. The short prints are 40 Rookies (1:4) and 10 Super Bowl XXXIII (1:8). Ultra has two parallel sets with Gold and Platinum Medallions. Other inserts include: As Good As It Gets, Caught in the Draft, Counterparts, Damage Inc. and Over the Top.

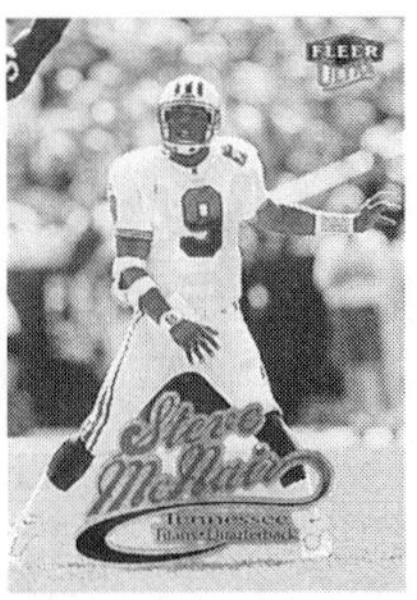

		MT
Complete Set (300):		200.00
Common Player:		.15
Minor Stars:		.30
Common Rookie (261-300):		1.50
Inserted 1:4		
Common Back 2 Back:		3.00
Inserted 1:8		
Pack (10):		3.50
Wax Box (24):		75.00
1	Terrell Davis	2.50
2	Courtney Hawkins	.15
3	Cris Carter	.50
4	Darnay Scott	.15
5	Darrell Green	.15
6	Jimmy Smith	.30
7	Doug Flutie	.75
8	Michael Jackson	.15
9	Warren Sapp	.15
10	Greg Hill	.15
11	Karim Abdul	.50
12	Greg Ellis	.15
13	Dan Marino	2.00
14	Napoleon Kaufman	.50
15	Peyton Manning	2.50
16	Simeon Rice	.15
17	Tony Simmons	.30
18	Carlester Crumpler	.15
19	Charles Johnson	.15
20	Derrick Alexander	.15
21	Kent Graham	.15
22	Randall Cunningham	.50
23	Trent Green	.50
24	Chris Spielman	.15
25	Carl Pickens	.30
26	Bill Romanowski	.15
27	Jermaine Lewis	.15
28	Ahman Green	.30
29	Bryan Still	.15
30	Dorsey Levens	.50
31	Frank Wycheck	.15
32	Jerome Bettis	.50
33	Reidel Anthony	.30
34	Robert Jones	.15
35	Terry Glenn	.50
36	Tim Brown	.50
37	Eric Metcalf	.15
38	Kevin Greene	.15
39	Takeo Spikes	.15
40	Brian Mitchell	.15
41	Duane Starks	.15
42	Eddie George	1.00
43	Joe Jurevicius	.15
44	Kimble Anders	.15
45	Kordell Stewart	1.00
46	Leroy Hoard	.15
47	Rod Smith	.30
48	Terrell Owens	.75
49	Tony McGee	.15
50	Charles Woodson	.50
51	Andre Rison	.15
52	Chris Slade	.15
53	Frank Sanders	.30
54	Michael Irvin	.30
55	Jerome Pathon	.15
56	Desmond Howard	.15
57	Billy Davis	.15
58	Anthony Simmons	.15
59	James Jett	.15
60	Jake Plummer	1.50
61	John Avery	.30
62	Marvin Harrison	.50
63	Merton Hanks	.15
64	Ricky Proehl	.15
65	Steve Beuerlein	.15
66	Willie McGinest	.15
67	Bryce Paup	.15
68	Brett Favre	3.00
69	Brian Griese	1.00
70	Curtis Martin	.75
71	Drew Bledsoe	1.25
72	Jim Harbaugh	.30
73	Joey Galloway	.50
74	Natrone Means	.50
75	O.J. McDuffie	.15
76	Tiki Barber	.15
77	Wesley Walls	.15
78	Will Blackwell	.15
79	Bert Emanuel	.15
80	J.J. Stokes	.30
81	Steve McNair	1.00
82	Adrian Murrell	.15
83	Dexter Coakley	.15
84	Jeff George	.30
85	Marshall Faulk	.30
86	Tim Biakabutuka	.30
87	Troy Drayton	.15
88	Ty Law	.15
89	Brian Simmons	.15
90	Eric Allen	.15
91	Jon Kitna	.75
92	Junior Seau	.30
93	Kevin Turner	.15
94	Larry Centers	.15
95	Robert Edwards	.50
96	Rocket Ismail	.15
97	Sam Madison	.15
98	Stephen Alexander	.15
99	Trent Dilfer	.30
100	Vonnie Holliday	.30
101	Charlie Garner	.15
102	Deion Sanders	.75
103	Jamal Anderson	.75
104	Mike Vanderjagt	.15
105	Aeneas Williams	.15
106	Daryl Johnston	.15
107	Hugh Douglas	.15
108	Torrance Small	.15
109	Amani Toomer	.15
110	Amp Lee	.15
111	Germane Crowell	.30
112	Marco Battaglia	.15
113	Michael Westbrook	.15
114	Randy Moss	4.00
115	Ricky Watters	.50
116	Rob Johnson	.30
117	Tony Gonzalez	.30
118	Charles Way	.15
119	Chris Penn	.15
120	Eddie Kennison	.15
121	Elvis Grbac	.15
122	Eric Moulds	.50
123	Terry Fair	.15
124	Tony Banks	.30
125	Chris Chandler	.30
126	Emmitt Smith	2.00
127	Herman Moore	.50
128	Irv Smith	.15
129	Kyle Brady	.15
130	Lamont Warren	.15
131	Troy Davis	.15
132	Andre Reed	.30
133	Justin Armour	.15
134	James Hasty	.15
135	Johnnie Morton	.15
136	Reggie Barlow	.15
137	Robert Holcombe	.30
138	Sean Dawkins	.15
139	Steve Atwater	.15
140	Tim Dwight	.50
141	Wayne Chrebet	.50
142	Alonzo Mayes	.15
143	Mark Brunell	1.25
144	Antowain Smith	.50
145	Bam Morris	.15
146	Isaac Bruce	.50
147	Bryan Cox	.15
148	Bryant Westbrook	.15
149	Duce Staley	.15
150	Barry Sanders	3.00
151	La'Roi Glover	.15
152	Ray Crockett	.15
153	Tony Brackens	.15
154	Roy Barker	.15
155	Kerry Collins	.30
156	Andre Wadsworth	.30
157	Cameron Cleeland	.30
158	Koy Detmer	.15
159	Marcus Pollard	.15
160	*Patrick Jeffers*	7.00
161	Aaron Glenn	.15
162	Andre Hastings	.15
163	Bruce Smith	.15
164	David Palmer	.15
165	Erik Kramer	.15
166	Orlando Pace	.15
167	Robert Brooks	.30
168	Shawn Springs	.15
169	Terance Mathis	.15
170	Chris Calloway	.15
171	Gilbert Brown	.15
172	Charlie Jones	.15
173	Curtis Enis	.75
174	Eugene Robinson	.15
175	Garrison Hearst	.50
176	Jason Elam	.15
177	John Randle	.15
178	Keith Poole	.15
179	Kevin Hardy	.15
180	Keyshawn Johnson	.75
181	O.J. Santiago	.15
182	Jacquez Green	.30
183	Bobby Engram	.15
184	Damon Jones	.15
185	Freddie Jones	.15
186	Jake Reed	.15
187	Jerry Rice	1.50
188	Joey Kent	.15
189	Lamar Smith	.15
190	John Elway	2.00
191	Leon Johnson	.15
192	Mark Chmura	.30
193	Peter Boulware	.15
194	Zach Thomas	.30
195	Marc Edwards	.15
196	Mike Alstott	.75
197	Yancey Thigpen	.30
198	Oronde Gadsden	.30
199	Rae Carruth	.15
200	Troy Aikman	1.50
201	Shawn Jefferson	.15
202	Rob Moore	.30
203	Rickey Dudley	.15
204	Jason Taylor	.15
205	Curtis Conway	.30
206	Darrien Gordon	.15
207	Eric Green	.15
208	Jesse Armstead	.15
209	Keenan McCardell	.30
210	Robert Smith	.50
211	Mo Lewis	.15
212	Ryan Leaf	1.00
213	Steve Young	1.00
214	Tyrone Davis	.15
215	Chad Brown	.15
216	Ike Hilliard	.15
217	Jimmy Hitchcock	.15
218	Kevin Dyson	.30
219	Levon Kirkland	.15
220	Neil O'Donnell	.15
221	Ray Lewis	.15
222	Shannon Sharpe	.50
223	Skip Hicks	.50
224	Brad Johnson	.50
225	Charlie Batch	1.00
226	Corey Dillon	.75
227	Dale Carter	.15
228	John Mobley	.15
229	Hines Ward	.30
230	Leslie Shepherd	.15
231	Michael Strahan	.15
232	R.W. McQuarters	.15
233	Mike Pritchard	.15
234	Antonio Freeman	.75
235	Ben Coates	.50
236	Michael Bates	.15
237	Ed McCaffrey	.50
238	Gary Brown	.15
239	Mark Bruener	.15
240	Mikhael Ricks	.15
241	Muhsin Muhammad	.15
242	Priest Holmes	.75
243	Stephen Davis	.15
244	Vinny Testaverde	.50
245	Warrick Dunn	1.00
246	Derrick Mayes	.15
247	Fred Taylor	1.50
248	Drew Bledsoe CL	.50
249	Eddie George CL	.50
250	Steve Young CL	.50
251	Back-2-Back - Super Bowl XXXIII	3.00
252	Back-2-Back - Super Bowl XXXIII	3.00
253	Back-2-Back - Super Bowl XXXIII	3.00
254	Back-2-Back - Super Bowl XXXIII	3.00
255	Back-2-Back - Super Bowl XXXIII	3.00
256	Back-2-Back - Super Bowl XXXIII	3.00
257	Back-2-Back - Super Bowl XXXIII	3.00
258	Back-2-Back - Super Bowl XXXIII	3.00
259	Back-2-Back - Super Bowl XXXIII	3.00
260	Back-2-Back - Super Bowl XXXIII	3.00
261	*Ricky Williams*	12.00
262	*Tim Couch*	12.00
263	*Chris Claiborne*	3.00
264	*Champ Bailey*	4.00
265	*Torry Holt*	8.00
266	*Donovan McNabb*	12.00
267	*David Boston*	8.00
268	*Chris McAlister*	3.00
269	*Brock Huard*	5.00
270	*Daunte Culpepper*	15.00
271	*Matt Stinchcomb*	1.50
272	*Edgerrin James*	25.00
273	*Jevon Kearse*	7.00
274	*Ebenezer Ekuban*	1.50
275	*Kris Farris*	1.50
276	*Chris Terry*	1.50
277	*Jerame Tuman*	1.50
278	*Akili Smith*	7.00
279	*Aaron Gibson*	3.00
280	*Rahim Abdullah*	1.50
281	*Peerless Price*	4.00
282	*Antoine Winfield*	3.00
283	*Antwan Edwards*	3.00
284	*Rob Konrad*	3.00
285	*Troy Edwards*	5.00
286	*John Thornton*	1.50
287	*James Johnson*	3.00
288	*Gary Stills*	1.50
289	*Mike Peterson*	1.50
290	*Kevin Faulk*	5.00
291	*Jared DeVries*	1.50
292	*Martin Gramatica*	3.00
293	*Montae Reagor*	1.50
294	*Andy Katzenmoyer*	3.00
295	*Sedrick Irvin*	3.00
296	*D'Wayne Bates*	3.00
297	*Amos Zereoue*	3.00
298	*Dre' Bly*	1.50
299	*Kevin Johnson*	6.00
300	*Cade McNown*	6.00

1999 Ultra Gold Medallion Parallel

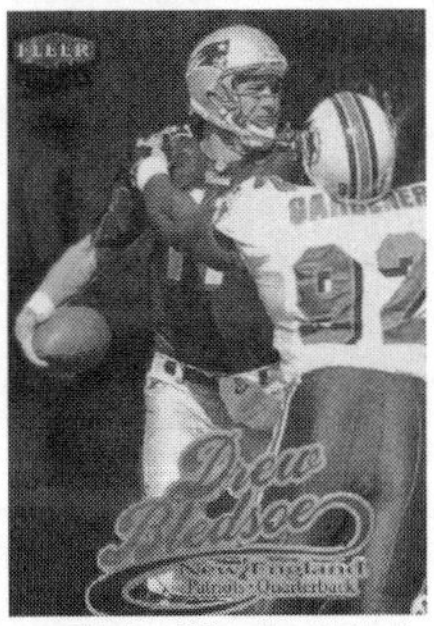

This is a 300-card parallel to the base and is the same except for each card is printed on gold foil and stamped Gold Medallion Edition on the back. Veterans were inserted 1:1, Rookies 1:25 and Super Bowl singles at 1:50.

	MT
Complete Set (300):	600.00
Gold Cards:	2x-4x
Inserted 1:1	
Gold Rookies:	1.5x
Inserted 1:25	
Gold Back 2 Back:	5x-10x
Inserted 1:50	

1999 Ultra Platinum Medallion Parallel

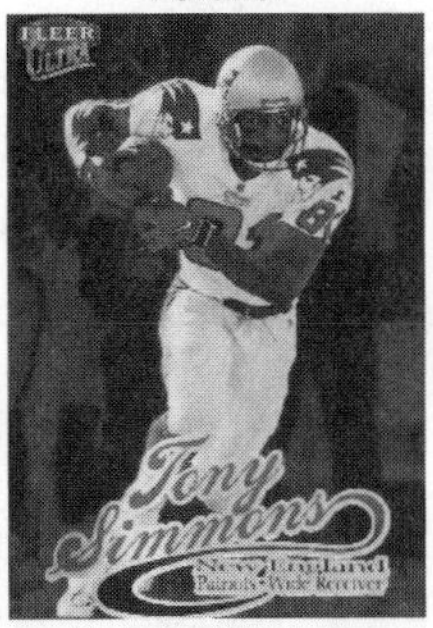

This is a parallel to the base and is the same except for each card is printed on a silver stock and on the backs are sequentially numbered and have a Platinum Medallion stamp. Veterans are numbered to 99, Rookies to 65 and Super Bowl singles to 40.

	MT
Platinum Cards:	35x-70x
Production 99 Sets	
Platinum Rookies:	3x-6x
Production 65 Sets	
Platinum Back 2 Back:	25x-50x
Production 40 Sets	

1999 Ultra As Good As It Gets

Each of the 15 players in this set are the best in the NFL. Each is on a die-cut felt stock with silver and gold holofoil. Singles were inserted 1:288 packs.

		MT
Complete Set (15):		500.00
Common Player:		12.00
Inserted 1:288		
1	Warrick Dunn	12.00
2	Terrell Davis	50.00
3	Robert Edwards	12.00
4	Randy Moss	75.00
5	Peyton Manning	50.00
6	Mark Brunell	20.00
7	John Elway	50.00
8	Jerry Rice	30.00
9	Jake Plummer	25.00
10	Fred Taylor	30.00
11	Emmitt Smith	50.00
12	Dan Marino	50.00
13	Charlie Batch	20.00
14	Brett Favre	60.00
15	Barry Sanders	60.00

1999 Ultra Caught In The Draft

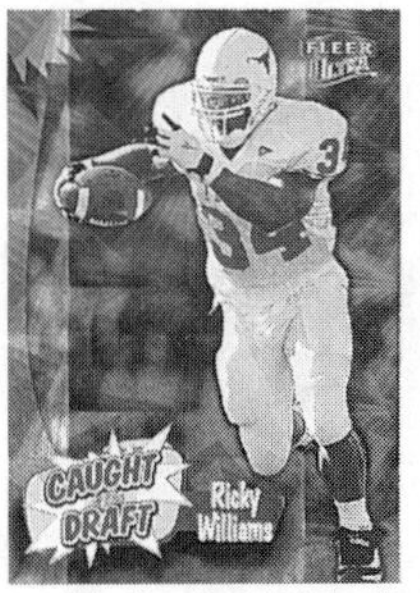

This 15-card set includes the top rookies from 1999 and captures them on a silver pattern holofoil card. They were inserted 1:18 packs.

		MT
Complete Set (15):		75.00
Common Player:		1.50
Minor Stars:		3.00
Inserted 1:18		
1	Ricky Williams	20.00
2	Tim Couch	25.00
3	Chris Claiborne	3.00
4	Champ Bailey	4.00
5	Torry Holt	6.00
6	Donovan McNabb	10.00
7	David Boston	6.00
8	Andy Katzenmoyer	1.50
9	Daunte Culpepper	8.00
10	Edgerrin James	12.00
11	Cade McNown	10.00
12	Troy Edwards	6.00
13	Akili Smith	10.00
14	Peerless Price	6.00
15	Amos Zereoue	3.00

1999 Ultra Counterparts

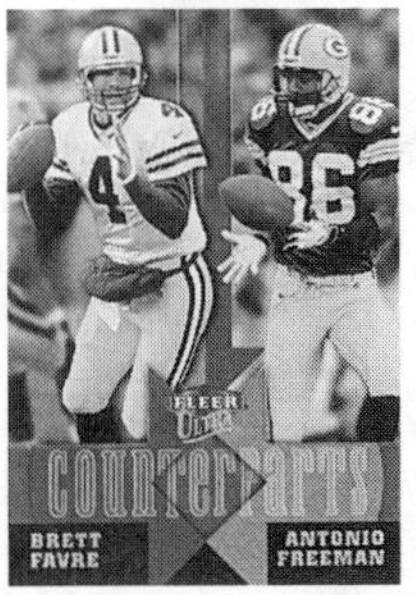

Each card in this 15-card set highlights two players from the same team and puts them on an embossed silver holofoil card. Singles were found 1:36 packs.

		MT
Complete Set (15):		100.00
Common Player:		4.00
Inserted 1:36		
1	Troy Aikman, Michael Irvin	10.00
2	Drew Bledsoe, Ben Coates	8.00
3	Terrell Davis, Howard Griffith	15.00
4	Warrick Dunn, Mike Alstott	6.00
5	Brett Favre, Antonio Freeman	20.00
6	Jake Plummer, Frank Sanders	8.00
7	Randy Moss, Randall Cunningham	25.00
8	Eddie George, Steve McNair	8.00
9	Keyshawn Johnson, Wayne Chrebet	4.00
10	Ryan Leaf, Mikhael Ricks	6.00
11	Peyton Manning, Marshall Faulk	15.00
12	Barry Sanders, Tommy Vardell	20.00
13	Charlie Batch, Herman Moore	8.00
14	Emmitt Smith, Daryl Johnston	15.00
15	Kordell Stewart, Jerome Bettis	8.00

1999 Ultra Damage Inc.

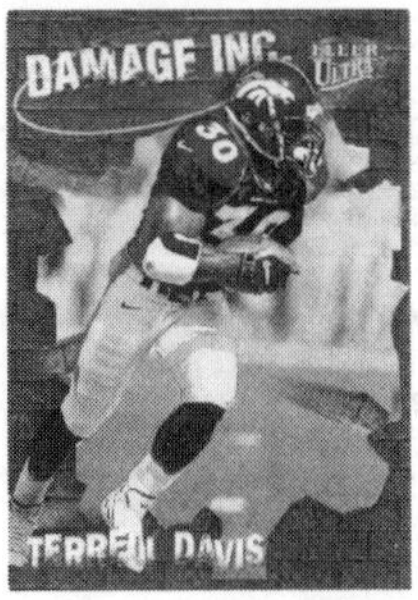

This 15-card set includes the top players in the league and showcases them on a sculpted special silver foil card. Singles were found 1:72 packs.

		MT
Complete Set (15):		180.00
Common Player:		6.00
Inserted 1:72		
1	Brett Favre	30.00
2	Dan Marino	20.00
3	John Elway	20.00
4	Mark Brunell	12.00
5	Peyton Manning	20.00
6	Robert Edwards	6.00
7	Terrell Davis	20.00
8	Troy Aikman	15.00
9	Randy Moss	35.00
10	Kordell Stewart	10.00
11	Jerry Rice	15.00
12	Fred Taylor	15.00
13	Emmitt Smith	20.00
14	Charlie Batch	10.00
15	Barry Sanders	30.00

1999 Ultra Over The Top

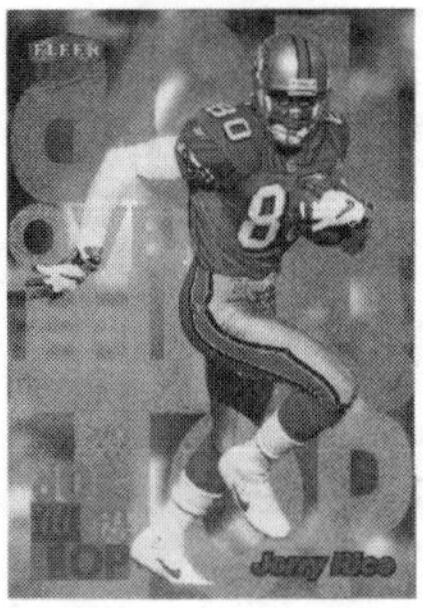

This was a 20-card set that included gold foil stamping and was inserted 1:6 packs.

		MT
Complete Set (20):		40.00
Common Player:		1.00
Minor Stars:		2.00
Inserted 1:6		
1	Troy Aikman	5.00
2	Drew Bledsoe	4.00
3	Mark Brunell	4.00
4	Randall Cunningham	2.00
5	Jamal Anderson	2.00
6	Warrick Dunn	3.00
7	Robert Edwards	2.00
8	John Elway	8.00
9	Eddie George	4.00
10	Eric Moulds	1.00
11	Keyshawn Johnson	2.00
12	Ryan Leaf	1.00
13	Dan Marino	8.00
14	Steve McNair	3.00
15	Jake Plummer	4.00
16	Jerry Rice	5.00
17	Deion Sanders	2.00
18	Kordell Stewart	4.00
19	Fred Taylor	8.00
20	Steve Young	3.00

Post-1980 cards in Near Mint condition will generally sell for about 75% of the quoted Mint value. Excellent-condition cards bring no more than 40%.

2000 Ultra

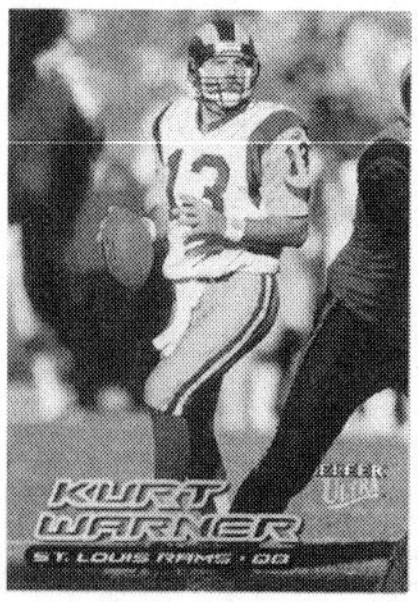

		MT
Complete Set (249):		150.00
Common Player:		.15
Minor Stars:		.30
Common Rookie:		1.25
Inserted 1:4		
Pack (10):		3.00
Wax Box (24):		60.00
1	Kurt Warner	3.00
2	Derrick Alexander	.15
3	Aaron Craver	.15
4	Kevin Faulk	.30
5	Marcus Robinson	.50
6	Tony Banks	.30
7	Jon Ritchie	.15
8	Torry Holt	.50
9	Joe Horn	.15
10	Eddie George	.60
11	Michael Westbrook	.30
12	Gus Frerotte	.15
13	Tim Brown	.30
14	Tamarick Vanover	.15
15	David Sloan	.15
16	Darnay Scott	.30
17	Junior Seau	.30
18	Warren Sapp	.30
19	Priest Holmes	.50
20	Jerry Rice	1.25
21	Cade McNown	.75
22	Johnnie Morton	.30
23	Vinny Testaverde	.30
24	James Jett	.15
25	Tony Gonzalez	.30
26	Charlie Batch	.50
27	Tony Simmons	.15
28	James Stewart	.30
29	Corey Dillon	.50
30	Ricky Williams	1.25
31	Ryan Leaf	.50
32	Terry Allen	.30
33	Freddie Jones	.15
34	Terry Kirby	.15
35	Charles Johnson	.15
36	William Henderson	.15
37	Stephen Alexander	.15
38	Moe Williams	.15
39	David Boston	.50
40	Emmitt Smith	1.75
41	Ken Oxendine	.15
42	Byron Hanspard	.15
43	Dwight Stone	.15
44	Jim Harbaugh	.30
45	Curtis Enis	.30
46	Peerless Price	.30
47	Terance Mathis	.15
48	Mike Alstott	.50
49	Rod Smith	.30
50	Marshall Faulk	.50
51	Derrick Mayes	.30
52	Keenan McCardell	.30
53	Curtis Martin	.50
54	Bobby Engram	.15
55	Carl Pickens	.30
56	Robert Smith	.50
57	Ike Hilliard	.30
58	Reidel Anthony	.30
59	Jeff Graham	.15
60	Mark Brunell	1.00
61	Joe Montgomery	.15
62	Ed McCaffrey	.50
63	Kenny Bynum	.15
64	Curtis Conway	.30
65	Trent Dilfer	.30
66	Jake Reed	.30
67	Jake Plummer	.75
68	Tony Martin	.15
69	Yatil Green	.15
70	Keyshawn Johnson	.50
71	Leroy Hoard	.15
72	Skip Hicks	.30
73	Marvin Harrison	.50
74	Steve Beuerlein	.30
75	Will Blackwell	.15
76	Derek Loville	.15
77	Warrick Dunn	.50
78	Amos Zereoue	.30
79	Ray Lucas	.50
80	Randy Moss	2.50
81	Wesley Walls	.30
82	Jimmy Smith	.50
83	Kordell Stewart	.50
84	Brian Griese	.50
85	Martin Gramatica	.15
86	Chris Chandler	.30
87	Reggie Barlow	.15
88	Jeff George	.30
89	Tavian Banks	.15
90	Muhsin Muhammad	.30
91	Steve McNair	.60
92	Hines Ward	.30
93	Brian Mitchell	.15
94	Daunte Culpepper	.75
95	Tim Dwight	.50
96	Terrence Wilkins	.30
97	Fred Lane	.15
98	Brett Favre	2.50
99	Richie Anderson	.15
100	Jamal Anderson	.50
101	Doug Flutie	.75
102	Charles Woodson	.50
103	Jacquez Green	.30
104	Olandis Gary	.50
105	Steve Young	.75
106	Wayne Chrebet	.50
107	Karim Abdul	.30
108	Andre Rison	.30
109	Eddie Kennison	.30
110	Jevon Kearse	.60
111	Tony Richardson	.15
112	*Jake Delhomme*	2.50
113	Errict Rhett	.30
114	Akili Smith	.75
115	Tyrone Wheatley	.30
116	Corey Bradford	.30
117	J.J. Stokes	.30
118	Simeon Rice	.15
119	Brad Johnson	.50
120	Edgerrin James	2.50
121	Amani Toomer	.30
122	O.J. McDuffie	.30
123	Az-Zahir Hakim	.30
124	Troy Edwards	.50
125	Tim Biakabutuka	.30
126	Jason Tucker	.50
127	Charles Way	.15
128	Terrell Davis	1.75
129	Garrison Hearst	.30
130	Fred Taylor	.75
131	Robert Holcombe	.15
132	Frank Sanders	.15
133	Morten Andersen	.15
134	Cris Carter	.50
135	Patrick Jeffers	.50
136	Antonio Freeman	.50
137	Jonathon Linton	.30
138	Rashaan Shehee	.15
139	Luther Broughton	.15
140	Tim Couch	1.25
141	Keith Poole	.15
142	Champ Bailey	.50
143	Yancey Thigpen	.30
144	Joey Galloway	.50
145	Mac Cody	.15
146	Damon Huard	.30
147	Dorsey Levens	.50
148	Donovan McNabb	.75
149	Jamie Asher	.15
150	Peyton Manning	2.00
151	Leslie Shepherd	.15
152	Charlie Rogers	.15
153	Tony Horne	.15
154	Jim Miller	.15
155	Richard Huntley	.15
156	Germane Crowell	.30
157	Natrone Means	.30
158	Justin Armour	.15
159	Drew Bledsoe	.75
160	Dedric Ward	.15
161	Allen Rossum	.15
162	Ricky Watters	.30
163	Kerry Collins	.30
164	J.J. Johnson	.30
165	Elvis Grbac	.30
166	Larry Centers	.15
167	Rob Moore	.30
168	Jay Riemersma	.15
169	Bill Schroeder	.15
170	Deion Sanders	.50
171	Jerome Bettis	.50
172	Dan Marino	1.75
173	Terrell Owens	.50
174	Kevin Carter	.15
175	Lamar Smith	.15
176	Ken Dilger	.15
177	Napoleon Kaufman	.30
178	Kevin Williams	.15
179	Tremain Mack	.15
180	Troy Aikman	1.25
181	Glyn Milburn	.15
182	Pete Mitchell	.15
183	Cameron Cleeland	.30
184	Qadry Ismail	.15
185	Michael Pittman	.15
186	Kevin Dyson	.30
187	Matt Hasselbeck	.30
188	Kevin Johnson	.50
189	Rich Gannon	.30
190	Stephen Davis	.50
191	Frank Wycheck	.15
192	Eric Moulds	.50
193	Jon Kitna	.50
194	Mario Bates	.15
195	Na Brown	.15
196	Jeff Blake	.30
197	Charles Evans	.15
198	Oronde Gadsden	.15
199	Donell Bennett	.15
200	Isaac Bruce	.50
201	Olindo Mare	.15
202	Darnell McDonald	.30
203	Charlie Garner	.30
204	Shawn Jefferson	.15
205	Adrian Murrell	.30
206	Peter Boulware	.15
207	LeShon Johnson	.15
208	Herman Moore	.30
209	Duce Staley	.50
210	Sean Dawkins	.15
211	Antowain Smith	.30
212	Albert Connell	.30
213	Jeff Garcia	.50
214	Kimble Anders	.15
215	Shaun King	.75
216	Raghib Ismail	.15
217	Andrew Glover	.15
218	Rickey Dudley	.15
219	Michael Basnight	.15
220	Terry Glenn	.30
221	*Peter Warrick*	10.00
222	*Ron Dayne*	12.50
223	*Thomas Jones*	5.00
224	*Joe Hamilton*	2.50
225	*Tim Rattay*	2.50
226	*Chad Pennington*	8.00
227	*Dennis Northcutt*	2.50
228	*Troy Walters*	1.25
229	*Travis Prentice*	4.00
230	*Shaun Alexander*	7.00
231	*J.R. Redmond*	3.00
232	*Chris Redman*	5.00
233	*Tee Martin*	2.50
234	*Tom Brady*	6.00
235	*Travis Taylor*	3.00
236	*R. Jay Soward*	2.50
237	*Jamal Lewis*	15.00
238	*Giovanni Carmazzi*	2.50
239	*Dez White*	2.50
240	*LaVar Arrington*	150.00
241	*Laveranues Coles*	3.00
242	*Sherrod Gideon*	1.25
243	*Trung Canidate*	2.50
244	*Michael Wiley*	2.50
245	*Anthony Lucas*	1.25
246	*Darrell Jackson*	2.50
247	*Plaxico Burress*	6.00
248	*Reuben Droughns*	1.25
249	*Marc Bulger*	1.25
250	*Danny Farmer*	2.50

2000 Ultr Gold Medallion Parallel

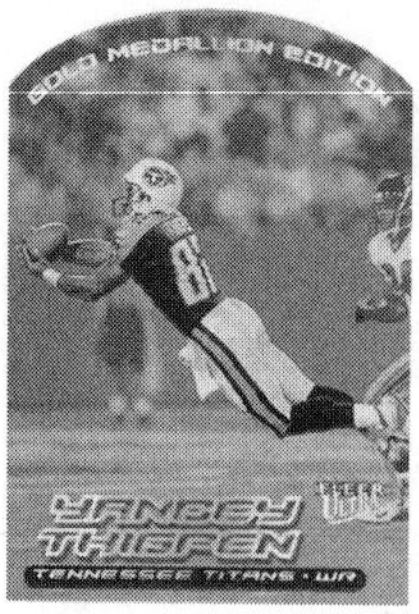

	MT
Complete Set (249):	300.00
Gold Cards:	2x-4x
Inserted 1:1	
Gold Rookies:	1.5x
Inserted 1:24	

2000 Ultra Masterpiece Parallel

MT

Production 1 Set

2000 Ultra Platinum Medallion Parallel

	MT
Platinum Cards:	35x-70x
Production 50 Sets	
Platinum Rookies:	6x-12x
Production 25 Sets	

2000 Ultra Autographics

	MT
Common Player:	10.00
Minor Stars:	20.00
Inserted 1:72	
Troy Aikman	10.00
Jamal Anderson	10.00
Jerome Bettis	20.00
Tim Biakabutuka	10.00
David Boston	20.00
Peter Boulware	10.00
Tom Brady	20.00
Isaac Bruce	20.00
Mark Brunell	45.00
Cris Carter	30.00
Germane Crowell	20.00
Terrell Davis	10.00
Ron Dayne	100.00
Tim Dwight	30.00
Deon Dyer	10.00
Kevin Dyson	10.00
Troy Edwards	10.00
Marshall Faulk	30.00
Christian Fauria	10.00
Jermaine Fazande	10.00
Rich Gannon	10.00
Jeff Garcia	25.00
Charlie Garner	10.00
Jeff Graham	10.00
Damon Griffin	10.00
Marvin Harrison	25.00
Tony Horne	20.00
Damon Huard	30.00
Darrell Jackson	20.00
Edgerrin James	100.00
Patrick Jeffers	20.00
Brad Johnson	25.00
Kevin Johnson	30.00
Rob Johnson	10.00
Terry Kirby	10.00
Jon Kitna	25.00
O.J. McDuffie	20.00
Rondell Mealey	20.00
Joe Montgomery	10.00
Herman Moore	20.00
Sylvester Morris	40.00
Eric Moulds	20.00
Muhsin Muhammad	20.00
Chad Pennington	75.00
Travis Prentice	35.00
Tim Rattay	20.00
Jon Ritchie	10.00
Antowain Smith	10.00
Kurt Warner	100.00
Chris Watson	10.00

2000 Ultra Dream Team

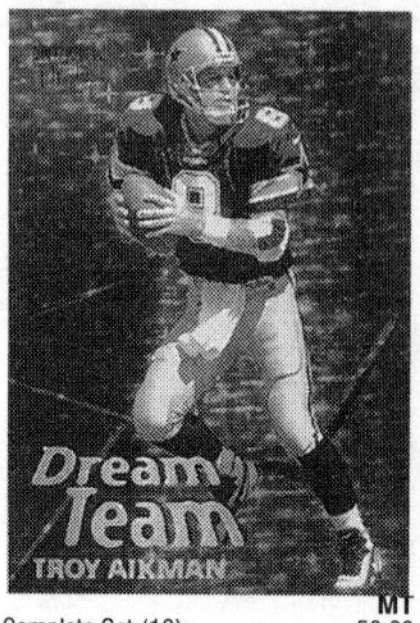

		MT
Complete Set (10):		50.00
Common Player:		2.50
Inserted 1:24		
1	Terrell Davis	8.00
2	Brett Favre	12.00
3	Troy Aikman	6.00
4	Keyshawn Johnson	2.50
5	Edgerrin James	12.00
6	Randy Moss	12.00
7	Marvin Harrison	2.50
8	Kurt Warner	15.00
9	Fred Taylor	6.00
10	Ricky Williams	8.00

2000 Ultra Fast Lane

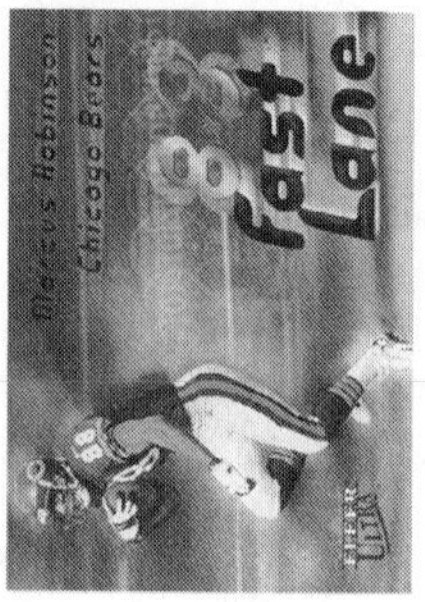

		MT
Complete Set (15):		12.00
Common Player:		.50
Minor Stars:		1.00
Inserted 1:3		
1	Jimmy Smith	1.00
2	Cris Carter	1.00
3	Marvin Harrison	1.00
4	Tim Brown	1.00
5	Muhsin Muhammad	1.00
6	Isaac Bruce	1.00
7	Bobby Engram	.50
8	Terance Mathis	.50
9	Randy Moss	3.00
10	Raghib Ismail	.50
11	Keyshawn Johnson	1.00
12	Terry Glenn	1.00
13	Jerry Rice	2.00
14	Marcus Robinson	1.50
15	Antonio Freeman	1.00

2000 Ultra Feel the Game

	MT
Complete Set (21):	500.00
Common Player:	20.00
Inserted 1:144	
Gold Cards:	2x
Production 50 Sets	
Karim Abdul	20.00
Mark Brunell	50.00
Chris Chandler	20.00
Tim Couch	75.00
Curtis Enis	20.00
Doug Flutie	50.00
Terry Glenn	30.00
Trent Green	20.00
Brian Griese	40.00
Az-Zahir Hakim	20.00
Terry Kirby	20.00
Dorsey Levens	30.00
Rob Moore	20.00
Jake Plummer	50.00
Frank Sanders	20.00
Emmitt Smith	100.00
Jimmy Smith	30.00
J.J. Stokes	20.00
Amani Toomer	20.00
Kurt Warner	150.00
Charles Woodson	30.00

2000 Ultra Feel the Game Gold Parallel

	MT
Gold Cards:	2x
Production 50 Sets	

2000 Ultra Head of the Class

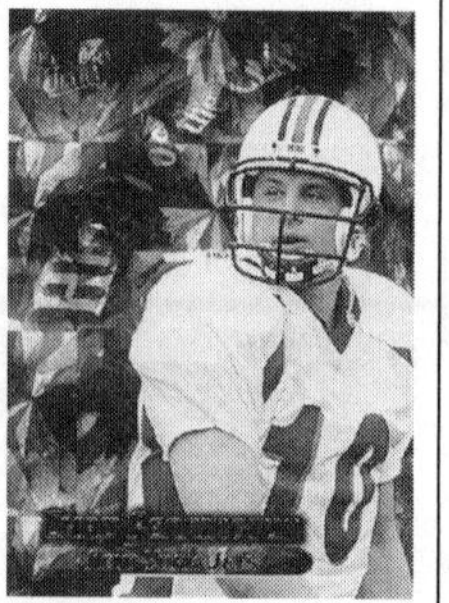

		MT
Complete Set (10):		15.00
Common Player:		.75
Inserted 1:6		
1	Peter Warrick	6.00
2	Ron Dayne	5.00
3	Thomas Jones	3.00
4	Chad Pennington	3.00
5	Joe Hamilton	.75
6	Shaun Alexander	2.00
7	J.R. Redmond	1.25
8	Troy Walters	.75
9	Travis Prentice	1.25
10	Chris Redman	1.50

2000 Ultra Instant 3 Play

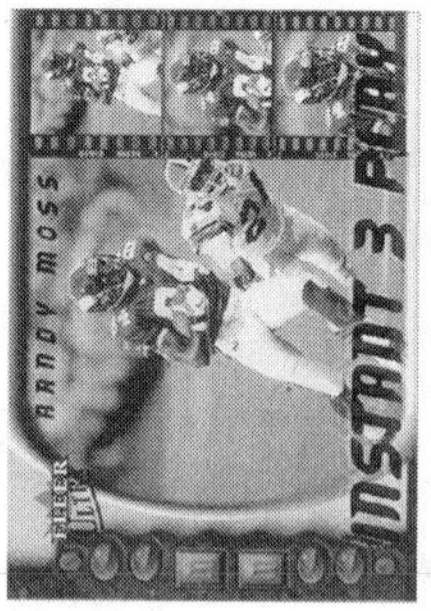

		MT
Complete Set (15):		12.00
Common Player:		.50
Minor Stars:		1.00
1	Peyton Manning	3.00
2	Curtis Enis	1.00
3	Charlie Batch	1.25
4	Fred Taylor	1.50
5	Az-Zahir Hakim	.50
6	Randy Moss	3.00
7	Jacquez Green	.50
8	Kevin Dyson	.50
9	Brian Griese	1.25
10	Rashaan Shehee	.50
11	Tony Simmons	.50
12	Charles Woodson	1.00
13	Hines Ward	.50
14	Skip Hicks	.50
15	Tim Dwight	1.00

2000 Ultra Millenium Monsters

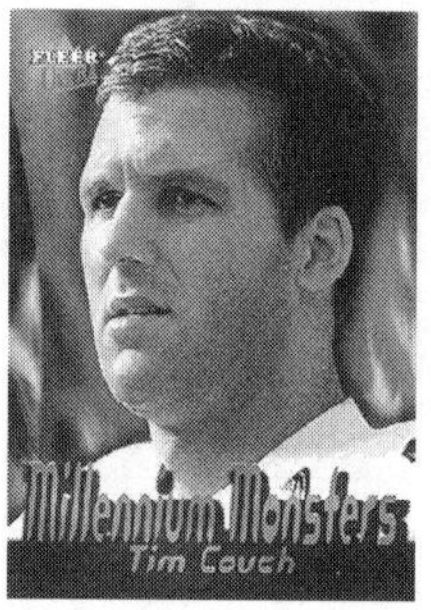

		MT
Complete Set (10):		20.00
Common Player:		1.00
Inserted 1:12		
1	Tim Couch	4.00
2	Eddie George	1.00
3	Brian Griese	1.00
4	Keyshawn Johnson	1.00
5	Peyton Manning	5.00
6	Randy Moss	5.00
7	Ricky Williams	4.00
8	Edgerrin James	5.00
9	Cade McNown	2.50
10	Donovan McNabb	2.50

2000 Ultra Season Pass

		MT
Complete Set (6):		20.00
Common Player:		2.00
1	Tim Couch	10.00
2	Troy Aikman	4.00
3	Mark Brunell	4.00
4	Drew Bledsoe	2.00
5	Chad Pennington	5.00
6	Chris Redman	2.00

2000 Ultra Won by One

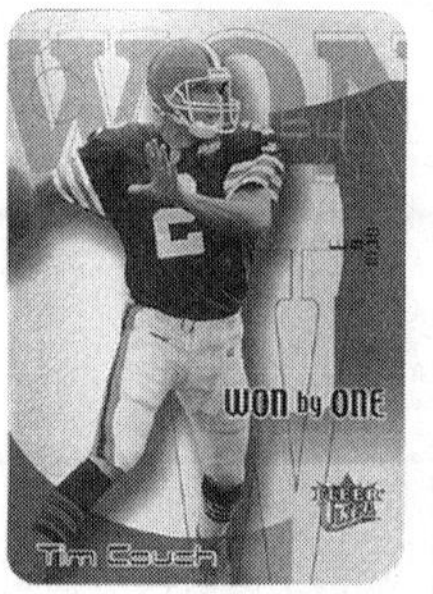

		MT
Complete Set (10):		100.00
Common Player:		4.00
Inserted 1:72		
1	Peyton Manning	20.00
2	Randy Moss	20.00
3	Brett Favre	20.00
4	Terrell Davis	12.00
5	Dan Marino	12.00
6	Jake Plummer	6.00
7	Tim Couch	10.00
8	Eddie George	4.00
9	Brian Griese	4.00
10	Kurt Warner	25.00

2001 Ultra

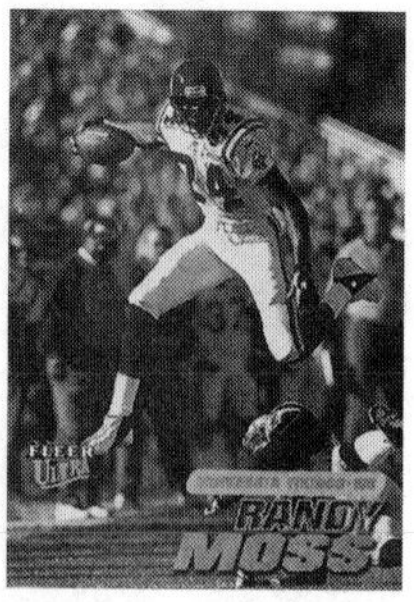

		MT
Complete Set (300):		250.00
Common Player:		.15
Minor Stars:		.30
Common Rookie:		2.00
Production 2,499 Sets		
Pack (10):		3.00
Wax Box (24):		60.00
1	Daunte Culpepper	1.25
2	Kurt Warner	2.00
3	Emmitt Smith	1.50
4	Eddie George	.75
5	Ron Dayne	1.25
6	Zach Thomas	.30
7	Itula Mili	.15
8	Jake Reed	.30
9	James Stewart	.50
10	Terrence Wilkins	.30
11	Jeff Blake	.30
12	Kerry Collins	.50
13	Christian Fauria	.15
14	Jackie Harris	.15
15	Kevin Johnson	.50
16	Tony Martin	.15
17	Joey Galloway	.50
18	Junior Seau	.30
19	Jason Tucker	.30
20	Steve Beuerlein	.30
21	Mike Cloud	.15
22	Kevin Faulk	.30
23	Az-Zahir Hakim	.30
24	Charles Johnson	.15
25	Curtis Martin	.50
26	Eric Moulds	.50
27	Bill Schroeder	.30
28	Amani Toomer	.30
29	Obafemi Ayanbadejo	.15
30	Aaron Shea	.15
31	Ken Dilger	.15
32	Terry Glenn	.50
33	Raghib Ismail	.30
34	Dorsey Levens	.50
35	Brian Mitchell	.15
36	Tony Richardson	.30
37	Sam Madison	.15
38	Darren Sharper	.15
39	Derrick Alexander	.30
40	Aaron Brooks	.75
41	Casey Crawford	.15
42	Terrell Fletcher	.15
43	William Henderson	.15
44	Thomas Jones	.50
45	Keenan McCardell	.30
46	Chad Pennington	1.25
47	Akili Smith	.50
48	Hines Ward	.30
49	Champ Bailey	.30
50	Cris Carter	.50
51	Corey Dillon	.50
52	Tony Gonzalez	.30
53	Darrell Jackson	.30
54	Chad Lewis	.30
55	Dave Moore	.15
56	Jay Riemersma	.15
57	J.J. Stokes	.30
58	Frank Wycheck	.30
59	Tiki Barber	.30
60	Tony Carter	.15
61	Rickey Dudley	.15
62	John Lynch	.15
63	Larry Foster	.15
64	Willie Jackson	.15
65	Jamal Lewis	1.75
66	Herman Moore	.30
67	Andre Rison	.30
68	Michael Strahan	.15
69	Charlie Batch	.50
70	Larry Centers	.15
71	Ron Dugans	.15
72	Jeff Graham	.15
73	Edgerrin James	1.75
74	Jermaine Lewis	.30
75	Charles Woodson	.30
76	Chris Redman	.75
77	Jon Ritchie	.15
78	Fred Taylor	.75
79	Jamal Anderson	.50
80	Isaac Bruce	.50
81	Terrell Davis	1.50
82	Rich Gannon	.30
83	Joe Horn	.30
84	Eddie Kennison	.30
85	Steve McNair	.50
86	Travis Prentice	.50
87	Rod Smith	.50
88	Ricky Watters	.30
89	Michael Bates	.15
90	Byron Chamberlain	.15
91	Warrick Dunn	.50
92	Elvis Grbac	.30
93	Patrick Jeffers	.50
94	Ray Lewis	.30
95	Sammy Morris	.50
96	Marcus Robinson	.50
97	Travis Taylor	.50
98	Fred Beasley	.15
99	Chris Chandler	.30
100	Tim Dwight	.50
101	Ahman Green	.50

102	Shawn Jefferson	.15
103	Jeremy McDaniel	.15
104	Sylvester Morris	.50
105	John Randle	.30
106	Vinny Testaverde	.50
107	Anthony Becht	.15
108	Wayne Chrebet	.50
109	Stephen Boyd	.15
110	Jacquez Green	.15
111	Mar Tay Jenkins	.15
112	Jason Gildon	.15
113	Chad Morton	.15
114	Deion Sanders	.50
115	Yancey Thigpen	.30
116	Marty Booker	.15
117	Curtis Conway	.30
118	Jermaine Fazande	.30
119	Matthew Hatchette	.30
120	Pat Johnson	.15
121	Terance Mathis	.15
122	Terrell Owens	.50
123	Corey Simon	.30
124	Darrick Vaughn	.15
125	Drew Bledsoe	.75
126	Albert Connell	.30
127	Brett Favre	2.50
128	Marvin Harrison	.50
129	Keyshawn Johnson	.50
130	Derrick Mason	.50
131	Dennis Northcutt	.30
132	Shannon Sharpe	.30
133	Brian Urlacher	1.25
134	Mike Anderson	1.75
135	Mark Bruener	.15
136	Sean Dawkins	.15
137	Jeff Garcia	.50
138	Tony Horne	.15
139	Shaun King	.50
140	Cade McNown	.50
141	Peerless Price	.30
142	R. Jay Soward	.30
143	Tyrone Wheatley	.50
144	Richie Anderson	.15
145	Mark Brunell	.75
146	JaJuan Dawson	.30
147	Charlie Garner	.30
148	Desmond Howard	.15
149	Jon Kitna	.30
150	Duane Starks	.15
151	J.R. Redmond	.50
152	Duce Staley	.50
153	Dez White	.30
154	David Boston	.50
155	Tim Couch	.75
156	Jay Fiedler	.30
157	Jessie Armstead	.15
158	Rob Johnson	.30
159	Brad Johnson	.50
160	Derrick Mayes	.30
161	Jerome Pathon	.15
162	David Sloan	.15
163	Wesley Walls	.15
164	Shaun Alexander	.50
165	Derrick Brooks	.15
166	Germane Crowell	.50
167	Doug Flutie	.50
168	Ike Hilliard	.15
169	Hugh Douglas	.15
170	Wane McGarity	.15
171	Michael Pittman	.15
172	Shawn Bryson	.15
173	Richard Huntley	.15
174	Darnell Autry	.15
175	Plaxico Burress	.50
176	Trent Dilfer	.30
177	Jeff George	.30
178	Qadry Ismail	.15
179	Ryan Leaf	.50
180	Jim Miller	.15
181	Jerry Rice	1.25
182	Kordell Stewart	.50
183	Ricky Williams	1.00
184	James Allen	.50
185	Courtney Brown	.50
186	Reidel Anthony	.15
187	Bubba Franks	.50
188	Priest Holmes	.50
189	Napoleon Kaufman	.30
190	Trevor Pryce	.15
191	Jake Plummer	.50
192	Jimmy Smith	.50
193	Michael Wiley	.30
194	Brock Huard	.30
195	Troy Brown	.15
196	Stephen Davis	.50
197	Oronde Gadsden	.30
198	Brad Hoover	.50
199	La'Roi Glover	.15
200	Donovan McNabb	1.00
201	Jerry Porter	.30
202	Robert Smith	.50
203	J.D. Watson	.15
204	Tim Biakabutuka	.30
205	Laveranues Coles	.50
206	Marshall Faulk	.75
207	Jim Harbaugh	.30
208	Doug Johnson	.30
209	Tee Martin	.30
210	Muhsin Muhammad	.30
211	Darnay Scott	.30
212	Jeremiah Trotter	.15
213	Troy Aikman	1.25
214	Kyle Brady	.15
215	Sam Cowart	.15
216	Darren Howard	.15
217	Donald Hayes	.30
218	Freddie Jones	.30
219	Ed McCaffrey	.50
220	David Patten	.15
221	Brian Griese	.75
222	Dedric Ward	.15
223	Jerome Bettis	.50
224	Greg Clark	.15
225	Bobby Engram	.15
226	Matt Hasselbeck	.50
227	James Jett	.15
228	Peyton Manning	1.75
229	Randy Moss	1.75
230	Warren Sapp	.30
231	James Thrash	.30
232	Mike Alstott	.50
233	Tim Brown	.30
234	Randall Cunningham	.30
235	Antonio Freeman	.50
236	Torry Holt	.50
237	Jevon Kearse	.50
238	James McKnight	.15
239	Marcus Pollard	.15
240	Lamar Smith	.50
241	Peter Warrick	1.25
242	Donnell Bennett	.15
243	Joe Johnson	.15
244	Troy Edwards	.30
245	Trent Green	.50
246	Jason Taylor	.15
247	Aeneas Williams	.15
248	Johnnie Morton	.30
249	Frank Sanders	.30
250	Jason Sehorn	.15
251	*Chris Weinke*	15.00
252	*Bobby Newcombe*	4.00
253	*LaDainian Tomlinson*	30.00
254	*Chad Johnson*	6.00
255	*Derrick Gibson*	2.00
256	*Sage Rosenfels*	6.00
257	*LaMont Jordan*	6.00
258	*Mike McMahon*	6.00
259	*Vinny Sutherland*	4.00
260	*Drew Brees*	30.00
261	*Deuce McAllister*	15.00
262	*Kevan Barlow*	2.00
263	*Jamar Fletcher*	4.00
264	*Gerard Warren*	2.00
265	*Todd Heap*	6.00
266	*Travis Henry*	10.00
267	*Quincy Morgan*	6.00
268	*Anthony Thomas*	30.00
269	*Andre Carter*	2.00
270	*Freddie Mitchell*	8.00
271	*Richard Seymour*	2.00
272	*Josh Booty*	4.00
273	*Robert Ferguson*	6.00
274	*Marques Tuiasosopo*	10.00
275	*Reggie Wayne*	10.00
276	*Jabari Holloway*	4.00
277	*Rudi Johnson*	6.00
278	*Michael Bennett*	15.00
279	*Marvin "Snoop" Minnis*	8.00
280	*Dan Morgan*	2.00
281	*Rod Gardner*	12.00
282	*Jesse Palmer*	4.00
283	*Michael Vick*	45.00
284	*Chris Chambers*	8.00
285	*James Jackson*	8.00
286	*David Terrell*	20.00
287	*Koren Robinson*	12.00
288	*Travis Minor*	8.00
289	*Santana Moss*	20.00
290	*Josh Heupel*	15.00
291	*Jamal Reynolds*	2.00
292	*Ken-Yon Rambo*	4.00
293	*Cedrick Wilson*	2.00
294	*Alge Crumpler*	2.00
295	*Fred Smoot*	4.00
296	*Dan Alexander*	2.00
297	*Tim Hasselbeck*	5.00
298	*Will Allen*	2.00
299	*Keith Adams*	2.00
300	*Heath Evans*	2.00

2001 Ultra Ball Hawks

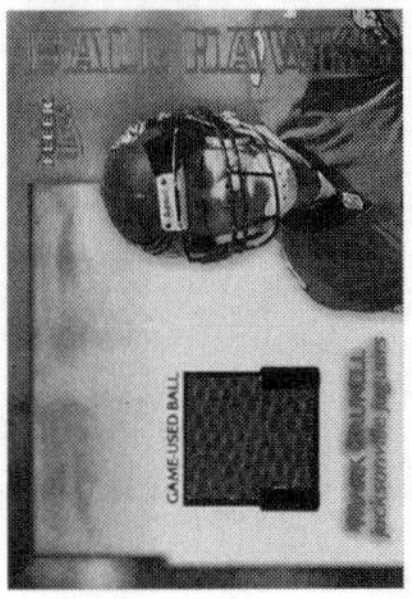

	MT
Common Player:	6.00
Inserted 1:144	
Troy Aikman	30.00
Derrick Alexander	6.00
Jamal Anderson	8.00
Charlie Batch	8.00
Courtney Brown	8.00
Mark Brunell	10.00
Tim Couch	12.00
Eddie George	8.00
Tony Gonzalez	6.00
Elvis Grbac	6.00
Marvin Harrison	8.00
Edgerrin James	35.00
Kevin Johnson	8.00
Jevon Kearse	8.00
Peyton Manning	40.00
Donovan McNabb	25.00
Steve McNair	8.00
Cade McNown	8.00
Herman Moore	6.00
Travis Prentice	8.00
Marcus Robinson	8.00
Emmitt Smith	35.00
Jimmy Smith	6.00
Duce Staley	8.00
Brian Urlacher	35.00

2001 Ultra Gold Medallion Parallel

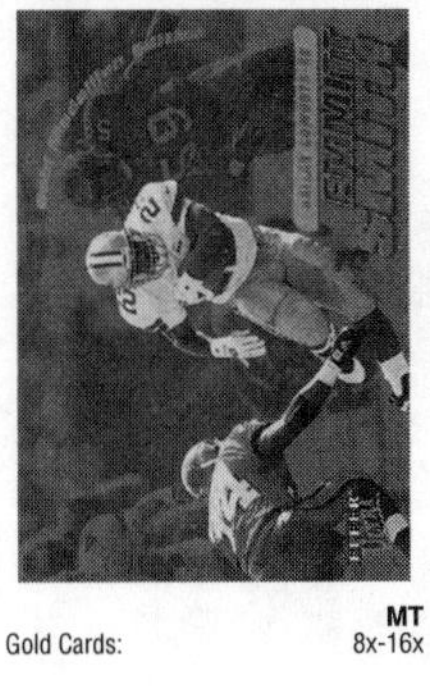

	MT
Gold Cards:	8x-16x
Production 250 Sets	
Gold Rookies:	2x-4x
Production 100 Sets	

2001 Ultra Ground Command

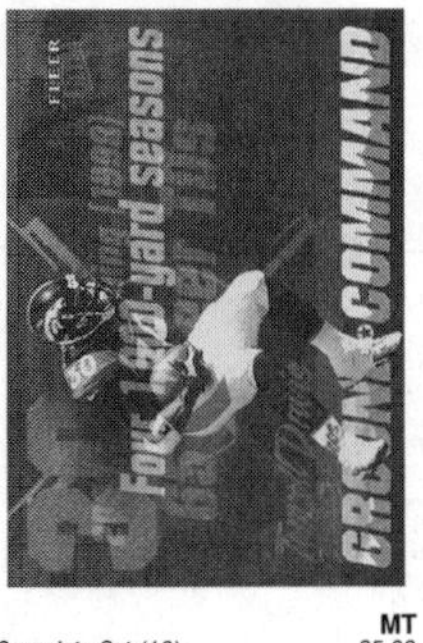

		MT
Complete Set (10):		25.00
Common Player:		1.50
Inserted 1:22		
Gold Cards:		2x-4x
Production 250 Sets		
Platinum Cards:		5x-10x
Production 50 Sets		
1GC	Emmitt Smith	4.00
2GC	Edgerrin James	6.00
3GC	Marshall Faulk	2.00
4GC	Jamal Lewis	7.00
5GC	Mike Anderson	7.00
6GC	Duce Staley	1.50
7GC	Jamal Anderson	1.50
8GC	Ricky Williams	3.00
9GC	Corey Dillon	1.50
10GC	Terrell Davis	4.00

2001 Ultra Head of the Class

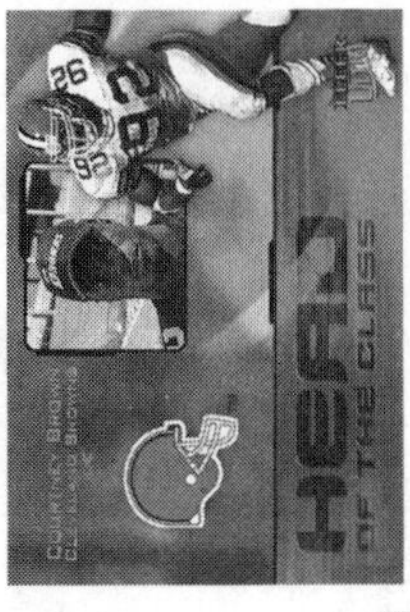

		MT
Complete Set (25):		65.00
Common Player:		1.50
Minor Stars:		3.00
Inserted 1:22		
1HC	Trung Canidate	1.50
2HC	Thomas Jones	3.00
3HC	Curtis Keaton	1.50
4HC	Courtney Brown	3.00
5HC	Chris Redman	4.00
6HC	Dennis Northcutt	3.00
7HC	Sylvester Morris	5.00
8HC	Shaun Alexander	5.00
9HC	Dez White	1.50
10HC	Laveranues Coles	4.00
11HC	R. Jay Soward	3.00
12HC	Jamal Lewis	10.00
13HC	J.R. Redmond	3.00
14HC	Travis Taylor	4.00
15HC	Plaxico Burress	5.00
16HC	Peter Warrick	7.00
17HC	Joe Hamilton	3.00
18HC	Ron Dugans	1.50
19HC	Tee Martin	3.00
20HC	Brian Urlacher	6.00
21HC	Ron Dayne	6.00
22HC	Travis Prentice	4.00
23HC	Chad Pennington	6.00
24HC	Corey Simon	1.50
25HC	Mike Anderson	10.00

2001 Ultra Head of the Class Hats

		MT
Common Player:		25.00
Production 100 Sets		
1HC	Trung Canidate	25.00
2HC	Thomas Jones	40.00
3HC	Curtis Keaton	25.00
4HC	Courtney Brown	35.00
5HC	Chris Redman	50.00
6HC	Dennis Northcutt	35.00
7HC	Sylvester Morris	60.00
8HC	Shaun Alexander	60.00
9HC	Dez White	25.00
10HC	Laveranues Coles	35.00
11HC	R. Jay Soward	25.00
12HC	Jamal Lewis	125.00
13HC	J.R. Redmond	35.00
14HC	Travis Taylor	40.00
15HC	Plaxico Burress	60.00
16HC	Peter Warrick	85.00
17HC	Joe Hamilton	35.00
18HC	Ron Dugans	25.00
19HC	Tee Martin	35.00
20HC	Brian Urlacher	100.00
21HC	Ron Dayne	75.00
22HC	Travis Prentice	45.00
23HC	Chad Pennington	100.00
24HC	Corey Simon	35.00
25HC	Mike Anderson	100.00

2001 Ultra Platinum Medallion Parallel

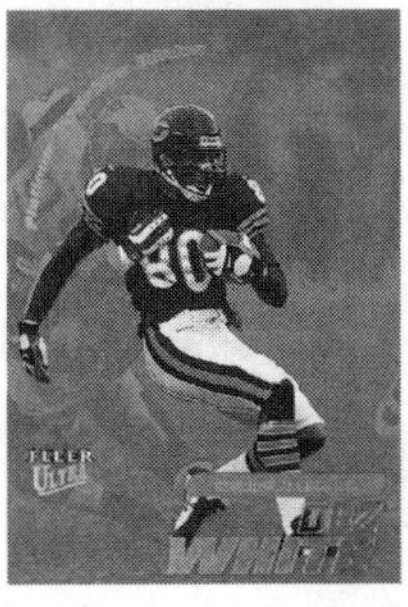

	MT
Platinum Cards:	50x-100x
Production 50 Sets	
Platinum Rookies:	4x-8x
Production 25 Sets	

2001 Ultra Quick Strike

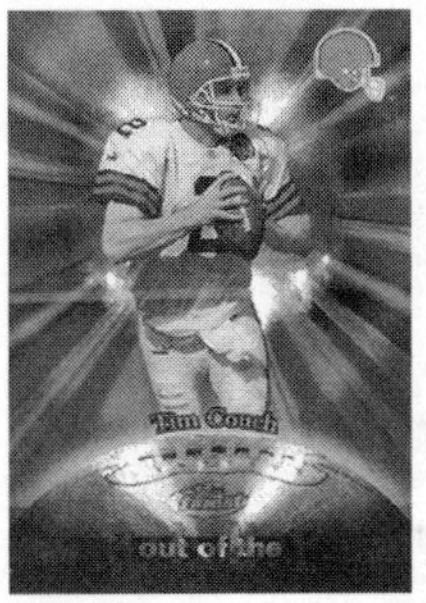

		MT
Complete Set (20):		80.00
Common Player:		1.50
Minor stars:		3.00
Inserted 1:22		
Gold Cards:		2x-4x
Production 250 Sets		
Platinum Cards:		5x-10x
Production 50 Sets		
1QS	Kurt Warner	10.00
2QS	Mark Brunell	4.00
3QS	Fred Taylor	4.00
4QS	Emmitt Smith	7.00
5QS	Jerry Rice	6.00
6QS	Eddie George	4.00
7QS	Cade McNown	3.00
8QS	Randy Moss	8.00
9QS	Donovan McNabb	5.00
10QS	Peyton Manning	8.00
11QS	Edgerrin James	8.00
12QS	Shaun King	5.00
13QS	Troy Aikman	6.00
14QS	Tim Couch	5.00
15QS	Jamal Lewis	7.00
16QS	Daunte Culpepper	7.00
17QS	Brett Favre	10.00
18QS	Drew Bledsoe	5.00
19QS	Terrell Davis	7.00
20QS	Marshall Faulk	4.00

2001 Ultra Sunday's Best

	MT
Common Player:	4.00
Inserted 1:63	
Jamal Anderson	6.00
Jerome Bettis	6.00
Drew Bledsoe	10.00
Isaac Bruce	6.00
Mark Brunell	10.00
Trung Canidate	4.00
Tim Couch	12.00
Stephen Davis	6.00
Ron Dayne	15.00
Warrick Dunn	4.00
Marshall Faulk	8.00
Doug Flutie	8.00
Antonio Freeman	6.00
Brian Griese	6.00
Kevin Johnson	6.00
Thomas Jones	6.00
Napoleon Kaufman	4.00
Curtis Martin	6.00
Keenan McCardell	4.00
Terrell Owens	6.00
Jake Plummer	6.00
Jerry Rice	25.00
Jimmy Smith	6.00
Rod Smith	6.00
R. Jay Soward	4.00
Fred Taylor	10.00
Brian Urlacher	20.00
Kurt Warner	35.00

2001 Ultra Two Minute Thrill

		MT
Complete Set (20):		50.00
Common Player:		1.50
Inserted 1:22		
Gold Cards:		2x-4x
Production 250 Sets		
Platinum Cards:		5x-10x
Production 50 Sets		
1TT	Troy Aikman	4.00
2TT	Terrell Davis	5.00
3TT	Keyshawn Johnson	1.50
4TT	Peyton Manning	6.00
5TT	Donovan McNabb	3.00
6TT	Steve McNair	1.50
7TT	Cade McNown	1.50
8TT	Ricky Williams	3.00
9TT	Brett Favre	8.00
10TT	Edgerrin James	6.00
11TT	Tim Couch	2.50
12TT	Fred Taylor	2.00
13TT	Rich Gannon	1.50
14TT	Kurt Warner	8.00
15TT	Randy Moss	6.00
16TT	Peter Warrick	4.00
17TT	Ron Dayne	3.00
18TT	Mark Brunell	2.00
19TT	Daunte Culpepper	4.00
20TT	Marshall Faulk	2.00

1991 Upper Deck Promos

These two promo card preview Upper Deck's 1991 debut football set. The design is similar to that which was used for the regular set, but the photos and card numbers for the two players' corresponding cards are different. Cards were also available through 900-number promotion by Upper Deck. The Montana card is $4; the Sanders card is $2.50.

		MT
Complete Set (2):		12.00
Common Player:		7.00
1	Joe Montana	7.00
500	Barry Sanders	8.00

1991 Upper Deck

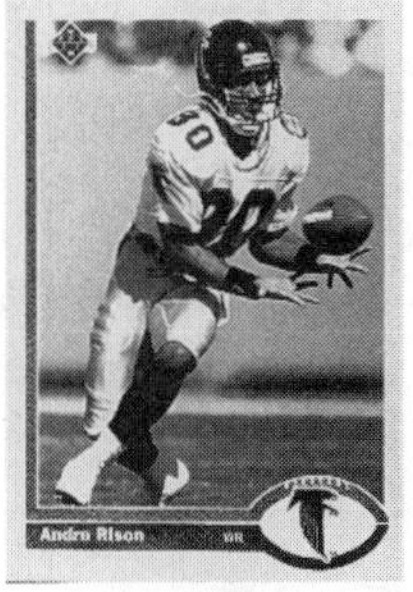

Issued in August, Upper Deck's premier football set was issued on foil packs. Upper Deck also randomly issued 2,500 autographed Joe Montana Heroes of Football cards. The set includes many of the elements from the baseball and hockey sets, including a "Star Rookies" subset. (Key: SR - star rookie, SL - season leader)

		MT
Complete Set (700):		15.00
Complete Lo Series (500):		10.00
Complete Hi Series (200):		5.00
Complete Factory Set (700):		20.00
Common Player:		.05
Low or High Pack (12):		.30
Low or High Wax Box (36):		10.00
1	Star Rookie Checklist	.10
2	*Eric Bieniemy* (SR)	.15
3	Mike Dumas (SR)	.05
4	*Mike Croel* (SR)	.15
5	*Russell Maryland* (SR)	.50
6	*Charles McRae* (SR)	.10
7	*Dan McGwire* (SR)	.10
8	*Mike Pritchard* (SR)	.35
9	*Ricky Watters* (SR)	1.75
10	*Chris Zorich* (SR)	.30
11	*Browning Nagle* (SR)	.20
12	*Wesley Carroll* (SR)	.10
13	*Brett Favre* (SR)	5.00
14	*Rob Carpenter* (SR)	.15
15	*Eric Swann* (SR)	.25
16	*Stanley Richard*	.35
17	*Herman Moore* (SR)	3.50
18	*Todd Marinovich* (SR)	.10
19	Aaron Craver (SR)	.10
20	Chuck Webb (SR)	.05
21	*Todd Lyght* (SR)	.10
22	*Greg Lewis* (SR)	.15
23	*Eric Turner* (SR)	.20
24	*Alvin Harper* (SR)	.30
25	*Jarrod Bunch* (SR)	.10
26	*Bruce Pickens* (SR)	.10
27	*Harvey Williams* (SR)	.50
28	*Randal Hill* (SR)	.40
29	*Nick Bell* (SR)	.15
30	Jim Everett, Henry Ellard	.05
31	Randall Cunningham, Keith Jackson	.10
32	Steve DeBerg, Stephone Paige	.05
33	Warren Moon, Drew Hill	.10
34	Dan Marino, Mark Clayton	.20
35	Montana, Rice	.40
36	Percy Snow	.05
37	Kelvin Martin	.05
38	Scott Case	.05
39	*John Gesek*	.10
40	*Barry Word*	.15
41	Cornelius Bennett	.05
42	Mike Kenn	.05
43	Andre Reed	.15
44	Bobby Hebert	.05
45	William Perry	.05
46	Dennis Byrd	.05
47	Martin Mayhew	.05
48	Issiac Holt	.05
49	William White	.05
50	JoJo Townsell	.05
51	Jarvis Williams	.05
52	Joey Browner	.05
53	Pat Terrell	.05
54	Joe Montana	1.00
55	Jeff Jerrod	.05
56	Cris Carter	.05
57	Jerry Rice	.75
58	Brett Perriman	.05
59	Kevin Fagen	.05
60	Wayne Haddix	.05
61	Tommy Kane	.05
62	Pat Beach	.05
63	Jeff Lageman	.05
64	Hassan Jones	.05
65	Bennie Blades	.05
66	Tim McGee	.05
67	Robert Blackmon	.05
68	*Fred Stokes*	.20
69	*Barney Bussey*	.10
70	Eric Metcalf	.05
71	Mark Kelso	.05
72	Bears Checklist (Neal Anderson)	.05
73	Bengals Checklist (Boomer Esiason)	.05
74	Bills Checklist (Thurman Thomas)	.25
75	Broncos Checklist (John Elway)	.15
76	Browns Checklist (Eric Metcalf)	.05
77	Buccaneers Checklist (Vinny Testaverde)	.05
78	Cardinals Checklist (Johnny Johnson)	.10
79	Chargers Checklist (Anthony Miller)	.05
80	Chiefs Checklist (Derrick Thomas)	.12
81	Colts Checklist (Jeff George)	.12
82	Cowboys Checklist (Troy Aikman)	.65
83	Dolphins Checklist (Dan Marino)	.30
84	Eagles Checklist (Randall Cunningham)	.10
85	Falcons Checklist (Deion Sanders)	.12
86	49ers Checklist (Jerry Rice)	.40
87	Giants Checklist (Lawrence Taylor)	.08
88	Jets Checklist (Al Toon)	.05
89	Lions Checklist (Barry Sanders)	.50
90	Oilers Checklist (Warren Moon)	.10
91	Packers Checklist (Sterling Sharpe)	.20
92	Patriots Checklist (Andre Tippett)	.05
93	Rams Checklist (Jim Everett)	.05
94	Raiders Checklist (Bo Jackson)	.25
95	Redskins Checklist (Art Monk)	.05
96	Saints Checklist (Morten Andersen)	.05
97	Seahawks Checklist (John L. Williams)	.05
98	Steelers Checklist (Rod Woodson)	.05
99	Vikings Checklist (Herschel Walker)	.05
100	Checklist	.05
101	Steve Young	.75
102	Jim Lachey	.05
103	Tom Rathman	.05
104	Earnest Byner	.05
105	Karl Mecklenburg	.05
106	Wes Hopkins	.05
107	Michael Irvin	.20
108	Burt Grossman	.05
109	Jay Novacek	.25
110	Ben Smith	.05
111	Rod Woodson	.05
112	Ernie Jones	.05
113	Bryan Hinkle	.05
114	Vai Sikahema	.05
115	Bubby Brister	.05
116	Brian Blades	.05
117	Don Majkowski	.05
118	Rod Bernstine	.05
119	Brian Noble	.05
120	Eugene Robinson	.05
121	John Taylor	.12
122	Vance Johnson	.05
123	Art Monk	.05
124	John Elway	.35
125	Dexter Carter	.05
126	Anthony Miller	.05
127	Keith Jackson	.15
128	Albert Lewis	.05
129	Bill Ray Smith	.05
130	Clyde Simmons	.05
131	Merril Hoge	.05
132	Ricky Proehl	.12
133	Tim McDonald	.05
134	Louis Lipps	.05
135	Ken Harvey	.05
136	Sterling Sharpe	.20
137	Gill Byrd	.05
138	Tim Harris	.05
139	Derrick Fenner	.10
140	Johnny Holland	.05
141	Ricky Sanders	.05
142	Bobby Humphrey	.05
143	Roger Craig	.05
144	Steve Atwater	.05
145	Ickey Woods	.05
146	Randall Cunningham	.15
147	Marion Butts	.05
148	Reggie White	.15
149	Ronnie Harmon	.05
150	Mike Saxon	.05
151	Greg Townsend	.05
152	Troy Aikman	1.00
153	Shane Conlan	.05
154	Deion Sanders	.25
155	Bo Jackson	.35
156	Jeff Hostetler	.20
157	Albert Bentley	.05
158	James Williams	.05
159	Bill Brooks	.05
160	Nick Lowery	.05
161	Ottis Anderson	.05
162	Kevin Greene	.05
163	Neil Smith	.05

164	Jim Everett	.05
165	Derrick Thomas	.25
166	John L. Williams	.05
167	Timm Rosenbach	.05
168	Leslie O'Neal	.05
169	Clarence Verdin	.05
170	Dave Krieg	.05
171	Steve Broussard	.05
172	Emmitt Smith	2.00
173	Andre Rison	.25
174	Bruce Smith	.05
175	Mark Clayton	.05
176	Christian Okoye	.05
177	Duane Bickett	.05
178	Stephone Paige	.05
179	Fredd Young	.05
180	Mervyn Fernandez	.05
181	Phil Simms	.10
182	Pete Holohan	.05
183	Pepper Johnson	.05
184	Jackie Slater	.05
185	Stephen Baker	.05
186	Frank Cornish	.05
187	Dave Waymer	.05
188	Terance Mathis	.10
189	Darryl Talley	.05
190	James Hasty	.05
191	Jay Schroeder	.05
192	Kenneth Davis	.05
193	Chris Miller	.05
194	Scott Davis	.05
195	Tim Green	.05
196	Dan Saleaumua	.05
197	Rohn Stark	.05
198	John Alt	.05
199	Steve Tasker	.05
200	Checklist	.05
201	Freddie Joe Nunn	.05
202	Jim Breech	.05
203	Roy Green	.05
204	Gary Anderson (T.B.)	.05
205	Rich Camarillo	.05
206	Mark Bortz	.05
207	Eddie Brown	.05
208	Brad Muster	.05
209	Anthony Munoz	.05
210	Dalton Hilliard	.05
211	Erik McMillan	.05
212	Perry Kemp	.05
213	Jim Thornton	.05
214	Anthony Dilweg	.05
215	Cleveland Gary	.05
216	Leo Goeas	.05
217	Mike Merriweather	.05
218	Courtney Hall	.05
219	Wade Wilson	.05
220	Billy Joe Tolliver	.05
221	Harold Green	.10
222	Al Baker	.05
223	Carl Zander	.05
224	Thane Gash	.05
225	Kevin Mack	.05
226	Morten Andersen	.05
227	Dennis Gentry	.05
228	Vince Buck	.05
229	Mike Singletary	.05
230	Rueben Mayes	.05
231	Mark Carrier (T.B.)	.05
232	Tony Mandarich	.05
233	Al Toon	.05
234	Renaldo Turnbull	.05
235	Broderick Thomas	.05
236	Anthony Carter	.05
237	Flipper Anderson	.05
238	Jerry Robinson	.05
239	Vince Newsome	.05
240	Keith Millard	.05
241	Reggie Langhorne	.05
242	James Francis	.05
243	Felix Wright	.05
244	Neal Anderson	.10
245	Boomer Esiason	.15
246	Pat Swilling	.05
247	Richard Dent	.05
248	Craig Heyward	.05
249	Ron Morris	.05
250	Eric Mann	.05
251	Jim Jensen	.05
252	Anthony Toney	.05
253	Sammie Smith	.05
254	Calvin Williams	.20
255	Dan Marino	.75
256	Warren Moon	.20
257	Tommie Agee	.05
258	Haywood Jeffires	.25
259	Eugene Lockhart	.05
260	Drew Hill	.05
261	Vinny Testaverde	.10
262	Jim Arnold	.05
263	Steve Christie	.05
264	Chris Spielman	.05
265	Reggie Cobb	.25
266	John Stephens	.05
267	Jay Hilgenberg	.05
268	Brent Williams	.05
269	Rodney Hampton	.75
270	Irving Fryar	.05
271	Terry McDaniel	.05
272	Reggie Roby	.05
273	Allen Pinkett	.05
274	Tim McKyer	.05
275	Bob Golic	.05
276	Wilber Marshall	.05
277	Ray Childress	.05
278	Charles Mann	.05
279	*Cris Dishman*	.15
280	Mark Rypien	.15
281	Michael Cofer (Det.)	.05
282	Keith Byars	.05
283	Mike Rozier	.05
284	Seth Joyner	.05
285	Jessie Tuggle	.05
286	Mark Bavaro	.05
287	Eddie Anderson	.05
288	Sean Landeta	.05
289	Howie Long	.12
290	Reyna Thompson	.05
291	Ferrell Edmunds	.05
292	Willie Gault	.05
293	John Offerdahl	.05
294	Tim Brown	.12
296	Kevin Ross	.05
297	Lorenzo White	.10
298	Dino Hackett	.05
299	Curtis Duncan	.05
300	Checklist	.05
301	Andre Ware	.12
302	David Little	.05
303	Jerry Ball	.05
304	Dwight Stone	.05
305	Rodney Peete	.05
306	Mike Baab	.05
307	Tim Worley	.05
308	Paul Farren	.05
309	Carnell Lake	.05
310	Clay Matthews	.05
311	Alton Montgomery	.05
312	Ernest Givins	.05
313	Mike Horan	.05
314	Sean Jones	.05
315	Leonard Smith	.05
316	Carl Banks	.05
317	Jerome Brown	.05
318	Everson Walls	.05
319	Ron Heller	.05
320	Mark Collins	.05
321	Eddie Murray	.05
322	Jim Harbaugh	.10
323	Mel Gray	.05
324	Keith Van Horne	.05
325	Lomas Brown	.05
326	Carl Lee	.05
327	Ken O'Brien	.05
328	Dermontti Dawson	.05
329	Brad Baxter	.15
330	Chris Doleman	.05
331	Louis Oliver	.05
332	Frank Stams	.05
333	Mike Munchak	.05
334	Fred Strickland	.05
335	Mark Duper	.05
336	Jacob Green	.05
337	Tony Paige	.05
338	Jeff Bryant	.05
339	Lemuel Stinson	.05
340	David Wyman	.05
341	Lee Williams	.05
342	Trace Armstrong	.05
343	Junior Seau	.30
344	John Roper	.05
345	Jeff George	.30
346	Herschel Walker	.05
347	Sam Clancy	.05
348	Steve Jordan	.05
349	Nate Odomes	.05
350	Martin Bayless	.05
351	Brent Jones	.05
352	Ray Agnew	.05
353	Charles Haley	.05
354	Andre Tippett	.05
355	Ronnie Lott	.10
356	Thurman Thomas	.50
357	Fred Barnett	.15
358	James Lofton	.05
359	*William Frizzell*	.10
360	Keith McKeller	.05
361	Rodney Holman	.05
362	Henry Ellard	.05
363	David Fulcher	.05
364	Jerry Gray	.05
365	James Brooks	.05
366	Tony Stargell	.05
367	Keith McCants	.05
368	Lewis Billups	.05
369	Ervin Randle	.05
370	Pat Leahy	.05
371	Bruce Armstrong	.05
372	Steve DeBerg	.05
373	Guy McIntyre	.05
374	Deron Cherry	.05
375	Fred Marion	.05
376	Michael Haddix	.05
377	Kent Hull	.05
378	Jerry Holmes	.05
379	Jim Richter	.05
380	Ed West	.05
381	Richmond Webb	.05
382	Mark Jackson	.05
383	Tom Newberry	.05
384	Ricky Nattiel	.05
385	Keith Sims	.05
386	Ron Hall	.05
387	Ken Norton	.05
388	Paul Gruber	.05
389	Danny Stubbs	.05
390	Ian Beckles	.05
391	Hoby Brenner	.05
392	Tory Epps	.05
393	Sam Mills	.05
394	Chris Hinton	.05
395	Steve Walsh	.05
396	Simon Fletcher	.05
397	Tony Bennett	.05
398	Aundray Bruce	.05
399	Mark Murphy	.05
400	Checklist	.05
401	Barry Sanders (SL)	.50
402	Jerry Rice (SL)	.35
403	Warren Moon (SL)	.10
404	Derrick Thomas (SL)	.12
405	Nick Lowery (SL)	.05
406	Mark Carrier (Chi., SL)	.05
407	Michael Carter	.05
408	Chris Singleton	.05
409	Matt Millen	.05
410	Ronnie Lippett	.05
411	E.J. Junior	.05
412	Ray Donaldson	.05
413	Keith Willis	.05
414	Jessie Hester	.05
415	Jeff Cross	.05
416	Greg Jackson	.10
417	Alvin Walton	.05
418	Bart Oates	.05
419	Chip Lohmiller	.05
420	John Elliott	.05
421	Randall McDaniel	.05
422	Richard Johnson	.05
423	Al Noga	.05
424	Lamar Lathon	.05
425	Ricky Fenney	.05
426	Jack Del Rio	.05
427	Don Mosebar	.05
428	Luis Sharpe	.05
429	Steve Wisniewski	.05
430	Jimmie Jones	.05
431	Freeman McNeil	.05
432	Ron Rivera	.05
433	Hart Lee Dykes	.05
434	Mark Carrier (Chi.)	.05
435	Rob Moore	.15
436	Gary Clark	.12
437	Heath Sherman	.10
438	Darrell Greem	.05
439	Jessie Small	.05
440	Monte Coleman	.05
441	Leonard Marshall	.05
442	Richard Johnson	.05
443	Dave Meggett	.05
444	Barry Sanders	1.25
445	Lawrence Taylor	.10
446	Marcus Allen	.05
447	Johnny Johnson	.25
448	Aaron Wallace	.05
449	Anthony Thompson	.05
450	Garry Lewis	.05
451	Andre Rison (MVP)	.12
452	Thurman Thomas (MVP)	.25
453	Neal Anderson (MVP)	.05
454	Boomer Esiason (MVP)	.05
455	Eric Metcalf (MVP)	.05
456	Emmitt Smith (MVP)	1.00
457	Bobby Humphrey (MVP)	.05
458	Barry Sanders (MVP)	.50
459	Sterling Sharpe (MVP)	.20
460	Warren Moon (MVP)	.10
461	Albert Bentley (MVP)	.05
462	Steve DeBerg (MVP)	.05
463	Greg Townsend (MVP)	.05
464	Henry Ellard (MVP)	.05
465	Dan Marino (MVP)	.40
466	Anthony Carter (MVP)	.05
467	John Stephens (MVP)	.05
468	Pat Swilling (MVP)	.05
469	Ottis Anderson (MVP)	.05
470	Dennis Byrd (MVP)	.05
471	Randall Cunningham (MVP)	.10
472	Johnny Johnson (MVP)	.10
473	Rod Woodson (MVP)	.05
474	Anthony Miller (MVP)	.05
475	Jerry Rice (MVP)	.35
476	John L. Williams (MVP)	.05
477	Wayne Haddix (MVP)	.05
478	Earnest Byner (MVP)	.05
479	Doug Widell	.05
480	Tommy Hodson	.05
481	Shawn Collins	.05
482	Rickey Jackson	.05
483	Tony Casillas	.05
484	Vaughan Johnson	.05
485	Floyd Dixon	.05
486	Eric Green	.12
487	Harry Hamilton	.05
488	Gary Anderson (Pit.)	.05
489	Bruce Hill	.05
490	Gerald Williams	.05
491	Cortez Kennedy	.30
492	Chet Brooks	.05
493	Dwayne Harper	.15
494	Don Griffin	.05
495	Andy Heck	.05
496	David Treadwell	.05
497	Irv Pankey	.05
498	Dennis Smith	.05
499	Marcus Dupree	.05
500	Checklist	.05
501	Wendell Davis	.10
502	Matt Bahr	.05
503	*Rob Burnett*	.12
504	Maurice Carthon	.05
505	Donnell Woolford	.05
506	Howard Ballard	.05
507	Mark Boyer	.05
508	Eugene Marve	.05
509	Joe Kelly	.05
510	Will Wolford	.05
511	Robert Clark	.05
512	*Matt Brock*	.12
513	Chris Warren	.50
514	Ken Willis	.05
515	*George Jamison*	.12
516	Rufus Porter	.05
517	*Mark Higgs*	.25
518	Thomas Everett	.05
519	Robert Brown	.05
520	Gene Atkins	.05
521	Hardy Nickerson	.05
522	Johnny Bailey	.05
523	William Frizzell	.05
524	Steve McMichael	.05
525	Kevin Porter	.05
526	Carwell Gardner	.05
527	Eugene Daniel	.05
528	Vestee Jackson	.05
529	Chris Goode	.05
530	Leon Seals	.05
531	Darion Conner	.05
532	Stan Brock	.05
533	*Kirby Jackson*	.10
534	Marv Cook	.05
535	Bill Fralic	.05
536	Keith Woodside	.05
537	Hugh Green	.05
538	Grant Feasel	.05
539	Bubba McDowell	.05
540	Vai Sikahema	.05
541	Aaron Cox	.05
542	Roger Craig	.05
543	Robb Thomas	.05
544	Ronnie Lott	.05
545	Robert Delpino	.05
546	Greg McMurtry	.05
547	*Jim Morrissey*	.10
548	Johnny Rembert	.05
549	*Markus Paul*	.12
550	*Karl Wilson*	.12
551	Gaston Green	.05
552	Willie Drewrey	.05
553	Michael Young	.05
554	Tom Tupa	.05
555	John Friesz	.15
556	*Cody Carlson*	.35
557	Eric Allen	.05
558	Tom Bensen	.05
559	*Scott Mersereau*	.10
560	Lionel Washington	.05
561	Brian Brennan	.05
562	Jim Jeffcoat	.05
563	Jeff Jaeger	.05
564	David Johnson	.05
565	Danny Villa	.05
566	Don Beebe	.05
567	Michael Haynes	.30
568	Brett Faryniarz	.05
569	Mike Prior	.05
570	*John Davis*	.12
571	*Vernon Turner*	.12
572	Michael Brooks	.05
573	Mike Gann	.05
574	Ron Holmes	.05
575	Gary Plummer	.05
576	Bill Romanowski	.05
577	Chris Jacke	.05
578	Gary Reasons	.05
579	*Tim Jorden*	.08
580	Tim McKyer	.05
581	Johnny Jackson	.05
582	Ethan Horton	.05
583	Pete Stoyanovich	.05
584	Jeff Query	.05
585	Frank Reich	.05
586	Riki Ellison	.05
587	Eric Hill	.05
588	Anthony Shelton	.05
589	Steve Smith	.05
590	*Garth Jax*	.08
591	*Greg Davis*	.10
592	Bill Maas	.05
593	*Henry Rolling*	.10
594	Keith Jones	.05
595	Tootie Robbins	.05
596	*Brian Jordan*	.25
597	*Derrick Walker*	.12
598	Jonathan Hayes	.05
599	*Nate Lewis*	.25
600	Checklist 501-600	.05
601	AFC Checklist RF (Greg Lewis, Keith Traylor, Kenny Walker, Denver Broncos)	.15
602	*James Jones*	.15
603	*Tim Barnett*	.15
604	*Ed King*	.10
605	Shane Curry	.05
606	Mike Croel	.20
607	*Bryan Cox*	.50
608	*Shawn Jefferson*	.12
609	*Kenny Walker*	.25
610	*Michael Jackson*	.75
611	*Jon Vaughn*	.20
612	Greg Lewis	.05
613	Joe Valerio	.05
614	*Pat Harlow*	.10
615	*Henry Jones*	.20
616	*Jeff Graham*	.75
617	*Darryll Lewis*	.12
618	*Keith Traylor*	.10
619	Scott Miller	.05
620	Nick Bell	.10
621	*John Flannery*	.12
622	*Leonard Russell*	.50
623	*Alfred Williams*	.10
624	Browning Nagle	.15
625	Harvey Williams	.10
626	Dan McGwire	.10
627	Brett Favre, Moe Gardner, Eric Pegram, Bruce Pickens, Mike Pritchard (CL)	.50
628	*William Thomas*	.10
629	*Lawrence Dawsey*	.15
630	*Aeneas Williams*	.10
631	Stan Thomas	.05
632	Randal Hill	.15
633	*Moe Gardner*	.10
634	Alvin Harper	.25
635	*Esera Tuaolo*	.08
636	Russell Maryland	.20
637	Anthony Morgan	.15
638	*Erric Pegram*	1.00
639	Herman Moore	.75
640	*Ricky Ervins*	.20
641	*Kelvin Pritchett*	.10
642	*Roman Phifer*	.10
643	*Antone Davis*	.10
644	Mike Pritchard	.40
645	*Vinnie Clark*	.10
646	*Jake Reed*	1.00
647	Brett Favre	2.00
648	Todd Lyght	.10
649	Bruce Pickens	.05
650	*Darren Lewis*	.25
651	Wesley Carroll	.10
652	*James Joseph*	.25
653	Robert Delpino	.05
654	Vencie Glenn	.05
655	Jerry Rice	.20
656	Barry Sanders	.50
657	Ken Tippins	.05
658	Christian Okoye	.05
659	Rich Gannon	.05
660	Johnny Meads	.05
661	*J.J. Birden*	.10
662	Bruce Kozerski	.05
663	Felix Wright	.05
664	Al Smith	.05
665	Stan Humphries	.30
666	Alfred Anderson	.05
667	Nate Newton	.05
668	*Vince Workman*	.10
669	Ricky Reynolds	.05
670	*Bryce Paup*	.75
671	Gill Generty	.05
672	Darrell Thompson	.20
673	Anthony Smith	.05
674	*Darryl Henley*	.08
675	Brett Maxie	.05
676	Craig Taylor	.05
677	Steve Wallace	.05
678	*Jeff Feagles*	.08
679	*James Washington*	.10
680	Tim Harris	.05
681	Dennis Gibson	.05
682	*Toi Cook*	.10
683	Lorenzo Lynch	.05
684	*Brad Edwards*	.10
685	*Ray Crockett*	.10
686	Harris Barton	.05
687	Byron Evans	.05
688	Eric Thomas	.05
689	Jeff Criswell	.05
690	Eric Ball	.05
691	Brian Mitchell	.20
692	Quinn Early	.05
693	Aaron Jones	.05
694	Jim Dombrowski	.05
695	Jeff Bostic	.05
696	Tony Casillas	.05
697	Ken Lanier	.05
698	Henry Thomas	.05
699	Steve Beuerlein	.20
700	Checklist 601-700	.05
SP1	Darrell Green	.50

1991 Upper Deck Game Breaker Holograms

Nine top running backs are featured on these insert cards, which were randomly included in 1991 Upper Deck packs. Series I packs contained cards 1-6; Series II packs had cards 7-9. Each card front has an action hologram against a background with a diagramed football play. "Gamebreakers" is in the bottom right corner, next to a stripe which has the player's name in it. The card backs are numbered with a "GB" prefix and contain the player's team logo and a career summary.

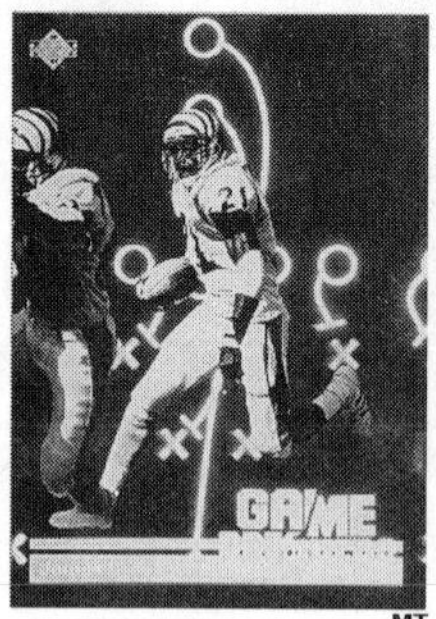

		MT
Complete Set (9):		8.00
Common Player:		.60
1	Barry Sanders	4.00
2	Thurman Thomas	1.25
3	Bobby Humphrey	.60
4	Earnest Byner	.60
5	Emmitt Smith	4.50
6	Neal Anderson	.60
7	Marion Butts	.60
8	James Brooks	.60
9	Marcus Allen	.75

1991 Upper Deck Joe Montana Heroes

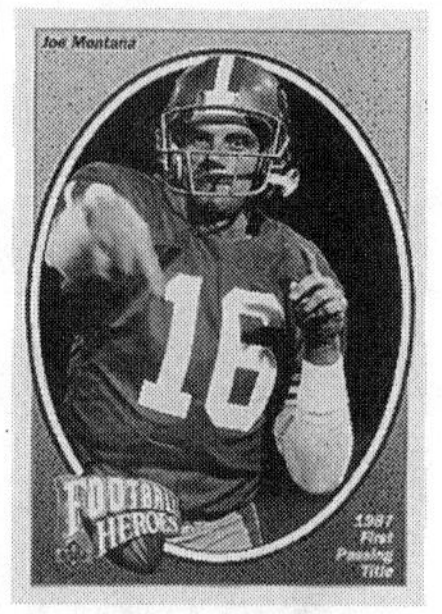

This is the first set of Upper Deck's Football Heroes series. These 10 cards are devoted to 49er quarterback Joe Montana. Each card front has an oval framed with white and blue borders. A color photo is inside the oval. The card is two-toned - it shades from mustard to brown, and has the set logo in the bottom left corner. The card back is designed like a football field and includes a career summary and card number (1 of 9, etc.). Cards were random inserts in 1991 Upper Deck Series I packs. Montana autographed 2,500 of the cards. The tenth card is an unnumbered header card. A title appears on each card, too.

		MT
Complete Set (10):		15.00
Common Player:		1.50
Montana Header SP (NNO):		6.00
Montana Auto/2500:		200.00
1	1974-78 College Years (Joe Montana)	1.50
2	1981 A Star is Born (Joe Montana)	1.50
3	1984 Super Bowl MVP (Joe Montana)	1.50
4	1987 1st Passing Title (Joe Montana)	1.50
5	1988 Rematch (Joe Montana)	1.50
6	1989 NFL's MVP (Joe Montana)	1.50
7	1989 Back-to-Back (Joe Montana)	1.50
8	1990 Career Highs (Joe Montana)	1.50
9	Checklist Heroes 1-9 (Joe Montana) (Vernon Wells potrait of Montana)	1.50
----	Title/Header card SP (Joe Montana) (Unnumbered)	6.00

1991 Upper Deck Heroes Montana Box Bottoms

This eight-card set is identical to the Montana Heroes insert except they have blank backs and are oversized. Cards measure 5-1/4" x 7-1/4" and were found on the bottom of 1991 Upper Deck low series wax boxes.

		MT
Complete Set (8):		5.00
Common Player:		1.00
1	1974-78 College Years	1.00
2	1981 A Star is Born	1.00
3	1984 Super Bowl MVP	1.00
4	1987 1st Passing Title	1.00
5	1988 Rematch	1.00
6	1989 NFL's MVP	1.00
7	1989 Back-to-Back	1.00
8	1990 Career Highs	1.00

1991 Upper Deck Joe Namath Heroes

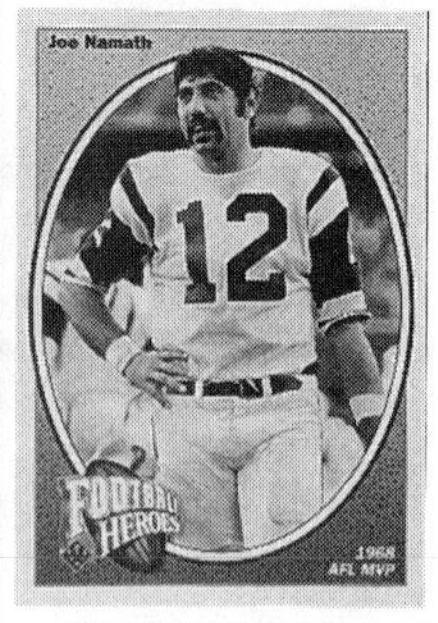

Hall of Fame quarterback Joe Namath is featured in this Football Heroes set which starts where the similar Joe Montana set ended. Cards are numbered 10-18 and were randomly inserted in 1991 Upper Deck Series II packs. The front has an oval with a picture in it, bordered with a white and blue frame. The player's name is in the bottom right corner, along with a title. A "Football Heroes" logo is in the lower left corner. The back has a football field design and includes a career summary and card number. Namath autographed 2,500 cards; he autographed every 100th card "Broadway Joe."

		MT
Complete Set (10):		15.00
Common Player:		1.50
Namath Header SP (NNO):		6.00
Namath Auto/2500:		200.00
10	1962-65 Crimson Tide (Joe Namath)	1.50
11	1965 Broadway Joe (Joe Namath)	1.50
12	1967 4,000 Yards Passing (Joe Namath)	1.50
13	1968 AFL MVP (Joe Namath)	1.50
14	1969 Super Bowl III (Joe Namath)	1.50
15	1969 All-Pro (Joe Namath)	1.50
16	1972 400 Yards (Joe Namath)	1.50
17	1985 Hall of Fame (Joe Namath)	1.50
18	Checklist Heroes 10-18 (Joe Namath)	1.50
----	Title/Header Card SP (Joe Namath) (Unnumbered)	6.00

1991 Upper Deck Heroes Namath Box Bottoms

This eight-card set has identical photos to the Namath Heroes insert, but has blank backs and printed on an oversized format. The cards measure 5-1/4" x 7-1/4" and are found on the bottom of 1991 Upper Deck high series football wax boxes.

		MT
Complete Set (8):		5.00
Common Player:		1.00
10	1962-65 Crimson Tide	1.00
11	1965 Broadway Joe	1.00
12	1967 4,000 Yards Passing	1.00
13	1968 AFL MVP	1.00
14	1969 Super Bowl III	1.00
15	1969 All-Pro	1.00
16	1972 400 Yards	1.00
17	1985 Hall of Fame	1.00

1991 Upper Deck Sheets

Upper Deck offered two 8-1/2" x 11" sheets, with one commemorating the New York Giants Super Bowl XXV Champions and the second commemorating the 40th anniversary of the 1951 Rams championship team. The Giants sheet has the issue date, production run and issue number in the lower right hand corner. The Rams sheet was limited to 60,000.

		MT
Complete Set (2):		10.00
Common Player:		5.00
1	Los Angeles Rams Commemorative Sheet October 1991 (60,000)	5.00
2	New York Giants vs. Washington Redskins October 27, 1991 (Rodney Hampton, Lawrence Taylor, Dave Meggett, Jeff Hostetler, Mark Collins, Ottis Anderson) (SB XXV Champions) (72,000)	5.00

1992 Upper Deck

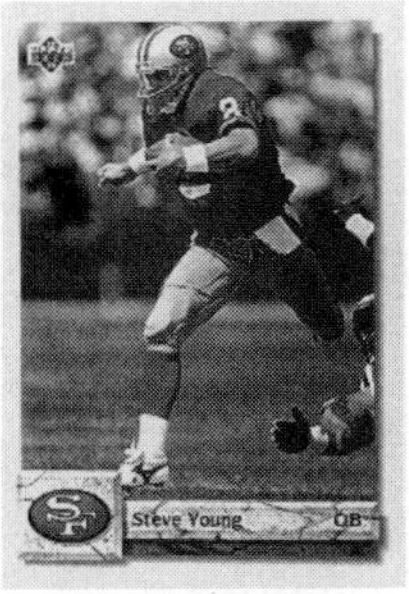

Upper Deck's 1992 set was issued in two series - 440 and 220 cards each. The card front has an action photo with a shadowed border framed by a white border. The player's name is at the bottom left; his position and team logo are on the right. Both are encompassed by a granite bar with a team color-coded bar accent. The back has another photo, plus stats and a biography. Subsets include Star Rookies, All-Rookies, Team Checklists, Season Leaders, Team MVP, Rookie Force and NFL Scrapbook. Insert sets include a Gold set of 50 (each card has a gold hologram); Pro Bowlers; Game Breakers; Walter Payton; Football Heroes (Dan Marino); NFL Fanimation and Coach's Report, which features comments from former Pittsburgh Steelers coach Chuck Noll about top rookies and second-year players.

		MT
Complete Set (620):		17.00
Complete Series 1 (400):		10.00
Complete Series 2 (220):		7.00
Common Player:		.05
Series 1 or 2 Pack (15):		.75
Series 1 or 2 Wax Box (36):		22.00
1	Star Rookie CL	.25
2	*Edgar Bennett*	.50
3	*Eddie Blake*	.08
4	*Brian Bollinger*	.08
5	*Joe Bowden*	.08
6	*Terrell Buckley*	.25
7	*Willie Clay*	.10
8	*Ed Cunningham*	.10
9	*Matt Darby*	.10
10	*Will Furrer*	.20
11	*Chris Hakel*	.10
12	*Carlos Huerta*	.10
13	*Amp Lee*	.30
14	*Ricardo McDonald*	.10
15	*Dexter McNabb*	.10
16	*Chris Mims*	.30
17	*Derrick Moore*	.50
18	*Robert Porcher*	.05
19	*Patrick Rowe*	.08
20	*Leon Searcy*	.08
21	*Torrance Small*	.08
22	*Jimmy Smith*	4.00
23	*Tony Smith*	.08
24	*Siran Stacy*	.08
25	*Kevin Turner*	.08
26	*Tommy Vardell*	.20
27	*Bob Whitfield*	.10
28	*Darryl Williams*	.10
29	*Jeff Sydner*	.10
30	All-Rookie Checklist	.10
31	Todd Marinovich	.10
33	Nick Bell	.10
34	Alvin Harper	.30
35	Mike Pritchard	.15
36	Lawrence Dawsey	.10
37	Tim Barnett	.05
38	John Flannery	.05
39	Stan Thomas	.05
40	Ed King	.05
41	Charles McRae	.08
42	Eric Moten	.08
43	Moe Gardner	.08
44	Kenny Walker	.08
45	Esera Tuaolo	.08
46	Alfred Williams	.10
47	Bryan Cox	.15
48	Mo Lewis	.05
49	Mike Croel	.08
50	Stanley Richard	.08
51	Tony Covington	.05
52	Larry Brown	.05
53	Aeneas Williams	.05
54	John Kasay	.05
55	Jon Vaughn	.08
56	David Fulcher	.05
57	Barry Foster	.40
58	Terry Wooden	.05
59	Gary Anderson	.05
60	Alfred Williams	.05
61	Robert Blackmon	.05
62	Brian Noble	.05
63	Terry Allen	.40
64	Darrell Green	.05
65	Darren Comeaux	.05
66	Rob Burnett	.05
67	Jerrod Bunch	.05
68	Michael Jackson	.15
69	Greg Lloyd	.05
70	Richard Brown	.05
71	Harold Green	.05
72	William Fuller	.05
73	Mark Carrier (TC)	.05
74	David Fulcher (TC)	.05
75	Cornelius Bennett (TC)	.05
76	Steve Atwater (TC)	.05
77	Kevin Mack (TC)	.05
78	Mark Carrier (TC)	.05
79	Tim McDonald (TC)	.05
80	Marion Butts (TC)	.05
81	Christian Okoye (TC)	.05
82	Jeff Herrod (TC)	.05
83	Emmitt Smith (TC)	1.00
84	Mark Duper (TC)	.05
85	Keith Jackson (TC)	.05
86	Andre Rison (TC)	.10
87	John Taylor (TC)	.05
88	Rodney Hampton (TC)	.10
89	Rob Moore (TC)	.05
90	Chris Spielman (TC)	.05
91	Haywood Jeffires (TC)	.05
92	Sterling Sharpe (TC)	.15
93	Irving Fryar (TC)	.05
94	Marcus Allen (TC)	.05
95	Henry Ellard (TC)	.05
96	Mark Rypien (TC)	.05
97	Pat Swilling (TC)	.05
98	Brian Blades (TC)	.05
99	Eric Green (TC)	.05
100	Anthony Carter (TC)	.05
101	Burt Grossman	.05
102	Gary Anderson	.05
103	Neil Smith	.05
104	Jeff Feagles	.05
105	Shane Conlon	.05
106	Jay Novacek	.05
107	Billy Brooks	.05
108	Mark Ingram	.05
109	Anthony Munoz	.05
110	Wendell Davis	.05
111	Jim Everett	.05
112	Bruce Matthews	.05
113	Mark Higgs	.05
114	Chris Warren	.10
115	Brad Baxter	.05
116	Greg Townsend	.05
117	Al Smith	.05
118	Jeff Cross	.05
119	Terry McDaniel	.05
120	Ernest Givins	.05
121	Fred Barnett	.05
122	Flipper Anderson	.05
123	Floyd Turner	.05
124	Stephen Baker	.05
125	Tim Johnson	.05
126	Brent Jones	.05
127	Leonard Marshall	.05
128	Jim Price	.05
129	Jessie Hester	.05
130	Mark Carrier	.05
131	Bubba McDowell	.05
132	Andre Tippett	.05
133	James Hasty	.05
134	Mel Gray	.05
135	Christian Okoye	.05
136	Earnest Byner	.05
137	Ferrell Edmunds	.05
138	Henry Ellard	.05
140	Brian Jordan	.05
141	Clarence Verdin	.05
142	Cornelius Bennett	.05
143	John Taylor	.05
144	Derrick Thomas	.05
145	Thurman Thomas	.25
146	Warren Moon	.25
147	Vinny Testaverde	.05
148	*Steve Bono*	.50
149	Robb Thomas	.05
150	John Friesz	.05
151	Richard Dent	.05
152	Eddie Anderson	.05
153	Kevin Greene	.05
154	Marion Butts	.05
155	Barry Sanders	1.25
156	Andre Rison	.25
157	Ronnie Lott	.10
158	Eric Allen	.05
159	Mark Clayton	.05
160	Terance Mathis	.05
161	Darryl Talley	.05
162	Eric Metcalf	.05
163	Reggie Cobb	.10
164	Ernie Jones	.05
165	David Griggs	.05
166	Tom Rathman	.05
167	Bubby Brister	.05
168	Broderick Thomas	.05
169	Chris Doleman	.05
170	Charles Haley	.05
171	Michael Haynes	.30
172	Rodney Hampton	.35
173	Nick Bell	.10
174	Gene Atkins	.05
175	Mike Merriweather	.05
176	Reggie Roby	.05
177	Bennie Blades	.05
178	John L. Williams	.05
179	Rodney Peete	.05
180	Greg Montgomery	.15
181	Vince Newsome	.05
182	Andre Collins	.05
183	Erik Kramer	.05
184	Bryan Hinkle	.05
185	Reggie White	.20
186	Bruce Armstrong	.05
187	Anthony Carter	.05
188	Pat Swilling	.05
189	Robert Delpino	.05
190	Brent Williams	.05
191	Johnny Johnson	.05
192	Aaron Craver	.05
193	Vincent Brown	.05
194	Herschel Walker	.10
195	Tim McDonald	.05
196	Gaston Green	.05
197	Brian Blades	.05
198	Rod Bernstine	.05
199	Brett Perriman	.05
200	John Elway	.40
201	Michael Carter	.05
202	Mark Carrier	.05
203	Cris Carter	.05
204	Kyle Clifton	.05
205	Alvin Wright	.10
206	Andre Ware	.05
207	Dave Waymer	.05
208	Darren Lewis	.05
209	Joey Browner	.05
210	Rich Miano	.05
211	Marcus Allen	.05
212	Steve Broussard	.05
213	Joel Hilgenberg	.05
214	*Bo Orlando*	.05
215	Clay Matthews	.05
216	Chris Hinton	.05
217	Al Edwards	.05
218	Tim Brown	.05
219	Sam Mills	.05
220	Don Majkowski	.05
221	James Francis	.05
222	Steve Hendrickson	.05
223	James Thornton	.05
224	Byron Evans	.05
225	Pepper Johnson	.05
226	Darryl Henley	.05
227	Simon Fletcher	.05
228	Hugh Millen	.05
229	Tim McGee	.05
230	Richmond Webb	.05
231	Tony Bennett	.05
232	Nate Odomes	.05
233	Scott Case	.05
234	Dalton Hilliard	.05
235	Paul Gruber	.05
236	Jeff Lageman	.05
237	Tony Mandarich	.05
238	Cris Dishman	.05
239	Steve Walsh	.05
240	Moe Gardner	.05
241	Bill Romanowski	.05
242	Chris Zorich	.05
243	Stephone Paige	.05
244	Mike Croel	.05
245	Leonard Russell	.30
246	Mark Rypien	.10
247	Aeneas Williams	.05
248	Steve Atwater	.05
249	Michael Stewart	.05
250	Pierce Holt	.05
251	Kevin Mack	.05
252	Sterling Sharpe	.10
253	Lawrence Dawsey	.05
254	Emmitt Smith	2.00
255	Todd Marinovich	.20
256	Neal Anderson	.10
257	Mo Lewis	.05
258	Vance Johnson	.05
259	Rickey Jackson	.05
260	Esera Tuaolo	.05
261	Wilber Marshall	.05
262	Keith Henderson	.05
263	William Thomas	.05
264	Rickey Dixon	.05
265	Dave Meggett	.05
266	Gerald Riggs	.05
267	Tim Harris	.05
268	Ken Harvey	.05
269	Clyde Simmons	.05
270	Irving Fryar	.05
271	Darion Conner	.05
272	Vince Workman	.05
273	Jim Harbaugh	.05
274	Lorenzo White	.05
275	Bobby Hebert	.05
276	Duane Bickett	.05
277	Jeff Bryant	.05
278	Scott Stephen	.05
279	Bob Golic	.05
280	Steve McMichael	.05
281	Jeff Graham	.05
282	Keith Jackson	.05
283	Howard Ballard	.05
284	Michael Brooks	.05
285	Freeman McNeil	.05
286	Rodney Holman	.05
287	Eric Bieniemy	.05
288	Seth Joyner	.05
289	Carwell Gardner	.05
290	Brian Mitchell	.05
291	Chris Miller	.05
292	Ray Berry	.05
293	Matt Brock	.05
294	Eric Thomas	.05
295	John Kasay	.05
296	Jay Hilgenberg	.05
297	Darrell Thompson	.05
298	Rich Gannon	.05
299	Steve Young	1.00
300	Mike Kenn	.05
301	Emmitt Smith (SL)	1.00
302	Haywood Jeffires (SL)	.05
303	Michael Irvin (SL)	.25
304	Warren Moon (SL)	.15
305	Chip Lohmiller (SL)	.05
306	Barry Sanders (SL)	.50
307	Ronnie Lott (SL)	.05
308	Pat Swilling (SL)	.05
309	Thurman Thomas (SL)	.25
310	Reggie Roby (SL)	.05
311	Season Leader Checklist	.05
312	Jacob Green	.05
313	Stephen Braggs	.05
314	Haywood Jeffires	.15
315	Freddie Joe Nunn	.05
316	Gary Clark	.05
317	Tim Barnett	.05
318	Mark Duper	.05
319	Eric Green	.05
320	Robert Wilson	.05
321	Michael Ball	.05
322	Eric Martin	.05
323	Alexander Wright	.05
324	Jessie Tuggle	.05
325	Ronnie Harmon	.05
326	Jeff Hostetler	.20
327	Eugene Daniel	.05
328	Ken Norton	.05
329	Reyna Thompson	.05
330	Jerry Ball	.05
331	Leroy Hoard	.05
332	Chris Martin	.05
333	Keith McKeller	.05
334	Brian Washington	.05
335	Eugene Robinson	.05
336	Maurice Hurst	.05
337	Dan Saleaumua	.05
338	Neil O'Donnell	.40
339	Dexter Davis	.05
340	Keith McCants	.05
341	Steve Beuerlein	.10
342	Roman Phifer	.05
343	Bryan Cox	.05
344	Art Monk	.05
345	Michael Irvin	.25
346	Vaughn Johnson	.05
347	Jeff Herrod	.05
348	Stanley Richard	.05
349	Michael Young	.05
350	Team MVP Checklist	.05
351	Jim Harbaugh (MVP)	.05
352	David Fulcher (MVP)	.05
353	Thurman Thomas (MVP)	.25
354	Gaston Green (MVP)	.05
355	Leroy Hoard (MVP)	.05
356	Reggie Cobb (MVP)	.05
357	Tim McDonald (MVP)	.05
358	Ronnie Harmon (MVP)	.05
359	Derrick Thomas (MVP)	.15
360	Jeff Herrod (MVP)	.05
361	Michael Irvin (MVP)	.25
362	Mark Higgs (MVP)	.10
363	Reggie White (MVP)	.10
364	Chris Miller (MVP)	.05
365	Steve Young (MVP)	.50
366	Rodney Hampton (MVP)	.10
367	Jeff Lageman (MVP)	.05
368	Barry Sanders (MVP)	.50
369	Haywood Jeffires (MVP)	.10
370	Tony Bennett	.05
371	Leonard Russell	.05
372	Jeff Jaeger	.05
373	Robert Delpino	.05
374	Mark Rypien	.05
375	Pat Swilling	.05
376	Cortez Kennedy	.05
377	Eric Green	.05
378	Cris Carter	.05
379	John Roper	.05
380	Barry Word	.05
381	Shawn Jefferson	.05
382	Tony Casillas	.05
383	*John Baylor*	.10
384	Al Noga	.05
385	Charles Mann	.05
386	Gil Byrd	.05
387	Chris Singleton	.05
388	James Joseph	.05
389	Larry Brown	.05
390	Chris Spielman	.05
391	Anthony Thompson	.05
392	Karl Mecklenburg	.05
393	Joe Kelly	.05
394	Kanavis McGhee	.05
395	Bill Maas	.05
396	Marv Cook	.05
397	Louis Lipps	.05
398	*Marty Carter*	.25
399	Louis Oliver	.05
400	Eric Swann	.05
401	*Troy Auzenne*	.10
402	Kurt Barber	.05
403	*Mark Boutte*	.10
404	*Dale Carter*	.10
405	*Marco Coleman*	.25
406	Quentin Coryatt	.40
407	*Shane Dronett*	.20
408	Vaughn Dunbar	.20
409	Steve Emtman	.15
410	*Dana Hall*	.10
411	*Jason Hansen*	.10
412	*Courtney Hawkins*	.30
413	Terrell Buckley	.10
414	*Robert Jones*	.10
415	David Klingler	.20
416	Tommy Maddox	.15
417	*Johnny Mitchell*	.50
418	Carl Pickens	1.00
419	Tracy Scroggins	.10
420	*Tony Sacca*	.15
421	Kevin Smith	.10
422	Alonzo Spellman	.10
423	*Troy Vincent*	.15
424	*Sean Gilbert*	.40
425	*Larry Webster*	.10
426	Rookie Force Checklist	.20
427	Bill Fralic	.05
428	Kevin Murphy	.05
429	Lemuel Stinson	.10
430	Harris Barton	.05
431	Dino Hackett	.10
432	John Stephens	.05
433	*Keith Jennings*	.10
434	Derrick Fenner	.05
435	*Kenneth Gant*	.25
436	Willie Gault	.05
437	Steve Jordan	.05
438	Charles Haley	.05
439	Keith Kartz	.05
440	Nate Lewis	.05
441	Doug Widell	.05
442	William White	.05
443	Eric Hill	.05
444	Melvin Jenkins	.05
445	David Wyman	.05
446	Ed West	.05
447	Brad Muster	.05
448	Ray Childress	.05
449	Kevin Ross	.05
450	Johnnie Jackson	.05
451	Tracy Simien	.05
452	Don Mosebar	.05
453	Jay Hilgenberg	.05
454	Wes Hopkins	.05
455	Jay Shoreder	.05
456	Jeff Bostic	.05
457	Bryce Paup	.05
458	Dave Waymer	.05
459	Toi Cook	.05
460	Anthony Smith	.05
461	Don Griffin	.05
462	Bill Hawkins	.05
463	Courtney Hall	.05
464	Jeff Ulenhake	.05
465	Mike Sherrard	.05
466	James Jones	.05
467	Jerrol Williams	.05
468	Eric Ball	.05
469	Randall McDaniel	.05
470	Alvin Harper	.40
471	Tom Waddle	.10
472	Tony Woods	.05
473	Kelvin Martin	.05
474	Jon Vaughn	.10
475	Gill Fenerty	.05
476	Aundray Bruce	.05
477	Morton Anderson	.05
478	Lamar Lathon	.05
479	Steve DeOssie	.05
480	Marvin Washington	.05
481	Herschel Walker	.05
482	Howie Long	.05
483	Calvin Williams	.10
484	Brett Favre	2.00
485	Johnny Bailey	.05
486	Jeff Gossett	.05
487	Carnell Lake	.05
488	*Michael Zordich*	.10
489	Henry Rolling	.05
490	Steve Smith	.05
491	Vestee Jackson	.05
492	Ray Crockett	.05
493	Dexter Carter	.05
494	Nick Lowery	.05
495	Cortez Kennedy	.15
496	Cleveland Gary	.05
497	Kelly Stouffer	.05
498	Carl Carter	.05
499	Shannon Sharpe	.30
500	Roger Craig	.05
501	Willie Drewrey	.05
502	Mark Schlereth	.05
503	Tony Martin	.05
504	Tom Newberry	.05
505	Ron Hall	.05
506	Scott Miller	.05
507	Donnell Woolford	.05
508	Dave Krieg	.05
509	Erric Pegram	.50
510	Checklist	.05
511	Barry Sanders (ScpBk)	.50
512	Thurman Thomas (ScpBk)	.25
513	Warren Moon (ScpBk)	.10
514	John Elway (ScpBk)	.20
515	Ronnie Lott (ScpBk)	.10
516	Emmitt Smith (ScpBk)	1.00
517	Andre Rison (ScpBk)	.20
518	Steve Atwater (ScpBk)	.05
519	Steve Young (ScpBk)	.20
520	Mark Rypien (ScpBk)	.05
521	Rich Camarillo	.05
522	Mark Bavaro	.05
523	Brad Edwards	.05
524	*Chad Hennings*	.05
525	Tony Paige	.05
526	Shawn Moore	.05
527	*Sidney Johnson*	.05
528	*Sanjay Beach*	.05
529	Kelvin Pritchett	.05
530	Jerry Holmes	.05
531	Al Del Greco	.05
532	Bob Gagliano	.05
533	Drew Hill	.05
534	*Donald Frank*	.05
535	*Pio Sagapolutele*	.05
536	Donald Hollas	.05
537	Vernon Turner	.05
538	Bobby Humphrey	.05
539	Audray McMillen	.05
540	*Gary Brown*	.25
541	Wesley Carroll	.05
542	Nate Newton	.05
543	Vai Sikahema	.05
544	Chris Chandler	.05
545	*Nolan Harrison*	.10
546	Mark Green	.05
547	Ricky Watters	.50
548	J.J. Birden	.05
549	Cody Carlson	.05
550	Tim Green	.05
551	Mark Jackson	.05
552	Vince Buck	.05
553	George Jamison	.05
554	Anthony Pleasant	.05
555	Reggie Johnson	.05
556	John Jackson	.05
557	Ian Beckles	.05
558	Buford McGee	.05
559	Fuad Reveiz	.05
560	Joe Montana	1.00
561	Phil Simms	.05
562	Greg McMurtry	.05
563	Gerald Williams	.05
564	Dave Cadigan	.05
565	Rufus Porter	.05
566	Jim Kelly	.25
567	Deion Sanders	.50
568	Mike Singletary	.05
569	Boomer Esiason	.10
570	Andre Reed	.15
571	James Washington	.05
572	Jack Del Rio	.05
573	Gerald Perry	.05
574	Vinnie Clark	.05
575	Mike Piel	.05
576	Michael Dean Perry	.05
577	Rickey Proel	.05
578	Leslie O'Neal	.05
579	Russell Maryland	.15
580	Eric Dickerson	.05
581	Fred Strickland	.05
582	Nick Lowery	.05
583	*Joe Milinichik*	.06
584	Mark Vlasic	.05
585	James Lofton	.05
586	Bruce Smith	.15
587	Harvey Williams	.15
588	Bernie Kosar	.05
589	Carl Banks	.05
590	Jeff George	.05
591	*Fred Jones*	.10
592	Todd Scott	.05
593	Keith Jones	.05
594	Tootie Robbins	.05
595	*Todd Philcox*	.25
596	Browning Nagle	.05
597	Troy Aikman	1.25
598	Dan Marino	1.50
599	Lawrence Taylor	.15
600	Webster Slaughter	.05
601	Aaron Cox	.05
602	Matt Stover	.05
603	Keith Sims	.05
604	Dennis Smith	.05
605	Kevin Porter	.05
606	Anthony Miller	.10
607	Ken O'Brien	.05
608	Randall Cunningham	.20
609	Timm Rosenbach	.05
610	Junior Seau	.15
611	Johnny Rembert	.05
612	Rick Tuten	.05
613	Willie Green	.15
614	*Sean Salisbury*	.40
615	Martin Bayless	.05
616	Jerry Rice	.75
617	Randal Hill	.10
618	Dan McGwire	.05
619	Merril Hoge	.05
620	Checklist	.05

1992 Upper Deck Gold

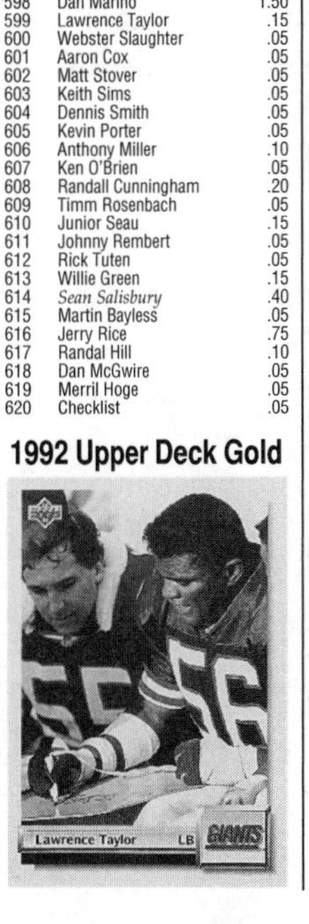

These inserts, numbered with a G prefix, feature cards from three subsets - NFL Top Prospects (1-20), Quarterback Club (21- 25) and veterans (26-50). Each 1992 Upper Deck Series I foil box contained a 15-card foil pack of these cards. Jerry Rice and Andre Reed Game Breaker holograms were also randomly included in these packs. All players were licensed by NFL Properties. Each card front has a color action photo with a white border. The player's name and position are at the bottom for cards 1-20 and 26-50; Quarterback Club cards have the player's name printed along the left side in a black stripe. The backs have a closeup photo, statistics, biography or profile, except for the Prospects cards, which only have a summary of the player's career. The NFL Properties logo is on the back of the card, along with a gold Upper Deck hologram football, instead of the usual silver design.

		MT
Complete Set (50):		15.00
Common Player:		.10
1	*Steve Emtman*	.25
2	*Carl Pickens*	3.50
3	*Dale Carter*	.60
4	*Greg Skrepenak*	.10
5	*Kevin Smith*	.50
6	*Marco Coleman*	.50
7	*David Klingler*	.50
8	*Phillippi Sparks*	.10
9	*Tommy Maddox*	.40
10	*Quentin Coryatt*	.50
11	Ty Detmer	.25
12	*Vaughn Dunbar*	.40
13	Ashley Ambrose	.10
14	Kurt Barber	.10
15	Chester McGlockton	.10
16	*Todd Collins*	.35
17	*Steve Israel*	.10
18	*Marquez Pope*	.25
19	*Alonzo Spellman*	.50
20	*Tracy Scroggins*	.60
21	Jim Kelly	.50
22	Troy Aikman	1.00
23	Randall Cunningham	.50
24	Bernie Kosar	.10
25	Dan Marino	2.00
26	Andre Reed	.35
27	Deion Sanders	.50
28	Randall Hill	.40
29	Eric Dickerson	.10
30	Jim Kelly	.75
31	Bernie Kosar	.10
32	Mike Singletary	.10
33	Anthony Miller	.10
34	Harvey Williams	.10
35	Randall Cunningham	.50
36	Joe Montana	1.00
37	Dan McGwire	.10
38	Al Toon	.10
39	Carl Banks	.10
40	Troy Aikman	1.00
41	Junior Seau	.50
42	Jeff George	.50
43	Michael Dean Perry	.10
44	Lawrence Taylor	.30
45	Dan Marino	2.00
46	Jerry Rice	1.00
47	Boomer Esiason	.10
48	Bruce Smith	.10
49	Leslie O'Neal	.10
50	Form Checklist	.10

1992 Upper Deck Coach's Report

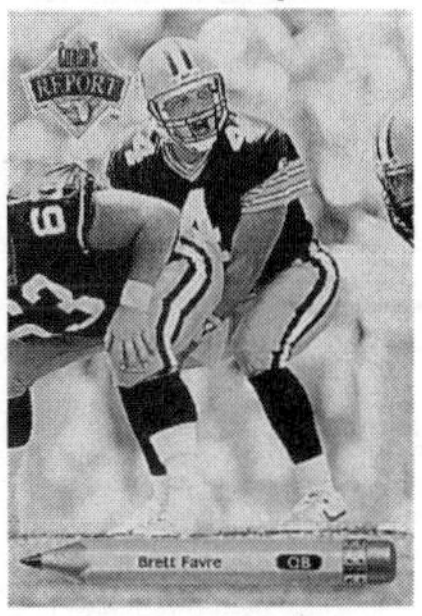

Top rookies and second-year players are analyzed by former Pittsburgh Steelers Coach Chuck Noll for this 20-card insert set. The set's logo is on the card front, along with a color full-bleed action photo and the player's name and position, which are printed on a pencil at the bottom of the card. The card back has a spiral notebook on top of a chalkboard and wooden desk. "From the desk of Chuck Noll" is written at the top; Noll's evaluation is on the notebook paper. The card number uses a "CR" prefix and appears at the top of the card in a white bar. Cards were randomly inserted in 1992 Upper Deck Series II hobby foil packs only.

		MT
Complete Set (20):		25.00
Common Player:		1.00
1	Mike Pritchard	1.00
2	Will Furrer	1.00
3	Alfred Williams	1.00
4	Tommy Vardell	1.00
5	Brett Favre	10.00
6	Alvin Harper	1.00
7	Mike Croel	1.00
8	Herman Moore	5.00
9	Edgar Bennett	3.00

10 Todd Marinovich 1.00
11 Aeneas Williams 1.00
12 Ricky Watters 4.00
13 Amp Lee 2.00
14 Terrell Buckley 1.00
15 Tim Barnett 1.00
16 Nick Bell 1.00
17 Leonard Russell 2.00
18 Lawrence Dawsey 1.00
19 Robert Porcher 1.00
20 Ricky Watters (CL) 2.00

1992 Upper Deck Fanimation

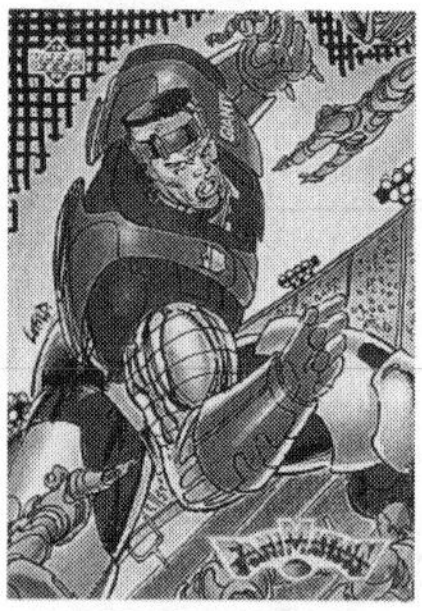

The artwork of artists Jim Lee and Rob Liefeld are featured on these 10 insert cards, available in 1992 Upper Deck Series II retail packs. Each card front features a color cartoon portraying the player, plus a "Fanimation" logo at the bottom. The back has a mug shot, biography and analysis of the player's strengths. The background has shades of red, orange and yellow. A card number, using an "F" for a prefix, also appears.

		MT
Complete Set (10):		30.00
Common Player:		2.00
1	Jim Kelly	2.00
2	Dan Marino	8.00
3	Lawrence Taylor	2.00
4	Deion Sanders	4.00
5	Troy Aikman	6.00
6	Junior Seau	2.00
7	Mike Singletary	2.00
8	Eric Dickerson	2.00
9	Jerry Rice	6.00
10	Checklist	2.00

1992 Upper Deck Game Breaker Holograms

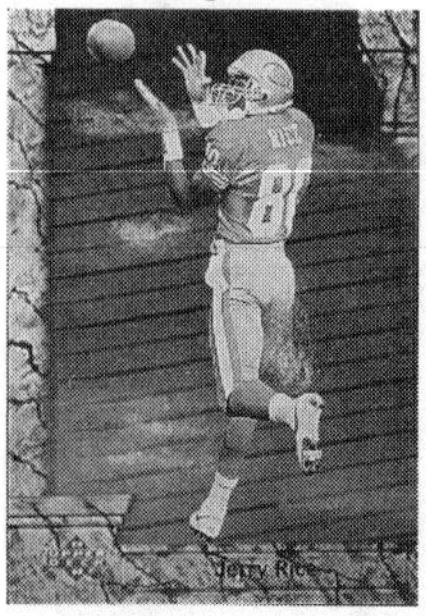

Some of the NFL's top wide receivers are featured in this nine-card hologram set. The front has a hologram image against a football field background. The player's name is at the bottom, along with the Upper Deck logo. The back has a marble-like tablet which contains career highlights. The player's name and "Game Breakers" are at the top of the card. Each card back is also numbered, using a "GB" prefix. Cards 1, 3, 4, 6, 8 and 9 were random inserts in 1992 Upper Deck Series I packs; cards 2, 5, and 7 were in Series II packs.

		MT
Complete Set (9):		15.00
Common Player:		1.50
1	Art Monk	1.50
2	Drew Hill	1.50
3	Haywood Jeffires	1.50
4	Andre Rison	1.50
5	Mark Clayton	1.50
6	Jerry Rice	5.00
7	Michael Haynes	1.50
8	Andre Reed	1.50
9	Michael Irvin	2.00

1992 Upper Deck Dan Marino Heroes

These 10 cards are a continuation of Upper Deck's Football Heroes set and starts with number 28, where the Walter Payton set left off. Cards, random inserts in 1992 Upper Deck Series II foil packs, have an oval picture on the front, featuring Dan Marino in a different stage in his career. The card's title is in the bottom right corner. The back has a marble-like background with career highlights, plus an Upper Deck hologram and card number. There is a checklist card in the set which is unnumbered.

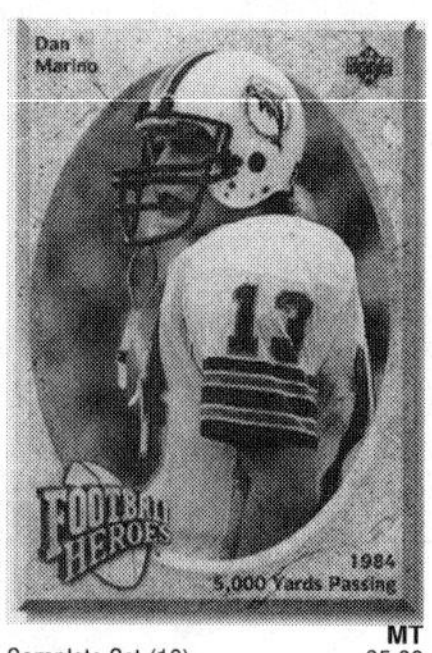

		MT
Complete Set (10):		35.00
Common Marino:		3.50
Marino Header (NNO):		6.00
28	College Years (Dan Marino)	3.50
29	Rookie of the Year (Dan Marino)	3.50
30	5,000 Yards Passing (Dan Marino)	3.50
31	Super Bowl XIX (Dan Marino)	3.50
32	4,000 Yards Passing (Dan Marino)	3.50
33	200th Touchdown (Dan Marino)	3.50
34	30,000 Yards (Dan Marino)	3.50
35	Still Counting (Dan Marino)	3.50
36	Checklist (Dan Marino)	3.50

1992 Upper Deck Walter Payton Heroes

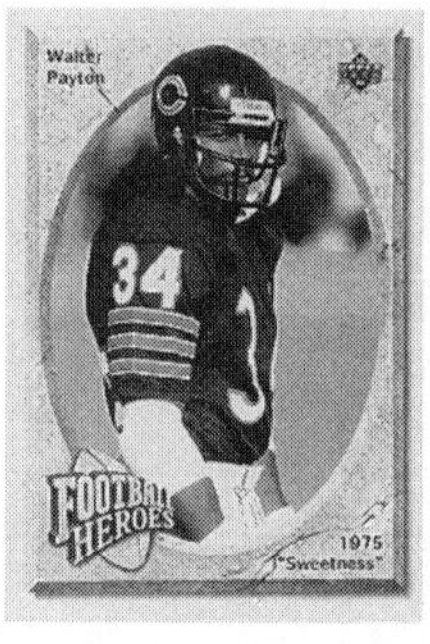

These insert cards feature Hall of Fame running back Walter Payton and continue with card 19, where the Joe Namath Football Heroes series ended. Cards were random inserts in 1992 Upper Deck football Series II foil packs. Each card front has an oval with a picture of Payton in it during a different point in his career. The picture is bordered by a marble-like frame. The card title appears in the lower right corner. Each card back has a career summary on a marble background with dark gray borders. The back is numbered and includes an Upper Deck hologram football. An unnumbered header card was also made.

		MT
Complete Set (10):		30.00
Common Payton:		3.00
Payton Header (NNO):		6.00
19	College Years (Walter Payton)	3.00
20	Sweetness (Walter Payton)	3.00
21	Career Year (Walter Payton)	3.00
22	NFL Rushing Record (Walter Payton)	3.00
23	2,000 Yard Seasons (Walter Payton)	3.00
24	Super Bowl XX (Walter Payton)	3.00
25	Walter Payton Day (Walter Payton)	3.00
26	Hall of Fame Bound (Walter Payton)	3.00
27	Checklist (Walter Payton)	3.00

1992 Upper Deck Heroes Payton Box Bottoms

Much like the Montana and Namath Heroes inserts were printed on a 5-1/4" x 7-1/4" format in 1991, Walter Payton Heroes were printed on the bottoms of 1992 Upper Deck Series I boxes. All box bottoms are blank on the back and feature identical fronts to the Payton Heroes insert.

		MT
Complete Set (8):		5.00
Common Payton:		1.00
19	College Years 1971-74	1.00
20	Sweetness 1975	1.00
21	Career Year 1977	1.00
22	NFL Rushing Record 1984	1.00
23	2,000 Yard Seasons 1983-85	1.00
24	Super Bowl XX 1986	1.00
25	Walter Payton Day 1987	1.00
26	Hall of Fame Bound 1992	1.00

1992 Upper Deck Pro Bowl

Players from the 1992 Pro Bowl are featured on these insert cards randomly included in 1992 Upper Deck Series I foil packs. The front is horizontally designed and features pictures of two different players; the AFC player is on the left, while the NFC player appears on the right. "Pro Bowl" is written in silver foil on a rainbow colored panel which separates the two photos. The rainbow colored band creates a prism-like effect when held under a light. The players' names are at the bottom of the card in silver foil. Each back is in a horizontal format and includes a summary paragraph about each player. Cards are numbered with a PB prefix and include an Upper Deck hologram football.

		MT
Complete Set (16):		30.00
Common Player:		1.50
1	Jeffires, Irvin	4.00
2	Mark Clayton, Gary Clark	4.00
3	Anthony Munoz, Jim Lachey	1.50
4	Moon, Rypien	4.00
5	Thomas, Sanders	8.00
6	Butts, Smith	12.00
7	Townsend, White	4.00
8	Cornelius Bennett, Seth Joyner	1.50
9	Thomas, Swilling	1.50
10	Darryl Talley, Chris Spielman	1.50
11	Ronnie Lott, Mark Carrier	1.50
12	Steve Atwater, Shaun Gayle	1.50
13	Rod Woodson, Darrell Green	1.50
14	Jeff Gossett, Chip Lohmiller	1.50
15	Tim Brown, Mel Gray	1.50
16	Checklist	3.00

1992 Upper Deck NFL Sheets

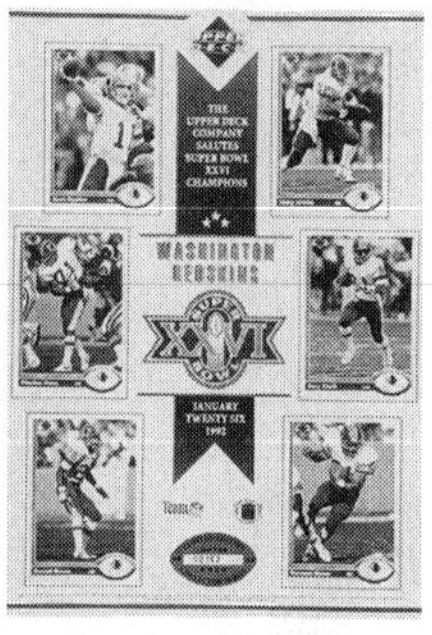

Upper Deck produced four different NFL Sheets in 1992. They commemorated the AFC Championship, NFC Championship, Super Bowl XXVI and Comic Ball IV, with each having a blank back. The AFC and NFC Championship sheets were given away at Upper Deck's Super Bowl Card Show III and at the NFL Experience in Minneapolis. The Super Bowl XXVI sheet was given away at various locations in the Minneapolis area during the week of the Super Bowl.

		MT
Complete Set (4):		30.00
Common Player:		5.00
1	AFC Championship vs. Buffalo Bills Jan 12, 1992 (Thurman Thomas, Cornelius Bennett, Andre Reed, John Elway, Steve Atwater, Gaston Green) (30,000)	5.00
2	NFC Championship vs. Washington Redskins Jan. 12, 1992 (Mark Rypien, Ricky Ervins, Charles Mann, Barry Sanders, Chris Spielman, Mel Gray) (30,000)	5.00
3	Super Bowl XXVII Jan. 26, 1992 (Mark Rypien, Ricky Ervins, Charles Mann, Gary Clark, Darrell Green, Earnest Byner) (15,000)	10.00
4	Comic Ball IV Looney Tunes Characters (Lawrence Taylor, Jerry Rice, Thurman Thomas, Dan Marino) (15,000)	12.00

1992 Upper Deck SCD Sheets

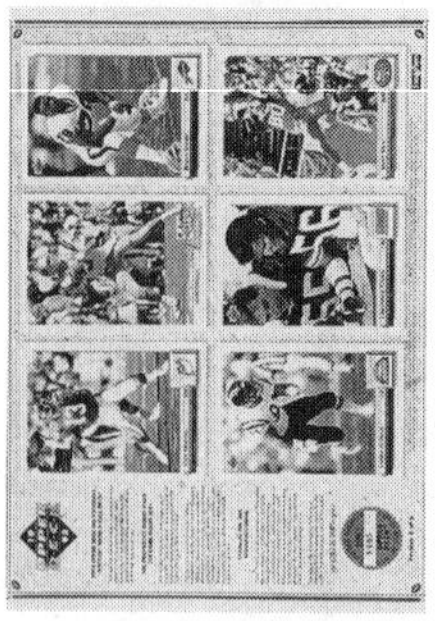

This eight-card set of 8-1/2" x 11" sheets was produced by Upper Deck and included in the Sept. 18, 1992 issue of Sports Collector's Digest at a rate of one per issue. Each sheet contained six cards and sheets were numbered 1-8. Sheet backs were covered with the repeated phrase "Upper Deck Limited Edition Commemorative Sheet."

		MT
Complete Set (8):		75.00
Common Player:		8.00
1	Randall Cunningham, David Klingler, Dan Marino, Troy Aikman, Jim Kelly, Bernie Kosar	15.00
2	Phillippi Sparks, Dale Carter, Steve Emtman, Kevin Smith, Marco Coleman, Carl Pickens	8.00
3	Quentin Coryatt, Greg Skrepenak, Chester McGlockton, Kurt Barber, Vaughn Dunbar, Ashley Ambrose	8.00
4	Ty Detmer, Steve Israel, Tracy Scroggins, Todd Collins, Alonzo Spellman, Marquez Pope	8.00
5	Eric Dickerson, Randal Hill, Jim Kelly, Bernie Kosar, Deion Sanders, Andre Reed	10.00
6	Joe Montana, Mike Singletary, Randall Cunningham, Anthony Miller, Dan McGwire, Harvey Williams	10.00
7	Al Toon, Michael Dean Perry, Troy Aikman, Jeff George, Carl Banks, Junior Seau	10.00
8	Dan Marino, Tommy Maddox, Bruce Smith, Leslie O'Neal, Lawrence Taylor, Jerry Rice	15.00

1992-93 Upper Deck NFL Experience

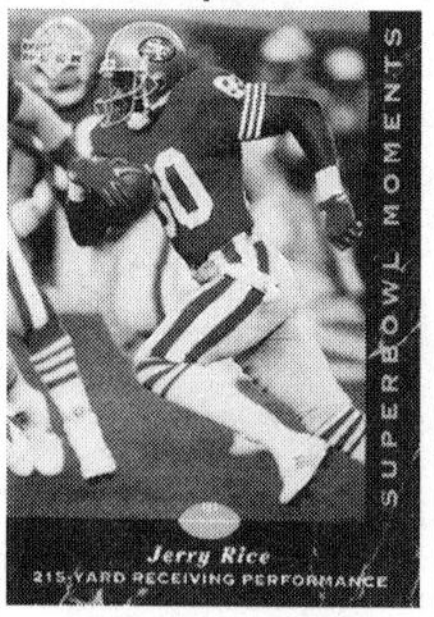

This 50-card set was distributed during the NFL Experience/ Super Bowl Card Show held during the Super Bowl XXVII week Pasadena, Calif. Two designs are used for the card fronts. Cards 1-20 have color photos bordered by different colored stripes on the left and bottom sides. Cards 21-50 have the photos slanted to the left, edged by a ghosted background. Each card back has another photo of the player close up, plus a quote, profile or game summary. The cards, which have a Super Bowl theme, are numbered on the back and include the NFL Experience logo. Some cards were stamped with silver foil; others were stamped in gold. The gold foils are about five times more valuable.

		MT
Complete Set (50):		13.00
Common Player:		.20
1	Joe Montana	1.25
2	Roger Staubach	.25
3	Bart Starr	.25
4	Len Dawson	.20
5	Fred Biletnikoff	.20
6	Jim Plunkett	.20
7	Terry Bradshaw	.25
8	Jerry Rice	.75
9	Doug Williams	.20
10	Dan Marino	.85
11	David Klingler	.60
12	Steve Emtman	.20
13	Dale Carter	.20
14	Quentin Coryatt	.25
15	Tommy Maddox	.50
16	Vaughn Dunbar	.20
17	Marco Coleman	.30
18	Carl Pickens	.50
19	Sean Gilbert	.50
20	Tony Smith	.20
21	Jim Kelly	.80
22	Dan Marino	1.00
23	Boomer Esiason	.35
24	Bernie Kosar	.25
25	Ken O'Brien	.20
26	Deion Sanders	.30
27	Mike Singletary	.20
28	Andre Reed	.35
29	Michael Dean Perry	.20
30	Ricky Proehl	.30
31	Leslie O'Neal	.25
32	Jerry Rice	1.00
33	Eric Dickerson	.20
34	Troy Aikman	2.00
35	Bruce Smith	.45
36	Browning Nagle	.20
37	Carl Banks	.20
38	Harvey Williams	.20
39	Jeff George	.20
40	Lawrence Taylor	.25
41	Webster Slaughter	.20
42	Anthony Miller	.30
43	Randall Cunningham	.35
44	Timm Rosenbach	.20
45	Russell Maryland	.40
46	Randal Hill	.20
47	Dan McGwire	.20
48	Merril Hoge	.20
49	Kevin Fagan	.20
50	Junior Seau	.50

1993 Upper Deck

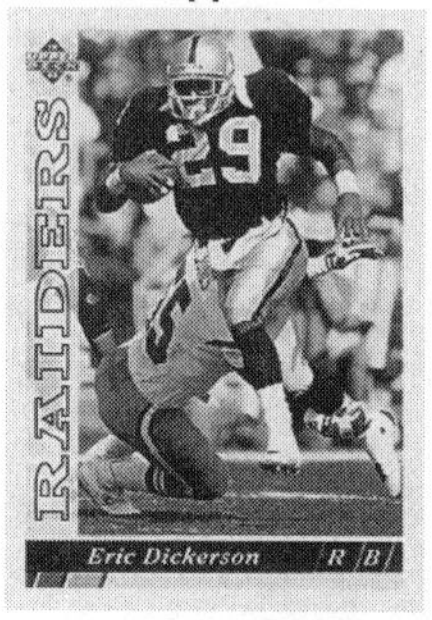

Upper Deck issued its 530-card 1993 set in one series. Each standard-size card has an action photo on the front, with two team color-coded stripes at the bottom with the player's name and position. His team name runs along the left side using team colors. The card back has a hologram, close-up photo, statistics and biographical information. Subsets include Star Rookies, All Rookie Team, NFL Hitmen, Team Checklist, Season Leaders and Berman's Best. Insert sets include America's Team, Future Heroes, Pro Bowlers and Team MVPs.

		MT
Complete Set (530):		25.00
Common Player:		.05
Minor Stars:		.10
Pack (12):		1.50
Wax Box (36):		36.00
1	Star Rookie Checklist	.25
2	*Eric Curry* (SR)	.10
3	*Rick Mirer* (SR)	.30
4	*Dan Williams* (SR)	.10
5	*Marvin Jones* (SR)	.10
6	*Willie Roaf* (SR)	.10
7	*Reggie Brooks* (SR)	.10
8	*Horace Copeland* (SR)	.50
9	*Lincoln Kennedy* (SR)	.10
10	*Curtis Conway* (SR)	1.00
11	*Drew Bledsoe* (SR)	3.00
12	*Patrick Bates* (SR)	.10
13	*Wayne Simmons* (SR)	.10
14	*Irv Smith* (SR)	.10
15	*Robert Smith* (SR)	1.50
16	*O.J. McDuffie* (SR)	1.00
17	*Darrien Gordon* (SR)	.10
18	*John Copeland* (SR)	.10
19	*Derek Brown* (SR)	.10
20	*Jerome Bettis* (SR)	1.50
21	*Deion Figures* (SR)	.20
22	*Glyn Milburn* (SR)	.50
23	*Garrison Hearst* (SR)	1.00
24	*Qadry Ismail* (SR)	.50
25	*Terry Kirby* (SR)	.50
26	*Lamar Thomas* (SR)	.10
27	*Tom Carter* (SR)	.10
28	*Andre Hastings* (SR)	.25
29	*George Teague* (SR)	.20
30	All Rookie Checklist	.10
31	David Klingler (ART)	.05
32	Tommy Maddox (ART)	.05
33	Vaughn Dunbar (ART)	.05
34	Rodney Culver (ART)	.05
35	Carl Pickens (ART)	.05
36	Courtney Hawkins (ART)	.05
37	Tyji Armstrong (ART)	.05
38	Ray Roberts (ART)	.05
39	Troy Auzenne (ART)	.05
40	Shane Dronett (ART)	.05
41	Chris Mims (ART)	.05
42	Sean Gilbert (ART)	.05
43	Steve Emtman (ART)	.05
44	Robert Jones (ART)	.05
45	Marco Coleman (ART)	.05
46	Ricardo McDonald (ART)	.05
47	Quentin Coryatt (ART)	.05
48	Dana Hall (ART)	.05
49	Derren Perry (ART)	.05
50	Darryl Williams (ART)	.05
51	Kevin Smith (ART)	.05
52	Terrell Buckley (ART)	.05
53	Troy Vincent (ART)	.05
54	Lin Elliot (ART)	.05
55	Dale Carter (ART)	.05
56	Steve Atwater (NFL)	.05
57	Junior Seau (NFL)	.10
58	Ronnie Lott (NFL)	.05
59	Louis Oliver (NFL)	.05
60	Cortez Kennedy (NFL)	.05
61	Pat Swilling	.05
62	NFL Hitmen Checklist	.05
63	Curtis Conway (TC)	.05
64	Alfred Williams (TC)	.05
65	Jim Kelly (TC)	.10
66	Simon Fletcher (TC)	.05
67	Eric Metcalf (TC)	.05
68	Lawrence Dawsey (TC)	.05
69	Garrison Hearst (TC)	.40
70	Anthony Miller (TC)	.05
71	Neil Smith (TC)	.05
72	Jeff George (TC)	.05
73	Emmitt Smith (TC)	1.00
74	Dan Marino (TC)	1.00
75	Clyde Simmons (TC)	.05
76	Deion Sanders (TC)	.25
77	Ricky Watters (TC)	.10
78	Rodney Hampton (TC)	.05
79	Brad Baxter (TC)	.05
80	Barry Sanders (TC)	.50
81	Warren Moon (TC)	.10
82	Brett Favre (TC)	.50
83	Drew Bledsoe (TC)	1.00
84	Eric Dickerson (TC)	.05
85	Cleveland Gary (TC)	.05
86	Earnest Byner (TC)	.05
87	Wayne Martin (TC)	.05
88	Rick Mirer (TC)	.50
89	Barry Foster (TC)	.05
90	Terry Allen (TC)	.05
91	Vinnie Clark	.05
92	Howard Ballard	.05
93	Eric Ball	.05
94	Marc Boutte	.05
95	*Larry Centers*	.25
96	Gary Brown	.05
97	Hugh Millen	.05
98	*Anthony Newman*	.05
99	Darrell Thompson	.05
100	George Jamison	.05
101	James Francis	.05
102	Leonard Harris	.05
103	Lomas Brown	.05
104	James Lofton	.05
105	Jamie Dukes	.05
106	Quinn Early	.05
107	Ernie Jones	.05
108	Torrance Small	.05
109	Michael Carter	.05
110	Aeneas Williams	.05
111	Renaldo Turnbull	.05
112	Al Smith	.05
113	Troy Auzenne	.05
114	Stephen Baker	.05
115	Daniel Stubbs	.05
116	Dana Hall	.05
117	Lawrence Taylor	.10
118	Ron Hall	.05
119	Derrick Fenner	.05
120	Martin Mayhew	.05
121	Jay Schroeder	.05
122	Michael Zordich	.05
123	Ed McCaffery	.05
124	John Stephens	.05
125	Brad Edwards	.05
126	Don Griffin	.05
127	Broderick Thomas	.05
128	Ted Washington	.05
129	Haywood Jeffires	.05
130	Gary Plummer	.05
131	Mark Wheeler	.05
132	Ty Detmer	.50
133	Derrick Walker	.05
134	Henry Ellard	.05
135	Neal Anderson	.05
136	Bruce Smith	.05
137	Cris Carter	.10
138	Vaughn Dunbar	.05
139	Dan Marino	2.00
140	Troy Aikman	.75
141	Randall Cunningham	.10
142	Darryl Johnston	.05
143	Mark Clayton	.05
144	Rich Gannon	.05
145	Nate Newton	.05
146	Willie Gault	.05
147	Brian Washington	.05
148	Fred Barnett	.05
149	Gill Byrd	.05
150	Art Monk	.05
151	Stan Humphries	.10
152	Charles Mann	.05
153	Greg Lloyd	.05
154	Marvin Washington	.05
155	Bernie Kosar	.05
156	Pete Metzelaars	.05
157	Chris Hinton	.05
158	Jim Harbaugh	.05
159	Willie Davis	.05
160	Leroy Thompson	.05
161	Scott Miller	.05
162	Eugene Robinson	.05
163	David Little	.05
164	Pierce Holt	.05
165	James Hasty	.05
166	Dave Krieg	.05
167	Gerald Williams	.05
168	Kyle Clifton	.05
169	Bill Brooks	.05
170	Vance Johnson	.05
171	Greg Townsend	.05
172	Jason Belser	.05
173	Brett Perriman	.05
174	Steve Jordan	.05
175	Kelvin Martin	.05
176	Greg Kragen	.05
177	Kerry Cash	.05
178	Chester McGlockton	.05
179	Jim Kelly	.10
180	Todd McNair	.05
181	Leroy Hoard	.05
182	Seth Joyner	.05
183	*Sam Gash*	.05
184	Joe Nash	.05
185	*Lin Elliott*	.05
186	Robert Porcher	.05
187	Tom Hodson	.05
188	Greg Lewis	.05
189	Dan Saleaumua	.05
190	Chris Goode	.05
191	Henry Thomas	.05

192 Bobby Hebert .05
193 Clay Matthews .05
194 Mark Carrier .05
195 Anthony Pleasant .05
196 Eric Dorsey .05
197 Clarence Verdin .05
198 Marc Spindler .05
199 Tommy Maddox .05
200 Wendell Davis .05
201 John Fina .05
202 Alonzo Spellman .05
203 Darryl Williams .05
204 Mike Croel .05
205 Ken Norton .05
206 Mel Gray .05
207 Chuck Cecil .05
208 John Flannery .05
209 Chip Banks .05
210 Chris Martin .05
211 Dennis Brown .05
212 Vinny Testaverde .05
213 Nick Bell .05
214 Robert Delpino .05
215 Mark Higgs .05
216 Al Noga .05
217 Andre Tippett .05
218 Pat Swilling .05
219 Phil Simms .05
220 Ricky Proehl .05
221 William Thomas .05
222 Jeff Graham .05
223 Darion Conner .05
224 Mark Carrier .05
225 Willie Green .05
226 *Reggie Rivers* .05
227 Andre Reed .10
228 Deion Sanders .40
229 Chris Doleman .05
230 Jerry Ball .05
231 Eric Dickerson .05
232 Carlos Jenkins .05
233 Mike Johnson .05
234 Marco Coleman .05
235 Leslie O'Neal .05
236 Browning Nagle .05
237 Carl Pickens .10
238 Steve Emtman .05
239 Alvin Harper .10
240 Keith Jackson .05
241 Jerry Rice .75
242 Cortez Kennedy .10
243 Tyji Armstrong .05
244 Troy Vincent .05
245 Randal Hill .05
246 Robert Blackmon .05
247 Junior Seau .10
248 Sterling Sharpe .10
249 Thurman Thomas .10
250 David Klingler .05
251 Jeff George .20
252 Anthony Miller .05
253 Earnest Byner .05
254 Eric Swann .05
255 Jeff Herrod .05
256 Eddie Robinson .05
257 Eric Allen .05
258 John Taylor .05
259 Sean Gilbert .05
260 Ray Childress .05
261 Michael Haynes .05
262 Greg McMurtry .05
263 Bill Romanowski .05
264 Todd Lyght .05
265 Clyde Simmons .05
266 Webster Slaughter .05
267 J.J. Birden .05
268 Aaron Wallace .05
269 Carl Banks .05
270 Richardo McDonald .05
271 Michael Brooks .05
272 Dale Carter .05
273 Mike Pritchard .05
274 Derek Brown .05
275 Burt Grossman .05
276 Mark Schlereth .05
277 Karl Mecklenburg .05
278 Ricky Jackson .05
279 Ricky Ervins .05
280 Jeff Bryant .05
281 Eric Martin .05
282 Eric Martin .05
283 Kevin Mack .05
284 Brad Muster .05
285 Kelvin Pritchett .05
286 Courtney Hawkins .05
287 Levon Kirkland .05
288 Steve DeBerg .05
289 Edgar Bennett .10
290 Michael Dean Perry .05
291 Richard Dent .05
292 Howie Long .05
293 Chris Mims .05
294 Kurt Barber .05
295 Wilber Marshall .05
296 Ethan Horton .05
297 Tony Bennett .05
298 Johnny Johnson .05
299 Craig Heyward .05
300 Steve Isreal .05
301 Kenneth Gant .05
302 Eugene Chung .05
303 Harvey Williams .05
304 Jerrod Bunch .05
305 Darren Perry .05
306 Steve Christie .05
307 John Randle .05
308 Warren Moon .10
309 Charles Haley .05
310 Tony Smith .05
311 Steve Broussard .05
312 Alfred Williams .05
313 Terrell Buckley .05
314 Trace Armstrong .05
315 Brian Mitchell .05
316 Steve Atwater .05
317 Nate Lewis .05
318 Richard Brown .05
319 Rufus Porter .05
320 Pat Harlow .05
321 Anthony Smith .05
322 Jack Del Rio .05
323 Darryl Talley .05
324 Sam Mills .05
325 Chris Miller .05
326 Ken Harvey .05
327 Rod Woodson .10
328 Tony Tolbert .05
329 Todd Kinchen .05
330 *Brian Noble* .05
331 David Meggett .05
332 Chris Spielman .05
333 Barry Word .05
334 Jessie Hester .05
335 Michael Jackson .05
336 Mitchell Price .05
337 Michael Irvin .10
338 Simon Fletcher .05
339 Keith Jennings .05
340 Vai Sikahema .05
341 Roger Craig .05
342 Ricky Watters .10
343 Reggie Cobb .05
344 Kanavis McGhee .05
345 Barry Foster .10
346 Marion Butts .05
347 Bryan Cox .05
348 Wayne Martin .05
349 Jim Everett .10
350 Nate Odomes .05
351 Anthony Johnson .05
352 Rodney Hampton .10
353 Terry Allen .05
354 Derrick Thomas .10
355 Calvin Williams .05
356 Pepper Johnson .05
357 John Elway .30
358 Steve Young .75
359 Emmitt Smith 2.00
360 Brett Favre 2.00
361 Cody Carlson .05
362 Vincent Brown .05
363 Gary Anderson .05
364 Jon Vaughn .05
365 Todd Marinovich .05
366 Carnell Lake .05
367 Kurt Gouveia .05
368 Lawrence Dawsey .05
369 Neil O'Donnell .15
370 Duane Bickett .05
371 Ronnie Harmon .05
372 Rodney Peete .05
373 Cornelius Bennett .05
374 Brad Baxter .05
375 Ernest Givins .05
376 Keith Byars .05
377 Eric Bieniemy .05
378 Mike Brim .05
379 Darren Lewis .05
380 Heath Sherman .05
381 Leonard Russell .05
382 Brent Jones .05
383 David Whitmore .05
384 Ray Roberts .05
385 John Offerdahl .05
386 Keith McCants .05
387 John Baylor .05
388 Amp Lee .05
389 Chris Warren .20
390 Herman Moore .50
391 Johnny Bailey .05
392 Tim Johnson .05
393 Eric Metcalf .05
394 Chris Chandler .05
395 Mark Rypien .05
396 Christian Okoye .05
397 Shannon Sharpe .10
398 Eric Hill .05
399 David Lang .05
400 Bruce Matthews .05
401 Harold Green .05
402 Moe Lewis .05
403 Terry McDaniel .05
404 Wesley Carroll .05
405 Richmond Webb .05
406 Andre Rison .10
407 Lonnie Young .05
408 Tommy Vardell .05
409 Gene Atkins .05
410 Sean Salisbury .05
411 Kenneth Davis .05
412 John L. Williams .05
413 Roman Phifer .05
414 Bennie Blades .05
415 Tim Brown .10
416 Lorenzo White .05
417 Tony Casillas .05
418 Tom Waddle .05
419 David Fulcher .05
420 Jessie Tuggle .05
421 Emmitt Smith (SL) .75
422 Clyde Simmons (SL) .05
423 Sterling Sharpe (SL) .10
424 Sterling Sharpe (SL) .10
425 Emmitt Smith (SL) .75
426 Dan Marino (SL) .75
427 Jones, McMillan (SL) .05
428 Thurman Thomas (SL) .10
429 Greg Montgomery (SL) .05
430 Pete Stoyanovich (SL) .05
431 Emmitt Smith (CL) .50
432 Steve Young (BB) .50
433 Jerry Rice (BB) .40
434 Ricky Watters (BB) .10
435 Barry Foster (BB) .10
436 Cortez Kennedy (BB) .10
437 Warren Moon (BB) .10
438 Thurman Thomas (BB) .10
439 Brett Favre (BB) .50
440 Andre Rison (BB) .10
441 Barry Sanders (BB) .50
442 Chris Berman (CL) .05
443 Moe Gardner .05
444 Robert Jones .05
445 Reggie Langhorne .05
446 Willie Anderson .05
447 James Washington .05
448 Aaron Craver .05
449 Jack Trudeau .05
450 Neil Smith .05
451 Chris Burkett .05
452 Darren Woodson .05
453 Drew Hill .05
454 Barry Sanders 1.25
455 Jeff Cross .05
456 Bennie Thompson .05
457 Marcus Allen .10
458 Tracy Scroggins .05
459 Leroy Butler .05
460 Joe Montana 1.25
461 Eddie Anderson .05
462 Tim McDonald .05
463 Ronnie Lott .05
464 Gaston Green .05
465 Shane Conlan .05
466 Leonard Marshall .05
467 Melvin Jenkins .05
468 Don Beebe .05
469 Johnny Mitchell .05
470 Darryl Henley .05
471 Boomer Esiason .10
472 Mark Kelso .05
473 John Booty .05
474 Pete Stoyanovich .05
475 *Thomas Smith* .10
476 *Carlton Gray* .10
477 *Dana Stubblefield* .50
478 *Ryan McNeil* .10
479 *Natrone Means* 1.00
480 *Carl Simpson* .10
481 *Robert O'Neal* .10
482 *Demetrius Dubose* .10
483 *Darrin Smith* .20
484 *Michael Barrow* .10
485 *Chris Slade* .40
486 *Steve Tovar* .10
487 *Ron George* .10
488 Steve Tasker .05
489 Will Furrer .05
490 Reggie White .10
491 Sean Jones .05
492 Gary Clark .05
493 Donnell Woolford .05
494 Steve Beuerlein .05
495 Anthony Carter .05
496 Louis Oliver .05
497 Chris Zorich .05
498 Bubba McDowell .05
500 Adrian Cooper .05
501 Bill Johnson .05
502 Shawn Jefferson .05
503 Siran Stacy .05
504 James Jones .05
505 Tom Rathman .05
506 Vince Buck .05
507 *Kent Graham* .30
508 *Darren Carrington* .10
509 Ricky Dixon .05
510 Toi Cook .05
511 Steve Smith .05
512 Ostell Miles .05
513 Phil Sparks .05
514 Lee Williams .05
515 Gary Reason .05
516 Shane Dronett .05
517 Jay Novacek .05
518 Kevin Greene .05
519 Derek Russell .05
520 Quentin Coryatt .10
521 Santana Dotson .05
522 Donald Frank .05
523 Mike Prior .05
524 *Dwight Hollier* .05
525 Eric Davis .05
526 Dalton Hilliard .05
527 Rodney Culver .05
528 Jeff Hostetler .10
529 Ernie Mills .05
530 Craig Erickson .05

1993 Upper Deck America's Team

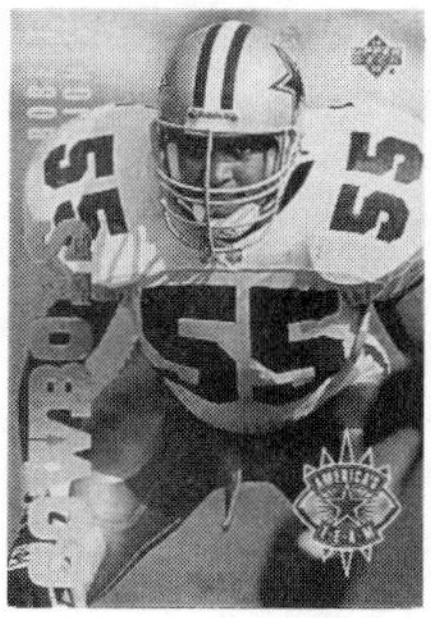

This 15-card insert set is devoted to the players from Super Bowl Championship Dallas Cowboys teams. Cards 1-6 feature Cowboys from Super Bowl XII; players from Super Bowl XXVII are featured on cards 7-13. The front has a color action photo, plus the player's name and team stamped in silver foil along the left side of the card. An "America's Team" logo is also on the front. The back has this logo as a background, with a paragraph devoted to the player's accomplishments in the Super Bowl game. Cards are numbered with an "AT" prefix and were random inserts in 1993 Upper Deck hobby foil packs. There is also an unnumbered title card which features Emmitt Smith.

		MT
Complete Set (15):		125.00
Common Player:		5.00
E. Smith Header:		15.00
1	Roger Staubach	12.00
2	Chuck Howley	5.00
3	Harvey Martin	5.00
4	Randy White	5.00
5	Bob Lilly	5.00
6	Drew Pearson	5.00
7	Emmitt Smith	45.00
8	Troy Aikman	25.00
9	Ken Norton	5.00
10	Robert Jones	5.00
11	Russell Maryland	5.00
12	Jay Novacek	5.00
13	Michael Irvin	7.00
14	Troy Aikman (CL)	10.00

1993 Upper Deck Future Heroes

These cards feature color action photos on the front, along with the team color-coded stripe on the left which contains the player's name. A 1993 "Future Heroes" logo is in gold foil in the bottom left corner, too. The back has another small color photo and player profile against a team color-coded background. The player's name and card number are at the top of the card. Numbering begins with #37, where the Upper Deck Football Series ended. These inserts, which were randomly included in all types of packs, also include an unnumbered title card which features Ricky Watters.

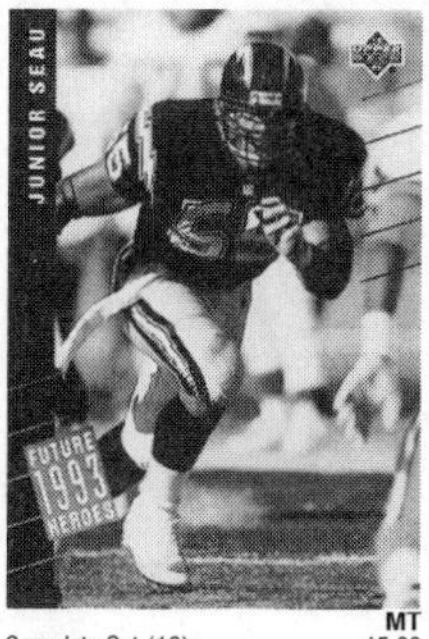

		MT
Complete Set (10):		15.00
Common Player:		1.00
37	Barry Foster	1.00
38	Junior Seau	1.00
39	Emmitt Smith	5.00
40	Troy Aikman	3.00
41	David Klingler	1.00
42	Ricky Watters	1.50
43	Barry Sanders	5.00
44	Brett Favre	5.00
45	Checklist	2.00

1993 Upper Deck Pro Bowl

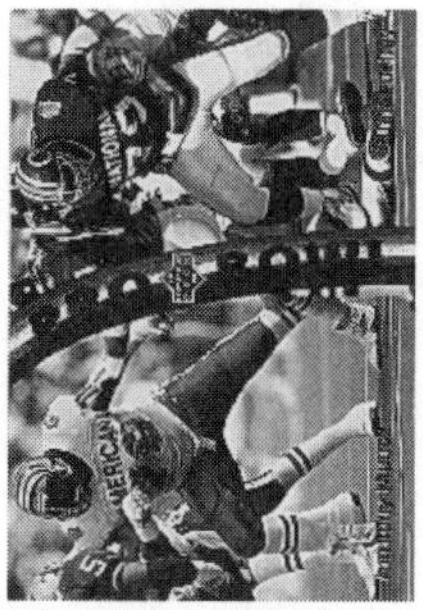

These glossy cards feature two photos on the horizontally-designed front - a color photo on the left with holographic borders on the left and bottom, and a second photo on the right. Each player was a Pro Bowl selection; the Pro Bowl logo is on the front in the lower left corner. The card back has a blue- and-white background with a career profile on it. A card number, using a "PB" prefix, also appears. Cards were random inserts in retail foil packs.

		MT
Complete Set (20):		160.00
Common Player:		5.00
1	Andre Reed	5.00
2	Dan Marino	30.00
3	Warren Moon	5.00
4	Anthony Miller	5.00
5	Barry Foster	5.00
6	Steve Atwater	5.00
7	Cortez Kennedy	5.00
8	Junior Seau	5.00
9	Jerry Rice	20.00
10	Michael Irvin	5.00
11	Sterling Sharpe	5.00
12	Steve Young	20.00
13	Troy Aikman	20.00
14	Brett Favre	30.00
15	Emmitt Smith	30.00
16	Rodney Hampton	5.00
17	Barry Sanders	25.00
18	Ricky Watters	5.00
19	Pat Swilling	5.00
20	Checklist	5.00

1993 Upper Deck Rookie Exchange

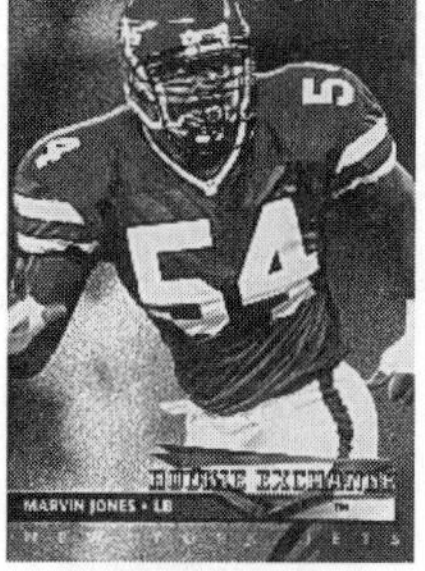

This set could be obtained by redeeming a "Trade Upper Deck" card, available randomly in every 72nd pack of Upper Deck football card packs. The card front uses Upper Deck's Electric printing, which gives it a metallic quality. A player photo is featured on the front, along with the player's name and position in a team color-coded bar at the bottom. His team name is also given, in silver letters. The back has another color photo on the left, plus a recap of the player's previous season. The background is in team colors. The player's name, position and card number, using an "RE" prefix, also appears on the card back.

		MT
Complete Set (7):		15.00
Common Player:		1.00
1	Rookie Trade Card	1.00
2	Drew Bledsoe	7.00
3	Rick Mirer	1.00
4	Garrison Hearst	2.00
5	Marvin Jones	1.00
6	Curtis Conway	1.50
7	Jerome Bettis	2.00

1993 Upper Deck Team MVPs

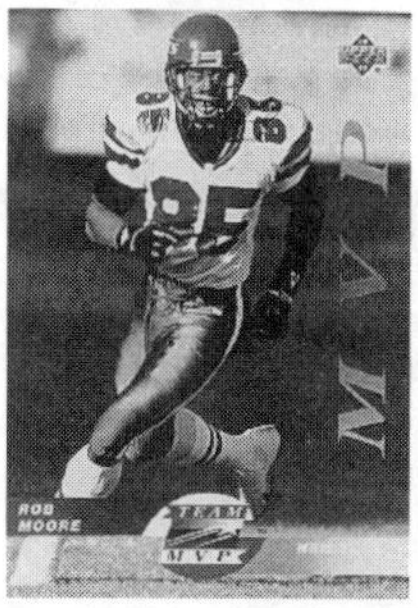

The Most Valuable Player on each of the 28 NFL teams is represented in this 29-card insert set. Each card front has a full-bleed color action photo, plus two team color-coded stripes at the bottom which contain the player's name and team. A Team MVP logo is also at the bottom of the card. Team color-coded stripes are also used on the back, which features another player photo and career highlights. A card number, using a "TM" prefix, is also given. Cards were random inserts in jumbo foil packs.

		MT
Complete Set (29):		20.00
Common Player:		.50
Minor Stars:		1.00
1	Neal Anderson	.50
2	Harold Green	.50
3	Thurman Thomas	1.00
4	John Elway	2.00
5	Eric Metcalf	.50
6	Reggie Cobb	.50
7	Johnny Bailey	.50
8	Junior Seau	1.00
9	Derrick Thomas	1.00
10	Steve Emtman	.50
11	Troy Aikman	4.00
12	Dan Marino	7.00
13	Clyde Simmons	.50
14	Andre Rison	1.00
15	Steve Young	3.00
16	Rodney Hampton	1.00
17	Rob Moore	.50
18	Barry Sanders	5.00
19	Warren Moon	1.00
20	Sterling Sharpe	1.00
21	Jon Vaughn	.50
22	Tim Brown	1.00
23	Jim Everett	.50
24	Gary Clark	.50
25	Wayne Martin	.50
26	Cortez Kennedy	1.00
27	Barry Foster	1.00
28	Terry Allen	.50
29	Checklist	.50

1993 Upper Deck Kansas City Chiefs

This 25-card team set is devoted to the Kansas City Chiefs. The cards use the same design format as Upper Deck's main 1993 issue. However, the cards, which are standard size, are numbered on the back using a "KC" prefix. The photos used on both sides are identical to those used for the regular set.

		MT
Complete Set (25):		8.00
Common Player:		.20
1	Nick Lowery	.25
2	Lonnie Marts	.20
3	Marcus Allen	1.00
4	Bennie Thompson	.20
5	Bryan Barker	.20
6	Christian Okoye	.25
7	Dale Carter	.25
8	Dan Saleaumua	.25
9	Dave Krieg	.25
10	Derrick Thomas	1.00
11	Doug Terry	.20
12	Fred Jones	.20
13	Harvey Williams	.60
14	J.J. Birden	.25
15	Joe Montana	3.00
16	John Alt	.25
17	Leonard Griffin	.20
18	Matt Blundin	.30
19	Neil Smith	.35
20	Tim Barnett	.25
21	Tim Grunhard	.20
22	Todd McNair	.25
23	Tracy Simien	.20
24	Willie Davis	.35
25	Joe Montana (Checklist back)	2.00

1993 Upper Deck Dallas Cowboys

This 25-card team set is devoted to the Dallas Cowboys. The cards are standard size and use the same design as Upper Deck's regular 1993 set. These cards, however, are numbered on the back using a "D" prefix. But the photos on both sides are the same as those used for the regular set.

		MT
Complete Set (25):		10.00
Common Player:		.25
1	Alvin Harper	1.00
2	Charles Haley	.50
3	Jimmy Smith	.25
4	Darrin Smith	.25
5	Jim Jeffcoat	.25
6	Darryl Johnston	.75
7	Dixon Edwards	.25
8	Emmitt Smith	3.00
9	James Washington	.25
10	Jay Novacek	.40
11	Ken Norton	.40
12	Kenneth Gant	.25
13	Larry Brown	.25
14	Leon Lett	.35
15	Lin Elliott	.25
16	Mark Tuinei	.25
17	Michael Irvin	1.50
18	Nate Newton	.25
19	Robert Jones	.25
20	Thomas Everett	.25
21	Tony Casillas	.25
22	Tony Tolbert	.25
23	Troy Aikman	3.00
24	Russell Maryland	.50
25	Troy Aikman (Checklist back)	2.00

1993 Upper Deck San Francisco 49ers

The San Francisco 49ers are represented in this 25-card team set from Upper Deck. The cards are standard size and follow the design format used in Upper Deck's regular 1993 issue. However, the card backs are numbered using an "SF" prefix. This set uses the same photos on each side as those which were used for the regular issue.

		MT
Complete Set (25):		8.00
Common Player:		.20
1	Amp Lee	.40
2	Bill Romanowski	.25
3	Brent Jones	.50
4	Dana Hall	.25
5	Dana Stubblefield	1.00
6	Dennis Brown	.20
7	Dexter Carter	.25
8	Don Griffin	.20
9	Eric Davis	.25
10	Guy McIntyte	.20
11	Jamie Williams	.20
12	Jerry Rice	2.00
13	John Taylor	.35
14	Keith DeLong	.25
15	Marc Logan	.25
16	Michael Walters	.20
17	Mike Cofer	.20
18	Odessa Turner	.20
19	Ricky Watters	.75
20	Steve Bono	.50
21	Steve Young	2.00
22	Ted Washington	.25
23	Tom Rathman	.35
24	Jesse Sapolu	.20
25	Steve Young (Checklist back)	1.00

1993 Upper Deck Authenticated Classic Confrontations

The 3-1/2" x 5" card features Montana and Marino. "Classic Confrontations XIX" is printed on the right side of the card. The card back is sequentially numbered as "x of 20,000."

		MT
Complete Set (1):		20.00
Common Player:		20.00
1	Classic Confrontation (Joe Montana, Dan Marino)	20.00

1993-94 Upper Deck Miller Lite SB

The five-card, 5" x 3-1/2" set was sponsored by Miller and Tombstone Pizza. One card was issued in each 12-pack of Miller Lite. The set was available through mail-in UPC offers. All entries received were entered in a drawing for 1,000 Montana autographed sheets. The card fronts feature two quarterbacks from a past Super Bowl on a horizontal design. The backs include highlight info over a ghosted Super Bowl logo.

		MT
Complete Set (5):		20.00
Common Player:		2.50
1	Super Bowl XXVII (Troy Aikman, Jim Kelly)	5.00
2	Super Bowl XXVI (Jim Kelly, Mark Rypien)	2.50

3	Super Bowl XXIV (John Elway, Joe Montana)	7.00
4	Super Bowl XXI (John Elway, Phil Simms)	3.00
5	Super Bowl XIX (Joe Montana, Dan Marino)	8.00

1994 Upper Deck Pro Bowl Samples

The six-card, standard-size set was distributed at the National Convention in Houston. The cards are very similar to the basic insert issue, except that the card backs have "Sample Card" printed diagonally.

		MT
Complete Set (6):		25.00
Common Player:		2.50
1	Jerome Bettis	2.50
2	Brett Favre	10.00
3	John Elway	4.00
4	Thurman Thomas	2.50
5	Jerry Rice	6.00
6	Steve Young	4.00

1994 Upper Deck

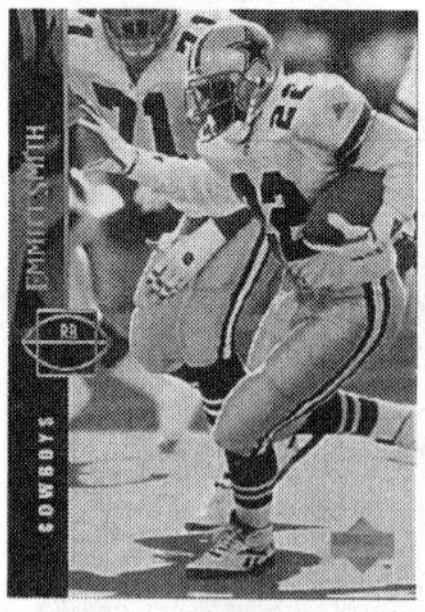

The Upper Deck Co. kicked off its 1994 football campaign, with a 330-card, single series issue. Upper Deck also introduced an upgraded card design and an interactive 50-card insert set, called Predictor Series. Two parallel Electric Field sets were also available. All 330 regular-issue cards will also be printed using gold and silver foil. These sets-within-a-set are called Silver Electric and Gold Electric, respectively. There are two other insert sets, called Then and Now and Pro Bowl Holoview.

		MT
Complete Set (330):		35.00
Common Player:		.10
Minor Stars:		.20
Silver Cards:		3x
Silver Rookies:		2x
Inserted 1:1		
Gold Cards:		12x-24x
Gold Rookies:		6x-12x
Inserted 1:35		
Pack (12):		1.50
Wax Box (36):		40.00
1	*Dan Wilkinson*	.20
2	*Antonio Langham*	.20
3	*Derrick Alexander*	.50
4	*Charles Johnson*	.50
5	*Bucky Brooks*	.20
6	*Trev Alberts*	.20
7	*Marshall Faulk*	6.00
8	*Willie McGinest*	.50
9	*Aaron Glenn*	.20
10	*Ryan Yarborough*	.20
11	*Greg Hill*	.50
12	*Sam Adams*	.20
13	John Thierry	.20
14	*Johnnie Morton*	.50
15	*LeShon Johnson*	.20
16	*David Palmer*	.20
17	*Trent Dilfer*	2.00
18	*Jamir Miller*	.20
19	*Thomas Lewis*	.20
20	*Heath Shuler*	.50
21	*Wayne Gandy*	.20
22	*Isaac Bruce*	4.00
23	*Joe Johnson*	.20
24	*Mario Bates*	.30
25	*Bryant Young*	.50
26	*William Floyd*	.50
27	*Errict Rhett*	.75
28	*Chuck Levy*	.20
29	*Darnay Scott*	.75
30	*Rob Fredrickson*	.20
31	Jamir Miller	.10
32	Thomas Lewis	.25
33	John Thierry	.10
34	Sam Adams	.25
35	Joe Johnson	.10
36	Bryant Young	.25
37	Wayne Gandy	.10
38	LaShon Johnson	.25
39	Mario Bates	.50
40	Greg Hill	.75
41	Andy Heck	.10
42	Warren Moon	.40
43	Jim Everett	.10
44	Bill Romanowski	.10
45	Michael Haynes	.10
46	Chris Doleman	.10
47	Merril Hoge	.10
48	Chris Miller	.10
49	Clyde Simmons	.10
50	Jeff George	.20
51	Jeff Burris	.20
52	Ethan Horton	.10
53	Scott Mitchell	.20
54	Howard Ballard	.10
55	Lawyer Tillman	.10
56	Marion Butts	.10
57	Erik Kramer	.10
58	Ken Norton	.10
59	Anthony Miller	.20
60	Chris Hinton	.10
61	Ricky Proehl	.10
62	Craig Heyward	.10
63	Darryl Talley	.10
64	Tim Worley	.10
65	Derrick Fenner	.10
66	Jerry Ball	.10
67	Darren Woodson	.10
68	Mike Croel	.10
69	Ray Crockett	.10
70	Tony Bennett	.10
71	Webster Slaughter	.10
72	Anthony Johnson	.10
73	Charles Mincy	.10
74	*Calvin Jones*	.40
75	Henry Ellard	.10
76	Troy Vincent	.10
77	Sean Salisbury	.10
78	Pat Harlow	.10
79	James Williams	.10
80	Derek Brown	.20
81	Marvin Jones	.10
82	Seth Joyner	.10
83	Deion Figures	.10
84	Stanley Richards	.10
85	Tom Rathman	.10
86	Rod Stephens	.10
87	Ray Seals	.10
88	Andre Collins	.10
89	Cornelius Bennett	.10
90	Richard Dent	.10
91	Louis Oliver	.10
92	Rodney Peete	.10
93	Jackie Harris	.10
94	Tracy Simien	.10
95	Greg Townsend	.10
96	Michael Stewert	.10
97	Irving Fryar	.10
98	Todd Collins	.10
99	Irv Smith	.10
100	Chris Calloway	.10
101	Kevin Greene	.10
102	John Friesz	.10
103	Steve Bono	.10
104	Brian Blades	.10
105	Reggie Cobb	.10
106	Eric Swann	.10
107	Mike Pritchard	.10
108	Bill Brooks	.10
109	Jim Harbaugh	.10
110	David Whitmore	.10
111	Eddie Anderson	.10
112	Ray Crittenden	.25
113	Mark Collins	.10
114	Brian Washington	.10
115	Barry Foster	.25
116	Gary Plummer	.10
117	Marc Logan	.10
118	John L. Williams	.20
119	Marty Carter	.10
120	Marvin Jones	.10
121	Ron Moore	.25
122	Pierce Holt	.10
123	Henry Jones	.10
124	Donnell Woolford	.10
125	Steve Tovar	.10
126	Anthony Pleasant	.10
127	Jay Novacek	.10
128	Dan Williams	.10
129	Barry Sanders	2.00
130	Robert Brooks	.10
131	Lorenzo White	.10
132	Kerry Cash	.10
133	Joe Montana	2.00
134	Jeff Hostetler	.10
135	Jerome Bettis	.75
136	Dan Marino	3.00
137	Vencie Glenn	.10
138	Vincent Brown	.10
139	Ricky Jackson	.10
140	Carlton Bailey	.10
141	Jeff Lageman	.10
142	William Thomas	.10
143	Neil O'Donnell	.20
144	Shawn Jefferson	.10
145	Steve Young	1.00
146	Chris Warren	.10
147	Courtney Hawkins	.10
148	Brad Edwards	.10
149	O.J. McDuffie	.25
150	David Lang	.10
151	Chuck Cecil	.10
152	Norm Johnson	.10
153	Pete Metzelaars	.10
154	Shaun Gayle	.10
155	Alfred Williams	.10
156	Eric Turner	.10
157	Emmitt Smith	3.00
158	Steve Atwater	.10
159	Robert Porcher	.10
160	Edgar Bennett	.10
161	Bubba McDowell	.10
162	Jeff Herrod	.10
163	Keith Cash	.10
164	Patrick Bates	.10
165	Todd Lyght	.10
166	Mark Higgs, Rob Burnett	.10
167	Carlos Jenkins	.10
168	Drew Bledsoe	2.00
169	Wayne Martin	.10
170	Mike Sherrard	.10
171	Ronnie Lott	.10
172	Fred Barnett	.10
173	Eric Green	.10
174	Leslie O'Neal	.10
175	Brent Jones	.10
176	John Vaughn	.10
177	Vince Workman	.10
178	Ron Middleton	.10
179	Terry McDaniel	.10
180	Willie Davis	.10
181	Gary Clark	.10
182	Bobby Hebert	.10
183	Russell Copeland	.10
184	Chris Gadney	.10
185	Tony McGhee	.10
187	Charles Haley	.10
188	Shannon Sharpe	.20
189	Mel Gray	.10
190	George Teague	.10
191	Ernest Givins	.10
192	Ray Buchannan	.10
193	J.J. Birden	.10
194	Tim Brown	.20
195	Tim Lester	.10
196	Marco Coleman	.10
197	Randall McDaniel	.10
198	Bruce Armstrong	.10
199	Willie Roaf	.10
200	Greg Jackson	.10
201	Johnny Mitchell	.10
202	Calvin Williams	.10
203	Jeff Graham	.10
204	Darren Carrington	.10
205	Jerry Rice	1.00
206	Cortez Kennedy	.20
207	Charles Wilson	.10
208	James Jenkins	.10
209	Ray Childress	.10
210	Leroy Butler	.10
211	Randal Hill	.10
212	Lincoln Kennedy	.10
213	Kenneth Davis	.10
214	Terry Obee	.10
215	Richardo McDonald	.10
216	Pepper Johnson	.10
217	Alvin Harper	.20
218	John Elway	.50
219	Derrick Moore	.10
220	Terrell Buckley	.10
221	Haywood Jeffires	.10
222	Jessie Hester	.10
223	Kimble Anders	.10
224	Raghib Ismail	.10
225	Roman Phifer	.10
226	Bryan Cox	.10
227	Cris Carter	.20
228	Sam Gash	.10
229	Renaldo Turnbull	.10
230	Rodney Hampton	.20
231	Johnny Johnson	.10
232	Tim Harris	.10
233	Leroy Thompson	.10
234	Junior Seau	.20
235	Tim McDonald	.10
236	Eugene Robinson	.10
237	Lawrence Dawsey	.10
238	Tim Johnson	.10
239	Jason Elam	.10
240	Willie Green	.10
241	Larry Centers	.10
242	Erric Pegram	.15
243	Bruce Smith	.10
244	Alonzo Spellman	.10
245	Carl Pickens	.30
246	Michael Jackson	.10
247	Kevin Williams	.25
248	Glyn Milburn	.15
249	Herman Moore	.50
250	Brett Favre	3.00
251	Al Smith	.10
252	Roosevelt Potts	.10
253	Marcus Allen	.20
254	Anthony Smith	.10
255	Sean Gilbert	.10
256	Keith Byars	.10
257	*Scottie Graham*	.50
258	Leonard Russell	.10
259	Eric Martin	.10
260	Jerrod Bunch	.10
261	Rob Moore	.10
262	Herschel Walker	.10
263	Levon Kirkland	.10
264	Chris Mims	.10
265	Ricky Watters	.25
266	Rick Mirer	.75
267	Santana Dotson	.10
268	Reggie Brooks	.15
269	Garrison Hearst	.50
270	Thurman Thomas	.25
271	Johnny Bailey	.10
272	Andre Rison	.20
273	Jim Kelly	.25
274	Mark Carrier	.10
275	David Klingler	.10
276	Eric Metcalf	.10
277	Troy Aikman	1.25
278	Simon Fletcher	.10
279	Pat Swilling	.10
280	Sterling Sharpe	.25
281	Cody Carlson	.10
282	Steve Emtman	.10
283	Neil Smith	.10
284	James Jett	.10
285	Shane Conlan	.10
286	Keith Jackson	.10
287	Qadry Ismail	.15
288	Chris Slade	.15
289	Derek Brown	.10
290	Phil Simms	.10
291	Boomer Esiason	.10
292	Eric Allen	.10
293	Rod Woodson	.20
294	Ronnie Harmon	.10
295	John Taylor	.20
296	Ferrell Edmunds	.10
297	Craig Erickson	.15
298	Brian Mitchell	.10
299	Dante Jones	.10
300	John Copeland	.10
301	Steve Beuerlein	.10
302	Deion Sanders	.75
303	Andre Reed	.20
304	Curtis Conway	.20
305	Harold Green	.10
306	Vinny Testaverde	.10
307	Michael Irvin	.50
308	Rod Bernstine	.10
309	Chris Spielman	.10
310	Reggie White	.20
311	Gary Brown	.10
312	Quentin Coryatt	.10
313	Derrick Thomas	.20
314	Greg Robinson	.10
315	Troy Drayton	.10
316	Terry Kirby	.15
317	John Randle	.10
318	Ben Coates	.50
319	Tyrone Hughes	.10
320	Corey Miller	.10
321	Brad Baxter	.10
322	Randall Cunningham	.25
323	Greg Lloyd	.10
324	Stan Humphries	.20
325	Dana Stubblefield	.20
326	Kelvin Martin	.10
327	Hardy Nickerson	.10
328	Desmond Howard	.10
329	Mark Carrier	.10
330	Darryl Johnston	.10

1994 Upper Deck Electric Silver

The 330-card, standard-size set was a parallel to the basic Upper Deck set. The cards differ from the gold versions by the logo that was produced with a foil finish instead of prismatic finish.

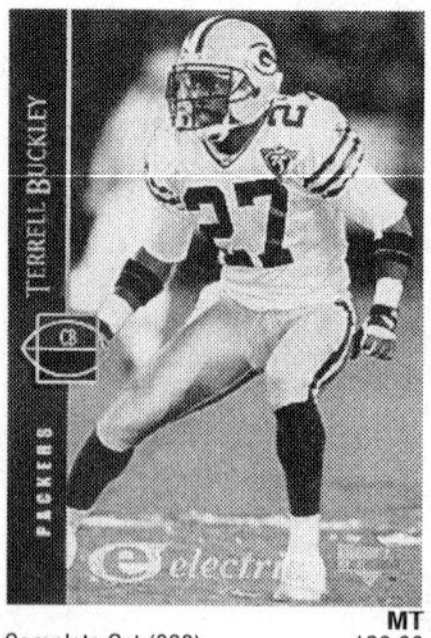

	MT
Complete Set (330):	120.00
Common Player:	.25
Veteran Stars:	2x-4x
Young Stars:	1.5x-3x
RCs:	1.25x-2.5x

1994 Upper Deck Electric Gold

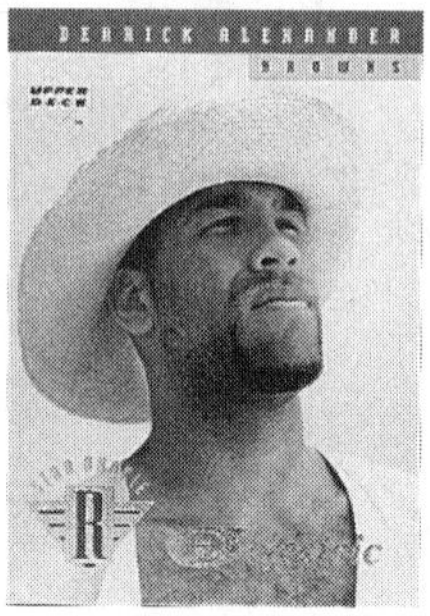

The Upper Deck Co. kicked off its 1994 football campaign, with a 330-card, single series issue. Upper Deck also introduced an upgraded card design and an interactive 50-card insert set, called Predictor Series. Two parallel Electric Field sets were also available. All 330 regular-issue cards will also be printed using gold and silver foil. These sets-within-a-set are called Silver Electric and Gold Electric, respectively. There are two other insert sets, called Then and Now and Pro Bowl Holoview.

		MT
Complete Set (330):		1700.
Common Player:		3.00
Minor Stars:		6.00
Unlisted Stars:		20x-40x
1	*Dan Wilkinson*	10.00
2	*Antonio Langham*	15.00
3	*Derrick Alexander*	6.00
4	*Charles Johnson*	30.00
5	*Bucky Brooks*	10.00
6	*Trev Alberts*	8.00
7	*Marshall Faulk*	100.00
8	*Willie McGinest*	10.00
9	*Aaron Glenn*	6.00
10	*Ryan Yarborough*	6.00
11	*Greg Hill*	30.00
12	*Sam Adams*	10.00
13	John Thierry	10.00
14	*Johnnie Morton*	10.00
15	*LeShon Johnson*	10.00
16	*David Palmer*	15.00
17	*Trent Dilfer*	40.00
18	*Jamir Miller*	6.00
19	*Thomas Lewis*	15.00
20	*Heath Shuler*	15.00
21	*Wayne Gandy*	6.00
22	*Isaac Bruce*	80.00
23	*Joe Johnson*	6.00
24	*Mario Bates*	25.00
25	*Bryant Young*	20.00
26	*William Floyd*	30.00
27	*Errict Rhett*	80.00
28	*Chuck Levy*	6.00
29	*Darnay Scott*	55.00
30	*Rob Fredrickson*	10.00
31	Jamir Miller	3.00
32	Thomas Lewis	6.00
33	John Thierry	6.00
34	Sam Adams	6.00
35	Joe Johnson	3.00
36	Bryant Young	6.00
37	Wayne Gandy	3.00
38	LaShon Johnson	6.00
39	Mario Bates	6.00
40	Greg Hill	15.00
41	Andy Heck	3.00
42	Warren Moon	8.00
43	Jim Everett	3.00
44	Bill Romanowski	3.00
45	Michael Haynes	3.00
46	Chris Doleman	3.00
47	Merril Hoge	3.00
48	Chris Miller	3.00
49	Clyde Simmons	3.00
50	Jeff George	6.00
51	Jeff Burris	10.00
52	Ethan Horton	3.00
53	Scott Mitchell	6.00
54	Howard Ballard	3.00
55	Lawyer Tillman	3.00
56	Marion Butts	3.00
57	Erik Kramer	3.00
58	Ken Norton	3.00
59	Anthony Miller	6.00
60	Chris Hinton	3.00
61	Ricky Proehl	3.00
62	Craig Heyward	3.00
63	Darryl Talley	3.00
64	Tim Worley	3.00
65	Derrick Fenner	3.00
66	Jerry Ball	3.00
67	Darren Woodson	3.00
68	Mike Croel	3.00
69	Ray Crockett	3.00
70	Tony Bennett	3.00
71	Webster Slaughter	3.00
72	Anthony Johnson	3.00
73	Charles Mincy	3.00
74	*Calvin Jones*	10.00
75	Henry Ellard	3.00
76	Troy Vincent	3.00
77	Sean Salisbury	3.00
78	Pat Harlow	3.00
79	James Williams	3.00
80	Derek Brown	6.00
81	Marvin Jones	3.00
82	Seth Joyner	3.00
83	Deion Figures	3.00
84	Stanley Richards	3.00
85	Tom Rathman	3.00
86	Rod Stephens	3.00
87	Ray Seals	3.00
88	Andre Collins	3.00
89	Cornelius Bennett	3.00
90	Richard Dent	3.00
91	Louis Oliver	3.00
92	Rodney Peete	3.00
93	Jackie Harris	3.00
94	Tracy Simien	3.00
95	Greg Townsend	3.00
96	Michael Stewert	3.00
97	Irving Fryar	3.00
98	Todd Collins	3.00
99	Irv Smith	3.00
100	Chris Calloway	3.00
101	Kevin Greene	3.00
102	John Friesz	3.00
103	Steve Bono	3.00
104	Brian Blades	3.00
105	Reggie Cobb	3.00
106	Eric Swann	3.00
107	Mike Pritchard	3.00
108	Bill Brooks	3.00
109	Jim Harbaugh	3.00
110	David Whitmore	3.00
111	Eddie Anderson	3.00
112	Ray Crittenden	6.00
113	Mark Collins	3.00
114	Brian Washington	3.00
115	Barry Foster	6.00
116	Gary Plummer	3.00
117	Marc Logan	3.00
118	John L. Williams	6.00
119	Marty Carter	3.00
120	Marvin Jones	3.00
121	Ron Moore	6.00
122	Pierce Holt	3.00
123	Henry Jones	3.00
124	Donnell Woolford	3.00
125	Steve Tovar	3.00
126	Anthony Pleasant	3.00
127	Jay Novacek	3.00
128	Dan Williams	3.00
129	Barry Sanders	70.00
130	Robert Brooks	3.00
131	Lorenzo White	3.00
132	Kerry Cash	3.00
133	Joe Montana	80.00
134	Jeff Hostetler	3.00
135	Jerome Bettis	25.00
136	Dan Marino	125.00
137	Vencie Glenn	3.00
138	Vincent Brown	3.00
139	Ricky Jackson	3.00
140	Carlton Bailey	3.00
141	Jeff Lageman	3.00
142	William Thomas	3.00
143	Neil O'Donnell	6.00
144	Shawn Jefferson	3.00
145	Steve Young	60.00
146	Chris Warren	3.00
147	Courtney Hawkins	3.00
148	Brad Edwards	3.00
149	O.J. McDuffie	6.00
150	David Lang	3.00
151	Chuck Cecil	3.00
152	Norm Johnson	3.00
153	Pete Metzelaars	3.00
154	Shaun Gayle	3.00
155	Alfred Williams	3.00
156	Eric Turner	3.00
157	Emmitt Smith	125.00
158	Steve Atwater	3.00
159	Robert Porcher	3.00
160	Edgar Bennett	3.00
161	Bubba McDowell	3.00
162	Jeff Herrod	3.00
163	Keith Cash	3.00
164	Patrick Bates	3.00
165	Todd Lyght	3.00
166	Mark Higgs, Rob Burnett	3.00
167	Carlos Jenkins	3.00
168	Drew Bledsoe	75.00
169	Wayne Martin	3.00
170	Mike Sherrard	3.00
171	Ronnie Lott	3.00
172	Fred Barnett	3.00
173	Eric Green	3.00
174	Leslie O'Neal	3.00
175	Brent Jones	3.00
176	John Vaughn	3.00
177	Vince Workman	3.00
178	Ron Middleton	3.00
179	Terry McDaniel	3.00
180	Willie Davis	3.00
181	Gary Clark	3.00
182	Bobby Hebert	3.00
183	Russell Copeland	3.00
184	Chris Gadney	3.00
185	Tony McGhee	3.00
187	Charles Haley	3.00
188	Shannon Sharpe	6.00
189	Mel Gray	3.00
190	George Teague	3.00
191	Ernest Givins	3.00
192	Ray Buchannan	3.00
193	J.J. Birden	3.00
194	Tim Brown	6.00
195	Tim Lester	3.00
196	Marco Coleman	3.00
197	Randall McDaniel	3.00
198	Bruce Armstrong	3.00
199	Willie Roaf	3.00
200	Greg Jackson	3.00
201	Johnny Mitchell	3.00
202	Calvin Williams	3.00
203	Jeff Graham	3.00
204	Darren Carrington	3.00
205	Jerry Rice	60.00
206	Cortez Kennedy	6.00
207	Charles Wilson	3.00
208	James Jenkins	3.00
209	Ray Childress	3.00
210	Leroy Butler	3.00
211	Randal Hill	3.00
212	Lincoln Kennedy	3.00
213	Kenneth Davis	3.00
214	Terry Obee	3.00
215	Richardo McDonald	3.00
216	Pepper Johnson	3.00
217	Alvin Harper	6.00
218	John Elway	25.00
219	Derrick Moore	3.00
220	Terrell Buckley	3.00
221	Haywood Jeffires	3.00
222	Jessie Hester	3.00
223	Kimble Anders	3.00
224	Raghib Ismail	3.00
225	Roman Phifer	3.00
226	Bryan Cox	3.00
227	Cris Carter	6.00
228	Sam Gash	3.00
229	Renaldo Turnbull	3.00
230	Rodney Hampton	6.00
231	Johnny Johnson	3.00
232	Tim Harris	3.00
233	Leroy Thompson	3.00
234	Junior Seau	6.00
235	Tim McDonald	3.00
236	Eugene Robinson	3.00
237	Lawrence Dawsey	3.00
238	Tim Johnson	3.00
239	Jason Elam	3.00
240	Willie Green	3.00
241	Larry Centers	3.00
242	Erric Pegram	6.00
243	Bruce Smith	3.00
244	Alonzo Spellman	3.00
245	Carl Pickens	3.00
246	Michael Jackson	3.00
247	Kevin Williams	6.00
248	Glyn Milburn	6.00
249	Herman Moore	6.00
250	Brett Favre	125.00
251	Al Smith	3.00
252	Roosevelt Potts	3.00
253	Marcus Allen	6.00
254	Anthony Smith	3.00
255	Sean Gilbert	3.00
256	Keith Byars	3.00
257	*Scottie Graham*	10.00
258	Leonard Russell	3.00
259	Eric Martin	3.00
260	Jerrod Bunch	3.00
261	Rob Moore	3.00
262	Herschel Walker	3.00
263	Levon Kirkland	3.00
264	Chris Mims	3.00
265	Ricky Watters	6.00
266	Rick Mirer	30.00
267	Santana Dotson	3.00
268	Reggie Brooks	3.00
269	Garrison Hearst	25.00
270	Thurman Thomas	6.00
271	Johnny Bailey	3.00
272	Andre Rison	6.00
273	Jim Kelly	8.00
274	Mark Carrier	3.00
275	David Klingler	3.00
276	Eric Metcalf	3.00
277	Troy Aikman	60.00
278	Simon Fletcher	3.00
279	Pat Swilling	3.00
280	Sterling Sharpe	8.00
281	Cody Carlson	3.00
282	Steve Emtman	3.00
283	Neil Smith	3.00
284	James Jett	3.00
285	Shane Conlan	3.00
286	Keith Jackson	3.00
287	Qadry Ismail	6.00
288	Chris Slade	6.00
289	Derek Brown	3.00
290	Phil Simms	3.00
291	Boomer Esiason	3.00
292	Eric Allen	3.00
293	Rod Woodson	6.00
294	Ronnie Harmon	3.00
295	John Taylor	6.00
296	Ferrell Edmunds	3.00
297	Craig Erickson	6.00
298	Brian Mitchell	3.00
299	Dante Jones	3.00
300	John Copeland	3.00
301	Steve Beuerlein	3.00
302	Deion Sanders	45.00
303	Andre Reed	6.00
304	Curtis Conway	6.00
305	Harold Green	3.00
306	Vinny Testaverde	3.00
307	Michael Irvin	20.00
308	Rod Bernstine	3.00
309	Chris Spielman	3.00
310	Reggie White	6.00
311	Gary Brown	3.00
312	Quentin Coryatt	3.00
313	Derrick Thomas	6.00
314	Greg Robinson	3.00
315	Troy Drayton	3.00
316	Terry Kirby	6.00
317	John Randle	3.00
318	Ben Coates	10.00
319	Tyrone Hughes	3.00
320	Corey Miller	3.00
321	Brad Baxter	3.00
322	Randall Cunningham	6.00
323	Greg Lloyd	3.00
324	Stan Humphries	3.00
325	Dana Stubblefield	6.00
326	Kelvin Martin	3.00
327	Hardy Nickerson	3.00
328	Desmond Howard	3.00
329	Mark Carrier	3.00
330	Darryl Johnston	3.00

1994 Upper Deck Predictor Award Winners

Hobby Predictor cards predicted what player would win the 1994 Most Valuable Player and Rookie of the Year. Each category included nine players and a longshot card. If the player pictured won that category, the

card was redeemable for a gold foil set of Hobby Predictors. If the the pictured player finished second in his category, the card could be redeemed for a 10-card, gold foil set of his specific category.

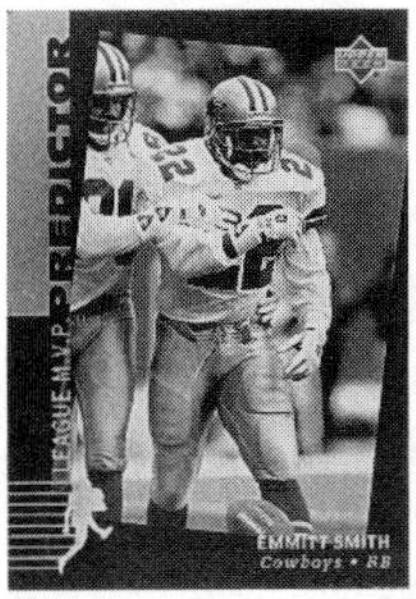

		MT
Complete Set (20):		60.00
Common Player:		1.00
Minor Stars:		2.00
Inserted 1:20 Hobby		
1	Emmitt Smith	7.50
2	Barry Sanders	10.00
3	Jerome Bettis	2.00
4	Joe Montana	6.00
5	Dan Marino	7.50
6	Marshall Faulk	2.00
7	Dan Wilkinson	1.00
8	Sterling Sharpe	2.00
9	Thurman Thomas	2.00
10	The Longshot	2.00
11	Marshall Faulk	2.00
12	Trent Dilfer	2.00
13	Heath Shuler	1.00
14	David Palmer	1.00
15	Charles Johnson	1.00
16	Greg Hill	1.00
17	Johnnie Morton	1.00
18	Errict Rhett	1.00
19	Darney Scott	2.00
20	The Longshot	2.00

1994 Upper Deck Predictor League Leaders

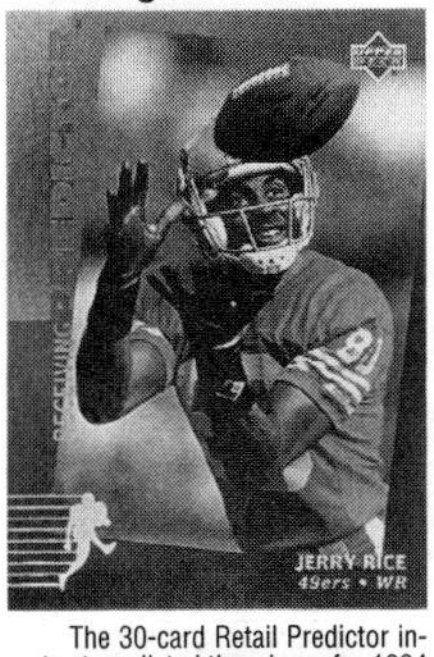

The 30-card Retail Predictor insert set predicted the winner for 1994 rushing yardage, passing yardage and receiving yardage. As with the Hobby Predictors, a winner could be exchanged for the entire Retail Predictor set, while a second place finisher could be redeemed for his specific category 10-card set.

		MT
Complete Set (30):		80.00
Common Player:		1.00
Minor Stars:		2.00
Inserted 1:20 Retail		
1	Troy Aikman	5.00
2	Steve Young	4.00
3	John Elway	6.00
4	Joe Montana	6.00
5	Brett Favre	10.00
6	Heath Shuler	1.00
7	Dan Marino	7.50
8	Rick Mirer	2.00
9	Drew Bledsoe	5.00
10	The Longshot	1.00
11	Emmitt Smith	7.50
12	Barry Sanders	10.00
13	Jerome Bettis	2.00
14	Rodney Hampton	1.00
15	Thurman Thomas	2.00
16	Marshall Faulk	2.00
17	Barry Foster	1.00
18	Reggie Brooks	1.00
19	Ricky Watters	2.00
20	The Longshot	1.00
21	Jerry Rice	5.00
22	Sterling Sharpe	2.00
23	Andre Rison	2.00
24	Michael Irvin	2.00
25	Tim Brown	2.00
26	Shannon Sharpe	2.00
27	Andre Reed	1.00
28	Irving Fryar	1.00
29	Charles Johnson	1.00
30	The Longshot	2.00

1994 Upper Deck Pro Bowl

The Upper Deck Pro Bowl insert set was randomly inserted into hobby and retail packs of 1994 Upper Deck football. It marked the debut of Holoview cards, which feature a three-dimensional image.

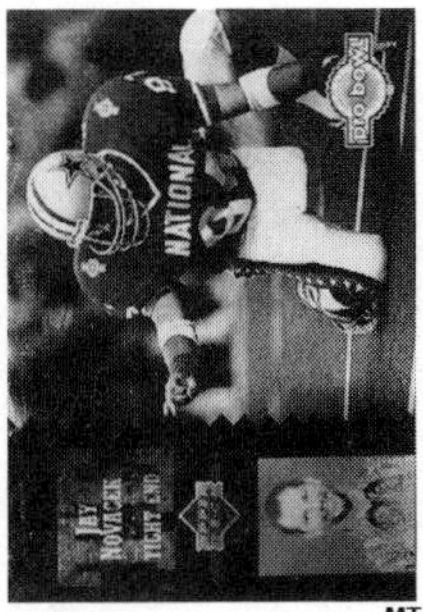

		MT
Complete Set (20):		100.00
Common Player:		2.00
Minor Stars:		4.00
Inserted 1:20		
1	Jerome Bettis	4.00
2	Jay Novacek	2.00
3	Shannon Sharpe	4.00
4	Brent Jones	2.00
5	Andre Rison	4.00
6	Tim Brown	4.00
7	Anthony Miller	2.00
8	Jerry Rice	12.00
9	Brett Favre	25.00
10	Emmitt Smith	18.00
11	Steve Young	10.00
12	John Elway	16.00
13	Warren Moon	4.00
14	Thurman Thomas	4.00
15	Ricky Watters	4.00
16	Rod Woodson	2.00
17	Reggie White	4.00
18	Tyrone Hughes	2.00
19	Derrick Thomas	4.00
20	Checklist	2.00

1994 Upper Deck 24K Gold

The eight-card, standard-size set has horizontal fronts with player facsimile autographs on the left and an etched portrait on the right. Even though the cards are numbered on the back out of 2,500, reportedly just 1,500 of each card was produced.

		MT
Complete Set (8):		550.00
Common Player:		40.00
1	Troy Aikman	75.00
2	Drew Bledsoe	75.00
3	Dan Marino	125.00
4	Rick Mirer	40.00
5	Joe Montana	80.00
6	Emmitt Smith	125.00
7	Thurman Thomas	40.00
8	Steve Young	60.00

1994-95 Upper Deck Sheets

The four-sheet, 8-1/2" x 11" set was issued at the Super Bowl Card Show VI in 1995.

		MT
Complete Set (4):		30.00
Common Sheet:		4.00
NNO	Rookie Class 1994	8.00
NNO	Super Bowl XXIX Autograph Sheet Jan. 26-29, 1995	4.00
NNO	Upper Deck Salutes / St. Louis Rams (Sean Gilbert, Kevin Carter, Isaac Bruce, Jerome Bettis, Chris Miller, Shane Conlan) (Undated numbered of 30,000)	8.00
NNO	1995 Record Breaker (Dan Marino) (Numbered of 30,000)	12.00

1995 Upper Deck

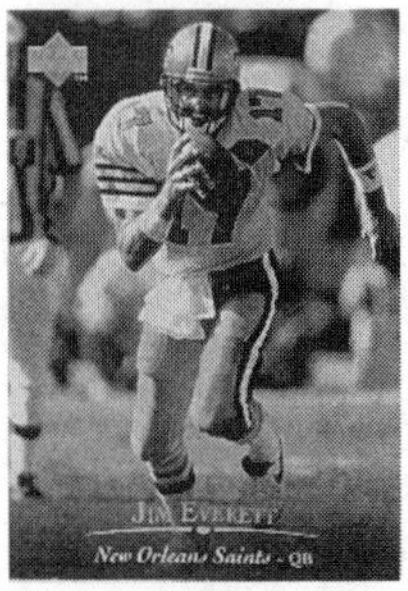

This 300-card 1995 Upper Deck football set contains 270 regular cards and 30 Star Rookies. In addition, retail packs have each card featured in an Electric (one per pack) and Electric Gold (one per box) parallel sets. Each regular card front has a full-bleed color photo, with the Upper Deck logo in the upper left corner and the player's name at the bottom stamped in gold foil. The player's team name and his position are in white letters, below his name. The card back has an action photo, with statistics and a brief recap of his 1994 season underneath. A black panel along the left side of the card has a card number, with a team logo under it. The player's name and biographical information are also included in the panel. A set-within-a-set, Special Edition, was also created. These cards, featuring photos by Walter Iooss Jr., have a different design from the base brand and were found in hobby packs only, one per pack. Gold versions were also created for the Special Edition cards; they were available one per box. Continued from Collector's Choice are the Joe Montana Trilogy cards, numbers MT9-16, plus a header card. Pro Bowl and Hobby and Retail Predictors also return. In addition, one in 144 packs is a Predictor Pack, which contain certain types of insert cards, depending on if the pack is retail or hobby.

		MT
Complete Set (300):		30.00
Common Player:		.10
Minor Stars:		.20
Comp. Elec. Gold Set (300):		600.00
Electric Gold Cards: 7x-14x		
Comp. Elec. Silv. Set (300):		120.00
Electric Silver Cards: 2x-4x		
Pack (12):		1.00
Wax Box (36):		30.00
1	*Ki-Jana Carter*	.50
2	*Tony Boselli*	.20
3	*Steve McNair*	5.00
4	*Michael Westbrook*	1.50
5	*Kerry Collins*	2.00
6	*Kevin Carter*	.20
7	*James Stewart*	.20
8	*Joey Galloway*	4.00
9	*Kyle Brady*	.50
10	*J.J. Stokes*	1.50
11	*Derrick Alexander*	.20
12	*Warren Sapp*	1.00
13	*Mark Fields*	.10
14	*Tyrone Wheatley*	1.00
15	*Napoleon Kaufman*	1.00
16	*James Stewart*	2.50
17	*Luther Elliss*	.10
18	*Rashaan Salaam*	.50
19	*Ty Law*	.20
20	*Mark Bruener*	.50
21	*Derrick Brooks*	.20
22	*Christian Fauria*	.20
23	*Ray Zellars*	.20
24	*Todd Collins*	.20
25	*Sherman Williams*	.20
26	*Frank Sanders*	.30
27	*Rodney Thomas*	.20
28	*Rob Johnson*	3.00
29	*Steve Stenstrom*	.20
30	*Curtis Martin*	5.00
31	Gary Clark	.10
32	Troy Aikman	1.00
33	Mike Sherrard	.10
34	Fred Barnett	.10
35	Henry Ellard	.10
36	Terry Allen	.10
37	Jeff Graham	.10
38	Herman Moore	.40
39	Brett Favre	3.00
40	Trent Dilfer	.20
41	Derek Brown	.10
42	Andre Rison	.10
43	Willie Anderson	.10
44	Jerry Rice	1.25
45	Andre Reed	.10
46	Sean Dawkins	.10
47	Irving Fryar	.10
48	Vincent Brisby	.10
49	Rob Moore	.10
50	Carl Pickens	.20
51	Vinny Testaverde	.10
52	Ray Childress	.10
53	Eric Green	.10
54	Anthony Miller	.10
55	Lake Dawson	.20
56	Tim Brown	.20
57	Stan Humphries	.10
58	Rick Mirer	.20
59	Randal Hill	.10
60	Charles Haley	.10
61	Chris Calloway	.10
62	Calvin Williams	.10
63	Ethan Horton	.10
64	Cris Carter	.20
65	Curtis Conway	.20
66	Scott Mitchell	.10
67	Edgar Bennett	.10
68	Craig Erickson	.10
69	Jim Everett	.10
70	Terance Mathis	.10
71	Robert Young	.10
72	Brent Jones	.10
73	Thurman Thomas	.20
74	Marshall Faulk	1.50
75	O.J. McDuffie	.10
76	Ben Coates	.10
77	Johnny Mitchell	.10
78	Darnay Scott	.50
79	Derrick Alexander	.10
80	Lorenzo White	.10
81	Charles Johnson	.20
82	John Elway	.40
83	Willie Davis	.10
84	James Jett	.10
85	Mark Seay	.10
86	Brian Blades	.10
87	Ronald Moore	.10
88	Alvin Harper	.10
89	Dave Brown	.10
90	Randall Cunningham	.10
91	Heath Shuler	.75
92	Jake Reed	.10
93	Donnell Woolford	.10
94	Barry Sanders	2.00
95	Reggie White	.20
96	Lawrence Dawsey	.10
97	Michael Haynes	.10
98	Bert Emanuel	.40
99	Troy Drayton	.10
100	Steve Young	1.25
101	Bruce Smith	.10
102	Roosevelt Potts	.10
103	Dan Marino	3.00
104	Michael Timpson	.10
105	Boomer Esiason	.10
106	David Klingler	.10
107	Eric Metcalf	.10
108	Gary Brown	.10
109	Neil O'Donnell	.20
110	Shannon Sharpe	.10
111	Joe Montana	1.25
112	Jeff Hostetler	.10
113	Ronnie Harmon	.10
114	Chris Warren	.20
115	Larry Centers	.10
116	Michael Irvin	.20
117	Rodney Hampton	.10
118	Herschel Walker	.10
119	Reggie Brooks	.10
120	Qadry Ismail	.10
121	Chris Zorich	.10
122	Chris Spielman	.10
123	Sean Jones	.10
124	Errict Rhett	.20
125	Tyrone Hughes	.10
126	Jeff George	.20
127	Chris Miller	.10
128	Ricky Watters	.20
129	Jim Kelly	.20
130	Tony Bennett	.10
131	Terry Kirby	.10
132	Drew Bledsoe	1.25
133	Johnny Johnson	.10
134	Dan Wilkinson	.10
135	Leroy Hoard	.10
136	Darryl Lewis	.10
137	Barry Foster	.10
138	Shane Dronett	.10
139	Marcus Allen	.10
140	Harvey Williams	.10
141	Tony Martin	.10
142	Rod Stephens	.10
143	Eric Swann	.10
144	Daryl Johnston	.10
145	Dave Meggett	.10
146	Charlie Garner	.10
147	Ken Harvey	.10
148	Warren Moon	.20
149	Steve Walsh	.10
150	Pat Swilling	.10
151	Terrell Buckley	.10
152	Courtney Hawkins	.10
153	Willie Roaf	.10
154	Chris Doleman	.10
155	Jerome Bettis	.20
156	Dana Stubblefield	.10
157	Cornelius Bennett	.10
158	Quentin Coryatt	.10
159	Bryan Cox	.10
160	Marion Butts	.10
161	Aaron Glenn	.10
162	Louis Oliver	.10
163	Eric Turner	.10
164	Cris Dishman	.10
165	John L. Williams	.10
166	Simon Fletcher	.10
167	Neil Smith	.10
168	Chester McGlockton	.10
169	Natrone Means	.20
170	Sam Adams	.10
171	Clyde Simmons	.10
172	Jay Novacek	.10
173	Keith Hamilton	.10
174	William Fuller	.10
175	Tom Carter	.10
176	John Randle	.10
177	Lewis Tillman	.10
178	Mel Gray	.10
179	George Teague	.10
180	Hardy Nickerson	.10
181	Mario Bates	.40
182	D.J. Johnson	.10
183	Sean Gilbert	.10
184	Bryant Young	.10
185	Jeff Burris	.10
186	Floyd Turner	.10
187	Troy Vincent	.10
188	Willie McGinest	.10
189	James Hasty	.10
190	*Jeff Blake*	.50
191	Stevon Moore	.10
192	Ernest Givins	.10
193	Bam Morris	.20
194	Ray Crockett	.10
195	Dale Carter	.10
196	Terry McDaniels	.10
197	Leslie O'Neal	.10
198	Cortez Kennedy	.10
199	Seth Joyner	.10
200	Emmitt Smith	3.00
201	Thomas Lewis	.10
202	Andy Harmon	.10
203	Ricky Ervins	.10
204	Fuad Reveiz	.10
205	John Thierry	.10
206	Johnnie Morton	.10
207	LeShon Johnson	.10
208	Charles Wilson	.10
209	Joe Johnson	.10
210	Charles Smith	.10
211	Roman Phifer	.10
212	Ken Norton	.10
213	Bucky Brooks	.10
214	Ray Buchanan	.10
215	Tim Bowens	.10
216	Vincent Brown	.10
217	Marcus Turner	.10
218	Derrick Fenner	.10
219	Antonio Langham	.10
220	Cody Carlson	.10
221	Greg Lloyd	.10
222	Steve Atwater	.10
223	Donnell Bennett	.10
224	Raghib Ismail	.10
225	John Carney	.10
226	Eugene Robinson	.10
227	Aeneas Williams	.10
228	Darrin Smith	.10
229	Phillipi Sparks	.10
230	Eric Allen	.10
231	Brian Mitchell	.10
232	David Palmer	.10
233	Mark Carrier	.10
234	Dave Krieg	.10
235	Robert Brooks	.10
236	Eric Curry	.10
237	Wayne Martin	.10
238	Craig Heyward	.10
239	Isaac Bruce	1.00
240	Deion Sanders	1.00
241	Steve Tasker	.10
242	Jim Harbaugh	.10
243	Aubrey Beavers	.10
244	Chris Slade	.10
245	Mo Lewis	.10
246	Alfred Williams	.10
247	Michael Dean Perry	.10
248	Marcus Robertson	.10
249	Kevin Greene	.10
250	Leonard Russell	.10
251	Greg Hill	.20
252	Rob Fredrickson	.10
253	Junior Seau	.20
254	Rick Tuten	.10
255	Garrison Hearst	.30
256	Russell Maryland	.10
257	Michael Brooks	.10
258	Bernard Williams	.10
259	Reggie Roby	.10
260	DeWayne Washington	.10
261	Raymont Harris	.10
262	Brett Perriman	.10
263	LeRoy Butler	.10
264	Santana Dotson	.10
265	Irv Smith	.10
266	Ron George	.10
267	Marquez Pope	.10
268	William Floyd	.20
269	Matt Darby	.10
270	Jeff Herrod	.10
271	Bernie Parmalee	.20
273	Leroy Thompson	.10
274	Marvin Jones	.10
275	Michael Jackson	.10
276	Al Smith	.10
277	Rod Woodson	.10
278	Glyn Milburn	.10
279	Kimble Anders	.10
280	Anthony Smith	.10
281	Andre Coleman	.10
282	Terry Wooden	.10
283	Ernest Givins	.10
284	Steve Beuerlein	.10
285	Mark Brunell	1.50
286	Keith Goganious	.10
287	Desmond Howard	.10
288	Darren Carrington	.10
289	Derek Brown	.10
290	Reggie Cobb	.10
291	Jeff Lageman	.10
292	Lamar Lathon	.10
293	Sam Mills	.10
294	Carlton Bailey	.10
295	Mark Carrier	.10
296	Willie Green	.10
297	Frank Reich	.10
298	Don Beebe	.10
299	Tim McKyer	.10
300	Pete Metzelaars	.10

1995 Upper Deck Electric Silver

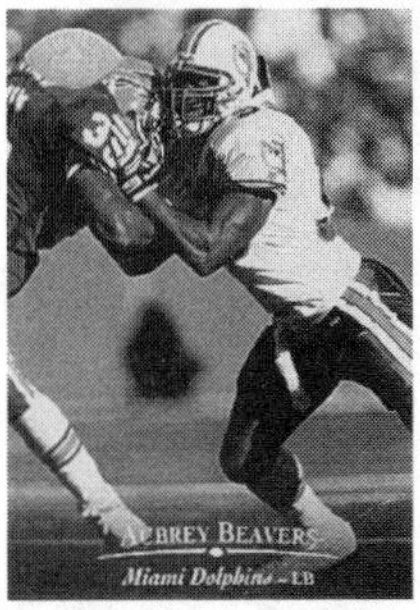

The 300-card, standard-size parallel set was inserted every pack and features a silver-foil "Electric" stamp on the card front.

	MT
Complete Set (300):	125.00
Common Player:	.20
Veteran Stars:	2x-4x
Young Stars:	1.5x-3x
RCs:	1.25x-2.5x

1995 Upper Deck Electric Gold

The 300-card, standard-size set was a parallel to the base set and was inserted every 35 packs. The card fronts have a gold-foil "Electric" logo.

	MT
Complete Set (300):	1200.
Common Player:	1.50
Veteran Stars: 20x-35x	
Young Stars: 15x-25x	
RCs: 10x-18x	

1995 Upper Deck Montana Trilogy

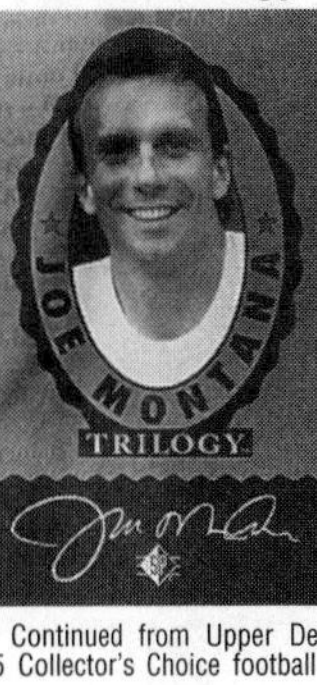

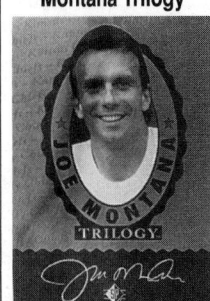

Continued from Upper Deck's 1995 Collector's Choice football are eight more Joe Montana Trilogy cards, seeded one per 12 packs. These cards, numbered 9-16 with an "MT" prefix, feature a metallic-like front background, with gold foil for the brand logo and a panel at the bottom of the card which describes the card's title. The title is listed above in a black strip. The Montana Trilogy logo also appears on the front. The card back has a player photo and a recap of the play being depicted on the front.

		MT
Complete Set (9):		40.00
Common Player:		6.00
Header Card:		6.00
9	The Drive	6.00
10	Super Bowl XXII	6.00
11	1989 - Dream Season	6.00
12	NFL MVP Back-to-Back	6.00
13	Super Bowl XXIV	6.00
14	Super Bowl XXIV MVP	6.00
15	Back-to-Back Super Bowls	6.00
16	The Comeback	6.00
UDH	Trilogy Header	6.00

1995 Upper Deck Hobby Predictor

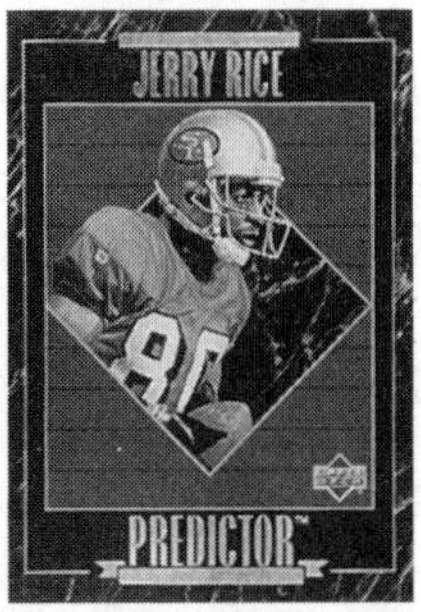

These 20 cards, random inserts in 1995 Upper Deck hobby packs, feature 18 players who were potential MVP and Rookie of the Year Award winners. Two longshot cards were also made. Cards were in one per every 30 packs. If the player featured won the category, or finished second in the voting, collectors could redeem the cards for prizes. Card backs, numbered using an "HP" prefix, explained the rules of the game.

		MT
Complete Set (20):		100.00
Common Player:		3.00
1	Dan Marino	15.00
2	Steve Young	7.00
3	Drew Bledsoe	7.00
4	Troy Aikman	7.00
5	Barry Sanders	7.00
6	Emmitt Smith	15.00
7	Jerry Rice	15.00
8	Ki-Jana Carter	5.00
9	John Elway	6.00
10	The Longshot	3.00
11	Ki-Jana Carter	5.00
12	Steve McNair	8.00
13	Michael Westbrook	4.00
14	Kerry Collins	3.00
15	Joey Galloway	7.00
16	Kyle Brady	3.00
17	Napoleon Kaufman	6.00
18	Tyrone Wheatley	6.00
19	Rashaan Salaam	5.00
20	The Longshot	3.00

1995 Upper Deck Retail Predictor

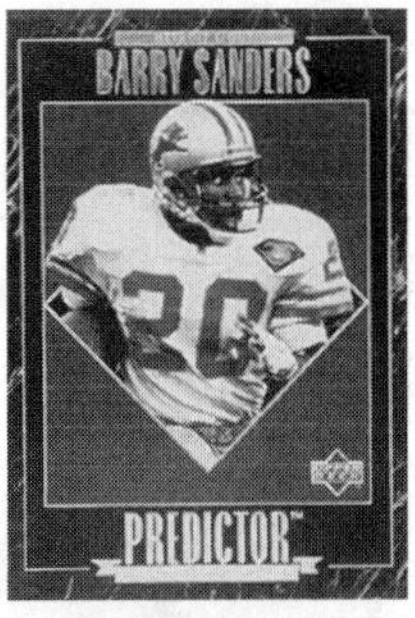

These 30 1995 Upper Deck football cards feature 28 players with the potential to win either the rushing yardage, passing efficiency and receiving yardage categories. Cards were randomly inserted one per every 30 retail packs. The card back, numbered using an "RP" prefix, explained the rules for if a player finished first or second in a category, and what prizes collectors could receive if they redeemed a winning card.

		MT
Complete Set (30):		75.00
Common Player:		1.00
Minor Stars:		2.00
Inserted 1:30 Retail		
1	Dan Marino	7.50
2	Steve Young	4.00

3	Drew Bledsoe	5.00
4	Troy Aikman	5.00
5	John Elway	7.50
6	Brett Favre	10.00
7	Stan Humphries	1.00
8	Jeff George	2.00
9	Kerry Collins	2.00
10	Longshot	1.00
11	Barry Sanders	10.00
12	Chris Warren	1.00
13	Emmitt Smith	7.50
14	Natrone Means	2.00
15	Rodney Hampton	1.00
16	Marshall Faulk	3.00
17	Errict Rhett	1.00
18	Napoleon Kaufman	5.00
19	Ki-Jana Carter	1.00
20	Longshot	1.00
21	Jerry Rice	5.00
22	Ben Coates	1.00
23	Cris Carter	2.00
24	Andre Reed	1.00
25	Andre Rison	1.00
26	Tim Brown	1.00
27	Michael Irvin	2.00
28	Irving Fryar	1.00
29	Michael Westbrook	2.00
30	Longshot	1.00

1995 Upper Deck Pro Bowl

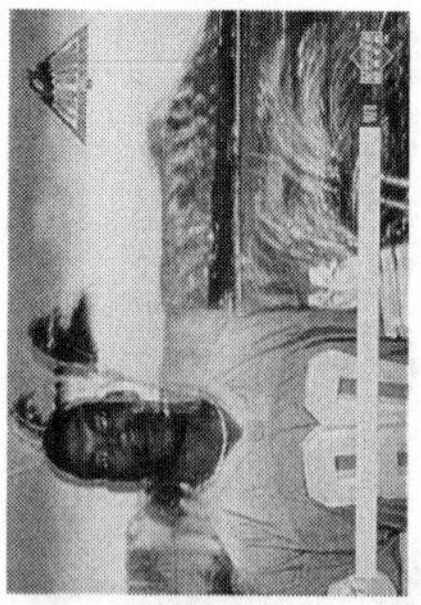

These 25 cards, random inserts one per every 35 packs of 1995 Upper Deck football, use the Holoview process. Top players from the 1995 Pro Bowl are included. In addition to the hologram front, which shows the player against a Hawaiian setting with palm trees, the Pro Bowl logo is in the upper right corner. The player's name, team, position and Upper Deck logo are along the bottom of the card, which uses a horizontal format for the front. The horizontal back has a photo of the player in his Pro Bowl uniform, against a ghosted action photo as a background. A recap of the player's 1994 season is also included, as is a card number, which uses a "PB" prefix.

		MT
Complete Set (25):		150.00
Common Player:		3.00
1	Barry Sanders	15.00
2	Brent Jones	3.00
3	Cris Carter	3.00
4	Emmitt Smith	30.00
5	Jay Novacek	3.00
6	Jerome Bettis	3.00
7	Jerry Rice	15.00
8	Michael Irvin	7.00
9	Ricky Watters	3.00
10	Steve Young	15.00
11	Troy Aikman	15.00
12	Warren Moon	3.00
13	Terance Mathis	3.00
14	Ben Coates	3.00
15	Chris Warren	3.00
16	Dan Marino	30.00
17	Drew Bledsoe	15.00
18	Irving Fryar	3.00
19	Jeff Hostetler	3.00
20	John Elway	10.00
21	Leroy Hoard	3.00
22	Marshall Faulk	8.00
23	Natrone Means	4.00
24	Tim Brown	3.00
25	Checklist	3.00

1995 Upper Deck Special Edition

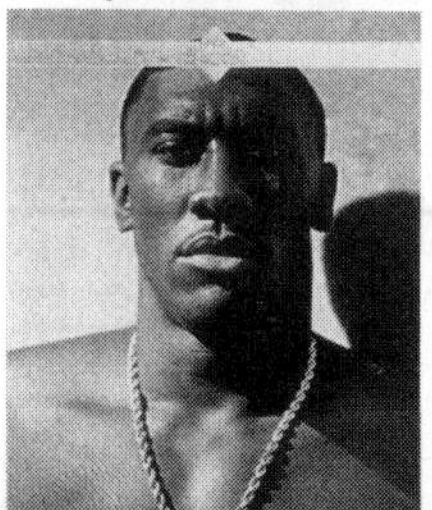

This set-within-a-set features the photography of Walter Iooss Jr. The cards, random inserts one per every 1995 Upper Deck hobby pack, use a different design from the base brand. Each card front has a full-bleed color action photo on it, with Special Edition written at the top of the card. The player's name is at the bottom of the card. Card backs are numbered using an "SE" prefix. Special Edition Gold versions were also created for each card in the set; these cards were seeded one per every box.

		MT
Complete Set (90):		45.00
Common Player:		.25
Minor Stars:		.50
Complete Gold Set (90):		600.00
Common Gold Player:		2.00
Minor Gold Stars:		4.00
Unlisted Gold Stars:		5x-10x
1	Terry Kirby	.25
2	Marcus Allen	.50
3	Bernie Parmalee	.50
4	Vernon Turner	.25
5	Dolphins Defense	.25
6	Kevin Turner	.25
7	Henry Thomas	.25
8	Barry Sanders	3.00
9	Marshall Faulk	2.00
10	Bill Bates	.25
11	Stan Humphries	.50
12	Barry Foster	.25
13	Shannon Sharpe	.50
14	Joe Montana	2.00
15	Bryan Cox	.25
16	Dale Carter	.25
17	Drew Bledsoe	2.00
18	Dan Marino	4.00
19	Ricky Watters	.50
20	Alvin Harper	.50
21	49ers Offensive Line	.25
22	Dan Marino	4.00
23	Ronnie Harmon	.25
24	Michael Irvin	.50
25	Emmitt Smith	4.00
26	Jeff Christie	.25
27	Terry Allen	.25
28	Randall Cunningham	.50
29	Todd Steussie	.25
30	Warren Moon	.50
31	Vikings Defense	.25
32	Tony Tolbert	.25
33	William Fuller	.25
34	Bernard Williams	.25
35	Charlie Garner	.25
36	Troy Aikman	2.00
37	Alvin Harper	.50
38	Kenneth Gant	.25
39	Daryl Johnston	.25
40	Ben Coates	.25
41	Rickey Jackson	.25
42	O.J. McDuffie	.25
43	Marion Butts	.25
44	NFL Offenses	.25
45	Kimble Anders	.25
46	Natrone Means	.50
47	Richmond Webb	.25
48	Carlos Jenkins	.25
49	James Harris	.25
50	Dexter Carter	.25
51	Qadry Ismail	.25
52	Jeff Herrod	.25
53	Sean Jones	.25
54	Keith Sims	.25
55	William Floyd	.50
56	Don Majkowski	.25
57	Charger Defense	.25
58	Byron Evans	.25
59	Chad Hennings	.25
60	Eric Allen	.25
61	Curtis Martin	5.00
62	Napoleon Kaufman	1.00
63	Kevin Carter	.50
64	Luther Elliss	.25
65	Frank Sanders	2.00
66	Rob Johnson	1.00
67	Christian Fauria	.25
68	Kyle Brady	.50
69	Michael Westbrook	1.50
70	James A. Stewart	.50
71	Ty Law	.25
72	Rodney Thomas	.25
73	Jimmy Oliver	.25
74	James O. Stewart	.50
75	Dave Barr	.25
76	Kordell Stewart	4.00
77	Michael Westbrook	1.50
78	Bobby Taylor	.25
79	Mark Fields	.25
80	Kerry Collins	1.00
81	Natrone Means	.50
82	Chargers Offense	.25
83	Deion Sanders	1.50
84	Dana Stubblefield	.25
85	49ers Defense	.25
86	Alfred Pupunu	.25
87	Tim Harris	.25
88	Jerry Rice	2.00
89	Steve Young	2.00
90	Super Bowl XXIX Champs.	2.00

1995 Upper Deck GTE Phone Cards AFC

The 15-card, 3-3/8" x 2-1/8" prepaid set has rounded corners and color action photos on the fronts. The card backs have instructions for usage on the five-unit cards.

		MT
Complete Set (15):		80.00
Common Player:		3.00
1	Marcus Allen	4.00
2	Drew Bledsoe	10.00
3	Gary Brown	3.00
4	Tim Brown	4.00
5	John Elway	7.00
6	Marshall Faulk	6.00
7	Barry Foster	3.00
8	Jim Kelly	4.00
9	Ronnie Lott	3.00
10	Dan Marino	20.00
11	Rick Mirer	4.00
12	Carl Pickens	4.00
13	Junior Seau	4.00
14	Vinny Testaverde	3.00
15	Title Card	3.00

A player's name in *italic type* indicates a rookie card.

1995 Upper Deck GTE Phone Cards NFC

The 15-card, 3-3/8" x 2-1/8" set is identical to the AFC set in design, but with NFC players. The card backs feature card usage instructions.

		MT
Complete Set (15):		60.00
Common Player:		3.00
1	Jerome Bettis	4.00
2	Gary Clark	3.00
3	Curtis Conway	4.00
4	Randall Cunningham	3.00
5	Rodney Hampton	4.00
6	Michael Haynes	3.00
7	Michael Irvin	4.00
8	Warren Moon	4.00
9	Hardy Nickerson	3.00
10	Jerry Rice	8.00
11	Andre Rison	4.00
12	Barry Sanders	8.00
13	Sterling Sharpe	4.00
14	Heath Shuler	6.00
15	Title Card	4.00

1995 Upper Deck Joe Montana Box Set

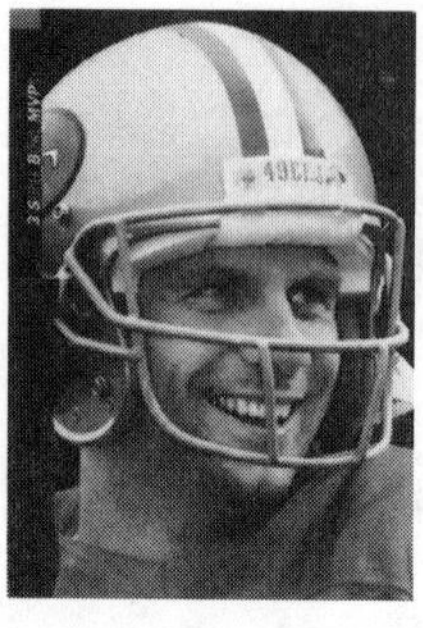

The 45-card, over-sized set highlights Montana's career from childhood through the pros. The card fronts feature gold foil with commentary text on the backs. The set was limited to 38,000 sets.

		MT
Complete Set (45):		20.00
Common Player:		.60
1	A Star Is Born	.60
2	Quarterback State	.60
3	Making Of A Hero	.60
4	National Champion	.60
5	Never-Say-Die	.60
6	The Protege	.60
7	New Orleans - The First Victim	.60
8	The Catch	.60
9	Super Bowl Fever	.60
10	Super Bowl XVI	.60
11	Emergence Of A/Record-Breaker	.60
12	Career-Year	.60
13	Heroic Comeback	.60
14	Super Bowl XIX	.60
15	Repeat Performance	.60
16	First Passing Crown	.60
17	Super Bowl XXIII	.60
18	Super Leader	.60
19	Best Of The Best	.60
20	Super Bowl XXIV	.60
21	Four-Time Champs	.60
22	Team Of The 80's	.60
23	Back-To-Back MVP's	.60
24	Down, But Far From Out	.60
25	Farewell Performance	.60
26	The Trade	.60
27	First K.C. Comeback	.60
28	Playoff Magic	.60
29	Dueling Quaterbacks	.60
30	Another Milestone Falls	.60
31	39 300-Yard Games	.60
32	273 Touchdowns	.60
33	112.4 Pass Efficiency Rating	.60
34	92.3 Pass Efficiency Rating	.60
35	117 Wins	.60
36	31 Comeback Victories	.60
37	5,391 Attempts	.60
38	3 Super Bowl MVP's	.60
39	3,409 Completions	.60
40	40,551 Yards	.60
41	Bill Walsh	.60
42	Russ Francis	.60
43	Roger Craig	.60
44	Jerry Rice	.60
45	Dwight Clark	.60
NNO	Super Bowl XIX / Quarterbabck Duel (Numbered of 38,000)	5.00
JM16	Joe Montana (Promo)	2.00

1995 Upper Deck Authenticated Joe Montana Jumbos

The four-card, 5" x 3-1/2" set was offered to collectors through UDA's catalog. Each card shows Montana playing in a different Super Bowl. The card backs feature regular and post season statistics.

		MT
Complete Set (4):		35.00
Common Player:		10.00
1	Super Bowl XVI (Joe Montana)	10.00
2	Super Bowl XIX (Joe Montana)	10.00
3	Super Bowl XXIII (Joe Montana)	10.00
4	Super Bowl XXIV (Joe Montana)	10.00

1996 Upper Deck

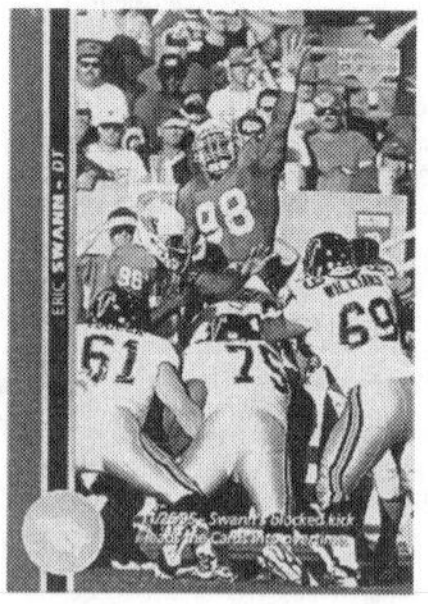

Upper Deck's Series I football has 300 cards in it, with more than 90 percent of them highlighting the actual game date of the photo on the card front. Silver foil stamping is used for an Upper Deck logo, team logo and the player's last name, which appears between two parallel foiled stripes. The back has a close-up shot of the player, statistics, a recap of the featured game and season highlights. Series I inserts include Game Jersey, Hobby and Retail Predictor cards, Team Trio, Hot Properties and Meet the Stars promotional scratch-off cards. These trivia cards give collectors a chance to meet Dan Marino and win Upper Deck merchandise. Cards were seeded one per every four packs.

		MT
Complete Set (300):		35.00
Common Player:		.10
Minor Stars:		.20
Pack (12):		2.50
Wax Box (24):		55.00
1	*Keyshawn Johnson*	2.50
2	*Kevin Hardy*	.20
3	*Simeon Rice*	.20
4	*Jonathan Ogden*	.10
5	*Cedric Jones*	.10
6	*Lawrence Phillips*	.75
7	*Tim Biakabutuka*	1.00
8	*Terry Glenn*	2.00
9	*Rickey Dudley*	.75
10	*Willie Anderson*	.10
11	*Alex Molden*	.10
12	*Regan Upshaw*	.10
13	*Walt Harris*	.20
14	*Eddie George*	4.00
15	*John Mobley*	.10
16	*Duane Clemons*	.10
17	*Eddie Kennison*	.30
18	*Marvin Harrison*	3.00
19	*Daryl Gardener*	.10
20	*Leeland McElroy*	.30
21	*Eric Moulds*	2.00
22	*Alex Van Dyke*	.20
23	*Mike Alstott*	1.50
24	*Jeff Lewis*	.75
25	*Bobby Engram*	.30
26	*Derrick Mayes*	1.00
27	*Karim Abdul-Jabbar*	.75
28	*Bobby Hoying*	.75
29	*Stepfret Williams*	.10
30	*Chris Darkins*	.20
31	*Stephen Davis*	4.00
32	*Danny Kanell*	.75
33	*Tony Brackens*	.40
34	Leslie O'Neal	.10
35	Chris Doleman	.10
36	Larry Brown	.10
37	Ronnie Harmon	.10
38	Chris Spielman	.10
39	John Jurkovic	.10
40	Shawn Jefferson	.10
41	Tommy Vardell	.10
42	Eric Davis	.10
43	Willie Clay	.10
44	Marco Coleman	.10
45	Lorenzo White	.10
46	Neil O'Donnell	.20
47	Natrone Means	.20
48	Cornelius Bennett	.10
49	Steve Walsh	.10
50	Jerome Bettis	.10
51	Boomer Esiason	.10
52	Glyn Milburn	.10
53	Kevin Greene	.10
54	Seth Joyner	.10
55	Jeff Harrod	.10
56	Darren Woodson	.10
57	Dale Carter	.10
58	Lorenzo Lynch	.10
59	Tim Brown	.10
60	Jerry Rice	1.50
61	Garrison Hearst	.20
62	Eric Metcalf	.10
63	Leroy Hoard	.10
64	Thurman Thomas	.20
65	Sam Mills	.10
66	Curtis Conway	.20
67	Carl Pickens	.20
68	Deion Sanders	.75
69	Shannon Sharpe	.10
70	Herman Moore	.40
71	Robert Brooks	.20
72	Rodney Thomas	.20
73	Ken Dilger	.10
74	Mark Brunell	1.00
75	Marcus Allen	.20
76	Dan Marino	3.00
77	Robert Smith	.10
78	Drew Bledsoe	1.25
79	Jim Everett	.10
80	Rodney Hampton	.10
81	Adrien Murrell	.10
82	Daryl Hobbs	.10
83	Ricky Watters	.20
84	Yancey Thigpen	.50
85	Roman Phifer	.10
86	Tony Martin	.10
87	Dana Stubblefield	.10
88	Joey Galloway	1.00
89	Errict Rhett	.75
90	Terry Allen	.10
91	Aeneas Williams	.10
92	Craig Heyward	.10
93	Vinny Testaverde	.10
94	Bryce Paup	.10
95	Kerry Collins	.30
96	Rashaan Salaam	.30
97	Dan Wilkinson	.10
98	Jay Novacek	.10
99	John Elway	.30
100	Bennie Blades	.10
101	Edgar Bennett	.10
102	Darryll Lewis	.10
103	Marshall Faulk	.50
104	Bryan Schwartz	.10
105	Tamarick Vanover	.75
106	Terry Kirby	.10
107	John Randle	.10
108	Ted Johnson	.10
109	Mario Bates	.10
110	Philippi Sparks	.10
111	Marvin Washington	.10
112	Terry McDaniel	.10
113	Bobby Taylor	.10
114	Carnell Lake	.10
115	Troy Drayton	.10
116	Darren Bennett	.10
117	J.J. Stokes	.30
118	Rick Mirer	.20
119	Jackie Harris	.10
120	Ken Harvey	.10
121	Rob Moore	.10
122	Jeff George	.20
123	Andre Rison	.10
124	Darick Holmes	.20
125	Tim McKyer	.10
126	Alonzo Spellman	.10
127	Jeff Blake	.75
128	Kevin Williams	.10
129	Anthony Miller	.10
130	Barry Sanders	1.75
131	Brett Favre	3.00
132	Steve McNair	1.00
133	Jim Harbaugh	.20
134	Desmond Howard	.10
135	Steve Bono	.10
136	Bernie Parmalee	.10
137	Warren Moon	.10
138	Curtis Martin	2.00
139	Irv Smith	.10
140	Thomas Lewis	.10
141	Kyle Brady	.10
142	Napoleon Kaufman	.10
143	Mike Mamula	.10
144	Erric Pegram	.10
145	Isaac Bruce	1.00
146	Andre Coleman	.10
147	Merton Hanks	.10
148	Brian Blades	.10
149	Hardy Nickerson	.10
150	Michael Westbrook	.20
151	Larry Centers	.10
152	Morten Andersen	.10
153	Michael Jackson	.10
154	Bruce Smith	.10
155	Derrick Moore	.10
156	Mark Carrier	.10
157	John Copeland	.10
158	Emmitt Smith	3.00
159	Jason Elam	.10
160	Scott Mitchell	.10
161	Mark Chmura	.30
162	Blaine Bishop	.10
163	Tony Bennett	.10
164	Pete Mitchell	.10
165	Dan Saleaumua	.10
166	Pete Stoyanovich	.10
167	Cris Carter	.10
168	Vincent Brisby	.10
169	Wayne Martin	.10
170	Tyrone Wheatley	.10
171	Mo Lewis	.10
172	Harvey Williams	.10
173	Calvin Williams	.10
174	Norm Johnson	.10
175	Mark Rypien	.10
176	Stan Humphries	.10
177	Derek Loville	.10
178	Christian Fauria	.10
179	Warren Sapp	.10
180	Henry Ellard	.10
181	Jamir Miller	.10
182	Jessie Tuggle	.10
183	Stevon Moore	.10
184	Jim Kelly	.20
185	Mark Carrier	.10
186	Chris Zorich	.10
187	Harold Green	.10
188	Chris Boniol	.10
189	Allen Aldridge	.10
190	Brett Perriman	.10
191	Chris Jackie (Jacke)	.10
192	Todd McNair	.10
193	Floyd Turner	.10
194	Jeff Lageman	.10
195	Derrick Thomas	.10
196	Eric Green	.10
197	Orlanda Thomas	.10
198	Ben Coates	.10
199	Tyrone Hughes	.10
200	Dave Brown	.10
201	Brad Baxter	.10
202	Chester McGlockton	.10
203	Rodney Peete	.10
204	Willie Williams	.10
205	Kevin Carter	.10
206	Aaron Hayden	.20
207	Steve Young	1.00
208	Chris Warren	.20
209	Eric Curry	.10
210	Brian Mitchell	.10
211	Frank Sanders	.10
212	Terance Mathis	.10
213	Eric Turner	.10
214	Bill Brooks	.10
215	John Kasay	.10
216	Erik Kramer	.10
217	Darnay Scott	.20
218	Charles Haley	.10
219	Steve Atwater	.10
220	Jason Hanson	.10
221	LeRoy Butler	.10
222	Cris Dishman	.10
223	Sean Dawkins	.10
224	James O. Stewart	.10
225	Greg Hill	.10
226	Jeff Cross	.10
227	Qadry Ismail	.10
228	Dave Meggett	.10
229	Eric Allen	.10
230	Chris Calloway	.10
231	Wayne Chrebet	.10
232	Jeff Hostetler	.10
233	Andy Harmon	.10
234	Greg Lloyd	.10
235	Toby Wright	.10
236	Junior Seau	.10
237	Bryant Young	.10
238	Robert Blackmon	.10
239	Trent Dilfer	.10
240	Leslie Shepherd	.10
241	Eric Swann	.10
242	Bert Emanuel	.10
243	Antonio Langham	.10
244	Steve Christie	.10
245	Tyrone Poole	.10
246	Jim Flanigan	.10
247	Tony McGee	.10
248	Michael Irvin	.20
249	Bam Morris	.10
250	Terrell Davis	1.50
251	Johnnie Morton	.10
252	Sean Jones	.10
253	Chris Sanders	.30
254	Quentin Coryatt	.10
255	Willie Jackson	.10
256	Mark Collins	.10
257	Randal Hill	.10
258	David Palmer	.10
259	Will Moore	.10
260	Michael Haynes	.10
261	Mike Sherrard	.10
262	William Thomas	.10
263	Kordell Stewart	1.50
264	D'Marco Farr	.10
265	Terrell Fletcher	.10
266	Lee Woodall	.10
267	Eugene Robinson	.10
268	Alvin Harper	.10
269	Gus Frerotte	.10
270	Antonio Freeman	.10
271	Clyde Simmons	.10
272	Chuck Smith	.10
273	Steve Tasker	.10
274	Kevin Butler	.10
275	Steve Tovar	.10
276	Troy Aikman	1.00
277	Aaron Craver	.10
278	Henry Thomas	.10
279	Craig Newsome	.10
280	Brent Jones	.10
281	Michael Barrow	.10
282	Ray Buchanan	.10
283	Jimmy Smith	.10
284	Neil Smith	.10
285	O.J. McDuffie	.10
286	Jake Reed	.10
287	Ty Law	.10
288	Torrance Small	.10
289	Hugh Douglas	.10
290	Pat Swilling	.10
291	Charlie Garner	.10
292	Ernie Mills	.10
293	John Carney	.10
294	Ken Norton	.10
295	Cortez Kennedy	.10
296	Derrick Brooks	.10
297	Heath Shuler	.20
298	Reggie White	.10
299	Kimble Anders	.10
300	Willie McGinest	.10

1996 Upper Deck Game Jersey

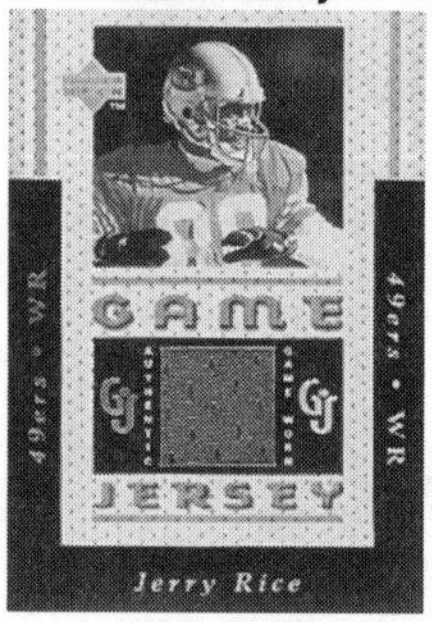

Each of these 1996 Upper Deck insert cards features an actual piece of a player's game-worn uniform. Cards, seeded one per every 2,500 Series I packs, are numbered using a "GJ" prefix. There are two different cards of Jerry Rice and Dan Marino.

		MT
Complete Set (10):		4000.
Common Player:		150.00
1	Dan Marino	575.00
2	Jerry Rice	350.00
3	Joe Montana	550.00
4	Jerry Rice	350.00
5	Rashaan Salaam	150.00
6	Marshall Faulk	200.00
7	Dan Marino	575.00
8	Steve Young	300.00
9	Barry Sanders	650.00
10	Mark Brunell	325.00

1996 Upper Deck Predictor

All new die-cut F/X designs grace the fronts of these 1996 Upper Deck Series I inserts, which are now based on personal goals. For example, if Dan Marino passes for 450 or more yards in a game, a collector can mail in the Marino card for a special TV-CEL redemption card. The player's goal and the word "Predictor" are

stamped in silver foil along the sides of the card. The back of the card explains the rules for the promotion. A maximum of 500 of each player's winning TV-CEL cards will be randomly inserted in packs. The same 20 players are represented in both retail and hobby versions, but the personal goals are different. The cards also use the corresponding "PH" or "PR" prefix for the card number.

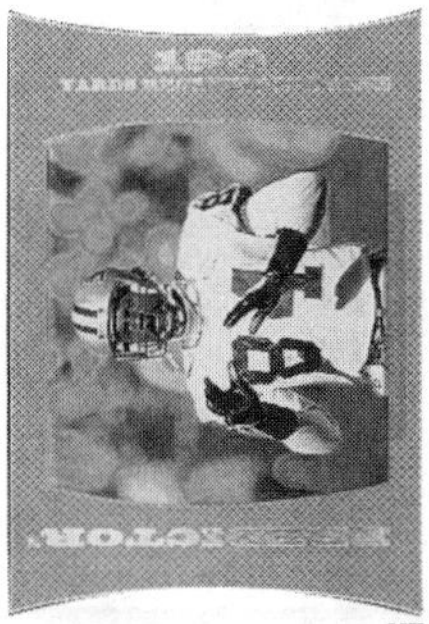

		MT
Comp. Hobby Set (20):		200.00
Comp. Retail Set (20):		200.00
Common Player:		2.00
PH1	Dan Marino	10.00
PH2	Steve Young	5.00
PH3	Brett Favre	50.00
PH4	Drew Bledsoe	30.00
PH5	Jeff George	2.00
PH6	John Elway	20.00
PH7	Barry Sanders	50.00
PH8	Curtis Martin	8.00
PH9	Marshall Faulk	5.00
PH10	Emmitt Smith	10.00
PH11	Terrell Davis	30.00
PH12	Errict Rhett	4.00
PH13	Lawrence Phillips	4.00
PH14	Jerry Rice	5.00
PH15	Michael Irvin	10.00
PH16	Joey Galloway	5.00
PH17	Herman Moore	3.00
PH18	Isaac Bruce	3.00
PH19	Carl Pickens	3.00
PH20	Keyshawn Johnson	4.00
PR1	Dan Marino	10.00
PR2	Steve Young	25.00
PR3	Brett Favre	10.00
PR4	Drew Bledsoe	30.00
PR5	Jeff George	2.00
PR6	John Elway	20.00
PR7	Barry Sanders	6.00
PR8	Curtis Martin	30.00
PR9	Marshall Faulk	5.00
PR10	Emmitt Smith	10.00
PR11	Terrell Davis	30.00
PR12	Errict Rhett	2.00
PR13	Lawrence Phillips	2.00
PR14	Jerry Rice	6.00
PR15	Michael Irvin	10.00
PR16	Joey Galloway	5.00
PR17	Herman Moore	15.00
PR18	Isaac Bruce	15.00
PR19	Carl Pickens	10.00
PR20	Keyshawn Johnson	5.00

1996 Upper Deck Pro Bowl

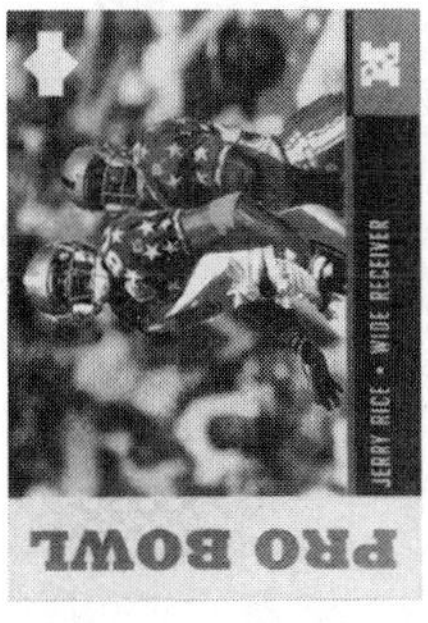

The 20-card Pro Bowl set was inserted every 33 packs of Upper Deck's Series One football. Cards are numbered and carry a "PB" prefix.

		MT
Complete Set (20):		125.00
Common Player:		3.00
1	Warren Moon	3.00
2	Brett Favre	20.00
3	Steve Young	10.00
4	Barry Sanders	18.00
5	Emmitt Smith	20.00
6	Jerry Rice	12.00
7	Herman Moore	6.00
8	Michael Irvin	3.00
9	Mark Chmura	3.00
10	Reggie White	3.00
11	Jim Harbaugh	3.00
12	Jeff Blake	8.00
13	Curtis Martin	18.00
14	Marshall Faulk	7.00
15	Chris Warren	3.00
16	Bryan Cox	3.00
17	Junior Seau	3.00
18	Carl Pickens	3.00
19	Yancey Thigpen	3.00
20	Ben Coates	3.00

1996 Upper Deck Proview

One Proview card was inserted in each Upper Deck Tech retail pack. The cards feature a cel window with a player close up. The fronts include another photo and the backs have basic player information. Silver (1:35) and Gold (1:143) parallel versions were also created.

		MT
Complete Set (40):		120.00
Common Player:		1.00
Minor Stars:		2.00
1	Warren Moon	1.00
2	Jerry Rice	7.00
3	Brett Favre	16.00
4	Jim Harbaugh	1.00
5	Junior Seau	1.00
6	Jeff Blake	2.00
7	John Elway	5.00
8	Troy Aikman	7.00
9	Steve Young	5.00
10	Kordell Stewart	7.00
11	Drew Bledsoe	7.00
12	Jim Kelly	2.00
13	Dan Marino	14.00
14	Kerry Collins	2.00
15	Jeff Hostetler	1.00
16	Terry Allen	1.00
17	Carl Pickens	1.00
18	Mark Brunell	7.00
19	Keyshawn Johnson	4.00
20	Barry Sanders	10.00
21	Deion Sanders	4.00
22	Emmitt Smith	14.00
23	Curtis Conway	1.00
24	Herman Moore	2.00
25	Joey Galloway	2.00
26	Robert Smith	1.00
27	Eddie George	10.00
28	Curtis Martin	7.00
29	Marshall Faulk	2.00
30	Terrell Davis	7.00
31	Rashaan Salaam	1.00
32	Jamal Anderson	2.00
33	Karim Abdul-Jabbar	6.00
34	Edgar Bennett	1.00
35	Thurman Thomas	2.00
36	Jerome Bettis	2.00
37	Tim Brown	1.00
38	Chris Sanders	1.00
39	Eddie Kennison	4.00
40	Shannon Sharpe	1.00

1996 Upper Deck Hot Properties

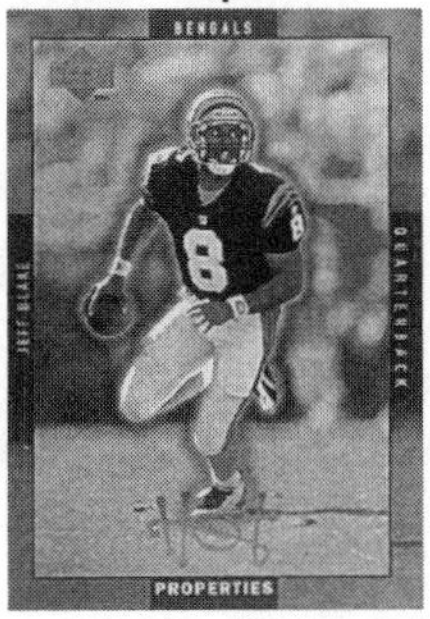

Each of these 1996 Upper Deck Series I inserts features a different player on each side. The card design features a color action photo (outlined with a red glow) against a silver metallic background. Red foil is used for the Upper Deck logo and the word "Hot" in the set's logo. The card number, using an "HT" prefix, is on one side, above an Upper Deck football-shaped hologram. Cards were seeded one per every 11 Series I packs.

		MT
Complete Set (20):		125.00
Common Player:		2.00
Comp. Gold Set (20):		375.00
Gold Cards:		1.5x-3x
1	Dan Marino, Drew Bledsoe	20.00
2	Jerry Rice, J.J. Stokes	10.00
3	Kordell Stewart, Deion Sanders	10.00
4	Brett Favre, Rick Mirer	20.00
5	Jeff Blake, Steve McNair	8.00
6	Emmitt Smith, Errict Rhett	20.00
7	John Elway, Warren Moon	6.00
8	Steve Young, Mark Brunell	10.00
9	Troy Aikman, Kerry Collins	12.00
10	Joey Galloway, Chris Sanders	8.00
11	Herman Moore, Cris Carter	2.00
12	Rodney Hampton, Terrell Davis	12.00
13	Carl Pickens, Isaac Bruce	5.00
14	Rashaan Salaam, Michael Westbrook	8.00
15	Marshall Faulk, Curtis Martin	12.00
16	Tamarick Vanover, Eric Metcalf	8.00
17	Keyshawn Johnson, Terry Glenn	12.00
18	Lawrence Phillips, Tim Biakabutuka	4.00
19	Kevin Hardy, Simeon Rice	2.00
20	Barry Sanders, Thurman Thomas	12.00

1996 Upper Deck Hot Properties Gold

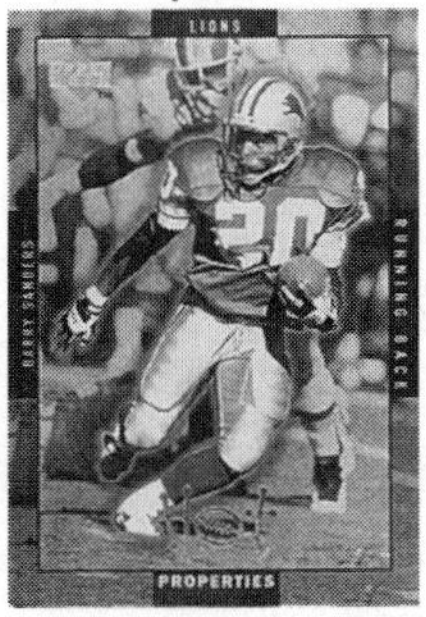

This insert paralleled the 20-card Hot Properties insert, but the letters "Hot Properties" were printed in gold foil. Hot Properties Gold were seeded one per 71 packs.

	MT
Complete Set (20):	375.00
Gold Cards:	3x

1996 Upper Deck Game Face

Game Face inserts were only found in special retail packs, and were numbered GF1-GF10. They included a close-up shot of the player, who had his intense, "game face" on.

		MT
Complete Set (10):		10.00
Common Player:		1.00
1	Dan Marino	4.00
2	Barry Sanders	2.00
3	Jerry Rice	2.00
4	Stan Humphries	1.00
5	Drew Bledsoe	2.00
6	Greg Lloyd	1.00
7	Jim Harbaugh	1.00
8	Rashaan Salaam	1.00
9	Jeff Blake	1.00
10	Reggie White	1.00

1996 Upper Deck TV Cels

TV Cels were available by redeeming winner Predictor cards. They include a television-like frame with cel technology inside, which reveals the player's image when held to light. Cards are numbered and carry a "PH" prefix.

		MT
Complete Set (20):		500.00
Common Player:		10.00
1	Dan Marino	125.00
2	Steve Young	15.00
3	Brett Favre	35.00
4	Drew Bledsoe	20.00
5	Jeff George	10.00
6	John Elway	25.00
7	Barry Sanders	35.00
8	Curtis Martin	15.00
9	Marshall Faulk	10.00
10	Emmitt Smith	100.00
11	Terrell Davis	35.00
12	Errict Rhett	10.00
13	Lawrence Phillips	10.00
14	Jerry Rice	60.00
15	Michael Irvin	10.00
16	Joey Galloway	15.00
17	Herman Moore	10.00
18	Isaac Bruce	10.00
19	Carl Pickens	10.00
20	Keyshawn Johnson	45.00

1996 Upper Deck Silver

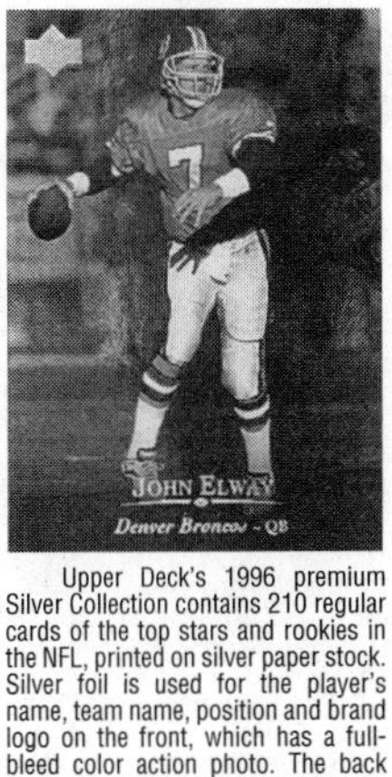

Upper Deck's 1996 premium Silver Collection contains 210 regular cards of the top stars and rookies in the NFL, printed on silver paper stock. Silver foil is used for the player's name, team name, position and brand logo on the front, which has a full-bleed color action photo. The back has a black strip along the left side, with the player's name, position and biographical information in it, plus a team logo and card number toward the top. A color action photo is at the top of the card, with statistics underneath. Subset cards are devoted to top players in certain offensive and defensive statistical leaders from the 1995 NFL season. Insert sets include All-NFL Team, All-Rookie Team, team helmet cards, Dan Marino Record Season, and a Rookie Draft Trade card, which is redeemable for 20-card Light F/X Rookie Redemption set from the 1996 NFL Draft. Cards were seeded one per every 103 packs.

		MT
Complete Set (225):		30.00
Common Player:		.10
Minor Stars:		.20
Pack (10):		1.00
Wax Box (28):		22.00
1	Larry Centers	.10
2	Terance Mathis	.10
3	Justin Armour	.10
4	Kerry Collins	.30
5	Mike Flanagan	.10
6	Dan Wilkinson	.10
7	Eric Zeier	.75
8	Deion Sanders	.75
9	Steve Atwater	.10
10	Johnnie Morton	.10
11	Craig Newsome	.10
12	Denver Broncos Offensive Line	.10
13	Ken Dilger	.10
14	Mark Brunell	.50
15	Tamarick Vanover	.50
16	Bernie Parmalee	.10
17	Orlanda Thomas	.10
18	Will Moore	.10
19	Mark Fields	.10
20	Tyrone Wheatley	.20
21	Kyle Brady	.10
22	Napoleon Kaufman	.50
23	Mike Mamula	.10
24	Erric Pegram	.10
25	Brent Jones	.10
26	*Aaron Hayden*	.50
27	Christian Fauria	.10
28	Dallas Cowboys Offensive Lines	.10
29	Derrick Brooks	.10
30	Brian Mitchell	.10
31	Garrison Hearst	.20
32	Devin Bush	.10
33	Andre Reed	.10
34	Derrick Moore	.10
35	Erik Kramer	.10
36	Jeff Blake	.75
37	Andre Rison	.10
38	Troy Aikman	1.50
39	Anthony Miller	.10
40	Scott Mitchell	.10
41	Reggie White	.20
42	Chris Sanders	.40
43	Ellis Johnson	.10
44	Willie Jackson	.10
45	Steve Bono	.20
46	Terry Kirby	.10
47	Jake Reed	.10
48	Vincent Brisby	.10
49	Quinn Early	.10
50	Thomas Lewis	.10
51	Wayne Chrebet	.10
52	Pat Swilling	.10
53	Bobby Taylor	.10
54	Mark Bruener	.10
55	Jerry Rice	1.50
56	Natrone Means	.25
57	Rick Mirer	.10
58	Kevin Carter	.10
59	Hardy Nickerson	.10
60	Detroit Lions Offensive Lines	.10
61	Eric Swann	.10
62	Eric Metcalf	.10
63	Russell Copeland	.10
64	Pete Metzelaars	.10
65	Curtis Conway	.10
66	Darnay Scott	.20
67	Leroy Hoard	.10
68	Darren Woodson	.10
69	John Elway	.50
70	Brett Perriman	.10
71	Mark Chmura	.10
72	Chris Chandler	.10
73	Marshall Faulk	1.00
74	Pete Mitchell	.10
75	Willie Davis	.10
76	Irving Fryar	.10
77	Robert Smith	.10
78	Drew Bledsoe	1.00
79	Mario Bates	.30
80	Chris Calloway	.10
81	Boomer Esiason	.10
82	Harvey Williams	.10
83	Fred Barnett	.10
84	Neil O'Donnell	.20
85	Lee Woodall	.10
86	Junior Seau	.20
87	Brian Blades	.10
88	Chris Miller	.10
89	Warren Sapp	.10
90	Terry Allen	.10
91	Dave Krieg	.10
92	Bert Emanuel	.10
93	Jim Kelly	.20
94	Mark Carrier	.10
95	Jeff Graham	.10
96	Tony McGee	.10
97	Vinny Testaverde	.10
98	Michael Irvin	.30
99	Shannon Sharpe	.10
100	Chris Spielman	.10
101	Edgar Bennett	.10
102	Haywood Jeffires	.10
103	Quentin Coryatt	.10
104	Jeff Lageman	.10
105	Neil Smith	.10
106	O.J. McDuffie	.10
107	Warren Moon	.10
108	Ben Coates	.10
109	Michael Haynes	.10
110	Mike Sherrard	.10
111	Adrian Murrell	.10
112	Jeff Hostetler	.10
113	Charlie Garner	.10
114	Yancey Thigpen	.10
115	Steve Young	1.50
116	Tony Martin	.10
117	San Francisco Offensive Lines	.10
118	Jerome Bettis	.10
119	Alvin Harper	.10
120	Heath Shuler	.40
121	Rob Moore	.10
122	Chris Doleman	.10
123	Bruce Smith	.10
124	Sam Mills	.10
125	Donnell Woolford	.10
126	Harold Green	.10
127	Antonio Langham	.10
128	Charles Haley	.10
129	Aaron Craver	.10
130	Barry Sanders	1.50
131	Sean Jones	.10
132	Steve McNair	1.00
133	Tony Bennett	.10
134	Miami Dolphins Offensive Lines	.10
135	Greg Hill	.10
136	Eric Green	.10
137	John Randle	.10
138	Dave Meggett	.10
139	Irv Smith	.10
140	Dave Brown	.10
141	Oakland Raiders Offensive Lines	.10
142	Raghib Ismail	.10
143	Rodney Peete	.10
144	Kevin Greene	.10
145	Derek Loville	.10
146	Leslie O'Neal	.10
147	Cortez Kennedy	.10
148	Sean Gilbert	.10
149	Jackie Harris	.10
150	Henry Ellard	.10
151	Frank Sanders	.30
152	Jeff George	.20
153	Darick Holmes	.75
154	Tyrone Poole	.10
155	Rashaan Salaam	.75
156	Carl Pickens	.20
157	Eric Turner	.10
158	Jay Novacek	.10
159	Terrell Davis	1.50
160	Herman Moore	.40
161	Robert Brooks	.10
162	Rodney Thomas	.40
163	Sean Dawkins	.10
164	James O. Stewart	.10
165	Marcus Allen	.10
166	Dan Marino	3.00
167	Cris Carter	.20
168	Curtis Martin	3.00
169	Tyrone Hughes	.10
170	Rodney Hampton	.10
171	Hugh Douglas	.10
172	Tim Brown	.10
173	Ricky Watters	.10
174	Kordell Stewart	2.00
175	J.J. Stokes	.75
176	Stan Humphries	.10
177	Joey Galloway	.50
178	Isaac Bruce	.75
179	Errict Rhett	.50
180	Michael Westbrook	.75
181	Pittsburgh Steelers Offensive Lines	.10
182	Craig Heyward	.10
183	Bryce Paup	.10
184	Brett Maxie	.10
185	Kevin Butler	.10
186	John Copeland	.10
187	Keenan McCardell	.10
188	Emmitt Smith	3.00
189	Glyn Milburn	.10
190	Jason Hanson	.10
191	Brett Favre	3.00
192	Darryll Lewis	.10
193	Jim Harbaugh	.10
194	Desmond Howard	.10
195	Derrick Thomas	.10
196	Bryan Cox	.10
197	Amp Lee	.10
198	Ty Law	.10
199	Jim Everett	.10
200	Vencie Glenn	.10
201	Charles Wilson	.10
202	Terry McDaniel	.10
203	Calvin Williams	.10
204	Greg Lloyd	.10
205	Merton Hanks	.10
206	Andre Coleman	.10
207	Chris Warren	.20
208	D'Marco Farr	.10
209	Trent Dilfer	.20
210	Ken Harvey	.10
211	Jim Harbaugh	.10
212	Brett Favre SL	1.00
213	Curtis Martin SL	1.50
214	Carl Pickens	.10
215	Norm Johnson	.10
216	Bryce Paup	.10
217	Herman Moore	.10
218	Jerry Rice SL	.75
219	Orlanda Thomas	.10
220	Emmitt Smith SL	1.50
221	Tyrone Hughes	.10
222	Tamarick Vanover	.30
223	Rick Tuten	.10
224	San Francisco 49ers	.10
225	Detroit Lions	.10
NNO	Draft Trade Card	20.00

1996 Upper Deck Silver All-NFL

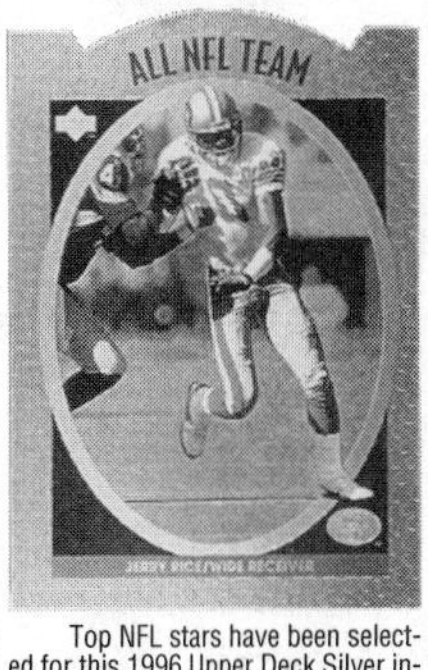

Top NFL stars have been selected for this 1996 Upper Deck Silver insert set. The 20 cards, seeded one per every five packs, are produced as a special Light F/X die-cut card. The front of the card has a gold foil border, with a photo in the center framed by a silver foil oval. The player's name is in a team color-coded bar below the photo. The Upper Deck logo and a team logo are stamped in silver foil on the front too, with All NFL Team written at the top. The back has a border which looks like a pigskin football. A square in the center has a color action photo in the top half, with the player's name and position given below. Then, a recap of the player's 1995 season and "All NFL Team" and a team logo follow. A card number, using an "AN" prefix, is in the upper left corner of the card.

		MT
Complete Set (20):		45.00
Common Player:		2.00
1	Herman Moore	3.00
2	Isaac Bruce	4.00
3	Jerry Rice	6.00
4	Michael Irvin	3.00
5	Eric Metcalf	2.00
6	Ben Coates	2.00
7	Brett Favre	10.00
8	Jim Harbaugh	2.00
9	Emmitt Smith	10.00
10	Barry Sanders	6.00
11	Chris Warren	3.00
12	Curtis Martin	8.00
13	Hugh Douglas	2.00
14	Neil Smith	2.00
15	Reggie White	2.00
16	Bryce Paup	2.00
17	Greg Lloyd	2.00
18	Carnell Lake	2.00
19	Merton Hanks	2.00
20	Tamarick Vanover	4.00

1996 Upper Deck Silver All-Rookie Team

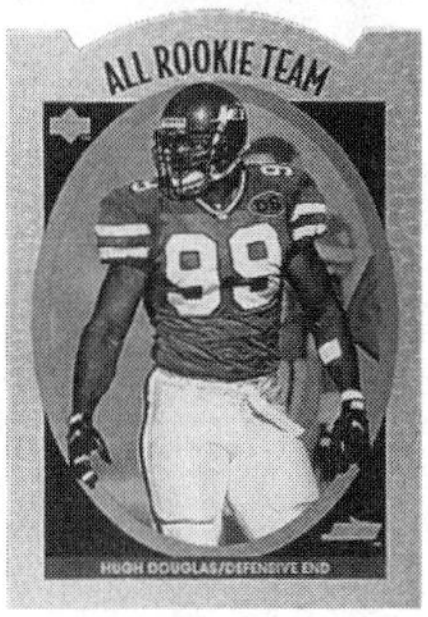

These 1996 Upper Deck Silver Collection insert cards, seeded one per every 18 packs, feature 20 of the top rookies selected to Upper Deck's "All-Rookie Team." The die-cut cards use Upper Deck's Light F/X technology. Cards are numbered and carry an "AR" prefix.

		MT
Complete Set (20):		120.00
Common Player:		3.00
1	Joey Galloway	12.00
2	Chris Sanders	6.00
3	J.J. Stokes	10.00
4	Ken Dilger	3.00
5	Pete Mitchell	3.00
6	Kordell Stewart	20.00
7	Kerry Collins	6.00
8	Tony Boselli	3.00
9	Terrell Davis	20.00
10	Rodney Thomas	6.00
11	Rashaan Salaam	6.00
12	Curtis Martin	24.00
13	Napoleon Kaufman	6.00
14	Hugh Douglas	3.00
15	Ellis Johnson	3.00
16	Kevin Carter	3.00
17	Derrick Brooks	3.00
18	Craig Newsome	3.00
19	Orlanda Thomas	3.00
20	Tamarick Vanover	3.00

1996 Upper Deck Silver Dan Marino

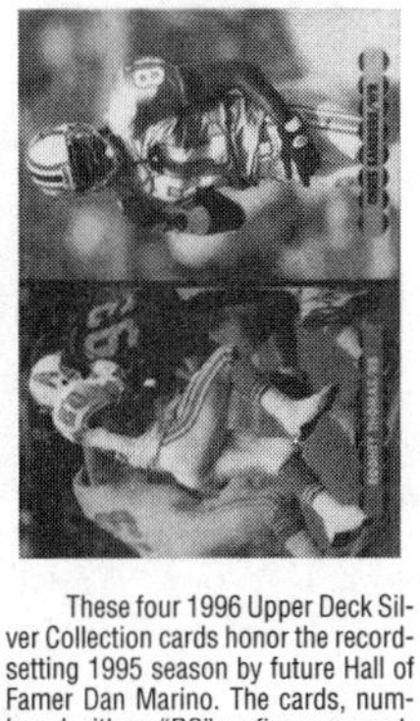

These four 1996 Upper Deck Silver Collection cards honor the record-setting 1995 season by future Hall of Famer Dan Marino. The cards, numbered with an "RS" prefix, were seeded one per every 81 packs.

	MT
Complete Set (4):	60.00
Common Player:	15.00

1	All-Time Completions 3,686	15.00
2	All-Time Passing Yards 47,003	15.00
3	All-Time Touchdown Pts. 342	15.00
4	300-Yards Passing Games 52	15.00

1996 Upper Deck Silver Helmet Cards

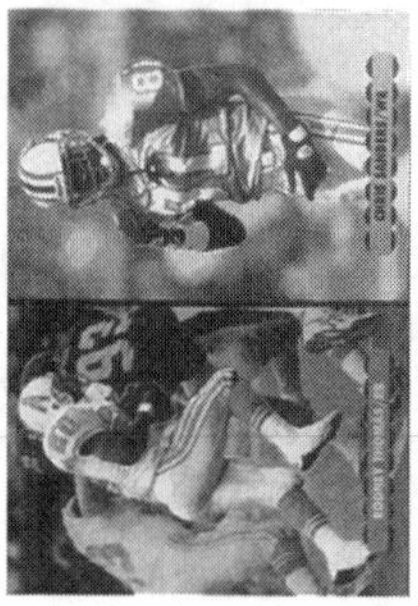

These 1996 Upper Deck Silver Collection insert cards were seeded one per every 23 packs. The cards, the first to use double-sided Light F/X technology, have a team helmet on one side, bordered on either side by a team color-coordinated panel which lists the team name or respective conference. A card number, using an "AC" or "NC" prefix, is also on this side. The opposite side has two action photos of teammates from that team, with their names below the photos in color-coded strips.

		MT
Complete Set (30):		275.00
Common Player:		3.00
NE1	Arizona Cardinals (Garrison Hearst, Frank Sanders)	3.00
NW1	Atlanta Falcons (Jeff George, Devin Bush)	3.00
NW2	Carolina Panthers (Sam Mills, Kerry Collins)	6.00
NC1	Chicago Bears (Erik Kramer, Rashaan Salaam)	6.00
AC1	Cincinnati Bengals (Jeff Blake, David Dunn)	8.00
AC2	Cleveland Browns (Vinny Testaverde, Eric Zeier)	3.00
NC2	Detroit Lions (Herman Moore, Luther Elliss)	6.00
AC3	Houston Oilers (Rodney Thomas, Chris Sanders)	6.00
AE1	Indianapolis Colts (Marshall Faulk, Ken Dilger)	8.00
AC4	Jacksonville Jaguars (Mark Brunell, James O. Stewart)	10.00
AW1	Kansas City Chiefs (Steve Bono, Tamarick Vanover)	3.00
NC3	Minnesota Vikings (Cris Carter, Orlanda Thomas)	3.00
NW3	New Orleans Saints (Mario Bates, Mark Fields)	3.00
NE2	New York Giants (Rodney Hampton, Tyrone Wheatley)	3.00
AE2	New York Jets (Wayne Chrebet, Hugh Douglas)	3.00
NE3	Philadelphia Eagles (Ricky Watters, Mike Mamula)	3.00
AW2	Seattle Seahawks (Chris Warren, Joey Galloway)	6.00
NW4	St. Louis Rams (Isaac Bruce, Kevin Carter)	8.00
NC4	Tampa Bay Buccaneers (Errict Rhett, Derrick Brooks)	6.00
NE4	Washington Redskins (Terry Allen, Michael Westbrook)	8.00
AC5	Pittsburgh Steelers (Greg Lloyd, Kordell Stewart)	18.00
AW4	San Diego Chargers (Natrone Means, Terrance Shaw)	6.00
NW5	San Francisco 49ers (Jerry Rice, J.J. Stokes)	20.00
AW4	Oakland Raiders (Tim Brown, Napoleon Kaufman)	6.00
AE3	Miami Dolphins (Dan Marino, Billy Milner)	40.00
NE5	Dallas Cowboys (Emmitt Smith, Sherman Williams)	40.00
AE4	Buffalo Bills (Jim Kelly, Darick Holmes)	6.00
NC5	Green Bay Packers (Robert Brooks, Craig Newsome)	6.00
AW5	Denver Broncos (John Elway, Terrell Davis)	20.00
AE5	New England Patriots (Drew Bledsoe, Curtis Martin)	25.00

1996 Upper Deck Silver Prime Choice Rookies

This 20-card set was available via redemption of a special trade card inserted in 1996 Upper Deck Silver. The card fronts feature a foil-accented photo and an inset photo of the player. The backs contain another player photo and biographical information.

		MT
Complete Set (20):		45.00
Common Player:		.50
Minor Stars:		1.00
1	Keyshawn Johnson	6.00
2	Kevin Hardy	.50
3	Simeon Rice	.50
4	Tim Biakabutuka	1.50
5	Terry Glenn	4.00
6	Rickey Dudley	1.00
7	Alex Molden	.50
8	Regan Upshaw	.50
9	Eddie George	15.00
10	John Mobley	.50
11	Eddie Kennison	1.00
12	Marvin Harrison	3.00
13	Leeland McElroy	1.00
14	Eric Moulds	6.00
15	Mike Alstott	5.00
16	Bobby Engram	1.00
17	Derrick Mayes	1.00
18	Karim Abdul-Jabbar	4.00
19	Stepfret Williams	.50
20	Jeff Lewis	.50
NNO	Redemption Card Expired	1.00

1997 Upper Deck

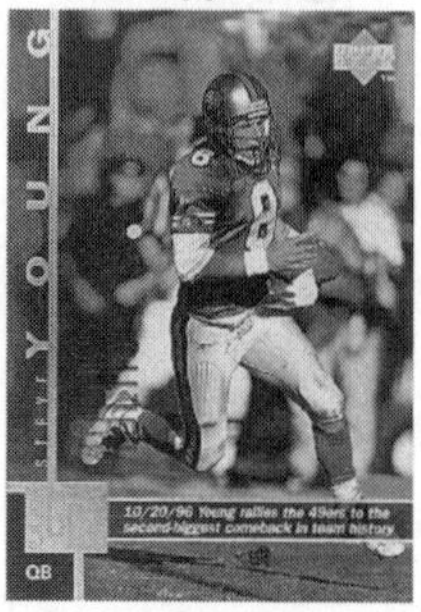

The 300-card set includes subsets of Star Rookies (35 cards), Star Rookie Flashback (10 cards) and Game Dated Moments (30 cards). The base cards have the player's name printed vertically along the left border, with the Upper Deck logo and player's position in the lower left corner. The team's name is to the right of the Upper Deck logo on the card front.

		MT
Complete Set (300):		40.00
Common Player:		.10
Minor Stars:		.20
Game Dated Foils:		40x-80x
Inserted 1:1,500		
Pack (12):		2.00
Wax Box (24):		45.00
1	*Orlando Pace*	.50
2	*Darrell Russell*	.10
3	*Shawn Springs*	.75
4	*Bryant Westbrook*	.30
5	*Ike Hilliard*	1.50
6	*Peter Boulware*	.10
7	*Tom Knight*	.10
8	*Yatil Green*	.50
9	*Tony Gonzalez*	1.00
10	*Reidel Anthony*	1.50
11	*Warrick Dunn*	2.00
12	*Kenny Holmes*	.10
13	*Jim Druckenmiller*	2.50
14	*James Farrior*	.10
15	*David LaFleur*	1.00
16	*Antowain Smith*	2.00
17	*Rae Carruth*	1.25
18	*Dwayne Rudd*	.10
19	*Jake Plummer*	4.00
20	*Reinard Wilson*	.10
21	*Byron Hanspard*	1.25
22	*Will Blackwell*	.50
23	*Troy Davis*	.50
24	*Corey Dillon*	4.00
25	*Joey Kent*	.75
26	*Renaldo Wynn*	.10
27	*Pat Barnes*	1.00
28	*Kevin Lockett*	.10
29	*Darnell Autry*	1.00
30	*Walter Jones*	.10
31	(Trevor Pryce)	.10
32	(Dan Marino SRF)	2.00
33	(Steve Young SRF)	1.00
34	(John Elway SRF)	1.00
35	(Jerry Rice SRF)	1.00
36	Tim Brown SRF	.10
37	Deion Sanders SRF	.50
38	Troy Aikman SRF	1.00
39	Barry Sanders SRF	1.00
40	Emmitt Smith SRF	2.00
41	Junior Seau SRF	.10
42	Neil Smith	.10
43	Brett Perriman	.10
44	Jim Everett	.10
45	Qadry Ismail	.10
46	Dana Stubblefield	.10
47	Bryant Young	.10
48	Ken Norton Jr.	.10
49	Terrell Owens	.75
50	Jerry Rice	1.50
51	Steve Young	.75
52	Terry Kirby	.10
53	Chris Doleman	.10
54	Lee Woddall	.10
55	Merton Hanks	.10
56	Garrison Hearst	.10
57	Rashaan Salaam	.20
58	Raymont Harris	.10
59	Curtis Conway	.10
60	Bobby Engram	.10
61	Bryan Cox	.10
62	Walt Harris	.10
63	Tyrone Hughes	.10
64	Rick Mirer	.10
65	Jeff Blake	.20
66	Carl Pickens	.10
67	Darnay Scott	.10
68	Tony McGee	.10
69	Ki-Jana Carter	.10
70	Ashley Ambrose	.10
71	Dan Wilkinson	.10
72	Chris Spielman	.10
73	Todd Collins	.10
74	Andre Reed	.10
75	Quinn Early	.10
76	Eric Moulds	.10
77	Darrick Holmes	.10
78	Thurman Thomas	.20
79	Bruce Smith	.10
80	Bryce Paup	.10
81	John Elway	2.00
82	Terrell Davis	2.00
83	Anthony Miller	.10
84	Shannon Sharpe	.10
85	Alfred Williams	.10
86	John Mobley	.10
87	Tory James	.10
88	Steve Atwater	.10
89	Darrien Gordon	.10
90	Mike Alstott	.10
91	Errict Rhett	.20
92	Trent Dilfer	.10
93	Courtney Hawkins	.10
94	Warren Sapp	.10
95	Regan Upshaw	.10
96	Hardy Nickerson	.10
97	Donnie Abraham	.10
98	Larry Centers	.10
99	Aeneas Williams	.10
100	Kent Graham	.10
101	Rob Moore	.10
102	Frank Sanders	.10
103	Leeland McElroy	.10
104	Eric Swann	.10
105	Simeon Rice	.10
106	Seth Joyner	.10
107	Stan Humphries	.10
108	Tony Martin	.10
109	Charlie Jones	.10
110	Andre Coleman ERR.#103	.10
111	Terrell Fletcher	.10
112	Junior Seau	.20
113	Eric Metcalf	.10
114	Chris Penn	.10
115	Marcus Allen	.20
116	Greg Hill	.10
117	Tamarick Vanover	.10
118	Lake Dawson	.10
119	Derrick Thomas	.10
120	Dale Carter	.10
121	Elvis Grbac	.10
122	Aaron Bailey	.10
123	Jim Harbaugh	.10
124	Marshall Faulk	.20
125	Sean Dawkins	.10
126	Marvin Harrison	.50
127	Ken Dilger	.10
128	Tony Bennett	.10
129	Jeff Herrod	.10
130	Chris Gardocki	.10
131	Cary Blanchard	.10
132	Troy Aikman	1.50
133	Emmitt Smith	2.00
134	Sherman Williams	.10
135	Michael Irvin	.20
136	Eric Bjornson	.10
137	Herschel Walker	.10
138	Tony Tolbert	.10
139	Deion Sanders	.50
140	Daryl Johnston	.10
141	Dan Marino	2.00
142	O.J. McDuffie	.10
143	Troy Drayton	.10
144	Karim Abdul-Jabbar	.75
145	Stanley Pritchett	.10
146	Fred Barnett	.10
147	Zach Thomas	.20
148	Sean Wooden	.10
149	Ty Detmer	.10
150	Derrick Witherspoon	.10
151	Ricky Watters	.20
152	Charlie Garner	.10
153	Chris T. Jones	.10
154	Irving Fryar	.10
155	Mike Mamula	.10
156	Troy Vincent	.10
157	Bobby Taylor	.10
158	Chris Boniol	.10
159	Devin Bush	.10
160	Bert Emanuel	.10
161	Jamal Anderson	.20
162	Terance Mathis	.10
163	Cornelius Bennett	.10
164	Ray Buchanan	.10
165	Chris Chandler	.10
166	Dave Brown	.10
167	Danny Kanell	.10
168	Rodney Hampton	.10
169	Tyrone Wheatley	.10
170	Amani Toomer	.10
171	Chris Calloway	.10
172	Thomas Lewis	.10
173	Phillippi Sparks	.10
174	Mark Brunell	1.25
175	Keenan McCardell	.10
176	Willie Jackson	.10
177	Jimmy Smith	.10
178	Pete Mitchell	.10
179	Natrone Means	.20
180	Kevin Hardy	.10
181	Tony Brackens	.10
182	James O. Stewart	.10
183	Wayne Chrebet	.10
184	Keyshawn Johnson	.50
185	Adrian Murrell	.10
186	Neil O'Donnell	.10
187	Hugh Douglas	.10
188	Mo Lewis	.10
189	Marvin Washington	.10
190	Aaron Glenn	.10
191	Barry Sanders	3.00
192	Scott Mitchell	.10
193	Herman Moore	.20
194	Johnnie Morton	.10
195	Glyn Milburn	.10
196	Reggie Brown	.10
197	Jason Hanson	.10
198	Steve McNair	.75
199	Eddie George	1.25
200	Ronnie Harmon	.10
201	Chris Sanders	.10
202	Willie Davis	.10
203	Frank Wycheck	.10
204	Darryll Lewis	.10
205	Blaine Bishop	.10
206	Robert Brooks	.10
207	Brett Favre	3.00
208	Edgar Bennett	.10
209	Dorsey Levens	.20
210	Derrick Mayes	.10
211	Antonio Freeman	.30
212	Mark Chmura	.10
213	Reggie White	.20
214	Gilbert Brown	.10
215	LeRoy Butler	.10
216	Craig Newsome	.10
217	Kerry Collins	1.00
218	Wesley Walls	.10
219	Muhsin Muhammad	.10
220	Anthony Johnson	.10
221	Tshimanga Biakabutuka	.20
222	Kevin Greene	.10
223	Sam Mills	.10
224	John Kasay	.10
225	Michael Barrow	.10
226	Drew Bledsoe	1.25
227	Curtis Martin	.75
228	Terry Glenn	.50
229	Ben Coates	.10
230	Shawn Jefferson	.10
231	Willie McGinest	.10
232	Ted Johnson	.10
233	Lawyer Milloy	.10
234	Ty Law	.10
235	Willie Clay	.10
236	Tim Brown	.10
237	Rickey Dudley	.10
238	Napoleon Kaufman	.10
239	Chester McGlockton	.10
240	Rob Fredrickson	.10
241	Terry McDaniel	.10
242	Desmond Howard	.10
243	Jeff George	.10
244	Isaac Bruce	.20
245	Tony Banks	.50
246	Lawrence Phillips ERR.#247	.20
247	Kevin Carter	.10
248	Roman Phifer	.10
249	Keith Lyle	.10
250	Eddie Kennison	.50
251	Craig Heyward	.10
252	Vinny Testaverde	.10
253	Derrick Alexander	.10
254	Michael Jackson	.10
255	Bam Morris	.10
256	Eric Green	.10
257	Ray Lewis	.10
258	Antonio Langham	.10
259	Michael McCreary	.10
260	Gus Frerotte	.10
261	Terry Allen	.10
262	Brian Mitchell	.10
263	Michael Westbrook	.10
264	Sean Gilbert	.10
265	Rich Owens	.10
266	Ken Harvey	.10
267	Jeff Hostetler	.10
268	Michael Haynes	.10
269	Mario Bates	.10
270	Eric Allen ERR.#273	.10
271	Ray Zellars	.10
272	Joe Johnson	.10
273	Renaldo Turnbull	.10
274	Heath Shuler	.10
275	Daryl Hobbs	.10
276	John Friesz	.10
277	Brian Blades	.10
278	Joey Galloway	.30
279	Chris Warren	.10
280	Lamar Smith	.10
281	Cortez Kennedy	.10
282	Chad Brown	.10
283	Warren Moon	.10
284	Jerome Bettis	.20
285	Charles Johnson	.10
286	Kordell Stewart	1.00
287	Erric Pegram	.10
288	Norm Johnson	.10
289	Levon Kirkland	.10
290	Greg Lloyd	.10
291	Carnell Lake	.10
292	Brad Johnson	.10
293	Cris Carter	.10
294	Jake Reed	.10
295	Robert Smith	.10
296	Derrick Alexander	.10
297	John Randle	.10
298	Dixon Edwards	.10
299	Orlanda Thomas	.10
300	DeWayne Washington	.10

1997 Upper Deck Game Jersey

The 10-card set includes a piece of the player's jersey. The cards were inserted 1:2,500 packs. Cards are numbered with a "GM" prefix.

		MT
Complete Set (10):		3000.
Common Player:		150.00
1	Warren Moon	150.00
2	Joey Galloway	225.00
3	Terrell Davis	375.00
4	Brett Favre	650.00
5	Brett Favre	650.00
6	Reggie White	200.00
7	John Elway	425.00
8	Troy Aikman	350.00
9	Carl Pickens	150.00
10	Herman Moore	150.00

1997 Upper Deck MVP

The 20-card set featured the players on gold Light F/X Cel Chrome cards. Upper Deck produced 100 of each card. Cards are numbered with a "MP" prefix.

		MT
Complete Set (20):		2000.
Common Player:		40.00
Minor Stars:		80.00
1	Jerry Rice	200.00
2	Carl Pickens	40.00
3	Terrell Davis	200.00
4	Mike Alstott	80.00
5	Vinny Testaverde	40.00
6	Junior Seau	40.00
7	Marcus Allen	80.00
8	Troy Aikman	200.00
9	Dan Marino	300.00
10	Ricky Watters	40.00
11	Mark Brunell	200.00
12	Barry Sanders	300.00
13	Eddie George	200.00
14	Brett Favre	350.00
15	Kerry Collins	100.00
16	Drew Bledsoe	200.00
17	Napoleon Kaufman	100.00
18	Isaac Bruce	80.00
19	Terry Allen	40.00
20	Jerome Bettis	40.00

1997 Upper Deck Star Crossed

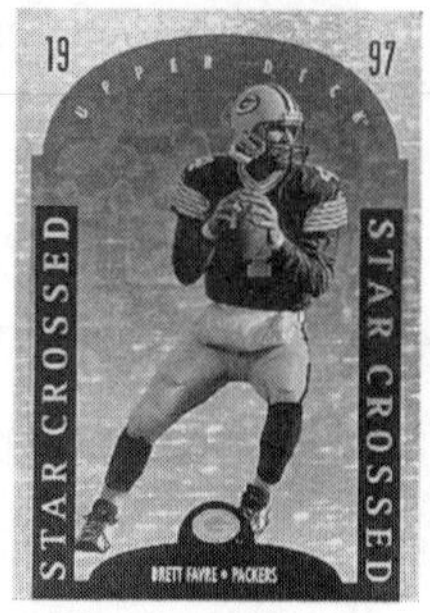

The 27-card set was inserted 1:27 packs. The player's photo is superimposed over an etched-foil starry background on the Light F/X cards. The cards are numbered on the back with an "SC" prefix.

		MT
Complete Set (30):		70.00
Common Player:		.75
Minor Stars:		1.50
1	Dan Marino	8.00
2	Mark Brunell	4.00
3	Kerry Collins	1.50
4	Jerry Rice	4.00
5	Kevin Greene	.75
6	Curtis Martin	3.00
7	Isaac Bruce	1.50
8	Eddie George	4.00
9	Deion Sanders	2.00
10	Troy Aikman	4.00
11	John Elway	4.00
12	Steve Young	3.00
13	Barry Sanders	6.00
14	Jerome Bettis	1.50
15	Herman Moore	1.50
16	Keyshawn Johnson	1.50
17	Simeon Rice	.75
18	Bruce Smith	.75
19	Drew Bledsoe	4.00
20	Kordell Stewart	4.00
21	Brett Favre	10.00
22	Emmitt Smith	8.00
23	Terrell Davis	4.00
24	Carl Pickens	.75
25	Terry Glenn	1.50
26	Reggie White	1.50
27	Rod Woodson	.75

1997 Upper Deck Team Mates

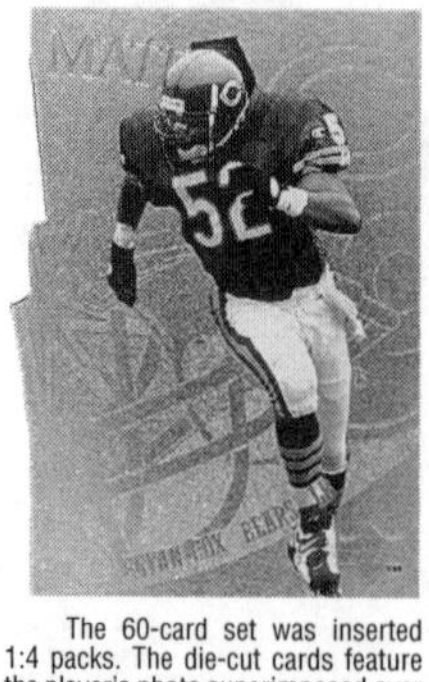

The 60-card set was inserted 1:4 packs. The die-cut cards feature the player's photo superimposed over a silver etched foil background. The die-cut cards fit together to show the two teammates from each team. The player's name, team, position and Upper Deck logo are printed in gold foil at the bottom. The cards are numbered on the back with a "TM" prefix.

		MT
Complete Set (60):		45.00
Common Player:		.25
Minor Stars:		.50
1	Simeon Rice	.25
2	Eric Swann	.25
3	Jamal Anderson	.50
4	Terance Mathis	.25
5	Vinny Testaverde	.25
6	Michael Jackson	.25
7	Thurman Thomas	.50
8	Bruce Smith	.25
9	Kerry Collins	.50
10	Anthony Johnson	.25
11	Bobby Engram	.25
12	Rashaan Salaam	.50
13	Carl Pickens	.25
14	Jeff Blake	.50
15	Troy Aikman	2.00
16	Emmitt Smith	4.00
17	John Elway	1.25
18	Terrell Davis	2.00
19	Herman Moore	.50
20	Barry Sanders	2.50
21	Brett Favre	5.00
22	Reggie White	.50
23	Eddie George	3.00
24	Steve McNair	1.00
25	Marshall Faulk	.50
26	Jim Harbaugh	.25
27	Mark Brunell	2.00
28	Keenan McCardell	.25
29	Marcus Allen	.50
30	Derrick Thomas	.25
31	Dan Marino	4.00
32	Karim Abdul-Jabbar	.75
33	Cris Carter	.75
34	Jake Reed	.25
35	Curtis Martin	2.00
36	Drew Bledsoe	2.00
37	Mario Bates	.25
38	Ray Zellars	.25
39	Keyshawn Johnson	.50
40	Adrian Murrell	.25
41	Tyrone Wheatley	.25
42	Rodney Hampton	.25
43	Napoleon Kaufman	.25
44	Tim Brown	.25
45	Ricky Watters	.50
46	Chris T. Jones	.25
47	Kordell Stewart	1.50
48	Jerome Bettis	.50
49	Junior Seau	.50
50	Tony Martin	.25
51	Steve Young	1.25
52	Jerry Rice	2.00
53	Joey Galloway	.50
54	Chris Warren	.25
55	Eddie Kennison	.75
56	Tony Banks	.75
57	Mike Alstott	.25
58	Errict Rhett	.50
59	Terry Allen	.25
60	Gus Frerotte	.25

1997 Upper Deck Crash the Game Super Bowl XXXI

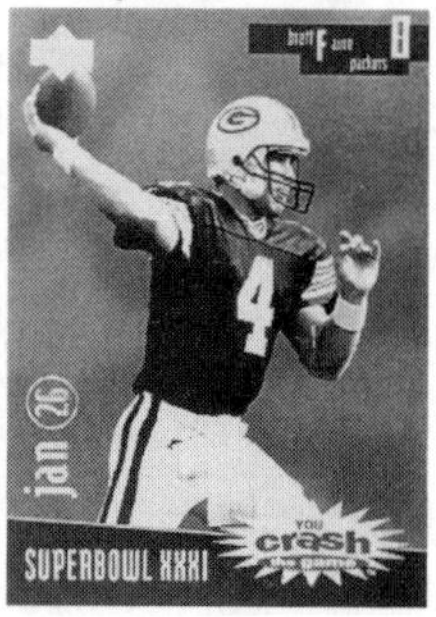

Upper Deck produced this special You Crash the Game set for Super Bowl XXXI. The cards were inserted in issues of Sports Collectors Digest. If the player pictured on the card scored a touchdown in the Super Bowl, collectors could redeem the card for a complete parallel set printed on foil stock. The game cards feature a player photo on a purple background with the Super Bowl date printed in gold foil.

		MT
Complete Set (8):		15.00
Common Player:		.75
Comp. Foil Prize Set (9):		10.00
Common Foil Prize:		.75
A1	Drew Bledsoe	1.50
A2	Curtis Martin	1.50
A3	Ben Coates	.75
A4	Terry Glenn	1.50
N1	Brett Favre	3.00
N2	Edgar Bennett	.75
N3	Don Beebe	.75
N4	Antonio Freeman	1.00

1997 Upper Deck Black Diamond

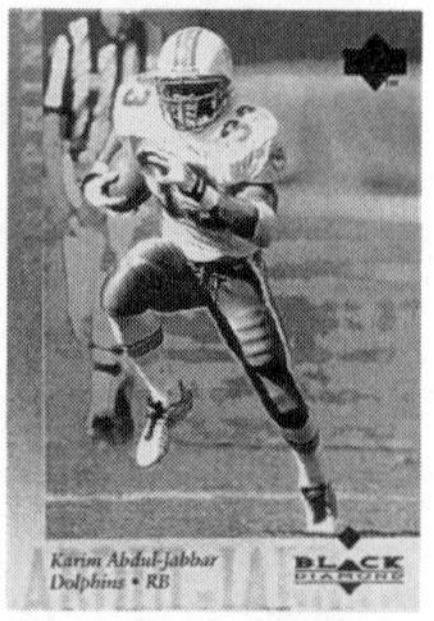

The 180-card, regular-sized set was released in six-card packs. The set was tiered in three levels: 90 single diamond, 60 double diamonds (1:4) and 30 triple diamonds (1:30). A parallel gold version was issued for each card: single diamond (1:15), double diamonds (1:46) and triple di-

amonds (limited to a production of 50). One insert set was included, Title Quest.

	MT
Complete Set (180):	400.00
Comp. Single Diamond (90):	20.00
Comp. Double Diamond (60):	80.00
Comp. Triple Diamond (30):	320.00
Common Diamond (1-90):	.10
Common Double Diamond (91-150):	.75
Common Triple Diamond (151-180):	4.00
Gold Diamond (1-90):	4x-8x
Gold Double Diamond (91-150):	2x-4x
Gold Triple Diamond (151-180):	5x-10x
Pack (6):	3.50
Wax Box (36):	100.00
1 Alfred Williams	.10
2 Alvin Harper	.10
3 Andre Hastings	.10
4 Andre Reed	.10
5 Anthony Johnson	.10
6 Anthony Miller	.10
7 Bam Morris	.10
8 Bobby Hebert	.10
9 Bobby Taylor	.10
10 Boomer Esiason	.10
11 Brett Perriman	.10
12 Brian Blades	.10
13 Bryan Cox	.10
14 Bryant Young	.10
15 Bryce Paup	.10
16 Carnell Lake	.10
17 Cedric Jones	.10
18 Chad Brown	.10
19 Charlie Garner	.10
20 Chris Chandler	.10
21 Cornelius Bennett	.10
22 Cortez Kennedy	.10
23 Cris Carter	.10
24 Dale Carter	.10
25 Daryl Gardner	.10
26 Derrick Alexander	.10
27 Derrick Mayes	.10
28 Don Beebe	.10
29 Eric Allen	.10
30 Eric Moulds	.10
31 Errict Rhett	.20
32 Frank Sanders	.10
33 Glyn Milburn	.10
34 Henry Ellard	.10
35 Jamal Anderson	.75
36 James O. Stewart	.10
37 Jason Dunn	.10
38 Jerry Rice	2.00
39 Jim Everett	.10
40 Jim Kelly	.10
41 Joey Galloway	1.00
42 John Carney	.10
43 John Elway	1.50
44 John Randle	.10
45 Karim Abdul-Jabbar	2.00
46 Keenan McCardell	.10
47 Ken Dilger	.10
48 Ken Norton	.10
49 Ki-Jana Carter	.10
50 Kordell Stewart	2.00
51 Lawrence Phillips	.10
52 Leslie O'Neal	.10
53 Mark Chmura	.10
54 Marshall Faulk	.25
55 Michael Haynes	.10
56 Michael Irvin	.20
57 Michael Jackson	.10
58 Michael Westbrook	.10
59 Mike Tomczak	.10
60 Napoleon Kaufman	1.00
61 Neil O'Donnell	.10
62 Neil Smith	.10
63 O.J. McDuffie	.10
64 Orlanda Thomas	.10
65 Rashaan Salaam	.20
66 Regan Upshaw	.10
67 Rick Mirer	.10
68 Rob Moore	.10
69 Ronnie Harmon	.10
70 Sam Mills	.10
71 Sean Dawkins	.10
72 Shawn Jefferson	.10
73 Stan Humphries	.10
74 Stepfret Williams	.10
75 Stephen Davis	.10
76 Steve Atwater	.10
77 Terance Mathis	.10
78 Terrell Fletcher	.10
79 Terry Glenn	2.50
80 Terry McDaniel	.10
81 Tony McGee	.10
82 Trent Dilfer	.10
83 Troy Drayton	.10
84 Ty Detmer	.10
85 Tyrone Hughes	.10
86 Walt Harris	.10
87 Wayne Chrebet	.10
88 Wesley Walls	.10
89 Willie Davis	.10
90 Willie McGinest	.10
91 Adrian Murrell	.75
92 Alex Molden	.75
93 Alex Van Dyke	.75
94 Andre Coleman	.75
95 Ben Coates	.75
96 Bobby Engram	.75
97 Bruce Smith	.75
98 Charles Johnson	.75
99 Chris Sanders	.75
100 Chris T. Jones	.75
101 Chris Warren	.75
102 Darnay Scott	.75
103 Dave Brown	.75
104 Derrick Thomas	.75
105 Drew Bledsoe	7.00
106 Edgar Bennett	.75
107 Emmitt Smith	14.00
108 Eric Bjornson	.75
109 Eric Metcalf	.75
110 Garrison Hearst	.75
111 Gus Frerotte	.75
112 Hardy Nickerson	.75
113 Herman Moore	1.50
114 Hugh Douglas	.75
115 Irving Fryar	.75
116 J.J. Stokes	.75
117 Jake Reed	.75
118 Jeff Hostetler	.75
119 Jeff Lewis	.75
120 Jim Harbaugh	.75
121 Johnnie Morton	.75
122 Jonathan Ogden	.75
123 Kevin Carter	.75
124 Kevin Greene	.75
125 Kevin Hardy	.75
126 Leeland McElroy	.75
127 Mike Alstott	1.50
128 Muhsin Muhammad	2.50
129 Natrone Means	.75
130 Quentin Coryatt	.75
131 Ray Lewis	.75
132 Ray Zellars	.75
133 Rickey Dudley	.75
134 Ricky Watters	.75
135 Robert Smith	.75
136 Scott Mitchell	.75
137 Sean Gilbert	.75
138 Shannon Sharpe	.75
139 Simeon Rice	.75
140 Stanley Pritchett	.75
141 Steve McNair	4.00
142 Steve Young	5.00
143 Tamarick Vanover	1.50
144 Terry Allen	.75
145 Thurman Thomas	.75
146 Tony Banks	3.00
147 Tony Martin	.75
148 Tyrone Wheatley	.75
149 Vinny Testaverde	.75
150 Zach Thomas	4.00
151 Amani Toomer	4.00
152 Barry Sanders	40.00
153 Bobby Hoying	4.00
154 Brett Favre	50.00
155 Carl Pickens	4.00
156 Curtis Conway	4.00
157 Curtis Martin	25.00
158 Dan Marino	50.00
159 Deion Sanders	10.00
160 Eddie George	40.00
161 Eddie Kennison	10.00
162 Elvis Grbac	4.00
163 Isaac Bruce	6.00
164 Jeff Blake	8.00
165 Jerome Bettis	4.00
166 Junior Seau	4.00
167 Kerry Collins	20.00
168 Keyshawn Johnson	10.00
169 Larry Centers	4.00
170 Marcus Allen	4.00
171 Mark Brunell	25.00
172 Marvin Harrison	10.00
173 Reggie White	4.00
174 Rodney Hampton	4.00
175 Terrell Davis	25.00
176 Tim Brown	4.00
177 Todd Collins	4.00
178 Troy Aikman	25.00
179 Tim Biakabutuka	4.00
180 Warren Moon	4.00

1997 Upper Deck Black Diamond Gold

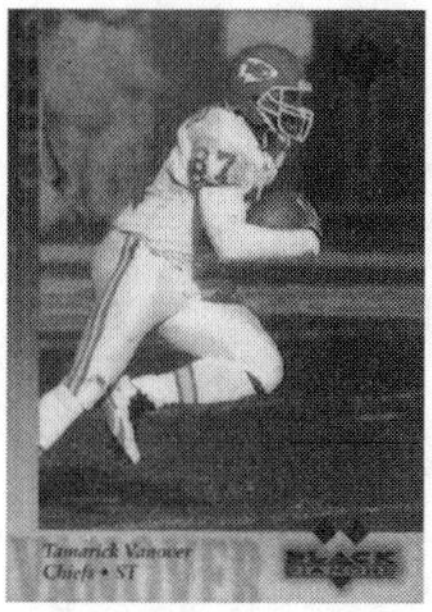

Gold parallel cards were available for all 180 cards in the 1997 Black Diamond set. The only difference between regular and gold versions is that the silver foil that is used on regular-issue cards is replaced by gold foil. Gold version of Single Black Diamond cards (1-90) were seeded one per 15 packs, while gold versions of Double Black Diamond cards (91-150) were inserted every 46 packs and gold Triple Black Diamond cards (151-180) were limited to 50 each.

	MT
Complete Set (180):	2900.
Comp. Single Diamond (90):	150.00
Comp. Double Diamond (60):	250.00
Comp. Triple Diamond (30):	2500.
Gold Single Diamonds: 4x-8x	
Gold Double Diamonds: 2x-4x	
Gold Triple Diamonds: 5x-10x	

1997 Upper Deck Black Diamond Title Quest

The 20-card, regular-sized, die-cut set was inserted into packs of 1997 Black Diamond football and was limited to a production of 100. The card fronts feature a square color action shot with a gold border.

	MT
Complete Set (20):	3000.
Common Player:	40.00
Minor Stars:	75.00
1 Dan Marino	350.00
2 Jerry Rice	200.00
3 Drew Bledsoe	200.00
4 Emmitt Smith	350.00
5 Troy Aikman	200.00
6 Steve Young	150.00
7 Brett Favre	350.00
8 John Elway	150.00
9 Barry Sanders	225.00
10 Jerome Bettis	75.00
11 Deion Sanders	100.00
12 Karim Abdul-Jabbar	125.00
13 Terrell Davis	225.00
14 Marshall Faulk	75.00
15 Curtis Martin	225.00
16 Eddie George	250.00
17 Steve McNair	125.00
18 Terry Glenn	75.00
19 Joey Galloway	40.00
20 Keyshawn Johnson	40.00

1997 Upper Deck Legends

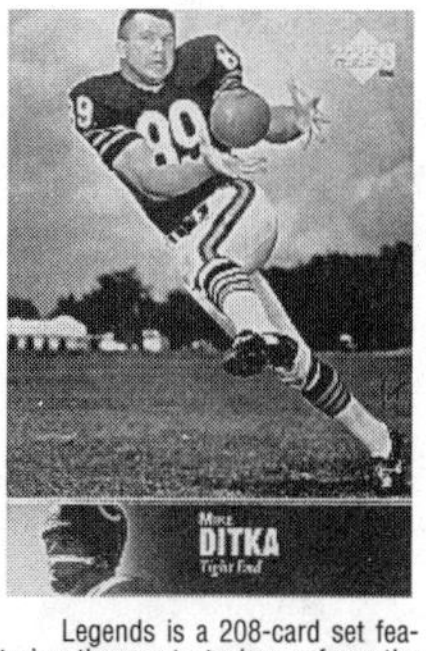

Legends is a 208-card set featuring the greatest players from the NFL's past. Besides the 168 regular cards, a 30-card Super Bowl Memories by Walter Iooss, Jr. subset and a 10-card Legendary Leaders subset were added. A parallel of the 168 regular cards featuring player autographs was inserted 1:5. The insert sets are Sign of the Times, Big Game Hunters and Marquee Matchups.

	MT
Complete Set (208):	45.00
Common Player:	.10
Minor Stars:	.20
Pack (10):	5.00
Wax Box (20):	80.00
1 Bart Starr	1.50
2 Jim Brown	2.50
3 Joe Namath	2.50
4 Walter Payton	2.50
5 Terry Bradshaw	2.50
6 Franco Harris	.50
7 Dan Fouts	.20
8 Steve Largent	.20
9 Johnny Unitas	1.50
10 Gale Sayers	1.00
11 Roger Staubach	2.50
12 Tony Dorsett	.50
13 Fran Tarkenton	1.00
14 Charley Taylor	.10
15 Ray Nitschke	.20
16 Jim Ringo	.10
17 Dick Butkus	1.00
18 Fred Biletnikoff	.20
19 Lenny Moore	.10
20 Len Dawson	.10
21 Lance Alworth	.10
22 Chuck Bednarik	.10
23 Raymond Berry	.10
24 Donnie Shell	.10
25 Mel Blount	.10
26 Willie Brown	.10
27 Ken Houston	.10
28 Larry Csonka	.50
29 Mike Ditka	.75
30 Art Donovan	.50
31 Sam Huff	.10
32 Lem Barney	.10
33 Hugh McElhenny	.10
34 Otto Graham	.75
35 Joe Greene	.10
36 Mike Rozier	.10
37 Lou Groza	.10
38 Ted Hendricks	.10
39 Elroy Hirsch	.10
40 Paul Hornung	.75
41 Charlie Joiner	.10
42 Deacon Jones	.20
43 Bill Bradley	.10
44 Floyd Little	.10
45 Willie Lanier	.10
46 Bob Lilly	.10
47 Sid Luckman	.10
48 John Mackey	.10
49 Don Maynard	.10
50 Mike McCormack	.10
51 Bobby Mitchell	.10
52 Ron Mix	.10
53 Marion Motley	.10
54 Leo Nomellini	.10
55 Mark Duper	.10
56 Mel Renfro	.10
57 Jim Otto	.10
58 Alan Page	.10
59 Joe Perry	.10
60 Andy Robustelli	.10
61 Lee Roy Selmon	.10
62 Jackie Smith	.10
63 Art Shell	.10
64 Jan Stenerud	.10
65 Gene Upshaw	.10
66 Y.A. Tittle	.50
67 Paul Warfield	.10
68 Kellen Winslow	.20
69 Randy White	.10
70 Larry Wilson	.10
71 Willie Wood	.10
72 Jack Ham	.10
73 Jack Youngblood	.10
74 Dan Abramowicz	.10
75 Dick Anderson	.10
76 Ken Anderson	.10
77 Steve Bartkowski	.10
78 Bill Bergey	.10
79 Rocky Bleier	.10
80 Cliff Branch	.10
81 John Brodie	.10
82 Bobby Bell	.10
83 Billy Cannon	.10
84 Gino Capelletti	.10
85 Harold Carmichael	.10
86 Dave Casper	.10
87 Wes Chandler	.10
88 Todd Christensen	.10
89 Dwight Clark	.10
90 Mark Clayton	.10
91 Cris Collinsworth	.10
92 Roger Craig	.10
93 Randy Cross	.10
94 Isaac Curtis	.10
95 Mike Curtis	.10
96 Ben Davidson	.10
97 Fred Dean	.10
98 Tom Dempsey	.10
99 Eric Dickerson	.10
100 Lynn Dickey	.10
101 John McKay	.10
102 Carl Eller	.10
103 Chuck Foreman	.10
104 Russ Francis	.10
105 Joe Gibbs	.10
106 Gary Garrison	.10
107 Randy Gradishar	.10
108 L.C. Greenwood	.10
109 Roosevelt Grier	.10
110 Steve Grogan	.10
111 Ray Guy	.10
112 John Hadl	.10
113 Jim Hart	.10
114 George Halas	.10
115 Mike Haynes	.10
116 Charlie Hennigan	.10
117 Chuck Howley	.10
118 Harold Jackson	.10
119 Tom Jackson	.10
120 Ron Jaworski	.10
121 John Jefferson	.10
122 Billy Johnson	.10
123 Ed "Too Tall" Jones	.10
124 Jack Kemp	1.50
125 Jim Kiick	.10
126 Billy Kilmer	.10
127 Jerry Kramer	.10
128 Paul Krause	.10
129 Daryle Lamonica	.10
130 Bill Walsh	.10
131 James Lofton	.10
132 Hank Stram	.10
133 Archie Manning	.10
134 Jim Marshall	.10
135 Harvey Martin	.10
136 Tommy McDonald	.10
137 Max McGee	.10
138 Reggie McKenzie	.10
139 Karl Mecklenberg	.10
140 Tom Landry	.20
141 Terry Metcalf	.10
142 Matt Millen	.10
143 Earl Morrall	.10
144 Mercury Morris	.10
145 Chuck Noll	.10
146 Joe Morris	.10
147 Mark Moseley	.10
148 Haven Moses	.10
149 Chuck Muncie	.10
150 Anthony Munoz	.10
151 Tommy Nobis	.10
152 Babe Parilli	.10
153 Drew Pearson	.10
154 Ozzie Newsome	.10
155 Jim Plunkett	.20
156 William Perry	.10
157 Johnny Robinson	.10
158 Ahmad Rashad	.30
159 George Rogers	.10
160 Sterling Sharpe	.10
161 Billy Sims	.10
162 Sid Gillman	.10
163 Mike Singletary	.10
164 Charlie Sanders	.10
165 Bubba Smith	.10
166 Ken Stabler	1.50
167 Freddie Soloman	.10
168 John Stallworth	.10
169 Dwight Stephenson	.10
170 Vince Lombardi	.30
171 Weeb Ewbank	.10
172 Lionel Taylor	.10
173 Otis Taylor	.10
174 Joe Theismann	.20
175 Bob Trumpy	.10
176 Mike Webster	.10
177 Jim Zorn	.10
178 Joe Montana	3.00
179 Packer Defense	.10
180 Bart Starr	.75
181 Max McGee	.10
182 Joe Namath	1.25
183 Johnny Unitas	.75
184 Len Dawson	.10
185 Chuck Howley	.10
186 Roger Staubach	.75
187 Paul Warfield	.10
188 Larry Csonka	.20
189 Fran Tarkenton	.20
190 Joe Green	.10
191 Ken Stabler	.10
192 Fred Biletnikoff	.10
193 Dick Anderson	.10
194 Harvey Martin	.10
195 Tony Dorsett	.20
196 Terry Bradshaw	1.00
197 John Stallworth	.10
198 Franco Harris	.20
199 Ken Anderson	.10
200 Joe Theismann	.10
201 Jim Plunkett	.10
202 Roger Craig	.10
203 William Perry	.10
204 Joe Morris	.10
205 Karl Mecklenberg	.10
206 Joe Montana	1.50
207 Joe Montana	1.50
208 Joe Montana	1.50

1997 Upper Deck Legends Big Game Hunters

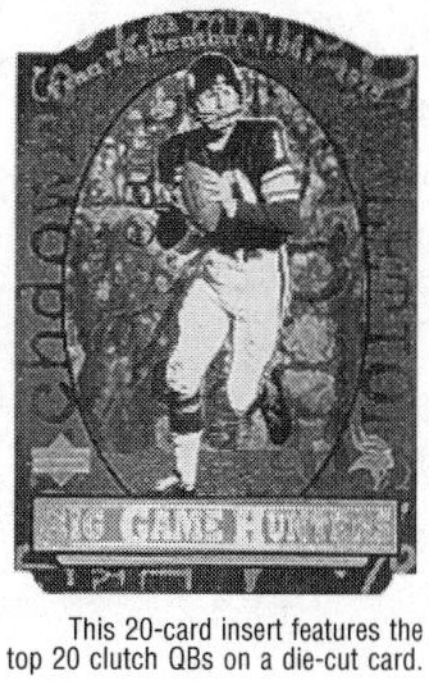

This 20-card insert features the top 20 clutch QBs on a die-cut card. They were inserted 1:75. Cards are numbered with the "BG" prefix.

	MT
Complete Set (20):	800.00
Common Player:	20.00
Minor Stars:	40.00
1 Joe Montana	100.00
2 Bart Starr	50.00
3 Roger Staubach	75.00
4 Johnny Unitas	50.00
5 Terry Bradshaw	75.00
6 Ken Stabler	50.00
7 Jim Plunkett	40.00
8 Len Dawson	20.00
9 Fran Tarkenton	50.00
10 Dan Fouts	40.00
11 Daryle Lamonica	20.00
12 Y.A. Tittle	20.00
13 Joe Namath	80.00
14 Kenny Anderson	20.00
15 John Brodie	20.00
16 Billy Kilmer	20.00
17 Earl Morrall	20.00
18 Jack Kemp	50.00
19 Steve Grogan	20.00
20 Joe Theismann	40.00

1997 Upper Deck Legends Marquee Matchups

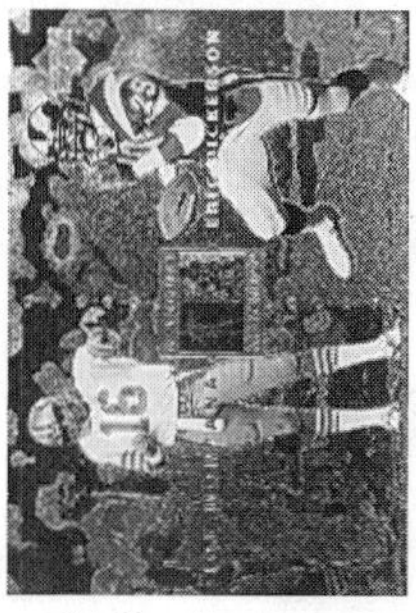

This 30-card insert features two of the NFL's greatest and creates a classic matchup. The cards use Light F/X technology and were inserted 1:17. Cards are numbered with a "MM" prefix.

	MT
Complete Set (30):	500.00
Common Player:	7.00
Minor Stars:	14.00
1 Joe Namath, Dan Fouts	30.00
2 Johnny Unitas, Joe Namath	40.00
3 Len Dawson, Bart Starr	25.00
4 Roger Staubach, Fran Tarkenton	30.00
5 Terry Bradshaw, Ken Stabler	30.00
6 Joe Montana, Kenny Anderson	45.00
7 Bart Starr, Johnny Unitas	30.00
8 Joe Greene, Jim Kiick	7.00
9 Franco Harris, Walter Payton	35.00
10 Ken Stabler, Dan Fouts	20.00
11 Charlie Joiner, Steve Largent	14.00
12 James Lofton, Drew Pearson	7.00
13 John Brodie, Deacon Jones	7.00
14 Fred Biletnikoff, Don Maynard	7.00
15 Jim Brown, Chuck Bednarik	30.00
16 Ray Nitschke, Gale Sayers	25.00
17 Paul Hornung, Dick Butkus	20.00
18 Joe Montana, Eric Dickerson	45.00
19 Tony Dorsett, Mike Singletary	14.00
20 Billy Sims, Chuck Foreman	7.00
21 Len Dawson, Willie Brown	7.00
22 Johnny Robinson, Larry Wilson	7.00
23 Marion Motley, Raymond Berry	7.00
24 Ron Mix, Jim Otto	7.00
25 Roger Staubach, Terry Bradshaw	35.00
26 Bob Lilly, Billy Kilmer	7.00
27 Ted Hendricks, Russ Francis	7.00
28 Babe Parilli, Jack Kemp	14.00
29 Deacon Jones, Alan Page	7.00
30 Dick Butkus, Ray Nitschke	25.00

1997 Upper Deck Legends Sign of the Times

This 10-card insert features autographs from some of the greatest players ever. The set was limited to less than 1,000 total cards. Cards were numbered with a "ST" prefix.

	MT
Complete Set (10):	2500.
Common Player:	125.00
1 Joe Montana	400.00
2 Fran Tarkenton	225.00
3 Johnny Unitas	275.00
4 Joe Namath	300.00
5 Terry Bradshaw	250.00
6 Jim Brown	200.00
7 Franco Harris	125.00
8 Walter Payton	300.00
9 Steve Largent	125.00
10 Bart Starr	275.00

1997 Upper Deck UD3

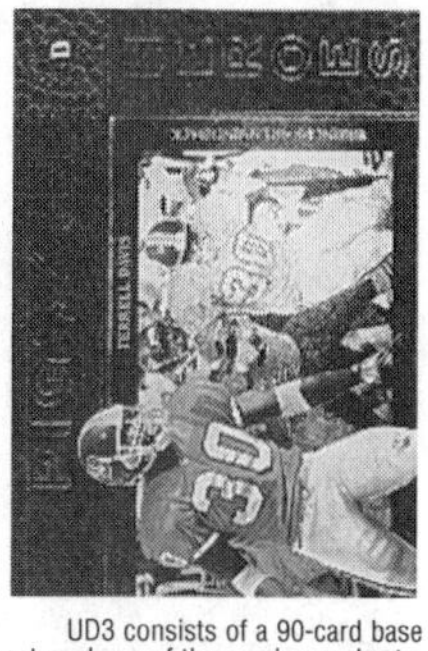

UD3 consists of a 90-card base set made up of three unique subsets. The first 30 cards are Prime Choice Rookies. The rookies are all featured with Light F/X technology. Cards 31-60 are Eye of a Champion. This subset features Cel-Chrome technology. The final subset is Pigskin Heroes. These cards feature two player shots on the front with an embossed, pigskin feel to the card. The inserts for UD3 are Generation eXcitement, Marquee Attraction and Signature Performers.

	MT
Complete Set (90):	75.00
Common Player:	.20
Minor Stars:	.40
Pack (3):	4.00
Wax Box (24):	80.00
1 *Orlando Pace*	.50
2 *Walter Jones*	.20
3 *Tony Gonzalez*	1.00
4 *David LaFleur*	1.00
5 *Jim Druckenmiller*	4.00
6 *Jake Plummer*	6.00
7 *Pat Barnes*	1.00
8 *Ike Hilliard*	1.50
9 *Reidel Anthony*	2.00
10 *Rae Carruth*	1.50
11 *Yatil Green*	.50
12 *Joey Kent*	.50
13 *Will Blackwell*	.50
14 *Kevin Lockett*	.50
15 *Warrick Dunn*	3.00
16 *Antowain Smith*	3.00
17 *Troy Davis*	.50
18 *Byron Hanspard*	1.50
19 *Corey Dillon*	5.00
20 *Darnell Autry*	1.00
21 *Peter Boulware*	.20
22 *Darrell Russell*	.20
23 *Kenny Holmes*	.20
24 *Reinard Wilson*	.20
25 *Renaldo Wynn*	.20
26 *Dwayne Rudd*	.20
27 *James Farrior*	.20
28 *Shawn Springs*	.40
29 *Bryant Westbrook*	.20
30 *Tom Knight*	.20
31 Barry Sanders	6.00
32 Brett Favre	6.00
33 Brian Mitchell	.20
34 Curtis Martin	2.00
35 Dan Marino	5.00
36 Deion Sanders	1.50
37 Drew Bledsoe	3.00
38 Eddie George	4.00
39 Edgar Bennett	.20
40 Emmitt Smith	5.00
41 Isaac Bruce	.40
42 Jerome Bettis	.40
43 Jerry Rice	3.00
44 John Elway	3.00
45 Junior Seau	.20
46 Karim Abdul-Jabbar	.50
47 Kerry Collins	.50
48 Marshall Faulk	.50
49 Marvin Harrison	.50
50 Michael Irvin	.40
51 Natrone Means	.40
52 Reggie White	.40
53 Ricky Watters	.40
54 Stan Humphries	.20
55 Steve Young	2.00
56 Terry Glenn	.50
57 Thurman Thomas	.40
58 Tony Martin	.20
59 Troy Aikman	3.00
60 Vinny Testaverde	.20
61 Anthony Johnson	.20
62 Bobby Engram	.20
63 Carl Pickens	.20
64 Cris Carter	.20
65 Derrick Witherspoon	.20
66 Eddie Kennison	.50
67 Eric Swann	.20
68 Gus Frerotte	.20
69 Herman Moore	.40
70 Irving Fryar	.20
71 Jamal Anderson	.40
72 Jeff Blake	.40
73 Jim Harbaugh	.20
74 Joey Galloway	.40
75 Keenan McCardell	.20
76 Kevin Greene	.20
77 Keyshawn Johnson	.50
78 Kordell Stewart	3.00
79 Marcus Allen	.40
80 Mario Bates	.20
81 Mark Brunell	3.00
82 Michael Jackson	.20
83 Mike Alstott	.40
84 Scott Mitchell	.20
85 Shannon Sharpe	.20
86 Steve McNair	2.50
87 Terrell Davis	3.00
88 Tim Brown	.20
89 Ty Detmer	.20
90 Tyrone Wheatley	.20

1997 Upper Deck UD3 Generation Excitement

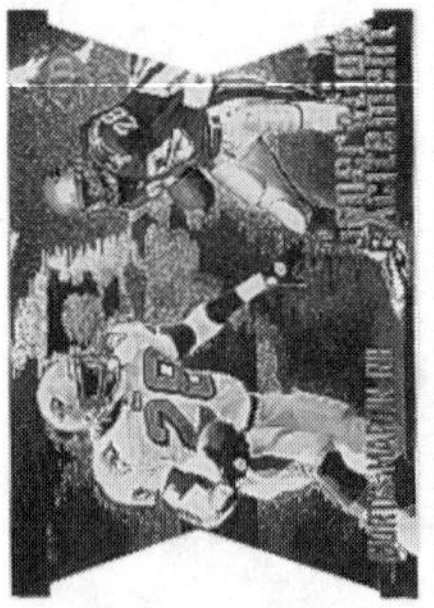

This 15-card insert features the NFL's most spectacular players. Each card has a die-cut, Light F/X design and features two action shots of the player on the front. The cards were inserted 1:11. Cards are numbered with a "GE" prefix.

		MT
Complete Set (15):		130.00
Common Player:		3.00
1	Jerry Rice	15.00
2	Carl Pickens	3.00
3	Curtis Conway	3.00
4	John Elway	15.00
5	Ike Hilliard	8.00
6	Marvin Harrison	5.00
7	Emmitt Smith	25.00
8	Barry Sanders	20.00
9	Deion Sanders	7.00
10	Rae Carruth	7.00
11	Curtis Martin	12.00
12	Terry Glenn	6.00
13	Napoleon Kaufman	5.00
14	Kordell Stewart	15.00
15	Jake Plummer	10.00

1997 Upper Deck UD3 Marquee Attraction

Marquee Attraction features the most collectible NFL players in a 15-card insert set. The cards are die-cut and feature Cel-Chrome technology. They were inserted 1:144 in UD3. Cards were numbered with a "MA" prefix.

		MT
Complete Set (15):		425.00
Common Player:		10.00
Minor Stars:		20.00
Inserted 1:144		
1	Steve Young	30.00
2	Troy Aikman	35.00
3	Keyshawn Johnson	20.00
4	Marcus Allen	10.00
5	Dan Marino	50.00
6	Mark Brunell	35.00
7	Eddie George	35.00
8	Brett Favre	70.00
9	Drew Bledsoe	35.00
10	Eddie Kennison	10.00
11	Terrell Davis	50.00
12	Warrick Dunn	35.00
13	Yatil Green	10.00
14	Troy Davis	10.00
15	Shawn Springs	10.00

1997 Upper Deck UD3 Signature Performers

Signature Performers is a four-card insert featuring special electric technology. The cards were autographed by the players in the set: Curtis Martin, Troy Aikman, Marcus Allen and Eddie George. The cards were inserted 1:1,500. Cards are numbered with a "PF" prefix.

		MT
Complete Set (4):		1100.
Common Player:		125.00
1	Curtis Martin	250.00
2	Troy Aikman	350.00
3	Marcus Allen	125.00
4	Eddie George	450.00

1998 UD3

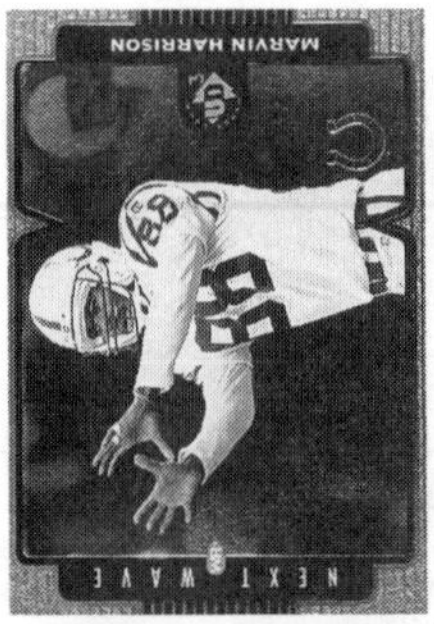

UD Cubed Football consists of a 270-card base set built from three 30-card subsets. Each subset is printed on three different technologies. Future Shock features rookies, Next Wave has young stars and Upper Realm highlights the established stars. Future Shock Embossed cards are inserted 1:6, Light F/X is seeded 1:12 and Rainbow Foil cards are found 1:1.33. Next Wave Embossed are seeded 1:4, Light F/X are found 1:1.5 and Rainbow Foil cards are inserted 1:12. Upper Realm Embossed cards are seeded 1:1.25, Light F/X are found 1:6 and Rainbow Foil cards are inserted 1:24. Die-cut versions of each card were also produced.

		MT
Complete Set (270):		750.00
Common Player (1-30):		2.50
#1-30 Inserted 1:6		
Common Player (31-60):		1.25
#31-60 Inserted 1:4		
Common Player (61-90):		.50
#61-90 Inserted 1:1.25		
Common Player (91-120):		5.00
#91-120 Inserted 1:12		
Common Player (121-150):		.50
#121-150 Inserted 1:1.5		
Common Player (151-180):		2.50
#151-180 Inserted 1:6		
Common Player (181-210):		.75
#181-210 Inserted 1:1.33		
Common Player (211-240):		5.00
#211-240 Inserted 1:12		
Common Player (241-270):		7.00
#241-270 Inserted 1:24		
Pack (3):		4.00
Wax Box (24):		90.00
1	Peyton Manning	25.00
2	Ryan Leaf	10.00
3	Andre Wadsworth	5.00
4	Charles Woodson	7.00
5	Curtis Enis	7.00
6	Grant Wistrom	2.50
7	Greg Ellis	2.50
8	Fred Taylor	12.00
9	Duane Starks	5.00
10	Keith Brooking	2.50
11	Takeo Spikes	5.00
12	Jason Peter	5.00
13	Anthony Simmons	5.00
14	Kevin Dyson	8.00
15	Brian Simmons	5.00
16	Robert Edwards	10.00
17	Randy Moss	25.00
18	John Avery	8.00
19	Marcus Nash	8.00
20	Jerome Pathon	5.00
21	Jacquez Green	6.00
22	Robert Holcombe	8.00
23	Patrick Johnson	5.00
24	Germane Crowell	8.00
25	Joe Jurevicius	5.00
26	Skip Hicks	5.00
27	Ahman Green	8.00
28	Brian Griese	8.00
29	Hines Ward	8.00
30	Tavian Banks	10.00
31	Warrick Dunn	8.00
32	Jake Plummer	8.00
33	Derrick Mayes	1.25
34	Napoleon Kaufman	2.50
35	Jamal Anderson	1.25
36	Marvin Harrison	1.25
37	Jermaine Lewis	1.25
38	Corey Dillon	6.00
39	Keyshawn Johnson	2.50
40	Mike Alstott	2.50
41	Bobby Hoying	2.50
42	Keenan McCardell	1.25
43	Will Blackwell	1.25
44	Peter Boulware	1.25
45	Tony Banks	2.50
46	Rod Smith	1.25
47	Tony Gonzalez	1.25
48	Antowain Smith	4.00
49	Rae Carruth	1.25
50	J.J. Stokes	1.25
51	Brad Johnson	2.50
52	Shawn Springs	1.25
53	Elvis Grbac	1.25
54	Jimmy Smith	2.50
55	Terry Glenn	2.50
56	Tiki Barber	1.25
57	Gus Frerotte	1.25
58	Danny Wuerffel	1.25
59	Fred Lane	2.50
60	Todd Collins	1.25
61	Barry Sanders	8.00
62	Troy Aikman	4.00
63	Dan Marino	6.00
64	Drew Bledsoe	4.00
65	Dorsey Levens	1.00
66	Jerome Bettis	1.00
67	John Elway	6.00
68	Steve Young	3.00
69	Terrell Davis	4.00
70	Kordell Stewart	3.00
71	Jeff George	1.00
72	Emmitt Smith	6.00
73	Irving Fryar	.50
74	Brett Favre	8.00
75	Eddie George	3.00
76	Terry Allen	.50
77	Warren Moon	1.00
78	Mark Brunell	3.00
79	Robert Smith	1.00
80	Jerry Rice	4.00
81	Tim Brown	1.00
82	Carl Pickens	1.00
83	Joey Galloway	1.00
84	Herman Moore	1.00
85	Adrian Murrell	1.00
86	Thurman Thomas	1.00
87	Robert Brooks	.50
88	Michael Irvin	1.00
89	Andre Rison	1.00
90	Marshall Faulk	1.00
91	Peyton Manning	45.00
92	Ryan Leaf	12.00
93	Andre Wadsworth	8.00
94	Charles Woodson	10.00
95	Curtis Enis	10.00
96	Grant Wistrom	5.00
97	Greg Ellis	5.00
98	Fred Taylor	20.00
99	Duane Starks	8.00
100	Keith Brooking	8.00
101	Takeo Spikes	8.00
102	Jason Peter	8.00
103	Anthony Simmons	8.00
104	Kevin Dyson	10.00
105	Brian Simmons	5.00
106	Robert Edwards	15.00
107	Randy Moss	45.00
108	John Avery	12.00
109	Marcus Nash	12.00
110	Jerome Pathon	8.00
111	Jacquez Green	10.00
112	Robert Holcombe	12.00
113	Patrick Johnson	8.00
114	Germane Crowell	10.00
115	Joe Jurevicius	8.00
116	Skip Hicks	8.00
117	Ahman Green	12.00
118	Brian Griese	20.00
119	Hines Ward	12.00
120	Tavian Banks	15.00
121	Warrick Dunn	4.00
122	Jake Plummer	4.00
123	Derrick Mayes	.50
124	Napoleon Kaufman	1.00
125	Jamal Anderson	1.00
126	Marvin Harrison	1.00
127	Jermaine Lewis	.50
128	Corey Dillon	3.00
129	Keyshawn Johnson	1.00
130	Mike Alstott	1.00
131	Bobby Hoying	1.00
132	Keenan McCardell	.50
133	Will Blackwell	.50
134	Peter Boulware	.50
135	Tony Banks	1.00
136	Rod Smith	.50
137	Tony Gonzalez	.50
138	Antowain Smith	2.00
139	Rae Carruth	.50
140	J.J. Stokes	.50
141	Brad Johnson	1.00
142	Shawn Springs	.50
143	Elvis Grbac	.50
144	Jimmy Smith	1.00
145	Terry Glenn	1.00
146	Tiki Barber	1.00
147	Gus Frerotte	.50
148	Danny Wuerffel	.50
149	Fred Lane	1.00
150	Todd Collins	.50
151	Barry Sanders	20.00
152	Troy Aikman	10.00
153	Dan Marino	15.00
154	Drew Bledsoe	10.00
155	Dorsey Levens	5.00
156	Jerome Bettis	5.00
157	John Elway	15.00
158	Steve Young	8.00
159	Terrell Davis	10.00
160	Kordell Stewart	8.00
161	Jeff George	5.00
162	Emmitt Smith	15.00
163	Irving Fryar	2.50
164	Brett Favre	20.00
165	Eddie George	10.00
166	Terry Allen	2.50
167	Warren Moon	5.00
168	Mark Brunell	8.00
169	Robert Smith	5.00
170	Jerry Rice	10.00
171	Tim Brown	5.00
172	Carl Pickens	5.00
173	Joey Galloway	5.00
174	Herman Moore	5.00
175	Adrian Murrell	5.00
176	Thurman Thomas	5.00
177	Robert Brooks	2.50
178	Michael Irvin	5.00
179	Andre Rison	2.50
180	Marshall Faulk	5.00
181	*Peyton Manning*	15.00
182	*Ryan Leaf*	5.00
183	*Andre Wadsworth*	1.50
184	*Charles Woodson*	4.00
185	*Curtis Enis*	4.00
186	*Grant Wistrom*	.75
187	*Greg Ellis*	1.50
188	*Fred Taylor*	7.00
189	*Duane Starks*	1.50
190	*Keith Brooking*	1.50
191	*Takeo Spikes*	1.50
192	*Jason Peter*	1.50
193	*Anthony Simmons*	1.50
194	*Kevin Dyson*	3.00
195	*Brian Simmons*	1.00
196	*Robert Edwards*	4.00
197	*Randy Moss*	15.00
198	*John Avery*	3.00
199	*Marcus Nash*	3.00
200	*Jerome Pathon*	1.50
201	*Jacquez Green*	3.00
202	*Robert Holcombe*	3.00
203	*Patrick Johnson*	1.50
204	*Germane Crowell*	5.00
205	*Joe Jurevicius*	1.50
206	*Skip Hicks*	1.50
207	*Ahman Green*	3.00
208	*Brian Griese*	6.00
209	*Hines Ward*	3.00
210	*Tavian Banks*	4.00
211	Warrick Dunn	18.00
212	Jake Plummer	18.00
213	Derrick Mayes	4.00
214	Napoleon Kaufman	6.00
215	Jamal Anderson	6.00
216	Marvin Harrison	6.00
217	Jermaine Lewis	4.00
218	Corey Dillon	12.00
219	Keyshawn Johnson	6.00
220	Mike Alstott	6.00
221	Bobby Hoying	6.00
222	Keenan McCardell	4.00
223	Will Blackwell	4.00
224	Peter Boulware	4.00
225	Tony Banks	6.00
226	Rod Smith	6.00
227	Tony Gonzalez	4.00
228	Antowain Smith	10.00
229	Rae Carruth	4.00
230	J.J. Stokes	4.00
231	Brad Johnson	6.00
232	Shawn Springs	4.00
233	Elvis Grbac	4.00
234	Jimmy Smith	6.00
235	Terry Glenn	6.00
236	Tiki Barber	6.00
237	Gus Frerotte	4.00
238	Danny Wuerffel	4.00
239	Fred Lane	6.00
240	Todd Collins	4.00
241	Barry Sanders	50.00
242	Troy Aikman	25.00
243	Dan Marino	40.00
244	Drew Bledsoe	25.00
245	Dorsey Levens	10.00
246	Jerome Bettis	10.00
247	John Elway	25.00
248	Steve Young	18.00
249	Terrell Davis	25.00
250	Kordell Stewart	20.00
251	Jeff George	10.00
252	Emmitt Smith	40.00
253	Irving Fryar	7.00
254	Brett Favre	50.00
255	Eddie George	20.00
256	Terry Allen	7.00
257	Warren Moon	10.00
258	Mark Brunell	20.00
259	Robert Smith	10.00
260	Jerry Rice	25.00
261	Tim Brown	7.00
262	Carl Pickens	7.00
263	Joey Galloway	10.00
264	Herman Moore	10.00
265	Adrian Murrell	7.00
266	Thurman Thomas	7.00
267	Robert Brooks	7.00
268	Michael Irvin	10.00
269	Andre Rison	7.00
270	Marshall Faulk	10.00

1998 UD3 Die Cuts

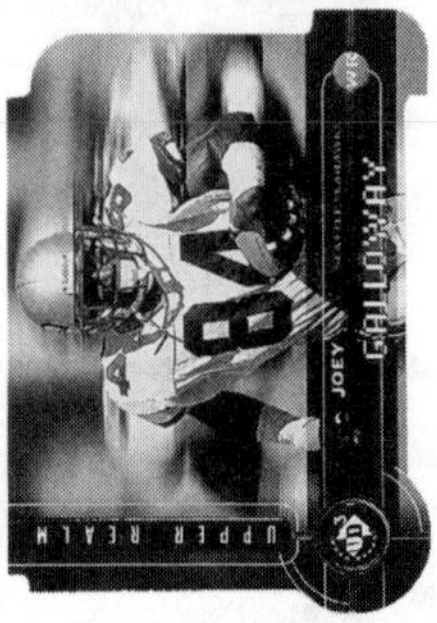

Die-cut versions were produced of each UD Cubed base card. The Embossed Die-Cut parallel is numbered to 2,000, Light F/X Die-Cut parallel cards are numbered to 1,000 and Rainbow Foil Die-Cuts are numbered to 100.

		MT
Common Player (1-90):		3.00
Production 2,000 Sets		
Common Player (91-180):		5.00
Production 1,000 Sets		
Common Player (181-270):		20.00
Production 100 Sets		
1	Peyton Manning	35.00
2	Ryan Leaf	12.00
3	Andre Wadsworth	6.00
4	Charles Woodson	15.00
5	Curtis Enis	15.00
6	Grant Wistrom	3.00
7	Greg Ellis	3.00
8	Fred Taylor	15.00
9	Duane Starks	6.00
10	Keith Brooking	3.00
11	Takeo Spikes	6.00
12	Jason Peter	6.00
13	Anthony Simmons	6.00
14	Kevin Dyson	10.00
15	Brian Simmons	6.00
16	Robert Edwards	10.00
17	Randy Moss	40.00
18	John Avery	10.00
19	Marcus Nash	10.00
20	Jerome Pathon	6.00
21	Jacquez Green	10.00
22	Robert Holcombe	10.00
23	Patrick Johnson	6.00
24	Germane Crowell	6.00
25	Joe Jurevicius	6.00
26	Skip Hicks	6.00
27	Ahman Green	10.00
28	Brian Griese	10.00
29	Hines Ward	10.00
30	Tavian Banks	12.00
31	Warrick Dunn	12.00
32	Jake Plummer	12.00
33	Derrick Mayes	3.00
34	Napoleon Kaufman	6.00
35	Jamal Anderson	3.00
36	Marvin Harrison	3.00
37	Jermaine Lewis	3.00
38	Corey Dillon	10.00
39	Keyshawn Johnson	6.00
40	Mike Alstott	6.00
41	Bobby Hoying	6.00
42	Keenan McCardell	3.00
43	Will Blackwell	3.00
44	Peter Boulware	3.00
45	Tony Banks	6.00
46	Rod Smith	3.00
47	Tony Gonzalez	3.00
48	Antowain Smith	8.00
49	Rae Carruth	3.00
50	J.J. Stokes	3.00
51	Brad Johnson	6.00
52	Shawn Springs	3.00
53	Elvis Grbac	3.00
54	Jimmy Smith	6.00
55	Terry Glenn	6.00
56	Tiki Barber	3.00
57	Gus Frerotte	3.00
58	Danny Wuerffel	3.00
59	Fred Lane	6.00
60	Todd Collins	3.00
61	Barry Sanders	25.00
62	Troy Aikman	12.00
63	Dan Marino	20.00
64	Drew Bledsoe	12.00
65	Dorsey Levens	6.00
66	Jerome Bettis	6.00
67	John Elway	12.00
68	Steve Young	10.00
69	Terrell Davis	12.00
70	Kordell Stewart	10.00
71	Jeff George	6.00
72	Emmitt Smith	20.00
73	Irving Fryar	3.00
74	Brett Favre	25.00
75	Eddie George	10.00
76	Terry Allen	3.00
77	Warren Moon	6.00
78	Mark Brunell	10.00
79	Robert Smith	6.00
80	Jerry Rice	12.00
81	Tim Brown	6.00
82	Carl Pickens	6.00
83	Joey Galloway	6.00
84	Herman Moore	6.00
85	Adrian Murrell	6.00
86	Thurman Thomas	6.00
87	Robert Brooks	3.00
88	Michael Irvin	6.00
89	Andre Rison	3.00
90	Marshall Faulk	6.00
91	Peyton Manning	50.00
92	Ryan Leaf	35.00
93	Andre Wadsworth	10.00
94	Charles Woodson	20.00
95	Curtis Enis	20.00
96	Grant Wistrom	5.00
97	Greg Ellis	10.00
98	Fred Taylor	20.00
99	Duane Starks	10.00
100	Keith Brooking	10.00
101	Takeo Spikes	10.00
102	Jason Peter	10.00
103	Anthony Simmons	10.00
104	Kevin Dyson	12.00
105	Brian Simmons	5.00
106	Robert Edwards	15.00
107	Randy Moss	55.00
108	John Avery	12.00
109	Marcus Nash	12.00
110	Jerome Pathon	10.00
111	Jacquez Green	15.00
112	Robert Holcombe	15.00
113	Patrick Johnson	10.00
114	Germane Crowell	10.00
115	Joe Jurevicius	10.00
116	Skip Hicks	10.00
117	Ahman Green	15.00
118	Brian Griese	15.00
119	Hines Ward	12.00
120	Tavian Banks	15.00
121	Warrick Dunn	20.00
122	Jake Plummer	20.00
123	Derrick Mayes	5.00
124	Napoleon Kaufman	10.00
125	Jamal Anderson	8.00
126	Marvin Harrison	8.00
127	Jermaine Lewis	5.00
128	Corey Dillon	15.00
129	Keyshawn Johnson	8.00
130	Mike Alstott	8.00
131	Bobby Hoying	8.00
132	Keenan McCardell	5.00
133	Will Blackwell	5.00
134	Peter Boulware	5.00
135	Tony Banks	8.00
136	Rod Smith	5.00
137	Tony Gonzalez	5.00
138	Antowain Smith	12.00
139	Rae Carruth	5.00
140	J.J. Stokes	5.00
141	Brad Johnson	8.00
142	Shawn Springs	5.00
143	Elvis Grbac	5.00
144	Jimmy Smith	8.00
145	Terry Glenn	8.00
146	Tiki Barber	8.00
147	Gus Frerotte	5.00
148	Danny Wuerffel	5.00
149	Fred Lane	8.00
150	Todd Collins	5.00
151	Barry Sanders	50.00
152	Troy Aikman	25.00
153	Dan Marino	40.00
154	Drew Bledsoe	25.00
155	Dorsey Levens	8.00
156	Jerome Bettis	8.00
157	John Elway	25.00
158	Steve Young	20.00
159	Terrell Davis	25.00
160	Kordell Stewart	20.00
161	Jeff George	8.00
162	Emmitt Smith	40.00
163	Irving Fryar	5.00
164	Brett Favre	50.00
165	Eddie George	20.00
166	Terry Allen	5.00
167	Warren Moon	8.00
168	Mark Brunell	20.00
169	Robert Smith	8.00
170	Jerry Rice	25.00
171	Tim Brown	8.00
172	Carl Pickens	8.00
173	Joey Galloway	8.00
174	Herman Moore	8.00
175	Adrian Murrell	8.00
176	Thurman Thomas	8.00
177	Robert Brooks	5.00
178	Michael Irvin	8.00
179	Andre Rison	5.00
180	Marshall Faulk	8.00
181	Peyton Manning	200.00
182	Ryan Leaf	100.00
183	Andre Wadsworth	40.00
184	Charles Woodson	60.00
185	Curtis Enis	75.00
186	Grant Wistrom	20.00
187	Greg Ellis	20.00
188	Fred Taylor	75.00
189	Duane Starks	20.00
190	Keith Brooking	20.00
191	Takeo Spikes	20.00
192	Jason Peter	20.00
193	Anthony Simmons	20.00
194	Kevin Dyson	50.00
195	Brian Simmons	20.00
196	Robert Edwards	50.00
197	Randy Moss	300.00
198	John Avery	50.00
199	Marcus Nash	50.00
200	Jerome Pathon	20.00
201	Jacquez Green	50.00
202	Robert Holcombe	60.00
203	Patrick Johnson	20.00
204	Germane Crowell	40.00
205	Joe Jurevicius	20.00
206	Skip Hicks	40.00
207	Ahman Green	50.00
208	Brian Griese	50.00
209	Hines Ward	50.00
210	Tavian Banks	50.00
211	Warrick Dunn	85.00
212	Jake Plummer	85.00
213	Derrick Mayes	20.00
214	Napoleon Kaufman	40.00
215	Jamal Anderson	30.00
216	Marvin Harrison	30.00
217	Jermaine Lewis	20.00
218	Corey Dillon	60.00
219	Keyshawn Johnson	30.00
220	Mike Alstott	30.00
221	Bobby Hoying	30.00
222	Keenan McCardell	20.00
223	Will Blackwell	20.00
224	Peter Boulware	20.00
225	Tony Banks	30.00
226	Rod Smith	20.00
227	Tony Gonzalez	20.00
228	Antowain Smith	50.00
229	Rae Carruth	20.00
230	J.J. Stokes	20.00
231	Brad Johnson	30.00
232	Shawn Springs	20.00
233	Elvis Grbac	20.00
234	Jimmy Smith	30.00
235	Terry Glenn	30.00
236	Tiki Barber	30.00
237	Gus Frerotte	20.00
238	Danny Wuerffel	20.00
239	Fred Lane	30.00
240	Todd Collins	20.00
241	Barry Sanders	200.00
242	Troy Aikman	100.00
243	Dan Marino	175.00
244	Drew Bledsoe	100.00
245	Dorsey Levens	30.00
246	Jerome Bettis	30.00
247	John Elway	100.00
248	Steve Young	85.00
249	Terrell Davis	100.00
250	Kordell Stewart	100.00
251	Jeff George	30.00
252	Emmitt Smith	175.00
253	Irving Fryar	20.00
254	Brett Favre	200.00
255	Eddie George	85.00
256	Terry Allen	20.00
257	Warren Moon	30.00
258	Mark Brunell	100.00
259	Robert Smith	30.00
260	Jerry Rice	100.00
261	Tim Brown	30.00
262	Carl Pickens	30.00
263	Joey Galloway	30.00
264	Herman Moore	30.00
265	Adrian Murrell	30.00
266	Thurman Thomas	30.00
267	Robert Brooks	20.00
268	Michael Irvin	30.00
269	Andre Rison	20.00
270	Marshall Faulk	30.00

1998 UD Choice Preview

Upper Deck released a 55-card UD Choice Preview set at retail outlets. The set consists of cards from the regular 1998 UD Choice set.

		MT
Complete Set (55):		10.00
Common Player:		.10
Minor Stars:		.20
Wax Box:		10.00
2	Rob Moore	.10
4	Larry Centers	.10
7	Jamal Anderson	.50
12	Byron Hanspard	.10
15	Jermaine Lewis	.10
20	Eric Moulds	.20
22	Bruce Smith	.10
26	Rae Carruth	.10
28	Winslow Oliver	.10
32	Bryan Cox	.10
35	Curtis Conway	.20
39	Jeff Blake	.10
40	Carl Pickens	.20
49	Deion Sanders	.30
53	Ed McCaffrey	.20
55	John Mobley	.10
58	Scott Mitchell	.10
62	Bryant Westbrook	.10
67	Reggie White	.20
70	LeRoy Butler	.10
72	Marshall Faulk	.50
76	Quentin Coryatt	.10
77	Keenan McCardell	.10
80	Jimmy Smith	.20
84	Andre Rison	.10
86	Tony Gonzalez	.10
92	Yatil Green	.10
96	Brad Johnson	.30
98	Jake Reed	.10
103	Troy Davis	.10
104	Andre Hastings	.10
110	Terry Glenn	.20
111	Ben Coates	.20
115	Danny Kanell	.10
119	Tiki Barber	.20
122	Glenn Foley	.20
124	Adrian Murrell	.20
129	Jeff George	.20
131	Darrell Russell	.10
136	Irving Fryar	.10
137	Mike Mamula	.10
143	Levon Kirkland	.10
147	Greg Lloyd	.10
150	Orlando Pace	.20
151	Isaac Bruce	.20
155	Eric Metcalf	.10
157	Tony Martin	.10
161	Merton Hanks	.10
165	J.J. Stokes	.20
168	Chad Brown	.10
173	Trent Dilfer	.30
175	Warren Sapp	.10
180	Steve McNair	.50
186	Gus Frerotte	.10
191	Chris Dishman	.10

1998 UD Choice

UD Choice was released in two series. Series One consists of a 255-card base set. The set has 165 regular cards featuring white borders and 27 full-bleed regular cards. Subsets include 30 Rookie Class cards and 30 Draw Your Own Trading Card contest winners. Three checklists round out the set. The base set is paralleled in Choice Reserve and Prime Choice Reserve. Inserts include StarQuest and Mini Bobbing Head cards. A Draw Your Own Trading Card entry was inserted in each pack. UD Choice Series Two consists of a 183-card base set,

featuring the 30-card Domination Next subset (1:4). Series Two also has Choice Reserve and Prime Choice Reserve parallels. Inserts include NFL GameDay '99, StarQuest-RookQuest and Domination Next SE.

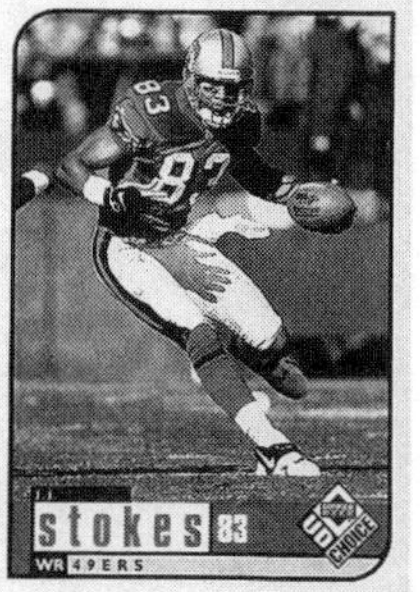

	MT
Complete Set (438):	70.00
Complete Series 1 (255):	35.00
Complete Series 2 (183):	35.00
Common Player:	.10
Minor Stars:	.20
Common Domination Next:	.75
Inserted 1:4	
Domination Next SE:	3x
Production 2,000 Sets	
Choice Reserve Stars:	5x-10x
Choice Reserve Rookies:	3x
Inserted 1:6	
PC Reserve Stars:	40x-80x
PC Reserve Rookies:	12x-25x
Production 100 Sets	
Pack (12):	1.40
Wax Box (36):	50.00

1 Jake Plummer .75
2 Rob Moore .10
3 Simeon Rice .10
4 Larry Centers .10
5 Aeneas Williams .10
6 Chris Gedney .10
7 Jamal Anderson .20
8 Michael Booker .10
9 Ronnie Bradford .10
10 Cornelius Bennett .10
11 Terance Mathis .10
12 Byron Hanspard .20
13 Peter Boulware .10
14 Jonathan Ogden .10
15 Jermaine Lewis .10
16 Tony Siragusa .10
17 Brian Kinchen .10
18 Michael Jackson .10
19 Doug Flutie .50
20 Eric Moulds .10
21 Antowain Smith .40
22 Bruce Smith .10
23 Jay Riemersma .10
24 Ruben Brown .10
25 Fred Lane .20
26 Rae Carruth .10
27 Wesley Walls .10
28 Winslow Oliver .10
29 Tyrone Poole .10
30 Lamar Lathon .10
31 Anthony Johnson .10
32 Erik Kramer .10
33 Darnell Autry .20
34 Bobby Engram .10
35 Curtis Conway .20
36 Jeff Jaeger .10
37 Chris Penn .10
38 Corey Dillon .50
39 Jeff Blake .20
40 Carl Pickens .10
41 Ki-Jana Carter .10
42 Reinard Wilson .10
43 Tremain Mack .10
44 Troy Aikman 1.00
45 Larry Allen .10
46 Darren Woodson .10
47 Anthony Miller .10
48 Erik Williams .10
49 Deion Sanders .50
50 Rick Cunningham .10
51 John Elway 1.00
52 Steve Atwater .10
53 Ed McCaffrey .10
54 Maa Tanuvasa .10
55 John Mobley .10
56 Bill Romanowski .10
57 Shannon Sharpe .20
58 Scott Mitchell .10
59 Jason Hansen .10
60 Herman Moore .20
61 Luther Elliss .10
62 Bryant Westbrook .10
63 Kevin Abrams .10
64 Brett Favre 2.00
65 Gilbert Brown .10
66 Antonio Freeman .20
67 Reggie White .20
68 Mark Chmura .10
69 Seth Joyner .10
70 LeRoy Butler .10
71 Marvin Harrison .20
72 Marshall Faulk .20
73 Ken Dilger .10
74 Steve Morrison .10
75 Zack Crockett .10
76 Quentin Coryatt .10
77 Keenan McCardell .10
78 Mark Brunell .75
79 Renaldo Wynn .10
80 Jimmy Smith .10
81 James O. Stewart .10
82 Kevin Hardy .10
83 Marcus Allen .20
84 Andre Rison .10
85 Pete Stoyanovich .10
86 Tony Gonzalez .20
87 Derrick Thomas .10
88 Rich Gannon .10
89 Elvis Grbac .10
90 Dan Marino 1.50
91 Lawrence Phillips .10
92 Yatil Green .20
93 Zach Thomas .10
94 Olindo Mare .10
95 Charles Jordan .10
96 Brad Johnson .20
97 Cris Carter .20
98 Jake Reed .10
99 Ed McDaniel .10
100 Dwayne Rudd .10
101 Leroy Hoard .10
102 Danny Wuerffel .10
103 Troy Davis .10
104 Andre Hastings .10
105 Nicky Savoie .10
106 Willie Roaf .10
107 Ray Zellars .10
108 Tedy Bruschi .10
109 Drew Bledsoe 1.00
110 Terry Glenn .20
111 Ben Coates .10
112 Willie Clay .10
113 Chris Slade .10
114 Larry Whigham .10
115 Danny Kanell .10
116 Jessie Armstead .10
117 Phillipi Sparks .10
118 Michael Strahan .10
119 Tiki Barber .20
120 Charles Way .10
121 Chris Calloway .10
122 Glenn Foley .10
123 Wayne Chrebet .10
124 Kyle Brady .10
125 Keyshawn Johnson .20
126 Aaron Glenn .10
127 James Farrior .10
128 Victor Green .10
129 Jeff George .20
130 Rickey Dudley .10
131 Darrell Russell .10
132 Tim Brown .10
133 James Trapp .10
134 Napoleon Kaufman .40
135 Bobby Hoying .10
136 Irving Fryar .10
137 Mike Mamula .10
138 Troy Vincent .10
139 Bobby Taylor .10
140 Chris Boniol .10
141 Jerome Bettis .20
142 Charles Johnson .10
143 Levon Kirkland .10
144 Carnell Lake .10
145 Will Blackwell .10
146 Tim Lester .10
147 Greg Lloyd .10
148 Tony Banks .20
149 Ryan McNeil .10
150 Orlando Pace .10
151 Isaac Bruce .20
152 Eddie Kennison .20
153 Leslie O'Neal .10
154 Darren Bennett .10
155 Natrone Means .20
156 Junior Seau .20
157 Tony Martin .10
158 Rodney Harrison .10
159 Freddie Jones .10
160 Terrell Owens .20
161 Merton Hanks .10
162 Chris Doleman .10
163 Steve Young .50
164 Chuck Levy .10
165 J.J. Stokes .20
166 Ken Norton .10
167 Bennie Blades .10
168 Chad Brown .10
169 Warren Moon .20
170 Cortez Kennedy .10
171 Darryl Williams .10
172 Michael Sinclair .10
173 Trent Dilfer .20
174 Mike Alstott .40
175 Warren Sapp .10
176 Reidel Anthony .20
177 Derrick Brooks .10
178 Horace Copeland .10
179 Hardy Nickerson .10
180 Steve McNair .50
181 Anthony Dorsett .10
182 Chris Sanders .10
183 Derrick Mason .10
184 Eddie George 1.00
185 Blaine Bishop .10
186 Gus Frerotte .10
187 Terry Allen .10
188 Darrell Green .10
189 Ken Harvey .10
190 Matt Turk .10
191 Chris Dishman .10
192 Keith Thibodeaux .10
193 *Peyton Manning* 10.00
194 *Ryan Leaf* 3.00
195 *Charles Woodson* 2.00
196 *Andre Wadsworth* 1.00
197 *Keith Brooking* .50
198 *Jason Peter* .30
199 *Curtis Enis* 2.50
200 *Randy Moss* 10.00
201 *Tre Thomas* .10
202 *Robert Edwards* 1.00
203 *Kevin Dyson* 1.00
204 *Fred Taylor* 4.00
205 *Corey Chavous* .10
206 *Grant Wistrom* .10
207 *Vonnie Holliday* .40
208 *Brian Simmons* .10
209 *Jeremy Staat* .10
210 *Alonzo Mayes* .10
211 *Anthony Simmons* .10
212 *Sam Cowart* .10
213 *Flozell Adams* .10
214 *Terry Fair* .10
215 *Germane Crowell* 1.50
216 *Robert Holcombe* 1.00
217 *Jacquez Green* 1.50
218 *Skip Hicks* .50
219 *Takeo Spikes* .40
220 *Az-Zahir Hakim* 1.00
221 *Ahman Green* 1.00
222 *Chris Fuamatu-Ma'afal* .75
223 Darnell Autry .10
224 John Randle .10
225 Scott Mitchell .10
226 Troy Aikman .30
227 Terrell Davis .30
228 Kordell Stewart .30
229 Warrick Dunn .20
230 Craig Newsome .10
231 Brett Favre .60
232 Kordell Stewart .30
233 Barry Sanders .50
234 Dan Marino .50
235 Dan Marino .50
236 Tamarick Vanover .10
237 Warrick Dunn .20
238 Andre Rison .10
239 Dan Marino .50
240 Reggie White .10
241 Tim Brown .10
242 Joe Montana .30
243 Robert Brooks .10
244 Danny Kanell .10
245 Emmitt Smith .50
246 Barry Sanders .50
247 Brett Favre .60
248 Brett Favre .60
249 Jerome Bettis .10
250 Kordell Stewart .30
251 Terrell Davis .30
252 Drew Bledsoe .30
253 Troy Aikman .30
254 Dan Marino .50
255 Warrick Dunn .10
256 Peyton Manning 10.00
257 Ryan Leaf 3.00
258 Andre Wadsworth 1.00
259 Charles Woodson 3.00
260 Curtis Enis 2.50
261 Grant Wistrom .75
262 Greg Ellis .75
263 Fred Taylor 4.00
264 Duane Starks 1.00
265 Keith Brooking .75
266 Takeo Spikes .75
267 Anthony Simmons .75
268 Kevin Dyson 2.00
269 Robert Edwards 1.25
270 Randy Moss 10.00
271 *John Avery* 1.50
272 *Marcus Nash* 1.50
273 *Jerome Pathon* 1.50
274 Jacquez Green 2.00
275 Robert Holcombe 1.00
276 *Patrick Johnson* .75
277 *Germane Crowell* 3.00
278 *Tony Simmons* 1.50
279 *Joe Jurevicius* 1.00
280 Skip Hicks .50
281 Sam Cowart .50
282 *Rashaan Shehee* .50
283 *Brian Griese* 10.00
284 *Tim Dwight* 4.00
285 Ahman Green .50
286 Adrian Murrell .20
287 Corey Chavous .10
288 Eric Swann .10
289 Frank Sanders .10
290 Eric Metcalf .10
291 *Jammi German* .50
292 Eugene Robinson .10
293 Chris Chandler .10
294 Tony Martin .10
295 Jessie Tuggle .10
296 Errict Rhett .10
297 Jim Harbaugh .10
298 Eric Green .10
299 Ray Lewis .10
300 Jamie Sharper .10
301 *Fred Coleman* .30
302 Rob Johnson .20
303 Quinn Early .10
304 Thurman Thomas .20
305 Andre Reed .10
306 Sean Gilbert .10
307 Kerry Collins .20
308 Jason Peter .10
309 Michael Bates .10
310 William Floyd .10
311 *Alonzo Mayes* .30
312 *Tony Parrish* .30
313 Walt Harris .10
314 Edgar Bennett .10
315 Jeff Jaeger .10
316 Brian Simmons .20
317 David Dunn .10
318 Ashley Ambrose .10
319 Darnay Scott .10
320 Neil O'Donnell .10
321 Flozell Adams .10
322 Stepfret Williams .10
323 Emmitt Smith 1.50
324 Michael Irvin .20
325 Chris Warren .10
326 *Eric Brown* .20
327 Rod Smith .20
328 Terrell Davis 1.50
329 Neil Smith .10
330 Darrien Gordon .10
331 *Curtis Alexander* .20
332 Barry Sanders 2.00
333 David Sloan .10
334 Johnnie Morton .10
335 Robert Porcher .10
336 Tommy Vardell .10
337 Vonnie Holliday .20
338 Dorsey Levens .20
339 Derrick Mayes .10
340 Robert Brooks .10
341 Raymont Harris .10
342 *E.G. Green* .75
343 Torrance Small .10
344 Carlton Gray .10
345 Aaron Bailey .10
346 Jeff Burris .10
347 *Donovin Darius* .20
348 *Tavian Banks* .75
349 *Aaron Beasley* .20
350 Tony Brackens .10
351 Bryce Paup .10
352 Chester McGlockton .10
353 Leslie O'Neal .10
354 Derrick Alexander .10
355 Kimble Anders .10
356 Tamarick Vanover .10
357 Brock Marion .10
358 *Larry Shannon* .20
359 Karim Abdul-Jabbar .30
360 Troy Drayton .10
361 O.J. McDuffie .10
362 John Randle .10
363 David Palmer .10
364 Robert Smith .20
365 *Kailee Wong* .20
366 Duane Clemons .10
367 *Kyle Turley* .20
368 Sean Dawkins .10
369 Lamar Smith .10
370 *Cameron Cleeland* .50
371 Keith Poole .10
372 *Tebucky Jones* .20
373 Willie McGinest .10
374 Ty Law .10
375 Lawyer Milloy .10
376 Tony Carter .10
377 *Shaun Williams* .20
378 *Brian Alford* .20
379 Tyrone Wheatley .10
380 Jason Sehorn .10
381 *David Patten* .20
382 *Scott Frost* .20
383 Mo Lewis .10
384 Kevin Williams .10
385 Curtis Martin .30
386 Vinny Testaverde .20
387 *Mo Collins* .20
388 James Jett .10
389 Eric Allen .10
390 *Jon Ritchie* .20
391 Harvey Williams .10
392 Tre Thomas .10
393 Rodney Peete .10
394 Hugh Douglas .10
395 Charlie Garner .10
396 *Karl Hankton* .20
397 Kordell Stewart .75
398 George Jones .10
399 Earl Holmes .10
400 *Hines Ward* .75
401 Jason Gildon .10
402 Ricky Proehl .10
403 Az-Zahir Hakim .20
404 Amp Lee .10
405 Eric Hill .10
406 *Leonard Little* .20
407 Charlie Jones .10
408 Craig Whelihan .10
409 Terrell Fletcher .10
410 *Kenny Bynum* .20
411 *Mikhael Ricks* .75
412 *R.W. McQuarters* .50
413 Jerry Rice 1.00
414 Garrison Hearst .20
415 Ty Detmer .10
416 Gabe Wilkins .10
417 *Michael Black* .20
418 James McKnight .10
419 Darrin Smith .10
420 Joey Galloway .20
421 Ricky Watters .20
422 Warrick Dunn .75
423 Brian Kelly .10
424 Bert Emanuel .10
425 John Lynch .10
426 Regan Upshaw .10
427 Yancey Thigpen .10
428 Kenny Holmes .10
429 Frank Wycheck .10
430 *Samari Rolle* .20
431 Brian Mitchell .10
432 Stephen Alexander .10
433 Jamie Asher .10
434 Michael Westbrook .10
435 Dana Stubblefield .10
436 Dan Wilkinson .10
437 Checklist (Dan Marino) .75
438 Checklist (Jerry Rice) .50

1998 UD Choice Choice Reserve

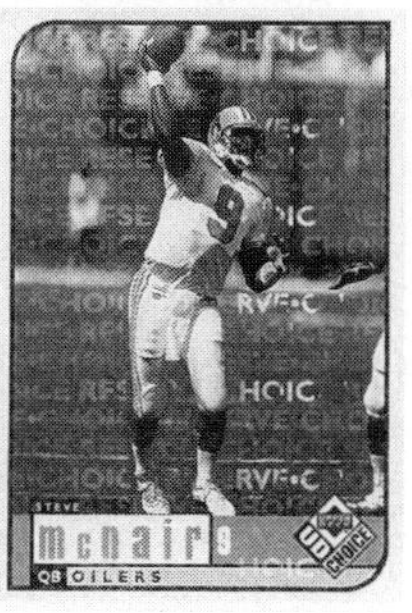

Choice Reserve is a parallel of the entire 438-card UD Choice set (255 cards from Series One and 183 from Series Two). The parallel was inserted one per six packs in each series.

	MT
Choice Reserve Cards:	5x-10x
Choice Reserve Rookies:	3x

1998 UD Choice Prime Choice Reserve

Prime Choice Reserve is a parallel of the complete 438-card UD Choice base set (255 cards from Series One and 183 from Series Two). This hobby-only set has "Prime Choice Reserve" foil-stamped on the card fronts and is numbered to 100.

	MT
PC Reserve Cards:	40x-80x
PC Reserve Rookies:	12x-25x

1998 UD Choice Mini Bobbing Head

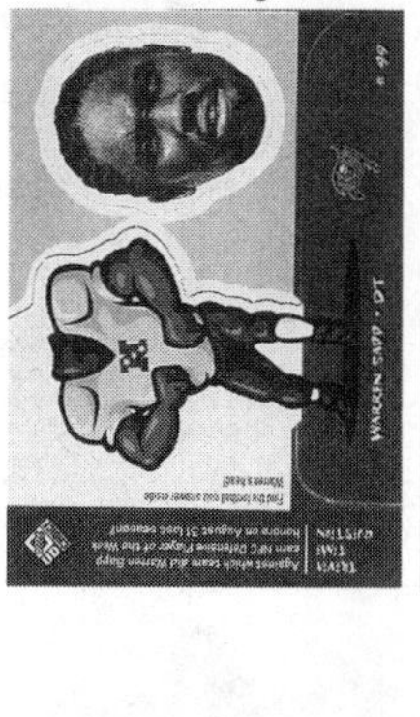

Mini Bobbing Head cards were an insert in Series One. The 30-card set consists of cards that can be folded into a stand-up figure with a removable bobbing head. The cards were inserted one per four packs.

		MT
Complete Set (30):		15.00
Common Player:		.25
Minor Stars:		.50
M1	Jake Plummer	1.25
M2	Jamal Anderson	.25
M3	Michael Jackson	.25
M4	Bruce Smith	.25
M5	Rae Carruth	.25
M6	Curtis Conway	.25
M7	Jeff Blake	.50
M8	Troy Aikman	1.50
M9	Michael Irvin	.50
M10	Terrell Davis	1.50
M11	Barry Sanders	3.00
M12	Herman Moore	.50
M13	Reggie White	.50
M14	Dorsey Levens	.50
M15	Marvin Harrison	.25
M16	Keenan McCardell	.25
M17	Andre Rison	.25
M18	Dan Marino	3.00
M19	Curtis Martin	1.00
M20	Keyshawn Johnson	.25
M21	Tim Brown	.25
M22	Kordell Stewart	1.50
M23	Gregg Lloyd	.25
M24	Junior Seau	.25
M25	Jerry Rice	1.50
M26	Merton Hanks	.25
M27	Joey Galloway	.50
M28	Warrick Dunn	1.25
M29	Warren Sapp	.25
M30	Darrell Green	.25

1998 UD Choice Starquest Blue

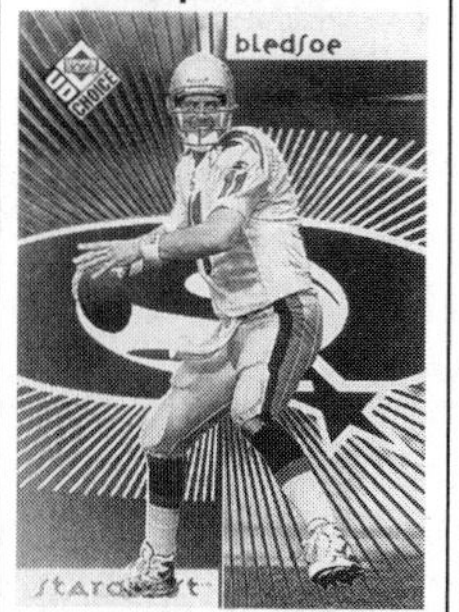

StarQuest is a 30-card, four-tiered insert in UD Choice Series One. Each tier has a different insertion rate and foil color. StarQuest 1-Star cards were seeded 1:1, 2-Star cards were found 1:7, 3-Stars were inserted 1:23 and 4-Star cards are numbered to 100.

		MT
Complete Set (30):		15.00
Common Player:		.25
Minor Stars:		.50
Green Cards:		2x-4x
Red Cards:		5x-10x
Gold Cards:		40x-80x
W1	Warren Moon	.25
W2	Jerry Rice	1.00
W3	Jeff George	.25
W4	Brett Favre	2.00
W5	Junior Seau	.25
W6	Cris Carter	.25
W7	John Elway	1.00
W8	Troy Aikman	1.00
W9	Steve Young	.75
W10	Kordell Stewart	1.00
W11	Drew Bledsoe	1.00
W12	Dorsey Levens	.50
W13	Dan Marino	1.75
W14	Joey Galloway	.50
W15	Antonio Freeman	.50
W16	Jake Plummer	1.00
W17	Corey Dillon	.75
W18	Mark Brunell	.75
W19	Andre Rison	.25
W20	Barry Sanders	1.50
W21	Deion Sanders	.60
W22	Emmitt Smith	1.75
W23	Antowain Smith	.60
W24	Herman Moore	.50
W25	Napoleon Kaufman	.60
W26	Jerome Bettis	.50
W27	Eddie George	1.00
W28	Warrick Dunn	1.00
W29	Adrian Murrell	.25
W30	Terrell Davis	1.00

Values quoted in this guide reflect the retail price of a card — the price a collector can expect to pay when buying a card from a dealer. The wholesale price — that which a collector can expect to receive from a dealer when selling cards — will be significantly lower, depending on desirability and condition.

1998 Upper Deck

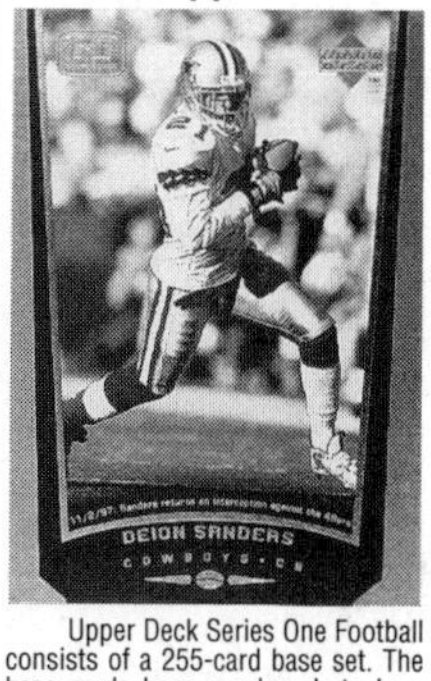

Upper Deck Series One Football consists of a 255-card base set. The base cards have a color photo bordered on three sides, with the player's name, team and position printed at the bottom. The set consists of 210 regular cards, 42 Star Rookie subset cards (1:4) and three checklists. The set is paralleled in UD Exclusives. Inserts include SuperPowers, Constant Threat, Define the Game (each with a tiered Quantum parallel), Game Jerseys and Hobby-Exclusive Game Jerseys.

	MT
Complete Set (255):	250.00
Common Player:	.15
Minor Stars:	.30
Common Rookie (1-42):	2.50
Bronze Cards:	40x-80x
Bronze Rookies:	2x-4x
Pack (10):	6.00
Wax Box (24):	125.00

1 *Peyton Manning* 40.00
2 *Ryan Leaf* 12.00
3 *Andre Wadsworth* 5.00
4 *Charles Woodson* 10.00
5 *Curtis Enis* 5.00
6 *Grant Wistrom* 2.50
7 *Greg Ellis* 2.50
8 *Fred Taylor* 15.00
9 *Duane Starks* 2.50
10 *Keith Brooking* 2.50
11 *Takeo Spikes* 4.00
12 *Jason Peter* 4.00
13 *Anthony Simmons* 2.50
14 *Kevin Dyson* 8.00
15 *Brian Simmons* 2.50
16 *Robert Edwards* 12.00
17 *Randy Moss* 40.00
18 *John Avery* 6.00
19 *Marcus Nash* 6.00
20 *Jerome Pathon* 4.00
21 *Jacquez Green* 8.00
22 *Robert Holcombe* 12.00
23 *Patrick Johnson* 2.50
24 *Germane Crowell* 12.00
25 *Joe Jurevicius* 4.00
26 *Skip Hicks* 6.00
27 *Ahman Green* 15.00
28 *Brian Griese* 20.00
29 *Hines Ward* 6.00
30 *Tavian Banks* 10.00
31 *Tony Simmons* 4.00
32 *Victor Riley* 2.50
33 *Rashaan Shehee* 4.00
34 *R.W. McQuarters* 2.50
35 *Flozell Adams* 2.50
36 *Tre Thomas* 2.50
37 *Greg Favors* 2.50
38 *Jon Ritchie* 2.50
39 *Jessie Haynes* 2.50
40 *Ryan Sutter* 2.50
41 *Mo Collins* 2.50
42 *Tim Dwight* 8.00
43 Chris Chandler .15
44 Byron Hanspard .15
45 Jessie Tuggle .15
46 Jamal Anderson .30
47 Terance Mathis .15
48 Morten Andersen .15
49 Jake Plummer 2.00
50 Mario Bates .15
51 Frank Sanders .15
52 Adrian Murrell .30
53 Simeon Rice .15
54 Aeneas Williams .15
55 Eric Swann .15
56 Jim Harbaugh .15
57 Michael Jackson .15
58 Peter Boulware .15
59 Errict Rhett .15
60 Jermaine Lewis .15
61 Eric Zeier .15
62 Rod Woodson .15
63 Rob Johnson .30
64 Antowain Smith 1.00
65 Bruce Smith .15
66 Eric Moulds .15
67 Andre Reed .15
68 Thurman Thomas .30
69 Lonnie Johnson .15
70 Kerry Collins .50
71 Kevin Greene .15
72 Fred Lane .30
73 Rae Carruth .15
74 Michael Bates .15
75 William Floyd .15
76 Sean Gilbert .15
77 Erik Kramer .15
78 Edgar Bennett .15
79 Curtis Conway .30
80 Darnell Autry .15
81 Ryan Wetnight .15
82 Walt Harris .15
83 Bobby Engram .15
84 Jeff Blake .30
85 Carl Pickens .30
86 Darnay Scott .15
87 Corey Dillon 1.25
88 Reinard Wilson .15
89 Ashley Ambrose .15
90 Troy Aikman 1.50
91 Michael Irvin .30
92 Emmitt Smith 2.50

93	Deion Sanders	.50
94	David LaFleur	.15
95	Chris Warren	.15
96	Darren Woodson	.15
97	John Elway	1.50
98	Terrell Davis	1.50
99	Rod Smith	.30
100	Shannon Sharpe	.30
101	Ed McCaffrey	.15
102	Steve Atwater	.15
103	John Mobley	.15
104	Darrian Gordon	.15
105	Barry Sanders	3.00
106	Scott Mitchell	.15
107	Herman Moore	.30
108	Johnnie Morton	.15
109	Robert Porcher	.15
110	Bryant Westbrook	.15
111	Tommy Vardell	.15
112	Brett Favre	3.00
113	Dorsey Levens	.30
114	Reggie White	.30
115	Antonio Freeman	.30
116	Robert Brooks	.15
117	Mark Chmura	.30
118	Derrick Mayes	.15
119	Gilbert Brown	.15
120	Marshall Faulk	.30
121	Torrance Small	.15
122	Marvin Harrison	.30
123	Quentin Coryatt	.15
124	Ken Dilger	.15
125	Zack Crockett	.15
126	Mark Brunell	1.25
127	Bryce Paup	.15
128	Tony Brackens	.15
129	Renaldo Wynn	.15
130	Keenan McCardell	.15
131	Jimmy Smith	.30
132	Kevin Hardy	.15
133	Elvis Grbac	.15
134	Tamarick Vanover	.15
135	Chester McGlockton	.15
136	Andre Rison	.15
137	Derrick Alexander	.15
138	Tony Gonzalez	.15
139	Derrick Thomas	.15
140	Dan Marino	2.50
141	Karim Abdul-Jabbar	.30
142	O.J. McDuffie	.15
143	Yatil Green	.15
144	Charles Jordan	.15
145	Brock Marion	.15
146	Zach Thomas	.15
147	Brad Johnson	.30
148	Cris Carter	.30
149	Jake Reed	.15
150	Robert Smith	.30
151	John Randle	.15
152	Dwayne Rudd	.15
153	Randall Cunningham	.15
154	Drew Bledsoe	1.25
155	Terry Glenn	.30
156	Ben Coates	.15
157	Willie Clay	.15
158	Chris Slade	.15
159	Derrick Cullors	.15
160	Ty Law	.15
161	Danny Wuerffel	.30
162	Andre Hastings	.15
163	Troy Davis	.30
164	Billy Joe Hobert	.15
165	Eric Guliford	.15
166	Mark Fields	.15
167	Alex Molden	.15
168	Danny Kanell	.15
169	Tiki Barber	.30
170	Charles Way	.15
171	Amani Toomer	.15
172	Michael Strahan	.15
173	Jesse Armstead	.15
174	Jason Sehorn	.15
175	Glenn Foley	.30
176	Curtis Martin	1.00
177	Aaron Glenn	.15
178	Keyshawn Johnson	.30
179	James Farrior	.15
180	Wayne Chrebet	.15
181	Keith Byars	.15
182	Jeff George	.30
183	Napoleon Kaufman	.50
184	Tim Brown	.30
185	Darrell Russell	.15
186	Rickey Dudley	.15
187	James Jett	.15
188	Desmond Howard	.15
189	Bobby Hoying	.15
190	Charlie Garner	.15
191	Irving Fryar	.15
192	Chris T. Jones	.15
193	Mike Mamula	.15
194	Troy Vincent	.15
195	Kordell Stewart	1.50
196	Jerome Bettis	.30
197	Will Blackwell	.15
198	Levon Kirkland	.15
199	Carnell Lake	.15
200	Charles Johnson	.15
201	Greg Lloyd	.15
202	Donnell Woolford	.15
203	Tony Banks	.30
204	Amp Lee	.15
205	Isaac Bruce	.30
206	Eddie Kennison	.30
207	Ryan McNeil	.15
208	Craig Heyward	.15
209	Ernie Conwell	.15
210	Natrone Means	.30
211	Junior Seau	.30
212	Tony Martin	.15
213	Freddie Jones	.15
214	Bryan Still	.15
215	Rodney Harrison	.15
216	Steve Young	1.00
217	Jerry Rice	1.50
218	Garrison Hearst	.15
219	J.J. Stokes	.15
220	Ken Norton	.15
221	Greg Clark	.15
222	Bryant Young	.15
223	Gabe Wilkins	.15
224	Warren Moon	.30
225	Jon Kitna	.30
226	Ricky Watters	.30
227	Chad Brown	.15
228	Joey Galloway	.30
229	Shawn Springs	.15
230	Cortez Kennedy	.15
231	Trent Dilfer	.30
232	Warrick Dunn	2.00
233	Mike Alstott	.30
234	Warren Sapp	.15
235	Bert Emanuel	.15
236	Reidel Anthony	.15
237	Hardy Nickerson	.15
238	Derrick Brooks	.15
239	Steve McNair	.50
240	Yancey Thigpen	.15
241	Anthony Dorsett	.15
242	Blaine Bishop	.15
243	Kenny Holmes	.15
244	Eddie George	1.25
245	Chris Sanders	.15
246	Gus Frerotte	.15
247	Terry Allen	.15
248	Dana Stubblefield	.15
249	Michael Westbrook	.15
250	Darrell Green	.15
251	Brian Mitchell	.15
252	Ken Harvey	.15
253	Checklist A (Troy Aikman)	.75
254	Checklist B (Dan Marino)	1.25
255	Checklist C (Herman Moore)	.15

1998 Upper Deck Bronze

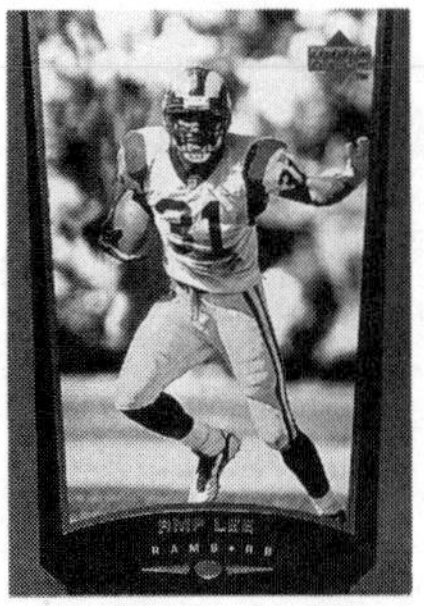

The UD Exclusives set parallels the Upper Deck Series One base set. One level is numbered to 100 and the other is a 1-of-1 set.

	MT
Bronze Cards:	40x-80x
Bronze Rookies:	2x-4x

1998 Upper Deck Constant Threat

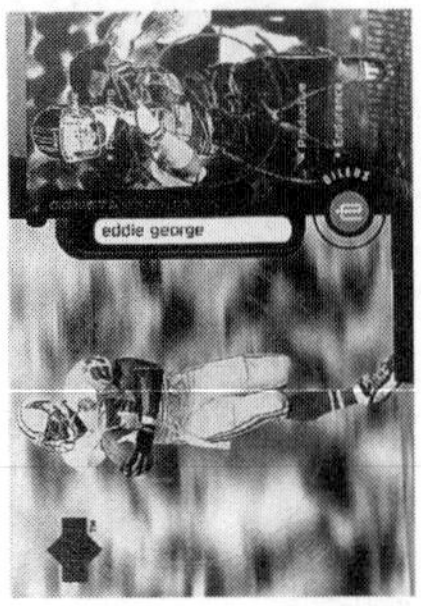

Constant Threat is a 30-card insert seeded one per 12 packs. The cards have a horizontal layout and two player photos. The color player photo is on the left and a negative exposure is on the right. The cards also feature blue foil highlights. Cards are numbered with a "CT" prefix.

		MT
Complete Set (30):		150.00
Common Player:		1.50
Minor Stars:		3.00
Bronze Cards:		20x-40x
Silver Cards:		2x
1	Dan Marino	12.00
2	Peyton Manning	15.00
3	Randy Moss	20.00
4	Brett Favre	15.00
5	Mark Brunell	6.00
6	Keyshawn Johnson	1.50
7	John Elway	6.00
8	Troy Aikman	7.00
9	Steve Young	5.00
10	Kordell Stewart	6.00
11	Drew Bledsoe	7.00
12	Joey Galloway	3.00
13	Elvis Grbac	1.50
14	Marvin Harrison	3.00
15	Napoleon Kaufman	4.00
16	Ryan Leaf	8.00
17	Jake Plummer	7.00
18	Terrell Davis	10.00
19	Steve McNair	5.00
20	Barry Sanders	15.00
21	Deion Sanders	4.00
22	Emmitt Smith	12.00
23	Antowain Smith	4.00
24	Herman Moore	3.00
25	Curtis Martin	6.00
26	Jerry Rice	7.00
27	Eddie George	6.00
28	Warrick Dunn	7.00
29	Curtis Enis	8.00
30	Michael Irvin	3.00

1998 Upper Deck Constant Threat Bronze/Silver

The Constant Threat insert has a three-tiered Quantum parallel. The cards are die-cut and sequentially numbered. Tier One features silver foil and is numbered to 1,000, Tier Two has bronze foil and numbering to 25 and Tier Three has gold foil and is a 1-of-1 set.

	MT
Bronze Cards:	20x-40x
Silver Cards:	2x-4x

1998 Upper Deck Define the Game

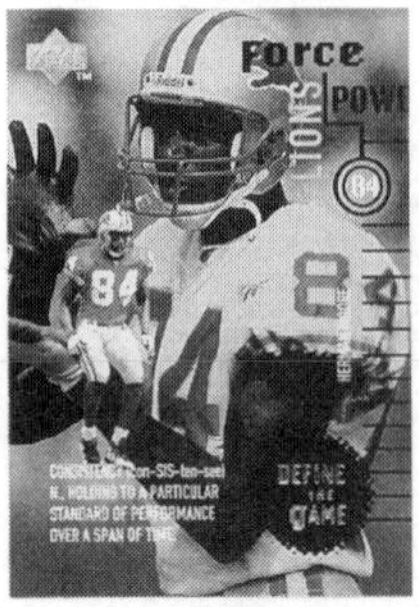

Define the Game is a 30-card insert seeded one per eight packs. The cards feature a small color photo of the player with a larger black-and-white photo in the background. The front of each card has a word that describes the player and the definition. Cards are numbered with a "DG" prefix.

		MT
Complete Set (30):		100.00
Common Player:		1.00
Minor Stars:		2.00
Bronze Cards:		15x-30x
Silver Cards:		2x
1	Dan Marino	10.00
2	Curtis Enis	6.00
3	Dorsey Levens	2.00
4	Charles Woodson	4.00
5	Junior Seau	1.00
6	Tiki Barber	1.00
7	Randy Moss	12.00
8	Troy Aikman	6.00
9	Jake Plummer	6.00
10	Corey Dillon	4.00
11	Jerry Rice	6.00
12	Emmitt Smith	10.00
13	Herman Moore	2.00
14	Brad Johnson	2.00
15	Gus Frerotte	1.00
16	Ryan Leaf	7.00
17	Shannon Sharpe	1.00
18	Jermaine Lewis	1.00
19	Jerome Bettis	2.00
20	Barry Sanders	12.00
21	Terry Allen	1.00
22	Reidel Anthony	1.00
23	Isaac Bruce	2.00
24	Mike Alstott	3.00
25	Rae Carruth	1.00
26	Tamarick Vanover	1.00
27	Eddie George	5.00
28	Warrick Dunn	6.00
29	Tony Gonzalez	1.00
30	Keenan McCardell	1.00

1998 Upper Deck Define the Game Bronze/Silver

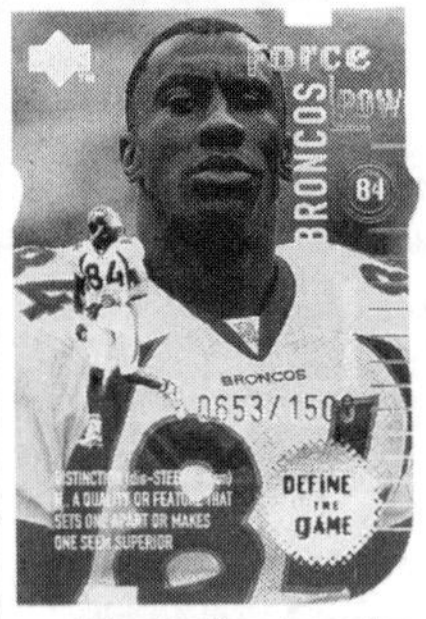

Define the Game has a three-tiered Quantum parallel. The cards are die-cut and sequentially numbered. Tier One is numbered to 1,500, Tier Two to 50 and Tier Three to 1.

	MT
Bronze Cards:	15x-30x
Silver Cards:	2x

1998 Upper Deck Game Jersey

The Game Jersey insert features 10 cards inserted 1:2,500. The set contains both veterans and rookies. The veteran cards feature a piece of game-used jersey and the rookie cards have a piece of jersey worn during the NFL rookie photo shoot. Dan Marino signed 13 of his cards. Cards are numbered with "GJ" prefix.

		MT
Complete Set (10):		3000.
Common Player:		150.00
1	Brett Favre	600.00
2	Reggie White	150.00
3	Barry Sanders	625.00
4	John Elway	425.00
5	Mark Brunell	300.00
6	Mike Alstott	200.00
7	Ryan Leaf	200.00
8	Andre Wadsworth	150.00
9	Robert Edwards	175.00
10	Kevin Dyson	150.00

1998 Upper Deck Hobby Exclusive Game Jerseys

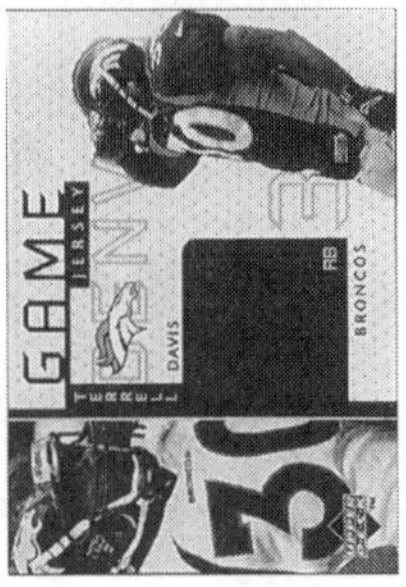

The Hobby-Exclusive Game Jersey insert features 10-cards inserted 1:288. The set features veterans and rookies. The veteran cards have a piece of game-worn jersey and the rookie cards have a piece of jersey from the NFL rookie photo shoot. Cards are numbered with "GJ" prefix.

		MT
Complete Set (10):		900.00
Common Player:		40.00
11	Dan Marino	250.00
12	Deion Sanders	100.00
13	Steve Young	110.00
14	Terrell Davis	140.00
15	Tim Brown	40.00
16	Peyton Manning	250.00
17	Takeo Spikes	40.00
18	Curtis Enis	100.00
19	Fred Taylor	125.00
20	John Avery	85.00

1998 Upper Deck SuperPowers

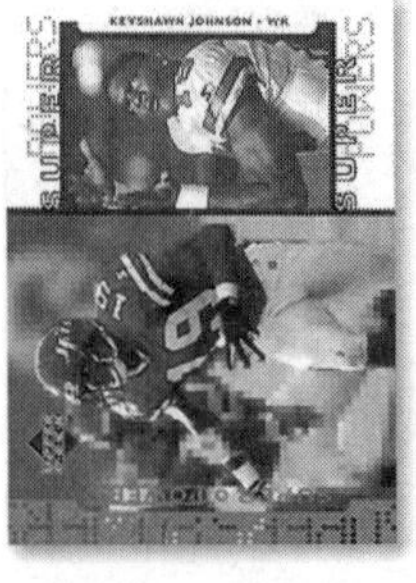

SuperPowers is a 30-card insert seeded one per four packs. The cards have a horizontal layout and feature a color photo on the left with a black-and-white photo on the right.

		MT
Complete Set (30):		45.00
Common Player:		.50
Minor Stars:		1.00
Bronze Cards:		10x-20x
Silver Cards:		2x
S1	Dan Marino	5.00
S2	Jerry Rice	3.00
S3	Napoleon Kaufman	1.50
S4	Brett Favre	6.00
S5	Andre Rison	.50
S6	Jerome Bettis	1.00
S7	John Elway	2.00
S8	Troy Aikman	3.00
S9	Steve Young	1.50
S10	Kordell Stewart	3.00
S11	Drew Bledsoe	3.00
S12	Antonio Freeman	1.00
S13	Mark Brunell	2.00
S14	Shannon Sharpe	.50
S15	Trent Dilfer	1.00
S16	Peyton Manning	6.00
S17	Cris Carter	.50
S18	Michael Irvin	1.00
S19	Terry Glenn	1.00
S20	Keyshawn Johnson	1.00
S21	Deion Sanders	1.50
S22	Emmitt Smith	5.00
S23	Marcus Allen	1.00
S24	Dorsey Levens	1.00
S25	Jake Plummer	3.00
S26	Eddie George	3.00
S27	Tim Brown	.50
S28	Warrick Dunn	3.00
S29	Reggie White	1.00
S30	Terrell Davis	3.00

1998 Upper Deck SuperPowers Bronze/Silver

The SuperPowers insert has a three-tiered Quantum parallel. The cards are die-cut and sequentially numbered. Tier One is numbered to 2,000, Tier Two to 100 and Tier Three is a 1-of-1 set.

	MT
Bronze Cards:	10x-20x
Silver Cards:	2x

1998 Upper Deck Black Diamond

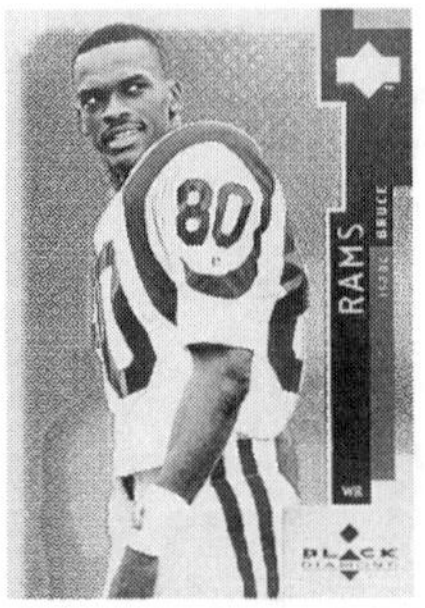

The Black Diamond Football base set consists of 150 cards designated by the Black Diamond logo and a single Black Diamond in the lower right corner. Three parallel versions were produced. Double Black Diamond cards (inserted 1:1) have two diamonds and red Light F/X backgrounds. Triple Black Diamonds (1:5) have gold Light F/X backgrounds and Quadruple Black Diamonds (50 total sets) have black Light F/X backgrounds. The Premium Cuts insert (30 cards) features the same four diamond levels of scarcity and a special die-cut. Single Diamond (1:7), Double Diamond (1:15), Triple Diamond (1:30) and Quadruple Diamond (1:180) versions were created. Upper Deck also included a hobby-only "Mystery Premium Cut" insert in Black Diamond. The 30 cards feature Black Light F/X backgrounds, embossing and a horizontal die-cut design. The cards in the "Mystery" insert have different insertion rates.

		MT
Complete Set (150):		50.00
Common Player:		.25
Minor Stars:		.50
Doubles:		2x
Triples:		3x-6x
Quadruples:		40x-80x
Pack (6):		4.00
Wax Box (30):		95.00
1	Kent Graham	.25
2	Darrell Russell	.25
3	Jim Harbaugh	.25
4	Cornelius Bennett	.25
5	Troy Vincent	.25
6	Natrone Means	.50
7	Michael Jackson	.25
8	Will Blackwell	.25
9	Greg Hill	.25
10	Andre Reed	.25
11	Darren Bennett	.25
12	Dan Marino	5.00
13	Tshimanga Biakabutuka	.25
14	Terrell Owens	.75
15	Cris Carter	.25
16	Darnell Autry	.50
17	Joey Galloway	.50
18	Terry Glenn	1.00
19	Ki-Jana Carter	.25
20	Isaac Bruce	.50
21	Shawn Jefferson	.25
22	Michael Irvin	.50
23	Warren Sapp	.25
24	Dave Brown	.25
25	Terrell Davis	2.50
26	Frank Wycheck	.25
27	Neil O'Donnell	.25
28	Scott Mitchell	.25
29	Michael Westbrook	.25
30	Tim Brown	.50
31	Antonio Freeman	.75
32	Jake Plummer	2.00
33	Irving Fryar	.25
34	Quentin Coryatt	.25
35	Jamal Anderson	.50
36	Jerome Bettis	.50
37	Keenan McCardell	.25
38	Derrick Alexander	.25
39	Stan Humphries	.25
40	Andre Rison	.25
41	Bruce Smith	.25
42	Garrison Hearst	.25
43	Zach Thomas	.50
44	Rae Carruth	.50
45	Kevin Greene	.25
46	Robert Smith	.25
47	Curtis Conway	.50
48	Christian Fauria	.25
49	Curtis Martin	2.00
50	Dan Wilkinson	.25
51	Eddie Kennison	.75
52	Mark Fields	.25
53	Anthony Miller	.25
54	Mike Alstott	1.00
55	Tiki Barber	.75
56	Neil Smith	.25
57	Gus Frerotte	.25
58	Adrian Murrell	.50
59	Johnnie Morton	.25
60	O.J. McDuffie	.25
61	Napoleon Kaufman	.50
62	Robert Brooks	.25
63	Byron Hanspard	.75
64	Ty Detmer	.25
65	Mark Brunell	2.00
66	Bam Morris	.25
67	Kordell Stewart	2.50
68	Elvis Grbac	.25
69	Antowain Smith	1.50
70	Junior Seau	.50
71	Tony Gonzalez	.50
72	Anthony Johnson	.25
73	Steve Young	1.50
74	Brian Manning	.25
75	Rick Mirer	.25
76	Warren Moon	.50
77	Torrian Gray	.25
78	Carl Pickens	.25
79	Tony Banks	1.00
80	Willie McGinest	.25
81	Deion Sanders	1.25
82	Warrick Dunn	3.00
83	Danny Wuerffel	.75
84	Rod Smith	.25
85	Steve McNair	1.75
86	Danny Kanell	.25
87	Herman Moore	.50
88	Brian Mitchell	.25
89	James Farrior	.25
90	Reggie White	.50
91	Simeon Rice	.25
92	James Jett	.25
93	Marshall Faulk	.50
94	Chris Chandler	.25
95	Mike Mamula	.25
96	Jimmy Smith	.25
97	Jamie Sharper	.25
98	Carnell Lake	.25
99	Marcus Allen	.50
100	Thurman Thomas	.50
101	Freddie Jones	.25
102	Karim Abdul-Jabbar	1.00
103	Kerry Collins	.50
104	Jerry Rice	2.50
105	Brad Johnson	.50
106	Raymont Harris	.25
107	Lamar Smith	.25
108	Drew Bledsoe	2.00
109	Corey Dillon	2.00
110	Lawrence Phillips	.25
111	Heath Shuler	.25
112	Emmitt Smith	4.00
113	Reidel Anthony	1.00
114	Ike Hilliard	.75
115	Shannon Sharpe	.25
116	Chris Sanders	.25
117	Keyshawn Johnson	.75
118	Barry Sanders	3.00
119	Cris Dishman	.25
120	Jeff George	.50
121	Dorsey Levens	.50
122	Rob Moore	.25
123	Ricky Watters	.50
124	Marvin Harrison	.75
125	Vinny Testaverde	.25
126	Charles Johnson	.25
127	Renaldo Wynn	.25
128	Todd Collins	.25
129	Tony Martin	.25
130	Derrick Thomas	.25
131	Wesley Walls	.25
132	Rod Woodson	.25
133	Troy Drayton	.25
134	Bryan Cox	.25
135	Shawn Springs	.25
136	Jake Reed	.25
137	Jeff Blake	.50
138	Craig Heyward	.25
139	Ben Coates	.25
140	Troy Aikman	2.50
141	Trent Dilfer	1.00
142	Troy Davis	.75
143	John Elway	2.00
144	Eddie George	2.50
145	Rodney Hampton	.25
146	Ed McCaffrey	.25
147	Terry Allen	.25
148	Wayne Chrebet	.25
149	Brett Favre	5.00
150	Daryl Johnston	.25

1998 Upper Deck Black Diamond Premium Cut

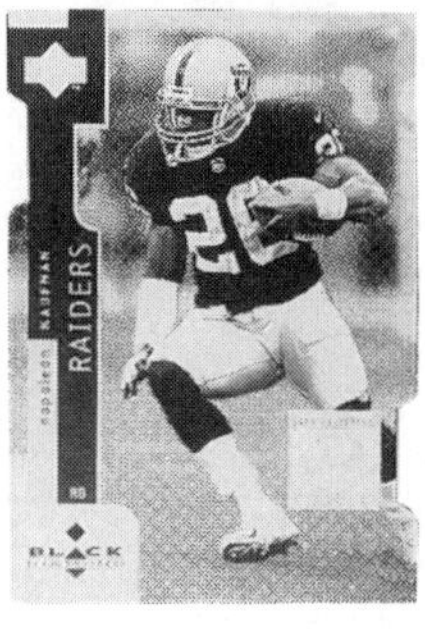

Premium Cut is a 30-card insert with four diamond versions. The cards have a special die-cut and Light F/X technology. Single Diamond (inserted 1:7), Double Diamond (1:15), Triple Diamond (1:30) and Quadruple Diamond (1:180) versions were produced. Cards are numbered with a "PC" prefix.

		MT
Complete Set (30):		225.00
Common Player:		3.00
Minor Stars:		6.00
Doubles:		2x
Triples:		2x-4x
Quad Horizontals:		2x-4x
Quad Verticals:		5x-10x
1	Karim Abdul-Jabbar	6.00
2	Troy Aikman	12.00
3	Kerry Collins	6.00
4	Drew Bledsoe	12.00
5	Barry Sanders	20.00
6	Marcus Allen	6.00
7	John Elway	12.00
8	Adrian Murrell	3.00
9	Junior Seau	3.00
10	Eddie George	12.00
11	Antowain Smith	8.00
12	Reggie White	6.00
13	Dan Marino	24.00
14	Joey Galloway	6.00
15	Kordell Stewart	12.00
16	Terry Allen	3.00
17	Napoleon Kaufman	6.00
18	Curtis Martin	12.00
19	Steve Young	10.00
20	Rod Smith	3.00
21	Mark Brunell	12.00
22	Emmitt Smith	24.00
23	Rae Carruth	6.00
24	Brett Favre	30.00
25	Jeff George	6.00
26	Terry Glenn	6.00
27	Warrick Dunn	12.00
28	Herman Moore	6.00
29	Cris Carter	3.00
30	Terrell Davis	12.00

1998 Upper Deck Black Diamond Rookies

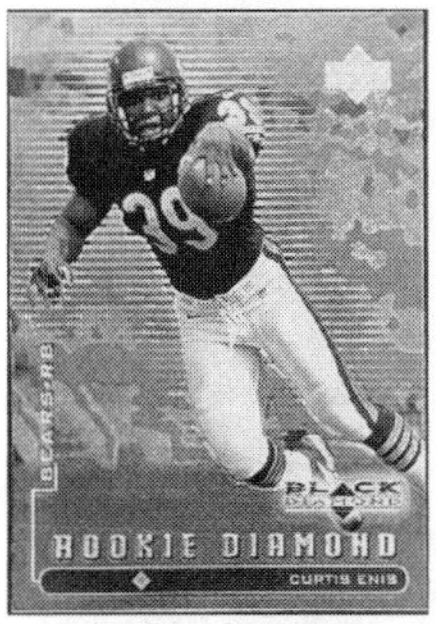

This 120-card set includes 90 regular player cards (all possessing Light F/X foil treatment) with each card sporting a Single Black Diamond, along with a 30-card, short-printed "Rookie Single Black Diamond" subset (1:4 packs). The parallel Double Black Diamond singles feature red Light F/X technology with veterans numbered to 3,000 and rookies to 2,500. The Triple Black Diamond parallel set has veterans numbered to 1,500 and rookies to 1,000. The Quadruple Black Diamond set has veterans numbered to 150 and rookies to 100.

		MT
Complete Set (120):		100.00
Common Player:		.15
Minor Stars:		.30
Common Rookie (91-120):		1.00
Inserted 1:4		
Double Cards:		2x-4x
Production 3,000 Sets		
Double Rookies:		1x
Production 2,500 Sets		
Triple Cards:		4x-8x
Production 1,500 Sets		
Triple Rookies:		2x
Production 1,000 Sets		
Quad. Cards:		20x-40x
Production 150 Sets		
Quad. Rookies:		3x-6x
Production 100 Sets		
Pack (6):		4.00
Wax Box (30):		110.00
1	Jake Plummer	1.25
2	Adrian Murrell	.15
3	Frank Sanders	.15
4	Jamal Anderson	.75
5	Chris Chandler	.30
6	Tony Martin	.15
7	Jim Harbaugh	.30
8	Errict Rhett	.15
9	Michael Jackson	.15
10	Rob Johnson	.30
11	Antowain Smith	.50
12	Thurman Thomas	.30
13	Fred Lane	.15
14	Kerry Collins	.30
15	Rae Carruth	.15
16	Erik Kramer	.15
17	Edgar Bennett	.15
18	Curtis Conway	.30
19	Corey Dillon	.75
20	Neil O'Donnell	.15
21	Carl Pickens	.30
22	Troy Aikman	1.50
23	Emmitt Smith	2.00
24	Deion Sanders	.50
25	John Elway	1.50
26	Terrell Davis	2.50
27	Rod Smith	.30
28	Barry Sanders	3.00
29	Johnnie Morton	.15
30	Herman Moore	.30
31	Brett Favre	3.00
32	Antonio Freeman	.50
33	Dorsey Levens	.30
34	Marshall Faulk	.50
35	Marvin Harrison	.30
36	Zack Crockett	.15
37	Mark Brunell	1.25
38	Jimmy Smith	.30
39	Keenan McCardell	.30
40	Elvis Grbac	.30
41	Andre Rison	.30
42	Derrick Alexander	.15
43	Dan Marino	2.00
44	Karim Abdul-Jabbar	.30
45	Zach Thomas	.30
46	Brad Johnson	.50
47	Cris Carter	.50
48	Robert Smith	.50
49	Drew Bledsoe	1.25
50	Terry Glenn	.30
51	Ben Coates	.30
52	Danny Wuerffel	.30
53	Lamar Smith	.15
54	Sean Dawkins	.15
55	Danny Kanell	.15
56	Tiki Barber	.15
57	Ike Hilliard	.15
58	Curtis Martin	.50
59	Vinny Testaverde	.30
60	Keyshawn Johnson	.50
61	Napoleon Kaufman	.50
62	Jeff George	.30
63	Tim Brown	.30
64	Bobby Hoying	.30
65	Charlie Garner	.15
66	Duce Staley	.15
67	Kordell Stewart	1.25
68	Jerome Bettis	.50
69	Charles Johnson	.15
70	Tony Banks	.30
71	Isaac Bruce	.30
72	Eddie Kennison	.30
73	Natrone Means	.30
74	Bryan Still	.15
75	Junior Seau	.30
76	Steve Young	1.00
77	Jerry Rice	1.50
78	Garrison Hearst	.50
79	Ricky Watters	.30
80	Joey Galloway	.50
81	Warren Moon	.30
82	Warrick Dunn	1.00
83	Trent Dilfer	.30
84	Bert Emanuel	.15
85	Steve McNair	.75
86	Eddie George	1.25
87	Yancey Thigpen	.15
88	Leslie Shepherd	.15
89	Terry Allen	.30
90	Michael Westbrook	.15
91	*Peyton Manning*	25.00
92	*Jacquez Green*	5.00
93	*Fred Taylor*	15.00
94	*Terry Fair*	3.00
95	*Patrick Johnson*	3.00
96	*Corey Chavous*	2.00
97	*Randy Moss*	25.00
98	*Curtis Enis*	5.00
99	*Rashaan Shehee*	3.00
100	*Kevin Dyson*	4.00
101	*Shaun Williams*	1.00
102	*Grant Wistrom*	2.00
103	*John Avery*	6.00
104	*Brian Griese*	12.00
105	*Ryan Leaf*	7.00
106	*Jerome Pathon*	4.00
107	*Sam Cowart*	1.00
108	*Germane Crowell*	6.00
109	*Ahman Green*	6.00
110	*Greg Ellis*	1.00
111	*Robert Holcombe*	6.00
112	*Marcus Nash*	6.00
113	*Duane Starks*	3.00
114	*Andre Wadsworth*	3.00
115	*Takeo Spikes*	3.00
116	*Eric Brown*	1.00
117	*Robert Edwards*	10.00
118	*Charlie Batch*	10.00
119	*Mikhael Ricks*	2.50
120	*Charles Woodson*	4.00

1998 Upper Deck Black Diamond Rookies Sheer Brilliance

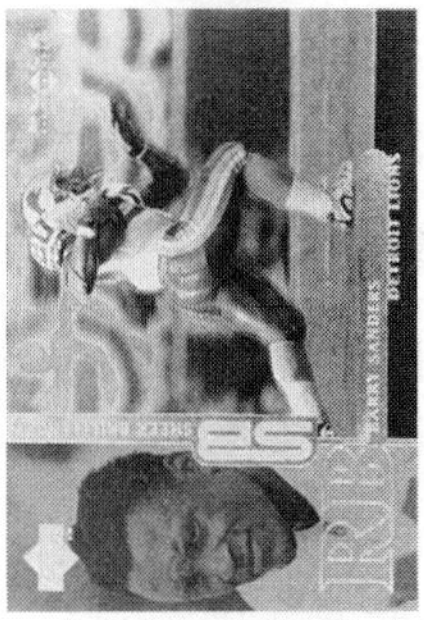

Each of these hobby-only singles has the Quadruple Black Diamond stamp on the front and each is sequentially numbered to the player's uniform number multiplied by 100. Cards are numbered with a "B" prefix.

		MT
Complete Set (30):		325.00
Common Player:		4.00
Hobby Only		
1	Dan Marino (1300)	25.00
2	Troy Aikman (800)	20.00
3	Brett Favre (400)	50.00
4	Ryan Leaf (1600)	25.00
5	Peyton Manning (1800)	45.00
6	Barry Sanders (2000)	25.00
7	Emmitt Smith (2200)	15.00
8	John Elway (700)	30.00
9	Steve Young (800)	15.00
10	Steve McNair (900)	12.00
11	Antowain Smith (2300)	4.00
12	Corey Dillon (2800)	6.00
13	Terrell Davis (3000)	10.00
14	Mark Brunell (800)	15.00
15	Charles Woodson (2400)	12.00
16	Brian Griese (1400)	15.00
17	Curtis Martin (2800)	4.00
18	Keyshawn Johnson (1900)	6.00
19	Kordell Stewart (1000)	15.00
20	Eddie George (2700)	6.00
21	Drew Bledsoe (1100)	15.00
22	Jake Plummer (1600)	12.00
23	Warren Moon (100)	30.00
24	Curtis Enis (3900)	6.00
25	John Avery (2000)	6.00
26	Randy Moss (1800)	80.00
27	Rob Johnson (1100)	6.00
28	Warrick Dunn (2800)	4.00
29	Terry Allen (2100)	4.00
30	Robert Smith (2600)	4.00

1998 Upper Deck Black Diamond Rookies White Onyx

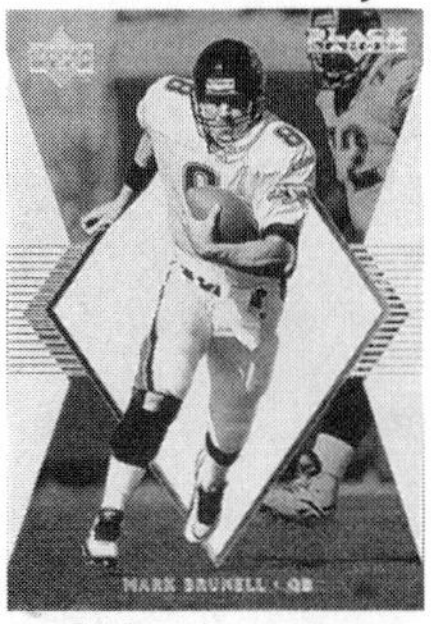

This insert incorporates a new design with Pearl Light F/X treatment and also has the Quadruple Black Diamond logo. Each is sequentially numbered to 2,250. Cards have an "ON" prefix.

		MT
Complete Set (30):		200.00
Common Player:		2.00
Minor Stars:		4.00
Production 2,250 Sets		
1	Peyton Manning	30.00
2	Corey Dillon	6.00
3	Jerome Bettis	4.00
4	Brett Favre	20.00
5	Napoleon Kaufman	4.00
6	Joey Galloway	4.00
7	John Elway	10.00
8	Troy Aikman	10.00
9	Robert Smith	2.00
10	Kordell Stewart	8.00
11	Garrison Hearst	4.00
12	Curtis Enis	8.00
13	Dan Marino	15.00
14	Jimmy Smith	2.00
15	Steve Young	6.00
16	Ryan Leaf	12.00
17	Steve McNair	6.00
18	Randy Moss	60.00
19	Curtis Martin	4.00
20	Barry Sanders	20.00
21	Rob Johnson	4.00
22	Emmitt Smith	15.00
23	Jake Plummer	8.00
24	Antonio Freeman	4.00
25	Mark Brunell	8.00
26	Warrick Dunn	8.00
27	Eddie George	8.00
28	Jerry Rice	10.00
29	Drew Bledsoe	8.00
30	Terrell Davis	15.00

1998 Upper Deck Encore

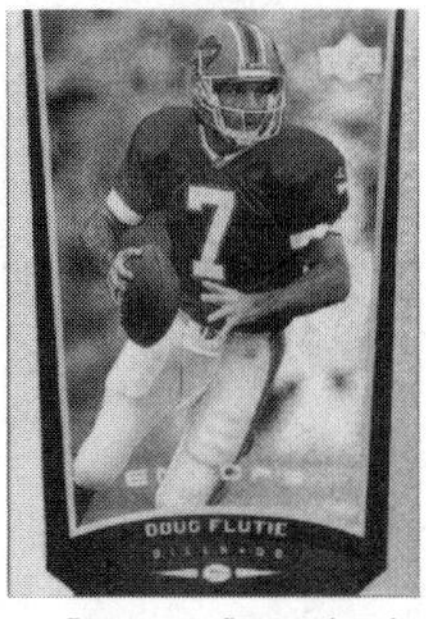

Encore was a fine-tuned version of Upper Deck's 1998 NFL Series I product that utilized a special rainbow-foil treatment on 150 of the earlier set's 255 cards (120 regular player cards and 30 Star Rookie subset cards). The rookies could be found 1:4 packs. The F/X set is a direct parallel of the entire Encore set. The differentiation comes in a color shift with a special "Encore F/X" call-out featured on the card fronts and backs. Singles are sequentially numbered to 125.

		MT
Complete Set (150):		275.00
Common Player:		.20
Minor Stars:		.40
Common Rookie:		2.00
Inserted 1:4		
F/X Gold Cards:		25x-50x
F/X Gold Rookies:		2x-4x
Production 125 Sets		
Pack (6):		4.00
Wax Box (24):		100.00
1	*Peyton Manning*	35.00
2	*Ryan Leaf*	12.00
3	*Andre Wadsworth*	3.00
4	*Charles Woodson*	10.00
5	*Curtis Enis*	5.00
6	*Fred Taylor*	12.00
7	*Duane Starks*	4.00
8	*Keith Brooking*	4.00
9	*Takeo Spikes*	4.00
10	*Kevin Dyson*	10.00
11	*Robert Edwards*	10.00
12	*Randy Moss*	35.00
13	*John Avery*	8.00
14	*Marcus Nash*	10.00
15	*Jerome Pathon*	4.00
16	*Jacquez Green*	10.00
17	*Robert Holcombe*	8.00
18	*Pat Johnson*	4.00
19	*Skip Hicks*	10.00
20	*Ahman Green*	12.00
21	*Brian Griese*	15.00
22	*Hines Ward*	6.00
23	*Tavian Banks*	6.00
24	*Tony Simmons*	6.00
25	*Rashaan Shehee*	4.00
26	*R.W. McQuarters*	4.00
27	*Jon Ritchie*	2.00
28	*Ryan Sutter*	2.00
29	*Tim Dwight*	8.00
30	*Charlie Batch*	15.00
31	Chris Chandler	.40
32	Jamal Anderson	1.00
33	Terance Mathis	.20
34	Jake Plummer	2.00
35	Mario Bates	.20
36	Frank Sanders	.20
37	Adrian Murrell	.20
38	Jim Harbaugh	.40
39	Michael Jackson	.20
40	Jermaine Lewis	.20
41	Doug Flutie	1.50
42	Rob Johnson	.40
43	Antowain Smith	1.00
44	Eric Moulds	1.00
45	Thurman Thomas	.40
46	Kevin Greene	.20
47	Fred Lane	.40
48	Rae Carruth	.20
49	William Floyd	.20
50	Erik Kramer	.20
51	Edgar Bennett	.20
52	Curtis Conway	.40
53	Bobby Engram	.20
54	Jeff Blake	.40
55	Carl Pickens	.75
56	Darnay Scott	.20
57	Corey Dillon	1.50
58	Troy Aikman	2.50
59	Michael Irvin	.40
60	Emmitt Smith	3.50
61	Deion Sanders	1.00
62	John Elway	3.00
63	Terrell Davis	4.00
64	Rod Smith	.40
65	Shannon Sharpe	.40
66	Ed McCaffrey	.75
67	Barry Sanders	5.00
68	Scott Mitchell	.40
69	Herman Moore	.75
70	Johnnie Morton	.20
71	Brett Favre	5.00
72	Dorsey Levens	.40
73	Reggie White	1.00
74	Antonio Freeman	1.00
75	Robert Brooks	.20
76	Marshall Faulk	1.00
77	Marvin Harrison	.40
78	Mark Brunell	2.00
79	Keenan McCardell	.40
80	Jimmy Smith	.75
81	Elvis Grbac	.20
82	Andre Rison	.40
83	Tony Gonzalez	.20
84	Derrick Thomas	.20
85	Dan Marino	3.50
86	Karim Abdul	1.00
87	O.J. McDuffie	.40
88	Zach Thomas	.40
89	Brad Johnson	1.00
90	Cris Carter	1.00
91	Jake Reed	.20
92	Robert Smith	.40
93	John Randle	.20
94	Randall Cunningham	1.00
95	Drew Bledsoe	2.00
96	Terry Glenn	1.00
97	Ben Coates	.40
98	Danny Wuerffel	.20
99	Andre Hastings	.20
100	Troy Davis	.20
101	Danny Kanell	.20
102	Tiki Barber	.20
103	Amani Toomer	.20
104	Vinny Testaverde	.40
105	Glenn Foley	.40
106	Curtis Martin	1.00
107	Keyshawn Johnson	1.00
108	Wayne Chrebet	.75
109	Jeff George	.40
110	Napoleon Kaufman	1.00
111	Tim Brown	.40
112	James Jett	.20
113	Bobby Hoying	.20
114	Charlie Garner	.20
115	Irving Fryar	.20
116	Kordell Stewart	2.00
117	Jerome Bettis	1.00
118	Will Blackwell	.20
119	Charles Johnson	.20
120	Tony Banks	.40
121	Amp Lee	.20
122	Isaac Bruce	.40
123	Eddie Kennison	.40
124	Natrone Means	.75
125	Junior Seau	.40
126	Bryan Still	.20
127	Steve Young	1.50
128	Jerry Rice	2.50
129	Garrison Hearst	.75
130	J.J. Stokes	.40
131	Terrell Owens	1.00
132	Warren Moon	.40
133	Jon Kitna	.40
134	Ricky Watters	.40
135	Joey Galloway	1.00
136	Trent Dilfer	.40
137	Warrick Dunn	2.00
138	Mike Alstott	1.00
139	Bert Emanuel	.20
140	Reidel Anthony	.20
141	Steve McNair	1.25
142	Yancey Thigpen	.20
143	Eddie George	2.00
144	Chris Sanders	.20
145	Gus Frerotte	.20
146	Terry Allen	.40
147	Michael Westbrook	.20
148	Troy Aikman CL	1.50
149	Dan Marino CL	1.50
150	Randy Moss CL	5.00

1998 Upper Deck Encore Constant Threat

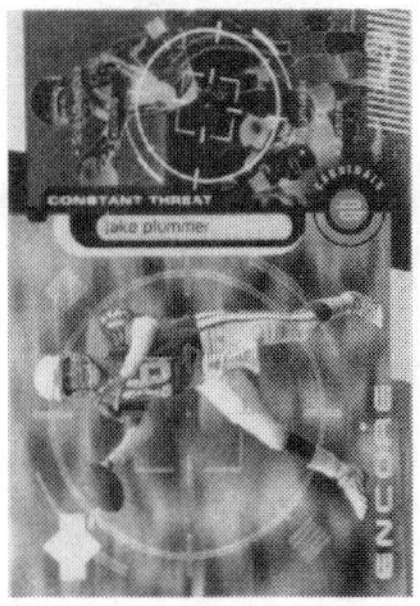

This lineup showcases high-impact players who could affect the outcome of a game in the blink of an eye. Singles have the prefix "CT" before the card number and were inserted 1:11 packs.

		MT
Complete Set (15):		85.00
Common Player:		2.00
Inserted 1:11		
1	Dan Marino	10.00
2	Peyton Manning	15.00
3	Randy Moss	25.00
4	Brett Favre	12.00
5	Mark Brunell	5.00
6	John Elway	8.00
7	Ryan Leaf	7.00
8	Jake Plummer	5.00
9	Terrell Davis	10.00
10	Barry Sanders	12.00
11	Emmitt Smith	10.00
12	Curtis Martin	2.00
13	Eddie George	5.00
14	Warrick Dunn	5.00
15	Curtis Enis	4.00

1998 Upper Deck Encore Driving Forces

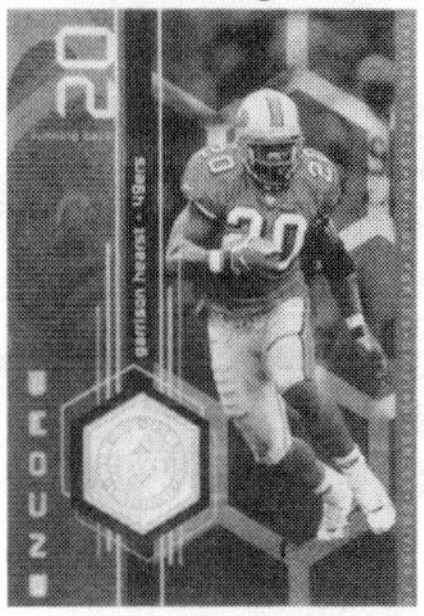

This insert consists of 14 NFL superstars, including top QB's, running backs and wide receivers. Singles have the prefix "F" before the card number and were inserted 1:23. The parallel F/X Golds are in gold foil and were sequentially numbered to 1,500.

		MT
Complete Set (14):		85.00
Common Player:		3.00
Inserted 1:23		
F/X Golds:		2x
Production 1,500 Cards		
1	Terrell Davis	15.00
2	Barry Sanders	20.00
3	Doug Flutie	7.00
4	Mark Brunell	8.00
5	Garrison Hearst	3.00
6	Jamal Anderson	5.00
7	Jerry Rice	10.00
8	John Elway	12.00
9	Robert Smith	3.00
10	Kordell Stewart	8.00
11	Eddie George	8.00
12	Antonio Freeman	3.00
13	Dan Marino	15.00
14	Steve Young	7.00

A player's name in *italic type* indicates a rookie card.

1998 Upper Deck Encore Milestones

This collection includes cards that will boast special "UD Milestones" stamps. Designated sequential numbering for each gold-foil card signifies a remarkable milestone reached by that player for the '98 season. For example, Dan Marino (400th touchdown pass thrown on 11/28/98) will be crash-numbered to 400.

		MT
Complete Set (8):		1500.
Common Player:		50.00
1	Peyton Manning/26	325.00
12	Randy Moss/17	850.00
60	Emmitt Smith/124	75.00
62	John Elway/50	150.00
63	Terrell Davis/30	250.00
67	Barry Sanders/100	125.00
85	Dan Marino/400	60.00
128	Jerry Rice/184	50.00

1998 Upper Deck Encore Rookie Encore

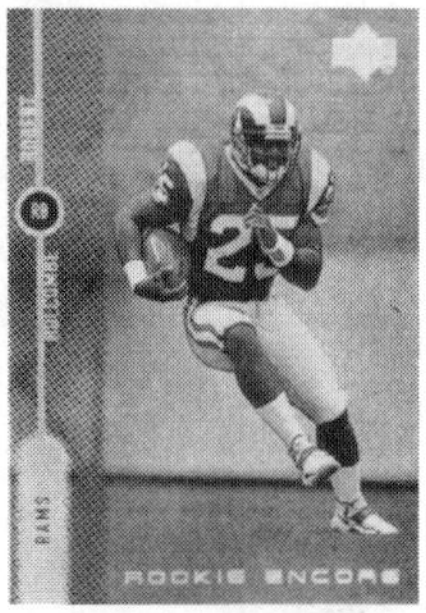

The 1998 season produced a host of solid first-year players and this lineup captures the best of the best. Each card has the prefix "RE" before the number and were found 1:23 packs. The FX Gold parallel singles are in gold foil and are sequentially numbered to 500.

		MT
Complete Set (10):		80.00
Common Player:		2.00
Inserted 1:23		
F/X Golds:		2x-4x
Production 500 Sets		
1	Randy Moss	40.00
2	Peyton Manning	20.00
3	Charlie Batch	12.00
4	Fred Taylor	12.00
5	Robert Edwards	7.00
6	Curtis Enis	6.00
7	Robert Holcombe	2.00
8	Ryan Leaf	8.00
9	John Avery	4.00
10	Tim Dwight	4.00

1998 Upper Deck Encore Super Powers

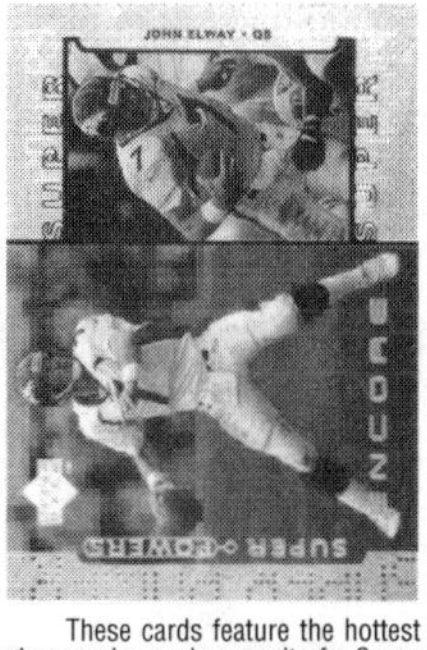

These cards feature the hottest players who are in pursuit of a Super Bowl ring. Singles are on rainbow-foil stock and were inserted 1:11 packs. Cards are numbered with a "S" prefix.

		MT
Complete Set (15):		85.00
Common Player:		2.00
Inserted 1:11		
1	Dan Marino	10.00
2	Napoleon Kaufman	2.00
3	Brett Favre	12.00
4	John Elway	8.00
5	Randy Moss	25.00
6	Kordell Stewart	5.00
7	Mark Brunell	5.00
8	Peyton Manning	15.00
9	Emmitt Smith	10.00
10	Jake Plummer	5.00
11	Eddie George	5.00
12	Warrick Dunn	5.00
13	Jerome Bettis	2.00
14	Terrell Davis	10.00
15	Fred Taylor	10.00

1998 Upper Deck Encore Superstar Encore

This insert includes the top six players in the league including rookie

Randy Moss. Each single has the prefix "RR" before the card number and were inserted 1:23 packs. The F/X Gold parallel singles were limited to only 25 of each.

		MT
Complete Set (6):		50.00
Common Player:		4.00
Inserted 1:23		
F/X Gold Cards:		20x-40x
F/X Gold Rookies:		10x-20x
Production 25 Sets		
1	Brett Favre	12.00
2	Barry Sanders	12.00
3	Mark Brunell	4.00
4	Emmitt Smith	8.00
5	Randy Moss	25.00
6	Terrell Davis	10.00

1998 Upper Deck Encore UD Authentics

This collection includes autographed cards of five NFL superstars: Mark Brunell, Dan Marino, Randy Moss, Terrell Davis and Joe Montana. Singles were inserted 1:288 packs.

		MT
Complete Set (5):		750.00
Common Player:		75.00
Inserted 1:288		
MB	Mark Brunell	75.00
DM	Dan Marino	200.00
RM	Randy Moss	275.00
TD	Terrell Davis	150.00
JM	Joe Montana	150.00

1999 UD Ionix

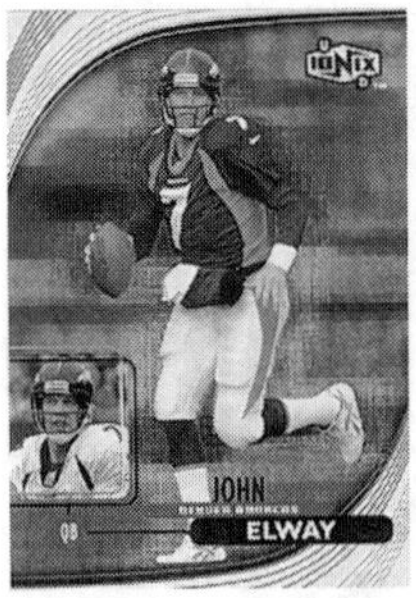

UD Ionix is a 90-card set with 30 seeded rookies found 1:4 packs. Each card is super thick, double laminated and metalized. Inserts include: Reciprocal, Astronomix, Electric Forces, HoloGrFX, Power F/X, UD Authentics and Warp Zone.

		MT
Complete Set (90):		125.00
Common Player:		.25
Minor Stars:		.50
Common Rookie:		1.50
Inserted 1:4		
Pack (4):		6.00
Wax Box (20):		110.00
1	Jake Plummer	2.00
2	Adrian Murrell	.25
3	Jamal Anderson	1.00
4	Chris Chandler	.50
5	Priest Holmes	1.00
6	Michael Jackson	.50
7	Antowain Smith	1.00
8	Doug Flutie	1.50
9	Tshimanga Biakabutuka	.25
10	Muhsin Muhammad	.25
11	Erik Kramer	.25
12	Curtis Enis	1.00
13	Corey Dillon	1.00
14	Ty Detmer	.50
15	Justin Armour	.25
16	Troy Aikman	2.00
17	Emmitt Smith	3.00
18	John Elway	3.00
19	Terrell Davis	3.00
20	Barry Sanders	4.00
21	Charlie Batch	1.50
22	Brett Favre	4.00
23	Dorsey Levens	1.00
24	Marshall Faulk	1.00
25	Peyton Manning	3.00
26	Mark Brunell	1.50
27	Fred Taylor	2.00
28	Elvis Grbac	.50
29	Andre Rison	.50
30	Dan Marino	3.00
31	Karim Abdul	.75
32	Randall Cunningham	1.00
33	Randy Moss	5.00
34	Drew Bledsoe	1.50
35	Terry Glenn	.75
36	Danny Wuerffel	.25
37	Kent Graham	.25
38	Gary Brown	.25
39	Vinny Testaverde	.50
40	Keyshawn Johnson	1.00
41	Napoleon Kaufman	1.00
42	Tim Brown	.50
43	Koy Detmer	.25
44	Duce Staley	.25
45	Kordell Stewart	1.25
46	Jerome Bettis	1.00
47	Isaac Bruce	.75
48	Robert Holcombe	.75
49	Jim Harbaugh	.50
50	Natrone Means	.75
51	Steve Young	1.50
52	Jerry Rice	2.00
53	Jon Kitna	1.25
54	Joey Galloway	1.00
55	Warrick Dunn	1.25
56	Trent Dilfer	.75
57	Steve McNair	1.25
58	Eddie George	1.25
59	Skip Hicks	1.00
60	Michael Westbrook	.50
61	*Tim Couch*	12.00
62	*Ricky Williams*	12.00
63	*Daunte Culpepper*	15.00
64	*Akili Smith*	5.00
65	*Donovan McNabb*	10.00
66	*Michael Bishop*	3.00
67	*Brock Huard*	4.00
68	*Torry Holt*	6.00
69	*Cade McNown*	4.00
70	*Shaun King*	8.00
71	*Champ Bailey*	3.00
72	*Chris Claiborne*	4.00
73	*Jevon Kearse*	5.00
74	*D'Wayne Bates*	2.50
75	*David Boston*	5.00
76	*Edgerrin James*	25.00
77	*Sedrick Irvin*	2.50
78	*Dameane Douglas*	2.50
79	*Troy Edwards*	3.00
80	*Ebenezer Ekuban*	1.50
81	*Kevin Faulk*	4.00
82	*Joe Germaine*	2.50
83	*Kevin Johnson*	4.00
84	*Andy Katzenmoyer*	2.50
85	*Rob Konrad*	1.50
86	*Chris McAlister*	2.50
87	*Peerless Price*	3.00
88	*Tai Streets*	2.50
89	*Autry Denson*	2.50
90	*Amos Zereoue*	2.50

1999 UD Ionix Reciprocal Parallel

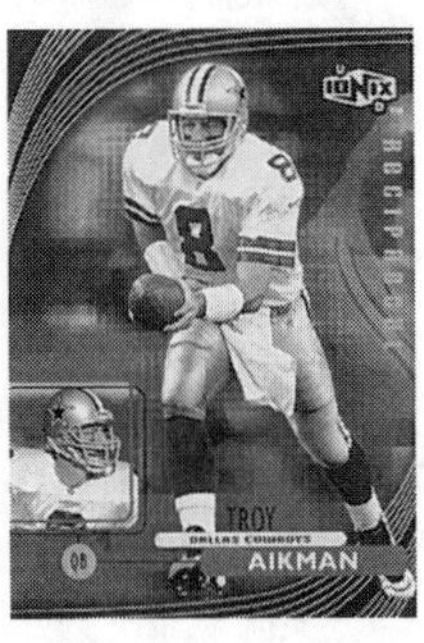

This is a parallel to the base and has the prefix R before the card number. Cards #1-60 were found 1:6 packs and the rookies #61-90 were inserted 1:19 packs. The word "Reciprocal" is printed on the fronts of each card.

	MT
Complete Set (90):	400.00
Reciprocal Cards:	2x-4x
Inserted 1:6	
Reciprocal Rookies:	2x
Inserted 1:19	

1999 UD Ionix Astronomix

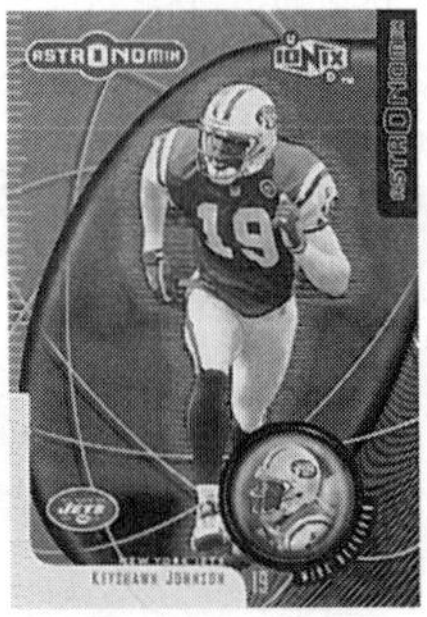

Each card in this 25-card set highlights a statistical achievement by that particular player. Singles were inserted 1:23 packs.

		MT
Complete Set (25):		200.00
Common Player:		5.00
Inserted 1:23		
1	Keyshawn Johnson	5.00
2	Emmitt Smith	18.00
3	Eddie George	6.00
4	Fred Taylor	12.00
5	Peyton Manning	18.00
6	John Elway	18.00
7	Brett Favre	25.00
8	Terrell Davis	18.00
9	Mark Brunell	8.00
10	Dan Marino	18.00
11	Randall Cunningham	5.00
12	Steve McNair	5.00
13	Jamal Anderson	5.00
14	Barry Sanders	25.00
15	Jake Plummer	12.00
16	Drew Bledsoe	8.00
17	Jerome Bettis	5.00
18	Jerry Rice	12.00
19	Warrick Dunn	6.00
20	Steve Young	8.00
21	Terrell Owens	5.00
22	Ricky Williams	30.00
23	Akili Smith	12.00
24	Cade McNown	12.00
25	David Boston	10.00

1999 UD Ionix Electric Forces

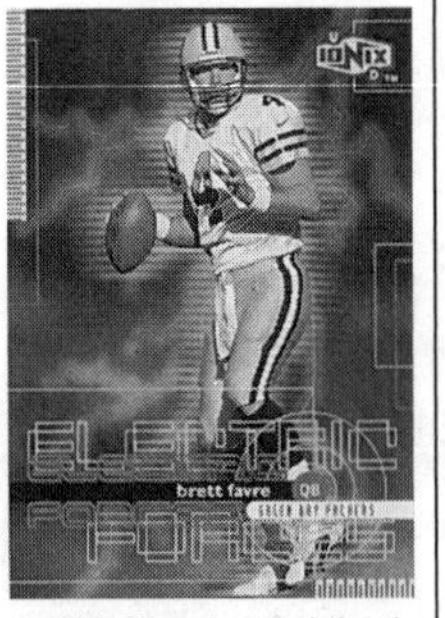

This 20-card set includes the most collectible NFL stars of today. Singles were inserted 1:6 packs.

		MT
Complete Set (20):		60.00
Common Player:		2.00
Inserted 1:6		
1	Ricky Williams	15.00
2	Tim Couch	15.00
3	Daunte Culpepper	5.00
4	Akili Smith	5.00
5	Cade McNown	5.00
6	Donovan McNabb	5.00
7	Brock Huard	2.00
8	Michael Bishop	3.00
9	Torry Holt	4.00
10	Peerless Price	3.00
11	Peyton Manning	6.00
12	Jake Plummer	4.00
13	John Elway	6.00
14	Mark Brunell	3.00
15	Steve Young	2.50
16	Jamal Anderson	2.00
17	Kordell Stewart	2.50
18	Eddie George	2.50
19	Fred Taylor	4.00
20	Brett Favre	8.00

1999 UD Ionix HoloGrFX

The top NFL stars and rookies are included in this 10-card set. Singles were issued at 1:1,500 packs.

		MT
Complete Set (10):		1200.
Common Player:		75.00
Inserted 1:1,500		
1	Ricky Williams	250.00
2	Tim Couch	250.00
3	Cade McNown	100.00
4	Peyton Manning	150.00
5	Jake Plummer	125.00
6	Randy Moss	250.00
7	Barry Sanders	250.00
8	Jamal Anderson	75.00
9	Terrell Davis	175.00
10	Brett Favre	250.00

1999 UD Ionix Power F/X

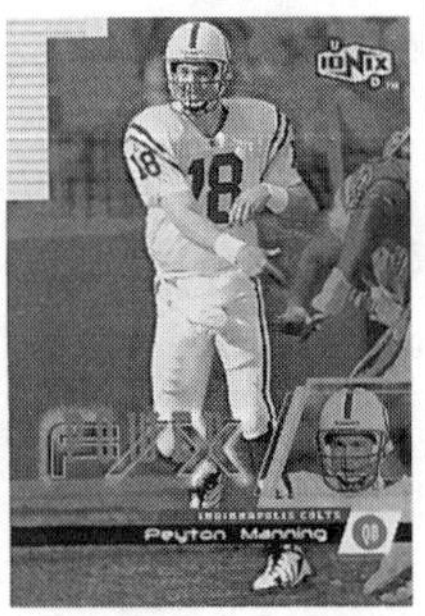

The game's most impressive talents, with a mix of rookies and veterans are highlighted in this 9-card set. Singles were inserted 1:11 packs.

		MT
Complete Set (9):		40.00
Common Player:		2.00
Inserted 1:11		
1	Peyton Manning	7.00
2	Randy Moss	10.00
3	Terrell Davis	8.00
4	Steve Young	3.00
5	Dan Marino	8.00
6	Warrick Dunn	2.00
7	Keyshawn Johnson	2.00
8	Barry Sanders	10.00
9	Tim Couch	12.00

1999 UD Ionix UD Authentics

This 10-card set includes autographs from the top rookies from the 1999 draft. Each player signed 100 cards each except for Ricky Williams who signed only 50.

		MT
Complete Set (10):		1300.
Common Player:		60.00
Production 100 Sets		
Ricky Williams Only Signed 50		
MB	Michael Bishop	75.00
TC	Tim Couch	250.00
DC	Daunte Culpepper	125.00
TH	Torry Holt	85.00
BH	Brock Huard	60.00
SK	Shaun King	60.00
DM	Donovan McNabb	125.00
CM	Cade McNown	125.00
AS	Akili Smith	125.00
RW	Ricky Williams	500.00

1999 UD Ionix Warp Zone

A mix of stars and rookies from the NFL make up this 15-card set that was inserted 1:108 packs.

		MT
Complete Set (15):		375.00
Common Player:		10.00
Inserted 1:108		
1	Ricky Williams	75.00
2	Tim Couch	75.00
3	Cade McNown	25.00
4	Daunte Culpepper	25.00
5	Akili Smith	25.00
6	Brock Huard	10.00
7	Donovan McNabb	25.00
8	Jake Plummer	25.00
9	Jamal Anderson	10.00
10	John Elway	40.00
11	Randy Moss	50.00
12	Terrell Davis	40.00
13	Troy Aikman	25.00
14	Barry Sanders	50.00
15	Fred Taylor	25.00

1999 Upper Deck

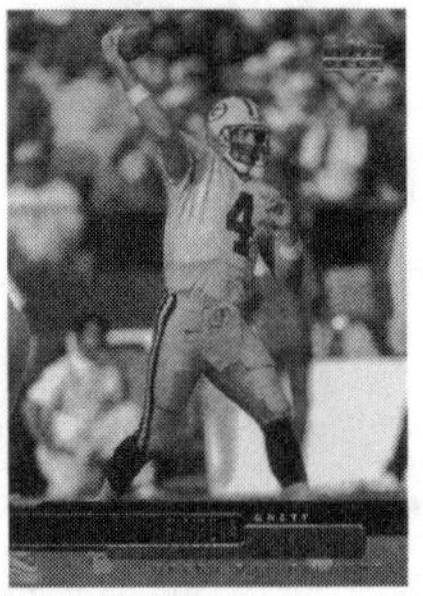

Upper Deck is a 270-card set that includes 45 seeded rookies found 1:4 packs. Each base card has a parallel Exclusive Silver and Exclusive Gold. Other inserts include: 21 TD Salute, Game Jersey, Game Jersey Patch, Highlight Zone, Livewires, PowerDeck, Quarterback Class and Strike Force.

		MT
Complete Set (270):		250.00
Common Player:		.15
Minor Stars:		.30
Common Rookie:		1.25
Inserted 1:4		
Pack (10):		3.50
Wax Box (24):		80.00
1	Jake Plummer	1.25
2	Adrian Murrell	.15
3	Rob Moore	.30
4	Larry Centers	.15
5	Simeon Rice	.15
6	Andre Wadsworth	.15
7	Frank Sanders	.30
8	Tim Dwight	.50
9	Ray Buchanan	.15
10	Chris Chandler	.30
11	Jamal Anderson	.50
12	O.J. Santiago	.15
13	Danny Kanell	.15
14	Terance Mathis	.15
15	Priest Holmes	.50
16	Tony Banks	.30
17	Ray Lewis	.15
18	Patrick Johnson	.15
19	Michael Jackson	.15
20	Michael McCrary	.15
21	Jermaine Lewis	.30
22	Eric Moulds	.50
23	Doug Flutie	.75
24	Antowain Smith	.50
25	Rob Johnson	.30
26	Bruce Smith	.15
27	Andre Reed	.15
28	Thurman Thomas	.15
29	Fred Lane	.15
30	Wesley Walls	.15
31	Tshimanga Biakabutuka	.15
32	Kevin Greene	.15
33	Steve Beuerlein	.15
34	Muhsin Muhammad	.15
35	Rae Carruth	.15
36	Bobby Engram	.15
37	Curtis Enis	.30
38	Edgar Bennett	.15
39	Erik Kramer	.15
40	Steve Stenstrom	.15
41	Alonzo Mayes	.15
42	Curtis Conway	.30
43	Tony McGee	.15
44	Darnay Scott	.15
45	Jeff Blake	.30
46	Corey Dillon	.50
47	Ki-Jana Carter	.15
48	Takeo Spikes	.15
49	Carl Pickens	.30
50	Ty Detmer	.15
51	Leslie Shepherd	.15
52	Terry Kirby	.15
53	Marquez Pope	.15
54	Antonio Langham	.15
55	Jamir Miller	.15
56	Derrick Alexander	.15
57	Troy Aikman	1.25
58	Raghib Ismail	.15
59	Emmitt Smith	2.00
60	Michael Irvin	.30
61	David LaFleur	.15
62	Chris Warren	.15
63	Deion Sanders	.50
64	Greg Ellis	.15
65	John Elway	2.00
66	Bubby Brister	.30
67	Terrell Davis	2.00
68	Ed McCaffrey	.30
69	John Mobley	.15
70	Bill Romanowski	.15
71	Rod Smith	.30
72	Shannon Sharpe	.30
73	Charlie Batch	.75
74	Germane Crowell	.30
75	Johnnie Morton	.15
76	Barry Sanders	2.50
77	Robert Porcher	.15
78	Stephen Boyd	.15
79	Herman Moore	.50
80	Brett Favre	2.50
81	Mark Chmura	.30
82	Antonio Freeman	.50
83	Robert Brooks	.15
84	Vonnie Holliday	.15
85	Bill Schroeder	.15
86	Dorsey Levens	.50
87	Santana Dotson	.15
88	Peyton Manning	2.00
89	Jerome Pathon	.15
90	Marvin Harrison	.30
91	Ellis Johnson	.15
92	Ken Dilger	.15
93	E.G. Green	.15
94	Jeff Burris	.15
95	Mark Brunell	1.00
96	Fred Taylor	1.25
97	Jimmy Smith	.30
98	James Stewart	.15
99	Kyle Brady	.15
100	Dave Thomas	.15
101	Keenan McCardell	.15
102	Elvis Grbac	.30
103	Tony Gonzalez	.30
104	Andre Rison	.30
105	Donnell Bennett	.15
106	Derrick Thomas	.15
107	Warren Moon	.30
108	Derrick Alexander	.15
109	Dan Marino	2.00
110	O.J. McDuffie	.30
111	Karim Abdul	.30
112	John Avery	.30
113	Sam Madison	.15
114	Jason Taylor	.15
115	Zach Thomas	.30
116	Randall Cunningham	.50
117	Randy Moss	3.00
118	Cris Carter	.50
119	Jake Reed	.15
120	Matthew Hatchette	.15
121	John Randle	.15
122	Robert Smith	.30
123	Drew Bledsoe	1.00
124	Ben Coates	.30
125	Terry Glenn	.30
126	Ty Law	.15
127	Tony Simmons	.30
128	Ted Johnson	.15
129	Tony Carter	.15
130	Willie McGinest	.15
131	Danny Wuerffel	.15
132	Cameron Cleeland	.15
133	Eddie Kennison	.15
134	Joe Johnson	.15
135	Andre Hastings	.15
136	La'Roi Glover	.15
137	Kent Graham	.15
138	Tiki Barber	.15
139	Gary Brown	.15
140	Ike Hilliard	.15
141	Jason Sehorn	.15
142	Michael Strahan	.15
143	Amani Toomer	.15
144	Kerry Collins	.30
145	Vinny Testaverde	.30
146	Wayne Chrebet	.30
147	Curtis Martin	.50
148	Mo Lewis	.15
149	Aaron Glenn	.15
150	Steve Atwater	.15
151	Keyshawn Johnson	.50
152	James Farrior	.15
153	Rich Gannon	.15
154	Tim Brown	.30
155	Darrell Russell	.15
156	Rickey Dudley	.15
157	Charles Woodson	.50
158	James Jett	.15
159	Napoleon Kaufman	.50
160	Duce Staley	.30
161	Doug Pederson	.15
162	Bobby Hoying	.15
163	Koy Detmer	.15
164	Kevin Turner	.15
165	Charles Johnson	.15
166	Mike Mamula	.15
167	Jerome Bettis	.50
168	Courtney Hawkins	.15
169	Will Blackwell	.15
170	Kordell Stewart	.75
171	Richard Huntley	.15
172	Levon Kirkland	.15
173	Hines Ward	.30
174	Trent Green	.30
175	Marshall Faulk	.50
176	Az-Zahir Hakim	.15
177	Amp Lee	.15
178	Robert Holcombe	.30
179	Isaac Bruce	.30
180	Kevin Carter	.15
181	Jim Harbaugh	.30
182	Junior Seau	.30
183	Natrone Means	.50
184	Ryan Leaf	.50
185	Charlie Jones	.15
186	Rodney Harrison	.15
187	Mikhael Ricks	.15
188	Steve Young	.75
189	Terrell Owens	.50
190	Jerry Rice	1.25
191	J.J. Stokes	.30
192	Irv Smith	.15
193	Bryant Young	.15
194	Garrison Hearst	.30
195	Jon Kitna	.75
196	Ahman Green	.30
197	Joey Galloway	.50
198	Ricky Watters	.30
199	Chad Brown	.15
200	Shawn Springs	.15
201	Mike Pritchard	.15
202	Trent Dilfer	.30
203	Reidel Anthony	.30
204	Bert Emanuel	.15
205	Warrick Dunn	.50
206	Jacquez Green	.30
207	Hardy Nickerson	.15
208	Mike Alstott	.50
209	Eddie George	.75
210	Steve McNair	.75
211	Kevin Dyson	.30
212	Frank Wycheck	.15
213	Jackie Harris	.15
214	Blaine Bishop	.15
215	Yancey Thigpen	.15
216	Brad Johnson	.50
217	Rodney Peete	.15
218	Michael Westbrook	.30
219	Skip Hicks	.50
220	Brian Mitchell	.15
221	Dan Wilkinson	.15
222	Dana Stubblefield	.15
223	Set Checklist #1	.15
224	Checklist #2	.15
225	Checklist #3	.15
226	*Champ Bailey*	5.00
227	*Chris McAlister*	2.50
228	*Jevon Kearse*	7.00
229	*Ebenezer Ekuban*	1.25
230	*Chris Claiborne*	2.50
231	*Andy Katzenmoyer*	2.50
232	*Tim Couch*	15.00
233	*Daunte Culpepper*	20.00
234	*Akili Smith*	8.00
235	*Donovan McNabb*	12.00
236	*Sean Bennett*	2.50
237	*Brock Huard*	6.00
238	*Cade McNown*	6.00
239	*Shaun King*	12.00
240	*Joe Germaine*	2.50
241	*Ricky Williams*	15.00
242	*Edgerrin James*	25.00
243	*Sedrick Irvin*	2.50
244	*Kevin Faulk*	5.00
245	*Rob Konrad*	2.50
246	*James Johnson*	2.50
247	*Amos Zereoue*	2.50
248	*Torry Holt*	8.00
249	*D'Wayne Bates*	2.50
250	*David Boston*	8.00
251	*Dameane Douglas*	1.25
252	*Troy Edwards*	5.00
253	*Kevin Johnson*	5.00
254	*Peerless Price*	4.00
255	*Antoine Winfield*	2.50
256	*Michael Cloud*	2.50
257	*Joe Montgomery*	2.50
258	*Jermaine Fazande*	2.50
259	*Scott Covington*	1.25
260	*Aaron Brooks*	12.00
261	*Patrick Kerney*	1.25
262	*Cecil Collins*	2.50
263	*Chris Greisen*	1.25
264	*Craig Yeast*	1.25
265	*Karsten Bailey*	1.25
266	*Reginald Kelly*	1.25
267	*Travis McGriff*	1.25
268	*Jeff Paulk*	1.25
269	*Jim Kleinsasser*	2.50
270	*Darrin Chiaverini*	2.50

1999 Upper Deck Exclusives Silver Parallel

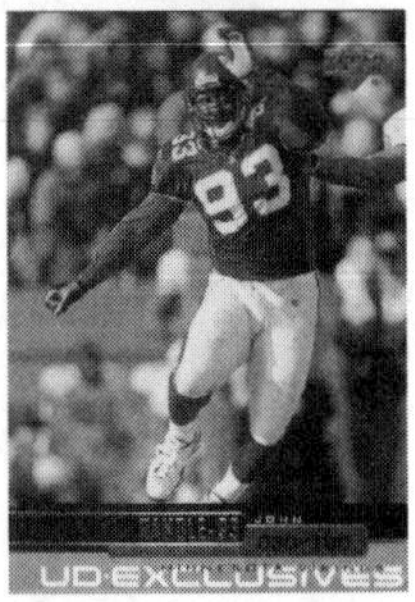

This is a parallel to the base set and is the same card except for on the bottom of the card the words "UD Exclusives" are printed on it along with the sequential numbering to 100 on gold foil.

	MT
UDE Cards:	20x-40x
UDE Rookies:	3x
Production 100 Sets	

1999 Upper Deck Exclusives Gold Parallel

This is a parallel to the base set with each single sequentially numbered to only 1.

	MT
Production 1 Set	

1999 Upper Deck 21 TD Salute

This 10-card insert is a salute to Denver running back Terrell Davis for becoming the fourth NFL player in history to run for more than 2,000 yards in a single season. He also set a Broncos' franchise record with 21 rushing touchdowns. Singles were found 1:23 packs. A parallel Silver set was made and sequentially numbered to 100 and a Gold limited to only one.

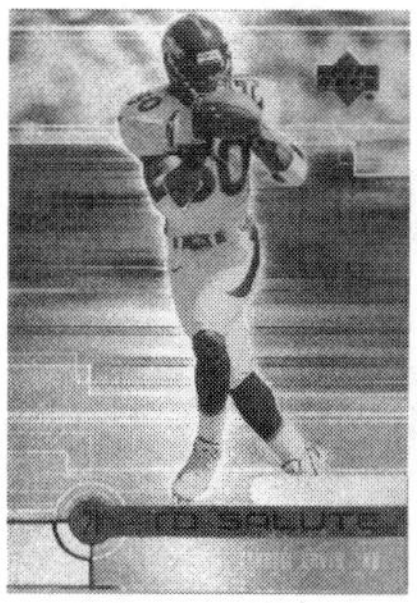

	MT
Complete Set (10):	60.00
Common Player:	6.00
Inserted 1:23	
Quantum Silver:	8x-16x
Production 100 Sets	
Quantum Gold	
Production 1 Set	
1 Terrell Davis	6.00
2 Terrell Davis	6.00
3 Terrell Davis	6.00
4 Terrell Davis	6.00
5 Terrell Davis	6.00
6 Terrell Davis	6.00
7 Terrell Davis	6.00
8 Terrell Davis	6.00
9 Terrell Davis	6.00
10 Terrell Davis	6.00

1999 Upper Deck Game Jersey

Singles from this 11-card set were inserted in both hobby and retail product at 1:2,500 packs. Each single has a piece of actual game-used (or rookie photo shoot-used) jersey on the fronts of the cards. Both Terrell Davis and Cade McNown signed cards to their jersey numbers of 30 and 8.

	MT
Complete Set (11):	2500.
Common Player:	100.00
Inserted 1:2,500	
JA Jamal Anderson	100.00
DB Drew Bledsoe	225.00
TC Tim Couch	425.00
TC-A Tim Couch Auto.	
TD Terrell Davis	400.00
TD-A Terrell Davis Auto.	
DF Doug Flutie	175.00
EJ Edgerrin James	350.00
KJ Keyshawn Johnson	150.00
DM Dan Marino	400.00
RM Randy Moss	500.00
AS Akili Smith	200.00
SY Steve Young	175.00

1999 Upper Deck Game Jersey Hobby

This 12-card insert could only be found in hobby product at 1:288 packs. Each single includes a piece of game-used (or rookie photo shoot-used) jersey on the fronts of the cards. Both Tim Couch and Brock Huard signed cards to their jersey number of 2 and 5.

	MT
Complete Set (12):	1700.
Common Player:	60.00
Inserted 1:288	
TA Troy Aikman	200.00
DV David Boston	100.00
DC Daunte Culpepper	150.00
JE John Elway	250.00
BH Brock Huard	60.00
BH-A Brock Huard Auto.	
PM Peyton Manning	250.00
MC Donovan McNabb	150.00
CM Cade McNown	150.00
CM-A Cade McNown Auto.	
EM Eric Moulds	60.00
JP Jake Plummer	200.00
JR Jerry Rice	200.00
BS Barry Sanders	300.00

1999 Upper Deck Game Jersey Patch

Each single in this 20-card set has a piece of the team logo from the jersey on the card. Singles were inserted 1:7,500 packs.

	MT
Common Player:	150.00
Inserted 1:7,500	
TA Troy Aikman	450.00
JA Jamal Anderson	150.00
DB Drew Bledsoe	400.00
DV David Boston	200.00
TC Tim Couch	700.00
DC Daunte Culpepper	300.00
TD Terrell Davis	600.00
JE John Elway	700.00
DF Doug Flutie	350.00
BH Brock Huard	150.00
EJ Edgerrin James	800.00
PM Peyton Manning	600.00
DM Dan Marino	600.00
DV Donovan McNabb	300.00
CM Cade McNown	300.00
RM Randy Moss	800.00
JR Jerry Rice	450.00
BS Barry Sanders	800.00
AS Akili Smith	300.00
SY Steve Young	375.00

1999 Upper Deck Highlight Zone

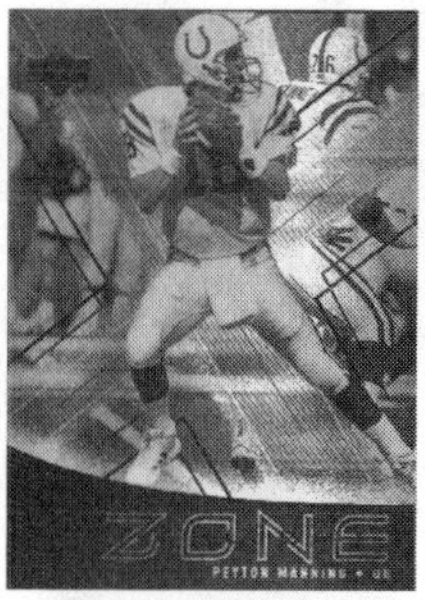

This 20-card insert spotlights the top players in the NFL. Singles were printed on a foil board and found 1:23 packs. A Silver parallel was printed and sequentially numbered to 100, along with a Gold numbered to only 1.

	MT
Complete Set (20):	170.00
Common Player:	2.00
Minor Stars:	4.00
Inserted 1:23	
Quantum Silver:	5x-10x
Production 100 Sets	
Quantum Gold	
Production 1 Set	
1 Terrell Davis	15.00
2 Ricky Williams	20.00
3 Akili Smith	8.00
4 Charlie Batch	4.00
5 Jake Plummer	10.00
6 Emmitt Smith	15.00
7 Dan Marino	15.00
8 Tim Couch	20.00
9 Randy Moss	20.00
10 Troy Aikman	10.00
11 Barry Sanders	20.00
12 Jerry Rice	10.00
13 Mark Brunell	8.00
14 Jamal Anderson	2.00
15 Peyton Manning	12.00
16 Jerome Bettis	2.00
17 Donovan McNabb	8.00
18 Steve Young	6.00
19 Keyshawn Johnson	4.00
20 Brett Favre	20.00

1999 Upper Deck Livewires

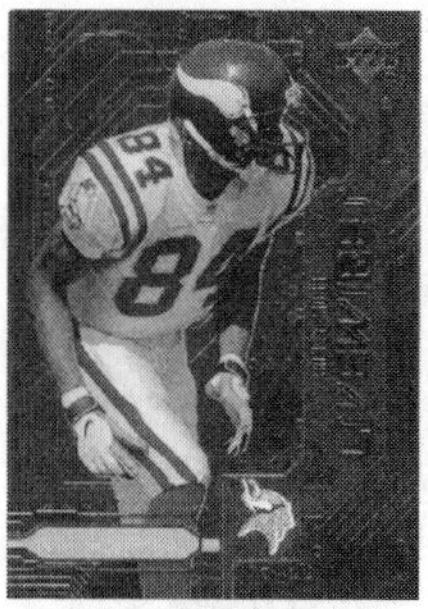

Each card in this 15-card set has actual printed transcripts of statements made by big-name players during games. Singles were inserted 1:10 packs. A Silver parallel was produced and numbered to 100, along with a Gold that was limited to only one set.

	MT
Complete Set (15):	50.00
Common Player:	1.00
Minor Stars:	2.00
Inserted 1:10	
Quantum Silver:	10x-20x
Production 100 Sets	
Quantum Gold:	
Production 1 Set	
1 Jake Plummer	4.00
2 Jamal Anderson	1.00
3 Emmitt Smith	6.00
4 John Elway	6.00
5 Barry Sanders	8.00
6 Brett Favre	8.00
7 Mark Brunell	3.00
8 Fred Taylor	4.00
9 Randy Moss	8.00
10 Drew Bledsoe	3.00
11 Keyshawn Johnson	2.00
12 Jerome Bettis	2.00
13 Kordell Stewart	2.00
14 Terrell Owens	2.00
15 Eddie George	2.00

Values quoted in this guide reflect the retail price of a card — the price a collector can expect to pay when buying a card from a dealer. The wholesale price — that which a collector can expect to receive from a dealer when selling cards — will be significantly lower, depending on desirability and condition.

1999 Upper Deck PowerDeck I

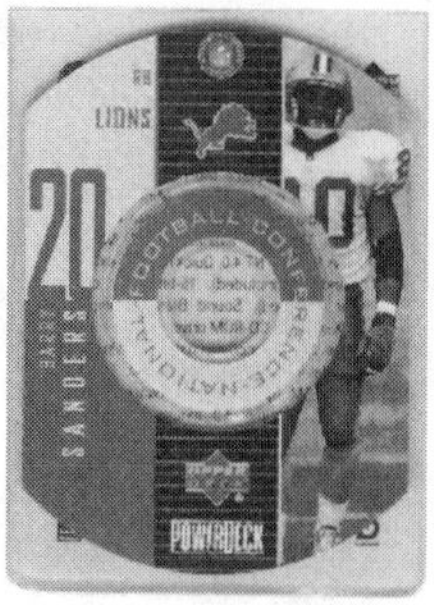

Each of these singles are an interactive card that comes to life with game-action footage, sound, photos and career highlights of the featured player. Singles were found 1:288 packs.

	MT
Complete Set (8):	325.00
Common Player:	25.00
Inserted 1:288	
TC-PD Tim Couch	60.00
DC-PD Daunte Culpepper	25.00
JE-PD John Elway	60.00
PM-PD Peyton Manning	60.00
DM-PD Dan Marino	60.00
CM-PD Cade McNown	25.00
BS-PD Barry Sanders	75.00
AS-PD Akili Smith	25.00

1999 Upper Deck PowerDeck II

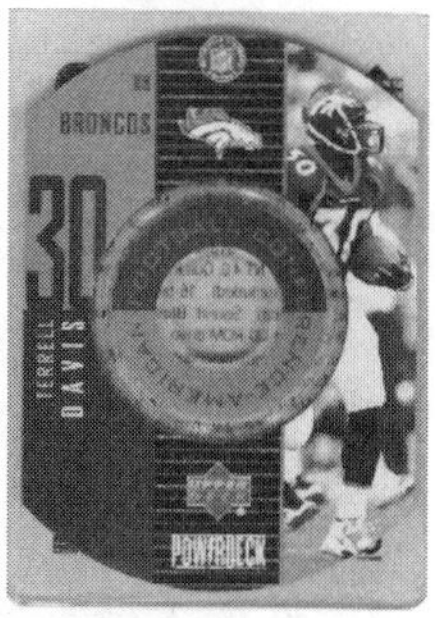

Each single in this set is a interactive card with game-action footage, sound, photos and career highlights of that featured player. Singles were found 1:24 packs.

	MT
Complete Set (8):	45.00
Common Player:	2.00
Inserted 1:24	
TA-PD Troy Aikman	8.00
TD-PD Terrell Davis	12.00
JG-PD Joe Germaine	2.00
BH-PD Brock Huard	2.00
SK-PD Shaun King	4.00
Mc-PD Donovan McNabb	8.00
JM-PD Joe Montana	8.00
RM-PD Randy Moss	16.00

1999 Upper Deck Quarterback Class

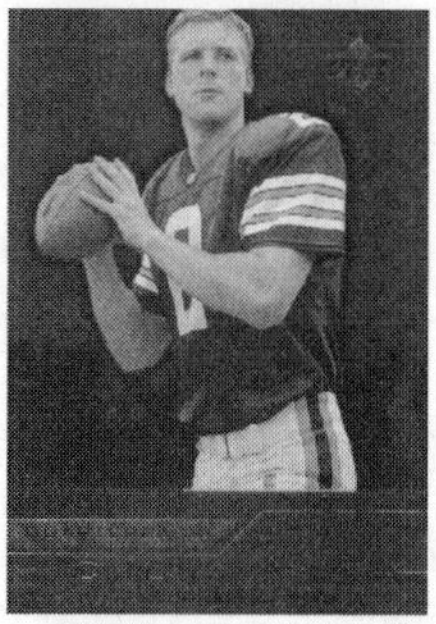

This 15-card insert includes the top QB's in the NFL along with rookies from 1999. Singles were found 1:10 packs. A parallel Silver was numbered to 100 and a parallel Gold was limited to only one set.

	MT
Complete Set (15):	50.00
Common Player:	1.00
Minor Stars:	2.00
Inserted 1:10	
Quantum Silver:	10x-20x
Production 100 Sets	
Quantum Gold	
Production 1 Set	
1 Tim Couch	10.00
2 Akili Smith	4.00
3 Daunte Culpepper	4.00
4 Cade McNown	4.00
5 Donovan McNabb	4.00
6 Brock Huard	1.00
7 John Elway	6.00
8 Dan Marino	6.00
9 Brett Favre	8.00
10 Charlie Batch	2.00
11 Steve Young	2.50
12 Jake Plummer	4.00
13 Peyton Manning	6.00
14 Mark Brunell	3.00
15 Troy Aikman	4.00

1999 Upper Deck Strike Force

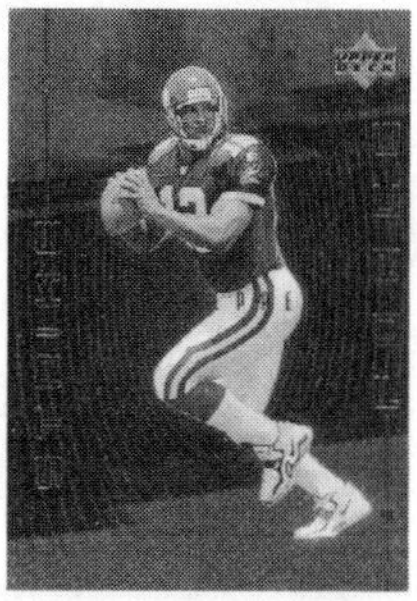

This 30-card set includes the top scoring threats in the NFL and brings them to life on a silver-foil board card. Singles were inserted 1:4 packs. A parallel Silver was sequentially numbered to 100 and a Gold parallel was issued with only one set made.

	MT
Complete Set (30):	50.00
Common Player:	1.00
Minor Stars:	2.00
Inserted 1:4	
1 Jamal Anderson	1.00
2 Keyshawn Johnson	2.00
3 Eddie George	2.50
4 Steve Young	2.50
5 Emmitt Smith	4.00
6 Karim Abdul	1.00
7 Kordell Stewart	2.50
8 Cade McNown	3.50
9 Tim Couch	8.00
10 Corey Dillon	2.00
11 Peyton Manning	5.00
12 Curtis Martin	2.00
13 Jerome Bettis	2.00
14 Jon Kitna	2.00
15 Dan Marino	5.00
16 Eric Moulds	2.00
17 Charlie Batch	2.50
18 Ricky Williams	8.00
19 Terrell Owens	2.00
20 Ty Detmer	1.00
21 Curtis Enis	2.00
22 Doug Flutie	2.50
23 Randall Cunningham	2.00
24 Donovan McNabb	3.50
25 Steve McNair	2.50
26 Terrell Davis	5.00
27 Daunte Culpepper	3.50
28 Warrick Dunn	2.00
29 Akili Smith	3.50
30 Barry Sanders	6.00

1999 Upper Deck Black Diamond

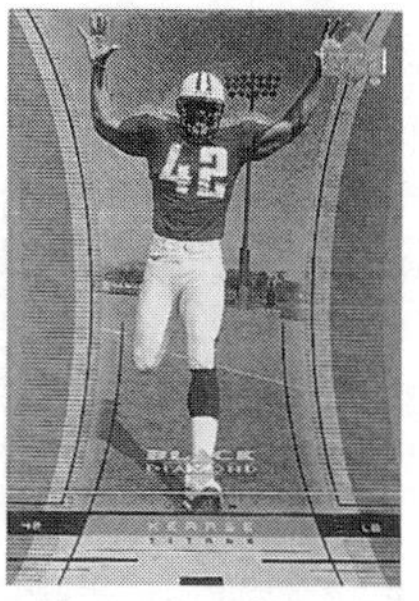

This was a 150-card set that included 40 rookies that were inserted 1:4 packs. Each single has a parallel Diamond Cut card with veterans inserted 1:7 packs and rookies inserted 1:12. Each also has a parallel Final Cut single with veterans numbered to 100 and rookies numbered to 50. Other insert sets included: A Piece of History, Diamonation, Gallery, Might, Myriad, Skills and the Walter Payton Autograph Game Jersey card. SRP was $3.99 for six-card packs.

	MT
Complete Set (150):	140.00
Common Player:	.20
Minor Stars:	.40
Common Rookie:	1.50
Inserted 1:4	
Pack (6):	4.00
Wax Box (30):	90.00
1 Adrian Murrell	.20
2 Jake Plummer	1.50
3 Rob Moore	.40
4 Frank Sanders	.40
5 Jamal Anderson	.75
6 Terance Mathis	.20
7 Chris Chandler	.40
8 Tim Dwight	.75
9 Jermaine Lewis	.20
10 Priest Holmes	.75
11 Peter Boulware	.20
12 Doug Flutie	1.25
13 Antowain Smith	.75
14 Eric Moulds	.75
15 Bruce Smith	.20
16 Rae Carruth	.20
17 Muhsin Muhammad	.40
18 Wesley Walls	.40
19 Tshimanga Biakabutuka	.40
20 Curtis Enis	.75
21 Curtis Conway	.40
22 Bobby Engram	.20
23 Darnay Scott	.40
24 Corey Dillon	.75
25 Jeff Blake	.40
26 Ty Detmer	.20
27 Terry Kirby	.20
28 Leslie Shepherd	.20
29 Emmitt Smith	3.00
30 Troy Aikman	2.00
31 Michael Irvin	.40
32 Raghib Ismail	.20
33 Brian Griese	1.50
34 Terrell Davis	3.00
35 Shannon Sharpe	.40
36 Rod Smith	.50
37 Barry Sanders	4.00
38 Herman Moore	.75
39 Charlie Batch	1.00
40 Johnnie Morton	.20
41 Brett Favre	4.00
42 Dorsey Levens	.75
43 Antonio Freeman	.75
44 Mark Chmura	.40
45 Peyton Manning	3.00
46 Jerome Pathon	.20
47 Marvin Harrison	.75
48 Fred Taylor	2.00
49 Mark Brunell	1.50
50 Jimmy Smith	.75
51 Keenan McCardell	.40
52 Andre Rison	.40
53 Elvis Grbac	.40
54 Derrick Alexander	.20
55 Tony Gonzalez	.40
56 Dan Marino	3.00
57 Oronde Gadsden	.40
58 O.J. McDuffie	.40
59 Randy Moss	4.00
60 Randall Cunningham	.75
61 Cris Carter	.75
62 Robert Smith	.75
63 Drew Bledsoe	1.50
64 Terry Glenn	.75
65 Ben Coates	.40
66 Billy Joe Hobert	.20
67 Eddie Kennison	.20
68 Cam Cleeland	.40
69 Gary Brown	.20
70 Ike Hilliard	.40
71 Amani Toomer	.40
72 Vinny Testaverde	.40
73 Keyshawn Johnson	.75
74 Curtis Martin	.75
75 Wayne Chrebet	.75
76 Tim Brown	.50
77 Rickey Dudley	.20
78 Napoleon Kaufman	.75
79 Charles Woodson	.75
80 Duce Staley	.75
81 Doug Pederson	.20
82 Charles Johnson	.20
83 Kordell Stewart	.75
84 Jerome Bettis	.75
85 Courtney Hawkins	.20
86 Isaac Bruce	.75
87 Marshall Faulk	.75
88 Trent Green	.50
89 Jim Harbaugh	.40
90 Junior Seau	.40
91 Natrone Means	.50
92 Lawrence Phillips	.40
93 Steve Young	1.25
94 Terrell Owens	.75
95 Jerry Rice	2.00
96 Jon Kitna	1.00
97 Ricky Watters	.50
98 Joey Galloway	.75
99 Shawn Springs	.20
100 Warrick Dunn	.75
101 Trent Dilfer	.40
102 Reidel Anthony	.40
103 Mike Alstott	.75
104 Steve McNair	1.00
105 Eddie George	1.00
106 Kevin Dyson	.40
107 Yancey Thigpen	.40
108 Michael Westbrook	.40
109 Brad Johnson	.75
110 Skip Hicks	.40
111 *Tim Couch*	15.00
112 *Akili Smith*	7.00
113 *Ricky Williams*	15.00
114 *Donovan McNabb*	12.00
115 *Edgerrin James*	25.00
116 *Cade McNown*	6.00
117 *Daunte Culpepper*	20.00
118 *Shaun King*	10.00
119 *Brock Huard*	5.00
120 *Joe Germaine*	3.00
121 *Troy Edwards*	5.00
122 *Champ Bailey*	5.00
123 *Kevin Faulk*	5.00
124 *David Boston*	7.00
125 *Kevin Johnson*	7.00
126 *Torry Holt*	8.00
127 *James Johnson*	3.00
128 *Peerless Price*	5.00
129 *D'Wayne Bates*	3.00
130 *Cecil Collins*	3.00
131 *Na Brown*	1.50
132 *Rob Konrad*	3.00
133 *Joel Makovicka*	1.50
134 *Dameane Douglas*	1.50
135 *Scott Covington*	1.50
136 *Daylon McCutcheon*	1.50
137 *Chris Claiborne*	3.00
138 *Karsten Bailey*	3.00
139 *Mike Cloud*	3.00
140 *Sean Bennett*	3.00
141 *Jermaine Fazande*	3.00
142 *Chris McAlister*	3.00
143 *Ebenezer Ekuban*	1.50
144 *Jeff Paulk*	1.50
145 *Jim Kleinsasser*	3.00
146 *Bobby Collins*	1.50
147 *Andy Katzenmoyer*	3.00
148 *Jevon Kearse*	7.00
149 *Amos Zereoue*	3.00
150 *Sedrick Irvin*	3.00

1999 Upper Deck Black Diamond Diamond Cut Parallel

This was a 150-card parallel to the base set. Each of these singles was printed on a die-cut card with a rainbow foil design. Veterans were inserted 1:7 packs and rookies were found 1:12.

	MT
Complete Set (150):	225.00
Diamond Cut Cards:	2x-4x
Inserted 1:7	
Diamond Cut Rookies:	1.5x
Inserted 1:12	

1999 Upper Deck Black Diamond Final Cut Parallel

This was a 150-card parallel to the base set. Each single was printed with gold foil and sequentially numbered. Veterans were numbered to 100 and rookies to 50.

	MT
Final Cut Cards:	15x-30x
Production 100 Sets	
Final Cut Rookies:	4x-8x
Production 50 Sets	

1999 Upper Deck Black Diamond A Piece of History

This was a 30-card insert set that displayed a single piece of a game-used football. Some singles were only found in hobby product and were inserted 1:179 packs. Others were inserted in both hobby and retail and they were found 1:359 packs. Each single had a parallel Double Diamond single that featured two pieces of a game-used football. Hobby singles were found 1:1,079 and hobby/retail singles were also inserted 1:1,079.

	MT
Complete Set (30):	1350.
Common Player:	25.00
H Inserted 1:179	
HR Inserted 1:359	
Double Diamond Cards:	2x
H Inserted 1:1,079	
HR Inserted 1:1,079	
TA Troy Aikman	75.00
CB Charlie Batch	35.00
DBl Drew Bledsoe	45.00
DBo David Boston	35.00
TB Tim Brown	25.00
TC Tim Couch	100.00
DC Daunte Culpepper	65.00
TD Terrell Davis	60.00
WD Warrick Dunn	25.00
BF Brett Favre	100.00
DF Doug Flutie	60.00
BG Brian Griese	45.00
TH Torry Holt	50.00
BH Brock Huard	35.00
EJ Edgerrin James	125.00
KJ Keyshawn Johnson	25.00
PM Peyton Manning	100.00
DM Dan Marino	100.00
CMa Curtis Martin	25.00
DMc Donovan McNabb	65.00
CM Cade McNown	65.00
HM Herman Moore	25.00
RM Randy Moss	100.00
JP Jake Plummer	50.00
JR Jerry Rice	75.00
DS Deion Sanders	25.00
AS Akili Smith	60.00
ES Emmitt Smith	75.00
RW Ricky Williams	100.00
SY Steve Young	60.00

1999 Upper Deck Black Diamond Diamonation

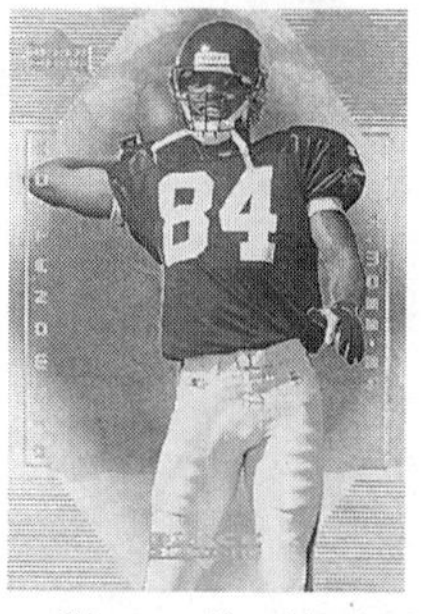

This was a 20-card insert set that included the most dominant players in the game. Singles were inserted 1:6 packs.

	MT
Complete Set (20):	50.00
Common Player:	1.50
Inserted 1:6	
1 Brett Favre	8.00
2 Eddie George	2.00
3 Terrell Davis	6.00
4 Jerome Bettis	1.50

5	Randall Cunningham	1.50
6	Jon Kitna	2.00
7	Troy Aikman	4.00
8	Marshall Faulk	2.00
9	Steve Young	3.00
10	Warrick Dunn	1.50
11	Jake Plummer	3.00
12	Fred Taylor	4.00
13	Antonio Freeman	1.50
14	Peyton Manning	6.00
15	Randy Moss	8.00
16	Steve McNair	2.00
17	Emmitt Smith	6.00
18	Terrell Owens	1.50
19	Kordell Stewart	1.50
20	Ricky Williams	8.00

1999 Upper Deck Black Diamond Gallery

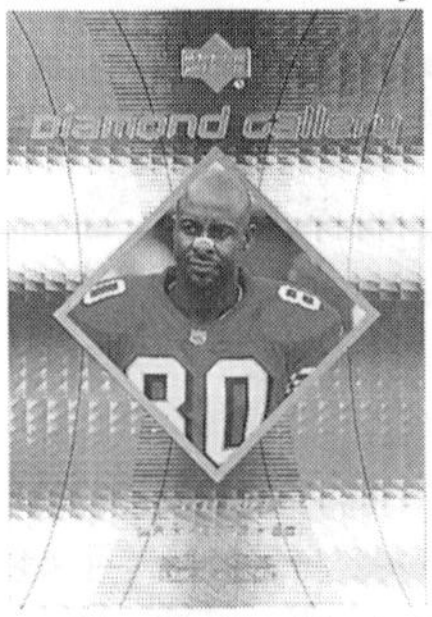

This was a 10-card insert set that featured candid gallery, portrait-style photography of the most collectible players in the NFL. Singles were inserted 1:14 packs.

		MT
Complete Set (10):		50.00
Common Player:		2.50
Inserted 1:14		
1	Akili Smith	6.00
2	Barry Sanders	12.00
3	Curtis Martin	2.50
4	Drew Bledsoe	5.00
5	Emmitt Smith	10.00
6	Keyshawn Johnson	2.50
7	Jerry Rice	8.00
8	Tim Couch	12.00
9	Terrell Owens	2.50
10	Troy Aikman	8.00

1999 Upper Deck Black Diamond Might

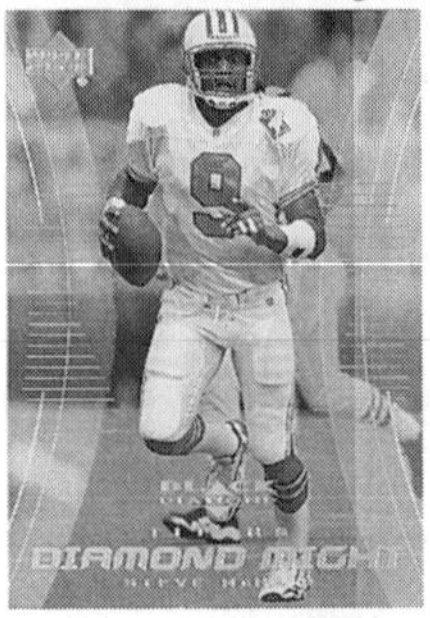

This was a 10-card insert set that included ten powerhouse players. Singles were inserted 1:12 packs.

		MT
Complete Set (10):		20.00
Common Player:		2.00
Inserted 1:12		
1	Antowain Smith	2.00
2	Steve McNair	3.00
3	Corey Dillon	3.00
4	Dan Marino	8.00
5	Eddie George	3.00
6	Jerome Bettis	2.00
7	Jerry Rice	6.00
8	Randall Cunningham	2.00
9	Brian Griese	3.50
10	Joey Galloway	2.00

1999 Upper Deck Black Diamond Myriad

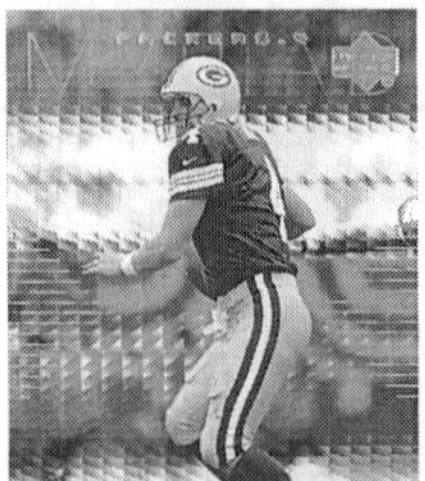

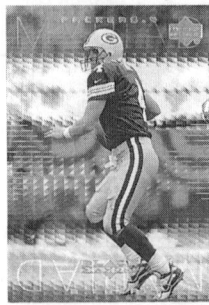

This was a 10-card insert set that captured the electrifying exploits of NFL standouts in action. Singles were inserted 1:29 packs.

		MT
Complete Set (10):		65.00
Common Player:		3.00
Inserted 1:29		
1	Barry Sanders	12.00
2	Randy Moss	12.00
3	Terrell Davis	8.00
4	Brett Favre	12.00
5	Jamal Anderson	3.00
6	Mark Brunell	5.00
7	Edgerrin James	15.00
8	Steve Young	5.00
9	Ricky Williams	10.00
10	Warrick Dunn	3.00

1999 Upper Deck Black Diamond Skills

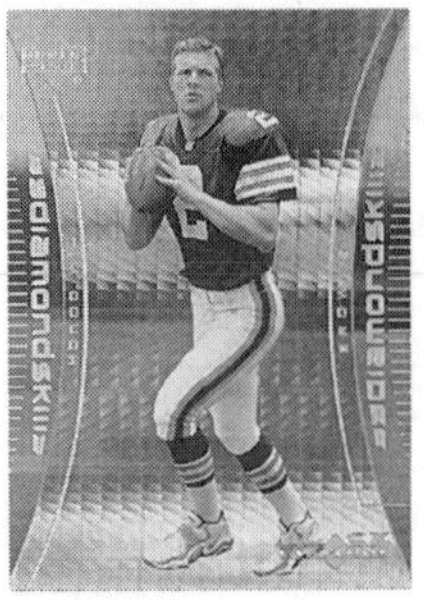

This was a 10-card insert set that included the most versatile and skilled athletes in the game. Singles were found 1:29 packs.

		MT
Complete Set (10):		85.00
Common Player:		3.00
Inserted 1:29		
1	Drew Bledsoe	5.00
2	Fred Taylor	7.00
3	Dan Marino	10.00
4	Jake Plummer	6.00
5	Kurt Warner	30.00
6	Marshall Faulk	3.00
7	Randy Moss	12.00
8	Peyton Manning	12.00
9	Keyshawn Johnson	3.00
10	Tim Couch	12.00

1999 Upper Deck Black Diamond W. Payton Jersey Auto.

Walter Payton signed 34 of these singles that included a piece of a game-used jersey. Singles were randomly inserted.

		MT
WPA	Walter Payton 34	2000.

1999 Upper Deck Century Legends

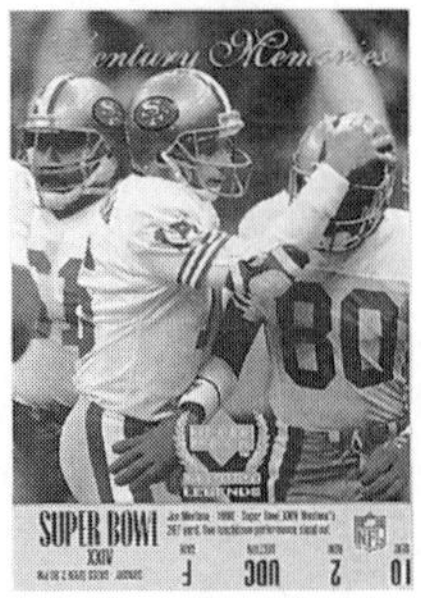

This was a 173-card set that included both past and present NFL players. Cards #4,6,14, 26,31,38 and 43 were never produced. Each single has a parallel Century Collection die-cut that was numbered to 100. Other insert sets included: 20th Century Superstars, Epic Milestones, Epic Signatures, Jerseys of the Century, Tour de France and Walter Payton signed cards. SRP was $4.99 for 12-card packs.

		MT
Complete Set (173):		65.00
Common Player:		.15
Minor Stars:		.30
Common Rookie:		.50
#4,6,14,26,31,38 & 43 never produced		
Pack (5):		5.00
Wax Box (24):		110.00
1	Jim Brown	2.00
2	Jerry Rice	1.00
3	Joe Montana	3.00
5	Johnny Unitas	1.00
7	Otto Graham	.30
8	Walter Payton	3.00
9	Dick Butkus	1.00
10	Bob Lilly	.15
11	Sammy Baugh	.30
12	Barry Sanders	2.00
13	Deacon Jones	.50
15	Gino Marchetti	.15
16	John Elway	1.50
17	Anthony Munoz	.15
18	Ray Nitschke	.30
19	Night Train Lane	.15
20	John Hannah	.15
21	Gale Sayers	1.00
22	Reggie White	.30
23	Ronnie Lott	.30
24	Jim Parker	.15
25	Merlin Olsen	.30
27	Dan Marino	1.50
28	Forrest Gregg	.15
29	Roger Staubach	1.50
30	Jack Lambert	.15
32	Marion Motley	.15
33	Earl Campbell	.50
34	Alan Page	.15
35	Bronko Nagurski	.30
36	Mel Blount	.15
37	Deion Sanders	.30
39	Sid Luckman	.15
40	Raymond Berry	.15
41	Bart Starr	1.00
42	Willie Lanier	.15
44	Terry Bradshaw	1.50
45	Herb Adderley	.30
46	Steve Largent	.30
47	Jack Ham	.15
48	John Mackey	.15
49	Bill George	.15
50	Willie Brown	.15
51	Jerry Rice	1.00
52	Barry Sanders	2.00
53	John Elway	1.50
54	Reggie White	.30
55	Dan Marino	1.50
56	Deion Sanders	.30
57	Bruce Smith	.15
58	Steve Young	.75
59	Emmitt Smith	1.50
60	Brett Favre	2.00
61	Rod Woodson	.15
62	Troy Aikman	1.00
63	Terrell Davis	1.50
64	Michael Irvin	.30
65	Andre Rison	.15
66	Warren Moon	.30
67	Thurman Thomas	.30
68	Randall Cunningham	.30
69	Jerome Bettis	.50
70	Junior Seau	.30
71	Drew Bledsoe	.75
72	Andre Reed	.30
73	Tim Brown	.30
74	Derrick Thomas	.15
75	Jake Plummer	.75
76	Kordell Stewart	.50
77	Herman Moore	.30
78	Shannon Sharpe	.30
79	Antonio Freeman	.50
80	Ricky Watters	.30
81	Warrick Dunn	.50
82	Mark Brunell	.75
83	Randy Moss	2.00
84	Fred Taylor	1.00
85	Curtis Martin	.50
86	Keyshawn Johnson	.50
87	Eddie George	.60
88	Marshall Faulk	.50
89	Joey Galloway	.50
90	Vinny Testaverde	.30
91	Garrison Hearst	.30
92	Jimmy Smith	.50
93	Doug Flutie	.75
94	Napoleon Kaufman	.50
95	Natrone Means	.30
96	Peyton Manning	1.50
97	Steve McNair	.60
98	Corey Dillon	.50
99	Terrell Owens	.50
100	Charlie Batch	.75
101	Brett Favre	2.00
102	Terrell Davis	1.50
103	Roger Staubach	1.00
104	Terry Bradshaw	1.00
105	Fran Tarkenton	.50
106	Walter Payton	3.00
107	Mark Brunell	.75
108	Jim Brown	1.50
109	Kordell Stewart	.50
110	Bart Starr	1.00
111	Steve Largent	.30
112	Raymond Berry	.15
113	Emmitt Smith	1.50
114	Forrest Gregg	.15
115	Drew Bledsoe	.75
116	Dick Butkus	.50
117	Johnny Unitas	1.00
118	Joe Montana	3.00
119	Deacon Jones	.30
120	Steve Young	.50
121	Bob Lilly	.15
122	Troy Aikman	1.00
123	Alan Page	.15
124	Earl Campbell	.50
125	Deion Sanders	.30
126	Ronnie Lott	.30
127	Reggie White	.30
128	Marshall Faulk	.50
129	Gale Sayers	1.00
130	Night Train Lane	.15
131	*Ricky Williams*	6.00
132	*Tim Couch*	8.00
133	*Donovan McNabb*	4.00
134	*Daunte Culpepper*	6.00
135	*Edgerrin James*	12.00
136	*Cade McNown*	3.00
137	*Torry Holt*	2.50
138	*David Boston*	2.50
139	*Champ Bailey*	1.75
140	*Peerless Price*	2.00
141	*D'Wayne Bates*	.75
142	*Joe Germaine*	.75
143	*Brock Huard*	1.25
144	*Chris Claiborne*	.75
145	*Jevon Kearse*	2.00
146	*Troy Edwards*	2.50
147	*Amos Zereoue*	.75
148	*Aaron Brooks*	3.00
149	*Andy Katzenmoyer*	.75
150	*Kevin Faulk*	1.50
151	*Shaun King*	4.00
152	*Kevin Johnson*	2.50
153	*Dameane Douglas*	.50
154	*Mike Cloud*	.50
155	*Sedrick Irvin*	1.50
156	*Akili Smith*	4.00
157	*Rob Konrad*	.50
158	*Scott Covington*	.50
159	*Jeff Paulk*	.50
160	*Shawn Bryson*	.50
161	Joe Montana	3.00
162	John Elway	1.50
163	Joe Namath	1.50
164	Jerry Rice	1.00
165	Terry Bradshaw	1.00
166	Jim Brown	2.00
167	Paul Warfield	.30
168	Herman Moore	.50
169	Walter Payton	3.00
170	Roger Staubach	1.00
171	Ken Stabler	1.00
172	Steve Young	.75
173	Troy Aikman	1.00
174	Fran Tarkenton	.50
175	Doug Williams	.15
176	Steve Largent	.30
177	Marcus Allen	.30
178	Mike Singletary	.30
179	Earl Campbell	.30
180	Dan Fouts	.30

1999 Upper Deck Century Legends Century Collection Parallel

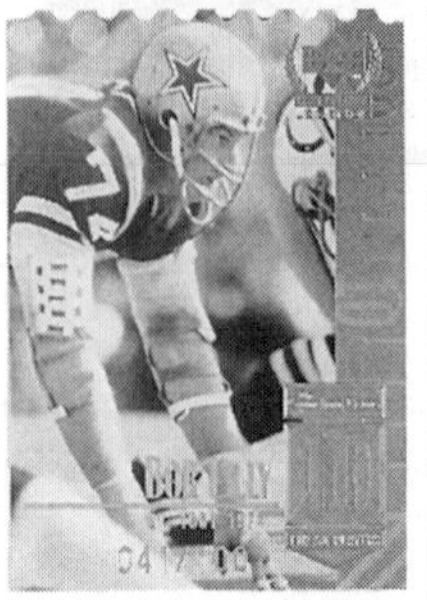

This was a 173-card parallel to the base set. Each single was die-cut and sequentially numbered to 100.

	MT
Century Cards:	10x-20x
Century Rookies:	5x-10x
Production 100 Sets	

1999 Upper Deck Century Legends 20th Century Superstars

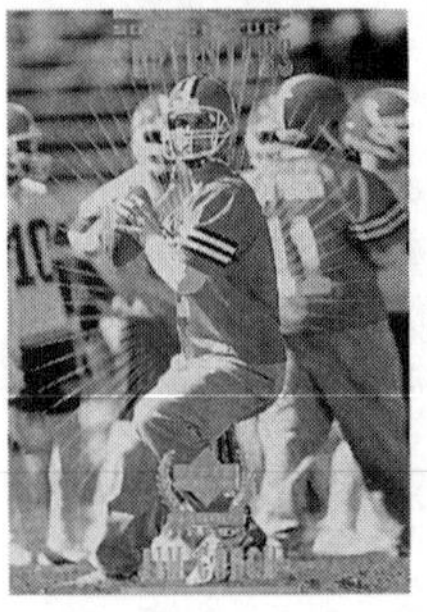

This 10-card insert set focused on the NFL's most-talked about players. Singles were inserted 1:11 packs.

		MT
Complete Set (10):		35.00
Common Player:		1.50
Inserted 1:11		
1	Tim Couch	8.00
2	Ricky Williams	6.00
3	Akili Smith	4.00
4	Donovan McNabb	4.00
5	Jake Plummer	3.00
6	Brett Favre	6.00
7	Steve Young	2.00
8	Randy Moss	6.00
9	Kordell Stewart	1.50
10	Peyton Manning	5.00

1999 Upper Deck Century Legends Epic Milestones

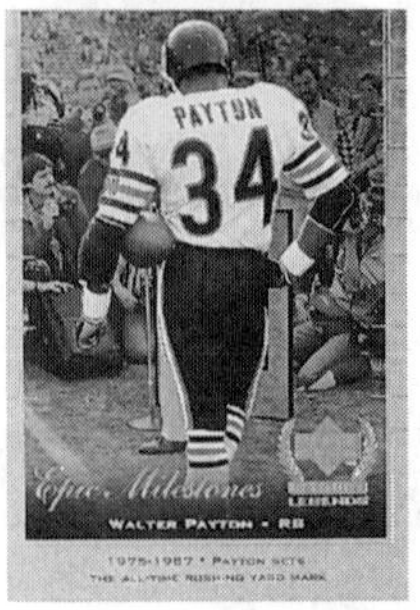

This was a 10-card insert set that pinpointed ten of the most impressive NFL milestones ever reached. Singles were inserted 1:11 packs.

		MT
Complete Set (10):		45.00
Common Player:		1.50
Inserted 1:11		
1	John Elway	5.00
2	Joe Montana	7.00
3	Randy Moss	7.00
4	Terrell Davis	5.00
5	Dan Marino	5.00
6	Jamal Anderson	1.50
7	Jerry Rice	4.00
8	Barry Sanders	7.00
9	Emmitt Smith	5.00
10	Walter Payton	7.00

1999 Upper Deck Century Legends Epic Signatures

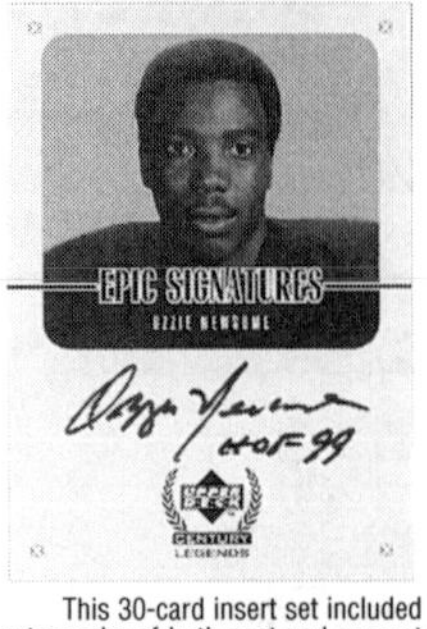

This 30-card insert set included autographs of both past and present stars. Singles were inserted 1:23 packs. A parallel Gold version was also released for every player except for Johnny Unitas. Each of those singles were numbered to 100.

		MT
Complete Set (30):		1750.
Common Player:		10.00
Minor Stars:		20.00
Inserted 1:23		
Century Gold Cards:		2x
Unitas never produced		
Production 100 Sets		
TA	Troy Aikman	75.00
RB	Raymond Berry	10.00
TB	Terry Bradshaw	125.00
DB	Dick Butkus	75.00
EC	Earl Campbell	50.00
HC	Harold Carmichael	20.00
CC	Cris Carter	20.00
TD	Terrell Davis	85.00
LD	Len Dawson	20.00
DF	Dan Fouts	20.00
CJ	Charlie Joiner	20.00
SL	Steve Largent	25.00
FL	Floyd Little	10.00
DM	Dan Marino	180.00
MY	Don Maynard	20.00
AM	Art Monk	20.00
JM	Joe Montana	250.00
RM	Randy Moss	175.00
JN	Joe Namath	250.00
ON	Ozzie Newsome	10.00
DR	Dan Reeves	20.00
JR	Jerry Rice	250.00
GS	Gale Sayers	30.00
MS	Michael Singletary	10.00
RS	Roger Staubach	100.00
FT	Fran Tarkenton	65.00
JU	Johnny Unitas	125.00
PW	Paul Warfield	10.00
DW	Doug Williams	20.00
JY	Jack Youngblood	10.00

1999 Upper Deck Century Legends Jerseys of the Century

This nine-card insert set included swatches of game jerseys from both past and present NFL stars. Singles were inserted 1:418 packs.

		MT
Complete Set (9):		1600.
Common Player:		75.00
#9 never produced		
Inserted 1:418		
1	Jerry Rice	225.00
2	Roger Staubach	200.00
3	Warren Moon	75.00
4	Ken Stabler	125.00
5	Reggie White	75.00
6	Dan Marino	275.00
7	Doug Flutie	125.00
8	Bob Lilly	75.00
9	Jim Brown	250.00

1999 Upper Deck Century Legends Tour de Force

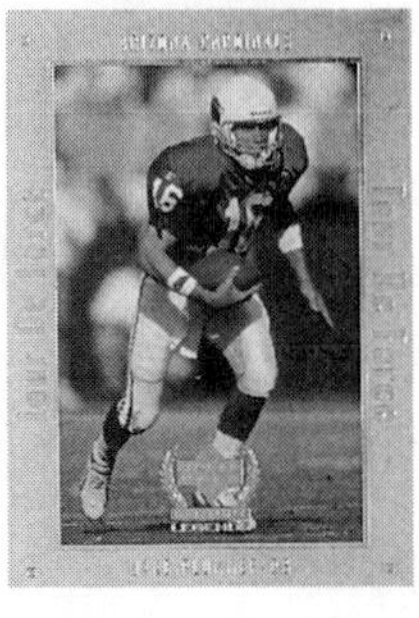

This was a 10-card insert set that highlighted the ten most important players in the NFL. Singles were inserted 1:23 packs.

		MT
Complete Set (10):		45.00
Common Player:		2.50
Inserted 1:23		
1	Tim Couch	12.00
2	Ricky Williams	10.00
3	Peyton Manning	8.00
4	Troy Aikman	6.00
5	Jake Plummer	5.00
6	Jamal Anderson	2.50
7	Terrell Davis	8.00
8	Barry Sanders	10.00
9	Fred Taylor	6.00
10	Keyshawn Johnson	2.50

1999 Upper Deck Century Legends Walter Payton

Walter Payton signed 50 UD Authentic cards and 34 Game-Used Jersey cards. Singles were randomly inserted.

		MT
WPAC	W.Payton AUTO/50	650.00
WPCL	W.Payton Jersey AUTO/34	2200.

1999 Upper Deck Encore

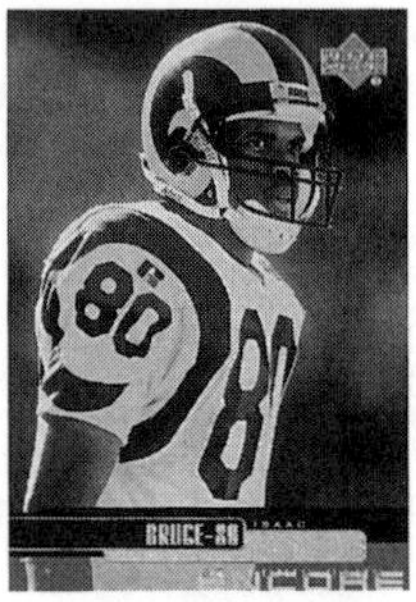

This was a 225-card set that included 45 rookies found 1:8 packs. Parallel sets included F/X and F/X Gold. Other insert sets included: Electric Currents, Game Used Helmets, Live Wires, Seize the Game, UD Authentics, Upper Realm and the Walter Payton Game Jersey card. SRP was $3.99 for six-card packs.

		MT
Complete Set (225):		275.00
Common Player:		.20
Minor Stars:		.40
Common Rookie:		3.00
Inserted 1:8		
Pack (6):		4.00
Wax Box (24):		70.00
1	Jake Plummer	1.25
2	Adrian Murrell	.20
3	Rob Moore	.40
4	Simeon Rice	.20
5	Andre Wadsworth	.20
6	Frank Sanders	.20
7	Tim Dwight	.75
8	Chris Chandler	.40
9	Jamal Anderson	.75
10	O.J. Santiago	.20
11	Tony Graziani	.20
12	Terance Mathis	.20
13	Priest Holmes	.75
14	Stoney Case	.40
15	Ray Lewis	.20
16	Peter Boulware	.20
17	Scott Mitchell	.20
18	Jermaine Lewis	.20
19	Eric Moulds	.75
20	Doug Flutie	1.00
21	Antowain Smith	.75
22	Rob Johnson	.40
23	Bruce Smith	.20
24	Andre Reed	.40
25	Wesley Walls	.40
26	Tshimanga Biakabutuka	.40
27	Fred Lane	.20
28	Steve Beurlein	.40
29	Muhsin Muhammad	.40
30	Rae Carruth	.20
31	Bobby Engram	.20
32	Curtis Enis	.75
33	Edgar Bennett	.20
34	Curtis Conway	.40
35	Shane Matthews	.20
36	Tony McGee	.20
37	Darnay Scott	.40
38	Jeff Blake	.40
39	Corey Dillon	.75
40	Ki-Jana Carter	.20
41	Ty Detmer	.20
42	Leslie Shepherd	.20
43	Terry Kirby	.20
44	Antonio Langham	.20
45	Jamir Miller	.20
46	Marc Edwards	.20
47	Troy Aikman	1.50
48	Raghib Ismail	.20
49	Emmitt Smith	2.00
50	Michael Irvin	.40
51	Deion Sanders	.75
52	Greg Ellis	.20
53	Bubby Brister	.40
54	Terrell Davis	2.00
55	Ed McCaffrey	.75
56	Rod Smith	.75
57	Shannon Sharpe	.40
58	Brian Griese	1.50
59	Charlie Batch	1.00

60 Germane Crowell .40
61 Johnnie Morton .20
62 Robert Porcher .20
63 Ron Rivers .20
64 Herman Moore .75
65 Brett Favre 3.00
66 Bill Schroeder .40
67 Antonio Freeman .75
68 Dorsey Levens .75
69 Desmond Howard .20
70 Vonnie Holliday .20
71 Peyton Manning 2.00
72 Jerome Pathon .20
73 Marvin Harrison .75
74 Ken Dilger .20
75 E.G. Green .20
76 Cornelius Bennett .20
77 Mark Brunell 1.25
78 Fred Taylor 1.50
79 Jimmy Smith .75
80 James Stewart .75
81 Keenan McCardell .40
82 Carnell Lake .20
83 Elvis Grbac .40
84 Tony Gonzalez .40
85 Andre Rison .40
86 Derrick Thomas .40
87 Warren Moon .40
88 Derrick Alexander .20
89 Dan Marino 2.00
90 O.J. McDuffie .40
91 Karim Abdul .40
92 Sam Madison .20
93 Zach Thomas .40
94 Tony Martin .20
95 Randall Cunningham .75
96 Randy Moss 3.00
97 Cris Carter .75
98 Jake Reed .40
99 John Randle .40
100 Robert Smith .75
101 Drew Bledsoe 1.25
102 Ben Coates .40
103 Terry Glenn .75
104 Tony Simmons .40
105 Terry Allen .40
106 Danny Wuerffel .40
107 Cameron Cleeland .40
108 Eddie Kennison .20
109 Billy Joe Hobert .20
110 Andre Hastings .20
111 Kent Graham .20
112 Tiki Barber .40
113 Gary Brown .20
114 Ike Hilliard .40
115 Jason Sehorn .20
116 Kerry Collins .40
117 Vinny Testaverde .40
118 Wayne Chrebet .75
119 Curtis Martin .75
120 Rick Mirer .20
121 Aaron Glenn .20
122 Keyshawn Johnson .75
123 Rich Gannon .40
124 Tim Brown .40
125 Darrell Russell .20
126 Tyrone Wheatley .40
127 Charles Woodson .75
128 Napoleon Kaufman .75
129 Duce Staley .75
130 Doug Pederson .20
131 Kevin Turner .20
132 Charles Johnson .20
133 Jerome Bettis .75
134 Courtney Hawkins .20
135 Kordell Stewart .75
136 Richard Huntley .40
137 Levon Kirkland .20
138 Hines Ward .40
139 *Kurt Warner* 25.00
140 Marshall Faulk .75
141 Az Hakim .40
142 Amp Lee .20
143 Isaac Bruce .75
144 Kevin Carter .20
145 Jim Harbaugh .40
146 Junior Seau .40
147 Natrone Means .40
148 Rodney Harrison .20
149 Mikhael Ricks .20
150 Erik Kramer .20
151 Steve Young 1.00
152 Terrell Owens .75
153 Jerry Rice 1.50
154 J.J. Stokes .40
155 *Jeff Garcia* 12.00
156 Lawrence Phillips .40
157 Jon Kitna 1.00
158 Derrick Mayes .40
159 Ricky Watters .40
160 Chad Brown .20
161 Shawn Springs .20
162 Sean Dawkins .20
163 Trent Dilfer .40
164 Reidel Anthony .40
165 Bert Emanuel .20
166 Warrick Dunn .75
167 Jacquez Green .40
168 Mike Alstott .75
169 Eddie George 1.00
170 Steve McNair 1.00
171 Kevin Dyson .40
172 Frank Wycheck .20
173 Blaine Bishop .20
174 Yancey Thigpen .40
175 Brad Johnson .75
176 Michael Westbrook .40
177 Skip Hicks .75
178 Brian Mitchell .20
179 Dana Stubblefield .20
180 Stephen Davis .75
181 *Champ Bailey* 5.00
182 *Chris McAlister* 4.00
183 *Jevon Kearse* 8.00
184 *Ebenezer Ekuban* 3.00
185 *Chris Claiborne* 4.00
186 *Andy Katzenmoyer* 4.00
187 *Tim Couch* 15.00
188 *Daunte Culpepper* 20.00
189 *Akili Smith* 7.00
190 *Donovan McNabb* 12.00
191 *Sean Bennett* 4.00
192 *Brock Huard* 5.00
193 *Cade McNown* 7.00
194 *Shaun King* 10.00
195 *Joe Germaine* 4.00
196 *Ricky Williams* 15.00
197 *Edgerrin James* 35.00
198 *Sedrick Irvin* 4.00
199 *Kevin Faulk* 5.00
200 *Rob Konrad* 4.00
201 *James Johnson* 4.00
202 *Amos Zereoue* 4.00
203 *Torry Holt* 8.00
204 *D'Wayne Bates* 3.00
205 *David Boston* 8.00
206 *Dameane Douglas* 3.00
207 *Troy Edwards* 6.00
208 *Kevin Johnson* 7.00
209 *Peerless Price* 5.00
210 *Antoine Winfield* 3.00
211 *Michael Cloud* 4.00
212 *Joe Montgomery* 4.00
213 *Jermaine Fazande* 4.00
214 *Scott Covington* 3.00
215 *Aaron Brooks* 12.00
216 *Terry Jackson* 4.00
217 *Cecil Collins* 4.00
218 *Olandis Gary* 10.00
219 *Craig Yeast* 3.00
220 *Karsten Bailey* 4.00
221 *Reginald Kelly* 3.00
222 *Travis McGriff* 3.00
223 *Jeff Paulk* 3.00
224 *Jim Kleinsasser* 4.00
225 *Jason Tucker* 6.00

1999 Upper Deck Encore F/X Parallel

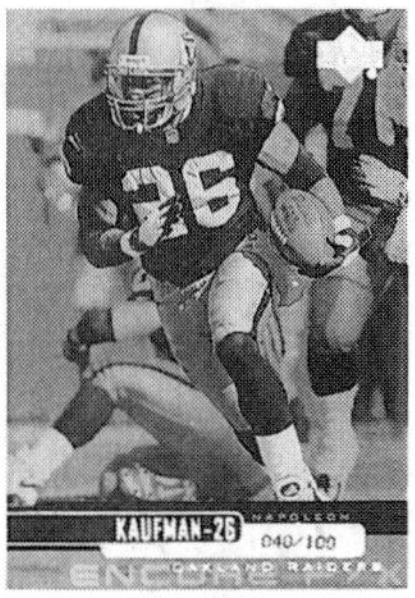

This was a 225-card parallel to the base set. Each single from this set was numbered to 100.

	MT
F/X Cards:	15x-30x
F/X Rookies:	2x-4x
Production 100 Sets	
F/X Gold Cards:	
Production 1 Set	

1999 Upper Deck Encore F/X Gold Parallel

This was a 225-card parallel to the base set. Only one of each card was produced.

	MT
F/X Gold Cards:	
Production 1 Set	

1999 Upper Deck Encore Electric Currents

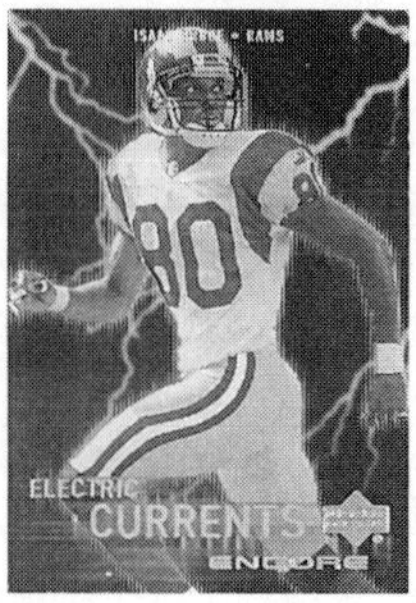

This was a 20-card insert set that featured the NFL's premier offensive stars. Singles were inserted 1:6 packs.

		MT
Complete Set (20):		25.00
Common Player:		.75
Minor Stars:		1.50
Inserted 1:6		
1	Steve Young	3.00
2	Doug Flutie	3.00
3	Jon Kitna	2.00
4	Randall Cunningham	1.50
5	Curtis Enis	1.50
6	Jerry Rice	5.00
7	Antonio Freeman	1.50
8	Keyshawn Johnson	1.50
9	Steve McNair	2.00
10	Kordell Stewart	1.50
11	Drew Bledsoe	3.00
12	Corey Dillon	1.50
13	Vinny Testaverde	.75
14	Tim Brown	.75
15	Antowain Smith	1.50
16	Charlie Batch	2.50
17	Stephen Davis	1.50
18	Isaac Bruce	1.50
19	Curtis Martin	1.50
20	Ricky Watters	.75

1999 Upper Deck Encore Game-Used Helmets

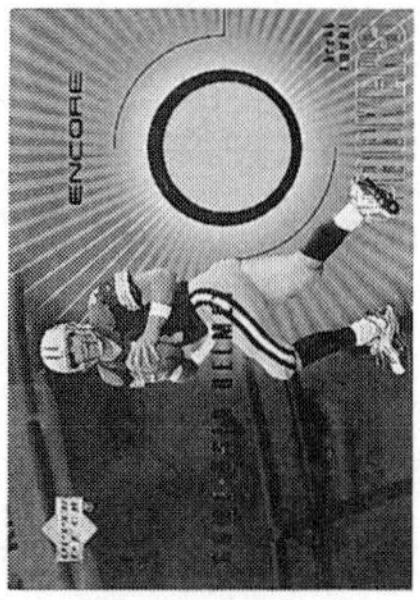

This was a six-card insert set that included a piece of a game-used helmet of that respected player. Singles were inserted 1:575 packs.

		MT
Complete Set (6):		450.00
Common Player:		30.00
Inserted 1:575		
MB	Mark Brunell	60.00
TD	Terrell Davis	75.00
MF	Marshall Faulk	30.00
BF	Brett Favre	150.00
DM	Dan Marino	120.00
JR	Jerry Rice	100.00

1999 Upper Deck Encore Game-Used Rookie Helmets

This 15-card insert set included pieces of helmets used in NFL Rookie Shoot. Singles were inserted 1:575 packs.

		MT
Complete Set (15):		1000.
Common Player:		30.00
Inserted 1:575		
CB	Champ Bailey	70.00
DW	D'Wayne Bates	30.00
DB	David Boston	80.00
CC	Cecil Collins	80.00
TC	Tim Couch	150.00
DC	Daunte Culpepper	125.00
TE	Troy Edwards	80.00
KF	Kevin Faulk	60.00
TH	Torry Holt	80.00
BH	Brock Huard	60.00
EJ	Edgerrin James	200.00
KJ	Kevin Johnson	80.00
Mc	Donovan McNabb	100.00
CM	Cade McNown	100.00
AS	Akili Smith	100.00

1999 Upper Deck Encore Live Wires

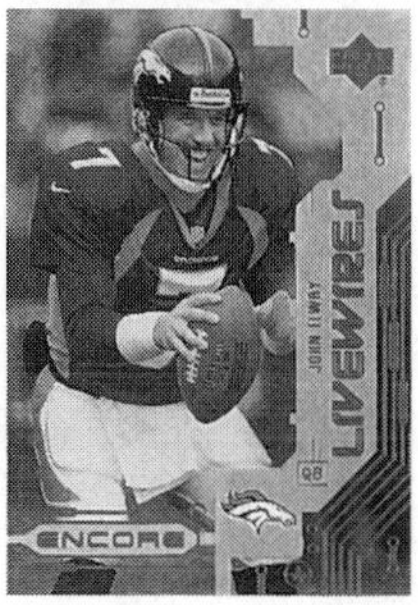

This 15-card insert set included the top stars in the NFL and inserted them 1:11 packs.

		MT
Complete Set (15):		45.00
Common Player:		2.00
Inserted 1:11		
1	Jake Plummer	3.00
2	Jamal Anderson	2.00
3	Emmitt Smith	6.00
4	John Elway	6.00
5	Barry Sanders	8.00
6	Brett Favre	8.00
7	Mark Brunell	3.00
8	Fred Taylor	4.00
9	Randy Moss	8.00
10	Drew Bledsoe	3.00
11	Keyshawn Johnson	2.00
12	Jerome Bettis	2.00
13	Kordell Stewart	2.00
14	Terrell Owens	2.00
15	Eddie George	3.00

1999 Upper Deck Encore Seize the Game

This 30-card insert set included the game's biggest game-breakers. Cards #1-#20 were inserted 1:20 packs and cards #21-#30 were inserted 1:23 packs. Each single also has a parallel Gold version and each was numbered to 250.

		MT
Complete Set (30):		100.00
Common Player (1-20):		2.50
Inserted 1:20		
Common Player (21-30):		4.00
Inserted 1:23		
F/X Gold Cards:		3x
Production 250 Sets		
1	Donovan McNabb	5.00
2	Keyshawn Johnson	2.50
3	Eddie George	2.50
4	Randall Cunningham	2.50
5	Charlie Batch	4.00
6	Curtis Martin	2.50
7	Edgerrin James	15.00
8	Jake Plummer	5.00
9	Drew Bledsoe	5.00
10	Marshall Faulk	2.50
11	Fred Taylor	6.00
12	Terrell Owens	2.50
13	Jerome Bettis	2.50
14	Antonio Freeman	2.50
15	Corey Dillon	2.50
16	Jerry Rice	8.00
17	Curtis Enis	2.50
18	Warrick Dunn	2.50
19	Kordell Stewart	2.50
20	Jamal Anderson	2.50
21	Terrell Davis	8.00
22	Randy Moss	10.00
23	Troy Aikman	6.00
24	Dan Marino	8.00
25	Ricky Williams	10.00
26	Peyton Manning	8.00
27	Steve Young	4.00
28	Tim Couch	10.00
29	Emmitt Smith	8.00
30	Brett Favre	10.00

1999 Upper Deck Encore UD Authentics

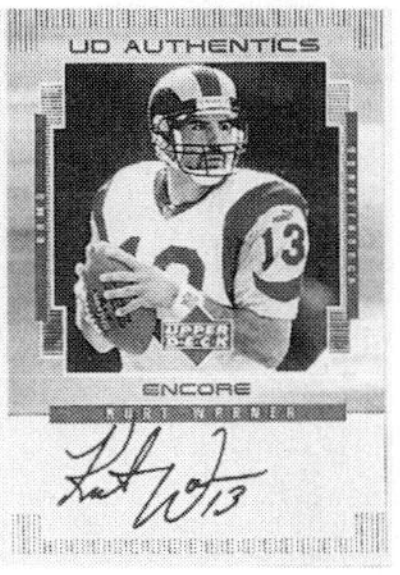

This 15-card insert set included autographs of the top current NFL stars. Singles were inserted 1:144 packs.

		MT
Complete Set (15):		1200.
Common Player:		25.00
Inserted 1:144		
TA	Troy Aikman	85.00
DB	David Boston	40.00
MB	Mark Brunell	70.00
TC	Tim Couch	125.00
TE	Troy Edwards	40.00
KF	Kevin Faulk	25.00
TH	Torry Holt	40.00
BH	Brock Huard	25.00
EJ	Edgerrin James	150.00
SK	Shaun King	60.00
PM	Peyton Manning	150.00
CM	Cade McNown	60.00
RM	Randy Moss	125.00
JN	Joe Namath	125.00
KW	Kurt Warner	200.00

1999 Upper Deck Encore Upper Realm

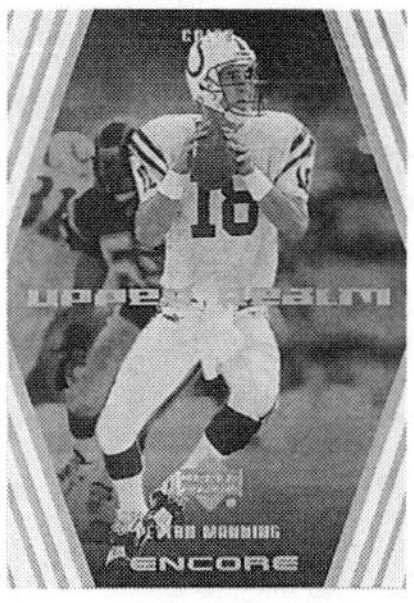

This 10-card insert set pays tribute to ten of the NFL's current elite stars. Singles were inserted 1:12 packs.

		MT
Complete Set (10):		25.00
Common Player:		.75
Minor Stars:		1.50
Inserted 1:12		
1	Randy Moss	7.00
2	Warrick Dunn	1.50
3	Stephen Davis	1.50
4	Peyton Manning	5.00
5	Tim Biakabutuka	.75
6	Steve Young	2.50
7	Kurt Warner	12.00
8	Steve McNair	1.50
9	Dan Marino	5.00
10	Jake Plummer	2.50

A player's name in *italic type* indicates a rookie card.

1999 Upper Deck Encore Walter Payton

Walter Payton signed 34 Game Jersey cards. Each single included a swatch of a game-used jersey and his signature. Singles were randomly inserted into the product.

		MT
WPE	W.Payton Jersey AUTO/34	2500.

1999 Upper Deck HoloGrFX

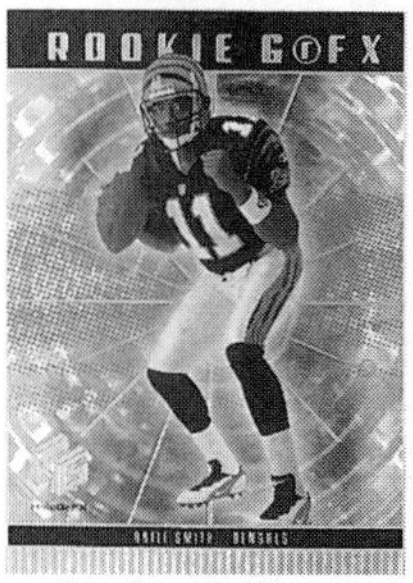

This was a 90-card set that included 30 rookies found 1:2 packs. Each single had an Ausome parallel with veterans inserted 1:8 packs and rookies inserted 1:17. Other insert sets included: 24/7, Future Fame, Star View and UD Authentics. SRP was $1.99 for three-card packs.

		MT
Complete Set (90):		65.00
Common Player:		.20
Minor Stars:		.40
Common Rookies:		.75
Pack (3):		1.75
Wax Box (36):		40.00
1	Jake Plummer	1.25
2	Jamal Anderson	.75
3	Priest Holmes	.75
4	Antowain Smith	.75
5	Doug Flutie	1.00
6	Tshimanga Biakabutuka	.40
7	Curtis Enis	.75
8	Corey Dillon	.75
9	Darnay Scott	.40
10	Leslie Shepherd	.20
11	Troy Aikman	1.50
12	Emmitt Smith	2.00
13	Michael Irvin	.40
14	Terrell Davis	2.00
15	Shannon Sharpe	.40
16	Rod Smith	.75
17	Barry Sanders	3.00
18	Charlie Batch	1.25
19	Herman Moore	.75
20	Brett Favre	3.00
21	Dorsey Levens	.75
22	Antonio Freeman	.75
23	Peyton Manning	2.00
24	Mark Brunell	1.25
25	Fred Taylor	1.50
26	Jimmy Smith	.75
27	Andre Rison	.40
28	Tony Gonzalez	.40
29	Dan Marino	2.00
30	Karim Abdul	.40
31	Randy Moss	3.00
32	Randall Cunningham	.75
33	Drew Bledsoe	1.25
34	Terry Glenn	.75
35	Cameron Cleeland	.40
36	Andre Hastings	.20
37	Amani Toomer	.20
38	Kent Graham	.20
39	Curtis Martin	.75
40	Keyshawn Johnson	.75
41	Vinny Testaverde	.40
42	Napoleon Kaufman	.75
43	Tim Brown	.40
44	Duce Staley	.75
45	Kordell Stewart	.75
46	Jerome Bettis	.75
47	Marshall Faulk	.75
48	Natrone Means	.50
49	Ryan Leaf	.75
50	Steve Young	1.00
51	Jerry Rice	1.50
52	Terrell Owens	.75
53	Joey Galloway	.75
54	Ricky Watters	.40
55	Jon Kitna	.75
56	Warrick Dunn	.75
57	Trent Dilfer	.40
58	Steve McNair	.75
59	Eddie George	.75
60	Brad Johnson	.75
61	*Tim Couch*	8.00
62	*Donovan McNabb*	4.00
63	*Akili Smith*	4.00
64	*Edgerrin James*	12.00
65	*Ricky Williams*	6.00
66	*Torry Holt*	2.50
67	*Champ Bailey*	1.50
68	*David Boston*	2.50
69	*Daunte Culpepper*	8.00
70	*Cade McNown*	3.00
71	*Troy Edwards*	2.50
72	*Kevin Johnson*	2.50
73	*James Johnson*	1.50
74	*Rob Konrad*	.75
75	*Kevin Faulk*	1.50
76	*Shaun King*	4.00
77	*Peerless Price*	2.00
78	*Michael Cloud*	.75
79	*Jermaine Fazande*	1.25
80	*D'Wayne Bates*	.75
81	*Brock Huard*	1.50
82	*Marty Booker*	.75
83	*Karsten Bailey*	.75
84	*Al Wilson*	.75
85	*Joe Germaine*	1.00
86	*Dameane Douglas*	.75
87	*Sedrick Irvin*	1.50
88	*Aaron Brooks*	3.00
89	*Cecil Collins*	1.75
90	*Michael Bishop*	1.50

1999 Upper Deck HoloGrFX Ausome Parallel

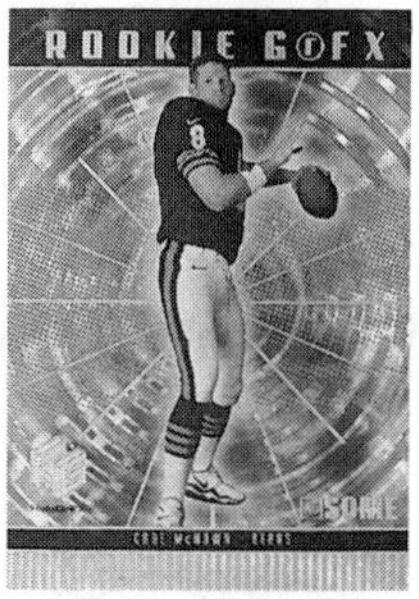

This was a 90-card parallel to the base set. Each single had gold foil added to the background. Veterans were inserted 1:8 packs and rookies were found 1:17.

	MT
Complete Set (90):	150.00
Ausome Cards:	2x-4x
Inserted 1:8	
Ausome Rookies:	2x
Inserted 1:17	

1999 Upper Deck HoloGrFX 24/7

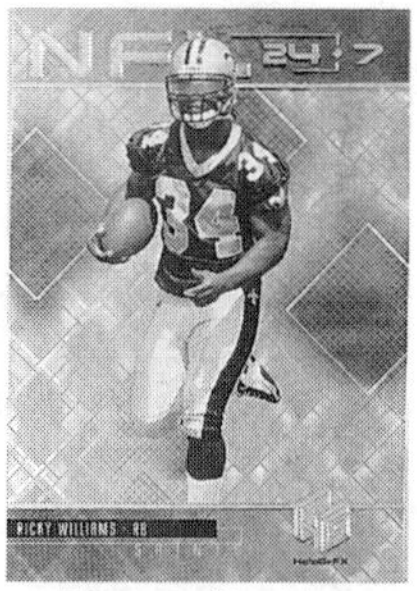

This was a 15-card insert set that captured the most exciting players in the NFL today. Singles were inserted 1:3 packs. A parallel Gold version was also made and singles were inserted 1:105 packs.

		MT
Complete Set (15):		35.00
Common Player:		1.00
Inserted 1:3		
Gold Cards:		4x-8x
Inserted 1:105		
1	Jake Plummer	2.00
2	Emmitt Smith	4.00
3	Terrell Davis	4.00
4	Peyton Manning	4.00
5	Drew Bledsoe	2.00
6	Troy Aikman	3.00
7	Ricky Williams	6.00
8	Keyshawn Johnson	1.00
9	Akili Smith	3.00
10	Eddie George	1.00
11	Edgerrin James	10.00
12	David Boston	1.50
13	Cade McNown	3.00
14	Jerome Bettis	1.00
15	Herman Moore	1.00

1999 Upper Deck HoloGrFX 24/7 Gold Parallel

This was a 15-card parallel to the 24/7 insert set. Singles were inserted 1:105 packs.

	MT
Gold Cards:	4x-8x
Inserted 1:105	

1999 Upper Deck HoloGrFX Future Fame

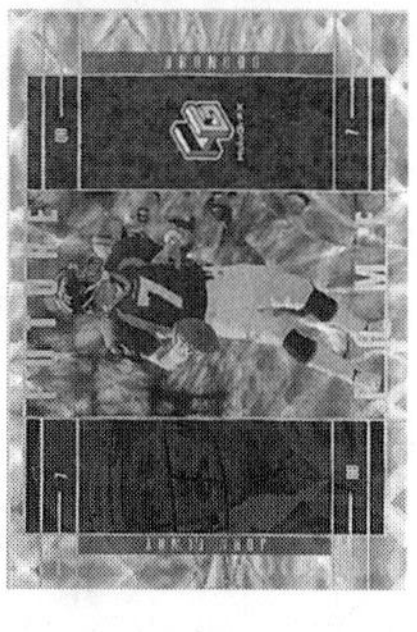

This was a six-card insert set that included the most impressive talents in the NFL. Singles were inserted 1:34 packs. A parallel Gold version was also released and inserted 1:431 packs.

		MT
Complete Set (6):		40.00
Common Player:		3.00
Inserted 1:34		
Gold Cards:		3x
Inserted 1:431		
1	John Elway	10.00
2	Dan Marino	10.00
3	Emmitt Smith	10.00
4	Randy Moss	12.00
5	Tim Brown	3.00
6	Barry Sanders	12.00

1999 Upper Deck HoloGrFX Future Fame Gold Parallel

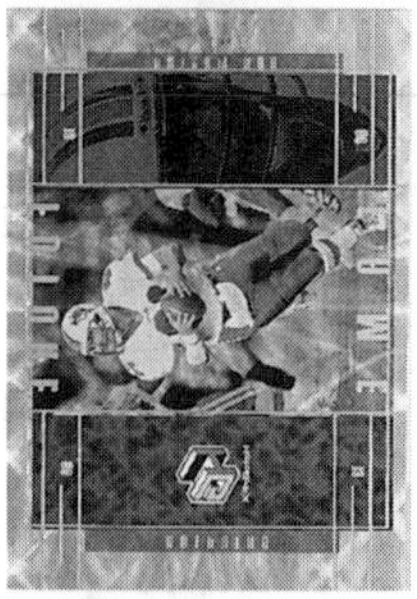

This was a six-card parallel to the Future Fame insert. Singles were inserted 1:431 packs.

	MT
Gold Cards:	3x
Inserted 1:431	

1999 Upper Deck HoloGrFX Star View

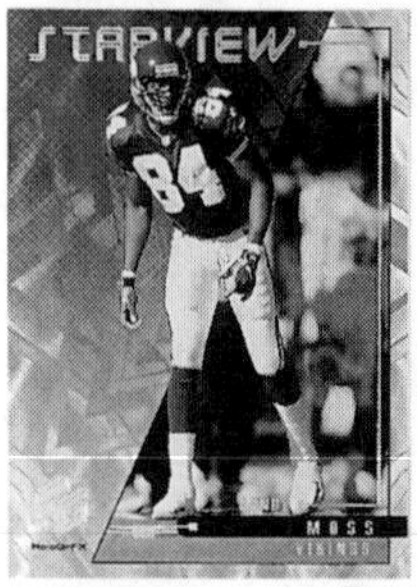

This was a nine-card insert set that focused on the NFL's marquee players. Singles were found 1:17 packs. A parallel Gold version was also released with singles inserted 1:210 packs.

		MT
Complete Set (9):		35.00
Common Player:		2.50
Inserted 1:17		
Gold Cards:		3x
Inserted 1:210		
1	Dan Marino	5.00
2	Brett Favre	7.00
3	Barry Sanders	7.00
4	Terrell Davis	5.00
5	Mark Brunell	3.00
6	Eddie George	2.50
7	Fred Taylor	5.00
8	Tim Couch	7.00
9	Randy Moss	7.00

1999 Upper Deck HoloGrFX Star View Gold Parallel

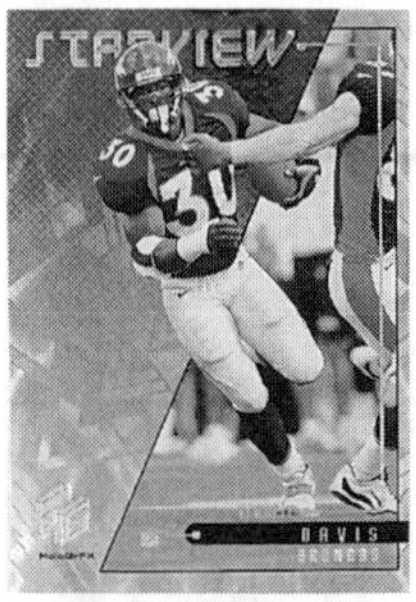

This was a nine-card parallel to the Star View insert. Singles were inserted 1:210 packs.

	MT
Gold Cards:	3x
Inserted 1:210	

1999 Upper Deck HoloGrFX UD Authentics

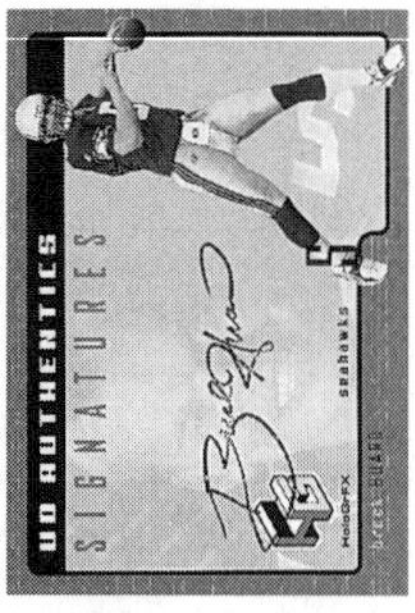

This was a 19-card insert set that included autographs of the top standouts in the league. Singles were inserted 1:144 packs.

		MT
Common Player:		25.00
Inserted 1:432		
TA	Troy Aikman	100.00
JA	Jamal Anderson	25.00
TC	Tim Couch	125.00
DC	Daunte Culpepper	100.00
TD	Terrell Davis	100.00
EG	Eddie George	60.00
TH	Torry Holt	50.00
BH	Brock Huard	25.00
EJ	Edgerrin James	200.00
SK	Shaun King	70.00
PM	Peyton Manning	175.00
DM	Donovan McNabb	70.00
CM	Cade McNown	70.00
EM	Eric Moulds	25.00
JP	Jake Plummer	100.00
JR	Jerry Rice	150.00
AS	Akili Smith	70.00
RW	Ricky Williams	125.00
SY	Steve Young	75.00

1999 Upper Deck MVP

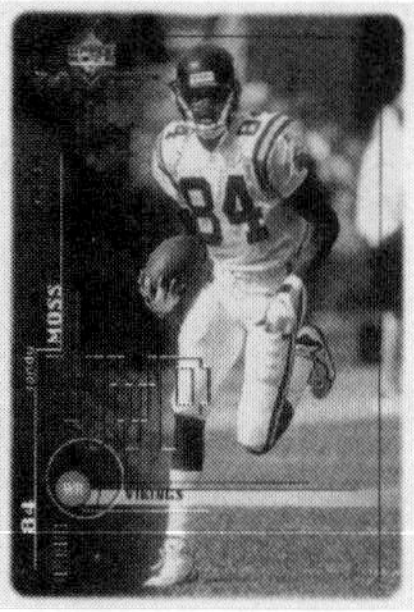

MVP Football is a 220-card set that includes 20 unseeded rookie cards. Three different parallel sets were made with Gold Script, Silver Script and Super Script. Other inserts include: Draw Your Own Card, Drive Time, Dynamics, Game Used Souvenirs, Power Surge, Strictly Business and Theatre.

		MT
Complete Set (220):		40.00
Common Player:		.10
Minor Stars:		.20
Hobby Pack (10):		2.00
Hobby Wax Box (28):		50.00
1	Jake Plummer	1.00
2	Adrian Murrell	.10
3	Larry Centers	.10
4	Frank Sanders	.10
5	Andre Wadsworth	.20
6	Rob Moore	.20
7	Simeon Rice	.10
8	Jamal Anderson	.50
9	Chris Chandler	.20
10	Chuck Smith	.10
11	Terance Mathis	.10
12	Tim Dwight	.50
13	Ray Buchanan	.10
14	O.J. Santiago	.10
15	Eric Zeier	.10
16	Priest Holmes	.50
17	Michael Jackson	.10
18	Jermaine Lewis	.20
19	Michael McCrary	.10
20	Rob Johnson	.20
21	Antowain Smith	.50
22	Thurman Thomas	.20
23	Doug Flutie	.75
24	Eric Moulds	.30
25	Bruce Smith	.10
26	Andre Reed	.20
27	Fred Lane	.10
28	Tshimanga Biakabutuka	.20
29	Rae Carruth	.10
30	Wesley Walls	.10
31	Steve Beuerlein	.10
32	Muhsin Muhammad	.10
33	Erik Kramer	.10
34	Edgar Bennett	.10
35	Curtis Conway	.20
36	Curtis Enis	.50
37	Bobby Engram	.10
38	Alonzo Mayes	.10
39	Corey Dillon	.50
40	Jeff Blake	.20
41	Carl Pickens	.20
42	Darnay Scott	.10
43	Tony McGee	.10
44	Ki-Jana Carter	.20
45	Ty Detmer	.20
46	Terry Kirby	.10
47	Justin Armour	.10
48	Freddie Solomon	.10
49	Marquez Pope	.10
50	Antonio Langham	.10
51	Troy Aikman	1.00
52	Emmitt Smith	1.50
53	Deion Sanders	.50
54	Raghib Ismail	.10
55	Michael Irvin	.20
56	Chris Warren	.20
57	Greg Ellis	.10
58	John Elway	1.50
59	Terrell Davis	1.50
60	Rod Smith	.20
61	Shannon Sharpe	.20
62	Ed McCaffrey	.20
63	John Mobley	.10
64	Bill Romanowski	.10
65	Barry Sanders	2.00
66	Johnnie Morton	.10
67	Herman Moore	.50
68	Charlie Batch	.75
69	Germane Crowell	.20
70	Robert Porcher	.10
71	Brett Favre	2.00
72	Antonio Freeman	.50
73	Dorsey Levens	.50
74	Mark Chmura	.20
75	Vonnie Holliday	.20
76	Bill Schroeder	.10
77	Marshall Faulk	.50
78	Marvin Harrison	.20
79	Peyton Manning	1.50
80	Jerome Pathon	.10
81	E.G. Green	.10
82	Ellis Johnson	.10
83	Mark Brunell	.75
84	Jimmy Smith	.20
85	Keenan McCardell	.10
86	Fred Taylor	1.00
87	James Stewart	.10
88	Kevin Hardy	.10
89	Elvis Grbac	.10
90	Andre Rison	.20
91	Derrick Alexander	.10
92	Tony Gonzalez	.20
93	Donnell Bennett	.10
94	Derrick Thomas	.20
95	Tamarick Vanover	.10
96	Dan Marino	1.50
97	Karim Abdul	.50
98	Zach Thomas	.20
99	O.J. McDuffie	.20
100	John Avery	.20
101	Sam Madison	.10
102	Randall Cunningham	.50
103	Cris Carter	.50
104	Robert Smith	.50
105	Randy Moss	2.00
106	Jake Reed	.10
107	Matthew Hatchette	.10
108	John Randle	.20
109	Drew Bledsoe	.75
110	Terry Glenn	.50
111	Ben Coates	.20
112	Ty Law	.10
113	Tony Simmons	.20
114	Ted Johnson	.10
115	Danny Wuerffel	.20
116	Lamar Smith	.10
117	Sean Dawkins	.10
118	Cameron Cleeland	.20
119	Joe Johnson	.10
120	Andre Hastings	.10
121	Kent Graham	.10
122	Gary Brown	.10
123	Amani Toomer	.10
124	Tiki Barber	.20
125	Ike Hilliard	.20
126	Jason Sehorn	.10
127	Vinny Testaverde	.20
128	Curtis Martin	.50
129	Keyshawn Johnson	.50
130	Wayne Chrebet	.50
131	Mo Lewis	.10
132	Steve Atwater	.10
133	Donald Hollas	.10
134	Napoleon Kaufman	.50
135	Tim Brown	.20
136	Darrell Russell	.10
137	Rickey Dudley	.20
138	Charles Woodson	.50
139	Koy Detmer	.10
140	Duce Staley	.10
141	Charlie Garner	.10
142	Doug Pederson	.10
143	Jeff Graham	.10
144	Charles Johnson	.10
145	Kordell Stewart	.75
146	Jerome Bettis	.50
147	Hines Ward	.20
148	Courtney Hawkins	.10
149	Will Blackwell	.10
150	Richard Huntley	.10
151	Levon Kirkland	.10
152	Trent Green	.30
153	Tony Banks	.20
154	Isaac Bruce	.30
155	Eddie Kennison	.20
156	Az-Zahir Hakim	.20
157	Amp Lee	.10
158	Robert Holcombe	.20
159	Ryan Leaf	.75
160	Natrone Means	.50
161	Jim Harbaugh	.20
162	Junior Seau	.20
163	Charlie Jones	.10
164	Rodney Harrison	.10
165	Steve Young	.75
166	Jerry Rice	1.00
167	Garrison Hearst	.30
168	Terrell Owens	.50
169	J.J. Stokes	.20
170	Bryant Young	.10
171	Ricky Watters	.30
172	Joey Galloway	.50
173	Jon Kitna	.50
174	Ahman Green	.20
175	Mike Pritchard	.10
176	Chad Brown	.10
177	Warrick Dunn	.75
178	Trent Dilfer	.20
179	Mike Alstott	.50
180	Reidel Anthony	.20
181	Bert Emanuel	.10
182	Jacquez Green	.20
183	Hardy Nickerson	.10
184	Steve McNair	.50
185	Eddie George	.75
186	Yancey Thigpen	.20
187	Frank Wycheck	.10
188	Kevin Dyson	.20
189	Jackie Harris	.10
190	Blaine Bishop	.10
191	Skip Hicks	.20
192	Michael Westbrook	.20
193	Stephen Alexander	.10
194	Leslie Shepherd	.10
195	Casey Weldon	.10
196	Brian Mitchell	.10
197	Dan Wilkinson	.10
198	Checklist Card #1 (Terrell Davis CL)	.50
199	Checklist Car #2 (Troy Aikman CL)	.30
200	Checklist Card #3 (Tim Couch CL)	3.00
201	*Ricky Williams*	5.00
202	*Tim Couch*	5.00
203	*Akili Smith*	2.00
204	*Daunte Culpepper*	5.00
205	*Torry Holt*	2.50
206	*Edgerrin James*	8.00
207	*David Boston*	2.50
208	*Peerless Price*	1.75
209	*Chris Claiborne*	1.00
210	*Champ Bailey*	1.25
211	*Cade McNown*	2.00
212	*Jevon Kearse*	2.00
213	*Joe Germaine*	1.50
214	*D'Wayne Bates*	.75
215	*Dameane Douglas*	.75
216	*Troy Edwards*	2.50
217	*Sedrick Irvin*	1.25
218	*Brock Huard*	1.50
219	*Amos Zereoue*	1.75
220	*Donovan McNabb*	4.00

1999 Upper Deck MVP Gold Script Parallel

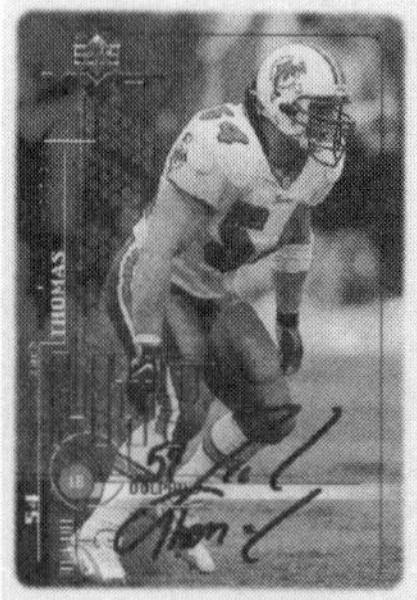

This is a parallel to the base set and is the same except for the players facsimile signature on the front in gold foil along with all the other foil in gold too. On the back the hologram is in gold foil and each single is sequentially numbered to 100.

	MT
Gold Cards:	30x-60x
Gold Rookies:	10x-20x
Production 100 Sets	

1999 Upper Deck MVP Silver Script Parallel

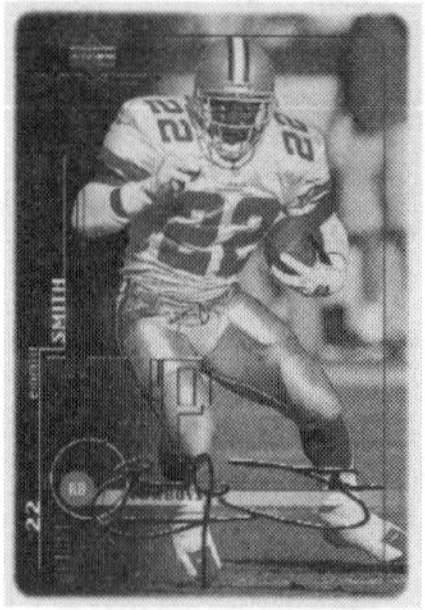

This is a parallel to the base and is the same except for the players facsimile autograph on the front in silver foil and the words Silver Script on the back. Singles were inserted 1:2 packs.

	MT
Complete Set (220):	120.00
Silver Cards:	4x
Silver Rookies:	2x
Inserted 1:2	

1999 Upper Deck MVP Super Script Parallel

This is a parallel to the base set and each single has a holo foil facsimile signature of the player on the front and and each is sequentially numbered to 25.

	MT
Super Cards:	75x-150x
Super Rookies:	20x-40x
Production 25 Sets	

A card number in parentheses ( ) indicates the set is unnumbered.

1999 Upper Deck MVP Draw Your Own

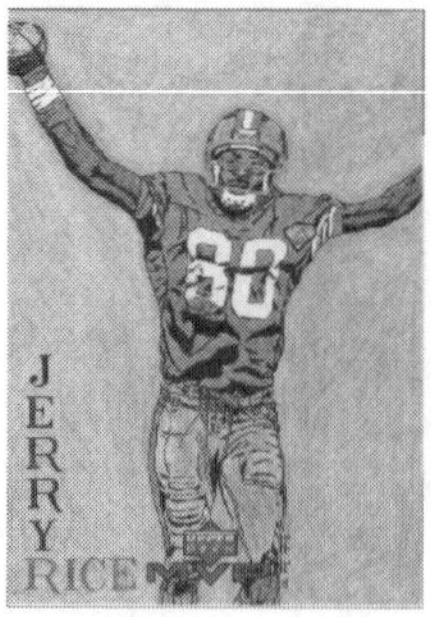

Each single from this 30-card set is a drawing from a young collector from a previous contest winner. Singles were inserted 1:6 packs.

		MT
Complete Set (30):		18.00
Common Player:		.20
Minor Stars:		.40
Inserted 1:6		
1	Brett Favre	2.00
2	Emmitt Smith	1.50
3	John Elway	1.50
4	Emmitt Smith	1.50
5	Randy Moss	2.00
6	Terrell Davis	1.50
7	Steve Young	.75
8	Drew Bledsoe	.75
9	Troy Aikman	1.00
10	Terry Allen	.20
11	Warrick Dunn	.75
12	Kimble Anders	.20
13	Joey Galloway	.40
14	Barry Sanders	2.00
15	Mark Brunell	.75
16	Bruce Smith	.20
17	Randy Moss	2.00
18	Jerome Bettis	.40
19	John Elway	1.50
20	Jerome Bettis	.40
21	Brett Favre	2.00
22	Troy Aikman	1.00
23	Cris Carter	.75
24	Jason Gildon	.20
25	Randall Cunningham	.75
26	Thurman Thomas	.40
27	Jerry Rice	1.00
28	Jerome Bettis	.40
29	Steve Young	.75
30	Reggie White	.40

1999 Upper Deck MVP Drive Time

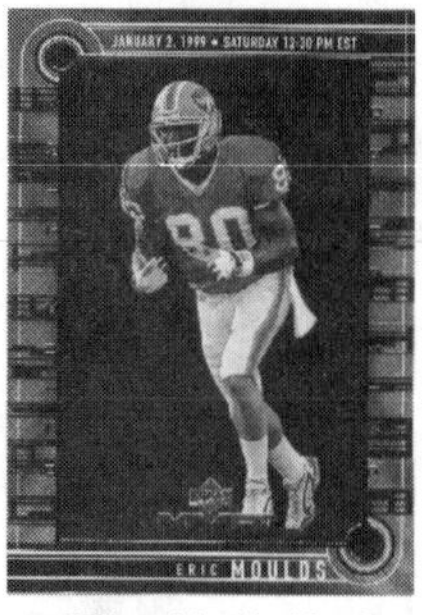

Each card in this 14-card set pays tribute to a star player who led the best offensive drive during the 1998 season. Singles were found 1:6 packs.

		MT
Complete Set (14):		10.00
Common Player:		.50
Minor Stars:		1.00
Inserted 1:6		
1	Steve Young	1.50
2	Kordell Stewart	1.25
3	Eric Moulds	1.00
4	Corey Dillon	1.00
5	Doug Flutie	1.50
6	Charlie Batch	1.50
7	Curtis Martin	1.00
8	Marshall Faulk	1.00
9	Terrell Owens	1.25
10	Antowain Smith	1.00
11	Troy Aikman	2.50
12	Drew Bledsoe	1.50
13	Keyshawn Johnson	1.00
14	Steve McNair	1.25

Values quoted in this guide reflect the retail price of a card — the price a collector can expect to pay when buying a card from a dealer. The wholesale price — that which a collector can expect to receive from a dealer when selling cards — will be significantly lower, depending on desirability and condition.

1999 Upper Deck MVP Dynamics

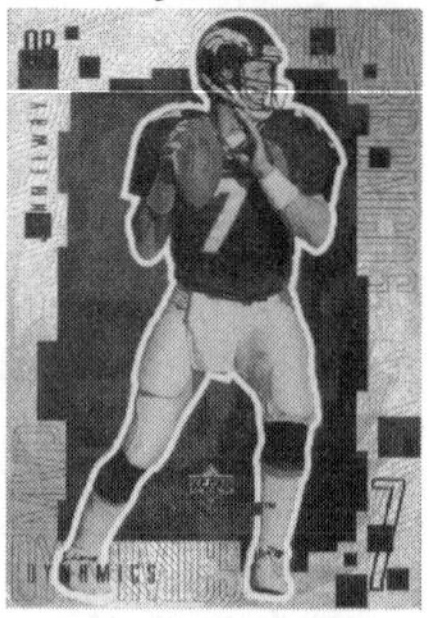

This 15-card set includes the top players in the NFL and puts them on a holo foil card. Singles were inserted 1:28 packs.

		MT
Complete Set (15):		65.00
Common Player:		2.00
Minor Stars:		4.00
Inserted 1:28		
1	John Elway	10.00
2	Steve Young	6.00
3	Jake Plummer	7.50
4	Fred Taylor	7.50
5	Mark Brunell	6.00
6	Joey Galloway	2.00
7	Terrell Davis	10.00
8	Randy Moss	15.00
9	Charlie Batch	5.00
10	Peyton Manning	10.00
11	Barry Sanders	15.00
12	Eddie George	5.00
13	Warrick Dunn	4.00
14	Jamal Anderson	2.00
15	Brett Favre	15.00

1999 Upper Deck MVP Game-Used Souvenirs

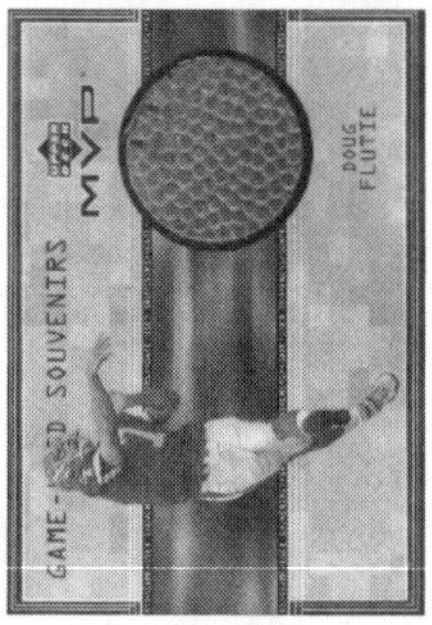

Each card in this 21-card set includes a piece of a game-used football by that player pictured on the card. Singles were inserted 1:130 packs.

		MT
Complete Set (21):		1400.
Common Player:		50.00
Inserted 1:130		
BS	Barry Sanders	160.00
ES	Emmitt Smith	120.00
DF	Doug Flutie	65.00
KJ	Keyshawn Johnson	60.00
JP	Jake Plummer	85.00
JE	John Elway	150.00
PM	Peyton Manning	125.00
RM	Randy Moss	175.00
TD	Terrell Davis	125.00
JA	Jamal Anderson	60.00
MC	Donovan McNabb	75.00
AS	Akili Smith	65.00
EJ	Edgerrin James	85.00
BH	Brock Huard	50.00
TH	Torry Holt	60.00
CB	Champ Bailey	50.00
DB	David Boston	60.00
DC	Daunte Culpepper	80.00
CM	Cade McNown	80.00
DM	Dan Marino	150.00

1999 Upper Deck MVP Power Surge

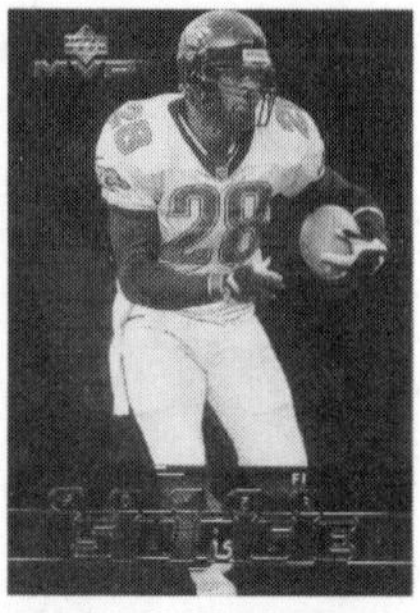

The game's most impressive talents are highlighted in this 15-card

set. Each foil card was inserted 1:9 packs.

		MT
Complete Set (15):		20.00
Common Player		.75
Minor Stars:		1.50
Inserted 1:9		
1	Jerome Bettis	1.50
2	Eddie George	2.00
3	Karim Abdul	.75
4	Curtis Martin	1.50
5	Antowain Smith	1.75
6	Kordell Stewart	1.75
7	Curtis Enis	1.50
8	Joey Galloway	1.50
9	Mark Brunell	2.50
10	Peyton Manning	4.00
11	Antonio Freeman	1.50
12	Jerry Rice	3.50
13	Eric Moulds	1.50
14	Drew Bledsoe	2.00
15	Fred Taylor	3.50

1999 Upper Deck MVP Strictly Business

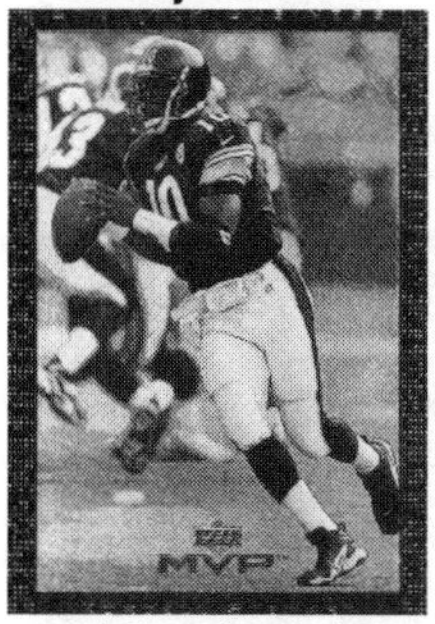

Only the top players in the game were included in this 13-card insert. Singles were found 1:14 packs.

		MT
Complete Set (15):		45.00
Common Player:		2.00
Inserted 1:14		
1	Eddie George	3.00
2	Curtis Martin	2.00
3	Fred Taylor	5.00
4	Steve Young	3.00
5	Kordell Stewart	3.00
6	Corey Dillon	2.00
7	Dan Marino	7.50
8	Jake Plummer	4.00
9	Jerry Rice	5.00
10	Warrick Dunn	3.00
11	Jerome Bettis	2.00
12	John Elway	7.50
13	Randy Moss	10.00
14	Troy Aikman	5.00
15	Brett Favre	10.00

1999 Upper Deck MVP Theatre

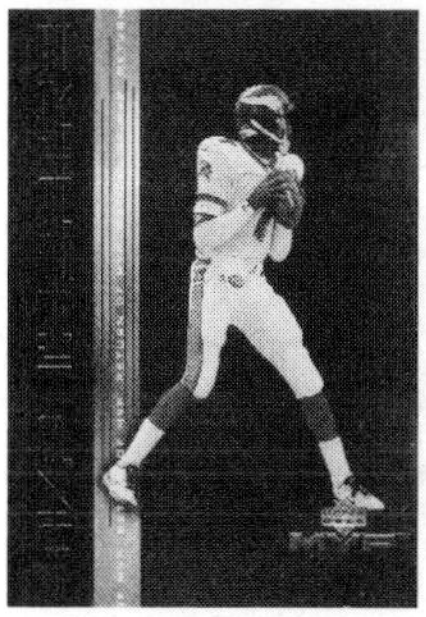

Each card in this 15-card set pictures a star player in action. Singles were inserted 1:9 packs.

		MT
Complete Set (15):		20.00
Common Player:		.75
Minor Stars:		1.50
Inserted 1:9		
1	Terrell Davis	5.00
2	Corey Dillon	1.50
3	Brett Favre	6.00
4	Jerry Rice	3.00
5	Emmitt Smith	4.00
6	Dan Marino	4.00
7	Jerome Bettis	.75
8	Napoleon Kaufman	1.50
9	Keyshawn Johnson	1.50
10	Warrick Dunn	1.50
11	Barry Sanders	6.00
12	Troy Aikman	3.00
13	Jamal Anderson	1.50
14	Randall Cunningham	.75
15	Doug Flutie	1.75

1999 Upper Deck Ovation

This was a 90-card set that included 30 rookies found 1:4 packs. Each single had a parallel Standing Ovation that was sequentially numbered to 50. Other insert sets included: A Piece of History, Center Stage, Curtain Calls, Spotlight, Star Performers, Super Signatures Silver and the Walter Payton Autographed Game Jersey. SRP was $3.99 for five-card packs.

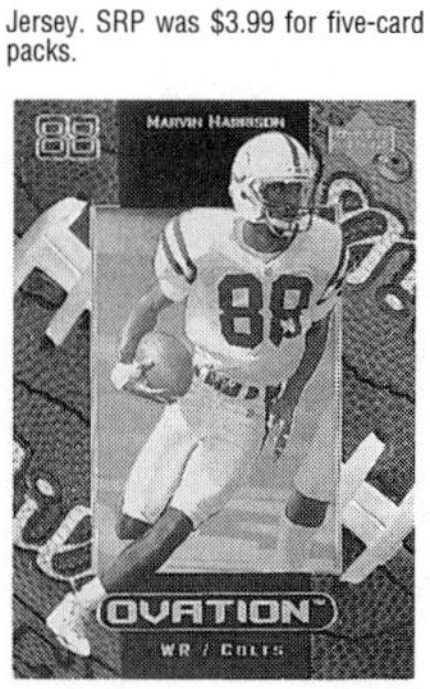

		MT
Complete Set (90):		125.00
Common Player:		.25
Minor Stars:		.50
Common Rookie:		1.50
Inserted 1:4		
Pack (5):		4.00
Wax Box (20):		90.00
1	Jake Plummer	1.25
2	Adrian Murrell	.25
3	Jamal Anderson	.75
4	Chris Chandler	.50
5	Tony Banks	.50
6	Antowain Smith	.50
7	Doug Flutie	1.00
8	Tshimanga Biakabutuka	.50
9	Steve Beuerlein	.25
10	Curtis Conway	.50
11	Curtis Enis	.75
12	Corey Dillon	.75
13	Jeff Blake	.50
14	Ty Detmer	.25
15	Troy Aikman	1.50
16	Emmitt Smith	2.00
17	Terrell Davis	2.00
18	Bubby Brister	.50
19	Barry Sanders	3.00
20	Charlie Batch	1.00
21	Brett Favre	3.00
22	Dorsey Levens	.50
23	Peyton Manning	2.00
24	Marvin Harrison	.75
25	Mark Brunell	1.25
26	Fred Taylor	1.50
27	Elvis Grbac	.25
28	Andre Rison	.25
29	Dan Marino	2.00
30	Karim Abdul	.50
31	Randall Cunningham	.75
32	Randy Moss	3.00
33	Drew Bledsoe	1.25
34	Terry Glenn	.75
35	Danny Wuerffel	.50
36	Cameron Cleeland	.50
37	Kerry Collins	.50
38	Amani Toomer	.25
39	Curtis Martin	.75
40	Keyshawn Johnson	.75
41	Napoleon Kaufman	.75
42	Tim Brown	.50
43	Doug Pederson	.25
44	Charles Johnson	.25
45	Kordell Stewart	1.00
46	Jerome Bettis	.75
47	Trent Green	.50
48	Marshall Faulk	.75
49	Natrone Means	.75
50	Jim Harbaugh	.50
51	Steve Young	1.00
52	Jerry Rice	1.50
53	Joey Galloway	.75
54	Jon Kitna	.75
55	Warrick Dunn	.75
56	Trent Dilfer	.50
57	Steve McNair	.75
58	Eddie George	.75
59	Brad Johnson	.50
60	Skip Hicks	.50
61	*Tim Couch*	12.00
62	*Donovan McNabb*	10.00
63	*Akili Smith*	6.00
64	*Edgerrin James*	25.00
65	*Ricky Williams*	12.00
66	*Torry Holt*	7.00
67	*Champ Bailey*	4.00
68	*David Boston*	7.00
69	*Daunte Culpepper*	15.00
70	*Cade McNown*	5.00
71	*Troy Edwards*	4.00
72	*Kevin Johnson*	6.00
73	*James Johnson*	4.00
74	*Rob Konrad*	3.00
75	*Kevin Faulk*	4.00
76	*Shaun King*	8.00
77	*Peerless Price*	4.00
78	*Michael Cloud*	3.00
79	*Jermaine Fazande*	3.00
80	*D'Wayne Bates*	3.00
81	*Brock Huard*	4.00
82	*Marty Booker*	1.50
83	*Karsten Bailey*	1.50
84	*Al Wilson*	3.00
85	*Joe Germaine*	4.00
86	*Dameane Douglas*	1.50
87	*Sedrick Irvin*	4.00
88	*Amos Zereoue*	4.00
89	*Cecil Collins*	4.00
90	*Ebenezer Ekuban*	1.50

A player's name in *italic type* indicates a rookie card.

1999 Upper Deck Ovation Standing Ovation Parallel

This was a 90-card parallel to the base set. Each single was sequentially numbered to 50.

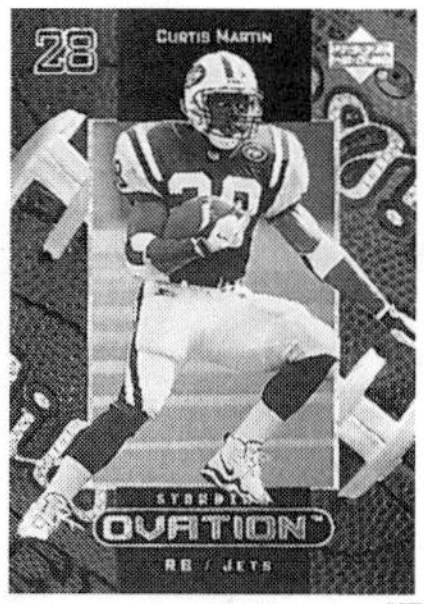

	MT
Standing Ovation Cards:	35x-70x
Standing Ovation Rookies:	5x-10x
Production 50 Sets	

1999 Upper Deck Ovation A Piece of History

This 13-card insert set included pieces of game-used footballs. A total of 4,560 cards were produced and randomly inserted.

		MT
Complete Set (13):		1250.
Common Player:		50.00
Production 4,560 Total Cards		
DC	Daunte Culpepper	85.00
BF	Brett Favre	200.00
JG	Joe Germaine	50.00
TH	Torry Holt	65.00
BH	Brock Huard	50.00
EJ	Edgerrin James	180.00
DM	Dan Marino	180.00
MC	Donovan McNabb	85.00
CM	Cade McNown	60.00
JR	Jerry Rice	100.00
AS	Akili Smith	85.00
RW	Ricky Williams	200.00
SY	Steve Young	85.00

1999 Upper Deck Ovation Center Stage

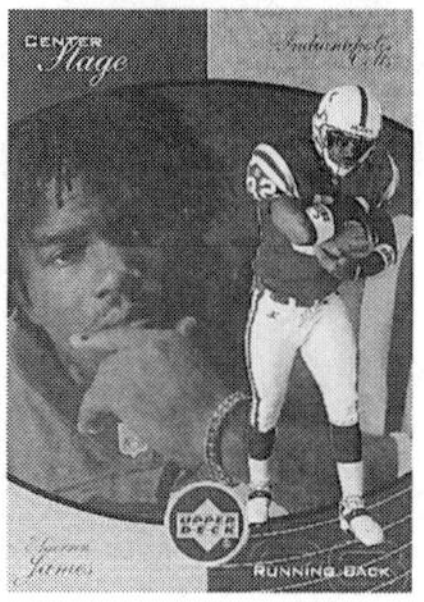

This 24-card insert set was a three-tiered collection focusing on eight great running backs from the NFL's past to present. Cards #1-#8 were inserted 1:9, cards #9-#16 were found 1:25 and cards #17-#24 were pulled 1:99 packs.

		MT
Complete Set (24):		225.00
Common Player #1-8:		1.00
Inserted 1:9		
Common Player #9-16:		3.00
Inserted 1:25		
Common Player #17-24:		6.00
Inserted 1:99		
1	Walter Payton	3.00
2	Barry Sanders	5.00
3	Emmitt Smith	3.00
4	Terrell Davis	3.00
5	Jamal Anderson	1.00
6	Fred Taylor	2.00
7	Ricky Williams	8.00
8	Edgerrin James	6.00
9	Walter Payton	6.00
10	Barry Sanders	10.00
11	Emmitt Smith	6.00
12	Terrell Davis	6.00
13	Jamal Anderson	3.00
14	Fred Taylor	4.00
15	Ricky Williams	15.00
16	Edgerrin James	12.00
17	Walter Payton	18.00
18	Barry Sanders	30.00
19	Emmitt Smith	18.00
20	Terrell Davis	18.00
21	Jamal Anderson	6.00
22	Fred Taylor	12.00
23	Ricky Williams	45.00
24	Edgerrin James	35.00

Post-1980 cards in Near Mint condition will generally sell for about 75% of the quoted Mint value. Excellent-condition cards bring no more than 40%.

1999 Upper Deck Ovation Curtain Calls

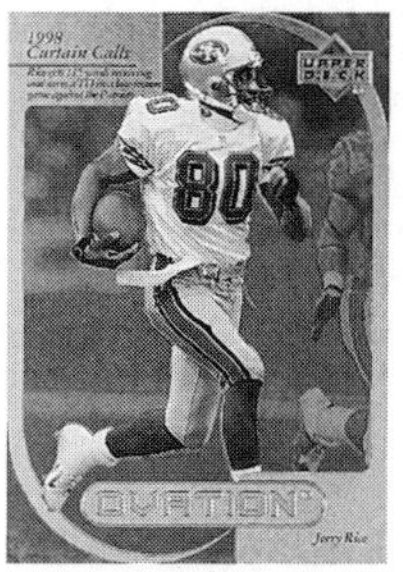

This 30-card insert set focused on some of the most memorable accomplishments posted during the 1998 NFL season. Inserted 1:4 packs.

		MT
Complete Set (30):		85.00
Common Player:		1.00
Minor Stars:		2.00
Inserted 1:4		
1	Peyton Manning	7.00
2	Fred Taylor	5.00
3	Randy Moss	10.00
4	Cris Carter	2.00
5	Troy Aikman	5.00
6	Randall Cunningham	2.00
7	Mark Brunell	3.00
8	Jon Kitna	2.00
9	Steve McNair	2.00
10	Jake Plummer	5.00
11	Jerry Rice	5.00
12	Kordell Stewart	3.00
13	Warrick Dunn	2.00
14	Emmitt Smith	7.00
15	Jerome Bettis	2.00
16	Terrell Owens	2.00
17	Antonio Freeman	2.00
18	Joey Galloway	2.00
19	Curtis Martin	2.00
20	Tim Brown	1.00
21	Charlie Batch	2.00
22	Doug Flutie	3.00
23	Barry Sanders	10.00
24	Drew Bledsoe	3.00
25	Corey Dillon	2.00
26	Eddie George	2.00
27	Keyshawn Johnson	2.00
28	Steve Young	3.00
29	Brett Favre	10.00
30	Terrell Davis	7.00

1999 Upper Deck Ovation Spotlight

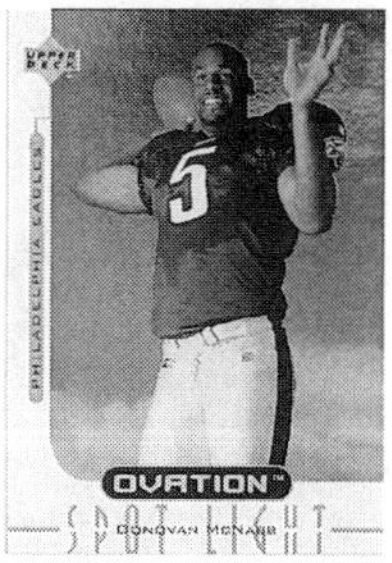

This was a 15-card insert set that featured the top players from the 1999 NFL Draft. Singles were inserted 1:9 packs.

		MT
Complete Set (15):		85.00
Common Player:		3.00
Inserted 1:9		
1	Tim Couch	15.00
2	Donovan McNabb	8.00
3	Akili Smith	8.00
4	Edgerrin James	12.00
5	Ricky Williams	15.00
6	Torry Holt	5.00
7	Champ Bailey	4.00
8	David Boston	5.00
9	Daunte Culpepper	8.00
10	Cade McNown	8.00
11	Troy Edwards	5.00
12	Kevin Johnson	5.00
13	Joe Germaine	3.00
14	Brock Huard	3.00
15	Kevin Faulk	4.00

1999 Upper Deck Ovation Star Performers

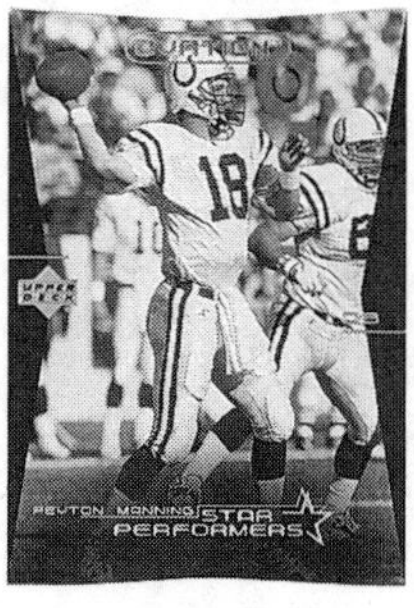

This was a 15-card insert set that included some of the top names in the NFL. Singles were inserted 1:39 packs.

		MT
Complete Set (15):		135.00
Common Player:		5.00
Inserted 1:39		
1	Terrell Davis	15.00
2	Peyton Manning	15.00
3	Brett Favre	20.00
4	Dan Marino	15.00
5	Barry Sanders	20.00
6	Jamal Anderson	5.00
7	Mark Brunell	8.00
8	Jerome Bettis	5.00
9	Charlie Batch	6.00
10	Antowain Smith	5.00
11	Jake Plummer	8.00
12	Joey Galloway	5.00
13	Randy Moss	20.00
14	Steve Young	8.00
15	Warrick Dunn	5.00

1999 Upper Deck Ovation Super Signatures

This was a three-card insert set that included autographs from three retired NFL superstars. Each single was sequentially numbered to 300. A parallel Gold version was also released and each of those were numbered to 150. A parallel Rainbow version was made and each was sequentially numbered to 10.

		MT
Complete Set (3):		600.00
Common Player:		200.00
Production 300 Sets		
Gold Cards:		1.5x
Production 150 Sets		
Rainbow Cards:		
Production 10 Sets		
NA	Joe Namath	200.00
MN	Joe Montana	225.00
WP	Walter Payton	200.00

1999 Upper Deck Ovation Walter Payton Auto. Jersey

Walter Payton signed a total of 34 Game Jersey cards. Each came with a swatch of a game-used jersey and were sequentially numbered to 34. Singles were randomly inserted.

		MT
Complete Set (1):		
WPJ	Walter Payton	2000.

1999 Upper Deck PowerDeck

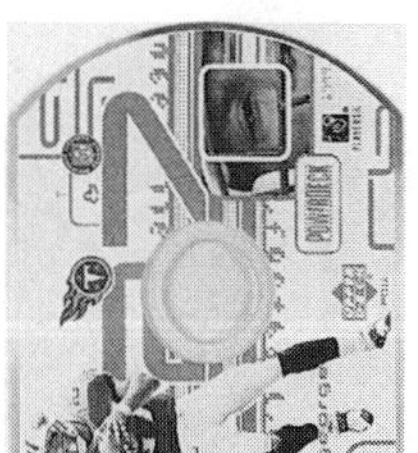

This was a 30-card set that pictured each player on a digital trading card. Each card was to be used on a CD-Rom and contained complete stats, bios, 20 to 30 images, music, audio clips and game highlights. Each single also had a parallel Auxiliary single. The CD singles were issued one-per-pack and the Auxiliary cards were issued two-per-pack. Other insert sets included: Autographs, Most Valuable Performances, Powerful Moments, Time Capsule and Walter Payton Autograph Game Jersey. SRP was $4.99 for three-card packs.

		MT
Complete Set (30):		150.00
Common Player:		2.50
Inserted 1:1		
Pack (3):		5.00
Wax Box (24):		90.00
1	Troy Aikman	6.00
2	Drew Bledsoe	5.00
3	Randy Moss	10.00
4	Barry Sanders	10.00
5	Brett Favre	10.00
6	Terrell Davis	8.00
7	Peyton Manning	8.00
8	Emmitt Smith	8.00
9	Dan Marino	8.00
10	Jake Plummer	5.00
11	Eddie George	4.00
12	Jerry Rice	6.00
13	Steve Young	4.00
14	Mark Brunell	5.00
15	Kordell Stewart	2.50
16	Keyshawn Johnson	2.50
17	Fred Taylor	6.00
18	Jamal Anderson	2.50
19	*Cecil Collins*	4.00
20	*Ricky Williams*	12.00
21	*Tim Couch*	12.00
22	*Donovan McNabb*	8.00
23	*Akili Smith*	7.00
24	*Edgerrin James*	20.00
25	*Daunte Culpepper*	12.00
26	*Brock Huard*	4.00
27	*Torry Holt*	6.00
28	*David Boston*	6.00
29	*Cade McNown*	5.00
30	*Champ Bailey*	3.50

1999 Upper Deck PowerDeck Auxiliary

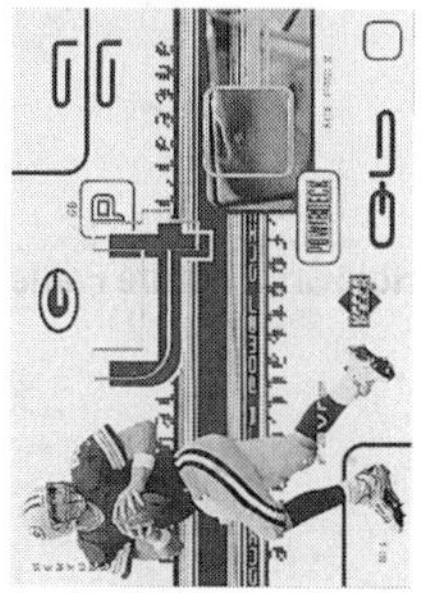

Each card in this 30-card set was printed on regular cardboard stock. Singles were issued two-per-pack. Each single had a parallel one-of-one Gold card.

		MT
Complete Set (30):		30.00
Common Player:		.50
1	Troy Aikman	1.00
2	Drew Bledsoe	.75
3	Randy Moss	2.00
4	Barry Sanders	2.00
5	Brett Favre	2.00
6	Terrell Davis	1.50
7	Peyton Manning	1.50
8	Emmitt Smith	1.50
9	Dan Marino	1.50
10	Jake Plummer	.75
11	Eddie George	.50
12	Jerry Rice	1.00
13	Steve Young	.75
14	Mark Brunell	.75
15	Kordell Stewart	.50
16	Keyshawn Johnson	.50
17	Fred Taylor	1.00
18	Jamal Anderson	.50
19	Cecil Collins	1.50
20	Ricky Williams	5.00
21	Tim Couch	5.00
22	Donovan McNabb	3.50
23	Akili Smith	3.00
24	Edgerrin James	8.00
25	Daunte Culpepper	3.50
26	Brock Huard	1.50
27	Torry Holt	2.00
28	David Boston	2.00
29	Cade McNown	2.00
30	Champ Bailey	1.50

1999 Upper Deck PowerDeck Autographed Cards

This was a 12-card insert set that included autographs from both veterans and prospects. Each single was sequentially numbered to 50.

		MT
Complete Set (12):		1250.
Common Player:		75.00
Production 50 Sets		
TA	Troy Aikman	175.00
CB	Champ Bailey	75.00
DB	David Boston	75.00
TC	Tim Couch	200.00
DC	Daunte Culpepper	125.00
TH	Torry Holt	75.00
BH	Brock Huard	75.00
EJ	Edgerrin James	300.00
DM	Dan Marino	250.00
CM	Cade McNown	125.00
JP	Jake Plummer	100.00
AS	Akili Smith	100.00

1999 Upper Deck PowerDeck Most Valuable Performances

This seven-card insert set highlighted historic performances in the Super Bowl and other notable games. Singles were inserted 1:287 packs. Each card also had a parallel Auxiliary single and they were also issued 1:287.

		MT
Complete Set (7):		300.00
Common Player:		15.00
Inserted 1:287		
Auxiliary Cards:		1x
Inserted 1:287		
1	Joe Montana	75.00
2	John Elway	45.00
3	Emmitt Smith	45.00
4	Jamal Anderson	15.00
5	Randy Moss	75.00
6	Brett Favre	75.00
7	Terrell Davis	45.00

1999 Upper Deck PowerDeck Powerful Moments

This six-card insert set showcased some of the most significant

games in pro football history. Singles were inserted 1:23 packs. Each card had an Auxiliary single that was also issued 1:23 packs.

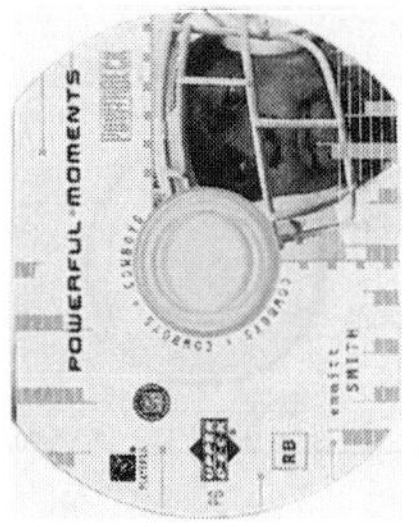

		MT
Complete Set (6):		60.00
Common Player:		8.00
Inserted 1:23		
Auxiliary Cards:		1x
Inserted 1:23		
1	Joe Montana	15.00
2	Terrell Davis	8.00
3	John Elway	10.00
4	Randy Moss	15.00
5	Dan Marino	10.00
6	Emmitt Smith	10.00

1999 Upper Deck PowerDeck Time Capsule

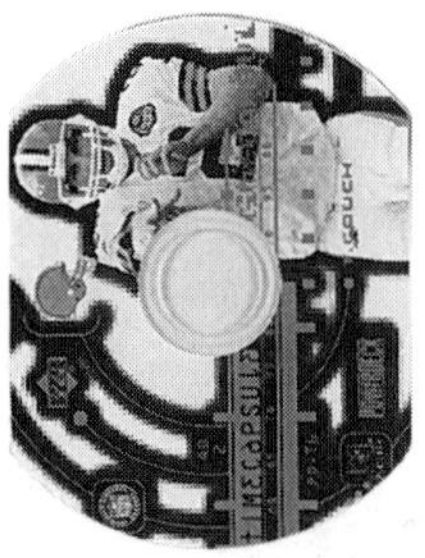

This was a six-card insert set that included flashbacks of the greatest superstars' rookie seasons. Singles were found 1:7 packs. Each single had a parallel Auxiliary card that was also inserted 1:7 packs.

		MT
Complete Set (6):		40.00
Common Player:		7.00
Inserted 1:7		
Auxiliary Cards:		1x
Inserted 1:7		
1	Edgerrin James	15.00
2	Barry Sanders	12.00
3	Terrell Davis	7.00
4	Emmitt Smith	10.00
5	Dan Marino	10.00
6	Tim Couch	10.00

1999 Upper Deck Retro

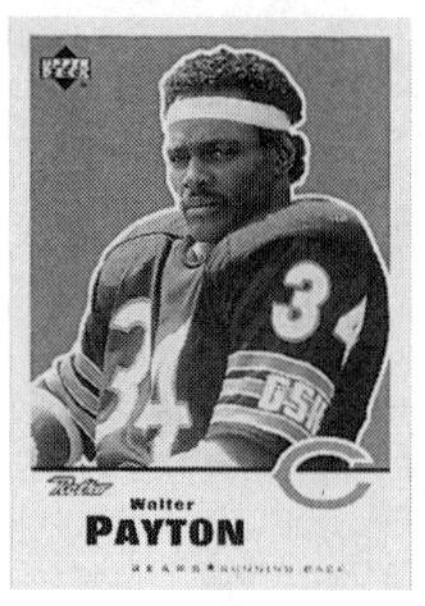

This was a 165-card set that pictured both past and present NFL stars. Each card had a classic oldtime look and feel. Each single had a parallel Gold card that was numbered to 175. Other insert sets included: Inkredible, Legends of the Fall, Old School/New School, Smashmouth and Throwback Attack.The packaging was unique in that each of the 24 packs were inserted into an actual lunch box. SRP was $4.99 for six-card packs.

		MT
Complete Set (165):		60.00
Common Player:		.15
Minor Stars:		.30
Common Rookie:		.75
Pack (6):		5.00
Wax Box (24):		110.00
1	Jake Plummer	1.25
2	Adrian Murrell	.15
3	Rob Moore	.30
4	Frank Sanders	.15
5	*David Boston*	2.50
6	Tim Dwight	.75
7	Chris Chandler	.30
8	Jamal Anderson	.75
9	O.J. Santiago	.15
10	Terance Mathis	.15
11	Priest Holmes	.75
12	Tony Banks	.30
13	Patrick Johnson	.15
14	Scott Mitchell	.15
15	Jermaine Lewis	.15
16	Eric Moulds	.75
17	Doug Flutie	1.00
18	Antowain Smith	.50
19	Thurman Thomas	.30
20	*Peerless Price*	2.00
21	Fred Lane	.15
22	Tshimanga Biakabutuka	.30
23	Steve Beurlein	.30
24	Muhsin Muhammad	.50
25	Rae Carruth	.15
26	Curtis Enis	.75
27	Walter Payton	5.00
28	Bobby Engram	.15
29	*Cade McNown*	3.00
30	Curtis Conway	.30
31	Darnay Scott	.30
32	Jeff Blake	.30
33	Corey Dillon	.75
34	*Akili Smith*	4.00
35	Carl Pickens	.30
36	*Tim Couch*	7.00
37	Ty Detmer	.15
38	Jim Brown	3.00
39	*Kevin Johnson*	2.50
40	Ozzie Newsome	.30
41	Troy Aikman	1.50
42	Raghib Ismail	.15
43	Emmitt Smith	2.00
44	Michael Irvin	.30
45	Deion Sanders	.50
46	Roger Staubach	2.00
47	John Elway	2.00
48	Bubby Brister	.30
49	Terrell Davis	2.00
50	Ed McCaffrey	.50
51	Rod Smith	.50
52	Shannon Sharpe	.30
53	Charlie Batch	1.00
54	Johnnie Morton	.15
55	Barry Sanders	3.00
56	*Sedrick Irvin*	1.50
57	Herman Moore	.50
58	Brett Favre	3.00
59	Mark Chmura	.30
60	Antonio Freeman	.75
61	Robert Brooks	.15
62	Dorsey Levens	.75
63	Peyton Manning	2.00
64	Jerome Pathon	.15
65	Marvin Harrison	.75
66	*Edgerrin James*	10.00
67	Ken Dilger	.15
68	Mark Brunell	1.25
69	Fred Taylor	1.50
70	Jimmy Smith	.75
71	James Stewart	.50
72	Keenan McCardell	.30
73	Elvis Grbac	.30
74	*Michael Cloud*	.75
75	Andre Rison	.30
76	Tony Gonzalez	.30
77	Warren Moon	.30
78	Derrick Alexander	.15
79	Dan Marino	2.00
80	O.J. McDuffie	.30
81	*James Johnson*	1.50
82	Paul Warfield	.30
83	*Cecil Collins*	2.50
84	Randall Cunningham	.75
85	Randy Moss	3.00
86	Cris Carter	.75
87	Fran Tarkenton	1.00
88	*Daunte Culpepper*	6.00
89	Robert Smith	.75
90	Drew Bledsoe	1.25
91	Terry Glenn	.75
92	*Kevin Faulk*	1.50
93	Tony Simmons	.30
94	Ben Coates	.30
95	Billy Joe Hobert	.15
96	Cameron Cleeland	.30
97	Eddie Kennison	.15
98	Andre Hastings	.15
99	*Ricky Williams*	6.00
100	Kerry Collins	.30
101	*Joe Montgomery*	.75
102	Gary Brown	.15
103	Ike Hilliard	.15
104	Amani Toomer	.15
105	Vinny Testaverde	.30
106	Wayne Chrebet	.75
107	Curtis Martin	.75
108	Joe Namath	2.50
109	Keyshawn Johnson	.75
110	Don Maynard	.50
111	Rich Gannon	.30
112	Tim Brown	.30
113	Charles Woodson	.75
114	Rickey Dudley	.15
115	Darrell Russell	.15
116	Napoleon Kaufman	.75
117	*Donovan McNabb*	4.00
118	Doug Pederson	.15
119	Duce Staley	.75
120	Torrance Small	.15
121	Charles Johnson	.15
122	Jerome Bettis	.75
123	Courtney Hawkins	.15
124	Kordell Stewart	.75
125	*Troy Edwards*	2.50
126	*Amos Zereoue*	.75
127	Trent Green	.50
128	Marshall Faulk	.75
129	Az Hakim	.30
130	*Joe Germaine*	.75
131	*Torry Holt*	2.50
132	Isaac Bruce	.75
133	Jim Harbaugh	.30
134	Junior Seau	.30
135	Natrone Means	.30
136	Ryan Leaf	.50
137	Dan Fouts	.50
138	Mikhael Ricks	.15
139	Steve Young	1.00
140	Terrell Owens	.75
141	Jerry Rice	1.50
142	J.J. Stokes	.30
143	Lawrence Phillips	.30
144	Joe Montana	3.50
145	Jon Kitna	.75
146	Ahman Green	.30
147	Joey Galloway	.75
148	Ricky Watters	.30
149	*Brock Huard*	1.50
150	Steve Largent	.75
151	Trent Dilfer	.50
152	Reidel Anthony	.30
153	Warrick Dunn	.75
154	Mike Alstott	.75
155	*Shaun King*	4.00
156	Eddie George	1.00
157	Steve McNair	1.00
158	Kevin Dyson	.30
159	Frank Wycheck	.15
160	Yancey Thigpen	.30
161	Brad Johnson	.75
162	Rodney Peete	.15
163	Michael Westbrook	.50
164	Skip Hicks	.30
165	*Champ Bailey*	1.50

1999 Upper Deck Retro Gold Parallel

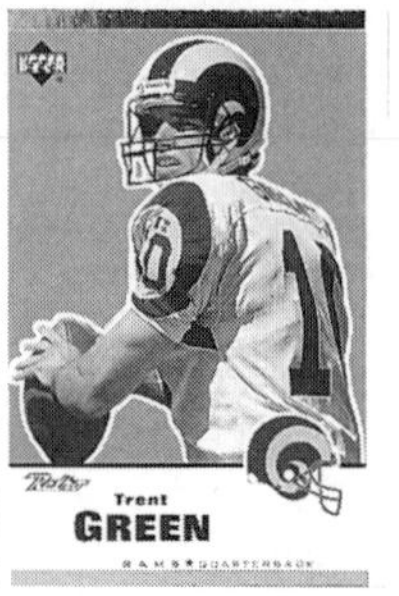

This was a 165-card parallel to the base set. Each card included gold foil and was sequentially numbered to 175.

	MT
Gold Cards:	6x-12x
Gold Rookies:	3x-6x
Production 175 Sets	

1999 Upper Deck Retro Inkredible

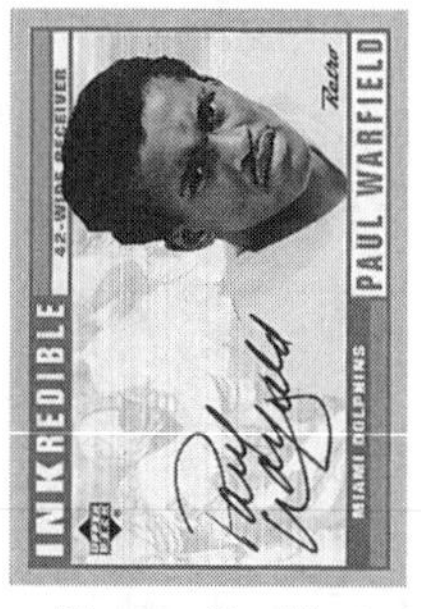

This was a 30-card insert set that featured authentic autograph cards of past and present NFL stars. Singles were inserted 1:23 packs. Each single also had a parallel Gold version that was sequentially numbered to the player's jersey number.

		MT
Complete Set (30):		1500.
Common Player:		10.00
Minor Stars:		20.00
1:Box		
DB	David Boston	35.00
CC	Cris Carter	30.00
WC	Wayne Chrebet	20.00
TC	Tim Couch	100.00
DC	Daunte Culpepper	45.00
TD	Terrell Davis	75.00
DF	Dan Fouts	20.00
GH	Garrison Hearst	10.00
TH	Torry Holt	35.00
BH	Brock Huard	20.00
SK	Shaun King	45.00
JK	Jon Kitna	20.00
SL	Steve Largent	20.00
DL	Dorsey Levens	20.00
MC	Donovan McNabb	45.00
CM	Cade McNown	45.00
JM	Joe Montana	180.00
RM	Randy Moss	150.00
AM	Adrian Murrell	10.00
JN	Joe Namath	180.00
OZ	Ozzie Newsome	10.00
TO	Terrell Owens	20.00
WP	Walter Payton	275.00
AK	Akili Smith	45.00
AS	Antowain Smith	20.00
RS	Rod Smith	20.00
RG	Roger Staubach	100.00
FT	Fran Tarkenton	50.00
PW	Paul Warfield	10.00
RW	Ricky Williams	120.00

1999 Upper Deck Retro Legends of the Fall

This was a 30-card insert set that focused on both current and former NFL stars who transcended their eras. Singles were inserted 1:11 packs. Each card had a parallel Silver version that was sequentially numbered to 75.

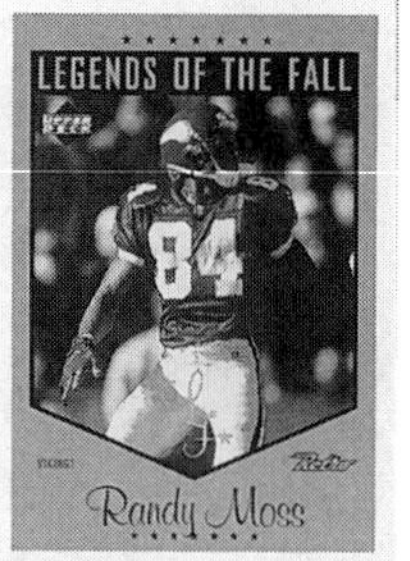

		MT
Complete Set (30):		45.00
Common Player:		.75
Minor Stars:		1.50
Inserted 1:11		
Silver Cards:		10x-20x
Production 75 Sets		
1	Jake Plummer	2.50
2	Corey Dillon	1.50
3	Curtis Martin	1.50
4	Vinny Testaverde	.75
5	Brett Favre	6.00
6	Randy Moss	6.00
7	John Elway	4.50
8	Jerry Rice	3.00
9	Troy Aikman	3.00
10	Ricky Watters	.75
11	Keyshawn Johnson	1.50
12	Mark Brunell	2.00
13	Dorsey Levens	.75
14	Steve McNair	1.50
15	Emmitt Smith	4.50
16	Marshall Faulk	1.50
17	Priest Holmes	.75
18	Steve Young	2.00
19	Skip Hicks	.75
20	Eddie George	1.50
21	Garrison Hearst	.75
22	Drew Bledsoe	2.50
23	Warrick Dunn	1.50
24	Eric Moulds	1.50
25	Joey Galloway	1.50
26	Tim Brown	.75
27	Chris Chandler	.75
28	Peyton Manning	4.50
29	Antonio Freeman	1.50
30	Deion Sanders	1.50

1999 Upper Deck Retro Lunch Boxes

This was a 16-box set that was used for the packing of the packs. Each box was a usable lunch box that featured a player or players on both sides. Dual player boxes were inserted one-per-case.

	MT
Complete Set (16):	225.00
Common Player:	8.00
One dual box per case	
Joe Montana	20.00
Ricky Williams	15.00
Randy Moss	15.00
Barry Sanders	15.00
John Elway	12.00
Terrell Davis	8.00
Dan Marino	12.00
Joe Namath	15.00
Joe Montana, John Elway	20.00
Joe Montana, Dan Marino	20.00
John Elway, Dan Marino	20.00
Joe Montana, Joe Namath	20.00
Ricky Williams, Tim Couch	20.00
Joe Namath, Dan Marino	20.00
Tim Couch, Joe Montana	20.00
Barry Sanders, Terrell Davis	20.00

1999 Upper Deck Retro Old School/New School

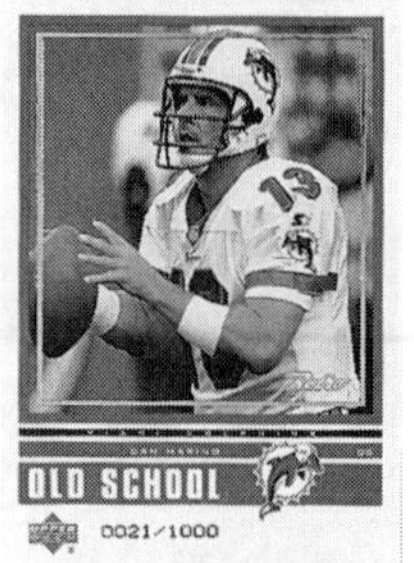

This was a 30-card insert set that focused on the NFL's top stars of yesterday and today and paired one of each player on one card. Each of these singles were sequentially numbered to 1,000. A parallel Level 2 was issued and each was numbered to 50.

		MT
Complete Set (30):		200.00
Common Player:		2.00
Minor Stars:		4.00
Production 1,000 Sets		
Level 2 Cards:		5x-10x
Production 50 Sets		
1	Terrell Davis, Ricky Williams	15.00
2	Joe Montana, Jake Plummer	18.00
3	Cris Carter, Randy Moss	15.00
4	Randall Cunningham, Daunte Culpepper	7.00
5	Brett Favre, Jon Kitna	15.00
6	Emmitt Smith, Fred Taylor	12.00
7	Mark Brunell, Brock Huard	6.00
8	John Elway, Peyton Manning	15.00
9	Steve Young, Cade McNown	8.00
10	Don Maynard, Keyshawn Johnson	4.00
11	Dan Marino, Tim Couch	15.00
12	Jerry Rice, Terrell Owens	10.00
13	Marshall Faulk, Edgerrin James	20.00
14	Dan Fouts, Akili Smith	6.00
15	Barry Sanders, Jamal Anderson	15.00
16	Terry Glenn, David Boston	4.00
17	Deion Sanders, Champ Bailey	4.00
18	Andre Reed, Eric Moulds	2.00
19	Junior Seau, Chris Claiborne	2.00
20	Steve Largent, Joey Galloway	4.00
21	Kordell Stewart, Shaun King	6.00
22	Ricky Watters, Kevin Faulk	4.00
23	Thurman Thomas, Warrick Dunn	2.00
24	Tim Brown, Troy Edwards	4.00
25	Jerome Bettis, Cecil Collins	5.00
26	Isaac Bruce, Torry Holt	5.00
27	Fran Tarkenton, Donovan McNabb	7.00
28	Warren Moon, Charlie Batch	5.00
29	Herman Moore, D'Wayne Bates	2.00
30	Roger Staubach, Troy Aikman	12.00

1999 Upper Deck Retro Smashmouth

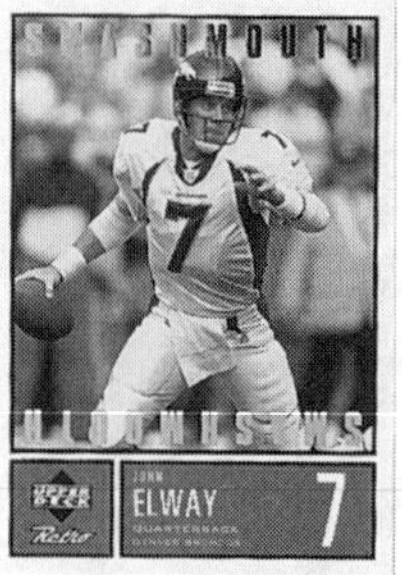

This was a 15-card insert set that took a look at 15 of the game's most aggressive players. Singles were inserted 1:8 packs. A parallel Level 2 was also released and each was sequentially numbered to 100.

		MT
Complete Set (15):		20.00
Common Player:		.75
Minor Stars:		1.50
Inserted 1:8		
Level 2 Cards:		6x-12x
Production 100 Sets		
1	Fred Taylor	2.50
2	Jamal Anderson	1.50
3	John Elway	4.00
4	Brock Huard	1.50
5	Daunte Culpepper	3.00
6	Charlie Batch	1.50
7	Steve McNair	1.50
8	Corey Dillon	1.50
9	Natrone Means	.75
10	Randall Cunningham	.75
11	Drew Bledsoe	2.00
12	Jerome Bettis	1.50
13	Antowain Smith	.75
14	Steve Young	2.00
15	Eddie George	1.50

1999 Upper Deck Retro Throwback Attack

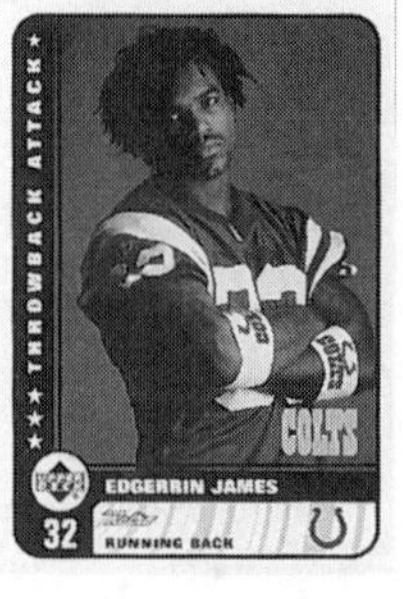

This was a 15-card insert set that showcased collectible, modern players with playing styles of the bygone era of football. Singles were inserted 1:5 packs. Each card had a parallel Gold single that was sequentially numbered to 500.

		MT
Complete Set (15):		25.00
Common Player:		.75
Minor Stars:		1.50
Inserted 1:5		
Gold Cards:		3x-6x
Production 500 Sets		
1	Brett Favre	4.00
2	Herman Moore	.75
3	Troy Aikman	2.50
4	Eric Moulds	1.50
5	Tim Couch	4.00
6	Terrell Owens	1.50
7	Champ Bailey	1.50
8	Kordell Stewart	1.50
9	Mark Brunell	2.00
10	Curtis Martin	1.50
11	Torry Holt	1.75
12	David Boston	1.75
13	Doug Flutie	1.75
14	Edgerrin James	6.00
15	Akili Smith	3.00

1999 Upper Deck Retro Walter Payton

Walter Payton signed 200 UD Authentic cards and each was sequentially numbered.

		MT
WP1	W.Payton AUTO	300.00

1999 Victory

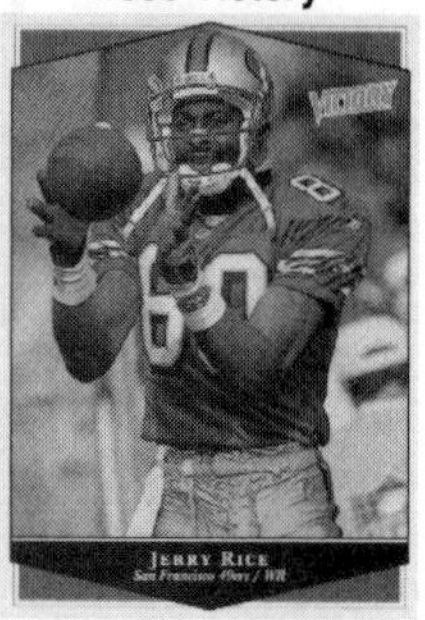

This was the premiere edition of Victory Football. The 440-card set included 60 rookie cards found one-per-pack. This was a retail-only release that didn't include any inserts. Subsets included: All-Victory, Season Leaders, Victory Parade, Rookie Flashback and '99 Rookie Class.

		MT
Complete Set (440):		70.00
Common Player:		.10
Minor Stars:		.20
Common Rookie:		.50
Inserted 1:1		
Pack (12):		1.00
Wax Box (36):		30.00
1	Arizona Cardinals visit	.10
2	Jake Plummer	.75
3	Adrian Murrell	.10
4	Michael Pittman	.10
5	Frank Sanders	.20
6	Andre Wadsworth	.10
7	Rob Moore	.20
8	Simeon Rice	.10
9	Kwamie Lassiter	.10
10	Mario Bates	.10
11	Atlanta Falcons visit	.10
12	Jamal Anderson	.30
13	Chris Chandler	.20
14	Chuck Smith	.10
15	Terance Mathis	.10
16	Tim Dwight	.30
17	Ray Buchanan	.10
18	O.J. Santiago	.10
19	Lester Archambeau	.10
20	Baltimore Ravens visit	.10
21	Tony Banks	.20
22	Priest Holmes	.30
23	Michael Jackson	.10
24	Jermaine Lewis	.20
25	Michael McCrary	.10
26	Rod Woodson	.10
27	Buffalo Bills visit	.10
28	Rob Johnson	.20
29	Antowain Smith	.30
30	Thurman Thomas	.20
31	Doug Flutie	.50
32	Eric Moulds	.30
33	Bruce Smith	.10
34	Andre Reed	.20
35	Phil Hansen	.10
36	Carolina Panthers visit	.10
37	Fred Lane	.10
38	Tshimanga Biakabutuka	.10
39	Rae Carruth	.10
40	Wesley Walls	.10
41	Steve Beuerlein	.10
42	Muhsin Muhammad	.10
43	Kevin Greene	.10
44	Chicago Bears visit	.10
45	Erik Kramer	.10
46	Edgar Bennett	.10
47	Curtis Conway	.20
48	Curtis Enis	.30
49	Bobby Engram	.10
50	Alonzo Mayes	.10
51	Tony Parrish	.10
52	Glyn Milburn	.10
53	Cincinnati Bengals visit	.10
54	Corey Dillon	.30
55	Jeff Blake	.20

56 Carl Pickens .20
57 Darnay Scott .10
58 Tony McGee .10
59 Ki-Jana Carter .10
60 Takeo Spikes .10
61 Cleveland Browns visit .10
62 Ty Detmer .10
63 Terry Kirby .10
64 Derrick Alexander .10
65 Leslie Shepherd .10
66 Marquez Pope .10
67 Antonio Langham .10
68 Marc Edwards .10
69 Dallas Cowboys visit .10
70 Troy Aikman 1.00
71 Emmitt Smith 1.50
72 Deion Sanders .30
73 Raghib Ismail .10
74 Michael Irvin .20
75 Chris Warren .10
76 Greg Ellis .10
77 Kavika Pittman .10
78 David LaFleur .10
79 Denver Broncos visit .10
80 John Elway 1.50
81 Terrell Davis 1.50
82 Rod Smith .20
83 Shannon Sharpe .20
84 Ed McCaffrey .20
85 John Mobley .10
86 Bill Romanowski .10
87 Jason Elam .10
88 Howard Griffith .10
89 Detroit Lions visit .10
90 Barry Sanders 2.00
91 Johnnie Morton .10
92 Herman Moore .30
93 Charlie Batch .50
94 Germane Crowell .20
95 Robert Porcher .10
96 Stephen Boyd .10
97 Green Bay Packers visit .10
98 Brett Favre 2.00
99 Antonio Freeman .30
100 Dorsey Levens .30
101 Mark Chmura .20
102 Vonnie Holliday .20
103 Bill Schroeder .10
104 LeRoy Butler .10
105 William Henderson .10
106 Indianapolis Colts visit .10
107 Peyton Manning 1.50
108 Marvin Harrison .30
109 Ken Dilger .10
110 Jerome Pathon .10
111 E.G. Green .10
112 Ellis Johnson .10
113 Jeff Burris .10
114 Jacksonville Jaguars visit .10
115 Mark Brunell .75
116 Jimmy Smith .20
117 Keenan McCardell .10
118 Fred Taylor 1.00
119 James Stewart .10
120 Dave Thomas .10
121 Kyle Brady .10
122 Bryce Paup .10
123 Kansas City Chiefs visit .10
124 Elvis Grbac .20
125 Andre Rison .20
126 Derrick Alexander .10
127 Tony Gonzalez .20
128 Donnell Bennett .10
129 Derrick Thomas .20
130 Tamarick Vanover .10
131 Donnie Edwards .10
132 Miami Dolphins visit .10
133 Dan Marino 1.50
134 Karim Abdul .30
135 Zach Thomas .20
136 O.J. McDuffie .20
137 John Avery .20
138 Sam Madison .10
139 Terrell Buckley .10
140 Jason Taylor .10
141 Oronde Gadsden .20
142 Minnesota Vikings visit .10
143 Randall Cunningham .30
144 Cris Carter .30
145 Robert Smith .20
146 Randy Moss 2.00
147 Jake Reed .10
148 Leroy Hoard .10
149 Matthew Hatchette .10
150 John Randle .10
151 Gary Anderson .10
152 New England Patriots visit .10
153 Drew Bledsoe .75
154 Terry Glenn .30
155 Ben Coates .20
156 Ty Law .10
157 Tony Simmons .20
158 Ted Johnson .10
159 Willie McGinest .10
160 Tony Carter .10
161 Shawn Jefferson .10
162 New Orleans Saints visit .10
163 Danny Wuerffel .20
164 Lamar Smith .10
165 Keith Poole .10
166 Cameron Cleeland .20
167 Joe Johnson .10
168 Andre Hastings .10
169 La'Roi Glover .10
170 Aaron Craver .10
171 New York Giants visit .10
172 Kent Graham .20
173 Gary Brown .20
174 Amani Toomer .10
175 Tiki Barber .10
176 Ike Hilliard .10
177 Jason Sehorn .10
178 Michael Strahan .10
179 Charles Way .10
180 New York Jets visit .10
181 Vinny Testaverde .20
182 Curtis Martin .30
183 Keyshawn Johnson .30
184 Wayne Chrebet .30
185 Mo Lewis .10
186 Steve Atwater .10
187 Leon Johnson .10
188 Bryan Cox .10
189 Oakland Raiders visit .10
190 Rich Gannon .10
191 Napoleon Kaufman .30
192 Tim Brown .30
193 Darrell Russell .10
194 Rickey Dudley .10
195 Charles Woodson .30
196 Harvey Williams .10
197 James Jett .10
198 Philadelphia Eagles visit .10
199 Koy Detmer .10
200 Duce Staley .20
201 Bobby Taylor .10
202 Doug Pederson .10
203 Karl Hankton .10
204 Charles Johnson .10
205 Kevin Turner .10
206 Hugh Douglas .10
207 Pittsburgh Steelers visit .10
208 Kordell Stewart .50
209 Jerome Bettis .30
210 Hines Ward .20
211 Courtney Hawkins .10
212 Will Blackwell .10
213 Richard Huntley .10
214 Levon Kirkland .10
215 Jason Gildon .10
216 St. Louis Rams visit .10
217 Trent Green .30
218 Isaac Bruce .20
219 Az Hakim .20
220 Amp Lee .10
221 Robert Holcombe .20
222 Ricky Proehl .10
223 Kevin Carter .10
224 Marshall Faulk .30
225 San Diego Chargers visit .10
226 Ryan Leaf .30
227 Natrone Means .30
228 Jim Harbaugh .20
229 Junior Seau .20
230 Charlie Jones .10
231 Rodney Harrison .10
232 Terrell Fletcher .10
233 Tremayne Stephens .10
234 San Francisco 49ers visit .10
235 Steve Young .75
236 Jerry Rice 1.00
237 Garrison Hearst .30
238 Terrell Owens .30
239 J.J. Stokes .20
240 Bryant Young .10
241 Tim McDonald .10
242 Merton Hanks .10
243 Travis Jervey .10
244 Seattle Seahawks visit .10
245 Ricky Watters .20
246 Joey Galloway .30
247 Jon Kitna .30
248 Ahman Green .20
249 Mike Pritchard .10
250 Chad Brown .10
251 Christian Fauria .10
252 Michael Sinclair .10
253 Tampa Bay Bucs visit .10
254 Warrick Dunn .30
255 Trent Dilfer .20
256 Mike Alstott .30
257 Reidel Anthony .20
258 Bert Emanuel .10
259 Jacquez Green .20
260 Hardy Nickerson .10
261 Derrick Brooks .10
262 Dave Moore .10
263 Tennessee Titans visit .10
264 Steve McNair .30
265 Eddie George .50
266 Yancey Thigpen .20
267 Frank Wycheck .10
268 Kevin Dyson .20
269 Jackie Harris .10
270 Blaine Bishop .10
271 Willie Davis .10
272 Washington 'Skins visit .10
273 Skip Hicks .20
274 Michael Westbrook .20
275 Stephen Alexander .10
276 Dana Stubblefield .10
277 Brad Johnson .30
278 Brian Mitchell .10
279 Dan Wilkinson .10
280 Stephen Davis .20
281 John Elway (All-Victory Team) .50
282 Dan Marino (All-Victory Team) .50
283 Troy Aikman (All-Victory Team) .30
284 Vinny Testaverde (All-Victory Team) .10
285 Corey Dillon (All-Victory Team) .10
286 Steve Young (All-Victory Team) .20
287 Randy Moss (All-Victory Team) .75
288 Drew Bledsoe (All-Victory Team) .30
289 Jerome Bettis (All-Victory Team) .10
290 Antonio Freeman (All-Victory Team) .10
291 Fred Taylor (All-Victory Team) .30
292 Doug Flutie (All-Victory Team) .10
293 Jerry Rice (All-Victory Team) .30
294 Peyton Manning (All-Victory Team) .50
295 Brett Favre (All-Victory Team) .50
296 Barry Sanders (All-Victory Team) .50
297 Keyshawn Johnson (All-Victory Team) .10
298 Mark Brunell (All-Victory Team) .20
299 Jamal Anderson (All-Victory Team) .10
300 Terrell Davis (All-Victory Team) .50
301 Randall Cunningham (All-Victory Team) .10
302 Kordell Stewart (All-Victory Team) .10
303 Warrick Dunn (All-Victory Team) .10
304 Jake Plummer (All-Victory Team) .20
305 Junior Seau (All-Victory Team) .10
306 Antowain Smith (All-Victory Team) .10
307 Charlie Batch (All-Victory Team) .20
308 Eddie George (All-Victory Team) .20
309 Michael Irvin (All-Victory Team) .10
310 Joey Galloway (All-Victory Team) .10
311 Randall Cunningham (Season Leaders) .10
312 Vinny Testaverde (Season Leaders) .10
313 Steve Young (Season Leaders) .20
314 Chris Chandler (Season Leaders) .10
315 John Elway (Season Leaders) .50
316 Steve Young (Season Leaders) .20
317 Randall Cunningham (Season Leaders) .10
318 Brett Favre (Season Leaders) .50
319 Vinny Testaverde (Season Leaders) .10
320 Peyton Manning (Season Leaders) .50
321 Terrell Davis (Season Leaders) .50
322 Jamal Anderson (Season Leaders) .10
323 Garrison Hearst (Season Leaders) .10
324 Barry Sanders (Season Leaders) .50
325 Emmitt Smith (Season Leaders) .30
326 Terrell Davis (Season Leaders) .50
327 Fred Taylor (Season Leaders) .30
328 Jamal Anderson (Season Leaders) .10
329 Emmitt Smith (Season Leaders) .30
330 Ricky Watters (Season Leaders) .10
331 O.J. McDuffie (Season Leaders) .10
332 Frank Sanders (Season Leaders) .10
333 Rod Smith (Season Leaders) .10
334 Marshall Faulk (Season Leaders) .10
335 Antonio Freeman (Season Leaders) .10
336 Randy Moss (Season Leaders) .75
337 Antonio Freeman (Season Leaders) .10
338 Terrell Owens (Season Leaders) .10
339 Cris Carter (Season Leaders) .10
340 Terance Mathis (Season Leaders) .10
341 Jake Plummer (Victory Parade) .20
342 Steve McNair (Victory Parade) .10
343 Randy Moss (Victory Parade) .75
344 Peyton Manning (Victory Parade) .50
345 Mark Brunell (Victory Parade) .20
346 Terrell Owens (Victory Parade) .10
347 Antowain Smith (Victory Parade) .10
348 Jerry Rice (Victory Parade) .30
349 Troy Aikman (Victory Parade) .30
350 Fred Taylor (Victory Parade) .30
351 Charlie Batch (Victory Parade) .10
352 Dan Marino (Victory Parade) .50
353 Eddie George (Victory Parade) .20
354 Drew Bledsoe (Victory Parade) .20
355 Kordell Stewart (Victory Parade) .10
356 Doug Flutie (Victory Parade) .10
357 Deion Sanders (Victory Parade) .10
358 Keyshawn Johnson (Victory Parade) .10
359 Jerome Bettis (Victory Parade) .10
360 Warrick Dunn (Victory Parade) .10
361 John Elway (Rookie Flashback) .50
362 Dan Marino (Rookie Flashback) .50
363 Brett Favre (Rookie Flashback) .50
364 Andre Rison (Rookie Flashback) .10
365 Rod Woodson (Rookie Flashback) .10
366 Jerry Rice (Rookie Flashback) .30
367 Barry Sanders (Rookie Flashback) .50
368 Thurman Thomas (Rookie Flashback) .10
369 Troy Aikman (Rookie Flashback) .30
370 Ricky Watters (Rookie Flashback) .10
371 Jerome Bettis (Rookie Flashback) .10
372 Reggie White (Rookie Flashback) .10
373 Junior Seau (Rookie Flashback) .10
374 Deion Sanders (Rookie Flashback) .10
375 Chris Chandler (Rookie Flashback) .10
376 Curtis Martin (Rookie Flashback) .10
377 Kordell Stewart (Rookie Flashback) .10
378 Mark Brunell (Rookie Flashback) .20
379 Cris Carter (Rookie Flashback) .10
380 Emmitt Smith (Rookie Flashback) .30
381 *Tim Couch* 8.00
382 *Donovan McNabb* 5.00
383 *Akili Smith* 4.00
384 *Edgerrin James* 10.00
385 *Ricky Williams* 8.00
386 *Torry Holt* 3.00
387 *Champ Bailey* 2.00
388 *David Boston* 3.00
389 *Chris Claiborne* 1.00
390 *Chris McAlister* 1.00
391 *Daunte Culpepper* 5.00
392 *Cade McNown* 3.00
393 *Troy Edwards* 3.00
394 *John Tait* .50
395 *Anthony McFarland* 1.00
396 *Jevon Kearse* 3.00
397 *Damien Woody* .50
398 *Matt Stinchcomb* .50
399 *Luke Petitgout* .50
400 *Ebenezer Ekuban* 1.00
401 *L.J. Shelton* .50
402 *Marty Booker* .50
403 *Antoine Winfield* 1.00
404 *Scott Covington* .50
405 *Antwan Edwards* 1.00
406 *Fernando Bryant* .50
407 *Aaron Gibson* .50
408 *Andy Katzenmoyer* 1.00
409 *Dimitrius Underwood* 1.00
410 *Patrick Kerney* .50
411 *Al Wilson* .50
412 *Kevin Johnson* 3.00
413 *Joel Makovicka* .50
414 *Reginald Kelly* .50
415 *Jeff Paulk* 1.00
416 *Brandon Stokley* 1.00
417 *Peerless Price* 2.00
418 *D'Wayne Bates* 1.50
419 *Travis McGriff* 1.00
420 *Sedrick Irvin* 1.50
421 *Aaron Brooks* 4.00
422 *Michael Cloud* 1.00
423 *Joe Montgomery* 1.50
424 *Shaun King* 5.00
425 *Dameane Douglas* 1.00
426 *Joe Germaine* 1.50
427 *James Johnson* 2.00
428 *Michael Bishop* 2.00
429 *Karsten Bailey* 1.00
430 *Craig Yeast* 1.00
431 *Jim Kleinsasser* 1.00
432 *Martin Gramatica* 1.00
433 *Jermaine Fazande* 1.00
434 *Dre' Bly* 1.00
435 *Brock Huard* 1.50
436 *Rob Konrad* 1.00
437 *Tony Bryant* 1.00
438 *Sean Bennett* 1.50
439 *Kevin Faulk* 2.00
440 *Amos Zereoue* 1.00

2000 UD Graded

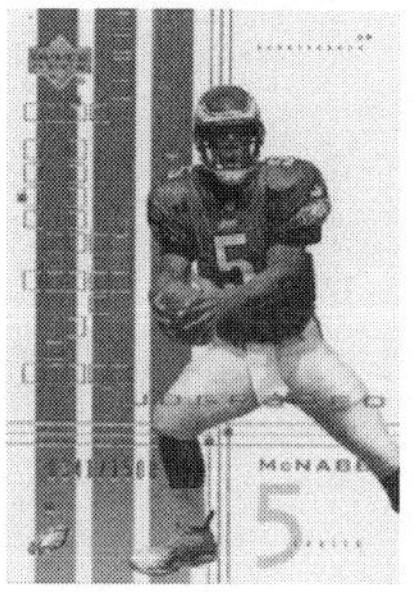

	MT
Complete Set (160):	1500.
Common Player (1-90):	1.50
Minor Stars (1-90):	3.00
Production 1,500 Sets	
Common Rookie (91-135):	5.00
Production 1,325 Sets	
Common Rookie Auto (136-155):	15.00
Production 500 Sets	
Common Rookie Auto (156-165):	25.00
Production 250 Sets	
Cards 138,139,147,148 & 163 never issued	
Pack (3+SGC):	50.00
Wax Box (6):	250.00

1 Jake Plummer 3.00
2 David Boston 3.00
3 Jamal Anderson 3.00
4 Shawn Jefferson 1.50
5 Qadry Ismail 1.50
6 Tony Banks 1.50
7 Priest Holmes 3.00
8 Rob Johnson 1.50
9 Eric Moulds 3.00
10 Steve Beuerlein 1.50
11 Muhsin Muhammad 1.50
12 Donald Hayes 1.50
13 Tim Biakabutuka 1.50
14 Cade McNown 3.00
15 Marcus Robinson 3.00
16 James Allen 3.00
17 Akili Smith 3.00
18 Corey Dillon 3.00
19 Tim Couch 5.00
20 Kevin Johnson 3.00
21 Troy Aikman 7.00
22 Emmitt Smith 8.00
23 Raghib Ismail 1.50
24 Terrell Davis 8.00
25 Rod Smith 3.00
26 Brian Griese 4.00
27 Charlie Batch 3.00
28 James O. Stewart 1.50
29 Germane Crowell 3.00
30 Brett Favre 12.00
31 Antonio Freeman 3.00
32 Dorsey Levens 3.00
33 Peyton Manning 10.00
34 Edgerrin James 10.00
35 Marvin Harrison 3.00
36 Mark Brunell 5.00
37 Jimmy Smith 3.00
38 Fred Taylor 5.00
39 Elvis Grbac 1.50
40 Tony Gonzalez 3.00
41 Lamar Smith 3.00
42 Jay Fiedler 3.00
43 Randy Moss 10.00
44 Daunte Culpepper 6.00
45 Robert Smith 3.00
46 Cris Carter 3.00
47 Drew Bledsoe 5.00
48 Kevin Faulk 3.00
49 Terry Glenn 3.00
50 Ricky Williams 7.00
51 Jeff Blake 3.00
52 Joe Horn 3.00
53 Kerry Collins 3.00
54 Amani Toomer 1.50
55 Tiki Barber 3.00
56 Wayne Chrebet 3.00
57 Curtis Martin 3.00
58 Vinny Testaverde 3.00
59 Tyrone Wheatley 3.00
60 Tim Brown 3.00
61 Rich Gannon 1.50
62 Duce Staley 3.00
63 Charles Johnson 1.50
64 Donovan McNabb 4.50
65 *Bobby Shaw* 4.00
66 Kordell Stewart 3.00
67 Jerome Bettis 3.00
68 Marshall Faulk 4.00
69 Isaac Bruce 3.00
70 Torry Holt 3.00
71 Kurt Warner 12.00
72 Neil Smith 1.50
73 Ryan Leaf 3.00
74 Curtis Conway 1.50
75 Jeff Garcia 3.00
76 Charlie Garner 1.50
77 Jerry Rice 7.00
78 Ricky Watters 3.00
79 Brock Huard 3.00
80 Jon Kitna 3.00
81 Keyshawn Johnson 3.00
82 Jacquez Green 1.50
83 Mike Alstott 3.00
84 Shaun King 4.00
85 Eddie George 4.00
86 Kevin Dyson 1.50
87 Steve McNair 3.00
88 Brad Johnson 3.00
89 Stephen Davis 3.00
90 Jeff George 3.00
91 *Ronald Dixon* 12.00
92 *Avion Black* 5.00
93 *Hank Poteat* 5.00
94 *Doug Chapman* 12.00
95 *Drew Haddad* 5.00
96 *Rondell Mealey* 7.00
97 *Spergon Wynn* 10.00
98 *Keith Bulluck* 5.00
99 *John Abraham* 5.00
100 *Rob Morris* 5.00
101 *Jerry Porter* 10.00
102 *Laveranues Coles* 15.00
103 *Jarious Jackson* 10.00
104 *Tom Brady* 10.00
105 *Jonas Lewis* 5.00
106 *Todd Husak* 7.00
107 *Shyrone Stith* 7.00
108 *Sammy Morris* 12.00
109 *Corey Simon* 12.00
110 *Chad Morton* 12.00
111 *Brian Urlacher* 25.00
112 *Anthony Becht* 7.00
113 *Chris Cole* 5.00
114 *Anthony Lucas* 5.00
115 *Charles Lee* 5.00
116 *JaJuan Dawson* 12.00
117 *Darrell Jackson* 12.00
118 *Gari Scott* 5.00
119 *Windrell Hayes* 5.00
120 *Paul Smith* 5.00
121 *Mareno Philyaw* 5.00
122 *Trevor Gaylor* 10.00
123 *Muneer Moore* 5.00
124 *Michael Wiley* 10.00
125 *Ronney Jenkins* 5.00
126 *Frank Moreau* 7.00
127 *Dante Hall* 5.00
128 *Darren Howard* 5.00
129 *Todd Pinkston* 12.00
130 *Mike Anderson* 45.00
131 *Doug Johnson* 10.00
132 *Shaun Ellis* 5.00
133 *James Williams* 5.00
134 *Ron Dugans* 5.00
135 *Frank Murphy* 5.00
136 *Dez White* 25.00
137 *Danny Farmer* 20.00
140 *Reuben Droughns* 15.00
141 *Jamal Lewis* 225.00
142 *J.R. Redmond* 35.00
143 *Tee Martin* 40.00
144 *Giovanni Carmazzi* 45.00
145 *Tim Rattay* 45.00
146 *Trung Canidate* 25.00
149 *Chris Coleman* 15.00
150 *Corey Moore* 15.00
151 *Troy Walters* 20.00
152 *Joe Hamilton* 30.00
153 *Kwame Cavil* 15.00
154 *Dennis Northcutt* 35.00
155 *Travis Taylor* 40.00
156 *Curtis Keaton* 20.00
157 *Shaun Alexander* 135.00
158 *Chad Pennington* 180.00
159 *Sylvester Morris* 75.00
160 *Plaxico Burress* 75.00
161 *Ron Dayne* 150.00
162 *Courtney Brown* 50.00
164 *Peter Warrick* 180.00
165 *Chris Redman* 120.00

2000 UD Graded SGC Blue Labels

	MT
Complete Set (165):	
Common Player:	
#'s 1-90 1x of base set	
Cards Graded 92	1x
Cards Graded 96	1x to 3x
Cards Graded 98	3x to 10x

2000 UD Graded Jerseys

		MT
Complete Set (21):		
Common Player:		10.00
TA	Troy Aikman	25.00
DB	Drew Bledsoe	20.00
IB	Isaac Bruce	40.00
MB	Mark Brunell	20.00
CC	Cris Carter	15.00
RD	Ron Dayne	20.00
BF	Brett Favre	50.00
TH	Torry Holt	10.00
EJ	Edgerrin James	40.00
KJ	Keyshawn Johnson	20.00
RJ	Rob Johnson	10.00
TJ	Thomas Jones	10.00
SK	Shaun King	10.00
PM	Peyton Manning	40.00
DM	Dan Marino	50.00
SM	Steve McNair	20.00
RM	Randy Moss	40.00
JR	Jerry Rice	40.00
ES	Emmitt Smith	50.00
KW	Kurt Warner	50.00
PW	Peter Warrick	10.00

2000 UD Graded Jerseys SGC Blue Labels

		MT
Complete Set (21):		
Common Player:		
Cards Graded 92 1x of base Jersey set		
Cards Graded 96 1x to 5x base Jersey set		
G-TA	Troy Aikman 96	
G-TA	Troy Aikman 92	
G-DB	Drew Bledsoe 96	
G-DB	Drew Bledsoe 92	
G-IB	Isaac Bruce 96	
G-IB	Isaac Bruce 92	
G-MB	Mark Brunell 96	
G-MB	Mark Brunell 92	
G-CC	Cris Carter 96	
G-CC	Cris Carter 92	
G-RD	Ron Dayne 96	
G-RD	Ron Dayne 92	
G-BF	Brett Favre 96	
G-BF	Brett Favre 92	
G-TH	Torry Holt 96	
G-TH	Torry Holt 92	
G-EJ	Edgerrin James 96	
G-EJ	Edgerrin James 92	
G-KJ	Keyshawn Johnson 96	
G-KJ	Keyshawn Johnson 92	
G-RJ	Rob Johnson 96	
G-RJ	Rob Johnson 92	
G-TJ	Thomas Jones 96	
G-TJ	Thomas Jones 92	
G-SK	Shaun King 96	
G-SK	Shaun King 92	
G-PM	Peyton Manning 96	
G-PM	Peyton Manning 92	
G-DM	Dan Marino 96	
G-DM	Dan Marino 92	
G-SM	Steve McNair 96	
G-SM	Steve McNair 92	
G-RM	Randy Moss 96	
G-RM	Randy Moss 92	
G-JR	Jerry Rice 96	
G-JR	Jerry Rice 92	
G-ES	Emmitt Smith 96	
G-ES	Emmitt Smith 92	
G-KW	Kurt Warner 96	
G-KW	Kurt Warner 92	
G-PW	Peter Warrick 96	
G-PW	Peter Warrick 92	

2000 UD Ionix

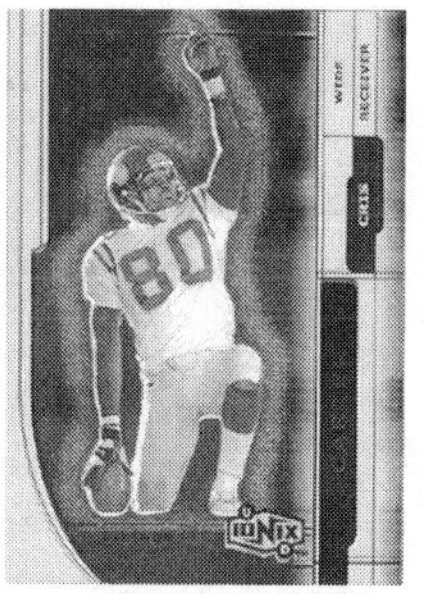

	MT
Complete Set (120):	400.00
Common Player:	.15
Minor Stars:	.30
Common Rookie:	3.00
Production 2,000 Sets	
Pack (4):	4.00
Wax Box (24):	70.00

1 Jake Plummer .50
2 Jamal Anderson .50
3 Qadry Ismail .15
4 Rob Johnson .30
5 Eric Moulds .50
6 Muhsin Muhammad .30
7 Patrick Jeffers .50
8 Cade McNown .75
9 Marcus Robinson .50
10 Akili Smith .60
11 Corey Dillon .50
12 Tim Couch 1.00
13 Kevin Johnson .50
14 Troy Aikman 1.00
15 Emmitt Smith 1.25
16 Raghib Ismail .15
17 Terrell Davis 1.25
18 Olandis Gary .60
19 Charlie Batch .50
20 James O. Stewart .50
21 Brett Favre 1.75
22 Antonio Freeman .50
23 Peyton Manning 1.50
24 Edgerrin James 1.75

25	Marvin Harrison	.50
26	Mark Brunell	.60
27	Fred Taylor	.75
28	Elvis Grbac	.30
29	Tony Gonzalez	.30
30	O.J. McDuffie	.15
31	Damon Huard	.30
32	Randy Moss	1.75
33	Cris Carter	.50
34	Drew Bledsoe	.60
35	Terry Glenn	.50
36	Ricky Williams	1.00
37	Kerry Collins	.30
38	Amani Toomer	.30
39	Keyshawn Johnson	.50
40	Vinny Testaverde	.50
41	Tim Brown	.30
42	Rich Gannon	.30
43	Duce Staley	.50
44	Donovan McNabb	.75
45	Troy Edwards	.50
46	Jerome Bettis	.30
47	Marshall Faulk	.50
48	Kurt Warner	2.00
49	Junior Seau	.30
50	Jeff Graham	.15
51	Charlie Garner	.30
52	Jerry Rice	1.00
53	Ricky Watters	.30
54	Jon Kitna	.50
55	Mike Alstott	.50
56	Shaun King	.75
57	Eddie George	.60
58	Steve McNair	.60
59	Brad Johnson	.50
60	Stephen Davis	.50
61	*Ahmed Plummer*	3.00
62	*Courtney Brown*	6.00
63	*Delthea O'Neal*	3.00
64	*Chad Morton*	5.00
65	*Corey Simon*	6.00
66	*Hank Poteat*	3.00
67	*Raynoch Thompson*	3.00
68	*Darren Howard*	3.00
69	*Rondell Mealey*	4.00
70	*Marcus Knight*	3.00
71	*Keith Bulluck*	3.00
72	*John Abraham*	3.00
73	*Rob Morris*	3.00
74	*Chris Redman*	12.00
75	*Joe Hamilton*	6.00
76	*Jarious Jackson*	6.00
77	*Tom Brady*	6.00
78	*Chad Pennington*	25.00
79	*Tee Martin*	6.00
80	*Giovanni Carmazzi*	6.00
81	*Tim Rattay*	6.00
82	*Marc Bulger*	3.00
83	*Todd Husak*	3.00
84	*Curtis Keaton*	4.00
85	*Ron Dayne*	30.00
86	*Shaun Alexander*	20.00
87	*Thomas Jones*	12.00
88	*Reuben Droughns*	4.00
89	*Jamal Lewis*	40.00
90	*J.R. Redmond*	8.00
91	*Travis Prentice*	10.00
92	*Shyrone Stith*	3.00
93	*Chris Hovan*	3.00
94	*Michael Wiley*	6.00
95	*Trung Canidate*	4.00
96	*Sebastian Janikowski*	6.00
97	*Brian Urlacher*	20.00
98	*Bubba Franks*	6.00
99	*Anthony Becht*	4.00
100	*Chris Cole*	3.00
101	*R. Jay Soward*	6.00
102	*Peter Warrick*	30.00
103	*Plaxico Burress*	15.00
104	*Sylvester Morris*	15.00
105	*Dez White*	6.00
106	*Travis Taylor*	8.00
107	*Trevor Gaylor*	5.00
108	*Anthony Lucas*	3.00
109	*Sherrod Gideon*	3.00
110	*Todd Pinkston*	6.00
111	*Dennis Northcutt*	6.00
112	*Jerry Porter*	6.00
113	*Ron Dugans*	6.00
114	*Laveranues Coles*	7.00
115	*Darrell Jackson*	7.00
116	*Danny Farmer*	6.00
117	*Gari Scott*	3.00
118	*JaJuan Dawson*	6.00
119	*Troy Walters*	3.00
120	*Quinton Spotwood*	3.00

2000 UD Ionix Game Jersey Greats

		MT
Production 375 Sets		
DM	Dan Marino AUTO	250.00

2000 UD Ionix High Voltage

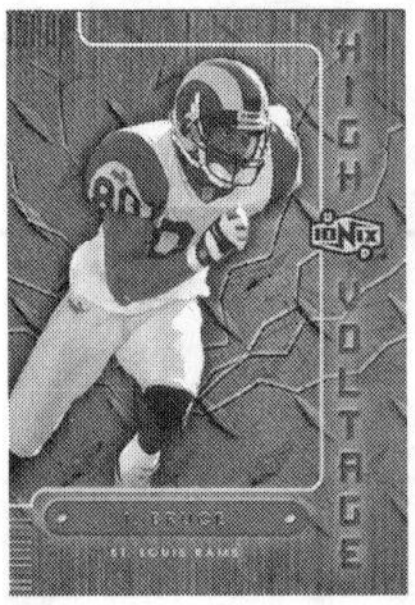

		MT
Complete Set (15):		8.00
Common Player:		.50
Minor Stars:		1.00
Inserted 1:4		
HV1	Fred Taylor	1.75
HV2	Michael Westbrook	.50
HV3	James O. Stewart	.50
HV4	Keyshawn Johnson	1.00
HV5	Marcus Robinson	1.00
HV6	Charlie Batch	1.00
HV7	Marvin Harrison	1.00
HV8	Olandis Gary	1.25
HV9	Curtis Martin	1.00
HV10	Isaac Bruce	1.00
HV11	Jake Plummer	1.00
HV12	Shaun King	1.50
HV13	Jimmy Smith	1.00
HV14	Muhsin Muhammad	.50
HV15	Raghib Ismail	.50

2000 UD Ionix Majestix

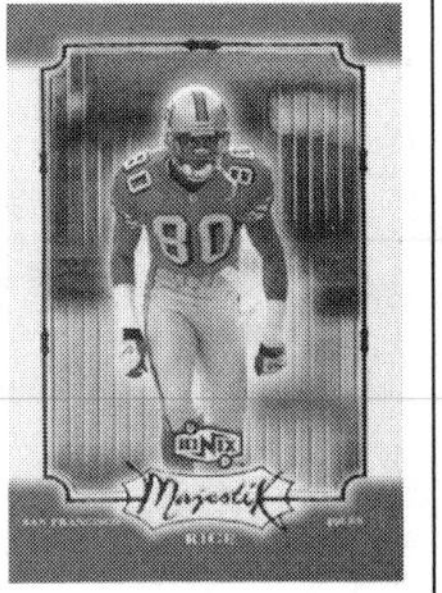

		MT
Complete Set (15):		20.00
Common Player:		.75
Minor Stars:		1.50
Inserted 1:11		
M1	Steve Young	2.00
M2	Jerry Rice	3.50
M3	Troy Aikman	3.50
M4	Emmitt Smith	4.00
M5	Vinny Testaverde	.75
M6	Cris Carter	1.50
M7	Brett Favre	5.00
M8	Eddie George	1.75
M9	Herman Moore	.75
M10	Drew Bledsoe	2.50
M11	Tim Brown	.75
M12	Steve Beuerlein	.75
M13	Brad Johnson	1.50
M14	Mark Brunell	2.50
M15	Randy Moss	5.00

2000 UD Ionix Rookie Xtreme

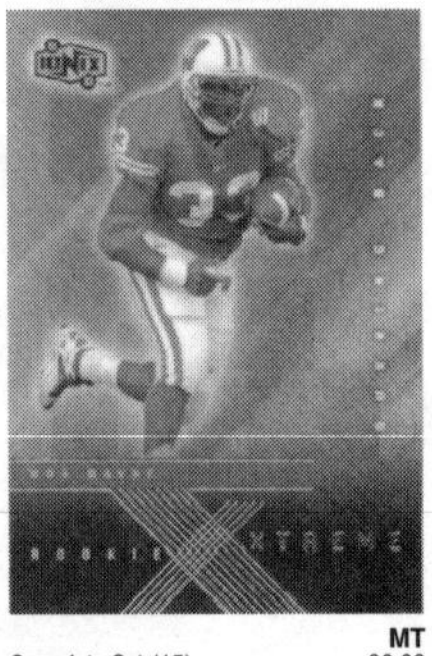

		MT
Complete Set (15):		30.00
Common Player:		1.00
Inserted 1:11		
RX1	Trung Canidate	1.00
RX2	Peter Warrick	6.00
RX3	Plaxico Burress	4.50
RX4	Jamal Lewis	3.50
RX5	Thomas Jones	3.50
RX6	Chad Pennington	4.50
RX7	Chris Redman	2.00
RX8	Ron Dayne	6.00
RX9	Courtney Brown	2.00
RX10	Corey Simon	1.00
RX11	Shaun Alexander	3.50
RX12	Dez White	1.00
RX13	J.R. Redmond	2.00
RX14	Shyrone Stith	1.00
RX15	Travis Taylor	2.50

2000 UD Ionix Sunday Best

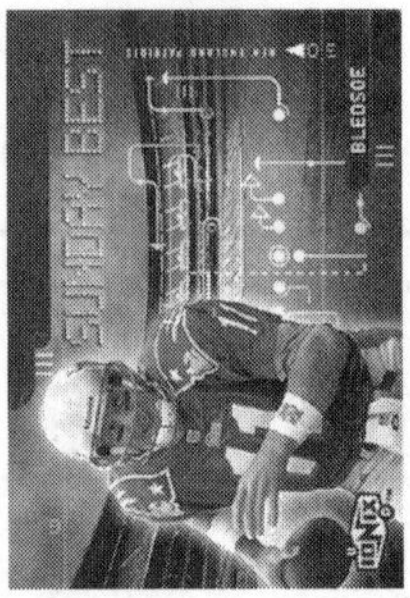

		MT
Complete Set (15):		20.00
Common Player:		1.00
Minor Stars:		2.00
Inserted 1:23		
SB1	Stephen Davis	2.00
SB2	Brian Griese	2.50
SB3	Corey Dillon	2.00
SB4	Muhsin Muhammad	1.00
SB5	Charlie Batch	2.00
SB6	Shaun King	3.00
SB7	Germane Crowell	2.00
SB8	Drew Bledsoe	3.50
SB9	Jake Plummer	2.00
SB10	Torry Holt	2.00
SB11	Marcus Robinson	2.00
SB12	Ricky Williams	4.50
SB13	Tim Couch	4.50
SB14	Kevin Johnson	2.00
SB15	Warrick Dunn	2.00

2000 UD Ionix Super Trio

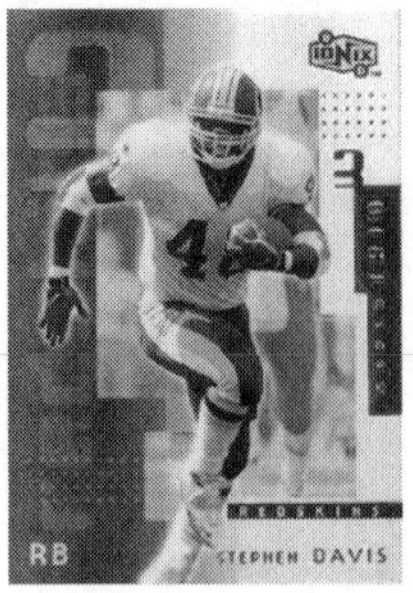

		MT
Complete Set (15):		30.00
Common Player:		1.00
Minor Stars:		2.00
Inserted 1:23		
ST1	Peyton Manning	6.00
ST2	Edgerrin James	6.00
ST3	Marvin Harrison	2.00
ST4	Kurt Warner	8.00
ST5	Marshall Faulk	2.00
ST6	Isaac Bruce	2.00
ST7	Mark Brunell	3.00
ST8	Fred Taylor	3.00
ST9	Jimmy Smith	2.00
ST10	Troy Aikman	4.00
ST11	Emmitt Smith	5.00
ST12	Raghib Ismail	1.00
ST13	Brad Johnson	2.00
ST14	Stephen Davis	2.00
ST15	Michael Westbrook	1.00

2000 UD Ionix UD Authentics Blue

		MT
Common Player:		10.00
Minor Stars:		20.00
Production 300 Sets		
SA	Shaun Alexander	50.00
CA	Champ Bailey	20.00
CB	Charlie Batch	25.00
DA	David Boston	25.00
TB	Tim Brown	25.00
IB	Isaac Bruce	25.00
CC	Cris Carter	25.00
WC	Wayne Chrebet	20.00
CN	Chris Coleman	10.00
DF	Danny Farmer	20.00
KF	Kevin Faulk	25.00
FR	Bubba Franks	30.00
OG	Olandis Gary	25.00
SG	Sherrod Gideon	10.00
BG	Brian Griese	30.00
JH	Joe Hamilton	20.00
TH	Torry Holt	25.00
RJ	Rob Johnson	20.00
RL	Ray Lucas	25.00
TM	Tee Martin	25.00
DN	Dennis Northcutt	25.00
TO	Terrell Owens	25.00
TP	Travis Prentice	30.00
TR	Tim Rattay	30.00
RS	R. Jay Soward	25.00
BU	Brian Urlacher	25.00
TW	Troy Walters	10.00
MW	Michael Wiley	25.00

2000 UD Ionix UD Authentics Gold

		MT
Common Player:		20.00
Minor Stars:		40.00
Production 100 Sets		
TA	Troy Aikman	85.00
MB	Mark Brunell	60.00
TC	Tim Couch	85.00
TD	Terrell Davis	100.00
RD	Ron Dayne	150.00
MF	Marshall Faulk	50.00
AF	Antonio Freeman	20.00
MH	Marvin Harrison	40.00
EJ	Edgerrin James	125.00
BJ	Brad Johnson	40.00
KJ	Keyshawn Johnson	40.00
TJ	Thomas Jones	100.00
DL	Dorsey Levens	20.00
JL	Jamal Lewis	100.00
PM	Peyton Manning	125.00
MC	Cade McNown	60.00
SL	Sylvester Morris	50.00
RM	Randy Moss	125.00
EM	Eric Moulds	40.00
CP	Chad Pennington	125.00
JP	Jake Plummer	40.00
CR	Chris Redman	65.00
KW	Kurt Warner	125.00
PW	Peter Warrick	150.00

2000 UD Ionix Warp Zone

		MT
Complete Set (15):		200.00
Common Player:		10.00
Inserted 1:239		
WZ1	Marshall Faulk	10.00
WZ2	Kurt Warner	45.00
WZ3	Peyton Manning	30.00
WZ4	Edgerrin James	30.00
WZ5	Brett Favre	40.00
WZ6	Tim Couch	20.00
WZ7	Ricky Williams	20.00
WZ8	Mark Brunell	15.00
WZ9	Fred Taylor	15.00
WZ10	Terrell Davis	25.00
WZ11	Dan Marino	30.00
WZ12	Randy Moss	40.00
WZ13	Emmitt Smith	25.00
WZ14	Eddie George	12.00
WZ15	Steve McNair	10.00

2000 Upper Deck

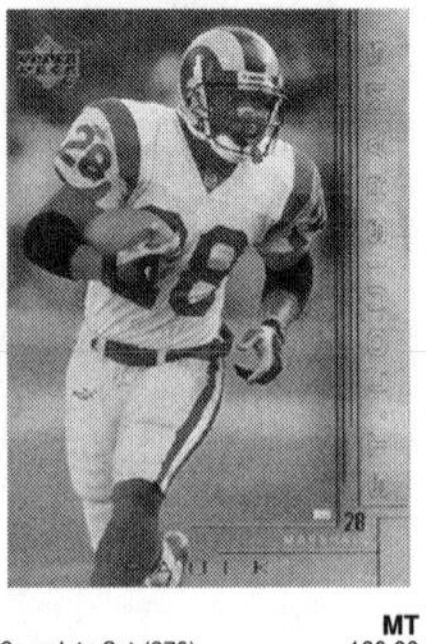

		MT
Complete Set (270):		180.00
Common Player:		.15
Minor Stars:		.30
Common Rookie:		2.00
Inserted 1:4		
Pack (10):		3.00
Wax Box (24):		60.00
1	Jake Plummer	.50
2	Michael Pittman	.15
3	Rob Moore	.30
4	David Boston	.50
5	Frank Sanders	.30
6	Aeneas Williams	.15
7	Kwamie Lassiter	.15
8	Rob Fredrickson	.15
9	Tim Dwight	.50
10	Chris Chandler	.30
11	Jamal Anderson	.50
12	Shawn Jefferson	.15
13	Ken Oxendine	.15
14	Terance Mathis	.15
15	Bob Christian	.15
16	Qadry Ismail	.15
17	Jermaine Lewis	.15
18	Rod Woodson	.15
19	Michael McCrary	.15
20	Tony Banks	.30
21	Peter Boulware	.15
22	Shannon Sharpe	.30
23	Peerless Price	.30
24	Rob Johnson	.30
25	Eric Moulds	.50
26	Doug Flutie	.75
27	Jay Riemersma	.15
28	Antowain Smith	.30
29	Jonathon Linton	.15
30	Muhsin Muhammad	.30
31	Patrick Jeffers	.50
32	Steve Beuerlein	.30
33	Natrone Means	.15
34	Tim Biakabutuka	.15
35	Michael Bates	.15
36	Chuck Smith	.15
37	Wesley Walls	.30
38	Cade McNown	1.00
39	Curtis Enis	.50
40	Marcus Robinson	.50
41	Eddie Kennison	.15
42	Bobby Engram	.15
43	Glyn Milburn	.15
44	Marty Booker	.15
45	Akili Smith	.75
46	Corey Dillon	.50
47	Darnay Scott	.30
48	Tremain Mack	.15
49	Damon Griffin	.15
50	Takeo Spikes	.15
51	Tony McGee	.15
52	Tim Couch	1.50
53	Kevin Johnson	.30
54	Darrin Chiaverini	.15
55	Jamir Miller	.15
56	Errict Rhett	.15
57	Terry Kirby	.15
58	Marc Edwards	.15
59	Troy Aikman	1.25
60	Emmitt Smith	1.75
61	Raghib Ismail	.15
62	Jason Tucker	.15
63	Dexter Coakley	.15
64	Joey Galloway	.50
65	Wane McGarity	.15
66	Terrell Davis	1.75
67	Olandis Gary	.75
68	Brian Griese	.75
69	Gus Frerotte	.15
70	Byron Chamberlain	.15
71	Ed McCaffrey	.30
72	Rod Smith	.30
73	Al Wilson	.15
74	Charlie Batch	.50
75	Germane Crowell	.50
76	Sedrick Irvin	.15
77	Johnnie Morton	.30
78	Robert Porcher	.15
79	Herman Moore	.50
80	James O. Stewart	.50
81	Brett Favre	2.50
82	Antonio Freeman	.50
83	Bill Schroeder	.50
84	Dorsey Levens	.50
85	Corey Bradford	.15
86	Demond Parker	.15
87	Vonnie Holliday	.15
88	Peyton Manning	2.00
89	Edgerrin James	2.00
90	Marvin Harrison	.50
91	Ken Dilger	.15
92	Terrence Wilkins	.30
93	Marcus Pollard	.15
94	Fred Lane	.15
95	Mark Brunell	1.00
96	Fred Taylor	1.00
97	Jimmy Smith	.50
98	Keenan McCardell	.30
99	Carnell Lake	.15
100	Tavian Banks	.15
101	Kyle Brady	.15
102	Hardy Nickerson	.15
103	Elvis Grbac	.30
104	Tony Gonzalez	.30
105	Derrick S. Alexander	.15
106	Donnell Bennett	.15
107	Mike Cloud	.15
108	Donnie Edwards	.15
109	Jay Fiedler	.30
110	James Johnson	.30
111	Tony Martin	.15
112	Damon Huard	.30
113	O.J. McDuffie	.30
114	Thurman Thomas	.30
115	Zach Thomas	.30
116	Oronde Gadsden	.15
117	Randy Moss	2.00
118	Robert Smith	.50
119	Cris Carter	.50
120	Matthew Hatchette	.15
121	Daunte Culpepper	1.00
122	Leroy Hoard	.15
123	Drew Bledsoe	1.00
124	Terry Glenn	.50
125	Troy Brown	.15
126	Kevin Faulk	.30
127	Lawyer Milloy	.15
128	Ricky Williams	1.50
129	Keith Poole	.15
130	Jake Reed	.15
131	Cameron Cleeland	.30
132	Jeff Blake	.30
133	Andrew Glover	.15
134	Kerry Collins	.50
135	Amani Toomer	.30
136	Joe Montgomery	.15
137	Ike Hilliard	.30
138	Tiki Barber	.30
139	Pete Mitchell	.15
140	Ray Lucas	.50
141	Mo Lewis	.15
142	Curtis Martin	.50
143	Vinny Testaverde	.50
144	Wayne Chrebet	.30
145	Dedric Ward	.15
146	Tim Brown	.30
147	Rich Gannon	.30
148	Tyrone Wheatley	.30
149	Napoleon Kaufman	.50
150	Charles Woodson	.50
151	Darrell Russell	.15
152	James Jett	.15
153	Rickey Dudley	.15
154	Jon Ritchie	.15
155	Duce Staley	.50
156	Donovan McNabb	1.00
157	Torrance Small	.15
158	Allen Rossum	.15
159	Mike Mamula	.15
160	Na Brown	.15
161	Charles Johnson	.15
162	Kent Graham	.15
163	Troy Edwards	.50
164	Jerome Bettis	.50
165	Hines Ward	.30
166	Kordell Stewart	.50
167	Levon Kirkland	.15
168	Richard Huntley	.15
169	Marshall Faulk	.50
170	Kurt Warner	2.75
171	Torry Holt	.50
172	Isaac Bruce	.50
173	Kevin Carter	.15
174	Az-Zahir Hakim	.30
175	Ricky Proehl	.15
176	Jermaine Fazande	.30
177	Curtis Conway	.30
178	Freddie Jones	.30
179	Junior Seau	.30
180	Jeff Graham	.15
181	Jim Harbaugh	.15
182	Rodney Harrison	.15
183	Steve Young	1.00
184	Jerry Rice	1.50
185	Charlie Garner	.50
186	Terrell Owens	.50
187	Jeff Garcia	.50
188	Fred Beasley	.15
189	J.J. Stokes	.30
190	Ricky Watters	.30
191	Jon Kitna	.50
192	Derrick Mayes	.15
193	Sean Dawkins	.15
194	Charlie Rogers	.15
195	Mike Pritchard	.15
196	Cortez Kennedy	.15
197	Christian Fauria	.15
198	Warrick Dunn	.50
199	Shaun King	1.00
200	Mike Alstott	.50
201	Warren Sapp	.30
202	Jacquez Green	.30
203	Reidel Anthony	.30
204	Dave Moore	.15
205	Keyshawn Johnson	.50
206	Eddie George	.75
207	Steve McNair	.60
208	Kevin Dyson	.30
209	Jevon Kearse	.60
210	Yancey Thigpen	.15
211	Frank Wycheck	.15
212	Isaac Byrd	.15
213	Neil O'Donnell	.15
214	Brad Johnson	.50
215	Stephen Davis	.50
216	Michael Westbrook	.30
217	Albert Connell	.15
218	Brian Mitchell	.15
219	Bruce Smith	.15
220	Stephen Alexander	.15
221	Jeff George	.50
222	Adrian Murrell	.15
223	*Courtney Brown*	3.00
224	*John Engleberger*	2.00
225	*Deltha O'Neal*	2.00
226	*Corey Simon*	3.00
227	*R. Jay Soward*	3.00
228	*Marc Bulger*	2.00
229	*Raynoch Thompson*	2.00
230	*Deon Grant*	2.00
231	*Darrell Jackson*	4.00
232	*Chris Cole*	2.00
233	*Trevor Gaylor*	2.00
234	*John Abraham*	2.00
235	*Chris Redman*	6.00
236	*Joe Hamilton*	3.00
237	*Chad Pennington*	12.00
238	*Tee Martin*	3.00
239	*Giovanni Carmazzi*	3.00
240	*Tim Rattay*	3.00
241	*Ron Dayne*	15.00
242	*Shaun Alexander*	10.00
243	*Thomas Jones*	6.00
244	*Reuben Droughns*	2.00
245	*Jamal Lewis*	20.00
246	*Michael Wiley*	2.00
247	*J.R. Redmond*	4.00
248	*Travis Prentice*	5.00
249	*Todd Husak*	2.00
250	*Trung Canidate*	2.00
251	*Brian Urlacher*	10.00
252	*Anthony Becht*	2.00
253	*Bubba Franks*	3.00
254	*Tom Brady*	2.00
255	*Peter Warrick*	15.00
256	*Plaxico Burress*	8.00
257	*Sylvester Morris*	8.00
258	*Dez White*	2.00
259	*Travis Taylor*	4.00
260	*Todd Pinkston*	3.00
261	*Dennis Northcutt*	3.00
262	*Jerry Porter*	2.00
263	*Laveranues Coles*	4.00
264	*Danny Farmer*	2.00
265	*Curtis Keaton*	2.00
266	*Sherrod Gideon*	2.00
267	*Ron Dugans*	2.00
268	Checklist (Steve McNair)	.30
269	Checklist (Jake Plummer)	.30
270	Checklist (Antonio Freeman)	.15

2000 Upper Deck Exclusives Gold Parallel

	MT
Gold Cards:	40x-80x
Gold Rookies:	6x-12x
Production 25 Sets	

2000 Upper Deck Exclusives Silver Parallel

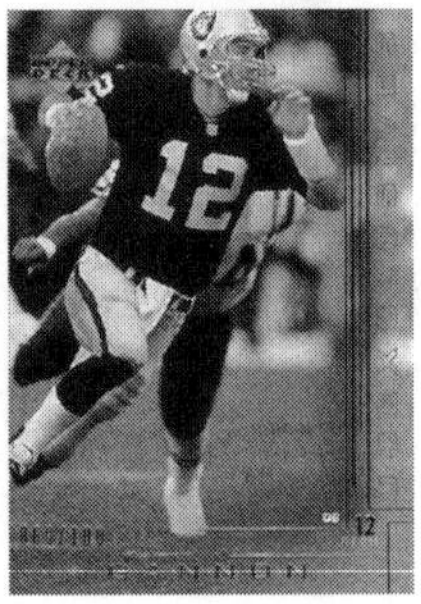

	MT
Silver Cards:	10x-20x
Silver Rookies:	3x-6x
Production 100 Sets	

2000 Upper Deck e-Card

		MT
Complete Set (6):		25.00
Common Player:		2.50
Inserted 2:Box		
SA	Shaun Alexander	6.00
TJ	Thomas Jones	6.00
JL	Jamal Lewis	6.00
CP	Chad Pennington	8.00
CR	Chris Redman	2.50
TT	Travis Taylor	4.00

2000 Upper Deck Game Jersey

		MT
Common Player:		20.00
Minor Stars:		40.00
Inserted 1:287		
MA	Mike Alstott	40.00
JA	Jamal Anderson	40.00
BO	David Boston	40.00
CB	Courtney Brown	50.00
TB	Tim Brown	20.00
PB	Plaxico Burress	65.00
DC	Daunte Culpepper	80.00
BF	Brett Favre	125.00
FR	Bubba Franks	20.00
AF	Antonio Freeman	40.00
OG	Olandis Gary	40.00
BG	Brian Griese	50.00
TH	Torry Holt	40.00
TJ	Thomas Jones	60.00
SK	Shaun King	50.00
DL	Dorsey Levens	20.00
JL	Jamal Lewis	125.00
RL	Ray Lucas	20.00
CM	Curtis Martin	40.00
TM	Tee Martin	60.00
DO	Donovan McNabb	60.00
SM	Steve McNair	50.00
HM	Herman Moore	20.00
SL	Sylvester Morris	60.00
EM	Eric Moulds	40.00
TO	Terrell Owens	40.00
CR	Chris Redman	65.00
JR	Jerry Rice	100.00
ES	Emmitt Smith	100.00
RJ	R. Jay Soward	40.00
JJ	J.J. Stokes	20.00
TT	Travis Taylor	65.00

RW	Ricky Williams	85.00
SY	Steve Young	60.00

2000 Upper Deck Game Jersey Autographs

		MT
Common Player:		80.00
Inserted 1:287 Hobby		
TA	Troy Aikman	125.00
JA	Jamal Anderson	80.00
DB	Drew Bledsoe	125.00
BO	David Boston	80.00
TB	Tim Brown	80.00
IB	Isaac Bruce	100.00
MB	Mark Brunell	125.00
TC	Tim Couch	125.00
TD	Terrell Davis	150.00
RD-A	Ron Dayne	150.00
MF	Marshall Faulk	120.00
AF	Antonio Freeman	80.00
OG	Olandis Gary	80.00
EG	Eddie George	120.00
BG	Brian Griese	100.00
MH	Marvin Harrison	80.00
TH	Torry Holt	80.00
EJ	Edgerrin James	150.00
JO	Kevin Johnson	80.00
KJ	Keyshawn Johnson	80.00
DL	Dorsey Levens	80.00
RL	Ray Lucas	80.00
PM	Peyton Manning	150.00
DM	Dan Marino	200.00
MC	Cade McNown	100.00
RM	Randy Moss	200.00
CP-A	Chad Pennington	150.00
KW	Kurt Warner	200.00
SY	Steve Young	100.00

2000 Upper Deck Game Jersey-Hobby Autographs

		MT
Complete Set (25):		
Common Player:		80.00
TA	Troy Aikman	125.00
SA	Shaun Alexander	100.00
DB	Drew Bledsoe	125.00
CB	Courtney Brown	80.00
IB	Isaac Bruce	100.00
MB	Mark Brunell	125.00
TC	Tim Couch	125.00
TD	Terrell Davis	100.00
RD	Ron Dayne	100.00
FA	Danny Farmer	80.00
MF	Marshall Faulk	125.00
EG	Eddie George	125.00
MH	Marvin Harrison	80.00
EJ	Edgerrin James	150.00
JO	Kevin Johnson	80.00
KJ	Keyshawn Johnson	100.00
TJ	Thomas Jones	80.00
PM	Peyton Manning	150.00
DM	Dan Marino	200.00
MC	Cade McNown	100.00
RM	Randy Moss	200.00
CP	Chad Pennington	150.00
CR	Chris Redman	80.00
KW	Kurt Warner	200.00
PW	Peter Warrick	100.00

2000 Upper Deck Game Jersey Greats

		MT
Production 200 Sets		
BS	Bart Starr AUTO	225.00

2000 Upper Deck Game Jersey Patch

		MT
Common Player:		100.00
Inserted 1:7,500		
JA	Jamal Anderson	100.00
DB	Drew Bledsoe	175.00
BO	David Boston	100.00
TB	Tim Brown	100.00
MB	Mark Brunell	200.00
TC	Tim Couch	225.00
DA	Daunte Culpepper	250.00
TD	Terrell Davis	225.00
BF	Brett Favre	375.00
AF	Antonio Freeman	100.00
MF	Marshall Faulk	225.00
OG	Olandis Gary	100.00
EG	Eddie George	225.00
BG	Brian Griese	100.00
MH	Marvin Harrison	100.00
TH	Torry Holt	100.00
EJ	Edgerrin James	325.00
JO	Kevin Johnson	100.00
KJ	Keyshawn Johnson	100.00
SK	Shaun King	100.00
DL	Dorsey Levens	100.00
RL	Ray Lucas	100.00
PM	Peyton Manning	350.00
DM	Dan Marino	450.00
CM	Curtis Martin	100.00
MC	Cade McNown	125.00
RM	Randy Moss	350.00
TO	Terrell Owens	100.00
ES	Emmitt Smith	300.00
FT	Fred Taylor	150.00

2000 Upper Deck Game Jersey Patch Autographs

		MT
Complete Set (6):		
Common Player:		
TC	Tim Couch	200.00
MF	Marshall Faulk	250.00
EG	Eddie George	200.00
EJ	Edgerrin James	250.00
RM	Randy Moss	300.00
KW	Kurt Warner	300.00

2000 Upper Deck Headline Heroes

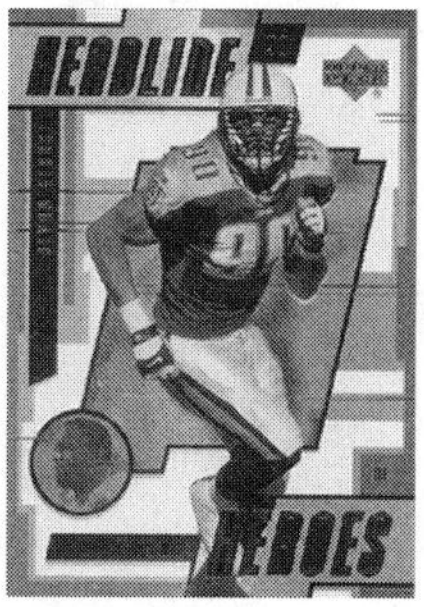

		MT
Complete Set (15):		25.00
Common Player:		1.00
Minor Stars:		2.00
Inserted 1:23		
HH1	Mark Brunell	3.00
HH2	Damon Huard	2.00
HH3	Ricky Williams	5.00
HH4	Jevon Kearse	2.50
HH5	Keyshawn Johnson	2.00
HH6	Ricky Watters	1.00
HH7	Michael Westbrook	2.00
HH8	Charlie Batch	2.00
HH9	Warren Sapp	1.00
HH10	Muhsin Muhammad	1.00
HH11	Brett Favre	8.00
HH12	Jeff George	2.00
HH13	Germane Crowell	2.00
HH14	Troy Aikman	5.00
HH15	Jimmy Smith	2.00

2000 Upper Deck Highlight Zone

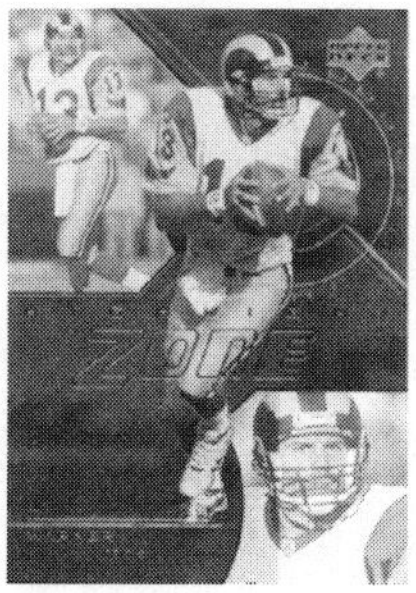

		MT
Complete Set (10):		10.00
Common Player:		.50
Minor Stars:		1.00
Inserted 1:11		
HZ1	Eddie George	1.50
HZ2	Steve McNair	1.25
HZ3	Kevin Dyson	.50
HZ4	Kurt Warner	5.00
HZ5	Emmitt Smith	3.00
HZ6	Brad Johnson	1.00
HZ7	Curtis Martin	1.00
HZ8	Ray Lucas	.50
HZ9	Akili Smith	1.00
HZ10	Jake Plummer	1.00

2000 Upper Deck New Guard

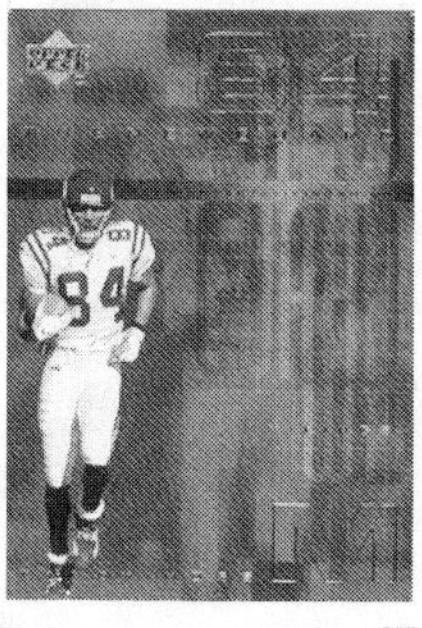

		MT
Complete Set (15):		35.00
Common Player:		1.25
Minor Stars:		2.50
Inserted 1:23		
NG1	Tim Couch	5.00
NG2	Ricky Williams	5.00
NG3	Shaun King	3.00
NG4	Brian Griese	2.50
NG5	Rob Johnson	1.25
NG6	Marcus Robinson	2.50
NG7	Troy Edwards	1.25
NG8	Kevin Johnson	1.25
NG9	Cade McNown	3.00
NG10	Jon Kitna	1.25
NG11	Peyton Manning	10.00
NG12	Edgerrin James	10.00
NG13	Akili Smith	2.50
NG14	Donovan McNabb	3.00
NG15	Randy Moss	10.00

2000 Upper Deck Proving Ground

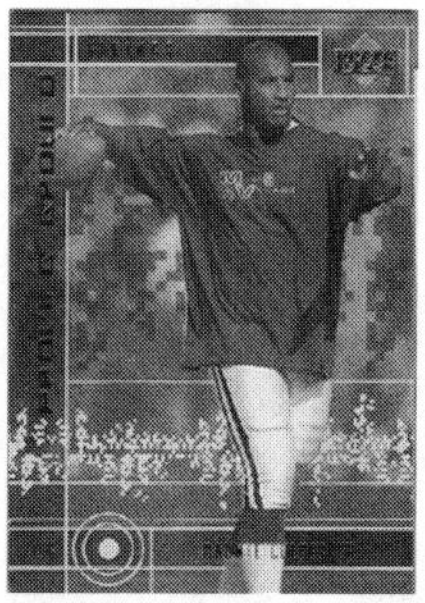

		MT
Complete Set (10):		7.00
Common Player:		.50
Minor Stars:		1.00
Inserted 1:11		
PG1	Marcus Robinson	1.00
PG2	Stephen Davis	1.00
PG3	Daunte Culpepper	2.00
PG4	Jevon Kearse	1.00
PG5	Marshall Faulk	1.00
PG6	Marvin Harrison	1.00
PG7	Germane Crowell	1.00
PG8	Darnay Scott	.50
PG9	Duce Staley	1.00
PT10	Warrick Dunn	1.00

2000 Upper Deck Strike Force

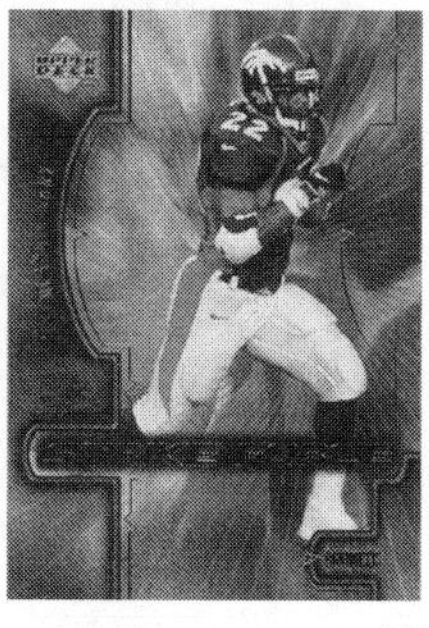

		MT
Complete Set (15):		5.00
Common Player:		.30
Minor Stars:		.60
Inserted 1:4		
SF1	Fred Taylor	1.50
SF2	Muhsin Muhammad	.60
SF3	Tony Gonzalez	.30
SF4	Marcus Robinson	.60
SF5	Charlie Garner	.30
SF6	Torry Holt	.60
SF7	Germane Crowell	.60
SF8	Amani Toomer	.30
SF9	Patrick Jeffers	.30
SF10	Albert Connell	.30
SF11	Olandis Gary	.60
SF12	Robert Smith	.60
SF13	Napoleon Kaufman	.30
SF14	Tim Biakabutuka	.30
SF15	Priest Holmes	.30

2000 Upper Deck Wired

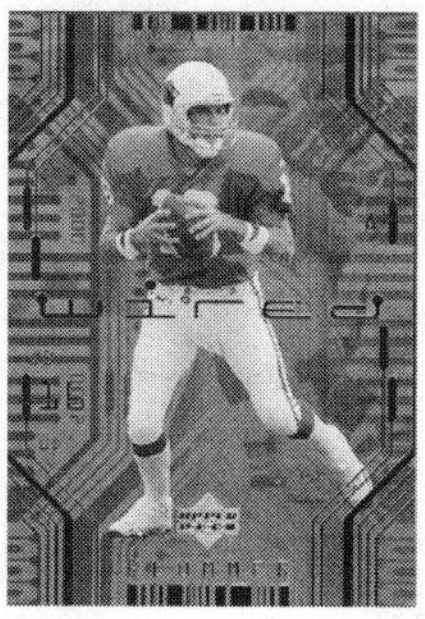

		MT
Complete Set (15):		12.00
Common Player:		.75
Minor Stars:		1.50
Inserted 1:8		
W1	Charlie Batch	1.50
W2	Terrell Davis	3.00
W3	Jake Plummer	1.50
W4	Cris Carter	1.50
W5	James O. Stewart	1.50
W6	Corey Dillon	1.50
W7	Ricky Watters	.75
W8	Curtis Enis	1.50
W9	Errict Rhett	.75
W10	Stephen Davis	1.50
W11	Mike Alstott	1.50
W12	Steve Beuerlein	.75
W13	Michael Westbrook	.75
W14	Terry Glenn	1.50
W15	Bill Schroeder	.75

2000 Upper Deck Black Diamond

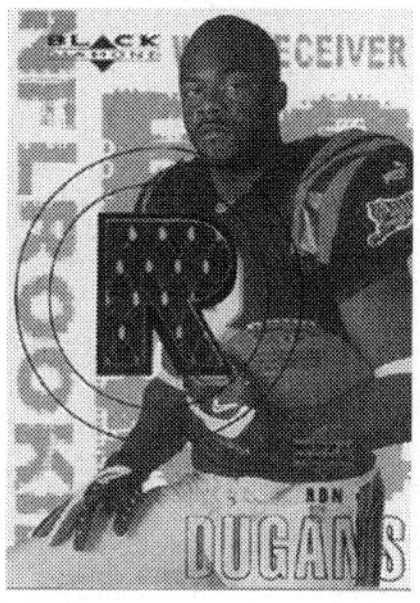

		MT
Complete Set (180):		850.00
Common Player:		.15
Minor Stars:		.30
Common Rookie (121-150):		1.50
Inserted 1:8		
Common Rookie Jersey (151-180):		12.00
Inserted 1:23		
Pack (6):		4.00
Wax Box (24):		65.00
1	Jake Plummer	.50
2	David Boston	.50
3	Frank Sanders	.30
4	Tim Dwight	.50
5	Chris Chandler	.30
6	Jamal Anderson	.50
7	Shawn Jefferson	.15
8	Terance Mathis	.15
9	Qadry Ismail	.15
10	Tony Banks	.30
11	Shannon Sharpe	.30
12	Peerless Price	.30
13	Rob Johnson	.30
14	Eric Moulds	.50
15	Antowain Smith	.30
16	Muhsin Muhammad	.30
17	Patrick Jeffers	.30
18	Steve Beuerlein	.30
19	Tim Biakabutuka	.30
20	Cade McNown	.30
21	Marcus Robinson	.50
22	Eddie Kennison	.15
23	Bobby Engram	.15
24	Akili Smith	.50
25	Corey Dillon	.50
26	Darnay Scott	.30
27	Tim Couch	1.25
28	Kevin Johnson	.50
29	Errict Rhett	.30
30	Troy Aikman	1.25
31	Emmitt Smith	1.75
32	Raghib Ismail	.15
33	Joey Galloway	.50
34	Terrell Davis	1.75
35	Olandis Gary	.60
36	Brian Griese	.60
37	Ed McCaffrey	.50
38	Rod Smith	.50
39	Charlie Batch	.50
40	Germane Crowell	.50
41	Johnnie Morton	.30
42	James O. Stewart	.50
43	Brett Favre	2.50
44	Antonio Freeman	.50
45	Dorsey Levens	.50
46	Peyton Manning	2.50
47	Edgerrin James	2.50
48	Marvin Harrison	.50
49	Terrence Wilkins	.50
50	Mark Brunell	1.00
51	Fred Taylor	1.00
52	Jimmy Smith	.50
53	Keenan McCardell	.30
54	Elvis Grbac	.30
55	Tony Gonzalez	.30
56	Derrick S. Alexander	.15
57	James Johnson	.30
58	Tony Martin	.15
59	Damon Huard	.50
60	Oronde Gadsden	.30
61	Randy Moss	2.50
62	Robert Smith	.50
63	Cris Carter	.50
64	Daunte Culpepper	1.50
65	Drew Bledsoe	1.00
66	Terry Glenn	.75
67	Sean Morey	.15
68	Ricky Williams	1.50
69	Keith Poole	.15
70	Jake Reed	.30
71	Jeff Blake	.30
72	Kerry Collins	.30
73	Amani Toomer	.30
74	Joe Montgomery	.15
75	Ike Hilliard	.30
76	Ray Lucas	.50
77	Curtis Martin	.50
78	Vinny Testaverde	.50
79	Wayne Chrebet	.50
80	Tim Brown	.50
81	Rich Gannon	.30
82	Tyrone Wheatley	.30
83	Rickey Dudley	.30
84	Napoleon Kaufman	.50
85	Duce Staley	.50
86	Donovan McNabb	1.00
87	Torrance Small	.15
88	Charles Johnson	.30
89	Kent Graham	.15
90	Troy Edwards	.50
91	Jerome Bettis	.50
92	Kordell Stewart	.60
93	Marshall Faulk	.50
94	Kurt Warner	2.50
95	Torry Holt	.50
96	Isaac Bruce	.50
97	Jermaine Fazande	.30
98	Ryan Leaf	.50
99	Jeff Graham	.15
100	Moses Moreno	.30
101	Jerry Rice	1.25
102	Terrell Owens	.50
103	Jeff Garcia	.50
104	Ricky Watters	.30
105	Jon Kitna	.50
106	Derrick Mayes	.30
107	Charlie Rogers	.15
108	Warrick Dunn	.50
109	Shaun King	1.00
110	Mike Alstott	.50
111	Keyshawn Johnson	.50
112	Eddie George	.75
113	Steve McNair	.60
114	Kevin Dyson	.30
115	Kevin Daft	.15
116	Jevon Kearse	.50
117	Brad Johnson	.50
118	Stephen Davis	.50
119	Michael Westbrook	.30
120	Jeff George	.50
121	*Kwame Cavil*	1.50
122	*Corey Moore*	1.50
123	*Sebastian Janikowski*	4.00
124	*Troy Walters*	3.00
125	*Mike Anderson*	15.00
126	*Tom Brady*	3.50
127	*Spergon Wynn*	4.00
128	*Tim Rattay*	5.50
129	*Giovanni Carmazzi*	5.50
130	*Chris Cole*	1.50
131	*Demario Brown*	1.50
132	*Chris Coleman*	1.50
133	*Michael Wiley*	4.00
134	*JaJuan Dawson*	5.00
135	*Deon Dyer*	3.00
136	*Trevor Gaylor*	4.00
137	*Todd Husak*	4.00
138	*Darrell Jackson*	6.00
139	*Erron Kinney*	3.00
140	*Anthony Lucas*	1.50
141	*Rondell Mealey*	3.00
142	*Chad Morton*	4.00
143	*Leon Murray*	1.50
144	*Mareno Philyaw*	1.50
145	*Gari Scott*	3.00
146	*Paul Smith*	1.50
147	*Terrelle Smith*	1.50
148	*Shyrone Stith*	3.00
149	*Bashir Yamini*	1.50
150	*Windrell Hayes*	1.50
151	*Courtney Brown*	20.00
152	*Corey Simon*	15.00
153	*R. Jay Soward*	15.00
154	*Chris Redman*	30.00
155	*Joe Hamilton*	20.00
156	*Chad Pennington*	60.00
157	*Tee Martin*	15.00
158	*Ron Dayne*	75.00
159	*Shaun Alexander*	50.00
160	*Thomas Jones*	30.00
161	*Reuben Droughns*	12.00
162	*Jamal Lewis*	100.00
163	*J.R. Redmond*	20.00
164	*Travis Prentice*	25.00
165	*Trung Canidate*	15.00
166	*Brian Urlacher*	50.00
167	*Anthony Becht*	15.00
168	*Bubba Franks*	15.00
169	*Peter Warrick*	75.00
170	*Plaxico Burress*	40.00
171	*Sylvester Morris*	40.00
172	*Dez White*	15.00
173	*Travis Taylor*	20.00
174	*Todd Pinkston*	20.00
175	*Dennis Northcutt*	20.00
176	*Jerry Porter*	15.00
177	*Laveranues Coles*	25.00
178	*Danny Farmer*	15.00
179	*Curtis Keaton*	12.00
180	*Ron Dugans*	15.00

2000 Upper Deck Black Diamond Gold Parallel

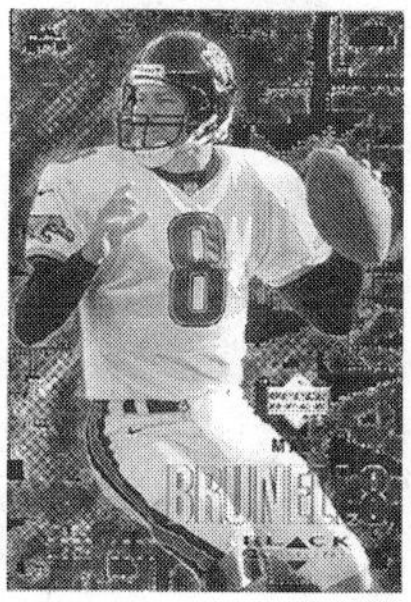

	MT
Gold Cards:	4x
#1-120 Production 1,000 Sets	
Gold Rookies:	1.5x
#121-150 Production 500 Sets	
Gold Rookie Jersey:	2x
#151-180 Production 100 Sets	

2000 Upper Deck Black Diamond Diamonation

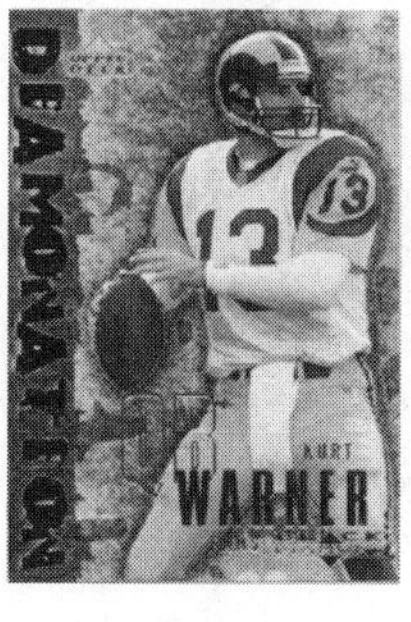

		MT
Complete Set (10):		8.00
Common Player:		.50
Minor Stars:		1.00
Inserted 1:8		
D1	Marshall Faulk	1.00
D2	Marcus Robinson	1.00
D3	Eddie George	1.25
D4	Kurt Warner	3.50
D5	Amani Toomer	.50
D6	Muhsin Muhammad	.50
D7	Jevon Kearse	1.00
D8	Jon Kitna	1.00
D9	Terrell Davis	2.75
D10	Tony Gonzalez	.50

2000 Upper Deck Black Diamond Might

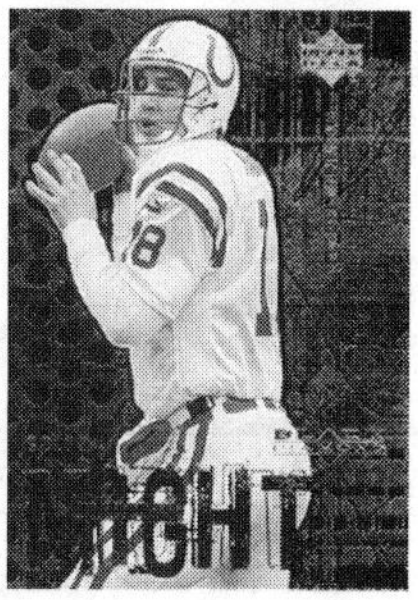

		MT
Complete Set (15):		25.00
Common Player:		1.00
Inserted 1:11		
DM1	Fred Taylor	1.75
DM2	Edgerrin James	4.00
DM3	Cade McNown	1.50
DM4	Randy Moss	4.00
DM5	Shaun King	1.50
DM6	Keyshawn Johnson	1.00
DM7	Jamal Anderson	1.00
DM8	Ricky Williams	3.00
DM9	Jerry Rice	3.00
DM10	Isaac Bruce	1.00
DM11	Peyton Manning	4.00
DM12	Mark Brunell	2.00
DM13	Tim Couch	3.00
DM14	Akili Smith	1.00
DM15	Emmitt Smith	3.00

2000 Upper Deck Black Diamond Skills

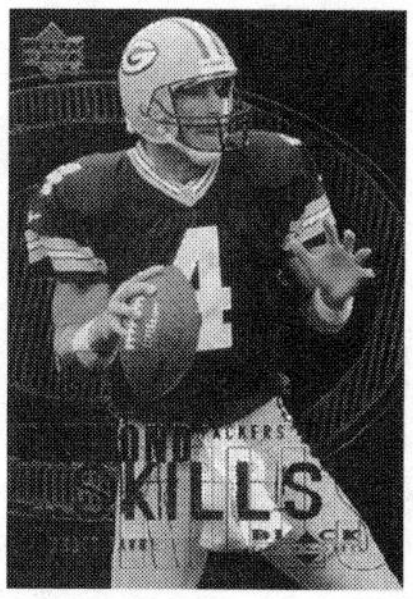

		MT
Complete Set (15):		25.00
Common Player:		1.00
Inserted 1:11		
DS1	Eddie George	1.50
DS2	Brett Favre	4.00
DS3	Marshall Faulk	1.00
DS4	Rob Johnson	1.00
DS5	Kevin Johnson	1.00
DS6	Randy Moss	4.00
DS7	Peyton Manning	4.00
DS8	Kurt Warner	5.00
DS9	Jake Plummer	1.50
DS10	Troy Aikman	3.00
DS11	Daunte Culpepper	2.50
DS12	Drew Bledsoe	2.00
DS13	Vinny Testaverde	1.00
DS14	Marvin Harrison	1.00
DS15	Charlie Batch	1.00

2000 Upper Deck Black Diamond Super Bowl

		MT
Complete Set (14):		60.00
Common Player:		3.00
CB	Champ Bailey	3.00
DB	David Boston	3.00
CC	Cecil Collins	3.00
TC	Tim Couch	10.00
DC	Daunte Culpepper	10.00
TH	Torry Holt	3.00
EJ	Edgerrin James	10.00
JJ	James Johnson	3.00
JK	Jevon Kearse	3.00
DM	Donovan McNabb	5.00
CM	Cade McNown	3.00
PP	Peerless Price	3.00
AS	Akili Smith	3.00
RW	Ricky Williams	5.00

A card number in parentheses ( ) indicates the set is unnumbered.

2000 Upper Deck Encore

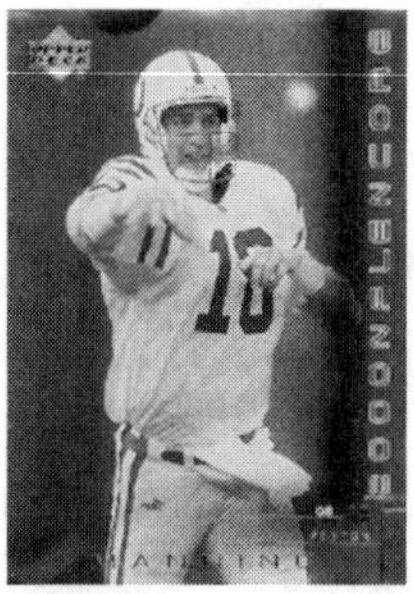

MT
Complete Set (270): 125.00
Common Player: .15
Minor Stars: .30
Common Rookie: 1.00
Inserted 1:6
Pack (5): 4.00
Wax Box (24): 75.00
Common Player (271-283): 2.00
Production 2,000 Sets

1 Jake Plummer .50
2 Michael Pittman .30
3 Rob Moore .30
4 David Boston .50
5 Frank Sanders .30
6 Aeneas Williams .15
7 Kwamie Lassiter .15
8 Rob Fredrickson .15
9 Tim Dwight .50
10 Chris Chandler .30
11 Jamal Anderson .50
12 Shawn Jefferson .15
13 Brian Finneran .15
14 Terance Mathis .15
15 Bob Christian .15
16 Qadry Ismail .15
17 Jermaine Lewis .15
18 Rod Woodson .15
19 Michael McCrary .15
20 Tony Banks .30
21 Peter Boulware .15
22 Shannon Sharpe .30
23 Peerless Price .30
24 Rob Johnson .30
25 Eric Moulds .50
26 Doug Flutie .75
27 Jeremy McDaniel .15
28 Antowain Smith .30
29 Shawn Bryson .15
30 Muhsin Muhammad .30
31 Donald Hayes .30
32 Steve Beuerlein .30
33 Reggie White .30
34 Tshimanga Biakabutuka .30
35 Michael Bates .15
36 Chuck Smith .15
37 Wesley Walls .30
38 Cade McNown .50
39 Curtis Enis .30
40 Marcus Robinson .50
41 Eddie Kennison .15
42 Bobby Engram .15
43 Glyn Milburn .15
44 Marty Booker .15
45 Akili Smith .50
46 Corey Dillon .50
47 James Allen .30
48 Tremain Mack .15
49 Damon Griffin .15
50 Takeo Spikes .15
51 Tony McGee .15
52 Tim Couch 1.00
53 Kevin Johnson .50
54 Darrin Chiaverini .15
55 Jamir Miller .15
56 Errict Rhett .30
57 Aaron Shea .15
58 Kevin Thompson .15
59 Troy Aikman 1.25
60 Emmitt Smith 1.50
61 Raghib Ismail .15
62 Jason Tucker .30
63 Chris Brazzell .15
64 Joey Galloway .50
65 Wane McGarity .15
66 Terrell Davis 1.50
67 Olandis Gary .50
68 Brian Griese .75
69 Gus Frerotte .30
70 Byron Chamberlain .15
71 Ed McCaffrey .30
72 Rod Smith .50
73 Al Wilson .15
74 Charlie Batch .50
75 Germane Crowell .50
76 Sedrick Irvin .15
77 Johnnie Morton .30
78 Robert Porcher .15
79 Herman Moore .50
80 James O. Stewart .30
81 Brett Favre 2.50
82 Antonio Freeman .50
83 Bill Schroeder .30
84 Dorsey Levens .50
85 Herbert Goodman .15
86 Ahman Green .30
87 Matt Hasselbeck .15
88 Peyton Manning 2.00
89 Edgerrin James 2.00
90 Marvin Harrison .50
91 Basil Mitchell .15
92 Terrence Wilkins .30
93 Kareem Abdul Jabbar .15
94 Ken Dilger .15
95 Mark Brunell .75
96 Fred Taylor .75
97 Jimmy Smith .50
98 Keenan McCardell .30
99 Stacey Mack .15
100 Jonathan Quinn .15
101 Kyle Brady .15
102 Hardy Nickerson .15
103 Elvis Grbac .30
104 Tony Gonzalez .30
105 Derrick S. Alexander .15
106 Tony Richardson .15
107 Michael Cloud .15
108 Donnie Edwards .15
109 Jay Fiedler .30
110 James Johnson .30
111 Tony Martin .15
112 Damon Huard .30
113 Lamar Smith .30
114 Thurman Thomas .30
115 Mike Quinn .15
116 Oronde Gadsden .30
117 Randy Moss 2.00
118 Robert Smith .50
119 Cris Carter .50
120 Matthew Hatchette .30
121 Daunte Culpepper 1.00
122 Moe Williams .15
123 Drew Bledsoe .75
124 Terry Glenn .50
125 Troy Brown .15
126 Kevin Faulk .30
127 Lawyer Milloy .15
128 Ricky Williams 1.25
129 Keith Poole .15
130 Jake Reed .30
131 *Jake Delhomme* 2.00
132 Jeff Blake .30
133 Andrew Glover .15
134 Kerry Collins .30
135 Amani Toomer .15
136 Joe Montgomery .15
137 Ike Hilliard .30
138 Tiki Barber .30
139 Pete Mitchell .15
140 Ray Lucas .30
141 Mo Lewis .15
142 Curtis Martin .50
143 Vinny Testaverde .30
144 Wayne Chrebet .50
145 Dedric Ward .30
146 Tim Brown .50
147 Rich Gannon .30
148 Tyrone Wheatley .30
149 Napoleon Kaufman .50
150 Charles Woodson .50
151 Darrell Russell .15
152 James Jett .15
153 Rickey Dudley .15
154 Jon Ritchie .15
155 Duce Staley .50
156 Donovan McNabb .75
157 Torrance Small .15
158 Ron Powlus .50
159 Mike Mamula .15
160 Dameane Douglas .15
161 Charles Johnson .30
162 Kent Graham .15
163 Troy Edwards .30
164 Jerome Bettis .30
165 Hines Ward .30
166 Kordell Stewart .50
167 Levon Kirkland .15
168 *Bobby Shaw* .75
169 Marshall Faulk .50
170 Kurt Warner 2.50
171 Torry Holt .50
172 Isaac Bruce .50
173 Kevin Carter .15
174 Az-Zahir Hakim .30
175 Ricky Proehl .15
176 Robert Chancey .15
177 Curtis Conway .30
178 Freddie Jones .30
179 Junior Seau .30
180 Jeff Graham .15
181 Reggie Jones .50
182 Rodney Harrison .15
183 Rick Mirer .30
184 Jerry Rice 1.25
185 Charlie Garner .30
186 Terrell Owens .30
187 Jeff Garcia .50
188 Fred Beasley .15
189 J.J. Stokes .30
190 Ricky Watters .50
191 Jon Kitna .50
192 Derrick Mayes .30
193 Sean Dawkins .15
194 Charlie Rogers .15
195 Brock Huard .50
196 Cortez Kennedy .15
197 Christian Fauria .15
198 Warrick Dunn .50
199 Shaun King .50
200 Mike Alstott .50
201 Warren Sapp .30
202 Jacquez Green .30
203 Reidel Anthony .30
204 Dave Moore .15
205 Keyshawn Johnson .50
206 Eddie George .75
207 Steve McNair .50
208 *Billy Volek* .50
209 Jevon Kearse .50
210 Yancey Thigpen .30
211 Frank Wycheck .30
212 Carl Pickens .30
213 Neil O'Donnell .30
214 Brad Johnson .30
215 Stephen Davis .50
216 Michael Westbrook .30
217 Albert Connell .30
218 *Aaron Stecker* .30
219 Bruce Smith .15
220 Stephen Alexander .15
221 Jeff George .30
222 Adrian Murrell .30
223 *Courtney Brown* 2.00
224 *John Engleberger* 1.00
225 *Deltha O'Neal* 1.00
226 *Corey Simon* 2.00
227 *R. Jay Soward* 2.00
228 *Chris Samuels* 2.00
229 *Avion Black* 1.00
230 *Doug Chapman* 1.00
231 *Darrell Jackson* 3.00
232 *Chris Cole* 1.00
233 *Trevor Gaylor* 2.00
234 *Chad Morton* 2.00
235 *Chris Redman* 5.00
236 *Joe Hamilton* 2.00
237 *Chad Pennington* 10.00
238 *Tee Martin* 2.00
239 *Giovanni Carmazzi* 2.00
240 *Tim Rattay* 2.00
241 *Ron Dayne* 12.00
242 *Shaun Alexander* 8.00
243 *Thomas Jones* 5.00
244 *Reuben Droughns* 1.00
245 *Jamal Lewis* 15.00
246 *Michael Wiley* 2.00
247 *J.R. Redmond* 3.00
248 *Travis Prentice* 3.50
249 *Todd Husak* 2.00
250 *Trung Canidate* 2.00
251 *Brian Urlacher* 8.00
252 *Anthony Becht* 2.00
253 *Bubba Franks* 2.00
254 *Tom Brady* 2.00
255 *Peter Warrick* 12.00
256 *Plaxico Burress* 6.00
257 *Sylvester Morris* 6.00
258 *Dez White* 2.00
259 *Travis Taylor* 3.00
260 *Todd Pinkston* 2.00
261 *Dennis Northcutt* 2.00
262 *Jerry Porter* 2.00
263 *Laveranues Coles* 3.00
264 *Danny Farmer* 2.00
265 *Curtis Keaton* 1.00
266 *Windrell Hayes* 1.00
267 *Ron Dugans* 2.00
268 Steve McNair CL .30
269 Jake Plummer CL .30
270 Antonio Freeman CL .30
271 *Brad Hoover* 10.00
272 *Charles Lee* 2.00
273 *Deon Dyer* 2.00
274 *Doug Johnson* 5.00
275 *JaJuan Dawson* 4.00
276 *Jarious Jackson* 5.00
277 *Larry Foster* 4.00
278 *Mike Anderson* 25.00
279 *Ron Dixon* 6.00
280 *Sammy Morris* 7.00
281 *Shyrone Stith* 2.00
282 *Spergon Wynn* 3.00
283 *Troy Walters* 4.00

2000 Upper Deck Encore SGC Blue Label Rookies

MT
Common SGC 98: 15.00
SGC 96: 30%
SGC 92: 20%
Inserted 1:Box

223 Courtney Brown 20.00
224 John Engleberger 20.00
225 Deltha O'Neal 15.00
226 Corey Simon 20.00
227 R. Jay Soward 15.00
228 Chris Samuels 20.00
229 Avion Black 15.00
230 Doug Chapman 15.00
231 Darrell Jackson 30.00
232 Chris Cole 15.00
233 Trevor Gaylor 20.00
234 Chad Morton 20.00
235 Chris Redman 35.00
236 Joe Hamilton 50.00
237 Chad Pennington 50.00
238 Tee Martin 25.00
239 Giovanni Carmazzi 20.00
240 Tim Rattay 20.00
241 Ron Dayne 80.00
242 Shaun Alexander 50.00
243 Thomas Jones 35.00
244 Reuben Droughns 25.00
245 Jamal Lewis 100.00
246 Michael Wiley 20.00
247 J.R. Redmond 35.00
248 Travis Prentice 45.00
249 Todd Husak 25.00
250 Trung Canidate 20.00
251 Brian Urlacher 55.00
252 Anthony Becht 25.00
253 Bubba Franks 30.00
254 Tom Brady 20.00
255 Peter Warrick 70.00
256 Plaxico Burress 35.00
257 Sylvester Morris 40.00
258 Dez White 20.00
259 Travis Taylor 30.00
260 Todd Pinkston 30.00
261 Dennis Northcutt 20.00
262 Jerry Porter 20.00
263 Laveranues Coles 25.00
264 Danny Farmer 15.00
265 Curtis Keaton 20.00
266 Windrell Hayes 20.00
267 Ron Dugans 40.00

2000 Upper Deck Encore Highlight Zone

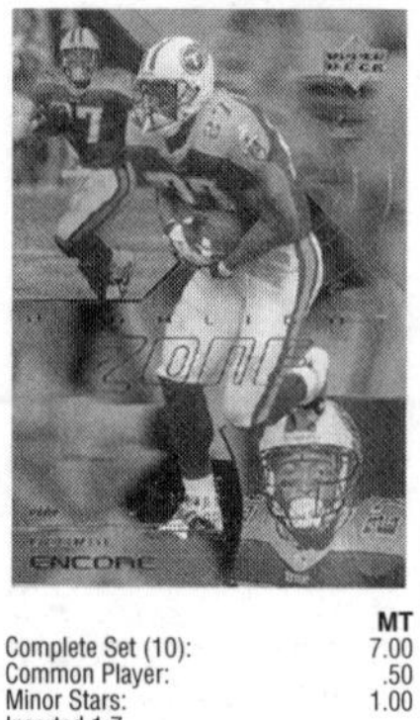

MT
Complete Set (10): 7.00
Common Player: .50
Minor Stars: 1.00
Inserted 1:7

HZ1 Eddie George 1.50
HZ2 Steve McNair 1.00
HZ3 Kevin Dyson .50
HZ4 Kurt Warner 4.00
HZ5 Emmitt Smith 3.00
HZ6 Brad Johnson .50
HZ7 Curtis Martin 1.00
HZ8 Ray Lucas .50
HZ9 Akili Smith 1.00
HZ10 Jake Plummer 1.00

2000 Upper Deck Encore Proving Ground

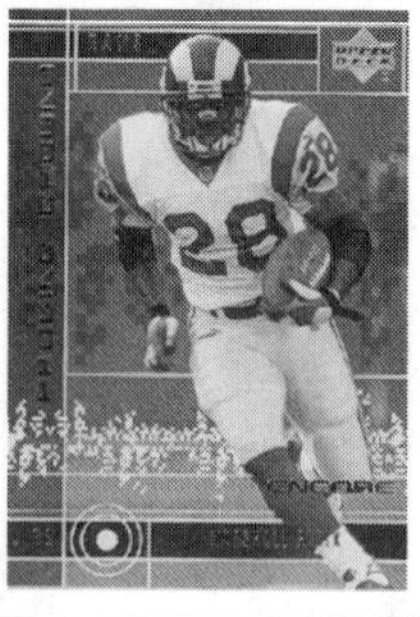

MT
Complete Set (10): 5.00
Common Player: .50
Minor Stars: 1.00
Inserted 1:7

PG1 Marcus Robinson 1.00
PG2 Stephen Davis 1.00
PG3 Daunte Culpepper 2.00
PG4 Jevon Kearse 1.00
PG5 Marshall Faulk 1.00
PG6 Marvin Harrison 1.00
PG7 Germane Crowell 1.00
PG8 Darnay Scott .50
PG9 Duce Staley 1.00
PG10 Warrick Dunn 1.00

2000 Upper Deck Encore Rookie Combo Jerseys

MT
Complete Set (9): 450.00
Common Player: 25.00
Inserted 1:287

RC1 Dez White, Brian Urlacher 60.00
RC2 Tee Martin, Plaxico Burress 45.00
RC3 Jerry Porter, Sylvester Morris 45.00
RC4 Peter Warrick, Courtney Brown 70.00
RC5 Peter Warrick, Curtis Keaton 70.00
RC6 Travis Prentice, Dennis Northcutt 25.00
RC7 Travis Taylor, Jamal Lewis, Chris Redman 150.00
RC8 Ron Dayne, Thomas Jones, Shaun Alexander 125.00
RC9 Chad Pennington, Laveranues Coles, Anthony Becht 100.00

2000 Upper Deck Encore Rookie Helmets

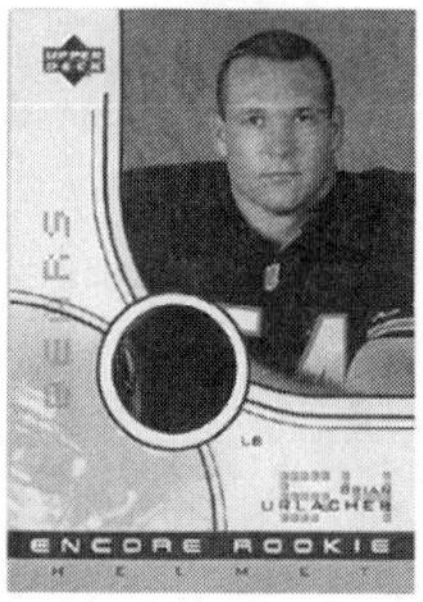

MT
Complete Set (28): 700.00
Common Player: 15.00
Inserted 1:287
Autographed Cards: 3x
Production 25 Sets

HSA Shaun Alexander 50.00
HTW Anthony Becht 15.00
HCB Courtney Brown 20.00
HPB Plaxico Burress 40.00
HLC Laveranues Coles 25.00
HRD Ron Dayne 75.00
HDR Reuben Droughns 15.00
HDU Ron Dugans 20.00
HDF Danny Farmer 20.00
HBF Bubba Franks 20.00
HTJ Thomas Jones 35.00
HCK Curtis Keaton 20.00
HJL Jamal Lewis 100.00
HTM Tee Martin 20.00
HSM Sylvester Morris 40.00
HDN Dennis Northcutt 20.00
HCP Chad Pennington 60.00
HPI Todd Pinkston 20.00
HJP Jerry Porter 20.00
HTP Travis Prentice 30.00
HCR Chris Redman 35.00
HJR J.R. Redmond 25.00
HCS Corey Simon 20.00
HRJ R. Jay Soward 20.00
HTT Travis Taylor 25.00
HBU Brian Urlacher 50.00
HPW Peter Warrick 75.00
HDW Dez White 20.00

2000 Upper Deck Encore Signed Rookie Helmets

MT
Complete Set (15):
Common Player:

SA Shaun Alexander 150.00
CB Courtney Brown 100.00
PB Plaxico Burress
LC Laveranues Coles 50.00
RD Ron Dayne 100.00
DU Ron Dugans 25.00
DF Danny Farmer 25.00
TM Tee Martin
SM Sylvester Morris 50.00
DN Dennis Northcutt 50.00
CP Chad Pennington 100.00
TP Travis Prentice 25.00
CR Chris Redman 100.00
BU Brian Urlacher 275.00
DW Dez White 50.00

2000 Upper Deck Encore UD Authentics

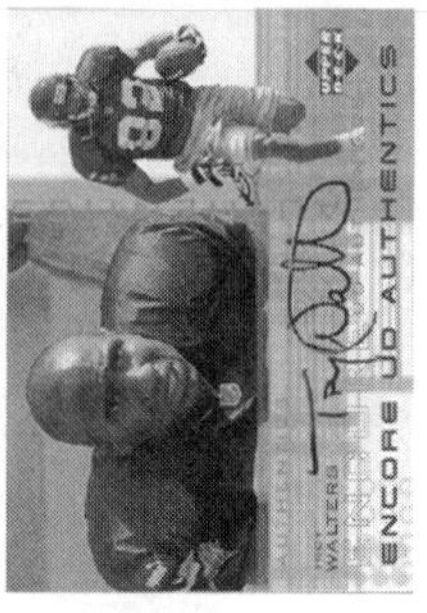

MT
Complete Set (28): 375.00
Common Player: 10.00
Inserted 1:23

SA Shaun Alexander 30.00
MA Mike Anderson 65.00
CB Courtney Brown 15.00
PB Plaxico Burress 25.00
TC Trung Canidate 10.00
KC Kwame Cavil 10.00
CC Chris Coleman 10.00
LC Laveranues Coles 15.00
RD Ron Dayne 45.00
DX Ron Dixon 15.00
DU Ron Dugans 10.00
DF Danny Farmer 10.00
TG Trevor Gaylor 10.00
SG Sherrod Gideon 10.00
DJ Darrell Jackson 15.00
JO Doug Johnson 15.00
TM Tee Martin 15.00
CM Corey Moore 10.00
SM Sylvester Morris 25.00
DN Dennis Northcutt 15.00
CP Chad Pennington 45.00
TP Travis Prentice 20.00
TR Tim Rattay 15.00
CR Chris Redman 25.00
BU Brian Urlacher 35.00
TW Troy Walters 10.00
DW Dez White 10.00
MW Michael Wiley 10.00

2000 Upper Deck Gold Reserve

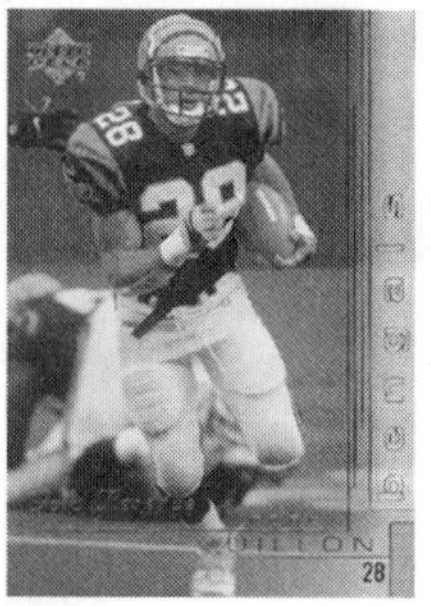

MT
Complete Set (222): 200.00
Common Player: .15
Minor Stars: .30
Common Rookie: 2.00
Production 2,500 Sets
Pack (10): 3.00
Wax Box (24): 50.00

1 Jake Plummer .50
2 Rob Moore .30
3 David Boston .50
4 Frank Sanders .30
5 Chris Chandler .30
6 Jamal Anderson .50
7 Shawn Jefferson .15
8 Terance Mathis .15
9 Qadry Ismail .15
10 Jermaine Lewis .15
11 Tony Banks .30
12 Peter Boulware .15
13 Shannon Sharpe .30
14 Peerless Price .30
15 Rob Johnson .30
16 Eric Moulds .50
17 Doug Flutie .75
18 Antowain Smith .30
19 Muhsin Muhammad .30
20 Patrick Jeffers .50
21 Steve Beuerlein .30
22 Natrone Means .30
23 Tshimanga Biakabutuka .30
24 Wesley Walls .15
25 Cade McNown .75
26 Curtis Enis .30
27 Marcus Robinson .50
28 Eddie Kennison .15
29 Bobby Engram .15
30 Akili Smith .50
31 Corey Dillon .50
32 Damon Griffin .15
33 Takeo Spikes .15
34 Tony McGee .15
35 Tim Couch 1.25
36 Kevin Johnson .30
37 Darrin Chiaverini .15
38 Errict Rhett .30
39 Troy Aikman 1.25
40 Emmitt Smith 1.75
41 Raghib Ismail .15
42 Jason Tucker .15
43 Joey Galloway .50
44 Wane McGarity .15
45 Terrell Davis 1.75
46 Olandis Gary .50
47 Brian Griese .75
48 Gus Frerotte .15
49 Ed McCaffrey .30
50 Rod Smith .50
51 Charlie Batch .50
52 Germane Crowell .50
53 Johnnie Morton .30
54 Robert Porcher .15
55 Herman Moore .50
56 James O. Stewart .30
57 Brett Favre 2.50
58 Antonio Freeman .50
59 Bill Schroeder .15
60 Dorsey Levens .50
61 Corey Bradford .15
62 Vonnie Holliday .15
63 Peyton Manning 2.00
64 Edgerrin James 2.50
65 Marvin Harrison .50
66 Ken Dilger .15
67 Terrence Wilkins .30
68 Marcus Pollard .15
69 Mark Brunell 1.00
70 Fred Taylor 1.00
71 Jimmy Smith .50
72 Keenan McCardell .30
73 Carnell Lake .15
74 Kyle Brady .15
75 Hardy Nickerson .15
76 Elvis Grbac .30
77 Tony Gonzalez .30
78 Derrick S. Alexander .15
79 Donnell Bennett .15
80 Mike Cloud .15
81 Donnie Edwards .15
82 Jay Fiedler .50
83 James Johnson .15
84 Tony Martin .15
85 Damon Huard .50
86 O.J. McDuffie .30
87 Thurman Thomas .30
88 Oronde Gadsden .30
89 Randy Moss 2.00
90 Robert Smith .50
91 Cris Carter .50
92 Daunte Culpepper 1.25
93 Matthew Hatchette .30
94 Drew Bledsoe 1.00
95 Terry Glenn .50
96 Troy Brown .15
97 Kevin Faulk .30
98 Lawyer Milloy .15
99 Ricky Williams 1.50
100 Keith Poole .15
101 Jake Reed .15
102 Jeff Blake .30
103 Andrew Glover .15
104 Kerry Collins .30
105 Amani Toomer .15
106 Joe Montgomery .15
107 Ike Hilliard .30
108 Tiki Barber .30
109 Ray Lucas .50
110 Mo Lewis .15
111 Curtis Martin .50
112 Vinny Testaverde .30
113 Wayne Chrebet .50
114 Dedric Ward .30
115 Tim Brown .50
116 Rich Gannon .30
117 Tyrone Wheatley .30
118 Napoleon Kaufman .50
119 Charles Woodson .30
120 James Jett .15
121 Rickey Dudley .30
122 Duce Staley .50
123 Donovan McNabb 1.00
124 Torrance Small .15
125 Allen Rossum .15
126 Na Brown .15
127 Charles Johnson .30
128 Kent Graham .15
129 Troy Edwards .30
130 Jerome Bettis .50
131 Hines Ward .30
132 Kordell Stewart .60
133 Richard Huntley .15
134 Marshall Faulk .50
135 Kurt Warner 3.00
136 Torry Holt .50
137 Isaac Bruce .50
138 Kevin Carter .15
139 Az-Zahir Hakim .30
140 Jermaine Fazande .15
141 Curtis Conway .30
142 Freddie Jones .15
143 Junior Seau .30
144 Jeff Graham .15
145 Jim Harbaugh .30
146 Jerry Rice 1.25
147 Charlie Garner .30
148 Terrell Owens .50
149 Jeff Garcia .50
150 J.J. Stokes .30
151 Ricky Watters .30
152 Jon Kitna .50
153 Derrick Mayes .30
154 Sean Dawkins .15
155 Charlie Rogers .15
156 Cortez Kennedy .15
157 Warrick Dunn .50
158 Shaun King 1.00
159 Mike Alstott .50
160 Warren Sapp .30
161 Jacquez Green .15

162	Reidel Anthony	.15
163	Keyshawn Johnson	.50
164	Eddie George	.75
165	Steve McNair	.50
166	Kevin Dyson	.15
167	Jevon Kearse	.50
168	Yancey Thigpen	.30
169	Isaac Byrd	.15
170	Neil O'Donnell	.15
171	Brad Johnson	.30
172	Stephen Davis	.50
173	Michael Westbrook	.30
174	Albert Connell	.15
175	Bruce Smith	.15
176	Stephen Alexander	.15
177	Jeff George	.30
178	*Bubba Franks*	3.00
179	*Brian Urlacher*	10.00
180	*Chad Pennington*	12.00
181	*Tim Rattay*	3.00
182	*Chris Redman*	6.00
183	*Corey Simon*	2.50
184	*Courtney Brown*	3.00
185	*Curtis Keaton*	2.00
186	*Danny Farmer*	2.00
187	*Erron Kinney*	2.00
188	*Deltha O'Neal*	2.00
189	*Dennis Northcutt*	3.00
190	*Dez White*	2.00
191	*Frank Murphy*	2.00
192	*Gari Scott*	2.00
193	*Giovanni Carmazzi*	3.00
194	*J.R. Redmond*	4.00
195	*JaJuan Dawson*	3.00
196	*Jamal Lewis*	20.00
197	*Jerry Porter*	3.00
198	*Joe Hamilton*	3.00
199	*Laveranues Coles*	3.00
200	*Michael Wiley*	2.00
201	*Peter Warrick*	15.00
202	*Plaxico Burress*	8.00
203	*R. Jay Soward*	2.00
204	*Reuben Droughns*	2.00
205	*Rob Morris*	4.00
206	*Ron Dayne*	18.00
207	*Ron Dugans*	2.00
208	*Sebastian Janikowski*	2.50
209	*Shaun Alexander*	10.00
210	*Sylvester Morris*	8.00
211	*Tee Martin*	3.00
212	*Thomas Jones*	6.00
213	*Todd Husak*	2.00
214	*Todd Pinkston*	2.50
215	*Tom Brady*	2.50
216	*Travis Prentice*	5.00
217	*Travis Taylor*	4.00
218	*Trevor Gaylor*	2.00
219	*Trung Canidate*	2.00
223	Peyton Manning CL	1.00
224	Randy Moss CL	1.00
225	Kurt Warner CL	1.50

2000 Upper Deck Gold Reserve Face Masks

		MT
Complete Set (15):		650.00
Common Player:		20.00
Production 100 Sets		
Gold Cards: 2x		
Production 25 Sets		
FMSA	Shaun Alexander	60.00
FMCB	Courtney Brown	20.00
FMPB	Plaxico Burress	45.00
FMRD	Ron Dayne	100.00
FMDR	Reuben Droughns	20.00
FMTJ	Thomas Jones	40.00
FMCK	Curtis Keaton	20.00
FMJL	Jamal Lewis	120.00
FMSM	Sylvester Morris	45.00
FMCP	Chad Pennington	75.00
FMCR	Chris Redman	40.00
FMJR	J.R. Redmond	25.00
FMRJ	R. Jay Soward	20.00
FMTT	Travis Taylor	25.00
FMPW	Peter Warrick	85.00

2000 Upper Deck Gold Reserve Face Masks Gold

		MT
Complete Set (6):		
Common Player:		
PB	Plaxico Burress	60.00
RD	Ron Dayne	100.00
TJ	Thomas Jones	50.00
JL	Jamal Lewis	150.00
CP	Chad Pennington	100.00
PW	Peter Warrick	100.00

2000 Upper Deck Gold Reserve Gold Mine

		MT
Complete Set (12):		15.00
Common Player:		1.50
Inserted 1:12		
GM1	Dez White	1.50
GM2	Peter Warrick	4.00
GM3	Plaxico Burress	2.50
GM4	Bubba Franks	1.50
GM5	Jamal Lewis	6.00
GM6	Travis Taylor	2.00
GM7	Chris Redman	2.25
GM8	Sylvester Morris	2.50
GM9	Courtney Brown	1.50
GM10	Shaun Alexander	3.00
GM11	Trung Canidate	1.50
GM12	J.R. Redmond	1.75

2000 Upper Deck Gold Reserve Gold Strike

		MT
Complete Set (12):		15.00
Common Player:		1.50
Inserted 1:12		
GS1	Eddie George	1.75
GS2	Edgerrin James	5.00
GS3	Terrell Davis	3.50
GS4	Jamal Anderson	1.50
GS5	Ricky Williams	2.50
GS6	Marshall Faulk	1.50
GS7	Keyshawn Johnson	1.50
GS8	Brett Favre	5.00
GS9	Cade McNown	1.50
GS10	Emmitt Smith	3.50
GS11	Peyton Manning	4.00
GS12	Kurt Warner	5.00

2000 Upper Deck Gold Reserve Setting the Standard

		MT
Complete Set (12):		15.00
Common Player:		1.50
Inserted 1:12		
SS1	Randy Moss	5.00
SS2	Peyton Manning	5.00
SS3	Stephen Davis	1.50
SS4	Cris Carter	1.50
SS5	Jevon Kearse	1.50
SS6	Jerry Rice	3.00
SS7	Troy Aikman	3.00
SS8	Edgerrin James	5.00
SS9	Daunte Culpepper	2.50
SS10	Shaun King	1.75
SS11	Mark Brunell	2.00
SS12	Fred Taylor	2.00

2000 Upper Deck Gold Reserve Solid Gold Gallery

		MT
Complete Set (6):		20.00
Common Player:		3.00
Inserted 1:23		
SG1	Jamal Lewis	8.00
SG2	Peter Warrick	5.00
SG3	Ron Dayne	6.00
SG4	Chad Pennington	4.00
SG5	Thomas Jones	3.00
SG6	Plaxico Burress	3.50

2000 Upper Deck Gold Reserve UD Authentics

		MT
Common Player:		10.00
Inserted 1:160		
Gold Cards:		4x
Production 25 Sets		
TA	Troy Aikman	50.00
SA	Shaun Alexander	40.00
KC	Kwame Cavil	10.00
CC	Chris Coleman	10.00
RD	Ron Dayne	70.00
DU	Ron Dugans	10.00
FA	Danny Farmer	10.00
DF	Doug Flutie	25.00
SG	Sherrod Gideon	10.00
JH	Joe Hamilton	20.00
BJ	Brad Johnson	10.00
TJ	Thomas Jones	25.00
TM	Tee Martin	20.00
CP	Chad Pennington	50.00
TR	Tim Rattay	20.00
CR	Chris Redman	25.00
TW	Troy Walters	10.00
DW	Dez White	10.00
MW	Michael Wiley	10.00

2000 Upper Deck Legends

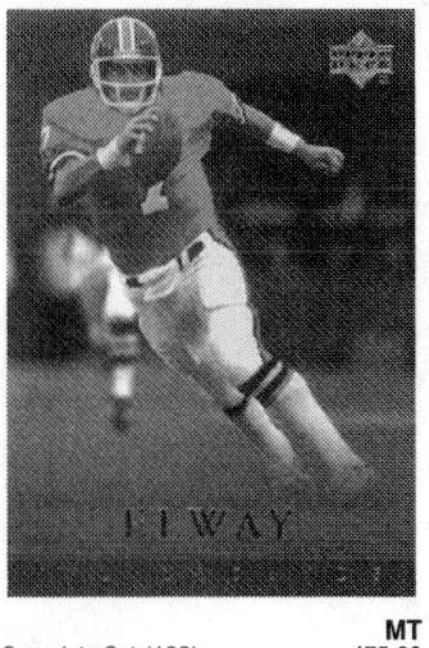

		MT
Complete Set (132):		475.00
Common Player:		.15
Minor Stars:		.30
Common 20th Century:		8.00
Production 2,500 Sets		
Common Rookie:		5.00
Production 2,000 Sets		
Pack (5):		5.00
Wax Box (24):		100.00
1	Jake Plummer	.50
2	Jamal Anderson	.50
3	Doug Flutie	.75
4	Jim Kelly	.50
5	Dick Butkus	.75
6	Mike Singletary	.30
7	Gale Sayers	.75
8	Boomer Esiason	.30
9	Anthony Munoz	.15
10	Otto Graham	.50
11	Jim Brown	1.00
12	Ozzie Newsome	.30
13	Bob Lilly	.30
14	Troy Aikman	1.25
15	Emmitt Smith	1.50
16	Roger Staubach	1.25
17	Deion Sanders	.50
18	Tony Dorsett	.50
19	Terrell Davis	1.50
20	John Elway	1.75
21	Charlie Batch	.50
22	Brett Favre	2.50
23	Bart Starr	1.50
24	Reggie White	.30
25	Earl Campbell	.50
26	Peyton Manning	2.00
27	Edgerrin James	2.50
28	Johnny Unitas	1.25
29	Marvin Harrison	.50
30	Mark Brunell	.75
31	Fred Taylor	.75
32	Len Dawson	.50
33	Dan Marino	1.75
34	Bob Griese	.50
35	Mark Duper	.15
36	Thurman Thomas	.30
37	Fran Tarkenton	.75
38	Randy Moss	2.00
39	Cris Carter	.50
40	Gary Anderson	.15
41	John Randle	.15
42	Drew Bledsoe	.75
43	Archie Manning	.30
44	Ricky Williams	1.25
45	Frank Gifford	.50
46	Kerry Collins	.30
47	Phil Simms	.30
48	Vinny Testaverde	.30
49	Curtis Martin	.50
50	Keyshawn Johnson	.50
51	Joe Namath	2.00
52	Marcus Allen	.50
53	Bruce Smith	.15
54	Ken Stabler	.75
55	Fred Biletnikoff	.15
56	Howie Long	.50
57	Ron Jaworski	.50
58	Harold Carmichael	.30
59	Kordell Stewart	.50
60	Levon Kirkland	.15
61	Mel Blount	.15
62	Jerome Bettis	.50
63	John Stallworth	.30
64	Franco Harris	.50
65	Jim Harbaugh	.30
66	Kellen Winslow	.30
67	Charlie Joiner	.30
68	Junior Seau	.30
69	Jerry Rice	1.25
70	Steve Young	.75
71	Joe Montana	2.50
72	Roger Craig	.30
73	Ronnie Lott	.30
74	Jon Kitna	.50
75	Steve Largent	.50
76	Ricky Watters	.30
77	Kurt Warner	3.00
78	Marshall Faulk	.50
79	Isaac Bruce	.50
80	Merlin Olsen	.50
81	Lee Roy Selmon	.15
82	Tim Brown	.50
83	Tim Couch	1.25
84	Mike Alstott	.50
85	Eddie George	.60
86	Steve McNair	.50
87	Brad Johnson	.50
88	Sonny Jurgensen	.50
89	Art Monk	.50
90	Joe Theismann	.50
91	Ray Nitschke TCL	8.00
92	Doak Walker TCL	8.00
93	Thurman Thomas TCL	8.00
94	Jim Brown TCL	10.00
95	Sammy Baugh TCL	10.00
96	Reggie White TCL	8.00
97	Eric Dickerson TCL	8.00
98	Paul Hornung TCL	8.00
99	Deion Sanders TCL	10.00
100	Bronko Nagurski TCL	8.00
101	Walter Payton TCL	25.00
102	Jim Thorpe TCL	10.00
103	*Ron Dayne*	30.00
104	*Tim Rattay*	6.00
105	*Brian Urlacher*	20.00
106	*Bubba Franks*	6.00
107	*Chad Pennington*	25.00
108	*Chris Cole*	5.00
109	*Chris Redman*	12.00
110	*Courtney Brown*	6.00
111	*Curtis Keaton*	5.00
112	*Dennis Northcutt*	6.00
113	*Dez White*	6.00
114	*Giovanni Carmazzi*	6.00
115	*J.R. Redmond*	8.00
116	*JaJuan Dawson*	6.00
117	*Jamal Lewis*	40.00
118	*Jerry Porter*	6.00
119	*Laveranues Coles*	7.00
120	*Peter Warrick*	30.00
121	*Plaxico Burress*	15.00
122	*R. Jay Soward*	6.00
123	*Reuben Droughns*	5.00
124	*Ron Dixon*	6.00
125	*Ron Dugans*	6.00
126	*Shaun Alexander*	20.00
127	*Sylvester Morris*	15.00
128	*Thomas Jones*	12.00
129	*Todd Pinkston*	6.00
130	*Travis Prentice*	10.00
131	*Travis Taylor*	15.00
132	*Trung Canidate*	6.00

2000 Upper Deck Legends Autographs

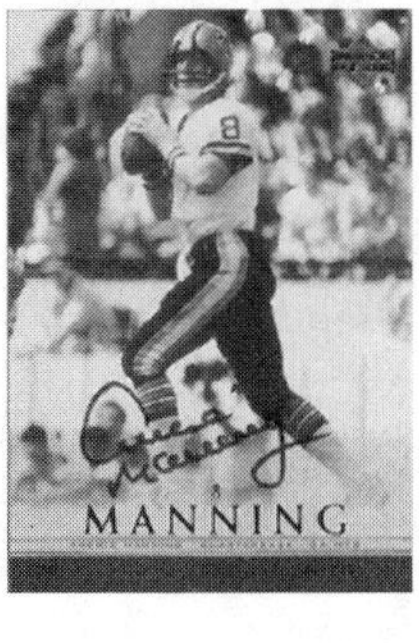

		MT
Common Player:		10.00
Minor Stars:		20.00
Inserted 1:47		
Gold Cards:		3x
Production 25 Sets		
TA	Troy Aikman	60.00
MA	Marcus Allen	35.00
JA	Jamal Anderson	30.00
BU	Jerome Bettis	40.00
FB	Fred Biletnikoff	30.00
DR	Drew Bledsoe	50.00
MB	Mel Blount	20.00
JB	Jim Brown	125.00
TB	Tim Brown	30.00
IB	Isaac Bruce	30.00
BR	Mark Brunell	45.00
DB	Dick Butkus	75.00
EC	Earl Campbell	30.00
HC	Harold Carmichael	10.00
CC	Cris Carter	40.00
TC	Tim Couch	60.00
RC	Roger Craig	10.00
DA	Terrell Davis	70.00
LD	Len Dawson	25.00
TD	Tony Dorsett	50.00
MD	Mark Duper	10.00
BE	Boomer Esiason	30.00
FL	Doug Flutie	25.00
EG	Eddie George	40.00
FG	Frank Gifford	100.00
OG	Otto Graham	20.00
BG	Bob Griese	40.00
FH	Franco Harris	50.00
MH	Marvin Harrison	30.00
EJ	Edgerrin James	125.00
RJ	Ron Jaworski	25.00
BJ	Brad Johnson	25.00
KJ	Keyshawn Johnson	30.00
CJ	Charlie Joiner	10.00
SJ	Sonny Jurgensen	40.00
JK	Jim Kelly	50.00
KI	Jon Kitna	20.00
SL	Steve Largent	20.00
BL	Bob Lilly	25.00
HL	Howie Long	50.00
RL	Ronnie Lott	50.00
AM	Archie Manning	20.00
PM	Peyton Manning	125.00
DM	Dan Marino	200.00
RG	Art Monk	25.00
JM	Joe Montana	200.00
RM	Randy Moss	125.00
AZ	Anthony Munoz	20.00
JN	Joe Namath	175.00
ON	Ozzie Newsome	10.00
JP	Jake Plummer	20.00
GS	Gale Sayers	50.00
LR	Lee Roy Selmon	10.00
PS	Phil Simms	20.00
MS	Mike Singletary	20.00
KS	Ken Stabler	40.00
JS	John Stallworth	20.00
ST	Bart Starr	200.00
RS	Roger Staubach	75.00
FT	Fran Tarkenton	50.00
VT	Vinny Testaverde	20.00
JT	Joe Theismann	30.00
JU	Johnny Unitas	150.00
WA	Kurt Warner	125.00
RI	Ricky Watters	20.00
KW	Kellen Winslow	20.00
SY	Steve Young	50.00

2000 Upper Deck Legends Canton Calling

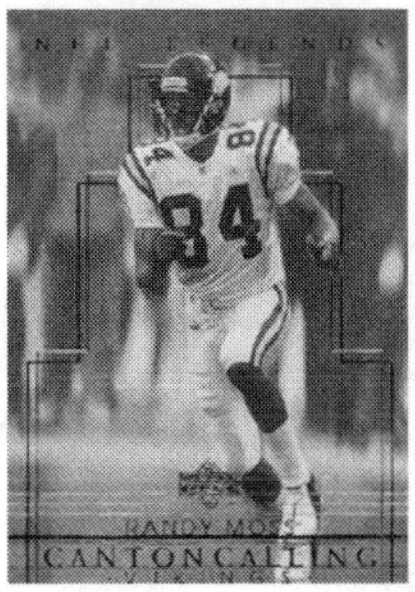

		MT
Complete Set (6):		15.00
Common Player:		1.50
Inserted 1:18		
CC1	Peyton Manning	6.00
CC2	Steve Young	3.00
CC3	Jerry Rice	4.00
CC4	Randy Moss	6.00
CC5	Cris Carter	1.50
CC6	Emmitt Smith	5.00

2000 Upper Deck Legends Defining Moments

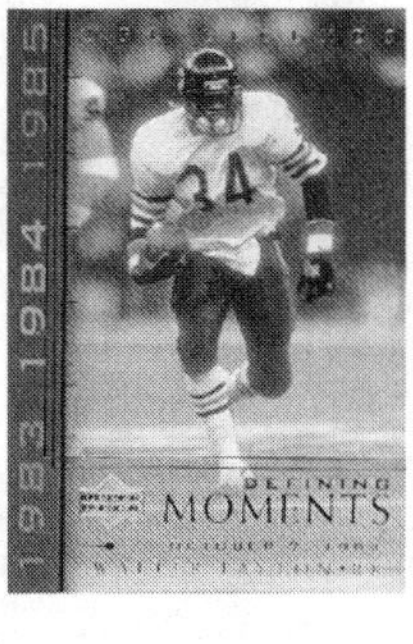

		MT
Complete Set (10):		25.00
Common Player:		1.50
Inserted 1:9		
DM1	Terrell Davis	4.50
DM2	Troy Aikman	3.00
DM3	Jerry Rice	3.00
DM4	Walter Payton	7.00
DM5	Joe Namath	4.00
DM6	Emmitt Smith	4.50
DM7	Steve Young	1.50
DM8	Franco Harris	1.50
DM9	Kurt Warner	7.00
DM10	Brett Favre	6.00

2000 Upper Deck Legends Game Jersey Greats

		MT
Production 400 Sets		
RS	Roger Staubach 400	175.00

2000 Upper Deck Legends Legendary Jerseys

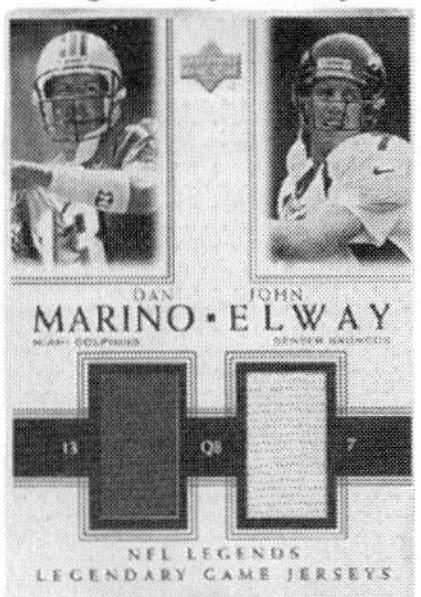

		MT
Common Player:		20.00
Inserted 1:23		
LJTA	Troy Aikman	60.00
LJLJ-MA	Marcus Allen	40.00
LJSE-MA	Marcus Allen	40.00
LJJA	Jamal Anderson	20.00
LJFB	Fred Biletnikoff	40.00
LJDB	Drew Bledsoe	40.00
LJCB	Cliff Branch	20.00
LJJB	John Brodie	30.00
LJMB	Mark Brunell	40.00
LJTC	Todd Christensen	20.00
LJTD	Terrell Davis	75.00
LJED	Eric Dickerson	40.00
LJJE	John Elway	85.00
LJEM	John Elway, Dan Marino	425.00
LJMF	Marshall Faulk	40.00
LJBF	Brett Favre	100.00
LJDF	Doug Flutie	30.00
LJCH	Charles Haley	20.00
LJLJ-TH	Ted Hendricks	20.00
LJSE-TH	Ted Hendricks	20.00
LJMI	Michael Irvin	30.00
LJDJ	Daryl Johnston	20.00
LJBL	Bob Lilly	30.00
LJHL	Howie Long	40.00
LJRL	Ronnie Lott	40.00
LJPM	Peyton Manning	100.00
LJDM	Dan Marino	85.00
LJJM	Joe Montana	150.00
LJWM	Warren Moon	30.00
LJRM	Randy Moss	100.00
LJJN	Joe Namath	150.00
LJKN	Ken Norton Jr.	20.00
LJNO	Jay Novacek	20.00
LJWP	Walter Payton	150.00
LJLJ-JP	Jim Plunkett	25.00
LJSE-JP	Jim Plunkett	25.00
LJJR	Jerry Rice	75.00
LJDS	Deion Sanders	40.00
LJOS	Otis Sistrunk	20.00
LJSM	Bruce Smith	20.00
LJES	Emmitt Smith	85.00
LJKS	Ken Stabler	40.00
LJRS	Roger Staubach	85.00
LJFT	Fran Tarkenton	60.00
LJGU	Gene Upshaw	20.00
LJVE	Mark Van Eeghen	20.00
LJHW	Herschel Walker	35.00
LJKW	Kurt Warner	125.00
LJRW	Reggie White	30.00
LJSY	Steve Young	50.00

2000 Upper Deck Legends Millennium QBs

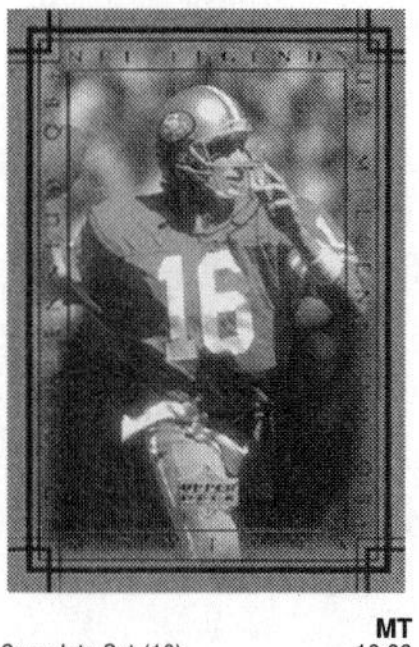

		MT
Complete Set (10):		10.00
Common Player:		.50
Inserted 1:5		
M1	Joe Montana	3.00
M2	Dan Marino	2.50
M3	John Elway	2.50
M4	Fran Tarkenton	1.00
M5	Sammy Baugh	1.00
M6	Joe Namath	2.50
M7	Warren Moon	.50
M8	Mark Brunell	.75
M9	Brett Favre	2.50
M10	Drew Bledsoe	.75

2000 Upper Deck Legends Reflections in Time

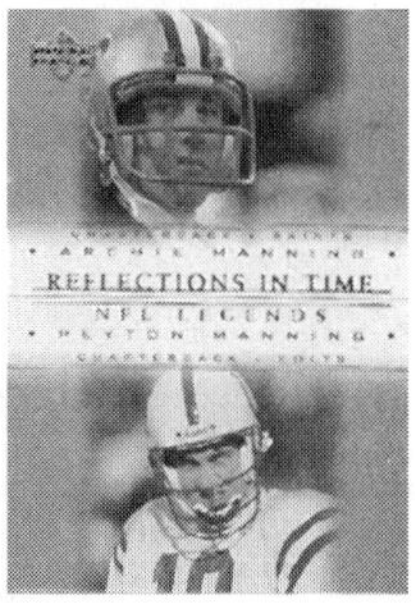

		MT
Complete Set (10):		15.00
Common Player:		1.50
Inserted 1:11		
R1	Earl Campbell, Eddie George	2.00
R2	Mike Singletary, Junior Seau	1.50
R3	Doak Walker, Ricky Williams	3.00
R4	Archie Manning, Peyton Manning	6.00
R5	Reggie White, Jevon Kearse	1.50
R6	Harold Carmichael, Randy Moss	6.00
R7	Gale Sayers, Edgerrin James	6.00
R8	Warren Moon, Daunte Culpepper	2.50
R9	Roger Staubach, Troy Aikman	4.00
R10	Thurman Thomas, Marshall Faulk	1.50

2000 Upper Deck Legends Rookie Gallery

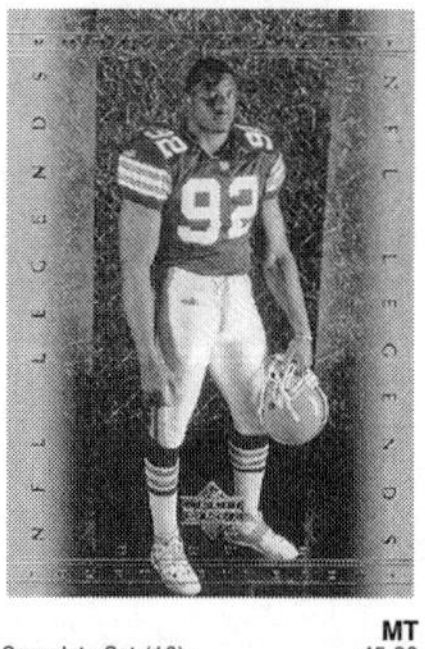

		MT
Complete Set (10):		45.00
Common Player:		3.00
Inserted 1:21		
RG1	Peter Warrick	10.00
RG2	Chris Redman	4.00
RG3	Courtney Brown	3.00
RG4	Thomas Jones	6.00
RG5	Chad Pennington	8.00
RG6	Jamal Lewis	7.00
RG7	Plaxico Burress	6.00
RG8	Ron Dayne	10.00
RG9	Sylvester Morris	5.00
RG10	Shaun Alexander	7.00

2000 Upper Deck MVP

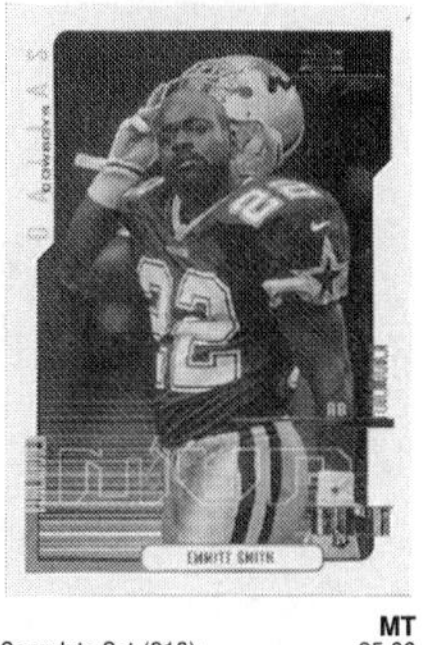

		MT
Complete Set (218):		25.00
Common Player:		.10
Minor Stars:		.20
Common Rookie:		.30
Pack (10):		1.50

Wax Box (28): 38.00
Cards #189 & #220 aren't included in the set price.
1 Jake Plummer .40
2 Michael Pittman .10
3 Rob Moore .20
4 David Boston .40
5 Frank Sanders .20
6 Aeneas Williams .10
7 Kwamie Lassiter .10
8 Tim Dwight .40
9 Chris Chandler .20
10 Jamal Anderson .40
11 Shawn Jefferson .10
12 Qadry Ismail .10
13 Jermaine Lewis .20
14 Rod Woodson .10
15 Michael McCrary .10
16 Tony Banks .20
17 Peter Boulware .10
18 Shannon Sharpe .20
19 Peerless Price .40
20 Rob Johnson .20
21 Eric Moulds .40
22 Doug Flutie .50
23 Muhsin Muhammad .20
24 Patrick Jeffers .30
25 Steve Beuerlein .20
26 Tshimanga Biakabutuka .20
27 Michael Bates .10
28 Cade McNown .60
29 Curtis Enis .30
30 Marcus Robinson .40
31 Shane Matthews .10
32 Bobby Engram .10
33 Glyn Milburn .10
34 Akili Smith .50
35 Corey Dillon .20
36 Darnay Scott .20
37 Tremain Mack .10
38 Tim Couch 1.00
39 Kevin Johnson .40
40 Darrin Chiaverini .10
41 Jamir Miller .10
42 Errict Rhett .20
43 Troy Aikman 1.00
44 Emmitt Smith 1.25
45 Raghib Ismail .10
46 Jason Tucker .30
47 Dexter Coakley .10
48 Joey Galloway .40
49 Greg Ellis .10
50 Terrell Davis 1.25
51 Olandis Gary .50
52 Brian Griese .50
53 Ed McCaffrey .30
54 Rod Smith .30
55 Trevor Pryce .10
56 Charlie Batch .40
57 Germane Crowell .20
58 Johnnie Morton .10
59 Robert Porcher .10
60 Luther Ellis .10
61 James O. Stewart .20
62 Brett Favre 1.50
63 Antonio Freeman .40
64 Bill Schroeder .10
65 Dorsey Levens .40
66 Peyton Manning 1.25
67 Edgerrin James 1.50
68 Marvin Harrison .40
69 Ken Dilger .10
70 Terrence Wilkins .20
71 Mark Brunell .60
72 Fred Taylor .60
73 Jimmy Smith .30
74 Keenan McCardell .20
75 Carnell Lake .10
76 Tony Brackens .10
77 Kevin Hardy .10
78 Hardy Nickerson .10
79 Elvis Grbac .20
80 Tony Gonzalez .20
81 Derrick Alexander .10
82 Donnell Bennett .10
83 James Hasty .10
84 Jay Fiedler .20
85 James Johnson .20
86 Tony Martin .20
87 Damon Huard .40
88 O.J. McDuffie .20
89 Oronde Gadsden .20
90 Zach Thomas .20
91 Sam Madison .10
92 Jeff George .30
93 Randy Moss 1.50
94 Robert Smith .30
95 Cris Carter .40
96 Matthew Hatchette .10
97 Drew Bledsoe .60
98 Terry Glenn .40
99 Troy Brown .10
100 Kevin Faulk .30
101 Lawyer Milloy .10
102 Ricky Williams 1.00
103 Keith Poole .10
104 Jake Reed .10
105 Cameron Cleeland .20
106 Jeff Blake .20
107 Andrew Glover .10
108 Kerry Collins .20
109 Amani Toomer .20
110 Joe Montgomery .20
111 Ike Hilliard .20
112 Michael Strahan .10
113 Jessie Armstead .10
114 Ray Lucas .30
115 Keyshawn Johnson .40
116 Curtis Martin .40
117 Vinny Testaverde .30
118 Wayne Chrebet .40
119 Dedric Ward .10
120 Tim Brown .30
121 Rich Gannon .20
122 Tyrone Wheatley .20
123 Napoleon Kaufman .30
124 Charles Woodson .30
125 Darrell Russell .10
126 Duce Staley .30
127 Donovan McNabb .60
128 Torrance Small .10
129 Allen Rossum .10
130 Brian Dawkins .10
131 Troy Vincent .10
132 Troy Edwards .40
133 Jerome Bettis .30
134 Hines Ward .20
135 Kordell Stewart .40
136 Levon Kirkland .10
137 Kent Graham .10
138 Marshall Faulk .40
139 Kurt Warner 2.00
140 Torry Holt .40
141 Isaac Bruce .40
142 Kevin Carter .10
143 Az-Zahir Hakim .30
144 Todd Lyght .10
145 Jermaine Fazande .20
146 Curtis Conway .20
147 Freddie Jones .20
148 Junior Seau .30
149 Jeff Graham .10
150 Ryan Leaf .40
151 Rodney Harrison .10
152 Steve Young .60
153 Jerry Rice 1.00
154 Charlie Garner .20
155 Terrell Owens .40
156 Jeff Garcia .30
157 Bryant Young .10
158 Lance Schulters .10
159 Ricky Watters .30
160 Jon Kitna .40
161 Derrick Mayes .20
162 Sean Dawkins .10
163 Cortez Kennedy .10
164 Chad Brown .10
165 Warrick Dunn .40
166 Shaun King .60
167 Mike Alstott .40
168 Warren Sapp .20
169 Jacquez Green .20
170 Derrick Brooks .10
171 John Lynch .10
172 Donnie Abraham .10
173 Eddie George .50
174 Steve McNair .50
175 Kevin Dyson .20
176 Jevon Kearse .40
177 Yancey Thigpen .20
178 Frank Wycheck .10
179 Eddie Robinson .10
180 Samari Rolle .10
181 Brad Johnson .40
182 Stephen Davis .40
183 Michael Westbrook .30
184 Albert Connell .20
185 Brian Mitchell .10
186 Bruce Smith .10
187 Stephen Alexander .10
188 *Peter Warrick* 3.00
189 *LaVar Arrington cutout* 25.00
190 *Chris Redman* 1.50
191 *Courtney Brown* .50
192 *Brian Urlacher* 2.00
193 *Plaxico Burress* 1.75
194 *Corey Simon* .50
195 *Bubba Franks* .50
196 *Deon Grant* .30
197 *Michael Wiley* .50
198 *Tim Rattay* .50
199 *Ron Dayne* 3.00
200 *Sylvester Morris* 1.75
201 *Shaun Alexander* 2.00
202 *Dez White* .50
203 *Thomas Jones* 1.50
204 *Reuben Droughns* .30
205 *Travis Taylor* .75
206 *Trevor Gaylor* .30
207 *Jamal Lewis* 4.00
208 *Chad Pennington* 2.50
209 *J.R. Redmond* .75
210 *Laveranues Coles* .75
211 *Travis Prentice* 1.00
212 *R. Jay Soward* .50
213 *Todd Pinkston* .50
214 *Dennis Northcutt* .50
215 *Shyrone Stith* .30
216 *Tee Martin* .50
217 *Giovanni Carmazzi* .50
218 Drew Bledsoe CL .30
219 Steve Young CL .20
220 Donovan McNabb CL SP 25.00

2000 Upper Deck MVP Gold Script Parallel

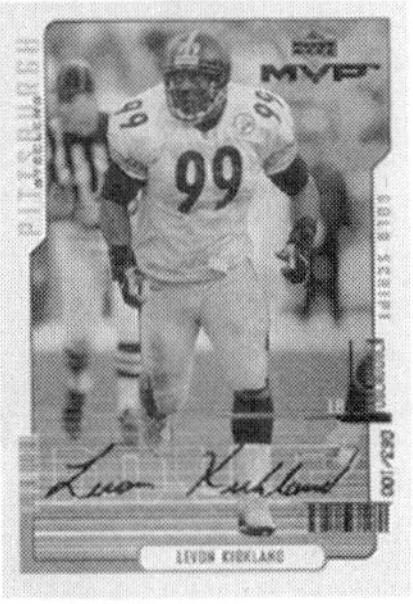

MT
Gold Script Cards: 15x-30x
Gold Script Rookies: 10x-20x
Production 100 Sets

2000 Upper Deck MVP Silver Script Parallel

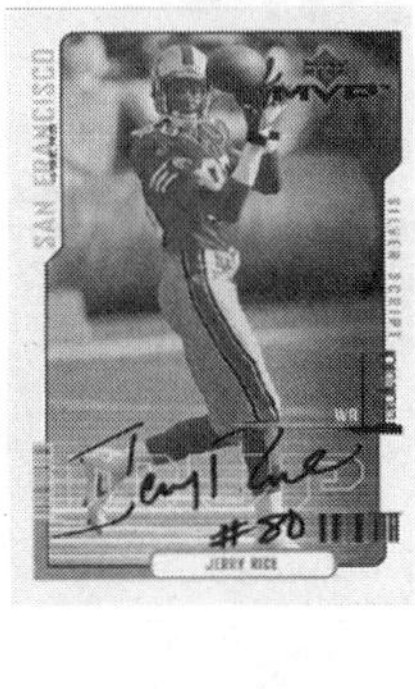

MT
Complete Set (218): 75.00
Silver Script Cards: 3x
Silver Script Rookies: 2x
Inserted 1:2

2000 Upper Deck MVP Super Script Parallel

MT
Super Script Cards: 50x-100x
Super Script Rookies: 25x-50x
Production 25 Sets

2000 Upper Deck MVP Air Show

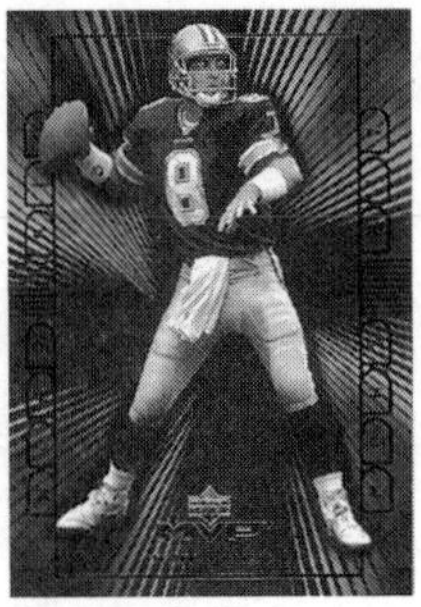

MT
Complete Set (10): 10.00
Common Player: .75
Minor Stars: 1.50
Inserted 1:14
AS1 Brian Griese 2.00
AS2 Drew Bledsoe 2.50
AS3 Rob Johnson .75
AS4 Jeff Garcia 1.50
AS5 Ray Lucas 1.50
AS6 Jon Kitna 1.50
AS7 Jeff George 1.50
AS8 Shaun King 2.50
AS9 Troy Aikman 4.00
AS10 Steve Beuerlein .75

2000 Upper Deck MVP Game-Jersey Greats

MT
JM Joe Montana 350.00

2000 Upper Deck MVP Game-Used Souvenirs

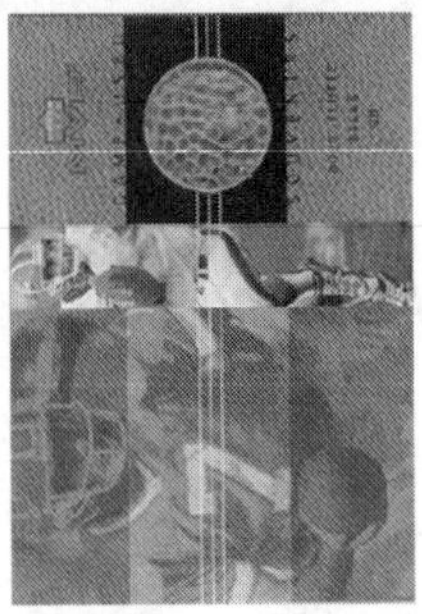

MT
Common Player: 20.00
Inserted 1:229 Hobby
TA Troy Aikman 40.00
MA Mike Alstott 30.00
CB Charlie Batch 20.00
MB Mark Brunell 35.00
CC Cris Carter 30.00
TC Tim Couch 45.00
SD Stephen Davis 30.00
TD Terrell Davis 45.00
MF Marshall Faulk 30.00
BF Brett Favre 70.00
DF Doug Flutie 30.00
EG Eddie George SB/40 100.00
BG Brian Griese 30.00
EJ Edgerrin James 60.00
BJ Brad Johnson 20.00
KJ Kevin Johnson 30.00
KE Keyshawn Johnson 30.00
SK Shaun King 35.00
JK Jon Kitna 20.00
PM Peyton Manning 60.00
DM Dan Marino 70.00
DM Donovan McNabb 40.00
CM Cade McNown 40.00
RM Randy Moss 70.00
JP Jake Plummer 30.00
JR Jerry Rice 40.00
AS Akili Smith 30.00
ES Emmitt Smith 50.00
FT Fred Taylor 35.00
KW Kurt Warner SB/40 250.00
RW Ricky Williams 45.00

2000 Upper Deck MVP Game-Used Souvenirs Autographs

MT
Common Player: 100.00
Production 25 Sets
TA Troy Aikman 250.00
CB Charlie Batch 100.00
MB Mark Brunell 150.00
CC Cris Carter 100.00
TC Tim Couch 275.00
SD Stephen Davis 100.00
TD Terrell Davis 275.00
MF Marshall Faulk 125.00
DF Doug Flutie 150.00
BG Brian Griese 100.00
EJ Edgerrin James 300.00
BJ Brad Johnson 100.00
KJ Kevin Johnson 125.00
KE Keyshawn Johnson 125.00
JK Jon Kitna 100.00
PM Peyton Manning 300.00
DM Dan Marino 350.00
RM Randy Moss 300.00
JP Jake Plummer 125.00
AS Akili Smith 150.00
KW Kurt Warner 450.00
RW Ricky Williams 275.00

2000 Upper Deck MVP Headliners

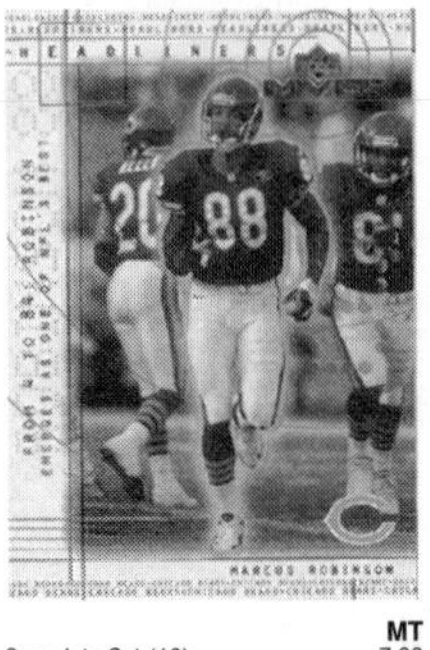

MT
Complete Set (10): 7.00
Common Player: .50
Minor Stars: 1.00
Inserted 1:6
H1 Isaac Bruce 1.00
H2 Michael Westbrook .50
H3 James O. Stewart .50
H4 Keyshawn Johnson 1.00
H5 Marcus Robinson 1.00
H6 Charlie Batch 1.00
H7 Marvin Harrison 1.00
H8 Olandis Gary 1.00
H9 Curtis Martin 1.00
H10 Jevon Kearse 1.00

2000 Upper Deck MVP Highlight Reel

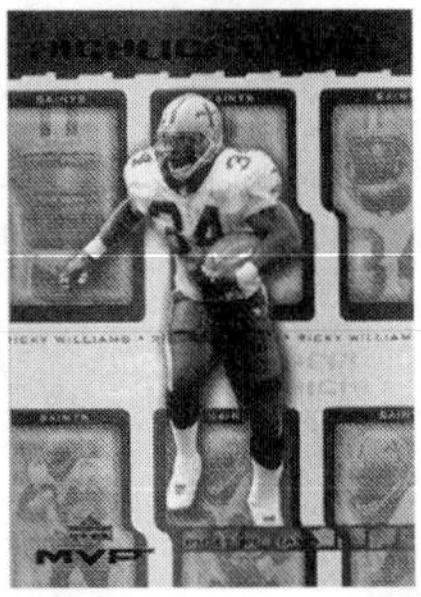

MT
Complete Set (7): 15.00
Common Player: 1.50
Inserted 1:28
HR1 Marvin Harrison 2.50
HR2 Isaac Bruce 2.50
HR3 Cris Carter 2.50
HR4 Ray Lucas 2.50
HR5 Muhsin Muhammad 1.50
HR6 Eddie George 3.00
HR7 Ricky Williams 5.00

2000 Upper Deck MVP Prolifics

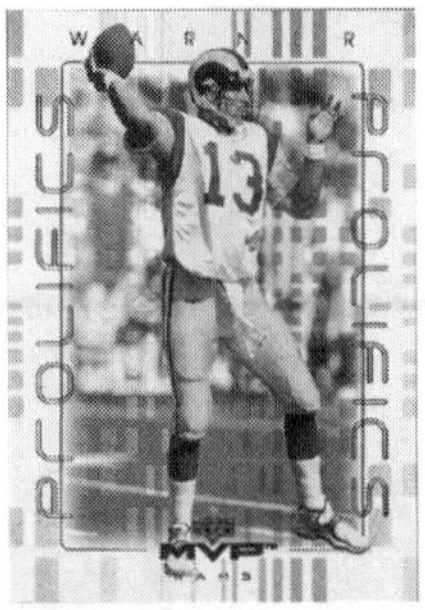

MT
Complete Set (7): 30.00
Common Player: 2.00
Inserted 1:28
P1 Brett Favre 7.00
P2 Marshall Faulk 2.00
P3 Edgerrin James 6.00
P4 Peyton Manning 6.00
P5 Tim Couch 4.00
P6 Dan Marino 6.00
P7 Kurt Warner 8.00

2000 Upper Deck MVP ProSign

MT
Common Player: 25.00
Inserted 1:215 Retail
Gold Cards: 4x
Production 25 Sets
SA Shaun Alexander 45.00
CB Charlie Batch 35.00
IB Isaac Bruce 30.00
MB Mark Brunell 40.00
KC Kwame Cavil 25.00
TC Tim Couch 50.00
HT Ron Dayne 75.00
RD Ron Dugans 30.00
MF Marshall Faulk 30.00
BG Brian Griese 35.00
TH Torry Holt 30.00
EJ Edgerrin James 85.00
KJ Keyshawn Johnson 30.00
TJ Thomas Jones 35.00
JK Jon Kitna 30.00
JL Jamal Lewis 100.00
PM Peyton Manning 85.00
DM Dan Marino Gold 350.00
TM Tee Martin 30.00
RM Randy Moss 85.00
CP Chad Pennington 60.00
JP Jake Plummer 30.00
CR Chris Redman 35.00
TT Travis Taylor 30.00
KW Kurt Warner 125.00
PW Peter Warrick 85.00
DW Dez White 30.00
RW Ricky Williams 60.00

2000 Upper Deck MVP Theatre

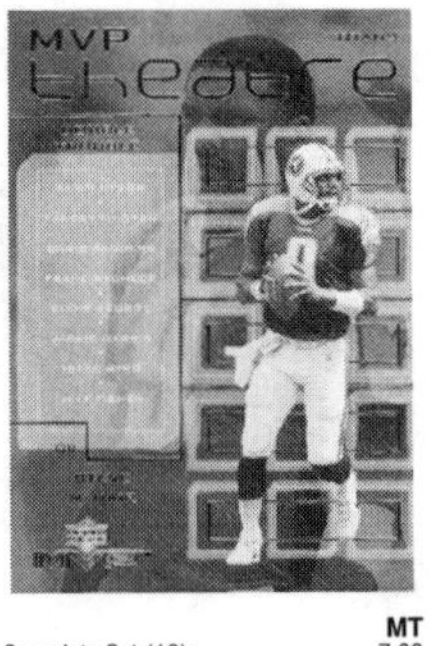

MT
Complete Set (10): 7.00
Common Player: .50
Minor Stars: 1.00
Inserted 1:6
M1 Troy Edwards 1.00
M2 Ed McCaffrey .50
M3 Stephen Davis 1.00
M4 Corey Dillon 1.00
M5 Steve McNair 1.00
M6 Jimmy Smith .50
M7 Fred Taylor 1.75
M8 Terrell Davis 3.00
M9 Jon Kitna 1.00
M10 Germane Crowell .50

2000 Upper Deck Ovation

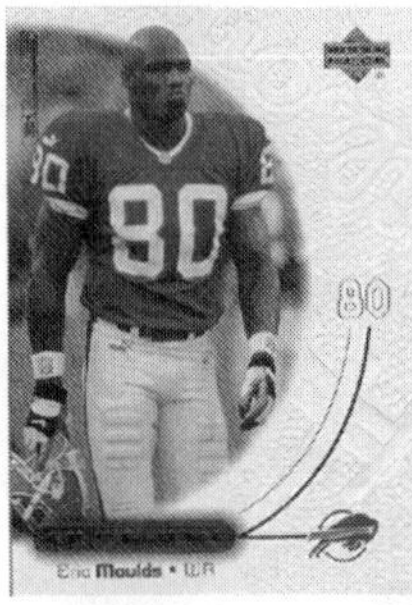

MT
Complete Set (90): 220.00
Common Player: .15
Minor Stars: .30
Common Rookie: 4.00
Production 2,500 Sets
Pack (5): 4.00
Wax Box (20): 60.00
1 Jake Plummer .50
2 Frank Sanders .30
3 Chris Chandler .30
4 Jamal Anderson .50
5 Qadry Ismail .15
6 Eric Moulds .50
7 Muhsin Muhammad .30
8 Steve Beuerlein .30
9 Cade McNown .75
10 Marcus Robinson .50
11 Akili Smith .50
12 Corey Dillon .50
13 Tim Couch 1.25
14 Kevin Johnson .30
15 Troy Aikman 1.00
16 Emmitt Smith 1.50
17 Terrell Davis 1.50
18 Olandis Gary .60
19 Charlie Batch .50
20 Germane Crowell .50
21 Brett Favre 2.00
22 Antonio Freeman .50
23 Peyton Manning 1.75
24 Edgerrin James 2.00
25 Mark Brunell .75
26 Fred Taylor .75
27 Elvis Grbac .30
28 Tony Gonzalez .30
29 Tony Martin .15
30 Damon Huard .50
31 Randy Moss 1.75
32 Daunte Culpepper 1.00
33 Drew Bledsoe .75
34 Terry Glenn .50
35 Ricky Williams 1.25
36 Jeff Blake .30
37 Kerry Collins .30
38 Amani Toomer .15
39 Curtis Martin .50
40 Vinny Testaverde .30
41 Tim Brown .30
42 Rickey Dudley .15
43 Duce Staley .50
44 Donovan McNabb .75
45 Troy Edwards .50
46 Jerome Bettis .50
47 Marshall Faulk .50
48 Kurt Warner 2.50
49 Freddie Jones .30
50 Junior Seau .30
51 Jerry Rice 1.00
52 Steve Young .75
53 Ricky Watters .30
54 Jon Kitna .50
55 Shaun King .75
56 Keyshawn Johnson .50
57 Eddie George .60
58 Steve McNair .50
59 Brad Johnson .50
60 Stephen Davis .50
61 *Courtney Brown* 7.00
62 *Corey Simon* 5.00
63 *R. Jay Soward* 6.00
64 *Anthony Becht* 5.00
65 *Chris Redman* 12.00
66 *Chad Pennington* 25.00
67 *Tee Martin* 7.00
68 *Giovanni Carmazzi* 8.00
69 *Ron Dayne* 30.00
70 *Shaun Alexander* 20.00
71 *Thomas Jones* 12.00
72 *Reuben Droughns* 4.00
73 *Jamal Lewis* 40.00
74 *J.R. Redmond* 10.00
75 *Travis Prentice* 10.00
76 *Trung Canidate* 5.00
77 *Brian Urlacher* 20.00
78 *Bubba Franks* 8.00
79 *Peter Warrick* 30.00
80 *Plaxico Burress* 15.00
81 *Sylvester Morris* 15.00
82 *Dez White* 5.00
83 *Travis Taylor* 10.00
84 *Todd Pinkston* 5.00
85 *Dennis Northcutt* 6.00
86 *Jerry Porter* 5.00
87 *Laveranues Coles* 7.00
88 *Danny Farmer* 4.00
89 *Curtis Keaton* 4.00
90 *Ron Dugans* 5.00

2000 Upper Deck Ovation Standing Ovation Parallel

MT
Standing Cards: 20x-40x
Standing Rookies: 2x-4x
Production 50 Sets

2000 Upper Deck Ovation A Piece of History

MT
Production 4,800 total cards
IB Isaac Bruce Helmet 45.00
TC Tim Couch 45.00
DC Daunte Culpepper 40.00
RD Ron Dayne Helmet 85.00
RD Ron Dayne 70.00
BF Brett Favre 70.00
EJ Edgerrin James 70.00
TJ Thomas Jones 35.00
SK Shaun King Helmet 85.00
PM Peyton Manning 70.00
DM Dan Marino 70.00
RM Randy Moss 70.00
CP Chad Pennington 50.00
CR Chris Redman 30.00
JR Jerry Rice 45.00
KW Kurt Warner Helmet 200.00
PW Peter Warrick Helmet 85.00
PW Peter Warrick 70.00

2000 Upper Deck Ovation A Piece of History Autographs

MT
Complete Set (8):
Common Player:
MB Mark Brunell 100.00
RD Ron Dayne 100.00
TJ Thomas Jones 100.00
PM Peyton Manning 200.00
RM Randy Moss 200.00
CP Chad Pennington 150.00
CR Chris Redman 100.00
PW Peter Warrick 100.00

Values quoted in this guide reflect the retail price of a card — the price a collector can expect to pay when buying a card from a dealer. The wholesale price — that which a collector can expect to receive from a dealer when selling cards — will be significantly lower, depending on desirability and condition.

2000 Upper Deck Ovation Center Stage

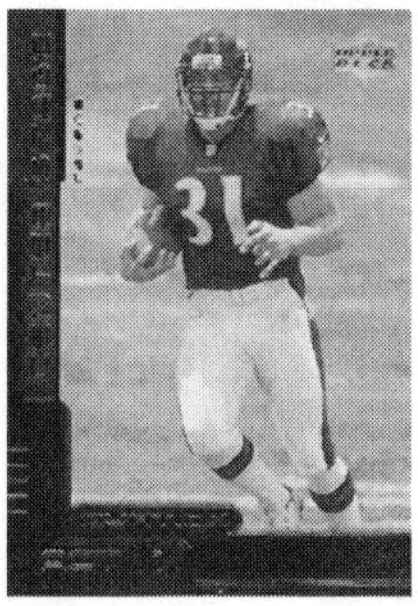

MT
Complete Set (10): 35.00
Common Player: 3.00
Inserted 1:19
Act 2 Cards: 3x
Inserted 1:79
Act 3 Cards: 6x-12x
Production 50 Sets
CS1 Tim Couch 4.00
CS2 Fred Taylor 3.00
CS3 Kurt Warner 8.00
CS4 Edgerrin James 7.00
CS5 Ron Dayne 8.00
CS6 Jamal Lewis 5.00
CS7 Thomas Jones 4.00
CS8 Peter Warrick 8.00
CS9 Plaxico Burress 4.50
CS10 Chad Pennington 6.00

2000 Upper Deck Ovation Curtain Calls

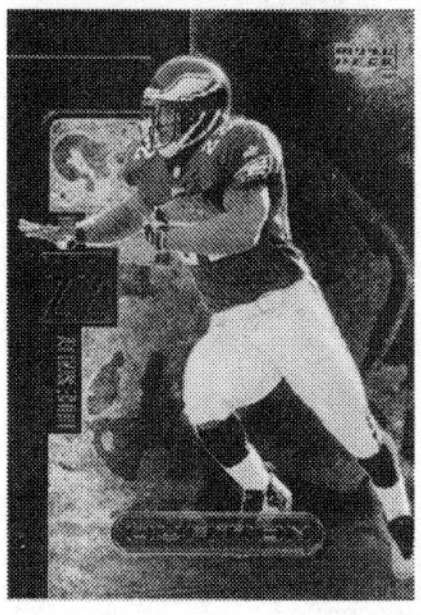

MT
Complete Set (15): 8.00
Common Player: .50
Minor Stars: 1.00
Inserted 1:3
CC1 Eddie George 1.25
CC2 Muhsin Muhammad .50
CC3 Marvin Harrison 1.00
CC4 Marcus Robinson 1.00
CC5 Duce Staley 1.00
CC6 Isaac Bruce 1.00
CC7 Germane Crowell 1.00
CC8 Amani Toomer .50
CC9 Fred Taylor 1.50
CC10 Michael Westbrook .50
CC11 Olandis Gary 1.25
CC12 Stephen Davis 1.00
CC13 Cade McNown 1.50
CC14 Priest Holmes .50
CC15 Corey Dillon 1.00

2000 Upper Deck Ovation Game-Jersey Greats

MT
Production 175 Cards
1 Joe Namath 175 300.00

2000 Upper Deck Ovation Spotlight

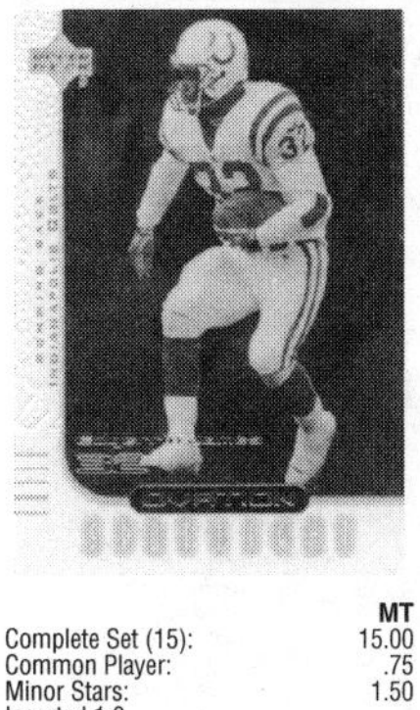

MT
Complete Set (15): 15.00
Common Player: .75
Minor Stars: 1.50
Inserted 1:9
OS1 Edgerrin James 6.00
OS2 Rob Johnson .75
OS3 Jake Plummer 1.50
OS4 Jamal Anderson 1.50
OS5 James O. Stewart .75
OS6 Shaun King 2.00
OS7 Jon Kitna 1.50
OS8 Ricky Williams 3.50
OS9 Errict Rhett .75
OS10 Stephen Davis 1.50
OS11 Daunte Culpepper 2.50
OS12 Donovan McNabb 2.00
OS13 Kevin Johnson 1.50
OS14 Akili Smith 1.50
OS15 Cade McNown 2.00

2000 Upper Deck Ovation Star Performers

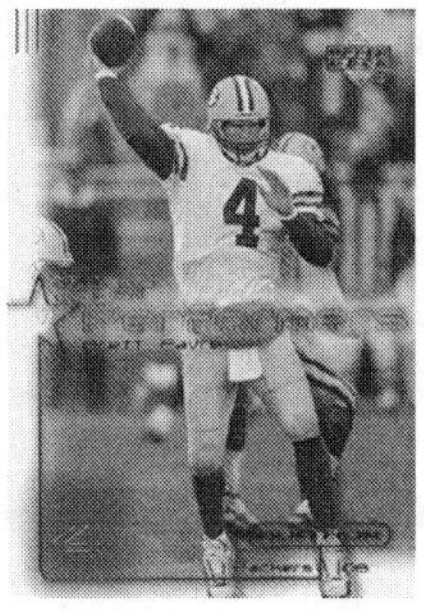

MT
Complete Set (15): 25.00
Common Player: .75
Minor Stars: 1.50
Inserted 1:9
SP1 Mark Brunell 2.50
SP2 Eddie George 2.00
SP3 Brad Johnson 1.50
SP4 Vinny Testaverde .75
SP5 Marshall Faulk 1.50
SP6 Tim Couch 3.00
SP7 Brett Favre 6.00
SP8 Ricky Williams 3.50
SP9 Peyton Manning 6.00
SP10 Keyshawn Johnson 1.50
SP11 Emmitt Smith 4.50
SP12 Jerry Rice 3.00
SP13 Tim Brown 1.50
SP14 Randy Moss 6.00
SP15 Jamal Anderson 1.50

2000 Upper Deck Ovation Super Signatures

MT
Production 100 Sets
Gold Cards: 1.5x
Production 50 Sets
Rainbow Cards:
Production 10 Sets
JB Jim Brown 125.00
MB Mark Brunell 50.00
TD Terrell Davis 85.00
MF Marshall Faulk 50.00
EG Eddie George 50.00
PM Peyton Manning 150.00
RM Randy Moss 125.00
JN Joe Namath 225.00

2000 Upper Deck Pros & Prospects

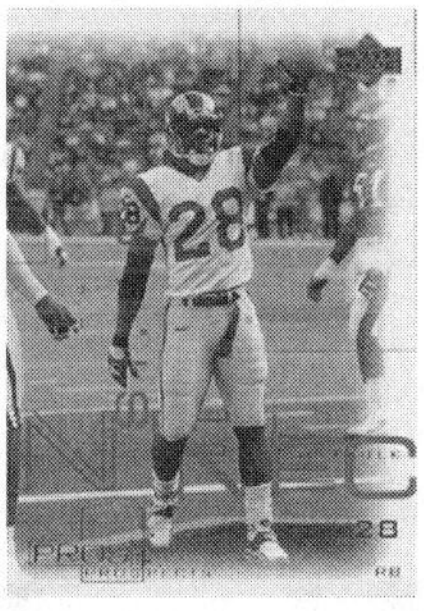

MT
Complete Set (126): 1700.
Common Player: .15
Minor Stars: .30
Common Rookie: 15.00
Production 1,000 Sets
Pack (5): 7.00
Wax Box (24): 150.00
Common Rookie (127-152): 8.00
Production 1,000 Sets
1 Jake Plummer .50
2 Michael Pittman .15
3 Tim Dwight .30
4 Chris Chandler .30
5 Qadry Ismail .15
6 Shannon Sharpe .30
7 Peerless Price .30
8 Rob Johnson .30
9 Eric Moulds .30
10 Muhsin Muhammad .30
11 Patrick Jeffers .30
12 Steve Beuerlein .30
13 Cade McNown .75
14 Curtis Enis .30
15 Marcus Robinson .50
16 Akili Smith .50
17 Corey Dillon .30
18 Tim Couch 1.00
19 Kevin Johnson .50
20 Errict Rhett .30
21 Troy Aikman 1.00
22 Emmitt Smith 1.25
23 Raghib Ismail .15
24 Terrell Davis 1.25
25 Olandis Gary .50
26 Brian Griese .50
27 Ed McCaffrey .30
28 Charlie Batch .50
29 Germane Crowell .30
30 James O. Stewart .30
31 Brett Favre 1.50
32 Antonio Freeman .30
33 Dorsey Levens .30
34 Peyton Manning 1.25
35 Edgerrin James 1.50
36 Marvin Harrison .50
37 Mark Brunell .75
38 Fred Taylor .75
39 Jimmy Smith .30
40 Elvis Grbac .30
41 Tony Gonzalez .30
42 Damon Huard .50
43 James Johnson .30
44 Jay Fiedler .30
45 Randy Moss 1.25
46 Robert Smith .30
47 Cris Carter .50
48 Drew Bledsoe .75
49 Terry Glenn .30
50 Ricky Williams 1.00
51 Jeff Blake .30
52 Keith Poole .15
53 Kerry Collins .30
54 Amani Toomer .30
55 Vinny Testaverde .30
56 Keyshawn Johnson .50
57 Curtis Martin .50
58 Tim Brown .30
59 Rich Gannon .30
60 Tyrone Wheatley .30
61 Duce Staley .50
62 Donovan McNabb .75
63 Troy Edwards .50
64 Jerome Bettis .30
65 Marshall Faulk .50
66 Kurt Warner 2.00
67 Torry Holt .50
68 Isaac Bruce .50
69 Junior Seau .30
70 Jeff Graham .15
71 Steve Young .75
72 Jerry Rice 1.00
73 Charlie Garner .30
74 Ricky Watters .30
75 Jon Kitna .50
76 Warrick Dunn .50
77 Shaun King .75
78 Mike Alstott .50
79 Eddie George .50
80 Steve McNair .30
81 Kevin Dyson .30
82 Brad Johnson .30
83 Stephen Davis .50
84 Michael Westbrook .30
85 *Peter Warrick* 150.00
86 *LaVar Arrington* 85.00
87 *Chris Redman* 60.00
88 *Courtney Brown* 30.00
89 *Plaxico Burress* 75.00
90 *Corey Simon* 20.00
91 *Bubba Franks* 30.00
92 *Deon Grant* 15.00
93 *Brian Urlacher* 100.00
94 *Ron Dayne* 150.00
95 *Sylvester Morris* 75.00
96 *Shaun Alexander* 100.00
97 *Dez White* 30.00
98 *Thomas Jones* 60.00
99 *Travis Taylor* 40.00
100 *Kwame Cavil* 15.00
101 *Jamal Lewis* 200.00
102 *Chad Pennington* 125.00
103 *J.R. Redmond* 40.00
104 *Sebastian Janikowski* 30.00
105 *Anthony Lucas* 25.00
106 *Travis Prentice* 50.00
107 *Danny Farmer* 25.00
108 *Sherrod Gideon* 15.00
109 *Todd Pinkston* 30.00
110 *Dennis Northcutt* 30.00
111 *Tim Rattay* 30.00
112 *Troy Walters* 25.00
113 *Michael Wiley* 25.00
114 *R. Jay Soward* 30.00
115 *Trung Candidate* 25.00
116 *Reuben Droughns* 20.00
117 *Rondell Mealey* 15.00
118 *Chris Coleman* 15.00
119 *Giovanni Carmazzi* 30.00
120 *Trevor Insley* 15.00
121 *Shyrone Stith* 20.00
122 *Gari Scott* 15.00
123 *Tee Martin* 30.00
124 *Tom Brady* 50.00
125 *Marcus Knight* 15.00
126 *Jerry Porter* 30.00
127 *Brad Hoover* 40.00
128 *Chad Morton* 12.00
129 *Charles Lee* 8.00
130 *Damon Hodge* 8.00
131 *Darrell Jackson* 30.00
132 *Doug Johnson* 15.00
133 *Frank Moreau* 12.00
134 *JaJuan Dawson* 15.00
135 *Jake Delhomme* 15.00
136 *Jarious Jackson* 25.00
137 *Joe Hamilton* 25.00
138 *Larry Foster* 10.00
139 *Laveranues Coles* 35.00
140 *Aaron Shea* 8.00
141 *Matt Lytle* 12.00
142 *Mike Anderson* 100.00
143 *Ron Dixon* 20.00
144 *Ronney Jenkins* 8.00
145 *Sammy Morris* 25.00
146 *Shockmain Davis* 8.00
147 *Spergon Wynn* 12.00
148 *Todd Husak* 20.00
149 *Trevor Gaylor* 15.00
150 *Tywan Mitchell* 8.00
151 *Windrell Hayes* 8.00
152 *Bobby Shaw* 12.00

Post-1980 cards in Near Mint condition will generally sell for about 75% of the quoted Mint value. Excellent-condition cards bring no more than 40%.

2000 Upper Deck Pros & Prospects Future Fame

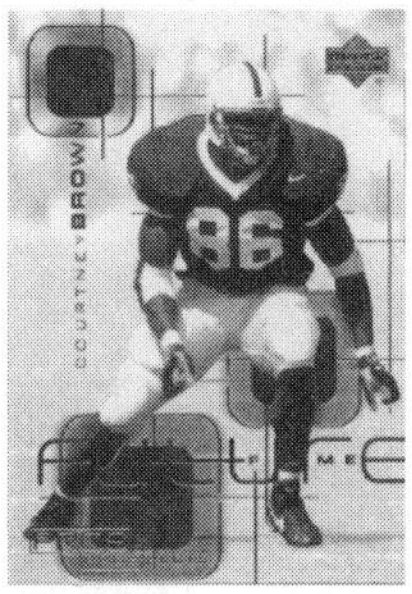

MT
Complete Set (10): 25.00
Common Player: 2.00
Inserted 1:6
FF1 Peter Warrick 7.00
FF2 Lavar Arrington 3.00
FF3 Courtney Brown 2.00
FF4 Travis Taylor 3.00
FF5 Plaxico Burress 4.00
FF6 Ron Dayne 6.00
FF7 Jamal Lewis 4.00
FF8 Thomas Jones 4.00
FF9 Chad Pennington 4.00
FF10 Chris Redman 2.00

2000 Upper Deck Pros & Prospects Elway Autograph Jersey

MT
JE John Elway 250.00

2000 Upper Deck Pros & Prospects Mirror Image

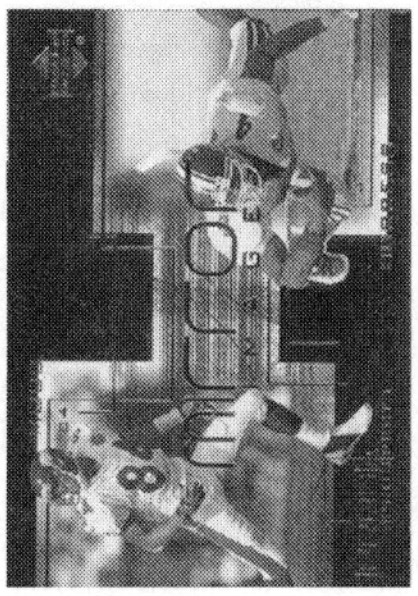

MT
Complete Set (10): 25.00
Common Player: 2.00
Inserted 1:12
M1 Thomas Jones, Fred Taylor 3.00
M2 Ron Dayne, Jerome Bettis 6.00
M3 Plaxico Burress, Randy Moss 6.00
M4 Peter Warrick, Marvin Harrison 6.00
M5 Tee Martin, Peyton Manning 7.00
M6 Chris Redman, Brett Favre 6.00
M7 Lavar Arrington, Junior Seau 4.00
M8 Dez White, Jimmy Smith 2.00
M9 Chad Pennington, Kurt Warner 8.00
M10 Shaun Alexander, Marshall Faulk 3.00

2000 Upper Deck Pros & Prospects ProMotion

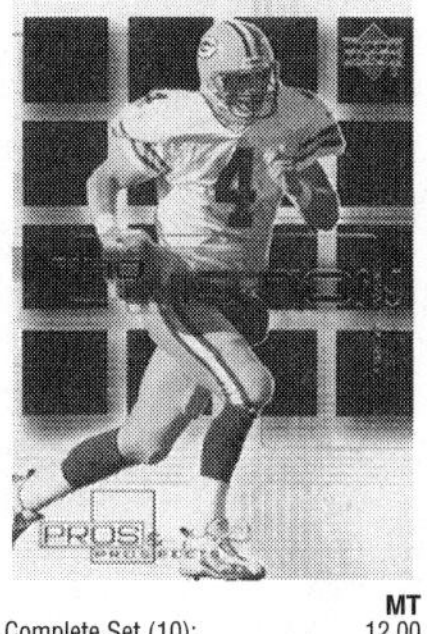

MT
Complete Set (10): 12.00
Common Player: 1.00
Inserted 1:6
P1 Kurt Warner 5.00
P2 Eddie George 1.50
P3 Marshall Faulk 1.00
P4 Keyshawn Johnson 1.00
P5 Emmitt Smith 3.00
P6 Randy Moss 4.00
P7 Marvin Harrison 1.00
P8 Mark Brunell 2.00
P9 Curtis Martin 1.00
P10 Brett Favre 4.00

2000 Upper Deck Pros & Prospects Report Card

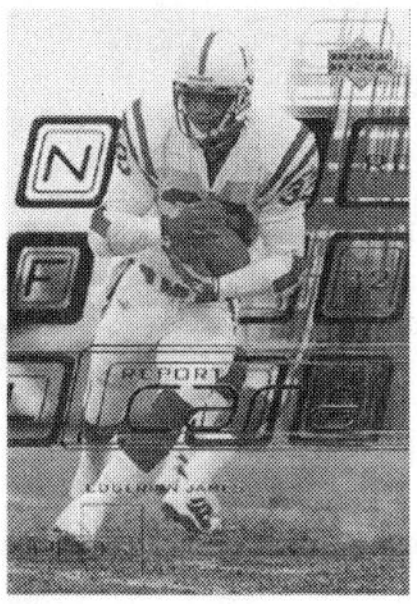

MT
Complete Set (12): 18.00
Common Player: 1.00
Inserted 1:12
RC1 Edgerrin James 5.00
RC2 Tim Couch 3.00
RC3 Cade McNown 2.50
RC4 Champ Bailey 1.00
RC5 Donovan McNabb 2.50
RC6 Kevin Johnson 2.00
RC7 Shaun King 2.50
RC8 Peerless Price 1.00
RC9 David Boston 1.00
RC10 Ricky Williams 3.00
RC11 Akili Smith 2.50
RC12 Jevon Kearse 2.00

2000 Upper Deck Pros & Prospects Signature Piece 1

MT
Complete Set (23): 2300.
Common Player: 30.00
Inserted 1:96
SPCB Champ Bailey 45.00
SPDB Drew Bledsoe 100.00
SPIB Isaac Bruce 60.00
SPMB Mark Brunell 100.00
SPCC Chris Claiborne 30.00
SPRD Ron Dayne 275.00
SPDF Danny Farmer 60.00
SPMF Marshall Faulk 60.00
SPOG Olandis Gary 70.00
SPBG Brian Griese 70.00
SPMH Marvin Harrison 60.00
SPTH Torry Holt 70.00
SPEG Edgerrin James 275.00
SPWR Kevin Johnson 70.00
SPDL Dorsey Levens 45.00
SPRL Ray Lucas 45.00
SPRM Randy Moss 250.00
SPTO Terrell Owens 60.00
SPKW Kurt Warner 350.00
SPTA Troy Aikman 150.00
SPKJ Keyshawn Johnson 70.00
SPPM Peyton Manning 250.00
SPDM Dan Marino 300.00

2000 Upper Deck Pros & Prospects Signature Piece 2

Too uncommon to price.

MT
Complete Set (20):
Common Player:
IB Isaac Bruce
MB Mark Brunell
CC Chris Claiborne
RD Ron Dayne
DF Danny Farmer
MF Marshall Faulk
OG Olandis Gary
BG Brian Griese
MH Marvin Harrison
TH Torry Holt
EG Edgerrin James
WR Kevin Johnson
RL Ray Lucas
RM Randy Moss
TO Terrell Owens
KW Kurt Warner
TA Troy Aikman
KJ Keyshawn Johnson
PM Peyton Manning
DM Dan Marino

Values quoted in this guide reflect the retail price of a card — the price a collector can expect to pay when buying a card from a dealer. The wholesale price — that which a collector can expect to receive from a dealer when selling cards — will be significantly lower, depending on desirability and condition.

2000 Upper Deck Ultimate Victory

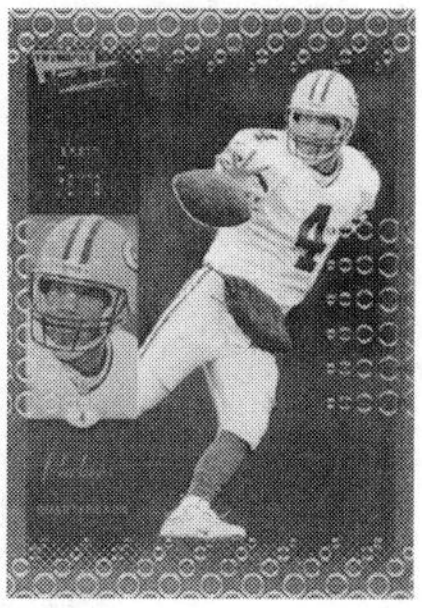

MT
Complete Set (150): 325.00
Common Player: .15
Minor Stars: .30
Common Rookie: 2.50
Production 2,000 Sets
Pack (5): 3.00
Wax Box (24): 45.00
1 Jake Plummer .50
2 David Boston .50
3 Frank Sanders .30
4 Chris Chandler .30
5 Jamal Anderson .50
6 Shawn Jefferson .15
7 Qadry Ismail .15
8 Tony Banks .30
9 Shannon Sharpe .15
10 Peerless Price .30
11 Rob Johnson .30
12 Eric Moulds .50
13 Muhsin Muhammad .30
14 Steve Beuerlein .30
15 Tshimanga Biakabutuka .30
16 Cade McNown .75
17 Curtis Enis .30
18 Marcus Robinson .50
19 Akili Smith .50
20 Corey Dillon .50
21 Darnay Scott .30
22 Tim Couch 1.00
23 Kevin Johnson .30
24 Errict Rhett .15
25 Troy Aikman 1.00
26 Emmitt Smith 1.25
27 Raghib Ismail .15
28 Joey Galloway .50
29 Terrell Davis 1.25
30 Olandis Gary .60
31 Ed McCaffrey .30
32 Charlie Batch .50
33 Germane Crowell .50
34 James O. Stewart .30
35 Brett Favre 1.50
36 Antonio Freeman .50
37 Dorsey Levens .50
38 Peyton Manning 1.50
39 Edgerrin James 1.50
40 Marvin Harrison .50
41 Mark Brunell .75
42 Fred Taylor .75
43 Jimmy Smith .50
44 Elvis Grbac .30
45 Tony Gonzalez .30
46 Derrick Alexander .15
47 Tony Martin .15
48 Damon Huard .30
49 O.J. McDuffie .30
50 Randy Moss 1.50
51 Robert Smith .50
52 Daunte Culpepper 1.00
53 Drew Bledsoe .75
54 Terry Glenn .50
55 Ricky Williams 1.00
56 Jake Reed .30
57 Jeff Blake .30
58 Kerry Collins .30
59 Amani Toomer .15
60 Ike Hilliard .15
61 Ray Lucas .30
62 Curtis Martin .50
63 Vinny Testaverde .30
64 Tim Brown .30
65 Rich Gannon .30
66 Tyrone Wheatley .30
67 Duce Staley .50
68 Donovan McNabb .75
69 Troy Edwards .50
70 Jerome Bettis .50
71 Marshall Faulk .50
72 Kurt Warner 2.00
73 Isaac Bruce .50
74 Curtis Conway .30
75 Freddie Jones .30
76 Jeff Graham .15
77 Jeff Garcia .50
78 Jerry Rice 1.00
79 Ricky Watters .30
80 Jon Kitna .50
81 Derrick Mayes .30
82 Keyshawn Johnson .50
83 Shaun King .75
84 Mike Alstott .50
85 Eddie George .60
86 Steve McNair .50
87 Jevon Kearse .50
88 Brad Johnson .50
89 Stephen Davis .50
90 Michael Westbrook .30
91 *Anthony Becht* 4.00
92 *Anthony Lucas* 2.50
93 *Bashir Yamini* 2.50
94 *Brian Urlacher* 15.00
95 *Chad Morton* 4.00
96 *Chad Pennington* 20.00
97 *Chris Cole* 2.50
98 *Chris Hovan* 3.00
99 *Tim Rattay* 5.00
100 *Chris Redman* 10.00
101 *Chris Samuels* 4.00
102 *Corey Simon* 5.00
103 *Courtney Brown* 5.00
104 *Curtis Keaton* 2.50
105 *Danny Farmer* 3.50

106	*Erron Kinney*	2.50
107	*Darren Howard*	2.50
108	*Deltha O'Neal*	2.50
109	*Dennis Northcutt*	5.00
110	*Demario Brown*	2.50
111	*Dez White*	3.50
112	*Frank Murphy*	2.50
113	*Gari Scott*	2.50
114	*Giovanni Carmazzi*	5.00
115	*J.R. Redmond*	6.00
116	*JaJuan Dawson*	5.00
117	*Jamal Lewis*	30.00
118	*Leon Murray*	2.50
119	*Jerry Porter*	5.00
120	*Joe Hamilton*	5.00
121	*John Abraham*	2.50
122	*John Engleberger*	2.50
123	*Keith Bulluck*	2.50
124	*Kwame Cavil*	2.50
125	*Laveranues Coles*	5.00
126	*Marc Bulger*	2.50
127	*Marcus Knight*	2.50
128	*Mareno Philyaw*	2.50
129	*Michael Wiley*	4.00
130	*Na'il Diggs*	2.50
131	*Peter Warrick*	25.00
132	*Plaxico Burress*	12.00
133	*Raynoch Thompson*	2.50
134	*Reuben Droughns*	2.50
135	*Rob Morris*	2.50
136	*Ron Dayne*	25.00
137	*Ron Dugans*	3.50
138	*Sebastian Janikowski*	4.00
139	*Shaun Alexander*	15.00
140	*Sherrod Gideon*	2.50
141	*Sylvester Morris*	12.00
142	*Tee Martin*	5.00
143	*Thomas Jones*	10.00
144	*Todd Husak*	3.50
145	*Todd Pinkston*	5.00
146	*Tom Brady*	3.50
147	*Travis Prentice*	8.00
148	*Travis Taylor*	6.00
149	*Trevor Gaylor*	3.50
150	*Trung Canidate*	4.00

2000 Upper Deck Ultimate Victory Collection Parallel

	MT
Collection Cards:	5x-10x
Inserted 1:11	
Collection Rookies:	1x
Inserted 1:23	

2000 Upper Deck Ultimate Victory Collection 100 Paralle

	MT
Collection 100 Cards:	15x-30x
Collection 100 Rookies:	3x
Production 100 Sets	

2000 Upper Deck Ultimate Victory Collection 25 Parallel

	MT
Collection 25 Cards:	35x-70x
Collection 25 Rookies:	3x-6x
Production 25 Sets	

2000 Upper Deck Ultimate Victory Battle Ground

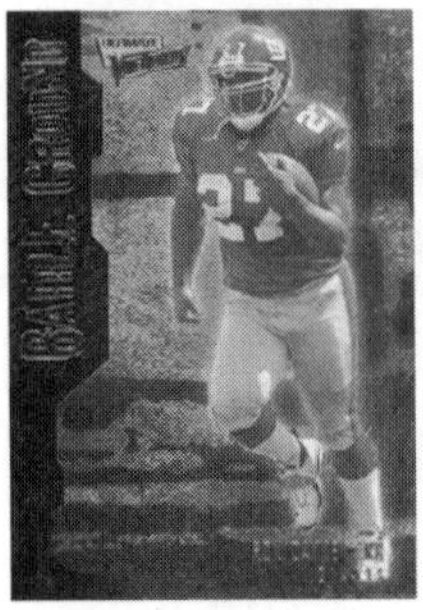

		MT
Complete Set (10):		20.00
Common Player:		1.00
Inserted 1:11		
BG1	Eddie George	1.50
BG2	Edgerrin James	5.00
BG3	Terrell Davis	3.50
BG4	Jamal Anderson	1.00
BG5	Ricky Williams	3.00
BG6	Thomas Jones	3.00
BG7	Jamal Lewis	4.00
BG8	Ron Dayne	6.00
BG9	Shaun Alexander	4.00
BG10	Trung Canidate	1.00

Post-1980 cards in Near Mint condition will generally sell for about 75% of the quoted Mint value. Excellent-condition cards bring no more than 40%.

2000 Upper Deck Ultimate Victory Competitors

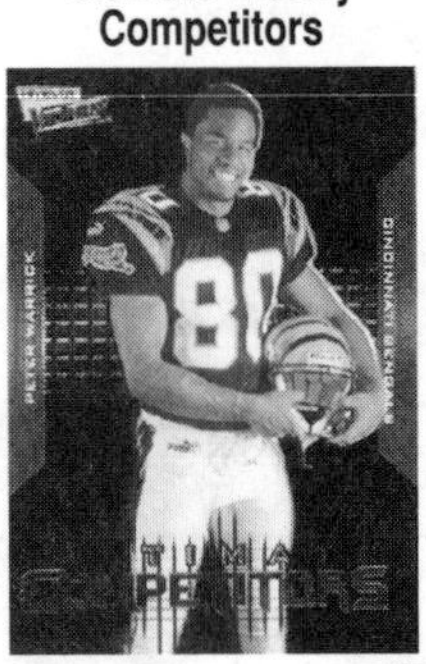

		MT
Complete Set (10):		15.00
Common Player:		1.00
Inserted 1:11		
UC1	Randy Moss	5.00
UC2	Peyton Manning	5.00
UC3	Stephen Davis	1.00
UC4	Cris Carter	1.00
UC5	Jevon Kearse	1.00
UC6	Peter Warrick	6.00
UC7	Plaxico Burress	3.50
UC8	Travis Taylor	2.50
UC9	Sylvester Morris	2.00
UC10	R. Jay Soward	1.00

2000 Upper Deck Ultimate Victory Crowning Glory

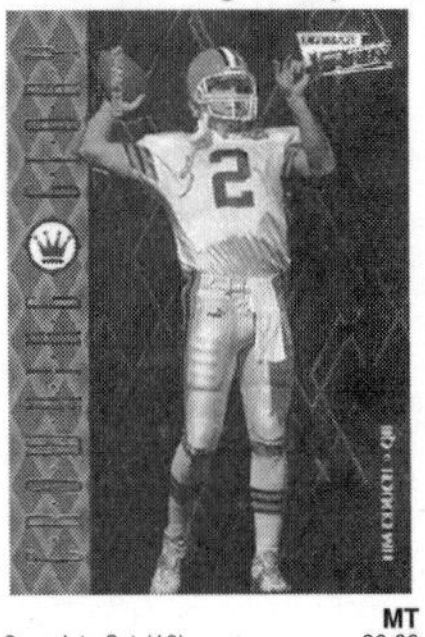

		MT
Complete Set (10):		30.00
Common Player:		2.00
Inserted 1:23		
CG1	Peyton Manning	8.00
CG2	Edgerrin James	8.00
CG3	Randy Moss	8.00
CG4	Tim Couch	5.00
CG5	Eddie George	2.50
CG6	Terrell Davis	6.00
CG7	Marcus Robinson	2.00
CG8	Marvin Harrison	2.00
CG9	Charlie Batch	2.00
CG10	Shaun King	3.00

2000 Upper Deck Ultimate Victory Fabric

		MT
Common Player:		20.00
Inserted 1:239		
IB	Isaac Bruce	30.00
KC	Kevin Carter	20.00
MF	Marshall Faulk	40.00
MF-KW	Marshall Faulk, Kurt Warner 50	
AZ	Az Hakim	20.00
TH	Torry Holt	30.00
TH-IB	Torry Holt, Isaac Bruce 100	85.00
RAMS	Torry Holt, Isaac Bruce, Marshall Faulk, Kurt Warner 10	
KW	Kurt Warner	100.00

2000 Upper Deck Ultimate Victory Legendary Fabrics

		MT
Common Player:		75.00
HL	Howie Long 250	75.00
RL	Ronnie Lott 250	75.00
JM	Joe Montana 250	200.00
HoF	Joe Montana, Ronnie Lott, Howie Long 100	300.00

Values quoted in this guide reflect the retail price of a card — the price a collector can expect to pay when buying a card from a dealer. The wholesale price — that which a collector can expect to receive from a dealer when selling cards — will be significantly lower, depending on desirability and condition.

2000 Upper Deck Vintage Preview

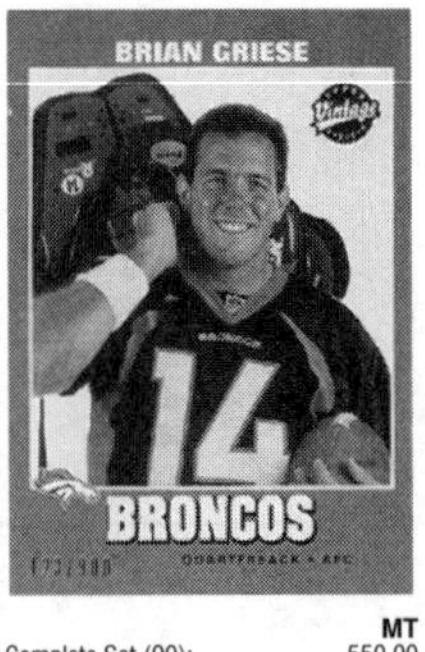

		MT
Complete Set (90):		550.00
Common Player:		.75
Minor Stars:		1.50
Common Rookie (#1-10):		15.00
Production 500 Sets		
Common Rookie (#11-20):		6.00
Production 1,000 Sets		
Common Rookie (#21-40):		4.00
Production 1,500 Sets		
1	*Jamal Lewis*	75.00
2	*Sammy Morris*	15.00
3	*Peter Warrick*	50.00
4	*Travis Prentice*	18.00
5	*Mike Anderson*	75.00
6	*Sylvester Morris*	25.00
7	*Ron Dayne*	60.00
8	*Chad Pennington*	50.00
9	*Plaxico Burress*	25.00
10	*Laveranues Coles*	18.00
11	*Spergon Wynn,Dennis Northcutt*	8.00
12	*Courtney Brown,JaJuan Dawson*	8.00
13	*Raynoch Thompson,Thomas Jones*	15.00
14	*Tom Brady,J.R. Redmond*	10.00
15	*John Abraham,Windrell Hayes*	6.00
16	*Todd Husak,Chris Samuels*	7.00
17	*Giovanni Carmazzi,Tim Rattay*	8.00
18	*Shaun Alexander,Darrell Jackson*	25.00
19	*Rob Morris,Kevin McDougal*	6.00
20	*Brian Urlacher,Dez White*	25.00
21	*Doug Johnson,Darrick Vaughn,Mark Simoneau*	6.00
22	*Chris Redman,John Jones,Travis Taylor*	25.00
23	*Kwame Cavil,Corey Moore,Erik Flowers*	4.00
24	*Ray Green,Lester Towns,Brad Hoover*	25.00
25	*Curtis Keaton,Danny Farmer,Ron Dugans*	6.00
26	*Scottie Montgomery,KaRon Coleman,Deltha O'Neal*	4.00
27	*Bubba Franks,Na'il Diggs,Charles Lee*	8.00
28	*Troy Walters,Chris Hovan,Doug Chapman*	8.00
29	*Chad Morton,Darren Howard,Terrelle Smith*	6.00
30	*Gari Scott,Todd Pinkston,Corey Simon*	8.00
31	*Chris Coleman,Keith Bulluck,Erron Kinney*	4.00
32	*Peter Sirmon,Billy Volek,Bashir Yamini*	4.00
33	*Jason Webster,Ahmed Plummer,Julian Peterson*	6.00
34	*Shockmain Davis,Patrick Pass,Antwan Harris*	4.00
35	*R. Jay Soward,Shyrone Stith,T.J. Slaughter*	8.00
36	*Trevor Gaylor,Ronney Jenkins,Rogers Beckett*	6.00
37	*Tee Martin,Joe Hamilton,Jarious Jackson*	10.00
38	*Chris Cole,Ron Dixon,James Williams*	8.00
39	*Reuben Droughns,Trung Canidate,Frank Moreau*	8.00
40	*Mike Brown,Jerry Porter,Michael Wiley*	8.00
41	Jake Plummer	1.50
42	Jamal Anderson	1.50
43	Qadry Ismail	.75
44	Doug Flutie	2.00
45	Rob Johnson	1.50
46	Steve Beuerlein	.75
47	Marcus Robinson	1.50
48	Cade McNown	1.50
49	Tim Couch	4.00
50	Corey Dillon	1.50
51	Troy Aikman	5.00
52	Emmitt Smith	7.00
53	Charlie Batch	1.50
54	Brian Griese	3.00
55	Terrell Davis	6.00
56	Brett Favre	10.00
57	Antonio Freeman	1.50
58	Peyton Manning	8.00
59	Edgerrin James	8.00
60	Marvin Harrison	1.50
61	Mark Brunell	3.50
62	Fred Taylor	3.50
63	Elvis Grbac	1.50
64	Derrick Alexander	.75
65	Lamar Smith	2.00
66	Daunte Culpepper	5.00
67	Randy Moss	8.00
68	Drew Bledsoe	3.50
69	Vinny Testaverde	1.50
70	Curtis Martin	1.50
71	Kerry Collins	1.50
72	Amani Toomer	.75
73	Jeff Blake	1.50
74	Ricky Williams	5.00
75	Rich Gannon	1.50
76	Tim Brown	1.50
77	Jerome Bettis	1.50
78	Kurt Warner	12.00
79	Marshall Faulk	2.00
80	Junior Seau	1.50
81	Jeff Garcia	1.50
82	Terrell Owens	1.50
83	Jerry Rice	5.00
84	Ricky Watters	1.50
85	Shaun King	2.00
86	Keyshawn Johnson	1.50
87	Steve McNair	1.50
88	Eddie George	3.00
89	Stephen Davis	1.50
90	Brad Johnson	1.50

2001 UD Game Gear

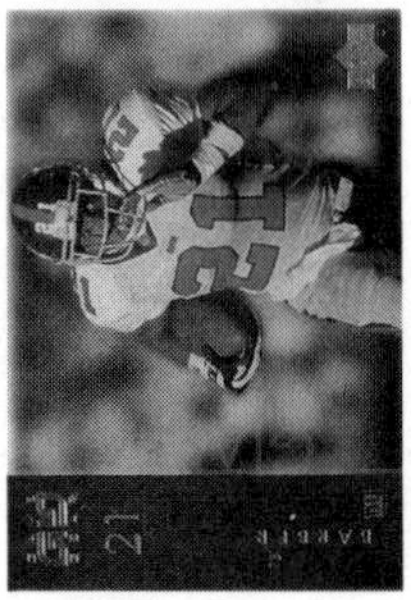

		MT
Complete Set (110):		300.00
Common Player:		.25
Minor Stars:		.50
Common Rookie (91-100):		7.00
Production 1,000 Sets		
Common Rookie (101-110):		10.00
Production 500 Sets		
Pack (4):		10.00
Wax Box (18):		140.00
1	Jake Plummer	1.00
2	David Boston	1.00
3	Jamal Anderson	1.00
4	Shawn Jefferson	.25
5	Jamal Lewis	2.50
6	Elvis Grbac	.50
7	Ray Lewis	.50
8	Rob Johnson	.50
9	Shawn Bryson	.25
10	Muhsin Muhammad	.50
11	Jeff Lewis	.50
12	Marcus Robinson	1.00
13	James Allen	.75
14	Brian Urlacher	2.00
15	Cade McNown	1.00
16	Peter Warrick	1.25
17	Akili Smith	1.00
18	Corey Dillon	1.00
19	Tim Couch	1.25
20	Kevin Johnson	1.00
21	Emmitt Smith	2.50
22	Raghib Ismail	.50
23	Joey Galloway	1.00
24	Terrell Davis	2.50
25	Brian Griese	1.25
26	Ed McCaffrey	1.00
27	Mike Anderson	2.50
28	Charlie Batch	1.00
29	Germane Crowell	1.00
30	James O. Stewart	.75
31	Brett Favre	4.00
32	Dorsey Levens	.75
33	Ahman Green	.75
34	Peyton Manning	3.00
35	Edgerrin James	2.50
36	Marvin Harrison	1.00
37	Mark Brunell	1.25
38	Jimmy Smith	1.00
39	Fred Taylor	1.25
40	Tony Gonzalez	.75
41	Derrick Alexander	.50
42	Trent Green	1.00
43	Lamar Smith	1.00
44	Oronde Gadsden	.50
45	Zach Thomas	.50
46	Randy Moss	3.00
47	Daunte Culpepper	2.00
48	Doug Chapman	.50
49	Cris Carter	1.00
50	Drew Bledsoe	1.25
51	Terry Glenn	1.00
52	Troy Brown	.50
53	Ricky Williams	1.50
54	Jeff Blake	.50
55	Aaron Brooks	1.25
56	Joe Horn	.75
57	Kerry Collins	.75
58	Ron Dayne	1.50
59	Amani Toomer	.50
60	Tiki Barber	.75
61	Vinny Testaverde	.75
62	Curtis Martin	1.00
63	Wayne Chrebet	.75
64	Rich Gannon	.75
65	Jerry Rice	2.00
66	Tim Brown	1.00
67	Duce Staley	1.00
68	Donovan McNabb	1.50
69	Jerome Bettis	1.00
70	Kordell Stewart	1.00
71	Marshall Faulk	1.25
72	Kurt Warner	3.00
73	Torry Holt	1.00
74	Isaac Bruce	1.00
75	Doug Flutie	1.25
76	Junior Seau	.75
77	Jeff Garcia	1.00
78	Terrell Owens	1.00
79	Matt Hasselbeck	1.00
80	Shaun Alexander	1.00
81	Ricky Watters	.75
82	Keyshawn Johnson	1.00
83	Brad Johnson	.75
84	Warrick Dunn	1.00
85	Mike Alstott	1.00
86	Eddie George	1.25
87	Steve McNair	1.00
88	Jeff George	.75
89	Michael Westbrook	.75
90	Stephen Davis	1.00
91	*Mike McMahon*	10.00
92	*James Jackson*	12.00
93	*Quincy Morgan*	12.00
94	*Travis Minor*	7.00
95	*Chris Chambers*	12.00
96	*Jesse Palmer*	7.00
97	*Santana Moss*	15.00
98	*Marques Tuiasosopo*	15.00
99	*Freddie Mitchell*	15.00
100	*Kevan Barlow*	10.00
101	*Michael Vick*	75.00
102	*Chris Weinke*	30.00
103	*Reggie Wayne*	20.00
104	*Robert Ferguson*	10.00
105	*Michael Bennett*	30.00
106	*Deuce McAllister*	35.00
107	*Drew Brees*	65.00
108	*LaDainian Tomlinson*	65.00
109	*Koren Robinson*	30.00
110	*Rod Gardner*	30.00

2001 UD Game Gear Autographs

		MT
Common Player:		10.00
Inserted 1:18		
MB-GS	Michael Bennett	50.00
DB-GS	Drew Brees	75.00
JB-GS	Jim Brown 295	75.00
CC-GS	Chris Chambers	20.00
TD-GS	Terrell Davis 95	40.00
RD-GS	Ron Dayne	25.00
GA-GS	Rich Gannon 360	20.00
JG-GS	Jeff Garcia	25.00
RG-GS	Rod Gardner 150	40.00
AZ-GS	Az-Zahir Hakim	10.00
CJ-GS	Chad Johnson	15.00
JL-GS	Jamal Lewis 295	35.00
PM-GS	Peyton Manning	60.00
DU-GS	Deuce McAllister	25.00
DM-GS	Dan Morgan	15.00
RM-GS	Randy Moss 95	150.00
SM-GS	Santana Moss	25.00
JN-GS	Joe Namath 295	100.00
KY-GS	Ken-Yon Rambo	15.00
JR-GS	John Riggins 395	85.00
KR-GS	Koren Robinson	25.00
DT-GS	David Terrell	25.00
AT-GS	Anthony Thomas	20.00
LT-GS	LaDainian Tomlinson	85.00
MV-GS	Michael Vick 195	100.00
GW-GS	Gerard Warren	15.00
PW-GS	Peter Warrick	20.00
RW-GS	Reggie Wayne	25.00
CW-GS	Chris Weinke 390	50.00

2001 UD Game Gear Jerseys

		MT
Common Player:		10.00
Inserted 1:18		
TA-J	Troy Aikman	30.00
DB-J	Drew Bledsoe	20.00
MB-J	Mark Brunell	20.00
WC-J	Wayne Chrebet	10.00
TC-J	Tim Couch	25.00
RD-J	Ron Dayne	15.00
WD-J	Warrick Dunn	10.00
MF-J	Marshall Faulk	20.00
BF-J	Brett Favre	45.00
RG-J	Rich Gannon	15.00
EG-J	Eddie George	20.00
TG-J	Terry Glenn	10.00
AH-J	Az-Zahir Hakim	10.00
PM-J	Peyton Manning	40.00
SM-J	Steve McNair	20.00
JR-J	Jerry Rice	25.00
ES-J	Emmitt Smith	35.00
RW-J	Ricky Williams	25.00

2001 UD Game Gear Helmets

		MT
Common Player:		18.00
Inserted 1:108		
TA-H	Troy Aikman	50.00
TB-H	Tiki Barber	18.00
KB-H	Kevan Barlow	25.00
MBe-H	Michael Bennett	60.00
DBo-H	David Boston	18.00
DBr-H	Drew Brees	75.00
IB-H	Isaac Bruce	25.00
MBr-H	Mark Brunell	30.00
CD-H	Corey Dillon	25.00
MF-H	Marshall Faulk	30.00
RG-H	Rod Gardner	30.00
TJ-H	Thomas Jones	18.00
PM-H	Peyton Manning	85.00
DM-H	Deuce McAllister	50.00
KM-H	Keenan McCardell	18.00
SM-H	Santana Moss	45.00
JR-H	Jerry Rice	60.00
KR-H	Koren Robinson	30.00
JS-H	Jason Sehorn	18.00
AS-H	Akili Smith	18.00
ES-H	Emmitt Smith	75.00
FT-H	Fred Taylor	30.00
DT-H	David Terrell	30.00
LT-H	LaDainian Tomlinson	65.00
AT-H	Amani Toomer	18.00
MV-H	Michael Vick	125.00
KW-H	Kurt Warner	75.00
PW-H	Peter Warrick	25.00
RW-H	Reggie Wayne	25.00
CW-H	Chris Weinke	50.00

2001 UD Game Gear Uniforms

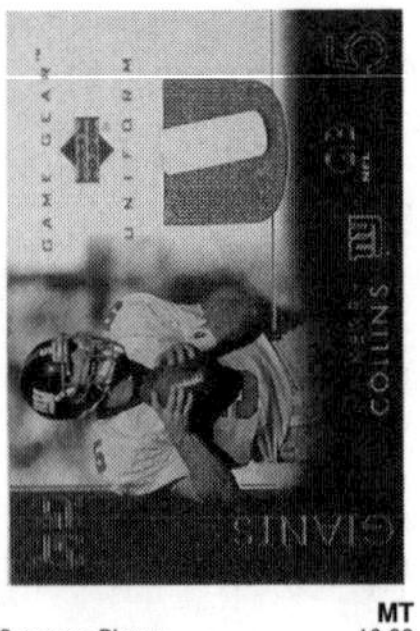

		MT
Common Player:		10.00
Inserted 1:18		
JA-U	Jesse Armstead	10.00
CB-U	Courtney Brown	10.00
JB-U	Jim Brown	50.00
KC-U	Kerry Collins	15.00
RD-U	Ron Dayne	15.00
TH-U	Torry Holt	15.00
JL-U	Jamal Lewis	25.00
RL-U	Ray Lewis	15.00
DM-U	Dan Marino SP	60.00
FM-U	Freddie Mitchell	20.00
RM-U	Randy Moss	45.00
WP-U	Walter Payton	85.00
JP-U	Jim Plunkett	15.00

2001 UD Graded

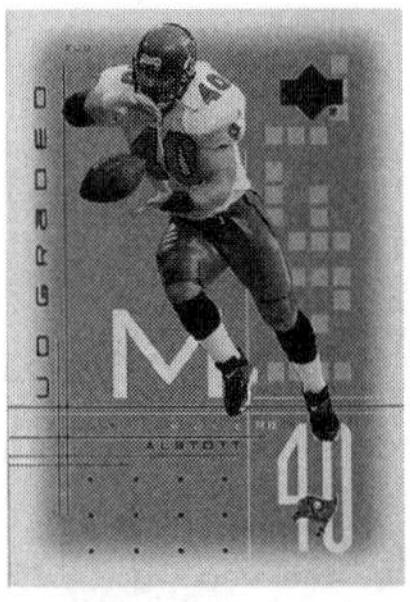

		MT
Complete Set (90):		500.00
Common Player:		.50
Minor Stars:		1.00
Common Rookie:		5.00
Production 900 Sets		
Pack (4plus BGS):		50.00
Wax Box (6):		225.00
1	Jake Plummer	2.00
2	Jamal Anderson	2.00
3	Jamal Lewis	5.00
4	Rob Johnson	1.00
5	Muhsin Muhammad	1.00
6	Marcus Robinson	2.00
7	Peter Warrick	2.50
8	Corey Dillon	2.00
9	Tim Couch	2.50
10	Emmitt Smith	5.00
11	Terrell Davis	4.00
12	Brian Griese	2.50
13	Charlie Batch	2.00
14	Brett Favre	8.00
15	Peyton Manning	7.00
16	Edgerrin James	6.00
17	Mark Brunell	2.50
18	Fred Taylor	2.50
19	Tony Gonzalez	1.00
20	Trent Green	2.00
21	Lamar Smith	1.00
22	Randy Moss	7.00
23	Daunte Culpepper	4.00
24	Drew Bledsoe	2.50
25	Ricky Williams	3.00
26	Kerry Collins	1.00
27	Ron Dayne	3.00
28	Vinny Testaverde	1.00
29	Curtis Martin	2.00
30	Rich Gannon	1.00
31	Charlie Garner	1.00
32	Duce Staley	2.00
33	Donovan McNabb	3.00
34	Jerome Bettis	2.00
35	Marshall Faulk	2.50
36	Kurt Warner	7.00
37	Doug Flutie	2.50
38	Jeff Garcia	2.00
39	Terrell Owens	2.00
40	Matt Hasselbeck	2.00
41	Keyshawn Johnson	2.00
42	Mike Alstott	2.00
43	Eddie George	2.50
44	Steve McNair	2.00
45	Stephen Davis	2.00
46	*Michael Bennett*	30.00
47	*Drew Brees*	50.00
48	*Chad Johnson*	10.00
49	*Deuce McAllister*	25.00
50	*Santana Moss*	20.00
51	*Koren Robinson*	20.00
52	*David Terrell*	25.00
53	*LaDainian Tomlinson*	80.00
54	*Michael Vick*	100.00
55	*Chris Weinke*	30.00
56	*Reggie Wayne*	12.00
57	*Anthony Thomas*	40.00
58	*Sage Rosenfels*	10.00
59	*Rod Gardner*	20.00
60	*Quincy Morgan*	12.00
61	*Freddie Mitchell*	12.00
62	*Gerard Warren*	10.00
63	*James Jackson*	12.00
64	*Travis Henry*	20.00
65	*Chris Chambers*	12.00
66	*Vinny Sutherland*	5.00

67	*Todd Heap*	8.00
68	*Dan Morgan*	5.00
69	*Rudi Johnson*	8.00
70	*Quincy Carter*	20.00
71	*Kevin Kasper*	8.00
72	*Scotty Anderson*	5.00
73	*Mike McMahon*	8.00
74	*Robert Ferguson*	8.00
75	*Marvin "Snoop" Minnis*	12.00
76	*Josh Heupel*	12.00
77	*Travis Minor*	8.00
78	*Justin Smith*	8.00
79	*Jesse Palmer*	8.00
80	*Marques Tuiasosopo*	15.00
81	*A.J. Freely*	5.00
82	*Correl Buckhalter*	12.00
83	*Kevan Barlow*	12.00
84	*Alex Bannister*	8.00
85	*Josh Booty*	8.00
86	*Eddie Berlin*	5.00
87	*Andre Carter*	8.00
88	*LaMont Jordan*	10.00
89	*Ken-Yon Rambo*	7.00
90	*Alge Crumpler*	7.00

2001 UD Graded Jerseys

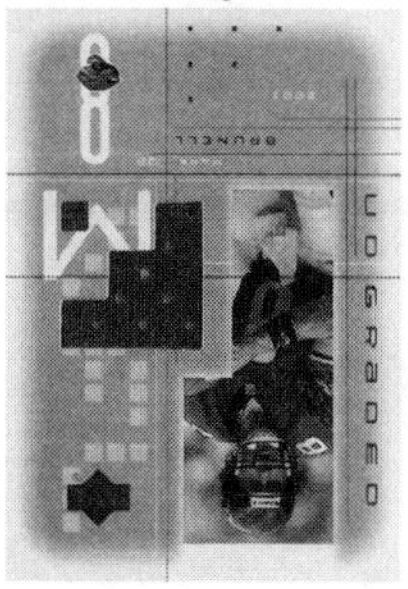

		MT
Common Player:		10.00
Inserted 1:2		
Blue Cards:		1.5x
Production 125 Sets		
TB	Tiki Barber	10.00
CB	Charlie Batch	10.00
DB	David Boston	10.00
MB	Mark Brunell	15.00
CC	Cris Carter	15.00
CH	Chris Chandler	10.00
DC	Daunte Culpepper	25.00
RD	Ron Dayne	15.00
MF	Marshall Faulk	20.00
BF	Brett Favre	45.00
TH	Torry Holt BLUE	30.00
KJ	Keyshawn Johnson	15.00
JL	Jamal Lewis	25.00
PM	Peyton Manning	40.00
KM	Keenan McCardell	10.00
RM	Randy Moss	40.00
JR	Jerry Rice	25.00
SS	Shannon Sharpe	10.00
JS	Jimmy Smith	10.00
KW	Kurt Warner	35.00
PW	Peter Warrick	15.00

2001 UD Graded Rookie Autographs

		MT
Complete Set (20):		
Common Player:		20.00
46	Michael Bennett	125.00
47	Drew Brees	175.00
48	Chad Johnson	30.00
49	Deuce McAllister	65.00
50	Santana Moss	50.00
51	Koren Robinson	50.00
52	David Terrell	50.00
53	LaDainian Tomlinson	175.00
54	Michael Vick	200.00
55	Chris Weinke	100.00
56	Reggie Wayne	25.00
57	Anthony Thomas	30.00
58	Sage Rosenfels	20.00
59	Rod Gardner	30.00
60	Quincy Morgan	30.00
61	Freddie Mitchell	35.00
62	Gerard Warren	20.00
63	James Jackson	40.00
64	Travis Henry	40.00
65	Chris Chambers	35.00

2001 UD Graded Rookie Jerseys

		MT
Common Player:		15.00
46	Michael Bennett	60.00
47	Drew Brees	80.00
48	Chad Johnson	20.00
49	Deuce McAllister	30.00
50	Santana Moss	25.00
51	Koren Robinson	30.00
52	David Terrell	40.00
53	LaDainian Tomlinson	80.00
54	Michael Vick	100.00
55	Chris Weinke	50.00
56	Reggie Wayne	25.00
57	Anthony Thomas	25.00
58	Sage Rosenfels	15.00
59	Rod Gardner	25.00
60	Quincy Morgan	20.00
61	Freddie Mitchell	25.00
62	Gerard Warren	15.00
63	James Jackson	30.00
64	Travis Henry	25.00
65	Chris Chambers	20.00

2001 UD Graded Rookie Series

		MT
Common Player:		10.00
46A	Michael Bennett A Gem Mt	150.00
46A	Michael Bennett A Mt	50.00
46P	Michael Bennett P Gem Mt	200.00
46P	Michael Bennett P Mt	60.00
47A	Drew Brees A Gem Mt	200.00
47A	Drew Brees A Mt	60.00
47P	Drew Brees P Gem Mt	200.00
47P	Drew Brees P Mt	60.00
48A	Chad Johnson A Gem Mt	30.00
48A	Chad Johnson A Mt	10.00
48P	Chad Johnson P Gem Mt	30.00
48P	Chad Johnson P Mt	10.00
49A	Deuce McAllister A Gem Mt	80.00
49A	Deuce McAllister A Mt	30.00
49P	Deuce McAllister P Gem Mt	80.00
49P	Deuce McAllister P Mt	30.00
50A	Santana Moss A Gem Mt	60.00
50A	Santana Moss A Mt	30.00
50P	Santana Moss P Mt	30.00
51A	Koren Robinson A Gem Mt	60.00
51A	Koren Robinson A Mt	30.00
51P	Koren Robinson P Gem Mt	60.00
51P	Koren Robinson P Mt	30.00
52A	David Terrell A Gem Mt	80.00
52A	David Terrell A Mt	30.00
52P	David Terrell P Gem Mt	80.00
52P	David Terrell P Mt	30.00
53A	LaDainian Tomlinson A Gem Mt	250.00
53A	LaDainian Tomlinson A Mt	100.00
53P	LaDainian Tomlinson P Gem Mt	250.00
53P	LaDainian Tomlinson P Mt	100.00
54A	Michael Vick A Gem Mt	275.00
54A	Michael Vick A Mt	110.00
54P	Michael Vick P Gem Mt	300.00
54P	Michael Vick P Mt	120.00
55A	Chris Weinke A Gem Mt	225.00
55A	Chris Weinke A Mt	60.00
55P	Chris Weinke P Gem Mt	175.00
55P	Chris Weinke P Mt	50.00
56A	Reggie Wayne A Mt	10.00
56P	Reggie Wayne P Gem Mt	40.00
56P	Reggie Wayne P Mt	10.00
57A	Anthony Thomas A Gem Mt	50.00
57A	Anthony Thomas A Mt	20.00
57P	Anthony Thomas P Gem Mt	50.00
57P	Anthony Thomas P Mt	20.00
58A	Sage Rosenfels A Gem Mt	30.00
58A	Sage Rosenfels A Mt	10.00
58P	Sage Rosenfels P Gem Mt	30.00
58P	Sage Rosenfels P Mt	10.00
59A	Rod Gardner A Gem Mt	50.00
59A	Rod Gardner A Mt	20.00
59P	Rod Gardner P Gem Mt	50.00
59P	Rod Gardner P Mt	20.00
60A	Quincy Morgan A Gem Mt	30.00
60A	Quincy Morgan A Mt	15.00
60P	Quincy Morgan P Gem Mt	30.00
60P	Quincy Morgan P Mt	15.00
61A	Freddie Mitchell A Gem Mt	40.00
61A	Freddie Mitchell A Mt	20.00
61P	Freddie Mitchell P Gem Mt	40.00
61P	Freddie Mitchell P Mt	20.00
62A	Gerard Warren A Gem Mt	20.00
62A	Gerard Warren A Mt	10.00
62P	Gerard Warren P Gem Mt	20.00
62P	Gerard Warren P Mt	10.00
63A	James Jackson A Gem Mt	40.00
63A	James Jackson A Mt	15.00
63P	James Jackson P Gem Mt	40.00
63P	James Jackson P Mt	15.00
64A	Travis Henry A Gem Mt	60.00
64A	Travis Henry A Mt	25.00
64P	Travis Henry P Gem Mt	60.00
64P	Travis Henry P Mt	25.00
65A	Chris Chambers A Gem Mt	40.00
65A	Chris Chambers A Mt	20.00
65P	Chris Chambers P Gem Mt	40.00
65P	Chris Chambers P Mt	20.00
66A	Vinny Sutherland A Gem Mt	20.00
66A	Vinny Sutherland A Mt	10.00
66P	Vinny Sutherland P Gem Mt	20.00
66P	Vinny Sutherland P Mt	10.00
67A	Todd Heap A Gem Mt	25.00
67A	Todd Heap A Mt	10.00
67P	Todd Heap P Gem Mt	25.00
67P	Todd Heap P Mt	10.00
68A	Dan Morgan A Gem Mt	20.00
68A	Dan Morgan A Mt	10.00
68P	Dan Morgan P Gem Mt	20.00
68P	Dan Morgan P Mt	10.00
69A	Rudi Johnson A Gem Mt	20.00
69A	Rudi Johnson A Mt	10.00
69P	Rudi Johnson P Gem Mt	20.00
69P	Rudi Johnson P Mt	10.00
70A	Quincy Carter A Gem Mt	60.00
70A	Quincy Carter A Mt	25.00
70P	Quincy Carter P Gem Mt	80.00
70P	Quincy Carter P Mt	30.00
70P	Quincy Carter P NmMt+	20.00
71A	Kevin Kasper A Gem Mt	20.00
71A	Kevin Kasper A Mt	10.00
71P	Kevin Kasper P Gem Mt	20.00
71P	Kevin Kasper P Mt	10.00
72A	Scotty Anderson A Gem Mt	20.00
72A	Scotty Anderson A Mt	10.00
72P	Scotty Anderson P Gem Mt	20.00
72P	Scotty Anderson P Mt	10.00
73A	Mike McMahon A Gem Mt	25.00
73A	Mike McMahon A Mt	12.00
73P	Mike McMahon P Gem Mt	25.00
73P	Mike McMahon P Mt	12.00
74A	Robert Ferguson A Gem Mt	20.00
74A	Robert Ferguson A Mt	10.00
74P	Robert Ferguson P Gem Mt	20.00
74P	Robert Ferguson P Mt	10.00
75A	Marvin "Snoop" Minnis A Gem Mt	40.00
75A	Marvin "Snoop" Minnis A Mt	20.00
75P	Marvin "Snoop" Minnis P Gem Mt	40.00
75P	Marvin "Snoop" Minnis P Mt	20.00
76A	Josh Heupel A Gem Mt	35.00
76A	Josh Heupel A Mt	15.00
76P	Josh Heupel P Gem Mt	35.00
76P	Josh Heupel P Mt	15.00
77A	Travis Minor A Gem Mt	30.00
77A	Travis Minor A Mt	12.00
77P	Travis Minor P Gem Mt	30.00
77P	Travis Minor P Mt	12.00
78A	Justin Smith A Gem Mt	20.00
78A	Justin Smith A Mt	10.00
78P	Justin Smith P Gem Mt	20.00
78P	Justin Smith P Mt	10.00
79A	Jesse Palmer A Gem Mt	30.00
79A	Jesse Palmer A Mt	12.00
79P	Jesse Palmer P Gem Mt	30.00
79P	Jesse Palmer P Mt	12.00
80A	Marques Tuiasosopo A Gem Mt	40.00
80A	Marques Tuiasosopo A Mt	20.00
80P	Marques Tuiasosopo P Gem Mt	40.00
80P	Marques Tuiasosopo P Mt	20.00
81A	A.J. Feeley A Gem Mt	20.00
81A	A.J. Feeley A Mt	10.00
81P	A.J. Feeley P Gem Mt	20.00
81P	A.J. Feeley P Mt	10.00
82A	Correll Buckhalter A Gem Mt	30.00
82A	Correll Buckhalter A Mt	15.00
82P	Correll Buckhalter P Gem Mt	30.00
82P	Correll Buckhalter P Mt	15.00
83A	Kevan Barlow A Gem Mt	40.00
83A	Kevan Barlow A Mt	20.00
83P	Kevan Barlow P Gem Mt	40.00
83P	Kevan Barlow P Mt	20.00
84A	Alex Bannister A Gem Mt	20.00
84A	Alex Bannister A Mt	10.00
84P	Alex Bannister P Gem Mt	20.00
84P	Alex Bannister P Mt	10.00
85A	Josh Booty A Gem Mt	20.00
85A	Josh Booty A Mt	10.00
85P	Josh Booty P Gem Mt	20.00
85P	Josh Booty P Mt	10.00
86A	Eddie Berlin A Gem Mt	20.00
86A	Eddie Berlin A Mt	10.00
86P	Eddie Berlin P Gem Mt	20.00
86P	Eddie Berlin P Mt	10.00
87A	Andre Carter A Gem Mt	20.00
87A	Andre Carter A Mt	10.00
87P	Andre Carter P Gem Mt	20.00
87P	Andre Carter P Mt	10.00
88A	LaMont Jordan A Gem Mt	25.00
88A	LaMont Jordan A Mt	12.00
88P	LaMont Jordan P Gem Mt	25.00
88P	LaMont Jordan P Mt	12.00
89A	Ken-Yon Rambo A Gem Mt	20.00
89A	Ken-Yon Rambo A Mt	10.00
89P	Ken-Yon Rambo P Gem Mt	20.00
89P	Ken-Yon Rambo P Mt	10.00
90A	Alge Crumpler A Gem Mt	20.00
90A	Alge Crumpler A Mt	10.00
90P	Alge Crumpler P Gem Mt	20.00
90P	Alge Crumpler P Mt	10.00

2001 UD Graded Rookie Series Autographs Graded

		MT
Common Player:		20.00
46	Michael Bennett Mt	180.00
46	Michael Bennett NmMt+	120.00
47	Drew Brees Mt	200.00
47	Drew Brees NmMt+	150.00
48	Chad Johnson Mt	40.00
48	Chad Johnson NmMt+	30.00
49	Deuce McAllister Mt	80.00
49	Deuce McAllister NmMt+	60.00
50	Santana Moss Mt	60.00
50	Santana Moss NmMt+	50.00
51	Koren Robinson Mt	50.00
51	Koren Robinson NmMt+	40.00
52	David Terrell Mt	60.00
52	David Terrell NmMt+	50.00
53	LaDainian Tomlinson Mt	200.00
53	LaDainian Tomlinson NmMt+	150.00
54	Michael Vick Mt	300.00
54	Michael Vick NmMt+	200.00
55	Chris Weinke Mt	125.00
55	Chris Weinke NmMt+	100.00
56	Reggie Wayne Gem Mt	100.00
56	Reggie Wayne Mt	40.00
56	Reggie Wayne NmMt+	25.00
57	Anthony Thomas Mt	50.00
57	Anthony Thomas NmMt+	30.00
58	Sage Rosenfels Mt	35.00
58	Sage Rosenfels NmMt+	25.00
59	Rod Gardner Mt	40.00
59	Rod Gardner NmMt+	30.00
60	Quincy Morgan Mt	40.00
60	Quincy Morgan NmMt+	30.00
61	Freddie Mitchell Mt	50.00
61	Freddie Mitchell NmMt+	40.00
62	Gerard Warren Mt	25.00
62	Gerard Warren NmMt+	20.00
63	James Jackson Mt	50.00
63	James Jackson NmMt+	40.00
64	Travis Henry Mt	50.00
64	Travis Henry NmMt+	40.00
65	Chris Chambers Mt	40.00
65	Chris Chambers NmMt+	30.00

2001 UD Graded Rookie Series Jerseys Graded

		MT
Common Player:		15.00
46	Michael Bennett Mt	100.00
46	Michael Bennett NmMt+	60.00
47	Drew Brees Gem Mt	275.00
47	Drew Brees Mt	130.00
47	Drew Brees NmMt+	70.00
48	Chad Johnson Mt	25.00
48	Chad Johnson NmMt+	20.00
49	Deuce McAllister Gem Mt	100.00
49	Deuce McAllister Mt	40.00
49	Deuce McAllister NmMt+	30.00
50	Santana Moss Gem Mt	80.00
50	Santana Moss Mt	30.00
50	Santana Moss NmMt+	25.00
51	Koren Robinson Gem Mt	100.00
51	Koren Robinson Mt	40.00
51	Koren Robinson NmMt+	30.00
53	LaDainian Tomlinson Gem Mt	275.00
53	LaDainian Tomlinson Mt	130.00
53	LaDainian Tomlinson NmMt+	70.00
54	Michael Vick Gem Mt	300.00
54	Michael Vick Mt	150.00
54	Michael Vick NmMt+	100.00
55	Chris Weinke Gem Mt	180.00
55	Chris Weinke Mt	70.00
55	Chris Weinke NmMt+	50.00
56	Reggie Wayne Gem Mt	60.00
56	Reggie Wayne Mt	30.00
56	Reggie Wayne NmMt+	25.00
58	Sage Rosenfels Mt	25.00
58	Sage Rosenfels NmMt+	15.00
59	Rod Gardner Gem Mt	80.00
59	Rod Gardner Mt	30.00
59	Rod Gardner NmMt+	25.00
60	Quincy Morgan Mt	25.00
60	Quincy Morgan NmMt+	20.00
61	Freddie Mitchell Gem Mt	70.00
61	Freddie Mitchell Mt	25.00
61	Freddie Mitchell NmMt+	20.00
62	Gerard Warren Gem Mt	40.00
62	Gerard Warren Mt	25.00
62	Gerard Warren NmMt+	15.00
63	James Jackson Mt	40.00
63	James Jackson NmMt+	30.00
64	Travis Henry Mt	30.00
64	Travis Henry NmMt+	25.00
65	Chris Chambers Gem Mt	60.00
65	Chris Chambers Mt	25.00
65	Chris Chambers NmMt+	20.00

2001 UD Top Tier

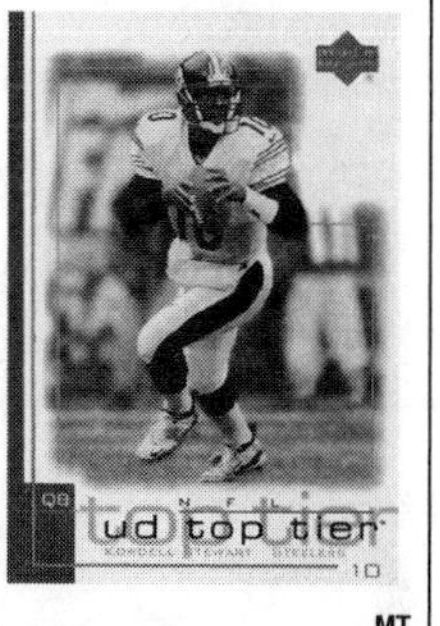

		MT
Complete Set (280):		450.00
Common Player:		.25
Minor Stars:		.50
Common Rookie:		2.00
Pack (5):		3.00
Wax Box (24):		50.00
1	Jake Plummer	.75
2	David Boston	.75
3	Thomas Jones	.50
4	Frank Sanders	.50
5	Tony Martin	.25
6	Jamal Anderson	.75
7	Chris Chandler	.50
8	Shawn Jefferson	.25
9	Jammi German	.25
10	Terance Mathis	.25
11	Jamal Lewis	2.00
12	Shannon Sharpe	.50
13	Elvis Grbac	.50
14	Ray Lewis	.75
15	Qadry Ismail	.25
16	Sam Gash	.25
17	Rob Johnson	.50
18	Eric Moulds	.75
19	Sammy Morris	.50
20	Shawn Bryson	.25
21	Jeremy McDaniel	.25
22	Muhsin Muhammad	.50
23	Brad Hoover	.50
24	Tim Biakabutuka	.25
25	Donald Hayes	.25
26	Dameyune Craig	.25
27	Wesley Walls	.50
28	Cade McNown	.75
29	James Allen	.50
30	Marcus Robinson	.75
31	Brian Urlacher	1.50
32	Bobby Engram	.25
33	Shane Matthews	.50
34	Peter Warrick	1.00
35	Corey Dillon	.75
36	Akili Smith	.75
37	Scott Mitchell	.50
38	Jon Kitna	.50
39	Tim Couch	1.00
40	Kevin Johnson	.75
41	Travis Prentice	.50
42	Spergon Wynn	.25
43	Jamel White	.25
44	JaJuan Dawson	.50
45	Courtney Brown	.50
46	Tony Banks	.50
47	Emmitt Smith	2.00
48	Joey Galloway	.75
49	Raghib Ismail	.25
50	Anthony Wright	.50
51	Darren Woodson	.25
52	Terrell Davis	1.50
53	Mike Anderson	2.00
54	Brian Griese	1.00
55	Rod Smith	.75
56	Ed McCaffrey	.50
57	Eddie Kennison	.25
58	Olandis Gary	.75
59	Charlie Batch	.75
60	Germane Crowell	.75
61	James O. Stewart	.50
62	Johnnie Morton	.50
63	Desmond Howard	.25
64	Brett Favre	3.00
65	Antonio Freeman	.75
66	Dorsey Levens	.50
67	Ahman Green	.75
68	Bill Schroeder	.50
69	Bubba Franks	.25
70	Peyton Manning	2.50
71	Edgerrin James	2.00
72	Marvin Harrison	.75
73	Jerome Pathon	.25
74	Lennox Gordon	.25
75	Terrence Wilkins	.25
76	Mark Brunell	1.00
77	Fred Taylor	1.00
78	Jimmy Smith	.75
79	Keenan McCardell	.50
80	Kevin Hardy	.25
81	Stacey Mack	.25
82	Tony Gonzalez	.75
83	Derrick Alexander	.50
84	Priest Holmes	.50
85	Trent Green	.75
86	Tony Horne	.25
87	Oronde Gadsden	.50
88	Lamar Smith	.75
89	Jay Fiedler	.75
90	Zach Thomas	.50
91	Ray Lucas	.50
92	O.J. McDuffie	.50
93	Randy Moss	2.50
94	Cris Carter	.75
95	Daunte Culpepper	1.50
96	Robert Griffith	.25
97	Jake Reed	.50
98	Drew Bledsoe	1.00
99	Terry Glenn	.50
100	Kevin Faulk	.25
101	Michael Bishop	.50
102	Troy Brown	.25
103	Ricky Williams	1.25
104	Jeff Blake	.50
105	Joe Horn	.50
106	Willie Jackson	.25
107	Aaron Brooks	1.00
108	Albert Connell	.50
109	Kerry Collins	.50
110	Amani Toomer	.50
111	Ron Dayne	1.25
112	Tiki Barber	.50
113	Ike Hilliard	.50
114	Ron Dixon	.25
115	Michael Strahan	.50
116	Vinny Testaverde	.50
117	Wayne Chrebet	.50
118	Curtis Martin	.75
119	Richie Anderson	.25
120	Laveranues Coles	.50
121	Chad Pennington	1.50
122	Tim Brown	.75
123	Rich Gannon	.50
124	Tyrone Wheatley	.25
125	Charlie Garner	.50
126	Jerry Rice	1.75
127	Charles Woodson	.75
128	Duce Staley	.75
129	Donovan McNabb	1.25
130	Todd Pinkston	.50
131	Chad Lewis	.25
132	Brian Mitchell	.25
133	Kordell Stewart	.75
134	Jerome Bettis	.75
135	Plaxico Burress	.75
136	Bobby Shaw	.25
137	Hines Ward	.50
138	Marshall Faulk	1.00
139	Kurt Warner	2.75
140	Isaac Bruce	.75
141	Torry Holt	.75
142	Justin Watson	.25
143	Az-Zahir Hakim	.50
144	Junior Seau	.50
145	Curtis Conway	.50
146	Doug Flutie	1.00
147	Jeff Graham	.25
148	Freddie Jones	.50
149	Rodney Harrison	.25
150	Jeff Garcia	.75
151	Tai Streets	.50
152	Terrell Owens	.75
153	J.J. Stokes	.50
154	Garrison Hearst	.50
155	Paul Smith	.25
156	Ricky Watters	.50
157	Shaun Alexander	1.00
158	Matt Hasselbeck	.75
159	Brock Huard	.50
160	Darrell Jackson	.75
161	Karsten Bailey	.25
162	Warrick Dunn	.75
163	Shaun King	.50
164	Reidel Anthony	.25
165	Mike Alstott	.75
166	Jacquez Green	.25
167	Brad Johnson	.50
168	Keyshawn Johnson	.75
169	Eddie George	1.00
170	Steve McNair	.75
171	Neil O'Donnell	.25
172	Derrick Mason	.50
173	Frank Wycheck	.25
174	Chris Sanders	.25
175	Jevon Kearse	.75
176	Jeff George	.50
177	Stephen Davis	.75
178	Kevin Lockett	.25
179	Michael Westbrook	.50
180	Stephen Alexander	.25
181	*Arnold Jackson 2,000*	3.00
182	*Bobby Newcombe 2,000*	5.00
183	*Vinny Sutherland 2,000*	5.00
184	*Michael Vick 1,500*	40.00
185	*Quentin McCord 2,500*	2.00
186	*Todd Heap 1,500*	6.00
187	*Chris Barnes 2,000*	4.00
188	*Travis Henry 1,500*	12.00
189	*Reggie Germany 2,500*	4.00
190	*Tim Hasselbeck 2,000*	5.00
191	*Dan Morgan 2,500*	3.00
192	*Dadrian "Dee" Brown 2,000*	3.00
193	*Chris Weinke 2,000*	20.00
194	*David Terrell 1,500*	20.00
195	*Anthony Thomas 1,500*	30.00
196	*Rudi Johnson 2,500*	6.00
197	*Chad Johnson 1,500*	7.00
198	*Quincy Morgan 2,500*	7.00
199	*James Jackson 1,500*	10.00
200	*Quincy Carter 2,000*	12.00
201	*Kevin Kasper 2,500*	5.00
202	*Scotty Anderson 2,000*	3.00
203	*Mike McMahon 1,500*	7.00
204	*Robert Ferguson 1,500*	6.00
205	*David Martin 2,000*	3.00
206	*Reggie Wayne 2,000*	8.00
207	*Kabeer Gbaja-Biamila 2,500*	15.00
208	*Marvin "Snoop" Minnis 2,000*	8.00
209	*Derrick Blaylock 1,500*	4.00
210	*Josh Heupel 2,500*	5.00
211	*Travis Minor 2,000*	5.00
212	*Chris Chambers 2,000*	10.00
213	*Michael Bennett 1,500*	20.00
214	*Justin Smith 1,500*	5.00
215	*Deuce McAllister 2,000*	12.00
216	*Moran Norris 2,500*	2.00
217	*Onomo Ojo 2,500*	3.00
218	*Jesse Palmer 1,500*	5.00
219	*Santana Moss 2,000*	10.00
220	*LaMont Jordan 2,000*	5.00
221	*Marques Tuiasosopo 2,000*	10.00
222	*A.J. Feeley 1,500*	4.00
223	*Correl Buckhalter 1,500*	10.00
224	*Freddie Mitchell 2,000*	10.00
225	*Chris Taylor 2,500*	2.00
226	*Drew Brees 1,500*	30.00
227	*LaDainian Tomlinson 1,500*	30.00
228	*Dave Dickenson 2,000*	7.00
229	*Kevan Barlow 2,000*	10.00
230	*Andre Carter 2,000*	6.00
231	*Cedrick Wilson 2,000*	5.00
232	*David Allen 2,500*	3.00
233	*Alex Bannister 1,500*	5.00
234	*Josh Booty 2,000*	5.00
235	*Koren Robinson 2,500*	10.00
236	*Damione Lewis 2,000*	4.00
237	*Eddie Berlin 2,500*	2.00
238	*Darnerian McCants 1,500*	4.00
239	*Sage Rosenfels 2,500*	5.00
240	*Rod Gardner 1,500*	12.00
241	*Billy Baber 2,500*	2.00
242	*Dan Alexander 2,000*	5.00
243	*Reggie White 2,500*	3.00
244	*Adam Archuleta 2,000*	6.00
245	*Derrick Gibson 2,500*	2.00
246	*Hakim Akbar 2,000*	2.00
247	*Brandon Manumaleuna 2,500*	3.00
248	*Andre King 2,500*	2.00
249	*Corey Alston 2,500*	2.00
250	*Fred Smoot 1,500*	6.00
251	*Kyle Vanden Bosch 2,500*	4.00
252	*Richard Seymour 1,500*	5.00
253	*Derek Combs 2,000*	4.00
254	*Ken-Yon Rambo 2,500*	5.00
255	*Joey Getherall 2,000*	4.00
256	*Jonathan Carter 1,500*	4.00
257	*Gerard Warren 1,500*	8.00
258	*Carlos Polk 2,000*	3.00
259	*Milton Wynn 2,500*	3.00
260	*Ronney Daniels 2,000*	3.00
261	*Edgerton Hartwell 1,500*	4.00
262	*Steve Smith 2,000*	4.00
263	*T.J. Houshmandzadeh 1,500*	4.00
264	*Alge Crumpler 2,000*	5.00
265	*Torrance Marshall 1,500*	5.00
266	*Tommy Polley 2,000*	3.00
267	*Sedrick Hodge 2,000*	2.00
268	*Kendrell Bell 2,500*	6.00
269	*Jamie Winborn 1,500*	4.00
270	*Brian Allen 2,000*	2.00
271	*Brandon Spoon 1,500*	5.00
272	*Paul Toviessa 2,000*	2.00
273	*Aaron Schobel 2,500*	2.00
274	*Will Allen 2,500*	5.00
275	*Jamar Fletcher 1,500*	5.00
276	*Andre Dyson 2,000*	2.00
277	*Nate Clements 2,500*	3.00
278	*Willie Middlebrooks 2,500*	2.00
279	*Ken Lucas 2,500*	2.00
280	*Jamal Reynolds 2,000*	5.00

2001 UD Top Tier Home/Away Jerseys

		MT
Common Player:		15.00
Inserted 1:239		
HA-KB	Kevan Barlow	20.00
HA-MB	Michael Bennett	30.00
HA-DB	Drew Brees	40.00
HA-CC	Chris Chambers	20.00
HA-RF	Robert Ferguson	15.00
HA-RG	Rod Gardner	20.00
HA-TH	Travis Henry	20.00
HA-JH	Josh Heupel	15.00
HA-JJ	James Jackson	20.00
HA-RJ	Rudi Johnson	15.00
HA-MC	Deuce McAllister	25.00
HA-MM	Mike McMahon	18.00
HA-TM	Travis Minor	15.00
HA-FM	Freddie Mitchell	20.00
HA-DM	Dan Morgan	15.00
HA-QM	Quincy Morgan	18.00
HA-SM	Santana Moss	20.00
HA-JP	Jesse Palmer	15.00
HA-KR	Koren Robinson	20.00
HA-LT	LaDainian Tomlinson	50.00
HA-MT	Marques Tuiasosopo	18.00
HA-MV	Michael Vick	50.00
HA-RW	Reggie Wayne	18.00

2001 UD Top Tier Rookie Duos

		MT
Common Player:		15.00
Inserted 1:239		
RD-BT	Drew Brees, LaDainian Tomlinson	45.00
RD-HC	Josh Heupel, Chris Chambers	18.00
RD-TT	David Terrell, Anthony Thomas	30.00
RD-WM	Chris Weinke, Dan Morgan	20.00
RD-JJ	Chad Johnson, Rudi Johnson	15.00
RD-RG	Sage Rosenfels, Rod Gardner	20.00
RD-MJ	Quincy Morgan, James Jackson	20.00
RD-VB	Michael Vick, Drew Brees	45.00
RD-GR	Koren Robinson, Rod Gardner	20.00
RD-MW	Reggie Wayne, Santana Moss	20.00

2001 UD Top Tier Then and Now Jerseys

		MT
Common Player:		15.00
Inserted 1:239		
TN-TA	Troy Aikman	50.00
TN-RD	Ron Dayne	30.00
TN-KJ	Keyshawn Johnson	15.00
TN-DM	Deuce McAllister	20.00
TN-FM	Freddie Mitchell	20.00
TN-JS	Junior Seau	15.00
TN-JJ	J.J. Stokes	15.00

2001 UD Top Tier Two of a Kind

		MT
Common Player:		15.00
Inserted 1:239		
2K-UM	Brian Urlacher, Dan Morgan	20.00
2K-DB	Ron Dayne, Michael Bennett	20.00
2K-NO	Ricky Williams, Deuce McAllister	20.00
2K-MT	Randy Moss, David Terrell	30.00
2K-CV	Daunte Culpepper, Michael Vick	35.00
2K-WM	Peter Warrick, Marvin "Snoop" Minnis	15.00
2K-FF	Brett Favre, Robert Ferguson	35.00
2K-JT	Edgerrin James, LaDainian Tomlinson	35.00
2K-JJ	Keyshawn Johnson, Chad Johnson	15.00

2001 UD Top Tier Tri-Stars

		MT
Common Player:		20.00
Inserted 1:239		
3S-SF	Jeff Garcia, Terrell Owens, J.J. Stokes	20.00
3S-CH	Cade McNown, Brian Urlacher, David Terrell	30.00
3S-IC	Edgerrin James, Peyton Manning, Marvin Harrison	40.00
3S-MV	Daunte Culpepper, Randy Moss, Cris Carter	40.00
3S-MD	Josh Heupel, Travis Minor, Chris Chambers	25.00
3S-NO	Aaron Brooks, Ricky Williams, Joe Horn	25.00
3S-GB	Brett Favre, Ahman Green, Antonio Freeman	50.00
3S-TB	Warrick Dunn, Mike Alstott, Keyshawn Johnson	20.00

Post-1980 cards in Near Mint condition will generally sell for about 75% of the quoted Mint value. Excellent-condition cards bring no more than 40%.

2001 UD Vintage

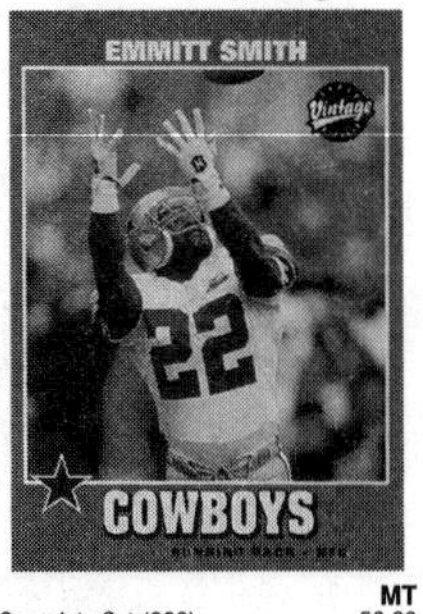
EMMITT SMITH
COWBOYS

		MT
Complete Set (290):		50.00
Common Player:		.10
Minor Stars:		.20
Common Rookies:		.50
Pack (10):		2.00
Wax Box (24):		35.00
1	Jake Plummer	.50
2	David Boston	.50
3	Thomas Jones	.30
4	Frank Sanders	.20
5	Bob Christian	.10
6	Jamal Anderson	.50
7	Chris Chandler	.20
8	Shawn Jefferson	.10
9	Brian Finneran	.10
10	Terance Mathis	.20
11	Jamal Lewis	1.00
12	Shannon Sharpe	.30
13	Elvis Grbac	.30
14	Ray Lewis	.50
15	Qadry Ismail	.30
16	Brandon Stokely	.30
17	Rob Johnson	.50
18	Eric Moulds	.50
19	Sammy Morris	.30
20	Shawn Bryson	.30
21	Jeremy McDaniel	.10
22	Muhsin Muhammad	.30
23	Brad Hoover	.50
24	Tim Biakabutuka	.30
25	Donald Hayes	.30
26	Jeff Lewis	.30
27	Wesley Walls	.30
28	Cade McNown	.50
29	James Allen	.50
30	Marcus Robinson	.50
31	Brian Urlacher	1.50
32	Jim Miller	.30
33	Peter Warrick	1.50
34	Corey Dillon	.50
35	Akili Smith	.50
36	Danny Farmer	.30
37	Ron Dugans	.30
38	Jon Kitna	.50
39	Tim Couch	.75
40	Kevin Johnson	.50
41	Travis Prentice	.50
42	Spergon Wynn	.30
43	Errict Rhett	.30
44	Dennis Northcutt	.30
45	Courtney Brown	.30
46	Tony Banks	.30
47	Emmitt Smith	1.00
48	Joey Galloway	.50
49	Raghib Ismail	.30
50	Anthony Wright	.30
51	Jackie Harris	.10
52	Terrell Davis	1.00
53	Mike Anderson	1.00
54	Brian Griese	.60
55	Rod Smith	.50
56	Ed McCaffrey	.50
57	Howard Griffith	.10
58	Olandis Gary	.30
59	Charlie Batch	.50
60	Germane Crowell	.50
61	James O. Stewart	.30
62	Johnnie Morton	.30
63	Desmond Howard	.10
64	Brett Favre	1.50
65	Antonio Freeman	.50
66	Dorsey Levens	.30
67	Ahman Green	.30
68	Bill Schroeder	.30
69	Bubba Franks	.30
70	Peyton Manning	1.25
71	Edgerrin James	1.25
72	Marvin Harrison	.50
73	Jerome Pathon	.10
74	Ken Dilger	.10
75	Terrence Wilkins	.30
76	Mark Brunell	.60
77	Fred Taylor	.60
78	Jimmy Smith	.30
79	Keenan McCardell	.20
80	R. Jay Soward	.20
81	Todd Collins	.10
82	Tony Gonzalez	.30
83	Derrick Alexander	.20
84	Trent Green	.40
85	Sylvester Morris	.30
86	Oronde Gadsden	.30
87	Lamar Smith	.40
88	Jay Fiedler	.50
89	Zach Thomas	.30
90	Ray Lucas	.30
91	O.J. McDuffie	.30
92	Randy Moss	1.25
93	Cris Carter	.50
94	Daunte Culpepper	.75
95	Robert Griffith	.10
96	Jake Reed	.60
97	Drew Bledsoe	.60
98	Terry Glenn	.30
99	Kevin Faulk	.30
100	Michael Bishop	.30
101	Troy Brown	.10
102	Ricky Williams	.30
103	Jeff Blake	.30
104	Joe Horn	.30
105	Willie Jackson	.20
106	Aaron Brooks	.50
107	Keith Poole	.10
108	Kerry Collins	.30
109	Amani Toomer	.20
110	Ron Dayne	.75
111	Tiki Barber	.30
112	Ike Hilliard	.20
113	Ron Dixon	.20
114	Michael Strahan	.10
115	Vinny Testaverde	.30
116	Wayne Chrebet	.30
117	Curtis Martin	.50
118	Richie Anderson	.10
119	Laveranues Coles	.50
120	Chad Pennington	.75
121	Tim Brown	.40
122	Rich Gannon	.30
123	Tyrone Wheatley	.30
124	Charlie Garner	.30
125	Andre Rison	.30
126	Charles Woodson	.30
127	Jon Ritchie	.10
128	Duce Staley	.50
129	Donovan McNabb	.60
130	Darnell Autry	.20
131	Chad Lewis	.20
132	Brian Mitchell	.10
133	Kordell Stewart	.40
134	Jerome Bettis	.40
135	Plaxico Burress	.40
136	Bobby Shaw	.20
137	Hines Ward	.20
138	Marshall Faulk	.60
139	Kurt Warner	1.50
140	Isaac Bruce	.50
141	Torry Holt	.50
142	Justin Watson	.10
143	Az-Zahir Hakim	.20
144	Junior Seau	.30
145	Curtis Conway	.20
146	Doug Flutie	.50
147	Jeff Graham	.10
148	Freddie Jones	.30
149	Rodney Harrison	.10
150	Jeff Garcia	.50
151	Jerry Rice	1.00
152	Jonas Lewis	.10
153	Terrell Owens	.50
154	J.J. Stokes	.20
155	Garrison Hearst	.30
156	Ricky Watters	.30
157	Shaun Alexander	.50
158	Matt Hasselbeck	.50
159	Brock Huard	.30
160	Darrell Jackson	.50
161	Itula Mili	.10
162	Warrick Dunn	.50
163	Shaun King	.40
164	Reidel Anthony	.20
165	Mike Alstott	.50
166	Jacquez Green	.20
167	Brad Johnson	.40
168	Keyshawn Johnson	.50
169	Eddie George	.60
170	Steve McNair	.50
171	Neil O'Donnell	.20
172	Derrick Mason	.40
173	Frank Wycheck	.10
174	Chris Sanders	.10
175	Jevon Kearse	.50
176	Jeff George	.30
177	Stephen Davis	.50
178	Skip Hicks	.30
179	Michael Westbrook	.30
180	Stephen Alexander	.10
181	Vinny Testaverde	.10
182	Trent Green	.20
183	Brian Griese	.30
184	Kerry Collins	.20
185	Aaron Brooks	.25
186	Jamal Lewis	.50
187	Jeff Garcia	.20
188	Warrick Dunn	.20
189	Mike Anderson	.50
190	Lamar Smith	.20
191	Daunte Culpepper	.40
192	Darren Sharper	.10
193	Marvin Harrison	.20
194	Torry Holt	.20
195	Trent Green	.20
196	Peyton Manning	.50
197	Muhsin Muhammad	.20
198	La'Roi Glover	.10
199	Brian Griese	.30
200	Darrick Vaughn	.10
201	*Bobby Newcombe*	1.00
202	*Leonard Davis*	.50
203	*Alge Crumpler*	1.00
204	*Michael Vick*	8.00
205	*Vinny Sutherland*	1.00
206	*Chris Barnes*	1.00
207	*Todd Heap*	1.00
208	*Travis Henry*	2.50
209	*Tim Hasselbeck*	1.00
210	*Nate Clements*	.50
211	*Chris Weinke*	4.00
212	*Dan Morgan*	1.00
213	*Anthony Thomas*	6.00
214	*David Terrell*	3.50
215	*Chad Johnson*	1.25
216	*Justin Smith*	1.00
217	*Rudi Johnson*	1.25
218	*T.J. Houshmandzadeh*	.50
219	*Gerard Warren*	1.00
220	*James Jackson*	1.25
221	*Quincy Morgan*	1.25
222	*Quincy Carter*	3.00
223	*Tony Dixon*	.50
224	*Kevin Kasper*	.75
225	*Willie Middlebrooks*	.75
226	*Mike McMahon*	1.25
227	*Shaun Rogers*	.50
228	*Jamal Reynolds*	.75
229	*Robert Ferguson*	1.25
230	*Reggie Wayne*	2.00
231	*Marcus Stroud*	.75
232	*Dustin McClintock*	.75
233	*Marvin "Snoop" Minnis*	1.75
234	*Chris Chambers*	1.50
235	*Josh Heupel*	2.50
236	*Travis Minor*	1.25
237	*Michael Bennett*	5.00
238	*Richard Seymour*	.75
239	*Hakim Akbar*	.50
240	*Deuce McAllister*	3.00
241	*Moran Norris*	.50
242	*Jesse Palmer*	1.00
243	*Will Allen*	.75
244	*LaMont Jordan*	1.25
245	*Santana Moss*	3.00
246	*Marques Tuiasosopo*	2.00
247	*Correl Buckhalter*	1.50
248	*Freddie Mitchell*	2.00
249	*A.J. Feeley*	.75
250	*Dave Dickenson*	1.00
251	*Drew Brees*	6.00
252	*LaDainian Tomlinson*	6.00
253	*David Allen*	.75
254	*Andre Carter*	1.00
255	*Kevan Barlow*	1.50
256	*Josh Booty*	1.00
257	*Koren Robinson*	2.50
258	*Adam Archuleta*	1.00
259	*Rod Gardner*	2.50
260	*Sage Rosenfels*	1.25
261	*Reggie Germany, Ken-Yon Rambo*	2.00
262	*Edgerton Hartwell, Gary Baxter*	.75
263	*Aaron Schobel, Brandon Spoon*	.75
264	*John Capel, Karon Riley*	.75
265	*Billy Baber, Derrick Blaylock*	.75
266	*Jamar Fletcher, Morlon Greenwood*	1.00
267	*Andre King, Ronney Daniels*	.75
268	*Arthur Love, Jabari Holloway*	.75
269	*Jonas Jennings, Kenyatta Walker*	.50
270	*Ben Hamilton, Paul Toviessa*	.50
271	*Chris Taylor, Joey Getherall*	1.00
272	*Casey Hampton, Kendrell Bell*	.75
273	*Cedrick Wilson, Jamie Winborn*	.75
274	*Alex Bannister, Heath Evans*	1.25
275	*Damione Lewis, Ryan Pickett*	1.00
276	*Tommy Polley, Brian Allen*	.75
277	*Jamie Henderson, Reggie White*	1.00
278	*Eddie Berlin, Justin McCareins*	.75
279	*Andre Dyson, Dan Alexander*	1.00
280	*Quentin McCord, Robert Garza*	.75
281	*Scotty Anderson, Eric Kelly, Willie Howard*	.75
282	*Bhawoh Jue, David Martin, Torrance Marshall*	1.00
283	*Stevonne Smith*, Dee Brown, *Jarrod Cooper*	1.00
284	*DeLawrence Grant, Derek Combs, Derrick Gibson*	1.00
285	*Carlos Polk, Tay Cody, Zeke Moreno*	.75
286	*David Rivers, Francis St. Paul, Milton Wynn*	.50
287	*Ennis Davis, Kenny Smith, Sedrick Hodge*	.50
288	*Ken Lucas, Orlando Huff, Steve Hutchinson*	.75
289	*Marcellus Rivers, Derrick Burgess, Tony Driver*	.75
290	*Darnerian McCants, Fred Smoot, Mike Cerimele*	1.00

2001 UD Vintage Franchise Players

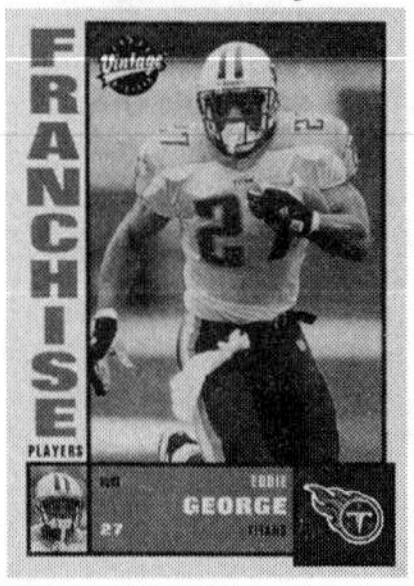
FRANCHISE
PLAYERS
GEORGE

		MT
Complete Set (7):		18.00
Common Player:		1.50
Inserted 1:24		
FP1	Charlie Batch	1.50
FP2	Ricky Williams	3.50
FP3	Brett Favre	10.00
FP4	Emmitt Smith	6.00
FP5	Terrell Davis	5.00
FP6	Jerome Bettis	1.50
FP7	Eddie George	2.00

2001 UD Vintage Matinee Idols

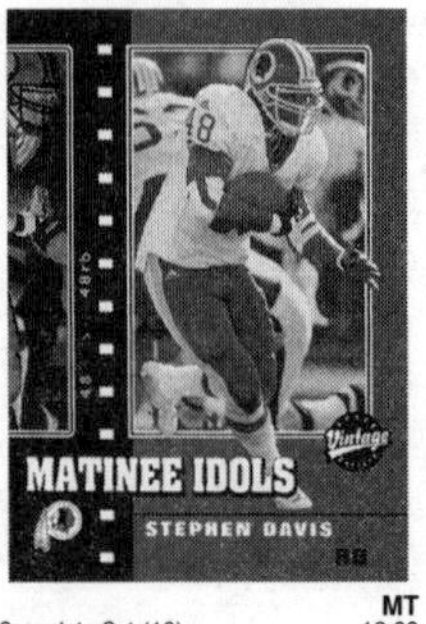
MATINEE IDOLS
STEPHEN DAVIS

		MT
Complete Set (10):		18.00
Common Player:		1.00
Inserted 1:18		
M1	Stephen Davis	2.00
M2	Mike Alstott	2.00
M3	Ricky Williams	3.00
M4	Ricky Watters	1.00
M5	Donovan McNabb	3.50
M6	Charlie Batch	1.00
M7	Jamal Lewis	5.00
M8	Drew Bledsoe	2.50
M9	Aaron Brooks	2.50
M10	Vinny Testaverde	1.00

2001 UD Vintage Old School Attitude

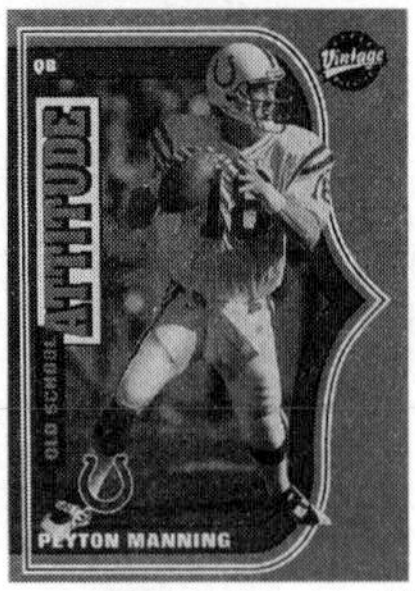
PEYTON MANNING

		MT
Complete Set (10):		18.00
Common Player:		1.00
Inserted 1:18		
OS1	Tim Brown	1.00
OS2	Peyton Manning	7.00
OS3	Jamal Anderson	1.00
OS4	Doug Flutie	2.50
OS5	Emmitt Smith	5.00
OS6	Cris Carter	1.00
OS7	Ed McCaffrey	1.00
OS8	Fred Taylor	2.50
OS9	Curtis Martin	1.00
OS10	Tim Couch	3.00

2001 UD Vintage Rookie Vintage Threads

		MT
Common Player:		10.00
KB-VT	Kevan Barlow	12.00
BE-VT	Michael Bennett	45.00
DR-VT	Drew Brees	50.00
RG-VT	Rod Gardner	25.00
JJ-VT	James Jackson	12.00
CJ-VT	Chad Johnson	10.00
DM-VT	Deuce McAllister	30.00
FM-VT	Freddie Mitchell	20.00
QM-VT	Quincy Morgan	12.00
SM-VT	Santana Moss	20.00
KR-VT	Koren Robinson	25.00
LT-VT	LaDainian Tomlinson	50.00
MV-VT	Michael Vick	70.00
RW-VT	Reggie Wayne	20.00
CW-VT	Chris Weinke	30.00

2001 UD Vintage Signed Vintage Threads

		MT
Common Player:		50.00
Production 100 Sets		
TA-SVT	Troy Aikman	100.00
MA-SVT	Mike Alstott	50.00
DB-SVT	Drew Bledsoe	60.00
MB-SVT	Mark Brunell	60.00
TC-SVT	Tim Couch	60.00
DC-SVT	Daunte Culpepper	85.00
SD-SVT	Stephen Davis	50.00
CD-SVT	Corey Dillon	50.00
JG-SVT	Jeff Garcia	50.00
PM-SVT	Peyton Manning	150.00
JM-SVT	Joe Montana	300.00
RM-SVT	Randy Moss	150.00
JR-SVT	Jerry Rice	125.00
KW-SVT	Kurt Warner	150.00

2001 UD Vintage Smashmouth

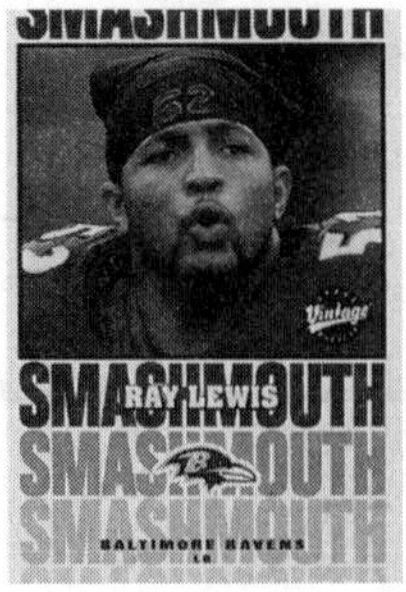
SMASHMOUTH
RAY LEWIS
BALTIMORE RAVENS

		MT
Complete Set (15):		12.00
Common Player:		.75
Inserted 1:12		
S1	Ray Lewis	1.50
S2	Junior Seau	.75
S3	Eddie George	2.50
S4	Jerome Bettis	1.50
S5	Ricky Williams	3.00
S6	Terrell Owens	1.50
S7	Warren Sapp	.75
S8	John Lynch	.75
S9	Brian Urlacher	3.00
S10	Zach Thomas	.75
S11	Tyrone Wheatley	.75
S12	Stephen Davis	1.50
S13	Mike Alstott	1.50
S14	Fred Taylor	2.00
S15	Cris Carter	1.50

2001 UD Vintage Vintage Signatures

		MT
Common Player:		12.00
Inserted 1:144		
MA-VS	Mike Anderson	35.00
CB-VS	Charlie Batch	18.00
NO-VS	Jeff Blake	12.00
TB-VS	Terry Bradshaw	100.00
AB-VS	Aaron Brooks	30.00
JB-VS	Jim Brown	125.00
IB-VS	Isaac Bruce	20.00
MB-VS	Mark Brunell	20.00
TC-VS	Tim Couch	30.00
WC-VS	Wayne Chrebet	12.00
TD-VS	Terrell Davis	35.00
DI-VS	Trent Dilfer	18.00
CD-VS	Corey Dillon	18.00
DF-VS	Doug Flutie	20.00
MF-VS	Marshall Faulk	30.00
TG-VS	Tony Gonzalez	20.00
PH-VS	Paul Hornung	30.00
EJ-VS	Edgerrin James	30.00
PM-VS	Peyton Manning	60.00
JN-VS	Joe Namath	175.00
JR-VS	John Riggins	175.00
MR-VS	Marcus Robinson	15.00
JS-VS	Junior Seau	20.00
VT-TS	Vinny Testaverde	12.00

2001 UD Vintage Vintage Threads

		MT
Common Player:		10.00
Inserted 1:144		
TA-VT	Troy Aikman	30.00
MB-VT	Mark Brunell	20.00
RD-VT	Ron Dayne	20.00
CD-VT	Corey Dillon	12.00
BF-VT	Brett Favre	50.00
JG-VT	Jeff Garcia	20.00
IH-VT	Ike Hilliard	10.00
RL-VT	Ray Lewis	20.00
RM-VT	Randy Moss	40.00
JR-VT	Jerry Rice	30.00
WS-VT	Warren Sapp	12.00
AS-VT	Akili Smith	10.00
ZT-VT	Zach Thomas	20.00
KW-VT	Kurt Warner	40.00
PW-VT	Peter Warrick	20.00

2001 UD Vintage Vintage Threads Combos

		MT
Common Player:		50.00
Production 50 Sets		
AM-VTC	Troy Aikman, Cade McNown	60.00
BF-VTC	Mark Brunell, Brett Favre	100.00
DB-VTC	Ron Dayne, Michael Bennett	85.00
FM-VTC	Marshall Faulk, Deuce McAllister	50.00
MJ-VTC	Peyton Manning, Edgerrin James	125.00

2001 Upper Deck

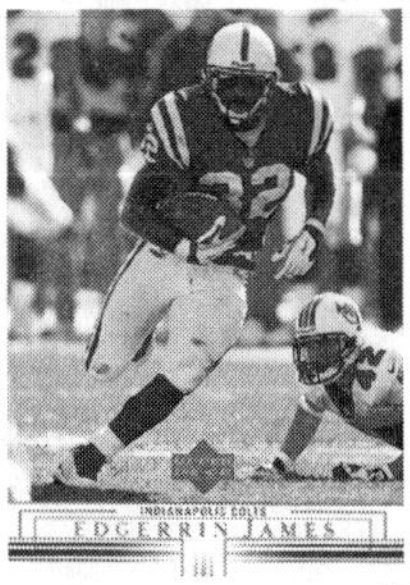
EDGERRIN JAMES

		MT
Complete Set (280):		325.00
Common Player:		.15
Minor Stars:		.30
Common Rookie:		1.50
Inserted 1:4		
Pack (8):		3.00
Wax Box (24):		55.00
1	Jake Plummer	.50
2	David Boston	.50
3	Thomas Jones	.15
4	Frank Sanders	.15
5	Eric Zeier	.15
6	Jamal Anderson	.50
7	Chris Chandler	.15
8	Shawn Jefferson	.15
9	Darrick Vaughn	.15
10	Terance Mathis	.15
11	Jamal Lewis	1.50
12	Shannon Sharpe	.15
13	Elvis Grbac	.15
14	Ray Lewis	.50
15	Qadry Ismail	.15
16	Chris Redman	.15
17	Rob Johnson	.50
18	Eric Moulds	.15
19	Sammy Morris	.15
20	Shawn Bryson	.15
21	Jeremy McDaniel	.15
22	Muhsin Muhammad	.15
23	Brad Hoover	.50
24	Tim Biakabutuka	.15
25	Steve Beuerlein	.15
26	Jeff Lewis	.15
27	Wesley Walls	.15
28	Cade McNown	.50
29	James Allen	.15
30	Marcus Robinson	.50
31	Brian Urlacher	1.25
32	Bobby Engram	.15

33	Peter Warrick	1.25
34	Corey Dillon	.50
35	Akili Smith	.50
36	Danny Farmer	.50
37	Ron Dugans	.15
38	Jon Kitna	.15
39	Tim Couch	.75
40	Kevin Johnson	.50
41	Travis Prentice	.15
42	Spergon Wynn	.15
43	Errict Rhett	.15
44	Dennis Northcutt	.15
45	Courtney Brown	.15
46	Tony Banks	.15
47	Emmitt Smith	1.75
48	Joey Galloway	.50
49	Raghib Ismail	.15
50	Randall Cunningham	.30
51	James McKnight	.15
52	Terrell Davis	1.50
53	Mike Anderson	1.50
54	Brian Griese	.75
55	Rod Smith	.15
56	Ed McCaffrey	.50
57	Eddie Kennison	.15
58	Olandis Gary	.15
59	Charlie Batch	.50
60	Germane Crowell	.15
61	James O. Stewart	.15
62	Johnnie Morton	.15
63	Brett Favre	2.50
64	Antonio Freeman	.50
65	Dorsey Levens	.15
66	Ahman Green	.15
67	Bill Schroeder	.15
68	Peyton Manning	2.00
69	Edgerrin James	1.75
70	Marvin Harrison	.50
71	Jerome Pathon	.15
72	Ken Dilger	.15
73	Mark Brunell	.75
74	Fred Taylor	.75
75	Jimmy Smith	.15
76	Keenan McCardell	.15
77	R. Jay Soward	.15
78	Todd Collins	.15
79	Tony Gonzalez	.15
80	Derrick Alexander	.15
81	Tony Richardson	.15
82	Sylvester Morris	.15
83	Oronde Gadsden	.15
84	Lamar Smith	.15
85	Jay Fiedler	.50
86	Jason Taylor	.15
87	Ray Lucas	.15
88	O.J. McDuffie	.15
89	Randy Moss	2.00
90	Cris Carter	.50
91	Daunte Culpepper	1.25
92	Moe Williams	.15
93	Troy Walters	.15
94	Drew Bledsoe	.75
95	Terry Glenn	.15
96	Kevin Faulk	.15
97	J.R. Redmond	.15
98	Troy Brown	.15
99	Ricky Williams	1.00
100	Jeff Blake	.15
101	Joe Horn	.15
102	Albert Connell	.15
103	Aaron Brooks	.75
104	Chad Morton	.15
105	Kerry Collins	.15
106	Amani Toomer	.15
107	Ron Dayne	1.25
108	Tiki Barber	.15
109	Ike Hilliard	.15
110	Ron Dixon	.15
111	Jason Sehorn	.15
112	Vinny Testaverde	.15
113	Wayne Chrebet	.15
114	Curtis Martin	.50
115	Dedric Ward	.15
116	Laveranues Coles	.50
117	Windrell Hayes	.15
118	Tim Brown	.50
119	Rich Gannon	.50
120	Tyrone Wheatley	.15
121	Charlie Garner	.15
122	Andre Rison	.15
123	Charles Woodson	.15
124	Trace Armstrong	.15
125	Duce Staley	.50
126	Donovan McNabb	1.00
127	Darnell Autry	.15
128	Charles Johnson	.15
129	Torrance Small	.15
130	Kordell Stewart	.50
131	Jerome Bettis	.50
132	Plaxico Burress	.50
133	Bobby Shaw	.15
134	Troy Edwards	.15
135	Marshall Faulk	.75
136	Kurt Warner	2.00
137	Isaac Bruce	.50
138	Torry Holt	.50
139	Trent Green	.15
140	Az-Zahir Hakim	.15
141	Junior Seau	.15
142	Curtis Conway	.15
143	Doug Flutie	.75
144	Jeff Graham	.15
145	Freddie Jones	.15
146	Marcelius Wiley	.15
147	Jeff Garcia	.50
148	Jerry Rice	1.50
149	Fred Beasley	.15
150	Terrell Owens	.50
151	J.J. Stokes	.15
152	Garrison Hearst	.15
153	Ricky Watters	.15
154	Shaun Alexander	.75
155	Matt Hasselbeck	.15
156	Brock Huard	.15
157	Darrell Jackson	.50
158	John Randle	.15
159	Warrick Dunn	.50
160	Shaun King	.30
161	Ryan Leaf	.50
162	Mike Alstott	.50
163	Jacquez Green	.15
164	Brad Johnson	.50
165	Keyshawn Johnson	.50
166	Eddie George	.75
167	Steve McNair	.50
168	Neil O'Donnell	.15
169	Derrick Mason	.15
170	Frank Wycheck	.15
171	Kevin Dyson	.15
172	Jevon Kearse	.30
173	Jeff George	.15
174	Stephen Davis	.30
175	Larry Centers	.15
176	Michael Westbrook	.15
177	Stephen Alexander	.15
178	Ron Dayne	1.25
179	Donovan McNabb	1.00
180	Jimmy Smith	.15
181	*Adam Archuleta*	3.00
182	*A.J. Feeley*	1.50
183	*Alex Bannister*	4.00
184	*Alge Crumpler*	3.00
185	*Andre Carter*	3.00
186	*Andre Dyson*	1.50
187	*Anthony Thomas*	20.00
188	*Arthur Love*	1.50
189	*Bobby Newcombe*	3.00
190	*Brandon Spoon*	3.00
191	*Carlos Polk*	1.50
192	*Casey Hampton*	1.50
193	*Cedrick Wilson*	3.00
194	*Chad Johnson*	5.00
195	*Chris Chambers*	10.00
196	*Chris Taylor*	3.00
197	*Chris Weinke*	12.00
198	*Correl Buckhalter*	4.00
199	*Damione Lewis*	3.00
200	*Dan Alexander*	3.00
201	*Dan Morgan*	4.00
202	*Willie Middlebrooks*	1.50
203	*David Terrell*	15.00
204	*Derrick Gibson*	1.50
205	*Deuce McAllister*	12.00
206	*Drew Brees*	20.00
207	*Edgerton Hartwell*	1.50
208	*Fred Smoot*	3.00
209	*Freddie Mitchell*	8.00
210	*Gary Baxter*	1.50
211	*Gerard Warren*	3.00
212	*Hakim Akbar*	1.50
213	*Heath Evans*	1.50
214	*Jabari Holloway*	1.50
215	*Jamal Reynolds*	3.00
216	*Jamar Fletcher*	3.00
217	*James Jackson*	5.00
218	*Jamie Winborn*	1.50
219	*Jesse Palmer*	4.00
220	*Josh Booty*	4.00
221	*Josh Heupel*	12.00
222	*Justin Smith*	4.00
223	*Karon Riley*	1.50
224	*Ken Lucas*	1.50
225	*Kenyatta Walker*	1.50
226	*Ken-Yon Rambo*	3.00
227	*Kevan Barlow*	4.00
228	*Kevin Kasper*	4.00
229	*Koren Robinson*	10.00
230	*LaDainian Tomlinson*	20.00
231	*LaMont Jordan*	5.00
232	*Leonard Davis*	1.50
233	*Marcus Stroud*	3.00
234	*Marques Tuiasosopo*	8.00
235	*Marvin "Snoop" Minnis*	6.00
236	*Michael Bennett*	10.00
237	*Michael Stone*	1.50
238	*Mike McMahon*	5.00
239	*Michael Vick*	25.00
240	*Moran Norris*	1.50
241	*Morlon Greenwood*	1.50
242	*Nate Clements*	3.00
243	*Orlando Huff*	1.50
244	*Quincy Morgan*	6.00
245	*Reggie Wayne*	10.00
246	*Richard Seymour*	3.00
247	*Robert Ferguson*	5.00
248	*Rod Gardner*	12.00
249	*Rudi Johnson*	5.00
250	*Sage Rosenfels*	5.00
251	*Santana Moss*	12.00
252	*Scotty Anderson*	1.50
253	*Sedrick Hodge*	1.30
254	*Shaun Rogers*	1.30
255	*Steve Hutchinson*	3.00
256	*T.J. Houshmandzadeh*	3.00
257	*Tay Cody*	1.50
258	*George Layne*	1.50
259	*Todd Heap*	4.00
260	*Tommy Polley*	1.50
261	*Tony Dixon*	1.50
262	*Brian Allen*	1.50
263	*Torrance Marshall*	3.00
264	*Travis Henry*	8.00
265	*Travis Minor*	8.00
266	*Vinny Sutherland*	3.00
267	*Will Allen*	3.00
268	*Derrick Blaylock*	1.50
269	*Zeke Moreno*	1.50
270	*Chris Barnes*	1.50
271	Dee Brown	3.00
272	*Reggie White*	4.00
273	*Derek Combs*	3.00
274	*Stevonne Smith*	3.00
275	*Milton Wynn*	3.00
276	*Justin McCareins*	3.00
277	*Darnerian McCants*	3.00
278	*Eddie Berlin*	3.00
279	*Francis St. Paul*	3.00
280	*Quincy Carter*	8.00

2001 Upper Deck Gold

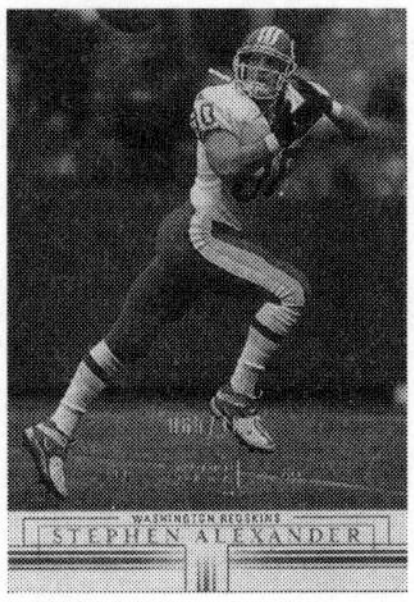

	MT
Gold Stars:	5x-10x
Production 100 Sets	
Gold Rookies:	2x-4x
Production 50 Sets	

2001 Upper Deck Championship Threads

		MT
Common Player:		10.00
Inserted 1:144		
CT-IB	Isaac Bruce	15.00
CT-TD	Terrell Davis	30.00
CT-DI	Trent Dilfer	15.00
CT-MF	Marshall Faulk	25.00
CT-BF	Brett Favre	60.00
CT-AF	Antonio Freeman	15.00
CT-TH	Torry Holt	15.00
CT-DL	Dorsey Levens	15.00
CT-JL	Jamal Lewis	35.00
CT-RL	Ray Lewis	20.00
CT-EM	Ed McCaffrey	15.00
CT-JR	Jerry Rice	40.00
CT-SS	Shannon Sharpe	10.00
CT-RS	Rod Smith	10.00
CT-KW	Kurt Warner	50.00

2001 Upper Deck Classic Drafts-Jersey

		MT
Common Player:		20.00
Inserted 1:288		
DB-CD	Drew Bledsoe	35.00
MB-CD	Mark Brunell	25.00
TC-CD	Tim Couch	30.00
DC-CD	Daunte Culpepper	50.00
JE-CD	John Elway	100.00
BG-CD	Brian Griese	30.00
KE-CD	Jevon Kearse	20.00
JK-CD	Jim Kelly	60.00
DM-CD	Dan Marino	100.00
FT-CD	Fred Taylor	25.00

2001 Upper Deck Constant Threat

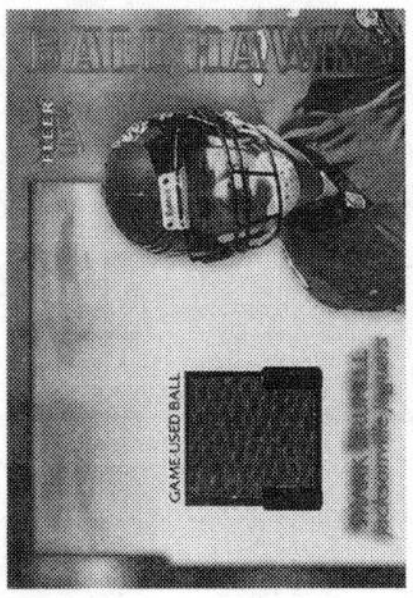

		MT
Complete Set (10):		12.00
Common Player:		2.00
Inserted 1:36		
CT1	Aaron Brooks	3.00
CT2	Charlie Batch	2.00
CT3	Donovan McNabb	3.50
CT4	Mark Brunell	3.00
CT5	Akili Smith	2.00
CT6	Ray Lucas	1.00
CT7	Jake Plummer	2.00
CT8	Steve McNair	2.00
CT9	Trent Green	1.00
CT10	Doug Flutie	2.50

2001 Upper Deck Game Jersey Autographs

		MT
Common Player:		40.00
Inserted 1:288		
MA-AJ	Mike Alstott	40.00
IB-AJ	Isaac Bruce	40.00
DC-AJ	Daunte Culpepper	125.00
JG-AJ	Jeff Garcia	50.00
BJ-AJ	Brad Johnson	40.00
JL-AJ	Jamal Lewis	85.00
PM-AJ	Peyton Manning	150.00
RM-AJ	Randy Moss	150.00
JP-AJ	Jake Plummer	40.00

2001 Upper Deck Power Surge

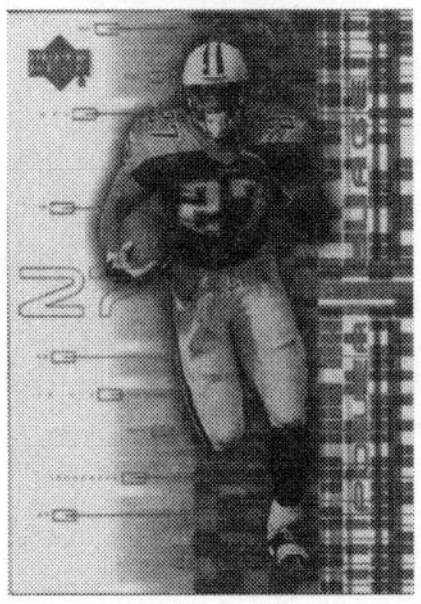

		MT
Complete Set (10):		20.00
Common Player:		2.00
Inserted 1:36		
PS1	Eddie George	2.50
PS2	Cris Carter	2.00
PS3	Curtis Martin	2.00
PS4	Jerry Rice	5.00
PS5	Jamal Anderson	2.00
PS6	Keyshawn Johnson	2.00
PS7	Ricky Williams	3.00
PS8	Randy Moss	7.00
PS9	Marvin Harrison	2.00
PS10	Corey Dillon	2.00

2001 Upper Deck Proving Ground

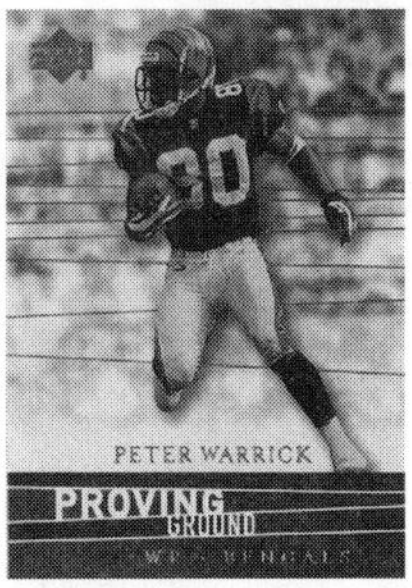

		MT
Complete Set (20):		15.00
Common Player:		.50
Inserted 1:9		
PG1	Mike Anderson	2.50
PG2	Tim Couch	1.75
PG3	Donovan McNabb	2.00
PG4	Aaron Brooks	1.50
PG5	Trent Dilfer	.50
PG6	Brian Griese	1.50
PG7	Kevin Johnson	1.00
PG8	Ahman Green	.50
PG9	Sylvester Morris	.50
PG10	Peter Warrick	2.00
PG11	Tiki Barber	.50
PG12	Torry Holt	1.25
PG13	Trent Green	.50
PG14	Ed McCaffrey	1.25
PG15	Joe Horn	.50
PG16	Muhsin Muhammad	.50
PG17	Kerry Collins	.50
PG18	Edgerrin James	4.00
PG19	Brad Hoover	1.25
PG20	Ron Dayne	2.00

2001 Upper Deck Rookie Threads

		MT
Common Player:		20.00
Inserted 1:144		
RT-KB	Kevan Barlow	20.00
RT-MB	Michael Bennett	50.00
RT-DB	Drew Brees	60.00
RT-CC	Chris Chambers	20.00
RT-RF	Robert Ferguson	20.00
RT-RG	Rod Gardner	30.00
RT-TH	Travis Henry	20.00
RT-CJ	Chad Johnson 102	25.00
RT-DM	Deuce McAllister	50.00
RT-FM	Freddie Mitchell	25.00
RT-KR	Koren Robinson	30.00
RT-LT	LaDainian Tomlinson 50	100.00
RT-MV	Michael Vick	100.00
RT-RW	Reggie Wayne	25.00
RT-CW	Chris Weinke	40.00

2001 Upper Deck Running Wild

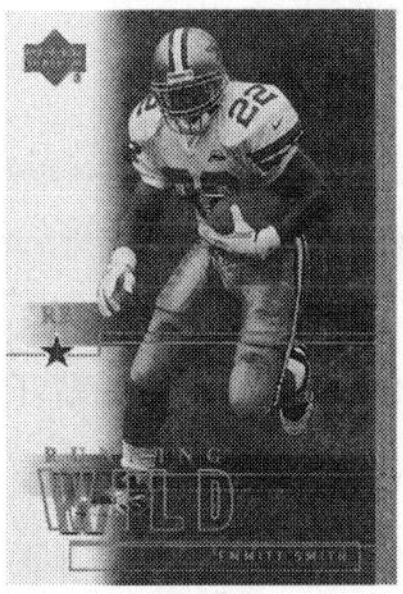

		MT
Complete Set (15):		25.00
Common Player:		1.00
Inserted 1:24		
RW1	Eddie George	2.50
RW2	Corey Dillon	2.00
RW3	Edgerrin James	6.00
RW4	Charlie Garner	1.00
RW5	Jamal Anderson	2.00
RW6	Emmitt Smith	6.00
RW7	Terrell Davis	5.00
RW8	Mike Anderson	5.00
RW9	James O. Stewart	1.00
RW10	Ricky Watters	1.00
RW11	Lamar Smith	1.00
RW12	Curtis Martin	2.00
RW13	Ricky Williams	3.00
RW14	Stephen Davis	2.00
RW15	Jerome Bettis	2.00

Post-1980 cards in Near Mint condition will generally sell for about 75% of the quoted Mint value. Excellent-condition cards bring no more than 40%.

2001 Upper Deck Starstruck

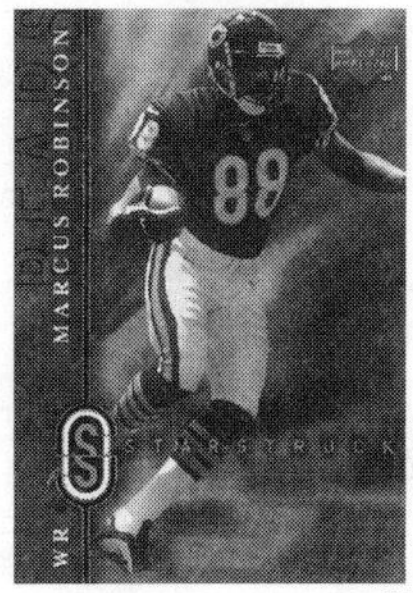

		MT
Complete Set (15):		20.00
Common Player:		1.00
Inserted 1:24		
S1	Curtis Martin	2.00
S2	Keyshawn Johnson	2.00
S3	Tim Brown	2.00
S4	Terrell Owens	2.00
S5	Duce Staley	2.00
S6	Rich Gannon	1.00
S7	Mike Anderson	5.00
S8	Stephen Davis	2.00
S9	Emmitt Smith	6.00
S10	Steve McNair	2.00
S11	Ricky Williams	3.00
S12	Marcus Robinson	2.00
S13	Vinny Testaverde	1.00
S14	Rod Smith	1.00
S15	Drew Bledsoe	2.50

2001 Upper Deck Teammates-Jersey

		MT
Common Player:		20.00
Inserted 1:144		
CM-T	Daunte Culpepper, Randy Moss	85.00
KJ-T	Shaun King, Keyshawn Johnson	20.00
MJ-T	Peyton Manning, Edgerrin James	100.00
MH-T	Peyton Manning, Marvin Harrison	75.00
FS-T	Brett Favre, Dorsey Levens	60.00
AS-T	Troy Aikman, Emmitt Smith	125.00
WF-T	Kurt Warner, Marshall Faulk	80.00
BM-T	Charlie Batch, Herman Moore	25.00
GO-T	Jeff Garcia, Terrell Owens	25.00
DB-T	Ron Dayne, Tiki Barber	30.00

2001 Upper Deck UD Lettermen Patches

		MT
Complete Set (9):		75.00
Common Player:		125.00
MB-LP	Michael Bennett	125.00
DB-LP	Drew Brees	150.00
DM-LP	Deuce McAllister	125.00
FM-LP	Freddie Mitchell	75.00
AT-LP	Anthony Thomas	225.00
LT-LP	LaDainian Tomlinson	125.00
MT-LP	Marques Tuiasosopo	75.00
MV-LP	Michael Vick	225.00
CW-LP	Chris Weinke	125.00

2001 Upper Deck UD Premium Patch Cards

		MT
Complete Set (20):		25.00
Common Player:		75.00
TA-PP	Troy Aikman	75.00
AF-PP	Drew Bledsoe	50.00
IB-PP	Isaac Bruce	40.00
MB-PP	Mark Brunell	50.00
TC-PP	Tim Couch	75.00
TDa-PP	Terrell Davis	50.00
MF-PP	Marshall Faulk	100.00
BF-PP	Brett Favre	225.00
EG-PP	Eddie George	75.00
BG-PP	Brian Griese	50.00
TH-PP	Torry Holt	25.00
DL-PP	Dorsey Levens	25.00
JL-PP	Jamal Lewis	100.00
EM-PP	Ed McCaffrey	25.00
SM-PP	Steve McNair	25.00
JR-PP	Jerry Rice	125.00
SS-PP	Shannon Sharpe	25.00
RS-PP	Rod Smith	25.00
FT-PP	Fred Taylor	40.00
KW-PP	Kurt Warner	125.00

Values quoted in this guide reflect the retail price of a card — the price a collector can expect to pay when buying a card from a dealer. The wholesale price — that which a collector can expect to receive from a dealer when selling cards — will be significantly lower, depending on desirability and condition.

2001 Upper Deck E-card

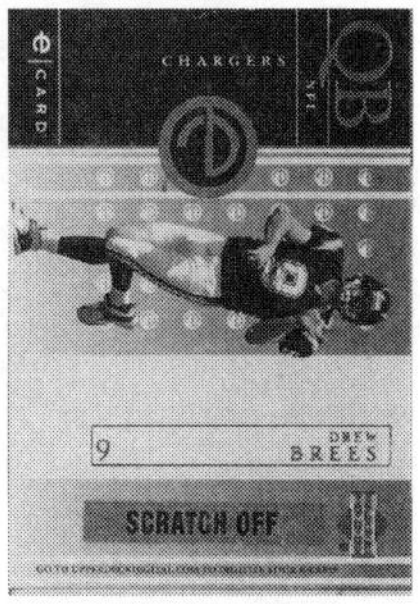

	MT
Complete Set (6):	30.00
Common Player:	4.00
Inserted 1:12	

2001 Upper Deck E-card-Autographed

		MT
Complete Set (6):		
Common Player:		
EA-MB	Michael Bennett	75.00
EA-DB	Drew Brees	75.00
EA-FM	Freddie Mitchell	50.00
EA-LT	LaDainian Tomlinson	75.00
EA-MV	Michael Vick	75.00
EA-CW	Chris Weinke	50.00

2001 Upper Deck E-card-Graded Rookie Watch

		MT
Complete Set (6):		
Common Player:		
EA-MB	Michael Bennett	40.00
EA-DB	Drew Brees	40.00
EA-FM	Freddie Mitchell	30.00
EA-LT	LaDainian Tomlinson	40.00
EA-MV	Michael Vick	40.00
EA-CW	Chris Weinke	30.00

2001 Upper Deck E-card-Jersey

		MT
Complete Set (6):		
Common Player:		
EJ-MB	Michael Bennett	50.00
EJ-DB	Drew Brees	50.00
EJ-FM	Freddie Mitchell	40.00
EJ-LT	LaDainian Tomlinson	60.00
EJ-MV	Michael Vick	50.00
EJ-CW	Chris Weinke	40.00

2001 Upper Deck Legends

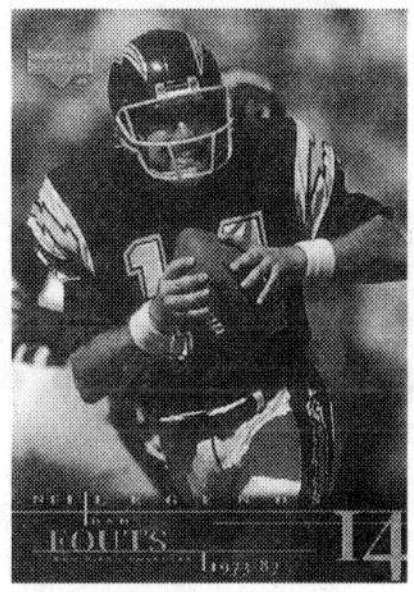

		MT
Complete Set (180):		275.00
Common Player:		.25
Minor Stars:		.50
Common Rookie:		2.50
Production 750 Sets		
Pack (5):		5.00
Wax Box (18):		70.00
1	Jake Plummer	.50
2	Jamal Anderson	.50
3	Ray Lewis	.50
4	Johnny Unitas	1.50
5	Jamal Lewis	1.50
6	Andre Reed	.50
7	Jim Kelly	.75
8	Thurman Thomas	.50
9	Rob Johnson	.25
10	Brian Urlacher	1.50
11	Dick Butkus	1.00
12	Gale Sayers	1.25
13	James Allen	.25
14	Corey Dillon	.50
15	Jim Brown	2.00
16	Tim Couch	1.00
17	Joey Galloway	.50
18	Emmitt Smith	2.00
19	Randy White	.25
20	Roger Staubach	2.00
21	Troy Aikman	1.50
22	Tony Dorsett	.75
23	Brian Griese	1.00
24	Floyd Little	.25
25	John Elway	3.00
26	Mike Anderson	1.25
27	Terrell Davis	1.50
28	Barry Sanders	2.50

29	Charlie Batch	.25
30	Bart Starr	2.00
31	Paul Hornung	1.00
32	Reggie White	.75
33	Warren Moon	.50
34	Edgerrin James	2.00
35	Peyton Manning	2.50
36	Mark Brunell	.50
37	Tony Gonzalez	.50
38	Eric Dickerson	.75
39	Jack Youngblood	.25
40	Jay Fiedler	.50
41	Lamar Smith	.25
42	Dan Marino	3.00
43	Oronde Gadsden	.25
44	Cris Carter	.75
45	Fran Tarkenton	1.00
46	Daunte Culpepper	1.50
47	Randy Moss	2.50
48	Robert Smith	.25
49	Drew Bledsoe	1.00
50	Archie Manning	.50
51	Jeff Blake	.25
52	Ricky Williams	1.25
53	Kerry Collins	.50
54	Ron Dayne	.50
55	Lawrence Taylor	.75
56	Wayne Chrebet	.50
57	Vinny Testaverde	.50
58	Joe Namath	2.00
59	Jim Plunkett	.50
60	George Blanda	.75
61	Tim Brown	.75
62	Jerry Rice	2.00
63	Ken Stabler	.50
64	Marcus Allen	.75
65	Donovan McNabb	1.50
66	Harold Carmichael	.50
67	Franco Harris	.75
68	Jerome Bettis	.50
69	Terry Bradshaw	2.00
70	Doug Flutie	1.00
71	Lance Alworth	.50
72	Junior Seau	.50
73	Kellen Winslow	.75
74	Dan Fouts	.75
75	Joe Montana	5.00
76	Terrell Owens	.75
77	Jeff Garcia	1.00
78	Steve Young	1.00
79	Matt Hasselbeck	.25
80	Kurt Warner	2.50
81	Marshall Faulk	1.00
82	Brad Johnson	.50
83	Eddie George	1.00
84	Charlie Taylor	.50
85	Stephen Davis	.50
86	Jeff George	.25
87	John Riggins	.75
88	Joe Theismann	.75
89	Michael Westbrook	.50
90	Sonny Jurgensen	.75
91	*Andre Carter*	3.00
92	*Cedrick Wilson*	3.00
93	*Kevan Barlow*	10.00
94	*Anthony Thomas*	30.00
95	*David Terrell*	20.00
96	*Chad Johnson*	8.00
97	*Justin Smith*	5.00
98	*Rudi Johnson*	5.00
99	*T.J. Houshmandzadeh*	3.00
100	*Brandon Spoon*	3.00
101	*Nate Clements*	3.00
102	*Travis Henry*	10.00
103	*Kevin Kasper*	8.00
104	*Willie Middlebrooks*	3.00
105	*Gerard Warren*	5.00
106	*James Jackson*	8.00
107	*Quincy Morgan*	8.00
108	*Bobby Newcombe*	5.00
109	*Arnold Jackson*	3.00
110	*Carlos Polk*	3.00
111	*Drew Brees*	25.00
112	*LaDainian Tomlinson*	25.00
113	*Tay Cody*	3.00
114	*Zeke Moreno*	3.00
115	*Marvin "Snoop" Minnis*	10.00
116	*George Layne*	3.00
117	*Derrick Blaylock*	3.00
118	*Reggie Wayne*	12.00
119	*Tony Dixon*	3.00
120	*Quincy Carter*	15.00
121	*Chris Chambers*	15.00
122	*Jamar Fletcher*	3.00
123	*Josh Heupel*	8.00
124	*Travis Minor*	8.00
125	*A.J. Feeley*	6.00
126	*Correll Buckhalter*	10.00
127	*Freddie Mitchell*	12.00
128	*Alge Crumpler*	5.00
129	*Michael Vick*	30.00
130	*Vinny Sutherland*	5.00
131	*Marcus Stroud*	3.00
132	*Mike McMahon*	12.00
133	*Scotty Anderson*	3.00
134	*Shaun Rogers*	3.00
135	*Jesse Palmer*	8.00
136	*Will Allen*	3.00
137	*Lamont Jordan*	6.00
138	*Santana Moss*	12.00
139	*Reggie White*	3.00
140	*Jamal Reynolds*	3.00
141	*Robert Ferguson*	5.00
142	*Torrance Marshall*	3.00
143	*Chris Weinke*	12.00
144	*Dan Morgan*	3.00
145	*Steve Smith*	5.00
146	*Dee Brown*	3.00
147	*Arthur Love*	3.00
148	*Hakim Akbar*	3.00
149	*Jabari Holloway*	3.00
150	*Derek Combs*	3.00
151	*Derrick Gibson*	3.00
152	*Ken-Yon Rambo*	3.00
153	*Marques Tuiasosopo*	12.00
154	*Adam Archuleta*	5.00
155	*Tommy Polley*	6.00
156	*Brian Allen*	3.00
157	*Milton Wynn*	3.00
158	*Francis St. Paul*	3.00
159	*Edgerton Hartwell*	3.00
160	*Gary Baxter*	3.00
161	*Todd Heap*	5.00
162	*Chris Barnes*	3.00
163	*Fred Smoot*	3.00
164	*Rob Gardner*	12.00
165	*Sage Rosenfels*	8.00
166	*Darnerian McCants*	3.00
167	*Deuce McAllister*	12.00
168	*Moran Norris*	3.00
169	*Sedrick Hodge*	5.00
170	*Alex Bannister*	5.00
171	*Heath Evans*	3.00
172	*Josh Booty*	5.00
173	*Ken Lucas*	3.00
174	*Koren Robinson*	12.00
175	*Chris Taylor*	3.00
176	*Andre Dyson*	3.00
177	*Dan Alexander*	5.00
178	*Justin McCareins*	3.00
179	*Eddie Berlin*	3.00
180	*Michael Bennett*	15.00

2001 Upper Deck Legends Legendary Artwork

		MT
Complete Set (15):		70.00
Common Player:		3.00
Inserted 1:18		
LA1	Jim Thorpe	4.00
LA2	Jerry Rice	6.00
LA3	Bart Starr	6.00
LA4	Fran Tarkenton	3.00
LA5	Barry Sanders	6.00
LA6	Jim Brown	6.00
LA7	Joe Montana	12.00
LA8	Joe Namath	7.00
LA9	John Elway	8.00
LA10	Johnny Unitas	6.00
LA11	Roger Staubach	5.00
LA12	Terry Bradshaw	5.00
LA13	Walter Payton	12.00
LA14	Dan Marino	8.00
LA15	Dick Butkus	3.00

2001 Upper Deck Legends Legendary Autographs

		MT
Complete Set (52):		
Common Player:		10.00
Inserted 1:54		
Some are SP's runs of 50 or 100		
TA	Troy Aikman	50.00
MA	Marcus Allen	25.00
LA	Lance Alworth	50.00
JB	Jeff Blake	10.00
TB	Terry Bradshaw	50.00
JB	Jim Brown	200.00
TB	Tim Brown	25.00
DB	Dick Butkus	50.00
HC	Harold Carmichael	10.00
WC	Wayne Chrebet	10.00
DC	Daunte Culpepper	75.00
ED	Eric Dickerson	50.00
TD	Tony Dorsett	25.00
JE	John Elway	75.00
DF	Doug Flutie	50.00
DF	Dan Fouts	25.00
JG	Jeff Garcia	10.00
JG	Jeff George	10.00
FH	Franco Harris	50.00
PH	Paul Hornung	50.00
EJ	Ed Jones	10.00
JK	Jim Kelly	50.00
AM	Archie Manning	25.00
PM	Peyton Manning	50.00
DM	Dan Marino	100.00
CM	Cade McNown	25.00
JM	Joe Montana	125.00
WM	Warren Moon	25.00
RM	Randy Moss	125.00
JN	Joe Namath	75.00
JP	Jake Plummer	25.00
JP	Jim Plunkett	10.00
AR	Andre Reed	10.00
JR	John Riggins	75.00
BS	Barry Sanders	100.00
GS	Gale Sayers	50.00
KS	Ken Stabler	50.00
BS	Bart Starr	100.00
RS	Roger Staubach	50.00
FT	Fran Tarkenton	50.00
CT	Charlie Taylor	10.00
LT	Lawrence Taylor	75.00
VT	Vinny Testaverde	50.00
JT	Joe Theismann	10.00
TT	Thurman Thomas	25.00
JU	Johnny Unitas	75.00
BU	Brian Urlacher	50.00
KW	Kurt Warner	50.00
RW	Ricky Williams	75.00
KW	Kellen Winslow	10.00
SY	Steve Young	100.00
JY	Jack Youngblood	10.00

2001 Upper Deck Legends Legendary Cuts

		MT
"Too Uncommon To Price"		
Complete Set (17):		
Common Player:		
LC-RB	Red Badgro	
LC-WE	Weeb Ewbanks 10	
LC-TF	Tom Fears 6	
LC-RG	Red Grange 10	
LC-GH	George Halas	
LC-TL	Tom Landry 8	
LC-BL	Bobby Layne 10	
LC-VL	Vince Lombardi 5	
LC-SL	Sid Luckman 9	
LC-MM	Marion Motley 6	
LC-BN	Bronko Nagurski 28	
LC-EN	Ernie Nevers 63	
LC-RN	Ray Nitschke 10	
LC-PR	Pete Rozelle 3	
LC-JT	Jim Thorpe 1	
LC-ET	Emlen Tunnell 22	
LC-VB	Norm Van Brocklin 3	

2001 Upper Deck Legends Memorable Materials

		MT
Common Player:		12.00
Inserted 1:36		
MM-CB	Charlie Batch	12.00
MM-DB	Drew Bledsoe	15.00
MM-IB	Isaac Bruce	15.00
MM-MB	Mark Brunell	12.00
MM-ED	Eric Dickerson/150	25.00
MM-JE	John Elway	40.00
MM-MF	Marshall Faulk	30.00
MM-DF	Doug Flutie	20.00
MM-DM	Dan Marino	50.00
MM-SM	Steve McNair	12.00
MM-WP	Walter Payton/150	125.00
MM-BS	Barry Sanders	30.00

2001 Upper Deck Legends Past Patterns

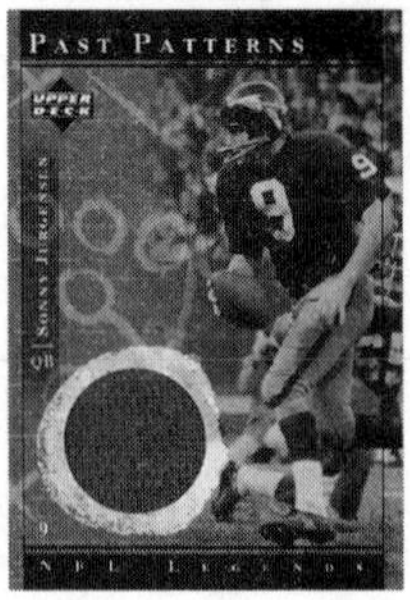

		MT
Common Player:		10.00
Inserted 1:18		
PP-TA	Troy Aikman	25.00
PP-MA	Mike Alstott	12.00
PP-GB	George Blanda	15.00
PP-TB	Terry Bradshaw/150	60.00
PP-CC	Cris Carter	12.00
PP-KC	Kerry Collins	12.00
PP-TC	Tim Couch	15.00
PP-SD	Stephen Davis	10.00
PP-WD	Warrick Dunn	12.00
PP-BF	Brett Favre	40.00
PP-DF	Doug Flutie	20.00
PP-JG	Jeff George	10.00
PP-PH	Paul Hornung	25.00
PP-SJ	Sonny Jurgensen	20.00
PP-JK	Jim Kelly	20.00
PP-SK	Shaun King	10.00
PP-AM	Archie Manning	20.00
PP-PM	Peyton Manning	30.00
PP-DM	Dan Marino	50.00
PP-JM	Joe Montana/150	100.00
PP-WM	Warren Moon	15.00
PP-JN	Joe Namath/150	60.00
PP-KN	Ken Norton	10.00
PP-JP	Jim Plunkett	15.00
PP-AR	Andre Reed	12.00
PP-JR	Jerry Rice	30.00
PP-JS	Junior Seau	12.00
PP-SS	Shannon Sharpe	15.00
PP-ES	Emmitt Smith	40.00
PP-RS	Robert Smith	10.00
PP-RS	Roger Staubach/95	60.00
PP-FT	Fred Taylor	12.00
PP-JT	John Taylor	10.00
PP-LT	Lawrence Taylor	20.00
PP-RW	Reggie White	15.00
PP-RW	Rod Woodson	15.00
PP-SY	Steve Young	20.00

2001 Upper Deck Legends Timeless Tributes

		MT
Common Player:		12.00
Inserted 1:6		
TT-JB	Jerome Bettis	12.00
TT-DG	Darrell Green	15.00
TT-HM	Harvey Martin	20.00
TT-JM	Joe Montana	75.00
TT-KN	Ken Norton Jr.	12.00
TT-WS	Warren Sapp	12.00
TT-BS	Bruce Smith	15.00
TT-LT	Lawrence Taylor	20.00
TT-DT	Derrick Thomas	25.00
TT-TT	Thurman Thomas	12.00
TT-RW	Randy White	12.00

2001 Upper Deck MVP

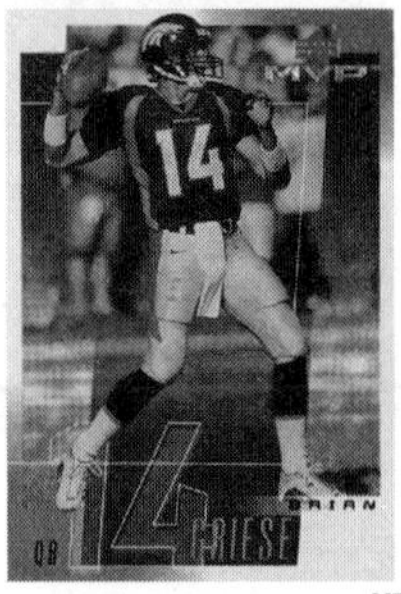

		MT
Complete Set (330):		35.00
Common Player:		.10
Minor Stars:		.20
Common Rookie:		.30
Pack (8):		2.00
Wax Box (24):		35.00
1	Jake Plummer	.40
2	David Boston	.20
3	Thomas Jones	.40
4	Michael Pittman	.20
5	Frank Sanders	.20
6	Mar Tay Jenkins	.10
7	Pat Tilman	.10
8	Tywan Mitchell	.10
9	Jamal Anderson	.40
10	Doug Johnson	.20
11	Ephraim Salaam	.10
12	Chris Chandler	.20
13	Shawn Jefferson	.10
14	Tim Dwight	.20
15	Terance Mathis	.10
16	Jamal Lewis	1.25
17	Shannon Sharpe	.20
18	Trent Dilfer	.20
19	Ray Lewis	.20
20	Qadry Ismail	.10
21	Travis Taylor	.40
22	Chris Redman	.40
23	Priest Holmes	.20
24	Rod Woodson	.10
25	Jamie Sharper	.10
26	Doug Flutie	.50
27	Rob Johnson	.20
28	Eric Moulds	.40
29	Sammy Morris	.20
30	Shawn Bryson	.10
31	Antowain Smith	.20
32	Jeremy McDaniel	.10
33	Sam Cowart	.20
34	Muhsin Muhammad	.20
35	Brad Hoover	.40
36	Tim Biakabutuka	.20
37	Steve Beuerlein	.20
38	Donald Hayes	.20
39	Jeff Lewis	.20
40	Dameyune Craig	.20
41	Wesley Walls	.20
42	Isaac Byrd	.10
43	Cade McNown	.40
44	James Allen	.40
45	Marcus Robinson	.40
46	Brian Urlacher	.75
47	Jim Miller	.20
48	Curtis Enis	.20
49	Eddie Kennison	.20
50	Marty Booker	.10
51	Bobby Engram	.10
52	Peter Warrick	.75
53	Corey Dillon	.40
54	Akili Smith	.40
55	Danny Farmer	.20
56	Brandon Bennett	.10
57	Curtis Keaton	.20
58	Ron Dugans	.20
59	Takeo Spikes	.10
60	Scott Mitchell	.20
61	Tim Couch	.50
62	Kevin Johnson	.20
63	Travis Prentice	.40
64	Spergon Wynn	.10
65	Errict Rhett	.10
66	David Patten	.10
67	Dennis Northcutt	.20
68	Aaron Shea	.10
69	Courtney Brown	.20
70	Troy Aikman	.75
71	Emmitt Smith	1.25
72	Joey Galloway	.40
73	Raghib Ismail	.10
74	Randall Cunningham	.20
75	Anthony Wright	.20
76	James McKnight	.10
77	Dexter Coakley	.10
78	Terrell Davis	1.25
79	Mike Anderson	1.25
80	Brian Griese	.50
81	Rod Smith	.20
82	Ed McCaffrey	.20
83	Olandis Gary	.40
84	Trevor Pryce	.10
85	John Mobley	.10
86	Charlie Batch	.40
87	Germane Crowell	.30
88	James O. Stewart	.30
89	Johnnie Morton	.30
90	Herman Moore	.30
91	Mario Bates	.10
92	Desmond Howard	.10
93	Stephen Boyd	.10
94	Chris Claiborne	.10
95	Kurt Schulz	.10
96	Brett Favre	1.75
97	Antonio Freeman	.30
98	Dorsey Levens	.30
99	Ahman Green	.30
100	Matt Hasselbeck	.40
101	De'Mond Parker	.20
102	Bill Schroeder	.20
103	Bubba Franks	.30
104	Donald Driver	.10
105	Darren Sharper	.10
106	Peyton Manning	1.25
107	Edgerrin James	1.25
108	Marvin Harrison	.40
109	Jerome Pathon	.20
110	Terrence Wilkins	.20
111	Ken Dilger	.10
112	Marcus Pollard	.10
113	Brad Scioli	.10
114	Mark Brunell	.50
115	Fred Taylor	.50
116	Jimmy Smith	.30
117	Jamie Martin	.10
118	Keenan McCardell	.20
119	Kyle Brady	.10
120	R. Jay Soward	.20
121	Alvis Whitted	.10
122	Brant Boyer	.10
123	Elvis Grbac	.30
124	Tony Gonzalez	.30
125	Derrick Alexander	.20
126	Tony Richardson	.20
127	Frank Moreau	.10
128	Sylvester Morris	.40
129	Kevin Lockett	.10
130	Donnie Edwards	.10
131	Oronde Gadsden	.20
132	Lamar Smith	.40
133	Jay Fiedler	.40
134	J.J. Johnson	.10
135	Thurman Thomas	.30
136	Leslie Shepherd	.10
137	Tony Martin	.10
138	O.J. McDuffie	.10
139	Zach Thomas	.30
140	Randy Moss	1.50
141	Bubby Brister	.10
142	Cris Carter	.40
143	Daunte Culpepper	1.75
144	Moe Williams	.10
145	Troy Walters	.10
146	Chris Walsh	.10
147	Matthew Hatchette	.10
148	Kailee Wong	.10
149	Robert Griffith	.10
150	Drew Bledsoe	.50
151	Terry Glenn	.30
152	Kevin Faulk	.20
153	J.R. Redmond	.30
154	Tony Carter	.10
155	Patrick Pass	.20
156	Troy Brown	.10
157	Tony Simmons	.10
158	Michael Bishop	.30
159	Lawyer Milloy	.10
160	Ricky Williams	.60
161	Jeff Blake	.20
162	Joe Horn	.20
163	Aaron Brooks	.40
164	La'Roi Glover	.10
165	Chad Morton	.10
166	Keith Mitchell	.10
167	Willie Jackson	.10
168	Robert Wilson	.10
169	Jake Reed	.20
170	Kerry Collins	.30
171	Amani Toomer	.20
172	Ron Dayne	.75
173	Tiki Barber	.30
174	Greg Comella	.10
175	Ike Hilliard	.20
176	Joe Jurevicius	.10
177	Ron Dixon	.20
178	Jason Sehorn	.10
179	Michael Strahan	.10
180	Vinny Testaverde	.30
181	Wayne Chrebet	.30
182	Curtis Martin	.40
183	Richie Anderson	.10
184	Dedric Ward	.20
185	Laveranues Coles	.40
186	Windrell Hayes	.10
187	Chad Pennington	.75
188	Tim Brown	.30
189	Rich Gannon	.30
190	Tyrone Wheatley	.30
191	Napoleon Kaufman	.20
192	Jon Ritchie	.10
193	James Jett	.10
194	Rickey Dudley	.10
195	Andre Rison	.20
196	Eric Allen	.10
197	Charles Woodson	.20
198	Duce Staley	.40
199	Donovan McNabb	.50
200	Darnell Autry	.10
201	Chad Lewis	.10
202	Charles Johnson	.10
203	Torrance Small	.10
204	Todd Pinkston	.20
205	Brian Mitchell	.10
206	Hugh Douglas	.10
207	David Akers	.10
208	Kordell Stewart	.40
209	Jerome Bettis	.40
210	Bobby Shaw	.10
211	Hines Ward	.30
212	Plaxico Burress	.40
213	Courtney Hawkins	.10
214	Troy Edwards	.20
215	Earl Holmes	.10
216	Richard Huntley	.10
217	Marshall Faulk	.50
218	Kurt Warner	1.75
219	Isaac Bruce	.40
220	Torry Holt	.40
221	Trent Green	.30
222	Justin Watson	.10
223	Trung Canidate	.20
224	Az-Zahir Hakim	.20
225	Ricky Proehl	.10
226	Dexter McCleon	.10
227	London Fletcher	.10
228	Junior Seau	.20
229	Curtis Conway	.20
230	Rodney Harrison	.10
231	Jeff Graham	.10
232	Freddie Jones	.20
233	Reggie Jones	.20
234	Ronney Jenkins	.10
235	Trevor Gaylor	.10
236	Jeff Garcia	.40
237	Jerry Rice	1.00
238	Charlie Garner	.30
239	Terrell Owens	.40
240	J.J. Stokes	.20
241	Fred Beasley	.10
242	Tim Rattay	.30
243	Garrison Hearst	.30
244	Ricky Watters	.30
245	Shaun Alexander	.50
246	Jon Kitna	.30
247	Brock Huard	.30
248	Darrell Jackson	.20
249	James Williams	.10
250	Sean Dawkins	.10
251	John Hilliard	.10
252	Warrick Dunn	.30
253	Shaun King	.40
254	Ryan Leaf	.40
255	Mike Alstott	.40
256	Jacquez Green	.20
257	Reidel Anthony	.20
258	Derrick Brooks	.10
259	John Lynch	.20
260	Warren Sapp	.30
261	Eddie George	.50
262	Steve McNair	.40
263	Rodney Thomas	.10
264	Derrick Mason	.25
265	Yancey Thigpen	.20
266	Frank Wycheck	.10
267	Chris Sanders	.10
268	Carl Pickens	.20
269	Kevin Dyson	.20
270	Jevon Kearse	.40
271	Jeff George	.30
272	Stephen Davis	.40
273	Brad Johnson	.30
274	Albert Connell	.20
275	James Thrash	.25
276	Michael Westbrook	.30
277	Stephen Alexander	.10
278	Deion Sanders	.40
279	Champ Bailey	.30
280	Todd Husak	.30
281	*Dan Morgan*	.30
282	*Josh Booty*	.30
283	*Michael Vick*	6.00
284	*Mike McMahon*	.75
285	*Reggie White*	.30
286	*Chris Weinke*	2.50
287	*Drew Brees*	4.50
288	*Sage Rosenfels*	.75
289	*Marques Tuiasosopo*	1.50
290	*Josh Heupel*	2.25
291	*David Rivers*	.30
292	*Kevin Kasper*	.30
293	*Jesse Palmer*	.50
294	*LaDainian Tomlinson*	4.00
295	*Deuce McAllister*	2.50
296	*Kevan Barlow*	.50
297	*LaMont Jordan*	1.00
298	*James Jackson*	1.00
299	*Anthony Thomas*	4.00
300	*Correl Buckhalter*	.30
301	*Travis Henry*	1.50
302	*Dan Alexander*	.30
303	*Travis Minor*	1.00
304	*Derrick Gibson*	.50
305	*Rudi Johnson*	1.00
306	*Michael Bennett*	3.00
307	*Alge Crumpler*	.30
308	*Todd Heap*	.50
309	*Marvin "Snoop" Minnis*	1.00
310	*Santana Moss*	3.00
311	*Reggie Wayne*	1.50
312	*Koren Robinson*	2.25
313	*Chris Chambers*	3.00
314	*David Terrell*	3.00
315	*Rod Gardner*	2.25
316	*Quincy Morgan*	1.00
317	*Ken-Yon Rambo*	.50
318	*Vinny Sutherland*	.50
319	*David Allen*	.30
320	*Bobby Newcombe*	.50
321	*Ronney Daniels*	.30
322	*T.J. Houshmandzadeh*	.50
323	*Chad Johnson*	1.00
324	*Freddie Mitchell*	1.25
325	*Moran Norris*	.30
326	Ron Dayne	.30
327	Mike Anderson	.50
328	Jamal Lewis	.50
329	Brian Urlacher	.40
330	Darren Howard	.10

2001 Upper Deck MVP Campus Classics

		MT
Common Player:		15.00
Multi-Color Swatches:		1.5x
Inserted 1:144		
Autographs:		2.5x
Production 25 Sets		
CC-TA	Troy Aikman	50.00
CC-MB	Michael Bennett	35.00
CC-DB	Drew Brees	60.00
CC-RD	Ron Dayne	35.00
CC-MF	Marshall Faulk	35.00
CC-JF	Jamar Fletcher	20.00
CC-KJ	Keyshawn Johnson	15.00
CC-PM	Peyton Manning	85.00
CC-DM	Deuce McAllister	35.00
CC-CM	Cade McNown	15.00
CC-FM	Freddie Mitchell	25.00
CC-AT	Anthony Thomas	50.00
CC-LT	LaDainian Tomlinson	85.00
CC-MT	Marques Tuiasosopo	20.00
CC-MV	Michael Vick	85.00
CC-CW	Chris Weinke	40.00

2001 Upper Deck MVP Souvenirs

		MT
Common Player:		8.00
Inserted 1:48		
Autographs:		5x
Production 25 Sets		
CB-S	Charlie Batch	8.00
AB-S	Aaron Brooks	12.00
BW-S	Aaron Brooks, Kurt Warner	35.00
DC-S	Daunte Culpepper	20.00
CM-S	Daunte Culpepper, Randy Moss	40.00
SD-S	Stephen Davis	8.00
RD-S	Ron Dayne	15.00
BF-S	Brett Favre	30.00
FM-S	Brett Favre, Donovan McNabb	35.00
GB-S	Rich Gannon, Tim Brown	15.00
GR-S	Jeff Garcia, Jerry Rice	30.00
GD-S	Jeff George, Stephen Davis	10.00
EJ-S	Edgerrin James	30.00
KJ-S	Keyshawn Johnson	8.00
TJ-S	Thomas Jones	8.00
TB-S	Shaun King, Keyshawn Johnson	10.00
JL-S	Jamal Lewis	25.00
PM-S	Peyton Manning	30.00
MJ-S	Peyton Manning, Edgerrin James	45.00
DM-S	Donovan McNabb	15.00
MC-S	Donovan McNabb, Daunte Culpepper	40.00
MR-S	Cade McNown, Marcus Robinson	10.00
RM-S	Randy Moss	30.00
RE-S	J.R. Redmond	8.00
JR-S	Jerry Rice	20.00
TM-S	Vinny Testaverde, Curtis Martin	10.00
BU-S	Brian Urlacher	18.00
KW-S	Kurt Warner	25.00
WF-S	Kurt Warner, Marshall Faulk	40.00
PW-S	Peter Warrick	15.00

2001 Upper Deck MVP Team MVP

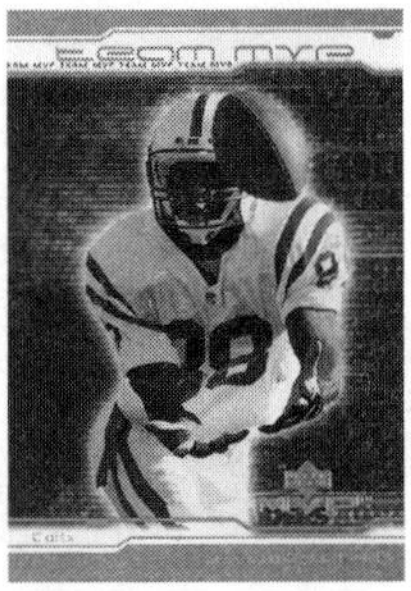

MT
Complete Set (20): 15.00
Common Player: .50
Minor Stars: 1.00
Inserted 1:6
MVP1 Brian Griese 1.25
MVP2 Rich Gannon .50
MVP3 Marshall Faulk 1.25
MVP4 Edgerrin James 6.00
MVP5 Eddie George 1.25
MVP6 Mike Anderson 3.00
MVP7 Ed McCaffrey .50
MVP8 Marvin Harrison 1.00
MVP9 Isaac Bruce 1.00
MVP10 Eric Moulds 1.00
MVP11 Tony Gonzalez .50
MVP12 Mike Alstott 1.00
MVP13 Ray Lewis .50
MVP14 Junior Seau 1.00
MVP15 Warren Sapp 1.00
MVP16 La'Roi Glover .50
MVP17 Derrick Brooks .50
MVP18 Charles Woodson 1.00
MVP19 Champ Bailey 1.00
MVP20 John Lynch .50

2001 Upper Deck MVP Top 10 Performers

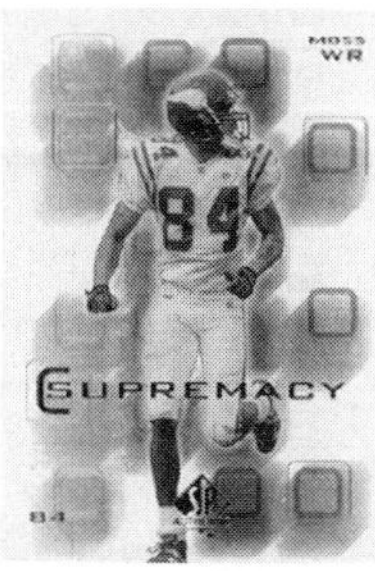

MT
Complete Set (10): 18.00
Common Player: .75
Minor Stars: 1.50
Inserted 1:13
TOP1 Mike Anderson 5.00
TOP2 Vinny Testaverde 1.50
TOP3 Terrell Owens 1.50
TOP4 Aaron Brooks 1.50
TOP5 Jamal Lewis 6.00
TOP6 Fred Taylor 2.50
TOP7 Randy Moss 6.00
TOP8 Ricky Williams 3.00
TOP9 Jason Sehorn .75
TOP10 Shannon Sharpe .75

2001 Upper Deck NFL Rookie FX

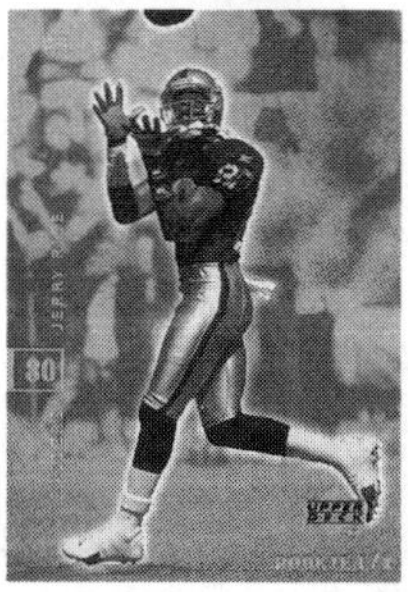

MT
Complete Set (225): 35.00
Common Player: .20
Minor Stars: .40
Common Player (226-338): 1.00
Common F/X (226-338): 3.00
Production 750 Sets
Only F/X Cards Are Rookies
Pack (5): 3.00
Box (24): 70.00
1 Jake Plummer .40
2 Thomas Jones .20
3 David Boston .60
4 Jamal Anderson .40
5 Chris Chandler .20
6 Tony Martin .20
7 Jamal Lewis 1.25
8 Elvis Grbac .40
9 Ray Lewis .50
10 Rob Johnson .40
11 Eric Moulds .50
12 Muhsin Muhammad .40
13 Tim Biakabutuka .40
14 James Allen .20
15 Marcus Robinson .50
16 Brian Urlacher 1.25
17 Jon Kitna .20
18 Peter Warrick .60
19 Corey Dillon .50
20 Kevin Johnson .40
21 Dennis Northcutt .20
22 Tim Couch .75
23 Raghib Ismail .20
24 Emmitt Smith 1.50
25 Joey Galloway .40
26 Terrell Davis 1.25
27 Rod Smith .40
28 Brian Griese .75
29 Mike Anderson 1.00
30 Charlie Batch .40
31 James O. Stewart .40
32 Germane Crowell .40
33 Brett Favre 2.50
34 Antonio Freeman .50
35 Ahman Green .60
36 Peyton Manning 2.00
37 Edgerrin James 1.50
38 Marvin Harrison .60
39 Jerome Pathon .20
40 Mark Brunell .60
41 Fred Taylor .75
42 Jimmy Smith .40
43 Tony Gonzalez .50
44 Priest Holmes .40
45 Trent Green .40
46 Oronde Gadsden .40
47 Jay Fiedler .40
48 Lamar Smith .40
49 Randy Moss 2.00
50 Cris Carter .50
51 Daunte Culpepper 1.25
52 Drew Bledsoe .75
53 Antowain Smith .20
54 Tom Brady 5.00
55 Ricky Williams 1.00
56 Joe Horn .20
57 Aaron Brooks .75
58 Kerry Collins .40
59 Tiki Barber .40
60 Ron Dayne .40
61 Vinny Testaverde .50
62 Wayne Chrebet .40
63 Curtis Martin .50
64 Tyrone Wheatley .20
65 Rich Gannon .40
66 Jerry Rice 1.50
67 Duce Staley .40
68 Donovan McNabb 1.25
69 Kordell Stewart .60
70 Jerome Bettis .40
71 Marshall Faulk .75
72 Kurt Warner 2.00
73 Torry Holt .60
74 Doug Flutie .75
75 Freddie Jones .20
76 Jeff Garcia .50
77 Garrison Hearst .40
78 Terrell Owens .50
79 Tai Streets .40
80 Ricky Watters .40
81 Matt Hasselbeck .40
82 Darrell Jackson .20
83 Brad Johnson .40
84 Warrick Dunn .40
85 Keyshawn Johnson .50
86 Eddie George .75
87 Steve McNair .50
88 Tony Banks .20
89 Michael Westbrook .40
90 Stephen Davis .60
91 Bob Christian .20
92 Brian Finneran .20
93 Brandon Stokely .20
94 Jeremy McDaniel .20
95 Brad Hoover .20
96 Donald Hayes .20
97 Jim Miller .40
98 Danny Farmer .20
99 Anthony Wright .40
100 Jackie Harris .20
101 Howard Griffith .20
102 Desmond Howard .20
103 Bill Schroeder .40
104 Terrence Wilkins .20
105 Todd Collins .20
106 Sylvester Morris .40
107 Zach Thomas .20
108 Robert Griffith .20
109 Kevin Faulk .40
110 Willie Jackson .20
111 Ron Dixon .20
112 Michael Strahan .20
113 Richie Anderson .20
114 Chad Pennington 1.00
115 Charles Woodson .20
116 Chad Lewis .20
117 Az-Zahir Hakim .40
118 Rodney Harrison .20
119 Mike Alstott .50
120 Jevon Kearse .50
121 MarTay Jenkins .20
122 Pat Tillman .20
123 Rod Woodson .40
124 Marty Booker .20
125 Scott Mitchell .20
126 John Mobley .20
127 Stephen Boyd .20
128 Kurt Schultz .20
129 Kyle Brady .20
130 Donnie Edwards .20
131 J.J. Johnson .20
132 Chris Walsh .20
133 J.R. Redmond .20
134 Keith Mitchell .20
135 Joe Jurivicius .20
136 Eric Allen .20
137 Todd Pinkston .20
138 Bobby Shaw .20
139 Hines Ward .40
140 Ricky Proehl .20
141 London Fletcher .20
142 Jeff Graham .20
143 Tim Rattay .20
144 Fred Beasley .20
145 James Williams .20
146 Derrick Brooks .20
147 Warren Sapp .40
148 Derrick Mason .20
149 Kevin Dyson .20
150 Champ Bailey .20
151 Michael Pittman .20
152 Kwamie Lassiter .20
153 Maurice Smith .20
154 Keith Brooking .20
155 Travis Taylor .40
156 Tony Siragusa .20
157 Alex Van Pelt .20
158 Shane Matthews .20
159 Darnay Scott .40
160 Aaron Shea .20
161 JaJuan Dawson .20
162 Clint Stoerner .50
163 Dat Nguyen .20
164 Bill Romanowski .20
165 Robert Porcher .20
166 Bubba Franks .20
167 Rob Morris .20
168 Stacey Mack .20
169 Chris Hovan .20
170 Lawyer Milloy .20
171 La'Roi Glover .20
172 Jessie Armstead .20
173 Mo Lewis .20
174 Jon Ritchie .20
175 James Thrash .40
176 Trung Canidate .40
177 Grant Wistrom .20
178 Curtis Conway .40
179 Ronney Jenkins .20
180 John Lynch .20
181 Frank Sanders .40
182 Shawn Jefferson .20
183 Darrick Vaughn .20
184 Terance Mathis .20
185 Shannon Sharpe .40
186 Qadry Ismail .40
187 Sammy Morris .20
188 Shawn Bryson .20
189 Wesley Walls .20
190 Akili Smith .50
191 Ron Dugans .20
192 Travis Prentice .40
193 Courtney Brown .20
194 Ed McCaffrey .50
195 Olandis Gary .40
196 Johnnie Morton .40
197 Dorsey Levens .40
198 Ken Dilger .20
199 Keenan McCardell .40
200 Derrick Alexander .40
201 Tony Richardson .20
202 Jason Taylor .20
203 O.J. McDuffie .40
204 Troy Walters .20
205 Troy Brown .40
206 Jeff Blake .40
207 Albert Connell .40
208 Amani Toomer .40
209 Ike Hilliard .20
210 Jason Sehorn .20
211 Laveranues Coles .40
212 Tim Brown .60
213 Charlie Garner .40
214 Plaxico Burress .60
215 Troy Edwards .40
216 Isaac Bruce .60
217 Junior Seau .40
218 Marcellus Wiley .20
219 J.J. Stokes .40
220 Shaun Alexander 1.00
221 John Randle .20
222 Jacquez Green .40
223 Neil O'Donnell .20
224 Frank Wycheck .20
225 Stephen Alexander .20
226 A.J. Feeley 2.50
227 Adam Archuleta 2.00
228 Willie Middlebrooks 2.00
229 Alex Bannister 2.50
230 Alge Crumpler 2.00
231 Andre Carter 1.00
232 Andre Dyson 1.00
233 Anthony Thomas 10.00
234 Arthur Love 1.00
235 Bobby Newcombe 2.00
236 Zeke Moreno 2.00
237 Brandon Spoon 1.00
238 Brian Allen 1.00
239 Carlos Polk 1.00
240 Casey Hampton 1.00
241 Cedrick Wilson 1.00
242 Chad Johnson 2.50
243 Chris Barnes 1.00
244 Chris Chambers 6.00
245 Chris Taylor 1.00
246 Chris Weinke 5.00
247 Correll Buckhalter 4.00
248 Damione Lewis 1.00
249 Dan Alexander 2.00
250 Dan Morgan 1.00
251 Darnerian McCants 1.00
255 David Terrell 6.00
256 Dee Brown 1.00
257 Derek Combs 1.00
258 Derrick Blaylock 1.00
259 Derrick Gibson 1.00
260 Deuce McAllister 5.00
263 Drew Brees 8.00
265 Eddie Berlin 1.00
266 Edgerton Hartwell 1.00
267 Francis St. Paul 1.00
268 Fred Smoot 2.00
269 Freddie Mitchell 5.00
270 Gary Baxter 1.00
271 George Layne 1.00
272 Gerard Warren 1.00
273 Hakim Akbar 1.00
274 Heath Evans 1.00
275 Jabari Holloway 1.00
276 Jamal Reynolds 2.00
277 Jamar Fletcher 2.00
278 James Jackson 3.00
279 Jamie Winborn 1.00
280 Jesse Palmer 3.00
281 John Capel 2.00
282 Josh Booty 2.50
283 Josh Heupel 3.00
284 Justin McCareins 1.00
285 Justin Smith 2.00
286 Karon Riley 1.00
287 Ken Lucas 1.00
288 Ken-Yon Rambo 2.00
289 Kenyatta Walker 1.00
290 Kevan Barlow 4.00
291 Kevin Kasper 2.00
292 Koren Robinson 5.00
293 LaDainian Tomlinson 8.00
294 Lamont Jordon 2.50
295 Leonard Davis 1.00
296 Marcus Stroud 1.00
297 Marques Tuiasosopo 5.00
298 Marvin "Snoop" Minnis 4.00
299 Michael Bennett 6.00
300 Michael Stone 1.00
301 Michael Vick 10.00
302 Mike McMahon 5.00
303 Moran Norris 1.00
304 Morlon Greenwood 1.00
305 Nate Clements 1.00
307 Orlando Huff 1.00
308 Quincy Carter 6.00
309 Quincy Morgan 3.00
310 Reggie Wayne 5.00
311 Reggie White 1.00
312 Richard Seymour 1.00
313 Robert Ferguson 2.50
314 Rod Gardner 5.00
316 Rudi Johnson 2.50
317 Sage Rosenfels 3.00
318 Santana Moss 5.00
319 Scotty Anderson 1.00
320 Sedrick Hodge 2.00
321 Shaun Rogers 1.00
322 Steve Hutchinson 1.00
323 Stevonne Smith 1.00
324 T.J. Houshmandzadeh 1.00
325 Tay Cody 1.00
327 Todd Heap 2.00
328 Tommy Polley 3.00
329 Tony Dixon 1.00
330 Torrance Marshall 1.00
331 Travis Henry 4.00
332 Travis Minor 3.00
333 Vinny Sutherland 2.50
334 Will Allen 2.00

MVP
230 Alge Crumpler 2.00
233 Anthony Thomas 10.00
235 Bobby Newcombe 2.00
242 Chad Johnson 2.50
244 Chris Chambers 6.00
246 Chris Weinke 5.00
247 Correll Buckhalter 4.00
249 Dan Alexander 2.00
250 Dan Morgan 1.00
253 David Allen 1.00
254 David Rivers 1.00
255 David Terrell 6.00
259 Derrick Gibson 1.00
260 Deuce McAllister 5.00
263 Drew Brees 8.00
269 Freddie Mitchell 5.00
278 James Jackson 3.00
280 Jesse Palmer 3.00
282 Josh Booty 2.50
283 Josh Heupel 3.00
288 Ken-Yon Rambo 2.00
290 Kevan Barlow 4.00
291 Kevin Kasper 2.00
292 Koren Robinson 5.00
293 LaDainian Tomlinson 8.00
294 LaMont Jordan 2.50
297 Marques Tuiasosopo 5.00
298 Marvin "Snoop" Minnis 4.00
299 Michael Bennett 6.00
301 Michael Vick 10.00
302 Mike McMahon 5.00
303 Moran Norris 1.00
309 Quincy Morgan 3.00
310 Reggie Wayne 5.00
311 Reggie White 1.00
314 Rod Gardner 5.00
315 Ronney Daniels 1.00
316 Rudi Johnson 2.50
317 Sage Rosenfels 3.00
318 Santana Moss 5.00
324 T.J. Houshmandzadeh 1.00
327 Todd Heap 2.00
331 Travis Henry 4.00
332 Travis Minor 3.00
333 Vinny Sutherland 2.50

Rookie F/X
226 *A.J. Feeley* 4.00
233 *Anthony Thomas* 15.00
241 *Cedrick Wilson* 3.00
242 *Chad Johnson* 4.00
244 *Chris Chambers* 10.00
246 *Chris Weinke* 8.00
247 *Correll Buckhalter* 6.00
250 *Dan Morgan* 3.00
255 *David Terrell* 10.00
260 *Deuce McAllister* 8.00
261 *Dominic Rhodes* 10.00
262 *Drew Bennett* 6.00
263 *Drew Brees* 12.00
269 *Freddie Mitchell* 8.00
278 *James Jackson* 5.00
280 *Jesse Palmer* 5.00
282 *Josh Booty* 4.00
284 *Justin McCareins* 3.00
290 *Kevan Barlow* 6.00
291 *Kevin Kasper* 4.00
292 *Koren Robinson* 8.00
293 *LaDainian Tomlinson* 12.00
294 *LaMont Jordan* 4.00
297 *Marques Tuiasosopo* 8.00
298 *Marvin "Snoop" Minnis* 6.00
299 *Michael Bennett* 10.00
301 *Michael Vick* 15.00
302 *Mike McMahon* 8.00
306 *Nick Goings* 3.00
308 *Quincy Carter* 10.00
309 *Quincy Morgan* 5.00
310 *Reggie Wayne* 8.00
313 *Robert Ferguson* 4.00
314 *Rod Gardner* 8.00
316 *Rudi Johnson* 4.00
318 *Santana Moss* 8.00
323 *Steve Smith* 3.00
327 *Todd Heap* 3.00
331 *Travis Henry* 6.00
332 *Travis Minor* 5.00

Victory
227 Adam Archuleta 2.00
229 Alex Bannister 2.50
230 Alge Crumpler 2.00
233 Anthony Thomas 10.00
235 Bobby Newcombe 2.00
241 Cedrick Wilson 1.00
242 Chad Johnson 2.50
243 Chris Barnes 1.00
244 Chris Chambers 6.00
246 Chris Weinke 5.00
247 Correll Buckhalter 4.00
249 Dan Alexander 2.00
250 Dan Morgan 1.00
255 David Terrell 6.00
259 Derrick Gibson 1.00
260 Deuce McAllister 5.00
263 Drew Brees 8.00
265 Eddie Berlin 1.00
269 Freddie Mitchell 5.00
270 Gary Baxter 1.00
272 Gerard Warren 1.00
274 Heath Evans 1.00
275 Jabari Holloway 1.00
276 Jamal Reynolds 2.00
277 Jamar Fletcher 2.00
278 James Jackson 3.00
280 Jesse Palmer 3.00
282 Josh Booty 2.50
283 Josh Heupel 3.00
285 Justin Smith 2.00
288 Ken-Yon Rambo 2.00
290 Kevan Barlow 4.00
291 Kevin Kasper 2.00
292 Koren Robinson 5.00
293 LaDainian Tomlinson 8.00
294 LaMont Jordan 2.50
297 Marques Tuiasosopo 5.00
298 Marvin "Snoop" Minnis 4.00
299 Michael Bennett 6.00
302 Mike McMahon 5.00
303 Moran Norris 1.00
305 Nate Clements 1.00
308 Quincy Carter 6.00
309 Quincy Morgan 3.00
310 Reggie Wayne 5.00
313 Robert Ferguson 2.50
314 Rod Gardner 5.00
316 Rudi Johnson 2.50
317 Sage Rosenfels 3.00
318 Santana Moss 5.00
319 Scotty Anderson 1.00
323 Steve Smith 2.00
324 T.J. Houshmandzadeh 1.00
326 Tim Hasselbeck 2.00
327 Todd Heap 2.00
331 Travis Henry 4.00
332 Travis Minor 3.00
333 Vinny Sutherland 2.50
334 Will Allen 1.00
338 Troy Hambrick 12.00

Vintage Rookies-Singles
226 A.J. Feeley 2.50
227 Adam Archuleta 2.00
228 Willie Middlebrooks 2.00
230 Alge Crumpler 2.00
231 Andre Carter 1.00
233 Anthony Thomas 10.00
235 Bobby Newcombe 2.00
242 Chad Johnson 2.50
243 Chris Barnes 1.00
244 Chris Chambers 6.00
246 Chris Weinke 5.00
247 Correll Buckhalter 4.00
250 Dan Morgan 1.00
252 Dave Dickenson 3.00
253 David Allen 1.00
255 David Terrell 6.00
260 Deuce McAllister 5.00
263 Drew Brees 8.00
264 Dustin McClintock 1.00
269 Freddie Mitchell 5.00
272 Gerard Warren 1.00
273 Hakim Akbar 1.00
276 Jamal Reynolds 2.00
278 James Jackson 3.00
280 Jesse Palmer 3.00
282 Josh Booty 2.50
283 Josh Heupel 3.00
285 Justin Smith 2.00
290 Kevan Barlow 4.00
291 Kevin Kasper 2.00
292 Koren Robinson 5.00
293 LaDainian Tomlinson 8.00
294 LaMont Jordan 2.50
295 Leonard Davis 1.00
296 Marcus Stroud 1.00
297 Marques Tuiasosopo 5.00
298 Marvin "Snoop" Minnis 4.00
299 Michael Bennett 6.00
301 Michael Vick 10.00
302 Mike McMahon 5.00
303 Moran Norris 1.00
305 Nate Clements 1.00
308 Quincy Carter 6.00
309 Quincy Morgan 3.00
310 Reggie Wayne 5.00
312 Richard Seymour 1.00
313 Robert Ferguson 2.50
314 Rod Gardner 5.00
316 Rudi Johnson 2.50
317 Sage Rosenfels 3.00
318 Santana Moss 5.00
321 Shaun Rogers 1.00
324 T.J. Houshmandzadeh 1.00
326 Tim Hasselbeck 2.00
327 Todd Heap 2.00
329 Tony Dixon 1.00
331 Travis Henry 4.00
332 Travis Minor 3.00
333 Vinny Sutherland 2.50
334 Will Allen 1.00
335 Jason Brookins 3.00
336 Dominic Rhodes 10.00
337 Benjamin Gay 5.00
338 Troy Hambrick 12.00

2001 Upper Deck NFL Rookie FX Heroes of Football

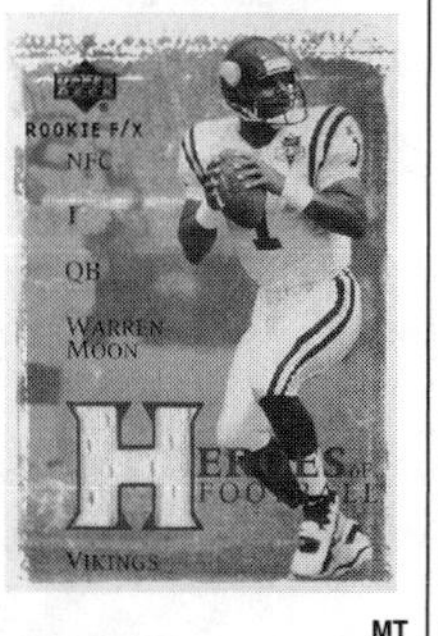

MT
Common Player: 15.00
Inserted 1:48
HF-HA Herb Adderly 15.00
HF-JE John Elway 40.00
HF-JK Jim Kelly 20.00
HF-RL Ronnie Lott 15.00
HF-TM Tom Mack 15.00
HF-DM Dan Marino 50.00
HF-MA Jim Marshall 15.00
HF-WM Warren Moon 15.00
HF-ON Ozzie Newsome 15.00
HF-JR John Riggins 40.00
HF-JT Jim Taylor 25.00
HF-TT Thurman Thomas 15.00
HF-DW Danny White 15.00
HF-RW Reggie White 15.00
HF-SY Steve Young 25.00

2001 Upper Deck NFL Rookie FX Legendary Combos

MT
Common Player: 25.00
Production 100 Sets
LC-FG Brett Favre, Ahman Green 75.00
LC-GM Brian Griese, Ed McCaffrey 25.00
LC-WF Kurt Warner, Marshall Faulk 75.00
LC-TB LaDainian Tomlinson, Drew Brees 75.00
LC-MH Peyton Manning, Marvin Harrison 50.00
LC-DB Ron Dayne, Tiki Barber 25.00
LC-YR Steve Young, Jerry Rice 60.00

2001 Upper Deck NFL Rookie FX Legends in the Making

MT
Common Player: 10.00
Inserted 1:48
LM-JA Jamal Anderson 10.00
LM-DB Drew Bledsoe 15.00
LM-DBr Drew Brees 25.00
LM-TB Tim Brown 10.00
LM-KC Kerry Collins 10.00
LM-TC Tim Couch 10.00
LM-TD Terrell Davis 20.00
LM-BF Brett Favre 40.00
LM-EG Eddie George 15.00
LM-EG Elvis Grbac 10.00
LM-PM Peyton Manning 30.00
LM-JR Jerry Rice 30.00
LM-WS Warren Sapp 10.00
LM-JrS Junior Seau 12.00
LM-JS Jimmy Smith 10.00
LM-LT LaDainian Tomlinson 20.00

2001 Upper Deck Ovation

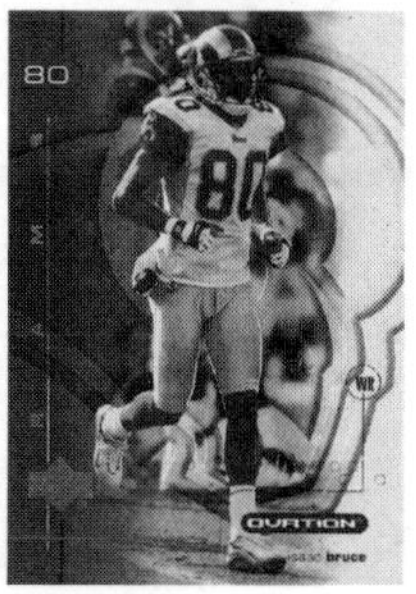

MT
Complete Set (150): 600.00
Common Player: .15
Minor Stars: .30
Common Rookie: 3.00
Black & White Rookie: 80%
Embossed Rookie: 1x
Pack (5): 4.00
Wax Box (20): 55.00
1 Jake Plummer .50
2 Thomas Jones .30
3 Frank Sanders .30
4 Jamal Anderson .50
5 Chris Chandler .30
6 Terance Mathis .15
7 Jamal Lewis 1.25
8 Elvis Grbac .30
9 Travis Taylor .50
10 Shawn Bryson .15
11 Rob Johnson .30
12 Eric Moulds .50
13 Muhsin Muhammad .30
14 Donald Hayes .30
15 Tim Biakabutuka .30
16 Cade McNown .50
17 Marcus Robinson .50
18 Brian Urlacher 1.00
19 Akili Smith .50
20 Peter Warrick .60
21 Corey Dillon .50
22 Kevin Johnson .50
23 Spergon Wynn .15
24 Tim Couch .60
25 Tony Banks .30
26 Emmitt Smith 1.25
27 Anthony Wright .30
28 Terrell Davis 1.00
29 Mike Anderson 1.25
30 Brian Griese .60
31 Ed McCaffrey .50
32 Charlie Batch .50
33 Germane Crowell .50
34 Johnnie Morton .30
35 Brett Favre 2.00
36 Antonio Freeman .50
37 Dorsey Levens .30
38 Ahman Green .50
39 Peyton Manning 1.50
40 Edgerrin James 1.25
41 Marvin Harrison .50
42 Mark Brunell .60
43 Fred Taylor .60
44 Jimmy Smith .50
45 Tony Gonzalez .30
46 Trent Green .50
47 Derrick Alexander .30
48 Oronde Gadsden .30
49 Tony Martin .15
50 Lamar Smith .50
51 Randy Moss 1.50
52 Cris Carter .50
53 Daunte Culpepper 1.00
54 Drew Bledsoe .60
55 Terry Glenn .30
56 Ricky Williams .75
57 Jeff Blake .30
58 Aaron Brooks .60
59 Kerry Collins .30
60 Tiki Barber .50
61 Ron Dayne .75
62 Vinny Testaverde .30
63 Wayne Chrebet .50
64 Curtis Martin .50
65 Tim Brown .30
66 Rich Gannon .30
67 Jerry Rice 1.00
68 Duce Staley .50
69 Donovan McNabb .75
70 Kordell Stewart .50
71 Jerome Bettis .50
72 Marshall Faulk .60
73 Kurt Warner 1.50
74 Isaac Bruce .50
75 Doug Flutie .60
76 Junior Seau .30
77 Jeff Garcia .50
78 Garrison Hearst .30
79 Terrell Owens .50

80	Ricky Watters	.30
81	Matt Hasselbeck	.50
82	Keyshawn Johnson	.50
83	Warrick Dunn	.50
84	Mike Alstott	.50
85	Kevin Dyson	.30
86	Eddie George	.60
87	Steve McNair	.50
88	Jeff George	.30
89	Michael Westbrook	.30
90	Stephen Davis	.50
91	*Milton Wynn*	4.00
92	*Dan Alexander*	6.00
93	*Rudi Johnson*	8.00
94	*Ken-Yon Rambo*	7.00
95	*Alex Bannister*	6.00
96	*Adam Archuleta*	8.00
97	*Andre Dyson*	3.00
98	*Cedrick Wilson*	6.00
99	*Chris Taylor*	5.00
100	*Eddie Berlin*	5.00
101	*Gary Baxter*	5.00
102	*Heath Evans*	5.00
103	*Jabari Holloway*	6.00
104	*Jamal Reynolds*	7.00
105	*Jamar Fletcher*	6.00
106	*Justin Smith*	4.00
107	*Kevin Kasper*	10.00
108	*Moran Norris*	3.00
109	*Nate Clements*	5.00
110	*Scotty Anderson*	5.00
111	*T.J. Houshmandzadeh*	5.00
112	*Travis Minor*	8.00
113	*Vinny Sutherland*	7.00
114	*Will Allen*	5.00
115	*Derrick Gibson*	3.00
116	*Kevan Barlow*	15.00
117	*LaMont Jordan*	12.00
118	*Todd Heap*	10.00
119	*Quincy Morgan*	15.00
120	*Dan Morgan*	10.00
121	*Gerard Warren*	10.00
122	*Mike McMahon*	12.00
123	*Sage Rosenfels*	12.00
124	*Marques Tuiasosopo*	20.00
125	*Josh Heupel*	15.00
126	*Jesse Palmer*	10.00
127	*Quincy Carter*	25.00
128	*Josh Booty*	10.00
129	*Correl Buckhalter*	15.00
130	*Travis Henry*	25.00
131	*Alge Crumpler*	10.00
132	*Marvin "Snoop" Minnis*	15.00
133	*Bobby Newcombe*	7.00
134	*Robert Ferguson*	8.00
135	*James Jackson*	15.00
136	*Michael Bennett*	30.00
137	*Drew Brees*	60.00
138	*Chris Chambers*	20.00
139	*Rod Gardner*	30.00
140	*Chad Johnson*	15.00
141	*Freddie Mitchell*	20.00
142	*Deuce McAllister*	35.00
143	*Santana Moss*	20.00
144	*Koren Robinson*	25.00
145	*David Terrell*	30.00
146	*LaDainian Tomlinson*	60.00
147	*Anthony Thomas*	60.00
148	*Reggie Wayne*	20.00
149	*Michael Vick*	75.00
150	*Chris Weinke*	30.00

2001 Upper Deck Ovation Rookie Gear

		MT
Common Player:		12.00
Inserted 1:20		
R-KB	Kevan Barlow	20.00
R-MB	Michael Bennett	30.00
R-DB	Drew Brees	40.00
R-MM	Chris Chambers	15.00
R-RF	Robert Ferguson	12.00
R-RG	Rod Gardner	20.00
R-JJ	James Jackson	15.00
R-DM	Deuce McAllister	25.00
R-QM	Quincy Morgan	15.00
R-SM	Santana Moss	20.00
R-KR	Koren Robinson	15.00
R-MV	Michael Vick	50.00
R-CW	Chris Weinke	30.00

2001 Upper Deck Ovation Train for the Game

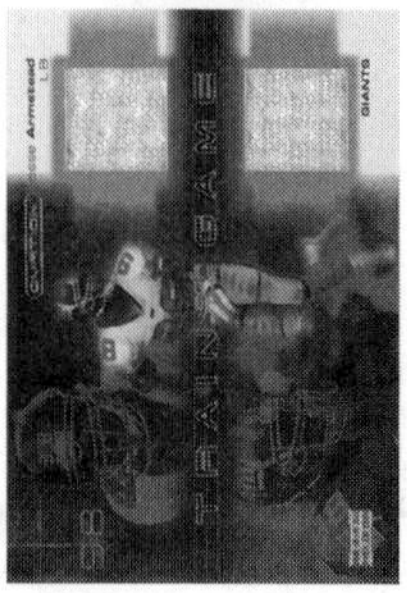

		MT
Common Player:		15.00
Inserted 1:120		
TG-JA	Jesse Armstead	15.00
TG-MB	Mark Brunell	30.00
TG-BF	Brett Favre	65.00
TG-DF	Doug Flutie	40.00
TG-JS	Junior Seau	20.00

Post-1980 cards in Near Mint condition will generally sell for about 75% of the quoted Mint value. Excellent-condition cards bring no more than 40%.

2001 Upper Deck Ovation Training Gear

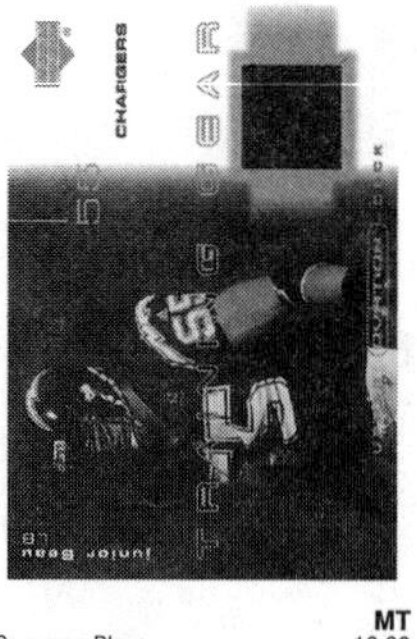

		MT
Common Player:		10.00
Inserted 1:20		
T-TB	Tiki Barber	10.00
T-BO	David Boston	15.00
T-DB	Drew Brees	40.00
T-MB	Mark Brunell	15.00
T-CC	Curtis Conway	10.00
T-TC	Tim Couch	20.00
T-RD	Ron Dayne	15.00
T-CD	Corey Dillon	15.00
T-BF	Brett Favre	45.00
T-RG	Rich Gannon	15.00
T-JG	Jeff Garcia	15.00
T-CG	Charlie Garner	10.00
T-EG	Elvis Grbac	15.00
T-JH	Jim Harbaugh	10.00
T-TJ	Thomas Jones	15.00
T-CK	Curtis Keaton	10.00
T-KM	Keenan McCardell	10.00
T-TO	Terrell Owens	15.00
T-MP	Michael Pittman	10.00
T-JP	Jake Plummer	15.00
T-JR	Jerry Rice	30.00
T-FS	Frank Sanders	10.00
T-JrS	Junior Seau	15.00
T-JS	Jason Sehorn	15.00
T-AS	Akili Smith	15.00
T-JJ	J.J. Stokes	10.00
T-FT	Fred Taylor	20.00
T-PW	Peter Warrick	15.00
T-TW	Tyrone Wheatley	10.00
T-CW	Charles Woodson	15.00

2001 Upper Deck Ovation Training Gear Trios

		MT
Common Player:		25.00
Inserted 1:240		
TT-J	Mark Brunell, Fred Taylor, Keenan McCardell	45.00
TT-C	Akili Smith, Corey Dillon, Peter Warrick	40.00
TT-A	Jake Plummer, Thomas Jones, David Boston	25.00
TT-NY	Jesse Armstead, Tiki Barber, Ron Dayne	30.00
TT-SD	Junior Seau, Drew Brees, Doug Flutie	85.00
TT-GB	Jeff Garcia, Terrell Owens, J.J. Stokes	40.00
TT-O	Rich Gannon, Tyrone Wheatley, Jerry Rice	60.00

2001 Upper Deck Pros & Prospects

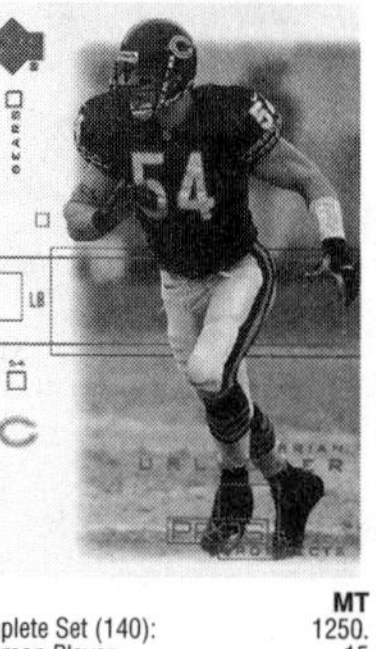

		MT
Complete Set (140):		1250.
Common Player:		.15
Minor Stars:		.30
Common Rookie:		12.00
Production 1,000 Sets		
Pack (5):		5.00
Wax Box (24):		100.00
1	Jake Plummer	.50
2	David Boston	.50
3	Jamal Anderson	.50
4	Doug Johnson	.50
5	Maurice Smith	.15
6	Jamal Lewis	1.50
7	Shannon Sharpe	.30
8	Trent Dilfer	.30
9	Doug Flutie	.75
10	Rob Johnson	.30
11	Eric Moulds	.50
12	Muhsin Muhammad	.30
13	Brad Hoover	.50
14	Tim Biakabutuka	.30
15	Cade McNown	.50
16	James Allen	.30
17	Marcus Robinson	.50
18	Brian Urlacher	1.00
19	Peter Warrick	1.00
20	Corey Dillon	.50
21	Tim Couch	.75
22	Kevin Johnson	.30
23	Travis Prentice	.50
24	Troy Aikman	1.00
25	Emmitt Smith	1.25
26	Terrell Davis	1.25
27	Mike Anderson	1.25
28	Brian Griese	.50
29	Charlie Batch	.30
30	Germane Crowell	.30
31	James O. Stewart	.30
32	Brett Favre	2.00
33	Antonio Freeman	.30
34	Dorsey Levens	.30
35	Ahman Green	.30
36	Peyton Manning	1.50
37	Edgerrin James	1.50
38	Marvin Harrison	.50
39	Mark Brunell	.75
40	Fred Taylor	.50
41	Jimmy Smith	.30
42	Elvis Grbac	.30
43	Tony Gonzalez	.30
44	Derrick Alexander	.15
45	Oronde Gadsden	.15
46	Lamar Smith	.50
47	Jay Fiedler	.30
48	Randy Moss	1.50
49	Moe Williams	.15
50	Cris Carter	.50
51	Daunte Culpepper	1.00
52	Drew Bledsoe	.75
53	Terry Glenn	.50
54	Ricky Williams	.75
55	Jeff Blake	.30
56	Joe Horn	.30
57	Aaron Brooks	.50
58	LaRoi Glover	.15
59	Kerry Collins	.30
60	Amani Toomer	.30
61	Ron Dayne	1.00
62	Vinny Testaverde	.30
63	Wayne Chrebet	.30
64	Curtis Martin	.50
65	Tim Brown	.30
66	Rich Gannon	.30
67	Tyrone Wheatley	.30
68	Duce Staley	.50
69	Donovan McNabb	.75
70	Kordell Stewart	.50
71	Jerome Bettis	.50
72	Marshall Faulk	.50
73	Kurt Warner	1.75
74	Isaac Bruce	.50
75	Junior Seau	.30
76	Curtis Conway	.30
77	Jeff Garcia	.50
78	Jerry Rice	1.00
79	Charlie Garner	.30
80	Terrell Owens	.50
81	Ricky Watters	.30
82	Shaun Alexander	.50
83	Warrick Dunn	.30
84	Shaun King	.30
85	Derrick Brooks	.15
86	Eddie George	.50
87	Steve McNair	.50
88	Brad Johnson	.30
89	Jeff George	.30
90	Stephen Davis	.50
91	*Jamal Reynolds*	12.00
92	*Justin Smith*	12.00
93	*Dan Morgan*	12.00
94	*Deuce McAllister*	35.00
95	*Drew Brees*	80.00
96	*Josh Booty*	15.00
97	*Mike McMahon*	30.00
98	*Sage Rosenfels*	15.00
99	*Marques Tuiasosopo*	30.00
100	*Josh Heupel*	15.00
101	*Heath Evans*	12.00
102	*Reggie White*	12.00
103	*Tim Hasselbeck*	15.00
104	*LaDainian Tomlinson*	85.00
105	*Kevan Barlow*	12.00
106	*LaMont Jordan*	25.00
107	*James Jackson*	12.00
108	*Anthony Thomas*	80.00
109	*Correl Buckhalter*	12.00
110	*Travis Henry*	30.00
111	*Dan Alexander*	12.00
112	*Travis Minor*	12.00
113	*Rudi Johnson*	20.00
114	*Michael Bennett*	40.00
115	*Todd Heap*	12.00
116	*Marvin "Snoop" Minnis*	12.00
117	*Santana Moss*	30.00
118	*Reggie Wayne*	30.00
119	*Koren Robinson*	30.00
120	*Chris Chambers*	30.00
121	*David Terrell*	40.00
122	*Rod Gardner*	30.00
123	*Quincy Morgan*	25.00
124	*Ken-Yon Rambo*	12.00
125	*Ronney Daniels*	12.00
126	*Ja'Mar Toombs*	12.00
127	*Bobby Newcombe*	12.00
128	*Cedrick Wilson*	12.00
129	*Chad Johnson*	30.00
130	*Shaun Rogers*	12.00
131	*Robert Ferguson*	25.00
132	*Kevin Kasper*	12.00
133	*Chris Weinke JERSEY*	50.00
134	*Freddie Mitchell JERSEY*	50.00
135	*Michael Vick JERSEY*	150.00
136	*Chris Taylor*	12.00
137	*Vinny Sutherland*	15.00
138	*Gerard Warren*	20.00
139	*Torrance Marshall*	12.00
140	*Jesse Palmer*	12.00

Values quoted in this guide reflect the retail price of a card — the price a collector can expect to pay when buying a card from a dealer. The wholesale price — that which a collector can expect to receive from a dealer when selling cards — will be significantly lower, depending on desirability and condition.

2001 Upper Deck Pros & Prospects Centerpiece

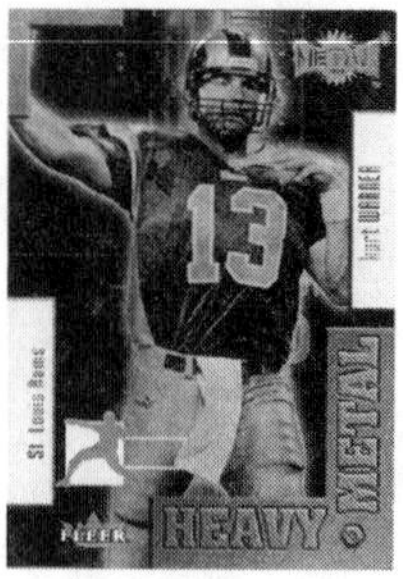

		MT
Complete Set (6):		25.00
Common Player:		2.00
Inserted 1:22		
C1	Randy Moss	7.00
C2	Donovan McNabb	3.00
C3	Kurt Warner	8.00
C4	Jamal Lewis	6.00
C5	Eddie George	2.00
C6	Mike Anderson	3.50

2001 Upper Deck Pros & Prospects Combo Jersey

		MT
Common Player:		200.00
Production 25 Sets		
SU-C	Bart Starr, Johnny Unitas	250.00
SB-C	Terry Bradshaw, Roger Staubach	250.00
MY-C	Joe Montana, Steve Young	300.00
AS-C	Troy Aikman, Emmitt Smith	250.00
JM-C	Edgerrin James, Peyton Manning	250.00
MC-C	Daunte Culpepper, Randy Moss	225.00
FW-C	Marshall Faulk, Kurt Warner	200.00

2001 Upper Deck Pros & Prospects Future Fame

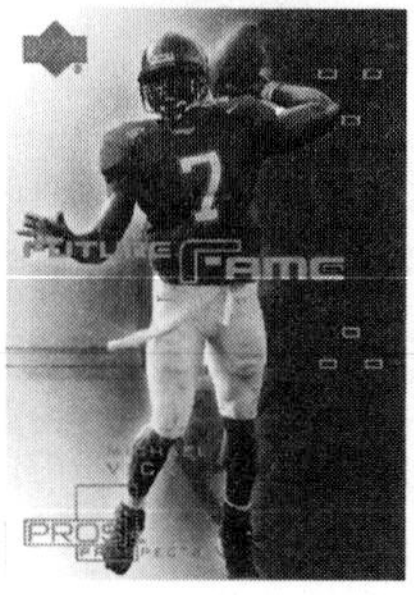

		MT
Complete Set (6):		25.00
Common Player:		3.00
Inserted 1:22		
F1	Michael Vick	12.00
F2	Deuce McAllister	6.00
F3	Drew Brees	10.00
F4	LaDainian Tomlinson	7.00
F5	Chris Weinke	4.00
F6	Santana Moss	3.00

2001 Upper Deck Pros & Prospects Game-Worn Jersey

		MT
Common Player:		15.00
Inserted 1:23		
Parallel Cards:		2x
Production 50 Sets		
TA-J	Troy Aikman	30.00
MA-J	Marcus Allen	25.00
AN-J	Mike Anderson	
BA-J	Tiki Barber	15.00
TB-J	Terry Bradshaw	70.00
MB-J	Mark Brunell	20.00
KC-J	Kerry Collins	25.00
DC-J	Daunte Culpepper	40.00
RD-J	Ron Dayne	25.00
CD-J	Corey Dillon	25.00
WD-J	Warrick Dunn	20.00
JE-J	John Elway	85.00
MF-J	Marshall Faulk	35.00
BF-J	Brett Favre	50.00
JG-J	Jeff Garcia	35.00
TH-J	Torry Holt	25.00
PH-J	Paul Hornung	75.00
EJ-J	Edgerrin James	45.00
KJ-J	Keyshawn Johnson	15.00
TJ-J	Thomas Jones	20.00
SK-J	Shaun King	15.00
DL-J	Dorsey Levens	15.00
PM-J	Peyton Manning	45.00
KM-J	Keenan McCardell	15.00
JM-J	Joe Montana	100.00
RM-J	Randy Moss	45.00
JN-J	Joe Namath	100.00
WP-J	Walter Payton	150.00
JP-J	Jake Plummer	15.00
PL-J	Jim Plunkett	25.00
JR-J	Jerry Rice	35.00
JS-J	Junior Seau	15.00
PS-J	Phil Simms	20.00
ES-J	Emmitt Smith	40.00
KS-J	Kordell Stewart	15.00
FT-J	Fred Taylor	20.00
KW-J	Kurt Warner	70.00

2001 Upper Deck Pros & Prospects ProActive

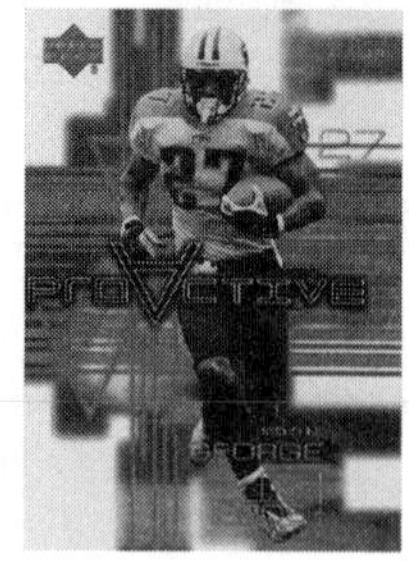

		MT
Complete Set (9):		20.00
Common Player:		1.00
Minor Stars:		2.00
Inserted 1:15		
PA1	Kurt Warner	6.00
PA2	Eddie George	2.00
PA3	Marshall Faulk	2.00
PA4	Corey Dillon	2.00
PA5	Emmitt Smith	5.00
PA6	Randy Moss	5.00
PA7	Marvin Harrison	2.00
PA8	Rich Gannon	1.00
PA9	Brett Favre	7.00

2001 Upper Deck Pros & Prospects ProMotion

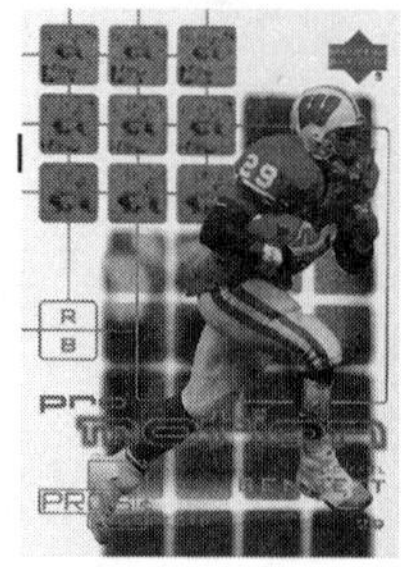

		MT
Complete Set (9):		25.00
Common Player:		1.00
Inserted 1:15		
PM1	Michael Vick	10.00
PM2	Michael Bennett	4.00
PM3	Reggie Wayne	2.00
PM4	Chad Johnson	2.00
PM5	Chris Chambers	2.00
PM6	David Terrell	5.00
PM7	Marvin "Snoop" Minnis	1.00
PM8	Koren Robinson	4.00
PM9	Rod Gardner	4.00

2001 Upper Deck Pros & Prospects Signed Jersey

		MT
Common Player:		25.00
Inserted 1:192		
Parallel Cards:		2x
Production 50 Sets		
JK-AJ	Jim Kelly	125.00
AM-AJ	Art Monk	
BS-AJ	Bart Starr	150.00
RS-AJ	Roger Staubach	100.00
FT-AJ	Fran Tarkenton	75.00
CT-AJ	Charlie Taylor	25.00
JT-AJ	Joe Theismann	45.00
JU-AJ	Johnny Unitas	125.00
SY-AJ	Steve Young SP	150.00
JY-AJ	Jack Youngblood	25.00

2001 Upper Deck Victory

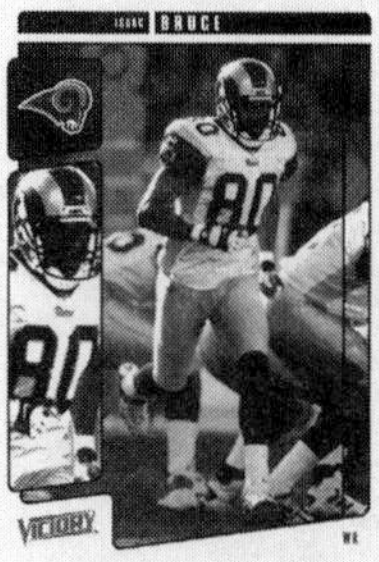

		MT
Complete Set (440):		70.00
Common Player:		.10
Minor Stars:		.20
Common Rookie:		.25
Pack (10):		1.00
Wax Box (36):		25.00
1	Jake Plummer	.40
2	David Boston	.40
3	Thomas Jones	.30
4	Michael Pittman	.20
5	Frank Sanders	.20
6	Joel Makovicka	.10
7	Corey Chavous	.10
8	Kwamie Lassiter	.10
9	Rob Moore	.20
10	Jamal Anderson	.40
11	Tony Martin	.20
12	Travis Jervey	.10
13	Chris Chandler	.20
14	Shawn Jefferson	.10
15	Rodney Thomas	.10
16	Terance Mathis	.10
17	Jessie Tuggle	.10
18	Ashley Ambrose	.10
19	Brian Finneran	.10
20	Maurice Smith	.40
21	Keith Brooking	.10
22	Jamal Lewis	1.00
23	Shannon Sharpe	.20
24	Brandon Stokley	.20
25	Ray Lewis	.40
26	Qadry Ismail	.20
27	Travis Taylor	.40
28	Chris Redman	.40
29	Rod Woodson	.20
30	Patrick Johnson	.10
31	Jermaine Lewis	.20
32	Elvis Grbac	.30
33	Tony Siragusa	.10
34	Larry Centers	.10
35	Rob Johnson	.30
36	Eric Moulds	.40
37	Sammy Morris	.20
38	Shawn Bryson	.10
39	Alex Van Pelt	.10
40	Jeremy McDaniel	.10
41	Sam Cowart	.10
42	Peerless Price	.30
43	Avion Black	.10
44	Phil Hansen	.10
45	Muhsin Muhammad	.30
46	Brad Hoover	.30
47	Tim Biakabutuka	.20
48	Wesley Walls	.20
49	Donald Hayes	.20
50	Jeff Lewis	.10
51	Dameyune Craig	.20
52	Mike Minter	.10
53	Isaac Byrd	.10
54	Patrick Jeffers	.20
55	Cade McNown	.40
56	James Allen	.40
57	Marcus Robinson	.40
58	Brian Urlacher	.75
59	Shane Matthews	.20
60	Glyn Milburn	.10
61	Scott Dragos	.10
62	Marty Booker	.20
63	Bobby Engram	.20
64	Kaseem Sinceno	.10
65	Ted Washington	.10
66	Peter Warrick	.50
67	Corey Dillon	.40
68	Akili Smith	.40
69	Danny Farmer	.20
70	Scott Mitchell	.20
71	Darryl Williams	.10
72	Ron Dugans	.20
73	Takeo Spikes	.10
74	Jon Kitna	.30
75	Darnay Scott	.20
76	Tony McGee	.10
77	Tim Couch	.75
78	Kevin Johnson	.40
79	Travis Prentice	.30
80	Spergon Wynn	.20
81	Errict Rhett	.20
82	Ty Detmer	.10
83	Dennis Northcutt	.30
84	Aaron Shea	.10
85	Courtney Brown	.30
86	JaJuan Dawson	.10
87	Rickey Dudley	.10
88	Jamir Miller	.10
89	Clint Stoerner	.40
90	Emmitt Smith	.75
91	Joey Galloway	.40
92	Raghib Ismail	.20
93	Ebenezer Ekuban	.10
94	Anthony Wright	.20
95	David LaFleur	.10
96	Dexter Coakley	.10
97	Jackie Harris	.10
98	Michael Wiley	.20
99	Wane McGarity	.10
100	Dat Nguyen	.10
101	Terrell Davis	.75
102	Mike Anderson	1.00
103	Brian Griese	.50
104	Rod Smith	.40
105	Ed McCaffrey	.30
106	Olandis Gary	.40
107	Kavika Pittman	.10
108	Bill Romanowski	.10
109	Gus Frerotte	.10
110	Howard Griffith	.10
111	Eddie Kennison	.20
112	Charlie Batch	.40
113	Germane Crowell	.30
114	James O. Stewart	.30
115	Johnnie Morton	.20
116	Herman Moore	.30
117	Larry Foster	.10
118	Desmond Howard	.10
119	Cory Schlesinger	.10
120	Robert Porcher	.10
121	Sedrick Irvin	.10
122	David Sloan	.10
123	Jim Harbaugh	.20
124	Brett Favre	1.50
125	Antonio Freeman	.40
126	Dorsey Levens	.30
127	Ahman Green	.30
128	Leroy Butler	.10
129	De'Mond Parker	.10
130	Bill Schroeder	.20
131	Bubba Franks	.20
132	Donald Driver	.10
133	Darren Sharper	.10
134	Corey Bradford	.10

135 Charles Lee .10
136 Peyton Manning 1.25
137 Edgerrin James 1.00
138 Marvin Harrison .40
139 E.G. Green .20
140 Terrence Wilkins .30
141 Ken Dilger .10
142 Jerome Pathon .10
143 Rob Morris .10
144 Lennox Gordon .10
145 Chad Bratzke .10
146 Mark Brunell .50
147 Fred Taylor .50
148 Jimmy Smith .30
149 Jamie Martin .10
150 Keenan McCardell .20
151 Kyle Brady .10
152 R. Jay Soward .20
153 Alvis Whitted .10
154 Stacey Mack .10
155 Damon Jones .10
156 Carnell Lake .10
157 Kevin Hardy .10
158 Trent Green .40
159 Tony Gonzalez .40
160 Derrick Alexander .10
161 Tony Richardson .10
162 Frank Moreau .10
163 Sylvester Morris .40
164 Priest Holmes .30
165 Donnie Edwards .10
166 Marvcus Patton .10
167 Larry Parker .10
168 Tony Horne .10
169 Bubby Brister .20
170 Oronde Gadsden .20
171 Lamar Smith .40
172 Jay Fiedler .40
173 J.J. Johnson .20
174 Rob Konrad .10
175 James McKnight .10
176 Dedric Ward .10
177 O.J. McDuffie .20
178 Zach Thomas .30
179 Ray Lucas .30
180 Sam Madison .10
181 Randy Moss 1.25
182 Jake Reed .20
183 Cris Carter .40
184 Daunte Culpepper .75
185 Moe Williams .10
186 Troy Walters .10
187 Todd Bouman .10
188 Jim Kleinsasser .20
189 Ed McDaniel .10
190 Robert Griffith .10
191 Byron Chamberlain .20
192 Chris Hovan .10
193 Drew Bledsoe .50
194 Terry Glenn .30
195 Kevin Faulk .30
196 J.R. Redmond .30
197 Antowain Smith .20
198 Bert Emanuel .10
199 Troy Brown .10
200 Tony Simmons .10
201 Michael Bishop .20
202 Lawyer Milloy .10
203 Torrence Small .10
204 Ty Law .10
205 Charles Johnson .10
206 Willie McGinest .10
207 Ricky Williams .60
208 Jeff Blake .20
209 Joe Horn .30
210 Aaron Brooks .60
211 LaRoi Glover .10
212 Chad Morton .10
213 Keith Mitchell .10
214 Willie Jackson .20
215 Robert Wilson .10
216 Norman Hand .10
217 Albert Connell .20
218 Joe Johnson .20
219 Kerry Collins .40
220 Amani Toomer .20
221 Ron Dayne .75
222 Tiki Barber .40
223 Greg Comella .10
224 Ike Hilliard .20
225 Joe Jurevicius .10
226 Ron Dixon .10
227 Jason Sehorn .10
228 Michael Strahan .30
229 Jessie Armstead .10
230 Mike Barrowman .10
231 Jason Garrett .10
232 Vinny Testaverde .30
233 Wayne Chrebet .40
234 Curtis Martin .40
235 Richie Anderson .10
236 Mo Lewis .10
237 Laveranues Coles .30
238 Windrell Hayes .10
239 Chad Pennington .40
240 Matthew Hatchette .10
241 Anthony Becht .10
242 Marvin Jones .10
243 Tim Brown .40
244 Rich Gannon .30
245 Tyrone Wheatley .20
246 Charlie Garner .20
247 Jon Ritchie .10
248 James Jett .10
249 Roland Williams .10
250 Jerry Porter .20
251 Darrell Russell .10
252 Charles Woodson .30
253 Jerry Rice 1.00
254 Greg Biekert .10
255 Duce Staley .40
256 Donovan McNabb .60
257 Darnell Autry .20
258 Chad Lewis .20
259 Na Brown .10
260 Koy Detmer .10
261 Todd Pinkston .30
262 Brian Mitchell .10
263 Hugh Douglas .10
264 James Thrash .20
265 Ron Powlus .10
266 Corey Simon .10
267 Kordell Stewart .40
268 Jerome Bettis .40
269 Bobby Shaw .10
270 Hines Ward .30
271 Plaxico Burress .40
272 Courtney Hawkins .10
273 Troy Edwards .10
274 Earl Holmes .10
275 Richard Huntley .10
276 Kent Graham .10
277 Tee Martin .30
278 Jon Witman .10
279 Marshall Faulk .50
280 Kurt Warner 1.25
281 Isaac Bruce .40
282 Torry Holt .40
283 Joe Germaine .20
284 Ernie Conwell .10
285 Trung Canidate .30
286 Az-Zahir Hakim .20
287 Ricky Proehl .10
288 Grant Wistrom .10
289 London Fletcher .10
290 Paul Justin .10
291 Robert Holcombe .10
292 Junior Seau .30
293 Curtis Conway .20
294 Rodney Harrison .10
295 Jeff Graham .10
296 Freddie Jones .20
297 Reggie Jones .20
298 Ronney Jenkins .10
299 Robert Gaylor .40
300 Tim Dwight .20
301 Fred McCrary .10
302 Terrell Fletcher .10
303 Doug Flutie .50
304 *Dave Dickenson* .40
305 Marcellus Wiley .10
306 Jeff Garcia .40
307 Jonas Lewis .10
308 Tai Streets .20
309 Terrell Owens .40
310 J.J. Stokes .20
311 Fred Beasley .10
312 Tim Rattay .20
313 Garrison Hearst .30
314 Giovanni Carmazzi .30
315 Bryant Young .10
316 Ricky Watters .30
317 Shaun Alexander .40
318 Matt Hasselbeck .40
319 Brock Huard .20
320 Darrell Jackson .20
321 James Williams .10
322 Charlie Rogers .10
323 Christian Fauria .10
324 Karsten Bailey .10
325 Travis Brown .10
326 Chad Brown .10
327 John Randle .20
328 Warrick Dunn .40
329 Shaun King .40
330 Rahib Abdullah .10
331 Mike Alstott .40
332 Jacquez Green .20
333 Reidel Anthony .20
334 Derrick Brooks .10
335 John Lynch .20
336 Warren Sapp .30
337 Brad Johnson .30
338 Keyshawn Johnson .40
339 Mark Royals .10
340 Dave Moore .10
341 Simeon Rice .10
342 Ronde Barber .10
343 Eddie George .50
344 Steve McNair .40
345 Samari Rolle .10
346 Derrick Mason .30
347 Randall Godfrey .10
348 Frank Wycheck .10
349 Chris Sanders .10
350 Neil O'Donnell .20
351 Kevin Dyson .20
352 Jevon Kearse .40
353 Chris Coleman .10
354 Mike Green .10
355 Blaine Bishop .10
356 Eddie Robinson .10
357 Jeff George .20
358 Stephen Davis .40
359 Donnell Bennett .10
360 Kevin Lockett .10
361 Derrius Thompson .10
362 Michael Westbrook .30
363 Stephen Alexander .20
364 Ki-Jana Carter .20
365 Champ Bailey .30
366 Todd Husak .20
367 Dan Wilkinson .10
368 Darrell Green .20
369 Sam Shade .10
370 Bruce Smith .20
371 *Bobby Newcombe* .40
372 *Vinny Sutherland* .40
373 *Alge Crumpler* .50
374 *Michael Vick* 5.00
375 *Gary Baxter* .50
376 *Todd Heap* .50
377 *Nate Clements* .50
378 *Travis Henry* 1.50
379 *Dan Morgan* .50
380 *Chris Weinke* 2.50
381 *David Terrell* 2.00
382 *Anthony Thomas* 2.75
383 *Rudi Johnson* .75
384 *Justin Smith* .50
385 *T.J. Houshmandzadeh* .50
386 *Chad Johnson* .75
387 *Quincy Morgan* 1.25
388 *Gerard Warren* .75
389 *James Jackson* 1.00
390 *Quincy Carter* 1.75
391 *Kevin Kasper* .75
392 *Scotty Anderson* .75
393 *Mike McMahon* .75
394 *Jamal Reynolds* .75
395 *Robert Ferguson* .60
396 *Reggie Wayne* 1.00
397 *Marvin "Snoop" Minnis* 1.00
398 *Chris Chambers* 1.25
399 *Jamar Fletcher* .50
400 *Travis Minor* .75
401 *Josh Heupel* 1.00
402 *Michael Bennett* 2.25
403 *Jabari Holloway* .50
404 *Moran Norris* .25
405 *Deuce McAllister* 1.50
406 *Will Allen* .50
407 *Jesse Palmer* .50
408 *LaMont Jordan* .75
409 *Santana Moss* 1.25
410 *Ken-Yon Rambo* .50
411 *Derrick Gibson* .25
412 *Marques Tuiasosopo* 1.25
413 *Correll Buckhalter* 1.25
414 *Freddie Mitchell* 1.25
415 *Drew Brees* 3.00
416 *LaDainian Tomlinson* 4.00
417 *Cedrick Wilson* .50
418 *Kevan Barlow* 1.00
419 *Alex Bannister* .50
420 *Heath Evans* .50
421 *Josh Booty* .50
422 *Koren Robinson* 1.25
423 *Adam Archuleta* .75
424 *Dan Alexander* .50
425 *Eddie Berlin* .50
426 *Rod Gardner* 1.50
427 *Sage Rosenfels* .75
428 *Steve Smith* .50
429 *Chris Barnes* .60
430 *Tim Hasselbeck* .60
431 Peyton Manning .50
432 Mike Anderson .50
433 Jamal Lewis .50
434 Randy Moss .50
435 Donovan McNabb .30
436 Daunte Culpepper .30
437 Kurt Warner .50
438 Eddie George .30
439 Marshall Faulk .30
440 Brett Favre .75

2001 Upper Deck Victory Gold

	MT
Gold Cards:	2x-4x
Gold Rookies:	3x
Inserted 1:2	

2000 Victory

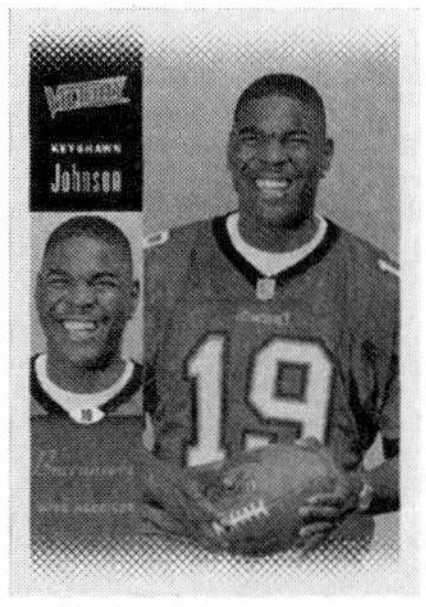

	MT
Complete Set (330):	45.00
Common Player:	.10
Minor Stars:	.20
Common Rookie:	.30
Inserted 1:1	
Pack (12):	1.00
Wax Box (36):	25.00

1 Jake Plummer .30
2 Michael Pittman .10
3 Rob Moore .20
4 David Boston .30
5 Frank Sanders .10
6 Aeneas Williams .10
7 Tim Dwight .30
8 Chris Chandler .20
9 Jamal Anderson .30
10 Shawn Jefferson .10
11 Ken Oxendine .10
12 Terance Mathis .10
13 Qadry Ismail .10
14 Jermaine Lewis .10
15 Rod Woodson .10
16 Michael McCrary .10
17 Tony Banks .20
18 Peter Boulware .10
19 Shannon Sharpe .20
20 Peerless Price .30
21 Rob Johnson .20
22 Eric Moulds .30
23 Doug Flutie .30
24 Jay Riemersma .10
25 Antowain Smith .30
26 Sam Cowart .10
27 Muhsin Muhammad .20
28 Patrick Jeffers .30
29 Steve Beuerlein .20
30 Natrone Means .20
31 Tim Biakabutuka .10
32 Michael Bates .10
33 Wesley Walls .20
34 Cade McNown .50
35 Curtis Enis .30
36 Marcus Robinson .30
37 Bobby Engram .10
38 Glyn Milburn .10
39 Marty Booker .10
40 Akili Smith .40
41 Corey Dillon .30
42 Darnay Scott .20
43 Tremain Mack .10
44 Michael Bankston .10
45 Tony McGee .10
46 Tim Couch .75
47 Kevin Johnson .30
48 Darrin Chiaverini .10
49 Jamir Miller .10
50 Errict Rhett .10
51 Ty Detmer .10
52 Terry Kirby .10
53 Troy Aikman .60
54 Emmitt Smith .75
55 Raghib Ismail .10
56 Chris Warren .10
57 Joey Galloway .30
58 Terrell Davis .75
59 Olandis Gary .60
60 Brian Griese .40
61 Gus Frerotte .10
62 Glenn Cadrez .10
63 Ed McCaffrey .20
64 Rod Smith .20
65 Charlie Batch .30
66 Germane Crowell .20
67 Stephen Boyd .10
68 Johnnie Morton .10
69 Robert Porcher .10
70 James O. Stewart .20
71 Brett Favre 1.25
72 Antonio Freeman .30
73 Bill Schroeder .10
74 Dorsey Levens .30
75 Darren Sharper .10
76 Peyton Manning 1.00
77 Edgerrin James 1.25
78 Marvin Harrison .30
79 Ken Dilger .10
80 Terrence Wilkins .20
81 Cornelius Bennett .10
82 E.G. Green .10
83 Mark Brunell .50
84 Fred Taylor .50
85 Jimmy Smith .30
86 Keenan McCardell .20
87 Carnell Lake .10
88 Kevin Hardy .10
89 Elvis Grbac .20
90 Tony Gonzalez .20
91 Derrick S. Alexander .10
92 Donnell Bennett .10
93 James Hasty .10
94 Kevin Lockett .10
95 Trace Armstrong .10
96 Terrell Buckley .10
97 Tony Martin .10
98 Damon Huard .20
99 O.J. McDuffie .20
100 Brock Marion .10
101 Zach Thomas .20
102 Randy Moss 1.00
103 Robert Smith .30
104 Cris Carter .30
105 Bubby Brister .10
106 Daunte Culpepper .50
107 John Randle .10
108 Drew Bledsoe .50
109 Terry Glenn .30
110 Willie McGinest .10
111 Kevin Faulk .20
112 Tedy Bruschi .10
113 Ricky Williams .75
114 Keith Poole .10
115 Jake Reed .10
116 Mark Fields .10
117 Jeff Blake .20
118 Andrew Glover .10
119 Kerry Collins .20
120 Amani Toomer .20
121 Jesse Armstead .10
122 Ike Hilliard .10
123 Ray Lucas .30
124 Curtis Martin .20
125 Vinny Testaverde .20
126 Wayne Chrebet .20
127 Dedric Ward .10
128 Tim Brown .20
129 Rich Gannon .20
130 Tyrone Wheatley .10
131 Napoleon Kaufman .30
132 Charles Woodson .20
133 Greg Biekert .10
134 Rickey Dudley .10
135 Duce Staley .30
136 Donovan McNabb .50
137 Torrance Small .10
138 Mike Mamula .10
139 Brian Dawkins .10
140 Troy Vincent .10
141 Kent Graham .10
142 Troy Edwards .30
143 Jerome Bettis .30
144 Hines Ward .20
145 Kordell Stewart .30
146 Levon Kirkland .10
147 Richard Huntley .20
148 Marshall Faulk .30
149 Kurt Warner 1.50
150 Torry Holt .30
151 Isaac Bruce .30
152 Kevin Carter .10
153 Az-Zahir Hakim .20
154 Todd Lyght .10
155 Jermaine Fazande .20
156 Curtis Conway .10
157 Freddie Jones .10
158 Junior Seau .20
159 Jeff Graham .10
160 Moses Moreno .10
161 Rodney Harrison .10
162 Steve Young .50
163 Jerry Rice .60
164 Ken Norton .10
165 Terrell Owens .30
166 Jeff Garcia .20
167 Ricky Watters .20
168 Jon Kitna .30
169 Derrick Mayes .20
170 Sean Dawkins .10
171 Chad Brown .10
172 Warrick Dunn .30
173 Keyshawn Johnson .30
174 Shaun King .50
175 Mike Alstott .30
176 Warren Sapp .10
177 Jacquez Green .20
178 Derrick Brooks .10
179 John Lynch .10
180 Eddie George .40
181 Steve McNair .30
182 Kevin Dyson .20
183 Jevon Kearse .30
184 Yancey Thigpen .10
185 Frank Wycheck .10
186 Eddie Robinson .10
187 Jeff George .20
188 Brad Johnson .30
189 Stephen Davis .30
190 Michael Westbrook .20
191 Albert Connell .20
192 Brian Mitchell .10
193 Bruce Smith .10
194 Champ Bailey .20
195 Sam Shade .10
196 Marvin Harrison .20
197 Jimmy Smith .20
198 Randy Moss .50
199 Marcus Robinson .20
200 Tim Brown .10
201 Jimmy Smith .20
202 Marvin Harrison .20
203 Muhsin Muhammad .10
204 Tim Brown .10
205 Cris Carter .20
206 Edgerrin James .50
207 Curtis Martin .20
208 Stephen Davis .20
209 Emmitt Smith .40
210 Marshall Faulk .20
211 Kurt Warner .60
212 Steve Beuerlein .10
213 Jeff George .10
214 Peyton Manning .50
215 Brad Johnson .10
216 Kurt Warner .60
217 Peyton Manning .50
218 Edgerrin James .50
219 Marshall Faulk .20
220 Randy Moss .50
221 Jimmy Smith .20
222 Tony Gonzalez .10
223 Tony Boselli .10
224 Orlando Pace .10
225 Larry Allen .10
226 Randall McDaniel .10
227 Tom Nalen .10
228 Kevin Carter .10
229 Jevon Kearse .10
230 Warren Sapp .10
231 Darrell Russell .10
232 Derrick Brooks .10
233 Peter Boulware .10
234 Junior Seau .10
235 Sam Madison .10
236 Charles Woodson .10
237 John Lynch .10
238 Carnell Lake .10
239 Mitch Berger .10
240 Jason Hanson .10
241 Randy Moss .50
242 Kurt Warner .60
243 Peyton Manning .50
244 Marshall Faulk .20
245 Edgerrin James .50
246 Eddie George .20
247 Stephen Davis .20
248 Keyshawn Johnson .20
249 Brad Johnson .20
250 Ricky Williams .40
251 Jimmy Smith .20
252 Isaac Bruce .20
253 Muhsin Muhammad .10
254 Marcus Robinson .20
255 Kevin Johnson .10
256 Tim Couch .20
257 Curtis Martin .20
258 Charlie Batch .20
259 Tim Brown .10
260 Jerry Rice .30
261 Drew Bledsoe .25
262 Brett Favre .50
263 Mark Brunell .25
264 Fred Taylor .25
265 Troy Edwards .20
266 Marvin Harrison .20
267 Germane Crowell .10
268 Terry Glenn .20
269 Qadry Ismail .10
270 Jake Plummer .10
271 *Anthony Becht* .50
272 *Anthony Lucas* .30
273 *Bashir Yamini* .30
274 *Brian Urlacher* 2.00
275 *Chad Morton* .50
276 *Chad Pennington* 2.50
277 *Chris Cole* .30
278 *Chris Hovan* .50
279 *Tim Rattay* .50
280 *Chris Redman* 1.25
281 *Chris Samuels* .50
282 *Corey Simon* .50
283 *Courtney Brown* .50
284 *Curtis Keaton* .30
285 *Danny Farmer* .50
286 *Erron Kinney* .30
287 *Darren Howard* .30
288 *Deltha O'Neal* .30
289 *Dennis Northcutt* .50
290 *Demario Brown* .30
291 *Dez White* .50
292 *Frank Murphy* .30
293 *Gari Scott* .30
294 *Giovanni Carmazzi* .50
295 *J.R. Redmond* 1.00
296 *JaJuan Dawson* .50
297 *Jamal Lewis* 4.00
298 *Leon Murray* .30
299 *Jerry Porter* .50
300 *Joe Hamilton* .50
301 *John Abraham* .30
302 *John Engleberger* .30
303 *Keith Bulluck* .30
304 *Kwame Cavil* .30
305 *Laveranues Coles* .75
306 *Marc Bulger* .30
307 *Marcus Knight* .30
308 *Mareno Philyaw* .30
309 *Michael Wiley* .30
310 *Na'il Diggs* .30
311 *Peter Warrick* 3.00
312 *Plaxico Burress* 1.75
313 *Raynoch Thompson* .30
314 *Reuben Droughns* .30
315 *Rob Morris* .30
316 *Ron Dayne* 3.00
317 *Ron Dugans* .50
318 *Sebastian Janikowski* .50
319 *Shaun Alexander* 2.00
320 *Sherrod Gideon* .30
321 *Sylvester Morris* 1.75
322 *Tee Martin* .50
323 *Thomas Jones* 1.25
324 *Todd Husak* .50
325 *Todd Pinkston* .50
326 *Tom Brady* .50
327 *Travis Prentice* 1.00
328 *Travis Taylor* .75
329 *Trevor Gaylor* .50
330 *Trung Canidate* .50

1993 U.S. Playing Cards Ditka's Picks

The 56-card, standard-size set, with rounded corners, are actually playing cards. The fronts have a borderless action shot with each card having the same generic back. "Ditka's Picks," "NFL," and other logos appear on the backs.

	MT
Complete Set (56):	5.00
Common Player:	.05

1C Steve Young .30
1D Joe Montana .50
1H Dan Marino .05
1S Troy Aikman .50
2C Jim Lachey .05
2D Richmond Webb .05
2H Wilber Marshall .05
2S Ronnie Lott .10
3C Sean Gilbert .10
3D Clay Matthews .10
3H Jeff Lageman .05
3S Audray McMillian .05
4C Morten Andersen .05
4D Pete Stoyanovich .05
4H Rohn Stark .05
4S Sean Landeta .05
5C Broderick Thomas .05
5D James Francis .05
5H Derrick Thomas .20
5S Tony Bennett .05
6C Seth Joyner .10
6D Percy Snow .05
6H Junior Seau .20
6S Chris Spielman .10
7C Pierce Holt .05
7D Rod Woodson .20
7H Ray Childress .10
7S Deion Sanders .40
8C Jay Novacek .20
8D Eric Green .05
8H Marv Cook .05
8S Brent Jones .10
9C Randall McDaniel .05
9D Mike Munchak .05
9H Bruce Matthews .05
9S Mark Stepnoski .05
10C Harris Barton .05
10D Steve Atwater .05
10H Henry Jones .05
10S Chuck Cecil .05
11C Sterling Sharpe .20
11D Anthony Miller .10
11H Haywood Jeffires .10
11S Jerry Rice .50
12C Reggie White .20
12D Howie Long .10
12H Cortez Kennedy .10
12S Chris Doleman .10
13C Emmitt Smith .05
13D Thurman Thomas .20
13H Barry Foster .10
13S Barry Sanders 1.00
WILD Tom Waddle .05
WILD Steve Wisniewski .05
NNO Ditka's AFC Picks .10
NNO Ditka's NFC Picks .10

1994 U.S. Playing Cards Ditka's Picks

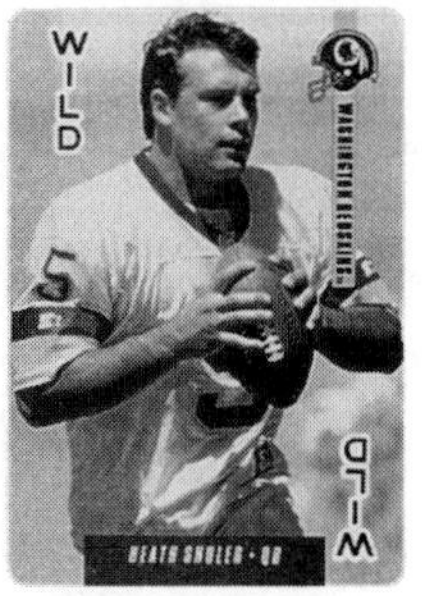

The U.S. Playing Card Co. released a 56-card deck of playing cards, featuring a cast of NFL stars, as well as rookies expected to shine in the 1994 season. Each card in the four-color deck contains an action shot of the player with the denomination in the upper left and lower right hand corners.

	MT
Complete Set (56):	5.00
Common Player:	.05

1C Sterling Sharpe .20
1D Rickey Jackson .05
1H Emmitt Smith 1.00
1S Rod Woodson .20
2C Marcus Robertson .05
2D Rohn Stark .05
2H Dave Cadigan .05
2S Kevin Williams .20
3C John Kasay .05
3D Carlton Haselrig .05
3H Donnell Woolford .05
3S Dan Wilkinson .20
4C Marshall Faulk 1.00
4D Greg Montgomery .05
4H Leslie O'Neal .10
4S Eric Curry .10
5C Eric Turner .10
5D Rick Mirer .25
5H Kevin Smith .10
5S Troy Vincent .10
6C Cornelius Bennett .10
6D Seth Joyner .10
6H Gary Zimmerman .05
6S LeRoy Butler .05
7C Tommy Vardell .05
7D Richmond Webb .05
7H Ben Coates .20
7S Steve Everitt .05
8C Tom Rathman .05
8D Ray Childress .05
8H Tim Brown .20
8S Mark Bavaro .05
9C Bennie Blades .05
9D John "Jumbo" Elliott .05
9H Jim Lachey .05
9S Neil Smith .20
10C Sean Gilbert .10
10D Steve Tasker .10
10H Chris Zorich .10
10S Haywood Jeffires .10
11C Troy Aikman .50
11D Jeff Hostetler .10
11H Junior Seau .20
11S Mark Stepnoski .05
12C Chris Spielman .10
12D Marcus Allen .20
12H Reggie White .20
12S Harris Barton .05
13C Andre Rison .20
13D Randall McDaniel .05
13H Cortez Kennedy .10
13S Norm Johnson .05

WILD Heath Shuler .60
WILD Shannon Sharpe .10
NNO Ditka's AFC Picks .10
NNO Ditka's NFC Picks .10

1995 U.S. Playing Cards Ditka's Picks

The 56-card, standard-size set, with rounded edges, is similar in design to the 1994 set, with color photos on the card fronts and a generic card back.

MT
Complete Set (56): 5.00
Common Player: .05
1C Randall McDaniel .05
1D Dan Marino 1.00
1H Drew Bledsoe .40
1S Steve Young .50
2C Renaldo Turnbull .05
2D Tony Boselli .10
2H Ki-Jana Carter .20
2S Todd Sauerbrun .05
3C Aeneas Williams .05
3D Bruce Smith .20
3H Shawn Jefferson .10
3S Andy Harmon .05
4C Donnell Woolford .05
4D Ronnie Lott .20
4H Tim Brown .20
4S Charles Haley .10
5C Merton Hanks .05
5D Eric Turner .10
5H Ben Coates .20
5S Brian Williams .05
6C Eric Metcalf .20
6D Dave Meggett .10
6H Neil Smith .10
6S Ian Beckles .05
7C Herman Moore .20
7D Mel Gray .10
7H Ray Childress .05
7S Jim Lachey .05
8C Bennie Blades .05
8D Kevin Greene .10
8H Gary Zimmerman .05
8S Willie Roaf .10
9C Bryant Young .10
9D Bruce Matthews .05
9H Richmond Webb .05
9S Howard Cross .05
10C Seth Joyner .05
10D Marshall Faulk .50
10H Jeff Dellenbach .05
10S Cris Carter .20
11C Sean Gilbert .10
11D John Carney .05
11H Rohn Stark .05
11S Jerry Rice .50
12C Reggie White .20
12D Terry McDaniel .05
12H Rod Woodson .20
12S Daryl Johnston .10
13C Norm Johnson .05
13D Cortez Kennedy .10
13H Cornelius Bennett .10
13S Barry Sanders 1.00
WILD Junior Seau .20
WILD Chris Spielman .10
NNO Ditka's NFC Picks .10
NNO Ditka's AFC Picks .10

V

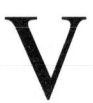

1967-68 Vikings

The 29-card, 8" x 10" set features black-and-white photos with blank backs.

NM
Complete Set (29): 120.00
Common Player: 4.00
1 Grady Alderman (Tackle) 4.00
2 Grady Alderman (Offensive lineman) 4.00
3 John Beasley 4.00
4 Bob Berry 4.00
5 Larry Bowie 4.00
6 Gary Cuozzo 5.00
7 Doug Davis 4.00
8 Paul Dickinson 4.00
9 Paul Flatley 5.00
10 Bob Grim 5.00
11 Dale Hackbart 4.00
12 Don Hansen 4.00
13 Jim Hargrove 4.00
14 Clint Jones 5.00
15 Jeff Jordan 4.00
16 Joe Kapp 8.00
17 John Kirby 4.00
18 Gary Larsen 5.00
19 Earsell Mackbee 4.00
20 Marlin McKeever 5.00
21 Milt Sunde 5.00
22 David Tobey 4.00
23 Ron Vanderkelen 5.00
24 Jim Vellone 4.00
25 Bobby Walden 4.00
26 Lonnie Warwick 4.00
27 Gene Washington (Wide receiver) 5.00
28 Gene Washington (End) 5.00
29 Roy Winston 5.00

1969 Vikings Team Issue

The 27-card, 5" x 6-7/8" set features black-and-white borderless player portraits with blank backs.

NM
Complete Set (27): 75.00
Common Player: 3.00
1 Bookie Bolin 3.00
2 Bobby Bryant 4.00
3 John Beasley 3.00
4 Gary Cuozzo 4.00
5 Doug Davis 3.00
6 Paul Dickson 3.00
7 Bob Grim 4.00
8 Dale Hackbart 3.00
9 Jim Hargrove 3.00
10 John Henderson 3.00
11 Wally Hilgenberg 4.00
12 Clinton Jones 4.00
13 Karl Kassulke 4.00
14 Kent Kramer 3.00
15 Gary Larsen 4.00
16 Bob Lee 3.00
17 Jim Lindsey 3.00
18 Earsell Mackbee 3.00
19 Mike McGill 3.00
20 Oscar Reed 3.00
21 Ed Sharockman 3.00
22 Steve Smith 3.00
23 Milt Sunde 3.00
24 Jim Vellone 3.00
25 Lonnie Warwick 3.00
26 Gene Washington 5.00
27 Charlie West 4.00

1971 Vikings Photos

The 52-card, 5" x 7-7/16" set consists of color close-up shots with blank backs. The player's name, position, and team name appear on the bottom border.

NM
Complete Set (52): 125.00
Common Player: 2.00
1 Grady Alderman 2.00
2 Neil Armstrong (CO) 2.00
3 John Beasley 2.00
4 Bill Brown 4.00
5 Bob Brown 2.00
6 Bobby Bryant 3.00
7 Jerry Burns (CO) 3.00
8 Fred Cox 3.00
9 Gary Cuozzo 3.00
10 Doug Davis 2.00
11 Al Denson 2.00
12 Paul Dickson 2.00
13 Carl Eller 10.00
14 Bud Grant (CO) 12.00
15 Bob Grim 3.00
16 Leo Hayden 2.00
17 John Henderson 2.00
18 Wally Hilgenberg 3.00
19 Noel Jenke 2.00
20 Clint Jones 2.00
21 Karl Kassulke 3.00
22 Paul Krause 5.00
23 Gary Larsen 2.00
24 Bob Lee 2.00
25 Jim Lindsey 2.00
26 Jim Marshall 10.00
27 Bus Mertes (CO) 2.00
28 John Michels (CO) 2.00
29 Jocko Nelson (CO) 2.00
30 Dave Osborn 4.00
31 Alan Page 12.00
32 Jack Patera (CO) 3.00
33 Jerry Patton 2.00
34 Pete Perreault 2.00
35 Oscar Reed 2.00
36 Ed Sharockman 2.00
37 Norm Snead 6.00
38 Milt Sunde 3.00
39 Doug Sutherland 2.00
40 Mick Tingelhoff 4.00
41 Stu Voigt 4.00
42 John Ward 2.00
43 Lonnie Warwick 2.00
44 Gene Washington 6.00
45 Charlie West 2.00
46 Ed White 4.00
47 Carl Winfrey 2.00
48 Roy Winston 3.00
49 Jeff Wright 2.00
50 Nate Wright 2.00
51 Ron Yary 4.00
52 Godfrey Zaunbrecher 2.00

1971 Vikings Postcards

The 19-card, 5" x 7-7/16" set features color posed close-ups with the backs containing a typical postcard layout. Bio information appears in the upper left corner of the horizontal backs. The set was issued during the season.

NM
Complete Set (19): 45.00
Common Player: 2.00
1 Grady Alderman 2.00
2 Neil Armstrong (CO) 2.00
3 John Beasley 2.00
4 Paul Dickson 2.00
5 Bud Grant (CO) 12.00
6 Wally Hilgenburg 2.00
7 Noel Jenke 2.00
8 Paul Krause 5.00
9 Gary Larsen 2.00
10 Dave Osborn 4.00
11 Alan Page 12.00
12 Jerry Patton 2.00
13 Doug Sutherland 2.50
14 Mick Tingelhoff 4.00
15 Lonnie Warwick 2.00
16 Charlie West 2.00
17 Jeff Wright 2.00
18 Nate Wright 2.00
19 Godfrey Zaunbrecher 2.00

1978 Vikings Country Kitchen

The seven-card, 5" x 7" set features a black-and-white player headshot with bio and stat information on the backs. The card fronts have a white border with the player's name and "Minnesota Vikings" printed.

NM
Complete Set (7): 35.00
Common Player: 4.00
1 Bobby Bryant 4.00
2 Tommy Kramer 6.00
3 Paul Krause 6.00
4 Ahmad Rashad 12.00
5 Jeff Siemon 4.00
6 Mick Tingelhoff 5.00
7 Sammie White 6.00

1983 Vikings Police

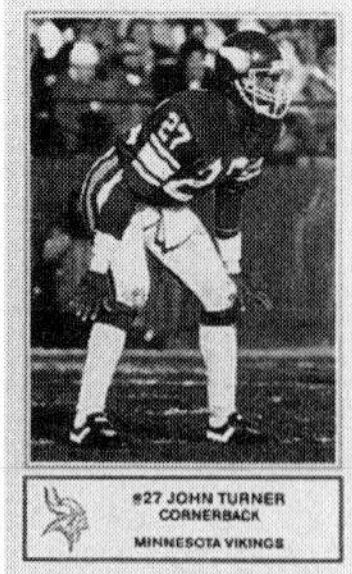

The 17-card, 2-5/8" x 4-1/8" set was sponsored by Green Giant, Burger King, Pillsbury and Minnesota Crime Prevention Officers Association. The fronts contain an action photo with the back including bio and stat information.

MT
Complete Set (17): 10.00
Common Player: .50
1 Checklist Card .75
2 Tommy Kramer 1.00
3 Ted Brown .50
4 Joe Senser .50
5 Sammie White 1.00
6 Doug Martin .50
7 Matt Blair 1.00
8 Bud Grant (CO) 2.00
9 Scott Studwell .75
10 Greg Coleman .50
11 John Turner .50
12 Jim Hough .50
13 Joey Browner 1.00
14 Dennis Swilley .50
15 Darrin Nelson .75
16 Mark Mullaney .50
17 Fran Tarkenton (All-Time Great) 3.00

1984 Vikings Police

The 18-card, 2-5/8" x 4-1/8" set, sponsored by Pillsbury, Burger King, the Minnesota Crime Prevention Officers Association and Green Giant, features an action shot on the card front with a crime prevention tip on the back.

MT
Complete Set (18): 8.00
Common Player: .40
1 Checklist Card .50
2 Keith Nord .40
3 Joe Senser .40
4 Tommy Kramer 1.25
5 Darrin Nelson .50
6 Tim Irwin .40
7 Mark Mullaney .40
8 Les Steckel (CO) .40
9 Greg Coleman .40
10 Tommy Hannon .40
11 Curtis Rouse .40
12 Scott Studwell .50
13 Steve Jordan 1.00
14 Willie Teal .40
15 Ted Brown .40
16 Sammie White 1.00
17 Matt Blair .40
18 Jim Marshall (All-Time Great) 2.50

1985 Vikings Police

The 16-card, 2-5/8" x 4-1/8" set was sponsored by Frito- Lay, Pepsi-Cola, KS95-FM and local law enforcement. The cards are similar in design to previous Police sets, with crime prevention tips on the backs.

MT
Complete Set (16): 8.00
Common Player: .40
1 Checklist Card .50
2 Bud Grant (CO) 1.50
3 Matt Blair .50
4 Alfred Anderson .50
5 Fred McNeill .40
6 Tommy Kramer .75
7 Jan Stenerud 1.25
8 Sammie White .75
9 Doug Martin .40
10 Greg Coleman .40
11 Steve Riley .40
12 Walker Lee Ashley .40
13 Tim Irwin .40
14 Scott Studwell .50
15 Darrin Nelson .50
16 Mick Tingelhoff (All-Time Great) .75

1986 Vikings Police

The 14-card, 2-5/8" x 4-1/8" set is similar to Police sets from previous years with a "Crime Prevention Tip" on the card back.

MT
Complete Set (14): 8.00
Common Player: .40
1 Jerry Burns (CO) (Checklist back) .50
2 Darrin Nelson .50
3 Tommy Kramer .75
4 Anthony Carter 1.50
5 Scott Studwell .50
6 Chris Doleman 1.50
7 Joey Browner .75
8 Steve Jordan .50
9 David Howard .40
10 Tim Newton .40
11 Leo Lewis .40
12 Keith Millard 1.00
13 Doug Martin .40
14 Bill Brown (All-Time Great) .75

1987 Vikings Police

The 14-card, 2-5/8" x 4-1/8" set features a color action shot on the front with a "Crime Prevention Tip" on the back. Card No. 1, Purple Power '87, is a Vikings montage by artist Cliff Spohn. Over 2 million sets were distributed over a 14-week period by the Vikings, Campbell's Soup, Frito-Lay, KSTP-FM and the Minnesota Crime Prevention Association.

MT
Complete Set (14): 8.00
Common Player: .40
1 Purple Power '87 (checklist back) .50
2 Jerry Burns (CO) .50
3 Scott Studwell .50
4 Tommy Kramer .75
5 Gerald Robinson .40
6 Wade Wilson 1.75
7 Anthony Carter 1.00
8 Terry Tausch .40
9 Leo Lewis .40
10 Keith Millard .75
11 Carl Lee .50
12 Steve Jordan .50
13 D.J. Dozier .75
14 Alan Page (ATG) 1.75

1988 Vikings Police

The 12-card, 2-5/8" x 4-1/8" set featured nine current players, one offense card, one defense card and one all-time great card (Paul Krause). The cards are similar in design to previous Police issues.

MT
Complete Set (12): 5.00
Common Player: .40
1 Vikings Offense (Checklist on back) .50
2 Jesse Solomon .50
3 Kirk Lowdermilk .40
4 Darrin Nelson .50
5 Chris Doleman 1.00
6 D.J. Dozier .50
7 Gary Zimmerman .75
8 Allen Rice .40
9 Joey Browner .75
10 Anthony Carter 1.00
11 Vikings Defense .50
12 Paul Krause (All-Time Great) 1.00

1989 Vikings Police

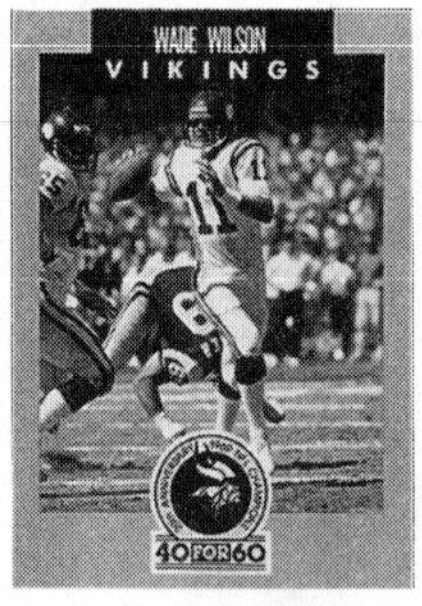

The 10-card, standard-size set features color photos on the gray-border fronts. The card backs are horizontal and contain safety tips, bio information and career highlights. Production was limited to 175,000 for each card.

MT
Complete Set (10): 5.00
Common Player: .50
1 Team Card (schedule on back) .75
2 Henry Thomas 1.00
3 Rick Fenney .50
4 Chuck Nelson .50
5 Jim Gustafson .50
6 Wade Wilson 1.00
7 Randall McDaniel .75
8 Jesse Solomon .50
9 Anthony Carter 1.00
10 Joe Kapp (All-Time Great) 1.00

1989 Vikings Taystee Discs

The 12-disc, 2-3/4" in diameter set, features Minnesota players in closeups on the fronts with bio and stat information on the backs. Each disc was issued with a Taystee product in the Minnesota area.

MT
Complete Set (12): 5.00
Common Player: .50
1 Anthony Carter 1.00
2 Chris Doleman 1.00
3 Joey Browner .75
4 Steve Jordan .75
5 Scott Studwell .50
6 Wade Wilson 1.00
7 Kirk Lowdermilk .50
8 Tommy Kramer .75
9 Keith Millard .75
10 Rick Fenney .50
11 Gary Zimmerman .50
12 Darrin Nelson .75

1990 Vikings Police

The 10-card, standard-size set was sponsored by Gatorade, WCCO Radio and local law enforcement and contained a crime prevention tip on the card backs.

MT
Complete Set (10): 5.00
Common Player: .50
1 Raymond Berry .50
2 Anthony Carter 1.00
3 Chris Doleman .75
4 Rick Fenney .50
5 Hassan Jones .75
6 Carl Lee .50
7 Mike Merriweather .50
8 Scott Studwell .50
9 Herschel Walker 1.50
10 Wade Wilson 1.00

1991 Vikings Police

The 10-card, standard-size set was sponsored by KFAN Radio, Gatorade, K102 Radio and Super Bowl XXVI. The cards were distributed on a weekly basis by area police departments in the order listed below.

MT
Complete Set (10): 5.00
Common Player: .40
1 Rick Fenney .40
2 Wade Wilson .75
3 Mike Merriweather .40
4 Hassan Jones .40
5 Rich Gannon 1.00
6 Mark Dusbabek .40
7 Sean Salisbury .75
8 Reggie Rutland .40
9 Tim Irwin .40
10 Chris Doleman .75

1992 Vikings Gatorade

Gatorade and the Minnesota Vikings teamed up to produce this 10-card team set.

MT
Complete Set (10): 8.00
Common Player: .50
1 Dennis Green .75
2 John Randle .75
3 Todd Scott .50
4 Anthony Carter .50
5 Steve Jordan .50
6 Terry Allen 2.00
7 Brian Habib .50
8 Fuad Reveiz .50
9 Roger Craig 1.00
10 Cris Carter 2.00

1992 Vikings Police

The 10-card, standard-size set was sponsored by Gatorade, KFAN Radio, K102 Radio and local law enforcement. The card fronts have a color action shot framed by a purple border with the Gatorade logo centered on the card front bottom edge. The card backs have a black and white headshot and other sponsor logos.

MT
Complete Set (10): 5.00
Common Player: .40
1 Dennis Green (CO) (Schedule on back) .75
2 John Randle .75
3 Todd Scott .40
4 Anthony Carter 1.00
5 Steve Jordan .40
6 Terry Allen 2.00
7 Brian Habib .40
8 Fuad Reveiz .40
9 Roger Craig 1.00
10 Cris Carter 1.50

1993 Vikings Police

The 10-card, standard-size set is similar in design to the 1992 Police set, complete with the Gatorade logo on the card fronts and a black and white headshot on the horizontal card back.

MT
Complete Set (10): 5.00
Common Player: .40
1 Dennis Green (CO) (CL/Schedule on back) .60
2 Henry Thomas .60
3 Todd Scott .40
4 Jack Del Rio .60
5 Vencie Glenn .40
6 Fuad Reveiz .40
7 Cris Carter 1.25
8 Terry Allen 1.50
9 Roger Craig .60
10 Carlos Jenkins .40

1995 Vikings Police

The 10-card, standard-size set features a purple border on the card front with the Gatorade logo appearing in the left lower corner. The Vikings 35th anniversary logo is printed in the lower right corner of the card front, with the player's name and "Vikings" appearing centered along the top edge in a gray box. The card backs feature a black and white headshot with brief bio information.

MT
Complete Set (10): 5.00
Common Player: .40
1 Warren Moon (CL/Schedule on the back) 1.00
2 Randall McDaniel .40
3 Jake Reed .75
4 Jack Del Rio .60
5 Cris Carter .75
6 Fuad Reveiz .40
7 Amp Lee .40
8 John Randle .60
9 Andrew Jordan .40
10 DeWayne Washington .60

1997 Vikings Police

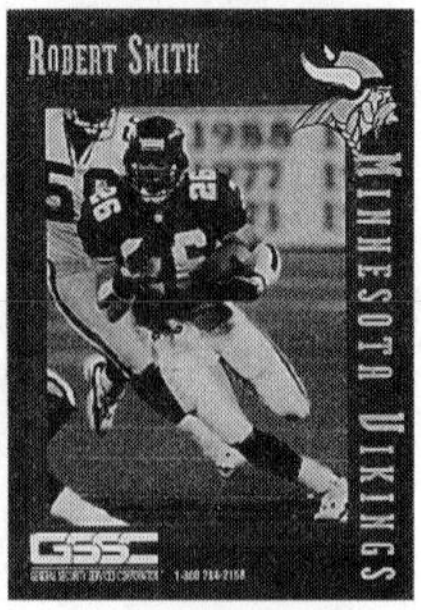

The Minnesota Vikings were featured in this eight-card set, which was bordered in purple, with the Vikings logo in the upper right and the words "Minnesota Vikings" printed down the right side. Fronts also feature a color shot of the player with a General Security Services Corp. logo and a toll free number in the bottom left corner. Card backs feature a head shot of the player, stats and Vikadontis Rex and McGruff the Crime Dog logos along with The Minnesota Crime Prevention Association logo. Card No. 1 features a set checklist and 1997 team schedule.

MT
Complete Set (8): 5.00
Common Player: .40
1 Cris Carter, Jake Reed 1.00
2 Robert Smith 1.00
3 Jeff Brady .40
4 Brad Johnson 1.50
5 Robert Griffith .40
6 Randall McDaniel .40
7 Leroy Hoard .40
8 John Randle .50

W

1986 Waddingtons Game

Produced in England, this NFL card game consists of 40 cards measuring 3-1/2" x 5-11/16". The card fronts feature color illustrations of NFL teams. Five different teams are portrayed on seven cards each. The other five cards in the set are interception cards, which have the NFL logo on the front. The backs of all the cards feature the NFL logo.

MT
Complete Set (40): 60.00
Common Player: .50
1 Bears 10 (Walter Payton) 3.00
2 Bears 20 (Walter Payton) 3.00
3 Bears 40 (Walter Payton) 3.00
4 Bears 50 (Walter Payton) 3.00
5 Bears First Down (Walter Payton) 3.00
6 Bears Punt (Walter Payton) 3.00
7 Bears Touchdown (Walter Payton) 3.00
8 Cowboys 10 (Danny White, Tony Dorsett) 1.00
9 Cowboys 20 (Danny White, Tony Dorsett) 1.00
10 Cowboys 40 (Danny White, Tony Dorsett) 1.00
11 Cowboys 50 (Danny White, Tony Dorsett) 1.00
12 Cowboys First Down (Danny White, Tony Dorsett) 1.00
13 Cowboys Punt (Danny White, Tony Dorsett) 1.00
14 Cowboys Touchdown (Danny White, Tony Dorsett) 1.00
15 Dolphins 10 (Lorenzo Hampton, Eric Laakso) .50
16 Dolphins 20 (Lorenzo Hampton, Eric Laakso) .50
17 Dolphins 40 (Lorenzo Hampton, Eric Laakso) .50
18 Dolphins 50 (Lorenzo Hampton, Eric Laakso) .50
19 Dolphins First Down (Lorenzo Hampton, Eric Laakso) .50

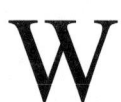

20	Dolphins Punt (Lorenzo Hampton, Eric Laakso)	.50
21	Dolphins Touchdown (Lorenzo Hampton, Eric Laakso)	.50
22	Redskins 10 (John Riggins, Joe Theismann)	1.00
23	Redskins 20 (John Riggins, Joe Theismann)	1.00
24	Redskins 40 (John Riggins, Joe Theismann)	1.00
25	Redskins 50 (John Riggins, Joe Theismann)	1.00
26	Redskins First Down (John Riggins, Joe Theismann)	1.00
27	Redskins Punt (John Riggins, Joe Theismann)	1.00
28	Redskins Touchdown (John Riggins, Joe Theismann)	1.00
29	Steelers 10 (Terry Bradshaw, Lynn Swann)	2.00
30	Steelers 20 (Terry Bradshaw, Lynn Swann)	2.00
31	Steelers 40 (Terry Bradshaw, Lynn Swann)	2.00
32	Steelers 50 (Terry Bradshaw, Lynn Swann)	2.00
33	Steelers First Down (Terry Bradshaw, Lynn Swann)	2.00
34	Steelers Punt (Terry Bradshaw, Lynn Swann)	2.00
35	Steelers Touchdown (Terry Bradshaw, Lynn Swann)	2.00
36	Interception Card	.50
37	Interception Card	.50
38	Interception Card	.50
39	Interception Card	.50
40	Interception Card	.50

1988 Wagon Wheel

The eight-card, 6-5/16" x 4-5/16" set was issued in the United Kingdom by Burtons and each card was included in boxes of Chocolate Biscuits. Players are not specifically identified as the purpose of the set was to explain American football to the British by giving examples of positions.

		MT
Complete Set (8):		60.00
Common Player:		6.00
1	Defensive Back (Todd Bowles covering Mark Bavaro)	6.00
2	Defensive Lineman (Ed "Too Tall" Jones, Neil Lomax)	8.00
3	Kicker (Kevin Butler)	6.00
4	Linebacker (Bob Brudzinski)	6.00
5	Offensive Lineman (Keith Van Horne leading Walter Payton)	15.00
6	Quarterback (John Elway)	20.00
7	Receiver (Steve Largent between Vann McElroy and Mike Haynes)	10.00
8	Running Back (Rodney Carter of the Steelers)	6.00

1964 Wheaties Stamps

These unnumbered stamps, which measure 2-1/2" x 2-3/4", were created to be stored in an accompanying stamp album titled "Pro Bowl Football Player Stamp Album." Each stamp has a color photo of the player, plus his facsimile signature, bordered by a white frame. The stamps were in panels of 12 inside the album and were perforated so they could be put on the corresponding spot within the album. Two stickers were attached to the inside front cover. Four team logo stamps and 70 players are represented on the stamps, but there were no spots in the album for the logo stamps or those for Y.A. Tittle or Joe Schmidt.

		NM
Complete Set (74):		250.00
Common Player:		2.00
(1)	Herb Adderley	6.00
(2)	Grady Alderman	2.00
(3)	Doug Atkins	4.00
(4)	Sam Baker	2.00
(5)	Erich Barnes	2.00
(6)	Terry Barr	2.00
(7)	Dick Bass	2.00
(8)	Maxie Baughan	3.00
(9)	Raymond Berry	6.00
(10)	Charley Bradshaw	2.50
(11)	Jim Brown	35.00
(12)	Roger Brown	2.50
(13)	Timmy Brown	3.00
(14)	Gail Cogdill	2.00
(15)	Tommy Davis	2.00
(16)	Willie Davis	6.00
(17)	Bob DeMarco	2.00
(18)	Darrell Dess	2.00
(19)	Buddy Dial	3.00
(20)	Mike Ditka	18.00
(21)	Galen Fiss	2.00
(22)	Lee Folkins	2.00
(23)	Joe Fortunato	2.00
(24)	Bill Glass	3.00
(25)	John Gordy	2.00
(26)	Ken Gray	2.50
(27)	Forrest Gregg	5.00
(28)	Rip Hawkins	2.00
(29)	Charlie Johnson	3.00
(30)	John Henry Johnson	5.00
(31)	Henry Jordan	3.00
(32)	Jim Katcavage	2.00
(33)	Jerry Kramer	5.00
(34)	Joe Krupa	2.00
(35)	John LoVetere	2.00
(36)	Dick Lynch	3.00
(37)	Gino Marchetti	5.00
(38)	Joe Marconi	2.00
(39)	Tommy Mason	3.00
(40)	Dale Meinert	2.00
(41)	Lou Michaels	2.00
(42)	Minnesota Vikings Emblem	3.00
(43)	Bobby Mitchell	6.00
(44)	John Morrow	2.00
(45)	New York Giants Emblem	3.00
(46)	Merlin Olsen	10.00
(47)	Jack Pardee	4.00
(48)	Jim Parker	4.00
(49)	Bernie Parrish	2.00
(50)	Don Perkins	3.00
(51)	Richie Petitbon	2.00
(52)	Vince Promuto	2.00
(53)	Myron Pottios	2.00
(54)	Mike Pyle	2.00
(55)	Pete Retzlaff	3.00
(56)	Jim Ringo	5.00
(57)	Joe Rutgens	2.00
(58)	St. Louis Cardinals Emblem	3.00
(59)	San Francisco 49ers Emblem	3.00
(60)	Dick Schafrath	2.00
(61)	Joe Schmidt	6.00
(62)	Del Shofner	3.00
(63)	Norm Snead	3.00
(64)	Bart Starr	15.00
(65)	Jim Taylor	6.00
(66)	Roosevelt Taylor	2.00
(67)	Clendon Thomas	2.00
(68)	Y.A. Tittle	12.50
(69)	Johnny Unitas	18.00
(70)	Bill Wade	3.00
(71)	Wayne Walker	2.00
(72)	Jesse Whittenton	2.00
(73)	Larry Wilson	5.00
(74)	Abe Woodson	2.00

1987 Wheaties

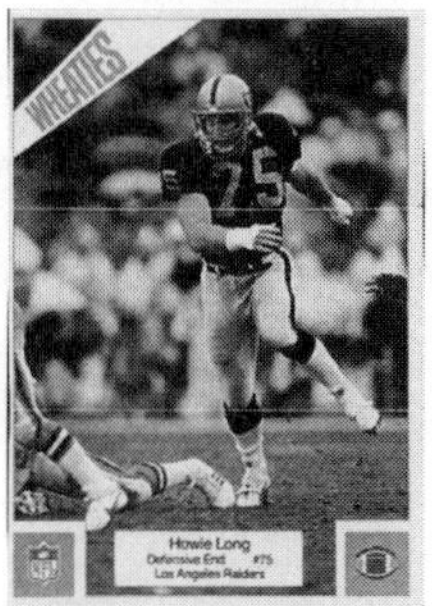

Specially-marked boxes of Wheaties cereal each contained one of these 5" x 7" posters. The posters, which were wrapped in cellophane, were produced by Starline Inc. with the cooperation of the NFLPA and organizational efforts of Michael Schechter Associates. Each front has a color action photo, with the player's name, team, position and uniform number listed in a white box at the bottom. "Wheaties" is written in a banner in the upper left corner. The poster back is numbered and includes biographical information and career summary notes. Bernie Kosar's card was not listed in the set on the checklist Wheaties provided on the box. It is assumed Kosar was pulled from the set at some point - his card is listed as a short print.

		MT
Complete Set (26):		130.00
Common Player:		2.50
1	Tony Dorsett	5.00
2	Herschel Walker	5.00
3	Marcus Allen	5.00
4	Eric Dickerson	6.00
5	Walter Payton	12.00
6	Phil Simms	4.00
7	Tommy Kramer	2.50
8	Joe Morris	2.50
9	Roger Craig	4.00
10	Curt Warner	3.50
11	Andre Tippett	2.50
12	Joe Montana	20.00
13	Jim McMahon	3.00
14	Bernie Kosar	25.00
15	Jay Schroeder	2.50
16	Al Toon	2.50
17	Mark Gastineau	2.50
18	Kenny Easley	2.50
19	Howie Long	2.50
20	Dan Marino	15.00
21	Karl Mecklenburg	3.25
22	John Elway	10.00
23	Boomer Esiason	5.00
24	Dan Fouts	4.00
25	Jim Kelly	10.00
26	Louis Lipps	3.00

1991 Wild Card National Promos

This three-card set was given away as a promo at the 12th Annual National Covention in Anaheim. The cards are numbered on the back, starting with the Dan McGwire card as "Prototype-2". Striped versions of the cards with a hologram in the upper left corner were also issued.

		MT
Complete Set (3):		12.00
Common Player:		2.50
2	Dan McGwire	6.00
3	Randal Hill	2.50
4	Todd Marinovich	6.00

1991 Wild Card College Draft Picks

Each of these cards features a glossy color action photo of a player in his college uniform. The card is black with an orange frame, which has different denominations running on top and down the right side. A circle with "1st Edition" appears in the lower left corner. The purple back has statistics, biographical information and a color photo. Striped, limited-edition Wild Card random inserts of each card were also produced (1 out of every 100 is wild). These cards had denominations of 5, 10, 20, 50, 100 and 1,000; the higher numbers were made in scarcer numbers. The finder was able to redeem the card for a like amount of the player's regular card.

		MT
Complete Set (160):		15.00
Common Player:		.05
1	Wild Card 1 (Todd Lyght)	.60
2	Kelvin Pritchett	.20
3	Robert Young	.05
4	Reggie Johnson	.05
5	Eric Turner	.50
6	Pat Tyrance	.10
7	Curvin Richards	.20
8	Calvin Stephens	.10
9	Corey Miller	.05
10	Michael Jackson	.30
11	Simmie Carter	.05
12	Roland Smith	.10
13	Pat O'Hara	.20
14	Scott Conover	.05
15	Wild Card 2 (Russell Maryland)	.75
16	Greg Amsler	.10
17	Moe Gardner	.30
18	Howard Griffith	.20
19	David Daniels	.10
20	Henry Jones	.10
21	Don Davey	.10
22	Wild Card 3 (Raghib (Rocket) Ismail)	1.00
23	Richie Andrews	.05
24	Shawn Moore	.25
25	Anthony Moss	.10
26	Vince Moore	.05
27	Leroy Thompson	.15
28	Darrick Brownlow	.20
29	Mel Agee	.10
30	Darryll Lewis	.25
31	Hyland Hickson	.05
32	Leonard Russell	1.00
33	Floyd Fields	.05
34	Esera Tuaolo	.15
35	Todd Marinovich	1.25
36	Gary Wellman	.10
37	Ricky Ervins	2.50
38	Pat Harlow	.20
39	Mo Lewis	.25
40	John Kasay	.30
41	Phil Hansen	.10
42	Kevin Donnalley	.10
43	Dexter Davis	.10
44	Vance Hammond	.05
45	Chris Gardocki	.10
46	Bruce Pickens	.20
47	Godfrey Myles	.15
48	Ernie Mills	.25
49	Derek Russell	.35
50	Chris Zorich	.50
51	Alfred Williams	.25
52	Jon Vaughn	.45
53	Adrian Cooper	.25
54	Eric Bieniemy	.05
55	Robert Bailey	.05
56	Ricky Watters	.25
57	Mark Vander Poel	.10
58	James Joseph	.50
59	Darren Lewis	.45
60	Wesley Carroll	.40
61	Dave Key	.10
62	Mike Pritchard	.75
63	Craig Erickson	.40
64	Browning Nagle	.75
65	Mike Dumas	.20
66	Andre Jones	.05
67	Herman Moore	.75
68	Greg Lewis	.60
69	James Goode	.05
70	Stan Thomas	.10
71	Jerome Henderson	.10
72	Doug Thomas	.10
73	Tony Covington	.10
74	Charles Mincy	.10
75	Kanavis McGhee	.20
76	Tom Backes	.05
77	Fernandus Vinson	.05
78	Marcus Robertson	.05
79	Eric Harmon	.05
80	Rob Selby	.10
81	Ed King	.20
82	William Thomas	.10
83	Mike Jones	.10
84	Paul Justin	.20
85	Robert Wilson	.20
86	Jesse Campbell	.10
87	Hayward Haynes	.05
88	Mike Croel	.75
89	Jeff Graham	.20
90	Vinnie Clark	.25
91	Keith Cash	.20
92	Tim Ryan	.10
93	Jarrod Bunch	.20
94	Stanley Richard	.30
95	Alvin Harper	.60
96	Bob Dahl	.10
97	Mark Gunn	.05
98	Frank Blevins	.05
99	Harvey Williams	1.00
100	Dixon Edwards	.20
101	Blake Miller	.05
102	Bobby Wilson	.25
103	Chuck Webb	.25
104	Randal Hill	.75
105	Shane Curry	.05
106	Barry Sanders	.75
107	Richard Fain	.15
108	Joe Garten	.05
109	Dean Dingham	.05
110	Mark Tucker	.05
111	Dan McGwire	1.00
112	Paul Glonek	.05
113	Tom Dohring	.05
114	Joe Sims	.05
115	Bryan Cox	.30
116	Bobby Olive	.05
117	Blaise Bryant	.15
118	Charles Johnson	.15
119	Brett Favre	2.00
120	Luis Cristobal	.05
121	Don Gibson	.05
122	Scott Ross	.05
123	Huey Richardson	.15
124	Chris Smith	.10
125	Duane Young	.05
126	Eric Swann	.30
127	Jeff Fite	.05
128	Eugene Williams	.05
129	Harlan Davis	.05
130	James Bradley	.05
131	Rob Carpenter	.20
132	Dennis Ransom	.05
133	Mike Arthur	.05
134	Chuck Weatherspoon	.30
135	Darrell Malone	.05
136	George Thornton	.10
137	Lamar McGriggs	.05
138	Alex Johnson	.05
139	Eric Moten	.10
140	Joe Valerio	.10
141	Jake Reed	.20
142	Ernie Thompson	.10
143	Roland Poles	.05
144	Randy Bethel	.05
145	Terry Bagsby	.05
146	Tim James	.05
147	Kenny Walker	.60
148	Nolan Harrison	.05
149	Keith Traylor	.20
150	Nick Subis	.05
151	Scott Zolak	.25
152	Pio Sagapolutele	.15
153	James Jones	.10
154	Mike Sullivan	.05
155	Joe Johnson	.05
156	Todd Scott	.10
157	Checklist 1	.05
158	Checklist 2	.05
159	Checklist 3	.05
160	Checklist 4	.05

1991 Wild Card NFL Prototypes

The six-card set promoted Wild Card's upcoming 1991 NFL set. The card fronts showcase an action photo bordered in black with different colored numbers around the top and right border. The Wild Card logo is in the upper left, with "NFL Premier Edition" printed inside a football in the lower left. The player's name and position are in the lower right. The card backs, numbered by a prefix of "prototype," have a photo of the player, his name, position and bio at the top. The player's stats are included inside a box at the bottom.

		MT
Complete Set (6):		40.00
Common Player:		5.00
1	Troy Aikman	9.00
2	Barry Sanders	10.00
3	Thurman Thomas	9.00
4	Emmitt Smith	12.50
5	Jerry Rice	7.50
6	Lawrence Taylor	5.00

1991 Wild Card NFL

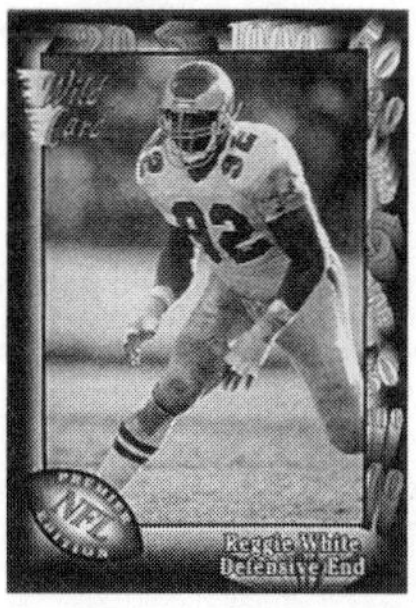

These cards, similar in design to Wild Cards' collegiate draft picks set, have a full-color glossy action photo on the front, with a black and yellow border. Multi-color numbers appear in the upper right corner and along the right side of the card. The player's name and position are in the lower right corner, opposite a football with the words "NFL Premier Edition" inside. The card back has a mug shot, statisitics, a card number and biographical information. Striped "Wild Cards," printed in limited editions, were also created for each card, in denominations of 10, 20, 50, 100 and 1,000. The card could be redeemed for a similar amount of the player's regular card, according to the denomination number in the stripe. A surprise Wild Card, #126, was also created; finders could redeem it for a 10-card NFL Experience subset which featured players from the Buffalo Bills and Washington Redskins. Also created were three bonus cards, which enabled finders to redeem them for the item pictured - either a case of cards, a box of cards, or a Wild Card cap.

		MT
Complete Set (160):		10.00
Common Player:		.03
Wax Box:		6.00
1	Jeff George	.35
2	Sean Jones	.03
3	Duane Bickett	.03
4	John Elway	.15
5	Christian Okoye	.08
6	Steve Atwater	.06
7	Anthony Munoz	.08
8	Dave Krieg	.08
9	Nick Lowery	.06
10	Albert Bentley	.06
11	Mark Jackson	.06
12	Jeff Bryant	.03
13	Johnny Hector	.03
14	John L. Williams	.08
15	Jim Everett	.15
16	Mark Duper	.06
17	Drew Hill	.08
18	Randal Hill	.60
19	Ernest Givins	.10
20	Ken O'Brien	.08
21	Blair Thomas	.40
22	Derrick Thomas	.15
23	Harvey Williams	.75
24	Simon Fletcher	.03
25	Stephone Paige	.06
26	Barry Wood	.25
27	Warren Moon	.20
28	Derrick Fenner	.12
29	Shane Conlan	.06
30	Karl Mecklenburg	.06
31	Gary Anderson	.06
32	Sammie Smith	.08
33	Steve DeBerg	.08
34	Dan McGwire	1.25
35	Roger Craig	.10
36	Tom Tupa	.10
37	Rod Woodson	.08
38	Junior Seau	.08
39	Bruce Pickens	.20
40	Greg Townsend	.03
41	Gary Clark	.12
42	Broderick Thomas	.06
43	Charles Mann	.06
44	Browning Nagle	.75
45	James Joseph	.45
46	Emmitt Smith	2.00
47	Cornelius Bennett	.08
48	Maurice Hurst	.03
49	Art Monk	.10
50	Louis Lipps	.06
51	Mark Rypien	.20
52	Bubby Brister	.08
53	John Stephens	.06
54	Merril Hoge	.03
55	Kevin Mack	.06
56	Al Toon	.08
57	Ronnie Lott	.10
58	Eric Metcalf	.06
59	Vinny Testaverde	.08
60	Darrell Green	.10
61	Randall Cunningham	.15
62	Charles Haley	.06
63	Mark Carrier	.08
64	Jim Harbaugh	.10
65	Richard Dent	.08
66	Stan Thomas	.08
67	Neal Anderson	.15
68	Troy Aikman	1.25
69	*Mike Pritchard*	.40
70	Deion Sanders	.20
71	Andre Rison	.15
72	Keith Millard	.06
73	Jerry Rice	.85
74	Johnny Johnson	.25
75	Tim McDonald	.06
76	*Leonard Russell*	1.25
77	Keith Jackson	.08
78	Keith Byars	.06
79	Ricky Proehl	.10
80	Dexter Carter	.08
81	*Alvin Harper*	.75
82	Irving Fryar	.06
83	Marion Butts	.10
84	Alfred Williams	.15
85	Timm Rosenbach	.10
86	Steve Young	.60
87	Albert Lewis	.06
88	Rodney Peete	.08
89	Barry Sanders	.85
90	Bennie Blades	.06
91	Chris Spielman	.06
92	John Friesz	.35
93	Jerome Brown	.06
94	Reggie White	.08
95	Michael Irvin	.20
96	Keith McCants	.08
97	Vinnie Clark	.10
98	Louis Oliver	.03
99	Mark Clayton	.08
100	John Offerdahl	.03
101	Michael Carter	.06
102	John Taylor	.12
103	William Perry	.08
104	Gill Byrd	.06
105	Burt Grossman	.03
106	*Herman Moore*	1.50
107	Howie Long	.06
108	Bo Jackson	.35
109	Kelvin Pritchett	.12
110	Jacob Green	.06
111	Chris Doleman	.06
112	Herschel Walker	.12
113	Russell Maryland	.45
114	Anthony Carter	.08
115	Joey Browner	.06
116	Tony Mandarich	.06
117	Don Majkowski	.08
118	Ricky Ervins	1.50
119	Sterling Sharpe	.75
120	Tim Harris	.06
121	Hugh Millen	.75
122	Mike Rozier	.06
123	Chris Miller	.15
124	Morten Andersen	.06
125	*Neil O'Donnell*	1.50
126	Surprise Wild Card	.25
127	Eddie Brown	.06
128	James Francis	.08
129	James Brookss	.08
130	David Fulcher	.03
131	*Michael Jackson*	.75
132	Clay Matthews	.03
133	Scott Norwood	.03
134	Wesley Carroll	.40
135	Thurman Thomas	.40
136	Mark Ingram	.03
137	Bobby Hebert	.08
138	Bobby Wilson	.08
139	Craig Heyward	.08
140	Dalton Hilliard	.06
141	Jeff Hostetler	.20
142	Dave Meggett	.10
143	Cris Dishman	.20
144	Lawrence Taylor	.10
145	Leonard Marshall	.06
146	Pepper Johnson	.06
147	Todd Marinovich	1.25
148	Mike Croel	.75
149	Erik McMillan	.06
150	Flipper Anderson	.06
151	Cleveland Gary	.06
152	Henry Ellard	.08
153	Kevin Greene	.06
154	Michael Cofer	.03
155	Todd Lyght	.40
156	Bruce Smith	.08
157	Checklist 1	.06
158	Checklist 2	.06
159	Checklist 3	.06
160	Checklist 4	.06

1991 Wild Card NFL Redemption Cards

This surprise Wild Card, #126, inserted randomly in 1991 Wild Card NFL packs, could be redeemed for the 10-card NFL Experience subset which is listed below. The cards feature members of the Buffalo Bills and Washington Redskins.

		MT
Complete Set (10):		3.50
Common Player:		.12
126A	Mark Rypien	.60
126B	Ricky Ervins	1.50
126C	Darrell Green	.25
126D	Charles Mann	.12
126E	Art Monk	.30
126F	Thurman Thomas	.90
126G	Bruce Smith	.30
126H	Cornelius Bennett	.25
126I	Scott Norwood	.12
126J	Shane Conlan	.18

1991 Wild Card NFL Super Bowl Promos

Super Bowl XXVI is honored on this 10-card set, which spotlights five players from each team. The cards were handed out to attendees at the Super Bowl Card Show. The card fronts have an action photo borded in black, with different colored numbers on the top and right borders. The NFL Experience logo is in the lower left. The player's name and position are located in the lower right. The card backs showcase a player photo, his name, position and bio at the top of the card. A text box at the bottom of the card explains that Wild Card was a corporate sponsor of the Super Bowl Card Show III.

		MT
Complete Set (10):		30.00
Common Player:		1.00
1	Mark Rypien	5.00
2	Ricky Ervins	10.00
3	Darrell Green	2.00
4	Charles Mann	1.00
5	Art Monk	2.50
6	Thurman Thomas	7.50
7	Bruce Smith	2.50
8	Cornelius Bennett	2.00
9	Scott Norwood	1.00
10	Shane Conlan	1.50

1991-92 Wild Card Redemption Prototypes

The six-card, standard-size set was available to collectors via a redemption mail-in offer. In exchange for three Collegiate Football Surprise wild cards before April 30, 1992, collectors also received the set, which is similar to the 1992 Wild Card NFL set. The cards are numbered with the "P" prefix.

		MT
Complete Set (6):		2.00
Common Player:		.20
1	Edgar Bennett (Florida State)	1.00
2	Jimmy Smith (Jackson State)	.75
3	Will Furrer (Virginia Tech)	.20
4	Terrell Buckley (Florida State)	.30
5	Tommy Vardell (Stanford)	.30
6	Amp Lee (Florida State)	.30

1992 Wild Card Prototypes

Picking up where the 1991 Wild Card Prototypes left off, this 12-card set begins with card No. P7. The card fronts include a color photo, bordered

with colored numbers on the top and right border. The Wild Card logo is in the upper left, with the player's team name along the left side. His name and position are in the lower right. The team's helmet is printed in the lower left of the photo. The backs have the player's name, picture and bio on the right side of the card. The player's stats are located inside a box on the left side. The cards are numbered with the "P" prefix.

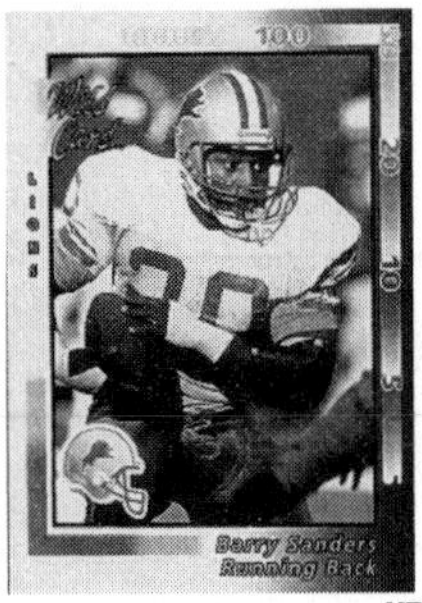

MT
Complete Set (12): 25.00
Common Player: 1.00
7 Barry Sanders 4.00
8 John Taylor 2.00
9 John Elway 3.00
10 Erik Kramer 2.00
11 Christian Okoye 1.00
12 Leonard Russell 1.00
13 Barry Sanders 4.00
14 Earnest Byner 1.00
15 Warren Moon 2.50
16 Ronnie Lott 2.00
17 Michael Irvin 2.50
18 Haywood Jeffires 2.00

1992 Wild Card

This 460-card set showcased a color photo on the front, with the Wild Card logo in the upper left, the team name along the left border, team helmet in the lower left of the photo and player's name and position in the lower right. The border of the card front changes from white to gray to black. The card backs have the card number in the upper right, with the player's name, bio and photo along the right side. His stats are located in a box along the left border. Reportedly, Wild Card produced 30,000 10-box cases of the 250-card Series I product. Overall, 100 case cards and 1,000 box cards were seeded in foil packs. A numbered stripe on the front of the cards would carry denominations of 5, 10, 20, 50, 100 and 1,000. The Surprise Cards could be redeemed for a four-card set which included a P1 Barry Sanders (with Surprise Card No. 1) or P2 Emmitt Smith Stat Smasher card (with Series II Suprise Card No. 251), Red-Hot rookie card, Field Force card and a silver or gold Field Force card. In addition, a Barry Sanders promo card was handed out at the 1992 National Convention. It featured the National logo and had value stripes of 5, 10, 20, 50 and 100.

MT
Complete Set (460): 15.00
Complete Series 1 (250): 7.50
Complete Series 2 (210): 7.50
Common Player: .05
Minor Stars: .10
Series 1/2 Wax Box: 8.00
1 Surprise Card .10
2 Marcus Dupree .05
3 Jackie Slater .05
4 Robert Delpino .05
5 Jerry Gray .05
6 Jim Everett .05
7 Roman Phifer .05
8 Alvin Wright .05
9 Todd Lyght .05
10 Reggie White .20
11 Randal Hill .05
12 Keith Byars .05
13 Clyde Simmons .05
14 Keith Jackson .05
15 Seth Joyner .05
16 James Joseph .05
17 Eric Allen .05
18 Sammie Smith .05
19 Mark Clayton .05
20 Aaron Craver .05
21 Hugh Green .05
22 John Offerdahl .05
23 Jeff Cross .05
24 Ferrell Edmunds .05
25 Mark Duper .05
26 Ronnie Harmon .05
27 Derrick Walker .05
28 Gary Plummer .05
29 Rod Bernstine .05
30 Burt Grossman .05
31 Donnie Elder .05
32 John Friesz .10
33 Bill Ray Smith .05
34 Luis Sharpe .05
35 Aeneas Williams .10
36 Ken Harvey .05
37 Johnny Johnson .05
38 Eric Swann .05
39 Tom Tupa .05
40 Anthony Thompson .05
41 Broderick Thomas .05
42 Vinny Testaverde .20
43 Mark Carrier .05
44 Gary Anderson .05
45 Keith McCants .05
46 Reggie Cobb .05
47 Lawrence Dawsey .05
48 Kevin Murphy .05
49 Keith Woodside .05
50 Darrell Thompson .05
51 Vinnie Clark .05
52 Sterling Sharpe .20
53 Mike Tomczak .05
54A Dan Majikowski (err) .05
54B Don Majikowski (cor) .05
55 Tony Mandarich .05
56 Mark Murphy .05
57 Dexter McNabb .05
58 Rick Fenney .05
59 Cris Carter .30
60 Wade Wilson .05
61 Mike Merriweather .05
62 Rich Gannon .05
63 Herschel Walker .05
64 Chris Doleman .05
65 UER (Al Noga) (On front, he's a DE; on back, he's a DT) .05
66 *Chris Mims* .10
67 Ed Cunningham .05
68 Marcus Allen .20
69 *Kevin Turner* .10
70 Howie Long .10
71 Tim Brown .20
72 Nick Bell .05
73 Todd Marinovich .05
74 Jay Schroeder .05
75 Mervyn Fernandez .05
76 Tony Smith .05
77 John Alt .05
78 Christian Okoye .05
79 Nick Lowery .05
80 Derrick Thomas .10
81 Bill Maas .05
82 Dino Hackett .05
83 Deron Cherry .05
84 Barry Word .05
85 Mike Mooney .05
86 Cris Dishman .05
87 Bruce Matthews .05
88 Tony Jones .05
89 William Fuller .05
90 Ray Childress .05
91 Warren Moon .10
92 Lorenzo White .05
93 Joe Bowden .05
94 Tom Rathman .05
95 Keith Henderson .05
96 Jesse Sapolu .05
97 Charles Haley .05
98 Steve Young .50
99 John Taylor .05
100 Tim Harris .05
101 Scott Davis .05
102 *Steve Bono* .30
103 Mike Kenn .05
104 Mike Farr .05
105 Rodney Peete .05
106 Jerry Ball .05
107 Chris Spielman .05
108 Barry Sanders 1.50
109 Bennie Blades .05
110 Herman Moore .50
111 Erik Kramer .05
112 Vance Johnson .05
113 Mike Croel .05
114 Mark Jackson .05
115 Steve Atwater .05
116 Gaston Green .05
117 John Elway 1.00
118 Simon Fletcher .05
119 Karl Mecklenburg .05
120 Hart Lee Dykes .05
121 Jerome Henderson .05
122 Chris Singleton .05
123 Marv Cook .05
124 Leonard Russell .05
125 Hugh Millen .05
126 Pat Harlow .05
127 Andre Tippett .05
128 Bruce Armstrong .05
129 Gary Clark .05
130 Art Monk .10
131 Darrell Green .05
132 Wilber Marshall .05
133 Jim Lachey .05
134 Earnest Byner .05
135 Chip Lohmiller .05
136 Mark Rypien .10
137 Ricky Sanders .05
138 Stan Thomas .05
139 Neal Anderson .05
140 Trace Armstrong .05
141 Kevin Butler .05
142 Mark Carrier .05
143 Dennis Gentry .05
144 Jim Harbaugh .10
145 Richard Dent .10
146 Andre Rison .20
147 Bruce Pickens .05
148 UER (Chris Hinton) (Dealt to Falcons in 1990, not 1989) .05
149 Brian Jordan .10
150 Chris Miller .05
151 Moe Gardner .05
152 Bill Fralic .05
153 Michael Haynes .10
154 Mike Pritchard .10
155 Dan Biasucci .05
156 Clarence Verdin .05
157 Donnell Thompson .05
158 Duane Bickett .05
159 Jon Hand .05
160 Sam Graddy .05
161 Emmitt Smith 1.50
162 Michael Irvin .20
163 Danny Noonan .05
164 Jack Del Rio .05
165 Jim Jeffcoat .05
166 Alexander Wright .05
167 Frank Minnifield .05
168 Ed King .05
169 Reggie Langhorne .05
170 Mike Baab .05
171 Eric Metcalf .05
172 Clay Matthews .05
173 Kevin Mack .05
174 Mike Johnson .05
175 Jeff Lageman .05
176 Freeman McNeil .05
177 Erik McMillan .05
178 James Hasty .05
179 Kyle Clifton .05
180 Joe Kelly .05
181 Phil Simms .10
182 Everson Walls .05
183 Jeff Hostetler .10
184 Dave Meggett .05
185 Matt Bahr .05
186 Mark Ingram .05
187 Rodney Hampton .10
188 Kanavis McGhee .05
189 Tim McGee .05
190 Eddie Brown .05
191 Rodney Holman .05
192 Harold Green .05
193 James Francis .05
194 Anthony Munoz .05
195 David Fulcher .05
196 Tim Krumrie .05
197 Bubby Brister .05
198 Rod Woodson .05
199 Louis Lipps .05
200 Carnell Lake .05
201 Don Beebe .05
202 Thurman Thomas .20
203 Cornelius Bennett .05
204 Mark Kelso .05
205 James Lofton .10
206 Darryl Talley .05
207 Morten Andersen .05
208 Vince Buck .05
209 Wesley Carroll .05
210 Bobby Hebert .05
211 Craig Heyward .05
212 Dalton Hilliard .05
213 Rickey Jackson .05
214 Eric Martin .05
215 Pat Swilling .05
216 Steve Walsh .05
217 Torrance Small .05
218 Jacob Green .05
219 Cortez Kennedy .05
220 John L. Williams .05
221 Terry Wooden .05
222 Grant Feasel .05
223 Siran Stacy .05
224 Chris Hakel .05
225 Todd Harrison .05
226 Bob Whitfield .05
227 Eddie Blake .05
228 *Keith Hamilton* .10
229 *Darryl Williams* .10
230 Ricardo McDonald .05
231 Alan Haller .05
232 Leon Searcy .05
233 Patrick Rowe .05
234 *Edgar Bennett* .30
235 *Terrell Buckley* .30
236 Will Furrer .05
237 *Amp Lee* .20
238 *Jimmy Smith* 2.00
239 *Tommy Vardell* .20
240 Leonard Russell .05
241 Mike Croel .05
242 Warren Moon .10
243 Mark Rypien .05
244 Thurman Thomas .10
245 Emmitt Smith .75
246 Checklist 1 .05
247 Checklist 2 .05
248 Checklist 3 .05
249 Checklist 4 .05
250 Checklist 5 .05
251 Surprise Card .10
252 Erric Pegram .10
253 Anthony Carter .05
254 Roger Craig .10
255 Hassan Jones .05
256 Steve Jordan .05
257 Randall McDaniel .05
258 Henry Thomas .05
259 Carl Lee .05
260 Ray Agnew .05
261 Irving Fryar .05
262 Tom Waddle .05
263 Greg McMurtry .05
264 Stephen Baker .05
265 Mark Collins .05
266 Howard Cross .05
267 Pepper Johnson .05
268 Fred Barnett .05
269 Heath Sherman .05
270 William Thomas .05
271 Bill Bates .05
272 Issiac Holt .05
273 Emmitt Smith 3.00
274 Eric Bieniemy .05
275 Marion Butts .05
276 Gill Byrd .05
277 Robert Blackmon .05
278 Brian Blades .05
279 Joe Nash .05
280 Bill Brooks .05
281 Mel Gray .05
282 Andre Ware .05
283 Steve McMichael .05
284 Brad Muster .05
285 Ron Rivera .05
286 Chris Zorich .05
287 Chris Burkett .05
288 Irv Eatman .05
289 Rob Moore .20
290 Joe Mott .05
291 Brian Washington .05
292 Michael Carter .05
293 Dexter Carter .05
294 Don Griffin .05
295 John Taylor .05
296 Ted Washington .05
297 Monte Coleman .05
298 Andre Collins .05
299 Charles Mann .05
300 Shane Conlon .05
301 Keith McKeller .05
302 Nate Odomes .05
303 Riki Ellison .05
304 Willie Gault .05
305 Bob Golic .05
306 Ethan Horton .05
307 Ronnie Lott .10
308 Don Mosebar .05
309 Aaron Wallace .05
310 Wymon Henderson .05
311 Vance Johnson .05
312 Ken Lanier .05
313 Steve Sewell .05
314 Dennis Smith .05
315 Kenny Walker .05
316 Chris Martin .05
317 Albert Lewis .05
318 Todd McNair .05
319 *Tracy Simien* .05
320 Percy Snow .05
321 Mark Rypien .05
322 Bryan Hinkle .05
323 David Little .05
324 Dwight Stone .05
325 *Van Waiters* .05
326 *Pio Sagapolutele* .05
327 Michael Jackson .10
328 Vestee Jackson .05
329 Tony Paige .05
330 Reggie Roby .05
331 Haywood Jeffires .10
332 Lamar Lathon .05
333 Bubba McDowell .05
334 Doug Smith .05
335 Dean Steinkuhler .05
336 Jessie Tuggle .05
337 Freddie Joe Nunn .05
338 Pat Terrell .05
339 Tom McHale .05
340 Sam Mills .05
341 John Tice .05
342 Brent Jones .05
343 *Robert Porcher* .20
344 *Mark D'Onofrio* .05
345 David Tate .05
346 *Courtney Hawkins* .10
347 Ricky Watters .20
348 Amp Lee .10
349 Steve Young .50
350 Natu Tuatagaloa .05
351 Alfred Williams .05
352 *Derek Brown* .10
353 *Marco Coleman* .10
354 *Tommy Maddox* .10
355 Siran Stacy .05
356 Greg Lewis .05
357 Paul Gruber .05
358 *Troy Vincent* .10
359 Robert Wilson .05
360 Jessie Hester .05
361 Shaun Gayle .05
362 Deron Cherry .05
363 Wendell Davis .05
364 *David Klingler* .20
365 *Jason Hanson* .10
366 *Marquez Pope* .10
367 *Robert Williams* .05
368 Kelvin Pritchett .05
369 Dana Hall .05
370 *David Brandon* .05
371 Tim McKyer .05
372 Darion Conner .05
373 Derrick Fenner .05
374 Hugh Millen .05
375 Bill Jones .05
376 J.J. Birden .05
377 Ty Detmer .10
378 *Alonzo Spellman* .20
379 Sammie Smith .05
380 Al Smith .05
381 *Louis Clark* .05
382 *Vernice Smith* .05
383 Tony Martin .20
384 Willie Green .05
385 *Sean Gilbert* .20
386 *Eugene Chung* .05
387 Tol Cook .05
388 Brett Maxie .05
389 Steve Israel .05
390 Mike Mularkey .05
391 Barry Foster .05
392 Hardy Nickerson .05
393 *Johnny Mitchell* .10
394 Thurman Thomas .20
395 *Tony Smith* .10
396 *Keith Goganious* .05
397 *Matt Darby* .05
398 *Nate Turner* .05
399 *Keith Jennings* .05
400 *Mitchell Benson* .05
401 *Kurt Barber* .05
402 *Tony Sacca* .05
403 *Steve Hendrickson* .05
404 Johnny Johnson .05
405 Lorenzo Lynch .05
406 Luis Sharpe .05
407 Jim Everett .05
408 Neal Anderson .05
409 *Ashley Ambrose* .10
410 *George Williams* .05
411 Clarence Kay .05
412 Dave Krieg .05
413 Terrell Buckley .10
414 Ricardo McDonald .05
415 Kelly Stouffer .05
416 Barney Bussey .05
417 Ray Roberts .05
418 *Fred McAfee* .05
419 Fred Banks .05
420 Tim McDonald .05
421 *Darryl Williams* .05
422 *Bobby Abrams* .05
423 Tommy Vardell .10
424 William White .05
425 Billy Ray Smith .05
426 Lemuel Stinson .05
427 *Brad Johnson* 20.00
428 Herschel Walker .05
429 Eric Thomas .05
430 Anthony Thompson .05
431 Ed West .05
432 Edgar Bennett .10
433 Warren Powers .05
434 Byron Evans .05
435 Rodney Culver .05
436 Ray Horton .05
437 Richmond Webb .05
438 *Mark McMillian* .05
439 Subset checklist .05
440 *Lawrence Pete* .05
441 *Rodney Smith* .05
442 *Mark Rodenhauser* .05
443 *Scott Lockwood* .05
444 *Charles Davenport* .05
445 Terry McDaniel .05
446 *Darren Perry* .10
447 *Darrick Owens* .10
448 Alvin Wright .05
449 Frank Stams .05
450 *Santana Dotson* .20
451 Mark Carrier .05
452 Kevin Murphy .05
453 Jeff Bryant .05
454 Eric Allen .05
455 *Brian Bollinger* .05
456 Elston Ridgle .05
457 Jim Riggs .05
458 Series II, checklist #6 .05
459 Series II, checklist #7 .05
460 Series II, checklist #8 .05

1992 Wild Card Class Back Attack

Inserted in 1992 Wild Card WLAF foil packs, the five-card set showcases a color action photo on the front. A green and black border surrounds the photo, with different colored numbers running along the right side of the card. In a football in the lower left is printed "Class Back Attack" or "Red Hot Rookie." The player's name and team are listed in the lower right. The card backs, numbered with an "SP" prefix, feature the player's photo and bio at the top. A text box at the bottom invites collectors to collect all singles and then continue to collect sets of the different value denominations.

MT
Complete Set (5): 16.00
Common Player: 1.25
1 Vaughn Dunbar 1.25
2 Barry Sanders 4.00
3 Emmitt Smith 7.50
4 Thurman Thomas 2.00
5 David Klingler (Red Hot Rookie; Surprise Card Redemption) 2.00

1992 Wild Card Field Force

Randomly seeded in 1992 Wild Card Series II foil packs, the 30-card set was also issued in both gold and silver foil versions. Each card front includes a photo which is bordered by a dark purple border on the left. It changes to purple and light purple as it runs to the right side of the card. The dark purple area on the left features gold or silver horizontal lines which run the length of the card. The Field Force logo is in the lower left, with the player's name and position in the lower right. The card back includes a photo on the left side and the player's stats on the right. The card number is located in the upper right.

MT
Complete Set (30): 18.00
Common Player: .25
1 Joe Montana 3.00
2 Quentin Coryatt .75
3 Tommy Vardell .50
4 Jim Kelly 1.00
5 John Elway 1.25
6 Ricky Watters 1.50
7 Vinny Testaverde .25
8 Randal Hill .25
9 Amp Lee .50
10 Vaughn Dunbar .25
11 Troy Aikman 3.50
12 Deion Sanders .50
13 Rodney Hampton 1.50
14 Brett Favre 2.00
15 Warren Moon .75
16 Browning Nagle .25
17 Terrell Buckley .30
18 Barry Sanders 3.00
19 Dan Marino 2.50
20 Carl Pickens .60
21 Herschel Walker .25
22 Ronnie Lott .25
23 Steve Emtman .30
24 Mark Rypien .25
25 Bobby Hebert .25
26 Dan McGwire .25
27 Neil O'Donnell 1.00
28 Cris Carter .25
29 Randall Cunningham .60
30 Jerry Rice 2.00

1992 Wild Card Pro Picks

Randomly seeded in 1992 Wild Card Series II foil packs, the 30-card chase set includes a Red Hot Rookies' logo inside a football in the lower left corner. Different colored numbers border the top and right of the photo. The player's name and position are at the lower right. The backs, numbered "of 30," have the player's name, bio and photo on the right, with his highlights in a box on the left. Gold and silver editions were inserted one per jumbo pack.

MT
Complete Set (8): 10.00
Common Player: .30
1 Emmitt Smith 4.00
2 Mark Rypien .50
3 Warren Moon .50
4 Leonard Russell .30
5 Thurman Thomas .50
6 John Elway 1.00
7 Barry Sanders 2.00
8 Steve Young 1.50

1992 Wild Card Red Hot Rookies

This 30-card set is identified by a flaming football with the words "Red Hot Rookies" in the lower right corner. The set was inserted into Series II packs of Wild Card, with gold and silver versions also available one per jumbo pack. Red Hot Rookies were also available in 5, 10, 20, 50, 100 and 1,000 stripe varieties, with the stripe placed in the upper right hand corner of the photo.

MT
Complete Set (30): 15.00
Complete Series 1 (10): 5.00
Complete Series 2 (20): 10.00
Common Player: .50
1 Darryl Williams .50
2 Amp Lee .75
3 Will Furrer .50
4 Edgar Bennett 1.50
5 Terrell Buckley .50
6 Bob Whitfield .50
7 Siran Stacy .50
8 Jimmy Smith 1.00
9 Kevin Turner .50
10 Tommy Vardell .75
11 Surprise Card 1.00
12 Derek Brown .50
13 Marco Coleman 1.00
14 Quentin Coryatt 1.00
15 Rodney Culver .50
16 Ty Detmer .50
17 Vaughn Dunbar .50
18 Steve Emtman .50
19 Sean Gilbert 1.00
20 Courtney Hawkins 1.25
21 David Klingler 1.00
22 Amp Lee .90
23 Tommy Maddox .50
24 Johnny Mitchell 1.25
25 Darren Perry .50
26 Carl Pickens 1.00
27 Robert Porcher .50
28 Tony Smith .50
29 Alonzo Spellman .50
30 Troy Vincent .50

1992 Wild Card Running Wild Silver

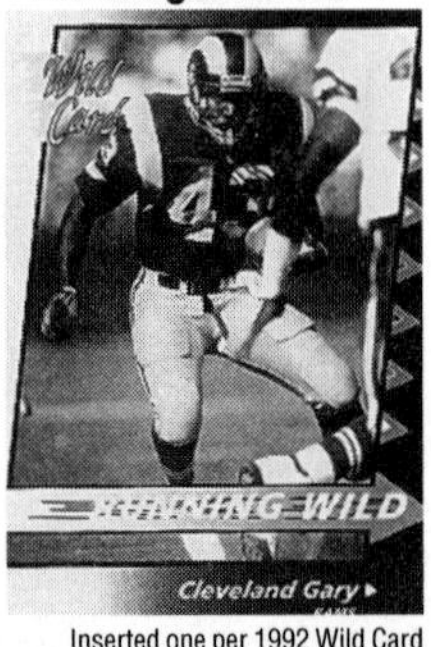

Inserted one per 1992 Wild Card Series II jumbo pack, the 40-card set showcased the Running Wild logo inside an arrow which overlapped the photo. Arrows also ran the length of the card from the top to the Running Wild logo. The player's name and team are located in the lower right. The card backs have a player photo on the left side, with his stats in a box on the right.

MT
Complete Set (40): 18.00
Common Player: .30
1 Terry Allen .75
2 Neal Anderson .50
3 Eric Ball .30
4 Nick Bell .30
5 Edgar Bennett .75
6 Rod Bernstine .30
7 Marion Butts .50
8 Keith Byars .30
9 Earnest Byner .30
10 Reggie Cobb .50
11 Roger Craig .50
12 Rodney Culver .50
13 Barry Foster .50
14 Cleveland Gary .30
15 Harold Green .50
16 Gaston Green .30
17 Rodney Hampton .75
18 Mark Higgs .30
19 Dalton Hilliard .30
20 Bobby Humphrey (UER) (Misspelled Humphries) .30
21 Amp Lee .50
22 Kevin Mack .30
23 Eric Metcalf .75
24 Brad Muster .30
25 Christian Okoye .50
26 Tom Rathman .30
27 Leonard Russell .50
28 Barry Sanders 2.50
29 Heath Sherman .30
30 Emmitt Smith 4.00
31 Blair Thomas .30
32 Thurman Thomas .75
33 Tommy Vardell .50
34 Herschel Walker .50
35 Chris Warren .75
36 Ricky Watters .75
37 Lorenzo White .50
38 John L. Williams .30
39 Barry Word .30
40 Vince Workman .50

1992 Wild Card Stat Smashers

Card Nos. 1-16 were randomly seeded in Series II foil packs, while card Nos. 17-52 were found one per pack in Series II jumbo packs. The card fronts have the Stat Smashers' logo in the upper right, while the player's name, team and position are in stripes near the bottom. A photo of the player is placed over a foil background. The card backs, numbered with a prefix of "SS," include the player's name, bio and photo on the left, while a highlights box appears on the right. A Barry Sanders card could be received in exchange for a Surprise Card in Series I. A Series II Surprise

Card could be redeemed for an Emmitt Smith card.

		MT
Complete Set (52):		55.00
Complete Series 1 (16):		30.00
Complete Series 2 (36):		25.00
Common Player (1-16):		1.25
Common Player (17-52):		.45
1	Barry Sanders	6.00
2	Leonard Russell	2.00
3	Thurman Thomas	3.00
4	John Elway	4.00
5	Steve Young	4.00
6	Warren Moon	2.00
7	Terrell Buckley	1.25
8	Randall Cunningham	2.00
9	Steve Emtman	1.25
10	Dan Marino	10.00
11	Joe Montana	8.00
12	Carl Pickens	1.25
13	Jerry Rice	6.00
14	Deion Sanders	2.50
15	Tommy Vardell	2.00
16	Ricky Watters	3.00
17	Troy Aikman	6.00
18	Dale Carter	.60
19	Quentin Coryatt	.75
20	Vaughn Dunbar	.50
21	Mark Duper	.45
22	Eric Metcalf	.45
23	Brett Favre	10.00
24	Barry Foster	2.25
25	Jeff George	.75
26	Sean Gilbert	1.00
27	Jim Harbaugh	.45
28	Courtney Hawkins	1.25
29	Charles Haley	.45
30	Bobby Hebert	.50
31	Stan Humphries	.55
32	Michael Irvin	2.50
33	Jim Kelly	1.50
34	David Klingler	1.50
35	Ronnie Lott	.45
36	Tommy Maddox	1.00
37	Todd Marinovich	.45
38	Hugh Millen	.60
39	Art Monk	.60
40	Browning Nagle	.65
41	Neil O'Donnell	1.00
42	Tom Rathman	.50
43	Andre Rison	1.00
44	Mike Singletary	.50
45	Tony Smith	.45
46	Emmitt Smith	10.00
47	Pete Stoyanovich	.45
48	John Taylor	.65
49	Troy Vincent	.60
50	Herschel Walker	.60
51	Lorenzo White	.80
52	Rodney Culver	1.00

1992 Wild Card NASDAM

Produced for and handed out at the 1992 NASDAM trade show in Orlando, this five card set features a color action photo on a white-bordered card front. Different colored numbers surround the photo on the top and right borders. The NASDAM logo appears in the lower left of the photo, while the player's name and position are in the lower right. The player's team's nickname is printed along the left border. The backs feature a photo of the player, along with his name, bio and stats.

		MT
Complete Set (5):		3.00
Common Player:		.40
1	Edgar Bennett	1.50
2	Amp Lee	.60
3	Terrell Buckley	.60
4	Tony Smith	.40
5	Will Furrer (UER) (Misspelled Furer)	.40

1992 Wild Card NASDAM/SCAI Miami

Produced and handed out at the 1992 NASDAM/SCAI conference in Miami, the six-card set showcases only Miami Dolphins. The card fronts feature a color action photo, with the NASDAM/SCAI logo in the lower left of the photo. "Dolphins" is printed along the left side of the photo. The top and right borders of the photo include different colored numbers. The player's name and position are located in the lower right. The card backs feature the player's name, bio and photo inside a football shape on the right side of the card. His stats are listed inside a box on the left side.

		MT
Complete Set (6):		4.00
Common Player:		.75
1	Mark Clayton	1.50
2	Aaron Craver	.75
3	Tony Paige	.75
4	Mark Duper	1.25
5	Tony Martin	1.25
6	Reggie Roby	.75

1992 Wild Card Sacramento CardFest

This six-card San Francisco 49ers set was given out at Sacramento CardFest in 1992, and contains the logo for the event in the lower left hand corner. The design is consistent with other 1992 Wild Card designs, with a white framed background that includes multi-colored trim on the top and right edge.

		MT
Complete Set (6):		3.00
Common Player:		.40
1	Tom Rathman	.40
2	Steve Young	1.00
3	Steve Bono	1.00
4	Brett Jones	.40
5	Ricky Watters	.60
6	Amp Lee	.40

1992 Wild Card WLAF

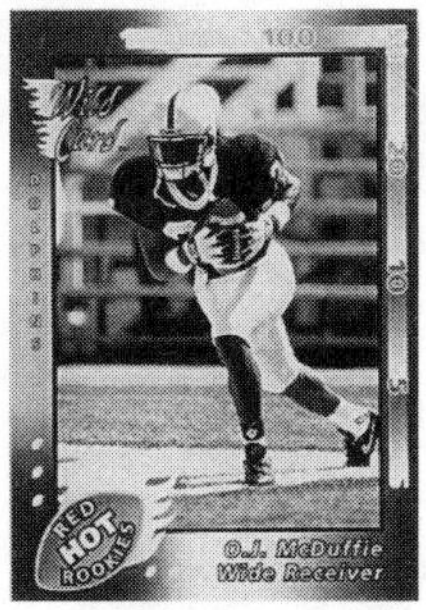

With a reported press run of 6,000 10-box cases, this 150-card set featured players from the World League of American Football. Card fronts featured a color photo surrounded by black, gray and white. The city the player performed in is printed like a postmark on the left, while the team's logo is located in the lower left. The World League logo is included with the Wild Card logo inside a stamp in the upper right. The player's name and team are in the lower right. The card backs have the player's name printed under the photo, while his bio and card number are to the right of his photo. His highlights are listed in a box near the bottom of the card.

		MT
Complete Set (150):		9.00
Common Player:		.05
1	World Bowl Champs	.10
2	Pete Mandley	.10
3	Steve Williams	.05
4	Dee Thomas	.05
5	Emanuel King	.10
6	Anthony Dilweg	.25
7	Ben Brown	.05
8	Darryl Harris	.05
9	Aaron Emanuel	.20
10	Andre Brown	.10
11	Reggie McKenzie	.10
12	Darryl Holmes	.05
13	Michael Proctor	.05
14	Ricky Johnson	.05
15	Ray Savage	.05
16	George Searcy	.05
17	Titus Dixon	.05
18	Willie Fears	.10
19	Terrence Cooks	.05
20	Ivory Lee Brown	.20
21	Mike Johnson	.05
22	Doug Williams	.10
23	Brad Goebel	.20
24	Tony Boles	.15
25	Cisco Richard	.05
26	Robb White	.05
27	Darrell Colbert	.05
28	Wayne Walker	.10
29	Ronnie Williams	.05
30	Erik Norgard	.05
31	Darren Willis	.05
32	Kent Wells	.05
33	Phil Logan	.05
34	Pat O'Hara	.05
35	Melvin Patterson	.05
36	Amir Rasul	.05
37	Tom Rouen	.10
38	Chris Cochrane	.05
39	Randy Bethel	.05
40	Eric Harmon	.05
41	Archie Herring	.05
42	Tim James	.05
43	Babe Laufenberg	.15
44	Herb Welch	.05
45	Stefon Adams	.05
46	Tony Burse	.10
47	Carl Parker	.05
48	Mike Prugle	.05
49	Michael Jones	.05
50	David Archer	.25
51	Corian Freeman	.05
52	Eddie Brown	.15
53	Paul Green	.05
54	Basil Proctor	.05
55	Mike Sinclair	.05
56	Louis Riddick	.05
57	Roman Matuez	.05
58	Darryl Clack	.10
59	Willie Davis	.05
60	Glen Rodgers	.05
61	Grantis Bell	.05
62	Joe Howard-Johnson	.15
63	Rocen Keeton	.05
64	Dean Witkowski	.05
65	Stacey Simmons	.10
66	Roger Vick	.10
67	Scott Mitchell	.20
68	Todd Krumm	.05
69	Kerwin Bell	.15
70	Richard Carey	.05
71	Kip Lewis	.05
72	Andre Alexander	.05
73	Reggie Slack	.20
74	Falanda Newton	.10
75	Tony Woods	.10
76	Chris McLemore	.05
77	Eric Wilkerson	.10
78	Cornell Burbage	.10
79	Doug Pederson	.05
80	Brent Pease	.15
81	Monty Gilbreath	.05
82	Wes Pritchett	.05
83	Byron Williams	.05
84	Ron Sancho	.10
85	Tony Jones	.10
86	Anthony Wallace	.05
87	Mike Perez	.15
88	Steve Bartalo	.05
89	Teddy Garcia	.05
90	Joe Greenwood	.05
91	Tony Baker	.05
92	Glenn Cobb	.05
93	Mark Tucker	.05
94	Lyneil Mayo	.05
95	Alex Espinoza	.05
96	Mike Norseth	.15
97	Steve Avery	.05
98	John Brantley	.05
99	Eddie Britton	.05
100	Philip Doyle	.05
101	Elroy Harris	.05
102	John R. Holland	.10
103	Mark Hopkins	.05
104	Arthur Hunter	.05
105	Paul McGowan	.05
106	John Miller	.05
107	Shawn Moore	.05
108	Phil Ross	.05
109	Eugene Rowell	.05
110	Joe Valerio	.10
111	Harvey Wilson	.05
112	Irvin Smith	.05
113	Tony Sargent	.05
114	Ricky Shaw	.05
115	Curtis Moore	.05
116	Fred McNair	.05
117	Danny Lockett	.10
118	William Kirksey	.05
119	Stan Gelbaugh	.25
120	Judd Garrett	.15
121	Dedrick Dodge	.05
122	Dan Crossman	.05
123	Jeff Alexander	.05
124	Lew Barnes	.05
125	Willie Don Wright	.05
126	Johnny Thomas	.05
127	Richard Buchanan	.05
128	Chad Fortune	.05
129	Eric Lindstrom	.05
130	Ron Goetz	.05
131	Bruce Clark	.10
132	Anthony Greene	.10
133	Demetrius Davis	.10
134	Mike Roth	.05
135	Tony Moss	.05
136	Scott Erney	.10
137	Brad Henke	.05
138	Malcolm Frank	.05
139	Sean Foster	.05
140	Michael Titley	.05
141	Rickey Williams	.05
142	Karl Dunbar	.05
143	Carl Bax	.05
144	Willie Bouyer	.05
145	Howard Feggins	.05
146	David Smith	.05
147	Bernard Ford	.10
148	Checklist 1	.05
149	Checklist 2	.05
150	Checklist 3	.05

1992-93 Wild Card San Francisco

Originally produced for the Sports Collectors Card Expo in San Francisco in 1992, the six-card set focused solely on 49ers. The set was later reissued with a different logo for the 1993 Spring National Sports Collectors Convention in San Francisco. The 1993 set also had different card numbers and two different players. The card fronts have the show's logo in the lower left of the photo. The usual Wild Card denominations are printed along the top and right borders of the photo. The player's name and position are listed in the lower right. The card backs, numbered "of 6," have the player's name, bio and photo on the right, with stats listed in a box on the left. Cards listed below with an "A" are from the 1992 set, while those with a "B" are from the 1993 set.

		MT
Complete Set (6):		4.00
Common Player:		.30
1A	John Taylor	.30
1B	Tom Rathman	.30
2A	Amp Lee	.30
2B	Steve Young	.75
3A	Steve Bono	.60
3B	Steve Bono	.60
4A	Steve Young	.75
4B	Brent Jones	.30
5A	Tom Rathman	.30
5B	Ricky Watters	.50
6A	Don Griffin	.30
6B	Amp Lee	.30

1993 Wild Card Prototypes

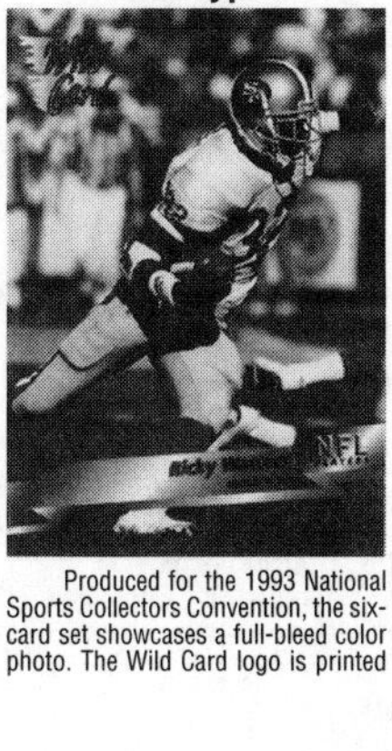

Produced for the 1993 National Sports Collectors Convention, the six-card set showcases a full-bleed color photo. The Wild Card logo is printed in the upper left, with the player's name, team and position printed inside a gold 3-D band at the bottom. "NFL players" is printed on the right side of the band. The card backs have a photo of the player on the right side, with his name, bio and stats printed over a photo of the team's city skyline. The card numbers are prefixed by a "P." The numbers begin at P19, which is where the 1992 Wild Card promos ended.

		MT
Complete Set (6):		5.00
Common Player:		.50
19	Emmitt Smith	2.00
20	Ricky Watters	.50
21	Drew Bledsoe	1.50
22	Garrison Hearst	.50
23	Barry Foster	.50
24	Rick Mirer	.75

1993 Wild Card Superchrome Promos

The six-card foil set features the same design as the 1993 Wild Card Prototypes, except the card fronts are printed in chrome. The card backs are also designed the same as the 1993 Prototypes, except the card numbers carry an "SCP" prefix.

		MT
Complete Set (6):		7.00
Common Player:		.50
1	Emmitt Smith	3.00
2	Ricky Watters	.75
3	Drew Bledsoe	2.50
4	Garrison Hearst	.50
5	Barry Foster	.50
6	Rick Mirer	1.00

1993 Wild Card

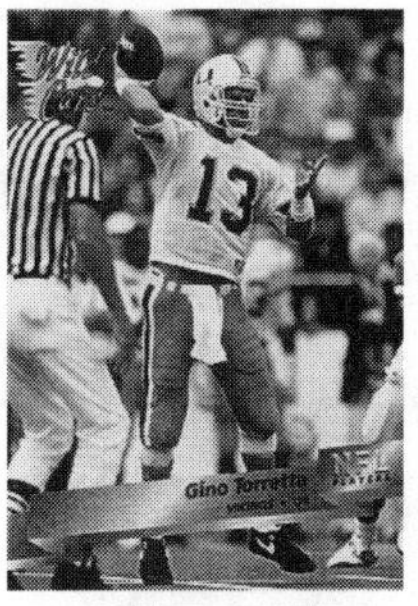

The 260-card set features full-bleed photos, with the Wild Card logo in the upper left and the player's name, team and position printed in a gold 3-D band at the bottom. The card backs have a photo on the right side. The player's name, bio and stats are located to the left of the player photo and printed over a skyline of the team's city. Series I boasted Field Force, Red Hot Rookies and Stat Smashers chase cards. In 1994, Wild Card changed its packages by adding Superchrome cards to packs. The Superchrome parallel cards were seeded in Superchrome 15-card low-series packs and 13-card high-series hobby packs. They are valued at four to nine times the value of the regular cards. In addition, denomination striped cards were randomly seeded into packs. Denominations fell between 5-1,000.

		MT
Complete Set (260):		10.00
Complete Series 1 (200):		6.00
Complete Series 2 (60):		4.00
Common Player:		.05
Minor Stars:		.10
Stripes 5/10/20: 2x-4x		
Stripes 50/100: 10x-20x		
Stripes 1000: 80x-160x		
Superchrome 1 Set (200):		20.00
Superchrome 2 Set (60):		15.00
Superchromes: 1.5x-3x		
Wax Box:		10.00
1	Surprise card	.05
2	Steve Young	.50
3	John Taylor	.05
4	Jerry Rice	.75
5	Brent Jones	.05
6	Ricky Watters	.20
7	*Elvis Grbac*	1.00
8	Amp Lee	.05
9	Steve Bono	.20
10	Wendell Davis	.05
11	Mark Carrier	.05
12	Jim Harbaugh	.05
13	*Curtis Conway*	.40
14	Neal Anderson	.05
15	Tom Waddle	.05
16	Jeff Query	.05
17	David Klingler	.10
18	Eric Ball	.05
19	Derrick Fenner	.05
20	Steve Tovar	.05
21	Carl Pickens	.20
22	Ricardo McDonald	.05
23	Harold Green	.05
24	Keith McKeller	.05
25	Steve Christie	.05
26	Andre Reed	.10
27	Kenneth Davis	.05
28	Frank Reich	.05
29	Jim Kelly	.15
30	Bruce Smith	.05
31	Thurman Thomas	.20
32	*Glyn Milburn*	.30
33	John Elway	.40
34	Vance Johnson	.05
35	Greg Lewis	.05
36	Steve Atwater	.05
37	Shannon Sharpe	.05
38	Mike Croel	.05
39	Kevin Mack	.05
40	Lawyer Tillman	.05
41	Tommy Vardell	.05
42	Bernie Kosar	.05
43	Eric Metcalf	.05
44	Clay Matthews	.05
45	Keith McCants	.05
46	Broderick Thomas	.05
47	Lawrence Dawsey	.05
48	Reggie Cobb	.05
49	*Lamar Thomas*	.10
50	Courtney Hawkins	.05
51	*Ivory Lee Brown*	.05
52	Ernie Jones	.05
53	Freddie Joe Nunn	.05
54	Chris Chandler	.05
55	Randal Hill	.05
56	Lorenzo Lynch	.05
57	*Garrison Hearst*	1.00
58	Marion Butts	.05
59	Anthony Miller	.05
60	Eric Bieneimy	.05
61	Ronnie Harmon	.05
62	Junior Seau	.15
63	Gill Byrd	.05
64	Stan Humphries	.15
65	John Friesz	.05
66	J.J. Birden	.05
67	Joe Montana	1.00
68	Christian Okoye	.05
69	Dale Carter	.05
70	Barry Wood	.05
71	Derrick Thomas	.10
72	Todd McNair	.05
73	Harvey Williams	.05
74	Jack Trudeau	.05
75	Rodney Culver	.05
76	Anthony Johnson	.05
77	Steve Emtman	.05
78	Quentin Coryatt	.05
79	Keith Cash	.05
80	Jeff George	.10
81	*Darrin Smith*	.10
82	Jay Novacek	.05
83	Michael Irvin	.30
84	Alvin Harper	.20
85	*Kevin Williams*	.50
86	Troy Aikman	.60
87	Emmitt Smith	1.25
88	*O.J. McDuffie*	.50
89	*Mike Williams*	.05
90	Dan Marino	1.25
91	Aaron Craver	.05
92	Troy Vincent	.05
93	Keith Jackson	.05
94	Marco Coleman	.05
95	Mark Higgs	.05
96	Fred Barnett	.05
97	Wes Hopkins	.05
98	Randall Cunningham	.10
99	Heath Sherman	.05
100	Vai Sikahema	.05
101	Tony Smith	.05
102	Andre Rison	.10
103	Chris Miller	.05
104	Deion Sanders	.30
105	Mike Pritchard	.05
106	Steve Broussard	.05
107	Stephen Baker	.05
108	Carl Banks	.05
109	Jarrod Bunch	.05
110	Phil Simms	.05
111	Rodney Hampton	.10
112	Dave Meggett	.05
113	Pepper Johnson	.05
114	*Coleman Rudolph*	.05
115	Boomer Esiason	.10
116	Browning Nagle	.05
117	Rob Moore	.05
118	*Marvin Jones*	.10
119	Herman Moore	.25
120	Bennie Blades	.05
121	Erik Kramer	.05
122	Mel Gray	.05
123	Rodney Peete	.05
124	Barry Sanders	.75
125	Chris Spielman	.05
126	Lamar Lathon	.05
127	Ernest Givins	.05
128	Lorenzo White	.05
129	*Michael Barrow*	.05
130	Warren Moon	.10
131	Cody Carlson	.05
132	Reggie White	.10
133	Terrell Buckley	.05
134	Ed West	.05
135	*Mark Brunell*	2.00
136	Brett Favre	1.25
137	Edgar Bennett	.10
138	Sterling Sharpe	.10
139	*George Teague*	.10
140	Leonard Russell	.05
141	*Drew Bledsoe*	2.00
142	Eugene Chung	.05
143	Walter Stanley	.05
144	Scott Zolak	.05
145	Jon Vaughn	.05
146	Andre Tippett	.05
147	Alexander Wright	.05
148	*Billy Joe Hobert*	.20
149	Terry McDaniel	.05
150	Tim Brown	.10
151	Willie Gault	.05
152	Howie Long	.05
153	Todd Marinovich	.05
154	Jim Everett	.05
155	David Lang	.05
156	Henry Ellard	.05
157	Cleveland Gary	.05
158	Steve Israel	.05
159	*Jerome Bettis*	1.00
160	Jackie Slater	.05
161	Art Monk	.10
162	Ricky Sanders	.05
163	Brian Mitchell	.05
164	*Reggie Brooks*	.15
165	Mark Rypien	.05
166	Earnest Byner	.05
167	Andre Collins	.05
168	Quinn Early	.05
169	Fred McAfee	.05
170	Wesley Carroll	.05
171	Gene Atkins	.05
172	*Derek Brown*	.15
173	Vaughn Dunbar	.05
174	Ricky Jackson	.05
175	John L. Williams	.05
176	*Carlton Gray*	.10
177	Cortez Kennedy	.10
178	Kelly Stouffer	.05
179	*Rick Mirer*	.50
180	Dan McGwire	.05
181	Chris Warren	.15
182	Barry Foster	.05
183	Merril Hoge	.05
184	Darren Perry	.05
185	*Deon Figures*	.10
186	Jeff Graham	.15
187	Dwight Stone	.05
188	Neil O'Donnell	.10
189	Rod Woodson	.05
190	*Alex Van Pelt*	.05
191	Steve Jordan	.05
192	Roger Craig	.05
193	*Qadry Ismail*	.40
194	*Robert Smith*	.50
195	*Gino Torretta*	.10
196	Anthony Carter	.05
197	Terry Allen	.05
198	Rich Gannon	.05
199	Checklist #1	.05
200	Checklist #2	.05
201	*Victor Bailey*	.15
202	*Michael Barrow*	.05
203	*Patrick Bates*	.05
204	Jerome Bettis	.30
205	Drew Bledsoe	.75
206	*Vincent Brisby*	.75
207	Reggie Brooks	.10
208	*Derek Brown*	.10
209	Keith Byars	.05
210	*Tom Carter*	.15
211	Curtis Conway	.20
212	*Russell Copeland*	.10
213	*John Copeland*	.10
214	*Eric Curry*	.10
215	*Troy Drayton*	.30
216	*Jason Elam*	.10
217	*Steve Everitt*	.10
218	Deon Figures	.05
219	Irving Fryar	.05
220	Darrien Gordon	.20
221	Carlton Gray	.05
222	Kevin Greene	.05
223	*Andre Hastings*	.20
224	Michael Haynes	.05
225	Garrison Hearst	.40
226	Bobby Hebert	.05
227	Lester Holmes	.05
228	Jeff Hostetler	.10
229	Desmond Howard	.05
230	*Tyrone Hughes*	.20
231	Quadry Ismail	.20
232	Rocket Ismail	.10
233	*James Jett*	.20
234	Marvin Jones	.05
235	*Todd Kelly*	.10
236	*Lincoln Kennedy*	.10
237	*Terry Kirby*	.40
238	Bernie Kosar	.05
239	*Derrick Lassic*	.10
240	Wilber Marshall	.05
241	O.J. McDuffie	.30
242	*Ryan McNeil*	.05
243	*Natrone Means*	1.00
244	Glyn Milburn	.10
245	Rick Mirer	.40
246	Scott Mitchell	.10
247	*Ron Moore*	.30
248	*Lorenzo Neal*	.20
249	Erric Pegram	.20
250	*Roosevelt Potts*	.20
251	*Leonard Renfro*	.10
252	*Greg Robinson*	.10
253	Wayne Simmons	.10
254	*Chris Slade*	.25
255	*Irv Smith*	.20
256	Robert Smith	.25
257	*Dana Stubblefield*	.40
258	George Teague	.10
259	Kevin Williams	.20
260	Checklist	.05

1993 Wild Card Bomb Squad

According to reports, 10,000 of these 30-card sets were produced. They were seeded in high-number (201-260) packs. The chromium fronts feature an action shot of a wide receiver inside a football shape. "Bomb Squad" is printed on the left side of the football. The player's name, team and position are printed in a rectangle at the bottom of the card. The orange-colored backs showcase the player's name, team and position at the top. His stats are listed horizontally along the left side of the card, while a player photo is on the right.

		MT
Complete Set (30):		12.00
Common Player:		.30
1	Jerry Rice	2.00
2	John Taylor	.50
3	J.J. Birden	.50
4	Stephen Baker	.30
5	Victor Bailey	.50
6	O.J. McDuffie	.50
7	Haywood Jeffires	.50
8	Eric Green	.30
9	Johnny Mitchell	.50
10	Art Monk	.50
11	Quinn Early	.50
12	Troy Drayton	.50
13	Vincent Brisby	.50
14	Courtney Hawkins	.50
15	Tom Waddle	.30
16	Curtis Conway	.50
17	Andre Reed	.50
18	Carl Pickens	.50
19	Sterling Sharpe	.50
20	Shannon Sharpe	.50
21	Qadry Ismail	.50
22	Rocket Ismail	.50
23	Andre Rison	.50
24	Michael Haynes	.50
25	Alvin Harper	.50
26	Michael Irvin	.50
27	Michael Jackson	.50
28	Herman Moore	.75
29	Anthony Miller	.50
30	Gary Clark	.50

1993 Wild Card Bomb Squad B/B

This 15-card set is a double-front version of the Bomb Squad chase set. The same design is featured for each player on the front and back. Inserted one per 20-pack box of the 1993 Wild Card high-number jumbo packs, the cards were part of the 1,000 sets which were reportedly produced.

		MT
	Complete Set (15):	20.00
	Common Player:	1.25
1	Jerry Rice, John Taylor	4.00
2	Tom Waddle, Curtis Conway	1.25
3	Andre Reed, Carl Pickens	2.00
4	Sterling Sharpe, Shannon Sharpe	2.00
5	Qadry Ismail, Rocket Ismail	2.00
6	Andre Rison, Michael Haynes	2.00
7	Alvin Harper, Michael Irwin	2.00
8	Michael Jackson, Herman Moore	1.25
9	Anthony Miller, Gary Clark	1.25
10	J.J. Birden, Stephen Baker	1.25
11	Victor Bailey, O.J. McDuffie	1.25
12	Haywood Jeffires, Eric Green	1.25
13	Johnny Mitchell, Art Monk	1.25
14	Quinn Early, Troy Drayton	1.25
15	Vincent Brisby, Courtney Hawkins	2.00

1993 Wild Card Field Force

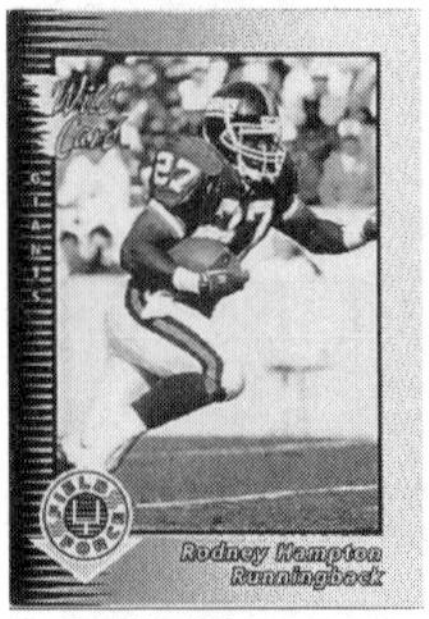

The 90-card chase set was randomly seeded into packs, however, it was released in three 30-card series based on Divisional alignment. The Field Force logo appears at the bottom left of the card fronts, while the player's name and position are located in the lower right. The Wild Card logo is in the upper left. The left border has black and blue jagged lines, while the rest of the card is blue and white. The card backs, numbered with either a "WFF," "EFF" or "CFF," depending on divisions, have a photo on the left and stats on the right. The card number is at the top right.

		MT
	Complete Set (90):	30.00
	Complete West Series (30):	10.00
	Complete East Series (30):	10.00
	Complete Cent. Series (30):	10.00
	Common Player:	.25
	Minor Stars:	.50
	Stripes 5/10/20:	1.5x-3x
	Stripes 50/100:	8x-16x
	Stripes 1000:	70x-140x
	Silver Cards:	1x-1.5x
	Gold Cards:	1x-2x
	Superchrome Set (10):	20.00
	Superchrome Cards:	1x-2x
31	Jerry Rice	2.00
32	Ricky Watters	.50
33	Steve Bono	1.00
34	Amp Lee	.25
35	Steve Young	2.00
36	Tommy Maddox	.25
37	Cleveland Gary	.25
38	John Elway	1.00
39	Glyn Milburn	.50
40	Stan Humphries	.75
41	Junior Seau	.75
42	Natrone Means	2.00
43	Dale Carter	.25
44	Joe Montana	2.00
45	Christian Okoye	.25
46	Deion Sanders	1.00
47	Roger Harper	.25
48	Steve Broussard	.25
49	Todd Marinovich	.25
50	BIlly Joe Hobert	.50
51	Patrick Bates	.25
52	Jerome Bettis	1.00
53	Willie Anderson	.25
54	Irv Smith	.25
55	Quinn Early	.25
56	Vaughn Dunbar	.25
57	Rick Mirer	2.00
58	Carlton Gary	.25
59	Chris Warren	.50
60	Dan McGwire	.25
61	Pete Metzelaars	.25
62	Kenneth Davis	.25
63	Thurman Thomas	.75
64	Chris Chandler	.25
65	Garrison Hearst	1.25
66	Ricky Proehl	.25
67	Steven Emtman	.25
68	Jeff George	.75
69	Clarence Verdin	.25
70	Troy Aikman	1.50
71	Emmitt Smith	2.50
72	Alvin Harper	.50
73	Michael Irvin	1.00
74	O.J. McDuffie	.50
75	Troy Vincent	.25
76	Keith Jackson	.25
77	Dan Marino	2.50
78	Leonard Renfro	.25
79	Heath Sherman	.25
80	Derek Brown	.25
81	Rodney Hampton	.50
82	James Hasty	.25
83	Johnny Mitchell	.25
84	Brad Baxter	.25
85	Leonard Russell	.25
86	Marv Cook	.25
87	Drew Bledsoe	5.00
88	Ricky Ervins	.25
89	Art Monk	.50
90	Earnest Byner	.25
91	Tom Waddle	.25
92	Neal Anderson	.25
93	Curtis Conway	.75
94	Harold Green	.25
95	Jeff Query	.25
96	Carl Pickens	1.00
97	David Klingler	.50
98	Michael Jackson	.25
99	Eric Metcalf	.25
100	Courtney Hawkins	.25
101	Eric Curry	.25
102	Reggie Cobb	.25
103	Mel Gray	.25
104	Barry Sanders	1.75
105	Rodney Peete	.25
106	Haywood Jeffires	.25
107	Cody Carlson	.25
108	Curtis Duncan	.25
109	Edgar Bennett	.50
110	George Teague	.25
111	Terrell Buckley	.25
112	Brett Favre	2.50
113	Deon Figures	.25
114	Rod Woodson	.25
115	Neil O'Donnell	.50
116	Barry Foster	.25
117	Cris Carter	.75
118	Gino Torretta	.25
119	Terry Allen	.25
120	Qadry Iamail	.25

1993 Wild Card Field Force Superchrome

A 10-card partial parallel set to the Field Force chase set, this featured the same design as the regular Field Force, except this set had chromium fronts. The card backs have a photo on the left, with stats on the right. The card number is printed in the upper right, prefixed by "SCF."

		MT
	Complete Set (10):	12.00
	Common Player:	.40
1	Jerry Rice	1.50
2	Glyn Milburn	.40
3	Joe Montana	1.50
4	Rick Mirer	.75
5	Troy Aikman	1.50
6	Emmitt Smith	3.00
7	Dan Marino	3.00
8	Drew Bledsoe	2.00
9	Barry Sanders	1.50
10	Brett Favre	3.00

1993 Wild Card Red Hot Rookies

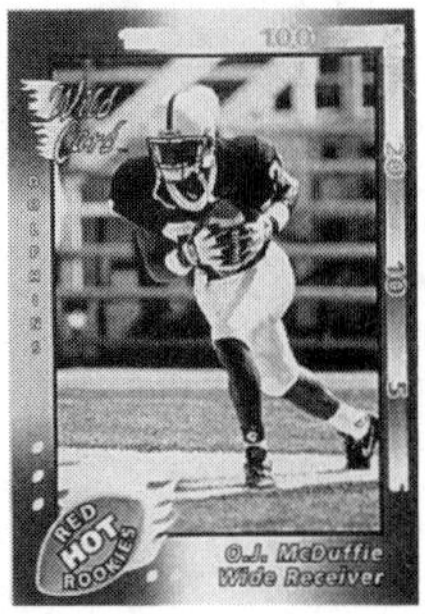

Randomly seeded into packs, the 30-card set was divided into three 10-card sets based on NFL divisions. The card fronts have the Red Hot Rookies logo in the lower left, with the Wild Card logo in the upper left. Various colored numbers border the photo on the top and right. The player's name and position are printed at the bottom. The backs -- numbered with a prefix of "WRHR," "ERHR" and "CRHR," depending on divisions -- have stats on the left. The player's name, bio and headshot are along the right side.

		MT
	Complete Set (30):	18.00
	Complete West Series (10):	8.00
	Complete East Series (10):	5.00
	Comp. Central Series (10):	5.00
	Common Player (31-60):	.25
31	Dana Stubblefield	.60
32	Todd Kelly	.25
33	Dan Williams	.25
34	Glyn Milburn	.60
35	Natrone Means	1.00
36	Lincoln Kennedy	.25
37	Patrick Bates	.25
38	Jerome Bettis	1.00
39	Irv Smith	.60
40	Rick Mirer	1.00
41	Garrison Hearst	1.50
42	Kevin Williams	1.25
43	Terry Kirby	.60
44	O.J. McDuffie	.60
45	Leonard Renfro	.25
46	Victor Bailey	.40
47	Marvin Jones	.40
48	Drew Bledsoe	3.00
49	Reggie Brooks (UER) (Missing career college stats)	.40
50	Tom Carter	.40
51	Curtis Conway	1.25
52	Dan Footman	.25
53	Lamar Thomas	.40
54	Eric Curry	.60
55	Ryan McNeil	.40
56	Michael Barrow	.40
57	Wayne Simmons	.40
58	George Teague	.40
59	Robert Smith	1.25
60	Qadry Ismail	.60

1993 Wild Card Red Hot Rookies Superchrome

This 10-card partial parallel set of Red Hot Rookies has the same design as the regular set, except it is done in chromium. The card backs are numbered with the "SCR" prefix. In addition, 20 high-number Superchrome Red Hot Rookies could be received by sending $29.95 to the company. Reportedly, 10,000 sets were produced.

		MT
	Complete Set (10):	20.00
	Common Player:	1.00
1	Dana Stubblefield	1.25
2	Glyn Milburn	1.00
3	Jerome Bettis	5.00
4	Rick Mirer	2.50
5	Garrison Hearst	3.00
6	Terry Kirby	1.50
7	Victor Bailey	1.00
8	Drew Bledsoe	6.00
9	Reggie Brooks	1.00
10	Qadry Ismail	1.25

1993 Wild Card Stat Smashers

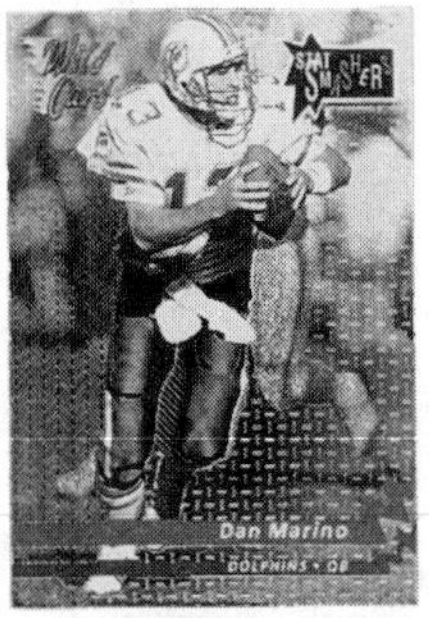

This 20-card set features a silver foil front, with the Stat Smashers' logo in the upper right. The player's name, team and position are located in stripes at the bottom. The card backs, numbered with a "CSS" prefix, have the player's name, bio, headshot and highlights. The backs are black-bordered. In addition, a gold version was also randomly inserted. This set features players who play with teams in the AFC and NFC Central Divisions.

		MT
	Complete Set (60):	60.00
	Complete West Series (20):	20.00
	Complete East Series (20):	20.00
	Complete Central Series (20):	20.00
	Common Player:	.50
	Gold Cards:	.75x-1.25x
53	Ricky Watters	1.00
54	Jerry Rice	3.00
55	Steve Young	2.50
56	Shannon Sharpe	1.00
57	John Elway	1.50
58	Glyn Milburn	1.00
59	Marion Butts	.75
60	Junior Seau	1.00
61	Natrone Means	1.50
62	Joe Montana	4.00
63	J.J. Birden	.50
64	Michael Haynes	.75
65	Deion Sanders	2.00
66	Billy Joe Hobert	1.00
67	Nick Bell	.50
68	Jerome Bettis	1.50
69	Vaughn Dunbar	.50
70	Quinn Early	.75
71	Dan McGwire	.50
72	Rick Mirer	1.50
73	Kenneth Davis	.50
74	Thurman Thomas	1.00
75	Garrison Hearst	2.00
76	Ricky Proehl	.50
77	Jeff George	1.00
78	Rodney Culver	.50
79	Troy Aikman	3.00
80	Emmitt Smith	6.00
81	Michael Irvin	1.00
82	O.J. McDuffie	1.00
83	Keith Jackson	.75
84	Dan Marino	6.00
85	Heath Sherman	.50
86	Fred Barnett	.75
87	Rodney Hampton	1.00
88	Marvin Jones	.75
89	Brad Baxter	.50
90	Drew Bledsoe	5.00
91	Ricky Ervins	.50
92	Art Monk	.75
93	Neal Anderson	.75
94	Curtis Conway	1.75
95	John Copeland	1.00
96	Carl Pickens	1.00
97	David Klingler	.75
98	Michael Jackson	.75
99	Kevin Mack	.50
100	Eric Curry	1.00
101	Reggie Cobb	.50
102	Willie Green	.50
103	Barry Sanders	3.00
104	Haywood Jeffires	.75
105	Lorenzo White	.75
106	Sterling Sharpe	1.00
107	Brett Favre	3.00
108	Neil O'Donnell	1.00
109	Barry Foster	.75
110	Rich Gannon	.75
111	Robert Smith	1.75
112	Qadry Ismail	1.00

1993 Wild Card Stat Smashers Rookies

Produced in gold and silver foil versions, the 52-card set was randomly seeded one per jumbo pack. The designs of the card fronts and backs resemble the other Stat Smasher set.

		MT
	Complete Set (52):	15.00
	Common Player:	.25
	Complete Gold Set (52):	25.00
	Gold Cards:	.75x-1.5x
1	Todd Kelly	.25
2	Dana Stubblefield	.60
3	Curtis Conway	.60
4	John Copeland	.60
5	Russell Copeland	.40
6	Thomas Smith	.40
7	Glyn Milburn	.60
8	Jason Elam	.40
9	Steve Everitt	.40
10	Eric Curry	.60
11	Horace Copeland	.40
12	Ronald Moore	.60
13	Garrison Hearst	1.50
14	Natrone Means	1.00
15	Darrien Gordon	.40
16	Roosevelt Potts	.40
17	Kevin Williams	1.25
18	Derrick Lassic	.40
19	O.J. McDuffie	.60
20	Terry Kirby	.60
21	Scott Mitchell	.60
22	Victor Bailey	.40
23	Vaughn Hebron	.40
24	Lincoln Kennedy	.25
25	Michael Strahan	.25
26	Marvin Jones	.40
27	Tony McGee	.60
28	Ryan McNeil	.40
29	Micheal Barrow	.40
30	Wayne Simmons	.40
31	George Teague	.40
32	Vincent Brisby	.60
33	Drew Bledsoe	3.00
34	Rocket Ismail	.40
35	Patrick Bates	.25
36	James Jett	.40
37	Jerome Bettis	.60
38	Troy Drayton	.60
39	Tom Carter	.40
40	Reggie Brooks	.40
41	Lorenzo Neal	.40
42	Derek Brown (BB)	.60
43	Tyrone Hughes	.60
44	Rick Mirer	1.00
45	Carlton Gray	.25
46	Andre Hastings	.60
47	Deon Figures	.60
48	Qadry Ismail	.60
49	Robert Smith	.60
50	Irv Smith	.60
51	Chris Slade	.60
52	Willie Roaf	.60

1993 Wild Card Superchrome FF/RHR B/B

Wild Card doubled up card fronts from the Red Hot Rookies and Field Force on these back-to-back cards. The designs of both card fronts resemble the regular chase set design. This 10-card set was randomly seeded in Superchrome Series II packs. The cards are unnumbered.

		MT
	Complete Set (10):	25.00
	Common Player:	1.25
1	Troy Aikman, Dana Stubblefield	2.50
2	Drew Bledsoe, Drew Bledsoe	3.00
3	Brett Favre, Terry Kirby	5.00
4	Dan Marino, Reggie Brooks	5.00
5	Glyn Milburn, Rick Mirer	1.25
6	Rick Mirer, Glyn Milburn	1.25
7	Joe Montana, Jerome Bettis	3.00
8	Jerry Rice, Garrison Hearst	2.50
9	Barry Sanders, Victor Bailey	2.50
10	Emmitt Smith, Qadry Ismail (UER) (Misspelled Quadry)	5.00

A card number in parentheses ( ) indicates the set is unnumbered.

1993 Wild Card Superchrome Rookies Promos

This five-card set featured purple chromium borders with the player photos inside a gold chrome oval. "Superchrome" is printed at the top, while "Rookies" is printed at the bottom. The player's name, team and position are printed within the gold oval at the top. In addition, "Wild Card sample" is printed on the card front. The card backs, numbered with a prefix of "P," are bordered in black and purple. The player's name, bio and highlights are included on the left, with a player photo on the right.

		MT
	Complete Set (5):	6.00
	Common Player:	.75
1	Rick Mirer	1.25
2	Reggie Brooks	.75
3	Glyn Milburn	.75
4	Drew Bledsoe	3.00
5	Jerome Bettis	1.25

1993 Wild Card Superchrome Rookies

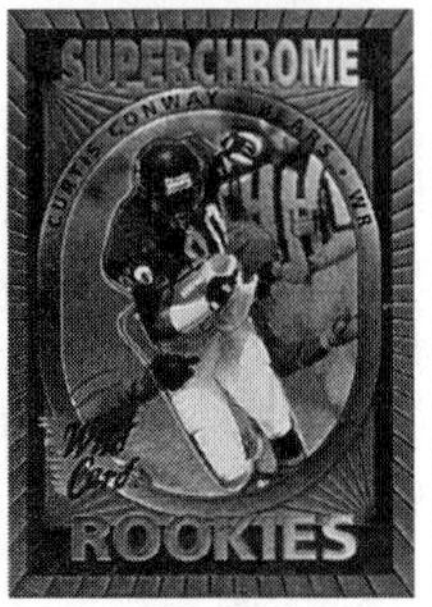

This 50-card set, released in early 1994, was inserted six cards per Superchrome Rookies 15-card foil pack. The other nine cards were 1993 Wild Card cards. The chromium fronts showcase "Superchrome" at the top and "Rookies" at the bottom. A photo is located inside a gold oval, with the player's name, team and position printed inside. The card backs include a player photo on the right, while his name, bio and stats are listed on the left.

		MT
	Complete Set (50):	20.00
	Common Player:	.20
1	Dana Stubblefield	.50
2	Todd Kelly	.20
3	Curtis Conway	1.00
4	John Copeland	.50
5	Tony McGee	.50
6	Russell Copeland	.30
7	Thomas Smith	.30
8	Jason Elam	.30
9	Glyn Milburn	.50
10	Steve Everitt	.30
11	Demetrius DuBose	.20
12	Eric Curry	.50
13	Garrison Hearst	1.25
14	Ronald Moore	.50
15	Darrien Gordon	.30
16	Natrone Means	.75
17	Roosevelt Potts	.30
18	Derrick Lassic	.30
19	Kevin Williams	1.00
20	Scott Mitchell (UER) (Text indicates drafted in '91; should be '90)	1.00
21	O.J. McDuffie	.75
22	Terry Kirby	.50
23	Vaughn Hebron	.30
24	Victor Bailey	.30
25	Lincoln Kennedy	.20
26	Michael Strahan	.20
27	Marvin Jones	.30
28	Will Shields	.20
29	Ryan McNeil	.30
30	Micheal Barrow	.30
31	George Teague	.30
32	Wayne Simmons	.30
33	Vincent Brisby	.50
34	Drew Bledsoe	3.00
35	Patrick Bates	.20
36	James Jett	.30
37	Rocket Ismail	.30
38	Troy Drayton	.30
39	Jerome Bettis	.75
40	Tom Carter	.30
41	Reggie Brooks	.30
42	Tyrone Hughes	.50
43	Derek Brown	.50
44	Willie Roaf	.50
45	Carlton Gray	.20
46	Rick Mirer	.75
47	Andre Hastings	.50
48	Deon Figures	.50
49	Qadry Ismail	.50
50	Robert Smith	.50

1993 Wild Card Superchrome Rookies B/B

These 25 double-fronted back-to-back cards were randomly seeded in Superchrome Rookies foil packs. The unnumbered cards carry the same design as the regular Superchrome Rookies cards.

		MT
	Complete Set (25):	30.00
	Common Player:	.75
1	Victor Bailey, Vaughn Hebron	.75
2	Micheal Barrow, Ryan McNeil	.75
3	Patrick Bates, Vincent Brisby	.75
4	Jerome Bettis, Natrone Means	2.00
5	Drew Bledsoe, Rick Mirer	5.00
6	Reggie Brooks, Glyn Milburn	.75
7	Derek Brown RB, Tyrone Hughes	1.25
8	Tom Carter, Jason Elam	.75
9	Curtis Conway, Steve Everitt	2.50
10	John Copeland, Tony McGee	1.25
11	Russell Copeland, Thomas Smith	.75
12	Eric Curry, Demetrius DuBose	1.25
13	Troy Drayton, Darrien Gordon	1.25
14	Deon Figures, Andre Hastings	1.25
15	Carlton Gray, Willie Roaf	.75
16	Garrison Hearst, Ronald Moore	2.50
17	Qadry Ismail, Rocket Ismail	1.25
18	James Jett, Robert Smith	2.00
19	Marvin Jones, Will Shields	.75
20	Todd Kelly, Dana Stubblefield	1.25
21	Lincoln Kennedy, Michael Strahan	.75
22	Terry Kirby, O.J. McDuffie	2.00
23	Derrick Lassic, Kevin Williams	2.00
24	Scott Mitchell, Roosevelt Potts	2.00
25	Wayne Simmons, George Teague	.75

1967 Williams Portraits

Measuring 8" x 10", these 512 charcoal portraits of NFL players were a Kraft Cheese promotion. Sold in eight-portrait sets for $1 and a proof of purchase from various Kraft Cheese products, the set was broken down into four eight-portrait groups for each of the 16 NFL teams. In addition, an album which held 32 portraits was available for $2. The unnumbered portraits featured the player's name and position under the player portrait. The backs of the portraits were blank. An 8" x 10" checklist sheet was also issued, but it is not considered a card.

		NM
	Complete Set (512):	5000.
	Common Player:	6.00
1	Taz Anderson	10.00
2	Gary Barnes	10.00
3	Lee Calland	10.00
4	Junior Coffey	12.00
5	Ed Cook	10.00
6	Perry Lee Dunn	10.00
7	Dan Grimm	10.00
8	Alex Hawkins	15.00
9	Randy Johnson	12.00
10	Lou Kirouac	10.00
11	Errol Linden	10.00
12	Billy Lothridge	10.00
13	Frank Marchlewski	10.00
14	Richard Marshall	10.00
15	Billy Martin	10.00
16	Tom Moore	12.00
17	Tommy Nobis	20.00
18	Jim Norton	10.00
19	Nick Rassas	10.00
20	Ken Reaves	10.00
21	Bobby Richards	10.00
22	Jerry Richardson	15.00
23	Bob Riggle	10.00
24	Karl Rubke	10.00
25	Marion Rushing	10.00
26	Chuck Sieminski	10.00
27	Steve Sloan	12.00
28	Ron Smith	10.00
29	Don Talbert	10.00
30	Ernie Wheelwright	12.00
31	Sam Williams	10.00
32	Jim Wilson	10.00
33	Sam Ball	10.00
34	Raymond Berry	30.00
35	Bob Boyd	12.00
36	Ordell Braase	10.00
37	Barry Brown	10.00
38	Bill Curry	12.00
39	Mike Curtis	15.00
40	Alvin Haymond	10.00
41	Jerry Hill	10.00
42	David Lee	10.00
43	Jerry Logan	10.00
44	Tony Lorick	10.00
45	Lenny Lyles	10.00
46	John Mackey	18.00
47	Tom Matte	15.00
48	Lou Michaels	12.00
49	Fred Miller	10.00
50	Lenny Moore	30.00
51	Jimmy Orr	12.00
52	Jim Parker	18.00
53	Glenn Ressler	10.00
54	Willie Richardson	12.00
55	Don Shinnick	10.00
56	Billy Ray Smith	12.00
57	Bubba Smith	20.00
58	Dan Sullivan	10.00
59	Dick Szymanski	10.00
60	Johnny Unitas	50.00
61	Bob Vogel	10.00
62	Rick Volk	10.00
63	Jim Welch	10.00
64	Butch Wilson	10.00
65	Charlie Bivins	10.00

66	Charlie Brown	10.00
67	Doug Buffone	12.00
68	Rudy Bukich	12.00
69	Ron Bull	12.00
70	Dick Butkus	50.00
71	Jim Cadile	10.00
72	Jack Concannon	12.00
73	Frank Cornish	10.00
74	Don Croftcheck	10.00
75	Dick Evey	10.00
76	Joe Fortunato	12.00
77	Curtis Gentry	10.00
78	Bobby Joe Green	10.00
79	John Henry Johnson	15.00
80	Bob Jones	10.00
81	Jimmy Jones	10.00
82	Ralph Kurek	10.00
83	Roger LeClerc	10.00
84	Andy Livingston	10.00
85	Bennie McRae	10.00
86	Johnny Morris	12.00
87	Richie Petitbon	12.00
88	Loyd Phillips	10.00
89	Brian Piccolo	45.00
90	Jim Purnell	10.00
91	Mike Pyle	10.00
92	Mike Reilly	10.00
93	Gale Sayers	50.00
94	George Seals	10.00
95	Roosevelt Taylor	12.00
96	Bob Wetoska	10.00
97	Erich Barnes	12.00
98	Johnny Brewer	10.00
99	Monte Clark	10.00
100	Gary Collins	15.00
101	Larry Conjar	10.00
102	Vince Costello	10.00
103	Ross Fichtner	10.00
104	Bill Glass	12.00
105	Ernie Green	15.00
106	Jack Gregory	10.00
107	Charlie Harraway	12.00
108	Gene Hickerson	12.00
109	Fred Hoaglin	12.00
110	Jim Houston	12.00
111	Mike Howell	10.00
112	Joe Bob Isbell	10.00
113	Walter Johnson	12.00
114	Jim Kanicki	10.00
115	Ernie Kellerman	12.00
116	Leroy Kelly	20.00
117	Dale Lindsey	10.00
118	Clifton McNeil	12.00
119	Milt Morin	10.00
120	Nick Pietrosante	10.00
121	Frank Ryan	15.00
122	Dick Schafrath	12.00
123	Randy Schultz	10.00
124	Ralph Smith	10.00
125	Carl Ward	10.00
126	Paul Warfield	20.00
127	Paul Wiggin	12.00
128	John Wooten	12.00
129	George Andrie	10.00
130	Jim Boeke	10.00
131	Frank Clarke	12.00
132	Mike Connelly	10.00
133	Buddy Dial	12.00
134	Leon Donohue	10.00
135	Dave Edwards	12.00
136	Mike Gaechter	10.00
137	Walt Garrison	15.00
138	Pete Gent	12.00
139	Cornell Green	15.00
140	Bob Hayes	20.00
141	Chuck Howley	15.00
142	Lee Roy Jordan	18.00
143	Bob Lilly	30.00
144	Tony Liscio	10.00
145	Warren Livingston	10.00
146	Dave Manders	10.00
147	Don Meredith	30.00
148	Ralph Neely	12.00
149	John Niland	10.00
150	Pettis Norman	12.00
151	Don Perkins	15.00
152	Jethro Pugh	12.00
153	Dan Reeves	30.00
154	Mel Renfro	18.00
155	Jerry Rhome	15.00
156	Les Shy	10.00
157	J.D. Smith	10.00
158	Willie Townes	10.00
159	Danny Villanueva	10.00
160	John Wilbur	10.00
161	Mike Alford	10.00
162	Lem Barney	18.00
163	Charley Bradshaw	10.00
164	Roger Brown	12.00
165	Ernie Clark	10.00
166	Gail Cogdill	12.00
167	Nick Eddy	12.00
168	Mel Farr	12.00
169	Bobby Felts	10.00
170	Ed Flanagan	10.00
171	Jim Gibbons	12.00
172	John Gordy	12.00
173	Larry Hand	10.00
174	Wally Hilgenberg	10.00
175	Alex Karras	20.00
176	Bob Kowalkowski	10.00
177	Ron Kramer	12.00
178	Mike Lucci	15.00
179	Bruce Maher	10.00
180	Amos Marsh	10.00
181	Darris McCord	10.00
182	Tom Nowatzke	10.00
183	Milt Plum	15.00
184	Wayne Rasmussen	10.00
185	Roger Shoals	10.00
186	Pat Studstill	12.00
187	Karl Sweetan	10.00
188	Bobby Thompson	10.00
189	Doug Van Horn	10.00
190	Wayne Walker	12.00
191	Tommy Watkins	10.00
192	Garo Yepremian	15.00
193	Herb Adderley	12.00
194	Lionel Aldridge	6.00
195	Donny Anderson	8.00
196	Ken Bowman	6.00
197	Zeke Bratkowski	8.00
198	Bob Brown (DT)	6.00
199	Tom Brown	6.00
200	Lee Roy Caffey	6.00
201	Don Chandler	7.00
202	Tommy Crutcher	6.00
203	Carroll Dale	8.00
204	Willie Davis	15.00
205	Boyd Dowler	8.00
206	Marv Fleming	7.00
207	Gale Gillingham	6.00
208	Jim Grabowski	6.00
209	Forrest Gregg	15.00
210	Doug Hart	6.00
211	Bob Jeter	6.00
212	Hank Jordan	12.00
213	Ron Kostelnik	6.00
214	Jerry Kramer	15.00
215	Bob Long	6.00
216	Max McGee	8.00
217	Ray Nitschke	18.00
218	Elijah Pitts	7.00
219	Dave Robinson	7.00
220	Bob Skoronski	7.00
221	Bart Starr	25.00
222	Fred Thurston	7.00
223	Willie Wood	18.00
224	Steve Wright	6.00
225	Dick Bass	15.00
226	Maxie Baughan	12.00
227	Joe Carollo	10.00
228	Bernie Casey	15.00
229	Don Chuy	10.00
230	Charlie Cowan	10.00
231	Irv Cross	12.00
232	Willie Ellison	12.00
233	Roman Gabriel	18.00
234	Bruce Gossett	10.00
235	Roosevelt Grier	18.00
236	Anthony Guillory	10.00
237	Ken Iman	10.00
238	Deacon Jones	20.00
239	Les Josephson	12.00
240	Jon Kilgore	10.00
241	Chuck Lamson	10.00
242	Lamar Lundy	12.00
243	Tom Mack	15.00
244	Tommy Mason	12.00
245	Tommy McDonald	15.00
246	Ed Meador	12.00
247	Bill Munson	15.00
248	Bob Nichols	10.00
249	Merlin Olsen	25.00
250	Jack Pardee	15.00
251	Bucky Pope	10.00
252	Joe Scibelli	10.00
253	Jack Snow	15.00
254	Billy Truax	12.00
255	Clancy Williams	10.00
256	Doug Woodlief	10.00
257	Grady Alderman	12.00
258	John Beasley	10.00
259	Bob Berry	12.00
260	Larry Bowie	10.00
261	Bill Brown	15.00
262	Fred Cox	12.00
263	Doug Davis	10.00
264	Paul Dickson	10.00
265	Carl Eller	18.00
266	Paul Flatley	12.00
267	Dale Hackbart	10.00
268	Don Hansen	10.00
269	Clint Jones	12.00
270	Jeff Jordan	10.00
271	Karl Kassulke	12.00
272	John Kirby	10.00
273	Gary Larsen	12.00
274	Jim Lindsey	10.00
275	Earsell Mackbee	10.00
276	Jim Marshall	18.00
277	Marlin McKeever	10.00
278	Dave Osborn	15.00
279	Jim Phillips	10.00
280	Ed Sharockman	10.00
281	Jerry Shay	10.00
282	Milt Sunde	12.00
283	Archie Sutton	10.00
284	Mick Tingelhoff	15.00
285	Ron Vanderkelen	10.00
286	Jim Vellone	10.00
287	Lonnie Warwick	10.00
288	Roy Winston	12.00
289	Doug Atkins	20.00
290	Vern Burke	10.00
291	Bruce Cortez	10.00
292	Gary Cuozzo	12.00
293	Ted Davis	10.00
294	John Douglas	10.00
295	Jim Garcia	10.00
296	Tom Hall	10.00
297	Jim Heidel	10.00
298	Leslie Kelley	10.00
299	Billy Kilmer	18.00
300	Kent Kramer	10.00
301	Jake Kupp	10.00
302	Earl Leggett	10.00
303	Obert Logan	10.00
304	Tom McNeill	10.00
305	John Morrow	10.00
306	Ray Ogden	10.00
307	Ray Rissmiller	10.00
308	George Rose	10.00
309	David Rowe	10.00
310	Brian Schweda	10.00
311	Dave Simmons	10.00
312	Jerry Simmons	10.00
313	Steve Stonebreaker	12.00
314	Jim Taylor	20.00
315	Mike Tilleman	10.00
316	Phil Vandersea	10.00
317	Joe Wendryhoski	10.00
318	Dave Whitsell	12.00
319	Fred Whittingham	10.00
320	Gary Wood	10.00
321	Ken Avery	10.00
322	Bookie Bolin	10.00
323	Henry Carr	12.00
324	Pete Case	10.00
325	Clarence Childs	10.00
326	Mike Ciccolella	10.00
327	Glen Condren	10.00
328	Bob Crespino	10.00
329	Don Davis	10.00
330	Tucker Frederickson	15.00
331	Charlie Harper	10.00
332	Phil Harris	10.00
333	Allen Jacobs	10.00
334	Homer Jones	12.00
335	Jim Katcavage	12.00
336	Tom Kennedy	10.00
337	Ernie Koy	12.00
338	Greg Larson	12.00
339	Spider Lockhart	12.00
340	Chuck Mercein	12.00
341	Jim Moran	10.00
342	Earl Morrall	15.00
343	Joe Morrison	12.00
344	Francis Peay	10.00
345	Del Shofner	12.00
346	Jeff Smith	10.00
347	Fran Tarkenton	40.00
348	Aaron Thomas	12.00
349	Larry Vargo	10.00
350	Freeman White	10.00
351	Sidney Williams	10.00
352	Willie Young	10.00
353	Sam Baker	10.00
354	Gary Ballman	10.00
355	Randy Beisler	10.00
356	Bob Brown (OT)	12.00
357	Timmy Brown	15.00
358	Mike Ditka	45.00
359	Dave Graham	10.00
360	Ben Hawkins	10.00
361	Fred Hill	10.00
362	King Hill	12.00
363	Lynn Hoyem	10.00
364	Don Hultz	10.00
365	Dwight Kelley	10.00
366	Israel Lang	10.00
367	Dave Lloyd	10.00
368	Aaron Martin	10.00
369	Ron Medved	10.00
370	John Meyers	10.00
371	Mike Morgan	10.00
372	Al Nelson	10.00
373	Jim Nettles	10.00
374	Floyd Peters	12.00
375	Gary Pettigrew	10.00
376	Ray Poage	10.00
377	Nate Ramsey	10.00
378	Dave Recher	10.00
379	Jim Ringo	15.00
380	Joe Scarpati	10.00
381	Jim Skaggs	10.00
382	Norm Snead	18.00
383	Harold Wells	10.00
384	Tom Woodeshick	12.00
385	Bill Asbury	10.00
386	John Baker	10.00
387	Jim Bradshaw	10.00
388	Rod Breedlove	10.00
389	John Brown	10.00
390	Amos Bullocks	10.00
391	Jim Butler	10.00
392	John Campbell	10.00
393	Mike Clark	10.00
394	Larry Gagner	10.00
395	Earl Gros	12.00
396	John Hilton	10.00
397	Dick Hoak	12.00
398	Roy Jefferson	12.00
399	Tony Jeter	10.00
400	Brady Keys	10.00
401	Ken Kortas	10.00
402	Ray Mansfield	10.00
403	Paul Martha	10.00
404	Ben McGee	10.00
405	Bill Nelsen	15.00
406	Kent Nix	10.00
407	Fran O'Brien	10.00
408	Andy Russell	15.00
409	Bill Saul	10.00
410	Don Shy	10.00
411	Clendon Thomas	12.00
412	Bruce Van Dyke	10.00
413	Lloyd Voss	10.00
414	Ralph Wenzel	10.00
415	J.R. Wilburn	10.00
416	Marv Woodson	10.00
417	Jim Bakken	12.00
418	Don Brumm	10.00
419	Vidal Carlin	10.00
420	Bobby Joe Conrad	12.00
421	Willis Crenshaw	10.00
422	Bob DeMarco	10.00
423	Pat Fischer	12.00
424	Billy Gambrell	10.00
425	Prentice Gault	12.00
426	Ken Gray	10.00
427	Jerry Hillebrand	10.00
428	Charlie Johnson	15.00
429	Bill Koman	10.00
430	Dave Long	10.00
431	Ernie McMillan	10.00
432	Dave Meggysey	12.00
433	Dale Meinert	10.00
434	Mike Melinkovich	10.00
435	Dave O'Brien	10.00
436	Sonny Randle	12.00
437	Bob Reynolds	10.00
438	Joe Robb	10.00
439	Johnny Roland	12.00
440	Roy Shivers	10.00
441	Sam Silas	10.00
442	Jackie Smith	18.00
443	Rick Sortun	10.00
444	Jerry Stovall	10.00
445	Chuck Walker	10.00
446	Bobby Williams	10.00
447	Dave Williams	12.00
448	Larry Wilson	18.00
449	Kermit Alexander	10.00
450	Cas Banaszek	10.00
451	Bruce Bosley	10.00
452	John Brodie	20.00
453	Joe Cerne	10.00
454	John David Crow	12.00
455	Tommy Davis	12.00
456	Bob Harrison	10.00
457	Matt Hazeltine	10.00
458	Stan Hindman	10.00
459	Charlie Johnson	10.00
460	Jim Johnson	18.00
461	Dave Kopay	10.00
462	Charlie Krueger	12.00
463	Roland Lakes	10.00
464	Gary Lewis	10.00
465	Dave McCormick	10.00
466	Kay McFarland	10.00
467	Clark Miller	10.00
468	George Mira	12.00
469	Howard Mudd	10.00
470	Frank Nunley	10.00
471	Dave Parks	12.00
472	Walt Rock	10.00
473	Len Rohde	10.00
474	Steve Spurrier	35.00
475	Monty Stickles	10.00
476	John Thomas	10.00
477	Bill Tucker	10.00
478	Dave Wilcox	10.00
479	Ken Willard	12.00
480	Dick Witcher	10.00
481	Willie Adams	6.00
482	Walt Barnes	6.00
483	Jim Carroll	6.00
484	Dave Crossan	6.00
485	Charlie Gogolak	7.00
486	Tom Goosby	6.00
487	Chris Hanburger	8.00
488	Rickie Harris	6.00
489	Len Hauss	7.00
490	Sam Huff	18.00
491	Steve Jackson	6.00
492	Mitch Johnson	6.00
493	Sonny Jurgensen	18.00
494	Carl Kammerer	6.00
495	Paul Krause	12.00
496	Joe Don Looney	12.00
497	Ray McDonald	6.00
498	Bobby Mitchell	15.00
499	Jim Ninowski	7.00
500	Brig Owens	6.00
501	Vince Promuto	6.00
502	Pat Richter	7.00
503	Joe Rutgens	6.00
504	Lonnie Sanders	6.00
505	Ray Schoenke	6.00
506	Jim Shorter	6.00
507	Jerry Smith	8.00
508	Ron Snidow	6.00
509	Jim Snowden	6.00
510	Charley Taylor	18.00
511	Steve Thurlow	6.00
512	A.D. Whitfield	6.00

1994 Ted Williams Card Co. NFL Football

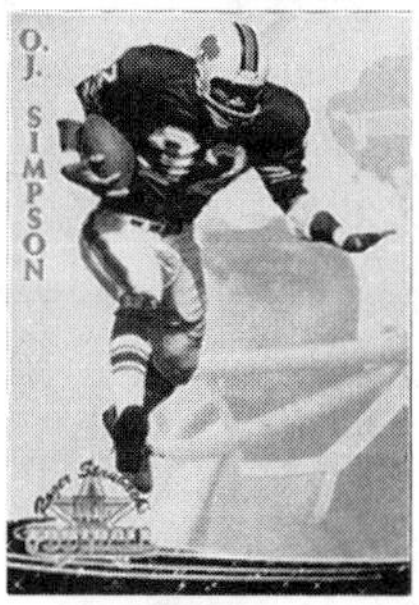

The Ted Williams Card Co., associated with the famous baseball Hall of Famer, followed up its debut baseball set with a 90-card set devoted to NFL greats from the past. Football Hall of Famer Roger Staubach lends his name to the set - the "Roger Staubach's NFL Football '94" set. The cards are numbered and grouped by teams first, followed by the set's three subsets - Chalkboard Legends (famous coaches), Golden Arms (great quarterbacks) and Dawning of a Legacy (two active quarterbacks). Cards were sold in packs of 10, or jumbo packs of 18. The set is limited to 5,000 numbered cases, meaning perhaps 200,000 of each card was made. There were also random inserts from six different sets available - Path to Greatness; Etched in Stone; the Walter Payton Collection; the Auckland Collection; Instant Replays; and limited print cards for Charles Barkley, Fred Dryer and Ted Williams throwing a football. Roger Staubach and Terry Bradshaw promo cards were also issued to preview the 1994 set. Also produced for the set were 18 different POG cards, which were inserted one per pack. Each case of cards also included a "Trade For Roger" card, which enabled collectors to obtain a 9-card Roger Staubach set available only through the mail.

		MT
Complete Set (90):		15.00
Common Player:		.10
Wax Box:		15.00
1	Roger Staubach	1.75
2	Tony Dorsett	.50
3	Bob Lilly	.35
4	Art Donovan	.25
5	Bert Jones	.30
6	Johnny Unitas	1.25
7	Jack Kemp	1.25
8	O.J. Simpson	1.75
9	Dick Butkus	.60
10	Gale Sayers	1.00
11	Mike Singletary	.25
12	Bronko Nagurski	.35
13	Ken Anderson	.25
14	Otto Graham	.35
15	Louis Groza	.25
16	Marion Motley	.30
17	Floyd Little	.15
18	Haven Moses	.10
19	Lem Barney	.25
20	Night Train Lane	.25
21	Bobby Layne	.40
22	Ray Nitschke	.25
23	Willie Wood	.25
24	White Shoes Johnson	.20
25	Mike Bell	.10
26	Buck Buchanan	.30
27	Len Dawson	.35
28	Roman Gabriel	.20
29	Leroy Irvin	.10
30	Deacon Jones	.30
31	Bob Waterfield	.35
32	Bob Griese	1.00
33	Carl Eller	.25
34	Fran Tarkenton	1.00
35	John Hannah	.25
36	Jim Plunkett	.20
37	Tom Dempsey	.15
38	Archie Manning	.25
39	Charlie Conerly	.25
40	Sam Huff	.25
41	Andy Robustelli	.25
42	Don Maynard	.25
43	Matt Snell	.15
44	Wesley Walker	.15
45	George Blanda	.40
46	Ben Davidson	.15
47	Jim Otto	.25
48	Norm Van Brocklin	.35
49	Harold Carmichael	.20
50	Joe Greene	.30
51	L.C. Greenwood	.15
52	Jack Lambert	.35
53	Lance Alworth	.35
54	Dan Fouts	.45
55	John Brodie	.30
56	Steve Largent	.35
57	Jim Zorn	.15
58	Jim Hart	.15
59	Mel Gray	.15
60	Lee Roy Selmon	.15
61	Sammy Baugh	.30
62	Sonny Jurgensen	.60
63	Checklist	.10
64	George Allen	.15
65	George Halas	.40
66	Tom Landry	.60
67	Vince Lombardi	.60
68	John Madden	.40
69	Chuck Noll	.20
70	Don Shula	.30
71	Hank Stram	.15
72	Checklist	.10
73	Terry Bradshaw	.85
74	Len Dawson	.35
75	Dan Fouts	.35
76	Bart Starr	.60
77	Roger Staubach	1.50
78	Fran Tarkenton	.75
79	Y.A. Tittle	.35
80	Johnny Unitas	1.25
81	Checklist	.10
82	Brett Favre	.50
83	Brett Favre	.65
84	Brett Favre	.65
85	Brett Favre	.65
86	Neil O'Donnell	.20
87	Neil O'Donnell	.20
88	Neil O'Donnell	.20
89	Neil O'Donnell	.20
90	Checklist	.10

1994 Ted Williams Card Co. Auckland Collection

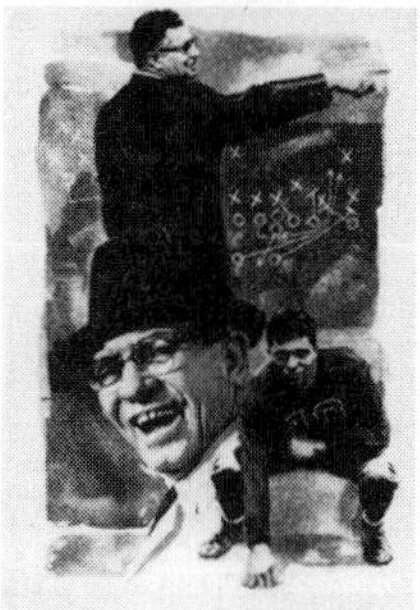

The Auckland Collection of insert cards features artwork by sports artist Jim Auckland. The cards have a special paper stock. The color illustration on each front is framed by a white border. The card back, numbered using an "AC" prefix, has a collage of ghosted player illustrations, plus a player profile, all bordered with a red and white frame. Cards were random inserts.

		MT
Complete Set (9):		30.00
Common Player:		3.00
1	Brett Favre	6.00
2	Vince Lombardi	7.00
3	Walter Payton	8.00
4	Phil Simms	5.00
5	Bart Starr	7.00
6	Roger Staubach	8.00
7	Jim Thorpe	6.00
8	Johnny Unitas	7.00
9	Checklist	3.00

1994 Ted Williams Card Co. Charles Barkley

These limited-edition inserts, devoted to NBA star Charles Barkley, were randomly included in Roger Staubach's NFL Football '94 packs. The cards are numbered with a "CB" prefix.

		MT
Complete Set (1)		5.00
1	Charles Barkley (LP)	5.00

1994 Ted Williams Card Co. Etched in Stone

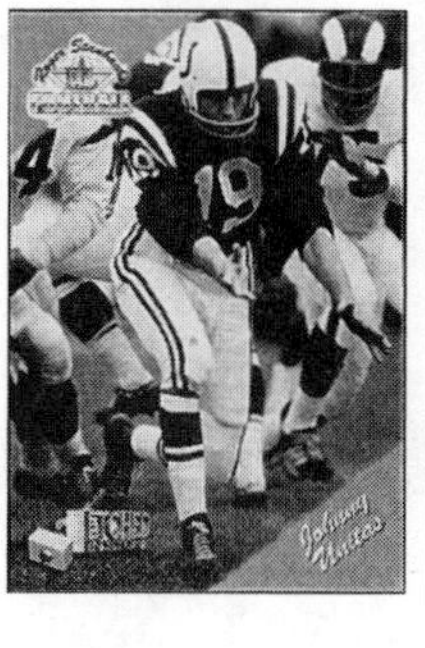

This 9-card insert set highlights the Hall of Fame career of quarterback Johnny Unitas. Each card front has either a color action photo or sepia-toned photo against a full-bleed background. However, gold triangles are located in the upper left corner, with the set logo in it, and the lower right corner, where Unitas' name is located. Each card back is numbered with a "ES" prefix and presents text which traces Unitas' career. The brick red background of the cards form a puzzle which says "Etched in Stone" and shows a chisel and gold star.

		MT
Complete Set (9):		20.00
Common Unitas:		2.50
1	(Johnny Unitas) (1970 Championship Game)	2.50
2	Johnny Unitas (Super Bowl V)	2.50
3	Johnny Unitas (Memories)	2.50
4	Johnny Unitas (Injuries)	2.50
5	Johnny Unitas (1959 Rematch)	2.50
6	Johnny Unitas (College Days)	2.50
7	Johnny Unitas (1972)	2.50
8	Johnny Unitas (Greatest Game Ever)	2.50
9	Checklist	2.50

1994 Ted Williams Card Co. Instant Replays

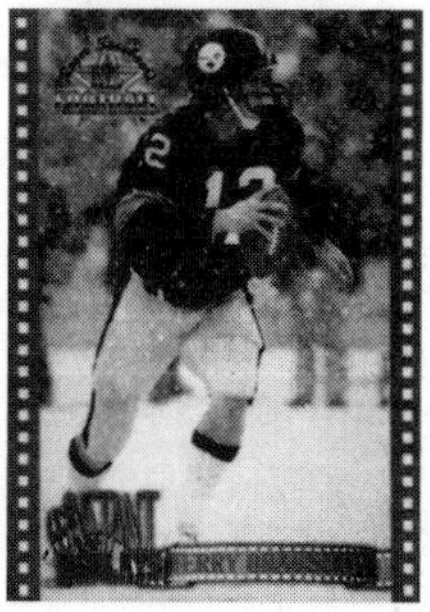

Four great teams from the NFL's past are featured on these inserts, which were randomly included in Roger Staubach's NFL Football '94 packs. The cards, available in hobby stores on a regional basis, feature players from the New York Giants, Green Bay Packers, Pittsburgh Steelers and Raiders. Each card front has either a sepia-toned or color photo, with gold filmstrip borders on the right and left side. The set logo is in the lower left corner, next to the player's name, which is in a filmstrip at the bottom. The orange back, numbered using an "IR" prefix, has the player's name at the top in a gold banner. A ghosted roll of film is in the background. Cards were random inserts in hobby packs only.

		MT
Complete Set (17):		40.00
Common Player:		1.50
1	Phil Simms	2.50
2	Y.A. Tittle	3.00
3	Sam Huff	2.00
4	Brad Van Pelt	1.50
5	Brett Favre	4.00
6	Bart Starr	6.00
7	Paul Hornung	4.00
8	Ray Nitschke	3.00
9	Neil O'Donnell	2.00
10	Terry Bradshaw	6.00
11	Joe Greene	3.00
12	Jack Lambert	3.00
13	Jeff Hostetler	2.00
14	Lyle Alzado	1.50
15	Dave Casper	1.50
16	Ken Stabler	3.00
17	Replays Checklist	1.50

1994 Ted Williams Card Co. Path to Greatness

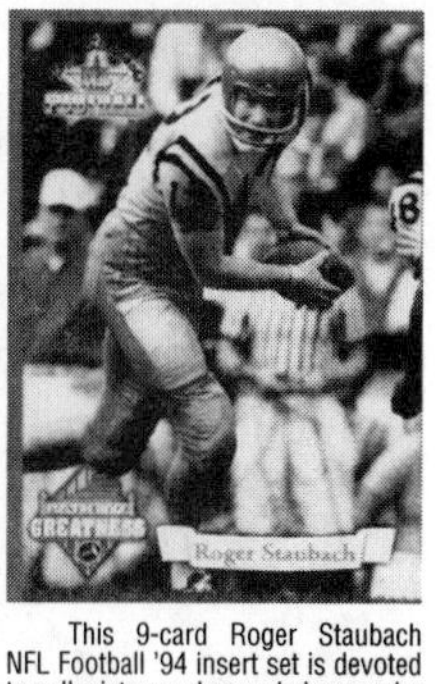

This 9-card Roger Staubach NFL Football '94 insert set is devoted to collegiate coaches and players who

went on to star in the NFL. Each card front has a gold framed border along the top and left side of the photo, which is either sepia toned or in color. The player's name is stamped in gold foil in a white banner at the bottom of the card, next to the set's logo. The backs, numbered using a "PG" prefix, have a summary of the player's collegiate accomplishments.

		MT
Complete Set (9):		35.00
Common Player:		1.25
1	Tony Dorsett	5.00
2	Red Grange	3.00
3	Bob Griese	4.00
4	Jeff Hostetler	2.00
5	Neil O'Donnell	1.75
6	Jim Plunkett	2.50
7	O.J. Simpson	12.00
8	Roger Staubach	8.00
9	Checklist	1.25

1994 Ted Williams Card Co. Sweetness - Walter Payton

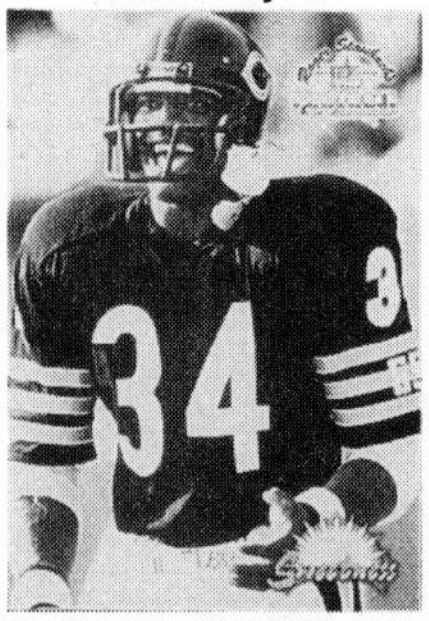

These insert cards, devoted to "Sweetness," Walter Payton, were random inserts in jumbo packs only. Each card front has a full-bleed color photo of Payton, with the set logos appearing in the corners on the right side of the card. The card back, numbered using a "WP" prefix, is blue. It includes an explanation about the card's title, which covers a specific point in the Hall of Famer's career.

		MT
Complete Set (9):		15.00
Common Player:		2.00
1	Ditka On Payton (Walter Payton)	2.00
2	Winning It All (Walter Payton)	2.00
3	Rookie (Walter Payton)	2.00
4	1977 (Walter Payton)	2.00
5	College (Walter Payton)	2.00
6	Payton vs. O.J. (Walter Payton)	4.00
7	Sweetness (Walter Payton)	2.00
8	The Records (Walter Payton)	2.00
9	Checklist Card	2.00

1994 Ted Williams Card Co. POG Cards

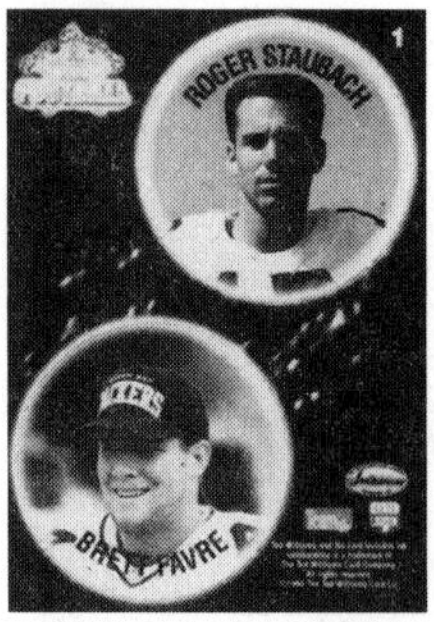

Each of these cards contains two POGs, measuring 1-5/8" in diameter. The POGs were intended to be punched out of the blue card, which is standard size. Each POG has a closeup shot of the player on the front, in either black-and-white or color, plus his name. A card number also appears on the front; the backs are blank. Each pack of 1994 Ted Williams Roger Staubach football cards contained one of these POG cards.

		MT
Complete Set (18):		5.00
Common Player:		.20
1	Roger Staubach, Brett Favre	.75
2	Roman Gabriel, Lee Roy Jordan	.25
3	Dan Fouts, John Brodie	.35
4	Terry Bradshaw, Bart Starr	.75
5	O.J. Simpson, Floyd Little	1.00
6	Pete Pihos, Larry Csonka	.25
7	Dick "Night Train" Lane, Carl Eller	.35
8	Sam Huff, Ben Davidson	.35
9	Jack Lambert, Jethro Pugh	.30
10	Mike Singletary, Harold Carmichael	.25
11	Chuck Noll, Bud Grant	.20
12	John Madden, Lyle Alzado	.20
13	Walter Payton, Gale Sayers	1.00
14	Fred Dryer, Ron Mix	.25
15	Bob Griese, Doug Williams	.30
16	Tony Dorsett, Red Grange	.50
17	Sonny Jurgensen, Jeff Hostetler	.30
18	Checklist Card	.20

1994 Ted Williams Card Co. Trade for Staubach

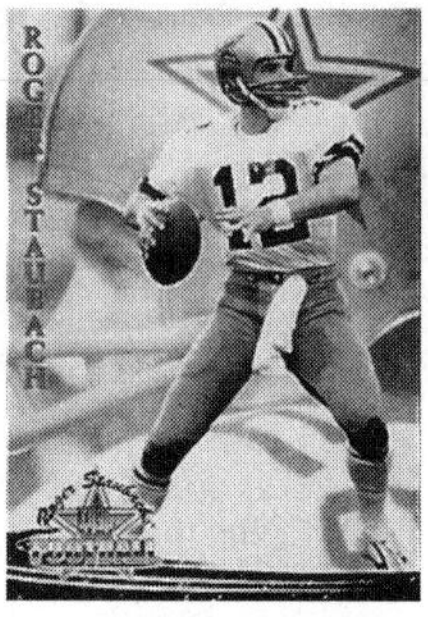

A "Trade for Roger" redemption card was randomly seeded one per case in the 5,000 cases. The redemption card, along with $3, entitled the collector to receive a nine-card set. The redemption card was returned to collectors with a validation stamp on it. Card fronts include borderless color or black-and-white photos, with the Roger Staubach NFL Football logo at the top right and the Ted Williams Card Co. logo in the lower left. Staubach's name is printed in foil along the right border. The card backs include a write-up of various highlights of Staubach's life. Cards are numbered with a "TR" prefix.

		MT
Complete Set (10):		30.00
Common Player:		3.00
1	The Dodger (Roger Staubach)	3.00
2	College Years (Roger Staubach)	3.00
3	The Heisman Trophy (Roger Staubach)	3.00
4	The Draft (Roger Staubach)	3.00
5	Coach's Decision (Roger Staubach)	3.00
6	A Leader (Roger Staubach)	3.00
7	MVP Year (Roger Staubach)	3.00
8	Hall of Fame (Roger Staubach)	3.00
9	Checklist	3.00
10	Trade for Roger Redemption Card	3.00

1974 Wonder Bread

Topps printed these 30 cards to be randomly included inside packages of Wonder Bread. Players from 18 NFL teams are represented on the cards, which have a closeup shot of the player and either a bright yellow or red border. The card back has biographical and statistical information about the player, plus a description and photograph illustrating a particular football play.

		NM
Complete Set (30):		25.00
Common Player:		.40
1	Jim Bakken	.45
2	Forrest Blue	.40
3	Bill Bradley	.40
4	Willie Brown	1.50
5	Larry Csonka	4.00
6	Ken Ellis	.40
7	Bruce Gossett	.40
8	Bob Griese	4.00
9	Chris Hanburger	.75
10	Winston Hill	.40
11	Jim Johnson	1.25
12	Paul Krause	1.00
13	Ted Kwalick	.85
14	Willie Lanier	1.50
15	Tom Mack	1.00
16	Jim Otto	1.50
17	Alan Page	1.75
18	Frank Pitts	.40
19	Jim Plunkett	1.50
20	Mike Reid	1.00
21	Paul Smith	.40
22	Bob Tucker	.75
23	Jim Tryer	.75
24	Eugene Upshaw	1.50
25	Phil Villapiano	1.00
26	Paul Warfield	2.00
27	Dwight White	.50
28	Steve Owens	.75
29	Jerrel Wilson	.40
30	Ron Yary	.75

1975 Wonder Bread

Once again, Topps produced this set for Wonder Bread to include the cards in specially-marked loaves of bread. The card front has a closeup shot of the player, with either a red or blue border surrounding it. The card back has statistics and biographical information about the player, plus questions and answers about the player and the game of football. The answers were written upside down.

		NM
Complete Set (24):		25.00
Common Player:		.35
1	Alan Page	1.50
2	Emmitt Thomas	.40
3	John Mendenhall	.35
4	Ken Houston	1.25
5	Jack Ham	1.25
6	L.C. Greenwood	.75
7	Tom Mack	.75
8	Winston Hill	.35
9	Isaac Curtis	.50
10	Terry Owens	.50
11	Drew Pearson	.60
12	Don Cockroft	.35
13	Bob Griese	2.50
14	Riley Odoms	.50
15	Chuck Foreman	.75
16	Forrest Blue	.35
17	Franco Harris	3.50
18	Larry Little	1.00
19	Bill Bergey	.60
20	Ray Guy	.90
21	Ted Hendricks	1.25
22	Levi Johnson	.35
23	Jack Mildren	.50
24	Mel Tom	.35

1976 Wonder Bread

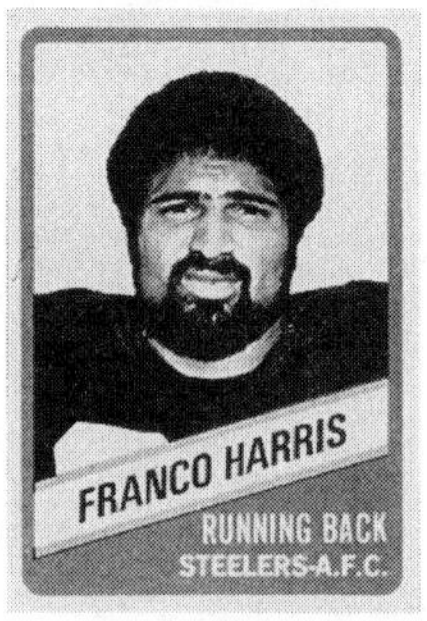

These 24 cards use two different frames for the card front; red frames are used for defensive players, while blue frames are used for the offensive players in the set. A close-up shot of the player is featured prominently on the front. Each back has biographical information about the player, plus a diagram of a favorite play of coach Hank Stram. The corresponding text indicates the offensive players' assignments for that particular play. Topps produced the cards for Wonder Bread to insert into loaves of bread.

		NM
Complete Set (24):		5.00
Common Player:		.20
1	Craig Morton	.35
2	Chuck Foreman	.35
3	Franco Harris	1.00
4	Mel Gray	.35
5	Charley Taylor	.60
6	Rich Caster	.20
7	George Kunz	.20
8	Rayfield Wright	.20
9	Gene Upshaw	.75
10	Tom Mack	.50
11	Len Hauss	.35
12	Garo Yepremian	.20
13	Cedrick Hardman	.20
14	Jack Youngblood	1.00
15	Wally Chambers	.20
16	Jerry Sherk	.20
17	Bill Bergey	.35
18	Jack Ham	.75
19	Fred Carr	.20
20	Jack Tatum	.35
21	Cliff Harris	.35
22	Emmitt Thomas	.20
23	Ken Riley	.20
24	Ray Guy	1.00

1984 Wranglers Carl's Jr.

The 10-card, 2-1/2" x 3-5/8" set was sponsored by Carl's Jr. restaurants and the Tempe Police Department in Arizona and featured top players from the USFL Arizona Wranglers football team. Included in the set is coach George Allen and former longtime NFL quarterback Greg Landry. The card fronts have a black and white posed photo with bio information appearing on the back.

		MT
Complete Set (10):		30.00
Common Player:		2.50
1	George Allen (CO)	8.00
2	Luther Bradley (27)	3.50
3	Trumaine Johnson (2)	3.50
4	Greg Landry (11)	6.00
5	Kit Lathrop (70)	2.50
6	John Lee (64)	2.50
7	Keith Long (33)	2.50
8	Alan Risher (7)	2.50
9	Tim Spencer (46)	3.50
10	Lenny Willis (89)	2.50

1984 Wranglers 8x10 Arizona

The eight-sheet, 8" x 10" set features two rows of four black and white cards, with the player's name printed below each card. The sheets are numbered.

		MT
Complete Set (8):		40.00
Common Panel:		5.00
1	Edward Diethrich PRES, Bill Harris VP, George Allen CO, G. Bruce Allen GM, Robert Barnes, Dennis Bishop, Mack Boatner, Luther Bradley	8.00
2	Clay Brown, Eddie Brown, Wamon Buggs, Bob Clasby, Frank Corral, Doug Cozen, Doug Dennison, Robert Dillon	6.00
3	Larry Douglas, Joe Ehrmann, Nick Eyre, Jim Fahnhorst, Doak Field, Bruce Gheesling, Frank Giddens, Alfondia Hill	5.00
4	David Huffman, Hubert Hurst, Donnie Johnson, Randy Johnson, Trumaine Johnson, Jeff Kiewel, Bruce Laird, Greg Landry	7.00
5	Kit Lathrop, John Lee, Alva Liles, Dan Lloyd, Kevin Long, Karl Lorch, Andy Melontree, Frank Minnifield	5.00
6	Tom Piette, Tom Porras, Paul Ricker, Alan Risher, Don Schwartz, Bobby Scott, Lance Shields, Ed Smith	5.00
7	Robert Smith, Tim Spencer, John Stadnik, Mark Stevenson, Dave Steif, Gerry Sullivan, Ted Sutton, Motrandy Taylor	5.00
8	Rob Taylor, Tom Thayer, Todd Thomas, Ted Walton, Stan White, Lenny Willis, Tim Wrightman, Wilbur Young	5.00

Z

1995 Zenith Promos

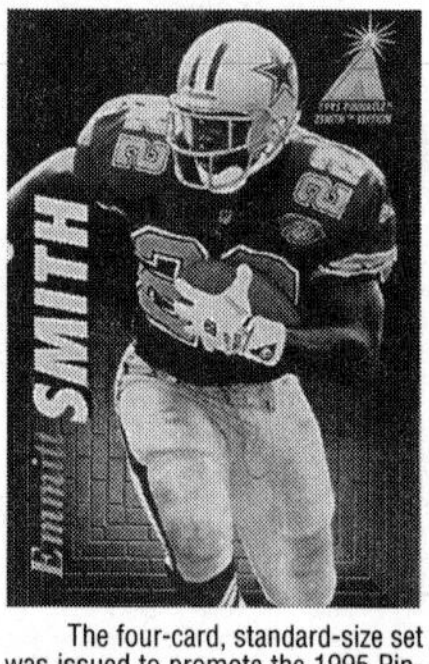

The four-card, standard-size set was issued to promote the 1995 Pinnacle Zenith set. "Promo" is printed across the card back but otherwise they are similar to the regular-issue cards.

		MT
Complete Set (4):		25.00
Common Player:		1.00
1	Emmitt Smith	10.00
94	Steve Young	5.00
97	Dan Marino	10.00
NNO	Title Card	1.00

1995 Zenith

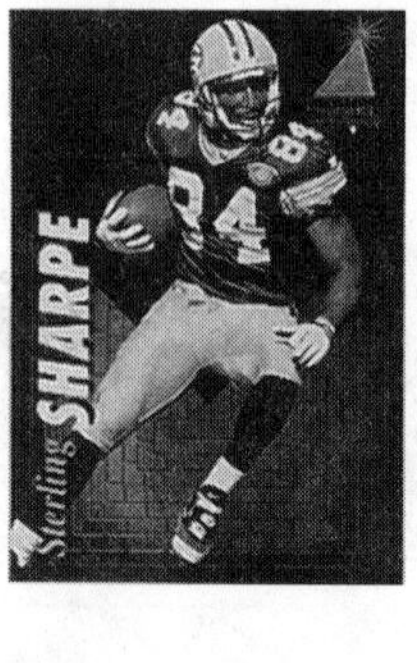

This 1995 Pinnacle Football Series II-Zenith Edition is a super-premium set that was the most limited of all Pinnacle football releases. All 150 cards in the set are printed on gold foil and noticeably thicker card stock. Each card front has a player action photo, with the set logo in the upper right corner. The player's first name is stamped in gold along the right side, next to his last name in white letters. The card back is horizontal and includes another action photo and analysis/breakdown of where the player makes his yardage or other types of plays. The cards are numbered using a Z prefix. Three types of inserts were randomly included in packs - Second Season, Rookie Roll Call and Z-Team.

		MT
Complete Set (150):		50.00
Common Player:		.25
Minor Stars:		.50
Pack (6):		7.00
Wax Box (24):		130.00
1	Emmitt Smith	10.00
2	Mark Carrier	.25
3	Johnny Mitchell	.25
4	Boomer Esiason	1.00
5	Jackie Harris	.25
6	Warren Moon	1.00
7	Harvey Williams	.25
8	Steve Walsh	.25
9	Cris Carter	1.00
10	Natrone Means	1.00
11	Art Monk	1.00
12	Johnny Johnson	.25
13	Adrian Murrell	.25
14	John Elway	4.00
15	Larry Centers	.25
16	Ricky Ervins	.25
17	Jeff Graham	.25
18	Ricky Watters	1.00
19	Eric Green	.25
20	Curtis Conway	.25
21	Jake Reed	.25
22	Michael Timpson	.25
23	Marcus Allen	1.00
24	Andre Rison	1.00
25	Terry Kirby	.25
26	Reggie White	1.00
27	Randall Cunningham	1.00
28	Jim Kelly	1.00
29	Robert Brooks	2.00
30	Terance Mathis	.25
31	Anthony Miller	1.00
32	Neil O'Donnell	1.00
33	Jeff Hostetler	.25
34	Drew Bledsoe	5.00
35	Irving Spikes	1.00
36	Keith Byars	.25
37	Rod Woodson	.25
38	Rob Moore	1.00
39	Scott Mitchell	.25
40	Cody Carlson	.25
41	Alvin Harper	1.00
42	Chris Warren	1.00
43	Ben Coates	1.00
44	Jim Everett	.25
45	Vinny Testaverde	.25
46	Glyn Milburn	.25
47	Calvin Williams	.25
48	Fred Barnett	.25
49	Tim Brown	1.00
50	Lorenzo White	.25
51	Brent Jones	.25
52	Henry Ellard	.25
53	Rick Mirer	1.00
54	Junior Seau	1.00
55	Jeff Blake	1.00
56	Desmond Howard	.25
57	Jerry Rice	6.00
58	Lewis Tillman	.25
59	Roosevelt Potts	.25
60	Raghib Ismail	1.00
61	Eric Hill	.25
62	Brett Favre	10.00
63	Haywood Jeffires	.25
64	Barry Foster	1.00
65	Willie Anderson	.25
66	Troy Aikman	6.00
67	Herschel Walker	1.00
68	Sean Dawkins	1.00
69	Erric Pegram	.25
70	Irving Fryar	.25
71	Thurman Thomas	1.00
72	Eric Metcalf	.25
73	John Taylor	.25
74	Jeff George	1.00
75	Courtney Hawkins	.25
76	Carl Pickens	.25
77	Mike Sherrard	.25
78	Rodney Hampton	.25
79	Joe Montana	7.00
80	Willie Davis	.25
81	Chris Penn	.25
82	Dave Brown	.25
83	Gary Brown	.25
84	Andre Reed	1.00
85	Michael Irvin	1.00
86	Vincent Brisby	.25
87	Barry Sanders	7.00
88	Qadry Ismail	1.00
89	Reggie Brooks	.25
90	Bruce Smith	.25
91	David Klingler	.25
92	Michael Haynes	.25
93	Derek Russell	.25
94	Steve Young	6.00
95	Terry Allen	.25
96	Mark Seay	.25
97	Dan Marino	10.00
98	All-Time TD Record (Jerry Rice)	6.00
99	Single-Season Recp. (Cris Carter)	1.00
100	Consecutive Games (Art Monk)	1.00
101	Cortez Kennedy	1.00
102	Stan Humphries	1.00
103	Herman Moore	1.00
104	Ron Moore	1.00
105	Chris Miller	.25
106	Jerome Bettis	1.00
107	Craig Erickson	.25
108	Keith Jackson	.25
109	Sterling Sharpe	1.00
110	Ronnie Harmon	.25
111	Deion Sanders	4.00
112	Steve Beuerlein	.25
113	Bernie Parmalee	.50
114	Leroy Hoard	.25
115	O.J. McDuffie	1.00
116	Garrison Hearst	2.00
117	Reggie Cobb	.25
118	Derek Brown	.25
119	David Palmer	.75
120	Gus Frerotte	1.00
121	Dan Wilkinson	.50
122	Chuck Levy	.25
123	Derrick Alexander	.50
124	Aaron Bailey	.25
125	Thomas Lewis	.25
126	Antonio Langham	.25
127	Bryan Reeves	.25
128	William Floyd	.75
129	Lake Dawson	.50
130	Bert Emanuel	1.00
131	Marshall Faulk	2.00
132	Heath Shuler	1.00
133	Mark Brunell	5.00
134	Willie McGinest	.50
135	Mario Bates	.50
136	Byron Morris	.75
137	Tim Bowens	.25
138	Errict Rhett	.50
139	Charlie Garner	1.00
140	Darnay Scott	.75
141	Greg Hill	1.00
142	LeShon Johnson	.25
143	Charles Johnson	.50
144	Trent Dilfer	3.00
145	Gus Frerotte	1.00
146	Johnnie Morton	1.00
147	Glenn Foley	1.00
148	Perry Klein	.25
149	Ryan Yarborough	.25
150	Tydus Winans	.25

1995 Zenith Rookie Roll Call

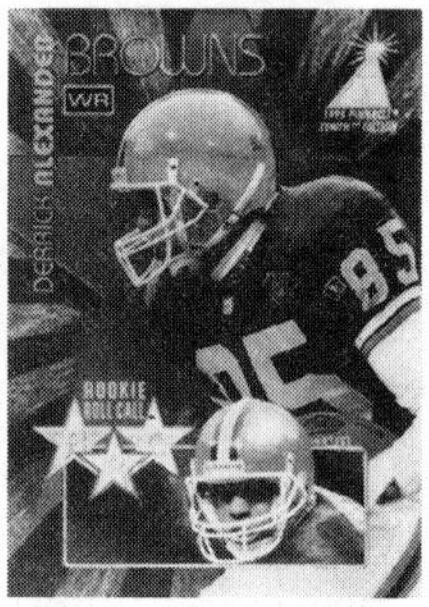

These cards were randomly inserted in 1995 Pinnacle Series II-Zenith Edition packs, one per 72 packs. The 18-card set features some of the league's top rookies on an all-foil Dufex design. The front has an action photo, plus a second photo in a rectangle at the bottom with the insert set's starry logo in its upper left corner. Card backs are numbered using an "RC" prefix.

		MT
Complete Set (18):		250.00
Common Player:		7.50
Minor Stars:		15.00
Inserted 1:72		
1	Marshall Faulk	50.00
2	Charlie Garner	15.00
3	Derrick Alexander	7.50
4	Heath Shuler	15.00
5	Glenn Foley	15.00
6	Trent Dilfer	30.00
7	David Palmer	7.50
8	Gus Frerotte	15.00
9	Byron Morris	7.50
10	Mario Bates	7.50
11	Greg Hill	15.00
12	Errict Rhett	15.00
13	Darnay Scott	15.00
14	Lake Dawson	7.50
15	Bert Emanuel	15.00
16	LeShon Johnson	7.50
17	William Floyd	7.50
18	Charles Johnson	15.00

1995 Zenith Z-Team

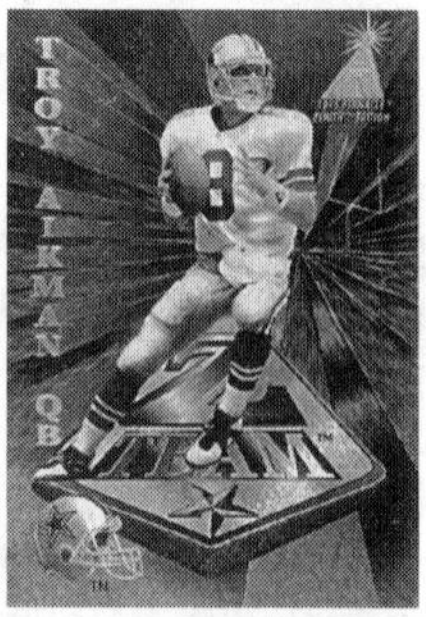

Z-Team inserts in 1995 Pinnacle Series II-Zenith packs could be found one per every 24 packs. The cards feature 18 of today's legends, utilizing an all-new 3D Dufex printing technology. The card front has a photo of the player standing on the Z Team logo, with his name and position running down the left side of the card. A team helmet is in the lower left corner; the Zenith logo is in the upper right. The

card back is numbered using a "ZT" prefix.

		MT
Complete Set (18):		450.00
Common Player:		10.00
1	Dan Marino	70.00
2	Troy Aikman	35.00
3	Emmitt Smith	70.00
4	Barry Sanders	35.00
5	Joe Montana	35.00
6	Jerry Rice	35.00
7	John Elway	25.00
8	Marshall Faulk	15.00
9	Brett Favre	70.00
10	Steve Young	25.00
11	Sterling Sharpe	10.00
12	Drew Bledsoe	35.00
13	Ricky Watters	10.00
14	Cris Carter	10.00
15	Warren Moon	10.00
16	Natrone Means	10.00
17	Michael Irvin	10.00
18	Chris Warren	10.00

1995 Zenith Second Season

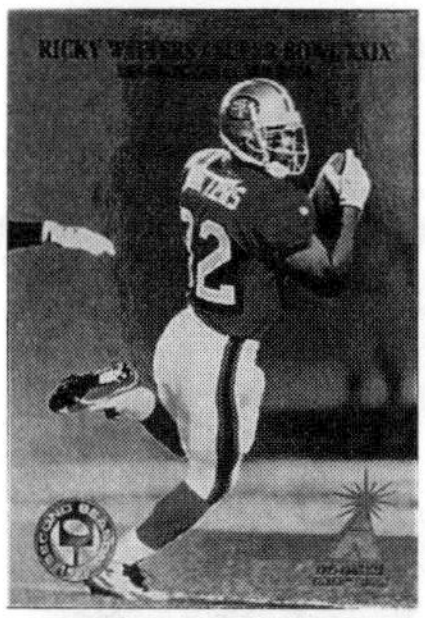

These Pinnacle Series II-Zenith Edition inserts pay tribute to the greatest moments from the 1994 post season, and the 25 players who made the plays happen. Included among the cards is one devoted to Joe Montana's final game. The front has the names of the teams and players involved in a game at the top; the insert set logo appears in the bottom left corner, opposite the Pinnacle logo. Card backs are numbered using an "SS" prefix. Cards were inserted one per six packs.

		MT
Complete Set (25):		140.00
Common Player:		3.00
Minor Stars:		6.00
1	Brett Favre	20.00
2	Dan Marino	20.00
3	Marcus Allen	6.00
4	Joe Montana	10.00
5	Vinny Testaverde	3.00
6	Emmitt Smith	20.00
7	Troy Aikman	10.00
8	Steve Young	10.00
9	William Floyd	3.00
10	Yancey Thigpen	6.00
11	Barry Foster	3.00
12	Natrone Means	6.00
13	Mark Seay	3.00
14	Stan Humphries	3.00
15	Tony Martin	3.00
16	Jerry Rice	10.00
17	Deion Sanders	7.00
18	Steve Young	10.00
19	Steve Young	10.00
20	Emmitt Smith	20.00
21	Troy Aikman	10.00
22	Jerry Rice (Super Bowl)	10.00
23	Ricky Watters (Super Bowl)	3.00
24	Steve Young (Super Bowl)	10.00
25	Jerry Rice, Steve Young (Super Bowl)	10.00

1996 Zenith Promos

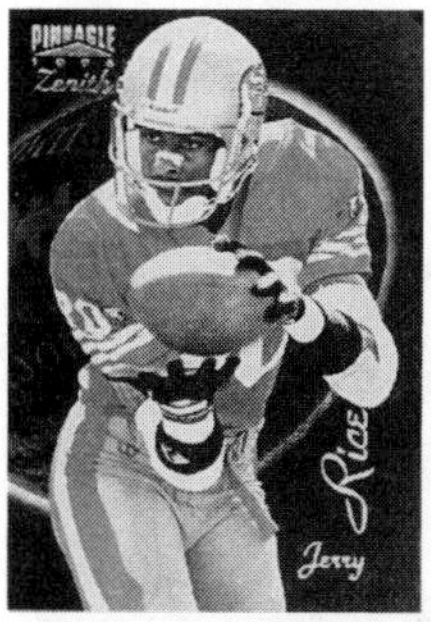

The four-card, standard-size set was issued to promote the 1996 Zenith release. The cards are basically identical to the regular-issue cards, except for "Promo" which is printed on the card backs.

		MT
Complete Set (4):		30.00
Common Player:		.50
4	Z-Team (Emmitt Smith)	25.00
32	Jerry Rice	4.00
36	John Elway	2.00
NNO	Title Card	.50

1996 Zenith

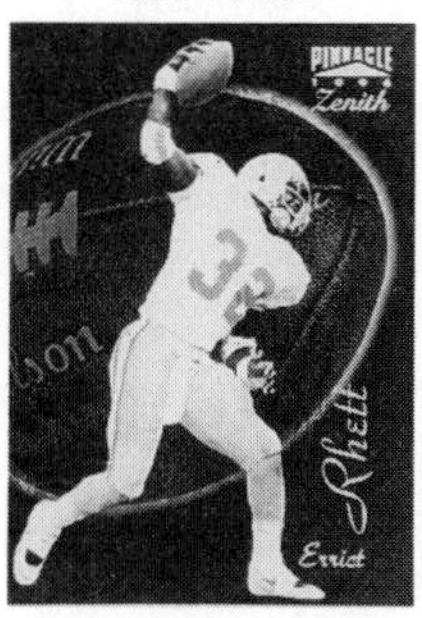

This 1996 Pinnacle Zenith set includes a 35-card Rookies subset, 15 Proof Positive cards, three checklists and one Triple Trouble card featuring Troy Aikman, Emmitt Smith and Michael Irvin. Each regular card has extra-thick stock. The front has a color action photo of the player against a foil football with a silver glow around it. The player's name is in gold foil in the lower right corner; the brand logo is in gold foil in the upper left corner. The card back has a photo on the right side, with the player's name, position and team underneath. A card number, using a "Z" prefix, is in the upper left corner. A football field grid appears on the left, containing statistical achievement breakdowns by yardage increments. Each card in the regular set is also printed as part of an Artist's Proof parallel set. These cards use rainbow holographic gold foil stamping in the design and are seeded one per 23 packs. There were also three insert sets available: Noteworthy '95, Rookie Rising and Z Team.

		MT
Complete Set (150):		40.00
Common Player:		.25
Minor Stars:		.50
Artist Proof Cards: 6x-12x		
Inserted 1:23		
Pack (6):		4.50
Wax Box (24):		85.00
1	Dan Marino	4.00
2	Yancey Thigpen	.50
3	Marcus Allen	.50
4	Curtis Conway	.50
5	Troy Aikman	2.50
6	William Floyd	.25
7	Ricky Watters	.50
8	Herman Moore	.75
9	Jim Harbaugh	.25
10	Isaac Bruce	.50
11	Drew Bledsoe	2.50
12	Jeff Blake	.50
13	Tim Brown	.50
14	Deion Sanders	1.50
15	Greg Hill	.25
16	Ben Coates	.25
17	Errict Rhett	.25
18	Barry Sanders	5.00
19	Erik Kramer	.25
20	Emmitt Smith	4.00
21	Brett Favre	5.00
22	Jerome Bettis	.75
23	Garrison Hearst	.50
24	Michael Irvin	.50
25	Chris Warren	.25
26	Steve Young	2.00
27	Cris Carter	.75
28	Carl Pickens	.50
29	Lake Dawson	.25
30	Marshall Faulk	.75
31	Vincent Brisby	.25
32	Jerry Rice	2.50
33	Eric Metcalf	.25
34	Natrone Means	.50
35	Steve Bono	.25
36	John Elway	4.00
37	Jeff Hostetler	.25
38	Scott Mitchell	.25
39	Andre Rison	.50
40	Daryl Johnston	.25
41	Mark Brunell	2.50
42	Jeff George	.50
43	Mario Bates	.25
44	Erric Pegram	.25
45	Brent Jones	.25
46	Trent Dilfer	.75
47	Larry Centers	.25
48	Anthony Miller	.25
49	Reggie White	.75
50	Bill Brooks	.25
51	Chris Zorich	.25
52	Jim Kelly	.75
53	Junior Seau	.50
54	Chris Miller	.25
55	Gus Frerotte	.50
56	Andre Reed	.50
57	Darnay Scott	.50
58	Brett Perriman	.25
59	Edgar Bennett	.25
60	Warren Moon	.50
61	Neil O'Donnell	.50
62	Jay Novacek	.25
63	Bam Morris	.25
64	Jim Everett	.25
65	Ken Norton Jr.	.25
66	Tony Martin	.50
67	Steve Atwater	.25
68	Henry Ellard	.25
69	Rodney Hampton	.25
70	Derrick Thomas	.25
71	Stan Humphries	.25
72	Harvey Williams	.25
73	Greg Lloyd	.25
74	Jake Reed	.25
75	Charles Haley	.25
76	Quinn Early	.25
77	Rodney Peete	.25
78	Brian Blades	.25
79	Robert Brooks	.25
80	Terry Allen	.50
81	Dave Brown	.25
82	Derrick Alexander	.25
83	Terance Mathis	.25
84	Rick Mirer	.50
85	Herschel Walker	.25
86	Charlie Garner	.50
87	Jeff Graham	.25
88	Bruce Smith	.25
89	Terry Kirby	.25
90	Craig Heyward	.25
91	Bernie Parmalee	.25
92	Adrian Murrell	.50
93	Derek Loville	.25
94	Heath Shuler	.50
95	Shannon Sharpe	.50
96	Bert Emanuel	.50
97	Hugh Douglas	.25
98	Lovell Pinkney	.25
99	Sherman Williams	.25
100	Tony Boselli	.25
101	Wayne Chrebet	.75
102	Orlanda Thomas	.25
103	Darick Holmes	.50
104	Tyrone Wheatley	.50
105	Christian Fauria	.25
106	Frank Sanders	.50
107	Chad May	.25
108	James Stewart	.50
109	Ken Dilger	.25
110	Kyle Brady	.25
111	Todd Collins	.50
112	Terrell Fletcher	.50
113	Eric Bjornson	.25
114	Justin Armour	.25
115	Rob Johnson	.75
116	Terrell Davis	8.00
117	J.J. Stokes	.75
118	Rashaan Salaam	.50
119	Chris Sanders	.50
120	Kerry Collins	.75
121	Michael Westbrook	.50
122	Eric Zeier	.50
123	Curtis Martin	3.00
124	Rodney Thomas	.25
125	Kordell Stewart	4.00
126	Joey Galloway	1.00
127	Steve McNair	1.50
128	Napoleon Kaufman	1.50
129	Tamarick Vanover	.50
130	Stoney Case	.25
131	James Stewart	.25
132	Carl Pickens	.25
133	Jim Harbaugh	.25
134	Yancey Thigpen PP	.25
135	Ricky Watters	.25
136	Isaac Bruce PP	.25
137	Kordell Stewart PP	2.00
138	Jeff Blake PP	.25
139	Terrell Davis PP	4.00
140	Scott Mitchell	.25
141	Rodney Thomas	.25
142	Robert Brooks	.25
143	Joey Galloway PP	.50
144	Brett Favre PP	2.50
145	Kerry Collins PP	.25
146	Herman Moore	.25
147	Michael Irvin, Emmitt Smith, Troy Aikman	2.00
148	Dan Marino CL	1.00
149	Jerry Rice CL	.50
150	Emmitt Smith CL	.75

1996 Zenith Artist's Proofs

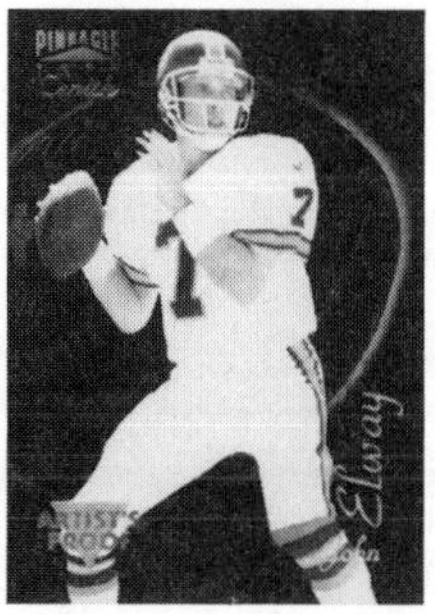

Each card in Pinnacle's 1996 Zenith football has a parallel Artist's Proof version. The cards, seeded one per 23 packs, use a rainbow holographic gold foil stamping in the design.

		MT
Complete Set (150):		2000.
Common Player:		5.00
Minor Stars:		10.00
Artist's Proof Cards: 15x-30x		
1	Dan Marino	125.00
2	Yancey Thigpen	15.00
3	Marcus Allen	10.00
4	Curtis Conway	10.00
5	Troy Aikman	80.00
6	William Floyd	10.00
7	Ricky Watters	10.00
8	Herman Moore	20.00
9	Jim Harbaugh	5.00
10	Isaac Bruce	15.00
11	Drew Bledsoe	80.00
12	Jeff Blake	15.00
13	Tim Brown	5.00
14	Deion Sanders	50.00
15	Greg Hill	5.00
16	Ben Coates	5.00
17	Errict Rhett	15.00
18	Barry Sanders	80.00
19	Erik Kramer	5.00
20	Emmitt Smith	125.00
21	Brett Favre	125.00
22	Jerome Bettis	10.00
23	Garrison Hearst	10.00
24	Michael Irvin	25.00
25	Chris Warren	10.00
26	Steve Young	80.00
27	Cris Carter	5.00
28	Carl Pickens	20.00
29	Lake Dawson	10.00
30	Marshall Faulk	70.00
31	Vincent Brisby	5.00
32	Jerry Rice	80.00
33	Eric Metcalf	5.00
34	Natrone Means	25.00
35	Steve Bono	10.00
36	John Elway	60.00
37	Jeff Hostetler	5.00
38	Scott Mitchell	5.00
39	Andre Rison	5.00
40	Daryl Johnston	5.00
41	Mark Brunell	60.00
42	Jeff George	10.00
43	Mario Bates	10.00
44	Erric Pegram	5.00
45	Brent Jones	5.00
46	Trent Dilfer	10.00
47	Larry Centers	5.00
48	Anthony Miller	5.00
49	Reggie White	10.00
50	Bill Brooks	5.00
51	Chris Zorich	5.00
52	Jim Kelly	10.00
53	Junior Seau	10.00
54	Chris Miller	5.00
55	Gus Frerotte	10.00
56	Andre Reed	5.00
57	Darnay Scott	20.00
58	Brett Perriman	5.00
59	Edgar Bennett	5.00
60	Warren Moon	10.00
61	Neil O'Donnell	10.00
62	Jay Novacek	5.00
63	Bam Morris	10.00
64	Jim Everett	5.00
65	Ken Norton Jr.	5.00
66	Tony Martin	5.00
67	Steve Atwater	5.00
68	Henry Ellard	5.00
69	Rodney Hampton	5.00
70	Derrick Thomas	5.00
71	Stan Humphries	5.00
72	Harvey Williams	5.00
73	Greg Lloyd	5.00
74	Jake Reed	5.00
75	Charles Haley	5.00
76	Quinn Early	5.00
77	Rodney Peete	5.00
78	Brian Blades	5.00
79	Robert Brooks	20.00
80	Terry Allen	5.00
81	Dave Brown	5.00
82	Derrick Alexander	5.00
83	Terance Mathis	5.00
84	Rick Mirer	10.00
85	Herschel Walker	5.00
86	Charlie Garner	5.00
87	Jeff Graham	5.00
88	Bruce Smith	5.00
89	Terry Kirby	5.00
90	Craig Heyward	5.00
91	Bernie Parmalee	5.00
92	Adrian Murrell	5.00
93	Derek Loville	5.00
94	Heath Shuler	15.00
95	Shannon Sharpe	5.00
96	Bert Emanuel	20.00
97	Hugh Douglas	5.00
98	Lovell Pinkney	5.00
99	Sherman Williams	20.00
100	Tony Boselli	5.00
101	Wayne Chrebet	5.00
102	Orlanda Thomas	5.00
103	Darick Holmes	30.00
104	Tyrone Wheatley	20.00
105	Christian Fauria	5.00
106	Frank Sanders	20.00
107	Chad May	5.00
108	James Stewart	20.00
109	Ken Dilger	5.00
110	Kyle Brady	5.00
111	Todd Collins	10.00
112	Terrell Fletcher	10.00
113	Eric Bjornson	5.00
114	Justin Armour	5.00
115	Rob Johnson	5.00
116	Terrell Davis	75.00
117	J.J. Stokes	50.00
118	Rashaan Salaam	15.00
119	Chris Sanders	20.00
120	Kerry Collins	75.00
121	Michael Westbrook	40.00
122	Eric Zeier	15.00
123	Curtis Martin	90.00
124	Rodney Thomas	15.00
125	Kordell Stewart	75.00
126	Joey Galloway	60.00
127	Steve McNair	60.00
128	Napoleon Kaufman	30.00
129	Tamarick Vanover	15.00
130	Stoney Case	5.00
131	James Stewart	5.00
132	Carl Pickens	5.00
133	Jim Harbaugh	5.00
134	Yancey Thigpen PP	20.00
135	Ricky Watters	5.00
136	Isaac Bruce PP	12.00
137	Kordell Stewart PP	40.00
138	Jeff Blake PP	20.00
139	Terrell Davis PP	40.00
140	Scott Mitchell	5.00
141	Rodney Thomas	5.00
142	Robert Brooks	5.00
143	Joey Galloway PP	30.00
144	Brett Favre PP	60.00
145	Kerry Collins PP	35.00
146	Herman Moore	5.00
147	Michael Irvin, Emmitt Smith, Troy Aikman	125.00
148	Dan Marino CL	60.00
149	Jerry Rice CL	30.00
150	Emmitt Smith CL	60.00

1996 Zenith Noteworthy '95

This 18-card insert set recaps some of the top events from the 1995 season. Each card front has a closeup photo of the player on the top half, against a silver-foiled background which says Noteworthy '95. The brand logo is in the upper right corner. The bottom half of the card has gold foil to show an action photo. The player's name and accomplishment are in silver foil above it. The card back is horizontal and is numbered in the upper left corner. A player photo appears on the card's left side, between two parallel gold bars. A recap of the player's 1995 season is on the right side. The player's name and team name are in the top gold bar; his accomplishment is in the lower bar. Cards were random inserts, one per 12 packs of 1996 Pinnacle Zenith football.

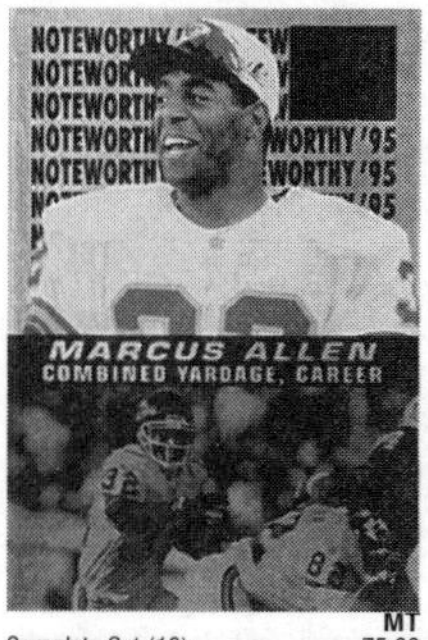

		MT
Complete Set (18):		75.00
Common Player:		1.50
Minor Stars:		3.00
Inserted 1:12		
1	Dan Marino	8.00
2	Jerry Rice	6.00
3	Michael Irvin	3.00
4	Emmitt Smith	8.00
5	Michael Irvin, Emmitt Smith	6.00
6	Herman Moore	3.00
7	Brett Favre	12.00
8	Barry Sanders	12.00
9	Marcus Allen	3.00
10	Steve Young	5.00
11	John Elway	8.00
12	Warren Moon	3.00
13	Jim Kelly	3.00
14	Jim Everett	1.50
15	Charles Haley	1.50
16	Emmitt Smith	8.00
17	Troy Aikman	6.00
18	Larry Brown	1.50

1996 Zenith Rookie Rising

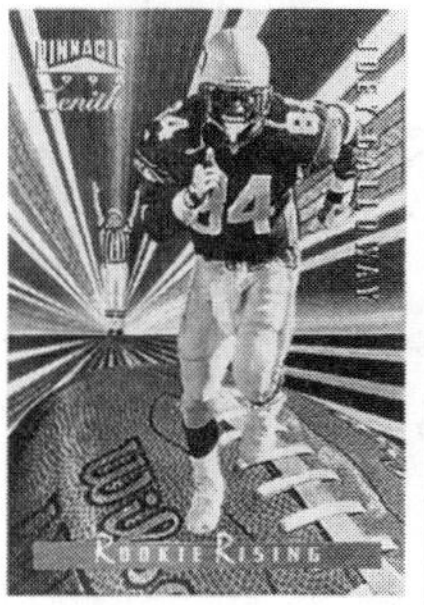

Pinnacle's 1996 version of Rookie Roll Call is its 18-card Rookie Rising set. The cards, randomly inserted one per 24 packs of 1996 Pinnacle Zenith football, feature players from the 1995 rookie class. The cards use a double-sided Dufex process, which gives each card a 3-D look. The front has an action photo of the player on top of a football. An official is on the horizon, signalling a touchdown. The player's name along the left side is stamped in gold foil, as are the brand logo in the upper left corner and the insert set name, in a colored panel at the bottom. The horizontal back has a closeup shot of the player, along with his team's helmet. A card number is in the upper right corner in a black rectangle.

		MT
Complete Set (18):		75.00
Common Player:		2.50
Minor Stars:		5.00
Inserted 1:24		
1	Sherman Williams	5.00
2	Curtis Martin	10.00
3	Michael Westbrook	7.00
4	Darick Holmes	5.00
5	James Stewart	5.00
6	Eric Zeier	5.00
7	Tamarick Vanover	5.00
8	J.J. Stokes	7.00
9	Kordell Stewart	15.00
10	Rodney Thomas	2.50
11	Kerry Collins	7.00
12	Terrell Davis	30.00
13	Steve McNair	12.00
14	Rashaan Salaam	7.00
15	Joey Galloway	7.00
16	Wayne Chrebet	7.00
17	Chris Sanders	5.00
18	Frank Sanders	7.00

1996 Zenith Z-Team

These 1996 Pinnacle inserts, using clear plastic for the card design, have a see-through design that includes gold foil-stamping and etched highlights. The card front has a black Z running through it, with an action player photo on it. See-through etched action photos appear on each side of the Z. Gold foil is used for the brand logo, which appears in the upper right corner, and the set icon, which is in the lower left corner, next to the gold foil-stamped player's name. The back repeats the photo design from the front, except the Z cuts through the main photo and has a brief career summary inside it. A card number is in the upper left corner.

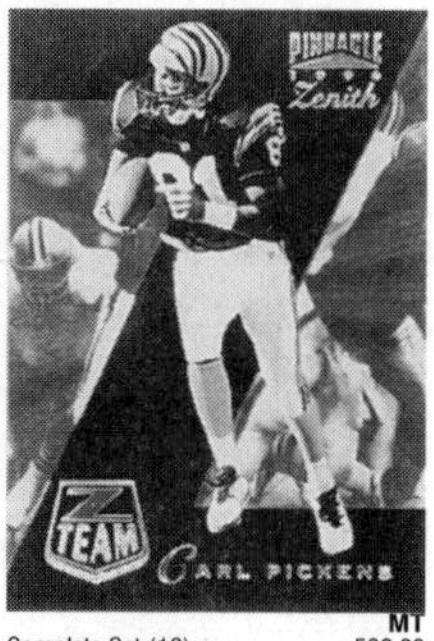

		MT
Complete Set (18):		500.00
Common Player:		6.00
Minor Stars:		12.00
Inserted 1:72		
1	Troy Aikman	30.00
2	Drew Bledsoe	30.00
3	Errict Rhett	6.00
4	Emmitt Smith	45.00
5	Jerry Rice	30.00
6	Cris Carter	12.00
7	Curtis Martin	25.00
8	Deion Sanders	20.00
9	Brett Favre	60.00
10	Michael Irvin	12.00
11	Chris Warren	6.00
12	Dan Marino	45.00
13	Steve Young	25.00
14	Marshall Faulk	15.00
15	Barry Sanders	60.00
16	John Elway	45.00
17	Isaac Bruce	12.00
18	Carl Pickens	6.00

1997 Zenith

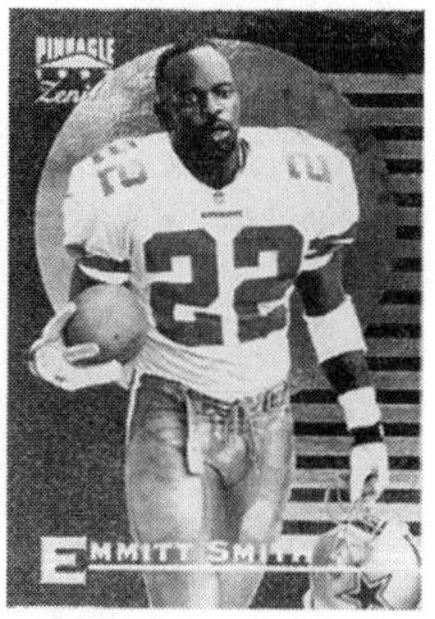

The 150-card, regular-sized set included Season Highlights (15), Awesome Foursome (1) and Rookies (35) subsets and was available in six-card packs. The base cards feature the player's image over a gold foil circle. The player's name is also printed in gold foil on the card face bottom. The card backs feature another photo with in-depth statistical information. Insert sets include Rookie Rising, V2, Z Team, Gold Mirror Mylar Z Team and the base-set parallel Artist's Proof.

		MT
Complete Set (150):		50.00
Common Player:		.15
Minor Stars:		.30
Artist's Proof Cards:		15x-30x
Pack (6):		5.00
Wax Box (24):		95.00
1	Brett Favre	4.00
2	Jerry Rice	2.00
3	Shannon Sharpe	.15
4	Dan Marino	4.00
5	James Stewart	.15
6	Warren Moon	.15
7	Emmitt Smith	4.00
8	Kordell Stewart	2.00
9	Kerry Collins	.40
10	Ricky Watters	.15
11	Gus Frerotte	.15
12	Barry Sanders	3.00
13	Joey Galloway	.75
14	Marshall Faulk	.40
15	Todd Collins	.15
16	Steve McNair	.50
17	Tyrone Wheatley	.15
18	Isaac Bruce	.50
19	Troy Aikman	2.00
20	Larry Centers	.15
21	Alvin Harper	.15
22	Rashaan Salaam	.15
23	Eric Metcalf	.15
24	Jim Everett	.15
25	Ken Dilger	.15
26	Curtis Martin	3.00
27	Neil O'Donnell	.15
28	Thurman Thomas	.15
29	Andre Rison	.15
30	Steve Bono	.15
31	Garrison Hearst	.15

32	Junior Seau	.15		100	Eddie George	3.00
33	Napoleon Kaufman	.15		101	Karim Abdul-Jabbar	.50
34	Jerome Bettis	.15		102	Amani Toomer	.15
35	Frank Wycheck	.15		103	Tony Banks	.30
36	Lamar Smith	.15		104	Regan Upshaw	.15
37	Derrick Alexander	.15		105	Leeland McElroy	.15
38	Steve Young	1.50		106	Jason Dunn	.15
39	Cris Carter	.15		107	Keyshawn Johnson	.40
40	O.J. McDuffie	.15		108	Winslow Oliver	.15
41	Deion Sanders	1.25		109	Walt Harris	.15
42	Robert Brooks	.15		110	Stanley Pritchett	.15
43	Jeff Blake	.50		111	Eddie Kennison	.30
44	Marcus Allen	.15		112	Terrell Owens	1.75
45	Herman Moore	.15		113	Duane Clemons	.15
46	Ray Zellars	.15		114	John Mobley	.15
47	Tim Brown	.15		115	Simeon Rice	.15
48	John Elway	1.50		116	Ernie Conwell	.15
49	Charles Johnson	.15		117	Eric Moulds	.30
50	Rodney Peete	.15		118	Marvin Harrison	.40
51	Curtis Conway	.15		119	Rickey Dudley	.30
52	Kevin Greene	.15		120	Mike Alstott	.30
53	Andre Reed	.15		121	Terry Glenn	.50
54	Mark Brunell	2.00		122	Brian Dawkins	.15
55	Tony Martin	.15		123	Kevin Hardy	.15
56	Elvis Grbac	.15		124	Bobby Engram	.30
57	Wayne Chrebet	.15		125	Alex Van Dyke	.15
58	Vinny Testaverde	.15		126	Zach Thomas	.75
59	Terry Allen	.15		127	Bryan Still	.15
60	Dave Brown	.15		128	Detron Smith	.15
61	LaShon Johnson	.15		129	Jerome Woods	.15
62	Trent Dilfer	.15		130	Muhsin Muhammad	.50
63	Chris Warren	.15		131	Lawrence Phillips	.30
64	Chris Sanders	.15		132	Alex Molden	.15
65	Kevin Carter	.15		133	Steve Young	.75
66	Jim Harbaugh	.15		134	Troy Aikman	1.00
67	Terance Mathis	.15		135	Junior Seau	.15
68	Ben Coates	.15		136	John Elway	.75
69	Robert Smith	.15		137	Dan Marino	2.00
70	Drew Bledsoe	2.00		138	Lawrence Phillips	.15
71	Henry Ellard	.15		139	Brett Favre	2.00
72	Scott Mitchell	.15		140	Jerry Rice	1.00
73	Andre Hastings	.15		141	Kerry Collins	.40
74	Rodney Hampton	.15		142	Barry Sanders	1.50
75	Michael Jackson	.15		143	Mark Brunell	1.00
76	Jeff Hostetler	.15		144	Drew Bledsoe	1.00
77	Reggie White	.15		145	Eddie Kennison	.50
78	Kent Graham	.15		146	Marvin Harrison	.50
79	Adrian Murrell	.15		147	Emmitt Smith	2.00
80	Carl Pickens	.15		148	Eddie George, Terry Glenn, Rickey Dudley, Bobby Hoying	2.00
81	Erik Kramer	.15				
82	Terrell Davis	2.50				
83	Sean Dawkins	.15		149	Emmitt Smith	2.00
84	Jamal Anderson	.50		150	Dan Marino	2.00
85	Stan Humphries	.15				
86	Chris T. Jones	.15				
87	Hardy Nickerson	.15				
88	Anthony Johnson	.15				
89	Michael Haynes	.15				
90	Irving Spikes	.15				
91	Bruce Smith	.15				
92	Keenan McCardell	.15				
93	Chris Chandler	.15				
94	Tamarick Vanover	.15				
95	Cortez Kennedy	.15				
96	Roman Phifer	.15				
97	Michael Irvin	.15				
98	Tim Biakabutuka	.50				
99	Stepfret Williams	.15				

1997 Zenith Artist's Proofs

Artist's Proofs paralled all 150 cards in the regular-issue set. The cards are distinguished by a holographic foil Artist's Proof stamp, and are inserted every 47 packs.

	MT
Complete Set (150):	1500.
Artist's Proof Cards:	15x-30x

1997 Zenith V2

The 18-card, regular-sized set features full-motion lenticular printing along with a conventional player photo. Inserted every 23 packs, the die-cut cards have "V2" printed underneath a motion picture with the player's name and team on the top and bottom of the horizontal card, respectively. The card backs are numbered with the "V" prefix and contain 1996 statistics and a brief highlight.

		MT
Complete Set (18):		350.00
Common Player:		6.00
1	Troy Aikman	25.00
2	John Elway	20.00
3	Jim Harbaugh	6.00
4	Barry Sanders	35.00
5	Deion Sanders	25.00
6	Drew Bledsoe	25.00
7	Dan Marino	45.00
8	Terrell Davis	30.00
9	Isaac Bruce	10.00
10	Jerome Bettis	6.00
11	Emmitt Smith	45.00
12	Brett Favre	50.00
13	Steve Young	15.00
14	Mark Brunell	25.00
15	Joey Galloway	6.00
16	Kordell Stewart	20.00
17	Jerry Rice	25.00
18	Curtis Martin	30.00

1997 Zenith Rookie Rising

The 24-card, regular-sized set was inserted every 23 packs of Pinnacle Zenith. The cards are individually numbered and feature the rookie on the card face in Dufex printing over a common stadium. The horizontal cards have "Rookie Rising" printed in gold script on the front with the player's name written in script in the upper left corner. The backs feature a player shot over a football.

		MT
Complete Set (24):		160.00
Common Player:		3.00
1	Eddie Kennison	5.00
2	Marvin Harrison	8.00
3	Keyshawn Johnson	8.00
4	Leeland McElroy	3.00
5	Terrell Owens	12.00
6	Terry Glenn	18.00
7	Bobby Engram	3.00
8	Karim Abdul-Jabbar	15.00
9	Lawrence Phillips	3.00
10	Amani Toomer	3.00
11	Eric Moulds	3.00
12	Jason Dunn	3.00
13	Stanley Pritchett	3.00
14	Eddie George	20.00
15	Muhsin Muhammad	5.00
16	Rickey Dudley	3.00
17	Tony Banks	5.00
18	Bryan Still	3.00
19	Tim Biakabutuka	3.00
20	Simeon Rice	3.00
21	Zach Thomas	8.00
22	Kevin Hardy	3.00
23	Jerris McPhail	3.00
24	Mike Alstott	6.00

1997 Zenith Z-Team

The 18-card, regular-sized set was inserted every 71 packs of Pinnacle Zenith while the parallel Gold Mirror Mylar Z Team set was found every 191 packs. The standard Z Team cards feature the player's image on a horizontal card with a "Z" printed on the left side over a large football backdrop. The card backs are numbered with the "Z" prefix and feature another player shot over a large football. A large black "Z" with a highlight text insert is on the left side. The Gold Mirror Mylar Z Team inserts are distinguishable by the reflective gold background on the card fronts. The card backs are essentially the same, with the exception of the words "Mirror Gold" printed along the left border.

		MT
Complete Set (18):		650.00
Common Player:		15.00
Mirror Gold Cards:		2x-3x
1	Emmitt Smith	80.00
2	Dan Marino	80.00
3	Jerry Rice	40.00
4	John Elway	30.00
5	Curtis Martin	50.00
6	Deion Sanders	25.00
7	Tony Banks	15.00
8	Jim Harbaugh	15.00
9	Joey Galloway	15.00
10	Troy Aikman	40.00
11	Brett Favre	80.00
12	Keyshawn Johnson	25.00
13	Eddie George	50.00
14	Barry Sanders	50.00
15	Kordell Stewart	40.00
16	Steve Young	30.00
17	Terrell Davis	50.00
18	Drew Bledsoe	40.00

1997 Zenith Z-Team Mirror Golds

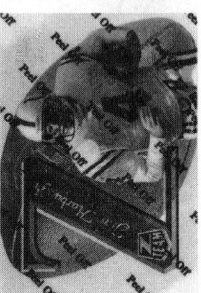

Z-Team Mirror Golds feature all 18 cards in the regular Z-Team set, but these inserts feature a Mirror Gold finish, and are inserted every 191 packs.

	MT
Complete Set (18):	1600.

COLLEGE

1993 Air Force Smokey

		MT
Complete Set (16):		15.00
Common Player:		.75
1	Fisher DeBerry (CO)	1.00
2	Dee Dowler	2.50
3	Chad Hennings	5.00
4	Carlton MacDonald	1.00
5	Terry Maki	1.00
6	Reggie Minton	1.00
7	Air Force Falcon	.75
8	Air Force Thunderbirds	.75
9	Cadet Field House	.75
10	Chapel	.75
11	Color Guard	.75
12	Commander-in-Chief's Trophy	.75
13	Drum and Bugle Corp	.75
14	Falcon Stadium	.75
15	Parachute Team	.75
16	Talon T-38	.75

1971 Alabama Team Sheets

		NM
Complete Set (6):		45.00
Common Player:		6.00
1	Mike Raines, Pat Raines, Terry Rowell, Gary Rutledge, Bubba Sawyer, Bill Sexton, Wayne Wheeler, Jack White, Steve Williams, Dexter Wood	8.00
2	Johnny Musso, Lanny Norris, Robin Parkhouse, Jim Patterson, Steve Root, Jimmy Rosser, Jeff Rouzie, Robby Rowan, Chuck Strickland, Tom Surlas, Steve Wade, David Watkins	10.00
3	Fred Marshall, Noah Miller, John Mitchell, Randy Moore, Gary Reynolds, Benny Rippetoe, Ronny Robertson, John Rogers, Jim Simmons, Paul Spivey, Steve Sprayberry, Rod Steakley	6.00
4	Richard Bryan, Chip Burke, Jerry Cash, Don Cokely, Greg Gantt, Jim Grammer, Wayne Hall, John Hannah, Rand Lambert, Tom Lusk, Bobby McKinney, David McMakin	8.00
5	Ellis Beck, Steve Bisceglia, Jeff Blitz, Buddy Brown, Steve Dean, Mike Denson, Joe Doughty, Mike Eckenrod, Pat Keever, David Knapp, Jim Krapf, Joe LaBue	6.00
6	Wayne Adkinson, David Bailey, Marvin Barron, Jeff Beard, Andy Cross, John Croyle, Bill Davis, Terry Davis, Steve Higginbotham, Ed Hines, Jimmy Horton, Wilbur Jackson	7.00

1972 Alabama

		NM
Complete Set (54):		95.00
Common Player:		1.50
1C	Skip Kubelius	1.50
1D	Terry Davis	2.50
1H	Robert Fraley	1.50
1S	Paul "Bear" Bryant (CO)	25.00
2C	David Watkins	1.50
2D	Bobby McKinney	1.50
2H	Dexter Wood	1.50
2S	Chuck Strickland	1.50
3C	John Hannah	15.00
3D	Tom Lusk	1.50
3H	Jim Krapf	1.50
3S	Warren Dyar	1.50
4C	Greg Gantt	2.50
4D	Johnny Sharpless	1.50
4H	Steve Wade	1.50
4S	John Rogers	1.50
5C	Doug Faust	1.50
5D	Jeff Rouzie	1.50
5H	Buddy Brown	1.50
5S	Randy Moore	1.50
6C	David Knapp	2.50
6D	Lanny Norris	1.50
6H	Paul Spivey	1.50
6S	Pat Raines	1.50
7C	Pete Pappas	1.50
7D	Ed Hines	1.50
7H	Mike Washington	1.50
7S	David McMakin	2.50
8C	Steve Dean	1.50
8D	Joe LaBue	1.50
8H	John Croyle	1.50
8S	Noah Miller	1.50
9C	Bobby Stanford	1.50
9D	Sylvester Croom	2.50
9H	Wilbur Jackson	6.00
9S	Ellis Beck	1.50
10C	Steve Bisceglia	1.50
10D	Andy Cross	1.50
10H	John Mitchell	2.50
10S	Bill Davis	1.50
11C	Gary Rutledge	2.50
11D	Randy Billingsley	1.50
11H	Randy Hall	1.50
11S	Ralph Stokes	1.50
12C	Jeff Blitz	1.50
12D	Robby Rowan	1.50
12H	Mike Raines	1.50
12S	Wayne Wheeler	1.50
13C	Steve Sprayberry	1.50
13D	Wayne Hall	2.50
13H	Morris Hunt	1.50
13S	Butch Norman	1.50
JK	Denny Stadium	1.50
JK	Memorial Coliseum	1.50

1973 Alabama

		NM
Complete Set (54):		80.00
Common Player:		1.50
1C	Skip Kubelius	1.50
1D	Mark Prudhomme	1.50
1H	Robert Fraley	1.50
1S	Paul "Bear" Bryant (CO)	20.00
2C	David Watkins	1.50
2D	Richard Todd	12.00
2H	Buddy Pope	1.50
2S	Chuck Strickland	1.50
3C	Bob Bryan	1.50
3D	Gary Hanrahan	1.50
3H	Greg Montgomery	1.50
3S	Warren Dyar	1.50
4C	Greg Gantt	2.50
4D	Johnny Sharpless	1.50
4H	Rick Watson	1.50
4S	John Rogers	1.50
5C	George Pugh	2.50
5D	Jeff Rouzie	1.50
5H	Buddy Brown	1.50
5S	Randy Moore	1.50
6C	Ray Maxwell	1.50
6D	Alan Pizzitola	1.50
6H	Paul Spivey	1.50
6S	Ron Robertson	1.50
7C	Pete Pappas	1.50
7D	Steve Kulback	1.50
7H	Mike Washington	1.50
7S	David McMakin	2.50
8C	Steve Dean	1.50
8D	Jerry Brown	1.50
8H	John Croyle	1.50
8S	Noah Miller	1.50
9C	Leroy Cook	1.50
9D	Sylvester Croom	2.50
9H	Wilbur Jackson	6.00
9S	Ellis Beck	1.50
10C	Tyrone King	1.50
10D	Mike Stock	1.50
10H	Mike Dubose	1.50
10S	Bill Davis	1.50
11C	Gary Rutledge	2.50
11D	Randy Billingsley	1.50
11H	Randy Hall	1.50
11S	Ralph Stokes	1.50
12C	Woodrow Lowe	6.00
12D	Marvin Barron	1.50
12H	Mike Raines	1.50
12S	Wayne Wheeler	1.50
13C	Steve Sprayberry	1.50
13D	Wayne Hall	2.50
13H	Morris Hunt	1.50
13S	Butch Norman	1.50
JKO	Denny Stadium	1.50
JKO	Memorial Coliseum	1.50

1988 Alabama Winners

		MT
Complete Set (73):		10.00
Common Player:		.15
1	Title Card (Schedule on back)	.25
2	Charlie Abrams	.15
3	Sam Atkins	.15
4	Marco Battle	.15
5	George Bethune	.15
6	Scott Bolt	.15
7	Tommy Bowden	.25
8	Danny Cash	.15
9	John Cassimus	.15
10	David Casteal	.15
11	Terrill Chatman	.15
12	Andy Christoff	.15
13	Tommy Cole	.15
14	Tony Cox	.15
15	Howard Cross	.75
16	Bill Curry (CO)	.25
17	Johnny Davis	.25
18	Vantreise Davis	.15
19	Joe Demos	.15
20	Philip Doyle	.15
21	Jeff Dunn	.15
22	John Fruhmorgen	.15
23	Jim Fuller	.15
24	Greg Gilbert	.15
25	Pierre Goode	.25
26	John Guy	.15
27	Spencer Hammond	.15
28	Stacy Harrison	.15
29	Murry Hill	.15
30	Byron Holdbrooks	.15
31	Ben Holt	.15
32	Bobby Humphrey	.75
33	Gene Jelks	.50
34	Kermit Kendrick	.15
35	William Kent	.15
36	David Lenoir	.15
37	Butch Lewis	.15
38	Don Lindsey	.15
39	John Mangum	.50
40	Tim Matheny	.15
41	Mac McWhorter	.25
42	Chris Mohr	.25
43	Larry New	.15
44	Gene Newberry	.15
45	Lee Ozmint	.15
46	Trent Patterson	.15
47	Greg Payne	.15
48	Thomas Rayam	.15
49	Chris Robinette	.15
50	Larry Rose	.15
51	Derrick Rushton	.15
52	Lamonde Russell	.15
53	Craig Sanderson	.15
54	Wayne Shaw	.15
55	Willie Shepherd	.15
56	Roger Shultz	.15
57	David Smith	.15
58	Homer Smith	.15
59	Mike Smith	.15
60	Byron Sneed	.15
61	Robert Stewart	.15
62	Vince Strickland	.15
63	Brian Stutson	.15
64	Vince Sutton	.15
65	Derrick Thomas	5.00
66	Steve Turner	.15
67	Alan Ward	.15
68	Lorenzo Ward	.15
69	Steve Webb	.15
70	Woody Wilson	.15
71	Chip Wisdom	.15
72	Willie Wyatt	.15
73	Mike Zuga	.15

1989 Alabama Coke 20

		MT
Complete Set (20):		10.00
Common Player:		.35
C1	Paul "Bear" Bryant (CO)	1.50
C2	John Hannah	.75
C3	Fred Sington	.35
C4	Derrick Thomas	1.50
C5	Dwight Stephenson	.75
C6	Cornelius Bennett	1.00
C7	Ozzie Newsome	1.00
C8	Joe Namath (Art)	2.00
C9	Steve Sloan	.60
C10	Bill Curry (CO)	.35
C11	Paul "Bear" Bryant (CO)	1.50
C12	Big Al (Mascot)	.35
C13	Scott Hunter	.50
C14	Lee Roy Jordan	.75
C15	Walter Lewis	.35
C16	Bobby Humphrey	.35
C17	John Mitchell	.35
C18	Johnny Musso	.75
C19	Pat Trammell	.35
C20	Ray Perkins (CO)	.60

1989 Alabama Coke 580

		MT
Complete Set (580):		35.00
Common Player:		.08
1	Paul "Bear" Bryant (CO)	.75
2	W.T. Van De Graff	.08
3	A.T.S. Hubert	.08
4	Bill Buckler	.08
5	Hoyt (Wu) Winslett	.08
6	Tony Holm	.08
7	Fred Sington Sr.	.15
8	John Suther	.08
9	Johnny Cain	.08
10	Tom Hupke	.15
11	Millard Howell	.25
12	Steve Wright	.08
13	Bill Searcey	.08
14	Riley Smith	.08
15	Arthur "Tarzan" White	.08
16	Joe Kilgrow	.08
17	Leroy Monsky	.08
18	James Ryba	.08
19	Carey Cox	.08
20	Holt Rast	.08
21	Joe Domnanovich	.08
22	Don Whitmire	.15
23	Harry Gilmer	.25
24	Vaughn Mancha	.08
25	Ed Salem	.08
26	Bobby Marlow	.30
27	George Mason	.08
28	Billy Neighbors	.25
29	Lee Roy Jordan	.50
30	Wayne Freeman	.08
31	Dan Kearley	.08
32	Joe Namath	1.00
33	David Ray	.15
34	Paul Crane	.08
35	Steve Sloan	.25
36	Richard Cole	.08
37	Cecil Dowdy	.15
38	Bobby Johns	.08
39	Ray Perkins	.30
40	Dennis Homan	.25
41	Ken Stabler	.60
42	Robert W. Boylston	.08
43	Mike Hall	.08
44	Alvin Samples	.08
45	Johnny Musso	.25
46	Bryant-Denny Stadium	.08
47	Tom Surlas	.08
48	John Hannah	.30
49	Jim Krapf	.08
50	John Mitchell	.15
51	Buddy Brown	.08
52	Woodrow Lowe	.15
53	Wayne Wheeler	.08
54	Leroy Cook	.08
55	Sylvester Croom	.15
56	Mike Washington	.08
57	Ozzie Newsome	.50
58	Barry Krauss	.15
59	Marty Lyons	.25
60	Jim Bunch	.08
61	Don McNeal	.15
62	Dwight Stephenson	.30
63	Bill Davis	.08
64	E.J. Junior	.15
65	Tommy Wilcox	.15
66	Jeremiah Castille	.15
67	Bobby Swafford	.08
68	Cornelius Bennett	.50
69	David Knapp	.15
70	Bobby Humphrey	.30
71	Van Tiffin	.08
72	Sid Smith	.08
73	Pat Trammell	.25
74	Mickey Andrews	.08
75	Steve Bowman	.08
76	Bob Baumhower	.25
77	Bob Cryder	.08
78	Bryan Braggs	.15
79	Warren Lyles	.08
80	Steve Mott	.08
81	Walter Lewis	.15
82	Ricky Moore	.08
83	Wes Neighbors	.08
84	Derrick Thomas	.75
85	Kermit Kendrick	.08
86	Larry Rose	.08
87	Charlie Marr	.08
88	James Whatley	.08
89	Erin Warren	.08
90	Charlie Holm	.08
91	Fred Davis	.08
92	John Wyhonic	.08
93	Jimmy Nelson	.08
94	Roy Steiner	.15
95	Tom Whitley	.08
96	John Wozniak	.08
97	Ed Holdnak	.08
98	Al Lary	.08
99	Mike Mizerany	.08
100	Pat O'Sullivan	.08
101	Jerry Watford	.08
102	Cecil Ingram	.15
103	Mike Fracchia	.08
104	Benny Nelson	.08
105	Tommy Tolleson	.08
106	Creed Gilmer	.08
107	John Calvert	.08
108	Derrick Slaughter	.08
109	Mike Ford	.08
110	Bruce Stephens	.08
111	Danny Ford	.25
112	Jimmy Grammer	.08
113	Steve Higginbotham	.08
114	David Bailey	.08
115	Greg Gantt	.25
116	Terry Davis	.15
117	Chuck Strickland	.08
118	Bobby McKinney	.08
119	Wilbur Jackson	.25
120	Mike Raines	.08
121	Steve Sprayberry	.08
122	David McMakin	.15
123	Ben Smith	.08
124	Steadman Shealy	.25
125	John Rogers	.08
126	Ricky Davis	.15
127	Conley Duncan	.08
128	Wayne Rhodes	.08
129	Buddy Seay	.08
130	Alan Pizzitola	.08
131	Richard Todd	.25
132	Charlie Ferguson	.08
133	Charley Hannah	.15
134	Wiley Barnes	.08
135	Mike Brock	.08
136	Murray Legg	.08
137	Wayne Hamilton	.08
138	David Hannah	.08
139	Jim Bob Harris	.08
140	Bart Krout	.08
141	Bob Cayavec	.08
142	Joe Beazley	.08
143	Mike Adcock	.08
144	Albert Bell	.08
145	Mike Shula	.40
146	Curt Jarvis	.08
147	Freddie Robinson	.08
148	Bill Condon	.08
149	Howard Cross	.30
150	Joe Demyanovich	.08
151	Major Ogilvie	.25
152	Perron Shoemaker	.08
153	Ralph Jones	.08
154	Vic Bradford	.08
155	Ed Hickerson	.08
156	Mitchell Olenski	.08
157	George Hecht	.08
158	Russ Craft	.08
159	Joey Jones	.25
160	Jack Green	.08
161	Lowell Tew	.15
162	Lamar Moye	.08
163	Jesse Richardson	.15
164	Harold Lutz	.08
165	Travis Hunt	.08
166	Ed Culpepper	.08
167	Nick Germanos	.08
168	Billy Rains	.08
169	Don Cochran	.08
170	Cotton Clark	.08
171	Gaylon McCollogh	.08
172	Tim Bates	.08
173	Wayne Cook	.08
174	Jerry Duncan	.08
175	Steve Davis	.08
176	Donnie Sutton	.08
177	Randy Barron	.08
178	Frank Mann	.08
179	Jeff Rouzie	.08
180	John Croyle	.08
181	Skip Kubelius	.08
182	Steve Bisceglia	.08
183	Gary Rutledge	.15
184	Mike Dubose	.08
185	Johnny Davis	.25
186	K.J. Lazenby	.08
187	Jeff Rutledge	.25
188	Mike Tucker	.08
189	Tony Nathan	.25
190	Buddy Aydelette	.08
191	Steve Whitman	.08
192	Ricky Tucker	.08
193	Randy Scott	.08
194	Warren Averitte	.08
195	Doug Vickers	.08
196	Jackie Cline	.08
197	Wayne Davis	.08
198	Hardy Walker	.08
199	Paul Ott Carruth	.15
200	Paul "Bear" Bryant (CO)	.75
201	Randy Rockwell	.08
202	Chris Mohr	.15
203	Walter Merrill	.08
204	Johnny Sullivan	.08
205	Harold Newman	.08
206	Erskine Walker	.08
207	Ted Cook	.08
208	Charles Compton	.08
209	Bill Cadenhead	.08
210	Butch Avinger	.08
211	Bobby Wilson	.08
212	Sid Youngelman	.25
213	Leon Fuller	.08
214	Tommy Brooker	.15
215	Richard Williamson	.25
216	Riggs Stephenson	.25
217	Al Clemens	.08
218	Grant Gillis	.08
219	Johnny Mack Brown	.40
220	Major Ogilvie	.25
221	Fred Pickhard	.08
222	Herschel Caldwell	.08
223	Emile Barnes	.08
224	Mike McQueen	.08
225	Ray Abruzzese	.15
226	Jesse Bendross	.25
227	Lew Bostick	.08
228	Jimmy Bowdoin	.08
229	Dave Brown	.08
230	Tom Calvin	.08
231	Ken Emerson	.08
232	Calvin Frey	.08
233	Thornton Chandler	.15
234	George Weeks	.08
235	Randy Edwards	.08
236	Phillip Brown	.08
237	Clay Whitehurst	.08
238	Chris Goode	.08
239	Preston Gothard	.08
240	Herb Hannah	.08
241	John M. Snoderly	.08
242	Scott Hunter	.25
243	Bobby Jackson	.08
244	Bruce Jones	.08
245	Robbie Jones	.08
246	Terry Jones	.08
247	Leslie Kelley	.08
248	Larry Lauer	.08
249	'61 National Champs (Tommy Brooker, Pat Trammell, Lee Roy Jordan, Paul "Bear" Bryant, Mike Fracchia, Billy Neighbors)	.25
250	Bobby Luna	.08
251	Keith Pugh	.08
252	Alan McElroy	.08
253	'25 National Champs (Team Photo)	.15
254	Curtis McGriff	.25
255	Norman Mosley	.08
256	Herky Mosley	.08
257	Ray Ogden	.15
258	Pete Jilleba	.08
259	Benny Perrin	.08
260	Claude Perry	.08
261	Tommy Cole	.08
262	Ed Versprille	.08
263	'30 National Champs (Team Photo)	.15
264	Don Jacobs	.08
265	Robert Skelton	.08
266	Joe Curtis	.08
267	Bart Starr	.75
268	Young Boozer	.08
269	Tommy Lewis	.15
270	Woody Umphrey	.08
271	Carney Laslie	.08
272	Russ Wood	.08
273	David Smith	.08
274	Paul Spivey	.08
275	Linnie Patrick	.08
276	Ron Durby	.08
277	'26 National Champs (Team Photo)	.15
278	Robert Higginbotham	.08
279	William Oliver	.08
280	Stan Moss	.08
281	Eddie Propst	.08
282	Laurien Stapp	.08
283	Clem Gryska	.08
284	Clark Pearce	.08
285	Pete Cavan	.08
286	Tom Newton	.08
287	Rich Wingo	.15
288	Rickey Gilliland	.08
289	Conrad Fowler	.08
290	Rick Neal	.08
291	James Blevins	.08
292	Dick Flowers	.08
293	Marshall Brown	.08
294	Jeff Beard	.08
295	Pete Moore	.08
296	Vince Boothe	.08
297	Charley Boswell	.08
298	Van Marcus	.08
299	Randy Billingsley	.15
300	Paul "Bear" Bryant (CO)	.75
301	Gene Blackwell	.08
302	Johnny Mosley	.08
303	Ray Perkins (CO)	.25
304	Harold Drew (CO)	.08
305	Frank Thomas (CO) (Not the Frank Thomas that went to Auburn)	.25
306	Wallace Wade	.15
307	Newton Godfree	.08
308	Steve Williams	.08
309	Al Lewis	.08
310	Fred Grant	.08
311	Jerry Brown	.08
312	Mal Moore	.15
313	Tilden Campbell	.08
314	Jack Smalley	.08
315	Paul "Bear" Bryant (CO)	.75
316	C.B. Clements	.08
317	Billy Piper	.08
318	Robert Lee Hamner	.08
319	Donnie Faust	.08
320	Gary Bramblett	.08
321	Peter Kim	.08
322	Fred Berrey	.08

323 Paul "Bear" Bryant (CO) .75
324 John Fruhmorgen .08
325 Jim Fuller .08
326 Doug Allen .08
327 Russ Mosley .08
328 Ricky Thomas .08
329 Vince Sutton .08
330 Larry Roberts .15
331 Rick McLain .08
332 Charles Eckerly .08
333 '34 National Champs (Team Photo) .15
334 Eddie McCombs .08
335 Scott Allison .08
336 Vince Cowell .08
337 David Watkins .08
338 Jim Duke .08
339 Don Harris .08
340 Lanny Norris .08
341 Thad Flanagan .08
342 Albert Elmore .08
343 Alan Gray .08
344 David Gilmer .08
345 Hal Self .08
346 Ben McLeod .08
347 Clell (Butch) Hobson .50
348 Jimmy Carroll .08
349 Frank Canterbury .08
350 John Byrd Williams .08
351 Marvin Barron .08
352 William Stone .08
353 Barry Smith .15
354 Jerrill Sprinkle .08
355 Hank Crisp (CO) .08
356 Bobby Smith .08
357 Charles Gray .08
358 Marlin Dyess .08
359 '41 National Champs (Team Photo) .15
360 Robert Moore .08
361 1961 National Champs (Billy Neighbors, Pat Trammell, Darwin Holt) (Team Photo) .15
362 Tommy White .08
363 Earl Wesley .08
364 John O'Linger .08
365 Bill Battle .08
366 Butch Wilson .08
367 Tim Davis .08
368 Larry Wall .08
369 Hudson Harris .08
370 Mike Hopper .08
371 Jackie Sherrill .40
372 Tom Somerville .08
373 David Chatwood .08
374 George Ranager .08
375 Tommy Wade .25
376 '64 National Champs (Joe Namath) .60
377 Reid Drinkard .08
378 Mike Hand .08
379 Ed White .25
380 Angelo Stafford .08
381 Ellis Beck .08
382 Wayne Hall .15
383 Randy Lee Hall .08
384 Jack O'Rear .08
385 Colenzo Hubbard .08
386 Gus White .08
387 Rich Watson .08
388 Steve Allen .08
389 John David Crow Jr. .15
390 Britton Cooper .08
391 Mike Rodriguez .08
392 Steve Wade .08
393 William J. Rice .08
394 Greg Richardson .08
395 Joe Jones .15
396 Todd Richardson .08
397 Anthony Smiley .08
398 Duff Morrison .08
399 Jay Grogan .08
400 Steve Booker .08
401 Larry Abney .08
402 Bill Abston .08
403 Wayne Adkinson .08
404 Charles Allen .08
405 Phil Allman .08
406 1965 National Champs (1965 Seniors) .25
407 James Angelich .08
408 Troy Barker .08
409 George Bethune .08
410 Bill Blair .08
411 Clark Boler .08
412 Duffy Boles .08
413 Ray Bolden .08
414 Bruce Bolton .08
415 Alvin Davis .08
416 Baxter Booth .08
417 Paul Boschung .08
418 1979 National Champs (Team Photo) .25
419 Richard Brewer .08
420 Jack Brown .08
421 Larry Brown .08
422 David Brungard .08
423 Jim Burkett .08
424 Auxford Burks .08
425 Jim Cain .08
426 Dick Turpin .08
427 Neil Callaway .08
428 David Casteal .08
429 Phil Chaffin .08
430 Howard Chappell .08
431 Bob Childs .08
432 Knute Rockne Christian .08
433 Richard Ciemny .08
434 J.B. Whitworth .08
435 Mike Clements .08
436 1973 National Champs (Coaching Staff) .08
437 Rocky Colburn .08
438 Danny Collins .08
439 James Taylor .08
440 Joe Compton .08
441 Bob Conway .08
442 Charlie Stephens .08
443 Kerry Goode .15
444 Joe LaBue .08
445 Allen Crumbley .08
446 Bill Curry (CO) .15
447 David Bedwell .08
448 Jim Davis .08
449 Mike Dean .08
450 Steve Dean .08
451 Vince DeLaurentis .08
452 Gary Deniro .08
453 Jim Dildy .08
454 Joe Dildy .08
455 Jimmy Dill .08
456 Jamie Dismuke .08
457 Junior Davis .08
458 Warren Dyar .08
459 Hugh Morrow .08
460 Grady Elmore .08
461 1978 National Champs (Jeff Rutledge, Tony Nathan, Barry Krauss, Marty Lyons, Rich Wingo) .25
462 Ed Hines .08
463 D. Joe Gambrell .08
464 Kavanaugh (Kay) Francis .08
465 Robert Fraley .08
466 Milton Frank .08
467 Jim Franko .08
468 Buddy French .08
469 Wayne Rhoads .08
470 Ralph Gandy .08
471 Danny Gilbert .08
472 Greg Gilbert .08
473 Joe Godwin .08
474 Richard Grammer .08
475 Louis Green .08
476 Gary Martin .08
477 Bill Hannah .08
478 Allen Harpole .08
479 Neb Hayden .08
480 Butch Henry .08
481 Norwood Hodges .08
482 Earl Smith .08
483 Darwin Holt .08
484 Scott Homan .08
485 Nathan Rustin .08
486 Gene Raburn .08
487 Ellis Houston .08
488 Frank Howard .08
489 Larry Hughes .08
490 Joe Kelley .08
491 Charlie Harris .08
492 Legion Field .08
493 Tim Hurst .08
494 Hunter Husband .08
495 Lou Ikner .08
496 Craig Epps .08
497 Jug Jenkins .08
498 Billy Johnson .08
499 David Johnson .08
500 Jon Hand .25
501 Max Kelley .08
502 Terry Killgore .08
503 Eddie Lowe .08
504 Noah Langdale .08
505 Ed Lary .08
506 Foy Leach .08
507 Harry Lee .08
508 Jim Loftin .08
509 Curtis Lynch .08
510 John Mauro .08
511 Ray Maxwell .08
512 Frank McClendon .08
513 Tom McCrary .08
514 Sonny McGahey .08
515 John McIntosh .08
516 David McIntyre .08
517 Wes Thompson .08
518 James Melton .08
519 John Miller .08
520 Fred Mims .08
521 Dewey Mitchell .08
522 Lydell Mitchell (Linebacker) .08
523 Greg Montgomery .15
524 Jimmie Moore .08
525 Randy Moore .08
526 Ed Morgan .08
527 Norris Hamer .08
528 Frank Mosely .08
529 Sidney Neighbors .08
530 Rod Nelson .08
531 James Nisbet .08
532 Mark Nix .08
533 L.W. Noonan .08
534 Louis Thompson .08
535 William Oliver .08
536 Gary Otten .08
537 Wayne Owen .08
538 Steve Patterson .08
539 Charley Pell .25
540 Bob Pettee .08
541 Gordon Pettus .08
542 Gary Phillips .08
543 Clay Walls .08
544 Douglas Potts .08
545 Mike Stock .08
546 John Mark Prudhomme .08
547 George Pugh .15
548 Pat Raines .08
549 Joe Riley .08
550 Wayne Trimble .08
551 Darryl White .08
552 Bill Richardson .08
553 Ray Richeson .08
554 Danny Ridgeway .08
555 Terry Sanders .08
556 Kenneth Roberts .08
557 Jimmy Watts .08
558 Ronald Robertson .08
559 Norbie Ronsonet .08
560 Jimmy Lynn Rosser .08
561 Terry Rowell .08
562 Larry Joe Ruffin .08
563 Jack Rutledge .08
564 Al Sabo .08
565 David Sadler .08
566 Donald Sanford .08
567 Hayward Sanford .08
568 Paul Tripoli .08
569 Lou Scales .08
570 Kurt Schmissrauter .08
571 Willard Scissum .08
572 Joe Sewell .15
573 Jimmy Sharpe .08
574 Willie Shepherd .08
575 Jack Smalley Jr. .08
576 Jim Simmons (Tight End) .08
577 Jim Simmons (Tackle) .08
578 Malcolm Simmons .08
579 Dave Sington .08
580 Fred Sington Jr. .15

A player's name in *italic* type indicates a rookie card.

1992 Alabama Greats Hoby

MT
Complete Set (42): 12.00
Common Player: .25
1 Bob Baumhower .50
2 Cornelius Bennett .75
3 Buddy Brown .25
4 Paul "Bear" Bryant (CO) .75
5 Johnny Cain .25
6 Jeremiah Castille .35
7 Leroy Cook .25
8 Paul Crane .35
9 Philip Doyle .25
10 Harry Gilmer .35
11 Jon Hand .50
12 Herb Hannah .25
13 John Hannah .75
14 Dennis Homan .35
15 Dixie Howell .35
16 Bobby Humphrey .35
17 Don Hutson .75
18 Curt Jarvis .35
19 Lee Roy Jordan .75
20 Barry Krauss .35
21 Woodrow Lowe .35
22 Marty Lyons .35
23 Vaughn Mancha .25
24 John Mangum .35
25 Bobby Marlow .35
26 Don McNeal .35
27 Chris Mohr .35
28 Johnny Musso .50
29 Billy Neighbors .35
30 Ozzie Newsome .75
31 Ray Perkins .50
32 Fred Sington .25
33 Ken Stabler .75
34 Siran Stacy .35
35 Dwight Stephenson .50
36 Robert Stewart .25
37 Derrick Thomas 1.00
38 Van Tiffin .25
39 Mike Washington .25
40 Arthur "Tarzan" White .25
41 Tommy Wilcox .35
42 Willie Wyatt .25

1980 Arizona Police

NM
Complete Set (24): 90.00
Common Player: 3.00
1 Brian Clifford 3.00
2 Mark Fulcher 3.00
3 Bob Gareeb 3.00
4 Marcellus Green 4.00
5 Drew Hardville 3.00
6 Neal Harris 3.00
7 Richard Hersey 3.00
8 Alfondia Hill 3.00
9 Tim Holmes 3.00
10 Jack Housley 3.00
11 Glenn Hutchinson 3.00
12 Bill Jensen 3.00
13 Frank Kalil 3.00
14 Dave Liggins 3.00
15 Tom Manno 3.00
16 Bill Nettling 3.00
17 Hubert Oliver 6.00
18 Glenn Perkins 3.00
19 John Ramseyer 3.00
20 Mike Robinson 3.00
21 Chris Schultz 4.00
22 Larry Smith (CO) 4.00
23 Reggie Ware (SP) 30.00
24 Bill Zivic 3.00

1981 Arizona Police

MT
Complete Set (27): 40.00
Common Player: 2.00
1 Moe Ankney (ACO) 3.00
2 Van Brandon 2.00
3 Bob Carter 2.00
4 Brian Christiansen 2.00
5 Mark Fulcher 2.00
6 Bob Gareeb 2.00
7 Gary Gibson 2.00
8 Mark Gobel 2.00
9 Alfred Gross 2.00
10 Kevin Hardcastle 2.00
11 Neal Harris 2.00
12 Brian Holland 2.00
13 Ricky Hunley 4.00
14 Frank Kalil 2.00
15 Jeff Kiewel 2.00
16 Chris Knudsen 2.00
17 Ivan Lesnik 2.00
18 Tony Neely 2.00
19 Glenn Perkins 2.00
20 Randy Robbins 2.00
21 Gerald Roper 2.00
22 Chris Schultz 3.00
23 Gary Shaw 2.00
24 Larry Smith (CO) 3.00
25 Tom Tunnicliffe 2.00
26 Sergio Vega 2.00
27 Brett Weber 3.00

1982 Arizona Police

MT
Complete Set (26): 35.00
Common Player: 1.50
1 Brad Anderson 1.50
2 Steve Boadway 1.50
3 Bruce Bush 1.50
4 Mike Freeman 1.50
5 Marsharne Graves 1.50
6 Courtney Griffin 1.50
7 Al Gross 2.00
8 Julius Holt 1.50
9 Lamonte Hunley 2.00
10 Ricky Hunley 2.50
11 Vance Johnson 5.00
12 Chris Kaesman 1.50
13 John Kaiser 1.50
14 Mark Keel 1.50
15 Jeff Kiewell 1.50
16 Ivan Lesnik 1.50
17 Glenn McCormick 1.50
18 Ray Moret 1.50
19 Tony Neely 1.50
20 Byron Nelson 2.00
21 Glenn Perkins 1.50
22 Randy Robbins 1.50
23 Larry Smith (CO) 2.00
24 Tom Tunnicliffe 2.00
25 Kevin Ward 1.50
26 David Wood 1.50

1983 Arizona Police

MT
Complete Set (24): 35.00
Common Player: 1.50
1 John Barthalt 1.50
2 Steve Boadway 1.50
3 Chris Brewer 1.50
4 Lynnden Brown 1.50
5 Charlie Dickey 1.50
6 Jay Dobins 1.50
7 Joe Drake 1.50
8 Allan Durden 2.00
9 Byron Evans 5.00
10 Nils Fox 1.50
11 Mike Freeman 1.50
12 Marsharne Graves 1.50
13 Lamonte Hunley 2.00
14 Vance Johnson 4.00
15 John Kaiser 1.50
16 Ivan Lesnik 1.50
17 Byron Nelson 2.00
18 Randy Robbins 1.50
19 Craig Schiller 1.50
20 Larry Smith (CO) 2.00
21 Tom Tunnicliffe 2.00
22 Mark Walczak 1.50
23 David Wood 1.50
24 Max Zendejas 2.00

1984 Arizona Police

MT
Complete Set (25): 15.00
Common Player: .75
1 Alfred Jenkins 2.00
8 John Connor 1.00
13 Max Zendejas 1.00
15 Gordon Bunch .75
19 Allen Durden 1.00
23 Lynnden Brown .75
25 Vance Johnson 2.00
28 Tom Bayse .75
35 Brent Wood .75
40 Greg Turner .75
47 Steve Boadway .75
52 Nils Fox .75
54 Craig Vesling .75
62 David Connor .75
67 Charlie Dickey .75
71 Brian Denton .75
78 John DuBose .75
79 Joe Drake .75
82 Joy Dobyns .75
85 Mark Walczak .75
86 Jon Horton .75
92 David Wood .75
98 Lamonte Hunley 1.00
99 John Barthalt .75
NNO Larry Smith (CO) 1.00

1985 Arizona Police

MT
Complete Set (23): 15.00
Common Player: .75
1 Alfred Jenkins 1.50
2 David Adams .75
6 Chuck Cecil 2.00
13 Max Zendejas 1.00
15 Gordon Bunch .75
18 Jeff Fairholm 1.00
19 Allen Durden 1.00
29 Don Be'ans .75
32 Joe Prior .75
42 Blake Custer .75
44 Boomer Gibson .75
48 Byron Evans 3.00
50 Val Bichekas .75
52 Joe Tofflemire 1.00
54 Craig Vesling .75
59 Jim Birmingham .75
72 Curt DiGiacomo .75
73 Lee Brunelli .75
78 John DuBose .75
83 Gary Parrish .75
95 Cliff Thorpe .75
96 Glenn Howell .75
NNO Larry Smith (CO) 1.00

1986 Arizona Police

MT
Complete Set (24): 15.00
Common Player: .75
1 David Adams .75
2 Frank Arriola .75
3 Val Biehekas .75
4 Jim Birmingham .75
5 Chuck Cecil 1.50
6 James Debow .75
7 Brian Denton .75
8 Byron Evans 2.00
9 Jeff Fairholm 1.00
10 Boomer Gibson .75
11 Eugene Hardy .75
12 Derek Hill 1.50
13 Jon Horton .75
14 Alfred Jenkins 1.25
15 Danny Lockett 1.00
16 Stan Mataele .75
17 Chris McLemore .75
18 Jeff Rinehart .75
19 Ruben Rodriguez 1.00
20 Martin Rudolph .75
21 Larry Smith (CO) 1.00
22 Joe Tofflemire 1.00
23 Dana Wells .75
24 Brent Wood .75

1987 Arizona Police

MT
Complete Set (23): 15.00
Common Player: .75
2 Bobby Watters 1.00
3 Doug Pfaff .75
6 Chuck Cecil 1.50
11 Gary Coston .75
18 Jeff Fairholm 1.00
22 Eugene Hardy .75
26 Troy Cephers .75
34 Charles Webb .75
38 James Debow .75
40 Art Greathouse .75
43 Jerry Beasley .75
44 Boomer Gibson .75
47 Gallen Allen .75
52 Joe Tofflemire 1.00
60 Jeff Rinehart .75
64 Kevin McKinney .75
68 Tom Lynch .75
82 Derek Hill 1.25
84 Kevin Singleton 1.00
87 Chris Singleton 3.00
97 George Hinkle .75
99 Dana Wells .75
NNO Dick Tomey (CO) 1.25

1988 Arizona Police

MT
Complete Set (25): 15.00
Common Player: .75
2 Bobby Watters 1.00
4 Darryl Lewis 2.00
5 Durrell Jones .75
8 Reggie McGill .75
10 Ronald Veal 1.00
15 Jeff Hammerschmidt .75
22 Scott Geyer .75
24 R. Groppenbacher .75
25 David Eldridge .75
35 Mario Hampton .75
38 James Debow .75
40 Art Greathouse .75
50 Darren Case .75
51 Doug Penner .75
52 Joe Tofflemire 1.00
63 John Brandom .75
65 Ken Hakes .75
74 Glenn Parker 1.25
78 Rob Woods .75
82 Derek Hill 1.25
84 Kevin Singleton 1.00
87 Chris Singleton 2.00
96 Brad Henke .75
99 Dana Wells .75
NNO Dick Tomey (CO) 1.00

1989 Arizona Police

MT
Complete Set (26): 12.00
Common Player: .60
1 Zeno Alexander .60
2 John Brandom .60
3 Todd Burden .60
4 Darren Case .60
5 David Eldridge .60
6 Nick Fineanganofo .60
7 Scott Geyer .60
8 Art Greathouse .60
9 Richard Griffith .60
10 Ken Hakes .60
11 Jeff Hammerschmidt .60
12 Mario Hampton .60
13 Darryl Lewis 1.50
14 Kip Lewis .60
15 George Malauulu .75
16 Reggie McGill .60
17 John Nies .60
18 Glenn Parker 1.00
19 Mike Parker .60
20 Doug Pfaff .60
21 David Roney .60
22 Pete Russell .60
23 Chris Singleton 1.50
24 Paul Tofflemire .60
25 Dick Tomey (CO) .75
26 Ronald Veal .75

1992 Arizona Police

MT
Complete Set (21): 10.00
Common Player: .50
1 Tony Bouie 1.00
2 Heath Bray .50
3 Charlie Camp .50
4 Ontiwaun Carter .60
5 Richard Griffith .50
6 Sean Harris .75
7 Mike Heemsbergen .50
8 Jimmy Hopkins .50
9 Billy Johnson .50
10 Keshon Johnson .50
11 Chuck Levy 1.25
12 Richard Maddox .50
13 George Malauulu .60
14 Darryl Morrison .75
15 Mani Ott .50
16 Ty Parten .50
17 Mike Scurlock .60
18 Warner Smith .50
19 Dick Tomey (CO) .60
20 Terry Vaughn .50
21 Rob Waldrop .75

1993 Army Smokey

MT
Complete Set (15): 12.00
Common Player: .75
1 Paul Andrzejewski .75
2 Kevin Czarnecki .75
3 Chad Davis .75
4 Glenn Davis 3.00
5 Mark Escobedo .75
6 Gary Graves .75
7 Leamon Hall 1.00
8 Jason Miller 1.00
9 Mike Plaia .75
10 Rick Roper 1.00
11 Jim Slomka .75
12 Bob Sutton (CO) .75
13 Jason Sutton .75
14 Pat Zelley .75
15 Army Mule (Mascot) .75

1972 Auburn Tigers

NM
Complete Set (54): 70.00
Common Player: 1.50
1C Ken Calleja 1.50
1D James Owens 1.50
1H Mac Lorendo 1.50
1S Ralph (Shug) Jordan (CO) 6.00
2C Rick Neel 1.50
2D Ted Smith 1.50
2H Eddie Welch 1.50
2S Mike Neel 1.50
3C Larry Taylor 1.50
3D Rett Davis 1.50
3H Rusty Fuller 1.50
3S Lee Gross 1.50
4C Bruce Evans 1.50
4D Rusty Deen 1.50
4H Johnny Simmons 1.50
4S Bill Newton 1.50
5C David Beverly 2.00
5D Dave Lyon 1.50
5H Mike Fuller 3.00
5S Bill Luka 1.50
6C Ken Bernich 1.50
6D Andy Steele 1.50
6H Wade Whatley 1.50
6S Bob Newton 2.00
7C Benny Sivley 2.00
7D Gardner Jett 2.00
7H Rob Spivey 2.00
7S Jay Casey 1.50
8C David Langner 1.50
8D Terry Henley 1.50
8H Thomas Gossom 1.50
8S Joe Tanory 1.50
9C Chris Linderman 1.50
9D Harry Unger 1.50
9H Kenny Burks 1.50
9S Sandy Cannon 1.50
10C Roger Mitchell 1.50
10D Jim McKinney 1.50
10H Gaines Lanier 1.50
10S Dave Beck 1.50
11C Bob Farrior 1.50
11D Miles Jones 1.50
11H Tres Rogers 1.50
11S David Hughes 1.50
12C Sherman Moon 1.50
12D Danny Sanspree 1.50
12H Steve Taylor 1.50
12S Randy Walls 1.50
13C Steve Wilson 1.50
13D Bobby Davis 1.50
13H Hamlin Caldwell 1.50
13S Dan Nugent 1.50
JK Joker - Auburn Memorial Coliseum 1.50
JK Joker - Cliff Hare Stadium 1.50

1973 Auburn Tigers

NM
Complete Set (54): 60.00
Common Player: 1.50
1C Ken Calleja 1.50
1D Chris Wilson 1.50
1H Lee Hayley 1.50
1S Ralph (Shug) Jordan (CO) 5.00
2C Rick Neel 1.50
2D Johnny Sumner 1.50
2H Mitzi Jackson 1.50
2S Jim Pitts 1.50
3C Steve Stanaland 1.50
3D Rett Davis 1.50
3H Rusty Fuller 1.50
3S Lee Gross 1.50
4C Bruce Evans 1.50
4D Rusty Deen 1.50
4H Liston Eddins 1.50
4S Bill Newton 1.50
5C Jimmy Sirmans 1.50
5D Harry Ward 1.50
5H Mike Fuller 2.50
5S Bill Luka 1.50
6C Ken Bernich 1.50
6D Andy Steele 1.50
6H Wade Whatley 1.50
6S Bob Newton 2.00
7C Benny Sivley 2.00
7D Rick Telhiard 2.00
7H Rob Spivey 2.00
7S David Williams 1.50
8C David Langner 1.50
8D Chuck Fletcher 1.50
8H Thomas Gossom 1.50
8S Holley Caldwell 1.50
9C Chris Linderman 1.50
9D Ed Butler 1.50
9H Kenny Burks 1.50
9S Mike Flynn 1.50
10C Roger Mitchell 1.50
10D Jim McKinney 1.50
10H Gaines Lanier 1.50
10S Carl Hubbard 1.50
11C Bob Farrior 1.50
11D Ronnie Jones 1.50
11H Billy Woods 1.50
11S David Hughes 1.50
12C Sherman Moon 1.50
12D Mike Gates 1.50
12H Steve Taylor 1.50
12S Randy Walls 1.50
13C Roger Pruett 1.50
13D Bobby Davis 1.50
13H Hamlin Caldwell 1.50
13S Dan Nugent 1.50
JK Joker - Auburn Memorial Coliseum 1.50
JK Joker - Cliff Hare Stadium 1.50

1989 Auburn Coke 20

MT
Complete Set (20): 8.00
Common Player: .35
C1 Pat Dye (CO) .50
C2 Zane Smith .35
C3 War Eagle (Mascot) .50
C4 Tucker Frederickson .50
C5 John Heisman .50
C6 Ralph (Shug) Jordan (CO) .50
C7 Pat Sullivan .50
C8 Terry Beasley .35
C9 Punt Bama Punt (Ralph (Shug) Jordan, Paul "Bear" Bryant) .50
C10 Retired Jerseys (Pat Sullivan, Terry Beasley) .50
C11 Bo Jackson 2.00
C12 Lawyer Tillman .75
C13 Gregg Carr .35

C14 Lionel James .50
C15 Joe Cribbs .60
C16 Heisman Winners (Pat Sullivan, Bo Jackson, Pat Dye CO) 1.00
C17 Aundray Bruce .50
C18 Aubie (Mascot) .35
C19 Tracy Rocker .35
C20 James Brooks 1.00

1989 Auburn Coke 580

MT
Complete Set (580): 30.00
Common Player: .07
1 Pat Dye (CO) (His First Game) .25
2 Auburn's First Team (1892 Team Photo) .15
3 Pat Sullivan .25
4 Over The Top (Bo Jackson) .75
5 Jimmy Hitchcock .07
6 Walter Gilbert .07
7 Monk Gafford .07
8 Frank D'Agostino .07
9 Joe Childress .15
10 Jim Pyburn .15
11 Tex Warrington .07
12 Travis Tidwell .15
13 Fob James .07
14 Jim Phillips .15
15 Zeke Smith .07
16 Mike Fuller .15
17 Ed Dyas .07
18 Jack Thornton .07
19 Ken Rice .07
20 Freddie Hyatt .07
21 Jackie Burkett .15
22 Jimmy Sidle .15
23 Buddy McClinton .07
24 Larry Willingham .15
25 Bob Harris .07
26 Bill Cody .07
27 Lewis Colbert .07
28 Brent Fullwood .25
29 Tracy Rocker .15
30 Kurt Grain .07
31 Walter Reeves .15
32 Jordan-Hare Stadium .07
33 Ben Tamburello .07
34 Benji Roland .07
35 Chris Knapp .07
36 Dowe Aughtman .07
37 Auburn Tigers Logo .07
38 Tommie Agee .15
39 Bo Jackson .75
40 Freddy Weygand .15
41 Rodney Garner .07
42 Brian Shulman .07
43 Jim Thompson .07
44 Shan Morris .07
45 Ralph (Shug) Jordan (CO) .15
46 Stacy Searels .07
47 1957 Champs (Team Photo) .15
48 Mike Kolen .15
49 A Challenge Met (Pat Dye) .15
50 Mark Dorminey .07
51 Greg Staples .07
52 Randy Campbell .07
53 Duke Donaldson .07
54 Yann Cowart .07
55 Second Blocked Punt (vs. Alabama 1972) .15
56 Keith Uecker .15
57 David Jordan .07
58 Tim Drinkard .07
59 Connie Frederick .07
60 Pat Arrington .07
61 Willie Howell .07
62 Terry Page .07
63 Ben Thomas .07
64 Ron Stallworth .15
65 Charlie Trotman .07
66 Ed West .15
67 James Brooks .50
68 Changing of the Guard (Doug Barfield, Ralph (Shug) Jordan) .15
69 Ken Bernich .07
70 Chris Woods .07
71 Ralph (Shug) Jordan (CO) .15
72 Steve Dennis (CO) .07
73 Reggie Herring (CO) .07
74 Al Del Greco .15
75 Wayne Hall (CO) .07
76 Langdon Hall .07
77 Donnie Humphrey .07
78 Jeff Burger .15
79 Vernon Blackard .07
80 Larry Blakeney (CO) .07
81 Doug Smith .07
82 Two Eras Meet (Ralph (Shug) Jordan, Vince Dooley) .15
83 Kyle Collins .07
84 Bobby Freeman .07
85 Pat Sullivan (CO) .25
86 Neil Callaway (CO) .07
87 William Andrews .25
88 Curtis Kuykendall .07
89 David Campbell .07
90 Seniors of '83 .25
91 Bud Casey (CO) .07
92 Jay Jacobs (CO) .07
93 Al Del Greco .15
94 Pate Mote .07
95 Rob Shuler .07
96 Jerry Beasley .07
97 Pat Washington .07
98 Ed Graham .07
99 Leon Myers .07
100 Paul Davis (CO) .07
101 Tom Banks Jr. .15
102 Mike Simmons .07
103 Alex Bowden .07
104 Jim Bone .07
105 Wincent Harris .07
106 James Daniel .07
107 Jimmy Carter .07
108 Leading Passers (Pat Sullivan) .25
109 Alvin Mitchell .07
110 Mark Clement .07
111 Bob Brown .07
112 Shot Senn .07
113 Loran Carter .07
114 Pat Dye's First Team (Team Photo) .15
115 Bob Hix .07
116 Bo Russell .07
117 Mike Mann .07
118 Mike Shirey .07
119 Pat Dye (CO) .15
120 Kevin Greene .25
121 Auburn Creed .07
122 Jordan's All-Americans (Ralph (Shug) Jordan, Tucker Frederickson, Jimmy Sidle) .15
123 Dave Blanks .07
124 Scott Bolton .07
125 Vince Dooley .15
126 Tim Jessie .07
127 Joe Davis .07
128 Clayton Beauford .07
129 Wilbur Hutsell (AD) .07
130 Joe Whit (CO) .07
131 Gary Kelley .07
132 Bo Jackson .75
133 Aundray Bruce .25
134 Ronny Bellew .07
135 Hindman Wall .07
136 Frank Warren .07
137 Abb Chrietzberg .07
138 Collis Campbell .07
139 Randy Stokes .07
140 Teedy Faulk .07
141 Reese McCall .15
142 Jeff Jackson .07
143 Bill Burgess .15
144 Willie Huntley .07
145 Doug Huntley .07
146 Bacardi Bowl (Walter Gilbert) .07
147 Russ Carreker .07
148 Joe Moon .07
149 A Look Ahead (Pat Dye) (CO) .15
150 Joe Sullivan .07
151 Scott Riley .07
152 Larry Ellis .07
153 Jeff Parks .07
154 Gerald Williams .07
155 Mike Griffith .07
156 First Blocked Punt (vs. Alabama 1972) .15
157 Bill Beckwith (ADMIN) .07
158 Celebration (1957 Action Photo) .15
159 Tommy Carroll .15
160 John Dailey .07
161 George Stephenson .07
162 Danny Arnold .07
163 Mike Edwards .07
164 1894 Auburn-Alabama Trophy .15
165 Don Anderson .07
166 Alvin Briggs .07
167 Herb Waldrop (CO) .07
168 Jim Skuthan .07
169 Alan Hardin .07
170 Coaching Generations (Pat Sullivan, Bobby Freeman) .25
171 Georgia Celebration (1971 Locker Room) .07
172 Auburn 17, Alabama 16 (1972) .15
173 Nat Ceasar .07
174 Billy Hitchcock .15
175 SEC Championship Trophy .15
176 Dr. James E. Martin (PRES) .07
177 Ricky Westbrook .15
178 Fob James .15
179 Stacy Dunn .07
180 Tracy Turner .07
181 Pat Dye (CO) .15
182 In the Record Book (Terry Beasley) .07
183 Ed "Foots" Bauer .07
184 1984 Sugar Bowl Scoreboard .07
185 Mark Robbins .07
186 Paul White (CO) .07
187 Hindman Wall (AD) .07
188 David Beverly .15
189 Sugar Bowl Trophy .07
190 Edmund Nelson .07
191 Edmund Nelson .07
192 Cliff Hare .07
193 Byron Franklin .15
194 Richard Manry .07
195 Malcolm McCary .07
196 Patrick Waters (ADMIN) .07
197 Chester Willis .07
198 Alex Dudchock .07
199 In the Record Book (Pat Sullivan) .25
200 Victory Ride (Pat Dye) (CO) .15
201 Dr. George Petrie (CO) .07
202 D.M. Balliet (CO) .07
203 G.H. Harvey (CO) .07
204 F.M. Hall (CO) .07
205 John Heisman (CO) .25
206 Billy Watkins (CO) .07
207 J.R. Kent (CO) .07
208 Mike Harvey (CO) .07
209 Billy Bates (CO) .07
210 Mike Donahue (CO) .07
211 W.S. Kienholz (CO) .07
212 Mike Donahue (CO) .07
213 Boozer Pitts (CO) .07
214 David Morey (CO) .07
215 George Bohler (CO) .07
216 John Floyd (CO) .07
217 Chet Wynne (CO) .07
218 Jack Meagher (CO) .07
219 Carl Voyles (CO) .07
220 Earl Brown (CO) .07
221 Ralph (Shug) Jordan (CO) .15
222 Doug Barfield (CO) .15
223 Most Career Points (Bo Jackson) .35
224 Sonny Ferguson .07
225 Ronnie Ross .07
226 Gardner Jett .15
227 Jerry Wilson .07
228 Dick Schmatz .07
229 Morris Savage .07
230 James Owens .07
231 Eddie Welch .07
232 Lee Hayley .07
233 Dick Hayley .07
234 Jeff McCollum .07
235 Rick Freeman .07
236 Bobby Freeman (CO) .07
237 Auburn 32, Alabama 22 (Trophy) .15
238 Chip Powell .07
239 Nick Ardillo .07
240 Don Bristow .07
241 Bucky Waid .07
242 Greg Robert .07
243 Ray Rollins .07
244 Tommy Hicks .07
245 Steve Wallace .15
246 David Hughes .07
247 Chuck Hurston .07
248 Jimmy Long .07
249 John Cochran (AD) .07
250 Bobby Davis .07
251 G.W. Clapp .07
252 Jere Colley .07
253 Tim James .07
254 Joe Dolan .07
255 Jerry Gordon .07
256 Billy Edge .07
257 Lawyer Tillman .25
258 John McAfee .07
259 Scotty Long .07
260 Billy Austin .07
261 Tracy Rocker .15
262 Mickey Sutton .07
263 Tommy Traylor .07
264 Billy Van Dyke .07
265 Sam McClurkin .07
266 Mike Flynn .07
267 Jim Sirmans .07
268 Reggie Ware .15
269 Bill Luke .07
270 Don Machen .07
271 Bill Grisham .07
272 Bruce Evans .07
273 Hank Hall .07
274 Tommy Lunceford .07
275 Pat Thomas .07
276 Marvin Trott .07
277 Brad Everett .07
278 Frank Reeves .07
279 Bishop Reeves .07
280 Carver Reeves .07
281 Billy Haas .07
282 Dye's First AU Bowl (Pat Dye) (CO) .15
283 Nate Hill .07
284 Bucky Howard .07
285 Tim Christian .07
286 Tim Christian (CO) .07
287 Tom Nettleman .07
288 Carl Hubbard .07
289 Auburn's Biggest Wins (Chart) .07
290 Jay Jacobs .07
291 Jimmy Pettus .07
292 Cliff Hare Stadium .07
293 Richard Wood .15
294 Sandy Cannon .07
295 Bill Braswell .07
296 Foy Thompson .07
297 Robert Margeson .07
298 Pipeline to the Pros (Seven Pro Players) .25
299 Bill Evans .07
300 Marvin Tucker .07
301 Jack Locklear .07
302 Mike Locklear .07
303 Harry Wright .07
304 Lee Marke Sellers .07
305 Ted Foret .07
306 Bobby Foret .07
307 Mike Neel .07
308 Rick Neel .07
309 Mike Alford .07
310 Mac Crawford .07
311 Bill Cunningham .07
312 Legends (Pat Sullivan, Jeff Burger) .25
313 Frank LaRussa .07
314 Chris Vacarella .07
315 Gerald Robinson .15
316 Ronnie Baynes .07
317 Dave Edwards .07
318 Steve Taylor .07
319 Phillip Gilchrist .07
320 Ben McCurdy .07
321 Dave Hill .07
322 Jimmy Reynolds .07
323 Chuck Fletcher .07
324 Bogue Miller .07
325 Dave Beck .07
326 Johnny Simmons .07
327 Howard Simpson .07
328 Benny Sivley .15
329 1953 SEC Champions (Team Photo) .15
330 Frank Cox .07
331 Phil Gargis .07
332 Don Webb .07
333 Dan Presley .07
334 Al Giffin .07
335 Don Lewis .07
336 Eric Floyd .15
337 Stadium (Ralph (Shug) Jordan) .15
338 Terry Hendly .07
339 Billy Atkins .07
340 Tony Long .07
341 Jimmy Clemmer .07
342 John Valentine .07
343 Bruce Bylsma .07
344 Merrill Shirley .07
345 Kenny Howard (CO) .07
346 Hal Hamrick .07
347 Greg Zipp .07
348 Mac Champion .07
349 Most Tackles in One Game (Kurt Crain) .07
350 Leading Career Rushers (Bo Jackson) .35
351 Homer Williams .07
352 Mike Gates .07
353 Rusty Fuller .07
354 Rusty Deen .07
355 Stalwart Defenders (Bob Harris, Mark Dorminey) .07
356 Heroes of '56 (Ralph (Shug) Jordan, Jerry Elliott, Frank Reeves) .15
357 Road to the Top (Cartoon) .15
358 Cleve Wester .07
359 Line Stars (Jackie Burkett, Zeke Smith) .15
360 Bob Scarbrough .07
361 Jimmy Speigner .07
362 Danny Speigner .07
363 Alvin Bresler .07
364 Wade Whatley .07
365 Lance Hill .07
366 Andy Steele .07
367 John Whatley .07
368 Alton Shell .07
369 Larry Blakeney .07
370 Mickey Zofko .07
371 Gene Lorendo (CO) .07
372 Mac Lorendo .07
373 Buddy Davidson (CO) .07
374 Dave Woodward .07
375 Richard Guthrie .07
376 George Rose .07
377 Alan Bollinger .07
378 Danny Sanspree .07
379 Winky Giddens .07
380 Franklin Fuller .07
381 Charles Collins .07
382 Auburn, 23-22 (Scoreboard) .07
383 Jeff Weekley .07
384 Larry Haynie .07
385 Miles Jones .07
386 Bobby Wilson .15
387 Bobby Lauder .07
388 Charlie Glenn .07
389 Claude Saia .07
390 Tom Bryan .07
391 Lee Gross .07
392 Jerry Popwell .07
393 Tommy Groat .07
394 Neal Dettmering .07
395 Dr. W.S. Bailey (ADMIN) .07
396 Jim Pitts .07
397 College Football History (Cliff Hare Stadium) .07
398 Doc Griffith .07
399 Liston Eddins .07
400 Woody Woodall .07
401 Auburn Helmet .07
402 Skip Johnston .07
403 Trey Gainous .07
404 Randy Walls .07
405 Jimmy Partin .07
406 Dick Ingwerson .07
407 David Shelby .07
408 Harry Ward .07
409 Thomas Gossom .07
410 Sanford T. Gower .07
411 Architects of the Future (Jeff Beard, Ralph (Shug) Jordan) .15
412 Ed Butler .07
413 Bob Butler .07
414 Ben Strickland .07
415 Jeff Lott .07
416 Harris Rabren .07
417 Mike McQuaig .07
418 Steve Wilson .07
419 Jorge Portela .07
420 Dave Middleton .15
421 Tommy Yearout .07
422 Gusty Yearout .07
423 The Auburn Stadium .07
424 Cliff Hare Stadium .07
425 Oscar Burford .07
426 Cliff Hare Stadium .07
427 Cliff Hare Stadium .07
428 Jordan-Hare Stadium .07
429 Jack Meagher (CO) .07
430 Jeff Beard (AD) .07
431 Frank Young (ADMIN) .07
432 Frank Riley .07
433 Ernie Warren .07
434 Brian Atkins .07
435 George Atkins .07
436 Ricky Sanders .35
437 George Kenmore .07
438 Don Heller .07
439 Pat Meagher .07
440 Tim Davis .07
441 Tiger Meat (Cooks) .07
442 Joe Connally (CO) .07
443 Bob Newton .15
444 Bill Newton .07
445 David Langner .07
446 Charlie Langner .07
447 Brownie Flournoy (ADMIN) .07
448 Mike Hicks .07
449 Larry Hill .07
450 Tim Baker .07
451 Danny Bentley .07
452 Tommy Lowry .07
453 Jim Price .07
454 Lloyd Nix .07
455 Kenny Burks .07
456 Rusty Deen, Sallie Deen (ADMIN) .07
457 Johnny Sumner .07
458 Scott Blackmon .07
459 Chuck Maxime .07
460 Big SEC Wins (Chart) .07
461 Bo Davis .07
462 George Rose .07
463 Bob Bradley .07
464 Steve Osburne .07
465 George Gross .07
466 Andy Gross .07
467 M.L. Brackett .07
468 Herman Wilkes .07
469 Roger Mitchell .07
470 Bobby Beaird .07
471 Sammy Oates .07
472 Jimmy Ricketts .07
473 Bucky Ayters .07
474 Bill James .07
475 Johnny Wallis .07
476 Chris Jornson .07
477 Joe Overton .07
478 Tommy Lorino .07
479 James Warren .07
480 Lynn Johnson .07
481 Sam Mitchell .07
482 Sedrick McIntyre .07
483 Mike Holtzclaw .07
484 Dave Ostrowski .07
485 Jim Walsh .07
486 Mike Henley .07
487 Roy Tatum .07
488 Al Parks .07
489 Billy Wilson .15
490 Ken Luke .07
491 Phillip Hall .07
492 Bruce Yates .07
493 Dan Hataway .07
494 Joe Leichtnam .07
495 Danny Fulford .07
496 Ken Hardy .07
497 Rob Spivey .07
498 Rick Telhiard .07
499 Ron Yarbrough .07
500 Leo Sexton .07
501 Dick McGowen (CO) .07
502 Lee Kidd .07
503 Rex McKissick .07
504 Fagen Canzoneri, Zach Jenkins .07
505 Jim Bouchillon .07
506 Forrest Blue .25
507 Mike Helms .07
508 Bobby Hunt .15
509 John Liptak .07
510 James McKinney .07
511 Ed Baker .07
512 Heisman Trophies .25
513 Eddy Jackson .07
514 Jimmy Powell .07
515 Jerry Elliott .07
516 Jimmy Jones .07
517 Jimmy Laster .07
518 Larry Laster .07
519 Jerry Sansom .07
520 Don Downs .07
521 Danny Skutack .07
522 Keith Green .07
523 Spence McCracken .07
524 Lloyd Cheatton .07
525 Mike Shows .07
526 Spec Kelley .07
527 Dick McGowen .07
528 Jon Kilgore .07
529 Frank Gatski .25
530 Joel Eaves .07
531 John Adcock .07
532 Jimmy Fenton .07
533 Mike McCartney .07
534 Harrison McCraw .07
535 Mailon Kent .07
536 Dickie Flournoy .07
537 Coker Barton .07
538 Scotty Elam .07
539 Tim Wood .07
540 Terry Fuller .07
541 Johnny Kern .07
542 Mike Currier .07
543 Richard Cheek .07
544 Dan Dickerson .07
545 Arnold Fagen .07
546 John "Rat" Riley .07
547 Jimmy Burson .15
548 Bob Fleming .07
549 Mike Fitzhugh .07
550 Jim Patton .25
551 Bryant Harvard .07
552 Leon Cochran .07
553 Wayne Frazier .07
554 Phillip Dembowski .07
555 Alex Spurlin, Ed Spurlin .07
556 Bill Kilpatrick .07
557 Gaines Lanier .07
558 Johnny McDonald .07
559 Ray Powell .07
560 Jimmy Putman .07
561 Bobby Wasden .07
562 Roger Pruett .07
563 Don Braswell .07
564 Jim Jeffery .07
565 Auburn - A TV Favorite (Pat Dye) (CO) .15
566 Lamar Rawson .07
567 Larry Rawson .07
568 David Rawson .07
569 Hal Herring (CO) .07
570 Pat Sullivan .25
571 John Cochran .07
572 Jerry Gulledge .07
573 Steve Stanaland .15
574 Greg Zipp .07
575 John Trotman .07
576 Clyde Baumgartner .07
577 Jay Casey .07
578 Ralph O'Gwynne .07
579 Sid Scarborough .07
580 Tom Banks Sr. .07

1991 Auburn Hoby

MT
Complete Set (42): 9.00
Common Player: .25
523 Thomas Bailey .25
524 Corey Barlow .35
525 Reggie Barlow .35
526 Fred Baxter .35
527 Eddie Blake .35
528 Herbert Casey .25
529 Pedro Cherry .25
530 Darrel Crawford .25
531 Tim Cromartie .35
532 Juan Crum .25
533 Karekin Cunningham .25
534 Alonzo Etheridge .25
535 Joe Frazier .25
536 Pat Dye (AD/CO) .35
537 Thery George .35
538 Chris Gray .35
539 Victor Hall .25
540 Randy Hart .25
541 Chris Holland .25
542 Chuckie Johnson .25
543 Anthony Judge .25
544 Corey Lewis .25
545 Reid McMillion .25
546 Bob Meeks .25
547 Dale Overton .25
548 Mike Pelton .35
549 Bennie Pierce .25
550 Mike Pina .25
551 Anthony Redmon .25
552 Tony Richardson .25
553 Richard Shea .25
554 Fred Smith .35
555 Otis Mounds .25
556 Ricky Sutton .25
557 Alex Thomas .25
558 Greg Thompson .25
559 Tim Tillman .25
560 Jim Von Wyl .25
561 Stan White .50
562 Darrell Williams .25
563 James Willis .25
564 Jon Wilson .25

1993 Baylor

MT
Complete Set (21): 15.00
Common Player: .75
1 Lamone Alexander .75
2 Joseph Asbell .75
3 Marvin Callies .75
4 Todd Crawford .75
5 Earnest Crownover .75
6 Will Davidson 1.00
7 Chris Dull .75
8 Raynor Finley .75
9 J.J. Joe 2.00
10 Phillip Kent .75
11 David Leaks .75
12 Scotty Lewis 1.00
13 Fred Miller 1.00
14 Bruce Nowak .75
15 Mike Oatis .75
16 Chuck Pope .75
17 Adrian Robinson 2.00
18 Tyrone Smith .75
19 Andrew Swasey .75
20 Byron Thompson .75
21 Tony Tubbs .75

1984 BYU All-Time Greats

MT
Complete Set (15): 18.00
Common Player: .50
1 Steve Young 10.00
2 Eldon Fortie .50
3 Bart Oates 1.50
4 Pete Van Valkenburg .60
5 Mike Mees .50
6 Wayne Baker .50
7 Gordon Gravelle .60
8 Gordon Hudson .60
9 Kurt Gunther .50
10 Todd Shell .60
11 Chris Farasopoulos 1.00
12 Paul Howard .50
13 Dave Atkinson .50
14 Paul Linford .50
15 Phil Odle .60

1984-85 BYU ational Champions

MT
Complete Set (15): 25.00
Common Player: 1.50
1 Mark Allen 1.50
2 Adam Hysbert 1.50
3 Larry Hamilton 1.50
4 Jim Hermann 1.50
5 Kyle Morrell 2.00
6 Lee Johnson 1.50
7 David Mills 1.50
8 Garrick Wright, Match Wright, Anae Wright, Louis Wong 3.00
9 Jim Hermann, Larry Hamilton 2.00
10 Louis Wong 1.50
11 Bosco in Holiday Bowl (Robbie Bosco) 5.00
12 BYU Cougar Stadium 1.50
13 UPI Final Top 20 1.50
14 BYU National Championship Roster 1.50
15 Schedule and Scores For 1984 1.50

1990 BYU Safety

MT
Complete Set (12): 15.00
Common Player: 1.00
1 Rocky Beigel 1.00
2 Matt Bellini 1.50
3 Tony Crutchfield 1.00
4 Ty Detmer 6.00
5 Norm Dixon 1.00
6 Earl Kauffman 1.50
7 Rich Kaufusi 1.50
8 Bryan May 1.00
9 Brent Nyberg 1.00
10 Chris Smith 1.50
11 Mark Smith 1.00
12 Robert Stephens 1.00

1991 BYU Safety

MT
Complete Set (16): 10.00
Common Player: .75
1 Josh Arnold .75
2 Rocky Biegel .75
3 Scott Charlton .75
4 Tony Crutchfield .75
5 Ty Detmer 3.00
6 LaVell Edwards (CO) 1.50
7 Scott Giles .75
8 Derwin Gray 1.00
9 Shad Hansen .75
10 Brad Hunter .75
11 Earl Kauffman .75
12 Jared Leavitt .75
13 Micah Matsuzaki .75
14 Bryan May .75

15	Peter Tuipulotu	.75
16	Matt Zundel	.75

1992 BYU Safety

		MT
Complete Set (16):		10.00
Common Player:		.60
1	Tyler Anderson	.60
2	Randy Brock	.60
3	Brad Clark	.60
4	Eric Drage	1.00
5	LaVell Edwards (CO)	1.00
6	Mike Empey	.60
7	Lenny Gomes	.60
8	Derwin Gray	1.00
9	Shad Hansen	.60
10	Eli Herring	.75
11	Micah Matsuzaki	.60
12	Patrick Mitchell	.75
13	Garry Pay	.60
14	Greg Pitts	.60
15	Byron Rex	.75
16	Jamal Willis	1.00

1993 BYU

		MT
Complete Set (20):		12.00
Common Player:		.60
1	Tyler Anderson	.60
2	Randy Brock	.75
3	Frank Christianson	.60
4	Eric Drage	1.00
5	LaVell Edwards	.75
6	Mike Empey	.60
7	Lenny Gomes	.75
8	Kalin Hall	.60
9	Nathan Hall	.60
10	Hema Heimuli	.75
11	Todd Herget	.60
12	Eli Herring	.75
13	Micah Matsuzaki	.60
14	Casey Mazzota	.60
15	Patrick Mitchell	.60
16	Evan Pilgrim	1.00
17	Greg Pitts	.60
18	Vic Tarleton	.60
19	John Walsh	3.00
20	Jamal Willis	1.00

1988 California Smokey

		MT
Complete Set (12):		12.00
Common Player:		1.25
1	Rob Bimson	1.25
2	Joel Dickson	1.25
3	Robert DosRemedios	1.25
4	Mike Ford	1.25
5	Darryl Ingram	1.25
6	David Ortega	1.25
7	Chris Richards	1.25
8	Bruce Snyder (CO)	1.50
9	Troy Taylor	2.00
10	Natu Tuatagaloa	2.00
11	Majett Whiteside	1.25
12	Dave Zawatson	1.25

1989 California Smokey

		MT
Complete Set (16):		12.00
Common Player:		1.00
1	John Hardy	1.00
2	Mike Ford	1.00
10	Robbie Keen	1.00
11	Troy Taylor	1.25
20	Dwayne Jones	1.00
21	Travis Oliver	1.00
34	Darrin Greer	1.00
40	David Ortega	1.00
41	Dan Slevin	1.00
52	Troy Auzenne	3.00
69	Tony Smith	1.00
80	Junior Tagaloa	1.00
83	Michael Smith	1.00
95	DeWayne Odom	1.00
99	Joel Dickson	1.00
NNO	Bruce Snyder (CO)	1.25

1990 California Smokey

		MT
Complete Set (16):		10.00
Common Player:		.75
1	Troy Auzenne (52)	2.00
2	John Belli (61)	.75
3	Joel Dickson (99)	.75
4	Ron English (42)	.75
5	Rhett Hall (57)	2.00
6	John Hardy (1)	.75
7	Robbie Keen (10)	.75
8	DeWayne Odom (95)	.75
9	Mike Pawlawski (9)	1.50
10	Castle Redmond (37)	.75
11	James Richards (64)	.75
12	Ernie Rogers (68)	.75
13	Bruce Snyder (CO)	1.00
14	Brian Treggs (3)	1.00
15	Anthony Wallace (6)	.75
16	Greg Zomalt (28)	.75

1991 California Smokey

		MT
Complete Set (16):		14.00
Common Player:		.75
1	Troy Auzenne	1.50
2	Chris Cannon	.75
3	Cornell Collier	.75
4	Sean Dawkins	3.00
5	Steve Gordon	.75
6	Mike Pawlawski	1.25
7	Bruce Snyder (CO)	1.00
8	Todd Steussie	2.00
9	Mack Travis	.75
10	Brian Treggs	1.00
11	Russell White	2.00
12	Jason Wilborn	.75
13	David Wilson	.75
14	Brent Woodall	.75
15	Eric Zomalt	1.25
16	Greg Zomalt	.75

1992 California Smokey

		MT
Complete Set (16):		10.00
Common Player:		.60
1	Chidi Ahanotu	.60
2	Wolf Barber	.60
3	Mick Barsala	.60
4	Doug Brien	1.50
5	Al Casner	.60
6	Lindsey Chapman	.60
7	Sean Dawkins	2.50
8	Keith Gilbertson (CO)	.75
9	Eric Mahlum	1.00
10	Chris Noonan	.60
11	Todd Steussie	1.50
12	Mack Travis	.60
13	Russell White	1.50
14	Jerrott Willard	1.00
15	Eric Zomalt	1.00
16	Greg Zomalt	.60

1993 California Smokey

		MT
Complete Set (16):		10.00
Common Player:		.60
1	Dave Barr	2.00
2	Doug Brien	1.25
3	Mike Caldwell	.60
4	Lindsey Chapman	.60
5	Jerod Cherry	1.00
6	Michael Davis	.60
7	Tyrone Edwards	.60
8	Keith Gilbertson (CO)	.60
9	Jody Graham	.60
10	Marty Holly	.60
11	Paul Joiner	.60
12	Eric Mahlum	.75
13	Damien Semien	.60
14	Todd Steussie	1.25
15	Jerrott Willard	.75
16	Eric Zomalt	.75

1995 California Smokey

		MT
Complete Set (16):		8.00
Common Player:		.50
1	Pat Barnes	.50
2	Nai'il Benjamin	.60
3	Sean Bullard	.50
4	Je'Rod Cherry	.50
5	Duane Clemons	1.00
6	Dante Depaola	.50
7	Kevin Devine	.50
8	Keith Gilbertson (CO)	.60
9	Andy Jacobs	.50
10	Ryan Longwell	.50
11	Ben Lynch	.50
12	Reynard Rutherford	.50
13	James Stallworth	.50
14	Regan Upshaw	2.00
15	Iheanyi Uwaezuoke	.75
16	Brandon Whiting	.50

1989 Clemson

		MT
Complete Set (32):		20.00
Common Player:		.75
1	Wally Ake (CO)	.75
2	Larry Beckman (CO)	.75
3	Mitch Belton (32)	.75
4	Scott Beville (61)	.75
5	Doug Brewster (92)	.75
6	Larry Brinson (CO)	1.00
7	Reggie Demps (30)	.75
8	Robin Eaves (44)	.75
9	Barney Farrar (CO)	.75
10	Stacy Fields (46)	.75
11	Vance Hammond (90)	.75
12	Eric Harmon (76)	.75
13	Ken Hatfield (CO)	1.50
14	Jerome Henderson (36)	1.50
15	Les Herrin (CO)	.75
16	Roger Hinshaw (CO)	.75
17	John Johnson (12)	1.50
18	Reggie Lawrence (34)	.75
19	Stacy Long (67)	.75
20	Eric Mader (82)	.75
21	Arlington Nunn (39)	.75
22	David Puckett (68)	.75
23	Danny Sizer (54)	.75
24	Robbie Spector (2)	.75
25	Rick Stockstill (CO)	1.00
26	Bruce Taylor (6)	.75
27	Doug Thomas (41)	.75
28	The Tiger (Mascot)	.75
29	Tiger Paw Title Card	.75
30	Bob Trott (CO)	.75
31	Larry Van Der Heyden (CO)	.75
32	Richard Wilson (CO)	.75

1950 C.O.P. Betsy Ross

		NM
Complete Set (6):		75.00
Common Player:		8.00
1	Don Campora	8.00
2	Don Hardey	8.00
3	Robert Klein	8.00
4	Eddie LeBaron	35.00
5	Eddie Macon	15.00
6	John Rohde	8.00

1990 Colorado Smokey

		MT
Complete Set (16):		16.00
Common Player:		.75
1	Eric Bieniemy	2.50
2	Joe Garten	1.00
3	Darian Hagan	2.00
4	George Hemingway	.75
5	Garry Howe	.75
6	Tim James	.75
7	Charles Johnson	2.50
8	Bill McCartney (CO)	2.00
9	Dave McCloughan	1.00
10	Kanavis McGhee	1.00
11	Mike Pritchard	5.00
12	Tom Rouen	1.00
13	Michael Simmons	.75
14	Mark Vander Poel	1.00
15	Alfred Williams	2.50
16	Ralphie (Mascot)	.75

1992 Colorado Pepsi

		MT
Complete Set (12):		15.00
Common Player:		1.00
1	Greg Biekert	2.00
2	Pat Blottiaux	1.00
3	Ronnie Bradford	1.50
4	Chad Brown	2.50
5	Marcellous Elder	1.50
6	Deon Figures	2.50
7	Jim Hansen	1.00
8	Jack Keys	1.00
9	Bill McCartney (CO)	2.00
10	Clint Moles	1.00
11	Jason Perkins	1.00
12	Scott Starr	1.00

1993 Colorado Smokey

		MT
Complete Set (16):		15.00
Common Player:		1.00
1	Craig Anderson	1.00
2	Mitch Berger	1.50
3	Jeff Brunner	1.00
4	Dennis Collier	1.00
5	Dwayne Davis	1.00
6	Brian Dyet	1.00
7	Sean Embree	1.00
8	Garrett Ford	1.00
9	James Hill	1.00
10	Charles Johnson	3.00
11	Greg Lindsey	1.00
12	Sam Rogers	1.00
13	Mark Smith	1.00
14	Duke Tobin	1.00
15	Ron Woolfork	1.50
16	Derek Agnew	1.00

1994 Colorado Smokey

		MT
Complete Set (16):		18.00
Common Player:		.75
1	Blake Anderson	.75
2	Norm Barnett	.75
3	Tony Berti	1.00
4	Ken Browne	.75
5	Christian Fauria	2.00
6	Darius Holland	1.50
7	Chris Hudson	1.00
8	Ted Johnson	1.50
9	Vance Joseph	.75
10	Jon Knutson	.75
11	Bill McCartney (CO)	1.50
12	Erik Mitchell	.75
13	Kordell Stewart	8.00
14	Derek West	.75
15	Michael Westbrook	4.00
16	Team Logo	.75

1973 Colorado State

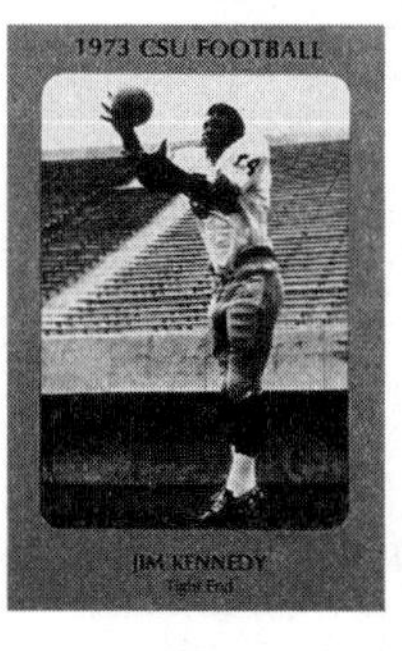
1973 CSU FOOTBALL
JIM KENNEDY
Tight End

		NM
Complete Set (8):		75.00
Common Player:		6.00
1	Wes Cerveny	6.00
2	Mark Driscoll	6.00
3	Jim Kennedy	6.00
4	Greg Kuhn	6.00
5	Willie Miller	20.00
6	Al Simpson (SP)	12.00
7	Jan Stuebbe (SP)	12.00
8	Tom Wallace	6.00

1987 Duke Police

		MT
Complete Set (16):		25.00
Common Player:		1.50
1	Andy Andreasik (60)	1.50
2	Brian Bernard (93)	1.50
3	Bob Calamari (31)	1.50
4	Jason Cooper (22)	1.50
5	Dave Demore (92)	1.50
6	Mike Dimitrio (21)	1.50
7	Jim Godfrey (56)	1.50
8	Doug Green (5)	1.50
9	Stanley Monk (24)	1.50
10	Chris Port (73)	2.00
11	Steve Ryan (63)	1.50
12	Steve Slayden (7)	2.00
13	Steve Spurrier (CO)	9.00
14	Dewayne Terry (27)	1.50
15	Fonda Williams (19)	1.50
16	Blue Devil (Mascot)	2.00

1988 Florida Burger King

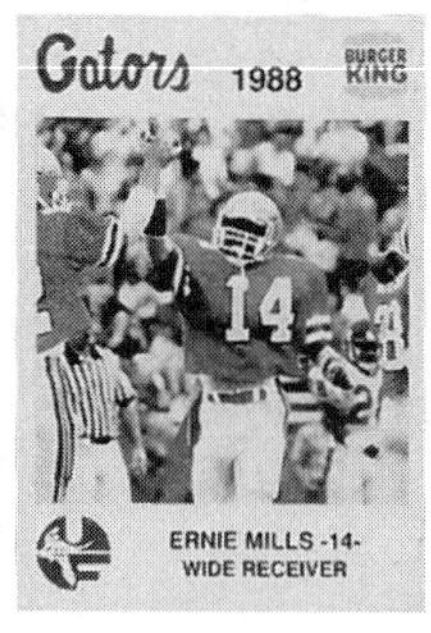
Gators 1988
BURGER KING
ERNIE MILLS -14-
WIDE RECEIVER

		MT
Complete Set (16):		60.00
Common Player:		.75
1	Florida Gators Team	5.00
2	Emmitt Smith (22)	45.00
3	David Williams (73)	1.25
4	Jeff Roth (96)	.75
5	Rhondy Weston (68)	1.00
6	Stacey Simmons (25)	1.00
7	Huey Richardson (90)	1.25
8	Wayne Williams (23)	1.00
9	Charlie Wright (79)	.75
10	Tracy Daniels (63)	.75
11	Ernie Mills (14)	3.00
12	Willie McGrady (38)	.75
13	Chris Bromley (52)	.75
14	Louis Oliver (18)	2.00
15	Galen Hall (CO)	1.25
16	Albert the Alligator (Mascot)	.75

1989 Florida

		MT
Complete Set (22):		16.00
Common Player:		.50
1	Dale Van Sickle	.50
2	Cris Collinsworth	1.00
3	Wilber Marshall	1.50
4	Jack Youngblood	1.00
5	Steve Spurrier	4.00
6	David Little	.75
7	Bruce Bennett	.50
8	Charlie LaPradd	.50
9	John L. Williams	1.50
10	Steve Tannen	.75
11	Neal Anderson	1.50
12	Larry Dupree	.50
13	Guy Dennis	.50
14	Jarvis Williams	.75
15	Bill Carr	.50
16	Clifford Charlton	.50
17	Wes Chandler	1.00
18	David Galloway	.50
19	Carlos Alvarez	.50
20	Lomas Brown	1.00
21	Larry Smith	.50
22	Ricky Nattiel	.75

1989 Florida Smokey

		MT
Complete Set (16):		35.00
Common Player:		1.00
1	Chris Bromley (52)	1.00
2	Richard Fain (28)	1.25
3	John David Francis (7)	1.00
4	Galen Hall (CO) (SP)	7.00
5	Tony Lomack (20)	1.00
6	Willie McClendon (5)	1.00
7	Pat Moorer (45)	1.00
8	Kyle Morris (1)	1.00
9	Huey Richardson (90)	1.25
10	Stacey Simmons (25)	1.00
11	Emmitt Smith (22)	25.00
12	Richard Starowesky (75)	1.00
13	Kerry Watkins (4)	1.00
14	Albert (Mascot)	1.00
15	Cheerleaders	1.25
16	Gator Helmet	1.00

1990 Florida Smokey

		MT
Complete Set (12):		15.00
Common Player:		1.00
1	Terence Barber (3)	1.00
2	Chris Bromley (52)	1.00
3	Richard Fain (28)	1.25
4	Willie McClendon (5)	1.25
5	Dexter McNabb (21)	1.25
6	Ernie Mills (14)	2.50
7	Mark Murray (54)	1.00
8	Jerry Odom	1.00
9	Huey Richardson (90)	1.25
10	Steve Spurrier (CO)	4.00
11	Albert and Alberta (Mascots)	1.00
12	Mr. Two-Birts (Fan)	1.00

1991 Florida Smokey

		MT
Complete Set (12):		12.00
Common Player:		1.00
1	Ephesians Bartley	1.25
2	Mike Brandon	1.00
3	Brad Culpepper	1.50
4	Arden Czyzewski	1.00
5	Cal Dixon	1.25
6	Tre Everett	1.00
7	Hesham Ismail	1.00
8	Shane Matthews	2.50
9	Steve Spurrier (CO)	4.00
10	Mark White	1.00
11	Will White	1.00
12	Albert and Alberta (Mascots)	1.00

1993 Florida State

		MT
Complete Set (6):		85.00
Common Player:		6.00
1	Bobby Bowden (CO)	15.00
2	Derrick Brooks	15.00
3	Corey Sawyer	10.00
4	Tamarick Vanover	30.00
5	Charlie Ward	25.00
6	Chief Osceola (Mascot)	6.00

1996 Florida State

		MT
Complete Set (12):		10.00
Common Player:		.50
1	Chad Bates, Todd Fordham	.50
2	Scott Bentley	1.00
3	Byron Capers	.75
4	James Colzie	.75
5	Andre Cooper	1.00
6	Henri Crockett	1.00
7	Warrick Dunn	5.00
8	Sean Hamlet	.75
9	Sean Liss	.75
10	Wayne Messam	1.00
11	Connell Spain	1.00
12	Reinard Wilson	2.00

1986 Fort Hayes State

		MT
Complete Set (27):		30.00
Common Player:		1.25
1	Kelly Barnard	1.25
2	James Bess	1.25
3	Eric Busenbark	1.25
4	Sylvester Butler	1.25
5	Channing Day	1.25
6	Edward Faagai	1.25
7	Randy Fayette	1.25
8	Gerald Hall	1.25
9	Mike Hipp	1.25
10	Sam Holloway	1.25
11	Howard Hood	1.25
12	James Jermon	1.25
13	Randy Jordan	1.25
14	John Kelsh	1.25
15	Randy Knox	1.25
16	Robert Long	1.25
17	Les Miller	1.25
18	Frankie Neal	1.25
19	Paul Nelson	1.25
20	Darryl Pittman	1.25
21	Mike Shoff	1.25
22	Kip Stewart	1.25
23	Rod Timmons	1.25
24	Rob Ukleya	1.25
25	John Vincent (CO)	1.25
26	Rick Wheeler	1.25
27	Mike Worth	1.25

1987 Fresno State Burger King

		MT
Complete Set (16):		25.00
Common Player:		1.50
1	Gene Taylor	1.50
5	Michael Stewart	3.00
9	Kevin Sweeney	3.00
12	Eric Buechele	1.50
19	Rod Webster	1.50
26	Kelly Skipper	1.50
27	Barry Belli	1.50
32	Kelly Brooks	1.50
45	David Grayson	2.00
67	Jethro Franklin	1.50
71	Jeff Truschel	1.50
80	John O'Leary	1.50
81	Stephen Baker	3.00
83	Henry Ellard	6.00
86	Stephone Paige	4.00
NNO	Jim Sweeney (CO)	2.00

1989 Fresno State Smokey

		MT
Complete Set (16):		15.00
Common Player:		1.00
1	Mark Barsotti	1.00
2	Rich Bartlewski	1.00
3	Ron Cox	2.50
4	Myron Jones	1.00
5	Steve Loop	1.00
6	Fil Lujan	1.00
7	Darrel Martin	1.00
8	Lance Oberparleiter	1.00
9	Dwight Pickens	1.00
10	Marquez Pope	3.00
11	Nick Ruggeroli	1.00
12	Jim Sweeney CO	1.50
13	Jeff Thiesen	1.00
14	Paul Vial	1.00
15	James Williams	1.00
16	Bulldog Stadium	1.00

1990 Fresno State Smokey

		MT
Complete Set (16):		15.00
Common Player:		1.00
1	Mark Barsotti	1.25
2	Ron Cox	1.50
3	Aaron Craver	1.50
4	DeVonne Edwards	1.00
5	Courtney Griffin	1.00
6	Jesse Hardwick	1.00
7	Melvin Johnson	1.00
8	Brian Lasho	1.00
9	Kelvin Means	1.00
10	Marquez Pope	2.50
11	Zack Rix	1.00
12	Nick Ruggeroli	1.00
13	Jim Sweeney (CO)	1.25
14	Erick Tanuvasa	1.00
15	Jeff Thiesen	1.00
16	James Williams	1.50

1988 Georgia McDag

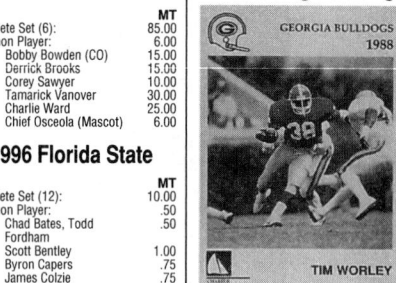

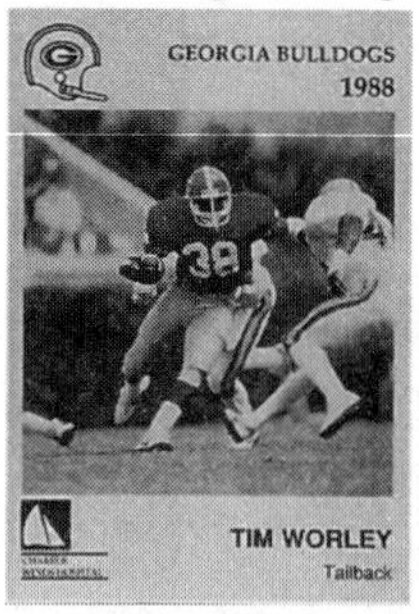
GEORGIA BULLDOGS
1988
TIM WORLEY
Tailback

		MT
Complete Set (16):		65.00
Common Player:		1.00
1	UGA IV (Mascot)	1.00
2	Vince Dooley (AD/CO)	3.00
3	Steve Crumley	1.00
4	Aaron Chubb	1.00
5	Keith Henderson	2.00
6	Steve Harmon	1.00
7	Terrie Webster	1.00
8	John Kasay	4.00
9	Wayne Johnson	1.00
10	Tim Worley	2.00
11	Wycliffe Lovelace	1.00
12	Brent Collins	1.00
13	Vince Guthrie	1.00
14	Todd Wheeler	1.00
15	Bill Goldberg	50.00
16	Rodney Hampton	7.00

1989 Georgia 200

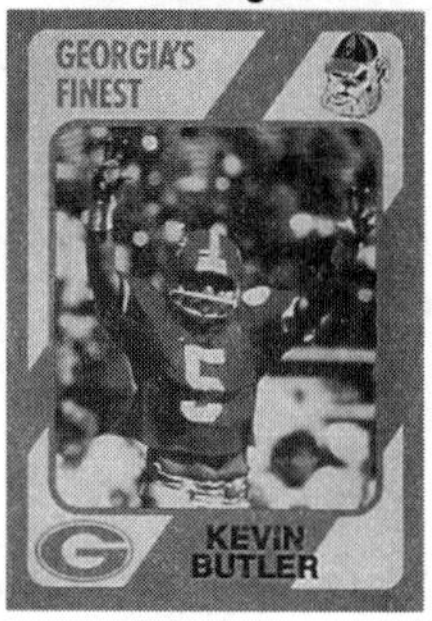
GEORGIA'S FINEST
KEVIN BUTLER

		MT
Complete Set (200):		18.00
Common Player:		.10
1	Vince Dooley (AD)	.20
2	Ivy M. Shiver	.10
3	Vince Dooley (CO)	.20
4	Vince Dooley (CO)	.20
5	Ray Goff (CO)	.20
6	Ray Goff (CO)	.20
7	Wally Butts (CO)	.20
8	Wally Butts (CO)	.20
9	Herschel Walker	.75
10	Frank Sinkwich	.20
11	Bob McWhorter	.10
12	Joe Bennett	.10
13	Dan Edwards	.10
14	Tom A. Nash	.10
15	Herb Maffett	.10
16	Ralph Maddox	.10
17	Vernon Smith	.10
18	Bill Hartman Jr.	.10
19	Frank Sinkwich	.20
20	Joe O'Malley	.10
21	Mike Castronis	.10
22	Aschel M. Day	.10
23	Herb St. John	.10
24	Craig Hertwig	.10
25	Johnny Rauch	.20
26	Harry Babcock	.10
27	Bruce Kemp	.10
28	Pat Dye	.20
29	Fran Tarkenton	1.00
30	Larry Kohn	.10
31	Ray Rissmiller	.10
32	George Patton	.20
33	Mixon Robinson	.10
34	Lynn Hughes	.10
35	Bill Stanfill	.20
36	Robert Dicks	.10
37	Lynn Hunnicutt	.10
38	Tommy Lyons	.10
39	Royce Smith	.10
40	Steve Greer	.10
41	Randy Johnson	.20
42	Mike Wilson	.10
43	Joel Parrish	.10
44	Ben Zambiasi	.20
45	Allan Leavitt	.10
46	George Collins	.10
47	Rex Robinson	.10
48	Scott Woerner	.10
49	Herschel Walker	.75
50	Bob Burns	.10
51	Jimmy Payne	.10
52	Fred Brown	.10
53	Kevin Butler	.20
54	Don Porterfield	.10
55	Mac McWhorter	.10
56	John Little	.10
57	Marion Campbell	.20
58	Zeke Bratkowski	.30
59	Buck Belue	.20
60	Duward Pennington	.10
61	Lamar Davis	.10
62	Steve Wilson	.10
63	Leman L. Rosenberg	.10
64	Dennis Hughes	.10
65	Wayne Radloff	.10
66	Lindsay Scott	.20
67	Wayne Swinford	.10
68	Kim Stephens	.10

69 Willie McClendon .20
70 Ron Jenkins .10
71 Jeff Lewis .10
72 Larry Rakestraw .10
73 Spike Jones .20
74 Tom Nash Jr. .10
75 Vassa Cate .10
76 Theron Sapp .20
77 Claude Hipps .20
78 Charley Trippi .30
79 Mike Weaver .10
80 Anderson Johnson .10
81 Matt Robinson .20
82 Bill Krug .10
83 Todd Wheeler .10
84 Mack Guest .10
85 Frank Ros .10
86 Jeff Hipp .10
87 Milton Leathers .10
88 George Morton .10
89 Jim Broadway .10
90 Tim Morrison .10
91 Homer Key .10
92 Richard Tardits .20
93 Tommy Thurson .10
94 Bob Kelley .10
95 Bob McWhorter .10
96 Vernon Smith .10
97 Eddie Weaver .10
98 Bill Stanfill .20
99 Scott Williams .10
100 Checklist Card .10
101 Len Hauss .20
102 Jim Griffith .10
103 Nat Dye .10
104 Quinton Lumpkin .10
105 Mike Garrett .10
106 Glynn Harrison .10
107 Aaron Chubb .10
108 John Brantley .10
109 Pat Hodgson .10
110 Guy McIntyre .30
111 Keith Harris .10
112 Mike Cavan .10
113 Kevin Jackson .10
114 Jim Cagle .10
115 Charles Whittemore .10
116 Graham Batchelor .10
117 Art DeCarlo .20
118 Kendall Keith .10
119 Jeff Pyburn .20
120 James Ray .10
121 Mack Burroughs .10
122 Jimmy Vickers .10
123 Charley Britt .10
124 Matt Braswell .10
125 Jake Richardson .10
126 Ronnie Stewart .10
127 Tim Crowe .10
128 Troy Sadowski .10
129 Robert Honeycutt .10
130 Warren Gray .10
131 David Guthrie .10
132 John Lastinger .20
133 Chip Wisdom .10
134 Butch Box .10
135 Tony Cushenberry .10
136 Vince Guthrie .10
137 Floyd Reid .20
138 Mark Hodge .10
139 Joe Happe .10
140 Al Bodine .10
141 Gene Chandler .10
142 Tommy Lawhorne .10
143 Bobby Walden .20
144 Douglas McFalls .10
145 Jim Milo .10
146 Billy Payne .75
147 Paul Holmes .10
148 Bob Clemens .10
149 Kenneth Sims .10
150 Reid Moseley Jr. .10
151 Tim Callaway .10
152 Rusty Russell .10
153 Jim McCollough .10
154 Wally Williamson .10
155 John Bond .10
156 Charley Trippi .30
157 The Play (Lindsay Scott) .20
158 Joe Boland .10
159 Michael Babb .10
160 Jimmy Poulos .10
161 Chris McCarthy .10
162 Billy Mixon .10
163 Dicky Clark .10
164 David Rholetter .10
165 Chuck Heard .10
166 Pat Field .10
167 Preston Ridlehuber .10
168 Heyward Allen .10
169 Kirby Moore .10
170 Chris Welton .10
171 Bill McKenny .10
172 Steve Boswell .10
173 Bob Towns .10
174 Anthony Towns .10
175 Porter Payne .10
176 Bobby Garrard .10
177 Jack Griffith .10
178 Herschel Walker .75
179 Andy Perhach .10
180 Dr. Charles Herty (CO) .10
181 Kent Lawrence .20
182 David McKnight .10
183 Joe Tereshinski .10
184 Cicero Lucas .10
185 Glenn "Pop" Warner (CO) .20
186 Tony Flack .10
187 Kevin Butler .20
188 Bill Mitchell .10
189 Poulos vs. Tech (Jimmy Poulos) .10
190 Pete Case .20
191 Pete Tinsley .10
192 Joe Tereshinski .20
193 Jimmy Harper .10
194 Don Leebern .10
195 Harry Mehre (CO) .10
196 Retired Jerseys (Herschel Walker, Theron Sapp, Charley Trippi, Frank Sinkwich) .30
197 Terrie Webster .10
198 George Woodruff (CO) .10
199 First Georgia Team (1892 Team Photo) .10
200 Checklist Card .10

1989 Georgia Police

MT
Complete Set (16): 60.00
Common Player: .75
1 Hiawatha Berry (58) .75
2 Brian Cleveland (37) .75
3 Demetrius Douglas (53) .75
4 Alphonso Ellis (33) .75
5 Ray Goff (CO) 1.00
6 Bill Goldberg (95) 50.00
7 Rodney Hampton (7) 6.00
8 David Hargett (25) .75
9 Joey Hester (1) .75
10 John Kasay (3) 3.00
11 Mo Lewis 3.00
12 Arthur Marshall (12) 1.50
13 Curt Mull (50) .75
14 Ben Smith (26) 1.50
15 Greg Talley (11) .75
16 Kirk Warner (83) .75

1990 Georgia Police

MT
Complete Set (14): 10.00
Common Player: .75
1 John Allen (44) .75
2 Brian Cleveland (37) .75
3 Norman Cowins (59) .75
4 Alphonso Ellis (33) .75
5 Ray Goff (CO) 1.00
6 David Hargett (25) .75
7 Sean Hunnings (6) .75
8 Preston Jones (14) 1.00
9 John Kasay (3) 1.50
10 Arthur Marshall (12) 1.50
11 Jack Swan (76) .75
12 Greg Talley (11) .75
13 Lemonte Tellis (77) .75
14 Chris Wilson (16) .75

1991 Georgia Police

MT
Complete Set (16): 15.00
Common Player: .75
1 John Allen .75
2 Chuck Carswell .75
3 Russell DeFoor .75
4 Ray Goff (CO) 1.00
5 David Hargett .75
6 Andre Hastings 2.50
7 Garrison Hearst 6.00
8 Arthur Marshall 1.25
9 Kevin Maxwell .75
10 DeWayne Simmons .75
11 Jack Swan .75
12 Greg Talley .75
13 Lemonte Tellis .75
14 Chris Wilson .75
15 George Wynn .75
16 UGA V (Mascot) .75

1992 Georgia Police

MT
Complete Set (15): 12.00
Common Player: .50
1 Mitch Davis .60
2 Damon Evans .50
3 Torrey Evans .50
4 Ray Goff (CO) .60
5 Andre Hastings 2.00
6 Garrison Hearst 5.00
7 Donnie Maib .50
8 Alec Millen .50
9 Shannon Mitchell .50
10 Mack Strong 1.00
11 Jack Swan .50
12 UGA (Mascot) .50
13 Bernard Williams .60
14 Chris Wilson .50
15 Eric Zeier 6.00

1993 Georgia Police

MT
Complete Set (16): 18.00
Common Player: .50
1 Scott Armstrong .50
2 Brian Bohannon .50
3 Carlo Butler .50
4 Charlie Clemons .50
5 Mitch Davis .60
6 Terrell Davis 12.00
7 Randall Godfrey .75
8 Ray Goff (CO) .60
9 Frank Harvey .50
10 Travis Jones .50
11 Shannon Mitchell .50
12 Greg Tremble .50
13 Bernard Williams .60
14 Chad Wilson .50
15 Eric Zeier 3.00
16 UGA (Mascot) .50

1991 Georgia Southern

MT
Complete Set (45): 30.00
Common Player: .60
1 Tracy Ham 4.00
2 Tim Foley 1.50
3 Vance Pike .60
4 Dennis Franklin .60
5 Ernest Thompson .60
6 Giff Smith .60
7 Flint Matthews .60
8 Joe Ross .60
9 Gerald Harris .60
10 Monty Sharpe .60
11 The Beginning (Erskine "Erk" Russell) (CO) 1.00
12 Mike West .60
13 Jessie Jenkins .60
14 '85 Championship (Ring) .60
15 Erskine "Erk" Russell (CO) 1.00
16 Tim Brown .75
17 Taz Dixon .60
18 '86 Championship .60
19 Sean Gainey .60
20 James "Peanut" Carter .75
21 Ricky Harris .75
22 Fred Stokes 2.00
23 Randell Boone .60
24 Ronald Warnock .60
25 Raymond Gross .60
26 Robert Underwood .60
27 Frank Johnson .60
28 Darren Alford .60
29 Darrell Hendrix .60
30 Raymond Gross .60
31 Hugo Rossignol .60
32 Charles Carper .60
33 Melvin Bell .60
34 The Catch (Tracy Ham to Frank Johnson) 1.50
35 Karl Miller .60
36 Our House - Allen E. Paulson Stadium .60
37 Danny Durham .60
38 '89 Championship .60
39 Tony Belser .60
40 Nay Young .60
41 Steve Bussoletti .60
42 Tim Stowers (CO) .60
43 Rodney Oglesby .60
44 '90 Championship .60
45 Tracy Ham 4.00

1989 Hawaii

MT
Complete Set (25): 10.00
Common Player: .50
3 Michael Coulson .50
4 Walter Briggs .50
5 Gavin Robertson .50
7 Jason Elam 3.00
16 Clayton Mahuka .50
18 Garrett Gabriel .60
19 Kim McCloud .50
27 Kyle Ah Loo .50
28 Dane McArthur .50
30 Travis Sims .50
31 David Maeva .50
37 Mike Tresler .50
43 Jamal Farmer .60
56 Mark Odom .50
61 Allen Smith .50
66 Manly Williams .50
67 Larry Jones .50
71 Sean Robinson .50
72 Shawn Alivado .50
79 Leo Goeas 1.00
86 Larry Khan-Smith .50
89 Chris Roscoe .50
91 Augie Apelu .50
97 Dana Directo .50
NNO Bob Wagner (CO) .60

1990 Hawaii 7-Eleven

MT
Complete Set (50): 15.00
Common Player: .35
1 Sean Abreu (40) .35
2 Joaquin Barnett (53) .35
3 Darrick Branch (87) .35
4 David Brantley (9) .35
5 Akili Calhoun (98) .35
6 Michael Carter (3) .35
7 Shawn Ching (72) .35
8 Jason Elam (7) 2.00
9 Jamal Farmer (43) .50
10 Garrett Gabriel (18) .50
11 Brian Gordon (15) .35
12 Kenny Harper (6) .35
13 Mitchell Kaaialii (57) .35
14 Larry Khan-Smith (86) .35
15 Haku Kahoano (94) .35
16 Nuuanu Kaulia (94) .35
17 Eddie Kealoha (38) .35
18 Zerin Khan (14) .35
19 David Maeva (31) .35
20 Dane McArthur (28) .35
21 Kim McCloud (19) .35
22 Jeff Newman (1) .35
23 Mark Odom (56) .35
24 Louis Randall (51) .35
25 Gavin Robertson (5) .35
26 Sean Robinson (71) .35
27 Tavita Sagapolu (77) .35
28 Lyno Samana (45) .35
29 Walter Santiago (12) .35
30 Joe Sardo (21) .35
31 Travis Sims (30) .35
32 Allen Smith (61) .35
33 Jeff Snyder (26) 1.50
34 Richard Stevenson (33) .35
35 David Tanuvasa (44) .35
36 Mike Tresler (37) .35
37 Lemoe Tua (60) .35
38 Peter Viliamu (69) .35
39 Bob Wagner (CO) .50
40 Terry Whitaker (2) .35
41 Manly Williams (66) .35
42 Jerry Winfrey (90) .35
43 Aloha Stadium .35
44 Assistant Coaches .35
45 Defense (Nuuanu Kaulia) .35
46 Offense (Jamal Farmer) .50
47 Special Teams (Jason Elam) .75
48 BYU Victory (Jamal Farmer) .50
49 UH Logo .35
50 WAC Logo .35

1991 Hoby SEC Stars

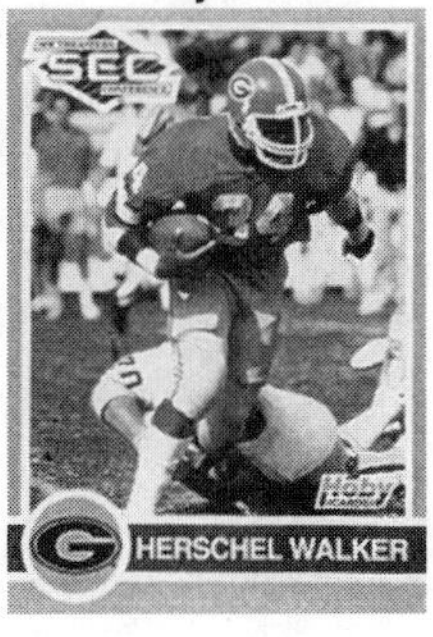

MT
Complete Set (396): 50.00
Common Player: .15
1 Paul "Bear" Bryant (CO) 2.00
2 Johnny Musso .50
3 Keith McCants .25
4 Cecil Dowdy .15
5 Thomas Rayam .15
6 Van Tiffin .15
7 Efrum Thomas .15
8 Jon Hand .25
9 David Smith .15
10 Larry Rose .15
11 Lamonde Russell .15
12 Mike Washington .15
13 Tommy Cole .15
14 Roger Shultz .15
15 Spencer Hammond .15
16 John Fruhmorgen .15
17 Gene Jelks .25
18 John Mangum .25
19 George Thornton .15
20 Billy Neighbors .25
21 Howard Cross .40
22 Jeremiah Castille .25
23 Derrick Thomas 1.00
24 Terrill Chatman .15
25 Ken Stabler 1.25
26 Lee Ozmint .15
27 Philip Doyle .15
28 Kermit Kendrick .15
29 Chris Mohr .15
30 Tommy Wilcox .15
31 Gary Hollingsworth .15
32 Sylvester Croom .25
33 Willie Wyatt .15
34 Pooley Hubert .15
35 Bobby Humphrey .25
36 Vaughn Mancha .15
37 Reggie Slack .40
38 Vince Dooley (CO) .40
39 Ed King .25
40 Connie Frederick .15
41 Jeff Burger .25
42 Monk Gafford .15
43 David Rocker .25
44 Jim Pyburn .15
45 Bob Harris .15
46 Travis Tidwell .15
47 Ralph (Shug) Jordan (CO) .40
48 Zeke Smith .25
49 Terry Beasley .25
50 Pat Sullivan .40
51 Stacy Danley .25
52 Jimmy Hitchcock .15
53 John Wiley .15
54 Greg Taylor .15
55 Lamar Rogers .25
56 Rob Selby .15
57 James Joseph .25
58 Mike Kolen .15
59 Kevin Greene .50
60 Ben Thomas .15
61 Shayne Wasden .15
62 Tex Warrington .15
63 Tommie Agee .25
64 Jim Phillips .15
65 Lawyer Tillman .40
66 Mark Dorminey .15
67 Steve Wallace .25
68 Ed Dyas .15
69 Alexander Wright .25
70 Lionel James .25
71 Aundray Bruce .25
72 Edmund Nelson .15
73 Jack Youngblood .50
74 Carlos Alvarez .25
75 Ricky Nattiel .25
76 Bill Carr .15
77 Guy Dennis .15
78 Charles Casey .15
79 Louis Oliver .40
80 John Reaves .25
81 Wayne Peace .25
82 Charlie LaPradd .15
83 Wes Chandler .40
84 Richard Trapp .15
85 Ralph Ortega .15
86 Tommy Durrance .15
87 Burton Lawless .25
88 Bruce Bennett .15
89 Huey Richardson .25
90 Larry Smith .15
91 Trace Armstrong .40
92 Nat Moore .40
93 James Jones .40
94 Kay Stephenson .25
95 Scot Brantley .15
96 Ray Criswell .15
97 Steve Tannen .25
98 Ernie Mills .40
99 Bruce Vaughn .15
100 Steve Spurrier 2.50
101 Crawford Ker .25
102 David Galloway .25
103 David Williams .25
104 Lomas Brown .40
105 Fernando Jackson .15
106 Jeff Roth .15
107 Mark Murray .15
108 Kirk Kirkpatrick .15
109 Ray Goff (CO) .25
110 Quinton Lumpkin .15
111 Royce Smith .15
112 Larry Rakestraw .25
113 Kevin Butler .25
114 Aschel M. Day .25
115 Scott Woerner .25
116 Herb St. John .15
117 Ray Rissmiller .15
118 Buck Belue .25
119 George Collins .15
120 Joel Parrish .15
121 Terry Hoage .25
122 Frank Sinkwich .40
123 Billy Payne .50
124 Zeke Bratkowski .25
125 Herschel Walker 1.00
126 Pat Dye (CO) .40
127 Vernon Smith .15
128 Rex Robinson .15
129 Mike Castronis .15
130 Pop Warner (CO) .40
131 George Patton .25
132 Harry Babcock .15
133 Lindsay Scott .25
134 Bill Stanfill .25
135 Bill Hartman Jr. .25
136 Eddie Weaver .15
137 Tim Worley .40
138 Ben Zambiasi .40
139 Bob McWhorter .15
140 Rodney Hampton 1.00
141 Len Hauss .25
142 Wallace Butts .25
143 Andy Johnson .25
144 I.M. Shiver Jr. .15
145 Clyde Johnson .15
146 Steve Meilinger .15
147 Howard Schnellenberger (CO) .50
148 Irv Goode .25
149 Sam Ball .15
150 Babe Parilli .40
151 Rick Norton .25
152 Warren Bryant .15
153 Mike Pfeifer .15
154 Sonny Collins .15
155 Mark Higgs .40
156 Randy Holleran .15
157 Bill Ransdell .15
158 Joey Worley .15
159 Jim Kovach .25
160 Joe Federspiel .25
161 Larry Seiple .25
162 Darryl Bishop .15
163 George Blanda 1.00
164 Oliver Barnett .25
165 Paul Calhoun .15
166 Dicky Lyons .15
167 Tom Hutchinson .25
168 George Adams .15
169 Derrick Ramsey .25
170 Rick Kestner .15
171 Art Still .40
172 Rick Nuzum .15
173 Richard Jaffe .15
174 Rodger Bird .15
175 Jeff Van Note .40
176 Herschel Turner .15
177 Lou Michaels .25
178 Ray Correll .15
179 Doug Moseley .15
180 Bob Gain .25
181 Tommy Casanova .40
182 Mike Anderson .15
183 Craig Burns .15
184 A.J. Duhe .25
185 Lyman White .15
186 Paul Dietzel (CO) .40
187 Paul Lyons .15
188 Eddie Ray .15
189 Roy Winston .15
190 Brad Davis .15
191 Mike Williams .15
192 Karl Wilson .25
193 Ronnie Estay .15
194 Malcolm Scott .15
195 Greg Jackson .15
196 Willie Teal .25
197 Eddie Fuller .15
198 Ralph Norwood .15
199 Bert Jones .40
200 Y.A. Tittle .50
201 Jerry Stovall .40
202 Henry Thomas .40
203 Lance Smith .15
204 Doug Moreau .25
205 Tyler LaFauci .15
206 George Bevan .15
207 Robert Dugas .15
208 Carlos Carson .25
209 Andy Hamilton .15
210 James Britt .15
211 Wendell Davis .40
212 Ron Sancho .15
213 Johnny Robinson .40
214 Eric Martin .40
215 Michael Brooks .25
216 Toby Caston .25
217 Jesse Anderson .15
218 Jimmy Webb .15
219 Mardye McDole .15
220 David Smith .15
221 Dana Moore .15
222 Cedric Corse .15
223 Louis Clark .15
224 Walter Packer .15
225 George Wonsley .25
226 Billy Jackson .15
227 Bruce Plummer .15
228 Aaron Pearson .15
229 Glen Collins .15
230 Paul Davis (CO) .15
231 Wayne Jones .15
232 John Bond .15
233 Johnnie Cooks .25
234 Robert Young .15
235 Don Smith .15
236 Kent Hull .40
237 Tony Shell .15
238 Steve Freeman .15
239 James Williams .15
240 Tom Goode .25
241 Stan Black .15
242 Bo Russell .15
243 Ricky Byrd .15
244 Frank Dowsing .15
245 Wayne Harris .40
246 Richard Keys .15
247 Artie Cosby .15
248 Dave Marler .15
249 Michael Haddix .15
250 Jerry Clower .25
251 Bill Bell .15
252 Jerry Bouldin .15
253 Parker Hall .15
254 Allen Brown .15
255 Bill Smith .15
256 Freddie Joe Nunn .25
257 John Vaught (CO) .25
258 Buford McGee .25
259 Kenny Dill .15
260 Jim Miller .15
261 Doug Jacobs .15
262 John Dottley .25
263 Willie Green .40
264 Tony Bennett .40
265 Stan Hindman .15
266 Charles Childers .15
267 Harry Harrison .15
268 Todd Sandroni .15
269 Glynn Griffing .15
270 Chris Mitchell .15
271 Shawn Cobb .15
272 Doug Elmore .15
273 Dawson Pruett .15
274 Warner Alford .15
275 Archie Manning 1.00
276 Kelvin Pritchett .25
277 Pat Coleman .15
278 Stevon Moore .25
279 John Darnell .15
280 Wesley Walls .25
281 Billy Brewer .25
282 Mark Young .15
283 Andre Townsend .25
284 Billy Ray Adams .15
285 Jim Dunaway .25
286 Paige Cothren .25
287 Jake Gibbs .40
288 Jim Urbanek .15
289 Tony Thompson .15
300 Johnny Majors (CO) .40
301 Roland Poles .15
302 Alvin Harper .50
303 Doug Baird .15
304 Greg Burke .15
305 Sterling Henton .15
306 Preston Warren .15
307 Stanley Morgan .50
308 Bobby Scott .25
309 Doug Atkins .40
310 Bill Young .15
311 Bob Garmon .15
312 Herman Weaver .15
313 Dewey Warren .15
314 John Boynton .25
315 Bob Davis .15
316 Pat Ryan .15
317 Keith DeLong .25
318 Bobby Dodd (CO) .25
319 Ricky Townsend .15
320 Eddie Brown .25
321 Herman Hickman (CO) .25
322 Nathan Dougherty .15
323 Mickey Marvin .15
324 Reggie Cobb .40
325A Condredge Holloway .50
325B Josh Cody .15
326A Anthony Hancock .40
326B Jack Jenkins .15
327A Steve Kiner .15
327B Bob Goodridge .15
328A Mike Mauck .15
328B Chris Gaines .15
329A Bill Bates .40
329B Willie Geny .15
330A Austin Denney .25
330B Bob Laws .15
331A Robert Neyland (CO) .40
331B Rob Monaco .15
332A Bob Suffridge .15
332B Chuck Scott .15
333A Abe Shires .15
333B Hek Wakefield .15
334A Robert Shaw .40
334B Ken Stone .15
335 Mark Adams .15
336 Ed Smith .15
337 Dan McGugin (CO) .15
338 Doug Mathews .15
339 Whit Taylor .40
340 Gene Moshier .15
341 Christine Hauck .15
342 Lee Nalley .15
343 Wamon Buggs .15
344 Jim Arnold .25
345 Buford Ray .25
346 Will Wolford .25
347 Steve Bearden .15
348 Frank Mordica .15
349 Barry Burton .15
350 Bill Wade .40
351 Tommy Woodroof .15
352 Steve Wade .15
353 Preston Brown .15
354 Ben Roderick .15
355 Charles Horton .15
356 DeMond Winston .15
357 John North .15
358 Don Orr .15
359 Art Demmas .15
360 Mark Johnson .15
361 Hootie Ingram (AD) .25
362 Gene Stallings (CO) .50
363 Alabama Checklist .15
364 Pat Dye (CO) .25
365 Auburn Checklist .15
366 Vince Dooley (AD) .25
367 Ray Goff (CO) .25
368 Georgia Checklist .15
369 C.M. Newton (AD) .25
370 Bill Curry (CO) .25
371 Kentucky Checklist .15
372 Joe Dean (AD) .15
373 Curley Hallman (CO) .25
374 LSU Checklist .15
375 Warner Alford (AD) .15
376 Billy Brewer (CO) .25
377 Ole Miss Checklist .15
378 Larry Templeton (AD) .15
379 Jackie Sherrill (CO) .40
380 Mississippi State Checklist .15
381 Bill Arnsparger (AD) .25
382 Steve Spurrier (CO) 1.25
383 Florida Checklist .15
384 Doug Dickey (AD) .15
385 Johnny Majors (CO) .25
386 Tennessee Checklist .15
387 Paul Hoolahan (AD) .15
388 Gerry DiNardo (CO) .25
389 Vanderbilt Checklist .15
390 The Iron Bowl - Alabama vs. Auburn .40
391 Largest Outdoor Cocktail Party Florida vs. Georgia .15
392 The Egg Bowl Mississippi State vs. Ole Miss .15
393 The Beer Barrel - Kentucky vs. Tennessee .15
394 Drama on Halloween - LSU vs. Ole Miss .15
395 Tennessee Hoedown Tennessee vs. Vanderbilt .15
396 Roy Kramer (COMM) .15

1991 Hoby SEC Stars Signature

MT
Complete Set (10): 375.00
Common Player: 15.00
1 Carlos Alvarez 15.00
2 Zeke Bratkowski 25.00

3 Jerry Clower 15.00
4 Condredge Holloway 25.00
5 Bert Jones 50.00
6 Archie Manning 75.00
7 Ken Stabler 100.00
8 Pat Sullivan 50.00
9 Jeff Van Note 20.00
10 Bill Wade 25.00

1992 Houston Motion Sports

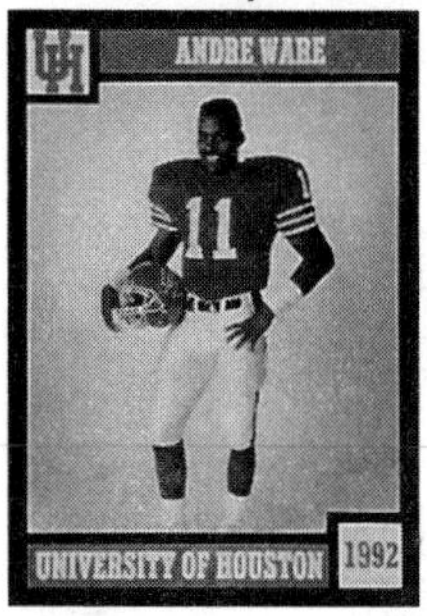

MT
Complete Set (66): 30.00
Common Player: .50
1 Freddie Gilbert .60
2 Lorenzo Dickson .50
3 Sherman Smith 1.00
4 Brad Whigham .50
5 Allen Aldridge 1.00
6 Truett Akin .50
7 Nahala Johnson .60
8 1980 Garden State Bowl (Terald Clark) .50
9 1977 Cotton Bowl .60
10 Tyrone Davis .50
11 Kevin Bleier .50
12 Nigel Ventress .50
13 Darren Woods .50
14 Linton Weatherspoon .50
15 John R. Morris .50
16 Kevin Batiste .60
17 Kelvin McKnight .50
18 Stewart Carpenter .50
19 Ron Peters .50
20 Stephen Dixon .60
21 Chandler Evans .50
22 Tyler Mucho .50
23 Kevin Labay .50
24 Steve Clarke .50
25 Keith Jack .50
26 Steve Matejka .50
27 The Astrodome .50
28 Roman Anderson .50
29 Quarterback U (Andre Ware, David Klingler) 1.50
30 Cougar Pride (Andre Ware, David Klingler) 1.50
31 Bayou Bucket (Annual Houston vs. Rice game) .50
32 Jeff Tait .50
33 Donald Douglas .50
34 Victor Mamich .50
35 John W. Brown .50
36 Zach Chatman .50
37 Jason Youngblood .50
38 David Klingler 2.00
39 John H. Brown .50
40 Tommy Guy .50
41 1980 Cotton Bowl (Game action) .60
42 1973 Bluebonnet Bowl (Game action) .60
43 Chris Pezman .50
44 Tracy Good .50
45 Stephen Harris .50
46 Ryan McCoy .60
47 Michael Newhouse .50
48 Jimmy Klingler 1.50
49 Joe Wheeler .50
50 Eric Harrison .50
51 Craig Hall .50
52 Shasta (Mascot) .50
53 NCAA Records (Passing and Receiving) .60
54 Darrell Clapp .60
55 Eric Blount .50
56 Tiandre Sanders .50
57 Kyle Allen .50
58 Brisket Howard .50
59 Greg Thornburgh .50
60 Wilson Whitley 1.00
61 Andre Ware 2.00
62 John Jenkins (CO) .60
NNO Ad Card Motion Sports .50
NNO Front Card .50
NNO Back Card .50
NNO Checklist .50

1988 Humboldt State Smokey

MT
Complete Set (11): 12.00
Common Player: 1.25
1 Richard Ashe (1) 1.25
2 Darin Bradbury (64) 1.25
3 Rodney Dorsett (7) 1.25
4 Dave Harper (55) 1.25
5 Earl Jackson (6) 1.25
6 Derek Mallard (82) 1.25
7 Scott Reagan (60) 1.25
8 Wesley White (1) 1.25
9 Paul Wienecke (40) 1.25
10 William Williams (14) 1.25
11 Kelvin Windham (30) 1.25

1989 Idaho

MT
Complete Set (12): 12.00
Common Player: .75
3 Brian Smith .75
11 Tim S. Johnson .75
16 Lee Allen .75
17 John Friesz 5.00
20 Todd Hoiness .75
25 David Jackson .75
53 Steve Unger .75
58 John Rust .75
63 Troy Wright .75
67 Todd Neu .75
83 Michael Davis .75
93 Mike Zeller .75

1990 Illinois Centennial

MT
Complete Set (45): 25.00
Common Player: .35
1 Harold "Red" Grange 3.00
2 Dick Butkus 2.50
3 Ray Nitschke 1.50
4 Jim Grabowski .50
5 Alex Agase .50
6 Claude Young .50
7 Scott Studwell .50
8 Tony Eason .50
9 John Mackovic .75
10 Jack Trudeau .75
11 Jeff George 2.00
12 Rose Bowl Coaches (Ray Eliot, Pete Elliott, Mike White) .35
13 George Huff .35
14 David Williams .35
15 Bob Zuppke .50
16 George Halas 2.00
17 Dike Eddleman .35
18 Dave Wilson .35
19 Tab Bennett .35
20 Jim Juriga .35
21 John Karras .35
22 Bobby Mitchell 1.00
23 Dan Beaver .35
24 Joe Rutgens .50
25 Bill Burrell .35
26 J.C. Caroline .50
27 Al Brosky .35
28 Don Thorp .35
29 First Football Team .35
30 Harold "Red" Grange (Retired) 1.00
31 Memorial Stadium .35
32 Chris White .35
33 Early Stars (Ralph Chapman, Perry Graves, Bart Macomber) .35
34 Early Stars (John Depler, Jim McMillen) .35
35 Early Stars (Burt Ingwerson, Butch Nowack, Bernie Shively) .35
36 Great Quarterbacks (Fred Custardo, Mike Wells, Tom O'Connell) .35
37 Great Running Backs (Thomas Rooks, Abe Woodson, Keith Jones) .50
38 Great Receivers (Mike Bellamy, Doug Dieken, John Wright) .50
39 Great Offensive (Forrest Van Hook, Larry McCarren, Chris Babyar) .35
40 Great Defensive Backs (Craig Swope, George Donnelly, Mike Gower) .35
41 Great Linebackers (Charles Boerio, Don Hansen, John Sullivan) .35
42 Defensive Linemen (Archie Sutton, Chuck Studley, Scott Davis) .35
43 Great Kickers (Mike Bass K, Bill Brown, Frosty Peters) .35
44 Retired Numbers (Dick Butkus) 1.50
45 Football Centennial Logo .35

1992 Illinois

MT
Complete Set (48): 18.00
Common Player: .35
1 Derek Allen .35
2 Jeff Arneson .35
3 Randy Bierman .35
4 Darren Boyer .35
5 Rod Boykin .35
6 Mike Cole .35
7 Chad Copher .35
8 Fred Cox .50
9 Robert Crumpton .50
10 Ken Dilger 2.00
11 Jason Edwards .35
12 Greg Engel .35
13 Steve Feagin .35
14 Erik Foggey .35
15 Kevin Hardy 3.00
16 Jeff Hasenstab .35
17 John Holecek .50
18 Brad Hopkins .75
19 John Horn .35
20 Dana Howard 1.00
21 Filmel Johnson .35
22 Jon Kerr .35
23 Jeff Kinney .50
24 Jim Klein .35
25 Todd Leach .35
26 Wagner Lester .35
27 Lashon Ludington .35
28 Clinton Lynch .35
29 Tim McCloud .35
30 David Olson .35
31 Antwoine Patton .50
32 Jim Pesek .35
33 Alfred Pierce .35
34 Mark Qualls .35
35 Phil Rathke .35
36 Chris Richardson .50
37 Derrick Rucker .35
38 Aaron Shelby .35
39 John Sidari .35
40 J.J. Strong .35
41 Mike Suarez .35
42 Lou Tepper (CO) .50
43 Scott Turner .35
44 Jason Verduzco 1.00
45 Tyrone Washington .35
46 Forry Wells .35
47 Pat Wendt .35
48 John Wright .35

1982 Indiana State Police

MT
Complete Set (64): 175.00
Common Player: 3.00
1 David Allen 3.00
2 Doug Arnold 3.00
3 James Banks 3.00
4 Scott Bartel 3.00
5 Kurt Bell 3.00
6 Terry Bell 3.00
7 Steve Bidwell 3.00
8 Keith Bonney 3.00
9 Mark Boster 3.00
10 Bobby Boyce 3.00
11 Steve Brickey (CO) 3.00
12 Mark Bryson 3.00
13 Steve Buxton 3.00
14 Ed Campbell 3.00
15 Jeff Campbell 5.00
16 Tom Chapman 3.00
17 Cheerleaders (Ruth Ann Medworth DIR) 4.00
18 Darrold Clardy 3.00
19 Wayne Davis 3.00
20 Herbert Dawson 3.00
21 Richard Dawson 4.00
22 Chris Delaplaine 3.00
23 Max Dillon 3.00
24 Rick Dwenger 3.00
25 Ed Foggs 3.00
26 Allen Hartwig 3.00
27 Pat Henderson (CO) 3.00
28 Don Hitz 3.00
29 Pete Hoener (CO) 3.00
30 Bob Hopkins 3.00
31 Kris Huber (Baton Twirler) 4.00
32 Leroy Irvin 20.00
33 Mike Johannes 3.00
34 Anthony Kimball 3.00
35 Gregg Kimbrough 3.00
36 Bob Koehne 3.00
37 Jerry Lasko (CO) 3.00
38 Kevin Lynch 3.00
39 Dan Maher 3.00
40 Ed Martin 3.00
41 Regis Mason 3.00
42 Rob McIntyre 3.00
43 Quintin Mikell 3.00
44 Jeff Miller 3.00
45 Mark Miller 3.00
46 Mike Osborne 3.00
47 Max Payne (CO) 3.00
48 Scott Piercy 3.00
49 Dennis Raetz (CO) 3.00
50 Kevin Ramsey 3.00
51 Dean Reader 3.00
52 Eric Robinson 3.00
53 Walter Seaphus 3.00
54 Sparkettes (Marthann Markler DIR) 4.00
55 John Spradley 3.00
56 Manual Studway 3.00
57 Sam Suggs 3.00
58 Larry Swart 3.00
59 Bob Tyree 3.00
60 Bob Turner (CO) 3.00
61 Brad Verdun 3.00
62 Keith Ward 3.00
63 Sean Whiten 3.00
64 Perry Willett 3.00

1971 Iowa Team Photos

NM
Complete Set (4): 25.00
Common Sheet: 6.00
1 Geoff Mickelson, Craig Clemons, Frank Holmes, Levi Mitchell, Charles Podolak, Lorin Lynch, Steve Penney, Larry Horton 8.00
2 Alan Schaefer, Dave Triplett, John Muller, Jim Kaiser, Wendell Bell, Clark Malmer, Rich Solomon, Kelly Disser 6.00
3 Bill Schoonover, Frank Sunderman, Craig Darling, Tom Cabalka, Dave Simms, Bill Rose, Buster Hoinkes, Charles Cross 6.00
4 Kyle Skogman, Jerry Reardon, Dave Harris, Rob Fick, Mike Dillner, Ike White, Mark Nelson, Harry Kokolus 6.00

1984 Iowa

MT
Complete Set (60): 50.00
Common Player: .75
1 Kevin Angel .75
2 Kerry Burt .75
3 Fred Bush .75
4 Craig Clark .75
5 Zane Corbin .75
6 Nate Creer .75
7 Dave Croston .75
8 George Davis .75
9 Jeff Drost .75
10 Quinn Early 4.00
11 Mike Flagg .75
12 Hayden Fry (CO) 2.50
13 Bruce Gear .75
14 Owen Gill 2.00
15 Bill Glass 1.00
16 Mike Haight 1.50
17 Bill Happel .75
18 Kevin Harmon 1.00
19 Ronnie Harmon 4.00
20 Craig Hartman .75
21 Jon Hayes 2.00
22 Erric Hedgeman .75
23 Scott Helverson .75
24 Mike Hooks .75
25 Paul Hufford .75
26 Keith Hunter .75
27 George Little .75
28 Chuck Long 2.00
29 J.C. Love-Jordan .75
30 George Millett .75
31 Devon Mitchell 1.00
32 Tom Nichol .75
33 Kelly O'Brien .75
34 Hap Peterson .75
35 Joe Schuster 1.00
36 Tim Sennott .75
37 Ken Sims .75
38 Mark Sindlinger .75
39 Robert Smith .75
40 Kevin Spitzig .75
41 Larry Station .75
42 Mike Stoops .75
43 Dave Strobel .75
44 Mark Vlasic 2.00
45 Jon Vrieze .75
46 Tony Wancket .75
47 Herb Webster .75
48 Coaching Staff 1.00
49 Captains 1.50
50 Bowl Players 1.00
51 Harmon Brothers (Kevin Harmon, Ronnie Harmon) 1.50
52 Cheerleaders 1.00
53 Pompons 1.00
54 Kinnick Stadium .75
55 Herky the Hawk (Mascot) .75
56 Rose Bowl Ring .75
57 Peach Bowl Trophy .75
58 Gator Bowl Stadium .75
59 Floyd of Rosedale (Trophy) .75
60 Checklist Card .75

1987 Iowa

MT
Complete Set (63): 40.00
Common Player: .60
1 Mark Adams .60
2 Dave Alexander 1.00
3 Bill Anderson .60
4 Tim Anderson .60
5 Rick Bayless .60
6 Jeff Beard .60
7 Mike Burke .60
8 Kerry Burt .60
9 Malcolm Christie .60
10 Craig Clark .60
11 Marv Cook 2.00
12 Jeff Croston .60
13 Greg Divis .60
14 Quinn Early 2.50
15 Greg Fedders .60
16 Mike Flagg .60
17 Melvin Foster .60
18 Hayden Fry (CO) 2.00
19 Grant Goodman .60
20 Dave Haight 1.00
21 Merton Hanks 3.00
22 Deven Harberts .60
23 Kevin Harmon .75
24 Chuck Hartlieb 1.25
25 Tork Hook .60
26 Rob Houghtlin .60
27 David Hudson .60
28 Myron Keppy .60
29 Jeff Koeppel .60
30 Bob Kratch 1.50
31 Peter Marciano .60
32 Jim Mauro .60
33 Marc Mazzeri .60
34 Dan McGwire 2.00
35 Mike Miller .60
36 Joe Mott 1.00
37 James Pipkins .60
38 Tom Poholsky .75
39 Jim Poynton .60
40 J.J. Puk .75
41 Brad Quast .60
42 Jim Reilly .60
43 Matt Ruhland .60
44 Bob Schmitt .60
45 Joe Schuster .75
46 Dwight Sistrunk .75
47 Mark Stoops .60
48 Steve Thomas .60
49 Kent Thompson .60
50 Travis Watkins .60
51 Herb Wester .60
52 Anthony Wright .60
53 Big 10 Championship Ring and Rose Bowl Ring .60
54 Cheerleaders .75
55 Floyd of Rosedale (Trophy) .60
56 Freedom Bowl (Game Action Photo) .75
57 Herky the Hawk (Mascot) .60
58 Holiday Bowl (Game Action Photo) .75
59 Indoor Practice Facility .60
60 Iowa Team Captains (Quinn Early and five others) 1.50
61 Kinnick Stadium .60
62 Peach Bowl (Game Action Photo) .60
63 Pom Pons (Cheerleaders) 1.00

1988 Iowa

MT
Complete Set (64): 30.00
Common Player: .50
2 Travis Watkins .60
4 James Pipkins .50
5 Mike Burke .50
8 Chuck Hartlieb 1.00
10 Anthony Wright .50
14 Tom Poholsky .60
16 Deven Harberts .50
18 Leroy Smith .50
20 David Hudson .50
21 Tony Stewart .50
22 Sean Smith .50
23 Richard Bass .50
26 Peter Marciano .50
29 Greg Brown .50
30 Grant Goodman .50
31 John Derby .50
32 Mike Saunders 1.00
35 Brad Quast .50
38 Chet Davis .50
40 Marc Mazzeri .50
41 Mark Stoops .50
42 Tork Hook .50
44 Keaton Smiley .50
45 Merton Hanks 2.00
48 Tyrone Berrie .50
50 Bill Anderson .50
51 Jeff Koeppel .50
53 Greg Fedders .50
57 Matt Ruhland .50
58 Greg Davis .50
60 Bob Schmitt .50
61 Dave Turner .50
64 Dave Haight .75
66 Melvin Foster .50
67 Jim Poynton .50
68 Tim Anderson .50
70 Bob Kratch 1.00
71 Jim Johnson .50
74 George Hawthorne .50
75 Greg Aegerter .50
77 Paul Glonek .50
80 Steve Green .50
81 Brian Wise .50
82 Jon Filloon .50
84 Marv Cook 1.50
85 John Palmer .60
87 Jeff Skillett .50
88 Tom Ward .50
95 Jim Reilly .50
96 Ron Geater .50
97 Joe Mott .75
99 Moses Santos .50
NNO Team Captains (Marv Crook and four others) 1.00
NNO Hayden Fry (CO) 1.00
NNO Holiday Bowl 1987 (Hayden Fry) (CO) .75
NNO Peach Bowl (Game Action Photo) .60
NNO Holiday Bowl 1986 (Game Action Photo) .60
NNO Herky the Hawk (Mascot) .50
NNO Cheerleaders .60
NNO Kinnick Stadium .50
NNO Pom Pons (Cheerleaders) .60
NNO Championship Rings .50
NNO Indoor Practice Facility .50
NNO Symbolic Tiger Hawk (Helmet) .50

1989 Iowa

MT
Complete Set (90): 30.00
Common Player: .40
1 Greg Aegerter .40
2 Kevin Allendorf .40
3 Bill Anderson .40
4 Richard Bass .40
5 Rob Baxley .40
6 Nick Bell 1.50
7 Phil Bradley .40
8 Greg Brown .40
9 Doug Buch .40
10 Gary Clark .40
11 Roderick Davis .40
12 Scott Davis 1.00
13 John Derby .50
14 Mike Devlin .40
15 Jason Dumont .40
16 Mike Ertz .40
17 Ted Faley .40
18 Greg Fedders .40
19 Mike Ferroni .50
20 Jon Filloon .40
21 Melvin Foster .40
22 Hayden Fry (CO) 1.00
23 Ron Geater .40
24 Ed Gochenour .40
25 Merton Hanks 2.00
26 Jim Hartlieb .50
27 George Hawthorne .40
28 Tork Hook .40
29 Danan Hughes 1.00
30 Jim Johnson .40
31 Jeff Koeppel .40
32 Marvin Lampkin .40
33 Peter Marciano .40
34 Ed Marshall .40
35 Kirk McGowan .40
36 Mike Miller .40
37 Lew Montgomery .40
38 George Murphy .40
39 John Palmer .50
40 James Pipkins .40
41 Tom Poholsky .50
42 Eddie Polly .40
43 Jim Poyton .40
44 Brad Quast .40
45 Matt Rodgers .75
46 Matt Ruhland .40
47 Ron Ryan .40
48 Moses Santos .40
49 Mike Saunders .75
50 Doug Scott .40
51 Jeff Skillett .40
52 Leroy Smith .40
53 Sean Smith .40
54 Sean Snyder .40
55 Tony Stewart .40
56 Mark Stoops .40
57 Dave Turner .40
58 Darrin Vande Zande .40
59 Ted Velicer .40
60 Travis Watkins .40
61 Dusty Weiland .40
62 Ladd Wessles .40
63 Matt Whitaker .40
64 Brian Wise .40
65 Anthony Wright .40
66 100 Years of Iowa Football (Logo) .40
67 The Tigerhawk (School Logo) .40
68 Herky the Hawk (Mascot) .40
69 Kinnick Stadium .40
70 Hawkeye Fans .40
71 NFL Tradition (Logo) .40
72 1982 Beach Bowl (Logo) .40
73 1982 Rose Bowl (Logo) .40
74 1983 Gator Bowl (Logo) .40
75 1984 Freedom Bowl (Logo) .40
76 1986 Holiday Bowl (Logo) .40
77 1986 Rose Bowl (Logo) .40
78 1987 Holiday Bowl (Logo) .40
79 1988 Beach Bowl (Logo) .40
80 Big Ten Conference (Logo) .40
81 Iowa Marching Band .40
82 Indoor Practice Facility .40
83 Iowa Locker Rooms .40
84 Iowa Weight Room .40
85 Iowa Class Rooms .40
86 Players' Lounge .40
87 Floyd of Rosedale (Trophy) .40
88 Medical Facilities .40
89 Media Coverage .40
90 Television Coverage (Camera) .40

1993 Iowa

MT
Complete Set (64): 25.00
Common Player: .40
1 Ryan Abraham .50
2 Greg Allen .40
3 Jeff Andrews .40
4 Jeff Anttila .40
5 Jefferson Bates .40
6 George Bennett .40
7 Lloyd Bickham .40
8 Larry Blue .40
9 Pat Boone .40
10 Tyrone Boudreaux .40
11 Paul Burmeister .75
12 Tyler Casey .40
13 Billy Coats .40
14 Maurea Crain .40
15 Ernest Crank .50
16 Mike Dailey .40
17 Anthony Dean .50
18 Bobby Diaco .40
19 Mike Duprey .40
20 Billy Ennis-Inge .40
21 Matt Eyde .40
22 Fritz Fequiere .75
23 Hayden Fry (CO) 1.00
24 Willie Guy .40
25 John Hartlieb .50
26 Jason Henlon .40
27 Matt Hilliard .40
28 Mike Hornaday .40
29 Rob Huber .40
30 Chris Jackson .40
31 Harold Jasper .75
32 Jamar Jones .40
33 Kent Kahl .40
34 Cliff King .40
35 John Kline .40
36 Tom Knight .40
37 Aaron Kooiker .40
38 Andy Kreider .40
39 Bill Lange .40
40 Doug Laufenberg .40
41 Hal Mady .50
42 Brian McCullouch .40
43 Jason Olejniczak .40
44 Chris Palmer .40
45 Scott Plate .50
46 Marquis Porter .50
47 Matt Purdy .40
48 Matt Quest .40
49 Damien Robinson .50
50 Todd Romano .40
51 Mark Roussell .40
52 Ted Serama .40
53 Scott Sether .40
54 Sedrick Shaw .50
55 Scott Slutzker .50
56 Ryan Terry .50
57 Mike Wells .40
58 Casey Wiegmann .40
59 Parker Wildeman .40
60 Big Ten Conference (Logo card) .40
61 Hawkeyes Schedule .40
62 Herky (Mascot) .40
63 Indoor Practice Facility .40
64 Kinnick Stadium .40

1997 Iowa

MT
Complete Set (19): 30.00
Common Player: 1.50
1 Brett Chambers 1.50
2 Billy Coats 1.50
3 Ryan Driscoll 2.00
4 Bill Ennis-Inge 2.50
5 Rodney Flier 1.50
6 Hayden Fry 2.50
7 Nick Gallery 1.50
8 Aaron Granquist 1.50
9 Brion Hurley 1.50
10 Tom Knight 3.00
11 Mark Mitchell 1.50
12 Demo Odems 1.50
13 Jon Ortlieb 1.50
14 Bill Reardon 1.50
15 Damien Robinson 2.00
16 Ted Serama 1.50
17 Ross Verba 3.00
18 Hawk Watch (1996 Seniors Iowa Hawkeyes Football) 2.00
19 Hawkeyes Logo 1.50

Post-1980 cards in Near Mint condition will generally sell for about 75% of the quoted Mint value. Excellent-condition cards bring no more than 40%.

1989 Kansas

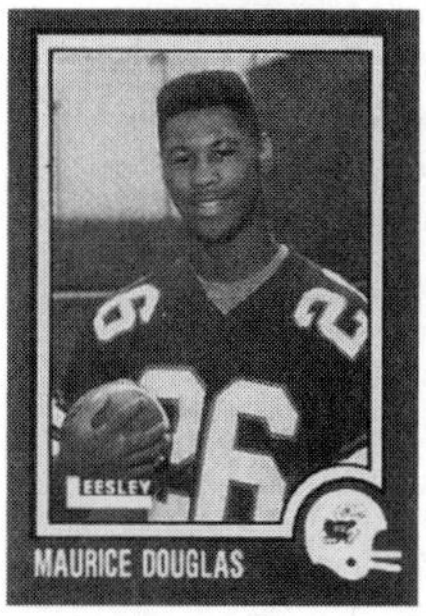
MAURICE DOUGLAS

		MT
Complete Set (40):		12.00
Common Player:		.35
1	Kelly Donohoe	.75
2	Roger Robben	.35
3	Tony Sands	.35
4	Paul Zaffaroni	.35
5	Lance Flachsbarth	.35
6	Brad Fleeman	.35
7	Chip Budde	.50
8	Bill Hundelt	.35
9	Dan Newbrough	.35
10	Gary Oatis	.35
11	B.J. Lohsen	.50
12	John Fritch	.35
13	Russ Bowen	.35
14	Smith Holland	.35
15	Jason Priest	.50
16	Scott McCabe	.35
17	Jason Tyrer	.35
18	Mongo Allen	.35
19	Glen Mason (CO)	1.00
20	Deral Boykin	.35
21	Quintin Smith	.35
22	Mark Koncz	.50
23	John Baker	.50
24	Football Staff (schedule on back)	.50
25	Maurice Hooks	.35
26	Frank Hatchett	.35
27	Paul Friday	.35
28	Doug Terry	.35
29	Kenny Drayton	.35
30	Jim New	.35
31	Chris Perez	.35
32	Maurice Douglas	1.25
33	Curtis Moore	.35
34	David Gordon	.35
35	Matt Nolen	.35
36	Dave Walton	.35
37	King Dixon	.50
38	Memorial Stadium	.35
39	Jayhawks in Action (Kelly Donohoe)	.50
40	Jayhawks in Action (John Baker) (OL)	.50
NNO	Title Card	.75

1992 Kansas

		MT
Complete Set (52):		20.00
Common Player:		.40
1	Mark Allison	.40
2	Hassan Bailey	.50
3	Greg Ballard	.40
4	Martin Blakeney	.40
5	Kristopher Booth	.40
6	Charley Bowen	.40
7	Gilbert Brown	1.00
8	Dwayne Chandler	.40
9	Brian Christian	.40
10	David Converse	.40
11	Monte Cozzens	.40
12	Don Davis	.40
13	Maurice Douglas	1.00
14	Dan Eichloff	.40
15	Chad Fette	.40
16	Matt Gay	.40
17	Harold Harris	.40
18	Rodney Harris	.40
19	Steve Harvey	.40
20	Hessley Hempstead	.40
21	Chip Hilleary	1.00
22	Dick Holt	.40
23	Guy Howard	.40
24	Chaka Johnson	.40
25	John Jones	.40
26	Rod Jones	.40
27	Kwamie Lassiter	.50
28	Rob Licursi	.40
29	Trace Liggett	.40
30	Keith Loneker	.40
31	Dave Marcum	.40
32	Glen Mason (CO)	.75
33	Chris Maumalanga	1.00
34	Gerald McBurrows	.40
35	Robert Mitchell	.40
36	Ty Moeder	.40
37	Kyle Moore	.40
38	Ron Page	.40
39	Chris Powell	.40
40	Dan Schmidt	.40
41	Ashaundai Smith	.40
42	Mike Steele	.40
43	Dana Stubblefield	4.00
44	Wes Swinford	.40
45	Larry Thiel	.40
46	Frederick Thomas	.50
47	Pete Vang	.40
48	Robert Vaughn	.40
49	George White	.50
50	Sylvester Wright	.40
NNO	Schedule Card	.40
NNO	Coaching Staff	.40

1982 Kentucky Schedules

		MT
Complete Set (19):		45.00
Common Player:		3.00
1	Richard Abraham	3.00
2	Glenn Amerson	3.00
3	Effley Brooks	3.00
4	Shawn Donigan	3.00
5	Rod Francis	3.00
6	Terry Henry	3.00
7	Ben Johnson	3.00
8	Dave Lyons	3.00
9	John Maddox	3.00
10	Rob Mangas	4.00
11	David "Buzz" Meers	3.00
12	Andy Molls	3.00
13	Tom Petty	3.00
14	Don Roe	3.00
15	Todd Shadowen	3.00
16	Gerald Smyth	3.00
17	Pete Venable	3.00
18	Allan Watson	3.00
19	Steve Williams	3.00

1986 Kentucky Schedules

		MT
Complete Set (4):		15.00
Common Player:		4.00
1	Jerry Claiborne (CO)	4.00
2	Mark Higgs	7.50
3	Marc Logan	6.00
4	Bill Ransdell	4.00

1981 Louisville Police

		MT
Complete Set (64):		125.00
Common Player:		1.00
1	Title Card SP (Catch That Cardinal Spirit)	50.00
2	Bob Weber (CO)	1.00
3	Assistant Coaches	1.00
4	Jay Trautwein	1.00
5	Darrell Wimberly	1.00
6	Jeff Van Camp	1.00
7	Joe Welch	1.00
8	Fred Blackmon	1.00
9	Lamar "Toot" Evans	1.00
10	Tom Blair	1.00
11	Joe Kader	1.00
12	Mike Trainor	1.00
13	Richard Tharpe	1.00
14	Gene Hagan	1.00
15	Greg Jones	1.00
16	Leon Williams	1.00
17	Ellsworth Larkins	1.00
18	Sebastian Curry	1.00
19	Frank Minnifield	6.00
20	Roger Clay	1.00
21	Mark Blasinsky	1.00
22	Mike Cruz	1.00
23	David Arthur	1.00
24	Johnny Unitas (In front background, list of Cardinals who played pro ball)	15.00
25	John DeMarco	1.00
26	Eric Rollins	1.00
27	Jack Pok	1.00
28	Pete McCartney	1.00
29	Mark Clayton	15.00
30	Jeff Hortert	1.00
31	Pete Bowen	1.00
32	Robert Niece	1.00
33	Todd McMahan	1.00
34	John Wall	1.00
35	Kelly Stickrod	1.00
36	Jim Miller	1.00
37	Tom Moore	1.00
38	Kurt Knop	1.00
39	Mark Musgrave	1.00
40	Tony Campbell	1.00
41	Mark Wilson	1.00
42	Robert Mitchell	1.00
43	Courtney Jeter	1.00
44	Wayne Taylor	1.00
45	Jeff Speedy	1.00
46	Donald Craft	1.00
47	Glenn Hunter	1.00
48	1981 Louisville Schedule	1.00
49	Greg Hickman	1.00
50	Nate Dozier	1.00
51	Pat Patterson	1.00
52	Scott Gannon	1.00
53	Dean May	1.00
54	David Hatfield	1.00
55	Mike Nuzzolese	1.00
56	John Ayers	1.00
57	Lamar Cummins	1.00
58	Bill Olsen (AD)	1.00
59	Tailgating	1.00
60	Football Complex	1.00
61	Marching Band	1.00
62	Cheerleaders	1.00
63	Administration Bldg.	1.00
64	Cardinal Bird	1.00

1990 Louisville Smokey

		MT
Complete Set (16):		25.00
Common Player:		1.25
1	Greg Brohm	1.25
2	Jeff Brohm	1.50
3	Pete Burkey	1.25
4	Mike Flores	1.25
5	Dan Gangwer	1.25
6	Reggie Johnson	1.50
7	Scott McAllister	1.25
8	Ken McKay	1.25
9	Browning Nagle	4.00
10	Ed Reynolds	1.25
11	Mark Sander	1.25
12	Howard Schnellenberger (CO)	5.00
13	Ted Washington	2.50
14	Klaus Wilmsmeyer	2.00
15	Cardinal Bird (Mascot)	1.25
16	Cardinal Stadium	1.25

1992 Louisville Kraft

		MT
Complete Set (30):		15.00
Common Player:		.60
1	Jamie Asher	1.50
2	Xzavia Atkins	.60
3	Kevin Blumeier	.60
4	Greg Brohm	.75
5	Jeff Brohm	.75
6	Brandon Brookfield	.60
7	Ray Buchanan	2.00
8	Rawle Bynoe	.60
9	Tom Cavallo	.60
10	Kevin Cook	.60
11	Andy Culley	.75
12	Ralph Dawkins	.75
13	Dave Debold	.60
14	Chris Fitzpatrick	.60
15	Kevin Gaines	.60
16	Jose Gonzalez	.60
17	Jim Hanna	.60
18	Ken Harnden	.60
19	Ivey Henderson	.60
20	Joe Johnson	1.50
21	Robert Knuutila	.60
22	Marty Lowe	1.00
23	Roman Oben	1.25
24	Garin Patrick	.60
25	Leonard Ray	.60
26	Shawn Rodriguez	.60
27	Anthony Shelman	1.00
28	Brevin Smith	.60
29	Jason Stinson	.75
30	Ben Sumpter	.75

1993 Louisville Kraft

		MT
Complete Set (30):		15.00
Common Player:		.60
1	Jamie Asher	1.25
2	Aaron Bailey	.60
3	Zoe Barney	.60
4	Anthony Bridges	.60
5	Jeff Brohm	.75
6	Brandon Brookfield	.60
7	Kendall Brown	.60
8	Tom Carrol	.60
9	Tom Cavallo	.60
10	Kevin Cook	.60
11	Ralph Dawkins	.75
12	Dave Debold	.60
13	Reggie Ferguson	.60
14	Chris Fitzpatrick	.60
15	Johnny Frost	.60
16	Jim Hanna	.60
17	Ivey Henderson	.60
18	Marcus Hill	.60
19	Shawn Jackson	.60
20	Joe Johnson	1.25
21	Marty Lowe	.75
22	Vertis McKinney	.60
23	Greg Minnis	.60
24	Roman Oben	1.00
25	Garin Patrick	.60
26	Terry Quinn	.75
27	Leonard Ray	.60
28	Anthony Shelman	.75
29	Jason Stinson	.60
30	Ben Sumpter	.60

1983 LSU Sunbeam

		MT
Complete Set (100):		12.00
Common Player:		.10
1	1958 LSU National Championship Team	.20
2	Abe Mickal	.10
3	Carlos Carson	.20
4	Charles Alexander	.20
5	Steve Ensminger	.10
6	Ken Kavanaugh Sr.	.20
7	Bert Jones	.50
8	David Woodley	.20
9	Jerry Marchand	.10
10	Clyde Lindsey	.10
11	James Britt	.10
12	Warren Rabb	.20
13	Mike Hillman	.10
14	Nelson Stokley	.10
15	Abner Wimberly	.10
16	Terry Robiskie	.20
17	Steve Van Buren	.30
18	Doug Moreau	.20
19	George Tarasovic	.10
20	Billy Cannon	.30
21	Jerry Stovall	.20
22	Joe Labruzzo	.10
23	Mickey Mangham	.10
24	Craig Burns	.10
25	Y.A. Tittle	.75
26	Wendell Harris	.20
27	Leroy Labat	.10
28	Hokie Gajan	.20
29	Mike Williams	.10
30	Sammy Grezaffi	.20
31	Clinton Burrell	.10
32	Orlando McDaniel	.10
33	George Bevan	.10
34	Johnny Robinson	.20
35	Billy Masters	.10
36	J.W. Brodnax	.10
37	Tommy Casanova	.20
38	Fred Miller	.10
39	George Rice	.10
40	Earl Gros	.20
41	Lynn LeBlanc	.10
42	Jim Taylor	.40
43	Joe Tumenello	.10
44	Tommy Davis	.20
45	Alvin Dark	.30
46	Richard Picou	.10
47	Chaille Percy	.10
48	John Garlington	.20
49	Mike Morgan	.10
50	Charles "Bo" Strange	.10
51	Max Fugler	.30
52	Don Schwab	.10
53	Dennis Gaubatz	.20
54	Jimmy Field	.10
55	Warren Capone	.10
56	Albert Richardson	.10
57	Charley Cusiman	.10
58	Brad Davis	.10
59	Gaynell "Gus" Kinchen	.10
60	Roy "Moonie" Winston	.20
61	Mike Anderson	.10
62	Jesse Fatherree	.10
63	Gene "Red" Knight	.10
64	Tyler LaFauci	.10
65	Emile Fournet	.10
66	Gaynell "Gus" Tinsley	.20
67	Remi Prudhomme	.20
68	Marvin "Moose" Stewart	.10
69	Jerry Guillot	.10
70	Steve Cassidy	.10
71	Bo Harris	.20
72	Robert Dugas	.10
73	Malcolm Scott	.10
74	Charles "Pinky" Rohm	.10
75	Gerald Keigley	.10
76	Don Alexander	.10
77	A.J. Duhe	.20
78	Ronnie Estay	.10
79	John Wood	.10
80	Andy Hamilton	.20
81	Jay Michaelson	.10
82	Kenny Konz	.20
83	Tracy Porter	.10
84	Billy Truax	.20
85	Alan Risher	.10
86	John Adams	.10
87	Tommy Neck	.10
88	Brad Boyd	.10
89	Greg LaFluer	.10
90	Bill Elko	.10
91	Binks Miciotto	.10
92	Lew Sibley	.10
93	Willie Teal	.10
94	Lyman White	.10
95	Chris Williams	.10
96	Sid Fournet	.10
97	Leonard Marshall	.20
98	Ramsey Dardar	.10
99	Kenny Bordelon	.10
100	Fred "Skinny" Hall	.10

1985 LSU Police

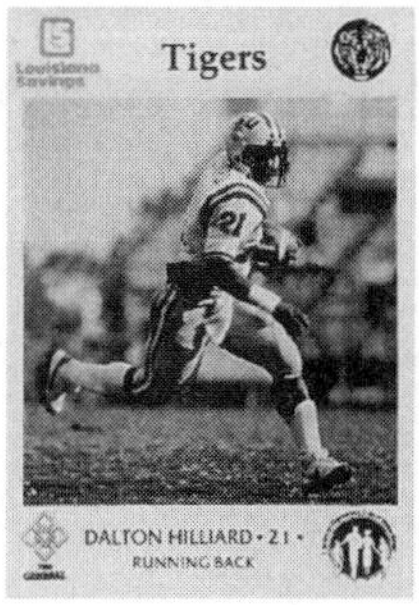
Tigers
DALTON HILLIARD • 21 •
RUNNING BACK

		MT
Complete Set (16):		8.00
Common Player:		.50
1	Mitch Andrews	.50
2	Bill Arnsparger (CO)	.75
3	Roland Barbay	.50
4	Michael Brooks	1.00
5	Shawn Burks	.50
6	Tommy Clapp	.50
7	Matt DeFrank	.50
8	Kevin Guidry	.50
9	Dalton Hilliard	1.50
10	Garry James	.75
11	Norman Jefferson	.50
12	Rogie Magee	.50
13	Mike the Tiger (Mascot)	.50
14	Craig Rathjen	.50
15	Jeff Wickersham	.75
16	Karl Wilson	.75

1986 LSU Police

		MT
Complete Set (16):		8.00
Common Player:		.50
1	Nacho Albergamo	.50
2	Eric Andolsek	1.00
3	Bill Arnsparger (CO)	.75
4	Roland Barbay	.50
5	Michael Brooks	1.00
6	Chris Carrier	.50
7	Toby Caston	1.00
8	Wendell Davis	1.50
9	Kevin Guidry	.50
10	John Hazard	.50
11	Oliver Lawrence	.50
12	Rogie Magee	.50
13	Sam Martin	.75
14	Darrell Phillips	.50
15	Steve Rehage	.50
16	Ron Sancho	.75

1987 LSU Police

		MT
Complete Set (16):		10.00
Common Player:		.50
1	Nacho Albergamo	.50
2	Eric Andolsek	.75
3	Mike Archer (CO)	.75
4	David Browndyke	.50
5	Chris Carrier	.50
6	Wendell Davis	1.00
7	Matt DeFrank	.50
8	Nicky Hazard	.50
9	Eric Hill	1.00
10	Tommy Hodson	1.50
11	Greg Jackson	1.00
12	Brian Kinchen	1.00
13	Darren Malbrough	.50
14	Sam Martin	.50
15	Ron Sancho	.50
16	Harvey Williams	3.50

1988 LSU Police

		MT
Complete Set (16):		8.00
Common Player:		.50
1	Mike the Tiger (Mascot)	.50
2	Mike Archer (CO)	.75
3	Tommy Hodson	1.50
4	Harvey Williams	2.50
5	David Browndyke	.50
6	Karl Dunbar	.50
7	Eddie Fuller	.50
8	Mickey Guidry	.50
9	Greg Jackson	.75
10	Clint James	.50
11	Victor Jones	.50
12	Tony Moss	.50
13	Ralph Norwood	.50
14	Darrell Phillips	.50
15	Ruffin Rodrigue	.50
16	Ron Sancho	.50

1989 LSU Police

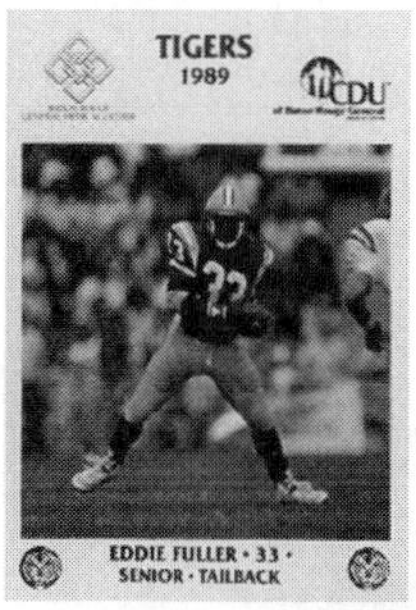
TIGERS
1989
EDDIE FULLER • 33 •
SENIOR • TAILBACK

		MT
Complete Set (16):		8.00
Common Player:		.50
1	Mike the Tiger (Mascot)	.50
2	David Browndyke	.50
3	Mike Archer (CO)	.75
4	Ruffin Rodrigue (68)	.50
5	Marc Boutte (95)	1.00
6	Clint James (70)	.50
7	Jimmy Young (5)	.50
8	Alvin Lee (26)	.50
9	Eddie Fuller (33)	.50
10	Tiger Stadium	.50
11	Harvey Williams (22)	2.00
12	Verge Ausberry (98)	.50
13	Karl Dunbar (63)	.50
14	Tommy Hodson (13)	1.25
15	Tony Moss (6)	.50
16	The Golden Girls (Cheerleaders)	.75

1992 LSU McDag

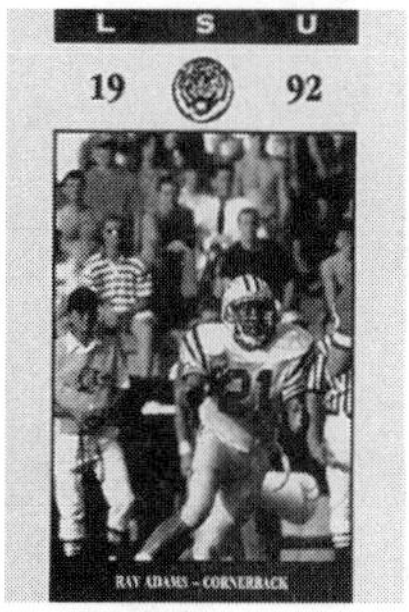
L S U
19 92
RAY ADAMS • CORNERBACK

		MT
Complete Set (16):		6.00
Common Player:		.50
1	Curley Hallman (CO)	.75
2	Ray Adams	.50
3	Chad Loup	.75
4	Odell Beckham	.50
5	Wesley Jacob	.50
6	Kevin Mawae	1.00
7	Clayton Mouton	.50
8	Roovelroe Swan	.50
9	Ricardo Washington	.50
10	David Walkup	.50
11	Jessie Daigle	.50
12	Carlton Buckles	.50
13	Anthony Williams	.50
14	Darron Landry	.50
15	Frank Godfrey	.50
16	Pedro Suarez	.50

1969 Maryland Team Sheets

		NM
Complete Set (6):		25.00
Common Panel:		6.00
1	Bill Backus, Lou Bracken, Sonny Demczuk, Roland Merritt, Rich Slaninka, Ralph Sonntag, Mike Stubljar, Jim Stull	6.00
2	Bill Bell CO, George Boutselis CO, Albert Ferguson CO, James Kehoe CO, Roy Lester CO, Dim Montero CO, Lee Royer CO	6.00
3	Pat Burke, John Dyer, Craig Gienger, Tony Greene, Bob MacBride, Bill Meister, Russ Nolen, Ray Soporowski	6.00
4	Steve Ciambor, Kenny Dutton, Dan Kecman, Bob Mahnic, Len Santacroce, David Seifert, Len Spicer, Rick Stoll	6.00
5	Bob Colbert, John Dill, Henry Gareis, Bill Grant, Glenn Kubany, Bill Reilly, Wally Stalnaker, Gary Vansickler	6.00
6	Paul Fitzpatrick, Larry Marshall, Tom Miller, Will Morris, Dennis O'Hara, Scott Shank, Jeff Shugars, Al Thomas	6.00

1991 Maryland HS Big 33

		MT
Complete Set (34):		18.00
Common Player:		.75
1	Asim Penny	1.00
2	Louis Jason	1.00
3	Mark McCain	1.00
4	Matthew Byrne	.75
5	Mike Gillespie	.75
6	Ricky Rowe	.75
7	David DeArmas	1.00
8	Duane Ashman	.75
9	James Cunningham	.75
10	Keith Kormanik	.75
11	Leonard Green	.75
12	Larry Washington	.75
13	Raphael Wall	.75
14	Kai Hebron	.75
15	Coy Gibbs	1.00
16	Lenard Marcus	.75
17	John Taliaferro	1.00
18	J.C. Price	.75
19	Jamal Cox	1.00
20	Rick Budd	.75
21	Shaun Marshall	.75
22	Allan Jenkins	.75
23	Bryon Turner	.75
24	Ryan Foran	.75
25	John Summerday	.75
26	Joshua Austin	.75
27	Emile Palmer	.75
28	John Teter	.75
29	John Kennedy	.75
30	Clarence Collins	.75
31	Daryl Smith	.75
32	David Wilkins	.75
33	David Thomas	.75
34	Russell Thomas	1.00

1988 McNeese State McDag/Police

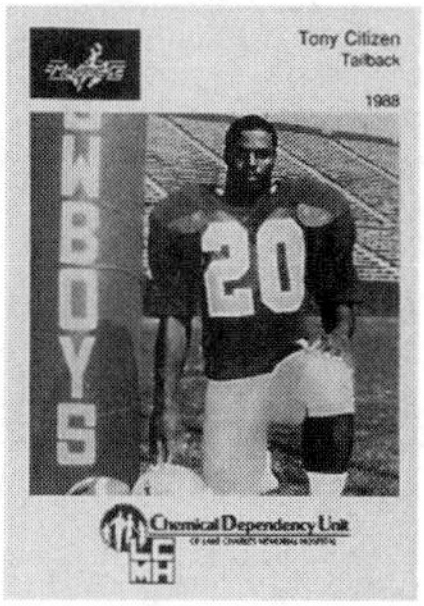
Tony Citizen
Tailback
1988

		MT
Complete Set (16):		6.00
Common Player:		.50
1	Sonny Jackson (CO)	.50
2	Lance Wiley	.50
3	Brian McZeal	.50
4	Berwick Davenport	.50
5	Gary Irvin	.50
6	Glenn Koch	.50
7	Chad Habetz	.50
8	Pete Sinclair	.50
9	Tony Citizen	.50
10	Scott Dieterich	.50
11	Hud Jackson	.50
12	Darrin Andrus	.50
13	Jeff Mathews	.50
14	Devin Babineaux	.50
15	Jeff Delhomme	.50
16	Eric LeBlanc, Mike Pierce	.50

1989 McNeese State McDag/Police

		MT
Complete Set (16):		6.00
Common Player:		.50
1	Marc Stampley	.50
2	Mark LeBlanc	.50
3	Kip Texada	.50
4	Brian Champagne	.50
5	Ronald Scott	.50
6	Jimmy Poirier	.50
7	Cliff Buckner	.50
8	Jericho Loupe	.50
9	Vaughn Calbert	.50
10	Rodney Burks	.50
11	Troy Jones	.50
12	Chris Andrus	.50
13	Robbie Vizier	.50
14	Kenneth Pierce	.50
15	Bobby Smith	.50
16	Trent Lee	.50

1990 McNeese State McDag/Police

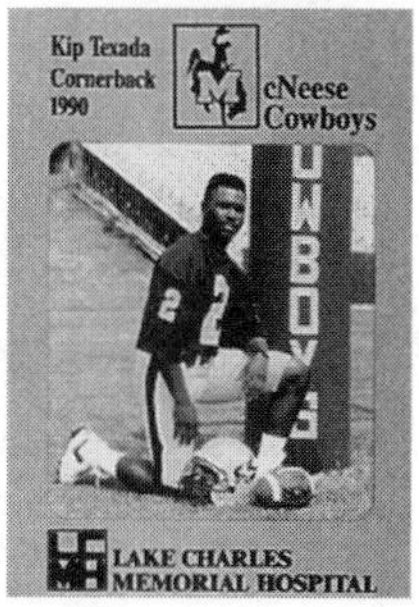
Kip Texada
Cornerback
1990
cNeese
Cowboys
LAKE CHARLES
MEMORIAL HOSPITAL

		MT
	Complete Set (16):	6.00
	Common Player:	.50
1	Hud Jackson	.50
2	Wes Watts	.50
3	Mark LeBlanc	.50
4	Jeff Delhomme	.50
5	Mike Reed	.50
6	Chuck Esponge	.50
7	Ronald Scott	.50
8	Ken Naquin	.50
9	Steve Aultman	.50
10	Sean Judge	.50
11	Greg Rayson	.50
12	Kip Texada	.50
13	Mike Pierce	.50
14	Jimmy Poirier	.50
15	Ronald Solomon	.50
16	Eric Foster	.50

1991 McNeese State McDag/Police

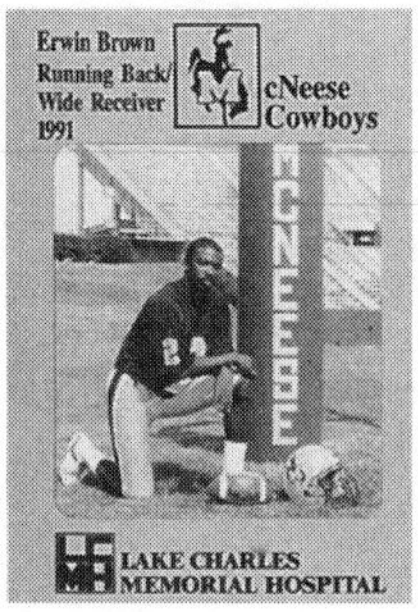

		MT
	Complete Set (16):	6.00
	Common Player:	.50
1	Eric Roberts	.50
2	Irwin Brown	.50
3	Marcus Bowie	.50
4	Wes Watts	.50
5	Brian Brumfield	.50
6	Marc Stampley	.50
7	Sean Judge	.50
8	Joey Bernard	.50
9	Ken Naquin	.50
10	Bobby Smith	.50
11	Sam Breaux	.50
12	Ronald Scott	.50
13	Edward Dyer	.50
14	Blayne Rush	.50
15	Ronald Solomon	.50
16	Steve Aultman	.50

1992 McNeese State McDag/Police

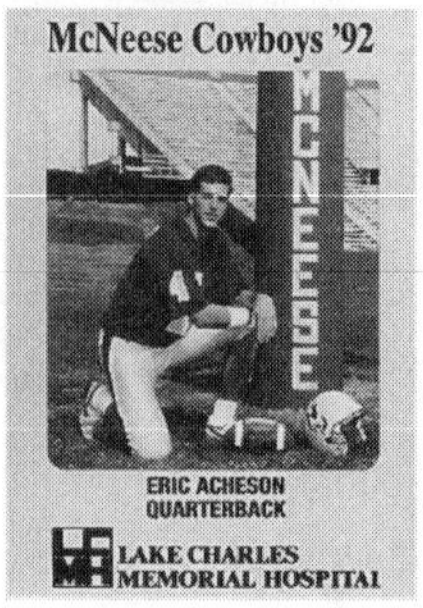

		MT
	Complete Set (16):	6.00
	Common Player:	.50
1	Eric Acheson	.50
2	Pat Neck	.50
3	Marcus Bowie	.50
4	Marty Posey	.50
5	Brian Brumfield	.50
6	Terry Irving	.75
7	Eric Fleming	.50
8	Lance Guidry	.50
9	Ken Naquin	.50
10	Chris Fontenette	.50
11	Sam Breaux	.50
12	Dana Scott	.50
13	Edward Dyer	.50
14	Blayne Rush	.50
15	Ronald Solomon	.50
16	Steve Aultman	.50

1990 Miami Smokey

		MT
	Complete Set (16):	18.00
	Common Player:	.75
1	Randy Bethel (93)	.75
2	Wesley Carroll (81)	2.00
3	Rob Chudzinski (84)	.75
4	Leonard Conley (28)	1.50
5	Luis Cristobal (59)	.75
6	Maurice Crum (49)	.75
7	Shane Curry (44)	1.50
8	Craig Erickson (7)	4.00
9	Dennis Erickson (CO)	2.00
10	Darren Handy (66)	.75
11	Randal Hill (3)	4.00
12	Carlos Huerta (27)	1.50
13	Russell Maryland (67)	3.00
14	Stephen McGuire (30)	1.50
15	Roland Smith (16)	.75
16	Mike Sullivan (79)	.75

1991 Miami Police

		MT
	Complete Set (16):	15.00
	Common Player:	1.00
1	Jessie Armstead	1.50
2	Micheal Barrow	2.00
3	Hurlie Brown	1.00
4	Dennis Erickson (CO)	2.00
5	Anthony Hamlet	1.00
6	Carlos Huerta	1.50
7	Herbert James	1.00
8	Claude Jones	1.00
9	Stephen McGuire	1.50
10	Eric Miller	1.00
11	Joe Moore	1.00
12	Charles Pharms	1.00
13	Leon Searcy	2.00
14	Darrin Smith	2.00
15	Lamar Thomas	1.50
16	Gino Torretta	2.00

1992 Miami Police

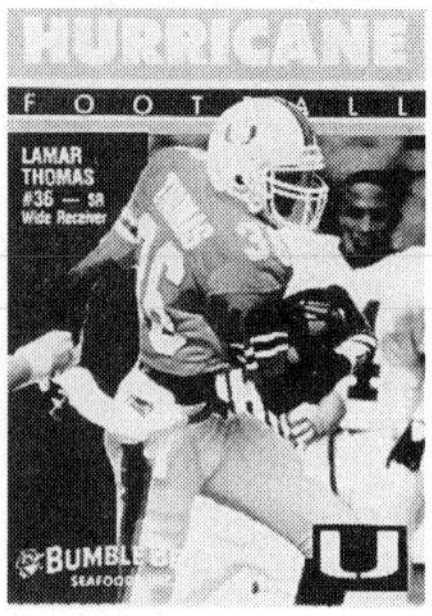

		MT
	Complete Set (16):	15.00
	Common Player:	.75
1	Jessie Armstead	1.00
2	Micheal Barrow	1.50
3	Coleman Bell	.75
4	Mark Caesar	.75
5	Horace Copeland (UER) (Name misspelled Horrace on front)	2.00
6	Mario Cristobal	.75
7	Dennis Erickson (CO)	1.50
8	Casey Greer	.75
9	Stephen McGuire	1.00
10	Ryan McNeil	1.50
11	Rusty Medearis	.75
12	Darrin Smith	1.50
13	Darryl Spencer	.75
14	Lamar Thomas	2.00
15	Gino Torretta	2.00
16	Kevin Williams (WR)	3.00

1993 Miami Bumble Bee

		MT
	Complete Set (16):	12.00
	Common Player:	.60
1	Rudy Barber	.60
2	Robert Bass	.60
3	Donnell Bennett	2.00
4	Jason Budroni	.60
5	Marcus Carey	.60
6	Ryan Collins	.60
7	Frank Costa	1.00
8	Dennis Erickson (CO)	1.00
9	Terris Harris	.60
10	Chris T. Jones	2.00
11	Larry Jones	1.50
12	Darren Krein	1.00
13	Kenny Lopez	.60
14	Kevin Patrick	.60
15	Dexter Seigler	.60
16	Paul White	.60

1907 Michigan Postcards

		NM
	Complete Set (15):	600.00
	Common Player:	30.00
1	Dave Allerdice	40.00
2	William Casey	30.00
3	William Embs	30.00
4	Keene Fitzpatrick (TR)	30.00
5	Flanagan	30.00
6	Walter Graham	30.00
7	H.S. Hammond	30.00
8	John Loell	30.00
9	Paul Magoffin	40.00
10	James Miller	30.00
11	Walter Rheinschild	30.00
12	Mason Rumney	30.00
13	Adolph "Germany" Schultz	125.00
14	William Wasmund	30.00
15	Fielding Yost (CO)	125.00

1977 Michigan

		NM
	Complete Set (21):	25.00
	Common Player:	.75
1	John Anderson	1.25
2	Russell Davis	1.25
3	Mark Donahue	.75
4	Walt Downing	.75
5	Bill Dufek	1.25
6	Jon Giesler (SP)	2.00
7	Steve Graves	.75
8	Curtis Greer	2.00
9	Dwight Hicks	2.50
10	Derek Howard	.75
11	Harlan Huckleby	2.50
12	Gene Johnson	.75
13	Dale Keitz	.75
14	Mike Kenn	2.50
15	Rick Leach	2.50
16	Mark Schmerge	.75
17	Ron Simpkins	1.25
18	Curt Stephenson (SP)	2.00
19	Gerry Szara (SP)	2.00
20	Rick White	.75
21	Gregg Willner	.75

1989 Michigan

		MT
	Complete Set (22):	12.00
	Common Player:	.50
1	H.O. "Fritz" Crisler (CO)	.60
2	Anthony Carter	1.50
3	Willie Heston	.50
4	Reggie McKenzie	.50
5	Bo Schembechler (CO)	1.50
6	Dan Dierdorf	1.50
7	Jim Harbaugh	1.50
8	Bennie Oosterbaan	.50
9	Jamie Morris	.60
10	Gerald R. Ford	1.50
11	Curtis Greer	.60
12	Ron Kramer	.60
13	Calvin O'Neal	.50
14	Bob Chappuis	.50
15	Fielding Yost (CO)	.60
16	Dennis Franklin	.50
17	Benny Friedman	.60
18	Jim Mandich	.60
19	Rob Lytle	.60
20	Bump Elliott	.60
21	Harry Kipke	.50
22	Dave Brown	.60

1988 Mississippi McDag

		MT
	Complete Set (2):	4.00
	Common Player:	2.00
15	Mark Young	2.00
16	Bryan Owen	2.00

1991 Mississippi Hoby

		MT
	Complete Set (42):	9.00
	Common Player:	.25
439	Gary Abide	.25
440	Dwayne Amos	.25
441	Tyji Armstrong	1.00
442	Tyrone Ashley	.25
443	Darron Billings	.25
444	Danny Boyd	.25
445	Billy Brewer (CO)	.35
446	Chad Brown	.35
447	Tony Brown	.25
448	Vincent Brownlee	.25
449	Jeff Carter	.35
450	Richard Chisolm	.25
451	Clint Conlee	.25
452	Marvin Courtney	.25
453	Cliff Dew	.25
454	Johnny Dixon	.25
455	Artis Ford	.25
456	Chauncey Godwin	.25
457	Brian Harper	.25
458	David Harris	.25
459	Pete Harris	.25
460	David Herring	.25
461	James Holcombe	.25
462	Kevin Ingram	.25
463	Phillip Kent	.35
464	Derrick King	.25
465	Brian Lee	.25
466	Jim Lentz	.25
467	Everett Lindsay	.25
468	Tom Luke	.25
469	Thomas McLeish	.25
470	Wesley Melton	.25
471	Tyrone Montgomery	.75
472	Deano Orr	.25
473	Darrick Owens	.35
474	Lynn Ross	.25
475	Russ Shows	.25
476	Eddie Small	.35
477	Trea Southerland	.25
478	Gerald Vaughn	.25
479	Abner White	.25
480	Sebastian Williams	.25

1991 Mississippi State Hoby

		MT
	Complete Set (42):	9.00
	Common Player:	.25
481	Lance Aldridge	.25
482	Treddis Anderson	.25
483	Shea Bell	.25
484	Chris Bosarge	.25
485	Daniel Boyd	.25
486	Jerome Brown	.25
487	Torrance Brown	.25
488	Keith Carr	.25
489	Herman Carroll	.25
490	Keo Coleman	.35
491	Michael Davis	.25
492	Trenell Edwards	.25
493	Chris Firle	.25
494	Lee Ford	.25
495	Tay Galloway	.25
496	Chris Gardner	.25
497	Arleye Gibson	.25
498	Tony Harris	.25
499	Willie Harris	.25
500	Kevin Henry	.35
501	Jackie Sherrill (CO)	.50
502	John James	.25
503	Tony James	.25
504	Todd Jordan	.25
505	Keith Joseph	.25
506	Kelvin Knight	.25
507	Lee Lipscomb	.25
508	Juan Long	.25
509	Kyle McCoy	.25
510	Tommy Morrell	.25
511	Kelly Ray	.25
512	Mike Riley	.25
513	Kenny Roberts	.25
514	William Robinson	.25
515	Bill Sartin	.25
516	Kenny Stewart	.25
517	Rodney Stowers	.50
518	Anthony Thames	.25
519	Edward Williams	.25
520	Nate Williams	.25
521	Karl Williamson	.25
522	Marc Woodard	.25

1992 Mobil Cotton Bowl

		MT
	Complete Set (24):	35.00
	Common Player:	1.00
1	The Cotton Bowl	1.00
2	Sammy Baugh	2.50
3	Doak Walker	2.00
4	Dicky Moegle	1.00
5	Bobby Layne	2.50
6	Curtis Sanford (Founder)	1.00
7	John Kimbrough	1.00
8	Ernie Davis	5.00
9	Lance Alworth	2.00
10	James Street, Darrell Royal CO	1.50
11	Mike Singletary	1.50
12	Roger Staubach	4.00
13	Earl Campbell	3.50
14	Wilson Whitley	1.00
15	Jim Swink	1.00
16	Martin Ruby	1.00
17	Davey O'Brien	1.50
18	Gene Stallings, Paul "Bear" Bryant (CO)	2.50
19	Bo Jackson	2.00
20	Joe Theismann	1.50
21	Mr. Cotton Bowl (Field Scovell)	1.00
22	Ken Hatfield	1.00
23	Joe Montana	5.00
24	Mobil Cotton Bowl Classic CL	1.00

1974 Nebraska

		NM
	Complete Set (54):	65.00
	Common Player:	1.00
1	Tom Osborne (CO)	20.00
2	Terry Rogers	1.00
3	Tom Ruud	1.50
4	Jeff Schneider	1.00
5	Mark Heydorff	1.00
6	Dean Gissler	1.00
7	Jim Burrow	1.00
8	Al Eveland	1.00
9	Chuck Jones	1.00
10	Brad Jenkins	1.00
11	Dave Butterfield	1.00
12	Rich Duda	1.50
13	Steve Hoins	1.00
14	Ron Pruitt	1.00
15	Tony Davis	1.50
16	Mike Fultz	1.00
17	Chad Leonardi	1.00
18	John Starkebaum	1.00
19	Marvin Crenshaw	1.50
20	Larry Mushinskie	1.00
21	Tom Pate	1.00
22	David Humm	4.00
23	Willie Thornton	1.50
24	Dave Redding	1.00
25	Dave Shamblin	1.00
26	Earl Everett	1.00
27	Rik Bonness	1.50
28	Mark Doak	1.00
29	John Lee	1.00
30	Mike Coyle	1.00
31	George Kyros	1.00
32	Gary Higgs	1.00
33	Dennis Pavelka	1.00
34	Jeff Moran	1.00
35	John O'Leary	1.00
36	Percy Eichelberger	1.00
37	Greg Jorgensen	1.00
38	George Mills	1.00
39	Terry Luck	1.00
40	Don Westbrook	1.00
41	Mike Offner	1.00
42	Stan Waldemore	1.00
43	Stan Hegener	1.00
44	Bobby Thomas	1.00
45	Bob Martin	1.00
46	Ritch Bahe	1.00
47	Tom Heiser	1.00
48	Steve Wieser	1.00
49	Ardell Johnson	1.00
50	Chuck Malito	1.00
51	Bob Lingenfelter	1.00
52	Wonder Monds	1.50
53	Bob Nelson	1.50
54	Memorial Stadium	1.50

1977 Nebraska

		NM
	Complete Set (54):	65.00
	Common Player:	1.00
1	Tom Osborne (CO)	15.00
2	Tom Alward	1.00
3	Dan Anderson	1.00
4	Frosty Anderson	1.00
5	Al Austin	1.00
6	Ritch Bahe	1.00
7	John Bell	1.00
8	Rik Bonness	1.50
9	Randy Borg	1.00
10	Rich Costanzo	1.00
11	Maury Damkroger	1.50
12	Tony Davis	1.50
13	Mark Doak	1.00
14	Richard Duda	1.50
15	John Dutton	3.00
16	Pat Fischer	3.00
17	Marvin Crenshaw	1.50
18	Dean Gissler	1.00
19	Dave Goeller	1.00
20	Percy Eichelberger	1.00
21	Stan Hegener	1.00
22	Dave Humm	2.50
23	Ardell Johnson	1.00
24	Doug Johnson	1.00
25	Chuck Jones	1.00
26	Wonder Monds	1.50
27	Terry Rogers	1.00
28	Bob Revelle	1.00
29	Tom Pate	1.00
30	Mike O'Holleran	1.00
31	Ron Pruitt	1.00
32	Bob Nelson	1.50
33	Larry Mushinskie	1.00
34	Jeff Moran	1.00
35	Bob Martin	1.00
36	Ralph Powell	1.00
37	Steve Manstedt	1.00
38	Brent Longwell	1.00
39	George Kyros	1.00
40	Zaven Yaralian	1.00
41	Bob Wolfe	1.00
42	Steve Wieser	1.00
43	Daryl White	1.00
44	Bob Thornton	1.00
45	John Starkebaum	1.00
46	Dave Shamblin	1.00
47	Don Westbrook	1.50
48	Bob Schmit	1.50
49	Rich Sanger	1.00
50	Willie Thornton	1.50
51	Tom Ruud	1.50
52	Steve Runty	1.00
53	Stadium (Red)	1.50
54	Stadium (Black)	1.50

1989 Nebraska 100

		MT
	Complete Set (100):	40.00
	Common Player:	.35
1	Tony Davis	.50
2	Keith Jones	.35
3	Turner Gill	1.25
4	Dave Butterfield	.35
5	Wonder Monds	.50
6	Dave Rimington	.75
7	John Dutton	.75
8	Irving Fryar	3.00
9	Dean Steinkuhler	.75
10	Mike Rozier	1.25
11	Jarvis Redwine	.75
12	Randy Schleusener	.35
13	Junior Miller	.50
14	Broderick Thomas	1.25
15	Steve Taylor	.50
16	Neil Smith	2.00
17	John McCormick	.35
18	Danny Noonan	.50
19	Mike Fultz	.35
20	Vince Ferragamo	1.00
21	Jerry Tagge	.75
22	Jeff Kinney	.50
23	Rich Glover	.50
24	Johnny Rodgers	1.25
25	Rik Bonness	.50
26	Dave Humm	.50
27	Mark Traynowicz	.50
28	Harry Grimminger	.35
29	Bill Lewis	.50
30	Jim Skow	.50
31	Larry Kramer	.35
32	Tony Jeter	.50
33	Robert Brown	.35
34	Larry Wachholtz	.35
35	Wayne Meylan	.50
36	Bob Newton	.35
37	Willie Harper	.50
38	Bob Martin	.35
39	Jerry Murtaugh	.50
40	Daryl White	.35
41	Larry Jacobson	.35
42	Joe Armstrong	.35
43	Laverne Allers	.35
44	Freeman White	.50
45	Marvin Crenshaw	.50
46	Forrest Behm	.35
47	Jerry Minnick	.35
48	Tom Davis	.35
49	Kelvin Clark	.50
50	Tom Rathman	1.25
51	Sam Francis	.35
52	Joe Orduna	.50
53	Ed Weir	.35
54	Bill Thornton	.35
55	Bob Devaney (CO)	.75
56	Bret Clark	.35
57	Frank Solich	.35
58	Tim Smith	.35
59	George Andrews	.35
60	Rick Berns	.50
61	Monte Johnson	.50
62	Walt Barnes	.35
63	Jim McFarland	.35
64	Jimmy Williams	.35
65	Vic Halligan	.35
66	Guy Chamberlin	.35
67	Hugh Rhea	.35
68	George Sauer	.50
69	E.O. Stiehm (CO)	.35
70	Walter G. Booth (CO)	.35
71	First Night Game (Memorial Stadium)	.35
72	Memorial Stadium	.35
73	M-Stadium Expansions	.35
74	Andra Franklin	.75
75	Ron McDole	.50
76	Pat Fischer	.50
77	Dan McMullen	.35
78	Charles Brock	.35
79	Verne Lewellen	.35
80	Bob Nelson	.50
81	Roger Craig	3.00
82	Fred Shirey	.35
83	Tom Novak	.35
84	Ray Richards	.35
85	Warren Alfson	.35
86	Lawrence Ely	.35
87	Mike Rozier	1.25
88	Dean Steinkuhler	.75
89	John Dutton	.75
90	Dave Rimington	.75
91	Johnny Rodgers	1.25
92	Herbie Husker (Mascot)	.35
93	Tom Osborne (CO)	1.25
94	Broderick Thomas	1.25
95	Bob Reynolds	.35
96	Mike Tingelhoff (UER) (Name misspelled Tinglehoff)	.75
97	Lloyd Cardwell	.35
98	Johnny Rodgers	1.25
99	'70 National Champs (Team Photo)	.50
100	'71 National Champs (Team Photo)	.50
NNO	Title Card (Contest on back)	.50

1993 Nebraska

		MT
	Complete Set (25):	15.00
	Common Player:	.50
1	Trev Alberts	2.00
2	Mike Anderson	.75
3	Ernie Beler	.75
4	Byron Bennett	.75
5	Troy Bromawn (Men's baseball)	.50
6	NaFeesah Brown (Women's basketball)	.50
7	Jed Dalton (Men's baseball)	.50
8	Sumner Darling (Men's gymnastics)	.50
9	Corey Dixon	.75
10	Troy Dumas	.75
11	Nicole Duval (Women's gymnastics)	.50
12	Mike Eierman (Wrestling)	.50
13	Amy Erlenbusch (Women's softball)	.50
14	Dennis Harrison (Men's gymnastics)	.50
15	Jamar Johnson (Men's basketball)	1.00
16	Calvin Jones	1.50
17	Laura Luther (Women's volleyball)	.50
18	Denise McMillen (Women's softball)	.50
19	Bruce Moore	.75
20	David Noonan	1.00
21	Lori Phillips (Women's gymnastics)	.50
22	Eric Piatkowski (Men's basketball)	2.00
23	Nikki Stricker (Women's volleyball)	.50
24	Frank Velazquez (Wrestling)	.50
25	Meggan Yedsena (Women's basketball)	.50

1994 Nebraska

		MT
	Complete Set (21):	12.00
	Common Player:	.50
1	Kelly Aspergren (Women's volleyball)	.50
2	Jaron Boone (Men's basketball)	1.00
3	Terry Connealy	.75
4	Jed Dalton (Men's basketball)	.50
5	Troy Dumas	.75
6	Cody Dusenberry (Women's softball)	.50
7	Nicole Duval (Women's gymnastics)	.50
8	Richard Grace (Men's gymnastics)	.50
9	Donta Jones	1.50
10	Rick Kieffer (Men's gymnastics)	.50
11	Barron Miles	1.00
12	Darin Petersen (Men's baseball)	.50
13	Cory Schlesinger	2.00
14	Ed Stewart	.75
15	Erick Strickland (Men's basketball)	.75
16	Joy Taylor (Women's gymnastics)	.50
17	Emily Thompson (Women's basketball)	.50
18	Tanya Upthegrove (Women's basketball)	.50
19	Zach Wiegert	1.50
20	Billie Winsett (Women's volleyball)	.50
21	Rob Zatechka	1.50

1996 Nebraska

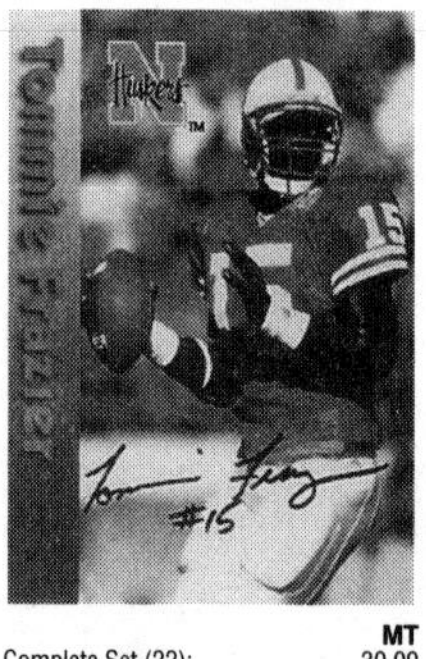

		MT
	Complete Set (22):	30.00
	Common Player:	1.00
1	Jacques Allen	1.00
2	Reggie Baul	1.50
3	Brook Berringer	3.00
4	Clinton Childs	2.00
5	Doug Colman	1.00
6	Phil Ellis	1.00
7	Tommie Frazier	5.00
8	Mark Gilman	1.00
9	Aaron Graham	1.50
10	Luther Hardin	1.00
11	Jason Jenkins	1.00
12	Chester Johnson	1.00
13	Jeff Makovicka	1.50
14	Brian Nunns	1.00
15	Steve Ott	1.00
16	Aaron Penland	1.00
17	Christian Peter	1.50
18	Darren Schmadeke	1.50
19	Tony Veland	1.00
20	Steve Volin	1.00
21	Tyrone Williams	1.00
22	Checklist Card Team Logo	1.00

1979 North Carolina Schedules

		NM
	Complete Set (4):	12.00
	Common Player:	3.00
1	Ricky Barden	3.00
2	Steve Junkman	3.00
3	Matt Kupec	5.00
4	Doug Paschal	3.00

1982 North Carolina Schedules

MT
Complete Set (8): 25.00
Common Player: 3.00
1 Kelvin Bryant 7.50
2 Alan Burrus 3.00
3 David Drechsler 3.00
4 Rod Elkins 4.00
5 Jack Parry 3.00
6 Greg Poole 3.00
7 Ron Spruill 3.00
8 Mike Wilcher 4.00

1986 North Carolina Schedules

MT
Complete Set (4): 15.00
Common Player: 3.00
1 Walter Bailey 3.00
2 Harris Barton 6.00
3 C.A. Brooks 3.00
4 Eric Streater 4.00

1988 North Carolina

MT
Complete Set (16): 15.00
Common Player: 1.00
1 Mack Brown (CO) 1.50
2 Pat Crowley 1.00
3 Torin Dorn 2.00
4 Jeff Garnica 1.00
5 Antonio Goss 1.25
6 Jonathan Hall 1.25
7 Darrell Hamilton 1.00
8 Creighton Incorminias 1.00
9 John Keller 1.00
10 Randy Marriott 1.00
11 Deems May 1.00
12 John Reed 1.00
13 James Thompson 1.25
14 Steve Steinbacher 1.00
15 Dan Vooletich 1.00
16 Mitch Wike 1.00

1991 North Carolina Schedules

MT
Complete Set (3): 7.00
Common Player: 2.00
1 Eric Gash 2.00
2 Dwight Hollier 4.00
3 Tommy Thigpen 2.00

1993 North Carolina State

MT
Complete Set (56): 25.00
Common Player: .50
1 John Akins .75
2 Darryl Beard .50
3 Ricky Bell .50
4 Geoff Bender .50
5 Chuck Browning .50
6 Chuck Cole .50
7 Chris Cotton .50
8 Eric Counts .50
9 Damien Covington 1.00
10 Dallas Dickerson .50
11 Gary Downs .50
12 Brian Fitzgerald .50
13 Ed Gallon .50
14 Ledel George .50
15 Walt Gerard .50
16 Gregg Giannamore .50
17 Eddie Goines 1.00
18 Ray Griffis .50
19 Mike Harrison .50
20 Terry Harvey .50
21 George Hegamin 1.00
22 Chris Hennie-Roed .50
23 Adrian Hill .50
24 Robert Hinton .50
25 David Inman .50
26 Dave Janik .50
27 Shawn Johnson .50
28 Tyler Lawrence .50
29 Miller Lawson .50
30 Sean Maguire .50
31 Drea Major .50
32 Mike Moore .50
33 James Newsome .50
34 Mike O'Cain (CO) .50
35 Loren Pinkney .50
36 Carlos Pruitt .50
37 Carl Reeves 1.00
38 Jon Rissler .50
39 Chad Robinson .50
40 Ryan Schultz .75
41 William Strong .75
42 Jimmy Sziksai .50
43 Eric Taylor .50
44 Pat Threatt .50
45 Steve Videtich .75
46 James Walker .75
47 Todd Ward .75
48 DeWayne Washington 2.00
49 Heath Woods .50
50 Scott Woods .50
51 Defensive Coaches (Buddy Green, Kent Briggs, Ken Pettus, Jeff Snipes, Henry Trevathan) .50
52 Offensive Coaches (Ted Cain, Robbie Caldwell, Jimmy Kiser, Brette Simmons, Dick Portee) .50
53 Tri-Captains (John Akins, Todd Ward, DeWayne Washington) .50
54 Carter-Finley Stadium .50
55 Checklist .50
56 Title Card .75

1989 North Texas McDag

MT
Complete Set (16): 7.00
Common Player: .50
1 Clay Bode .50
2 Scott Bowles .50
3 Keith Chapman .50
4 Darrin Collins .50
5 Tony Cook .50
6 Scott Davis 1.00
7 Byron Gross .50
8 Larry Green .50
9 Major Greene 1.00
10 Carl Brewer .50
11 J.D. Martinez .50
12 Charles Monroe .50
13 Kregg Sanders .50
14 Lou Smith .50
15 Jeff Tutson .50
16 Trent Touchstone .50

1990 North Texas McDag

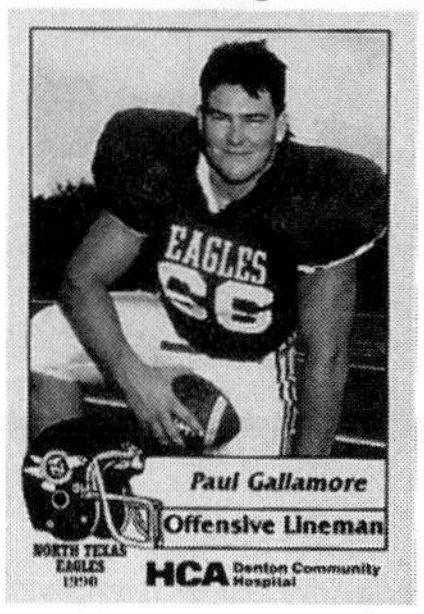
EAGLES
Paul Gallamore
Offensive Lineman
NORTH TEXAS EAGLES 1990
HCA Denton Community Hospital

MT
Complete Set (16): 9.00
Common Player: .50
1 Scott Davis .75
2 Byron Gross .50
3 Tony Cook .50
4 Walter Casey .50
5 Erric Pegram 4.00
6 Clay Bode .50
7 Scott Bowles .50
8 Shawn Wash .50
9 Isaac Barnett .50
10 Paul Gallamore .50
11 J.D. Martinez .50
12 Velton Morgan .50
13 Major Greene .75
14 Bart Helsley .50
15 Jeff Tutson .50
16 Tony Walker .50

1992 Northwestern Louisiana State

MT
Complete Set (16): 7.00
Common Player: .50
1 Darius Adams .50
2 Paul Arevalo .50
3 Brad Brown .60
4 Steve Brown .60
5 J.J. Eldridge .50
6 Sam Goodwin (CO) .60
7 Adrian Hardy .60
8 Guy Hedrick .50
9 Brad Laird .60
10 Lawann Latson .50
11 Deon Ridgell .50
12 Bryan Roussell .50
13 Brannon Rowlett .60
14 Marcus Spears .60
15 Carlos Treadway .60
16 Vic (Team Mascot) .50

1930 Notre Dame Postcards

NM
Complete Set (25): 800.00
Common Player: 30.00
1 Marty Brill 35.00
2 Frank Carideo 35.00
3 Tom Conley 30.00
4 Al Culver (October 25) 30.00
5 Dick Donaghue (October 18) 30.00
6 Nordy Hoffmann 30.00
7 Al Howard (November 15) 30.00
8 Chuck Jaskwich (November 22) 30.00
9 Clarence Kaplan (October 18) 30.00
10 Tom Kassis 30.00
11 Ed Koska (November 22) 30.00
12 Joe Kurth 35.00
13 Bernie Leahy 50.00
14 Bernie Leahy 125.00
15 Dick Mahoney (November 8) 30.00
16 Art McManmon (November 1) 30.00
17 Bert Metzger 30.00
18 Larry "Moon" Mullins 50.00
19 John O'Brien 30.00
20 Bucky O'Connor 30.00
21 Joe Savoldi 35.00
22 Marchmont Schwartz 35.00
23 Robert Terlaak (November 8) 30.00
24 George Vik (October 25) 30.00
25 Tom Yarr 35.00

1988 Notre Dame

MT
Complete Set (60): 20.00
Common Player: .25
1 Golden Dome .50
2 Lou Holtz (CO) 2.00
3 Mark Green .50
4 Andy Heck .75
5 Ned Bolcar .50
6 Anthony Johnson .50
7 Flash Gordon .25
8 Pat Eilers .25
9 Raghib Ismail 5.00
10 Ted FitzGerald .25
11 Ted Healy .25
12 Braxston Banks .50
13 Steve Belles .25
14 Steve Alaniz .25
15 Chris Zorich 2.00
16 Kent Graham 1.00
17 Mike Brennan .25
18 Marty Lippincott .25
19 Rod West .25
20 Dean Brown .25
21 Tom Gorman .25
22 Tony Rice 1.50
23 Steve Roddy .25
24 Reggie Ho .50
25 Pat Terrell .75
26 Joe Jarosz .25
27 Mike Stonebreaker 1.00
28 David Jandric .25
29 Jeff Alm .75
30 Pete Graham .25
31 Corny Southall .25
32 Joe Allen .25
33 Jim Sexton .25
34 Michael Crounse .25
35 Kurt Zackrison .25
36 Stan Smagala .50
37 Mike Heidt .25
38 Frank Stams .75
39 D'Juan Francisco .50
40 Tim Ryan .50
41 Arnold Ale .25
42 Andre Jones .25
43 Wes Pritchett .25
44 Tim Grunhard .75
45 Chuck Killian .25
46 Scott Kowalkowski .50
47 George Streeter .25
48 Donn Grimm .25
49 Ricky Watters 6.00
50 Ryan Mihalko .25
51 Tony Brooks .75
52 Todd Lyght 1.00
53 Winston Sandri .25
54 Aaron Robb .25
55 Derek Brown (TE) 1.00
56 Bryan Flannery .25
57 Kevin McShane .25
58 Billy Hackett .25
59 George Williams .25
60 Frank Jacobs .25

1988 Notre Dame Smokey

MT
Complete Set (14): 30.00
Common Player (1-10): 1.50
Common Sport (11-14): 1.50
1 Braxston Banks (39) 2.00
2 Ned Bolcar (47) 2.00
3 Tom Gorman (87) 1.50
4 Mark Green (24) 2.00
5 Andy Heck (66) 2.00
6 Lou Holtz (CO) 3.50
7 Anthony Johnson (22) 2.00
8 Wes Pritchett (34) 1.50
9 George Streeter (27) 1.50
10 Ricky Watters (12) 9.00
11 Men's Soccer 1.50
12 Volleyball 1.50
13 Women's Basketball 1.50
14 Women's Tennis 1.50

1989 Notre Dame 1903-32

MT
Complete Set (22): 7.00
Common Player: .35
1 Hunk Anderson .50
2 Bert Metzger .35
3 Roger Kiley .35
4 Nordy Hoffman .35
5 Knute Rockne (CO) 2.00
6 Elmer Layden .75
7 Gus Dorais .50
8 Ray Eichenlaub .35
9 Don Miller .50
10 Moose Krause .75
11 Jesse Harper .50
12 Jack Cannon .35
13 Eddie Anderson .35
14 Louis Salmon .35
15 John Smith .35
16 Harry Stuhldreher .75
17 Joe Kurth .35
18 Frank Carideo .35
19 Marchy Schwartz .35
20 Adam Walsh .35
21 George Gipp 2.00
22 Jim Crowley .75

1989 Notre Dame 1935-59

MT
Complete Set (22): 7.00
Common Player: .35
1 Frank Leahy (CO) .75
2 John Lattner .75
3 Jim Martin .50
4 Joe Heap .35
5 Paul Hornung 1.25
6 Bill Shakespeare .35
7 Bob Dove .35
8 Bob Williams .35
9 Al Ecuyer .35
10 George Connor .75
11 Leon Hart .75
12 Joe Beinor .35
13 Bill Fischer .35
14 Angelo Bertelli .75
15 Ralph Guglielmi .50
16 Pat Filley .35
17 Emil (Red) Sitko .50
18 Don Schaefer .35
19 Monty Stickles .50
20 Creighton Miller .35
21 Chuck Sweeney .35
22 John Lujack 1.00

1989 Notre Dame 1964-87

MT
Complete Set (22): 7.00
Common Player: .35
1 Dan Devine (CO) .50
2 Joe Theismann 1.00
3 Tom Gatewood .50
4 Timmy Brown 1.25
5 Ara Parseghian (CO) .75
6 Jim Lynch .50
7 Luther Bradley .35
8 Ross Browner .50
9 John Huarte 1.00
10 Bob Crable .50
11 Ken MacAfee .50
12 Alan Page .75
13 Vagas Ferguson .50
14 Dick Arrington .35
15 Bob Golic .50
16 Mike Townsend .35
17 Walt Patulski .50
18 Allen Pinkett .50
19 Terry Hanratty .75
20 Dave Casper .75
21 Jack Snow .75
22 Nick Eddy .50

1990 Notre Dame Promos

MT
Complete Set (10): 7.00
Common Player: .50
1 Knute Rockne (CO) 1.00
2 Joe Theismann 1.00
3 Joe Montana 4.00
4 George Gipp 1.00
5 Notre Dame Stadium .50
6 Ara Parseghian (CO) .75
7 Frank Leahy (CO) .50
8 Lou Holtz (CO) .75
9 Tony Rice .50
10 Rocky Bleier .75

1990 Notre Dame 200

MT
Complete Set (200): 18.00
Common Player: .10
1 Joe Montana 1.25
2 Tim Brown .50
3 Reggie Barnett .20
4 Joe Theismann .50
5 Bob Clasby .10
6 Dave Casper .20
7 George Kunz .20
8 Vince Phelan .10
9 Tom Gibbons .10
10 Tom Thayer .10
11 Notre Dame Helmet .10
12 John Scully .10
13 Lou Holtz (CO) .30
14 Larry Dinardo .20
15 Greg Marx .10
16 Greg Dingens .10
17 Jim Seymour .20
18 1979 Cotton Bowl (Program) .10
19 Mike Kadish .20
20 Bob Crable .20
21 Tony Rice .20
22 Phil Carter .10
23 Ken MacAfee .20
24 Nick Eddy .20
25 1988 National Champs (Trophies) .20
26 Clarence Ellis .20
27 Joe Restic .10
28 Dan Devine (CO) .20
29 John K. Carney .10
30 Stacey Toran .20
31 47th Sugar Bowl (Program) .10
32 J. Heavens .10
33 Mike Fanning .10
34 Dave Vinson .10
35 Ralph Guglielmi .10
36 Reggie Ho .10
37 Allen Pinkett .20
38 Jim Browner .20
39 Blair Kiel .20
40 Joe Montana 1.25
41 Rocky Bleier .30
42 Terry Hanratty .20
43 Tom Regner .20
44 Pete Holohan .10
45 Greg Bell .20
46 Dave Duerson .20
47 Frank Varrichione .20
48 1988 Championship (Team Photo) .20
49 Ted Burgmeier .10
50 Ara Parseghian (CO) .30
51 Mike Townsend .10
52 Liberty Bowl 1983 (Program) .10
53 Tony Furjanic .10
54 Luther Bradley .20
55 Steve Niehaus .20
56 56th Orange Bowl (Program) .10
57 32nd Gator Bowl (Program) .10
58 40th Sugar Bowl (Program) .10
59 52nd Cotton Bowl (Program) .10
60 1975 Orange Bowl (Program) .10
61 Wayne Bullock .10
62 Larry Moriarty .10
63 Jim Lynch .20
64 Mike McCoy .20
65 Tony Hunter .20
66 1984 Aloha Bowl (Program) .10
67 Dave Huffman .10
68 John Lattner .20
69 Tom Gatewood .20
70 Knute Rockne (CO) .35
71 Phil Pozderac .10
72 Ross Browner .20
73 Pete Demmerle .10
74 Sunkist Fiesta Bowl (Program) .10
75 Walt Patulski .20
76 George Gipp .50
77 LeRoy Leopold .10
78 John Huarte .30
79 Tony Yelovich (CO) .10
80 John Lujack .30
81 Cotton Bowl Classic (Program) .10
82 Tim Huffman .10
83 Bob Golic .20
84 Tom Clements .20
85 39th Orange Bowl (Program) .10
86 James J. White (ADMIN) .10
87 Frank Carideo .10
88 Vinny Cerrato .10
89 Louis Salmon .10
90 Bob Burger .10
91 Gerry Dinardo .20
92 Mike Creaney .10
93 John Krimm .10
94 Vagas Ferguson .10
95 Kris Haines .10
96 Gus Dorais .20
97 Tom Schoen .10
98 Jack Robinson .10
99 Joe Heap .10
100 Checklist 1-99 .10
101 Gary Darnell (CO) .10
102 Peter Vaas (CO) .10
103 1924 National Champs (Team Photo) .20
104 Wayne Millner .20
105 Moose Krause .20
106 Jack Cannon .10
107 Christy Flanagan .10
108 Bob Lehmann .10
109 1947 Champions (Team Photo) .20
110 Joe Kurth .10
111 Tommy Yarr .10
112 Nick Buoniconti .30
113 Jim Smithberger .10
114 Joe Beinor .10
115 Pete Cordelli (CO) .10
116 Daryle Lamonica .30
117 Kevin Hardy .10
118 Creighton Miller .20
119 Bob Gladieux .20
120 Fred Miller (Later Miller Brewing) .20
121 Gary Potempa .10
122 Bob Kuechenberg .20
123 Jesse Harper (CO) .10
124 1929 National Champs (Team Photo) .20
125 Alan Page .30
126 Don Miller .20
127 1943 National Champs (Team Photo) .20
128 Bob Wetoska .10
129 Skip Holtz (CO) .10
130 Hunk Anderson (CO) .10
131 Bob Williams .10
132 1966 National Champs (Team Photo) .10
133 Jim Reilly .10
134 Earl "Curly" Lambeau .20
135 Ernie Hughes .10
136 Dick Bumpas (CO) .10
137 Jay Haynes (CO) .10
138 Harry Stuhldreher .20
139 1971 Cotton Bowl (Game Photo) .20
140 1930 National Champs (Team Photo) .20
141 Larry Conjar .20
142 1977 National Champs (Team Photo) .20
143 Pete Duranko .20
144 Heisman Winners (Seven Trophy Winners) .30
145 Bill Fisher .10
146 Marchy Schwartz .10
147 Chuck Heater (CO) .10
148 Bert Metzger .10
149 Bill Shakespeare .20
150 Adam Walsh .10
151 Nordy Hoffman .10
152 Ted Gradel .10
153 Monty Stickles .20
154 Neil Worden .10
155 Pat Filley .10
156 Angelo Bertelli .20
157 Nick Pietrosante .20
158 Art Hunter .10
159 Ziggy Czarobski .10
160 1925 Rose Bowl (Program) .10
161 Al Ecuyer .10
162 1949 Notre Dame Champs (Team Photo) .10
163 Elmer Layden .20
164 Joe Moore (CO) .10
165 1946 National Champs (Team Photo) .10
166 Frank Rydzewski .10
167 Bud Boeringer .10
168 Jerry Groom .10
169 Jack Snow .20
170 Joe Montana 1.25
171 John Smith .10
172 Frank Leahy (CO) .30
173 Emil "Red" Sitko .20
174 Dick Arrington .10
175 Eddie Anderson .10
176 1928 Army (Logo and score) .10
177 1913 Army (Logo and score) .10
178 1935 Ohio State (Logo and game score) .10
179 1946 Army (Logo and game score) .10
180 1953 Georgia Tech (Logo and game score) .10
181 Don Schaefer .10
182 1973 Football Team (Team Photo) .20
183 Bob Dove .10
184 Dick Szymanski .10
185 Jim Martin .20
186 1957 Oklahoma (Logo and game score) .10
187 1966 Michigan State (Logo and game score) .10
188 1973 USC (Logo and game score) .10
189 1980 Michigan (Logo and game score) .10
190 1982 Michigan (Logo and game score) .10
191 Chuck Sweeney .10
192 Notre Dame Stadium .10
193 Roger Kiley .10
194 Ray Eichenlaub .10
195 George Connor .20
196 1982 Pittsburgh (Logo and game score) .10
197 1986 USC (Logo and game score) .10
198 1988 Miami (Logo and game score) .10
199 1988 USC (Logo and game score) .10
200 Checklist 101-199 .10

1990 Notre Dame 60

MT
Complete Set (60): 25.00
Common Player: .35
1 Joe Allen .35
2 William Pollard .35
3 Tony Smith .35
4 Tony Brooks .75
5 Kenny Spears .35
6 Mike Heldt .35
7 Derek Brown (TE) .75
8 Rodney Culver .75
9 Ricky Watters 3.00
10 Raghib Ismail 2.50
11 Lou Holtz (CO) .75
12 Chris Zorich 1.00
13 Erik Simien .35
14 Shawn Davis .35
15 Greg Davis .35
16 Walter Boyd .35
17 Tim Ryan .50
18 Lindsay Knapp .35
19 Junior Bryant .35
20 Mike Stonebreaker .50
21 Randy Scianna .35
22 Rick Mirer 6.00
23 Ryan Mihalko .35
24 Todd Lyght .75
25 Andre Jones .35
26 Rod Smith (DB) .50
27 Winston Sandri .35
28 Bob Dahl .50
29 Stuart Tyner .35
30 Brian Shannon .35
31 Shawn Smith .35
32 Jim Sexton .35
33 Dorsey Levens 1.00
34 Lance Johnson .35
35 George Poorman .35
36 Irv Smith 1.00
37 George Williams .35
38 George Marshall .35
39 Reggie Brooks 2.00
40 Scott Kowalkowski .50
41 Jerry Bodine .35
42 Karmeelyah McGill .35
43 Donn Grimm .35
44 Billy Hackett .35
45 Jordan Halter .35
46 Mirko Jurkovic .75
47 Mike Callan .35
48 Justin Hall .35
49 Nick Smith .35
50 Brian Ratigan .35
51 Eric Jones .35
52 Todd Norman .35
53 Devon McDonald .50
54 Marc deManigold .35
55 Bret Hankins .35
56 Adrian Jarrell .35
57 Craig Hentrich .50
58 Demetrius DuBose .75
59 Gene McGuire .75
60 Ray Griggs .35

1990 Notre Dame Greats

MT
Complete Set (22): 8.00
Common Player: .35
1 Clarence Ellis .50
2 Rocky Bleier .75
3 Tom Regner .50
4 Jim Seymour .35
5 Joe Montana 3.00
6 Art Hunter .50
7 Mike McCoy .50
8 Bud Boeringer .35
9 Greg Marx .35
10 Nick Buoniconti .75
11 Pete Demmerle .35
12 Fred Miller .35
13 Tommy Yarr .35
14 Frank Rydzewski .35
15 Dave Duerson .50
16 Ziggy Czarobski .35
17 Jim White .50
18 Larry DiNardo .50
19 George Kunz .50
20 Jack Robinson .35
21 Steve Niehaus .50
22 John Scully .50

1992 Notre Dame

MT
Complete Set (59): 25.00
Common Player: .35
1 Lou Holtz (CO) 1.00
2 Rick Mirer 4.00
3 Demetrius DuBose .75
4 Lee Becton 1.25
5 Pete Bercich .50
6 Jerome Bettis 4.00
7 Reggie Brooks 1.50
8 Junior Bryant .35
9 Jeff Burris 1.25
10 Tom Carter 1.00
11 Willie Clark .35
12 John Covington .50
13 Travis Davis .35
14 Lake Dawson 1.50
15 Mark Zataveski .35
16 Paul Failla .75
17 Jim Flanigan .75
18 Oliver Gibson .35
19 Justin Goheen .50
20 Tracy Graham .35
21 Ray Griggs .35
22 Justin Hall .35

23 Jordan Halter .35
24 Brian Hamilton .50
25 Craig Hentrich .50
26 Germaine Holden .35
27 Adrian Jarrell .50
28 Clint Johnson .50
29 Lance Johnson .35
30 Lindsay Knapp .50
31 Ryan Leahy (Not alphabetical order) .50
32 Greg Lane .50
33 Dean Lytle .35
34 Bernard Mannelly .35
35 Oscar McBride .35
36 Devon McDonald .50
37 Kevin McDougal 1.00
38 Karl McGill .35
39 Mike McGlinn .35
40 Mike Miller .75
41 Jeremy Nau .35
42 Todd Norman .50
43 Tim Ruddy (Not alphabetical order) .50
44 William Pollard .35
45 Brian Ratigan .35
46 Leshane Saddler .35
47 Jeremy Sample .35
48 Irv Smith 1.00
49 Laron Moore (Not alphabetical order) .35
50 Anthony Peterson (No alphabetical order) .50
51 Charles Stafford .35
52 Nick Smith .35
53 Greg Stec .35
54 John Taliaferro .35
55 Aaron Taylor 1.00
56 Stuart Tyner .35
57 Ray Zellars (Not alphabetical order) 1.50
58 Tyler Young (Not alphabetical order) .35
59 Bryant Young 1.50

1993 Notre Dame

MT
Complete Set (72): 20.00
Common Player: .25
1 Jeremy Akers .35
2 Joe Babey .25
3 Huntley Bakich .25
4 Jason Beckwith .25
5 Lee Becton .75
6 Pete Bercich .35
7 Jeff Burris 1.25
8 Pete Chryplewicz .25
9 Willie Clark .25
10 John Covington .35
11 Travis Davis .25
12 Lake Dawson 1.25
13 Paul Failla .50
14 Jim Flanigan .50
15 Reggie Fleurima .25
16 Ben Foos .25
17 Herbert Gibson .25
18 Oliver Gibson .50
19 Justin Goheen .35
20 Tracy Graham .25
21 Paul Grasmanis .35
22 Jordan Halter .25
23 Brian Hamilton .35
24 Germaine Holden .25
25 Lou Holtz (CO) 1.00
26 Robert Hughes .25
27 Adrian Jarrell .35
28 Clint Johnson .35
29 Lance Johnson .25
30 Thomas Knight .35
31 Jim Kordas .25
32 Greg Lane .35
33 Ryan Leahy .35
34 Will Lyell .35
35 Dean Lytle .25
36 Brian Magee .25
37 Alton Maiden .25
38 Derrick Mayes 1.50
39 Oscar McBride .35
40 Mike McCullough .50
41 Kevin McDougal .50
42 Mike McGlinn .25
43 Brian Meter .25
44 Mike Miller .25
45 Steve Misetic .25
46 Jeremy Nau .35
47 Todd Norman .35
48 Kevin Pendergast .35
49 Anthony Peterson .25
50 David Quist .25
51 Jeff Riney .25
52 Tim Ruddy .35
53 Leshane Saddler .25
54 Jeremy Sample .25
55 Charles Stafford .25
56 Greg Stec .25
57 Cliff Stroud .25
58 John Taliaferro .25
59 Aaron Taylor 1.00
60 Bobby Taylor 1.25
61 Bill Wagasy .25
62 Leon Wallace .25
63 Shawn Wooden .25
64 Renaldo Wynn .35
65 Bryant Young 1.25
66 Mark Zataveski .35
67 Dusty Zeigler .35
68 Ray Zellars 1.25
69 Blue Roster Checklist .25
70 Gold Roster Checklist .25
71 Green Roster Checklist .25
72 White Roster Checklist .25

1961 Nu-Card

NM
Complete Set (80): 175.00
Common Player: 2.00
101 Bob Ferguson 5.00
102 Ron Snidow 3.00
103 Steve Barnett 2.00
104 Greg Mather 2.00
105 Vern Von Sydow 2.00
106 John Hewitt 2.00
107 Eddie Johns 2.00
108 Walt Rappold 2.00
109 Roy Winston 4.00
110 Bob Boyda 2.00
111 Bill Neighbors 5.00
112 Don Purcell 2.00
113 Ken Byers 2.00
114 Ed Pine 2.00
115 Fred Oblak 2.00
116 Bobby Iles 2.00
117 John Hadl 18.00
118 Charlie Mitchell 2.00
119 Bill Swinford 2.00
120 Bill King 2.00
121 Mike Lucci 5.00
122 Dave Sarette 2.00
123 Alex Kroll 3.00
124 Steve Bauwens 2.00
125 Jimmy Saxton 3.00
126 Steve Simms 2.00
127 Andy Timura 2.00
128 Gary Collins 6.00
129 Ron Taylor 2.00
130 Bobby Dodd 8.00
131 Curtis McClinton 6.00
132 Ray Poage 3.00
133 Gus Gonzales 2.00
134 Dick Locke 2.00
135 Larry Libertore 2.00
136 Stan Sczurek 2.00
137 Pete Case 3.00
138 Jesse Bradford 2.00
139 Coolidge Hunt 2.00
140 Walter Doleschal 2.00
141 Bill Williamson 2.00
142 Pat Trammell 6.00
143 Ernie Davis 65.00
144 Chuck Lamson 2.00
145 Bobby Plummer 3.00
146 Sonny Gibbs 3.00
147 Joe Ellers 2.00
148 Roger Kochman 2.00
149 Norman Beal 2.00
150 Sherwyn Torson 2.00
151 Russ Hepner 2.00
152 Joe Romig 2.00
153 Larry Thompson 2.00
154 Tom Perdue 2.00
155 Ken Bolin 2.00
156 Art Perkins 2.00
157 Jim Sanderson 2.00
158 Bob Asack 2.00
159 Dan Celoni 2.00
160 Bill McGuirt 2.00
161 Dave Hoppmann 2.00
162 Gary Barnes 2.00
163 Don Lisbon 3.00
164 Jerry Cross 2.00
165 George Pierovich 2.00
166 Roman Gabriel 25.00
167 Billy White 2.00
168 Gale Weidner 2.00
169 Charles Rieves 2.00
170 Jim Furlong 2.00
171 Tom Hutchinson 3.00
172 Galen Hall 8.00
173 Wilburn Hollis 2.00
174 Don Kasso 2.00
175 Bill Miller 3.00
176 Ron Miller 2.00
177 Joe Williams 2.00
178 Mel Mellin 2.00
179 Tom Vassell 2.00
180 Mike Cotton 3.00

1961 Nu-Card Pennant Inserts

NM
Complete Set (264): 800.00
Common Player: 3.00
1 Air Force/Georgetown 3.00
2 Air Force/Queens 3.00
3 Air Force/Upsala 3.00
4 Alabama/Boston U 4.00
5 Alabama/Cornell 4.00
6 Alabama/Detroit 4.00
7 Alabama/Harvard 4.00
8 Alabama/Wisconsin 4.00
9 Allegheny/Colorado St. 3.00
10 Allegheny/Oregon 3.00
11 Allegheny/Piedmont 3.00
12 Allegheny/Wm. and Mary 3.00
13 Arizona/Kansas 3.00
14 Arizona/Mississippi 3.00
15 Arizona/Pennsylvania 3.00
16 Arizona/S.M.U. 3.00
17 Army/Ga. Tech 3.00
18 Army/Iowa 3.00
19 Army/Johns Hopkins 3.00
20 Army/Maryland 3.00
21 Army/Missouri 3.00
22 Army/Pratt 3.00
23 Army/Purdue 3.00
24 Auburn/Florida 4.00
25 Auburn/Gettysburg 3.00
26 Auburn/Illinois 4.00
27 Auburn/Syracuse 4.00
28 Auburn/Virginia 4.00
29 Barnard/Colombia 3.00
30 Barnard/Maine 3.00
31 Barnard/N. Carolina 3.00
32 Baylor/Colorado St. 3.00
33 Baylor/Drew 3.00
34 Baylor/Oregon 3.00
35 Baylor/Piedmont 3.00
36 Boston Coll./Minnesota 3.00
37 Boston Coll./Norwich 3.00
38 Boston Coll./Winthrop 3.00
39 Boston U./Cornell 3.00
40 Boston U./Rensselaer 3.00
41 Boston U./Stanford 3.00
42 Boston U./Temple 3.00
43 Boston U./Utah State 3.00
44 Bridgeport/Holy Cross 3.00
45 Bridgeport/N.Y.U. 3.00
46 Bridgeport/Northwestern 3.00
47 Bucknell/Illinois 3.00
48 Bucknell/Syracuse 3.00
49 Bucknell/Virginia 3.00
50 California/Delaware 3.00
51 California/Hofstra 3.00
52 California/Kentucky 3.00
53 California/Marquette 3.00
54 California/Michigan 4.00
55 California/Notre Dame 7.50
56 California/Wingate 3.00
57 Charleston/Dickinson 3.00
58 Charleston/Lafayette 3.00
59 Charleston/U. of Mass. 3.00
60 Cincinnati/Maine 3.00
61 Cincinnati/Ohio West 3.00
62 Citadel/Columbia 3.00
63 Citadel/Maine 3.00
64 Citadel/N. Carolina 3.00
65 Coast Guard/Drake 3.00
66 Coast Guard/Penn St. 3.00
67 Coast Guard/Yale 3.00
68 Coker/UCLA 3.00
69 Coker/Wingate 3.00
70 Colby/Kings Point 3.00
71 Colby/Queens 3.00
72 Colby/Rice 3.00
73 Colby/Upsala 3.00
74 Colgate/Dickinson 3.00
75 Colgate/Lafayette 3.00
76 Colgate/U. of Mass. 3.00
77 Colgate/Springfield 3.00
78 Colgate/Texas AM 3.00
79 C.O.P./Princeton 3.00
80 C.O.P./Oklahoma St. 3.00
81 C.O.P./Oregon St. 3.00
82 Colorado St./Drew 3.00
83 Colorado St./Oregon 3.00
84 Colorado St./Piedmont 3.00
85 Colorado St./Wm. and Mary 3.00
86 Columbia/Dominican 3.00
87 Columbia/Maine 3.00
88 Columbia/N. Carolina 3.00
89 Cornell/Harvard 3.00
90 Cornell/Rensselaer 3.00
91 Cornell/Stanford 3.00
92 Cornell/Wisconsin 3.00
93 Dartmouth/Michigan St. 3.00
94 Dartmouth/Ohio U. 3.00
95 Dartmouth/Wagner 3.00
96 Davidson/Ohio Wesl. 3.00
97 Davidson/S. Carolina 3.00
98 Davidson/Texas Tech 3.00
99 Delaware/Marquette 3.00
100 Delaware/Michigan 3.00
101 Delaware/Notre Dame 5.00
102 Delaware/UCLA 3.00
103 Denver/Florida State 4.00
104 Denver/Indiana 3.00
105 Denver/Iowa State 3.00
106 Denver/USC 3.00
107 Denver/VMI 3.00
108 Detroit/Harvard 3.00
109 Detroit/Rensselaer 3.00
110 Detroit/Stanford 3.00
111 Detroit/Utah State 3.00
112 Dickinson/U. of Mass. 3.00
113 Dickinson/Regis 3.00
114 Dickinson/Springfield 3.00
115 Dickinson/Texas AM 3.00
116 Dominican/North Carolina 3.00
117 Drake/Duke 3.00
118 Drake/Kentucky 3.00
119 Drake/Middlebury 3.00
120 Drake/Penn St. 3.00
121 Drake/St. Peters 3.00
122 Drake/Yale 3.00
123 Drew/Middlebury 3.00
124 Drew/Oregon 3.00
125 Drew/Piedmont 3.00
126 Drew/Wm. and Mary 3.00
127 Duke/Middlebury 3.00
128 Duke/Rhode Island 3.00
129 Duke/Seton Hall 3.00
130 Duke/Yale 3.00
131 Finch/Long Island AT 3.00
132 Finch/Michigan St. 3.00
133 Finch/Ohio U. 3.00
134 Finch/Wagner 3.00
135 Florida/Gettysburg 3.00
136 Florida/Illinois 4.00
137 Florida/Syracuse 4.00
138 Florida/Virginia 4.00
139 Florida St./Indiana 4.00
140 Florida St./Iowa St. 4.00
141 Florida St./So. Cal. 4.00
142 Florida St./VMI 4.00
143 Georgetown/Kings Point 3.00
144 Georgetown/Rice 3.00
145 Georgia/Missouri 4.00
146 Georgia/Ohio Wesleyan 3.00
147 Georgia/Rutgers 3.00
148 Georgia/So. Carolina 4.00
149 Ga. Tech/Johns Hopkins 3.00
150 Ga. Tech/Maryland 3.00
151 Ga. Tech/Missouri 3.00
152 Gettysburg/Syracuse 3.00
153 Harvard/Miami 4.00
154 Harvard/NC State 3.00
155 Harvard/Stanford 3.00
156 Harvard/Utah State 3.00
157 Harvard/Wisconsin 3.00
158 Hofstra/Marquette 3.00
159 Hofstra/Michigan 4.00
160 Hofstra/Navy 3.00
161 Hofstra/UCLA 3.00
162 Holy Cross/Navy 3.00
163 Holy Cross/New York 3.00
164 Holy Cross/Northwestern 3.00
165 Holy Cross/Nyack 3.00
166 Howard/Kentucky 3.00
167 Howard/Villanova 3.00
168 Illinois/Syracuse 3.00
169 Indiana/Iowa State 3.00
170 Indiana/VMI 3.00
171 Iowa/Maryland 3.00
172 Iowa/Missouri 3.00
173 Iowa/Pratt 3.00
174 Iowa State/So. Cal. 4.00
175 Johns Hopkins/Pratt 3.00
176 Johns Hopkins/Purdue 3.00
177 Kansas/St. Francis 3.00
178 Kansas/S.M.U. 3.00
179 Kansas State/N.Y.U. 3.00
180 Kansas State/T.C.U. 3.00
181 Kentucky/Maryland 3.00
182 Kentucky/Middlebury 3.00
183 Kentucky/New Hampshire 3.00
184 Kentucky/Penn State 5.00
185 Kentucky/St. Peter's 3.00
186 Kentucky/Seton Hall 3.00
187 Kentucky/Villanova 3.00
188 Kings Point/Queens 3.00
189 Kings Point/Rice 3.00
190 Kings Point/Upsala 3.00
191 Lafayette/U. of Mass. 3.00
192 Lafayette/Regis 3.00
193 Long Isl. AT/Michigan St. 3.00
194 Long Isl. AT/Ohio U. 3.00
195 Long Isl. At/Wagner 3.00
196 Loyola/Minnesota 3.00
197 Loyola/Norwich 3.00
198 Loyola/Winthrop 3.00
199 Marquette/Michigan 4.00
200 Marquette/Navy 3.00
201 Marquette/New Paltz 3.00
202 Marquette/Notre Dame 5.00
203 Marquette/UCLA 3.00
204 Maryland/Missouri 3.00
205 Mass./Regis 3.00
206 Mass./Springfield 3.00
207 Mass./Texas AM 3.00
208 Michigan/Navy 4.00
209 Michigan/New Paltz 3.00
210 Michigan/UCLA 4.00
211 Michigan St./Ohio U. 3.00
212 Michigan St./Wagner 3.00
213 Middlebury/Penn St. 3.00
214 Middlebury/Yale 3.00
215 Minnesota/Norwich 3.00
216 Minnesota/Winthrop 3.00
217 Mississippi/Penn 3.00
218 Mississippi/St. Francis 3.00
219 Missouri/Purdue 3.00
220 Navy/Notre Dame 7.50
221 Navy/UCLA 4.00
222 Navy/Wingate 3.00
223 New Hampshire/Villanova 3.00
224 N.Y.U./Northwestern 3.00
225 NCE/Temple 3.00
226 NCE/Wisconsin 3.00
227 NC State/Temple 3.00
228 Northwestern/TCU 3.00
229 Norwich/Winthrop 3.00
230 Notre Dame/UCLA 7.50
231 Notre Dame/Wingate 5.00
232 Ohio U./Wagner 3.00
233 Ohio Wesl./Roberts 3.00
234 Ohio Wesl./S. Carolina 3.00
235 Oklahoma St./Oregon St. 3.00
236 Oklahoma St./Princeton 3.00
237 Oregon/Piedmont 3.00
238 Oregon/Wm. and Mary 3.00
239 Oregon St./Princeton 3.00
240 Penn State/St. Peter's 3.00
241 Penn State/Seton Hall 3.00
242 Penn State/Yale 3.00
243 Penn/S.M.U. 3.00
244 Penn/St. Francis 3.00
245 Queens/Rice 3.00
246 Queens/Upsala 3.00
247 Rensselaer/Stanford 3.00
248 Rensselaer/Temple 3.00
249 Rensselaer/Utah State 3.00
250 Rhode Island/Yale 3.00
251 Rice/Upsala 3.00
252 Roberts/So. Carolina 3.00
253 Roberts/Texas Tech 3.00
254 Rutgers/So. Carolina 3.00
255 St. Francis/S.M.U. 3.00
256 St. Peter's/Villanova 3.00
257 St. Peter's/Yale 3.00
258 So. California/VMI 4.00
259 So. Carolina/Texas Tech 3.00
260 Syracuse/Virginia 3.00
261 Temple/Wisconsin 3.00
262 UCLA/Wingate 4.00
263 Utah State/Wisconsin 3.00
264 Villanova/Yale 3.00

1991 Oberlin College Heisman Club

MT
Complete Set (5): 5.00
Common Player: 1.00
1 50 Years, Two Careers (C.W. "Doc" Savage, J.H. Nichols) (Athletic Directors) 1.00
2 John W. Heisman (CO) 2.00
3 Oberline's 1892 Team 1.00
4 Oberlin's Fauver Twins (Doc Edgar Fauver, Doc Edwin Fauver) 1.00
5 Oberlin's Four Horsemen (Carl Semple, Carl Williams, H.K. Regal, C.W. "Doc" Savage) 1.00

1979 Ohio State Greats

NM
Complete Set (53): 35.00
Common Player: .75
1C Chris Ward .75
1D Jan White 1.00
1H Ernest R. Godfrey (ACO) .75
1S Ray Pryor .75
2C Ray Griffin 1.00
2D Tom Deleone 1.00
2H Francis A. Schmidt (CO) .75
2S Dave Foley .75
3C Tom Cousineau 1.25
3D Randy Gradishar 2.00
3H Jim Parker 2.00
3S Rufus Mayes 1.00
4C Aaron Brown 1.00
4D John Hicks 1.25
4H Vic Janowicz 1.50
4S Rex Kern 1.50
5C Chris Ward .75
5D Van Decree .75
5H Les Horvath 1.50
5S Jim Otis 1.50
6C Tom Skladany 1.25
6D Randy Gradishar 2.00
6H Bill Willis 1.25
6S Ted Provost .75
7C Bob Brudzinski 1.00
7D Archie Griffin 2.50
7H James Daniell .75
7S Jim Stillwagon 1.25
8C Ted Smith .75
8D John Hicks 1.25
8H Gust Zarnas .75
8S Jack Tatum 1.50
9C Tom Skladany 1.25
9D Neal Colzie 1.00
9H Gomer Jones .75
9S Tim Anderson .75
10C Archie Griffin 2.50
10D Pete Cusick .75
10H Wes Fesler 1.00
10S John Brockington 1.50
11C Tim Fox 1.00
11D Van Decree .75
11H Gaylord Stinchcomb .75
11S Mike Sensibaugh 1.00
12C Tom Skladany 1.25
12D Archie Griffin 2.50
12H Chic Harley .75
12S Jim Stillwagon 1.25
13C Kurt Schumacher 1.00
13D Steve Meyers 1.00
13H Tom Cousineau 1.25
13S Jack Tatum 1.50
JK Howard Jones (CO) 1.00

1988 Ohio State

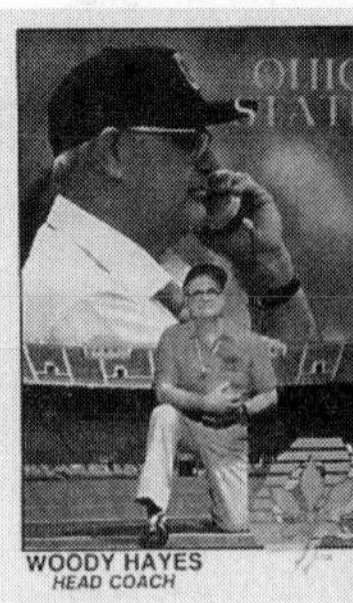

MT
Complete Set (22): 40.00
Common Player: .40
1 Bob Brudzinski .50
2 Keith Byars 1.50
3 Hopalong Cassady 1.00
4 Arnold Chonko .50
5 Wes Fesler .40
6 Randy Gradishar 1.00
7 Archie Griffin 1.50
8 Chic Harley .40
9 Woody Hayes (CO) 1.00
10 John Hicks .50
11 Les Horvath 1.00
12 Jim Houston .75
13 Vic Janowicz 1.00
14 Pepper Johnson .75
15 Ike Kelley .40
16 Rex Kern .75
17 Jim Lachey .75
18 Jim Parker 1.00
19 Tom Skladany .40
20 Chris Spielman 1.00
21 Jim Stillwagon .75
22 Jack Tatum 1.00

1989 Ohio State

MT
Complete Set (22): 8.00
Common Player: .40
1 Mike Tomczak 1.00
2 Paul Warfield 1.50
3 Kirk Lowdermilk .50
4 Bob Ferguson .50
5 Jack Graf .40
6 Tim Fox .50
7 Eric Kumerow .50
8 Neal Colzie .50
9 Jim Otis .75
10 John Brockington 1.00
11 Cornelius Greene .40
12 Jim Marshall 1.00
13 Tom Spencer .50
14 Don Scott .40
15 Chris Ward .50
16 Marcus Marek .50
17 Dave Foley .50
18 Bill Willis .75
19 John Frank .75
20 Rufus Mayes .50
21 Tom Tupa .75
22 Jan White .50

1990 Ohio State

MT
Complete Set (22): 8.00
Common Player: .35
1 Jeff Uhlenhake .50
2 Ray Ellis .35
3 Todd Bell .50
4 Jeff Logan .35
5 Pete Johnson .75
6 Van DeCree .35
7 Ted Provost .35
8 Mike Lanese .35
9 Aaron Brown .50
10 Pete Cusick .35
11 Vlade Janakievski .35
12 Steve Myers .35
13 Ted Smith .35
14 Doug Donley .50
15 Ron Springs .50
16 Ken Fritz .35
17 Jeff Davidson .35
18 Art Schlichter .75
19 Tom Cousineau .75
20 Call Murray .35
21 Brian Baschnagel .50
22 Joe Staysniak .35

1992 Ohio State

MT
Complete Set (59): 20.00
Common Player: .25
1 John Cooper (CO) .75
2 Kirk Herbstreit .50
3 Steve Tovar 1.00
4 Chico Nelson .25
5 Tim Patillo .25
6 Tito Paul .25
7 Jim Borchers .25
8 Craig Powell .75
9 Deron Brown .25
10 Alex Rodriguez .25
11 Chris Sanders 1.50
12 Cedric Saunders .25
13 Walter Taylor .40
14 Jack Thrush .25
15 Brian Stablein .50
16 Tim Walton .25
17 Rod Smith .50
18 Brad Pope .25
19 William Houston .25
20 Dan Wilkinson 1.50
21 Jason Winrow .40
22 Mark Williams .25
23 Jason Simmons .50
24 Luke Fickell .50
25 Tim Williams .25
26 Raymont Harris 1.50
27 Preston Harrison .25
28 Len Hartman .25
29 Eddie George 3.00
30 Jayson Gwinn .50
31 Korey Stringer 1.00
32 Tom Lease .25
33 Randall Brown .25
34 DeWayne Carter .25
35 Bryan Cook .25
36 Allen DeGraffenreid .50
37 Brian Stoughton .25
38 Derrick Foster .25
39 Butler By'not'e .75
40 Jeff Cothran .75
41 Robert Davis .25
42 Joey Galloway 5.00
43 Roger Harper .75
44 Bobby Hoying 1.50
45 C.J. Kelly .25
46 Brent Johnson .25
47 Paul Long .25
48 Joe Metzger .25
49 Jason Louis .25
50 Dave Monnot .25
51 Greg Beatty .25
52 Pete Beckman .25
53 Matt Bonhaus .25
54 Marlon Kerner .50
55 Alan Kline .25
56 Greg Kuszmaul .25
57 Buckeye Flashback - October 12, 1968 (Jim Otis) .40
58 Buckeye Flashback - September 30, 1972 .40
NNO Title Card (CL) .40

1997 Ohio State

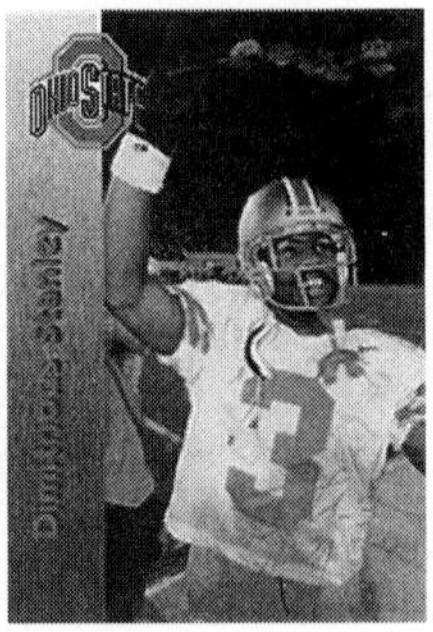

MT
Complete Set (24): 25.00
Common Player: 1.00
1 Greg Bellisari 1.50
2 Matt Calhoun 1.00
3 Shane Clark 1.00
4 Dan Colson 1.00
5 John Cooper CO 1.50
6 LeShun Daniels 1.00
7 Luke Fickell 1.00
8 Matt Finkes 2.00
9 Anthony Gwinn 1.50
10 Bob Houser 1.00
11 Ty Howard 1.50
12 Josh Jackson 1.00
13 D.J. Jones 1.00
14 Rob Kelly 1.50
15 Heath Knisely 1.00
16 Ryan Miller 1.00
17 Juan Porter 1.00
18 Chad Pulliam 1.00
19 Dimitrious Stanley 1.50
20 Buster Tillman 1.50
21 Mike Vrabel 2.00
22 American Marketing Associates 1.00
23 1997 Senior Rose Bowl Champions 1.50
24 Team Logo 1.00
25 Sponsor card 1.00

1982 Oklahoma Playing Cards

MT
Complete Set (56): 40.00
Common Player: .50
C1 Action Shot (Joe Washington) 1.00
C2 Coaches 1895-1934 .50
C3 All-Americans 1946-48 (Buddy Burris) 1.00
C4 All-Americans 1953-54 (Buck McPhail, J.D. Roberts, Max Boydston, Kurt Burris) 1.00
C5 All-Americans 1963-69 (Ralph Neely, Carl McAdams, Bob Kalsu, Steve Owens) 1.00
C6 All-Americans 1974-75 (Kyle Davis, Tinker Owens, Dewey Selmon, Lee Roy Selmon) 1.00
C7 1951 (Jim Weatherall) 1.00
C8 1952 (Billy Vessels) 1.00
C9 NCAA Champions 1955 1.00
C10 Action Shot (Uwe Von Schamann) .50
C11 Action Shot (Tony DiRienzo) .50

C12 Action Shot (Joe Washington) 1.00
C13 Action Shot (Tinker Owens) .50
D1 Action Shot (Joe Washington) 1.00
D2 Coaches 1935-1982 .50
D3 All-Americans 1949 (Jimmy Owens, Darrell Royal) 1.00
D4 All-Americans 1955-56 (Bo Bolinger, Ed Gray, Jerry Tubbs, Terry McDonald) 1.00
D5 All-Americans 1966-71 (Granville Liggins, Steve Zabel, Ken Mendenhall, Jack Mildren) 1.00
D6 All-Americans 1975-76 (Terry Webb, Billy Brooks, Jimbo Elrod, Mike Vaughan) 1.00
D7 1953 (J.D. Roberts) 1.00
D8 1969 (Steve Owens) 1.50
D9 NCAA Champions 1956 1.00
D10 Barry Switzer (CO) .50
D11 Action Shot (Lucius Selmon) .50
D12 Action Shot (Elvis Peacock) .50
D13 Action Shot (Billy Sims) 1.00
H1 Action Shot (Jimbo Elrod) .50
H2 All-Americans 1913-37 1.00
H3 All-Americans 1949-51 (Jim Weatherall) 1.00
H4 All-Americans 1957-59 (Bill Krisher, Clendon Thomas, Bob Harrison, Jerry Thompson) 1.00
H5 All-Americans 1971-74 (Greg Pruitt, Tom Brahaney, Derland Moore, Rod Shoate) 1.00
H6 All-Americans 1976-78 (Zac Henderson, Greg Roberts, Daryl Hunt, George Cumby) 1.00
H7 1975 (Lee Roy Selmon) 1.50
H8 1978 (Billy Sims) 1.50
H9 NCAA Champions 1974 1.00
H10 Action Shot (Lee Roy Selmon) 1.00
H11 Action Shot (Tinker Owens) .50
H12 Action Shot .50
H13 Action Shot (Lee Roy Selmon) 1.00
S1 Action Shot (Horace Ivory) .50
S2 All-Americans 1938-46 1.00
S3 All-Americans 1951-52 (Tom Catlin, Billy Vessels, Eddie Crowder) 1.00
S4 All-Americans 1962-63 (Leon Cross, Wayne Lee, Jim Grisham, Joe Don Looney) 1.00
S5 All-Americans 1973-75 (Lucius Selmon, Eddie Foster, John Roush, Joe Washington) 1.00
S6 All-Americans 1978-81 (Reggie Kinlaw, Billy Sims, Louis Oubre, Terry Crouch) 1.00
S7 1978 (Greg Roberts) 1.00
S8 NCAA Champions 1950 1.00
S9 NCAA Champions 1975 1.00
S10 Action Shot (Bobby Proctor) (CO) .50
S11 Action Shot (Steve Davis) .50
S12 Action Shot (Greg Pruitt) 1.00
S13 Action Shot (Elvis Peacock) .50
JK1 Sooner Schooner .50
JK2 Sooner Schooner .50
NNO Mail Order Card .50
NNO Mail Order Card .50

1986 Oklahoma

MT
Complete Set (16): 8.00
Common Player: .35
1 Championship Ring - 1985 National Champs .50
2 Orange Bowl (In Bowl Play) .35
3 On The Road To Record .35
4 Graduation Record .35
5 President of Exxon (Lawrence G. Rawl) .35
6 Barry Switzer (Winners) 1.50
7 Win Streaks Hold Records .35
8 Brian Bosworth 1.00
9 Heisman Trophy (Billy Vessels 1952, Steve Owens 1969, Billy Sims 1978) .75
10 All-America Sooners (Tony Casillas) .75
11 Jamelle Holieway .50
12 Sooner Strength .35
13 Sooner Support .35
14 Go Sonners (Crimson and Cream) .35
15 Border Battle (Oklahoma vs. Texas) .50
16 Barry Switzer (CO) (SP) (Caricature; "I Want You..."; '86 OU football schedule on back) 2.50

1986 Oklahoma McDag

MT
Complete Set (16): 20.00
Common Player: 1.00
1 Brian Bosworth 3.00
2 Sonny Brown 1.00
3 Steve Bryan 1.00
4 Lydell Carr 1.50
5 Patrick Collins 1.50
6 Jamelle Holieway 2.00
7 Mark Hutson 1.00
8 Keith Jackson 6.00
9 Troy Johnson 1.00
10 Dante Jones 3.00
11 Tim Lashar 1.00
12 Paul Migliazzo 1.00
13 Anthony Phillips 1.00
14 Darrell Reed 1.00
15 Derrick Shepard 1.50
16 Spencer Tillman 1.50

1987 Oklahoma Police

MT
Complete Set (16): 18.00
Common Player: .75
1 Eric Mitchel 1.25
4 Jamelle Holieway 2.00
10 David Vickers .75
25 Anthony Stafford 1.25
29 Rickey Dixon 2.00
33 Patrick Collins 1.25
40 Darrell Reed .75
45 Lydell Carr 1.25
50 Dante Jones 2.00
66 Jon Phillips .75
68 Anthony Phillips .75
75 Greg Johnson .75
79 Mark Hutson .75
80 Troy Johnson .75
88 Keith Jackson 6.00
98 Dante Williams .75
NNO Barry Switzer (CO) 3.00

1988 Oklahoma Greats

MT
Complete Set (30): 7.00
Common Player: .20
1 Jerry Anderson .20
2 Dee Andros .20
3 Dean Blevins .20
4 Rick Bryan .50
5 Paul (Buddy) Burris .20
6 Eddie Crowder .30
7 Jack Ging .20
8 Jim Grisham .30
9 Jimmy Harris .30
10 Scott Hill .20
11 Eddie Hinton .30
12 Earl Johnson .20
13 Don Key .20
14 Tim Lashar .20
15 Granville Liggins .50
16 Thomas Lott .30
17 Carl McAdams .30
18 Jack Mitchell .30
19 Billy Pricer .20
20 John Roush .20
21 Darrell Royal .50
22 Lucius Selmon .30
23 Ron Shotts .20
24 Jerry Tubbs .30
25 Bob Warmack .30
26 Joe Washington .50
27 Jim Weatherall .30
28 '86 Sooner Great Game .20
29 '75 Sooners .20
30 Checklist Card .30

1988 Oklahoma Police

MT
Complete Set (16): 18.00
Common Player: 1.00
1 Rotnei Anderson 2.00
2 Eric Bross 1.00
3 Mike Gaddis 2.50
4 Scott Garl 1.00
5 James Goode 1.00
6 Jamelle Holieway 2.00
7 Bob Latham 1.00
8 Ken McMichel 1.00
9 Eric Mitchel 1.50
10 Leon Perry 1.50
11 Anthony Phillips 1.00
12 Anthony Stafford 1.50
13 Barry Switzer (CO) 4.00
14 Mark Vankeirsbilck 1.00
15 Curtice Williams 1.00
16 Dante Williams 1.00

1989 Oklahoma Police

MT
Complete Set (16): 15.00
Common Player: 1.00
1 Tom Backes 1.00
2 Frank Blevins 1.00
3 Eric Bross 1.00
4 Adrian Cooper 3.00
5 Scott Evans 1.00
6 Mike Gaddis 2.00
7 Gary Gibbs (CO) 1.50
8 James Goode 1.00
9 Ken McMichel 1.00
10 Leon Perry 1.50
11 Mike Sawatzky 1.00
12 Don Smitherman 1.00
13 Kevin Thompson 1.00
14 Mark VanKeirsbilck 1.00
15 Mike Wise 1.00
16 Dante Williams 1.00

1991 Oklahoma Police

MT
Complete Set (16): 15.00
Common Player: 1.00
1 Gary Gibbs (CO) 1.50
2 Cale Gundy 2.00
3 Charles Franks 1.00
4 Mike Gaddis 1.50
5 Brad Reddell 1.00
6 Brandon Houston 1.00
7 Chris Wilson 1.00
8 Darnell Walker 1.00
9 Mike McKinley 1.00
10 Kenyon Rasheed 2.00
11 Joe Bowden 2.00
12 Jason Belser 2.00
13 Steve Collins 1.00
14 Reggie Barnes 1.00
15 Randy Wallace 1.00
16 Proctor Land 1.00

1953 Oregon

NM
Complete Set (20): 340.00
Common Player: 15.00
1 Farrell Albright 20.00
2 Ted Anderson 15.00
3 Len Berrie 15.00
4 Tom Elliott 15.00
5 Tim Flaherty 15.00
6 Cecil Hodges 15.00
7 Barney Holland 15.00
8 Dick James 25.00
9 Harry Johnson 15.00
10 Dave Lowe 15.00
11 Jack Patera 35.00
12 Ron Pheister 20.00
13 John Reed 15.00
14 Hal Reeve 20.00
15 Larry Rose 15.00
16 George Shaw 25.00
17 Lon Stiner Jr. 15.00
18 Ken Sweitzer 15.00
19 Keith Tucker 15.00
20 Dean Van Leuven 15.00

1956 Oregon

NM
Complete Set (19): 285.00
Common Player: 15.00
1 Bruce Brenn 15.00
2 Jack Brown 15.00
3 Reanous Cochran 15.00
4 Jack Crabtree 20.00
5 Tom Crabtree 15.00
6 Tom Hale 15.00
7 Spike Hillstrom 15.00
8 Jim Linden 15.00
9 Hank Loumena 15.00
10 Nick Markulis 15.00
11 Phil McHugh 15.00
13 Harry Mondale 15.00
14 Leroy Phelps 15.00
15 Jack Pocock 15.00
16 John Roventos 15.00
17 Jim Shanley 15.00
18 Ron Stover 20.00
19 J.C. Wheeler 15.00

1958 Oregon

NM
Complete Set (20): 260.00
Common Player: 15.00
1 Greg Altenhofen 15.00
2 Darrel Aschbacher 20.00
3 Dave Fish 15.00
4 Sandy Fraser 15.00
5 Dave Grosz 20.00
6 Bob Grottkau 20.00
7 Marlan Holland 15.00
8 Tom Keele 15.00
9 Alden Kimbrough 15.00
10 Don Laudenslager 15.00
11 Riley Mattson 25.00
12 Bob Peterson 15.00
13 Dave Powell 15.00
14 Len Read 15.00
15 Will Reeve 15.00
16 Joe Schaffeld 15.00
17 Charlie Tourville 15.00
18 Dave Urell 15.00
19 Pete Welch 15.00
20 Willie West 25.00

1991 Oregon Smokey

MT
Complete Set (12): 12.00
Common Player: 1.00
1 Bud Bowie 1.00
2 Rich Brooks (CO) 3.00
3 Sean Burwell 1.00
4 Eric Castle 1.50
5 Andy Conner 1.00
6 Joe Farwell 1.00
7 Matt LaBounty 1.50
8 Gregg McCallum 1.00
9 Daryle Smith 1.00
10 Jeff Thomason 1.50
11 Tommy Thompson 1.00
12 Marcus Woods 1.50

1988 Oregon State Smokey

MT
Complete Set (12): 12.00
Common Player: 1.25
1 Troy Bussanich 1.25
2 Andre Harris 1.25
3 Teddy Johnson 1.25
4 Jason Kent 1.25
5 Dave Kragthorpe (CO) 1.25
6 Mike Matthews 1.25
7 Phil Ross 1.25
8 Brian Taylor 1.25
9 Robb Thomas 2.50
10 Esera Tuaolo 2.50
11 Erik Wilhelm 2.50
12 Dowell Williams 1.25

1990 Oregon State Smokey

MT
Complete Set (16): 10.00
Common Player: 1.00
1 Brian Beck 1.00
2 Martin Billings 1.00
3 Matt Booher 1.00
4 George Breland 1.00
5 Brad D'Ancona 1.00
6 Dennis Edwards 1.00
7 Brent Huff 1.00
8 James Jones 1.00
9 Dave Kragthorpe (CO) 1.00
10 Todd McKinney 1.00
11 Torey Overstreet 1.00
12 Reggie Pitchford 1.00
13 Todd Sahlfeld 1.00
14 Scott Thompson 1.00
15 Esera Tuaolo 2.00
16 Maurice Wilson 1.00

1991 Oregon State Smokey

MT
Complete Set (12): 10.00
Common Player: 1.00
1 Adam Albaugh 1.00
2 Jamie Burke 1.00
3 Chad de Sully 1.00
4 Dennis Edwards 1.00
5 James Jones 1.00
6 Fletcher Keister 1.00
7 Tom Nordquist 1.00
8 Tony O'Billovich 1.00
9 Jerry Pettibone (CO) 1.25
10 Mark Price 1.00
11 Todd Sahlfeld 1.00
12 Earl Zackery 1.00

1992 Oregon State Smokey

MT
Complete Set (12): 9.00
Common Player: .75
1 Zechariah Davis .75
2 Chad De Sully .75
3 Michael Hale .75
4 Fletcher Keister .75
5 Chad Paulson .75
6 Rico Petrini .75
7 Jerry Pettibone (CO) 1.00
8 Sailusi Poulivaati .75
9 Tony O'Billovich .75
10 Dwayne Owens .75
11 J.J. Young 1.50
12 Maurice Wilson .75

1994 Oregon State Smokey

MT
Complete Set (12): 8.00
Common Player: .75
1 William Ephraim .75
2 Johnny Feinga .75
3 John Garrett .75
4 Michael Hale .75
5 Tom Holmes .75
6 Cory Huot .75
7 Rico Petrini .75
8 Cameron Reynolds .75
9 Kane Rogers .75
10 Don Shanklin 1.00
11 Reggie Tongue .75
12 J.J. Young 1.00

1988 Penn State Police

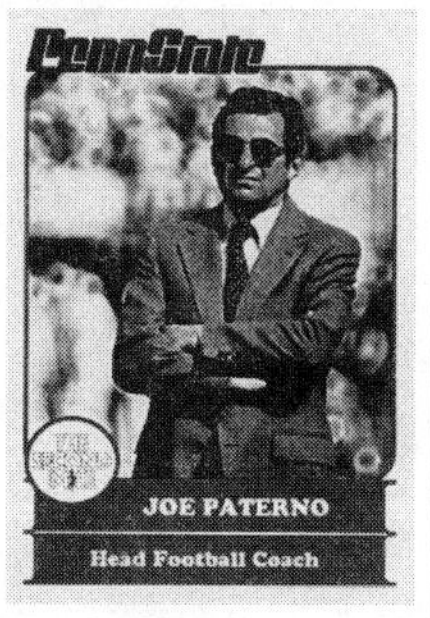

MT
Complete Set (12): 25.00
Common Player: 1.25
5 Michael Timpson 4.00
20 John Greene 1.25
28 Brian Chizmar 1.25
31 Andre Collins 4.00
32 Blair Thomas 4.00
39 Eddie Johnson 1.25
66 Steve Wisniewski 4.00
75 Rich Schonewolf 1.25
78 Roger Duffy 1.25
84 Keith Karpinski 1.25
NNO Joe Paterno (CO) 5.00
NNO Penn State Mascot - The Nittany Lion 1.50

1989 Penn State Police

MT
Complete Set (15): 20.00
Common Player: 1.00
1 Brian Chizmar 1.00
2 Andre Collins 2.50
3 David Daniels 2.50
4 Roger Duffy 1.00
5 Tim Freeman 1.00
6 Scott Gob 1.00
7 David Jakob 1.00
8 Geoff Japchen 1.00
9 Joe Paterno (CO) 4.00
10 Sherrod Rainge 1.00
11 Rich Schonewolf 1.00
12 Dave Szott 2.50
13 Blair Thomas 2.50
14 Leroy Thompson 4.00
15 Nittany Lion (Mascot) 1.00

1990 Penn State Police

MT
Complete Set (16): 15.00
Common Player: .75
1 Gerry Collins .75
2 David Daniels 1.25
3 Jim Deter .75
4 Mark D'Onofrio 1.25
5 Sam Gash 2.00
6 Frank Giannetti .75
7 Keith Goganious 1.25
8 Doug Helkowski .75
9 Hernon Henderson .75
10 Matt McCartin .75
11 Joe Paterno (CO) 3.00
12 Darren Perry 2.00
13 Tony Sacca 2.00
14 Terry Smith .75
15 Willie Thomas .75
16 Leroy Thompson 2.50

1991-92 Penn State Legends

MT
Complete Set (51): 15.00
Common Player: .35
1 Joe Paterno (CO) 2.00
2 Kurt Allerman .35
3 Chris Bahr .50
4 Matt Bahr .50
5 Bruce Bannon .35
6 Greg Buttle .50
7 John Capelletti .75
8 Bruce Clark .35
9 Andre Collins .75
10 Shane Conlan .75
11 Chris Conlin .35
12 Randy Crowder .35
13 Keith Dorney .50
14 D.J. Dozier .75
15 Bill Dugan .35
16 Chuck Fusina .50
17 Leon Gajecki .35
18 Jack Ham 1.25
19 Bob Higgins .35
20 John Hufnagel .75
21 Kenny Jackson .50
22 Tim Johnson .35
23 Dave Joyner .35
24 Roger Kochman .35
25 Ted Kwalick .50
26 Richie Lucas .75
27 Matt Millen .75
28 Lydell Mitchell .75
29 Bob Mitinger .35
30 John Nessel .35
31 Ed O'Neil .35
32 Dennis Onkotz .35
33 Darren Perry .50
34 Charlie Pittman .50
35A Tom Rafferty (ERR) (Photo actually T. Quinn) 5.00
35B Tom Rafferty (COR) 1.25
36 Mike Reid (UER) (Reversed negative) 1.25
37 Glenn Ressler .50
38 Dave Robinson .50
39 Mark Robinson .35
40 Randy Sidler .35
41 John Skorupan .50
42 Neal Smith .35
43 Steve Suhey .50
44 Sam Tamburo .35
45 Blair Thomas 1.25
46 Curt Warner 1.50
47 Steve Wisniewski .75
48 Charlie Zapiec .35
49 Michael Zordich .50
50 Harry Wilson, Joe Bedenk .35
P1 Joe Paterno (CO) (Promo) 4.00
P10 Shane Conlan (Promo) 2.00
P18 Jack Ham (Promo) 2.50
NNO Checklist Card .35

1992 Penn State Police

MT
Complete Set (16): 20.00
Common Player: .60
1 Richie Anderson 2.00
2 Lou Benfatti 1.00
3 Derek Bochna .60
4 Kyle Brady 4.00
5 Kerry Collins 8.00
6 Troy Drayton 2.00
7 John Gerak 1.00
8 Reggie Givens 1.00
9 Shelly Hammonds .60
10 Greg Huntington .60
11 Tyoka Jackson 1.00
12 O.J. McDuffie 4.00
13 Lee Rubin .60
14 E.J. Sandusky .60
15 Tisen Thomas .60
16 Brett Wright .60

1993 Penn State

MT
Complete Set (25): 18.00
Common Player: .50
1 Mike Archie, Ki-Jana Carter, Stephen Pitts 5.00
2 Lou Benfatti .75
3 Derek Bochna .50
4 Kyle Brady 3.00
5 Kerry Collins 5.00
6 Criag Fayak .50
7 Marlon Forbes .50
8 Brian Gelzheiser 1.00
9 Bucky Greeley .50
10 Ryan Grube .75
11 Shelly Hammonds .75
12 Jeff Hartings .75
13 Rob Holmberg 1.00
14 Tyoka Jackson .75
15 Mike Malinoski .75
16 Brian Monaghan .75
17 Brian O'Neal .75
18 Jeff Perry .50
19 Derick Pickett .50
20 Tony Pittman .50
21 Eric Ravotti .75
22 Lee Rubin .50
23 Vin Stewart .50
24 Tisen Thomas .50
25 Phil Yeboah-Kodie .75

1989 Pittsburgh

MT
Complete Set (22) 10.00
Common Player: .30
1 Tony Dorsett 2.00
2 Pop Warner (CO) .40
3 Hugh Green .60
4 Matt Cavanaugh .50
5 Mike Gottfried .40
6 Jimbo Covert .50
7 Bob Peck .30
8 Gibby Welch .30
9 Bill Daddio .40
10 Jock Sutherland (CO) .40
11 Joe Walton .40
12 Dan Marino 4.00
13 Russ Grimm .40
14 Mike Ditka 2.00
15 Marshall Goldberg .50
16 Bill Fralic .40
17 Paul Martha .40
18 Joe Schmidt .75
19 Rickey Jackson .60
20 Ave Daniell .30
21 Bill Maas .40
22 Mark May .40

1990 Pitt Foodland

MT
Complete Set (12): 8.00
Common Player: .50
1 Curtis Bray .50
2 Craig Gob .50
3 Paul Hackett (CO) .50
4 Keith Hamilton 1.50
5 Ricardo McDonald 1.50
6 Ronald Redmon .50
7 Curvin Richards .50
8 Louis Riddick 1.50
9 Chris Sestili .50
10 Olanda Truitt 1.50
11 Alex Van Pelt 1.50
12 Nelson Walker .50

1991 Pitt Foodland

MT
Complete Set (12): 7.00
Common Player: .75
1 Richard Allen .75
2 Curtis Bray .75
3 Jeff Christy .75
4 Steve Israel 1.00
5 Scott Kaplan .75
6 Ricardo McDonald 1.00
7 Dave Moore .75
8 Eric Seaman .75
9 Chris Sestili .75
10 Alex Van Pelt 1.50
11 Nelson Walker .75
12 Kevin Williams (HB) .75

1991 Pitt State

MT
Complete Set (18): 12.00
Common Player: .60
1 Chuck Broyles (CO) .60
2 Darren Dawson .60
3 Kendall Gammon .60
4 Jamie Goodson .60
5 Brian Hoover .60
6 James Jenkins .60
7 Ky Kiger .60
8 Phil McCoy .60
9 Kline Minniefield .60
10 Ron Moore 4.00
11 Jeff Mundhenke .60
12 Brian Pinamonti .60
13 Michael Rose .60
14 Shane Tafoya .60
15 Ronnie West 1.25
16 Michael Wilber .60
17 Troy Wilson 1.50
18 Team Photo 1.25
.60

1992 Pitt State

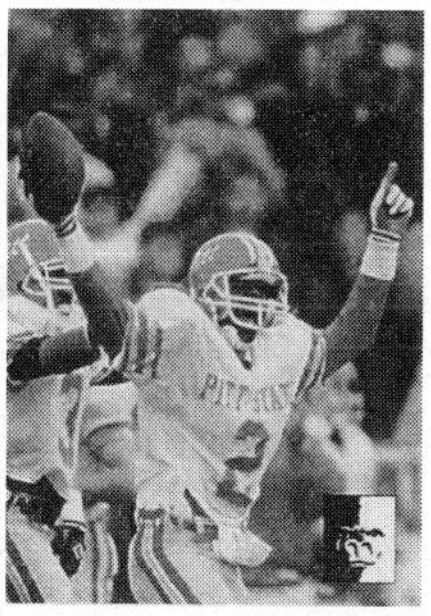

MT
Complete Set (18): 10.00
Common Player: .60
1 Ron Moore 2.00
2 Craig Jordan .60
3 Joel Thornton .60
4 Don Tolar .60
5 Andy Kesinger .60
6 Mike Brockel .60
7 Troy Wilson 1.25
8 Brian Hutchins .60
9 Chris Hanna .60
10 Coaching Staff .60
11 Gus Gorilla (Mascot) .60
12 Lance Gosch .60
13 Jerry Boone, Chad Watskey .60
14 Jeff Moreland, Scott Lutz .60
15 Ronnie Fuller, Mickey Beagle .60
16 Todd Hafner, Kevin Duncan .60
17 Duke Palmer, Eric Perks .60
18 Kris Mengarelli .60

1989 Purdue Legends Smokey

MT
Complete Set (16): 25.00

Common Player:		1.25
1	Fred Akers (CO)	1.50
2	Jim Everett (LEG)	4.00
3	Bob Griese (LEG)	6.00
4	Mark Herrmann (LEG)	2.00
5	Bill Hitchcock	1.25
6	Steve Jackson	1.50
7	Derrick Kelson	1.25
8	Leroy Keyes (LEG)	2.00
9	Shawn McCarthy	1.50
10	Dwayne O'Connor	1.25
11	Mike Phipps (LEG)	2.00
12	Darren Trieb	1.25
13	Tony Vinson	1.25
14	Calvin Williams	3.00
15	Rod Woodson (LEG)	5.00
16	Dave Young (LEG)	1.25

1990 Rice Aetna

		MT
Complete Set (12):		12.00
Common Player:		1.00
1	O.J. Brigance	1.50
2	Trevor Cobb	2.50
3	Tim Fitzpatrick	1.00
4	Fred Goldsmith (CO)	2.00
5	David Griffin	1.00
6	Eric Henley	1.50
7	Donald Hollas	2.50
8	Richard Segina	1.00
9	Matt Sign	1.00
10	Bill Stone	1.00
11	Trey Teichelman (UER) (Misspelled Tichelman on front and back)	1.00
12	Alonzo Williams	1.00

1991 Rice Aetna

		MT
Complete Set (12):		12.00
Common Player:		1.00
1	Mike Appelbaum	1.00
2	Louis Balady	1.00
3	Nathan Bennett	1.00
4	Trevor Cobb	2.00
5	Herschel Crowe	1.00
6	David Griffin	1.00
7	Eric Henley	1.50
8	Matt Sign	1.00
9	Larry Stuppy	1.00
10	Trey Teichelman	1.00
11	Alonzo Williams	1.00
12	Greg Willig	1.00

1992 Rice Taco Cabana

		MT
Complete Set (12):		12.00
Common Player:		1.00
1	Shawn Alberding	1.00
2	Mike Appelbaum	1.00
3	Louis Balady	1.00
4	Nathan Bennett	1.00
5	Trevor Cobb	2.00
6	Josh LaRocca	1.00
7	Jimmy Lee	1.50
8	Corey Seymour	1.00
9	Matt Sign	1.00
10	Emmett Waldron	1.50
11	Alonzo Williams	1.00
12	Taco Cabana (Advertisement)	1.00

1993 Rice Taco Cabana

		MT
Complete Set (12):		12.00
Common Player:		1.00
1	Nathan Bennett	1.00
2	Cris Cooley	1.50
3	Bert Emanuel	5.00
4	Jimmy Golden	1.00
5	Tom Hetherington	1.00
6	Ed Howard	1.00
7	Jimmy Lee	1.50
8	Corey Seymour	1.00
9	Clemente Torres	1.00
10	Emmett Waldron	1.50
11	Sean Washington	1.00
12	Taco Cabana Ad Card	1.00

1990 San Jose State Smokey

		MT
Complete Set (15):		10.00
Common Player:		.75
1	Bob Bleisch (90)	.75
2	Sheldon Canley (20)	.75
3	Paul Franklin (37)	.75
4	Anthony Gallegos (72)	.75
5	Steve Hieber (48)	.75
6	Everett Lampkins (43)	.75
7	Kelly Liebengood (21)	.75
8	Ralph Martini (9)	.75
9	Lyneil Mayo (62)	.75
10	Mike Powers (57)	.75
11	Mike Scialabba (46)	.75
12	Terry Shea (CO)	.75
13	Freddie Smith (4)	.75
14	Eddie Thomas (26)	.75
15	Brian Woods (64)	.75

1992 San Jose State

		MT
Complete Set (20):		10.00
Common Player:		.60
1	Maceo Barbosa	.60
2	Bobby Blackmon	.60
3	David Blakes	.60
4	Walter Brooks Jr.	.60
5	Greg Bruggeman	.60
6	Bryce Burnett	.60
7	Doug Calcagno	.60
8	Gary Charlton	.60
9	Chris Clarke	.60
10	Hesh Colar	.60
11	Jeff Greeney	.60
12	Leon Hawthorne	.60
13	Peni Iosefa	.60
14	Byron Jackson	.60
15	Robbie Miller	.60
16	Freddie Smith	.60
17	Spencer Smith	.60
18	Simon Vaoifi	.60
19	Matt Veatch	.60
20	Blair Zerr	.60

1969 South Carolina Team Sheets

		NM
Complete Set (6):		45.00
Common Player:		6.00
1	Tim Bice, Candler Boyd, Don Buckner, Ronald Bunch, Bob Cole, Carl Cowart, Don Dunning, Mike Fair, Tony Fusaro, Benny Galloway	6.00
2	Allen Brown, Don Somma, Billy Tharp, Scott Townsend, Pat Watson, Bob Wehmeyer, Bob White, Curtis Williams, Tom Wingard, Fred Zeigler	6.00
3	Andy Chavous, Wally Orrel, Ronnie Palmer, Hyrum Pierce, Jimmy Poole, Roy Don Reeves, Larry Royal, Gene Schwarting, Fletcher Spigner, Frank Tetterton	6.00
4	Paul Dietzel CO, Larry Jones CO, Johnny Menger CO, Pride Ratterree CO, Bill Rowe CO, Bill Shalosky CO, Lou Holtz CO, Don Purvis CO, Jack Powers CO, Dick Weldon CO	15.00
5	Ben Garnto, Gordon Gibson, Johnny Glass, Jimmy Gobble, Dave Grant, Johnny Gregory, Bob Harris, Rudy Holloman, Earl Hunter, Jack James	6.00
6	Jimmy Killen, Joe Komoroski, Dave Lucas, Bob Mauro, George McCarthy, Toy McCord, Wally Medlin, Bob Morris, Warren Muir, Jim Mulvihill	6.00

1974 Southern Cal Discs

		NM
Complete Set (30):		75.00
Common Player:		2.00
1	Bill Bain	2.50
2	Otha Bradley	2.50
3	Kevin Bruce	2.00
4	Mario Celotto	2.00
5	Marvin Cobb	4.00
6	Anthony Davis	8.00
7	Joe Davis	2.00
8	Shelton Diggs	2.50
9	Dave Farmer	2.50
10	Pat Haden	10.00
11	Donnie Hickman	2.00
12	Doug Hogan	2.00
13	Mike Howell	2.00
14	Gary Jeter	4.00
15	Steve Knutson	2.00
16	Chris Limahelu	2.50
17	Bob McCaffrey	2.00
18	J.K. McKay	4.00
19	John McKay (CO)	5.00
20	Jim O'Bradovich	4.00
21	Charles Phillips	2.50
22	Ed Powell	2.00
23	Marvin Powell	4.00
24	Danny Reece	2.50
25	Art Riley	2.00
26	Traveller II (Richard Sako)	2.50
27	Trojan Statue (Tommy Trojan)	2.50
28	USC Song Girls	2.50
29	USC Song Girls	2.50
30	Richard Wood	4.00

1988 Southern Cal Smokey

		MT
Complete Set (17):		12.00
Common Player:		.75
1	Erik Affholter	1.25
2	Gene Arrington	.75
3	Scott Brennan	.75
4	Jeff Brown	.75
5	Tracy Butts	.75
6	Martin Chesley	.75
7	Paul Green	.75
8	John Guerrero	.75
9	Chris Hale	.75
10	Rodney Peete	4.00
11	Dave Powroznik	.75
12	Mark Sager	.75
13	Mike Serpa	.75
14	Larry Smith (CO)	1.25
15	Chris Sperle	.75
16	Joe Walshe	.75
17	Steven Webster	.75

1988 Southern Cal Winners

		MT
Complete Set (73):		15.00
Common Player:		.15
1	Title Card (schedule on back)	.25
2	George Achica	.25
3	Marcus Allen	2.00
4	Jon Arnett	.35
5	Johnny Baker	.15
6	Damon Bame	.15
7	Chip Banks	.35
8	Mike Battle	.25
9	Hal Bedsole	.25
10	Ricky Bell	.35
11	Jeff Bregel	.15
12	Tay Brown	.15
13	Brad Budde	.25
14	Dave Cadigan	.25
15	Pat Cannamela	.15
16	Paul Cleary	.15
17	Sam Cunningham	.35
18	Anthony Davis	.50
19	Clarence Davis	.25
20	Morley Drury	.15
21	John Ferraro	.15
22	Bill Fisk	.15
23	Roy Foster	.25
24	Mike Garrett	.35
25	Frank Gifford	1.25
26	Ralph Heywood	.15
27	Pat Howell	.15
28	Gary Jeter	.25
29	Dennis Johnson	.15
30	Mort Kaer	.15
31	Grenny Lansdell	.15
32	Ronnie Lott	1.25
33	Paul McDonald	.25
34	Tim McDonald	.35
35	Ron Mix	.35
36	Don Mosebar	.35
37	Artimus Parker	.25
38	Charles Phillips	.15
39	Erny Pinckert	.15
40	Marvin Powell	.25
41	Aaron Rosenberg	.15
42	Tim Rossovich	.25
43	Jim Sears	.15
44	Gus Shaver	.15
45	Nate Shaw	.15
46	O.J. Simpson	5.00
47	Ernie Smith	.15
48	Harry Smith	.15
49	Larry Stevens	.15
50	Lynn Swann	1.00
51	Brice Taylor	.15
52	Dennis Thurman	.25
53	Keith Van Horne	.25
54	Cotton Warburton	.15
55	Charles White	.50
56	Elmer Willhoite	.15
57	Richard Wood	.25
58	Ron Yary	.35
59	Adrian Young	.15
60	Charles Young (UER) (listed as Adrian Young on card front)	.25
61	Pete Adams, John Grant	.15
62	Bill Bain, Jim O'Bradovich	.25
63	Nate Barrager, Francis Tappan	.15
64	Booker Brown, Steve Riley	.15
65	Al Cowlings, Jimmy Gunn, Charles Weaver	1.00
66	Jack Del Rio, Duane Bickett	.50
67	Clay Matthews, Bruce Matthews	.50
68	Marlin McKeever, Mike McKeever	.35
69	Orv Mohler, Garrett Arbelbide	.15
70	Sid Smith, Marv Montgomery	.15
71	John Vella, Willie Hall	.25
72	Don Williams, Jesse Hibbs	.15
73	Stan Williamson, Tony Slaton	.15

1989 Southern Cal Smokey

		MT
Complete Set (23):		10.00
Common Player:		.60
1	Dan Barnes	.60
2	Dwight Carner	.60
3	Delmar Chesley	.60
4	Cleveland Colter	.60
5	Aaron Emanuel	1.25
6	Scott Galbraith	1.25
7	Leroy Holt	.75
8	Randy Hord	.60
9	John Jackson	1.50
10	Brad Leggett	.60
11	Marching Band	.60
12	Dan Owens	1.50
13	Brent Parkinson	.60
14	Tim Ryan	1.50
15	Bill Schultz	.60
16	Larry Smith (CO)	.75
17	Ernest Spears	.60
18	J.P. Sullivan	.60
19	Cordell Sweeney	.60
20	Traveler (Horse Mascot)	.60
21	Marlon Washington	.60
22	Michael Williams	.60
23	Yell Leaders and Song Girls	.75

1991 Southern Cal College Classics

		MT
Complete Set (100):		30.00
Common Player:		.25
1	Charles White	.75
2	Anthony Davis	.75
3	Clay Matthews	.75
4	Hoby Brenner	.35
5	Mike Garrett	.50
6	Bill Sharman (Basketball)	1.25
7	Bob Seagren (Track)	.35
8	Mike McKeever	.35
9	Celso Kalache (Volleyball)	.25
10	John Williams (CO) (Water Polo)	.25
11	John Naber (Swimming)	.50
12	Brad Budde	.35
13	Tim Ryan	.35
14	Mark Tucker	.25
15	Rodney Peete	1.00
16	Art Mazmanian (Baseball)	.25
17	Red Badgro (Baseball)	.35
18	Sue Habernigg (Women's Swimming)	.25
19	Craig Fertig	.25
20	John Block (Basketball)	.50
21	Jen-Kai Liu (Volleyball)	.25
22	Kim Ruddins (Women's Volleyball)	.25
23	Al Cowlings	1.00
24	Ronnie Lott	1.00
25	Adam Johnson (Volleyball)	1.50
26	Fred Lynn (Baseball)	.50
27	Rick Leach (Tennis)	.35
28	Tim Rossovich	.50
29	Marvin Powell	.35
30	Ron Yary	.50
31	Ken Ruettgers	.50
32	Bob Yoder (CO) (Men's Volleyball)	.25
33	Megan McCallister (Women's Volleyball)	.25
34	Dave Cadigan	.35
35	Jeff Bregel	.25
36	Michael Wayman (Tennis)	.25
37	Sippy Woodhead-Kantzer (Women's Swimming)	.50
38	Tim Hovland (Volleyball)	1.00
39	Steve Busby (Baseball)	.50
40	Tom Seaver (Baseball)	2.00
41	Anthony Colorito	.25
42	Wayne Carlander (Basketball)	.35
43	Erik Affholter	.35
44	Jim Obradovich	.35
45	Duane Bickett	.50
46	Leslie Daland (Women's Swimming)	.25
47	Ole Oleson (Track)	.25
48	Ed Putnam (Baseball)	.25
49	Stan Smith (Tennis)	.75
50	Jeff Hart (Golf)	.25
51	Jack Del Rio	.50
52	Bob Boyd (CO) (Basketball)	.35
53	Pat Haden	1.00
54	John Lambert (Basketball)	.35
55	Pete Beathard	.75
56	Anna-Maria Fernandez (Women's Tennis)	.50
57	Marta Figueras-Dotti (Women's Golf)	.35
58	Don Mosebar	.35
59	Don Doll	.35
60	Dave Stockton (Golf)	.75
61	Trisha Laux (Women's Tennis)	.25
62	Roy Foster	.35
63	Bruce Matthews	.35
64	Steve Sogge	.35
65	Tracy Nakamura (Women's Golf)	.35
66	Marv Montgomery	.25
67	Jack Tingley (Swimming)	.25
68	Larry Stevens	.25
69	Harry Smith	.25
70	Bill Bain	.25
71	Mark McGwire (Baseball)	3.00
72	Brad Brink (Baseball)	.25
73	Richard Wood	.35
74	Rod Dedeaux (CO) (Baseball)	.50
75	Paul Westphal (Basketball)	1.25
76	Al Krueger	.25
77	James McConica (Swimming)	.25
78	Rod Martin	.35
79	Bill Yardley (Volleyball)	.25
80	Bill Stetson (Volleyball)	.25
81	Ray Looze (Swimming)	.25
82	Dan Jorgensen (Swimming)	.25
83	Anna-Lucia Fernandez (Women's Tennis)	.50
84	Terri O'Loughlin (Women's Swimming)	.25
85	John Grant	.25
86	Chris Lewis (Tennis)	.25
87	Steve Timmons (Volleyball)	2.00
88	Dr. Dallas Long (Track)	.35
89	John McKay (CO)	.50
90	Joe Bottom (Swimming)	.25
91	John Jackson	.35
92	Paul McDonald	.35
93	Jimmy Gunn	.25
94	Rod Sherman	.35
95	Cecilia Fernandez (Women's Tennis)	.25
96	Doug Adler (Tennis)	.25
97	Ron Orr (Swimming)	.25
98	Debbie Landreth Brown (Women's Volleyball)	.25
99	Debbie Green (Women's Volleyball)	.25
100	Pat Harrison (Baseball)	.25

1991 Southern Cal Smokey

		MT
Complete Set (16):		8.00
Common Player:		.60
1	Kurt Barber	1.25
2	Ron Dale	.60
3	Derrick Deese	1.00
4	Michael Gaytan	.60
5	Matt Gee	.60
6	Calvin Holmes	1.00
7	Scott Lockwood	1.00
8	Michael Moody	.60
9	Marvin Pollard	.60
10	Mark Raab	.60
11	Larry Smith (CO)	.75
12	Raoul Spears	.60
13	Matt Willig	.60
14	Alan Wilson	.60
15	James Wilson	.60
16	Traveler (The Trojan Horse)	.60

1992 Southern Cal Smokey

		MT
Complete Set (16):		8.00
Common Player:		.60
1	Wes Bender	.60
2	Estrus Crayton	.60
3	Eric Dixon	.60
4	Travis Hannah	1.50
5	Zuri Hector	.60
6	Lamont Hollinquest	.60
7	Yonnie Jackson	.60
8	Bruce Luizzi	.60
9	Mike Mooney	.60
10	Stephon Pace	.60
11	Joel Scott	.60
12	DeNail Sparks	.60
13	Titus Tuiasosopo	.60
14	Larry Wallace	.60
15	David Webb	.60
16	Title Card ART	.60

1988 Southwestern Louisiana McDag

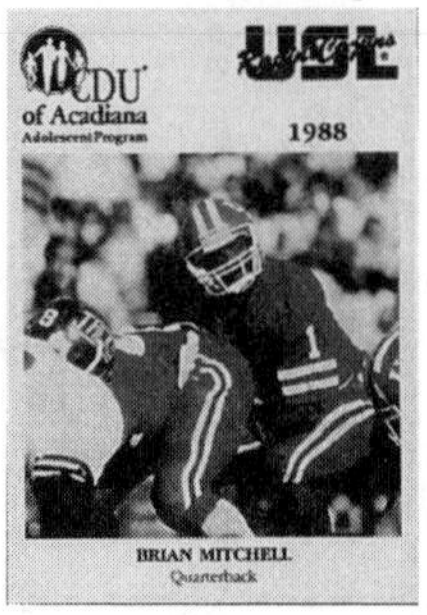
CDU
of Acadiana
Adolescent Program
USL
1988
BRIAN MITCHELL
Quarterback

		MT
Complete Set (12):		6.00
Common Player:		.50
1	Brian Mitchell (QB rolling out)	2.00
2	Brian Mitchell (QB over center)	2.00
3	Chris Gannon (DE signalling sideline)	.50
4	Chris Gannon (DE awaiting snap)	.50
5	Willie Culpepper	.75
6	Greg Eagles	.50
7	Steve McKinney	.50
8	Pat Decuir	.50
9	Leslie Luquette	.50
10	Robert Johnson	.50
11	Lisa McCoy (Cheerleader)	.50
12	Michelle Aubert (Cheerleader)	.50

1991 Stanford All-Century

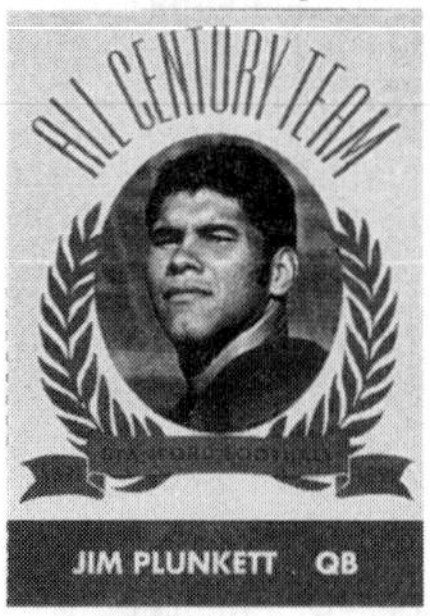
ALL CENTURY TEAM
JIM PLUNKETT QB

		MT
Complete Set (100):		100.00
Common Player:		.75
1	Frankie Albert	1.25
2	Lester Archambeau	1.00
3	Bruno Banducci	.75
4	Benny Barnes	1.00
5	Guy Benjamin	2.00
6	Mike Boryla	1.25
7	Marty Brill	.75
8	John Brodie	6.00
9	Jackie Brown	.75
10	George Buehler	1.00
11	Don Bunce	1.25
12	Chris Burford	1.25
13	Walter Camp (CO)	2.50
14	Gordy Ceresino	.75
15	Jack Chapple	.75
16	Toi Cook	2.00
17	Bill Corbus	.75
18	Steve Dils	2.50
19	Pat Donovan	1.25
20	John Elway	20.00
21	Chuck Evans	.75
22	Skip Face	.75
23	Hugh Gallarneau	.75
24	Rod Garcia	.75
25	Bob Garrett	.75
26	Rick Gervais	.75
27	John Gillory	.75
28	Bobby Grayson	1.00
29	Bones Hamilton	1.00
30	Ray Handley	2.00
31	Mark Harmon	.75
32	Marv Harris	.75
33	Emile Harry	1.25
34	Tony Hill	2.50
35	Brian Holloway	1.25
36	John Hopkins	.75
37	Dick Horn	.75
38	Jeff James	1.00
39	Gary Kerkorian	.75
40	Gordon King	1.00
41	Younger Klippert	.75
42	Pete Kmetovic	.75
43	Jim Lawson	.75
44	Pete Lazetich	.75
45	Dave Lewis	1.00
46	Vic Lindskog	.75
47	James Lofton	6.00
48	Ken Margerum	1.25
49	Ed McCaffrey	2.00
50	Charles McCloud	.75
51	Bill McColl	1.00
52	Duncan McColl	.75
53	Milt McColl	.75
54	Jim Merlo	1.00
55	Phil Moffatt	.75
56	Bob Moore	1.00
57	Sam Morley	.75
58	Monk Moscrip	.75
59	Brad Muster	2.50
60	Ken Naber	.75
61	Darrin Nelson	2.00
62	Ernie Nevers	3.00
63	Dick Norman	.75
64	Blaine Nye	1.25
65	Don Parish	.75
66	John Paye	2.00
67	Gary Pettigrew	1.00
68	Jim Plunkett	6.00
69	Randy Poltl	.75
70	Seraphim Post	.75
71	John Ralston (CO)	1.25
72	Bob Reynolds	.75
73	Don Robesky	.75
74	Doug Robison	.75
75	Greg Sampson	.75
76	John Sande	.75
77	Turk Schonert	2.00
78	Jack Schultz	.75
79	Clark Shaughnessy (CO)	1.25
80	Ted Shipkey	.75
81	Jeff Siemon	2.00
82	Andy Sinclair	.75
83	Malcolm Snider	1.00
84	Norm Standlee	1.00
85	Roger Stillwell	.75
86	Chuck Taylor (CO)	.75
87	Dink Templeton	.75
88	Tiny Thornhill (CO)	.75
89	Dave Tipton	.75
90	Keith Topping	.75
91	Randy Vataha	.75
92	Garin Veris	1.25
93	Jon Volpe	2.50
94	Bill Walsh (CO)	5.00
95	Pop Warner (CO)	2.00
96	Gene Washington	2.00
97	Vincent White	.75
98	Paul Wiggin	1.25
99	John Wilbur	1.00
100	Dave Wyman	1.25

1992 Stanford

		MT
Complete Set (35):		15.00
Common Player:		.35
1	Seyon Albert	.35
2	Estevan Avila	.50
3	Tyler Batson	.35
4	Guy Benjamin (ACO)	.60
5	David Calomese	.35
6	Mike Cook	.50
7	Chris Dalman	.50
8	Dave Garnett	.35
9	Ron George	1.00
10	Darrien Gordon	2.00
11	Tom Holmoe (ACO)	.60
12	Derron Klafter	.35
13	J.J. Lasley	.50
14	John Lynch	.60
15	Glyn Milburn	4.00
16	Fernando Montes (ACO)	.50
17	Vince Otoupal	.35
18	Rick Pallow	.35
19	Ron Redell	.35
20	Aaron Rembisz	.35
21	Bill Ring (ACO)	.50
22	Ellery Roberts	.60
23	Scott Schuhmann (ACO)	.35
24	Terry Shea (ACO)	.35
25	Bill Singler (ACO)	.35
26	Paul Stonehouse	.35
27	Dave Tipton (ACO)	.35
28	Keena Turner (ACO)	.75
29	Fred von Appen (ACO)	.35
30	Bill Walsh (CO)	3.00
31	Ryan Wetnight	2.00
32	Tom Williams	.35
33	Mike Wilson (ACO)	.50
34	Billy Wittman	.35
35	Checklist Card (J.J. Lasley)	.50

1993 Stanford

		MT
Complete Set (18):		10.00
Common Player:		.50
1	Jeff Bailey	.50
2	Parker Bailey	.50
3	Roger Boden	.50
4	Hartwell Brown	.50
5	Vaughn Bryant	.60
6	Brian Cassidy	.50
7	Glen Cavanaugh	.50
8	Kevin Garnett	.50
9	Mark Hatzenbuhler	.50
10	Steve Hoyem	.60
11	Mike Jerich	.50
12	Paul Nickel	.50
13	Toby Norwood	.60
14	Tyrone Parker	.60
15	Ellery Roberts	.60
16	David Shaw	.50
17	Bill Walsh (CO)	2.50
18	Josh Wright	.50

1989 Syracuse Burger King

		MT
Complete Set (15):		15.00
Common Player:		1.00
1	David Bavaro	1.50

2	Blake Bednars	1.00
3	Alban Brown	1.00
4	Dan Burey	1.00
5	Rob Burnett	2.50
6	Fred DeRiggi	1.00
7	John Flannery	2.00
8	Duane Kinnon	1.00
9	Dick MacPherson (CO)	2.00
10	Rob Moore	5.00
11	Michael Owens	1.50
12	Bill Scharr	1.00
13	Turnell Sims	1.00
14	Sean Whiteman	1.00
15	Terry Wooden	2.50

1991 Syracuse Program Cards

		MT
Complete Set (36):		30.00
Common Player:		.75
1	George Rooks	.75
2	Marvin Graves	4.00
3	Andrew Dees	.75
4	Glen Young	1.00
5	Chris Gedney	2.00
6	Paul Pasqualoni	1.00
7	Terrence Wisdom	.75
8	John Biskup	.75
9	Mark McDonald	.75
10	Dan Conley	1.00
11	Kevin Mitchell	.75
12	Qadry Ismail	6.00
13	John Lusardi	.75
14	David Walker	.75
15	John Capachione	.75
16	Shelby Hill	1.25
17	Dwayne Joseph	.75
18	Greg Walker	.75
19	Jerry Sharp	.75
20	Tim Sandquist	.75
21	Chuck Bull	.75
22	Jo Jo Wooden	.75
23	Terry Richardson	.75
24	Doug Womack	.75
25	Reggie Terry	.75
26	Garland Hawkins	.75
27	Tony Montemorra	.75
28	Chip Todd	.75
29	Pat O'Neill	1.00
30	Kevin Barker	.75
31	John Reagan	.75
32	Pat O'Rourke	.75
33	Jim Wentworth	.75
34	Ernie Brown	.75
35	John Nilsen	.75
36	Al Wooten	.75

1980 Tennessee Police

		NM
Complete Set (19):		37.00
Common Player:		1.50
1	Bill Bates	1.50
2	James Berry	1.50
3	Chris Bolton	1.50
4	Mike L. Cofer	1.50
5	Glenn Ford	1.50
6	Anthony Hancock	1.50
7	Brian Ingram	1.50
8	Tim Irwin	1.50
9	Kenny Jones	1.50
10	Wilbert Jones	1.50
11	Johnny Majors (CO)	1.50
12	Bill Marren	1.50
13	Danny Martin	1.50
14	Jim Noonan	1.50
15	Lee North	1.50
16	Hubert Simpson	1.50
17	Danny Spradlin	1.50
18	John Warren	1.50
19	Brad White	1.50

1990 Tennessee Centennial

		MT
Complete Set (294):		30.00
Common Player:		.10
1	Vince Moore	.20
2	Steve Matthews	.10
3	Joey Chapman	.10
4	Terence Cleveland	.10
5	Thomas Wood	.10
6	J.J. McCleskey	.10
7	Jason Julian	.10
8	Andy Kelly	.20
9	Derrick Folsom	.10
10	Chip McCallum	.10
11	Lloyd Kerr	.10
12	Cory Fleming	.30
13	Kevin Zurcher	.10
14	Lee England	.10
15	Carl Pickens	2.00
16	Sterling Henton	.10
17	Lee Wood	.10
18	Kent Elmore	.10
19	Craig Faulkner	.10
20	Keith Denson	.10
21	Preston Warren	.10
22	Floyd Miley	.10
23	Earnest Fields	.10
24	Tony Thompson	.10
25	Jeremy Lincoln	.30
26	David Bennett	.10
27	Greg Burke	.10
28	Tavio Henson	.10
29	Kevin Wendelboe	.10
30	Cedric Kline	.10
31	Keith Jeter	.10
32	Chris Russ	.10
33	DeWayne Dotson	.10
34	Mike Rapien	.10
35	Clemons McCroskey	.10
36	Mark Fletcher	.10
37	Chuck Smith	.20
38	Jeff Tullis	.10
39	Kelly Days	.10
40	Shazzon Bradley	.10
41	Reggie Ingram	.10
42	Roland Poles	.10
43	Tracy Smith	.10
44	Chuck Webb	.30
45	Shon Walker	.20
46	Eric Riffer	.10
47	Greg Amsler	.10
48	J.J. Surlas	.10
49	Brian Bradley	.10
50	Tom Myslinski	.20
51	John Fisher	.10
52	Craig Martin	.10
53	Carey Bailey	.10
54	Houston Thomas	.10
55	Ryan Patterson	.10
56	Chad Goodin	.10
57	Brian Spivey	.10
58	Todd Kelly	.10
59	Mike Stowell	.10
60	Jim Fenwick	.10
61	Marc Jones	.10
62	Chris Ragan	.10
63	Rodney Gordon	.10
64	Mark Needham	.10
65	Patrick Lenoir	.10
66	Martin Williams	.10
67	Brad Seiber	.10
68	Larry Smith	.10
69	Jerry Teel	.10
70	Charles McRae	.30
71	Rex Hargrove	.10
72	James Wilson	.10
73	Doug Baird	.10
74	Mark Moore	.10
75	Lance Nelson	.10
76	Robert Todd	.10
77	Greg Gerardi	.10
78	Antone Davis	.30
79	Eric Still	.10
80	Anthony Morgan	.75
81	Alvin Harper	1.00
82	Charles Longmire	.10
83	Mark Adams	.10
84	Chris Benson	.10
85	Horace Morris	.10
86	Harlan Davis	.10
87	Darryl Hardy	.10
88	Tracy Hayworth	.20
89	Von Reeves	.10
90	Marion Hobby	.10
91	John Ward (ANN)	.10
92	Roderick Lewis	.10
93	Orion McCants	.10
94	James Warren	.10
95	Mario Brunson	.10
96	Joe Davis	.10
97	Shawn Truss	.10
98	Keith Steed	.10
99	Kacy Rodgers	.10
100	Johnny Majors (CO)	.30
101	Phillip Fulmer (CO)	.30
102	Larry Lacewell (CO)	.20
103	Charlie Coe (CO)	.10
104	Tommy West (CO)	.10
105	David Cutcliffe (CO)	.10
106	Jack Sells (CO)	.10
107	Rex Norris (CO)	.10
108	John Chavis (CO)	.10
109	Tim Keane (CO)	.10
110	Recruiter (Tim Mingey)	.10
111	Sr. Admin. Asst. (Bill Higdon)	.10
112	Tim Kerin (TR)	.10
113	Bruno Pauletto (CO)	.10
114	Vols 17, Co. State 14 (Chuck Webb)	.20
115	Vols 24, UCLA 6 (Chuck Webb)	.20
116	Vols 28, Duke 6 (Game Action Photo)	.10
117	Vols 21, Auburn 14 (Game Action Photo)	.10
118	Vols 17, Georgia 14 (Jason Julian)	.10
119	Vols 30, Alabama 47 (Roland Poles)	.10
120	Vols 45, LSU 39 (Charles McRae)	.20
121	Vols 52, Akron 9 (Brian Spivey)	.10
122	Vols 33, Ole Miss 21 (Alvin Harper)	.30
123	Vols 31, Kentucky 10 (Kelly Days)	.10
124	Vols 17, Vanderbilt 10 (Game Action Photo)	.10
125	'90 Mobil Cotton Bowl 1 (Jason Julian)	.10
126	'90 Mobil Cotton Bowl 2 (Andy Kelly)	.10
127	'90 Mobil Cotton Bowl 3 (Chuck Webb)	.20
128	'90 Mobil Cotton Bowl 4 (Scoreboard)	.10
129	Eric Still	.10
130	Chris Benson	.10
131	Preston Warren	.10
132	Lee England	.10
133	Kent Elmore	.10
134	Eric Still	.10
135	Chuck Webb	.30
136	Marion Hobby	.10
137	Kent Elmore	.10
138	Antone Davis	.30
139	Thomas Woods	.10
140	Charles McRae	.30
141	Preston Warren	.10
142	Darryl Hardy	.10
143	Offense or Defense (Carl Pickens)	1.00
144	Carl Pickens	2.00
145	Chuck Webb	.30
146	Thomas Woods	.10
147	Total Offense Game (Andy Kelly)	.10
148	The TVA (Offensive Line)	.10
149	Smokey (Mascot)	.10
150	Director of Athletics (Doug Dickey)	.10
151	Neyland Stadium	.10
152	Neyland-Thompson Ctr	.10
153	Gibbs Hall (Dormitory)	.10
154	Asst. AD (Carmen Tegano) (Academics and Athletics)	.10
155	Gene McEver (HOF)	.10
156	Beattie Feathers (HOF)	.30
157	Robert Neyland (HOF) (CO)	.50
158	Herman Hickman (HOF)	.20
159	Bowden Wyatt (HOF)	.20
160	Hank Lauricella (HOF)	.20
161	Doug Atkins (HOF)	.30
162	Johnny Majors (HOF)	.30
163	Bobby Dodd (HOF)	.30
164	Bob Suffridge (HOF)	.10
165	Nathan Dougherty (HOF)	.10
166	George Cafego (HOF)	.10
167	Bob Johnson (HOF)	.20
168	Ed Molinski (HOF)	.10
169	Reggie White	2.00
170	Willie Gault	.60
171	Doug Atkins	.30
172	Keith DeLong	.30
173	Ron Widby	.20
174	Bill Johnson	.20
175	Jack Reynolds	.30
176	Tim McGee	.30
177	Harry Galbreath	.20
178	Roland James	.20
179	Abe Shires	.10
180	Ted Daffer	.10
181	Bob Foxx	.10
182	Richmond Flowers	.30
183	Beattie Feathers	.30
184	Condredge Holloway	.50
185	Larry Sievers	.20
186	Johnnie Jones	.10
187	Carl Zander	.20
188	Dale Jones	.10
189	Bruce Wilkerson	.20
190	Terry McDaniel	.30
191	Craig Colquitt	.20
192	Stanley Morgan	.75
193	Curt Watson	.10
194	Bobby Majors	.20
195	Steve Kiner	.20
196	Paul Naumoff	.20
197	Bud Sherrod	.10
198	Murray Warmath	.20
199	Steve DeLong	.20
200	Bill Pearman	.10
201	Bobby Gordon	.10
202	John Michels	.10
203	Bill Mayo	.10
204	Andy Kozar	.10
205	1892 Volunteers (Team Photo)	.10
206	1900 Volunteers (Team Photo)	.10
207	1905 Volunteers (Team Photo)	.10
208	1907 Volunteers (Individual player photos)	.10
209	1916 Volunteers (Team Photo)	.10
210	1914 Volunteers (Team Photo)	.10
211	1896 Volunteers (Team Photo)	.10
212	1908 Volunteers (Team Photo)	.10
213	1926 Volunteers (Team Photo)	.10
214	1930 Volunteers (Team Photo)	.10
215	1934 Volunteers (Team Photo)	.10
216	1938 Volunteers (Team Photo)	.10
217	1940 Volunteers (Team Photo)	.10
218	1944 Volunteers (Team Photo)	.10
219	1945 Volunteers (Team Photo)	.10
220	1954 Volunteers (Team Photo)	.10
221	1969 Volunteers (Team Photo)	.10
222	1962 Volunteers (Team Photo)	.10
223	1976 Volunteers (Team Photo)	.10
224	1985 Volunteers (Team Photo)	.10
225	1978 Volunteers (Team Photo)	.10
226	1980 Volunteers (Team Photo)	.10
227	1984 Volunteers (Team Photo)	.10
228	1988 Volunteers (Team Photo)	.10
229	James Baird	.10
230	Condredge Holloway	.50
231	J.G. Lowe	.10
232	E.A. McLean	.10
233	Lemont Holt Jeffers	.10
234	Howard Johnson	.10
235	Malcolm Aiken	.10
236	Toby Palmer	.10
237	Sam Bartholomew	.10
238	Ray Graves	.10
239	Billy Bevis	.10
240	Bert Rechichar	.20
241	Jim Beutel	.10
242	Mike Lucci	.30
243	Hal Wantland	.10
244	Jackie Walker	.10
245	Ron McCartney	.10
246	Robert Shaw	.30
247	Lee North	.10
248	James Berry	.10
249	Carl Zander	.20
250	Chris White	.10
251	Timmy Sims	.10
252	Tim McGee	.50
253	Keith DeLong	.30
254	1931 NY Charity Game (Program)	.10
255	1941 Super Bowl (Program)	.10
256	1945 Rose Bowl (Program)	.10
257	1957 Gator Bowl (Program)	.10
258	1968 Orange Bowl (Program)	.10
259	1972 Bluebonnet Bowl (Program)	.10
260	1981 Graden State Bowl (Program)	.10
261	1968 Sugar Bowl (Program)	.10
262	Checklist 1-76	.10
263	Checklist 77-152	.10
264	Checklist 153-228	.10
265	Checklist 229-294	.10
266	Chris White	.10
267	Kelsey Finch	.10
268	Johnnie Jones	.10
269	Johnnie Jones	.10
270	Curt Watson	.10
271	William Howard	.10
272	Bubba Wyche	.10
273	Tony Robinson	.30
274	Daryl Dickey	.30
275	Alan Cockrell, Willie Gault	.30
276	Alan Cockrell	.30
277	Bobby Scott	.30
278	Tony Robinson	.30
279	Jeff Francis	.20
280	Alvin Harper	1.00
281	Johnny Mills	.10
282	Thomas Woods	.10
283	Bob Lund	.10
284	Gene McEver	.10
285	Stanley Morgan	.75
286	Fuad Reveiz	.30
287	Kent Elmore	.10
288	Jimmy Colquitt	.10
289	Willie Gault	.60
290	100 Years Celebration (Reggie White)	.75
291	The 100 Years Kickoff (Group Photo)	.10
292	Like Father, Like Son (Keith DeLong, Steve DeLong)	.30
293	Offense and Defense (Raleigh McKenzie, Reggie McKenzie)	.20
294	It's Football Time (1990 schedule on back)	.20

1991 Tennessee Hoby

		MT
Complete Set (42):		25.00
Common Player:		.25
397	Mark Adams	.25
398	Carey Bailey	.25
399	David Bennett	.25
400	Shazzon Bradley	.25
401	Kenneth Campbell	.25
402	Dale Carter	1.50
403	Joey Chapman	.25
404	Jerry Colquitt	.50
405	Bernard Daffney	.50
406	Craig Faulkner	.25
407	Earnest Fields	.25
408	John Fisher	.25
409	Cory Fleming	.75
410	Mark Fletcher	.25
411	Tom Fuhler	.25
412	Johnny Majors (CO)	.50
413	Darryl Hardy	.25
414	Aaron Hayden	3.00
415	Tavio Henson	.25
416	Reggie Ingram	.25
417	Andy Kelly	.50
418	Todd Kelly	.75
419	Patrick Lenoir	.25
420	Roderick Lewis	.25
421	Jeremy Lincoln	1.50
422	J.J. McCleskey	.35
423	Floyd Miley	.25
424	Chris Mims	1.50
425	Tom Myslinski	.35
426	Carl Pickens	5.00
427	Roc Powe	.25
428	Von Reeves	.25
429	Eric Riffer	.25
430	Kacy Rodgers	.25
431	Steve Session	.25
432	Heath Shuler	6.00
433	Chuck Smith	.35
434	James O. Stewart	3.00
435	Mike Stowell	.25
436	J.J. Surlas	.25
437	Shon Walker	.35
438	James Wilson	.25

1991 Texas HS Legends

		MT
Complete Set (25):		18.00
Common Player:		.60
1	Marty Akins	.60
2	Gil Bartosh	.60
3	Bill Bradley	1.00
4	Chris Gilbert	1.25
5	Glynn Gregory	.75
6	Charlie Haas	.60
7	Craig James	2.00
8	Boody Johnson	.60
9	Ernie Koy Jr.	.75
10	Glenn Lippman	.60
11	Jack Pardee	1.00
12	Billy Patterson	.60
13	Billy Sims	3.00
14	Byron Townsend	.60
15	Doyle Traylor	.60
16	Joe Washington Jr.	1.00
17	Allie White	.60
18	Wilson Whitley	.75
19	Gordon Wood	.75
20	Willie Zapalac	.60
21	Cover Card 1	.60
22	Cover Card 2	.60
23	Cover Card 3	.60
24	Cover Card 4	.60
25	Cover Card 5	.60

1993 Texas Taco Bell

		MT
Complete Set (50):		25.00
Common Player:		.50
1	Mike Adams	2.00
2	Thomas Baskin	.50
3	Tony Brackens	2.00
4	Steve Bradley	.50
5	Blake Brockermeyer (Wearing home jersey)	1.50
6	Blake Brockermeyer (Wearing away jersey)	1.50
7	Phil Brown	.50
8	Chris Carter	.50
9	Stonie Clark	.75
10	Gerald Crawford	.50
11	Trent Elliot	.50
12	Joey Ellis	.75
13	John Elmore	.75
14	Jon Feick	.50
15	Victor Frazier	.50
16	Jimmy Hakes	.50
17	Anthony Holmes	.50
18	Brian Howard	.50
19	Jon Hunter	.50
20	Curtis Jackson	.75
21	Eric Jackson	.50
22	Bryan Johnson	.75
23	James Lane	.50
24	Doug Livingston	.50
26	Chad Lucas	.50
27	John Mackovic (CO)	1.00
28	Van Malone	1.25
29	Justin McLemore	.75
30	Shea Morenz	2.50
31	Dan Neil	.75
32	Cosmo Palmieri	.50
33	Joe Phillips	.50
34	Lovell Pinkney	2.50
35	Chris Rapp	.50
36	Robert Reed	.50
37	Jason Reeves	.50
38	Troy Riemer	.50
39	Scott Szeredy	.50
40	Tre Thomas	.75
41	Winfred Tubbs	1.50
42	Duane Vacek	.75
43	Brian Vasek	.75
44	Rodrick Walker	1.00
45	Norman Watkins	.50
46	Kevin Watler	.50
47	Pascal Watty	.50
48	Bryant Westbrook	.75
49	Longhorns Band	.50
50	Taco Bell Logo Card - 1993 Texas schedule	.50

1992 Texas A and M

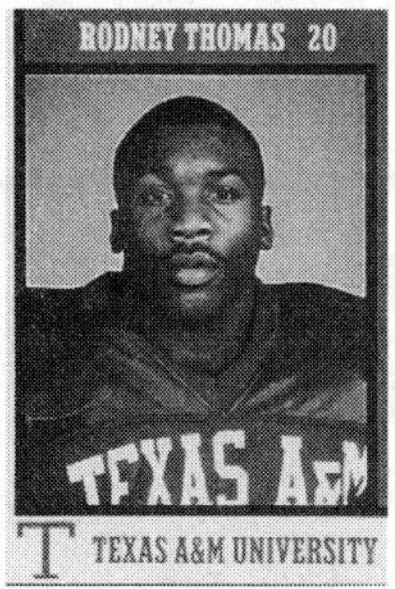

		MT
Complete Set (65):		25.00
Common Player:		.35
1	Matt Miller	.50
2	Steve Emerson	.35
3	Brad Cooper	.35
4	Mike Hendricks	.50
5	Dexter Wesley	.35
6	Darrell Red	.35
7	Antonio Shorter	1.00
8	Larry Wallace	.35
9	Kefa Chatham	.35
10	Billy Mitchell	.35
11	Patrick Bates	2.00
12	Greg Hill	5.00
13	Tommy Preston	.35
14	Ryan Mathews	.35
15	Steve Kenney	.35
16	John Richard	.35
17	John Ellisor	.35
18	Ryan Kern	.35
19	Jeff Jones	.35
20	Chris Sanders	.35
21	Reggie Graham	.35
22	David Davis	.35
23	Tony Harrison	.50
24	Jason Mathews	.50
25	Otis Nealy	.35
26	Kent Petty	.35
27	Rodney Thomas	5.00
28	Sam Adams	2.00
29	Clif Groce	.35
30	Tyler Harrison	.35
31	Eric England	.35
32	Jason Atkinson	.50
33	Lance Teichelman	.35
34	Marcus Buckley	2.00
35	Steve Solari	.35
36	Aggie Coaches	.50
37	Derrick Frazier	.50
38	James McKeehan	.50
39	Doug Carter	.35
40	Larry Jackson	.35
41	Brian Mitchell	.75
42	Greg Schorp	.50
43	Greg Cook	.35
44	Kyle Maxfield	.35
45	Todd Mathison	.35
46	Chris Dausin	.35
47	Junior White	.35
48	Wilbert Biggens	.35
49	Terry Venetoulias	.35
50	Jessie Cox	.35
51	R.C. Slocum (CO)	1.00
52	Defensive Coaches (Bob Davie, Kirk Doll, Bill Johnson, Trent Walters)	.35
53	Offensive Coaches (Mike Sherman, Shawn Slocum, Bob Toledo, Gary Kubiak, David Culley)	.50
54	Recruiting Coordinator (Tim Cassidy)	.35
55	Yell Leaders (Steve Scanlon, Adin Pfeuffer, Tim Isgitt, Ronnie McDonald, Mark Rollins)	.35
56	A and M Band	.35
57	Reveille V Mascot	.35
58	Twelfth Man Statue	.50
59	Bonfire	.35
60	Training Facility	.35
61	Kyle Field	.35
62	Texas A and M Campus	.35
NNO	Front Card (Texas A and M Logo)	.35
NNO	Back Card	.35
NNO	Checklist Card	.35

1995 Tony's Pizza College Mascots

		MT
Complete Set (20):		7.00
Common Player:		.25
1	Alabama Crimson Tide	.50
2	Auburn Tigers	.40
3	Arizona Wildcats	.25
4	Boston College Eagles	.25
5	Colorado Buffaloes	.40
6	Florida State Seminoles	.50
7	Florida Gators	.50
8	Kansas State Wildcats	.25
9	Miami Hurricanes	.50
10	Michigan Wolverines	.50
11	Nebraska Cornhuskers	.50
12	Notre Dame Fightin' Irish	.50
13	Penn State Nittany Lions	.50
14	Tennessee Volunteers	.50
15	Texas Longhorns	.40
16	Texas A M Aggies	.40
17	UCLA Bruins	.50
18	USC Trojans	.50
19	Washington Huskies	.40
20	Wisconsin Badgers	.25

1991 UNLV

		MT
Complete Set (12):		8.00
Common Player:		.75
1	Cheerleaders and Songleaders	.75
2	Gang Tackle	.75
3	Instant Offense (Hernandez Cooper)	.75
4	No Escape	.75
5	On The Move	.75
6	Punching It In	.75
7	Ready To Fire (Derek Stott)	.75
8	Rebel Fever	.75
9	Rebel Sack	.75
10	Silver Bowl (Sam Boyd)	.75
11	Jim Strong (CO)	.75
12	Team Photo	1.00

1990 Virginia

		MT
Complete Set (16):		25.00
Common Player:		1.25
1	Chris Borsari	1.25
2	Ron Carey	1.25
3	Paul Collins	1.25
4	Tony Covington	3.00
5	Derek Dooley	1.25
6	Joe Hall	1.25
7	Myron Martin	1.25
8	Bruce McGonnigal	1.50
9	Jake McInerney	1.25
10	Keith McMeans	1.25
11	Herman Moore	12.00
12	Shawn Moore	4.00
13	Trevor Ryals	1.25
14	Chris Stearns	1.25
15	Jason Wallace	1.25
16	George Welsh (CO)	1.50

1992 Virginia Coca-Cola

		MT
Complete Set (16):		15.00
Common Player:		1.00
1	Bobby Goodman	1.25
2	Michael Husted	2.00
3	Greg Jeffries	2.00
4	Charles Keiningham	1.00
5	Terry Kirby	5.00
6	Kenneth Miles	1.00
7	Tim Samec	1.00
8	Chris Slade	3.50
9	Alvin Snead	1.00
10	Gary Steele	1.00
11	Jeff Tomlin	1.00
12	Terrence Tomlin	1.00
13	David Ware	1.00
14	George Welsh (CO)	1.25
15	Virginia 20, Clemson 7; Sept. 8, 1990	1.00
16	Virginia 20, N.Carolina 17; Nov 14, 1987	1.00

1993 Virginia Coca-Cola

		MT
Complet Set (16):		15.00
Common Player:		1.00
1	Tom Burns	1.00
2	Peter Collins	1.00
3	Bill Curry	1.00
4	Mark Dixon	1.00
5	Bill Edwards	1.00
6	P.J. Killian	1.00
7	Keith Lyle	1.00
8	Greg McClellan	1.00
9	Matt Mikeska	1.00
10	Aaron Mundy	1.00
11	Jim Reid	1.00
12	Josh Schrader	1.00
13	Jerrod Washington	1.00
14	George Welsh (CO)	1.25
15	Cavalier Spirit (Cheerleaders)	1.00
16	Cavalier Mascot	1.00

1973 Washington KFC

		NM
Complete Set (30):		350.00
Common Player:		12.00
1	Jim Anderson	12.00
2	Jim Andrilenas	12.00
3	Glen Bonner	18.00
4	Bob Boustead	12.00
5	Skip Boyd	18.00
6	Gordie Bronson	12.00
7	Reggie Brown	12.00
8	Dan Celoni	12.00
9	Brian Daheny	12.00
10	Fred Dean	12.00
11	Pete Elswick	12.00
12	Dennis Fitzpatrick	12.00
13	Bob Graves	12.00
14	Pedro Hawkins	12.00
15	Rick Hayes	12.00
16	Barry Houlihan	12.00
17	Roberto Jourdan	12.00
18	Washington Keenan	12.00

19	Eddie King	12.00
20	Jim Kristoff	12.00
21	Murphy McFarland	12.00
22	Walter Oldes	12.00
23	Louis Quinn	12.00
24	Frank Reed	18.00
25	Dain Rodwell	12.00
26	Ron Stanley	12.00
27	Joe Tabor	12.00
28	Pete Taggares	12.00
29	John Whitacre	12.00
30	Hans Woldseth	12.00
NNO	Color Team Photo (Large 8x10)	18.00
NNO	Coaches Photo (Large 8x10)	25.00

1988 Washington Smokey

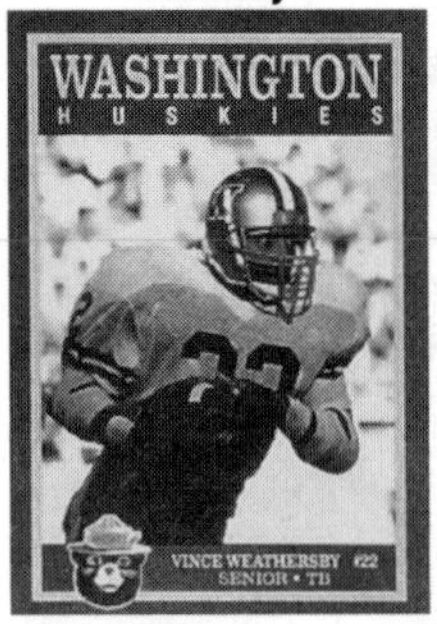

		MT
	Complete Set (16):	15.00
	Common Player:	1.00
1	Ricky Andrews	1.00
2	Bern Brostek	2.00
3	Dennis Brown	2.00
4	Cary Conklin	2.00
5	Tony Covington	1.00
6	Darryl Hall	1.00
7	Martin Harrison	2.00
8	Don James (CO)	2.00
9	Aaron Jenkins	1.00
10	Le-Lo Lang	2.00
11	Art Malone	1.00
12	Andre Riley	1.00
13	Brian Slater	1.00
14	Vince Weathersby	1.00
15	Brett Wiese	1.00
16	Mike Zandofsky	1.50

1990 Washington Smokey

		MT
	Complete Set (16):	15.00
	Common Player (1-12):	.75
	Common Player (13-16):	.75
1	Eric Briscoe (28)	.75
2	Mark Brunell (11)	6.00
3	James Clifford (53)	.75
4	John Cook (93)	.75
5	Ed Cunningham (79)	2.00
6	Dana Hall (5)	2.50
7	Don James (CO)	1.50
8	Donald Jones (48)	.75
9	Dean Kirkland (51)	.75
10	Greg Lewis (20)	2.00
11	Orlando McKay (4)	.75
12	Travis Richardson (58)	.75
13	Kelley Larsen (Women's Volleyball)	.75
14	Michelle Reid (Women's Volleyball)	.75
15	Ashleigh Robertson (Women's Volleyball)	.75
16	Gail Thorpe (Women's Volleyball)	.75

1991 Washington Smokey

		MT
	Complete Set (16):	15.00
	Common Player (1-12):	.75
	Common Player (13-16):	.75
1	Mario Bailey	1.50
2	Beno Bryant	1.50
3	Brett Collins	.75
4	Ed Cunningham	1.50
5	Steve Emtman	2.00
6	Dana Hall	2.00
7	Billy Joe Hobert	4.00
8	Dave Hoffmann	.75
9	Don James (CO)	1.25
10	Donald Jones	.75
11	Siupeli Malamala	1.50
12	Orlando McKay	.75
13	Diane Flick (Women's Volleyball)	.75
14	Kelley Larsen (Women's Volleyball)	.75
15	Ashleigh Robertson (Women's Volleyball)	.75
16	Dana Thompson (Women's Volleyball)	.75

Values quoted in this guide reflect the retail price of a card — the price a collector can expect to pay when buying a card from a dealer. The wholesale price — that which a collector can expect to receive from a dealer when selling cards — will be significantly lower, depending on desirability and condition.

1992 Washington Greats/Pacific

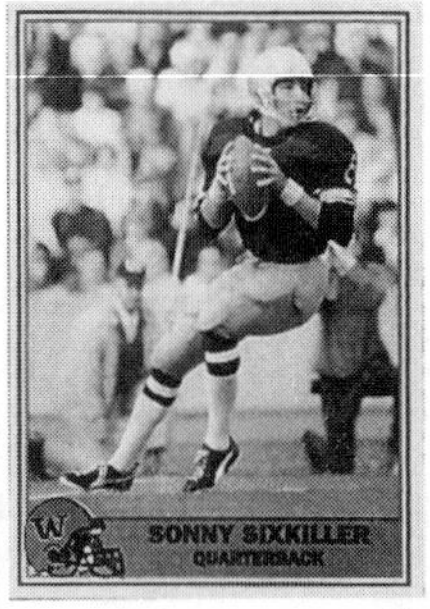

		MT
	Complete Set (110):	15.00
	Common Player:	.15
1	Don James (CO)	.50
2	Cary Conklin	.50
3	Tom Cowan	.15
4	Thane Cleland	.15
5	Steve Pelluer	.50
6	Sonny Sixkiller	.50
7	Koll Hagen	.15
8	Danny Greene	.15
9	George Black	.15
10	Mike Baldassin	.15
11	Bill Douglas	.15
12	Tom Flick	.25
13	Brian Slater	.15
14	Dick Sprague	.15
15	Bob Schloredt	.35
16	Bill Smith	.15
17	Marv Bergmann	.15
18	Sam Mitchell	.25
19	Bill Earley	.15
20	Clarence Dirks	.15
21	Jimmie Cain	.15
22	Don Heinrich	.35
23	Paul (Socko) Sulkosky	.15
24	By Haines	.15
25	Joe Steele	.15
26	Bob Monroe	.15
27	Roy McKasson	.15
28	Charlie Mitchell	.25
29	Ernie Steele	.15
30	Kyle Heinrich	.25
31	Travis Richardson	.15
32	Hugh McElhenny	1.00
33	George Wildcat Wilson	.15
34	Merle Hufford	.15
35	Steve Thompson	.15
36	Jim Krieg	.15
37	Chuck Olson	.15
38	Charley Russell	.15
39	Duane Wardlow	.15
40	Jay MacDowell	.15
41	Alf Hemstad	.15
42	Max Starcevich	.15
43	Ray Mansfield	.25
44	Brooks Biddle	.15
45	Toussaint Tyler	.35
46	Randy Van Diver	.15
47	John Cook	.15
48	Paul Skansi	.25
49	Tim Meamber	.15
50	Milt Bohart	.15
51	Curt Marsh	.25
52	Antowaine Richardson	.15
53	Jim Rodgers	.15
54	Mike Rohrbach	.15
55	Dan Agen	.15
56	Tom Turnure	.15
57	Ron Medved	.25
58	Vick Markov	.15
59	Carl (Bud) Ericksen	.15
60	Bill Kinnune	.15
61	Karsten (Corky) Lewis	.15
62	Sam Robinson	.25
63	Dave Nisbet	.15
64	Barry Bullard	.15
65	Norm Dicks	.15
66	Rick Redman	.25
67	Mark Jerue	.25
68	Jeff Toews	.15
69	Fletcher Jenkins	.15
70	Ray Horton	.25
71	Tom Erlandson	.15
72	Steve Alvord	.15
73	Dean Browning	.15
74	Scott Greenwood	.15
75	Bo Yates	.15
76	Jake Kupp	.25
77	Jim Owens (CO)	.15
78	Don McKeta	.15
79	Ben Davidson	.50
80	Tim Bullard	.15
81	Bill Albrecht	.15
82	Jim Cope	.15
83	Earl Monlux	.15
84	Paul Schwegler	.15
85	Steve Bramwell	.15
86	Ted Holzknecht	.15
87	Larry Hatch	.15
88	John Brady	.15
89	Bob Hivner	.15
90	Chuck Nelson	.25
91	Jeff Jaeger	.25
92	Rich Camarillo	.25
93	Jim Houston	.25
94	Jim Skaggs	.25
95	John Cherberg (CO)	.15
96	Bo Cornell	.25
97	Bill Cahill	.15
98	Dean McAdams	.15
99	Gil Dobie (CO)	.25
100	Walter Shiel	.15
101	Enoch Bagshaw (CO)	.15
102	Ray Eckmann	.15
103	Luther Carr	.15
104	Jimmy Bryan	.15
105	Darrell Royal	.35
106	Ray Frankowski	.15
107	Ray Pinney	.25
108	Skip Boyd	.15
109	Al Burleson	.15
110	Dennis Fitzpatrick	.25
NNO	Checklist Card	3.00
AU32	Hugh McElhenny (Certified Autograph, serially numbered of 1000)	50.00

1992 Washington Pay Less

		MT
	Complete Set (16):	15.00
	Common Player:	.75
1	Walter Bailey	.75
2	Jay Barry	.75
3	Mark Brunell	5.00
4	Beno Bryant	1.00
5	James Clifford	.75
6	Jaime Fields	.75
7	Travis Hanson	.75
8	Billy Joe Hobert (SP)	4.00
9	Dave Hoffmann	.75
10	Matt Jones	.75
11	Lincoln Kennedy	2.00
12	Andy Mason	.75
13	Shane Pahukoa	.75
14	Tommie Smith	.75
15	Darius Turner	.75
16	Team Photo (Schedule)	.75

1993 Washington Safeway

		MT
	Complete Set (16):	10.00
	Common Player:	.75
1	Beno Bryant	1.00
2	Hillary Butler	.75
3	D'Marco Farr	1.50
4	Jamal Fountaine	.75
5	Tom Gallagher	.75
6	Travis Hanson	.75
7	Damon Huard	1.50
8	Matt Jones	.75
9	Pete Kaligis	.75
10	Napoleon Kaufman	5.00
11	Joe Kralik	.75
12	Andy Mason	.75
13	Jim Nevelle	.75
14	Pete Pierson	.75
15	Steve Springstead	.75
16	John Werdel	.75

1994 Washington

		MT
	Complete Set (12):	12.00
	Common Player:	.60
1	Eric Bjornson	2.00
2	Mark Bruener	3.00
3	Richie Chambers	1.00
4	Frank Garcia	1.00
5	Russell Hairston	.60
6	Damon Huard	1.25
7	Napoleon Kaufman	3.50
8	David Killpatrick	.60
9	Lamar Lyons	.60
10	Andrew Peterson	1.00
11	Donovan Schmidt	.60
12	Richard Thomas	.60

1995 Washington

		MT
	Complete Set (16):	8.00
	Common Player:	.50
1	Ink Aleaga	.75
2	Eric Battle	.75
3	Ernie Conwell	.50
4	Deke Devers	.50
5	Mike Ewaliko	.50
6	Scott Greenlaw	.50
7	Trevor Highfield	.50
8	Stephen Hoffmann	.50
9	Damon Huard	1.00
10	Dave Janoski	.50
11	Patrick Kesi	.50
12	Jim Lambright (CO)	.50
13	Lawyer Milloy	1.50
14	Leon Neal	.50
15	Reggie Reser	.50
16	Richard Thomas	.50

1988 Washington State Smokey

		MT
	Complete Set (12):	12.00
	Common Player:	1.00
3	Timm Rosenbach	2.00
18	Shawn Landrum	1.00
19	Artie Holmes	1.00
31	Steve Broussard	2.00
42	Ron Lee	1.00
55	Tuineau Alipate	1.00
60	Mike Utley	4.00
68	Chris Dyko	1.00
74	Jim Michalczik	1.00
75	Tony Savage	1.00
76	Ivan Cook	1.00
82	Doug Wellsandt	1.00

1990 Washington State Smokey

		MT
	Complete Set (16):	8.00
	Common Player:	.75
1	Lewis Bush (48)	.75
2	Carrie Couturier (Women's Volleyball)	.75
3	Steve Cromer (70)	.75
4	C.J. Davis (1)	.75
5	John Diggs (22)	.75
6	Alvin Dunn (27)	.75
7	Aaron Garcia (9)	.75
8	Bob Garman (74)	.75
9	Brad Gossen (12)	1.00
10	Calvin Griggs (5)	.75
11	Kelly Hankins (Women's Volleyball)	.75
12	Jason Hanson (4)	2.50
13	Kristen Hovde (Women's Volleyball)	.75
14	Keri Killebrew (Women's Volleyball)	.75
15	Chris Moton (6)	.75
16	Ron Ricard (26)	.75

1991 Washington State Smokey

		MT
	Complete Set (16):	9.00
	Common Player (1-12):	.75
	Common Player (13-16):	.75
1	Lewis Bush	.75
2	Chad Cushing	.75
3	C.J. Davis	.75
4	Bob Garman	.75
5	Jason Hanson	2.00
6	Gabriel Oladipo	.75
7	Anthony Prior	1.50
8	Jay Reyna	.75
9	Lee Tilleman	.75
10	Kirk Westerfield	.75
11	Butch Williams	.75
12	Michael Wright	.75
13	Carrie Couturier (Women's Volleyball)	.75
14	Kelly Hankins (Women's Volleyball)	.75
15	Kristen Hovde (Women's Volleyball)	.75
16	Keri Killebrew (Women's Volleyball)	.75

1992 Washington State Smokey

		MT
	Complete Set (20):	20.00
	Common Player (1-12):	.50
	Common Player (13-20):	.50
1	Drew Bledsoe	12.00
2	Phillip Bobo	.75
3	Lewis Bush	.50
4	C.J. Davis	.50
5	Shaumbe Wright-Fair	.75
6	Bob Garman	.50
7	Ray Hall	.50
8	Torey Hunter	.50
9	Kurt Loertscher	.50
10	Anthony McClanahan	.50
11	John Rushing	.50
12	Clarence Williams	.75
13	Betty Bartram (Women's Volleyball)	.50
14	Krista Beightol (Women's Volleyball)	.50
15	Carrie Gilley (Women's Volleyball)	.50
16	Shannan Griffin (Women's Volleyball)	.50
17	Becky Howlett (Women's Volleyball)	.50
18	Kristen Hovde (Women's Volleyball)	.50
19	Keri Killebrew (Women's Volleyball)	.50
20	Cindy Fredrick CO, M. Farokhmanesh ACO, Gweyn Leabo ACO (Women's Volleyball)	.50

1974 West Virginia

		NM
	Complete Set (53):	80.00
	Common Player:	1.00
1C	Stu Wolpert	1.00
1D	Mountaineer Coaches	4.00
1H	Leland Byrd (AD)	1.00
1S	Bobby Bowden (CO)	25.00
2C	Jay Sheehan	1.00
2D	Tom Brandner	1.00
2H	Tom Bowden	1.00
2S	Chuck Smith	1.00
3C	Ray Marshall	1.00
3D	Randy Swinson	1.00
3H	Tom Loadman	1.00
3S	Bob Kaminski	1.00
4C	Ron Lee	3.00
4D	Kirk Lewis	1.00
4H	Greg Dorn	1.00
4S	Emil Ros	1.00
5C	Mark Burke	1.00
5D	Rory Fields	1.00
5H	Gary Lombard	1.00
5S	Brian Gates	1.00
6C	John Schell	1.00
6D	Paul Jordan	1.00
6H	Mike Hubbard	1.00
6S	Chuck Kelly	1.00
7C	Rick Pennypacker	2.00
7D	Heywood Smith	1.00
7H	Jack Eastwood	1.00
7S	Andy Peters	1.00
8C	Steve Dunlap	1.00
8D	Dave Wilcher	2.00
8H	Greg Anderson	1.00
8S	Ken Culbertson	1.00
9C	David Van Halanger	1.00
9D	Rick Shaffer	1.00
9H	Rich Lukowski	1.00
9S	Al Gluchoski	1.00
10C	Dwayne Woods	1.00
10D	Ben Williams	2.00
10H	John Adams	1.00
10S	Tom Florence	1.00
11C	Marcus Mauney	1.00
11D	John Spraggins	1.00
11H	Bruce Huffman	1.00
11S	Bernie Kirchner	1.00
12C	Artie Owens	2.00
12D	Charlie Miller	1.00
12H	1974 Cheerleaders	1.00
12S	Eddie Russell	1.00
13C	Danny Buggs	4.00
13D	Marshall Mills	1.00
13H	John Everly	1.00
13S	Jeff Merrow	1.00
JK	Student Foundation	1.00

1988 West Virginia

		MT
	Complete Set (16):	20.00
	Common Player:	1.00
1	Charlie Baumann	1.50
2	Anthony Brown	1.00
3	Willie Edwards	1.00
4	Theron Ellis	1.50
5	Chris Haering	1.00
6	Major Harris	4.00
7	Undra Johnson	1.50
8	Kevin Koken	1.00
9	Pat Marlatt	1.00
10	Eugene Napoleon	1.00
11	Don Nehlen (CO)	2.00
12	Bo Orlando	3.00
13	Chris Parker	1.00
14	Robert Pickett	1.00
15	Brian Smider	1.00
16	John Stroia	1.00

1990 West Virigina Program Cards

		MT
	Complete Set (49):	35.00
	Common Player:	.75
1	Tarris Alexander	.75
2	Leroy Axem	.75
3	Michael Beasley	.75
4	Calvin Bell	.75
5	Matt Bland	.75
6	John Brown	1.25
7	Brad Carroll	.75
8	Mike Collins	.75
9	Mike Compton	1.25
10	Cecil Doggette	.75
11	Rick Dolly	.75
12	Theron Ellis	1.25
13	Charlie Fedorco	.75
14	Garrett Ford	.75
15	Scott Gaskins	.75
16	Boris Graham	.75
17	Keith Graley	.75
18	Chris Gray	.75
19	Greg Hertzog	.75
20	Ed Hill	.75
21	Verne Howard	.75
22	James Jett	4.00
23	Greg Jones	.75
24	Jon James	.75
25	Ted Kester	.75
26	Darroll Mitchell	.75
27	John Murphy	.75
28	Don Nehlen (CO)	2.50
29	Tim Newsom	.75
30	Joe Pabian	.75
31	John Ray	.75
32	Steve Redd	.75
33	Joe Ruth	.75
34	Alex Shook	.75
35	Jeff Sniffen	.75
36	Ray Staten	.75
37	Rick Stead	.75
38	Darren Studstill	2.00
39	Lorenzo Styles	2.00
40	Gary Tillis	.75
41	Rico Tyler	.75
42	Darrell Whitmore	2.00
43	E.J. Wheeler	.75
44	Darrick Wiley	.75
45	Tim Williams	.75
46	Sam Wilson	.75
47	Dale Wolfley	.75
48	Rob Yachini	.75
49	Mountaineer Field	.75

1991 West Virginia ATG

		MT
	Complete Set (50):	15.00
	Common Player:	.35
1	Jeff Hostetler	2.50
2	Tom Allman	.35
3	Russ Bailey	.35
4	Paul Bischoff	.35
5	Bruce Bosley	.50
6	Jim Braxton	.50
7	Danny Buggs	.50
8	Harry Clarke	.35
9	Ken Culbertson	.35
10	Willie Drewrey	.50
11	Steve Dunlap	.35
12	Garrett Ford	.35
13	Dennis Fowlkes	.35
14	Bob Gresham	.50
15	Chris Haering	.50
16	Major Harris	1.00
17	Steve Hathaway	.35
18	Rick Hollins	.35
19	Chuck Howley	1.00
20	Sam Huff	1.25
21	Brian Jozwiak	.50
22	Gene Lamone	.35
23	Oliver Luck	.75
24	Kerry Marbury	.35
25	Joe Marconi	.50
26	Jeff Merrow	.50
27	Steve Newberry	.35
28	Bob Orders	.35
29	Artie Owens	.50
30	Tom Pridemore	.50
31	Mark Raugh	.35
32	Reggie Rembert	.50
33	Ira Rodgers	.35
34	Mike Sherwood	.35
35	Joe Stydahar	.50
36	Renaldo Turnbull	1.25
37	Paul Woodside	.35
38	Fred Wyant	.35
39	Carl Leatherwood	.35
40	Darryl Talley	1.00
41	David Grant	.35
42	Bobby Bowden (CO)	1.00
43	Jim Carlen (CO)	.35
44	Frank Cignetti (CO)	.35
45	Gene Corum (CO)	.35
46	Art Lewis (CO)	.35
47	Don Nehlen (CO)	.50
48	New Mountaineer Field	.35
49	Old Mountaineer Field	.35
50	Lambert Trophy	.50

1991 West Virginia Program Cards

		MT
	Complete Set (42):	25.00
	Common Player:	.75
1	Tarris Alexander	.75
2	Johnathan Allen	.75
3	Leroy Axem	.75
4	Joe Ayuso	.75
5	Michael Beasley	.75
6	Rich Braham	1.00
7	Tom Briggs	.75
8	John Cappa	.75
9	Mike Collins	1.00
10	Mike Compton	1.00
11	Doug Cooley	.75
12	Cecil Doggette	.75
13	Rick Dolly	.75
14	Garrett Ford	.75
15	Scott Gaskins	1.00
16	Boris Graham	.75
17	Keith Graley	.75
18	Chris Gray	.75
19	Barry Hawkins	.75
20	Ed Hill	1.00
21	James Jett	3.00
22	Jon Jones	.75
23	Jim LeBlanc	1.00
24	David Mayfield	1.00
25	Adrian Murrell	3.00
26	Sam Mustipher	.75
27	Tim Newsom	.75
28	Tommy Orr	.75
29	Joe Pabian	.75
30	John Ray	.75
31	Wes Richardson	1.00
32	Nate Rine	.75
33	Joe Ruth	.75
34	Alex Shook	.75
35	Kwame Smith	.75
36	Darren Studstill	2.00
37	Lorenzo Styles	1.50
38	Gary Tillis	.75
39	Ron Weaver	.75
40	Darrell Whitmore	2.50
41	Darrick Wiley	.75
42	Rodney Woodard	.75

1992 West Virginia Program Cards

		MT
	Complete Set (49):	25.00
	Common Player:	.75
1	Tarris Alexander	.75
2	Joe Avila	.75
3	Leroy Axem	.75
4	Mike Baker	.75
5	Sean Biser	.75
6	Mike Booth	.75
7	Rich Braham	1.00
8	Tom Briggs	.75
9	Tim Brown	.75
10	Darius Burwell	.75
11	John Cappa	.75
12	Matt Ceglie	.75
13	Mike Collins	.75
14	Mike Compton	1.00
15	Rick Dolly	.75
16	Garrett Ford	.75
17	Scott Gaskins	1.00
18	Boris Graham	.75
19	Dan Harless	.75
20	Barry Hawkins	.75
21	Ed Hill	1.00
22	James Jett	3.00
23	Mark Johnson	.75
24	Jon Jones	.75
25	Jake Kelchner	2.50
26	Harold Kidd	.75
27	Jim LeBlanc	1.00
28	David Mayfield	1.00
29	Brian Moore	.75
30	Adrian Murrell	2.50
31	Robert Nelson	.75
32	Tommy Orr	.75
33	Joe Pabian	.75
34	Brett Parise	.75
35	Steve Perkins	.75
36	Steve Redd	.75
37	Wes Richardson	1.00
38	Nate Rine	.75
39	Tom Robsock	.75
40	Kwame Smith	.75
41	Darren Studstill	1.50
42	Lorenzo Styles	1.50
43	Matt Taffoni	.75
44	Mark Ulmer	.75
45	Mike Vanderjagt	.75
46	Darrick Wiley	.75
47	Dale Williams	.75
48	Rodney Woodard	.75
49	James Wright	.75

1993 West Virginia

		MT
	Complete Set (49):	20.00
	Common Player:	.50
1	Zach Abraham	.50
2	Tarris Alexander	.50
3	Mike Baker	.50
4	Aaron Beasley	.50
5	Derrick Bell	.50
6	Mike Booth	.50
7	Rich Braham	.75
8	Tim Brown	.50
9	Mike Collins	.50
10	Doug Costin	.50
11	Calvin Edwards	.50
12	Jim Freeman	.50
13A	Big East Trophy	1.50
13B	Daymeian Gallimore	1.50
14	Jimmy Gary	.50
15	Scott Gaskins	.75
16	Buddy Hager	.50
17	Dan Harless	.50
18	John Harper	.50
19	Barry Hawkins	.75
20	Ed Hill	.75
21	Jon Jones	.50
22	Jay Kearney	.50
23	Jake Kelchner	2.00
24	Harold Kidd	.50
25	Chris Klick	.50
26	Jim LeBlanc	.75
27	Chris Ling	.50
28	David Mayfield	.75
29	Keith Morris	.50
30	Tommy Orr	.50
31	Joe Pabian	.50
32	Ken Painter	.50
33	Steve Perkins	.50
34	Maurice Richards	.50
35	Wes Richardson	.75
36	Nate Rine	.50
37	Tom Robsock	.50
38	Todd Sauerbrun	1.50
39	Darren Studstill	1.50

40	Matt Taffoni	.50
41	Keith Taparausky	.50
42	Mark Ulmer	.50
43	Robert Walker	1.25
44	Charles Washington	.50
45	Darrick Wiley	.50
46	Dale Williams	.50
47	James (Puppy) Wright	.50
48	Don Nehlen (CO)	1.00
49	Mountaineer Field	.50

1992 Wisconsin Program Cards

		MT
Complete Set (27):		20.00
Common Player:		.75
1	Troy Vincent	2.50
2	Tim Krumrie	1.25
3	Barry Alvarez (CO)	1.50
4	Pat Richter	1.25
5	Nate Odomes	1.25
6	Ron Vander Kelen	1.50
7	Don Davey	1.25
8	Alan Ameche	2.00
9	Randy Wright	1.25
10	Ken Bowman	1.00
11	Chuck Belin	.75
12	Elroy Hirsch	2.00
13	Paul Gruber	1.25
14	Al Toon	1.50
15	Richard Johnson	1.00
16	Pat Harder	1.00
17	Gary Casper	.75
18	Rufus Ferguson	.75
19	Pat O'Donahue	.75
20	Dennis Lick	.75
21	Jeff Dellenbach	1.00
22	Jim Bakken	1.00
23	Milt Bruhn (CO)	.75
24	Mike Webster	1.50
25	Dave McClain (CO)	.75
26	Bill Marek	.75
27	Rick Graf	.75

1990 Wyoming Smokey

		MT
Complete Set (16):		20.00
Common Player:		1.50
1	Tom Corontzos (18)	1.50
2	Jay Daffer (34)	1.50
3	Mitch Donahue (49)	2.00
4	Sean Fleming (42)	1.50
5	Pete Gosar (53)	1.50
6	Robert Midgett (57)	1.50
7	Bryan Mooney (9)	1.50
8	Doug Rigby (77)	1.50
9	Paul Roach (CO)	2.00
10	Mark Timmer (48)	1.50
11	Paul Wallace (29)	1.50
12	Shawn Wiggins (15)	1.50
13	Gordy Wood (95)	1.50
14	Willie Wright (96)	1.50
15	Cowboy Joe Mascot	1.50
16	Title Card Cowboy logo	1.50

1993 Wyoming Smokey

		MT
Complete Set (16):		12.00
Common Player:		.75
1	John Burrough	.75
2	Wade Constance	.75
3	Mike Fitzgerald	.75
4	Jarrod Heidmann	.75
5	Joe Hughes	.75
6	Kenny Johnson	1.00
7	Mike Jones	.75
8	Cody Kelly	.75
9	Rob Levin	.75
10	Prentice Rhone	.75
11	Greg Scanlan	1.00
12	Cory Talich	.75
13	Kurt Whitehead	.75
14	Thomas Williams	.75
15	Tyrone Williams	.75
16	Ryan Yarborough	3.00

1992 Youngstown State

		MT
Complete Set (54):		20.00
Common Player:		.40
1	Ramon Amill	.40
2	Dan Black	.40
3	Trent Boykin	.40
4	Reginald Brown	.40
5	Mark Brungard	1.00
6	Larry Bucciarelli	.40
7	David Burch	.40
8	Nick Cochran	.40
9	Brian Coman	.40
10	Ken Conatser (ACO)	.40
11	Darnell Clark	1.00
12	Dave DelBoccio	.40
13	Tom Dillingham	.40
14	John Englehardt	.40
15	Marcus Evans	.40
16	Malcolm Everette	.40
17	Drew Gerber	.40
18	Michael Ghent	.40
19	Aaron Green	.40
20	Jon Heacock (ACO)	.40
21	Alfred Hill (ACO)	.40
22	Terica Jones	.40
23	Craig Kertesz	.40
24	Paul Kokos Jr	.40
25	Reginald Lee	.50
26	Raymond Miller	.40
27	Brian Moore (ACO)	.40
28	Mike Nezbeth	.40
29	William Norris	.40
30	James Panozzo	.40
31	Derek Pixley	.40
32	Jeff Powers	.40
33	David Quick	.40
34	John Quintana	.40
35	Mike Rekstis	.40
36	Demario Ridgeway	.40
37	Dave Roberts	.40
38	Chris Sammarone	.40
39	Randy Smith	.40
40	Tamron Smith	.50
41	John Steele	.40
42	Jim Tressel (CO)	1.00
43	Chris Vecchione	.40
44	Lester Weaver	.50
45	Jeffrey Wilkins	.50
46	Herb Williams	.40
47	Ryan Wood	.40
48	Don Zwisler	.40
49	Penguin Pros Card 1	.50
50	Penguin Pros Card 2	.50
51	First-Team All-American	.50
52	Did You Know 1	.40
53	Did You Know 2	.40
54	Did You Know 3	.40

1991 Pennsylvania HS Big 33

		MT
Complete Set (36):		35.00
Common Player:		.50
PA1	Dietrich Jells	2.00
PA2	Mike Archie	3.00
PA3	Tony Miller	.50
PA4	Edmund Robinson	.50
PA5	Brian Miller	.75
PA6	Marvin Harrison	5.00
PA7	Mike Cawley	.50
PA8	Thomas Marchese	.50
PA9	Scott Milanovich	2.00
PA10	Shawn Wooden	1.00
PA11	Curtis Martin	12.00
PA12	William Khayat	.50
PA13	Jermell Fleming	.50
PA14	Ray Zellars	4.00
PA15	Jon Witman	.75
PA16	Chris McCartney	.50
PA17	David Rebar	.50
PA18	Mark Zataveski	.75
PA19	Todd Atkins	.75
PA20	Shannon Stevens	.50
PA21	Keith Conlin	.75
PA22	John Bowman	.50
PA23	Maurice Lawrence	.50
PA24	Mike Halapin	.50
PA25	Steve Keim	.50
PA26	Dennis Martin	.50
PA27	Keith Morris	.50
PA28	Chris Villarrial	.50
PA29	Thomas Tumulty	.50
PA30	Jason Augustino	.50
PA31	Gregory Delong	.50
PA32	James Moore	.50
PA33	Eric Clair	.75
PA34	Tyler Young	.50
PA35	Jeffrey Sauve	.50
PA36	Terry Hammons	.50

1995 Roox HS

		MT
Complete Set (39):		18.00
Common Player:		.50
1	Wesley Crane	.50
2	Nili Hammond	.50
3	Daniel Anglin	.50
4	Ronnie Williams	.50
5	Harold Blackmon	.50
6	Tim Lavery	.50
7	Babatunde Ridley	.50
8	Fred Wakefield	.50
9	Bobie Singleton	.50
10	Chris Janek	.50
11	Steffan Nicholson	.50
12	Scott Mullen	.50
13	Jason Scherer	.50
14	Kevin Beard Jr.	.50
15	Michael Sergeant	.50
16	Marcus Smith	.50
17	Eric Garrett	.50
18	Chris Pickett	.50
19	Michael Burden	.50
20	Nick Abruzzo	.50
21	Stanley Williams	.50
22	Joey Goodspeed	.50
23	Stephen Olien	.50
24	R.J. Luke	.50
25	Matt Kelly	.50
26	Ricardo King	.50
27	Tamaine Hills	.50
28	Michael Yarborough	.50
29	Brian Schmitz	.50
30	Joe Carroll	.50
31	Roy Sessions	.50
32	Marcus Hood	.50
33	Lorenzo Smith	.50
34	Karlton Thomas	.50
40	Carlos Polk	.50
41	Montinez Williams	.50
42	Neil Carroll	.50
43	Shaka Jones	.50
---	Cover Card - blankbacked	.10

1996 Roox Prep Star AT/EA/SE

		MT
Complete Set (142):		70.00
Common Player:		.50
AT1	David Garrard	.50
AT2	Erik Lipton	.50
AT3	Tim Olmstead	.50
AT4	Craig Powers	.50
AT5	Jason Thompson	.50
AT6	William Combs	.50
AT7	Gil Harris	.50
AT8	Golden Myers	.50
AT9	Chris Willetts	.50
AT10	Chris Ramseur	.50
AT11	Anthony Sanders	.50
AT12	Ali Culpepper	.50
AT13	Dominique Stevenson	.50
AT14	Rondell White	.50
AT15	David Foster	.50
AT16	Luis Moreno	.50
AT17	Sherman Scott	.50
AT18	Doug Bost	.50
AT19	Terry Denoon	.50
AT20	Dave Johnson	.50
AT21	Dain Lewis	.50
AT22	Chris McDaniel	.50
AT23	Chadwick Scott	.50
AT24	Brian Scott	.50
AT25	Bobby Graham	.50
AT26	Steve Shipp	.50
AT27	Jimmy Caldwell	.50
AT28	Rico Gladden	.50
AT29	Evan Kay	.50
AT30	Rashad Slade	.50
AT31	Nate Krill	.50
AT32	Chris Luzar	.50
AT33	Graham Manley	.50
AT34	Neely Page	.50
AT35	David Pugh	.50
AT36	Jason Cox	.50
AT37	Jason McFeasters	.50
AT38	John Miller	.50
AT39	Bobby Dameron	.50
AT40	Keith Esteppe	.50
AT41	Tim Falls	.50
AT42	Jeman Jacobs	.50
AT43	Scott McLain	.50
AT44	Ty Hunt	.50
AT45	Jeff Chambers	.50
AT46	Nick Gilliland	.50
AT47	Buddy Young	.50
AT48	DeAngelo Lloyd	.50
AT49	Ben Bacot	.50
AT50	Corey Nelson	.50
AT51	Jimi Massey	.50
AT52	Sam Scott	.50
AT53	Mike Winfield	.50
AT54	Jayvon McKinney	.50
EA1	Luke Richmond	.50
EA2	Mike Gaydosz	.50
EA3	Eddie Campbell	.50
EA4	Dan Ellis	.50
EA5	Darin Miller	.50
EA6	Ravon Anderson	.50
EA7	Jason Murray	.50
EA8	Brett Aurilla	.50
EA9	Tremayne Bendross	.50
EA10	Sean Fisher	.50
EA11	J.R. Johnson	.50
EA12	Victor Strader	.50
EA13	Dennis Thomas	.50
EA14	Quentin Harris	.50
EA15	Reggie Garrett	.50
EA16	Patrick O'Brien	.50
EA17	Guenter Kryszon	.50
EA18	Kareem McKenzie	.50
EA19	Martin Bibla	.50
EA20	Joe Collins	.50
EA21	John Kuchmek	.50
EA22	Greg Ransom	.50
EA23	Tim Sample	.50
EA24	Marty Wensel	.50
EA25	Jack Bloom	.50
EA26	Nate Ritzenhaler	.50
EA27	Charley Powell	.50
EA28	Ron Graham	.50
EA29	Joe McKinney	.50
EA30	Jeremiah Clarke	.50
EA31	Frank Fodera	.50
EA32	John Yura	.50
EA33	Jonathon Harris	.50
EA34	Ben Martin	.50
EA35	Cory Wire	.50
EA36	Sean Bell	.50
EA37	Brad Eissler	.50
EA38	Lavar Arrington	.50
SE1	Kenny Kelly	.50
SE2	Daniel Cobb	.50
SE3	Phillip Deas	.50
SE4	Adam Cox	.50
SE5	Ron Johnson	.50
SE6	Tommy Banks	.50
SE7	Sherrod Dickson	.50
SE8	Davey Ford Jr.	.50
SE9	Travis Henry	.50
SE10	William McCray	.50
SE11	Dan Morgan	.50
SE12	Adrian Peterson	.50
SE13	Darrell Jackson	.50
SE14	Orlando Iglesias	.50
SE15	Eddie Williams	.50
SE16	Matt Wright	.50
SE17	Fred Weary	.50
SE18	Braxton Anderson	.50
SE19	Romaro Miller	.50
SE20	Ronald Boldin	.50
SE21	Otis Duhart	.50
SE22	Jabari Ellison	.50
SE23	Tom Hillard	.50
SE24	Ryan Smith	.50
SE25	Erik Strange	.50
SE26	Sam Matthews	.50
SE27	Thomas Pittman	.50
SE28	Andrew Zow	.50
SE29	Gerard Warren	.50
SE30	Adrian Wilson	.50
SE31	Char-Ron Dorsey	.50
SE32	Kenard Ellis	.50
SE33	Jabari Holloway	.50
SE34	Melvin Richey	.50
SE35	Willie Sams	.50
SE36	Josh Weldon	.50
SE37	Travis Carroll	.50
SE38	Cortez Allen	.50
SE39	Andra Davis	.50
SE40	Matt Miller	.50
SE41	Whit Smith	.50
SE42	Stanford Simmons	.50
SE43	Tony Dixon	.50
SE44	Clifton Robinson	.50
SE45	Hugh Holmes	.50
SE46	Abdul Howard	.50
SE47	Rob Pate	.50
SE48	Matt Howard	.50
SE49	Terrence Trammell	.50
SE50	Earl Williams	.50
---	Jesse Palmer	.50

1996 Roox Prep Star C/W

		MT
Complete Set (145):		70.00
Common Player:		.50
C1	B.J. Tiger	.50
C2	Ryan Lown	.50
C3	Sherard Poteete	.50
C4	Eric Gooden	.50
C5	Ken Alsop	.50
C6	Levi Mehl	.50
C7	Justin Galimore	.50
C8	Dallas Davis	.50
C9	Ahmed Kabba	.50
C10	Aaron Lockett	.50
C11	Kevin Wendling	.50
C12	Ryan Humphrey	.50
C13	Brandon Stephens	.50
C14	Dan Engel	.50
C15	Jared Holland	.50
C16	Tango McCauley	.50
C17	Kyle Jenson	.50
C18	Kody Hergert	.50
C19	Jon Rutherford	.50
C20	John Teasdale	.50
C21	Steve Wiedower	.50
C22	Joshua Graham	.50
C23	John Robertson	.50
C24	Austin Lee	.50
C25	Brandon Washington	.50
C26	Andy Wisne	.50
C27	Bary Holleyman	.50
C28	Darren Palladino	.50
C29	Mike Burke	.50
C30	Thomas Fortune	.50
C31	Pete Battisti	.50
C32	Monty Beisel	.50
C33	John Paul Keserich	.50
C34	Garrett Masters	.50
C35	Bubba Babb	.50
C36	Marlon Guess	.50
C37	Stanley Peters	.50
C38	Harold Burgess	.50
C39	Courtney Hysaw	.50
C40	Darcey Levy	.50
C41	Zach Magalei	.50
C42	Drew Smith	.50
C43	Jeff Ferguson	.50
C44	Eric Rosel	.50
C45	Jeremy Toles	.50
C46	Jason Krause	.50
C47	Jeff Gloy	.50
C48	Brandan Kramer	.50
C49	Marques Spivey	.50
W1	Randy Fasani	.50
W2	Todd Mortensen	.50
W3	Spencer Brinton	.50
W4	Greg Cicero	.50
W5	Scott McEwan	.50
W6	Drew Miller	.50
W7	Austin Moherman	.50
W8	David Priestley	.50
W9	David Carr	.50
W10	Chris Czernek	.50
W11	Jared Flint	.50
W12	Josh Rogers	.50
W13	Damion Barton	.50
W14	Eddie Gayles	.50
W15	Mike Rhodes	.50
W16	Donovan Calhoun	.50
W17	Dante Clay	.50
W18	James Creason	.50
W19	Tony Elam	.50
W20	Brian Palmer	.50
W21	Roderick Walker	.50
W22	Terrynce White	.50
W23	Michael Yancy	.50
W24	Ken-Yon Rambo	.50
W25	Eddie Gorton	.50
W26	Ja'Warren Hooker	.50
W27	Jeff Johnson	.50
W28	Cody Joyce	.50
W29	Rossi Martin	.50
W30	Rashawn Owens	.50
W31	Joey Getherall	.50
W32	Jamien McCullum	.50
W33	Brandon Nash	.50
W34	Tafiti Uso	.50
W35	Lonnie Ford	.50
W36	Shon Jones	.50
W37	Corey Lee Smith	.50
W38	Donnell Burch	.50
W39	Lee Turner	.50
W40	Brian Polak	.50
W41	Mike Souza	.50
W42	Kurt Vollers	.50
W43	Craig Brooks	.50
W44	Ron Price	.50
W45	Mike Wambolt	.50
W46	Ralph Zarate	.50
W47	Jim Adams	.50
W48	Ed Anderson	.50
W49	Justin David	.50
W50	Brian Hart	.50
W51	Nic Hawkins	.50
W52	Brandon Hoopes	.50
W53	Kris Keene	.50
W54	Travis Pfeifer	.50
W55	Langston Walker	.50
W56	Andre Carter	.50
W57	John Jackson	.50
W58	Welton Kage	.50
W59	Anthony Thomas	.50
W60	Justin Bannan	.50
W61	Ryan Nielsen	.50
W62	Brandon Manumaleuna	.50
W63	Kyle Roselle	.50
W64	Darrell Daniels	.50
W65	Bobby Demars	.50
W66	Tracy Hunt	.50
W67	Zeke Moreno	.50
W68	Tim Shear	.50
W69	Kori Dickerson	.50
W70	Ty Gregorak	.50
W71	Malachi Keddington	.50
W72	Don Meyers	.50
W73	Tony Thompson	.50
W74	Ife Ohalete	.50
W75	Antuan Simmons	.50
W76	Albus Brooks	.50
W77	Dewey Hale	.50
W78	Kameron Jones	.50
W79	Lamont Thompson	.50
W80	Fred Washington	.50
W81	Shanga Wilson	.50
W82	Marques Anderson	.50
W83	DeMario Franklin	.50
W84	Melvin Justice	.50
W85	Kris Richard	.50
W86	Julius Thompson	.50
W87	Wes Tufaga	.50
W88	Zak Haselmo	.50
W89	Jeremy Kelly	.50
W90	John Gonzalez	.50
W91	Robert Jackson	.50
W92	Rod Perry Jr.	.50
W93	Charles Tharp	.50
W94	Ryan Brady	.50
W95	Merle Sango	.50

1996 Roox Prep Star MW/SW

		MT
Complete Set (115):		80.00
Common Player:		.75
MW1	Zack Kustock	.75
MW2	Tyler Evans	.75
MW3	Bob Johnson	.75
MW4	Chris Ludban	.75
MW5	Ken Stopka	.75
MW6	Kyle Van Sluys	.75
MW7	Sean Penny	.75
MW8	Bill Andrews	.75
MW9	James Harrison	.75
MW10	DeWayne Hogan	.75
MW11	Carlos Honare	.75
MW12	Ray Jackson	.75
MW13	Greg Simpson	.75
MW14	Israel Thompson	.75
MW15	Ernest Brown	.75
MW16	Sam Crenshaw	.75
MW17	Adrian Duncan	.75
MW18	Kahill Hill	.75
MW19	Teddy Johnson	.75
MW20	Omari Jordan	.75
MW21	Jason Kemble	.75
MW22	Jace Sayler	.75
MW23	Tim Stratton	.75
MW24	Adam Fay	.75
MW25	Josh Jakubowski	.75
MW26	Ben Mast	.75
MW27	Mike Collins	.75
MW28	Oliver King	.75
MW29	Rocky Nease	.75
MW30	Josh Parrish	.75
MW31	Clifton Reta	.75
MW32	Brian Wise	.75
MW33	Maurice Williams	.75
MW34	Kevin Bell	.75
MW35	Derek Burns	.75
MW36	Andre Cooper	.75
MW37	Jeremy Dox	.75
MW38	Raesche Hill	.75
MW39	Jason Ptak	.75
MW40	Ben Pulfer	.75
MW41	Heath Queen	.75
MW42	Bill Seymour	.75
MW43	Demetrius Smith	.75
MW44	Ben Sobieski	.75
MW45	Hubert Thompson	.75
MW46	Jake Frysinger	.75
MW47	Jason Ott	.75
MW48	Kyle Vanden Bosch	.75
MW49	Kurt Anderson	.75
MW50	Napoleon Harris	.75
MW51	Jason Manson	.75
MW52	Joel Mesman	.75
MW53	Jeff Skibitsky	.75
MW54	T.J. Turner	.75
MW55	Mike Clinkscale	.75
MW56	Jamie Grant	.75
MW57	Kyle Moffatt	.75
MW58	Abdullah Muhammad	.75
MW59	Eric Parker	.75
MW60	Mike Young	.75
MW61	Pat Gibson	.75
MW62	Brendan Rauh	.75
MW63	Antwan Randle El	.75
MW64	Levron Williams	.75
SW1	Edmond Stansbury	.75
SW2	Grant Elam	.75
SW3	Regan George	.75
SW4	Matt Schobel	.75
SW5	Hodges Mitchell	.75
SW6	Twone Simmons	.75
SW7	Donald Williams	.75
SW8	Jason Coffey	.75
SW9	Corey Harris	.75
SW10	Shon Jones	.75
SW11	Burnest Rhodes	.75
SW12	Adrian Thomas	.75
SW13	Robert Williams	.75
SW14	Daniel Belcha	.75
SW15	Damon Daniels	.75
SW16	Raymond Turner	.75
SW17	Chad Irwin	.75
SW18	Ed Kelly	.75
SW19	Miles Koon	.75
SW20	Luke Nichols	.75
SW21	Dennis Jones	.75
SW22	Rodney Endsley	.75
SW23	Norman McKinney	.75
SW24	Terry Williams	.75
SW25	David Warren	.75
SW26	Lonnie Madison	.75
SW27	Shaun Rogers	.75
SW28	Mike Minott	.75
SW29	Evan Perroni	.75
SW30	Grant Irons	.75
SW31	Josh Spoerl	.75
SW32	Tommy Tull	.75
SW33	Chad Chester	.75
SW34	Devon Lemons	.75
SW35	Antowan Alexander	.75
SW36	Jay Brooks	.75
SW37	Quenton Jammer	.75
SW38	Derrick Yates	.75
SW39	Gary Baxter	.75
SW40	Danny Black	.75
SW41	Brandon Couts	.75
SW42	Derek Dorris	.75
SW43	Mitchell Jameson	.75
SW44	Mickey Jones	.75
SW45	Kevon Morton	.75
SW46	Rod Sheppard	.75
SW47	J.R. Pouncey	.75
SW48	Sterlin Gilbert	.75
SW49	Terry Burrell	.75
SW50	Jason Stevenson	.75

1996 Roox Shrine Bowl HS

		MT
Complete Set (74):		35.00
Common Player (NC1-NC36):		.50
Common Player (SC1-SC36):		.50
NC1	Rocky Hunt	.50
NC2	Cam Holland	.50
NC3	Derrick Chambers	.50
NC4	Ramondo North	.50
NC5	Bo Manis	.50
NC6	Antonio Graham	.50
NC7	Clayton White	.50
NC8	Billy Young	.50
NC9	Joshua Tucker	.50
NC10	Rod Emery	.50
NC11	Matt Burdick	.50
NC12	Chad Gathings	.50
NC13	Brian Ray	.50
NC14	Brandon Spoon	.50
NC15	Dauntae Finger	.50
NC16	Raymond Massey	.50
NC17	Damien Bennett	.50
NC18	Bennie Griffin	.50
NC19	Randolph Galloway	.50
NC20	Titus Pettigrew	.50
NC21	Chris McCoy	.50
NC22	Virgil Johnson	.50
NC23	Marcus Reaves	.50
NC24	Scottie Stepp	.50
NC25	Julius Bell	.50
NC26	Robert Williams	.50
NC27	Rashad Burke	.50
NC28	Michael Cox	.50
NC29	Kwabena Greene	.50
NC30	Tim Burgess	.50
NC31	Scott Smith	.50
NC32	Steven Lindsey	.50
NC33	Charles Berry	.50
NC34	Chris Satterfield	.50
NC35	Eric Leak	.50
NC36	Nick Means MG	.50
SC1	Ikie Curry	.50
SC2	Shaun Ellis	.50
SC3	Zabeion McRoy	.50
SC4	Will McLaurin	.50
SC5	Jarvis Davis	.50
SC6	Justin Hill	.50
SC7	Antwon Black	.50
SC8	Justin Watts	.50
SC9	Ray Mazyck	.50
SC10	Chris McGee	.50
SC11	Stan Manning	.50
SC12	Micale Chandler	.50
SC13	Deveron Harper	.50
SC14	Brian Wolford	.50
SC15	Tim Winfield	.50
SC16	Donovan Norman	.50
SC17	Chip Brogden	.50
SC18	Seth Stoddard	.50
SC19	Nakia Adderson	.50
SC20	Adam Varnadore	.50
SC21	Lance Legree	.50
SC22	Scott Greer	.50
SC23	B.J. Little	.50
SC24	Kinte Wilson	.50
SC25	Rod Joseph	.50
SC26	Benji Wallace	.50
SC27	Don Moore	.50
SC28	Cecil Caldwell	.50
SC29	Thomas Washington	.50
SC30	Rory Gallman	.50
SC31	Courtney Brown	.50
SC32	Jermale Kelly	.50
SC33	Walsh Dingle	.50
SC34	Mal Lawyer	.50
SC35	Will Gainey	.50
SC36	Bird Bourne MG	.50
---	South Carolina Title Card	.10
---	North Carolina Title Card	.10

1991 Texas HS Legends

		MT
Complete Set (25):		18.00
Common Player:		.60
1	Marty Akins	.60
2	Gil Bartosh	.60
3	Bill Bradley	1.00
4	Chris Gilbert	1.25
5	Glynn Gregory	.75
6	Charlie Haas	.60
7	Craig James	2.00
8	Boody Johnson	.60
9	Ernie Koy Jr.	.75
10	Glenn Lippman	.60
11	Jack Pardee	1.00
12	Billy Patterson	.60
13	Billy Sims	3.00
14	Byron Townsend	.60
15	Doyle Traylor	.60
16	Joe Washington Jr.	1.00
17	Allie White	.60
18	Wilson Whitley	.75
19	Gordon Wood	.75
20	Willie Zapalac	.60
21	Cover Card 1	.60
22	Cover Card 2	.60
23	Cover Card 3	.60
24	Cover Card 4	.60
25	Cover Card 5	.60

1990 Versailles HS

		MT
Complete Set (20):		8.00
Common Player:		.50
1	Kevin Bergman	.50
2	A.J. Bey	.50
3	Brad Bey	.50
4	Ed Dingman	.75
5	Brian Griesdorn	.50
6	Al Hetrick (CO)	.75
7	Garth Hoelfrich	.50
8	Trent Huff	.50
9	Brian Keiser	.50
10	Lane Knore	.50
11	Brian Kunk	.50
12	Keenan Leichty	.50
13	Marc Litten	.50
14	Craig Oliver	.50
15	Jon Pothast	.50
16	Joe Rush	.50
17	Shane Schultz	.50
18	Mark Siekman	.50
19	Matt Stall	.50
20	Nathan Subler	.50

CANADIAN

1991 All-World CFL

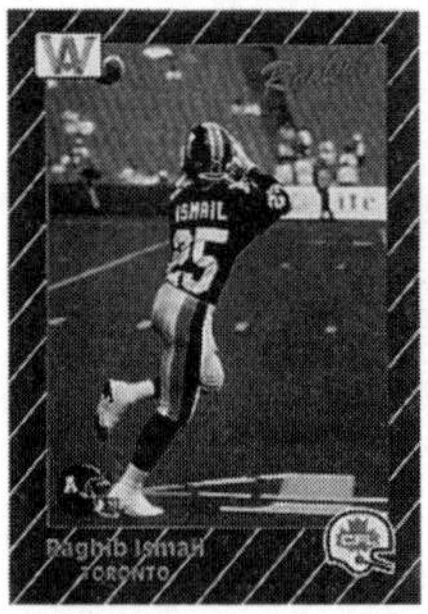

		MT
Complete Set (110):		3.00
Common Player:		.04
1	Raghib (Rocket) Ismail	.25
2	Bruce McNall (owner)	.04
3	Ray Alexander	.08
4	Matt Clark	.08
5	Bobby Jurasin	.08
6	Dieter Brock (LEG)	.08
7	Doug Flutie	.75
8	Stewart Hill	.04
9	James Mills	.08
10	Raghib (Rocket) Ismail, With Bruce McNall	.25
11	Tom Clements (LEG)	.15
12	Lui Passaglia	.20
13	Ian Sinclair	.08
14	Chris Skinner	.08
15	Joe Theismann (LEG)	.15
16	Jon Volpe	.30
17	Deatrich Wise	.04
18	Danny Barrett	.08
19	Warren Moon (LEG)	.25
20	Leo Blanchard	.04
21	Derrick Crawford	.08
22	Lloyd Fairbanks	.08
23	David Beckman (CO)	.04
24	Matt Finlay	.04
25	Darryl Hall	.04
26	Ron Hopkins	.08
27	Wally Buono (CO)	.04
28	Kenton Leonard	.08
29	Brent Matich	.04
30	Greg Peterson	.04
31	Steve Goldman (CO)	.04
32	Allen Pitts	.25
33	Raghib (Rocket) Ismail	.25
34	Danny Bass	.08
35	John Gregory (CO)	.04
36	Rod Connop	.04
37	Craig Ellis	.08
38	Raghib (Rocket) Ismail (Rookie)	.25
39	Ron Lancaster (CO)	.08
40	Tracy Ham	.25
41	Ray Macoritti	.08
42	Willie Pless	.08
43	Bob O'Billovich (CO)	.04
44	Michael Soles	.08
45	Reggie Taylor	.15
46	Henry Williams	.20
47	Adam Rita (CO)	.04
48	Larry Wruck	.08
49	Grover Covington	.08
50	Rocky DePietro	.08
51	Darryl Rogers (CO)	.04
52	Pete Giftopoulus	.08
53	Herman Heard	.08
54	Mike Kerrigan	.08
55	Reggie Barnes (AS)	.08
56	Derrick McAdoo	.08
57	Paul Osbaldiston	.08
58	Earl Winfield	.08
59	Greg Battle (AS)	.08
60	Damon Allen	.08
61	Reggie Barnes	.15
62	Bob Molle	.04
63	Raghib (Rocket) Ismail	.25
64	Irv Daymond	.04
65	Andre Francis	.04
66	Bart Hull	.15
67	Stephen Jones	.08
68	Raghib (Rocket) Ismail	.25
69	Glenn Kulka	.08
70	Loyd Lewis	.04
71	Rob Smith	.04
72	Roger Aldag	.08
73	Kent Austin	.25
74	Ray Elgaard	.08
75	Mike Clemons (AS)	.25
76	Jeff Fairholm	.08
77	Richie Hall	.04
78	Willis Jacox	.08
79	Eddie Lowe	.04
80	Ray Elgaard (AS)	.08
81	Donald Narcisse	.15
82	James Mills (AS)	.08
83	Dave Ridgway	.08
84	Ted Wahl	.08
85	Carl Brazley	.08
86	Mike Clemons	.35
87	Matt Dunigan	.35
88	Grey Cup (Checklist 1)	.04
89	Harold Hallman	.08
90	Rodney Harding	.08
91	Don Moen	.08
92	Raghib (Rocket) Ismail	.25
93	Reggie Pleasant	.08
94	Darrell Smith (UER) (One L on front, two on back)	.15
95	Group Shot (Checklist 2)	.04
96	Chris Schultz	.08
97	Don Wilson	.04
98	Greg Battle	.08
99	Lyle Bauer	.04
100	Less Browne	.08
101	Raghib (Rocket) Ismail	.25
102	Tom Burgess	.15
103	Mike Gray	.04
104	Rod Hill	.08
105	Warren Hudson	.08
106	Tyrone Jones	.15
107	Stan Mikawos	.04
108	Robert Mimbs	.15
109	James West	.08
110	Raghib (Rocket) Ismail	.25
P1	Rocket Ismail Promo# (numbered P)	1.00
NNO	Raghib (Rocket) Ismail (Autographed card/1600)	50.00

1992 All-World CFL

		MT
Complete Set (180):		10.00
Common Player:		.05
1	Checklist 1-90	.05
2	Draft Picks Checklist	.05
3	Western Final	.05
4	Eastern Final	.05
5	79th Grey Cup	.05
6	Grey Cup Most Outstanding Player (Rocket Ismail)	.20
7	Memorable Grey Cups 1909	.05
8	Memorable Grey Cups 1969	.05
9	Memorable Grey Cups 1982	.05
10	Memorable Grey Cups 1989	.05
11	Jeff Braswell	.05
12	Glenn Kulka	.05
13	Will Johnson	.20
14	Lance Chomyc	.10
15	Stan Mikawos	.05
16	Bobby Jurasin	.20
17	Terry Baker	.05
18	Tracy Ham	.50
19	Todd Wiseman	.05
20	Rob Crifo	.05
21	Chris Morris	.20
22	Jon Volpe	.50
23	Donald Narcisse	.20
24	David Williams	.20
25	Paul Clatney	.05
26	Willie Pless	.20
27	Rickey Foggie	.20
28	Denny Chronopoulos	.05
29	Darryl Sampson	.05
30	Patrick Wayne	.05
31	Terrence Jones	.20
32	Larry Wruck	.10
33	Angelo Snipes	.50
34	Tony Champion	.20
35	Steve Taylor	.20
36	Lorne King	.05
37	Roger Aldag	.10
38	Damon Allen	.30
39	Chris Walby	.10
40	Doug Davies	.05
41	Dan Rashovich	.05
42	Mark Scott	.05
43	Reggie Pleasant	.10
44	Bob Cameron	.05
45	Danny McManus	.20
46	Matt Clark	.10
47	Bart Hull	.10
48	Hank Llesic	.05
49	Pee Wee Smith	.30
50	Irv Daymond	.05
51	Greg Battle (J.P. McCaffrey Trophy)	.10
52	Will Johnson (Norm Fieldgate Trophy)	.10
53	Lance Chomyc (Lew Hayman Trophy)	.10
54	Jim Mills (DeMarco-Becket Memorial Trophy)	.10
55	Jon Volpe (Jackie Parker Trophy)	.20
56	Raghib (Rocket) Ismail (Frank M. Gibson Trophy)	.30
57	Dave Ridgway (David Dryburgh Memorial Trophy)	.10
58	Chris Walby (Leo Dandurand Trophy)	.10
59	Doug Flutie (Jeff Nicklin Memorial Trophy)	.75
60	Robert Mimbs (Jeff Russell Memorial Trophy)	.20
61	Jon Volpe (Eddie James Memorial Trophy)	.20
62	Blake Marshall (Dr. Beattie Martin Trophy)	.10
63	Eric Streater	.10
64	Carl Brazley	.05
65	Kent Warnock	.05
66	Brian Bonner	.05
67	Tom Burgess	.20
68	Bob Gordon	.05
69	Milson Jones	.10
70	Todd Dillon	.05
71	Keyvan Jenkins	.20
72	Ken Evraire	.20
73	Willis Jacox	.20
74	Carl Bland	.05
75	Daniel Hunter	.20
76	Chris Schultz	.05
77	Earl Winfield	.20
78	Henry Williams	.30
79	Matt Dunigan	.75
80	Mark McLoughlin	.05
81	Craig Ellis	.10
82	Rodney Harding	.20
83	Scott Douglas	.05
84	Ray Elgaard	.20
85	Doug Flutie	1.00
86	Gary Lewis	.05
87	Rod Hill	.10
88	Greg Stumon	.10
89	Ray Alexander	.20
90	Blake Dermott	.05
91	Checklist 91-180	.05
92	Trophy Winners CL	.10
93	British Columbia CL	.05
94	Calgary CL	.05
95	Edmonton CL	.05
96	Saskatchewan CL	.05
97	Hamilton CL	.05
98	Ottawa CL	.05
99	Toronto CL	.05
100	Winnipeg CL	.05
101	James West	.20
102	Jeff Fairholm	.20
103	Mike Campbell	.05
104	Darren Flutie	.40
105	Blake Marshall	.25
106	Loyd Lewis	.05
107	Enis Jackson	.05
108	John Motton	.20
109	Ken Walcott	.05
110	Richie Hall	.05
111	Greg Peterson	.05
112	Wally Zatylny	.05
113	Lui Passaglia	.25
114	Darryl Hall	.05
115	Michael Soles	.10
116	Doug Brewster	.05
117	Mike Gray	.05
118	Mike Trevathan	.05
119	Don Moen	.05
120	Chris Armstrong	.05
121	Lucius Floyd	.05
122	Ken Pettway	.05
123	Anthony Drawhorn	.20
124	Brian Walling	.05
125	Troy Westwood	.20
126	Reggie Barnes	.20
127	Raghib (Rocket) Ismail	.50
128	Rod Connop	.10
129	Chris Major	.20
130	David Bovell	.05
131	Quency Williams	.05
132	Michel Bourgeau	.05
133	Harold Hallman	.10
134	Junior Thurman	.20
135	Stewart Hill	.05
136	Brent Matich	.05
137	Leroy Blugh	.05
138	Nick Mazzoli	.05
139	Dave Ridgway	.20
140	Matt Finlay	.05
141	Mike Clemons	1.00
142	Jason Riley	.05
143	Stacey Hairston	.05
144	Jim Mills	.10
145	Paul Randolph	.05
146	David Sapunjis	.25
147	Charles Gordon	.05
148	Chris Tsangaris	.05
149	Darrell Smith	.20
150	Leo Groenewegen	.05
151	Greg Battle	.20
152	Bruce Covernton	.10
153	Paul Osbaldiston	.10
154	Don Wilson	.05
155	Kent Austin	.30
156	Jamie Morris	.20
157	Andre Francis	.05
158	O.J. Brigance	.20
159	Less Browne	.10
160	Alondra Johnson	.05
161	Dexter Manley	.20
162	Bob Poley	.05
163	Ed Berry	.05
164	Pete Giftopoulus	.05
165	Glen Suitor	.05
166	Eddie Thomas	.05
167	Danny Barrett	.20
168	Robert Mimbs	.20
169	Jim Sandusky	.20
170	Maurice Smith	.05
171	David Conrad	.05
172	Larry Willis	.05
173	Ian Sinclair	.05
174	Allen Pitts	.50
175	Don McPherson	.20
176	Ray Bernard	.05
177	Dale Sanderson	.05
178	Dan Ferrone	.10
179	Vic Stevenson	.05
180	Rob Smith	.05
P1	Doug Fluti Promo# (Numbered P)	1.50
P2	Rocket Ismail Promo# (Numbered P)	1.00

1982 Bantam/FBI CFL Discs

		MT
Complete Set (31):		300.00
Common Player:		5.00
1	Junior Ah You	10.00
2	Zenon Andrusyshyn	10.00
3	Leon Bright	10.00
4	Bob Cameron	5.00
5	Tom Clements	35.00
6	Jim Corrigall	10.00
7	Tom Cousineau	15.00
8	Carl Crennell	10.00
9	Dave Cutler	10.00
10	Peter Dalla Riva	15.00
11	Dave Fennell	5.00
12	Vince Ferragamo	25.00
13	Tom Forzani	10.00
14	Tony Gabriel	25.00
15	Gabriel Gregoire	5.00
16	Billy Hardee	5.00
17	Larry Highbaugh	10.00
18	Condredge Holloway	25.00
19	Mark Jackson	5.00
20	Billy Johnson (White Shoes)	25.00
21	Larry Key	5.00
22	Marc Lacelle	5.00
23	Ian Mofford	5.00
24	Gerry Organ	10.00
25	Tony Petruccio	5.00
26	Tony Proudfoot	10.00
27	Randy Rhino	15.00
28	Ian Santer	5.00
29	Jerry Tagge	15.00
30	Jim Washington	10.00
31	Tom Wilkinson	15.00

1954 Blue Ribbon Tea CFL

		NM
Complete Set (80):		9000.
Common Player:		100.00
1	Jack Jacobs	250.00
2	Neil Armstrong	150.00
3	Lorne Benson	100.00
4	Tom Casey	125.00
5	Vincent Drake	100.00
6	Tommy Ford	100.00
7	Bud Grant	500.00
8	Dick Huffman	125.00
9	Gerry James	150.00
10	Bud Korchak	100.00
11	Thomas Lumsden	100.00
12	Steve Patrick	100.00
13	Keith Pearce	100.00
14	Jesse Thomas	100.00
15	Buddy Tinsley	125.00
16	Alan Scott Wiley	100.00
17	Winty Young	100.00
18	Joseph Zaleski	100.00
19	Ron Vaccher	100.00
20	John Gramling	100.00
21	Bob Simpson	150.00
22	Bruno Bitkowski	125.00
23	Kaye Vaughan	125.00
24	Don Carter	100.00
25	Gene Roberts	100.00
26	Howie Turner	100.00
27	Avatus Stone	100.00
28	Tom McHugh	100.00
29	Clyde Bennett	100.00
30	Bill Berezowski	100.00
31	Eddie Bevan	100.00
32	Dick Brown	100.00
33	Bernie Custis	125.00
34	Merle Hapes	125.00
35	Tip Logan	100.00
36	Vince Mazza	125.00
37	Pete Neumann	125.00
38	Vince Scott	125.00
39	Ralph Toohy	100.00
40	Frank Anderson	100.00
41	Bob Dean	100.00
42	Leon Manley	100.00
43	Bill Zock	125.00
44	Frank Morris	150.00
45	Jim Quondamatteo	100.00
46	Eagle Keys	150.00
47	Bernie Faloney	400.00
48	Jackie Parker	500.00
49	Ray Willsey	100.00
50	Mike King	100.00
51	Johnny Bright	300.00
52	Gene Brito	125.00
53	Stan Heath	125.00
54	Roy Jenson	100.00
55	Don Loney	100.00
56	Eddie Macon	100.00
57	Peter Maxwell-Muir	100.00
58	Tom Miner	100.00
59	Jim Prewett	100.00
60	Lowell Wagner	100.00
61	Red O'Quinn	125.00
62	Ray Poole	125.00
63	Jim Staton	100.00
64	Alex Webster	200.00
65	Al Dekdebruin	100.00
66	Ed Bradley	100.00
67	Tex Coulter	150.00
68	Sam Etcheverry	500.00
69	Larry Grigg	100.00
70	Tom Hugo	100.00
71	Chuck Hunsinger	100.00
72	Herb Trawick	125.00
73	Virgil Wagner	125.00
74	Phil Adrian	100.00
75	Bruce Coulter	100.00
76	Jim Miller	100.00
77	Jim Mitchener	100.00
78	Tom Moran	100.00
79	Doug McNichol	100.00
80	Joey Pal	100.00

1988 Bootlegger B.C. Lions

		MT
Complete Set (13):		15.00
Common Player:		1.00
1	Jamie Buis	1.00
2	Jan Carinci	1.00
3	Dwayne Derban	1.00
4	Roy Dewalt	3.00
5	Andre Francis	1.25
6	Rick Klassen	2.00
7	Kevin Konar	1.25
8	Scott Lecky	1.00
9	James Parker	3.00
10	John Ulmer	1.00
11	Peter VandenBos	1.00
12	Todd Wiseman	1.00
13	NNO Title Card (Corporate Sponsors)	1.25

1971 Chevron B.C. Lions

		NM
Complete Set (50):		225.00
Common Player:		3.00
Common SP:		12.00
1	George Anderson	3.00
2	Josh Ashton	4.00
3	Ross Boice (SP)	12.00
4	Paul Brothers	3.00
5	Tom Cassese	3.00
6	Roy Cavallin	3.00
7	Rusty Clark (SP)	12.00
8	Owen Dejanovich (CO)	3.00
9	Dave Denny	3.00
10	Brian Donnelly	3.00
11	Steve Duich (SP)	12.00
12	Jim Duke	3.00
13	Dave Easley	3.00
14	Trevor Ekdahl	4.00
15	Jim Evenson	4.00
16	Greg Findlay	3.00
17	Ted Gerela	3.00
18	Dave Golinsky	3.00
19	Lefty Hendrickson	3.00
20	Lach Heron	3.00
21	Gerry Herron	3.00
22	Larry Highbaugh (SP)	12.00
23	Wayne Holm	3.00
24	Bob Howes	3.00
25	Max Huber	3.00
26	Garrett Hunsperger	3.00
27	Lawrence James (SP)	12.00
28	Brian Kelsey (SP)	12.00
29	Eagle Keys (CO)	4.00
30	Mike Leveille	3.00
31	John Love	3.00
32	Ray Lychak	3.00
33	Dick Lyons (SP)	12.00
34	Wayne Matherne	3.00
35	Ken McCullough (CO)	3.00
36	Don Moorhead	3.00
37	Peter Palmer	3.00
38	Jackie Parker (GM)	12.00
39	Ken Phillips	3.00
40	Cliff Powell	3.00
41	Gary Robinson	3.00
42	Ken Sugarman	4.00
43	Bruce Taupier	3.00
44	Jim Tomlin (SP)	12.00
45	Bud Tynes (CO)	3.00
46	Carl Weathers (SP)	12.00
47	Jim White	3.00
48	Mike Wilson	3.00
49	Jim Young	8.00
50	Contest Card (For Chevron)	3.00

1971 Chiquita CFL All-Stars

		NM
Complete Set (13):		200.00
Common Pair:		15.00
1	Bill Baker, 2 Ken Sugarman	20.00
3	Wayne Giardino, 4 Peter Dalla Riva	20.00
5	Leon McQuay, 6 Jim Thorpe	25.00
7	George Reed, 8 Jerry Campbell	20.00
9	Tommy Joe Coffey, 10 Terry Evanshen	25.00
11	Jim Young, 12 Mark Kosmos	20.00
13	Ron Forwick, 14 Jack Abendschan	15.00
15	Don Jonas, 16 Al Marcellin	20.00
17	Joe Theismann, 18 Jim Corrigall (Toronto Argonauts)	50.00
19	Ed George, 20 Dick Dupuis	15.00
21	Ted Dushinski, 22 Bob Swift	15.00
23	John Lagrone, 24 Bill Danychuk	15.00
25	Garney Henley, 26 John Williams	20.00
NNO	Yellow Viewer	40.00

1961 CKNW B.C. Lions

		NM
Complete Set (30):		200.00
Common Player:		6.00
1	By Bailey	15.00
2	Nub Beamer	6.00
3	Bob Belak (Kings Drive-In)	6.00
4	Neil Beaumont	6.00
5	Bill Britton (Nestle's Quik)	6.00
6	Tom Brown (Kings Drive-In)	8.00
7	Mike Cacic	6.00
8	Jim Carphin	6.00
9	Bruce Claridge	6.00
10	Pat Claridge	6.00
11	Steve Cotter	6.00
12	Lonnie Dennis (Nestle's Quik)	6.00
13	Norm Fieldgate	8.00
14	Willie Fleming	18.00
15	George Grant	6.00
16	Sonny Homer (Nestle's Quik)	8.00
17	Bob Jeter	10.00
18	Dick Johnson	6.00
19	Earl Keeley	6.00
20	Vic Kristopatis	6.00
21	Gordie Mitchell	6.00
22	Rae Ross (Nestle's Quik)	6.00
23	Bob Schloredt	8.00
24	Gary Schwertfeger	6.00
25	Mel Semenko (Kings Drive-In)	6.00
26	Ed Sullivan	8.00
27	Barney Therrien (Nestle's Quik)	6.00
28	Ed Vereb	6.00
29	Don Vicic	6.00
30	Ron Watton	6.00

1962 CKNW B.C. Lions

		NM
Complete Set (32):		200.00
Common Player:		5.00
1	By Bailey	15.00
2	Nub Beamer	5.00
3	Neil Beaumont	5.00
4	Bob Belak	5.00
5	Walt Bilicki	5.00
6	Tom Brown (Shop-Easy)	8.00

7 Mark Burton (Shop-Easy) 8.00
8 Mike Cacic 5.00
9 Jim Carphin 5.00
10 Pat Claridge 5.00
11 Steve Cotter 5.00
12 Lonnie Dennis 5.00
13 Norm Fieldgate 8.00
14 Willie Fleming (Shop-Easy) 18.00
15 Dick Fouts 8.00
16 George Grant 5.00
17 Ian Hagemoen 5.00
18 Tommy Hinton 8.00
19 Sonny Homer 8.00
20 Joe Kapp 25.00
21 Earl Keeley 5.00
22 Vic Kristopatis (Shop-Easy) 5.00
23 Tom Larscheid 5.00
24 Mike Martin 5.00
25 Gordie Mitchell 5.00
26 Baz Nagle 5.00
27 Bob Schloredt 8.00
28 Gary Schwertfeger 5.00
29 Willie Taylor 8.00
30 Barney Therrien 5.00
31 Don Vicic 5.00
32 Tom Walker 5.00

1965 Coke Caps CFL

NM
Complete Set (230): 600.00
Common Player: 3.00
1 Neal Beaumont 3.00
2 Tom Brown 6.00
3 Mack Burton 3.00
4 Mike Cacic 3.00
5 Pat Claridge 3.00
6 Steve Cotter 3.00
7 Norm Fieldgate 6.00
8 Greg Findlay 3.00
9 Willie Fleming 7.50
10 Dick Fouts 3.00
11 Tom Hinton 6.00
12 Sonny Homer 3.00
13 Joe Kapp 15.00
14 G. Kasapis 3.00
15 Peter Kempf 3.00
16 Bill Lasseter 3.00
17 Mike Martin 3.00
18 Ron Morris 3.00
19 Bill Munsey 3.00
20 Paul Seale 3.00
21 Steve Shafer 3.00
22 Ken Sugarman 3.00
23 Bob Swift 3.00
24 J. Williams 3.00
25 Ron Albright (UER) (misspelled Albright) 3.00
26 Lu Bain 3.00
27 Frank Budd 3.00
28 Lovell Coleman 4.00
29 Eagle Day 6.00
30 P. Dudley 3.00
31 Jim Furlong 3.00
32 George Hansen 3.00
33 Wayne Harris 9.00
34 Herman Harrison 6.00
35 Pat Holmes 3.00
36 Art Johnson 3.00
37 Jerry Keeling 6.00
38 Roger Kramer 4.00
39 Hal Krebs 3.00
40 Don Luzzi 6.00
41 Pete Manning 3.00
42 Dale Parsons 3.00
43 R. Payne 3.00
44 Larry Robinson 3.00
45 Gerry Shaw 3.00
46 Don Stephenson 3.00
47 Bob Taylor 3.00
48 Ted Woods 3.00
49 Jon Anabo 3.00
50 R. Ash 3.00
51 Jim Battle 3.00
52 Charlie Brown 3.00
53 Tommy Joe Coffey 9.00
54 Marcel Deleeuw 3.00
55 Al Ecuyer 3.00
56 Ron Forwick 3.00
57 Jim Higgins 3.00
58 H. Huth 3.00
59 R. Kerbow 3.00
60 Oscar Kruger 3.00
61 T. Machan 3.00
62 G. McKee 3.00
63 Bill Mitchell 3.00
64 Barry Mitchelson 3.00
65 Roger Nelson 6.00
66 Bill Redell 3.00
67 M. Rohliser 3.00
68 Howie Schumm 3.00
69 E.A. Sims 3.00
70 John Sklopan 3.00
71 Jim Stinnette 3.00
72 Barney Therrien 3.00
73 Jim Thomas 3.00
74 Neil Thomas 3.00
75 B. Tobin 3.00
76 Terry Wilson 3.00
77 Art Baker 3.00
78 John Barrow 6.00
79 Gene Ceppetelli 3.00
80 J. Cimba 3.00
81 Dick Cohee 3.00
82 Frank Cosentino 4.00
83 Johnny Counts 3.00
84 Stan Crisson 3.00
85 Tommy Grant 7.50
86 Garney Henley 7.50
87 H. Hoerster 3.00
88 Zeno Karcz 3.00
89 Ellison Kelly 7.50
90 Bob Krouse 3.00
91 Billy Ray Locklin 3.00
92 Chet Miksza 3.00
93 Angelo Mosca 15.00
94 Bronko Nagurski 7.50
95 Ted Page 3.00
96 Don Sutherin 6.00
97 Dave Viti 3.00
98 Dick Walton 3.00
99 Billy Wayte 3.00
100 Joe Zuger 3.00
101 Jim Andreotti 3.00
102 John Baker 4.00
103 G. Beretta 3.00
104 Bill Bewley 3.00
105 Garland Boyette 4.00
106 Doug Daigneault 3.00
107 George Dixon 7.50
108 D. Dolatri 3.00
109 Ted Elsby 3.00
110 Don Estes 3.00
111 Terry Evenshen 9.00
112 Clare Exelby 3.00
113 Larry Fairholm 4.00
114 Bernie Faloney 15.00
115 Don Fuell 3.00
116 M. Gibbons 3.00
117 Ralph Goldston 3.00
118 Al Irwin 3.00
119 John Kenerson 3.00
120 Ed Learn 3.00
121 Moe Levesque 3.00
122 Bob Minihane 3.00
123 Jim Reynolds 3.00
124 Billy Roy 3.00
125 L. Tominson 3.00
126 Ernie White 3.00
127 Rick Black 3.00
128 Mike Blum 3.00
129 Billy Joe Booth 3.00
130 Jim Cain 3.00
131 Bill Cline 3.00
132 Merv Collins 3.00
133 Jim Conroy 3.00
134 Larry DeGraw 3.00
135 Jim Dillard 3.00
136 Gene Gaines 6.00
137 Don Gilbert 3.00
138 Russ Jackson 15.00
139 Ken Lehmann 3.00
140 Bob O'Billovich 3.00
141 John Pentecost 3.00
142 Joe Poirier 3.00
143 Moe Racine 3.00
144 Sam Scoccia 3.00
145 Bo Scott 7.50
146 Jerry Selinger 3.00
147 Marshall Shirk 3.00
148 Bill Siekierski 3.00
149 Ron Stewart 7.50
150 Whit Tucker 6.00
151 Ron Atchison 6.00
152 Al Benecick 3.00
153 Clyde Brock 3.00
154 Ed Buchanan 3.00
155 R. Cameron 3.00
156 Hugh Campbell 7.50
157 Henry Dorsch 3.00
158 Larry Dumelie 3.00
159 Garner Ekstran 3.00
160 Martin Fabi 3.00
161 Bob Good 3.00
162 Bob Kosid 3.00
163 Ron Lancaster 9.00
164 Hal Ledyard 3.00
165 Len Legault 3.00
166 Ron Meadmore 3.00
167 Bob Ptacek 3.00
168 George Reed 9.00
169 Dick Schnell 3.00
170 Wayne Shaw 3.00
171 Ted Urness 6.00
172 Dale West 3.00
173 Reg Whitehouse 3.00
174 Gene Wlasiuk 3.00
175 Jim Worden 3.00
176 Dick Aldridge 3.00
177 Walt Balasiuk 3.00
178 Ron Brewer 3.00
179 W. Dickey 3.00
180 B. Dugan 3.00
181 L. Ferguson 3.00
182 Don Fuell 3.00
183 Ed Harrington 3.00
184 Ron Howell 3.00
185 F. Laroue 3.00
186 Sherman Lewis 7.50
187 Marv Luster 6.00
188 Dave Mann 4.00
189 Pete Martin 3.00
190 Marty Martinello 3.00
191 Lamar McHan 6.00
192 Danny Nykoluk 3.00
193 Jackie Parker 20.00
194 Dave Pivec 3.00
195 Jim Rountree 3.00
196 Dick Shatto 7.50
197 Billy Shipp 3.00
198 Len Sparks 3.00
199 D. Still 3.00
200 Norm Stoneburgh 3.00
201 Dave Thelan 6.00
202 J. Vilanus 3.00
203 J. Walter 3.00
204 P. Watson 3.00
205 John Wydareny 3.00
206 Billy Cooper 3.00
207 Wayne Dennis 3.00
208 Paul Desjardins 3.00
209 N. Dunford 3.00
210 Farrell Funston 3.00
211 Herb Gray 7.50
212 Roger Hamelin 3.00
213 Barrie Hansen 3.00
214 Henry Janzen 3.00
215 Hal Ledyard 3.00
216 Leo Lewis 7.50
217 Brian Palmer 3.00
218 Art Perkins 3.00
219 Cornel Piper 3.00
220 Ernie Pitts 3.00
221 Kenny Ploen 7.50
222 Dave Raimey 4.00
223 Norm Rauhaus 3.00
224 Frank Rigney 6.00
225 Roger Savoie 3.00
226 Jackie Simpson 6.00
227 Dick Thornton 4.00
228 Sherwyn Thorson 3.00
229 Ed Elmer 3.00
230 Bill Whisler 3.00

1952 Crown Brand

NM
Complete Set (48): 2000.
Common Player: 50.00
1 John Brown 50.00
2 Tom Casey 75.00
3 Tommy Ford 50.00
4 Ian Gibb 50.00
5 Dick Huffman 75.00
6 Jack Jacobs 100.00
7 Thomas Lumsden 50.00
8 George McPhail 50.00
9 Jim McPherson 50.00
10 Buddy Tinsley 75.00
11 Ron Vaccher 50.00
12 Al Wiley 50.00
13 Ken Charlton 75.00
14 Glenn Dobbs 75.00
15 Sully Glasser 50.00
16 Nelson Greene 50.00
17 Bert Iannone 50.00
18 Art McEwan 50.00
19 Jimmy McFaul 50.00
20 Bob Pelling 50.00
21 Chuck Radley 50.00
22 Martin Ruby 100.00
23 Jack Russell 50.00
24 Roy Wright 50.00
25 Paul Alford 50.00
26 Sugarfoot Anderson 50.00
27 Dick Bradley 50.00
28 Bob Bryant 50.00
29 Cliff Cyr 50.00
30 Cal Green 50.00
31 Stan Heath 50.00
32 Stan Kaluznick 50.00
33 Guss Knickerhm 50.00
34 Paul Salata 50.00
35 Murry Sullivan 50.00
36 Dave West 50.00
37 Joe Aquirre 50.00
38 Claude Arnold 50.00
39 Bill Briggs 50.00
40 Mario DeMarco 50.00
41 Mike King 50.00
42 Donald Lord 50.00
43 Frank Morris 75.00
44 Gayle Pace 50.00
45 Rod Pantages 50.00
46 Rollin Prather 50.00
47 Chuck Quilter 50.00
48 Jim Quondamatteo 50.00

1993 Dream Cards Winnipeg Bombers

MT
Complete Set (12): 6.00
Common Player: .50
1 Matt Dunigan 2.00
2 Greg Battle 1.00
3 Nathaniel Bolton .50
4 Stan Mikawos .50
5 Miles Gorrell .50
6 Troy Westwood 1.00
7 Michael Richardson 1.00
8 David Black .50
9 Chris Walby .75
10 David Williams .75
11 Blaise Bryant .75
12 Bob Cameron .50

1981 Edmonton Journal Eskimos

MT
Complete Set (16): 175.00
Common Player: 5.00
1 Dave Fennell 7.50
2 Brian Fryer 5.00
3 Jim Germany 6.00
4 Gary Hayes 5.00
5 Larry Highbaugh 10.00
6 Joe Hollimon 5.00
7 Ed Jones 5.00
8 Dan Kearns 5.00
9 Brian Kelly 15.00
10 Dan Kepley 10.00
11 Neil Lumsden 6.00
12 Warren Moon 75.00
13 James Parker 15.00
14 Tom Scott 10.00
15 Waddell Smith 5.00
16 Bill Stevenson 6.00

1984 Edmonton Journal Eskimos

MT
Complete Set (13): 40.00
Common Player: 3.50
1 Leo Blanchard 3.50
2 Marco Cyncar 5.00
3 Blake Dermott 3.50
4 Brian Fryer 3.50
5 Joe Hollimon 3.50
6 James Hunter 3.50
7 Greg Marshall 5.00
8 Mike Nelson (CO) 3.50
9 Hector Pothier 3.50
10 Paul Rudzinski (ACO) 3.50
11 Bill Stevenson 5.00
12 Tom Towns 3.50
13 Eric Upton 3.50

1981 JOGO CFL B/W

MT
Complete Set (51): 200.00
Common Player: 1.00
1 Richard Crump 2.00
2 Tony Gabriel 7.50
3 Gerry Organ 1.00
4A Greg Marshall 2.50
4B J.C. Watts (SP) 40.00
5 Mike Raines 1.00
6 Larry Brune 1.00
7 Randy Rhino 2.50
8 Bruce Clark 4.00
9 Condredge Holloway 7.50
10 Dave Newman 1.00
11 Cedric Minter 1.00
12 Peter Muller 1.00
13 Vince Ferragamo 8.00
14 James Scott 2.00
15 Billy Johnson (White Shoes) 6.00
16 David Overstreet 6.00
17 Keith Gary 1.50
18 Tom Clements 15.00
19 Keith Baker 1.00
20 David Shaw 1.00
21 Ben Zambiasi 3.00
22 John Priestner 1.00
23 Warren Moon 100.00
24 Tom Wilkinson 3.00
25 Brian Kelly 6.00
26 Dan Kepley 2.00
27 Larry Highbaugh 2.50
28 David Boone 1.00
29 John Henry White 1.00
30 Joe Paopao 3.00
31 Larry Key 1.00
32 Glen Jackson 1.00
33 Joe Hollimon 1.00
34 Dieter Brock 6.00
35 Mike Holmes 1.00
36 William Miller 1.00
37 John Helton 3.00
38 Joe Poplawski 1.50
39 Joe Barnes 5.00
40 John Hufnagel 6.00
41 Bobby Thompson 1.00
42 Steve Stapler 1.00
43 Tom Cousineau 6.00
44 Bruce Threadgill 1.00
45 Ed McAleney 1.00
46 Leif Petterson 1.50
47 Paul Bennett 1.00
48 James Reed 1.00
49 Gerry Dattilio 1.50
50 Checklist Card 1.50

1982 JOGO Ottawa

MT
Complete Set (24): 8.00
Common Player: .40
1 Jordan Case .50
2 Larry Brune .50
3 Val Belcher .50
4 Greg Marshall .75
5 Mike Raines .40
6 Rick Sowieta .40
7 John Glassford .40
8 Bruce Walker .40
9 Jim Reid .50
10 Kevin Powell .40
11 Jim Piaskoski .50
12 Kelvin Kirk .40
13 Gerry Organ .50
14 Carl Brazley .75
15 William Mitchell .40
16 Billy Hardee .40
17 Jonathan Sutton .40
18 Doug Seymour .40
19 Pat Staub .40
20 Larry Tittley .40
21 Pat Stoqua .40
22 Sam Platt .40
23 Gary Dulin .40
24 John Holland .50

1982 JOGO Ottawa Past

MT
Complete Set (16): 25.00
Common Player (1-12): 1.25
Common Player (13-16): 2.00
Common DP: .75
1 Tony Gabriel 3.00
2 Whit Tucker (DP) 1.50
3 Dave Thelen 2.00
4 Ron Stewart (DP) 1.50
5 Russ Jackson (DP) 3.50
6 Kaye Vaughan 2.00
7 Bob Simpson 2.00
8 Ken Lehmann 1.50
9 Lou Bruce 1.25
10 Wayne Giardino (DP) .75
11 Moe Racine 1.25
12 Gary Schreider 1.25
13 Don Sutherin 4.00
14 Mark Kosmos (DP) 1.25
15 Jim Foley (DP) 2.00
16 Jim Conroy .75

1983 JOGO CFL Limited

MT
Complete Set (110): 900.00
Common Player: 4.00
1 Steve Ackroyd 4.00
2 Joe Barnes 12.00
3 Bob Bronk 4.00
4 Jan Carinci 4.00
5 Gordon Elser 4.00
6 Dan Ferrone 5.00
7 Terry Greer 12.00
8 Mike Hameluck 4.00
9 Condredge Holloway 15.00
10 Greg Holmes 4.00
11 Hank Llesic 10.00
12 John Malinosky 4.00
13 Cedric Minter 4.00
14 Don Moen 4.00
15 Rick Mohr 4.00
16 Darrell Nicholson 4.00
17 Paul Pearson 5.00
18 Matthew Teague 4.00
19 Geoff Townsend 4.00
20 Tom Trifaux 4.00
21 Darrell Wilson 4.00
22 Earl Wilson 4.00
23 Ricky Barden 4.00
24 Roger Cattelan 4.00
25 Michael Collymore 4.00
26 Charles Corneilus 4.00
27 Mariet Ford 4.00
28 Tyron Gray 5.00
29 Steve Harrison 4.00
30 Tim Hook 4.00
31 Greg Marshall 5.00
32 Ken Miller 4.00
33 Dave Newman 4.00
34 Rudy Phillips 4.00
35 Jim Reid 4.00
36 Junior Robinson 4.00
37 Mark Seale 4.00
38 Rick Sowieta 4.00
39 Pat Stoqua 4.00
40 Skip Walker 10.00
41 Al Washington 4.00
42 J.C. Watts 50.00
43 Keith Baker 4.00
44 Dieter Brock 35.00
45 Rocky DiPietro 20.00
46 Howard Fields 4.00
47 Ron Johnson 6.00
48 John Priestner 4.00
49 Johnny Shepherd 4.00
50 Mike Walker 6.00
51 Ben Zambiasi 12.00
52 Nick Arakgi 5.00
53 Brian DeRoo 4.00
54 Denny Ferdinand 4.00
55 Willie Hampton 4.00
56 Kevin Starkey 4.00
57 Glen Weir 4.00
58 Larry Crawford 6.00
59 Tyrone Crews 4.00
60 James Curry 10.00
61 Roy DeWalt 12.00
62 Mervyn Fernandez 50.00
63 Sammy Green 4.00
64 Glen Jackson 4.00
65 Glenn Leonhard 4.00
66 Nelson Martin 4.00
67 Joe Paopao 8.00
68 Lui Passaglia 10.00
69 Al Wilson 4.00
70 Nick Bastaja 4.00
71 Paul Bennett 4.00
72 John Bonk 4.00
73 Aaron Brown 4.00
74 Bob Cameron 4.00
75 Tom Clements 60.00
76 Rick House 5.00
77 John Hufnagel 15.00
78 Sean Kehoe 4.00
79 James Murphy 12.00
80 Tony Norman 4.00
81 Joe Poplawski 4.00
82 Willard Reaves 15.00
83 Bobby Thompson 4.00
84 Wylie Turner 4.00
85 Dave Fennell 6.00
86 Jim Germany 5.00
87 Larry Highbaugh 6.00
88 Joe Hollimon 4.00
89 Dan Kepley 10.00
90 Neil Lumsden 4.00
91 Warren Moon 500.00
92 James Parker 12.00
93 Dale Potter 4.00
94 Angelo Santucci 4.00
95 Tom Towns 4.00
96 Tom Tuinei 5.00
97 Danny Bass 12.00
98 Ray Crouse 4.00
99 Gerry Dattilio 7.50
100 Tom Forzani 4.00
101 Mike Levenseller 4.00
102 Mike McTague 5.00
103 Bernie Morrison 4.00
104 Darrell Toussaint 4.00
105 Chris DeFrance 4.00
106 Dwight Edwards 5.00
107 Vince Goldsmith 10.00
108 Homer Jordan 4.00
109 Mike Washington 4.00
110A Darrell Moir (Set number on back) 12.00
110B Darrell Moir (Without set number) 50.00

1983 JOGO Quarterbacks

MT
Complete Set (9): 75.00
Common Player: 1.50
1 Dieter Brock 5.00
2 Tom Clements 7.50
3 Gerry Dattilio 1.50
4 Roy DeWalt 3.00
5 Johnny Evans 1.50
6 Condredge Holloway 4.00
7 John Hufnagel 4.00
8 Warren Moon 40.00
9 J.C. Watts 25.00

1984 JOGO CFL

MT
Complete Set (160): 275.00
Complete Series 1 (110): 150.00
Complete Series 2 (50): 125.00
Common Player (1-110): 1.00
Common Player (111-160): 2.50
1 Mike Hameluck 1.50
2 Bob Bronk 1.00
3 Paul Pearson 1.00
4 Dan Ferrone 1.50
5 Paul Bennett 1.00
6 Joe Barnes 4.00
7 Condredge Holloway 6.00
8 Terry Greer 5.00
9 Vince Goldsmith 3.00
10 Darrell Wilson 1.00
11 Tom Trifaux 1.00
12 Kelvin Pruenster 1.00
13 Earl Wilson 1.00
14 Hank Llesic 2.50
15 Stephen Del Col 1.00
16 Lamont Meacham 1.00
17 Lester Brown 1.00
18 Rob Forbes 1.00
19 Darrell Nicholson 1.00
20 James Curry 2.50
21 Skip Walker 2.50
22 J.C. Watts 25.00
23 Kevin Powell 1.00
24 Dean Dorsey 2.00
25 Tyron Gray 2.00
26 Mike Hudson 1.50
27 Dan Rashovich 1.50
28 Rudy Phillips 1.50
29 Larry Tittley 1.00
30 Ricky Barden (UER) (Number missing) 1.00
31 Mark Seale 1.00
32 Prince McJunkins 1.50
33 Kevin Dalliday 1.00
34 Rick Sowieta 1.00
35 Roger Cattelan 1.00
36 Damir Dupin 1.00
37 Jack Williams 1.00
38 Dave Newman 1.00
39 Maurice Doyle 1.00
40 Tim Hook 1.00
41 Dieter Brock 12.00
42 Rufus Crawford 5.00
43 Steve Kearns 1.00
44 Ross Francis 1.00
45 Henry Waszczuk 1.00
46 Mark Streeter 1.00
47 Mike McIntyre 1.00
48 John Priestner 1.00
49 Paul Palma 1.00
50 Mike Walker 1.50
51 Mike Barker 1.00
52 Todd Brown 1.00
53 Andre Francis 2.00
54 Glenn Keeble 1.00
55 Turner Gill 10.00
56 Eugene Belliveau 1.00
57 Willie Hampton 1.00
58 Ken Ciancone 1.00
59 Preston Young 1.00
60 Stanley Washington 1.00
61 Denny Ferdinand 1.00
62 Steve Smith 1.00
63 Rick Klassen 1.50
64 Larry Crawford 1.50
65 John Henry White 1.00
66 Bernie Glier 1.00
67 Don Taylor 1.00
68 Roy DeWalt 3.00
69 Mervyn Fernandez 25.00
70 John Blain 1.00
71 James Parker 4.00
72 Henry Vereen 1.00
73 Gerald Roper 1.00
74 Jim Sandusky 12.00
75 John Pankratz 1.00
76 Tom Clements 10.00
77 Vernon Pahl 1.00
78 Trevor Kennerd 2.50
79 Stan Mikawos 1.00
80 Ken Hailey 1.00
81 James Murphy 4.00
82 Jeff Boyd 2.00
83 Bob Cameron 1.00
84 Jerome Erdman 1.00
85 Tyrone Jones 2.50
86 John Bonk 1.00
87 John Sturdivant 1.00
88 Dan Huclack 1.00
89 Tony Norman 1.00
90 Kevin Neiles 1.00
91 Dave Kirzinger 1.00
92 Kevin Molle 1.00
93 Jerry DeBrouolny 1.00
94 Larry Hogue 1.00
95 Ken Moore 1.00
96 Jerry Friesen 1.00
97 Mike McTague 1.50
98 Jason Riley 1.00
99 Roger Aldag 2.00
100 Dave Ridgway 4.00
101 Eric Upton 1.00
102 Laurent DesLauriers 1.00
103 Brian Fryer 1.00
104 Brian DeRoo 1.00
105 Neil Lumsden 1.00
106 Hector Pothier 1.00
107 Brian Kelly 12.00
108 Dan Kepley 3.00
109 Danny Bass 5.00
110 Nick Arakgi 1.50
111 Lyle Bauer 2.50
112 Al Washington 2.50
113 Michel Bourgeau 3.00
114 Keith Gooch 2.50
115 Sean Kehoe 2.50
116 Ken Clark 3.00
117 Orlando Flanagan 2.50
118 Greg Vavra 2.50
119 Mark Bragagnolo 2.50
120 Dave Cutler 7.50
121 Nick Hebeler 2.50
122 Harry Skipper 5.00
123 Frank Robinson 3.00
124 DeWayne Jett 3.00
125 Mark Young 2.50
126 Felix Wright 25.00
127 Bob Poley 2.50
128 Leo Ezerins 2.50
129 Johnny Shepherd 3.00
130 Jeff Inglis 2.50
131 Dwaine Wilson 2.50
132 Aaron Hill 2.50
133 Brian Dudley 2.50
134 Ned Armour 2.50
135 Darryl Hall 2.50
136 Vince Phason 2.50
137 Terry Lymon 2.50
138 Jerry Dobrovolny 2.50
139 Richard Nemeth 2.50
140 Matt Dunigan 60.00
141 Rick Mohr 2.50
142 Lawrie Skolrood 2.50
143 Craig Ellis 6.00
144 Steve Johnson 2.50
145 Glen Suitor 3.00
146 Jeff Roberts 2.50
147 Greg Fieger 2.50
148 Sterling Hinds 2.50
149 Willard Reaves 9.00
150 John Pitts 2.50
151 Delbert Fowler 3.00
152 Mark Hopkins 2.50
153 Pat Cantner 2.50
154 Scott Flagel 3.00
155 Don Rose 2.50
156 David Shaw 2.50
157 Mark Moors 2.50
158 Chris Walby 5.00
159 Eugene Belliveau 2.50
160 Trevor Kennerd 10.00

1984 JOGO Ottawa Yesterday's Heroes

MT
Complete Set (22): 75.00
Common Player: 3.50
1 Tony Gabriel 5.00
2 Whit Tucker 3.50
3 Dave Thelen 3.50
4 Ron Stewart 3.50
5 Russ Jackson 10.00
6 Kaye Vaughan 3.50
7 Bob Simpson 3.50
8 Ken Lehmann 3.50
9 Lou Bruce 3.50
10 Wayne Giardino 3.50
11 Moe Racine 3.50
12 Gary Schreider 3.50
13 Don Sutherin 5.00
14 Mark Kosmos 3.50
15 Jim Foley 3.50
16 Jim Conroy 3.50
17 George Brancato 5.00
18 Art Green 5.00
19 Rudy Sims 5.00
20 Jim Coode 5.00
21 Jerry Campbell 5.00
22 Jim Piaskoski 5.00

1985 JOGO CFL

MT
Complete Set (110): 150.00
Common Player: 1.00
1 Mike Hameluck 1.50
2 Michel Bourgeau 1.50
3 Waymon Alridge 1.00
4 Daric Zeno 1.50
5 J.C. Watts 20.00
6 Kevin Gray 1.00
7 Steve Harrison 1.00
8 Ralph Dixon 1.00
9 Jo Jo Heath 1.00
10 Rick Sowieta 1.00
11 Brad Fawcett 1.00
12 Lamont Meacham 1.00
13 Dean Dorsey 1.50
14 Bernard Quarles 1.00
15 Mike Caterbone 1.00
16 Bob Stephen 1.00
17 Nick Benjamin 1.50
18 Tim McCray 1.50
19 Chris Sigler 1.00
20 Tony Johns 1.00
21 Jason Riley 1.00
22 Ralph Scholz 1.00
23 Ken Hobart 2.50
24 Paul Bennett 1.00
25 Dan Ferrone 1.50
26 Jim Kalafat 1.00
27 William Mitchell 1.00
28 Denny Ferdinand 1.00
29 James Curry 2.50
30 Jeff Inglis 1.00
31 Bob Bronk 1.00
32 Dan Petschenig 1.00
33 Terry Greer 4.00
34 Condredge Holloway 5.00
35 Ian Beckstead 1.00
36 James Parker 3.00
37 Tim Cowan 1.50
38 Roy DeWalt 2.50
39 Mervyn Fernandez 15.00
40 Bernie Glier 1.00
41 Keyvan Jenkins 3.00
42 Melvin Byrd 2.00
43 Ron Robinson 2.00
44 Andre Jones 1.00
45 Jim Sandusky 6.00
46 Darnell Clash 2.50
47 Rick Klassen 1.50
48 Brian Kelly 6.00
49 Rick House 1.50
50 Stewart Hill 3.00
51 Chris Woods 3.00
52 Darryl Hall 1.50
53 Laurent DesLauriers 1.00
54 Larry Cowan 1.00
55 Matt Dunigan 15.00
56 Andre Francis 1.50
57 Roy Kurtz 1.00
58 Steve Raquet 1.00
59 Turner Gill 5.00
60 Sandy Armstrong 1.00
61 Nick Arakgi 1.50
62 Mike McTague 1.50
63 Aaron Hill 1.00
64 Brett Williams 2.00
65 Trevor Bowles 1.50
66 Mark Hopkins 1.00
67 Frank Kosec 1.00
68 Ken Ciancone 1.00
69 Dwaine Wilson 1.00
70 Mark Stevens 1.00
71 George Voelk 1.00
72 Doug Scott 1.00
73 Rob Smith 1.00
74 Alan Reid 1.00
75 Rick Mohr 1.00
76 Dave Ridgway 3.50
77 Homer Jordan 1.00
78 Terry Leschuk 1.00
79 Rick Goltz 1.00
80 Neil Quilter 1.00
81 Joe Paopao 2.50
82 Stephen Jones 2.50
83 Scott Redl 1.00
84 Tony Dennis 1.00
85 Glen Suitor 1.50
86 Mike Anderson 1.00
87 Stewart Fraser 1.00
88 Fran McDermott 1.00
89 Craig Ellis 3.00
90 Eddie Ray Walker 2.00
91 Trevor Kennerd 3.00
92 Pat Cantner 1.00
93 Tom Clements 10.00
94 Glen Steele 1.00
95 Willard Reaves 4.00
96 Tony Norman 1.00
97 Tyrone Jones 2.50
98 Jerome Erdman 1.00
99 Sean Kehoe 1.00
100 Kevin Neiles 1.00
101 Ken Hailey 1.00
102 Scott Flagel 1.50
103 Mark Moors 1.00
104 Gerry McGrath 1.00
105 James Hood 1.00
106 Randy Ambrosie 1.00
107 Terry Irvin 1.00
108 Joe Barnes 3.00
109 Richard Nemeth 1.00
110 Darrell Patterson 1.00

1985 JOGO Ottawa Program Inserts

MT
Complete Set (9): 50.00
Common Player: 5.00
1 1960 Grey Cup Team 5.00
2 Russ Jackson 12.00
3 Angelo Mosca 10.00
4 Joe Poirier 5.00
5 Sam Scoccia 5.00
6 Gilles Archambeault 5.00
7 Ron Lancaster 5.00
8 Tom Jones 5.00
9 Gerry Nesbitt 5.00

1986 JOGO CFL

MT
Complete Set (169): 135.00
Common Series 1 (110): 75.00
Common Series 2 (59): 60.00
Common Player (1-110): .75
Common Player (111-169): .75
1 Ken Hobart 2.00
2 Tom Porras 1.25
3 Jason Riley .75
4 Ron Ingram .75
5 Steve Stapler 1.25
6 Mike Derks .75
7 Grover Covington 5.00
8 Lance Shields 1.25
9 Mike Robinson .75
10 Mark Napiorkowski .75
11 Romel Andrews .75
12 Ed Gataveckas .75
13 Tony Champion 5.00
14 Dale Sanderson .75
15 Mark Barousse .75
16 Nick Benjamin 1.25
17 Reginal Butts .75
18 Tom Burgess 6.00
19 Todd Dillon 3.00
20 Jim Reid 1.25
21 Robert Reid .75
22 Roger Cattelan .75
23 Kevin Powell .75
24 Randy Fabi .75
25 Gerry Hornett .75
26 Rick Sowieta .75
27 Warren Hudson 1.25
28 Steven Cox .75
29 Dean Dorsey 1.25
30 Michel Bourgeau 1.25
31 Ken Joiner .75
32 Mark Seale .75
33 Condredge Holloway 4.00
34 Bob Bronk .75
35 Jeff Inglis .75
36 Lance Chomyc 1.50
37 Craig Ellis 2.00
38 Marcellus Greene .75
39 David Marshall .75
40 Kerry Parker .75
41 Darrell Wilson .75
42 Walter Lewis 3.50
43 Sandy Armstrong .75
44 Ken Ciancone .75
45 Steve Raquet .75
46 Lemont Jeffers .75
47 Paul Gray .75
48 Jacques Chapdelaine .75
49 Rick Ryan .75
50 Mark Hopkins .75
51 Glenn Keeble .75
52 Roy Kurtz .75
53 Brian Dudley .75
54 Mike Gray .75
55 Tyrone Crews .75
56 Roy DeWalt 2.50
57 Mervyn Fernandez 6.00
58 Bernie Glier .75
59 James Parker 3.00
60 Bruce Barnett .75
61 Keyvan Jenkins 1.50
62 Alan Wilson .75
63 Delbert Fowler 1.25
64 James Jefferson 5.00
65 James West 7.50
66 Laurent DesLauriers .75
67 Damon Allen 10.00
68 Roy Bennett 3.00
69 Hasson Arbubakrr .75
70 Tom Clements 7.50
71 Trevor Kennerd 1.50
72 Perry Tuttle 3.50
73 Pat Cantner .75
74 Mike Hameluck .75
75 Rob Prodanovic .75
76 James Bell 1.25
77 Hector Pothier .75
78 Milson Jones 2.00
79 Craig Shaffer .75
80 Chris Skinner 1.25
81 Matt Dunigan 7.50
82 Tom Dixon .75
83 Brian Pillman 1.25
84 Randy Ambrosie .75
85 Rick Johnson 3.50
86 Larry Hogue .75
87 Garrett Doll .75
88 Stu Laird 1.25
89 Greg Fieger .75
90 Sean McKeown .75
91 Rob Bresciani .75
92 Harold Hallman 2.50
93 Jamie Harris .75
94 Dan Rashovich .75
95 David Conrad .75
96 Glen Suitor 1.25
97 Mike Siroishka .75
98 Michael McGruder 3.00
99 Brad Calip .75
100 Mike Anderson .75
101 Trent Bryant .75
102 Gary Lewis .75
103 Tony Dennis .75
104 Paul Tripoli .75
105 Daric Zeno .75
106 Michael Elarms .75
107 Donohue Grant .75
108 Ray Elgaard 15.00
109 Joe Paopao 2.00
110 Dave Ridgway 2.50
111 Rudy Phillips 1.25
112 Carl Brazley 1.25
113 Andre Francis .75
114 Mitchell Price 1.50
115 Wayne Lee .75
116 Tim McCray 1.50
117 Scott Virkus .75
118 Nick Hebeler .75
119 Eddie Ray Walker 1.25
120 Bobby Johnson .75
121 Mike McTague .75
122 Jeff Inglis .75
123 Joe Fuller .75
124 Steve Crane .75
125 Bill Henry .75
126 Ron Brown .75
127 Henry Taylor .75
128 Greg Holmes .75
129 Steve Harrison .75
130 Paul Osbaldiston 3.00
131 Craig Walls .75
132 Clorindo Grilli .75
133 Marty Palazeti .75
134 Darryl Hall .75
135 David Black .75
136 Bennie Thompson 2.50
137 Darryl Sampson .75
138 James Murphy 2.50
139 Scott Flagel .75
140 Trevor Kennerd 2.00
141 Bob Molle .75
142 Darrell Patterson .75
143 Stan Mikawos .75
144 John Sturdivant .75
145 Tyrone Jones 2.00
146 Jim Zorn 15.00
147 Steve Howlett .75
148 Jeff Volpe .75
149 Jerome Erdman .75
150 Ned Armour .75
151 Rick Klassen 1.25
152 Brett Williams 2.00
153 Richie Hall .75
154 Ray Alexander 2.50
155 Willie Pless 5.00
156 Marion Jones .75
157 Danny Bass 3.50
158 Frank Balkovec .75
159 Less Browne 4.00
160 Paul Osbaldiston 1.50
161 Trevor Bowles .75
162 David Daniels .75
163 Kevin Konar 1.50
164 Gary Allen 2.00
165 Karlton Watson .75
166 Ron Hopkins 1.25
167 Rob Smith .75
168 Garrett Doll .75
169 Rod Skillman 2.00

1987 JOGO CFL

MT
Complete Set (110): 90.00
Common Player: .60
1 Jim Reid 2.00
2 Nick Benjamin 1.00
3 Dean Dorsey 1.00
4 Hasson Arbubakrr .60
5 Gerald Alphin 6.00
6 Larry Willis 3.00
7 Rick Wolkensperg .60
8 Roy DeWalt 2.00
9 Michel Bourgeau 1.00
10 Anthony Woodson .60
11 Marv Allemang .60
12 Jerry Dobrovolny .60
13 Larry Mohr .60
14 Kyle Hall .60
15 Irv Daymond .60
16 Ken Ford .60
17 Leo Groenewegen .60
18 Michael Cline .60
19 Gilbert Renfroe 3.00
20 Danny Barrett 6.00
21 Dan Petschenig .60
22 Gill Fenerty (UER) (Misspelled Gil on card front) 10.00
23 Lance Chomyc 1.00
24 Jake Vaughan .60
25 John Congemi 2.00
26 Kelvin Pruenster .60
27 Mike Siroishka .60
28 Dwight Edwards 1.00
29 Darnell Clash 1.50
30 Glenn Kulka 1.50
31 Jim Kardash .60
32 Selwyn Drain .60
33 Ian Sinclair 1.00
34 Pat Cantner .60
35 Trevor Kennerd 2.50
36 Bob Cameron .60
37 Willard Reaves 3.00
38 Jeff Trefflin .60
39 David Black .60
40 Chris Walby 2.00
41 Tom Clements 4.00
42 Mike Gray .60
43 Bennie Thompson 1.50
44 Tyrone Jones 2.00
45 Ken Winey .60
46 Nick Arakgi 1.00
47 James West 2.50
48 Ken Pettway .60
49 James Murphy 2.50
50 Carl Fodor .60
51 Tom Muecke 2.00
52 Alvis Satele .60
53 Grover Covington 2.00
54 Tom Porras 1.00
55 Jason Riley .60
56 Jed Tommy .60
57 Bernie Ruoff 1.00
58 Ed Gataveckas .60
59 Wayne Lee .60
60 Ken Hobart 1.50
61 Frank Robinson 1.00
62 Mike Robinson .60
63 Ben Zambiasi (UER) (No team listed on front of card) 2.00
64 Byron Williams .60
65 Lance Shields 1.00
66 Ralph Scholz .60
67 Earl Winfield 5.00
68 Terry Lehne .60
69 Alvin Bailey .60
70 David Sauve .60
71 Bernie Glier .60
72 Nelson Martin .60
73 Kevin Konar 1.00
74 Greg Peterson .60
75 Harold Hallman 1.50
76 Sandy Armstrong .60
77 Glenn Harper .60
78 Rick Worman 1.50
79 Darrell Toussaint .60
80 Larry Hogue .60
81 Rick Johnson 2.50
82 Richie Hall .60
83 Stu Laird 1.00
84 Mike Emery .60
85 Cliff Toney .60
86 Matt Dunigan 6.00
87 Hector Pothier .60
88 Stewart Hill 1.50
89 Stephen Jones 1.50
90 Dan Huclack .60
91 Mark Napiorkowski .60
92 Mike Derks .60
93 Mike Walker 1.50
94 Michael McGruder 2.00
95 Terry Baker 3.00
96 Bobby Jurasin 4.00
97 James Curry 2.50
98 Tracey Mack .60
99 Tom Burgess 3.50
100 Steve Crane .60
101 Glen Suitor 1.00
102 Walter Bender .60
103 Jeff Bentrim 2.00
104 Eric Florence .60
105 Terry Cochrane .60
106 Tony Dennis .60
107 Dave Albright .60
108 David Sidoo .60
109 Harry Skipper 1.00
110 Dave Ridgway 2.00

1988 JOGO CFL

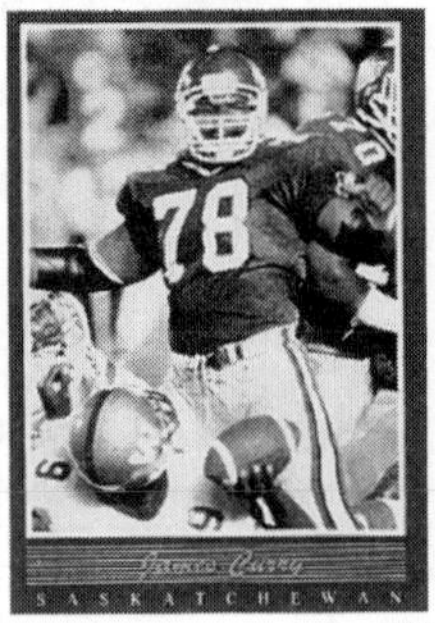
SASKATCHEWAN

MT
Complete Set (110): 110.00
Common Player: .60
1 Roy DeWalt 2.00
2 Jim Reid 1.25
3 Patrick Wayne .60
4 Jerome Erdman .60
5 Tom Dixon .60
6 Brad Fawcett .60
7 Tom Muecke 1.25
8 Mike Hudson .60
9 Orville Lee 1.50
10 Michel Bourgeau 1.00
11 Dan Sellers .60
12 Rob Pavan .60
13 Rae Robirtis .60
14 Rod Brown .60
15 Ken Evraire 1.00
16 Irv Daymond .60
17 Tim Jessie 1.00
18 Jim Sandusky 4.00
19 Blake Dermott 1.00
20 Brian Warren .60
21 Mike Walker 3.00
22 Tom Porras 1.00
23 Less Browne 1.25
24 Paul Osbaldiston 1.00
25 Vernell Quinn .60
26 Mike Derks .60
27 Arnold Grevious .60
28 Jim Lorenz .60
29 Mike Robinson .60
30 Doug Davies .60
31 Earl Winfield 3.00
32 Wally Zatylny 2.00
33 Martin Sartin .60
34 Lee Knight .60
35 Jason Riley .60
36 Darrell Gorbin .60
37 Tony Champion 2.50
38 Steve Stapler 1.00
39 Scott Flagel .60
40 Grover Covington 1.50
41 Mark Napiorkowski .60
42 Jacques Chapdelaine .60
43 Lance Shields 1.00
44 Donohue Grant .60
45 Henry Williams 25.00
46 Trevor Bowles 1.00
47 Don Wilson .60
48 Tracy Ham 15.00
49 Richie Hall 1.00
50 Rob Bresciani .60
51 James Curry 1.25
52 Kent Austin 15.00
53 Jeff Bentrim 1.00
54 Dave Ridgway 1.25
55 Terry Baker 1.00
56 Lance Chomyc 1.00
57 Paul Sandor .60
58 Kevin Cummings .60
59 John Congemi 1.25
60 Gilbert Renfroe 1.50
61 Jake Vaughan .60
62 Doran Major .60
63 Dwight Edwards 1.00
64 Bruce Elliott .60
65 Lorenzo Graham .60
66 Jim Kardash .60
67 Reggie Pleasant 1.50
68 Carl Brazley .60
69 Gill Fenerty 5.00
70 Selwyn Drain .60
71 Warren Hudson 1.00
72 Willie Fears .60
73 Randy Ambrosie .60
74 George Ganas .60
75 Glenn Kulka 1.00
76 Kelvin Pruenster .60
77 Darrell Smith 1.50
78 Jearld Baylis 1.50
79 Blaine Schmidt .60
80 Tony Visco 1.00
81 Carl Fodor .60
82 Rudy Phillips 1.00
83 Craig Watson 1.00
84 Kent Warnock 1.00
85 Ken Ford .60
86 Blake Marshall 2.00
87 Terry Cochrane .60
88 Shawn Faulkner .60
89 Marshall Toner .60
90 Darren Yewshyn .60
91 Eugene Belliveau .60
92 Jay Christensen .60
93 Anthony Parker 1.25
94 Walter Ballard .60
95 Matt Dunigan 6.00
96 Andre Francis 1.00
97 Rickey Foggie 6.00
98 Delbert Fowler .60
99 Michael Allen .60
100 Greg Battle 6.00
101 Mike Gray .60
102 Dan Wicklum .60
103 Paul Shorten .60
104 Paul Clatney .60
105 Rod Hill 2.00
106 Steve Rodehutskors .60
107 Sean Salisbury 4.00
108 Vernon Pahl .60
109 Trevor Kennerd 1.00
110 David Williams 2.50

1988 JOGO CFL League

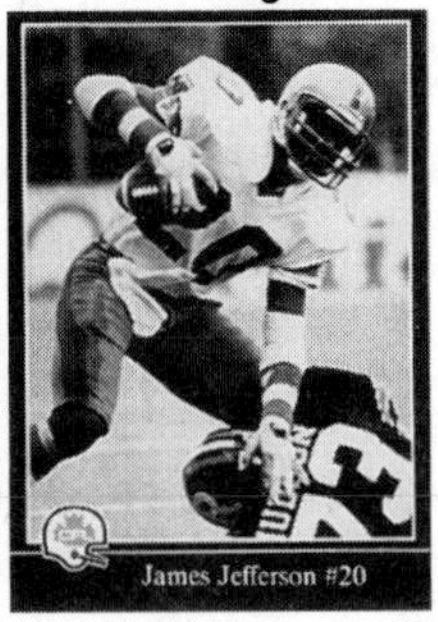
James Jefferson #20

MT
Complete Set (106): 250.00
Common Player: 1.25
1 Walter Ballard 1.25
2 Jan Carinci 1.25
3 Larry Crawford 1.25
4 Tyrone Crews 1.25
5 Andre Francis 2.00
6 Bernie Glier 1.25
7 Keith Gooch 1.25
8 Kevin Konar 1.25
9 Scott Lecky 1.25
10 James Parker 3.00
11 Jim Sandusky (Traded) 10.00
12 Greg Stumon 1.25
13 Todd Wiseman (Not listed on checklist card) 1.25
14 Gary Allen 2.00
15 Scott Flagel (Traded) 3.00
16 Harold Hallman 1.25
17 Larry Hogue (UER) (Misspelled Hogue) 1.25
18 Ron Hopkins 1.25
19 Stu Laird 2.00
20 Andy McVey 1.25
21 Bernie Morrison 1.25
22 Tim Petros 1.25
23 Bob Poley 1.25
24 Tom Spoletini 1.25
25 Emmanuel Tolbert 4.00
26 Larry Willis 2.00
27 Damon Allen 4.00
28 Danny Bass 4.00
29 Stanley Blair 1.25
30 Marco Cyncar 1.25
31 Tracy Ham 25.00
32 Milson Jones (Traded) 4.00
33 Stephen Jones 3.00
34 Jerry Kauric 3.00
35 Hector Pothier 1.25
36 Tom Richards 3.00
37 Chris Skinner 2.00
38 Henry Williams 40.00
39 Larry Wruck 1.25
40 Pat Brady 1.25
41 Grover Covington 3.00
42 Rocky DiPietro 4.00
43 Howard Fields 1.25
44 Miles Gorrell 1.25
45 Johnnie Jones 1.25
46 Tom Porras 2.00
47 Jason Riley 1.25
48 Dale Sanderson 1.25
49 Ralph Scholz 1.25
50 Lance Shields 2.00
51 Steve Stapler 1.25
52 Mike Walker 3.00
53 Gerald Alphin 4.00
54 Nick Arakgi (SP) (Retired before season) 20.00
55 Nick Benjamin 2.00
56 Tom Dixon 1.25
57 Leo Groenewegen 1.25
58 Will Lewis 2.00
59 Greg Marshall (Injured and retired) 5.00
60 Larry Mohr 1.25
61 Kevin Powell (Traded) 3.00
62 Jim Reid 2.00
63 Art Schlichter 8.00
64 Rick Wolkensperg 1.25
65 Anthony Woodson 1.25
66 Dave Albright 1.25
67 Roger Aldag 1.25
68 Mike Anderson 1.25
69 Kent Austin 25.00
70 Tom Burgess 6.00
71 James Curry 3.00
72 Ray Elgaard 4.00
73 Denny Ferdinand 1.25
74 Bobby Jurasin 6.00
75 Gary Lewis 1.25
76 Dave Ridgway 3.00
77 Harry Skipper 2.00
78 Glen Suitor 2.00
79 Ian Beckstead 2.00
80 Lance Chomyc 2.00
81 John Congemi 3.00
82 Gill Fenerty 8.00
83 Dan Ferrone 2.00
84 Warren Hudson 2.00
85 Hank Llesic 3.50
86 Jim Kardash 1.25
87 Glenn Kulka 2.00
88 Don Moen 1.25
89 Gilbert Renfroe 3.00
90 Chris Schultz 1.25
91 Darrell Smith 1.25
92 Lyle Bauer 1.25
93 Nick Bastaja 1.25
94 David Black 1.25
95 Bob Cameron 1.25
96 Randy Fabi 1.25
97 James Jefferson 6.00
98 Stan Mikawos 1.25
99 James Murphy 3.00
100 Ken Pettway 1.25
101 Willard Reaves (Signed with Redskins) 12.00
102 Darryl Sampson 1.25
103 Chris Walby 4.00
104 James West 5.00
105 Tom Clements (SP) (Retired before season) 20.00
106 Checklist Card SP 6.00

1989 JOGO CFL

MT
Complete Set (160): 95.00
Complete Series 1 (110): 60.00
Complete Series 2 (50): 35.00
Common Player (1-160): .50
1 Mike Kerrigan 2.50
2 Ian Beckstead .50
3 Lance Chomyc .75
4 Gill Fenerty 3.50
5 Lee Morris .50
6 Todd Wiseman .50
7 John Congemi .75
8 Harold Hallman .75
9 Jim Kardash .50
10 Kelvin Pruenster .50
11 Blaine Schmidt .50
12 Bruce Holmes .50
13 Ed Berry .50
14 Bobby McAllister 2.50
15 Frank Robinson .75
16 Darrell Corbin .50
17 Jason Riley .50
18 Darrell Patterson .50
19 Darrell Harle .50
20 Mark Napiorkowski .50
21 Derrick McAdoo 2.00
22 Sam Loucks .50
23 Ronnie Glanton .50
24 Lance Shields .75
25 Tony Champion 2.00
26 Floyd Salazar .50
27 Tony Visco .75
28 Glenn Kulka .75
29 Reggie Pleasant .75
30 Rod Skillman .50
31 Grover Covington 1.50
32 Gerald Alphin 2.00
33 Gerald Wilcox .75
34 Daniel Hunter .50
35 Tony Kimbrough .75
36 Willie Fears .75
37 Tyrone Thurman 4.00
38 Dean Dorsey .75
39 Tom Schimmer .50
40 Ken Evraire .75
41 Steve Wiggins .50
42 Donovan Wright .50
43 Tuineau Alipate .50
44 Richie Hall .50
45 Rob Bresciani .50
46 Tom Burgess 1.50
47 Jeff Fairholm 4.00
48 John Hoffman .50
49 Dave Ridgway 1.25
50 Terry Baker .75
51 Mike Hildebrand .50
52 Danny Bass 2.50
53 Jeff Braswell .50
54 Michel Bourgeau .75
55 Ken Ford .50
56 Enis Jackson .50
57 Tony Hunter 1.25
58 Andre Francis .75
59 Larry Wruck .75
60 Pierre Vercheval 1.00
61 Keith Wright .50
62 Andrew McConnell .50
63 Gregg Stumon .75
64 Steve Taylor 3.00
65 Brett Williams .75
66 Tracy Ham 5.00
67 Stewart Hill .75
68 Eugene Belliveau .50
69 Tom Porras .75
70 Jay Christensen .50
71 Michael Soles 1.00
72 John Mandarich 1.25
73 Dan Wicklum .50
74 Shawn Daniels .50
75 Marshall Toner .50
76 Kent Warnock .75
77 Terrence Jones 4.00
78 Damon Allen 2.00
79 Kevin Konar .75
80 Phillip Smith .50
81 Marcus Thomas .50
82 Jamie Taras .50
83 Rob Moretto .50
84 Eugene Mingo .50
85 Matt Dunigan 5.00
86 Jan Carinci .50
87 Anthony Parker 2.00
88 Keith Gooch .50
89 Ron Howard .50
90 David Williams 1.50
91 Less Browne .75
92 Quency Williams .50
93 Tim McCray .75
94 Jeff Croonen .50
95 Greg Battle 2.00
96 Moustafa Ali .50
97 Michael Allen .50
98 David Black .50
99 Paul Randolph .50
100 Trevor Kennerd .75
101 Ken Pettway .50
102 Sean Salisbury 2.50
103 Bob Cameron .50
104 Tim Jessie .75
105 Leon Hatziloannou .50
106 Matt Pearce .50
107 Paul Clatney .50
108 Randy Fabi .50
109 Mike Gray .50
110 James Murphy 2.00
111 Danny Barrett 1.50
112 Wally Zatylny .75
113 Tony Truelove .50
114 Leroy Blugh .50
115 Reggie Taylor 1.50
116 Mark Zeno 2.50
117 Paul Wetmore .50
118 Mark McLoughlin .50
119 Randy Ambrosie .50
120 Will Johnson .75
121 Brock Smith .50
122 Willie Gillus .50
123 Andy McVey .50
124 Wes Cooper .50

125 Tyrone Pope .50
126 Craig Ellis 1.50
127 Darrel Hopper .50
128 Brad Fawcett .50
129 Pat Miller .50
130 Irv Daymond .50
131 Bob Molle .50
132 James Mills 3.00
133 Darrell Wallace .75
134 Jerry Beasley .50
135 Loyd Lewis .50
136 Bernie Glier .50
137 Eric Streater 2.00
138 Gerald Roper .50
139 Brad Tierney .50
140 Patrick Wayne .50
141 Craig Watson .50
142 Doug Landry 3.50
143 Orville Lee 1.50
144 Rocco Romano .50
145 Todd Dillon 1.00
146 Michel Lamy .50
147 Tony Cherry 3.50
148 Flint Fleming .50
149 Kennard Martin .50
150 Lorenzo Graham .50
151 Junior Thurman 1.50
152 Darnell Graham .50
153 Dan Ferrone .75
154 Matt Finlay .50
155 Brent Matich .50
156 Kent Austin 5.00
157 Will Lewis .50
158 Mike Walker 1.50
159 Tim Petros .75
160 Stu Laird 1.50

1990 JOGO CFL

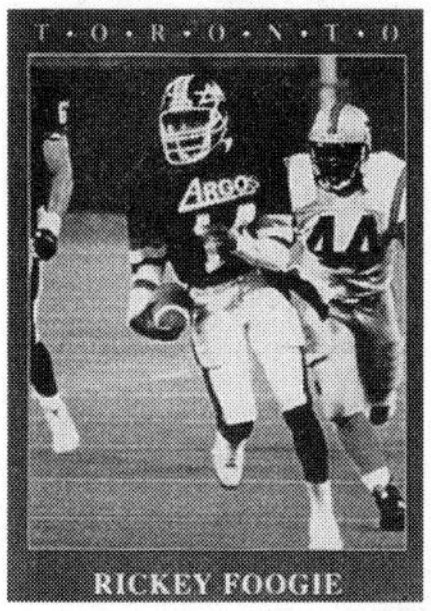

MT
Complete Set (220): 60.00
Complete Series 1 (110): 30.00
Complete Series 2 (110): 30.00
Common Player: .25
1 1989 Grey Cup Champs (Saskatchewan) 1.00
2 Kent Austin 2.50
3 James Ellingson .40
4 Vince Goldsmith .40
5 Gary Lewis .25
6 Bobby Jurasin 1.00
7 Tim McCray .40
8 Chuck Klingbeil 1.50
9 Albert Brown .25
10 Dave Ridgway .75
11 Tony Rice 3.00
12 Richie Hall .25
13 Jeff Fairholm 1.00
14 Ray Elgaard 1.25
15 Sonny Gordon .25
16 Peter Giftopoulos .75
17 Mike Kerrigan 1.00
18 Jason Riley .25
19 Wally Zatylny .40
20 Derrick McAdoo .40
21 Dale Sanderson .25
22 Paul Osbaldiston .40
23 Todd Dillon .40
24 Miles Gorrell .25
25 Earl Winfield .75
26 Bill Henry .25
27 Darrell Harle .25
28 Ernie Schramayr .25
29 Greg Peterson .25
30 Marshall Toner .25
31 Danny Barrett 1.50
32 Mike Palumbo .25
33 Ken Ford .25
34 Brock Smith .25
35 Tom Spoletini .25
36 Will Johnson .40
37 Terrence Jones 1.50
38 Darcy Kopp .25
39 Tim Petros .40
40 Mitchell Price .40
41 Junior Thurman 1.00
42 Kent Warnock .40
43 Darrell Smith 1.00
44 Chris Schultz (UER) (No team on back) .40
45 Kelvin Pruenster .25
46 Matt Dunigan 3.00
47 Lance Chomyc .40
48 John Congemi .75
49 Mike Clemons 10.00
50 Glenn Harper .25
51 Branko Vincic .25
52 Tom Porras .40
53 Reggie Pleasant .40
54 Randy Marriott .25
55 James Parker .75
56 Don Moen .40
57 James West 1.00
58 Trevor Kennerd .75
59 Warren Hudson .40
60 Tom Burgess 1.50
61 David Black .25
62 Matt Pearce .25
63 Steve Rodehutskors .40
64 Rod Hill .40
65 Nick Benjamin .40
66 Bob Cameron .25
67 Leon Hatziioannou .25
68 Robert Mimbs 2.50
69 Mike Gray .25
70 Ken Winey .25
71 Mike Hildebrand .25
72 Brett Williams .40
73 Tracy Ham 2.50
74 Danny Bass .75
75 Mark Norman .25
76 Andre Francis .40
77 Todd Storme .25
78 Henry Williams 5.00
79 Kevin Clark .75
80 Enis Jackson .25
81 Leroy Blugh .25
82 Jeff Braswell .40
83 Larry Wruck .25
84A Mike McLean (ERR) (Photo actually 24 Mike Hildebrand) 3.00
84B Mike McLean (COR) (Two players shown) 5.00
85 Leo Groenewegen (UER) (Misspelled Groenewegan on card bac k) .25
86 Mark Gastineau 1.50
87 Larry Clarkson .25
88 Major Harris 2.50
89 Ray Alexander .40
90 Joe Paopao .40
91 Ian Sinclair .40
92 Tony Visco (UER) (British Columbia on front, correct ly has team as Toronto on front) .25
93 Lui Passaglia .75
94 Doug Flutie 20.00
95 Glenn Kulka .40
96 Bruce Holmes .25
97 Stacey Dawsey .25
98 Damon Allen .75
99 Ken Evraire .40
100 David Williams .60
101 Gregg Stumon .40
102 Scott Flagel .40
103 Gerald Roper .25
104 Tony Cherry 1.00
105 Jim Mills .25
106 Dean Dorsey .40
107 Patrick Wayne .25
108 Reggie Barnes 2.00
109 Kari Yli-Renko .25
110 Ken Hobart .75
111 Doug Flutie 15.00
112 Grover Covington .75
113 Michael Allen .25
114 Mike Walker .75
115 Danny McManus 4.00
116 Greg Battle 1.25
117 Quency Williams .25
118 Jeff Croonen .25
119 Paul Randolph .25
120 Rick House .40
121 Rob Smith .40
122 Mark Napiorkowski .25
123 Ed Berry .25
124 Rob Crifo .25
125 Gord Weber .25
126 Jeff Boyd .40
127 Paul McGowan .40
128 Reggie Taylor .75
129 Warren Jones .25
130 Blake Marshall .40
131 Darrell Corbin .25
132 Jim Rockford .40
133 Richard Nurse .25
134 Bryan Illerbrun .25
135 Mark Waterman .25
136 Doug Landry 1.25
137 Ronnie Glanton .25
138 Mark Guy .40
139 Mike Anderson .25
140 Remi Trudel .25
141 Stephen Jones 1.00
142 Mike Derks .25
143 Michel Bourgeau (Edmonton Oilers) .40
144 Jeff Bentrim .40
145 Roger Aldag .40
146 Donald Narcisse 2.50
147 Troy Wilson .25
148 Glen Suitor .40
149 Stewart Hill 1.00
150 Chris Johnstone .25
151 Mark Mathis .25
152 Blaine Schmidt .25
153 Craig Ellis .75
154 John Mandarich .40
155 Steve Zatylny .25
156 Michel Lamy .25
157 Irv Daymond .25
158 Tom Porras .40
159 Rick Worman .40
160 Major Harris 1.50
161 Darryl Hall .40
162 Terry Andrysiak .40
163 Harold Hallman .40
164 Carl Brazley .25
165 Kevin Smellie .25
166 Mark Campbell .40
167 Andy McVey .25
168 Derrick Crawford .40
169 Howard Dell .25
170 Dave Van Belleghem .25
171 Don Wilson .25
172 Robert Smith .40
173 Keith Browner .40
174 Chris Munford .25
175 Gary Wilkerson .25
176 Rickey Foggie (UER) (Misspelled Foogie on card front) 1.25
177 Robin Belanger .25
178 Andrew Murray .25
179 Paul Masotti .40
180 Chris Gaines .25
181 Joe Clausi .25
182 Greg Harris .25
183 David Bovell .25
184 Eric Streater .40
185 Larry Hogue .25
186 Jan Carinci .25
187 Floyd Salazar .25
188 Alondra Johnson .40
189 Jay Christensen (UER) (Misspelled Christenson on card fro nt) .40
190 Rick Ryan .25
191 Willie Pless 1.50
192 Walter Ballard .25
193 Lee Knight .25
194 Ray Macoritti .40
195 Dan Payne .25
196 Dan Sellers .25
197 Rae Robirtis .25
198 Dave Mossman .25
199 Sam Loucks .25
200 Derek MacCready .25
201 Tony Cherry .75
202 Ali Moustafa .40
203 Terry Baker .40
204 Matt Finlay .25
205 Daniel Hunter .25
206 Chris Major 2.00
207 Henry Smith .25
208 David Sapunjis 4.00
209 Darrell Wallace .40
210 Mark Singer .25
211 Tuineau Alipate .25
212 Tony Champion 1.25
213 Mike Lazecki .25
214 Larry Clarkson .25
215 Lorenzo Graham .25
216 Tony Martino .25
217 Ken Watson .25
218 Paul Clatney .25
219 Ken Pettway .25
220 Tyrone Jones 1.00

1991 JOGO CFL

MT
Complete Set (220): 6.00
Complete Series 1 (110): 3.00
Complete Series 2 (110): 3.00
Common Player: .04
1 Tracy Ham .35
2 Larry Wruck .08
3 Pierre Vercheval .04
4 Rod Connop .04
5 Michel Bourgeau .04
6 Leroy Blugh .04
7 Mike Walker .04
8 Ray Macoritti .04
9 Michael Soles .04
10 Brett Williams .15
11 Blake Marshall .15
12 David Williams .08
13 Enis Jackson .04
14 Craig Ellis .15
15 Reggie Taylor .15
16 Mike McLean .04
17 Blake Dermott .04
18 Henry Williams .50
19 Jordan Gaertner .04
20 Willie Pless .15
21 Danny Bass .15
22 Trevor Bowles .04
23 Rob Davidson .04
24 Mark Norman .04
25 Ron Lancaster (CO) .10
26 Chris Johnstone .04
27 Randy Ambrosie .04
28 Glenn Kulka .04
29 Gerald Wilcox .15
30 Kari Yli-Renko .04
31 Daniel Hunter .04
32 Bryan Illerbrun .04
33 Terry Baker .04
34 Jeff Braswell .04
35 Andre Francis .04
36 Irv Daymond .04
37 Sean Foudy .04
38 Brad Tierney .04
39 Gregg Stumon .04
40 Scott Flagel .04
41 Gerald Roper .04
42 Charles Wright .04
43 Rob Smith .04
44 James Ellingson .04
45 Damon Allen .08
46 John Congemi .04
47 Reggie Barnes .20
48 Stephen Jones .15
49 Rob Prodanovic .04
50 Steve Goldman .04
51 Patrick Wayne .04
52 David Conrad .04
53 John Krupke .04
54 Loyd Lewis .04
55 Tony Cherry .20
56 Terrence Jones .25
57 Dan Wicklum .04
58 Allen Pitts .50
59 Junior Thurman .04
60 Ron Hopkins .04
61 Andy McVey .04
62 Leo Blanchard .04
63 Mark Singer .04
64 Darryl Hall .04
65 David McCrary .04
66 Mark Guy .04
67 Marshall Toner .04
68 Derrick Crawford .04
69 Danny Barrett .20
70 Kent Warnock .08
71 Brent Matich .04
72 Mark McLoughlin .04
73 Joe Clausi .04
74 Wally Buono (CO) .04
75 Will Johnson .04
76 Walter Ballard .04
77 Matt Finlay .04
78 David Sapunjis .35
79 Greg Peterson .04
80 Paul Clatney .04
81 Lloyd Fairbanks .04
82 Herman Heard .15
83 Richard Nurse .04
84 Dave Richardson .04
85 Ernie Schramayr .04
86 Todd Dillon .04
87 Tuineau Alipate .04
88 Peter Giftopoulos .04
89 Miles Gorrell .04
90 Earl Winfield .20
91 Paul Osbaldiston .04
92 Dale Sanderson .04
93 Jason Riley .04
94 Ken Evraire .04
95 Lee Knight .04
96 Tim Lorenz .04
97 Derrick McAdoo .15
98 Bobby Dawson .04
99 Rickey Royal .04
100 Ronald Veal .20
101 Grover Covington .20
102 Mike Kerrigan .20
103 Rocky DiPietro .20
104 Mark Dennis .04
105 Tony Champion .20
106 Tony Visco .04
107 Darrell Harle .04
108 Wally Zatylny .04
109 David Beckman (CO) .04
110 Checklist 1-110 .04
111 Jeff Fairholm .04
112 Roger Aldag .04
113 Dave Albright .04
114 Gary Lewis .04
115 Dan Rashovich .04
116 Lucius Floyd .04
117 Bob Poley .04
118 Donald Narcisse .20
119 Bobby Jurasin .15
120 Orville Lee .15
121 Stacey Hairston .04
122 Richie Hall .04
123 John Gregory (CO) .04
124 Rick Worman .04
125 Dave Ridgway .15
126 Wayne Drinkwater .04
127 Eddie Lowe .04
128 Mike Hogue .04
129 Larry Hogue .04
130 Milson Jones .15
131 Ray Elgaard .20
132 Dave Pitcher .04
133 Vic Stevenson .04
134 Albert Brown .04
135 Mike Anderson .04
136 Glen Suitor .04
137 Kent Austin .30
138 Mike Gray .04
139 Steve Rodehutskors .04
140 Eric Streater .04
141 David Black .04
142 James West .15
143 Danny McManus .30
144 Darryl Sampson .04
145 Bob Cameron .04
146 Tom Burgess .35
147 Rick House .04
148 Chris Walby .15
149 Michael Allen .04
150 Warren Hudson .04
151 David Bovell .04
152 Rob Crifo .04
153 Lyle Bauer .04
154 Trevor Kennerd .20
155 Troy Johnson .04
156 Less Browne .04
157 Nick Benjamin .04
158 Matt Pearce .04
159 Tyrone Jones .04
160 Rod Hill .04
161 Bob Molle .04
162 Lee Hull .04
163 Greg Battle .20
164 Robert Mimbs .30
165 Giulio Caravatta .04
166 James Mills .15
167 Ian Sinclair .04
168 Robin Belanger .04
169 Deatrich Wise .04
170 Chris Skinner .04
171 Norman Jefferson .04
172 Larry Clarkson .04
173 Chris Major .35
174 Stewart Hill .04
175 Tony Hunter .04
176 Stacey Dawsey .04
177 Doug Flutie 1.00
178 Mike Trevathan .04
179 Jearld Baylis .04
180 Matt Clark .25
181 Ken Pettway .04
182 Lloyd Joseph .04
183 Jon Volpe 1.00
184 Leo Groenewegen .04
185 Carl Coulter .04
186 O.J. Brigance .35
187 Ryan Hanson .04
188 Rocco Romano .04
189 Ray Alexander .04
190 Bob O'Billovich (CO) .04
191 Paul Wetmore .04
192 Harold Hallman .04
193 Ed Berry .04
194 Brian Warren .04
195 Matt Dunigan .40
196 Kelvin Pruenster .04
197 Ian Beckstead .04
198 Carl Brazley .04
199 Trevor Kennerd .15
200 Reggie Pleasant .04
201 Kevin Smellie .04
202 Don Moen .04
203 Blaine Schmidt .04
204 Chris Schultz .04
205 Lance Chomyc .04
206 Darrell Smith .20
207 Dan Ferrone .04
208 Chris Gaines .04
209 Keith Castello .04
210 Chris Munford .04
211 Rodney Harding .20
212 Darryl Ford .04
213 Rickey Foggie .20
214 Don Wilson .04
215 Andrew Murray .04
216 Jim Kardash .04
217 Mike Clemons 1.25
218 Bruce Elliott .04
219 Mike McCarthy .04
220 Checklist .04

1991 JOGO CFL Stamp Card Inserts

MT
Complete Set (3): 30.00
Common Player: 10.00
1 Albert H.G. Grey 10.00
2 Trevor Kennerd 10.00
NNO Grey Cup Trophy (Grey Cup Winners listed on card back) 10.00

Post-1980 cards in Near Mint condition will generally sell for about 75% of the quoted Mint value. Excellent-condition cards bring no more than 40%.

1992 JOGO CFL Promos

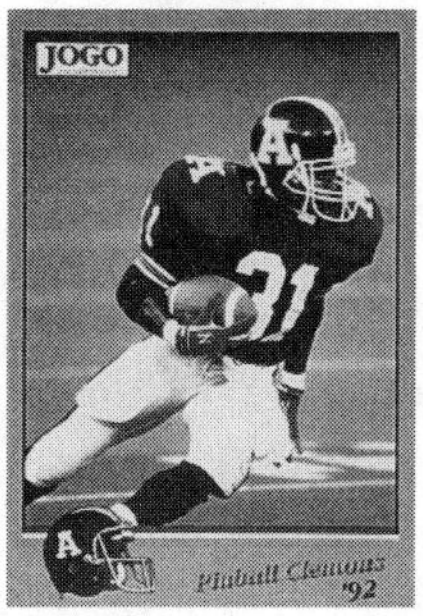

MT
Complete Set (7): 12.00
Common Player: .75
A1 Mike Clemons 2.00
A2 Jon Volpe 2.00
A3 Rocket Rat (Cartoon character) .75
P1 Mike Clemons 3.00
P2 Jon Volpe 3.00
CC1 Ken Danby Art Coll. Classic Library .75
CC2 Ken Danby Art Coll. Classic Library .75

1992 JOGO CFL

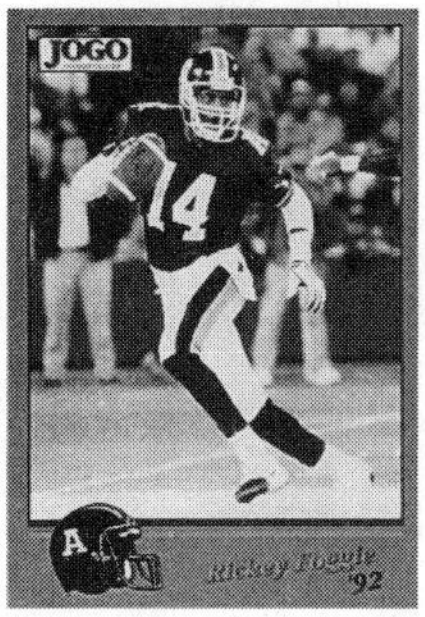

MT
Complete Set (220): 20.00
Common Player: .05
1 David Bovell .05
2 Don Moen .10
3 Ian Beckstead .05
4 David Williams .10
5 Hank Ilesic .10
6 Brian Warren .05
7 Paul Massotti .05
8 Kelvin Pruenster .05
9 Mike Clemons 1.00
10 Chris Schultz .10
11 Andrew Murray .05
12 Lance Chomyc .10
13 Ed Berry .05
14 Harold Hallman .10
15 Dave Van Belleghem .05
16 Rodney Harding .10
17 Rickey Foggie .20
18 Darrell Smith .25
19 Bob Skemp .05
20 Carl Brazley .10
21 J.P. Izquierdo .05
22 Mike Campbell .10
23 Reggie Pleasant .10
24 Dan Ferrone .10
25 Kevin Smellie .05
26 Don Wilson .05
27 Adam Rita (CO) .05
28 Greg Peterson .05
29 David Sapunjis .50
30 Srecko Zizakovic .05
31 Carl Bland .05
32 Errol Tucker .05
33 Allen Pitts .30
34 Pee Wee Smith .30
35 Will Johnson .30
36 Kent Warnock .10
37 Brent Matich .05
38 Stu Laird .10
39 Shawn Beals .05
40 Darcy Kopp .05
41 Ken Moore .05
42 Alondra Johnson .10
43 Matt Finlay .05
44 Andy McVey .05
45 Paul Clatney .05
46 Karl Anthony .05
47 Bruce Covernton .35
48 Mark McLoughlin (UER) (Name misspelled several times on t he card back) .10
49 Pat Hinds .05
50 Eric Mitchel (UER) (Misspelled Mitchell on both sides) .20
51 Dan Wicklum .05
52 Tim Cofield .25
53 Steve Taylor .35
54 Darryl Hall .10
55 Angelo Snipes .60
56 Shawn Daniels .05
57 Terrence Jones .25
58 Brian Bonner .05
59 Kari Yli-Renko .05
60 Denny Chronopoulos .05
61 Damon Allen .10
62 Reggie Barnes .30
63 Andre Francis (UER) (Misspelled Frances on card front) .10
64 Rob Smith .25
65 Anthony Drawhorn .20
66 David Conrad (UER) (Back text says team is Green Rider s) .05
67 Irv Daymond .05
68 Terry Baker .10
69 Daniel Hunter .05
70 Gord Weber .05
71 Tom Burgess .30
72 Charles Gordon .05
73 Bobby Gordon .05
74 Jock Climie .25
75 Patrick Wayne .05
76 Sean Foudy .05
77 James Ellingson .10
78 Gregg Stumon .10
79 John Kropke .10
80 Stephen Jones .25
81 Ron Smeltzer .05
82 Scott Campbell .50
83 Henry Williams 1.00
84 Willie Pless .25
85 Dan Murphy .05
86 Chris Armstrong .05
87 Tracy Ham .50
88 Larry Wruck .10
89 Rod Connop .05
90 Jim Sandusky .25
91 Randy Ambrosie .05
92 Michel Bourgeau .10
93 Bennie Goods (UER) (Misspelled Benny) .10
94 Rob Davidson .05
95 Leroy Blugh .05
96 Brian Walling .05
97 Michael Soles .10
98 Craig Ellis .25
99 Pierre Vercheval .10
100 Matt Dunigan .40
101 Enis Jackson .05
102 Tom Muecke .20
103 Jed Roberts .05
104 Steve Krupey .05
105 Blake Marshall .35
106 Trevor Bowles .10
107 Eddie Thomas .05
108 Rocket Ray (Jogo Mascot) .10
109 Checklist 1-110 (UER) (50 Eric Mitchell 93 Benny Goods) .10
110 Tom Burgess .35
111 Bob Cameron .05
112 James West .20
113 Chris Walby .15
114 David Black .05
115 Nick Benjamin .10
116 Matt Pearce .05
117 Bob Molle .05
118 Rod Hill .10
119 Kyle Hall .05
120 Danny McManus .35
121 Calvin Murphy .15
122 Stan Mikawos .05
123 Bobby Evans .05
124 Larry Willis .10
125 Eric Streater .10
126 Perry Tuttle .20
127 Leon Hatziioannou .05
128 Sammy Garza .05
129 Greg Battle .25
130 Elfrid Payton .25
131 Troy Westwood .20
132 Mike Gray .05
133 Dave Vankoughnett .05
134 Paul Randolph .05
135 Darryl Sampson .05
136 Less Browne .10
137 Quency Williams .05
138 Robert Mimbs .35
139 Matt Dunigan 1.50
140 Dan Rashovich .05
141 Dan Farthing .05
142 Bruce Boyko .05
143 Kim McCloud .05
144 Richie Hall .05
145 Paul Vajda .05
146 Willis Jacox .25
147 Glen Scrivner .05
148 Dave Ridgway .15
149 Lucius Floyd .10
150 James King .05
151 Kent Austin .50
152 Jeff Fairholm .10
153 Roger Aldag .10
154 Albert Brown .05
155 Chris Gioskos .05
156 Stacey Hairston .05
157 Glen Suitor .10
158 Milson Jones .10
159 Vic Stevenson .05
160 Bob Poley .05
161 Bobby Jurasin .20
162 Gary Lewis .05
163 Donald Narcisse .25
164 Mike Anderson .05
165 Nick Mazzoli .05
166 Lance Trumble .05
167 Dale Sanderson .05
168 Todd Wiseman .05
169 Mark Dennis .05
170 Peter Giftopoulos .05
171 Ken Evraire .10
172 Darrell Harle .05
173 Terry Wright .05
174 Jamie Morris .20
175 Corris Ervin .05
176 Don McPherson .30
177 Jason Riley .05
178 Tim Jackson .05
179 Todd Dillon .10
180 Lee Knight .05
181 Scott Douglas .05
182 Dave Richardson .05
183 Wally Zatylny .10
184 Rickey Martin .05
185 John Motton .30
186 Mark Waterman .05
187 Ernie Schramayr .05
188 Miles Gorrell .05
189 Tony Champion .20
190 Earl Winfield .25
191 John Zajdel .05
192 Danny Barrett .30
193 Ian Sinclair .10
194 Norman Jefferson .05
195 Ryan Hanson .05
196 Matt Clark .15
197 Leo Groenewegen .05
198 Ray Alexander .10
199 James Mills .20
200 Jon Volpe .60
201 Doug Hocking .05
202 Tony Kimbrough .05
203 Lui Passaglia .15

204	Bruce Holmes	.05
205	Jamie Taras	.05
206	Derek MacCready	.05
207	Jay Christensen	.10
208	O.J. Brigance	.30
209	Robin Belanger	.05
210	Stewart Hill	.10
211	Mike Marasco	.05
212	Mike Trevathan	.10
213	Chris Major	.25
214	Steve Rodehutskors	.10
215	Paul Wetmore	.05
216	Ken Pettway	.05
217	Darren Flutie	1.25
218	Giulio Caravatta	.05
219	Murray Pezim	.10
220	Checklist 111-220	.10

1992 JOGO CFL Missing Years

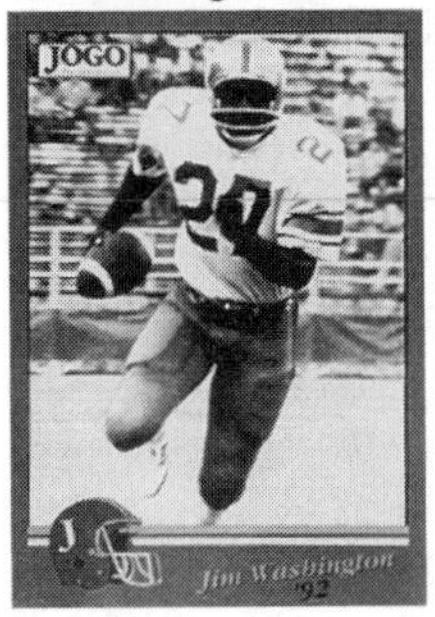

		MT
Complete Set (22):		20.00
Common Player:		1.00
1	Larry Smith	1.50
2	Mike Nelms	1.50
3	John Sciarra	2.00
4	Ed Chalupka	1.00
5	Mike Rae	1.50
6	Terry Metcalf (UER) (His CFL years were 78-80, not 78-9 0)	2.50
7	Chuck Ealey	5.00
8	Junior Ah-You	1.50
9	Mike Samples	1.00
10	Ray Nettles	1.00
11	Dickie Harris	1.00
12	Willie Burden	3.00
13	Johnny Rodgers	5.00
14	Anthony Davis	3.00
15	Joe Pisarcik (UER) (His CFL years were 74-76, not 74-7 5)	1.50
16	Jim Washington	1.00
17	Tom Scott (UER) (11 years in CFL, not 10)	1.50
18	Butch Norman	1.00
19	Steve Molnar	1.00
20	Jerry Tagge	2.50
21	Leon Bright (UER) (His CFL years were 77-80, not 77-7 9)	2.50
22	Waddell Smith	2.00

1992 JOGO CFL Stamp Cards

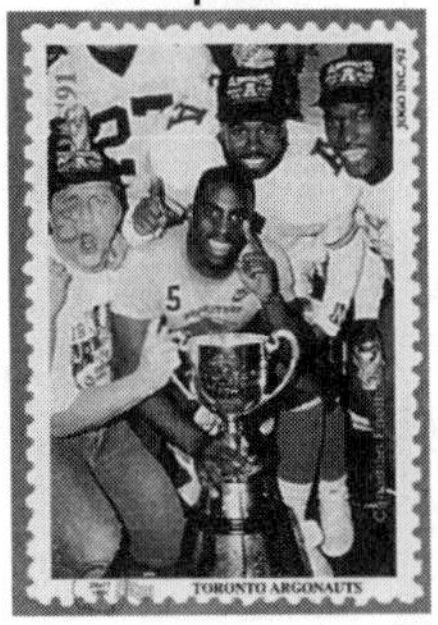

		MT
Complete Set (5):		30.00
Common Player:		6.00
1	CFL Hall of Fame Museum and Statue	6.00
2	Toronto Argonauts 1991 Grey Cup Champs	6.00
3	Tom Pate Memorial Trophy	6.00
4	Russ Jackson (MVP)	6.00
5	Oldest Trophy in The Hall of Fame (Montreal Football Challenge Cup)	6.00

Values quoted in this guide reflect the retail price of a card — the price a collector can expect to pay when buying a card from a dealer. The wholesale price — that which a collector can expect to receive from a dealer when selling cards — will be significantly lower, depending on desirability and condition.

1993 JOGO CFL

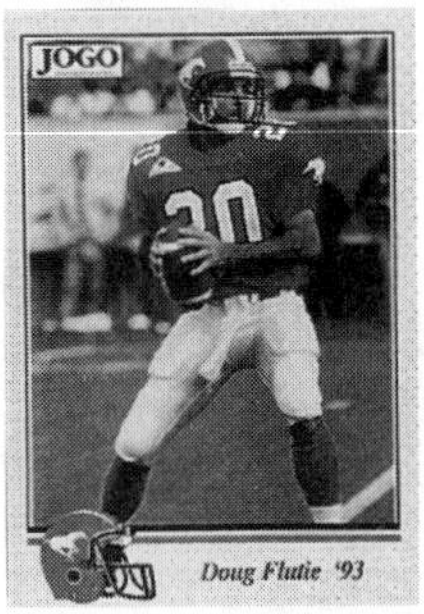

		MT
Complete Set (220):		60.00
Complete Series 1 (110):		35.00
Complete Series 2 (110):		25.00
Common Player:		.20
1	Stephen Jones	.50
2	Chris Gioskos	.20
3	Treamelle Taylor	.20
4	Irv Daymond	.20
5	Gord Weber	.20
6	James Ellingson	.35
7	Lybrant Robinson	.20
8	Michael Allen	.75
9	Greg Stumon	.35
10	Darren Joseph	.35
11	Terry Baker	.35
12	Denis Chronopoulos	.20
13	Tom Burgess	1.00
14	Wayne Walker	.50
15	Brendan Rogers	.20
16	Matt Pearce	.20
17	Chris Tsangaras	.20
18	Leon Hatziioannou	.20
19	Bob Cameron	1.00
20	Don Smith	.20
21	Michael Richardson	1.00
22	Jayson Dzikowicz	.20
23	Matt Dunigan	2.00
24	Steve Grant	.20
25	Rob Crifo	.20
26	Dave Vankoughnett	.20
27	Paul Massotti	.35
28	Blaine Schmidt	.20
29	Dave Van Belleghem	.20
30	Hank Ilesic	.20
31	Reggie Pleasant	.35
32	Tracy Ham	1.00
33	Mike Clemons	2.00
34	Lance Chomyc	.35
35	Ken Benson	.20
36	Chris Green	.20
37	Mike Campbell	.35
38	Chris Schultz	.35
39	Reggie Rogers	.35
40	John Hood	.35
41	Dave Richardson	.20
42	Mike Jovanovich	.35
43	Joey Jauch	.20
44	Lubo Zizakovich	.20
45	Don McPherson	.35
46	Brett Williams	.50
47	Tod Wiseman	.20
48	Jim Jauch	.20
49	Erus Sanchez	.35
50	Scott Walker	.20
51	Roger Hennig	.20
52	Glen Suitor	.35
53	Bobby Jurasin	.35
54	Scott Hendrickson	.20
55	Venson Donelson	.20
56	Dan Rahsovich	.20
57	Kent Austin	.75
58	Ray Elgaard	.35
59	Dave Ridgway	.50
60	Byron Williams	.20
61	Larry Ryckman (PRES)	.20
62	Karl Anthony	.20
63	Greg Knox	.20
64	Ken Moore	.20
65	Allen Pitts	.50
66	Matt Finlay	.35
67	Tony Martino	.20
68	Harold Hasselbach	1.00
69	David Sapunjis	1.00
70	Andy McVey	.20
71	Stu Laird	.35
72	Derrick Crawford	.35
73	Mark McLoughlin	.20
74A	Will Johnson (ERR) (Eskimo logo)	2.00
74B	Will Johnson (COR) (Stampeder logo)	.75
75	Don Wilson	.20
76	J.P. Izquierdo	.20
77	Henry Williams	1.25
78	Larry Wruck	.35
79	David Shelton	.35
80	Damion Lyons	.20
81	Jed Roberts	.20
82	Trent Brown	.20
83	Michel Bourgeau	.35
84	Blake Dermott	.35
85	Willie Pless	.50
86	Leroy Blugh	.20
87	Steve Krupey	.20
88	Jim Sandusky	.35
89	Danny Barrett	.50
90	James West	.50
91	Glen Scrivner	.20
92	Tyrone Jones	.35
93A	Jon Volpe (Photo has poor color)	2.00
93B	Jon Volpe (corrected)	.75
94	Less Browne	.35
95	Matt Clark	.35
96	Andre Francis	.35
97	Darren Flutie	1.25
98	Ray Alexander	.35
99	Rob Smith	1.00
100	Fred Anderson (Managing General Partner)	.35
101	Rob White	.20
102	Bobby Humphrey	.35
103	Willie Bouyer	.20
104	Titus Dixon	.35
105	John Wiley	.20
106	Kerwin Bell	1.00
107	Carl Parker	.20
108	Mike Oliphant	.75
109	David Archer	2.50
110	Freeman Baysinger	.35
111	Gerlad Alphin	.35
112	Gerald Wilcox	.35
113	Reggie Barnes	.50
114	Michel Raby	.20
115	Charles Wright	.20
116	Brett Young	.35
117	Charles Gordon	.20
118	Anthony Drawhorn	.35
119	Daved Benefield	.35
120	Patrick Burke	.20
121	Joe Sardo	.20
122	Dexter Manley	.35
123	Bruce Beaton	.20
124	Joe Fuller	.20
125	Michel Lamy	.20
126	Terrence Jones	.50
127	Jeff Croonen	.20
128	Leonard Johnson	.20
129	Dan Payne	.20
130	Carlton Lance	.20
131	Errol Brown	.20
132	Wayne Drinkwater	.20
133	Malvin Hunter	.20
134	Maurice Crum	.20
135	Brooks Findlay	.20
136	Ray Bernard	.20
137	Paul Osbaldiston	.35
138	Mark Dennis	.35
139	Glenn Kulka	.35
140	Lee Knight	.20
141	Mike O'Shea	1.00
142	Paul Bushey	.20
143	Nick Mazzoli	.20
144	Earl Winfield	.50
145	Gary Wilkerson	.20
146	Jason Riley	.20
147	Bob MacDonald	.35
148	Dale Sanderson	.20
149	Bobby Dawson	.20
150	Rod Connop	.20
151	Tony Woods	.20
152	Dan Murphy	.35
153	Mike DuMaresq	.20
154	Alan Boyko	.20
155	Vaughn Booker	.75
156	Elfrid Payton	.35
157	Mike Kerrigan	.50
158	Charles Anthony	.20
159	Brent Matich	.20
160	Craig Hendrickson	.20
161	Dave Pitcher	.20
162	Stewart Hill	.35
163	Terryl Ulmer	.20
164	Paul Cranmer	.35
165	Mike Saunders	1.50
166	Doug Flutie	2.00
167	Kelian Matthews	.20
168	Kip Texada	.20
169	Jonathan Wilson	.20
170	Bruce Dickson	.20
171	Mike Trevathan	.35
172	Vic Stevenson	.20
173	Keith Powe	.20
174	Eddie Taylor	.20
175	Tim Lorenz	.20
176	Sesan Millington	.35
177	Ryan Hanson	.20
178	Ed Berry	.20
179	Kent Warnock	.35
180	Spencer McLennan	.20
181	Brian Walling	.35
182	Danny McManus	.75
183	Donovan Wright	.20
184	Giulio Caravatta	.20
185	Derek MacCready	.20
186	Greg Eaglin	.20
187	Jim Mills	.20
188	Tom Europe	.20
189	Zock Allen	.30
190	Ian Sinclair	.20
191	O.J. Brigance	1.00
192	Steve Rodehutskors	.35
193	Lou Cafazzo	.20
194	Mark Dube	.20
195	Srecko Zizakovic	.20
196	Alondra Johnson	.35
197	Rocco Romano	.20
198	Raymond Biggs	.20
199	Frank Marof	.20
200	Brian Wiggins	.35
201	Marvin Pope	.20
202	Gerald Vaughn	.20
203	Todd Storme	.20
204	Blair Zerr	.20
205	Eric Johnson	.35
206	Mark Pearce	.20
207	Will Moore	2.00
208	Bruce Plummer	.20
209	Kari Yli-Renko	.20
210	Doug Parrish	.20
211	Warren Hudson	.35
212	Kevin Whitley	.20
213	Enis Jackson	.20
214	Wally Zatylny	.35
215	Bruce Elliott	.20
216	Harold Hallman	.35
217	Glenn Rogers	.20
218	Manny Hazard	.50
219	Robert Clark	.35
220	Doug Flutie (UER) (Three misspelled Tree on back)	2.00

1993 JOGO CFL Missing Years

		MT
Complete Set (22):		15.00
Common Player:		.60
1B	Jim Edwards	1.00
2B	Lou Harris	.75
3B	George Mira	1.25
4B	Fred Biletnikoff	3.50
5B	Randy Halsall	.60
6B	Don Sweet	.60
7B	Jim Coode	.60
8B	Steve Mazurak	.75
9B	Wayne Allison	.60
10B	Paul Williams	.60
11B	Eric Allen	1.25
12B	M.L. Harris	.75
13B	James Sykes	1.50
14B	Chuck Zapiec	.75
15B	George McGowan	.60
16B	Bob Macoritti	.75
17B	Chuck Walton	.60
18B	Willie Armstead	.75
19B	Rocky Long	.60
20B	Gene Mack	.60
21B	David Green	1.25
22B	Don Warrington	.75

1994 JOGO CFL Caravan

		MT
Complete Set (22):		40.00
Common Player:		1.00
1	Glenn Kulka	1.00
2	Jock Climie	2.00
3	Danny Barrett	3.00
4	Stephen Jones	2.00
5	Mike Clemons	4.00
6	Pierre Vercheval	1.50
7	Andre Evraire	1.50
8	Brett Williams (UER) (Misspelled Willians on card front)	1.50
9	Wally Zatylny	1.50
10	Mike O'Shea	2.50
11	Earl Winfield	2.00
12	Mike Oliphant	2.00
13	Matt Dunigan	4.00
14	Chris Walby	2.00
15	Tracy Ham	3.00
16	Darrell Smith	2.00
17	Glen Suitor	1.50
18	Mark McLoughlin	1.00
19	Bruce Covernton	1.50
20	Willie Pless	2.00
21	Henry Williams	4.00
22	Lui Passaglia	1.50

1994 JOGO CFL

		MT
Complete Set (310):		75.00
Complete Series 1 (110):		20.00
Complete Series 2 (110):		20.00
Complete Series 3 (90):		35.00
Common Player (1-110):		.15
Common Player (111-220):		.15
Common Player (221-310):		.30
1	Danny Barrett	.50
2	Remi Trudel	.15
3	Terry Baker	.15
4	Paul Clatney	.15
5	Michael Richardson	.75
6	John Kropke	.30
7	Glenn Kulka	.15
8	Daved Benefield	.30
9	Derek MacCready	.15
10	Jessie Small	.30
11	Chris Gioskos	.15
12	Gregg Stumon	.30
13	Lee Johnson	.30
14	Michael Jefferson Jr.	.15
15	Mario Perry	.15
16	Joe Mero	.15
17	Reggie Barnes	.30
18	Mike Stowell	.15
19	Tony Moss	.15
20	Antoine Worthman	.15
21	Joe Fuller	.15
22	Daniel Hunter	.15
23	Doug Flutie	2.50
24	Douglas Craft	.50
25	Lubo Zizakovic	.15
26	Srecko Zizakovic	.15
27	Stu Laird	.30
28	Brian Wiggins	.30
29	Will Johnson	.50
30	David Sapunjis	1.00
31	Rocco Romano	.15
32	Raymond Biggs	.15
33	Ken Moore	.15
34	Matt Finlay	.30
35	Ian Sinclair	.30
36	Glen Scrivner	.15
37	Less Browne	.30
38	Darren Flutie	1.00
39	Freeman Baysinger	.15
40	Kent Austin	.50
41	Donovan Wright	.15
42	Cory Philpot	1.50
43	Tom Europe	.15
44	Giulio Caravatta	.15
45	Mike Clemons	1.50
46	Leon Hatziioannou	.15
47	Blaine Schmidt	.15
48	Reggie Pleasant	.30
49	Paul Masotti	.30
50	Pierre Vercheval	.15
51	Duane Forde	.15
52	Jeff Fairholm	.30
53	Carl Coulter	.15
54	Bobby Gordon	.15
55	Mike Jovanovich	.15
56	Chris Johnstone	.15
57	Matt Pearce	.15
58	Bob Cameron	.75
59	Brett MacNeil	.15
60	Blaise Bryant	.40
61	Chris Tsangaris	.15
62	Dave Vankoughnett	.15
63	Gerald Alphin	.30
64	Alfred Jackson	.30
65	Jayson Dzikowicz	.15
66	Bobby Evans	.15
67	Dave Ridgway	.30
68	Bobby Jurasin	.30
69	Dan Payne	.15
70	Ray Elgaard	.50
71	Dan Farthing	.15
72	Glen Suitor	.30
73	Mike Saunders	1.00
74	Brent Matich	.15
75	Scott Hendrickson	.15
76	Dan Rashovich	.15
77	Wayne Drinkwater	.15
78	Larry Wruck	.30
79	J.P. Izquierdo	.15
80	Jed Roberts	.15
81	Michel Bourgeau	.30
82	Malvin Hunter	.15
83	Bruce Dickson	.15
84	Jim Sandusky	.50
85	Mike DuMaresq	.15
86	Tracy Gravely	.15
87	Tracy Ham	1.00
88	John Congemi	.30
89	Darrell Corbin	.15
90	Maurice Kelly	.30
91	Doug Flutie (MVP)	2.50
92	Alfred Jordan	.30
93	Curtis Mayfield	.40
94	David Hollis	.15
95	James Blake	.15
96	Anthony Blue	.30
97	Jeffrey Sawyer	.15
98	Al Whiting	.15
99	Brad LaCombe	.15
100	Wally Zatylny	.30
101	Bob Torrance	.15
102	Jeffery Fields	.15
103	John G. Motton Jr.	.30
104	Todd Wiseman	.15
105	Mike O'Shea	.75
106	Scott Douglas	.15
107	Dale Sanderson	.15
108	David Diaz-Infante	.30
109	Mike Kiselak	.15
110	Chris Thieneman	.15
111	Horace Brooks	.30
112	Andre Francis	.30
113	Nick Mazzoli	.15
114	Irv Daymond	.15
115	Alfred Smith	.15
116	Stephen Jones	.40
117	Bruce Beaton	.15
118	Corey Dowden	.15
119	Gerald Collins	.30
120	Joe Washington	.30
121	Irvin Smith	.15
122	Harold Nash Jr.	.30
123	Ray Savage Jr.	.15
124	Billy Scott	.15
125	Aaron Kanner	.15
126	Ben Williams	.40
127	Keith Browner	.30
128	Eros Sanchez	.30
129	Don Caparotti	.15
130	Earnest Fields	.15
131	O.J. Brigance	.75
132	Walter Wilson	.30
133	Allen Pitts	.50
134	Tony Stewart	.30
135	Marvin Pope	.15
136	Tony Martino	.15
137	Vince Danielsen	.15
138	Pee Wee Smith	.50
139	Bruce Covernton	.40
140	Greg Knox	.15
141	Gerald Vaughn	.15
142	Jay McNeil	.15
143	Larry Ryckman (OWN)	.15
144	Blair Zerr	.15
145	Danny McManus	.75
146	Jamie Taras	.15
147	Kelly Sims	.30
148	Denny Chronopoulos	.15
149	Enis Jackson	.15
150	Virgil Robertson	.15
151	Tyrone Chatman	.15
152	Brian Forde	.15
153	Andrew Stewart	.15
154	Ryan Hanson	.15
155	Francois Belanger	.15
156	Tony O'Billovich	.15
157	Erik White	.30
158	Kevin Whitley	.15
159	Chris Schultz	.30
160	Mike Campbell	.15
161	Wayne Lammie	.15
162	Keith Ballard	.15
163	Neil Fort	.15
164	Charles Anthony	.15
165	John Buddenberg	.15
166	Allan Boyko	.15
167	Paul Randolph	.15
168	Gerald Wilcox	.40
169	Brendan Rogers	.15
170	Kim Phillips	.15
171	David Williams	.30
172	James Pruitt	.30
173	Kevin O'Brien	.15
174	Tre Everett	.30
175	Hurlie Brown	.15
176	Malcolm Frank	.15
177	Sean Brantley	.15
178	Aaron Ruffin	.15
179	Anthony Drawhorn	.30
180	Larry Thompson	.75
181	Brooks Findlay	.15
182	Dallas Rysavy	.15
183	Ray Bernard	.15
184	Donald Narcisse	.75
185	Warren Jones	.30
186	Tom Gerhart	.15
187	David Robinson Jr.	.30
188	Damon Allen	.30
189	Henry Williams	1.00
190	Jay Christensen	.30
191	Trent Brown	.15
192	Rod Connop	.15
193	Michael Soles	.30
194	Vance Hammond	.15
195	Maurice Miller	.15
196	Shar Pourdanesh	.50
197	Elfrid Payton	.30
198	Ken Benson	.15
199	David Maeva	.15
200	Carlos Huerta	.30
201	Prince Wimbley III	.30
202	Anthony Calvillo	2.00
203	Kenny Wilhite	.30
204	Peter Shorts	.15
205	Willie Fears	.30
206	Rod Harris	.75
207	Terry Wright	.15
208	Stephen Bates	.30
209	John Hood	.30
210	Steven McKee	.15
211	Richard Nurse	.30
212	Lee Knight	.15
213	Joey Jauch	.30
214	Dave Richardson	.15
215	Paul Bushey	.15
216	Lou Cafazzo	.15
217	Don Odegard	.15
218	Mark Ledbetter	.15
219	Curtis Moore	.15
220	CFL Team Helmets (Set number card)	.30
221	Patrick Burke	.30
222	Dean Noel	.60
223	Leonard Johnson	.30
224	Darren Joseph	.60
225	Adam Rita (CO)	.60
226	Fred Ward	.60
227	Tony Bailey	.30
228	Frank Marof	.30
229	Andrew Thomas	.60
230	Peter Tuipulotu	.60
231	Shawn Beals	.30
232	Ken Watson	.30
233	Robert Holland	.30
234	John Terry	.30
235	Michael Philbrick	.30
236	Reggie Slack	1.25
237	Gary Wilkerson (UER) (First name misspelled Garry on bac k)	.30
238	Brett Young	.30
239	Eric Carter	.60
240	Sheldon Canley	.60
241	Lester Smith	.30
242	Donald Igwebuike	.60
243	Keith Ballard	.30
244	Roger Reinson	.30
245	Dwayne Dmytryshyn	.30
246	Marvin Coleman	.30
247	Ken Burress	.30
248	Jearld Baylis	.75
249	Rickey Foggie	.75
250	Dave Dinnall	.60
251	Darrell Harle	.30
252	Peter Martin	.60
253	Val St. Germain	.30
254	Tim Cofield	.75
255	Charles Gordon	.30
256	Keilly Rush	.30
257	James Pruitt	.60
258	Brian McCurdy	.60
259	Joe Johnson (UER) (Front says last name is Jackson)	.60
260	Joe Burgos	.30
261	Tim Jackson	.30
262	George Nimako	.60
263	Hency Charles	.30
264	Eric Drage	.60
265	Joe Sardo	.30
266	Norm Casola	.30
267	Dave Irwin	.60
268	Tommy Henry	.30
269	Taly Williams	.30
270	Swift Burch III	.30
271	Keita Crespina	.30
272	Michael Brooks	.60
273	Chris Armstrong	.30
274	Karl Anthony	.30
275	David Archer	3.00
276	Kevin Robson	.30
277	Jamie Holland	.60
278	Don Smith	.30
279	Norris Thomas	.60
280	Matt Dunigan	1.50
281	Greg Clarke	.30
282	Del Lyles	.30
283	Alan Wetmore	.30
284	Errol Brown	.30
285	Ryan Carey	.30
286	Rob Davidson	.30
287	Ed Kucy	.30
288	Tom Burgess	1.00
289	Peter Miller	.30
290	Dale Joseph	.30
291	Chris Burns	.30
292	Nathaniel Bolton	.60
293	Byron Williams	.15
294	David Harper	.30
295	Jason Wallace	.30
296	Greg Joelson	.15
297	Doug Parrish	.30
298	Sean Fleming	.30
299	Mike Lee	.60
300	Chris Morris	.60
301	Eddie Brown	.60
302	Blake Dermott	.30
303	Brian Walling	.60
304	Charles Miles	.60
305	Rob Crifo	.60
306	Nick Benjamin	.60
307	Jim Speros (PR/OWN)	.60
308	Robert Presbury	.30
309	Mike Pringle	2.50
310	Jon Volpe	1.00

1994 JOGO CFL Hall of Fame C

		MT
Complete Set (25):		18.00
Common Player:		.75
C1	Leo Lewis	2.00
C2	Tom Brown	.75
C3	Samuel Berger	.75
C4	David Fennell	1.25
C5	Arthur Chipman	.75
C6	Tony Gabriel	1.25
C7	Frank Clair	.75
C8	Dean Griffing	.75
C9	Hec Crighton	.75
C10	Eddie James	.75
C11	Andrew Currie	.75
C12	Ab Box	.75
C13	Gord Perry	.75
C14	Terry Evanshen	2.00
C15	Syd Halter	.75
C16	Don Luzzi	1.25
C17	Norm Kimball	.75
C18	Percival Molson	.75
C19	Bob Kramer	.75
C20	Angelo Mosca	2.50
C21	Ralph Cooper	.75
C22	Ken Charlton	.75
C23	Jim Young	1.25
C24	Joe Tubman	.75
C25	Virgil Wagner	1.25

1994 JOGO CFL Hall of Fame D

		MT
Complete Set (25):		18.00
Common Player:		.75
D1	Teddy Morris	.75
D2	John Ferraro	.75
D3	Len Back	.75
D4	Harold Ballard	1.25
D5	Seppi DuMoulin	.75
D6	Herman Harrison	1.25
D7	William Foulds	.75
D8	Peter Dalla Riva	1.25
D9	John Metras	.75
D10	Don Sutherin	1.25
D11	Ken Preston	.75
D12	Ellison Kelly	1.25
D13	Annis Stukus	.75
D14	Brian Timmis	.75
D15	Ralph Sazio	.75

D16	Hugh Stirling	.75
D17	Jimmie Simpson	.75
D18	Russ Rebholz	.75
D19	Seymour Wilson	.75
D20	Paul Rowe	.75
D21	Jeff Russel	.75
D22	Art Stevenson	.75
D23	Whit Tucker	1.25
D24	Dave Thelen	1.25
D25	Tom Wilkinson	2.00

1994 JOGO CFL Hall of Fame Inductees

		MT
	Complete Set (5):	5.00
	Common Player:	.75
1	Bill Baker	1.00
2	Tom Clements	2.50
3	Gene Gaines	1.00
4	Don McNaughton	.75
5	Title Card	.75

1994 JOGO CFL Missing Years

		MT
	Complete Set (20):	12.00
	Common Player:	.50
C1	Steve Ferrughelli (UER) (Photo actually John O'Leary)	1.50
C2	Rhome Nixon	.75
C3	Don Moorhead	.75
C4	Mike Widger	.75
C5	Pete Catan	.75
C6	Ron Meeks	.50
C7	Ezzret Anderson	1.25
C8	Bill Hatanaka	.50
C9	Joe Jackson	.75
C10	Tom Campana	.75
C11	Vernon Perry	1.00
C12	Ian Mofford	.75
C13	Walter Highsmith	.75
C14	Jake Dunlop	.75
C15	Bill Stevenson	.50
C16	Pete Lavorato	.50
C17	Cyril McFall	.50
C18	Maurice Butler	.50
C19	Tom Pate	1.25
C20	Eugene Clark	1.25

1995 JOGO CFL

		MT
	Complete Set (399):	145.00
	Complete Series 1 (110):	40.00
	Complete Series 2 (110):	40.00
	Complete Series 3 (110):	40.00
	Complete Update Set (69):	25.00
	Common Player:	.20
1	Doug Flutie	3.00
2	Lubo Zizakovic	.20
3	Srecko Zizakovic	.20
4	Greg Knox	.20
5	Kenny Walker	.35
6	Raymond Biggs	.20
7	Stu Laird	.35
8	Jeff Garcia	10.00
9	Alfred Jordan	.35
10	Tracy Gravely	.35
11	Tracy Ham	.75
12	O.J. Brigance	.75
13	Mike Pringle	1.50
14	Nick Subis	.20
15	Irvin Smith	.20
16	Shar Pourdanesh	.35
17	Lester Smith	.20
18	Josh Miller	.20
19	Jamie Taras	.20
20	Darren Flutie	1.00
21	Danny McManus	.75
22	Spencer McLennan	.20
23	Tony Collier	.20
24	Cory Philpot	1.00
25	Ian Sinclair	.35
26	Dave Chaytors	.20
27	Dave Ritchie (UER) (Richie on front)	.20
28	Rob Wallow	.20
29	Brad Breedlove	.50
30	Adrian Smith	.20
31	Stephen Bates	.20
32	Don Odegard	.20
33	Eric Nelson	.20
34	Danton Barto	.20
35	Donald Smith	.20
36	Gary Morris	.20
37	Mike Jovanovich	.20
38	Danny Barrett	.20
39	Ray Alexander	.35
40	John Kropke	.35
41	Remi Trudel	.20
42	Ray Bernard	.20
43	Pat Mahon	.20
44	Dan Murphy	.20
45	Stefen Reid	.20
46	Marcus Gates	.20
47	Tom Gerhard	.20
48	Mike Kiselak	.20
49	David Archer	2.00
50	Tommie Smith	.20
51	Roman Anderson	.20
52	Tony Burse	.20
53	Todd Jordan	.20
54	Peter Shorts	.20
55	Jimmy Klingler	.75
56	Mark Ledbetter	.20
57	Thomas Rayam	.20
58	Andre Strode	.20
59	Eddie Davis	.20
60	Jimmie Reed	.20
61	Fernando Thomas	.20
62	Craig Gibson	.20
63	Akaba Delaney	.20
64	Mike Clemons	1.25
65	Kent Austin	.75
66	Joe Burgos	.20
67	John Terry	.20
68	Don Wilson	.20
69	Eric Blount (DE)	.20
70	Reggie Barnes	.35
71	Darrick Branch	.20
72	P.J. Gleason	.20
73	Rod Connop	.20
74	J.P. Izquierdo	.20
75	Jed Roberts	.20
76	Jim Sandusky	.35
77	Chris Vargas	.20
78	Henry Williams	.75
79	Michael Soles	.35
80	Robert Holland	.20
81	Larry Wruck	.35
82	Dale Sanderson	.20
83	Anthony Calvillo	.75
84	Kalin Hall	.20
85	Sam Rogers	.20
86	Lee Knight	.20
87	Wally Zatylny	.35
88	Earl Winfield	.35
89	Dave Richardson	.20
90	Mike O'Shea	.75
91	Bruce Boyko	.20
92	Dave Ridgway	.35
93	Dave Van Belleghem	.20
94	Mike Anderson	.20
95	Ray Elgaard	.35
96	Dan Rashovich	.20
97	Wayne Drinkwalter	.20
98	Brent Matich	.20
99	Joe Fuller	.20
100	Freeman Baysinger	.20
101	Billy Joe Tolliver	.75
102	Martin Patton	.20
103	Wayne Walker	.35
104	Bjorn Nittmo	.75
105	Alan Wetmore	.20
106	K.D. Williams	.20
107	Bob Cameron	.75
108	Ken Burress	.20
109	Chris Johnstone	.20
110	Allan Boyko	.20
111	David Sapunjis	1.25
112	Matt Finlay	.35
113	Jamie Crysdale	.20
114	Marvin Pope	.20
115	Craig Brenner	.20
116	Vince Danielsen	.20
117	Will Johnson	.35
118	Tony Stewart	.20
119	Chris Wright	.50
120	Grant Carter	.20
121	Karl Anthony	.20
122	Elfrid Payton	.35
123	Ken Watson	.20
124	Cory Mantyka	.20
125	Todd Furdyk	.20
126	Keithen McCant	.20
127	Ryan Hanson	.20
128	Glen Scrivner	.20
129	Mike Trevathan	.35
130	Tom Europe	.20
131	Giulio Caravatta	.20
132	Eddie Thomas	.20
133	Shelton Quarles	.20
134	Robert E. Davis II	.20
135	Damon Allen	.35
136	Derek Brown	.20
137	Joe Horn	.50
138	John Tweet Martin	.20
139	Greg Battle	.35
140	Ed Berry	.20
141	Irv Daymond	.20
142	Jay Christensen	.35
143	Michael Richardson	.50
144	James Ellingson	.20
145	Brett Young	.35
146	Kai Bjorn	.20
147	James Monroe	.20
148	Eric Geter	.20
149	Emanuel Martin	.20
150	DeWayne Knight	.20
151	Mike Saunders	1.00
152	David Harper	.20
153	Bobby Humphrey	.35
154	Charles Franks	.20
155	Jeffrey Sawyer	.20
156	John Buddenberg	.20
157	Willie Fears	.35
158	Jason Wallace	.20
159	Robert Gordon	.20
160	Scott Player	.35
161	York Kurinsky	.20
162	Stephen Anderson	.20
163	Shonte Peoples	.20
164	Angelo Snipes	.50
165	Ted Long	.20
166	Anthony Drawhorn	.35
167	Marvin Graves	.20
168	Joe Sardo	.20
169	Duane Forde	.20
170	P.J. Martin	.20
171	Jock Climie	.20
172	Jeff Fairholm	.35
173	Tommy Henry	.20
174	Paul Masotti	.35
175	Chris Green	.20
176	Bruce Dickson	.20
177	Darian Hagan	.20
178	Malvin Hunter	.20
179	Steve Krupey	.20
180	Sean Fleming	.20
181	Blake Dermott	.35
182	Leroy Blugh	.20
183	Steve Taylor	.50
184	Eric Carter	.35
185	Jessie Small	.35
186	Blaine Schmidt	.20
187	Lou Cafazzo	.20
188	Doug Davies	.20
189	Kelvin Means	.20
190	Derek R. Grier	.20
191	Darren Joseph	.35
192	Aaron Ruffin	.20
193	Dan Farthing	.20
194	Dan Payne	.20
195	Brooks Findlay	.20
196	Paul Vajda	.20
197	Ron Goetz	.20
198	Tim Broady	.20
199	Terryl Ulmer	.20
200	Harold Nash Jr.	.35
201	Mike Stowell	.35
202	Ben Williams	.35
203	Curtis Mayfield	.35
204	Reggie Rogers	.35
205	Donnell Johnson	.20
206	Jon Heidenreich	.20
207	Ronald Perry	.20
208	Robbie Keen	.20
209	Alex Mash Jr.	.20
210	Jason Mallett	.20
211	Miles Gorrell	.20
212	Juran Bolden	.75
213	Greg Clark	.20
214	Ryan Carey	.20
215	Del Lyles	.20
216	Brendan Rogers	.20
217	Kevin Robson	.20
218	Paul Randolph	.20
219	Shannon Garrett	.20
220	Charlie Clemons	.20
221	Matt Dunigan	1.50
222	Jay McNeil	.20
223	Denny Chronopoulos	.20
224	Bobby Pandelidis	.20
225	Bruce Beaton	.20
226	Mark Pearce	.20
227	Rocco Romano	.20
228	Alondra Johnson	.35
229	Tony Martino	.20
230	John James	.20
231	Courtney Griffin	.20
232	Robert Davis	.20
233	Manny Hazard	.35
234	Joe Mero	.20
235	Maurice Kelly	.35
236	Michael Morreale	.20
237	Reggie Slack	.50
238	Greg Eaglin	.20
239	Noah Cantor	.20
240	Shawn Daniels	.20
241	Charles Gordon	.20
242	Enis Jackson	.20
243	Matt Clark	.35
244	Dave Lucas	.20
245	Roger Hennig	.20
246	Leonard Nelson	.20
247	George Bethune	.20
248	Maurice Miller	.20
249	Kenny Walker	.35
250	Andre Ware	1.00
251	Jay Macias	.20
252	Mark Ricks	.20
253	Chris Tsangaris	.20
254	Wayne Lammie	.20
255	Derek MacCready	.20
256	Paul Yatkowski	.20
257	Horace Brooks	.20
258	Kerry Brown	.20
259	Jude St. John	.20
260	Mike Schad	1.00
261	Malcolm Frank	.20
262	Kenny Wilhite	.35
263	Bill Hess	.20
264	Grady Cavness	.35
265	Roosevelt Collins Jr.	.20
266	Darren Muilenberg	.20
267	Kitrick Taylor	.75
268	Chuck Esty	.20
269	Myron M. Wise	.20
270	James King	.20
271	Jim Kemp	1.00
272	Oscar Giles	.35
273	Dave Ritchie (CO)	.20
274	Joe Kralik	.20
275	Troy Mills	.20
276	Mark Stock	.20
277	Pierre Vercheval	.35
278	Terry Baker	.35
279	Scott Douglas	.20
280	Leon Hatziioannou	.20
281	Jeff Cummins	.20
282	Allen Pitts	.50
283	Ken Walcott	.20
284	Swift Burch III	.20
285	Charles Davis	.20
286	Leo Groenewegen	.20
287	Bennie Goods	.35
288	Craig Hendrickson	.20
289	John Kalin	.20
290	Trent Brown	.20
291	Marc Tobert	.20
292	Nick Mazzoli	.20
293	Singor Mobley	.20
294	Dondre Owens	.20
295	Kerwin Bell	.75
296	Mike Kerrigan	.50
297	Hassan Bailey	.20
298	Frank Marof	.20
299	Derrick McAdoo	.35
300	Brian McCurdy	.35
301	Larry Thompson	.50
302	Errol Brown	.20
303	Troy Alexander	.20
304	Dave Pitcher	.20
305	Joey Jauch	.35
306	Gene Makowsky	.20
307	Ventson Donelson	.20
308	Gary Rogers	.20
309	Carl Coulter	.20
310	Chris Gioskos	.20
311	Mike DuMaresq	.20
312	Rob Crifo	.20
313	Terry Smith	.20
314	Don Robinson	.20
315	Uzooma Okeke	.20
316	Eldonta Osborne	.20
317	Rob Hitchcock	.20
318	Ray Savage Jr.	.20
319	Terry Beauford	.20
320	Cliff Baskerville	.20
321	David Gamble	.20
322	Darrius Watson	.20
323	Tim Daniel	.20
324	Len Johnson	.20
325	Blaise Bryant	.35
326	Doug Hocking	.20
327	Sean Graham	.20
328	Jamie Holland	.35
329	Matt Pearce	.20
330	Doug Flutie (C.F.L. MVP)	2.00
331	Donald Narcisse	.50
332	Chuck Reed	.20
333	Sheldon Benoit	.20
334	John Motton	.35
335	Franco Grilla	.20
336	Brett MacNeil	.20
337	Wade Miller	.20
338	Steven McKee	.20
339	Brad Elberg	.20
340	Greg Patrick	.20
341	Andrew Grigg	.20
342	Kevin McDougal	.20
343	Prince Wimbley III	.20
344	Sam Hairston	.20
345	Curtis Gordon	.35
346	Chris Keneally	.20
347	Michael Philbrick	.20
348	Keith Embray	.20
349	Steve Grant	.20
350	Taly Williams	.20
351	Garry Sawatzky	.20
352	Dean Noel	.35
353	Mike Armstrong	.20
354	David Pool	.20
355	Tyrone Edwards	.20
356	Tim Cofield	1.00
357	Gerald Vaughn	.20
358	Mark McLoughlin	.20
359	Robert Dougherty	.20
360	Norm Casola	.20
361	Shawn Knight	.20
362	Kelvin Means	.20
363	Reggie Pleasant	.35
364	Jim Smyrl	.20
365	Fred Montgomery	.20
366	Ron Perry	.20
367	Jami Anderson	.20
368	Jeff Reinebold	.20
369	Steve Brannon	.20
370	Jimmy Cunningham	.50
371	Damion Lyons	.20
372	John Tweet Martin	.20
373	Mike Campbell	.20
374	Jonathan Wilson	.20
375	Sandy Annunziata	.20
376	Brian Walling	.35
377	Eric Blount (RB)	.50
378	Tom Gerhart	.50
379	Milt Stegall	.20
380	Bob Kronenberg	.20
381	Barry Rose	.20
382	Tim Walton	.20
383	Kelvin Harris	.35
384	Dwayne Provo	.50
385	Jayson Dzikowicz	.20
386	Melendez Byrd	.20
387	Val St. Germain	.20
388	Dave Vankoughnett	.20
389	Aaron Kanner	.20
390	Nicky Richards	.20
391	Rohan Marley	.50
392	Chris Burns	.20
393	Joe Fuller	.20
394	Donovan Gans	.20
395	Jermaine Chaney	.20
396	Jackie Kellogg	.20
397	Ray Savage Jr.	.20
398	Oscar Giles	.35
399	Jeff Neal	.20

1995 JOGO CFL Athletes in Action

		MT
	Complete Set (21):	10.00
	Common Player:	.40
1	Kelly Sims	.60
2	Craig Hendrickson	.40
3	Kerwin Bell	1.50
4	Glenn Harper	.40
5	Jim Sandusky	.60
6	Eldonta Osborne	.40
7	Guy Earle	.40
8	Charles Anthony	.40
9	O.J. Brigance	1.50
10	Junior Thurman	.60
11	Erik White	.60
12	Henry Newby	.40
13	Darryl Sampson	.40
14	Tony Woods	.40
15	Sean Brantley	.40
16	Shalon Baker	.40
17	Greg Frers	.40
18	Danny Barrett	.60
19	John Earle	.40
20	Tracy Ham	2.00
21	Jimmy Klingler	1.00

1995 JOGO CFL Missing Years

		MT
	Complete Set (20):	12.00
	Common Player:	.50
1D	Jimmy Jones	.75
2D	Charlie Brandon	.50
3D	Erik Kramer (UER) (name spelled Krammer)	3.00
4D	Jeff Avery	.50
5D	Wally Buono	.50
6D	Mike Strickland	.75
7D	Bob Toogood	.75
8D	Joe Hernandez	.50
9D	Doug Battershill	.50
10D	Al Brenner	.50
11D	Tim Anderson	.50
12D	Ted Provost	.50
13D	Eugene Goodlow	.75
14D	Rudy Flurio	.50
15D	Joey Walters	.75
16D	Bob Viccars	.50
17D	Tyrone Walls	.75
18D	John Harvey	.75
19D	Dick Aldridge	.50
20D	Grady Cavness	.75

1996 JOGO CFL

This 220-card set features players from the Canadian Football League.

		MT
	Complete Set (220):	50.00
	Common Player:	.20
1	Jeff Garcia	.50
2	Jeff Cummins	.50
3	Terry Baker	.35
4	James Taras	.20
5	Eric Blount RB	.50
6	Dan Rashovich	.20
7	Dale Sanderson	.20
8	Paul Masotti	.35
9	Giulio Caravatta	.20
10	Stefen Reid	.20
11	Lee Knight	.20
12	Dave Vankoughnett	.20
13	Stu Laird	.35
14	Todd Storme	.20
15	Glenn Rogers Jr.	.20
16	Miles Gorrell	.20
17	Mike Kiselak	.20
18	Mike Trevathan	.50
19	Troy Westwood	.20
20	Michael Jovanovich	.20
21	Alan Wetmore	.20
22	Bruce Covernton	.35
23	Ryan Carey	.20
24	Larry Wruck	.35
25	Lou Cafazzo	.20
26	Mac Cody	1.00
27	Todd Furdyk	.20
28	Shannon Garrett	.20
29	Kenny Wilhite	.35
30	Bruce Beaton	.20
31	Tony Martino	.20
32	Brooks Findlay	.20
33	Matt Dunigan	1.00
34	Ed Kucy	.20
35	Mike Clemons	1.00
36	Cory Philpot	1.00
37	Steve Taylor	.50
38	Jackie Kellogg	.20
39	Spencer McLennan	.20
40	Jason Mallett	.20
41	Robert Mimbs	.75
42	Doug Davies	.20
43	Malvin Hunter	.20
44	Wayne Lammie	.20
45	David Maeva	.20
46	Jay McNeil	.20
47	Ed Berry	.20
48	Irvin Smith	.20
49	Wade Miller	.20
50	Dan Farthing	.20
51	Tom Gerhart	.20
52	Ray Bernard	.20
53	Jude St. John	.20
54	Terry Vaughn	.20
55	Shelton Quarles	.20
56	Kelvin Anderson	1.50
57	Mike Withycombe	.20
58	Sean Graham	.20
59	Errol Brown	.20
60	Swift Burch III	.20
61	Jed Roberts	.20
62	Ted Long	.20
63	Mike Morreale	.20
64	Tyrone Chatman	.20
65	Anthony McClanahan	.20
66	David Pitcher	.20
67	Shannon Baker	.20
68	Fred Childress	.20
69	John Terry	.20
70	Chris Morris	.50
71	Andrew Grigg	.20
72	Reggie Givens	.50
73	Cory Mantyka	.20
74	Alfred Jordan	.35
75	Harold Nash Jr.	.20
76	Brett MacNeil	.20
77	Brent Matich	.20
78	Gerry Collins	.20
79	Johnson Joseph	.20
80	Jimmy Cunningham	.50
81	Eddie Davis	.20
82	Tom Europe	.20
83	Darryl Hall	.35
84	Tracy Gravely	.20
85	Bob Cameron	.50
86	Paul McCallum	.20
87	Tyrone Williams	.20
88	Maurice Kelly	.35
89	Sammie Brennan	.20
90	Ken Benson	.20
91	Sean Millington	.20
92	Greg Knox	.20
93	Kevin Robson	.20
94	Rod Harris	.50
95	Charles Gordon	.20
96	Donald Smith	.20
97	Joe Mero	.20
98	Reggie Slack	.50
99	Garry Sawatzky	.20
100	Adrion Smith	.20
101	Allan Boyko	.20
102	Scott Hendrickson	.20
103	Eddie Britton	.20
104	Will Johnson	.50
105	John Raposo	.20
106	Chris Tsangaris	.20
107	Cooper Harris	.20
108	Quinn Magnuson	.20
109	Blaine Schmidt	.20
110	David Archer	2.00
111	David Sapunjis	.75
112	Stephen Anderson	.20
113	Raymond Biggs	.20
114	Jean-Agnes Charles	.20
115	Vince Danielsen	.20
116	Wayne Drinkwalter	.35
117	Farell Duclair	.20
118	Duane Forde	.20
119	Rohn Meyer	.20
120	Travis Moore	.20
121	Kevin Reid	.20
122	Roger Reinson	.20
123	Gonzalo Floyd	.20
124	Dwayne Provo	.20
125	Peter Tuipulotu	.20
126	Curtis Mayfield	.35
127	Ray Elgaard	.50
128	John James	.20
129	Dave Van Belleghem	.20
130	J.P. Izquierdo	.20
131	Darren Joseph	.35
132	Frank Jagas	.20
133	Heath Rylance	.20
134	Rick Walters	.20
135	Michael Philbrick	.20
136	Val St. Germain	.20
137	Justin Ring	.20
138	Mike Campbell	.20
139	Burt Thornton	.20
140	Jason Kaiser	.20
141	Tim Brown	.20
142	Ken Watson	.20
143	Tommie Frasier	2.50
144	Tyrone Rodgers	.20
145	Craig Hendrickson	.20
146	Johnny R. Scott	.20
147	Mark Pimiskern	.20
148	Frank Pimiskern	.20
149	Carl Coulter	.20
150	Reggie Carthon	.20
151	Ronald Williams	.20
152	Ted Alford	.20
153	Dave Chaytors	.20
154	Robert Gordon	.20
155	Jayson Dzikowicz	.20
156	Lubo Zizakovic	.20
157	Mike Hendricks	.20
158	Obie Spanic	.20
159	Andre Bolduc	.20
160	Robert Drummond	.50
161	Chuck Esty	.20
162	Tommy Henry	.20
163	Nick Richards	.20
164	Profail Grier	.20
165	Melvin Aldridge	.20
166	Uzooma Okeke	.20
167	Courtney Griffin	.20
168	Leonard Humphries	.20
169	Jason Wallace	.20
170	Derek MacCready	.20
171	Franky West	.20
172	Kelvin Means	.20
173	David Harper	.20
174	Rob Stevenson	.20
175	John Kalin	.20
176	Nigel Williams	.20
177	Chris Armstrong	.50
178	Douglas Craft	.50
179	Michael Soles	.35
180	Mike Saunders	1.00
181	Michel Lamy	.20
182	Jock Climie	.50
183	Grant Carter	.20
184	Hency Charles	.20
185	Jason Bryant	.20
186	Dexter Dawson	.20
187	Glen Scrivener	.20
188	K.D. Williams	.20
189	Dean Lytle	.20
190	Donovan Wright	.20
191	Andrew Henry	.20
192	Doug Flutie	3.50
193	Brendan Rogers	.20
194	Darian Hagan	.20
195	Jeff Fairholm	.35
196	Marcello Simmons	.20
197	Oscar Giles	.35
198	Chris Gioskos	.20
199	Dan Murphy	.20
200	Norm Casola	.20
201	Vic Stevenson	.20
202	Duane Dmytryshyn	.20
203	Christopher Perez	.20
204	Noah Cantor	.20
205	Mike Vanderjagt	.20
206	George Nimako	.35
207	Andrew Stewart	.20
208	Pierre Vercheval	.35
209	Chris Green	.20
210	Maurice Miller	.20
211	Leroy Blugh	.35
212	Jim Sandusky	.35
213	Thomas Rayam	.20
214	Cody Ledbetter	.20
215	Michael Sellers	.20
216	Reggie Pleasant	.50
217	Errol Martin	.20
218	Trent Brown	.20
219	Bruce Dickson	.20
220	Dan Payne	.20

1989 KFC Calgary

		MT
	Complete Set (24):	10.00
	Common Player:	.40
3	David McCrary	.40
4	Brent Matich	.40
8	Danny Barrett	1.50
9	Terrence Jones	1.25
12	Tim Petros	.60
13	Mark McLoughlin	.40
15	Ron Hopkins	.60
20	Chris Major	1.25
24	Greg Peterson	.40
25	Shawn Faulkner	.40
32	Darcy Kopp	.40
34	Andy McVey	.40
39	Doug (Tank) Landry	1.00
59	Leo Blanchard	.40
61	Tom Spoletini	.40
65	Mike Palumbo	.40
66	Dan Ferrone	.60
74	Mitchell Price	.60
76	Marshall Toner	.40
84	Eugene Belliveau	.60
85	Brock Smith	.40
89	Larry Willis	.75
93	Kent Warnock	.75
97	Ken Ford	.40

1990 KFC Calgary

		MT
	Complete Set (24):	10.00
	Common Player:	.50
1	Walter Ballard	.50
2	Danny Barrett	1.50
3	Eddie Brown	.75
4	Joe Clausi	.50
5	Lloyd Fairbanks	.75
6	Matt Finlay	.75
7	Ken Ford	.50
8	Ron Hopkins	.75
9	Keyvan Jenkins	1.25
10	Will Johnson	.75
11	Terrence Jones	1.25
12	David McCrary	.50
13	Mark McLoughlin	.50
14	Andy McVey	.50
15	Brent Matich	.50
16	Mike Palumbo	.50
17	Greg Peterson	.50
18	Tim Petros	.75
19	Mitchell Price	.75
20	Brock Smith	.50
21	Tom Spoletini	.50
22	Junior Thurman	1.25
23	Marshall Toner	.50
24	Kent Warnock	.75

1984 McDonald's Ottawa

		MT
	Complete Set (4):	10.00
	Common Player:	2.00
1	Ken Miller, Rudy Phillips, Jim Reid	2.00
2	Gary Dulin, Greg Marshall, Junior Robinson	2.00
3	Kevin Powell, Tyron Gray, Skip Walker	2.00
4	Rick Sowieta, Bruce Walker, J.C. Watts	5.00

1983 Mohawk B.C. Lions

		MT
	Complete Set (24):	18.00
	Common Player:	.60
1	John Blain	.60
2	Tim Cowan	.60
3	Larry Crawford	1.00
4	Tyrone Crews	.60

5 James Curry 1.00
6 Roy Dewalt 1.50
7 Mervyn Fernandez 3.00
8 Sammy Greene .60
9 Jo Jo Heath .60
10 Nick Hebeler .60
11 Glen Jackson .60
12 Tim Kearse .60
13 Rick Klassen 1.00
14 Kevin Konar 1.00
15 Glenn Leonhard .60
16 Nelson Martin .60
17 Mack Moore .60
18 John Pankratz .60
19 Joe Paopao 1.25
20 Lui Passaglia 2.00
21 Don Taylor .60
22 Mike Washburn .60
23 John Henry White .60
24 Al Wilson .60

1984 Mohawk B.C. Lions

MT
Complete Set (32): 18.00
Common Player: .50
1 Ned Armour .50
2 John Blain .50
3 Melvin Byrd .75
4 Darnell Clash 1.00
5 Tim Cowan .50
6 Larry Crawford .75
7 Tyrone Crews .50
8 Roy DeWalt 1.50
9 Mervyn Fernandez 3.00
10 Bernie Glier .50
11 Dennis Guevin .50
12 Nick Hebeler .50
13 Bryan Illerbrun .50
14 Glen Jackson .50
15 Andre Jones .50
16 Rick Klassen .75
17 Kevin Konar .75
18 Glenn Leonhard .50
19 Nelson Martin .50
20 Billy McBride .50
21 Mack Moore .50
22 John Pankratz .50
23 James Parker 1.25
24 Lui Passaglia 1.50
25 Ryan Potter .50
26 Gerald Roper .50
27 Jim Sandusky 2.00
28 Don Taylor .50
29 John Henry White .50
30 Al Wilson .50
31 Team Card .75
32 Checklist .75

1985 Mohawk B.C. Lions

MT
Complete Set (32): 18.00
Common Player: .50
1 John Blain .50
2 Jamie Buis .50
3 Melvin Byrd .75
4 Darnell Clash 1.00
5 Tim Cowan .75
6 Tyrone Crews .50
7 Mark DeBrueys .50
8 Roy Dewalt 1.50
9 Mervyn Fernandez 3.00
10 Bernie Glier .50
11 Keith Gooch .50
12 Dennis Guevin .50
13 Nick Hebeler .50
14 Bryan Illerbrun .50
15 Glen Jackson .50
16 Keyvan Jenkins 1.00
17 Andre Jones .50
18 Rick Klassen .75
19 Kevin Konar .75
20 Glenn Leonhard .50
21 Nelson Martin .50
22 John Pankratz .50
23 James Parker 1.25
24 Lui Passaglia 1.50
25 Ryan Potter .50
26 Ron Robinson .75
27 Gerald Roper .50
28 Jim Sandusky 2.00
29 John Henry White .50
30 Al Wilson .50
31 Team Photo .75
32 Checklist .75

1963 Nalley's Coins

NM
Complete Set (160): 2750.
Common Player: 4.00
1 Jackie Parker 20.00
2 Dick Shatto 8.00
3 Dave Mann 5.00
4 Danny Nykoluk 4.00
5 Billy Shipp 4.00
6 Doug McNichol 4.00
7 Jim Rountree 4.00
8 Art Johnson 4.00
9 Walt Radzick 4.00
10 Jim Andreotti 4.00
11 Gerry Philip 20.00
12 Lynn Bottoms 20.00
13 Ron Morris (SP) 100.00
14 Nobby Wirkowski (CO) 20.00
15 John Wydareny 20.00
16 Gerry Wilson 20.00
17 Gerry Patrick (SP) 50.00
18 Aubrey Linne 20.00
19 Norm Stoneburgh 20.00
20 Ken Beck 20.00
21 Russ Jackson 15.00
22 Kaye Vaughan 8.00
23 Dave Thelen 8.00
24 Ron Stewart 8.00
25 Moe Racine 4.00
26 Jim Conroy 4.00
27 Joe Poirier 4.00
28 Mel Seminko 4.00
29 Whit Tucker 8.00
30 Ernie White 4.00
31 Frank Clair (CO) 20.00
32 Marv Bevan 20.00
33 Jerry Selinger 20.00
34 Jim Cain 20.00
35 Mike Snodgrass 20.00
36 Ted Smale 20.00
37 Billy Joe Booth 20.00
38 Len Chandler 20.00
39 Rick Black 20.00
40 Allen Schau 20.00
41 Bernie Faloney 15.00
42 Bobby Kuntz 4.00
43 Joe Zuger 4.00
44 Hal Patterson 12.00
45 Bronko Nagurski 10.00
46 Zeno Karcz 4.00
47 Hardiman Cureton 4.00
48 John Barrow 8.00
49 Tommy Grant 8.00
50 Garney Henley 8.00
51 Dick Easterly 20.00
52 Frank Cosentino 20.00
53 Geno DeNobile 20.00
54 Ralph Goldston 20.00
55 Chet Miksza 20.00
56 Bob Minihane 20.00
57 Don Sutherin 40.00
58 Ralph Sazio (CO) 20.00
59 Dave Viti (SP) 35.00
60 Angelo Mosca (SP) 100.00
61 Sandy Stephens 8.00
62 George Dixon 8.00
63 Don Clark 4.00
64 Don Paquette 4.00
65 Billy Wayte 4.00
66 Ed Nickla 4.00
67 Marv Luster 8.00
68 Joe Stracina 4.00
69 Bobby Jack Oliver 4.00
70 Ted Elsby 4.00
71 Jim Trimble (CO) 20.00
72 Bob Leblanc 20.00
73 Dick Schnell 20.00
74 Milt Crain 20.00
75 Dick Dalatri 20.00
76 Billy Roy 20.00
77 Dave Hoppmann 20.00
78 Billy Ray Locklin 20.00
79 Ed Learn (SP) 125.00
80 Meco Poliziani (SP) 40.00
81 Leo Lewis 8.00
82 Kenny Ploen 8.00
83 Steve Patrick 4.00
84 Farrell Funston 4.00
85 Charlie Shepard 4.00
86 Ronnie Latourelle 4.00
87 Gord Rowland 4.00
88 Frank Rigney 5.00
89 Cornel Piper 4.00
90 Ernie Pitts 4.00
91 Roger Hagberg 30.00
92 Herb Gray 50.00
93 Jack Delveaux 20.00
94 Roger Savoie 20.00
95 Nick Miller 20.00
96 Norm Rauhaus 20.00
97 Cec Luining 20.00
98 Hal Ledyard 20.00
99 Neil Thomas 20.00
100 Bud Grant (CO) 75.00
101 Eagle Keys (CO) 8.00
102 Mike Wicklum 4.00
103 Bill Mitchell 4.00
104 Mike Lashuk 4.00
105 Tommy Joe Coffey 8.00
106 Zeke Smith 4.00
107 Joe Hernandez 4.00
108 Johnny Bright 8.00
109 Don Getty 8.00
110 Nat Dye 4.00
111 James Earl Wright 20.00
112 Mike Volcan (SP) 35.00
113 Jon Rechner 20.00
114 Len Vella 20.00
115 Ted Frechette 20.00
116 Larry Fleisher 20.00
117 Oscar Kruger 20.00
118 Ken Peterson 20.00
119 Bobby Walden 20.00
120 Mickey Ording 20.00
121 Pete Manning 4.00
122 Harvey Wylie 4.00
123 Tony Pajaczkowski 8.00
124 Wayne Harris 10.00
125 Earl Lunsford 8.00
126 Don Luzzi 4.00
127 Ed Buckanan 4.00
128 Lovell Coleman 5.00
129 Hal Krebs 4.00
130 Eagle Day 8.00
131 Bobby Dobbs (CO) 20.00
132 George Hansen 20.00
133 Roy Jokanovich (SP) 75.00
134 Jerry Keeling 30.00
135 Larry Anderson 20.00
136 Bill Crawford 20.00
137 Ron Albright 20.00
138 Bill Britton 20.00
139 Jim Dillard 20.00
140 Jim Furlong 20.00
141 Dave Skrien (CO) 5.00
142 Willie Fleming 10.00
143 Nub Beamer 4.00
144 Norm Fieldgate 8.00
145 Joe Kapp 35.00
146 Tom Hinton 8.00
147 Pat Claridge 4.00
148 Bill Munsey 4.00
149 Mike Martin 4.00
150 Tom Brown 8.00
151 Ian Hagemoen 20.00
152 Jim Carphin 20.00
153 By Bailey 40.00
154 Steve Cotter 20.00
155 Mike Cacic 20.00
156 Neil Beaumont 20.00
157 Lonnie Dennis 20.00
158 Barney Therrien 20.00
159 Sonny Homer 20.00
160 Walt Bilicki 20.00
S1 Toronto Shield 50.00
S2 Ottawa Shield 50.00
S3 Hamilton Shield 50.00
S4 Montreal Shield 50.00
S5 Winnipeg Shield 50.00
S6 Edmonton Shield 50.00
S7 Calgary Shield 50.00
S8 British Columbia Shield 50.00

1964 Nalley's Coins

NM
Complete Set (100): 720.00
Common Player: 4.00
1 Joe Kapp 30.00
2 Willie Fleming 10.00
3 Norm Fieldgate 8.00
4 Bill Murray 4.00
5 Tom Brown 10.00
6 Neil Beaumont 4.00
7 Sonny Homer 4.00
8 Lonnie Dennis 4.00
9 Dave Skrien 4.00
10 Dick Fouts (CO) 4.00
11 Paul Seale 4.00
12 Peter Kempf 4.00
13 Steve Shafer 4.00
14 Tom Hinton 8.00
15 Pat Claridge 4.00
16 By Bailey 8.00
17 Nub Beamer 5.00
18 Steve Cotter 4.00
19 Mike Cacic 4.00
20 Mike Martin 4.00
21 Eagle Day 12.00
22 Jim Dillard 4.00
23 Pete Murray 4.00
24 Tony Pajaczkowski 8.00
25 Don Luzzi 4.00
26 Wayne Harris 10.00
27 Harvey Wylie 4.00
28 Bill Crawford 4.00
29 Jim Furlong 4.00
30 Lovell Coleman 5.00
31 Pat Haines 4.00
32 Bob Taylor 4.00
33 Ernie Danjean 4.00
34 Jerry Keeling 8.00
35 Larry Robinson 4.00
36 George Hansen 4.00
37 Ron Albright 4.00
38 Larry Anderson 4.00
39 Bill Miller 4.00
40 Bill Britton 4.00
41 Lynn Amadee 8.00
42 Mike Lashuk 4.00
43 Tommy Joe Coffey 8.00
44 Junior Hawthorne 4.00
45 Nat Dye 4.00
46 Al Ecuyer 4.00
47 Howie Schumm 4.00
48 Zeke Smith 4.00
49 Mike Wicklum 4.00
50 Mike Volcan 4.00
51 E.A. Sims 4.00
52 Bill Mitchell 4.00
53 Ken Reed 4.00
54 Len Vella 4.00
55 Johnny Bright 8.00
56 Don Getty 8.00
57 Oscar Kruger 4.00
58 Ted Frechette 4.00
59 James Earl Wright 4.00
60 Roger Nelson 4.00
61 Ron Lancaster 10.00
62 Bill Clarke 4.00
63 Bob Shaw 4.00
64 Ray Purdin 4.00
65 Ron Atchison 8.00
66 Ted Urness 8.00
67 Bob Ptacek 4.00
68 Neil Habig 4.00
69 Garner Ekstran 4.00
70 Gene Wlasiuk 4.00
71 Jack Gotta 4.00
72 Dick Cohee 4.00
73 Ron Meadmore 4.00
74 Martin Fabi 4.00
75 Bob Good 4.00
76 Len Legault 4.00
77 Al Benecick 4.00
78 Dale West 4.00
79 Reg Whitehouse 4.00
80 George Reed 10.00
81 Kenny Ploen 8.00
82 Leo Lewis 10.00
83 Dick Thornton 5.00
84 Steve Patrick 4.00
85 Frank Rigney 5.00
86 Cornel Piper 4.00
87 Sherwyn Thorson 4.00
88 Ernie Pitts 4.00
89 Roger Hagberg 5.00
90 Bud Grant (CO) 50.00
91 Jack Delveaux 4.00
92 Farrell Funston 4.00
93 Ronnie Latourelle 4.00
94 Roger Hamelin 4.00
95 Gord Rowland 4.00
96 Herb Gray 10.00
97 Nick Miller 4.00
98 Norm Rauhaus 4.00
99 Bill Whisler 4.00
100 Hal Ledyard 4.00
S1 British Columbia Shield 45.00
S2 Calgary Shield 45.00
S3 Edmonton Shield 45.00
S4 Saskatchewan Shield 45.00
S5 Winnipeg Shield 45.00

1976 Nalley's Chips CFL

NM
Complete Set (30): 300.00
Common Player: 8.00
1 Bill Baker 20.00
2 Eric Guthrie 8.00
3 Lou Harris 10.00
4 Layne McDowell 8.00
5 Ray Nettles 8.00
6 Lui Passaglia 25.00
7 John Sciarra 15.00
8 Wayne Smith 8.00
9 Michael Strickland 8.00
10 Jim Young 20.00
11 Dave Cutler 15.00
12 Larry Highbaugh 12.00
13 John Koniszewski 8.00
14 Bruce Lemmerman 8.00
15 George McGowan 12.00
16 Dale Potter 8.00
17 Charlie Turner 8.00
18 Tyrone Walls 8.00
19 Don Warrington 8.00
20 Tom Wilkinson 25.00
21 Willie Burden 35.00
22 Larry Cates 8.00
23 Lloyd Fairbanks 12.00
24 Joe Forzani 8.00
25 Tom Forzani 8.00
26 Rick Galbos 8.00
27 John Helton 15.00
28 Harold Holton 8.00
29 Rudy Linterman 12.00
30 Joe Pisarcik 15.00

1968 O-Pee-Chee CFL

NM
Complete Set (132): 1100.
Common Player: 6.00
1 Roger Murphy 15.00
2 Charlie Parker 6.00
3 Mike Webster 6.00
4 Carroll Williams 6.00
5 Phil Brady 6.00
6 Dave Lewis 6.00
7 John Baker 6.00
8 Basil Bark 6.00
9 Donnie Davis 6.00
10 Pierre Desjardins 6.00
11 Larry Fairholm 6.00
12 Peter Paquette 6.00
13 Ray Lychak 6.00
14 Ted Collins 6.00
15 Margene Adkins 15.00
16 Ron Stewart 20.00
17 Russ Jackson 35.00
18 Bo Scott 15.00
19 Joe Poirier 6.00
20 Wayne Giardino 6.00
21 Gene Gaines 15.00
22 Billy Joe Booth 6.00
23 Whit Tucker 15.00
24 Rick Black 6.00
25 Ken Lehmann 12.00
26 Bob Brown 6.00
27 Moe Racine 6.00
28 Dick Thornton 8.00
29 Bob Taylor 6.00
30 Mel Profit 12.00
31 Dave Mann 8.00
32 Marv Luster 12.00
33 Ed Buchanan 6.00
34 Ed Harrington 8.00
35 Jim Dillard 6.00
36 Bob Taylor 6.00
37 Ron Arends 6.00
38 Mike Wadsworth 6.00
39 Wally Gabler 12.00
40 Pete Martin 6.00
41 Danny Nykoluk 6.00
42 Bill Frank 6.00
43 Gordon Christian 6.00
44 Tommy Joe Coffey 20.00
45 Ellison Kelly 20.00
46 Angelo Mosca 30.00
47 John Barrow 20.00
48 Bill Danychuk 12.00
49 Jon Hohman 6.00
50 Bill Redell 6.00
51 Joe Zuger 8.00
52 Willie Bethea 12.00
53 Dick Cohee 6.00
54 Tommy Grant 15.00
55 Garney Henley 20.00
56 Ted Page 6.00
57 Bob Krouse 6.00
58 Phil Minnick 6.00
59 Butch Pressley 6.00
60 Dave Raimey 8.00
61 Sherwyn Thorson 6.00
62 Bill Whisler 6.00
63 Roger Hamelin 6.00
64 Chuck Harrison 6.00
65 Ken Nielsen 12.00
66 Ernie Pitts 6.00
67 Mitch Zainasky 6.00
68 John Schneider 6.00
69 Ron Kirkland 6.00
70 Paul Desjardins 6.00
71 Luther Selbo 6.00
72 Don Gilbert 6.00
73 Bob Lueck 6.00
74 Gerry Shaw 6.00
75 Chuck Zickefoose 6.00
76 Frank Andruski 6.00
77 Lanny Boleski 6.00
78 Terry Evanshen 20.00
79 Jim Furlong 6.00
80 Wayne Harris 20.00
81 Jerry Keeling 15.00
82 Roger Kramer 8.00
83 Pete Liske 20.00
84 Dick Suderman 12.00
85 Granville Liggins 20.00
86 George Reed 30.00
87 Ron Lancaster 30.00
88 Alan Ford 6.00
89 Gordon Barwell 6.00
90 Wayne Shaw 6.00
91 Bruce Bennett 15.00
92 Henry Dorsch 6.00
93 Ken Reed 6.00
94 Ron Atchison 15.00
95 Clyde Brock 6.00
96 Alex Benecick 6.00
97 Ted Urness 12.00
98 Wally Dempsey 6.00
99 Don Gerhardt 6.00
100 Ted Dushinski 6.00
101 Ed McQuarters 12.00
102 Bob Kosid 6.00
103 Gary Brandt 6.00
104 John Wydareny 6.00
105 Jim Thomas 6.00
106 Art Perkins 6.00
107 Frank Cosentino 12.00
108 Earl Edwards 8.00
109 Garry Lefebvre 6.00
110 Greg Pipes 8.00
111 Ian MacLeod 6.00
112 Dick Dupuis 6.00
113 Ron Forwick 6.00
114 Jerry Griffin 6.00
115 John LaGrone 12.00
116 E.A. Sims 6.00
117 Greenard Poles 6.00
118 Leroy Sledge 6.00
119 Ken Sugarman 8.00
120 Jim Young 30.00
121 Garner Ekstran 12.00
122 Jim Evenson 12.00
123 Greg Findlay 6.00
124 Ted Gerela 8.00
125 Lach Heron 8.00
126 Mike Martin 6.00
127 Craig Murray 6.00
128 Pete Ohler 6.00
129 Sonny Homer 6.00
130 Bill Lasseter 6.00
131 John McDowell 6.00
132 Checklist Card 60.00

1968 O-Pee-Chee CFL Poster Inserts

NM
Complete Set (16): 325.00
Common Player: 15.00
1 Margene Adkins 20.00
2 Tommy Joe Coffey 25.00
3 Frank Cosentino 18.00
4 Terry Evanshen 25.00
5 Larry Fairholm 15.00
6 Wally Gabler 15.00
7 Russ Jackson 35.00
8 Ron Lancaster 30.00
9 Pete Liske 25.00
10 Dave Mann 18.00
11 Ken Nielsen 18.00
12 Dave Raimey 18.00
13 George Reed 30.00
14 Carroll Williams 15.00
15 Jim Young 30.00
16 Joe Zuger 15.00

1970 O-Pee-Chee CFL

NM
Complete Set (115): 300.00
Common Player: 2.00
1 Ed Harrington 5.00
2 Danny Nykoluk 2.00
3 Marv Luster 4.00
4 Dave Raimey 3.00
5 Bill Symons 3.00
6 Tom Wilkinson 20.00
7 Mike Wadsworth 2.00
8 Dick Thornton 3.00
9 Jim Tomlin 2.00
10 Mel Profit 3.00
11 Bob Taylor 4.00
12 Dave Mann 3.00
13 Tommy Joe Coffey 5.00
14 Angelo Mosca 15.00
15 Joe Zuger 3.00
16 Garney Henley 10.00
17 Mike Strofolino 2.00
18 Billy Ray Locklin 2.00
19 Ted Page 2.00
20 Bill Danychuk 3.00
21 Bob Krouse 2.00
22 John Reid 2.00
23 Dick Wesolowski 2.00
24 Willie Bethea 3.00
25 Ken Sugarman 3.00
26 Rich Robinson 2.00
27 Dave Tobey 2.00
28 Paul Brothers 2.00
29 Charlie Brown 2.00
30 Jerry Bradley 2.00
31 Ted Gerela 3.00
32 Jim Young 8.00
33 Gary Robinson 2.00
34 Bob Howes 2.00
35 Greg Findlay 2.00
36 Trevor Ekdahl 3.00
37 Ron Stewart 6.00
38 Joe Poirier 3.00
39 Wayne Giardino 2.00
40 Tom Schuette 2.00
41 Roger Perdrix 2.00
42 Jim Mankins 2.00
43 Jay Roberts 2.00
44 Ken Lehmann 3.00
45 Jerry Campbell 3.00
46 Billy Joe Booth 3.00
47 Whit Tucker 5.00
48 Moe Racine 2.00
49 Corey Colehour 3.00
50 Dave Gasser 2.00
51 Jerry Griffin 2.00
52 Greg Pipes 3.00
53 Roy Shatzko 2.00
54 Ron Forwick 2.00
55 Ed Molstad 2.00
56 Ken Ferguson 2.00
57 Terry Swarn 5.00
58 Tom Nettles 2.00
59 John Wydareny 2.00
60 Bayne Norrie 2.00
61 Wally Gabler 3.00
62 Paul Desjardins 2.00
63 Peter Francis 2.00
64 Bill Frank 2.00
65 Chuck Harrison 2.00
66 Gene Lakusiak 2.00
67 Phil Minnick 2.00
68 Doug Strong 2.00
69 Glen Schapansky 2.00
70 Ed Ulmer 2.00
71 Bill Whisler 2.00
72 Ted Collins 2.00
73 Larry DeGraw 2.00
74 Henry Dorsch 2.00
75 Alan Ford 2.00
76 Ron Lancaster 20.00
77 Bob Kosid 2.00
78 Bobby Thompson 2.00
79 Ted Dushinski 2.00
80 Bruce Bennett 4.00
81 George Reed 15.00
82 Wayne Shaw 2.00
83 Cliff Shaw 2.00
84 Jack Abendschan 2.00
85 Ed McQuarters 5.00
86 Jerry Keeling 5.00
87 Gerry Shaw 2.00
88 Basil Bark (UER) (Misspelled Back) 2.00
89 Wayne Harris 6.00
90 Jim Furlong 2.00
91 Larry Robinson 2.00
92 John Helton 10.00
93 Dave Cranmer 2.00
94 Lanny Boleski (UER) (Misspelled Larry) 2.00
95 Herman Harrison 5.00
96 Granville Liggins 5.00
97 Joe Forzani 3.00
98 Terry Evanshen 8.00
99 Sonny Wade 6.00
100 Dennis Duncan 2.00
101 Al Phaneuf 2.00
102 Larry Fairholm 2.00
103 Moses Denson 4.00
104 Gino Baretta 2.00
105 Gene Ceppetelli 2.00
106 Dick Smith 2.00
107 Gordon Judges 2.00
108 Harry Olszewski 2.00
109 Mike Webster 2.00
110 Checklist 1-115 30.00
111 Outstanding Player (list from 1953-1969) 8.00
112 Player of the Year (list from 1954-1969) 8.00
113 Lineman of the Year (list from 1955-1969) 6.00
114 CFL Coaches (listed on card front) 6.00
115 Identifying Player (explanation of uniform numbering system) 15.00

1970 O-Pee-Chee CFL Push-Out Inserts

NM
Complete Set (16): 200.00
Common Player: 10.00
1 Ed Harrington 10.00
2 Danny Nykoluk 10.00
3 Tommy Joe Coffey 25.00
4 Angelo Mosca 30.00
5 Ken Sugarman 12.00
6 Jay Roberts 10.00
7 Joe Poirier 12.00
8 Corey Colehour 10.00
9 Dave Gasser 10.00
10 Wally Gabler 15.00
11 Paul Desjardins 10.00
12 Larry DeGraw 10.00
13 Jerry Keeling 20.00
14 Gerry Shaw 10.00
15 Terry Evanshen 25.00
16 Sonny Wade 12.00

1971 O-Pee-Chee CFL

NM
Complete Set (132): 250.00
Common Player: 1.00
1 Bill Symons 5.00
2 Mel Profit 1.50
3 Jim Tomlin 1.00
4 Ed Harrington 1.50
5 Jim Corrigall 4.00
6 Chip Barrett 1.00
7 Marv Luster 3.00
8 Ellison Kelly 4.00
9 Charlie Bray 1.00
10 Pete Martin 1.00
11 Tony Moro 1.00
12 Dave Raimey 1.50
13 Joe Theismann 100.00
14 Greg Barton 6.00
15 Leon McQuay 6.00
16 Don Jonas 6.00
17 Doug Strong 1.00
18 Paul Brule 1.00
19 Bill Frank 1.00
20 Joe Critchlow 1.00
21 Chuck Liebrock 1.00
22 Rob McLaren 1.00
23 Bob Swift 1.00
24 Rick Shaw 1.00
25 Ross Richardson 1.00
26 Benji Dial 1.00
27 Jim Heighton 1.00
28 Ed Ulmer 1.00
29 Glen Schapansky 1.00
30 Larry Slagle 1.00
31 Tom Cassese 1.00
32 Ted Gerela 1.00
33 Bob Howes 1.00
34 Ken Sugarman 1.50
35 A.D. Whitfield 1.50
36 Jim Young 6.00
37 Tom Wilkinson 10.00
38 Lefty Hendrickson 1.00
39 Dave Golinsky 1.00
40 Gerry Herron 1.00
41 Jim Evenson 1.50
42 Greg Findlay 1.00
43 Garrett Hunsperger 1.00
44 Jerry Bradley 1.00
45 Trevor Ekdahl 1.50
46 Bayne Norrie 1.00
47 Henry King 1.00
48 Terry Swarn 1.50
49 Jim Thomas 1.50
50 Bob Houmard 1.00
51 Don Trull 3.00
52 Dave Cutler 8.00
53 Mike Law 1.00
54 Dick Dupuis 1.50
55 Dave Gasser 1.00
56 Ron Forwick 1.00
57 John LaGrone 1.50
58 Greg Pipes 1.50
59 Ted Page 1.00
60 John Wydareny 1.50
61 Joe Zuger 1.50
62 Tommy Joe Coffey 6.00
63 Rensi Perdoni 1.00
64 Bob Taylor 2.50
65 Garney Henley 6.00
66 Dick Wesolowski 1.00
67 Dave Fleming 1.00
68 Bill Danychuk 1.50
69 Angelo Mosca 15.00
70 Bob Krouse 1.00
71 Tony Gabriel 18.00
72 Wally Gabler 1.50
73 Bob Steiner 1.00
74 John Reid 1.00
75 Jon Hohman 1.00
76 Barry Ardern 1.00
77 Jerry Campbell 1.50
78 Billy Cooper 1.00
79 Dave Braggins 1.00
80 Tom Schuette 1.00
81 Dennis Duncan 1.00
82 Moe Racine 1.00
83 Rod Woodward 1.00
84 Al Marcelin 1.00
85 Garry Wood 5.00
86 Wayne Giardino 1.00
87 Roger Perdrix 1.00
88 Hugh Oldham 1.00
89 Rick Cassatta 2.50
90 Jack Abendschan 1.50
91 Don Bahnuik 1.00
92 Bill Baker 10.00
93 Gordon Barwell 1.00
94 Gary Brandt 1.00
95 Henry Dorsch 1.00
96 Ted Dushinski 1.00
97 Alan Ford 1.00
98 Ken Frith 1.00

99 Ralph Galloway 1.00
100 Bob Kosid 1.00
101 Ron Lancaster 15.00
102 Silas McKinnie 1.00
103 George Reed 8.00
104 Gene Ceppetelli 1.00
105 Merl Code 1.00
106 Peter Dalla Riva 8.00
107 Moses Denson 2.50
108 Pierre Desjardins 1.00
109 Terry Evanshen 6.00
110 Larry Fairholm 1.50
111 Gene Gaines 5.00
112 Ed George 1.50
113 Gordon Judges 1.00
114 Garry Lefebvre 1.00
115 Al Phaneuf 1.50
116 Steve Smear 5.00
117 Sonny Wade 3.00
118 Frank Andruski 1.00
119 Basil Bark 1.00
120 Lanny Boleski 1.00
121 Joe Forzani 1.50
122 Jim Furlong 1.00
123 Wayne Harris 6.00
124 Herman Harrison 4.00
125 John Helton 4.00
126 Wayne Holm 1.00
127 Fred James 1.00
128 Jerry Keeling 4.00
129 Rudy Linterman 1.50
130 Larry Robinson 1.50
131 Gerry Shaw 1.00
132 Checklist Card 25.00
1.00

1971 O-Pee-Chee CFL Poster Inserts

NM
Complete Set (16): 150.00
Common Player: 6.00
1 Tommy Joe Coffey 15.00
2 Herman Harrison 15.00
3 Bill Frank 6.00
4 Ellison Kelly 10.00
5 Charlie Bray 6.00
6 Bill Danychuk 7.50
7 Saskatchewan Roughriders (Ron Lancaster) 20.00
8 Bill Symons 7.50
9 Steve Smear 10.00
10 Angelo Mosca 20.00
11 Wayne Harris 15.00
12 Greg Findlay 6.00
13 John Wydareny 7.50
14 Garney Henley 15.00
15 Al Phaneuf 7.50
16 Ed Harrington 6.00

1972 O-Pee-Chee CFL

NM
Complete Set (132): 175.00
Common Player: 1.00
1 Bob Krouse 2.50
2 John Williams 1.00
3 Garney Henley 6.00
4 Dick Wesolowski 1.00
5 Paul McKay 1.00
6 Bill Danychuk 1.50
7 Angelo Mosca 10.00
8 Tommy Joe Coffey 5.00
9 Tony Gabriel 10.00
10 Mike Blum 1.00
11 Doug Mitchell 1.00
12 Emery Hicks 1.00
13 Max Anderson 1.00
14 Ed George 1.50
15 Mark Kosmos 1.50
16 Ted Collins 1.00
17 Peter Dalla Riva 5.00
18 Pierre Desjardins 1.00
19 Terry Evanshen 6.00
20 Larry Fairholm 1.50
21 Jim Foley 1.50
22 Gordon Judges 1.00
23 Barry Randall 1.00
24 Brad Upshaw 1.00
25 Jorma Kuisma 1.00
26 Mike Widger 1.00
27 Joe Theismann 50.00
28 Greg Barton 4.00
29 Bill Symons 3.00
30 Leon McQuay 4.00
31 Jim Corrigall 4.00
32 Jim Stillwagon 4.00
33 Dick Thornton 1.50
34 Marv Luster 4.00
35 Paul Desjardins 1.00
36 Mike Eben 1.00
37 Eric Allen 5.00
38 Chip Barrett 1.00
39 Noah Jackson 3.00
40 Jim Young 6.00
41 Trevor Ekdahl 1.50
42 Garrett Hunsperger 1.00
43 Willie Postler 1.00
44 George Anderson 1.00
45 Ron Estay 1.00
46 Johnny Musso 15.00
47 Eric Guthrie 1.00
48 Monroe Eley 1.00
49 Don Bunce 5.00
50 Jim Evenson 1.50
51 Ken Sugarman 1.50
52 Dave Golinsky 1.00
53 Wayne Harris 5.00
54 Jerry Keeling 4.00
55 Herman Harrison 4.00
56 Larry Robinson 1.50
57 John Helton 4.00
58 Gerry Shaw 1.00
59 Frank Andruski 1.00
60 Basil Bark 1.00
61 Joe Forzani 1.50
62 Jim Furlong 1.00
63 Rudy Linterman 1.50
64 Granville Liggins 4.00
65 Lanny Boleski 1.00
66 Hugh Oldham 1.00
67 Dave Braggins 1.00
68 Jerry Campbell 1.50
69 Al Marcelin 1.50
70 Tom Pullen 1.00
71 Rudy Sims 1.00
72 Marshall Shirk 1.00
73 Tom Laputka 1.00
74 Barry Ardern 1.00
75 Billy Cooper 1.00
76 Dan Deever 1.00
77 Wayne Giardino 1.00
78 Terry Wellesley 1.00
79 Ron Lancaster 12.00
80 George Reed 10.00
81 Bobby Thompson 1.00
82 Jack Abendschan 1.00
83 Ed McQuarters 3.00
84 Bruce Bennett 3.00
85 Bill Baker 5.00
86 Don Bahnuik 1.00
87 Gary Brandt 1.00
88 Henry Dorach 1.00
89 Ted Dushinski 1.00
90 Alan Ford 1.00
91 Bob Kosid 1.00
92 Greg Pipes 1.50
93 John LaGrone 1.50
94 Dave Gasser 1.00
95 Bob Taylor 1.50
96 Dave Cutler 5.00
97 Dick Dupuis 1.00
98 Ron Forwick 1.00
99 Bayne Norrie 1.00
100 Jim Henshall 1.00
101 Charlie Turner 1.00
102 Fred Dunn 1.00
103 Sam Scarber 1.00
104 Bruce Lemmerman 5.00
105 Don Jonas 6.00
106 Doug Strong 1.00
107 Ed Williams 1.00
108 Paul Markle 1.00
109 Gene Lakusiak 1.00
110 Bob LaRose 1.00
111 Rob McLaren 1.00
112 Pete Ribbins 1.00
113 Bill Frank 1.00
114 Bob Swift 1.00
115 Chuck Liebrock 1.00
116 Joe Critchlow 1.00
117 Paul Williams 1.00
118 Pro Action 1.00
119 Pro Action 1.00
120 Pro Action 1.00
121 Pro Action 1.00
122 Pro Action 1.00
123 Pro Action 1.00
124 Pro Action 1.00
125 Pro Action 1.00
126 Pro Action 1.00
127 Pro Action 1.00
128 Pro Action 1.00
129 Pro Action 1.00
130 Pro Action 1.00
131 Pro Action 1.00
132 Checklist Card 30.00
1.00

1972 O-Pee-Chee CFL Trio Sticker Insert

NM
Complete Set (24): 250.00
Common Player: 4.00
1 Johnny Musso, 2 Ron Lancaster, 3 Don Jonas 4.00
4 Jerry Campbell, 5 Bill Symons, 6 Ted Collins 4.00
7 Dave Cutler, 8 Paul McKay, 9 Rudy Sims 4.00
10 Wayne Harris, 11 Greg Pipes, 12 Chuck Ealey 4.00
13 Ron Estay, 14 Jack Abendschan, 15 Paul Markle 4.00
16 Jim Stillwagon, 17 Terry Evanshen, 18 Willie Postler 4.00
19 Hugh Oldham, 20 Joe Theismann, 21 Ed George 4.00
22 Larry Robinson, 23 Bruce Lemmerman, 24 Garney Henley 4.00
25 Bill Baker, 26 Bob LaRose, 27 Frank Andruski 4.00
28 Don Bunce, 29 George Reed, 30 Doug Strong 4.00
31 Al Marcelin, 32 Leon McQuay, 33 Peter Dalla Riva 4.00
34 Dick Dupuis, 35 Bill Danychuk, 36 Marshall Shirk 4.00
37 Jerry Keeling, 38 John LaGrone, 39 Bob Krouse 4.00
40 Jim Young, 41 Ed McQuarters, 42 Gene Lakusiak 4.00
43 Dick Thornton, 44 Larry Fairholm, 45 Garrett Hunsperger 4.00
46 Dave Braggins, 47 Greg Barton, 48 Mark Kosmos 4.00
49 John Helton, 50 Bobby Taylor, 51 Dick Wesolowski 4.00
52 Don Bahnuik, 53 Rob McLaren, 54 Granville Liggins 4.00
55 Monroe Eley, 56 Bob Thompson, 57 Ed Williams 4.00
58 Tom Pullen, 59 Jim Corrigall, 60 Pierre Desjardins 4.00
61 Ron Forwick, 62 Angelo Mosca, 63 Tom Laputka 4.00
64 Herman Harrison, 65 Dave Gasser, 66 John Williams 4.00
67 Trevor Ekdahl, 68 Bruce Bennett, 69 Gerry Shaw 4.00
70 Jim Foley, 71 Pete Ribbins, 72 Marv Luster 4.00

1952 Parkhurst CFL

NM
Complete Set (100): 3000.
Common Player (1-19): 20.00
Common Player (20-100): 30.00
1 Watch The Games 50.00
2 Teamwork 20.00
3 Football Equipment 20.00
4 Hang Onto The Ball 20.00
5 The Head On Tackle 20.00
6 The Football Field 20.00
7 The Lineman's Stance 20.00
8 Centre's Spiral Pass 20.00
9 The Lineman 20.00
10 The Place Kick 20.00
11 The Cross-Body Block 20.00
12 T Formation 20.00
13 Falling On The Ball 20.00
14 The Throw 20.00
15 Breaking From Tackle 20.00
16 How To Catch A Pass 20.00
17 The Punt 20.00
18 Shifting The Ball 20.00
19 Penalty Signals 20.00
20 Leslie Ascott 30.00
21 Robert Marshall 30.00
22 Tom Harpley 30.00
23 Robert McClelland 30.00
24 Rod Smylie 30.00
25 Bill Bass 30.00
26 Fred Black 30.00
27 Jack Carpenter 30.00
28 Bob Hack 30.00
29 Ulysses Curtis 30.00
30 Nobby Wirkowski 50.00
31 George Arnett 30.00
32 Lorne Parkin 30.00
33 Alex Toogood 30.00
34 Marshall Haymes 30.00
35 Shanty McKenzie 30.00
36 Byron Karrys 30.00
37 George Rooks 30.00
38 Red Ettinger 30.00
39 Al Bruno 40.00
40 Stephen Karrys 30.00
41 Herb Trawick 50.00
42 Sam Etcheverry 350.00
43 Marv Melrowitz 30.00
44 John Red O'Quinn 50.00
45 Jim Ostendarp 30.00
46 Tom Tofaute 30.00
47 Joey Pal 30.00
48 Ray Cicia 30.00
49 Bruce Coulter 35.00
50 Jim Mitchener 30.00
51 Lally Lalonde 30.00
52 Jim Staton 30.00
53 Glenn Douglas 30.00
54 Dave Tomlinson 30.00
55 Ed Salem 30.00
56 Virgil Wagner 50.00
57 Dawson Tilley 30.00
58A Cec Findlay 40.00
58B Tommy Manastersky 40.00
59 Frank Nable 30.00
60 Chuck Anderson 30.00
61 Charlie Hubbard 30.00
63 Benny MacDonnell 30.00
64 Peter Karpuk 30.00
65 Tom O'Malley 30.00
66 Bill Stanton 30.00
67 Matt Anthony 30.00
68 John Morneau 30.00
69 Howie Turner 30.00
70 Alton Baldwin 30.00
71 John Bovey 30.00
72 Bruno Bitkowski 35.00
73 Gene Roberts 30.00
74 John Wagoner 30.00
75 Ted MacLarty 30.00
76 Jerry Lefebvre 30.00
77 Buck Rogers 30.00
78 Bruce Cummings 30.00
79 Hal Wagner 40.00
80 Joe Shinn 30.00
81 Eddie Bevan 30.00
82 Ralph Sazio 50.00
83 Bob McDonald 30.00
84 Vince Scott 40.00
85 Jack Stewart 30.00
86 Ralph Bartolini 30.00
87 Blake Taylor 30.00
88 Richard Brown 30.00
89 Douglas Gray 30.00
90 Alex Muzyka 30.00
91 Pete Neumann 50.00
92 Jack Rogers 30.00
93 Bernie Custis 40.00
94 Cam Fraser 30.00
95 Vince Mazza 40.00
96 Pete Wooley 30.00
97 Earl Valiquette 30.00
98 Floyd Cooper 30.00
99 Louis DiFrancisco 30.00
100 Robert Simpson 125.00

1956 Parkhurst CFL

NM
Complete Set (50): 3500.
Common Player: 40.00
1 Art Walker 80.00
2 Frank Anderson 40.00
3 Normie Kwong 150.00
4 Johnny Bright 150.00
5 Jackie Parker 500.00
6 Bob Dean 40.00
7 Don Getty 125.00
8 Rollie Miles 100.00
9 Ted Tully 40.00
10 Frank Morris 90.00
11 Martin Ruby 80.00
12 Mel Beckett 80.00
13 Bill Clarke 40.00
14 John Wozniak 40.00
15 Larry Isbell 40.00
16 Ken Carpenter 80.00
17 Sully Glasser 40.00
18 Bobby Marlow 90.00
19 Paul Anderson 40.00
20 Gord Sturtridge 80.00
21 Alex Macklin 40.00
22 Duke Cook 40.00
23 Bill Stevenson 40.00
24 Lynn Bottoms 80.00
25 Aramis Dandoy 40.00
26 Peter Muir 40.00
27 Harvey Wylie 80.00
28 Joe Yamauchi 40.00
29 John Alderton 40.00
30 Bill McKenna 40.00
31 Edward Kotowich 40.00
32 Herb Gray 100.00
33 Calvin Jones 100.00
34 Herman Day 40.00
35 Buddy Leake 40.00
36 Robert McNamara 40.00
37 Bud Grant 300.00
38 Gord Rowland 80.00
39 Glen McWhinney 40.00
40 Lorne Benson 40.00
41 Sam Etcheverry 300.00
42 Joey Pal 40.00
43 Tom Hugo 40.00
44 Tex Coulter 80.00
45 Doug McNichol 40.00
46 Tom Moran 40.00
47 Red O'Quinn 80.00
48 Hal Patterson 200.00
49 Jacques Belec 40.00
50 Pat Abruzzi 100.00

1981 Police Saskatchewan

MT
Complete Set (10): 15.00
Common Player: 1.25
1 Roger Aldag (44) 2.00
2 Joe Barnes (7) 1.25
3 Lester Brown (22) 1.25
4 Dwight Edwards (33) 1.25
5 Vince Goldsmith (78) 2.00
6 John Hufnagel (12) 5.00
7 Ken McEachern (20) 1.25
8 Mike Samples (66) 1.25
9 Joey Walters (17) 1.25
10 Lyall Woznesensky (76) 1.25

1982 Police Hamilton

MT
Complete Set (35): 20.00
Common Player: .50
1 Marv Allemang .50
2 Jeff Arp .50
3 Keith Baker .50
4 Gerald Bess .75
5 Mark Bragagnolo .50
6 Carmelo Carteri .50
7 Tom Clements 7.50
8 Grover Covington 3.00
9 Rocky DiPietro 4.00
10 Howard Fields .50
11 Ross Francis .50
12 Ed Fulton .50
13 Peter Gales .50
14 Ed Gataveckas .50
15 Dave Graffi .50
16 Obie Graves .50
17 Hazen Henderson .50
18 Ron Johnson 1.25
19 Dave Marler .75
20 Jim Muller .50
21 Leroy Paul .50
22 John Priestner .75
23 Dave Purves .50
24 James Ramey .50
25 Doug Redl .50
26 Bernie Ruoff .75
27 David Sauve .50
28 David Shaw .50
29 Kerry Smith .50
30 Steve Stapler .75
31 Kyle Stevens .50
32 Mike Walker 2.00
33 Henry Waszczuk .50
34 Harold Woods .50
35 Ben Zambiasi 2.50

1982 Police Saskatchewan

MT
Complete Set (16): 12.00
Common Player: .75
2 Greg Fieger .75
7 Joe Adams .75
12 John Hufnagel 4.00
17 Joey Walters .75
20 Ken McEachern .75
21 Marcellus Greene .75
25 Steve Dennis .75
29 Fran McDermott .75
37 Frank Robinson 1.00
44 Roger Aldag 1.25
57 Bob Poley .75
66 Mike Samples .75
69 Don Swafford .75
74 Chris DeFrance .75
76 Lyall Woznesensky .75
78 Vince Goldsmith 1.50

1982 Police Winnipeg

MT
Complete Set (24): 10.00
Common Player: .40
1 Nick Bastaja .40
2 Paul Bennett .40
3 John Bonk .40
4 Dieter Brock 2.50
5 Peter Catan .40
6 Leo Ezerins .40
7 Eugene Goodlow .40
8 John Helton 1.50
9 Rick House .60
10 Mark Jackson .60
11 Ray Jauch (CO) .40
12 Milson Jones 1.00
13 Trevor Kennerd 1.25
14 Stan Mikawos .40
15 William Miller .60
16 Tony Norman .40
17 Vince Phason .40
18 Reggie Pierson .40
19 Joe Poplawski .60
20 James Reed .40
21 Franky Smith .40
22 Bobby Thompson .40
23 Chris Walby 1.00
24 Charles Williams .40

1983 Police Hamilton

MT
Complete Set (37): 20.00
Common Player: .50
1 Marv Allemang .50
2 Jeff Arp .50
3 Keith Baker .50
4 Harold E. Ballard (PRES) 2.00
5 Mike Barker .50
6 Gerald Bess .75
7 Pat Brady .50
8 Mark Bragagnolo .50
9 Tom Clements 7.50
10 Grover Covington 3.00
11 Rufus Crawford 2.00
12 Rocky DiPietro 4.00
13 Leo Ezerins .50
14 Howard Fields .50
15 Ross Francis .50
16 Peter Gales .50
17 Ed Gataveckas .50
18 Paul Gohier .50
19 Dave Graffi .50
20 Ron Johnson 1.25
21 Steve Kearns .50
22 Wayne Lee .50
23 Mike McIntyre .50
24 Paul Palma .50
25 George Piva .50
26 Mitchell Price .75
27 John Priestner .75
28 Bernie Ruoff .75
29 David Sauve .50
30 Johnny Shepherd .50
31 Steve Stapler 1.00
32 Mark Streeter .50
33 Jeff Tedford .50
34 Mike Walker 2.00
35 Henry Waszczuk .50
36 Felix Wright 2.50
37 Ben Zambiasi 2.50

1983 Police Saskatchewan

MT
Complete Set (16): 12.00
Common Player: .75
9 Ron Robinson 1.00
12 John Hufnagel 3.00
13 Ken Clark 1.00
18 Mike Washington 1.00
24 Marshall Hamilton .75
25 Mike Emery .75
30 Duane Galloway .75
33 Dwight Edwards 1.00
36 Dave Ridgway 2.00
42 Eddie Lowe .75
58 J.C. Pelusi .75
60 Karl Morgan .75
61 Bryan Illerbrun .75
65 Neil Quilter .75
72 Ray Elgaard 3.00
74 Chris DeFrance .75

1984 Police Ottawa

MT
Complete Set (10): 30.00
Common Player: .75
1 Greg Marshall 1.25
2 Dave Newman .75
3 Rudy Phillips 1.25
4 Jim Reid 1.25
5 Mark Seale (SP) 20.00
6 Rick Sowieta 1.25
7 Pat Stoqua 1.25
8 Skip Walker 2.50
9 Al Washington .75
10 J.C. Watts 8.00

1985 Police Ottawa

MT
Complete Set (10): 6.00
Common Player: .50
1 Ricky Barden .50
2 Michel Bourgeau .75
3 Roger Cattelan .50
4 Ken Clark .75
5 Dean Dorsey .75
6 Greg Marshall .75
7 Kevin Powell .50
8 Jim Reid .75
9 Rick Sowieta .75
10 J.C. Watts 3.00

1962 Post Cereal CFL

NM
Complete Set (137): 1600.
Common Player: 7.50
1A Don Clark (Brown Back) 20.00
1B Don Clark (SP) (White Back) 60.00
2 Ed Meadows 7.50
3 Meco Poliziani 7.50
4 George Dixon 20.00
5 Bobby Jack Oliver 10.00
6 Ross Buckle 7.50
7 Jack Espenship 7.50
8 Howard Cissell 7.50
9 Ed Nickla 7.50
10 Ed Learn 7.50
11 Billy Ray Locklin 7.50
12 Don Paquette 7.50
13 Milt Crain 7.50
14 Dick Schnell 7.50
15 Dick Cohee 7.50
16 Joe Francis 7.50
17 Gilles Archambeault 7.50
18 Angelo Mosca 25.00
19 Ernie White 7.50
20 George Brancato 7.50
21 Ron Lancaster 35.00
22 Jim Cain 7.50
23 Gerry Nesbitt 7.50
24 Russ Jackson 30.00
25 Bob Simpson 18.00
26 Sam Scoccia 7.50
27 Tom Jones 7.50
28 Kaye Vaughan 15.00
29 Chuck Stanley 7.50
30 Dave Thelen 15.00
31 Gary Schreider 7.50
32 Jim Reynolds 7.50
33 Doug Daigneault 7.50
34 Joe Poirier 10.00
35 Clare Exelby 7.50
36 Art Johnson 7.50
37 Menan Schriewer 7.50
38 Art Darch 7.50
39 Cookie Gilchrist 25.00
40 Brian Aston 7.50
41 Bobby Kuntz (SP) 50.00
42 Gerry Patrick 7.50
43 Norm Stoneburgh 7.50
44 Billy Shipp 7.50
45 Jim Andreotti 15.00
46 Tobin Rote 20.00
47 Dick Shatto 15.00
48 Dave Mann 10.00
49 Ron Morris 7.50
50 Lynn Bottoms 10.00
51 Jim Rountree 7.50
52 Bill Mitchell 7.50
53 Wes Gideon (SP) 50.00
54 Boyd Carter 7.50
55 Ron Howell 10.00
56 John Barrow 15.00
57 Bernie Faloney 30.00
58 Ron Ray 7.50
59 Don Sutherin 15.00
60 Frank Cosentino 10.00
61 Hardiman Cureton 7.50
62 Hal Patterson 20.00
63 Ralph Goldston 7.50
64 Tommy Grant 15.00
65 Larry Hickman 7.50
66 Zeno Karcz 10.00
67 Garney Henley 20.00
68 Gerry McDougall 10.00
69 Vince Scott 12.00
70 Gerry James 15.00
71 Roger Hagberg 10.00
72 Gord Rowland 10.00
73 Ernie Pitts 7.50
74 Frank Rigney 12.00
75 Norm Rauhaus 12.00
76 Leo Lewis 20.00
77 Mike Wright 7.50
78 Jack Delveaux 7.50
79 Steve Patrick 7.50
80 Dave Burkholder 7.50
81 Charlie Shepard 7.50
82 Kenny Ploen 20.00
83 Ronnie Latourelle 7.50
84 Herb Gray 15.00
85 Hal Ledyard 7.50
86 Cornel Piper (SP) 50.00
87 Farrell Funston 7.50
88 Ray Smith 7.50
89 Clair Branch 7.50
90 Fred Burket 7.50
91 Dave Grosz 7.50
92 Bob Golic 10.00
93 Billy Gray 7.50
94 Neil Habig 7.50
95 Reg Whitehouse 7.50
96 Jack Gotta 10.00
97 Bob Ptacek 10.00
98 Jerry Keeling 15.00
99 Ernie Danjean 7.50
100 Don Luzzi 12.00
101 Wayne Harris 20.00
102 Tony Pajaczkowski 15.00
103 Earl Lunsford 15.00
104 Ernie Warlick 12.00
105 Gene Filipski 12.00
106 Eagle Day 15.00
107 Bill Crawford 7.50
108 Oscar Kruger 7.50
109 Gino Fracas 10.00
110 Don Stephenson 7.50
111 Jim Letcavits 7.50
112 Howie Schumm 7.50
113 Jackie Parker 45.00
114 Rollie Miles 15.00
115 Johnny Bright 20.00
116 Don Getty 15.00
117 Bobby Walden 10.00
118 Roger Nelson 15.00
119 Al Ecuyer 7.50
120 Ed Gray 7.50
121 Vic Chapman (SP) 50.00
122 Earl Keeley 7.50
123 Sonny Homer 7.50
124 Bob Jetter 20.00
125 Jim Carphin 7.50
126 By Bailey 15.00
127 Norm Fieldgate 15.00
128 Vic Kristopaitis 7.50
129 Willie Fleming 20.00
130 Don Vicic 7.50
131 Tom Brown (SP) 50.00
132 Tom Hinton (SP) 50.00
133 Pat Claridge 7.50
134 Bill Britton 7.50
135 Neal Beaumont 10.00
136 Nub Beamer (SP) 50.00
137 Joe Kapp 60.00
NNO Post Album 75.00

1963 Post Cereal CFL

NM
Complete Set (160): 900.00
Common Player: 5.00
1 Larry Hickman 7.50
2 Dick Schnell 5.00
3 Don Clark 7.50
4 Ted Page 5.00
5 Milt Crain 7.50
6 George Dixon 10.00
7 Ed Nickla 5.00
8 Barrie Hansen 5.00
9 Ed Learn 5.00
10 Billy Ray Locklin 5.00
11 Bobby Jack Oliver 7.50
12 Don Paquette 5.00
13 Sandy Stephens 12.00
14 Billy Wayte 5.00
15 Jim Reynolds 5.00
16 Ross Buckle 5.00
17 Bob Geary 5.00
18 Bobby Lee Thompson 5.00
19 Mike Snodgrass 5.00
20 Billy Joe Booth 7.50
21 Jim Cain 5.00
22 Kaye Vaughan 10.00
23 Doug Daigneault 5.00
24 Millard Flemming 5.00
25 Russ Jackson 25.00
26 Joe Poirier 7.50
27 Moe Racine 5.00
28 Norb Roy 5.00
29 Ted Smale 5.00
30 Ernie White 5.00
31 Whit Tucker 10.00
32 Dave Thelen 10.00
33 Len Chandler 5.00
34 Jim Conroy 7.50
35 Jerry Selinger 5.00

36 Ron Stewart 12.00
37 Jim Andreotti 7.50
38 Jackie Parker 25.00
39 Lynn Bottoms 7.50
40 Gerry Patrick 5.00
41 Gerry Philip 5.00
42 Art Johnson 5.00
43 Aubrey Linne 5.00
44 Dave Mann 7.50
45 Marty Martinello 5.00
46 Doug McNichol 5.00
47 Ron Morris 5.00
48 Walt Radzick 5.00
49 Jim Rountree 5.00
50 Dick Shatto 10.00
51 Billy Shipp 5.00
52 Norm Stoneburgh 5.00
53 Gerry Wilson 5.00
54 Danny Nykoluk 5.00
55 John Barrow 10.00
56 Frank Cosentino 7.50
57 Hardiman Cureton 7.50
58 Bobby Kuntz 7.50
59 Bernie Faloney 20.00
60 Garney Henley 12.00
61 Zeno Karcz 7.50
62 Dick Easterly 5.00
63 Bronko Nagurski 12.00
64 Hal Patterson 15.00
65 Ron Ray 5.00
66 Don Sutherin 8.00
67 Dave Viti 5.00
68 Joe Zuger 7.50
69 Angelo Mosca 20.00
70 Ralph Goldston 5.00
71 Tommy Grant 10.00
72 Geno DeNobile 5.00
73 Dave Burkholder 5.00
74 Jack Delveaux 5.00
75 Farrell Funston 5.00
76 Herb Gray 10.00
77 Roger Hagberg 7.50
78 Henry Janzen 7.50
79 Ronnie Latourelle 5.00
80 Leo Lewis 10.00
81 Cornel Piper 5.00
82 Ernie Pitts 5.00
83 Kenny Ploen 10.00
84 Norm Rauhaus 7.50
85 Charlie Shepard 5.00
86 Gar Warren 5.00
87 Dick Thornton 7.50
88 Hal Ledyard 5.00
89 Frank Rigney 7.50
90 Gord Rowland 7.50
91 Don Walsh 5.00
92 Bill Burrell 5.00
93 Ron Atchison 9.00
94 Billy Gray 5.00
95 Neil Habig 5.00
96 Bob Ptacek 7.50
97 Ray Purdin 5.00
98 Ted Urness 8.00
99 Dale West 7.50
100 Reg Whitehouse 5.00
101 Clair Branch 5.00
102 Bill Clarke 5.00
103 Garner Ekstran 7.50
104 Jack Gotta 7.50
105 Len Legault 5.00
106 Larry Dumelie 5.00
107 Bill Britton 5.00
108 Ed Buchanan 5.00
109 Lovell Coleman 7.50
110 Bill Crawford 5.00
111 Ernie Danjean 5.00
112 Eagle Day 9.00
113 Jim Furlong 5.00
114 Wayne Harris 15.00
115 Roy Jakanovich 5.00
116 Phil Lohmann 5.00
117 Earl Lunsford 8.00
118 Don Luzzi 8.00
119 Tony Pajaczkowski 8.00
120 Pete Manning 7.50
121 Harvey Wylie 8.00
122 George Hansen 5.00
123 Pat Holmes 5.00
124 Larry Robinson 7.50
125 Johnny Bright 15.00
126 Jon Rechner 5.00
127 Al Ecuyer 5.00
128 Don Getty 12.00
129 Ed Gray 5.00
130 Oscar Kruger 5.00
131 Jim Letcavits 5.00
132 Mike Lashuk 7.50
133 Don Duncalfe 5.00
134 Bobby Walden 7.50
135 Tommy Joe Coffey 12.00
136 Nat Dye 5.00
137 Roy Stevenson 5.00
138 Howie Schumm 5.00
139 Roger Nelson 8.00
140 Larry Fleisher 7.50
141 Dunc Harvey 5.00
142 James Earl Wright 7.50
143 By Bailey 8.00
144 Nub Beamer 5.00
145 Neal Beaumont 7.50
146 Tom Brown 8.00
147 Pat Claridge 5.00
148 Lonnie Dennis 7.50
149 Norm Fieldgate 8.00
150 Willie Fleming 12.00
151 Dick Fouts 7.50
152 Tom Hinton 8.00
153 Sonny Homer 7.50
154 Joe Kapp 30.00
155 Tom Larscheid 5.00
156 Mike Martin 5.00
157 Mel Mein 5.00
158 Mike Cacic 5.00
159 Walt Bilicki 5.00
160 Earl Keeley 7.50
NNO Post Album 75.00

1991 Queen's University

MT
Complete Set (52): 12.00
Common Card (1-51): .30
Common Card (P1-P5): 3.00
1 First Rugby Team (Team Photo) .75
2 Grey Cup Years (Harry Batstone, Frank R. Leadlay) .75
3 1978 Vanier Cup Champs .30
4 1978 Vanier Cup Champs .30
5 Tim Pendergast .30
6 Brad Elberg .30
7 Ken Kirkwood .30
8 Kyle Wanzel .30
9 Brian Alford .30
10 Paul Kozan .30
11 Paul Beresford .30
12 Ron Herman .30
13 Mike Ross .30
14 Tom Black .30
15 Steve Yovetich .30
16 Mark Robinson .30
17 Don Rorwick .30
18 Ed Kidd .30
19 Jamie Galloway .30
20 Dan Wright .30
21 Scott Gray .30
22 Dan McCullough .30
23 Steve Othen .30
24 Doug Hargreaves (CO) .30
25 Sue Bolton (CO) .30
26 Coaching Staff .50
27 Joel Dagnone .30
28 Mark Morrison .30
29 Rob Krog .30
30 Dan Pawliw .30
31 Greg Bryk .30
32 Eric Dell .30
33 Mike Boone .30
34 James Paterson .30
35 Jeff Yach .30
36 Peter Pain .30
37 Aron Campbell .30
38 Chris McCormick .30
39 Jason Moller .30
40 Terry Huhtala .30
41 Matt Zarowny .30
42 David St. Amour .30
43 Frank Tindall .30
44 Ron Stewart 1.00
45 Jim Young 1.00
46 Bob Howes .30
47 Stu Lang .30
48 Mike Schad (In College Uniform) .75
49 Mike Schad (In Philadelphia Eagles Uniform) .75
50 Jock Climie 1.00
51 Checklist .30
P1 Jock Climie 3.00
P1AU Jock Climie (AU/100) 30.00
P2 Ron Stewart 4.00
P2AU Ron Stewart (AU/300) 30.00
P3 Jim Young 4.00
P4 Stu Lang 3.00
P5 Mike Schad 3.00
P5AU Mike Schad (AU/100) 30.00
NNO Title Card .75

1981 Red Rooster Calgary Stampeders

MT
Complete Set (40): 25.00
Common Player: .60
1 Willie Armstead .60
2 Doug Battershill .60
3 Willie Burden (From waist up) 3.00
4 Willie Burden (Head and shoulders) 3.00
5 Scott Burk (UER) (Misspelled Burke 4th line of bio) .60
6 Al Burleson .60
7 Ken Dombrowski .60
8 Lloyd Fairbanks 1.25
9 Rob Forbes .60
10 Tom Forzani 1.00
11 Miles Gorrell .60
12 J.T. Hay .60
13 John Holland 1.00
14 Norm Hopely .60
15 Jeff Inglis .60
16 Lepoleon Ingram .60
17 Terry Irvin .60
18 Ken Johnson 1.00
19 Franklin King .60
20 Dave Kirzinger .60
21 Frank Kosec .60
22 Tom Krebs .60
23 Reggie Lewis .60
24 Robert Lubig .60
25 Scott MacArthur .60
26 Ed McAleney .60
27 Mike McTague 1.00
28 Mark Moors .60
29 Bernie Morrison .60
30 Mark Nelson .60
31 Ray Odums .60
32 Ronnie Paggett .60
33 John Palazeti .60
34 John Prassas .60
35 Tom Reimer .60
36 James Sykes (Close-up) 3.00
37 James Sykes (From waist up) 3.00
38 Bruce Threadgill .60
39 Bob Viccars .60
40 Merv Walker .60

1981 Red Rooseter Edmonton Eskimos

MT
Complete Set (40): 50.00
Common Player: .60
1 Leo Blanchard .60
2 David Boone .60
3 Brian Broomell .60
4 Hugh Campbell (CO) 1.25
5 Dave Cutler 2.50
6 Marco Cyncar 1.00
7 Ron Estay .60
8 Dave Fennell 1.00
9 Emilio Fraietta .60
10 Brian Fryer .60
11 Jim Germany 1.00
12 Gary Hayes .60
13 Larry Highbaugh 1.25
14 Joe Hollimon .60
15 Hank Ilesic 1.25
16 Ed Jones .60
17 Dan Kearns .60
18 Sean Kehoe .60
19 Brian Kelly 2.50
20 Dan Kepley 1.25
21 Stu Lang .60
22 Pete Lavorato .60
23 Neil Lumsden 1.00
24 Bill Manchuk .60
25 Mike McLeod .60
26 Ted Milian .60
27 Warren Moon 25.00
28 James Parker 2.00
29 John Pointer .60
30 Hector Pothier .60
31 Dale Potter .60
32 Angelo Santucci .60
33 Tom Scott 1.00
34 Waddell Smith 1.00
35 Bill Stevenson .60
36 Tom Towns .60
37 Eric Upton .60
38 Mark Wald .60
39 Ken Walter .60
40 Tom Wilkinson 3.00

1995 R.E.L. CFL

MT
Complete Set (250): 35.00
Common Player: .10
1 Doug Flutie 1.25
2 Bruce Covernton .20
3 Jamie Crysdale .10
4 Matt Finlay .20
5 Alondra Johnson .20
6 Will Johnson .20
7 Greg Knox .10
8 Stu Laird .20
9 Kenton Leonard .10
10 Tony Martino .10
11 Mark McLoughlin .10
12 Allen Pitts .25
13 Marvin Pope .10
14 Rocco Romano .10
15 David Sapunjis .50
16 Pee Wee Smith .20
17 Tony Stewart .10
18 Srecko Zizakovic .10
19 Kerwin Bell .35
20 Leroy Blugh .10
21 Rod Connop .10
22 Blake Dermott .20
23 Lucius Floyd .10
24 Bennie Goods .20
25 Glenn Harper .10
26 Craig Hendrickson .10
27 Robert Holland .10
28 Malvin Hunter .10
29 John Kalin .10
30 Nick Mazzoli .10
31 Willie Pless .25
32 Jim Sandusky .20
33 Michael Soles .20
34 Marc Tobert .10
35 Henry Williams .35
36 Larry Wruck .20
37 Lee Knight .10
38 Shawn Prendergast .10
39 Richard Nurse .10
40 Eric Carter .20
41 Frank Marof .10
42 Roger Hennig .10
43 Derek Grier .10
44 Kelvin Means .10
45 Michael Philbrick .10
46 Jessie Small .20
47 Mike O'Shea .35
48 Marcus Cotton .10
49 Hassan Bailey .10
50 Anthony Calvillo .50
51 Mike Kerrigan .25
52 Hank Ilesic .10
53 Paul Osbaldiston .20
54 Earl Winfield .20
55 Danton Barto .10
56 Tim Cofield .25
57 Bruce Perkins .10
58 Damion Lyons .20
59 Joe Horn .25
60 Rickey Foggie .25
61 Bobby Dawson .10
62 Eddie Brown .20
63 Vance Hammond .10
64 Ed Berry .10
65 Stephen Bates .10
66 Greg Battle .20
67 Gary Anderson .10
68 Donald Smith .10
69 Adrion Smith .10
70 Rodney Harding .10
71 Damon Allen .20
72 Junior Robinson .10
73 Ken Watson .10
74 Nick Subis .10
75 Mike Pringle 1.00
76 Shar Pourdanesh .20
77 Elfrid Payton .20
78 Josh Miller .10
79 Carlos Huerta .20
80 Tracy Ham .50
81 Tracey Gravely .10
82 Matt Goodwin .10
83 Neil Fort .10
84 O.J. Brigance .35
85 Jearld Baylis .25
86 Mike Alexander .10
87 Shannon Culver .10
88 Robert Clark .20
89 Courtney Griffin .10
90 Demetrious Maxie .10
91 Dave Ridgway .20
92 Terryl Ulmer .10
93 Lybrant Robinson .10
94 Troy Alexander .10
95 Darren Joseph .20
96 Warren Jones .20
97 Dan Rashovich .10
98 Glenn Kulka .10
99 Dale Joseph .10
100 Scott Hendrickson .10
101 Ron Goetz .10
102 Ventson Donelson .10
103 Mike Anderson .10
104 Brent Matich .10
105 Donald Narcisse .25
106 Tom Burgess .35
107 Bobby Jurasin .25
108 Ray Elgaard .20
109 Brian Bonner .25
110 Robbie Keen .10
111 Bjorn Nittmo .35
112 Martin Patton .10
113 Rod Harris .25
114 Mike Johnson .10
115 Billy Joe Tolliver .35
116 Curtis Mayfield .20
117 Ben Jefferson .10
118 Jon Heidenreich .10
119 Mike Stowell .10
120 Alex Mash .10
121 Ray Savage .10
122 Mario Perry .10
123 Ron Perry .10
124 Joe Fuller .10
125 Jonathan Wilson .10
126 Anthony Shelton .10
127 Emanuel Martin .10
128 Ray Alexander .20
129 Michael Richardson .25
130 Irv Daymond .10
131 Terry Baker .20
132 Danny Barrett .20
133 James Ellingson .20
134 John Kropke .20
135 Garry Lewis .10
136 James Monroe .10
137 Brett Young .20
138 Remi Trudel .10
139 Jed Tommy .10
140 Odessa Turner .20
141 David Black .10
142 Eric Geter .10
143 Sammy Garza .10
144 Loyd Lewis .10
145 Enis Jackson .10
146 Danny McManus .35
147 Cory Philpot .75
148 Glen Scrivner .10
149 Ian Sinclair .20
150 Vic Stevenson .10
151 Andrew Stewart .10
152 Jamie Taras .10
153 Rob Gordon .10
154 Tom Europe .10
155 Spencer McLennan .10
156 Mike Trevathan .20
157 Matt Clark .20
158 Daved Benefield .20
159 Darren Flutie .50
160 Charles Gordon .10
161 Ryan Hanson .10
162 Kent Austin .25
163 Reggie Barnes .10
164 Mike Clemons .75
165 Jock Climie .10
166 Duane Forde .10
167 Leon Hatziioannou .10
168 Wayne Lammle .10
169 Paul Masotti .20
170 George Nimako .10
171 Calvin Tiggle .10
172 Don Wilson .10
173 Lui Passaglia .20
174 Chris Tsangaris .10
175 Darrick Branch .10
176 Carl Coulter .10
177 P.J. Martin .10
178 Eric Blount (DE) .10
179 Norm Casola .10
180 Joe Burgos .10
181 John Buddenberg .10
182 George Bethune .10
183 Oscar Giles .20
184 Myron Wise .10
185 Roman Anderson .10
186 Dave Harper .10
187 Mike Saunders .50
188 Roosevelt Collins .10
189 Peter Shorts .10
190 Willie Fears .20
191 Mike Kiselak .10
192 Malcolm Frank .10
193 Joe Kralik .10
194 David Archer 1.25
195 Billy Hess .10
196 Mark Stock .10
197 James King .10
198 Tony Burse .10
199 Donovan Gans .10
200 Keith Woodside .10
201 Anthony Drawhorn .20
202 Jimmy Klingler .35
203 Matt Dunigan .75
204 John Motton .20
205 Scott Player .20
206 Franco Grilla .10
207 Shonte Peoples .10
208 Derrick Crawford .20
209 Fernando Thomas .10
210 Delius Morris .10
211 Roosevelt Patterson .10
212 Willie McClendon .10
213 Jason Phillips .10
214 Mike James .10
215 Andre Strode .10
216 Chris Dyko .10
217 Chris Walby .10
218 Miles Gorrell .10
219 Dave Vankoughnett .10
220 Del Lyles .10
221 Bob Cameron .35
222 Troy Westwood .10
223 Reggie Slack .25
224 Blaise Bryant .20
225 Gerald Wilcox .20
226 David Williams .20
227 Keilly Rush .10
228 Stan Mikawos .10
229 Paul Randolph .10
230 Greg Clark .10
231 Jason Mallett .10
232 Juran Bolden .35
233 Brett MacNeil .10
234 Chris Johnstone .10
235 Toronto Argonauts Logo .10
236 Ottawa Rough Riders Logo .10
237 Hamilton Tiger-Cats Logo .10
238 Winnipeg Blue Bombers Logo .10
239 Saskatchewan Roughriders/Logo .10
240 Calgary Stampeders Logo .10
241 Edmonton Eskimos Logo .10
242 B.C. Lions Logo .10
243 Memphis Mad Dogs Logo .10
244 Birmingham Barracudas Logo .10
245 San Antonio Texans Logo .10
246 Shreveport Pirates Logo .10
247 Baltimore Stallions Logo .10
248 Grey Cup Logo .10
249 Checklist #1 .20
250 Checklist #2 .20
P1 (Doug Flutie) (Promo numbered one of 2500) 2.00
AU1 (Doug Flutie) (AUTO) (signed card) 50.00

1971 Royal Bank B.C. Lions

NM
Complete Set (16): 50.00
Common Player: 2.50
1 George Anderson 2.50
2 Paul Brothers 2.50
3 Brian Donnelly 2.50
4 Dave Easley 2.50
5 Trevor Ekdahl 3.50
6 Jim Evenson 3.50
7 Greg Findlay 2.50
8 Lefty Hendrickson 2.50
9 Bob Howes 2.50
10 Garrett Hunsperger 2.50
11 Wayne Matherne 2.50
12 Don Moorhead 2.50
13 Ken Phillips 2.50
14 Ken Sugarman 3.50
15 Tom Wilkinson 10.00
16 Jim Young 10.00

1973 Royal Bank B.C. Lions

NM
Complete Set (16): 50.00
Common Player: 2.50
1 Barry Ardern 2.50
2 Monroe Eley 3.50
3 Bob Friend 2.50
4 Eric Guthrie 2.50
5 Garrett Hunsperger 2.50
6 Wayne Matherne 2.50
7A Don Moorhead (Black border) 2.50
7B Don Moorhead (Silver border) 2.50
8 Johnny Musso 7.50
9 Ray Nettles 2.50
10 Pete Palmer 2.50
11 Gary Robinson (SP) 20.00
12 Al Wilson 2.50
13 Mike Wilson 2.50
14 Jim Young 7.50
15 Coaches (Bud Tynes, Ken McCullough, Owen Dejanovich, Eagle Keys) 2.50

1974 Royal Bank B.C. Lions

NM
Complete Set (14): 40.00
Common Player: 2.50
1 Bill Baker 6.00
2 Karl Douglas 2.50
3 Layne McDowell 2.50
4 Ivan MacMillan 2.50
5 Bud Magrum 2.50
6 Don Moorhead 2.50
7 Johnny Musso 7.50
8 Ray Nettles 2.50
9 Brian Sopatyk 2.50
10 Curtis Wester 3.50
11 Slade Willis 2.50
12 Al Wilson 2.50
13 Jim Young 7.50
14 Coaching Staff 3.50

1975 Royal Bank B.C. Lions

NM
Complete Set (14): 40.00
Common Player: 2.50
1 Brock Ansley 2.50
2 Terry Bailey 2.50
3 Bill Baker 6.00
4 Elton Brown 2.50
5 Grady Cavness 3.50
6 Ross Clarkson 2.50
7 Joe Fourqurean 2.50
8 Lou Harris 3.50
9 Layne McDowell 2.50
10 Don Moorhead 2.50
11 Tony Moro 2.50
12 Ray Nettles 2.50
13 Curtis Wester 3.50
14 Jim Young 7.50

1976 Royal Bank B.C. Lions

NM
Complete Set (15): 40.00
Common Player: 2.50
1 Terry Bailey 2.50
2 Bill Baker 6.00
3 Ted Dushinski 2.50
4 Eric Guthrie 2.50
5 Lou Harris 3.50
6 Glen Jackson 2.50
7 Rocky Long 2.50
8 Layne McDowell 2.50
9 Ray Nettles 2.50
10 Gary Robinson 2.50
11 John Sciarra 6.00
12 Wayne Smith 2.50
13 Michael Strickland 2.50
14 Al Wilson 2.50
15 Jim Young 7.50

1977 Royal Bank B.C. Lions

NM
Complete Set (12): 40.00
Common Player: 2.50
1 Doug Carlson 2.50
2 Sam Cvijanovich 2.50
3 Ted Dushinski 2.50
4 Paul Giroday 2.50
5 Glen Jackson 2.50
6 Frank Landy 2.50
7 Lui Passaglia 7.50
8 John Sciarra 6.00
9 Michael Strickland 2.50
10 Jerry Tagge 7.50
11 Al Wilson 2.50
12 Jim Young 7.50

1978 Royal Bank B.C. Lions

NM
Complete Set (12): 40.00
Common Player: 2.50
1 Terry Bailey 2.50
2 Leon Bright 5.00
3 Doug Carlson 2.50
4 Grady Cavness 3.50
5 Al Charuk 2.50
6 Paul Giroday 2.50
7 Larry Key 2.50
8 Frank Landy 2.50
9 Lui Passaglia 7.50
10 Jerry Tagge 7.50
11 Al Wilson 2.50
12 Jim Young 7.50

1987 Royal Studios Saskatchewan Roughriders

MT
Complete Set (40): 35.00
Common Player: .75
1 Dave Albright .75
2 Roger Aldag 1.00
3 Mike Anderson .75
4 Tron Armstrong .75
5 Terry Baker 1.00
6 Walter Bender 1.25
7 Jeff Bentrim 1.25
8 Todd Brown .75
9 Tom Burgess 3.00
10 Coaching Staff (John Hufnagel, Dick Adams, John Gregory, Ted Heath, Gary Hoffman, M. Samples) 1.00
11 Terry Cochrane .75
12 David Conrad .75
13 Steve Crane .75
14 James Curry 2.00
15 Tony Dennis .75
16 Ray Elgaard 3.00
17 Denny Ferdinand 1.00
18 Roderick Fisher .75
19 Joe Fuller .75
20 Gainer The Gopher (Team Mascot) .75
21 Norris Gibbs .75
22 Nick Hebeler .75
23 Bryan Illerbrun 1.00
24 Alan Johns .75
25 Bobby Jurasin 3.00
26 Eddie Lowe 1.00
27 Tracey Mack .75
28 Tim McCray 1.50
29 Mike McGruder 1.00
30 Ken Moore .75
31 Dan Rashovich .75
32 Scott Redl .75
33 Dave Ridgway 1.25
34 Dave Sidoo .75
35 Harry Skipper 1.00
36 Lawrie Skolrood .75
37 Vic Stevenson .75
38 Glen Suitor 1.00
39 Brendan Taman Asst. EQ MG, Ivan Gutfriend Athletic Therapist, Norm Fong EQ MG .75
40 Mark Urness .75

1988 Royal Studios Saskatchewan Roughriders

MT
Complete Set (54): 40.00
Common Player: .50
1 Dave Albright .50
2 Roger Aldag (DP) .75
3 Mike Anderson .50
4 Kent Austin (DP) 4.00
5 Terry Baker .75
6 Jeff Bentrim .75
7 Rob Bresciani .50
8 Albert Brown .50
9 Tom Burgess (DP) 2.50
10 Coaching Staff (Gary Hoffman, Dick Adams, Dan Daniel, Ted Heath, John Gregory, Steve Goldman) .75
11 Dick Cohee and The Store (and The Store) .50
12 David Conrad .50
13 Steve Crane .50
14 James Curry (DP) 1.25
15 Dream Team (Cheerleaders) 1.25
16 Ray Elgaard 2.50
17 James Ellingson .50
18 Jeff Fairholm 1.25
19 Denny Ferdinand .75
20 The Flame (Team Mascot) .50
21 Norm Fong, Ivan Gutfriend (Equipment/Trainer) .50
22 Joe Fuller .50
23 Gainer The Gopher (Team Mascot) .50
24 Vince Goldsmith 1.00
25 John Gregory (CO) .75
26 Richie Hall .50
27 Bill Henry .50
28 James Hood .50
29 Bryan Illerbrun (UER) (Name misspelled Brian on front and back) .75

30 Milson Jones 1.25
31 Bobby Jurasin (DP) 2.50
32 Tim Kearse .50
33 Rick Klassen .75
34 Gary Lewis .75
35 Eddie Lowe .75
36 Greg McCormack .50
37 Tim McCray 1.00
38 Ray McDonald .75
39 Mike McGruder .75
40 Ken Moore .50
41 Donald Narcisse 2.00
42 Dan Rambo, Brendan Taman (Rider Scouting) .50
43 Dan Rashovich .75
44 Dameon Reilly .75
45 Dave Ridgway (DP) 1.00
46 Rocco Romano .50
47 Harry Skipper .75
48 Vic Stevenson .50
49 Glen Suitor .75
50 Jeff Treftlin .50
51 Mark Urness .50
52 Eddie Ray Walker .50
53 John Walker .75
54 Jeff Watson .50

1989 Royal Studios Saskatchewan Roughriders

MT
Complete Set (54): 35.00
Common Player: .50
1 Dave Albright .50
2 Roger Aldag (DP) .75
3 Tuineau Alipate .75
4 Mike Anderson .50
5 Kent Austin 3.00
6 Terry Baker .75
7 Jeff Bentrim .75
8 Rob Bresciani .50
9 Albert Brown .50
10 Tom Burgess (DP) 2.50
11 Coaching Staff .75
12 Steve Crane .50
13 James Curry 1.25
14 Kevin Dixon .50
15 Dream Team (Cheerleaders sponsored by CKRM) 1.00
16 Wayne Drinkwalter .75
17 Ray Elgaard 2.00
18 James Ellingson .50
19 Jeff Fairholm .75
20 The Flame .50
21 Norm Fong, Ivan Gutfriend (Equipment/Trainer) .50
22 Gainer The Gopher (DP) (Team Mascot) .50
23 John Gregory (CO) .75
24 Vince Goldsmith .75
25 Mark Guy .50
26 Richie Hall (DP) .50
27 John Hoffman .50
28 Bryan Illerbrun (UER) (Name misspelled Brian on front and back) .75
29 Milson Jones .75
30 Bobby Jurasin (DP) 2.00
31 Chuck Klingbeil .75
32 Gary Lewis .75
33 Eddie Lowe .75
34 Greg McCormack .50
35 Tim McCray 1.00
36 Ray McDonald .50
37 Ken Moore .50
38 Cedric Moses .50
39 Donald Narcisse 1.50
40 Dan Payne .50
41 Bob Poley .50
42 Dan Rashovich .50
43 Dave Ridgway (DP) 1.00
44 Junior Robinson .75
45 Harry Skipper .75
46 Vic Stevenson .50
47 Glen Suitor 1.00
48 Jeff Treftlin .50
49 Kelly Trithart .50
50 Mark Urness .50
51 Lionel Vital .50
52 Eddie Ray Walker .75
53 Steve Wiggins .50
54 Donovan Wright .50

1990 Royal Studios Saskatchewan Roughriders

MT
Complete Set (60): 35.00
Common Player: .50
1 Dick Adams (CO) .50
2 Dave Albright .50
3 Roger Aldag .75
4 Tuineau Alipate .75
5 Mike Anderson .50
6 Kent Austin 3.00
7 Tony Belser .50
8 Jeff Bentrim .75
9 Bruce Boyko .75
10 Albert Brown .75
11 Paul Bushey .50
12 Larry Donovan (CO) .50
13 Dream Team (Cheerleaders sponsored by CKRM) .75
14 Wayne Drinkwalter .75
15 Sean Dykes .50
16 Ray Elgaard 2.00
17 Jeff Fairholm 1.00
18 Norman Fong MG, Ivan Gutfriend MG .50
19 Alan Ford (GM) .50
20 Lucius Floyd .75
21 Gainer The Gopher (Team Mascot) .50
22 Chris Gioskos .50
23 Vince Goldsmith 1.00
24 John Gregory (CO) .75
25 Mark Guy .75
26 Stacey Hairston .75
27 Richie Hall .75
28 Greg Harris .50
29 Ted Heath (CO) .50
30 Gary Hoffman (CO) .50
31 John Hoffman .50
32 Larry Hogue .75
33 Bobby Jurasin 2.00
34 Milson Jones 1.00
35 James King .50
36 Chuck Klingbeil 1.00
37 Mike Lazecki .50
38 Orville Lee 1.50
39 Gary Lewis .75
40 Eddie Lowe .75
41 Greg McCormack .50
42 Tim McCray 1.00
43 Ken Moore .50
44 Donald Narcisse 1.50
45 Dave Pitcher .50
46 Bob Poley .50
47 Brent Pollack .50
48 Dan Rashovich .50
49 Tony Rice 1.50
50 Dave Ridgway 1.00
51 Pal Sartori .50
52 Saskatchewan Roughriders 1.00
53 Glen Scrivner .50
54 Tony Simmons .50
55 Vic Stevenson .50
56 Glen Suitor 1.00
57 Jeff Treftlin .75
58 Kelly Trithart (UER) (Name misspelled Trihart on front and back) .75
59 Lionel Vital .50
60 Slater Zaleski .50

1991 Royal Studios Saskatchewan Roughriders

MT
Complete Set (66): 35.00
Common Player: .40
1 Dick Adams (CO) .40
2 Dave Albright .40
3 Roger Aldag .60
4 Mike Anderson .40
5 Kent Austin 3.00
6 John Bankhead .60
7 1990 Miss Grey Cup (Kerry Beutler) .60
8 Allan Boyko .60
9 Bruce Boyko .60
10 Doug Brewster .40
11 Albert Brown .60
12 Paul Bushey .40
13 Coaching Staff .40
14 Larry Donovan (CO) .40
15 Wayne Drinkwalter .60
16 Sean Dykes .40
17 Ray Elgaard 2.00
18 Jeff Fairholm 1.00
19 Dan Farthing .40
20 Lucius Ford .60
21 Gainer The Gopher (Team Mascot) .40
22 Chris Gioskos (UER) (Name misspelled Gioskas on front) .60
23 Sonny Gordon .40
24 John Gregory (CO) .60
25 Stacey Hairston .60
26 Richie Hall .60
27 Greg Harris .40
28 Major Harris 1.50
29 Ted Heath (CO) .40
30 Gary Hoffman (CO) .40
31 John Hoffman .40
32 Larry Hogue .40
33 Willis Jacox 1.50
34 Ray Jauch (CO) .40
35 Gene Jelks 1.50
36 Milson Jones .40
37 Bobby Jurasin 2.00
38 James King .40
39 Mike Lazecki .40
40 Orville Lee 1.50
41 Gary Lewis .60
42 Eddie Lowe .60
43 Paul Maines .40
44 Don Matthews (CO) .40
45 Dane McArthur .40
46 David McCrary .40
47 Don Narcisse 1.50
48 Offensive Line .40
49 David Pitcher .60
50 Bob Poley .40
51 Brent Pollack .40
52 Basil Proctor .40
53 Dan Rashovich .40
54 Dave Ridgway (UER) (Name misspelled Ridgeway on back) 1.00
55 Roughriders vs The Rocket 1.00
56 Roughriders Team .60
57 Glen Scrivner .40
58 Keith Stephens .40
59 Vic Stevenson .40
60 Glen Suitor 1.00
61 Chris Thieneman .40
62 Jeff Treftlin .60
63 Kelly Trithart .60
64 Paul Vaida .40
65 Ted Wahl .40
66 Rick Worman 1.00

1971 Sargent Promotions Stamps

NM
Complete Set (225): 240.00
Common Player: .75
1 Jim Young 7.50
2 Trevor Ekdahl 1.25
3 Ted Gerela 1.25
4 Jim Evenson 1.25
5 Ray Lychak .75
6 Dave Golinsky .75
7 Ted Warkentin .75
8 A.D. Whitfield 1.25
9 Lach Heron 1.25
10 Ken Phillips .75
11 Lefty Hendrickson .75
12 Paul Brothers .75
13 Eagle Keys (CO) 1.50
14 Garrett Hunsperger .75
15 Greg Findlay .75
16 Dave Easley .75
17 Barrie Hansen .75
18 Wayne Dennis .75
19 Jerry Bradley .75
20 Gerry Herron .75
21 Gary Robinson .75
22 Bill Whisler .75
23 Bob Howes .75
24 Tom Wilkinson 6.00
25 Tom Cassese .75
26 Dick Suderman 1.25
27 Jerry Keeling 4.00
28 John Helton 4.00
29 Jim Furlong .75
30 Fred James .75
31 Howard Starks .75
32 Craig Koinzan .75
33 Frank Andruski .75
34 Joe Forzani 1.25
35 Herb Schumn .75
36 Gerry Shaw .75
37 Lanny Boleski .75
38 Jim Duncan (CO) .75
39 Hugh McKinnis .75
40 Basil Bark .75
41 Herman Harrison 4.00
42 Larry Robinson 1.25
43 Larry Lawrence .75
44 Granville Liggins 2.00
45 Wayne Harris 4.00
46 John Atamian .75
47 Wayne Holm .75
48 Rudy Linterman 1.25
49 Jim Sillye .75
50 Terry Wilson .75
51 Don Trull 2.00
52 Rusty Clark .75
53 Ted Page .75
54 Ken Ferguson .75
55 Alan Pitcaithley .75
56 Bayne Norrie .75
57 Dave Gasser .75
58 Jim Thomas .75
59 Terry Swarn 1.25
60 Ron Forwick .75
61 Henry King .75
62 John Wydareny 1.25
63 Ray Jauch (CO) 1.25
64 Jim Henshall .75
65 Dave Cutler 4.00
66 Fred Dunn .75
67 Dick Dupuis 1.25
68 Fritz Greenlee .75
69 Jerry Griffin 1.25
70 Allen Ische .75
71 John LaGrone 1.25
72 Mike Law .75
73 Ed Molstad .75
74 Greg Pipes 1.25
75 Roy Shatzko .75
76 Joe Zuger 1.25
77 Wally Gabler 1.25
78 Tony Gabriel 6.00
79 John Reid .75
80 Dave Fleming .75
81 Jon Hohman .75
82 Tommy Joe Coffey 5.00
83 Dick Wesolowski .75
84 Gordon Christian .75
85 Steve Worster 6.00
86 Bob Taylor 1.50
87 Doug Mitchell .75
88 Al Dorow (CO) 1.25
89 Angelo Mosca 7.50
90 Bill Danychuk 1.25
91 Mike Blum .75
92 Garney Henley 6.00
93 Bob Steiner .75
94 John Manel .75
95 Bob Krouse .75
96 John Williams .75
97 Scott Henderson .75
98 Ed Chalupka .75
99 Paul McKay .75
100 Rensi Perdoni .75
101 Ed George 1.25
102 Al Phaneuf 1.25
103 Sonny Wade 2.00
104 Moses Denson 2.00
105 Terry Evanshen 6.00
106 Pierre Desjardins .75
107 Larry Fairholm .75
108 Gene Gaines 4.00
109 Bobby Lee Thompson .75
110 Mike Widger .75
111 Gene Ceppetelli .75
112 Barry Randall .75
113 Sam Etcheverry (CO) 2.50
114 Mark Kosmos 1.25
115 Peter Dalla Riva 4.00
116 Ted Collins .75
117 John Couture .75
118 Tony Passander .75
119 Garry Lefebvre .75
120 George Springate .75
121 Gordon Judges .75
122 Steve Smear 2.50
123 Tom Pullen .75
124 Merl Code .75
125 Steve Booras .75
126 Hugh Oldham .75
127 Moe Racine .75
128 John Kruspe .75
129 Ken Lehmann 1.25
130 Billy Cooper .75
131 Marshall Shirk .75
132 Tom Schuette .75
133 Doug Specht .75
134 Dennis Duncan .75
135 Jerry Campbell 1.25
136 Wayne Giardino .75
137 Roger Perdrix .75
138 Jack Gotta (CO) .75
139 Terry Wellesley .75
140 Dave Braggins .75
141 Dave Pivec .75
142 Rod Woodward .75
143 Garry Wood 2.00
144 Al Marcelin 1.25
145 Dan Dever .75
146 Ivan MacMillan .75
147 Wayne Smith .75
148 Barry Ardern .75
149 Rick Cassatta 1.25
150 Bill Van Burkleo .75
151 Ron Lancaster 5.00
152 Wayne Shaw .75
153 Bob Kosid .75
154 George Reed 7.50
155 Don Bahnuik .75
156 Gordon Barwell .75
157 Clyde Brock .75
158 Alan Ford .75
159 Jack Abendschan .75
160 Steve Molnar .75
161 Al Rankin .75
162 Bobby Thompson .75
163 Dave Skrien (CO) .75
164 Nolan Bailey .75
165 Bill Baker 5.00
166 Bruce Bennett 1.50
167 Gary Brandt .75
168 Charlie Collins .75
169 Henry Dorsch .75
170 Ted Dushinski .75
171 Bruce Gainer .75
172 Ralph Galloway .75
173 Ken Frith .75
174 Cliff Shaw .75
175 Silas McKinnie .75
176 Mike Eben .75
177 Greg Barton 2.00
178 Joe Theismann 20.00
179 Charlie Bray .75
180 Roger Scales .75
181 Bob Hudspeth .75
182 Bill Symons 1.50
183 Dave Raimey 1.25
184 Dave Cranmer 1.25
185 Mel Profit 1.25
186 Paul Desjardins .75
187 Tony Moro .75
188 Leo Cahill (CO) .75
189 Chip Barrett .75
190 Pete Martin .75
191 Walt Balasiuk .75
192 Jim Corrigall 1.50
193 Ellison Kelly 5.00
194 Jim Tomlin .75
195 Marv Luster 2.00
196 Jim Thorpe 2.00
197 Jim Stillwagon 4.00
198 Ed Harrington .75
199 Jim Dye .75
200 Leon McQuay 2.50
201 Rob McLaren .75
202 Benji Dial .75
203 Chuck Liebrock .75
204 Glen Schapansky .75
205 Ed Ulmer .75
206 Ross Richardson .75
207 Lou Andrus .75
208 Paul Robson .75
209 Paul Brule .75
210 Doug Strong .75
211 Dick Smith .75
212 Bill Frank .75
213 Jim Spavital (CO) .75
214 Rick Shaw .75
215 Joe Critchlow .75
216 Don Jonas 3.00
217 Bob Swift .75
218 Larry Kerychuk .75
219 Bob McCarthy .75
220 Gene Lakusiak .75
221 Jim Heighton .75
222 Chuck Harrison .75
223 Lance Fletcher .75
224 Larry Slagle .75
225 Wayne Giesbrecht .75

1956 Shredded Wheat CFL

NM
Complete Set (105): 9000.
Common Player: 80.00
A1 Peter Muir 80.00
A2 Harry Langford 80.00
A3 Tony Pajaczkowski 150.00
A4 Bob Morgan 80.00
A5 Baz Nagle 80.00
A6 Alex Macklin 80.00
A7 Bob Geary 80.00
A8 Don Klosterman 125.00
A9 Bill McKenna 80.00
A10 Bill Stevenson 80.00
A11 Charles Baillie 80.00
A12 Berdett Hess 80.00
A13 Lynn Bottoms 90.00
A14 Doug Brown 80.00
A15 Jack Hennemier 80.00
B1 Frank Anderson 80.00
B2 Don Barry 80.00
B3 Johnny Bright 200.00
B4 Kurt Burris 80.00
B5 Bob Dean 80.00
B6 Don Getty 150.00
B7 Normie Kwong 200.00
B8 Earl Lindley 80.00
B9 Art Walker 100.00
B10 Rollie Miles 125.00
B11 Frank Morris 125.00
B12 Jackie Parker 300.00
B13 Ted Tully 80.00
B14 Frank Ivy 90.00
B15 Bill Rowekamp 80.00
C1 Al Sherman 80.00
C2 Larry Cabrelli 80.00
C3 Ron Kelly 80.00
C4 Edward Kotowich 80.00
C5 Buddy Leake 100.00
C6 Thomas Lumsden 80.00
C7 Bill Smitiuk 80.00
C8 Buddy Tinsley 125.00
C9 Ron Vaccher 80.00
C10 Eagle Day 125.00
C11 Buddy Allison 80.00
C12 Bob Haas 90.00
C13 Steve Patrick 80.00
C14 Keith Pearce (UER) (Misspelled Pierce on front) 80.00
C15 Lorne Benson 80.00
D1 George Arnett 80.00
D2 Eddie Bevan 80.00
D3 Art Darch 80.00
D4 John Fedosoff 80.00
D5 Cam Fraser 80.00
D6 Ron Howell 90.00
D7 Alex Muzyka 80.00
D8 Chet Miksza 80.00
D9 Walt Nikorak 80.00
D10 Pete Neumann 125.00
D11 Steve Oneschuk 80.00
D12 Vince Scott 125.00
D13 Ralph Toohy 80.00
D14 Ray Truant 80.00
D15 Nobby Wirkowski 100.00
E1 Pete Bennett 80.00
E2 Fred Black 80.00
E3 Jim Copeland 80.00
E4 Al Pfeifer 90.00
E5 Ron Albright 80.00
E6 Tom Dublinski 80.00
E7 Billy Shipp 80.00
E8 Baz Mackie 80.00
E9 Bill McFarlane 80.00
E10 John Sopinka 100.00
E11 Dick Brown 80.00
E12 Gerry Doucette 80.00
E13 Dan Shaw 80.00
E14 Dick Shatto 175.00
E15 Bill Swiacki 100.00
F1 Ray Syrnyk 80.00
F2 Martin Ruby 125.00
F3 Bobby Marlow 125.00
F4 Doug Kiloh 80.00
F5 Gord Sturtridge 90.00
F6 Stan Williams 80.00
F7 Larry Isbell 80.00
F8 Ken Casner 80.00
F9 Mel Becket 100.00
F10 Reg Whitehouse 80.00
F11 Harry Lampman 80.00
F12 Mario DeMarco 90.00
F13 Ken Carpenter 100.00
F14 Dick Filchock 100.00
F15 Frank Tripucka 125.00
G1 Tom Tracy 150.00
G2 Pete Ladygo 80.00
G3 Sam Scoccia 80.00
G4 Joe Upton 80.00
G5 Bob Simpson 150.00
G6 Bruno Bitkowski 90.00
G7 Joe Stracini (UER) (Misspelled Straccini on card front) 80.00
G8 Hal Ledyard 80.00
G9 Milt Graham 80.00
G10 Bill Sowalski 80.00
G11 Avatus Stone 80.00
G12 John Boich 100.00
G13 Don Pinhey (UER) (Misspelled Bob Pinkney on card front) 80.00
G14 Peter Karpuk 80.00
G15 Frank Clair 125.00

1994 Smokey Sacramento

MT
Complete Set (18): 30.00
Common Player: 1.25
1 Fred Anderson (GEO) 1.25
2 David Archer 5.00
3 George Bethune 1.25
4 David Diaz-Infante 1.25
5 Willie Fears 1.50
6 Corian Freeman 1.25
7 Pete Gardere 1.50
8 Tom Gerhart 1.25
9 Rod Harris 1.25
10 Bobby Humphery 2.50
11 Mike Kiselak 1.25
12 Mark Ledbetter 1.25
13 Maurice Miller 1.25
14 Troy Mills 1.25
15 Mike Oliphant 2.50
16 James Pruitt 1.25
17 Junior Robinson 1.25
18 Kay Stephenson (CO) 1.25

1993 Sport Chek Calgary Stampeders

MT
Complete Set (24): 15.00
Common Player: .60
1 Karl Anthony .60
2 Raymond Biggs .60
3 Douglas Craft .60
4 Doug Davies .60
5 Mark Dube .60
6 Matt Finlay .60
7 Doug Flutie 4.00
8 Fred Gatlin .60
9 Keyvan Jenkins 1.00
10 Alondra Johnson .60
11 Pat Mahon .60
12 Tony Martino .60
13 Mark McLoughlin .60
14 Andy McVey .60
15 Will Moore 2.50
16 Mark Pearce .60
17 Allen Pitts 1.25
18 David Sapunjis 1.25
19 Junior Thurman 1.25
20 Gerald Vaughn .60
21 Ken Watson .60
22 Brian Wiggins 1.00
23 Blair Zerr .60
24 Srecko Zizakovic 1.00

1958 Topps CFL

NM
Complete Set (88): 500.00
Common Player: 5.00
1 Paul Anderson 12.00
2 Leigh McMillan 5.00
3 Vic Chapman 5.00
4 Bobby Marlow 12.00
5 Mike Cacic 5.00
6 Ron Pawlowski 5.00
7 Frank Morris 9.00
8 Earl Keeley 6.00
9 Don Walsh 5.00
10 Bryan Engram 5.00
11 Bobby Kuntz 6.00
12 Jerry Janes 5.00
13 Don Bingham 5.00
14 Paul Fedor 5.00
15 Tommy Grant 12.00
16 Don Getty 20.00
17 George Brancato 5.00
18 Jackie Parker 40.00
19 Alan Valdes 5.00
20 Paul Dekker 5.00
21 Frank Tripucka 12.00
22 Gerry McDougall 9.00
23 Duke Dewveall 6.00
24 Ted Smale 5.00
25 Tony Pajaczkowski 12.00
26 Don Pinhey 5.00
27 Buddy Tinsley 12.00
28 Cookie Gilchrist 35.00
29 Larry Isbell 5.00
30 Bob Kelley 5.00
31 Tom "Corky" Tharp 6.00
32 Steve Patrick 5.00
33 Hardiman Cureton 5.00
34 Joe Mobra 5.00
35 Harry Lunn 5.00
36 Gord Rowland 6.00
37 Herb Gray 15.00
38 Bob Simpson 15.00
39 Cam Fraser 5.00
40 Kenny Ploen 18.00
41 Lynn Bottoms 6.00
42 Bill Stevenson 5.00
43 Jerry Selinger 5.00
44 Oscar Kruger 9.00
45 Gerry James 15.00
46 Dave Mann 12.00
47 Tom Dimitroff 5.00
48 Vince Scott 12.00
49 Fran Rogel 6.00
50 Henry Hair 5.00
51 Bob Brady 5.00
52 Gerry Doucette 5.00
53 Ken Carpenter 6.00
54 Bernie Faloney 25.00
55 John Barrow 20.00
56 George Druxman 5.00
57 Rollie Miles 12.00
58 Jerry Cornelison 5.00
59 Harry Langford 5.00
60 Johnny Bright 20.00
61 Ron Clinkscale 5.00
62 Jack Hill 5.00
63 Ron Quillian 5.00
64 Ted Tully 5.00
65 Pete Neft 5.00
66 Arvyd Buntins 5.00
67 Normie Kwong 20.00
68 Matt Phillips 5.00
69 Pete Bennett 5.00
70 Vern Lofstrom 5.00
71 Norm Stoneburgh 5.00
72 Danny Nykoluk 5.00
73 Chuck Dubuque 5.00
74 John Varone 5.00
75 Bob Kimoff 5.00
76 John Pyeatt 5.00
77 Pete Neumann 12.00
78 Ernie Pitts 9.00
79 Steve Oneschuk 5.00
80 Kaye Vaughan 12.00
81 Joe Yamauchi 5.00
82 Harvey Wylie 9.00
83 Berdett Hess 5.00
84 Dick Shatto 20.00
85 Floyd Harrawood 5.00
86 Ron Atchison 12.00
87 Bobby Judd 5.00
88 Keith Pearce 9.00

1959 Topps CFL

NM
Complete Set (88): 400.00
Common Player: 4.00
1 Norm Rauhaus 10.00
2 Cornel Piper (UER) (Misspelled Cornell on both sides) 4.00
3 Leo Lewis 20.00
4 Roger Savoie 4.00
5 Jim Van Pelt 10.00
6 Herb Gray 10.00
7 Gerry James 10.00
8 By Bailey 12.00
9 Tom Hinton 8.00
10 Chuck Quilter 4.00
11 Mel Gillett 4.00
12 Ted Hunt 4.00
13 Sonny Homer 5.00
14 Bill Jessup 4.00
15 Al Dorow (Checklist 1-44 back) 20.00
16 Norm Fieldgate 12.00
17 Urban Henry 5.00
18 Paul Cameron 4.00
19 Bruce Claridge 4.00
20 Jim Bakhtiar 4.00
21 Earl Lunsford 12.00
22 Walt Radzick 4.00
23 Ron Albright 4.00
24 Art Scullion 4.00
25 Ernie Warlick 6.00
26 Nobby Wirkowski 5.00
27 Harvey Wylie 9.00
28 Gordon Brown 4.00
29 Don Luzzi 10.00
30 Hal Patterson 20.00
31 Jackie Simpson 15.00
32 Doug McNichol 4.00
33 Bob MacLellan 4.00
34 Ted Elsby 4.00
35 Mike Kovac 4.00
36 Bob Leary 4.00
37 Hal Krebs 4.00
38 Steve Jennings 4.00
39 Don Getty 12.00
40 Normie Kwong 12.00
41 Johnny Bright 15.00
42 Art Walker 5.00
43 Jackie Parker (UER) (Incorrectly listed as Tackle on card front) 35.00
44 Don Barry (Checklist 45-88 back) 20.00
45 Tommy Joe Coffey 25.00
46 Mike Volcan 4.00
47 Stan Renning 4.00
48 Gino Fracas 9.00
49 Ted Smale 4.00
50 Mack Yoho 5.00
51 Bobby Gravens 4.00
52 Milt Graham 4.00
53 Lou Bruce 4.00
54 Bob Simpson 12.00
55 Bill Sowalski 4.00
56 Russ Jackson 40.00
57 Don Clark 4.00
58 Dave Thelen 10.00
59 Larry Cowart 4.00
60 Dave Mann 4.00
61 Norm Stoneburgh (UER) (Misspelled Stoneburg) 4.00
62 Ronnie Knox 9.00
63 Dick Shatto 12.00
64 Bobby Kuntz 5.00
65 Phil Muntz 4.00
66 Gerry Doucette 4.00
67 Sam DeLuca 5.00

68 Boyd Carter 4.00
69 Vic Kristopaitis 9.00
70 Gerry McDougall (UER) 5.00
(Misspelled Jerry)
71 Vince Scott 10.00
72 Angelo Mosca 35.00
73 Chet Miksza 4.00
74 Eddie Macon 5.00
75 Harry Lampman 4.00
76 Bill Graham 4.00
77 Ralph Goldston 5.00
78 Cam Fraser 4.00
79 Ron Dundas 4.00
80 Bill Clarke 4.00
81 Len Legault 4.00
82 Reg Whitehouse 4.00
83 Dale Parsons 4.00
84 Doug Kiloh 4.00
85 Tom Whitehouse 4.00
86 Mike Hagler 4.00
87 Paul Anderson 4.00
88 Danny Banda 5.00

1960 Topps CFL

NM
Complete Set (88): 500.00
Common Player: 4.00
1 By Bailey 12.00
2 Paul Cameron 4.00
3 Bruce Claridge 4.00
4 Chuck Dubuque 4.00
5 Randy Duncan 12.00
6 Norm Fieldgate 10.00
7 Urban Henry 5.00
8 Ted Hunt 4.00
9 Bill Jessup 4.00
10 Ted Tully 4.00
11 Vic Chapman 4.00
12 Gino Fracas 5.00
13 Don Getty 10.00
14 Ed Gray 4.00
15 Oscar Kruger 20.00
(Checklist 1-44 back)
16 Rollie Miles 10.00
17 Jackie Parker 30.00
18 Joe-Bob Smith (UER) 4.00
(Misspelled Bob-Joe
on both sides)
19 Mike Volcan 4.00
20 Art Walker 5.00
21 Ron Albright 4.00
22 Jim Bakhtiar 4.00
23 Lynn Bottoms 5.00
24 Jack Gotta 8.00
25 Joe Kapp 50.00
26 Earl Lunsford 9.00
27 Don Luzzi 9.00
28 Art Scullion 4.00
29 Hugh Simpson 4.00
30 Ernie Warlick 8.00
31 John Barrow 12.00
32 Paul Dekker 4.00
33 Bernie Faloney 20.00
34 Cam Fraser 4.00
35 Ralph Goldston 5.00
36 Ron Howell 5.00
37 Gerry McDougall (UER) 4.00
(Misspelled Jerry)
38 Angelo Mosca 20.00
39 Pete Neumann 8.00
40 Vince Scott 8.00
41 Ted Elsby 4.00
42 Sam Etcheverry 25.00
43 Mike Kovac 4.00
44 Ed Learn 4.00
45 Ivan Livingstone 20.00
(Checklist 45-88 back)
46 Hal Patterson 18.00
47 Jackie Simpson 12.00
48 Veryl Switzer 4.00
49 Bill Bewley 9.00
50 Joel Wells 4.00
51 Ron Atchison 9.00
52 Ken Carpenter 5.00
53 Bill Clarke 4.00
54 Ron Dundas 4.00
55 Mike Hagler 4.00
56 Jack Hill 4.00
57 Doug Kiloh 4.00
58 Bobby Marlow 10.00
59 Bob Mulgado 4.00
60 George Brancato 5.00
61 Lou Bruce 4.00
62 Hardiman Cureton 4.00
63 Russ Jackson 25.00
64 Gerry Nesbitt 4.00
65 Bob Simpson 10.00
66 Ted Smale 4.00
67 Dave Thelen 9.00
68 Kaye Vaughan 8.00
69 Pete Bennett 4.00
70 Boyd Carter 4.00
71 Gerry Doucette 4.00
72 Bobby Kuntz 5.00
73 Alex Panton 4.00
74 Tobin Rote 18.00
75 Jim Rountree 5.00
76 Dick Shatto 10.00
77 Norm Stoneburgh 4.00
78 Tom "Corky" Tharp 5.00
79 George Druxman 4.00
80 Herb Gray 10.00
81 Gerry James 10.00
82 Leo Lewis 10.00
83 Ernie Pitts 4.00
84 Kenny Ploen 15.00
85 Norm Rauhaus 4.00
86 Gord Rowland 4.00
87 Charlie Shepard 5.00
88 Don Clark 10.00

1961 Topps CFL

NM
Complete Set (132): 900.00
Common Player: 6.00
1 By Bailey 15.00
2 Bruce Claridge 6.00
3 Norm Fieldgate 12.00
4 Willie Fleming 20.00
5 Urban Henry 7.50
6 Bill Herron 6.00
7 Tom Hinton 10.00
8 Sonny Homer 7.50
9 Bob Jeter 15.00
10 Vic Kristopaitis 6.00
11 Baz Nagle 6.00
12 Ron Watton 6.00
13 Joe Yamauchi 6.00
14 Bob Schloredt 15.00
15 B.C. Lions Team 12.00
16 Ron Albright 6.00
17 Gordon Brown 6.00
18 Gerry Doucette 6.00
19 Gene Filipski 12.00
20 Joe Kapp 30.00
21 Earl Lunsford 12.00
22 Don Luzzi 12.00
23 Bill McKenna 6.00
24 Ron Morris 6.00
25 Tony Pajaczkowski 12.00
26 Lorne Reid 6.00
27 Art Scullion 6.00
28 Ernie Warlick 10.00
29 Stampeders Team 12.00
30 Johnny Bright 15.00
31 Vic Chapman 6.00
32 Gino Fracas 7.50
33 Tommy Joe Coffey 18.00
34 Don Getty 15.00
35 Ed Gray 6.00
36 Oscar Kruger 7.50
37 Rollie Miles 12.00
38 Roger Nelson 12.00
39 Jackie Parker 35.00
40 Howie Schumm 6.00
41 Joe-Bob Smith (UER) 6.00
(Misspelled Bob-Joe
on both sides)
42 Art Walker 7.50
43 Eskimos Team 12.00
44 John Barrow 15.00
45 Paul Dekker 6.00
46 Tom Dublinski 6.00
47 Bernie Faloney 25.00
48 Cam Fraser 6.00
49 Ralph Goldston 7.50
50 Ron Howell 7.50
51 Gerry McDougall 7.50
52 Pete Neumann 12.00
53 Bronko Nagurski 15.00
54 Vince Scott 10.00
55 Steve Oneschuk 7.50
56 Hal Patterson 20.00
57 Jim Taylor 7.50
58 Tiger-Cats Team 12.00
59 Ted Elsby 6.00
60 Don Clark 7.50
61 Dick Cohee 10.00
62 George Dixon 20.00
63 Wes Gideon 6.00
64 Harry Lampman 6.00
65 Meco Poliziani 6.00
66 Charles Baillie 6.00
67 Howard Cissell 6.00
68 Ed Learn 6.00
69 Tom Moran 6.00
70 Jack Simpson 12.00
71 Bill Bewley 7.50
72 Tom Hugo 6.00
73 Alouettes Team 15.00
74 Gilles Archambeault 6.00
75 Lou Bruce 6.00
76 Russ Jackson 30.00
77 Tom Jones 6.00
78 Gerry Nesbitt 6.00
79 Ron Lancaster 40.00
80 Joe Kelly 6.00
81 Joe Poirier 7.50
82 Doug Daigneault 6.00
83 Kaye Vaughan 10.00
84 Dave Thelen 15.00
85 Ron Stewart 25.00
86 Ted Smale 6.00
87 Bob Simpson 15.00
88 Ottawa Rough Riders 12.00
Team
89 Don Allard 6.00
90 Ron Atchison 12.00
91 Bill Clarke 6.00
92 Ron Dundas 6.00
93 Jack Gotta 10.00
94 Bob Golic 7.50
95 Jack Hill 6.00
96 Doug Kiloh 7.50
97 Len Legault 6.00
98 Doug McKenzie 6.00
99 Bob Ptacek 6.00
100 Roy Smith 6.00
101 Saskatchewan 12.00
Roughriders Team
102 Checklist 1-132 90.00
103 Jim Andreotti 7.50
104 Boyd Carter 6.00
105 Dick Fouts 7.50
106 Cookie Gilchrist 25.00
107 Bobby Kuntz 7.50
108 Jim Rountree 7.50
109 Dick Shatto 15.00
110 Norm Stoneburgh 6.00
111 Dave Mann 10.00
112 Ed Ochiena 6.00
113 Bill Stribling 6.00
114 Tobin Rote 20.00
115 Stan Wallace 6.00
116 Billy Shipp 7.50
117 Argonauts Team 15.00
118 Dave Burkholder 6.00
119 Jack Delveaux 6.00
120 George Druxman 6.00
121 Farrell Funston 7.50
122 Herb Gray 12.00
123 Gerry James 12.00
124 Ronnie Latourelle 6.00
125 Leo Lewis 15.00
126 Steve Patrick 6.00
127 Ernie Pitts 6.00
128 Kenny Ploen 15.00
129 Norm Rauhaus 7.50
130 Gord Rowland 7.50
131 Charlie Shepard 7.50
132 Winnipeg Blue 20.00
Bombers Team Card

1961 Topps CFL Transfers

NM
Complete Set (24): 700.00
Common Player (1-15): 25.00
Common Team (19-27): 20.00
1 Don Clark 30.00
2 Gene Filipski 30.00
3 Willie Fleming 40.00
4 Cookie Gilchrist 45.00
5 Jack Hill 25.00
6 Bob Jeter 30.00
7 Joe Kapp 65.00
8 Leo Lewis 40.00
9 Gerry McDougall 25.00
10 Jackie Parker 50.00
11 Hal Patterson 40.00
12 Kenny Ploen 40.00
13 Bob Ptacek 25.00
14 Ron Stewart 40.00
15 Dave Thelen 40.00
16 British Columbia Lions 20.00
Logo/Pennant
20 Calgary Stampeders 20.00
Logo/Pennant
21 Edmonton Eskimos 20.00
Logo/Pennant
22 Hamilton Tiger-Cats 20.00
Logo/Pennant
23 Montreal Alouettes 20.00
Logo/Pennant
24 Ottawa Rough Riders 20.00
Logo/Pennant
25 Saskatchewan 20.00
Roughriders
Logo/Pennant
26 Toronto Argonauts 20.00
Logo/Pennant
27 Winnipeg Blue 20.00
Bombers
Logo/Pennant

1962 Topps CFL

NM
Complete Set (169): 500.00
Common Player: 2.00
1 By Bailey 6.00
2 Nub Beamer 2.00
3 Tom Brown 8.00
4 Mack Burton 2.00
5 Mike Cacic 2.00
6 Pat Claridge 2.00
7 Steve Cotter 2.00
8 Lonnie Dennis 2.00
9 Norm Fieldgate 5.00
10 Willie Fleming 10.00
11 Tom Hinton 4.00
12 Sonny Homer 3.00
13 Joe Kapp 14.00
14 Tom Larscheid 2.00
15 Gordie Mitchell 2.00
16 Baz Nagle 2.00
17 Norris Stevenson 2.00
18 Barney Therrien (UER) 2.00
(Misspelled Therien on
card front)
19 Don Vicic 2.00
20 B.C. Lions Team 8.00
21 Ed Buchanan 2.00
22 Joe Carruthers 2.00
23 Lovell Coleman 4.00
24 Barrie Cyr 2.00
25 Ernie Danjean 3.00
26 Gene Filipski 4.00
27 George Hansen 2.00
28 Earl Lunsford 5.00
29 Don Luzzi 4.00
30 Bill McKenna 2.00
31 Tony Pajaczkowski 4.00
32 Chuck Quilter 2.00
33 Lorne Reid 2.00
34 Art Scullion 2.00
35 Jim Walden 2.00
36 Harvey Wylie 4.00
37 Calgary Stampeders 8.00
Team Card
38 Johnny Bright 10.00
39 Vic Chapman 2.00
40 Marion Drew Deese 2.00
41 Al Ecuyer 2.00
42 Gino Fracas 3.00
43 Don Getty 6.00
44 Ed Gray 2.00
45 Urban Henry 3.00
46 Bill Hill 2.00
47 Mike Kmeche 2.00
48 Oscar Kruger 3.00
49 Mike Lashuk 2.00
50 Jim Letcavits 2.00
51 Roger Nelson 4.00
52 Jackie Parker 15.00
53 Howie Schumm 2.00
54 Jim Shipka 2.00
55 Bill Smith 2.00
56 Jo Bob Smith 2.00
57 Art Walker 3.00
58 Edmonton Eskimos 8.00
Team Card
59 John Barrow 8.00
60 Hardiman Cureton 2.00
61 Geno DeNobile 2.00
62 Tom Dublinski 2.00
63 Bernie Faloney 12.00
64 Cam Fraser 2.00
65 Ralph Goldston 3.00
66 Tommy Grant 7.00
67 Garney Henley 15.00
68 Ron Howell 3.00
69 Zeno Karcz 3.00
70 Gerry McDougall (UER) 3.00
(Misspelled Jerry)
71 Chet Miksza 2.00
72 Bronko Nagurski 6.00
73 Hal Patterson 10.00
74 George Scott 2.00
75 Vince Scott 4.00
76 Hamilton Tiger-Cats 8.00
Team Card
77 Ron Brewer 3.00
78 Ron Brooks 2.00
79 Howard Cissell 2.00
80 Don Clark 3.00
81 Dick Cohee 3.00
82 John Conroy 2.00
83 Milt Crain 3.00
84 Ted Elsby 2.00
85 Joe Francis 3.00
86 Gene Gaines 8.00
87 Barrie Hansen 2.00
88 Mike Kovac 2.00
89 Ed Learn 2.00
90 Billy Ray Locklin 2.00
91 Marv Luster 6.00
92 Bobby Jack Oliver 3.00
93 Sandy Stephens 8.00
94 Montreal Alouettes 10.00
Team Card
95 Gilles Archambeault 2.00
96 Bruno Bitkowski 3.00
97 Jim Conroy 3.00
98 Doug Daigneault 2.00
99 Dick Desmarais 2.00
100 Russ Jackson 15.00
101 Tom Jones 2.00
102 Ron Lancaster 20.00
103 Angelo Mosca 15.00
104 Gerry Nesbitt 2.00
105 Joe Poirier 3.00
106 Moe Racine 2.00
107 Gary Schreider 2.00
108 Bob Simpson 6.00
109 Ted Smale 2.00
110 Ron Stewart 7.00
111 Dave Thelen 6.00
112 Kaye Vaughan 4.00
113 Ottawa Rough Riders 8.00
Team Card
114 Ron Atchison (UER) 4.00
(Misspelled Atcheson
on card front)
115 Danny Banda 2.00
116 Al Benecick 2.00
117 Clair Branch 2.00
118 Fred Burket 2.00
119 Bill Clarke 2.00
120 Jim Copeland 2.00
121 Ron Dundas 2.00
122 Bob Golic 3.00
123 Jack Gotta 4.00
124 Dave Grosz 2.00
125 Neil Habig 3.00
126 Jack Hill 2.00
127 Len Legault 2.00
128 Bob Ptacek 2.00
129 Roy Smith 2.00
130 Saskatchewan 8.00
Roughriders Team
Card
131 Lynn Bottoms 3.00
132 Dick Fouts 3.00
133 Wes Gideon 2.00
134 Cookie Gilchrist 15.00
135 Art Johnson 2.00
136 Bobby Kuntz 3.00
137 Dave Mann 4.00
138 Marty Martinello 2.00
139 Doug McNichol 2.00
140 Bill Mitchell 2.00
141 Danny Nykoluk 2.00
142 Walt Radzick 2.00
143 Tobin Rote 10.00
144 Jim Rountree 3.00
145 Dick Shatto 8.00
146 Billy Shipp 3.00
147 Norm Stoneburgh 2.00
148 Toronto Argonauts 10.00
Team Card
149 Dave Burkholder 2.00
150 Jack Delveaux 2.00
151 George Druxman 2.00
152 Farrell Funston 3.00
153 Herb Gray 5.00
154 Roger Hagberg 3.00
155 Gerry James 6.00
156 Henry Janzen 3.00
157 Ronnie Latourelle 2.00
158 Hal Ledyard 2.00
159 Leo Lewis 6.00
160 Steve Patrick 2.00
161 Cornel Piper 2.00
162 Ernie Pitts 2.00
163 Kenny Ploen 8.00
164 Norm Rauhaus 3.00
165 Frank Rigney 6.00
166 Gord Rowland 3.00
167 Roger Savoie 2.00
168 Charlie Shepard 3.00
169 Winnipeg Blue 20.00
Bombers Team Card

1963 Topps CFL

NM
Complete Set (88): 300.00
Common Player: 2.50
1 Willie Fleming 12.00
2 Dick Fouts 3.50
3 Joe Kapp 15.00
4 Nub Beamer 2.50
5 By Bailey 6.00
6 Tom Walker 2.50
7 Sonny Homer 3.50
8 Tom Hinton 5.00
9 Lonnie Dennis 2.50
10 British Columbia Lions 7.50
Team Card
11 Ed Buchanan 2.50
12 Ernie Danjean 2.50
13 Eagle Day 6.00
14 Earl Lunsford 5.00
15 Don Luzzi 5.00
16 Tony Pajaczkowski 5.00
17 Jerry Keeling 15.00
18 Pat Holmes 2.50
19 Wayne Harris 15.00
20 Calgary Stampeders 7.50
Team Card
21 Tommy Joe Coffey 7.50
22 Mike Lashuk 2.50
23 Bobby Walden 5.00
24 Don Getty 8.00
25 Len Vella 2.50
26 Ted Frechette 2.50
27 E.A. Sims 2.50
28 Nat Dye 2.50
29 Edmonton Eskimos 7.50
Team Card
30 Bernie Faloney 10.00
31 Hal Patterson 8.00
32 John Barrow 6.00
33 Sam Fernandez 2.50
34 Garney Henley 12.00
35 Joe Zuger 5.00
36 Hardiman Cureton 2.50
37 Zeno Karcz 3.50
38 Bobby Kuntz 3.50
39 Hamilton Tiger-Cats 7.50
Team Card
40 George Dixon 6.00
41 Don Clark 3.50
42 Marv Luster 6.00
43 Bobby Jack Oliver 3.50
44 Billy Ray Locklin 2.50
45 Sandy Stephens 6.00
46 Milt Crain 3.50
47 Meco Poliziani 2.50
48 Ted Elsby 2.50
49 Montreal Alouettes 9.00
Team Card
50 Russ Jackson 15.00
51 Ron Stewart 8.00
52 Dave Thelen 6.00
53 Kaye Vaughan 5.00
54 Joe Poirier 3.50
55 Moe Racine 2.50
56 Whit Tucker 10.00
57 Ernie White 2.50
58 Ottawa Rough Ridgers 7.50
Team Card
59 Bob Ptacek 2.50
60 Ray Purdin 2.50
61 Dale West 3.50
62 Neil Habig 2.50
63 Jack Gotta 3.50
64 Billy Gray 2.50
65 Don Walsh 2.50
66 Bill Clarke 2.50
67 Saskatchewan 7.50
Roughriders Team
Card
68 Jackie Parker 15.00
69 Dave Mann 5.00
70 Dick Shatto 6.00
71 Norm Stoneburgh 2.50
(UER) (Misspelled
Stoneburg front)
72 Clare Exelby 2.50
73 Art Johnson 2.50
74 Doug McNichol 2.50
75 Danny Nykoluk 2.50
76 Walt Radzick 2.50
77 Toronto Argonauts 9.00
Team Card
78 Leo Lewis 6.00
79 Kenny Ploen 7.00
80 Henry Janzen 3.50
81 Charlie Shepard 3.50
82 Roger Hagberg 3.50
83 Herb Gray 6.00
84 Frank Rigney 5.00
85 Jack Delveaux 2.50
86 Ronnie Latourelle 2.50
87 Winnipeg Blue 7.50
Bombers Team Card
88 Checklist Card 50.00

1964 Topps CFL

NM
Complete Set (88): 300.00
Common Player: 2.50
1 Willie Fleming 12.00
2 Dick Fouts 3.50
3 Joe Kapp 15.00
4 Nub Beamer 2.50
5 Tom Brown 5.00
6 Tom Walker 2.50
7 Sonny Homer 3.50
8 Tom Hinton 5.00
9 Lonnie Dennis 2.50
10 B.C. Lions Team 7.50
11 Lovell Coleman 4.00
12 Ernie Danjean 2.50
13 Eagle Day 5.00
14 Jim Furlong 2.50
15 Don Luzzi 5.00
16 Tony Pajaczkowski 5.00
17 Jerry Keeling 6.00
18 Pat Holmes 2.50
19 Wayne Harris 7.50
20 Calgary Stampeders 7.50
Team Card
21 Tommy Joe Coffey 7.50
22 Al Ecuyer 2.50
23 Checklist Card 35.00
24 Don Getty 6.00
25 Len Vella 2.50
26 Ted Frechette 2.50
27 E.A. Sims 2.50
28 Nat Dye 2.50
29 Edmonton Eskimos 7.50
Team Card
30 Bernie Faloney 15.00
31 Hal Patterson 8.00
32 John Barrow 6.00
33 Tommy Grant 6.00
34 Garney Henley 9.00
35 Joe Zuger 3.50
36 Hardiman Cureton 2.50
37 Zeno Karcz 3.50
38 Bobby Kuntz 3.50
39 Hamilton Tiger-Cats 7.50
Team Card
40 George Dixon 7.50
41 Dave Hoppmann 2.50
42 Dick Walton 2.50
43 Jim Andreotti 3.50
44 Billy Ray Locklin 2.50
45 Fred Burket 2.50
46 Milt Crane 3.50
47 Meco Poliziani 2.50
48 Ted Elsby 2.50
49 Montreal Alouettes 9.00
Team Card
50 Russ Jackson 15.00
51 Ron Stewart 8.00
52 Dave Thelen 5.00
53 Kaye Vaughan 5.00
54 Joe Poirier 3.50
55 Moe Racine 2.50
56 Whit Tucker 6.00
57 Ernie White 2.50
58 Ottawa Roughriders 7.50
Team Card
59 Bob Ptacek 2.50
60 Ray Purdin 2.50
61 Dale West 3.50
62 Neil Habig 2.50
63 Jack Gotta 3.50
64 Billy Gray 2.50
65 Don Walsh 2.50
66 Bill Clarke 2.50
67 Saskatchewan 7.50
Roughriders Team
Card
68 Jackie Parker 15.00
69 Dave Mann 4.00
70 Dick Shatto 6.00
71 Norm Stoneburgh 2.50
72 Clare Exelby 2.50
73 Jim Christopherson 2.50
74 Sherman Lewis 6.00
75 Danny Nykoluk 2.50
76 Walt Radzick 2.50
77 Toronto Argonauts 9.00
Team Card
78 Leo Lewis 6.00
79 Kenny Ploen 6.00
80 Henry Janzen 3.50
81 Charlie Shepard 3.50
82 Roger Hagberg 3.50
83 Herb Gray 6.00
84 Frank Rigney 5.00
85 Jack Delveaux 2.50
86 Ronnie Latourelle 2.50
87 Winnipeg Blue 7.50
Bombers Team Card
88 Checklist Card 50.00

1965 Topps CFL

NM
Complete Set (132): 325.00
Common Player: 2.00
1 Neal Beaumont 6.00
2 Tom Brown 6.00
3 Mike Cacic 2.00
4 Pat Claridge 2.00
5 Steve Cotter 2.00
6 Lonnie Dennis 2.00
7 Norm Fieldgate 4.00
8 Willie Fleming 10.00
9 Dick Fouts 3.00
10 Tom Hinton 4.00
11 Sonny Homer 3.00
12 Joe Kapp 12.00
13 Paul Seale 2.00
14 Steve Shafer 2.00
15 Bob Swift 2.00
16 Larry Anderson 2.00
17 Lu Bain 2.00
18 Lovell Coleman 3.00
19 Eagle Day 4.00
20 Jim Furlong 2.00
21 Wayne Harris 6.00
22 Herman Harrison 12.00
23 Jerry Keeling 5.00
24 Hal Krebs 2.00
25 Don Luzzi 4.00
26 Tony Pajaczkowski 4.00
27 Larry Robinson 4.00
28 Bob Taylor 3.00
29 Ted Woods 2.00
30 Jon Anabo 2.00
31 Jim Battle 2.00
32 Charlie Brown 2.00
33 Tommy Joe Coffey 7.50
34 Marcel Deleeuw 2.00
35 Al Ecuyer 2.00
36 Jim Higgins 2.00
37 Oscar Kruger 3.00
38 Barry Mitchelson 2.00
39 Roger Nelson 4.00
40 Bill Redell 2.00
41 E.A. Sims 2.00
42 Jim Stinnette 2.00
43 Jim Thomas 2.00
44 Terry Wilson 2.00
45 Art Baker 2.00
46 John Barrow 6.00
47 Dick Cohee 3.00
48 Frank Cosentino 4.00
49 Johnny Counts 2.00
50 Tommy Grant 5.00
51 Garney Henley (See 9.00
also number 57)
52 Zeno Karcz 3.00
53 Ellison Kelly 12.00
54 Bobby Kuntz 3.00
55 Angelo Mosca 12.00
56 Bronko Nagurski 6.00
57 Don Sutherin (UER) 12.00
(number 51 on back)
58 Dave Viti 2.00
59 Joe Zuger 3.00
60 Checklist 1-60 25.00
61 Jim Andreotti 3.00
62 Harold Cooley 2.00
63 Nat Craddock 2.00
64 George Dixon 6.00
65 Ted Elsby 2.00
66 Clare Exelby 2.00
67 Bernie Faloney 12.00
68 Al Irwin 2.00
69 Ed Learn 2.00
70 Moe Levesque 2.00
71 Bob Minihane 2.00
72 Jim Reynolds 2.00
73 Billy Roy 2.00
74 Billy Joe Booth 3.00
75 Jim Cain 2.00
76 Larry DeGraw 2.00
77 Don Estes 2.00
78 Gene Gaines 5.00
79 John Kennerson 2.00
80 Roger Kramer 3.00
81 Ken Lehmann 3.00
82 Bob O'Billovich 2.00
83 Joe Poirier 3.00
84 Bill Quinter 2.00
85 Jerry Selinger 2.00
86 Bill Siekierski 2.00
87 Len Sparks 2.00
88 Whit Tucker 4.00
89 Ron Atchison 4.00
90 Ed Buchanan 2.00
91 Hugh Campbell 10.00
92 Henry Dorsch 2.00
93 Garner Ekstran 3.00
94 Martin Fabi 2.00
95 Bob Good 2.00
96 Ron Lancaster 12.00
97 Bob Ptacek 2.00
98 George Reed 25.00
99 Wayne Shaw 2.00
100 Dale West 3.00
101 Reg Whitehouse 2.00
102 Jim Worden 2.00
103 Ron Brewer 3.00
104 Don Fuell 2.00
105 Ed Harrington 3.00
106 George Hughley 2.00
107 Dave Mann 4.00
108 Marty Martinello 2.00
109 Danny Nykoluk 2.00
110 Jackie Parker 15.00
111 Dave Pivec 2.00
112 Walt Radzick 2.00
113 Lee Sampson 2.00
114 Dick Shatto 5.00
115 Norm Stoneburgh 2.00
116 Jim Vollenweider 2.00
117 John Wydareny 3.00
118 Billy Cooper 2.00
119 Farrell Funston 3.00
120 Herb Gray 5.00
121 Henry Janzen 3.00
122 Leo Lewis 6.00
123 Brian Palmer 2.00
124 Cornel Piper 2.00
125 Ernie Pitts 2.00
126 Kenny Ploen 6.00
127 Norm Rauhaus 3.00
128 Frank Rigney 4.00
129 Roger Savoie 2.00
130 Dick Thornton 4.00

131	Bill Whisler	2.00
132	Checklist 61-132	40.00

1965 Topps CFL Transfers

		NM
Complete Set (27):		500.00
Common Player:		20.00
1	British Columbia Lions Crest	20.00
2	British Columbia Lions Pennant	20.00
3	Calgary Stampeders Crest	20.00
4	Calgary Stampeders Pennant	20.00
5	Edmonton Eskimos Crest	20.00
6	Edmonton Eskimos Pennant	20.00
7	Hamilton Tiger-Cats Crest	20.00
8	Hamilton Tiger-Cats Pennant	20.00
9	Montreal Alouettes Crest	20.00
10	Montreal Alouettes Pennant	20.00
11	Ottawa Rough Riders Crest	20.00
12	Ottawa Rough Riders Pennant	20.00
13	Saskatchewan Roughriders Crest	20.00
14	Saskatchewan Roughriders Pennant	20.00
15	Toronto Argonauts Crest	20.00
16	Toronto Argonauts Pennant	20.00
17	Winnipeg Blue Bombers Crest	20.00
18	Winnipeg Blue Bombers Pennant	20.00
19	Quebec Provincial Crest	20.00
20	Ontario Provincial Crest	20.00
21	Manitoba Provincial Crest	20.00
22	Saskatchewan Provincial Crest	20.00
23	Alberta Provincial Crest	20.00
24	British Columbia Provincial Crest	20.00
25	Northwest Territories Territorial Crest	20.00
26	Yukon Territory Territorial Crest	20.00
27	Canada	30.00

1988 Vachon CFL

		MT
Complete Set (160):		135.00
Common Player:		.75
1	Dave Albright	1.00
2	Roger Aldag	1.00
3	Marv Allemang	.75
4	Damon Allen	2.50
5	Gary Allen	1.00
6	Randy Ambrosie	.75
7	Mike Anderson	.75
8	Kent Austin	4.00
9	Terry Baker	1.00
10	Danny Bass	3.00
11	Nick Bastaja	.75
12	Greg Battle	2.50
13	Lyle Bauer	.75
14	Jearld Baylis	2.00
15	Ian Beckstead	.75
16	Walter Bender	1.50
17	Nick Benjamin	1.00
18	David Black	.75
19	Leo Blanchard	.75
20	Trevor Bowles	.75
21	Ken Braden	.75
22	Rod Brown	.75
23	Less Browne	1.00
24	Jamie Buis	.75
25	Tom Burgess	3.50
26	Bob Cameron	1.00
27	Jan Carinci	.75
28	Tony Champion	2.50
29	Jacques Chapdelaine	.75
30	Tony Cherry	2.50
31	Lance Chomyc	1.00
32	John Congemi	2.00
33	Rod Connop	.75
34	David Conrad	.75
35	Grover Covington	2.00
36	Larry Crawford	1.25
37	James Curry	2.00
38	Marco Cyncar	1.00
39	Gabriel DeLaGarza	.75
40	Mike Derks	.75
41	Blake Dermott	1.00
42	Roy DeWalt (SP)	4.00
43	Todd Dillon	1.25
44	Rocky DiPietro	2.00
45	Kevin Dixon (SP)	2.00
46	Tom Dixon	.75
47	Selwyn Drain	.75
48	Matt Dunigan	7.50
49	Ray Elgaard	3.00
50	Jerome Erdman	.75
51	Randy Fabi	.75
52	Gill Fenerty	2.00
53	Denny Ferdinand	1.00
54	Dan Ferrone	1.00
55	Howard Fields	.75
56	Matt Finlay	.75
57	Rickey Foggie	2.00
58	Delbert Fowler	1.00
59	Ed Gataveckas	.75
60	Keith Gooch	.75
61	Miles Gorrell	.75
62	Mike Gray	.75
63	Leo Groenewegen	.75
64	Ken Hailey	.75
65	Harold Hallman	1.00
66	Tracy Ham	5.00
67	Rodney Harding	2.00
68	Glenn Harper	.75
69	J.T. Hay	.75
70	Larry Hogue	.75
71	Ron Hopkins (SP)	2.00
72	Hank Llesic	2.00
73	Bryan Illerbrun	.75
74	Lemont Jeffers	.75
75	James Jefferson	2.00
76	Rick Johnson	2.00
77	Chris Johnstone	.75
78	Johnnie Jones	.75
79	Milson Jones	1.50
80	Stephen Jones	2.00
81	Bobby Jurasin	2.50
82	Jerry Kauric	1.00
83	Dan Kearns	.75
84	Trevor Kennerd	2.00
85	Mike Kerrigan	4.00
86	Rick Klassen	2.00
87	Lee Knight	.75
88	Kevin Konar	1.00
89	Glenn Kulka	1.25
90	Doug (Tank) Landry	2.00
91	Scott Lecky	.75
92	Orville Lee	1.50
93	Marc Lewis	1.00
94	Eddie Lowe	.75
95	Lynn Madsen	.75
96	Chris Major	3.00
97	Doran Major	.75
98	Tony Martino	.75
99	Tim McCray	1.25
100	Michael McGruder	1.25
101	Sean McKeown (SP)	4.00
102	Andy McVey	.75
103	Stan Mikawos	.75
104	James Mills	2.00
105	Larry Mohr	.75
106	Bernie Morrison	.75
107	James Murphy	2.00
108	Paul Osbaldiston	1.00
109	Anthony Parker	1.50
110	James Parker	2.00
111	Greg Peterson	.75
112	Tim Petros	1.25
113	Reggie Pleasant	1.25
114	Willie Pless	2.00
115	Bob Poley	.75
116	Tom Porras	1.50
117	Hector Pothier	.75
118	Jim Reid	1.50
119	Robert Reid	.75
120	Gilbert Renfroe	2.00
121	Tom Richards	1.25
122	Dave Ridgway	2.00
123	Rae Robirtis	.75
124	Gerald Roper	.75
125	Darryl Sampson	.75
126	Jim Sandusky	2.50
127	David Sauve	.75
128	Art Schlichter	2.00
129	Ralph Scholz	.75
130	Mark Seale	1.00
131	Dan Sellers	.75
132	Lance Shields	1.00
133	Ian Sinclair	1.50
134	Mike Siroishka	.75
135	Chris Skinner	.75
136	Harry Skipper	1.00
137	Darrell Smith	3.00
138	Tom Spoletini	.75
139	Steve Stapler	1.00
140	Bill Stevenson	.75
141	Gregg Stumon	1.25
142	Glen Suitor	.75
143	Emmanuel Tolbert	2.50
144	Perry Tuttle (SP)	4.00
145	Peter VandenBos	.75
146	Jake Vaughan	.75
147	Chris Walby	1.50
148	Mike Walker	1.50
149	Patrick Wayne	.75
150	James West	2.00
151	Brett Williams	1.50
152	David Williams	2.50
153	Henry Williams	8.00
154	Tommy Williams	.75
155	Larry Willis	1.00
156	Don Wilson	.75
157	Earl Winfield	2.50
158	Rick Worman	2.00
159	Larry Wruck	.75
160	Kari Yli-Renko	.75

1989 Vachon CFL

		MT
Complete Set (160):		125.00
Common Player:		.75
1	Tony Williams	1.00
2	Sean Foudy	.75
3	Tom Schimmer	.75
4	Ken Evraire	1.00
5	Gerald Wilcox	1.00
6	Damon Allen	2.00
7	Tony Kimbrough	.75
8	Dean Dorsey	1.00
9	Rocco Romano	.75
10	Ken Braden	.75
11	Kari Yli-Renko	.75
12	Darrel Hopper	.75
13	Irv Daymond	.75
14	Orville Lee	1.00
15	Steve Howlett	.75
16	Kyle Hall	.75
17	Reggie Ward	.75
18	Gerald Alphin	2.00
19	Troy Wilson	.75
20	Patrick Wayne	.75
21	Harold Hallman	1.25
22	John Congemi	1.50
23	Doran Major	.75
24	Hank Llesic	1.50
25	Gilbert Renfroe	2.00
26	Rodney Harding	1.00
27	Todd Wiseman	.75
28	Chris Schultz	1.00
29	Carl Brazley	1.00
30	Darrell Smith	2.50
31	Glenn Kulka	1.00
32	Bob Skemp	.75
33	Don Moen	1.00
34	Jearld Baylis	2.00
35	Lorenzo Graham	.75
36	Lance Chomyc	1.00
37	Warren Hudson	.75
38	Gill Fenerty	2.00
39	Paul Masotti	1.00
40	Reggie Pleasant	1.25
41	Scott Flagel	.75
42	Mike Kerrigan	2.50
43	Frank Robinson	1.00
44	Jacques Chapdelaine	.75
45	Miles Gorrell	.75
46	Mike Walker	1.50
47	Jason Riley	.75
48	Grover Covington	1.50
49	Ralph Scholz	.75
50	Mike Derks	.75
51	Derrick McAdoo	1.50
52	Rocky DiPietro	2.00
53	Lance Shields	1.00
54	Dale Sanderson	.75
55	Tim Lorenz	.75
56	Rod Skillman	.75
57	Jed Tommy	.75
58	Paul Osbaldiston	1.00
59	Darrell Corbin	.75
60	Tony Champion	1.50
61	Romel Andrews	.75
62	Bob Cameron	1.00
63	Greg Battle	2.00
64	Rod Hill	1.00
65	Steve Rodehutskors	1.00
66	Trevor Kennerd	1.50
67	Moustafa Ali	1.00
68	Mike Gray	.75
69	Bob Molle	.75
70	Tim Jessie	1.00
71	Matt Pearce	.75
72	Will Lewis	.75
73	Sean Salisbury	2.50
74	Chris Walby	1.00
75	Jeff Croonen	.75
76	David Black	.75
77	Buster Rhymes	2.00
78	James Murphy	1.50
79	Stan Mikawos	.75
80	Lee Saltz	2.00
81	Bryan Illerbrun	.75
82	Donald Narcisse	3.00
83	Milson Jones	1.00
84	Dave Ridgway	1.50
85	Glen Suitor	.75
86	Terry Baker	1.00
87	James Curry	1.50
88	Harry Skipper	1.00
89	Bobby Jurasin	2.00
90	Gary Lewis	.75
91	Roger Aldag	1.00
92	Jeff Fairholm	2.00
93	Dave Albright	.75
94	Ray Elgaard	2.50
95	Kent Austin	3.50
96	Tom Burgess	3.00
97	Richie Hall	.75
98	Eddie Lowe	.75
99	Vince Goldsmith	1.00
100	Tim McCray	1.00
101	Leo Blanchard	.75
102	Tom Spoletini	.75
103	Dan Ferrone	1.00
104	Doug (Tank) Landry	1.50
105	Chris Major	1.50
106	Mike Palumbo	.75
107	Terrence Jones	2.00
108	Larry Willis	1.25
109	Kent Warnock	.75
110	Tim Petros	1.00
111	Marshall Toner	.75
112	Ken Ford	.75
113	Ron Hopkins	.75
114	Eric Kramer	7.50
115	Stu Laird	.75
116	Vernell Quinn	.75
117	Lemont Jeffers	.75
118	Derrick Taylor	.75
119	Jay Christensen	1.00
120	Mitchell Price	.75
121	Rod Connop	.75
122	Mark Norman	.75
123	Andre Francis	1.00
124	Reggie Taylor	1.50
125	Rick Worman	1.00
126	Marco Cyncar	1.00
127	Blake Dermott	.75
128	Jerry Kauric	1.00
129	Steve Taylor	2.00
130	Dave Richardson	.75
131	John Mandarich	1.00
132	Gregg Stumon	1.00
133	Tracy Ham	4.00
134	Danny Bass	2.50
135	Blake Marshall	1.50
136	Jeff Braswell	1.00
137	Larry Wruck	1.00
138	Warren Jones	.75
139	Stephen Jones	1.50
140	Tom Richards	1.00
141	Tony Cherry	1.50
142	Anthony Parker	1.50
143	Gerald Roper	.75
144	Lui Passaglia	2.00
145	Mack Moore	.75
146	Jamie Taras	.75
147	Rickey Foggie	1.50
148	Matt Dunigan	6.00
149	Anthony Drawhorn	1.00
150	Eric Streater	1.25
151	Marcus Thomas	.75
152	Wes Cooper	.75
153	James Mills	1.00
154	Peter VandenBos	.75
155	Ian Sinclair	1.00
156	James Parker	1.50
157	Andrew Murray	.75
158	Larry Crawford	1.25
159	Kevin Konar	1.00
160	David Williams	1.50

1959 Wheaties CFL

		NM
Complete Set (48):		4000.
Common Player:		60.00
1	Ron Adam	60.00
2	Bill Bewley	75.00
3	Lynn Bottoms	75.00
4	Johnny Bright	150.00
5	Ken Carpenter	75.00
6	Tony Curcillo	60.00
7	Sam Etcheverry	250.00
8	Bernie Faloney	200.00
9	Cam Fraser	75.00
10	Don Getty	125.00
11	Jack Gotta	75.00
12	Milt Graham	60.00
13	Jack Hill	60.00
14	Ron Howell	75.00
15	Russ Jackson	200.00
16	Gerry James	125.00
17	Doug Kiloh	60.00
18	Ronnie Knox	75.00
19	Vic Kristopaitis	60.00
20	Oscar Kruger	60.00
21	Bobby Kuntz	75.00
22	Normie Kwong	175.00
23	Leo Lewis	150.00
24	Harry Lunn	60.00
25	Don Luzzi	100.00
26	Dave Mann	75.00
27	Bobby Marlow	90.00
28	Gerry McDougall	75.00
29	Doug McNichol	60.00
30	Rollie Miles	100.00
31	Red O'Quinn	90.00
32	Jackie Parker	250.00
33	Hal Patterson	150.00
34	Don Pinhey	60.00
35	Kenny Ploen	125.00
36	Gord Rowland	75.00
37	Vince Scott	90.00
38	Art Scullion	60.00
39	Dick Shatto	125.00
40	Bob Simpson	125.00
41	Jackie Simpson (UER) (Misspelled Jacki)	100.00
42	Bill Sowalski	60.00
43	Norm Stoneburgh	60.00
44	Buddy Tinsley	90.00
45	Frank Tripucka	100.00
46	Jim Van Pelt	60.00
47	Ernie Warlick	75.00
48	Nobby Wirkowski	100.00

MEMORABILIA/FIGURINES

1964 Coke Caps All-Stars AFL

The 44-cap, 1-1/8" in diameter set, found on bottles of Coca-Cola, was distributed in AFL cities. The cap outsides have a Coke logo with a football icon, while the inside of the cap features the player's face in black with surrounding text. A cap saver sheet was issued and could be redeemed for various prizes. Other Coke products, such as Fresca and Tab, also had the football caps.

		NM
Complete Set (44):		175.00
Common Player:		2.50
1	Tommy Addison	2.50
2	Dalva Allen	2.50
3	Lance Alworth	10.00
4	Houston Antwine	2.50
5	Fred Arbanas	2.50
6	Tony Banfield	2.50
7	Stew Barber	2.50
8	George Blair	2.50
9	Mel Branch	2.50
10	Nick Buoniconti	8.00
11	Doug Cline	2.50
12	Eldon Danehauer	2.50
13	Clem Daniels	5.00
14	Larry Eisenhauer	2.50
15	Earl Faison	2.50
16	Cookie Gilchrist	5.00
17	Freddy Glick	2.50
18	Larry Grantham	5.00
19	Ron Hall	2.50
20	Charlie Hennigan	5.00
21	E.J. Holub	2.50
22	Ed Husmann	2.50
23	Jack Kemp	25.00
24	Dave Kocourek	2.50
25	Keith Lincoln	5.00
26	Charlie Long	2.50
27	Paul Lowe	5.00
28	Archie Matsos	2.50
29	Jerry Mays	5.00
30	Ron Mix	5.00
31	Tom Morrow	2.50
32	Billy Neighbors	2.50
33	Jim Otto	5.00
34	Art Powell	5.00
35	Johnny Robinson	5.00
36	Tobin Rote	2.50
37	Bob Schmidt	2.50
38	Tom Sestak	2.50
39	Billy Shaw	2.50
40	Bob Talamini	2.50
41	Lionel Taylor	5.00
42	Jim Tyrer	5.00
43	Dick Westmoreland	2.50
44	Fred Williamson	5.00

1964 Coke Caps All-Stars NFL

The 44-cap, 1-1/8" in diameter set is virtually identical to the 44-cap AFL set of the same year. The outside of each cap has the Coke logo with a football, with the inside having the player's facial image. As with the AFL set, a Cap Saver sheet was issued with potential prizes for collectors. Other Coke products, such as Fresca and Tab, also had the football caps.

		NM
Complete Set (44):		160.00
Common Player:		2.50
1	Doug Atkins	5.00
2	Terry Barr	2.50
3	Jim Brown	25.00
4	Roger Brown	5.00
5	Roosevelt Brown	6.00
6	Timmy Brown	5.00
7	Bobby Joe Conrad	5.00
8	Willie Davis	6.00
9	Bob DeMarco	2.50
10	Darrell Dess	2.50
11	Mike Ditka	15.00
12	Bill Forester	2.50
13	Joe Fortunato	2.50
14	Bill George	5.00
15	Ken Gray	2.50
16	Forrest Gregg	8.00
17	Roosevelt Grier	6.00
18	Hank Jordan	5.00
19	Jim Katcavage	5.00
20	Jerry Kramer	7.00
21	Ron Kramer	2.50
22	Dick Lane	5.00
23	Dick Lynch	2.50
24	Gino Marchetti	6.00
25	Tommy Mason	2.50
26	Ed Meador	2.50
27	Bobby Mitchell	7.00
28	Larry Morris	2.50
29	Merlin Olsen	8.00
30	Jim Parker	5.00
31	Jim Patton	5.00
32	Myron Pottios	2.50
33	Jim Ringo	5.00
34	Dick Schafrath	2.50
35	Joe Schmidt	5.00
36	Del Shofner	5.00
37	Bob St. Clair	5.00
38	Jim Taylor	8.00
39	Roosevelt Taylor	5.00
40	Y.A. Tittle	10.00
41	Johnny Unitas	16.00
42	Larry Wilson	5.00
43	Willie Wood	5.00
44	Abe Woodson	5.00

1964 Coke Caps Browns

The 35-cap, 1-1/8" in diameter set was issued in Ohio and featured top Browns players, including a a first-year cap of receiver Paul Warfield. The cap tops feature a football stamp while the inside depicts a Browns player. A Cap Saver sheet, featuring Frank Ryan, was also issued.

		NM
Complete Set (35):		125.00
Common Player:		2.50
1	Walter Beach	2.50
2	Larry Benz	2.50
3	Johnny Brewer	2.50
4	Jim Brown	30.00
5	John Brown	2.50
6	Monte Clark	5.00
7	Gary Collins	5.00
8	Vince Costello	5.00
9	Ross Fichtner	2.50
10	Galen Fiss	2.50
11	Bobby Franklin	2.50
12	Bob Gain	2.50
13	Bill Glass	5.00
14	Ernie Green	2.50
15	Lou Groza	8.00
16	Gene Hickerson	2.50
17	Jim Houston	2.50
18	Tom Hutchinson	2.50
19	Jim Kanicki	2.50
20	Mike Lucci	5.00
21	Dick Modzelewski	5.00
22	John Morrow	2.50
23	Jim Ninowski	2.50
24	Frank Parker	2.50
25	Bernie Parrish	5.00
26	Frank Ryan	5.00
27	Charlie Scales	2.50
28	Dick Schafrath	5.00
29	Roger Shoals	2.50
30	Jim Shorter	2.50
31	Billy Truax	5.00
32	Paul Warfield	16.00
33	Ken Webb	2.50
34	Paul Wiggin	2.50
35	John Wooten	5.00
NNO	Browns Saver Sheet Frank Ryan pictured	20.00

1964 Coke Caps Chargers

The 35-cap, 1-1/8" set was issued in Southern California and featured top players from the AFL Chargers. As with other cap sets, a Cap Saver sheet was also available and when completed, collectors could redeem it for various prizes.

		NM
Complete Set (35):		100.00
Common Player:		2.50
1	Chuck Allen	5.00
2	Lance Alworth	16.00
3	George Blair	2.50
4	Frank Buncom	2.50
5	Earl Faison	5.00
6	Kenny Graham	2.50
7	George Gross	2.50
8	Sam Gruneison	2.50
9	John Hadl	10.00
10	Dick Harris	2.50
11	Bob Jackson	2.50
12	Emil Karas	2.50
13	Dave Kocourek	2.50
14	Ernie Ladd	6.00
15	Bobby Lane	2.50
16	Keith Lincoln	5.00
17	Paul Lowe	5.00
18	Jacque MacKinnon	2.50
19	Gerry McDougall	2.50
20	Charlie McNeil	5.00
21	Bob Mitinger	2.50
22	Ron Mix	6.00
23	Don Norton	2.50
24	Ernie Park	2.50
25	Bob Petrich	2.50
26	Jerry Robinson	2.50
27	Don Rogers	2.50
28	Tobin Rote	5.00
29	Henry Schmidt	2.50
30	Pat Shea	2.50
31	Walt Sweeney	5.00
32	Jimmy Warren	2.50
33	Dick Westmoreland	2.50
34	Bud Whitehead	2.50
35	Ernie Wright	5.00
NNO	Chargers Saver Sheet	20.00

1964 Coke Caps Lions

The 35-cap, 1-1/8" set was distributed in Michigan and contains Detroit Lions players' images on the inside of each cap. A Cap Saver sheet was also issued and the caps could also be found on Coke products such as Fresca and Tab.

		NM
Complete Set (35):		100.00
Common Player:		2.50
1	Terry Barr	2.50
2	Carl Brettschneider	2.50
3	Roger Brown	5.00
4	Mike Bundra	2.50
5	Ernie Clark	2.50
6	Gail Cogdill	5.00
7	Larry Ferguson	2.50
8	Dennis Gaubatz	2.50
9	Jim Gibbons	5.00
10	John Gonzaga	2.50
11	John Gordy	2.50
12	Tom Hall	2.50
13	Alex Karras	10.00
14	Dick Lane	8.00
15	Dan LaRose	2.50
16	Yale Lary	8.00
17	Dick LeBeau	5.00
18	Dan Lewis	2.50
19	Gary Lowe	2.50
20	Bruce Maher	2.50
21	Darris McCord	2.50
22	Max Messner	2.50
23	Earl Morrall	7.00
24	Nick Pietrosante	2.50
25	Milt Plum	2.50
26	Daryl Sanders	2.50
27	Joe Schmidt	6.00
28	Bob Scholtz	2.50
29	J.D. Smith	5.00
30	Pat Studstill	5.00
31	Larry Vargo	2.50
32	Wayne Walker	5.00
33	Tom Watkins	2.50
34	Bob Whitlow	2.50
35	Sam Williams	2.50
NNO	Lions Saver Sheet	20.00

1964 Coke Caps Rams

The 35-cap, 1-1/8" set, issued in the Los Angeles area, had top Rams players and their image on the Coke bottle cap insides. The Cap Saver sheet could be redeemed for prizes and other Coke products also had the Rams bottle caps.

		NM
Complete Set (35):		85.00
Common Player:		2.50
1	Jon Arnett	5.00
2	Pervis Atkins	2.50
3	Terry Baker	5.00
4	Dick Bass	5.00
5	Charley Britt	2.50
6	Willie Brown	5.00
7	Joe Carollo	2.50
8	Don Chuy	2.50
9	Charlie Cowan	2.50
10	Lindon Crow	2.50
11	Carroll Dale	5.00
12	Roman Gabriel	6.00
13	Roosevelt Grier	6.00
14	Mike Henry	2.50
15	Art Hunter	2.50
16	Ken Iman	2.50
17	Deacon Jones	10.00
18	Cliff Livingston	2.50
19	Lamar Lundy	5.00
20	Marlin McKeever	2.50
21	Ed Meador	5.00
22	Bill Munson	5.00
23	Merlin Olsen	8.00
24	Jack Pardee	5.00
25	Art Perkins	2.50
26	Jim Phillips	2.50
27	Roger Pillath	2.50
28	Mel Profit	2.50
29	Joe Scibelli	2.50
30	Carver Shannon	2.50
31	Bobby Smith	2.50
32	Bill Swain	2.50
33	Frank Varrichione	2.50
34	Danny Villanueva	2.50
35	Nat Whitmyer	2.50
NNO	Rams Saver Sheet	20.00

1964 Coke Caps Redskins

The 32-cap, 1-1/8" in diameter set featured top players from the Redskins. Collectors who assembled the entire set before a specific expiration date could redeem it for prizes. The outside of the cap features the Coke logos with a stamp of a football, while the inside has the player's likeness. There may have been more of the 32 unnumbered caps issued than are listed below.

		NM
Complete Set (32):		85.00
Common Player:		2.50
1	Bill Barnes	2.50
2	Don Bosseler	2.50
3	Rod Breedlove	2.50
4	Frank Budd	2.50
5	Henry Butsko	2.50
6	Jimmy Carr	2.50
7	Angelo Coia	2.50
8	Fred Dugan	2.50
9	Fred Hageman	2.50
10	Sam Huff	8.00
11	Sonny Jurgensen	10.00
12	Carl Kammerer	2.50
13	Gordon Kelley	2.50
14	Bob Khayat	2.50
15	Paul Krause	5.00
16	J.W. Lockett	2.50
17	Riley Mattson	2.50
18	Bobby Mitchell	8.00
19	John Nisby	2.50
20	Fran O'Brien	2.50
21	John Paluck	2.50
22	Jack Pardee	5.00
23	Vince Promuto	2.50
24	Pat Richter	5.00
25	Johnny Sample	5.00
26	Lonnie Sanders	2.50
27	Dick Shiner	5.00
28	Ron Snidow	2.50
29	Jim Steffen	2.50
30	Charley Taylor	10.00
31	Tom Tracy	5.00
32	Fred Williams	2.50

1964 Coke Cap Team Emblems NFL

The 14-cap, 1-1/8" in diameter set features a cap for each of the NFL teams. The Cap Saver sheet had a section for collecting the team emblem caps which were also available with other Coke products such as Fresca and Tab.

		NM
Complete Set (14):		50.00
Common Player:		5.00
1	Baltimore Colts	5.00
2	Chicago Bears	5.00
3	Cleveland Browns	5.00
4	Dallas Cowboys	7.00
5	Detroit Lions	5.00
6	Green Bay Packers	7.00
7	Los Angeles Rams	5.00
8	Minnesota Vikings	5.00
9	New York Giants	5.00
10	Philadelphia Eagles	5.00
11	Pittsburgh Steelers	5.00
12	San Francisco 49ers	6.00
13	St. Louis Cardinals	5.00
14	Washington Redskins	6.00

1965 Coke Caps All-Stars AFL

The 34-cap, 1-1/8" set features All-Stars from the AFL and was distributed in AFL cities along with local team caps. As with other caps, the outside features a Coke logo with a football icon and the inside depicts a facial image of an AFL All-Star. The caps are numbered with the "C" prefix.

		NM
Complete Set (34):		130.00
Common Player:		2.50
37	Jerry Mays	2.50
38	Cookie Gilchrist	4.00
39	Lionel Taylor	2.50
40	Goose Gonsoulin	4.00
41	Gino Cappelletti	4.00
42	Nick Buoniconti	6.00
43	Larry Eisenhauer	2.50
44	Babe Parilli	2.50
45	Jack Kemp	20.00
46	Billy Shaw	2.50
47	Scott Appleton	2.50
48	Matt Snell	2.50
49	Charlie Hennigan	2.50
50	Tom Flores	5.00
51	Clem Daniels	2.50
52	George Blanda	8.00
53	Art Powell	2.50
54	Jim Otto	5.00
55	Larry Grantham	2.50
56	Don Maynard	8.00
57	Gerry Philbin	2.50
58	E.J. Holub	2.50
59	Chris Burford	2.50
60	Ron Mix	5.00
61	Ernie Ladd	8.00
62	Fred Arbanas	2.50
63	Tom Sestak	2.50
64	Elbert Dubenion	2.50
65	Mike Stratton	2.50
66	Willie Brown	5.00
67	Sid Blanks	2.50
68	Len Dawson	8.00
69	Lance Alworth	8.00
70	Keith Lincoln	2.50

1965 Coke Caps All-Stars NFL

The 34-cap, 1-1/8" set featured NFL All-Stars and was distributed in NFL cities along with a Cap Saver sheet and local player caps. The completed sheet could be redeemed for various prizes. The caps are numbered with the "C" prefix.

		NM
Complete Set (34):		125.00
Common Player:		2.50
37	Sonny Jurgensen	8.00
38	Fran Tarkenton	12.00
39	Frank Ryan	2.50
40	Johnny Unitas	12.00
41	Tommy Mason	2.50
42	Mel Renfro	5.00
43	Ed Meador	2.50
44	Paul Krause	4.00
45	Irv Cross	4.00
46	Bill Brown	2.50
47	Joe Fortunato	2.50
48	Jim Taylor	6.00
49	John Henry Johnson	5.00
50	Pat Fischer	2.50
51	Bob Boyd	2.50
52	Terry Barr	2.50
53	Charley Taylor	5.00
54	Paul Warfield	8.00
55	Pete Retzlaff	2.50
56	Maxie Baughan	2.50
57	Matt Hazeltine	2.50
58	Ken Gray	2.50
59	Ray Nitschke	6.00
60	Myron Pottios	2.50
61	Charlie Krueger	2.50
62	Deacon Jones	7.00
63	Bob Lilly	7.00
64	Merlin Olsen	7.00
65	Jim Parker	5.00
66	Roosevelt Brown	5.00
67	Jim Gibbons	2.50
68	Mike Ditka	12.00
69	Willie Davis	5.00
70	Aaron Thomas	2.50

1965 Coke Caps Bills

The 35-cap, 1-1/8" set featuring the Bills was issued in western New York with a Cap Saver sheet, which could be redeemed for prizes such as an AFL leather football, a mini Bills megaphone, or a set of mini plastic AFL helmets. The cap tops have the Coke logo and a football stamp while the insides have the player's likeness. Hall of Fame quarterback Jack Kemp was the key player featured in the cap set. The caps are numbered with the "B" prefix.

		NM
Complete Set (35):		120.00
Common Player:		2.50
1	Ray Abbruzzese	2.50
2	Joe Auer	2.50
3	Stew Barber	2.50
4	Glenn Bass	2.50
5	Dave Behrman	2.50
6	Al Bemiller	2.50
7	George (Butch) Byrd	2.50
8	Wray Carlton	2.50
9	Hagood Clarke	2.50
10	Jack Kemp	25.00
11	Oliver Dobbins	2.50
12	Elbert Dubenion	2.50
13	Jim Dunaway	2.50
14	Booker Edgerson	2.50
15	George Flint	2.50
16	Pete Gogolak	5.00
17	Dick Hudson	5.00
18	Harry Jacobs	2.50
19	Tom Keating	2.50
20	Tom Day	2.50
21	Daryle Lamonica	10.00
22	Paul Maguire	8.00
23	Roland McDole	2.50
24	Dudley Meredith	2.50
25	Joe O'Donnell	2.50
26	Willie Ross	2.50
27	Ed Rutkowski	2.50
28	George Saimes	5.00
29	Tom Sestak	5.00
30	Billy Shaw	5.00
31	Bobby Smith	2.50
32	Mike Stratton	2.50
33	Gene Sykes	2.50
34	John Tracey	2.50
35	Ernie Warlick	2.50
NNO	Bills Saver Sheet	20.00

1965 Coke Caps Giants

The 35-cap, 1-1/8" set was distributed in the metropolitan New York area and featured key players from the Giants. The outside of the cap features a Coke logo and a football while the inside depicts one of the Giants players. A Cap Saver sheet was also available and completed sheets could be redeemed for prizes (NFL leather football, mini plastic NFL helmet set, mini Giants megaphone). The caps are numbered with the "G" prefix.

		NM
Complete Set (35):		100.00
Common Player:		2.50
1	Joe Morrison	2.50
2	Dick Lynch	2.50
3	Andy Stynchula	2.50
4	Clarence Childs	2.50
5	Aaron Thomas	2.50
6	Mickey Walker	2.50
7	Bill Winter	2.50
8	Bookie Bolin	2.50
9	Tom Scott	2.50
10	John Lovetere	2.50
11	Jim Patton	5.00
12	Darrell Dess	2.50
13	Dick James	2.50
14	Jerry Hillebrand	2.50
15	Dick Personen	2.50
16	Del Shofner	2.50
17	Erich Barnes	2.50
18	Roosevelt Brown	6.00
19	Greg Larson	2.50
20	Jim Katcavage	2.50
21	Frank Lasky	2.50
22	Lou Slaby	2.50
23	Jim Moran	2.50
24	Roger Anderson	2.50
25	Steve Thurlow	2.50
26	Ernie Wheelwright	2.50
27	Gary Wood	5.00
28	Tony Dimidio	2.50
29	John Contoulis	2.50
30	Tucker Fredrickson	5.00
31	Bob Timberlake	2.50
32	Chuck Mercein	2.50
33	Ernie Koy	2.50
34	Tom Costello	2.50
35	Homer Jones	5.00
NNO	Giants Saver Sheet	20.00

1965 Coke Caps Jets

The 35-cap, 1-1/8" in diameter set was issued in the New York City area and was highlighted by top players from the Jets. Collectors who redeemed the complete set were awarded either a leather AFL football, a mini plastic AFL helmet set, or a Jets mini megaphone. The caps were numbered with the "J" prefix. Joe Namath's cap is the key to the set.

		NM
Complete Set (35):		150.00
Common Player:		2.50
1	Don Maynard	10.00
2	George Sauer Jr.	5.00
3	Cosmo Iacavazzi	2.50
4	Jim O'Mahoney	2.50
5	Matt Snell	5.00
6	Clyde Washington	2.50
7	Jim Turner	2.50
8	Mike Taliaferro	2.50
9	Marshall Starks	2.50
10	Mark Smolinski	2.50
11	Bob Schweickert	2.50
12	Paul Rochester	2.50
13	Sherman Plunkett	2.50
14	Gerry Philbin	2.50
15	Pete Perreault	2.50
16	Dainard Paulson	2.50
17	Joe Namath	50.00
18	Winston Hill	2.50
19	Dee Mackey	2.50
20	Curley Johnson	2.50

21 Mike Hudock 2.50
22 John Huarte 5.00
23 Gordy Holz 2.50
24 Gene Heeter 5.00
25 Larry Grantham 5.00
26 Dan Ficca 2.50
27 Sam DeLuca 2.50
28 Bill Baird 2.50
29 Ralph Baker 2.50
30 Wahoo McDaniel 10.00
31 Jim Evans 2.50
32 Dave Herman 2.50
33 John Schmitt 2.50
34 Jim Harris 2.50
35 Bake Turner 5.00
NNO Jets Saver Sheet 20.00

1965 Coke Caps Lions

NM
Complete Set (36): 100.00
Common Player: 2.50
1 Pat Studstill 5.00
2 Bob Whitlow 2.50
3 Wayne Walker 5.00
4 Tom Watkins 2.50
5 Jim Simon 2.50
6 Sam Williams 2.50
7 Terry Barr 2.50
8 Jerry Rush 2.50
9 Roger Brown 2.50
10 Tom Nowatzke 5.00
11 Dick Lane 7.00
12 Dick Compton 2.50
13 Yale Lary 5.00
14 Dick LeBeau 5.00
15 Dan Lewis 5.00
16 Wally Hilgenburg 5.00
17 Bruce Maher 2.50
18 Darris McCord 2.50
19 Hugh McInnis 2.50
20 Ernie Clark 2.50
21 Gail Cogdill 5.00
22 Wayne Rasmussen 2.50
23 Joe Don Looney 8.00
24 Jim Gibbons 5.00
25 John Gonzaga 2.50
26 John Gordy 2.50
27 Bobby Thompson 2.50
28 J.D. Smith 5.00
29 Earl Morrall 6.00
30 Alex Karras 8.00
31 Nick Pietrosante 2.50
32 Milt Plum 5.00
33 Daryl Sanders 2.50
34 Joe Schmidt 8.00
35 Bob Scholtz 2.50
36 Team Logo 2.50
NNO Lions Saver Sheet 20.00

1965 Coke Caps National NFL

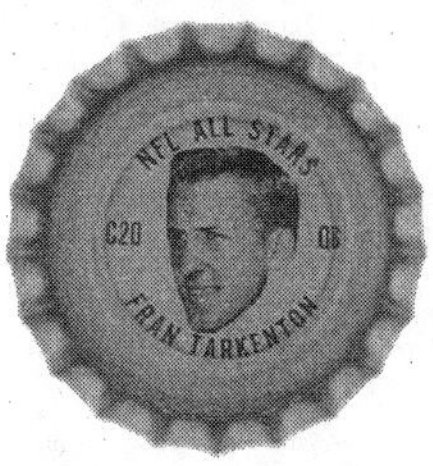

The 70-cap, 1-1/8" set was issued in metropolitan areas that did not have (in 1965) an NFL team. The caps have red liners and depict a player's facial image on the inside. The top of the cap had a Coke logo and a football icon. The caps are numbered with the "C" prefix.

NM
Complete Set (70): 200.00
Common Player: 2.50
1 Herb Adderley 5.00
2 Yale Lary 5.00
3 Dick LeBeau 2.50
4 Bill Brown 5.00
5 Jim Taylor 8.00
6 Joe Fortunato 2.50
7 Bill Boyd 2.50
8 Terry Barr 2.50
9 Dick Szymanski 2.50
10 Mick Tinglehoff 2.50
11 Wayne Walker 2.50
12 Matt Hazeltine 2.50
13 Ray Nitschke 7.00
14 Grady Alderman 2.50
15 Charlie Krueger 2.50
16 Tommy Mason 2.50
17 Willie Wood 5.00
18 Johnny Unitas 14.00
19 Lenny Moore 5.00
20 Fran Tarkenton 12.00
21 Deacon Jones 7.00
22 Bob Vogel 2.50
23 John Gordy 2.50
24 Jim Parker 2.50
25 Jim Gibbons 2.50
26 Merlin Olsen 7.00
27 Forrest Gregg 6.00
28 Roger Brown 2.50
29 Dave Parks 2.50
30 Raymond Berry 5.00
31 Mike Ditka 12.00
32 Gino Marchetti 5.00
33 Willie Davis 5.00
34 Ed Meador 2.50
35 Browns Logo 2.50
36 Colts Logo 2.50
37 Sam Baker 2.50
38 Irv Cross 5.00
39 Maxie Baughan 2.50
40 Vince Promuto 2.50
41 Paul Krause 5.00
42 Charley Taylor 5.00
43 John Paluck 2.50
44 Paul Warfield 8.00
45 Dick Modzelewski 2.50
46 Myron Pottios 2.50
47 Erich Barnes 2.50
48 Bill Koman 2.50
49 Art Thomas 2.50
50 Gary Ballman 2.50
51 Sam Huff 5.00
52 Ken Gray 2.50
53 Roosevelt Brown 6.00
54 Bobby Joe Conrad 2.50
55 Pat Fischer 2.50
56 Irv Goode 2.50
57 Floyd Peters 2.50
58 Charlie Johnson 5.00
59 John Henry Johnson 5.00
60 Charley Bradshaw 2.50
61 Jim Ringo 5.00
62 Pete Retzlaff 5.00
63 Sonny Jurgensen 8.00
64 Don Meredith 12.00
65 Bob Lilly 8.00
66 Bill Glass 2.50
67 Dick Schafrath 2.50
68 Mel Renfro 5.00
69 Jim Houston 2.50
70 Frank Ryan 2.50

1965 Coke Caps Packers

The 36-cap, 1-1/8" in diameter set featured Packers players and was issued in the greater metropolitan areas of Wisconsin, such as Milwaukee, Green Bay and Madison areas. Completed sets on a Cap Saver sheet could be redeemed for a variety of prizes before an expiration date. The caps are numbered with a "C" prefix.

NM
Complete Set (36): 160.00
Common Player: 2.50
1 Herb Adderley 5.00
2 Lionel Aldridge 2.50
3 Hank Gremminger 2.50
4 Willie Davis 6.00
5 Boyd Dowler 5.00
6 Marv Fleming 2.50
7 Ken Bowman 2.50
8 Tom Brown 2.50
9 Doug Hart 2.50
10 Steve Wright 2.50
11 Dennis Claridge 2.50
12 Dave Hanner 2.50
13 Tommy Crutcher 2.50
14 Fred Thurston 5.00
15 Elijah Pitts 5.00
16 Lloyd Voss 2.50
17 Lee Roy Caffey 5.00
18 Dave Robinson 5.00
19 Bart Starr 14.00
20 Ray Nitschke 10.00
21 Max McGee 6.00
22 Don Chandler 2.50
23 Norm Masters 2.50
24 Ron Kostelnik 2.50
25 Carroll Dale 5.00
26 Hank Jordan 5.00
27 Bob Jeter 2.50
28 Bob Skoronski 2.50
29 Jerry Kramer 6.00
30 Willie Wood 6.00
31 Paul Hornung 14.00
32 Forrest Gregg 8.00
33 Zeke Bratkowski 5.00
34 Tom Moore 2.50
35 Jim Taylor 10.00
36 Team Logo 2.50
NNO Packers Saver Sheet 20.00

1965 Coke Caps Patriots

The 36-cap, 1-1/8" set was issued in the New England area and a completed set on a Cap Saver sheet could be redeemed for a prize. The cap tops feature a Coke logo and an image of a football, while the inside has the facial image of a Patriots player. Other Coke products, such as Fresca and Tab, also had the player caps. The caps are numbered with a "C" prefix.

NM
Complete Set (36): 100.00
Common Player: 2.50
1 Jon Morris 5.00
2 Don Webb 2.50
3 Charles Long 5.00
4 Tony Romeo 2.50
5 Bob Dee 2.50
6 Tommy Addison 5.00
7 Bob Yates 2.50
8 Ron Hall 2.50
9 Billy Neighbors 2.50
10 Jack Rudolph 2.50
11 Don Oakes 2.50
12 Tom Yewcic 2.50
13 Ron Burton 5.00
14 Jim Colclough 2.50
15 Larry Garron 5.00
16 Dave Watson 2.50
17 Art Graham 5.00
18 Babe Parilli 5.00
19 Jim Hunt 2.50
20 Don McKinnon 2.50
21 Houston Antwine 2.50
22 Nick Buoniconti 8.00
23 Ross O'Hanley 2.50
24 Gino Cappelletti 5.00
25 Chuck Shonta 2.50
26 Dick Felt 2.50
27 Mike Dukes 2.50
28 Larry Eisenhauer 2.50
29 Bob Schmidt 2.50
30 Len St. Jean 2.50
31 J.D. Garrett 2.50
32 Jim Whalen 2.50
33 Jim Nance 5.00
34 Eddie Wilson 2.50
35 Lonnie Farmer 2.50
36 Boston Patriots Logo 2.50
NNO Patriots Saver Sheet 20.00

1965 Coke Caps Redskins

The 36-cap, 1-1/8" set was distributed in the Washington, D.C. area and featured top players from the Redskins. As with other Coke cap sets, the Redskins set could be collected on a Cap Saver sheet and redeemed for prizes. Other Coke products, such as Fresca and Tab, also had the player caps. The caps are numbered with a "C" prefix.

NM
Complete Set (36): 100.00
Common Player: 2.50
1 Jimmy Carr 2.50
2 Fred Mazurek 2.50
3 Lonnie Sanders 2.50
4 Jim Steffen 2.50
5 John Nisby 2.50
6 George Izo 5.00
7 Vince Promuto 2.50
8 Johnny Sample 5.00
9 Pat Richter 5.00
10 Preston Carpenter 2.50
11 Sam Huff 8.00
12 Pervis Atkins 2.50
13 Fred Barnett 2.50
14 Len Hauss 5.00
15 Bill Anderson 2.50
16 John Reger 2.50
17 George Seals 2.50
18 J.W. Lockett 2.50
19 Tom Walters 2.50
20 Joe Rutgens 2.50
21 John Paluck 2.50
22 Fran O'Brien 2.50
23 Joe Rutgens 2.50
24 Rod Breedlove 2.50
25 Bob Pellegrini 2.50
26 Bob Jencks 2.50
27 Joe Hernandez 2.50
28 Sonny Jurgensen 10.00
29 Bob Toneff 2.50
30 Charley Taylor 8.00
31 Bob Shiner 2.50
32 Bobby Williams 2.50
33 Angelo Coia 2.50
34 Ron Snidow 2.50
35 Paul Krause 5.00
36 Team Logo 2.50
NNO Redskins Saver Sheet 20.00

1966 Coke Caps All-Stars AFL

The 34-cap, 1-1/8" in diameter set was issued in AFL cities and could be collected on Cap Saver sheets, some of which had separate sections to place both the local and All-Star caps. The caps are virtually identical to previous Coke caps sets and were also found on Fresca and Tab products. The caps are numbered with a "C" prefix.

NM
Complete Set (34): 120.00
Common Player: 2.00
37 Babe Parilli 4.00
38 Mike Stratton 2.00
39 Jack Kemp 18.00
40 Len Dawson 8.00
41 Fred Arbanas 2.00
42 Bobby Bell 4.00
43 Willie Brown 4.00
44 Buck Buchanan 4.00
45 Frank Buncom 2.00
46 Nick Buoniconti 4.00
47 Gino Cappelletti 4.00
48 Eldon Danenhauer 2.00
49 Clem Daniels 4.00
50 Les Duncan 4.00
51 Willie Frazier 2.00
52 Cookie Gilchrist 4.00
53 Dave Grayson 2.00
54 John Hadl 5.00
55 Wayne Hawkins 2.00
56 Sherrill Headrick 2.00
57 Charlie Hennigan 4.00
58 E.J. Holub 2.00
59 Curley Johnson 2.00
60 Keith Lincoln 2.00
61 Paul Lowe 4.00
62 Don Maynard 6.00
63 Jon Morris 2.00
64 Joe Namath 20.00
65 Jim Otto 4.00
66 Dainard Paulson 2.00
67 Art Powell 4.00
68 Walt Sweeney 4.00
69 Bob Talamini 2.00
70 Lance Alworth (UER, Name misspelled Alsworth) 8.00

1966 Coke Caps All-Stars NFL

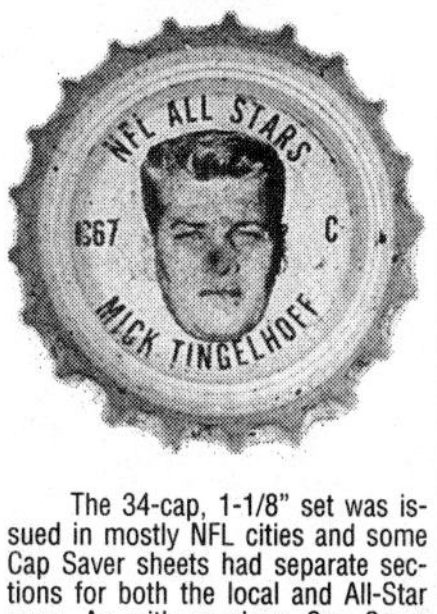

The 34-cap, 1-1/8" set was issued in mostly NFL cities and some Cap Saver sheets had separate sections for both the local and All-Star caps. As with previous Cap Saver sheets, collectors could turn in a completed set for prizes. The caps are identical in design with other caps issues and could be found with Tab and Fresca products as well. The caps are numbered with a "C" prefix.

NM
Complete Set (34): 120.00
Common Player: 2.00
37 Frank Ryan 4.00
38 Timmy Brown 4.00
39 Tucker Frederickson 2.00
40 Cornell Green 4.00
41 Bob Hayes 4.00
42 Charley Taylor 4.00
43 Pete Retzlaff 4.00
44 Jim Ringo 6.00
45 John Wooten 2.00
46 Dale Meinert 2.00
47 Bob Lilly 8.00
48 Sam Silas 2.00
49 Roosevelt Brown 6.00
50 Gary Ballman 2.00
51 Gary Collins 2.00
52 Sonny Randle 2.00
53 Charlie Johnson 2.00
54 Herb Adderley 4.00
55 Doug Atkins 4.00
56 Roger Brown 2.00
57 Dick Butkus 14.00
58 Willie Davis 4.00
59 Tommy McDonald 2.00
60 Alex Karras 6.00
61 John Mackey 4.00
62 Ed Meador 2.00
63 Merlin Olsen 6.00
64 Dave Parks 2.00
65 Gale Sayers 14.00
66 Fran Tarkenton 10.00
67 Mick Tingelhoff 2.00
68 Ken Willard 2.00
69 Willie Wood 4.00
70 Bill Brown 4.00

1966 Coke Caps Bills

The 36-cap, 1-1/8" in diameter set was distributed in western New York and was highlighted by Bills players. The caps are nearly identical in design as previous sets, except that the insides are numbered with a "B" prefix.

NM
Complete Set (36): 120.00
Common Player: 2.00
1 Bill Laskey 2.00
2 Marty Schottenheimer 8.00
3 Stew Barber 2.00
4 Glenn Bass 2.00
5 Remi Prudhomme 2.00
6 Al Bemiller 2.00
7 George (Butch) Byrd 3.00
8 Wray Carlton 2.00
9 Hagood Clarke 2.00
10 Jack Kemp 25.00
11 Charlie Warner 2.00
12 Elbert Dubenion 3.00
13 Jim Dunaway 2.00
14 Booker Edgerson 2.00
15 Paul Costa 2.00
16 Henry Schmidt 2.00
17 Dick Hudson 2.00
18 Harry Jacobs 2.00
19 Tom Janik 2.00
20 Tom Day 2.00
21 Daryle Lamonica 5.00
22 Paul Maguire 6.00
23 Roland McDole 2.00
24 Dudley Meredith 2.00
25 Joe O'Donnell 2.00
26 Charlie Ferguson 2.00
27 Ed Rutkowski 2.00
28 George Saimes 2.00
29 Tom Sestak 3.00
30 Billy Shaw 2.00
31 Bobby Smith 2.00
32 Mike Stratton 3.00
33 Gene Sykes 2.00
34 John Tracey 2.00
35 Ernie Warlick 2.00
36 Bills Logo 2.00
NNO Bills Saver Sheet 20.00

1966 Coke Caps Browns

The 36-cap, 1-1/8" set was part of Coke's 14-cap NFL set. The caps have a Coke logo and football icon on the outside with a the player's image on the inside. A Cap Saver sheet was also issued and, as with previous releases, a completed sheet could be redeemed for prizes. The caps are numbered with a "C" prefix.

NM
Complete Set (36): 100.00
Common Player: 2.00
1 Jim Ninowski 3.00
2 Leroy Kelly 6.00
3 Lou Groza 6.00
4 Gary Collins 3.00
5 Bill Glass 3.00
6 Dale Lindsey 2.00
7 Galen Fiss 2.00
8 Ross Fichtner 2.00
9 John Wooten 2.00
10 Clifton McNeil 2.00
11 Paul Wiggin 2.00
12 Gene Hickerson 3.00
13 Ernie Green 2.00
14 Mike Howell 2.00
15 Dick Schafrath 2.00
16 Sidney Williams 2.00
17 Frank Ryan 3.00
18 Bernie Parrish 3.00
19 Vince Costello 2.00
20 John Brown (CO) 2.00
21 Monte Clark 2.00
22 Walter Roberts 2.00
23 Johnny Brewer 2.00
24 Walter Beach 2.00
25 Dick Modzelewski 2.00
26 Gary Lane 2.00
27 Jim Houston 2.00
28 Milt Morin 2.00
29 Erich Barnes 2.00
30 Tom Hutchinson 2.00
31 John Morrow 2.00
32 Jim Kanicki 2.00
33 Paul Warfield 8.00
34 Jim Garcia 2.00
35 Walter Johnson 2.00
36 Browns Logo 2.00
NNO Browns Saver Sheet 20.00

1966 Coke Caps Cardinals

The 36-cap, 1-1/8" set was issued in conjunction with other NFL, AFL and All-Star sets. Cap Saver sheets were also issued and completed sheets could be redeemed for prizes. The caps are virtually identical in design to previous sets. The caps are numbered with a "C" prefix.

NM
Complete Set (36): 80.00
Common Player: 2.00
1 Pat Fischer 3.00
2 Sonny Randle 2.00
3 Joe Childress 2.00
4 Dave Meggysey (UER, Name misspelled Meggyesy) 4.00
5 Joe Robb 2.00
6 Jerry Stovall 3.00
7 Ernie McMillan 3.00
8 Dale Meinert 2.00
9 Irv Goode 2.00
10 Bob DeMarco 2.00
11 Mal Hammack 2.00
12 Jim Bakken 3.00
13 Bill Thornton 2.00
14 Buddy Humphrey 2.00
15 Bill Koman 2.00
16 Larry Wilson 5.00
17 Charles Walker 2.00
18 Prentice Gautt 3.00
19 Charlie Johnson (UER, Name misspelled Charley) 3.00
20 Ken Gray 2.00
21 Dave Simmons 2.00
22 Sam Silas 2.00
23 Larry Stallings 2.00
24 Don Brumm 2.00
25 Bobby Joe Conrad 3.00
26 Bill Triplett 2.00
27 Luke Owens 2.00
28 Jackie Smith 5.00
29 Bob Reynolds 2.00
30 Abe Woodson 3.00
31 Jim Burson 2.00
32 Willis Crenshaw 2.00
33 Billy Gambrell 2.00
34 Ray Ogden 2.00
35 Herschel Turner 2.00
36 Cardinals Logo 2.00
NNO Cardinals Saver Sheet 20.00

1966 Coke Caps Chiefs

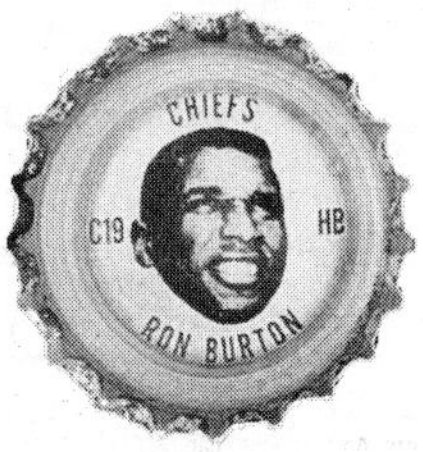

The 36-cap, 1-1/8" set featured key players from the Chiefs and had the Coke logo with a football stamp on the top and a player's image on the inside. Player caps could also be found on Fresca and Tab bottles. The caps are numbered with a "C" prefix.

NM
Complete Set (36): 100.00
Common Player: 2.00
1 E.J. Holub 3.00
2 Al Reynolds 2.00
3 Buck Buchanan 5.00
4 Curt Merz (SP) 8.00
5 Dave Hill 2.00
6 Bobby Hunt 2.00
7 Jerry Mays 3.00
8 Jon Gilliam 2.00
9 Walt Corey 2.00
10 Soloman Brannan 2.00
11 Aaron Brown 2.00
12 Bert Coan 2.00
13 Ed Budde 2.00
14 Tommy Brooker 2.00
15 Bobby Bell 5.00
16 Smokey Stover 2.00
17 Curtis McClinton 3.00
18 Jerrel Wilson 2.00
19 Ron Burton 3.00
20 Mike Garrett 5.00
21 Jim Tyrer 3.00
22 Johnny Robinson 3.00
23 Bobby Ply 2.00
24 Frank Pitts 2.00
25 Ed Lothamer 2.00
26 Sherrill Headrick 3.00
27 Fred Williamson 5.00
28 Chris Burford 3.00
29 Willie Mitchell 2.00
30 Otis Taylor 5.00
31 Fred Arbanas 2.00
32 Hatch Rosdahl 2.00
33 Reg Carolan 2.00
34 Len Dawson 8.00
35 Pete Beathard 3.00
36 Chiefs Logo 2.00
NNO Chiefs Saver Sheet 20.00

1966 Coke Caps Colts

The 36-cap, 1-1/8" in diameter set was issued along with a Cap Saver sheet that, when completed, could be redeemed for various prizes. The caps are numbered with the "C" prefix.

NM
Complete Set (36): 100.00
Common Player: 2.00
1 Ted Davis 2.00
2 Bob Boyd 2.00
3 Lenny Moore 8.00
4 Jackie Burkett 2.00
5 Jimmy Orr 3.00
6 Andy Stynchula 2.00
7 Mike Curtis 4.00
8 Jerry Logan 2.00
9 Steve Stonebreaker 2.00
10 John Mackey 6.00
11 Dennis Gaubatz 2.00
12 Don Shinnick 2.00
13 Dick Szymanski 2.00
14 Ordell Braase 2.00
15 Lenny Lyles 2.00
16 Rick Kestner 2.00
17 Dan Sullivan 2.00
18 Lou Michaels 3.00
19 Gary Cuozzo 3.00
20 Butch Wilson 2.00
21 Willie Richardson 3.00
22 Jim Welch 2.00
23 Tony Lorick 2.00
24 Billy Ray Smith 3.00
25 Fred Miller 2.00
26 Tom Matte 4.00
27 Johnny Unitas 12.00
28 Glenn Ressler 2.00
29 Alvin Haymond 3.00
30 Jim Parker 5.00
31 Butch Allison 2.00
32 Bob Vogel 2.00
33 Jerry Hill 2.00
34 Raymond Berry 8.00
35 Sam Ball 2.00
36 Colts Team Logo 2.00
NNO Colts Saver Sheet 20.00

1966 Coke Caps Cowboys

The 36-cap, 1-1/8" set was issued to highlight the Cowboys. A Cap Saver sheet was also available, and when completed, could be redeemed for prizes. Fresca and Tab bottles also had the player caps. Key players in the set are Don Meredith, Dan Reeves and Bob Hayes. The caps are numbered with a "C" prefix.

NM
Complete Set (36): 140.00
Common Player: 2.50
1 Mike Connelly 2.50
2 Tony Liscio 2.50
3 Jethro Pugh 2.50
4 Larry Stephens 2.50
5 Jim Colvin 2.50
6 Malcolm Walker 2.50
7 Danny Villanueva 2.50
8 Frank Clarke 4.00
9 Don Meredith 12.00
10 George Andrie 4.00
11 Mel Renfro 6.00
12 Pettis Norman 4.00
13 Buddy Dial 4.00
14 Pete Gent 4.00
15 Jerry Rhome 5.00
16 Bob Hayes 10.00
17 Mike Gaechter 2.50
18 Joe Bob Isbell 2.50
19 Harold Hays 2.50
20 Craig Morton 5.00
21 Jake Kupp 2.50
22 Cornell Green 4.00
23 Dan Reeves 12.00
24 Leon Donohue 2.50
25 Dave Manders 2.50
26 Warren Livingston 2.50
27 Bob Lilly 8.00
28 Chuck Howley 5.00
29 Don Bishop 2.50
30 Don Perkins 4.00
31 Jim Boeke 2.50
32 Dave Edwards 2.50
33 Lee Roy Jordan 5.00
34 Obert Logan 2.50
35 Ralph Neely 4.00
36 Cowboys Logo 2.50
NNO Cowboys Saver Sheet 20.00

1966 Coke Caps Eagles

The 36-card, 1-1/8" set was issued with a Cap Saver sheet that could be redeemed for various prizes. The top of the caps had the Coke logo and a football icon while the inside had the player's image. The caps are numbered with the "C" prefix.

NM
Complete Set (36): 75.00
Common Player: 2.00
1 Norm Snead 4.00
2 Al Nelson 2.00
3 Jim Skaggs 2.00

4	Glenn Glass	2.00
5	Pete Retzlaff	4.00
6	John Osmond	2.00
7	Ray Rissmiller	2.00
8	Lynn Hoyem	2.00
9	King Hill	4.00
10	Timmy Brown	4.00
11	Ollie Matson	6.00
12	Dave Lloyd	2.00
13	Jim Ringo	6.00
14	Floyd Peters	2.00
15	Gary Pettigrew	2.00
16	Frank Molden	2.00
17	Earl Gros	2.00
18	Fred Hill	2.00
19	Don Hultz	2.00
20	Ray Poage	2.00
21	Aaron Martin	2.00
22	Mike Morgan	2.00
23	Lane Howell	2.00
24	Ed Blaine	2.00
25	Jack Concannon	4.00
26	Sam Baker	2.00
27	Tom Woodeshick	4.00
28	Joe Scarpati	2.00
29	John Meyers	2.00
30	Nate Ramsey	2.00
31	Ben Hawkins	2.00
32	Bob Brown	4.00
33	Willie Brown	2.00
34	Ron Goodwin	2.00
35	Randy Beisler	2.00
36	Team Logo	2.00
NNO	Eagles Saver Sheet	20.00

1966 Coke Caps Falcons

The 36-cap, 1-1/8" in diameter set highlights top members of the Falcons. A Cap Saver sheet was also available which could be redeemed for prizes. Coke products, such as Fresca and Tab, also came with player caps. The final cap in the set, which is numbered with the "C" prefix, is the Falcons team cap.

		NM
Complete Set (36):		80.00
Common Player:		2.00
1	Tommy Nobis	7.00
2	Ernie Wheelwright	3.00
3	Lee Calland	2.00
4	Chuck Sieminski	2.00
5	Dennis Claridge	2.00
6	Ralph Heck	2.00
7	Alex Hawkins	3.00
8	Dan Grimm	2.00
9	Marion Rushing	2.00
10	Bobbie Johnson	2.00
11	Bobby Franklin	2.00
12	Bill McWatters	2.00
13	Billy Lothridge	3.00
14	Billy Martin	2.00
15	Tom Wilson	2.00
16	Dennis Murphy	2.00
17	Randy Johnson	3.00
18	Guy Reese	2.00
19	Frank Marchlewski	2.00
20	Don Talbert	2.00
21	Errol Linden	2.00
22	Dan Lewis	2.00
23	Ed Cook	2.00
24	Hugh McInnis	2.00
25	Frank Lasky	2.00
26	Bob Jencks	2.00
27	Bill Jobko	2.00
28	Nick Rassas	2.00
29	Bob Riggle	2.00
30	Ken Reaves	2.00
31	Bob Sanders	2.00
32	Steve Sloan	3.00
33	Ron Smith	2.00
34	Bob Whitlow	2.00
35	Roger Anderson	2.00
36	Falcons Logo	2.00
NNO	Falcons Saver Sheet	20.00

1966 Coke Caps 49ers

The 36-cap, 1-1/8" set was issued to highlight members of the 49ers. A Cap Saver sheet was also available and could be redeemed for prizes upon completion. Tab and Fresca also had player caps. The cap tops featured the Coke logo with a football icon while the bottom had the player's image. The caps are numbered with a "C" prefix.

		NM
Complete Set (36):		80.00
Common Player:		2.00
1	Bernie Casey	3.00
2	Bruce Bosley	2.00
3	Kermit Alexander	3.00
4	John Brodie	8.00
5	Dave Parks	3.00
6	Len Rohde	2.00
7	Walter Rock	2.00
8	George Mira	4.00
9	Karl Rubke	2.00
10	Ken Willard	3.00
11	John David Crow (UER, Name misspelled Crowe)	3.00
12	George Donnelly	2.00
13	Dave Wilcox	3.00
14	Vern Burke	2.00
15	Wayne Swinford	2.00
16	Elbert Kimbrough	2.00
17	Clark Miller	2.00
18	Dave Kopay	3.00
19	Joe Cerne	2.00
20	Roland Lakes	2.00
21	Charlie Krueger	2.00
22	Billy Kilmer	4.00
23	Jim Johnson	5.00
24	Matt Hazeltine	2.00
25	Mike Dowdle	2.00
26	Jim Wilson	2.00
27	Tommy Davis	3.00
28	Jim Norton	2.00
29	Jack Chapple	2.00
30	Ed Beard	2.00
31	John Thomas	2.00
32	Monty Stickles	2.00
33	Kay McFarland	2.00
34	Gary Lewis	2.00
35	Howard Mudd	2.00
36	49ers Logo	2.00
NNO	49ers Saver Sheet	20.00

1966 Coke Caps Giants

The 35-cap, 1-1/8" set highlights top Giants players and was issued with a Cap Saver sheet, which when completed, could be redeemed for various prizes. The cap is similar in design to previous cap issues, complete with the Coke logo. The caps are numbered with a "G" prefix.

		NM
Complete Set (35):		80.00
Common Player:		2.00
1	Joe Morrison	3.00
2	Dick Lynch	3.00
3	Pete Case	2.00
4	Clarence Childs	2.00
5	Aaron Thomas	2.00
6	Jim Carroll	2.00
7	Henry Carr	3.00
8	Bookie Bolin	2.00
9	Roosevelt Davis	2.00
10	John Lovetere	2.00
11	Jim Patton	3.00
12	Wendell Harris	2.00
13	Roger LaLonde	2.00
14	Jerry Hillebrand	2.00
15	Spider Lockhart	3.00
16	Del Shofner	3.00
17	Earl Morrall	5.00
18	Roosevelt Brown	5.00
19	Greg Larson	2.00
20	Jim Katcavage	3.00
21	Smith Reed	2.00
22	Lou Slaby	2.00
23	Jim Moran	2.00
24	Bill Swain	2.00
25	Steve Thurlow	2.00
26	Olen Underwood	2.00
27	Gary Wood	3.00
28	Larry Vargo	2.00
29	Jim Prestel (Cap saver sheet reads Ed Prestel)	2.00
30	Tucker Frederickson	3.00
31	Bob Timberlake	2.00
32	Chuck Mercein	3.00
33	Ernie Koy	3.00
34	Tom Costello	2.00
35	Homer Jones	3.00
NNO	Giants Saver Sheet	20.00

1966 Coke Caps Jets

The 35-cap, 1-1/8" in diameter set, distributed in western New York, featured key Jets players, including Joe Namath. A Cap Saver sheet was issued to help collectors complete the set and when completed, could be redeemed for prizes. The caps are numbered with a "J" prefix.

		NM
Complete Set (35):		120.00
Common Player:		2.00
1	Don Maynard	10.00
2	George Sauer Jr.	4.00
3	Paul Crane	2.00
4	Jim Colclough	2.00
5	Matt Snell	4.00
6	Sherman Lewis	2.00
7	Jim Turner	4.00
8	Mike Taliaferro	2.00
9	Cornell Gordon	2.00
10	Mark Smolinski	2.00
11	Al Atkinson	4.00
12	Paul Rochester	2.00
13	Sherman Plunkett	2.00
14	Gerry Philbin	4.00
15	Pete Lammons	4.00
16	Dainard Paulson	2.00
17	Joe Namath	45.00
18	Winston Hill	4.00
19	Dee Mackey	2.00
20	Curley Johnson	2.00
21	Verlon Biggs	2.00
22	Bill Mathis	4.00
23	Carl McAdams	2.00
24	Bert Wilder	2.00
25	Larry Grantham	4.00
26	Bill Yearby	2.00
27	Sam DeLuca	2.00
28	Bill Baird	2.00
29	Ralph Baker	2.00
30	Ray Abruzzese	2.00
31	Jim Hudson	2.00
32	Dave Herman	2.00
33	John Schmitt	2.00
34	Jim Harris	2.00
35	Bake Turner	4.00
NNO	Jets Saver Sheet	20.00

1966 Coke Caps National NFL

The 70-cap, 1-1/8" set was available in mostly non-NFL cities in addition to a Cap Saver sheet, which when redeemed, could earn collectors prizes. The cap tops have the Coke logo and a football icon, while the bottoms have the player's image in black. The caps are numbered with a "C" prefix.

		NM
Complete Set (70):		200.00
Common Player:		2.00
1	Larry Wilson	5.00
2	Frank Ryan	4.00
3	Norm Snead	4.00
4	Mel Renfro	4.00
5	Timmy Brown	4.00
6	Tucker Frederickson	2.00
7	Jim Bakken	2.00
8	Paul Krause	4.00
9	Irv Cross	2.00
10	Cornell Green	4.00
11	Pat Fischer	2.00
12	Bob Hayes	4.00
13	Charley Taylor	5.00
14	Pete Retzlaff	4.00
15	Jim Ringo	5.00
16	Maxie Baughan	2.00
17	Chuck Howley	4.00
18	John Wooten	2.00
19	Bob DeMarco	2.00
20	Dale Meinert	2.00
21	Gene Hickerson	2.00
22	George Andrie	2.00
23	Joe Rutgens	2.00
24	Bob Lilly	6.00
25	Sam Silas	2.00
26	Bob Brown (OT)	2.00
27	Dick Schafrath	2.00
28	Roosevelt Brown	6.00
29	Jim Houston	2.00
30	Paul Wiggin	2.00
31	Gary Ballman	2.00
32	Gary Collins	4.00
33	Sonny Randle	2.00
34	Charlie Johnson	4.00
35	Browns Logo	2.00
36	Packers Logo	2.00
37	Herb Adderley	6.00
38	Grady Alderman	2.00
39	Doug Atkins	4.00
40	Bruce Bosley	2.00
41	John Brodie	6.00
42	Roger Brown	2.00
43	Bill Brown	2.00
44	Dick Butkus	15.00
45	Lee Roy Caffey	2.00
46	John David Crow	4.00
47	Willie Davis	6.00
48	Mike Ditka	12.00
49	Joe Fortunato	2.00
50	John Gordy	2.00
51	Deacon Jones	6.00
52	Alex Karras	6.00
53	Dick LeBeau	2.00
54	Jerry Logan	2.00
55	John Mackey	4.00
56	Ed Meador	2.00
57	Tommy McDonald	4.00
58	Merlin Olsen	6.00
59	Jimmy Orr	4.00
60	Jim Parker	4.00
61	Dave Parks	2.00
62	Walter Rock	2.00
63	Gale Sayers	14.00
64	Pat Studstill	2.00
65	Fran Tarkenton	12.00
66	Mick Tinglehoff	2.00
67	Bob Vogel	2.00
68	Wayne Walker	2.00
69	Ken Willard	2.00
70	Willie Wood	5.00
NNO	National Saver Sheet	20.00

1966 Coke Caps Oilers

The 36-cap, 1-1/8" set featured the top players from the Oilers and was distributed in the Houston area. A Cap Saver sheet was also issued, and when redeemed, the collector could earn prizes. Fresca and Tab products also had the player caps. The caps are numbered with a "C" prefix.

		NM
Complete Set (36):		100.00
Common Player:		2.00
1	Scott Appleton	2.00
2	George Allen	4.00
3	Don Floyd	2.00
4	Ronnie Caveness	2.00
5	Jim Norton	2.00
6	Jacky Lee	4.00
7	George Blanda	10.00
8	Tony Banfield	4.00
9	George Rice	2.00
10	Charley Tolar	2.00
11	Bobby Jancik	2.00
12	Freddy Glick	2.00
13	Ode Burrell	2.00
14	Walt Suggs	2.00
15	Bob McLeod	2.00
16	Johnny Baker	2.00
17	Danny Bradshaw	2.00
18	Gary Cutsinger	2.00
19	Doug Cline	2.00
20	Hoyle Granger	2.00
21	Bob Talamini	2.00
22	Don Trull	4.00
23	Charlie Hennigan	4.00
24	Sid Blanks	2.00
25	Pat Holmes	2.00
26	John Frongillo	2.00
27	John Whitehorn	2.00
28	George Kinney	2.00
29	Charles Frazier	2.00
30	Ernie Ladd	6.00
31	W.K. Hicks	2.00
32	Sonny Bishop	2.00
33	Larry Elkins	2.00
34	Glen Ray Hines	2.00
35	Bobby Maples	4.00
36	Oilers Logo	2.00
NNO	Oilers Saver Sheet	20.00

1966 Coke Caps Packers

The 36-cap, 1-1/8" set, issued in metropolitan areas in Wisconsin, was virtually identical in design to previous Coke player cap sets. A Cap Saver sheet was also available and a collector could redeem the completed sheet for various prizes. The caps are numbered with a "C" prefix.

		NM
Complete Set (36):		150.00
Common Player:		2.50
1	Herb Adderley	6.00
2	Lionel Aldridge	4.00
3	Bob Long	2.50
4	Willie Davis	6.00
5	Boyd Dowler	4.00
6	Marv Fleming	2.50
7	Ken Bowman	2.50
8	Tom Brown	2.50
9	Doug Hart	2.50
10	Steve Wright	2.50
11	Bill Anderson	2.50
12	Bill Curry	4.00
13	Tommy Crutcher	2.50
14	Fred Thurston	5.00
15	Elijah Pitts	5.00
16	Lloyd Voss	2.50
17	Lee Roy Caffey	4.00
18	Dave Robinson	2.50
19	Bart Starr	14.00
20	Ray Nitschke	8.00
21	Max McGee	5.00
22	Don Chandler	2.50
23	Richard Marshall	2.50
24	Ron Kostelnik	2.50
25	Carroll Dale	4.00
26	Hank Jordan	5.00
27	Bob Jeter	4.00
28	Bob Skoronski	2.50
29	Jerry Kramer	6.00
30	Willie Wood	6.00
31	Paul Hornung	14.00
32	Forrest Gregg	8.00
33	Zeke Bratkowski	4.00
34	Tom Moore	2.50
35	Jim Taylor	12.00
36	Packers Team Emblem	2.50
NNO	Packers Saver Sheet	20.00

1966 Coke Caps Patriots

The 36-cap, 1-1/8" in diameter set, distributed in the New England area, featured key players from the Patriots roster. A Cap Saver sheet was also issued to aid collectors in completing the set, which could then be redeemed for various prizes. The caps are numbered with a "C" prefix.

		NM
Complete Set (36):		75.00
Common Player:		2.00
1	Jon Morris	2.00
2	Don Webb	2.00
3	Charles Long	2.00
4	Tony Romeo	2.00
5	Bob Dee	2.00
6	Tommy Addison	4.00
7	Tom Neville	2.00
8	Ron Hall	2.00
9	White Graves	2.00
10	Ellis Johnson	2.00
11	Don Oakes	2.00
12	Tom Yewcic	2.00
13	Tom Hennessey	2.00
14	Jay Cunningham	2.00
15	Larry Garron	4.00
16	Justin Canale	2.00
17	Art Graham	4.00
18	Babe Parilli	4.00
19	Jim Hunt	2.00
20	Karl Singer	2.00
21	Houston Antwine	2.00
22	Nick Buoniconti	6.00
23	John Huarte	4.00
24	Gino Cappelletti	4.00
25	Chuck Shonta	2.00
26	Dick Felt	2.00
27	Mike Dukes	2.00
28	Larry Eisenhauer	2.00
29	Jim Fraser	2.00
30	Len St. Jean	2.00
31	J.D. Garrett	2.00
32	Jim Whalen	2.00
33	Jim Nance	4.00
34	Rick Arrington	2.00
35	Lonnie Farmer	2.00
36	Patriots Logo	2.00
NNO	Patriots Saver Sheet	20.00

1966 Coke Caps Rams

The 36-cap, 1-1/8" set features a Coke logo and a football icon on the cap top, as do the previous player cap sets. The cap insides depict a facial image of the player in black. Other Coke products, such as Fresca and Tab, also had the player caps. The caps are numbered with a "C" prefix.

		NM
Complete Set (36):		100.00
Common Player:		2.00
1	Tom Mack	5.00
2	Tom Moore	2.00
3	Bill Munson	3.00
4	Bill George	5.00
5	Joe Carollo	2.00
6	Dick Bass	3.00
7	Ken Iman	2.00
8	Charlie Cowan	2.00
9	Terry Baker	4.00
10	Don Chuy	2.00
11	Jack Pardee	5.00
12	Lamar Lundy	3.00
13	Bill Anderson	2.00
14	Roman Gabriel	6.00
15	Roosevelt Grier	6.00
16	Billy Truax	3.00
17	Merlin Olsen	8.00
18	Deacon Jones	7.00
19	Joe Scibelli	2.00
20	Marlin McKeever	2.00
21	Doug Woodlief	2.00
22	Chuck Lamson	2.00
23	Dan Currie	2.00
24	Maxie Baughan	3.00
25	Bruce Gossett	3.00
26	Les Josephson	3.00
27	Ed Meador	2.00
28	Anthony Guillory	2.00
29	Irv Cross	4.00
30	Tommy McDonald	3.00
31	Bucky Pope	2.00
32	Jack Snow	4.00
33	Joe Wendryhoski	2.00
34	Clancy Williams	2.00
35	Ben Wilson	2.00
36	Rams Logo	2.00
NNO	Rams Saver Sheet	20.00

1966 Coke Caps Steelers

The 36-cap, 1-1/8" set featured key players from the Steelers squad with the Coke logo and a football stamp on the cap top. The player's image was printed in black on the cap inside. A Cap Saver sheet was also issued and a completed sheet could be redeemed for various prizes. The caps are numbered with a "C" prefix.

		NM
Complete Set (36):		80.00
Common Player:		2.00
1	John Baker	2.00
2	Mike Lind	3.00
3	Ken Kortas	2.00
4	Willie Daniel	2.00
5	Roy Jefferson	3.00
6	Bob Hohn	2.00
7	Dan James	2.00
8	Gary Ballman	3.00
9	Brady Keys	2.00
10	Charley Bradshaw	2.00
11	Jim Bradshaw	2.00
12	Jim Butler	2.00
13	Paul Martha	4.00
14	Mike Clark	2.00
15	Ray Lemek	2.00
16	Clarence Peaks	3.00
17	Theron Sapp	2.00
18	Ray Mansfield	2.00
19	Chuck Hinton	2.00
20	Bill Nelsen	3.00
21	Rod Breedlove	2.00
22	Frank Lambert	2.00
23	Ben McGee	2.00
24	Myron Pottios	2.00
25	John Campbell	2.00
26	Andy Russell	4.00
27	Mike Sandusky	2.00
28	Bob Schmitz	2.00
29	Riley Gunnels	2.00
30	Clendon Thomas	3.00
31	Tommy Wade	2.00
32	Dick Hoak	3.00
33	Marv Woodson	2.00
34	Bob Nichols	2.00
35	John Henry Johnson	5.00
36	Steelers Logo	2.00
NNO	Steelers Saver Sheet	20.00

1971 Coke Caps Packers

The 22-cap, 1-1/8" set, issued in 1971, featured twist-off caps as well as the basic bottle opener cap. The twist-off cap is valued at twice the listings below. As with past Coke player sets, a Cap Saver sheet was issued to help collectors in completing the set.

		NM
Complete Set (22):		50.00
Common Player:		1.50
1	Ken Bowman	1.50
2	John Brockington	3.00
3	Bob Brown (DT)	1.50
4	Fred Carr	1.50
5	Jim Carter	1.50
6	Carroll Dale	1.50
7	Ken Ellis	1.50
8	Gale Gillingham	1.50
9	Dave Hampton	1.50
10	Doug Hart	1.50
11	Jim Hill	1.50
12	Dick Himes	1.50
13	Scott Hunter	1.50
14	MacArthur Lane	3.00
15	Bill Lueck	1.50
16	Al Matthews	1.50
17	Rich McGeorge	1.50
18	Ray Nitschke	5.00
19	Francis Peay	1.50
20	Dave Robinson	3.00
21	Alden Roche	1.50
22	Bart Starr	14.00

1981 Coke Caps

The 15-cap set was issued by Coke in conjuction with a collector contest, which distributed prizes to consumers who completed a column on the Cap Saver sheet. The prize for finding all seven caps from the middle row was $1,000, while the five caps in the third row earned the collector a "Mean" Joe Greene jersey. The first column required four caps and awarded a T-shirt. The most difficult caps to obtain were of Ed "Too Tall" Jones, Steve Fuller and Gene Upshaw. The caps were skip numbered.

		MT
Complete Set (15):		30.00
Common Player:		1.00
1	Joe Greene	3.00
3	Steve Grogan	1.50
6	Mike Siani	1.00
11	Dan Fouts	3.00
12	Wesley Walker	1.50
23	Harold Carmichael	1.50
30	Greg Pruitt	1.00
38	Gene Upshaw (SP)	
47	Steve Fuller (SP)	
49	Walter Payton	7.00
53	Ed "Too Tall" Jones (SP)	
107	Benny Barnes	1.00
108	Billy Sims	2.00
127	Robert Newhouse	1.00
146	Charlie Waters	1.00

FIGURES PRICE GUIDE

STARTING LINEUPS FOOTBALL

1988 FOOTBALL

Complete Set (137)	$8,500.00
5-player stand w/box	60.00
5-player stand w/o box	40.00
Blue Collector's Showcase	60.00

Player	Mint
Allen, Marcus	70.00
Anderson, Neal	35.00
Banks, Chip	100.00
Bavaro, Mark	50.00
Bennett, Cornelius	150.00
Bentley, Albert	90.00
Bickett, Duane	120.00
Blackledge, Todd	70.00
Bosworth, Brian	42.00
Brennan, Brian	65.00
Brooks, Bill	110.00
Brooks, James	65.00
Brown, Eddie	60.00
Browner, Joey	100.00
Bruce, Aundray	60.00
Burkett, Chris	120.00
Byars, Keith	50.00
Campbell, Scott	140.00
Carson, Carlos	90.00
Carson, Harry	55.00
Carter, Anthony	80.00
Carter, Gerald	45.00
Carter, Michael	65.00
Casillas, Tony	75.00
Chadwick, Jeff	70.00
Cherry, Deron	85.00
Childress, Ray	100.00
Christiansen, Todd	100.00
Clark, Gary	80.00
Clayton, Mark	100.00
Collinsworth, Cris	100.00
Cosbie, Doug	130.00
Craig, Roger	40.00
Cunningham, Randall	80.00
Davis, Jeff	45.00
Davis, Ken	120.00
Dent, Richard	50.00
Dickerson, Eric	50.00
Dixon, Floyd	60.00
Dorsett, Tony	275.00
Duper, Mark	90.00
Eason, Tony	120.00
Ekern, Carl	85.00
Ellard, Henry	60.00
Elway, John	200.00
Epps, Phillip	120.00
Esiason, Boomer	80.00
Everett, Jim	50.00
Fullwood, Brent	100.00
Gastineau, Mark	45.00
Gault, Willie	120.00
Golic, Bob	100.00
Gray, Jerry	75.00
Green, Darrell	375.00
Green, Jacob	110.00
Green, Roy	85.00
Grogan, Steve	105.00
Harmon, Ronnie	160.00
Hebert, Bobby	150.00
Highsmith, Alonzo	40.00
Hill, Drew	40.00
Jackson, Earnest	85.00
Jackson, Rickey	125.00
Johnson, Vance	50.00
Jones, Ed	140.00
Jones, James	50.00
Jones, Rod	50.00
Jones, Rulon	60.00
Jordan, Steve	175.00
Junior, E.J.	125.00
Kelly, Jim	200.00
Kenney, Bill	80.00
Kosar, Bernie	40.00
Kramer, Tommy	120.00
Krieg, Dave	180.00
Krumrie, Tim	140.00
Lee, Mark	140.00
Lippett, Ronnie	50.00
Lipps, Louis	110.00
Lomax, Neil	120.00
Long, Chuck	60.00
Long, Howie	130.00
Lott, Ronnie	120.00
Mack, Kevin	40.00
Malone, Mark	175.00
Manley, Dexter	45.00
Marino, Dan	225.00
Martin, Eric	55.00
Mayes, Rueben	50.00
McMahon, Jim	50.00
McNeil, Freeman	40.00
Mecklenburg, Karl	50.00
Merriweather, Mike	170.00
Mitchell, Stump	75.00
Monk, Art	270.00
Montana, Joe	200.00
Moon, Warren	90.00
Morgan, Stanley	50.00
Morris, Joe	45.00
Nelson, Darrin	125.00
Newsome, Ozzie	110.00
O'Brien, Ken	40.00
Offerdahl, John	110.00
Okoye, Christian	50.00
Quick, Mike	40.00
Rice, Jerry	300.00
Riggs, Gerald	40.00
Rogers, Reggie	50.00
Rozier, Mike	40.00
Schroeder, Jay	90.00
Shuler, Mickey	40.00
Simms, Phil	45.00
Singletary, Mike	55.00
Smith, Billy Ray	180.00
Smith, Bruce	175.00
Smith, J. T.	85.00
Stradford, Troy	100.00
Taylor, Lawrence	60.00
Testaverde, Vinny	75.00
Tippett, Andre	40.00
Toney, Anthony	40.00
Toon, Al	40.00
Trudeau, Jack	125.00
Walker, Herschel	55.00
Warner, Curt	55.00
Waymer, Dave	100.00
White, Charles	55.00
White, Danny	120.00
White, Randy	225.00
White, Reggie	100.00
Wilder, James	50.00
Williams, Doug	55.00
Wilson, Marc	310.00
Winder, Sammy	50.00
Winslow, Kellen	375.00
Woodson, Rod	400.00
Wright, Randy	195.00

1989 FOOTBALL

Complete Set (123) $8,500.00

Player	Mint
Allen, Marcus	50.00
Anderson, Neal	30.00
Banks, Carl (R)	100.00
Bates, Bill (R)	350.00
Bavaro, Mark	45.00
Bennett, Cornelius	70.00
Bickett, Duane	140.00
Blades, Bennie (R)	125.00
Brister, Bubby (R)	60.00
Brooks, Bill	90.00
Brooks, James	40.00
Brown, Eddie	50.00
Brown, Jerome (R)	280.00
Brown, Tim (R)	100.00
Browner, Joey	100.00
Bryant, Kelvin (R)	50.00
Burt, Jim (R)	150.00
Byars, Keith	180.00
Cadigan, Dave (R)	300.00
Carter, Anthony	40.00
Carter, Michael	50.00
Chandler, Chris (R)	80.00
Clark, Gary	40.00
Conlan, Shane (R)	100.00
Covert, Jimbo (R)	300.00
Craig, Roger	30.00
Cunningham, Randall	50.00
Dent, Richard	35.00
Dixon, Hanford (R)	100.00
Doleman, Chris (R)	125.00
Dorsett, Tony (HOF)	110.00
Duerson, Dave (R)	70.00
Elway, John	200.00
Esiason, Boomer	50.00
Everett, Jim	30.00
Everett, Thomas (R)	185.00
Farrell, Sean (R)	220.00
Fralic, Bill (R)	250.00
Fryar, Irving (R)	170.00
Fulcher, David (R)	100.00
Givins, Ernest (R)	60.00
Gordon, Alex (R)	135.00
Haley, Charles (R)	200.00
Hebert, Bobby	50.00
Hector, Johnny (R)	100.00
Hill, Drew	30.00
Hilliard, Dalton (R)	40.00
Hinkle, Bryan (R)	300.00
Irvin, Michael (R)	125.00
Jackson, Keith (R)	60.00
James, Gary (R)	50.00
Jones, Sean (R)	100.00
Kelly, Jim	175.00
Kelly, Joe (R)	70.00
Kosar, Bernie	30.00
Krumrie, Tim	100.00
Lipps, Louis	160.00
Lockhart, Eugene (R)	170.00
Lofton, James (R)	90.00
Lomax, Neil	40.00
Long, Chuck	30.00
Long, Howie	110.00
Lott, Ronnie	100.00
Mack, Kevin	30.00
Mandley, Pete (R)	30.00
Manley, Dexter	30.00
Mann, Charles (R)	55.00
Manuel, Lionel (R)	35.00
Marino, Dan	225.00
Marshall, Leonard (R)	120.00
Martin, Eric	50.00
Mayes, Rueben	50.00
McElroy, Vann (R)	70.00
McKinnon, Dennis (R)	100.00
McMahon, Jim	35.00
McMichael, Steve (R)	220.00
McMillan, Eric (R)	80.00
McNeil, Freeman	30.00
Millard, Keith (R)	100.00
Miller, Chris (R)	60.00
Minnifield, Frank (R)	100.00
Monk, Art	85.00
Montana, Joe	110.00
Moon, Warren	75.00
Morris, Joe	45.00
Munoz, Anthony (R)	275.00
Nattiel, Ricky (R)	45.00
Nelson, Darrin	85.00
Noonan, Danny (R)	150.00
O'Brien, Ken	
(err. sp.)	100.00
(cor. sp.)	30.00
Pelleur, Steve (R)	100.00
Quick, Mike	30.00
Reed, Andre (R)	120.00
Rice, Jerry	65.00
Rozier, Mike	45.00
Schroeder, Jay	40.00
Settle, John (R)	65.00
Shuler, Mickey	100.00
Simms, Phil	30.00
Singletary, Mike	35.00
Slaughter, Webster (R)	50.00
Smith, Bruce	150.00
Spielman, Chris (R)	215.00
Stephens, John (R)	35.00
Stouffer, Kelly (R)	40.00
Swilling, Pat (R)	60.00
Taylor, Lawrence	60.00
Testaverde, Vinny	55.00
Thomas, Thurman (R)	120.00
Tippett, Andre	40.00
Toney, Anthony	50.00
Toon, Al	30.00
Veris, Garin (R)	275.00
Walker, Herschel	30.00
Warner, Curt	40.00
White, Reggie	60.00
Williams, Doug	50.00
Williams, John (R)	80.00
Wilson, Wade (R)	100.00
Woods, Ickey (R)	30.00
Woodson, Rod	320.00
Young, Steve (R)	325.00

1989 HELMET COLLECTION

Complete Set (4) $375.00

Player	Mint
AFC Offense Helmet	100.00
AFC Defense Helmet	100.00
NFC Offense Helmet	100.00
NFC Defense Helmet	100.00

1990 FOOTBALL

Complete Set (75) $2,000.00

Player	Mint
Aikman, Troy (R)	60.00
Anderson, Neal	
(blue '90)	20.00
(white '89)	20.00
Bavaro, Mark	65.00
Beuerlein, Steve (R)	50.00
Brister, Bubby	90.00
Brooks, James	30.00
Brown, Tim	85.00
Carter, Cris (R)	200.00
Craig, Roger	
(red '90)	25.00
(white '89)	50.00
Cunningham, Randall	
(green '90)	30.00
(white '89)	60.00
Dykes, Hart Lee (R)	60.00
Elway, John	
(orange '90)	85.00
(white '89)	85.00
Esiason, Boomer	
(black '89)	20.00
(white '90)	20.00
Everett, Jim	15.00
Fletcher, Simon (R)	150.00
Flutie, Doug (R)	175.00
Gentry, Dennis (R)	50.00
Hampton, Dan (R)	110.00
Harbaugh, Jim (R)	65.00
Holman, Rodney (R)	50.00
Humphrey, Bobby (R)	25.00
Irvin, Michael	80.00
Jackson, Bo (R)	16.00
Jackson, Keith	40.00
Johnson, Vance	140.00
Kelly, Jim	35.00
Kosar, Bernie	
(brown '90)	70.00
(white '89)	20.00
Lipps, Louis	120.00
Majkowski, Don (R)	20.00
Mann, Charles	50.00
Manuel, Lionel	20.00
Marino, Dan	150.00
McGee, Tim (R)	20.00
Meggett, Dave (R)	20.00
Merriweather, Mike	75.00
Metcalf, Eric (R)	25.00
Millard, Keith	40.00
Montana, Joe	
(red '90)	75.00
(white '89)	80.00
Moon, Warren	35.00
Okoye, Christian	20.00
Rathman, Tom (R)	50.00
Reed, Andre	30.00
Riggs, Gerald	18.00
Rypien, Mark (R)	22.00
Sanders, Barry (R)	100.00
Sanders, Deion (R)	45.00
Sanders, Ricky (R)	15.00
Simmons, Clyde (R)	70.00
Simms, Phil	15.00
Singletary, Mike	
(blue '90)	30.00
(white '89)	30.00
Slaughter, Webster	50.00
Smith, Bruce	80.00
Stephens, John	30.00
Taylor, John (R)	25.00
Thomas, Thurman	40.00
Tomczak, Mike (R)	20.00
Townsend, Greg (R)	70.00
Turner, Odessa (R)	25.00
Walker, Herschel	20.00
Walsh, Steve (R)	60.00
White, Reggie	
(green '90)	40.00
(white '89)	30.00
Wilson, Wade	70.00
Woods, Ickey	20.00
Woolford, Donnell (R)	60.00
Worley, Tim (R)	80.00
Wright, Felix (R)	110.00

1991 FOOTBALL

Complete Set (26) $650.00

Player	Mint
Aikman, Troy	75.00
Anderson, Flipper (R)	15.00
Anderson, Neal	15.00
Brooks, James	15.00
Brown, Eddie	15.00
Carrier, Mark (R)	15.00
Esiason, Boomer	15.00
Francis, James (R)	22.00
George, Jeff (R)	15.00
Hampton, Rodney (R)	20.00
Harbaugh, Jim	35.00
Hostetler, Jeff (R)	25.00
Humphrey, Bobby	14.00
Majkowski, Don	15.00
Marino, Dan	100.00
Meggett, Dave	14.00
Montana, Joe	40.00
Moon, Warren	24.00
Okoye, Christian	10.00
Rice, Jerry	45.00
Rison, Andre (R)	20.00
Sanders, Barry	65.00
Simms, Phil	15.00
Smith, Emmitt (R)	160.00
Thomas, Thurman	24.00
Walker, Herschel	15.00

1991 HEADLINE FOOTBALL

Complete Set (6) $275.00

Player	Mint
Elway, John	120.00
Esiason, Boomer	18.00
Marino, Dan	120.00
Montana, Joe	55.00
Rice, Jerry	70.00
Sanders, Barry	60.00

1992 FOOTBALL

Complete Set (26) $500.00

Player	Mint
Aikman, Troy	40.00
Byner, Earnest (R)	12.00
Cunningham, Randall	18.00
Hampton, Rodney	15.00
Hebert, Bobby	15.00
Hostetler, Jeff	15.00
Irvin, Michael	20.00
Jackson, Bo	15.00
Jeffires, Haywood (R)	12.00
Joyner, Seth (R)	15.00
Kelly, Jim	15.00
Lott, Ronnie	30.00
Marino, Dan	100.00
Montana, Joe	40.00
Moon, Warren	20.00
Moore, Rob (R)	12.00
Rice, Jerry	35.00
Rison, Andre	15.00
Rypien, Mark	10.00
Sanders, Barry	50.00
Sanders, Deion	24.00
Smith, Emmitt	75.00
Swilling, Pat	12.00
Thomas, Derrick (R)	35.00
Thomas, Thurman	15.00
Young, Steve	60.00

1992 HEADLINE FOOTBALL

Complete Set (6) $125.00

Player	Mint
Montana, Joe	25.00
Moon, Warren	18.00
Rypien, Mark	12.00
Sanders, Barry	50.00
Smith, Emmitt	65.00
Thomas, Thurman	20.00

1993 FOOTBALL

Complete Set (27) $350.00

Player	Mint
Aikman, Troy	30.00
Bennett, Cornelius	10.00
Cunningham, Randall	15.00
Doleman, Chris	18.00
Elway, John	80.00
Foster, Barry (R)	12.00
Irvin, Michael	15.00
Jackson, Rickey	8.00
Kennedy, Cortez (R)	15.00
Klingler, David (R)	10.00
Lohmiller, Chip (R)	15.00
Maryland, Russell (R)	12.00
Miller, Anthony (R)	15.00
Miller, Chris	10.00
Montana, Joe	50.00
Moon, Warren	
(white)	14.00
(blue)	20.00
Reed, Andre	12.00
Sanders, Barry	35.00
Sanders, Deion	15.00
Seau, Junior (R)	20.00
Sharpe, Sterling (R)	35.00
Smith, Emmitt	25.00
Smith, Neil (R)	10.00
Stoyanovich, Pete (R)	15.00
Watters, Ricky (R)	15.00
Woodson, Rod	20.00
Young, Steve	25.00

1994 FOOTBALL

Complete Set (32) $550.00

Player	Mint
Aikman, Troy	20.00
Bettis, Jerome (R)	35.00
Bledsoe, Drew (R)	40.00
Cunningham, Randall	12.00
Esiason, Boomer	10.00
Favre, Brett (R)	125.00
Foster, Barry	8.00
Hampton, Rodney	10.00
Harmon, Ronnie	8.00
Hearst, Garrison (R)	17.00
Ismail, Raghib (R)	15.00
Jones, Brent (R)	12.00
Kennedy, Cortez	10.00
Lowery, Nick (R)	12.00
Marino, Dan	40.00
Metcalf, Eric	10.00
Mirer, Rick (R)	10.00
Montana, Joe	35.00
Norton, Ken (R)	17.00
Rice, Jerry	20.00
Rison, Andre	10.00
Sanders, Barry	30.00
Sanders, Deion	10.00
Seau, Junior	10.00
Simms, Phil	10.00
Smith, Emmitt	35.00
Taylor, Lawrence	15.00
Warren, Chris (R)	12.00
White, Lorenzo (R)	10.00
White, Reggie	20.00
Woodson, Rod	15.00
Young, Steve	20.00

1995 FOOTBALL

Complete Set (33) $500.00

Player	Mint
Aikman, Troy	20.00
Bettis, Jerome	20.00
Bledsoe, Drew	23.00
Christie, Steve (R)	12.00
Coates, Ben (R)	15.00
Cunningham, Randall	10.00
Davis, Willie (R)	10.00
Everett, Jim	10.00
Faulk, Marshall (R)	50.00
Favre, Brett	40.00
Fryar, Irving	15.00
George, Jeff	10.00
Humphries, Stan (R)	12.00
Irvin, Michael	18.00
Johnson, Johnny (R)	10.00
Joyner, Seth	10.00
Lloyd, Greg (R)	20.00
Marino, Dan	30.00
McDaniel, Terry (R)	10.00
Means, Natrone (R)	15.00
Mitchell, Scott (R)	7.00
Montana, Joe	50.00
Moon, Warren	12.00
Nickerson, Hardy (R)	14.00
Perry, Michael Dean (R)	12.00
Rice, Jerry	16.00
Sanders, Barry	25.00
Sanders, Deion	12.00
Sharpe, Shannon (R)	20.00
Smith, Emmitt	30.00
Wilkinson, Dan (R)	14.00
Young, Steve	15.00
Zorich, Chris (R)	10.00

1996 FOOTBALL

Complete Set (40) $500.00

Player	Mint
Aikman, Troy	
(regular)	20.00
(Albertson's)	25.00
(Blue sleeves w/stars)	175.00
Allen, Terry (R)	18.00
Beuerlein, Steve	20.00
Blake, Jeff (R)	15.00
Bledsoe, Drew	15.00
Bono, Steve (R)	10.00
Brady, Kyle (R)	12.00
Brooks, Robert (R)	15.00
Brown, Dave (R)	10.00
Bruce, Isaac (R)	30.00
Brunell, Mark (R)	25.00
Carrier, Mark (R)	10.00
Carter, Cris	15.00

Collins, Kerry (R) 20.00
Elway, John 30.00
Faulk, Marshall 20.00
Favre, Brett (Shopko) 35.00
Galloway, Joey (R) 24.00
Greene, Kevin (R) 15.00
Marino, Dan 35.00
McNair, Steve (R) 25.00
Metcalf, Eric 10.00
Novacek, Jay (R) 17.00
Paup, Bryce (R) 15.00
Pickens, Carl (R) 10.00
Reich, Frank (R) 14.00
Rhett, Errict (R) 12.00
Rice, Jerry 15.00
Salaam, Rashaan (R) 8.00
Sanders, Barry 25.00
Sanders, Deion 10.00
Seau, Junior 10.00
Smith, Emmitt 35.00
Spielman, Chris 15.00
Stewart, Kordell (R) 40.00
Watters, Ricky 15.00
White, Reggie 15.00
Williams, Harvey (R) 12.00
Young, Steve 12.00

1997 FOOTBALL

Complete Set (46) $550.00
Player **Mint**
Abdul-Jabbar, Karim (R) 10.00
Aikman, Troy 12.00
Anderson, Jamal (R) 18.00
Bettis, Jerome 12.00
Blake, Jeff 10.00
Bledsoe, Drew 15.00
Bradshaw, Terry (Hill's) 18.00
Brunell, Mark 12.00
Carter, Dale (R) 8.00
Centers, Larry (R) 10.00
Chmura, Mark (R) 8.00
Collins, Kerry 10.00
Cox, Brian (R) 12.00
Davis, Terrell (R)
(w/mustache) 60.00
Early, Quinn (R) 10.00
Elway, John 20.00
Favre, Brett 20.00
George, Eddie (R) 30.00
George, Jeff 10.00
Grbac, Elvis (R) 15.00
Greene, Kevin 10.00
Harbaugh, Jim 10.00
Harrison, Marvin (R) 35.00
Johnson, Brad (R) 25.00
Johnson, Keyshawn (R) 25.00
Johnston, Daryl (R) 14.00
Marino, Dan 15.00
Martin, Curtis (R) 45.00
Martin, Tony (R) 10.00
Moore, Herman (R) 20.00
Rice, Jerry 10.00
Roaf, William (R) 15.00
Sanders, Deion 10.00
Seau, Junior (Super Bowl) 25.00
Smith, Bruce 10.00
Smith, Emmitt
(regular) 15.00
(Albertson's) 20.00
Sparks, Phillippi (R) 10.00
Stewart, Kordell 18.00
Testaverde, Vinny 10.00
Turner, Eric (R) 10.00
Warren, Chris 10.00
Watters, Ricky 10.00
Westbrook, Michael (R) 16.00
White, Reggie 10.00
Young, Steve 14.00

1997 FOOTBALL CLASSIC DOUBLES

Complete Set (8) $250.00
Player **Mint**
Sanders, B./Payton, W. 100.00
Clark, D./Montana, J. 25.00
Rice, J./Montana, J. 30.00
Marino, D./Griese, B. 28.00
Favre, B./Starr, B. 28.00
Aikman, T/Staubach, R. 35.00
Brown, T./Biletnikoff, F. 35.00
Smith, E./Dorsett, T. 35.00

1997 GRIDIRON GREATS

Complete Set (9) $175.00
Player **Mint**
Favre, Brett 30.00
Greene, Kevin 15.00
Marino, Dan 30.00
Montana, Joe 30.00
Rice, Jerry 30.00
Sanders, Deion 20.00
Smith, Emmitt 35.00
Thomas, Thurman 15.00
Watters, Ricky 15.00

1997 HEISMAN

Complete Set (9) $90.00
Player **Mint**
Dorsett, Tony 15.00
Flutie, Doug 15.00
George, Eddie 20.00
Griffin, Archie 10.00
Jackson, Bo 12.00
Owens, Steve 12.00
Rodgers, Johnny 10.00
Sanders, Barry 20.00
Wuerffel, Danny (R) 12.00

1998 FOOTBALL

Complete Set (44) $475.00
Player **Mint**
Aikman, Troy 12.00
Allen, Terry 10.00
Bettis, Jerome 15.00
Bledsoe, Drew 10.00
Boselli, Tony (R) 20.00
Brooks, Derrick (R) 25.00
Brunell, Mark 12.00
Collins, Kerry 12.00
Davis, Terrell 20.00
Dilfer, Trent (R) 18.00
Dillon, Corey (R) 22.00
Elway, John 16.00
Favre, Brett 14.00
Freeman, Antonio (R) 15.00
Frerotte, Gus (R) 12.00
Galloway, Joey 14.00
George, Eddie 16.00
Glenn, Terry (R) 12.00
Grbac, Elvis
(correct jersey number) 50.00
(incorrect jersey number) 10.00
Harris, Raymont (R) 10.00
Hoying, Bobby (R) 10.00
Lake, Carnell (R) 22.00
Lathon, Lamar (R) 10.00
Marino, Dan
(regular) 15.00
(Super Bowl) 20.00
McDaniel, Randall (R) 25.00
McGlockton, Chester (R) 20.00
Mitchell, Scott 7.00
Murrell, Adrian (R) 15.00
Newton, Nate (R) 12.00
Odgen, Jonathan (R) 25.00
Pace, Orlando (R) 25.00
Pickens, Carl 12.00
Rice, Jerry 12.00
Rice, Simeon (R) 10.00
Sanders, Barry (Meijers) 25.00
Sanders, Deion 12.00
Smith, Antowain (R) 20.00
Smith, Emmitt 10.00
Stewart, Kordell (Hills) 20.00
Stubblefield, Dana (R) 15.00
Testaverde, Vinny 10.00
Wheatley, Tyrone (R) 18.00
White, Reggie 10.00
Young, Steve 12.00

EXTENDED

Complete Set (10) $150.00
Player **Mint**
Alstott, Mike (R) 24.00
Davis, Terrell 18.00
Harbaugh, Jim 10.00
Leaf, Ryan (R) 10.00
Manning, Peyton (R) 50.00
Martin, Curtis 20.00
McNair, Steve 20.00
Sanders, Deion 15.00
Sharpe, Shannon 16.00
Woodson, Charles (R) 20.00

1998 FOOTBALL 12" FIGURES

Complete Set (6) $150.00
Player **Mint**
Aikman, Troy (Serv. Mer.) 30.00
Bledsoe, Drew 25.00
Elway, John 30.00
Favre, Brett 30.00
Marino, Dan 30.00
Rice, Jerry 30.00
Stewart, Kordell (Hills) 25.00

1998 FOOTBALL CLASSIC DOUBLES

Complete Set (8) $125.00
Player **Mint**
Rice, J./Young, S. 25.00
Elway, J./Marino, D. 35.00
Seau, J./Butkus, D. 15.00
Allen, T./Garrett, E. 15.00
Aikman, T./Smith, E. 28.00
Tittle, Y./Huff, S. 15.00
Namath, J./Maynard, D. 20.00
Sanders, D./Adderly, H. 15.00

QB CLUB

Complete Set (6) $125.00
Player **Mint**
Bledsoe, Drew 15.00
Elway, John 25.00
Harbaugh, Jim 15.00
Marino, Dan 30.00
Smith, Emmitt 28.00
Young, Steve 25.00

1998 GRIDIRON GREATS

Complete Set (8) $160.00
Player **Mint**
Aikman, Troy 20.00
Bledsoe, Drew 25.00
Brunell, Mark 25.00
Elway, John 28.00
Sanders, Barry 30.00
Seau, Junior 20.00
Starr, Bart (Shopko) 25.00
Young, Steve 20.00

1998 FOOTBALL HALL OF FAME

Complete Set (11) $100.00
Player **Mint**
Butkus, Dick 12.00
Csonka, Larry 14.00
Greene, Joe 12.00
Jones, Deacon 10.00
Lilly, Bob 12.00
Lombardi, Vince 18.00
Nitschke, Ray 25.00
Sayers, Gale 12.00
Starr, Bart 12.00
Tittle, Y. A. 10.00
Upshaw, Gene 15.00

1998 HEISMAN

Complete Set (10) $80.00
Player **Mint**
Allen, Marcus 10.00
Campbell, Earl 15.00
Cappelletti, John 10.00
Davis, Glenn 8.00
Hornung, Paul 17.00
Howard, Desmond 8.00
Salaam, Rashaan 8.00
Staubach, Roger 12.00
Walker, Herschel 15.00
Woodson, Charles 15.00

1999 FOOTBALL

Complete Set (34) $500.00
Player **Mint**
Aikman, Troy 10.00
Bledsoe, Drew 10.00
Brunell, Mark 12.00
Chandler, Chris 12.00
Chrebet, Wayne (R) 20.00
Cunningham, Randall 12.00
Davis, Terrell 15.00
Dawson, Dermontti (R) 25.00
Dillon, Corey 10.00
Dunn, Warrick (R) 20.00
Elway, John 12.00
Enis, Curtis (R) 8.00
Favre, Brett 10.00
Flutie, Doug 12.00
George, Eddie
Oilers 15.00
Titans 25.00
Kaufman, Napoleon (R) 12.00
Kelly, Jim (Ames) 15.00
Leaf, Ryan 8.00
Levens, Dorsey (R) 10.00
Manning, Peyton 18.00
Marino, Dan 12.00
Martin, Curtis 12.00
Moss, Randy (R) 25.00
Plummer, Jake (R) 18.00
Rice, Jerry 10.00
Rison, Andre 10.00
Sanders, Barry
(regular) 12.00
(Meijers) 16.00
Sapp, Warren (R) 35.00
Smith, Emmitt 10.00
Smith, Jimmy (R) 24.00
Smith, Neil 10.00
Smith, Robert (R) 25.00
Staubach, R. (Albertson's) 20.00
Stewart, Kordell 10.00
Swann, Eric (R) 12.00
Thomas, Zach (R) 50.00
Watters, Ricky 10.00
Young, Steve 10.00

EXTENDED

Complete Set (8) $120.00
Player **Mint**
Anderson, Jamal 12.00
Batch, Charlie (R) 10.00
Couch, Tim (R) 25.00
McCaffery, Ed (R) 12.00
McNabb, Donovan (R) 35.00
Randle, John (R) 15.00
Taylor, Fred (R) 18.00
Williams, Ricky (R) 25.00

1999 FOOTBALL 12" FIGURES

Complete Set (5) $125.00
Player **Mint**
Davis, Terrell 30.00
Favre, Brett 25.00
Sanders, Barry 30.00
Stewart, Kordell 25.00
Young, Steve 25.00

1999 FOOTBALL CLASSIC DOUBLES

Complete Set (10) $150.00
Player **Mint**
Alstott, M./Dunn, W. 15.00
Campbell, E./George, E. 18.00
Carter, C./Moss, R. 35.00
Elway, J./Davis, T. 20.00
Harris, F./Bettis, J. 18.00
Lambert, J./Ham, J. 20.00
Manning, A./Manning, P. 30.00
Munoz, A./Esiason, B. 15.00
Stabler, K./Casper, D. 18.00
Unitas, J./Berry, R. 15.00

QB CLUB

Complete Set (5) $75.00
Player **Mint**
Aikman, Troy 18.00
Davis, Terrell 20.00
Favre, Brett 20.00
Plummer, Jake 18.00
Stewart, Kordell 18.00

1999 FOOTBALL HEROES OF THE GRIDIRON

Complete Set (9) $75.00
Player **Mint**
Batch, Charlie 10.00
Brunell, Mark 8.00
Davis, Ernie 8.00
Dunn, Warrick 8.00
Martin, Curtis 15.00
Moss, Randy 20.00
Plunkett, Jim 10.00
Ward, Charlie 8.00
Williams, Ricky 15.00

1999 FOOTBALL GRIDIRON GREATS

Complete Set (8) $110.00
Player **Mint**
Butkus, Dick 18.00
Davis, Terrell 20.00
Dunn, Warrick 12.00
George, Eddie 20.00
Marino, Dan 20.00
Martin, Curtis 20.00
Sanders, Barry 15.00
Stewart, Kordell 15.00

2000 FOOTBALL

Complete Set (40) $600.00
Player **Mint**
Aikman, Troy
8.00
Alstott, Mike 10.00
Armstead, Jesse (R) 20.00
Bailey, Champ (R) 15.00
Bledsoe, Drew 9.00
Brackens, Tony (R) 12.00
Brunell, Mark 8.00
Couch, Tim
(Regular) 12.00
(Ames Exclusive) 15.00
Culpepper, Daunte (R) 105.00
Davis, Stephen (R) 15.00
Davis, Terrell 10.00
Elway, John 12.00
Favre, Brett 12.00
Flutie, Doug 12.00
Freeman, Antonio 10.00
Gonzalez, Tony (R) 18.00
Griese, Brian (R) 25.00
Holt, Torry (R) 25.00
James, Edgerrin (R) 25.00
Johnson, Brad 10.00
Johnson, Keyshawn
(NY Jets uniform) 12.00
(TB Buccaneers uniform) .17.00
King, Shaun (R) 20.00
Kitna, Jon (R) 15.00
Manning, Peyton 14.00
Marino, Dan 40.00
McNair, Steve 12.00
Montana, Joe 15.00
Moss, Randy 15.00
Newsome, Ozzie 15.00
Otto, Jim (R) 40.00
Owens, Terrell (R) 20.00
Plummer, Jake 10.00
Spikes, Takeo (R) 12.00
Taylor, Fred 10.00
Testaverde, Vinny 10.00
Warner, Kurt
(old uniform) (R) 30.00
(new uniform) 35.00
(Wal-Mart Exclusive) 25.00
Williams, Ricky
(old uniform) 12.00
(uniform variation) 12.00

EXTENDED

Complete Set (10) $140.00
Player **Mint**
Alexander, Shaun (R) 20.00
Bruce, Isaac 12.00
Carter, Cris 10.00
Dayne, Ron (R) 18.00
Harrison, Marvin 18.00
Kearse, Jevon (R) 20.00
Sehorn, Jason (R) 18.00
Springs, Shawn (R) 12.00
Warrick, Peter (R)
(white uniform) 18.00
(black uniform) 15.00

2000 FOOTBALL CLASSIC DOUBLES

Complete Set (7) $100.00
Player **Mint**
Aikman, T./Kelly, J. 18.00
Davis, T./Anderson, J. 15.00
Elway, J./Favre, B. 20.00
Favre, B./Bledsoe, D. 18.00
George, E./Faulk, M. 25.00
Montana, J./Marino, D. 35.00
Simms, P./Elway, J. 18.00
Manning, Peyton
college/pro(Wilk's) 20.00

2000 FOOTBALL ELITE

Complete Set (6) $80.00
Player **Mint**
Davis, Terrell 15.00
Favre, Brett 15.00
Manning, Peyton 20.00
Montana, Joe 25.00
Moss, Randy 20.00
Smith, Emmitt 25.00

2000 FOOTBALL HOBBY SET

Complete Set (9) $85.00
Player **Mint**
Aikman, Troy 8.00
Davis, Terrell 9.00
Faulk, Marshall 25.00
Manning, Peyton 14.00
Moss, Randy 14.00
Plummer, Jake 8.00
Smith, Akili (R) 10.00
Williams, Ricky 10.00
Woodson, Darren (R) 22.00

MCFARLANE FOOTBALL

2001 FOOTBALL SERIES 1

Complete Set (6) $75.00
Player **Mint**
George, Eddie
(blue jersey) 12.00
(white jersey) 30.00
(helmetless) 85.00
James, Edgerrin
(white jersey) 15.00
(blue jersey) 35.00
(helmetless) 90.00
Moss, Randy
(purple jersey) 15.00
(white jersey) 45.00
(helmetless) 100.00
Sapp, Warren
(red jersey) 10.00
(white jersey) 33.00
(helmetless) 65.00
Smith, Emmitt
(white jersey) 20.00
(blue jersey) 65.00
(blue jersey - no stars) .. 90.00
(helmetless) 225.00
Warner, Kurt
(white jersey) 18.00
(blue jersey) 40.00
(helmetless) 135.00

2001 FOOTBALL SERIES 2

Complete Set (6) $75.00
Player **Mint**
Brunell, Mark
(blue jersey) 10.00
(white jersey) 25.00
(helmetless) 60.00
Chrebet, Wayne
(white jersey) 12.00
(green jersey) 30.00
(helmetless) 60.00
Culpepper, Daunte
(white jersey) 18.00
(purple jersey) 40.00
(helmetless) 80.00
Faulk, Marshall
(blue jersey) 25.00
(white jersey) 55.00
(helmetless) 100.00
Harrison, Marvin
(blue jersey) 10.00
(white jersey) 30.00
(helmetless) 60.00
Urlacher, Brian
(black jersey) (R) 50.00
(white jersey) 100.00
(helmetless) 200.00

2002 FOOTBALL SERIES 3

Complete Set (4) $30.00
Player **Mint**
Bennett, Michael (R) 20.00
Jackson, James (R) 10.00
Tomlinson, LaDainian (R) 15.00
Weinke, Chris (R) 10.00

HALL OF FAMERS AUTOGRAPH GUIDE

Includes pricing for items that were not certified via an authentication system, including a sticker or hologram on the item, at the time of signing.

Player (born-died)	Year Inducted	Signed Cut/3x5	Signed 8x10 Photo	Signed Goal Line Art	Signed Mini Helmet	Signed Footbll	Signed Helmet
Adderley, Herb (1939-)	1980	$5	$15	$15	$40	$85	$180
Allen, George (1918-1990)	2002	60	150	*	*	300	*
Alworth, Lance (1940-)	1978	10	30	45	75	125	225
Atkins, Doug (1930-)	1982	6	20	15	40	85	180
Badgro, Red (1902-1998)	1981	10	25	25	70	135	190
Barney, Lem (1945-)	1992	5	15	15	40	85	180
Battles, Cliff (1910-1981)	1968	65	250	*	*	*	*
Baugh, Sammy (1914-)	1963	15	50	40	70	200	300
Bednarik, Chuck (1925-)	1967	5	20	15	40	100	200
Bell, Bert (1895-1959)	1963	125	500	*	*	*	*
Bell, Bobby (1940-)	1983	5	18	15	40	85	180
Berry, Raymond (1933-)	1973	5	18	20	40	85	180
Bidwill, Charles (1895-1947)	1967	400	800	*	*	*	*
Biletnikoff, Fred (1943-)	1988	10	25	25	40	110	200
Blanda, George (1927-)	1981	10	40	50	95	125	225
Blount, Mel (1948-)	1989	5	20	25	50	85	200
Bradshaw, Terry (1948-)	1989	10	60	75	125	200	300
Brown, Jim (1936-)	1971	10	60	60	100	300	300
Brown, Paul (1908-1991)	1967	15	100	150	*	300	*
Brown, Roosevelt (1932-)	1975	10	15	15	40	85	180
Brown, Willie (1940-)	1984	6	15	20	40	85	180
Buchanan, Buck (1940-1992)	1990	20	60	60	*	200	*
Buoniconti, Nick (1940-)	2001	5	25	40	60	110	225
Butkus, Dick (1942-)	1979	10	30	40	50	150	225
Campbell, Earl (1955-)	1991	10	30	35	60	125	225
Canadeo, Tony (1919-)	1974	4	20	20	50	85	180
Carr, Joe (1880-1939)	1963	500	1000	*	*	*	*
Casper, Dave (1951-)	2002	5	20	30	50	85	200
Chamberlain, Guy (1894-1967)	1965	200	500	*	*	*	*
Christiansen, Jack (1928-1986)	1970	40	200	*	*	*	*
Clark, Dutch (1906-1978)	1963	40	150	*	*	*	*
Connor, George (1925-)	1975	6	20	25	50	85	180
Conzelman, Jim (1898-1970)	1964	75	500	*	*	*	*
Creekmur, Lou (1927-)	1996	5	10	15	40	80	180
Csonka, Larry (1946-)	1987	6	35	40	60	150	225
Davis, Al (1929-)	1992	50	100	150	175	300	350
Davis, Willie (1934-)	1981	7	15	20	50	85	200
Dawson, Len (1935-)	1987	8	25	25	50	125	200
Dickerson, Eric (1960-)	1999	5	25	35	60	90	275
Dierdorf, Dan (1949-)	1996	5	20	30	60	90	180
Ditka, Mike (1939-)	1988	10	30	30	50	125	225
Donovan, Art (1925-)	1968	7	20	20	40	85	200
Dorsett, Tony (1954-)	1994	3	30	40	60	150	225
Driscoll, Paddy (1896-1968)	1965	100	400	*	*	*	*
Dudley, Bill (1921-)	1966	6	20	20	40	75	170

Player (born-died)	Year Inducted	Signed Cut/3x5	Signed 8x10 Photo	Signed Goal Line Art	Signed Mini Helmet	Signed Footbll	Signed Helmet
Edwards, Turk (1907-1973)	1969	80	300	*	*	*	*
Ewbank, Weeb (1907-1998)	1978	5	30	40	75	125	200
Fears, Tom (1923-2000)	1970	7	20	25	60	125	180
Finks, Jim (1927-1994)	1995	35	100	*	*	200	*
Flaherty, Ray (1904-1994)	1976	5	40	25	*	200	*
Ford, Len (1926-1972)	1976	100	250	*	*	*	*
Fortmann, Dan (1916-1995)	1965	25	75	*	*	*	*
Fouts, Dan (1951-)	1993	5	30	25	60	150	225
Gatski, Frank (1922-)	1985	3	20	15	40	85	180
George, Bill (1930-1982)	1974	50	300	*	*	*	*
Gibbs, Joe (1940-)	1996	6	30	30	75	125	225
Gifford, Frank (1930-)	1977	15	45	60	85	170	235
Gillman, Sid (1911-)	1983	5	20	30	50	85	180
Graham, Otto (1921-)	1965	3	20	40	60	125	225
Grange, Red (1903-1991)	1963	50	175	195	*	600	*
Grant, Bud (1927-)	1994	3	25	30	50	100	180
Greene, Joe (1946-)	1987	3	25	30	50	125	200
Gregg, Forrest (1933-)	1977	9	25	35	50	100	200
Griese, Bob (1945-)	1990	7	25	35	50	125	220
Groza, Lou (1924-2000)	1974	6	25	35	50	100	210
Guyon, Joe (1892-1971)	1966	35	300	*	*	*	*
Halas, George (1895-1983)	1963	50	250	*	*	500	*
Ham, Jack (1948-)	1988	3	20	25	45	100	200
Hampton, Dan (1957-)	2002	5	20	25	50	85	190
Hannah, John (1951-)	1991	6	30	35	60	100	225
Harris, Franco (1950-)	1990	10	40	60	90	150	300
Haynes, Mike (1953-)	1997	7	18	30	40	75	180
Healy, Ed (1894-1978)	1964	60	250	*	*	*	*
Hein, Mel (1909-1992)	1963	20	60	*	*	175	*
Hendricks, Ted (1947-)	1990	6	20	20	40	85	180
Henry, Pete (1897-1952)	1963	100	350	*	*	*	*
Herber, Arnie (1910-1969)	1966	75	500	*	*	*	*
Hewitt, Bill (1909-1947)	1971	100	600	*	*	*	*
Hinkle, Clarke (1909-1988)	1964	25	100	*	*	200	*
Hirsch, Elroy (1923-)	1968	5	20	15	50	125	225
Hornung, Paul (1935-)	1986	5	20	25	50	125	225
Houston, Ken (1944-)	1986	4	20	20	40	85	180
Hubbard, Cal (1900-1977)	1963	50	250	*	*	*	*
Huff, Sam (1934-)	1982	3	20	30	50	100	200
Hunt, Lamar (1932-)	1972	8	25	60	100	150	250
Hutson, Don (1913-1997)	1963	10	50	85	150	200	300
Johnson, Jimmy (1938-)	1994	3	20	25	40	85	180
Johnson, John Henry (1929-)	1987	7	15	20	40	85	180
Joiner, Charlie (1947-)	1996	5	18	15	40	85	180
Jones, Deacon (1938-)	1980	6	15	20	45	100	200
Jones, Stan (1931-)	1991	3	15	20	40	85	180
Jordan, Henry (1935-1976)	1995	150	500	*	*	*	*
Jurgensen, Sonny (1934-)	1983	5	30	35	60	125	235

Player (born-died)	Year Inducted	Signed Cut/3x5	Signed 8x10 Photo	Signed Goal Line Art	Signed Mini Helmet	Signed Footbll	Signed Helmet
Kelly, Jim (1960-)	2002	10	35	65	75	135	225
Kelly, Leroy (1942-)	1994	3	15	15	40	85	200
Kiesling, Walt (1903-1962)	1966	75	500	*	*	*	*
Kinard, Frank (1914-1965)	1971	60	500	*	*	*	*
Krause, Paul (1942-)	1998	3	15	25	50	85	200
Lambeau, Curly (1898-1965)	1963	150	600	*	*	*	*
Lambert, Jack (1952-)	1990	5	30	40	60	150	250
Landry, Tom (1924-2000)	1990	15	50	75	125	200	350
Lane, Dick (1928-2002)	1974	5	20	25	50	100	200
Langer, Jim (1948-)	1987	8	15	20	40	85	180
Lanier, Willie (1945-)	1986	3	15	20	40	85	180
Largent, Steve (1954-)	1995	8	35	45	75	125	225
Lary, Yale (1930-)	1979	3	15	15	40	85	180
Lavelli, Dante (1923-)	1975	3	15	15	40	85	180
Layne, Bobby (1926-1986)	1967	50	175	*	*	500	*
Leemans, Tuffy (1912-1979)	1978	100	250	*	*	*	*
Levy, Marv (1928-)	2001	6	25	30	50	85	200
Lilly, Bob (1939-)	1980	3	15	20	45	100	200
Little, Larry (1945-)	1993	5	15	15	40	85	180
Lombardi, Vince (1913-1970)	1971	150	500	*	*	2000	*
Long, Howie (1960-)	2000	10	30	60	85	150	250
Lott, Ronnie (1959-)	2000	6	30	50	75	100	170
Luckman, Sid (1916-1998)	1965	10	35	40	100	150	275
Lyman, Link (1898-1972)	1964	75	300	*	*	*	*
Mack, Tom (1943-)	1999	4	15	25	40	85	150
Mackey, John (1941-)	1992	3	15	20	40	85	180
Mara, Tim (1887-1959)	1963	200	700	*	*	*	*
Mara, Wellington (1916-)	1997	5	20	20	50	85	225
Marchetti, Gino (1927-)	1972	3	15	20	40	85	180
Marshall, George P. (1887-1969)	1963	125	400	*	*	*	*
Matson, Ollie (1930-)	1972	5	20	30	50	100	200
Maynard, Don (1935-)	1987	7	15	25	45	100	200
McAfee, George (1918-)	1966	7	15	20	40	85	180
McCormack, Mike (1930-)	1984	5	15	15	40	85	180
McDonald, Tommy (1934-)	1998	6	15	20	40	85	180
McElhenny, Hugh (1928-)	1970	5	20	25	40	100	200
McNally, Johnny (1903-1985)	1963	50	200	*	*	500	*
Michalske, Mike (1903-1983)	1964	30	200	*	*	400	*
Millner, Wayne (1913-1976)	1968	75	300	*	*	*	*
Mitchell, Bobby (1935-)	1983	3	20	20	40	85	180
Mix, Ron (1938-)	1979	6	15	20	40	85	180
Montana, Joe (1956-)	2000	20	50	85	125	175	275
Moore, Lenny (1933-)	1975	7	15	20	40	85	180
Motley, Marion (1920-1999)	1968	8	20	40	75	100	180
Munchak, Mike (1960-)	2001	6	25	30	40	85	180
Munoz, Anthony (1958-)	1998	3	20	20	40	85	250
Musso, George (1910-2000)	1982	5	25	25	60	100	180
Nagurski, Bronko (1908-1990)	1963	40	125	*	*	400	*

Player (born-died)	Year Inducted	Signed Cut/3x5	Signed 8x10 Photo	Signed Goal Line Art	Signed Mini Helmet	Signed Footbll	Signed Helmet
Namath, Joe (1943-)	1985	20	60	75	150	225	400
Neale, Greasy (1891-1973)	1969	75	400	*	*	*	*
Nevers, Ernie (1903-1976)	1963	50	250	*	*	*	*
Newsome, Ozzie (1956-)	1999	5	20	15	40	85	250
Nitschke, Ray (1936-1998)	1978	10	40	60	125	175	300
Noll, Chuck (1932-)	1993	3	15	20	40	85	180
Nomellini, Leo (1924-2000)	1969	10	25	25	60	100	180
Olsen, Merlin (1940-)	1982	7	30	40	60	125	200
Otto, Jim (1938-)	1980	6	20	20	40	85	180
Owen, Steve (1898-1964)	1966	200	750	*	*	*	*
Page, Alan (1945-)	1988	3	20	25	50	100	180
Parker, Ace (1912-)	1972	3	15	20	40	85	180
Parker, Jim (1934-)	1973	3	15	20	40	85	180
Payton, Walter (1954-1999)	1993	30	75	150	200	300	350
Perry, Joe (1927-)	1969	8	120	25	40	100	200
Pihos, Pete (1923-)	1970	3	15	20	40	85	180
Ray, Hugh (1884-1956)	1966	200	1000	*	*	*	*
Reeves, Dan (1912-1971)	1967	75	400	*	*	*	*
Renfro, Mel (1941-)	1996	5	15	20	40	85	180
Riggins, John (1949-)	1992	20	100	150	150	225	325
Ringo, Jim (1931-)	1981	5	15	20	40	85	180
Robustelli, Andy (1925-)	1971	3	20	20	50	100	200
Rooney, Art (1901-1988)	1964	40	125	*	*	300	*
Rooney, Dan (1932-)	2000	5	25	30	75	100	200
Rozelle, Pete (1926-1996)	1985	20	75	150	200	250	300
St. Clair, Bob (1931-)	1990	6	20	30	40	85	180
Sayers, Gale (1943-)	1977	7	25	30	45	125	200
Schmidt, Joe (1932-)	1973	3	15	20	40	85	180
Schramm, Tex (1920-)	1991	6	15	20	40	85	180
Selmon, Lee Roy (1954-)	1995	3	20	20	50	85	180
Shaw, Billy (1938-)	1999	3	15	20	35	85	175
Shell, Art (1946-)	1989	4	25	35	60	100	180
Shula, Don (1930-)	1997	15	35	60	85	150	250
Simpson, O. J. (1947-)	1985	25	45	60	75	150	275
Singletary, Mike (1958-)	1998	7	20	30	50	100	275
Slater, Jackie (1955-)	2001	3	20	40	40	85	180
Smith, Jackie (1940-)	1994	3	15	20	40	85	180
Stallworth, John (1952-)	2002	8	25	40	50	100	200
Starr, Bart (1934-)	1977	20	50	60	100	150	250
Staubach, Roger (1942-)	1985	10	40	60	100	150	225
Stautner, Ernie (1925-)	1969	4	15	20	40	85	180
Stenerud, Jan (1942-)	1991	5	15	15	50	85	195
Stephenson, Dwight (1957-)	1998	3	15	20	45	85	190
Strong, Ken (1906-1979)	1967	40	200	*	*	*	*
Stydahar, Joe (1912-1977)	1967	40	250	*	*	*	*
Swann, Lynn (1952-)	2001	20	50	125	100	150	250
Tarkenton, Fran (1940-)	1986	10	30	60	75	150	235
Taylor, Charley (1941-)	1984	4	15	20	50	85	195

Player (born-died)	Year Inducted	Signed Cut/3x5	Signed 8x10 Photo	Signed Goal Line Art	Signed Mini Helmet	Signed Footbll	Signed Helmet
Taylor, Jim (1935-)	1976	5	25	60	60	100	225
Taylor, Lawrence (1959-)	1999	8	30	40	70	125	210
Thorpe, Jim (1888-1953)	1963	1500	6000	*	*	*	*
Tittle, Y.A. (1926-)	1971	4	25	25	50	100	225
Trafton, George (1896-1971)	1964	75	300	*	*	*	*
Trippi, Charley (1922-)	1968	3	15	15	45	85	175
Tunnell, Emlen (1925-1975)	1967	75	300	*	*	*	*
Turner, Clyde "Bulldog" (1919-1998)	1966	10	35	40	150	150	250
Unitas, Johny (1933-)	1979	20	40	50	100	170	220
Upshaw, Gene (1945-)	1987	7	20	25	50	85	200
Van Brocklin, Norm (1926-1983)	1971	60	225	*	*	350	*
Van Buren, Steve (1920-)	1965	3	15	20	30	85	175
Walker, Doak (1927-1998)	1986	10	40	60	75	150	225
Walsh, Bill (1931-)	1993	10	25	50	80	125	200
Warfield, Paul (1942-)	1983	3	20	20	30	100	175
Waterfield, Bob (1920-1983)	1965	75	250	*	*	350	*
Webster, Mike (1952-)	1997	4	20	25	50	85	200
Weinmeister, Arnie (1923-2000)	1987	4	20	25	60	100	200
White, Randy (1953-)	1994	4	20	25	50	85	175
Wilcox, Dave (1942-)	2000	6	15	20	30	85	175
Willis, Bill (1921-)	1977	6	20	25	40	85	175
Wilson, Larry (1938-)	1978	3	15	25	30	85	175
Winslow, Kellen (1957-)	1995	3	15	25	50	100	200
Wojciechowicz, Alex (1915-1992)	1968	10	50	800	*	225	*
Wood, Willie (1936-)	1989	3	15	20	30	85	175
Yary, Ron (1946-)	2001	6	20	25	50	85	200
Youngblood, Jack (1950-)	2001	6	20	30	50	100	200

FOOTBALL PLAYERS AUTOGRAPH GUIDE

"Auth." refers to an item certified by an authentication system, including a sticker or hologram on the item that was applied at the time of signing.

Player	Signed 8x10 Photo	Signed MiniHel.	Auth. Mini	Signed FBall	Auth. FBall	Sig'd Helm.	Auth. Helm.
ACTIVE PLAYERS							
Alexander, Derrick	15	40		75		200	
Alexander, Shaun	20	45		85		225	
Alstott, Mike	25	60		95		250	
Anderson, Jamal	25	75		120		250	
Anderson, Mike	20	45	90	85		200	
Arrington, Lavar	20	80		100		200	
Atwater, Steve	10	40		75		250	
Bailey, Champ	20	40		75		200	
Banks, Tony	12	40		75		200	
Barber, Tiki	15	40		75		250	
Batch, Charlie	15	40		75		200	
Bennett, Cornelius	15	50		75		200	
Bettis, Jerome	15	75		75		275	
Beuerlien, Steve	15	40		75		200	
Biakabutuka, Tim	12	40		75		200	
Blake, Jeff	12	40		75		200	
Bledsoe, Drew	25	65	90	85	200	250	
Boselli, Tony	20	50		85		225	
Boston, David	20	50	60	85		200	
Brady, Kyle	15	40		75		200	
Brady, Tom	40	75		150			
Brees, Drew	20	45	80	80		225	
Brooks, Aaron	12	40	80	75		225	
Brown, Tim	30	60	90	85		260	
Brown, Troy	20	50		85		200	
Bruce, Isaac	15	50	75	75		250	
Brunell, Mark	25	70	100	100	200	250	550
Burress, Plaxico	15	40	60	75		200	
Carr, David	40	50	75	125		250	
Carter, Quincy	15	40		75		200	
Chambers, Chris	15	50		75		200	
Chandler, Chris	20	60		100		225	
Chrebet, Wayne	15	50		75		200	
Coles, Laveranues	15	40		75		200	
Collins, Kerry	15	50		85		225	
Conway, Curtis	8	40		75		225	
Couch, Tim	25	60	100	100	180	250	500
Cox, Bryan	15	40		75		200	
Crowell, Germaine	12	40		75		200	
Culpepper, Daunte	20	60	100	90	200	275	
Cunningham, Ra.	25	50	190	90		250	450
Davis, Stephen	20	40	75	85		225	
Davis, Terrell	40	100		175	200	300	575
Dayne, Ron	20	50	200	90	200	225	575
Dilfer, Trent	(15)	45		85		225	
Dilger, Ken	12	40		75		225	
Dillon, Corey	20	60		100		275	
Dudley, Rickey	12	40		75		225	
Dunn, Warrick	35	75		125		300	
Dwight, Tim	15	40		75		200	
Dyson, Kevin	15	40	50	75		200	
Elam, Jason	20	40		85		200	
Emanuel, Bert	12	40		75		250	
Faulk, Kevin	40	85		135		225	
Faulk, Marshall	50	100		135		300	
Favre, Brett	60	125	150	175	250	350	650
Fiedler, Jay	15	40		75		200	
Flutie, Doug	25	65		125		300	
Freeman, Antonio	15	45		85		225	
Galloway, Joey	20	55		90		260	
Gannon, Rich	20	50	90	100	170	225	
Garcia, Jeff	20	55		90		250	
Gardner, Rod	15	40		75		200	
Garner, Charlie	15	40		75		200	
Gary, Olandis	20	40		85		200	
George, Eddie	25	60	125	100	220	325	550
George, Jeff	15	40		75		225	
Glenn, Terry	15	40		75		225	
Gonzalez, Tony	15	40		75		250	
Green, Ahman	15	45		85		250	
Green, Trent	15	40		75		200	
Griese, Brian	25	60		100	150	250	
Harbaugh, Jim	12	40		75		250	
Harrington, Joey	25	50		100		225	
Harrison, Marvin	20	60		100		275	
Hasselback, Matt	15	40		75		200	
Hearst, Garrison	20	45		85		250	
Henry, Travis	15	40		75		200	
Hilliard, Ike	12	40		75		250	
Holmes, Priest	15	40		75		200	
Holt, Torry	15	50	75	75		250	
Horn, Joe	15	40		75		200	
Howard, Desmond	15	45		75		250	
Ismail, Qadry	15	40		75		200	
Ismail, Rocket	15	40		75		200	
James, Edgerrin	35	75		100	350	325	600
Jett, James	12	40		75		250	
Johnson, Brad	20	50		75	150	250	
Johnson, Key.	25	55	125	80	180	275	
Johnson, Rob	15	45		85		250	
Kennison, Eddie	15	50		100		250	
Kirkland, Levon	12	40		75		250	
Kirby, Terry	12	40		75		250	
Kitna, John	15	40		75		200	
Leaf, Ryan	15	40	50	75		200	
Levens, Dorsey	15	40		75		200	
Lewis, Jamal	12	50		75		250	
Lewis, Jermaine	15	40		75		200	
Lewis, Ray	30	60		100		250	
Manning, Peyton	40	90	160	115	300	325	625
Martin, Curtis	25	75		100		275	
Martin, Tony	15	40		75		250	
Mason, Derrick	15	40	55	75		200	
Mathis, Terrance	12	40		75		250	
McAllister, Deuce	15	40		75		200	
McCaffrey, Ed	12	40		75		250	
McCardell, Keenan	15	40		85		250	
McDuffie, O.J.	15	40		75		250	
McNabb, Donovan	30	75	90	100	200	300	
McNair, Steve	18	50		95		275	
McNown, Cade	18	45		90		250	
Moore, Herman	15	40		75		250	
Moore, Rob	10	40		75		250	
Morris, Sylvester	15	40		75		200	
Morton, Johnnie	12	40		75		225	
Moss, Randy	35	80		125		275	650
Moss, Santana	15	40		75		200	
Moulds, Eric	20	50		85		250	
Muhammad, Muh.	15	40		75		200	
Nguyen, Dat.	20	40		85		200	
Owens, Terrell	20	65		100		275	
Pace, Orlando	20	45		85		200	
Pennington, Chad	20	45		85		225	
Peppers, Julius	20	50		100		225	
Plummer, Jake	20	50	80	90		200	
Price, Peerless	15	40		75		200	
Proehl, Ricky	15	40		75		200	
Redman, Chris	15	40		75		200	
Redmond, J.R.	15	40		75		200	
Reed, Jake	15	45		85		200	
Rice, Jerry	45	115	150	150	230	275	700

Player	Signed 8x10 Photo	Signed MiniHel.	Auth. Mini	Signed FBall	Auth. FBall	Sig'd Helm.	Auth. Helm.
Rice, Simeon	12	40		75		250	
Rison, Andre	15	45		80		225	
Roaf, Willie	20	45		85		200	
Romanowski, Bill	20	45		85		225	
Sanders, Chris	12	40		75		250	
Sanders, Frank	12	40		75		250	
Sapp, Warren	20	65		90		275	
Schroeder, Bill	15	40		75		200	
Seau, Junior	20	50		75		250	
Sehorn, Jason	20	45		85		225	
Sharpe, Shannon	20	60		75		225	
Smith, Akili	20	35		85		225	
Smith, Antowain	15	40		85		250	
Smith, Bruce	25	50		100		250	
Smith, Emmitt	35	100		120		300	650
Smith, Jimmy	18	50		90		250	
Smith, Lamar	15	40		75		200	
Smith, Neil	15	45		85		250	
Smith, Rod	20	40		85		225	
Staley, Duce	15	40		85		200	
Stewart, James	15	40		75		250	
Stewart, Kordell	25	55		100		225	
Stokes, J.J.	12	45		75		200	
Strahan, Michael	20	45		85		200	
Taylor, Fred	25	50	75	85	150	250	
Taylor, Travis	15	40		75		200	
Terrell, David	15	40		75		200	
Testaverde, V.	25	45	75	90		250	
Thomas, Anthony	20	50		75		200	
Tomlinson, LaD.	20	50	75	90		250	
Urlacher, Brian	20	50		100		225	
Vick, Michael	40	75	120	100	200	250	
Walls, Wesley	12	40		85		250	
Warner, Kurt	40	90	175	125	225	275	
Warrick, Peter	15	40	55	75		200	
Watters, Ricky	15	50		85		200	
Weinke, Chris	20	40		100		225	
Westbrook, Mi.	15	40		75		200	
Wheatley, Tyrone	15	40		75		200	
Wilkins, Terrence	15	40		75		200	
Williams, Ricky	30	75		125		250	
Woodson, Charles	20	50	75	100		275	
Woodson, Rod	15	50		100		250	
Wright, Anthony	15	40		75		200	

RETIRED PLAYERS

*Asterisk denotes deceased player

Player	Signed 8x10 Photo	Signed MiniHel.	Auth. Mini	Signed FBall	Auth. FBall	Sig'd Helm.	Auth. Helm.
Aikman, Troy	30	75	150	125	250	275	625
Allen, Marcus	30	60		80		250	
Alzado, Lyle*	100	*		250		*	
Ameche, Alan*	100	*		400		*	
Bleier, Rocky	15	40		75		225	
Carter, Cris	15	55		85		250	
Craig, Roger	15	40	50	85		225	
Elway, John	40	120		150	350	350	
Esiason, Boomer	20	55		85	330	300	650
Fryar, Irving	15	40		85		225	
Gabriel, Roman	15	40		85		225	
Grbac, Elvis	15	45		75		225	
Greene, Kevin	15	45		85		225	
Greenwood, L.C.	18	40		85		200	
Irvin, Michael	25	45	65	80		250	
Jackson, Bo	30	75	110	100	150	275	550
Jackson, Tom	20	50		100		250	
Johnston, Daryl	15	40		75		225	
Jones, Brent	15	40		75		250	
Jones, Ed	18	40		75		225	

Player	Signed 8x10 Photo	Signed MiniHel.	Auth. Mini	Signed FBall	Auth. FBall	Sig'd Helm.	Auth. Helm.
Karras, Alex	20	50		100		225	
Kemp, Jack	25	40		100		250	
LeBaron, Eddie	18	40		85		200	
Marino, Dan	50	100	170	175	300	300	650
Matuszek, John*	75	*		250		*	
McMahon, Jim	20	50		75		225	
Meredith, Don	50	100		150		300	
Monk, Art	22	50		135		275	
Moon, Warren	25	50		80		250	
Morrall, Earl	12	40		85		225	
Norton, Ken	15	40		85		250	
Piccolo, Brian*	275	*		*		*	
Pickens, Carl	15	45		85		225	
Plunkett, Jim	25	45		85		250	
Rashad, Ahmad	25	55		100		250	
Sanders, Barry	50	100		150	450	300	650
Sanders, Deion	40	80		150		300	
Scott, Jake	50	75		150		275	
Sharpe, Sterling	30	60		90		250	
Simms, Phil	25	50		85		275	
Stabler, Ken	25	45		90		250	
Summerall, Pat	15	40		85		250	
Taylor, John	10	40		85		250	
Theismann, Joe	20	45		85		250	
Young, Steve	40	75		125		250	

COACHES & OWNERS

Player	Signed 8x10 Photo	Signed MiniHel.	Auth. Mini	Signed FBall	Auth. FBall	Sig'd Helm.	Auth. Helm.
Cowher, Bill	15	40		85		250	
Dungy, Tony	15	40		85		225	
Fisher, Jeff	15	40		85		225	
Green, Dennis	15	40		85		225	
Holmgren, Mike	15	45		100		250	
Jones, Jerry	15	45		85		225	
Madden, John	30	75		150		275	
Mariucci, Steve	15	40		85		225	
Parcells, Bill	25	55		125		250	
Reeves, Dan	15	45		85		225	
Schottenheimer, M.	15	45		85		200	
Seifert, George	15	40		75		200	
Shanahan, Mike	15	45		100		250	
Spurrier, Steve	30	60	75	125		225	
Vermeil, Dick	15	40		85		225	
Wannstedt, Dave	12	40		85		225	

CHRONOLOGICAL INDEX